Dictionary of Christ and the Gospels

Dictionary of Christ and the Gospels

EDITED BY

JAMES HASTINGS, D.D.

WITH THE ASSISTANCE OF

JOHN A. SELBIE, D.D.

AND (IN THE READING OF THE PROOFS) OF

JOHN C. LAMBERT, D.D.

VOLUME I

AARON — KNOWLEDGE

BAKER BOOK HOUSE
GRAND RAPIDS, MICHIGAN

ISBN: 0-8010-4095-7
© 1906 by Charles Scribner's Sons, New York. Reprinted 1973 by Baker Book House Company, Grand
Rapids, Michigan, with the permission of the
copyright holder.

PHOTOLITHOPRINTED BY CUSHING - MALLOY, INC.
ANN ARBOR, MICHIGAN, UNITED STATES OF AMERICA
1973

Publisher's Preface

THIS complete and independent *Dictionary of the New Testament* originally appeared as two separate titles: *A Dictionary of Christ and the Gospels* and *A Dictionary of the Apostolic Church*. The present volumes follow the original format. Volumes I and II comprise a dictionary concerned with the person, life, work, and teachings of Christ as presented in the Four Gospels. Volumes III and IV are a dictionary that covers the history of the Christian church as detailed in Acts through Revelation, to the end of the first century.

In some cases, entry words or phrases found in Volumes I and II are also included in Volumes III and IV, yet there is rarely any duplication, for the first entry is concerned with the Gospels and the second with the remainder of the New Testament. Often the second entry fleshes out the first.

Users of this *Dictionary of the New Testament* should not overlook the valuable indexes which are found at the ends of Volumes II and IV. Here are indexes of subjects (including cross-references), Greek terms, and Scripture texts. Each index adds to the usefulness of the set.

Baker Book House is pleased to make these four volumes available once again, for ministers who have been fortunate enough to have them on the library shelf have found them very helpful in sermon preparation. They have been described as "far more practical than many other reference works." In fact, some have labeled them as "indispensable."

PREFACE

THE Purpose of this DICTIONARY is to give an account of everything that relates to CHRIST—His Person, Life, Work, and Teaching.

It is in a sense complementary to the *Dictionary of the Bible*, in which, of course, Christ has a great place. But a Dictionary of the Bible, being occupied mainly with things biographical, historical, geographical, or antiquarian, does not give attention to the things of Christ sufficient for the needs of the preacher, to whom Christ is everything. This is, first of all, a preacher's Dictionary. The Authors of the articles have been carefully chosen from among those Scholars who are, or have been, themselves preachers. And even when the articles have the same titles as articles in the *Dictionary of the Bible*, they are written by new men, and from a new standpoint. It is thus a work which is quite distinct from, and altogether independent of, the *Dictionary of the Bible*.

It is called a DICTIONARY OF CHRIST AND THE GOSPELS, because it includes everything that the Gospels contain, whether directly related to CHRIST or not. Its range, however, is far greater than that of the Gospels. It seeks to cover all that relates to Christ throughout the Bible and in the life and literature of the world. There will be articles on the Patristic estimate of Jesus, the Mediæval estimate, the Reformation and Modern estimates. There will be articles on Christ in the Jewish writings and in the Muslim literature. Much attention has been given to modern thought, whether Christian or anti-Christian. Every aspect of modern life, in so far as it touches or is touched by Christ, is described under its proper title.

Still, the Gospels are the main source of our knowledge of Christ, and it will be found that the contents of the Gospels, especially their spiritual contents, have never before been so thoroughly investigated and set forth.

It will be observed at once that a large number of the titles of the articles are new. Thus—to take the first letter of the alphabet—there are no articles in the *Dictionary of the Bible* (unless the word happens to be used in some obsolete sense) on ABGAR, ABIDING, ABOVE AND BELOW, ABSOLUTION, ACCOMMODATION, ACTIVITY, AFFLICTION, AGONY, AMAZEMENT, AMBASSAGE, AMBITION, ANNOUNCEMENTS OF DEATH, ANNUNCIATION, ARBITRATION, ARISTEAS, ARISTION, ARREST, ASCETICISM, ATTRACTION OF CHRIST, ATTRIBUTES OF CHRIST, AUTHORITY OF CHRIST, AUTHORITY IN RELIGION, AWE. These articles are enough to give the present work distinction.

Again, there are certain topics which are treated more fully here than in the *Dictionary of the Bible*, because they have specially to do with Christ. In the letter A may be named ACCEPTANCE, ACCESS, ALPHA AND OMEGA, ANGER, ANOINTING, ASCENSION, ASSURANCE, ATONEMENT.

All these articles, moreover, have a range which is greater than the corresponding articles in the *Dictionary of the Bible*, if they occur there. They describe some aspect of Christ's Person or Work, not only as it is presented in the Bible, but also as it has been brought out in the history of the Church, and in Christian experience.

And even when the articles are confined to the Gospels they have a character of their own. The ground that has to be covered being less, the treatment can be fuller. It has also been found possible to make it more expository. Take the following examples—ABBA, AMEN, ANGELS, APOSTLES, ARCHELAUS, ART, AUGUSTUS.

Thus, in a word, there are three classes of topics, each of which contributes something towards the distinction of this work. There are topics, like AUTHORITY OF CHRIST, which are wholly new. There are topics which may or may not be wholly new, like ATTRACTION (which is new) and ATONEMENT (which is not), but which have a wider range than any topics in the *Dictionary of the Bible*. And there are topics, like ANGELS, which have a narrower range, having no occasion to go beyond the limits of the Gospels, but within that range are fuller, and of more practical value for the preacher.

The subject is inexhaustible. It has not been exhausted in this work. Perhaps the most that has been done is to show how great Christ is.

Many scholars have rendered valuable assistance. In addition to the services of Dr. Selbie and Dr. Lambert, the Editor desires especially to acknowledge those of Professor Howard Osgood of Rochester Theological Seminary, New York, who examined the Gospels minutely to see that no topic had been omitted, and added some useful titles to the list.

The Dictionary will be completed in two volumes, of which this is the first.

LIST OF ABBREVIATIONS

I. GENERAL

Alex. = Alexandrian.
Apoc. = Apocalypse, Apocalyptic.
Apocr. = Apocrypha, Apocryphal.
Aq. = Aquila.
Arab. = Arabic.
Aram. = Aramaic.
Assyr. = Assyrian.
Bab. = Babylonian.
c. = *circa*, about.
Can. = Canaanite.
cf. = compare.
ct. = contrast.
D = Deuteronomist.
E = Elohist.
edd. = editions or editors.
Egyp. = Egyptian.
Eng. = English.
Eth. = Ethiopic.
f. = and following verse or page : as Ac 10^{34f}.
ff. = and following verses or pages : as Mt 11^{28ff}.
Gr. = Greek.
H = Law of Holiness.
Heb. = Hebrew.
Hel. = Hellenistic.
Hex. = Hexateuch.
Isr. = Israelite.
J = Jahwist.
J″ = Jehovah.
Jerus. = Jerusalem.
Jos. = Josephus.

LXX = Septuagint.
MSS = Manuscripts.
MT = Massoretic Text.
n. = note.
NT = New Testament.
Onk. = Onkelos.
OT = Old Testament.
P = Priestly Narrative.
Pal. = Palestine, Palestinian.
Pent. = Pentateuch.
Pers. = Persian.
Phil. = Philistine.
Phœn. = Phœnician.
Pr. Bk. = Prayer Book.
R = Redactor.
Rom. = Roman.
Sam. = Samaritan.
Sem. = Semitic.
Sept. = Septuagint.
Sin. = Sinaitic.
Symm. = Symmachus.
Syr. = Syriac.
Talm. = Talmud.
Targ. = Targum.
Theod. = Theodotion.
TR = Textus Receptus.
tr. = translate or translation
VSS = Versions.
Vulg. = Vulgate.
WH = Westcott and Hort's text.

II. BOOKS OF THE BIBLE

Old Testament.

Gn = Genesis.
Ex = Exodus.
Lv = Leviticus.
Nu = Numbers.
Dt = Deuteronomy
Jos = Joshua.
Jg = Judges.
Ru = Ruth.
1 S, 2 S = 1 and 2 Samuel.
1 K, 2 K = 1 and 2 Kings.
1 Ch, 2 Ch = 1 and 2 Chronicles
Ezr = Ezra.
Neh = Nehemiah.
Est = Esther.
Job.
Ps = Psalms.
Pr = Proverbs.
Ec = Ecclesiastes.

Ca = Canticles.
Is = Isaiah.
Jer = Jeremiah.
La = Lamentations.
Ezk = Ezekiel.
Dn = Daniel.
Hos = Hosea.
Jl = Joel.
Am = Amos.
Ob = Obadiah.
Jon = Jonah.
Mic = Micah.
Nah = Nahum.
Hab = Habakkuk.
Zeph = Zephaniah.
Hag = Haggai.
Zec = Zechariah.
Mal = Malachi.

Apocrypha.

1 Es, 2 Es = 1 and 2 Esdras.
To = Tobit.
Jth = Judith.

Ad. Est = Additions to Esther.
Wis = Wisdom.
Sir = Sirach or Ecclesiasticus.
Bar = Baruch.
Three = Song of the Three Children.

Sus = Susanna.
Bel = Bel and the Dragon.
Pr. Man = Prayer of Manasses.
1 Mac, 2 Mac = 1 and 2 Maccabees.

New Testament.

Mt = Matthew.
Mk = Mark.
Lk = Luke.
Jn = John.
Ac = Acts.
Ro = Romans.
1 Co, 2 Co = 1 and 2 Corinthians.
Gal = Galatians.
Eph = Ephesians.
Ph = Philippians.
Col = Colossians.

1 Th, 2 Th = 1 and 2 Thessalonians.
1 Ti, 2 Ti = 1 and 2 Timothy.
Tit = Titus.
Philem = Philemon.
He = Hebrews.
Ja = James.
1 P, 2 P = 1 and 2 Peter.
1 Jn, 2 Jn, 3 Jn = 1, 2, and 3 John.
Jude.
Rev = Revelation.

III. English Versions

Wyc. = Wyclif's Bible (NT *c.* 1380, OT *c.* 1382, Purvey's Revision *c.* 1388).
Tind. = Tindale's NT 1526 and 1534, Pent. 1530.
Cov. = Coverdale's Bible 1535.
Matt. or Rog. = Matthew's (*i.e.* prob. Rogers') Bible 1537.
Cran. or Great = Cranmer's 'Great' Bible 1539.
Tav. = Taverner's Bible 1539.
Gen. = Geneva NT 1557, Bible 1560.

Bish. = Bishops' Bible 1568.
Tom. = Tomson's NT 1576.
Rhem. = Rhemish NT 1582.
Dou. = Douay OT 1609.
AV = Authorized Version 1611.
AVm = Authorized Version margin.
RV = Revised Version NT 1881, OT 1885.
RVm = Revised Version margin.
EV = Auth. and Rev. Versions.

IV. For the Literature

AHT = Ancient Hebrew Tradition.
AJSL = American Journal of Sem. Lang. and Literature.
AJTh = American Journal of Theology.
AT = Altes Testament.
BL = Bampton Lecture.
BM = British Museum.
BRP = Biblical Researches in Palestine.
CIG = Corpus Inscriptionum Græcarum.
CIL = Corpus Inscriptionum Latinarum.
CIS = Corpus Inscriptionum Semiticarum.
COT = Cuneiform Inscriptions and the OT.
DB = Dictionary of the Bible.
DCA = Dictionary of Christian Antiquities.
DRE = Dictionary of Religion and Ethics.
EHH = Early History of the Hebrews.
ExpT = Expository Times.
GAP = Geographie des alten Palästina.
GGA = Göttingische Gelehrte Anzeigen.
GGN = Nachrichten der königl. Gesellschaft der Wissenschaften zu Göttingen.
GJV = Geschichte des Jüdischen Volkes.
GVI = Geschichte des Volkes Israel.
HCM = Higher Criticism and the Monuments.
HE = Historia Ecclesiastica.
HGHL = Historical Geog. of Holy Land.
HI = History of Israel.
HJP = History of the Jewish People.
HPM = History, Prophecy, and the Monuments.
HPN = Hebrew Proper Names.
IJG = Israelitische und Jüdische Geschichte.
JBL = Journal of Biblical Literature.
JDTh = Jahrbücher für deutsche Theologie.
JQR = Jewish Quarterly Review.
JRAS = Journal of the Royal Asiatic Society.
JSL = Journal of Sacred Literature.
JThSt = Journal of Theological Studies.
KAT = Die Keilinschriften und das Alte Test.
KGF = Keilinschriften u. Geschichtsforschung.
KIB = Keilinschriftliche Bibliothek.
LB = The Land and the Book.
LCBl = Literarisches Centralblatt.
LOT = Introd. to the Literature of the Old Test.

MNDPV = Mittheilungen u. Nachrichten d. deutschen Pal.-Vereins.
NHWB = Neuhebräisches Wörterbuch.
NTZG = Neutestamentliche Zeitgeschichte.
ON = Otium Norvicense.
OP = Origin of the Psalter.
OTJC = The Old Test. in the Jewish Church
PB = Polychrome Bible.
PEF = Palestine Exploration Fund.
PEFSt = Quarterly Statement of the same.
PSBA = Proceedings of Soc. of Bibl. Archæology.
PRE = Real-Encyklopädie für protest. Theologie und Kirche.
QPB = Queen's Printers' Bible.
RB = Revue Biblique.
REJ = Revue des Études Juives.
RP = Records of the Past.
RS = Religion of the Semites.
SBE = Sacred Books of the East.
SBOT = Sacred Books of Old Test.
SK = Studien und Kritiken.
SP = Sinai and Palestine.
SWP = Memoirs of the Survey of W. Palestine.
ThL or *ThLZ* = Theol. Literaturzeitung.
ThT = Theol. Tijdschrift.
TS = Texts and Studies.
TSBA = Transactions of Soc. of Bibl. Archæology.
TU = Texte und Untersuchungen.
WAI = Western Asiatic Inscriptions.
WZKM = Wiener Zeitschrift für Kunde des Morgenlandes.
ZA = Zeitschrift für Assyriologie.
ZAW or *ZATW* = Zeitschrift für die Alttest. Wissenschaft.
ZDMG = Zeitschrift der Deutschen Morgenländischen Gesellschaft.
ZDPV = Zeitschrift des Deutschen Palästina-Vereins.
ZKSF = Zeitschrift für Keilschriftforschung.
ZKW = Zeitschrift für kirchliche Wissenschaft.
ZNTW = Zeitschrift für die Neutest. Wissenschaft.
ZThK = Zeitschrift f. Theologie u. Kirche.

A small superior number designates the particular edition of the work referred to : as *KAT*[2], *LOT*[6].

AUTHORS OF ARTICLES IN VOL. I

Rev. ROBERT M. ADAMSON, M.A., Ardrossan.

Rev. WALTER F. ADENEY, D.D., Professor of Theology and Principal of the Lancashire College, Manchester.

Rev. P. HENDERSON AITKEN, B.Sc., B.D., Glasgow.

Rev. GROSS ALEXANDER, S.T.D., late Professor of New Testament Greek and Exegesis in Vanderbilt University, Nashville.

Rev. WILLOUGHBY C. ALLEN, M.A., Chaplain, Fellow, and Lecturer in Theology and Hebrew, Exeter College, Oxford.

Rev. WILLIAM P. ARMSTRONG, D.D., Professor of New Testament Literature and Exegesis in Princeton Theological Seminary, N.J.

Rev. BENJAMIN WISNER BACON, D.D., Professor of New Testament Criticism and Interpretation in Yale University, New Haven.

Rev. P. MORDAUNT BARNARD, B.D., late Rector of Headley, Epsom.

Rev. FRANCIS R. BEATTIE, Ph.D., D.D., LL.D., Professor of Apologetics and Systematic Theology in the Presbyterian Theological Seminary of Kentucky.

Very Rev. JOHN HENRY BERNARD, D.D., Dean of St. Patrick's, Fellow of Trinity College, and Archbishop King's Lecturer in Divinity in the University of Dublin.

Rev. HARRY BISSEKER, M.A., The Leysian Mission, London.

Rev. ARCHIBALD BISSET, Ratho.

Rev. ANDREW N. BOGLE, M.A., Leith.

Rev. ALBERT BONUS, M.A., Alphington, Exeter.

Rev. GEORGE H. BOX, M.A., late Hebrew Master, Merchant Taylors' School, London, Rector of Linton, Ross.

Rev. E. P. BOYS-SMITH, M.A., Vicar of Hordle, Brockenhurst.

Rev. J. B. BRISTOW, B.D., Rector of Clondalkin, Co. Dublin.

Rev. MORISON BRYCE, Baldernock, Milngavie.

Rev. A. E. BURN, D.D., Rector of Handsworth, Birmingham, and Prebendary of Lichfield.

Rev. DUGALD CLARK, B.D., Glassary, Lochgilphead.

Rev. JOHN S. CLEMENS, M.A., Principal of Ranmoor College, Sheffield.

Rev. ARTHUR W. COOKE, M.A., Newcastle-on-Tyne.

Rev. JAMES COOPER, D.D., Professor of Ecclesiastical History in the University of Glasgow.

Rev. HUGH H. CURRIE, B.D., Keig, Aberdeenshire.

Rev. EDGAR DAPLYN, London.

Right Rev. CHARLES FREDERICK D'ARCY, D.D., Bishop of Clogher.

Rev. EDWIN CHARLES DARGAN, D.D., LL.D., Professor of Homiletics and Ecclesiology in the Southern Baptist Theological Seminary, Louisville, Ky.

Rev. W. THEOPHILUS DAVISON, D.D., Professor of Theology in Richmond Theological College, Surrey.

Rev. PERCY DEARMER, M.A., Vicar of St. Mary's the Virgin, Primrose Hill, London.

Rev. FRANCIS BRIGHAM DENIO, D.D., Professor of Old Testament Language and Literature in Bangor Theological Seminary, Maine.

Rev. JAMES DENNEY, D.D., Professor of New Testament Language, Literature, and Theology in the United Free Church College, Glasgow.

Rev. C. T. DIMONT, M.A., Vicar of Holy Trinity, Halifax.

Rev. MARCUS DODS, D.D., Professor of Exegetical Theology in the New College, Edinburgh.

Rev. HENRY E. DOSKER, D.D., Professor of Church History in the Presbyterian Theological Seminary of Kentucky.

Rev. F. HOMES DUDDEN, B.D., Fellow of Lincoln College, Oxford.

Rev. ALEXANDER A. DUNCAN, B.D., Auchterless, Aberdeenshire.

Rev. HUGH DUNCAN, B.D., Garturk, Coatbridge.

Rev. W. H. DUNDAS, B.D., Curate Assistant of St. Thomas's, Belfast.

Rev. WILLIAM HENRY DYSON, Edgerton, Huddersfield.

Rev. GEORGE BOARDMAN EAGER, D.D., Professor of Biblical Introduction and Pastoral Theology in the Southern Baptist Theological Seminary, Louisville, Ky.

Rev. WILLIAM EWING, M.A., Edinburgh, formerly of Tiberias, Palestine.

Rev. J. W. FALCONER, B.D., Halifax, Nova Scotia.

Rev. R. A. FALCONER, D.Litt., D.D., Principal of the Presbyterian Theological College, Halifax, Nova Scotia.

Rev. GEORGE FARMER, formerly Vicar of Hartlip, Kent.

Rev. J. H. FARMER, Professor in M‘Master University, Toronto.

Rev. C. L. FELTOE, D.D., Rector of Duxford, Cambridge.

Rev. ADAM FYFE FINDLAY, M.A., Arbroath.

Rev. J. DICK FLEMING, B.D., Tranent.

Rev. FRANK HUGH FOSTER, Ph.D., D.D., lately Professor of Systematic Theology in the Pacific Seminary, Berkeley, Cal.

Rev. WILLIAM BARRETT FRANKLAND, M.A., late Fellow of Clare College, Cambridge, and Assistant-Chaplain at Giggleswick School.

Rev. ROBERT SLEIGHTHOUSE FRANKS, M.A., B.Litt., Birmingham.

Rev. NORMAN FRASER, B.D., Edinburgh.

Rev. HENRY WILLIAM FULFORD, M.A., Fellow of Clare College, Cambridge.

Rev. C. E. GARRAD, M.A., Fellow of Clare College, and Vice-Principal of the Clergy Training School, Cambridge.

Rev. ALFRED ERNEST GARVIE, D.D., Professor of Ethics, Theism, and Comparative Religion in New and Hackney Colleges, London.

Rev. OWEN H. GATES, Ph.D., Professor in Andover Theological Seminary, Mass.

Rev. LUCIEN GAUTIER, Ph.D., Honorary Professor of Old Testament Exegesis and History, Geneva.

Rev. ALFRED S. GEDEN, M.A., Professor of Biblical Literature and Exegesis in Richmond College, Surrey.

Rev. GEORGE HOLLEY GILBERT, Ph.D., D.D., late Professor of New Testament Literature and Interpretation in Chicago Theological Seminary.

Rev. RICHARD GLAISTER, B.D., Kirkcudbright.

TERROT REAVELEY GLOVER, M.A., Fellow and Classical Lecturer, St. John's College, Cambridge.

Rev. CALVIN GOODSPEED, D.D., Professor of Systematic Theology in Baylor University, Waco, Texas.

Rev. GEORGE PEARCE GOULD, M.A., Principal of Regent's Park College, London.

Rev. JAMES GORDON GRAY, D.D., Rome.

Rev. THOMAS GREGORY, M.A., Kilmalcolm.

Rev. Canon CHARLES T. P. GRIERSON, B.D., Rector of Seapatrick, Banbridge, Co. Down.

Rev. JAMES O. HANNAY, M.A., Rector of Aughaval, Westport, Co. Mayo.

Rev. CHARLES HARRIS, D.D., Vicar of Claverley, Wolverhampton, late Lecturer in Theology in St. David's College, Lampeter.

Rev. JOHN HERKLESS, D.D., Professor of Church History in the University of St. Andrews.

Rev. F. R. MONTGOMERY HITCHCOCK, B.D., Rector of Kinnitty, King's Co.

Rev. CASPAR WISTAR HODGE, D.D., Lecturer in Systematic Theology in Princeton Theological Seminary, N.J.

Rev. A. MITCHELL HUNTER, M.A., Cardross, Dumbartonshire.

Rev. WILLIAM RALPH INGE, D.D., Vicar of All Saints', Ennismore Gardens, London, late Fellow and Tutor of Hertford College, Oxford.

Rev. JAMES IVERACH, D.D., Professor of Apologetics and Dogmatics, Principal of the United Free Church College, Aberdeen.

Rev. H. L. JACKSON, M.A., Vicar of St. Mary's, Huntingdon.

Rev. ARTHUR JENKINSON, Innellan, Greenock.

A. J. JENKINSON, M.A., Fellow of Brasenose College, Oxford.

Rev. E. GRIFFITH-JONES, B.A., London.

Rev. W. S. KERR, B.D., Vicar of Ballywalter, Co. Down.

Rev. THOMAS B. KILPATRICK, D.D., Professor of Systematic Theology in Knox College, Toronto.

Rev. RICHARD JOHN KNOWLING, D.D., Canon of Durham, and Professor of Divinity in the University of Durham.

Rev. DAVID M. W. LAIRD, M.A., Edinburgh.

Rev. JOHN C. LAMBERT, D.D., Fenwick, Kilmarnock.

Rev. ROBERT LEGGAT, Berwick-on-Tweed.

Rev. JOHN ROBERT LEGGE, M.A., Buckhurst Hill, Essex.

Rev. WILLIAM F. LOFTHOUSE, M.A., Professor in the Theological College, Handsworth, Birmingham.

Rev. CHARLES SCOTT MACALPINE, B.D., Manchester.

Rev. A. B. MACAULAY, M.A., Dundee.

Rev. GEORGE M‘HARDY, D.D., Kirkcaldy.

Rev. GEORGE M. MACKIE, D.D., Chaplain to the Church of Scotland at Beyrout, Syria.

Rev. DUNCAN A. MACKINNON, M.A., Marykirk, Kincardineshire.

Rev. ROBERT MACKINTOSH, D.D., Professor of Christian Ethics, Apologetics, and Sociology in the Lancashire Independent College, Manchester.

Right Rev. ARTHUR JOHN MACLEAN, D.D., Bishop of Moray.

Rev. A. H. M‘NEILE, B.D., Fellow and Dean of Sidney Sussex College, Cambridge.

Rev. JAMES EDMOND M‘OUAT, B.D., Logiealmond, Perthshire.

Rev. WILLIAM M. M‘PHEETERS, D.D., Professor of Old Testament Literature and Exegesis, Columbia Theological Seminary, S.C.

Rev. ROBERT MACPHERSON, D.D., Elgin.

Rev. JOSEPH T. L. MAGGS, D.D., Leeds.

Rev. JOHN TURNER MARSHALL, D.D., Principal of the Baptist College, Manchester.

Rev. A. STUART MARTIN, B.D., Scone, Perth.

Rev. G. CURRIE MARTIN, D.D., Professor of New Testament Theology and Patristics in the United College, Bradford.

E. W. GURNEY MASTERMAN, M.D., F.R.C.S., F.R.G.S., D.P.H., Jerusalem, Syria.

Rev. SHAILER MATHEWS, D.D., Professor of New Testament History and Interpretation in the University of Chicago.

Rev. J. H. MAUDE, M.A., Rector of Hilgay, Downham Market.

Late Rev. PREBENDARY F. MEYRICK, M.A., Rector of Blickling, Aylesham.

Rev. ANDREW MILLER, M.A., Glasgow.

Rev. W. J. S. MILLER, B.D., Houndwood, Reston.

Rev. GEORGE MILLIGAN, D.D., Caputh, Perthshire.

Rev. JAMES MOFFATT, D.D., Dundonald, Ayrshire.

Rev. W. S. MONTGOMERY, B.D., Abbeyleix, Queen's County.

Rev. W. W. MOORE, D.D., President of Union Theological Seminary, Richmond, Va.

Rev. W. MORGAN, M.A., Tarbolton, Ayrshire.

Rev. R. WADDY MOSS, D.D., Professor of Classics in the Didsbury College, Manchester.

Rev. JOHN MUIR, B.D., Kirkcowan, Wigtownshire.

Rev. JOSEPH MUIR, B.D., Edinburgh.

Rev. LEWIS A. MUIRHEAD, D.D., Broughty Ferry.

Rev. GEORGE MURRAY, B.D., Sauchie, Alloa.

Rev. JAMES ROSS MURRAY, M.A., Manchester.

EBERHARD NESTLE, Ph.D., D.D., Professor at Maulbronn.

Rev. M. R. NEWBOLT, B.A., Vicar of Iffley, Oxford.

Rev. ALBERT HENRY NEWMAN, D.D., LL.D., Professor of Church History in Baylor University, Texas.

Rev. THOMAS NICOL, D.D., Professor of Biblical Criticism in the University of Aberdeen.

Rev. W. O. E. OESTERLEY, B.D., Organizing Secretary of the Parochial Missions to the Jews at Home and Abroad.

Rev. J. W. OMAN, D.Phil., Alnwick.

Rev. JAMES PATRICK, B.D., B.Sc., Burntisland.

Rev. WILLIAM PATRICK, D.D., Principal of Manitoba College, Winnipeg.

ARTHUR S. PEAKE, B.D., Professor of Biblical Exegesis and Dean of the Faculty of Theology, Victoria University, Manchester.

Rev. JOHN ROBERT VAN PELT, Ph.D., Lewisburg, Pa.

Rev. ALFRED PLUMMER, D.D., late Master of University College, Durham.

Rev. E. B. POLLARD, Georgetown, Ky.

Rev. CYRIL HENRY PRICHARD, M.A., Rector of Wiston, Steyning, Sussex.

Rev. F. S. RANKEN, M.A., Rector of South Walsham, Norwich.

Rev. W. M. RANKIN, B.D., Glasgow.

Rev. JOHN REID, M.A., Inverness.

Rev. J. S. RIGGS, D.D., Professor of Biblical Criticism in the Theological Seminary of Auburn, N.Y.

Rev. C. W. RISHELL, D.D., Professor of Historical Theology in Boston University, Mass.

Rev. JOHN EDWARD ROBERTS, B.D., Manchester.

Rev. ARCHIBALD THOMAS ROBERTSON, D.D., Professor of Interpretation of the New Testament in the Southern Baptist Theological Seminary, Louisville, Ky.

Rev. JAMES ROBERTSON, D.D., Whittingehame.

Rev. F. E. ROBINSON, B.D., Professor of Hebrew in the Baptist College, Bristol.

Rev. GEORGE LIVINGSTON ROBINSON, Ph.D., Professor of Old Testament Literature and Exegesis in the M'Cormick Theological Seminary, Chicago.

Rev. ANDREW E. ROSS, B.D., Rector of Portrush, Co. Antrim.

Rev. ALFRED NORMAN ROWLAND, M.A., London.

Rev. JOHN RICHARD SAMPEY, D.D., LL.D., Professor of Interpretation of the Old Testament in the Southern Baptist Theological Seminary, Louisville, Ky.

Rev. WILLIAM SANDAY, D.D., LL.D., D.Sc., Lady Margaret Professor of Divinity, and Canon of Christ Church, Oxford, Chaplain in Ordinary to H.M. the King.

Rev. CHARLES ANDERSON SCOTT, M.A., London.

Rev. ERNEST F. SCOTT, B.A., Prestwick.

Rev. ROBERT SCOTT, M.A., Professor in Wilson College, Bombay.

Rev. HENRY CLAY SHELDON, D.D., Professor of Systematic Theology in Boston University.

Rev. EDWARD SHILLITO, M.A., Brighton.

Rev. S. J. RAMSAY SIBBALD, B.D., Crathie, Ballater.

Rev. J. G. SIMPSON, M.A., Principal of the Clergy School, Leeds.

Rev. DAVID SMITH, M.A., Tulliallan.

Rev. HAROLD SMITH, M.A., Rector of Grimley, Worcester.

Rev. J. CROMARTY SMITH, B.D., Coatdyke, Coatbridge.

W. TAYLOR SMITH, M.A., Sevenoaks, Kent.

Rev. HARRY HERBERT SNELL, B.A., Reading.

Late Rev. J. SOUTAR, M.A., Tiberias, Palestine.

ALEXANDER SOUTER, M.A., Litt.D., Yates Professor of New Testament Exegesis in Mansfield College, Oxford.

Rev. W. B. STEVENSON, B.D., Professor of Hebrew and Old Testament Introduction in the Theological College, Bala.

Rev. GEORGE WAUCHOPE STEWART, B.D., Aberdeen.

Rev. ROBERT LAIRD STEWART, D.D., Professor in Lincoln University, Chester Co., Penn.

Rev. DARWELL STONE, M.A., Pusey Librarian, Oxford.

Rev. G. GORDON STOTT, B.D., London.

Rev. R. H. STRACHAN, M.A., Elie.

Rev. A. POLLOK SYM, B.D., Lilliesleaf.

Rev. JOHN G. TASKER, D.D., Professor of Biblical Literature and Exegesis in Handsworth College, Birmingham.

Rev. R. BRUCE TAYLOR, M.A., Aberdeen.

Rev. MILTON SPENCER TERRY, D.D., LL.D., Professor of Christian Doctrine in the Garrett Biblical Institute, Northwestern University.

Rev. G. W. THATCHER, B.D., Professor of Hebrew and Old Testament History in Mansfield College, Oxford.

Rev. W. H. GRIFFITH THOMAS, D.D., Principal of Wycliffe Hall, Oxford.

Rev. WILLIAM D. THOMSON, M.A., Edinburgh.

Rev. EDWARD HARPER TITCHMARSH, M.A., Sheffield.

Rev. GEERHARDUS VOS, Ph.D., D.D., Professor of Biblical Theology in Princeton Theological Seminary, N.J.

Rev. G. H. S. WALPOLE, D.D., Rector of Lambeth.

Rev. BENJAMIN BRECKINRIDGE WARFIELD, D.D., LL.D., Professor of Theology in Princeton Theological Seminary, N.J.

Rev. GEORGE C. WATT, B.D., Edinkillie.

Rev. THOMAS H. WEIR, B.D., M.R.A.S., Lecturer in Hebrew and Arabic in the University of Glasgow.

Professor Dr. JOHANNES WEISS of the University of Marburg.

Rev. NEWPORT J. D. WHITE, D.D., Lecturer in Hebrew and Divinity in the University of Dublin, and Canon of St. Patrick's Cathedral.

Rev. B. WHITEFOORD, D.D., Prebendary of Salisbury Cathedral and Principal of the Theological College, Salisbury.

Rev. A. R. WHITHAM, M.A., Principal of the Culham Training College, Abingdon.

Rev. J. R. WILLIS, B.D., Rector of Preban and Moyne, Rathdrum, Co. Wicklow.

HERBERT G. WOOD, M.A., Fellow of Jesus College, Cambridge.

Rev. NATHAN E. WOOD, President of the Theological Seminary, and Professor of Christian Theology, Newton Centre, Mass.

Rev. ARTHUR W. WOTHERSPOON, M.A., Glasgow.

Rev. T. H. WRIGHT, Edinburgh.

Rev. ANDREW C. ZENOS, D.D., Professor of Biblical Theology in the M'Cormick Theological Seminary, Chicago.

DICTIONARY OF CHRIST
AND THE GOSPELS

A

AARON.—The name occurs only 5 times in the NT. Three of the passages contain historical references only : Lk 1⁵ where Elisabeth is described as ' of the daughters of Aaron ' ; Ac 7⁴⁰ which refers to the request of the Israelites that Aaron would 'make them gods'; and He 9⁴ 'Aaron's rod that budded.' The other two passages refer to Aaron's office as high priest, and are directly concerned with the Christian doctrine of the priesthood of Christ. In He 5⁴ we read, ' And no man taketh the honour unto himself, but when he is called of God, even as was Aaron ' ; and He 7¹¹ speaks of another priest after the order of Melchizedek, who should ' not be reckoned after the order of Aaron.' It is as the representative high priest that Aaron has been regarded as a type of Christ.

The two points on which the writer of Hebrews insists are, one of comparison, and one of contrast. On the one hand, Christ, like Aaron, did not take His priestly office on Himself, but was directly appointed by God (5⁵) ; on the other, the Aaronic type of priesthood is sharply distinguished from that of our Lord in certain fundamental respects. Christ was indeed divinely appointed : He was prepared for service, in being made like His brethren (2¹⁷), and fitted by His sympathy (4¹⁵) and fidelity to undertake priestly work on their behalf ; through His death on the cross He offered Himself as a sacrifice, apparently on earth and certainly in heaven as a temple not made with hands (9²⁴) ; He is able to save to the uttermost those who come to God through Him as priest, seeing He ever lives to make priestly intercession for them (7²⁵). Thus far He was Aaron's antitype. But the analogy fails most seriously in certain important features, as the writer of Hebrews shows. Christ's priesthood was not according to the Law. If He were on earth, He would not be a priest at all, springing as He did from Judah, not from Levi (7¹⁴). He did not hold His office in virtue of earthly descent, nor was He limited to an earthly sanctuary, nor did He present to God a sin-offering which could be, or needed to be, frequently repeated (9²⁴ᶠ·). None of the sacrifices of the Law could ' make perfect as pertaining to the conscience ' (9⁹). At best they procured only a limited access to God. Into the holiest place the high priest was permitted to enter only once a year, and then in virtue of sacrifices offered for

his own sins, as well as the people's (9⁷). Christ's priesthood was 'after the order of Melchizedek' (6²⁰), eternal : His sacrifice was a spiritual one, offered once for all ; it is impossible to think of the repetition on earth of that offering which 'through (the) eternal Spirit' (9¹⁴) our glorified High Priest presents continually in 'a more perfect tabernacle' (v.¹¹) in heaven itself, for us. He was made a priest, not according to any legal enactment belonging to earth and finding its expression in the flesh ; but dynamically, according to the enduring power of an indissoluble life (7¹⁶).

Thus Christ may well be spoken of as the second Adam, but not as a second Aaron. The lines of Bishop Wordsworth's hymn, ' Now our heavenly Aaron enters, Through His blood within the veil,' can be defended only in so far as the name Aaron is synonymous with high priest. The personal name suggests just those limitations which the generic name avoids, and which the writer of Hebrews expressly warns us must on no account be attributed to our great High Priest who has passed into the heavens. So far as the doctrine of Christ is concerned, it is well to follow Scripture usage and to speak of Him as our Eternal High Priest, rather than to press an analogical or typical relation to Aaron, which fails at many cardinal points.

LITERATURE.—For the further discussion of the subject see Westcott and A. B. Davidson on *Hebrews*, especially the detached note of the latter on the Priesthood of Christ ; also Milligan's Baird Lectures on *The Ascension and Heavenly Priesthood of our Lord*, and the art. of Dr. Denney on 'Priesthood in NT' in Hastings' *DB*, vol. iv.   W. T. DAVISON.

ABBA.—An Aramaic word preserved by St. Mark in our Lord's prayer in Gethsemane (14³⁶ Ἀββᾶ ὁ πατήρ, πάντα δυνατά σοι), and given twice in the same association with ὁ πατήρ by St. Paul (Ro 8¹⁵ ἐλάβετε πνεῦμα υἱοθεσίας ἐν ᾧ κράζομεν, Ἀββᾶ ὁ πατήρ ; and Gal 4⁶ ἐξαπέστειλεν ὁ Θεὸς τὸ Πνεῦμα τοῦ υἱοῦ αὐτοῦ εἰς τὰς καρδίας ἡμῶν κρᾶζον, Ἀββᾶ ὁ πατήρ). A difficulty arises both as to the spelling and the pronunciation of the word Abba, and also as to its being found in all the above passages joined to ὁ πατήρ.

1. Abba (ἀββᾶ) corresponds to the Aramaic אַבָּא *abbâ*, which is the definite state of אַב *âbh* (construct state אַב *abh*), and means 'Father,' unless it is used for 'my Father' (אַבָּא for אָבִי) as in Gn 19³⁴ᵃ (Targ. of Onkelos and pseudo-Jonathan ; see Dal-

man, *Aramäisch-Neuhebräisches Wörterbuch*, s.v.,
Gramm. p. 162, and *Words of Jesus*, p. 192 [Dalman says that the suffix of 1 pers. sing. is 'deliberately avoided with אַב and is supplied by the determinative form']). It is not, however, quite certain that the word was pronounced *abbâ* in Palestine in our Lord's time. As the points were not invented till many centuries after, we cannot be sure that *abbâ* was then the definite state rather than *abhâ* as in Syriac; and we have no indication except the Greek transliteration that the *b* was then doubled. But the fact that, when points were first used (A.D. 700?), the *daghesh* was employed for the definite state of this word in the Targumic literature, coupled with the doubling of the β in the Greek, affords a presumption that the *b* was hard and doubled in this word at the beginning of our era [Dalman gives for the definite state אַבָּא Gn 44¹⁹, or אָב Nu 25¹⁴, or in Palestinian Targum also אַבָּא; with other pronominal suffixes we have אֲבוּהִי etc., and the pl. definite state is אֲבָהָתָא]. The Syriac, on the other hand, has *b* aspirated throughout, ܐܰܒ *abh*, ܐܰܒܳܐ *abhâ* (pron. *av*, *avâ*, or *aw*, *awâ*), etc., and the distinction between ܐܰܒܳܐ *abâ*, *a spiritual father*, and ܐܰܒܳܐ *avâ*, *a natural father*, which the grammarians make, appears not to be founded on any certain basis, nor to agree with the manuscripts (Payne-Smith, *Thesaurus Syriacus*, s.v.). The proper name ܐܰܒܳܐ also in Syriac has always aspirated *b*, while Dalman (*Wörterbuch*) gives for Targumic אַבָּא, and says it is an abbreviation of אֲבָיָה. In Mk 14³⁶ (Peshiṭta) Pusey and Gwilliam give ܐܰܒܳܐ as in Massora 1 in the British Museum (Codex Additionalis 12138, Nestorianus, A.D. 899); the American edition prints ܐܰܒܳܐ (*i.e.* with ܳ) in all three NT places; but this is rather a following of the grammarians than of good manuscripts. It is very noteworthy, however, that the Ḥarkleian version in the Markan passage spells the word ܐܰܒܒܳܐ, transliterating the Greek directly back into Syriac, rather than using the Syriac word itself.

John Lightfoot (*Horæ Hebraicæ* on Mk 14³⁶) remarks that the Targum, in translating the OT, never renders a 'civil' father, *i.e.* a master, prince, lord, etc., by אַבָּא, but only a natural father, or a father who adopts; in the former sense they use some other word. But this throws no light on the pronunciation of Abba.

It is to be noticed that it is not certain how the Greeks of the 1st cent. themselves pronounced ἀββᾶ, whether *abbâ* or, as the modern Greeks pronounce it, *avvâ*. The word is not found in the LXX. It passed into ecclesiastical Latin with a doubled *b*, and gave us such words as 'abbot,' 'abbacy,' etc.

But does it mean 'Father' or 'my Father'? If it be a Jewish formula or fixed manner of beginning prayer, it may well be the latter. We must, however, note that whatever be the way of accounting for 'Αββᾶ ὁ πατήρ (see below), the originators or originator of that phrase in Greek, whether the Jews, or our Lord, or St. Paul, or the Second Evangelist, seem to have taken 'Αββᾶ to mean merely 'Father.' And the same is probably true of the translators of the Peshiṭta. The Sinaitic Syriac, however, appears tó read ܐܰܒܝ *my Father* (see below). The Curetonian Syriac is wanting here.

2. We have next to account for the association of 'Αββᾶ in its Greek dress with ὁ πατήρ in all the three places where it occurs in NT. In Mk 14³⁶ the Peshiṭta reads ܐܰܒܐ ܐܰܒܐ ܐܰܒܝ 'Father, my Father,' and the Sinaitic Syriac has simply ܐܰܒܝ 'my Father.' In Ro 8¹⁵ and Gal 4⁶ the Peshiṭta reads ܐܰܒܐ ܐܰܒܐ ܐܰܒܘܢ. All these appear to be mere expedients adopted to avoid the awkwardness of repeating ܐܰܒܐ, and they do not really throw light on the origin of the Greek phrase.

We may first take as a supposition that our Lord, praying in Gethsemane, used the Aramaic language, and therefore said 'Abba' only, and that ὁ πατήρ is the Evangelist's explanation, for Greek readers, of the Aramaic word. St. Mark undoubtedly reports several Aramaic words, and except in the case of the well-known 'Rabbi,' 'Rabboni' (9⁵ 10⁵¹ etc.), explains them. But then he always uses a formula, ὅ ἐστιν (3¹⁷ 7¹¹. ³⁴) or ὅ ἐστι μεθερμηνευόμενον (5⁴¹ 15³⁴). It is suggested that in the case of Abba the familiarity of the word would make the connecting formula unnecessary; but the same consideration would make it unnecessary to explain it at all. Another suggestion is that the solemnity of the context would make the formula incongruous. The strongest argument for ὁ πατήρ being an addition of the Evangelist is that, whatever view we take of our Lord's having made use of Greek in ordinary speech, it is extremely unlikely that His prayers were in that language; and if He prayed in Aramaic, He would only say 'Abba.' It is the common experience of bilingual countries that though the acquired language may be in constant use for commerce or the ordinary purposes of life, the native tongue is tenaciously retained for devotion and prayer. Sanday-Headlam's supposition (*Romans*, in loc.), that our Lord used both words spontaneously, with deep emotion, might be quite probable if He prayed in the foreign tongue, Greek; but scarcely so if He prayed in the native Aramaic (see, however, below).

If ὁ πατήρ be due to St. Mark, it is probably not a mere explanation for the benefit of Greek readers. The suggestion that 'Αββᾶ ὁ πατήρ had become a quasi-liturgical formula, possibly even among the Jews, or more probably among the Christians, would account for its introduction in a prayer, where interpretations would be singularly out of place. And this suggestion would account for St. Paul's using the phrase twice, in two Epistles written about the same time, indeed, but to two widely distant Churches. St. Paul is not in the habit of introducing Aramaic words ('Maran atha' in 1 Co 16²² is an exception), and if he were not quoting a well-known form, it is unlikely that he would have introduced one in writing to the Romans and Galatians. It is not probable, however, that he is quoting or thinking of our Lord's words in Gethsemane, for there is nothing in the context to suggest this.

If the phrase be a liturgical formula, we may account for it in various ways. J. B. Lightfoot (*Galatians*, in loc.) suggests that it may have originated among Hellenistic Jews; or else among Palestinian Jews, after they had learned Greek, as 'an expression of importunate entreaty.' He prefers the latter view, thinking that perhaps our Lord Himself used both words. He apparently means that Jesus took the Greek word into His Aramaic prayer; and he quotes from Schöttgen a similar case where a woman entreats a judge and addresses him as מרי כירי 'My lord, lord,' the second word being equivalent to the first, except for the possessive suffix, and being a transliteration of κύριε. Chase ('The Lord's Prayer in the Early Church,' in the Cambridge *Texts and Studies*, vol. ⅼ p. 23) has suggested another origin for the phrase, which would place its home, not among the Jews (for which there is no evidence), but among the Christians. He suggests that it is due to the shorter or Lukan form of the Lord's Prayer (Lk 11²ᶠᶠ·). The Aramaic shorter form would begin with Abba, for the Greek begins with Πάτερ; and the hypothesis is that the early Christians in the intensity of their devotion repeated the first word of the prayer in either language. A somewhat similar phenomenon is seen in the repetitions for emphasis in Rev 9¹¹ 12⁹ 20², where the names are given in both languages. Such a repetition is possible only in a bilingual country. That it is the shorter form of the Lord's Prayer that is used (if Dr. Chase's hypothesis be true), is seen from the Aramaic אַבָּא Abba. If the longer form had been in question, Πάτερ ἡμῶν, the initial word of the Aramaic would have had the possessive pronominal suffix of 1 pers. pl., and would be אֲבוּנָא *ăbhúná*. It is a confirmation of this theory that the words which follow, 'Not what I will but what thou wilt,' recall 'Thy will be done' of the Lord's Prayer; compare especially Mt 26⁴² γενηθήτω τὸ θέλημά σου, the exact words of the longer form of the Lord's Prayer. This shows that both Evangelists had that prayer in their minds when relating the agony. The only consideration which militates against the theory is that ὁ πατήρ is used for Πάτερ. The nominative with the article is, however, often used in NT, by a Hebrew analogy, for an emphatic vocative, and the desire for emphasis may account for its use here.   A. J. MACLEAN.

ABEL (הֶבֶל, Ἄβελ).—**1.** The name occurs in the Gospels only in Mt 23³⁵ ‖ Lk 11⁵¹, where Jesus declares that the blood of the prophets will be required of this generation. The passage is one of a series of invectives against Pharisaism, collected in Mt 23, parts of which are preserved in Lk 11. 13. 14. 20. 21. Abel is named as the first of the long line of martyrs whose blood had been shed during the period covered by the OT, the last being Zachariah (which see). 'In both cases the ἐκζήτησις is indicated: "the voice of thy brother's blood crieth unto me from the ground" (Gn 4¹⁰); "the Lord look upon it, and require it" (2 Ch 24²²).' In St. Matthew the words are addressed to the Pharisees in the 2nd person: 'that upon you may come every righteous blood [*i.e.* the blood of each righteous person] shed upon the earth, from the blood of Abel the righteous, until the blood of Zachariah . . . etc.' In St. Luke the passage is thrown into the 3rd person: 'that the blood of all the prophets which hath been shed from the foundation of the world may be required of this generation, from the blood of Abel until the blood of Zachariah . . . etc.'

The description of Abel in St. Matthew as 'the righteous' is noteworthy, and should be compared with He 11⁴. In the story of Abel nothing whatever is said as to his moral character; the contrast between him and his brother lay in the fact that 'Jehovah had respect unto Abel and to his offering; but unto Cain and to his offering he had not respect.' The writer of the Epistle to the Hebrews says that it was faith which led Abel to offer the more excellent sacrifice; but wherein the excellence consisted the narrative of Genesis does not explain. But the expression τοῦ δικαίου seems to reflect the Pharisaic conception of righteousness as that which 'consisted primarily in the observance of all the rites and ceremonies prescribed in the law' (cf. Lk 1⁶). Abel's offering must have been preferred presumably because it was in some way more to

God's liking—more correct. This, however, was not consonant with Christ's idea of righteousness—'except your righteousness shall abound beyond that of the scribes and Pharisees, ye shall not enter into the kingdom of heaven' (Mt 5²⁰). It may be concluded, therefore, that St. Luke has preserved the more original form of Christ's words, and that 'the righteous' is an addition in Mt 23³⁵ due to current Jewish conceptions.

2. It is possible that Christ had the story of Abel in mind when He spoke of the devil as being 'a murderer (ἀνθρωποκτόνος) from the beginning,' *i.e.* the instigator of murder as he is of lies (Jn 8⁴⁴). But the passage may be a reference to the introduction of death into the world by the fall of Adam.

3. In He 12²⁴ the 'blood of Abel' is contrasted with the 'blood of sprinkling' under the new dispensation. In Gn 4¹⁰ God says: 'Hark! (קוֹל) thy brother's blood crieth unto me from the ground,' *i.e.* it pleads for vengeance. But the blood of sprinkling 'speaketh something better' (κρεῖττον λαλοῦντι): it is the blood shed in ratification of a New Covenant, whose mediator is Jesus.

LITERATURE.—The most recent commentaries on Matthew and Luke (*ad locc.*); Wright, *Synopsis of the Gospels in Greek*, p. 232; Sanday-Headlam, *Romans*, pp. 28–31, on δίκαιος and its cognates; Driver, *Genesis* (in Westminster commentaries); Dillmann, 'Genesis,' in *Kurzgef. exeget. Handb. z. AT* [Eng. tr. by Stevenson, Edinburgh, 1897]; Marcus Dods, 'Genesis' in *Expositor's Bible*.   A. H. M'NEILE.

ABGAR.—Between the years B.C. 99 and A.D. 217 eight (or ten) kings or toparchs of Edessa in Osrhoëne bore this name. It is with the toparch that ruled in the time of our Saviour, Abgar Ukkâmâ ('the Black,' *c.* B.C. 13 to A.D. 50 [Gutschmid], B.C. 9 to A.D. 46 [Dionysius of Telmahar]), that we are here concerned, owing to the legendary accounts of his correspondence with Jesus, accepted as historical fact by Eusebius, and by him given wide currency. Eusebius (*HE* i. 13) relates, without any suggestion of scepticism, that 'king Abgar, who ruled with great glory the nations beyond the Euphrates, being afflicted with a terrible disease which it was beyond the power of human skill to cure, when he heard of the name of Jesus and His miracles, . . . sent a message to Him by a courier and begged Him to heal the disease.' Eusebius proceeds to impart the letter of Abgar and the answer of Jesus, which he claims to have derived directly from the archives of Edessa, and to have translated (or caused to be translated) literally from Syriac into Greek. The letter of Abgar reads as follows:—

'Abgar, ruler of Edessa, to Jesus the excellent Saviour who has appeared in the country of Jerusalem, greeting. I have heard the reports of thee and of thy cures as performed by thee without medicines or herbs. For it is said that with a word only thou makest the blind to see and the lame to walk, that thou cleansest lepers and castest out impure spirits and demons, and that thou healest those afflicted with lingering diseases, and also that thou raisest the dead. And having heard all these things concerning thee, I have concluded that one of two things must be true: either thou art God and hast come down from heaven to do these things, or else thou who doest these things art the Son of God. Wherefore I have written to thee to ask thee that thou wouldest take the trouble to come even to me and heal the disease which I have. For I have been informed that the Jews are murmuring against thee and are plotting to injure thee. But I have a city, small indeed yet honourable, which may suffice for us both.'

The answer of Jesus runs—

'Blessed art thou who hast believed in me when thou thyself hast not seen me. For it stands written concerning me, that they who have seen me will not believe in me, and that they who have not seen me will believe and be saved. But in regard to what thou hast written me, that I should come to thee, it is necessary for me to fulfil all things here for which I have been sent, and after I have fulfilled them thus to be taken up again to Him that sent me. But after I have been taken up I will send to thee one of my disciples, that he may heal thy disease and give life to thee and those who are with thee.'

From an accompanying narrative in the Syriac language, giving an account of the fulfilment of Christ's promise, Eusebius quotes at considerable length. A brief summary of the contents of this document must here suffice. Judas, also called Thomas, is said to have sent Thaddæus, one of the Seventy, to Edessa, soon after the ascension of Jesus. Arriving in Edessa he took lodgings, and without reporting himself at the court engaged extensively in works of healing. When the king heard thereof he suspected that he was the disciple promised by Jesus, and had him brought to court. On the appearance of Thaddæus 'a great vision appeared to Abgar in the countenance of Thaddæus,' which led the former to prostrate himself before the latter, to the astonishment of the courtiers, who did not see the vision. Having become assured that his guest is the promised disciple of Jesus, and that he has come fully empowered to heal and to save on condition of his exercise of faith, Abgar assures Thaddæus that his faith is so strong that, had it not been for the presence of the Romans, he would have sent an army to destroy the Jews that crucified Jesus. Thaddæus assures him that in fulfilment of the Divine plan of redemption Jesus has been taken up to His Father, and, on a further profession of faith in Father and Son, Thaddæus lays his hands upon the king and heals him. Many other healings follow, accompanied by the preaching of the gospel. At Thaddæus' suggestion the king summons the citizens as a body to hear the preaching of the word, and afterwards offers him a rich reward, which is magnanimously refused. According to the Syriac document from which Eusebius quotes, the visit of Thaddæus occurred in the year 340 of the era of the Seleucidæ (corresponding, according to K. Schmidt in *PRE*[2], *sub voc.*, to A.D. 29; according to others, A.D. 30, 31, or 32).

From the same Edessene materials Moses of Chorene, the Armenian historian of the middle of the 5th cent., prepared independently of Eusebius an account of the intercourse between Abgar and Christ and His disciples, which attests the general correctness of Eusebius' work. The fact that Moses was for several years a student in Edessa enhances the value of his account. He represents the reply of Jesus as having been written on His behalf by Thomas the Apostle. In Moses' account occurs the statement that after his conversion Abgarus wrote letters to the emperor Tiberius, to Narses, king of Assyria, to Ardaches, king of Persia, and others, recommending Christianity (*Hist. Arm.* ii. 30–33). Here also appears the legend that Christ sent by Ananias, the courier of Abgar, a picture of Himself impressed upon a handkerchief. This part of the story was still further elaborated by Cedrenus (*Hist. Comp.* p. 176), who represents Ananias, the courier of Abgar, as himself an artist, and as so overcome by the splendour of the countenance of Jesus when attempting to depict it that he was obliged to desist; whereupon Christ, having washed His face, wiped it with a towel which retained His likeness. This picture was taken by Ananias to his master, and it became for the city a sort of talisman. This miraculously produced portrait, or what purported to be such, is said to have been transferred to the church of St. Sophia at Constantinople in the 10th cent., and later to have passed thence to the church of St. Sylvester in Rome, where it is still exhibited for the edification of the faithful. A church in Genoa makes a rival claim to the possession of the original handkerchief portrait.

Any suspicion that Eusebius fabricated the documents that he professes to translate was set aside by the discovery and publication of what have been accepted as the original Syriac documents (*The Doct. of Addai the Apostle*, with an English Translation and Notes, by G. Phillips, London, 1876). The Syriac document contains the story of the portrait, which was probably already current in the time of Eusebius. The Syriac version of the story given by Cureton in his *Ancient Syriac Documents* seems to be an elaborate expansion of that of Eusebius, and to have been composed considerably later.

The letter of Christ to Abgar was declared by a Roman Council in 494 or 495 to be spurious. Tillemont sought to prove the genuineness of the correspondence (*Memoirs*, i. pp. 362, 615), and similar attempts have been made by Welte (*Tübingen Quartalschr.* 1842, p. 335 ff.), Rinck (*Zeitschr. f. Hist. Theol.* 1843, ii. pp. 3–26), Phillips (preface to *The Doct. of Addai*), and Cureton (*Anc. Syr. Doc.*).

It may be assumed that the documents were forged some time before Eusebius used them. Christianity seems to have been introduced into Osrhoëne during the 2nd cent. A.D. The first king known to have favoured Christianity was Abgar VIII. (bar-Manu), who reigned 176–213, and is said to have been on very intimate terms with Bardesanes, the scholarly Gnostic. A Christian church building modelled after the temple in Jerusalem existed in Edessa some time before 202, until, according to the Edessene Chronicle, it was destroyed (middle of the 6th cent.) by flood. As Edessa grew in importance as a Christian centre, with its theological school, its ambition for distinction may have led some not over-scrupulous ecclesiastic to fabricate these documents and to palm them off on the too credulous authorities. The forgery may have occurred early in the 3rd cent. (Zahn), but more probably early in the 4th. The only piece of real information that has come down to us regarding the Abgar of the time of Christ is a very uncomplimentary reference in Tacitus (*Ann.* xii. 12. 14).

LITERATURE.—In addition to the works already mentioned, special reference should be made to Lipsius, *Die edessenische Abgarsage*, 1880, where the available materials are brought under review and critically tested; cf. also Matthes, *Die edessenische Abgarsage auf ihre Fortbildung untersucht*, 1882; Tixeron, *Les origines de l'église d'Edesse et la légende d'Abgar*, 1888; Farrar, *Christ in Art*, p. 79 f.

ALBERT HENRY NEWMAN.

ABIA (AV of Mt 1[7], Lk 1[5]).—See ABIJAH.

ABIATHAR.—The son of Ahimelech, the son of Ahitub, the son of Phinehas, the son of Eli. He is mentioned in Mk 2[25. 26] 'Have ye never read what David did, when he had need, and was an hungred, he, and they that were with him? How he went into the house of God in the days of Abiathar the high priest, and did eat the shewbread?' The RV, however, translates, 'when Abiathar was high priest.' The reference is evidently to 1 S 21, where, according to the Hebrew text, *Ahimelech* gives David the sacred bread. There is thus a discrepancy between the two passages. The facts are these :—The AV, cited above, follows the reading of A and C (ἐπὶ 'Αβιαθὰρ τοῦ ἀρχιερέως), RV follows that of B and א (which omit the article) and the Vulgate ('sub Abiathar principe sacerdotum'). The clause is omitted altogether by D. In the MT of 1 S 21 and 22 and in Ps 52[2] (title) the high priest is Ahimelech the son of Ahitub and the father of David's friend Abiathar. In the Greek text of all these passages, however, the name is *Abimelech*. In 2 S 8[17] and 1 Ch 24[6] Ahimelech (in 1 Ch 18[16] Abimelech) the son of Abiathar is priest along with Zadok, but it is generally supposed that Abiathar the son of Ahimelech is meant. Ahimelech is usually held to be identical also with Ahijah the son of Ahitub of 1 S 14[3. 18].

The discrepancy between Mk 2²⁶ and 1 S 21 f. has been sought to be accounted for in several ways. It may readily be due to a mere *lapsus memoriæ* or *calami*, Abiathar, David's high priest, being a much more familiar figure than his father, just as in Jer 27¹ 'Jehoiakim' is a slip for Zedekiah. It is not impossible that father and son may each have borne both names, according to Arab usage, Abiathar corresponding to the Arab *kunyah*, and Ahimelech being the *ism* or *lakab*, or name proper. It has been suggested that the reference in St. Mark is not to 1 S 21 at all, but to some later unrecorded incident, such as might have occurred during the flight from Absalom. But this is very improbable.*   T. H. WEIR.

ABIDING.—Of the three possible renderings of the Greek μονή and μένω, 'remaining, to remain,' 'dwelling, to dwell,' 'abiding, to abide,' the last is the most satisfactory. The first has the advantage of being akin to the Greek in derivation, but it is too passive in its sense, and in so far as it includes the conception of expectation it is misleading; the second is too local, and is rather the fitting rendering of κατοικία, κατοικέω; the last is an adequate though not a perfect rendering. 'Mansions' (RVm 'abiding-places') is the stately rendering (AV and RV), through the Vulg. *mansiones*, of the noun in Jn 14²; but it becomes impossible in v.²³ of the same chapter when the translators fall back on 'abode.' Further, in the English of to-day 'mansion' suggests merely a building, and that of an ostentatious type. The Scottish 'manse,' self-contained, modest, and secure, would be a nearly exact equivalent if it carried with it more than the idea of a dwelling-house; yet neither it nor 'mansion' has any correspondent verb.

Students who desire to get at the full meaning of verb or noun will find all that is needful in the etymological paragraph *sub voc.* μένω in the larger edition of Liddell and Scott's *Greek Lexicon*. They will discover how rich in language product is the root of this word. The inquiry cannot be pursued further here. It is enough to say that locality enters very slightly into its conception, and that what is dominant is ethical. The leading idea is that of steadfast continuance. This is apparent the moment one turns to the derivative ὑπομονή (cf. Ro 2⁷), the term of Stoic virtue boldly incorporated and transmuted in Christian usage and experience. The primitive noun, however (μονή), reminds Christians more clearly of the sphere in which it is contained, of a life in which it survives, of a power not its own on which it depends, and which in turn it exercises. If, as will be shown, the ethical import of μένω and μονή is dominant in the Gospels, the instances where the verb has a purely local sense, the sense of stopping or staying, may be dismissed. As a matter of fact, the instances are almost entirely confined to the Synoptists, and occur but in twelve passages; the use of the noun is purely Johannine. Only twice in the Synoptists does the verb occur in relation to persons, viz. Lk 24²⁹ in the pathetic appeal of Cleopas and his anonymous comrade, and the gracious response of the risen Christ; and even here there is no ethical significance, for the prepositions which link the verb and the personal pronouns imply only association (μεῖνον μεθ' ἡμῶν), or joint action (εἰσῆλθεν τοῦ μεῖναι σὺν αὐτοῖς).

As soon as the student turns from the Synoptists to the Johannine literature, the idea of 'mansion' (one could wish it were a theological term) becomes full, luminous, and suggestive. St. John uses the verb μένω only thrice in its literal sense in the

Gospel (2¹² 4⁴⁰ 10⁴⁰); he seems almost jealously to reserve it for metaphorical, *i.e.* ethical, application. We are not here concerned with St. John's letters, but it is pertinent to observe that μένω occurs 23 times therein, while it is used in the Gospel some 35 times. Moreover, as if the Evangelist and letter-writer would not suffer the spiritual point to be lost, he perpetually reminds his readers and children of the sphere of 'mansion,' and the source of its power. With a singular and marked uniformity, he employs the preposition ἐν in connexion with the verb. The Evangelist presses the idea not only of intimate relationship, but also of resultant power and blessing.

It is to be observed that, until we reach the great discourses in the chamber and on the way (chs. 14 and 15), we have only passing hints of the nature of the Abiding. The former chapter unfolds its meaning. The difficulties besetting the interpretation of these discourses are familiar to all students of the Fourth Gospel, and need not be dealt with here. They are not adequately met by references to the subjectivity or mysticism of the Evangelist. Our modes of thought, as Bishop Westcott reminds us,* follow a logical sequence; Hebrew modes of thought follow a moral sequence. The sermon to the Apostles in the chamber, especially, bears this moral impress throughout, and is rightly interpreted as the complement to the Sermon on the Mount. But while the connexion is thus somewhat precarious to the reader, certain great ideas or conceptions of the Abiding stand luminously forth for the devout mind. Here is set forth—(1) the Abiding of Christ in the Father; (2) the Abiding of Christ in the Church, as in the individual believer; (3) the issues of the Abiding.

1. *The Abiding of Christ in the Father.*—Here the student is, indeed, on ground most holy. He may not add to the Lord's words, he trembles as he ventures to interpret them. He feels with the patriarch that this place in the Scriptures is dreadful—full of a holy awe. Thus much, however, may be said, that the abiding of Christ in the Father belongs wholly to the operation and energy of the Holy Spirit. The keynote of this truth is struck by the testimony of the Baptist in the preamble of the Gospel (Jn 1³²ᶠ·). It is important to notice that that which was the object of sight to the Baptist was not merely the descent of the Holy Spirit, but the Abiding. And here the careful student will observe that, though the preposition used in these verses is not ἐν but ἐπί, yet the employment of the latter is necessary as linking the descent and the continuous indwelling of the Spirit in the Son. But if any hesitation remains as to the view that the character and sphere of Christ's abiding in the Father lies in and through the indwelling Spirit, it must disappear on consideration of our Lord's words (Jn 14²⁰), 'At that day [the day of *realized life*] ye shall come to know [by the Spirit what is at present a matter of faith only] that I am in my Father.' The thought is inevitably linked with the Spirit's work both in Him and for them. When, therefore, the Lord invites His own to abide in His love (15¹⁰), He does not merely imply that His love is the atmosphere of their discipleship, but, as St. Augustine† suggests, He invites them to abide in that Holy Spirit whose love as fully permeates Him as it is imperfectly exhibited in His disciples.

2. *The Abiding of Christ in the Church, as in the individual believer.*—Our Lord's teaching as to the Abiding in Him refers even more closely to the Church than to the individual. Jn 14 and 15 are penetrated through and through by Pente-

---

* Swete (*St. Mark, ad loc.*) suggests that the clause ἐπὶ Ἀβιαθὰρ ἀρχιερέως, which is peculiar to Mark, may be an editorial note.

* *Introd. to the Gospel of St. John,* ii. 7.
† *Hom. in Joan.* xiv. No. lxxiv, *ad fin.*

costal thought and Pentecostal expectations.
Christ looked eagerly forward to the birthday of
the Spirit-bearing body. He could and does,
indeed, fully abide in the heart of each individual
believer; but that believer is not a mere unit
standing solitary and unsupported. The individual disciple will be a terrible loser unless he
realize his incorporation, his oneness with the
universal body, the body of Christ. But as if to
make sure that this great truth should never
escape His own down the ages, Christ introduces
the great figure of the Vine and the branches (15¹⁻⁶).
The vine was already the symbol of the ancient
Church; * Christ speaks of Himself as the true,
the ideal Vine. But it is as a formula incomplete
without the complement of v.⁵ 'I am the Vine, ye
are the branches.' As a vine is inconceivable
without branches,† so in all devoutness it may be
said He is inconceivable without His disciples.
Again, they draw their life from abiding in Him.
The life may be imperfectly realized, the fruitage
may be disappointing, it may be nothing but
leaves (Mt 21¹⁹); the task of discipline, or of
cleansing (καθαίρειν, Jn 15²ᶠ·) is in the hands of the
Great Husbandman. Thus as in ancient Israel
union with the Church nation was the condition of
life, so in the new dispensation the condition of
life was to be the abiding in Christ. As apart
from the vine the branches are useless since the
living sap is therein no longer, so separated from
Christ there can be no productiveness in Christian
lives. St. John bears record of one more thought
of the highest consolation to Christian hearts.
There is a true analogy and correspondence between
the abiding of Christ in the Father and the abiding
of believers in Him (15¹⁰). Our abidings in Christ,
often so sadly brief, uncertain, precarious, through
the consequences of sin, have still their sublime
counterpart in the abiding of Christ in the
Father.

3. *The issues of the Abiding.*—We have seen that
the Abiding finally depends upon the Spirit's work,
whether in the Church or in the individual heart.
The first fruit of that Spirit is love. The Spirit
moves in this sphere, He manifests and expresses
Himself in love. Thus love furnishes the test of
the indwelling, as truly as it contains the pledge
of a fruitful issue. According, moreover, to
Johannine teaching, this love spread abroad in
the hearts of believers is not a stagnant or sentimental affection. Of the basal or abiding virtues
(1 Co 13¹³) it is the greatest because of its fruitful
action. St. John presents another aspect of this
truth when he shows that obedience and love are
strictly correlated (Jn 15¹⁰). This love is seen in
action. It doeth the will, and the reward of such
loving obedience is final and complete. Those
who in this dutiful and affectionate temper keep
the commandments are raised by Christ from the
base of bond-service to the height of friendship. It
is enough—the fiat has gone forth—'such ones I
have called friends.' ‡

LITERATURE.—A. Maclaren, *Holy of Holies*, 190; A. Murray,
Abide in Christ; T. D. Bernard, *Central Teaching of Jesus
Christ*, 219; J. H. Jowett, *Apostolic Optimism*, 225; B. F.
Westcott, *Peterborough Sermons*, 49, 61; Sir A. Blackwood,
Christian Service, 46; G. B. Stevens, *Johannine Theology*, 258.
                                             B. WHITEFOORD.

ABIJAH (אֲבִיָּה, 'Αβιά, ' Jah is my father'; or more
probably without the particularizing pronoun, 'Jah
is father').—**1.** Son of Rehoboam (Mt 1⁷) by Maacah
(2 Ch 11²⁰—see art. 'Maacah' No. **3** in Hastings' *DB*
iii. 180). Abijah reigned over Judah from about
B.C. 920, and the impressions made by him are
given with some variety in 1 K 15³ and by a later
tradition in 2 Ch 13⁴⁻²². His name is introduced
by St. Matthew simply as a link in the pedigree,

* Hos 10¹, Is 51ff, Jer 22¹.
† Westcott's Commentary, *in loco.*   ‡ Jn 15¹⁵.

in which it is shown that Jesus was both of Jewish
and of royal stock.

2. A descendant of Eleazar, son of Aaron. The
name was attached to the eighth of the twenty-
four courses into which the priests were alleged
to have been divided by David (1 Ch 24¹⁰). Members of only four courses seem to have returned
from the Captivity (Neh 7³⁹⁻⁴², Ezr 2³⁶⁻³⁹ 10¹⁸⁻²²).
According to Jerus. Talm. *Taanith*, iv. 68, these
men were divided into twenty-four courses with a
view to restore the ancient arrangement. The
authority for this statement is not of the best
kind; but the statement itself is substantially
confirmed by Neh 12¹⁻⁷, where twenty-two groups
are referred to (in Neh 12¹²⁻²¹ the number has fallen
to twenty-one, and two of the courses are grouped
under a single representative), and by Ezr 8², where
two other priestly families are mentioned. Slight
changes were probably made in the classification during the process of the resettlement of the country;
but by the time of the Chronicler the arrangement
seems to have become fixed. The course of Abijah
is not mentioned amongst those that returned from
the Exile; but in one of the later rearrangements
the name was attached to a course that afterwards
included Zacharias (Lk 1⁵). Each course was on
duty for a week at a time, but all were expected
to officiate as needed at the three great annual
festivals. It is not possible with our present
materials to determine exactly how the various
services were divided amongst the members of a
course, or at what times in the year Zacharias
would be on duty. Nor does his inclusion in the
course of Abijah carry with it lineal descent
through that line from Aaron.   R. W. MOSS.

ABILENE.—Mentioned in Lk 3¹ as the district
of which Lysanias was tetrarch in the 15th year
of Tiberius. It was called after its capital Abila,
situated on the Barada, about 18 miles from Damascus, and represented by the modern village of
Suk. The identity of *Suk* with Abila is confirmed
by a Roman rock-inscription to the west of the
town. According to popular tradition, the name
Abila is derived from Abel, who was buried by
Cain in a tomb which is still pointed out in the
neighbourhood. Little is known of the history of
Abilene at the time referred to by St. Luke; but
when Tiberius died in A.D. 37, some ten years
later, the tetrarchy of Lysanias was bestowed by
Caligula on Herod Agrippa I. (Jos. *Ant.* XVIII. vi.
10), and this grant was confirmed in A.D. 41 by
Claudius (XIX. v. 1; *BJ* II. xi. 5). On the death
of Agrippa I. (A.D. 44) his dominions passed into
the charge of Roman procurators (*Ant.* XIX. ix. 2;
BJ II. xi. 6), but in A.D. 53 some parts of them,
including Abilene, were granted by Claudius to
Agrippa II. (*Ant.* XX. vii. 1; *BJ* II. xii. 8), and
remained in his possession till his death in A.D.
100. See LYSANIAS.

LITERATURE.—Schürer, *HJP* I. ii. 335 ff.; Robinson, *Later
BRP* 479 ff.; Porter, *Giant Cities of Bashan*, 352 f.; Conder,
Tent Work in Pal. 127; *SWP*, Special Papers.
                                             JAMES PATRICK.

ABIUD ('Αβιούδ).—A son of Zerubbabel, Mt 1¹³.
The name appears in the OT in the form *Abihud*
(אֲבִיהוּד ' Father is glory'), 1 Ch 8³.

ABOMINATION OF DESOLATION (τὸ βδέλυγμα
τῆς ἐρημώσεως).—This phrase is found in the NT
only in Mt 24¹⁵ and Mk 13¹⁴, in both cases forming
part of the passage in which Christ predicts the
woes to come on the Jews, culminating in the destruction of Jerusalem. St. Mark's words, which
are probably more exact than those of St. Matthew,
are: ὅταν δὲ ἴδητε τὸ βδέλυγμα τῆς ἐρημώσεως ἐστηκότα
ὅπου οὐ δεῖ (ὁ ἀναγινώσκων νοείτω), τότε οἱ ἐν τῇ Ἰουδαίᾳ
φευγέτωσαν εἰς τὰ ὄρη, κ.τ.λ. Three points in this

account are to be noticed : (1) the change of gender *
τὸ βδέλυγμα—ἑστηκότα (cf. 2 Th 2⁶·⁷, Rev 21¹⁴) ; (2)
the 'editorial note' ὁ ἀναγινώσκων νοείτω, calling
special attention to the prophecy (cf. Dn 9²⁵, Rev
2⁷ 13¹⁸) ; (3) the command to flee to the mountains,
which seems to have been obeyed by the Christians
who escaped to Pella (Euseb. *HE* iii. 5 ; Epiphan.
Hæres. xxix. 7). St. Matthew characteristically
adds the words (absent from the best MSS [אBL] of
St. Mark) τὸ ῥηθὲν διὰ Δανιὴλ τοῦ προφήτου; substitutes the neuter ἑστός for the masc. ἑστηκότα ; and
instead of the quite general phrase ὅπου οὐ δεῖ has
the more definite ἐν τόπῳ ἁγίῳ,—an expression which
may refer to the Temple (cf. Ac 6¹³ 21²⁸), but (without the article) may mean nothing more than 'on
holy ground.' To the Jews all Jerusalem (and,
indeed, all Palestine) was holy (2 Mac 1⁷ 3¹). St.
Luke, writing most probably after the destruction
of Jerusalem, omits the 'editorial note'; and for
ὅταν ἴδητε τὸ βδέλυγμα τῆς ἐρημώσεως substitutes
ὅταν ἴδητε κυκλουμένην ὑπὸ στρατοπέδων Ἱερουσαλήμ (21²⁰).

The phrase we are considering occurs three times
in the LXX of Daniel : † 9²⁷ (βδ. τῶν ἐρημώσεων), 11³¹
(βδ. ἐρημώσεως) and 12¹¹ (cf. 8¹³), and is quoted in
1 Mac 1⁵⁴. The original reference is clearly to the
desecration of the Temple by the soldiers of Antiochus Epiphanes, the ceasing of the daily burnt-
offering, and the erection of an idol-altar upon the
great Altar of Sacrifice in B.C. 168 (1 Mac 1³³⁻⁵⁹;
Jos. *Ant.* XII. v. 4, *BJ* I. i. 1). Thus it is plain
that Christ, in quoting the words of Daniel,
intends to foretell a desecration of the Temple (or
perhaps of the Holy City) resembling that of
Antiochus, and resulting in the destruction of the
national life and religion. Josephus (*Ant.* X. xi. 7)
draws a similar parallel between the Jewish misfortunes under Antiochus and the desolation caused
by the Romans (ὁ Δανίηλος καὶ περὶ τῆς Ῥωμαίων
ἡγεμονίας ἀνέγραψε, καὶ ὅτι ὑπʼ αὐτῶν ἐρημωθήσεται).
But the precise reference is not so clear.

(1) Bleek, Alford, Mansel, and others explain it
of the desecration of the Temple by the Zealots
just before the investment of Jerusalem by Titus
(Jos. *BJ* IV. iii. 6–8, vi. 3). Having seized the
Temple, they made it a stronghold, and 'entered
the sanctuary with polluted feet' (μεμιασμένοις τοῖς
ποσὶ παρῄεσαν εἰς τὸ ἅγιον). In opposition to Ananus,
they set up as high priest one Phannias, 'a man
not only unworthy of the high priesthood, but
ignorant of what the high priesthood was' (ἀνὴρ οὐ
μόνον ἀνάξιος ἀρχιερεὺς ἀλλʼ οὐδʼ ἐπιστάμενος σαφῶς τί
ποτʼ ἦν ἀρχιερωσύνη). The Temple precincts were
defiled with blood, and Ananus was murdered.
His murder, says Josephus, was the beginning of
the capture of the city (οὐκ ἂν ἁμάρτοιμι δʼ εἰπὼν
ἁλώσεως ἄρξαι τῇ πόλει τὸν Ἀνάνου θάνατον). In support of this view it is urged (a) that the 'little
Apocalypse' (2 Th 2¹⁻¹², a passage closely resembling this) clearly contemplates a *Jewish* apostasy ;
(b) that the word used in Daniel (שִׁקּוּץ = βδέλυγμα) is
properly used not of idolatry in the abstract, but of
idolatry or false worship *adopted by Jews* (1 K 11⁵,
2 K 23¹³, Ezk 5¹¹) ; (c) that there was among the
Jews a tradition to the effect that Jerusalem would
be destroyed if their own hands should pollute the
Temple of God (ἐὰν χεῖρες οἰκεῖαι προμιάνωσι τὸ τοῦ
θεοῦ τέμενος, Jos. *BJ* IV. vi. 3).

* Dr. A. Wright (*Synopsis*², 131) says that the masculine indicates that St. Mark interprets τὸ βδέλυγμα to signify a man.
But this does not seem necessary. The masc. appears to denote
a personification rather than a person. Such personifications
are not uncommon in prophetic and apocalyptic literature
(Ezk 38, Rev 21 [ἄγγελος] 2²⁰ [Ἰεζάβελ] 12³ [δράκων]). In 2 Th 2³
ὁ ἄνθρωπος τῆς ἀνομίας (אִישׁ בְּלִיַּעַל = Βελίαρ) may denote not a
person, but a sin (ἀποστασία); see Nestle in *Expos. Times*, July
1905, p. 472 f.

† The Hebrew text and its meaning are doubtful (see A. A.
Bevan, *Daniel*, p. 192). Our Lord adopted the current view
with which the LXX had made the Jews familiar.

(2) Others (Bengel, Swete, Weiss) explain it
by reference to the investment of Jerusalem by
the Roman armies. A modification of this view
is that of H. A. W. Meyer, who explains it of the
'doings of the heathen conquerors during and
after the capture of the Temple.' When the city
was taken, sacrifices were offered in the Temple
to the standards (*BJ* VI. vi. 1, cf. Tertullian,
Apol. 16). Between the first appearance of the
Roman armies before Jerusalem (A.D. 66) and the
final investment by Titus (just before Passover
A.D. 70), there would be ample time for flight 'to
the mountains.' Even after the final investment
there would be opportunities for 'those in Judæa'
to escape. St. Luke's words (21²⁰) are quoted in
support of this view.

(3) Theodoret and other early Commentators
refer the prophecy to the attempt of Pilate to set
up effigies of the emperor in Jerusalem (*BJ* II.
ix. 2).

(4) Spitta (*Offenb. des Joh.* 493) thinks it has to
do with the order of Caligula to erect in the
Temple a statue of himself, to which Divine
honours were to be paid (*Ant.* XVIII. viii. 8). This
order, though never executed, caused widespread
apprehension among the Jews.

(5) Jerome (Commentary on Mt 24) suggests
that the words may be understood of the equestrian statue of Hadrian, which in his time stood
on the site of the Holy of Holies. Similarly,
Chrysostom and others refer them to the statue of
Titus erected on the site of the Temple.

(6) Bousset treats the passage as strictly eschatological, and as referring to an Antichrist who
should appear in the 'last days.' *

Of these views (1) and (2) are the most probable.
Considerations of chronology make (3), (4), and (5)
more than doubtful, while the warnings that the
events predicted should come to pass soon (Mt
24³³·³⁴, Mk 13²⁸⁻³⁰, Lk 21²⁹⁻³³) and the command to
flee 'to the mountains' seem fatal to (6). Between
(1) and (2) the choice is not easy, though the
balance of evidence is on the whole in favour of (1).
St. Luke's language (ὅταν ἴδητε κυκλουμένην ὑπὸ
στρατοπέδων Ἱερουσαλήμ) is not decisive. He may
not have intended his words to be an exact reproduction of Christ's words so much as an accommodation of them which would be readily understood
by his Gentile readers.

LITERATURE.—R. W. Newton on Mt 24 (1879); Bousset, *Der
Antichrist* (1885), English tr. by A. H. Keane, 1896 ; J. H. Russell,
The Parousia (1887); articles in Hastings' *DB* (by S. R. Driver),
Encyc. Bibl. (by T. K. Cheyne), Smith's *DB*² (by W. L. Bevan)
the Commentaries of Bengel, Cornelius a Lapide, H. A. W.
Meyer, Alford, Wordsworth, Mansel (in *Speaker's Commentary
on NT*, i. 139), H. B. Swete, *St. Mark, ad loc.* ; A. A. Bevan,
The Book of Daniel, ad loc.   H. W. FULFORD.

ABOVE AND BELOW.—**1.** *As cosmological terms.*
Like all similar expressions (ascent, descent, etc.),
they presented to early ages a clear-cut image,
which has disappeared with the rise of modern
astronomy. But this is rather a gain than a loss.
Here, as in so many other cases, the later knowledge is an aid to faith. At the beginning of the
Christian era the earth was still regarded as a
fixed body placed at the centre of the Universe,
with the heavens surrounding it as vast spheres.
But we know now that it is only a small planet
revolving round the sun, which also has a 'solar
way,' so immense and obscure that it is not yet
determined : while the whole sidereal system—of
which our constellation forms a 'mere speck'—is
'alive with movements' too complex to be under-

* Some (Keim, Holtzmann, Cheyne) hold the passage to be
part of an independent Jewish (or Jewish-Christian) Apocalypse
inserted subsequently in the Gospels. But it occurs in all the
Synoptists, and 'it is difficult to think that even these words
. . . are without a substantial basis in the words of Christ'
(Driver).

stood. While, therefore, 'above and below' (like 'east,' 'west,' 'north,' 'south') would have for the ancients an absolute and cosmic, they can have for us only a relative and phenomenal, significance. We still use the old terms, just as we still speak of the rising sun, but we do so with a new interpretation. They have no meaning in a boundless Universe save in relation to our observation, and appearances are misleading. But these wider views of the Universe should help us to realize that all language involving conceptions of time and space is utterly inadequate to express spiritual realities.

2. For the *spiritual* significance of these and kindred terms we turn first of all to Jn $8^{23. 42. 44}$. Manifestly, 'I am from above' ($\dot{\epsilon}\kappa \tau \hat{\omega}\nu \ \dot{\alpha}\nu\omega$)='I came forth and am come from God'; and clearly also, 'Ye are from beneath' ($\dot{\epsilon}\kappa \tau \hat{\omega}\nu \ \kappa \dot{\alpha}\tau\omega$)='Ye are of this world,' 'Ye are of your father, the devil.' 'The source of My life is above, *i.e.* in My Father; ye draw your inspiration from below, *i.e.* from a malign spirit of darkness.' This is the spiritual significance of 'above and below.' To be 'born again,' or 'born from above' ($\dot{\alpha}\nu\omega\theta\epsilon\nu$) (Jn 3^3), is to be 'born of God' (Jn 1^{13}). To receive power 'from above' ($\dot{\alpha}\nu\omega\theta\epsilon\nu$), as in the case of Pilate (Jn 19^{11}), is to receive it from God (Ro 13^1). The wisdom which is from *beneath* is 'earthly, sensual, devilish' (Ja 3^{15}); while the wisdom which is 'from above' 'is of God' (cf. 1^5 3^{17}). The following passages may also be consulted: Jn $3^{13. 31}$ 6^{38} 16^{28} 20^{17}, Ro 10^{6-8}, Col $3^{1. 2}$.

3. But, as has been already suggested, in using these and all similar terms, it is important to bear in mind their inadequacy and limitations. Not merely has theology suffered to an extent that is little realized, but the spiritual life of thousands has been impoverished through a tenacious clinging to an order of ideas in a region where they no longer apply. The difficulty, of course, is that we must employ such categories of thought even though we are compelled to recognize their inadequacy. 'A danger besets us in the gravest shape when we endeavour to give distinctness to the unseen world. We transfer, and we must transfer, the language of earth, the imagery of succession in time and space, to an order of being to which, as far as we know, it is wholly inapplicable. We cannot properly employ such terms as "before" and "after," "here" and "there," of God or of Spirit. All *is*, is at once, is present, to Him; and the revelations of the Risen Lord seem to be designed in part to teach us that, though He resumed all that belongs to the perfection of man's nature, He was not bound by the conditions which we are forced to connect with it' (Westcott, *The Historic Faith*, p. 74). We invoke 'our Father in heaven,' not as One who is divided from us by immeasurable tracts of space, but as far beyond our ignorance and sin—infinitely above us, yet unspeakably near.

'Speak to Him thou for He hears, and Spirit with Spirit can meet,—
Closer is He than breathing, and nearer than hands and feet.'

So, when the Apostle bids us 'seek those things which are above, where Christ sitteth at the right hand of God' (Col 3^1), we must shake off the incumbent thought of immeasurable distances to be crossed. And when we think of Christ's Ascension into heaven, we must not conceive of it as a flight into some far-off region, but as His passing into a state of existence (of which we gain hints during the great forty days) which we can describe only by employing words which, in the very act of using them, we see to be utterly inadequate. He has gone into a state which we cannot even imaginatively picture to ourselves without robbing it of much of its truth.

LITERATURE.—Westcott, *Gospel of St. John*; F. D. Maurice, *The Gospel of St. John* [especially valuable]. If the reader

wishes to pursue the subject of the inadequacy of the categories of the understanding, and of the concepts of time and space in relation to spiritual realities, he will find an ample field of investigation by beginning with Kant's *Critique of the Pure Reason*, and then, if he cares to, following the discussion into more recent works of Philosophy. He will find two valuable chapters (vi. and vii.) in Caird's *Introduction to the Philosophy of Religion*, dealing with the subject.   ARTHUR JENKINSON.

ABRAHAM.—It is noteworthy that while in the Synoptic Gospels references to the patriarch Abraham are comparatively frequent, and his personality and relation to Israel form part of the historical background which they presuppose, and of the thoughts and conceptions which are their national inheritance, in the Gospel of St. John his name does not appear except in ch. 8. In the Synoptists he is the great historical ancestor of the Jews, holding a unique place in their reverence and affections; he is their father, as they each of them his children (Mt 3^9 ‖ Lk 3^8, Lk 13^{16} $16^{24. 30}$ 19^9). To this the introductory title of St. Matthew's Gospel testifies; it is 'the book of the generation of Jesus Christ, the son of David, *the son of Abraham*.' And in the genealogical record that follows, his name stands at the head (Mt 1^2), and through equally graduated stages,—epochs marked by the name of Israel's most famous king, and by the nation's most bitter humiliation (v.^{17}), —the ascent of the Christ is traced to the great fountain and source of all Jewish privilege and life. It is otherwise in the genealogy of St. Luke; and the difference indicates the different standpoints of Jewish and Gentile thought. Here the historian records no halting-places in his genealogy, but carries it back in an uninterrupted chain, of which the patriarch Abraham forms but one link (Lk 3^{34}), to its ultimate source in God. See art. GENEALOGIES.

Other references in the Synoptists are on the same plane of thought, and presuppose a prevalent and accepted faith, which not only knew Abraham as the forefather and founder of their national life in the far-off ages of the past, but realized that in some sort or other he was still alive; and it was believed that to be with him, to be received into his bosom (Lk 16^{22}), was the highest felicity that awaited the righteous man after death. Both St. Matthew and St. Mark bear emphatic testimony to this belief, in their narrative of the incident of our Lord's solution of the dilemma presented by the Sadducees with their tale of the seven brothers. Jesus quotes Ex 3^6 in proof of the fact of the patriarchs' resurrection and continued existence (Mt 22^{32} ‖ Mk 12^{26} Lk 20^{37}), inasmuch as the Divine sovereignty here asserted over Abraham, Isaac, and Jacob necessarily implies the conscious life of those who are its subjects. In the Songs of Mary and Zacharias, again (Lk $1^{46-55. 68-79}$), Abraham is the forefather of the race, the recipient of the Divine promises (confirmed by an oath, Lk 1^{73}) of mercy and goodwill to himself and his descendants (cf. Gal $3^{16. 18}$, He 6^{13}, Ac 7^{17}, Ro 4^{13}); and his name is a pledge that the same mercy will not overlook or cease to care for his children (Lk 1^{55}). And, finally, to be with Abraham and his great sons, to 'sit down with Abraham and Isaac and Jacob in the kingdom of heaven' (Mt 8^{11}), is the desire and reward of the faithful Israelite. This reward, however, Christ teaches, is not confined to the Jews, the sons of Abraham according to the flesh, still less is it one to which they have any right by virtue of the mere fact of physical descent from him; it is one that will be enjoyed by 'many' faithful ones from other lands, even to the exclusion of the 'sons of the kingdom,' if they prove themselves, like His present opponents, faithless and unworthy (Lk 13^{28}).

The expression '**Abraham's bosom**' (Lk 16^{22}) or

'bosoms' (v.[23]) * is hardly to be understood as conveying the idea of an eminent or unusual degree of happiness. It is practically equivalent to 'Paradise.' And the new condition of blessedness in which Lazarus finds himself is pre-eminent only in the sense that it is so striking a reversal of the relations previously existing between Dives and himself. The parable says nothing of any superior piety or faith exhibited by Lazarus, which might win for him a more exalted position than others. As far as his present and past are concerned, it but sets forth retributive justice redressing for him and Dives alike the unequal balance of earth. 'Abraham's bosom,' like the Hades in which the rich man lifts up his eyes, is part of the figurative or pictorial setting of the parable, and indicates no more than a haven of repose and felicity, the home and resting-place of the righteous with Abraham, who is the typical example of righteousness. The parable is on the plane of popular belief, and of set purpose employs the imagery which would be most familiar and intelligible to the hearers.†

In conformity with the general character of St. John's Gospel, the references to Abraham there would seem to imply a more mystical, less matter of fact and as it were prosaic manner of regarding the great patriarch. He is spoken of in the 8th chapter alone, in the course of a discussion with Jews who are said to be believers in Jesus (v.[31]). Here also Abraham is the father of the Jews, and they are his children, his seed (vv.[37, 39, 56]); and this position they claim with pride (vv.[33, 39, 53]). It is a name and position, however, which Christ declares is belied by their conduct, in that, though nominally Abraham's seed, they do not Abraham's works, in particular when they conceive and plot the death of an innocent man (vv.[39, 40]). To the charge itself they have no answer, except to reassert their sonship, in this instance of God Himself (v.[41f.]), and to repeat the offensive imputation of demoniacal possession (v.[42]). But with almost startling abruptness, taking advantage of a phrase quietly introduced, which they interpret to imply freedom from physical death for those who accept Christ's teaching, they interrupt with the assertion that Abraham died 'and the prophets' (v.[52]), in apparent contradiction to the tenor and assumption of the language which a moment before they had employed. Probably they meant no more than that he and they, like all other men, had passed through the gate of death which terminates life on earth; and were more intent on gaining a dialectic advantage than on weighing the implications of their own words. But, in spite of them, for the few moments that are left the discourse preserves the high level of otherworldliness, to which Christ's last words have raised it; and gives occasion for one of the most striking and emphatic assertions in which He is recorded to have passed beyond the boundaries and limitations of mere earthly experience. Abraham has seen His day (v.[56]). And by silence He concedes and affirms the half-indignant, half-contemptuous and protesting question of the Jews; He has seen Abraham, and is greater even than their father (vv.[53, 57]). The climax is reached in v.[58],—in a brief sentence, which, if it did not bear so evidently the stamp of simplicity and truth, would be said to have been constructed with the most consummate skill and the finest touch of artistic feeling and insight. 'Before Abraham came into being,'—the speaker gathers up and

* The plural form is frequently used by the Greek Fathers, e.g. Chrys. *Hom. XL in Gen.*: πάντες οἱ δίκαιοι . . . εὐχῆς ἔργον ποιοῦνται εἰς τοὺς κόλπους τοῦ πατριάρχου καταντῆσαι.

† On the phrase 'Abraham's bosom,' see Trench, *Parables* 13, p. 461 ff., and the references there given; Lightfoot, *Horæ Heb. et Talm.* iii. p. 167 ff.; Stevens, *Theology of the New Testament*, p. 82; Meyer, and the commentators, *in loc.* Cf. also Salmond in Hastings' *DB* i. 17b f.

utilizes Jewish belief in its past and reverence for its head,—'I am.' Abraham ἐγένετο; Christ *is*. Thus was conveyed the answer to their question, 'Art thou greater?' (v.[53]); and thus was reasserted with emphasis the measureless distance between Himself and the greatest of the Jews, and *a fortiori*, as it would appear to the company around, of the whole human race.

It is remarkable and suggestive that in the only notice of the patriarch Jacob that is contained in the Fourth Gospel, ch. 45f. 12, the same question is addressed by the woman of Samaria to Christ: 'Art thou greater than our father Jacob,'—the Dispenser of the new water with its marvellous properties than the actual giver of the well? It was natural and inevitable that one of the questions that more particularly forced itself upon the attention of His contemporaries should be the relation of the Teacher, who had arisen in their midst and who claimed so great things, not only to the earlier prophets, but to the patriarchs and ancestors of the Jewish nation. See further art. JACOB.

The figure of Abraham, therefore, in the Gospels is idealized, and invested with a simple grandeur as the head and founder of the race in the indistinct ages of the past, to whom are owing its present privileges, and around whom gather its future hopes. There is, however, no indication of hero-worship, as in the case of the more or less mythical ancestors of other peoples. This conception, moreover, apart from St. John's Gospel, is purely patriarchal. The characteristic Pauline presentation of Abraham as the father of the faithful in a moral and spiritual sense, as the type and pattern of all righteousness and obedience, as it is developed in the Epistles to the Romans and Galatians, is absent (cf. also He 11[8ff.], Ja 2[21, 23]). References to the details of his history are not indeed wanting in the remaining books of the New Testament, but they are all, as it were, with a moral and didactic purpose: Gal 4[22], the two covenants; He 7[1ff.], Abraham and Melchizedek; Ro 4[18f.] and He 11[8, 17], faith exhibited in the abandonment of his fatherland, in the birth and offering up of Isaac; Ac 7[2, 16], the same abandonment of his country and the purchase of a tomb from the sons of Emmor in Sychem; cf. 1 P 3[6], with a possible reference to Gn 18[12].

Later Hebrew literature discussed especially this aspect of his character, and the historical view was superseded by the ethical or theological. Cf., for example, *Pirke Aboth* v. 4, of the ten testings or trials (נסיונות) of Abraham, and Taylor, *in loc.*; 'Testament of Abraham,' ed. M. R. James, *Texts and Studies*, ii. 2.

LITERATURE.—The authorities cited above, with articles on 'Abraham' in Bible Dictionaries, and the Commentaries.

A. S. GEDEN.

ABSOLUTION.—**1.** *Our Lord's words on Absolution.*—We find these in the following passages: Mt 16[16-19], especially this word spoken to Peter, 'I will give unto thee the keys of the kingdom of heaven: and whatsoever thou shalt bind on earth shall be bound in heaven: and whatsoever thou shalt loose on earth shall be loosed in heaven'; Mt 18[18] (spoken to all the Apostles), 'Verily I say unto you, What things soever ye shall bind on earth shall be bound in heaven: and what things soever ye shall loose on earth shall be loosed in heaven'; Jn 20[21ff.] 'Jesus therefore said to them again, Peace be unto you: as the Father hath sent me, even so send I you. And when he had said this he breathed on them, and said unto them, Receive ye the Holy Ghost: whose soever sins ye forgive, they are forgiven unto them: whose soever sins ye retain, they are retained.'

The first of the sayings—that about the keys and the binding and loosing—we might have been under some compulsion to take as for Peter alone, if it had not been that the like saying is repeated to all the Apostles afterwards. The words were special to Peter, as the early history of the Acts shows; but they were not limited to him. And following as they do on his great confession—being a prize and reward of that confession—they belong to him as a man who had attained by the revelation of the Father to a true faith that Jesus was the Christ the Son of God : they belonged to all the Apostles as men of like faith : and they belong to the whole Church of which these twelve were the nucleus, in proportion as that faith is alive in it. In regard to the saying (in Jn 20^{23}) about the forgiveness and retaining of sins, it was spoken in 'a general gathering of the believers in Jerusalem' (see Lk 24^{33}), and 'there is nothing in the context to show that the gift was confined to any particular group (as the Apostles) among the whole company present. The commission, therefore, must be regarded properly as the commission of the Christian society and not as that of the Christian ministry' (Westcott, *in loco*).

The 'keys' may be understood as the keys of the porter at the outer door of the house, and as symbolic of authority to admit into the kingdom of heaven or to exclude from it. Or they may be taken as the keys of the steward for use inside the house, and as symbolic of authority to open the stores or treasuries of the household of God and to give forth from these treasuries according to the requirements of the household. It is rather in this second sense that authority is given to bind and to loose, which in Rabbinical usage meant to forbid and to allow in matters of conduct ; that is to say, to interpret the will of God and to enjoin rules of life in harmony with that will. This is the work of the steward of the mysteries of God, and has to do directly with things, not persons. But the first sense, that of admitting and excluding, which has to do with persons, is what is chiefly meant by the power of the keys, and it is as an exercise of this power and of the power given in the words, 'Whose soever sins ye forgive, they are forgiven unto them,' that absolution must be considered.

Our Lord's words seem at first reading to invest the Church with absolute authority, and to promise that Heaven will follow and ratify the action of the Church on earth, whatever that action may be, in forgiving or judging, in admitting into the kingdom of heaven or excluding from it. But we recoil from this as impossible. There is no Church, how great soever its claims in regard to absolution, which does not admit that God alone forgives sin. We feel, however, that we must find a great sense in which to understand so great words as those of our Lord in these commissions. And we observe that before the words in Jn 20^{23} our Lord breathed upon His disciples and said, 'Receive ye the Holy Ghost.' He imparted to them His own very Spirit, so enabling them to be His representatives and equipping them to continue His work. (The faith which Peter had by revelation of the Father, that is to say, by the same Spirit, was an equivalent endowment before he received the promise of the keys). It was evidently the purpose of the Lord Jesus that His Church should continue the exercise on earth of the power which He constantly exercised and set in the forefront of His ministry, the power of saying to the penitent, 'Thy sins are forgiven thee' ; and of saying this with such assured knowledge of the truth of God and such sympathetic discernment of the spirits of men, that what was done by the Church on earth should be valid in heaven, and the word of Christ by the Church powerful to give comfort to truly penitent souls.

The Lord is concerned not only that men be forgiven, but that His disciples should know that they are forgiven. The grace of forgiveness has not its proper power in transforming their lives unless they know that they have it. As long as men are under fear and doubt they are not Christ's freemen : their religion is still only regulative. It

is when they have an assured sense of forgiveness and reconciliation to God that a great impulse of gratitude, with a new life in their souls, makes them free indeed, and strong in their freedom to serve God. Christ accordingly equips His Church to convey this assurance of forgiveness, and if a Church does not succeed in doing this, especially if, as often, the current idea in the Church is that to be assured of forgiveness is abnormal and unusual, the Church is greatly failing in its mission. If the form of our Lord's promise in Jn 20^{23} 'Whose soever sins ye forgive,' etc., seem too absolute, we must remember that the gift of the Holy Spirit, which He then gave the sign of imparting, is a gift of exceeding power, and that no limit can be set to the degree in which God through Christ is willing to give the Spirit. 'He giveth not the Spirit by measure' (Jn 3^{34}). And our Lord is speaking, according to His wont, to the ideal Church, to the Church which receives in the fulness with which He is willing to bestow. Just as, speaking at the high level of the ideal, He says to His servants in another place (Lk 10^{16}), 'He that heareth you heareth me : and he that despiseth you despiseth me' ; so He says here, 'Whose soever sins ye forgive, they are forgiven,' etc. But all these and such like promises depend for their fulfilment on the Spirit of Christ working, nay, reigning, in the Church. This power and reign of the Spirit ebbs and flows according to the faith and receptivity of the Church ; and while it is the duty of the Church to believe in God being with it, and while the Church ought to clothe itself with the mighty assurance of heaven assenting to its judgments, it can dare to do so, and will be able to do so, only in proportion as it has sought and obtained the indwelling of the Spirit.

The words of our Lord before us certainly do not mean that forgiveness by the mouth and at the will of man is always to be followed by a ratification of God in heaven, even though that man be an apostle. But they do imply that when Christ's servants do their work in the enlightenment and guidance of the Spirit, they will be able to convey messages of grace which will be according to the truth of things, and therefore valid in heaven : they will be able also to convey assurances of forgiveness, which will be owned of God as true, and will be made effective by His Spirit in penitent souls. So then the great and chief means by which the Church has in all ages fulfilled the work which is sustained by these startling promises, is the preaching of the gospel of reconciliation by Jesus Christ. By preaching in the power of the Spirit, thousands of souls have been in all ages receiving remission of sins and an assurance of forgiveness. Although the preaching is public, and the preacher has little or no separate knowledge of individual hearts, there is a 'privacy of publicity' in which whatever message he has from God is made an absolution Divine in power and assurance to one and another of the hearers. So effectual is preaching in the Spirit, that it may perhaps be found that in the Churches in which there is no ordinance with the title of 'private absolution,' the sense of forgiveness of sins is truer, deeper, and more widely spread than in those which have such an ordinance, and count it necessary. Obviously another means by which the Church carries out the Lord's purpose of conveying absolution to the penitent is by the sacraments. But there is great occasion also for the Church to afford full opportunity for individual help to souls in spiritual trouble, and such individual dealing as may in its issue amount to private absolution. In every revival of religion the need for this is felt. There are souls in doubt whether their repentance and faith are true, and whether they are themselves accepted of God. Such souls seek the help of the Church, and often greatly profit by it. 'Inquiry-rooms' have been of notable service in modern 'missions,' and it is a common thing for people in trouble of conscience about some special sin to long to unbosom themselves about it to one whom they feel to have spiritual authority. Evangelical religious newspapers have found that they supply a demand by setting apart a column, often largely used, for the answers of some minister of reputation to men who open their minds to him, confess their chief sins, doubts, or temptations, and seek comfort through him. All the Churches, to a greater or less extent, supplement the preaching of the word by 'discipline,' and their admission to communion and exclusion from it tell powerfully on the individual conscience. The effectiveness of all such dealing has a natural basis in the fact of experience that a man's judgment of himself is greatly influenced by the judgment of his fellow-men. It belongs to human nature that the judgment of the community in which a man lives so tells upon his spirit that it is hard for him to bear up against it. This is carried to a higher power in the Church, in the sphere wherein the Spirit of Christ works. The testimony of men who are spiritually minded and in communion with God is felt to have an authority such that great relief is given to souls by the Church's absolution, and great burden imposed by its refusal. And justly, for the discernment of spirits is one of the gifts of the Spirit of Christ to His servants. They all have it in some measure, some in a wonderful measure (1 Co 2^{15}, 1 Jn 2^{20} 4^{1}), and it may be recalled that after our Lord promised to Peter that on him He would build His Church, He did not say, as we should have expected, 'I will give thee the keys of the Church,' but 'the keys of the kingdom of heaven': from which we infer that, while the Church and the kingdom are not conterminous, the Church is meant to be a true realization of the kingdom, and its judgments valid for that kingdom. In an ideal Church this would be fulfilled. In any actual Church the power spoken of, at once gracious and awful, varies in its effectiveness according to the fulness of the Spirit in its office-bearers and members.

2. *History of Absolution in the Church.*—In the NT age there is no trace of the practice of private confession to ministers of the Church for private absolution (Ja 5^{16} cannot be so interpreted). But very early in the history of the Church it became customary for those who, after baptism, had fallen into gross sins, especially the sins of idolatry, adultery, or murder, to be cut off from fellowship, and to be readmitted after repentance manifested by public confession in the church. This readmission was an absolution, which came to be spoken of as the Church's power to forgive sins,—a power, however, declared by Tertullian (*de Pudic.* xxi.) to belong to the Church only in so far as she is composed of spiritual men. This power in the 2nd cent. was claimed as vested in the whole episcopate, and, by and by, in every single bishop; still later, in every priest. And from the time of Leo the Great (Bishop of Rome A.D. 440), the custom grew of private confession and private absolution.

In the Middle Ages there were many discussions as to whether the priest had power simply to declare the forgiveness of sins, God alone having power to forgive, or whether the priest truly himself exercises a power to forgive as representative of God.

The final doctrine of the Church of Rome, as fixed by the Council of Trent, combines both these views. God alone forgives sins, and He does this solely on account of the sinner's repentance. But the priest is the necessary instrument of God. God has been pleased to make the priest's absolution the means by which the grace is conveyed, and the word of the priest is a judicial act in which he passes sentence on the penitent. The priest is entitled to use the words of the ritual, 'I absolve thee from thy sins in the name of the Father, the Son, and the Holy Ghost.' It is admitted that 'perfect sorrow for sin without addition of external rite blots out the stains, and restores the peace of God in the soul'; yet this perfect sorrow involves in a well-instructed Catholic the intention of confessing and receiving the priest's absolution when opportunity offers. Protestants truly penitent may indeed receive the peace of God, because this desire of confession may be regarded as implicit in them. But confession to the priest is a necessary duty, and priestly absolution may not be omitted without loss of salvation.

The Lutheran Church did not entirely abolish confession and absolution; but Luther made changes which very greatly altered its character. Confession was not made compulsory: it was a free opportunity that might be used in case of sins about which the penitent could not otherwise attain to peace. Luther made it unnecessary in confession to enumerate every individual sin; and so little was absolution sacerdotal that it might be given by a Christian layman. In course of time, private confession to the pastor mostly died out in the Lutheran Church. But it has often been spontaneously resumed in times of religious revival, of which interesting examples may be found in Dr. Büchsel's *Erinnerungen*. He testifies strongly to the benefit both to pastor and people of the *Privatbeichte*, as he calls the Lutheran method, in contradistinction to the Roman Catholic *Ohrbeichte* (vol. ii. p. 113ff.). And he justifies the word of absolution spoken by the minister, 'I absolve thee,' etc., defending it from the objection that it is falsified and of no effect if the absolved has not truth and faith, by saying that in that case it is still effectual for judgment, as in the case of the misuse of the Lord's Supper, or, indeed, of the preached gospel.

In regard to the Anglican Church, in its ordinary service 'the absolution or remission of sins to be pronounced by the priest alone, the people still kneeling,' is no more than a gospel proclamation of God's pardon to the penitent, ending in a prayer for true repentance. The exhortation before the Communion contains this invitation, to be pronounced by the curate : 'If there be any of you who . . . cannot quiet his own conscience, let him come to me, or to some other discreet and learned minister of God's word, and open his grief, that by the ministry of God's holy word he may receive the benefit of absolution, together with ghostly counsel and advice to the quieting of his conscience, and avoiding of all scruple and doubtfulness.' From this, the teaching of the Church of England appears to be similar to that of the Lutheran, making confession exceptional not compulsory, and absolution not sacerdotal, but a part of the ministry of the Word.

In the service for the visitation of the sick, the minister is enjoined 'to move the sick person to make a special confession of his sins if he feel his conscience troubled with any weighty matter. After which confession the priest shall absolve him (if he humbly and heartily desire it) after this sort : "Our Lord Jesus Christ, who hath left power to His Church to absolve all sinners who truly repent and believe in Him, of His great mercy forgive thee thine offences : and by His authority committed to me, I absolve thee from all thy sins in the name of the Father, and of the Son, and of the Holy Ghost."

In the Presbyterian Churches the words 'absolve' and 'absolution' are used only of the restoration to Communion by the minister and elders—*i.e.* the Kirk-Session—of those members of the Church who have fallen into any scandalous sin by which Christ is publicly dishonoured. These are usually dealt with first by the minister in private : then they appear before the Session, or before a delegation of it, to make acknowledgment, and profess repentance. Thereupon they may be addressed and 'absolved,' by which is meant restored to Communion. This dealing has been undoubtedly, when used with spiritual tact and tenderness, a great means of deepening both the sense of sin and the trust of God's forgiveness, and it has the effect of giving many who had lost character a new spiritual start. The value, however, of this discipline depends wholly on the measure in which those who administer it are Christian, not legal, in their spirit, and on the support which the discipline receives from the spiritual level of the general body of the Church.

3. *Conclusion.*—Absolution, in the full meaning of bringing men into the sense of God's forgiveness and keeping them in that sense, may be said to be the primary work of the Church and its ministry. This work is carried out mainly by preaching, sacraments, and individual dealing with souls. The short history given above indicates the more or less fitting and successful methods by which the Christian Church has endeavoured to fulfil especially the duty of individual dealing. In order that a Church may be truly successful in this work of grace, it must be largely and widely pervaded by the Spirit of Christ in its whole membership. The gift of power in this work is not confined to the ministry; it is found wherever there is a deeply spiritual mind and Christian experience. Men in spiritual trouble do not betake themselves to a priest or minister unless they feel him to have the spiritual authority that belongs to Christ-like character. A merely official spiritual authority is not seriously believed in. What comforts and assures in time of soul-trouble is the word or sign of acknowledgment from the Christian company speaking by those who truly represent it—those who are truly called of God to the ministry, or who are shown by their goodness to be in the fellowship of God. On the training-ship *Shaftesbury* a bad boy met with an accident; he was taken to the little hospital. When he was awake at night he talked to the nurse. One night he said, 'Sister, I think I am dying, and it is so hard ; but I think if you kissed me as if I was a good boy, I could bear it.' This boy, conscious of an evil past and struggling to escape from it, felt as if the kiss of that good woman would give him cheer, and hope of acceptance with God—would be, in fact, an absolution. A Christian minister, in converse with a dying man in whom he discerns a true repentance, may be able to say with great power, 'Brother, be assured thy sins are forgiven thee,' and great blessing of comfort to the man may follow, may indeed be looked for. Only in a high moment of spiritual impulse and assurance could the minister venture to say, 'In the name of the Lord Jesus I absolve thee from thy sins.'

LITERATURE.—The Commentaries on the Gospels, especially Westcott on St. John, Bruce on St. Matthew, Dods on St. John ; Bishop Harold Browne's *Exposition of the Thirty-nine Articles* ; *A Catholic Dictionary* by Addis and Arnold, art. 'Penance' ; Canon Carter's *The Doctrine of Confession in the Church of England* ; Dean Wace's *Confession and Absolution* ; Dr. Drury's *Confession and Absolution* ; Dr. Büchsel's *Erinnerungen aus dem Leben eines Landgeistlichen* ; F. W. Robertson, of Brighton, *Sermons*, 3rd series, v. ; Selby, *The Imperfect Angel*, etc., xii.   J. ROBERTSON.

ABYSS (ἡ ἄβυσσος).—The word 'abyss,' which we find in several places in the RV of the NT, is not found in the AV. There we find instead, in St. Luke (8³¹) and in Romans (10⁷) 'the deep,' and in the Apocalypse 'the bottomless pit.' In Rev 9¹· ² we find (RV) 'the pit of the abyss' (τὸ φρέαρ τῆς ἀβύσσου), a somewhat peculiar expression, but not having, it would seem, a different signification from the simple word 'abyss.'

It is not easy to see that the word 'abyss' has the same signification in Romans as it has in St. Luke and the Apocalypse. In a general way, of course, the word may be taken as meaning the underworld, the world of departed spirits and of things dim and mysterious,—a world conceived of as deeply hidden away from that of things seen and known, even as the interior of the earth and the depths of the ocean are hidden. The abyss is certainly the realm of the departed in Ro 10⁷, where St. Paul himself interprets the word for us : 'Who shall descend into the abyss (that is, to bring up Christ from the dead)?' But a more specific meaning than that of simply the underworld must be given to the word in Lk 8³¹ and in the various passages in the Apocalypse where it occurs. The abyss is not even in Lk 8³¹, perhaps, the ultimate place of punishment, but it is there assuredly a place of restraint and of terror, as it is also so far in the Apocalypse. The abyss in the latter is the Satanic underworld, the dark and mysterious region out of which evil comes, but also the prison in which during the millennial period Satan is confined. Of course much that is given in the Apocalypse is given under poetic imagery. The abyss is rather a condition of spiritual beings than a region of space. But under the imagery there is fact, the fact that there are spiritual beings setting themselves in opposition to the Kingdom of God, and yet in their very opposition conscious of His restraining power. Satan is bound for a season in the abyss. He has no absolute power, but must submit to such restraint as is put upon him. Evil comes from the abyss, but the very Spirit of evil has to submit to being bound there.

LITERATURE.—The Commentaries on the passages above cited ; the art. 'Abyss' in Hastings' *DB* and in the *Encyc. Biblica.*
                                    GEORGE C. WATT.

ACCEPTANCE.—The state or relation of being in favour, especially with God. It is a common OT conception that has been carried over into the NT. In the former it has both a ceremonial significance, involving the presence of an approved offering or

a state of ceremonial purity, and also an ethical significance, involving divinely approved conduct. The Hebrew expression פָּנִים אֵשָּׂנ, 'to lift up or accept the face or person of one,' becomes in NT πρόσωπον λαμβάνειν, 'to accept the person or presence,' which, however, with its derivatives, προσωπολημπτεῖν and προσωπολήμπτης, always implies the acceptance of the outward presence, without regard to the inward or moral qualities ; hence, in a bad sense, partiality, as in Lk 20²¹ (cf. Mt 22¹⁶ and Mk 12¹⁴). In a good sense the idea is expressed by εὐάρεστος, 'well-pleasing' (Mt 3¹⁷ 'This is my beloved Son, in whom I am well pleased' ; cf. Mt 17⁵) ; cf. also δεκτός, 'acceptable' (Lk 4²⁴, Ph 4¹⁸), used with ἐνιαυτός, 'acceptable year' (Lk 4¹⁹) and with καιρός, 'acceptable time' (2 Co 6²), of a period or time when God's favour is specially manifest. In numerous passages in the Gospels and Epistles acceptance with God comes only through and in Jesus Christ (Jn 14⁶, Eph 1⁶ 'accepted in the Beloved,' Ro 14¹⁸, He 13²¹). So also the disciple's conduct and service are to be such as will find acceptance with Christ (Eph 5¹⁰, 2 Co 5⁹ ; cf. He 12²⁸). See, further, art. ACCESS.

As applied to our Lord Himself, the idea of His acceptance both with God and man is of frequent occurrence in the Gospels. Of Jesus as a growing boy this twofold acceptance on earth and in heaven is expressly affirmed (Lk 2⁵²). His perfect acceptance with the Father is testified to, not only by a voice from heaven both at the beginning of His ministry (Mt 3¹⁷ ‖) and towards its close (Mt 17⁵ ‖), but by the constant affirmations of His own self-consciousness (Mt 11²⁷ ‖, Mk 12⁶ ‖, Jn 5²⁰ 8²⁹ 10¹⁷, 15⁹ etc.). The favour with which He was regarded by the people when He first came declaring 'the acceptable year of the Lord,' is proved not only by such notices as, 'The common people heard him gladly' (Mk 12³⁷), but by the crowds which followed Him constantly all through the period of public favour. So far as acceptance with men is concerned, there is, of course, another side to the picture. 'No prophet,' He said, 'is acceptable in his own country' (Lk 4²⁴). His own brethren did not believe on Him (Jn 7³⁻⁵), His own townsmen thrust Him out of their city (Lk 4²⁸· ²⁹), His own people were guilty at last of that great act of rejection which found utterance in the shouts, 'Not this man, but Barabbas' (Jn 18⁴⁰), and 'Crucify him, crucify him' (Lk 23²¹), and was visibly set forth to all coming time when He was nailed to a cross in full sight of Jerusalem (see REJECTION). He who had been accepted for a time was now 'a root out of a dry ground,' the 'despised and rejected of men' (Is 53²· ³). And yet it was from this same root of rejection and sorrow that the acceptance of Christ was to grow into universal forms. Being lifted up from the earth, He drew all men unto Him (Jn 12³²). And though as the well-beloved Son He had never for a moment lost favour in His Father's sight, it was through enduring the cross and despising the shame that He sat down at the right hand of the throne of God (He 12² ; cf. Ph 2⁸⁻¹¹).   E. B. POLLARD.

ACCESS (προσαγωγή).—No word in the English language expresses the double meaning of προσαγωγή. While the AV translates it invariably 'access,' the RV more accurately renders 'our access' in Ro 5² and Eph 2¹⁸.

The προσαγωγεύς at Eastern courts acted as official introducer in conducting strangers to a king's presence.* Whether there were any allusion to this or not in the minds of our New Testament writers, the custom *illustrates* appropriately one use of the word 'access.' Christ as our Introducer obtains admission for us into the favour and

* Tholuck, *Rom. l.c.*, and Usteri, *Lehrb.* II. i. 1, p. 101.

presence of God. προσαγωγή is '*aditus ad rem vel personam*' (Grotius). It means (1) 'introduction,' 'admission' (see references to classical Greek authors, and to Chrysostom in Ellicott on Eph 2[18]); (2) 'liberty of approach.'

'Access' (προσαγωγή) occurs in three passages in the New Testament, Ro 5[2], Eph 2[18], and 3[12]. An examination of these passages will best explain what 'access' meant in the thought of St. Paul. Then it will be necessary to consider 1 P 3[18] 'For Christ also hath once suffered for sins, the just for the unjust, that he might bring us (προσαγάγῃ) to God'; and afterwards, the idea of the author of the Epistle to the Hebrews regarding 'access' as the act of drawing near to God through the great High Priest must be stated.

1. **Ro 5[2]** 'Through whom we have also [καί, 'copulat et auget' (Toletus), 'answering almost to our "as might be expected"' (Alf.)] got [ἐσχήκαμεν] our [τήν] access (introduction) by our [τῇ] faith, into this grace wherein we stand.' The Perfect tense is used in connexion with that justifying act referred to in v.[1]. Access is not here a second privilege of the justified, but introduction to the very grace of justification itself. We owe to Christ not only peace as the primary blessing of justification, but admission to that state which is the atmosphere of peace.

This paragraph, beginning with v.[1] and descriptive of the life of the justified, is founded on the doctrinal basis just laid down. The Apostle has examined the world of men, as it appeared in the prevalent antithesis of Jew and Gentile. His spiritual diagnosis revealed the fact of universal sin and universal condemnation. A guilty race, a holy God, and a broken law, with its death penalty, were factors in the problem for solution. This problem, insoluble by man, is taken in hand by Christ. Christ provided a solution as effectual as the need for it is clamant. The summary of that solution as contained in 4[24f.] is the Divine certificate of its efficacy. It was written not for the sake of Abraham alone (a typical case of its application), but for us also, to whom it shall be imputed, if we believe on Him that raised up Jesus our Lord from the dead; who was delivered for our offences, and was raised again for our justification. Based on this, ch. 5 begins: 'Therefore being justified by faith, we have peace with God through our Lord Jesus Christ.' Before getting further, the Apostle 'harks back' in v.[2] to the thought of justifying grace, access to which is by Christ.

Into the state of justifying grace we have access through Christ's Passion. His introduction includes, nay, is the starting-point of, liberty of approach. The need of an introduction implies that we were outside the state into which we are introduced. St. Paul himself had experienced transition from the condition of a condemned, to that of a justified, sinner. 'Barnabas introduced him to the apostles (Ac 9[27]), and there were others "that led him by the hand to Damascus" (v.[8]); but it was Christ that introduced and led him by the hand into this grace' (M. Henry). Christ *introduces*, 'Contigit nobis ut perduceremur' (Erasmus). He does not drag unwilling followers. Faith is the following foot. If He draws us, we run after Him.

2. **Eph 2[18]** 'For through him we both have our access in one Spirit unto the Father.' 3[12] 'In whom we have our boldness and our access with confidence by the faith of him.' The old controversy as to whether access means in these verses introduction or liberty of approach, still survives. Among moderns, Alford and Ellicott take opposite sides. Alford contends for the latter as 'better representing the *repetition*, the *present* liberty of approach which ἔχομεν implies, but which "*introduc-*

tion" does not give.' While pressing the point that as 'boldness' (παρρησία) is subjective in 3[12], 'access' there coupled with it must also be subjective, he gives away his case by admitting that the second term (προσαγωγή) is 'less purely so than the first' (παρρησία). Ellicott argues for 'introduction' on grounds of lexical and classical usage, but also makes the significant admission that the *transitive* meaning of προσαγωγή is a little less certain in 3[12] than it is in 2[18], on account of its union with the intransitive παρρησία.

Where equally competent critical authorities thus differ, the context of the passages may be allowed to decide between them. In the paragraph 2[11-22], where '*access*' (v.[18]) appears, the Apostle writes of a change in the Ephesians' relations corresponding to the change already described as having taken place in their moral and spiritual condition. At one time they were afar off, aliens, strangers, hopeless, godless. A change was effected by the blood of Christ. Those for whom His death procured peace are now declared to be fellow-citizens of the saints, members of the household of God, stones in that living temple in which God dwells through the Spirit. There is surely something more implied by 'access' in such a setting than mere liberty of approach to God. The Church is Christ's body, sharing the privileges of its Head. The reconciliation effected by His blood is not a mere potential one. Very definite language is used to express change of relationship: v.[13] 'were brought nigh' (historic). To become citizens of a kingdom, members of a household, stones in a building, implies a definite act performed on behalf of the persons or things thus brought into these new relations. *Access* in the sense of *introduction* seems to express most fitly the alteration thus contextually described.

The argument for 'introduction' is not quite so strong in 3[12]. In the context preceding, St. Paul has been speaking of his own office as Apostle of the Gentiles. He was made a minister of the gospel in order by its means to bring the Gentiles into the fellowship of the saints, and instruct men as to the eternal purpose of God in Redemption. That purpose, executed in Christ, manifested to principalities and powers in heaven the wisdom of God. Had the 'access' been used by itself in v.[12] after the above line of thought, that would not point to *introduction* rather than to *liberty of approach*. But standing as it does between 'boldness' (παρρησίαν) and 'with confidence' (ἐν πεποιθήσει), 'liberty of approach' scarcely expresses all the author's thought. The multiplication of terms indicates an attempt to give utterance to something besides this. And so, according to the analogy of Ro 5[2] and Eph 2[18], we are warranted here also in translating προσαγωγή, by 'introduction.' 'While the former of the parallel terms (boldness) describes the liberty with which the newborn Church of the redeemed address themselves to God the Father and the unchecked freedom of their petitions, the latter (admittance) takes us back to the act of Christ by which He introduced us to the Father's presence and gave us the place of sons in the house' (Findlay in *Expos. Bible*, 'Ephesians').

Confusion has been created by expositors insisting that 'access' must, in the three passages where the word occurs, always mean either *introduction*, or *liberty of approach* exclusively. But the larger concept, 'introduction,' includes the lesser, 'liberty of approach.' To put it in another way—the latter term follows from the former. Presentation at the Court of Heaven gives one the right to return there. It secures habitual access to God at all times.

3. **1 P 3[18]** 'Because Christ also suffered for sins

once, the righteous for the unrighteous, that he
might bring us (προσαγάγῃ) to God.' The Apostle
does not set himself in this Epistle to expound the
theology of the Passion. His general purpose is to
comfort and sustain Christians who are suffering
persecutions. Some of them were slaves, enduring
wrongs from cruel masters because of their faith
in Christ. These were directed to the exemplary
character of Christ's sufferings. In 3¹³ St. Peter
assures them that it is better to suffer for well-
doing than for evil-doing. Then in v.¹⁸ he links
them in thought with the suffering Saviour. But
it is not on the exemplary significance of Christ's
sufferings that he enlarges. That is left behind.
The writer is spellbound by the very mention of
the Cross, and for a moment he forgets his purpose of directing some wronged slaves to Christ as
the supreme example of suffering innocence, that
he may state again the wider and deeper meaning
of his Lord's Passion. Christ suffered in connexion
with sin once for all (ἅπαξ). The unique significance of His death consisted in its being the
death of a righteous person for the unrighteous
(δίκαιος ὑπὲρ ἀδίκων); and His action had this end
in view, that He might conduct us (προσαγάγῃ) to
God : ' ut nos, qui abalienati fueramus, ipse abiens
ad Patrem, secum una, justificatos adduceret in
cœlum, v.²², per eosdem gradus quos ipse emensus
est, exinanitionis et exaltationis ' (Bengel). 'And
if the soul bear back still through distrust, He
takes it by the hand and draws it forward ; leads
it unto His Father ; presents it to Him, and leaves
not the matter till it [the reconciliation between a
sinner and God] be made a full and sure agreement ' (Leighton).

4. The word προσαγωγή is not found in the Epistle
to the Hebrews. *Access* is expressed there in
different language from that in the passages considered, because it is associated with somewhat
different ideas. The author of Hebrews, writing
as a pastor, not as an evangelist, aims at con-
serving rather than initiating faith. Instead
of the Pauline and Petrine idea of the Saviour
leading in a sinner, we have the sinner coming to
the Saviour. *Introduction* (προσαγωγή) becomes
access, liberty of approach, approximation. Sinners
are represented in the very act of approaching—
are exhorted to approach. The worshippers under
the law were τοὺς προσερχομένους, 'the comers'
(He 10¹) ; ' not those that come to the worship, but
those who by the worship come to God' (Owen).
Under the gospel (Judaism evolved) their attitude
and character remained the same : 7²⁵ 11⁶ (singular)
or 4¹⁶ 10²², where believers are exhorted to draw
near (προσερχώμεθα).

As a Hebrew Christian addressing Hebrew
Christians, the writer of Hebrews makes large use
of Old Testament conceptions and Old Testament
rites familiar to himself and his correspondents.
Urging upon them the truth 'that the faith of
Christ is the true and final religion' (Davidson),
he presents a series of contrasts between what was
elementary in Judaism and the finished product of
Christianity. Modern readers are apt to lose
themselves amid unfamiliar details here. But it
is possible to set these details in the background,
and yet grasp the permanent truths, which are as
important for us as for the readers to whom such
details became the most effective illustrations.
We shall keep this in view when attempting now
to summarize the great facts associated with the
idea of access in the four Epistles already referred
to.

(1) The need of *access to* implies *separation from*
God—want of fellowship like that enjoyed by
those who walk in the light. We are by nature
afar off (Eph 2¹³), aliens (v.¹²). There is an enmity which must be slain before peace is effected.

The wrath of God is revealed against all ungodliness and unrighteousness of men (Ro 1¹⁸). The
Ephesians were by nature children of wrath (Eph
2³). That exhortation used in Hebrews to draw
near (4¹⁶ 10²²) could be addressed only to those
who are at a distance from God. 'Whereas it
is emphatically affirmed that He is able to save
unto the uttermost, it is supposed that great
oppositions and difficulties do lie in the way of
its accomplishment' (Owen).

(2) The great separating barrier is *sin*. All
have sinned (Ro 3²⁵): and the correlative of universal sin is universal condemnation. Sin and
death are so associated as to be completely one
(Ro 5¹². ¹⁴. ¹⁵. ¹⁷. ²¹). The Ephesians are represented
as dead in trespasses and sins (2¹).

(3) All three Persons of the Godhead conspired
to deal with the problem of sin, in a way corresponding to its magnitude. Access is (*a*) *to* (πρός)
the Father (Eph 2¹⁸)—representing the God to
whom we are to be reconciled and introduced, and
into whose family we are to be adopted ; (*b*) *through*
(διά) the Son (Ro 5², Eph 2¹⁸); (*c*) *by* (ἐν) the
Spirit (Eph 2¹⁸).

(4) This is the special work of Christ. He bridges
the gulf which sin has created between God and
man. We have access into the grace of justification through the redemption that is in Christ
Jesus, whom God hath set forth to be a propitiation through faith in His blood (Ro 3²⁴. ²⁵). The
double alienation from God and His Church discussed in Ephesians is removed through Christ—by
His blood (2¹³), by His flesh (v.¹⁵), by His Cross
(v.¹⁶).

The steps whereby access was effected by Christ
are clearly laid down in 1 P 3¹⁸. His death has
a connexion with sin. He suffered once for all
(ἅπαξ), 'so that to them who lay hold on Him this
holds sure, that sin is never to be suffered for in the
way of strict justice again, as not by Him, so not by
them who are in Him' (Leighton). The unique
significance of Christ's suffering in connexion with
sins is expressed in the words 'the just for the
unjust' (δίκαιος ὑπὲρ ἀδίκων). In dying, the righteous One took on Himself the liability of the
unrighteous. Access to God was, in St. Peter's
estimation, thus purchased at an unspeakable
price. 'A righteous One has once for all faced,
and in death taken up and exhausted, the responsibilities of the unrighteous, so that they no more
stand between them and God' (Denney, *The Death
of Christ*, p. 102).

The author of Hebrews explains and illustrates
by a method *sui generis*, how Christ obtains access
for us. Christ is the great High Priest interceding for men in the heavenly sanctuary, and the function
which He discharges in heaven is based on the
death which He died on earth. A priest's duty is
to establish and represent fellowship between God
and man. Christ found that sin barred the way to
this fellowship, and accordingly dealt with sin.
He was appointed with a view to this end—to
make propitiation for the sins of the people (He
2¹⁷). In contrast with the Levitical priests and
their duties, Christ's Person and work are perfect
(τέλειος). He deals with sin by way of sacrifice.
This He did *once* when He offered up Himself
(7²⁷). 'Once in the end of the world hath he
appeared to put away sin by the sacrifice of himself' (9²⁶). 'Christ was once offered to bear the
sins of many' (v.²⁸). 'For by one offering he hath
perfected for ever ['to perfect,' τελειοῦν, 'is to bring
into the true condition of those in covenant']
them that are sanctified' ['to sanctify,' ἁγιάζειν,
'is to make to belong to God,' Davidson].

Associated with the same conception of sacrifice
are the references in the Epistle to the blood of
Christ. He entered into the Holy Place by (διά)

His blood (9^{12}). The blood of Christ, who offered Himself to God, purges the conscience from dead works (v.[14]). We have boldness to enter into the Holiest by the blood of Christ (10^{19}). Access is therefore dependent on Christ's Person and work. In reliance on His sacrifice (10^{19}), along a way consecrated by His death (v.[20]), mindful of their High Priest (v.[21]) in heaven, believers are exhorted to *draw near* to God. The exhortation in 4^{16} to come boldly unto the throne of grace is also founded on Jesus having passed into the heavens as our great High Priest: and it adds the thought of Christ's sympathy, as having experienced infirmities and temptations Himself, in order to encourage suppliants for mercy and grace. The truth put hortatively in these passages is also taught directly in 7^{25}, where access is linked with intercession. This intercession, of which an example is preserved in Jn 17, is continued in heaven, and derives its power from the sacrifice which Christ offered on earth.

(5) Faith is the subjective condition of those who have access (Ro 3^{25} 5^2, Eph 3^{12}). 'He who comes to God must believe that he is' (He 11^6). The eleventh chapter of Hebrews is a record of faith in action, faith as illustrated in the lives of saints, who first came to God, and then acted and endured, because sustained by the strength of God.

LITERATURE.—The Commentaries on the passages discussed, especially Sanday-Headlam on *Romans*; Ellicott, Meyer, H. G. Miller, and Armitage Robinson on *Ephesians*; Delitzsch, Davidson, Westcott, and Bruce on *Hebrews*; also Calvin's *Institutes*, III. xiii. 5, xx. 12; Cremer's *Biblico-Theol. Lex.*; Denney, *The Death of Christ*; *Expositor*, 4th series [1890], ii. 131; 2nd series [1882], iv. 321.

D. A. MACKINNON.

ACCOMMODATION.—

i. The Incarnation as the supreme example.
   (*a*) The birth and childhood of Jesus.
   (*b*) The temptations to which He was subjected.
   (*c*) The mental and spiritual sufferings experienced by Him.
ii. Incidents inferentially valuable.
   (*a*) His education in a pious Jewish home.
   (*b*) The deliberate acceptance and public avowal by Him of the limitations conditioning human life.
   (*c*) Revelation of these limitations involved in the spontaneity of His attitude towards (1) His fellow-men, (2) His Father.
iii. Jesus' activity as Teacher.
   (*a*) Repeated assertions as to nature of the authority wielded by Him.
   (*b*) Objective of His message defined by (1) the national characteristics of His fellow countrymen; (2) their theological and traditional beliefs—
      (α) Messianic kingdom.
      (β) Doctrine of angel-mediation.
      (γ) Current conceptions of the power of Satan and of evil spirits.
   (*c*) Methods employed by Jesus in His teaching: (1) parables purposely and economically utilized; (2) use of popular figurative expressions; (3) employment of aphorism, allegory, etc.; (4) acceptance of current conceptions as to—
      (α) Natural phenomena.
      (β) Anthropology.
iv. Attitude of Jesus towards the Messianic hopes of His day.
   (*a*) Assumption of the title 'Son of Man.'
   (*b*) Attitude towards the Jewish Canon of Scripture observable in His acceptance of (1) its general historicity; (2) the traditional view of the authorship and interpretation of Ps 110.
v. Summary and practical conclusion.
   Literature.

The term 'accommodation' may be defined as the principle or law according to which God adapts His Self-revelation to the capacities and limitations of created intelligences. In every age, from the earliest onwards, this Self-revelation of God has been made, and has its own characteristic features. Between the time when men conceived of God in the rudimentary anthropomorphism of Gn 3^8 and the time of the highest attainment by the human mind of His Nature and Being (Jn $4^{23f.}$), every conceivable gradation occurs in the extent and character of God's revelation of Himself to men.

i. THE INCARNATION AS THE SUPREME EXAMPLE.

—This is not the place to enter into a detailed inquiry as to the nature and extent of the self-imposed limitations of Christ, or how far the modern theories of the *kenosis* (wh. see) are justified by revelation, directly or by implication. It will be sufficient here to indicate how far the Gospels, as we have them, point to a real adoption by Him of the conditions of that life which He assumed, and involved Him *ex necessitate* in the limitations of a real human life.

(*a*) So complete is the accommodation to the capacities and requirements of infanthood, that St. Luke scruples not to record, as part of the angelic message, the finding by the shepherds of . . . 'a babe wrapped in swaddling clothes and lying in a manger' (Lk 2^{12}), and St. Matthew makes the safety of His childhood depend on the vigilance and care of Joseph and His mother, their return from enforced exile being conditioned by the fact that 'they are dead that sought the young child's life' (Mt 2^{20}). All this presupposes, of course, His development along the lines of human growth, which is boldly outlined by St. Luke in the much debated passage, 'Jesus advanced in wisdom and stature, and in favour with God and men' (Lk 2^{52}). If these words are to be interpreted according to their obvious meaning, they imply a moral and spiritual as well as a physical advancement along lines as normal as, for example, those which marked the growth of the child Samuel. We may say, indeed, that there is a marked reference to the words . . . καὶ ἀγαθὸν καὶ μετὰ Κυρίου καὶ μετὰ ἀνθρώπων of 1 S 2^{26} [LXX]. 'Christ's growth was from His birth a holy growth' (Martensen, *Christian Dogmatics*, Eng. tr. p. 282); but the words 'the child grew and waxed strong' (Lk 2^{40}) point to the essentially human conditions under which that growth was effected.

The sole incident in connexion with His boyhood which has come down to us in our reliable authorities is that of His visit to the temple (Lk $2^{41ff.}$). Short, however, as it is, it throws a clear light on the nature and reality of the advance 'in wisdom and favour,' and its uninterrupted continuity is well expressed in v.[40], if we give the word πληρούμενον its proper significance. Day by day He was being filled with wisdom. Even at this age, His marvellous intellectual powers displayed themselves, and already He exhibited that keen insight which in after life He so frequently showed. The verb used to express the amazement of the learned teachers (ἐξίσταντο) shows how much these men wondered at the Boy's knowledge and at the depth of His understanding (ἐπὶ τῇ συνέσει). Notwithstanding this feature of the narrative, the historian is far from leading us to suppose that there was anything supernatural in the matter. He rather represents Jesus as a boy of a singularly inquiring turn of mind, who deliberately determines to find out for Himself the solution of many problems which puzzled Him during the course of His home education, and for which He could find no satisfactory explanation from His teachers in Nazareth. He sits down (καθιζόμενον) at the feet of these great teachers (διδασκάλων) as a learner (cf. St. Paul's description of his own education in the Law, Ac 22^3). Nor are we to look upon the circumstance in the temple as constituting an exhibition of miraculous intellectual acquirements in the ordinary sense of that word. All Jewish children from their 'earliest infancy' (Jos. *c. Apion.* ii. 18) were made to acquire a knowledge of and to practise the precepts of the Law. We have only to compare the Lukan narrative with that given in the Arabic *Gospel of the Infancy* to see how completely natural and human is the whole incident, and how entirely the boyhood of Jesus was subject to boyhood's conditions and limitations. In the latter He is represented as cross-examining each of the doctors, and instructing them not only in matters appertaining to the Law and the Prophets, but in astronomy, physics, metaphysics, and other branches of current erudition (see chs. xlviii.–lii.).

Without entering into an examination of the words contained in His answer to His mother's gentle rebuke, or what relation they bear to His subsequent complete and developed self-consciousness, it may be said that they do not necessarily involve all that is sometimes imported into them. Even the implied antithesis ὁ πατήρ σου of v.48 and ἐν τοῖς τοῦ πατρός μου of v.49 probably means nothing more than a reminder that the claims of His heavenly Father take precedence of all others, and bears testimony to a profound appreciation of the transcendent reality of His Divine Sonship (cf. B. Weiss, *Leben Jesu*, Eng. tr. vol. i. p. 278 ff.). It is true, we have no right to assume that the Boy Jesus had no knowledge of His unique relationship to God (cf. Gore, *Diss.* p. 78, n. 1). The use of the possessive particle μου points to the probability that His powers of realization in this respect were as wonderful as the development of His mental faculties in another. This is, however, far from saying that Jesus at this early age possessed the consciousness of His Messiahship, which only came to full maturity at the next turning-point of His life (see Sanday's art. 'Jesus Christ' in Hastings' *DB*, vol. ii. p. 609); and the short but graphic touch with which St. Luke portrays for us His surprise at His parents' method of search (τί ὅτι ἐζητεῖτέ με;), and His sustained subordination (ἦν ὑποτασσόμενος αὐτοῖς gives the idea of a continuance of His subjection to the conditions of His home life) to the authority of Joseph and Mary shows how completely the Son of God 'emptied Himself,' μορφὴν δούλου λαβών, Ph 27.

One incidental reference to this period of Jesus' life in the Synoptic narrative further deepens the impressiveness of this self-humiliation. St. Mark relates that on the occasion of one of His visits to Nazareth (Mk 6[1]) His teaching was met by His fellow-townsmen with the scornful question, 'Is not this the carpenter?' (ὁ τέκτων).* This single question gives point to the more general remark of St. Luke mentioned above, and interprets his use of the analytical or periphrastic tense (ἦν ὑποτασσόμενος: for the use of this form of the verb the reader is recommended to see Burton's *NT Moods and Tenses*, p. 11 f. and p. 16 ; see also Blass, *Gram. of NT Greek*, p. 203).

His whole life, then, previous to the events which led to His public ministry, was lived under the simple conditions which obtained in a humble but pious country home, and His answer to the Baptist's remonstrance, 'it becometh us (πρέπον ἐστὶν ἡμῖν) to fulfil all righteousness' (Mt 3[15]), is the result of a training characteristic in its naïveté of a house whose inmates 'waited for the redemption of Israel' (Lk 2[25]), and were strict observers of the laws governing the religious life of the Jews. See, further, artt. BOYHOOD and CHILDHOOD.

It may not be out of place to note a slight but significant difference in the method of introducing the narrative of Jesus' baptism between the Lukan and the other two Synoptic versions. The latter speak of Jesus as coming from Galilee for the special purpose of being baptized (see fragment of Gosp. Heb. in Jerome's *adv. Pelag.* 3)—τοῦ βαπτισθῆναι ὑπ' αὐτοῦ (Mt 3[13]), καὶ ἐβαπτίσθη ὑπὸ Ἰωάννου (Mk 19),—and seem to be conscious of a certain amount of astonishment on account of the act. The Lukan narrative, on the other hand, gives the story an incidental character ; and by its uses of the participle, both in describing the act of baptism and also His prayer which immediately followed (καὶ Ἰησοῦ βαπτισθέντος καὶ προσευχομένου, Lk 3[21]), the Evangelist gives a human touch to the whole scene which harmonizes well with the style of his history in this place.

(*b*) It is, however, when we come to the scene of His temptation, and study it in connexion with the revelation which He had just received from His Father, that we begin to appreciate the full meaning of the words of He 4[15] that Jesus was One who 'in all points' (κατὰ πάντα) was tempted like ourselves. Whatever be the interpretation we are inclined to put upon the nature and method of the temptations (see art. TEMPTATION) to which He was subjected, one thing must be uncompromis-

* This would seem to be the original and correct form of the expression, though the Matthæan record has ὁ τοῦ τέκτονος υἱός (Mt 13[55]), to which the Western text (ll) of St. Mark has conformed (see Wright, *Synopsis of the Gospels in Greek*, p. 52 f.).

ingly insisted on—the struggle was a real one, it was intense, it was necessary (ἔπρεπεν γὰρ αὐτῷ . . . διὰ παθημάτων τελειῶσαι, He 2[10]). It is necessary that we should be on our guard against falling into the errors which mar, for example, the work of Hilary of Poitiers in his controversy with the Arians (see especially his *Libri XII. de Trinitate*, Liber x.). To explain away the reality of the sufferings of Jesus arising out of His different temptations, whether these sufferings are mental or physical, is of the essence of Docetism ; and a docetic Christ has never yet appealed, and we are confident never will appeal, to the conscious needs of humanity. Jesus Himself must have been the ultimate source from which the story of the Temptation became known, and it is very evident that the impression made upon His mind by the terrible ordeal was most profound. He had just received from His Father the revelation of His unique Sonship.* St. Matthew and St. Luke agree in prefixing to two of the temptations the words, 'If thou art the Son of God,' the essence of the trial consisting in the danger of doubting the truth which had been disclosed to His consciousness, and of testing the fidelity of God by a thaumaturgical exhibition. There is also a subtle psychological and spiritual fitness in the character of the first of the series, which speaks, perhaps, more for its real force than any direct statement could do. The appeal came to Jesus in the hour and on the side of His physical exhaustion, and this is in direct accordance with the general experience of humanity. Temptation becomes infinitely stronger and more dangerous when physical weakness comes to the aid of the external promptings of the Evil One.

That Jesus believed, and led those to whom He recounted His experiences to believe, in the near presence of a personal spirit of evil during this critical period of conflict, is very evident (see Gore, *Diss.* p. 24 ff.). Moreover, this Evil One (ὁ διάβολος, Mt 4[5. 8. 11], Lk 4[3. 6. 13] ; ὁ Σατανᾶς, Mk 1[13]) is a prince standing at the head of a kingdom which is the direct antithesis of the kingdom of God. According to the Lukan version of this incident, Jesus expected to meet again in personal conflict this great spiritual enemy. The devil left Him only till further opportunity for assault should arise (ἄχρι καιροῦ, Lk 4[13]) ; and towards the end of His ministry we find Him giving expression to the consciousness that the great struggle with His arch-foe was about to recommence—'The prince of the world (ὁ τοῦ κοσμου ἄρχων, Jn 14[30]) is (now) coming' (cf. 12[1]). When His arrest, following upon His betrayal, was about to become an accomplished fact, He recognized the return of the spirit of evil, and that the return was with power (ἡ ἐξουσία τοῦ σκότους, Lk 22[53]).

Perhaps there is no more vivid presentation of the profound reality of His subjection to temptation than that afforded by the narrative dealing with the events which occurred in Cæsarea Philippi. It is almost possible to see the startled look of horror on Jesus' face as He listens to Peter's well-meant, if indiscreet, remonstrance. In the words of His chief Apostle He hears again the voice of Satan (cf. Mt 16[23] and Mk 8[33]), and the almost fierce way in which He rebukes Peter points to the conclusion that this is not the first time the suggestion has whispered itself into His ear, to forego the bitter taste which He knows He must experience before His work is ended.

(*c*) Before passing from the consideration of this aspect of the Incarnation viewed as the self-adaptation of the Son of God to the conditions of humanity, we must refer shortly to some of the details of the last, greatest, and most awful of the temptations to which Jesus was exposed. Some have sought to explain away the reality both of the temptations and the sufferings, through a vain desire to exalt His Divine at the expense of

* For our present purpose it is immaterial whether we reject the words of the Textus Receptus Σὺ εἶ ὁ υἱός μου ὁ ἀγαπητός, ἐν σοὶ ηὐδόκησα in favour of the Western reading of Lk 3[22] υἱός μου εἶ σύ, ἐγὼ σήμερον γεγέννηκά σε, which Resch and Blass as well as others seem to prefer (cf. Blass, *Ev. secundum Lucam*, etc., Præfatio, pp. xxxvi–xxxvii).

His human nature; but this is not the method of interpreting the life of Christ which brings out of it God's answer to man's deepest and most conscious needs. There can hardly be a doubt in the mind of any unprejudiced reader that the Synoptists place on record their accounts of the Passion believing the facts detailed to be real and objective. The words of Jesus are the expressions of a mind torn with the mental and spiritual conflict; and if Lk 22⁴³· ⁴⁴ be not a mere Western interpolation, the element of awful fear entered into and heightened His sufferings. It is only in this way that we can interpret the words ἐν ἀγωνίᾳ. See art. AGONY. The thrice-repeated prayer of Jesus, in which He speaks of His own will as distinct from, but completely subordinate to, His Father's, adds to the impression, already gained, of the purely human feelings exhibited by Him in His struggle, and recalls to our mind the words in His own form of prayer, 'Thy will be done' (Mt 6¹⁰); thus connecting, in the greatest crisis of His life, His own with our absolute dependence upon the expressed will of His Father.

The writer of the Fourth Gospel records sayings of Jesus which are very similar to this. After the conversation of Jesus with the woman of Samaria, He explains to His disciples the all-absorbing, satisfying character of His life's work, which is to do the will (τὸ θέλημα) of His Father (Jn 4³⁴). In other places He distinguishes between His own θέλημα and that of His Father (Jn 5³⁰ 6³⁸); and this is the word used by the Synoptic writers when recording the words of Jesus' prayer in Gethsemane. On what grounds St. Luke employs the verb βούλομαι (22⁴²) in this connexion we do not know. If the choice is not accident, it is evidence that even in His great affliction Jesus bowed Himself to the *deliberate* determination of God (for the connexion between βούλομαι and θέλω see Cremer, pp. 143 ff. and 726 f.).

A very pathetic touch is given by St. Matthew to the portraiture of this scene in the garden. Both he and St. Mark relate how Jesus expressed a wish that His three disciples should be on their guard. St. Mark, however, leaves the impression that He is bidding them watch against the too sudden intrusion of their enemies upon His privacy. Twice He uses the imperative 'Watch.' On the other hand, St. Matthew twice adds to this same verb the expression 'with me,' as if anxious to show the very human desire of Jesus to have the companionship of faithful friends in the hour of His need and solitude. The same two writers have recorded a saying of Jesus to His sleeping companions ('Sleep on now, and take your rest') which is omitted by St. Luke. In these words it is possible to discover a tinge of bitter sadness and disappointment, as if the reflection were forced upon Him that He was bereft even of that loyal friendship which had left all and followed Him; and that, too, at a time when it was most precious, and when He stood in sorest need of its help and sympathy. The truth is, He felt the full force of the temptation to leave undone the last and hardest part of the work which He came to do, or to find a way of fulfilling His Father's will other than by treading the path of suffering and death. It was in the very act of submission that He found His most effective weapon of resistance; and we have here at the same time a verification of the reality of His human nature, and an example of Himself carrying out to fulfilment the principle which He inculcated as a guide to others—'He that humbleth himself shall be exalted' (Lk 18¹⁴ 14¹¹).

ii. INCIDENTS INFERENTIALLY VALUABLE.—(a) If we scrutinize carefully the method of resistance which Jesus adopted in His first great conflict, we cannot fail to see the results of that moral and spiritual education which was the characteristic element of His domestic surroundings, and with which we become incidentally acquainted by the tone of His remark to His mother in the temple. The words ἐν τοῖς τοῦ πατρός μου (Lk 2⁴⁹) show how profoundly He was impressed with the sense of His Divine Sonship; and, we must believe, they were the outcome of His familiarity with the thought underlying much of the language of the OT. In repelling the Satanic attacks of the Temptation He reveals to us a mind steeped in the

literature of, and full to overflowing with spiritual principles culled from, the Book of Deuteronomy. Nor was it only when He felt the sore stress of temptation that His belief in the truth of God's revelation given in the OT, and His profound knowledge of its contents, came to His aid. In the hour of His intensest bodily and mental agony, the words of Ps 22 leaped instinctively to His mind, and gave expression to the feeling of awful loneliness which then hung over Him like a black cloud. If in moments of deepest feeling, when the soul almost without conscious effort turns to the sources whence it drew its early sustenance, Jesus had recourse to the words of the OT, and was able to extract from that wide field of literature all that was purest and most spiritual, it was not, we feel sure, without long, deep study and pondering over the meaning of the different writers from His childhood onwards. Remembering, then, this feature in the mental and spiritual equipment of Christ, it will not be surprising if we find Him displaying the same habit of mind in almost every variety of circumstance of which He found Himself the centre. St. Matthew and St. Mark tell us that, at the time of St. Peter's confession at Cæsarea Philippi, He for the first time spoke to His disciples of the fatal end in store for Him. St. Matthew clearly points out that this was a new departure—ἀπὸ τότε ἤρξατο, κ.τ.λ. (16²¹),—and that He continually reverted to the subject as if desirous of impressing the disciples with the impossibility of His escape. We do not know at what precise period Jesus was convinced that there could inevitably be only one ending to His work, or whether He knew from the beginning, and merely waited for a fitting time to prepare His disciples for the shock. We do, however, know that at this period He was convinced not merely by the 'signs of the times' (Mt 16³), which all pointed in this direction, but also by His knowledge and interpretation of the things which were written 'in the law of Moses, and the prophets, and the psalms' (Lk 24⁴⁴), concerning Him, that the way of glory was the way of the cross. St. Mark makes a pointed reference to the connexion, which evidently existed in Jesus' mind, between the death of the Baptist and His own coming end (9¹²f·); and we know that the murder of John made a profound impression upon Him (Mt 14¹³, cf. Jn 6¹). Perhaps we may be allowed to conjecture that this circumstance marked an advance in the mind of Christ towards a great synthesis—the identification of the Conquering with the Suffering Messiah.

The question πῶς γέγραπται, κ.τ.λ., of Mk 9¹², shows what it was that strengthened His resolve to pursue His mission to its consummation. That He dwelt long and deliberately on this aspect of His work is seen by the way in which He again refers to it towards the end of His journey to Jerusalem (Mk 10³³, to which St. Luke adds the characteristic formula . . . τελεσθήσεται πάντα τὰ γεγραμμένα διὰ τῶν προφητῶν, Lk 18³¹; cf. also Mt 26²⁴ καθὼς γέγραπται, Lk 22²² κατὰ τὸ ὡρισμένον, 24²⁵f· ⁴⁴· ⁴⁶, Mt 26⁵⁴.

(b) One of the most widely canvassed, and, indeed, the most difficult passage in the Gospel history is that in which Jesus is said to have disclaimed the knowledge of the time of His glorious Return. St. Matthew and St. Mark record His disavowal in almost identical words, except that the former emphasizes it by the addition of μόνος to the words εἰ μὴ ὁ πατήρ, which are common to both (cf. Mt 24³⁶ and Mk 13³²). In both narratives Jesus is represented as speaking in the 3rd person (οὐδὲ ὁ υἱός, by which we are doubtless to understand His usual self-designation 'Son of Man,' occurring as this title does in the context of both passages, Mt 24³⁷· ³⁹, Mk 13²⁶). How are we to interpret, then, this self-revelation which emanates from the consciousness of Jesus? Many expedients have been tried to get over the logical conclusion derivable from a literal exegesis, some even going so far as to suggest that the passage is an Arian interpolation.

Athanasius would almost dichotomize the Person of Christ in his effort at explanation. Indeed, he plainly asserts that the Son did know 'the hour of the end of all things.' But as being the Word (ὡς μὲν λόγος) He knew, though at the same time as man (ὡς δὲ ἀνθρωπος) He is ignorant of it (ἀγνοεῖ). In the same context he maintains that Jesus acted deliberately in speaking of His ignorance for the sake of 'economy' (φανερὸν πεποίηκεν ὅτι περὶ τῆς ἀνθρωπίνης αὐτοῦ λειτουργίας ἔλεγεν, 'οὐδὲ ὁ Τίος'). See his Orations against the Arians, bk. ii. chapters xliii. and xliv., where these passages occur (Bright's ed.). Cyril of Alexandria, in his capacity of malleus Arianorum, speaks in much the same strain, and sometimes more unguardedly, as if he were unwilling, as indeed most of the Fathers were, to face the theological and exegetical difficulties of this whole question. Most of us will sympathize with the strong and vigorous language of Theodoret with respect to the evasions so commonly current. 'If,' he says, 'He knew the day, but being desirous to conceal it said He did not know, you see in what blasphemy the inference lands us. For the Truth lies' (Repr. XII. capp. Cyril in Anath. IV.).

There is also a considerable body of modern thought which seems to reject all serious consideration of this aspect of the Incarnation as being dangerous to a right and reverent attitude towards the claims of Christ. We have only to read such a book as Hall's The Kenotic Theory, or several articles in the Ch. Q. Review (e.g. vols. xliv., xlv., and lii.), to see how earnestly men contend against the frank acceptance, in their most obvious meaning, of the words of Jesus.

However mysterious the conclusion at which we are forced to arrive may be, and however inconsistent the different parts of our Christological system may appear, it is necessary for us candidly to accept this self-revelation of Jesus as being strictly in accord with His personal consciousness, and, moreover, as being an infallible indication of the complete and perfect manner in which the Divine Word accommodated Himself to the conditions of the race whose nature He took.

It would, again, be impossible and absurd to treat the incident of the barren fig-tree, related by both St. Matthew (21$^{18-22}$) and St. Mark (11$^{12-14}$), as if it were a mere scenic display for the purpose of solemnly inculcating a moral lesson. Yet this is practically what we are asked to do by writers who refuse to believe that the mind of Jesus was no more exempt from human characteristics than His body was from the sufferings incident to earthly life. On this occasion He felt the pangs of hunger, and He believed He saw the natural means of satisfying His need. We could look for no more convincing example, in His life, of the complete adaptation of Himself to all the laws governing mortal existence. Other instances there are in abundance which point in the same direction, viz. to His complete and willing submission to the limitations which condition the human mode of life. He hungered, as we have seen (Mt 4^2, Mk 11^{12} = Mt 21^{18}, Jn 4^{31}), and sympathized with those who suffered thus (Mt 15^{32} = Mk 8^2, cf. Mt. 12$^{1ff.}$ and 25$^{35. 42}$). He suffered the pangs of thirst (Jn 4^7 and 19^{28}). He experienced physical weariness after prolonged exertion (Jn 4^6, cf. Mt 8^{24} = Mk 4^{38}). Notwithstanding O. Holtzmann's interpretation of Lk 9^{58} (= Mt 8^{20}) it is very certain that there is a personal reference to His homeless condition in these words, and we notice a quiet sadness, as if He felt the loneliness attaching to a life of continued wandering (cf. O. Holtzmann's Leben Jesu, Eng. tr. p. 169, note 3, and p. 303 f.).

(c) The element of spontaneity discoverable in the words and actions of Jesus, expressive of His attitude either towards His fellow-men or towards God, lends force to what we have been saying about limitations involved in His manhood. (1) He experienced feelings of keen disappointment with the people of His country for their lack of spirituality (Mk 8^{12} 6^6, Jn 11$^{33. 38}$, cf. Mk 9^{19}, Jn 14^9, Mk 8$^{17ff.}$ 6^4 = Lk 4^{24}, Lk 8^{25} = Mk 4^{40} = Mt 8^{26}, Mk 3^5 7^{18} 8^{12} 10$^{21ff.}$ = Lk 18$^{18-30}$ = Mt 19$^{16-24}$). On the other hand, He expressed astonishment at the spiritual

receptivity of some who had no claim to be amongst the number of the chosen people of God (Mt 8^{10} = Lk 7^9, cf. Mt 15^{28} = Mk 7^{29}), though He recognizes the fact that this phenomenon was not confined to His own experience (Mt 12$^{41f.}$ = Lk 11$^{31f.}$, Lk 4$^{22-27}$). The legitimate inference to be drawn from the passage last mentioned is not so much that the Divine love flowed over spontaneously towards those who were outside the Abrahamic covenant, as that faith and trust, often found amongst the heathen, drew towards them God's gracious intervention, just as the lack of these spiritual graces amongst His own people tended to dry up the fountain of God's active love (Mk 6$^{1-6}$ = Mt 13$^{54-58}$ = Lk 4$^{16-24}$ [cf. Plummer, in loc.]).

One of the methods adopted by Jesus for purposes of instruction was that with which the name of Socrates is usually linked. Starting from premises universally recognized as valid, He leads His hearers onwards by question and answer to the result He wishes to establish (Mk 8$^{14-21}$ = Mt 16$^{5-12}$, Mk 12$^{14ff.}$, Mt 12^{48} 22$^{31ff.}$ 22$^{41-46}$ = Mk 12$^{35-37}$ = Lk 20$^{41-44}$). With these examples we may also compare the merciless way in which Jesus employed this method to involve His enemies in an awkward dilemma (Mt 21$^{24-26}$), driving home His argument against their moral dishonesty by the parable of the Two Sons, and the question arising out of it (Mt 21$^{28-31}$; cf. 21$^{40-45}$, 12^{27} and 15^3). Not all the questions, however, asked by Jesus were of this character. Some are of the nature of ordinary inquiry—a demand for some needed information. Such are the questions addressed to the sisters of Bethany (Jn 11^{34}), to the Gerasene demoniac (Lk 8^{30} = Mk 5^9), to the father of the epileptic boy (Mk 9^{21}), to the disciples on the two occasions (if, indeed, they are not different versions of the same occurrence) of His feeding the multitude (Mk 6^{38}, 8^5 = Mt 15^{34}; cf., however, Jn 6^6, which is the author's gloss).

(2) Not very far removed from this phenomenon in Jesus' life is the habit of prayer and quiet communion with God which He habitually and sedulously cultivated (Mt 11$^{25-30}$ = Lk 10$^{21f.}$, Lk 3^{21}, Mk 1^{35}, Mt 14^{23}, Lk 5^{16} 6^{12} 9^{28} 22^{32} 22$^{42ff.}$ = Mt 26$^{36ff.}$ = Mk 14$^{32ff.}$, with which we may compare Jn 17$^{9-15. 20}$ 14^{16} 12$^{27f.}$). Of the three Synoptists, St. Luke seems to be the one who most appreciates this feature of Jesus' attitude to His Father. No truer comment has ever been made on it than that of the writer of the Epistle to the Hebrews (5^7) in referring to His supplications in Gethsemane—the 'obedience' of Christ was slowly fashioned through prayer, which was answered for His reverent devotion (Westcott, Ep. to Heb. in loc.). The two descriptive words employed by this writer (δεήσεις τε καὶ ἱκετηρίας) illustrate well the intense nature of these supplications (μετὰ κραυγῆς ἰσχυρᾶς καὶ δακρύων), reminding us of the vivid representation of Mk 14^{35}. We have here 'the spectacle of true man, weighted with a crushing burden, the dread of a catastrophe awful and unfathomed' (Gore, Diss. p. 82 f.).

iii. JESUS' ACTIVITY AS TEACHER.—(a) When we look at the position of Teacher occupied by Jesus, we not merely see Him assuming tacitly to be the ultimate authority upon the ethical value of OT laws, and giving instruction from that standpoint suitable to the receptive powers of His hearers, we are also confronted with His confessed subordination even in this sphere. His is a delegated authority conferred on Him by an unction from God. He was sent with a definite message, the contents of which He identified with that given in Deutero-Isaiah (ch. 42, cf. 61$^{1f.}$). We are reminded of the words of the Apostle Peter at Cæsarea (Ac 10^{38}), where he uses the same word to express this unction, and adds as the secret of the marvellous power exhibited by the Anointed that God was with Him. This thought is most frequently and plainly dwelt on in the Fourth Gospel, and this is the more surprising as it appears alongside of claims the most far-reaching as to the significance of His life and teaching. In His conversation with Nicodemus, Jesus sets forth His place in the scheme of world-salvation. He is the object of men's faith and belief. It is through Him that life is brought into the world. At the same time He is the Sent of God (. . . ἀπέστειλεν ὁ θεὸς τὸν υἱὸν εἰς τὸν κόσμον, κ.τ.λ., Jn 3^{17}, cf. 3^{34} 4^{34} 5$^{23.}$ $^{24. 30. 36-38}$ 6$^{29. 38. 39. 44. 57}$ 7$^{16. 18. 28. 29. 33}$ 8$^{16. 18. 26. 29. 42}$ 9^{4} 10^{36} 11^{42} 12$^{44. 45. 49}$ 14^{24} 15^{21} 16^{5} 17^{3} and 20^{21}, Lk 10^{16} 9^{48}, Mt 10^{40}, cf. Mk 9^{37} and Jn 13^{20}).

(*b*) Not only has He received His commission as a Teacher from God, but there is a limitation defined for Him in the scope of the delivery of His message (Jn 1^{11}, Mt 15^{24} 21$^{37f.}$). (1) This limit He not only observed Himself, but imposed also on His disciples. During His ministry their preaching was confined to the borders of Israel by His direct orders (Mt 10$^{5f.}$); and this limitation was considered of binding force at the time (Ac 3^{26}), though it was abrogated in the light of further development (cf. Mt 28^{18}, Mk 16$^{15f.}$, Lk 24^{47}, Ac 1^{4}). It is important, then, to recognize that Jesus Himself consciously set national and local bounds to His missionary activity, and was willing to adapt His methods of work to suit the conditions which governed the time and place of His incarnate life. It is difficult to see how He could have approached, with any hope of success, a people so hide-bound in traditionalism as were His countrymen, in any other way than He did. Discrimination in the choice, rather than originality in the creation and presentment of fundamental ideas, characterizes His teaching. And in this we discover His Divine wisdom and greatness. With conscious deliberation He refused, so far as His own personal work was concerned, to break with the best and truest tradition as it was embodied in the teaching and institutions of His time. (2) There is a line of development observable in the Jewish mind from the days of the earliest prophets right onwards to the time of Jesus, and He did not break off at a sharp angle from its continuation. He rather set His face towards the direction in which that line travelled, and unswervingly refused to turn aside at the bidding of a childish literalism or of a debased legalism. That He did not confine His recognition of truth to what was overtly taught in the OT is shown by the whole-hearted way in which He accepted the doctrine of individual resurrection, and pressed home the truth of this latter-day Judaistic development upon those who refused to accept it, by a magnificent *argumentum ad hominem* (Lk 20$^{37f.}$ = Mk 12$^{26f.}$ = Mt 22$^{31f.}$). With this doctrinal disputation between Jesus and the Sadducees we may compare that on the same subject between Gamaliel and the 'scribes of the Sadducees' (see Edersheim, *Life and Times of Jesus the Messiah*, vol. i. p. 316 n.). This Rabbi bases his argument also on a passage out of the Pentateuch (Dt 1^{8}, cf. 11^{9}), but misses the opportunity so well utilized by Jesus of emphasizing the spiritual side of that truth. It is significant in respect of this, that Jesus very seldom makes a formal declaration or revelation of the truth of the resurrection doctrine (Jn 5$^{25. 28}$); and, except on this occasion when He was challenged to prove it, He never attempts to give any reasons for its acceptance. He found the belief prevalent amongst the best spirits of His time, and He simply refers to it as a matter of course by taking for granted that His hearers will understand the allusion, and accept the consequences He deduces (Lk 14^{14}, cf. Jn 11^{24}). On the one hand, He lays stress on His own judicial

functions as finding their final scope when that wondrous result is achieved (cf. Jn 5$^{21. 27}$, Mt 24^{31} 16^{27} 25$^{31ff.}$ 19^{28} 13$^{49f.}$, Mk 13$^{23f.}$). Then, again, He incidentally refers to the resurrection as a future event of universal significance, to be brought into objective existence by the power of God (Mt 22^{29}) exercised through Himself, who will employ angels as the executors of His final decrees (Mt 13$^{41ff. 49f.}$, Mk 13^{27}).

(*a*) In these passages we are able to observe a double object in the teaching of Jesus about two distinct contemporary beliefs. As we have seen, there was a current belief, existent amongst the best religious thought, in the resurrection of the dead. This was, however, intimately connected with Jewish hopes as to the future earthly national Messianic kingdom (cf. Is 26$^{14. 19}$, Ezk 37^{11}, Dn 12^{2}, where its extent is limited to those who have distinguished themselves on one side or other of the national conflict, mainly with Antiochus Epiphanes [see Driver, *Daniel, in loc.* and Introd. xci f., and Salmond, *Christian Doctrine of Immortality*^{4}, p. 213; cf. Dn 11$^{32f.}$]).

The imperfection and uncertainty of the hold which this doctrine had on the Jewish mind is evidenced by such passages as 2 Mac 7$^{9. 14. 23. 36}$, 2 Es 7$^{(79)-(100)}$; Jos. *Ant.* xviii. i. 3; Bar 2^{17}, Sir 17$^{27f. 414}$. In the Apocalypse of Baruch, in answer to the question as to the changes which are to take place (49^{3}), the writer affirms his belief in the resurrection of the body, and the subsequent transformation of the bodies of the righteous in order to the enjoyment of unending spiritual happiness (chs. 50 and 51 [ed. by Prof. Charles]). The authors of the Book of Enoch vary as to the extent of the resurrection, but all are agreed as to the restoration of the righteous Israelite to the fulness of a glorious life in the new Messianic kingdom which God shall establish on earth.

Now, as we have just said, Jesus, in His allusions to the doctrine of the resurrection, while accommodating His language to the received Jewish opinions, emphasizes the truth and discards the excrescences which had deformed the popular belief. In His eschatological references and discourses, connexions with current thought are easily discovered, even when He is engaged in contradicting the presumptuous expectations of those whom He is addressing. Compare His use of apocalyptic figures when speaking of His Parousia (Mt 8^{11}, Lk 13$^{28f.}$ 22^{16}, Mt 26^{29}), where the future kingdom is likened to a banquet where the guests recline at the table with the fathers of the Jewish nation (cf. *e.g.* Mt 22$^{1-14}$ and Lk 14$^{15-24}$). This is the more remarkable that it is accompanied by a stern reminder that the real heirs of the kingdom shall find themselves outside their heritage. The reference to the judgment of the tribes of Israel is also to be noted in Mt 19^{28}, Lk 22^{30}, and Rev 20^{4}, reminding us of the idea expressed in Dn 7^{22}, 1 Co 6$^{2f.}$, Wis 3^{8}, Sir 4^{15}.

The imagery in which Jesus clothed His description of the events which were to precede the destruction of Jerusalem (Mt 24$^{1-31}$ = Mk 13$^{1-27}$ = Lk 21$^{5-28}$), and His subsequent Return, finds many parallels in Jewish literature (cf. 2 Es 5$^{1-13}$ 6$^{18-28}$ 9$^{1-12}$ 13$^{29-31}$, 2 Mac 5$^{2f.}$, Apoc. Bar 70$^{2-8}$; Mishna, *Sota*, ix. 15; and Jos. *BJ* vi. v. 3). It is probable that in Mt 24^{28} we have the quotation of a current proverb which may or may not have had its origin in the detestation in which the symbols of Roman power and authority were held (see Plummer on Lk 17^{37}; and Farrar, *Life of Christ*, vol. ii. p. 262). In any event we know that the phrase οἱ ἀετοί was known to His hearers as symbolical of God's judgments wrought by means of heathen enemies and oppressors (see Charles' ed. of *Enoch* [92]; cf. Dt 28^{49}, Job 9^{26}, Hab 1^{8} etc.). The same may be said of the reference to the trumpet (σάλπιγξ) as the instrument by which the resurrection of the dead is immediately effected (cf. 1 Th 4^{16}, 1 Co 15^{52}, Mt 24^{31}, and 2 Es 6^{22}). In this connexion, and intimately related to the subject of the destruction of Jerusalem, we may note the simile used by Jesus in His lamentation over that city. The similitude of the hen and her brood (Mt 23^{37}) 'is not found in the OT, but is frequent in Rabbinical literature' (Plummer on Lk 13^{34}). Compare, *e.g.*, 2 Es 1^{30}, in which context are also to be found very similar references to the righteous wrath of God and its terrible consequences. He will require the blood of all His servants and prophets slain by the hands of those to whom they were sent (2 Es 1^{32}). Their house is left unto them desolate (v.^{33}). These words remind us of the language of Jesus in Mt 23$^{35f. 38}$ (cf. Lk 11$^{49ff.}$), where Wendt thinks there is a reference to a Jewish apocalyptic writing (ἡ σοφία τοῦ θεοῦ εἶπεν) on the part of Jesus (*Lehre Jesu*, Eng. tr. ii. 362). See, further, MESSIAH, PAROUSIA.

(β) The other contemporary belief referred to above had to do with the part played by angels in the Divine economy of revelation and grace. Amongst the Jews of the time of Jesus there was a tendency to emphasize the importance of the functions ascribed to these beings. This tendency arose out of the growing habit of thought which removed God farther and farther from that active participation in the world's concerns which was characteristic of early Israelitish belief (Ex 3[7ff.], Gn 11[7] 18[21] [cf. G. B. Stevens, *The Theology of the NT*, p. 11 f.]). To them angels were the necessary media connecting a transcendental God with the world and men. (For the external influences which helped the growth of this development see art. [by Whitehouse] 'Demon, Devil,' in Hastings' *DB*, vol. i. p. 592). Over against God and His kingdom, thus conceived, stood Satan and his dominion, ruled after the same method by means of dependent demoniacal beings. It is important to note that, although these dualistic conceptions held a large place in the current thought of His day, Jesus has let fall no hint as to His ideas on the subject of angelology. By Him God is conceived as in direct living contact with men, guiding their affairs, and interesting Himself in their welfare (Mt 5[45], Lk 6[35], Mt 6[4. 6. 18. 32] 7[11]). Perhaps in no way does this come out so clearly as in the stress laid by Him on the Fatherhood of God (cf. *e.g.* Lk 15[11ff.]). What was halting, spasmodic, and inferential in the OT becomes in the teaching of Jesus a central, illuminating truth which He would have His hearers emphasize during the most sacred moments of their lives—Πάτερ ἡμῶν (Mt 6[9], cf. the Πάτερ of Lk 11[2]). At the same time the Gospels furnish us with many references by Jesus to angels and their work, all of which are intimately related to contemporary ideas. It is unimportant for our present purpose whether we interpret these references literally, or, as Beyschlag and others do, metaphorically; viz. as poetical and figurative expressions.

From Himself must have come the information noted by the Synoptists as to angelic ministrations (cf. Mt 4[11]=Mk 1[13], Lk 22[43]); and He must have been thinking of these services when He rebuked St. Peter with the question recorded in Mt 26[53] (cf. Jn 18[36], where οἱ ὑπηρέται οἱ ἐμοί may refer to them also). That He believed in the reality of their existence is, of course, true. That He ascribed to them functions suitable to their state of being is also true. They are described as 'holy,' possessed of a knowledge of the ways of God in a higher degree than the sons of men (οὐδὲ οἱ ἄγγελοι), and interested in the spiritual condition of mankind (cf. Mk 8[38], Mt 16[27] 25[31], Mk 13[32], Lk 15[10], with which we may compare 2 Es 16[66] and Lk 12[8]). Jesus in the parable of Dives and Lazarus, utilizes the Rabbinical belief that the souls of the righteous are carried to paradise by the angels, but in a way so incidental that we are not justified in affirming or denying His belief in that tenet (Lk 16[22], with which may be compared the description of Elijah's translation in 2 K 2[11]). In Mt 18[10] there is a deliberate assertion by Jesus that God's care over the least important of His people is exercised through the media of angels. This is an extension or development of the idea of national guardian angels in Dn 10[13. 20]. He makes an incidental reference to their supersensual nature in His discussion with the Sadducees on the subject of the Resurrection (Mk 12[25]=Mt 22[30]=Lk 20[36]), where He employs a well-known Jewish opinion (with the Lukan ἰσάγγελοι compare Apoc. Bar 51[10] and Eth. Enoch 104[4. 6]) in order to enforce a fundamental spiritual truth. The same didactic purpose is discoverable in all the references of Jesus to these beings; and we are therefore led to the conclusion that there is, in His attitude towards this question, evidence of that *deliberate* economy by which He set to Himself the task of accommodation to the limited knowledge of His fellow-men. It seems to the present writer to be very evident that Jesus knowingly refrained from correcting their ideas on this subject because He had an infinitely more important work to perform. To say with Bishop Gore that His 'language certainly reaches the level of positive teaching' about good spirits, seems to import more significance into that language than it can bear (cf. *Diss.* p. 23 f.). The work of Jesus lay on a far higher plane than this—the correcting and revealing of details as to the nature, position, and employment of subordinate spiritual agencies. It was sufficient for His purpose that a general belief existed in the

loving activity of God, though that activity might be somewhat too rigorously conceived of as mediated by certain personal forces—λειτουργικὰ πνεύματα (He 1[14]). A comparison of one pair of parallel passages may throw some light on the way in which Jesus' attitude towards this belief was interpreted by those who heard Him. In Mt 10[32] we read of those who accept, and are loyal in their adherence to, His Messianic claims, that the Son of Man will confess them before His Father in heaven; while in Lk 12[8] the words run, 'Him shall the Son of Man also confess before the angels of God.' From this it would appear that 'the angels of God' is a popular synonym for the Sacred Presence, and is employed by Jesus as such (cf. also Lk 15[7. 10]). But see art. ANGELS, p. 57[b] f.

(γ) On coming to the consideration of the kindred question arising out of Jesus' language respecting Satan, demons, and demoniacal possession, we are confronted with a more intricate and difficult problem. There can be no doubt, the present writer thinks, that as He believed in the personal existence of good, so He also believed in that of evil angels. How far, on the other hand, we are bound to accept the views which a literal interpretation of the passages where reference to them is found would convey, is another question, and one which demands some care in determining. In the first place, there are several instances where the language of Jesus respecting these beings is obviously figurative, and intended to be interpreted as such. In relating His experiences during the Temptation period, it would certainly seem as if He intended to convey, in language vividly symbolical, an idea of the tremendous difficulties which beset Him in His choice of two alternatives. The popular Jewish Messianic expectations He embodied in a personified form, and Satan appears in the narrative because of the didactic purpose which He had in view.

A similar interpretation seems necessary in Jesus' explanation of the parable of the Sower (Mt 13[19] ἔρχεται ὁ πονηρός; Mk 4[15] ἔρχεται ὁ Σατανᾶς; Lk 8[12] ἔρχεται ὁ διάβολος), though Plummer (note on Lk 8[12]) insists that Jesus is here emphasizing His belief in the Personality of the evil there described as working. The whole passage, however, is highly figurative, and it seems somewhat arbitrary to pick and choose in that way. A very remarkable instance of similar personification is found in the Lukan narrative of the healing of St. Peter's mother-in-law. Just as St. Luke seems to be the most deeply impressed of the Synoptists with this aspect of Jesus' power and work, so he is the only one of the three to note this. By using the verb ἐπετίμησεν (4[39]), which he had employed immediately before (v.[35]) in describing the healing of the demoniac in the synagogue, he links the two acts together by an inward connexion. The same verb, indeed, is found in all three Synoptists in their narratives of the stilling of the tempest on the Lake of Gennesaret (cf. Lk 8[24], Mt 8[26], Mk 4[39]), and we cannot resist the conclusion that the disciples saw behind the storm the work of a living personal agent, and that Jesus acted in the spirit of that presupposition (cf. O. Holtzmann's *Leben Jesu*, Eng. tr. p. 268). Similarly in His rebuke of St. Peter (Mk 8[33]=Mt 16[23]), Jesus sees behind the language of that chief Apostle that spirit of evil which all through His work strove to thwart and hinder Him. He addresses him directly and personally as 'Satan' (Σατανᾶ), just as He addressed the last and fiercest temptation in the first dangerous crisis of His life (Mt 4[10]).

A striking and illustrative example of this figure is discovered in Jesus' words to His returned missionary disciples (Lk 10[18]). These, in their report, referred specially to the power over demons, recently conferred upon the Twelve, as being also possessed by themselves, which elicited from Him the following reply, 'I beheld Satan fallen (AV fall) as lightning from heaven' (cf. Is 14[12]). Some see in these words a reference by Jesus to the original Fall of the Angels, and an implied rebuke to the disciples, warning them against the sin which caused that catastrophe. On the other hand, the use of the aorist participle (πεσόντα) in the place of emphasis points to the conclusion that Jesus is speaking of an event occurring during the time of the successful missionary tour (cf. Blass, *Gram. of NT Greek*, §58, 4, p. 197 f.; and Burton, *NT Moods and Tenses*, §146 ff., p. 67 f.). Be that as it may, the simile is a familiar one to the Jews (cf. Is 14[12-15], Rev 12[7-9]), and is used by Jesus to point to the overthrow of the kingdom of evil, as it was foreshadowed by the success which attended His disciples' first efforts (cf. Jn 12[31]).

A very remarkable instance of this method is peculiar to the Lukan narrative. Jesus, in warning St. Peter of his coming fall, informs him in solemn language that Satan 'obtained him by asking' (ἐξητήσατο, Lk 22[31]) for the purpose of testing him (cf. Job 1[6-12] and 2[1-6]). He puts Himself in direct personal opposition (ἐγὼ δὲ ἐδεήθην) to the Prince of Evil by praying for His Apostle. No less remarkable and instructive is the allegory, common to St. Matthew and St. Luke, by which He teaches the danger of and tendency towards reverting to a former state of sin. He speaks of the unclean spirit or demon (τὸ ἀκάθαρτον πνεῦμα) which, having been cast out of his victim, goes in search of rest through dry and desert regions (δι' ἀνύδρων τόπων). Failing in his quest, he deliberates with himself as to his future line of action, and finally makes up his mind to return to the place whence he was driven. With himself he brings seven other spirits, and they all take up their abode in the empty chamber, which was all too ready to receive them (Lk 11²⁴⁻²⁶, Mt 12⁴³⁻⁴⁵). For the belief that more than one demon might possess a human being, compare Mk 5¹ᶠ, Mt 8²⁸ᶠ, Lk 8²⁶ᶠ, and Lk 8² (ἑπτὰ δαιμόνια). The teaching of Jesus is not only based on the popular belief in the active connexion between evil spirits and the children of men, but there is a reference in it to the generally accepted idea that wild and desert regions are the special habitat of these beings (see art. 'Demon, Devil' in Hastings' *DB*, vol. i. p. 593ᵇ).

Jesus, on more than one occasion, seems to sanction the current conception of the malignant influence of demons on the human body, their activity in this respect being controlled and guided by their chief, Satan (ὁ ἄρχων τῶν δαιμονίων, Mt 12²⁴). St. Luke's diagnosis of the woman's case who was afflicted for eighteen years, is simply that she was possessed of a 'spirit of infirmity' (πνεῦμα ἀσθενείας, Lk 13¹¹); and Jesus apparently countenanced the belief by the words contained in His reproof (ἣν ἔδησεν ὁ Σατανᾶς, v.¹⁶). A similar instance of His countenancing popular beliefs occurs in the healing of the deaf and dumb epileptic (Mk 9¹⁷⁻²⁷). The boy's father believes his son to be the victim of demoniac malignity (ἔχοντα πνεῦμα ἄλαλον, v.¹⁷); and Jesus addresses the spirit by an authoritative command (τὸ ἄλαλον καὶ κωφὸν πνεῦμα, ἐγὼ ἐπιτάσσω σοι, v.²⁵).

Perhaps the surest evidence we have that Jesus *deliberately* suited His language to the notions of His day arises out of the way in which He wrought His cures, depending as He did on the moral and spiritual forces inherent in His own Person. A word, a command, a touch of the hand suffices His purpose (cf. Mt 8¹⁶, Mk 1²⁷, Lk 13¹³). There is no trace of His ever having employed any of the current methods of exorcism—the use of certain magic formulæ, such as 'the ineffable Name,' etc. (see Edersheim's *Life and Times of Jesus the Messiah*, bk. iii. ch. xiv. and Ap. XVI. Cf. the astonishment which Jesus' method created amongst His countrymen [Lk 4³⁶; cf. Ac 19¹³]). That He knew of such methods is evident from the ironical question He put to the Pharisees who accused Him of collusion with Beelzebub (Mt 12²⁷=Lk 11¹⁹). For evidence that Jesus believed in power over evil spirits exercised by others not directly commissioned by Him, cf. Mt 7²², Mk 9³⁸ᶠ=Lk 9⁴⁹ᶠ.

On the other hand, signs are not wanting that Jesus recognized an essential difference between the casting out of demons and the curing of bodily disease—' I cast out demons and perform cures' (Lk 13³², cf. Mt 10⁸, Mk 6¹³, Lk 9¹ 6¹⁷ᶠ). St. Matthew, moreover, records the same distinction in his account of the early Galilæan ministry (δαιμονιζομένους καὶ σεληνιαζομένους, 4²⁴, with which cf. Mk 1³²⁻³⁴). We may also note in passing that instances are not wanting of references to disease without mention of these agents (cf. e.g. Mt 9²⁷⁻³¹, Mk 7³²⁻³⁷, Lk 17¹¹⁻¹⁹).

Looking then at this last aspect of the question, and noting the way in which He employed the language current in His day about this mysterious phenomenon, we perceive Jesus' knowledge to be in advance of that possessed by His countrymen. We see the workings of that love which, while it appeals to man as he is, yet ever strives to draw him upwards by gradually stripping him of the clogging weights of superstition and of false conceptions. See artt. DEMON, LUNATIC, POSSESSION.

(*c*) In harmony with this characteristic habit of Jesus is His general method of imparting definite instruction. It is impossible not to be struck with the way in which He, not content with telling His hearers directly what He wishes them to know, approaches them from another side — the side of reason and its resultant freedom and independence of thought. The Sermon on the Mount is not a body of precepts like the Mosaic code, so much as a series of paradoxes which arrest and fix the attention, calling out and developing the powers of rational deduction. The same

feature runs through the parabolic form which His teaching so largely took, and which was so admirably suited to maintain the studied reserve in the content of His communications. Notice the way in which He keeps back, all through the earliest period of His ministry, the revelation of His claims to be the Messiah (Mk 1²⁵ 3¹² 8³⁰, Lk 4⁴¹, cf. Mt 12¹⁶ 8⁴ etc.); and even to the Twelve He does not impart the nature of those claims till they slowly worked out for themselves the conviction to which St. Peter gave such emphatic expression at Cæsarea Philippi (Mk 8²⁹=Mt 16¹⁶=Lk 9²⁰).

(1) Popularly intelligible and highly impressive, the parables of Jesus have been the wonder and admiration of every age. The OT is not without examples of this mode of teaching (2 S 12¹ᶠ 14⁶ᶠ, 1 K 20³⁹ᶠ, Is 5¹⁻⁶), and the Rabbinical writings afford numerous examples of parables (see Edersheim, *Life and Times of Jesus the Messiah*, vol. i. p. 580 f.) some of which bear a striking resemblance to those of Jesus (cf. Midrash on Ca 1¹). The object of parabolic teaching was twofold, and was thus purposely employed by Him (Mt 13¹⁰⁻¹⁷). By it He meant to conceal the truth 'from the wise and clever' (ἀπὸ σοφῶν καὶ συνετῶν, Mt 11²⁵ [see Moffatt's *Histor. NT*², p. 316 f.]). By it He at the same time intended to unfold the same truth 'to babes' (νηπίοις). According to the Markan narrative, there was an adaptation to the capacities of His hearers even within the zone of His parabolic teaching. He did not, that is to say, employ this method indiscriminately or harshly, but in a tentative and gentle fashion, proportionate to the intelligences of those who heard Him (Mk 4³³).

Such was the aim and intention of Jesus; and in connexion with this it will not be unimportant to note how, as His experience widened, and the stress of opposition increased, and the bitterness of the enmity to which He was exposed intensified, the parable enters more and more largely into His public teaching, and gradually assumes a more admonitory, controversial, and sometimes a warning judicial tone. It is impossible to draw up any hard and fast rule exemplifying this statement, but a comparison of the parables grouped in Mt 13 with those in Lk 14⁷⁻¹¹ 13⁶⁻⁹ 14¹⁶⁻²⁴ 16¹⁻¹³ 19⁻³¹ 19¹²⁻²⁷ etc. will show the gradual development of method in the employment of the parable by Jesus to drive home the meaning of His message to the heart and understanding of His hearers. See PARABLE.

(2) Without entering into a discussion as to the difference between the parable, the fable, the allegory, and other forms of instruction by figure, it is important to note that Jesus never disdains to use popular figurative expressions in order to point the truth He is aiming to disclose. Just as in its outward form and method He conformed to the usages of His time (cf. Mt 5¹, Lk 4²⁰, Jn 8², Mt 13¹ᶠ etc.), so in His choice of language He did not disdain to employ what He found ready to His hand, though it was manifestly imperfect. He did not, for example, correct the popular notions as to the local positions of Heaven and Hades. The one was regarded as being situated at an indefinite height above the earth (see Ac 1⁹ᶠ), the other 'as a dark deep underworld in which the deceased continued to exist' (Salmond, art. 'Hades' in Hastings' *DB* ii. 275). The ethical teaching of Jesus is not disturbed by these crudities. On more than one occasion He uses them as illustrations of His meaning. Capernaum, because it rejected the unparalleled opportunities afforded by His presence and works, He addressed with the question, 'Shalt thou be exalted unto heaven?' answering it Himself at the same time, 'Thou

shalt go down to Hades.' The idea was that a complete moral and spiritual overthrow awaited her, whereas she might have enjoyed the full and lofty freedom characteristic of the atmosphere of God's presence (see Mt 11^{23} = Lk 10^{15}).

The expression 'gates of Hades' (Mt 16^{18}) is similarly figurative, and in this place has reference to the forces of death and spiritual decay. Here there is an incidental reference to the general belief that Hades is an enclosed prison-like (cf. the ἐν φυλακῇ of 1 P 3^{19}) abode whose inhabitants are locked and detained inside its gates (cf. Rev 1^{18} 'I have the keys of Hades'), while there is added to this notion the further thought that there is even in Hades a broad impassable line of demarcation ('between us and you a great gulf is fixed,' Lk 16^{26}) between the souls of those who have lived piously here and those whose lives were selfish (cf. Lk 23^{43} where the former department of Hades is called 'Paradise'). In connexion with this subject it is instructive to note such ideas as are found in Enoch 22. 51. 63^{10} 102^5 etc., where, with the single exception of the *locale* of Sheol, the general description is very similar to that we have been discussing.

(3) One of the traditional forms of teaching was by the employment of aphoristic sayings, such as we have before us in the gnomic wisdom of the Son of Sirach, or of the *Pirḳe Aboth* in the Mishna (Schürer, *HJP* II. iii. pp. 23–32). Jesus uses this method with wonderful effect, as we see especially in the list of utterances grouped in Mt 5–7, which were collected, we may feel sure, from many different periods of His ministry. All four Gospels afford examples of these proverbial expressions. Cf. e.g. Mk $2^{17. 27}$ $9^{35. 40}$ 12^{17} 14^{38}, Mt 22^{14} 12^{30}, Lk 12^{48} 16^{10}, and the unrecorded saying in Ac 20^{35}, Jn 3^6 4^{24} 12^{25}, while, in this Gospel, Jesus refers explicitly to a proverb current in His time ('Herein is the saying true,' Jn 4^{37}). Very striking and vivid also are such figures as those by which the doctrine or teaching of the Pharisees is referred to by the word 'leaven' (Mk 8^{15}), His own suffering by the words 'cup' and 'baptism' (Mk 10^{38}, cf. Lk $12^{49f.}$), the relative positions of Jew and Gentile in the kingdom of grace by the words 'children' and 'dogs' (Mk 7^{27}). In the Fourth Gospel there is a striking frequency in this mode of expression. It is in this writing that Jesus speaks of Himself as 'the way' (ἡ ὁδός, Jn 14^6), 'the light of the world' (8^{12}), 'the bread of life' (6^{35}), 'the vine' (15^1), 'the door' (10^7). He speaks of His work as His 'meat' (4^{34}), of His body as 'this temple' (2^{19}). Cf. also such passages as those which deal with the second birth (3^3), the living water (4^{10}), the heavenly mansions (14^2), and so on. In all this we observe a method which is peculiarly adapted to the intelligence of those He meant to instruct; and this is still more emphatically the case when, as He sometimes does, He expands these figures and similes until they assume the shape of allegories. We see examples of this in His use of the figure of 'the shepherd' ($10^{10ff.}$), 'the vine' ($15^{1ff.}$), 'the light' ($12^{35f.}$), etc. No one who has ever heard these can fail to admire 'the wonderful art and power of popular eloquence' which He possessed. It was precisely the power to gain the attention and arouse and retain the interest of the people which Jesus wielded, and we can appreciate the reasons for the willingness and eagerness with which He was listened to by the proletariat (Mk 12^{37}). See art. WISDOM.

(4) The references in the discourses of Jesus to natural or world-phenomena, and to the psychological features of man's being, exhibit the same reserve, the same restraint in correcting popular notions, the same frank acceptance of current thought. A few examples will be sufficient to show how completely He adapted His language to the limitations of contemporary knowledge. (α) God makes His sun to rise (Mt 5^{45}); lightning comes out of the east and takes its swift journey towards the west (Mt 24^{27}), or it falls down straight from heaven (Lk 10^{18}); the germ of life in the wheat-grain is brought into active play only

by the death of the seed (Jn 12^{24}). Even the signs which enabled men to forecast the weather were laid by Him under contribution to emphasize a contrast (Lk $12^{54ff.}$). The wind blows hither and thither, but men know neither its beginning nor its ending (Jn 3^8), any more than they can point to the origin or the destiny of the mysterious ζωή ἄνωθεν, the reality of whose existence He nevertheless insists cannot be doubted. The gradual growth of the kingdom of God eludes men's observation, just as that of the planted seed does, which receives the vital principle of its growth from the earth, and advances steadily though secretly (Mk 4^{27}).

It seems to the present writer that in the last two cases Jesus is pointing to the existence of a wider field of knowledge into which man has not as yet entered. At the same time He seems to include Himself in the number of those who 'know not' the how or the wherefore. Ages were yet to pass over the world before men discovered the laws which govern the relations of natural phenomena, and which enable them, in some cases at least, to predict with almost infallible certainty their regular sequence. Jesus consciously recognized that it was no part of His work to add to the sum total of human knowledge of these subjects.

(β) The same trait is observable in His references to the anthropological ideas of His time; but for the illustration of this we must refer the reader to artt. FLESH, HEART, SOUL, SPIRIT.

iv. THE ATTITUDE OF JESUS TOWARDS THE MESSIANIC EXPECTATIONS OF HIS TIME. — A discussion of the question of Jesus' attitude towards Messianic hopes and longings is of the utmost importance, on account of its bearing upon the subject with which we are dealing. The attention of the student is at once arrested by His obvious anxiety during the early periods of His ministry to conceal from the general public His claims to the Messiahship. This He did expressly by forbidding the open proclamation of the truth not merely by the demoniacally possessed (Mk 1^{25} 3^{12}, Mt 12^{16}, Lk 4^{41}), but also by those amongst His circle of disciples who grasped the purport of His teaching and the secret of His Personality (Mt 16^{20} = Mk 8^{30} = Lk 9^{21}; Mt 17^9 = Mk 9^9 = Lk 9^{36}). For the same reason He courted secrecy in the performance of miraculous cures, and enjoined silence on those who were healed (Mk $1^{43f.}$ 5^{43} 7^{36} $8^{23. 26}$, Mt 9^{30} 8^4). Indeed, there is no part of the message which Jesus came to deliver where the words of Mk 4^{33} ('He spake the word unto them as they were able to hear it') are more appropriate. The declaration of His Messiahship was gradual; and even those who were nearest His Person, and in closest touch with His teaching, were left by Him to work out the truth slowly and by degrees.

(a) Perhaps the self-chosen title 'Son of Man,' by which He is styled early in His first Galilæan ministry, might at first sight contradict this statement (cf. Mk 2^{10} = Mt 9^6 = Lk 5^{24}; Mk 2^{28} = Mt 12^8 = Lk 6^5; Mt 12^{32} = Lk 12^{10}). On further consideration, however, it will be seen that Jesus, by this designation of Himself, had a twofold object in view—the concealment of His Messiahship from the many who were not ready to accept His interpretation of its meaning and purpose; and at the same time, the unfolding to the few who could bear the revelation, of the character of His Person and His work as shadowed by the title 'Son of Man.' See art. SON OF MAN.

(b) The attitude of Jesus to the Jewish Canon of the OT must not be left out of account when considering the methods of His public teaching. Frankly, the belief is at once confessed that here also He 'used the common language of His contemporaries in regard to the OT' (Sanday, *Bampton Lect.* p. 414), and in accordance with this we can explain the words which St. Luke puts into the mouth of the risen Jesus, where the tripartite division of the Hebrew Bible is recognized—the Law of Moses, the Prophets, and the Psalms (24[44]). With this we may compare the division given in the Prologue of the grandson of Jesus ben Sirach. Other divisions were also current, as 'Moses and the Prophets' (Lk 16[29. 31] 24[27]), 'the Law and the Prophets' (Lk 16[6], Mt 7[12]), where the idea is the same, namely, the entire OT as then existing. In perfect harmony with this is the acceptance by Jesus of the Mosaic authorship of the Pentateuch (Lk 16[29. 31] 24[27. 44], Mt 19[8] = Mk 10[3-5], Mk 12[26] = Lk 20[37], Jn 5[45-47] 7[19. 22f.]), and the Davidic authorship, if not of the whole Jewish Psalter, at least of many of the Psalms contained therein (Mk 12[36f.] = Mt 22[43ff.] = Lk 20[42ff.]).

(1) Several other indications there are which show that He accepted not only the general popular belief in the authenticity of the OT books as a whole, but also the literal genuineness of the stories with which they abound. The details of the narratives of the Flood and Noah (Mt 24[37ff.] = Lk 17[26f.]), the story of Jonah and his adventures by sea as well as in Nineveh (Mt 12[40f.] 16[4], Lk 11[29f.]), are utilized by Jesus on the assumption of their genuine historicity. The glory of Solomon's reign, that heyday of Israelitish prosperity, is incidentally mentioned by Him without any reserve (Mt 6[29] = Lk 12[27]). The question is not, as Dr. Sanday puts it (*The Oracles of God* [5], p. 111), whether Jesus 'accommodated His language to current notions, *knowing them to be false*,' but rather, was His 'accommodation' or 'condescension' so complete that He never entertained any other idea as to the character of these narratives than the one currently held? It certainly seems that it never entered into His mind to question their historical truth; and if we seek for the estimation in which He held 'the Law and the Prophets,' we find it expressed in words which, if genuine,* are as emphatic as any that are to be had. Not 'one jot or one tittle' (ἰῶτα ἓν ἢ μία κεραία) was to be done away with until all was fulfilled (Mt 5[18]). Into this Jewish idea of the abiding nature of the Law, Jesus characteristically imported a depth of meaning which, while it did not destroy, transmuted its whole tenor, giving it the eternal significance of which He speaks (ἕως ἂν παρέλθῃ ὁ οὐρανὸς καὶ ἡ γῆ), and which it could never otherwise have had. This habitual method, by which Jesus based His teaching on the foundations of existing knowledge, receives some illustration from the way in which He treats the story of Moses and the Bush (Mk 12[26] = Lk 20[37], cf. Mt. 22[31]). He says nothing whatever of the nature of this vision beyond what the letter of the narrative expresses. He does not tell us whether the sight was visible to the outward eye or to the inward spiritual understanding alone. Cf. also His references to the brazen serpent (Jn 3[14] 12[32]).

(2) In the same way, it seems to the present writer, we are to interpret the reference to the authorship of Ps 110 (Mt 22[41-45] = Mk 12[35-37] = Lk 20[41-44]). There were three distinct ideas current about this Psalm which Jesus adopts as the groundwork of His argument: (i.) it was Davidic, (ii.) it was written by David under the influence of inspiration (Δαβὶδ ἐν πνεύματι), (iii.) it was explicitly Messianic. If Jesus placed the *imprimatur* of His Divine authority upon any one of these notions, we are bound to believe that He did so on all, and by consequence on the Messianic ideas which were popularly held, and which doubtless were supposed to be favoured by Ps 110. We know, however, that He habitually discouraged the popular belief in a Messiah who was to be an earthly Sovereign of all-conquering power, which was held to be countenanced by the words of this

* See Hastings' *DB*, Extra Vol. p. 24 f.

Psalm (cf. Jn 6[15] 18[36f.] and Lk 17[20f.]). There is no hint given by any of the three Synoptists that Jesus corrected these Messianic expectations during the course of the argument. His purpose was other than this, 'to argue from the contents' of the Psalm, and not at all to correct ideas as to authorship and interpretation (cf. Driver, *LOT* [3] p. 363 n. ; and A. F. Kirkpatrick, 'Psalms,' in the *Cambridge Bible*, Introd. to Ps 110).

The whole edifice so laboriously constructed by the opponents of a rational criticism, on the basis of Jesus' references to this Psalm as well as to other portions of OT Scriptures, falls to the ground when considered beneath 'the dry light of reason.' The following words of Bishop Gore are so moderate and reasonable in connexion with this reference of Jesus to the Davidic authorship of Ps 110, that we may be pardoned for quoting them in full. 'On the face of it, the argument suggests that the Messiah could not be David's Son,—"if David calleth him Lord, how is he his Son?"—but, in fact, its purpose is not to prove or disprove anything, to affirm or deny anything, but simply to press upon the Pharisees an argument which their habitual assumptions ought to have suggested to them : to confront them with just that question, which they, with their principles, ought to have been asking themselves' (*Bampton Lect.* p. 198). In a word, nothing can be truer than that both 'the Saviour and the Apostles have quoted a body of sacred Scriptures, and it does not appear that in their teaching they had any wish to introduce a novel theory as to the meaning and authority of that collection. Neither the Apostolic writings nor the tradition of the Christian Church bear any trace of an explicit decision given by Jesus Christ or the Apostles with respect to the Canon of the Old Testament, and still less of a decision which would have the effect of formally correcting opinions which obtained in the Jewish world' (Loisy, *Canon de l'Ancien Testament*, p. 97).

v. SUMMARY AND CONCLUSION.—In summing up and reviewing the conditions under which the teaching of Jesus was ushered into the world, and the relation in which that teaching stood to the human race, we cannot do better than quote a passage from a little work of the last-named writer (*L'Évangile et l'Église*), though he is there dealing with a very different problem :—

'Nothing could make Jesus other than a Jew. He was only man under condition of belonging to one branch of humanity. In that in which He was born, the branch that may well be said to have carried in it the religious future of the world, this future was known in quite a precise manner, by the hope of the reign of God, by the symbol of the Messiah. He who was to be the Saviour of the world could enter on His office only by assuming the position of Messiah and by presenting Himself as the Founder of the Kingdom, come to accomplish the hope of Israel. The Gospel, appearing in Judæa, and unable to appear elsewhere, was bound to be conditioned by Judaism. Its Jewish exterior is the human body, whose Divine soul is the Spirit of Jesus. But take away the body, and the soul will vanish in the air like the lightest breath. Without the idea of the Messiah, the Gospel would have been but a metaphysical possibility, an invisible, intangible essence, even unintelligible, for want of a definition appropriate to the means of knowledge, not a living and conquering reality. The Gospel will always need a body to be human. Having become the hope of Christian people, it has corrected in the interpretation certain parts of its Israelitish symbolism. None the less it remains the shadowy representation of the great mystery, God and the Providential destiny of man and of humanity, because it is a representation always striving after perfection, inadequate and insufficient. This is the mystery that Jesus revealed, as far as it could be revealed, and under the conditions which made revelation possible. It may be said that Christ lived it as much as He made it manifest.'

The present writer has no intention of entering into the very difficult and much-debated question of the connexion between Jesus' ideas of 'the kingdom of God' (or 'of heaven') during the early and the later periods of His active ministry, or how far the latter was a development of the former ; nor again to inquire as to the period when it dawned upon His consciousness that His death was the condition upon which its inauguration and subsequent life rested. Broadly speaking, a line of demarcation might be drawn through the life as it is presented to us, cutting it into two fairly well marked divisions at the time of the Petrine confession and the Transfiguration. After these events Jesus began to concentrate His teaching more especially upon the circle of disciples gathered closely round Him. It was then that He, in solemn and almost sad foreboding, warned His followers of the events which were soon to try His own fidelity to the cause which He so constantly and fearlessly championed, and which were to put their faith to a most cruel test. We are indebted to the writer of the Fourth Gospel for the series of discourses in which He endeavoured to strengthen and encourage His disciples against the coming time of trial. From these we gather that Jesus looked forward to the establishment, on the basis of His own life, of a kingdom amongst men which was to carry on His teaching, even as it received the truth at the hands of His Spirit. The time had not as yet arrived when they could assimilate the full self-revelation of God (Jn 16[12]), but as their experience widened and their understandings became enlarged, they would be made the recipients of 'all the truth' (v.[13], cf. also 15[26]). That He looked beyond the lives of those whom He thus addressed will not, we think, be disputed (cf. εἰς τὸν αἰῶνα, 14[16]). Certainly His words were so interpreted by His followers (see Mt 28[20]; cf. 18[20], Jn 14[3] 17[24], Ac 2[39]). We are thus emboldened to state our belief that this plan of Divine self-accommodation enters into the very centre of the life of Jesus Himself, and that it is the plan by which the world has received its education from the beginning even till these latter days.

'Each of them [Baptism, Temptation, and Transfiguration of Jesus] constitutes a moment, and a moment important, nay supreme, in the development of the Humanity of our Lord. That for the ultimate, Divine consummation accomplished in the garden and on the cross He was preparing all His life long, and that we can see in these three events a scheme divinely prepared, by which that development was set forward ; that we can see Him in each of the three pass from stage to well-defined stage of that incomprehensible process which is indicated in the Epistle to the Hebrews, when He is spoken of as "learning obedience." . . . That this growth . . . should have gone on to the end of His life is in itself no more marvellous or more mysterious than that it should ever have been possible, and have taken place' (Ch. Quart. Rev., July 1901, pp. 303–4).

The question naturally arises at this stage, How far is this Divine method of educating humanity to enter into the conscious active life of the teaching 'Body of Christ' (Eph. 4[12])? How is the Church to exercise her functions as the guide and instructress of the race? Is she to draw lines of distinction between those who 'are able to bear' the fulness of the faith delivered to her keeping, and those whose receptive faculties she considers are not fitted to receive such revelation? How far is she to practise the doctrine of economy or reserve in disclosing to men 'the faith which was once for all delivered to the saints'? (Jude [3]). That grave dangers await a policy which seems to put such judicial authority into the hands of men, is not to be denied ; nor can we shut our eyes to the tendency which such a course fosters, to hold up different standards of belief and practice before different minds. At the same time, we cannot shut our eyes to the sad phenomenon of a rent and distracted Christendom, which necessarily implies inability somewhere to grasp the fundamental verity of Christian life (cf. Jn 13[35]). Imperfect belief and faith are the causes to which must be attributed the vital as well as the minor differences separating those who ought to belong to the same household. The bearing with each other, the sympathetic endeavour on each side to understand the other's point of view, seem to be the only worthy methods of continuing the work of love begun by Jesus. It seems, indeed, to be the method which, springing from the love for men which He inculcated, He bequeathed to His teaching Body. We are, however, bound to admit that those occupying the position of *Doctores ecclesiæ* have not always marched in the van of human progress, and that often they have adopted the rôle of obscurantists where the discoveries of

science ran counter to preconceived ideas. The Church, at times, seemed to have been committed almost irrevocably to a false and transient philosophy, to a weak and untenable exegetical process, when she was forced by the onward march of God's self-revelation, grasped and promulgated in the teeth of opposition and obloquy by the brightest intellects amongst her children, to review her position, to reject old prejudices, and to bring her interpretation of the life and teaching of Jesus into line with the newer discoveries which are so constantly revealing to men's minds wider and profounder ideas of the condescending love of God. The chief object for which the Church exists is, while 'reproving, rebuking, exhorting' (cf. 2 Ti 4[2]), to interpret the Incarnation as it bears on man's life, and on the destiny of the world and the race, in the light of an ever-increasing knowledge. Her business is not so much to keep back the profounder mysteries of a gradually accumulating revelation from the minds of 'the weak' (1 Co 8[9]), as to build up and strengthen the entire man, intellectual and spiritual, so that all may learn that there is no department of human life which has not its own intimate relationship with the Incarnate Son of God.

LITERATURE.—The following works, most of which are either quoted or referred to in the course of this article, are specially recommended as throwing light on a difficult problem :— Schürer, *HJP*, which is a veritable mine from which we may excavate an immense amount of information about contemporary beliefs, customs, modes of thought and of teaching ; J. B. Mozley, *Ruling Ideas in Early Ages* ; Edersheim, *The Life and Times of Jesus the Messiah* ; B. Weiss, *Leben Jesu*, Eng. tr., and *Bibl. Theol. NT*, Eng. tr. (T. & T. Clark) ; H. J. Holtzmann, *Neutest. Theol.* ; O. Holtzmann, *Leben Jesu*, Eng. tr. (A. & C. Black) ; Farrar, *The Life of Christ* ; Gore, *The Incarnation* (*BL*, 1891), and *Dissertations on Subjects connected with the Incarnation* ; Plummer, *St. Luke* (Internat. Crit. Com.) ; Gould, *St. Mark* (Internat. Crit. Com.) ; Salmond, *Christian Doctrine of Immortality* [4] ; Jülicher, *Die Gleichnisreden Jesu*, and §§ 28–29 of his *Einleitung in das NT*, which are incidentally rather than directly useful ; Trench, *Notes on the Parables*, and *Notes on the Miracles* ; V. Rose, *Studies on the Gospels* ; Loisy, *L'Évangile et l'Église* [1], and *Autour d'un petit livre*, especially two letters therein entitled 'Sur la critique des Évangiles et spécialement sur l'Évangile de Saint Jean,' and 'Sur la divinité de Jésus-Christ' ; T. H. Wright, *The Finger of God* ; Wendt, *Lehre Jesu*, Eng. tr. (T. & T. Clark) ; Stevens, *The Theology of the NT* ; Bruce, *The Humiliation of Christ* ; Sanday, *Inspiration* (*BL*, 1893), and *The Oracles of God* ; A. Robertson, *Regnum Dei* (*BL*, 1901) ; J. Lightfoot, *Horæ Hebraicæ et Talmudicæ* (ed. Gandell, Oxford 1859) ; several articles in Hastings' *DB*, especially Sanday's 'Jesus Christ' ; Driver's art. 'Son of Man,' which ought to be studied in conjunction with two papers on 'The use and meaning of the phrase *The Son of Man* in the Gospels,' by J. Drummond in the *Journ. of Theol. Studies* (Apr. and July 1901) ; Fairweather, 'Development of Doctrine' in Extra Vol. of *DB* ; R. L. Ottley, 'Incarnation' in vol. ii. ; A. B. Davidson, 'Angel' in vol. i. ; and Whitehouse, 'Demon, Devil' in vol. i., and 'Satan' in vol. iv.

The reader is also recommended to refer to such articles in the *Encyc. Bibl.* as 'Demons,' §§ 6–10, and 'Satan,' §§ 5–8, by J. Massie, and Jülicher's art. 'Parables.' See also Charles, *The Book of Enoch* and *The Apocalypse of Baruch*, which are useful for a comparative study of some of the subjects treated in this article, and in conjunction with these read his two articles on 'Eschatology' in Hastings' *DB* and in the *Encyc. Biblica*.

J. R. WILLIS.

ACCUSATIONS.—See TRIAL (OF JESUS).

ACHIM ('Αχείμ).—An ancestor of Joseph, according to the genealogy of our Lord in St. Matthew's Gospel (1[14]). The name may be a shortened form of *Jehoiachim*, or it may be for *Ahiam* (cf. 1 Ch 11[35]) or *Jachin* (cf. Gn 46[10]).

ACTIVITY.—1. The period of our Lord's activity is, in other words, that of His ministry, in the fulfilment of which His activity was exhibited. Its duration is a matter of dispute, relevant only so far as it compresses into one year the recorded details, or extends them to the traditional three. In any case the records are in no sense exhaustive. Manifold ministries are expressed in few words (Mt 4[23. 24] 15[30], Lk 4[43] 8[1], Jn 4[1] etc.) ; a complete account is beyond an Evangelist's scope (Jn 20[30. 31]), and would be voluminous (21^{25}). This is said of things done 'in the presence of the disciples' (Jn 20^{30}), and we cannot suppose they saw or knew all that Jesus did. See art. MINISTRY.

In fact, we possess no more than specimens of Christ's labours; but these, no doubt, are so selected as to give us a general idea of the whole. In this connexion the first Sabbath at Capernaum (of which a detailed account is given in Mk 1^{21-34}, Lk 4^{31-43}) has well been pointed to as a specimen day. Some details of the Son of Man's toilsome life—wearying journeys (Jn 4^6), rising 'a great while before day' (Mk 1^{35})—may be in themselves not much more than features of Oriental life: others—'nowhere to lay his head' (Mt 8^{20})—cannot be so explained. Day to Him meant work. The Father's work was both a daily necessity (Jn 9^4) and His very 'meat' (4^{34}). Its substance was twofold : (1) the *general* work of evangelizing and healing ; (2) the *special* work of training others, the Twelve (Mk 3^{14} 6^7 etc.) and the Seventy (Lk 10^1), and superintending their efforts. Similarly we may regard as twofold the conditions under which it was carried on : (1) the *normal* conditions, ever varying, of the day (Sabbath or week-day), the place (synagogue, Temple or open-air) and the hearers (multitudes or individuals) ; (2) the *abnormal* conditions, created by the presence of opponents (Mt $12^{10-14. \ 24-42}$ etc.), or of crowds who clung to Him sometimes for days together (Mt 15^{32}, Mk 8^2). Under such pressure there was often no leisure to eat (Mk 3^{20} 6^{31}). Night did not mean sleep, but was given largely to prayer (Mt 14^{23}, Lk 6^{12} 9^{28} 22^{39-41}), till His exhausted nature, finding opportunity for repose, could sleep undisturbed even by a storm (Mk 4^{38}, Lk 8^{23}). More than once His disciples (accustomed by their trade to night-watches, Lk 5^5) proved unequal to the strain of wakefulness (Lk 9^{32}, Mk $14^{37. \ 40}$). His friends, fearing a mental breakdown, came to restrain Him by force (Mk 3^{21}). It would be hazardous to estimate degrees of spiritual activity by the precarious test of numerical results (Jn 12^{37-40}), but it is noticeable that at one time He made more disciples than John the Baptist (Jn 4^1).

Certain limitations of Christ's activity are clear and significant. (1) In scope it was confined to 'the house of Israel,' more especially its 'lost sheep' (Jn 1^{31}, Mt 15^{24}). A few outsiders (Gentiles and proselytes) came within its range ; but these were exceptional (Mt 8^{5-13} 15^{22}, Lk 17^{16}, Jn 4^9 $12^{20. \ 21}$). (2) In development it was regulated by the unfolding of a Divine plan, frequently referred to by such expressions as 'my hour' (Jn 2^4 7^{30} 8^{20} 13^1 etc.), 'my time' (Mt 26^{18}, Jn 7^6). (3) In operation it was morally conditioned by the existence (or otherwise) of a certain measure of receptiveness (Mk 6^5).

In reference to the source of His activity, it must be noted : (1) that it was always and essentially associated with times of retirement and prayer (Mk 1^{35} 3^{13} 6^{46} 9^2 etc.) ; (2) that its manifestation is directly ascribed to the power of the Spirit (Mt 12^{28}, Lk 4^{14} etc.) ; and (3) that, in its miraculous exercise, there is indicated (at least once) a perception that 'power had gone out' (Mk 5^{30}, Lk 8^{46}).

2. In the Christian course, energy is constantly commanded (Mt 11^{12}, Mk 13^{33}, Lk 13^{24}). Yet it is worthy of remark that in Christ's estimate of human character the active qualities seem sometimes to be depreciated in comparison with the passive, contemplative, and devotional. The latter attain to 'the good part' (Lk 10^{38-42}), and find their place in the Beatitudes (Mt 5^{3-12}). See, further, CHARACTER (Christian).

3. Finally, the believer's view of Christ is not, in the Gospels, primarily directed to His active labours. Such things are the record of an Apostle (2 Cor $6^{4. \ 5}$ etc.) rather than a Saviour : accord-ingly, if with the account of our Lord's active labours we measure that of His Passion, both as to general proportion and minutiæ of detail, there can be no doubt that in the Gospel picture the Passion, and not the activity, occupies the foreground.   F. S. RANKEN.

ACTS OF THE APOSTLES.—The aim of this article is to answer the question, What does the Acts of the Apostles say of Christ ? ; otherwise expressed, How is the Book of Acts related to 'the gospel ?' or, What is 'the gospel' of the Acts ? We do not know the name of the author of the book—for St. Luke or some other disciple of St. Paul did not compose it, but merely supplied valuable materials for its composition—but his religious individuality may be ascertained from his work with sufficient clearness to enable us to answer the questions just stated. The problem is all the more interesting because the author can hardly have written before the end of the 1st cent., and thus cannot reckon himself among the first eye-witnesses and ministers of the word (Lk 1^2). What then is the picture of Christ that stamps itself on the heart of a man of the second generation ? Has this man anything new, anything unique, to tell us of Him ?

Before we go on to answer this question, we must make it clear to ourselves that our author, in what he writes, does not always speak *in his own person*. From the Gospel of St. Luke we know to what an extent he is dependent on sources. This may be observed and proved in particular instances by a close comparison with St. Mark and (in the case of the discourses) with St. Matthew. In the Gospel he is almost entirely a mere retailer of older tradition, and the lineaments of his own personality scarcely come into view. There can be no doubt that likewise in the Acts he largely reproduces early tradition, that he makes use of sources, sometimes copying them in full, at other times abbreviating or expanding them, grouping them and editing both their language and their contents. Modern criticism, however, has reached the conviction that in this second work more of the author's idiosyncrasy is to be detected than in his Gospel. Hence it will be necessary to make the attempt to distinguish the notions which reveal to us the educated writer of the last decade of the 1st cent. from those passages in which the rôle is played by early popular tradition.

The author's personality undoubtedly shows itself more strongly in the second than in the first part of the book, but most clearly in the way in which the work is arranged in these two parts, so that the first is dominated by the person of Peter and the second by that of Paul. To him the Church rests upon the foundation of the Apostles and prophets (cf. Eph 2^{20} 3^5)—not upon *one* Apostle, as in Mt 16^{18}, but upon the two great leaders, the head of the primitive Church who by a Divine dispensation was led to engage in a mission to the Gentiles, and the great Apostle of the heathen world who by Divine guidance had to turn his back on his own people and betake himself to the Gentiles. 'Peter and Paul' is the watchword, the shibboleth of the Roman Church, as we find again in the First Epistle of Clement.

It is especially in the *speeches* contained in the second part of the book that the author reveals his conception of Christianity. When St. Paul discourses (Ac 24^{24}) of 'the faith in Christ Jesus,' the subjects of his address are given in v. ^{25} as 'righteousness, temperance, and judgment to come.' This future and not distant judgment is also the point that forms the climax of St. Paul's address at Athens (17^{31}) : 'He hath appointed a day in the which he will judge the world in righteousness,' and immediately thereafter, 'by a man whom he hath (thereto) ordained, having given him his credentials before all men by having raised him from the dead.' This last is the essentially new point in contradistinction from the Jewish preaching in the Diaspora. That there is to be a judgment of the world had, indeed, been already declared, but that the Judge 'appointed by God over living and dead' (10^{42}) is already present in heaven (3^{21}), has already been manifested on earth (1^3 $10^{40f.}$), and accredited by God through an unprecedented miracle—this is the cardinal and significant message of the Apostles. Now, it is noteworthy how the author of the Acts gives point and practical application to this generally accepted idea. The resurrection of *Jesus* is the main content of the Apostolic preaching, so much so that in 1^{22} the Apostles are roundly designated 'witnesses of the resurrection.' In the eyes of our author it comes to this, that in the gospel of the resurrection of *Jesus* is implied the doctrine of the resurrection of the dead *in general*. What St. Paul (1 Co 15^{12-19}) seeks to prove to his readers, is to our author self-evident : the one special case implies the general. This is plainly declared in Ac 4^2 'they proclaimed *in Jesus* the resurrection from the dead.' So also in 17^{18} 'he preached Jesus *and the resurrection*,' and in v.^{32} 'the resurrection of the dead' is the point in St. Paul's address on which the Athenians fix. Before the Sanhedrin St. Paul declares : 'Touching the hope and *resurrection of the dead* I am called in question' (23^6) ; to Felix he says : 'I have the hope that there shall be a resurrection both of the just and of the unjust' (24^{15}). The latter passage is specially important because in it the relation of Christianity to Judaism is defined to the effect that there is really no essential difference between them. St. Paul, like his accusers, serves, although after the new 'Way,' the God of the fathers (v.^{13}) ; 'for the hope of Israel' he bears his chain (28^{20}). All Jews who believe in the resurrection ought really to be Christians. 'Why is it judged incredible with you if God doth raise the dead ?' (26^8). Hence also the Pharisees, who believe in the resurrection of the dead, appear as the party favourable to Christianity; whereas the Sadducees, who say that 'there is no resurrection,' are its enemies (23^8). Resurrection, then, is the main theme of the new message, hence the preaching of the Apostles bears the designation 'words of this Life' (5^{20}). The Risen One is 'the Prince of Life' (3^{15}). By His resurrection and exaltation He is proved to be the Saviour ($\sigma\omega\tau\eta\rho$, the term best answering our author's purpose, and most intelligible to the Greeks of the time, $5^{30f.}$ 13^{23}) ; the 'word' is the 'word of salvation' (13^{26}) ; and the whole of the Acts of the Apostles might have this motto prefixed : 'In none other is there salvation, and neither is there any other name under heaven, that is given among men, wherein we must be saved' (4^{12}). This religion is proved to be the superior of all earlier ones, superior alike to the darkness of heathendom (26^{18}) and to Judaism, in this, that it tells of a *Saviour* who saves *alive*. The method is described in 10^{43} $13^{38f.}$ 26^{18} as the forgiveness of sins, or, to use the designation adopted in one of St. Paul's addresses, 'justification' (13^{39}).

But who now is the Judge and Saviour accredited by the resurrection ? It is very characteristic of our author that in those passages where for the most part it is himself that speaks, *e.g.* in the speeches put into the mouth of St. Paul before Agrippa or Felix or Festus (chs. 22. 23), we scarcely hear of the earthly Jesus but of the heavenly Lord. The appearance of the Exalted One near Damascus is the great matter which St. Paul has to communicate to his countrymen and to the Jewish

king. It is the heavenly Lord that permeates the life of His Church and His apostles, the Κύριος on whom Christians believe. This Divine name is very often applied in the Acts to God, but not infrequently also to Christ. Thus the Exalted Christ, working miracles from heaven by His name (9^{34}), accredited by the miracle of the resurrection, and destined to come again with judgment and salvation, occupies the central point of the faith of our author.

But it would be a mistake to suppose that our author had no interest in the earthly Jesus of Nazareth. As the heavenly Christ says to Saul, 'I am Jesus of Nazareth whom thou persecutest' (22^8), so to the writer of the Acts 'the Christ' and 'Jesus' constitute an inseparable unity. He interchanges freely such expressions as 'proclaimed unto them the Christ' (8^5) and 'preached unto him Jesus' (v.^{35}) ; cf. 5^{42} 'to preach Christ Jesus' (RV 'Jesus [as] the Christ'), 9^{20} 'proclaimed Jesus that he is the Son of God,' 18^5 'testifying to the Jews that Jesus was the Christ.' And as our author in his Gospel narrative already calls Jesus 'Lord,' it is always of the Exalted One that he thinks even when communicating what he knows of the earthly life of Jesus. More than once he defines the contents of the Apostolic preaching as 'the things concerning Jesus' (18^{25}) or 'the things concerning the Lord Jesus Christ' (28^{31}), and this concise formula embraces far more than one might infer from the meagre sketches of St. Paul's address in 13^{24-30} or St. Peter's in 10^{37-43}. We must keep in mind that the first readers of the Acts, Theophilus in particular, when this work came into their hands, were already acquainted with the Third Gospel, and would thus, by means of the full details supplied in it, unconsciously clothe with meaning the brief formulæ in question. Still more varied was the knowledge which *our author* possessed of the life of Jesus, for he was acquainted not only with St. Mark's Gospel, but with other writings which he utilized merely for extracts ; and how manifold may have been the oral tradition current at the same time, which he made use of in an eclectic fashion ! The whole of this copious tradition we must think of as forming the background of the Acts if we are to appreciate rightly its picture of Christ.

A special charm of the Lukan writings arises from the fact that the author, with all his culture and Greek sympathies, has had the good taste to retain in large measure the peculiar, un-Greek, popular Palestinian character of his sources, and that both in language and contents. Some scholars, indeed, are of opinion that he himself deliberately produced the colouring appropriate to place and time, as in the case of an artificial *patina*. But this view is untenable. The more thoroughly the Third Gospel and the Acts are examined, the deeper becomes the conviction that the author worked upon a very ancient tradition which he has preserved in his own style. As in the early narratives of his Gospel he preserves almost unimpaired the colouring and tone of Jewish-Christian piety without any admixture of Græco-Gentile-Christian elements, so also in the Acts, especially in the first part of the book, he has succeeded in presenting the original picture of the religious conceptions and the piety of the earliest Christian community in Jerusalem. We are far from believing that everything here related is 'historical' in the strict sense. For instance, it is in the highest degree improbable that the actual speeches of St. Peter have been preserved *verbatim* ; all we assert is that these chapters are a true representation of the spirit of early Jewish Christianity. Very specially is this the case with the Christology. For such a doctrine of Christ as is represented by the Petrine discourses was scarcely to be found in the Church after the time of St. Paul and at the time when the Fourth Gospel was written. After the *kenosis* doctrine of St. Paul had been propounded, and then, as its counterpart, the Johannine picture of Christ, in which also the earthly Jesus wears the 'form of God,' had taken hold of men's minds, a Christology such as the first part of the Acts exhibits could not have been devised. But we are grateful to the author for having preserved to us a picture of that earliest mode of thought. Let us examine its main features.

We may use as a collateral witness the words of the disciples on the way to Emmaus (Lk 24^{19}), for it is a mere accident, so to speak, that this story is found in the Gospel and not in the Acts : 'Jesus of Nazareth, which was a prophet (ἀνὴρ προφήτης), mighty in deed and word before God and all the people.' So also He is described by St. Peter : 'Jesus of Nazareth, a man approved of God unto you by mighty works and wonders and signs, which God did by him in the midst of you' (Ac 2^{22}). The peculiarity of this last statement is that the wonders and signs are not attributed to Jesus Himself : *God* wrought them through Him ; He was simply God's organ or instrument. The same thing is expressed in another passage (10^{38}), where it is declared that in His going about and in His deeds God was *with Him.* In both instances the conception comes out clearly that Jesus was a man chosen and specially favoured of God. There is not a word in all these discourses of a Divine birth, no word of a coming down from heaven or of a 'Son of God' in a physical or supernatural sense. On the contrary, Jesus is called more than once 'the Servant of God' (3$^{13. 26}$ 4^{27}). This designation suggests a prophet, and as a matter of fact Jesus is directly characterized as a prophet when in 4^{22} the words of Dt 18$^{15. 18f.}$ are applied to Him. At the same time He is no ordinary prophet, but *the* prophet like unto Moses ; He is the second Moses predicted by Moses himself.

But it may be asked, Was Jesus then nothing more than this to the earliest disciples, was He not to them *the Messiah*? In a certain sense—yes, and in another sense—no. Certainly He had received the kingly anointing (10^{38}) ; but, as David was anointed long before he received the kingdom, so Jesus was from the time of His baptism a king, indeed, but a secret one with an invisible crown. The primitive Jewish-Christian Church was far from saying : Jesus of Nazareth, as He journeyed through the land teaching and healing, *was* the Messiah ; no, He was then merely the One destined for lordship. It was only at a later period that He received the crown, namely at His resurrection and exaltation. Here comes into view the saying of St. Peter in Ac 2^{36}, which is a gem to the historian of primitive Christianity : 'This Jesus hath God made *both Lord and Christ,*' namely by exalting Him to His right hand (v.^{33}) and thereby fulfilling the words of Ps 110^1 'Sit thou at my right hand.' The exaltation of Jesus marks His ascension of the throne ; now He has become in reality what since His baptism He was in claim and anticipation—'the Anointed.' Now for the first time the name 'Lord' is fully appropriate to Him. This is the principal extant proof passage for the *earliest Christology.* It reveals to us the conceptions of the primitive Church, which, as a matter of fact, still underlie the teaching even of St. Paul. For, in spite of his advanced speculations on the subject of Christ, in spite of his doctrine of preexistence and his cosmological Christology, the Apostle holds fast in Ro 1^4 and Ph 2^9 to the notion that Jesus became 'Son of God in power' through His resurrection from the dead, and was invested with the title 'Lord' at His exaltation. To the

same effect St. Paul in Ac 13^{33} applies the words of Ps 2^7 ('Thou art my Son, *this day* have I begotten thee') not to the birth nor to the baptism of Jesus, but to the day of His resurrection and exaltation. With this fundamental passage corresponds another. When in Ac 3$^{19f.}$, speaking of the future, it is said 'that there may come the times of refreshing from the presence of the Lord, and that he may send the Christ who hath been appointed for you, even Jesus,' this assumes that Jesus has not yet made His appearance *as Messiah* ; in that capacity He belongs to the future ; there is not a word of coming *again* or of a *second* sending. Such is the earliest primitive Christian conception, and it is this alone which is in harmony with the preaching and the self-estimate of Jesus when these are rightly understood.

But what now are the contents and the significance of the life-work of Jesus? Thoroughly in harmony with important words of Jesus, Ac 10^{38} replies : 'He went about doing good, and healing all that were oppressed *of the devil.*' Just as the Third Gospel delights to represent the work of Jesus as a conflict with the devil, the brief formula we have quoted reproduces accurately the contents of His life work. Along with this, indeed, should be taken also 3^{26} 'God sent him to bless you in turning away every one of you from your iniquities.' He was 'the Holy and Righteous One' (3^{14}), or, absolutely, 'the Righteous One' (7^{52}). The latter expression is chosen no doubt in order to emphasize His innocence in His sufferings and death, but it is certainly not contrary to the spirit of the Acts to find in it the testimony that it was He that was called to break the sway of sin in the world. Less clear is Ac 10^{36}, according to which God caused 'peace to be preached by Jesus to the children of Israel,' a form of expression which recalls Eph 2^{17}, and in its abrupt conciseness no doubt reflects the conceptions of the author more than those of the early Church.

This brings us to the question, What view, judging from the evidence of the Acts, did the early Church take of the death of Christ? Repeatedly in the addresses of St. Peter it is urged upon opponents that *this* Jesus, the Holy and Righteous One, was put to death by the Jews (2^{23} 3^{13} 4$^{10. 25ff.}$ 5$^{28ff.}$ 7^{52} 10^{39} 13^{28}), by the hands of wicked men (2^{23}), although Pilate was prepared to acquit Him (3^{13}). In all these instances, as was fitting in addresses meant to lead the hearers to conviction and repentance, the innocence of Jesus is emphasised as a point to awaken conscience, not as an element in a doctrine of the atoning death of Christ. Such an element is entirely lacking in these chapters, for in the passage from Is 53 about the Suffering Servant, which Philip expounded to the Ethiopian eunuch, it is precisely the expressions about bearing our sins that are wanting. The early theology of the death of Christ confines itself entirely to the point that this event was in no way contrary to God's saving purpose ; on the contrary, it had long been foreseen (2^{23} 3^{18} 4^{28} 13^{29}). Hence the copious Scripture proofs, which, however, deal more with the resurrection than with the sufferings and death (2$^{25ff. 34f.}$ 4$^{11. 25f.}$ 8$^{32f.}$ 13$^{33ff.}$).

The resurrection is not in these passages, as with St. Paul, regarded as a clothing of the Risen One with a glorified body, but as the revivification, or, to put it better, the conservation of the very same body of flesh which was laid in the grave. The principle that governs the conception is found in Ps 16^{10} (quoted in Ac 2^{27}), 'Thou wilt not leave my soul to Sheol, neither wilt thou suffer thine holy one to see corruption.' For, if Christ did descend to Hades, He was not given over to its power (2^{31}), God 'having loosed "the pangs of death," because it was not possible that he should be holden of it' (v.[24]), 'nor did his flesh see corruption' (v.[31]). This is the essential point, that the same body which was laid in the grave was that which rose again. For this reason, as in St. Luke's Gospel (24[39-43]), such emphasis is laid upon the eating and drinking of the Risen One (Ac 10[41]); hence also the forty days' intercourse with the disciples (1[3]). Jesus, in short, actually returned again to earth in complete corporeality; hence the necessity, at the end of the forty days, of yet another special miracle, that of the Ascension (1[9]). Like Moses or Elijah, He is carried up by a cloud, as He still walks on earth and still belongs to earth. This tradition says nothing about the necessary change whereby this fleshly body that rose from the grave was transformed into the glorified heavenly body that appeared to Saul of Tarsus in kingly splendour. We have here before us the popular view of the Resurrection in its crudest form. That an author whose ideas otherwise are cast in such a Greek mould should reproduce it, shows that the popular conceptions cannot have been so strange to him as we should have supposed. Conceptions which *our* intelligence thinks it necessary to separate, and which a St. Paul did separate, appear to have found a place in the same mind side by side.

We owe a special debt of gratitude to the author of the Acts for having drawn for us several pictures illustrating the prominent part played in the early Church by the Spirit and the Name of the exalted Christ. The Spirit sent by the latter is the proof of His exaltation and Messiahship (2[33-36]). This is the culminating point of St. Peter's Pentecostal address (2[14-36]), whose *order* of thought forms a very interesting study for the historian of primitive Christianity. This proof is addressed primarily to the house of Israel (2[36]). The Jews have not, indeed, seen the Risen One (10[41]), but for that very reason His exaltation is designed as a final means of leading Israel to repentance (5[31]), for the coming of the era of salvation is bound up with this repentance (3[19f.]). Through this Spirit the exalted Lord is ever present with His own; He imparts power and success to the words of the Apostles (2[37] 5[33] 6[5]); and miracles are wrought by the power of God (6[8]). It is noteworthy, however, that it is only rarely that the Spirit of God is introduced in this connexion; far more frequently it is the Name of Christ that, like a present representative of the Lord, works miracles (3[16] 4[30]). Specially instructive are 9[34] where the *pronouncing* of the Name effects healing, and 19[13] where the use of the Name is resorted to even by unbelievers.

Literature.—Johannes Weiss, *Absicht u. literar. Charakter der Apostelgeschichte*; Weizsäcker, *Apostolic Age*; Pfleiderer, *Urchristentum*; McGiffert, *Hist. of Christianity in the Apostol. Age*; Hort, *Judaistic Christianity*; Chase, *Credibility of Acts*; *Expositor*, IV. iv. [1891] 178 ff.　　　　　J. WEISS.

ADAM.—1. In Lk 3[38] the ancestry of Jesus is traced up to Adam. From what source the Evangelist drew his genealogy it is impossible to say. But when compared with that in the First Gospel, it clearly shows the purpose with which St. Luke wrote. As a Gentile, writing for a Gentile, he took every opportunity of insisting upon the universal power of the gospel. The effects of the life and Person of Jesus are not confined to the Jews; for Jesus is not, as in St. Matthew's Gospel, a descendant of Abraham only, but of the man to whom all mankind trace their origin. See art. GENEALOGY OF JESUS CHRIST. But further, St. Luke closes his genealogy with the significant words 'the son of Adam, the son of God' (τοῦ Ἀδάμ, τοῦ Θεοῦ). Adam, and therefore all mankind, had a Divine origin. The same Evangelist who relates the fact of the virgin birth, and records that Christ was, in His own proper

Person, υἱὸς Θεοῦ (1[35]), claims that the first man, and hence every human being, is υἱὸς Θεοῦ. Thus the genealogy, which might at first sight appear to be a useless addition to the Gospel narrative, possesses a lasting spiritual value.

The truth placed by St. Luke in the forefront of his Gospel is treated in its redemptive aspect by his master St. Paul, who in four passages brings Adam and Christ into juxtaposition:

(*a*) 1 Co 15[22]. The solidarity of mankind in their physical union with Adam involves universal death as a consequence of Adam's sin. Similarly the solidarity of mankind in their spiritual union with Christ involves universal life as a consequence of Christ's perfect work.

(*b*) In Ro 5[12-21] this solidarity and its results are treated in fuller detail. (i.) Vv.[12-14]. *There is a parallelism between Adam and Christ.* Adam 'is a type of him who was to come' (v.[14]), in the sense that his act affected all men. Adam committed a παράπτωμα, a lapse, a false step—commonly termed the Fall. By this lapse, sin was as 'a malignant force let loose among mankind'; and through sin came physical death. (St. Paul sees no occasion for proof of the connexion between sin and physical death; he unhesitatingly bases his position on the narrative in Genesis; see 2[17] 3[3. 19. 21]). Were this all, the passage would implicitly annul human responsibility. But St. Paul, without attempting fully to reconcile them, places side by side the two aspects of the truth—the hereditary transmission of guilt, and moral responsibility: 'and thus death made its way (διῆλθεν) to every individual man, *because all sinned* (ἐφ' ᾧ πάντες ἥμαρτον)'. Controversy has raged hotly round this phrase, Augustine and many other writers having understood the relative ω as masculine, and as referring to Adam; so Vulg. *in quo*. But there can be no doubt that ἐφ' ᾧ must be taken in its usual meaning 'because.' Adam's fall involved all men in sin, and therefore in death; but this was because all men (in full exercise of their free will) sinned. It would be out of place here to discuss the attempts that have been made to combine these two factors in the moral history of man (see Literature): strictly speaking, they cannot fully and logically be combined; but many of the most fundamental truths of the Christian religion can be arrived at only by the balancing of complementary statements. In vv.[13. 14] a qualification is entered, which causes St. Paul to ruin his construction, and omit the apodosis of which v.[12] forms the protasis. He feels obliged to explain that, sin being an offence against law, those who lived between Adam and Moses had no law, and thus did not transgress an explicit command as Adam had done. But the fact that death reigned throughout that period only shows that—not the guilt of individuals, but—the transmitted effects of Adam's sin were at work. And it is this that makes him a type of the Messiah. (ii.) Vv.[15-17]. *The contrast is far greater than the similarity.* The contrast between Adam and Christ is great:—In *quality* (v.[15]). The one representative man, Adam, committed a παράπτωμα; but over-against that must be placed the undeserved kindness (χάρις) of God, and the gift of righteousness arising from the kindness of the other representative Man, Jesus Christ. In *quantity* (v.[16]). 'One act tainting the whole race with sin, and a multitude of sins collected together in one only to be forgiven.' In *character* and *consequences* (v.[17]). Adam's fall ushered in a reign of death; Christ's work ensures that all who have received His kindness and His gift of righteousness shall themselves reign in life. (iii.) Vv.[18-21]. *Summary* of the argument, in which it is further shown that Law 'came in as an afterthought' (παρεισῆλθεν), multiplying sin, but thereby only increasing the abundance of God's kindness.

(*c*) 1 Co 15[44-47]. The two foregoing passages from St. Paul's writings deal with the practical moral results of union with Adam and Christ respectively. These verses (i.) go back behind that, and show that there is a complete and radical difference between the *nature* of each; (ii.) look forward, and show that this difference has a vital bearing on the truth of man's resurrection.

(i.) St. Paul maintains (vv.[36-44a]), by a series of illustrations from the natural world, the reasonableness of a resurrection from death. In Nature 'every seed has its own particular body'—'all flesh is not the same flesh'—the terrestrial differs from the celestial—there is a different glory of the sun, the moon, and the stars. So also it may be rightly held that it is possible for *man* to exist in two different states, one far higher than the other. Not only so, but (vv.[44b. 45]) there actually exists such an analogous distinction between man and man, as Scripture shows. The thought in v.[45] is arrived at by an adaptation of Gn 2[7]: ⑤ καὶ ἐγένετο ὁ ἄνθρωπος εἰς ψυχὴν ζῶσαν. These words relate only that after being lifeless clay, man was by God's breath transformed into a living being. But St. Paul reads into the statement the doctrinal significance that the body of the first representative man became the vehicle of a 'psychical' nature, while the body of the Second is the organ of a 'pneumatical' nature. St. Paul's trichotomy of man may be represented thus:

$$\text{ΠΝΕΥΜΑ}$$
$$\text{ΨΥΧΗ} = \begin{cases} \text{ΝΟΥΣ} \\ \text{ΣΩΜΑ} \end{cases} = \text{ΣΑΡΞ}$$

Everything in man that is not πνεῦμα may be called 'psychical' in so far as it is considered as 'intellect,' and 'carnal' in so far as it is thought of as the seat of the animal passions; both the adjectives ψυχικός and σαρκικός thus mean 'non-spiritual.' The second half of St. Paul's statement—'the last Adam became a life-giving spirit'—finds no exact parallel in the OT, but seems to be based on a reminiscence of Messianic passages which speak of the work of the Divine Spirit, *e.g.* Is 11¹· ², Jl 2²⁸⁻³².

(ii.) But as the ψυχὴ ζῶσα came first and the πνεῦμα ζωοποιοῦν last, so it is with the development of mankind ; the spiritual must follow the psychical (v.⁴⁶). As the first man was formed from the clay, and had a nature in conformity with his origin, while the second Man has His origin 'from heaven' (v.⁴⁷), so among mankind there are those whose nature remains low and mean, tied to the clods of earth, and there are those whose nature has become heavenly (v.⁴⁸). But this implies more (v.⁴⁹). In his present state man is an exact counterpart, he visibly reproduces the lineaments and character, of the first man, because of his corporate union with him (ἐφορέσαμεν τὴν εἰκόνα τοῦ χοϊκοῦ). But the time is coming when we shall become the exact counterpart or image of the second Man (cf. Gn 2²⁶ᶠ·), because of our spiritual union with Him (φορέσομεν καὶ τὴν εἰκόνα τοῦ ἐπουρανίου). The above follows the text of B a c g 17 aeth.

arm. [syr. ‎ـــــــــــ‎ is indeterminate] ; and Theodoret distinctly says τὸ γὰρ φορέσομεν προρρητικῶς οὐ παραινετικῶς εἴρηκεν. The mass of authorities read φορέσωμεν, 'from a desire to turn what is really a physical assertion into an ethical exhortation' (Alf.) ; so Chrys., τοῦτ᾽ ἐστιν, ἄριστα πράξωμεν . . . συμβουλευτικῶς εἰσάγει τὸν λόγον. But it is difficult to conceive how St. Paul, who has from v.³⁵ been leading up to the thought of the resurrection, could at the critical moment throw his argument to the winds, and content himself with saying, 'according as we have been earthly in our thoughts, let us strive to be heavenly.'

It has been suggested that St. Paul adopted the designation of Christ as 'the last Adam' and 'the second Adam' from Rabbinic theology. But such a comparison between Adam and the Messiah was unknown to the earlier Jewish teachers. Passages adduced to support it belong to the Middle Ages, and are influenced by the Ḳabbala. See G. F. Moore, *JBL* xvi. (1897), 158–161 ; Dalman, *The Words of Jesus*, Eng. tr. 248 f., 251 f.

(*d*) Ph 2⁶. St. Paul speaks of 'Christ Jesus, who being [in His eternal and inherent nature, ὑπάρχων] in the form of God, deemed it not a thing to be snatched at (ἁρπαγμόν) to be on an equality with God.' There is here an implied contrast with Adam, who took fruit from the tree of knowledge of good and evil, which God said had made him 'as one of us' (Gn 3²²).

2. In Mt 19⁴⁻⁶ ǁ Mk 10⁶⁻⁸ reference is made by Jesus to the account of Adam and Eve in Gn 1²⁷ 'male and female created he them' (ἄρσεν καὶ θῆλυ ἐποίησεν αὐτούς). Pharisees came and asked Him whether divorce was allowable ['for any cause,' Mt.]. Our Lord's answer is intended to show that the provision made for divorce in the Mosaic law (Dt 24¹) was only a concession to the hardness of men's hearts. The truer and deeper view of marriage which Christians should adopt must be based on a nobler morality,—on a morality which takes its stand on the primeval nature of man and woman as God made them. 'To suit (πρός) your hardness of heart he wrote for you this commandment. But from the beginning of the creation "he made them male and female."' And with this quotation is coupled one from Gn 2²⁴ (see also Eph 5³¹), 'For this cause shall a man leave his father and mother [and shall cleave to his wife (Mt.)], and they twain shall become one flesh.' The same result is reached in Mt., but with a transposition of the two parts of the argument. See Wright's *Synopsis, in loc.* Thus Jesus bases the absolute indissolubility of the marriage tie on the union of man and woman from the first. In Mt 19⁹ 5³² this pronouncement is practically annulled by the admission of the words 'except for fornication' (μὴ ἐπὶ πορνείᾳ, and παρεκτὸς λόγου πορνείας). See Wright, *in loc.*, who contends that 'the Church (of Alexandria?) introduced these two clauses into the Gospel in accordance with the permission to legislate which our Lord gave to all Churches (Mt 18¹⁸).' See art. MARRIAGE.

3. In Jn 8⁴⁴ ἀνθρωποκτόνος may refer to the introduction of death into the world by the fall of Adam. But see art. ABEL.

4. The parallel drawn by St. Paul between Adam and Christ may have been the origin of the tradition that Adam was buried under Golgotha. Jer. (*Com. in Mat.* § iv. 27) rejects it, saying that it arose from the discovery of an ancient human skull at that spot. He also declines to see any reference to it in Eph 5¹⁴. But in Ep. 46 he says, 'The place where our Lord was crucified is called Calvary, because the skull of the primitive man was buried there. So it came to pass that the second Adam, that is the blood of Christ (a play on ארם and הרם), as it

dropped from the Cross, washed away the sins of the buried protoplast,* the first Adam, and thus the words of the apostle were fulfilled,'—quoting Eph 5¹⁴. Epiphanius (*contra Hær.* xlvi. 5) goes farther, stating that Christ's blood dropped upon Adam's skull, and restored him to life. The tradition is mentioned also by Basil, Ambrose, and others.

LITERATURE.—Besides the works cited in the article, the following may be consulted on the relation between Adam and Christ : Sanday-Headlam, *Com. on Epistle to Romans* (pp. 130– 153) ; Bethune-Baker, *An Introduction to the Early History of Christian Doctrine*, ch. xvii. ; Tennant, *The Sources of the Doctrine of the Fall and Original Sin* ; Sadler, *The Second Adam and the New Birth* ; Thackeray, *The Relation of St. Paul to Contemporary Jewish Thought*, ch. ii.

A. H. M'NEILE.

ADDI.—An ancestor of Jesus Christ, Lk 3²⁸.

ADULTERY (μοιχεία).—This word is used to denote the sexual intercourse of a married man or woman with any other than the person to whom he or she is bound by the marriage tie. It has sometimes been maintained that μοιχεία is confined in its use to the misdemeanours, in this respect, of the woman. That it has, however, a wider sense is evidenced by the reference which Jesus makes to the inward lust of *any* man after *any* woman (ὅτι πᾶς ὁ βλέπων γυναῖκα πρὸς τὸ ἐπιθυμῆσαι αὐτῆς ἤδη ἐμοίχευσεν αὐτήν, κ.τ.λ., Mt 5²⁸). The word πορνεία is also employed to describe this sin, though it has been contended that it refers solely to pre-nuptial immorality ; and again we have a reference made by Jesus in His teaching to this sin, which disposes of that contention, and which establishes the fact that the *married* woman who commits herself in this way was said to be guilty of πορνεία (cf. παρεκτὸς λόγου πορνείας, Mt 5³², and (εἰ) μὴ ἐπὶ πορνείᾳ, Mt 19⁹). In both passages just quoted Jesus makes the woman's guilt the ground of His teaching on divorce. With these examples we may compare the words of Am 7¹⁷ (LXX) . . . ἡ γυνή σου ἐν τῇ πόλει πορνεύσει, κ.τ.λ., where the form of the expression incidentally but conclusively carries out our argument.

A very favourite figure of speech, by which the intimate relations of Jehovah and Israel were denoted by OT writers, was that of marriage (see, *e.g.*, Is 54⁵ 62⁵, Jer 3¹⁴, Hos 2⁷· ¹⁹· ²⁰) ; and accordingly in the prophetic books the defection of the Jewish people from the altars of Jehovah, and their repeated reversions to the worship and practices of their heathen neighbours, were stigmatized as 'adultery' (ni'úph or ni'úphîm, Jer 13²⁷, Ezk 23⁴³ ; cf. Is 57³, Jer 3⁸ᶠ·, Ezk 23³⁷). This transference of an idea from the daily social life to the life spiritual finds its place in the teaching of Jesus, whose example in this respect is followed by writers of a subsequent period (cf. Ja 4⁴). The generation in which He lived was denounced by Him, for its continued rejection of His claims, as 'wicked and adulterous' (γενεὰ πονηρὰ καὶ μοιχαλίς, Mt 12³⁹ 16⁴ ; cf. also Mk 8³⁸). It is, of course, possible that Jesus by these words had in view the social evils of His day, as well as the general lack of spiritual religion. 'That nation and generation might be called *adulterous* literally ; for what else, I beseech you, was their irreligious polygamy than continual adultery ? And what else was their ordinary practice of divorcing their wives, no less irreligious, according to every man's foolish or naughty will ?' (Lightfoot, *Hor. Heb. et Talmud. ad* Mt 12³⁹). It is not necessary, however, in the interpretation of His teaching in this and similar places to insist on such a view of His words. The entire body of the recorded teaching of Jesus betrays the most intimate acquaintance with the literature and ethical tendencies of the OT.

That exceedingly lax and immoral views of this sin were held generally by the generation in which Jesus lived, becomes evident not only from His casual references to the subject, but also from His

* Cf. Wis. 7¹.

positive teaching in answer to hostile questions addressed to Him about adultery and the kindred subject of divorce. We are also confronted with the same phenomenon in the writings, *e.g.*, of Josephus (cf. *Ant.* IV. viii. 23; *Vita*, § 76), Sir 7²⁶ 25²⁶ 42⁹, and in the Talmud. The result of the teaching of Hillel was of the worst description, reducing as it did the crime of adultery to the level of an ordinary or minor fault. This Rabbi actually went the length, in his interpretation of the Deuteronomic law of divorce as stated in Dt 24¹, of laying down the rule that a man might put away his wife 'if she cook her husband's food badly by salting or roasting it too much' (see Lightfoot, *Hor. Heb. et Talmud. ad* Mt 5³¹), and R. 'Aḳiba, improving on this instruction, interpreted the words 'if she find no favour in his eyes' as giving permission to a man to divorce his wife 'if he sees a woman fairer than her.'

On the other hand, R. Shammai refused to take a view so loose and immoral, and in his exposition of the Deuteronomic permission confined the legality of divorce to cases of proved unchastity on the part of the wife. Other celebrated Rabbins took a similarly rigid view of this question, while all, of every school, were agreed that the crime of adultery demanded divorce as its punishment. The form of the question addressed to Jesus by the Pharisees (κατὰ πᾶσαν αἰτίαν) in Mt 19³ shows the nature of the controversy between the rival Rabbinical schools, and also lets us see how far the pernicious teaching of the school of Hillel had permeated the social fabric. Men's ideas about this sin were also debased by the polygamous habits then prevalent. Of Herod the Great we read that he had ten wives; which, according to Josephus, was not only permissible, but had actually become a common occurrence amongst the Jews, 'it being of old permitted to the Jews to marry many wives' (*BJ* I. xxiv. 2). In another place the same historian remarks, in connexion with the story of the Herodian family, that 'it is the ancient practice among us to have many wives at the same time' (*Ant.* XVII. i. 2). There seems to have been no hard and fast rule limiting the number of wives permissible to each man, but their teachers advised them to restrict themselves to four or five (cf. Schürer, *HJP* I. i. 455, note 125).

From these observations we see what an important bearing the teaching of Jesus had on the current conceptions of sexual morality obtaining amongst His countrymen. It is quite in harmony with His method of instruction to reduce the overt commission of a sin to the element out of which it originates and takes its shape. 'A corrupt tree cannot bring forth good fruit' (Mt 7¹⁷ᶠ·, cf. 12³³ and Lk 6⁴³ᶠ·), and the heart corrupted by evil desire fructifies, just as surely, by an inexorable law of nature. There exists within the man whose inner life is thus tainted not merely latent or germinal sin, such as may or may not yet issue in deeds of wrong. The lustful eye gazing with sinful longing is the consummation,—the fruit of the corrupt tree, —and so far as the man's will is concerned, the sinful act is completed (Mt 5²⁸). The note of sternness which characterizes this teaching is not altogether original, as will be seen if we refer to such commands as are found, *e.g.*, in Ex 20¹⁷, Pr 6²⁵, Sir 9⁸ etc., and to such interpretative sayings in the Talmud as forbade the gazing upon 'a woman's heel' or even upon her 'little finger' (cf. Lightfoot, *Hor. Heb. et Talmud. ad* Mt 5²⁸). The ethical foundation, however, upon which Jesus based His doctrine strikes the reader as being the deepest and the firmest of any that had as yet been revealed on the subject; and this must have seemed to His hearers to be not the least remarkable of those luminous addresses by which He contra-

dicted the laboriously minute guidance of their moral and religious guides. We are not concerned here to inquire whether Jesus put no difference between the guilt of the man who, though he has lustful desires, abstains from carrying them into practice, and that of the man who completes them by the sinful act. Common sense forbids us to suppose that Jesus put out of sight the social aspects of the question when He discussed it. What is of importance is to note the lofty tone assumed by Him when engaged in inculcating the absolute necessity of sexual purity. Nor is it possible to infer that Jesus confined His remarks to the case of those who were married. The general terms into which He casts His instruction (πᾶς ὁ βλέπων) forbids us to assume that γυναῖκα and ἐμοίχευσεν are to be limited to the post-nuptial sin with a married woman. It gives a much more fitting as well as a truer meaning to Jesus' words if we think of Him as giving directions for the guidance of the entire social and ethical life to all members of society whether married or otherwise.

According to the laws of the ancients, those guilty of adultery were to be put to death, whether by burning (Gn 38²⁴) or by stoning (Jn 8⁵, cf. Dt 22²³ᶠᶠ·, Lv 20¹⁰, Ezk 18¹¹ᶠᶠ·). This punishment was not, however, universally prescribed; for where the woman was a slave, and consequently not the owner of her own person, the man was exonerated by presenting a guilt-offering (Lv 19²⁰ᶠᶠ·). It is doubtful, indeed, if ever capital punishment was insisted on. Lightfoot, for example, says: 'I do not remember that I have anywhere in the Jewish pandect read any example of a wife punished with death for adultery' (*Horæ Heb. et Talmud. ad* Mt 19⁸). This statement is borne out by such incidental references as we have in Mt 1¹⁹, where Joseph receives the praise of his contemporaries (δίκαιος ὤν) for his merciful intention; and if the story of Hosea's wife is to be taken literally, we have an OT example of mercy towards the guilty being recommended, and even of divorce not being suggested as a punishment. Jesus Himself also leaned to the side of mercy; and nowhere does the tenderness of His solicitude for the guilty sinner appear so deep as in the traditional, yet doubtless genuine, narrative incorporated in the Fourth Gospel (Jn 7⁵³-8¹¹). For a discussion of the 'pericope adulteræ' see Blass, *Ev. sec. Lucam*, Pref. p. xlvii, and his *Philology of the Gospels*, pp. 155-163.

A closer examination than we have as yet attempted in this place, of the words and teaching of Jesus Christ will reveal some startling results, and furnish obvious reasons to explain the difficulties which have been always felt on the relations of adultery, divorce, and remarriage, by Christian thinkers and legislators. A comparative examination of the passages in the Synoptic writers (Mt 5³² 19⁹, Mk 10¹¹ᶠ·, Lk 16¹⁸) discloses a peculiar addition to the words and teaching in the first of these places. According to Mt 5³², Jesus asserts that the wife who is wrongfully divorced is involved compulsorily in the guilt of her husband. He is not only an adulterer himself (Lk 16¹⁸), but 'he causes her to be an adulteress,' or rather 'he makes her to commit adultery' (ποιεῖ αὐτὴν μοιχευθῆναι). The interpretation which would explain these words as if they meant that the divorced wife is placed in such a position that she probably will commit adultery by marrying another man, is manifestly unsatisfactory. The statement is unqualified even if we are absolutely convinced of the genuineness of the succeeding words, ' καὶ ὃς ... μοιχᾶται.' [They are omitted by D 11, see WH, *New Test. in Greek*]. It is as if Jesus said: 'The wife who is divorced is, in virtue of her false position, an adulteress though she be innocent, and the man who marries her while she occupies that position becomes a willing partner in her guilt.' It is not too much to say that, in this place, we have a glimpse of the profound depth which Jesus was accustomed to sound in His ethical teaching. Marriage is a Divine institution, and has its roots in the eternal order of things (cf. Mt 19⁴⁻⁶). It results in a mystical union so close that the married pair are no longer two ; they have become 'one flesh.' With this we may compare the teaching which St. Paul embodies in a few luminous words based on his Christological doctrine (Eph 5²²⁻³³, especially vv.²⁸ and ²⁹), and of which he says 'this mystery is great.'

We have thus a clue to the meaning of the difficult expression ποιεῖ αὐτὴν μοιχευθῆναι. Any mode of conduct or action which tends to mar or set at nought the mysterious relationship of marriage is of the essence of adultery. Perhaps we shall not be considered to be importing more meaning into words than they were originally intended to convey, if we press the Markan addition ἐπὶ αὐτήν into our service here. Jesus, according to St. Mark, seems to teach His hearers that the husband in wrongfully divorcing his wife is guilty of the aggravated sin of dragging her into the slough where he is himself already wallowing. On him falls the woe pronounced in another connexion by Jesus (Mt 18⁶⁻⁷) ; for he compels his wife to occupy a position which is a living contradiction of the Divine law. A course of action tending to the dissolution of that which in the Divine intention is indissoluble, Jesus places in the category of adulterous acts. He mentions nothing as to His view of the case of the remarriage of a woman justifiably divorced, but to the present writer He appears plainly to assert that the man who marries an innocent divorced woman is guilty of adultery.

In our critical examination of these passages we are confronted with a still greater and no less remarkable variety. St. Matthew differs from the other two Synoptists by giving a place in Jesus' teaching to an implied ground for legitimate divorce. He alone includes the exceptive clauses παρεκτὸς λόγου πορνείας (5³²) and μὴ ἐπὶ πορνείᾳ (19⁹). It is this variety in the records of Jesus' words which has introduced so much difficulty, doctrinal and legislative, into the questions of divorce and the remarriage of divorced persons. We are not, of course, without that form of conjectural criticism which would delete these clauses as mere glosses or unsuitable interpolations (see Bacon, The Sermon on the Mount, ad loc.). In the absence, however, of external or textual evidence we are not entitled to invent textual emendations in the interests of a preconceived theory (cf. Wright, Synopsis of the Gospels in Greek, p. 98 f.). It is but fair to add that the Codex Vaticanus (B) and some less important authorities manifest a strong desire to make Mt 19⁹ conform literally to Mt 5³², and thereby create some uncertainty as to the textual purity of these passages. The evidential value, however, of these variations is too slight to be of any avail against the unanimity of all our other witnesses ; they are transparent and later attempts at assimilation or harmony. The argumentum e silentio is in this case too strong to admit the validity of conjecture. A forcible statement of the other side of the case may be found in the art. 'Sermon on the Mount' (Votaw) in the Extra Vol. of Hastings' DB p. 27.

At all periods of the history of Christian teaching, differences of opinion have existed within the Church as to the practical application of Jesus' words concerning adultery, divorce, and remarriage. These differences have been stereotyped in the Eastern and Western branches of the Catholic Church. The former takes the more lenient view, and permits the remarriage of the innocent divorcé(e), while the latter has always maintained the more stringent and (shall we say ?) the more strictly literal conclusion from Jesus' words, that inequality of treatment is not to be tolerated, interpreting the conclusion by refusing the right of remarriage to either during the life of the other.

On the other hand, the general consensus of theological opinion amongst English-speaking divines since the Reformation has leaned towards the view held by the Eastern Church, and the resolutions of the bishops in the Pan-Anglican Conference of 1888 on this subject were but the

formal expressions of a traditional mode of interpretation. When we turn from the words of Jesus to see what were the ideas of those who taught in His name during the ages immediately subsequent, we have St. Paul's teaching on, and references to, the question of divorce. In one place he treats marriage as indissoluble, and he has no hesitation in saying that the woman who marries another man during the lifetime of her husband is guilty of adultery (Ro 7¹⁻³). On the other hand, we must not forget that the Apostle in this place is dealing with the Jewish law and with Jews who did not admit the absolute indissolubility of the marriage tie. The fact that he has made no reference to this Jewish law of divorce forbids us drawing any certain conclusion as to the length St. Paul was willing to go in stating a universal principle which would guide the legislative activity of the Christian Church. In another place he speaks of separation as the possible outcome of an unhappy or unequal marriage, and gives permission, if not encouragement, to that contingent result (χωρι-ζέσθω). In this he goes farther than Jesus, so far as we have His teaching recorded for us, went. According to Jesus, adultery is the only crime of sufficient enormity to warrant divorce ; according to St. Paul, the law of marriage does not govern the deserted wife or husband (οὐ δεδούλωται ὁ ἀδελφὸς ἢ ἡ ἀδελφὴ ἐν τοῖς τοιούτοις, 1 Co 7¹⁵ [cf. Newman Smyth, Christian Ethics³, p. 412 f. and note]).

The Shepherd of Hermas (Mand. iv. 1. 6) lays down the rule that adultery demands separation or divorce (ἀπολυσάτω αὐτήν), because by continuing to live with his wife after she has been convicted of guilt, the husband becomes 'an accomplice in her adultery.' On the other hand, he is equally insistent that the man thus wronged must not marry another, lest he cut his guilty partner off from the hope of repentance, and lest he involve himself likewise in the sin of adultery (ἐὰν δὲ ἀπολύσας τὴν γυναῖκα ἑτέραν γαμήσῃ, καὶ αὐτὸς μοιχᾶται).

Amongst the number of those who are debarred from inheriting the kingdom of God, St. Paul mentions fornicators and adulterers (πόρνοι καὶ μοιχοί, 1 Co 6⁹ ; cf. Eph 5⁵, 1 Ti 1¹⁰, He 13⁴, Rev 21⁸ 22¹⁵).

The universal conclusion is that this sin creates a breach of the marriage relation so grave and far-reaching that it makes divorce the only legitimate sequel—divorce a mensâ et thoro. The question, however, remains whether the Christian Church has the right to go farther and say that, as the result of an adulterous act, the aggrieved party has a just claim to divorce a vinculo ; has a right, that is to say, to be placed in a position as if the marriage had never taken place. This will, no doubt, be answered differently by different minds, and the difficulty is not decreased by merely appealing to the authority of Jesus. Different answers are given to the more fundamental questions, Did Jesus intend to occupy the position of legislator when He spoke of adultery and divorce ? or was He simply enunciating a general principle, leaving future generations to deal with social conditions as they arose ? The present writer has no hesitation in saying that his own opinion leans strongly to the side of those who believe that Jesus affirmed solemnly the indissolubility of the marriage tie, and that He meant His followers to understand that the remarriage of either party during the life of the other constitutes adultery. At the same time he is not unaware of the fact that there is a strong body of sober modern thought which tends towards a relaxation of this view in favour of the innocent (see Gore, The Sermon on the Mount, p. 73).

If Jesus in Mt 5²⁷⁻³² is making a categorical statement of universal application, then the opinion, given by the present writer as his own, can scarcely be disputed ; but if He is interpreted as dealing with the foundations rather than making structural alterations in the ethical beliefs of His countrymen, we must conclude that He leaves His followers to deal with the question as it arises. In the latter case it is, of course, competent for the Church in each age to treat the question *de novo*. The conditions of society alter, and what constitutes danger to the social welfare at one time, may have comparatively little peril for the people of another period. At the same time it must not be forgotten that the tendency of human legislation has been and is likely to be, for some time to come at least, towards the loosening of the marriage bond, and the minimizing of the seriousness of that guilt by which men uproot the foundations of their social and domestic life.

LITERATURE.—Newman Smyth's *Christian Ethics*[3] contains a very fair and cautious discussion of this whole question, and along with that work it will be found useful to study the more abstract volume of Bampton Lectures on the same subject (1895) by T. B. Strong ; cf. G. B. Stevens' *The Theology of the NT.* Gore's *The Sermon on the Mount* may be read along with Bacon's volume of the same title, and Votaw's article 'Sermon on the Mount' in the Extra Volume of Hastings' *DB.* In the latter work (vols. i. and iii.) are also to be found useful references under artt. 'Crimes,' 'Marriage.' A very suggestive art., 'The Teaching of Christ about Divorce,' by the Rev. the Hon. E. Lyttelton, will be found in the *Journal of Theol. Studies* for July 1904. Cf. also H. M. Luckock's *History of Marriage* (1894), and O. D. Watkins' *Holy Matrimony* (1895).

J. R. WILLIS.

ADVENT.—In its primary application the term is used to denote the first visible coming of Jesus into the world. His coming again at an after period is distinguished as the Second, or the Final, Coming (see COMING AGAIN and PAROUSIA).

The term is also employed to designate one of the ecclesiastical seasons,—that immediately preceding the Festival of the Nativity,—during which, in certain sections of the Church, the thoughts of believers are turned to the first appearance of their Lord in the flesh. This season includes four Sundays, commencing on the one nearest St. Andrew's Day (Nov. 30) and lasting till Christmas Eve. With Advent the appointed order of Church services is renewed, and the ecclesiastical year begins.

Dealing here specially with the primary historical application, the first coming of Jesus possesses a unique significance as marking the entrance into the world of a moral force altogether unparalleled, a momentous turning-point in the religious progress of mankind. As the Son of God (Mt 10^{32}, Jn $3^{16. 17}$), revealing and representing God in His own person (Jn 5^{30} $14^{9. 10}$), whose mission it was to redeem men from sin (Mt 18^{11}, Lk 4^{43} 17^{21}), Jesus was to prove Himself in the truest sense the Messiah whom the Jewish people had long been expecting,—'a Saviour, who is Christ the Lord' (Lk 2^{11}).

1. *The foreshadowing Promise.*—The expectation entertained by the Jews had its roots in a promise enshrined in their earliest literature and dating from the dawn of history, that a signal deliverance from sin should be brought to the human race,— the promise contained in the sentence pronounced on the tempter, that the seed of the woman should bruise his head (Gn 3^{15}). This brighter outlook for fallen humanity was confirmed by the assurance given to Abraham that in the line of his descendants the original promise was destined to be fulfilled (Gn $12^{2. 3}$),—an assurance which was further strengthened when, under Moses, Israel was formed into a nation and entered at Sinai into covenant with Jehovah as His chosen people (Ex 20–24). It was not, however, till David's prosperous reign, with its recognition of ruling power held in the name of Jehovah, had passed, and when the idea of the theocratic kingship had been deeply implanted in the national consciousness, that the conception of the blessing to be looked for took definite shape. Then, as successive rulers failed

and the nation's fortunes became embarrassed, the splendours of David's time, glorified by the halo which memory and distance cast around them, were projected into the future, forming a picture full of allurement and charm. It fired the imagination of the prophets amid the troubles of the later monarchy.

The promise, as thus transformed, was that of a king, or line of kings, sprung from David's house, who, endowed with transcendent gifts, and acting by special authority as the Anointed of the Lord, should reign in righteousness, introduce an era of Divine salvation for Israel, and draw all other nations round them in loyalty to Jehovah's law (Is 2^2 11^{5-9} 27^1, Mic 4^{1-4}). This was the blossoming out of the Messianic idea.

During the period of the Exile, with the fall of the monarchy and the collapse of the expectations based upon it, the figure of the victorious and righteous king was thrown into the background ; yet the prospect of a future glorious manifestation of Divine mercy, rescuing the people from their iniquities and miseries, kept its hold on susceptible minds (Is 55^5 60^{1-8}). It was in this period that the distinctively spiritual character of the coming deliverance emerged into prominence. As delineated in Ezekiel and the Second Isaiah, it was to consist in an inward regeneration, wrought by penitence and the impartation of a new spirit and a new heart (Is $65^{6. 7}$, Ezk $11^{19. 20}$ 36^{25-30}). In those prophecies of the Exile, Jehovah Himself is set forth as the true and ever-living King of Israel ; and collective Israel, the nation regarded poetically as an individual, is conceived as the Anointed Servant of Jehovah, who, amid manifold afflictions, is to bear witness for Jehovah, and be the medium of accomplishing His saving purpose for mankind. On the return from the Exile the hope of salvation through a Davidic kingship revived, as is evident from the prophetic utterances of Haggai ($2^{22. 23}$) and Zechariah (3^8 6^{12}) ; but in Malachi's day it had again disappeared.

With the Maccabæan struggle against Antiochus Epiphanes (B.C. 167–135) the Messianic idea entered on a fresh course of development. In the Book of Daniel, which dates presumably from that time, we find supernatural elements more freely introduced. The writer in vision beholds an ancient of days, seated on his throne to judge the great world-kingdoms and their rulers. Before him appears, coming with the clouds of heaven, 'one like unto a son of man,' and to him is given everlasting dominion and a kingdom which shall not be destroyed ($7^{13. 14}$). This dominion is passed over to 'the saints of the Most High,' to be theirs for ever and ever ($7^{18. 27}$). There is thus a picture of the Messianic future in which the triumph and rule of the godly over the nations are the distinguishing features.

We look in vain in the books of the Apocrypha for any expansion of these ideas. Their allusions to the Messianic hope are somewhat meagre, and do not expressly refer to the appearance of a personal Messiah. It is in the Apocalyptic literature, which sprang up in imitation of the Book of Daniel, that we find the conceptions which gave peculiar shape and colour to the Messianic expectations entertained in later times. We see there, amid the stress of national misfortunes, the predictions of the prophets interpreted and expanded in such a way as to furnish elaborately drawn out schemes of future glory. The coming of the God-sent king is depicted (*Sib. Orac.* iii. 652 ff.), the supernatural Son of Man, who was hidden with God before the world was created, and who, clothed with Divine attributes, will suddenly appear along with the Head of Days to execute judgment on men and angels (*Similitudes* of Enoch $46^{1. 2}$ $48^{2. 3}$). The dispersed of Israel will be restored, and the Gentiles drawn into submission (Enoch 90^{30}) ; sin and wrong will be banished (*Simil.* 49^2) ; the faithful dead will be raised to life again, and the righteous will dwell in everlasting joy (Enoch 51^1 90^{37}). In the Psalter of Solomon, written under the pressure of the Roman domination (B.C. 70–40), the idea of a king of the Davidic line is once more revived. The Messiah is regarded as 'the Son of David,' 'the Anointed of the Lord,' free from sin and endowed with miraculous powers, who will conquer, not by force of arms, but will smite the earth by the rod of His mouth (17$^{28f.}$), and bring to an end all unrighteousness (17^{36}).

In those Apocalyptic writings peculiar prominence is given to the spiritual content of the Messianic hope. Notwithstanding the supernatural elements they so largely introduce, they throw into strong relief the higher religious conceptions which the best of the prophets had insisted on as essentially bound up with the great period of blessing expected; while the scope of the ancient promise is widened out beyond national and temporal limitations to embrace the world and the life to come.

Meanwhile the scribes were at work, hardening the Messianic idea into scholastic form, and reducing the poetic language and bold imagery of the prophets to dogmatic statements and literal details, with the result, on the whole, of a restoration of the theocratic idea that God was to vindicate His authority as the true Sovereign of the nation, and to send His vicegerent in the line of David to establish His law and introduce the rule of righteousness under His anointed King.

Such was the form which the long-cherished hope had assumed when Jesus appeared. It was largely mixed up with expectations of political deliverance, yet the thoughts of many earnest spirits were centred mainly on the prospect of a spiritual emancipation for Israel. He came to meet the great hope by fulfilling in their ideal and spiritual significance the prophecies that had kindled and kept it alive. Leaving aside the merely earthly, time-coloured features that bulked so largely in the popular imagination, He entered the world to offer Himself as the true representative of God, in and through whom all that was eternal and most precious in the Messianic idea was destined to be realized. See art. MESSIAH.

2. *The state of Religion at the date of Christ's Advent.*—In many respects the way had been prepared for the appearance of Jesus and the spread of His influence as Messiah and Saviour. There were national, political, social, and other conditions existing in the world at the time, which rendered His coming and work singularly opportune (see FULNESS OF TIME); but here we are specially concerned with the prevailing aspects of religious life in the immediate scene in which He appeared. Undoubtedly, among the Jewish people at that period religion was a dominating interest, and was based on principles far higher than any that obtained in other nations. Yet its quality was vitiated by certain serious defects. There was—

(1) Its *partisanship*. Scribes and Pharisees on the one hand, and Sadducees on the other, stood in mutual antagonism, striving for ascendency as leaders of national religious feeling,—the scribes and Pharisees combining to enforce the mass of stringent precepts which the former had elaborated to supplement the original written word; the Sadducees entirely rejecting those precepts, and contending that the Law as written was sufficient, and that the observance of the temple ordinances, its worship and sacrifices, was the central element in religion. The controversies that arose over those points of difference, and over the doctrine of the resurrection, created a fierce party spirit, bitter and bigoted on the one side, haughty and contemptuous on the other, while the smaller sect of the Essenes, with their extremist views and rigid austerity, maintained an inflexible protest against both these classes of religionists.

(2) Then there was its *legalism*. By their insistence on conformity to the regulations they had added to the Law as a condition of Divine favour, the scribes and Pharisees, who were the most numerous and aggressive party, converted religion itself into a matter of slavish obedience, in which the instigating motives were the hope of reward and the fear of punishment. The calculating temper thus engendered rendered the religious life a taskwork of anxious scrupulosity and constraint, want-

ing in spontaneous action from the higher impulses of the soul; while in the case of those less sincere it introduced an element of prudential self-regard concerned only with the prospect of future benefit and safety.

(3) Closely allied to this was the *externalization* of piety. The Rabbinical regulations were held to be so binding, and their multiplicity was so great, that the effort to observe them inevitably involved a machine-like routine and formality. The Jew in his fulfilment of the Law found himself at every turn brought under the pressure of hard and fast exacting rules,—in his food, his clothes, his daily occupations, his devotions, and the smallest acts of his life. The endeavour to yield obedience under such circumstances necessarily led to a laborious outward punctiliousness; a tendency to ostentation and spiritual pride was fostered; and many were ensnared into hypocrisy by finding they could obtain a reputation for exceptional piety by an obtrusive parade of their ceremonial performances. The most precise minuteness was observed in trifles, the tithing of mint and cummin, but in matters of greater import the principles of morality were surrendered.

These are the darker shades of the picture. Nevertheless, it is clear that a very considerable measure of religious earnestness was preserved in the nation. It was fed by the ancient Scriptures, which were regularly read in the synagogues and committed to memory in the synagogue schools. Thus in the body of the people there was kept alive a sense of the holy character and mighty doings of Jehovah; and although, owing to the decayed influence of the priesthood, the Temple itself was not a centre of spiritual life, yet the hallowed memories it recalled in the breasts of the multitudes assembled at the religious festivals were calculated to inspire the higher emotions. At all events, there is evidence enough to show that many hearts throughout the nation were imbued with a deep-seated reverence for God and a true spiritual longing for the hope of Israel. The soul of religion might be sadly crushed by legality and formalism, but it was not utterly dead. Devout men and women in varied ranks of society were holding a pure faith and leading lives of simple sincerity, vaguely dissatisfied with the bondage of legal observances and Rabbinical rules, and yearning to rise into a more spiritual atmosphere, a closer communion with the Divine mind and will. Of these Zacharias and Elisabeth (Lk 1$^{5.6}$), Anna (2$^{36.37}$), and the aged Simeon (2^{25}) may be taken as examples; while the numbers who responded to the living preaching of John the Baptist and became his followers are an index of the extent to which genuine piety survived in the land. It was amongst such that the spiritual preparation was found for the recognition and welcome of the promised Saviour when He appeared. The coming of Jesus brought the birth of a new spirit in religion, a spirit of fresh vitality and power; and the life of absolute devotion to righteousness which He began to live, and which He was ultimately to close in a death of sacrificing love, infused into religion an inspiring energy destined on a scale of vast magnitude to regenerate and redeem.

3. *The national unrest of the period.*—The Jewish people, fretting under political depression, had flung themselves with impassioned eagerness on the hope that the long-desired Messiah and His kingdom must be drawing nigh. It was even thought by many that He was hidden somewhere in obscurity, only waiting for a more penitent disposition in the national mind; and so inflamed was the common imagination with these ideas, that popular excitement was easily aroused, and any bold spirit, rising in revolt against the existing state of things, could find a group of followers ready to believe in him as the one who should deliver Israel. In the broader world outside, too, the expectation of a powerful king, issuing from Judæa, who was to conquer the world, appears to have been widely spread ; and the references to this given by Tacitus (*Hist.* v. 13) and by Suetonius (*Vesp.* 4) may be taken at least as an echo of views disseminated throughout the Roman Empire by the Jews of the Dispersion. When Jesus was born into the world, however, an event had transpired vastly grander than Jewish expectation at the time conceived. The day at last had dawned to which the original promise to fallen humanity pointed forward, and for which the best minds of the nation had for ages yearned ; the divinely-pledged Deliverer from sin and its curse had arrived, to set up the kingdom of righteousness, love, and peace.

Literature.—For a lengthened treatment of the Messianic hope and its transformations, see Riehm, *Messianic Prophecy*[3] (Eng. tr. 1900); Drummond, *The Jewish Messiah* (1877); Stanton, *The Jewish and Christian Messiah* (1886); Briggs, *Messianic Prophecy* (1886); Orelli, *OT Prophecy of the Consummation of God's Kingdom* (Eng. tr.); and for a more condensed survey, Schürer, *HJP* II. ii., and Schultz, *OT Theol.* (Eng. tr. 1898) vol. ii. For the Apocalyptic writings, see Charles' editions of the *Book of Enoch*, etc. On the religious condition of the Jewish nation at the date of the Advent, see Stapfer, *Palestine in the Time of Christ* (Eng. tr. 1886); Edersheim, *Life and Times of Jesus the Messiah*, II. v. (1883); Keim, *Jesus of Nazara* (Eng. tr.), vol. i.; Wellhausen, *Die Pharisäer und die Sadducäer* (1874); Ewald, *Hist. of Israel* (Eng. tr.), vol. vi.; and Cheyne, *Jewish Religious Life after the Exile.*

G. M'HARDY.

ADVERSARY.—In the Gospels the word 'adversary' stands twice (Lk 13[17] 21[15]) for ἀντικείμενος, and thrice (Mt 5[25], Lk 12[58] 18[3]) for ἀντίδικος. The first two passages require no comment, as they describe the opponents of the gospel in the simplest terms, as adversaries. Thus we read that when Jesus triumphantly vindicated His actions, His adversaries were ashamed and could not answer Him. Similarly Jesus assured His disciples that none of their adversaries in the approaching time of persecution should be able to gainsay or resist the words of wisdom which the Holy Spirit would put into their mouths.

In Mt 5[25] (∥ Lk 12[58]), and again in the parable of the Unjust Judge (Lk 18[3]), the question suggests itself, 'Who is the adversary referred to?' The passage from the Sermon on the Mount occurs as one of a series of maxims of Christian prudence, and the key to its interpretation is suggested by that which immediately precedes it (Mt 5[23f.]), where Christ says that reconciliation with an offended brother must go before the offering of a gift at God's altar.

Alienation from the brother offended must operate as a hindrance to true worship. Therefore he who would be accepted of God must do justly by his brother and have all cause of difference with him removed, for if he regards iniquity in his heart, has upon his conscience the guilt of wrong-doing or ill-will, or a grudge, the Lord will not hear him (Ps 66[18]). Thus a certain order must be observed in connexion with this matter of worship. Still more, Jesus appears to suggest, does this principle of order hold in respect of the controversy between God and sinners. Reconciliation with God must be for every man the first business to be attended to. That antagonism must be removed, and he must satisfy the claim which the law of God has against him in the first place, else if he fails to avail himself of the present opportunity of ending the controversy, the law must take its course. The adversary referred to is thus the broken law, or God Himself as the Author of the law, whom the unreconciled sinner treats as an adversary (cf. Lk 14[31f.]).

In the parable of the Unjust Judge the widow's petition against her opponent at law, and her importunity in pressing it upon the attention of the judge, are used to illustrate the prayers of God's elect. The reference seems to be to the opposition which, in her efforts to promote the cause and kingdom of God, the Church is obliged to encounter, some adverse influence to which she has long been exposed, and against which she fears she is left to struggle alone. Here there is no special reason for identifying this adversary with Satan (cf. Alford, *in loc.* ; Trench, *Parables*, 488, etc.) or with the Jewish persecutors of the Early Church (Weizsäcker, who regards the passage as a late addition ; cf. Weiss in Meyer's Commentary, *in loc.*). We must not forget that the word occurs in a parable which was spoken with a special didactic purpose, that being, as St. Luke is careful to explain, the encouragement not of the Church only, but especially of individual believers, to persevere in their efforts by faith and prayer to withstand the power of evil in the world, in whatever form it may assail them or thwart their endeavours. Christ's object was to assure them that their importunity must prevail with God, who shall soon respond to their prayers and grant them the victory over all that would frustrate their efforts for the advancement of His cause. See also art. SATAN.

Literature.—Cremer, *Bib.-Theol. Lex. s.vv.* ἀντίδικος, ἀντικείμενος ; Trench, *Notes on the Parables* ; Bruce, *The Parabolic Teaching of Christ* ; Comm. of Meyer, Alford, Bengel, etc. ; Schmid, *Biblical Theology of the NT*, p. 175 ff. ; Beyschlag, *NT Theology* (2nd Eng. ed.), i. 90 ; H. J. Holtzmann, *Lehrbuch der neutest. Theologie*, i. 179 ff. ; Weizsäcker, *Apostolic Age*, ii. 61 ; Wernle, *The Beginnings of Christianity*, i. 76 ff.

H. H. CURRIE.

ADVOCATE (παράκλητος). — A term applied to Christ in 1 Jn 2[1] (AV and RV ; RVm 'Or *Comforter* or *Helper*,' Gr. *Paraclete*'), and to the Holy Spirit in RVm of Jn 14[16. 26] 15[26] 16[7], where both AV and RV have 'Comforter' in the text. For an examination of the Greek word and its cognates, see art. 'Paraclete' in Hastings' *DB* iii. 665–668. The verb παρακαλέω occurs in the papyri in the contrasted senses of 'encourage' (*Oxyr. Pap.* 663. 42) and of 'entreat' (*ib.* 744. 6) ; but the passive verbal form has not been found. The term in its Latinized form came originally from the Itala or one of the Old Latin versions through the Vulgate. And Wyclif introduced it into the English versions, translating 1 Jn 2[1] 'we han avoket' in 1382 ; so Purvey 'an aduocat' in 1388.

Etymologically the word means 'called to one's side,' especially for the purposes of help, and, in its technical usage, for advice in the case of judicial procedure, with the further suggestion of endeavouring to enlist the sympathy of the judge in favour of the accused. In 1 Jn 2[1] the last is generally taken to be the only sense ; and the meaning evidently is that, if any believer sin, Jesus Christ in person intercedes in his behalf with the Father, and, representing the believer, carries on his cause in the courts of heaven. Similarly, according to the passage in the Fourth Gospel, the Holy Spirit may be regarded as God's Advocate both with and in man, promoting the Divine interests in the human sphere, from repentance (Jn 16[7-11], cf. Job 33[23-30]) to perfecting. But here the technical legal sense of the word disappears, and the Spirit becomes, according to another marginal rendering, the God-sent 'Helper' of a man who is struggling against everything within or around him that makes godly living difficult. Whilst, therefore, the provisions of grace include the twofold advocacy, — Christ as the Advocate of a believer with God, and the Spirit as the Advocate of God with man, whether believing or unregenerate, — the two functions differ both in range and in relation ; and the term

'Advocate' is too specialized to characterize or to cover the operations attributed to the Spirit. The Spirit, as an Advocate sent from God, entreats and helps a man (see art. COMFORTER), but does not represent him before God as Judge or as Father, and does not appeal to anything in man of final and supreme authority.   R. W. MOSS.

ÆNON (Αἰνών, probably from Aramaic עֵינָן 'springs').—Mentioned only in Jn 3²³ 'And John also was baptizing in Ænon near to Salim, because there were many waters there' (RVm). The place cannot be identified with certainty. Four sites have been proposed, two in Samaria and two in Judæa.

1. Eusebius and Jerome (*Onomast.*² 229. 91, 99. 25) place Ænon in the Jordan Valley, 8 miles south of Scythopolis (*Beisân*), 'juxta Salem et Jordanem.' About 7 miles south of Beisân and 2 miles west of the Jordan there are seven springs, all lying within a radius of a quarter of a mile, and numerous rivulets. Three-quarters of a mile to the north of these springs van de Velde found a tomb bearing the name of *Sheikh Salim*. But the fact that a modern sheikh bore the name *Salim* is far from satisfactory proof that the *Salim* of our narrative was at this place. If we are to find Salim in Samaria at all, does not the mention of it as a well-known place suggest the well-known *Salim* 4 miles east of Shechem? And would it not be gratuitous for the Evangelist to say of a place so near the Jordan that there was much water there? But, in spite of these objections, Sanday (*Sacred Sites of the Gospels*, p. 36) and others still think this site has the best claim.

2. Tristram (*Bible Places*, p. 234) and Conder (*Tent Work in Palestine*, i. pp. 91–93) place Ænon at 'Ainun on a hill near the head of the great Fâr'ah valley, the open highway from the Damieh ford of the Jordan to Shechem. Four miles south-west of the village of 'Ainun, in the Wady Fâr'ah, is a succession of springs, yielding a copious perennial stream, with flat meadows on either side, where great crowds might gather. Three miles south of the valley (7 miles from 'Ainun) stands Salim. Conder says: 'The site of Wady Fâr'ah is the only one where all the requisites are met— the two names, the fine water supply, the proximity of the desert, and the open character of the ground.' The situation is a central one also, accessible by roads from all quarters, and it agrees well with the new identification of Bethabara. But (*a*) 'Ainun is not 'near to Salim,' the two places being 7 miles apart, and separated by the great Wady Fâr'ah. (*b*) There is not a drop of water at 'Ainun (Robinson, *Bib. Res.* iii. 305). (*c*) It is not likely that John the Baptist was labouring among the Samaritans, with whom the Jews had no dealings (cf. Mt 3⁵ 10⁵). (*d*) It appears that both Jesus and John were baptizing in Judæa (Jn 3²²·²³), and their proximity gave occasion to the remarks referred to in Jn 3²⁵, and that Jesus left Judæa for Galilee with the intention of getting out of the neighbourhood of John and removing the appearance of rivalry (Jn 4¹). But if Ænon was in Samaria, Jesus was nearer John than before.

3. Ewald and Hengstenberg prefer *Shilhim* (LXX Σελεείμ) in the extreme south of Judæa, mentioned (Jos 15³²) in connexion with Ain. Godet says the reason given for John's baptizing in Ænon would have greater force as applied to a generally waterless region like the southern extremity of Judah than if the reference were to a well-watered district like Samaria. But elsewhere (Jos 19⁷, 1 Ch 4³², Neh 11²⁹) Ain is connected with Rimmon and not with Shilhim.

4. More probable as a Judæan site for Ænon is *Wady Fâr'ah*, a secluded valley with copious springs about 6 miles north-east of Jerusalem (quite different, of course, from the great *Wady Fâr'ah* of Samaria). This is the view adopted by Professor Konrad Furrer in his article on the geographical allusions in the Gospel of St. John in the *ZNTW*, 1902, Heft 4, p. 258. The suggestion is not new. It was put forward nearly fifty years ago by Barclay (*City of the Great King*, pp. 558–570), but has never received the attention it deserves. Barclay says that 'of all the fountains in the neighbourhood of Jerusalem, the most copious and interesting by far are those that burst forth within a short distance of each other in Wady Fâr'ah.' He quotes the following description from *The History of the Jerusalem Mission*:—

'From the brow at Wady Fâr'ah we descended with some difficulty into that "Valley of Delight,"—for such is the literal signification of its name,—and truly I have seen nothing so delightful in the way of natural scenery, nor inviting in point of resources, etc., in all Palestine. Ascending its bold stream from this point, we passed some half-dozen expansions of the stream, constituting the most beautiful natural *natatoria* I have ever seen ; the water, rivalling the atmosphere itself in transparency, of depth varying from a few inches to a fathom or more, shaded on one or both sides by umbrageous fig-trees, and sometimes contained in naturally-excavated basins of red mottled marble —an occasional variegation of the common limestone of the country. These pools are supplied by some half-dozen springs of the purest and coldest water, bursting from rocky crevices at various intervals. Verily, thought I, we have stumbled upon Enon ! . . . Portions of aqueducts, both of pottery and stone, and in a tolerable state of preservation, too, in many places, are still found remaining on each side of the valley, indicating the extent to which the valley was at one time irrigated ; and richer land I have never seen than is much of this charming valley. . . . Several herds of cattle were voraciously feeding on the rich herbage near the stream ; and thousands of sheep and goats were[seen approaching the stream, or "resting at noonday" in the shadow of the great rock composing the overhanging cliff here and there. . . . Rank grasses, luxuriant reeds, tall weeds, and shrubbery and trees of various kinds, entirely conceal the stream from view in many places. . . . Higher up, the valley becomes very narrow, and the rocky precipices tower to a sublime height.'

The name Ænon does not seem to have survived in connexion with these springs, but within 2 miles of them there is another valley called by the Arabs *Wady Saleim*. It is at least possible that this name was once borne by one of the towns whose ruins still crown the neighbouring heights. A town thus placed would have been a conspicuous object from many parts of Judæa, and would have been naturally referred to by the Evangelist when describing the location of Ænon.

LITERATURE.—In addition to writers cited above, see artt. 'Ænon' in Smith's *DB* ², and 'Salim' in *Encyc. Biblica*.
                     W. W. MOORE.

AFFLICTION.—In AV of the Gospels 'affliction' occurs only twice (Mk 4¹⁷ 13¹⁹), corresponding both times to θλῖψις in the original. RV gives 'tribulation'—its invariable rendering of θλῖψις except in Jn 16²¹, where, like AV, it has 'anguish.' In Mt 24⁹ AV translates εἰς θλίψιν 'to be afflicted' (RV 'unto tribulation'). In all remaining cases it renders θλῖψις by 'tribulation' (Mt 13²¹ 24²¹·²⁹, Mk 13²⁴, Jn 16³³). The Greek θλῖψις (WH θλίψις) signifies literally 'pressing together,' 'pressure' (cf. ὁδὸς τεθλιμμένη in Mt 7¹⁴ of the 'straitened way' ; ἵνα μὴ θλίβωσιν αὐτόν, 'lest they should throng him,' in Mk 3⁹). In classical Greek it is found infrequently, and with its literal meaning only. In Biblical Greek, where the metaphorical significance prevails, it is of much commoner occurrence, always possessing a passive sense, and usually suggesting 'sufferings inflicted from without' (Lightfoot).

In the sayings of Christ the word bears three references. It denotes the persecution to which His followers will be subjected, and by which their loyalty will be tested (Mk 4¹⁷=Mt 13²¹ ; Mt 24⁹, Jn 16³³). It describes the privations and sufferings (not, as above, necessarily induced by His service) attendant upon a great national or universal crisis (Mk 13¹⁹·²⁴=Mt 24²¹·²⁹). And, finally, it is employed in one of His illustrations to indicate a woman's pangs in childbirth (Jn 16²¹, AV and RV 'anguish'). See, further, artt. PERSECUTION, SUFFERING, TRIBULATION. H. BISSEKER.

AGE.—The word 'age' is a vague term, as may be seen by its doing duty as a possible translation for αἰών (Lat. *ævum*, an unmeasured period of existence), for γενεά (Lat. *generatio*), and even for the more precise and exact terms χρόνος (Lat. *tempus*), and καιρός (Lat. *occasio*). Its strictest Greek equivalent, however, is ἡλικία (Lat. *ætas*). An examination into the significance of the term shows a remarkable parallel between its employment in classical literature and in the Greek of the New Testament. Ἡλικία marks a normal development of life; such development may be registered in the individual by years, or by physique. In classical Greek, the former is the usual reference of the term, and hence the most ordinary meaning of the word is, like the poetical ἥβη, the flower or prime of life. The significance, however, of ἡλικία as *stature* or *height*, that feature of physical development which mostly attracts the eye, is quite classical; and this sense occurs in Herodotus (iii. 16),* Plato, and Demosthenes. Turning to the New Testament, we find the same oscillation of meaning in ἡλικία. In the Fourth Gospel the parents of the blind man for fear of excommunication evade the question of the Jews, and shift the responsibility of answering upon their son : 'Therefore said his parents, He is of age,† ask him.' In the Sermon on the Mount 'age'‡ appears to be the true rendering of ἡλικία. A **cubit** would be a prodigious addition to a man's height, while a span was already a proverbial expression§ to signify the brevity of life. **'Stature'** is, of course, the only possible rendering in the interesting note about Zacchæus; ‖ and this is the only place in the Gospel where, as will be seen, ἡλικία bears this meaning with an absolute certainty.

The idea of periodicity, which is largely foreign to the meaning of ἡλικία in classical Greek, appears only once, and that doubtfully, in the New Testament.¶ The different 'ages of man'** and so of our Lord,†† are indicated by the classical formula of time, 'years' being in the genitive case. Hence the word yields no suggestion as to those characteristic periods, or epochs in the earthly life of our Lord— the infancy, childhood, manhood of Christ. Nor would the word deserve a place in this Dictionary were it not for two passages in which it occurs or is referred to when its interest is a real one, as is evident by the attention paid to them by all commentators on St. Luke's Gospel.‡‡ Both passages appear as a postscript to the narrative of the Holy Child with the doctors in the temple. It is an incident in the regular equable development of His life upon earth. This development is shown in two aspects. The Evangelist declares that Jesus increased (or advanced) in wisdom and stature, and in favour (or grace) with God and man. St. Luke's phraseology was no doubt influenced by his recollection of a similar encomium passed upon the youthful Samuel,§§ and already he had found it not unsuitable to be quoted in reference to the Baptist.‖‖ The key to the meaning of ἡλικία in Lk 2⁵² may

be discovered by a comparison of these four passages—

1 S 2²⁶ Καὶ τὸ παιδάριον Σαμουὴλ ἐπορεύετο [+ μεγαλυνόμενον], καὶ ἀγαθὸν καὶ μετὰ Κυρίου καὶ μετὰ ἀνθρώπων (LXX, B, said of Samuel).

Lk 1⁸⁰ τὸ δὲ παιδίον ηὔξανε καὶ ἐκραταιοῦτο πνεύματι (said of the Baptist).

Lk 2⁴⁰ τὸ δὲ παιδίον ηὔξανεν καὶ ἐκραταιοῦτο πληρούμενον σοφίᾳ, καὶ χάρις θεοῦ ἦν ἐπ᾽ αὐτό (said of Christ).

Lk 2⁵² καὶ Ἰησοῦς προέκοπτεν ἐν τῇ σοφίᾳ καὶ ἡλικίᾳ καὶ χάριτι παρὰ θεῷ καὶ ἀνθρώποις (said of Christ).

A careful comparison of these passages appears determinative of the sense of ἡλικία in the last as 'stature,' not 'age.' What was noticeable in a measure in Samuel and in the Baptist, was supremely characteristic of the Holy Child, namely, an equal development both on the physical and spiritual side. Translate it as RVm, and it is little more than a truism. 'Stature' is not only not superfluous, but an interesting and unexpected contribution to that group of references which lay stress on our Lord's humanity. It helps to explain His 'favour with men' with which it stands in parallel. It suggests that our Lord's personality, even His appearance, may have had a fascination about it. Even more, it may make the student of Messianic prophecy cautious in attaching a too physical meaning to the description of the countenance of Jehovah's Servant (Is 52¹⁴ 53²). B. WHITEFOORD.

AGONY.—This word is used in Lk 22⁴⁴ to describe the sorrow, suffering, and struggle of Jesus in Gethsemane. The Greek word *agōnia* (ἀγωνία) is derived from *agōn* (ἀγών), meaning: (1) an assembly of the people (cf. ἀγορά); (2) a place of assembly, especially the place in which the Greeks assembled to celebrate solemn games; (3) a contest of athletes, runners or charioteers. Ἀγών is used in a figurative sense in He 12¹ 'let us run with patience the *race* that is set before us.' The word has the general sense of *struggle* in 1 Th 2² 'in much conflict'; Ph 1³⁰ 'having the same conflict'; 1 Ti 6¹² 'the good fight of faith'; 2 Ti 4⁷ 'I have fought the good fight.' It means *solicitude* or *anxiety* in Col 2¹ 'how greatly I strive for you' (literally, 'how great an *agōn* I have for you').

The state of Jesus in Gethsemane is described in the following phrases : Mt 26³⁷ 'he began to be sorrowful and sore troubled'; Mk 14³³ 'he began to be greatly amazed and sore troubled'; Lk 22⁴⁴ 'And being in an agony he prayed more earnestly : and his sweat became as it were great drops of blood falling down upon the ground.' * Jesus confesses His own feelings in the words, 'My soul is exceeding sorrowful, even unto death' (Mt 26³⁸, Mk 14³⁴). That He regarded the experience as a temptation is suggested by His warning words to His disciples : 'Watch and pray, that ye enter not into temptation : the spirit indeed is willing, but the flesh is weak' (Mt 26⁴¹, Mk 14³⁸; cf. Lk 22⁴⁰·⁴⁶). That He was conscious of human weakness, and desired Divine strength for the struggle, is evident from the prayers, in reporting the words of which the Evangelists do not verbally agree, as the following comparison shows :—

Mt 26³⁹.	Mk 14³⁶.	Lk 22⁴².
'O my Father, if it be possible, let this cup pass away from me : nevertheless not as I will, but as thou wilt.'	'Abba, Father, all things are possible unto thee; remove this cup from me : howbeit not what I will, but what thou wilt.'	'Father, if thou be willing, remove this cup from me : nevertheless, not my will, but thine, be done.'

St. Mark and St. Luke give the words of one prayer only, although the former evidently intends to report three distinct acts of prayer (vv.³⁵·³⁹·⁴¹),

* On the genuineness of this passage see the 'Notes on Select Readings' in Westcott and Hort's *NT in Greek*.

* ἔχων τὴν αὐτὴν ἡλικίην Ἀμάσι. † ἡλικίαν ἔχει (Jn 9²¹·²³).
‡ Mt 6²⁷, Lk 12²⁵. § Ps 39⁵.
‖ Lk 19³, cf. Eph 4¹³. ¶ He 11¹¹.
** Mk 5⁴², Lk 8⁴². †† Lk 3²³.
‡‡ Lk 2⁴⁰·⁵². §§ 1 S 2²⁶.
‖‖ Lk 1⁸⁰.

and the latter apparently only two (vv.[41. 44]).
But St. Matthew gives the words of the second
prayer, which he reports as repeated the third
time (vv.[42. 44]) : ' O my Father, if this cannot pass
away, except I drink it, thy will be done.' It is
not at all improbable that there was such progress
in Jesus' thoughts. At first He prayed for the
entire removal of the cup, if possible (Mt.), because
possible to God (Mk.), if God were willing (Lk.) ;
and then, having been taught that it could not be
taken away, He prayed for strength to take the
cup. It is not necessary for us to decide which of
the reports is most nearly verbally correct, as the
substance of the first prayer is the same in all
reports. Although St. John gives no report of the
scene in Gethsemane, yet in his account of the
interview of Jesus with the Greeks there is introduced what seems to be a faint reminiscence :
' Now is my soul troubled ; and what shall I say ?
Father, save me from this hour : but for this
cause came I unto this hour. Father, glorify thy
name ' (Jn 12[27. 28]). It is substantially the same
request, expressed in the characteristically Johannine language. But even if this conjecture be
unwarranted, and this be an utterance on the
occasion to which the Fourth Evangelist assigns
it, the words serve to illustrate Jesus' struggle in
view of His death. Much more confident can we
be that Gethsemane is referred to in He 5[7. 8]
' Who in the days of his flesh, having offered up
prayers and supplications with strong crying and
tears unto him that was able to save him from
death, and having been heard for his godly fear ;
though he was a Son, yet learned obedience by
the things which he suffered.' Having passed in
review the material which is offered us in dealing
with the question of the nature of the agony in
Gethsemane, we may now concentrate our attention upon it, excluding all reference to other
matters which are dealt with in their own place.

Many answers have been given to the question,
What was the cup which Jesus desired to be taken
away ?

(1) The most obvious, but not on that account
the most intelligent and reverent, answer is that
in Gethsemane Jesus was overcome by the fear of
death, from which He longed to escape. But this
is to place Christ on a lower plane of manhood
than many men, even among the lowest races. If
the love of Christ has constrained many martyrs
for His name to face rack and block, water and
flame, and many other painful modes of death
without shrinking, and even with the song of
praise upon the lips, is it at all likely that He
Himself shrank back ?

(2) A more ingenious view, which has an apparent
verbal justification in Mt 26[38], Mk 14[34] (' even unto
death '), and He 5[7] (' to save him from death '), is
that Jesus felt Himself dying, and that He feared
He would die before He could offer the great
sacrifice for the sin of the world. But to this
suggestion there are three objections. Firstly,
there is no evidence of such physical exhaustion on
the part of Jesus as would justify such a fear ;
although the stress of His work and suffering had
undoubtedly put a severe strain upon His bodily
strength, yet we have no proof that His health
had given way so far as to make death appear at
all probable. Secondly, only a very superficial
and external view of His work as Saviour warrants
the supposition that His sacrifice could be accomplished only on the Cross ; that its efficacy depended
in any way on its outward mode ; that His death,
if it had come to Him in Gethsemane, would have
had less value for God and man than His crucifixion has. Thirdly, even if this supposition be
admitted, we may be sure of this, that Jesus was
so confident of His Father's goodness and guardian-

ship in every step of His path, that it was impossible for Him to fear that the great purpose of His
life would be left unfulfilled on account of His
premature death. His rebuke of the ' little faith '
(Mt 8[26]) of His disciples during the storm at sea
would have been applicable to Himself had He
cherished any such fear.

(3) A much more profound view is offered to our
consideration, when not the death itself, but the
circumstances of the death, are represented as the
cause of Jesus' agony. He regarded His death not
only as a sacrifice which He was willing to offer,
not only as a tragedy which He was ready to
endure, but as a crime of man against God from
which He shrank with horror. That the truth
and grace of God in Him should meet with this
insult and injury from the race which He had
come to save and bless—this it was that caused
His agony. He could not endure to gaze into ' the
abysmal depths ' of human iniquity and impiety,
which the murder of the Holy One and the Just
opened to view. Surely this apocalypse of sin was
not necessary as a condition of the apocalypse of
grace. If we look more closely at the conduct of
the actors in this drama, we shall better understand how appalling a revelation of sin it must have
appeared to Jesus. The fickleness of the multitude, the hypocrisy and bigotry of the Pharisees,
the worldliness and selfishness of the priesthood,
the treachery of Judas, the denial by Peter, the
antagonism of the disciples generally to the Master's
saving purpose, the falsehood of His accusers, the
hate and the craft of His persecutors,—all these
were present to the consciousness of Jesus as an
intolerable offence to His conscience, and an unspeakable grief to His heart. To His moral
insight and spiritual discernment these were not
single misdeeds, but signs and proofs of a wickedness and godlessness spreading far and wide in the
life of mankind, reaching deep into the soul of
man. Must this antagonism of sin to God be
forced to its ultimate issue ? Could He not save
mankind by some mode of sacrifice that would
involve the men concerned in it in less heinous
guilt ? Must He by persevering in His present
course drive His enemies to do their worst against
Him, and thus by His fidelity to His vocation
must He involve all who opposed Him in this
greater iniquity ? That such questions cannot
have been present to the mind of Jesus, who can
confidently affirm ? He foresaw the doom of the
guilty nation, and He also saw that it was the
crime about to be committed against Him that
would seal its doom. That He shrank from
being thus the occasion of its judgment cannot be
doubted. But if in Gethsemane Jesus anticipated
distinctly and accepted deliberately what He so
intensely experienced on the Cross, then this solicitude for all who were involved in the crime of His
death does not at all exhaust His agony. The
words of darkness and desolation on the Cross,
' My God, my God, why hast thou forsaken me ? '
(Mt 27[46]), must be our clue to the mystery of this
experience.

(4) The only view that seems to the present
writer at all adequate is that what Jesus dreaded
and prayed to be delivered from in the experience
of death was the sense of God's distance and
abandonment. His sorrow unto death was not
the fear of death as physical dissolution, nor of
dying before He could finish His work on the
Cross, but the shrinking of His filial soul from
the sting of death, due to sin, the veiling in darkness of His Father's face from Him. His prayer
was answered, for He was saved from death,
inasmuch as the experience of darkness and
desolation was momentary, and ere He gave up
the ghost He was able to commit Himself with

childlike trust unto His Father. 'Father, into thy hands I commend my spirit' (Lk 23[46]). His agony in Gethsemane was worthy of Him as the Son of God, for it was the recoil of His filial spirit from the interruption of His filial communion with His Father, which appeared to Him to be necessarily involved in the sacrifice which He was about to offer for the sins of the world.

It is not the function of this article to offer a theological interpretation of Jesus' experience in Gethsemane; but a justification of the above answer to the question of the nature of Jesus' agony may be briefly offered in a psychological analysis of His experience. First of all, then, we note Jesus' sense of solitude. He must leave behind Him the disciples except three, and even from these three He must withdraw Himself (Mt 26[36, 39]). He sought this outward isolation because He felt this inner solitude. Since His announcement of His Passion (Mt 16[21]) the disciples had been becoming less and less His companions, as they were being more and more estranged from His purpose. At last He knew that they would abandon Him altogether, their outer distance but the sign and proof of their inward alienation. Yet the comfort of the Father's presence would remain with Him: 'Behold, the hour cometh, yea, is come, that ye shall be scattered every man to his own, and shall leave me alone: and yet I am not alone, because the Father is with me' (Jn 16[32]). But now in Gethsemane He began to realize that it might be necessary for the accomplishment of His sacrifice that even the Father's presence should be withdrawn from Him. That dread drives Him to the Father's presence, but the assurance that there is no ground for this fear does not come to Him. Again He turns to His disciples. Secondly, therefore, we note His need of sympathy. When He withdrew from the three, He asked them to watch with Him; when, returning, He found them sleeping, His words are a pathetic reproach: 'What, could ye not watch with me one hour?' (Mt 26[40]). He craved sympathy, not only because He felt solitary, but because this solitude was due to His love for man. The sacrifice He was about to offer, in which the sense of His Father's abandonment was the sting of death, was on behalf of, and instead of man; and yet not even the men He had chosen would sorrow with Him, although He was suffering for all mankind. Thus man's denial of sympathy must have made Him feel more keenly the dread that even God's comfort and help might be withheld from Him. Thirdly, we note that this dread was not groundless, but was rooted deep in His experience and vocation. We must then go beyond any of the words uttered in Gethsemane itself to discover all that was involved in His agony there. As the incarnate love, mercy, and grace of God, His experience was necessarily vicarious. He suffered with and for man. He so identified Himself with sinful mankind, that He shared its struggle, bore its burden, felt its shame. Himself sinless, knowing no sin, He was made sin for mankind in feeling its sin as it were His very own. The beloved of God, He became a curse in experiencing in His own agony and desolation the consequences of sin, although as innocent He could neither feel the guilt nor bear the penalty of sin. So completely had He become one with mankind in being made sin and a curse for man, that even His consciousness of filial union and communion with God as His Father was obscured and interrupted, if even for only a moment, by His consciousness of the sin of man. God did not withdraw Himself from, or abandon His only-begotten and well-beloved Son, but was with Him to sustain Him in His sacrifice; but the Son of

God was so overshadowed and overwhelmed by His consciousness of the sin and the consequent curse of the race which He so loved as to make Himself one with it, that He dreaded in Gethsemane to lose, and did on Calvary lose for a moment, the comfort and help of His Father's love. In this experience He exhibited the antagonism of God and sin, the necessary connexion between the expulsion of God and the invasion of sin in any consciousness, since His self-identification with sinful man involved His self-isolation from the Holy Father. This, then, was the agony in Gethsemane, such a sense of the sorrow, shame, and curse of mankind's sin as His very own as became a dread of the loss of God's fatherly presence. Although He at first prayed to be delivered from this, to Him, most terrible and grievous experience, yet He afterward submitted to God's will, as God's purpose in the salvation of mankind was dearer to Him than even the joy of His filial communion with God His Father. In this surrender He was endowed with such strength from above that He finished the work His Father had given Him to do, and in His obedience even unto death offered the sacrifice of His life, which is a ransom for many, and the seal of the new covenant of forgiveness, renewal, and fellowship with God for all mankind. See also art. DERELICTION.

LITERATURE.—The standard Commentaries and Lives of Christ; Hastings' *DB* ii. 712 f.; Jonathan Edwards, *Works*, ii. 866 ff.; *Expos. Times*, vi. [1894–1895], 433 f., 522; *Expositor*, 3rd ser. v. 180 ff.; Fairbairn, *Studies in the Life of Christ*, 'Gethsemane,' where the explanation numbered (3) above is fully elaborated.
ALFRED E. GARVIE.

AGRAPHA.—See SAYINGS.

AGRICULTURE.—The influence of the physical and climatic characteristics of a land upon the character of its people has been a favourite theme with many writers. But we are more concerned here with another marked feature—the profound influence exerted by the occupations of a people on their manner of thought and their modes of expressing it. Nowhere was this subtle influence more manifest than in the case of the Hebrews. Their occupations were largely determined by the characteristics of the land they inhabited, but their thought and the language that was its vehicle were equally moulded by their occupations.

1. *The place of Agriculture in the life and thought of the Hebrews.* — From the first the Hebrews were a pastoral, and from very early times an agricultural people; and these twin employments have lent their colour and tone to their literature, and shaped their profoundest thoughts and utterances regarding God and man. God is the Shepherd of Israel (Ps 80[1]); Israel is 'the people of his pasture, and the sheep of his hand' (95[7], cf. 74[1] 79[13] 100[3]). God is the Husbandman; Israel is His vineyard (Is 5[1ff.]). God is the Ploughman; Israel is the land of His tillage (Is 28[25ff.], cf. 1 Co 3[9]).

When we turn to the Gospels we find the same stream of thought in full flow. The highest Christian virtue is enforced by appeal to Him who 'maketh his sun to rise on the evil and on the good, and sendeth rain on the just and on the unjust' (Mt 5[45]). The kingdom of God is set forth under such emblems as the sower going forth to sow (13[3ff.]), the wheat and the tares growing together until the harvest (v.[24ff.]), the lord of the vineyard going out early in the morning to hire labourers (20[1ff.]), or sending to demand its fruits (21[33ff.]). Christ compares Himself to the shepherd who seeks his lost sheep until he finds it (Lk 15[4]), or lays down his life for the sheep (Jn 10[11]). The multitude are, to His compassionate eye, as 'sheep not having a shepherd' (Mt 9[36], Mk 6[34]). The world appears to Him as a great field 'white unto harvest' (Jn 4[35]), and awaiting the labour of the reapers (Mt 9[37f.]). His relation to His disciples is expressed under the figure of the vine and its branches (Jn 15[1ff.]) See also art. HUSBANDMAN.

Noteworthy also is the place assigned by Biblical writers to the cultivation of the soil. It is represented as the duty of the first man. Adam, placed in the Garden of Eden, is 'to dress it and to keep it' (Gn 2[15]); driven from it, he is sent 'to till the ground from whence he was taken' (3[23]). To Noah the promise is given that 'while the earth remaineth, seedtime and harvest . . . shall not cease' (8[22]). The land of promise is 'a land of wheat and barley' (Dt 8[8]). The Golden Age will be a time when men 'shall beat their swords into ploughshares, and their spears into pruning-hooks,' and 'they shall sit every man under his vine and under his fig-tree' (Is 2[4], Mic 4[3. 4]). The gladness of the Messianic age is 'joy according to the joy in harvest' (Is 9[3]).

Nor was it only in their conception of the past and their anticipation of the future that the influence of agriculture made itself felt: it was the very foundation of their national and religious life. A pastoral age, it is true, preceded the agricultural, and the patriarchs are represented, for the most part, as herdsmen rather than cultivators (Gn 37[12] 47[3]); and even as late as the beginning of the settlement in Canaan, the trans-Jordanic tribes are said to have had a great multitude of cattle (Nu 32[1]). But, on the other hand, we learn that Isaac, who had gone to Gerar, 'sowed in that land, and found in the same year an hundredfold' (Gn 26[12]); while the first dream of Joseph shows that if he did not actually follow, he was at least familiar with, agricultural pursuits (37[5-7]). But it was not till after their conquest of the Land of Promise that the Hebrews became an agricultural people on any large scale. Prior to that time, however, agriculture was highly developed among the Canaanites (Dt 8[8]); and it may have been from the conquered race that they acquired it. Once learned, it became the staple industry of the country.

The Mosaic legislation presupposes a people given to agricultural pursuits. That is sufficiently attested by the laws anent the three annual festivals (Ex 23[14-16]), the septennial fallow (23[11]), the gleanings of the harvest field (Lv 19[9. 10]), the year of Jubilee (25[10ff.] 27[17ff.]), and many others. Further attestation of the same fact is found in the blessings that were to attend the faithful observance of the Law, and the curses that would follow disobedience (Lv 26[3-5. 14-20], Dt 28[1-5. 15-18]).

2. *The soil of Palestine.*—The fertility of the soil of Palestine was remarkable, as is testified by Josephus (*c. Apion.* i. 22; *BJ* ii. 3) and others (Diod. xl. 3, 7; Tac. *Hist.* v. 6). The soil varies in character. In the Jordan Valley and the maritime plains it consists of a very rich alluvial deposit; in the regions lying at a higher elevation it has been formed from decomposing basaltic rock and cretaceous limestone. This, however, was greatly enriched by the system of 'terracing,' low walls of 'shoulder-stones' being built along the mountain slopes, and the ledges behind them filled with the alluvial soil of the valleys. These walls gave protection against the heavy rains, and prevented the soil from being washed away. It was to this system that districts such as Lebanon, Carmel, and Gilboa owed the wonderful fertility that formerly characterized them.

All parts were not, of course, equally productive. Thus we find the Mishna (*Giṭṭin*, v. 1) enumerating several classes of soil according to their quality or the degree of moisture. Such a classification is quite distinct from that of the parable of the Sower, where the wayside, the rocky places, etc., are all within the limits of a single field (Mt 13[5], Mk 4[3], Lk 8[5]). It may be noted here that ground which yielded thorns was considered specially good for wheat-growing, while that which was overrun with weeds was assigned to barley. The most productive fields were often marked by the presence of large stones, some of which were beyond a man's own strength to remove. Their presence was regarded as a token that the soil was fertile. Smaller stones, which were also plentiful, were often used for making rude walls along the side of the fields. In some districts they were so numerous that they had to be removed every year after ploughing had taken place.

3. *Agricultural operations*, etc.—The work of preparing the land for cultivation was the first concern of the farmer. Where virgin soil had to be reclaimed, a beginning was made by clearing it of timber, brushwood, or stones (Jos 17[18], Is 5[2]). It was then ready to receive the plough (which see).

(*a*) *Ploughing* began immediately after the 'early rain' had softened the ground, *i.e.* towards the end of September or beginning of October, and went on right through the winter, provided the soil had not become too wet and, therefore, too heavy. Usually a single ploughing sufficed, but if the soil was very rough it was ploughed twice.

In some cases the *hoe* or *mattock* took the place of the plough. That is the common practice in modern times where there is a rocky bottom and only a sparse covering of earth. In ancient times the same course was followed where hillsides were brought under cultivation (Is 7[25]). The same implement was employed for breaking up large clods of earth (Is 28[24], Hos 10[11]), but whether the reference includes the clods upturned by the plough, or merely those occurring in 'stony ground,' is not quite certain.

(*b*) **Dung** was employed for increasing the productiveness of fruit trees (Lk 13[8]), but not, as a rule, for grain fields. The most common forms were house and farmyard refuse mixed with straw (Is 25[10]), withered leaves, oil-scum, and woodashes. The blood of slaughtered animals was also used for this purpose.

(*c*) The *principal crops* were wheat, barley, spelt, millet, beans, and lentils (see articles on the first two of these). Oats were little cultivated. From Jos 2[6] we learn that flax was grown. It was sometimes sown as an experiment for testing the quality of the soil, for a field which had yielded good flax was regarded as specially suitable for wheat-growing.

(*d*) The *sowing* season began in the early days of October. A beginning was made with pulse varieties, barley came next, and wheat followed. Millet was sown in summer, the land being prepared for it by irrigation. When the winter set in cold and wet, barley was not sown till the beginning of February.

The sower carries the seed in a basket or bag, from which he scatters it broadcast. Where a single ploughing suffices, the seed is sown first and then ploughed in. When it is sown on ploughed ground, the usual course is also to plough it in, but sometimes a light harrow (not infrequently a thorn-bush) is used to cover it. Seed that falls on the footpath or 'wayside' cannot be covered owing to the hardness of the ground, and is picked up by the birds (Mt 13[4] and parallels).

(*e*) The crops thus sown were exposed, as they grew, to various *dangers*, such as the inroads of roaming cattle, the depredations of birds, or the visitation of locusts; and also to such adverse natural and climatic influences as drought, east wind, and mildew. Some of these will be separately treated, and need not be dwelt upon now. But it may be convenient to say a few words at this stage regarding—

(f) *The water supply of the country.*—Unlike Egypt, which owed its fertility exclusively to the Nile, Palestine had its time of rain (Dt 11[10. 11. 14], Jer 5[24] etc.). The 'early rain' (מוֹרֶה) of the Bible is that of October, which precedes ploughing and sowing : the 'latter rain' (מַלְקוֹשׁ) denotes the refreshing showers that fall in March and April, and give much-needed moisture to the growing crops. The intervening period is marked by the heavy rains of winter (גֶּשֶׁם), the wettest month being January. The rainfall is not uniform over the country. In the Jordan Valley it is very slight ; at Jerusalem it averages about 20 inches annually ; in some other upland regions it is almost twice as much. In the highest lying parts, as Lebanon, there is a considerable fall of **snow**. There are also many brooks and springs (Dt 8[7]), and irrigation is employed, especially in gardening, though naturally on a much smaller scale than in Egypt. The summer months are hot and rainless.

(g) *Harvest.*—Barley harvest (2 S 21[9]) began in April or May, according as the district was early or late ; wheat and spelt were ripe a few weeks after (Ex 9[31. 32]). The grain was cut with a sickle (Jl 3[13], Dt 16[9], Mk 4[29] ; see art. SICKLE), or pulled up by the roots (Mishna, *Peah* iv. 10). The latter method was followed both in Palestine and in Egypt, and is so still ; but the use of the sickle goes back to very early times, as the excavations at Tell el-Ḥesy have shown. Ordinarily the stalks were cut about a foot beneath the ear, but in some instances even higher (Job 24[24]). The reaper grasped them in handfuls (Ru 2[16]), reaped them with his arm (Is 17[5]), and laid them behind him ; while the binder, following him, gathered them in his bosom (Ps 129[7]), tied them with straw into sheaves (Gn 37[7]), and set them in heaps (עֲמָרִים * Ru 2[7]).

(h) *Threshing.*—The sheaves thus prepared were carried to the *threshing-floor* on the backs of men or of beasts of burden, such as donkeys, horses, or camels. Am 2[13] has been taken by some as implying that they were sometimes removed in carts, but this is very doubtful. The reference is more probably to the threshing-sledge (Is 28[28]).

The **threshing-floor** is simply a circle of level ground which has been carefully cleaned and beaten hard, and is enclosed with a row of big stones to prevent the straw from being too widely scattered. The spot selected always stood higher than the surrounding ground, so that it should be open to the air currents, and that rain, if it occurred, though 'it was rare in harvest time (1 S 12[17]), might run off without doing injury. The sheaves were unbound and scattered over the floor, till a heap was formed about a foot high. Cattle (Hos 10[11]) were then driven over it repeatedly, or a threshing-wain drawn by cattle. The Pentateuchal law provided that the cattle engaged in this operation should not be muzzled (Dt 25[4]). It was also the custom to blindfold them, as otherwise, moving continually in a circle, they became dizzy (Talmud, *Kelim* xvi. 7). Certain crops, however, were threshed by being beaten with a stick (Is 28[27]).

Two kinds of threshing machines were employed, the drag and the waggon. The drag (מוֹרַג, חָרוּץ) was a heavy wooden board,† the under-surface of which was studded with nails or sharp fragments of stone (Is 41[15]). It was further weighted with

---

* See Vogelstein, *Landwirthschaft in Pal.* 61.
† See illustration in Driver's *Joel and Amos* (Camb. Bible), p. 227.

---

large stones, and by the driver himself, who stood, sat, or even lay upon it. The waggon (עֲגָלָה Is 28[28]) was provided with sharp metal discs. These were affixed to revolving rollers set in a rude waggon-frame.

(i) *Winnowing.*—The operation of threshing yielded a confused mass of grain, chaff, and broken straw, which required to be winnowed. Two implements were used for this process—the shovel and the fan (Is 30[24]). With these the mixed mass was tossed into the air, against the wind. The chaff was blown away (Ps 1[4]), the straw fell a little distance off, and the grain at the feet of the winnower. Where, as at large public threshing-floors, there was an accumulation of chaff, it was burned (Mt 3[12]). The chopped straw (תֶּבֶן Is 11[7]) was used as fodder for cattle.

(j) *Sifting.*—The winnowed grain still contained an admixture of small stones and particles of clay, stubble, and unbruised ears, and also of smaller poisonous seeds such as tares, and so stood in need of yet further cleansing. This was effected by means of **sifting**. In modern Palestine the sieve in common use is a wooden hoop with a mesh made of camel-hide. This implement probably corresponds to the כְּבָרָה (*kĕbhārāh*) of ancient times (Am 9[9]). The mesh was wide enough to allow the separated grains to pass through, but retained the unthreshed ears, which were cast again on the threshing-floor.* In Is 30[28] another implement is mentioned, נָפָה (*nāphāh*), which both AV and RV render 'sieve.' It is not quite certain, however, that the *nāphāh* was really a sieve. If it was, it may have resembled the modern *ghirbal*, which is of smaller mesh than the *kĕbhārāh* (Arab. *kirbal*), and permits only broken grains and dust to pass through, while retaining the unbruised kernels.

The sifted grain was collected in large heaps, and, pending its removal to the granary, slept by the owner, to guard against thieving, slept by the threshing-floor (Ru 3[7]). In the Gospels there is one reference to sifting (Lk 22[31]).

(k) *Storage.*—In the NT a granary is called ἀποθήκη (Mt 6[26] 13[30], Lk 12[18. 24]). In the OT quite a variety of names occurs (מִסְכְּנוֹת Ex 1[11] ; אֲסָמִים Dt 28[8] ; מַאֲבֻסִים Jer 50[26] ; מְזָוִים Ps 144[13] ; אֹצָרוֹת and מַמְּגֻרוֹת Jl 1[17]). But though the nomenclature is so rich, of the construction and character of those granaries we know nothing. Some of them were probably sheds, and may have resembled the flat-roofed buildings used in Egypt for storing grain. Others may have been dry wells, or cisterns, or caves hewn out of the rock, such as are common in modern times. The grain stored in these magazines will remain good for years.

LITERATURE.—Ugolinus, *Thesaurus*, vol. xxix. ; Benzinger, *Heb. Arch.* 207 ff.; Nowack, *Lehrbuch der Heb. Archäologie*, i. 228 ff.; Vogelstein, *Die Landwirthschaft in Palästina zur Zeit der Mischna* ; Stade, *Geschichte d. Volkes Israel*, i. vii.; Wilkinson, *Ancient Egyptians*, *passim* ; Thomson, *The Land and the Book* ; van Lennep, *Bible Lands and Customs* ; *ZDPV* ix. ; *PEFSt*, *passim* ; Ungewitter, *Die landwirthschaftlichen Bilder und Metaphern i. d. poet. Büch. d. Alt. Test.* ; Hastings' *DB*, and *Encyc. Bibl. s.v.* 'Agriculture.'

HUGH DUNCAN.

AHAZ.—One of the kings of Judah (*c.* 735-720 B.C.), named in St. Matthew's genealogy of our Lord (Mt 1[9]).

AHIMELECH.—See ABIATHAR.

AKELDAMA.—The name given in Ac 1[19] to the field purchased with the price of Judas' treachery.

---

* In this case the meaning of 'the least *grain*' in Am 9[9] must be 'the least pebble' (so Preuschen, *ZATW*, 1895, p. 24). Others (e.g. Driver, *Joel and Amos*, p. 221 ; Nowack and Marti in their Comm. *ad loc.*) take the word צְרוֹר (*zĕrôr*, lit. 'pebble') to stand here for a grain of wheat, while admitting that the word is not elsewhere so used. On this supposition the action of the *kĕbhārāh* would be similar to that of the modern *ghirbal* described above.

The true reading seems to be ἀκελδαμάχ (B; cf. ἀχελδαμάχ, אA 61, etc.; ἀκελδαιμάχ, D; ἀκελδαμὰκ, E) rather than the TR ἀκελδαμά; and the final aspirate is here of importance, as will be seen.

The two accounts of the death of Judas (Mt 27³ᵗ· and Ac 1¹⁸ᶠ·) are hard to reconcile (see JUDAS, and art. in *Expositor* for June 1904, by the present writer); but it is sufficient to note here that they are clearly independent of each other. The salient features of the Matthæan tradition are—(a) Judas stricken with remorse returned the money paid to him as the price of his treachery; (b) he hanged himself in despair, nothing being said as to the scene of his suicide; (c) the priests bought with the money a field known as 'the Potter's Field,' which (d) thenceforth was called ἀγρὸς αἵματος, the allusion being to the blood of Christ, shed through the treachery of Judas; (e) the field was devoted to the purpose of a cemetery for foreigners. In Acts, on the other hand, (a) nothing is said of a refunding of the money by Judas; (b) his death was not self-inflicted, nor was it caused by hanging; it is described as due to a fall and a consequent rupture of the abdomen; (c) the field was bought by Judas himself, and not by the priests; (d) nothing is said of its former use as a 'potter's field,' nor (e) of the purpose for which it was used after the death of Judas; (f) the blood which gave its name to the field was that of Judas, by which it was defiled, for (g) the field Akeldama is identified with the place of his death, a fact of which there is no mention in Matthew.

The only point common to the two accounts is that the name by which the field was known in the next generation after Judas' death was an Aramaic word which was variously rendered ἀγρὸς αἵματος and χωρίον αἵματος by Mt. and Luke. Lk. gives a transliteration of this Aramaic name; he says it was ἀκελδαμάχ, that is, he understands it as equivalent to חֲקֵל דְּמָא, 'Field of Blood.' And ἀκελδαμάχ is, no doubt, a possible transliteration of these Hebrew words, for we have other instances of final א being represented by the Greek χ, as, e.g., in the equation Σιράχ = סִירָא. But we should not *expect* a final χ, although it might be defended, if the last part of the Aramaic title were דְּמָא; the presence of χ suggests rather that the Aramaic title ended with the letters דמך. Now it is remarkable that דְּמֵך = κοιμᾶσθαι, so that κοιμητήριον 'cemetery' would be the exact equivalent of חֲקֵל דְּמָך. And Klostermann (*Probleme im Aposteltexte*, p. 6 ff.) has suggested that this was really the name by which the field was known to the native Jews, and that we have here a corroboration of St. Matthew's tradition 'to bury strangers in' (Mt 27⁷). This conjecture is confirmed by the fact, which has been pointed out above, that the significance of the name 'Field of Blood' was differently understood by Mt. and Luke. When we have two rival explanations offered of a place-name, it is probable that the name itself is a corruption of some other, akin in sound, but not in sense.

The evidence, then, points to the following conclusions. The field which was purchased with the wages of Judas was originally a 'potter's field,' or pit, in the neighbourhood of Jerusalem. It may have been (as Christian tradition had it afterwards) the place in the Valley of Hinnom where the potter of Jeremiah's day pursued his craft (Jer 18² 19²); but of this there is no hint in the NT, for the reference to Jeremiah in the text of Mt 27⁹ is an inadvertence, the passage quoted by the Evangelist being Zec 11¹³. This 'potter's field' was used as a burial-ground for strangers, and so was called חֲקֵל דְּמָך = cœmeterium. Within half a century the name became corrupted to חֲקֵל דְּמָא 'the Field of Blood,' the allusion being variously interpreted of the blood of Christ and the blood of Judas.

There is no good reason to doubt the identity of the modern Ḥakḳ ed-Dumm, on the south bank of the Valley of Hinnom, with the 'Akeldamach' of Lk. and the ἀγρὸς αἵματος of Matthew. The early pilgrims, e.g. Antoninus (570) and Arculf (685), describe its site with sufficient accuracy, and so do the later mediæval travellers.

Tradition has distinguished Akeldama, the field purchased with Judas' thirty pieces of silver, from the scene of his death —a distinction of sites which, though inconsistent with Ac 1, is compatible with Mt., as has been pointed out above. Thus Antoninus places 'Akeldemac, hoc est, ager sanguinis, in quo omnes peregrini sepeliuntur' (§ 26), near Siloam; but the fig-tree 'on which Judas hanged himself' was shown him on the N.E. of the city (§ 17). Arculf seems to place the latter upon the Hill of Evil Counsel (§ 18), where it is shown at the present day; but the tradition has not been constant, the 'elder-tree' of Judas having been pointed out to Sir J. Maundeville (in 16th cent.) near Absalom's pillar.

The best description of Ḥakḳ ed-Dumm, and of the buildings which remain of the old charnel house, will be found in an article by Schick (*PEFSt*, 1892, p. 283 ff.). It is quite possible, as he says, that this was once the site of a potter's cave; and clay used to be taken, up to quite recent times, from a place a little higher up the Hill of Evil Counsel. This burial-place was much used in Crusading times; indeed, it came to be regarded as an honour to be buried in Akeldama, so completely were the old associations of horror forgotten or ignored.

J. H. BERNARD.

ALABASTER (ἀλάβαστρος or ἀλάβαστρον; in secular writers always ἀλάβαστρος [more correctly ἀλάβαστος], though with a heterog. plur. ἀλάβαστρα; in NT only in accus., and only once with art., which is found in different MSS in all the genders —τήν, τόν, τό [Tisch., Treg., WH, Meyer, Alford prefer τήν]).—The word occurs four times in the Gospels: Mt 26⁷, Mk 14³ᵇⁱˢ, Lk 7³⁷. The Oriental alabaster, so called from the locality in Egypt (the town of Alabastron, near Tell el-Amarna) * where it is found in greatest abundance, is a species of marble softer and more easily worked than the ordinary marble. It was so frequently used for holding precious ointment that ἀλάβαστρος came to be a synonym for an unguent box (Theocr. xv. 114; Herod. iii. 20). Horace (*Od.* iv. 12. 17) uses *onyx* in the same way.

In all three of the Gospel narratives emphasis is laid on the costliness of the offering made to our Lord. The ointment was that with which monarchs were anointed. Judas valued it at three hundred pence. If we bear in mind that a *denarius* was a day's wage for ordinary labour, it would represent about four shillings of our money, and unguent and box would have a value of something like £60. Mary 'brake the box.' This is generally interpreted as merely meaning 'unfastened the seal'; but is it not in accordance alike with a profound instinct of human nature and with Oriental ideas to interpret the words literally? The box which had been rendered sacred by holding the ointment with which Jesus was anointed would never be put to a lower use.

This incident is the gospel protest against philanthropic utilitarianism. 'Man shall not live by bread alone, but by every word that proceedeth out of the mouth of God.' We have here the warrant for the expenditure of money on everything that makes for the higher life of man. Whatever tends to uplift the imagination, to ennoble and purify the emotions, to refine the taste, and thus to add to the spiritual value of life, is good, and is to be encouraged. Jesus claims our best. He inspires us to be and do our best, and the first-fruits of all the higher faculties of the soul are to be devoted to Him. See, further, art. ANOINTING i. 2.

A. MILLER.

* The reverse supposition is possible, that the town derived its name from the material (see *Encyc. Bibl.* i. 108).

ALEXANDER AND RUFUS.—The Synoptists all record that the Saviour's cross was borne by one Simon of Cyrene. St. Mark (15²¹) alone adds that he was 'the father of Alexander and Rufus.' From this we gather that, when the Second Gospel was written, the sons of him who bore the cross were followers of the Crucified, and men of prominence and note in the Church. This information as to the two sons of Simon being Alexander and Rufus, is also found in the Gospel of Nicodemus (ch. 4). The name Alexander appears in Ac 4⁶ 19³³, 1 Ti 1²⁰, 2 Ti 4¹⁴, but there is not the slightest ground for identifying any one of these with the Alexander of Mk 15²¹.

In the case of Rufus, however, it has generally been considered that he is probably the same as the Rufus who, with his mother, is saluted by St. Paul in Ro 16¹³ (Ῥοῦφον τὸν ἐκλεκτὸν ἐν Κυρίῳ). And if this is so, it tells us that not only the sons of Simon of Cyrene, but his wife also, were members of the Church. Lightfoot supports this view, and Swete considers that it has 'some probability.' In St. Paul's Epistle to the Philippians, written from Rome, occurs a salutation sent to the Church at Philippi from Cæsar's household (4²²). Lightfoot has compared the list of names of those to whom St. Paul sends greeting in his letter to the Romans (ch. 16) with the names in the lists of the household which occur in the inscriptions, and on the name Rufus he writes (*Philippians*⁷, p. 176)—

'Rufus is a very ordinary name, and would have claimed notice here but for its occurrence in one of the Gospels. There seems no reason to doubt the tradition that St. Mark wrote especially for the Romans; and if so, it is worth remarking that he alone of the Evangelists describes Simon of Cyrene as the "father of Alexander and Rufus" (15²¹). A person of this name, therefore, seems to have held a prominent place among the Roman Christians: and thus there is at least fair ground for identifying the Rufus of St. Paul with the Rufus of St. Mark. The inscriptions exhibit several members of the household bearing the names Rufus and Alexander, but this fact is of no value where both names are so common.'

In connexion with Bishop Lightfoot's note, it is worthy of notice that in Polycarp's Epistle to the Philippians (9) we find Ignatius, Zozimus, and Rufus adduced as examples, with St. Paul and the rest of the Apostles, of men who had obeyed the word of righteousness and exercised all patience, 'and are gone to the place that was due to them from the Lord with whom also they suffered; for they loved not this present world, but Him who died and was raised again by God for us.' In the *Acts of Andrew* and *of Peter*, Rufus and Alexander appear as the companions of Peter, Andrew, and Matthias, but no further information is given.   J. B. BRISTOW.

ALLEGORY.—See PARABLE.

ALMSGIVING (ἐλεημοσύνη).—[For the history of the word, and Jewish teaching, see Hastings' *DB* i. 67]. Only on three occasions does our Lord in the NT employ the word (Mt 6¹⁻⁴, Lk 11⁴¹ and 12³³). But these texts by no means exhaust His teaching on the subject. All the Gospels witness to His interest in it. Mk. contains the incidents of the Rich Young Man whom He told, 'Yet one thing thou lackest: go, sell all that thou hast, and give to the poor, and thou shalt have treasure in heaven' (10²¹); the Widow's Mite (12⁴³); and the emphatic praise of Mary of Bethany (14⁷). Jn. again exhibits all Christ's miracles as so many charities (*e.g.* 2¹⁻¹¹), 'good works' which Christ 'showed you from the Father' (10³²); tells the Lord's defence of Mary's act (12⁸); and drops a hint twice over (12⁶ and 13²⁹) of Christ's own practice of giving something to the poor out of His scanty wallet. But it is St. Matthew the converted tax-gatherer who left all and followed Him, and St. Luke the beloved physician, with his abounding

sympathy for wretchedness of every sort, who have preserved to us the most numerous and striking of His sayings on the subject.

The general character of our Lord's teaching concerning Almsgiving has been described as in close accordance with the Jewish thought of the time, even in points where we should have least expected it. Certainly He endorses and very much enhances the praise of Almsgiving which we find in the OT (*e.g.* Ps 41¹, Pr 19¹⁷, Dn 4²⁷). But in dealing with the teachings of the Apocrypha, which probably reflect more closely the views He found prevailing, He discriminates. If, on the one hand, He combines (Mt 6²· ⁵· ¹⁶) Almsgiving, Prayer, and Fasting, as in To 12⁸, and describes Almsgiving as providing a treasure in the heavens which faileth not (Lk 12³³), as in Sir 40¹⁷; yet, on the other hand, He explicitly condemns (Mt 6²) the notion countenanced in Sir 31¹¹ [LXX, 34¹¹] that alms may be done to gain a reputation for piety; while in Mt 5⁴⁵ He directly contradicts both the precept and the doctrine of Sir 12⁵⁻⁷ 'Give *not* to the ungodly . . . for the Most High hateth sinners, and will repay vengeance.'

Almsgiving is, according to Christ, a duty even towards our enemies, and those with whom we have little to do (Mt 5⁴²⁻⁴⁵, Lk 6³³⁻³⁶ 10³⁷); it is a means whereby we may conform ourselves to the example of our Father which is in heaven (Mt 5⁴⁵, Lk 6³⁵); it is the first exercise of righteousness (Mt 6¹⁻⁴). As eliminating from our enjoyment of material things the elements of unthankfulness and selfishness, it is the true way to purify them for our use (Lk 11⁴¹). To obtain the means of almsgiving, we may profitably part with earthly goods, because we shall thereby provide ourselves with 'purses which wax not old,' and raise our hearts, with our treasures, to heaven (Lk 12³³· ³⁴). In certain cases, like that of the Rich Young Ruler, it may be needful for a man to sell all and distribute to the poor (Mt 19²¹, Mk 10²¹, Lk 18²²); while the poor whom we may make our friends by using 'the mammon of unrighteousness,' for their benefit, are able, by their grateful prayers for us, to 'receive us, when *it* (our wealth) has failed us, into the eternal tabernacles' (Lk 16¹⁻¹³ parable of the Unjust Steward). Even trifling alms, given in the name of a disciple, are to be rewarded (Mt 10⁴²). And surely in those words of the Good Samaritan to the innkeeper, 'Whatsoever thou spendest more, *when* (not, if) I come again I will repay thee' (Lk 10³⁵), we must discern the voice of our Lord Himself: since no one but He can be certain either of returning (Ja 4¹³), or of ability to reward the ministrations of love. His rewards, when He does come, will surprise some, who did not realize that in ministering to 'his brethren' they ministered to Him (Mt 25³⁷ff.). On the other hand, for the rich to indulge themselves, and neglect their poor neighbour, is the way for them to Gehenna (Lk 16¹⁹⁻³¹ parable of the Rich Man and Lazarus); and the omission of the duty will be a ground of condemnation at the Last Day (Mt 25⁴⁵).

Other notices, though less direct, are worth considering, *e.g.* our Lord's injunction to the Twelve, 'Freely ye have received, freely give' (Mt 10⁸); His own compassionate feeding of the hungry multitudes (Mt 14¹⁶ 15³², Mk 6³⁷ 8³, Lk 9¹³); His rebuke of the Rabbis' rule, that when sons had rashly or selfishly taken the vow of Corban, they must no longer be suffered to do aught for their father or their mother (Mt 15⁵, Mk 7¹¹); His acceptance of the Jews' intercession for the Gentile who had built them a synagogue (Lk 7⁵); the praise of the women who ministered unto Him of their substance (8³); His advice, when we make a feast, to invite the poor (14¹³); and the vow of the penitent Zacchæus, 'The half of my goods I give to the poor' (19[8]). Nor may we omit 'the words of the Lord Jesus,' quoted by St. Paul, but preserved by St. Luke (Ac 20[35]), 'It is more blessed to give than to receive.'

We do not find in the teaching of our Lord Himself any of those cautions, which are so dear to the present day, against excessive almsgiving; though doubtless St. Paul 'had the mind of Christ' (1 Co 2[16]) when he laid down his rule, 'If any man *will* not work, neither let him eat' (2 Th 3[10]). Not far, at any rate, from this is His parable of the Labourers in the Vineyard (Mt 20[1-16]), where Jesus describes God under the figure of a rich and generous householder who gives work and wages (not mere alms) to those who are able to work, asks with surprise of such, 'Why stand ye here all the day idle?' and, on learning it was their misfortune and not their fault, makes them work for the last hour, yet pays them a whole day's wages.

We have seen how Christ condemns the doing of alms to have glory of men. He exposes also the ugliness of boasting of our giving before God (Lk 18[11] parable of the Pharisee and the Publican); insists that justice, mercy, and truth are of infinitely greater importance than minute scrupulousness in tithing, and lays down the comprehensive principle that, however there may be opportunities for us to do more than we have been explicitly *commanded*, yet we never can do more than we *owe* to God: 'When ye have done all, say, We are unprofitable servants: we have done that which it was our duty to do' (Lk 17[10]). Again, by His own example, in the case of the woman of Canaan (Mt 15[21-28]), He cuts off another unworthy motive, too often active in our so-called almsgiving, the wish to get rid of a beggar's importunity; while, both in the case of this woman and of her with the issue of blood (Mt 9[20], Mk 5[25], Lk 8[43]), He shows by His own example that true kindness is not indiscriminate, but takes the most careful account, not so much of the immediate and material, as of the ultimate and spiritual benefit which may be done, by its assistance, to the afflicted or the needy. The soul's wellbeing is higher than the body's. And, of course, our almsgiving, like all our works, is to be done in subjection to the two commandments which are the standing law of His kingdom, that we love the Lord our God with all our heart and all our mind, and that we love our neighbour as ourself (Mt 22[37ff.] ||).

LITERATURE.—Besides the Commentaries on passages referred to, consult O. Cone, *Rich and Poor in the New Testament*, 112 ff.; B. F. Westcott, *Incarnation and Common Life*, 195–208; A. T. Lyttelton, *College and University Sermons*, 256; W. C. E. Newbolt, *Counsels of Faith and Practice*, 227; F. Temple, *Rugby Sermons*, 2nd ser. 7; Pusey, *Sermons*.

JAMES COOPER.

ALOES.—We have in the NT only one reference to aloes, Jn 19[39], where Nicodemus brings myrrh and aloes with him, when he joins Joseph of Arimathea in taking away the body of Jesus for burial. In English, 'aloe' is used to designate (1) *Aloe vulgaris*, *A. spicata*, etc., of the natural order Liliaceæ, from which the medicine known as 'bitter aloes' is obtained; (2) *Agave Americana*, or American aloe, of the order Amaryllidaceæ, a plant which is noted for its long delay in flowering, and for the rapidity with which it at length puts forth its flowering stalk; and (3) *Aquilaria Agallocha*, *Aq. secundaria*, etc., of the order Aquilariaceæ, from which is obtained the aloes-wood or eagle-wood of commerce. The substance so named is the result of disease occurring in the wood of the tree. To obtain it, the tree has to be split, as it is found in the centre. With this eaglewood are probably to be identified the aloes of the Bible.

The grounds on which this identification rests are chiefly these :—(1) Under the name ἀγάλλοχον

Dioscorides (i. 21) describes an aromatic wood which was imported from India and Arabia, and was not only used for medicinal purposes, but also burned instead of frankincense. Similarly Celsius (*Hierobot.* i. 135 ff.) discusses references of Arab writers to many varieties of *aghâlûji* found in India and Ceylon which gave off, when burned, a sweet fragrance, and which were used as a perfume for the very same purposes as those which 'aloes' served among the Jews (Ps 45[8], Pr 7[17], Ca 4[14]). Quite analogous is the employment of aloes for perfuming the coverings of the dead (Jn 19[39]; cf. 2 Ch 16[14]).

(2) It is practically certain that ἀγάλλοχον and *a'jhâlûji*, and also the Hebrew אֲהָלִים (*ăhālîm*) and אֲהָלוֹת (*ăhālôth*), are derivatives of the Sanskrit word *aguru*, of which the term 'eagle-wood' is itself a corruption. If this etymology is correct, it indicates that both the name and the commodity were brought from the Far East (cf. נֵרְדְּ, Sanskrit *narada*). The Greek ἀλόη and our own 'aloe' may be from the same root.

(3) There was an active trade in spices carried on in ancient times, not only through Phœnicia but also through the Syrian and Arabian deserts, so that there is no great difficulty in supposing that 'aloes' were brought from India. These considerations seem to afford sufficient justification for the belief that eagle-wood was the aloes of the Biblical writers.   HUGH DUNCAN.

ALPHA AND OMEGA.—A solemn designation of divinity, of Jewish origin, peculiar to the Book of Revelation. In Rev 1[8] it is applied to Himself by 'the Almighty,' with obvious relation to Ex 3[14] (cf. v.[4]) and Is 41[4] 44[6] (for the LXX rendering of יהוה צְבָאוֹת by παντοκράτωρ, cf. Am 3[13] 4[13]). In Rev 21[6] also the epithet is applied not to the Son but to the Father, as shown by the context (cf. verses [3] 'a voice out of the throne,' [5] 'He spake that is seated on the throne,' [7] 'I will be his God and he shall be my son'). In 22[13] it is placed in a derived sense (*i.e.* 'I, the primary object and ultimate fulfilment of God's promise') in the mouth of the glorified Jesus. This transfer of a Divine title to the Son furnishes a problem of great interest for the early development of Christology; for, as R. H. Charles points out (Hastings' *DB* i. p. 70), 'although in Rev 1[8] [add 21[6]] this title is used of God the Father, it seems to be confined to the Son in Patristic and subsequent literature.'

1. *Origin and Significance.* — (*a*) The simplest and most primary use of this figure, derived as it is from the first and last terms of the alphabet, which with Greeks and Hebrews were also those of numerical notation, is common to several languages. Thus in English we have the expression 'from A to Z.' Schoettgen (*Hor. Heb.* i. 1086) adduced from *Jalkut Rubein*, fol. 17. 4, 'Adam transgressed the whole law from א to ת'; and 48. 4, 'Abraham kept the law from א to ת.' As Cremer shows (*Theol. Wörterbuch*, p. 1), this has no bearing on the case except linguistically. In *Jalkut Rub.* 128. 3, God is said to bless Israel from א to ת (because Lv 16[3. 16] begins with א and ends with ת), but to curse only from ו to ם (because Lv 16[14-43] begins with ו and ends with ם). R. H. Charles (*l.c.*) adds examples of this (general) use from Martial (v. 26 and ii. 57) and Theodoret (*HE* iv. 8).

(*b*) In the later, more philosophical, period of Hebrew literature similar expressions are applied to God, as indicative of His omnipresence and eternal existence. God, as the Being *from* whom all things proceed and *to* whom they tend, is thus contrasted in Deutero-Isaiah with heathen divinities (41[4] 43[10] [cf. Ex 3[14]] 44[6] 48[12]). Here the best example is the Ḳabbalistic designation of the

Shekinah as אח, according to Buxtorf = 'principium et finis' (*Lex. Chald. Talm. et Rabb.*).

But a threefold designation of God as the Eternal is also employed. The *Jerusalem Targum* on Ex 3[14] so interprets the Divine name ('qui fuit, est, et erit, dixit mundo'), and the *Targ. Jonathan* on Dt 32[9] ('ego ille est, qui est, et qui fuit, et qui erit'). So also, according to Bousset (*ad* Rev 1[4]), *Shemoth R.* iii. f. 105. 2, *Midrash Tillim* 117. 2, *Bereshith R.* on Dn 10[21] (the 'writing of אמח—truth = the seal of God.' See below). Thus in He 2[10] God is both end and *means* of all things (δι' ὅν, δι' οὗ τὰ πάντα); in Ro 11[36] 'Of him, *through* him, and unto him are all things'; cf. Rev 1[4].

Instances of expressions of like implication applied to the Deity (ὁ θεός), or to individual divinities, are naturally still more common in Greek philosophical literature, so that, as Justin says (*ad Grœcos*, xxv.), 'Plato, when mystically expressing the attributes of God's eternity, said, "God is, as the old tradition runs, the end and the middle of all things"; plainly alluding to the Law of Moses.' The tradition was indeed 'old' in Plato's day, but there are many more probable sources than Ex 3[14] for Plato. We need refer only to the song of the Peleiadæ at Dodona : Ζεὺς ἦν, Ζεὺς ἔστιν, Ζεὺς ἔσσεται (*Paus.* x. 12. 5) ; and the Orphic saying, Ζεὺς πρῶτος γένετο, Ζεὺς ὕστατος ἀρχικέραυνος, Ζεὺς κεφαλή, Ζεὺς μέσσα, κ.τ.λ. (Lobeck, *Aglaophamus*, 521, 523, 530 f.). Similar attributes are applied to Athene and Asclepius in examples quoted by Wetstein. Notoriously the Jewish apologists had been beforehand with Justin Martyr in ascribing to Moses the larger and more philosophical conceptions of Deity enunciated by the philosophers ; and from these writings of the period of Revelation and earlier it is possible to demonstrate the existence of a Jewish *kerygma* (formula of missionary propaganda) defining the true nature of the Deity and of right worship, wherein Is 44[6ff.] with the expression borrowed in Rev 1[8] 21[6], or its equivalent, is the central feature. Josephus (*c. Apion.* ii. 190–198 [ed. Niese]), contrasting the law of Moses on this subject with heathenism, calls it 'our doctrine (λόγος) concerning God and His worship.' What he designated 'the first commandment' is easily recognizable as part of such a *kerygma*, and seems to be derived from the same Jewish apologist, pseudo-Hecatæus (*c.* 60 B.C.) whom he quotes in *c. Apion.* i. § 183–204, and ii. 43. It is traceable already in the diatribes against idolatry in the *Ep. of Aristeas* (132–141) and the *Wisdom of Solomon* (chapters 13–14). The Proœmium of the oldest Jewish Sibyl (*Sib. Or.* v. 7–8, 15) has : 'There is one God Omnipotent, immeasurable, eternal, almighty, invisible, alone all-seeing, Himself unseen. . . . Worship Him, the alone existent, the Ruler of the world, who alone is from eternity to eternity.' It appears again in Christian adaptation in Ac 17[24-31] (cf. 14[15-17], 1 Th 1[9. 10], Ro 1[18-32] Wis 11[23] 13[6. 10] 14[12. 22-27]) ; in the fragment of the *Kerygma Petri*, quoted in Clem. *Strom.* vi. 5. 39–43 (Frags. 2 and 3 *ap.* Preuschen, *Antileg.* p. 52 : εἰς θεός ἐστιν, ὃς ἀρχὴν πάντων ἐποίησεν καὶ τέλους ἐξουσίαν ἔχων, κ.τ.λ.) : in the *Apology of Aristides* ; Tatian's *Oration* iv. ; Athenagoras, *Leg.* xiii., and the *Ep. to Diogn.* iii. It begins in Josephus : ὅτι θεὸς ἔχει τὰ σύμπαντα παντελὴς καὶ μακάριος, αὐτὸς αὑτῷ καὶ πᾶσιν αὐτάρκης, ἀρχὴ καὶ μέσα καὶ τέλος οὗτος τῶν πάντων—'He is the beginning and middle and end of all things' (*c. Apion.* ii. 190).

On the other hand, the apologetic and eschatological literature, which Rabbinic Judaism after the rise of Christian speculation more and more excluded from canonical use, shows a marked tendency to offset these heathen demiurgic ascriptions by similar ones applied not directly to God but to a hypostatized creative Wisdom (Pr 8[22-36], Wis 7[21] 8[1] 9[4. 9], Sir 24[9. 28], Bar 3[9-37]), or to an angelic Being endowed with the same demiurgic attributes (2 Es 5[56-6[6]).

The statement of Rabbi Kohler (*Jewish Encycl.* i. p. 438) is therefore correct regarding the phrase in Rev 1[8] and 21[6] if not in 22[13] : 'This is not simply a paraphrase of Is 44[6] "I am the first and the last," but the Hellenized form of a well-known Rabbinical dictum, "The seal of God is *Emet*, which means Truth, and is derived from the letters א מ ח the first, the middle, and the last letters of the Hebrew alphabet, the beginning, the middle, and the end of all things."' In other words, we must realize the metaphysical development of Jewish theology which had taken place between Deutero-Isaiah and Revelation. The passages adduced by Kohler from *Joma* 69b and *Sanh.* 64a, and in particular Jerus. *Jeb.* xii. 13a, *Gen. R.* lxxxi., show the early prevalence of this interpretation of Dn 10[21] 'I shall show thee what is marked upon the writing of truth (בכחב אמח), as the *signum* of God ; for, says Simon ben Laḳish, "א is the first, מ the middle, and ח the last letter of the alphabet."' This being the name of God according to Is 44[6], explained Jerus. *Sanh.* i. 18a, 'I am the first [having had none from whom to receive the kingdom] ; I am the middle, there being none who shares the kingdom with me ; [and I am the last], there being none to whom I shall hand the kingdom of the world.' It would seem probable, however, considering the connexion with Is 44[6] ('first and last,' the passage is a commonplace of early Christian-Jewish polemic), that the Ḳabbalistic form את is the earlier, the middle term having perhaps been inserted in opposition to Jewish angelological and Christian cosmological speculation. Cf. Rev 11[17] and 16[5] with 1[4] 4[8] ; and 2 Es 6[1-6] (where Uriel, speaking in the name of the Creator, says, 'In the beginning, when the earth was made . . . then did I design these things, and they all were through me alone, and through none other : as by me also they shall be ended, and by none other') with He 2[10].

In 1 Co 8[6] we have a significant addition to the two-term ascription, 'One God, the Father, *of* (ἐξ) whom are all things, and we *unto* (εἰς) him.' St. Paul (or his Corinthian converts) adds, 'And one Lord Jesus Christ, *through* whom are all things, and we *through* him.' This addition marks the parting of the ways for Jewish and Christian theology, implying a mediating hypostasis identified with Christ, that is, a Wisdom-Logos doctrine. That in Rev 1[8] and 21[6] the phrase is still applied in the purely Jewish sense to God the Father alone, is placed beyond all doubt by the connected ascriptions, especially ὁ ὢν καὶ ὁ ἦν καὶ ὁ ἐρχόμενος (not = ἐσόμενος) connecting 1[8] with 1[4].

Why, and in what sense, the term A–Ω is applied in Rev 22[12] by the glorified Christ to Himself, is the problem remaining ; and this independently of the question of composite authorship ; for to the final redactor, whose date can scarcely be later than A.D. 95, there was no incompatibility.

(*c*) Besides the metaphysical or *cosmological* development, which we have traced in connexion with the Divine title A–Ω from Deutero-Isaiah through Wisdom and pseudo-Aristeas to its bifurcation in Jewish and Christian theology contemporary with the Book of Revelation, we have a parallel development of *eschatological* character. Jehovah is contrasted with the gods of the heathen in Is 41[26. 27] 42[9] 43[9. 10] 44[6. 7. 26] 45[21] 46[9. 10] 48[3. 5. 12], also, and indeed primarily, as '**first and last**' in the sense of director of all things to the fulfilment of His predeclared purpose, *i.e. confirmer and fulfiller of His promise of redemption* (44[7]). And manifestly the development of this idea of Jehovah as 'first and last' in the redemptive or soteriological sense, would be more congenial to Hebrew thought than the metaphysical, although cosmology plays a great and increasing part in apocalyptic literature. In the substitution of ὁ ἐρχόμενος for the anticipated ὁ ἐσόμενος in Rev 1[4] 4[8] (cf. 11[17] 16[5]) recalling Mt 11[3] and He 10[37], we have evidence of the apocalyptic tendency to conceive of God by preference soteriologically.

But the final redemptive intervention of Jehovah is necessarily conceived as through some personal, human, or at least angelic (Mal 3[1], 2 Es 5[56]) agency, even when creative and cosmological functions are still attributed to Jehovah directly, without any, or with no more than an impersonal, intermediate agency. Hence, while in Rev 1[8] as in 1[4] and 21[6] Jehovah Himself, 'the Alpha and Omega, the beginning and the end,' is also ὁ ἐρχόμενος, there is no escape for any believer in Jesus from transferring the title in this soteriological sense to Him as Messiah. This will be the case whether his cosmology requires a Logos-doctrine for demiurgic functions, as with St. Paul, the Epistle to the Hebrews, and the Fourth Evangelist, or not. (The only trace of a true Logos-doctrine is the very superficial touch Rev 19[13b]). Thus in Rev 1[17] 2[8] the Isaian title 'the first and the last' is applied to Christ, and in 3[14] He is called 'the Amen . . . the beginning of the creation of God.' The titles are combined in 22[13], where we should perhaps render (Benson, *Apocalypse*, 1900, p. 26), 'I, the Alpha and the Omega (am coming), the first and the last, the beginning and the end.' As Hengstenberg maintained (on Rev 1[8]), 'In this declaration the Omega is to be regarded as emphatic. It is equivalent to saying, As I am the Alpha, so am I also the Omega. The beginning is surety for the end' (cf. Ph 1[6]). For this reason it is perhaps also better to connect the words Ναί, Ἀμήν of 1[7] with v.[8] 'Verily, verily, I am the Alpha and the Omega' (Terry, *Bibl. Apocalyptics*, 1898, p. 281).

The true sense, and at the same time the origin and explanation of this application of the Divine title, is to be found, as before, in the Epistles of St. Paul. In 2 Co 1[20] the promises of God, howsoever many they be, are said all to have their Yea in Christ. And, because this is so, it is further declared, 'the Amen is also through him.' The conception that Christ is the Amen or fulfilment of all the promises of God, as 'heir of all things' and we 'joint heirs with him' (Ro 4[13] 8[17], 1 Co 3[22], He 1[2], Rev 21[7]), is comparatively familiar to us. It represents the significance of the term Ω in the eschatological application. We are much less familiar with the idea expressed in the A, though it is equally well attested in primitive Christian and contemporary Jewish thought. In Pauline language it represents that the people of Messiah were 'blessed with every spiritual blessing in the heavenly places in Christ, inasmuch as God chose them in his person before the foundation of the world . . . and foreordained them to be an adoption of sons,' Eph 1[4. 5]; cf. Is 44[1. 2. 7], Wis 18[13], He 2[5-10], Rev 21[7], and the doctrine of the apocalyptic writers, Jewish and Christian, that 'the world was created for the sake of man'— resp. 'Israel,' 'the righteous,' 'the Church' (*Assump. Mos.* 1[12-14]; 2 Es 6[55-59] 7[10. 11] 9[13]; Hermas, *Vis.* ii. 4[1] etc. The doctrine rests on Gn 1[26f.], Ps 8[4-8], Ex 4[22] etc.). Harnack has shown (*History of Dogma*, vol. i. Appendix 1, 'The Conception of Pre-existence') how pre-existence is for the Jewish mind in some sense involved in that of ultimate persistence. The heir 'for whom' all things were created was in a more or less real sense (according to the disposition of the thinker) conceived as present to the mind of the Creator before all things. Thus in Rabbinic phrase Messiah is one of the 'seven

pre-existent things,' or His 'soul is laid up in Paradise before the foundation of the world.' Apocalyptic eschatology demanded a representative 'Son,' the 'Beloved,' chosen 'in the beginning' to be head of the 'Beloved' people of 'sons' in the end, with at least as much logical urgency as speculative cosmology demanded an agent of the creation itself. It is this which is meant when St. Paul says that 'however many be the promises of God, they are in Christ Yea.' This is 'the mystery which from all ages hath been hid in God who created all things . . . according to the eternal purpose which he purposed in Christ Jesus.' In Pauline language, Christ 'the Beloved,' the 'Son of his love,' is the Yea and the Amen of the promises of God. Cosmologically, He is the precreative Wisdom, 'the firstborn of all creation, in whom all things were created' (cf. Rev 3[14], Pr 8[22]). But it is not only that 'he is before all things, and in him all things consist' (cf. Sir 24[9], Wis 1[7]), not only that 'all things have been created *through* him,' but also eschatologically '*unto* him' (Col 1[15-17]; cf. He 1[2. 3] and Wis 7[22-27]), logically subsequent to Him because made for His sake. In Revelation we have only the latter. The cosmological 'through' Him practically disappears. It is only in the eschatological sense that Christ becomes the original object and the ultimate fulfilment of the Divine purpose and promises, 'the Yea, the Amen,' 'the Alpha and the Omega, the first and the last, the beginning and the end.'

2. *The Later History.* — It is doubtless from Revelation that the use of the term in Patristic literature and Christian epigraphy is mainly derived, though its popularity may well have been partly due to oral currency in Jewish-Christian circles before the publication of Revelation. The eschatological interest is still apparent in the hymn of Prudentius (*Cathem.* ix. 10-12), wherein the first line contains a reference to Ps 45[1] Vulg. ('Eructavit cor meum Verbum bonum'), treated as Messianic by the Fathers—

> 'Corde natus ex Parentis
> Ante mundi exordium
> Alpha et Ω cognominatus
> Ipse fons et clausula
> Omnium quæ sunt, fuerunt
> Quæque post futura sunt.'

But in Clem. Alex. (*Strom.* iv. 25 and vi. 16) and Tertullian (*de Monog.* 5) the cosmological predominates. Ambrose (*Expositio in VII visiones*, i. 8) presents a different interpretation. In Gnostic circles speculative and cosmological interpretations are unbridled. Thus Marcus (*ap.* Irenæus, *Hær.* I. xiv. 6, xv. 1) maintained that Christ designated Himself A Ω to set forth His own descent as the Holy Ghost on Jesus at His baptism, because by Gematria A Ω (= 800 + 1) and περιστερά (= 80 + 5 + 100 + 10 + 200 + 300 + 5 + 100 + 1) are equivalent.

LITERATURE.—For the great mass of later epigraphic material the reader is referred to N. Müller in Herzog-Hauck's *Realencykl.* i. pp. 1-12, and the article 'Monogram' in Smith and Cheetham's *Dict. of Christian Antiquities.* Besides the works already cited, articles on A and Ω may be found in the various Bible Dictionaries and Encyclopædias. Its use in Rev 1[8] 21[6] and 22[13] should be studied in the critical commentaries. On Divine epithets and the doctrine of hypostases see Bousset, *Religion des Judenthums*, iv. chs. 2 and 5 (1903). Older monographs in J. C. Wolfe, *Curæ Philolog. et Crit.* on Rev 1[8].

B. W. BACON.

ALPHÆUS (Ἀλφαῖος).—In the NT this name is borne by (1) the father of the Levi who is commonly identified with Matthew the Apostle (Mk 2[14]); (2) the father of the second James in the lists of the Apostles (Mt 10[3], Mk 3[18], Lk 6[15], Ac 1[13]). The desire to connect as many of the Twelve as possible by ties of natural relationship has led some (*e.g.* Weiss) to identify the two. But in the lists Matthew and James are separated by Thomas in St. Mark and St. Luke; and even in St. Matthew, where one follows the other, there is no note that they were brothers, similar to that attached to the names of the sons of Zebedee.

The identification of (2) with the **Clopas** of Jn 19^{25} rests on two hypotheses: (a) The assumption that as a Mary is given as the mother of James, and consequently as the wife of Alphæus, she must be the same as Mary the wife of Clopas who stood by the Cross. Jerome (*de Perpet. Virg.* v. 16) adopted this argument. But Mary is a name of far too common occurrence in the NT to make this theory of any value. (β) The alleged derivation of the names Alphæus and Clopas from a common Aramaic original. But this has not been satisfactorily established: there is even a lack of agreement as to the form of the original. WH hold that its initial letter would be ח, and print 'Αλφαῖος accordingly; but Edersheim quotes the Babylonian Talmud to show that the letter would be א. Jerome, although predisposed by his view of the Brethren of the Lord in favour of finding the same man under both names, rejects the linguistic identification; and the Syriac versions also represent them by different words. Delitzsch held Alphæus to be a Grecized form of an Aramaic word, but Clopas and Cleopas to be abbreviations of a Greek name Cleopatros (against this see Deissmann, *Bible Studies*, Eng. tr. p. 315 n.).

Nothing is known of either Alphæus beyond the name; for such details as that (2) was the brother of Joseph, the reputed father of the Lord, stand or fall with his identification with Clopas to whom they really belong. See art. CLOPAS, below.

LITERATURE. — Lightfoot, Essay on 'The Brethren of the Lord' in his Commentary on *Galatians*, also in *Dissertations on the Apost. Age*, p. 1; Mayor, *The Epistle of St. James*, Introd. p. xxi; Edersheim, *Life and Times of Jesus the Messiah*, bk. v. ch. 15; Andrews, *Life of our Lord upon Earth*, 114, 115; Weiss, *Life of Christ*, bk. iv. ch. 7 [Eng. tr.].

C. T. DIMONT.

ALTAR (θυσιαστήριον, a word of Hellenistic usage, applied to Jewish altars as distinguished from βωμός, the ordinary word for heathen altars [cf. Ex 34^{13}, Nu 23^1, Dt 7^5, Ac 17^{23}]).—The raised structure on which sacrifices and oblations were presented. As used in the Jewish ritual, the word was applied not only to the great altar of burnt-offering before the temple, but also to the altar of incense within the holy place, and on one or two occasions even to the table of shewbread (cf. Mal 1$^{7.12}$, Ezk 41^{22}). When no further specification was added, it denoted the altar of burnt-offering, the altar κατ' ἐξοχήν.

The Jewish altar of Christ's day was the last term of a long development, the history of which remains still in many points obscure. In the primitive Semitic worship it seems that no altar, properly speaking, was in use; unless we choose to give that name to the sacred stone or pillar beside which the victim was slain, and on which the blood or fat of the sacrifice was smeared (cf. 1 S 14^{33} 6$^{14.15}$, 1 K 1^9). In such cases the victims were slain (or slain and burnt), not on the sacred stone, but beside it. No doubt the significant part of the offering lay in the smearing of the stone, which was more or less identified with the Deity (Gn 28$^{18-22}$), and might thus be considered as both altar and temple. Later the burning of the victim came to be an integral part of the ceremony, and the hearth of burning acquired more importance. The hearth was originally the bare ground, or a rock (Jg 6^{20} 13$^{19.20}$), but later it was artificially formed. In the earliest law (Ex 20$^{24-26}$) it was prescribed that the altar should be of earth, or of unhewn stone, and be made without steps, evidently a reversion to a simpler custom than prevailed in many of the Canaanite altars, or in the altars of the high places. That the stone was not to be hewn may also be connected with the primitive idea that the deity which inhabited the stone might be offended or injured by the dressing. These regulations were respected in a modified degree in the building of the altars of the temple at Jerusalem. The altar built by Ahaz, on an Assyrian model, was probably designed in total disregard of the early prescriptions; but the later altars endeavoured to conform somewhat to the original ideal. Thus the altars of the second temple — both that of Zerubbabel and that built by Judas Maccabæus— were built of unhewn stone. In all probability there were steps up to the altar of the first temple * (cf. the altar of Ezekiel's vision [43^{17}], which had steps on the eastern side); but the altars of the second temple were ascended by means of a gradual acclivity.

The altar of Herod's temple, though larger than all former altars, preserved their main characteristics. It stood in front of the temple, in the innermost court. It was built of unhewn stone; no iron tool was used in its construction. In this the letter of the law in Exodus was adhered to, while its evident intention was evaded. A new interpretation of the law against the use of hewn stone was given by Jewish tradition in the words of Johanan ben Zakkai: 'The altar is a means of establishing peace between the people of Israel and their Father in heaven; therefore iron, which is used as an instrument of murder, should not be swung over it.' The altar was of huge dimensions. According to Josephus (*BJ* v. v. 6) it was 15 cubits high and 50 cubits square at the base; according to the more reliable tradition of the Mishna, which enters into precise details, it was 32 cubits square at the base and correspondingly less in height.† Like the earlier altars, it rose up in a series of terraces or stages, contracting at irregular intervals. (The first landing was a cubit from the ground, and a cubit in breadth; while 5 cubits higher came a second landing). The hearth on the top still measured 24 cubits in length and breadth. The altar-hearth was made accessible to the ministering priests by a structure on the south side, built in the form of a very gradual acclivity, and making a pathway 32 cubits long by 16 broad. Beside this main ascent were small stairs to the several stages of the altar. Round the middle of the entire altar ran a red line as an indication to the priest when he sprinkled with the blood the upper and lower parts of the altar. At the southwest corners of the hearth and of the altar's base were openings to carry off the wine of the drink-offerings or the blood sprinkled on the side of the altar. These openings led into a subterranean canal which connected with the Ḳidron. At the corners of the altar-hearth were projections, called **horns**. The supposition that these were a survival of the time when the victims were slain as well as burnt on the altar, and required to be bound upon the hearth, has at least the recommendation of simplicity; but it scarcely explains the peculiar sacredness attached to the altar-horns, or the important part they had in the ritual (1 K 1^{51} 2^{28}, Lv 8^{15} 9^9 16^{18}; in certain cases they were sprinkled with blood, Ex 29^{12}, Lv 4^7). The explanation given by Stade and others connects them with the worship of Jahweh as symbolized by a young bull. Northward from the altar was the place of slaughtering, with rings fastened in the ground, to which the animals were tied; it was

---

* *i.e.* the altar of Ahaz. For the ' brazen altar' of Solomon see the daring hypothesis of W. R. Smith (*RS*, note L), and A. R. S. Kennedy's note in Hastings' *DB* i. 76^b.

† The dimensions given by pseudo-Hecatæus (Jos. *c. Apion.* i. 22)—20 cubits square and 10 cubits high—are not adducible here; they refer to an altar of the second temple. The altar of Ezekiel's vision was 18 cubits square at the base and 11 cubits high. The altar of Solomon, according to 2 Ch 4^1, was 20 cubits square at the base and 10 high; dimensions perhaps taken, by the author who inserted them, from the altar of the second temple, with which he was acquainted.

provided also with pillars and tables for purposes of hanging, flaying, and washing. The temple, together with the altar and the place of slaughter, were separated from the rest of the inner court by a wall of partition, a cubit high, to mark off the part reserved for the priests from that free to Israelites generally.

On this great altar the fire was kept burning night and day; it was the centre of the Jewish ritual. On it, morning and evening, was offered the daily burnt-offering in the name of the people, accompanied with meal-offerings and drink-offerings. On the Sabbaths and during the festival days, the public offerings were greatly augmented. Still more vast was the number of private sacrifices which were offered day by day; and on the festival days, when Jerusalem was crowded with worshippers, thousands of priests officiated, and the great altar was scarcely sufficient to burn the masses of flesh that were heaped continuously upon it.

The altar of incense, or the golden altar, stood within the Holy Place. It was of very modest dimensions, and was used chiefly for the offering of incense, which took place twice daily, in the morning before the burnt-offering, and in the evening after it.

Besides an incidental mention of the altar (Mt 23^{35}, Lk 11^{51}), there are two pregnant sayings of Christ in the Gospels where the altar is concerned. In the first (Mt $5^{23. 24}$) He opposes to the mere externalism of the altar-worship the higher claims of brotherhood, teaching that what God requires is mercy and not sacrifice. In the other (Mt 23^{18-20}) He exposes the puerility of the distinction made, in swearing, between the altar and the gift upon it. It was by such miserable casuistry that the scribes and Pharisees evaded the most solemnly assumed obligations.

LITERATURE.—Benzinger's and Nowack's *Heb. Arch.* (Index, *s.v.* 'Altar'); Josephus, *BJ* v. v. 6, and *c. Apion.* i. 22; Mishna, *Middoth* iii. 1–4; Schenkel, *Bibellexicon*, 'Brandopferaltar'; Lightfoot, *The Temple Service*; Schürer, *HJP* II. i. 24; Wellhausen, *Prolegomena* ('Die Opfer'), and *Reste des Arab. Heidenthums* [2], 101 f.; W. R. Smith, *RS* (Index, *s.v.* 'Altar'); Perrot and Chipiez, *Histoire de l'Art* (Eng. tr., sections on Phœnicia and Judæa). See also Lightfoot (J. B.), 'Essay on the Chr. Ministry' in *Phil.* pp. 251, 261, 265, and in *Dissertations*, pp. 217, 229, 234; Westcott (B. F.), *Hebrews*, pp. 453–461.

J. DICK FLEMING.

AMAZEMENT.—The interest of this word to students of the Gospels is twofold, and arises out of its employment, on the one hand, as one of the terms used to express the effect upon the people of our Lord's supernatural manifestation, and on the other, in one unique instance, to describe an emotion which tore the heart of the God-man Himself.

The nominal form, 'amazement,' is of rare occurrence in EV (only Ac 3^{10}, 1 P 3^6 [for πτόησις] in AV; Mk 5^{42}, Lk 4^{36} 5^{26}, Ac 3^{10} in RV); the passive verb, 'to be amazed,' occurs not infrequently in the narrative books of NT (rarely in OT, *e.g.* Ex 15^{15}). They are especially characteristic of the Synoptic Gospels, and are currently employed in their narratives, along with several kindred terms, to describe the impression made by our Lord's wonderful teaching and His miraculous works. In the AV they translate in these narratives a number of Gr. words: θάμβος, θαμβέομαι, ἐκθαμβέομαι; ἴστασις, ἐξίσταμαι; ἐκπλήσσομαι. But the RV, studying greater uniformity of rendering, omits ἐκπλήσσομαι from this list, and makes 'amazement,' 'to be amazed,' the stated representatives of the other two groups [exceptions are: Mk 16^8 where ἔκστασις is rendered 'astonishment'; Ac $3^{10f.}$ where θάμβος, ἐκθαμβος are represented by 'wonder': passages like Mk 3^{21}, 2 Co 5^{13}, and again Ac 10^{10} 11^{15} 22^{17} are, of course, not in question]. To ἐκπλήσσομαι it uniformly assigns 'astonish,' 'astonishment'; and to the accompanying terms of kindred implications similarly appropriate renderings: to θαυμάζω (ἐκθαυμάζω, Mk 12^{17}) generally 'to marvel' (but 'to wonder,' Mt 15^{31}, Lk 2^{18} 4^{22} 9^{43} $24^{12.41}$, also Ac 7^{31}), and to φοβέομαι (φόβος Mt 14^{26}, Mk 4^{41}, Lk 5^{26} 7^{16} 8^{37}; cf. ταράσσω Mt 14^{26}, Mk 6^{50}, τρόμος Mk 16^8, τρέμω Mk 5^{33}, Lk 8^{47}) 'to be afraid,' varied to 'to fear.' The constant recurrence in the Synoptic narrative of one or another of these terms as a comment upon the effect of our Lord's teaching or works, imparts to the reader a vivid sense of the supernaturalness of His manifestation and of the deep impression which it made as such on the people.

Sometimes it appears to have been the demeanour or bearing of our Lord which awoke wonder or struck with awe (Mt 27^{14} ‖ Mk 15^5, Mk 9^{15} 10^{32}; cf. Lk 2^{48}). Sometimes the emotion was aroused rather by the tone of His teaching, as, with His great 'I say unto you' He 'taught them as having authority, and not as the scribes' (Mk 1^{22} ‖ Lk 4^{32}, Mt 7^{28}; cf. Mk 11^{18}, Mt 22^{33}). At other times it was more distinctly what He said, the matter of His discourse, that excited the emotions in question —its unanticipated literalness, or its unanticipatable judiciousness, wisdom, graciousness, or the radical paradox of its announcements (Lk $2^{47. 48}$ 4^{22}; Mt 13^{54} ‖ Mk 6^2; Jn 7^{15}; Mt 19^{25} ‖ Mk 10^{26}; Mt 22^{22} ‖ Mk 12^{17}, Lk 20^{26}). Most commonly, however, it was one of His wonderful works which brought to the spectators the dread sense of the presence of the supernatural (Lk 5^9; Mk 1^{27} ‖ Lk 4^{36}; Mk 2^{12} ‖ Lk 5^{26}, Mt 9^8; Lk 7^{16} 11^{14}; Mt 12^{23}; Mt 8^{27} ‖ Mk 4^{41}; Mk 5^{15} ‖ Lk $8^{32. 37}$; Mk $5^{30. 33. 42}$ ‖ Lk 8^{35}; Mt 9^{33}; Mk 6^{51}; Jn 6^{19} ‖ Mt 14^{26}; Mk 7^{37}; Lk 9^{43}; Mt 21^{20}), and filled the country with wonder (Mt 15^{31}).

The circle affected, naturally, varies from a single individual (Mk 5^{33}), or the few who happened to be concerned (Lk 2^{48} 5^9), or the body of His immediate followers (Mt 17^6, Mk $10^{24. 26}$, Mt 19^{25} 21^{20}), up to a smaller or larger assemblage of spectators (Lk 2^{47} 4^{22}; Mk 1^{22} ‖ Lk 4^{32}; Mk 1^{27} ‖ Lk 4^{36}; Mk 2^{12}, Lk 7^{16} $8^{25. 37}$, Mk 5^{42}, Mt 13^{54}, Mk 6^{51}; Jn 6^{19} ‖ Mt 14^{26}, Mk 6^{50}; Mk 7^{27}, Lk 9^{43}, Mk 16^8; Mt 22^{22} ‖ Mk 12^{17}, Lk 20^{26}). These spectators are often expressly declared to have been numerous: they are described as 'the multitudes' or 'all the multitudes,' 'all the people of the country,' or quite generally, when not a single occasion but a summary of many is in question, 'great multitudes' (Mt 9^8 ‖ Lk 5^{26}; Mt 7^{28} 12^{23}, Lk 11^{14}; 8^{35} ‖ Mk 5^{15}; Mk 8^{20}; Mt 9^{33} 15^{31}, Mk 9^{15}, Jn 7^{15}, Mk 11^{18}, Mt 22^{33}).

The several terms employed by the Evangelists to describe the impression on the people of these supernatural manifestations, express the feelings natural to man in the presence of the supernatural. In their sum they leave on the reader's mind a very complete sense of the reality and depth of the impression made. Their detailed synonymy is not always, however, perfectly clear. The student will find discriminating discussions of the two groups of terms which centre respectively around the notions of 'wonder' and 'fear' in J. H. Heinrich Schmidt's well-known *Synonymik der griechischen Sprache*, at Nos. 168 and 139. It will probably suffice here to indicate very briefly the fundamental implication of each term in its present application.

Θαυμάζω is a broad term, primarily expressing the complete engagement of the mind with an object which seizes so powerfully upon the attention as to compel exclusive occupation with it. It is ordinarily used in a good sense, and readily takes on the implication of 'admiration'; but it often occurs also when the object contemplated arouses internal opposition and displeasure. What it always implies is that its object is remarkable, extraordinary, beyond not so much expectation as ready comprehension, and therefore irresistibly engages attention and awakens 'wonder.' It does not import 'surprise,' but rather, if you will, 'curiosity,' or better, 'interestedness.' In this it separates itself from θαμβέομαι, in which the notion of 'unexpectedness' is, at least originally, inherent.

This latter term gives expression to the sense of mental helplessness which oppresses us on the occurrence of an unanticipated and astonishing phenomenon. The affection of the mind it suggests is one of mingled admiration and fear; and in the usage of the word this passes both downward into 'consternation,' strengthened to 'fright' and 'terror,' and upward into 'awe' and 'veneration.' In the LXX the lower senses are predominant (*e.g.* Sir 12^5, Ca 3^8 $6^{3[4]}$ 9^{10}, Ezk 7^{18}; 1 K 14^{15}, 2 S 7^{15}, Wis 17^3, Dn $8^{17. 18}$; 1 Mac 6^8, Dn 77, Sir 30^9). In the Evangelical passages now before us, on the other hand, the higher senses come forward, and the idea expressed lies near to 'awe,' and the term comes thus into close synonymy with φοβέομαι.

The notion of 'surprise' which underlies θαμβέομαι seems to be much more prominent in ἐξίσταμαι. This term, broad enough to be applied to any 'derangement,' bodily or mental, was particularly employed, with or without a defining adjunct, to describe that aberration of the mind, the subjects of which in English too we speak of simply as 'demented' (2 Co 5[13]). In its more ordinary usage the implication is no more than that the subject is thrown out of his normal state into a condition of 'ecstasy,' or extreme emotion,—the emotion in question being of varied kind, but more commonly an 'amazement' which carries with it at least a suggestion of perplexity, if not of bewilderment.

When this 'surprise' rises to its height, however, especially if it is informed with alarm, the appropriate term to express it would seem to be ἐκπλήσσομαι, although this term is used so frequently for purely intellectual effects arising from intellectual causes, that it falls readily into the sense of pure 'astonishment.' Nevertheless, the element of 'alarm' inherent in it places it among the synonyms of φοβέομαι, from which it differs as a sudden access of fright differs from an abiding state of fear, or as, in connexions like those at present engaging our attention, to be 'awestruck' differs from the continuous sense of 'awful reverence' which prompts to withdrawal from the dread presence.

The same fundamental emotion of fear which finds its most natural expression in φοβέομαι is more rarely given expression also in such terms as ταράσσω, the basal implication of which is 'agitation,' 'perturbation,' passing on into the 'disquietude,' on the one side, of that 'troubled worry' the extreme of which is expressed by ἀδημονέω, and on the other into that terrified 'consternation' which finds its extreme expression in πτοέομαι (Lk 24[37]): or as τρέμω, which in its application to the trembling of the mind—to mental 'shivering'—draws near to the notions of 'anxiety' and 'horror.'

The emotions signalized as called out by the manifestation of Jesus in His word and work, it will be seen, run through the whole gamut of the appropriate responses of the human spirit in the presence of the supernatural. Men, seeing and hearing Him, wondered, were awestruck, amazed, astonished, made afraid, with a fear which disquieted their minds and exhibited itself in bodily trembling. The confusion by RV under the common rendering 'amaze,' 'amazement' of two of these groups of terms (θάμβος, θαμβέομαι, ἔκθαμβος, ἐκθαμβέομαι, and ἔκστασις, ἐξίσταμαι), seems scarcely to do justice to the distinctive implications of either, and especially fails to mark the clear note of the higher implication of 'awe' that sounds in the former. The interest of noting how completely the notion of 'surprise,' originally present in θάμβος, has in usage retired into the background in favour of deeper conceptions, is greatly increased by the employment of the strengthened form of the verb ἐκθαμβέομαι by St. Mark (14[33]) to describe an element in our Lord's agony in Gethsemane.

When St. Matthew (26[37]) tells us that Jesus 'began to be sorrowful (λυπεῖσθαι) and sore troubled' (ἀδημονεῖν), St. Mark, varying the phraseology, says (in the RV) that He 'began to be greatly amazed (ἐκθαμβεῖσθαι) and sore troubled (14[33]).' Surely the rendering 'amazed,' however, misses the mark here: the note of the word, as a parallel to ἀδημονεῖν and λυπεῖσθαι, is certainly that of anguish not of unexpectedness, and the commentators appear, therefore, to err when they lay stress on the latter idea. The usage in the LXX, both of the word itself (Sir 30[9], where also, oddly enough, it is paralleled with λυπέω) and of its cognates, seems decisively to suggest a sense for it which will emphasize not the unexpectedness of our Lord's experience, but its dreadfulness, and will attribute to our Saviour on this awful occasion, therefore, not 'surprise,' but 'anguish and dread,' 'depression and alarm' (J. A. Alexander), or even 'inconceivable awe' (Swete).

The difficulty of the passage, let it be remarked, is not a dogmatic, but an exegetical one. There is no reason why we should not attribute to the human soul of the Lord all the emotions which are capable of working in the depths of a sinless human spirit (cf. J. A. Alexander's excellent note on Mk 8[10] and Swete's on Mk 6[6]). But certainly the employment of the verb ἐκθαμβέομαι here by St. Mark affords no warrant for thinking of the agony of Gethsemane as if it exceeded the expectation of our Lord, and as if it consisted in large part of the surprise and perplexity incident upon discovering it to be worse than He had anticipated (cf. the otherwise admirable note of Dr. Swete, in loc.—'long as He had foreseen the Passion, when it came clearly into view its terrors exceeded His anticipations'; A. J. Mason, The Conditions of our Lord's Life on Earth, pp. 135–138—'when the hour came, it exceeded all His expecta-

tions'). On the contrary, the usage of the word combines with the context here to suggest that its whole force is absorbed in indicating the depths of soul-agony through which our Lord was called upon to pass in this mysterious experience. On the terms employed, the note of Pearson, On the Creed, ed. 1835, p. 281 ; ed. New York, 1847, pp. 288–289, is still worth consulting.

In studying the emotional life of our Lord's human spirit during His life on earth, as it is exhibited to us in the Gospel narratives, nothing in point of fact is more striking than the richness of the vocabulary by means of which He is pictured to us as the 'man of sorrows and acquainted with grief,' and the slenderness of the suggestion that He may have been subject to the surprises which constitute so large an element in the lives of mere men. So far as the explicit assertions of the Evangelic narratives go, it would seem that the unexpected never happened to Jesus. Neither surprise, nor astonishment, nor amazement, nor suspense, nor embarrassment, nor perplexity, nor distraction, is ever, in so many words, attributed to Him. Those who would discover in the narratives, nevertheless, some ground for supposing that He may have experienced these emotions (e.g. A. J. Mason, The Conditions of our Lord's Life on Earth, pp. 135–138 ; T. Adamson, Studies of the Mind in Christ, pp. 11, 12, 167 : and in its extremity, E. A. Abbott, Philomythus, on which see Southern Presbyterian Review, Oct. 1884, 'Some Recent Apocryphal Gospels,' p. 733 ff.), must needs depend on an inferential method, the inconclusiveness of which has been repeatedly pointed out of old, as, for example, by Augustine (e.g. c. Faust. Manich. xxii. 13), who remarks upon its equal applicability to the anthropomorphisms of the OT.

'Wonder' (AV ; RV 'marvelling'), to be sure, is attributed to Jesus on two occasions (Mt 8[10] ‖ Lk 7[9], Mk 6[6]). But the term used (θαυμάζω) is on both occasions precisely that one which least of all implies 'surprise,' which declares its object rather extraordinary than unexpected. 'Θαυμάζω,' remarks Schmidt (op. cit. p. 184), 'is perfectly generally "to wonder" or "to admire," and is distinguished from θαμβεῖν precisely as the German sich wundern or bewundern is from staunen ; that is, what has specially seized on us is in the case of θαυμάζειν the extraordinary nature of the thing, while in the case of θαμβεῖν it is the unexpectedness and suddenness of the occurrence.' All that needs be imported by these passages is that the circumstances adverted to were in themselves remarkable ; and that Jesus recognized, felt, and remarked upon their remarkableness,—in the one instance with the implication of admiration, in the other with that of reprobation. That the circumstances which called out His sense of the incongruity in the situations He remarks upon were unanticipated by our Lord, and therefore when observed struck Him with a shock of surprise, we are not told. BENJAMIN B. WARFIELD.

AMBASSAGE.—This term is used in Lk 14[32] (AV and RV) and in RV of Lk 19[14] (more accurately instead of AV 'message'). The Greek is πρεσβεία. Both in the original and the translation the abstract is used for the concrete ; a term meaning the office or message of an ambassador or body of ambassadors for the ambassadors themselves.

The formation of the word is not fully explained. The earlier form both in English and French was ambassade. The French suffix -age (= Lat. -aticum) is usually found in words transferred from France, but [sometimes it was added to English words. Ambassage seems to be an exception to both. It may be either a formation from a French root or a softening of ambassade by the influence of analogy. The word was accented by some on the first syllable, by others on the second. An alternative spelling was embassage. Both forms are obsolete, being supplanted by embassy, the direct equivalent of ambassade.

In Lk 14[26-35] Jesus is speaking of discipleship and the necessary condition of entire surrender to spiritual authority. And He gives in illustration the parable which teaches the folly of entering on an enterprise without counting the cost. A prince who has provoked to war a superior power will do well to send an ambassage to sue for peace—peace without honour. The man whose force of character is not able to withstand and overcome the worldly obstacles, must in some form or other make compromise with the worldly powers. He is not fit for the kingdom of God. (For other interpretations see Trench and the Commentators).

The second occurrence (Lk 19[14]) is in the parable of the Pounds ; not in the main part, which bears resemblance to the parable of the Talents, but in one of two verses (vv. [14, 27]) directed to a subsidiary aspect of the situation. While the servants of the distant dignitary are, in his absence, carrying out instructions and using opportunities, a section of his subjects resolve to cast off his authority. To this effect they send an embassy. When he returns he rewards the faithful and executes punishment on the disloyal. The application is to the Second Coming of the Lord.

The term πρεσβεία (from πρέσβυς, 'old') belongs to classical Greek, and it contains an expression of the rule that responsible duties of statecraft are naturally entrusted to approved elders and heads of families. St. Paul uses the corresponding verb in 2 Co 5²⁰, where he describes the Christian preachers as 'ambassadors for Christ,' and in Eph 6²⁰ the idea is repeated. Perhaps we may connect the occurrence of πρεσβεία in the Third Gospel with St. Luke's apparent preference of 'presbyter' to 'bishop' (Ac 20¹⁷), and his repeated use of *presbyterion* for the body of Jewish elders (Lk 22⁶⁶, Ac 4⁵ 22⁵). For the terms are expressive of dignity, and in St. Luke's literary style a sense of dignity is clearly shown.

It is further notable that commentators are able to refer the suggestion of both these parables to contemporary history. The former corresponds with the struggle between Antipas and his father-in-law, Hareth, king of Arabia; the latter is illustrated by Herod, by Archelaus, and by Antipas, each of whom went to Rome to obtain an enhancement of power. But details apply to the case of Archelaus, who put his friends in command of cities, and against whom the Jews sent to the emperor an embassy of fifty men (Jos. *Ant.* XVII. xi. 1).   R. Scott.

AMBITION.—The word 'ambition' is not found in the AV or RV, but the propensity signified is, of course, represented in the New Testament. Its derivation is Latin [*ambi*, 'about,' and *ire*, *itum*, 'to go'], meaning *a going about in all directions*, especially with a view to collecting votes. It thus means to have *such a desire as to make one go out of one's way to satisfy it*, and, in a secondary sense, denotes the object which arouses such desire and effort. As a psychological fact, Ambition may be defined as a natural spring of action which makes for the increment of life. Ethically speaking, it takes its colour from the object towards which it is directed. In ordinary use it implies blame; but in true Christianity, where the utmost is given for the highest, it is otherwise.

In the Epistles the verbs διώκω, σπουδάζω, ζητέω are used figuratively for this propensity (Ph 3¹², 2 P 3¹⁴, Ro 10³); but perhaps a nearer synonym is ζηλόω with its corresponding substantive ζῆλος (as in 1 Co 14¹· ¹²· ³⁹, cf. Weymouth's *NT in Modern Speech*), though ζῆλος in a good sense is generally translated 'zeal,' and in a bad sense 'jealousy,' both words being of rather broader significance than 'ambition.'

It is in accordance with the literary characteristics of the Gospel narratives that such an abstract idea as *ambition* can be found only under some picturesque phrase, *e.g.* 'lamp of the body' (Mt 6²²· ²³), 'food' (Jn 4³⁴). 'To cut off the right hand' or 'to pluck out the right eye' is the expression used by our Lord for destroying one's dearest ambition, whether it is controlling one's energies or directing one's imagination (Mk 9⁴³ᶠ·, cf., as Trench points out, the use of ὀφθαλμὸς πονηρός [Mt 6²³, Mk 7²²] for 'envy').

But although there is no explicit reference to Ambition in the NT, it is so characteristic a fact of human nature that a large part of the teaching of Christ might be exhibited in relation to it. And because it is capable of being bent towards lofty as well as sinister, or at least selfish ends, Christian ethics seems from one point of view to be the exaltation of Ambition, from another its deposition.

1. *For Ambition.*—Christ's method was to use the fact of Ambition and purify it by exercising

it on the highest objective. The call to the first disciples was an appeal to their ambition for a higher life: 'Follow me, and I will make you fishers of men' (Mt 4¹⁹). He gave primacy to an ambition for the ends of the Kingdom over all worldly ambitions in the words: 'Seek ye first the kingdom of God and His righteousness' (Mt 6³³). He compared the earnestness of true followers with the ambition of a pearl-merchant (Mt 13⁴⁵), and encouraged the religious ambition of the young ruler by trying to turn it into a new and deeper channel (Mt 19²¹): 'If thou wouldest be perfect, sell . . . give . . . and thou shalt have treasure in heaven.' It was part of His teaching to set before His disciples a prize to aim at (Lk 22²⁹· ³⁰, Mt 5¹³· ¹⁴, Jn 12²⁶); and He expected them to go out of their way in devotion, and to all lengths in fidelity (Lk 9⁶² 14²⁶ᶠ· 19¹⁵⁻¹⁹, Mt 25¹⁴⁻²³), in order to win the truest praise and most lasting success. 'The Christian moral reformation may indeed be summed up in this—humanity changed from a restraint to a motive' (*Ecce Homo*).

2. *Against Ambition.*—But it may with equal truth be said that the aim of the life and teaching of Christ was to depose Ambition from its ruling place. He was always rebuking (1) inordinate desires for any kind of selfish satisfaction, whether they were associated with *greed* (Jn 6²⁷ 'food that perisheth'; Lk 6²⁴, and esp. 12¹⁵⁻²¹) or with *pride* (Mt 6¹⁻⁴ 'glory of men,' 20²⁵⁻²⁸ 'lord it,' 23⁵⁻¹² 'seen of men and called Rabbi'); or (2) even a high-placed desire if it was held thoughtlessly and without counting the cost (Lk 14²⁸⁻³³ the builder and the king who failed in their ambition; Mk 10³⁵⁻⁴⁰ the sons of Zebedee who 'knew not what they asked'). Moreover, Christ cut away the very tap-root of Ambition by turning self out of its place at the seat of the motives of life, in favour of a living trust in the Father and an undivided allegiance to Himself. The virtues which are most prominent in the Christian ideal leave no room at all for Ambition in the generally accepted use of the word. For Christianity demands *humility* (Mt 5³ etc., Lk 14⁷⁻¹¹ etc., Jn 13¹²⁻¹⁵), *generosity* (Mk 12⁴³· ⁴⁴, Lk 6³⁰· ³¹ 12³³ etc.), and *self-renouncement* (Mt 10³⁸· ³⁹, Mk 10²⁹· ³⁰, Jn 12²⁴⁻²⁶).

On the whole, the influence of Christ's teaching and inspiration on Ambition has been not to extirpate it, but to control and chasten it by the discovery and establishment of other standpoints, such as the outlook of other-worldliness, the sense of brotherhood, and personal allegiance to Himself.

Literature.—Lightfoot (J. B.), *Cambridge Sermons*, 217; Moore (A. L.), *Advent to Advent*, 239; Shedd (W. G. T.), *Sermons to the Spiritual Man*, 371; Mozley (W. B.), *University Sermons*, 262.   A. Norman Rowland.

AMEN.—Like the Greek ἀμήν, this is practically a transliteration of the Heb. אמן, which itself is a verbal adjective connected with a root signifying *to make firm, establish.* In the last instance, and as we are concerned with it, it is an indeclinable particle. Barth treats it as originally a substantive (= 'firmness,' 'certainty'). For the derivation, cf. our Eng. 'yes,' 'yea,' which is also connected with an old verbal root of similar significance.

As a formula of solemn confirmation, asseveration and assent, it was established in old and familiar usage amongst the Jews in the time of our Lord. Its function is specially associated with worship, prayer, the expression of will and desire, the enunciation of weighty judgments and truths. Four modes in which Amen is used may be distinguished—(1) *Initial*, when it lends weight to the utterance following. (2) *Final*, when used by the speaker himself in solemn confirmation of what precedes. (3) *Responsive*, when used to express assent to the utterance of another, as in prayers, benedictions, oaths, etc. (4) *Subscriptional*, when used to mark the close of a writing, but hardly amounting to much more than a peculiar variant of 'Finis.'

The subscriptional Amen requires but a brief notice. No instance of it is found in the OT; and as regards the closing Amen in the several Scriptures of the NT there is for the most part a lack of textual authority. The AV, following the TR, in most instances has it; the RV in most instances omits it. Where it is found, in the Epistles and the Apocalypse, it is rather due to the fact that these writings close with a doxology, prayer, or benediction. The variations of authority in such cases seem to a large extent capricious: else why, *e.g.*, Amen at the end of 1 Corinthians and not at the end of 2 Corinthians? The closing Amen in each of the Gospels, though without authority, is a genuine instance of the subscriptional use of later times. This use has a further curious illustration in the practice of copyists of MSS who wrote 99 at the end of their work, this being the total numerical value of the characters in ἀμήν. For the purposes of the present article it will be necessary to examine the whole Biblical usage of 'Amen.'

1. *Amen in the OT.*—The formula is found in (*a*) the Pentateuch (Nu 5[22], Dt 27 *passim*) as a ritual injunction (LXX γένοιτο throughout). (*b*) In 1 K 1[36], 1 Ch 16[36], Neh 5[13], Jer 11[5] 28[6] it is mentioned as being actually used (LXX in 1 K 1[36] γένοιτο οὕτως, Jer 28[6] ἀληθῶς, elsewhere ἀμήν). (*c*) In the Psalms (41[13] 72[19] 89[53] 106[48]) we meet with its liturgical use (LXX γένοιτο). The most common equivalent for Amen in the LXX is γένοιτο; and with this may be compared St. Paul's familiar μὴ γένοιτο, the negative formula of dissent and deprecation.

No clear instance of the use of an *initial* Amen occurs. Hogg thinks we have such in 1 K 1[36], Jer 11[5] and 28[6]; but in each of these cases it will be found that the Amen is a *responsive* assent to something that precedes. It is true that the LXX rendering in Jer 28[6] (ἀληθῶς) shows that the translators were inclined to regard this as an instance of an initial Amen; but even here the term is really an ironical response to the false prophecy of Hananiah in vv.[2-4]. Almost all the instances, indeed, in which Amen is met with in the OT are examples of the responsive use; the only considerable instances of the *final* use being found at the end of each of the first three divisions of the Psalter. In the Apocrypha we have further instances of the responsive Amen in To 8[8] and in Jth 13[20] and 15[10] (EV in the latter book renders 'So be it'). The doubled formula ('Amen, Amen,' cf. Jth 13[20]) thus used is naturally explained as an expression of earnestness. It may here be added that among the Jews at a much later period Amen has a responsive and desiderative use in connexion with every kind of expression of desire and felicitation; *e.g.* 'May he live to see good days: Amen!'

2. *Amen in the Gospels.*—We must set aside the instances of *subscriptional* Amen (see above) as without authority. In Mt 6[13] some ancient authorities support the conclusion of the Lord's Prayer with doxology and Amen; but it can hardly be doubted that Amen here, along with the doxology which it closes, is not original, but due to liturgical use (see 'Notes on Select Readings' in Westcott-Hort's *NT in Greek, ad loc.*). In all the other instances in the Gospels it is the *initial* Amen that is found, given always and only as a *usus loquendi* of Christ in the formula, ἀμὴν λέγω ὑμῖν (σοι), according to the Synoptists,

and ἀμὴν ἀμὴν λέγω ὑμῖν (σοι), according to St. John.

Now, whilst final Amen as a formula of conclusion or response remains unaltered throughout in NT in the various versions, it is of interest to notice the different ways in which this initial Amen is treated. The Vulgate, *e.g.*, invariably keeps the untranslated form, and reads *Amen* (or *Amen, Amen*) *dico vobis*. The modern Greek equivalent is ἀληθῶς (ἀληθῶς ἀληθῶς); and with this accords our EV 'Verily,' and also Luther's *Wahrlich*. And, indeed, among the Synoptists themselves there are indications that an initial Amen has sometimes been replaced by another term. This is specially so in the case of St. Luke, who has only 6 instances of ἀμήν as against 30 in St. Matthew, and 13 in St. Mark. We have, *e.g.*, ναί in Lk 11[51] for ἀμήν in the parallel Mt 23[36]; ἀληθῶς in Lk 9[27] (cf. Mt 16[28], Mk 9[1]). All this goes to show that this use of Amen on the part of Jesus was quite a peculiarity.

The very λέγω ὑμῖν alone would have been noticeable as a mode of assertion: the addition of ἀμήν does but intensify this characteristic, as an enforcement and corroboration of the utterances that are thus prefaced. The Heb. אָמֵן, which in our Lord's time was usual only in responses, thus appears to have been taken by Him as an expedient for confirming His own statement 'in the same way as if it were an oath or a blessing.' Formulæ of protestation and affirmation involving an oath were in use among Rabbinical teachers to enforce teachings and sayings, and with these the mode of Jesus invites comparison and contrast.

The attempt of Delitzsch to explain this Amen (particularly in the double form) through the Aramaic אֲמַר אֲנָא 'I say,' cannot be sustained. Jannaris, again (*Expos. Times*, Sept. 1902, p. 564), has ventured the suggestion that ἀμήν thus used is a corruption of ἦ μήν (εἶ μήν); but interesting and ingenious as this may be, it lacks confirmation, and amongst the instances of the use of ἦ μήν which he adduces from the LXX, the papyri, etc., not one suits the case here by showing any such construction as ἦ μὴν λέγω ὑμῖν in use.

A parallel between Amen and our 'Yes' has been already suggested: and in the NT we similarly find ἀμήν and ναί closely associated (2 Co 1[20], Rev 1[7]), whilst we have before noticed how in St. Luke ναί is found as a substitute for ἀμήν. It may not therefore be out of place here to suggest that we have an illustration and analogy as regards the use of an initial Amen in the use of an introductory 'Yes' sometimes found in English (see, *e.g.*, Shakspeare, *2 Hen. IV.* I. iii. 36; Pope, *Moral Essays*, i. 1).

The double Amen, which occurs 25 times in St. John, and is peculiar to that Gospel, has provoked much curiosity as to how it is to be explained. If Jesus used as a formula in teaching now ἀμὴν λέγω ὑμῖν and again ἀμὴν ἀμὴν λέγω ὑμῖν, it is very strange that the Synoptics should invariably represent Him as using the former, and the Fourth Gospel invariably as using the latter. Why not instances of both promiscuously through all the Gospels if the two were thus alike used? The statement that the Johannine form 'introduces a truth of special solemnity and importance' (as Plummer in *Camb. Gr. Test. for Schools*, etc., 'St. John,' note on ch. 1[51]) is quite gratuitous, as a comparison of the sayings and discourses of our Lord will show. It is too obviously a *dictum* for the purpose of explanation. The truth is, if we have regard to the exclamatory character of ἀμήν as a particle in this special use, there is nothing surprising in its being thus repeated; and we have the analogy of the repeated Amen in responses, as noticed above. Why St. John alone should give the formula in this particular way is a further question. If a consideration of the phenomena connected with the composition of the Fourth

Gospel leads to the conclusion that in the *form* in which the utterances of Jesus are there presented we have not His *ipsissima verba*, we may most naturally regard the repetition of ἀμήν as a peculiarity due to the Evangelist, and (taking the evidence of the Synoptists into account) not necessarily a form actually used by Jesus.

3. *Amen in the rest of the NT.*—In the numerous instances in which Amen occurs in the NT outside the Gospels, it is almost entirely found in connexion with prayers, doxologies, or benedictions, as a solemn corroborative conclusion (*final* use). In addition, we have the *responsive* use of Amen illustrated in 1 Co 14[16] (see below, s. 'Liturgical use') and Rev 5[14]: and ἀμήν in Rev 22[20] is responsive to the ἔρχομαι ταχύ preceding. Extra-canonical writings furnish plentiful examples of the same use. Two instances, again, of an *introductory* Amen in the Apocalypse (7[12] 19[4]), as a form of exultant acclamation, are interesting, but are quite distinct from the initial Amen in the utterances of Jesus in the Gospels.

Amen as a substantive appears in two forms: (1) τὸ ἀμήν, (2) ὁ ἀμήν. We meet with the former in 1 Co 14[16] and 2 Co 1[20]. In both cases there appears to be a reference to a liturgical Amen. In the latter passage, indeed, it might be contended that ἀμήν is merely in correspondence with ναί, both simply conveying the idea of confirmation and assurance; but if we follow the better supported reading (as in RV) the presence of such a reference can hardly be denied.

The use of ὁ ἀμήν as a name for our Lord in Rev 3[14] is striking and peculiar. The attempt, however, to explain it by reference to 2 Co 1[20] is not satisfactory. The curious expression 'the God of Amen' (EV 'the God of truth') in Is 65[16] is not sufficiently parallel to afford an explanation, for the Amen in this case is not a personal name, but the EV furnishes a satisfactory equivalent in the rendering 'truth.' Surely, however, there need be little difficulty about the use of such a term as a designation of Jesus. Considering the wealth of descriptive epithets applied to Him in the NT and other early Christian writings, and also the terminology favoured by the author of the Apocalypse, we must feel that this use of Amen, if bold, is not unnatural or unapt, so suggestive as the term is of truth and firmness. Another but very different use of Amen as a proper name may be mentioned. Among certain of the Gnostics ἀμήν figured as the name of an angel (Hippolytus, *Philosophumena*, ccxviii. 79, ccciv. 45).

4. *Amen in liturgical use.*—(*a*) *Jewish.*—In the Persian period Amen was in use as 'the responsory of the people to the doxology of the Priests and the Levites' (see Neh 8[6], 1 Ch 16[36], Ps 106[48]). In the time of Christ it had become an established and familiar formula of the synagogue worship in particular, the response used in the Temple being a longer form : 'Blessed be the Name of the glory of His kingdom for ever and ever !' In still later times a formula of response was used which was apparently a combination of the synagogue Amen with the Temple responsory : 'Amen : praised be the great Name for ever and ever !' In the synagogue service the Amen was said by the people in response to the reader's doxology. (In the great synagogue of Alexandria the attendant used to signal the congregation with a flag when to give the response). Amen was also the responsory to the priestly blessing.

Responsive Amen at the end of prayers was evidently an old custom among the Jews. In later times they are said to have discouraged this, because Amen at the end of every prayer had become the habit of Christians. The use of Amen in this connexion was thus considerably restricted ;

but certain synagogue prayers were still specified as to be followed by the Amen.

The Rabbis in their liturgical exactness rigorously determined the sense of Amen, and, among other things, enjoined that every doxology, on whatever occasion, must be followed by this response. Curious sayings were current among them, emphasizing the significance and value of Amen. Should, *e.g.*, the inhabitants of hell exclaim 'Amen !' when the holy Name of God is praised, it will secure their release (*Yalk.* ii. 296 to Is 26[2]).

(*b*) *Christian.* — This use of Amen was undoubtedly borrowed by the Christians from the Jewish synagogue, as, indeed, other liturgical features were. St. Paul's words in 1 Co 14[16] are of special interest here. The reader is so to recite his prayers that the ignorant should have the boon of answering the Amen to the doxology. The ἰδιώτης (הֶדְיוֹט) for whom he pleads is similarly considered by the Rabbis, and they give the same instruction. It cannot be maintained that the term εὐχαριστία used here by St. Paul has that special and, so to speak, technical sense which it afterwards acquires as applied to the Lord's Supper, and that so 'the Amen' (τὸ ἀμήν) intended is specifically the response connected with the observance of that institution. At the same time, the whole reference clearly indicates that Amen as a responsory in Christian worship was already a regular and familiar usage.

It is, however, in connexion with the Eucharist, in the special sense of the term, that the Fathers particularly mention the responsive Amen, and refer to it as said after the doxology with which the long Prayer of Consecration closed. Justin Martyr (*Apol.* 2), Tertullian (*de Spectacul.* 25), Dionysius of Alexandria (*ap.* Euseb. *HE*), and Chrysostom (*Hom. 35 in* 1 Cor.) make such reference. This prayer, of course, was at first said aloud, so as to be heard by all ; but in the course of time (after the 8th cent.) the custom grew for the officiating minister to say it *sotto voce*. Even then, such importance was attached to the response of the people that the priest was required to say the closing words ('world without end') aloud, so that then the 'Amen' might be said. This in the West : in the Greek Church it was similarly required that the words of the institution should be said aloud, though the first part of the prayer was said inaudibly, so that the people might hear them and make their response. A writer of the 9th cent. (Florus Magister), referring to this usage, says : 'Amen, which is responded by the whole church, means *It is true*. This, therefore, the faithful respond at the consecration of so great a mystery, as also in every prayer duly said, and by responding declare assent.' A similar use of Amen at the end of the Exhortation (which is not a prayer), commencing the second part of the eucharistic service (see Book of Common Prayer), and at the end of the corresponding 'Preface' in the old Gallican Liturgy, may also be pointed out.

Jerome has an interesting reference to the loud congregational Amen, which he describes as resounding like thunder ('ad similitudinem cœlestis tonitrui' — *Com. ad Galat.*). This corresponds to a synagogue custom of uttering the 'Amen with the full power' of the voice (*Shab.* 119b).

The modern practice of singing Amen at the close of hymns in public worship is partly due to a musical demand for a suitable cadence to conclude the tune : but it is also in harmony with the most ancient practice of closing hymns with doxologies, which naturally carried an Amen with them. The discrimination observable in some hymnals, whereby hymns containing a prayer or a doxology are closed with Amen and others not, arises from misapprehension. Amen not only means 'So be it,' but equally 'So it is,' and should thus be suitable as a conclusion to all hymns that are appropriate for Christian worship.

(c) *Mohammedan.*—Among the Mohammedans Amen is used liturgically, but only to a slight extent. It is universally used by them after every recital of the first *Sura* of the Koran—the so-called *Surat al-Fâtihat* (= Preface or Introduction). This brief, prayer-like form is held in great veneration, and has among them a place corresponding to that of the Paternoster amongst Christians.

LITERATURE.—The Bible Dictionaries, *s.v.*; *Jewish Encyclopedia*, *s.v.*; *Berakhoth* i. 11–19; H. W. Hogg, *Jewish Quart. Review*, Oct. 1896; articles in *Expository Times*, by Nestle (Jan. 1897), and Jannaris (Sept. 1902); Dalman, *Die Worte Jesu* (Eng. tr. 1902, p. 226 ff.); Scudamore, *Notitia Eucharistica*.

J. S. CLEMENS.

AM HA'AREZ (עַם הָאָרֶץ) means literally 'the people of the land.' Sometimes—particularly in later books of OT—it is found in the plural '*ammê hā'ārez* or '*ammê hā'ărāzôth.* Its use in the time of Christ indicates the following development :—From being (1) applied to the ordinary inhabitants of the land (Gn 23[7. 12. 13]) or to the people at large as a body (2 K 11[14. 18. 19. 20] 15[5] 16[15] 21[24] etc.), the term came (2) to be used to designate the common people as distinguished from the king, princes, priests, etc. (Jer 44[21], Hag 2[4], Zec 7[5]), and (3) like 'pagan' from *pagus*, was applied to those remote from or untouched by the culture (particularly religious culture) of the time, till it became (4) finally, an expression of contempt meaning 'uncultured,' 'rude,' 'barbarous,' 'irreligious,' applied to a certain class or even to a member of that class. To the '*am hā'ārez* the Pharisees directly refer in Jn 7[49] 'This multitude which knoweth not the Law are accursed.'

The origin of this cleavage is found in the OT. At the Exile we are told 'none were left save the very poor of the people of the land' (דַּלַּת עַם הָאָרֶץ) 2 K 24[14]). These mingled with the neighbouring non-Israelites and perhaps also with the settlers from Assyria, intermarrying with them, and probably adopting their customs. Hence at the Return both Ezra and Nehemiah demanded a complete separation (Ezr 9[1. 12], Neh 10[28-31]) between the returned exiles who observed the Law strictly, and those settlers who constituted 'the people of the land.'

This idea developed and led to the formation of a party called 'Separatists,' *Ḥăsîdîm* or *Pĕrûshîm* (Aram. *Pĕrîshayyā'* ; see art. 'Pharisees' in Hastings' *DB* iii. p. 826[b]), who regarded all contact with the vulgar crowd ('*am hā'ārez*) as defiling, observed a strict *régime* of ceremonial purity, and called each other *ḥābēr* (*i.e.* 'brother'). The '*am hā'ārez* was the antithesis of the *ḥābēr*, outside the pale of this higher Judaism, poor, ignorant of the Law, despised. In Rabbinical literature, where he is always regarded as a Jew, many definitions of the '*am hā'ārez* are given. Thus in the Talmud (*Berakhôth* 47*b*) he is described as one 'who does not give his tithes regularly,' or 'who does not read the Shema morning and evening,' or 'who does not wear *tĕphillîm*,' or 'who has no *mĕzúzāh* on his doorposts,' or 'who fails to teach his children the Law,' or 'who has not associated with the learned.' Montefiore in his *Hibbert Lectures* denies that such sharp cleavage between the *Ḥăsîdîm* and the '*am hā'ārez* ever existed save in the minds of later Rabbis who had difficulty in defining '*am hā'ārez*, and consequently he questions the authenticity of Jn 7[49], but on insufficient grounds. A great gulf and much bitterness existed between the two. A Pharisee would not accept the evidence of an '*am hā'ārez* as a witness, nor give him his daughter

in marriage. Even the touch of the garment of an '*am hā'ārez* was defiling ; and Lazarus (*Ethics of Judaism*) quotes a saying, 'An '*am hā'ārez* may be killed on the Sabbath of Sabbaths, or torn like a fish.' This can hardly be taken literally ; yet it illustrates the feeling which doubtless prevailed in the time of Christ towards the '*am hā'ārez.* The mind of Jesus triumphed over this narrow spirit. In these poor despised outcasts He saw infinite possibilities for goodness. They were the objects of His special care. To them had the Father sent Him, for at the very worst they were only 'the lost sheep of the house of Israel' (Mt 10[6]).

LITERATURE. — *Jewish Encyclopedia* (art. Am - haaretz'); Schürer, *GJV*[3] ii. 40 [Eng. *HJP* II. ii. 22] ; Weber, *Jüd. Theol.*[2] (Index, *s.* 'Am haarez'); Edersheim, *Life and Times of Jesus the Messiah*, i. 85 ; Wünsche, *Der Bab. Talm.* II. i. 295 ; Lazarus, *Ethics of Judaism*, Eng. tr. i. Appendix, note 48[a], 258 ; C. G. Montefiore, *Hibbert Lectures*, 1892, 'Origin and Growth of Hebrew Religion,' pp. 497–502 ; Rosenthal, *Vier Apokryphische Bücher*, pp. 25–29 ; Hamburger, *RE* ii. 54–56.

G. GORDON STOTT.

AMMINADAB.—An ancestor of our Lord, Mt 1[4].

AMON.—A king of Judah (*c.* 640 B.C.) mentioned in our Lord's genealogy, Mt 1[10] (Gr. Ἀμώς, RVm **Amos**).

ANDREW (Ἀνδρέας, 'manly').—In the Synoptic Gospels, Andrew is little more than a name ; but the references to him in the Fourth Gospel are of such a character as to leave upon our minds a wonderfully clear impression of the manner of man he was, and of the service which he rendered to the Church of Christ. Andrew was a native of Bethsaida (Jn 1[44]), but afterwards shared the same house (Mk 1[29]) at Capernaum (v.[21]) with his better known brother Simon Peter. By trade he was a fisherman (Mt 4[18]), but, attracted by all that he had heard or seen of John the Baptist, for a time at least he left his old work, and, following the Baptist into the wilderness, came to be recognized as one of his disciples (Jn 1[35. 40]). A better teacher Andrew could not have had ; for if from John he first learned the exceeding sinfulness of sin, by him also he was pointed to the promised Deliverer, the Lamb of God, who was to take away the sin of the world. And when, accordingly, the Christ did come, it was to find Andrew with a heart ready and eager to welcome Him. Of that first interview between the Lord and His new disciple the Fourth Evangelist, who was himself present, has preserved the record (Jn 1[35-40]), and he it is also who tells us that no sooner had Andrew realized for himself the truth regarding Jesus, than he at once went in search of his brother Peter (vv.[41. 42]). And thus to the first-called of Christ's disciples (πρωτόκλητος, according to a common designation of Andrew in early ecclesiastical writers) was given the joy of bringing next his own brother to the Lord. The call of James and of John, if they had not been previously summoned, would seem to have followed ; but in none of these instances did this imply as yet more than a personal relationship to the Saviour. The actual summons to work came later, when, by the Sea of Galilee, Jesus bade Andrew, along with the same three companions, leave his nets and come after Him (Mt 4[18ff.]). And this in turn was followed shortly afterwards by Andrew's appointment to a place in the Apostolic Band (Mt 10[2ff.]). His place, moreover, was a place of honour, for his name always occurs in the first group of four, and it is with Peter and James and John that he is again associated in the 'private' inquiries to Jesus regarding the time of the Last Things (Mk 13[3]).

Still more interesting, however, as illustrating Andrew's character, are the two occasions on which he is specially associated with Philip, the only other Apostle who bore a Greek name. The first incident occurred at the Feeding of the Five Thousand, when, in contrast to the anxious, calculating Philip, the downright, practical Andrew thought it worth while to draw the Saviour's attention to the lad's little store, even though he too was at a loss as to what it could effect (Jn 6$^{5\mathrm{ff.}}$). And the second occurred when to Philip, again perplexed by the desire of certain Greeks (Gentiles, therefore) to see Jesus, Andrew suggested that the true course was at least to lay the request before Jesus Himself, and leave Him to decide whether or not it could be granted (Jn 12$^{20\mathrm{ff.}}$).

After this, with the exception of the incident already referred to (Mk 13^3), Andrew is not again mentioned in the Gospels, and the only subsequent reference to him in Scripture is the mere mention of his name in Ac 1^{13}. Tradition, however, has been busy with his after-history; and he is represented as labouring, according to one account, in Scythia (Eus. *HE* iii. 1), whence he has been adopted as the patron-saint of Russia; or, according to another, in Achaia. In any case, there is general agreement that he was martyred at Patræ in Achaia, being bound, not nailed, to the cross, in order to prolong his sufferings. There is, however, no warrant for the belief that the cross was of the decussate shape (✗), as this cross, usually associated with his name, is of a much later date.

A striking tradition preserved in the *Muratorian Fragment* brings Andrew and John together in their old age as they had been in their youth: 'The fourth Gospel [was written by] John, one of the disciples (*i.e.* Apostles). When his fellow-disciples and bishops urgently pressed him, he said, "Fast with me [from] to-day, for three days, and let us tell one another any revelation which may be made to us, either for or against [the plan of writing]." On the same night it was revealed to Andrew, one of the Apostles, that John should relate all in his own name, and that all should review [his writing]' (see Westcott, *Gospel of St. John*, p. xxxv; *History of NT Canon*, p. 523).

It is also deserving of mention that about 740 Andrew became the patron-saint of Scotland, owing to the belief that his arm had been brought by St. Regulus to the town on the East Coast that now bears his name.

The character of Andrew, as it appears in the few scattered notices that we have of him, is that of a simple, kindly man who had the courage of his opinions, as proved by his being the first of the Baptist's disciples openly to follow Jesus; who was eager to share with others the privileges he himself enjoyed (witness his search for Peter, and his treatment of the Greeks); and who, his work done, was always ready to efface himself (see especially Lightfoot, *Sermons on Special Occasions*, p. 160 ff.). Again, when we think of the Apostle in his more official aspect, it is sufficient to recall that he was not only the first home-missionary (Jn 1^{41}), but also the first foreign-missionary (12^{22}) —evidence, if evidence be wanted, of the close connexion between the two spheres of work.

LITERATURE.—In addition to what has been noted above, and the references to Andrew in the different Lives of Christ, see H. Latham, *Pastor Pastorum*, p. 156 ff.; the present writer's *The Twelve Apostles* (J. M. Dent), p. 24 ff.; *Expositor*, 1st ser. vii. [1882], 424 ff.; Ker, *Sermons*, 2nd ser. 100 ff. The principal authority on Andrew's traditional history is Lipsius, *Die Apokryphen Apostelgeschichten und Apostellegenden*, i. p. 543 ff.; cf. M. R. James in Hastings' *DB*, vol. i. p. 93. His place in Art is discussed by Mrs. Jameson, *Sacred and Legendary Art*, i. p. 226 ff. We may refer also to Keble's poem on 'St. Andrew's Day' in *The Christian Year*, and to the poem on 'St. Andrew and his Cross' in the *Lyra Innocentium*.

GEORGE MILLIGAN.

ANGELS.—The statements as to angels which meet us in the Gospels are in most respects the same as are found in the Jewish literature of the period, both Biblical and extra-Biblical. In the main, Christ and His Apostles appropriated the Angelology of current Judaism — but not without critical selection. It would be difficult

to point to a time when the Jews, as a people, did not believe in angels; yet there were exceptions. Possibly it was the exuberance of the belief that produced in some minds a reaction. At all events, it is a fact that the portion of the OT known to criticism as the Priests' Code is silent on the subject of angels; and it is also noteworthy that the Sadducees, who were the descendants of the high-priestly families, protested in the time of our Lord against some, if not all, of the popular notions respecting angels (Ac 23^8).

It is probable that belief in angels is originally a corollary from the conception of God as King. A lone king—a king without a court—is almost a contradiction in terms. And inasmuch as the recognition of God *as King* is the earliest and most prevalent of Israel's conceptions of God, we naturally expect the belief in angels, as God's court, serving Him in His palace and discharging the function of messengers, to be ancient and pervasive. We have then, doubtless, a very primitive conception of angels in the words of Micaiah to Ahab, in 1 K 22^{19} 'I saw Jahweh sitting on his throne, and all the host of heaven standing by him, on his right hand and on his left.' A second and quite distinct feature of the Angelology of the OT is found in the appearances of one who is called '*the* Angel of Jahweh'—who is described as undistinguishable from man in appearance, and yet claims to speak and act in the name of Jahweh Himself (Gn 18$^{2. 16. 17}$ 32$^{24. 30}$, Jg 13$^{3. 6. 22}$). It is noteworthy as a feature of OT criticism, that, as P is *silent* as to angels, so the appearances of an angel as a manlike manifestation of God and not a mere messenger, are confined to those portions of the OT which, on quite other grounds, are assigned to JE. Thirdly, when the Jews came to have more exalted views of God, and of the incompatibility between Divinity and humanity, spirit and matter, good and evil, and, in consequence, conceived of God as aloof from the world and incapable of immediate contact and intercourse with sinful mortals, the doctrine of angels received more attention than ever before. The same influences which led the Persians to frame such an elaborate system of Angelology, led the Jews, during and after the Exile, to frame a similar system, or in some respects to borrow from the Persian system; to believe in gradations among the angelic hosts; to give names to those who were of high rank, and to assign to each of these some definite kind of work to do among men, or some province on the earth to administer as satrap under 'the King of Heaven' (see art. 'Zoroastrianism' in vol. iv. of Hastings' *DB*).

In the Gospels there are clear indications of the first and third of these phases of belief. The second is of interest to the NT student as a preparatory discipline in the direction of Christology; and as such has no further importance for us at present. Ewald has said (*OT and NT Theology*, p. 79) that in Christianity there is 'no denial of the existence of angels, but a return to the simpler colouring of the early narratives.' So far as simplicity of narrative is concerned, there is certainly a close resemblance between the angel-incidents of St. Luke and Acts on the one hand, and of Genesis on the other; but in the NT the angel never identifies himself with Jahweh as is done in Genesis; and there are in the NT some phases of Angelology which belong, not to 'the early narratives,' but to post-exilic conceptions.

We wish now, with the help of Jewish literature, more or less contemporary, to make a systematic presentation of those beliefs as to angels which are found in the discourses and narratives of the four Gospels. It might be supposed that we should find it helpful to keep apart the utterances of our

Lord from the descriptions of the Evangelists; but, in fact, there is such complete unity of conception underlying both discourses and narratives, that no useful purpose can be served by treating them separately.

i. ANGELS IN HEAVEN.—1. They form an *army* or *host*. Lk 2¹³ 'There was with the angel (who appeared to the shepherds) a multitude of the heavenly host' (στρατιά). Our Lord carries the military metaphor even further when He speaks of 'more than 12 legions of angels' (Mt 26⁵³). Oriental hyperbole was fully employed in expressing the magnitude of the heavenly army. Rev 5¹¹ speaks of 'myriads of myriads and thousands of thousands'; and He 12²² speaks of 'the myriads of angels'—both in probable allusion to Dn 7¹⁰. In Job 25³ also the question is asked: 'Is there any number of his armies?' Similarly the Pal. Targ. to Ex 12¹² tells of 90,000 myriads of destroying angels; and in Dt 34⁵ the same Targum speaks of the glory of the Shekinah being revealed to the dying Moses, with 2000 myriads of angels and 42,000 chariots; as 2 K 6¹⁷ tells of a 'mountain full of horses and chariots of fire round about Elisha.'

2. They form a *court*. Heaven is 'God's throne' (Mt 5³⁴ 23²²), and there also 'the Son of Man shall sit on the throne of his glory' (Mt 19²⁸). The angels, as courtiers, stand in vast multitudes before the throne (Rev 5¹¹ 7¹¹). As in earthly courts there are gradations of rank and dignity, so in heaven. It is St. Paul who speaks most explicitly of 'the principalities and powers in the heavenly places' (Eph 3¹⁰), and of Christ's being 'exalted far above all rule, and authority, and power, and dominion' (Eph 1²¹); and 'evidently Paul regarded them as actually existent and intelligent forces' (Robinson, *in loco*); but the same conception presents itself in the Gospels in the reference to archangels, who were four, or in some authors seven, in number: Gabriel, Raphael, Michael, and Uriel being those most frequently mentioned. In Lk 1¹⁹ the angel who appears to Zacharias says: 'I am Gabriel, that stand in the presence of God'; as in To 12¹⁵ the angel says to Tobit: 'I am Raphael, one of the seven holy angels, which present the prayers of the saints and go in before the glory of the Holy One.' Even in the OT the angels are spoken of as forming 'a *council*': *e.g.* in Ps 89⁷, where God is said to be 'very terrible in the council of the holy ones,' and in Ps 82¹ where He is said to 'judge amidst the Elohim.' This idea was a great favourite with later Jews, who maintained that 'God does nothing without consulting the family above' (*Sanhedrin*, 38b). To the same circle of ideas belong the words of the Lord Jesus: 'Every one that shall confess me before men, him will the Son of Man confess before the angels of God; but he that denieth me in the presence of men shall be denied in the presence of the angels of God' (Lk 12⁸·⁹). Evidently the angels are interested spectators of men's behaviour, responsive to their victories and defeats, their sins and struggles; and we are here taught that to be denied before such a vast responsive assembly intensifies the remorse of the apostate, as to be confessed before them intensifies the joy of those who are 'faithful unto death.' Again, in many courts, and particularly in that of the Persians, there were secretaries or scribes, whose business it was to keep a 'book of records' (Est 6¹), in which the names and deeds of those who had deserved well of the king were honourably recorded. The metaphor of heaven as a palace and court is so far kept up, that the Jews often spoke of *books* in heaven in which men's deeds are recorded. Not only do we read in Slavonic Enoch 19⁵ of 'angels who are over the souls of men, and who write down all their works

and their lives before the face of the Lord'; and in the Apocalypse of John, where symbolism abounds, of 'books' being 'opened,' and of the 'dead' being 'judged according to what was written in the books': but even in an Epistle of St. Paul we read of those 'whose names are in the book of life' (Ph 4³), and in He 12²³, of 'the church of the firstborn who are enrolled in heaven'; and precisely in accord with the above our Lord bade His disciples rejoice, because their names 'are written in heaven,' *i.e.* enrolled for honour (Lk 10²⁰).

3. They form a *choir* in the heavenly temple. The description of heaven in the Apocalypse is quite as much that of a temple as a palace. Heaven contains its altar (8⁵ 9¹³), its censers (5⁸ 8³), its musicians (5⁸ 15²), and its singers (5⁹ 14³ 15³). In extra-Biblical literature the veil is often mentioned, concealing the abode of God in the Most Holy Place, within which the archangels are permitted to enter (To 12¹²·¹⁵, Enoch 40²). The only reference in the Gospels under this head is the song of the angels, described in Lk 2¹³ᶠ. It is possible, in spite of the reading of some very ancient Greek MSS (א*ABD), that this song, like that of the seraphim in Is 6², is a triple antiphonal one—

' Glory to God in the highest [heaven],
    Peace on earth,
    Among men [Divine] good pleasure.'

4. They are '*sons of God*.' In this respect the saints who are raised again are 'equal to the angels' (Lk 20³⁶). They are sons of God by creation and by obedience (Job 1⁶ 2¹ 38⁷). They 'do not owe their existence to the ordinary process of filiation, but to an immediate act of creation' (Godet, *OT Studies*, 7); thus resembling in their origin the bodily nature of those who are 'sons of the resurrection.' Hence we find that they are frequently described as 'holy' (Mt 25³¹, Mk 8³⁸, Lk 9²⁶, Job 5¹ 15¹⁵, Dn 8¹³), and by implication we learn that angels obey God's will in heaven, since we are taught by our Lord to pray that God's holy will may be done on earth as it is in heaven (Mt 6¹⁰, cf. Ps 103²⁰).

5. They are *free from sensuous feelings*. This is taught in Mt 22³⁰ 'In the resurrection they neither marry [as men] nor are given in marriage [as women], but are as the angels of God in heaven.' These words were spoken by our Lord in response to the doubts of the Sadducees on the subject of the resurrection. Christ's reply is in effect this: The source of your error is that you do not fully recognize the power of God. You seem to think that God can make only one kind of body, with one sort of functions, and dependent on one means of life. In that way you limit unduly the power of God. 'In that age' (Lk 20³⁵), 'when they rise from the dead' (Mk 12²⁵), men do not eat and drink (Ro 14¹⁷). Not being mortal, they are not dependent on food for nourishment, nor have they, by nature, sensuous appetites, but are ἰσάγγελοι ('equal to the angels'). Thus skilfully did Jesus give a double-edged reply to the teachings of the Sadducees (Ac 23⁸). While answering their objection against the resurrection, He affirms that 'those who are accounted worthy to attain to that αἰών, and the resurrection from the dead . . . are equal to the angels'—thus plainly disclosing His belief in angels and setting it over against their disbelief. As to the spiritual nature of angels, Philo speaks of them as ἀσώματοι καὶ εὐδαίμονες ψυχαί ('incorporeal and happy souls'); and again, as 'bodiless souls, not mixtures of rational and irrational natures as ours are, but having the irrational nature cut out, wholly intelligent throughout, pure-thoughts (λογισμοί, elsewhere λόγοι) like a monad' (Drummond's *Philo*, 145–147; cf. Philo's

Confusion of Tongues, p. 8, *Allegory*, iii. 62). The Rabbis interpreted Dn 7[10] to teach that the nature of the angels is fire. 'They are nourished by the radiance which streams from the presence of God. They need no material nourishment, and their nature is not responsive to bodily pleasures' (Weber, *Jüd. Theol.*[2] 167; *Pesiḳta*, 57*a*; *Exodus R.* 32). They are also said to be 'spiritual beings' (*Lev. R.* 24), 'without sensuous requirements' (*Yoma*, 74*b*), 'without hatred, envy, or jealousy' (*Chag.* 14). The Jewish legends which interpret Gn 6[4] as teaching a commingling of angels with women, so as to produce 'mighty men, men of renown,' seem at variance with the above belief as to the immunity of celestial intelligences from all passion. It is true that Jude [6] and Enoch 15[3-7] both speak of the angels as having first 'left their habitation' in heaven; but the fact that they were deemed *capable* of sexual intercourse implies a much coarser conception of the angelic nature than is taught in the words of our Lord, of Philo, and of the Talmud.

6. They have *extensive, and yet limited, knowledge.* This is clearly taught in one utterance of Christ's, recorded in Mt 24[36] || Mk 13[32] 'Of that day and hour knoweth no man, *not even* the angels of heaven.' The implications clearly are (1) that angels know most things, far better than men; but (2) that there are some things, including the day of the Second Advent, which they do *not* know. Both these propositions admit of copious illustration from Jewish literature. First, as to their extensive knowledge. There are numerous intimations of the scientific skill of the angels, their acquaintance with the events of human lives, and their prescience of future events. The Book of Jubilees, a pre-Christian work extensively read, affirms (1[27]) that Moses was taught by Gabriel concerning Creation and the things narrated in Genesis; that angels taught Noah herbal remedies (10[12]), and brought to Jacob seven tablets recording the history of his posterity (32[21]). In Enoch 8[1] Azazel is said to have taught men metallurgy and other sciences; as Prometheus was said to have taught the Greeks. In To 12[12] the angel assures Tobit that he was familiar with all the events of his troublous days: as in 2 S 14[17. 20] the woman of Tekoa flatters Joab that he was 'as wise as an angel of God to know all things that are in the earth.' But this knowledge has its *limits.* Angels were supposed to understand no language but Hebrew (*Chagigah*, 16*a*). In 2 Es 4[52], in revealing eschatological events, the angel gives the tokens of the coming end, but confesses his ignorance as to whether Esdras will be alive at the time. The Midrash on Ps 25[14] affirms that 'nothing is hidden from the angels'; but according to *Sanhedrin*, 99*a*, and other Talmudic passages, 'they know not the time of Israel's redemption.' In 1 P 1[12] we are told that 'the angels desire' (but in vain) 'to look into' some of the NT mysteries; and in Slav. Enoch 24[3] 40[2], Enoch tells his children that not even the angels know the secrets which he discloses to them.

7. They *take a deep interest in the salvation of men.* We gather this from the evident joy with which angels announced the advent of the Messiah to the shepherds at Bethlehem. The angel who brought the 'tidings of great joy' (Lk 2[10]) clearly felt the joy himself; and the song which the heavenly host sang in praise to God was the outcome of joyous hearts. Even more explicitly is this taught in Lk 15[10] 'There is joy in the presence of the angels of God over one sinner that repenteth.' The word ἐνώπιον seems here to mean 'in the midst of,' 'among.' 'Joy is manifest on every countenance.' Even if the joy intended be 'the joy *of* God, which breaks forth in presence of

the angels' (Godet, *in loco*), still the implication would be that the heart of the angelic throng is *en rapport* with the heart of 'the happy God.' On this point the words of the angel are instructive which are recorded in Rev 22[10] 'I am a fellow-servant with thee and with thy brethren the prophets, and with them that keep the words of this book.' The interpreting angel confesses to unity of service with the Church, and in so doing implies a oneness of sympathy and love with the saints. So also when, in 1 P 1[12], we read that 'the angels desire to look into' the marvels of redemption, there is, as Dr. Hort says, 'a glimpse of the fellowship of angels with prophets and evangelists, and implicitly with the suffering Christians to whom St. Peter wrote.' The same deep interest in the progress of the Church appears in Eph 3[10], where we are taught that one great purpose which moved God to enter on the work of human salvation was, that 'through the Church the manifold wisdom of God might be made known to the principalities and powers in heavenly places.' The Church on earth is the arena on which the attributes of God are displayed for the admiration and adoration of 'the family in heaven' (Eph 3[15]).

ii. ANGELS AS VISITANTS TO EARTH. — **1.** To *convey messages from God to man.*—(*a*) In dreams. It is a peculiarity of the Gospel of the Infancy, as recorded by St. Matthew, that the appearances of the angels are in dreams to Joseph, bidding him acknowledge Mary as his wife (Mt 1[20]), take the young child and His mother to Egypt (2[13]), and return to Palestine on the death of Herod (2[19]). The only OT parallel to this is Gn 31[11], where Jacob tells his wives that 'the angel of God spake' to him 'in a dream.'

(*b*) In other instances the message of the angel is brought in full, wakeful consciousness. It was while Zacharias was ministering at the altar of incense in the Holy Place that an angel who called himself Gabriel appeared, foretelling the birth of John (Lk 1[11]). It was while the shepherds were keeping watch over their flock that the angel stood near them and directed them to the babe in Bethlehem (Lk 2[9. 11]); and it is narrated by the three Synoptists that it was through angelic agency that the disciples were informed of the Resurrection. St. Matthew narrates that it was an angel who had 'descended from heaven' (28[2]), that spoke to the women at the tomb (28[5. 7]). St. Mark speaks of a young man 'arrayed in a white robe' (16[5]), and St. Luke of 'two men in dazzling apparel' (24[4]), who assured the women that Christ was risen. The author of the Fourth Gospel is silent as to angelic appearances at the Resurrection, but he bears testimony to the popular belief in angelic voices (Jn 12[29]). When a voice came from heaven, saying, 'I have glorified and will again glorify (my name),' the Evangelist records: 'Some of the people said, An angel spake to him.'

We reserve for special consideration the sacredly mysterious interview of the angel Gabriel with the Virgin Mary (Lk 1[26-38]). The salutation of the angel was: 'Hail, thou favoured one! The Lord is with thee.' When she was perplexed at the saying, the angel announced: 'Thou shalt conceive in thy womb and bear a son, and shalt call his name Jesus.' This Son is further described as 'Son of the Most High' and He to whom 'the Lord God will give the throne of his father David.' Then, in reply to the Virgin's further doubts and perplexities, the angel vouchsafes the dread explanation, 'The Holy Ghost shall come upon thee, and the power (δύναμις) of the Most High shall overshadow thee. . . . No word from God shall be devoid of power.' The full consideration of these words will be fittingly considered under ANNUNCIATION (which see). On us it seems to devolve to speak of the view which arose very early in Jewish Christian circles, and which regarded the angel as not merely the messenger, but the *cause* of the conception. It was a general belief among the Jews that a spoken word has causal efficacy. This lay at the root of the belief in the potency of spells and charms. And if every spoken word is mighty, the words of God are almighty. The expression 'No word from (παρά) God shall be devoid of power' (Lk 1³⁷) was accordingly interpreted to mean that the message brought from God through the angel had causal efficacy: the Divine word spoken by the angel caused the conception. In the *Protevangelium of James* (11²) the angel is recorded to have said: 'Thou shalt conceive from His word' (ἐκ τοῦ λόγου αὐτοῦ), and the same expression occurs in the Arabic *Gospel of the Infancy*. This is the origin of the curious doctrine of the ancient Church, that the Virgin conceived *through the ear*. The word of the angel, which was a Divine message, reached the Virgin through the ear. The ear was thus believed to be the channel through which the Divine potency was operative. Even Augustine says: 'Virgo per aurem impregnabatur.' As bearing on this subject, we may note that in the *Ascension of Isaiah* the angel Gabriel is called 'the angel of the Holy Spirit' (3¹⁶ 7²³ 9³⁶). In *pseudo-Matthew* (c. 10), Joseph says: 'Why do ye mislead me to believe that an angel of the Lord hath made her pregnant?' and in the *Protevangelium of James* the Virgin explains her condition to Joseph in these words: 'The case is the same as it was with Adam whom God created. He said, "Let him be"; and he was.'

2. Angels as *performing physical actions.* This is an ancient representation of which the OT furnishes many instances: Ps 91¹¹ᶠ· (cited Mt 4⁶, Lk 4¹⁰ᶠ·), 'angels ... shall bear thee up on their hands'; in Dn 6²² angels shut the lions' mouths; in Ps 34⁷ angels encamp round about them that fear God; so in Apocrypha (Bel ³⁶, Three ²⁶). It is therefore precisely in accord with Jewish modes of thought that we read in Mt 28² 'There was a great earthquake: for an angel of the Lord descended from heaven, and came and *rolled away the stone*'; and in Mk 1¹³ 'He was with the wild beasts; and the angels *ministered* unto him' (cf. Mt 4¹¹).

3. As *performing psychical actions.* When Jesus was in the garden, and 'being in an agony prayed more earnestly,' we are told that 'there appeared to him an angel from heaven *strengthening* him' (Lk 22⁴³).* So in Dn 10¹⁷ᶠ· Daniel records that there was 'no strength in him, and no breath left in him,' and an angel 'touched him and strengthened him.' The Hebrews drew no distinction between the physical and the psychical. It was in their regard just as easy for these spiritual existences to roll away a stone as to infuse vigour into the system, and give power to the enfeebled nerves and will.

4. Angels are deputed to *guard the righteous from danger.* In Gn 24⁷ Abraham prays for his servant: 'May God send his angel before thee'; and Jacob saw angels 'ascending and descending' over him in his sleep (Gn 28¹²). In the time of Christ it was a Jewish belief not merely that angels are sent to guide and guard men, but also that every man has his *own* guardian spirit, or, as others teach, two guardians. In the Talmudic treatise *Berakhoth* (60b), when a man goes into an unclean place, he prays his guardian angels to wait outside till he returns. In Pal. Targum to Gn 33¹⁰ Jacob says to Esau, 'I have seen thy face as if I saw the face of *thy* angel'; on Gn 48¹⁶ the same Targum reads: 'May the angel whom thou hast assigned to me bless the lads.' Similarly the *Sohar*

---

* On the question of the genuineness of this passage see the 'Notes on Select Readings' in Westcott and Hort's *NT in Greek.*

---

to Exodus (p. 190) says: 'From the 13th year of a man and onwards, God assigns to every man two angels, one on the right hand and one on the left; and the *Testament of Joseph* (c. 6) names the angel of Abraham as the guardian of Joseph. It is here more than elsewhere that we seem to recognize the influence of Persia on Jewish beliefs.

The question now occurs, What connexion is there between the above and Mt 18¹⁰ 'See that ye despise not one of these little ones, for I say unto you, that their angels in heaven continually behold the face of my Father who is in heaven'? It is evident that 'their angels' means angels that watch over them. But did our Lord refer to the 'angels of the presence' or to individual guardian angels? The former is more probable for two reasons—(1) It was not part of the Jewish creed that any angels behold the face of God except the archangels; (2) the guardian spirits accompanying men on earth could hardly at the same time be said to be *in heaven* continually beholding the face of the Father who is in heaven. The allusion probably is, then, to the 'angels of the presence,' and especially to Michael the guardian of the pious and the helpless. It must be admitted that in Ac 12¹⁵ we seem to have the popular Jewish notion in all its later development. When many brethren were met in the house of Mary, mother of John Mark, and were unable to believe that Peter had really been delivered, they said to Rhoda, first, 'Thou art mad,' and then, 'It is his angel.' This, if pushed to its apparent implications, seems to contain an allusion to a notion which occurs in some Jewish writings, that heaven is a counterpart of earth, and every man has his double in the celestial sphere; or at all events the guardian angel is *like* him whom he guards. It is quite likely, however, that on the lips of the disciples these words might be merely an allusion to a popular conception, without carrying with them any literal belief.

5. Angels *visit wrath on the adversaries of the righteous.* This is implied in Christ's words: 'See that ye despise not one of these little ones' (Mt 18¹⁰). The word ὁρᾶτε implies 'beware!' and the teaching clearly is that angels are capable of punishing any who injure those whom it is their business to guard. The OT contains instances of their punitive abilities. It was an angel of the Lord who smote 185,000 in the camp of the Assyrians (2 K 19³⁵), and who destroyed the children of Israel till, when he came to Jerusalem, the Lord said to him, 'It is enough' (2 S 24¹⁶); and Ps 35⁵ᶠ· presents a picture calculated to inspire terror in every breast: 'Let them be as chaff before the wind, the angel of the Lord driving them on. Let their way be dark and slippery, the angel of the Lord pursuing them.' It is very noteworthy that the Lord Jesus, even in His hour of intensest agony, drew comfort from the thought of angelic help. It was a real comfort to Him that the angels were at His control, if He needed them. The military band led by Judas could not arrest or injure Him unless He voluntarily submitted Himself to them. He had 'authority to lay down' His 'life'; and when the struggle was over, and the resolve retaken that the path of the cross was the path of duty, He conveyed to the Eleven the fact of His self-surrender by saying to Peter, who had impetuously used the sword in his Lord's defence, 'Thinkest thou that I cannot now beseech the Father, and he would even now send me more than twelve legions of angels'? (Mt 26⁵³). We note here that the prayer is not to be addressed to angels. There are very few instances of Jews praying to angels. The Rabbis discouraged it. Every pious Jew would, as Jesus did, pray to God that He would *send* angelic ministry; as in 2 Mac

15²³, where Judas is said to have prayed: 'O sovereign Lord, send a good angel before us to bring terror and trembling.'

6. Angels *render aid at death.* Lk 16²² 'Lazarus was carried away *by* the angels into Abraham's bosom.' We come here upon a widespread belief among Jews and Jewish Christians—that angels convey the souls of the righteous to Paradise. Michael is usually the one entrusted with this duty. If he has a companion, it is Gabriel. The *Gospel of Nicodemus* records that when Jesus descended into Hades and released the righteous dead from captivity, He delivered Adam and all the righteous to the archangel Michael, and all the saints followed Michael; and he led them all into the glorious gate of Paradise: among them being the penitent thief. The *History of Joseph the Carpenter* records that Michael and Gabriel drew out the soul of Joseph and wrapped it in a silken napkin, and amid the songs of angels took him to his good Father, even to the dwelling-place of the just. In the *Testament of Abraham* we have a similar account of the death of Abraham. The *Ascension of Isaiah* (7²⁵) affirms that 'those who love the Most High and His Beloved will ascend to heaven by the Angel of the Holy Spirit.'

7. Angels are to be *the ministrants of Christ at His Second Advent.* 'The reapers' in the great Harvest 'are angels'; and they separate the tares from the wheat (Mt 13³⁹). 'The Son of Man will send forth his angels to gather out all that offend' (Mt 13⁴¹). 'He shall come in his glory, and all the holy angels with him' (Mt 25³¹). 'He shall send forth his angels with the great sound of a trumpet to gather the elect' (Mt 24³¹; cf. 1 Th 4¹⁷, 2 Th 1⁷).

8. To complete our survey, we must add one word as to *the appearance of angels* when men were conscious of their presence. It is taken for granted that there needs to be a preparation of vision before man can recognize their presence. As Balaam was unaware that the angel confronted him until the Lord opened his eyes (Nu 22³¹), and as Elisha prayed that God would open the eyes of his servant (2 K 6¹⁷), so when the risen Jesus appeared to Saul of Tarsus, those who travelled with him 'saw no man' (Ac 9⁷). (*a*) Angels had a manlike appearance. As Abraham and Manoah's wife mistook them for men (Gn 18¹⁶, Jg 13⁶), so, in describing the Resurrection, St. Mark says that the women 'saw a young man' (16⁵), and St. Luke that 'two men stood by them' (24⁴).—(*b*) Their appearance was usually with brilliant light or 'glory.' When the angel appeared to the shepherds, 'the glory of the Lord shone round about them' (Lk 2⁹), and when the Son of Man cometh, He will come 'in the glory of the holy angels' (Lk 9²⁶). So in To 3¹⁶, Cod. B reads: 'The prayer of both was heard before the glory of the great Raphael'; in 2 Mac 3²⁶ two young men appeared, 'notable in their strength and beautiful in their glory'; and the *Protevangelium of James* narrates that 'an angel of the Lord appeared in the great light to Joachim.'—(*c*) They wear raiment of great luminousness. Mt 28³ 'His appearance was like lightning, and his raiment white as snow'; cf. Dn 10⁶, Ezk 1¹³, Rev 1¹⁴ 19¹². So *Apoc. of Peter* says of the angels, 'their body was whiter than any snow.'

iii. DIFFERENCES BETWEEN NT AND RABBINISM AS TO ANGELS.—We undertook to show that 'in the main Christ and His Apostles appropriated the Angelology of Judaism'; and the above systematic treatment has surely rendered this evident. It has often been observed that 'Jesus says very little about angels'; and, so far as the bulk of His sayings is concerned, this is quite true; but when we *classify* His utterances, we find that they constitute almost a complete Angelology; and so far as it goes, it is in harmony with the Jewish beliefs of the period. The Jews believed all that the NT says of angels, but they also believed much more.

1. It is very significant that the Gospels are silent as to *the mediation of angels.* In Judaism this was very prominent. In Tobit, *e.g.*, one great function of angels is said to be to carry the prayers of saints within the veil, before the glory of the Holy One (12¹². ¹⁵). In Enoch 40⁶ the seer says: 'And the third voice heard I pray and intercede for those who dwell on the earth, and supplicate in the name of the Lord of spirits.' In the Greek *Apoc. of Baruch* (c. 11), Michael is said to have a great receptacle in which the prayers of men are placed to be carried through the gates into the presence of the Divine glory (*Texts and Studies*, v. i. 100). In the Midrash *Exodus Rabba* 21 an angel set over the prayers of men is said to weave them into crowns for the Most High.—But not only are the Gospels *silent* as to the need of angels to be mediators in carrying the prayers and necessities of saints into the unapproachable chamber of the Most High, the teaching of Jesus was designed to counteract such a view of God. When our Lord said: 'Your heavenly Father knoweth that ye have need of all these things' (Mt 6³²); 'Your heavenly Father feedeth the fowls' (6²⁶); 'Thy Father seeth in secret' (6¹⁸); 'Pray to thy Father who *is* in secret' (6⁶),—He certainly wished to break down the barriers which the Jewish mind had placed between itself and God, and encourage men to come direct to the Father in childlike confidence.

2. In other respects the only difference is, that the Gospels are free from the extravagant embellishment in which the Rabbis indulged, when speaking of angels: (*a*) as to their *size*. The Talmudic treatise *Chagigah* (13*b*) says that Sandalfon is taller than his fellows by the length of a journey of 500 years; and the *Gospel of Peter* (c. 9) tells how the Roman soldiers saw two men descend from heaven, and the head of the two reached unto heaven, but that of Him whom they released from the tomb overpassed the heavens.—(*b*) As to a fondness for the marvellous in describing their appearance and actions. For instance, *Yoma* 21*a* narrates how a high priest was killed by an angel in the Holy of Holies, and the impress of a calf's foot was found between his shoulders. Joshua ben Hananiah is reported to have told the Emperor Hadrian that God hears the song of new angels every day. When asked whence they come, he replied, 'From the fiery stream which issues from the throne of God' (Dn 7¹⁰); see Bacher, *Agada der Tannaiten*, i. 178.—(*c*) The Jews also speculated much as to the origin of the angels, their connexion with the four elements, etc.; and they had ingenious methods of computing their number by Kabbalistic *Gematria*—the whole thing being the extravaganza of Oriental phantasy.

iv. THE OBJECTIVE VALUE OF THE NT DOCTRINE OF ANGELS.—The most difficult part of our task now awaits us, to give some account of modern views as to the *reality* of angels, and to discuss whether there are valid reasons why we, as Christians, are bound to accept the *prima facie* NT teaching as to the angelic ministry. Every Christian must feel that it is of very great importance to decide whether the Lord Jesus really believed in the objective existence and ministrations of angels. To this question the present writer feels obliged to give an affirmative reply [but see art. ACCOMMODATION, above, p. 20], and that for the following reasons: (1) Though Jesus did not speak much concerning angels, yet His recorded sayings cover, with some intentional exceptions, almost the complete Angelology of the Jews—which is evidence that He was, in the main, in agreement with it. (2) If the disciples had been radically mistaken on this subject, surely this is a matter as to which Christ's words were applicable : ' If it were not so, I would have told you,' Jn 14[2]. (3) In controversy with the Sadducees, who were sceptical as to angels, He adroitly gave them such a reply to their objection against the resurrection as to show that the existence and nature of angels was to Him a settled matter, and might be used to elucidate the nature of the resurrection body. There is a wealth of conviction in the words of Jesus : ' Those who rise again are like the angels.' (4) Christ made mention of angels not merely in the parables, where we expect symbolism and pictorial illustration, but also in the interpretation (Mt 13[39. 41. 49]). (5) He used the punitive ability of angels to warn men against despising the little ones in His kingdom (Mt 18[10]). Apart from a literal belief in angels, such words are an empty threat. (6) In the time of His most intense agony He evidently derived comfort from the loving sympathy of the ' cloud of witnesses' ; for when He emerges from the trial and its bitterness is past, He assures Peter that, had He permitted it, more than twelve legions of angels would readily have intervened to deliver Him (Mt 26[53]). — Stevens (*Theology of NT*, p. 80) is impressed by other passages. ' In several places,' he says, ' Christ seems to refer to angels in such a way as to show that He believed in their *real existence*. He will " come in the glory of his Father with his holy angels " (Mk 8[38]). " Angels in heaven " neither marry nor are given in marriage (Mk 12[25]). Of the hour of his Advent " not even the angels in heaven " know (Mk 13[32]).'

In recent times the views of scholars are much divided on this subject. **1.** There are large sections of the universal Church to whom the existence of angels is very real, not only as a matter of theoretical belief, but as a matter of religious experience. They set great value on the services of angels as mediators between themselves, in their sins and needs and miseries, and the holy, infinite God ; and they delight to think that the spiritual strength and light and succour which come to them in answer to prayer, reach their low estate through the mediation of angels. We might readily quote from saints of the Greek and Roman Churches on this head, but we prefer to give the ' disclosures ' of Swedenborg. ' According to him, we are every moment in the most vital association with the spirits both of heaven and hell. They are the perpetual prompters of our thoughts : they incessantly work by insinuating influences on our loves ; and they give force on the one hand to the power of temptation, and on the other fortify the soul, by hidden influx, to resist temptation' (Rev. G. Bush, *Disclosures of Swedenborg*, 79).

2. There are many who believe in angels theoretically. They take the teaching of the NT in a thoroughly literal sense. They are prepared to maintain and contend that Jesus Christ believed in the real existence of angels ; and, in consequence, a belief in angels forms part of their ' creed' ; but angels have no part in their inner religious life. Some admit, not without regret and self-reproach, that angels do not seem so real to them as they did to Jesus ; while others are reluctant to admit that it can be a fault to yearn as they do for heart-to-heart fellowship with God Himself, without the intervention of an angel ministry — to seek for direct interaction with God, without even the holiest angel intervening in the sacredness of the communion. As a specimen of this attitude, we quote from an article in the First Series of the *Expositor* (viii. 409 ff.) by R. Winterbotham : ' I do not mean to imply that we *disbelieve* either the existence or the ministry of angelic beings : we

cannot do so without rejecting and denying point blank the unquestioned and unquestionable dicta of our Lord and of His apostles. But I do say that our belief in angels is formal only, or at the best merely poetic. It does not strike its roots down into our religious consciousness, into that inner and unseen, but most real and often passionate, life of the soul towards God and the powers of the world to come.'

3. There are others yet again who set such a high value on the immediacy of the interaction of fellowship with God, believing, as they do, that it was the chief feature of Christ's teaching to reveal the possibility of fellowship with God as our Father —or led perhaps by scientific predilections to feel that there is now no room for angels in our modern world—that they sweep away the intervention of angels, and are reluctant to admit that the Lord Jesus really believed in their existence. They would believe rather that He accommodated Himself in this matter to current popular notions. For instance, Beyschlag maintains that ' the immediate relation to the world in which Jesus viewed His heavenly Father left no room for such personal intermediate beings' [as the Jews of that time believed in]. In passages like Lk 12[8] and 15[10] angels are ' a poetic paraphrase for God Himself.' ' The holy angels of the Son of Man, with whom He will come again in His glory, are the rays of Divine majesty which is then to surround Him with splendour : they are the Divine powers with which He is to waken the dead.' And again, ' The most remarkable passage is Mt 18[10], and it is the very passage which we can least of all take in prosaic literalness. According to it, even the least of the children of men has his guardian angel who at all times has access to the Heavenly Father, viz. to complain to Him of the offences done to his protégé on earth. But as God, according to Jesus, knows what happens to each of His children without needing to be told, in what other way can we conceive this entirely poetical passage, than that in every child of man a peculiar thought of God has to be realized, which stands over his history, like a genius, or guardian spirit, and which God always remembers, so that everything which opposes its realization on earth comes before Him as a complaint ?' (*New Test. Theology*, i. 86 f.). Dr. Bruce is even more pronounced. In his *Epistle to the Hebrews* (p. 45) he says : ' For modern men, the angels are very much a dead theological category. Everywhere in the old Jewish world, they are next to nowhere in our world. They have practically disappeared from the universe in thought and in fact.' Then, with a strange lapse of the historic sense, he adds : ' This subject was probably a weariness to the writer of our Epistle. A Jew, and well acquainted with Jewish opinion, and obliged to adjust his argument to it, he was tired, I imagine, of the angelic régime. Too much had been made of it in Rabbinical teaching and in popular opinion. It must not be supposed that he was in sympathy with either.'

A belief in angels among men of to-day depends entirely on one's religious outlook, one's general view of God and the world. The man who has *scientific* proclivities, who has toiled through much doubt and uncertainty before he can sincerely affirm the first article of the Christian creed, ' I believe in God the Father Almighty,' will probably be reluctant to take more cargo aboard than his faith can carry. In other words, he will employ the Law of Parsimony, ' Entia præter necessitatem non multiplicanda sunt,' and, finding the full satisfaction of his religious needs in direct intercourse with God the Father, will reject, or ignore as superfluous, the ministry of angels. So also the man of *mystical* tendencies, whose eager desire is to have communion with the Divine—who claims to be endowed with a faculty by which he can cognize God, and receive immediate communications from Him, is also likely to regard the intervention of angels between his spirit and the Divine Spirit as an intrusion. And not less so is this the case with one who has leanings to *Pantheism*—whether he regards God as altogether immanent in the world, or as both immanent and transcendent. In proportion as one's thoughts centre on Divine immanence, and as one regards God as more or less identical with Force, variant but transmutable, present everywhere, and everywhere causative, in that proportion are one's thoughts drawn away from every theological conception but that of the One Great Cause of motion, life, and mind. There is no room for angels.

The only scientific conception which to some minds seems to foster the belief in angels is the Law of Evolution, or, to speak more accurately, the anticipation of gradation of being, encouraged by that law. T. G. Selby, in his volume of sermons headed by one on 'The Imperfect Angel,' contends that a true science welcomes the belief in angels as intervening between man and God. 'It is surely not unscientific,' he says, 'to assume the existence of the pure and mighty beings spoken of by seers and prophets of the olden time.' 'The spirit of inspiration, in seeking to convey to us some faint hint of the strict and awful and absolute holiness of God, depicts ranks of angels indefinitely higher and better than the choicest saints on earth: and then tells us that these angels, which seem so lofty and stainless and resplendent, are creatures of unwisdom and shortcoming in comparison with the ineffable wisdom and surpassing holiness of God' (p. 7). Godet in his *Biblical Studies on the OT* has elaborated a scientific *apologia* on behalf of angels. He contends that science recognizes three forms of being: species without individuality, in the vegetable world; individuality under bondage to species, in the animal world; individuality overpowering species, in the human race. He holds, therefore, that it is antecedently probable that there is a *fourth* form of being—individuality without species — each individual owing his existence no longer to parents like himself, but immediately to the Creative Will. This fourth form would exactly be the angel (p. 2 ff.).

It remains now to show that a belief in angels is in precise accord with the fundamental views of God and the world which present themselves in the recorded life and teaching of the Lord Jesus. Were the belief in angels at variance with Christ's personal religious outlook, we might readily regard it as an excrescence which modern thought might lop off without much detriment ; but if it is closely allied to our Lord's fundamental doctrines, then this will surely confirm the impression arrived at from other evidence, that Jesus sincerely believed in the reality of angels, and would have us derive from the belief the same comfort and support which He did. Where shall we look with more assurance for the first principles of the doctrine of Jesus than to the Lord's Prayer? There our Saviour taught His disciples to say, 'Our Father which art in heaven. Hallowed be Thy name. . . . Thy will be done on earth as it is in heaven.' Beyond all contradiction, then, it is an axiom of the creed of Jesus that there are beings in heaven who do God's will. It is generally recognized that Jesus presented to men a conception of God which meets the needs of man's religious nature, rather than of his reason and intellect. Men of culture and philosophical training may aspire to know God as 'the One in all,' 'the Absolute,' 'the First Cause' ; and may appeal for support to isolated

sayings of the Apostles, but *not* to sayings of the Master. His sayings owe their eternal permanence to the fact that they appeal to that which is common to all men—the innermost in all men—the heart—the religious nature. To conceive of God as the Absolute, or the First Cause, may satisfy the reason ; but before the heart can be satisfied, it must know God as Father, the 'Father in heaven.' But the very phrase 'Father in heaven' seems to imply that He has *sons* in heaven. And that this implication is warranted, is irrefragably substantiated by the words which follow : 'Thy will be done on earth as it is in heaven.' Surely no one can deny that Christ firmly believed that there are beings in heaven who do God's will, to say the least, far more perfectly than we do, since their obedience is the model to which we are constantly taught to pray that we may attain. Again, it was the outstanding feature of Judaism to push God aloof from men and the world, whereas Jesus brought God nearer to men, as a Father who takes a minute interest in all that concerns us. But if Jesus thus brought heaven nearer to man, He must, in the very act, have brought the occupants of heaven nearer, and must wish us to believe that they also are deeply interested in our welfare. There is no need that angels should *tell* God anything that concerns us. He knows already far more than they can tell. Those who object to the doctrine of angels because it interposes a barrier between our prayers and our Father's love, misunderstand Christ's teaching. His disclosure of the Fatherliness of God was meant to correct Judaism, in so far as it made angels the bearers of our prayers and the informants to God of our requirements. Those Christians also who approach God through angels contravene in this way Christ's teaching : and also His *example*, for in the garden He said to Peter (Mt 26[53]): 'I could pray the *Father*, and he would *send* . . . angels.' Christ's teaching and example both show that it is our duty and privilege to have direct intercourse with God in prayer and fellowship. But this is not to say that there is no room for the *ministry* of angels. We may still believe that angels are *sent* on errands of mercy. Indeed, we may well say to those who on this subject are of doubtful mind, as the writer of the Epistle to the Hebrews said : 'Are they not all ministering spirits, sent forth to do service on behalf of those who shall inherit salvation ? ' (1[14]). There is nothing at all in the Gospel doctrine of angels which is at variance with the religious needs of the most cultured among us. It may present difficulties to reason, as everything which is supernatural does ; but the heart of man which loves God must surely rejoice to think that the heavenly Father has also a 'family in heaven ' as on earth (Eph 3[15]). It must always find a responsive chord in the nature of men who allow the heart a place in their creed, to be told that there are beings who 'continually behold the face of our Father,' who are deeply interested in us (Mt 18[10]) ; that our penitence gives the angels joy (Lk 15[10]) ; that in our times of depression and anguish it may be our privilege to have 'an angel sent from heaven, strengthening ' us (Lk 22[43]), as in our times of gladness it is our privilege to 'give thanks to the Father from whom the whole family in heaven and earth is named ' (Eph 3[14f.]).

LITERATURE. — Articles on 'Angels' in Hastings' *DB* (by Davidson ; cf. also Extra Vol. p. 285 ff.), Schenkel's *Bibellexicon* (by Schenkel), Riehm's *HWB* (by Delitzsch), *Encyclopædia Britannica* (by Robertson Smith). For Jewish beliefs see *Jewish Encyclopedia*, vol. i. p. 583 ff. ; Edersheim, *Life and Times of Jesus*, vol. ii. Appendix xiii. ; Bousset, *Religion des Judenthums*, 313–325 ; Gfrörer, *Urchristenthum*, i. 352–378 ; Weber, *Jüdische Theologie*[2] (see Index *s.* 'Engel') ; Donehoo, *Apocryphal and Legendary Life of Christ* ; Schiefer, *Die religiösen und ethischen Anschauungen des IV Ezrabuches* ; Kohut, *Die Jüdische Angelologie*. On the general subject see Everling,

Die Paulinische Angelologie ; Latham, *The Service of Angels* ; Martensen, *Christian Dogmatics*, 127 ff. ; *Expositor*, First Series, viii. 409 ff. ; *Expository Times*, iii. 437, vi. 145, 193 ; Davidson, *Theology of OT*, 289–306 ; Beyschlag, *NT Theology*[2], i. 86 ff.

J. T. MARSHALL.

ANGER.—Anger is the instinctive resentment or reaction of the soul against anything which it regards as wrong or injurious. It is part of its equipment for self-preservation, and the promptitude and energy with which it comes into play are a fair measure of the soul's power to protect itself from the evil which is in the world. If there is not an instant and indignant repulsion of evil, it creeps into the apathetic soul, and soon makes it not only its victim but its instrument. The child's anger with the fire which burns him is in a sense irrational ; but one true meaning and purpose of anger in the moral world is illustrated by it. It is the vehement repulsion of that which hurts, and there is no spiritual, as there is no natural, life without it.

An instinct, however, when we come into the world of freedom and responsibility, always needs education ; and the radical character of the education required by the instinct of anger is apparent from the fact that the first thought of almost all men is that anger is a vice. Taking human nature as it is, and looking at the actual manifestations of anger, this is only too true. There is, as a rule, something vicious in them. They are self-regarding in a selfish way. Men are angry, as Aristotle puts it (*Ethics*, iv. 5. 7), on wrong grounds, or with the wrong people, or in a wrong way, or for too long a time. Their anger is natural, not spiritual ; selfish, not guided by consideration of principle ; the indulgence of a temper, not the staking of one's being for a cause. In the NT itself there are far more warnings against anger than indications of its true place and function. Yet when we read the Gospels with the idea of anger in our minds, we can easily see that justice is done to it both as a virtue and a vice. There is a certain arbitrariness in trying to systematize the teaching of Jesus on this or on any other subject, but most of the matter can be introduced if we examine (1) the occasions on which Jesus Himself is represented as being angry ; (2) those in which He expresses His judgment on moral questions with a vehemence which is undoubtedly inspired by indignation ; and (3) those in which He gives express teaching about anger.

1. *Occasions on which Jesus Himself is represented as being angry.*—(*a*) The most explicit is Mk 3[5] 'He looked round on them with anger (μετ' ὀργῆς), being grieved (συνλυπούμενος) over the hardening of their heart.' The objects of Christ's anger here are the people in the synagogue, who maintained an obstinate and prejudiced silence when He asked them, 'Is it lawful on the Sabbath day to do good or to do evil, to save life or to kill ?' What roused His anger was partly their inhumanity, which cared nothing for the disablement of the man with the withered hand, but even more, perhaps, the misrepresentation of God of which they were guilty, when in His honour (as they would have it) they justified inhumanity on the Sabbath day. To be inhuman themselves was bad enough, but to impute the same inhumanity to the Heavenly Father was far worse, and the indignation of Jesus was visible as He looked round on them. He passionately resented their temper, and repelled it from Him with vehemence, as injurious at once to God and to man. Yet His indignation was expressed in one indignant glance (περιβλεψάμενος, aorist), while it was accompanied by a deep pain, which did not pass away (συνλυπούμενος, present), over the hardening of their heart. This combination, in which resentment of wrong is accompanied with a grief which makes the

offender's case one's own, and seeks to win him by reaching the inner witness to God in his soul before insensibility has gone too far, is characteristic of Jesus, and is the test whether anger is Christian.

(*b*) The next occasion on which we see our Lord display an emotion akin to anger is found in Mk 10[13ff.]. He was 'moved with indignation' (RV ἠγανάκτησεν) when the disciples forbade the children to be brought to Him. The other instances in which the same word is used (Mk 10[41] 14[4], Mt 21[15], Lk 13[14]) show that a natural feeling of being hurt or annoyed is what the word specifically means. The disciples should have known Him better than to do what they did : they wronged Him in forbidding the approach of the children. Hence doctrines and practices which refuse to children, and to the intellectually and morally immature in general, their place and interest in the kingdom of God, are proper subjects of resentment. In one aspect of it, the kingdom of God is a protest against nature, and to enter into it we must be born again ; but in another, there is a real analogy between them ; the order of nature is constituted with a view to the order of grace ; man is made in God's image and for God, and it is his true nature to welcome God ; if the children are 'suffered,' and not forbidden, they will go to Jesus. They wrong God who deny this, and therefore the denial is to be resented.

(*c*) There is a striking passage in Luke (14[25ff.]), where, although anger is not mentioned, it is impossible not to feel that Jesus is speaking with a profound and even passionate resentment. 'Great multitudes followed with him, and he turned, and said to them, If any man cometh to me, and hateth not his father, and mother, and wife, and children, and brothers, and sisters, yea, and his own life also, he cannot be my disciple.' Jesus was on His way to die ; and it moved Him as an indignity, which He was entitled to resent, that on the very path to the cross He should be attended by a shallow throng who did not have it in them to do the slightest violence to themselves for the sake of the kingdom of God. The whole passage, in which the moral demands of discipleship are set at the highest, vibrates with indignation. To follow Christ is a great enterprise, like building a tower, or going to war ; it requires the painful sacrifice of the tenderest natural affections, the renunciation of the most valued possessions ; and when it is affected by people who have no moral salt in them—who could not win it from themselves to give up anything for God and His cause—the resentment of Jesus rises into scorn (v.[34f.]). With all His love for men, there was a kind of man whom He did not shrink from describing as 'good for nothing.'

(*d*) The last passage is that in which Jesus cleanses the Temple : Mk 11[15] and parallels. What stirred His indignation here was in part the profanity to which sacred places and their proper associations had lost all sacredness ; in part, the covetousness which on the pretext of accommodating the pilgrims had turned the house of prayer into a den of thieves ; in part, again, the inhumanity which, by instituting a market so noisy in the Court of the Gentiles, must have made worship for these less privileged seekers after God difficult, if not impossible. The text quoted in Jn 2[17] (Ps 69[9]), as remembered by the disciples in connexion with this event—'the zeal of thy house shall eat me up'—sums up as well as anything could do the one characteristic which is never wanting in the anger of Jesus, and which alone renders anger just. It is jealousy for God—the identification of oneself with His cause and interest on earth, especially as it is represented in human beings, and resentment of everything which does it wrong.*

2. *The occasions on which Jesus expresses His judgment on moral questions with a vehemence which is undoubtedly inspired by indignation.*— Every moral judgment, of course, contains feeling: it is not merely the expression of assent or dissent, but of consent or resentment. We are all within the moral world, not outside of it ; we cannot be spectators merely, but in every thought we are actors as well ; to deny this is to deny that there is a moral world at all. Hence all dissent is condemnation, and all condemnation, if real, is resentment ; but there are circumstances in which the condemnation is so emphatic that the resentment becomes vivid and contagious, and it is illustrations of this that we wish to find in the life of Jesus.

(*a*) The most conspicuous is perhaps that which we find in the passage on σκάνδαλα (Mt 18⁶ᶠ·). Jesus has taken a little child to rebuke the ambitious strife of the Twelve ; but ' these little ones who believe in me' are not children, but the disciples generally (cf. Mt 10⁴²). 'To make one of them stumble' (σκανδαλίζειν) is to perplex him, to put him out about Christ, to create misunderstanding and estrangement, such as we hear of for a time in the case of the Baptist (11²ᶠᶠ·) and the Nazarenes (13⁵⁷), and so to make his discipleship void. In a more general sense it means to mislead, or to be the cause that another falls into sin which his better conscience condemns. If we are to judge from His language, nothing ever moved Jesus to such passionate indignation as this. The sin of sins was that of leading others into sin, especially ' the little ones'—the weak, the untaught, the easily perplexed and easily misled—whose hearts were otherwise naturally right with Him. Every word in Jesus' sentence is laden with indignation : ' Better for him that a great millstone were hanged about his neck, and that he were drowned in the depth of the sea.' This anger of Jesus is exactly what is meant in the OT by ' the jealousy of God,' *i.e.* His love pledged to His own, and resenting with all the intensity of the Divine nature any wrong inflicted on them (cf. Zec 8²ᶠ·). Though anger is often sinful, the absence of anger may be due to the absence of love : and the man who can see the ' little ones' being made to stumble and who takes it quite coolly is very far from the kingdom of God.

(*b*) It is possibly an instance of this same indignation that we find in Mt 16²³. Peter tempts Jesus to decline the cross—in other words, tries to make Him stumble at the will of the Father ; and the indignant vehemence with which he is repelled —' Get thee behind me, Satan'—shows how real the temptation was, and how a prompt and decisive resentment is the natural security in such trials. We have a right and a duty to be angry with the tempter.

(*c*) In the answer of Jesus to the Sadducees in Mk 12²⁴ᶠᶠ· we have another light on what moved Him to indignation. In the scornful πολὺ πλανᾶσθε with which the discussion closes, resuming the πλανᾶσθε of v.²⁴, Jesus' resentment shines out. The question at issue, that of man's immortality, was a great and solemn question. It involved the whole character of God—what He was, and what in His power, His goodness, and His faithfulness He could and would do for the souls He had made

* In Mt 21³¹ Wellhausen adopts the reading ὁ ὕστερος instead of ὁ πρῶτος. This makes the Jews deride Jesus, instead of seriously answering Him ; and Wellhausen, taking it so, finds in the words which follow—' The publicans and the harlots go into the kingdom of God before you'—not an explanation of the parable, but a *Zornesausbruch*, an outburst of wrath, which could hardly be cleared of petulance (*Das Evangelium Matthæi*, 106 f.). O. Holtzmann's idea that Jesus cursed the fig-tree in a momentary fit of temper is only worth mentioning as a warning (see his *Leben Jesu*, p. 324).

in His own image. The Sadducees had tried to degrade it and make it ridiculous, and the indignation of Jesus is unmistakable. It is an example which justifies indignation with those who by unworthy controversial methods profane or render ridiculous subjects in which the dearest concernments of humanity are involved.

(*d*) To these passages may be added Jesus' denunciation of the Pharisees in Mt 23¹³ᶠᶠ·. The long series of woes is not merely a revelation of things which in the mind of Jesus are illegitimate, it is a revelation of the passionate resentment which these things evoke in Him. They are the things with which God is angry every day, and it is a sin in men if they can look at them without indignation. To keep people ignorant of religious truth, neither living by it ourselves, nor letting them do so (v.¹³) ; to make piety or the pretence of it a cloak for avarice (v.¹⁴, only introduced here from ‖ Mark) ; to raise recruits for our own faction on the pretext of enlisting men for the kingdom of God (v.¹⁵) ; to debauch the simple conscience by casuistical sophistries (vv.¹⁶⁻²²) ; to destroy the sense of proportion in morals by making morality a matter of law in which all things stand on the same level (v.²³ᶠ·) ; to put appearance above reality, and reduce life to a play, at once tragedy and farce (vv.²⁵⁻²⁸) ; to revive the spirit and renew the sins of the past, while we affect a pious horror of them, crucifying the living prophets while we build monuments to the martyred (v.²⁹ᶠᶠ·) : these are the things which made a storm of anger sweep over the soul of Jesus, and burst in this tremendous denunciation of His enemies. Yet it is entirely in keeping with the combination of ideas in Mk 3⁵ (μετ’ ὀργῆς . . . συνλυπούμενος) when the Evangelist attaches to this our Lord's lament over Jerusalem (v.³⁷ᶠᶠ·, cf. Lk 13³⁴ᶠ·). His anger does not extinguish His compassion, and if the city could be moved to repentance He would still gather her children together as a hen gathers her chickens under her wings.

Putting the whole of the passages together, and generalizing from them, we may infer that the two things in human conduct which moved Jesus most quickly and deeply to anger, were (1) inhumanity, wrong done to the needs or rights of men ; and (2) misrepresentation of God by professedly religious people, and especially by religious teachers. He stood in the world for the rights and interests, or, we may say, for the truth of God and of human nature ; and His whole being reacted immediately and vehemently against all that did wrong to either.

3. Something may further be learned from *the passages in which Jesus gives express teaching about anger.*—(*a*) The chief of these is Mt 5²¹⁻²⁷. Here our Lord interprets the sixth commandment for the citizens of the kingdom of God. It is not only the act of murder which is condemned, but the first movement of the passions which leads in that direction. 'He who murders shall be liable to the judgment? I tell you, every one who is angry with his brother shall be liable to the judgment.' The reading εἰκῆ (' without cause,' *temere*) is no doubt erroneous here ; but the introduction of it is rather a rhetorical than an exegetical blunder. As Tholuck observed, to bring in the idea that there is such a thing as lawful anger would only weaken the condemnation passed here upon such anger as men are familiar with in themselves and others ; but after what has been said under (1) and (2), it does not need to be proved that there is a place for anger in the Christian in the world in which we live. What Jesus condemns here is not any kind of anger, but anger with a brother, which forgets that he is a brother, and that we have a brother's duty to him ; the anger which leads straight to contemptuous and insulting words (the ῥακά and μωρέ of v.[22]), and ends in irreconcilable bitterness (v.[25f.]). Anger like this on the part of one Christian toward another is sin, and sin so deadly that no words could exaggerate the urgency of escape from it. No religious duty, not even the most sacred, can take precedence of the duty of reconciliation. If a man should be offering his gift at the altar—if he should actually be seated at the communion table with the communion cup in his hand, let him put it down, and go first, and get out of these angry relations with his brother, and then come and have fellowship with God (v.[23f.]). How can an angry man, with the temper of a quarrel in him, have communion with the God of peace? It is possible to raise casuistical questions in all such situations as are here supposed, but as these questions present themselves only to the spectators, not to the responsible actors, it is not worth while to raise them. The one duty insisted on here, as in the partly parallel passage in Mt 18[15-18], is the duty of placability. The person who has suffered the wrong—that is, who is in the right, who is entitled to be angry—is for that very reason to take the initiative in reconciliation, and to bear the expense of it. That is how God deals with us, who have offended Him, and that is how we are to deal with those who offend us. There is to be no anger in the sense of a selfish resentment into which the bad passions of unregenerate human nature can pour themselves; and the lawful anger of the soul, whose wrong is a wrong done to the kingdom of God, will pass away at once when he who has done the wrong is brought to repentance. The penitence and the resentment are the guilty and the innocent index of the reality of the wrong; and each is as inevitable as the other if the Christian life is to be morally sincere.

(b) It is natural to take account here of the passage on retaliation and non-resistance in Mt 5[38ff.]. Anger seems to be unconditionally precluded by such a saying as, 'Whosoever smiteth thee on the right cheek, turn to him the other also.' It is difficult to believe that any one was ever struck on the face unjustly (as is assumed in the connexion) without resenting it, and just as difficult to believe that it would be for the good of humanity or of the kingdom of God that it should be so. But Jesus, who came to abolish one literalism, did not come to institute another. His words are never to be read as statutes, but as appeals to conscience. What He teaches in this place is that there is no limit to be laid down beforehand beyond which love is no longer to regulate the conduct of His disciples. No provocation can be so insulting, no demand can be so unjust, so irrational, so exasperating, as that His disciples shall be entitled to cast love overboard, and meet the world with weapons like its own. Love must to all extremities be the supreme and determining principle in their conduct, the same love, with the same interests in view, as that of their Father in heaven (v.[45]); but no more in them than in Him does it exclude all manifestation of anger. What it does exclude is the selfish anger which is an alternative to love, not the Divine resentment which is a mode of love, and expresses its sense of the reality of wrong. If this died out of the world, society would swiftly rot to extinction; but the gospel, in the sense of the words, the example, and the spirit of Jesus, is so far from proscribing this that it is the greatest of all powers for keeping it alive. For those who have learned that where the spirit of the Lord is there is liberty, the literal interpretation of words like Mt 5[39-42] is a combination of pedantry and fanaticism which no genius will ever make anything else than absurd.

Echoes of the teaching of Jesus on anger are probably to be traced at various points in the teaching of the Apostles. E.g. in Ro 12, a chapter which often recalls the Sermon on the Mount, vv.[18-21] are entirely in the key of Mt 5[38ff.]. 'The wrath' of Ro 12[19], to which Christians are to leave room, is the wrath of God which will be revealed at the last day. God has reserved for Himself (ἐμοὶ ἐκδίκησις, ἐγὼ ἀνταποδώσω) the vindication of the wronged, and they are not to forestall Him or take His work out of His hands; in the day of wrath, when His righteous judgment is revealed, all wrongs will be rectified; meanwhile, as Christ teaches, love is to rule all our conduct, and we must overcome evil with good. It is perhaps with a vague recollection of Mt 5[23f.] that men are directed in 1 Ti 2[8] to pray χωρὶς ὀργῆς: an angry man cannot pray. Accordingly a bishop must not be ὀργίλος, given to anger, or of an uncontrollable temper (Tit 1[7]). Exhortations like those in Eph 4[31], Col 3[8], Ja 1[19], show that anger was known to the Church mainly in forms which the Christian conscience condemned. Ja 1[19] is particularly interesting, because it reminds us of the danger (in anger) of enlisting self in the service of God, calling on the old man to do what can be done only by the new: 'The wrath of *man* worketh not the righteousness of *God*.' But though it is difficult, it need not be impossible that the wrath which a man feels, and under the impulse of which he expresses himself, should be, not 'the wrath of man,' but a Divine resentment of evil. The words of Mt 18[6] or Mt 23[13ff.] fell from human lips, but they are the expression and the instrument of the jealousy of God. To be angry without sin is difficult for men, but it is a difficult duty (Eph 4[26]).

Apart from anything yet alluded to is the use of the verb ἐμβριμᾶσθαι to describe some kind of emotion in Jesus (Mk 1[43], Mt 9[30], Jn 11[33, 38]). Ordinarily the word conveys the idea of indignation which cannot be repressed; but this, though found elsewhere in the Gospels (e.g. Mk 14[5]), is not obviously appropriate in the passages quoted. In the first two it may be due to our Lord's consciousness of the fact that the persons on whom He had conferred a great blessing were immediately going to disregard His command to keep silent about it; the sense of this put something severe and peremptory into His tones. In the last two it has been explained as expressing Jesus' sense of the indignity of death; He resented, as something not properly belonging to the Divine idea of the world, such experiences as He was confronted with on the way to the grave of Lazarus. But this is precarious, and on the whole there is little stress to be laid on any inference we can draw from the use of ἐμβριμᾶσθαι in the Gospels.

LITERATURE.—Butler, *Sermons*, viii., ix.; Law, *Serious Call*, ch. xxi.; Seeley, *Ecce Homo*, chs. xxi.-xxiii.; Dale, *Atonement*[7], p. 338 ff.; *Expos. Times*, iv. [1893], pp. 256 ff., 492 ff.; *Expositor*, 1st ser. i. [1875], 133 ff.   JAMES DENNEY.

ANIMALS.—It cannot be said that animals play a very important part in the life and teaching of our Lord; yet the Gospel references cover a wider range than is usually imagined. The Evangelists use no fewer than 40 different Greek words denoting animals, and, apart from such general terms as 'birds of the air,' 'wild beasts,' and 'serpents,' they mention at least 20 particular kinds. The references may best be classified under the headings 'Domestic' and 'Wild.'

i. DOMESTIC ANIMALS.—**1.** The *beasts of burden* in Palestine in the time of our Lord were the ass and the camel. The horse is not mentioned in the Gospels, its use in the East being restricted to purposes of war. Thus the horse becomes prominent in the military imagery of the Apocalypse.

A general term for 'beast of burden' occurs in the parable of the Good Samaritan (Lk 10³⁴ κτῆνος). In Rev 18¹³ 'beasts of burden' are distinguished from horses. Josephus (Ant. IV. vi. 3) uses the word of asses in particular. In Ac 23²⁴ a 'beast' is provided to carry St. Paul to Cæsarea; in the NT therefore κτῆνος is clearly some 'beast of burden' which is not a horse. Probably the Good Samaritan rode on an ass, or possibly on a mule.

The **ass** is denoted by four other words in the Gospels, viz. πῶλος, ὀνάριον, ὄνος, and ὑποζύγιον. The animal on which our Lord made His triumphal entry into Jerusalem is described by all four Evangelists as a **colt** (πῶλος, Mt 21². ⁵. ⁷, Mk 11². ⁴. ⁵. ⁷, Lk 19³⁰. ³³. ³⁵, Jn 12¹⁵). The word is not used elsewhere in the Gospels, and in John it occurs only in the quotation from Zechariah. St. John describes the colt as ὀνάριον, a young ass. St. Matthew introduces the she-ass, the mother of the colt, into the story. In the Matthæan form of the quotation from Zechariah (Mt 21⁵) the mother ass is further described as a draught beast (ὑποζύγιον).

The meaning of this fulfilment of prophecy is well brought out by Chrysostom. Jesus entered Jerusalem riding on an ass, 'not driving chariots like the rest of the kings, not demanding tributes, not thrusting men off, and leading about guards, but displaying His great meekness even hereby' (Hom. 66 in Mt.).

The triumphal entry into Jerusalem is the only incident in the life of our Lord in which an ass is concerned; but in His teaching, as reported by St. Luke, there are two other references. The synagogue-ruler, who forbade people to come to be healed on the Sabbath, received the rebuke, 'Hypocrites, does not each one of you loose his ox or his ass (τὸν ὄνον) from the stall on the Sabbath and lead him away to watering?' (Lk 13¹⁵). On another occasion, with reference to the same question of Sabbath healing, our Lord asked, 'Which of you shall have an ass or an ox fallen into a well, and will not straightway draw him up on a Sabbath day' (Lk 14⁵).

The text of the latter passage is uncertain, the evidence of א and B being divided. B reads υἱός, adopted by Westcott and Hort; while א reads ὄνος, retained by the Revisers. Possibly neither is the correct text; but if we follow the Revisers, we may notice that on the only two occasions when the ass is mentioned in our Lord's teaching, it is coupled with the ox, as if to imply that the Jewish farmer took equal care of each. 'The ox, the ass, and the sheep are the (chief) domestic animals with which an Israelite household is provided' (O. Holtzmann).

The ass occupies a much more important place in the farm life of the East than his neglected descendant occupies in England to-day. The finer breeds are regularly used for riding, while the commoner breeds draw the plough and carry burdens. 'The ass is still the most universal of all beasts of burden in Bible lands' (Post, in Hastings' DB).

The **camel** (κάμηλος) figures in two sayings of our Lord which have a proverbial ring. (Thomson notes that the camel is still the subject of many Arabian proverbs). The three Synoptics record the saying, 'It is easier for a camel to pass through a needle's eye than for a rich man to enter the kingdom of God' (Mt 19²⁴, Mk 10²⁵, Lk 18²⁵). There is no need to stumble at the hyperbole involved in 'a needle's eye,' nor is it necessary to explain the phrase as a reference to a particularly small gate (see art. 'Camel' in Hastings' DB). The second reference is found in the denunciation of the Pharisees, who strain out a gnat while they gulp down a camel (Mt 23²⁴). A camel-caravan would be one of the sights of our Lord's boyhood, and the awkwardness of meeting a camel in the narrow street, which modern travellers experience, was not unknown nineteen hundred years ago. The camel must have been the largest animal with which our Lord was familiar, and in both sayings it is mentioned for its size.

The only other reference to the camel occurs in the description of the dress of John the Baptist, whose garment, like that of Elijah, was of camel's hair (Mt 3⁴, Mk 1⁶).

On this Sir Thomas Browne notes: 'a coarse garment, a cilicious or sackcloth garment, suitable to the austerity of his life—the severity of his doctrine, repentance—and the place thereof, the wilderness—his food and diet, locusts and wild honey.'

2. Of *larger cattle,** oxen, bulls, and calves find a place in the Gospels.

The **ox** (βοῦς) is mentioned three times in Luke, twice in connexion with the ass in the passages previously cited (Lk 13¹⁵ 14⁵), and again in the parable of the Great Supper, when one of the invited guests excuses himself on the ground that he has bought five yoke of oxen which need to be tested (Lk 14¹⁹). The ox was employed in the East for ploughing and threshing; it was also used for sacrifice, as appears from the only other passage in the Gospels where oxen are mentioned, viz. St. John's account of the cleansing of the Temple court. Sheep and oxen (Jn 2¹⁴f.) were driven out along with their vendors.

Bulls (ταῦροι) and **fat beasts** (σιτιστά) † are mentioned only in Mt 22⁴. They form samples of the rich dainties prepared for the marriage feast of the king's son, and illustrate the magnificent scale of the entertainment which those summoned to partake so insolently spurned. Similarly the **fatted calf** (ὁ μόσχος ὁ σιτευτός), which appears only in the parable of the Prodigal Son (Lk 15²³. ²⁷. ³⁰), indicates an unusual feast, made to celebrate an unusual joy. The fatted calf is contrasted with the kid, the customary repast, which Oriental hospitality provides to this day. The elder brother complains that he has never been allowed to offer his friends the entertainment which his father is wont to provide for any chance visitor; while for the graceless prodigal is killed the fatted calf, which is destined only for high festivals. The bulls and fatlings in the parable of the Marriage Feast, and the fatted calf in the parable of the Returning Prodigal, alike stand for the lavish generosity of God's love, which the Scribes and Pharisees could not appreciate, even when offered to themselves, the king's invited guests, much less when those prodigals, the publicans and sinners, were likewise embraced therein.

3. Of *smaller cattle,* goats and sheep are mentioned.

Goats (ἔριφος, ἐρίφιον, lit. 'kid,' a meaning retained in Lk 15²⁹; in LXX the word = 'goat' as well as 'kid') appear only in the picture of the Last Judgment (Mt 25³²f.), where they are contrasted with sheep. The point of the contrast lies in the colour rather than the character of the animals, the sheep being pure white, while the goats are covered with long jet-black hair. So in the Song of Solomon (4¹) the locks of the beloved are compared to 'a flock of goats that appear from Mt. Gilead.' The Son of Man shall separate all the nations 'as a shepherd separateth the sheep from the goats,' and the simile is quite true to pastoral life. Tristram (Nat. Hist. p. 89) says that sheep and goats pasture together, but never trespass on each other's domains; they are folded together, but they do not mix; they may be seen to enter the fold in company, but once inside they are kept separate.

The Syrian goat, *Capra mambrica*, is the most common breed in Palestine. It is distinguished by long pendant ears, stout recurved horns, and long black silky hair. Flocks of goats are most frequent in hilly districts from Hebron to Lebanon, where their habit of browsing on young trees tends to deforest the country.

---

* The word 'cattle' is used to tr. θρέμματα in Jn 4¹². The word is also found in the AV of Lk 177.

† Wyclif, following the Vulg. *altilia*, translates 'my volatilis (fowls)'; but fatted cattle are probably meant.

A **kid** (ἔριφος, some MSS ἐρίφιον) is mentioned in the parable of the Prodigal Son (Lk 15²⁹). The kid formed the ordinary dish at an Eastern feast, as lambs were preserved for the sake of wool, and were, as a rule, slain only in sacrifice. For the contrast between the kid and the fatted calf see above, s. 'fatted calf.' There is no other direct mention of the goat in the Gospels, though the wine-bottles (ἀσκοί) referred to in Mt 9¹⁷ (‖ Mk 2²², Lk 5³⁷ᶠ·) were doubtless made of goat-skin. These bottles were made by cutting off the head and legs, and drawing the carcass out by the neck, and then tying the neck, legs, and vent, and tanning the skin, with the hairy side out (Post, in Hastings' *DB* ii. 195).

The word for **sheep** (πρόβατον) is to be found in the Gospels no fewer than 36 times, while words connected with sheep, e.g. ποίμνη, ποίμνιον, 'a flock,' are not infrequent. Sheep were so often in the thoughts of Jesus that we have postponed fuller consideration of these passages to § iv.

Of the two words for **lamb**, one, ἀμνός, is applied only to our Lord, whom John the Baptist twice describes as 'the Lamb of God,' adding in one case 'which taketh away the sin of the world' (Jn 1²⁹· ³⁶). The title implies sacrifice.

Whether the Baptist was thinking of the Paschal lamb or of the lamb daily offered in the temple matters little. In Jesus he saw 'the reality of which all animal sacrifice was the symbol' (Marcus Dods). No doubt the patience of the lamb is implied in the title, as unfolded in Is 53⁷ 'as a lamb before its shearer is dumb, so he opened not his mouth.' The purity of the lamb, without spot and without fault, on which St. Peter dwells (1 P 1¹⁹), is also involved. But the idea of redemption through sacrifice is fundamental in the Baptist's words.

The second word for 'lamb' occurs in two forms, ἄρνας (acc. pl.) and ἀρνίον. The diminutive form is found only in Jn 21¹⁵, where our Lord bids Peter feed His lambs. 'Lambs' is used instead of 'sheep,' to bring out more strongly the appeal to care, and the consequent complete confidence in Peter (M. Dods). In the Apocalypse our Lord is called 'the Lamb' (τὸ ἀρνίον) no fewer than 27 times. The form ἄρνας is confined to Lk 10³ 'Behold, I send you forth as lambs into the midst of wolves.'

The parallel Mt 10¹⁶ reads 'sheep,' but the Lukan form is supported by Clement of Rome, *Ep.* ii. 5, 'Ye shall be as lambs (ἀρνία) in the midst of wolves. But Peter answered him, saying, If then the wolves tear the lambs in pieces? Jesus said to Peter, Let not the lambs fear the wolves, after they (the lambs) are dead.' Further support for the reading 'lambs' may perhaps be derived from Justin's casual description of Marcionites as lambs torn by wolves (ἄρνες συνηρπασμένοι, *Apol.* c. 58).

4. *Poultry* were kept in Palestine in the time of our Lord, as is clear from the references to the **cock** (ἀλέκτωρ) and the **hen** (ὄρνις). If we except the mention of cock-crow (see sep. art.) in Mk 13³⁵, the cock appears only in the story of Peter's denial, and our Lord's prediction of it (Mt 26³⁴· ⁷⁴ᶠ·, Mk 14³⁰ ⁽⁶⁸⁾· ⁷², Lk 22³⁴· ⁶⁰ᶠ·, Jn 13³⁸ 18²⁷). The hen (ὄρνις) affords a simile in the lament over Jerusalem. 'How often would I have gathered thy children together, as a hen gathereth her chickens (Lk. 'her brood') under her wings!' (Mt 23³⁷, Lk 13³⁴). The action by which the hen gives rest and protection to the chickens under the shelter of her wings is too well known to need comment. The tenderness of the simile witnesses to the love of Jesus for His own countrymen, and His longing to avert national disaster. The words used for 'chickens' and 'brood' (νοσσίον and νοσσιά) are found here only, though a word from the same root is employed in the phrase 'two young pigeons' (νοσσοὺς περιστερῶν, Lk 2²⁴).

5. To the list of domestic animals we may add dogs and swine, which were classed together as unclean.

Dogs (κύνες) are mentioned twice. In the Sermon on the Mount the disciples are warned not to give that which is holy to dogs (Mt 7⁶). The pariah dogs that infest Eastern towns, and have to be cleared off periodically with poison, are 'a lean, mangy, and sinister brood,' acting as scavengers and living on offal. Naturally these animals do not possess a fastidious palate, and their manner of life is disgusting enough to justify the Jews' contempt for them. To call a man a dog is throughout the Bible a customary form of abuse. These wild dogs, says Tristram (*Nat. Hist.* p. 80), were the only dogs known in Palestine, with the exception of the Persian greyhound; and though they could be trained enough to act as watch-dogs for the sheep-folds,* they hardly became companions to man [the dog of To 5¹⁶ 11⁴ is altogether an exceptional case]. To the Jew the dog was a very fitting symbol of the man who had depraved his moral and spiritual taste by evil living. In the *Didache*, 'Give not that which is holy to dogs' is interpreted to mean, Do not administer the Eucharist to the unbaptized; but the principle involved in the text is capable of wider application. A Christian is not required to wear his heart on his sleeve! In the parable of Dives and Lazarus it is said that these street-dogs came and licked the beggar's sores (Lk 16²¹). This is an aggravation rather than an alleviation of Lazarus' suffering. It shows his destitute and defenceless condition, that he could not even keep the dogs away! A diminutive form of κύων, viz. κυνάριον, occurs in the story of the Syro-Phœnician woman. 'It is not right,' said the Master, 'to take the children's bread and cast it to dogs.' 'Yea, Lord,' replied the woman, 'yet the dogs eat of the crumbs that fall from their masters' table' (Mt 15²⁷ᶠ·, Mk 7²⁷ᶠ·). Bochart treats the diminutive κυνάριον as doubling the contempt inherent in the word. But it is clear from the woman's reply that the dogs in question are kept within the house; they are household pets. Tristram says that he found no difficulty in making a pet of a puppy taken from among the pariah dogs (*Nat. Hist.* p. 80). Probably the κυνάρια were puppies which had been taken into Jewish households as pets in a similar way. The word is not intended to add to the harshness of our Lord's saying; the woman saw in it her ground for appeal.

Swine (χοῖρος, not ὗς) appear in the story of the Gadarene demoniac (Mt 8³⁰ᶠᶠ·, Mk 5¹¹ᶠᶠ·, Lk 8³²ᶠ·). 'The fact that swine were kept in Palestine at all is evidence of the presence of the foreigner ' (O. Holtzmann). Cf. Lv 11⁷, Dt 14⁸, Is 65⁴. The country on the east side of the Lake was much under Gentile influence. The Prodigal Son is put to tend swine. The nature of the task is evidence at once of the difference between his home and the far country, and of the want and degradation into which he has fallen (Lk 15¹⁵ᶠ·) The only further reference to swine is the saying, 'Cast not your pearls before swine' (Mt 7⁶), in which our Lord emphasizes the necessity of tact in religious work.

ii. WILD ANIMALS.—**1.** θηρίον, the general word for *wild beast*, is found in the Gospels only once. Mk 1¹³ tells us that during the Temptation our Lord was with the wild beasts. Thomson says that 'though there are now no lions (in Palestine), wolves, leopards, and panthers still prowl about the wild wadys' (*Land and Book*, 'Central Palestine,' p. 594). 'In the age of Jesus, the chief beast of prey in Palestine was, as to-day, the jackal. Mark's addition indicates Jesus' complete severance from human society' (O. Holtzmann, *Life of Jesus*, p. 143 f.).

The word θηρίον is now to be found in the second of the five new Sayings recently recovered by Messrs. Grenfell and Hunt: 'The birds of the air and whatever of the beasts are on the earth or under it are they who draw us into the kingdom.'

---

* It would be truer to say that the pariah dogs have degenerated from the sheep-dogs than that the latter have developed from the former.

ANIMALS

ANIMALS 65

Here the word is not confined to 'beasts of prey'; it stands for the whole kingdom of wild animals. There is a similar use of the word in a saying of our Lord as given by Justin Martyr: 'Be not anxious as to what ye shall eat or what ye shall put on: are ye not much better than the birds and the beasts?' (1 *Apol.* 15). These considerations support the conclusion that St. Mark's addition does not imply physical danger, but is rather intended to suggest that our Lord was alone with Nature.

Two beasts of prey mentioned by name in the Gospels are the fox (ἀλώπηξ) and the wolf (λύκος). The **fox**, which has at least a hole to live in, is contrasted with the homeless Son of Man (Mt 8²⁰, Lk 9⁵⁸). In Lk 13³² our Lord speaks of Herod as 'that fox.' The cunning and perhaps the cowardice of the animal are the basis of the comparison. 'The name,' says O. Holtzmann, 'must have been given to Herod because he was inimical, yet, not daring to make any open attack, timidly prowled about until he found an opportunity to murder in secret' (*Life of Jesus*, p. 364).

The **wolf** is mentioned only in connexion with or in contrast to sheep. The wolf is the chief enemy against which the shepherd has to guard his flock. 'A single wolf,' says Tristram, 'is far more destructive than a whole pack of jackals' (*Nat. Hist.* p. 153). Eastern shepherds employ dogs (if they employ them at all) not to help in herding the sheep, but to ward off wolves. In contrast to the hireling, the Good Shepherd faces the wolf even at the risk of his life (Jn 10¹²). False prophets are wolves in sheep's clothing (Mt 7¹⁵). The contrast between outward profession and inward character could not be more vividly expressed. The same antithesis is used by our Lord to portray the contrast between the Church and the world, between the patient non-resistance of the one and the brutal violence of the other. The disciples are sent forth as sheep (Lk. as lambs) into the midst of wolves (Mt 10¹⁶, Lk 10³).

2. The general term for *wild birds* is τὰ πετεινά, '**the birds**,' often τὰ πετεινὰ τοῦ οὐρανοῦ, 'the birds of heaven.' They are mentioned in the Sermon on the Mount: 'Consider the birds: they do not sow, nor reap, nor gather into barns' (Mt 6²⁶; in the parallel passage, Lk 12²⁴, the reading is κόρακας, 'ravens,' which, however, are themselves called πετεινά at the end of the verse). Dean Stanley says that the birds most in evidence round the Sea of Galilee are partridges and pigeons. Finches and bulbuls are also abundant, according to Thomson. For the doctrine of providence involved in this and similar sayings of our Lord, we must refer our readers to § iv. Like the foxes, the birds are contrasted with the Son of Man; they have nests, while He hath not where to lay His head (Mt 8²⁰, Lk 9⁵⁸). The birds appear in the parable of the Sower, where they pick up the seed that falls by the wayside (Mt 13⁴, Mk 4⁴, Lk 8⁵). No doubt the fields round the lake, with the birds busy upon them, could be seen from the place where Jesus stood to teach the people. Probably the parable was spoken early in the year. The parable of the Mustard Seed also introduces the birds, which come and lodge in the branches of the full-grown tree (Mt 13³², Mk 4³², Lk 13¹⁹). Here the imagery seems to be drawn from Dn 4¹². ²¹, where the kingdom of Nebuchadrezzar is likened to a tree 'upon whose branches the birds of the heavens had their habitations.' Daniel interprets the tree to represent the greatness of Nebuchadrezzar's dominion, which is to reach to the end of the earth. The description in the parable carries with it the same implication with regard to the kingdom of heaven. There is one other reference to 'the birds' in Lk 12²⁴ 'How much better are ye than the birds!'

The following particular wild birds are mentioned in the Gospels:—dove (pigeon), eagle, raven, sparrow, turtle-dove.

VOL. I.—5

In all four Gospels the **dove** appears as the symbol of the Holy Ghost at our Lord's Baptism. In Mt 3¹⁶ the vision of the Holy Ghost descending in the form of a dove (ὡσεὶ περιστεράν) seems to have been granted to all present at the Baptism. In Mk 1¹⁰ and Lk 3²² the vision is apparently addressed more especially to Jesus Himself. In Jn 1³² it is a sign given to John the Baptist. In the story of the Creation, a metaphor from bird-life is employed to describe the Spirit of God fluttering (RVm 'brooding') over the waters (Gn 1²). The same Spirit rests on the Saviour with whom begins God's new creation. But the mention of the dove naturally carries us back to the story of the Flood (Gn 8¹¹). For Jesus the dove with olive-leaf after the Flood is the emblem of the Spirit (A. B. Bruce in *Expositor's Greek Testament*, on Mt 3¹⁶). The Holy Ghost in the form of a dove typifies the hope of the gospel, peace between man and God. In cleansing the Temple-court our Lord came upon them that sold doves for sacrifice. It is to these dove-sellers that the words in Jn 2¹⁶ are addressed, 'Take these things hence.' The cattle can be driven out: the doves must be carried out. This detail, which is perfectly natural, is recorded only in John, who consequently mentions 'doves' twice (Jn 2¹⁴. ¹⁶), while Matthew and Mark have only one reference each (Mt 21¹², Mk 11¹⁵).

The word περιστερά is used in the LXX where the EV reads '**pigeon**' as well as where it reads 'dove.' The same bird is probably meant by the two English words. But in the directions for sacrifice in Leviticus, the word 'pigeon' is regularly used, and in Lk 2²⁴ περιστερά is translated 'pigeon,' though elsewhere in the Gospels it is rendered 'dove.' In Lv 12⁸ a poor woman, 'if she be not able to bring a lamb, shall bring two turtles or two young pigeons.' The mother of Jesus brings the poor woman's sacrifice.

To the ancients the dove symbolized purity (Aristotle mentions the chastity of the dove), and this fact perhaps made birds of this class suitable for sacrifice. The only other reference to the dove in the Gospels is found in Mt 10¹⁶, where the disciples are bidden to be as pure (ἀκέραιοι) as doves, a command which St. Paul echoes in Ro 16¹⁹ and Ph 2¹⁵.

The **turtle-dove** (τρυγών) is mentioned only in the quotation from Lv 12⁸ in Lk 2²⁴. There are three species of turtle-doves in Palestine. The collared turtle (*T. risorius*) is the largest, and frequents the shores of the Dead Sea. The palm turtle (*T. Senegalensis*) 'resorts much to the gardens and enclosures of Jerusalem.' 'It is very familiar and confiding in man, and is never molested.' The common turtle (*T. auritus*) is the most abundant of the three species.

The **eagle** (ἀετός) is the subject of a proverbial saying recorded in Mt 24²⁸ ‖ Lk 17³⁷ 'where the carcass is, there shall the eagles be gathered together.' According to Post, there are four kinds of vultures and eight kinds of eagles to be found in the Holy Land. Here the term 'eagle' is generic. Thomson describes the eagles' flight as majestic, and their eyesight and, apparently, sense of smell, are both extremely keen.

The exact force of the above saying is hard to determine. Some old commentators, following the Fathers, take it to refer to 'the conflux of the godly to the light and liberty of the Gospel' (Master Trapp). More modern exegesis regards the passage as hinting at the gathering of the Roman eagles round the moribund Jewish nation. But Bengel rightly observes that in Mt 24 the reference of v.²⁸ goes back to the false prophets and false Christs of v.²³. In the decay of Judaism as a religious faith, such men will find their opportunity, and will turn popular fanaticism to their own profit. In Matthew the proverb is perfectly general in form, and is capable of wider application. National ruin and feverish religiosity go hand in hand. False Messianism marked the final overthrow of the Jews in A.D. 135; and when the barbarians laid siege to Rome in 408, even a Pope consented to resort to Etruscan magic rites! (Milman, *Latin*

Christianity, i. 126). In Lk 17³⁷ the 'wheresoever' becomes 'where,' and the saying is in answer to a definite question regarding the signs that are to mark the sudden return of the Son of Man. Here it is difficult to interpret the eagles of the Roman standards. For St. Luke evidently does not take the saying as a statement of a general law. The Matthæan form and position give the more attractive interpretation.

The **raven** (κόραξ) is mentioned only in Lk 12²⁴, 'Consider the ravens how they neither sow nor reap.' The parallel Mt 6²⁶ reads, 'birds.' The whole passage and the force of Luke's change will be considered in § iv. The term 'raven' includes the numerous tribes of crows. Tristram mentions eight different species as common in Palestine. God's care for the ravens is twice mentioned in OT (Job 38⁴¹, Ps 147⁹). These passages may have influenced Luke, if he changed 'birds' into 'ravens.' Again, they may have been in the mind of our Lord, if Luke gives the original form of the saying.

The **sparrow** (στρουθίον) is twice mentioned in sayings recorded both in Matthew and Luke. In Mt 10²⁹ we read, 'Are not two sparrows sold for a farthing?' and in Lk 12⁶ 'Are not five sparrows sold for two farthings?' In Tatian's *Diatessaron* the words *in taberna*, 'in the cookshop,' are added. Doubtless we have here the prices current in popular eating-houses in the time of our Lord. 'Sparrows, two a farthing; five a halfpenny.' In Mt 10²¹ and Lk 12⁷ our Lord adds, 'Ye are much more worth than many sparrows.' For a discussion of these references to sparrows and of their bearing on our Lord's teaching, we must again refer our readers to § iv.

3. For *fish*, three words are used, ἰχθύς, ἰχθύδιον, and ὀψάριον. The latter term is confined to John. In the feeding of the five thousand, the Synoptics speak of 'two fishes' (δύο ἰχθύας, Mt 14¹⁷. ¹⁹, Mk 6³⁸. ⁴¹. ⁴³, Lk 9¹³. ¹⁶). The parallel narrative in John reads δύο ὀψάρια, which is also translated 'two fishes' (Jn 6⁹. ¹¹). But while the Syn. ἰχθύς is a general term, ὀψάριον, says Edersheim, 'refers, no doubt, to those small fishes (probably a kind of sardine) of which millions were caught in the lake, and which, dried and salted, would form the most common savoury, with bread, for the fisher-population along the shore' (*Life and Times of Jesus the Messiah*, i. 682). The parable of the Drag-net (Mt 13⁴⁷⁻⁵⁰) is taken from the life of the Galilæan fisherfolk. But this definite meaning of ὀψάριον cannot always be maintained: for in John's narrative of the miraculous draught of fishes, ὀψάριον and ἰχθύς are interchanged as equivalents (ὀψάριον, Jn 21⁹. ¹⁰. ¹³; ἰχθύς, vv.⁶. ⁸. ¹¹). Jesus says to the disciples, 'Bring of the fish (ὀψαρίων) which ye have now caught. Simon Peter went up, and dragged the net to shore full of great fishes' (ἰχθύων). Both in the narratives of the miraculous multiplication of loaves and fishes and in His post-resurrection appearance by the lake, our Lord makes use of the disciples' own resources, while adding to them something of His own. In the similar miracle recorded in Lk 5, ἰχθύς is the word used (vv.⁶. ⁹). When narrating the feeding of the four thousand, both Matthew and Mark speak of a few small fishes (ὀλίγα ἰχθύδια, Mt 15³⁴, Mk 8⁷). These are probably the same as the ὀψάρια of Jn 6. In Mt 15³⁶ ἰχθύς reappears. The remaining references to fish do not require much comment. Mt 17²⁷ is concerned with the stater in the fish's mouth. This passage contains the only reference to line-fishing in the Gospels : 'Cast a hook and take the first fish (ἰχθύν) that cometh up.' In Lk 24⁴² we read that our Lord convinced the disciples of the reality of His resurrection by eating before them a piece of cooked fish (ἰχθύος ὀπτοῦ μέρος). In Mt 7¹⁰ ‖ Lk 11¹¹ the word ἰχθύς, 'fish,' is found in the teaching of Jesus. In Matthew the passage runs thus : 'What man is there among you who, if his son ask for bread, will give him a stone? or if he ask for fish, will give him a serpent?' Here fish and bread are the subject of joint reference, as in the narratives of the feeding of the five and four thousands. Bread and fish are clearly the customary diet of the common people of Galilee, and in the form of these questions, as in so many other details, the teaching of Jesus closely reflects the daily life of His countrymen.

In the Catacombs the figure of a fish was often used as a symbol of Christ. The letters which make up ἰχθύς form the initial letters of Ἰησοῦς Χριστὸς Θεοῦ Υἱὸς Σωτήρ, so that the word served as a summary of the faith. See art. CHRIST IN ART.

4. The general word for *serpent* (ὄφις) occurs 7 times in the Gospels. No human father will give his son a serpent as a substitute for fish (Mt 7¹⁰, Lk 11¹¹). Some small reptile as common as the scorpion must be meant, as Luke twice (10¹⁹ 11¹²) couples scorpions and serpents (ὄφεις). The disciples are to be as wise as serpents [or 'as the serpent,' reading ὁ ὄφις for οἱ ὄφεις : the sense is the same in either case] (Mt 10¹⁶). The ideal of discipleship is a combination of the prudence of the serpent with the guilelessness of doves. As in the saying about not casting one's pearls before swine, our Lord here condemns recklessness and tactlessness in religious work. 'Religion without policy is too simple to be safe : Policy without religion is too subtle to be good' (Trapp). In Mt 23³³ the word 'serpents' is applied to the Pharisees.

In the later appendix to Mark's Gospel, power to take up serpents is numbered among the signs that are to follow faith in Christ (16¹⁸). The passage is paralleled in Lk 10¹⁹ 'Behold, I have given you power to tread upon serpents and scorpions, and upon all the might of the evil one.' WH here note a reference to Ps 91¹³ 'Thou shalt tread upon the lion and the adder.' Possibly the passage is to be interpreted metaphorically, and the 'serpents' are to be explained by the might of the Evil One. The words, however, find a more literal fulfilment in St. Paul's experience at Melita (Ac 28³· ⁶).

The **viper** (ἔχιδνα) is referred to only in the phrase γεννήματα ἐχιδνῶν, 'offspring of vipers,' and the phrase is applied only to scribes and Pharisees. John the Baptist thus addressed the Pharisees that came to his baptism, 'O offspring of vipers, who hath warned you to flee from the wrath to come?' (Mt 3⁷, Lk 3⁷). According to Mt., our Lord on two occasions adopted the same mode of address (Mt 12³⁴ 23³³). Sand-vipers about 1 foot long are common in Palestine. The young are said to feed upon the mother. But the force of the phrase, Bochart observes, is not to be derived from any such special characteristic; the sense implied is simply 'bad sons of bad fathers.' This comment satisfactorily interprets Mt 23³³ : but perhaps we may read a little more into the phrase. The words of John the Baptist suggest the familiar picture of vipers roused from torpor into activity by the approach of heat (cf. Ac 28³). In Mt 12³⁴ the phrase receives added point from the fact that the Pharisees have just been attempting to poison the popular mind against Christ by suggesting that the miracles were the work of Beelzebub ; there is something spiteful and venomous about their attacks on our Lord.

5. Scorpions (σκορπίος), which we are told may be found under every third stone in Palestine, are twice mentioned in Luke. The disciples are to tread on scorpions with impunity (Lk 10¹⁹). However we interpret the passage, the addition of 'scorpion' seems to imply that the disciples are to be protected against some small, frequent, and at the same time serious danger. The other reference is in Lk 11¹². If a son asks for an egg, the father will not give him a scorpion. In both passages the scorpion and the serpent are mentioned together, being common objects of the country in Palestine. The scorpion at rest is said closely to resemble an egg in appearance.

6. The **worm** (σκώληξ) is mentioned only in Mk 9[48] in the phrase ' where their worm dieth not,' a description of Gehenna based on the last verse of Isaiah (66[24]).

In the TR the verse appears 3 times, Mk 9[44. 46. 48], and there is something impressive in the repetition : WH, however, retain only 9[48]. Whether literally or metaphorically understood, the phrase must not be taken as the basis of a Christian doctrine of future retribution. The worm does not stand for remorse : it is simply part of a picture of complete physical corruption. A man has sometimes to choose between losing a limb and losing his life : the part has to be sacrificed to save the whole. The same law of sacrifice, says Christ, holds good in the spiritual world.

7. Of *insects* the bee is indirectly referred to, while the gnat, the locust, and the moth are all mentioned. In Lk 24[42], the Western Text says the disciples gave our Lord part of a **bees'** honeycomb (ἀπὸ μελισσίου κηρίον), *i.e.* the product of hived bees. John the Baptist, on the other hand, lived on wild rock honey, *i.e.* honey deposited in clefts of the rock by wild bees ; this honey was often very difficult to get.

Bees, wild and hived, are very common in Palestine. Tristram (*Nat. Hist.* p. 325) says : ' Many of the Bedouin obtain their subsistence by bee-hunting, bringing into Jerusalem skins and jars of the wild honey on which John the Baptist fed.' Bee-keeping is much practised, especially in Galilee. The hives are very simple in construction ; being ' large tubes of sun-dried mud, about 8 inches in diameter and 4 feet long, closed with mud at each end, having only a small aperture in the centre.'

The **gnat** (κώνωψ) is mentioned in Mt 23[24]. As one of the smallest animals, it is contrasted with the camel, one of the largest. The Pharisees strain out a gnat with scrupulous care, while they will swallow a camel. They are careful to tithe mint, but they fail to do justice. The Pharisees may have adopted a practice which is still in use among the Brahmans, viz. of drinking through muslin in order to avoid swallowing any fly or insect present in the water.

Locusts (ἀκρίδες) formed part of the food of John the Baptist (Mt 3[4], Mk 1[6]). The LXX uses ἀκρίς for the third of the four kinds of edible locusts mentioned in Lv 11[22]. They formed a common article of diet in Palestine, and there is no need to alter the text, as one or two MSS have done, reading ἐγκρίδες, ' cakes.'

The **moth** (σής) is mentioned as disfiguring earthly treasures (Mt 6[19. 20], Lk 12[33]). The common clothes-moth is meant, of which there are many species in Palestine. ' In this warm climate it is almost impossible to guard against their ravages ' (Post). There is an indirect reference to the saying of Jesus in Ja 5[2].

8. A **sponge** (σπόγγος) full of vinegar was offered to our Lord on the cross (Mt 27[48]). Of sponges, the finest in texture and the most valued is the Turkish or Levant sponge. The sponge-fisheries of the Mediterranean have always been and still are very considerable. For the method of diving for sponges see Post in Hastings' *DB* iv. 612[b].

iii. THE PLACE OF ANIMALS IN THE LIFE OF OUR LORD.—In this connexion it may be worth while to point out that the part played by animals in many of the incidents in which their presence is recorded, serves to emphasize the humility of Jesus. The two young pigeons which Mary brings as an offering when she presents Jesus in the Temple (Lk 2[24]), are a mark of her poverty. Jesus belonged to a poor family. The peaceful character of Christ's teaching, which is marked at the outset by the descent of the dove at His baptism, is confirmed at the close by the fact that He rode into Jerusalem (Mt 21[2-7]||) not on the warrior's horse, but on the ass, which, as prophecy foretold, was to be a sign of the lowliness of the coming Messiah.

iv. THE PLACE OF ANIMALS IN THE TEACHING OF OUR LORD.—We have reserved for discussion under this head the imagery drawn from pastoral life in which Jesus described His own mission, and the doctrine of providence unfolded more especially in His sayings about the birds of the air.

1. *Our Lord's mission illustrated.*—(*a*) Jesus confined His earthly ministry to ' the lost sheep of the house of Israel ' (Mt 15[24]). When He sent forth the Twelve on a preaching tour, He bade them observe the same limits (Mt 10[6]). We need not suppose from this phrase that the work of Jesus embraced only the outcasts of Israel. ' The lost sheep of the house of Israel ' describes the nation as a whole [grammatically the words ' of the house of Israel ' (οἴκου 'I.) are best taken as a defining genitive, *i.e.* ' the lost sheep who are the house of Israel ']. The very sight of a Galilæan crowd touched the heart of Jesus, for they were like worried and scattered sheep that have no shepherd (Mt 9[36], Mk 6[34]). In the eyes of Jesus, the spiritual condition of His countrymen agreed with the description of the shepherdless people given in Ezk 34. More particularly the Jews needed guidance in their national and religious aspirations. They had mistaken alike the character of the coming Messiah and the nature of the coming kingdom. The hope to re-establish by force the throne of David made the people the helpless victims of political agitators like Judas the Gaulonite (Ac 5[37]), and led at length to the chastisement inflicted on the nation by the Roman power.

The exact interpretation of Jn 10 is exceedingly difficult, but it may in part be understood, in relation to this view given in Matthew and Mark, of the nation as a shepherdless flock. Jesus speaks of Himself as the door of the sheep, through which if a man enters, he shall be saved (vv.[7. 9]). The only hope of salvation for the Jews lay in their realizing, through the teaching of Jesus, that God's kingdom was not of this world. Those who offered themselves as leaders before Christ, and who proposed to subdue Rome by arms, were thieves and robbers who came only to steal and destroy (vv.[8. 10]). The best comment on these thieves and robbers, and their treatment of those helpless sheep, the house of Israel, is perhaps Josephus' account of the Judas above mentioned—

'There was one Judas a Gaulonite, . . . who, taking with him Sadduc, a Pharisee, became zealous to draw (the people) to a revolt ; who both said that this taxation (under Cyrenius) was no better than an introduction of slavery, and exhorted the nation to assert their liberty ; as if they could procure them happiness and security for what they possessed, and an assured enjoyment of a still greater good, which was that of the honour and glory they would thereby acquire for magnanimity. . . . All sorts of misfortunes also sprang from these men, and the nation was infected with this doctrine to an incredible degree : one violent war came upon us after another, and we lost our friends, who used to alleviate our pains ; *there were also very great robberies and murders of our principal men. This was done in pretence of the public welfare, but in reality from the hopes of gain to themselves*' (Jos. *Ant.* XVIII. i. 1).

If Barabbas was one of these robbers (cf. Jn 18[40] with 10[8]), the fact that the Jews chose Barabbas in preference to the Good Shepherd shows the bewilderment of the popular mind, which led Jesus to compare the house of Israel to lost sheep. Jesus further describes Himself as the Good Shepherd in contrast to the hirelings, who care nothing for the sheep (Jn 10[11. 15]). If the thieves and robbers betoken political agitators like Barabbas and Judas, ' the hirelings ' are probably the Pharisees and Sadducees, the shepherds who, in the words of Ezekiel, ' fed themselves and did not feed the sheep.'

The interpretation here suggested is not usually adopted. Godet, for example, understands the thieves and robbers to be the Pharisees. The wolf (v.[12]) he takes as a further symbol of the same party, the hirelings being the scribes and priests, whom cowardice kept from opposing Pharisaic domination. This latter interpretation fits in well with the context, *i.e.* with ch. 9 (see Godet, *St. John*, vol. ii. pp. 375–397).

But without attempting to decide questions of exposition, it is sufficient for us to point out that the imagery of the parable is true to life.

'A **sheep-fold** in the East is not a covered building like our stables, but a mere enclosure surrounded by a wall or palisade. The sheep are brought into it in the evening, several flocks being generally assembled within it. The shepherds, after committing them to the care of a common keeper, a **porter**, who is charged with their safe keeping during the night, retire to their homes. In the morning they return, and knock at the closely barred door of the enclosure, which the porter opens. They then separate each his own sheep, by calling them: and after having thus collected their flocks, lead them to the pastures. As to robbers, it is by scaling the wall that they penetrate into the fold' (Godet, *l.c.* p. 378).

The details are confirmed by all Eastern travellers. Thus, speaking of the power of the sheep in distinguishing between the voice of the shepherd and that of a stranger, Thomson tells us that, if a stranger calls, they stop, lift up their heads in alarm; and if the call is repeated, they turn and flee from him. 'This is not the fanciful costume of a parable, but a simple fact. I have made the experiment often' ('Central Palestine,' p. 594).

Godet cites 'the well-known anecdote of a Scotch traveller, who, meeting under the walls of Jerusalem a shepherd bringing home his flock, changed garments with him, and thus disguised proceeded to call the sheep. They, however, remained motionless. The true shepherd then raised his voice, when they all hastened towards him, in spite of his strange garments' (*l.c.* p. 382).

All the sheep distinguish the voice of a shepherd from that of a stranger: a shepherd's own sheep distinguish his voice from that of any other shepherd (v.³). The practice of naming sheep (φωνεῖ κατ' ὄνομα, v.³) is common in the East. The picture of the shepherd thrusting his sheep out of the enclosure (ἐκβάλῃ, v.⁴, implies the use of a certain amount of force) and then placing himself at the head of the flock, is likewise a simple fact, and not fanciful imagery.

Though the historical application of the parable in Jn 10 is not easy to determine, yet it is clear that the chapter deals with the relation of Christ to the Church and to the individual Christian, and it is unnecessary to draw out in detail the lessons that follow from the fact that Christ is for us the door of the sheep and the Good Shepherd. It is, however, important to notice that in Jn 10 our Lord speaks of the Jewish nation as a whole and of His disciples alike as sheep ('his own sheep,' *i.e.* the disciples, are distinguished from the other flocks in the fold, *i.e.* the Jewish people), and that He compares His mission towards both to the work of a shepherd. These ideas are common to St. John and the Synoptists, and the pastoral imagery we are considering links the Fourth Gospel to the other three.

(*b*) We have seen that in the Synoptics our Lord spoke of the people as lost sheep. But though the Matthæan phrase 'the lost sheep of the house of Israel' applies to the nation as a whole, the parable of the Lost Sheep in Mt 18¹²ᶠ· is a defence of Christ's view of children, and in Lk 15³⁻⁶ (where alone in Luke the word πρόβατον is used) a similar parable forms an answer to the criticism of the Pharisees, who could not understand our Lord's eating with publicans and sinners. In a sense all the Jews were like lost sheep; in a very special sense the comparison applied to these social outcasts. 'No animals are more helpless than sheep that have strayed from the flock: they become utterly bewildered, for sheep are singularly destitute of the bump of locality. They have to be brought back' (Thomson). The figure of the lost sheep illustrates to some extent the character of the publicans and sinners. In the East, says Thomson, the sheep have to be taught to follow

the shepherd: they would otherwise leave the pasture lands and stray into the corn-fields. Naturally some sheep follow the shepherd closely, while others straggle and have to be recalled to the path by means of the crook. So a lost and wandering sheep is an ill-trained and troublesome one. But the main point of the parable is the action of the shepherd, who would regard it as part of his ordinary duty to seek the lost. Though Jesus does not call Himself the Good Shepherd in the Synoptics, yet the parable recorded in Mt. and Lk. shows us how naturally He came to compare His ministry to the work of a shepherd, and how He used the comparison to justify His friendly attitude to publicans and sinners. According to Mt 12¹¹ᶠ·, our Lord also adduced an owner's care for a single sheep as a defence of His healing a man with a withered hand on the Sabbath-day.

(*c*) If the weakness and the helplessness of sheep supplied Jesus with similes whereby to describe the Jewish people as a whole, the purity symbolized by their white wool, their harmlessness and patience, led Him to speak of His own disciples in similar terms. The disciples are sent forth as sheep (or as lambs) into the midst of wolves (Mt 10¹⁶, Lk 10³; Clem. Rom. *Ep.* ii. 5). Christians are to be ready even to suffer death without resistance, so at least the epistle attributed to Clement interprets the saying (see above under 'lamb').

(*d*) In the Synoptics the few other passages where the disciples are described as sheep throw little light on the subject. In Mt 25 the righteous and the wicked are contrasted as sheep and goats; but, as has already been pointed out, the character of the animals concerned has little to do with the comparison. The words 'I will smite the shepherd, and the sheep shall be scattered' (quoted from Zec 13⁷ in Mt 26³¹, Mk 14²⁷), serve only to show that the death of Christ would place the disciples in the same leaderless bewilderment which, in the eyes of our Lord, marked the nation as a whole. But in a somewhat different connexion (Lk 12³²) our Lord spoke of His disciples as a little flock. After bidding them forego anxiety about earthly goods and seek the kingdom, our Lord adds, 'Fear not, little flock: for it is your Father's good pleasure to give you the kingdom.' The reassuring words were needed, no doubt, because the disciples were but a little feeble band. But surely the little flock implies something as to character as well as number. It is the duty of the shepherd at all times to find suitable pasture, and in the autumn and winter he has to provide fodder. Sheep cannot fend for themselves. Similarly the disciples, intrusting to God the care of their earthly interests, will appear to the world at once foolish and ineffectual; yet this little flock is to inherit the kingdom. God chooses the weak things of this world (1 Co 1²⁷).

Further references to sheep in the Gospels are less important. Mt 7¹⁵ speaks of the false prophets who are sheep in appearance and wolves in reality, a saying which also appears in Justin, *Dial.* 35. In Jn 21¹⁶ᶠ· Peter is bidden to tend (ποιμαίνειν) Christ's sheep (προβάτια, 'lambs,' is given as a variant in WH). Here we have in germ the pastoral view of the ministerial office. See art. SHEPHERD.

Jesus' description of Himself as the Good Shepherd laid hold from the first of the Christian imagination. In the NT Jesus is twice spoken of as the Shepherd (He 13²⁰, 1 P 2²⁵). In the Catacombs no symbol of Christ is more frequent than the picture of the Good Shepherd. See CHRIST IN ART.

2. Our Lord illustrates His teaching concerning *God's providence* by one or two sayings about the birds. He bids His disciples 'consider the birds of the air : for they neither sow nor reap nor gather into barns ; yet your heavenly Father feedeth them. Are ye not much better than they?' (Mt 6²⁶). In conjunction with this passage, we must examine the reference to sparrows in Mt 10²⁹· ³¹, Lk 12⁶ᵗ·. 'Are not two sparrows sold for a farthing? yet not one of them shall fall to the earth without your Father. . . . Fear not then : ye are of more value than many sparrows.' Bochart well brings out the force of Luke's mention of 'ravens' instead of 'birds of the air,' and he rightly discerns the bearing of the reference to the sparrows, when he says, 'Express mention is made of ravens and sparrows among the other birds, to make it clear that God's providence is not only concerned with birds in general, but even extends to the most worthless and the most despised among birds : so that men, especially those that believe, may the more certainly draw from this fact the conclusion that God cares for them, since He will not deny to those who worship Him and call upon Him, the care which He so graciously bestows on animals of the lowest order.' Bochart further dwells on the harsh grating voice, the ugly black colour, and the awkward movements of the raven, which make him a despicable bird. Concerning the sparrows, Thomson says they are 'a tame, troublesome, vivacious and impertinent generation : they nestle just where they are not wanted. Their nests stop up stove-pipes and water-gutters. They are destroyed eagerly as a worthless nuisance' ('Lebanon,' etc., p. 59). Jesus then insists that the birds which men hold cheap are not unthought of by God : 'our Lord has taught us that God providently caters for the sparrow, and Himself conducts its obsequies.'

By taking the references to sparrows and ravens closely together, we may save ourselves from a onesided interpretation of Mt 6²⁶ which has found favour with many. Thus O. Holtzmann (*Life of Jesus*, p. 102) says : 'With the drudgery and toil of human labour, Jesus contrasts the toilless life of nature, in which God feeds the raven and clothes the lilies.' A parallel saying from the Talmud is cited in Delitzsch's *Jewish Artisan Life*, which suggests the same view of our Lord's teaching. 'Didst thou ever see in all thy life,' says Rabbi Simeon, son of Eleazar, 'a bird or an animal working at a craft? And yet these creatures, made simply for the purpose of serving me, gain their living without difficulty. But I am created to serve my Creator : and if those who are created to serve can gain their livelihood without difficulty, shall not I, who am made to serve my Creator, earn my living without trouble?' If this saying is modelled on Mt 6²⁶, then Rabbi Simeon and O. Holtzmann seem to agree in interpreting our Lord's teaching to the effect that 'the birds are fed, without working : surely we may expect God to feed us too, without our toil.' Such an interpretation makes Mt 6²⁶ the magna charta of idleness. But the superiority of the birds does not lie in their not working, but in their not worrying. If we may paraphrase the passage, 'the birds do not engage in any methodical toil : yet they trust God for daily food, and praise Him for His care : men are better than birds, a superiority shown in the fact that men work in an orderly manner : now, if God feeds the birds, which live a haphazard kind of life, how much more will He reward men's patient labour without their needing to be anxious?' This section of the Sermon on the Mount is best interpreted by St. Peter's words, 'casting all your care (*i.e.* your worries and anxieties) on him ; for he careth for you' (1 P 5⁷), or by St. Paul's lesson of contentment under all circumstances (Ph 4¹¹⁻¹³). Our daily wants are the care of God. The saying about the sparrows for-

bids us to assume that daily needs will be met exactly in the way we expect. We are not to assume that food and raiment will be provided amply and at all times. Privation and suffering may fall to men's lot ; but suffering even unto death is not to be feared, because the very death of a sparrow is not forgotten before God.

Our Lord's teaching as to the trust in God's providence, which may be learnt from the animals, appears to be summed up in the second of the five new Sayings recently discovered by Grenfell and Hunt. They restore this logion as follows : 'Jesus saith (ye ask? who are those) that draw us (to the kingdom, if) the kingdom is in Heaven? . . . The fowls of the air, and all beasts that are under the earth or upon the earth, and the fishes of the sea (these are they which draw) you, and the kingdom of Heaven is within you ; and whoever shall know himself shall find it. (Strive therefore?) to know yourselves and ye shall be aware that ye are the sons of the (almighty?) Father ; (and?) ye shall know that ye are in (the city of God?) and ye are (the city?).' The restoration of the saying is highly conjectural, but it seems to be based in part on Job 12⁷· ⁸. 'Ask now the beasts and they shall teach thee ; and the fowls of the air and they shall tell thee. Or speak to the earth and it shall teach thee ; and the fishes of the sea shall declare unto thee.' And the conclusion which the saying is intended apparently to enforce may be stated in the following verses taken from the same passage in Job. 'Who knoweth not in all these that the hand of the Lord hath wrought this? In whose hand is the soul of every living thing and the breath of all mankind' (v.⁹ᶠ·). In effect we are taught that converse with nature should produce a calm trust in God.

It does not fall within the scope of this article to discuss the wider aspects of our Lord's attitude towards Nature. But the place taken by animals in His teaching bears out the truth of the following words of a recent writer. 'Jesus loved Nature as Nature : here as everywhere He was in touch with the actual. Plenty of people—from Æsop to Mrs. Gatty—have made or drawn parables from Nature, but not like His. His lost sheep have no proverbs : His lilies may be dressed more charmingly than Solomon, but they have not Solomon's wisdom : and His sparrows are neither moralists nor theologians, but sparrows,—two for a farthing, sparrows chirping and flying about and building their nests,—just sparrows ! But the least motion which they made seemed a thrill of pleasure. . . . Sparrows, lilies, lost sheep, hens and chickens, midnight stars and mountain winds,—they all entered into His mind and heart, and spoke to Him of the character of God, of His delight in beauty, and His love' (T. R. Glover).

LITERATURE. — Without attempting to provide a complete bibliography, it may be worth while to give a list of books that the present writer has found helpful. Bochart's *Hierozoicon* (ed. Rosenmüller) is encyclopædic. Tristram's *Natural History of the Bible* is a most handy manual of compact and accessible information. References to animals are frequent in books of Oriental travel : *e.g.* Stanley's *Sinai and Palestine* ; Robinson's *BRP* ; and Thomson's *Land and the Book* [the latest edition of Thomson's work in 3 vols. is especially valuable, though the information is widely scattered and is not always easy to find]. The articles on natural history and on particular animals in Hastings' *DB* and the *Encyc. Bibl.* may be consulted with advantage. The standard 'Lives of Jesus' deal with the references to animals incidentally ; Edersheim is perhaps the fullest and most reliable. There are some fresh, though not always accurate, observations on the subject in the *Life of Jesus* by O. Holtzmann. Of the many commentaries that expound the passages in the Gospels which concern our subject, the present writer has found vol. i. of the *Expositor's Greek Testament* ('Synoptics' by A. B. Bruce, 'St. John' by M. Dods) most useful. H. G. WOOD.

ANISE.—'Anise' is the translation given in AV and RV of ἄνηθον (Mt 23²³) : the marginal rendering 'dill' is the correct one. The true anise is the plant *Pimpinella anisum*, which is quite distinct from *Anethum graveolens*, the anise of the Bible.

By the Jews dill was cultivated as a garden plant, but in Egypt and Southern Europe, to which it was indigenous, it is often found growing wild in the cornfields. It possesses valuable carminative properties, and in the East the seeds are eaten with great relish as a condiment. It is a hardy annual or biennial umbellifer, and grows to a height of one, two, or even three feet. The stem is round, jointed, and striated; the leaves are finely divided; the flowers, which are small, are yellow; the fruits are brown, oval, and flat.

In Mt 23²³ dill is represented as subject to tithe. That is in strict accord with the provision of the Law (Lv 27³⁰, Dt 14²²), and is corroborated by the express statement of the Mishna (Ma'aseroth iv. 5). See, further, art. RUE; and cf. note by Nestle in Expos. Times, Aug. 1904, p. 528ᵇ.

HUGH DUNCAN.

ANNA ("Αννα, Heb. חַנָּה).—When His parents brought the infant Jesus to the temple to present Him to the Lord, two aged representatives of the OT Church received Him with songs of praise, Simeon and Anna (Lk 2²⁵ᶠᶠ·). Anna was the daughter of Phanuel, of the tribe of Asher (v.³⁶), which, though one of the Ten Tribes of the Dispersion, was still represented in Palestine. From it some beautiful women are said to have been chosen as wives for the priests (Edersheim, Life and Times of Jesus the Messiah, i. p. 200). Anna was a widow 84 years of age (AV), or more probably (RV) about 105, as 7 years of married life followed by 84 years of widowhood would make her to be. She was a devout and saintly woman, worshipping constantly in the temple, with fastings and supplications, night and day; and, like Deborah and Huldah of the OT, she had prophetic gifts. Her desire, like the Psalmist's (Ps 27⁴), was to dwell always in the house of God, though it is hardly likely that a woman would be allowed literally to dwell within the sacred precincts. Having entered the temple at the same time as Jesus was brought in, she followed up the song of Simeon in similar strains, and spake of the Holy Child 'to all them that were looking for the redemption of Jerusalem' (v.³⁸). Anna would seem to later times an ideal saint of the cloister, as such stress is laid on her virginity, her long life of widowhood, and her ceaseless devotions. Possibly her name may have had to do with the name Anna, given to the mother of the Virgin Mary, in the Protevangelium of James.

DAVID M. W. LAIRD.

ANNAS ("Αννας, Heb. חָנָן, Ḥanan, Jos. "Αναvos, Ananos).—High priest of the Jews from A.D. 6 to 15, and thereafter exercising commanding influence through his high priestly rank and his family connexions. The son of one named Sethi, who is otherwise unknown, he was appointed high priest by Quirinius, probably in A.D. 6, and exercised that office, which involved political as well as religious headship of the nation, until he was deposed by the procurator Valerius Gratus in A.D. 15 (Jos. Ant. XVIII. ii. 2). The duration of his rule, and the fact that of his sons no fewer than five succeeded him at intervals in the high priesthood ('which has never happened to any other of our high priests'), caused him to be regarded by his contemporaries as a specially successful man (Ant. XX. ix. 1). On the other hand, he incurred in an unusual degree the unpopularity for which the high priests were proverbial. In addition to their common faults of arrogance and injustice, Annas was notorious for his avarice, which found opportunity in the necessities of the Temple worshippers. It was he, probably, who established the 'bazaars of the sons of Annas' (ḥănnûyôth běnê Ḥānān), a Temple market for the sale of materials requisite for sacrifices, either within the Temple precinct (Keim, Jesus of Nazara, v. 116) or on the Mount of Olives (Derenbourg), the profits of which enriched the high priestly family. Beyond this, the house of Annas is charged with the special sin of 'whispering' or 'hissing like vipers, 'which seems to refer to private influence on the judges, whereby "morals were corrupted, judgment perverted, and the Shekinah withdrawn from Israel"' (Eders-

heim, Life and Times of Jesus the Messiah, i. 263).

Annas is referred to by St. Luke and by St. John. In Lk 3² ('in the high priesthood of Annas and Caiaphas') he is linked with Caiaphas, who alone was actually high priest at the time (A.D. 26). The explanation of this is found partly in the fact that the office having become to some extent the prerogative of a few families, it had acquired some degree of hereditary and indelible quality, and partly in the unusual personal authority exercised by Annas. The result was that even after his deposition he continued to enjoy much of the influence, and even to receive the title, of his former office (Schürer, HJP II. i. 195 ff.; against this Keim, l.c. vi. 36 ff.; H. Holtzmann, Hdcom. ad Lk 3²). In like manner in Ac 4⁶ Annas appears at the head of the chiefs of the Sanhedrin in its action against the Apostles, though the actual president was the high priest. See CHIEF PRIESTS.

The only other passage in which Annas is referred to is in the narrative of the trial of Jesus in the Fourth Gospel (Jn 18¹³⁻²⁴). The Evangelist, speaking with technical accuracy, refrains from calling him high priest, and assigns as a reason for Jesus being led before Annas the relationship between Annas and Caiaphas. The ex-highpriest had probably been the chief instigator of the plot against Jesus, and before him He was brought not for trial, but only for an informal and private examination (so Schürer, l.c. p. 182). 'The Lord Himself is questioned, but there is no mention of witnesses, no adjuration, no sentence, no sign of any legal process' (Westcott, ad loc.).

C. A. SCOTT.

ANNOUNCEMENTS OF DEATH.—It is certain that we have words from Jesus concerning His death; for such ruthless criticism as that of Schmiedel (Encyc. Bibl. 'Gospels'), who admits only nine genuine sayings of the Master, is uncritical and unscientific These words appear in the Synoptics as well as in the Fourth Gospel. The genuineness of the latter is here assumed, though there is a wide difference in character between it and the Synoptics.

The main point in the announcements of His death by Jesus rests on the time of their utterance. Hence the chronological grouping of these sayings of Jesus must be followed. If He spoke of His death only as a disappointed man after He saw the manifest hate of the rulers, there would be little ground for claiming Messianic consciousness concerning His death as an atonement for sin. And the heart of the whole problem turns on the Messianic consciousness. *When did He become conscious of His death? Why did He expect a violent death? What did He think was to be accomplished by His death? Was His death a voluntary sacrifice, or merely a martyr's crown?* These and similar questions can be answered only by a careful and comprehensive survey of Christ's own words upon the subject. It is noteworthy that Jesus put the emphasis in His career on His death rather than on His incarnation. That is so out of the ordinary as at once to challenge attention. Here is One who came to give life by dying. That is in deepest harmony with nature, but not in harmony with man's view of his own life.

1. *The first foreshadowings.*—(a) Jesus first exhibits knowledge of His death at the time of the Temptation, immediately after the Baptism and the formal entrance upon the Messianic ministry. The word 'death' or 'cross' is not mentioned between Jesus and Satan, but the point at issue was the easy or the hard road to conquest of the world. It is the unexpressed idea in this struggle for the mastery of men. Hence, before Jesus began to teach men, He had already wrestled with

His Messianic destiny and chosen the path that led to the cross. This tone of high moral conflict is never absent from Jesus till the end. The Synoptic Gospels thus give the first account of Christ's consciousness of His struggle to the death for the spiritual mastery of men.

(b) Another * occasion for the mention of His death by our Lord grew out of the failure of Nicodemus to understand the new birth and the spiritual nature of the kingdom of God (Jn 3⁹). If the teacher of Israel could not apprehend these aspects of what took place in the kingdom on earth, how could he lay hold of the purposes of God in heaven (v.¹²) about the work of the kingdom? One of the chief of these 'heavenly things' is the necessity of the death of Christ for the sin of the world. The brazen serpent of the older history serves as an illustration (v.¹⁴), but 'das göttliche "δεῖ" Todes-schicksals' (Schwartzkopff, *Die Weissagungen Jesu Christi*, p. 20) is grounded in the eternal love of God for the world (Jn 3¹⁶). The Son of Man (Jn 3¹⁴) who 'must' be lifted up is the Son of God (3¹⁶). It is not perfectly certain that 3¹⁶ is a word of Jesus and not of the Evangelist, but at any rate it is a correct interpretation of the preceding argument. The high religious necessity for His death, of which Jesus is here conscious, could come to Him by revelation from the Father (Schwartz-kopff, *l.c.* p. 22). The consciousness of Jesus is clear, but He finds in Nicodemus an inability to grasp this great truth. The word 'lifted up' (ὑψωθῆναι) refers to the cross, as is made plain afterwards (Jn 8²⁸ 12³²ᶠ·). Even when the multitudes heard Jesus use the word just before His death, they did not understand it (Jn 12³⁴), though the Evangelist gives the correct interpretation in the light of the after history (12³³). In itself the word could refer to spiritual glory (Paulus) or heavenly glory (Bleek), but not in view of the later developments. So then the cross is consciously before Jesus from the very beginning of His ministry.

(c) It is possibly nearly a year before we have the next allusion by the Master to His death. Again in parabolic phrase Jesus calls Himself the bridegroom who will be taken away from the disciples (Mk 2²⁰, Mt 9¹⁵, Lk 5³⁵). The Pharisees from Jerusalem (Lk 5¹⁷) are now in Galilee watching the movements of Jesus, so as to gain a case against Him. On this occasion they are finding fault because the disciples of Jesus do not observe stated seasons of fasting. The answer of Jesus is luminous in marking off the wide difference in spirit between a ceremonial system like Judaism and a vital personal spiritual religion like Christianity. There is a time to fast, but it is a time of real, not perfunctory, sorrow. Such a time will come to the disciples of Jesus when He is taken away. By itself this reference might allude merely to the death that would come to Christ as to other men, but the numerous other clear passages of a different nature preclude that idea here. Gould is right (*Internat. Crit. Com.* on Mk 2²⁰) in saying that 'even as a premonition it is not premature,' though there is more in it than this, for Jesus understood the significance of His death. Soon the historical developments confirm the prejudgment of Jesus, for the enmity of the historical conspiracy grows apace. At the next feast at which Jesus appears in Jerusalem (Jn 5¹) the rulers make a definite attempt to kill Him as a Sabbath-breaker and blasphemer, also for claiming equality with God the Father (Jn 5¹⁸). This decision to kill Jesus soon reappears in

Galilee (Mk 3⁶), and often in Jerusalem during the closing six months of the ministry.

(d) The use of the cross as a metaphor, as in Mt 10³⁸ (see also Mk 8²⁴, Mt 16²⁴, Lk 14²⁷), would not of itself constitute an allusion to the death of Jesus, since death on the cross was so common at this time. But in the light of the many allusions by Jesus Himself to His death, the background of the metaphor would seem to be personal, and so to imply His own actual cross. He is Himself the supreme example of saving life by losing it. Meyer, *in loco*, considers that this verse was transferred from the later period; but this is unnecessary; for it is eminently pertinent that in the directions to the Twelve, who are now sent out on their first mission, they should be urged to self-sacrifice by the figure of His own death on the cross. In this same address occurs an apocalyptic saying that presupposes the death of Christ (Mt 10²³). It is not an anachronism (J. Weiss) to find self-sacrifice and self-realization in the words of Jesus about losing life and finding it (Mt 10³⁹), for Jesus Himself gives the historical background of this image in the sublime justification of His own death in His resurrection (Jn 12²⁴).

(e) It is just a year (Jn 6⁴) before the death of Jesus that He is addressing the Galilæan populace in the synagogue at Capernaum. He explains that He is the bread of heaven, the true manna, the spiritual Messiah. It is the climax of the Galilæan ministry, for but yesterday they had tried to make Him king (v.¹⁵). To-day Jesus tests their enthusiasm by the supreme revelation of His gift of Himself 'for the life of the world' (v.⁵¹), a clear allusion to His atoning death on the cross. Thus will it be possible for men to make spiritual appropriation of Christ as the living bread. The people and many of the so-called disciples fall back at this saying (v.⁶⁶), and thus justify the wisdom of Jesus in having said no more as yet concerning His death, and life by His death. For at the first dim apprehension of this basal truth the people left Him. But it was time for the truth to be told to the flippant multitudes. Here Jesus reveals His consciousness of the character and work of Judas as the betrayer, a very devil (Jn 6⁷⁰ᶠ·). The bald truth of the betrayal is not at this point told to the Twelve, for John's comment is made afterwards; but Jesus expressly says that one of them is a devil. Jesus clearly knows more than He tells. There is this bitterness in His cup at the very time that the people desert Him. The shadow of the cross is growing closer and darker, but Christ will go on to meet His hour.

2. *The definite announcements.* — (a) The new departure at Cæsarea Philippi. Just after the renewed confession by Peter that Jesus is the Messiah, St. Matthew says that 'from that time began Jesus to show unto his disciples how that he must go unto Jerusalem, and suffer many things of the elders and chief priests and scribes, and be killed, and the third day be raised up' (Mt 16²¹). St. Mark (8³¹) also says that 'he began to teach them.' Clearly, then, this was an epoch in the teaching of Jesus concerning His death. When He withdrew from Galilee this last summer, he devoted Himself chiefly to the disciples, and especially to preparing them for His departure. The specific teaching concerning His death follows, therefore, the searching test of their fidelity to Him as the Messiah. This is not a new idea to Jesus, as we have already seen. It has been the keynote of His mission all the time, but He had to speak of it in veiled and restrained language till now, when 'he spake the saying openly' (Mk 8³²). Now Jesus told the details of His death, the place and the persecutors. He repeats the necessity (δεῖ) of His death as He had proclaimed it in

---

* Jn 2²⁹ and Mt 12³⁹ are passed over because of doubts (not shared by the present writer) as to their interpretation or genuineness. The case is strong enough without these disputed passages.

Jn 3¹⁴. The disciples are still unprepared for this plain truth, and Peter even dares to rebuke Jesus for such despondency (Mt 16²²). The sharp rebuke of Peter by Jesus (v.²³) shows how strong a hold the purpose to die had on His very nature. Peter had renewed the attack of Satan in the Temptation. The Gospels record the dulness of the disciples, thus disproving the late invention of these sayings attributed to Jesus. The principle of self-giving is a basal one for Jesus and for all His followers (Lk 9²³⁻²⁵). The disciples could not yet, any more than Nicodemus, grasp the moral necessity of the death of Jesus. They recoiled at the bare fact.

(b) On the Mount of Transfiguration a week later, somewhere on the spurs of Hermon, Peter, James, and John get a fresh word from Jesus about His death (Mk 9⁹). It is not necessary to suppose that they understood or even heard the conversation of Jesus with Moses and Elijah about 'his decease which he was about to accomplish at Jerusalem' (Lk 9³¹). Most likely they did not, if Peter's remarks are a criterion (Lk 9³²ᶠ·). There is a fitness both from the manner of the deaths of Moses and Elijah, and from their respective positions in law and prophecy, that these two should talk with Jesus about His atoning and predicted sacrificial death. This exalted scene lifts the curtain a little for us, so that we catch some glimpse of the consciousness of Jesus concerning His death, as He held high converse with Moses and Elijah. But the remark of Jesus (Mt 17⁹) was a caution to the three disciples to keep to themselves what they had seen till His resurrection, when they would need it. But ·the lesson of strength was lost on them for the present. Even the chosen three questioned helplessly with each other about the rising from the dead (Mk 9¹⁰). They could not understand a dying Messiah now or later till the risen Christ had made it clear.

(c) In Galilee Jesus renewed His earnest words about the certainty of His death (Mk 9³¹, Mt 17²²ᶠ·, Lk 9⁴⁴). He concealed His presence in Galilee as far as possible (Mk 9³⁰), but He was very insistent in urging, 'Let these words sink into your ears: for the Son of Man shall be delivered up into the hands of men' (Lk 9⁴⁴). But it was to no purpose, for they understood it not (Mk 9³²). St. Luke (9⁴⁵), in fact, says that it was concealed from them, thus raising a problem of God's purpose and their responsibility. They were sorry (Mt 17²³), but afraid to ask Jesus (Lk 9⁴⁵). Hence Jesus has not yet succeeded in making the disciples understand His purpose to die for men. So then He will have no human sympathy, and will have to tread the path to Calvary alone.

(d) At the feast of Tabernacles, or a few days afterwards, just six months before the end, in the midst of the hostile atmosphere of Jerusalem, Jesus emphasizes the voluntary character of His death for His sheep (Jn 10¹⁵). He does this to distinguish between Himself and the Pharisees, who have been vehemently attacking Him. They are robbers, wolves, and hirelings, while Jesus is the Good Shepherd. He is not merely caught in the maelstrom of historic forces, nor is He the victim of time and circumstance, for He has voluntarily put Himself into the vortex of sin (Jn 10¹⁷ᶠ·). The Father has given the Son the power or right (ἐξουσία) to lay down and to take up His life again. It was a 'commandment' from the Father, but not to the exclusion of the voluntary nature of His death; just as the necessity of His death was an inward necessity of love, not an outward compulsion of law. It is in the realm of spirit that we find the true value of the death of Jesus for our sins (He 9¹⁴), and the moral grandeur of it is seen in the fact

that He made a voluntary offering of His life for those who hated Him (Ro 5⁸).

(e) As the time draws nearer, Jesus even manifests eagerness to meet His death (Lk 12⁴⁹ᶠ·). It is only some three months till the end. However we take τί, whether as interrogative or exclamation, we see clearly the mingled eagerness and dread with which Jesus contemplated His death. It is a fire that will burn, but also attracts. He had come just for this purpose, to make this fire. It will be a relief when it is kindled. It is a baptism of death that presses as a Divine compulsion upon Him, like the 'must' of the earlier time (Jn 3¹⁴, Mk 8³¹). Here we feel the inward glow of the heart of Christ as it bursts out for a moment like a flame from the crater, unable to be longer restrained. So Jesus had a double point of view about His death, one of joy and one of shrinking, but He did not go now one way and now the other. He will pursue His way steadily, and as the time draws nigh, His view of His death will amount to rapture (Jn 17¹·³³). But Jesus was never more conscious and sane than when He spoke thus about His death. It was, in fact, His inner self speaking out. He thus gave us not only a new view of His own death, but a new view of death itself.

(f) Jesus even tells His enemies that He expects to be put to death in Jerusalem (Lk 13³³). They were posing as His friends, but were either representatives of Herod Antipas or of the Jerusalem Pharisees. Jesus asserted His independence of 'that fox' and of them, but announced the inward necessity ('I must') that He should ultimately at the right time meet the fate of other prophets in Jerusalem. His lament over Jerusalem reveals the depth of His love for that city, and demands a Judæan ministry such as that described by John.

(g) It is not till the death of Lazarus that the disciples realize that Jesus may be put to death (Jn 11⁸); and then as a dread growing out of the last attempt of the Jews to kill Him at the feast of Dedication (10³⁹). Thomas has the courage of despair (11¹⁶) in the gloomy situation, but Jesus speaks of His own glorification (11⁴·⁴⁰). One item in this glorification was the formal decision of the Sanhedrin to put Jesus to death (11⁵³). With this formal decision resting over Him, Jesus withdrew to the hills of Ephraim, near where in the beginning He had refused Satan's offer of a compromise, and had chosen His own way and the Father's. Had He made a mistake?

3. *Facing the end.*—(a) The relation between the death of Christ and the consummation of the kingdom. It is in the last journey to Jerusalem that the Pharisees ask when the kingdom of God comes (Lk 17²⁰). They are thinking of the apocalyptic conception current in their literature. There are two difficulties thus raised. One is their utter failure to understand the nature of the kingdom, for it is inner and spiritual, not external (the Papyri show that ἐντός means 'within,' not 'among').* But, though the kingdom had already come in this sense, there would be in the end a fuller and completer realization of the work of the kingdom. It is in this sense that Jesus addresses the disciples in Lk 17²⁵. The day when the Son of Man shall be revealed (Lk 17³⁰) will be the end. 'But first must he suffer many things, and be rejected of this generation.' Thus Jesus separates His own death from the final stage of the Messianic work on earth. The other difficulty is raised by the disciples, and concerns the place where the Son will manifest Himself (Lk 17³⁷). He will come when there are people for Him to come for.

(b) Jesus uses the word 'crucify' before He reaches Jericho on this last journey to Jerusalem

* Cf., however, *Expos. Times*, xv. [1904], 387.

(Mt 20[19]). Stapfer scouts this item as put in *post eventum* (*Jesus Christ during His Ministry*, p. 202), because it is expressly used by Christ only twice before His death (see also Mt 26[2]) ; but the Master particularizes beforehand other details, such as the mocking, scourging, spitting, delivering to the Gentiles (these all now mentioned for the first time, Mk 10[33f.], Mt 20[19], Lk 18[32f.]). Besides, now for the first time also Jesus claims that His death will be in fulfilment of the prophetic writings concerning the Son of Man (Lk 18[31]). See later Mt 21[42], Jn 13[18], Mk 14[27], Lk 22[37] 24[27]. Jesus is not, however, playing a part just to fulfil the Scripture, but He sees this objective confirmation of the inner witness of His spirit to the Father's will concerning His death. Besides, on this occasion Jesus had made a special point of talking about His coming death, taking the Twelve apart (Mt 20[17f.]), and explaining that He does so now because they are near Jerusalem. There was an unusual look on the Master's face, so much so that the disciples were amazed and afraid (Mk 10[32]). But with all this pain, they were hopelessly dull on this subject (Lk 18[34]).

(*c*) There is strange pathos in the next occasion Jesus had for speaking concerning His death. James and John and their mother (Mt 20[20], Mk 10[35]) seem hardly able to wait for the Master to cease telling about His death before they come and ask for the chief positions in the temporal kingdom for which they are still looking. It was a shock to Jesus. Waiving their ignorance, He asked if they could drink His cup of death and take His baptism of blood (Mt 20[22], Mk 10[38]). They actually said that they were able. And James was the first of the Twelve to die a martyr's death, and John the last ; for Jesus had said that they would have His cup and baptism (Mk 10[39]).

(*d*) It was on the same occasion, as Jesus proceeded to give the disciples a needed lesson in true greatness and taught the dignity of service, that He set forth in plain speech the purpose of His death (Mt 20[28], Mk 10[45]). Certainly Jesus had the right to tell the purpose of His voluntary death. Λύτρον is obviously 'ransom,' but it need not be said that this word exhausts all the content in the death of Christ. Jesus Himself elsewhere spoke of the vital connexion between Himself and the believer (Jn 15[1ff.]). This view of the redemptive death of Christ is further emphasized by the symbol of Baptism and also of the Supper, in both of which the vital aspect of mystic union is expressed. 'Αντί is here used to express the idea of substitution, though ὑπέρ is more common in this sense in the NT (Jn 11[50]) and in the earlier Greek (*Alcestis*, for instance). It is a ransom instead of many.

A distinction needs to be made between the atoning death of Christ as a basis for reconciliation and the consummation of reconciliation in the individual case by the Holy Spirit's work in the heart. The doctrine of the substitutionary atoning death of Jesus, with vital and mystic union of the believer with Him, is not a rabbinic and legal refinement of St. Paul. He simply echoes the words of the Master more at length, while true to the heart of the matter.

(*e*) The request of the Greeks during the last week brought forth one of the deepest words of Jesus concerning the necessity of His death (Jn 12[23-25]). He gives, in fact, the philosophy of grace about His death, which is, in truth, the same as the law of nature. It is the law of self-giving. Thus the wheat grows, and thus will Jesus establish the kingdom. By His death the middle wall of partition between Jew and Gentile, and between both and God, will be broken down (Eph 2[14-18]). The agitation of Jesus on this occasion is surpassed only by that in the Garden of Gethsemane, and the cause is the same. In facing His death He shrinks from it, but instantly submits to the Father (Jn 12[26f.]), and is comforted by the Father's voice. To the multitude Jesus boldly announces

that His lifting up (on the cross) will be the means of drawing all men (Gentile as well as Jew) to Him (v.[32]). And it has been so. Jesus gloried in His own cross as the means of saving the lost world.

(*f*) In the famous controversy with the Jewish rulers in the temple on the last Tuesday, Jesus identified Himself as the rejected Stone in the Messianic prophecy in Ps 118[22], and pronounced condemnation on those who collided with the rejected Stone (Mt 21[44]). At every turn during these last days the death of Jesus is in the background of His words and deeds ; especially is this true of the great eschatological discourse (Mt 24 f.), as well as of the third lament over Jerusalem (Mt 23[37-39]), and the previous defiance of His enemies (Mt 23[32]).

(*g*) It is on Tuesday night (beginning of Jewish Wednesday) that Jesus definitely foretells the time of His death (Mt 26[2]). It will be at the feast of the Passover, which begins after two days. Strangely enough, on this very night the rulers were in conference, and had decided, owing to the popularity of Jesus with the multitude at the feast, as shown by the triumphal entry and the temple teaching, to postpone the effort to kill Him till after the feast (Mt 26[3-5]). And so it would have been but for the treachery of one of Christ's own disciples, who this very night, after the doleful announcement by Jesus of His near death, and after a stern rebuke for his covetous stinginess (Jn 12[6f.]), went in disgust and showed the Sanhedrin how to seize Him during the feast (Lk 22[6]). But Jesus saw in the beautiful act of Mary a prophecy of His burial (Jn 12[7]).

(*h*) Jesus is fully conscious that the Paschal meal which He is celebrating is His last, is, in fact, taking place on the very day of His death (Jn 13[31-33. 38]). The material is now so rich and full, as the great tragedy draws near, that it can only be alluded to briefly. He is eager to eat this meal before He suffers (Lk 22[15f.]). He knows that now at last His hour has come (Jn 13[1]), and that He will conquer death (v.[3]). The contentious spirit of the Twelve at such a time occasions the object-lesson in humility. Jesus points out the betrayer, who leaves the room ; comforts the disciples, and warns them of their peril, though all fail to grasp the solemn fact or the moral greatness of the tragedy that is coming swiftly on them, actually producing two swords for a fight under the new policy of resistance now announced by Jesus (Lk 22[36-38]).

Pfleiderer (*Evolution and Theology*, p. 179) seeks to reconstruct the whole story of Jesus' attitude towards His death by the answer of Jesus, 'It is enough.' He forgets that this answer may be neither irony nor sober earnest, but rather an inability to make the disciples understand more about the matter before the time. It is chimerical for Pfleiderer to set up his view of this one passage against all the clear words of Jesus, and say that Jesus did not expect to die.

(*i*) When Jesus introduces the Supper just after the Passover meal, He speaks a strong word about His death. He calls the cup of this new ordinance 'my blood of the covenant' (Mk 14[24], Mt 26[28]) ; and it is the 'new' covenant, *i.e.* of grace (1 Co 11[25], Lk 22[20]). Not only so, but the blood of Jesus is shed for many (Mk 14[24], Mt 26[28]), as He had previously said (Mt 20[28], Lk 18[45]) ; and St. Matthew has the further clause 'unto remission of sins' (Mt 26[28]).

H. Holtzmann (*Hand-Com., in loco*) would expunge this phrase, while Spitta (*Urchristentum*, p. 266 ff.) denies that Jesus made any reference to His death on this occasion. Hollmann admits that He spoke of His death, but rejects the liturgical observance commanded in 1 Co 11[25f.]. Bruce (*Kingdom of God*, p. 247) bluntly calls all this 'criticism carried to an extreme in the interest of a theory.'

There is just doubt as to the true text of Lk 22[19f.], but this in no way affects any of the points above mentioned. Certainly expiation of sin by the shedding of His blood is the idea of Jesus here.

The world had long been familiar with blood sacrifice, but the new thing in His vicarious sacrifice is that it has real efficacy and is not mere type and shadow. The blood is the life, and Jesus gave Himself, a sinless and free self, the representative Man and God's own Son. The moral value of this voluntary and vicarious blood-offering comes from the worth of the spiritual self of Jesus. Jesus could see that this atoning sacrifice was in Is 53¹⁰, but it was also inwrought in His very consciousness.

(j) The very heart of Jesus is laid bare in Jn 14–17. The Master tries once more to prepare the Eleven for the tremendous fact of His death. Nothing in life or literature approaches the touch of Christ as He makes plain the awful truth of His separation, silences the doubt of Thomas, Philip, Judas, cheers them with the promise of another Paraclete, reminds them of their high dignity as His friends, exhorts them to courage against the world, and promises victory in spite of tribulation. In the prayer that follows, a halo is around the cross in the mind of Christ, for He asks for His glorification in death (Jn 17¹·⁵). He had already sanctified Himself to this mission (vv.¹⁷·¹⁹), and now the hour is at hand.

(k) And yet in Gethsemane Jesus Himself is 'greatly amazed' at His own agitation of spirit (Mk 14³³). He needs the Father's help, and for the moment has difficulty in finding Him fully, for Satan has renewed his temptation with fresh energy. For a moment Satan seemed indeed to triumph, but Jesus quickly surrendered to the Father's will and won supreme mastery over Himself (Mk 14³⁵ᶠ·). But Ritschl is in error in saying that Jesus 'is first of all a priest in His own behalf' (Justification and Reconciliation, p. 474). What broke the heart of Christ in Gethsemane was no thought of His own sin, but the sin of the world. Here in Gethsemane the heart of Jesus was touched to the quick by the essence of the redemptive sacrifice. The disciples gave Him no human sympathy, and Satan even sought to poison His heart toward the Father. The picture in Hebrews (5⁷⁻⁹) of the strong Son of God, having learned obedience through suffering, crying out to the Father for help, is the acme of soul agony. Jesus won the power to drink the cup, and in the dregs of the cup was the kiss of Judas. His hour has come at last, and His enemies take Him now only because He allows them. It is the hour and the power of darkness (Lk 22⁵³). The hour and the power of light will come later. Once again He speaks of the necessity of His death that the Scriptures may be fulfilled (Mt 26⁵²⁻⁵⁴).

(l) In the trial it is a foregone conclusion that Jesus will be condemned, and on the cross He 'sees what He foresaw.' He knows that His public confession of His Messiahship means His death, but He asserts His ultimate triumph over His enemies (Mt 26⁶³ᶠ·). He claims superiority over the world, and that He is now fulfilling His destiny (Jn 18³⁶ᶠ·). On the cross itself He practises the forgiveness of enemies which He had preached (Lk 23³⁴), exercises saving power though dying (v.⁴³), is in some sense forsaken by the Father (Mk 15³⁴), is conscious to the last of what He is performing (Jn 19²⁸), and proclaims the completion of His Messianic work (Jn 19³⁰) as He dies with submission to the Father (Lk 23⁴⁶).

After the resurrection Jesus had a new standpoint from which to teach the disciples the significance of His death (Lk 24²⁵⁻²⁷·³²·⁴⁵). But it is not till they receive the new light from the Holy Spirit at Pentecost that the disciples fully appreciate the moral greatness of the death of Christ, and see the glory of the cross, with something of the dignity with which Jesus Himself went into the shadow.

LITERATURE.—Schwartzkopff, Die Weissagungen Jesu Christi von seinem Tode, seiner Auferstehung und Wiederkunft (1895); Babut, La Pensée de Jésu sur la Mort (1897); Smeaton, Our Lord's Doctrine of the Atonement (1871); Fairbairn, 'Christ's Attitude to His Own Death,' Expositor (Oct. Dec. 1896; Jan. Feb. 1897); Denney, The Death of Christ (1902); Hollmann, Die Bedeutung des Todes Jesu; Dale, The Atonement (1881); Ritschl, Justification and Reconciliation (1900); Belser, Die Geschichte des Leidens und Sterbens, der Auferstehung und Himmelfahrt des Herrn (1903); Barth, Die Hauptprobleme des Lebens Jesu (1903); Baldensperger, Das Selbstbewusstsein Jesu (1892); Schürer, Das Messianische Selbstbewusstsein (1903); Hoffmann, Das Selbstbewusstsein Jesu nach den drei ersten Evangelien (1904); Appel, Die Selbstbezeichnung Jesu (1896); Bruce, Training of the Twelve, pp. 167 ff., 273 ff., 289 ff., 346 ff.   A. T. ROBERTSON.

ANNUNCIATION, THE (Annuntiatio, Εὐαγγελ-ισμός, Χαριτισμός).—The announcement of the fact that the Son of God was to be born of the Virgin Mary, who at the time was espoused to Joseph, the descendant and heir of David. St. Luke (1²⁶⁻³⁸) tells us that this announcement was made to Mary by the angel Gabriel at Nazareth six months after the same angel had told Zacharias in the Temple at Jerusalem that his wife Elisabeth should bear him a son, who was to be called John. St. Luke is our sole authority for this announcement by the angel to Mary. St. Mark and St. John are silent; and the narrative of St. Matthew, who is our other authority for the fact that Jesus was born of a virgin, is very different, being written as entirely from Joseph's point of view as St. Luke's is written from Mary's point of view (see below). Nevertheless there is no contradiction between the accounts, and in some important particulars they confirm one another. They are wholly independent narratives, as their wide differences show. Yet they agree, not only as to the central fact of the virgin birth, but also as to the manner of it, viz. that it took place through the operation of the Holy Spirit. This agreement is all the more remarkable when we remember that there is nothing like this effect of the Spirit of God upon a virgin in the Old Testament, and that, prior to the New Testament, the very expression 'Holy Spirit' is rare (see the art. in Hastings' DB ii. p. 402 ff.); also that the fact of the Incarnation is elsewhere indicated in quite other terms, as by St. John (1¹⁴). Moreover, the two narratives agree as to four other points, which are of some importance. Both state that at the time of the announcement Mary was espoused to Joseph, that the child was to be named 'Jesus,' that He was born at Bethlehem in Judæa, and that the parents brought Him up at Nazareth.

It is well to remember that there are stories, more or less analogous to what is told by the two Evangelists, in heathen mythologies. The historical probability of the Gospel narratives is not weakened but strengthened by such comparisons. St. Luke's Gentile readers must have felt the unspeakable difference between the coarse impurity of imagined intercourse between mortals and divinities, in the religious legends of paganism, and the dignity and delicacy of the spiritual narrative which St. Luke laid before them. And St. Matthew's Jewish readers, if they compared his story with their own national ideas, as illustrated in the Book of Enoch (6. 15. 69. 86. 106), would find a similar contrast. Nor should the legendary additions to the Gospel story, which are found in the Apocryphal Gospels, be forgotten. These show us what pitiful stuff the imagination of early Christians could produce, even when the Canonical Gospels were there as models. All these three classes of fiction, heathen, Jewish, and Christian, warn us that we must seek some source for the Gospel narrative other than the fertile imagination of some Gentile or Jewish Christian whose curiosity led him to speculate upon a mysterious subject. We should have had something very different, both in details and in tone, if there had been no better source than this. And this applies even more strongly to St. Luke's narrative than to that of St. Matthew. It required more delicacy to tell the story of the virgin birth from Mary's side than from Joseph's; and this greater delicacy is forthcoming. And it is all the more conspicuous because St. Luke's narrative is the richer in details. We conclude, therefore, that St. Luke had good authority for what he has told us, viz. an authority well acquainted with the facts. For if he was incapable of imagining what he has related, equally incapable was his informant. The narrative which he has handed on to us is what it is because in the main it sets forth what is true.

Then who was St. Luke's authority? Assuming the truth of the narrative, it is obvious that, in the last resort, the authority for it must have been Mary herself. No one else could know what St. Luke records. It does not follow from this that he got the information from her directly, although there is nothing incredible in the supposition that he and she had met. And the form of the narrative leads one to think that there cannot have been many persons between her and him. By frequent transmission from mouth to mouth details about the angel's outward appearance, his beauty and brightness, and about Mary's attitude and employment, would have crept in, and the conversation would have been expanded; all of which corruptions are found in the Apocryphal Gospels. Moreover, such touches as $2^{19. 51}$ would be likely to drop out; and they have dropped from the Apocryphal Gospels.

We may go a step farther, and say that if St. Luke did not get his information direct from Mary herself, the person who passed on the mysterious story from her to the Evangelist was almost certainly a woman. Mary would be much more likely to tell it to a woman than to a man; and, in spite of her habitual reticence, she would, after Joseph's death, be likely to confide it to some one. She would feel that such an astounding fact, so much in harmony with the life and death and resurrection of her Son, must not be allowed to die with her; and she would therefore communicate it to some intimate friend, who may have communicated it to St. Luke.

It is quite possible that this communication was at its first stage, or had not even started, when St. Mark composed his Gospel, so that when he wrote he was ignorant of the virgin birth. But as the plan of his Gospel excludes all that preceded the preaching of the Baptist, St. Mark's silence would be natural even if he already knew it. Probably most of the first generation of Christians were ignorant of this mystery, for the Book of Acts and the Epistles show us that what was preached by the Apostles was not the miraculous birth, but the death and resurrection of Christ (Ac 1^{22} $2^{23. 24. 32}$ 3^{15} 4^{10} $10^{39. 40}$ 13^{28-30} 17^{31} etc.).

That the Fourth Evangelist knew the Synoptic Gospels, and sometimes silently corrects them, is certain; but he does not correct the story of the virgin birth. On the contrary, what he says about the Incarnation and about the pre-existence of the Son of Man and His oneness with the Father, is in harmony with it. Such passages as 1^{14} 3^{13} $6^{38. 44. 51. 62}$ $8^{38. 46. 58}$ 10^{30} 11^{25} $20^{28. 31}$ are more intelligible if written by one who believed the virgin birth, than if written by one who knew the doctrine and rejected it. It is indeed urged that this Evangelist's beliefs about the Christ are such, that he must have stated the virgin birth, if he believed it. But, as the story had already been twice told, there was no need to repeat it. And the whole of his Gospel shows that he is reserved

about the Virgin Mother, whose name he alone among the Evangelists never mentions. She had become his mother (19^{27}), and he is reticent about all things connected with himself. He nowhere names his own brother.

Nevertheless, when the mystery became known through the diffusion of the First and Third Gospels, its importance as a completion and confirmation of the faith was recognized. Ignatius (c. A.D. 110), in a passage (*Eph.* 19) which is frequently quoted by later Fathers (Origen, Eusebius, Basil, Jerome, etc.), places the virgin birth in the front rank among Gospel truths; and we find it as an article of faith in the Old Roman Creed, which can be traced almost to the beginning of the second century, τὸν γεννηθέντα ἐκ πνεύματος ἁγίου καὶ Μαρίας τῆς παρθένου: *qui natus est de S.S. ex M.V.*

The antecedent probability that St. Luke derived the information respecting Mary either from herself, or from a woman to whom she had confided it, is confirmed by the characteristics of these first two chapters of his Gospel. The notes of time ($1^{26. 36. 56}$) are specially feminine; and competent critics find a feminine touch throughout ($1^{24. 25. 41-43. 57}$ $2^{5-7. 19. 35. 48. 51}$). Lange (*Life of Christ* [ed. 1872], i. p. 258) says: 'The colouring of a woman's memory and a woman's view is unmistakable in the separate features of this history. When it is once ascribed to a female narrator . . . we comprehend the indescribable grace, the quiet loveliness and sacredness of this narrative.' Ramsay (*Was Christ born at Bethlehem?* p. 88) says: 'There is a womanly spirit in the whole narrative which seems inconsistent with the transition from man to man.' Sanday (*Expository Times*, April 1903, p. 297) agrees that the narrative came not only *from* a woman, but *through* a woman, and he thinks that Joanna, the wife of Chuza, steward to Herod Antipas (Lk $8^{2. 3}$ 24^{10}; cf. 23^{49}, Ac 1^{14}), may have been the person through whom the information passed from Mary to St. Luke. Both Lange (confidently) and Sanday (less confidently) believe that St. Luke received the information *in writing*, and that he wrote the first two chapters with a document before him. On the whole, this is probable. It is quite true that the peculiarities and characteristics of St. Luke's very marked style are specially frequent in these two chapters (Plummer, *St. Luke*, p. lxx); but they are also very frequent in other places where he was working from a document. St. Luke seems never to have simply copied his authority. In using written material he freely altered the wording to expressions which were more natural to himself: so that mere frequency of marks of his style is no proof that he was not using what was already in writing. And, of course, when he was translating from an Aramaic document his own favourite words and constructions would come spontaneously.

But, while this is admitted because it admits of something like proof, we are not compelled to admit the unproved assertion that the hymns of praise with which these chapters are enriched have been composed by St. Luke himself, and have no more basis in fact than the speeches in Livy. Each of these canticles suits the time at which it is supposed to have been uttered better than the time at which St. Luke wrote, and it may be doubted whether he could in imagination have thrown himself back to the surroundings and anticipations of Zacharias and Mary and Simeon. There may have been on his part 'a free literary remodelling of material' (B. Weiss). Before anything was written down there may have been some modification in the wording as the result of reflexion upon what had been uttered and done. There may even have been conscious elaboration. But it is reasonable to believe that these exquisite and appropriate songs represent fairly accurately what was said and felt on each occasion. What was said and felt would be remembered, and perhaps was committed to writing long before St. Luke obtained the precious record, although not till many years after the events. And there is nothing extravagant in the belief that Mary herself may at last have thought it best to commit her recollections and meditations to writing. The feeling, *meum secretum mihi*, would prevail for a long time: 'she pondered these things in her heart.' Then, as the end of her life drew nearer, she might put on record what ought not to be lost. Finally, she committed the sacred mystery to another woman, or to a small group of women; and from them it passed to St. Luke. But we must be content to remain in ignorance as to whether Mary, or some confidante, or St. Luke himself, was the first to put the story in writing.

That St. Luke should be the Evangelist to receive this womanly story of women is not surprising. The rest of his Gospel shows a marked sympathy with the sex which was so commonly looked down upon by both Jews and Gentiles. To this day, in the public service of the synagogue, the men thank God that they have not been made women. No other Evangelist gives us so many types of women. Besides those in the first two chapters, we have the widow at Nain, the sinner in Simon's house, Mary Magdalene, Joanna, Susanna, the woman with the issue, Martha and Mary, the woman bowed down for eighteen years, the widow with her two mites, the daughters of Jerusalem, and the women at the tomb. And he alone gives us the parable of the Woman and the Lost Coin. We may believe that he was one in whom a woman might naturally confide.

While in St. Luke everything is grouped round Mary and her kinswoman Elisabeth, in St. Matthew everything is grouped round Joseph. Joseph's genealogy is given by way of preface. The Annunciation is made to him; and all revelations about the name of the Child, and the provisions to be taken for His safety, are made also to him. Obviously, if the story is true, Joseph must have been the ultimate source of a great deal of it; but it may have passed through many mouths before it took the form in which it appears in the First Gospel.

Doubt has been thrown upon the two narratives, because in the First Gospel the revelations are made by the angel of the Lord *in dreams*, whereas in the Third they are made by angels to persons *in their waking moments*. It is argued that in each case the miraculous agency is due to the imagination of the writer. This is possible. But it is also reasonable to believe that the special method of communication was in each case adapted to the character of the recipients. It cannot be said that St. Matthew always gives us dreams, or that St. Luke objects to such things. St. Matthew mentions the ministry of angels (4[11]), and communications made by means of them (28[5-7]); and St. Luke mentions communications made by means of visions in the night (Ac 16[9] 18[9. 10]). And if the writers had imagined the substance of the heavenly message, would not St. Matthew have given the promise of the Kingdom, and St. Luke the promise of Salvation? But it is St. Matthew who has the latter (1[21]), while St. Luke has the former (1[32. 33]). It is worth noting that in the New Testament we do not read of dreams or visions in the night anywhere but in St. Matthew and in Acts; cf. 2 Co 12[1].

Again, doubts have been raised about the two narratives, because in the one the revelation of the miraculous conception is made to Mary, in the other to Joseph; and either revelation, it is urged, would render the other unnecessary. On the contrary, both are necessary. If the virgin birth was to take place, God in His mercy would not leave Mary in ignorance of the mysterious manner in which He was about to deal with her. We may reverently say that the Annunciation to Mary was a necessity in order to save her from dreadful perplexity and suffering. And this rendered a revelation to Joseph also necessary. On the mere testimony of Mary he could not have accepted so extraordinary a story. The fact that, in spite of his inevitable suspicions, he took her in marriage, requires us to believe that to him also had been revealed God's purposes respecting his betrothed.

It is evident that St. Matthew and St. Luke give the narratives as historical. Each believed his own story, and expected that others would believe it also (Lk 1[4]). Indeed, the isolation in which these two very different intimations of the virgin birth stand in the New Testament makes the explanation of them very difficult unless there is an historical basis. They are not needed to explain anything else. They are intensely Jewish in tone; but we may be sure that Judaism, with its enthusiastic estimate of the blessings of marriage, would not have invented them. Moreover, at the time when these Gospels were written, Judaism was antagonistic to the new faith, and would not have tolerated such a glorifying of its Founder.

In the Annunciation to Mary we are not told that she saw anything, for the ἰδοῦσα read by A C in Lk 1[29] is almost certainly not genuine. Gabriel was sent, and entered some building in which she was living at Nazareth, and there delivered his message. The εἰσελθών is against the later tradition that she was at the fountain drawing water (*Protevangelium of James*, 11; *Gospel of pseudo-Matthew*, 9). The angelic message is given 'in three little pieces of trimeter poetry, which have become somewhat obscured by the Greek translation' (Briggs, *The Messiah of the Gospels*, p. 45 ff.), the first of which is the Ave Maria 'in the form of a distich'—

'Hail, thou that art endued with grace,
The Lord is with thee.'

The much discussed κεχαριτωμένη must mean 'endued with grace' (Sir 18[17]): πίστιν καὶ χάριν λαβοῦσα Μαρία (Justin Martyr, *Try.* 100); and both here and in 1[30] the usual translation 'grace' should be retained for χάρις. 'The Lord is with thee' is frequent in the Old Testament (Jos 1[9] 6[27], Jg 6[12], Is 43[5]). The RV is probably right in omitting 'Blessed (art) thou among women,' which may have come from 1[42]: אBL, with the Egyptian and Armenian Versions, omit.

By the first words of the angel, Mary was greatly disturbed (διεταράχθη) both in mind and heart: then her perplexity and emotion gave place to thought (διελογίζετο). But, although ποταπός originally meant 'from what country or nation,' she was not deliberating, like ♦Hamlet about the ghost, whether the message came from heaven or hell, *i.e.* whether it was Divine or diabolical. The Latin Versions rightly have *qualis*, not *cujas*, as an equivalent. Nowhere in the New Testament has ποταπός a local signification, but means simply 'of what kind or quality' (ποῖος), and implies astonishment (Lk 7[39], Mt 8[27], Mk 13[1], 2 P 3[11], 1 Jn 3[1]).

In his second address Gabriel calms the Virgin's fears and explains the purpose of his mission. 'Thou hast found grace with God' is another Old Testament expression (Gn 6[8] 18[3] 19[19] 39[4], Ex 33[12. 13. 16. 17]). This 'grace' is manifested in making her the mother of the longed-for Messiah, an unspeakable joy to a Jewish mother. In the promise which follows there are allusions to two prophecies. 'Son of the Most High' recalls Ps 2⁷, and 'the throne of his father David' recalls the great Messianic prediction in Is 9⁶·⁷.

By the second utterance of Gabriel, which contains the substance of the Annunciation, Mary is astounded. Yet she does not, like Zacharias, ask for proof (1¹⁸). Nor is her 'How?' a request for an explanation. Rather it is an exclamation of amazement. She is not married : how can she have a son? And how can a humble maiden like herself have such a son? This seems to be the natural import of her words. It is unlikely that 'I know not a man' means that she has already taken, or there and then takes, or intends to take, a vow of perpetual virginity. And can Mt 1²⁵, with its Imperfect tense (not Aorist, as in Gn 19⁸), be reconciled with any such vow? Mary's ἄνδρα οὐ γινώσκω is a confession of conscious purity, drawn from her by the surprising promise that she is to have a son before she is married (see Sadler, *ad loc.*).

Although Mary does not ask for an explanation or a sign, Gabriel gives both in a third utterance. As to the explanation, it is an influence that is spiritual and not carnal, that is holy and not sinful, that is to come upon her and enable her to become a mother, and the mother of the Messiah.

> 'Wherefore also the holy thing which shall be born
> Shall be called the Son of God.'

'Son of God' was a recognized title of the Messiah. Both in the Book of Enoch and frequently in 4 Ezra the Almighty speaks of the Messiah as His Son. Jesus rarely uses this title of Himself (Mt 27⁴³, Jn 10³⁶). But we have it in the voices from heaven (Lk 3²² 9³⁵) and in the devil's challenge (4³·⁹), in St. Peter's confession (Mt 16¹⁶), in the cries of the demoniacs (Mk 3¹¹ 5⁷), and in the centurion's exclamation (15³⁹). The primitive Church adopted it as a concise statement of the Divinity of Jesus Christ (Swete, *Apostles' Creed*, p. 24). It is worth noting, in connexion with the part assigned to the Holy Spirit in the virgin birth, that in a fragment of the Gospel according to the Hebrews quoted by Origen (*Com. in Johan.* iii. § 63) the words, 'My mother, the Holy Spirit, took Me,' are put into the mouth of Christ.

As to the sign, which was granted unasked, Mary receives one which is as convincing as the one given to Zacharias, but much more gracious. Another wonderful birth is about to take place, and by the mention of 'the sixth month' the angel assures Mary that all is known to him. Mary can verify his words respecting Elisabeth, and thereby know that this message to herself is true. He intimates that there is to be close relationship between Elisabeth's son and her own, and directs her to her kinswóman for confirmation and sympathy.

Mary's final response to the angel is not a prayer that what he has promised may be fulfilled, but an expression of absolute submission. She foresees the difficulty with Joseph and with all who know her. But she accepts, without reserve, God's decree respecting her, as made known to her by His messenger, and leaves the issue in His hands. She is the Lord's bondmaid, and His will must be done.

There is perhaps more irreverence than wisdom in speculating whether God could have redeemed mankind by one who was produced without human parent ; or, again, by one who had a human father as well as a human mother. But suggestions of this kind have been made, and perhaps call for comment. It may be pointed out that a new act of creation would have left no nexus between the Redeemer and those to be redeemed. He would

not have belonged to the same race as those whom He came to save. He would not have taken their flesh, and His life would have had little relation to theirs. It is difficult to see how the death and resurrection of such a being would have aided the human race. But the virgin birth avoided all violent breach with humanity. Just as the prophet (John the Baptist) who was to renovate Israel was taken from the old priesthood, so the Christ who was to redeem the whole of mankind was not created out of nothing, but 'born of a woman.'

Again, if the Christ had had two human parents, it is difficult to see how the hereditary contamination of the race could have been excluded. It may be said that such contamination remains even with only one human parent, and that the choice lies between admitting the contamination and severing the nexus with the human race altogether. But, in truth, there is no such dilemma. The choice is not between creation on the one hand and human parentage (whether with one or two parents) on the other. There is also the possibility of the substitution of Divine agency for the human father. It is conceivable that the presence of this Divine element would entirely exclude the possibility of contamination from the human mother. Indeed it is difficult to conceive that the Divine element could in any way receive contamination. But it is wiser to accept with reverent thankfulness what has been revealed to us respecting this mystery than to speculate needlessly, and perhaps fruitlessly, about what has not been revealed.

It has been pointed out already that the beauty, dignity, and delicacy of the story of the Annunciation are tokens of historic reality ; for the fictions about similar subjects in pagan, Jewish, and Christian literature are, in these respects, so very different. There is yet another mark of historic truth to be noted, viz. the extreme simplicity of the Christology. New Testament doctrine about the Christ is here found at a very early stage, earlier even than that in the Epistles to the Corinthians ; for there we have Christ's pre-existence implied as 'the second man from heaven' (1 Co 15⁴⁷), who 'became poor' when He became man for us (2 Co 8⁹, cf. 4⁴⁻⁶) ; and therefore much earlier than the more developed Christology of Colossians (1¹⁵) and Ephesians (1⁵⁻⁷ 4¹³), and than that of the writer to the Hebrews (1³), or that of the Fourth Gospel (1¹⁴ 3¹³ 17⁵). 'The power of the Most High shall overshadow thee' reminds us rather of the manifestations of the Divine presence in the Old Testament, especially the 'pillar of cloud' (Ex 13²¹ 40³⁴⁻³⁸, 1 K 8¹⁰·¹¹). If St. Luke had invented the story of the Annunciation, would he not have given us more of Pauline Christology, and that in its fullest form? That he has given us what is so rudimentary is evidence that he gives a record of what was revealed to Mary at the time, rather than what he himself knew and believed.

The couplet with which the narrative ends (1³⁸) balances that with which it opens (1²⁸), and it is one of deep spiritual significance to every believer. By her absolute submission to the will of God, in spite of the agony of shame and distress which this involved, Mary entered into an intimacy of relationship with Father, Son, and Holy Spirit, such as even angels cannot know. And yet it is precisely here that the humblest Christian may, by similar obedience, follow her. 'Blessed is the womb that bare thee,' said one to the Lord, 'and the breasts which thou didst suck. But he said, Yea rather, blessed are they that hear the word of God, and keep it' (Lk 11²⁷·²⁸).

It was natural that a special day should be set

apart to commemorate this mystery, but we do not know when this was first done. The earliest mention of such a festival is in the Acts of the Tenth Synod of Toledo (A.D. 656); and the next is in those of the Second Synod in Trullo (A.D. 692). But, just as the Purification was originally a feast in honour of our Lord rather than of the Virgin Mary, viz. of His presentation in the Temple and meeting with Simeon and Anna, so also this festival originally commemorated His miraculous conception rather than the announcement made to her. In the Ethiopian Calendar it is not called 'the Annunciation of the blessed Virgin Mary,' but 'the Conception of Christ': elsewhere the later name of the feast has driven out the original title, not only in the West, but also in the Eastern Churches.

LITERATURE.—Briggs, *The Messiah of the Gospels*, p. 41 ff., *New Light on the Life of Jesus*, 1904, p. 160 ff.; Ramsay, *Was Christ born at Bethlehem?*; Sanday, art. 'Jesus Christ' in Hastings' *DB* ii. p. 643 ff., also *Expository Times*, April 1903; Pearson, *On the Creed*, art. iii.; Swete, *The Apostles' Creed*, p. 41 ff., also *Expos. Times*, 1893; Westcott, *The Historic Faith*, p. 59 ff.; B. Weiss, *Leben Jesu*, ii. § 2 [Eng. tr. i. p. 222 ff.]; Loofs, *Leitfaden z. Studium d. Dogmengeschichte*; Soltau, *Geburtsgeschichte Jesu Christi*, 1902; J. A. Robinson, *Some Thoughts on the Incarnation*, 1903; Knowling, *Our Lord's Virgin Birth*; *Ch. Quart. Rev.*, July and Oct. 1904; Gore, *The Incarnation*, 77 ff., 251 f.; Garvie, *Expositor*, Feb. 1902. On the sceptical side: Keim, *Jesus of Nazara*, ii. p. 38 ff.; Hase, *Geschichte Jesu*, § 22 ff.; O. Holtzmann, *Leben Jesu*, cap. iv. [Eng. tr. p. 81 ff.]; P. Lobstein, *The Virgin-Birth of Christ*, 1903; Cheyne, *Bible Problems*, 1904.　　　A. PLUMMER.

ANOINTING.—I. In the ancient world, Jewish and pagan alike, it was customary to refresh guests at banquets by pouring cool and fragrant ointment on their heads. Cf. Mart. iii. 12; Ps 23[5], where Cheyne gives an Egyptian illustration: 'Every rich man had in his household an anointer, who had to place a cone of ointment on the head of his master, where it remained during the feast.' There are two instances of the usage in the Gospel history:

1. *The anointing in the house of Simon the Pharisee* (Lk 7[36-50]).—Impressed by the fame of Jesus and desirous of closer acquaintance with one who was certainly a prophet, perhaps more,[*] Simon bade Him to his table, inviting also a party of his friends. He was a Pharisee of the better sort, yet he shared the pride of his order and put a difference betwixt Jesus and the other guests, withholding from Him the customary courtesies: the kiss of welcome, the ablution of the feet, the anointing of the head. In the course of the meal a woman appeared in the room, wearing her hair loose, which in Jewish society was the token of a harlot.[†] What did she in a Pharisee's house? She had come, a sorrowful penitent, in quest of Jesus; and she brought an offering, an alabaster vase of ointment. As He reclined at table, she stole to His couch and, stooping over His feet, rained hot tears upon them, wiped them with her flowing tresses, kissed them, and anointed them with the ointment. She should have poured it on His head, but she durst not.[‡]

2. *The anointing in the house of Simon the Leper* (Jn 12[1-11] = Mk 14[3-9] = Mt 26[6-13]).—On His way up to the last Passover, Jesus stopped at the village of Bethany, where, a few weeks before, He had raised Lazarus; and, in defiance of the Sanhedrin's edict (Jn 11[57]), He was received with grateful reverence. One of the principal men of the village, named Simon, made a banquet in His honour. He had been a leper, and, if he had been healed by Jesus, it was fitting that his house should be

* According to the *v.l. ὁ προφήτης* in v.[39], Simon thought Jesus might be the prophet who should arise and herald the Messiah. Cf. Jn 1[21. 25] 6[14] 7[40].

† See Lightfoot on Jn 12[3].

‡ Orig. *in Matth. Comm. Ser.* § 77: 'Non fuit ausa ad caput Christi venire sed lacrymis pedes ejus lavit, quasi vix etiam ipsis pedibus ejus digna.'

the scene of the banquet.[*] But it was a public tribute, and others bore a part in it. Lazarus was present, and the good housewife Martha managed the entertainment. And what part did Mary take? She entered the room with her hair loose and an alabaster vase of precious ointment in her hand, and, approaching the Lord's couch, poured the ointment over His feet and wiped them with her hair. See MARY.

There are several points of difference between John's and Matthew-Mark's accounts of the anointing: (1) Matthew and Mark say that it happened in the house of Simon the Leper, and make no mention of Lazarus and his sisters. They simply say that the 'beautiful work' was wrought by 'a woman.' (2) They seem to put the incident two days (Mt 26[2] = Mk 14[1]), whereas John puts it six days before the Passover (12[1]). (3) They represent the nameless woman as pouring the ointment not on the Lord's feet but on His head, and say nothing of her wiping His feet with her hair. On the ground of these discrepancies it was generally maintained by the Fathers that there were two anointings at Bethany, the incidents recorded by Matthew-Mark and John being distinct. So Chrysostom (*in Matth.* lxxxi.), who apparently identified the anointing in the house of Simon the Leper (Mt.-Mk.) with that in the house of Simon the Pharisee (Lk.). Origen (*in Matth. Comm. Ser.* § 77) held that there were in all three anointings: (*a*) in the house of Simon the Leper (Mt.-Mk.); (*b*) in the house of Simon the Pharisee (Lk.); (*c*) at Bethany by Mary (Jn.); mentioning also the opinion that there were four, Matthew and Mark recording distinct incidents. Nowadays the tendency is rather to ignore the differences and identify all the narratives, reducing them to one. The Matthew-Mark narrative is regarded as authentic, the Lukan and Johannine narratives being adaptations thereof (Strauss, Ewald, Keim). Even in Origen's day a similar view prevailed: 'multi quidem existimant de una eademque muliere quatuor Evangelistas exposuisse.'

It hardly admits of reasonable doubt that there were two anointings, one in the house of Simon the Pharisee, and the other by Mary in the house of Simon the Leper at Bethany.[†] The discrepancies in the triple account of the latter are not inexplicable. (1) Matthew-Mark's omission of the names of Lazarus and his sisters belongs to the larger question of the Synoptic silence regarding the family at Bethany. (2) The position of the incident in Matthew-Mark is merely an example of the freedom wherewith the Synoptic editors were wont to handle the material of the Evangelic tradition, arranging it topically rather than chronologically. They have brought the story into juxtaposition with the betrayal (Mt 26[14-16] = Mk 14[10-11]), evidently by way of casting light on the traitor's action. The Lord's rebuke at the feast angered him, and, burning for revenge, he went and made his bargain with the high priests. Cf. Aug. *de Cons. Ev.* ii. § 153. (3) The difference regarding the manner of the anointing is an instance of John's habit of tacitly correcting his predecessors. His account is historical, and it would stand so in the Apostolic tradition; but the Synoptic editors or, more probably, the catechisers in their oral repetition of the tradition, wondering, since they did not know who the woman was, at the strangeness of her action, substituted 'head' for 'feet,' and then omitted the unintelligible circumstance of her wiping His feet with her hair. See MARY.

LITERATURE.—Andrews, *Life of our Lord*, pp. 281–283; Ramsay, *Was Christ Born at Bethlehem?* pp. 91–92; Hastings' *DB*, articles 'Anointing' and 'Mary,'; *Expositor*, 1st ser. vi. [1877] pp. 214–220; *Ecce Homo*[15], p. 232 ff.; Bruce, *Training of the Twelve*[5], pp. 289–308; Ker, *Sermons*, 1st ser. p. 16 ff.; Vinet, *Vital Christianity*, p. 294 ff. Reference may also be made to Bunyan, *Jerus. Sinner Saved* (ed. 1765), pp. 58–62; Herbert, *Marie Magdalane*; Hartley Coleridge's fine sonnet on Lk 7[47].

　　　　　　　　　　　　　　　　　　　DAVID SMITH.

II. Besides the two special incidents already described, some other references to 'anointing' may be briefly dealt with.

1. In Mt 6[17] Jesus tells His disciples that when they fast they are to anoint (ἀλείφω) the head as usual. The allusion is to that daily use of oil, as an application soothing and refreshing to the skin, which is common in hot countries, and was regularly practised by the Jews. The meaning of Jesus is that His disciples, when they feel it right to fast, should undertake the observance as in the sight of God, and not ostentatiously parade their performance of it before the eyes of men. They should wash and anoint themselves as usual, and not draw attention by any peculiarities of outward appearance to a matter lying between themselves and their heavenly Father.

* Lazarus was not the host, but one of the guests (Jn 12[2]). The notion that his house was the scene of the banquet has occasioned speculations about Simon. Theophylact mentions the opinion that he was Lazarus' father, lately deceased (Ewald).

† So Aug. *de Cons. Ev.* ii. § 154

2. In Mk 6[13] we read of the Twelve on their evangelistic mission, that they 'anointed (ἀλείφω) with oil many that were sick, and healed them.' The employment of oil as a medicinal agent was familiar in the time of Christ (cf. Lk 10[34], Ja 5[14]), and is doubtless referred to here; though the natural virtues of the oil were accompanied in this case by miraculous powers of healing. In Jn 9[6. 11] Jesus, before working the miracle upon the blind man, anoints (ἐπιχρίω) his eyes with clay which He had made by spitting on the ground. Here, also, the anointing may have had a medicinal aspect (see Meyer and *Expositor's Gr. Test. in loc.* on the ancient belief that both spittle and clay were beneficial to the eyes); though, of course, it is the miraculous agency of Jesus that is paramount in the narrative. In Rev 3[18] Jesus says to the Church of the Laodiceans, '. . . and anoint thine eyes with eyesalve, that thou mayest see,' where the effect of the application of collyrium is used as a figure of the healing and enlightenment which are found in the grace of the Lord Jesus Christ.

3. In Mk 14[8] Jesus says of the gracious act of Mary of Bethany in anointing Him at the feast, 'She hath anointed (μυρίζω fr. μύρον = 'ointment'; probably akin to μύρρα = 'myrrh') my body aforehand for the burying' (cf. Jn 12[7]). And in Mk 16[1] we read how Mary Magdalene and the other women went to the sepulchre to anoint (ἀλείφω) the dead body of the Saviour (cf. Lk 23[56], Jn 19[39. 40]). This application of ointments and spices (cf. Lk 24[1]) was an expression of reverence and affection for the departed, and may be compared with the modern custom of surrounding the beloved dead with fragrant and beautiful flowers. These unguents were not used for the purpose of embalming the dead, as among the Egyptians, but were only outwardly applied, and did not prevent decomposition (cf. Jn 11[39]).

4. When Jesus in the synagogue at Nazareth read from Is 61 the prophetic words, 'The Spirit of the Lord is upon me, because he anointed (χρίω) me to preach good tidings to the poor . . .' (Lk 4[18]), and went on to say, after closing the book, 'To-day hath this scripture been fulfilled in your ears' (v.[21]), He definitely claimed to be set apart to the Messianic calling. In the OT anointing was the symbol of consecration alike in the case of prophet (1 K 19[16]), priest (Lv 8[12]), and king (1 S 10[1]). And in the case of Jesus, who to His people is at once prophet, priest, and king, a spiritual anointing is distinctly affirmed by His Evangelists and Apostles as well as claimed by Himself (cf. Ac 4[27] 10[38], He 1[9]). The Hebrew word 'Messiah' (מָשִׁיחַ from מָשַׁח 'to anoint') means 'the anointed one'; and of this word 'Christ' is the Greek equivalent (χριστός, from χρίω, 'to anoint,' being employed in LXX to render מָשִׁיחַ).

5. In 1 Jn 2[20] the Apostle writes, 'And ye have an anointing (χρίσμα) from the Holy One, and ye know all things' (so RV; AV renders 'unction'). Again, in v.[27] he says, 'And as for you, the anointing (χρίσμα) which ye received of him abideth in you. . . .' (here AV as well as RV gives 'anointing'). That the 'Holy One' of this passage is Christ Himself, and that the 'anointing' He dispenses is the bestowal of the Holy Spirit, is held by nearly all commentators. Being Himself anointed with the Holy Ghost (Ac 10[38]), the Christ has power to impart the same gift to His disciples. Indeed, the bestowal of this gift is constantly represented as His peculiar function (cf. Jn 15[26] 16[7. 13-15], Ac 2[33]).

LITERATURE.—H. B. Swete, E. P. Gould, A. F. Hort, and esp. E. H. Plumptre on Mk 6[13]; also A. Plummer, and C. Watson on 1 Jn 2[20].   J. C. LAMBERT.

ANSWERS.—See QUESTIONS AND ANSWERS.

ANTIPAS.—See HEROD, No. 2.

ANTONIA (TOWER OF).—See TEMPLE.

ANXIETY.—See CARE.

APOCALYPTIC LITERATURE.—

  i. Name and Nature.
  ii. Origin and History.
  iii. The Apocalypses.
    1. The Ethiopic Enoch.
    2. The Slavonic Enoch.
    3. The Sibylline Oracles.
    4. The Assumption of Moses.
    5. Fourth Esdras.
    6. The Syriac Baruch.
    7. The Greek Baruch.
    8. The Psalter of Solomon.
    9. The Testaments of the XII Patriarchs.
    10. The Book of Jubilees.
    11. The Ascension of Isaiah.
    12. The Histories of Adam and Eve.
    13. The Apocalypse of Abraham.
    14. The Apocalypse of Elias.
    15. The Apocalypse of Zephaniah.
    16. Anonymous Apocalypse.
    17. The Prayer of Joseph.
    18. The Book of Eldad and Modad.
  iv. General Characteristics.
    1. The Vision Form.
    2. Dualism.
    3. Symbolism.
    4. Angelology.
    5. The Unknown as subject-matter.
    6 Pseudonymity.
    7. Optimism.
  v. Theological Ideas.
    1. The Doctrine of the two Æons.
    2. The Impending Crisis.
    3. The Conception of God.
    4. Complex Cosmology.
    5. Arch-enemy of God.
    6. Doctrine of Man.
    7. Doctrine of Sin.
    8. The coming Messiah.
    9. The Resurrection.
    10. The Judgment.
    11. Punishment of the Wicked.
    12. The Reward of the Righteous.
    13. The Renovation of the World.
    14. Predestination.
  vi. Contact with the New Testament.
    1. Apocalyptic Forms in the New Testament.
    2. Current Phraseology : Son of Man, etc.
    3. Quotations.
    4. Influence of Ideas.
    5. Treatment of Common Questions.
      Literature.

i. NAME AND NATURE.—The term 'apocalypse' (ἀποκάλυψις from ἀποκαλύπτω, *to uncover*) signifies in the first place the act of uncovering, and thus bringing into sight that which was before unseen, hence 'revelation.' It is predominantly a NT word. It occurs rather rarely in extra-biblical Greek, is used only once in the canonical portion of the LXX (1 S 20[30]), and thrice in Sirach (11[27] 22[22] 42[1] [41[23]]) In the NT it is used to designate the disclosing or communicating of knowledge by direct Divine act. The gospel is an apocalypse to the nations (Lk 2[32], Ro 16[25. 26]). St. Paul received it as an apocalypse (Gal 1[12]). The manifestation of Jesus Christ in glory is an apocalypse (Gal 2[2], 2 Co 12[1. 7], 2 Th 1[7], 1 P 1[7. 13] 4[13]).

An apocalypse is thus primarily the act of revelation; in the second place it is the subject-matter revealed; and in the third place a book or literary production which gives an account of revelation, whether real or alleged (*e.g.* 'The Apocalypse of St. John the Divine'). As a matter of history, the form in which the revelation purports to come is of the utmost importance in determining the question whether a writing should be called an apocalypse or not. In general, the form is like the drawing of the veil from before a picture, the result of which action presents to the eye a definite image. All imparting of Divine truth is revelation; but it is not all given in the apocalyptic form, *i.e.* it does not all come in grand imagery, as if portrayed on canvas or enacted in scenic representation. Some revelations come in sub-conscious convictions. Those who receive them do not feel called upon to give an account of the way in which they have received them. In fact they seem ignorant of the method of communication; they only know that they have received knowledge not previously possessed. Apocalypse and revelation thus, though primarily the same thing, come to be distinguished from each other.

The term 'apocalypse' is also sometimes used, with an effort at greater precision, to designate the pictorial portraiture of the future as foreshadowed by the seer. When so employed it becomes appropriate only as the title of certain passages in books otherwise not to be called apocalypses (so Bousset in Herzog-Hauck, *PRE*, *s.v.*, who enumerates the following passages: Dn 2^{7-12}; Eth. En 85–91. 37–71; Ps-Sol 2. 17. 18; the Assumption of Moses; Slav. En.; 4 Ezra; Syr. Bar.; Sibyl. Orac. iii. 286 to the end, iii. 36–92, iv., the Jewish source of i. and ii.; also certain sections of the Apoc. John and 2 Th 2^{3-12}; Mt 24 with parallels).

To constitute a writing an apocalypse, it is not necessary that the author should have actually seen or experienced what he portrays. It is enough that he write as one who has had a vision and is describing it. Thus apocalypse becomes a form of literature precisely in the same manner as an epistle. Strictly an epistle is simply a letter from one person, or many persons, to another, or others. But, as a matter of usage, it has often been adopted as a form into which men have chosen to cast their thoughts for the public. The same is true of the dialogue, of fiction, and many other species of literature. Such forms become favourites in certain ages, usually after some outstanding character has made successful use of them. The dialogue became fashionable when Plato made it such a telling medium for the teaching of his philosophical system. The epistle was used by Horace, and later by Seneca. The apocalypse form appears as a favourite about the beginning of the 2nd cent. B.C. The most illustrious specimen, and perhaps the prototype of later apocalyptic literature, is the Book of Daniel.

ii. ORIGIN AND HISTORY.—The question has been mooted as to the earlier antecedents of the apocalyptic form. Its ultimate source has been traced variously to Egypt, Greece, Babylonia, and Persia. In view of the fact, however, that the Hebrew prophets frequently incorporate visions into their writings (Is 6, Jer 24^{1-3}, Ezk 1^{37}, Is 24–27), it is scarcely necessary to go outside of Israel to search for its origins. Nevertheless, the Persians, the Babylonians, the Egyptians, and the Greeks had their apocalyptics. And it would be a mistake to ignore the influence especially of Persian forms during the period of the formation of Jewish apocalyptics. This was the very period when Jewish forms came most directly into touch with Persian. In any case, much of the material of the Jewish apocalypse has been adopted and naturalized from Persia (cf. Bousset, *Die Jüd. Apokalyptik*, 1903; Gunkel, *Schöpfung u. Chaos*, 1895). Apocalyptic literature in general begins before Christ. Soon after the Christian era it develops into the two naturally distinct forms of Christian and neo-Hebraic. Hence we may distinguish three classes of apocalypses:—(1) The earlier Jewish ones, or those which were published from B.C. 200 to A.D. 100. Within this class, however, may be included also such writings as proceed from Jewish sources purely, though not written until half a century, more or less, later than the last limit of the period. (2) Christian apocalypses, including the canonical book known as *the* Apocalypse (Revelation of St. John), and a series of apocryphal imitations. These are mostly pseudonymous, but include an occasional work in which the author does not conceal his name behind that of an apostle or older prophet (*The Shepherd of Hermas*). Apocalypses of this class pass into Patristics and culminate in Dante's immortal *Commedia*. (3) The neo-Hebraic apocalypses, beginning with the predominance of the Talmud (especially the Babylonian) and including a series of revelations to the great Rabbis (*The Revelation of R. Joshua b. Levi, The Alphabets of R. Akiba, The Hebrew Elijah Apocalypse, The Apocalypse of Zerubbabel, The Wars of King Messiah, The Revelations of R. Simon b. Yohai, The Prayer of R. Simon b. Yohai*, and the *Persian Apocalypse of Daniel*).

It would be somewhat beside the purpose of this article to do more than sketch the first of these three classes of apocalypses. On the other hand, as Christ emerged in history at a definite period and in a definite environment, and as in this environment nothing is more conspicuous and potent than the early Jewish apocalyptic literature, the importance of this literature cannot be overestimated. A flood of light is shed by the form and content of these writings upon His life, teaching, and work. Happily, considerable attention has been given in recent years to this as a field of investigation, and some definite results may be registered.

iii. THE APOCALYPSES.—Of the earlier Jewish apocalypse, the canonical Daniel forms the prototype. The proper place, however, for a particular treatment of Daniel is conventionally the sphere of Old Testament Introduction (see art. 'Daniel' in Hastings' *DB* vol. i.). Our list will begin with the Books of Enoch.

1. The Ethiopic Enoch.—The adjective 'Ethiopic' has been attached to the title of this work because of another Book of Enoch discovered in a Slavonic version. Outside the canonical Daniel, this is the best known of the apocalypses, because of the quotation from it in Jude $^{14f.}$. Tertullian knows it, believes in its genuineness, and attempts to account for its transmission through and survival under the vicissitudes of the Flood. It appears to have been neglected, however, through the Middle Ages, and lost until 1773, when two MS copies of an Ethiopic version of it were brought from Abyssinia by J. Bruce. A translation of one of these was made by Lawrence, and published in 1821. But its full importance and significance came to be realized only with Dillmann's critical edition of the Ethiopic text in 1851, which was followed in 1853 by a thorough German translation and commentary. A portion of the Greek text was discovered in 1886–7, and edited by H. B. Swete.

Contents.—As it stands to-day, the Book of Enoch can be subdivided into five main parts with an introduction and a conclusion, as follows: *Introductory Discourse*, in which the author announces his parable, and formally asks attention to the important matters which he is about to divulge (1–5).

(*a*) The first section is concerned with *Angelology* (6–36), beginning with the report of the fall of two hundred angels who were enticed by the beauty of the daughters of men, and left heaven in order to take them for wives. Out of these unions sprang giants 3000 cubits in height. The fallen angels, moreover, taught men all manner of secrets whereby they were led into sin. When the giants had consumed all the possessions of men, they turned against the men themselves and smote them until their cry went up to heaven. Ringleaders of the angels are Azazel and Semjâzâ (6–9). Through the intercession of the four archangels, Michael, Uriel, Raphael, and Gabriel, God is moved to arrest bloodshed upon earth. He sends Uriel to Noah to tell him that He has determined to destroy the world. He commands Raphael to bind Azazel and throw him into a pit in the wilderness, where he shall remain until the day of the great judgment, and then be cast into the fire. He commands Gabriel to rouse the giants against each other; and, finally, he commands Michael to announce to Semjâzâ the sentence of punishment, which is, that the fallen angels shall be kept enchained and imprisoned under the hills of the earth, waiting the last judgment, when they shall be cast into the fire (10). After the destruction of all impiety upon earth, the righteous shall flourish and live long, the earth shall yield abundantly, all people shall pray to God, and all evil shall be banished from the earth (11). The sentence upon the fallen angels is communicated to Enoch (12), and he reveals it to them; but, at their urgent request, he composes a petition on their behalf, that they might obtain forgiveness; while rehearsing this, preparatory to presenting it, he falls asleep and is informed in a dream that their request for forgiveness will not be granted, and once more makes known to the angels their impending doom (13–16). Enoch tells of a journey in which he learned of the places where thunders and lightnings originate, and saw the stream of Hades, the corner-stone and the pillars of the world, the seven mountains of precious stones, and the places of punishment of the disobedient angels, *i.e.* the stars (17–19). He gives the names and functions of the six (seven) archangels (20). He once more visits the place of punishment of the condemned angels, and the nether world (21), consisting of four parts (22). He travels to the West (23–25). From there he returns to the city of Jerusalem, which is the centre of the earth (26. 27); then he travels to the East (28–33), to the North (34. 35), and, lastly, to the South (36).

(*b*) The second section is *Christological*, and consists of chs. 37–71, subdivided into three Similitudes. A short introductory discourse (37) is followed by the first *Similitude*, including chs. 38–44. The appearance of the Messiah, the righteous One, brings an end of sinners upon earth (38). Enoch is carried by storm-clouds to the end of heaven, and there beholds the pre-existing Kingdom of God, the dwellings of the righteous and the elect, and of angels and archangels (39. 40). He then sees the weighing of men's actions in the balance, the rejection of sinners, the places prepared for the righteous, and certain physical mysteries (lightnings, thunders, winds, hail, mist, clouds, sun and moon, 41), also the place of Wisdom in heaven (42), and, finally, some more physical mysteries (43. 44). The second *Similitude* includes chs. 45–57. It begins with the Messianic Judgment (45). Enoch sees the Son of Man beside the Head of Days (46). An angel explains the vision (47, the Son of Man will overthrow and judge the kings and mighty ones of the ungodly). The task of the pre-existing Son of Man is outlined (48. 49), and the happy consequences of the judgment for the pious, together with the punishments of the wicked, and the resurrection of those who have died in righteousness (50. 51). In a vision of six mountains of metal which pass away, the destruction of the heathen world by the Messiah is portrayed. The heathen world endeavours through offerings to propitiate God, but fails. The angels of punishment go forth to do their work. The synagogue service may now be carried on unhindered (52–54[6]). An account of the coming flood and its occasion is inserted (54[7]–55[2]), and is followed by the final assault of the heathen world-power (55[3-56]) and the return of the dispersed Jews (57). The third *Similitude* comprises chs. 58–69, to which chs. 70 and 71 are added by way of an appendix. It begins with the picture of the blessedness of the righteous in heaven (58);

an account of the mystery of lightning and thunder follows (59). A vision of Noah, an account of Leviathan and Behemoth, and various nature-elements which take part in the Flood are then given (60). The judgment of the Son of Man over the angels in heaven, and the sentence of kings by Him, followed by vain pleas on their part for mercy, are given next (61–64). Then comes the revelation to Noah of the fall of the angels, the Flood, his own preservation, the punishment of the angels, and the judgment of men by the Son of Man (65–69). Enoch's translation to Paradise, his ascension to heaven, and his acceptance by the Son of Man, are then given in the appendix (70, 71).

(*c*) The third section is *Cosmological*, and consists of chs. 72–82. It has been called the 'Book of the Luminaries of Heaven.' It contains a revelation given by the angel Uriel on all sorts of astronomical and geographical matters, among others on the convulsions that will occur during the period of the wicked upon earth. The course of the sun is first described (72), next the course of the moon (73. 74); untoward days (75); the winds (76); the four quarters of heaven (77); further details regarding the rising and setting of the sun (78. 79), changes in the order of things to come in the last days (80), and the return of Enoch to the earth; and the committal of these matters to Methusaleh (81. 82).

(*d*) The fourth section is a *Historical forecast*. Enoch narrates to his son Methusaleh two visions which he saw before he had taken a wife to himself. The first of these (83. 84) came to him as he was learning to write. It placed before his eyes the picture of the Deluge. The second vision (85–90) unfolded before him the whole history of Israel from the creation of man to the end of time. The children of Israel appeared in this vision in the forms of the clean animals (bulls, sheep, lambs, and goats). Their enemies were in the form of dogs, foxes, swine, and all manner of birds of prey. In the conflict between the clean and unclean, the struggle of Israel against her enemies was portrayed. The chosen people were delivered into the hands of lions, tigers, wolves, and jackals (the Assyrians and Babylonians); then they were put under the care of seventy shepherds (angels). (From this fact this section of the book takes the title of 'Vision of the Seventy Shepherds'). The shepherds allowed more of the faithful to perish than was the will of God, but at the critical moment there appeared a white lamb in their midst and entered into a fierce combat with the birds of prey, while a heavenly being gave him assistance. Then the Lord Himself burst forth from heaven, the enemies of Israel were overthrown and exterminated, the judgment ensued, and the universal restoration; and the Messiah was born as a white bull.

(*e*) The fifth section (91–105) is a *Book of Exhortations*. Enoch commands his son Methusaleh to summon to his side all his other sons, and when they have come he delivers to them an address on righteousness, which is especially designed to instruct the righteous of all ages (91[1-11]). In this first discourse is inserted the prediction of the *Ten Weeks* (91[12-17] 93). The remainder of the book (92. 94. 105) is taken up with final encouragements and messages of hope.

The conclusion of the whole Book of Enoch (106–108) contains an account of the marvels destined to accompany the birth of Noah (106. 107), and a new description of the fiery tribulations reserved for the wicked and of the blessings that await those who 'loved eternal heaven better than their own lives' (108).

Literary features.—Thus far the Book of Enoch has been treated as it is extant. A closer inspection reveals the fact that it is composite. Criticism is still in a considerable state of flux as to the correct analysis of it. Charles believes it to consist of five primary documents. Clemen finds in it seven separate Enoch traditions or legends worked together by a redactor. The weight of probability, however, is rather in favour of three primitive documents : (1) A Book of Enoch, consisting of chs. 1–36 and 72–105 ; (2) A Book of Similitudes, including chs. 36–71 ; and (3) a Noachic document, broken up and inserted in various parts within the preceding two. The work of redaction appears to have been done after the two primary documents had undergone some modification, possibly accidental. The redactor used the lost Apocalypse of Noah, alluded to in Jubilees (10^{13} 21^{10}), supplementing what he deemed to be lacunæ. The passages inserted from the Book of Noah are the following : 54^7–55^2 60. 65^1–69^{25}, and 106. 107. To these some would add several other passages.

The date of the first of these documents is the first quarter of the 2nd cent. B.C. (200 to 175) ; that of the Book of Similitudes offers an as yet unsolved problem whose difficulty is somewhat enhanced by the importance of the issue involved, i.e. the relation the book sustains to the NT. The fact that this relation is undoubted and intimate has quickened interest and led to the perception of slight considerations otherwise easily left out of view. The weight of these considerations is, moreover, so well balanced that criticism seems unable to reach a general consensus on the subject. The views that divide the field are (1) that the book was composed in the Maccabæan period (Ewald, B.C. 144) ; (2) that it was produced between B.C. 95 and 64 (Dillmann, Sieffert, Charles) ; (3) that it was written during the days of Herod (Lücke, Hausrath, Lipsius, Schodde, Schürer, Baldensperger, Beer) ; (4) that it is a product of the 2nd cent., and written by a Christian who has used an older Jewish apocalypse as a basis (Hoffmann, Weisse, Hilgenfeld, Volkmar, Tideman) ; (5) that though a Jewish apocalypse and possibly written before the beginning of the Christian era, it was interpolated by a Christian through the insertion of the 'Son of Man' passages (Drummond, Stalker). That the book should have been composed as a Jewish apocalypse and as such adopted the Messianic title 'Son of Man' from the Christian Gospels, is not to be thought of. That it should have been originally a Jewish apocalypse and modified by a Christian, either with a free hand or by the mechanical interpolation of the 'Son of Man' passages, is credible. But a more natural hypothesis is that it was a pre-Christian work, inclusive of the 'Son of Man' passages. It has been demonstrated by Baldensperger and Dalman that the title 'Son of Man' occurs in Jewish rabbinical writings as the name of the Messiah (Das Selbstbewusstsein Jesu², p. 90 ; Words of Jesus, p. 234 f.) ; and there is therefore nothing in the occurrence of this phrase to lead to its being considered due to a Christian author. Upon the whole it is probable that the book was produced in the 1st cent. B.C. The redaction is difficult to locate with precision and may be post-Christian.

The originals of the book were undoubtedly Semitic (Hebrew or Aramaic). The fragment of the Greek version recently discovered shows clear evidences of being the translation of a Semitic original (the case is argued conclusively by Charles, Book of Enoch, pp. 21, 22, 325, and Halévy, Journal Asiat. 1887, pp. 352–395).

Editions.—(1) Ethiopic Text: Lawrence (1838), Dillmann (1851), Flemming (Texte u. Untersuch., Neue Folge, vii. 1, 1902). (2) Greek Fragments : Bouriant (1892), Lods (1892), Charles (1893), Swete (1897).

(3) Translations.—English : Lawrence (partial, 1821), Schodde (1882), Charles (1893).—German : Hoffmann (1833–1838), Dillmann (1853), Flemming and Radermacher (1901).—French : Lods (the Greek Fragments only, 1892).

LITERATURE.—(See Charles, Book of Enoch, pp. 9–21) ; Lücke, Einl. in d. Offenb. Johan. (1852) ; Ewald, Abhandl. üb. d. Eth. B. Henoch (1855) ; Hoffmann, 'Üb. d. Entstehungszeit d. B. Henoch' in ZDMG, 1852, pp. 87–91 ; Köstlin, 'Üb. d. Entstehung d. B. Henoch' in Theol. Jahrb. 1856, pp. 240–279, 370–386 ; Gebhardt, 'Die 70 Hirten d. B. Henoch' in Merx' Archiv, vol. ii. 1872, pp. 163–246 ; Wieseler, 'Zur Abfassungszeit d. B. Henoch' in ZDMG, 1882, pp. 185–195 ; Lawlor in Journ. of Philol. 1897, pp. 164–225 ; Clemen, 'Die Zusammensetzung d. B. Henoch, etc.' in SK, 1898, pp. 210–227 ; Stalker, The Christology of Jesus, 1899, App. B, pp. 269–294.

2. The Slavonic Enoch.—This is one of the most recent additions to our group of apocalypses. Its existence was not indeed suspected before its discovery. But this was due to the fact that a number of books were attributed to Enoch. In this very work Enoch is said to have written 366 ; cf. 23^6 68^1. And because some of those were extant in the Ethiopic book no one thought of seeking for more. Nevertheless, it was no source of surprise when it was announced that a new Enoch had been found. This came first as an intimation that a copy of a Slavonic version of the Ethiopic Enoch was in existence (Kozak in Jahrb. f. Prot. Theol. 1892). Prof. Charles started to investigate the matter, and with the assistance of Mr. Morfill procured and examined printed copies of the Slavonic text in question. The result was the publication of the altogether independent and

hitherto unknown pseudepigraph (1896). Prof. Charles' title for the book is The Book of the Secrets of Enoch, but it is likely to be known in the future by the more convenient title, The Slavonic Enoch,* which distinguishes it from the better known and older Ethiopic work.

Contents.—The book may be divided into three parts, viz. (1) The Ascension of Enoch and his travels in the Seven Heavens (1–38). (2) The Return and Instructions to his children (39–56). (3) Second Series of Instructions, including in his audience an assemblage of 2000 people, and final assumption (57–68).

(a) Chs. 1–38. The book opens with a short prologue, introducing the personality of Enoch, and giving the time and place of a dream he saw (1). Enoch then warns his children of his impending absence from them for a time (2) ; he is taken by two angels up to the first heaven (3), where he sees 200 angels who guard the treasuries of the snow, the dew, and the oil (4–6). He is next taken up into the second heaven, and beholds and converses with the fallen angels (7). In the third heaven, the paradise prepared for the righteous (8. 9), he is led to the northern region, where he sees the places of torture (10). From thence he is taken up into the fourth heaven, the habitation of the sun and moon, and there sees the phœnixes and chalkadris (chalkydries), mysterious composite beings with heads of crocodiles and bodies of serpents (11. 12). In the eastern portion of the fourth heaven he comes to the gates of the sun (13) ; thence he is led to the western regions, and hears a song by the phœnixes and chalkydries (14. 15). He is then taken to the eastern course, and hears indescribable music by angels (16. 17). Here his visit to the fourth heaven ends ; he is carried to the fifth heaven, where he sees the Grigori or Watchers (18). In the sixth heaven he delays only a short time, and thence passes to the seventh (19. 20), where the Lord is seated on a high throne. Here the ministering angels who have brought him take their departure ; Enoch falls down and worships the Lord ; he is stripped of his earthly clothing, anointed, and robed in suitable apparel ; he is given over to Vretil, the archangel (patron of literature), to be instructed (21. 22). Under the guidance of this archangel he writes 366 books (23). He returns into the presence of the Lord, and holds direct converse with Him, learning the secrets of creation (24–29²), and of the formation of 10,000 angels and the fall of Satanail (29³⁻⁵) ; also of the creation of man, i.e. Adam and Eve (30), his being placed in paradise, his fall and judgment (31. 32). God then declares His purposes for the future (33. 34), and sends him back to the earth to stay thirty days longer and teach his children the true knowledge of God (35–38).

(b) Chs. 39–56. Enoch now begins his admonitions and instructions to his children (39) ; he tells of the manner in which he was given his visions, and of how he wrote them down (40) ; of how he wept for the sins of Adam (41) ; of his visit to the gates of hell, and the impression produced upon him (42) ; of the judgment of the Lord (43) ; of the duty of charity (44) ; of the superiority of a contrite and broken heart to sacrifice as a means of pleasing God (45) ; of God's love of purity in heart and His rejection of the sacrifices of the impure (46) ; and commends his writing to them as a permanent means of knowing God's will (47. 48). He further instructs them not to swear by heaven or the earth, and deprecates vengeance (49. 50) ; he urges them to be generous to the poor, not to hoard up treasures on earth (51), to praise God, and to be at peace with men (52). He enjoins them not to

* Bousset quotes these two works as I and II Enoch respectively (Die Religion des Judenthums, 1903).

trust in his own intercession with God, but to give heed to his writings and be wise (53); and closes his address with an exhortation to circulate his writings, announcing at the same time that the hour for his ascension to heaven has come (54. 55).

(c) Chs. 56–67. The second series of Exhortations opens with a request by Methosalem for a blessing over the houses and children of Enoch (56); Enoch asks Methosalem to call his brothers together (57), and gives them his instructions (58), especially that they should not eat the flesh of cattle (59), nor kill any man through 'net,' 'weapon,' or 'tongue' (60); but practise righteousness, and trust in repentance for the future (61. 62), and not despise the humble and thus incur God's curse (63). At this point God calls Enoch with a loud voice, and 2000 persons come together to give him their greetings (64); he delivers his final exhortations to them, which are to the effect that they should fear and serve the Lord (65. 66). A thick darkness covers the earth, and while it lasts Enoch is taken up, but no one knows how (67). The book concludes with a summary of Enoch's life and work, and an account of Methosalem's building an altar upon the spot where his father was last seen before his ascension.

Literary questions.—The author of the work was an Alexandrian Jew. This is made clear by the affinities of his style and thought with those of Philo, his use of the LXX, his portraiture of phœnixes and chalkadris (chalkydries), and his syncretistic cosmogony. The date of composition cannot be later than A.D. 70. The temple was evidently still standing, and sacrifice was offered (59²). But the Ethiopic Enoch was also in existence (40⁵·⁹, cf. also 43². ³ 52⁸ 61². ⁴).

The original language was undoubtedly Greek. This is proved by the explanation of the name Adam, which is made upon the basis of the Greek form ΑΔΑΜ, each letter representing one of the cardinal points of the compass (ΑΝΑΤΟΛΗ, ΔΥΣΙΣ, ΑΡΚΤΟΣ, ΜΕΣΗΜΒΡΙΑ). The book was known and used by Barnabas, by the author of the *Ascension of Isaiah*, by the author of the *Testaments of the Twelve Patriarchs*, by some of the many Sibyls, and by Irenæus.

Editions.—The Slavonic text has been published from different manuscripts, varying more or less from one another, and not as yet fully collated (Popoff, 1880).

Translations.—English: Charles and Morfill, *The Book of the Secrets of Enoch*, 1896.—German: Bonwetsch, 'Das Slavische Henochbuch' in *Abhandl. d. Gött. Ges. d. Wiss.* (Phil.-hist. Klasse, Neue Folg. 1–3, 1896).

LITERATURE.—Harnack, *Gesch. d. Altchrist. Litt.* ii. 1, 1897, p. 564; Charles in Hastings' *DB*, 1898; Volz, *Jüd. Eschatologie*, 1903, pp. 29, 30.

3. The Sibylline Oracles.

The name 'sibyl' is of uncertain derivation. Even the spelling of the word varies in the earliest period. It is, however, a very ancient one, and occurs as early as in the works of Heraclitus. By the Romans a number (ten) of sibyls were distinguished. The one of Erythræ in Ionia is reckoned the oldest. The sibyl of Cumæ (Kyme) became the most famous. Large collections of verses were circulated under her name during the latter years of the commonwealth and the early empire. Sibylline verses became common in Egypt, and there arose a so-called Jewish sibyl simultaneously with the appearance of the spirit of proselytism among the Jews. Finally, a Christian sibyl came into existence in succession to and imitation of the Jewish one. The productions of the Jewish and Christian sibyls are for the most part blended into one body. They constitute a compilation of hexameters in twelve Books, besides some fragments. Each of these is evidently independent of the others, and may have circulated separately.

Contents.—Book I. opens with an account of the Creation, based upon Genesis. This is followed by the story of the Fall, the multiplication of mankind, the appearance of four successive races down to the days of the giants, the story of Noah and the Flood, a sixth race and the Titans, from whom the transition is made to Christ, and the dispersion of the Jews.—Book II. predicts a time of plagues and wickedness, which is succeeded by the tenth race (the Romans), and a period of peace. After an interpolation of a group of proverbs, the woes of the last generations are portrayed, and the events of the last day of judgment and resurrection are foretold. Then follows a picture of the punishment of the wicked and the blessedness of the righteous.—Book III. extols the unity and power of God, denounces idolatry, proclaims the coming of the Great King, and of his opponent Beliar, foreshadows the reign of a woman (Cleopatra), and the subjection of the world to Christ. At this point the sibyl returns to the origin of man, and beginning with the Tower of Babel recounts the story as given in the OT down to Roman days. She foretells the doom of Rome, and of many Asiatic cities, as well as of the islands of the Ægean. A general judgment and millennium (Messianic Day) closes the book. — Book IV. declares the blessedness of the righteous, sketches successively the Assyrian and Medo-Persian dominations, announcing the Greek conquest, which will bring woes on Phrygia, Asia, and Egypt; one great king especially will cause calamities to fall on Sicily and Greece. After the Macedonian will come a Roman conquest. The impious will suffer many evils, and a general resurrection, judgment and retribution will follow.—Book V. opens with a prophecy of the reign of the Roman emperors; it then passes in review the calamities impending on Egypt and Asia Minor; it breaks out into a felicitation of the Jews and Judæa, and of the heavenly Joshua, and once more returns to further details of judgment, such as the destruction of Serapis, Isis, and the Ethiopians.—Book VI. describes the pre-existence, incarnation, and baptism of the Son of God, His teaching and miracles, the miseries in store for the guilty land, and the glories of the Cross.—Book VII. is an account of the woes impending upon various lands and cities of Greece, Asia Minor, and Egypt, in which just one prediction of the signs of the Messiah is incorporated.—Book VIII. is a history of the world under five monarchies. The fifth of these furnishes the subject for a prophecy of misery, judgment, and destruction. From this the sibyl passes to the denunciation of woes upon Egypt, the islands of the Mediterranean, and Persia, and closes with a picture of the Messiah.—Books IX. and X. are in fragments.—Book XI. is an orderly story of the world-powers from the time of the Tower of Babel to the subjection of Egypt under Cleopatra.—Book XII. pictures the fortunes of the Cæsars, beginning with Augustus and closing with Alexander Severus.—Book XIII. concerns the times of the emperors of the 1st cent., beginning with Maximin. It touches more especially upon their relations with the Persians and Syrians, closing with an allegory of a bull, a stag, a lion, and a goat.—Book XIV. is the most obscure of the Sibylline productions. The writer evidently intends to unfold the fortunes of a long succession of emperors and conquerors. He gives the initial letter of the name of each, and suggests other ways of identification. But his descriptions are so wide of the historical figures that they cannot be safely identified. The period portrayed is generally the late Roman and possibly the early Byzantine.

Literary questions.—The above division into books was made in the 6th cent. of the Christian era (during the reign of Justinian). Whoever made it is also responsible for the collection of the oracles from various sources, and the insertion of certain verses of his own among them. It has been conjectured that he was a literary monastic and expert transcriber of manuscripts. Before his time the verses were circulated in a rude, undigested mass. The task of unravelling the confusion, which does not seem to have disturbed him, and of rearranging the material according to authorship and date of origin, is a very complex one, and not as yet fully accomplished. This much is evident, however, that there are four classes of utterances in the oracles: (1) those which issue from a Jewish source; (2) those which come from a Christian; (3) those which are of heathen origin; and (4) neutral elements. The last of these adds very much to the difficulty of the critical problem. The heathen elements are not very extensive, and attach themselves in general to the Jewish. For the rest, the analysis which results from the labours of Ewald and Alexandre may be safely adopted as workable, and is as follows :—

The Sibylline Oracles may be grouped into eight parts, each by a different author and from a different age, as follows—(1) The Prologue of Book I. and Book III., 97-828, belong to the age of Ptolemy Physcon (B.C. 140). They were therefore written by an Alexandrian Jew. They constitute the pith and kernel of the whole collection in point of value for the study of inter-Testamental conditions and modes of thought, and for the times of Jesus. (2) Book IV. was written about A.D. 80. Its author may have been either a Christian or a Jew, with the probability largely in favour of the former alternative. (3) Book V., with the possible exception of the first part, issued from the 1st cent. A.D., and is a mixture of Jewish and Christian fragments impossible to disentangle from each other. (4) Books VI. and VII. (to which Ewald adds the first part of Book V.) date from the early part of the 3rd century. The author was a heretical Christian. (5) Book VIII., 1-360, is also by a Christian, but not a heretic, probably of the middle of the 3rd century. (6) Book VIII., 361-501, is also by an orthodox Christian of the 3rd century. (7) Book I. (without the Prologue), Book II., and Book III., 1-35, come from the middle of the 3rd cent., and are of Christian origin. (8) Books XI., XII., XIII., and XIV. were writtten by a Jew resident in Egypt, who, however, lived in Christian times, and is acquainted with some Christian practices. According to this analysis, these oracles cover a period of more than 400 years in their production, and represent a wide variety of types of thought.

Editions.—The first eight books in the original Greek text were published in 1545 at Basel, and subsequently by others up to Angelo Mai (1819 and 1828, Milan). The first complete edition is that of Alexandre (1841, and again 1869). Recent critical editions by Rzach (1891), Geffcken (1902), and Heitz (1903).

Translations.—Latin: Sebastian Castalio (1546), Angelo Mai (1817).—English: Floyer (prose, 1731), M. S. Terry (metrical, 1899).— French: Bouché - Leclercq in *Revue de l'Histoire des Religions*, vols. vii. 1883, pp. 236-248; viii. 1883, pp. 619-635; ix. 1884, pp. 220-233 (left incomplete).—German: Friedlieb (1852), Blass (of III. IV. and V. in Kautzsch's *Pseudepigr.* 1900).

LITERATURE.—(See Englemann, *Bibliotheca Scriptorum Classicorum*, 1880, i. p 528); Bleek, 'Üb. d. Entstehung u. Zusammensetz. d. Sibyl. Or.' in *Theol. Zeitschr.*, herausg. v. Schleiermacher, de Wette, u. Lücke, i. 1819, pp. 120-246; ii. 1820, pp. 172-239; Hilgenfeld, 'Die Jüdische Sibyllen - Weissagung' in *ZWTh*, 1860, pp. 313-319; also 1871, pp. 30-50; Ewald, *Abhandlung üb. Entstehung, Inhalt u. Wert. d. Sibyll. Bücher*, 1858; Laroque, 'Sur la date du troisième Livre Sib.' in *Revue Archéolog.*, 1869, pp. 269-270; Bernhardy, *Grundriss der Griech. Litt.*, iii. (ii. 1, pp. 441-453, 1867); Buresch, 'Die Pseudosib. Or.' in *Jahrbb. f. Class. Phil.* 1891, pp. 529-555; 1892, pp. 273-308; Friedländer, 'La Sibylle Juive' in *REJ*, 1894, pp. 183-196; Harnack, *Gesch. d. Altchrist. Litt.* i. 762, 861-863; ii. 581-589; Schürer, *HJP* II. iii. 271-292.

4. The Assumption of Moses.

—There is some vagueness in the early Patristic references to the *Assumption of Moses.* Syncellus (ed. Dind. i. 48) mentions an *Apocalypse of Moses.* Clement of Alexandria (*Adumb. in Epist. Jud.* [*ap.* Zahn, *Supplementum Clementinum*, 84]) and Didymus (*Epist. Judæ Enarratio* [in Gallandi, *Bib. Patr.* vi. 307]), allude to an *Assumptio Moysi.* Origen (*de Princ.* III. ii. 1) refers to an *Adscensio Mosis.* In the Acts of the Nicene Synod (Mansi, *Sacror. Concil., Nova Collectio*, ii. 18, 20) there is mention again of an *Assumption of Moses.* In other lists of apocrypha, a *Testament* (Διαθήκη) *of Moses* is mentioned (*Stichometry* of Nicephorus and *Synopsis* of pseudo-Athanasius). It has been argued (by Schürer, followed by Charles) that these two titles represent two separate divisions of one and the same book, or two books fused together in one. The work was lost during the Middle Ages, and recovered by Ceriani in an old Latin version in the Ambrosian Library at Milan in 1861.

Contents.—Moses calls to himself Joshua, the son of Nun, and directs him to preserve his writings (1). He then forecasts the apostasy and distress of the twelve tribes of Israel and their divisions into the ten and two (2), their awakening to consciousness of their sin, their repentance (3), the restoration of the two tribes and the preservation of the ten among the Gentiles (4), their repeated backslidings (5), the tyranny of Herod (6), the prevalence of wicked leaders over them (7), the oppres-

sion by the Romans (8), the advent of the Levite Taxo,* who was destined to restore a better state of things among them (9). At this point the author inserts a Psalm of Hope and adds a few concluding words closing the discourse of Moses (10). Joshua then laments over the course of events revealed to him, and refuses to be comforted (11); but Moses urges him to take up his work, and conquer and destroy the Gentiles (12). At this point the book breaks off rather abruptly.

Literary questions.—The Patristic quotations from the *Assumption of Moses* identify the words of Jude [9] as from this book; but as the extant text does not contain the words, it can only be that it is either (1) wrongly entitled, or (2) that the quotation is made from the second part of it which is lost (Schürer), or (3) that two separate works entitled respectively *The Testament of Moses* and the *Assumption* (*Ascension*) *of Moses* were fused into one (Charles). The last position is most convincingly supported by its advocate, and seems the most probable. The present so-called *Assumption of Moses* is then the *Testament of Moses*, bearing within it traces of the addition to it of the original *Assumption of Moses.*

The text of the book exists in a single Latin manuscript of the 5th (6th) cent. A.D. This is undoubtedly a translation from a Greek text. It has been further conjectured that the Greek itself was a translation of a Hebrew or Aramaic original; but though the advocates of each of these languages, as also of the Greek, strenuously defend each his position, in the absence of definite data nothing can be dogmatically asserted on the point. Hilgenfeld and Drummond favour a Greek original; Ewald argues for a Semitic (either Hebrew or Aramaic); Wieseler and Langen, for a Hebrew; Hausrath, Schmidt-Merx, Dillmann, Thompson, for an Aramaic.

The author of the work was probably a devout Jew, a Pharisee, and a mystic who does not share but rather aims to defeat the purposes of the Zealots (so Charles, but it has been strenuously maintained that he was a Zealot). The date of the composition is fixed by the allusion to Herod the Great. At the earliest, it must be 44, but various dates down to 138 have been advocated. The design of the author seems to be to teach the lesson that God has foreseen and foreshadowed all things; hence Israel should entertain no fear. A deliverer is to come.

Editions.—Ceriani (*Monumenta Sacra et Profana*, vol. i. Fasc. 1, pp. 55-64), Hilgenfeld (*NT extra Canonem Receptum*, 1876, pp. 107-135), Schmidt-Merx (*Archiv*, I. ii. 1868, p. 111 ff.), Fritzsche (*Lib. Apoc. Vet. Test.* 1871, pp. 700 to 730), Charles (*Assumption of Moses*, 1897, pp. 54-101).

Translations.—Greek: Hilgenfeld (attempted restoration from the Latin, *Messias Judæorum*, 1869, pp. 435-468). — English: Charles, *Assumption of Moses* (1897). — German: Volkmar, *Mose Prophetie und Himmelfahrt* (1867), Clemen in Kautzsch's *Pseudepigr.* (1900).

LITERATURE.—Colani, 'L'Assomption de Moïse' in *Revue de Théol.* 1868, pp. 65-94; Wieseler, 'Die jüngst aufgefundene Aufnahme Moses,' etc., in *Jahrbb. f. deutsche Theol.* 1868, pp. 622-648; Heidenheim, 'Beiträge z. besser. Verständniss d. Ascensio Mosis' in *Vierteljahrschrift f. deutsche u. englische Theologie*, 1874, pp. 216-218; Hilgenfeld, *ZWTh*, 1886, pp. 132-139; Schürer, *HJP* II. iii. 73-83.

5. Fourth Ezra (Second Esdras).

—This pseudepigraph has been known from the earliest Christian days, and has been widely circulated under the name of Ezra as his second, third, fourth, or fifth book, according to the various ways of grouping and entitling the books that issue from the Restoration generation. (See explanation of these names by Thackeray in Hastings' *DB*, art. 'Esdras, First Book of'). Fourth Ezra, however, has come to be generally accepted as the name for it.

Contents.—This is given in seven visions. The First Vision (3^1-5^{19}) is granted to Ezra in answer to disturbing doubts arising in his mind. These concern the origin of sin and suffering in the world (3^{1-36}). An angel gives him the answer: God's ways are inscrutable. The human spirit can comprehend but little (4^{1-21}). But as he pleads that it is painful to be left in ignorance on such vital matters, he is assured of a change of æon to take place soon. Definite signs will mark the change. He must fast for seven days, and receive another revelation at the end of that time (4^{22}-5^{19}).

The Second Vision (5^{20}-6^{34}) is granted in answer

---

* After unsuccessful attempts by many others, a satisfactory explanation of this name has been given by Burkitt (see Hastings' *DB* iii. 449b). Taxo is a copyist's mistake for Taxok —Ταξώκ. And this is to be read by Gematria as Eleazar. אלעזר = תכסוף. Eleazar the father of seven sons is the great Levite (2 Mac 6^{19}).

to the question, Why has God given over His only chosen people into the hands of the heathen? ($5^{20\text{-}30}$). He receives the answer that God loves His people, and the problem must be regarded as not solvable for man : nevertheless deliverance is drawing near ; the generations of men are passing ; the world has become old ; the signs of the end are visible (5^{31}–6^{34}).

The Third Vision (6^{35}–9^{25}), like the second, is given after a period of seven days' fasting, and is in answer to the question, Why does not Israel possess the land which belongs to it ? ($6^{35\text{-}59}$). The answer is not direct. An evil age must necessarily precede the good that shall be in the future ($7^{1\text{-}16}$). The doom of sinners is grievous but well-deserved. The Son of God, the Christ, shall appear in judgment ($7^{17\text{-}44}$). Few are chosen, but all the greater is the honour conferred on them ($7^{45\text{-}74}$). A sevenfold suffering and a sevenfold joy await men in the intermediate state ($7^{75\text{-}101}$). Intercession for the condemned will be of no avail at the last judgment ($7^{102\text{-}115}$), they have deserved their doom ($7^{116\text{-}131}$). God's mercy is consistent with the sufferings of the condemned (7^{132}–8^{19}). At this point Ezra interposes a prayer and receives an answer ($8^{20\text{-}45}$). The saved shall rejoice at their own lot, and forget the sufferings of sinners ($8^{46\text{-}61}$). It is certain that the end of the world is nigh. The signs are not to be mistaken (8^{62}–9^{13}). There are more of the lost than of the saved ($9^{14\text{-}25}$).

The Fourth Vision (9^{26}–10^{58}) is given upon the Plain of Ardath. It consists of a symbolic picture of Zion's sorrow, followed by glory. The vision (9^{26}–10^{28}) presents a woman in tattered garments, weeping and wailing because of her lost son. The explanation by the angel ($10^{29\text{-}58}$) identifies the woman with Zion, and points out the lesson to the seer.

The Fifth Vision (10^{60}–12^{51}) presents the fourth world-empire under the figure of an eagle coming out of the sea, and like the fourth vision falls into two parts, i.e. the Vision (10^{60}–12^{3}) and the interpretation of it by the angel ($12^{4\text{-}40}$). This is followed by a Conclusion in story form. The people come out to seek for Ezra, they find him in the plain, and he sends them back into the city ($12^{40\text{-}51}$).

The Sixth Vision ($13^{1\text{-}58}$) portrays a man emerging out of a stormy sea and floating on a cloudless heaven ($13^{1\text{-}4}$). A countless multitude comes to wage war against him ; but by a stream of fire proceeding from his mouth he overcomes his enemies ($13^{5\text{-}11}$). Then another host of friendly men flock around him ($13^{12\text{-}13}$). The question is raised, Is it better to survive to the end of the world or to die beforehand ? It is answered in favour of the former alternative ($13^{14\text{-}24}$). The explanation of the vision follows. The man in the cloud is the Son of God, the events are those of the Messianic age ($13^{25\text{-}58}$).

The Seventh Vision ($14^{1\text{-}50}$) is given three days after the sixth, under an oak. This is the familiar legend of Ezra's restoring the lost Scriptures. But it begins with a command to keep his present vision secret ($14^{1\text{-}17}$). A prayer of Ezra follows, in which he beseeches the Lord for the privilege of rewriting the lost Scriptures ($14^{17\text{-}26}$). The prayer is answered, and Ezra reproduces the lost books together with seventy others ($14^{27\text{-}48}$). The book concludes with an account of Ezra's decease.

The above does not include chs. 1. 2 and 15. 16, found in the Latin Version, which is the basis of the chapter divisions of the book. The Latin Version has also served as the basis of some current translations into English (*The Variorum Apocrypha*, by C. J. Ball, and in Wace's *Holy Bible*, 'Apocrypha,' by Lupton). These four chapters are universally regarded as later additions by a strongly anti-Jewish Christian author,

appended respectively to the beginning and end of the Latin Version. The other versions do not contain them. They have been detached and published together as 5th Esdras by Fritzsche (*Lib. Apocr. Vet. Test.* 'Liber Esdræ Quintus,' pp. 640–653).

Literary questions.—The book is a unity, and comparatively free from interpolations and editorial tampering. The author was a devout man for whom problems of theodicy especially had a considerable fascination, but he is also interested in the broader and more constant questions which recur in the religious sphere with every generation. He naturally looks into his own age, and finds no sign of a restoration to righteousness and recognition of God in the forces that work there. He accordingly plants his hopes in the world to come. Kabisch has indeed analyzed the work into four different productions fused together into unity by clumsy redactors (*Das Vierte Buch Esra*, 1889), and his theory has been substantially accepted by de Faye, but his observations would lead rather to the composition of the book from pre-existing sources than to the bringing together of independent books of documents by a redactor. The impression of unity is too strong to be destroyed by such considerations as Kabisch alleges.

The date of the book cannot be earlier than the fall of Jerusalem, as that event is distinctly alluded to (3^2 10^{48} 12^{48}). The Temple is destroyed and the service in abeyance (10^{21}). A still later chronological starting-point is given in an allusion to the death of Titus (11^{35}); the author even expects the death of Domitian ($12^{2.28}$). It is safe, therefore, to set down the year 90 as approximately the time of composition.

Editions.—The book exists in Latin, Syriac, Ethiopic, Arabic (2), and Armenian versions. The original was in Greek. This is made evident by the characteristic differences of the versions. They are all easily accounted for by an original Greek. The Latin text was first edited critically by Volkmar (1863); also by Fritzsche (*Lib. Apocr. Vet. Test.* 1871). The Syriac was published in Ceriani's *Monumenta Sacra*, i. Fasc. 2 (1866); also in photolithographic reproduction, under the title *Translatio Syro-Pescitto Veteris Testamenti*, etc. (1876–1888); again by R. Bensly, with an introd. by M. R. James (*Texts and Studies*, Camb. iii. 2, 1895). The Ethiopic was published by Lawrence (1820), the Arabic by Gildemeister (1877), the Armenian by the Mechitharists in Venice (1806).

Translations.—English: Bissell (Lange's *Commentary*, 1880), Lupton (Wace's 'Apocrypha,' 1888).—German: Volkmar (1863), Ewald (*Abhandl. d. Gött. Gesellsch. d. Wiss.* xi. 1862–1863), Zöckler (*Kgf. Kom.* 1891). A translation into Greek was made and published by Hilgenfeld (*Messias Judæorum*, 1869).

LITERATURE.—Corrodi, *Krit. Gesch. d. Chiliasmus*, 1781, vol. i. pp. 179–230; Gudschmid, 'Die Apoc. des Esra,' etc. in *ZWTh*, 1860; Volkmar, *Handbuch d. Einleit. in die Apokr.* 1893; Wieseler, 'Das Vierte b. Ezra' in *SK*, 1870, pp. 263–304; Kabisch, *Das Vierte B. Ezra*, 1889; Schieffer, *Die religiösen und ethischen Anschauungen des IV Ezra Buches*, 1901; Clemen in *SK*, 1898, pp. 237–246; Schürer, *GJV*³ iii. 232 ff. [*HJP* II. iii. 93 ff.].

6. The Syriac Baruch.—Baruch is mentioned as Jeremiah's companion and helper during the trying days which ended in the destruction of Jerusalem and the deportations under Jehoiakim and Zedekiah (Jer $32^{12.13}$ 36. 45). The fact that he wrote under Jeremiah's direction seems to have stimulated the tendency to publish alleged prophecies and revelations in his name. The first of these was the book that passed into the group of OT Apocrypha. One of Ceriani's many contributions to apocalyptics was the discovery, translation into Latin (1866), and later publication of a Syriac text of a Book of Baruch (*Monumenta Sacra*, v. 1871, pp. 11–18).

Contents.—The book is divided into two main parts, i.e. the Apocalypse proper (chs. 1–77) and the Letter to the Nine Tribes and a Half (chs. 78–87).

Part I. may again be subdivided into seven sections. (1) The first section (1–12) begins with the announcement of the impending fall of Jerusalem, and the captivity of Judah ; next comes the portraiture of the advancing Chaldæans, the hiding of the treasures of the Temple, and the destruction of the walls by angels, so that the Chaldæans might not claim the glory of the capture of the city. The next day the city is occupied by the enemy (6–8). Baruch stays amid the ruins of the city, while Jeremiah, by Divine command, accompanies the exiles to Babylon (9–12).—(2) The second section (13–20) contains a vision given to Baruch while standing on Mount Zion. He is assured that the calamity just fallen on the chosen people has been inflicted in mercy (13) ; he complains that good men are no better than others, but is answered that sin in one who possesses the Law is worthy of being punished (14. 15). He expresses other misgivings which are answered. He is then promised a new revelation (16–20).—(3) The third section (21–34) opens with Baruch's appearance at the end of seven days in the place appointed. Here he expresses his thoughts in the form of a prayer (21) ; he is shown that his knowledge is imperfect, that the time is coming when God's judgment will mature (22–25) ; he wishes to know of the distresses of the last days (26), and is given a revelation concerning the order of the times. The tribulation will come in twelve stages (27) ; the whole earth will be affected, but those in the chosen land will escape ; the Messiah will appear, first to bring blessings to the righteous on the earth (28. 29), and then, as He returns to His glory, to raise from the dead both the righteous and the unrighteous, and consign them respectively to happiness and perdition (30). Baruch then summons the elders of the people, and announces to them that the ruined Zion shall be rebuilt and destroyed again, and finally restored in glory to last for ever (31–34).—(4) The fourth section (35–46) gives a vision which Baruch saw as he slept amid the ruins of the Holy Place. On one side there appeared a great forest in a valley surrounded with mountains ; on the other side a vine with a gentle spring streaming from beneath its roots. But the spring grew into a mighty river, and overwhelmed the forest, together with the mountains round about. A solitary cedar was left. The stream first addressed words of denunciation against the cedar, and then annihilated it. In the place of forest and mountains the vine grew, and the valley was filled with blossoms (35–37). The interpretation of the vision is given as requested by Baruch. The kingdoms which have oppressed Zion shall be overwhelmed by the Messiah. The cedar is the last king of the last kingdom ; he shall be slain by the Messiah, who shall then begin His eternal reign (38–40). Baruch is commanded to warn the people and prepare himself for further visions (41–43), which he accordingly does (44–46).—(5) The fifth section (47–52) also opens with a prayer of Baruch's offered seven days later (47–48²⁴). In answer Baruch receives a new revelation regarding the distress of the last days (48²⁵⁻⁵⁰), and of the resurrection both of the evil and the good, together with their punishment and reward (49–52).—(6) The sixth section (53–76) is again in the form of a vision. A cloud ascends from the sea, and pours forth upon the earth black and white (dark and bright) waters. Lightning illumines it, and twelve streams are put in subjection under it (53). Baruch prays that it may be explained to him (54), and the angel Ramael is sent to him to interpret the vision (55). The cloud pouring forth the waters represents mankind in its historical unfolding ; the dark waters stand for evil ages, the bright for good. The course of the world from Adam to the Exile is thus symbolized. The twelve periods are identified with the bright and dark streams (56–68). The twelfth is the age of the rebuilding of Jerusalem and of the restoration of the Temple service. These twelve are followed by a last black stream, which stands for the tribulation of the Messianic age. Then shall the Messiah take charge of the few saved ones (69–71). The lightning is the Messiah, and His eternal beneficent reign (72–74). Baruch thanks God, and is informed that he will shortly be taken from the earth, though not by death (75. 76).—(7) The seventh section tells how Baruch called the people together, told them of his impending departure, wrote two letters, one to the exiles in Babylon and the other to the nine and a

half tribes in the regions beyond, and how he sent the first by messengers and entrusted the second to an eagle (77).

Part II. This part of the book is taken up with the letter to the nine tribes and a half (78–87). In it Baruch recalls to the minds of the tribes God's mercy, and assures them that their sufferings are intended for their good (78–81). God has shown Baruch in visions the meaning of their experiences and the doom of their enemies (82–84) ; they should therefore be undismayed, and expect speedy deliverance, for the end is near (85). The letter then ends with formal instructions (86. 87).

Literary questions.—The extant text in Syriac is from an original Greek. This is shown by the use of such forms as Godolias Sedekias, etc., which could only have been made from the Greek. The word for 'splendour' in 3⁷ is manifestly a translation of κόσμος. But if the Syriac was made from a Greek text, was this Greek the original language of the book ? The answer demanded by the facts seems to be negative. There are traces of a Hebrew original behind the Greek. The most distinct of these is the occurrence of Hebrew idioms surviving through the two translations. Moreover, the quotations agree in all cases with the Hebrew text as distinguished from the LXX, which must have been used had the original been in Greek. Certain obscurities, too, can be cleared up by retranslation into Hebrew. (For the full argument see Charles, *The Apoc. of Baruch*, pp. xliii–liii.)

The relation of this apocalypse to 4 Ezra is very striking. Both books seem to be the products of the same environment. They deal with the same questions and in similar fashion. Their resemblances are indeed so marked that they have been denominated 'the twin apocalypses.'

The author of Baruch was evidently a Jew. The date when he wrote is determined partly from his relation to the author of 4 Ezra. There are other data in the case. Papias quotes one sentence from it, though attributing the expression to Jesus. This fixes the *terminus ad quem* as A.D. 180. The *terminus a quo* is an allusion to Eth. Enoch 56¹²·¹³, hence B.C. 160. Charles, however, following Kabisch, believes that it was put together out of five or six independent writings, composed between A.D. 50 and 90, some time about the year 100.

Editions.—The Syriac Text: Ceriani (*Monumenta Sacra*, v. fasc. 11, 1871 ; also in photolithographic reproduction of the entire MS of the Syriac OT, 1876).

Translations.—Latin: Ceriani (1866) ; Fritzsche, *Lib. Apocr.* 1861.—English : Charles, *The Apocalypse of Baruch*, 1896.—German : Rothstein in Kautzsch's *Pseudepigr.* 1900.

LITERATURE.—Langen, *de Apocalypsi Baruch*, 1867 ; Renan, 'L'Apocalypse de Baruch' in *Journal des Savants*, 1877, pp. 222–231 ; Kneucker, *Das Buch Bar.* 1879 ; Hilgenfeld, *ZWTh*, 1888, pp. 257–278 ; Kabisch, 'Die Quellen Baruchs' in *Jahrb. f. Prot. Theol.* 1892, pp. 66–107 ; Clemen, *SK*, 1898, pp. 227–237.

7. The Greek Baruch.—A hint as to the existence of another book bearing the name Baruch was long known to exist in a passage of Origen (*de Princ.* II. iii. 6), in which he alludes to Baruch's account of the Seven Heavens. No such account is to be found either in the OT apocryphon or in the Syriac apocalypse bearing the name of Baruch. But it was not until 1896 that the book alluded to by Origen was discovered and published in *Texts and Studies* (Camb. vol. v. 1, pp. 84–94).

Contents.—The book opens with Baruch's lamentation and prayer over the fallen kingdom of Judah. Forthwith an angel visits him and promises to show him wonderful secrets (1). The promise is fulfilled. He is taken up into the first heaven, where he sees creatures with the faces of bulls, the horns of stags, the feet of goats, and the haunches of lambs ; he then inquires as to the dimensions of this heaven, and is given some astounding figures (2). In the second heaven he sees men with the look of dogs and the feet of deer. They are those who have counselled the building of the tower [of Babel] (3). In the third heaven he sees a dragon which lives on the bodies of the wicked ; it is Hades. He further learns that the tree which caused Adam's fall was the vine, and therefore the abuse of the fruit of the vine has ever since been the source of fearful evils to men (4). He is told the nature of Hades (5), and is shown the Phœnix, which protects the earth from the burning rays of the sun (6). The approach of this monster terrifies him (7). He learns that the renewing of the crown of the sun is necessary, because the view of the sins of men daily dims and weakens this luminary; it must be cleansed and refreshed at the end of each day (8). The chariot of the moon and the explanation of its stages, together with the reason for its shining only at night, are then made known to Baruch (9). In the fourth heaven he comes into view of a vast plain and body of water which is the source of the ‘dew of heaven’ (10). The gates of the fifth heaven are closed as he and his guide come to them; but upon being opened they admit the archangel Michael, who receives the prayers and good works of the righteous and presents them before God (11, 12). The guardian angels of the unrighteous petition to be released from their hated work, but are told to wait (13). Michael departs, but returns again bringing oil, which he gives to the angels that had brought to him the virtues of men (14. 15). He addresses the angels who had brought no good works (16). The gate closes, and the prophet and angel return to the earth.

Literary questions.—Thus far there are two recensions of this apocalypse known, the Greek and the Slavonic. But neither of them is believed to be the original. Their relations to one another are those of a more and a less condensed version of the same story. That the original must have been fuller and larger is clear from Origen's intimation that it gave an account of seven heavens, whereas the Greek text before us stops with the fifth heaven, and the Slavonic knows of only two.

The relation of the book to the Syriac Baruch is probably explained by referring to 76³·⁴ of that work. Here God promises to give Baruch, after the lapse of forty days, a further revelation regarding the world of material elements (the cycle of the earth, the summits of the mountains, the depths of the valleys and of the seas, and the number of the rivers). The fulfilment of this promise is not recorded in what follows, and the Greek apocalypse was composed to show not only that it was fulfilled, but also in what way.

This dependence on the Syriac Baruch on the one side and the allusion of Origen to the work on the other, fix the date of its composition as between 100 and 175 A.D. It was written as a Jewish apocalypse, but shows traces of interpolation by Christians (cf. ch. 4, ‘The Vine’).

Editions.—Greek Text: James (*Texts and Studies*, Camb. 1897, v. 1, pp. 84–94).

Translations.—English: James (as above); the Slavonic text, pub. by Novakovitch, is given in English translation by Morfill in the same volume with the edition of the Greek text by James.—German: Bonwetsch (*Nachrichten von d. König. Gesell. d. Wiss. zu Gött.*, Phil. Klasse, 1896, pp. 94–101); Ryssel in Kautzsch's *Pseudepigr.* 1900.

LITERATURE.—This is limited almost altogether to the introductions accompanying the editions and translations. Of these, however, that by Prof. James is quite ample and thorough.

8. The Psalter of Solomon.

—The Psalter of Solomon is placed in the *Stichometry* of Nicephorus among the Antilegomena of the OT, and not among the Apocrypha; so also in pseudo-Athanasius' *Synopsis S. Scripturæ*. It is a collection of lyrics, each one independent of every other. Only the last two of these (the 17th and 18th), strictly speaking, fall into the group of apocalyptic writings. They were known and referred to as the ‘Odes of Solomon’ as early as the *Pistis Sophia* (200 to 250 A.D.), and frequently later than that date.

Contents.—Ps 17 is in general a prophecy of the restoration of the glory to the desolated throne of David. It opens with an expression of trust in the Lord, the Eternal King of Israel, addressed directly to Him (1–4). The Lord (still addressed in the second person) has chosen David to be king over Israel, and promised him and his seed perpetual dominion; but sinners have risen up against Israel and have desolated the throne of David (5–8); yet the Lord will cast these down and visit them according to their sins (9–12). They have done wickedly and acted proudly (13–17); the righteous fled before them and wandered in desert places (18–20); the sins of the wicked have abounded (21, 22); the Lord is to raise the son of David, His Servant, purge Jerusalem, cast down the unrighteous and lawless nation, gather together His people, and judge all the tribes of men (23–36). He will not put confidence in human weapons of warfare, but

in the Lord; and the Lord will bless him, will strengthen and give him dominion (37–44). He shall rule righteously and wisely (45–49). Blessed are they who shall live in his day (50. 51).

Ps 18 is on the Messianic Age. It begins with an ascription of praise to the Lord for His favour to Israel and His love to the seed of Abraham (1–5). It foreshadows a blessed day in which God shall purge Israel and raise His Messiah (6); it declares the blessedness of those who shall live in the days of the Anointed (7–10), and closes with a doxology for the constancy and perpetuity of the heavenly luminary (11–14).

Literary questions.—Though the Psalter of Solomon is a collection of independent compositions, these apparently issue from the same historical conditions and are pervaded by the same spirit and tone. They nowhere claim to be Solomon's composition. This claim was made for them by later copyists. In general, the conditions under which they were written are those of the period of thirty years between 70 and 40 B.C. Pompey is alluded to as ‘the mighty striker’ who comes ‘from the ends of the earth’ (8¹⁶). Certain princes of the land go forth to meet him and welcome him (8¹⁸). These are Aristobulus II. and Hyrcanus II. The Gentiles tread Jerusalem under foot (2²⁰ 8²³·²⁴); but he who has conquered it and inflicted severe sufferings on it is finally overtaken and suffers a shameful death in Egypt (2²⁹·³⁰). All this points directly to the Roman conquest under Pompey.

Some older critics read the allusions above indicated as having reference to Herod and his days (Movers, Keim); Ewald saw in them Antiochus Epiphanes and his times; but these identifications are manifestly far-fetched. The consensus of critics is now against them. But there are exceptions, such as Frankenberg, who advocates the age of Antiochus.

The original language of the Psalter was Hebrew. The radical difference between the type of Messianism held up in 17 and 18 and the eschatology of the rest of the collection points to a separate authorship of these two psalms. But apart from this, and the antecedent probability that lyrics of this class are apt to be independent contributions, there are no clear grounds for ascribing particular psalms to different authors. The author (or authors) belonged to the Pharisaic sect.

Editions.—Hilgenfeld, *ZWTh*, 1868; Geiger, *Der Psalter Salomos*, 1871; Fritzsche, *Libri Apocr. Gr.* 1871, pp. 569, 589; Pick, ‘The Psalter of Solomon’ in *Presb. Rev.*, 1883, pp. 775–812; Ryle and James, *The Psalms of the Pharisees*, 1891; O. von Gebhardt, *Die Psalmen Salomos*, 1895; Swete, *The Psalms of Solomon, with the Greek Fragments of the Book of Enoch*, 1899.

Translations.—English: Bissell in Lange's *Com.* ‘Apocrypha,’ 1880; Pick (above cited), Ryle and James (above cited).—German: Kittel in Kautzsch's *Pseudepigr.* 1900.

LITERATURE.—Ewald, *Gesch* iv., p. 392 f.; Movers in Wetzer u. Welte's *Kirchenlex.*¹ i. p. 340; Keim, *Gesch. von Jesu v. Nazara*, i. p. 243; Carriere, *de Psalterio Salomonis*, 1870; Kaulen in Wetzer u. Welte², i. p. 1060 f.; O. Holtzmann in Stade's *GVI*; Jacquier, ‘Les Psaumes de Salomon’ in *L'université Catholique*, Nouv. Série, xii. 1893, pp. 94–131, 251–275; Frankenberg, *Die Datirung d. Ps. Salomonis*, 1896.

9. The Testaments of the Twelve Patriarchs.

—This production was well known to the ancient Patristic writers. It is quoted by Irenæus (*Fragm.* 17, ed. Harvey, ii. 487), Origen (*Hom. in Jos.* 15⁶), and Tertullian (*adv. Marc.* v. 1). It is named in the *Synopsis* of pseudo-Athanasius and in the *Stichometry* of Nicephorus. In the 13th cent. Bishop Grosseteste made a translation of it into Latin. It has been very frequently translated both in ancient and in modern times.

Contents.—The book extends the idea of Gn 49 to the sons of Jacob. Just as the father had called his sons together before his death and told them his last thoughts, so each of the sons is made to summon his own children to his deathbed and to give them a retrospective and a prospective view. Each, however, centres his discourse in a dominant idea or topic. (1) Reuben, *on Thoughts*. This Testament begins with the confession by Reuben of his sin and the penance he performed therefor (1). Man has seven spirits given him to perform his work in the world, *i.e.* life, sight, hearing, smell, taste, speech, reproduction (2); an eighth is added to these; but Beliar has intermingled with these seven misleading spirits, *i.e.* fornication, gluttony, strife, vanity, arrogance, lying, and injustice; sleep is a counterfeit eighth (3). Beware of fornication (4). Women have always been seducers. They misled the *Grigori*, ‘watchers’ (5). Give heed to Levi, for he shall know the Law (6 and 7).—(2) Simeon, *on Envy*. This also opens with a confession, but the sin confessed is envy (1. 2). The patriarch warns his children against this sin (3), commends Joseph, and urges them to imitate him (4–8).—(3) Levi, *on the Priesthood and Arrogance*. This is the distinctively apocalyptic Testament. After introducing himself, the patriarch recounts the revelation given him of the seven heavens (1–4); then tells of being ushered into the presence of the Lord, who gave him the command to destroy the Shechemites (5). Contrary to the desire of his father, he executed the command (6. 7). He saw a second vision, in which he was invested with the priesthood and received instructions from his grandfather Isaac (8. 9). He foreshadows the corruption of the priesthood by his family (11. 12), instructs them in their duties and again warns against corruption (13. 14); foretells the destruction of the Temple, and indicates from the Book of Enoch that the Captivity will last seventy years (15–17); he announces the Messiah, His rejection and the dispersion of Israel, and closes with an exhortation to choose well (18. 19).—(4) Judah, *on Fortitude, Avarice, and Fornication*. After introducing himself, Judah gives a glowing account of his physical strength and agility, with many illustrative incidents (1–9). He tells of how he chose Tamar as the wife of his son Er, of the wickedness of his sons and their death, and of his own relations with Tamar (10–12). Ascribing his fall to drunkenness and covetousness, he warns his children against these vices, as well as against fornication (13–17); he foresees from the Books of Enoch the wickedness into which they shall fall in the last days, and warns them (18–21); he urges them to love Levi, and predicts with sorrow their apostasies from the Lord and the wars and commotions until the time of Messias (22–24). This shall be followed by the resurrection of the patriarchs (25).—(5) Issachar, *on Simplicity*. Beginning with the circumstances of his birth, this patriarch gives an account of his early life and marriage (1–3), and points out his simplicity and singleness of mind as virtues to be imitated (4–7).—(6) Zebulun, *on Compassion and Mercy*. After naming himself and the prosperous circumstances in which he was born, he claims not to have sinned except in thought. Only in the affair of Joseph, which he describes at length, he had conspired with his brothers, but with sorrow and compassion for Joseph (1–5). He was the first to construct a boat and go fishing. He used the fish he caught in feeding the needy (6. 7). He urges his children to be compassionate (8) and united in action (9. 10).—(7) Dan, *on Anger and Lying*. This patriarch also begins with a confession. He had planned to slay Joseph out of envy, but the Lord had withheld the opportunity (1). He warns his children against the spirit of lying and anger (2–4); he predicts evil days in the future, of which he had learned from the Books of Enoch (5), and exhorts them to stand firm in righteousness (6. 7). — (8) Naphtali, *on Natural Goodness*. This Testament opens with an account of the mother of the patriarch, Bilhah (1). It proceeds with a description of his fleetness of foot, which gives occasion for a speech on the fitness of the body to the character of the soul (2). He exhorts his children not to force the order of nature (3. 4), and tells of a vision he saw when forty years of age. It was on the Mount of Olives, to the east of Jerusalem. The sun and moon stood still; Jacob called his sons to go and seize them. Levi took hold of the sun, Judah of the moon; they were lifted up. A bull with two horns on its head and two wings on its back made its appearance. They tried to capture it, and Joseph succeeded. Finally, a holy writing appeared telling of the captivity of Israel (5). Seven months later he saw another vision. Jacob and his sons were standing by the Sea of Jamnia. A vessel full of dried fish appeared; but it had no rudder or sails. They embarked, and a storm arose. They were threatened with destruction; Levi prayed, and, though the vessel was wrecked, they were saved upon pieces of the wreckage (6). Naphtali told his visions to his father, who saw in them a token that Joseph was living (7). With the prediction of the Messiah (8. 9) the Testament closes.—(9) Gad, *on Hatred*. After the customary account of himself, Gad (1) confesses that he hated Joseph and brought about his sale to the Ishmaelites (2. 3). He warns his children against hatred, points out its evil, and urges them to cherish and exercise love (4–8).—(10) Asher, *on the Two Aspects of Vice and Virtue*. This patriarch begins with a portraiture of the two ways open before men, describing each carefully (1. 2). He commends simplicity of heart and devotion to virtue (3), gives reasons (4), and again commends the path of virtue (5, 6), closing with warnings and predictions (7. 8). —(11) Joseph, *on Chastity*. Joseph begins with the contrasts between his many-sided suffering and God's many-sided help and deliverance (1). He then proceeds to narrate the circumstances of his servitude in Egypt (2), his temptation (3–7), his imprisonment (8. 9), and exhorts to brotherly love (10) and the fear of God (11). He further goes back to tell the story once more of the circumstances of the temptation (12–15), and concludes with an exhortation to honour Levi and Judah, predicting that from them should arise the Lamb of God (17–20).—(12) Benjamin, *on a Pure Mind*. Benjamin begins by telling of his birth (1); then of the meeting with Joseph in Egypt (2). This leads to the exaltation of Joseph as the perfect man, who should be imitated (3. 4). A pure mind will be recognized by the wicked (5). Beliar himself cannot mislead the pure-minded (6). There is a sevenfold evil in wickedness, and a sevenfold punishment is to be measured out to those who practise it (7). Flee wickedness, he urges, and concludes with the prediction of corruption among his descendants (8. 9), and of the resurrection and the judgment which will follow.

Literary questions.—The book is extant in a Greek text, also in a complete Armenian and fragmentary Syriac and Aramaic versions. The Latin version, frequently reprinted from the 16th century onwards, is Grosseteste's. An ancient Latin translation is not known to exist. A Slavonic version of uncertain origin is also published by Tichonravoff (*Denkm. d. altruss. Apocr. Litt.*, St. Petersb. 1863). The original of the work was either Greek or Hebrew. Grabe (*Spicileg. Patr.* 2, 1714, 129–144) argued for the Hebrew. All other critics have favoured Greek until Prof. Charles' revival of Grabe's contention. Charles reasons mainly from the language (cf. also Gaster, 'The Heb. Text of One of the Twelve Testaments of the Patriarchs' in *PSBA*, Dec. 1893). As it stands, the book presents the anomaly of a work intensely Jewish upon the whole, but containing passages of quite as intensely Christian colour. To explain the anomaly, it must be assumed either that a Christian of late date adopted the mask of a Jew of an earlier period, or that the work was originally that of a Jew, and the Christian passages are later interpolations. The former of these alternatives is practically excluded by the type of Judaism running through the work as a whole. This is not such as one would assume for the sake of literary effect. Accordingly the tendency of all later writers has been towards the view that the main part of the Testaments was composed in the 1st cent. B.C. It is found, however, that the author incorporated into this work parts of an apocalyptic composition of the century preceding (B.C. 200–100). The whole was later interpolated by a Christian, or rather a number of Christians, at least one of whom held Docetic views. These interpolations were made during the first three centuries of the Christian era.

Editions. — Grabe (*Spicileg. Patr.* 1714), Fabricius (*Cod. Pseudepigr.* 1713), Gallandi (*Bib. Vet. Pat.* i. 1788), Migne (*Patrol. Græc.*), Sinker (*Test. XII. Patr.* 1869; Sinker also published an Appendix containing collating of readings and bibliographical notes, 1879).

LITERATURE.—Translations exist in English, French, German, Dutch, Bohemian, and Icelandic.—English: Sinker (*Ante-Nicene Christian Library*, vol. xxii. 1871).—French: Migne, *Dictionnaire des Apocryphes,* i. 1856.—German: Anonymous, *Aechte Apokryphische Bücher* (Tübing. 1875); Schnapp and Kautzsch in Kautzsch's *Pseudepigr.* 1900; Nitzsch, *Comm. Crit. de Test. XII Patr.* 1810; Reuss, *Gesch. d. Heil. Schrift. NT,* 257; Kayser, 'Die Test. der XII Patr.' in *Beitr. z. d. Theol. Wissenschaften,* herausg. v. Reuss und Cunitz, 1851; Vorstmann, *Disquisitio de Test. Patr.* 1857; Hilgenfeld, *ZWTh,* 1859, p. 395 ff., 1871, p. 302 ff.; van Hengel, ' De Testamenten der twaalf Patriarchen op nieuw ter sprake gebragt' in *Godgeleerde Bijdragen,* 1860; Geiger, *Jüd. Zeit. f. Wiss. u. Leben,* 1869, pp. 116–135, 1871, 123–125; *Presb. Rev.* 1880; Schnapp, *Test. der Zwölf Patr.* 1884.

10. The Book of Jubilees.—This book was known and often alluded to by the ancient and mediæval ecclesiastical writers up to the days of Theodorus Metochita (A.D. 1332). It was called 'Jubilees' ('The Book of Jubilees'), or 'Little Genesis' (*Parva Genesis,* Λεπτογένεσις). Some time after the middle of the 14th cent. it disappeared, and was known only through the references to it of the earlier writers. Its recovery in modern times was accomplished by the African missionary Krapf in 1844. Krapf found an Ethiopic version of it in Abyssinia, which he sent to Europe. Here it came into the hands of Dillmann, and was by him translated and published first in German and afterwards in Ethiopic.

Contents.—The general plan of this book follows so closely that of the canonical Genesis that it will suffice to designate some of its distinctive features only. The book gives a haggadistic version of the history contained in Genesis, including also Exodus as far as ch. 14. The main events are identical in all essential points, but very many additions and embellishments are introduced. First of all, the whole of time is represented as subdivided into jubilee periods, these into sabbatical periods, and these into years. This, it is said, was the original plan of God, and the knowledge of it was communicated to Moses by revelation. The account of the manner and time of the revelation is given in ch. 1, in which, further, the *angelus interpres* (who is in this case the Angel of the Presence) furnishes an outlook into the future and foretells the apostasy of Israel and her restoration to God. In the rest of the book the feasts and observances of the Mosaic ritual are transferred to the days of Noah and Abraham, and in general the events of this earlier period are treated with much freedom and illustrated by amplification and tradition. In the account of the Creation, an addition is made with reference to the creation of the angels. The luminaries created on the fourth day are said to be for Sabbaths and festivals. Eve was created during the second week. Therefore the command ' that their defilement is to be seven days for a male child and fourteen days for a female.' Adam is said to have been set to keep the garden from the incursions of the beasts of the field. Before the Fall animals could speak. It was between the 63rd and 70th year of Adam's life that Cain was born; between the 70th and 77th that Abel was born; between the 77th and 84th that Awan his only daughter was born. Adam and Eve had nine other sons (making twelve children altogether). The names of the wives of antediluvians are generally given. Enoch's wife was Edna, the daughter of Daniel. The corruption of mankind which led to the Flood is said to have spread through the whole creation, so that even animals were made subject to it, for which reason they perished in the waters. The *Nephilim,* who sprang from the union of the sons of God with the daughters of men, were set at enmity with one another, and ' slew each man his neighbour.' After the Flood, Noah offered a sacrifice which is described as in every particular conforming to the Levitical law. The feast of the first-fruits was observed by Noah. The feast of the New Moon also had its origin at this time. The year consists of 13 months, each of 28 days, or altogether 364 days. After the Flood, Mastema (Satan) led men to sin through the building of the Tower of Babel and the worship of graven images. Abraham did not fall into this sin. He tried to convert his father from idolatry, and failing to do so he burned the house of idols, in which his brother Haran perished, and then was called to leave his native land. When Abraham had established himself in the Land of Canaan, and Ishmael and Isaac were born, after Hagar and Ishmael had been sent away, Mastema appeared before God to move him to try Abraham by demanding the offering of his son Isaac. Nine other events in Abraham's life were trials, thus making the complete number ten. Before his death, Abraham addressed his son Isaac, advising and warning him against idolatry. When he was about to die, he called Jacob his grandson and, taking his fingers, closed his own eyes with them and stretched himself on his bed. Jacob fell asleep with his fingers on his grandfather's eyes. When he awoke, he found that Abraham was cold and dead. The affair of Jacob's obtaining Esau's blessing from his father is narrated so as to eliminate direct falsehood. When Isaac asks, ' Who art thou?' Jacob answers simply, ' I am thy son.' The story of the massacre of the Shechemites by Simeon and Levi is also softened, so as to justify the deed. The relations of Jacob and Esau are presented in a light entirely unfavourable to Esau, who is made to act the part of a cowardly and cunning traitor. In the story of Joseph, the elements of envy and cruelty on the part of his brethren are left out. The account of Jacob's death is given without his final addresses to his sons. It is simply said that he blessed his sons. The death of Joseph gives occasion for the mention of a new king who ruled over Egypt after Memkeron, thus intimating the end of the Shepherd dynasty. In the account of Moses' early life, Hebrew maidens are represented as serving Pharaoh's daughter. The last chapter is occupied altogether with the Sabbath law, which is given with great precision and rigidity.

Literary questions.—The book is preserved as a whole in an Ethiopic version. A fragment, containing about one-third of it, is also found in Latin, probably made from a Greek copy. In addition to these, some smaller Syriac and Greek fragments are known to exist. The original was evidently in a Semitic language, but whether Hebrew or Aramaic is not absolutely certain. Hebrew was more usually the language of such apocalyptic books. Jerome, moreover, alludes to the ' Little Genesis' as a book in Hebrew. But neither of these considerations is quite decisive. In using the term ' Hebrew,' Jerome did not always keep in mind the distinction between that language and Aramaic. He followed the NT habit of calling Aramaic Hebrew (Jn 19¹³). In favour of an Aramaic original, the use of the form Mastema as the name of Satan may be adduced. *Mastema* is the Aphel form from מטם ' to accuse,' and מַטְם is Aramaic for שׂטן. Further, it is said that when Abraham left Mesopotamia he took with him the books of his father (12²⁸), ' and they were written in Hebrew,' which would be uncalled for if the account itself was in Hebrew.

The date of the book is approximately fixed by its relation to Eth. Enoch on one side, and the Testaments of the Twelve Patriarchs on the other. The Ethiopic Enoch is undoubtedly known and used by the author of Jubilees (cf. Jub 21 = Enoch 3; Jub 7 = Enoch 7; Jub 10 = Enoch 10⁴·⁵; Jub 2 = Enoch 60¹⁶·²¹). On the other hand, in all probability, the author of the Testaments had used Jubilees (Jub 30. 33 = Test. Reub. 1. 3; Jub 32 = Test. Lev. 8; Jub 32 = Test. Lev. 5; Jub 34 = Test. Jud. 3–4; Jub 23 = Test. Zeb. 9). Its chronological place is therefore after the end of the 2nd cent. B.C. and before the end of the 1st cent. A.D.

The author has been held to be an Essene (Jellinek), a Hellenist (Frankel), or a Sadducee; but there are strong reasons against any of these views. He was more probably a Pharisee (Dillmann, Rönsch, Drummond).

Editions.—Dillmann, *Kufale, sive Liber Jubilæorum,* 1859; Ceriani, *Monumenta Sacra,* i. fasc. 1, 1861; Charles, *Anecdota Oxon.* viii., 1895.

Translations.—English: Schodde in *Biblioth. Sacra,* 1885–1887; Charles in *JQR,* 1893, pp. 703–708, 1894, pp. 184–217 and 710–745, 1895, pp. 297–328.—German: Dillmann (as above); Rönsch, *Das Buch der Jubiläen,* 1874; Littmann in Kautzsch's *Pseudepigr.* 1900. A translation into Hebrew was made and published with notes by Rubin (Vienna, 1870).

LITERATURE.—Jellinek, *Üb. d. Buch. d. Jub. u. das Noah-Buch.* 1885 ; Beer, *d. Buch. d. Jub. u. sein Verhältniss z. d. Midraschim,* 1856 ; Frankel in *Monatsschrift f. Gesch. u. Wiss. d. Jüd.* 1856 ; Hilgenfeld, *ZWTh,* 1874, pp. 435–441.

11. The Ascension of Isaiah.

— The ancients allude to non-canonical literature associated with the name of Isaiah under four different titles. Origen speaks of the *Martyrdom of Isaiah* ; Epiphanius names an *Anabatikon,* and Jerome an *Ascension* ; in the list of canonical and kindred books published by Montfaucon (given by Westcott, *Canon of the New Testament,* App. D, xvii), a *Vision* (ὅρασις) *of Isaiah* is included. Of these, the Vision is again named by Euthymius Zigabenus in the 11th cent., and a *Testament of Hezekiah* is spoken of by Georgius Cedrenus in the 12th century. Whatever the facts may have been as to the identity of these writings or their relations to one another, nothing was definitely known of them until 1819, when Archbishop Lawrence accidentally found an *Ascension of Isaiah* in a second-hand bookstore in London. It was an Ethiopic text, and Lawrence published it with a translation and notes. Upon this, together with two other MSS., later brought to light, Dillmann based his edition of the Ethiopic *Ascension of Isaiah* in 1877.

Contents.—The work consists of two parts.

Part I. (1–5). In the 26th year of Hezekiah, Isaiah predicts that Manasseh would be led by Satan to apostatize. Hezekiah wishes to slay his son, but is prevented by the prophet (1). After the death of Hezekiah, Manasseh does give himself up to the service of Satan and practises all manner of wickedness. Isaiah takes refuge in the desert (2). Balkira, a Samaritan, accuses the prophet of uttering threats against Jerusalem and raising himself above Moses in authority, whereupon Manasseh, possessed by Satan, causes the capture of Isaiah ($3^{1\cdot12}$). The reason for this is the wrath of Satan, roused by Isaiah's disclosures regarding the coming of Christ from the seventh heaven, regarding His death, His resurrection, His ascension, His second coming, the sending of the twelve disciples, the persecutions of the Church, the advent of Antichrist, and his destruction (3^{13}–4^{22}). Manasseh causes Isaiah to be sawn asunder, and the prophet endures the martyrdom with steadfast calmness in spite of the derision of Balkira and Satan (5).

Part II. (6–11). In the twentieth year of Hezekiah, Isaiah saw a vision which he narrated to the king and council of prominent men (6): an angel took him through the firmament and through the six lower heavens into the seventh. Here he saw the departed patriarchs—Adam, Abel, and Enoch—and God Himself. He learned that Christ should come into the earth ; and having received this information, he was led by the same angel back into the firmament (7–10). In the firmament he saw the future birth, life, suffering, death, resurrection and ascension of Jesus into the seventh heaven. The angel left him, and Isaiah's soul returned into his earthly body. It was because of this vision, which he had related to Hezekiah, that Manasseh caused Isaiah to be put to death (11).

Literary questions.—The signs of the compositeness of the book are too plain to require critical demonstration. The question is simply whether it consists of two, three, or four independent writings. The most obvious partition is into two. The Vision of Isaiah is complete in itself and distinct from the Martyrdom. Even its being put after the Martyrdom, which it would precede in historical sequence, is an evidence of independence. But these two main sections have been enlarged by the addition of a preface and two minor passages in the second part. Thus the analysis is : (1) the Martyrdom of Isaiah (1–5, exc. 1 and 3^{13}–5^1). (2) The Vision of Isaiah (6–11, exc. $11^{2\cdot22}$). (3) An introduction by a later hand (1). (4) Additions by a later Christian writer (3^{13}–5^1, and $11^{2\cdot22}$). This is Dillmann's analysis, and has been generally accepted.

The dates of these two sections are also widely apart. The

Vision belongs to the class and period of Christian apocalypses which culminate in Dante's *Divina Commedia.* It was probably produced in the 2nd cent. A.D. The *Martyrdom* is the embodiment of an ancient tradition regarding the death of the prophet, and was probably composed just before the Christian era.

Editions.—Ethiopic Text : Lawrence (1819), Dillmann (1877).

Translations.—Latin (with both the above). A Greek translation of a late Patristic origin has been published by von Gebhardt (*ZWTh,* 1878, pp. 330–353).—English : *Luth. Quar. Rev.* 1878, p. 513 ff.—French : Migne in *Dictionnaire des Apocryphes,* i., 1858 ; Basset, *Les Apocryphes Éthiopiens,* iii., 1894. — German : Jolowicz (based on Lawrence's text, 1854) ; Clemen in Kautzsch's *Pseudepigr.* 1900.

LITERATURE.—Gesenius, *Com. üb. Jesaja,* 1821 ; Stokes in Smith and Wace's *Dict. of Christ. Biogr.* ; Harnack, *Gesch. d. altchr. Litt.* i. p. 854 f., ii. pp. 573–579, 714 ff. ; Armitage Robinson in Hastings' *DB* ii. 499 ; Charles, *Ascension of Isaiah.*

12. The Histories of Adam and Eve.

—This work appears under two main forms, almost as distinct as two works : one in Greek and one in Latin. The Greek is entitled *Narrative and Citizenship of Adam and Eve* (Διήγησις). It was published by Tischendorf in 1866 (*Apocal. Apocr.* pp. 1–23) under the misleading title of 'The Apocalypse of Moses.' The Latin version is entitled *Vita Adæ et Evæ,* and was published by W. Meyer (*Abhandl. d. München. Akad. Phil.-Hist. Klasse* xiv. 3, 1878, pp. 185–250). A third slightly varying form exists in Slavonic, and a fourth in Armenian. Both of these are from the Greek narrative.

Contents.—The story opens with an account of the deeds of Adam and Eve immediately following the expulsion from the Garden of Eden. Adam and Eve seek for food, experience difficulties in obtaining it, and perform penance in order to secure God's mercy (1–8). Satan once more tempts Eve (9–11), and narrates at the request of Adam the circumstances of his own fall (12–17). Then follows an account of the birth of Cain and Abel, and Adam is taught how to cultivate the soil (18–22). Eve dreams of Abel's death, which presently occurs ; but Seth and other children are born to Adam and Eve (23. 24). Adam informs Seth of a vision given him through the archangel Michael, after he and Eve had been cast out of Eden. It was a chariot similar to the wind, but with wheels of fire. The Lord sat upon it, and many thousand angels stood on His right hand and on His left. Adam addressed a prayer to the Lord, and the Lord assured him that those who should know and serve Himself would not fail from the seed of Adam. Adam enjoins Seth to receive this knowledge and keep it (25–29). At the age of 930, Adam falls sick, and, calling his sons together, once more tells them of the circumstances of the Fall (30–34). He then sends Eve and Seth to the vicinity of Paradise in order that, putting dust upon their heads, they might plead for him and receive some of the oil of life to anoint him (35. 36). On the way they are met by the Serpent, which bites Seth, but is persuaded by Eve to let him go (37–39). They reach the gates of Paradise, present their petition, but, instead of the oil for which they had asked, they receive the promise of a blessing in the distant future (40–42). They return to Adam, and report their experiences (43. 44). Adam then dies and is buried (45–51).

The *Diegesis* gives a parallel account of the Fall by Eve (15–30), of Adam's last will and death (30, 31), of the intercession of the entire angel host in behalf of forgiveness for Adam (33–36), of the acceptance of the prayer (37), of the burial of Adam by the angel (38–42), and of Eve's death and burial (42, 43).

Literary questions.—This book (or couplet of books) is found in three recensions, Greek, Latin, and Slavonic. It is based on a Jewish original (Tischendorf, Conybeare, Spitta, Harnack, Fuchs). Others, however, do not believe in the Jewish original (Schürer, Gelzer).

The date of the composition is uncertain. The author was a Jew. [Hort, however, finds traces of Christian influence, and relegates the Adam story to post-Christian times.]

Editions.—Greek Text : Tischendorf, *Apocalypses Apocryphæ,*

1866; Wilh. Meyer, *Vita Adœ et Evœ.*—English translations: in Schaff and Wace's *Ante-Nicene Christicn Library*, vol. xxii.; Conybeare in *JQR* vii. 1895, pp. 216-235.—German : *Litteratur-blatt. d. Orients*, 1850, pp. 705 ff., 732 ff. ; Fuchs in Kautzsch's *Pseudepigr.* 1900.

LITERATURE.—Hort, art. 'Adam Books' in Smith and Wace's *Dict. of Christ. Biog.*; Gelzer, *Julius Africanus*, ii. 1, 1885.

13. The Apocalypse of Abraham.—This is a work preserved only in a Slavonic translation. It was published in that language (1863), but only made known more widely through a German translation by Bonwetsch (1897). It tells of how Abraham took offence at the idolatry of his father, how he despised both the wooden image Barisat and the stone statue Marumath, and was on that ground made the subject of a special visit on the part of the angel Jaoel, who taught him to offer sacrifice, and then took him into heaven on the wings of a dove. Here Abraham received many revelations. This work should not be mistaken for the *Testament of Abraham*, edited by James in the Cambridge *Texts and Studies* (ii. 2, 1892).

14. The Apocalypse of Elias.—Mention of this work occurs in Origen's *Com.* on Mt 27[9] (ed. de la Rue, iii. 916; ed. Lommatzsch, v. 29). Here it is said to be the source from which St. Paul quotes 1 Co 2[9] 'Eye hath not seen,' etc. Cf. also Epiphanius, *Hœr.* 42 [Dindorf, ii. 398]; and Jerome, *Epist.* 57 *ad Pammachium.* Fragments of this writing have been recovered in a Coptic manuscript brought from Akhmim. Some of these fragments were taken to Paris and some to Berlin. Those in the former place have been edited and published by Bouriant; those in Berlin by Steindorff (*Texte u. Unters.*, Neue Folge, ii. 3a). This editor thinks that the original was a Jewish apocalypse interpolated by a later Christian writer.

15. The Apocalypse of Zephaniah.—This was a larger work than the preceding, and was known to Clement of Alexandria (*Strom.* v. 11. 77). Among the Akhmim fragments published by Bouriant and Steindorff there are portions of this apocalypse also, but they are not extensive enough to serve as a basis of any trustworthy judgment as to its origin and nature. The extracts recovered do not, however, contain Christian interpolations.

16. An Anonymous Apocalypse.—The Akhmim fragments contain, in addition to the above, portions of a purely Jewish apocalypse, which cannot be identified or associated with any special name. The author, speaking in the first person, names Elias among other saints whom he has seen in heaven (14). The fragments are published along with Steindorff's above-named edition of the Akhmim manuscripts.

17. The Prayer of Joseph.—Origen (ed. de la Rue, iv. 84; Lommatzsch, i. 147) calls this 'a writing not to be despised, current among the Hebrews.' Nothing, however, besides Origen's quotations from it, is known of the contents of the work.

18. The Book of Eldad and Modad.—These names [EV *Medad*] occur in Nu 11[26-29]. A book bearing this name is mentioned in Hermas' *Shepherd* (*Vis.* ii. 3), but nothing more is known of it with certainty.

iv. GENERAL CHARACTERISTICS. — The general characteristics of apocalyptic literature may not all be found in ideal vividness in any single production of the class. Nevertheless, in so-called apocalypses, most of the following traits are predominant, and, with the majority of them, all appear in some degree of clearness.

1. *The Vision Form.* — This is what gives the name to the class, and, although not an indispensable feature, is quite determinative. The authors put themselves in the place of seers, and throw upon the canvas large, vivid, lifelike portraitures. The imagery is in many cases fantastic and unreal as compared with the actual world, but it is strik-

ing and clearly drawn. Conflicts and struggles, judicial assizes, conversations and debates, as well as cosmographical delineations, are placed before the eyes of the seer, and by him described more or less in detail.

2. *Dualism.*—The distinction between the world of sense and the world of Divine or spiritual realities is always prominently in the mind. The other world is, however, conceived as only imperceptible to the bodily senses, not as different in kind. A dualism as between matter and spirit underlies the philosophy of the apocalypse, but is necessarily ignored in the presentation of the realities of the spiritual. These are put before the bodily senses as if a simple heightening of the powers of the senses would bring them into view.

3. *Symbolism.*—The visions portrayed abound in conventional symbolical figures. Mixed organisms, partaking of the parts and characteristics of different creatures (beasts), frequently recur. Generally the different parts that enter into these mixed figures represent different abstract principles, and the mixed figure as a whole stands for combinations of powers. Mystic and symbolic numbers, too, constantly appear (seven heavens, seven archangels, ten shepherds). Sometimes this symbolism is explained in minute terms, but sometimes it is left for the seer to unravel. Sometimes the purpose of the use of such symbolism seems to be simply to harmonize the form of presentation to the mysterious nature of the subject-matter; but at other times it is evidently designed to conceal the exact import of the revelation from the uninitiated, and to keep it a secret within an esoteric circle. The method of interpretation known as Gematria is to this end frequently resorted to.

4. *Angelology.*—A system of mediators between the two worlds is pictured as establishing their connexion. In comparison with the angelology of the OT (with the exception of Daniel), this mediatorial hierarchy is complex and definite. It is, moreover, subdivided into two branches, the good and the evil, which are at enmity with one another. In some apocalypses one particular angel is commissioned to the task of acting as the companion and friendly interpreter of the seer (*angelus interpres*). To him the seer appeals in his ignorance of the meaning of the mystic visions, and from him he receives needed explanations. Here, too, a difference must be noted between the apocalypses and the earlier prophets (cf. Am 7-9), who see visions, but speak directly with the Almighty in person.

5. *The Unknown as subject-matter.*—The subject-matter revealed concerns one of two spheres, viz., either the inscrutable mechanism of the other world, or the purposes of God regarding the present world : (a) Under the first head are portrayed the characteristics, deeds, and destinies of angels, both good and evil, the secret forces and courses of the great nature-powers and elements, and the mode of the Creation. (b) Under the second head naturally two divisions are distinguishable, the historical and the eschatological. Such great landmarks in the history of the world as the entrance of sin, the fortunes of the first human pair, the Flood, the destinies of Israel, are given as known and decreed of God. The whole eschatology, including the final judgment, the Messianic Age, the fate of mankind, the resurrection of the dead, and the destruction of the world, are of the utmost interest to the apocalyptist. In fact, so prominent is this part of the world of mystery in the apocalypses, that some authorities have yielded to the temptation of making it the sole test of an apocalypse. Apocalyptic is, according to this view, synonymous with eschatological. (So Lücke, and, among more recent scholars, Bousset).

6. *Pseudonymity.*—The author of an apocalypse generally assumes the name of a very ancient person, preferably of some one who is represented in the canonical books as having enjoyed direct communication with the spiritual world. Enoch, Moses, and Elijah stand out as those who passed from this world to the other in a preternatural manner, and therefore were favoured even while here with apocalyptic glimpses of the other. Others, because of their exceptional holiness and nearness to God, are easily put into the same place of favour. Such are Isaiah, Ezra, Baruch, and Daniel. The name of Ezekiel, however, quite singularly does not seem to have drawn any of these writings to itself. Jeremiah's began to be used, but did not become very popular. That of Solomon was attached to a body of psalms for quite obvious reasons. The Sibyl was probably drafted into the service in order to gain the confidence of heathen readers through the use of the voice of a trusted prophetess of their own. It was intended to propagate Jewish doctrines among the Gentiles (Schürer). This pseudonymity is accompanied by a not altogether accidental tendency to tamper with the apocalypses. More than any other class of writings they show signs of having been edited and modified. Many of them are manifestly collections or compilations of smaller productions. Others abound in interpolations and additions designed to embellish, clarify, and expand their portraitures.

7. *Optimism.*—The design of the whole class is predominantly that of encouraging and comforting the chosen people under persecution. Some, of course, are more or less sectarian in their tendency, *i.e.* they address their words of encouragement and hope to a particular section of the people, who are regarded as faithful or righteous *par excellence*. The majority are meant to teach and comfort the whole nation.

v. THEOLOGICAL IDEAS.—The root of the apocalyptic theology is the sense of need. Though it may not be strictly accurate to call the apocalypses 'tracts for hard times,' it is quite true that they issue from a faith which looks to God for deliverance from evil days. The eye is turned into the future for the good which the God of the Covenant has promised to Israel. The darker the outlook, the brighter the hope which breaks through it and sees ultimate victory. The rallying point of thought is here furnished by the conception of the 'Day of Jahweh' in the prophets of the earlier period. But this hope for the future is impatient. It cannot await the working of the slow moral forces gradually evolving the consummation. It rather sees the Golden Age bursting forth in a sudden and supernatural manifestation of God's power and favour to His chosen people. Accordingly, the cardinal doctrines of the apocalyptic theology must begin with the contrast of the ages.

1. *The doctrine of the two Æons* (4 Ezr 7[50]).—This is developed from the older idea of the 'latter days' (אַחֲרִית הַיָּמִים) which the earlier prophets always held up as a source of comfort and encouragement whenever they were moved to denounce the existing evils of their day. A great day of Jehovah would bring about the righting of all that was wrong with the world. In the apocalypses, all that precedes the critical day is summed up under the conception of the present age (αἰὼν οὗτος, עוֹלָם הַזֶּה); the future, with its ideally good conditions, is the coming age (αἰὼν ὁ μέλλων, ἐρχόμενος, עוֹלָם הַבָּא). The noteworthy feature about the conception of the æons is that each is a coherent unity, and has a character of its own. The present age is unpropitious, evil (4 Ezr 7[12]); the future will be good. The past is the age of the world-kingdom, portrayed under the symbolic figure of beasts; the

future, the age of the Divine reign; it has a human aspect. All this is put forth as a source of comfort and encouragement to the faithful. The duration of the evil age is variously computed. Enoch makes it 10,000 years (Eth. Enoch 16[1] 18[16] 21[6]); in the Assumption of Moses it is 5000; at any rate, it is definite and near its end. It is soon to pass away. The question is even pertinent whether those living shall continue to the end of it. This question, however, is not answered (4 Ezr 4[37] 5[50f.] 6[20], Syr. Bar 44[9]).

2. *The impending Crisis.*—The passing of the old will be accompanied by great changes in nature. The order of things will be reversed. The moon will alter her course, and not appear at her appointed times; the stars shall wander from their orbits and be concealed (Eth. Enoch 80[3-7]). Trees will flow with blood, and stones will cry out (Syr. Bar 27). In the heavens, dread signs of portentous significance will appear (Sib. Or 3[796-806]). Fountains will dry up, the earth will refuse to yield; the heavens will be turned into brass; the rains will fail, and springs of waters will be dried up. Among men, wars and rumours of wars will prevail (Eth. Enoch 99[4], 4 Ezr 9[3]), and private feuds and recklessness of the life of men will be the rule (Eth. Enoch 100[2]; Sib. Or 3[633-647], Syr. Bar 48[32] 70[3]). Women will cease to be fruitful, and miscarriages will occur (4 Ezr 5[8] 6[21]). These are the ἀρχὴ ὠδίνων of Mt 24[8], Mk 13[8].

3. The *Conception of God* is more definitely anthropomorphic than in the earlier period. He is pictured by the apocalyptists as seated on the highest heaven, and surrounded by a host of attendants. In the Slavonic Enoch, in the Ascension of Isaiah, in the Greek Baruch, and in general in all the apocalypses, God is regarded as a monarch with an army to fight His battles, and a retinue of servants to execute His orders. Much of this is naturally a part of the drapery of the vision, but it all tends to accentuate the gulf which separates God from man. Especially where the anthropomorphism is conscious of its own inadequacy, and is combined with descriptions of the fearfulness of God's person, the idea of transcendency is accentuated, and begins to dominate the apocalyptists' thought of God.

4. The *cosmology* is a corollary of the transcendence of God. The distance between heaven, His dwelling-place, and earth, the abode of man, is enlarged and filled with six stages, making altogether seven heavens. These are minutely described in the Slavonic Enoch, the Ascension of Isaiah, the Greek Baruch (cf. also Test. Lev. 2 and 3). The substance of which these heavens are made is light, or rather luminous matter (Eth. En 14[8-25]). The language is not metaphorical. This light becomes fuller and more intense as one approaches the throne of God Himself. With God are to be found in this sphere the forces and persons that wage His warfare and serve to carry out His plans. Besides the hierarchy of angels (already spoken of), there are here the abodes of the sun, moon, stars, and nature-powers; also the Messiah, ready to be manifested at the proper time.

5. An *arch-enemy* called Beliar, Mastema, Azazel (Satan), at every point undertakes to thwart the purposes of God. It was he who tempted and misled Adam and Eve in the Garden of Eden (*Life of Adam and Eve*). As he takes on himself a body and appears on earth in order to defeat the Messiah, he is Antichrist. In this capacity he is sometimes represented as taking the form of a king (Antiochus Epiphanes, Nero, Caligula) and sometimes that of a false prophet (Sib. Or 3[63ff.])

6. *Man.*—There is a definite realization of the unity of the human race. Sin, need, and death

are looked upon as affecting all men. They have one cause for all. The world was created for the sake of man (4 Ezr 8[44], Syr. Bar 14[18]). Similarly, the plans of God have in view the welfare of men as such. The blessings of the Messianic age come to men in general, although with varying degrees of fulness (Sib. Or 3[367ff. 767ff.]). But the distinction between those who please God by obeying His law and those who do not is never lost sight of. Israel is His chosen people, and He has given it the Law; but the Israelite who transgresses the Law is punished, whereas the Gentile who observes the Sabbath shall be holy and blessed like 'us,' says the author of Jubilees.

7. *Sin.*—All misery among men is the result of sin, and the fall of the first pair in the Garden of Eden is the cause of it. This is predominantly the lesson of the *Life of Adam and Eve*; but it is also clearly put in 4 Ezra and in the Syriac Baruch (Tennant, *The Sources of the Doctrine of the Fall and Original Sin*, 1905).

8. *The coming Messiah.*—The central development of apocalyptic literature is the figure of the Messiah; but it is nowhere outlined so clearly as in the Ethiopic Enoch. He is here designated as the Son of Man; He is also called the Righteous One, the Elect One, the Elect of Righteousness and the Faithful One, and the Anointed One. He is not a mere human being; He has His home in heaven with the Ancient of Days (39[7] 46[1]). Enoch sees Him as pre-existing. This pre-existence is also implied in the declaration that His name was named by the Creator of spirits before the creation of the sun and stars (48[3]), that He was chosen and concealed before the foundation of the world (48[6] 62[6]). He will become manifest in the day of consummation, taking His seat beside the Lord of the Spirits, and all creatures shall fall down before Him (51[3. 4] 61[1] 63[3]). Other portraitures are to be found in 4 Ezr 13[3] ('One in the form of a man'), and in the Psalms of Solomon (17 and 18).

9. *The Resurrection.*—The doctrine of Dn 12[2] is that 'many of them that sleep in the dust of the earth shall awake, some to everlasting life, and some to shame and everlasting contempt.' In the Eth. Enoch (51[1]) this is broadened into a universal resurrection, the object of which is defined as judgment for the deeds done in the body (Eth. Enoch 22). This idea is also taught elsewhere (4 Ezr 7[32] 5[45] 14[35], Syr. Bar 42[7] 50[2], Test. Benj. 10, almost in the words of Dn 12[2], *Life of Adam*, 41. 10. 13. 28. 51).

10. *The Judgment.*—This undoubtedly developed from the prophetic conception of the Day of Jahweh. It is to be distinguished from the judgment which takes place during the course of the present age. It is called the Great Judgment (μεγάλη κρίσις, Eth. Enoch 10[6. 12] 25[4] 45[3. 6] 48[9] 50[4] 58[6] 60[5] 65[5. 10] 67[10], Jub 5[10] 32[11], Eth. En 91[7], Test. of Levi 3, Assump. Mos 1[18]); Eternal Judgment (Slav. Enoch 7[1] 40[12], 4 Ezr 7[70-73], Syr. Bar 20[4] 57[2] 59[2] 83[7] 85[12ff.], *Life of Adam*, 39). It consists in a spectacular revelation of the wickedness of God's opponents, and their condemnation and punishment for their enmity to Him. The subjects of the judgment are both heavenly and earthly powers. Satan and Antichrist (if these two be looked at as different), the fallen angels, the world-powers, and wicked men are all included. The judgment will be upon the ground of books in which either the names or the deeds of men have been inscribed according to their good or evil. Sometimes the deeds are represented as being weighed in the scales. Each person judged must stand upon his own merits. Intercession in his behalf by another is of no avail. The judge is God Himself. He appears as the Ancient of Days (one having a Head of Days),

with white hair and beard. He is seated on a glorious throne, and surrounded with myriads of angels (Eth. En 1[4. 9], Sib. Or 3[91. 92], Slav. En 20[1], Test. Levi 4, Assump. Mos 12[9]). In some representations it is the Messiah who acts as the judge (uniformly in the Book of Similitudes, Eth. Enoch 37-71, with the exception of 47[3]). His sphere of judgment, however, includes the fallen angels and demons, not men. For the most part, the Messiah appears either before or after the judgment (4 Ezr 7[33], before; Eth. Enoch 90, after). Again, Messiah is associated with God and acts as the judge while God executes sentence (Eth. En 62).

11. *The Punishment of the Wicked.*—The most manifest effect of the judgment is the overthrow of God's enemies and the infliction of fit penalties upon them. Of these enemies, three classes may be distinguished: (*a*) Spirits, including Satan and fallen angels (Test. Benj. 3, Sib. Or 3[73], Test. Sim. 6, Zeb. 9). (*b*) Heathen world-powers, looked at either in the abstract or as special individual kings 4 Ezr 11. 12[3], Sib. Or 3[250-380], Ps-Sol 17[22], Eth. En 51[4] 52[6] 53[7]). (*c*) Sinners in general. But special mention is made of Israelites who transgressed the law (Syr. Bar 85[15] 54[22]). Satan (Beliar) is cast into the fire (Test. Jud. 25), though he rules in hell with his angels (Eth. En 53[3] 56[1]). The fallen angels pass at the judgment into a permanent condition of damnation. The giants who sprang from the union of the angels with the daughters of men are also confined in eternal torment. The heathen who have opposed God and oppressed Israel are destroyed. Destruction (ἀπώλεια), however, is not conceived as equivalent to annihilation, but as involving existence in a wretched state.

12. *The Reward of the Righteous.*—The works of the pious are preserved as in a treasury in heaven (4 Ezr 7[77] 8[33], Syr. Bar 14[12] 24[1]). When they are raised from the dead, it is in order that they may come into eternal life (Ps-Sol 3[16]). This they are said to inherit (Eth. En 37[4] 40[9], Ps-Sol 9[9] 14[11. 3]). Eternal life is sometimes looked at as simply a prolonged bodily life (Eth. En 5[9] 10[10. 17] 62[14], Jub 23[27-.9]); but sometimes it appears as a superior kind of life in another world (4 Ezr 8[53], Syr. Bar 21[22], Test. Lev. 18.

13. *The Renovation of the World.*—This is the natural corollary of the idea that the world as at present constituted has been corrupted by rebellion against God and sin, and therefore cannot stand. Deutero-Isaiah (65[17] 66[22]) foreshadows the advent of 'a new heaven and a new earth.' The same world-reconstruction is held in prospect by the apocalyptists. The Ethiopic Enoch (91[16f.]) announces that 'the first heaven will vanish and pass away, and a new heaven will appear.' The present order of the material heavens will last only until the new eternal creation is brought into existence (Eth. En 72[1]). Time distinctions will cease when the new creation is accomplished (Jub 50[2]).

14. *Predestination.*—In the sense of the determination of the destiny of individuals beforehand, as elect or non-elect, the idea of predestination does not clearly appear in the apocalyptic literature. In the sense, however, that all the experiences of God's people are known and have always been known by Him, and do not come to pass without His consent, the doctrine is constant as the undertone of thought. All the events unfolded in the eschatological pictures are certain to come to pass because God wills that they should. Certainty of blessedness for the righteous is not dependent upon their own piety, but upon God's having foreordained it (Assump. Mos 12[8]). The age is as a whole fixed and measured (Book of Jubilees). When its course has run, it comes to

an end (4 Ezr 4[39] 7[74]). A certain number of righteous must be gathered in. Only when this takes place can the consummation occur. It was this doctrine that made the whole apocalyptic theory a practical effective scheme, because it enabled it to impart the assurance of the realization of that good in the future which was missed in the present.

vi. CONTACT WITH THE NEW TESTAMENT.— The significance of apocalyptic literature for the NT is very large. In general, apocalyptic furnishes the atmosphere of the NT. Its form, its language, and its material are extensively used.* In particular, this is true of the following main lines :—

1. The apocalyptic *form* is used as such in the literary composition of the NT. In the Apocalypse of John this becomes the form of the whole book. In other places it is introduced as a part of productions of a different literary type (cf. Mt 24 and parallels). Whether these passages were originally separate works and the Gospel writers incorporated them, or whether they make up integral parts of the plans of the Gospels, is a question for historical criticism to deal with. In their interpretation no satisfactory results will be reached if their formal affinity to the apocalypses be ignored. In 2 Th 2[2-12] the case is clear. The Apostle evidently weaves an apocalyptic passage of his own construction into his Epistle. A firm base of operations is thus furnished for the interpretation of the apocalyptic portions of the NT. These must be read as the apocalypses in general are read.

2. Some outstanding *phrases* in the NT terminology deserve special mention. The expression 'Son of Man' occurs first in Daniel (7[13]). From here, if the now predominant pre-Christian dating of the Book of Similitudes (Eth. En 37–71) be correct, it is adopted into that work, and this usage serves as the bridge of connexion between Daniel and Jesus, who treats this term constantly as His own title. Closely associated with this title is the phrase 'Head of Days' (Eth. En 47[3] 48[2-6]), as applied to God. Other phrases of this class are the 'Day of Judgment,' the 'Great Day of Judgment' (Eth. En 19[1] 22[4-11]).

3. *Quotations* from apocalyptic books are not very common in the NT. The most familiar is that in Jude [14f.] from Eth. En 1[9]. Jude[9] is also a quotation from the Assumption of Moses (Charles, *Testament of Moses*). The book is not named here, and the quotation is identified by ancient writers to whom this apocalypse was familiar. But coincidences of phraseology, suggesting quotations either of one from the other or of both from a common source, are quite frequent (cf. Charles, *Book of Enoch*, pp. 42–49 ; *Apocalypse of Baruch*, pp. lxxvi–lxxix ; *Book of the Secrets of Enoch*, pp. xxii, xxiii ; *Assumption of Moses*, pp. 113 ; also Sinker, *Testamenta XII Patriarcharum*, pp. 209–210). Some of these parallelisms must be ascribed to the nature of the thought expressed, which perhaps would not admit, or at least would not easily lend itself to very different phraseology ; but in a large number the coincidence can occur only where literary affiliation of some kind exists.

4. The most important point of contact, however, is that in *subject-matter*. And here it is no mere point of contact that we have to note, but a large and free adoption of the forms worked out by the apocalyptists. To undertake a list would be to repeat the summary given above of the apocalyptic theology. The simplest way to describe the relation is to say that Jesus and the writers of the NT found the forms of thought made use of in apo-

---

* This does not mean, however, that there are not in the fundamental matters sharp contrasts between the NT and the apocalypses. The New Testament is the New Testament. Its originality is beyond question.

calyptic literature convenient vehicles, and have cast the gospel of God's redemptive love into these as into moulds. The Messianism of the apocalyptists has thus become unfolded into the Christology of the NT. The theocratic judgment has passed into the universal ethical discrimination between individuals according to the deeds done in the body. Other doctrines, such as angelology and demonology, have likewise been used as the vehicles of great eternal verities.

5. Solutions of some *questions* which St. Paul faced are proposed in some of the apocalypses (notably 4 Ezr and Syr. Bar). These are often as different as they can possibly be. Whether they are meant to be a secret form of attack on Christianity or simply independent ways of approaching the same subjects, they are of the utmost importance. In the first case, they throw light on the growth of Christian belief and the manner of the polemic waged against it. In the latter, they illustrate the nature of the setting in which the gospel found itself as soon as preached.

LITERATURE.—Besides the special works (referred to above) on the individual apocalypses, the following comprehensive works may be consulted :—Grörer, *Das Jahrhundert d. Heils*, 1838 ; Hilgenfeld, *Jüd. Apokal.* 1857, and *Messias Judæorum*, 1869 ; Drummond, *The Jewish Messiah*, 1877 ; Smend, ' Jüd. Apok.' in *ZATW*, 1885, pp. 222–250 ; Deane, *Pseudepigrapha*, 1891 ; Thomson, *Books which Influenced Our Lord and His Apostles*, 1891 ; de Faye, *Les Apocalypses Juives*, 1892 ; Bousset, *Der Antichrist* [Eng. tr. by Keane, 1896], and the same author's *Offenbarung Johannis*, 1896, *Die Rel. d. Judentums*, 1903, and *Jüd. Apokal.* 1903 ; Charles, *Eschatology, Hebrew, Jewish, and Christian*, 1899 ; Schürer, *GJV*[3], 1898, iii. ; M. S. Terry, *Biblical Apocalyptics*, 1898 ; Wellhausen, *Skizzen u. Vorarbeiten*, 1899 ; Volz, *Jüd. Eschatologie*, 1903 ; Baldensperger, *Die Messianisch-Apokalyptischen Hoffnungen des Judentums*, 1903 [this is the 3rd ed. of his *Selbstbewusstsein Jesu*[1], 1888] ; H. A. A. Kennedy, *The Eschatology of Paul*, 1904 ; Muirhead, *The Eschatology of Jesus*, 1904 ; articles by Charles in Hastings' *DB* and in *Encyc. Biblica* ; Porter, *Messages of the Apocalyptical Writers*, 1905.

A. C. ZENOS.

APOCRYPHA.—This term is here used for those Jewish writings included in the Gr., Lat., and Eng. Bibles to which the title is commonly applied, *i.e.* the Biblical Apocrypha. For the literary history and characteristics of the Apocrypha see Hastings' *DB*, vol. i. *s.v.* 'Apocrypha.' The relation of the Apocrypha to Christ and Christianity, which is the subject of this article, comes especially under four heads—the Messianic idea, the doctrine of Wisdom, the anticipation of Christian doctrines other than that of the Person or mission of Christ, the use of the Apocrypha in the Christian Church.

i. THE MESSIANIC IDEA. —While this idea is luxuriantly developed in Apocalyptic literature, it is singularly neglected in most of the Apocrypha. The stream of prophecy which ran clear and strong in the OT became turbid and obscure in those degenerate successors of the prophets, the Apocalyptic visionaries. But it was in the line of the prophetic schools of teaching that the Messianic idea was cherished. Accordingly the treatment of the later stage of that teaching as erratic and unauthoritative, not fit for inclusion in the Canon, involved the result that the remaining more sober literature, which was recognized as nearer to the standard of Scripture, and in Egypt included in the later canon (at all events as in one collection of sacred books), was for the most part associated with those schools in which the Messianic hope was not cultivated. Therefore it is not just to say that this hope had faded away or suffered temporary obscurity during the period when the Apocrypha was written, the truth being that it was then more vigorous than ever in certain circles. But these circles were not those of our Old Testament Apocrypha. Thus the question is literary rather than historical. It concerns the editing of certain books, not the actual life and thought of Israel.

This will be evident if we compare the *Book of*

Daniel with *1 Maccabees*. These two books deal with the same period. Yet the former, although it does not know a personal Messiah, is the very fount and spring of the Messianic conception of the golden age in subsequent Apocalypses. On the other hand, 1 Maccabees ignores the Messianic hope, at all events in its usually accepted form.

Only two passages in this book can be pointed to as suggesting the Messianic idea, and they will not bear the strain that is sometimes put upon them. The first is 1 Mac 2⁵⁷ 'David for being merciful inherited the throne of a kingdom for ever and ever.' We have here that very elementary form of the Messianic idea, if we may so call it, the permanence of David's throne. But it is evident that David as the founder of the royal line, not the Messiah, is here referred to, and that the permanence of the throne is for the succession of his descendants, not for any one person. Not only is this the most reasonable interpretation of the passage, but it rests on OT promises to that effect, where the family of David and not the personal Messiah is intended (*e.g.* 2 S 7¹³· ¹⁶, cf. Ps 132¹²). Of this passage, however, as of the earlier Scriptures on which it rests, we may say that the idea contained in it is realized by the permanent reign of David's great Son, and in a much larger and higher way than had been anticipated. The other passage is 1 Mac 4⁴⁵· ⁴⁶ 'And there came into their mind a good counsel, that they should pull it [*i.e.* the sanctuary] down, lest it should be a reproach to them, because the Gentiles had defiled it : and they pulled down the altar, and laid up the stones in the mountain of the house in a convenient place, until there should come a prophet to give an answer concerning them.' This is not even a reference to '*the* prophet' of whom we read in Jn 1²⁵. It is merely a case of waiting for some prophet to come and say when the temple was to be rebuilt, with no definite assurance that one specifically anticipated prophet was thus destined to arise.

Nevertheless, though we cannot point to any Messianic prophecy in 1 Mac., some of the Psalms attributed to this period indicate a prevalence of ideas that belong to the same circle of thought. Passionate patriotism fired by martyrdom and crowned with temporary success naturally painted great hopes for the nation. The reason why these were not connected with a coming Messiah may be twofold. (1) For a time it seemed likely that the Maccabees themselves were realizing those hopes, that this remarkable family of patriots was really restoring the glory of Israel. (2) Since these men were of the priestly line, the splendour of their achievements eclipsed for the time being the national dreams of the house of David.

The reaction of the later *Ḥasidim*, out of whom the Pharisaic party emerged, against the worldly methods of the Hasmonæan family and their identification of the mission of Israel with military prowess, released the more spiritual religious hopes, and so prepared for a revival of Messianic ideas. This new movement, which saw the true good of the nation to lie in her religion and looked for her help from God, did not altogether coincide with the hope of a personal Christ, for God Himself was the Supreme King whose coming was to be expected by His people.

The book of *Judith* is a romance issuing from the Pharisaic reactionary party ; but it is devoid of all specific Messianic ideas. In this case the human saviour of Israel is a woman.

Of the three other popular tales, two, *The History of Susanna* and *Bel and the Dragon*, contain nothing bearing on the Messianic idea ; but the latter part of *Tobit* may be accounted Messianic in the general sense as giving a picture of the Golden Age of the future. Jerusalem is to be scourged for her children's works, but she is to give praise to the everlasting King that 'afterwards his tabernacle may be builded' in her 'again with joy.' Many nations are to come from far to the name of the Lord God with gifts in their hands. All generations shall praise her with great joy. The city is to be built and paved with precious stones. 'And all her streets shall say Hallelujah ; and they shall praise him, saying, Blessed be God, which hath exalted it for ever' (To 13⁹⁻¹⁸). In all this there is no mention of the son of David or any human king and deliverer. (In the Hebrew varia-

tion of the text of this chapter as rendered by Neubauer, we read of 'the coming of the Redeemer and the building of Ariel,' *i.e.* Jerusalem ; but evidently this Redeemer is Jahweh). We must go outside our Apocrypha to the *Psalms of Solomon* for the Pharisaic revival of the Messiah of the line of David.

Apocalyptic literature lends itself more readily to Messianic ideas, and these find full expression in the *Book of Enoch*, where—in the 'Similitudes' —the descriptions of the Messiah who appears in clouds as the Son of Man are assigned by Dr. Charles to the pre-Christian Jewish composition.

2 Esdras, also a Jewish Apocalyptic work, calls for closer examination, since it is contained in our Apocrypha, although its late date diminishes its value in the history of the development of thought. The Christian additions (chapters (*a*) 1. 2 ; (*b*) 15. 16) do not call for attention here ; they could only come into the study of the development of Christian thought if they were in any way contributions to that subject ; but the warnings of the supplanting of Israel by the Gentiles in (*a*), and the judgment of the nations in (*b*), cannot be regarded in that light. The original work (chapters 3–14) affords significant evidence of the melancholy condition into which Jewish Messianic hopes had sunk during the gloomy interval between the destruction of Jerusalem and the rise of Bar-Cochba, the reign of Domitian (A.D. 81–96) being its generally accepted date (see Hastings' *DB*, vol. i. p. 765). Unlike the other Apocryphal writings, since it does not illustrate the transition from the OT to the NT, it is serviceable only in the study of post-Christian Judaism. Its Christian interpolations do not materially hinder us from discovering the original text. The Messianic passages are in chapters 7. 12. and 13. The insertion of the name 'Jesus' in 7²⁸ (not found in the Oriental versions) by a Christian hand is not sufficient reason for discrediting the Jewish character of the composition. The picture of the Messiah is quite un-Christian. It is startling to read that he is to die (7²⁹) ; but (1) this is after reigning 400 years, and (2) without a subsequent resurrection. The first point indicates the visionary ideas of the Apocalyptic writer, not the known fact of our Lord's brief life on earth, and the second is in conflict with the great prominence which the early Christians gave to our Lord's resurrection. A Messiah who lived for 400 years and then died, and so ended his Messiahship, could not be Jesus Christ. Accordingly the Syriac reads '30' instead of '400,' evidently a Christian emendation. Undoubtedly this is a Jewish conception, and its mournful character, so unlike the triumphant tone of Enoch, is in keeping with the gloomy character of the book, and a reflection of the deep melancholy that took possession of the minds of earnest, patriotic Jews after the fearful scenes of the siege of Jerusalem and the overwhelming of their hopes in a deluge of blood. The reference to the death of the Messiah is not found in the Arabic or the Armenian versions ; but it is easy to see how it came to be omitted, while there is no likelihood that it would be inserted later, either by a Jew, to whom the idea would be unwelcome, or by a Christian, since the resurrection is not also mentioned. A noteworthy fact is that the Messiah is addressed by God as 'My son.' The Ethiopic of 7²⁸, instead of 'My son Jesus' reads 'My Messiah,' and the Armenian, 'the anointed of God.' But the reference to sonship occurs elsewhere frequently, *e.g.* 'My son Christ,' or 'My anointed son' (7²⁹ ; see also 13³²· ³⁷· ⁵² 14⁹, in most versions, but not in Arm. : see Dr. Sanday, art. 'Son of God' in Hastings' *DB*, vol. iv. p. 571). Since, as Dr. Sanday remarks in the article just referred to, the strongly Messianic passage in Ps-Sol 17²³⁻⁵¹ has not the title 'Son,' but clearly borrows from Ps 2 in v.²⁶, it is a likely inference that 2 Esdras is here based on that Psalm. Compare the words of the high priest in Mt 26⁶³.

In chs. 12 and 13 the writer names Daniel, and manifestly bases his elaboration of the Messianic picture on the Book of Daniel. The Messiah appears as a lion rising up out of a wood and roaring. A certain pre-existence is implied in the assertion that the Most High had *kept* him (12³²); the Latin has only 'for the end,' but the Syriac reads 'for the end of days, who shall spring up out of the seed of David.' He will come to upbraid and destroy the guilty people, but he will have mercy on a remnant and deliver them. Similar ideas are repeated in ch. 13, but in a different form. A man comes from the midst of the sea. This is unlike Daniel (7³· ¹³), where the four beasts come up from the sea, but the 'one like unto a son of man' from the clouds. The Most High has kept him for a great season (v.²⁶), another reference to pre-existence. Similarly later on we read, 'Like as one can neither seek out nor know what is in the depths of the sea, even so can no man upon earth see my Son, or those that be with him, but in the time of his day' (v.⁵²). He exists, but hidden till the time when God will reveal him. When he comes and is revealed, 'it will be as a man ascending.' 'When all the nations hear his voice' they will draw together to fight against him. But he will stand on the top of Mount Zion, and there he will taunt the nations to their face and destroy them without any effort on his part, the instrument of destruction being the Law, which is compared to fire. Then in addition to the saved remnant of the Jews already referred to, the lost ten tribes will be brought back from their exile beyond the Euphrates, whither they had gone by a miraculous passage through the river, and whence they will return by a similar miraculous staying of 'the springs of the river' again. Thus we have the idea of a restoration of all Israel under the Messiah, but with no further extension of the happy future so as to include other nations, as in the Christian Apocalyptic conceptions; on the contrary, those nations will be humiliated and chagrined at the spectacle of the glorification of the former victims of their oppression. On the whole we must conclude with Paul Volz (*Jüdische Eschatologie*, p. 202) that 2 Ezra adopts the traditional hope of the Messiah, but does not see in it the chief ground of assurance for the future. He is hailed as God's son, but he appears to have only a temporary existence. He does not bring deliverance from sin; nor is he to come for judgment. His death is the end of his mission.

ii. The Doctrine of Wisdom. — Unlike the Prophetic and Apocalyptic literature which confessedly anticipated a great future, and so furnished a hope which Christianity subsequently claimed to fulfil, the Hebrew Wisdom writings profess to give absolute truth, and betray no consciousness of further developments. Nevertheless the Church was quick to seize on them as teaching the essential Divinity of Christ. The historical method of more recent times sees in them the germs of ideas on this subject which were subsequently developed by Christian theologians of the Alexandrian school. For the doctrine of Wisdom in the OT see *DB*, art. 'Wisdom.' That doctrine in the Apocrypha is in direct succession from the Ḥokhmah teaching of Proverbs.

1. Sirach.—In the Palestinian school represented by Sirach it is difficult to see much, if any, advance on Proverbs. The idea of Wisdom itself is essentially the same, and the gnomic form of writing continues an identity of method.

(*a*) *Literary Form.*—There is no attempt at metaphysical analysis or philosophical argumentation. This Jewish philosophy is not elucidated by reasoning, or based on logical grounds. It is regarded as intuitive in origin and the treatment of it is didactic. Thus we have nothing like a philosophical or ethical treatise. Much of the writing is directly hortatory, and where the third person is used we have descriptions and reflections, accounts of the nature and function of wisdom, and illustrations of its operations in life and history.

(*b*) *Unity of Wisdom.* — In Sirach, as in Pr., Wisdom is described from two points of view: as found in God and His administration of the world, and as attainable by man in his own character and life. But it is not that God's wisdom is merely the model or the source of our wisdom. Wisdom throughout, though seen in such different relations, is taken as essentially one entity. It is wisdom, absolute wisdom, that God uses in the administration of the universe, and that man also is exhorted to pursue. This realism in dealing with an abstract notion is the first step towards personification.

(*c*) *Personification.*—As in Proverbs, wisdom is here personified. Wisdom is supposed to act, *e.g.* 'How exceeding harsh is she to the unlearned' (6²⁰). In a fine passage she celebrates her own praises, glorying in the midst of her people, saying—

'I came forth from the mouth of the Most High,
    And covered the earth as a mist.
    I dwelt in high places,
    And my throne is in the pillar of the cloud' (24³· ⁴);

and, further, after a rich description of the scenes of nature that she influences—

'In three things I was beautified,
    And stood up beautiful before the Lord and men,' etc. (25¹).

But there is nothing in this personification beyond a free use of the Oriental imagination. No doubt to this vivid imagination such writing presents wisdom as in some way a concrete entity, and more, as a gracious, queenly presence. But all along there are expressions which admit the imaginary character of the whole picture. For instance, the opening passage, describing how Wisdom stood up in the congregation of the Most High to celebrate her own praises, would lose all its force of appeal if it were taken in prosaic literalness. It is just because this is no actual person posing for admiration, but a truth set forth before us, that the whole picture appears to be sublime, and serves its purpose in leading to a high appreciation of wisdom. Then wisdom is identified with understanding: 'Whoso is wise, cleave thou unto him' (6³⁴) . . . 'If thou seest a man of understanding, get thee betimes unto him' (v.³⁶). Thus cultivation of friendship with a man of wisdom or understanding is part of the pursuit of wisdom itself. Even Philo's much more explicit personification of the Logos does not mean that he held the Logos to be an actual person in our sense of the term. Here all we can say of the subject is that the allegorizing is very vivid, so vivid as to be on the verge of the mythopœic, but still in the original intention of the writer not meant to be more than the glorification of a great quality found primarily in God, impressed on nature, and commended to mankind as a highly desirable attainment.

The difficulty of the question lies in the fact that the Oriental mind would not clearly face this question of personality. The imagination would so vividly realize the allegorical picture that the idea would seem to assume form and body, condensing to an apparently concrete and even personal presence, so that it would be regarded for the time being as a person, and yet in the course of the meditation this would melt again into an abstraction, and in the less imaginative passages be regarded in its original character purely as a mode of thought or action. To apply to the product of such a process the logic of the West, or to attempt to bring it into harmony, say, with Locke's theory of ideas, is unreasonable. The atmosphere does not allow of so hard a definition of personality as that which may be either affirmed or denied.

(d) *Source.* — Wisdom originates in God. She 'came forth from the mouth of the Most High' (24³). 'Wisdom was created together with the faithful in the womb' (1¹⁴). She exclaims, 'He created me from the beginning, before the world' (24⁹). As with Pr 8²², the Arian controversy has given a factitious importance to this sentence. Wisdom is identified with Christ; and thus the Arian doctrine that Christ is a creature, that He was created, not begotten by God and not eternal, appears to have clear support. It is probable that Sirach is dependent on Proverbs, and the rendering of LXX (ἔκτισε) is doubtful.* But the much debated point is of little real importance; indeed, it is of no value till we grant that Wisdom in Proverbs and Sirach is (1) personal, and (2) identical with Christ. The denial of (1) in the previous paragraph carries with it the exclusion of (2). Nevertheless, apart from the Arian conception, we still have the idea of the creation of wisdom to account for. This, however, is but a consequence of the allegorical personification in conjunction with the thought that wisdom proceeds from God. That has a twofold signification, corresponding to the two aspects of wisdom. First, God is the source of His own wisdom. He has not to learn; all His plans and purposes spring from His own mind. Secondly, mankind learns wisdom from God; it is His gift to His children. Wisdom is with all flesh according to God's 'gift' (1¹⁰).

(e) *Characteristics.* — There is an intellectual element in wisdom, which is the highest exercise of the mind. The opposite of wisdom is folly, a stupid and brutish thing. The Divine side of wisdom most clearly exhibits this character. Wisdom created by God is with God, and therefore is seen in His presence and works. Nevertheless, Sirach makes very little reference to the manifestation of wisdom in Nature or Providence. The whole stress is on this Divine gift as an object of aspiration for mankind. Wisdom is seen as the best of all human possessions. The sublimity of wisdom is set forth in order to fire the enthusiasm of men to have their lives enriched with the Divine grace. This is just the same as in Proverbs. So also are two further characteristics of Hebrew wisdom. First, it is moral. It is concerned with the practical reason, not the speculative. Its realm is ethics, not metaphysics. It is not a philosophy for solving the riddle of the universe; it is a guide to conduct. The ethics is not discussed theoretically; there is no theory of ethics. The aim of the book is practical, and the treatment of wisdom is didactic and hortatory. Sirach even discourages speculation, in directing the attention solely to conduct—

'Seek not things that are too hard for thee,
And search not out things that are above thy strength.
The things that have been commanded thee, think thereupon;
For thou hast no need of the things that are secret' (3²¹· ²²).

Second, it is religious. Wisdom here, as in Proverbs, is identified with the fear of the Lord. The way to attain wisdom is to keep the Law—

'If thou desire wisdom, keep the commandments,
And the Lord shall give her unto thee freely' (1²⁶).

---

* The Hebrew of Proverbs (קָנָה) is rendered in RV as well as AV 'possessed.' Still RVm has 'formed,' in agreement with Bertheau, Zöckler, Hitzig, and Ewald, and Delitzsch has the similar word 'produced'; moreover, Syr. and Targ. agree with the LXX. In Pr 4⁷ קָנָה is rendered 'get,' and certainly there it can only have that meaning.

Like Proverbs, Sirach contains a quantity of shrewd worldly wisdom, and it is eminently prudential in aim; but it is the better self that is considered, and the higher interests, rather than wealth and pleasure, that are studied. In this way the whole book is concerned with the exposition of the nature and merits of wisdom.

2. Baruch. — The eloquent celebration of the praises of wisdom in this book, which probably dates from the 1st cent. A.D. (see *DB*, art. 'Baruch'), is on similar lines to Sirach. Wisdom is like choice treasure, to be sought out from far. But since she is above the clouds or beyond the sea, no man can be expected to reach so far. There is only One who can do this. 'He that knoweth all things knoweth her' (3³²). Here the idea is different from that of Sirach. Wisdom is not created by God, but is found by Him, as though an independent pre-existence—'He found her out with His understanding' (*ib.*). But the personification is thinner and more pallid than in Sirach. There is no real dualism. The language is little more than a metaphorical expression of the idea that God has the wisdom which is above human reach. Still it goes on into a sort of myth, for Wisdom thus discovered by God hidden in some remote region afterwards appears on earth and becomes conversant with men (3³⁷). Here we have a curious parallel to the Johannine conception of the Word originally with God and then becoming incarnate and dwelling with men. But Baruch has no conception of incarnation, and the idea has no place in the Hebrew personification of wisdom.

3. Wisdom.—(a) *The nature of Wisdom.*—Although, as an Alexandrian work in touch with Greek philosophy, the Bk. of Wisdom carries the doctrine of Ḥokhmah a stage forward in the direction of Philo, it is essentially Jewish, and its idea of wisdom is fundamentally the same as that of Proverbs and Sirach, but with additions, some of which may be attributed to Hellenic influences. The essential Hebrew elements, however, remain. While a movement of intellect, wisdom is practical, moral, and religious. We are no more in the regions of metaphysics or even abstract ethical speculation than in the Palestinian literature. Thus we read—

'For her true beginning is desire of discipline;
And the care for discipline is love of her' (6¹⁷).

(b) *Personification.*—The personification of Wisdom, though still very shadowy, is a little more accentuated than in Sirach. Wisdom is described as 'a spirit' (1⁶), and as such seems to be identified with 'the spirit of God' (v.⁷). In answer to Solomon's prayer God gave him 'a spirit of wisdom' (7⁷). 'She is a breath of the power of God' (7²⁵). She sits as God's 'assessor' (Drummond) by His side on His throne (9⁴). When, however, various functions, such as Creation and Providence, seem to be ascribed to her, this cannot be as to a personal agent, because they are also ascribed to God (e.g. 9¹· ²). It must be, therefore, that God is thought of as doing these things by means of His wisdom.

(c) *Attributes.*—A string of 21 attributes, in thoroughly Greek style, is ascribed to the spirit of Wisdom (7²²ff.). Among other things, she is said to be 'only begotten' (μονογενές, the very word used of Christ in Jn 1¹⁴· ¹⁸ 3¹⁶· ¹⁸ and 1 Jn 4⁹, though RV of Wisdom renders it here 'alone in kind,' having 'sole born' in the margin). Further, wisdom is described as 'a clear effluence of the glory of the Almighty' and an 'effulgence (ἀπαύγασμα, whence He 1³) from everlasting light' (7²⁵· ²⁶). She is free from all defilement, beneficent, beautiful.

(d) *Functions.*—Divine functions are ascribed to Wisdom, since it is by His wisdom that God performs them. (1) Creation. She is 'the artificer of all things' (7^{22}), 'an artificer of the things that are' (8^6). (2) Providence. The function of wisdom in providence is much dwelt on. Wisdom is regarded as a sort of guardian angel watching over men and directing the course of history. Patriarchal history from Adam downward is described as thus under the charge of wisdom. (3) Revelation. The picture of Wisdom as the effulgence from everlasting light points to this. She is also described as 'an unspotted mirror of the working of God, and an image ($\epsilon i \kappa \omega \nu$, cf. 2 Cor 4^4, Col 1^{15}) of His goodness' (7^{26}) ; in attaining to wisdom we come to know the ways of God.

(e) *Wisdom as a human acquisition.* — While wisdom is described in its relation to God as co-extensive with the infinite range of the Divine activities, it is also represented from another point of view as a treasure which mankind is invited to seek. The difficulty of acquiring wisdom suggested in Baruch is not found here. On the contrary, we read that—

'Easily is she beheld of them that love her,
And found of them that seek her' (6^{12}).

Moreover, there is no limitation of Jewish exclusiveness in the privilege of enjoying this greatest of God's gifts, 'for wisdom is a spirit that loveth man' (1^6). When a little later we read that 'the spirit of the Lord hath filled the world' ($\tau \grave{\eta} \nu$ οἰκουμένην, 'the inhabited earth,' RVm), the breadth of Hellenism seen throughout the Alexandrian movement, first Jewish, later Christian, is here apparent. While Wisdom is identified with the Law in the Palestinian work Sirach, here all true enlightenment, pagan as well as Jewish, must be included in this far-reaching wisdom. At the same time, this widespread wisdom is very different from Greek philosophy. The practical, ethical element which is essential to the Hebrew Ḥokhmah is always its chief constituent. Moreover, the homelier conception of wisdom as an exalted prudence serviceable in worldly affairs, which is often apparent in Proverbs and Sirach, is also to be found in the Bk. of Wisdom.

(f) *Anticipations of Christology.*—With this conception of wisdom we cannot claim the identity of terms (ἀπαύγασμα, εἰκών, λόγος) which are here applied to wisdom and in the NT to Jesus Christ as an indication of any clear anticipation of Christian truth. It is rather the other way. St. Paul and the author of Hebrews knew Wisdom, and made use of expressions in the book for their own purposes, giving to them a richer Christian meaning. Nor can it be allowed that the use of the word λόγος as closely associated with wisdom is any real anticipation of the λόγος doctrine of Philo. In Wis 9^1 we read—

' O God of the fathers, and Lord who keepest thy mercy,
Who madest all things *by thy word*' (ὁ ποιήσας τὰ πάντα ἐν λόγῳ σου).

This is evidently an allusion to the Creation story in Gn 1, so that we must understand λόγος in the sense of 'word' (דָּבָר, in the familiar OT expression 'the word of the Lord'). But Philo uses λόγος in the Stoic sense of 'reason.' It may be conjectured that the transition to this meaning has begun in Wis., because the line immediately following that just quoted is, 'and by thy wisdom thou formedst man' (Wis 9^2). Thus λόγος is treated as parallel to wisdom. In any case λόγος is a rational word, not a mere utterance of the voice, but a word with thought, reason in it. Still, the author elsewhere uses the term in the sense of 'word' as the implied reference to Gn 1 indicates that he does here.* It

* λόγος occurs 15 times in Wisdom (viz. 1^9. 16 2^2. 17. 20 6^9. 11 7^{16} 8^5. 18 9^1 12^9 16^{12} 18^{15}. 22). In 13 of these instances there is no question that it means 'word.' Of the 2 remaining cases one is that now under consideration ; the other is 2^2—' And while our

would be nearer the mark to say that Jn 1^1 is an echo of Wis 9^1. Still there is much more in the prologue to the Fourth Gospel than can be derived in any way from this simple statement, and a great deal of that reminds us more of Philo than of Wisdom. The conclusion would seem to be that in John as in Wisdom λόγος is used in the common Biblical sense of 'word' ; but that there are also associations with Philo, the author of the Fourth Gospel ascribing to the λόγος as 'word' some of the attributes which Philo had ascribed to his λόγος as 'reason.' Accordingly the prologue to the Fourth Gospel may be said to combine reminiscences both of Wisdom and of Philo, together with its own original Christian ideas.

iii. ANTICIPATION OF CHRISTIAN DOCTRINES. —Anticipations of the Christ idea, either as Messiah or as Wisdom, have been dealt with in the previous sections. It remains to be seen for what other Christian doctrines preparation is made in the Apocrypha.

1. *The Doctrine of God.*—This subject is treated very fully in *DB*, Extra Vol. art. 'Development of Doctrine,' pp. 276–281. All that is called for here is to indicate those phases of the doctrine that approach the Christian idea. 1 Maccabees is remarkable for its omission of any direct reference to God. But although (according to the best text) the name of God does not appear, He is thought of under the euphemism 'heaven' (*e.g.* 1 Mac 3^{18}). Therefore we must take the omission of the sacred name as an indication of the reverence that feared to mention it, which was characteristic of a later Judaism. This went with the growing conception of the Divine transcendence which was not an anticipation of Christianity, but the reverse, and against which Christianity was a reaction. Still it prepared for Christianity by emphasizing the need of some intermediary power to bring man into contact with God, a mediating Christ. While no hint of anything of the kind is dropped in the historical part of the Apocrypha, the soil is here prepared for it by the very barrenness of religion in lack of it. The popular tales in the Apocrypha contribute nothing material to the conception of God. The fierce patriotism of Judith falls back on the ancient appropriation of Jehovah for Israel ; but this can scarcely be reckoned a theological narrowing, since the thought is not turned to any question concerning the nature of God. In the Wisdom literature, however, we may look for some development of the doctrine. Negatively we see this in the avoidance of the anthropomorphism that fearlessly asserted itself in the OT. Not only is there no approach to a theophany in human form, but the human features often poetically ascribed to God in the older literature do not appear. This, again, goes with the growing feeling of Divine transcendence, which is alien to Christianity. But it is also an indication of a spiritual conception that may be taken as anticipatory of the spiritual idea of God in the NT. In Sirach, God is not so much too remote, but rather too great for men to understand His nature—

' When ye glorify the Lord, exalt him as much as ye can;
For even yet will he exceed' (Sir 43^{30}).

God is addressed as 'Father and Master of my life' (23^1), and 'Father and God of my life' (v.^{4}), which implies the Divine fatherhood of the individual, a doctrine only just reached in the latest OT teaching. Moreover, the goodness of God extends to all mankind (18^{13}). In Wisdom, under the influence of Hellenic thought, the idealizing process is pushed further. God is the 'eternal light' (Wis 7^{26}), so that wisdom which irradiates the world is the

heart beateth, reason is a spark.' Here it is human reason that is referred to. In every case where λόγος is predicated of God the sense is 'word.' See especially 12^9 18^{22}.

effluence from this central fountain of light. On the other hand, there is a narrowing of the idea of creation under the influence of the Greek notion of pre-existent matter. God creates the world out of 'formless matter' (11[17]), and creation is described as being 'impressed,' like wax by the seal (19[6]). The motive of creation was love, and God hates nothing that He has made, loving all things that are (11[24]). Nevertheless, it is said in another place that God only loves him who dwells with wisdom (7[28]). The seeming inconsistency may be reconciled if we understand that here we have the more special personal affection of Divine friendship.

2. *The Fall and Original Sin.*—While Gn 3 contains the narrative of the fall of Adam, (1) it does not attribute this to the devil, not identifying the serpent with Satan, but treating it simply as the most subtle of beasts ; and (2) it does not affirm that either sin or death visits the whole race in consequence of this primary offence and its doom. But both of these ideas appear in Christianity ; and the latter is contained in the writings of St. Paul, who does not give it as part of the new teaching, but assumes that it is already an accepted belief. St. Paul simply appeals to it as a basis for his analogous teaching concerning Christ. Thus he writes, ' *as* through the one man's disobedience the many were made sinners ' (Ro 5[19]), and similarly with the second part of the doctrine, ' *as* in Adam all die ' (1 Co 15[22]). Therefore these ideas must have grown up apart from the OT. Now we find them in the Apocr. Wisdom literature, both Palestinian and Alexandrian, *e.g.* the Palestinian teaching—

'From a woman was the beginning of sin ;
And because of her we all die' (Sir 25[24])—

an easy inference from Gn 3, but never made in the OT. Then there is the Alexandrian teaching, ' By the envy of the devil, death entered into the world ' (Wis 2[24]).

Grätz regards this as a Christian interpolation ; but Dr. Drummond shows that his three reasons for this view do not appear to have much force. (1) Grätz objects that the clause disturbs the connexion of the passage, but it balances the previous statement—

'God created man for incorruption,
And made him an image of his own proper being' (v.[23]) ;

for thus we have the antithesis which is one of the common forms of Hebrew poetry. (2) For Grätz to assert that it has for him 'absolutely no sense,' is a criticism that would apply to it equally whoever wrote it. (3) The fact that it is without parallel in other Jewish writings must not be taken as condemning it. The idea is familiar in Christian literature ; yet there is nothing specifically Christian about it, since it simply results from an application of the doctrine of a devil to the Genesis narrative, with the exercise of some imagination as to the Evil Spirit's motive. Moreover, Milton's adoption of the idea of envy as that motive in *Paradise Lost*, shows that, to a great poet at all events, the expression is not without a reasonable meaning. The author of Wisdom is a sufficiently-brilliant writer to have struck out these ideas and made the inferences without any antecedent example. Dähne considers the passage to be allegorical, because the notion of 'an evil principle in opposition to the Divine is foreign to pure Alexandrianism.' Accordingly he applies Philo's interpretation of Gn 3 to it, and understands the word διάβολος to stand for the serpent as an image of carnal pleasure. But why should not the writer mention the serpent if he meant it ? Since ὁ διάβολος appears in the LXX for ' the Satan,' it is impossible that a Jew who was familiar with that version would use the word in an entirely original way for a reptile. The story of fallen angels was not unfamiliar to Jewish Apocalyptic literature (see Drummond, *Philo Judæus*, p. 195 f.). That, however, Wisdom does not teach the total depravity of the race, we may infer from its singling out the inhabitants of Canaan as deserving to be extirpated because of their innate vice. 'Their nature by birth was evil' (12[10]) ; 'they were a seed accursed from the beginning' (v.[11]). Here a doctrine of heredity is implied ; but it is applied only to the Canaanites, who are regarded as of an inveterately and hopelessly evil stock. It is to be inferred that other peoples are not so bad.

The late date of 2 Esdras removes it out of the category of anticipations of Christianity. Still, as a Jewish work it witnesses to Jewish thoughts which have their roots in an earlier period. Now this book distinctly teaches the doctrine of original sin. The angel Uriel undertakes to teach Esdras 'wherefore the heart is wicked' (2 Es 4[4]). In an earlier passage the sin of the race was traced to Adam (3[21]). The pessimism of the book is especially gloomy in regard to this subject. Esdras declares that 'it had been better that the earth had not given thee Adam, or else, when it had given him, to have restrained him from sinning' (7[46]). Though it was Adam who sinned, the evil did not fall on him alone, but on all of us who come from him (v.[48]).

3. *Redemption.*—There is nothing approaching the Christian doctrine of redemption in the Apocrypha. The NT teachers had to go back beyond all this literature to Is 53 for the seed thoughts of their specific teaching on this subject. In the Messianic ideas, as far as these appear in the Apocrypha, which we have seen is but meagrely, there are the two thoughts of God redeeming His people, and the Christ coming as a personal redemption. There is no anticipation of the doctrine of the cross. The sombre prediction of the death of the Christ in 2 Es. (later than the Christian gospel, as it is) contains no hint that this is either sacrificial or redemptive. The goodness and mercy of God in delivering His people are frequently celebrated ; but with no specific doctrine of salvation. The *Ḥokhmah* teaching would suggest that escape from sin is to be had through the acquisition of wisdom, which is rooted in the fear of the Lord. It was wisdom that brought the first man out of his fall (Wis 10[1]). Tobit has the great OT teaching of God's forgiveness for His penitent people whom He scourges for their iniquity, but to whom He will show mercy. If they turn to Him with all their heart and soul to do truth before Him, He will turn to them (To 13[5. 6]). Sinners must turn and do righteousness if they would receive His restoring grace. The Patristic idea that the ' blessed . . . wood . . . through which cometh righteousness ' (Wis 14[7], cf. Ac 5[30], 1 P 2[24]) is the cross, ignores the context, which plainly shows that the reference is to Noah's Ark (see v.[6]).

4. *Liberalizing of religion.*—In several respects the Apocrypha shows advance beyond the narrower exclusiveness of Judaism. The historical situation in 1 Mac. did not encourage this movement. When the Jews were struggling for freedom of life and worship against the forcible intrusion of paganism, they were not in a condition for missionary enthusiasm. Judith breathes a spirit of fiercest Jewish patriotism. But Tobit in his prayer of rejoicing declares that many nations shall come from far to the name of the Lord God with gifts in their hands (To 13[11]). That this is not the reluctant homage of subject peoples is shown by the sequel, where we read about 'generations of generations' praising God with songs of rejoicing. Still all this is ministering to the glory of Jerusalem. Israel is exalted in the honour shown to her God. The Palestinian *Ḥokhmah* literature is not free from Jewish narrowness. In Sirach, God is prayed to send His fear on all nations. But this is to be by lifting up His hand *against* them, so that they may see His mighty power. Still some gracious end even in this stern treatment of the heathen may be desired, since the prayer proceeds, ' And let them know thee, as we also have known thee ' (Sir 36[5]). God is asked to hear the prayer of His suppliants [Israel], in order that all on the earth may know that He is the Lord, the eternal God (v.[17]). This may not mean more than the acknowledgment of God for His glory and for the reflexion of that on His privileged people. On the other hand, the importance attached to wisdom has a widening tendency ; for this is an internal grace, not an external privilege. But the identification of wisdom in Sirach with interest in the Law (39¹) tends to limit this grace itself and confine it to Israel.

When we turn to the Alexandrian teaching of the Book of Wisdom we expect a wider outlook. Here also the national privileges of Israel are accentuated. God gave oaths and covenants of good promises to the nation's ancestors (12²¹ 18⁶). Moreover, 'the righteous' are to judge the nations and have rule over the people (3⁸). But since the domain of wisdom is world-wide and 'the spirit of God filleth the world' (1⁷), it might be supposed that the world at large would benefit by that gracious presence. Princes of peoples are invited to honour wisdom that they may reign for ever (6²¹), an invitation necessarily applying to the Gentile world. It is stated in a general way that 'the ways of *them which are on the earth*' [more than Israel] were corrected by wisdom (9¹⁸). There is a magnificent universalism in the great saying that God loves all things that are, and abhors none of the things that He has made (11²⁴). God's incorruptible spirit is in all things (12¹); there is no other God that careth for all (v.¹³); His sovereignty over all leads Him to forbear all (v.¹⁶). But further than this the book does not go. It contains no explicit promise of redemption or of the blessings of the future for the world outside Israel, though it would be no illegitimate inference from these large ideas concerning the presence and activity and graciousness of God the whole world over to conclude that such good things were not to be confined to Israel. On the other hand, not only were the Canaanites a helplessly evil race, but the more recent oppressors of Israel, whose gross idolatry is scornfully portrayed at large, after the manner of Deutero-Isaiah, are described as 'prisoners of darkness . . . exiled from the eternal providence' (17²). For other heathen people allowance is made on account of their ignorance. 'For these men there is but small blame: for they too, peradventure, do but go astray' (13⁶).

5. *Resurrection and Immortality.*—With regard to no other subject is advance from the OT standpoint towards that of the NT more apparent in the Apocrypha. The distinction between Palestinian and Alexandrian conceptions is here very marked, the Palestinian writings promising resurrection, the Alexandrian making no reference to a resurrection, but adopting the Greek idea of the immortality of the soul. The more conservative books of the former school, Tobit, Sirach, and 1 Mac., contain no reference to the resurrection or the future life in any form, retaining only the old gloomy Hebrew notion of Sheol, which, on the other hand, in these writings is not Gehenna, not a place of punishment. 'There are no chastisements in Sheol' (Sir 41⁴, Heb. mar., and LXX).* According to Tobit, Sheol is an 'eternal place' (3⁶) where life is extinct. 'All the rewards of faithfulness enumerated by the dying Mattathias (1 Mac 2⁵²⁻⁶¹) are limited to this life' (Charles, *Eschat.* p. 219). In Judith eternal punishment is threatened to the enemies of Israel (16¹⁷); but nothing is said about a future life for God's people. 2 Mac., an epitome of the five books of Jason of Cyrene (2²³), contains a clear doctrine of resurrection to eternal life (7⁹), which is denied to the non-Israelite (v.¹⁴); this is a bodily resurrection (7¹¹· ²²· ²³), and it will be enjoyed in the fellowship of brethren similarly privileged (v.²⁹). In 2 Esdras we have 'the day of judgment' (12³⁴). A first resurrection may be suggested by the reference to 'those that will be with him' in the day of God's Son (13⁵²). The end will come when the

number of those like Ezra is complete (4³⁶). Till then the spirits of the wicked shall wander about in torment while God's servants will be at rest (7⁷⁵). These spirits of the wicked will be tormented in seven ways (vv.⁸¹⁻⁸⁷), and after the final judgment even more grievously (v.⁸⁴). On the other hand, those who have kept the ways of the Most High shall have joy in seven ways, according to their seven orders, during the intermediate period, and after the judgment receive glory (v.⁹⁵), when 'their face shall shine as the sun,' and 'they shall be made like unto the light of the stars, being henceforth incorruptible' (v.⁹⁷).

In Wisdom there is no idea of resurrection. The body is the temporary earthly burden (9¹⁵) of a pre-existent soul (8²⁰). Immortality is for the soul, but not by nature or necessity. It is attained through wisdom (8¹³· ¹⁷). Still it was God's design that man should enjoy it, for He 'created man for incorruption' (2²³). 'The souls of the righteous are in the hand of God' (3¹), at peace, with a hope full of immortality. 'The righteous live for ever' (v.¹⁵). The wicked have no hope in their death. They will be dashed speechless to the ground; and yet their fate does not seem to be annihilation, for 'they shall lie utterly waste, and they shall be in anguish' (4¹⁹). But there is no definite statement of eternal punishment.

iv. Use of the Apocrypha in the Gospels and the Church.—Our Apocr., which consists of Jewish writings contained in the Vulg. but not found in the Hebrew OT, rests primarily on the LXX, and that was the version of the OT commonly used by the Greek-speaking Jews in the times of the Apostles, and subsequently by the Christians. Being thus the Scriptures in the hands of the NT writers, the LXX introduced the Apocr. to them together with the books of our OT. But most of the NT writers knew the Hebrew Bible. This is evident in the case of St. Paul, St. John, and St. Matthew. The only certain exception is the author of Hebrews, to whom probably we should add St. Luke; and it is reasonable to suppose that these two men, being the most scholarly NT writers, were not unacquainted with the limits of the Palestinian Canon. No NT writer names any book of the Apocr., nor is there any direct quotation from one of these books in the NT. Phrases from some of them indicate, however, that these books were used by the writers in whom they occur, although there is no evidence that they regarded them as authoritative. On the other hand, 2 Esdras borrows from the NT, especially from the Apocalypse. 2 Es 8³ is an echo of Mt 20¹⁶. The only books of our Apocr. to which reference can be manifestly traced in the NT are the works of Wisdom literature, *Wisdom* and *Sirach*, especially the former; and the NT writers who most evidently make allusion to phrases in those books are St. Paul, St. James, and the author of Hebrews. Since these writers are beyond the scope of this Dictionary, the inquirer is referred to *DB* articles, 'Wisdom,' 'Sirach,' 'Apocrypha,' and those on the various NT books.

Coming to the special subject of the present volume, we note that Jesus Christ never names or distinctly cites any of the books of the Apocr., nor are any of them mentioned or directly quoted by any of the Evangelists. Nevertheless there seem to be several reminiscences of Wisdom and Sirach, if not direct allusions to those books in the Gospels.

Wis 3⁷ has been connected with Mt 13⁴³; but the Gospel phrase can be better derived from Dn 12³, for in both cases the same verb is used — ἐκλάμψουσι[ν], while in Wis. the verb is ἀναλάμψουσιν. Wis 3⁸ 'They shall judge (κρινοῦσιν) the nations' may be alluded to in Mt 19²⁸ 'judging (κρίνοντες) the twelve tribes of Israel'; and, if so, the change is in accordance with our Lord's modifications of Jewish Messianic expectations, showing

---

* Dr. Charles points out that the reference to Gehenna in Sir 7¹⁷ is undoubtedly corrupt, since it is contrary to the whole outlook of the writer as to the future, and is not supported by the Heb., Syr., and best MSS of the Ethiopic (*Eschatology*, p. 164).

that the judgment which the Jews reserved for Gentiles was to come upon Israel. Possibly Wis 4⁴ is alluded to in Mt 7¹⁹. But Wis 9¹ (ὁ ποιήσας τὰ πάντα ἐν λόγῳ σου) may be more than anticipation of Jn 1³; it may have suggested the idea in the Gospel, though the entirely different language (πάντα δι' αὐτοῦ ἐγένετο) with reference to the function of the Logos in creation excludes the notion of actual quotation. Wis 15⁸ ' when he is required (ἀπαιτηθείς) to render back the soul (τῆς ψυχῆς) which was lent him ' is suggested by Lk 12²⁰ ' this night is thy soul (τὴν ψυχήν σου) required (ἀπαιτοῦσιν) of thee.' Perhaps 'the darkness that should afterwards receive them' (Wis 17²¹) suggested our Lord's image of 'outer darkness' (Mt 8¹²) as the fate of the lost; but the idea is too general to make any connexion evident. On the other hand, Mt 12⁴¹·⁴² should not be cited as a reference to Wis 4¹⁶ ; nor Lk 12⁴⁷·⁴⁸ for Wis 6⁶ ; nor Jn 7¹⁷ for Wis 6¹² ; nor Mt 25³⁴ for Wis 9⁸ ; nor Mt 4⁴ for Wis 16²⁶. The last instance is a declared quotation from the OT, and the other cases are too vague to allow of any identification.

Sir 2¹⁵ 'They that love (ἀγαπῶντες) him will keep (τηρήσουσιν) his ways ' may well have suggested the language in Jn 14²³ 'If a man love (ἀγαπᾷ) me he will keep (τηρήσει) my word.' Sir 4⁴ 'Turn not away (μὴ ἀποστρέψῃς) thy face from a poor man' suggests to us Mt 5⁴² 'From him that would borrow of thee, turn not thou away (μὴ ἀποστραφῆς).' Sir 7¹⁴ 'Repeat not thy words in thy prayer' suggests Mt 6⁷, but here the Greek is very different; Sir 10¹⁴ 'The Lord cast down the thrones of rulers, and set the meek in their stead,' is probably the source of Lk 1⁵², which is nearer to it than to Job 5¹¹ or Ps 147⁶, especially in the use of the word 'thrones.' Possibly Sir 11¹⁹ suggested Lk 12¹⁹ ; Sir 12¹ has been associated with Mt 7⁶, it is more likely to have suggested Didache 1 ; Sir 19²¹ is too general and obvious to have suggested Mt 21²⁹, which is more definite and specific; Sir 21¹¹ 'He that keepeth the law becometh master of the interest thereof ' is a fine anticipation of Jn 7¹⁷ ; Sir 23⁹ anticipates our Lord's rebuke of swearing (Mt 5³³·³⁴), but is less specific; the metaphor of the vine in Jn 15¹ff. is not to be referred to Sir 24¹⁷, it is more likely to have been suggested by Is 5¹ff., if by any passage ; Mt 6¹⁴ seems to be a reference to Sir 28² 'Forgive thy neighbour the hurt that he hath done thee ; and then thy sins shall be pardoned when thou prayest.' The association of Mt 6¹⁹ with Sir 29¹² proposed by Daubney, is very doubtful ; equally vague is that of Mt 16²⁷ with Sir 32²⁴ 'He that trusteth in the Lord shall suffer no loss.' In both of these cases the slight resemblances are probably purely accidental. Lk 1¹⁷ᵇ ἐπιστρέψαι καρδίας πατέρων ἐπὶ τέκνα evidently comes from Sir 48¹⁰ ἐπιστρέψαι καρδίαν πατρὸς πρὸς υἱόν. The peculiarity of thought and phrase is too striking for an accidental coincidence. But that it is a reminiscence and not a direct quotation is clear from the three changes of words for which no reason can be assigned since the sense remains the same, viz. singular for plural ; πρός for ἐπί ; υἱόν for τέκνα. The following clause in the parallelism is entirely different in the two texts, so that either the conclusion was quite forgotten or a new conclusion was deliberately formed. In Luke we have 'and the disobedient to walk in the wisdom of the just,' while the clause in Sir. is 'and to restore the tribes of Jacob.' The expression 'the wisdom of the just' in Luke seems to be a reference to the wisdom of Sirach, which was probably originally simply 'Wisdom.' In codex B this is called ΣΟΦΙΑ ΣΕΙΡΑΧ ; and in the Syriac, חכמתא דבר סירא. Similarly at the end of the Hebrew text it is described as 'the wisdom of Simeon ben Jeshua ben Eleazar ben Sirā.' On the other hand, St. Luke has not the LXX word for wisdom (σοφία), his phrase being ἐν φρονήσει δικαίων. The conclusion to be drawn from these data seems to be that both Wisdom and Sirach were known to Mat., Luke, John, or to collectors of Logia of Jesus earlier than those Gospels, that Sirach especially was used by the author of the Magnificat, and that our Lord seems to have made use of both books, Sirach more probably than Wisdom.

While the special subjects of this Dictionary do not call for a study of the Apocr. in later times, a topic exhaustively treated in DB, vol. i. pp. 120–123, a brief résumé of its history in the Church may be here added. The presence of the books which we designate Apocryphal in the LXX mixed up with the OT Scriptures of the narrower Heb. Canon would naturally tend to float them among the Greek-speaking Churches. Several of them are cited as Scripture by Irenæus and Clement of Alexandria in the Greek Church, and by Tertullian and Cyprian in the Latin Church. While Melito of Sardis held to the Hebrew Canon, Origen championed the more comprehensive Greek Canon. A century later, Cyril of Jerusalem condemned this wider Canon, holding to the Heb. 22 books ; and his position was confirmed by the Synod of Laodicea (c. 360 A.D.). Epiphanius and especially Athanasius introduced the intermediate course, a recognition of several of the Apocr., not, however, as in the Canon, but as good and useful. Since then, while from time to time scholars have declared the Apocryphal books to be non-canonical, the Eastern Church has used them, and they are in the Bible of the Greek Church. In the West, the Apocr. obtained acceptance as part of the Old Latin Version, which was based on the LXX, and as such formed part of Jerome's revision. But when Jerome translated the OT afresh from the Hebrew, seeing that the Apocr. was not there, he advised its rejection from the Canon. Still, he allowed it an intermediate position ; and, in spite of its translator's opinion to the contrary, the books of the Apocr. took their place in the Vulgate as integral parts of Scripture. At the Council of Trent the Vulgate being pronounced infallibly inspired, the Apocr. was canonized with the rest of that version, and therefore it is now regarded as Scripture in the Roman Catholic Church. Among Protestants it has either taken an intermediate position, or has been rejected as not being Scripture. Luther placed it between the OT and the NT with the title 'Apocrypha,' and a statement that it was 'not equal to the Sacred Scriptures,' but nevertheless 'useful and good to read.' The Reformed Church is more severe ; in the Zürich Bible the Apocryphal books come after the NT as 'not numbered among the canonical books,' and without a word of commendation. Coverdale translated the Apocr. and placed it between the OT and the NT with a statement that the books were in the Vulgate but not in the Hebrew. It has a similar position in subsequent revisions, including AV (1611), where it is marked 'Apocrypha.' But from 1629 onwards editions of the AV began to appear without it.

LITERATURE.—Swete, OT in Greek ; RV of Apocrypha ; Commentaries by Wace (Holy Bible with Com., Murray), Fritzsche, and Grimm (Kurzgefasstes Exegetisches Handbuch zu den Apocr. etc.); Bissell (Lange-Schaff); DB articles, 'Apocrypha,' 'Development of Doctrine,' also articles on the several books of Apocr. ; Drummond, Jewish Messiah and Philo Judæus ; Stanton, The Jewish and the Christian Messiah ; Deane, The Book of Wisdom ; Charles, Eschatology ; Paul Volz, Jüdische Eschatologie ; Bousset, Die Religion des Judentums ; Schürer, GJV³. The DB articles referred to contain lists of books, which therefore need not be repeated here.   W. F. ADENEY.

APOCRYPHAL GOSPELS.—See GOSPELS (APOCRYPHAL).

APOSTLES.—

Introduction.
1. The first disciples.
2. Beginning of our Lord's Galilæan ministry
3. Choice of the Twelve.
4. Training of the Apostles.
    Literature.

Introduction.—It is proposed to treat in this article the chief facts relating to that group of our Lord's personal disciples known to us by the name of 'apostles.' The sole authorities on the subject are the four Gospels and the first chapter of the Acts. The remaining books of the NT furnish no information as to the relations between Jesus and His Apostles during His ministry on earth ; and nothing that is found in the Apocryphal Gospels can be regarded as historical.

The assumption so often made that the Synoptics possess a greater trustworthiness than the Fourth Gospel is baseless, and its baselessness cannot be better seen than in the case of the Apostles. The Apostles of the Fourth Gospel are the Apostles of the first three. Their character, prejudices, limitations, ambitions, views, sympathies are the same in the four Gospels. How can this harmony be explained unless all our authorities draw from the life? But more than this. The Fourth Gospel contains information regarding the Twelve peculiar to itself which, properly weighed, enables us to understand much that is otherwise perplexing in the first three. How can this familiarity with the Apostles be accounted for if the writer was not himself one of them? What is the alternative hypothesis? That the writer of the Fourth Gospel, with the first three before him, was able to form so true and complete an apprehension of the intelligence, moral condition, modes of thought, and language of the Twelve as to be able to create situations where he represents them as speaking and acting with perfect verisimilitude, while all the time he was simply drawing on his imagination. The author of the Fourth Gospel was a man of genius, but his genius was religious, not intellectual or imaginative

The achievement attributed to him was wholly beyond his powers or the powers of any man who has ever lived. The disciples of the Fourth Gospel are the disciples of the first three; their portraits are firm, exact, striking, because the writer knew them personally.

When the attention of a reader is called to the numerous occasions on which the Apostles figure in the Gospels, he might feel disposed to contend that the Apostles are so prominent in the Gospels because they are their ultimate authors. But this supposition, however ingenious, is unsubstantial. Great as is the place filled by the Apostles in the Gospels, they are never magnified; it is Jesus alone who is magnified. The many references made to the Apostles correspond exactly to the position they held; the Gospels are so much occupied with them only because Jesus Himself was constantly occupied with them, not the least of the tasks of His life being to teach and train them to understand His mind and heart, and to transmit to others a correct representation of what He was and said and did.

The Gospel of St. Mark has been characterized as pre-eminently the Gospel of the disciples. But this language does injustice to the rest of the Gospels, which are equally Gospels of the disciples. A judicious reader sees at once that the Apostles hold substantially the same place in all the Gospels. There is nothing to prove that one of the Evangelists took a deeper interest in the Twelve than any of the rest.

1. *The first disciples.*—It is clear from the Gospels that several of the Apostles had been on the most intimate terms with our Lord before He selected them to become Apostles. In fact the most prominent among them passed through two stages of relationship to our Lord before they were chosen as Apostles. They were first called to become disciples in the most general sense of the term, and thereafter they were summoned to leave their usual occupations and to become the personal companions of Jesus. It is therefore desirable to learn the connexion in which the most distinguished of them stood to Jesus before their formal appointment to the apostolate.

After the Temptation our Lord returned to Bethany in Peræa. Whether this happened by arrangement betweeen Himself and His forerunner we cannot tell, but nothing was more natural than for Him to go thither. The Baptist could best fulfil his duty if He were by his side. On two occasions John, fixing a steadfast gaze on our Lord, said in the hearing of some of his disciples, 'Behold the Lamb of God' (Jn 1$^{29. 36}$). The remarkable expression doubtless suggested to his hearers that this was the Messiah. Two of them sought an interview with our Lord, and ere they quitted the house were convinced that they had found the Messiah. Not a word is related of the considerations which brought them to this conclusion, but the explanation is to be found partly in the testimony of the Baptist, partly and pre-eminently in the impression produced on them by the personality of Jesus. There was that in His character, aims, and language which distinguished Him from all other men. Hence Andrew and John, the two disciples in question, had no doubt that the Messiah stood before them (v.^{41}). It is not quite clear whether each started to find his brother; but Andrew, at anyrate, brought his brother Simon to Jesus. Reading his character and discerning its possibilities, Jesus bestowed on him the name by which he is now known to the world: the name Peter (v.^{42}). Our Lord, for reasons unknown to us, had determined to set out for Galilee, accompanied by His new disciples. On starting, He called Philip to follow Him, and the instant obedience rendered suggests that Philip had already believed that Jesus was the Messiah, probably through his friends and fellow-citizens Andrew and Peter. On the way Philip encountered his friend Nathanael,

who lived in the village of Cana, at no great distance from his own home at Bethsaida, and informed him of the discovery of the Messiah, in the person of Jesus of Nazareth. Nathanael hesitated, but he came and saw and heard, and the knowledge which Jesus displayed of his character and of his inmost life convinced him that He was indeed what Philip had declared Him to be (v.$^{43ff.}$). How many of these disciples accompanied Jesus to Cana and witnessed His first miracle (2$^{1ff.}$) is not certain; possibly the majority, if not all. The same uncertainty arises in connexion with the journey to Jerusalem at the Passover. We do not know who witnessed the expulsion of the traffickers from the temple, heard the mysterious words spoken regarding the destruction of the temple, or saw the many miracles which He performed in the capital (v.$^{13ff.}$), baptized at His command when He laboured in Judæa in the vicinity of the Baptist, and accompanied Him through Samaria on His return to Galilee (4$^{1ff.}$). It would seem as if thereafter the disciples returned to their usual occupations, and our Lord retired for a little from public life.

2. *Beginning of our Lord's Galilæan ministry.*—After a short interval our Lord resumed His labours, and continued them without interruption until His death. The Baptist had just been imprisoned (Mk 1^{14} and ‖), and He seemed to regard his imprisonment as a call to attempt more than He had yet done. So long as the Baptist laboured, the work done by Jesus does not seem to have differed much from his. Now that he was in prison, our Lord proceeded to develop a ministry of His own. This new type of ministry was marked by a change of residence from Nazareth to Capernaum (Mt 4^{13}). He wished to influence as many of the inhabitants of Galilee as He could, and there was no better centre from which to approach them than Capernaum. The town was large, and was near many others of the same character. It lay on several great roads, and was therefore easily reached from all quarters. The people were genuinely Jewish, and not given to Gentile tastes or customs. No more suitable position from which to command Galilee could have been chosen. It was soon after He settled in Capernaum that He renewed His summons to four of the men whom He had already chosen as His disciples. Walking along the shore of the Sea of Galilee, He saw the brothers Simon and Andrew, who were fishermen, engaged in casting their net. In words the significance of which they could not fail to discern, He commanded them to follow Him and become fishers of men. Proceeding a little farther, He found James with his brother John repairing their nets, and addressed to them the same command. They, like Peter and Andrew, instantly obeyed (Mk 1$^{16-20}$). It is clear that our Lord had a definite aim in calling these four disciples. The duty to which He now invited them was an advance on their former relationship. They were to be no longer fishermen. They must exchange their former calling for a new one. And the nature of that new calling was not wholly obscure. The allusion to the occupation which they were bidden to leave illustrated the character of the labours to which they were invited. They were to capture men instead of fish. Not one of the four could fail to perceive that they were to be employed continuously in the service of Jesus. The call would fill them with the less surprise because they had already served an apprenticeship to Jesus, when they baptized in obedience to His commands. It need not be inferred that Jesus intended to send the four immediately on a special mission. No particular time is specified in His command; and though St. Luke (5^{10}) marks the capture of men as beginning with the moment of the call, this can only mean that their new career began as soon as they obeyed the call addressed to them. Only one other call of the same kind is related in the Gospels, that of Levi or Matthew (Mk 2[16], Mt 9[9]). It, too, occurred in Capernaum. To the four fishermen a tax-gatherer was added. Capernaum was the seat of a customhouse, and the collector of customs, Levi by name, was called precisely as the two pairs of brothers had been. What previous acquaintance existed between Matthew and our Lord, what special qualities commended him we cannot tell; but the instant obedience he rendered to so extraordinary a command, and the feast which he gave in our Lord's honour as he bade farewell to his fellow-officials, suggest that they had known one another for some time. The interval which separated the call of Matthew from the call of the four cannot be ascertained, but as it is unlikely that he was a disciple of the Baptist, and as it is probable that he was not brought into contact with our Lord till He settled in Capernaum, some little time must have elapsed between his first knowledge of our Lord and his call. He could hardly have been with Jesus from the outset of His career in Galilee.

3. *Choice of the Twelve.*—It might have been supposed that our Lord would continue as He had begun, and summon disciple after disciple to His side until He had obtained the number He required for His purpose. But this was not to be. He had determined to make a formal selection of a definite number from the body of His disciples (Mk 3[13], Lk 6[13]). The importance of the step He was about to take is shown by the fact that He spent the preceding night in prayer (Lk 6[12]), doubtless seeking to learn His Father's will regarding the intention He had formed and the mode in which it was to be accomplished. One of the critical hours of His life was before Him. The nature of the selection He was about to make was of supreme consequence. A serious mistake would be followed by calamitous results. No wonder then that He sought specific guidance. He may even have gone over the names of all whom He judged competent, and have made His final choice.

The Gospels have not preserved any statement by our Lord Himself as to His aim in selecting a special group of disciples. That aim can be judged of only by the issue, for it is certain that what the Apostles proved to be, was what Jesus designed they should become. An account, indeed, is found in St. Mark's Gospel (3[14]), according to which the purpose of our Lord in choosing them was that they might be with Him and that He might send them forth to announce the approach of the Kingdom of God, endowed with the power to heal and to exorcize. That this is a correct description so far as it goes cannot be doubted, but it cannot be said to embrace the full scope of our Lord's purpose. It defines His immediate rather than His ultimate end. Its horizon is that of the first journey on which the Apostles were sent, not that world-wide commission afterwards committed to them. Hence when we speak of the reasons which induced our Lord to select the Twelve, we must look to the work actually entrusted to them. That work cannot be better described than by the words used by our Lord Himself to the Twelve on the eve of His death. He had been the envoy of the Father to earth. They were to be His envoys on earth. As He had interpreted the Father to men, so were they to interpret Him to men. Their chief, their supreme duty, was to bear witness to Him: to teach the world how He lived, what He said, what He wrought (Jn 17[18], Ac 1[8]).

A comparison has often been drawn between the disciples of Plato or of the Pharisees and the disciples of Jesus. And such comparisons are not without suggestiveness. But a sagacious

mind discerns that the apostolate of Jesus Christ is a unique institution. The Apostles differ from, far more than they agree with, the disciples of any thinker or teacher. They stand by themselves, devoted to the performance of an unexampled task. No one but Jesus could have conceived such a task; the Apostles were the fit instruments for its accomplishment.

It is a noteworthy circumstance that few writers have spent any time in describing the actual selection of the Twelve. The silence of the Gospels on this point is only what was to be expected, but it is surprising that those writers of our Lord's life who have given the freest rein to their imagination in endeavouring to reproduce the scenes of His career, have passed this event over as if it afforded no opportunity for their skill. Yet what materials lay ready to their hand! What were the sentiments with which our Lord addressed Himself to the task? What was His appearance as He stood on the mountain side and called His followers to Him? How did these followers feel as they perceived that He was about to make a choice among them? Was there excitement among the crowd? Was there strong desire on the part of many to be chosen? Was there any discussion as to the principles He followed in the choice, or did reverence prevent all debate? Was there much disappointment when the number was completed? Was there surprise at the persons named? Not less instructive would be some knowledge of the sentiments of the Apostles when they stood together for the first time in the presence of our Lord. What were their thoughts? Were they filled with exultation? Did they infer that the Kingdom of God would immediately appear? Did they anticipate a brilliant future for themselves? Or were there those among them who reflected with humility on their unfitness to be the generals and statesmen of the new Kingdom? Did it occur to even one of them that the choice just made was a fresh disclosure of the view taken by Jesus of the Kingdom of God and of the means by which it was to be extended?

Who now were the objects of our Lord's choice? With some of them we are already acquainted. Simon, Andrew, James, John, Philip, and Levi or Matthew are already known to us. So too possibly is Bartholomew (wh. see). *Bartholomew* is not a proper name, but means simply 'son of Tolmai,' and there is much probability in the opinion that he is to be identified with Nathanael. These seven disciples our Lord must have known for some time. The remaining five names—Thomas, James the son of Alphæus, Simon the Zealot, Judas or Lebbæus or Thaddæus, and Judas Iscariot are new. How long they had been known to Jesus is not told us; perhaps some of them had been in His company for several months. On the other hand, it is possible that He may have chosen some of the Twelve without much if any personal knowledge, relying on that power to read the heart which He undoubtedly possessed.

Who the **Alphæus** was of whom James was a son (Mk 3[18]) we cannot tell. There is no reason except the similarity of name for connecting him with the father of Levi; and the assumption that he is the same person as Clopas is gratuitous. The force of the epithet **Cananæan** is not free from doubt; the most likely meaning is that of *zealot*. But the sense of 'zealot' in turn is not perfectly clear. It may denote the political party known by that name; it may, again, simply designate unusual devotion to a cause. Reflexion shows that this latter view has but scanty recommendation, and that the former has nearly everything in its favour. The Apostle who bears a triple name is commonly known as **Jude**. That there were two Judes among the Apostles is plain from the language of Jn 14[22], where 'Judas not Iscariot' is mentioned. In two of the lists of the Apostles, those in Luke (6[16]) and Acts (1[13]), he is described as 'Judas of James'; that is almost certainly Judas the *son* not the *brother* of James. But who this James was is quite uncertain. In Mt 10[3] and Mk 3[18] this Judas is called **Thaddæus**, or, according to the Western text, **Lebbæus**; and he was probably known indifferently as Judas or as Thaddæus. The exact significance of the term **Iscariot** is still under discussion. Most commonly it is regarded as a geographical term signifying 'man of Kerioth,' but where Kerioth was situated is keenly canvassed, some placing it to the east of the Dead Sea and others in the south of Judah (see JUDAS ISCARIOT).

Attempts have often been made to prove that several of the Apostles were *related to our Lord*. Many of those who have sought for traces of this relationship have been governed by motives very different from those influencing our Lord, who would have been the last person to allow His selection of an Apostle to be determined by the ties of blood. Still there is no reason why relatives of our Lord should not have been among the Apostles. But what evidence is there to this effect? It has been conjectured that James and John were cousins of our Lord, Mary and Salome being sisters. This is one possible interpretation and by no means the least satisfactory of the well-known verse in St. John (19²⁵) which mentions the women at the cross. Whether the silence of Scripture regarding the relationship can outweigh the fitness of this interpretation will be answered variously, yet a reader will allow for the possibility that James and John were our Lord's cousins. But if he tolerate this view he will reject without hesitation the opinion once so common, that several of our Lord's brothers were among the Apostles. Practically nothing can be brought forward in support of this hypothesis; for who can attach any value to the fact that three of the Apostles bore the same names as three of our Lord's brothers, when it is known that these names were among the most common in the land? The statement made in Jn 7⁵ that six months before the Crucifixion none of our Lord's brothers believed on Him is wholly inconsistent with the view that two or even three of them were Apostles. Scarcely less decisive is the distinction traced in the Acts between the brothers of Jesus and the Apostles (1¹⁴). Much ingenuity and labour have been expended in the endeavour to prove that James the son of Alphæus was a cousin of our Lord, his father being a brother of Joseph. But the steps by which this identification is made are numerous and all open to challenge, so that no gain can arise from an examination of the question. See art. BRETHREN OF THE LORD.

Four lists of the Apostles are contained in the NT, one in each of the Synoptics and one in the Acts (Mt 10²⁻⁴, Mk 3¹⁶⁻¹⁹, Lk 6¹⁴⁻¹⁶, Ac 1¹³). A careful examination of these lists shows that each of them consists of three groups of quaternions, and that in each group the same person is mentioned first. The first group contains the names of Peter, James, John, and Andrew. The second is made up of Philip, Nathanael, Thomas, and Matthew. The third is formed of James the son of Alphæus, Simon the Zealot, Judas or Thaddæus, and Judas Iscariot. Is this arrangement due to accident, or does it rest on a perception of the historical importance of the disciples at the time at which it was drawn up? The places given to Peter and Judas and the contents of the different groups suggest that there is here an indication of the view taken of the Apostles in the early Church. By whom the catalogues were framed is unknown, but their value as historical witnesses is great. They form, as it were, a table of precedence dating from the earliest times, and embodying the verdict it may be of the Apostles themselves, or at least of those of them who survived when they were prepared. In all the lists the name of Peter occupies the first place. St. Matthew (10²) writes: 'Now the names of the twelve apostles are these; the first, Simon.' In what sense is this 'first' to be understood? It might refer to the fact that Peter was the first of the Apostles to be chosen. This is perfectly credible, but the fact that the order of the names is not uniform in the lists may be regarded as showing that the memory of the order in which the Twelve were called was not preserved in the Church. But why was Peter the first called? Must not an explanation of this fact be sought? And is it not to be found in the circumstance that he was the foremost of the Apostles, their leader, their spokesman? Primacy in the sense of jurisdiction or authority over his fellow-Apostles Peter never received and never exercised. His position is that of the foremost among equals; a position due not to any formal or official appointment, but to the ardour and force of his nature.

What kind of men were the Apostles? What was their character, education, social rank, ability, age? The Apostles were in an eminent sense religious men. The tie which bound them to Jesus was a religious tie. It was impossible for any person to become a follower of Jesus who did not

believe in obedience to the will of God as the first of all duties. The Apostles were men who desired to fulfil the demands of the law of God. Their aims were high; their morals were pure; whatever their ignorance, misconceptions, defects, they were men of integrity, justice, and mercy; diligent, candid, honest, pious, God-fearing. None of the Apostles had received more than a common education. The range of their knowledge was that of most of their fellow-countrymen. But they were in no sense illiterate. It is probable that all of them could read and write. Most if not all of them spoke Aramaic and Greek. Their minds had been quickened and nourished by the services in the Synagogue. The education that springs from the truest knowledge of God and of man was theirs. And the discipline of their daily lives had rendered them alert, considerate, patient, energetic.

The Apostles without exception belonged to the working classes as they would be called to-day. There was no man of rank or distinction or of social consideration among them. Four of them, we know, were fishermen. One of them was a collector of taxes. The rest belonged to the same rank in life, and followed similar occupations. All of them knew what it was to labour to maintain themselves; they were familiar with life as it presents itself to the great body of mankind. There is no evidence that any of the Apostles was specially distinguished by intellectual force. There was no man of genius among them: no original thinker; no man dowered with the imaginative faculty; no man of great powers of organization. It does not appear that any of them had an unusually impressive or attractive personality. As far as can be ascertained, they were all young men, about the same age as, or younger than, our Lord Himself. No man of middle life, no grey head was included in the circle. Variety of taste, temper, mode of life found full expression among the Apostles. No one was the same as another. Their experience of life had differed. Their anticipations of the future differed. Their habits of thought and action differed. Perhaps the only common elements were their piety and their devotion to Jesus. Such then were the Apostles. They were pious men belonging to the people, full of the plain sense and judgment which mark the common man: slow to learn, but teachable; free from social prejudices; untrammelled by any fixed systems of thought; with keen eyes for character; anxious to win the favour of Jesus.

The most discordant criticisms have been passed on the choice of the Apostles, many of these betraying a complete failure to grasp the circumstances and facts of the case. The vindication of the wisdom shown in the selection is the future career and achievements of the Twelve. In judging it is necessary to bear in mind the materials at our Lord's command and the purposes which He had in view. The man who realizes these has no difficulty in appreciating and admiring the sagacity exhibited by Jesus. Here, too, he will perceive that originality which marks His entire career. The Twelve would never have chosen one another. Had the selection been left to them individually or to any two or three among them, the persons included would have been very different. Nobody but Jesus Himself would have acted in disregard, as it would appear, of the motives by which men are constantly swayed. No one will suppose that our Lord had any aversion to intellect, wealth, rank, genius, experience, in themselves, or that He preferred fishermen to lawyers, and tax-collectors to priests. But He was equally free from the bias which leads so many to believe that the success of any movement depends on its being supported by the higher classes, whether of intellect or rank. His one test of men was fitness or capacity for the special objects He had in view. The number of adherents at His command as Apostles was limited. His primary aim was to discover men who could be taught and trained to comprehend His character, aims, and labours, who could describe His life to their fellows, who could inform them as to what He said and as to the deeds of mercy and power which He wrought. The defects and the limitations of the Apostles were far better known to our Lord than they are to us or to His critics. Yet He called them despite of these, for after all they were the best instruments within His reach. Their faults of intellect, taste, manner, speech, their stupidity, folly, their prejudices and prepossessions, their unbalanced judgment and intemperate zeal were all before His eyes; nevertheless He summoned them to be His Apostles in the confidence that He could make them become the very men best fitted to discharge the duties connected with the establishment of the Kingdom of God. He had no false anticipations as to the kind of men the Twelve would prove; He chose them knowing what they were and what they would become.

The Apostles were *twelve in number*. The number was intended to be significant. Its import could not have been lost on the Twelve themselves when they were first called, or on the multitude who witnessed their election. Our Lord was evidently thinking of the twelve tribes of Israel. Though ten of the tribes had largely disappeared, Israel still consisted ideally of twelve tribes, and the mission of the Messiah was to be to all the tribes of the nation. Hence the fitness of the number chosen by our Lord. There was one Apostle for each tribe. Nor should it be overlooked that the employment of this number was a fresh claim on the part of Jesus to be the Messiah. His disciples would argue thus: Who but the Messiah could venture to create a body or group of twelve disciples only? Nobody had done so before, no prophet, not even the Baptist. Jesus then must be the Messiah.

It has been suggested that the number twelve was, so to speak, accidental; that our Lord did not choose a definite number of disciples, but that He allowed all who desired to do so to remain beside Himself. The alleged choice of the Twelve is pronounced not historical. They chose our Lord, not He them. The Twelve is but a name for His closest and most devoted adherents. The only arguments advanced for this view are the silence of the Gospel of St. Matthew as to the selection of the Twelve, and the omission of the list of the Twelve from the Gospel of St. John. But St. Matthew furnishes a list of the Twelve, and therefore presupposes their selection. He assumes as self-evident that they had been appointed by our Lord. St. John not less than St. Matthew takes the selection of the Twelve (6^{67. 70}) as known, and even makes our Lord refer to His appointment of them (15¹⁶). To assert that the Twelve attached themselves to our Lord gradually and spontaneously is to misread the tenor of the statements regarding them.

The title 'Apostle' and its equivalents. — It is expressly stated that the Twelve received from our Lord the title 'apostles'; but it is doubtful whether the title was bestowed when they were chosen, and its exact sense has always been a subject of debate. It will be expedient at this point to examine the designations borne by the Apostles, because they are not called uniformly by one name.

The most common of all the appellations bestowed on them in the Gospels is that of **disciples.** This usage is as characteristic of the Fourth Gospel as of the Synoptics. And it is noteworthy that in none of the Gospels are the twelve disciples sharply discriminated from the other disciples of our Lord. They are called 'the disciples of Jesus,' 'his disciples,' 'the disciples,' but the context alone reveals whether the writer is speaking of a limited group or of the disciples of our Lord in general.

A peculiar usage appears in the Gospel of St. John. There the title is applied to those who first attached themselves to our Lord. 'The disciples' form a body or class by themselves long before the Apostles are chosen. From the narrative it looks as if no person belonged to this group who was not at a later stage included among the Apostles, but the point is not by any means certain.

The adoption of the term 'disciples' to denote the followers of our Lord requires no explanation. The primary sense of the word indicates the relation of a pupil to his teacher, and the designation was therefore the most natural and appropriate which could be employed.

The Twelve. This phrase explains itself. As soon as our Lord had selected a specific number of persons for a definite end, it was to be expected that they should be called by the number which they formed. They were twelve, and were accordingly known as 'the Twelve.' It is doubtful whether it is proper to supply such a substantive

as 'disciples' or 'apostles.' There is authority in the NT for the use of both of these phrases, but it does not follow that the name first given to this inmost circle of our Lord's adherents was 'the twelve disciples' or 'the twelve apostles' rather than 'the Twelve.' A time came when all three designations were current. St. Matthew mentions 'the Twelve' four times (10⁵ 26^{14. 20. 47}), St. Mark nine times (4¹⁰ 6⁷ 9³⁵ 10³² 11¹¹ 14^{10. 17. 20. 43}), St. Luke six times (8¹ 9^{1. 12} 18³¹ 22^{3. 47}), and St. John four times (6^{67. 70. 71} 20²⁴). St. Matthew speaks four times (10¹ 11¹ 20¹⁷ 26²⁰) of 'the twelve disciples,' but he stands alone in his use of this description. It is worth while to observe that after the death of Judas the phrase 'the Eleven' was employed precisely as 'the Twelve' had been. It is found absolutely in Lk 24⁹; it is found with the substantive 'disciples' in Mt 28¹⁶, and with the substantive 'apostles' in Ac 1²⁶.

The word ἀπόστολος occurs ten times in the Gospels. In the Gospel of St. John it is used only in its etymological sense of *a person sent forth* (13¹⁶); in the other three Gospels it refers to the twelve disciples of our Lord. But there is some doubt as to the meaning it bears in each of these Gospels. St. Matthew employs it once only —in the passage already quoted: 'The names of the twelve apostles are these' (10²). This language is used to introduce the list of the Apostles, together with the charge addressed to them. The term may be understood here in either of two senses: it may designate the Twelve as sent out on one special mission of evangelization, or it may bear the meaning which it has in Christendom to-day. A decision between these senses is hardly possible in the case of St. Matthew's Gospel. It is otherwise with the Gospel of St. Mark. Here the term is employed twice (3¹⁴.6³⁰), and apparently in both instances only with regard to the particular missionary tour or journey on which they were about to enter. The use of the term in St. Luke is noteworthy. It occurs six times. Once (11⁴⁹) it is possibly used in its etymological meaning of *messenger*; in two other places (6¹³ 9¹⁰) it may be used to designate the special mission on which the Twelve were first sent; but in the remaining three (17⁵ 22¹⁴ 24¹⁰) it is employed to designate the Twelve in their capacity as the representatives of Jesus, the sense which it commonly bears in the Acts.

It is unnecessary for our present purpose to enter on the history of the word 'apostle' in Greek. That the word was in use in NT times in its etymological sense of *messenger* is generally allowed. This fact is confirmed by the NT itself. Our Lord, in speaking to His disciples on the night of the betrayal, declared that the person sent (apostle) is not greater than he that sent him (Jn 13¹⁶). Again when our Lord is designated in He 3¹ as 'the apostle and high priest of our confession,' the reference is probably to His own description of Himself as 'the sent of God' (Jn. 17¹⁸). There is then clear evidence that the word was current in our Lord's time in its sense of *messenger, delegate, envoy*. Was it also in use in a technical sense to designate those who were despatched from the mother city by the rulers of the race on any foreign mission, especially such as were charged with collecting the tribute paid to the temple service? (Lightfoot, *Gal.* 93). And was it this usage which suggested to our Lord His own employment of the term? There is no evidence to show that the term was current in this technical sense before the Gospels were written. Besides, even though it had been in existence, it is doubtful whether our Lord would have employed a term which had already in the minds of His hearers distinct associations of its own. The absence of such associations would recommend a term to Him

It was the very simplicity and directness of the expression 'apostle' which won for it the favour of our Lord. The Twelve were simply to be His messengers or envoys. The analogy between His own case and that of the men He had selected was always present to His mind. He had been sent by the Father : they were to be sent by Himself. A technical term could only have served to bewilder the Twelve and lead them to misconceive the object of their mission. What was necessary for our Lord's purpose was a word which set forth simply and aptly the relations of the Twelve to Himself, and for this there was no more suitable term than 'messenger,' 'envoy.' The term 'apostle' then was not suggested to our Lord by its currency as a technical expression. He chose a common word and adapted it to His own purpose. He wished to give the most expressive title to the men whom He had chosen, and none seemed to Him so suitable as the word 'sent.' It reminded them perpetually that they were men with a mission.

It is generally held that the name 'apostles' was given to the Twelve on the occasion of their call. The language of St. Luke (6[13]) does not compel us to adopt this conclusion, nor is that of St. Mark (3[14]) decisive on the point.* The statements in both Gospels are consistent alike with the view that the Apostles were so named when they were first called, and with the view that this title was bestowed on them at a later date. The other considerations to which appeal may be made tell in opposite directions. It may be urged that the impression left on the mind of an ordinary reader is that the Apostles received their name at the time of their call, but it does not follow that this impression is correct. For it is said in the same context that our Lord gave to Simon the name Peter, and we know that this name was given to him long before he became an Apostle. This proves that the statements made in connexion with the appointment of the Twelve must not be pressed as if they referred to that event exclusively. Again, it may be contended with much propriety that there was a special fitness in our Lord assigning a new name to the men whom He had set apart for a new task. The new relation might well be designated by a new name. But it may be pointed out in reply that an interval elapsed between the choice of the Twelve and their being sent forth. Is it not probable that the new designation was given only when the new vocation was actually begun? Would the new title be understood apart from the experience by which it was illuminated? This argument is strengthened by the circumstance that St. Mark appears to employ the term 'apostle' only in connexion with the missionary journey of the Twelve. With him it is not so much a title belonging to them, as a term descriptive of the functions assigned to them on a special occasion. To decide between these conflicting opinions is not easy, but on the whole the suggestion that the disciples were not called 'apostles' till they were first sent out appears the more probable.

The Sermon on the Mount is regarded by many as an address delivered by our Lord when He chose the Twelve. The note of time in the Gospel of St. Luke ascribes it to this occasion, and there is no reason to reject this testimony. Besides, it has the greatest internal probability in its favour The appointment of the Apostles formed an epoch in the ministry of our Lord ; what more natural or suitable than that He should avail Himself of the occasion to explain and enforce His convictions as to the true life of man? The time was most opportune for such a deliverance. The hearts of the disciples were deeply moved ; their whole natures were quickened and alert ; why not sow seed which might afterwards bear abundant fruit? The character of the Sermon itself is another argument confirming this conclusion. It is didactic rather than hortatory. It expounds truth rather than proclaims the mercy of God. Finally, there is nothing in the Sermon which conflicts with this opinion. It may then be assumed with some confidence that the Sermon on the Mount was spoken in connexion with the call of the Twelve. Many writers go further and contend that it was spoken to them principally or exclusively. But this opinion is at variance with the statements of the Gospels of St. Matthew and St. Luke, and is not required by the contents of the Sermon. The truths it announces were not intended for the Twelve alone ; why then should they not have been heard by all the disciples? This result is in no way inconsistent with the opinion that the Sermon on the Mount formed, as it were, a special charge to the Twelve in view of the new position which they were henceforward to occupy. It is not necessary for our purpose to discuss the limits of the Sermon or do more than furnish a brief account of its teaching. Our Lord wished His followers to understand the meaning of righteousness ; to know what the will of God really was ; the true nature of the demands He made on them ; how to frame their conduct if they were to obtain His approval. The subject of the address then is the true life of man. The characteristic features of that life are set forth in a series of blessings pronounced on those who possess

*It should be noted that the words οὓς καὶ ἀποστόλους ὠνόμασεν do not occur in TR. See, however, RVm.

the qualities spoken of ; the mission of Christians as the light of the world and the salt of the earth is touched on ; and then our Lord proceeds to contrast the perfect requirements of the Law of God as understood by Himself with the requirements of that Law as contained in the OT or as sanctioned by tradition ; after which He illustrates the true nature of almsgiving, fasting, and prayer, and of devotion to the will of God. See SERMON ON THE MOUNT below, and in Hastings' DB, Ext. Vol. 1 ff.

It would have been most instructive had any record of the effect produced on the Apostles by this Sermon been preserved. Their surprise must have equalled their admiration. The severe requirements, the strictures on the Law, the novelty of the interpretations, the apparent paradoxes, must have astonished and perplexed them. It is doing them no injustice to say that much it contained was beyond their comprehension. They may have seen that the qualities required of them were embodied in our Lord's own life, and that the temper of the Beatitudes was exactly His temper. They may have felt that the sphere of the inner life was not less properly the sphere of law than that of speech and conduct. They may have discerned that the true greatness of man is to live not merely as God enjoins, but as God Himself lives. But they could hardly grasp what our Lord meant by the fulfilment of the Law. A fulfilment which was at the same time an abolition was a mystery to them. Nor would they perceive that He had transformed morality by reducing it to the principle of life according to God ; the one supreme rule of duty being to love God and man. The paradoxical expressions, too, would be as puzzling to them as they have proved to thousands since. In their discussions there would be champions of literalism, but these would soon be brought to acknowledge that a perfectly literal obedience to the commands given was impracticable.

4. Training of the Apostles.—From the call of the Apostles the mission of our Lord was more a mission to them than to His fellow-countrymen at large. He had waited until the time that a proper selection from His disciples could be made : now that the choice had taken place He devoted Himself to their instruction and training. The Apostles were to accompany Jesus from place to place ; they were to be with Him continually. This implied the relinquishment of their means of living. It was not possible for them to continue at their occupations and be Apostles of Jesus. The sacrifice made by each Apostle in obeying the summons to apostleship has seldom been adequately appreciated. In some instances the property left or sold, the income abandoned, might not be great intrinsically, but a man's all is great to him, hence the moral courage needed of every Apostle was not slight. How then were their wants supplied? Whence did they obtain money to meet their daily expenses? The arrangement followed was probably devised by our Lord, and formed one of the earliest lessons He intended them to master. In a sense this first lesson is the supreme and even the sole lesson which He sought to teach, that of absolute reliance on Himself for everything. Trust in the Father, trust in Himself, was the lesson which Jesus sought to inculcate at all times. The Twelve and our Lord formed, as it were, a single household, of which He was the head. He presided at the common meals, He gave directions as to their movements. The cost of their maintenance was borne by a common purse. One of the Twelve was the treasurer of the company (Jn 13[29]). The food needed was either carried with them, or purchased, or provided by the hospitality which is so characteristic of the East. The company could not only supply their own wants, but could minister to those of the poor (Jn 13[29]). The sources from which their supplies were drawn were doubtless various. Some among them had had or still had property, and the proceeds, contributed to the common stock, helped to defray the charges of each day. It is almost certain that presents were made to our Lord and the company from time to time by grateful friends and neighbours. But the principal source seems to have been the generosity of several women who accompanied them on some of their journeys, and placed their means and services at the command of our Lord. The names of some of these women have been preserved in a most instructive passage in St. Luke's Gospel (8[2, 3]), which is the chief authority on the subject under consideration. Among these are mentioned Mary of Magdala, Joanna (possibly a widow whose husband had been a steward of Herod Antipas), and Susanna. It is evident from St. Luke's statement that the number of such women was large, and it was probably owing to their generosity that our Lord and the Twelve were able to devote themselves untroubled and untrammelled to their task. It should be noticed that the kind of life lived by the Twelve was itself a practical illustration of some of the cardinal lessons which Jesus desired to teach. The subordinate value of earthly possessions could not have been more effectively taught than by the life of dependence on the liberality of others. Their journeys, too, from place to place had also their value. They were stimulated by new scenes and new persons; new conditions had to be faced, new duties performed. They had leisure to ponder on what was said to them; they were not distracted from the great work of their life, the knowledge of their Master. This was their duty, and it became their glory. For in understanding Him they came to resemble Him. The education of the Twelve, the transformation of them from the men they were into the men they became, is one of the greatest of our Lord's achievements. The Apostles were to be our Lord's witnesses, but the witnessing of which He thought demanded insight, sympathy, courage, self-command, tolerance, patience, charity. It was inseparable from the highest moral endowments. It involved great receptive and assimilative power, issuing in vigorous and unceasing obedience and service.

In order that the Apostles might become His witnesses, our Lord made use of three principal agencies: (a) His personality, (b) His miracles, and (c) His teaching.

(a) *To be with Jesus* was in itself the best of all education and training. It was on this account that the Apostles were chosen to be with Him habitually. A complete knowledge of Him could be attained only in this way. For knowledge is acquired insensibly not less than sensibly, and the Apostles learned much regarding Jesus when it never struck them that they were doing so. Gradually His influence told on them. His ideals, motives, ends became clear to them. His manners, looks, tones, words, ways became their inspiration and guide. They felt what goodness, truth, duty were. Above all, they came to know God as the Father. It would, however, be a serious error to hold that the Twelve from the first moment of their selection appreciated the true grandeur of the life of Jesus. On the contrary, that life must often have presented to them a problem of no little difficulty. It was not the type of life which they had been accustomed to regard as specifically religious, still less as embodying religion in its perfection and integrity. It is probable that those of the Apostles who had been disciples of the Baptist were at first more impressed by his austere and solitary life than by the life of Jesus, which was substantially that of ordinary men. He ate and drank as they did. He dressed like them. He moved freely among them. He never sought to protect Himself from the approach of men, but on the contrary invited them to draw near. Nothing in His bearing or speech betrayed that He regarded Himself as standing on a different plane from other men, or that He expected them to treat Him as belonging to a different order of existence. He was simple, genial, affable, accessible. His mode of life, too, viewed as religious, must have filled them with surprise. He had no fixed hours or forms of prayer. His approach to the Father was the expression of His habitual reverence, adoration, and trust, but it was not determined, much less fettered, by rule. He prayed as He was moved to pray.

Again, He departed from a usage which was one of the chief features of the piety of the time. He declined to fast. Not only had He no regular fast days, He neither fasted Himself nor did He inculcate the observance on them. Another respect in which He deviated widely from the religious practices of His time was His disregard of ceremonial ablutions. He paid no attention to the rules affecting ritual purity. There is no evidence that He violated the usages of His nation as to foods, but His attitude towards these showed that He attached no value to them. Even that rite which was fundamental and distinctive, the pledge of salvation because the assurance of being a member of the covenant, the rite of *circumcision*, was unnoticed in His teaching. In yet another and hardly less important respect our Lord's life was largely different from the accepted type of sanctity. The *Sabbath*, like circumcision, was one of the peculiar glories of Judaism, and the teachers of our Lord's age and of preceding generations had framed a code of rules to protect it from desecration. These He trampled under foot. The endless regulations intended to stop the performance of any work whatever on that day He brushed aside as at variance with the true end of the Sabbath institution. He rejoiced in the Sabbath, esteeming it to be one of God's best gifts to man, but He was everywhere denounced as a Sabbath-breaker by those who regarded themselves as the interpreters of the law (Jn 5[18]). Even in the matter of almsgiving He was not as the men who professed to be specially religious. He was beneficent in the highest degree, but He followed no systematic rules.

Hence it is plain that the tenor of our Lord's life must have formed a problem of no little complexity to the Twelve during the first stages of their apprenticeship. Was this life—so simple, so natural—a truly religious life? Was the religious life bright, sunny, cheerful, full of hope and joy? Was this life of simple trust in the Father and of obedience to His will in the fulfilment of the common duties of life—was this religion? Nor was the perplexity of the Apostles lessened by the classes with which our Lord preferred to associate. He addressed Himself to the sick, the poor, and the outcast. The solicitude of Jesus for the least necessitous of these classes was a difficulty to some of them, but their surprise rose to the height when they saw Him mix freely with those under a social ban.

Doubtless the eyes of the Apostles were opened gradually. They came to perceive, as we do to-day, that the life spent by their Master was the typical life of man. Its likeness to the common life of men is its glory. For by it the common life which all must live is transfigured and made the ideal life of men. Its freedom from rule is discerned to be the reason why it is capable of becoming the model of all lives without exception. For that freedom teaches men that true religion creates its own forms, while its essence of trust in God and devotion to His will remains unalterable. The sympathy which He exhibited for all classes was a revelation of the truth that He was the Saviour of the world.

(b) Perhaps nothing impressed our Lord's disciples more when they first became acquainted with Him than His *miracles*. The expectation that the Messiah would work miracles seems to have been general. The Gospels leave the impression that the common people anticipated that works of a most marvellous description would be performed by the Messiah. The nature of these works was undefined, but they transcended the ordinary endowments of man. The Twelve then may have felt little surprise when they saw their

Lord perform miracles, but every new miracle would serve to strengthen their conviction of His title to be the Messiah. It is not likely, however, that they were prepared for the kind of miracles which He worked. None of them could have foretold that the Messiah would confine Himself in great measure to the accomplishment of miraculous cures of body and mind; that He would spend many hours on many days in healing sickness and in expelling demons. The miracles of Jesus were as unexpected as His mode of life. The Apostles were dreaming of miracles of judgment at the very hour when He was performing miracles of mercy. Even the miracles over nature were not those of which they naturally thought.

The Apostles could not fail to perceive the range of the power wielded by their Master and be filled with amazement. No disease could withstand His word or touch. The very demons yielded to His sway. Death itself was powerless before Him. It is important to notice that some of the miracles were performed before the Apostles only. The miracles in which the Apostles as a whole or some of them were specially concerned are these : the Miraculous Draught of Fishes recorded by St. Luke (5^{1-7}), the Stilling of the Storm (Mk 4^{39}), the Walking on the Sea (6^{48}, Jn 6^{16}), the Stater in the Fish's Mouth (Mt 17^{27}), the Cursing of the Fig-tree (Mk 11^{20}), and the Second Miraculous Draught of Fishes (Jn 21^{11}). These signs had a peculiar value for the Twelve. They were proofs of knowledge and of power fitted to promote faith and to enforce truth. There is a fitness in the circumstance that most of the miracles on nature were wrought before or on behalf of the Apostles. For they more than others were prepared to embrace the truth that Jesus was the Lord of nature. It was indispensable that they should be taught this fact, and how could it have been better illustrated than by the miracles wrought on the Sea of Galilee? What a revelation of the knowledge or power of Jesus; what a prophecy of the success of the new vocation to which they were summoned, was the first draught of fishes! What a lesson concerning the might of Jesus was contained in the instant obedience of the raging waves and winds to His command! What a fresh disclosure of His power was His walking towards them on the sea as they toiled to make the western shore of the lake! What instruction to Peter and to the rest when Peter first succeeded in imitating his Master's walking on the water and then began to sink! How fraught with suggestions to Peter the coin found in the mouth of the first fish which came to his hook as he lowered it into the lake! What confirmation of all that they had learned was found in the second draught of fishes, that after the Resurrection! The cursing of the fig-tree occupies a place by itself among our Lord's miracles, but the lesson it teaches is most weighty. A miracle of judgment is as suitable as a parable of judgment. The lesson of the need of correspondence between profession and practice could not have been more impressively taught than by the fate of the fig-tree.

No one can doubt that the number and variety of the miracles witnessed by the Apostles enhanced their conception of our Lord's person and powers. Perhaps, too, they discerned, even if imperfectly, what is so clear to us to-day, that the miracles were indeed what He called them, *signs* : manifestations of the character and qualities of the kingdom which He had come to set up. The boundless sympathy and compassion of their Master must have struck them; His life not less than His teaching was mercy and service. His works of mercy were the living embodiment of the principles of mercy He inculcated. He healed all who sought His aid, making no inquiry into their past, their station, their gifts, but caring only for their needs. It was impossible for the Apostles not to discover that the miracles they beheld with such frequency were signs of the grace and love of the Father speaking to men through Jesus.

As the Apostles saw the miracles and heard what Jesus said respecting them, did they form a just conception of their nature and function? Were they able to compare them with the portents for which they had at one time longed? Did they perceive the relation of the signs to the person of Jesus? Did they discern that the signs could be fully understood only through His character? Did they recognize that the character and words of Jesus were greater than His signs, but that these were nevertheless such as to convince every impartial judge that His mission was of God? They knew that Jesus never regarded His miracles as the chief evidence for the validity of His claims; they were neither His sole nor His principal credentials; they were rather a part and element of His message and His work. Did they see clearly that the evidential value of the miracles did not consist in their departure from the established order of nature, in their capacity as marvels, but in their congruity with the character and aims of Jesus, and as illustrations of His spirit and ways? We would gladly learn whether the Apostles ever reflected on the use made by our Lord of His miraculous endowments. Believing in Him as the Lord of nature and of life, aware that He had unnumbered forces at His command, were they surprised that He never employed His powers to promote His advantage or to defend His disciples or Himself from injustice and violence? Whence this self-repression? Why was the sphere of the miraculous so strictly limited? Why were none of the miracles of a character to dazzle, compel, overwhelm? Why did Jesus refuse so often the request for a sign, and especially for a sign from heaven? Why was the thaumaturgic element wholly absent from His works? The fact that our Lord observed a peculiar temperance in the employment of His miraculous gifts must have imprinted itself on the minds of the Apostles, and it is probable that the significance of the fact became more and more obvious as their experience widened. Even before the Crucifixion they may have discerned that this self-restraint was in full harmony with His attitude towards the world, and only the corollary of His conception of the Kingdom. See, further, art. MIRACLES.

(c) From the first, the disciples had regarded Jesus as a *teacher*, and whatever more He became to them as their intercourse with Him deepened, a teacher He remained to the end. Or, to speak more correctly, from being *a* teacher He became *the* Teacher; and the greatest of teachers, measured by any proper standard, He certainly was and abides. The substance of His teaching is the truest, wisest, and best on the loftiest and weightiest of all topics—topics as to which all teachers before Him were as men groping in the dark. He and He alone speaks with the confidence of personal knowledge regarding the nature of God and His relations to man. It is sufficient for our present purpose to refer to the naturalness, the ease, the familiarity with which Jesus spoke concerning the Kingdom of God; the character and intentions of the Father; the righteousness He requires; the conditions on which entrance into the Kingdom depends; its history and its final issues; the testimony borne by Jesus to Himself; the place He assigns to His person and work. Never man so spake (Jn 7^{46}). Yet He speaks what He knows, and testifies of what He has seen (Jn 3^{11}). Here, if anywhere, the entire religious experience of mankind affirms the truth of the witness He bore. His message authenticates itself ; it bears the seal of its Divine origin upon it. Such views never sprang up within the mind of man ; they descended out of heaven from God.

And this teaching was conveyed to the disciples and to the people according to definite methods and in language which forms an epoch in human speech. It is unlikely that our Lord ever reflected on the problems which form the science and art of teaching, or that He ever laid down rules for His own guidance ; but the essence of all that is best in the writings of the great educators is embodied in His practice. Let a reader come to the Gospels full of what he has learned regarding education from Plato and Aristotle and their successors, and he can perceive without difficulty, in the relations between our Lord and the Apostles; in His attitude towards them ; in His modes of stimulating, enlarging, and enriching their minds ; in His tact, patience, and wisdom,—the signs of skill which is incomparable because so spontaneous, so flexible, and so fertile of resource. Never for a moment did He lose sight of His object, to qualify the Apostles to be His witnesses and representatives ; but He did not dwell on that purpose. He was aware that the power of personality is the strongest and most penetrating of all forces, and accordingly He separated the Apostles more and more, as the days went by, from their familiar scenes and labours, in order that they might, because of their complete intimacy with Him, breathe His spirit and share in His aims. They were ennobled, as it were, despite themselves. New ideals and motives took possession of them. He was so constantly before their eyes, so continually the subject of their speech, so much the centre of their interests and the goal of their hopes, that they grew into His image. Not less evident was His desire that the Apostles should not be mere echoes of Himself, but men of originality, courage, and resource. It was on this account that He delivered no systematic instruction ; that He caused nothing to be committed to memory ; that He did not store the minds of the Apostles with rules, lists of duties, tables of the forbidden and the permissible. Hence He gave no dogmas in fixed shape even on the greatest of all subjects. Hence, too, He furnished no directory for the duties of the day, and made no attempt to prescribe the hours to be employed in devotion or the words to be used, or to determine the provision to be made for the sick and the poor. Again, He taught only as His disciples were able to receive. Not that He never went beyond their capacity. This He frequently did, and of set purpose. But He observed an order in what He said. The most obvious illustration of this fact is His teaching regarding His person. He did not begin to tell at once who He was, nor did He open His lips as to His death until He had evoked from Peter's lips as the spokesman of the Twelve the confession that He was the Messiah (Mk 8²⁹, Mt 16¹⁶, Lk 9²⁰). It is expressly stated that He kept back much from His disciples, leaving them to the enlightenment of the Spirit, because they were unprepared to receive what He had to communicate (Jn 16¹²). If He spoke of what they did not comprehend at once, it was either that their intellects might be quickened or that they might treasure in their memories the truth mentioned, in view of their future experience. His references to His death had as their chief aim to render the Apostles certain of the fact and, above all, that it was foreknown by Him. Nor was He impatient for results. He never forced growth. He knew that to build durably is to build slowly ; and so He bore with ignorance, with misapprehension, with imperfect views, with partial and hasty

inferences, knowing that these would be corrected by the discipline of experience. He sought especially to preserve the individuality of His disciples, and to unfold the characteristic endowments of each. None of them was to be other than himself. No one was to be a model for the rest. He knew each so well that He could play on him as on an instrument, but this knowledge He used only to promote the welfare of the disciple. The manifestation of personal character, the personal discernment of truth, the exhibition of personal sympathy, appreciation, reverence, devotion, love, filled Him with delight.

The Gospels show on every page that our Lord encouraged the disciples to ask Him questions. Whatever difficulties presented themselves to their minds they were free to place before Him. This they did so constantly that the habit must have been created by our Lord. How large a portion of the Gospels is occupied with the questions and remarks of the Apostles ! It is to these questions that we are indebted for the explanation of the parable of the Sower (Mk 4¹⁰). The same is true of His teaching regarding defilement (Mt 15¹⁵). How much we owe to Peter's questions—'How often shall my brother sin against me and I forgive him?' (Mt 18²¹) ; 'What shall we have therefore?' (Mt 19²⁷). But perhaps the finest illustration of the relations of our Lord and the Apostles in this connexion is the intercourse on the night of the betrayal. No passage in the Gospels is so instructive as to the readiness of the disciples to break in by questions on what our Lord was saying, and the skill with which He availed Himself of these questions to open to them His deepest thoughts and purposes (Jn 13³⁶ff·).

The resources of human speech have been strained to the utmost to describe the grace and power of the language of Jesus, and yet the result is felt to be inadequate. Did the Apostles recognize the originality, the strength, the flexibility, the charm, the aptness, the simplicity, the depth of the words of Jesus? We cannot tell ; it may have been that their apprehension of the beauty and majesty of His language was much less than ours, but even they must have felt a strange thrill as they heard the most sublime of all truths clothed in terms which they were in the habit of using every day of their lives. It was a new experience to have religion speak the tongue of the home, the workshop, and the street. Then, too, the illustrations which He used ! The whole life of the ordinary man was laid under tribute to illustrate the Kingdom of God. The furniture of his home, his food, his clothing, his work, his intercourse with his fellows were made the symbol and the vesture of heavenly truths. Earth shone in the light of heaven. One form of speech is specially identified with the teaching of Jesus—the **parable.** The parable may be regarded as the creation of Jesus. The parables of the OT, and those found in Jewish writings, hardly deserve mention in this respect. Nor did Jesus teach in parables because the language of parable is the language of the East. He devised the parable to meet the requirements of His hearers. The parable is His own workmanship, the product of His mind and heart. The parables of Jesus are unique alike in literature and religion, and are as distinctive of Him as the miracles.

An ordinary reader of the Gospels is apt to suppose that the ministry of Jesus, from its beginning to its close, was distinguished by the use of parables. But this opinion is erroneous. No parables marked the opening of the ministry. The first use of the parable is noticed at length. To the question why Jesus finally adopted the parable most men would reply—to attract, to interest, to stimulate, to find the readiest and most direct access to the mind for truth and duty. But when the Gospels are consulted they give an answer altogether different. They tell that our Lord, when questioned on the subject, affirmed that He taught in parables, not to reveal but to conceal the truth; not to instruct but to condemn men (Mk 4¹²). These words have always been a stumbling-block to interpreters. Perhaps their true significance may never be ascertained; but the view which rejects them as the correct description of the parables as a whole is justified, because they are at variance with the Gospels themselves. The most cursory examination of the parables shows that many of them are messages of grace. Who can fail to discern that the heart of God is represented in the parable of the Prodigal Son as the heart of a Father? Is this truth meant to extinguish hope? Again, an examination reveals that many of the parables were spoken to the disciples themselves. Was this the penalty of their blindness and hardness of heart? Accordingly, the common view of the parable is the true view, and our Lord spoke in parables to render his teaching as simple, vivid, stimulating, and effective as possible. See PARABLES, and ILLUSTRATIONS.

The extent to which the parables were addressed to the Twelve has scarcely received adequate recognition. Indeed the parables are seldom spoken of in connexion with the education of the Twelve. Yet one-third of them were, to all appearance, directed to the Apostles exclusively. These cover the period from the time when our Lord first began to speak in parables till His death. The ten parables belonging to this class, following the order first of St. Matthew and then of St. Luke, are: the Hidden Treasure, the Pearl, the Drag-net, the Unmerciful Servant, the Labourers in the Vineyard, the Ten Virgins, the Talents, the Friend at Midnight, the Unprofitable Servant, the Unjust Judge. A slight acquaintance with these parables shows that the lessons they teach were those our Lord was most anxious that His disciples should learn. The measureless value of the kingdom of God, the certainty of a final severance between the evil and the good, the necessity of a forgiving disposition, the nature and conditions of the future recompense, the obligation of watchfulness, the reward of perseverance in prayer, the truth that no men have claims of merit on God, are the subjects with which these parables deal, and these subjects were constantly in the heart and on the lips of our Lord. A flood of light was thrown on all these topics by the parables. The truth was now clearer, more comprehensible, more affecting, more subduing.

Is it possible to discover the sentiments with which the Twelve listened to the parables? Perhaps they were too plain men to perceive their exquisite naturalness and beauty. In all their discussions concerning them not a word may have been spoken in praise of that perfect felicity which secures for them an unequalled place in the literature of the world. But they would at least perceive their appropriateness. How they must have lived in their memories and illuminated truth and duty! Did the Twelve find any difficulty in understanding the import of the parables? Presumably their condition was just that of the diligent and devout reader of to-day. Some parables bear their meanings, as it were, on their forehead. Nobody doubts what is the meaning of the parable of the Good Samaritan or of the Ten Virgins. It is true that there are questions connected with their interpretation which are still under discussion, but the lessons which they inculcate are obvious. But what of the parables which perplex expositors to-day? What of the Unjust Steward? What of the Labourers in the Vineyard? The same difficulties which occur to us must have occurred to the disciples. But they had this immense advantage over us that they could ask their Master questions as to His meaning, and we know that these questions were freely put. The interpretations of the parables of the Sower and of the Tares are said to have been replies made to the request of the disciples for an explanation. What strikes one in these answers is the point, depth, freshness of the meaning. These explanations have sometimes been assigned to the Apostles themselves,

but the supposition is without probability. Were it sound, it would form the most striking proof of the effect on them of their intercourse with Jesus, for it is impossible to suggest juster or more suitable interpretations of the parables concerned. One peculiarly instructive sentence was spoken by our Lord in this connexion (Mt 13⁵²). He had been expounding some of the parables to His disciples, and asked if He had been understood. When they replied affirmatively, He remarked that every teacher of the Law instructed regarding the kingdom of heaven was like a householder who produced from his stores things new and old. The Apostles were the scribes of Jesus, taught to understand the nature, characteristics, and history of the Kingdom of God, and hence capable of furnishing most profitable instruction to their hearers. The old and the new alike were at their command in their mutual relations and connexions. They did not despise the one nor vaunt themselves concerning the other. The Law and the Gospel, prophecy and its accomplishment, the Law and its fulfilment, furnished them with the subjects which they could treat with knowledge and power.

After the Twelve had been some time with our Lord, they were sent forth on a missionary journey (mission of the Apostles, Mk 6⁷, Mt 10⁵, Lk 9¹). The time at which the mission took place, the town from which they started, the duration of the mission, are uncertain. Two reasons probably influenced our Lord in despatching the Twelve on this enterprise. The first and most prominent was His profound sympathy for the condition of the people of Galilee. It was impossible for Him to evangelize all Galilee, to say nothing of the entire land; others must share His labours. This was one of the ends for which the Twelve had been chosen, and accordingly He sent them to announce everywhere that the Kingdom of God was nigh. A second reason was that He might in this way train them for their future career. The message which they were to proclaim corresponded with their own comparative immaturity on the one hand, and with the spiritual state of their audiences on the other. To have declared the Messiahship of Jesus would have led to misunderstanding, and have hindered rather than furthered the expansion of the kingdom; hence they were confined to the assertion, so full of promise and hope, that the Kingdom was at hand. To assist them in discharging their mission as the envoys of Jesus they were endowed with miraculous powers. They were enabled to cure disease and to expel demons. These powers they were to exercise gratuitously. This liberality was intended by Jesus to be an evidence of the nature of the kingdom, of which they announced the near approach. It was to be a kingdom of compassion, sympathy, tenderness. These endowments, besides serving to show the nature of the kingdom, were also a demonstration of the truth of their message. The Apostles were enjoined to make no special provision for the mission on which they were about to enter. They were to start on it just as they were. They were to take neither money, nor food, nor clothing for their journey. They were to rely for their maintenance on the providence of God, and on the hospitality which they were to seek. Because of the urgency of the case their attention was to be concentrated on the lost sheep of the house of Israel. It is, indeed, not probable that our Lord meant their mission to extend beyond Galilee, or even to the whole of the province, the Greek-speaking cities being excluded. The efforts of the Twelve were probably intended to be restricted to the homes of the people. No reference is made in the instructions given them to any appearance in the synagogue or in the market-place. Their inexperience did not permit them to deliver addresses in public. The Twelve were sent on their mission by twos; that is, six different enterprises were carried on by them at once. The wisdom of this arrangement is obvious. It was desirable that they should overtake as many of the population as possible, but it was not less important that they should be encouraged and strengthened by one another's presence. Had each of the Twelve entered on the work alone, he would have felt isolated and discouraged, and often have been at a loss how to act. No agreement exists among scholars as to the length of time occupied by the mission. Some consider that it lasted only a single day, others two days, others several weeks, and others again, several months. It may be pronounced with confidence that it took up some weeks at least.

The Twelve strictly followed the commands they received, passing through the villages, preaching repentance and the gospel, and casting out demons and healing everywhere. How their message was received does not appear. It is simply known that on their return they told our Lord what they had done and taught. No reference is made to the experience they had acquired or to the conclusions they had been led to form. It would have been most profitable had any information on these points reached us. Not less advantageous would it have been for us to know how they felt when they wrought their first miracles. Were they startled? Did they exult? Or were they grateful and humble? We can but speculate on these points, but we may feel assured that the Apostles profited not a little by this their first mission. Besides those lessons of confidence in the wisdom and power of their Master which they were always receiving, they were taught how to apply the truths they had learned, and how to use the powers with which they were clothed. They were forced to act for themselves, to reflect and decide in a way which elicited their latent capabilities.

From this point the education and training of the Apostles may be regarded as merged in the life of our Lord, and the further treatment of the subject must be sought under the relevant articles. The intercourse between our Lord and the Apostles should be regarded from their side if the work He accomplished in their case is to be fully appreciated and understood. To study the life and teaching of Jesus through the eyes and minds of the Apostles is advantageous in no common degree, because of the many new questions which are thus raised, and which cannot be determined without a clearer and fuller insight being obtained into the wisdom of the methods He followed in preparing them to expound His thoughts and to extend His kingdom. A list of some of the more important topics to be considered may be serviceable. They are such as these: the question put to the Twelve at the crisis in Galilee, 'Will ye also go away?' the confession of Peter, and its significance for the Apostles; the predictions of the death and resurrection made, it would appear, to the Apostles only; the strife for the first places in the Kingdom, and the action taken by our Lord regarding it; the words spoken to the Apostles on the night of the betrayal, some of which form a parting charge to them; the appearances to the Eleven; the final commands addressed to them. Two subjects besides are deserving of particular notice: the inner circle of the Apostles—Peter, James, and John, the Three within the Twelve; and the many questions connected with the name of Judas Iscariot.

The Christian Church rests on the Apostles, for the Christian Church is their creation. But they, in turn, were the creation of Jesus. That He trans-

formed them in so brief a space of time from the men they were when called, as to be able to convince the world that He was the Messiah of Israel, the Son of God, the Saviour of mankind, is not the least of His titles to the admiration and the gratitude of men; for His success proves what can be made of ordinary men when they surrender themselves to the guidance of His spirit.

LITERATURE.—The chief books to be consulted are the Commentaries on the Gospels and the Lives of Christ, together with art. 'Apostle' in the different *Bible Dictionaries* and *Encyclopædias*, though the best of these are meagre and inadequate for the purposes of the student of the Gospels. For a general treatment two valuable works in English should be named—Bruce's *Training of the Twelve* and Latham's *Pastor Pastorum*. On the name and office of an Apostle see Lightfoot, *Gal.*[5] 92–101; Hort, *Christian Ecclesia*, 22–41; and on the Apostolic group, *Expositor*, I. i. [1875] 29–43, III. ix. [1889] 100 ff., 187 ff., 434 ff.

W. PATRICK.

APPARITION.—

In AV this word occurs thrice, in the Apocr. only: Wis 17[3] (Gr. ἴνδαλμα, RV 'spectral form'), 2 Mac 3[24] (Gr. ἐπιφάνεια, RV 'apparition,' RVm 'manifestation'), and 5[4] (Gr. ἐπιφάνεια, RV 'vision,' RVm 'manifestation'). In RV it occurs thrice only: Mt 14[26] ‖ Mk 6[49] (φάντασμα, AV 'spirit'), and 2 Mac 3[24] (as above).

The Revisers have used this word in its ordinary current sense of 'an immaterial appearance, as of a real being, a spectre, phantom, or ghost.' There is always connected with this term the idea of a *startling* or *unexpected* appearance, which seems also associated with the original φάντασμα. The immaterial appearance of a person supposed to be seen before (*double*) or soon after death (*ghost*), is a *wraith*; but these three synonyms are often interchanged.

The Jews of Christ's time, like all unscientific minds (ancient and modern), believed in ghosts naturally, instinctively, uncritically. Dr. Swete (*The Gospel according to St. Mark*, London, 1898, p. 131) refers to Job 4[15ff. 20[8], and especially to Wis 17[3 (4)] and 17[14 (15)] for earlier evidence of a popular belief in apparitions among the Hebrew people. The disciples' sudden shriek of terror (ἀνέκραξαν, Mk 6[49]) shows that they thought the phantom was real; but if we try to realize their attitude and outlook, we shall understand the futility of attributing to such naïve intelligences the discrimination of modern psychological research. The suggestions of excitable imaginations were indistinguishable from the actual presentations of objective reality. The best illustrations of their habits of thought must be sought in ancient and modern records of Oriental beliefs.

A. Erman (*Life in Ancient Egypt*, London, 1894, pp. 307, 308) says that 'the Egyptians did not consider man as a simple individuality; he consisted of at least three parts, the body, the soul, and the ghost, the image, the double, or the genius, according as we translate the Egyptian word *Ka*. . . . After the death of a man, just as during his lifetime, the *Ka* was still considered to be the representative of his human personality, and so the body had to be preserved that the *Ka* might take possession of it when he pleased. . . . It is to their faith in the *Ka* that we owe all our knowledge of the home life of the people of ancient Egypt.'

E. J. W. Gibb (*History of Ottoman Poetry*, London, 1900, pp. 56–59) says that 'according to the Sufi theory of the human soul it is a spirit, and therefore, by virtue of its own nature, in reality a citizen of the Spirit World. Its true home is there, and hence, for a certain season, it descends into this Physical Plane, where, to enable it to act upon its surroundings, it is clothed in a physical body. . . . The power of passing from the Physical World into the Spiritual is potential in every soul, but is actualized only in a few.'

For the mediæval conception of the nature of ghosts see the *locus classicus*—Dante, *Purg.* xxv. 88–108—in which Dante explains his conception of the disembodied soul as having the power of operating on matter and impressing upon the surrounding air the shape which it animated in life (Aquinas), thus forming for itself an aerial vesture (Origen and St. Augustine). See also Dante, *Conv.* tr. ii. c. 9, and Thomas Aquinas, *Summa Theol.* pt. iii. suppl. qu. lxix, art. 1.

Keim (*Jesus of Nazara*, London, 1879, iv. 184–191) critically reviews the various explanations offered of the miracle of Jesus walking over the billows, but says nothing of the word φάντασμα, merely remarking (p. 190) : 'If we adhere to the actual narrative, the going on the water was far from being an act of an ordinary character—it was something divine or ghostly.' For the latest criticism of the popular belief of NT times in the manifestations of the spirit world, see P. Wernle, *Beginnings of Christianity*, London, 1903, pp. 1–11.

P. HENDERSON AITKEN.

APPEARANCE. See CHRIST IN ART, and POR-TRAITS.

APPEARANCES.—See RESURRECTION.

APPRECIATION (OF CHRIST).—The whole NT is one long appreciation of Christ. It is no blindfold acceptance of Him, no mere echo of a tradition, but a series of utterances of men personally convinced of the supreme value of Christ to the world. St. Paul speaks of Christ only as he himself has been influenced by the Lord, not as the disciples had described Jesus to him. His phrases—high, beautiful, and so often mystical—are the direct expressions of his own personal consciousness of Jesus Christ. No one has accused him of extravagance or of exaggeration. It is because he has felt that to be clothed with the Lord must be the perfection of power and joy, that he says, 'Put ye on the Lord Jesus Christ' (Ro 13^{14}). It is because he has seen the love eternal that nothing imaginable can utterly root out again from the awakened heart, that he says, 'Neither death, nor life, . . . nor any other creation, shall be able to separate us from the love of God, which is in Christ Jesus our Lord' (Ro 8$^{38f.}$). And St. John opens his first Epistle with the strongest personal declaration of the whole of the Epistles, 'that which we have heard, . . . seen with our eyes, . . . and our hands have handled of the word of life . . . declare we unto you' (1 Jn 1^1).

But the simplest appreciation of all—as natural as a bird's song or a child's praise—is that which threads its way through every page of the Gospels. In spite of all the enmity written there ; remembering that there were those who saw in Him an ally of Beelzebub (Mt 12^{24}), working with the devil's aid ; that some called Him 'a gluttonous man, a winebibber, friend of publicans and sinners' (11^{19}) ; that lawyers, and Pharisees, and Sadducees were ever watching to trip Him (22^{15}), and plotting with Herodians (v.^{16}) to destroy Him ; that the Galilæan cities, which should have known Him best,—Chorazin, Bethsaida, Capernaum (11$^{21. 23}$), and even Nazareth,—rejected Him (Lk 4$^{28f.}$) ; and remembering the awful and lonely agonies of the last hours, we can yet point to the Gospels as abounding with witness to the wide contemporary appreciation of Christ.

It was most natural that it should be so, even when He is thought of entirely apart from any doctrine of His Divine personality. His own sympathy for others, and indeed for all things, was sure to attract others to Him. His quick perception of the good in all, His tender response to the least wave of the world's infinite music, show Him as destined to be the desired of men. He came upon the most diverse types, the most opposite of characters, and instantly knew their possibilities and their worth. He sees through the pure-minded hesitancy of Nathanael (Jn 1^{47}), He recognizes the true value of the widow's mite (Lk 21$^{1-4}$), He draws Nicodemus the timid to Him (Jn 3^1), He knows what will satisfy Thomas (Jn 20^{27}), and what will please and win Zacchæus (Lk 19^5) ; and His immediate followers include a Mary Magdalene as well as a Mary of Bethany, a Judas as well as a John. Even the failures are appreciated by a standard of faith unknown to the world. He acknowledges

the longing of the heart though a weak will robs it of fruition ; He reads the zealous affection of Peter between the lines of a moment's Satanic pride (Mt 16^{22}), or a terror-stricken denial (Mt 26^{70}) ; He penetrates to the secret yearnings behind the materialistic questions of the woman at the well, and imparts to her His highest thought of God (Jn 4^{24}). He cannot even look upon the earth or sky but He must read into it the indwelling of the Eternal, find in all its pages picture and parable of spiritual realities. To His all-sensitive being the universe of things seen is but a symbol. The sower with his seed, the harvest-fields, the birds of the air, the fox in his hole, the sheep in the fold or lost on the hills, the wind that foretells heat or rain (Lk 12$^{54. 55}$), the prophecies of the sunset (Mt 16^2), or the springtide promise of the sprouting fig-tree (Mk 13^{28}),—all passing through His appreciative spirit is treasured as the visible manuscript of God.

We might expect that such a receptive, comprehensive, and understanding nature would compel confidence. Men could not help trusting such deep and ready sympathy. And, as we read the Evangelists, one of their most notable traits is this—that they succeed in bringing together, almost without form, and apparently without intention, a wonderful accumulation of witness to the appreciation Jesus inspired from the first. The record is so varied. It is from no one school, or type, or rank. Almost every grade of life in the community is there—from the outcast and the leper to the Sanhedrist and the Roman centurion. From the first His gifts of healing attract the sufferers, and none are more definite in their acknowledgment of Him. The villagers bring their sick on beds to the market-places (Mk 6$^{55. 56}$), or lower the palsied through the roof at Capernaum (Mk 2^4). The centurion in that town is satisfied that a word from Jesus will be enough to heal his sick servant (Mt 8^8). Martha says, with such simple trust, 'Lord, if thou hadst been here, my brother had not died' (Jn 11^{21}). The ruler of the synagogue feels that the touch of the Lord's hand would be enough to heal his dying daughter (Mt 9^{18}). The woman with the issue of blood would but touch the hem of His garment to be cured (Mk 5^{28}). The Syro-Phœnician woman persisted in her prayer for her sick daughter, eagerly claiming the rights, while bearing the reproach of being a Gentile 'dog' (Mk 7^{28}). With one cry is He greeted alike by blind Bartimæus (Mk 10^{47}), the two blind men (Mt 9^{27}), and the ten lepers (Lk 17^{13})—'Jesus, thou Son of David, have mercy on us' ; a cry the meaning of which is uttered by the leper (Mk 1^{40})—'Lord, if thou wilt, thou canst make me clean.' When sight is given to the man born blind, the parents testify to the Divine origin of the power that has been exercised (Jn 9^{33}). And the multitude at Nain, when they saw the dead raised, had no hesitation in crying—'A great prophet is risen among us' (Lk 7^{16}). It was a glad welcome from the sufferers and their friends that greeted Jesus as the manifestation of God in all these things. But not less earnest is the witness of the crowds to the popular estimate of the teacher. 'There went great multitudes with him' is the frequent note that leads up to some great doctrine of life (Mt 19^2, Lk 14^{25}, Mk 6). The house filled at Capernaum (Mk 2^2) is but the parallel of the occasion when His own mother 'could not come at him for the press' (Lk 8^{19}), or of the thousands by the seashore (Mk 4^1), or of the multitude that 'trod one upon another' (Lk 12^1). Lives that He changes from darkness to light bear willing evidence to His power and charm : Mary Magdalene will not be held back by false shame from entering the Pharisee's house to acknowledge her Saviour (Lk 7[36-50]), nor be repulsed by the charge of wastefulness through sentiment (Mk 14[4]); and Zacchæus will boldly profess a practical conversion before those who know him intimately (Lk 19[8]).

We look for appreciation from His nearest disciples, a quick obedience, a joy that has no place for fasting (Mk 2[18]), the mother's confidence at the marriage-feast at Cana (Jn 2[5]), the great utterances of His forerunner the Baptist (Jn 1[30] 3[30]), the exalted vision of the Transfiguration (Mk 9[5]), and that Petrine outburst, repeated by all, as they neared Gethsemane—'If I should die with thee, I will not deny thee.' From these His intimates we anticipate such trust. We look for it, too, from the band of holy women—Joanna, Susanna, Salome, the Marys, and those 'who ministered unto him of their substance' (Lk 8[3]). But beyond these we have the scribes (Mt 8[19], Mk 12[34]) earnestly approaching Him, Pharisees inviting Him to their houses (Lk 11[37] 14[1]); we have the confession of the council of priests and Pharisees—'If we let him alone, all will believe on him' (Jn 11[48]); we have the acknowledgment of Samaritans, convinced not by hearsay but by personal knowledge (Jn 4[42]), of centurions (Mt 8[5-13], Mk 15[39]), and of the rich young man 'running and kneeling' and saying, 'Good Master' (Mk 10[17]). Strangers seek Him out—'Sir, we would see Jesus' (Jn 12[20]); and the common people of His own race 'heard him gladly' (Mk 12[37]), and acclaimed His entry into Jerusalem (Mk 11[8-10]). In the beginning, shepherds and magi, angels and stars bear witness to the newborn King; so that to the last it is a strange mixed company, that seems to include (by his long faltering before judgment) Pilate himself, the lone, mysterious figure of Joseph of Arimathæa, and Nicodemus 'bringing myrrh and aloes' (Jn 19[29]).

This many-sided appreciation of our Lord in His own day, in addition to its obvious gain to the Christian preacher, is suggestive of the many differing points of view from which men may reverently regard Christ, each one expressive of a truth, though not the entirety of the truth. And it may also indicate the many successive ways of wonder, repentance, sympathy, and vision in which Christ speaks to each individual soul.

EDGAR DAPLYN.

ARAMAIC.—See LANGUAGE.

ARBITRATION.—The settlement of disputes by the acceptance of the judgment of a third party supposed to be impartial. The arrangement may be purely private, or in accordance with special statute; the application is multifarious. Some method of settlement by umpires is as old as civil government. In Job 9[33] the 'daysman' is perfectly described. The Greek term (μεσίτης) translated 'mediator' (or middleman) has the same meaning; though as applied, in the NT, to Moses and to Christ (Gal 3[19. 20], 1 Ti 2[5], He 8[6] 9[15] 12[24]), as standing between man and God (cf. Dt 5[5]), it belongs to an essentially different order of ideas, inasmuch as God is not man. The complexity of modern life has multiplied the occasions; but the most important recent advance has been the application to international differences. Thereby questions such as have often led to wars become capable of amicable settlement. The first notable instance was the Geneva arbitration under the Washington Treaty (1871) in the Alabama Question. The principle, then disputed, has now found universal acceptance. Treaties of arbitration already exist or are being negotiated between most nations that have mutual relations. And in the future, except where ambitions and strong passions are involved, this means of agreement will be largely resorted to.

The idea is based on the acknowledgment of the identity of moral law in the two spheres of individual and national life. Duty for persons or communities or nations is one. There is no valid distinction of private and public right; the code of ethics that is binding for the private individual is equally obligatory on kings and the representatives of peoples. This doctrine is opposed to the long history of statecraft, to the maxims of diplomatists, and to the passions of despotism. But few now openly deny its truth; and the acknowledgments already made in treaties of arbitration may be reckoned one of the greatest triumphs of Christian civilization.

The principle may be said to be based on the Golden Rule (Mt 7[12], Lk 6[31]), which teaches reciprocal obligation, or on the kindred command to love our neighbours as ourselves (Mt 22[39], Mk 12[31]). These fundamental laws are given as the sum of practical duty. They condemn the egoistic attitude. They teach us to regard the position of others with full sympathy, to seek an impartial standpoint, and to make the individual will harmonize with the general mind. The principle of arbitration is also an illustration of the grace of peaceableness. 'Blessed are the peacemakers' (Mt 5[9]). This truth finds full expression in the Epistles, where peace, the fruit of the Spirit (Gal 5[22]), and the concomitant of righteousness, is contrasted with the strife and envy of sin, and is noted as a mark of the kingdom of God, who is the God of peace. Once more, the principle may be based on prudence; for a willing settlement may prevent a legal defeat, or even a worse disaster (Mt 5[25. 26], Lk 12[58. 59], cf. Pr 25[8. 9]).

Christ declined on one occasion to be an arbiter (Lk 12[13f.]). He was addressing the multitude, when one of them said, 'Master, bid my brother divide the inheritance with me.' Jesus replied, 'Man, who made me a judge (κριτήν, so BDL and the crit. edd.; TR has δικαστήν) or a divider (μεριστήν, only here in NT) over you?' The words which follow (v. [15ff.]) show that Jesus knew that this man was moved by covetousness; but apart from His censure of a wrong motive, He here affirms that it was no business of His to arbitrate between men. He would not interfere in civil disputes which fell properly to be decided by the regular law (cf. Dt 21[17]). But His saying goes far beyond the sphere of jurisprudence. Christ lays down universal laws of justice and love, but does not apply them. Moral casuistry was no part of His mission, and decisions of the kind this man wanted could only have weakened the sense of personal responsibility, and hindered the growth of those spiritual dispositions it was His chief aim to create.

R. SCOTT.

ARCHELAUS ('Αρχέλαος) is named once in the NT (Mt 2[22]), and probably is referred to in the parable of the Pounds (Lk 19[12ff.]). He was the elder of the two sons of Herod the Great by Malthace, a Samaritan woman (Jos. BJ I. xxviii. 4, xxxiii. 7). Judæa, with the title of 'king,' was bequeathed to him by his father's will; but he would not assume the royal dignity till he had obtained confirmation of that will from the emperor Augustus (Ant. XVII. viii. 2–4). Before his departure to Rome a rebellion broke out in Jerusalem; and in quelling it his soldiers put three thousand men to death, among whom were pilgrims visiting the Holy City for the passover (ib. XVII. ix. 3). Thus at the beginning of his reign an evil reputation was gained by Archelaus, and the alarm of Joseph may be understood ('But when he heard that Archelaus did reign in Judæa in the room of his father Herod, he was afraid to go thither').

After the rebellion, Archelaus proceeded to Rome (Ant. XVII. ix. 3–7, cf. Lk 19[12]). Augustus, dealing with Herod's will, received a deputation from the people of Judæa, who begged that neither Archelaus nor any of his brothers should be appointed king (cf. Lk 19[14]). The emperor finally decided that Archelaus should receive Judæa, Samaria, and Idumæa, with the title not of 'king,' but of 'ethnarch' (*Ant.* XVII. xi. 1–4; *BJ* II. vi. 3). On his return from Rome the ethnarch sought vengeance against his enemies (cf. Lk 19[27]) in Judæa and Samaria. In the ninth or tenth year of his reign, after many acts of tyranny and violence, he was banished by the emperor to Vienne in Gaul (*Ant.* XVII. xiii. 2). According to Jerome, the tomb of Archelaus was pointed out near Bethlehem (*de Situ et Nomin. Loc. Hebraic.* 101. 11).

LITERATURE.—Josephus, *Antiquities of the Jews, Wars of the Jews* [*BJ*], as cited above; references *s.* 'Archelaus' in Index to Schürer's *Geschichte des Jüdischen Volkes im Zeitalter Jesu Christi*, 1898–1901 [Eng. tr. of 2nd ed. 1885–90]; and Hausrath's *Neutestamentliche Zeitgeschichte*, 1873–77 [Eng. tr. in 2 vols. 1878–80]. Of the last named work, vol. i. [German] was published in a 3rd ed. in 1879.   J. HERKLESS.

ARIMATHÆA ('Αριμαθαία) is mentioned in Mt 27[57], Mk 15[43], Lk 23[51], and Jn 19[38] as the place from which Joseph, who buried the body of Jesus, came up to Jerusalem. In the *Onomasticon* (225. 12) it is identified with 'Αρμαθὲμ Σειφά (Ramathaim-zophim*), the city of Elkanah and Samuel (1 S 1[1]), near Diospolis (Lydda) and in the district of Timnah (Tibneh). In 1 Mac 11[34], Ramathem is referred to along with Aphærema and Lydda as a Samaritan toparchy transferred, in 145 B.C., to Judæa. These notices of Ramathaim point to *Beit-Rima*, 13 miles E.N.E. of Lydda, and 2 miles N. of Timnah,—an identification adopted by G. A. Smith (*HGHL* 254 n. 7) and Buhl (*GAP* 170). Another possible site is *Râm-allah*, 3 miles S.W. of Bethel, suggested by Ewald (*Hist.* ii. 421). The proposed sites S. of Jerusalem are not 'in the hill-country of Ephraim' (1 S 1[1]). If Arimathæa, then, be identified with the Ramathaim of Elkanah, it may well be at the modern hill-village of *Beit-Rima*. The LXX form of Ramathaim is 'Αρμαθαίμ (1 S 1[1] and elsewhere), thus providing a link between Ramathaim and Arimathæa.

A. W. COOKE.

ARISTEAS (LETTER OF).—This interesting piece of fiction may find a place in this Dictionary, because it gives the first account of that work which more than any other paved the way for the gospel in early times, namely, the Greek translation of the OT, the so-called Septuagint. There is no agreement as yet about either the age or the aim of this composition. That it is a fiction is now generally admitted. The author pretends to have been one of the two ambassadors—Andreas, ἀρχισωματοφύλαξ of the king, being the other—sent by king Ptolemæus Philadelphus to the high priest Eleazar of Jerusalem in order to get for him a copy of the Law, and men to translate it for the Royal Library at Alexandria. The letter gives a long description of the gifts sent by Philadelphus to Jerusalem, of the city, its temple and the religious customs of the Jews, and of the table-talk between the king and each of the 72 interpreters. When the work was finished, a solemn curse was denounced on any one who should change anything in it (cf. Dt 4[2], Rev 22[18.19]). Schürer, I. Abrahams, and others fix the date about B.C. 200; Herriot (on Philo) dates it 170–150; Wellhausen (*Isr. und Jüd. Gesch.*[3] 1897, p. 232) in the 1st cent. B.C. (but in 4th ed. 1901, p. 236, he assigns it to the 2nd cent.); Wendland, between 96 and 63,† nearer to 96; L.

* On this name (which is almost certainly based on a textual corruption), see Hastings' *DB*, vol. iv. p. 198a note.
† In Hastings' *DB* iv. 438b, line 7 from bottom of text, read **63 for 93**.

Cohn doubts whether it was known to Philo; Graetz placed it in the reign of Tiberius, and Willrich (*Judaica*, 1900, pp. 111–130) brings its composition down to 'later than A.D. 33.' Lombroso was the first to show that the 'author was well acquainted with the details of court life in the times of the Ptolemies'; and recent researches have confirmed this; on the other hand, there are interesting connexions with the Greek of the NT; compare καταβολή used absolutely for 'creation' (Mt 13[35] and Aristeas, § 129 [a usage apparently unknown to Hort *ad* 1 P 1[20], and Swete, *Introd.* p. 397]); ἀνατάττεσθαι (Lk 1[1] and Aristeas, § 144; Mt 6[31.32] and Aristeas, § 140, etc.).

While Jerome had already called attention to the fact that Aristeas speaks only of the Law as having been translated by the 72 interpreters, in later times it became customary to consider the whole Greek OT as the work of the 'Septuagint.' Philo seems to follow a somewhat different tradition, and mentions that in his days the Jews of Alexandria kept an annual festival in honour of the spot where the light of this translation first shone forth, thanking God for an old but ever new benefit. He is sure that God heard the prayer of the translators 'that the greater part of mankind, or even the whole of it, may profit by their work, when men shall use philosophical and excellent ordinances for regulating their lives.'

On the use made of the Greek OT in the NT see Swete, pp. 381–405, 'Quotations from the LXX in the NT.' That Jesus Himself was acquainted with it would seem to follow from the quotation in Mt 15[9] = Mk 7[7]. For the words μάτην δὲ σέβονταί με are the Septuagint rendering of the Hebrew יְהִי וַתְּהִי יִרְאָתָם, which rendering rests on a confusing of the first word with יְהִי וַתְּהִי (noticed already by Grotius). But it is doubtful whether we are entitled to expect in our Greek Gospels such a *verbatim* report of the words of Jesus.

On the influence of the Septuagint on the spread of the Gospel, cf. (in addition to older works like Grinfield, Oikonomos, etc.) Alfred Deissmann, 'Die Hellenisierung des semitischen Monotheismus,' Leipzig, 1903 (reprinted from *Neue Jahrbücher für das klassische Altertum*, 1903).

LITERATURE.—The Letter of Aristeas was first published in Latin (Rome, 1471 fol.) in the famous Latin Bible of Sueynheim and Pannartz; first edition of the Greek text by Simon Schard, Basle, 1561; all subsequent editions superseded by that of (Mendelssohn-) Wendland (Lipsiae, Teubner, 1900), and that of H. St. J. Thackeray in H. B. Swete's *Introduction to the OT in Greek* (Cambridge, 1900, 2nd ed. 1902). English translations by J. Done, 1633 and 1685; Lewis, 1715; Whiston (*Authentic Records*, i. 423–584), 1727; recently by Thackeray (*JQR* xv., April 1903). Compare, further, Abrahams, 'Recent Criticism on the Letter of Aristeas' (*ib.* xiv. 321–342); the works on the Septuagint (Swete, *l.c.*; Nestle in Hastings' *DB* i.v.); Friedländer, *Geschichte der jüdischen Apologetik* (Zürich, 1903).

EB. NESTLE.

ARISTION (ARISTO).—One of the principal authorities from whom Papias derived (written?) 'narratives of the sayings of the Lord' (τῶν τοῦ Κυρίου λόγων διηγήσεις; cf. Lk 1[1]), and (indirectly) oral traditions.

1. *Importance and Difficulty of Identification.*—According to Eusebius (*HE* iii. 39), Papias of Hierapolis in his five books of *Interpretations* (var. *l.* Interpretation) *of the Lord's Oracles* 'referred frequently by name' to 'Aristion and the Elder John' as his authorities. From the Preface (προοίμιον) Eusebius cited the following sentence to prove that Irenæus had misunderstood Papias in taking him to refer to the *Apostle* John as his authority, whereas the 'John' in question was not the 'disciple of the Lord,' but a comparatively obscure 'Elder.' We abridge the sentence, but give the relevant variants: εἰ δέ που καὶ παρηκολουθηκώς τις τοῖς πρεσβυτέροις ἔλθοι, τοὺς τῶν πρεσβυτέρων ἀνέκρινον λόγους· τί Ἀνδρέας ἢ τί Πέτρος εἶπεν . . . ἢ τις ἕτερος τῶν τοῦ Κυρίου μαθητῶν, ἅτε Ἀριστίων καὶ ὁ πρεσβύτερος Ἰωάννης οἱ τοῦ Κυρίου μαθηταὶ λέγουσιν.

For Ἀριστίων Syr. and Arm. read Ἀρίστων, and omit the clause οἱ τοῦ Κυρίου μαθηταὶ λέγουσιν, Arm. by compensation rendering ' Aristo and John the Elders.' Nicephorus (*HE* ii. 46, but not iii. 20) makes the same omission. Rufinus renders *ceterique discipuli dicebant*. Jerome changes the tense (*loquebantur*). Four Greek MSS and Niceph. (iii. 20) omit οἱ

Deferring the question of the significance of the variant readings, it is apparent that 'Aristion and the Elder John' are in several ways placed in contrast with the group of 'disciples of the Lord' mentioned immediately before, by whom Papias certainly means the twelve Apostles, enumerating seven (including James the Lord's brother ; cf. Gal 1[19] 2[9]), from Andrew to 'John (author of the Revelation) and Matthew' (author of the *Logia*). The designation μαθηταί instead of ἀπόστολοι is employed because the function in consideration is that of transmitting μαθήματα—the precepts (ἐντολαί) learned from the Lord. The disciples (including James) of the Lord Himself are the first generation of *traditores*. The group next mentioned, 'Aristion and the Elder John,' are distinguished expressly and implicitly as belonging to a subsequent generation.

(1) As Eusebius points out, the John spoken of in connexion with Aristion is (*a*) 'mentioned after an interval,' (*b*) 'classed with others outside the number of the Apostles,' (*c*) has 'Aristion mentioned before him,' (*d*) is 'distinctly called an Elder' (in contrast with the John mentioned just before, who is called a 'disciple of the Lord'). Nowhere in the context should the term 'Elder' be taken as = 'Apostle.'

(2) A distinction not referred to by Eusebius, but at least equally important, is the contrast of tense (disregarded by Rufinus and Jerome), whereby Papias makes it apparent that at the time of his inquiries the Apostles, including John, were dead ; whereas Aristion and the *Elder* John were living. He 'used to inquire of those who came his way what *had been* said (τί εἶπεν) by Andrew, Peter, Philip, Thomas, James, John or Matthew, or any other of the Lord's disciples ; as well as what was *being* said (ἅτε λέγουσιν) by Aristion and the Elder John.' Hence, as an authority of note, and a transmitter of Gospel traditions earlier than the time of Papias' writing (A.D. 145–160), Aristion is a witness of the first importance for the history of Gospel tradition. On the other hand, great difficulty and dispute are caused by the descriptive clause attached in most texts to his name and that of John the Elder, because it is identical with that by which the Apostles are appropriately designated as *traditores* of the first generation; whereas the distinctions already noted, especially the contrast of tense τί εἶπεν—ἅτε λέγουσιν, make it certain that Papias did not regard Aristion and the Elder John as belonging to this group. For Lightfoot's proposal (*Essays on Sup. Rel.* p. 150, n. 3) to regard λέγουσιν as 'a historical present introduced for the sake of variety,' is confessedly advanced only to escape the 'chronological difficulty' of supposing two 'disciples of the Lord' still living at the time of Papias' inquiries. It is certainly inadmissible.

The Armenian version makes a natural inference when it forms the second group by reading 'Aristo and John *the Elders*.' But the change is clearly arbitrary. Papias applies the title 'the Elder' only to 'John' to distinguish him from the Apostle. It was doubtless applicable to Aristion as well (Conybeare, *Expositor*, 1893, p. 248, against Hilgenfeld, *Ztschr. f. wissenschaft. Theol.* xxxvii. 1894, p. 626), but was superfluous. The exegesis suggested above (Weiffenbach, Corssen, *et al.*) removes all difficulty by rendering τοὺς τῶν πρ. ἀνέκρινον λόγους as an ellipsis : 'I would inquire the utterances of

the Elders (reporting) what Andrew or Peter . . . had said,' because 'Elder' is then used consistently throughout the paragraph for *traditor* of the post-Apostolic generation (cf. Ac. 15[2, 4, 6] 21[18] and the Heb. וְ), though it is not relied on (as in Arm.) to make the distinction of the Apostolic from the post-Apostolic generation, but only of the two homonymous individuals, John the Apostle and John the Elder.

On this interpretation, Aristion and John were members of the group which perpetuated the traditions of the Apostles (in Palestine ?) until Papias' day (cf. Hegesippus *ap.* Eus. *HE* III. xxxii. 6–8, and Lk 1[1, 2], Ac 1[30] 15[2, 4, 6, 22, 23] 21[18]). But even if this exegesis be rejected, there is no escape from the following alternative : Either the descriptive phrase οἱ τοῦ Κυρίου μαθηταί, appended after 'Aristion and the Elder John' precisely as after the list of Apostles, is textually corrupt (assimilated to the preceding clause) ; or the desi‧‧‧tion is used in a different and very loose significance. On this view the only certainty is that Aristion was living at the time of Papias' inquiries (A.D. 120–140 ?) after 'Apostolic narratives' (ἀποστόλικας διηγήσεις), and in a region whence Papias could obtain them only from 'travellers who came his way.' For Eusebius' statement that 'Papias was himself a hearer, not of the Apostles, but of Aristion and the Elder John,' is made in the interest of his desire to find 'some other John in Asia' besides the Apostle (Zahn, *Forsch.* vi. 117 f.), and is corrected by himself in the next clause : 'At all events he mentions them frequently by name, and sets down their traditions in his writings.'

(3) A second difficulty of more importance for the true reading of Papias and the identification of 'Aristion' than is generally recognized, is the spelling of the name, which Syr. and Arm. give as 'Aristo.' For this spelling, in combination with the omission of the designation 'the disciples of the Lord,' is not only traceable to about A.D. 400 (Syr. is extant in a MS of A.D. 462), but these two main variations are accompanied by minor ones in Syriac, Armenian, and Latin authorities, which form a group in that they manifest a belief in common regarding the personality of Aristo-Aristion which differs from that of the received text of Eusebius.

2. *Text of Eusebius.* — Mommsen (*ZNTW* iii. 1902, p. 156 ff.) regarded this textual evidence as conclusive in conjunction with the admitted 'chronological difficulty.' He would therefore omit the epitheton *from the text of Eusebius.* Corssen (*ib.* iii. p. 242 ff.) rightly criticised Mommsen's proposal to omit, because some designation of this second link in the chain of *traditores* is indispensable in the sense. He thought Papias capable of the colossal anachronism of regarding his own contemporaries as 'disciples of the Lord.' The present writer had argued (*Journ. of Bibl. Lit.* xvii., 1898) for the reading οἱ τούτων μαθηταί (sc. τῶν ἀποστόλων) *as the true text of Papias*, on the internal evidence, and because 'the Elders' of Papias are twice referred to by Irenæus (*Hær.* v. v. 1 and V. xxxvi. 1) as 'the disciples of the Apostles.' The corruption followed by Eusebius (and probably even by Irenæus in this passage, though he transcribed others where 'the Elders' were correctly described as 'disciples of the Apostles'), involves only the change (by assimilation) of three letters, ΟΙΤΟΥ‐(ΤΩΝ)ΜΑΘΗΤΑΙ becoming ΟΙΤΟΥ(Κ͞Υ)ΜΑΘΗΤΑΙ. In the form wherein Edwin Abbott (*Enc. Bibl. s.v.* 'Gospels,' ii. col. 1815, n. 3) adopts the emendation, the change involves but two letters, ΟΙΤΟΥ‐(Τ͞Ω)ΜΑΘΗΤΑΙ becoming ΟΙΤΟΥ(Κ͞Υ)ΜΑΘΗΤΑΙ, as in Jg 4[24] (LXX) ΤΩΝ ΤΙΩΝ B becomes Κ͞Υ ΤΙΩΝ in A. This would largely explain the strange error

of Irenæus in taking Papias to belong to a generation even earlier than Polycarp (' some of them saw
not only John but other Apostles also, and heard
these same things from them and *testify* [present]
these things'). The difficulty experienced by
Eusebius in refuting it could hardly have been
so great if his text of Papias had not the same
corruption.

On this view the variants are of no help to
improve the text of *Eusebius*, which is correct
in the received form (Bacon, art. ' False Witness,'
etc., in *ZNTW* vi. 1905). They have some importance, even if arbitrary, as indicating that in
antiquity also the 'chronological difficulty' was
felt as well as (in Arm.) the incompleteness of
sense produced by simple omission of the descriptive clause and (in Rufinus) the incongruity of
applying to ' Aristion and John the Elder' the
same designation by which the Apostles had just
been distinguished. They would have great importance if it could be made probable that they
rest, directly or indirectly, upon a knowledge of
Papias (or, much less probably, of Aristion-Aristo)
independently of Eusebius.

3. *Origin of Variants.*—' Aristo' is not simply
'the Greek name Aristion badly spelt' (Conybeare, *l.c.* p. 243), nor even should it in strictness
be called ' an equivalent (*gleichbedeutende*) form of
the same proper name' (Hilgenfeld, *Ztschr. f.
wissenschaft. Theol.* 1875 ii. p. 256, 1883 i. p. 13,
1894 p. 626). It is at least the more usual, if not
more correct form, and ' occurs very frequently in
ancient writers. It has been calculated that about
thirty persons of this name may be distinguished.'
But Smith's *Dict. of Greek and Roman Biogr.*, the
authority for the statement just made (i. p. 310),
knows of but two occurrences of the form ' Aristion,' once as the nickname of the adventurer
Athenion (B.C. 87), once as designating a surgeon
of small repute *c.* 150 B.C. In Jewish literature
only the form 'Aristo' occurs (Jos. *Ant.* xix. 353
[ed. Niese]). Pape (*s.v.* Ἀριστίων) adds four others
from Antiph. vi. 12, Æsch. Πλαταικός 3. 162, Plut.
Num. 9, and Pausanias. Patristic literature
knows only the form ' Aristo' in Christian legend
(*Acta Barn.* xiv. ed. Tisch. p. 69, knows a Christian host Aristo in Cyprus; *Acta Petri*, ed. Lipsius,
p. 51, 14–53. 13, one in Puteoli; *Constit. Apost.* vii.
46, ed. Lagarde, p. 228, 21, gives to the first and
third bishops of Smyrna the name Aristo). The
form ' Aristion' is unknown. Eusebius himself
(*HE* iv. 6) draws his account of the devastation
of Judæa in the insurrection against Hadrian (132–
135) from a certain Aristo of Pella. This writer,
accordingly, would be a contemporary of Papias in
position to be referred to as a *traditor* of Apostolic
teaching. To speak of him and 'the Elder John,'
if by the latter were meant John the elder of the
Jerusalem Church (Eus. *HE* iv. 5; cf. Schlatter,
Kirche Jerusalems, 1898, p. 40), whose death is
dated by Epiphanius (*Hær.* lxvi. 20) in the 19th
year of Trajan, as 'disciples of the Apostles,'
would involve no greater looseness or exaggeration
than we should expect in Asia *c.* 150 A.D. But
as Eusebius gives no account of Aristo's writings,
although making it a principal object of his work
to describe early Christian authorities, it is probable that Aristo of Pella was not a Christian, but
a Jewish or (more probably) pagan writer. To
this supposition there is but one serious objection,
for the references of Nicephorus (*HE* iii. 24) and
the *Paschal Chronicle* may admittedly be disregarded as merely reproducing Eusebius. Maximus
Confessor, however, in his scholion on the *Theol.
Mystica* of Areopagiticus (c. i. p. 17, ed. Corder),
undoubtedly refers to the same 'Aristo of Pella'
(Ἀρίστωνι τῷ Πελλαίῳ) as author of the Christian
Dialogue of Jason and Papiscus, basing his state-

ment on 'the sixth book of the *Hypotyposeis* of
Clement of Alexandria,' who seems to have
referred to this 'Jason' as 'mentioned by (*l.
ὃν ἀναγράψαι*) Luke' (Ac 17⁵⁻⁹). Only, while the
Dialogue is known to Celsus (*c.* 167), Origen,
Tertullian, Cyprian, and Jerome, if not to pseudo-
Barnabas and Justin Martyr, and even probably
survives in more or less altered form in the *Altercatio Simonis et Theophili* (*TU* I. iii. p. 115 ff.;
P. Corssen, *Altercatio S. et Th.* 1890), it is known
to none of these as the work of Aristo, nor do
any of the later quotations, references, or other
evidences indicate that the work in question
contained διηγήσεις τῶν τοῦ Κυρίου λόγων (Eus. *l.c.*).
If the name ' Aristo' was ever properly connected
with the *Dialogue*, it circulated only anonymously
after A.D. 200, and without the introductory narrative portion which it may have once possessed.
The late and unsupported statement of Maximus
is therefore much more likely to be due to some
misunderstanding of the *Hypotyposeis*, especially
as we have the explicit quotation of the same
Aristo of Pella by Moses of Chorene (400–450?)
extending to considerable length beyond the portion quoted by Eusebius, accompanied by the
statement that Aristo was secretary of Ardasches,
king of Armenia, when the latter was sent by
Hadrian into Persia (Langlois, *Coll. des. Hist. de
l'Armenie*, i. p. 391 ff., cf. ii. 110, n. 3, and Le
Vaillant de Florival, *Hist. Arm.* ii. 57). Harnack
(*TU* i. 2, p. 125) and Zahn, it is true, reject Moses'
quotation as a fabrication; but it contains nothing 'fabulous,' and is defended with reason by
Hilgenfeld (*Zts. f. w. Th.* 1883, p. 8 ff.). Besides
this, Stephen of Byzantium, who knows of no
Aristo of Pella, mentions an Aristo of Gerasa (less
than 25 miles distant) simply as an ἀστεῖος ῥήτωρ.

Our conclusion must be that, while direct
acquaintance with Papias is quite conceivable, the
variant form 'Aristo' in Syriac and Armenian
sources is best accounted for by a mistaken identification of this Aristo of *HE* iv. 6 with the ' Elder
Aristion' of *HE* iii. 39 and Moses of Chorene.

4. *The Appendix of Mark.*—The most important
addition to our data regarding Aristo was made by
Conybeare's discovery at Eçmiadzin in 1893 of
an Armenian MS. of the Gospels dated A.D. 989,
in which the longer ending of Mark (Mk 16⁹⁻²⁰)
has the separate title in red ink, corresponding to
the other Gospel titles: 'From the Elder Aristo'
(*Expositor*, Oct. 1893, pp. 241–254). This representation, though late, Conybeare takes to be
based on very early authority (*Expositor*, Dec.
1895, pp. 401–421), appealing to the internal evidence of the verses in question. Undeniably the
reference in Mk 16¹⁸ to drinking of poison with
impunity must have literary connexion with
Papias' anecdote regarding Justus Barsabbas (Eus.
HE iii. 39), whatever the source. Conybeare's
citation of a gloss 'against the name Aristion' in
a Bodleian 12th cent. codex of Rufinus' translation
of this passage, which referred to this story of the
poison cup, was even (to the discoverer's eye) a
designation by the unknown glossator of Aristion
as author of this story. But, besides the precariousness of this inference, it would scarcely be possible
to write a gloss 'against the name Aristion'
which would not be equally 'against the name
of the Elder John' immediately adjoining; and as
mediæval legend reported the story of the poison
cup of *John* (*i.e.* the Apostle, identified with the
Elder in the glossator's period) this would seem to
be the more natural reference and meaning of the
gloss.

The evidence connecting the Appendix of Mark
with the name 'Aristo' is thus reduced to the
statement 'inserted by an afterthought' by the
Armenian scribe John, A.D. 989, over Mk 16⁹⁻²⁰,

which he had attached, contrary to Syriac and Armenian tradition, to his text of the Gospel. This, however, is unquestionably important, especially if, as Conybeare maintains, 'it must have stood in the older copy transcribed.' The statement has been generally received at its face value, but with different identifications of 'the Elder Aristo.' Resch ('Ausserkanonische Paralleltexte,' *TU* x. 3, 1894, p. 449; Eng. tr. by Conybeare in *Expos.* 4th ser. x. [1894], pp. 226–232) regards Aristo of Pella as the only personality open to consideration as author of the Appendix. Hilgenfeld (*Ztschr. f. wissenschaft. Theol.* xxxvii. 1894, p. 627) stands apparently alone in identifying the 'Aristion' of Papias with Aristo of Pella, 'a notable contemporary of Papias,' and refusing to the Aristo of the Eçmiadzin codex any significance beyond that of 'some Elder Aristo or other before *c.* 500 A.D., from whom a Syriac MS will have borrowed Mk 16^9-20' (regarded by Hilg. as the original ending). Other critics regard it as 'practically certain' that the Mark-Appendix is really taken from the authority referred to by Papias. Harnack sets the example of peremptorily refusing the suggestion of Resch (*TU* x. 2, p. 453 ff.), that this 'Elder Aristo' may be no other than Aristo of Pella, but gives no other reason than the date (*c.* 140); which, as he rightly says, is irreconcilable with the (disputed) phrase οἱ τοῦ Κυρίου μαθηταί (*Chron.* i. p. 269; on the textual question, see above, § 2). Zahn (*Theol. Literaturbl.* 22nd Dec. 1893 [Eng. tr. by Conybeare in *Expos. l.c.*] regards it as a conclusive objection to Resch's identification that 'Aristo of Pella, who wrote his (?) *Dialogue of Jason and Papiscus* after 135, and perhaps a good deal later, cannot be the author of a section (Mk 16^9-20) which Tatian already read in his Mark at the latest in 170, and which Justin had already known so early as 150, though perhaps not (N.B.) as an integral part of Mark.' We may inquire later what authority the scribe John may have had for his insertion of the title.

5. Internal evidence of the Appendix.—The impression of Westcott and Hort (*Gr. NT*, ii. p. 51), corroborated by Conybeare (*Expositor*, 1893, p. 241 ff.), that the Appendix to Mark is not the original full narrative, but an excerpt, constitutes the next step in the solution of our problem. In particular, a real contribution is made by Zahn (*Gesch. Kan.* ii. App. xiv. 1*a*, and *Forsch.* vi. § 3, p. 219) in the demonstration that Jerome (*c. Pelag.* ii. 15, ed. Vall. ii. 758) had access to it in a fuller, more original form; for he adds after v.^14 'Et illi satisfaciebant dicentes: Sæculum istud iniquitatis et incredulitatis substantia (cod. Vat. 1, 'sub Satana') est, quæ (*l.* qui) non sinit per immundos spiritus veram Dei apprehendi virtutem; idcirco jam nunc revela justitiam tuam' (cf. Ac 1^6). Jerome's source for this material, whose Hebraistic expressions and point of view confirm its authenticity, becomes a question of importance. This source can scarcely have been the *Dialogue of Jason and Papiscus*, whoever its author; for while Jerome was acquainted with this work (*Com.* on Gal 3^13, and *Quæst. Heb. in lib. Gen.*, beginning), and while Celsus, who also used it, twice quotes the substance of Mk 16^9 (*c. Cels.* ii. 55 and 70), the nature of the work, so far as ascertainable, was not such as to admit material of this kind. Besides, we have seen that by all early authorities it is treated as anonymous. Zahn's supposition (*Forsch.* vi. p. 219) has stronger evidence in its favour, and still leaves room to account for the points of contact between the Appendix, the *Dialogue*, Celsus, and Jerome. According to Zahn, 'The ancient book in which Mk 16^14-18 was extant independently of the Second Gospel, and whence it was drawn by transcribers of Mark, can only have been the

work of Papias, in which it was contained as a διήγησις of Aristion (*sic*).' But Jerome, he holds, obtained his version indirectly, through his teacher Apollinaris of Laodicea. This explanation has in its favour certain evidences adduced by Conybeare (*Expositor*, Dec. 1895), to connect the cancellation of Mk 16^9-20 in Armenian MSS with knowledge *derived from Papias* of its true origin. In particular, the same Eçmiadzin codex which attributes the Appendix to 'the Elder Aristo' has a version of the Pericope Adulteræ (Jn 7^53-8^11 TR) independent of the received form, briefer, but with the explanatory comment after Jn 8^6 'To declare their sins; and they were seeing their several sins on the stones.' Echoes of this addition are traceable in Jerome (*Pelag.* ii. 17), in uncial U, and perhaps elsewhere. Moreover, Conybeare's contention that this 'represents the form in which Papias . . . gave the episode,' is strongly supported by Eusebius' statement of what he found *in Papias* ('a story about a woman *accused of many sins* before the Lord, which the *Gospel according to the Hebrews* contains'). This applies to the Eçmiadzin text only ('A certain woman was *taken in sins*, against whom all bore witness,' etc. Cf. Eus. *HE* iii. 39). It has some further support in the express statement of Vartan (14th cent.) that this pericope was derived from Papias, though this may be merely dependent on Eusebius. Conybeare's suggestion that the story will have been one of the 'traditions of the Elder John,' and for this reason have become attached in most texts to the Fourth Gospel, is more probable than Zahn's attributing it to 'Aristion'; but see Blass, *Philology of the Gospels*, p. 156, who thinks it was simply appended at the end of the Gospel canon.

The Eçmiadzin Codex, accordingly, in the two most important questions of Gospel text makes deliberate departure from the received Armenian tradition, in both cases relying on authority which might conceivably go back indirectly to Papias himself. (1) Until about this date (A.D. 989) Armenian tradition followed the Sinaitic, or older Syriac, in omitting the Mark-Appendix. In the 10th cent. it begins to be inserted as in the Curetonian and Tatian, but with various scribal notes of its secondary character. Our codex is simply more exact and specific than others of its time in adding a datum which could never have gone with the Appendix, but must have been derived, like the comment of Vartan on the Pericope Adulteræ, from comparison of Eusebius, which in the Arm. spells the name 'Aristo' and expressly designates him as 'Elder.' (2) It also goes beyond current Armenian tradition regarding Jn 8^1-11. Instead of attaching the story after Lk 21^36, as the *Gosp. acc. to the Hebrews* probably suggested, it adopts the position usually assigned it after Jn 7^52, with the marginal scholion in red ink τῆς μοιχαλίδος, and an expurgated and embellished text, which Eusebius enables us to identify as that of Papias. To infer from this, however, that the scribe John had actual access to Papias would be rash in the extreme. On the contrary, the evidence is only too convincing that his title is based simply on a comparison of the two Eusebian passages regarding 'Aristo,' with the further statements of his own chief national historian, Moses of Chorene (400–450), regarding the Aristo of Pella quoted by Eusebius in *HE* iv. 6.

6. *Aristo of Pella.* — Moses of Chorene (cf. Langlois, *l.c.*), in writing of the death and obsequies of Ardasches, king and national hero of Armenia, transcribes first the quotation of Eusebius from Aristo of Pella regarding Hadrian's devastation of Jerusalem, to explain how Aristo came to be attached to his (Ardasches') person as secretary; for Ardasches had been sent by Hadrian into

Persia. He then continues, quoting professedly from 'the same historian,' an elaborate account of Ardasches' death and obsequies. The connexion of this supplementary quotation, however, is so awkwardly managed as to leave it quite ambiguous to whose person Aristo was attached as secretary. In the text it follows the statement that Hadrian 'established in Jerusalem a community of pagans and Christians whose bishop was Mark. Langlois accordingly makes him secretary of Mark (cf. Eus. *HE* iv. 6). Zahn understands of Hadrian himself (!). The Eçmiadzin scribe seems to have been of Langlois' opinion, and to have drawn the inference that this Aristo, secretary of Mark the bishop of Jerusalem under Hadrian, could be no other than 'the Elder Aristo' of Eus. *HE* iii. 39, as well as the natural completer of 'Mark's' Gospel.

If the attribution of Mk 16⁹⁻²⁰ to 'the Elder Aristo' be dismissed as untrustworthy, our knowledge of the 'Aristion' from whom Papias derived (indirectly) his 'accounts of the Lord's sayings' is reduced to a minimum. Eusebius clearly did not identify him with Aristo of Pella, and from his silence would seem to have known nothing more about him than the statement of Papias that he was an elder, one of the 'disciples of the Apostles'; or, as his text of Papias would seem already to have read (by assimilation to the preceding), 'of the Lord.' Aristo of Pella, Eusebius certainly did not include in his chain ᵇf Christian writers, and save for the late and improbable statement of Maximus Confessor, all that we know of Aristo indicates that he does not belong there. He may, or may not, be the same as 'the cultured rhetorician Aristo of Gerasa.'

7. Conclusions.—The following may be taken as more or less probable conclusions from the foregoing data. (1) In the famous extract of Eusebius from Papias and the adjoining context (*HE* iii. 39), there is no warrant for substituting the reading Ἀρίστων, the common form of the name, for the rarer form Ἀριστίων. The Syriac, followed by Arm., assimilates it to Ἀρίστων (ὁ Πελλαῖος), quoted a few paragraphs farther on by Eusebius himself (*HE* iv. 6), or perhaps merely falls into the ordinary spelling. The reverse process is inconceivable. Of this Aristion, Eusebius seems unable to relate anything beyond what he found in Papias. He certainly did not regard him as identical with Aristo of Pella, whose narrative of the revolt of Bar Cochba was in his hands. Papias, however, knew of Aristion as a *traditor* (orally; cf. οὐ γὰρ ἐκ τῶν βιβλίων, κ.τ.λ.) of the teachings of the Apostles, himself 'one of the disciples of these,' probably in Palestine, since Papias obtained his traditions (Eusebius to the contrary notwithstanding) only from 'those who came his way.' Aristion was still living at the period of Papias' (youthful? καλῶς ἐμνημόνευσα) inquiries.

(2) From this otherwise unknown 'Aristion' of Papias we must sharply distinguish 'Aristo of Pella,' the historian of the revolt of Bar Cochba, quoted by Eusebius. Had this been a Christian writer, it is inexplicable that Eusebius, in spite of the avowed purpose of his book, elsewhere so consistently followed, should have omitted all mention whatsoever of his works. The *Viri Illust.* of Jerome is equally silent.

(3) The process of confusion of Papias' Aristion with Eusebius' Aristo of Pella begins with the Syriac translator (*c.* 400), followed by the Armenian; or, if Maximus Confessor be right in attributing to Clement's *Hypotyposeis* the (conjectural?) assignment of the anonymous *Dialogue of Jason and Papiscus* to this author, perhaps with Clement. The late and unsupported statement of Maximus (*c.* 600), quite in conflict with all that is known either of the *Dialogue* or the writer, is really valueless.

(4) The Armenian historian Moses of Chorene (5th cent. ?) appears really to have known, as he claims, Aristo of Pella. His quotation, where it goes beyond that of Eusebius, shows more and more manifestly the secular, non-Christian writer. His statement that Aristo was secretary of Ardasches, which was so unfortunately ambiguous as to seem to make him secretary of Mark, bishop of Jerusalem, seems to be the starting-point for the last stage of the process.

(5) The scribe 'John' who wrote the Armenian Codex of the Gospels in A.D. 989 (found by Conybeare at Eçmiadzin), departed from previous Armenian tradition by appending, after the row of discs by which he had marked the end of the Gospel of Mark, at Mk 16⁸, the spurious ending vv.⁹⁻²⁰, literally translated from the ordinary Greek text. To justify this unusual insertion, he crowded in 'by an afterthought' between the first line and the row of discs, in small, cramped, red letters, the title 'Of the Elder Aristo.' That he knew the Eusebian passage about Papias' informant is indicated by his use of the title 'Elder' and the form 'Aristo'; for only the *Armenian* Eusebius has these peculiarities. That he should have identified the writer of the Markan appendix with 'the Elder Aristo' is most probably explained by his finding in Moses of Chorene what he took to be the statement that Aristo (of Pella) was secretary of Mark, the bishop of Jerusalem, in the time of Hadrian. Who indeed should venture to complete Mark's unfinished Gospel, if not his secretary ?

B. W. BACON.

ARMOUR.—Lk 11²² speaks of the πανοπλία (ἅπ. λεγ. in Gospels; also Eph 6¹¹·¹³, with which cf. 1 Th 5⁸) of 'the strong man' = the Wicked One —the def. art. ὁ (v.²¹) indicating a single and definite person. The 'armour' is the potent influences at his disposal, called by St. Paul (Eph 6¹¹) 'wiles' and (6¹⁶) 'fiery darts,' by which he deludes and overcomes. Trusting to these, he with his possessions is 'at peace' until 'the stronger than he' (ἰσχυρότερος αὐτοῦ [cf. Lk 3¹⁶]) comes on the scene, when the armour is taken away and he is spoiled of his possessions.

The passage has a soteriological and an eschatological bearing. (1) It points to the power of Christ as able to dislodge evil passions and habits from the heart (cf. Mt 10²⁸ *et pass.*). He is 'stronger' than 'the strong man,' and has 'power to heal' (Lk 5¹⁷). He thus fulfils the prophecy of Is 49²⁴·²⁵ and 53¹², delivering the prey and dividing the spoil. (2) Eschatologically it points to the final victory of good over evil. Cf. Col 2¹⁵, where we have the word ἀπεκδυσάμενος (cf. Lighfoot's note, *in loc.*). The 'stronger' had already come into the 'strong one's' house and had delivered many ; the conflict was continued by Him and against Him till His death, when He overcame him that had the power of death ; the same conflict of evil against good is still continued, His 'spoiling' is going on, He is still taking from His adversary one and another of his possessions, till in the end He shall bind him in the abyss and utterly destroy him (cf. esp. 1 Co 15²⁵⁻²⁷ and Rev 19⁶·¹¹ff.).

For passages descriptive of Roman armour of the time, in Polybius and Josephus, see Hastings' *DB, s.v.* ; cf. also Martial, *Epigr.* ix. 57. With these St. Paul's description of the Christian's armour is in close harmony ; but to find a 'diabolic' significance in the several details is rather fanciful than helpful.

LITERATURE.—Hastings' *DB, s.v.* ; *Ecce Homo*, ch. xiii. ; *Expos. Times*, iii. (1892) p. 349 ff. ; Bunyan, *Holy War*, ch. ii.

R. MACPHERSON.

ARMY.—'Armies' (στρατεύματα) are mentioned by Jesus as the natural instruments of discipline at the command of an Eastern king (Mt 22⁷). He also foretells (Lk 21[20]) the day when 'Jerusalem shall be compassed with armies' (στρατόπεδα). Otherwise there is little allusion to armies in the Gospels, and comparatively small use is made of lessons or figures drawn from military life. The Roman soldier, the legionary, did not loom very large in Palestine. When the Church spreads into the Province Asia, to Rome and Corinth, the impression of the army of Rome is much stronger both in the incidents of the Acts and in the figurative allusions of the Epistles.

John the Baptist found soldiers (see art. SOLDIER) among the crowds who came to him to be baptized (Lk 3[14]); and the most remarkable bond of union between the military character and the character conformed to God, that of discipline and orderly subordination, was suggested to our Lord by the conduct of a centurion (Lk 7[8]).

M. R. NEWBOLT.

ARNI.—An ancestor of Jesus, according to the genealogy given by St. Luke (3[33], AV *Aram*). In Mt 1[3f.] he is called *Ram* (AV *Aram*).

ARPHAXAD.—The spelling (in both AV and RV of Lk 3[36]) of the OT name which appears more correctly in the RV of OT as *Arpachshad*.

ARREST (Jn 18[2-11] = Mt 26[47-56] = Mk 14[43-52] = Lk 22[47-53]). — When Judas, withdrawing from the Supper, betook himself to the high priests and informed them that he was ready to implement his agreement (see BETRAYAL), their simplest way would have been to accompany him back to the upper room and there arrest Jesus. It was, however, impossible for them to proceed thus summarily. They had, indeed, the officers of the temple at their command (cf. Jn 7[32]); but these were insufficient, since the Law forbade them to go armed on the Passover day,[*] and, though Jesus and the Eleven were defenceless, He was the popular hero, and, should an alarm be raised, the multitude would be aroused and would come to the rescue. Moreover, had they taken such a step on their own authority, they would have offended the procurator, Pontius Pilate, who was ever jealous for the maintenance of order, especially at the festal seasons; and it was of the utmost moment that they should secure his sympathy and co-operation. Accordingly, though doubtless impatient of the delay, they first of all appealed to him and obtained from him a detachment of soldiers from Fort Antonia, under the command of a tribune.

The Roman garrison at Jerusalem consisted of a single cohort (σπεῖρα), i.e. 500 men (cf. Schürer, *HJP* I. ii. p. 55). λαβὼν τὴν σπεῖραν (Jn 18[3]) does not, of course, imply that the entire cohort was despatched on the errand. Cf. such phrases as 'call out the military,' 'summon the police.'

Ere all was arranged several hours had elapsed. Jesus had quitted the upper room and the city, but the traitor knew whither He had gone, and led the way to the garden on Mount Olivet, where each night during the Passion-week the Master had bivouacked with the Twelve in the open (Lk 22[39]). It was a motley band that followed Judas. The soldiers would march in order, but the temple-servants, armed with cudgels and carrying lamps and torches, gave it the appearance of a mere rabble (cf. Mt 26[47] = Mk 14[43] = Lk 22[47]). And with the rest, forgetting their dignity in their eagerness to witness the success of their machinations, went some of the high priests, the temple-captains,[†] and the elders.

---

[*] Mishna, *Shabb.* vi. 4: 'No one shall go out with sword or bow, with shield or sling or lance. But if he go out, he shall be guilty of sin.'

[†] Lk 22[4.52] στρατηγοὶ τοῦ ἱεροῦ, the סְגָנִים, officials next in dignity to the priests, charged with the preservation of order in the temple. Cf. Schürer, *HJP* II. i. p. 257 ff.

When he had guided the band to the garden, Judas doubtless would fain have kept in the background, but he was doomed to drink his cup of degradation to the dregs. It was the business of the soldiers to make the arrest, but they did not know Jesus, and, seeing not one man but twelve, they were at a loss which was He. It was necessary that Judas should come forward and resolve their perplexity. Casting shame to the winds, he gave them a sign: 'The one whom I shall kiss is he. Take him.' Then he advanced and, greeting Jesus with feigned reverence: 'Hail, Rabbi!' kissed Him effusively.[*] It was the climax of his villainy, and Jesus repulsed him with a stinging sentence. 'Comrade!' He cried, in that one word summing up the traitor's baseness; 'to thine errand.'[†] Brushing the traitor aside, He stepped forward and demanded of the soldiers: 'Whom are ye seeking?' 'Jesus the Nazarene,' they faltered. 'I am he,' He answered, making perhaps to advance towards them and surrender Himself; and, overawed by His tone and bearing, they retreated and fell on the ground.

'Unless,' says St. Jerome,[‡] 'He had had even in His countenance something sidereal, the Apostles would never have followed Him at once, nor would those who had come to arrest Him have fallen to the ground.' It is, however, unnecessary to assume a miracle. Cf. the consternation of the mercenary soldier who came, sword in hand, to kill C. Marius at Minturnæ. 'The chamber in which he happened to be lying having no very bright light but being gloomy, it is said that the eyes of Marius appeared to dart a great flame on the soldier, and a loud voice came from the old man: "Darest thou, fellow, to slay C. Marius?" So the barbarian immediately rushed out, crying: "I cannot kill C. Marius!"'[§] It is related of John Bunyan that once, as he was preaching, a justice came with several constables to arrest him. 'The justice commanded him to come down from his stand, but he mildly told he was about his Master's business, and must rather obey His voice than that of man. Then a constable was ordered to fetch him down; who coming up, and taking hold of his coat, no sooner did Mr. Bunyan fix his eyes stedfastly upon him, having his Bible then open in his hand, but the man let go, looked pale and retired; upon which said he to his auditors, "See how this man trembleth at the word of God!"' And John Wesley was once assailed by a gang of ruffians. 'Which is he? which is he?' they cried, not recognizing him in the press. 'I am he,' said Wesley, confronting them fearlessly; and they fell back and let him go unmolested.

Jesus reiterated His question: 'Whom are ye seeking?' and, when they answered again: 'Jesus the Nazarene,' He once more gave Himself up to arrest, adding an intercession for the Eleven: 'If ye are seeking *me*, let these men go their way.' Recovering themselves, the soldiers seized Him, and, as they were proceeding to bind Him, the more roughly perhaps that they were ashamed of their weakness, the indignation of the disciples mastered their alarm, and Peter, with the courage of despair, drew a sword which he carried under his cloak‖ and, assailing a slave of the high priest named Malchus, cut off his right ear. An uproar ensued, and the disciples must have paid the penalty of the rash act had not Jesus intervened. Working His hands free from the cords and craving a brief release: 'Let me go—just thus far,' He touched the wounded ear and healed it.¶ The miracle occasioned a diversion; and, while his mates were crowding about Malchus, Jesus reasoned with His excited followers. 'Put the sword into its sheath,' He commanded Peter. 'The cup which my Father hath given me, shall I not drink it? Dost thou suppose that I cannot appeal to my

---

[*] Mt 26[48-49] = Mk 14[44-45] φιλήσω, κατεφίλησεν. Cf. Lk 7[38. 45].

[†] Euth. Zig. τὸ δὲ ἐφ' ᾧ (Tisch., WH ἐφ' ὅ) πάρει οὐκ ἐρωτηματικῶς ἀναγνωστέον· ἐγίνωσκε γὰρ ἐφ' ᾧ παρεγίνετο· ἀλλ' ἀποφαντικῶς.

[‡] *Ad Principiam Explan. Psalm.* xliv.

[§] Plut. *C. Mar.* § 39.

‖ Cf. Lk 22[38]. Chrysostom thinks that these μάχαιραι were the knives (μάχαιρα may mean either *sword* or *knife*) which Peter and John (cf. Lk 22[8]) had used in slaying and dressing the Paschal lamb. It evinces their sense of impending peril that they carried the μάχαιραι despite the legal prohibition.

¶ This miracle is recorded by Luke alone, but the immunity of Peter from instant vengeance is inexplicable without it.

Father, and he will even now send to my support more than twelve legions of angels (*i.e.* one for Himself and one for each of the Eleven)? How then are the scriptures to be fulfilled that even thus it must come to pass?' St. Chrysostom [*] finds here an allusion to the destruction of Sennacherib's army (2 K 19[35]): If a single angel smote that host of 185,000 armed men, what could this rabble do against 72,000 angels?

Anxious to avert attention still further from the Eleven, Jesus addressed Himself to the Jewish rulers who with their officers had accompanied the soldiers. 'As though against a brigand,' He said scornfully, 'have ye come forth with swords and cudgels? Daily in the temple I was wont to sit teaching, and ye did not arrest me.' What had kept them from arresting Him in the temple-court? It was fear of the multitude (cf. Mt 26[3-5] = Mk 14[1-2] = Lk 22[1-2]). And they were cowards still, coming forth with an armed band against a defenceless man. It was a stroke of biting sarcasm, and they felt the sting of it. Apparently it provoked them to violence. At all events the Eleven were at that moment stricken with sudden panic, and 'all forsook him and fled.'

They made good their escape, but the infuriated rulers [†] laid hands on one who, though not a follower of Jesus, was evidently a friend and sympathizer. St. Mark alone has recorded the incident. A solitary figure (εἶς τις) strangely attired had been hovering near during the *rencontre*—'a young man arrayed in a linen sheet [‡] over his undress.' When the Eleven took to flight the rulers laid hold on him; and, dropping his garment, he left it in their grasp and escaped undressed. [§]

Who was he? and why should the Evangelist have recorded an incident which seems merely to introduce an incongruous element of comedy into the tragic narrative? Of all the conjectures which have been offered, [‖] the most reasonable seems to be that he was St. Mark himself (Olshaus., Godet). The conjecture is of recent date, but long ago it was alleged that he was from the house where Jesus had eaten the Passover (Euth. Zig., Theophyl.); and it may well have been, as Ewald suggests, the house of Mary, that widow lady who resided in Jerusalem with her son John Mark, and showed hospitality to the Apostles in after days (Ac 12[12]). Probably Mark had gone to rest that evening after the celebration of the Passover by his household, and, with a foreboding of trouble, had lain awake. He had heard Jesus and the Eleven descend after midnight from the upper room and quit the house, and, hastily rising and wrapping his sheet about him, had anxiously followed after them and witnessed all that passed in Gethsemane. And it may be that the incident was less trivial than it appears. In early days St. Mark bore a singular epithet. He was styled 'the stump-fingered,' [¶] and in the absence of any reasonable explanation of the epithet it may, perhaps, be conjectured that during the scuffle in Gethsemane his finger had been mutilated by the slash of a sword (see *Expos.* 1st ser. i. [1875] pp. 436–446).

DAVID SMITH.

ART.—There has been in Christian history no antagonism between religion and art as such; though there have been abuses of particular forms of art, and consequent reactions against those abuses. The NT affords little guidance, for it is not concerned with the subject. It is the revelation of a Person, not of a code of rules. It deals with fundamental spiritual facts, and it was not within the scope of the writers of its books to supply disquisitions on art or philosophy or science. Such problems were left to be settled from age to age

[*] *In Matth.* lxxxv.
[†] Mk 14[51] οἱ νεανίσκοι om. Tisch., WH.
[‡] The σινδών was a bed-sheet. Cf. Eus. *HE* vi. 40: μένων ἐπὶ τῆς εὐνῆς, ἧς ἤμην γυμνός, ἐν τῷ λινῷ ἐσθήματι, where Heinichen, comparing our passage, comments: 'ἐν τῷ λινῷ ἐσθήματι idem est quod alias vocatur σινδών.'
[§] γυμνός, not absolutely *naked.* Cf. Jn 21[7].
[‖] *John,* who recovered from his panic and followed Jesus to the high priest's palace (Gregory, *Moral.* xiv. 23). *James, the Lord's brother,* who, according to Eus. *HE* ii. 23, always after his conversion wore linen garments (Epiphan., Theophyl.). See Petavel in *Expositor,* March 1891.
[¶] Hippol. *Philosoph.* vii. 30: οὔτε Παῦλος ὁ ἀπόστολος οὔτε Μάρκος ὁ κολοβοδάκτυλος.

by the spiritual instinct of a Church, to which Christ promised the abiding presence of the Spirit: the NT has no more to say about art than it has to say about economics or natural science, and therefore it neither praises any of these things nor condemns them; it is concerned with that which underlies them all.

The NT is neutral also in regard to the use of art in the worship of the Temple. The Jews were not an inartistic nation, though they had not the genius for art of some other races: they had music, poetry, sculpture, architecture, and the usual minor arts of their time; and, though in sculpture they were under strict regulations for the prevention of idolatry, this did not prevent them from using graven images within the sanctuary itself, while in the ornaments of their worship they had been guided by elaborate regulations as to form and colour and symbolism. Christianity grew up in these surroundings, and did not find any fault with them. Our Lord condemned the ethical formalism of current religion, but not its art: He condemned the trafficking in the Temple, but not its beauty. Nor did His disciples have anything to say against the art of the pagan cities where they went, though they had much to say about the wickedness: they are silent on the subject, except for a few illustrations from engraving and painting in He 1[3] 8[5] and 10[1]. It is in the Apocalypse alone that we have any setting forth of visible beauty; and here there is a clearer recognition of the principle of art, because nothing else could express what the writer had to show forth. It is not enough to say that the imagery of the Apocalypse is merely symbolic: all religious art is symbolic. St. John envelops his conception of the highest form of being in an atmosphere of glowing beauty; and a Church which accepted his teaching could hardly mistrust material beauty as a handmaid of religion. It is not therefore to be wondered at that Christian worship, as we know of it after the Peace of the Church, was much influenced by the descriptions of the heavenly worship in the Apocalypse (see, *e.g.*, the recently discovered *Testament of our Lord,* A.D. 350).

But, if we would find in the NT the final argument in favour of art, we must turn, as Westcott says in his great essay on the subject, to the central message of Christianity—*the Word became flesh.* Here is the justification and the sanctification of all that is truly human: Christianity embraces all life, and 'the inspiration of the new birth extends to every human interest and faculty.' The old conflict between the spiritual and the material is reconciled by the Incarnation; for by it the visible became the sacrament, or outward sign, of that which is inward and spiritual. Thus, like the Incarnation itself, 'Christian art embodies the twofold conception of the spiritual destiny of the visible, and of a spiritual revelation through the visible. The central fact of the Christian faith gives a solid unity to both truths.' The office of art, Westcott continues, is 'to present the truth of things under the aspect of beauty': the effect of Christianity upon art is that of 'a new birth, a transfiguration of all human powers by the revelation of their divine connexions and destiny'; and thus 'Christian art is the interpretation of beauty in life under the light of the Incarnation.' Thus the Christian artist is a teacher, his art is ministerial, and when it appears to be an end in itself idolatry has begun; his true function is both to interpret the world as God has made it in its beauty, in the light of a deeper understanding of its meaning, and also to embody to men his own visions of the truth—'he is not a mirror but a prophet,' and love is his guide. Thus he is led 'through the most patient and reverent regard of phenomena to the contemplation of the eternal'; for 'the beauty which is the aim of Christian art is referred to a Divine ideal. It is not "of the world," as finding its source or its final measure there, but "of the Father," as corresponding to an unseen truth. The visible to the Christian eye is in every part a revelation of the invisible.'

Westcott, however, assumes an 'antagonism of early Christians to contemporary art,' and points to the central message of Christianity as establishing a reconciliation between supposed 'elements of contrast.' Was there, we must ask any such antagonism as a matter of history? When Westcott wrote, Christian archæology was still in its infancy; much that we now have was still undiscovered, and that which was known was uncertain in date and inaccurately reproduced; notions still held the field which have since been disproved, as, for instance, that which credits the early Church with the wanton destruction of pagan monuments, when, as a matter of fact, the ancient Roman temples were, after the triumph of Christianity, long kept in repair at the expense of the Christian State, as the chief glory of the city.

The question is of great importance, for modern writers frequently condemn Christianity because of its supposed depreciation of humanity. Thus the natural scientist Metchnikoff — writing, as people do, about matters which are outside his province — declares in *The Nature of Man* that Christianity lowered our conception of human nature, and gives as evidence this statement :— 'Sculpture, which played so great a part in the ancient world, and which was intimately associated with Greek ideals, began to decline in the Christian era,'—the real truth being, as we shall see, that sculpture had been declining for several generations in pagan hands, and that Christian artists did what they could with the decadent craft.

Now Westcott himself states that 'the literary evidence is extremely scanty' as regards the relation of Christianity to art; and, writing twenty-two years later, we may add that archæological evidence all points in the opposite direction to that which he supposed. The literary evidence, indeed, proves little as to the first two centuries, though recent discoveries have increased our knowledge of the 3rd century.

The usual quotations from the Fathers—such as Westcott gives—are, indeed, 'extremely scanty'; but the one extract which does deal directly and definitely with the subject has been curiously overlooked. It is from Clement of Alexandria in the chapter headed 'Human arts as well as Divine knowledge proceed from God' (*Strom.* i. 4), and is quite final as to Clement's opinion. After pertinently referring to the craftsman Bezalel the son of Uri (Ex 31²⁻⁶), whose 'understanding' was from God, he proceeds—

'For those who practise the common arts are in what pertains to the senses highly gifted: in hearing, he who is commonly called a musician; in touch, he who moulds clay; in voice, the singer; in smell, the perfumer; in sight, the engraver of devices on seals. ... With reason, therefore, the Apostle has called the wisdom of God "manifold," which has manifested its power "in many departments and in many modes" [Eph 3¹⁰, He 1¹]—by art, by knowledge, by faith, by prophecy—for our benefit. "For all wisdom is from the Lord and is with him for ever" [Sir 1¹], as says the Wisdom of Jesus.'

Though less comprehensive than this admirable statement, the passage to which Westcott himself alludes is also extremely interesting. Clement describes a number of subjects commonly engraved upon seals to which Christians could give a Christian meaning (see CHRIST IN ART), whilst he forbids the use of seals which bear idols, swords, bows, and drinking cups—condemning thus, not art, but idolatry, war, and drunkenness (*Pæd.* iii.

3). Origen's answer to Celsus (*c. Cels.* viii. 17–20) is often quoted as denying the use of art. He meets Celsus' charge that 'we shrink from raising altars, statues, and temples,' by saying that Celsus 'does not perceive that we regard the spirit of every good man as an altar,' and that Christ is 'the most excellent image in all creation,' and 'that we do refuse to build lifeless temples to the Giver of all life, let anyone who chooses learn how we are taught that our bodies are the temple of God.' This rhetorical answer cannot be taken as denying the use of art by the African Christians : it is a vindication of the spiritual nature of Christian worship, and the 'lifeless temples' must be referred to paganism, since there was nowhere any shrinking from the erection of church buildings. Origen is not concerned with the question of art : he merely denies 'altars, statues, and temples' in the heathen sense.

Even Tertullian, Montanist though he was, is clear in not condemning artists for practising their art, though he has a good deal to say about their making idols; the artist who makes idols works 'illicitly' like Hermogenes, who 'despises God's law in his painting' (*adv. Hermog.* 1). An artist's profession was full of temptation from heathen patrons : so Tertullian warns them that 'every artificer of an idol is guilty of one and the same crime' as he who worships it (*de Idol.* 3), since to make an idol is to worship it (*ib.* 6); and he advises them to practise their art in other directions—'gild slippers instead of statues'—'We urge men generally to such kinds of handicrafts as do not come in contact with an idol' (*ib.* 8). Elsewhere he gives useful testimony by his incidental mention of Christian art work in the painting of the Good Shepherd and other subjects upon chalices (*de Pudic.* 7 and 10).

This is, in fact, the conclusion to which the literary evidence leads us: the early Christians were told to keep clear of paganism, with which their daily work was often so closely involved, but they were not told to forswear art.

If we wish to find a condemnation of art as such, we must turn not to Christianity, but to pre-Christian philosophy, and—in spite of all that has been said about the opposition between Hebraism and Hellenism—not to a Jewish but to a Greek writer. **Plato** knew what art was; he belonged to a race with whom art was not a mere incident but a most important part of life; in describing his ideal city he had to deal with the problem of art, and he settled it by excluding the artist altogether. Beginning with dramatic art, he proceeds, towards the end of the *Republic*, with a consistent adherence to principle that is as rare now as it was then, to include every form of art in his condemnation. His reasons are three—The artist creates without knowing or caring what is good or bad, and thus separates himself from morality; he is an imitator of appearances, and therefore a long way off the truth; and art, whether poetry or painting or the drama, excites passions which ought to be curbed. Plato fully recognized that if painting is wrong, poetry must be wrong too; and he decided that poetry also must be excluded from the perfect city. He was right at least in this, that all art must stand or fall together; and in the light of his clear thought it is easy to see that the three movements which have appeared in Christendom—Asceticism, Iconoclasm, and Puritanism—were not really movements against art. The Christian Church never adopted Plato's position : the ascetic precursors of Monasticism came nearest it, but they formulated no principle beyond that of complete renunciation of the world for the benefit of their own souls, and they did little or nothing to check the lavish decoration of churches which characterized their age.

The Iconoclasts of the Byzantine Empire were often great patrons of architecture, poetry, and the minor arts; and, though they carried their special principle down to the forbidding of pictures of sacred subjects even in books, they did not carry it beyond the question of images. The Puritans, being Englishmen, were naturally less logical than the Greek iconoclasts; thus, they accepted Judaism when it forbade images, and ignored it when it commanded ceremonial: in fact, they disliked art in so far as it embodied ideas which were distasteful to them, and no further. Puritanism was a mingling of the two earlier reactions, asceticism and iconoclasm: it can hardly be taken as embodying a principle of opposition to art.

The question is not, then, one between Puritanism and Catholicism, or between Hebraism and Hellenism, but between Platonism and Aristotelianism. For it was Aristotle who answered Plato; and he did so by pointing out that a true philosophy must make the whole of human nature rationally intelligible; for, the Universe being rationally organized, the existence of art proves that it must have a proper function in life. This is surely the philosophy also of the Incarnation: the Word became flesh, and in that the whole of human nature becomes intelligible; it is good in itself, and in its unstained perfection can become a fit manifestation of the Divine.

Sin, indeed, mars this perfection; and while sin remains, asceticism continues to have its function in the world. The love of the beautiful may degenerate into the lust of the eye, because the inward and spiritual is forgotten, and the sacramentalism of art is lost. It may then become necessary to pluck out the eye that sees, or to cut off the fashioning hand, in order to enter into life; but it is a choice of evils,—the man escapes Gehenna, but he enters into life 'maimed.'

So, though it is better to be maimed than to be lost, better to hate art than to make it a god, hiding the eternal which it should reveal, better, indeed, to break images than to worship them; yet the fulness of truth lies not in the severance, but in the union of the good and the beautiful. They have often appeared as rival tendencies in history. Religious men have often been narrow and inhuman, artists have often been weak in will and the creatures of their emotions, as Aristotle found them; but the one-sidedness of men serves only to illustrate the manysidedness of truth. Christendom through all her struggles has loved righteousness, and has not forgotten to love art also. She has her fasts, but she has also her feasts.

It is certain as a historic fact that the early Church had no suspicion of art, but accepted without scruple the decorative motives and forms of the classical civilization to which, apart from religion and ethics, she belonged, eliminating only such themes as bore an idolatrous or immoral meaning. Limited at first in her resources, she did not for a while attain to magnificence; but all the evidence of archæology, which is yearly accumulating, shows that she made use of art so far as she had opportunity. Nor did she try to create an art of her own; she used the art as she used the languages of the empire. The art of the early Church is not Christian in its form, but in its inspiration.

Most of the earliest Christian art that has been discovered is in the Catacombs of Rome. This does not mean, as Westcott supposes, that the Church of Italy was artistic while the rest of the Church was not; still less does it show, as is popularly imagined, that the Roman Christians used the Catacombs as their churches and permanent hiding-places. The art of the Catacombs has survived because it has been preserved under-ground; but it was not the only art, and the early Christians worshipped above ground like everybody else, except in the case of occasional services for the departed. But hardly anything has survived of the art above ground: in literature we have only hints that stir but do not satisfy the imagination,—as when Eusebius tells us (*HE* viii. 12) that in times of persecution the churches were pulled down (as by Diocletian in 302), and mentions that the church at Nicomedia, destroyed in 303, was of great size and importance (*de Mort. Pers.* 12, 'fanum illud editissimum'). At a time when not the buildings only, but the very books of the Christians were destroyed, it was in the burial-places—immune by Roman law from molestation, and hidden away from the ravages of sun and air, and of barbarians ancient and modern—that works of art survived; and to the Catacombs we must turn for our evidence. There is every reason to suppose that the art which we find there is typical of that of the whole Church; for (1) the Christian Churches were bound together by remarkably close ties in the first three centuries; (2) the symbolism of the Catacombs is shown by the early literature to have been that of the rest of the Church also; and (3) there was a uniformity of art throughout the empire, of which Rome was the cosmopolitan centre,—an Italian city indeed in which most of the art was executed by Greeks.

Enough description for our present purpose of the **paintings** in the Catacombs will be found in the article on CHRIST IN ART. To that article, which deals with Christian art on its most important side (the Christological), reference may also be made for illustrations from the other arts which are here more briefly mentioned. It will suffice here to make a few general statements. (1) Pictorial art is found in the earliest catacombs, belonging to a period before the end of the 1st cent., as well as in those of later date; (2) the first Christians must have been fond of art to use it so freely in the dark: the *cubicula* of the Catacombs, which were only visited occasionally, and where nothing could be painted or seen except by lamp-light, must represent art at its minimum. Yet that art is both good and abundant. (3) Among the very earliest examples, figures are included as well as merely decorative subjects of animals, flowers, etc. (4) The art is the highly developed art of the Roman Empire, which was at its height in the 1st and 2nd centuries, and declined after the reign of Hadrian. (5) The art of the Catacombs is therefore Christian only in that it generally represents Christian subjects, and that it acquires almost at once a certain marked character of mystic symbolism which is peculiar to the ages of persecution. Certainly there is something about this early painting which at once distinguishes it as Christian. Its authors were intent on expressing ideas,—not the technical theology of an ecclesiastical system, but the faith and hope of ordinary Christian people,—therefore they use suggestion and symbol, and are fond of a conventional treatment even of Scripture subjects, and thus their work is marked by a quiet reserve that excludes all reference to the sufferings and death of the martyrs, and dwells upon the life and power of Christ, not upon His death and passion. This art is marked by simplicity, happiness, and peace; it deals only with such OT and NT and other subjects as could bear a mystical interpretation in connexion with the deliverance and happiness of the departed through the power of Christ and the grace of the sacraments. It is sometimes of a high technical order and of great beauty, though the difficulties of its execution led to its being often sketchy in character. Born full-grown in the 1st cent., it passed in the 2nd into this second mystical period, declining after the 2nd cent. gradually in technique, as the pagan art was declining. After the Peace of the Church in the 4th cent. it passes into its third period, when its symbolism is more obvious, more didactic and dogmatic.

Sculpture naturally does not appear so early as painting. The dark catacombs were no place for its display, though in them it has its beginnings in the *graffiti* or incised designs which are common on the tombs. These were easily to be seen, and could be wrought on the spot, which was an important consideration in days when it was difficult to order Christian sculpture from pagan shops. It would be an easier matter to have executed in the public studios a subject that could bear a pagan interpretation; and thus it is that we do find a statue of the Good Shepherd which probably belongs to the 3rd cent., though one would naturally expect Christians who lived in pagan times to be shy of the use of statuary. In the 4th cent. the growing custom of burial above ground, coupled with the prosperity of the Church, encouraged the use of sculptured sarcophagi (cf. CHRIST IN ART). Excellent carved ivories are also found at this period, but art had been steadily declining since Hadrian's time, and after the 6th cent. no good sculpture of any sort is found. There was no opposition to it in the West, but in the East the Iconoclastic controversy (716–867) led to the wholesale destruction of 'images,' whether painted or carved; and though it ended in the restoration of pictures, there was a tacit compromise by which statues were not restored, in spite of the decision in favour of 'images' by the Second Council of Nicæa (787). This renunciation of statuary in the Eastern Church grew into a passionate aversion to its use inside a place of worship,—an aversion which continues still.

Among the **minor arts** may be mentioned that of *gold-glass*, which commenced early in the 3rd cent., and has preserved for us many Christian pictures and symbols. Miniature illustration came into general use in the 4th cent. in MSS of books of the Bible; it was not decorative like that of the Middle Ages; the miniatures were separated from the text, and were devoted to giving pictures of the Scripture events described, much as in present-day book illustration. The handicrafts of pottery, metal, and jewel work, etc., gradually adopted Christian symbolism,—thus it first appears on lamps in the 3rd century. The magnificence of church plate after the Peace of the Church almost passes belief. An early instance is given in the *Pilgrimage of Sylvia* (A.D. 385), which was discovered in 1888.

'It is needless,' she says, describing her experiences in Syria, 'to write what was the ornamenting on that day of the Church of the Anastasis, or of the cross in Jerusalem or in Bethlehem; for there you would see nothing but gold and gems or silk; for if you see the vefls, they are all of silk, with stripes of gold; if you see the curtains, they are all the same. Every kind of gold and gemmed vessel is used on that day. It is impossible to relate the number and weight of the lights, tapers, and lamps and other utensils. And what shall I say of the adornment of the fabric, which Constantine, with all the power of his kingdom, in the presence of his mother, honoured with gold, mosaic, and precious stones?'

With this may be compared the gifts, recorded in the *Liber Pontificalis*, which Constantine made to certain churches: among them he gave to St. Peter's '3 golden chalices with emeralds and jacinths, each having 45 gems and weighing 12 pounds'; and 'a golden paten with a tower of purest gold, with a dove adorned with emeralds and jacinths, and 215 pearls, weighing 30 pounds'; while to St. John Lateran he gave no fewer than 174 candlesticks and chandeliers of various sorts, as to which Fleury reckons that altogether they furnished 8730 separate lights. These figures

suggest a magnificence of the surroundings of worship that is far removed from the simple two-handled cup of the 2nd cent. fresco of the *Fractio Panis*. None the less, the fact that Constantine's gift was made shows that there was no tradition of dislike to such magnificence. Such descriptions bear out the general impression that the early Church made free use of whatever richness of art her opportunities could provide, though when necessity required she was content, as Jerome says, 'to carry the body of Christ in a basket of osiers and His blood in a cup of glass.'

Mosaic art, of which there are extant such splendid examples in the churches of the Imperial cities, Rome and Ravenna and Constantinople, followed upon architecture, and flourished between the 4th and 7th centuries. Its magnificence and durability make it to us the most characteristic feature of the Christian art of that period. The principal subjects represented are the great figures of Christ enthroned, figures of the Apostles and other saints, apocalyptic and other symbolic subjects, scenes from the Old and New Testaments, and pictures of imperial personages and bishops.

In **architecture** there have been many theories as to the origin of the basilica. It is now very generally agreed that the Christian church is a development of the classical *atrium*, the central colonnaded court of dwelling-houses in the Imperial age. The earliest gatherings for worship took place in the *atrium* of some wealthy convert, and were thus surrounded with all the greater and lesser arts of the period. Now, the Greek and Roman temples were constructed for a worship in which both the altar and the worshippers stood outside. The Christian worship began in the home (Ro 16^5 and perhaps Ac 2^{46}), and the purpose of the earliest churches was to hold a large number of worshippers before the Lord's Table; thus, though the style was that of the age, the manner of its use was different from the first. The basilica is a distinctively Christian building, marked out by its oblong shape, clerestory, colonnaded aisles, and apse. It was probably in process of development in the centuries before the Peace of the Church,—we read, *e.g.*, of church buildings in the newly found *Canons of Hippolytus, c.* 220–250 A.D.,—though no extant edifice is known (unless the startling theory just put forth by Dr. Richter and Mr. C. Taylor in their books on S. Maria Maggiore in Rome comes to be accepted—the theory being that this church and its mosaics belong to the 2nd century). The churches destroyed by Diocletian were rebuilt under Constantine, and it is to the Constantinian period that the earliest surviving basilicas belong, whether in Italy, Syria, or Africa. In the East there was later one marked development, the use of the dome, which culminated under Justinian in St. Sofia, and has continued to be characteristic of the Greek and Russian churches down to our own day. In the West the basilica continued unchanged till the 8th, and in some parts till the 10th cent., when it was modified by the growth of what is called Romanesque architecture, of which Gothic is but a development; but the main features of the basilica—nave, clerestory, aisles, projecting sanctuary, and often transepts—remain unchanged to-day.

The decline of Western art in what are called the Dark Ages is often attributed to Christianity and its supposed hatred of human nature. The truth is, that while Byzantium maintained a high culture far better and longer than used to be supposed, the whole Roman civilization well-nigh disappeared under the invasions of the northern races; these peoples were converted and gradually civilized by Christianity, and, as their civilization grew up, their art developed from the barbaric stage till it culminated in the perfection of Gothic. That art in its development had the limitations of the young races; it developed more rapidly in architecture and architectural carving than in painting or statuary; but all this has nothing to do with Christianity, as writers like Taine suppose—'If one considers the stained glass windows, or the windows in the cathedrals, or the rude paintings, it appears as if the human race had become degenerate, and its blood had been impoverished: pale saints, distorted martyrs, hermits withered and unsubstantial,' etc. (*Phil. de l'Art*, 88, 352, 4th ed.). Passages like this are beside the mark; the art of the Middle Ages was full-blooded enough, and was admirable even in its rude beginnings, when it had not learnt the most difficult of lessons — the representation of the human form. In architecture and the kindred arts the Middle Ages brought a new revelation of beauty into the world,—an art that stands alone, not only for its lofty spirituality and technical excellence, but also for its homely democratic humanity.

Beyond this it is not necessary to go, since we are not dealing with the history of art in general, but only with the relation between it and Christianity. It has been necessary to sketch the beginnings because of the widespread idea that Christianity started with an aversion to the fine arts, and was reconciled to them only as worldliness increased upon her. Modern archæology has proved this idea to be mistaken; and, having pointed out what is now known as to the early use of art by the Church, we need not follow the subsequent history of painting and sculpture, of architecture and the handicrafts, in their developments and decadences, except to say that, though art in the Christian era has been sometimes rude and sometimes pagan, it has at its best—when most perfect in technique and most imbued with spiritual purpose—excelled all else that the world has been able to produce: even the perfect statuary of Greece was outrivalled by such an artist as Michael Angelo, who reveals not only the body but the soul within the body also. The best Christian art is better than anything that has gone before, because it has more to express.

Christendom, then, began its career in natural association with art; and art is Christian, not by reason of any peculiarity of style, but when it is informed by the Christian ideal. Art is not an end in itself, but a language; the greatest artificers, like the greatest writers, are those who have the greatest things to say, and the fineness of any art is, as Ruskin says, 'an index of the moral purity and majesty of the emotion it expresses.' Pagan reaction has, indeed, more than once taken refuge in art, as it has also taken refuge in science; but the fault does not lie in either. There must always be reaction when the Church refuses to recognize the truth of science or the seriousness of art. And art is serious, for it is one of man's primal gifts, and, like nature, one of his most constant educators. Art is necessary because, in Ruskin's words, 'life without industry is guilt, and industry without art is brutality'; and though, as he found, religious men in his time despised art, they despised it at the peril of religion. He was himself the greatest exponent of the religious mission of art and of its moral value. And his conclusion was that the root of all good art lies in 'the two essential instincts of humanity, the love of order and the love of kindness,' the one associated with righteousness, the other with charity. The 'love of beauty,' he proceeds, 'is an essential part of all healthy human nature, and though it can long coexist with states of life in many other respects unvirtuous, it is itself wholly good,—the direct ad-

versary of envy, avarice, mean worldly care, and especially of cruelty. It entirely perishes when these are wilfully indulged.' If this be so, it is indeed of the gospel, and excellent in so far as it is close to the spirit of Christ. If this be so,—and no man had a better right to make bold generalizations on the subject than Ruskin,—artists and preachers can agree in his conclusion that the great arts 'have had, and can have, but three principal directions of purpose: first, that of enforcing the religion of men; secondly, that of perfecting their ethical state; thirdly, that of doing them material service.'

LITERATURE.—The same authorities mainly as for the article on CHRIST IN ART. Special use has been made in the present article of: W. Lowrie's *Christian Art and Archæology* (1901); Westcott's essay on 'The Relation of Christianity to Art' in his *Commentary on the Epistles of St. John* (1883); A. J. Maclean's *Recent Discoveries Illustrating Early Christian Life and Worship* (1904); an article on 'Art and Puritanism' by J. W. Mackail in *Saint George*, vol. vii. (1904); while out of the multitude of Ruskin's works the concluding extract is taken from his *Lectures on Art* (1887). P. DEARMER.

ASA.—A king of Judah (c. 918–878 B.C.), named in our Lord's genealogy, Mt 1⁷ᶠ·.

ASCENSION.—The Ascension is the name applied to that event in which the Risen Christ finally parted from His disciples and passed into the heavens. The traditional view is based on the passage Ac 1¹·¹², supported by Mk 16¹⁹, Lk 24⁴⁹·⁵¹ (which narrate the event), Jn 6⁶² 20¹⁷ (which look forward to it), Eph 4⁸·¹⁰, 1 Ti 3¹⁶, 1 P 3²², He 4¹⁴ (which imply it). To the foregoing list many would add references of Christ to His departure (from the context not identifiable with His death), Mt 9¹⁵ 26¹¹· ²⁹· ⁶⁴, Jn 7³³ 14–16; and allusions in Acts, Epistles, Revelation, to Christ being 'seated at the right hand of God' (Ac 2³³ 3²¹ 5³¹ 7⁵⁶ 13³⁵·³⁷, Ph 2⁹, He 1³ 2⁹ 12², Rev 1¹³ 5⁶ etc.). The details are drawn from Ac 1: the scene, the Mt. of Olives; the time, forty days after the Resurrection; the occasion, a conversation concerning the Kingdom; the act of parting in being taken up; the vanishing in a cloud; the vision of two men in white apparel and their announcement of His coming again: all indicating a bodily disappearance by an upward movement into the sky.

The bodily Ascension is vindicated as possible, as necessary, and as adequately evidenced.

1. *Possibility.*—The wonderfulness of the event is not denied, but its acceptance is urged by a varied appeal. Sometimes the reference is to the Divine power operating in the fulfilment of the Divine purpose of salvation. The Ascension is then regarded as part and parcel of the redemptive scheme, and not more wonderful than the other redemptive facts, *e.g.* Incarnation, Resurrection, etc. Or the reference is to our ignorance of the physical universe and its constitution. 'Miraculous Christianity' does not 'imply an anti-scientific view of the world' (cf. Goldwin Smith, *Guesses at the Riddle of Existence*, p. 165). There is a vast uncomprehended region in nature not yet within the sweep of human faculties, which Science has not fathomed and to whose existence she has become recently profoundly sensitive. The world, as science interprets its phenomena, is not the complete world which may hold potentialities permissive of such an event as the Ascension. Or, again, the reference may be to our ignorance of the nature of the ascending body. Grant the cogency of the scientific objection to a body having gravity and normal dimensions rising in upward flight to a distance, is it certain that such was the body of Christ? There are hints which furnish the opposite suggestion. The only sure statement that may be affirmed with regard to it is that it was the same, yet not the same, as the pre-Resurrection body: it was a body which issued from the sepulchre with identity complete, yet physically changed, existing under new conditions of which we have only the faintest apprehension. Physically, the Ascension meant a complete change of conditions, the passing into a mode of existence having no longer direct physical relations with our ordinary experience, whither we cannot follow by the exercise of our sensitive intelligence, and which in our lack of material for comparison we cannot even imaginatively picture. The conjecture, further, is hazarded that if the process of spiritualizing the body was at the time of the Ascension so complete as to render it invisible to ordinary sense, the process of preparing the spiritual perception of the disciples was by that time also complete, so that what was hidden from others was manifested to them. Recent research also into psychical activities, both conscious and sub-conscious, has brought the question into renewed prominence especially among scientific men, and that in no spirit of hostility to the traditional view.

2. *Necessity.*—The necessity of the Ascension is obvious. It was at once the natural consequence of all that preceded and the only sufficient cause of the marvellous experiences that followed. The *risen state* and the forty days demanded its occurrence. Apart from any explicit teaching on the subject during those days, the situation of itself must have provoked reflection and pointed to an exit from earthly scenes not by way of mortal dissolution but rather of glorification. The interval is clearly transitory. The relationship between Jesus and the disciples evinces a certain reserve on His side, a certain surprise and perplexity on theirs. It partakes in all the mystery that hangs over the world of spirits in general, as well as in that pertaining specially to the borderland of that world, the region where thought and matter meet. His appearances are only occasional. His movements are mysterious. His life is not of the bodily order. Whether the theory of progressive spiritualizing be tenable or not,—the conception is very obscure, —the facts of physical transformation and spiritual enhancement are indubitable. The disciples are convinced by the empty tomb and the apparitional body that He had not seen corruption in the grave, yet do not always recognize Him as He appears. He is no longer of them. Their mind must have been challenged again and again to inquire, What next? It was neither fitting that He should die again, nor that He should remain on the earth in His then state: death He had already sounded and survived, while for His departure He had aforetime prepared them. Further, His *Person* claimed it. His self-consciousness during the earthly ministry, and the teaching it prompted; the definite impression of these on the minds of the disciples leading to the expectation of further developments of His Being; as well as the most distinct intimations of the preparatory character of His present activity, the specialty of His saving mission, the uniqueness of His relation to the Father and heaven,—all combined in an impressive witness to the assurance that not this world but the heavenly life was His proper and rightful sphere, and that until He had attained to it He was not in possession of His own, the glory He had with the Father before the world was, which was as yet for the most part hid, revealing itself only in hints, and which He was bound to reassume, accentuated, so to speak, with all that virtue He had won in His human nature for bestowal on men. In His human life He had been the subject of development in time,—a development, it is true, not from evil or imperfection to the good and perfect, but from strength to strength, involving living growth, a process pre-

sumably capable of reaching its end. Underlying that process lay His Divine Being, in its inherent power incapable of growth, no attainment but original endowment. The return to the Father in the Ascension-act marked the perfection of the human process in harmonious realization within the Divine powers of His Person.

Still further, the *work* of Christ remained incomplete without the Ascension. It has been objected against His teaching that it is incomplete as a system and incoherent in its details. There is ground for the complaint. His ministry bears traces throughout of its preparatory character. His teaching is at times parabolic, His acts often typical, His method as much an effort to create a new power of insight as to offer a new sum of truths. He holds out hopes of a more immediate personal, if spiritual, direction, under the force of which a richer fulness of His truth shall be gained. He anticipates future acts of His work which are not simply symbolic of His utterances, but necessary to their interpretation. A future is always with Him: separate from the present in its conditions and gifts and in the nature of His agency, so separate as justly to be entitled to the name of a new 'dispensation.' The Ascension marks the transition. It has no substantial independence. It closes the public ministry; it opens the continuation of that ministry in the new age of the Spirit. It announces that the great human facts necessary to redemption are finished, and that the results are henceforth to be increasingly realized. His saving energies are consummated in His incarnate and glorified Personality: the departure is necessitated that they may not remain a legacy of dead and inoperative information. For this reason the Ascension, as the passing into exaltation, stands at the beginning of the *fresh spiritual experiences* of the Apostolic age. It explains the extraordinary change in the mind of the Apostles. They felt an intense conviction. Because there had been no loss, their conception of Christ has been cleared, His exaltation seen, His perpetual action promised. Under the new light they proceed to organize the momentous work of the Church. On precisely the same basis they instruct their hearers and develop their doctrine. The centre of the missionary discourses is the Exalted Christ; intimate communion with Him exalted is normative to their thought. That truth fills up their entire consciousness and crushes out every other thought. It forms the firm foundation on which their whole life and mind are built up. They are witnesses to one great fact. The NT documents set forth much in the way of new truths and new ethics, but their distinctive testimony is to a new intense experience, which has altered the entire character of those who share it. That experience is everywhere traced in direct derivation from Christ glorified.

But the Christ glorified is the Jesus of history. The new experience is related to the acts of His life in a vital way. A distinction may be drawn between them, but only as two aspects of one reality, not as two terms, the one of which may be regarded as the mythic symbol of the other. Both terms must be safeguarded. Hence, if the Lord now glorified was once within the conditions of human experience, cognoscible to human faculties, and has passed from them, the question cannot be silenced, *How* did He pass? The essential point is His passage out of those earthly conditions of life within which He had hitherto been known. Must not such passing have been visible? The bodily Ascension is the answer.

3. *Historicity.*—The evidence for the Ascension is direct and indirect. (*a*) The *direct* witness is meagre. There is but one description that may serve as a basis of fact, viz. the narrative in Ac

$1^{1\text{-}12}$. The other passages (Mk 16^{19}, Lk 24^{51}) are under the highest critical suspicion as being not original to their texts. They suffer, moreover, under two further disadvantages: their vagueness, their summary character. They appear to give results, being less accounts of detail than confessions of faith. Their value is similar in character to that of the Epistles; they testify to the existence of a widespread crystallized tradition in the first century. Does the record in Ac $1^{1\text{-}12}$ give more? It belongs to the less authentic of the sources of the author. If the author be St. Luke, he cannot be reckoned an eye-witness; but he may furnish the information of an eye-witness. The narrative bears every trace of careful statement and of non-reflective features. Even if indications of idealization of the past occur in this first part of the book elsewhere, there are none here; the phrasing is simple and matter of fact; there is no sentiment, nor sorrow: only a glad vision evoking worship, challenging thought, inspiring courage. The discrepancies between this account and that in Lk. are probably superficial. Bethany lay on the further or eastern slope of the Mt. of Olives, about a mile down from the summit. The road from Jerusalem passed along over the lower wooded ridges, on one of which in all likelihood, just above the village (ἔως πρός) over against it, the Ascension took place. There was another route leading nearer the summit, on which later tradition sought the site and erected a church. Neither Acts nor Lk. means to give an exact spot. The fragmentariness of the narrative has created difficulty. Several considerations are adduced in reply. For one thing, the Ascension is plainly regarded as belonging to the Resurrection appearances, viz. as the appearance in which Christ's final vanishing took place, and notable simply on that ground. For another, it is pointed out that the NT writers take a view of history which does not correspond to modern requirements. They write not to prove truths denied, but to illustrate truths accepted. They do not seek to prove the occurrence of events or to escape 'discrepancies'; they seek rather to emphasize the significance of events. And to the significance of the Ascension there is abundant reference. A suggestion, again, of great interest as justifying the sparse particulars given in the Gospels, is that a sort of convention forbade the introduction of the theme into a narrative of Christ's life, the Resurrection being regarded as the culminating point of His earthly existence.

(b) The *indirect* evidence is remarkably strong. Both in the two Gospels which do not record the event and in the Epistles and discourses of Acts as well as in the visions of the Apocalypse it is implied. We thus have reference to the belief in sources for the greater part earlier than the Gospels. St. Matthew represents Christ as foretelling it (26^{64}); St. John puts similar foreshadowings into His mouth (6^{62} $13^{3.\ 33}$ 14^{28} $16^{5.\ 10.\ 17.\ 28}$); St. Paul and St. Peter habitually assume it as a fact (Ac 2^{33} 3^{21} 5^{31} $13^{30\text{-}37}$, Eph $4^{8\text{-}10}$, Ph 1^{23} 2^9 3^{20}, Col 3^1, 1 Th 1^{10} $4^{14\text{-}16}$, 1 Ti 3^{16}, 1 P 3^{22}); St. Stephen declares the same (Ac $7^{55.\ 56}$). The author of the Epistle to the Hebrews is equally explicit (He 2^9 4^{14} $6^{19.\ 20}$ 7^{26} 9^{24} $10^{12.\ 13}$ 12^2). In the Apocalypse many passages corroborate (Rev 1^{13} 5^6 14^{14} $19^{11\text{-}16}$ 22^1). The conviction of His Ascension fills the mind of the Apostolic age. It is nowhere insisted upon or proved, it is assumed as a fact among the other facts of Christ's life, as consistent with them, and as real. There is no suggestion that it is an idea less historical than the other features described.

4. *Modern departures from the traditional view.*—Within recent years the traditional view of the Ascension has been vigorously contested in various interests. From the side of naturalistic theory the *idea* of corporeal ascension has been assailed as absurd. Different rationalistic tendencies have scouted the *event* as delusion (classical representatives are Renan in France; Strauss in Germany; Baur, Schenkel), or myth, whose growth was natural from the presence of contributory elements in the intellectual and religious atmosphere of the age which were not only not inharmonious with such an idea and event, but even rendered it necessary (cf. Keim, M. Arnold, 'Supernatural Religion,' etc.). Even *the necessities of a true spiritual experience* have been urged against it by at least one considerable school (viz. that of Ritschl), which has vastly enriched present-day theological movements by a singularly impressive attempt to interpret the Christian facts through analysis of the ethical experience of the Christian personality, since such experience, it is maintained, best grows and is best explained by communion with the Exalted Christ, conceived not as 'reaching down within the realm of our earthly experience,' but as 'otherwise than we see Him in the mirror of history' (Herrmann, *Communion of the Christian with God*, Bks. ii., iii.),—a conception to which the Evangelical record as it stands is not adequate. In association with those attempts the relevant textual evidence has been painstakingly sifted and found insufficient (as, *e.g.*, latest by Schmiedel in his *Encyc. Bibl.* article on 'Resurrection and Ascension Narratives'). The departures from the traditional view here referred to are better dealt with under RESURRECTION. Here we may point merely to two considerations. First, the whole controversy between orthodox and liberal thought as to the miraculous features in the history of Christ's life has entered on a new phase. A separation is being made between the 'Jesus of history' and the 'Christ of faith' identified by ecclesiastical dogma. It is admitted that what we have in the Gospel narratives was written after the identification was practically complete. The 'Jesus of history,' therefore, can be resuscitated only by going behind even the oldest historical sources; where, the presumption is, it will be found that the miraculous incidents disappear. The various sources whence the 'myth of Christ' is derivable are inquired into; the ignorance of the times, the manifest prejudices of His biographers, and the natural tendency in Oriental minds to expand fact into fable.* The hypotheses of fraud, or delusion, or vision, previously entertained, are discarded and 'the intellectual atmosphere of the age' substituted. In particular, in the matter of the Ascension emphasis is laid on (a) current Jewish ideas concerning the departure of great men of God; (b) alleged similar ideas in ethnic religions; (c) contemporary apotheosis of the Roman emperors; (d) the natural working of the human mind, venerating a great name, to idealize the life and invest its close with marvel—as all contributory to the belief. Such analogies are pressed with ingenuity. It may be rejoined, however, that in reality they are not in point. Prevailing mental conceptions do not seem even to have favoured the acceptance of the doctrine, not to speak of having originated it. The narratives give the essential impression of its novelty. It appears as not native, but alien to the disciples' thought. Comparison with the assumption of Enoch and of Moses or the translation of Elijah, or with the deification of the Imperial representative, or with the Buddha-legend, only serves to demonstrate its striking originality. It has a character, place, and use that cannot be assigned to these. It is not in the same plane or in the same department of thought. It possesses an inevitableness, a conscious connexion with previous conditions, a naturalness as another and new

* Cf. Browning, *Christmas Eve*, xv.

aspect of Jesus' life yet continuous with and necessarily complementary to it, which they all alike lack. It lacks their formality, spectacular effect, incoherence with real life. The motives, moreover, which prompted the Senate to give each successive emperor a place among the gods, or the Hindu devotee to regard his hero as divine, are easy to trace : in the former instance political ; in the latter, religious indeed, but too naïve for the Jew, who had no natural tendency to deify—such a tendency has not been proved, it is incompatible with the exclusive and stubborn monotheism of the race. The belief enshrines in simple and reticent phrase the reception by the disciples of a new fact of His Person, which brings new light and adds new mystery, yet for which they had been prepared.

Secondly, the attempt to separate the Christian facts from Christian experience is not well based. We may rejoice to witness that the life of faith now is the being in Christ in a richer sense than the being with Him before He ascended. The acknowledgment, however, neither disproves the necessity for His life before the Ascension, nor proves the necessity to visualize it after the Ascension. The increase of faith may not, indeed, come by a mere ʻreturn to Jesus' as He was known before His death ; but how can He as ascended be fruitfully contemplated by ignoring His earthly existence? Then, again, wherein lay the need for the disciples to give outward form to their emotions more than for us now? The narratives they have given us, it is averred, are due to their spiritual imagination embodying in mythic form their spiritual experience. The disciple lives by faith and not by sight, it is argued, hence Christian experience must dispense with outward events.[*] There is in both statements a gross exaggeration. The full glory of Christ's Person is, of course, immeasurable : no vision or bodily appearance can possibly exhibit it except in faint traces. Is the vision therefore useless? The contrary is the very principle of the Incarnation ; God revealing Himself in personal, eventful form. ʻThe Christian facts underlie Christian faith, and make it progressively effective' (Westcott, ʻWork,' 2). And this because they manifest the Person of Christ, by them His Person is brought within the range of our experience ; they are the channel of His communicating His power to us. The facts and the faith are vitally related. They form one reality. They are distinguishable as aspects of that reality, but not to be separated. In explaining the reality it is not legitimate to make the distinction and then proceed to reject one of its terms, resolving, as may happen, on the one hand, the experience into an aftermath of the event ; or, on the other, the event into a vivid picture of the experience. In both cases the witness is invalidated by imagination. The second of those tendencies is aggressively in vogue. If carried to its logical issue, it must eviscerate the Ascension-experience of Christ of all objective substance, and expunge the narrative from the gospel. But to do this is to create a lacuna in the facts which will prove intolerable.

On the whole, the new method of psychological analysis of the primitive Church consciousness has brought no new danger. In at least three respects it is beneficial : it has given the *coup de grace* to earlier negations (cf. Schmiedel in above cited article) ; it has withdrawn attention from the details to the belief itself as the heart of the question, as the better mind of the Church insists ;

[*] The references in the foregoing section are to the school of Ritschl on the one hand (cf. Herrmann, *Communion with God*, etc.), and to such theistic theologians as Martineau and Estlin Carpenter (cf. the former's *Seat of Authority*, also sermon on ʻAscension' in vol. entitled *National Duties* ; and the latter's *The First Three Gospels*.

it has broadened the range of points to be considered, opening the door for a class familiar to traditionalists but hitherto excluded by advanced critical investigation.

5. *General consequences for Christian faith.*—Belief in Christ's Ascension involves several general consequences of an interesting kind. From the earliest time it was seen, *e.g.*, to be a type of the ascension of all believers. If Heaven is His true abode, it is also theirs ; and this as the natural goal of human nature, the end continuous with the beginnings of human life on earth. For Christ, His Ascension was the assumption of His own proper life, the orderly passing into its full exercise and enjoyment ; for the Christian, it is the orderly completion of his life recreated in Christ. It is not simply the ideal to be set before his natural life here, and to be realized by modification or development hereafter. The earthly life is renewed by being incorporated into Christ, through whose Spirit a new power enters into it ; he is a ʻnew creature.' But the new creation is his own proper life, to live below it is to degrade his nature. The renewed earthly nature is already begun to be taken into God ; like Christ, believers are ascending even here. To this process the ascension is but the natural close. As such it is at once the entering into the heavenly inheritance of blessing and the entering upon the triumph of them that endure.

Again, the Ascension of Christ assures and develops the desire for immortality. It has greatly quickened interest in the hope of life after death, and encouraged the conviction that it will be justified by the event. There are ʻnatural intimations of immortality.' There is a practically universal remonstrance of the human heart against the grave. The highest knowledge of this world has always been optimistic of reaching a world of solved problems and of realized ideals. The latest gift of science to mankind is the gospel of hope which is contained in the doctrine of evolution, ʻman is not man as yet, but in completed man begins anew, a tendency to God' (*Ascent through Christ*, iii. 3). But of all this there never has been real certainty. The hope is but a longing and an inference at the best. Did Christ actually ascend? The conviction that He did has for centuries been rooted in Christian minds, and has reacted on the general hope. It has assured them that the spirit in man is more powerful than death ; it has furnished the proof, as it is the illustration, of man's final destiny. That conviction, be it observed, is not an inference from the general hope. It is a fruit of fellowship with Christ. It is a religious experience : the experience, viz., of men who, united to Christ, share in the power of His Spirit, and by that power enter upon endless life. Further, Christ's Ascension offers a suggestion of important possibilities for the bodily nature. There is to be ʻa redemption of our body' (Ro 8^{23}) ; there is ʻan image of the heavenly' (1 Co 15^{49}) we must bear ; a ʻspiritual body' (v.^{44}), the ʻbody of glory' (Ph 3^{21}), that will be raised ; ʻour mortal bodies' are to be ʻquickened' (Ro 8^{11}). The future life is not to be one of pure spirit : it is to be ʻclothed upon' (2 Co 5^2). In no respect did Christ assume fundamental divergence between His nature and human nature. The Apostolic thought dwells on His oneness with His brethren. Later theology became audacious, and affirmed explicitly, ʻMan is to be made God.' Manhood is to be taken up into the Godhead. That the body in some mysterious manner is to participate in this glorification would appear to be necessary, however difficult the conception. The one precedent for the thought is Christ's, whose body was not dissolved but transfigured. See BODY.

LITERATURE.—Milligan's *The Ascension and Heavenly Priest-hood of Our Lord* still remains the most exhaustive book in English on the theological aspects of the subject. Every 'Life of Christ' deals, with more or less fulness, with the event in its historical details: see specially the studies of Fairbairn, Gilbert, Farrar, Edersheim. Of brochures, the following are important :—Knowling, *Witness of the Epistles*, 397–414 ; Bernard in *Expository Times*, 1900–1901, pp. 152–155. There may be consulted also : Bruce in *Expos. Gr. Test.* vol. i.; Swete, *Apostles' Creed* ; Westcott, *Historic Faith*, ch. vi., *Revelation of the Risen Lord*, chs. x., xi. ; art. 'Ascension' in Hastings' *DB*; Paget, *Studies in the Christian Character*, Sermons xxi., xxii. ; Findlay, *Things Above*, 119–138.

A. S. MARTIN.

ASCETICISM.—Asceticism may be defined as a form of self-discipline which consists in the habitual renunciation of the things of the flesh, with a view to the cultivation of the life of the spirit. It is a deliberate attempt to eliminate and uproot the sensuous, to banish it altogether from the sphere of consciousness. It is not content with a doctrine of mere subordination. It does not stop short with teaching men to govern their wants, to subject them to the service of a higher end and purpose. It bids men stifle and suppress them, or at least resist them to the utmost of their ability. The body is represented as the enemy of the soul, and the way of perfection is identified with the progressive extirpation of the natural instincts and inclinations by means of fasting, celibacy, voluntary poverty, and similar exercises of devotion. Hence asceticism may be described as the gospel of negation,—negation of the world and negation of the flesh, each of which is apt to be confounded with negation of the devil.

It is the purpose of the present article to inquire what traces, if any, of such asceticism are to be found in the practice and preaching of Jesus. As a preliminary, however, it will be necessary to notice briefly the main forms of asceticism which were prevalent in Palestine in the time of Christ.

The Jewish ascetics of the 1st cent. may be divided roughly into three classes. (1) First, there were the Essenes, who lived together in monastic colonies, shared all things in common, and practised voluntary poverty. Philo says that they were indifferent to money, pleasure, and worldly position. Their food was limited in quantity and carefully regulated in respect of quality. They ate no animal flesh, drank no wine, and abstained from the use of oil for purposes of anointing. The stricter members of the brotherhood eschewed marriage. The idea of this rigorous asceticism seems to have been that the objects of sense, as such, were unholy, and that man's natural cravings could not be gratified without sin. Hence the Essenes may be said to have prepared the way for the Gnostic doctrine of dualism and of matter as the seat and abode of evil. In this place, however, the principles of the Essenes need not further be discussed. They are not referred to in the Gospels, and the suggestion that John the Baptist or Jesus Himself came under their influence cannot for a moment be entertained. (2) Secondly, there was a class of hermit ascetics who fled away from the allurements and temptations of society, and gave themselves up to a life of rigid self-discipline in the solitude of the wilderness. We meet with an example of this class in the Banus, mentioned by Josephus, who lived in the desert, clothed himself with the leaves of trees, ate nothing save the natural produce of the soil, and bathed day and night in cold water for purity's sake (Jos. *Vit.* 2). A hermit of a somewhat different type was John the Baptist. He, too, dwelt in the desert, wore for dress a rough garment of camel's hair with a leathern girdle, and subsisted on carob-beans (?) and wild honey. We learn from a saying of Jesus that his rigorous mode of life astonished the people, who gave out that he was possessed by a demon (Mt 11¹⁸, Lk 7³³). But the asceticism of John seems to have been an incident of his environment and vocation, and was not regarded as an end in itself. He made no attempt to convert his hearers into ascetics. While it is true that his immediate disciples were addicted to fasting, presumably with his sanction (Mt 9¹⁴, Mk 2¹⁸, Lk 5³³), yet in the fragments of his popular sermons which have been preserved there is no trace of any exhortation to ascetic exercises. The moral preparation for the Kingdom, by repentance and works of righteousness, was the substance of his teaching (Mt 3⁷⁻¹², Lk 3¹⁻¹⁴). (3) Lastly, there were many pious Jews who cultivated asceticism of a milder and less striking kind, who, like Anna, 'served God with fasting and prayers night and day' (Lk 2³⁷). The more strict among the Pharisees paid particular attention to abstinence from food, and, in addition to ordinary fasts, were accustomed to observe all Mondays and Thursdays in the year as days of fasting (Lk 18¹²). The asceticism of the Pharisees, however, was a formal performance which resulted naturally from their legal and ceremonial conception of religion. It expressed itself chiefly in fasting, and did not include either voluntary poverty or abstinence from marriage.

Such being the principal types of contemporary asceticism, it remains to inquire, What attitude did Jesus Himself take up in relation to this asceticism? How far did He identify the life of righteousness with that 'vita religiosa' which has found its fullest expression in Monasticism? To answer this question we must consider (1) the practice of Jesus, and (2) the teaching of Jesus so far as it bears upon the subject.

1. *The practice of Jesus.*—Now it cannot be denied that from very early times there were circles of Christian ascetics who pointed to Jesus as the Founder and Example of the ascetic life (Clem. Alex. *Strom.* iii. 6). They emphasized His forty days' fast, His abstinence from marriage, His voluntary poverty, and leaped to the conclusion that the highest life, as exemplified by Jesus, was the life of asceticism or world-denial. Complete renunciation of the things of the present was 'the way of perfection according to the Saviour.' Even now large numbers of people are of this way of thinking ; but a closer and more detailed examination of Jesus' mode of life seems scarcely to bear out such a conclusion. Offering, as He did, a most wonderful example of self-forgetfulness and self-denial in the service of others, Jesus exhibited nothing of that asceticism which characterized the Essenes, or John the Baptist, or Christian saints like St. Bernard, St. John of the Cross, and even St. Francis, who of all ascetics approached most nearly to the spirit of his Master. He showed no disposition to flee from the world, or hold aloof from it ; He did not eschew the amenities of social life. He accepted the hospitality of rich men and poor, He was present at meals, He contributed to the gaiety of a marriage-feast, He permitted very precious ointment to be poured upon His feet, He had a love for children, welcomed the society of women, and clearly enjoyed the domestic life of the home in Bethany. There is no trace in the records that Jesus frowned on innocent pleasures. His life, entirely devoted to His mission, was undoubtedly hard and laborious in the highest degree ; but the motive of His renunciation—*e.g.* of marriage or property—seems to have been, not the desire to avoid these things as in themselves incompatible with spiritual perfection, but the desire to leave Himself perfect freedom in the prosecution of His work. He did not, so far as we know, impose upon Himself unnecessary austerities, or go out of His way to seek suffering. He accepted pleasures and pains as they came, neither avoiding the one nor courting the other, but, with a sublime serenity, subordinating both to His main end and purpose. The so-called 'forty days' fast' need not cause us to modify our view. This fast is not mentioned in the oldest authority (Mk 1[13]); and at any rate it can scarcely have been a ceremonial observance of fasting, but was rather a necessity imposed on Jesus by His situation in the wilderness. The key to its meaning may perhaps be found in St. Luke's expression, 'in those days he did eat nothing' (Lk 4[2]), with which we may compare Christ's own description of the life of John the Baptist, 'John came neither eating nor drinking' (Mt 11[18]). The phrase as applied to Jesus may, as in the case of John, mean merely that He ate no ordinary food, but supported life on such means of subsistence as the wilderness afforded. But even if St. Matthew's νηστεύσας (Mt 4[2]) be taken literally, yet, in the face of Christ's teaching on the subject (to be mentioned below), we cannot believe that He attributed any great importance to this abstinence from food. He was supremely indifferent to the traditional practices of asceticism; in the sphere of self-renunciation in which He moved, no one-sided principle of world-negation could find a place. Hence, while Jesus is presented to us by the Evangelists as the living type and embodiment of absolute self-denial,—self-sacrifice, as it were, incarnate,—yet the marks of the ascetic are not found in Him. And it is interesting to note that His unascetic deportment and manner of life attracted the observation of His contemporaries. 'John came neither eating nor drinking, and they say, He hath a devil. The Son of man came eating and drinking, and they say, Behold a man gluttonous and a wine-bibber, a friend of publicans and sinners' (Mt 11[18. 19], Lk 7[33. 34]). There can be no question that the Jews were right when they pointed out the absence of asceticism from the practice of Jesus. We have but to contrast the life of the Son of Man, who 'came eating and drinking,' with that of such an one as St. John of the Cross, and the fact will immediately become apparent.

2. The teaching of Jesus.—Passing now to the consideration of the teaching of Jesus, we remark at the outset that, from first to last, it is instinct with the spirit of self-denial. 'If any man will come after me, let him deny himself,' is the refrain which continually recurs. The principle laid down by Jesus is that the doing of the will of God and the promotion of His kingdom is the absolute duty of man, to which all private and particular aims must necessarily give place. 'Seek ye first the kingdom of God' (Mt 6[33], Lk 12[31]) is the categorical imperative. The Kingdom of God is the highest good, and as such establishes a claim on man's exclusive devotion. Hence all desires and strivings which have not righteousness as their ultimate goal must be ruthlessly suppressed; all lesser goods and blessings which hinder and obstruct a man in the pursuit of the *summum bonum* must unhesitatingly be sacrificed. Thus a man must sell all that he has in order to purchase the field with the treasure, or the pearl of great price (Mt 13[44-46]). If necessity arise, he must surrender all his possessions to come and follow Jesus (Mt 19[21], Mk 10[21]); he must even renounce the closest ties of earthly relationship,—father and mother, children and wife (Mt 10[37], Lk 14[26]), the last imperative duties of affection (Lk 9[59. 60]), the courtesies of farewell (Lk 9[61. 62]); nay, the most indispensable goods, the hand, the foot, the eye, must be abandoned if they cause offence (Mt 5[29. 30], Mk 9[43-47]); and, at the call of God, the very life itself must be laid down (Mt 16[24f.], Mk 8[34f.], Lk 9[23f.]). 'Whosoever he be of you that forsaketh not all that he hath, he cannot be my disciple' (Lk 14[33]). No teaching could be clearer or more forcible than

this. With the greatest possible plainness Jesus declares that every earthly blessing must be made subordinate to the service of God and contributory thereto. All lesser goods which come to be sought for their own sake, whether in preference to, or even independently of, the highest good, must be instantly sacrificed. In other words, when the individual realizes that the gratification of any desire will impede or distract him in the performance of his duties as a member of the Kingdom, he is bound to forego such gratification if he would still be in truth a disciple of Christ.

It is important to notice that, in all Jesus' precepts about the sacrifice of earthly goods, there is a condition, explicit or implied. The condition in any given case is, that the particular good to be sacrificed shall have been ascertained to be an obstacle to the attainment of righteousness on the part of its possessor—'if it cause thee to stumble.' Thus the necessity of every sacrifice is determined by the special circumstances of the particular case. The rich young man is bidden to part with all his possessions and follow Jesus; Zacchæus gives half, and is told 'this day is salvation come to this house' (Lk 19[9]); Martha and Mary are not asked to leave their home. To one man Jesus denies permission to bid farewell to his relatives (Lk 9[62]); to another He says, 'Return to thine own house' (Lk 8[39]). A sacrifice which is imperative for one man need not necessarily be the duty of another, but the general rule is laid down that all must be prepared, if occasion arise, to surrender their dearest and most cherished blessings for the sake of the Kingdom of God.

Now the note of this doctrine is self-denial, not asceticism. Jesus nowhere teaches that earthly goods are of the devil, or that the gratification of the natural cravings is fraught with sin. He does not recommend men to treat their bodies with contempt. He does not suggest that flight from the world and disengagement from physical conditions is sanctification. He does not say that those who, for duty's sake, renounce the world, are on a higher spiritual level than those who do their duty in the world. He does not hint that the only way of avoiding sin lies in an austere renunciation of all those things from which an occasion of sin might arise. He nowhere implies that the lower goods are of no value in themselves, or that they ought under all circumstances to be foregone. The doctrine of Jesus is a doctrine not of annihilation, but of subordination. He admits, indeed, that special circumstances may make it incumbent on an individual to abstain from certain things which others, otherwise situated, may lawfully enjoy; but He does not say that earthly goods, as such, are irreconcilable with righteousness. His teaching on the subject may be summarized in the word *subordination*. The main point is that earthly goods are not to be retained or enjoyed for their own sake, but must be made subordinate and subservient to a higher end, and must ultimately be directed towards the promotion of the righteousness of the Kingdom of God.

Further to illustrate this point of view, we may briefly allude to Jesus' teaching on three prominent characteristics of the ascetic life—voluntary poverty, celibacy, and bodily discipline as exercised in the practice of fasting.

(1) No one could have been more alive than Jesus was to the dangers of *wealth*, and to the peculiar psychological difficulties which hinder the rich from entering the Kingdom. His warnings on the subject are more than usually vigorous. Wealth is represented as an idol; care about material things as a kind of heathenism. He even goes so far as to say that, humanly speaking, it is impossible for a rich man to be saved (Mt 19[26], Mk

10^{27}, Lk 18^{27}). 'Woe unto you that are rich!' He cries again, 'for ye have received your consolation' (Lk 6^{24}). He bids men not lay up treasures upon earth (Mt 6^{19}), but rather sell what they have and give alms (Lk 12^{33}). He says, 'Ye cannot serve God and mammon' (Mt 6^{24}). Jesus knew that men tend to become absorbed in their property, to give their heart to it, to become its slaves instead of its masters; and the idea of such bondage filled Him with horror. Hence to those who were in danger of falling beneath the tyranny of money and material things He had but one word to say : 'Go and sell that thou hast, and give to the poor . . . and come, follow me' (Mt 19^{21}, Mk 10^{21}, Lk 18^{22}). This, however, is not a precept of universal validity; it is not, as some of the Fathers have wrongly conceived (*e.g.* Hieron. *c. Vigilant.* 14; Bæda, *Exp. in Marci Ev.* iii. 10), a *consilium evangelicum* of poverty. It was addressed primarily to a particular person, and it can properly be applied only to those who are in danger of forgetting that 'a man's life consisteth not in the abundance of the things which he possesseth' (Lk 12^{15}). The parables of the Unjust Steward (Lk 16^{1-12}), of the Talents (Mt 25^{14-30}), or the Pounds (Lk 19^{12-27}), prove that Jesus was far from regarding wealth as evil in itself, or requiring that people in general should renounce its use. On the contrary, He insisted that riches are a deposit from God, which can and ought to be employed in His service ; and He even declared that fidelity in such employment would be the standard for testing a man's capacity for higher tasks. 'If ye have not been faithful in the unrighteous mammon, who will commit to your trust the true riches?' (Lk 16^{11}). There is nothing ascetic in such teaching. What Jesus reprobates is not wealth, but the abuse of it; what He recommends is not alienation of wealth, but subordination of it. He recognizes, indeed, that there may be special cases where the retention of wealth is incompatible with the service of God, but in general He bids men keep and use it in accordance with the purposes of Him who has bestowed it on them. Neither wealth nor poverty is in itself meritorious : only the disposition which makes either minister to the coming of the Kingdom.

(2) So, too, in respect of *marriage*. Jesus certainly teaches that a spiritual vocation is sometimes inconsistent with the married state. 'There be eunuchs which have made themselves eunuchs for the kingdom of heaven's sake. He that is able to receive it, let him receive it' (Mt 19^{12}). 'This,' says Jerome, 'is the voice of the Lord exhorting and urging on His soldiers to the reward of chastity.' But to write thus is an exaggeration, if not a perversion of the truth. Nothing is more noticeable than the extremely guarded form of Christ's utterance here, in striking contrast with His very explicit injunctions concerning renunciation in other matters. Jesus weighs His words with the greatest care. He makes no general exhortation to celibacy. He merely points out that some people, in the enthusiasm of their heavenly calling, have suppressed the very instincts of nature, so that they have, as it were, undergone an operation of ethical self-emasculation, being dead to sexual desire; and He recommends those who have received the gift of abstinence, in this sense, not to neglect it. Just as elsewhere, in His pregnant, paradoxical way, Jesus bids men 'hate' father, and mother, and wife, and children (Lk 14^{26}), if their claims tend to supersede the claims of God (Mt 10^{37}); so here He bids those who are convinced that God's claims demand the whole of their time and energy, to refrain altogether from entering the marriage state. But this is no ascetic doctrine of celibacy. The Master who

taught that matrimony was a divinely ordered condition, and emphasized in the strongest terms the sanctity of the conjugal relation (Mt 5^{32} 19^{3-9}, Mk 10^{2-12}, Lk 16^{18}), who practised (Lk 2^{51}) and inculcated the duty of filial obedience and love towards parents (Mt 15^{4-6}, Mk 7^{10-13}), who habitually used the symbolism of the family to express the profoundest and holiest truths of religion, certainly did not mean to teach that family life, as such, was irreconcilable with righteousness. He uttered no word in disparagement of it ; He never implied that the married attain a lower grade of perfection than the continent. On the contrary, it is clear that Jesus regarded marriage as the right and natural course for the majority of people, and He even chose a married man as the chief of His apostles. In short, while recognizing that through special circumstances the individual might be called upon to renounce the gratifications of marriage, Jesus appears to indicate that such renunciation is an exceptional duty imposed on the few, not a general rule for the many. Marriage in itself is not to be avoided as a thing debasing ; it debases only when men refuse to subordinate it to the claims of the Kingdom.

(3) So, once more, towards the traditional *discipline* of asceticism Jesus took up an attitude of indifference. In His view, the value of such exercises depends solely upon the spirit in which they are undertaken. As forms through which devotion seeks to find expression, He does not condemn them ; but, on the other hand, He does not suggest that they are the necessary or inevitable concomitants of the holy life. This will appear from His teaching on fasting—one of the most distinguishing characteristics of the Jewish piety of His time. Jesus points out that true fasting is not a parade of piety before the eyes of men, but an outward expression of a personal relation of the individual soul to the 'Father which seeth in secret' (Mt 6^{16-18}). Hence fasting is not a matter of compulsion or prescription or external ordinance ; it has value solely as the appropriate manifestation of a state of mind. Thus Jesus refuses to impose fasts on His disciples in their days of gladness, but He foresees that 'the days will come when the bridegroom shall be taken from them,' and then the sorrow of their heart will seek an outlet through the forms of sorrow (Mt 9^{15}, Mk $2^{19. 20}$, Lk $5^{34. 35}$). In justification of His refusal to lay down fixed rules upon the subject, Jesus goes on to say that, just as no wise man would sew a new patch on to an old garment, or pour new wine into old bottles, so it would be foolish to graft the new-found liberty of the gospel on to the mass of old observances, and still more foolish to attempt to force the new system as a whole within the forms of the old. The new piety must develop new forms of its own (Mt $9^{16. 17}$, Mk $2^{21. 22}$, Lk 5^{36-38}). From all this we gather that Jesus refuses to bind religion to external acts of asceticism, or to declare such acts to be of obligation. Such performances as fasting, flagellation, or restriction of sleep may certainly have a conditional worth as the sincere expression of a sad and contrite spirit, but they are not of the essence of devotion. Jesus emphasizes the state of the heart, the self-denying disposition, the bent of the soul towards God ; with anything besides this He is not concerned.

Hence in answer to the question, Was Jesus an ascetic? we are bound to reply in the negative. Neither in His practice nor in His teaching did He adopt the tone of asceticism. He called indeed for self-denial, self-sacrifice, self-forgetfulness. He demanded that all lower goods should be subordinated to the highest good, that all human strivings should be directed ultimately towards righteousness. But He does not condemn the lower goods or attempt to tear out the human instincts and cravings. Nor does He make fellowship with God depend on any kind of outward ascetical observances. Indeed, as Harnack writes, 'Asceticism has no place in the gospel at all; what it asks is that we should struggle against mammon, against care, against selfishness; what it demands and disengages is love; the love that serves and is self-sacrificing. This struggle and this love are the kind of asceticism which the gospel means, and whoever encumbers Jesus' message with any other kind fails to understand it. He fails to understand its grandeur and importance; for there is something still more important than "giving one's body to be burned, and bestowing all one's goods to feed the poor," namely, self-denial and love' (Harnack, *What is Christianity?* p. 88). See also art. SELF-DENIAL and the Literature cited at end of that article.   F. HOMES DUDDEN.

ASHER (LXX and NT Ἀσήρ, Jos. Ἄσηρος) is the transliteration of the Heb. אָשֵׁר = 'fortunate.' In Gn 30¹³ the origin of the name Asher is connected by J with this adjective, but perhaps its source should be found rather in the name of some Semitic divinity (cf. the goddess Ashera and perhaps also the Assyrian god Ashur). In Rev 7⁶ Asher appears in the list of the twelve tribes of Israel (cf. Nu 1¹³·⁴⁰ᶠ· 2²⁷ᶠ· 7⁷²⁻⁷⁷ 10²⁶ 13¹³ [P], Dt 27¹³ [D]). The patronymic ancestor of the tribe is presented in Gn 30¹³ (J) and 35²⁶ (P) as the eighth son of Jacob: born (like Gad) of Zilpah, Leah's slave-girl. Asher is mentioned in the 'Blessings' of Jacob (Gn 49²⁰) and of Moses (Dt 33²⁴). It is put in possession of a territory in the land of Canaan (Jos 19²⁴⁻³¹ [P], cf. 21⁶·³⁰ᶠ· [P]), but does not succeed in making itself thoroughly master of it (Jg 1³¹ᶠ·); the result of which is that its territory is sometimes confused with that of Manasseh (Jos 17¹¹ [J]), and that it holds a precarious situation in the midst of the Canaanites (contrast Jg 1³²ᶠ· with v.²⁹ᶠ·). The district assigned to Asher corresponds to what was afterwards western Galilee, a very fertile country, but apparently never subdued completely by Israel; it is by a fiction that the possession of cities like Acco, Achzib, Tyre, and Sidon is attributed to it. Asher is named in the Song of Deborah (Jg 5¹⁷) as devoted to navigation; it figures also in the story of Gideon (Jg 6³⁵ 7²³). But it quickly disappears from the page of history, where after all it had played a very small part. It is still mentioned incidentally in 1 K 4¹⁶ under Solomon, and in 2 Ch 30¹¹ under Hezekiah, but there is no trace of it in the Books of Ezra and Nehemiah. The genealogical tables will be found in Gn 46¹⁷ (P), Nu 26⁴⁴⁻⁴⁷ (P), and 1 Ch 7³⁰⁻⁴⁰.

According to Lk 2³⁶ the prophetess Anna, the daughter of Phanuel, was of the tribe of Asher. The source of this genealogical statement is unknown. Its correctness has been suspected in view of similar claims made for some Jews elsewhere to illustrious origin (descent from Aaron, David, etc.). It may, however, be remarked, that there is a cardinal difference between these and the present instance: there was nothing particularly glorious in descent from Asher.   LUCIEN GAUTIER.

ASHES.—Used twice in the Gospels, referring to an ancient and widespread Eastern mourning custom. The mourner, or the penitent, would throw dust, or dust mixed with ashes (σποδός), into the air, as an expression of intense humiliation, due to penitence for sin, or grief because of affliction (Mt 11²¹; for this idea in the OT cf. Mic 1¹⁰, Job 42⁶). Such symbolic use of dust and ashes was not unnatural, since grief seems to call for a prostration of the body. These, being beneath the

feet, suggest humiliation, and when thrown into the air they were allowed to fall upon the person of the mourner, that he might carry the evidences of his grief with him. Sometimes ashes is associated with σάκκος, sackcloth; the penitent or mourner sitting upon the ash-heap, his face begrimed with the dust. To this custom Christ referred when He said of Tyre and Sidon, 'They would have repented long ago, sitting in sackcloth and ashes' (Lk 10¹³; cf. use of אֵפֶר in Job 2⁸, Jon 3⁶).
                    E. B. POLLARD.

ASS.—See ANIMALS, p. 63ª.

ASTONISHMENT, ASTONISHED.—These terms occur with some frequency in EV of OT, but in NT only in the historical books (except John), and in the RV only in the Synoptic Gospels (except Ac 3¹²). They are always used in NT as an expression of one of the emotions aroused by supernatural manifestations. The noun occurs once only in either version (but in different passages: AV Mk 5⁴²; RV Mk 16⁸): the verb more frequently. In AV the term translates sometimes ἐκπλήσσομαι (Mt 7²⁸ 13⁵⁴ 22³³, Mk 6² 7³⁷ 10²⁶ 11¹⁸, Lk 4³², Ac 13¹²); sometimes ἐξίσταμαι or ἔκστασις (Mk 5⁴², Lk 2⁴⁷ 8⁵⁶ 24²², Ac 10⁴⁵ 12¹⁶); and sometimes θαμβέομαι or θάμβος (Mk 10²⁴, Lk 5⁹, Ac 9⁶). In RV it is reserved for ἐκπλήσσομαι (except Mk 16⁸, where 'astonishment' represents ἔκστασις), of which it is the uniform rendering. In its etymological implication it very fairly represents ἐκπλήσσομαι, which is literally 'to be struck out (of the senses) by a blow,' and hence, to be 'stunned,' 'shocked,' 'astonished.' For its relation to words implying 'fear,' see Schmidt, *Synonymik d. gr. Sprache*, No. 139. For its place among the terms descriptive of the effect of our Lord's ministry on its witnesses, see art. AMAZEMENT.   BENJAMIN B. WARFIELD.

ASTROLOGY was an important element of all ancient astronomy. The scientific observation of the positions and movements of the heavenly bodies was closely associated with the belief in their Divine character, and their influence upon the destinies of men, and formed the basis of calculations and predictions of future events. Babylonia was the earliest home of this study, which continued to be prosecuted in that part of the world with special diligence, so that in later times the word 'Chaldæan' was equivalent to 'Eastern astrologer.' It is to this class that we must refer the Magi or Wise Men from the East, who are mentioned in Mt 2¹ᶠ· They had seen in their own home the rising (for so perhaps we should understand the words ἐν τῇ ἀνατολῇ, rendered 'in the east,' in v.²) of a star or constellation, which they connected with the expectation, already diffused in the East, of the birth of a great ruler among the Jews. Travelling to Palestine, they ascertained at Jerusalem that the Messiah was expected to be born in Bethlehem, and directing their steps thither they saw the 'star' in front of them all the way, till they came to the house where the infant Jesus was found. (This appears to be the only sense in which the popular and picturesque language of v.⁹ can be understood.)

The first two chapters of the First Gospel are recognized as being taken from another source than the rest of the book, and different views have been held as to their historic value. But so far as the astrological references in ch. 2 are concerned, no difficulty need be felt about the narrative. The Evangelist, it is true, does not raise any question as to the reality of the connexion between the 'star' and the birth of Jesus. On the possibility of such a connexion, no doubt he shared the common beliefs of his time. But we may accept his statement of the facts without being compelled to admit that there is any truth in astrological theories. The famous calculation of Kepler shows that an unusual conjunction of Mars, Jupiter, and Saturn took place about B.C. 7, and it is quite conceivable that this or some similar phenomenon may in God's providence have led the Wise Men, even through the mistaken principles of their science, actually to visit Palestine about the time when Jesus was born. See further, artt. MAGI and STAR.   JAMES PATRICK.

ASSURANCE.—This term stands for the fact and the doctrine of personal fellowship with God in Jesus Christ, made certain to the consciousness of the believer by the direct witness of the Holy Spirit. The prophetic ideal appears in the promise of a peaceful work of righteousness, the effect of which is quietness and confidence for ever (Is 32^{17}). In Mt 11^{27} Jesus declares that 'no one knoweth the Father save the Son, and he to whomsoever the Son willeth to reveal him.' Such a personal revelation of God to the believer in Christ would seem to be necessarily obvious and assuring to him who receives it. The immediate context also gives assurance of rest and comfort to the souls of all who labour and are heavy laden, and who come to Christ for help. This teaching is confirmed and enhanced by the doctrine of the Gospel of St. John concerning the Comforter. This heavenly Comforter, the Holy Spirit of truth, bears witness of Christ, and makes known the things of Christ, unto those who receive and love Him (Jn 15^{26} 16^{14}). The world cannot receive this Spirit of truth, for He is an invisible presence, known only to the believer with whom and in whom He abides (14^{17}). Those disciples in whom the Spirit thus dwells are loved by the Father and realize the manifestation of Christ, so that Father, Son, and Spirit come unto them and make their abode with them (14$^{21.\ 23}$). The doctrine also finds noteworthy confirmation in the First Epistle of St. John (3$^{19-24}$ 4^{13}), where it is said that the Spirit of God and of Christ abides in the believer, and assures (*persuades*) his heart with the Divine conviction of His immediate presence, so that he has great 'boldness toward God' (παρρησίαν πρὸς τὸν θεόν).

That the Holy Spirit bears immediate and direct witness within the human spirit to the fact of one's being a child of God, is the explicit teaching of St. Paul (Ro 8^{16}). In Col 2^2 we note the remarkable expression about Christian hearts being comforted and 'knit together in love unto all riches of the full assurance (πληροφορία, 'fulness') of understanding' in knowing the mystery of God. The same truth appears in the phrases 'full assurance of hope' and 'full assurance of faith' (He 6^{11} 10^{22}). The author of the Epistle to the Hebrews declares faith itself to be 'assurance of things hoped for, conviction of things not seen' (11^1).

This Biblical doctrine of Assurance presents one of the most precious truths of the gospel of Christ. It presupposes, as a matter of course, the believer's personal acquaintance with the saving truths of Christianity and the facts of Divine revelation; but it has been needlessly complicated with the dogmas of Election and the final Perseverance of the Saints. It should not be construed to involve a present assurance of final salvation, but it should be defined and guarded against the various delusions of mere subjective feeling. A spiritual conviction, however deep and assuring, needs the constant test of verification in a pure and upright life. It must have the 'testimony of our conscience, that in holiness and sincerity of God, not in fleshly wisdom but in the grace of God, we behaved ourselves in the world' (2 Co 1^{12}). The fruit of the Spirit (Gal 5$^{22-25}$) must supplement and

continuously establish the personal witness of the Spirit. Therefore Jesus Himself gave the important admonition that the real character of a tree is known by its fruit (Mt 7$^{15-20}$).

LITERATURE. — Calvin, *Institutes*, bk. III. ch. ii. §§ 15–17; Westminster Confession, ch. xviii.; W. Cunningham, 'The Reformers and the Doctrine of Assurance,' the third essay in his *Reformers and the Theology of the Reformation*; John Wesley, *Sermons* on 'The Witness of the Spirit,' and 'The Witness of our own Spirit'; Richard Watson, *Theol. Institutes*, vol. ii. pp. 269–284; Hodge, *Systematic Theology*, vol. iii. pp. 106, 107; Miley, *Systematic Theology*, vol. ii. pp. 339–353; Bishop Sherlock, *Works*, vol. i. Discourse 8; R. N. Young, *The Witness of the Spirit*, Fernley Lecture of 1882; Jonathan Edwards, *Religious Affections*, Part iii., Introd.; Dorner, *System of Christian Doctrine*, vol. iv. p. 184; J. Agar Beet, *Romans*, 231 ff.; J. H. Newman, *Parochial Sermons*, v. 239; J. Martineau, *National Duties*, 146 ff.   M. S. TERRY.

ATONEMENT. — The Atonement is the reconciling work of Jesus Christ the Son of God, in gracious fulfilment of the loving purpose of His Father; whereby, through the sacrifice of Himself upon the Cross once for all, on behalf and instead of sinful men, satisfaction was made for the sins of the world and communion between God and man restored.

The starting-point of Christian experience is the Resurrection of Jesus (1 Co 15^{17}, Ro 4^{25}). It may now be taken as accepted that the belief of the primitive community and the Apostolic preaching were based on this conviction (see Harnack, *What is Christianity?* Eng. tr. Lect. ix.; Schmiedel, *Encyc. Bibl.* art. 'Resurrection'). This fact, reinforced by successive appearances of the risen Christ whether to individuals or the assembled disciples, led to the further conviction, the ultimate root of the doctrine of the Atonement, that Jesus of Nazareth, crucified, risen, ascended, was present in the midst of the Christian congregation. He who in the days of His ministry had claimed authority on earth to forgive sins (Mt 9$^{2-8}$), confirming the word with signs following, who had awakened an implicit trust as alone having the words of eternal life (Jn 6^{68} 16^{30}), and who had manifested Himself as the one way by which men might come to the Father (Jn 14^6), had fulfilled His own promise to return to His elect and abide with them to the end of the days (Mt 28^{20}). The first corporate act of the disciples was to claim the promise to be present in the midst of two or three gathered in His name (Mt 18^{20}), by calling upon their Master to choose into the Apostolate one of two set before Him conceived as invisibly present (Ac 1$^{15-26}$). Moreover, He was present in power as exalted to God's right hand, not therefore limited by time and space, but acting under Divine, eternal conditions, arising to succour His martyr Stephen (Ac 7$^{55.\ 59}$), manifesting Himself as the Righteous One to St. Paul (22^{14}), giving specific revelations of His will to Ananias and to St. Paul himself (9$^{4-6.\ 10-16}$ 18$^{9.\ 10}$ 23^{11}), and performing those greater works of which He had spoken (Jn 14^{12}) through those who wrought in His name (Ac 3^6 9^{34}). This conviction, peculiarly vivid in the earlier ages, is clearly traced in the hymns addressed to Christ 'as to a god' (Pliny's *Letter to Trajan*), and in the records of early martyrdoms. And the realism with which it was held even as late as the 4th cent. is attested by apologetic like that of Athanasius (see *de Incarnatione*, 46 ff.), or traditions like that of the consecration of St. John Lateran.

But proclamation of forgiveness of sins through faith in the name of Jesus, though arising out of the conviction that the Absolver was Himself in the power of His deity still present on earth, was not made until the realization of the promise of the Spirit in the Pentecostal gift. To this fact, the external results of which were present in the experience of his hearers, St. Peter appealed as witnessing to the reality of Jesus' exaltation and His power to remit sins (Ac 2³³, cf. Gal 3¹⁴). This significant element in the first preaching of the Gospel answers by anticipation objections urged against the Atonement as involving immoral consequences and unworthy views of God. Not only in this passage but throughout the Acts the possession of the Spirit is emphasized as the essential mark of discipleship (Ac 2³⁸ 4³¹ 5³² 8¹⁴⁻¹⁹ 9¹⁷ 10⁴⁷ 11¹⁶ 13⁵² 19¹⁻⁶). The call to repentance, intimately associated with the gift of the Holy Spirit (Ac 2³⁸, cf. Mt 3¹¹), necessarily involved a life conformed to the image of the Son of God. The Gospel, though a message of God's free favour with no condition of antecedent righteousness, referred to moral results, the manifestation of an imparted spirit, as evidence of the truth of the promise (Ro 8¹³· ¹⁴, Gal 5²²⁻²⁴). And when the doctrine of justification by faith was challenged by imperfectly instructed Christians, St. Paul met the charge by an abrupt appeal not only to elementary moral convictions, but to the implications of baptism as a new and spiritual birth (Ro 6¹⁻⁴). Nor, again, was it possible for those to whom the possession of the Spirit was a fact of experience to regard God otherwise than as the Father. For He who dwelt within them was the Spirit of Christ Jesus (Ac 16⁷, Ro 8⁹, Ph 1¹⁹, 1 P 1¹¹), the promise of the Father (Ac 1⁴), whereby they had themselves attained the adoption, and were enabled to cry, 'Abba, Father' (Ro 8¹⁵⁻¹⁷, Gal 4⁶).

The fact of Pentecost was immediately explained as that outpouring of the Spirit upon all flesh which was to mark the establishment of the Messianic kingdom (Ac 2¹⁶⁻²¹ 5³¹· ³²). It stood directly related to the event of which the Apostles were the chosen witnesses, the Resurrection of Jesus, whereby He was exalted to be a Prince and a Saviour unto the remission of sins (Ac 2³³· ³⁸), of which, according to Hebrew expectation, the kingdom was to be the home (e.g. Jer 31, Ezk 36¹⁶⁻³⁶). The assurance that Christ was the ever present source of forgiveness gave its supreme significance to the Cross by which He entered into His glory (Jn 12³²). Later theologians have been charged with 'placing the emphasis too exclusively upon the death of Jesus as the means of redemption' (H. L. Wild, Contentio Veritatis, Essay iii.). But the evidence of the NT is irresistible. It is true that the earliest sermons lay stress rather upon the fact of the Resurrection, but always as closely following upon the Death, which, though inflicted by His enemies, resulted from the determinate counsel of God (Ac 2²³) who glorified 'his Servant' Jesus. The frequent repetition of this OT expression (παῖς θεοῦ) in the early chapters of Acts (3¹³· ²⁶ 4²⁷· ³⁰), taken in connexion with explicit references to the things which God foreshadowed by the prophets that His Messiah should suffer (Ac 2²³ 3¹⁸ 4¹¹· ²⁵⁻²⁸ 13²⁷; cf. 1 Co 15³, 1 P 1¹¹), leaves no room for doubt that Philip the Evangelist was not alone in beginning from the picture of Jehovah's Suffering Servant to preach Jesus (Ac 8³⁵), but that the Apostles gave their witness to the Resurrection by preaching what St. Paul called 'Christ crucified' (1 Co 1²³, cf. Gal 3¹). The Crucifixion was regarded neither as a bare fact nor as the symbol of a theological system, but as a 'gospel,' an event whose reality lay in its significance, a message of Divine favour and forgiveness. The central fact of Christ's life and work was complex, consisting of both the Cross and the Resurrection. The NT considers neither apart. The redeeming efficacy is attached to each in turn. While, according to the compressed formula in which St. Paul expresses the content of his gospel, 'Christ died for our sins and rose again the third day' (1 Co 15³· ⁴), the common form of the Petrine preaching represents God as raising up Jesus 'for

to give repentance and remission of sins' (Ac 5³⁰· ³¹; cf. 2³²⁻³⁶ 3¹⁵· ²⁶, 1 P 1²¹ 3²¹, also Ro 4²⁵ and 1 Co 15¹⁷). But it was the Cross that tended to fix itself as the central fact, and therefore the characteristic symbol of Christendom. It is the figure of Him 'who bare our sins in his body on the tree' which dominates the First Epistle of Peter (1 P 2²⁴). And the 2nd cent. Gospel according to Peter has contrived with singular fidelity to the Apostle's mind to give an imaginative picture of the Resurrection, wherein the Cross is curiously blended with the rending tomb (Gospel acc. to Peter, § 10, ed. Robinson and James). With St. Paul the gospel of Christ, which is the fixed point in his teaching (Gal 1¹¹, 1 Co 15¹, 1 Ti 1¹¹, 2 Ti 2⁸), the touchstone of all preaching (Gal 1⁸· ⁹, 1 Ti 1³ 6³), proclaimed alike to Jew and Gentile (1 Co 1²⁴), delivered whether to St. Peter or to himself as the deposit of Christian truth (1 Co 3¹¹, 2 Ti 1¹³· ¹⁴), is 'the word of the cross' (1 Co 1¹⁸· ²³). So remarkable is the unanimity of the two great primary preachers of Christianity that it leaves no room to question the statement of Harnack (What is Christianity? Eng. tr. Lect. ix.) that 'the primitive community called Jesus its Lord because He sacrificed His life for it, and because its members were convinced that He had been raised from the dead and was then sitting at the right hand of God.'

To this must be added the general symmetry of the NT and the evidence of Christian institutions and Church History. The story of the Passion is out of all proportion to the rest of the Synoptic narrative, as given in each of the three Gospels, unless the foreground is rightly occupied by the Cross. And here the Fourth Gospel, though it emphasizes the function of revelation in the incarnate life of the Son of God, is found in close and almost unexpected agreement with its predecessors. The Apocalypse rings with the praises of 'the Lamb' (Rev 5⁴· ⁶· ¹²· ¹³ 7¹⁰· ¹⁴⁻¹⁷ 12⁷⁻¹² 14¹⁻⁵ 19⁶⁻⁹; cf. 1⁵ 13⁸). The Epistle to the Hebrews, though it opens with one of the classical Christological passages, yet makes the Death of Jesus the pivot of its teaching (He 2⁹). And the Epistle to the Romans, which elaborates the great argument of Justification through a crucified and risen Saviour, is central to the theology of St. Paul.

Midway between the NT and Church History, as related in point of evidential value to either, come the Creed and Sacraments. The former represents the inviolable basis of the word concentrated in catechetical teaching. That its emphasis rested upon the Cross is apparent not only from such primitive formulæ as the Apostles' Creed, but from the NT itself (1 Co 15³· ⁴, 1 Ti 1¹⁵). Baptism is the initiatory Christian rite, and whether it conveys or only represents the forgiveness of sins, stood from the first in close relation to the Death and Resurrection of Christ (Mt 28¹⁹, Mk 16¹⁵· ¹⁶, Ac 2³⁸ 8¹³· ¹⁶· ³⁶ 9¹⁸ 10⁴⁷· ⁴⁸ 16⁵³ 19⁵ 22¹⁶, Ro 6³· ⁴, Gal 3²⁶· ²⁷, Eph 4⁴⁻⁶, Col 2¹², Tit 3⁴⁻⁶, 1 P 3²¹; cf. Jn 3⁵, Ac 11¹⁶, 1 Co 10², He 6¹⁻⁶ 10²², 1 Jn 5⁶⁻⁸). The Eucharist is the Christian counterpart of the sacrifice of the Passover, which commemorated the deliverance of God's people from Egypt; it is associated by the terms of its celebration with the Lord's Passion, and employs language of sacrificial import (Mt 26²⁶⁻²⁸, Lk 14²²⁻²⁴, Lk 22¹⁹· ²⁰, 1 Co 11¹⁸⁻³⁴ 10¹⁶⁻²² [for τράπεζα Κυρίου = θυσιαστήριον, cf. Mal 1⁷], cf. Jn 6⁵²⁻⁶⁸ [see Westcott, ad loc.], Ex 12²⁷, He 13¹⁰).

Following upon the Sacraments is the witness of Church History—the worship, the dogma, the art, the experience of the Christian centuries—which have all consistently gathered round the Cross. We are therefore entitled to hold that any interpretation of the Christian facts which shifts the focus from Calvary to Bethlehem or Galilee represents a departure from the historic faith, and tends to distort the Christian revelation.

Theories of the Atonement, of which the view that identifies it with the Incarnation may be taken as the norm, have inevitably been popular in an age dominated by two great influences, physical science and Hegelian philosophy. But it may be doubted whether they have taken their rise in a study of the facts of Scripture and not rather in a determinist conception of the Universe, to which the Incarnation seemed to give a religious and Christian form. A consequence of this method of thought has been the revival, in this country by Bishop Westcott and others, of speculations like those of Rupert of Deutz and the Scotists, which postulate an Incarnation independent of those conditions of human life which demand the forgiveness of sins.* It is perhaps enough to say of this line of thought, with Dr. A. B. Davidson (*OT Prophecy*, ch. x.), that it involves 'a kind of principle, according to which God develops Himself by an inward necessity,' and which 'is certainly not a Biblical principle.' Such thinking invariably regards the Atonement merely as a mode of the Incarnation required by the conditions under which it took place. And whether this theory be specifically held or not, it has been a tendency of recent theology to fix the mind rather upon the ethical principle of the Atonement, *i.e.* the obedience or penitence or assent to God's abhorrence of sin, of which death is the 'sacrament' or visible sign, than upon the Crucifixion as a work intrinsically efficacious apart from the moral qualities expressed in its accomplishment. Such views are defective, not because they fail to give expression to aspects of Christ's redeeming work, but because they stop short at the point where explanation is necessary, why these qualities of the spirit of Jesus should have been directed towards the particular end of the death of the Cross. The climax of the account which St. Paul gives in the Epistle to the Philippians of the exaltation of Jesus, is neither the assumption of human flesh nor the suffering of death, but the obedience which accepted the humiliation of the Cross as the act whereby He fulfilled, not the general, but the particular will of God (Ph 2^{5-11}, cf. 1 P 1^{11}).

The Apostles, as we have seen, saw the purpose, and therefore the explanation, of this concrete historical event through the medium of the OT. Whatever view it may be expedient to take of the relation between Hebrew prophecy and Jesus of Nazareth, this fact is of primary importance, because it exhibits what in the view of the first messengers of the Cross was the essential character of the good news it was their mission to proclaim ; nor would the case be materially altered if the language of Law and Prophets had merely been chosen to illustrate the central idea of the Gospel. What we find is the remarkable manner in which the idea of the King and the Kingdom, consonant with contemporary Jewish expectation, is combined with that of the suffering Messiah, so alien to the current interpretation of the Scriptures as to present 'to the Jews a stumbling-block.' The antithesis between the Cross and the Resurrection was, indeed, such as to suggest that the death of Jesus was united to its marvellous sequel by a chain of causation removing it from the ordinary category of dissolution, and making it the interpretative fact of a career otherwise the most unintelligible in history. But the main

---

* These speculations must be distinguished from the teaching of the Calvinistic Supralapsarians of the 17th cent., which, relying upon such passages as Eph 3^{11}, 1 P 1^{20}, Rev 13^8 (?), maintained that the Atonement was itself the fulfilment of an eternal purpose.

point to observe is that the Resurrection, being in the first instance the crucial fact of experience which marked off for the disciples their Master Jesus as the Son of God (Ro 1^4 ὁρισθέντος, cf. Ac 10^{36-43} $13^{23.\ 32.\ 33}$), ratified, in the minds of those who had continued with Him in His temptations, that view of His work which had been before the eye of the Divine Sufferer throughout His ministry, and which He had progressively disclosed to hearts slow of belief, until a hitherto invincible prejudice had succumbed to the decisive evidence of accomplishment.

The persistence with which early heresies connected themselves with the Baptism of Jesus reveals the prominence which the event assumed in the story of the ministry, and goes far to authenticate the details of the Synoptic narrative (Mt 3^{13-17}, Mk 1^{9-11}, Lk $3^{21.\ 22}$, cf. Jn 1^{32-34}), the correspondence of which with the Apostolic view of the Saviour's mission is too subtle to warrant the theory that they are the glosses of a later tradition. In this narrative Jesus is represented as doing something more than declaring the obligation which rested upon Him to fulfil that righteousness characteristic of the Hebrew covenant. ' *Thus* it becometh us to fulfil all righteousness,' *i.e.* by submitting to the baptism which John would have withheld because it involved repentance and provided for the remission of sins. The Voice from Heaven, and the Temptation endured in the power of the baptismal Spirit (Mt 4^1, Mk 1^{12}, Lk 4^1), even if they be regarded merely as the interpretation of the subjective consciousness of Jesus, witness to the identity between the scheme of the ministerial life accepted from the first by the Son of Man and the gospel of the redeeming work preached by the Apostles. For the Voice blends the prophecy of the royal Son (Ps 2^7) with that of the beloved Servant (Is 42^1), and the Temptation is essentially the refusal of Messianic royalty on any condition but that of suffering service. It is no accident that the same Voice is heard again on the Mount of Transfiguration (Mt 17^5 and Mk 9^7 ὁ υἱός μου ὁ ἀγαπητός, Lk 9^{35} ὁ υἱός μου ὁ ἐκλελεγμένος [*v.l.* ἀγαπητός], cf. Is 42^1), when the manner in which righteousness is to be fulfilled is made explicit in the subject of Jesus' converse with Moses and Elijah, ' the decease which he was about to fulfil' (Lk 9^{31} πληροῦν, cf. Mt 3^{15} πληρῶσαι) ; and that again, from the moment when He begins to make plain to the unwilling ears of His disciples that His throne can be reached only through resurrection after suffering and death, He has to cry, 'Get thee behind me, Satan' (Mt 16^{23}). And the taunt of the rulers on Calvary, when the crucified Jesus is bidden to prove Himself the Christ of God, the chosen (Lk 23^{35} ὁ ἐκλεκτός), makes it clear that the claim to be at once the Messiah and the Servant, if doubted by the disciples and derided by the Jews, was at least in the hour of its accomplishment sufficiently understood.

It is the Divine necessity of dying which is prominent in the later teaching of the Lord, beginning from that crisis of the ministry which is emphatically presented in all the Synoptics (Mt 16^{21-28}, Mk 8^{31-9^1}, Lk 9^{22-27}). He sets His face towards it as the end (Lk 22^{37} [cf. Is 53^{12}] τελεσθῆναι and τέλος ἔχει, cf. Jn $19^{28.\ 30}$), the goal to which His whole life moves. And in the hour when the things concerning Him had fulfilment, He singled out the leading feature in the portrait of the Servant as that which above all others fastened its application upon Himself. 'I say unto you that this which is written must be fulfilled in me, And he was reckoned with transgressors.' The Prophet, who at the outset of His ministry read in the synagogue of Nazareth the words foreshadowing the deliverance which was to issue in the Kingdom of God (Lk $4^{18.\ 19}$ = Is $61^{1.\ 2}$), knew that for Himself it meant the Man of

Sorrows, led like the lamb of the Hebrew ritual to the slaughter, and in the power of His healing wounds making intercession for the transgressors of His people (Is 53 ; for the connexion with the Ceremonial Law see Davidson, *OT Prophecy*, ch. xxii.) There is thus no inconsistency between the language of Jesus as recorded in the Synoptics and those utterances of the Fourth Gospel which seem to remove the Passion and Death from the immediate historical conditions, and to represent them as the decision of eternal issues by the voluntary activity of the Divine Sufferer, who lays down His life of Himself and judges the prince of this world on the uplifted throne of the Cross (Jn 3^{14} $10^{17. 18}$ 12^{31-33} 14^{30} $16^{11. 33}$).

These considerations give peculiar point to the declaration which, according to both St. Matthew and St. Mark, stands in close relation to the request of the sons of Zebedee for eminent places in the Messianic kingdom. Messiah's kingship is based on service which takes specific form in the death He goes to accomplish—'The Son of Man came to give his life a ransom for many'—a substitution which made His soul an offering for sin, fulfilling all that was foreshadowed not only in the redemption of the people from Egypt, but also in the redemptions of the Ceremonial Law (Mk 10^{45}, Mt 20^{28} λύτρον ἀντί not ὑπέρ, cf. ἀντίλυτρον 1 Ti 2^6, λυτρώσηται Tit 2^{14}, ἐλυτρώθητε 1 P 1^{18}, where also the τίμιον αἷμα of Christ is the price ; Is 53^{10}, 2 S 7^{23}, Ex 13^{13}, Nu 18^{15}, cf. Ps 49^8).

That Jesus should thus have recognized the true significance of His death as a fact possessing not an accidental but an inherent worth, is not inconsistent with a due acknowledgment of the historical circumstances which became its efficient cause. With regard to the prophecy of Jehovah's Servant, it must be remembered that the Sufferer, though offering a sacrifice for sin of which the liturgical oblation is the type, yet incurs pain and death only through setting his face as a flint (Is 50^{4-9}) in maintaining truth and righteousness under conditions which inevitably made this witness a martyrdom. And it would be misreading the phenomena of the Gospel narrative to represent the propitiatory death of Christ as wantonly sought by our Lord in a manner inconsistent with the dictates of common morality. The Cross could not have been mediatorial if Jesus had been an official and conventional Messiah reaching Calvary by any other road than that which in the first instance made Him one with His brethren (He 2^{10-18}) in the pursuit of His own moral end. His death, which affects the conscience (He 9^{14} 10^{22}), is not represented as self-immolation. He 'witnessed before Pontius Pilate a good confession' (1 Ti 6^{13}, cf. 'the faithful witness,' Rev 1^5 3^{14}). His mission being to establish the kingdom upon a basis of surrender (Mt 20^{28}, Jn $13^{4. 13-15}$), upon a gospel preached to the poor (Lk 4^{18}) by one who is Himself lowly in heart (Mt 11^{29}), He must not shrink till He send forth judgment unto victory (Mt 12^{20}). When there is no more risk of quenching the smoking flax by appearing openly as the uncompromising foe of the hierarchy, He recognizes that His hour is come (Jn 12^{23} 17^1 *al.*, Mk 14^{41}, cf. Jn 2^4, Lk 22^{53}), changing the method of His discourse so that they who reject Him may perceive that He speaks of them (Mt 21^{45}), and without further parley join the inevitable issue. There is, however, no warrant for Mr. F. W. Newman's theory, that Jesus' denunciation of scribes and Pharisees was a deliberate provocation of judicial murder ; though it must be remarked that, assuming the knowledge of power to rise again the third day, we could not judge even such an action entirely by the ordinary standard. Still, if the one necessity of the case was a sacrificial death upon the stage of history, the event might have been

accomplished amid accessories more suggestive of ritual than the Crucifixion. But this would have been something less than a moral act, whereas the NT shows the propitiation wrought by Jesus Christ 'the righteous' (1 Jn 2^1, Ac 3^{14} 7^{52} 22^{14}) to have been something more. The Agony in the Garden, followed by the Seven Words from the Cross, attests the naturalness of the Passion as suffering, though voluntarily endured, yet inflicted from without. It is only after the Resurrection that the human actors in the tragedy fall out of sight, and the Cross can be presented absolutely as that which it behoved the Christ to suffer, so entering into His glory (Lk 24^{26}).

From what has been already said, it follows that an adequate soteriology, or theology of the Atonement which is genuinely evangelical, must be the expression of a spiritual experience resting upon Christ's death as the expiation of sin. With a few notable exceptions, foremost among them Dr. R. W. Dale, the trend of modern theology, since the publication of M'Leod Campbell's treatise on *The Nature of the Atonement*, has been on the whole to develop the doctrine on its ethical side, and to find its spiritual principle either in the sinless penitence or the perfect obedience of Jesus (*e.g.* Westcott, Wilson, Moberly, Scott Lidgett). The tendency of these writings has been, while dissipating theories of a non-moral 'transaction,' to obscure to a greater or less extent 'the offering of the body of Christ,' and to give an insufficient value to the Biblical account of His death as an objective act of propitiation addressed to the Father by the incarnate Son. No doubt English writers for the most part maintain that the 'penitence' and obedience of Christ are imparted by grace to the believer. But between the obedience and the grace, as that which gives meaning to both, NT theology places the substitutionary sacrifice.

St. Peter connects obedience with the 'sprinkling of the blood of Christ' (1 P $1^{2. 14. 18. 19}$) and the sin-bearing of the tree (2^{24}). Involving as these expressions do 'the blood of the covenant' (Ex 24^{6-8}, Lv 16^{14-19} $17^{11. 12}$, Zec 9^{11} ; cf. He 10^{29} 13^{20}, and, for the 'new covenant,' Jer 31^{31-34} 33^8, Ezk 36^{25}), and the laying of hands upon the head of the sin-offering (Lv 16^{21}, cf. Is 53^6 ; the whole passage [Is 53^{4-7}] should be carefully compared with 1 P 2^{21-25}, and the influence of the Levitical code in moulding language and ideas noted), both familiar conceptions of the Hebrew ritual, they point undoubtedly to a real transfer of guilt, a genuine substitution, as the true meaning of the 'glad tidings' (1 P 1^{12}), of which the Apostle was the witness (5^1). The Christian society is the 'people of God's own possession' ($2^{9. 10}$), ransomed and brought into covenant by the precious blood. The obedience and sufferings of Christians are not, therefore, redemptive, for such are already dead to sin (2^{24}).

With this the Johannine writings agree. Fellowship with God is the eternal life which Christians enjoy, but this mystical union * is effected by the purifying blood of Jesus His Son (1 Jn 1^7), in whom is forgiveness ($1^{9. 10}$ 2^1 3^5), who is the propitiation for the sins of the whole world ($2^2,4^{10}$, cf. 5^6 [Jn 19^{34}], Jn 4^{42} 11^{51}, Ro 3^{25} ἱλαστήριον). The antecedent power of Christ's death is thus explained by the sacrificial term ἱλασμός to be an effectual means for turning away the wrath of God, which the impressive imagery of the Apocalypse represents as resting upon the wicked (Rev $6^{16. 17}$ 14^{19} and *passim*). Nowhere is the significant figure of the Lamb more

* The *unio mystica* must not be confounded with atonement by pressing the etymology of the latter word (at-one-ment), the Pauline equivalent of which (καταλλαγή) St. John never uses. According to its proper meaning, the verb 'atone' is not transitive, but is followed by the preposition 'for.' Mr. Inge in *Contentio Veritatis* constantly ignores this.

emphatically applied to Christ than in the Johannine books (Jn 1[29. 36] 19[36] [Ex 12[46]], the Apocalypse, *passim*).

With the Apostle Paul we reach the fullest statement of the doctrine of the Atonement. And here it must be noted that the Epistles of the first imprisonment, which develop the teaching concerning the Person of Christ in His eternal relation to the Universe and the Church, follow those which give detailed expression to the reconciliation of believers to God through the redemption which is in Christ Jesus. It would seem, therefore, that theologians like Westcott, who subordinate redemption to the Incarnation, are less true to Christian experience than those who reach the Incarnation through the Atonement. For St. Paul the Cross in its twofold aspect of Death and Resurrection is the central fact which forms the subject of his gospel (1 Co 1[18. 23] 2[2], Gal 5[11], 1 Ti 2[5-7]), the basis of Baptism (see above) and of the Eucharist (see above), the source of the forgiveness of sins (Col 2[13. 14], cf. 3[12], Eph 4[32]), the motive of Christian morality (Ro 6[4]), the spring of faith (1 Co 12[3], cf. Ro 10[9]) and of spiritual life (2 Co 4[10. 11], Gal 2[20]), and the assurance of immortality (2 Ti 1[10]). To this fact there is a corresponding personal experience, so that baptism may be represented as involving an identification of the believer with his Lord so intimate that not only is the figure of putting on Christ as a garment felt to be appropriate to the initiatory Christian rite (see above), but His death, burial, and resurrection are regarded as reproduced in the believer (see above). From the Cross the Christian life takes its specific complexion, so that 'the new man created in righteousness' (Eph 4[24]) becomes 'crucified unto the world' (Gal 6[14]), branded in the body with the marks of the Lord Jesus (Gal 6[17]); glories in the Cross (v.[14]); and fills up that which is lacking in the sufferings of Christ (Col 1[24]). Obviously, therefore, the interpretation of this fact and its consequent experience is from the point of view of St. Paul the primary task of the Christian theologian.

The interpretative word used in St. Paul's soteriology is καταλλαγή, 'reconciliation' (Ro 5[11] AV 'atonement'), the root idea of which is restoration of personal relations between parties hitherto estranged. This involves the explanation of the 'catastrophe in human life,' sufficiently evident in common experience but inexplicable apart from the Hebrew realization of the personal God, which is set forth in Ro 1[18-28] as the rebellion of the unthankful human will against the claim of the Divine Creator (v.[21]). The need is universal (Ro 3[9. 23]);* but the later Augustinian terminology, which, in spite of Luther's return to a fuller Paulinism, still dominates the language even of Protestant divinity, tends by the use of such figures as 'vice' (*vitium*), 'flaw,' 'disease,' to palliate the exceeding sinfulness of sin and to obscure the personal significance of the Cross, which is always uppermost in St. Paul. Three points must be noted.

1. *Christ died 'to reconcile the Father to us.'*—This phrase, if not strictly Biblical, conveys the essential idea of Scripture, which is quite obscured by the statement that His death reconciles men to God. Modern teachers, concerned to vindicate the love of God, have inclined to represent the Cross as intended to produce merely a change in the moral life of the sinner. Not only

is this inconsistent with the idea of reconciliation, but St. Paul, while, with the NT generally, always representing the work of Christ as arising in the gracious will of the Father (2 Co 5[18. 19], Ro 5[8] 8[32], Col 1[19. 20], Eph 1[9. 10], 1 Th 5[9], Tit 3[4]; cf. 1 P 1[3], Jn 3[16] and *passim*, 1 Jn 3[1]), yet invariably regards it as the loving act (2 Co 5[14] 8[9], Gal 1[4] 2[20], Ro 8[37], Eph 5[2], cf. Jn 10[11], Rev 1[5]) of a mediator (1 Ti 2[5. 6], cf. He 9[15]), producing in the first instance a change in God's attitude towards the sinner (2 Th 1[8. 9], Ro 8[1], cf. vv.[7. 8]), turning away wrath (1 Th 1[10], Ro 5[9]), removing trespasses (2 Co 5[19]), and providing a channel through which God might forgive sins as an act not only of mercy but of justice (Ro 3[26]).

It is perhaps unnecessary to argue with the formality which sets up an abstract Law * to which even God must do homage. At this point even Dale becomes somewhat cumbrous. But it is obvious that even the parable of the Prodigal Son would not ring true in human ears unless it was for ever interpreted by a transaction which gives due weight to the enormity of a sin that entailed the sacrifice of the Father's only Son. Nor would St. Paul have succeeded in commending the death of Christ to the Christian conscience save by insisting that only thus could God reconcile a world unto Himself and be alike just and the justifier of the believer.

2. *The death of Christ is the act of God* (Tit 2[13] [cf. 2 P 1[1]], Ro 1[4], 2 Co 4[4], Col 1[15], Ph 2[6], Ro 9[5 (?)], Ac 20[28]).—'It is at this point in the last resort that we become convinced of the deity of Christ' (Denney). 'God was in Christ,' who was 'marked off as the Son of God by the resurrection.' Grace is always in St. Paul the free act of God's favour (Ro 3[24] 4[4. 5] *al.*), and it is 'the grace of our Lord Jesus Christ' (Ro 5[15] 16[20], 2 Co 8[9] 13[14]), whereby we have been enriched. The love of Christ which constrains us, because He died for all, is Divine (2 Co 5[14. 19. 20] 'on behalf of Christ' = 'as though God were entreating by us'). The position of the justified sinner is that of a restored sonship, because his redemption from first to last is the action towards him of the eternal God Himself. His right relation to the Father is witnessed by, or rather is, the presence of the Spirit of the Son 'sent forth' into his heart by that same God who had 'sent forth' the Son Himself to work out a redemption under the conditions which imposed this necessity of love upon the paternal heart of God (Gal 4[4-6]). When this is once apprehended, the objections to a doctrine of substitution ('ego sum peccatum tuum, tu es justitia mea'—2 Co 5[21]) are seen to have no application in fact. They are valid only if the activity of the Mediator is separated sharply from that of the Father. Such a distinction is neither Pauline nor Christian. The threefoldness of God is a revelation incidental to 'the unfolding of the work of Divine Atonement' (see Moberly, *Atonement and Personality*, ch. viii.). With St. Paul, as with St. John, it is the Father who is revealed in the Son (see above), whose work is manifest in the work of Christ. Redemption is parallel to Creation (Gal 6[15], Col 1[18], Eph 1[10], 1 Co 15[20-28. 45]; cf. Jn 1[1-18], Rev 21[1. 5]). If the morality of the latter lies in the fact that 'God saw that it was good,' the justice of the former is witnessed not only by the 'new creation' but by the infinite worth of the Son (1 Co 6[20]), whom God gave up for us all and who endured the Cross.

<hr>

* Notice that St. Paul *more Hebraico* states sin as a universal fact—'all have sinned'—without developing a theory by physical analogy. No amount of 'originality' in sin detracts from full moral responsibility towards God in the individual. Mr. Tennant in his *Hulsean Lectures* speaks as though the traditional doctrine of sin neutralized personal disobedience; but this is not the case, as a right understanding of St. Paul's doctrine of reconciliation in Christ will show.

<hr>

* Such theories, like the attempt of Anselm in *Cur Deus Homo* to express the Atonement in terms of the feudal idea of society dominant in the Middle Age, to which they are akin, no doubt perform useful service in freeing the teaching of Scripture from unwarrantable and misleading accretions, but they are a method of expressing rather than of explaining the problem.

3. *Reconciliation is antecedent to the renewal of the individual.*—This is almost wholly ignored in modern German theology, which thereby goes far to forfeit its claim to be a true development of Lutheran teaching, losing touch with the NT generally and especially with St. Paul. Ritschl, for example, for whom the statement that 'Christ expiated sin by His passion' has 'very little warrant in the Biblical circle of thought,' regards the death of Jesus merely as 'the summary expression of the fact that Christ maintained His religious unity with God,' and places the forgiveness of sins in the 'effective union' of believers with God in that Divine kingdom which it was the vocation of Jesus to found (*Justification and Reconciliation,* Eng. tr. ch. viii.). Now, while Ritschl thus recovers a truly Apostolic conception in the Kingdom of God as the primary object of reconciliation (see below), he does so only at the expense of the 'finished work,' which is the glory of all true evangelicalism. St. Paul in particular leaves no doubt as to the objective character of the 'reconciliation' wrought by Christ, which stands complete before the preaching whereby comes hearing and faith. 'While we were enemies we were reconciled to God through the death of his Son' (Ro 5[10], cf. vv.[6. 8. 9], Col 1[21. 22]). He has previously shown (Ro 3[24-26]) that the vindication of God's righteousness (ἔνδειξις τῆς δικαιοσύνης αὐτοῦ), which conscience requires as a condition of the acquittal of sinners, has already been given in the redemption wrought by Christ, involving as it did the bloodshedding of the Son of God, which constituted the Redeemer a propitiation for sin. The equivalence adumbrated by the symbolic transfer of guilt to the head of the victim was consummated in Christ (Ro 8[3], 2 Co 5[21], Gal 3[13], cf. Lv 16[5] also Hebrews, *passim,* see below). The spectacle of such a substitution—not one man redeeming his brother, but God putting Himself in the sinner's place—was the manifestation of a Divine righteousness to which Law and Prophets, the Hebrew dispensation, had witnessed (Ro 3[21]). In Christ crucified that righteousness is complete, needing no human condition (ἔργον) to perfect it, but offered freely to him that believeth on the justifier of the ungodly, so that his faith can be reckoned instead of righteousness,* because through it the sinner appropriates Christ's finished work and becomes 'the righteousness of God in him' (2 Co 5[21]). Here the Atonement, as St. Paul interprets it, leads to the development of the doctrine of the Incarnation (Ro 5[12-21], cf. 1 Co 15[21. 22]). Christ is the second Adam; He 'recapitulates' (Eph 1[10], cf. *Protev. Jac.* 13, and Irenæus, bk. III. ch. xxx. 'recapitulans in se Adam') the human race, so that His redemptive, recreative act has more than a representative value. In Him 'all died' (2 Co 5[14]). This characteristic principle of Pauline theology—'in Christ'—expands on the other side into the doctrine of the new life through membership (Ro 12[4. 5], Eph 4[25]) in the body of Christ and fellowship of the one Spirit (1 Co 12[13], 2 Co 13[14]). The second Adam is a quickening spirit, endowed with the grace of unction (Hooker, *Eccl. Pol.*, bk. v. ch. lv.), imparting through the Resurrection a Spirit which dwells in the believer and finally quickens even his mortal body (Ro 8[11]).

That the communion of the elect people with God meant the indwelling of His Spirit, is a familiar idea of the OT (Is 63[9-14] Ezk 36[27]). So

* Much harm has resulted from insisting on the 'forensic' character of this justification. No doubt δικαιόω has associations of the law court; but it is as absurd to suppose that legal fictions were present to the mind of St. Paul as to ascribe these ideas to the compiler of Genesis (Gn 15[6]) or the author of the thirty-second Psalm (Ps 32[2]). The word expresses only the free forgiveness of the Father's love.

the body of Christ, which is the Church (Col 1[24]), being the primary object of redemption (Ac 20[28], Eph 1[14. 22] 2[11-16] 4[4-6], Tit 2[14]; cf. 1 P 2[9. 10]), reconciled through death (Eph 2[13]), becomes a habitation of the Spirit (Eph 2[21. 22]), distributed according to the measure of faith to the several members (Eph 4[7. 16], Ro 12[4]), which through the Presence ('Christ in you,' 'the Spirit of the Son shed abroad in your hearts,' 'the fulness of God,' Eph 3[19]) have a common access to the Father (Eph 2[18], cf. 3[12]), manifest the gifts of the Spirit (1 Co 12[4-11], Ro 12[6-8]), and in mutual dependence grow together to 'the measure of the stature of the fulness of Christ' (Eph 4[13. 15. 16], Col 2[19], Ro 12[4-6]). That this teaching, though given in St. Paul's individual manner, was no personal speculation of his own, may be gathered from its close relation to the great social sacraments of Baptism and the Eucharist, which would be startling if, in view of their generally accepted significance in the primitive community, it were not obvious (Eph 4[4. 5], 1 Co 10[17]).

To claim for the death of Christ that it is a completed act of reconciliation, the ground of the believing sinner's justification, and thus alike the subject of adoring gratitude and the source of renewed moral effort, is to establish a doctrine satisfactory to reason rather because it sets the several parts of Scripture and Christian teaching in an intelligible proportion to one another, than because it is itself rationally explained. The Cross establishes the Law (Ro 3[31]), and, as thus interpreted, manifests and supplies the need of the human spirit, and thus finds its justification in experience. But propitiatory sacrifice remains to be apprehended rather than understood. This is because it is a fact of religion rather than of ethics. Men have felt the need of something to set them right with God, even when they have been far from knowing that He is love. If this distinction be not perceived, we shall fail to see the true bearing of the evidence from Comparative Religion for the universality of the idea of atonement as manifested in myth, ritual, and custom. Thus Sir Oliver Lodge (see art. 'Suggestions towards the Reinterpretation of Christian Doctrine,' *Hibbert Journal,* vol. ii., No. 3), while admitting the cogency of the universal belief in immortality, sees in the crudities of the widespread practice of sacrifice only a reason for discounting this element in traditional Christianity. There can be no doubt that atonement is fundamental to the idea of sacrifice (see Robertson Smith, *Religion of the Semites,* Lect. vi. p. 219; Lect. xi. pp. 377–384), and that this idea of 'covering' is prominent in the ritual of the OT (see Schultz, *OT Theol.*, Eng. tr. vol. i. pp. 384–400).

Far from deprecating, or even ignoring the ancient sacrifices, the NT, as we have seen, presents Christ as the 'Lamb of God.' And in the Epistle to the Hebrews the Son is explicitly set forth as 'Himself the victim and Himself the priest,' manifested once at the consummation of the ages to put away sin by the sacrifice of Himself (He 9[26]). Though, unlike St. Paul, who sees the analogy between heathen sacrifices and the Christian Eucharist (1 Co 10[21]), the author of this Epistle confines his attention to the worship of the Hebrews, the argument may be legitimately extended to embrace the 'blood of bulls and goats' offered under any system for what in view of the Cross is seen to be a typical, conventional purification and approach to God. There is, however, one important point in which the Mosaic sacrifices differ from all others. They fulfilled the primary condition of Divine appointment, and therefore availed within the limits of the institution. They were inadequate, not because, like the oblations of the heathen, they were material, but because, unlike the offering of Christ, they were transitory (He 10[1. 11]), and alien to those who brought them (9[12. 25]). Christ, who elsewhere in the NT appears as the Mediator, Saviour, Word made flesh, here becomes specifically the Priest (2[11] [ὁ ἁγιάζων = 'priest'; the act of consecration is identified with the Cross in 13[12], cf. 2[9. 10]] 3[1] and *passim*), the appropriate scientific term, as we may call it, for whoever establishes the proper end of religion, communion with God. His is a 'finished work,' because by Divine appointment (3[2] 5[1. 4. 5]) He is 'a priest for ever' (5[10] 7[24. 28]), who 'through the eternal Spirit' (9[14]) obediently (5[8] 10[9]) fulfilled the priestly function (8[3]) in offering the body prepared for Him by the will of God (10[5-10]) as an eternal sacrifice (10[12], cf. 5[9]). This is no metaphorical self-sacrifice, the essence of which is undeviating conformity to the general law which conditions human life. It is 'through his own blood' (9[12]) that He enters once for all into heaven. This lays the emphasis on His death as the means through which He makes that purification of sins (1[3] 9[14]) whereby access is gained to the throne of grace (10[19] 4[14. 16]). The open way witnesses to a sacrifice already offered and accepted (10[10] ἡγιασμένοι not ἁγιαζόμενοι, 10[14] τετελείωκεν [cf. Jn 19[30]] τοὺς ἁγιαζομένους, which RV rightly translates 'them that are [not 'are being'] sanctified'). The new covenant is thus dedicated with blood (9[18-22]), not because life is liberated through death (for why should death effect this result except according to Oriental mysticism?), but because a death must have taken place for the redemption of transgressions (9[15] 10[29], cf. Mk 14[24] and parallels), which is, in the phraseology of sacrifice, what St. Peter says when he declares that 'Christ bore our sins in his body on the tree' (1 P 2[24]).

Minds to which sacerdotal ideas are repugnant will always resent such language as sophistical and superstitious, and, if they do not reject, will endeavour to explain away what is certainly the meaning of the Epistle to the Hebrews. No doubt this particular mould of thought is not necessary to the gospel, which is content to assert that Christ died for our sins. Yet the consequence of rejecting it is likely to be a denial of the atoning character of Christ's death. To describe the central fact of the gospel in ethical terms as a revelation of love, an exhibition of obedience, or a manifestation of the Divine character, expresses a side of truth, apart from which a doctrine of substitution may become, if not immoral, at least superstitious. But such descriptions cease to be true, if they are taken for definitions. The Cross is no longer a revelation, if it be not a redemption. If it be large enough to deal with a situation of which the factors are God, man, and sin; if it be a fact of religion through which men approach that Personality in whom they have their being, its significance cannot be understood unless it be recognized as a mystery, illuminating and illuminated by life and experience, but itself not reducible to simpler terms. It is at this point that 'mysteries,' in the Greek sense of the word, have their place. No organized religious system can entirely dispense with them. And Christianity with its sacraments of initiation and membership bears witness to the 'mystery of godliness' (1 Ti 3[16]) preached by it among the nations. Whatever may be the case with individuals, the race has found no language in which to express its need towards God but that of propitiatory sacrifice. To the method of its satisfaction many analogies point, but all taken together cannot sum up the Cross. For it is essentially an eternal fact, embracing but not embraced by experience; and its theory, though to the spiritual man increasingly rational, must ever be less than that which it seeks

to explain. It is not distrust of reason, but the confidence of intelligent faith which, the more surely it realizes the reasonableness of the evangelical doctrine of the Atonement, will the more readily make the words of Bp. Butler its own : 'Some have endeavoured to explain the efficacy of what Christ has done and suffered for us, beyond what the Scripture has authorized; others, probably because they could not explain it, have been for taking it away, and confining His office as Redeemer of the world to His instruction, example, and government of the Church. Whereas the doctrine of the Gospel appears to be . . . not only that He revealed to sinners that they were in a capacity of salvation . . . but . . . that He put them into this capacity of salvation by what He did and suffered for them. . . . And it is our wisdom thankfully to accept the benefit, by performing the conditions upon which it is offered, on our part, without disputing how it was procured on His' (*Analogy*, pt. ii. ch. v.).

LITERATURE.—Among English works, J. M'Leod Campbell, *The Nature of the Atonement*; H. N. Oxenham, *Catholic Doctrine of the A.*; R. W. Dale, *The Atonement*; J. M. Wilson, *Hulsean Lectures*; J. Denney, *The Death of Christ*, and *The A. and the Modern Mind*; J. Scott Lidgett, *The Spiritual Principle of the A.* (Appendix on 'The Doctrine of the A. in Church History'); R. C. Moberly, *Atonement and Personality*; B. F. Westcott, *The Victory of the Cross*; W. Alexander, *Verbum Crucis*; W. O. Burrows, *The Mystery of the Atonement*. The student should also consult A. M. Fairbairn, *Christ in Modern Theol.*, Div. III. ch. ii.; W. Sanday, *Priesthood and Sacrifice*; B. F. Westcott, *Com. on Ep. to the Heb.*, *passim*, also dissertation on 'The Gospel of Creation' in *The Epistles of St. John*; A. B. Davidson, *Theol. of the OT*, 350 ff.; S. R. Driver, art. 'Propitiation' in Hastings' *DB*; W. P. Paterson, art. 'Sacrifice,' *ib.* Among foreign writers may be mentioned A. Ritschl, *Die christl. Lehre von d. Rechtfertigung u. d. Versöhnung* (Eng. tr. *Justification and Reconciliation*); A. Seeberg, *Der Tod Christi*; W. Herrmann, *Der Verkehr d. Christen mit Gott* (Eng. tr. *Communion with God*); B. Weiss, *Lehrbuch d. biblisch. Theol. d. Neuen Test.* (Eng. tr. i. 419 ff. and ii. 220 ff.); A. Sabatier, *The Doctrine of the A. and its historical Evolution* (Eng. tr.). As landmarks in the development of doctrine Athanasius' *de Incarnatione* and Anselm's *Cur Deus Homo* are amongst the most important.   J. G. SIMPSON.

ATONEMENT, DAY OF.—See DAY OF ATONEMENT.

ATTRACTION.—Under this head we shall consider the attraction possessed and exerted by the character and the teaching of Christ as portrayed and expressed in the four Gospels. That character and that teaching are, of course, inseparable; for the work and the message of Christ are vitally and absolutely a personal work and a personal message. Thus the supreme appeal of the gracious invitation is : 'Come unto Me' (Mt 11[28]). Christ's character and teaching have an attraction, both extensive and intensive, which goes far beyond the merely æsthetic : it is a dynamical and spiritual attraction including and permeating man's personality. On the one hand, there is the uniqueness of the message (Jn 7[46]); on the other, the beauty of the character (Jn 1[14]); and yet the attraction of Christ for all men is something deeper than expression or analysis, the attraction of One *lifted up from the earth, drawing all men to Himself* (Jn 12[32]). This attraction is the continual directed pressure of His Holy Spirit in the hearts of men, and its reality is suggested by Ignatius' comparison of the Cross to a crane of which the Holy Spirit is the rope to draw mankind upwards to the Father in heaven (*Eph.* 9). The universality of this attraction is exemplified in the Gospel records. Jesus was the centre of attraction for multitudes, men and women and children (Mk 1[27] 2[2], Lk 19[48] etc.); and Zacchæus (Lk 19[4]), Nicodemus (Jn 3[2]), the 'Greeks' (Jn 12[21]) are only instances of this attractive power which had its culmination in the response of the Apostles to their Master's call. In these cases the attraction was visibly, audibly, and sensibly personal; the objects of it saw, heard, and often felt *the Man that is called JESUS* (Jn 9[11], 1 Jn 1[1]).

To-day, the attraction of the teaching must be held to be personal still, through that action of the Holy Spirit which is implied in the inspiration of the Gospels. This attraction may also be said to have its seat in the fact of the revelation of God-in-man vouchsafed to the race of men fashioned in the likeness of God. Thus no limits can be set to the efficacy of the attraction of Christ which starts from such a source : witness the unfailing attractiveness of the Sermon on the Mount (Mt 5-7) and the last discourses (Jn 13-17). The attraction, too, increases many-fold as it takes effect in drawing us nearer to the Master. One feature of this will be the more easy and quick perception of fresh beauties and glories in the four-fold Gospel of Christ, the acquisition of grace upon grace (Mt 11, Mk 10, Lk 15, Jn 9).

More difficult of expression, and intertwined with this attraction of the teaching, is the attraction of the *character*. Christ appealed to it. 'Me ye have not always' is the pathetic appeal He made as man (Mt 26[11]); 'I am with you all the days' is the glorious promise He makes as God (Mt 28[20]). Above all, however, it is the work of Christ in the sacrifice of self for love of others that draws the heart of man with cords stronger and surer than any variable and uncertain attractions. 'Having loved his own which were in the world, he loved them unto the end' (to the uttermost, εἰς τέλος, Jn 13[1]). It is the Cross of Christ which is the supreme instrument of the attraction, the Cross on which He was lifted up in glory and in shame.

LITERATURE.—Seeley, *Ecce Homo*[15], p. 156 f. ; Bruce, *Galilean Gospel*, p. 30 ff. and *passim* ; Dale, *Living Christ*, p. 42 ff., *Atonement*[7], p. 438 f.   W. B. FRANKLAND.

ATTRIBUTES OF CHRIST.

— In the Divine Person of Jesus Christ two perfect Natures were united. We shall therefore find attributes belonging to (1) His Divine Nature, (2) the union of the two Natures, (3) His true Human Nature. As in dealing with certain passages the extent of the Kenosis will weigh greatly, the present arrangement must be taken as largely provisional.

i. ATTRIBUTES BELONGING TO CHRIST'S DIVINE NATURE.—Jesus Christ is the manifestation of the Divine attributes. He is 'the image (εἰκών) of the invisible God' (Col 1[15]); 'the effulgence (ἀπαύγασμα) of his glory, and the very image (χαρακτήρ) of his substance' (He 1[3]); 'the power of God and the wisdom of God' (1 Co 1[24])—synonyms for Λόγος, in the phraseology of Jewish speculators. He applied to Himself words spoken of God, making the significant change of 'Me' to 'Thee' (Lk 7[27], cf. Mal 3[1] and Lk 1[17] 3[4]); He asserted that He came forth from God (ἐκ Jn 8[42], cf. παρά 17[8], ἀπό 13[3]), words which 'can only be interpreted of the true divinity of the Son of which the Father is the source and fountain' (Westcott); He claimed the power of interpreting and revising the Mosaic law (Mt 5[27f], Mk 10[4f]); He acted in the temple as its master (Jn 2[14f], Mt 21[12]); He accepted from Thomas the supreme title (Jn 20[28]), and joined His name permanently with that of the Father (Mt 28[19]). St John identified the Divine Person of Isaiah's vision with Christ (Jn 12[41]). St Paul charged the Ephesian elders to 'feed the Church of God which he purchased with his own blood' (Ac 20[28]) and applied to Christ the words of Joel, 'Whosoever shall call upon the name of the LORD shall be saved' (Ro 10[13]). Thus He is One to whom prayer is offered (Ac 7[59] 1[24] probably), cf. one of the earliest names for His disciples (Ac 9[14. 21], 1 Cor 1[2]). In the Epistles His Divinity is everywhere assumed and is 'present in solution in whole pages from

which not a single text could be quoted that explicitly declares it.' * His name is joined with that of the Father, and a singular verb follows (1 Th 3[11], 2 Th 2[16. 17]); the title 'Lord' in the highest sense is given (Ro 10[9], 1 Cor 12[3], etc.); He is 'God blessed for ever' † (Ro 9[5]), and 'in him dwelleth all the fulness (πλήρωμα) of the Godhead bodily' (Col 2[9], cf. 1[19] Jn 1[16]).

1. Eternal Existence.—Christ claimed that He came down from heaven without ceasing to be what He was before (Jn 3[13]). Existence without beginning is implied in 8[58] 'before Abraham was born (γενέσθαι) I am' (εἰμί), cf. Rev 21[6]; and He spoke of the glory which He had with the Father before the world was (Jn 17[5]). The Λόγος was in the beginning, He was the 'mediate Agent of Creation' (Jn 1[1. 3], Col 1[16], He 1[2. 10]); He is the upholder of all things (Col 1[17], He 1[3]), the 'first-born of all creation' and 'before all things' (Col 1[15. 17], cf. the use of 'manifested' (φανερούσθαι) in 1 Ti 3[16], 1 P 1[20], etc.

2. Unique Relation to God.—In a few passages only does Jesus call Himself the Son of God (Lk 22[70], Jn 5[25] 9[35] 11[4], cf. Mt 27[43], Jn 10[36]); yet He was early conscious of His Sonship (Lk 2[49]). He frequently accepted the title (cf. Mt 16[16]), and this led to the charge of blasphemy (Jn 19[7], cf. 5[18]). From the earliest time it was adopted as expressing the uniqueness of His Person (Ac 9[20], Ro 1[4], etc.). He is described as the 'Only-begotten' (μονογενής, Jn 1[14. 18] 3[16. 18], 1 Jn 4[9]). He spoke of 'My Father,' 'Your Father,' but not of 'Our Father' (except as a form of address to be used by His disciples in prayer, Mt 6[9], Lk 11[2] AV), 'thus drawing a sharp line of distinction between Himself and His disciples, from which,' says Dalman,‡ 'it may be perceived that it was not the veneration of those that came after that first assigned to Him an exceptional relation to God incapable of being transferred to others.' In this respect Mt 11[27], which forms the link between the Synoptics and the Fourth Gospel, is quite explicit (cf. Hastings' *DB* ii. 623); cf. also Mk 13[32] and the clear distinction made in Jn 20[17].

3. Union and Equality.—The Jews interpreted His words 'My Father worketh even until now and I work' as making Himself equal with God, and He did not correct them (Jn 5[17. 18]). 'I and the Father are one' (ἓν ἐσμεν) implies one essence not one Person (10[30]), cf. 5[23] 10[33] 14[7f.] 17[11. 21f.]. It is difficult to describe the manner in which St. Paul associates Him with the Father as the ground of the Church's being and the source of spiritual grace and peace, in any other terms than as ascribing to Him a coequal Godhead (1 Th 1[1] 3[11f.], 2 Th 1[1], 2 Co 13[14]), cf. Ph 2[6] (οὐχ ἁρπαγμὸν ἡγήσατο τὸ εἶναι ἴσα θεῷ).

4. Subordination and Dependence — such as belong to the filial relation—are also clearly implied in Jn 5[19] ('The Son can do nothing of himself, but what he seeth the Father doing : for what things soever he doeth, these the Son also doeth in like manner'), and in Jn 14[28] ('The Father is greater than I'), cf. also Jn 5[22. 26] 6[37]. So in Epp. 'All things are yours; and ye are Christ's; and Christ is God's' (1 Co 3[21. 23]), cf. 1 Co 11[3] 15[28].

5. Universal Power is frequently claimed by Christ as His even on earth, although it could not be fully exercised until after the Ascension (Lk 10[22] ‖ Jn 16[15]). He is given authority (ἐξουσία) over all flesh (Jn 17[2]); 'All authority hath been given unto me in heaven and on earth' (Mt 28[18]), cf. Jn 3[35] 13[3]. Accordingly St. Peter describes Him as 'Lord of all' (Ac 10[36]); He is 'over all' (Ro 9[5]); and the 'head of all principality and power' (Col 2[10]).

---

* Dale, *Christian Doctrine*, p. 87.
† See Sanday-Headlam, *Romans*, pp. 233-238.
‡ *The Words of Jesus*, p. 190 (Eng. tr.).

He is present still with His Church though invisible (Mt 18²⁰ 28²⁰, cf. 1 Co 5⁴), ruling and guiding (Ac 9¹⁰ 22¹⁸ 23¹¹, and cf. the letters to the Churches, Rev 2. 3).

6. Divine Consciousness and Knowledge. — Jesus claimed a unique knowledge of the Father and the exclusive power of revealing Him (Mt 11²⁷). He spoke of heavenly things which could only be known by Divine consciousness (Mt 18¹⁰· ¹⁹, Lk 15¹⁰, Jn 3¹² 14¹). He was the great Prophet which was to come (Jn 6¹⁴, Ac 3²²), the fullest revealer of God's will (He 1²), but He differed essentially from even the highest prophets, in that He spoke with authority as from Himself, and never introduced His message by such words as 'Thus saith the Lord.' 'In him are all the treasures of wisdom and knowledge hidden' (Col 2³). He knew (Jn 18⁴) and made known the details of His Passion and Resurrection (Mk 8³¹ 9³¹ 10³³ etc., cf. 14⁸· ⁹). He foretold the sufferings of His disciples (Mt 10¹⁸ᶠ·), the destruction of Jerusalem (Lk 19⁴³· ⁴⁴ 21²¹), events preceding the end of the world (Mt 24 ‖) and the judgment of mankind (see below). Here too may be mentioned His power of knowing the thoughts of men. Such knowledge is described both as relative, acquired (γινώσκειν, cf. Mk 2⁸), and absolute, possessed (εἰδέναι, cf. Jn 6⁶¹, Lk 11¹⁷), cf. Lk 7³⁹· ⁴⁰ 9⁴⁷. He seems to be addressed as καρδιογνώστης in Ac 1²⁴, which agrees with what is told as to His supernatural knowledge of the thoughts and lives of persons, cf. Jn 2²⁴· ²⁵ ('He knew all men. . . . he himself knew what was in man'), also Lk 19⁵, Jn 1⁴⁸ 4¹⁸· ²⁹ 6⁶⁴ 11¹¹· ¹⁴. It appears also with regard to things (Mt 17²⁷ 21² 26¹⁸, Lk 5⁴⁻⁶, cf. Jn 21⁶). Whether such passages imply absolute omniscience, or omniscience conditioned by human nature, depends upon the view taken of the Kenosis (see Westcott, Add. Note on Jn 2²⁴; Gore, *Bamp. Lect.* p. 147).

7. Self-assertion and Exclusive Claims. — His works were such as no other man did (Jn 15²⁴), His words shall outlast heaven and earth (Mt 24³⁵), men will be judged by their relation to Him (Mt 7²³ 10³²), and by their belief or unbelief on Him (Mk 16¹⁶, Jn 6⁴⁰ 12⁴⁸). He requires the forsaking of everything which may prove a hindrance to following Him (Mt 8²¹ 10³⁷, Mk 10²¹, Lk 14²⁶). Suffering and loss incurred for His Name's sake will be rewarded in the Regeneration (Mt 19²⁹ ‖), even now those who suffer for His sake are blessed (Mt 5¹⁰ᶠ·). He claims to be the Light of the world (Jn 8¹² 9⁵ 12⁴⁶), the Way, the Truth, and the Life (Jn 14⁶). Eternal life, spiritual strength, and growth can come only from union with Him and feeding on Him (Jn 5⁴⁰ 6⁵¹ᶠ· 10²⁸ 15⁴· ⁵ 17²). He is the Giver of rest and peace (Mt 11²⁸, Jn 14²⁷). And such claims are endorsed by St. John (Jn 1⁹, 1 Jn 5¹²) and St. Paul (Ro 8¹, Ph 4¹³, 1 Ti 1¹²).

ii. ATTRIBUTES BELONGING TO THE UNION OF THE TWO NATURES. — **1. Mediation.** — There is a twofold Mediatorial activity ascribed to the Son of God which must be distinguished ; that presented in the revelation of the Logos proceeding from God all-creating and all-sustaining ; and that exhibited in the work of the Christ, leading back to God and transforming the relation of contrast into one of union, that God may be all in all.* The former has been already mentioned, the latter appears in passages which speak of Christ as delivering us from sin and Satan (Jn 12³¹· ³², He 2¹⁴· ¹⁵, 1 Jn 3⁵· ⁸), as obtaining for us eternal life (Jn 3¹⁴ᶠ· 6⁵¹, Ro 6²³ etc.), as procuring the gracious influence of the Holy Spirit (Jn 14¹⁶· ²⁶, Ac 2³³, Tit 3⁵· ⁶ etc.), conferring Christian graces (1 Co 1⁴ᶠ·, Eph 1³· ⁴ etc.), and acting as our representative High Priest (He 4¹⁴ 7²⁵ᶠ· etc.).† The title 'Mediator' (μεσίτης) occurs in 1 Ti 2⁵, He 8⁶ 9¹⁵ 12²⁴.

* See Martensen, *Christian Dogmatics,* § 180.
† Dale, *Atonement,* p. 451.

2. Sovereignty. — One object of Christ's coming was to found a world-wide imperishable society, called the Kingdom of Heaven or the Kingdom of God. He was foretold in prophecy as King (Zec 9⁹, cf. Mt 21⁵). He Himself spoke of His Kingdom (Mt 13⁴¹ 16²⁸, Lk 22³⁰) and accepted the title from Pilate, but explained that it was 'not of this world' (Jn 18³⁶· ³⁷). Satan tempted Him to antedate it by a short but sinful method (Mt 4⁸· ⁹). He is 'King of Kings and Lord of Lords' (Rev 19¹⁶, cf. 11¹⁵).

Dalman (*Words of Jesus,* p. 133 f.) thinks, assuming an Aramaic original, that ἐν τῇ βασ. μου or αὐτοῦ would have to be rendered 'when I am King,' etc., and Lk 23⁴² 'as King' ; cf. Dn 6²⁹ בְּמַלְכוּת דָּרְיָוֶשׁ 'in the reign of Darius.' On the 'originality' and 'audacity' of Christ's design to form a world-wide kingdom see Liddon, *Bamp. Lect.* iii.; *Ecce Homo,* ch. v.

3. Consciousness of His Mission was ever present to His mind. Frequently He uses such expressions as 'the Father that sent me' (Jn 6⁴⁴ 8¹⁶, cf. 20²¹), 'Him that sent me' (Jn 7³³ 12⁴⁴ 16⁵), 'I am sent' (Mt 15²⁴, Lk 4⁴³). There was the sense of purpose in His life, 'To this end am I come into the world, that I should bear witness unto the truth' (Jn 18³⁷) ; it is implied in the repeated use of 'must' (δεῖ), implying 'moral obligation, especially that constraint which arises from Divine appointment' (Grimm-Thayer, see Mk 8³¹, Lk 24⁴⁶ TR, Jn 3¹⁴ etc.) ; and cf. Lk 9⁵¹ 'He steadfastly set (ἐστήριξε) his face to go to Jerusalem.'

4. Sinlessness. — While He had the most perfect appreciation of sin and holiness, while He prescribed repentance and conversion, rebuking all self-righteousness and pride, He was absolutely without any consciousness of sin or need of repentance in Himself. He claimed to be free from it (Jn 14³⁰) ; He challenged examination and conviction (Jn 8⁴⁶) ; He could say at the end : 'I glorified thee on the earth, having accomplished the work which thou hast given me to do' (Jn 17⁴, cf. Jn 8²⁹ 19³⁰, Mt 3¹⁷ 17⁵ ; and as to His best disciples, Lk 17¹⁰). The truth of His claim was testified by His forerunner (Mt 3¹⁴), most intimate friends (Jn 1¹⁴), enemies (Mk 14⁵⁵ᶠ·), judges (Jn 18³⁸, Mt 27²⁴ etc., Lk 23¹⁵), and betrayer (Mt 27⁴)—on Mk 10¹⁸ see the Commentaries. Christ's moral perfection is recognized everywhere in the Epistles : 'who knew no sin' (2 Co 5²¹) ; 'who did no sin, neither was guile found in his mouth' (1 P 2²²). He is holy (ἅγιος, Ac 3¹⁴, Rev 3⁷ ; ὅσιος, He 7²⁶), righteous (δίκαιος, 1 P 3¹⁸, 1 Jn 2¹), pure (ἁγνός, 1 Jn 3³), guileless and undefiled (ἄκακος, ἀμίαντος, He 7²⁶) ; cf. He 4¹⁵, 1 Jn 3⁵, 1 P 1¹⁹.

5. Glory. — St. John, summing up his experience, writes : 'We beheld his glory, glory as of the only-begotten from the Father' (Jn 1¹⁴) ; here many find a reference to the Shekinah (note ἐσκήνωσεν) and interpret δόξα as the 'totality of the Divine attributes' (cf. Liddon, *B L²* 232) ; others, as 'a glory which corresponded with His filial relation to the Father even when He had laid aside His divine glory' (Westcott). Isaiah in his vision saw His glory (Jn 12⁴¹), it was manifested in His 'signs' (Jn 2¹¹), and at the Transfiguration (2 P 1¹⁷). In some sense it was laid aside or veiled at the Incarnation (Jn 17⁵), but Christ constantly spoke of it as regained by means of His death and resurrection (Jn 12²³ 13³¹ 17¹· ⁵), cf. Jn 12¹⁶, Ph 3²¹, and Rev 5¹² ('Worthy is the Lamb that hath been slain to receive the power and riches . . . and glory and blessing'). He will come hereafter in His glory as Judge (Mt 25³¹), cf. Mt 19²⁸, 1 P 4¹³ ; and in Epp. He is styled 'the Lord of glory' (1 Co 2⁸, Ja 2¹).

6. Salvation. — His mission on earth was 'to seek and to save that which was lost' (Lk 19¹⁰, cf. 9⁵⁶, Jn 3¹⁷, 1 Ti 1¹⁵), it was implied in His very name (Mt 1²¹). He is the author (ἀρχηγός, He 2¹⁰ ; αἴτιος, 5⁹) of salvation. Twice only is the full title

'Saviour of the world' given (Jn 4⁴², 1 Jn 4¹⁴, cf. 1 Ti 4¹⁰), but 'Saviour' is found frequently (Lk 2¹¹, cf. 2³⁰, Ac 5³¹ 13²³, Ph 3²⁰, 2 P 3¹⁸ etc.). In this connexion may be noted the power of forgiving sins which He claimed on earth as Son of Man; see His words to the man sick of the palsy, with the comment of the bystanders (Mt 9²ᶠ·), and to the woman who was a sinner (Lk 7⁴⁸), cf. Ac 5³¹ 10⁴³.

7. Judgment.—One of the most momentous attributes is the power of judging mankind, involving complete and entire knowledge of the thoughts, actions, and circumstances of all men (cf. 1 Co 4⁵). That such should be His work was foretold by John the Baptist (Mt 3¹²) and asserted by Himself (Mt 16²⁷ 25³¹ etc., cf. Rev 22¹²). It is committed to Him by the Father (Jn 5²²), because He is a son of man (Jn 5²⁷ RVm), and His disciples should watch, making supplication that they may prevail . . . to stand before Him (Lk 21³⁶). He is 'ordained by God to be the judge of quick and dead' (Ac 10⁴², cf. 17³¹, 2 Ti 4¹), and before His judgment-seat we all must be made manifest (2 Co 5¹⁰, cf. Ro 14¹⁰).

8. Supreme Power.—He exercised power over *nature* (Jn 2⁹, Mt 8²⁶ 14²⁵ 21¹⁹, Mk 6³⁵ᶠ·, Lk 5⁴ᶠ·). His various miracles of healing showed His power over *disease*. Sometimes the cure was accompanied by His touch (Mt 8³· ¹⁵ 20³⁴, Lk 22⁵¹); sometimes the sufferer touched Him (Mk 5²⁸, Lk 6¹⁹); it was wrought by a word (Mt 12¹³); or by visible and tangible means (Jn 9⁶· ⁷); and even at a distance (Mt 8¹³, Mk 7³⁰, Jn 4⁵⁰). Three instances of power over *death* are recorded (Mk 5⁴¹, Lk 7¹⁴, Jn 11⁴³); cf. Mt 11⁵. His power also over *evil spirits* was shown in many cases and acknowledged by them (Mk 1²⁴ 5⁷, Lk 4³³ etc., cf. Ac 10³⁸). He was the One stronger than the strong man, Lk 11²², cf. Mt 4¹⁰· ¹¹. He *excited astonishment* in the people (noted chiefly in Mk. and Lk.). It was caused by His teaching (Mt 7²⁸, Mk 1²²), His words of grace (Lk 4²², cf. Jn 7¹⁵· ⁴⁶), and the authority with which He spoke (Lk 4³²); in these instances θαυμάζειν and ἐκπλήσσεσθαι are used. The effects produced by His miracles are expressed by similar words of amazement—θαυμάζειν (Mt 15³¹, Mk 5²⁰, Lk 11¹⁴, Jn 7²¹); ἐκπλήσσεσθαι (Mk 7³⁷, Lk 9⁴³); θάμβος and ἐκθαμβεῖσθαι (Mk 9¹⁵, Lk 4³⁶); ἔκστασις and ἐξίστασθαι (Mk 2¹², Lk 5²⁶ 8⁵⁶); φόβος (Lk 5²⁶ 7¹⁶). Among the disciples the same feelings were caused: 'they were sore amazed in themselves' (λίαν ἐξίσταντο, Mk 6⁵¹); 'being afraid they marvelled' (φοβηθέντες ἐθαύμασαν, Lk 8²⁵); 'they were amazed (ἐθαμβοῦντο) and astonished exceedingly' (ἐξεπλήσσοντο, Mk 10²⁴· ²⁶); 'they were amazed (ἐθαμβοῦντο) and afraid' (ἐφοβοῦντο) on the last journey to Jerusalem (Mk 10³²).

9. Dignity.—An attribute commanding respect and reverence is closely connected with the above. The Baptist declared Christ to be immeasurably above himself (Jn 1²⁷), while Christ described him as the greatest of the prophets because His forerunner (Mt 11⁹· ¹⁰); the disciples 'were afraid to ask him' (Mk 9³², cf. Jn 4²⁷); those who came to arrest Him fell to the ground (Jn 18⁶, cf 10³⁹ RV), and Pilate was the more afraid hearing His claim to be the Son of God (Jn 19⁸); note His silence (Mt 26⁶²ᶠ·, Mk 15³ᶠ·, Lk 23⁹). Other feelings, however, than reverence for His dignity were also excited, *e.g. repulsion* in the demoniacs (Lk 4³³) and in the Gerasenes (Mk 5¹⁷); *wrath* (Lk 4²⁸); *shame* in His adversaries, *joy* in the multitude (Lk 13¹⁷); *consciousness of unworthiness* in the centurion (Mt 8⁸), and *of sinfulness* in Peter (Lk 5⁸).

10. Restraint in the use of Power.—This attribute is strongly marked. Christ never used His Divine power for His own benefit (Mt 4²ᶠ·) nor for destroying life (on apparent exceptions, Mk 5¹³, Mt 21¹⁹, see Comm.). He restrained it that the

Scriptures might be fulfilled (Mt 26⁵⁴), and His exercise of it was often limited by want of faith on the part of those present (Mt 13⁵⁸).

iii. **Attributes belonging to Christ's true human nature.**—Becoming truly man, He took upon Him our nature as the Fall had left it, with its limitations, its weaknesses, and its ordinary feelings so far as they are not tainted by sin. He partook of flesh and blood, and in all things was made like unto His brethren (He 2¹⁴· ¹⁷, cf. Ro 8³). He possessed a true *human will*, but ever subject to the guidance of the Divine will (Jn 6³⁸, Mt 26³⁹); a *human soul* (ψυχή, Mt 26³⁸, Jn 12²⁷) and a *human spirit* (πνεῦμα, Mk 2⁸, Lk 23⁴⁶, Jn 11³³, 1 P 3¹⁸); He was representative Man (1 Co 15²²); all which is implied in 'the Word became flesh' (ὁ Λόγος σάρξ ἐγένετο, Jn 1¹⁴). The *Permanence of His Manhood* is evident since He was recognized after the Resurrection (cf. Jn 20²⁷) and ascended with His glorified body into Heaven; there He intercedes as our High Priest (He 4¹⁴ etc.), and will one day come again in like manner as He was seen to go into heaven (Ac 1¹¹).

1. Limitation of Power seems to be implied in the Incarnation; it is noted especially by St Mark, who has several passages expressing inability (οὐ δύνασθαι, Mk 1⁴⁵ 7²⁴ and 6⁵, which compare with Mt 13⁵⁸).

2. Limitation of Knowledge is distinctly asserted by Jesus Himself on one point (Mt 24³⁶ RV, Mk 13³², cf. Ac 1⁷, He 10¹³). In His childhood He grew, 'becoming full of wisdom' (πληρούμενον); He advanced (προέκοπτε) in wisdom (Lk 2⁴⁰· ⁵²); the story of the fig-tree implies that He expected to find fruit (ἦλθεν εἰ ἄρα εὑρήσει τι ἐν αὐτῇ, Mk 11¹³). He prayed as if the future were not clear (Mt 26³⁹); He asked questions for information (Mt 9²⁸, Mk 6³⁸ 8²³· ²⁷ 9²¹, Lk 8³⁰, Jn 11³⁴), cf. Mk 11¹¹.

3. Astonishment and Surprise.—In two cases only is Jesus said to have marvelled (θαυμάζειν, Mk 6⁶, Lk 7⁹), but surprise is implied at His parents (Lk 2⁴⁹); at the disciples' slowness of faith and understanding (Mk 4⁴⁰ 7¹⁸); at the sleep of Simon (Mk 14³⁷); cf. Mk 14³³ where a very strong word is used of the Agony (ἐκθαμβεῖσθαι, to be 'struck with amazement').

4. Need of Prayer and Communion with the Father is apparent from many passages. Sometimes He continued all night in prayer (Lk 6¹²). It was associated with great events in His life (Lk 3²¹ 6¹²· ¹³ 9¹⁸· ²⁸, Jn 12²⁷; Mt 26³⁶ᶠ·||, cf. He 5⁷); it is mentioned after days of busy labour (Mt 14²³, Mk 1³⁵, Lk 5¹⁶). He offered thanks also (Mt 11²⁵, Jn 11⁴¹). Jesus prayed for His disciples (Lk 22³², Jn 17), and taught them to pray (Mt 6⁹, Lk 11²), but He never gathered them to pray with Him. Compare also Mt 14¹⁹ 19¹³, Lk 11¹ 24³⁰ etc.

5. Temptation was a reality to Jesus (Mt 4¹⁻¹¹ ||), Satan left Him only for a season (Lk 4¹³; cf. Lk 22⁵³, Jn 14³⁰). It came also from Peter (Mt 16²³) and His enemies (Lk 11⁵³); cf. Lk 22²⁸ (ἐν τοῖς πειρασμοῖς μου); He was 'in all points tempted like as we are, yet without sin' (χωρὶς ἁμαρτίας, He 4¹⁵).

6. Suffering came from such temptation (He 2¹⁸); but the word πάσχειν is specially used of the last days of His earthly life. Thus the prophecy of the Suffering Servant in Isaiah was fulfilled (Mk 9¹², Lk 24²⁶· ⁴⁶; cf. εἰ παθητὸς ὁ Χριστός, Ac 26²³). Peter's confession at Cæsarea Philippi marked the time when Jesus began to emphasize this side of the Messianic prophecies (Mt 16²¹, cf. Mt 4¹⁷). The only absolute use of the word in the Gospels occurs in Lk 22¹⁵. (See 'Sorrow' below.) By suffering He learned the moral discipline of human experience, He was 'made *perfect*' and 'learned *obedience*' (He 2¹⁰ 5⁸· ⁹), so that He can be a *pattern* and *example* for Christians (1 P 2²¹, 1 Jn 2⁶ 3³). He exhibited *faith* (He 3²· ⁶) and *trust* (Jn 11⁴¹ᶠ·, He 2¹²) in the highest forms. He is the 'author and per-fecter (ἀρχηγὸς καὶ τελειωτής) of our faith' (He 12²), 'the perfect example—perfect in realization and effect—of that faith which we are to imitate trust-ing in Him' (Westcott). *Submission* and *Obedience* He showed to Mary and Joseph also (Lk 2⁵¹), and to His Heavenly Father (Mt 26⁴²); cf. Ro 5¹⁹. The purpose of His life was summed up in the words ' to do thy will, O God' (He 10⁷).

7. Liability to Human Infirmities.—Jesus experi-enced *hunger* (Mt 4² 21¹⁸, cf. Jn 4³¹); *thirst* (Jn 4⁷ 19²⁸, cf. Mt 27³⁴); *weariness* and *pain* : 'being wearied (κεκοπιακώς) with His journey He sat thus (οὕτως) by the well' (Jn 4⁶); in the boat He 'fell asleep' (ἀφύπνωσε, Lk 8²³); in the Garden there appeared an angel strengthening Him (ἐνισχύων, Lk 22⁴³); He was unable to carry His cross (Mk 15²¹), and it would seem that He Himself required support (cf. φέρουσι v.²² with ἐξάγουσι v.²⁰); cf. 2 Co 13⁴, He 4¹⁵. No sickness is mentioned (the quot. in Mt 8¹⁷ can hardly bear this meaning); He truly died, but it was a voluntary death (Jn 10¹⁷·¹⁸; and note that in no Gospel is the word 'died' used of His passing from life); cf. Ro 6⁹ 'death hath no more dominion over him' (οὐκέτι κυριεύει), and Ac 2²⁴.

8. Sorrow.—The prophecy was amply fulfilled that the Messiah should be ' a man of sorrows and acquainted with grief.' Sorrow was inevitable for one who had such insight into human nature, and so sympathized with its woes (cf. Jn 11³³⁻³⁸). It came also from 'the gainsaying' (ἀντιλογία) of sinners (He 12³, cf. 1 P 2²¹ᶠ·). One of the greatest causes of grief is misunderstanding of motive and action, which He experienced in abundance. On one occasion His relatives spoke of Him as 'mad' (ἐξέστη, Mk 3²¹); His enemies said He had a demon and was mad (Jn 10²⁰), and ascribed His works to Beelzebub (Lk 11¹⁵). There was disappointment also (Lk 13³⁴, Jn 5⁴⁰). The knowledge of what was coming cast a shadow on His life (Lk 12⁵⁰, Jn 12²⁷), it is implied in the description of the last journey to Jerusalem (Mk 10³²); at the Last Supper He was troubled in spirit (ἐταράχθη, Jn 13²¹); it is clearly expressed in the accounts of the Agony —Mt 26³⁷ ἤρξατο λυπεῖσθαι καὶ ἀδημονεῖν, the latter expressing 'utter loneliness, desertion, and desolate-ness' (Edersheim); Mk 14³³ ἤρξατο ἐκθαμβεῖσθαι καὶ ἀδημονεῖν; Lk 22⁴⁴ γενόμενος ἐν ἀγωνίᾳ, and the Bloody Sweat; His soul was περίλυπος ἕως θανάτου (Mt 26³⁸); the strong word ἀπεσπάσθη 'was parted' is used in Lk 22⁴¹ as if the separation itself caused grief; and the sorrow culminated in the heart-broken cry on the cross (Mt 27⁴⁶). Cf. He 5⁷ μετὰ κραυγῆς ἰσχυρᾶς καὶ δακρύων.

9. Joy.—It would be a great mistake, however, to regard His whole life as one of continuous over-whelming sorrow.* Our accounts deal almost entirely with the last three years, and surely there must have been much real happiness in the previous thirty years spent in honest work amid the beautiful surroundings of Nazareth, especially as He was conscious of no stain of guilt or failure in duty, and felt no remorse. Even in the Gospels we see His pure appreciation of nature and of children's games. It is once recorded that He rejoiced in spirit (ἠγαλλιάσατο, Lk 10²¹), and several times He used 'joy' (χαρά and χαίρω) of Himself (Jn 11¹⁵ 15¹¹ 17¹³, cf. Lk 15⁵·¹⁰). He must have felt joy in communion with His Father (Mt 11²⁵, Jn 11⁴¹), and in the consciousness of success (Lk 10¹⁸, Jn 16³³). Complaisance appears in His praise of the centurion (Mt 8¹⁰) and His words to Simon (Mt 16¹⁷); cf. Mt 21¹⁶, Lk 19⁴⁰, Jn 4³². So He 12² ('for the joy that was set before him he endured the cross'). See 'Sociability' (22).

10. Humility and Meekness.—These were shown in the circumstances of His childhood (Lk 2²⁴·⁵¹);

* See Brooks, *New Starts in Life*, Sermon on ' Joy and Sorrow.'

during His ministry He was homeless (Mt 8²⁰), and sometimes without money (Mt 17²⁷, cf. Lk 8³). He describes Himself as 'meek and lowly of heart' (πρᾷος καὶ ταπεινός, Mt 11²⁹); cf. Jn 1²⁹, 2 Co 10¹ (διὰ τῆς πρᾳότητος καὶ ἐπιεικείας τοῦ Χριστοῦ). 'Though he was rich, yet for your sakes he became poor' (ἐπτώχευσε, 2 Co 8⁹); He 'emptied himself' (ἑαυτὸν ἐκένωσε, Ph 2⁷, see whole passage). His life was one of unselfish ministry to others (Mt 20²⁸, Jn 13⁴ᶠ·, Lk 22²⁷·⁵¹; cf. 23²⁸ and the first three 'Words on the Cross'). He 'pleased not himself' (Ro 15³), and 'He gave himself up for us' (Eph 5²).

11. Patience and Longsuffering are seen in Lk 9⁵⁵ 23³⁴, Jn 18¹¹·²³; He left us the example of His patience (1 P 2²⁰·²¹, He 12¹·²); cf. 2 Th 3⁵ (Lightfoot's *Notes on Epp. of St. Paul, in loc.*) and 1 Ti 1¹⁶.

12. Compassion.—His compassion (σπλαγχνίζεσθαι) is often noticed; it led Him to send out the Twelve (Mt 9³⁶), to heal the sick (Mt 14¹⁴), to feed the 4000 (Mt 15³²), to give sight to the blind (Mt 20³⁴), to touch the leper (Mk 1⁴¹), to teach (Mk 6³⁴), and to restore the widow's son (Lk 7¹³). Cf. also Lk 1⁷⁸, Mk 9²², Ph 1⁸. In AV 'compassion' stands also for ἐλεεῖν (Mk 5¹⁹) and μετριοπαθεῖν (He 5²). His mercy is appealed to (ἐλεεῖν) by the Canaanite woman (Mt 15²²), Bartimæus (Mk 10⁴⁷), and the ten lepers (Lk 17¹³). He is a High Priest who can be 'touched with the feeling (συμπαθῆσαι) of our infirmities' (He 4¹⁵); cf. Mt 8¹⁷.

13. Tender Thoughtfulness appears in Mt 17⁷ 28¹⁰, Mk 6³¹·⁴⁸, Jn 6¹⁰ (RV) 18⁸ 20¹⁵. Cf. the story of Jairus' daughter, Mk 5³⁶·⁴⁰·⁴¹·⁴³ (on Mk 7²⁵ᶠ·, see Comm.).

14. Pity.—In the story of the man with the withered hand mingled pity and anger appear (συλλυπούμενος, Mk 3⁵). Twice He is recorded to have *sighed* (ἐστέναξε, Mk 7³⁴; ἀναστενάξας τῷ πνεύματι, 8¹²). Twice He wept for others (ἔκλαυσεν, Lk 19⁴¹; ἐδάκρυσεν, Jn 11³⁵; cf. He 5⁷, under 'Sorrow' above). He was accustomed to give alms to the poor (Jn 12⁵ 13²⁹). Cf. Lk 13³⁴ 22⁶¹.

15. Love.—He showed His affection for little children, taking them up in His arms (Mk 9³⁶ 10¹⁶, cf. Mt 21¹⁶); beholding the rich young ruler, He loved him (ἠγάπησεν, Mk 10²¹); He called the dis-ciples His friends (φίλοι, Lk 12⁴, Jn 15¹⁴·¹⁵), whom He loved (ἠγάπησεν) unto the end (Jn 13¹, cf. 13³⁴ 15⁹·¹²). Even in this select circle there was one of whom it was specially said 'Jesus loved him' (ἠγάπα, Jn 19²⁶ 21⁷·²⁰; ἐφίλει, Jn 20²). He also loved (ἐφίλει) Lazarus (Jn 11³·³⁶), and, with a sig-nificant change of word (ἠγάπα, Jn 11⁵), Martha and Mary. There are many reff. in Epp. to His love for His people and the Church; cf. Eph 5²·²⁵, Ro 8³⁵, 2 Co 5¹⁴, it 'passeth knowledge' (Eph 3¹⁹), from it true love may be learned (1 Jn 3¹⁶ RV).

16. Courage and Firmness appear under various circumstances in Mt 8²⁶, Mk 4³⁸⁻⁴⁰ 10³², Lk 4³⁰, Jn 11⁷ᶠ· 18⁴ᶠ· 19¹¹. His *independence* was well expressed by His questioners (Mt 22¹⁶).

17. Fear in any unworthy sense (φόβος) is not attributed to Him. In He 5⁷ it is said that He was 'heard for His godly fear' (εὐλάβεια). Westcott takes the word in 'its noblest sense,' so Alford 'reverent submission' (see note); but Grimm-Thayer prefers to render as 'fear, anxiety, dread'; 'by using this more select word, the writer, skilled as he was in the Greek tongue, speaks more rever-ently of the Son of God than if he had used φόβος.' *Caution*, however, is often noted; cf. His with-drawals before opposition (Mk 3⁷ 7²⁴, Jn 7¹ 11⁵⁴), also Jn 6¹⁵ and the directions about the place of the Last Supper (Lk 22¹⁰).

18. Desire (ἐπιθυμία, see art. DESIRE) is once used of Himself (Lk 22¹⁵), and a *longing for sym-pathy* is apparent in His bringing of the three into the Garden and His returning to them between

His prayers (Mt 26[37f.]) : 'in magnis tentationibus juvat solitudo, sed tamen ut in propinquo sint amici' (Bengel).

19. That he felt **shame** at hearing a foul story seems a fair inference from Jn 8[6f.] (see *Ecce Homo*, ch. ix. end). He Himself says, 'Whosoever shall be ashamed of me and of my words, of him shall the Son of Man be ashamed' ($\epsilon\pi\alpha\iota\sigma\chi\upsilon\nu\theta\dot{\eta}\sigma\epsilon\tau\alpha\iota$, Lk 9[26]); cf. He 12[2].

20. Anger and Indignation He often showed, though $\dot{o}\rho\gamma\dot{\eta}$ is attributed to Him in only one passage in the Gospels (Mk 3[5]; cf. $\dot{o}\rho\gamma\dot{\eta}$ $\tau o\hat{\upsilon}$ $\dot{'}A\rho\nu\dot{\iota}o\upsilon$, Rev 6[16]). He was 'moved with indignation' at the action of the disciples ($\dot{\eta}\gamma\alpha\nu\dot{\alpha}\kappa\tau\eta\sigma\epsilon$, Mk 10[14]); possibly this should also be the translation of $\dot{\epsilon}\mu\beta\rho\iota\mu\hat{\alpha}\sigma\theta\alpha\iota$ in Jn 11[33. 38] (RVm), on which see notes of Westcott and Godet. The same word is rendered 'strictly charge' ('threateningly to enjoin,' Grimm-Thayer) in Mt 9[30], Mk 1[43]. His rebukes ($\dot{\epsilon}\pi\iota\tau\iota\mu\hat{\alpha}\nu$) are noted (Mt 8[26], Mk 1[25], Lk 4[39]). Cf. also Mk 5[40] 11[21], Jn 2[15], Mt 21[12]. Sometimes he used *Irony* and *Sarcasm* : Lk 5[31], Mk 7[9] ($\kappa\alpha\lambda\hat{\omega}s$ $\dot{\alpha}\theta\epsilon\tau\epsilon\hat{\iota}\tau\epsilon$); Lk 13[32] ('that fox'); Lk 16[22] ('and was buried' ['a sublime irony,' Trench]). Hypocrisy excited His deepest abhorrence. Cf. the Woes on the Scribes and Pharisees, Mt 23[13f.] ‖ ending 'ye serpents, ye offspring of vipers'; also Mt 12[34].

21. Attractiveness appears in the readiness of many whom He called to forsake all and follow Him. The common people 'heard him gladly' (Mk 12[37], cf. Lk 19[48], Jn 12[19]); publicans and outcasts were drawn to the 'friend of publicans and sinners' (Mk 2[15], Lk 7[37] 19[3]); two members at least of the Sanhedrin became His disciples (Jn 19[38. 39]); and He foretold how by His Crucifixion and Resurrection this attractiveness would attain universal sway (Jn 12[32]). See art. ATTRACTION.

22. Sociability.—In this respect Jesus presented a marked contrast to the Baptist, which was commented upon (Lk 7[33. 34]). He accepted invitations from Pharisees (Lk 7[36] 11[37] 14[1]) and from Publicans (Mt 9[10], cf. Lk 19[5f.]). In the home at Bethany He was a welcome guest (Lk 10[38]). His first 'sign' was wrought at a marriage feast (Jn 2[1]), and much of His parabolic teaching was suggested by feasts and the incidents of ordinary life; cf. Mt 22[2] 25[1. 14], Lk 14[16] 19[12].

23. His **Catholicity** is to be noted finally. Though a Jew on the human side, yet He rose entirely above all merely national limits. 'He can be equally claimed by both sexes, by all classes, by all men of all nations.' * Even in His earthly ministry, though necessarily confined to His own nation (Mt 15[24]), His sympathy went beyond these bounds; cf. Mt 8[5f.] 15[22f.], Lk 10[33f.] 17[18], Jn 4[23. 35] 10[16] 12[20f. 47]. He looked forward to the time when 'they shall come from the east and west, and from the north and south' (Lk 13[29]); cf. Mk 13[10] and His last command, Mt 28[19]. So each race of men as it is gathered into the Church finds in Him its true ideal.

We have thus presented to us a Person in whom Divine power, wisdom, and goodness are joined with the highest and holiest type of manhood. The portrait is 'such as no human being could have invented. . . . We could not portray such an image without some features which would betray their origin, being introduced by our limited, erring, sinful minds. . . . And least of all could Jews have done so; for this was not by any means the ideal of their minds' (Luthardt, *Fundamental Truths of Christianity*, 295 f., and notes). See also artt. on DIVINITY and HUMANITY OF CHRIST, and on NAMES AND TITLES.

LITERATURE.—Sanday's 'Jesus Christ,' Ottley's 'Incarnation,' and other articles in Hastings' *DB*; Gore, *Bampton Lectures* and *Dissertations*; Liddon, *Bampton Lectures*; Stalker, *Imago*

* See Gore, *Bampton Lect.* 168 f.

Christi; Seeley, *Ecce Homo*; Dale, *Christian Doctrine* and *The Atonement*; Dalman, *The Words of Jesus*; Robinson (J. A.), *The Study of the Gospels*; Robinson (C. H.), *Studies in the Character of Christ*; D'Arcy, *Ruling Ideas of Our Lord*; Beet, *Through Christ to God*; Edersheim, *Life and Times of Jesus the Messiah*; Commentaries of Westcott, etc.

W. H. DUNDAS.

AUGUSTUS.—The designation usually applied to Caius Octavius, son of Caius Octavius and Atia, grandson of Julia the sister of C. Julius Cæsar, grand-nephew of the Dictator and ultimately his adopted son and heir. He was born 23rd Sept. B.C. 63, not far from the 'House' on the Palatine afterwards built for him; declared Emperor B.C. 29; honoured with the title of 'Augustus' B.C. 27; died 19th Aug. A.D. 14 at Nola, when he had almost reached the age of 77.

If we take B.C. 6 as the corrected date for the birth of Jesus, we find that Augustus was then in his 58th year, had already been Emperor 23 years, and had before him 20 more. Though his reign thus runs parallel with the Christian era for 20 years, there is but a single allusion to him in the Gospel history (Lk 2[1]). In the NT writings there are but three other instances of the use of the name Augustus. Of these one only (Ac 27[1]) can be held as possibly pointing to him, the other two (Ac 25[21] and 25[25]) mean the reigning Cæsar (RV 'Emperor'), in both cases Nero. Even that solitary allusion to Cæsar Augustus might have had no place in the Gospel record, had it not been St. Luke's aim to 'trace the course of all things accurately from the first.' In 'drawing up his narrative' he makes it evident that Nazareth, not Bethlehem, was the home of Joseph and Mary, and that the 'enrolment,' originating in a decree of Cæsar Augustus, was the occasion of the journey from Nazareth within a little time of the expected birth. The Syrian governor is named with the view of fixing the date, as was the custom in those days. Theophilus, as a Roman official, would have access to the list of provincial governors, and must have at once understood the exact period meant. Thus Augustus' contact with Jesus, so far as Scripture deals with it, begins and ends with Lk 2[1].

It need not surprise us that there is no further reference in the 20 years of contemporaneous history that followed. The birth of Jesus took place in a remote part of the Empire and in an insignificant town of Judah. The first 30 years of His life, with the exception of the brief sojourn in Egypt, were spent in the obscure, even despised, Nazareth. Among His townsmen He was known only as the carpenter (Mk 6[3]), or the carpenter's son (Mt 13[55]). Though the arrival of the wise men from the East, with the inquiry as to the birth of 'the King of the Jews,' 'troubled Herod' and 'all Jerusalem with him' (Mt 2[3]), the commotion caused by their advent soon passed with the tyrant's death in B.C. 4. Even the Massacre of the Innocents 'from two years old and under' in Bethlehem may never have been heard of in the palace of Augustus, or, if heard of, would have made very little impression, owing to the many acts of cruelty that had marked Herod's reign. It was about this very time that Augustus is reported to have said that it was 'better to be Herod's sow than his son' (Macrob. *Saturn.* ii. 4).

For St. Luke, with his wider outlook as a cultured Greek writing to a Roman official, it was quite natural to give a distinct place in his record to the decree about the census as leading up to the birth in Bethlehem. The object of the decree is given in the RV correctly as 'an enrolment' ($\dot{\alpha}\pi\sigma\gamma\rho\alpha\phi\dot{\eta}$), not necessarily involving 'a taxing' as well. As on this occasion it did not lead to any serious uprising of the Jews, as in A.D. 6, it must have been only a census in accordance with Jewish customs: 'all went to enrol themselves, every one to his own city.' The historian is careful to point out that it was part only of a world-wide enrolment ('all the world'). In the light of later research, we can add that this decree seems to have introduced a periodic census in the Roman Empire. The carefully chosen language of St. Luke distinguishes between the going up from Galilee as an act once for all completed (ἀνέβη), and an enrolment begun and having a continuance (ἐπορεύοντο πάντες ἀπογράφεσθαι).[*] The further description of the census as 'the first' accords with this, not the first under Quirinius, but the first of a series. For those to whom St. Luke wrote the decree was memorable as 'the first' that affected the Jews. Other enrolments may have taken place before it under Augustus, as the review by the Emperor himself in the celebrated *Monumentum Ancyranum* bears, but there is no contradiction between that and the Evangelist's testimony. Three distinct censuses are there named (in B.C. 28, B.C. 8, and in A.D. 14). Only the number of Roman citizens is given in each case, as all others might not have been considered worthy of being mentioned in the Emperor's Memorials. Important light has recently been thrown on the system of enrolments in the Roman Empire through the labours of various scholars referred to by Prof. W. M. Ramsay in his volume *Was Christ born at Bethlehem?* The tombs and even the dust-heaps of Egypt are proving that enrolments of households there were quite common, and even that a cycle of 14 years was observed. Applying this cycle to the period immediately before and after the Christian era, we bring out well-known dates, B.C. 8 and A.D. 6, the former marking a Roman-citizen census taken by Augustus, and the other that of the 'great census,' when the disturbances took place in Palestine which were quelled by Quirinius. There is thus a strong presumption, amounting almost to proof, that B.C. 8 is the most likely date for the issue of the decree referred to in Lk 2[1]. The delay between B.C. 8 and B.C. 6, so as to have it coincide with the corrected date for the birth of Jesus, may be accounted for by the strained relations existing about the time between Augustus and Herod, and also between Herod and his subjects. As it seems to have been the first enrolment of Jews under the Empire, it is easy to conceive that time was needed to overcome Jewish scruples.

The real difficulty, however, as to this alleged census under Quirinius lies in reconciling St. Luke's testimony with the facts of secular history. The Syrian governors in the period of B.C. 9–4 are given by Schürer as C. Sentius Saturninus (B.C. 9–6) and P. Quintilius Varus (B.C. 6–4). As B.C. 4 is the generally accepted year of Herod's death, the possibility of a governorship of Quirinius at the time of the execution of the decree of Cæsar Augustus is thereby excluded. Many therefore have been ready to say, with Mommsen, that St. Luke has 'erred.' Even Tertullian is quoted against the Evangelist, when he affirms that an 'enrolment' was made by Sentius Saturninus. And yet his testimony, while it differs from that of St. Luke as to the name of the governor of Syria, supports none the less the fact that there was a census earlier than the famous one of A.D. 6. The evidence in favour of an earlier as well as later governorship of Quirinius is now admitted to be so strong, that Mommsen and others have fully accepted it. The only question that remains is as to where we are to place it. Important help towards the solution of it has been found in the inscription discovered at Tivoli in 1764, now preserved in the Lateran Museum of Christian Antiquities. On it are recorded the exploits of a Roman official, with the honours awarded to him in the time of Augustus. While no name has been preserved, we are told that he was proconsul in Asia, and that he twice governed Syria and Phœnicia. The only one, known to us, who satisfies these conditions is Quirinius. Where then, in the interval immediately before the birth of Jesus in B.C. 6 or at latest B.C. 5, are we to find room for his earlier Syrian governorship? It must be between Saturninus and Varus, or as a contemporary of the one or the other. If we can find proofs in history of a double 'hegemony' in provincial government, we may consider that only *there* can the solution lie. In the history of Josephus we have a singular confirmation of this twofold governorship. A Volumnius is named in relation to Sentius Saturninus as 'the hegemon of Cæsar' (Schürer, *HJP* I. i. p. 350). Why might not Quirinius have been the military governor, while Saturninus was the civil administrator? In view of the progress of discovery in recent years, may we not hope that some additional fragment of the Tiburtine inscription will be found, and definitely settle the much debated question as to the historical accuracy of St. Luke? See art. CENSUS.

Though secular history from B.C. 6 to A.D. 14 furnishes us with no trace of any influence having been exerted by Augustus on Jesus or by Jesus on Augustus, we are able to trace, in the remarkable career of Augustus, a singular preparation for the Christian era. In nothing is this more manifest than in his unification of the Empire. When Augustus finally defeated Antony at Alexandria in B.C. 31, he was the one ruler left in the whole Roman world. The only adverse influence with which he had thereafter to contend was found among the heads of the old families in the Roman Senate. In the course of the next 10 or 12 years he so skilfully guided the affairs of the State, that he was clothed with every attribute of supremacy which it seemed possible for the State to bestow.

[*] It is true, indeed, that the imperf. may point, not to a repetition of the census, but simply to the fact of its going on for some time (cf. Winer, *Gram. of NT Greek* [Eng. tr.][9], p. 335).

The title of 'Princeps Senatus' was revived in B.C. 29, and had new significance given to it. In B.C. 27 the Senate conferred upon him the proconsular *imperium* for 10 years. This put into his hands an all but absolute military power throughout the empire. At this same time he received the title of 'Augustus,' a name having to do with the science of augury [or from *augeo*, as *an*-gustus from *ango*], and suggesting something akin to religious veneration. Though even then he wished himself to be considered as having a primacy only among equals, yet, as wielding the power both of purse and sword, he had become really the master of the Roman world. Nor was he content with this. The *tribunicia potestas* was granted to him in a sense more extended than ever before. While he appeared to assume it year by year, it really became his for life, and was the symbol of his sovereign authority, being used to mark the years of his reign. In B.C. 23 the whole machinery of the State had definitely and permanently passed into his hands. When the Christian era dawned, Augustus had for 17 years exercised a dominion unrivalled in its nature and extent, entitling it to be spoken of as over 'the whole world.' And yet there was no one in his day that felt so much the need of limiting the extension of the Empire. Among his last instructions there was one enjoining his successors not to seek enlargement, as it only made the work of guarding the frontiers more difficult. One of his greatest anxieties during his later years, owing to the deaths of Marcellus, Agrippa, Lucius, and Gaius, had to do with the succession to the Imperial throne. While the Christian era had not yet reached its first decade, he had only Tiberius, his step-son, to look to as his successor. At an early period of his reign Augustus had given himself to the development of a complete system of road-supervision for Italy and the provinces. The celebrated pillar of gilded bronze, the 'Milliarium Aureum,' of which but a fragment of the marble base can be seen to-day near the ascent of the Capitol, was set up by Augustus on 'his completion of the great survey and census of the Roman world' (Lanciani). On it were marked the distances of all the principal places along the main roads from the city gates. Where these roads led, civil government was found established, with a representative of the Emperor or the Senate, and with tribunals for the administration of justice. Anyone claiming to be a Roman citizen had the privilege of appeal to Cæsar, and could be assured of a safe conduct to Rome. Safe and comparatively speedy modes of travel were assured.

Our knowledge of the government of the provinces under Augustus is too limited to admit of any clear and full description of it. Suetonius (*August.* 47) has given us the principles on which he acted in dividing the provinces between himself and the Senate, in these words: 'The provinces which could neither be easily nor safely governed by annual magistrates he undertook himself.' In other words, those that required a strong force to hold them in subjection, or whose frontiers were exposed to attack on the part of restless and powerful enemies, he retained in his own hands. The others, which could be easily governed and had nothing to fear from surrounding peoples, he handed over to the Senate. This arrangement placed in his hands almost the whole military forces of the Empire. The Emperor's legates, commanding the provincial troops, were not only appointed by him, but could be suspended or dismissed at his pleasure. The provinces were divided into groups according as they were administered by consuls, prætors, or simply knights. Even those that appeared to be entirely under the control of the Senate were restricted in their appointments by the Emperor, as the list of those eligible had to be submitted to him, and all on the list must have served, with an interval of five years, as consuls or prætors. In the case of Syria we find an Imperial province exposed to inroads from warlike peoples on its Northern and Eastern borders, and therefore in need of a military more than a civil commander over it to act as its *hegemon*. The term answers best to our Viceroy. This was the position which Quirinius probably held, and he would have power from Augustus to allow in Herod's dominions a census that would as little as possible offend Jewish prejudices. Each set of provinces had its own separate treasury. The revenues from the Imperial provinces flowed into the Emperor's *fiscus*, and out of it were taken the enormous sums spent on the great military roads, which became the highways for Christianity. To the Senate, Augustus granted the right of minting copper only, reserving gold and silver for the Imperial treasury. As the result of these and other measures the Empire enjoyed unusual prosperity. Augustus also bestowed great care on the selection of his legates, closely watched over their administration, and made it all but impossible for a corrupt governor to escape swift punishment. To this in great measure the Empire owed its popularity in Augustus' time.

There was another remarkable preparation for the world-census in the ordnance survey initiated by Julius Cæsar, and completed only after 25 years of labour on the part of four of the greatest surveyors of the age. The main object of it, no doubt, was the taxation of land, the most profitable source of revenue under the Empire. Thus a completely organized and a world-wide Empire, in absolute dependence upon its supreme ruler in Rome, had become an accomplished fact ere the Christian era had dawned.

As this new era approached, signs were multiplying of a desire for peace on the part of ruler and ruled, though it is scarcely true that the actual year of the birth at Bethlehem was distinguished by the prevalence of universal peace. To the immediately preceding period, B.C. 13–9, belongs the famous 'Altar of Peace,' whose actual site has been laid bare within very recent years (1903–1904) under the Via in Lucina, a little way off from the Corso, the old Flaminian Way. The very same year in which Augustus became Pontifex Maximus owing to the death of his former co-triumvir Lepidus, the Senate decreed the erection of an 'Altar of Peace,' which at first was to have been set up in the Senate-house, but was afterwards placed on the edge of the Campus Martius. One of the chief features of the period to which it belongs was the closing of the temple of Janus. Horace, writing in B.C. 13 (*Epp.* II. i. 255 and *Odes* IV. xv. 9), speaks of the closing as a recent occurrence. Twice before in the reign of Augustus, in B.C. 29 and B.C. 25, this temple had been closed (*Mon. Anc.* 13), 'when peace throughout the whole dominions of the Roman people by land and sea had been obtained by victories,' and 'only twice before his birth since the foundation of the city,' in all five times up to the Christian era. The Gades (Cadiz) inscription is a remarkable confirmation of B.C. 13 as the date of the third closing of the temple of Janus in Augustus' time.

The monument entitled the 'Ara Pacis Augusti' is of unusual proportions and of exquisite workmanship. Within the walls of a massive marble screen there was placed the altar on an elevated base, pyramidal, and having marble steps leading up to it. The screen was splendidly decorated both within and without with sculptures in high relief. The outer side of the screen had two distinct bands of ornamentation : the lower floral, the upper a procession with figures, many of which might have been actual portraits. The best known of these processional reliefs are to be found in the Gallery of the Uffizi at Florence, one is in the Cortile Belvedere of the Vatican, and one in the Louvre, Paris.

The altar was a splendid tribute to Peace, but it was a peace after many and bloody victories, reminding us of the saying, 'where they make a desert they call it peace' (Tac. *Agricola*, 30), and it was also a peace that was not to last. Yet there the altar stood on the field of Mars, as the reign of the 'Prince of Peace' was ushered in, and became for ages thereafter a witness to the Pax Romana of the Augustan age. Far more of it remains to the present time than of the triple arch of Augustus set up in celebration of his victories, of which only the bare foundations can be seen between the temple of Julius and that of Castor and Pollux.

The energies of Augustus found scope for themselves in other lines, and all with the object of building up his world-wide Empire that he meant to last in the ages to come. At the beginning of his reign he put his hand to the restoration of the State religion. In B.C. 28 he claims to have 'repaired 82 temples of the gods' (*Mon. Anc.* 20), earning for himself the title given him by Livy (*Hist.* IV. xx. 7), 'the builder or restorer of all the temples.' The sacred images, we are told, had become actually 'foul with smoke' or were 'mouldering with mildew.' The ancestral religion was dead, belief in the gods had all but disappeared. Nor was it only the repair of edifices for religious worship that he took in hand ; from him the sacred colleges and brotherhoods received a new impulse by his becoming a member himself of one and all of them. Through him their endowments were greatly increased. With great ceremony was observed the centenary of the city, for which Horace prepared his well-known ode, as the inscription found in the Tiber in 1871 so strikingly confirms ('carmen composuit Q. Horatius Flaccus'). The worship of the Lares was restored. At crossways and street corners three hundred small shrines were set up, whose altars were adorned twice a year with flowers. One of the latest discoveries is that of a shrine of the Lares Publici in front of the Arch of Titus, on the branch of the Via Sacra leading up to the Palatine by the old Mugonian Gate. New temples were erected, the most notable being that of Apollo behind his own 'Domus.' A new spirit also was infused into the rites and ceremonies of the old worship, to which the writings of Virgil contributed in a special degree.

The hardest task yet remained in the social and moral reformation of his people. As early as B.C. 25 we find Horace (*Od.* III. vi.), in this reflecting probably the opinion of his master, affirming the necessity of 'a reformation of morals as well as a restoration of temples and a revival of religion.' In a later ode (xxiv.) he promises immortality to the statesman who shall bring back the morality of the olden time. The action taken by Augustus about that time was effective, temporarily at least, for his praises were celebrated as 'one who by his presence had cleansed the family from its foul stains, had curbed the licence of the age, and recalled the old morality.' The text of his laws enacted for this purpose has not come down to us, but their date may be taken as from B.C. 18 to 17, or about 12 years before the Christian era. His own example, unfortunately, did not enable him to take up a very high position on the subject of marriage. He had put away Scribonia in order to marry Livia, whom he took from her husband Tiberius Nero. Again and again he interposed to dissolve existing marriages, when his policy as to the succession required it. High motives, therefore, we do not expect to find in his legislation on marriage. Nothing could have brought out more clearly the impotence of such legislation than the openly scandalous character of his daughter Julia. In B.C. 2, the very year when he was hailed by the Senate as the father of his country, he became aware of what had long been in everyone's knowledge. So keenly did he feel the scandal that he shunned society for a time, and even absented himself from the city. His only remedy was her banishment to Pandataria. Never afterwards was she allowed to set foot in Rome. Nor did she see again the face of her father, whom she outlived only by a few short weeks. There were not wanting schools of philosophy that vied with each other in leading men to virtue. Greek philosophers of note were welcomed to the halls of the 'Domus Augusti.' But no system of morals or philosophy had yet appeared that could show the way of attaining to the Divine likeness by the bestowal of a new nature, until Christianity came upon the scene.

The same moulding hand that built up the Empire can be traced in the modification through which Cæsar - worship passed under Augustus. The deification of Julius by the Senate in B.C. 42 was only what was to be expected. The decree ran: 'To the Genius of the divine Julius, father of his country, whom the Senate and Roman people placed among the number of the gods.' In the very heart of the Roman Forum, from B.C. 29, there was to be seen, on an elevated platform, a most beautiful marble temple proclaiming the deification of the great Julius. Augustus never allowed such worship of himself during his lifetime as had been the case with Julius. From the earliest period of his reign there is evidence that he allowed it in the provinces, but only in conjunction with 'Rome,' and the formula enjoined for all that were not Roman citizens was 'Rome and Augustus.' In the case of citizens the one name allowed, along with Rome, was that of 'the divine Julius.' For his Roman subjects he would be neither 'rex' nor 'divus,' but outside the favoured circle of Roman citizenship he had less scruple in receiving for himself a share of divine honour, believing that it formed the binding link that was needed to knit all the parts of his wide Empire into one great unity.

As to the permanence of this 'cult' in the provinces, under the joint title of 'Rome and Augustus,' there is still a measure of uncertainty. Dr. Lindsay believes the balance of evidence is in favour of 'Rome' having been left out even in Augustus' lifetime. In that case 'Augustus' signified 'not the person of the Emperor, but the symbol of the deification of the Roman State, personified in its ruler.' Certainly that might have admirably served to establish his State policy, and make him believe that he had accomplished all that human ingenuity could to make his Empire as enduring as it was world-wide.

On his death in A.D. 14 a modification necessarily came, when the Senate decreed that thereafter he should be known as 'Divus Augustus.'

The priesthood of this Imperial 'cult' was divided into two classes, the one representing the State religion in a province, and the other having charge of religious ceremonies in the cities. The provincial priests were responsible only to the Emperor as Pontifex Maximus, and had, in the West at least, jurisdiction over the municipal priests. The way was thus prepared for the development of a full hierarchical system, which became afterwards the model for the Roman Church, with its Pontifex Maximus in Rome, its Metropolitans in each province, and the municipal priests in the cities. The 'cult' itself spread with great rapidity, was binding on every Roman subject with the exception of the Jews only, and prepared the way for the application of the prime test for the Christians of the early ages: 'Sacrifice to the Emperor or death.' The man of all others, who created the conditions in which Christianity was to find that supreme test, was Augustus. The Universal Empire, with its ruler as an object of worship, had not long become an accomplished fact when the God-man, in contrast with the man-god, appeared,—'the Word became flesh and dwelt among us.' No contrast could well be greater than that which distinguished (in B.C. 6–A.D. 14) this world-ruler from the Founder of Christianity:—Augustus, a perfect master in State-craft, merciful to his foes only when he had made his position absolutely sure, only somewhat more advanced in his morality than the men of his age, full of self-esteem, as the last scene of his life reveals, yet entitled to be considered by the world in which he lived as its 'chief benefactor' (Lk 22²⁵); Jesus, though in His twelfth year able to claim a relationship with the Father in heaven such as distinguishes Him from every other son of man, yet remaining for those 20 years of His life at Nazareth as the carpenter's son, all unknown to the great world without, subject to His reputed

father and His 'highly favoured' mother, 'advancing in wisdom' as in stature, and above all 'in favour with God and man.' Of the whole of Augustus' work there now remains little but crumbling or half-buried ruins, but the name of Jesus 'endures,' and gives evidence of the truth of the prophecy which points to the world's kingdom as becoming His, and His reign as being 'for ever and ever' (Rev 11¹⁵).

LITERATURE.—Mommsen, *Res Gestæ Divi Augusti*, also *The Roman Provinces*, and *History of Rome*; Schürer, *HJP* Index, *s.v.* 'Octavianus Augustus'; W. M. Ramsay, *Was Christ born at Bethlehem?*, *The Church in the Roman Empire*; Shuckburgh, *The Life and Times of the Founder of the Roman Empire*; John B. Firth, *Augustus Cæsar and the Organization of the Empire of Rome*; Baring Gould, *The Tragedy of the Cæsars*; T. M. Lindsay, *The Church and the Ministry in the Early Centuries*; Merivale, *History of the Romans under the Empire*.

J. GORDON GRAY.

AUTHORITY OF CHRIST.—The first recorded comment on the teaching of Jesus is that of Mt 7²⁸ᶠ· (‖Mk 1²², Lk 4³²): 'They were astonished at his teaching, for he taught them as one having authority, and not as their scribes.' The scribes said nothing of themselves: they appealed in every utterance to tradition (παράδοσις); the message they delivered was not self-authenticating; it had not the moral weight of the speaker's personality behind it; it was a deduction or application of some legal maxim connected with a respectable name. They claimed authority, of course, but men had no immediate and irresistible consciousness that the claim was just. With Jesus it was the opposite. He appealed to no tradition, sheltered Himself behind no venerable name, claimed no official status; but those who heard Him could not escape the consciousness that His word was with authority (Lk 4³²). He spoke a final truth, laid down an ultimate law.

In one respect, He continued, in so doing, the work and power of the prophets. There was a succession of prophets in Israel, but not a prophetic tradition. It was a mark of degeneration and of insincerity when self-styled prophets repeated each other, stealing God's words every one from his neighbour (Jer 23³⁰). The true prophet may have his mind nourished on earlier inspired utterances, but his own message must spring from an immediate prompting of God. It is only when his message is of this kind that his word is with power. No mind was ever more full than the mind of Jesus of all that God had spoken in the past, but no one was ever so spontaneous as He, so free from mere reminiscence, so completely determined in His utterance by the conditions to which it was addressed. It is necessary to keep both things in view in considering His authority as a teacher. Abstract formulæ about the seat of authority in religion are not of much service in this connexion. It is, of course, always true to say that truth and the mind are made for each other, and that the mind recognizes the authority of truth because in truth it meets its counterpart, that which enables it to realize its proper being. It is always correct, also, to apply this in the region of morals and religion, and to say that the words of Jesus and the prophets are authoritative because our moral personality instinctively responds to them. We have no choice, as beings made for morality and religion, to do anything but bow before them. The difficulty is that the 'mind,' or 'conscience,' or 'moral personality,' on which our recognition of the truth and authority of Jesus' teaching is here made dependent, is not a fixed quantity, and still less a ready-made faculty; it is rather a possibility or potentiality in our nature, which needs to be evoked into actual existence; and among the powers which are to evoke it and make it actual and valuable, by far the most important is that teaching of Jesus which it is in some sense allowed to judge. We may say in Coleridge's phrase that we believe the teaching of Jesus, or acknowledge its (or His) authority, because it 'finds' us more deeply than anything else ; but any Christian will admit that 'find' is an inadequate expression. The teaching of Jesus does not simply find, it evokes or creates the personality by which it is acknowledged. We are born again by the words of eternal life which come from His lips, and it is the new man so born to whom His word is known in all its power. There is a real analogy between this truth and the familiar phenomenon that a new poet or artist has to create the taste which is necessary for the appreciation of his work. Dismissing, therefore, the abstract and general consideration of the idea of authority in religion (see next art.), our course must be (1) to examine the actual exercise of authority by Jesus in the Gospels, referring especially to occasions on which His authority was challenged, or on which He gave hints as to the conditions on which alone it could be recognized ; (2) by way of supplement we can consider the authority of the exalted Christ as it is asserted in the Epistles and exercised in the Church through the NT as a whole.

1. *The exercise of authority by Jesus on earth.*— (*a*) The simplest but most far-reaching form in which Jesus exercised authority was the *practical* one. He claimed other men, other moral personalities, for Himself and His work, and required their unconditional renunciation of all other ties and interests that they might become His disciples. He said, 'Follow me,' and they rose, and left all and followed Him (Mt 4[18-22] 9[9]). He made this kind of claim because He identified Himself with the gospel (Mk 8[35] 10[29]) or with the cause of God and His Kingdom in the world, and for this cause no sacrifice could be too great, no devotion too profound. ' He that loveth father or mother more than me is not worthy of me. He that loveth son or daughter more than me is not worthy of me. Whosoever he be of you that renounceth not all that he hath, he cannot be my disciple' (Mt 10[37], Lk 14[33]). Nothing is less like Jesus than to do violence to anyone's liberty, or to invade the sacredness of conscience and of personal responsibility ; but the broad fact is unquestionable, that without coercing others Jesus dominated them, without breaking their wills He imposed His own will upon them, and became for them a supreme moral authority to which they submitted absolutely, and by which they were inspired. His authority was unconditionally acknowledged because men in His presence were conscious of His moral ascendency, of His own devotion to and identification with what they could not but feel to be the supreme good. We cannot explain this kind of moral or practical authority further than by saying that it is one with the authority which the right and the good exercise over all moral beings.

Not that Jesus was able in every case to carry His own will through in the wills of other men. Moral ascendency has to be exercised under moral conditions, and it is always possible, even for one who acknowledges its right, to fail to give it practical recognition by obedience. When Jesus said to the rich ruler, 'Sell all that thou hast, and give to the poor, and thou shalt have treasure in heaven : and come, follow me' (Mk 10[21]), He failed to win the will of one who nevertheless was conscious that in refusing obedience he chose the worse part. ' He went away sorrowful ' — his sorrow implying that was within the right on the part of Jesus to put him to this tremendous test. He acknowledges by his sorrow that he would have been a better man—in the sense of

the gospel a perfect man—if he had allowed the authority of Jesus to have its perfect work in him. These are the facts of the case, and they are ignored by those who argue that it is no man's business to part with all he has for the sake of the poor ; that property is a trust which we have to administer, not to renounce ; that the commandment to sell all cannot be generalized, and is therefore not moral ; and that it is, in short, an instance of fanaticism in Jesus, due to His belief in the nearness of the Kingdom, and the literal worthlessness of everything in comparison with entering into it at His side. There is nothing here to generalize about. There is a single case of conscience which Jesus diagnoses, and for which He prescribes heroic treatment ; but it is not in the patient to rise to such treatment. The high calling of God in Christ Jesus is too high for him ; he counts himself unworthy of the eternal life (Ac 13[46]). The authority of Jesus is in a sense acknowledged in this man ; it is felt and owned though it is declined. Where the authority lay is clear enough. It lay in the Good Master Himself, in His own identification with the good cause, in His own renunciation of all things for the Kingdom of God's sake ; it lay in His power to reveal to this man the weak spot in his moral constitution, and in the inward witness of the man's conscience (attested by his sorrow as he turned away) that the voice of Jesus was the voice of God, and that through obedience to it he would have entered into life. It lay in the whole relation of these two concrete personalities to each other, and it cannot be reduced to an abstract formula.

This holds true whenever we think of the moral or practical authority of Jesus. It is never legal : that is, we can never take the letter in which it is expressed and regard it as a statute, incapable of interpretation or modification, and binding in its literal meaning for all persons, all times, all social conditions. This is plain in regard to such a command of Jesus as the one given to the rich ruler : no one will say that this is to be obeyed to the letter by all who would enter into the Kingdom of God. But it is equally true of precepts which are addressed to a far wider circle, and which are sometimes supposed (like this one) to rest in a peculiar sense on the authority of Jesus. Take, *e.g.*, the case of the Sermon on the Mount in Mt 5[21-48]. From beginning to end this may be read as an assertion of the moral authority of Jesus, an authority which is conscious of transcending the highest yet known in Israel. ' It was said to them of old time . . . but I say unto you.' On what do the words of Jesus throughout this passage depend for their actual weight with men ? They depend on the consciousness of men that through these words the principle of morality, for which our nature has an abiding affinity, is finding expression. But just because we are conscious of this principle and of the affinity of our nature for it, we are free with regard to any particular expression of it ; the particular words in which it is embodied even by Jesus do not possess the authority of a statute to which we can only conform, but about which we must not think. When Jesus says, ' Whoso shall smite thee on the right cheek, turn to him also the other ; to him that would go to law with thee and take thy coat, leave also thy cloak ' : it is not to keep us from thinking about moral problems by giving us a rule to be blindly obeyed, it is rather to stimulate thought and deliver us from rules. His precepts are legal in form, but He came to abolish legalism, and therefore they were never meant to be literally read. When they are literally read, conscience simply refuses to take them in. They are casuistic in form, but anti-casuistic in intention, and their authority lies in the intention, not in the form. What the precepts of non-resistance and non-retaliation mean is that under no circumstances, under no provocation, must the disciple of Jesus allow his conduct to be determined by any other motive than that of love. He must be prepared to go all lengths with love, and no matter how love is tried, he must never renounce it for an inferior principle, still less for an instinctive natural passion, such as the desire for revenge. Put thus, the moral authority of Jesus is unquestionable, and it asserts itself over us the more, the more we feel that He embodied in His own life and conduct the principle which He proclaims. But there is nothing in this which binds us to take in the letter what Jesus says about oaths, or non-resistance, or revenge; and still less is there anything to support the idea that His words on these subjects are part of a fanatical renunciation of the world in the region of honour as well as of property,—a literal surrender, in view of the imminence of the Kingdom, of all that makes life on earth worth having. It is not uncommon now for those who regard the Kingdom of God as purely transcendent and eschatological to match this paradoxical doctrine with an ethical system equally paradoxical, a system made up purely of renunciation and negation, and to fasten it also upon Jesus; but it is hardly necessary to refute either the one paradox or the other. What commands conscience in the most startling words of Jesus is the truth and love which dictate them, but to recognize the truth and love is to recognize that no form of words is binding of itself. It is the supreme task of the moral being to discover what in his own situation truth and love require; and there is no short cut to the discovery of this, even in the Sermon on the Mount. Jesus is our authority, but His words are not our statutes: we are not under law, even the law of His words, but under grace—that is, under the inspiration of His personality; and though His words are one of the ways in which His moral ascendency is established over us, they are only one. There is an authority in Him to which no words, not even His own, can ever be equal.

The final form which this practical or moral authority of Jesus assumes in the NT is the recognition of Him as Judge of all. Probably in the generation before that in which He lived the Jews had come to regard the Messiah as God's vicegerent in the great judgment which ushered in the world to come; but what we find in the NT in this connexion is not the formal transference of a piece of Messianic dogmatic to Jesus; it is the moral recognition of the moral supremacy of Jesus, and of His right to pronounce finally on the moral worth of men and things. Experiences like that which inspired Lk 5[8] ('Depart from me, for I am a sinful man, O Lord'), Jn 4[29] ('Come see a man which told me all things that ever I did'), 21[17] ('Thou knowest all things, thou knowest that I love thee'), are the basis on which the soul recognizes Christ as Judge. The claim to be Judge appears also in His own teaching (Mt 7[22f.], Lk 13[25ff.], Mt 25[31ff.]); and if the form of the words in the first of these passages has been modified in tradition in order to bring out their bearing for those for whom the Evangelist wrote, no one doubts that their substance goes back to Jesus. It is He who contemplates the vain pleas which men will address to Him 'in that day'—men who with religious profession and service to the Church have nevertheless been morally unsound. The standard of judgment is variously represented: it is 'the will of my Father which is in heaven' (Mt 7[21]) or 'these sayings of mine' (7[24]) or it is what we might call in a word 'humanity' (25[35. 42]): and in its way each of these is a synonym for the moral

authority of Jesus. As far as we are sensitive to their demands we are sensitive to His moral claim. Into the representations of Jesus as Judge outside of the Gospels it is not necessary to enter.

(b) The authority of Jesus comes before us in another aspect when we think of Him not as commanding but as teaching, not as Legislator or Judge, but as Revealer. In the first case, authority means His title to obedience; in this case, it may be said to mean His title to belief.

Perhaps of all theological questions the nature and limits of this last authority are those which have excited the keenest discussion in recent times. On the one hand, there are those who, fixing their minds on the Divinity of Jesus, regard it as essentially un-Christian to question His utterances at any point. Whatever Jesus believed, or seemed to believe, on any subject is by that very fact raised above question. The mind has simply to receive it on His authority. Thus when He refers to Jonah (Mt 12[38ff.], Lk 11[29ff.]), the literal historicity of the Book of Jonah is guaranteed; when He ascribes the 110th Psalm to David (Mt 22[41ff.] and ‖), critical discussion of the authorship is foreclosed; when He recognizes possession by unclean spirits (Mk 1[23ff.] and often), possession is no longer a theory to explain certain facts, and therefore open to revision; it is itself a fact: it gives us a glimpse into the constitution of the spiritual universe which we are not at liberty to question. On the other hand, there are those who, while they declare their faith in the Incarnation, argue that it belongs to the very truth of the Incarnation that Jesus should not merely be man, but man of a particular time and environment; not man in the abstract, but man defined (and therefore in some sense limited) by the conditions which constitute reality. He had not simply intelligence, but intelligence which had been moulded by a certain education, and could only reveal itself through a certain language; and both of these are conditions which (while essential to historical reality) nevertheless involve limitation. Hence with regard to the class of subjects just referred to, those who are here in question feel quite at liberty to form their own opinions on relevant grounds. They do not, as they think, set aside the authority of Jesus in doing so: their idea rather is that in these regions Jesus never claimed to have or to exercise any authority. Thus in the first two instances adduced above, He simply takes the OT as it stands, and He appeals to it to confirm a spiritual truth which He is teaching on its own merits. In Mt 12[38ff.] He is reproaching an impenitent people, and He refers to the Book of Jonah for a great example of repentance, and that on the part of a heathen race; the men of Nineveh who repented will condemn His unrepentant contemporaries in the day of judgment. In Mt 22[41ff.] He is teaching that the essential thing in Messiahship is not a relation to David, but a relation to God; and He refers to the 110th Psalm, and to David as its author, as unintelligible except on this hypothesis. In both cases (it is argued) the truths which rest on the authority of Jesus are independent of the OT appeal which is associated with them. That repentance is an essential condition of entering into the Kingdom of God, and that there is no responsibility so heavy as that of those who will not repent even when Jesus calls, are truths which are not affected though the Book of Jonah is read as an allegory or a poem; that the fundamental thing in the person of Jesus is not His relation to David (which He shared with others) but His relation to God (which belonged to Him alone), is a truth which is not affected though the 110th Psalm is ascribed to the Maccabæan period. In other words, the authority of Jesus as a revealer of God and of the laws of His Kingdom is not touched, though we suppose Him to share on such matters as are here in question the views which were current among His contemporaries. It is not denying His Divinity to say this; it is rather denying His humanity if we say the opposite. Parallel considerations apply to the belief in possession which Jesus undoubtedly shared with His fellow-countrymen, and in fact with His contemporaries generally. Possession was the current theory of certain morbid conditions of human nature, physical, mental, and probably in some cases also moral; but the one thing of consequence in the Gospel is not that Jesus held this or any other theory about these morbid conditions, but that in Him the power of God was present to heal them. Our theory of them may be different, but that only means that we belong to a different age; it does not touch the truth that from these terrible and mysterious woes Jesus was mighty to save. It does not matter that His notions of medicine and psychology were different from ours; He did not come to reveal medicine or pyschology—to 'reveal' such things is a contradiction in terms; He came to reveal the Father, and His authority has its centre there.

There is, no doubt, great possibility of error in arguing from such abstract ideas as 'Divinity' and 'humanity,' especially when they are in some way opposed to one another in our minds : however we may define them, we must remember that they were in no sense opposed or inconsistent in Christ. He was at once and consistently all that we mean by Divine and all that we mean by human, but we cannot learn what that was by looking up 'divine' and 'human' in the dictionary, or in a book of dogmatic theology. We must look at Jesus Himself as He is presented to us in the Gospels. And further, we must consider that there is a vast region of things in which there neither is nor can be any such thing as authority —the region, namely, which is covered by science. Now questions of the kind to which reference has just been made all belong to the domain of science. The nature of the Book of Jonah, the date and authorship of the 110th Psalm, the explanation of the morbid phenomena which the ancients ascribed to evil spirits inhabiting the bodies of men : these are questions for literary, for historical, for medical science. It is a misleading way of speaking about them, and needlessly hurts some Christian feelings, to say that the authority of Jesus was limited, and did not extend to such matters. The truth rather is that such matters belong to a region where there is no such thing as authority, or where the only authority is that of facts, which those in quest of knowledge must apprehend and interpret for themselves. It is a negation of the very idea of science to suppose that any constituent of it could be revealed, or could rest upon authority, even the authority of Jesus. Hence in regard to all such subjects the question of Jesus' authority ought never to be raised : it is not only misleading, but unreal. On the other hand, when we come to the authority which Jesus actually claims as a revealer of God, and of the things of His Kingdom, we find that it is not only real but absolute—an authority to which the soul renders unreserved acknowledgment.

This is brought out most clearly in Mt 11^{27}. Here Jesus speaks in explicit terms of His function as Revealer, and we see at once the absoluteness of His authority, and its sphere. 'All things have been delivered unto me by my Father, and no one knoweth the Son save the Father, neither doth any know the Father save the Son, and he to whomsoever the Son willeth to reveal him.'

Whatever else these words express, they express Jesus' sense of absolute competence in His vocation : He had everything given to Him which belonged to the work He had to do, and He was conscious of being equal to His task. If we try to interpret 'all things' by reference to the context, then whether we look before or after we must say that the 'all things' in view are those involved in the revelation of God : in the work of revelation, and especially in the revelation of Himself as Father, God has no organ but Christ, and in Christ He has an adequate organ. The passage anticipates Jn 14^6 'I am the way, the truth, and the life : no man cometh unto the Father but by me.' It is in a word like this—*I am the truth*—that we find the key to the problems which have been raised about the authority of Jesus as a Teacher or Revealer. The truth which we accept on His authority is the truth which we recognize in Him. It is not announced by Him from a world into which we cannot enter : it is present here, in Him, in the world in which we live. It is not declared on authority to which we blindly surrender; it is exhibited in a Person and a Life which pass before us and win our hearts. To put it otherwise, the truth which we owe to Jesus, and for which He is our authority, is not information; it is not a contribution to science, physical or historical—for this we are cast by God on our own resources; it is the truth which is identical with His own being and life in the world, which is embodied or incarnate in Him. It is the truth which is involved in His own relation to God and man, and in His perfect consciousness of that relation : it is the truth of His own personality, not any casual scientific fact. He does not claim to know everything, and it would be difficult to reconcile such a claim with true manhood; but He does claim full knowledge of the Father, and not His words only, but His whole being and life are the justification of His claim.[*]

The authority of Christ as a Teacher and Revealer has been called in question mainly in connexion with His words about the future. There is no doubt that these present great difficulty to those who believe in Him. They seem to say quite unmistakably that certain things will happen, and happen within a comparatively short time, which (if we are to read literally) have not happened yet. 'Ye shall not have gone through the cities of Israel till the Son of man be come' (Mt 10^{23}); 'Verily I say unto you, there be some of them that stand here which shall in no wise taste of death till they see the Son of man coming in his kingdom' (Mt 16^{28}; cf. Mt 24^{29-35}, Mk $13^{30f.}$, Lk $21^{27f.}$). The coming of the Son of man in His kingdom was conceived quite definitely by the Apostolic Church as a supernatural visible coming on the clouds of

<hr/>

[*] Loisy (*L'Évangile et L'Église*, 45 f., *Autour d'un petit Livre*, 130 f.) has attacked Mt 11^{27} on the ground that the unique Divine Sonship which it ascribes to Jesus is of a sort which it was not historically possible for Him to conceive or assert. Jesus, he holds, could only have used 'Son of God' in the Messianic official sense of Ps 27; here, therefore, where the meaning is clearly more than official, it cannot be the voice of a Jewish Messiah which is heard, but the voice of the Christian consciousness in a Gentile environment : the larger Church has universalized the Jewish conception, elevated the official Son—the Messianic King—into a Son by nature, and put its own faith and its own experience of Jesus into Jesus' own lips. Perhaps it is enough to say in refutation of this, that the words here in question, as found both in Mt. and Lk., in all probability belong to Weiss's 'apostolic source,' the oldest record of words of Jesus; and that the same unique relation of 'the Father' and 'the Son' is implied in Mk 13^{32}, the genuineness of which no one doubts. Schmiedel (*Encyc. Bibl.* ii. 2527), without disputing the words in Mt 11^{27}, tries by recurring to the Western text to reduce them to the 'official' Messianic meaning which Loisy could recognize as possibly historical. Harnack, on the other hand, treats them as authentic, and indeed as the most important and characteristic words of Jesus on record for determining His thought regarding Himself (*Das Wesen des Christentums*, p. 81).

heaven, and it is a strong measure to assume that in cherishing this hope, by which the NT is inspired from beginning to end, the early Church was completely misapprehending the Master. He must have said something—when we consider the intensity of the Apostolic hope, surely we may say He must have said much—to create and sustain an expectation so keen. But there are considerations we must keep in mind if we would do justice to all the facts. (1) The final triumph of His cause, which was the cause of God and His kingdom, was not for Jesus an item in a list of dogmas, but a living personal faith and hope; in this sense it has the authority of His personality behind it. It was as sure to Him as His own being that the cause for which He stood in the world would triumph; and it is as sure for everyone who believes in Him. (2) He Himself, with all this assurance of faith, explicitly declares His ignorance of the day and hour at which the final triumph comes. He longed for it intensely; He felt that it was urgent that it should come; and urgency, when expressed in terms of time, means imminence; but the disclaimer of knowledge remains. The one thing certain is that He spoke of the time as uncertain, as sometimes sooner than men would expect, and sometimes later: the moral attitude required being always that of watching (Bruce, *Kingdom of God*, p. 278 ff.; Wendt, *Teaching of Jesus*, i. p. 127). (3) When Jesus bodied forth this hope of the future triumph of His cause, and of His own glorious coming, He did it in language borrowed mainly from the OT apocalypse, the Book of Daniel. It would be hard to say that the Apostles completely misunderstood Him when He did so, but it is hard for anyone in using such language to say what is literal in it and what has to be spiritualized. No one in reading Dn 7 takes the four great beasts, and the sea out of which they rise, literally; why, then, must we be compelled to take the human form and the clouds of heaven, literally? The Book of Acts (2$^{16-21}$) sees in the experience of the Church at Pentecost the fulfilment of a prophecy in Joel (2^{30}) which speaks of 'blood and fire and vapour of smoke, of the sun turning into darkness and the moon into blood,' though no such phenomena actually accompanied the gift of the Spirit. May not modern Christians, and even the early believers, have taken poetic expressions of the living hope of Jesus more prosaically than He meant them? (4) We must allow for the possibility that in the reports of Jesus' words which we possess, the reporters may sometimes have allowed the hopes kindled in their own hearts by Jesus to give a turn or a colour, quite involuntarily, to what they tell us. They might not be able to distinguish precisely between the hopes they owed to Him and the very words in which He had declared His own assurance of victory. And finally (5), we must remember that in a spiritual sense the prophecies of Jesus have been fulfilled. He came again in power. He came in the resurrection, and He came at Pentecost. He filled Jerusalem with His presence in the early days of the Church as He had never done while He lived on earth; from the very hour when they condemned Him (Mt 26^{64}) it was possible for His judges to be conscious of His exaltation and of His coming in power. It may be that in all prophecy, even in the prophecy of Jesus, there is the element which we can call illusive, without having to call it delusive. To be intelligible, it must speak the language of the age, but it is going to be fulfilled in another age, the realities and experiences of which transcend the conceptions and the speech of the present. Even if this be so, it does not shake our faith in Jesus and His authority. The truth which is incarnate in His person is the truth of the final—and who will not sometimes say the speedy?—triumph of His cause. We may misconceive the mode of it, even when we try to guide ourselves by His words; but the important thing is not the mode but the fact, and of that we are as sure as we are sure of Him.

(c) Besides the authority which He exercised in establishing His ascendency over men, and that which we recognize in Him as the Truth, we may distinguish (though it is but part of His revelation of the Father) the gracious authority exercised by Christ in *forgiving sins*. That He did forgive sins is not to be doubted. The narrative in Mk 2$^{1-12}$ makes this clear. Jesus no more *declared* that the paralytic's sins were forgiven than He declared that he was not lame: the meaning of the whole incident is that His word *conferred* with equal power the gift of pardon and the gift of bodily strength. The one miracle of redemption—'who forgiveth all thine iniquities, who healeth all thy diseases'—reaches through the whole of human nature, and Jesus has authority to perform it all. It is in this sense that we must interpret passages like Lk 7$^{47ff.}$ 23^{43} as well as Mk 2^{17}, Lk 15, and ultimately Mt 18^{18} and Jn 20^{23}. There is not anything to be said of this authority but that it must vindicate itself. No one can believe that Jesus has authority to forgive sins except the man who through Jesus has had the experience of forgiveness. The Divine love that dwelt in Jesus, that received sinners and ate with them, that spent itself to seek and save the lost, that saw what was of God in men and touched it: that Divine love made forgiveness not only credible to sinners, but real. It entered into their hearts with God's own authority, and in penitent faith and love the burden passed from their consciences and they were born again. When He was challenged by the scribes, Jesus appealed to the physical miracle, which was indisputable, in support of the spiritual one, which lay beyond the reach of sense; but it was only the scribes, not the forgiven man, who needed this seal of His authority to pardon. Those whom He forgave had the witness in themselves, and ultimately there can be no other. The authority which Jesus exercised in this gracious sense He extended to His disciples alike during their brief mission while He was on earth (Mk 3^{15} 6$^{7-13}$), and in view of their wider calling when He was exalted (Mt 18^{18}, Jn 20^{23}).

Some light is thrown upon the authority of Jesus if we consider the occasions on which it was challenged, and the way in which Jesus met them.

(a) It was tacitly challenged wherever men were 'offended' in Him. To be offended (σκανδαλίζεσθαι) is to stumble at His claims, to find something in Him which one cannot get over and which is incompatible with absolute surrender to Him; it is to deny His right to impose upon men the consequences (persecution, poverty, even death) which may be involved in accepting His authority (see Mt 11^6 13$^{21.\ 28ff.}$ 15^{12} 24^{10} 26^{31}: the other Gospels here add nothing to Mt.). Sometimes Jesus met this tacit challenge by pointing to the general character of His work as vindicating His claims. This is what He does in the case of John the Baptist (Mt 11$^{2-6}$). Whether we read this passage—'the blind receive their sight, the lame walk,' etc.—in the physical or the spiritual sense, the works in question are the signs that God's Anointed has come, and it can only mean loss and ruin to men if they fail to see and to acknowledge Him as what He is. Sometimes, again, Jesus encountered those who were 'offended' in Him with a severity amounting to scorn. When the Pharisees 'stumbled' because His word about things that do and do not defile cut straight across their traditional prejudices, He did nothing to conciliate them. 'Every plant that my heavenly Father hath not planted shall be rooted up. Let them alone. They are blind guides of blind men. And if the blind man leads the blind, both shall fall into the ditch' (Mt 15$^{13f.}$). In reality the 'offence' in this case meant that sham holiness would not acknowledge true; and in this situation it can only be war *à l'outrance*. As a rule, however, Jesus only speaks of men being offended, or offended in Him, by way of warning; and He assumes that to the solemn tones of His warning conscience will respond. His authority is inherent in Himself and His actions, and cannot with a good conscience be repudiated by any one who sees what He is. This is the tone of Mt 13^{21} 24^{10} 26^{31}.

(β) It is a more explicit challenge of His authority when Jesus is asked to show a sign, or a sign from heaven (Mt 12$^{38f.}$ 16$^{1f.}$, Lk 23^8, Jn 6^{30}). This was the recurrence of the temptation of the pinnacle, and Jesus consistently rejected it. He never consented (not even in the case of the paralytic of Mk 2$^{1-9}$, see above) to present the physical as evidence for the spiritual. The proof of the authority with which He spoke did not lie outside of His word, in something which could be attached to it, but in the word itself; if it was not self-attesting, nothing else could attest it. This is put with peculiar force in the Fourth Gospel. It is true that an evidential value is recognized in the miracles, but it is only by an afterthought, or as a second best: 'though ye believe not me, believe the works' (Jn 10^{38}); 'believe that I am in the Father and the Father in me; or else, believe for the very works' sake' (14^{11}). The main line of thought is that which deprecates faith based on signs and wonders (4^{48}). When the multitudes ask, 'What sign doest thou then? our fathers did eat the manna in the wilderness,' the answer of Jesus virtually is, '*I* am the bread of life. . . . He that eateth *me* shall live by me . . . the words that I speak unto you are spirit and are life' (Jn 6$^{30ff.}$). In other words, the authority of Jesus does not depend upon any external credentials; it is involved in what He is, and must be immediately apprehended and responded to by the soul. What enables men to recognize Jesus as what He is, and so to acknowledge His authority, is, according to the representation of the central chapters in John (chs. 6–10), a need in their nature or state which He can supply. If we wish to be sure that He is the Christ, the King in the Kingdom of God, the way to certainty is not to prove that He was born at Bethlehem of the seed of David (7^{42}), nor that He came into the world mysteriously (7^{27}), nor that He has done many miracles (7^{31}): it is to see in Him the living bread (ch. 6), the living water (ch. 4 and 7^{37}), the light of the world (chs. 8 and 9), the Good Shepherd (ch. 10), the Giver of Life (chs. 5 and 11). These are ideas or experiences which are relative to universal human needs, and therefore they are universally intelligible; every one who knows what it is to be hungry, thirsty, forlorn, in the dark, dead, knows how to appreciate Jesus; and apart from these experiences no cleverness in applying prophetic or other theological signs to Him is of any value. All this is strictly relevant, for it is through experiences in which we become debtors to Jesus for meat and drink, for light and life, that we become conscious of what His authority means.

(γ) Once, at least, the authority of Jesus was challenged in a quasi-legal fashion. When He drove the traders from the Temple, the chief priests and the elders of the people came to Him, saying, 'By what authority doest thou these things, and who gave thee this authority?' (Mt 21$^{23ff.}$, Mk 11$^{27ff.}$, Lk 20$^{1ff.}$). Formally, by His counter question about the Baptist, Jesus only silences His adversaries; but more than this is meant. If, He suggests, they had been true to the earlier messenger of God, they would have had no difficulty about His claims. If they had repented at John's summons, and been right with God, then to their simple and humble hearts Jesus' action would have vindicated itself: as it is, to their insincere souls He has no advance to make. The ambassador of an earthly king has credentials external to his person and his message, but not the ambassador in whom God Himself visits His people. His actions like His words speak for themselves. Throughout the Fourth Gospel it is an affinity of spirit with Jesus on which the recognition of His authority depends. It is those who are of God (Jn 8^{47}), of the truth (18^{37}), those who are His sheep (10$^{4f. 26}$), who hear His voice: those who are not of God, especially the insincere, who seek honour from one another (5^{44}), are inevitably offended in Him.

2. Thus far we have considered the authority of Christ as it was exercised, acknowledged, or declined during His life on earth. But the NT exhibits much more than this. It is not merely as historical, but as *exalted*, that Christ exercises authority—in the Church. In all its aspects the authority which we have studied in the Gospels reappears in the Epistles. It is perpetuated in the Christian society in an effective, if somewhat undefinable way.

What strikes one first in the NT literature, apart from the Gospels, is the almost complete absence of *literal* appeal to Jesus. The Apostles, whatever be the explanation, do not, except on rare occasions, *quote* the Lord. It is true that when they do so, His word is regarded as decisive in a sense in which even the word of an apostle is not (cf. 1 Co 7^{10} with vv.$^{12. 25. 40}$). It is true also that passages like Ro 12.13, and much in the Epistle of James, could only have been written (in all probability) by men who not only had the Spirit of Christ, but whose minds were full of echoes of His words. Nevertheless the fact remains that Jesus is hardly appealed to formally as an authority in the NT writings. There could be no more striking proof of the fact that Christianity was apprehended from the first as a free and spiritual religion to which everything statutory was alien. Not even the word of Jesus had legal character for it. What Jesus sought and found in His disciples was a spiritual remembrance of Himself. His words were preserved not in a phonograph, or in a stenographic report, but in the impression they made, in the insight they gave, in the thoughts and experiences they produced in the lives of living men. They were perpetuated not merely by being put on record, but still more by being preached. Now to preach is not only to report, but to apply; and the application of the word of Christ to new circumstances inevitably and unconsciously brings with it a certain or rather an uncertain amount of interpretation, of bringing out the point, of emphasis on this or that which at the moment demands it. What we wish to know is whether the men whose ministry perpetuated the word of Christ, and perpetuated it in this free and spiritual fashion, had the qualifications demanded by their task. Could Christ so fit them for their ministry that they should be under no legal constraint, and yet should never be unfaithful to His meaning, or misrepresent Him or His work? In other words, could He in any sense transmit His authority to His witnesses, so that it should be felt in them as in Him?

The answer of the NT is in the affirmative, and it is not too much to say that the NT as a whole is the proof that this answer is right. 'We have the mind of Christ,' says St. Paul (1 Co 2¹⁶), and again (in 2 Co 13³), 'Ye seek a proof of Christ speaking in me'—a proof which he is quite ready to give. He was conscious that in the discharge of his Apostolic ministry he was not alone : Christ was in him pleading His own cause. Of course the authority of Christ in this case cannot be other than we have already seen it to be in the earthly life of Christ. Its range is the same, and its recognition is conditioned in the same way. The Apostle is no more bound literally to reproduce Jesus than Jesus is bound literally to reproduce Himself. He is no more bound than Jesus is to prove the truth of his message by credentials external to it. He no more hesitates than Jesus does to trace the rejection of his message, the refusal to call Jesus Lord, to a want of moral affinity with Jesus which is the final definition of sin. 'If our gospel is veiled, it is veiled in them that are perishing, in whom the god of this world hath blinded the minds of the unbelieving' (2 Co 4³ᶠ·). It is not possible to say beforehand, on the basis of any doctrine of inspiration, whether there are elements in the Apostolic writings, and if so what, which have no authority for us. Nothing in them has legal or statutory authority, and spiritual authority must be trusted to win for itself the recognition which is its due. There is something to be said for the distinction that while the testimony of the Apostles to Jesus—a testimony resting on their experience of what He was and of what He had done for them—is perennially authoritative, the theology of the Apostles—a theology conditioned by the intellectual environment in which they lived and to which they had to vindicate their message—has only a transient importance. The difficulty is just to draw the distinction between testimony and theology ; as a matter of fact, the two things interpenetrate in the NT, and there is a point at which the distinction disappears. To insist upon it as if it were absolute is really to introduce again into Christianity (under the form of the Apostolic testimony) that legal or statutory or dogmatic element from which Jesus set all religion free. It is better to read the Apostles as men through whose minds Christ pleads His own cause in the Spirit. The minds may be more or less adequate instruments for His service ; they may be more adequate in some relations, and less so in others ; but they are indivisible, and it is not helpful in the long run to introduce into them the schism of testimony and theology. We must let them tell upon us in their integrity, and acknowledge their authority whenever it proves irresistible. (More detailed consideration of this point will be found in the article on PREACHING CHRIST).

The part of the NT which raises in the acutest form the question of the authority of Christ—or perhaps we should say here of His Apostle—is the Fourth Gospel. It is practically agreed among scholars that the style of the discourses in that Gospel is due to the author, not to the speakers. Every one speaks in the same style—John the Baptist, Jesus, the Evangelist himself. The words of an actor in the history (Jesus, for example, in the first part of ch. 3, and the Baptist in the latter part) pass over insensibly into words of the historian. The first person plural is used by Jesus (e.g. 3¹¹ 9⁴) where it is tempting to say that it is the Christian consciousness which is expressed, the common mind of the Church which owes its being to Him. Further, Jesus says things about Himself in the Fourth Gospel to which there is no parallel in the other three. He speaks plainly of His pre-existence, of the glory which He had with the Father before the world was, of an eternal being which was His before Abraham was born ; He makes Himself the content and the subject of His teaching—'I am the bread of life, the light of the world, the resurrection and the life' ; He identifies Himself in a mysterious way with the redeeming purpose and power of God—'I and the Father are one,' 'He that hath seen me hath seen the Father.' It may be difficult for the historian, on purely historical grounds, to prove that Jesus uttered all the words thus ascribed to Him, and if the difficulty presses, the authority of the words may seem to disappear. But is this really so? May not the Fourth Gospel itself be the fulfilment of one of the words in question—'I have many things to say unto you, but ye cannot bear them now. But when he is come, the Spirit of truth, he shall guide you into all the truth : for he shall not speak from himself, but whatsoever things he shall hear, these shall he speak . . . He shall take of mine, and shall announce it to you' (Jn 16¹²ᶠ·). These words would not be satisfied by a merely literal reproduction of what Jesus had uttered : they imply that with the gift of the Spirit will come a profounder insight into all that He had meant, and ability to render a more adequate testimony to the truth embodied in Him. Twice in the Gospel (2²² 12¹⁶) the writer tells us expressly that after Jesus was glorified the disciples remembered incidents in His career and saw a meaning in them unnoticed at the time ; and this principle may well reach further. When Jesus fed the multitudes, He did not, so far as the Synoptics record, say anything to explain His act ; all they were conscious of was that He had compassion on their hunger. But the Spirit-taught Apostle, long afterwards, saw what He meant, and felt that if they had only had ears to hear as the bread passed from hand to hand, they would have caught the voice of Jesus—'I am the bread of life.' So when He opened the eyes of the blind, what He meant was, 'I am the light of the world' ; and when He raised the dead, 'I am the resurrection and the life.' If John did not hear Him say so at the moment, he heard Him afterwards, and the authority of the words need not be less though we have to think of them as spoken, not by the historical Christ in Galilee or Judæa, but by the exalted Christ through His Spirit in the soul of the beloved disciple. They would be in this case a sublime illustration of what St. Paul calls 'Christ speaking in me.' The peculiarity that they are put into the lips of Jesus Himself, in connexion with definite scenes and incidents in His earthly life, was possibly quite intelligible to those who first read the Gospel ; they knew that it was a spiritual Gospel, and that it was never intended to be taken as a literal record of Jesus' discourses, but as an inspired interpretation of all that He was and did. Read in this light, it has its authority in itself, as the other NT books have, and as Jesus Himself had when He spoke with men face to face ; and it is an authority, as experience proves, not less potent than that which is claimed and wielded by Christ in any other of His witnesses. If we compare it with the other Gospels, which have in a higher degree the character of literal transcripts of word and deed, we may even say that it is a fulfilment of the words found in the lips of Jesus in 14¹² 'He that believeth on me, the works that I do shall he also do : and greater works than these shall he do ; because I go to the Father.' Faith in Jesus has never achieved anything surpassing the witness—the true witness — of this Gospel to the Son of God. The final and supremely authoritative testimony to Jesus is no doubt that which is given in His being and in His work in the world ; but so dull of eye and slow of heart were the disciples, that had He put all the import of this into words they could not have taken it in. What He could not say on earth, however, He was able to say by His Spirit from heaven ; and when that one of the disciples who was able to hear puts what he has heard into the Master's lips, he is only giving Him His own. The authority of the word of Jesus here, as everywhere in the NT, lies in itself, and in the fact which it interprets. It is an authority which has never failed to win recognition, and it may be said of it with emphasis, 'Every one that is of the truth heareth this voice.'

LITERATURE.—H. P. Liddon, *Bampton Lectures*, 166 ff. ; C. Gore, *Bampton Lectures*, ch. vii. ; A. B. Bruce, *Training of the Twelve*, 536 ff., *Apologetics*, 492 ff. ; J. Denney, *Studies in Theology*, ii., iii. ; A. Sabatier, *Religions of Authority and Religion of the Spirit*, 292 ff. ; H. H. Henson, *Value of the Bible*, 250 ff. ; M. Fuller, *In Terra Pax*, 124 ff.

JAMES DENNEY.

AUTHORITY IN RELIGION.—1. *Various connotations of the word 'authority.'*—The familiar distinction between legislative, judicial, and executive authority is one that is not only convenient, but rational and necessary. These several kinds of authority differ in their respective sources and appropriate modes of expression, and may differ also in their respective repositories. Again, authority may be original or delegated. The latter, moreover, while on a different plane, is not one whit less real than the former. And, passing by other uses of the word, it will be found that the idea lying at the heart of them all is that of *a right* on the part of somebody to submission of some sort and in some degree on the part of somebody else. In other words, the use of the term 'authority' implies the existence of an ethical standard. We shall not, therefore, have reached the ultimate authority along any line until we have arrived at this ultimate standard of right, by which the reality of all other authorities is tested. To avoid confusion, then, in considering Christ's teachings regarding authority in religion, we shall have at every step to take account of the particular kind of authority then being dealt with.

2. *Christ's conception of religion.*—That Christ's conception of religion must have conditioned and shaped His teachings upon authority in religion is too obvious to be questioned. Hence we must at least glance at His conception of religion ; but as this subject is itself a large one, we can at most merely glance at it. Our Lord, of course, has nowhere given us a formal definition of religion, nor has He anywhere formally discussed its nature. At the same time, few, we presume, will affirm that Christ has left us wholly at sea upon such a point. By common consent, religion is a term of relation. For present purposes we may, without unwarrantable assumption, say that the terms of this relation are God and man. Further, without undue assumption, we may add that true religion and right relation between God and man are equivalent expressions. Our present question, then, resolves itself into this, What, according to Christ, are the essentials of right relation between God and man ?

Now, for answering this question, three statements of our Lord seem to the writer to be of fundamental importance. (1) The first of these occurs in His high priestly prayer. 'This,' says He, 'is eternal life, that they should know thee the only true God, and him whom thou didst send, even Jesus Christ' (Jn 17³). Here the last clause may be an epexegetical addition of the Evangelist himself. With this statement naturally associate themselves, among others, those in Jn 10¹⁰ 3⁵, Mt 11²⁷. Now, certainly no one will even for a moment suppose that our Lord here lends any countenance to anything that can properly be called intellectualism. And yet it would be violent exegesis indeed that eradicated from His words the idea that right relations to God invariably imply, and

ground themselves on, right conceptions of God. On any other view, what would be the propriety of the pronoun 'thee,' which certainly singles out from all other possible individuals or entities Him in the knowledge of whom Christ declares that 'eternal life' consists ? If right conceptions of God are not essential to right relation between God and man, where, again, would be the propriety of the words 'the only true,' and the emphasis evidently centred upon them ? (cf. also Mt 11²⁷).

(2) A second passage of fundamental significance for Christ's conception of religion is Mt 22³⁷ff. ‖ Mk 12²⁸ff. 'Thou shalt love the Lord thy God, etc. Thou shalt love thy neighbour as thyself, etc. On these two commandments hangeth the whole law and the prophets.' But that, according to the teaching of Christ, there is an emotional element in religion, is so generally recognized that it would be superfluous to multiply references, especially in such an incidental treatment of the subject as the present.

(3) The third passage that may be regarded as fundamental for our Lord's conception of religion is Mt 7²¹ 'Not every one that saith unto me, Lord, Lord, shall enter into the kingdom of heaven ; but he that doeth the will of my Father which is in heaven.' This, like the last passage cited, is typical. It represents a group of statements that need not be reproduced here.

While, therefore, the first of these three great passages implicates man's understanding in religion, and the second his emotions, this last implicates his will, as controlling his conduct and finding its legitimate expression through it.

What may be called, then, a qualitative analysis of Christ's conception of religion reveals the fact, that it contains this trinity of elements bound together in the indissoluble unity of the rational soul. Were any of them totally lacking, there would be no real religion. On the other hand, the necessary interrelation and interaction between them are recognized by Christ in such declarations as, 'If any man willeth to do his will, he shall know of the teaching whether it be of God, or whether I speak from myself' (Jn 7¹⁷) ; 'How can ye believe which receive glory one of another, and the glory that cometh from the only God ye seek not' (Jn 5⁴⁴) ; 'While ye have the light, believe on the light, that ye may become sons of light' (Jn 12³⁶). Such is the essential unity of the soul, that it cannot experience depravation in one of its functions without all of the others being more or less affected thereby.

While, however, we can with a measure both of ease and of certainty make what we have ventured to call a qualitative analysis of Christ's conception of religion, it would not be so easy to arrive at a quantitative analysis of it, and say just how much knowledge, how much emotion, and how much volitional activity must be present in order to the existence in the soul of any real religion. Indeed, it is hard to conceive of Christ as elaborating any views upon such a subject. We may refrain, then, from pressing our investigation into what would only be a region of arid and empty speculation. It is enough, if it has been shown that Christ's conception of religion recognizes the essential unity of the soul, and involves its right relation to God in all its several powers or functions. To this conception His teachings regarding authority in religion will be found to conform. See, further, art. RELIGION.

i. CHRIST'S TEACHING AS TO THE ULTIMATE STANDARD OF RIGHT, AND THE ULTIMATE SOURCE OF RIGHTS.—Obviously we need not expect to find Christ dealing with the ultimate standard of right under the forms of Western dialectics, or in the abstract terms of philosophy. At the same time, we need not despair of obtaining some insight into His mind even upon this question. For one thing, His mode of addressing His Father is significant. Especially is it so when we take into account the circumstances under which it was employed. 'Holy Father,' He says in His intercessory prayer; and again, 'O righteous Father.' Now, under the circumstances, this language is more, far more, than the ascription to His Father of the possession of the qualities expressed by the words 'holy' and 'righteous.' For we must not forget that Christ's intercessory prayer was offered at the very crisis of His career. We cannot pretend to fathom the experiences of His soul in that hour. The prayer itself, however, as recorded in Jn 17, is tense with the emotions that wrought in our Lord's soul as He poured it forth. He was, so to speak, getting His footing as the floods of great waters gathered around Him in their mysterious energy. And the bed-rock upon which He plants Himself is one lying out of sight so far as the visible providence of God is concerned. He assures Himself of its existence as a reality by turning away from what is taking place under the providence of God, and fixing His mind upon the nature of God. God's nature is His voucher for the righteousness of the course of God's providence towards Himself. In the time of stress that was upon Him, He fixes His eye upon God's holiness and righteousness as His sole but sufficient guarantee for the existence of the qualities for which these words stand.

But, further, that Christ found the ultimate standard of right in God's nature as expressed through God's will, is clear also from such statements as these: 'Now is my soul troubled; and what shall I say? Father, save me from this hour? but for this cause came I unto this hour. Father, glorify thy name' (Jn 12[27f.]). Here, it will be seen, our Lord places Himself absolutely at the disposal of the Divine will. But this would have been sheer moral insanity, unless God's nature contained the final norm of righteousness. And this language is by no means exceptional; for, as all know, the Gospel of John abounds with expressions of Christ making the will of God the standard to which everything is to be referred (e.g. 4[34] 5[30] 6[38f.]). Nor is the case different when we turn to the Synoptics (cf. Mt 5[48] 6[10] 11[25f.], Lk 22[42]). All these passages and others leave no room to doubt that Christ taught that the nature of God, as finding expression through His will, is the ultimate standard of right.

And as, for Christ, God's nature is the ultimate norm of right, so for Him God's will is the fountain and source of all particular *rights*. Wherever there exists a right upon the part of anybody to submission of any kind or degree from anybody else, such right exists in virtue of God's ordering, and is delimited by God's will. These statements, it seems to us, are involved in the passages already cited. All authority, in other words, is simply *author*-ity writ short and differently pronounced. A free creature, like man, may be, in a limited sense, an original source of power, but never of *rights*. His rights are all derived from, and bear the stamp of, the author of his being. Not only the primary and all-comprehending dependence, but all subordinate dependences and interdependences ground themselves ultimately on the relation that subsists between the Creator, as Creator, and the creature, as creature.

ii. Legislative authority in religion. — 1. *Term defined.*—What we have called legislative authority is concerned primarily with *duty*. Its prescriptions, while mediated, at least so far as the knowledge of them goes, through the understanding, terminate upon the conscience and the will. It is the right to require or to forbid. It is the right to establish relations and define the duties or the privileges attaching to them. It is the first and most fundamental form of authority, cleaving closest to the etymological and logical sense of the word, which as already noted is simply *author*-ity. Legislative authority is really or approximately a creative function. In the case of God, of course, it is really creative. Behind it lies only the Divine nature, which alone conditions and regulates its exercise. From it arise all the relations of the creature to the Creator, and to his fellow-creatures, with the duties and the privileges that inhere in them, or that, in the wisdom of God, are, from time to time and under the particular circumstances, attached to them.

Now, according to our Lord's teaching, all legislative authority in religion vests exclusively in God. He represents God as in the most absolute sense 'Lord of the conscience.' To Him it belongs to say, 'Thou shalt,' and to Him also to say, 'Thou shalt not.' As He has determined the relations between Himself and His creatures ('Father, Lord of heaven and earth,' Mt 11[25]; cf. also 19[4]), it is for Him to define the duties emerging from those relations.

2. If, now, we pass to Christ's teaching as to how this legislative authority belonging exclusively to God comes to expression, we find—(1) That our Lord is wholly silent as to the manifestation of God's legislative authority in what we call 'the laws of nature,' using this phrase so as to include not only the laws of matter, but of mind as well, and also so as to include what St. Paul calls 'the law written in the heart.' For instance, nowhere does He directly advert to 'the ordinance of heaven' (Jer 31[35f.], Job 38[33]) as an expression of the Divine will; nowhere does He refer His hearers to the constitution of their own nature, physical, mental, or moral, as embodying an expression of the Divine will regarding this or that. There is, it may be, the glimmer of such a reference in passages like Jn 10[17ff.], Mt 10[29f.], but it is at most a glimmer, and need not detain us.

(2) But that the legislative authority of God is exercised mediately as well as immediately is also taught by Christ. (a) Thus *the preceptive portions of the OT*, though mediated by 'Moses and the prophets,' are really 'the commandments of God.' Moses and the prophets, *quoad* this matter, are, so to speak, merely the heralds of the 'Great King,' or, to borrow an OT account of the relation between the prophet and God, the former is the 'mouth' of the latter (Ex 4[16], cf. 7[1]). And so, while 'Moses said, Honour thy father and thy mother' (Mk 7[10]), this is still for Christ 'the commandment of God.' Further, that 'the law of Moses' was for Him the law of God appears from the fact that, when He was Himself tempted, and had to choose between two courses, what was written in Deuteronomy prescribed for Him the path of duty (Mt 4[4.7.10.11]). In the parable of Dives and Lazarus, our Lord puts these very significant words into the mouth of Abraham, 'They have Moses and the prophets; let them hear them' (Lk 16[29]). The law in Nu 28[9.10] (or perhaps in 1 Ch 9[32]), according to which 'the priests in the temple profane' (ironical thrust at His adversaries) 'the Sabbath and are guiltless' (Mt 12[5]), was for Christ determinative of duty and of privilege. Indeed, He virtually puts it upon the same plane for authority as the primary intuition and verdict of conscience, namely, that 'it is lawful to do good—on the Sabbath day' (Mt 12[12]). Further, Christ's summaries of 'the law and the prophets' (Mt 7[12] 22[37ff.]) bear impressive testimony to the fact that He regarded the whole preceptive portion of the OT as an expression of the will of God. 'Whatsoever ye would that men should do to you,

even so do ye also unto them,' is, according to our Lord, but a just summary of 'the law and the prophets' in terms that may be appreciated by the moral sense of all men. He teaches that the whole OT, so far as it has to do with duty towards man, is but an unfolding, in relation to this or that set of circumstances, of the 'Golden Rule,' whose Divine origin and authority are self-evidencing (cf. Mt 12[28ff.]).

(*b*) Whether Christ represents the *Apostles* also as organs through whom God exercises His legislative authority is, perhaps, not quite so clear. Doubtless they were. But even passages such as Mt 10[20] 16[18], Jn 20[23] 16[13] may refer to a grant of judicial rather than of strictly legislative authority. The authority conferred in these passages is, indeed, large and significant, but none of them necessarily implies that the Apostles were to be organs through whom God would make substantive additions to the commands laid upon the human conscience. Nor has the writer been able to satisfy himself that Christ anywhere uses of them language either demanding, or even susceptible of such an interpretation. In other words, while he thinks it unquestionable that the Apostles were media through whom God exercised His legislative authority, he is of opinion that we have to go outside of the Gospels for the evidence of this fact.

(*c*) With *Christ Himself*, however, the case is different. No doubt much of the authority we find Him using in the Gospels is judicial and not legislative. At the same time, intermingled with His judicial expositions of the law of God, we hear Him lay His own commands upon the conscience. Not only does He declare what is the Law, and what its meaning (see above), but He enunciates many specific precepts that stand related to His comprehensive summaries very much as the statutes of the land stand related to its constitution.

'Lay not up for yourselves treasures upon earth,' etc. (Mt 6[19ff.]); 'Give not that which is holy unto the dogs, neither cast your pearls before the swine,' etc. (Mt 7[6]); 'Love your enemies, do good to them that hate you,' etc. (Lk 6[27]); 'Repent ye, and believe in the gospel' (Mk 1[15])—will serve as samples. Very significant for Christ's claims to be a special organ of the legislative authority of the Godhead is such a statement as, 'The Son of man is Lord of the Sabbath' (Mt 12[8]), and equally so this other, 'Ye call me Teacher and Lord : and ye say well ; for so I am' (Jn 13[13]). In both these instances it is clear that Christ asserts for Himself an authority going beyond any that can with propriety be considered as merely judicial. The 'Lord' is a giver of law, not simply its interpreter. The same conclusion follows even more stringently, perhaps, when our Lord says, 'I and the Father are one,' thereby, as the Jews affirmed, and He Himself did not deny, 'making himself (thyself) equal with God' (Jn 10[30], cf. 10[33], Mt 11[27. 29] note the word 'yoke'). And, finally, here we must not overlook Mt 28[18b] 'All authority is given to me in heaven and on earth,' which certainly constitutes a claim comprehensive enough to include the authority to prescribe laws to the conscience. See preceding article.

(3) But to say that Christ teaches that all legislative authority in religion vests exclusively in God, is hardly to put the case either as fully or as strongly as it needs to be put. For not only does our Lord represent *God as 'Lord of the conscience,'* but with equal emphasis and great explicitness He teaches that 'God alone is Lord of the conscience, and hath left it free from the doctrines and commandments of men which are in anything contrary to His word, or beside it in matters of' religious truth and duty. (For the purposes of this article 'His word' here may be taken quite broadly for any form in which God has made His will known).

This explains His word at the baptism, when the Baptist 'would have hindered him,' and He said, 'Suffer it now : for thus it becometh us to fulfil all righteousness' (Mt 3[15]). So saying, He denies to the human reason the prerogative, by annulling or setting them aside, to pass judgment upon the propriety or the expediency of Divine prescriptions. Recognizing what is praiseworthy in the spirit of the Baptist, He at the same time sets the seal of His disapprobation upon all man-devised substitutions for, or modifications of, Divine ordinances. These are all either acts of open rebellion, or well meant but real usurpations of legislative functions pertaining exclusively to God. The same view finds yet more palpable and pungent expression in His rebuke to the Pharisees (Mk 7[6ff.]). And, as is well known, it was His resistance in word and deed to the traditions of the elders regarding the Sabbath—these being 'beside' God's word—that earned for Him, with the Pharisees, the odium of being Himself a Sabbath-breaker (Jn 5, Mt 12, Mk 3).

Indeed, at the beginning of His Galilæan ministry, our Lord is careful to disclaim, even for Himself, either purpose or authority to disannul any of God's commandments. 'Think not,' said He, 'that I am come to destroy the law or the prophets : I came not to destroy, but to fulfil' (Mt 5[17]). See, further, article COMMANDMENT, below. Thus He, as it were, anticipated and forestalled the malice of His own, and the mistaken zeal of a later day. The former made it a charge against Him that He taught contrary to Moses and the prophets ; and the latter, strangely enough, has supposed that it honours Him by affirming the same. And, lofty as were the claims that He made for Himself, Christ still impressed it upon His hearers that He not only did not assume to lay upon them anything contrary to God's revealed will but that He taught, and could teach nothing that was 'beside' that will (Jn 5[30], cf. 5[19] 8[28f.]). And that nothing 'contrary to or beside' the Scriptures correctly interpreted was to be tolerated, is abundantly evident from the finality attached to them in all Christ's appeals to the OT. For Him its declarations were an end of controversy (Mt 22[29] 19[4] 12[3ff.], Jn 10[35]).

iii. JUDICIAL AUTHORITY IN RELIGION. — 1. *Term defined.*—As legislative authority has particularly to do with *duty*, so judicial authority has particularly to do with *truth* : the former prescribes what one is *to do* or *to be* ; the latter, what he is *to believe* : the former *creates* and *defines* relation and obligations ; the latter *declares* and *interprets* them : the former is mainly concerned with the *conscience* ; the latter, with the *understanding*. It is worth noting further that legislative differs from judicial authority in that the former is original and the latter derivative. Legislative authority, along with other things, prescribes who is to interpret the laws it makes, and how much of finality shall attach to their interpretation by different persons. At the same time, we should not overlook the fact that the most limited judicial authority, so far as it goes, is no less real than the most absolute. Further, judicial authority, though derived, is just as real authority as is legislative authority. And, finally, when the judicial function vests in the same person as the legislative, then the maxim, 'The interpretation of the law is the law,' receives its highest exemplification ; for then the law and the interpretation of the law are but different modal manifestations of one and the same personal will or *author*-ity. For, in this case, the same character that guarantees to the conscience the righteousness of the relation or obligation created by the will of the lawgiver, guarantees also to the understanding the truth of the finding of the judge. And this, be it observed, is precisely the function of judicial authority, namely, not to create a right, not to make an idea correspond with reality, but to certify to the understanding the existence or non-existence of a right, the truth or the falsity of an idea or a statement. The vital importance of this distinction will appear more and more as the discussion proceeds.

2. *Repositories.*—As to judicial authority, our Lord teaches that it is distributed among a number of repositories, somewhat as the same kind of authority in a modern State is distributed

among a number of courts from the lowest to the highest.

In the case of such courts, no one thinks of denying to the least and lowest of them the character of a true court. Its jurisdiction may be limited, its decisions liable to reversal, but so long as it keeps within its jurisdiction, so long as the appeal from its decisions is pending, its authority is not only as real but as absolute as that of the highest court. Further, even the lowest court possesses a genuine independence: its functions cannot be discharged for it, nor can they be wrested from it by any other court. Further still, it is for each court, at least in the first instance, to interpret and declare the law by which it was created, and its duties and prerogatives under the law. Nor does the fact that it may err in the exercise of this right either nullify or invalidate the right itself. We elaborate this analogy thus in detail, because we believe that it will prove helpful in enabling us to understand our Lord's teachings concerning judicial authority in the sphere of religion.

Proceeding now to note His distribution itself, we find that He accords the fullest recognition (1) to what is commonly known as *the right of private judgment*. For Him each individual is clothed with a large, though not an absolute or final, judicial authority. Indeed, it is safe to say that no one has surpassed Christ in the honour, and even—if such words may be used of Him—in the deference with which in practice He treated the judicial rights of the darkest and humblest human souls. Despite the supreme claims that He made for Himself, He habitually permitted both Himself and His claims to be put upon proof at the bar of such souls. Not only did He consent, like any other man of His day, to plead at the bar of the ecclesiastical and civil authorities, but, while He always spake as one having authority, He never failed to submit His credentials along with His claims at the bar of the individual reason and conscience. But here we must particularize.

Christ taught, then, (a) That it is the inalienable prerogative of every man to verify for himself the truth of a proposition before assenting to it as true; and to verify for himself the rectitude of a command before yielding obedience to it as right (cf. Jn 15²⁴, Mt 16⁴ 11⁴ff. 9⁶ 11²⁰).

(b) Further, as is involved in what has been already said, Christ teaches that the conclusions reached in the exercise of this prerogative are not to be, if, indeed, we should not say *cannot* be, dictated by any form of external compulsion. In many ways He emphasizes the position that the individual is to be left wholly untrammelled in the exercise of his judicial rights. What else, after all, is the meaning of His words to Pilate, 'My kingdom is not of this world: if my kingdom were of this world, then would my servants fight, that I should not be delivered to the Jews: but now is my kingdom not from hence' (Jn 18³⁶)? If men were to be left free to deal with His own claims, including, of course, His teachings, without constraint or compulsion of any kind, and to do this even when the decision reached affected not only His liberty but His very life, certainly He would have them no less untrammelled in dealing with every other question of truth or of duty with which they might find themselves confronted. Nor was it only the compulsion of physical force that Christ declined to countenance. He set the seal of His disapproval upon the more subtle and spiritual, but no less real compulsion of a tyrannical public or ecclesiastical opinion, whether formulated into a tradition or into a usage.

His 'Do not your alms before men, to be seen of them' (Mt 6¹), was designed hardly more to eradicate pride from the souls of His disciples, than it was to hearten them to throw off the incubus of a perverted public and ecclesiastical sentiment which threatened to stifle Christian humility and Godwardness in their very birth. It was to disenthrall the souls of His disciples from all fear tending to paralyze the free action of the spirit in its quest for truth and in its witness to the truth, that He said, 'Be not afraid of them that kill the body, but are not able to kill the soul: but rather fear him,' etc. (Mt 10²⁸); cf. Mk 10²⁹f. 79ff., Mt 12¹ff., Jn 5. 9.

(c) If what has been said be true, we are not surprised to find Christ teaching that every mind is equipped for the exercise of this high prerogative, that in a certain very true sense the mind has 'the supreme norm of its ideas and acts, not outside of itself, but within itself, in its very constitution' (Sabatier, *Religions of Authority*, p. xvi).

This also is involved in the passages already quoted. And what else can we make of such statements as these: 'Ought not this woman, being a daughter of Abraham, whom Satan hath bound, lo, these eighteen years, to be loosed from this bond on the day of the Sabbath' (Lk 13¹⁶)? Where would have been the use of submitting such a case to 'the stupid country *archisynagogos*' (Edersheim), unless, stupid as he was, even he was so equipped as to be able to subject it to some sort of process of 'inner verification'? Or, take the question put to the disciples, 'Who do the multitudes say that I am?' and what propriety would there be in it, unless it carried with it the implication that men generally—'the multitudes'—were equipped for the forming of a rational judgment upon the truth and righteousness of His claims, and had some touchstone each within himself by which he could determine the truth or falsity of those claims, and the moral quality of the character and of the teachings that lay behind them? The possession of such a norm is involved in every argument framed, in every appeal made, and in every rebuke administered by Christ.

Not only does Christ recognize in every man the existence of such a norm, but He goes farther, and shows that He regards this norm as 'supreme,' in the sense, at least, that for the individual man there is no standard of truth or of right more ultimate than that embedded in his very constitution. Nothing can be substituted for it. Nothing can be used to supplement or to correct it. No appeal lies from it. Man has nought that he can do but to abide by the decisions reached in the use of it. 'If ye believe not that I am he, ye shall die in your sins' (Jn 8²⁴) is no arbitrary sentence; but simply the announcement of the momentous truth, that the beliefs or unbeliefs of those whom He addressed would involve certain consequences *for them*, precisely because those beliefs or unbeliefs were *theirs*. Christ does not teach, of course, that men can make or unmake truth or right for themselves any more than for others. But He does teach that the conclusions that men reach in the use of the norm that is embedded in the very constitution of the mind are for them severally and individually final. It is this fact that constitutes the very heart of the solemnity of His words, when He says, 'If the light that is in thee be darkness, how great is that darkness' (Mt 6²³). The light that is in a man is the only light that is available for him. It is the light in which he sees light. It cannot itself be tested, so far, at least, as the user of it is concerned, by any other light (cf. also Mt 13⁹ and the principle laid down in Ro 14³⁰).

(d) Christ, moreover, is equally clear in teaching that in the proper use of the equipment given them, men may and always will arrive at correct judgments in regard both to truth and to duty— that is, in all cases and as regards all matters in reference to which they are called upon, or indeed are entitled, to form judgments. He recognizes, to be sure, the sad fact that men not only may, but as a matter of fact often do, give hospitable entertainment both to error and to evil. He is very emphatic, however, in asserting that this is their fault, and in no sense their misfortune. Whatever the difficulties of the teaching, they need not leave the soul in error or even in doubt. 'If any man willeth to do his will,' says our Lord, 'he shall know of the teaching, whether it be of God, or whether I speak from myself' (Jn 7¹⁷).

Any account of Christ's teachings as to the judicial authority vested in the individual would be fatally defective if it overlooked a saying like Mt 11²⁷ (cf. Jn 14⁹b. 8¹⁹b. 17²⁶). 'No one knoweth the Son,' says Christ, 'save the Father; neither doth any know the Father, save the Son, and he to whomsoever the Son willeth to reveal him.' This is not the place for a detailed exposition of these remarkable words. So much, however, is clear upon their very face, namely, that there is a knowledge of

God for which men are *wholly dependent upon Christ*. Again, it is evident from Jn 14[9b.] that whatever other elements this knowledge of God contains, it is a knowledge that is mediated through the understanding. 'He that *hath seen* me,' says our Lord, 'hath seen the Father.'. The same conclusion follows inevitably from the great emphasis which Christ laid upon His teaching function. But how is a man to test the correctness of propositions for the very knowledge of the contents of which, and much more for their accuracy, he is *ex hypothesi* wholly dependent upon Christ? We have said that Christ teaches that it is the prerogative of every man to bring every proposition, to the truth of which he is expected to assent, to some sort of process of 'inner verification'; but here are matters which, *ex hypothesi*, men must accept upon testimony, albeit it is the testimony of no less a witness than Christ Himself. Have we here, then, an inconsistency in Christ's teaching? We think not. We test our telescope; we satisfy ourselves that the laws of its structure are the same as those that obtain in the structure of the eye itself. It is just as truly an organ of vision as is the eye itself, though, of course, an organ of vastly greater range. What it discloses to us we could not apprehend without it. Much that it discloses to us, we either only gradually come to comprehend, or find to be at present incomprehensible to us. But whether we comprehend what we apprehend through the telescope or not, we accept its disclosures, and at least refer them to the large and vague category of what we call facts of existence, and wait expecting to be able to make a closer classification with our advancing knowledge, or the further development of our powers. And, while we never reach the point where we are able with our own eyes to verify the facts given us through the telescope, yet, when we have used the norm in our eye upon the norm in the telescope, and have thus proved a complete correspondence between the two, we have an unshakable conviction that they are not two but one, and that what has been disclosed by the norm in the telescope is assented to by the norm in our eye, as much so as if we had been in a position to bring the norm in our eye to bear directly upon the phenomena revealed to us through the telescope. Just so it is in the case of the individual and Christ. For the knowledge of certain facts regarding God and Christ, and concerning God in Christ, we are absolutely dependent upon the testimony of Christ. We cannot verify the correspondence between that testimony and reality by ourselves comparing it with the reality. The reality here is as inaccessible to our immediate inspection as the phenomena of stellar space would be, apart from the telescope. What then? Does Christ call upon us to surrender the very badge of our individuality, when we are dealing with His statements? Does He claim that His statements must be accepted without our being able to subject them to any process of 'inner verification,' the latter being, of course, the only possible real verification? Not at all. What He does claim, however, is that when we have assented to His trustworthiness, we have assented to the trustworthiness of His statements. Obviously, if He is as He claims to be, 'the Truth,' and we have satisfied ourselves of this by the same rational and moral processes by which we satisfy ourselves of any other propositions whatever, then in verifying Him, so to speak, we have verified His statements, as truly and as certainly as if we were capable of comparing those statements with the great realities to which they relate. Otherwise, where would be the sense in examining witnesses in our courts? And how else do we verify the ultimate facts given us, in the frame of nature and in the constitution of our own being—which, be it observed, are after all but the testimony of God,—except by verifying God? That we can do, of which proposition the simple proof is that we do it. For nothing is more certain than that 'it is impossible for God to lie.' This is the ultimate axiom upon which not only all certainty, but the possibility of any certainty depends.

Christ's teaching in reference to an external revelation, and our absolute dependence upon His veracity for the truth and the righteousness of its contents, do not impinge in the least either upon His teaching as to the judicial authority with which each individual is invested, or upon the true and proper autonomy of the soul. For He constantly teaches both by implication and by direct assertion that it is possible for men to verify Him, so to speak, and that it is at once their privilege and their duty to do so. And how exquisitely tender is His subtle appeal to His disciples to apply to His moral being that norm embedded in the constitution of their minds, when He says, 'In my Father's house are many mansions; if it were not so, I would have told you' (14[2]).

(2) While Christ accords a large judicial authority to the individual, it is, as already stated, neither an unlimited, nor an absolutely final authority. In His famous words to St. Peter, He speaks of 'my *church*' (Mt 16[18]), and in His equally celebrated words to Pilate, of 'my kingdom' (Jn 18[36]). Now it is no doubt true, as Dr. Vos has shown (*The Kingdom of God and the Church*, ch. ix.), that these expressions are not absolutely coterminous in their respective connotations, the 'church' being but one phase of the 'kingdom.' Still, even this being true, it follows that the Church is an organized body, with officers, laws, and members. Now it is clear, from what Christ says of the Church,

that the authority vested in her, and exercised through her officers, is a purely judicial authority. The Lord is her lawgiver. From Him alone she receives all the laws by which she binds the consciences of men. Her sole functions are to declare and to apply the law of Christ. To make any laws for her own members or for others is beyond her prerogative.

That such is her authority as set forth in the teachings of Christ appears from such statements as, 'If thy brother sin against thee, go show him his fault between thee and him alone: . . . But if he hear thee not, take with thee one or two more, etc. And if he refuse to hear them, tell it unto the church: and if he refuse to hear the church also, let him be unto thee as the Gentile and the publican' (Mt 18[15ff.]); 'Go ye, therefore, and make disciples of all nations, etc.: teaching them to observe all things whatsoever I have commanded you,' etc. (Mt 28[19f.]).

The criticism of the former passage by B. Weiss can hardly be regarded as invalidating it as a proper source of information as to our Lord's teaching concerning the Church (see his *NT Theol.* i. p. 141). It is fair, we think, to assume that the charge contained in the latter passage was addressed to the Apostles, not as such, but as representatives of the Church in all ages.

As will be observed, the judicial authority ascribed to the Church in these sayings of our Lord has a twofold aspect. In Mt 28 she is authorized to declare the law of Christ to those without her fold with a view to bringing them into subjection to Him. And in both sayings she is empowered to unfold that law to those within her pale. The necessity for both aspects of her judicial authority is as obvious as is the grant of it. If it be her function to extend the Kingdom, then it must also be her prerogative authoritatively to declare the nature and laws of the Kingdom. And again, if the term 'kingdom' as applied to the Church is not a hopeless misnomer, then she must have authority to determine what the law of Christ demands of the citizens of the Kingdom, and when this or that citizen is conforming to the law. See, further, art. CHURCH.

(3) The supreme and final judicial authority belongs to the *Holy Spirit*, whose findings are mediated proximately through the Scriptures, and ultimately through the Prophets, Apostles, and Christ Himself. We have seen that, while both the individual and the Church may, in the proper use of their respective equipments, arrive at a knowledge of truth and right in reference to all matters of truth and duty upon which they are respectively entitled to formulate a judgment; yet, as a matter of fact, neither the Church nor the individual does always arrive at such knowledge. Now the very statement of this position implies the existence of some standard by the use of which faulty judgments, when reached, may be detected as such, and corrected. This standard, according to Christ, is, in the last resort, to be found nowhere else than in the teachings of the Prophets, Apostles, and Himself. The finality and the infallibility of these teachings are, so our Lord teaches, guaranteed by the fact that they proceed directly from the Godhead, through the immediate agency of its great executive, the Holy Spirit, whose instruments or organs the Prophets, Apostles, and He Himself were. If we may use the term 'Scriptures' as a somewhat loose synonym for the teachings of the Prophets, Apostles, and Christ, then the Scriptures are, or, as with admirable accuracy the Westminster Confession puts it, 'the Holy Spirit speaking in the Scripture' is, 'the Supreme Judge by which all controversies of religion are to be determined . . . and in whose sentence we are to rest' (ch. i. sec. x.).

(*a*) That Christ conceived of the teachings of the *Prophets*, or the OT, as constituting, as far as it went, a court of last appeal in matters of religion, is strikingly evinced in His two summaries of those teachings already referred to: 'Thou shalt love the Lord thy God, etc. . . . . Thou shalt love thy neighbour, etc. . . . On these two commandments hangeth the whole law and the prophets' (Mt 22³⁴ᶠᶠ·, Mk 12²⁸ᶠᶠ·, Mt 7¹²). But God being love, it is just in love that religion finds its highest and fullest expression. That standard, therefore, which being adhered to leads to love, is the final standard.

The same point of view as regards the OT finds expression in the words, 'They have Moses and the prophets; let them hear them. . . . If they hear not Moses and the prophets, neither will they be persuaded, if one rise from the dead' (Lk 16²⁹· ³¹). The implication in Dives' plea was that it was his misfortune that he had come to that place of torment. These words distinctly disallow that implication. They affirm both the sufficiency and the finality of the OT in all matters connected with the salvation of those to whom that revelation was given. And so the Sadducees are told (Mt 22²⁹), 'Ye do err, not knowing the Scriptures,' etc., which means, of course, that they need not have erred had they only gone to the Scriptures in the right spirit. Upon all questions raised by His adversaries, it was to the teachings of the OT that Christ Himself continually appealed as the final authority. Quoting Hosea, He said to the Pharisees, 'If ye had known what this meaneth, I desire mercy and not sacrifice, ye would not have condemned the guiltless' (Mt 12⁷). Thus the standard to which He brings their judgment of Himself and by which He exposes its falsity and wickedness, is the teaching of the OT. His 'Woe unto you, scribes and Pharisees, hypocrites! for ye tithe mint and anise and cummin, and have left undone the weightier matters of the law, judgment, mercy, and faith : but these ye ought to have done, and not to have left the other undone' (Mt 23²³), is but an application of the standard of the OT for the testing of Pharisaic teachings and practice. Further, He recognizes the *oughtness* of these teachings, when they concern the tithing of mint, anise, and cummin, as truly as in the weightier matters of judgment, mercy, and faith. Especially significant are words like those in Mk 12³⁵ᶠᶠ· (cf. Mt 22⁴¹ᶠᶠ·, Lk 20⁴¹ᶠᶠ·) : 'How say the scribes that the Christ is the son of David ? David himself said in the Holy Spirit, The Lord said unto my Lord, etc. David himself calleth him Lord, and whence is he his son?'

(*b*) Besides the passages already cited, the following show that Christ represents His *Apostles* as being the organs of the Holy Spirit in such sense that their teachings, *qua* Apostles, are ultimate and infallible in all matters of faith and duty : 'And I also say unto thee, That thou art Peter, etc. . . . I will give unto thee the keys of the kingdom of heaven : and whatsoever thou shalt bind on earth shall be bound in heaven : and whatsoever thou shalt loose upon earth shall be loosed in heaven' (Mt 16¹⁸ᶠ·). The same promise is made to the Apostles, no doubt to all of them, in Mt 18¹⁸. In Jn 20²²ᶠ· we read, 'And when he had said this he breathed on them, and saith unto them, Receive ye the Holy Spirit : whose soever sins ye forgive, they are forgiven ; whose soever sins ye retain, they are retained.'

B. Weiss (*NT Theol.* i. 142, footnote) regards Mt 18¹⁸ as addressed to 'the disciples in the wider sense,' and avoids bringing the statement into collision with the facts of history only by finding in them 'nothing else than the authorization of the Apostles to proclaim the message by means of which men are called into the Kingdom' (*ib.* p. 139, where he is commenting more particularly upon Mt 16¹⁹. On the other side see art. 'Power of the Keys' in Hastings' *DB*, vol. iv.). To most persons, however, such a view of this passage will appear inadequate. Dr. Chas. Hodge, believing that the grant of power made in these words was not designed to be limited to the Apostles, seeks to avoid collision with the facts of history by representing it as made to the invisible Church (*Church Polity*, p. 35 ff.). This, however, will seem to many as little satisfactory as is Weiss' view. That the words were addressed to the Apostles, and to no others, appears probable, not only from Mt 16¹⁸ᶠ· and Jn 20²²ᶠ·, but even more so from a comparison of Mt 18¹ᶠᶠ· with Mk 9³³ᶠᶠ·. That the Church also, according to Christ, was invested with a limited judicial authority, has already been shown.

The full character and extent of the power with which Christ represents His Apostles as being clothed appear conspicuously in the words, 'And whosoever shall not receive you nor hear your words, as ye go forth out of that house, or that city, shake off the dust of your feet. Verily, I say unto you, It shall be more tolerable for the land of Sodom and Gomorrah in the day of judgment than for that city' (Mt 10¹⁴ᶠ·. With this should be compared Mt 11²⁴). The sufficient

ground for such a statement is furnished by the words also spoken of the Apostles (and subsequently of 'the seventy,' who received a similar, but more temporary commission, Lk 10¹⁶) — 'He that receiveth you receiveth me, and he that receiveth me receiveth him that sent me' (Mt 10⁴⁰, cf. Jn 13²⁹).

(*c*) That Christ claimed for *Himself* a judicial authority that was absolute and final, needs hardly to be illustrated. It appears from such facts as that He taught as one having authority (Mk 1²²· ²⁷, Lk 4³⁶) ; He always commanded and never merely counselled (Mt 28²⁰, Lk 8⁵⁵, Mt 10⁵) ; while unfailingly tender, He did not tolerate even well-meant correction (Mt 16²²ᶠ·) ; He invited, expected, and demanded of His disciples the most complete and unreserved surrender to His teachings and to His will.

His 'hypocoristic expressions' or 'endearing diminutives' (see art. by Professor B. B. Warfield in *Bible Student and Teacher*, Sept. 1904, p. 515 ff.) indicate not only His attitude towards His disciples, but, indirectly, that He expected their attitude towards Him to be one of unquestioning docility, dependence, and submission (Lk 12³² 10³, Jn 10⁷· ¹⁶ 13¹⁵, Mt 18¹⁹ *et passim*). Both His authority and the nature of it are less veiled behind the very common designation of 'disciples.' 'A disciple,' says our Lord, using the figure of *meiosis*, 'is not above his teacher' (Mt 10²⁴). The very terms of discipleship demand the same absolute self-abnegation upon the disciple's part that Christ Himself had manifested towards His Father. 'If any man,' says He, 'will come after me, let him deny himself, and take up his cross and follow me' (Mk 8³⁴, Lk 9²³). In the saying, 'Ye call me Teacher and Lord : and ye say well : for so I am' (Jn 13¹³), 'teacher' is suggestively united with 'Lord.' And not less suited to arrest the attention is the statement, 'But be ye not called Rabbi : for one is your teacher, and all ye are brethren' (Mt 23⁸).

Once more, Christ declared Himself to be 'The Way, and the Truth, and the Life' (Jn 14⁶) ; He invited men to believe in Himself just as they believed in God (v.¹) ; He conditioned His blessings upon the acceptance of His 'yoke' and His teachings (Mt 11²⁹). Nay, He conditioned men's everlasting salvation upon their unquestioning acceptance of His statements about Himself (Jn 8²⁴ ; for the repetition of this thought in a slightly different form see Mt 23³⁷ᶠ·, Lk 13³⁴ᶠ· 19⁴¹ᶠ·). The word that He spake was to judge them at the last day (Jn 12⁴⁸). His words are God's words : 'The words that I say unto you, I speak not from myself : but the Father abiding in me he doeth the works' (Jn 14¹⁰). In a word, He and the Father are one (Jn 10³⁰) ; seeing Him, one sees the Father (14⁹) ; the 'Spirit of truth' in guiding into all truth was to glorify Him, 'for,' said our Lord, 'he shall take of mine, and shall declare it unto you. All things whatsoever the Father hath are mine : therefore said I that he shall take of mine and shall declare it unto you' (16¹⁴ᶠ·).

Thus when we reach Christ in the matter of religion, we have reached the fountainhead. It were idle to look for a court in which to review and put to the test His findings in regard either to truth or to duty. Such, certainly, is His own teaching upon the subject. See preceding article.

iv. EXECUTIVE AUTHORITY IN RELIGION. — **1.** *Term defined.*—The function of executive authority, as needs scarcely be said, is simply and solely to give effect to the legislative will and to judicial findings. Of itself it originates nothing, interprets and declares nothing. It simply *does*. More need not be said, because executive authority is so obviously and so markedly distinct from both legislative and judicial, that there is no danger of its being confused with either the one or the other.

2. *Repositories.*—(1) Our Lord obviously teaches that as every *individual* is a repository of judicial authority, so every individual was designed to be, and every individual Christian is, an executive agent of the Godhead. It is His constant contention that it is for *doing* the will of God that men exist, whether as creatures or as Christians. The end of His whole teaching function was to set men doing, and to guide them in doing, the will of God. It was the gravamen of His complaint against those, like the Pharisees, who ought to have been His disciples, but were not, that instead of doing the will of God, they did the lusts of their father, the devil (Jn 8[44]). The end that He set before those professing to be His disciples was, 'So let your light shine before men, that they may see your good works, and glorify your Father which is in heaven' (Mt 5[16]). The first three petitions that He puts on their lips are, 'Hallowed be thy name, Thy kingdom come, Thy will be done, as in heaven, so on earth.' The badge of discipleship (Mt 12[39]), the only accepted evidence of love and of loyalty (Jn 14[15]), a condition *sine qua non* to salvation (Mt 7[22ff.]), was that His followers should *do* the will of God. It was His ceaseless theme, elaborated now in this form and now in that, that the end of life is not getting, or having, or being ministered unto, or thinking, but *being and doing the will of God*. To go into details here would require the incorporation in this article of a very considerable part of all four Gospels, and would be superfluous.

(2) The passages already cited show that Christ represents *the Church* in her corporate capacity as the great executive agency of God for the preaching of the gospel of the Kingdom as a witness among all nations, making disciples of all nations, and teaching them to observe all things whatsoever He has commanded. Executive and judicial authority here complement each other.

(3) That Christ ascribes executive authority to the *Prophets* is perhaps a fair inference from such a passage as Mk 7[6], in which our Lord refers to Isaiah not merely as an interpreter of God's law, but as a teacher of God's people. But the inference is not to be strained. And for evidence of the executive authority unquestionably exercised by the Prophets, we have to turn elsewhere than to the Gospels. The case is different with the *Apostles*. The mission of 'the Twelve' (Mt 10) points clearly to the fact that they were invested with authority to diffuse the knowledge of the gospel, and to use a variety of agencies to gain men's attention and win their allegiance to it. The same follows from Lk 24[44ff.] and Ac 1[8]. But as to the details of their executive functions we learn but little from the Gospels. It is different, however, in the case of *Christ*. He applies to Himself (Lk 4[17ff.]) the famous passage from Is 61, 'The Spirit of the Lord is upon me,' etc. This is not the place to unfold in detail the several features of the wondrous programme outlined in the words of the prophet: it is hardly necessary, for they are as plain as they are precious. The title of 'The Good Shepherd,' which our Lord appropriated to Himself (perhaps from Ezk 34), is evidence both of the fact and of the nature of His executive functions (Jn 10). The same fact underlies such statements as 'I have a baptism to be baptized with, and how am I straitened until it be accomplished' (Lk 12[50]). This last passage also brings before us the central feature of the work committed to Christ. Here, again, we must forbear from going into details, which belong properly to another field of discussion. It must suffice merely to recall to the reader's mind such sayings of our Lord as 'Therefore doth my Father love me, because I lay down my life, that I may take it again. No one taketh it away from me, but I lay it down of myself. I have authority to lay it down, and I have authority to take it again. This commandment received I from my Father' (Jn 10[17ff.]); 'This is my body . . . for this is my blood of the covenant, which is shed for many unto the remission of sins' (Mt 26[26. 28]); and

the word from the cross, 'It is accomplished' (Jn 19[30]). Surely the prophet went not amiss when he spoke of Him as the great '*Ebhedh Jahweh* (עֶבֶד יְהֹוָה).

(4) According to our Lord, the great executive of the Godhead is the *Holy Spirit*. It belongs to another article (see HOLY SPIRIT) to unfold His doctrine of the Holy Spirit. But we may, without intruding into that discussion, call attention to passages like Jn 3[1ff.] 14[16] 16[7f. 13ff.] 20[22f.], Ac 1[4f. 8].

LITERATURE.—The literature bearing formally upon the teachings of Christ concerning authority in religion is very much scattered and somewhat meagre. We must content ourselves, therefore, with mentioning some works and articles that deal with the question of authority in religion without treating specifically of the teachings of our Lord upon this point. Dr. James Martineau's *The Seat of Authority in Religion* is still the first in its class. (Dr. Martineau denies, of course, the existence of any external authority in religion; and supports his contention with an acuteness and vigour that still remain not only unsurpassed, but wholly unequalled by any who have given in their adhesion to his general position). More recent works, representing substantially Dr. Martineau's view, but adding little to what may be called his historical, and nothing whatever to his psychological and philosophical defence of it, are : *Religions of Authority and the Religion of the Spirit*, by the late Prof. Auguste Sabatier; *Liberal Christianity*, by his pupil and after colleague, Prof. Jean Réville; *The Religion of a Mature Mind*, by Prof. George A. Coe. Prof. Sabatier and Dr. Coe both claim the support of Christ for their position. But Prof. Sabatier's presentation of the teachings of Christ is lacking not only in completeness, but in cogency, and Prof. Coe's comes perilously near being mere caricature. For an (in some vital particulars) opposite view of the general subject, the reader may be referred to Stanton, *The Place of Authority in Matters of Religious Belief*; Dale, *Protestantism* (ch. ii.); Ellicott, *Christus Comprobator*; Oman, *Vision and Authority*; Strong, *Authority in the Church*; and also to the following articles: 'The Philosophy of Authority in Religion,' by Wilfrid Ward in *The Hibbert Journal*, vol. i. pp. 677–692; 'The Right of Systematic Theology,' by Prof. B. B. Warfield in *The Presbyterian and Reformed Review*, July 1896; 'Authority in Religion,' by Dr. Henry Collin Minton, *ib.* April 1900. Dr. Warfield's article, besides the always valuable matter from his own pen, contains a number of useful references and extracts.

W. M. M'PHEETERS.

AVARICE.—See COVETOUSNESS.

AVE MARIA.—This well-known devotion of the Latin Church is based upon the salutations addressed to the Virgin Mary by the angel Gabriel and by Elisabeth the mother of John the Baptist (Lk 1[28. 42]). Its earlier and shorter form follows closely the words of Scripture, with the addition only of the names 'Mary' and 'Jesus'; 'Hail (Mary), full of grace; blessed art thou among women, and blessed is the fruit of thy womb (Jesus).' As thus recited, it cannot be called a prayer, but may be considered either as a memorial of thanksgiving for the Incarnation; or as one of those devotional apostrophes of departed saints which are found even in the writings of the Christian Fathers and in early Christian inscriptions.

The use of the *Ave Maria* in the fixed liturgical services of the Latin Church is of comparatively late origin. Its devotional use is, however, much older : it is even said to be traceable as far back as the 7th century. In the 14th cent. it is found in the popular handbooks of devotion. *The Mirror of our Lady* (first half of the 15th cent.) alludes to it as forming part of the preliminary prayers said privately by the worshipper before the office began. An interesting example of its use is given by Maskell (*Monumenta Ritualia*, ii. 71). The foundation statutes of the Abbey of Maxstoke in the reign of Edward III. order its recital daily.

But the *Ave* was not definitely placed in the offices of the Breviary until the 16th cent. ; and curiously enough by the liturgical reformer, Cardinal Quignonez. In the present Roman Breviary, dating from Pope Pius V. (1568), it is directed to be said with the Lord's Prayer at the beginning of each office, and after Compline.

The pre-Reformation *Ave* was usually the shorter and Scriptural form as given above. But as it stands now in the Breviary, it ends with a direct prayer addressed to the Virgin, said to date from the middle of the 15th cent.: 'Holy Mary, mother of God, pray for us sinners, now and in the hour of our death.'

It is fair to remember that, whatever lines the devotions to Mary ultimately followed, they were, in their original intention, undoubtedly devotions to Christ. Like the title *Theotokos*, sanctioned by the Third Œcumenical Council (Ephesus 431), they were intended to safeguard and emphasize the true humanity of Christ. Not only was Christ perfect God, but He was truly conceived and born of a human mother, so that the Son of Mary is indissolubly God and man in one person. The devotions addressed to His mother were therefore a commemoration of the intimate union between the Godhead and human nature, of which union Mary was both the willing instrument and the sign.

LITERATURE.—Addis and Arnold, *A Catholic Dictionary*, 1897; Wright and Neil, *A Protestant Dictionary*, 1904; Bodington, *Books of Devotion*, 1903; Procter, *A History of the Book of Common Prayer*, 1884; Maskell, *Monumenta Ritualia*, 1846; the *Breviarium Romanum; The Hours of the Blessed Virgin Mary* (Preface), Percival & Co. 1892; Bengel, Meyer, and Alford on Lk 1²⁸.   A. R. WHITHAM.

AWE.—The adoration of what is mysterious and sublime is an essential element in religion. When expressed towards unworthy objects the result is superstition, but the motive itself is the soul of worship. As the feeling is thus fundamental to the relationship between the human and the Divine, increase of knowledge, while testing and purifying this relationship, should protect and strengthen it.

In the service of the missionary gospel, the complaint is made to-day by Eastern heathen religions that our Western Christianity, which comes to them as the aggressive herald of a higher life, is gravely deficient in religious veneration. It becomes, therefore, of practical interest to inquire how Christ's first disciples were influenced in this direction by His presence among them, and to what extent the same feeling towards the person of the living Christ pervades the Church of modern times.

When Christ took upon Him our nature, it was under such circumstances of poverty and humble birth as could not inspire the conventional regard which the world bestows upon rank and title. Further, His life was lived in such daily intimacy with those around Him, and was so thoroughly affected by the local customs of Israel and the social conditions of the time, that His disciples could speak of their fellowship with Him in terms of exact knowledge and distinct impression. They could afterwards refer to His life as something that they had seen with their eyes and their hands had handled (1 Jn 1¹).

Nevertheless, there is nothing more evident in the story of the Evangelists than the fact that a permanent and increasing mystery, passing into reverence and awe, accompanied that familiar acquaintance. The feeling was usually called forth by some manifestation of knowledge or power, and deeper even than the impression thus produced by His wonderful teaching and miraculous works was the trustful consciousness of their being in contact with a personality that was altogether holy and separate from sin. Finally, the reverent submission thus instilled into the minds of the disciples was exemplified in Christ Himself towards the will of God, as in the temptation in the wilderness and in the Garden of Gethsemane.

As their power of spiritual perception increased, the disciples learnt to apprehend and accept the startling renovation, the sudden depth, and the delightful expansion that the Master gave to old religious truths, but there were always meanings about which they had to seek an interpretation in private, and to the end of their fellowship they had often to confess that they knew not what He said. The difficulty thus created by His personality and actions was so far recognized by the Lord Jesus, that on one occasion He encouraged His disciples to make known their own thoughts and the thoughts of others about Himself (Mt 16¹³). Thus Nathanael was overawed by the knowledge that He had been watching him in his place of seclusion (Jn 1⁴⁹); and this feeling soon became a general persuasion that He knew all men and what was in man (2²⁴·²⁵). Peter felt himself so immediately in the presence of Divine power that he confessed his own sinfulness, and he and James and John decided to leave all and follow Him (Lk 5¹⁻¹¹). The bereaved sisters at Bethany repeat the conviction that if He had been there, their brother would not have died (Jn 11²¹·³²). And among those who came into more incidental contact with Him by simple inquiry or importunate need, Nicodemus was attracted by the persuasion that He was a teacher come from God (Jn 3²); an admission to the same effect was made on one occasion by the Pharisees and Herodians (Mk 12¹⁴); the chief priests and scribes were driven to assign a Satanic origin to His unquestionable power (Mt 12²⁴); while the Pharisees reached a stage in their controversy with Him after which no man durst ask Him any question (Mt 22⁴⁶, Mk 12³⁴). The privileged traffickers in the temple quailed under His exposure and rebuke (Mt 21¹²(, and to the end the challenge to convict Him of sin remained unanswered (Jn 8⁴⁶). All the miracles of Christ, while expressing His pity and love, accentuated this Divine power, and His teaching bore the distinguishing mark of authority (Mt 7²⁹).

To His first Jewish disciples the name Messiah was the unveiling of a historical mystery, the justification of the calling, preservation, and discipline of Israel. They found in Him the fulfilment of the prophecy 'and his name shall be called Wonderful' (Is 9⁶). With so much that attracted them to His person and depended upon His presence, it is doubtful if they could have ventured upon our depersonalized formulæ about 'the plan of salvation.' And so, while the Fourth Gospel, like the ancient epics, begins with the introduction of its principal theme, namely, 'The Word became flesh, and dwelt among us' (Jn 1¹⁴), the Evangelist could add that even through that obscuring medium Christ's disciples were enabled to behold His glory (*ib.*).

After the Resurrection this veil was so completely removed, and the awe of Christ's presence became so unclouded and continuous, that one of the Apostles could write, 'Though we have known Christ after the flesh, yet now we know him so no more' (2 Co 5¹⁶).

Thereafter it became the commission of the Church to proclaim and teach and exemplify how the flesh may in turn become the Word, and every believer be a dwelling-place for the Spirit of Christ. The reverence that once gathered around His own visible person could still influence men through every witness in whom His Spirit dwelt. The condition of life and service was fixed, namely, 'As he is, so are we in this world' (1 Jn 4¹⁷). And so in the Apostolic preaching of the gospel the living personality of Christ was never lost in the analysis of His mind and nature. Instead of the parched abstractions that with us so often take the place of the mystical indwelling, they preached ' Jesus and the resurrection' (Ac 17¹⁸), 'Jesus Christ and him crucified' (1 Co 2²).

Can it be said to-day of Christian sainthood and the service of the missionary gospel, that the person of Christ is thus central, His presence an indispensable necessity, likeness to Him the recognition mark of His Church, and the conquest of the world the consummation of its appointed labours ? If it be otherwise, certain signs may be expected to manifest themselves. Christ will be little more than a beautiful name in His Church, an idea developed and resident in our minds. The work of the Holy Spirit in bringing and revealing the things of Christ will be shadowy and almost superfluous to those who have already reached a complete conception of Christ by philosophical method applied to the study of doctrine. The question, 'Is Christ divided ?' (1 Co 1¹³) will cease to startle and distress, and the loyalty due to the Head of the Church and to the universal kingdom will be pledged to sectarian trusts and the watchwords of exhausted controversy. When the one standard of elevation, the stature of Christ, is withdrawn, Church distinctions will be restricted to the superficial dimensions of mere historical length and doctrinal width. In the ideal picture of the future fold, the one flock still needs the presence of the one Shepherd (Jn 10¹⁶). Through this visible union in Him, Christ will be glorified (17¹⁰), and solely to its manifestation is promised the conquest of the world (v.²¹).

LITERATURE.—Fowler and Wilson's *Principles of Morals*, Oxf. 1894, p. 101 ; Kidd, *Morality and Religion*, Edin. 1895, p. 187 ; Davidson, *Theism and Human Nature*, p. 279 ; and on Christ's awe, Swete's *St. Mark*², 1902, p. 342 (on Mk 14³³).

G. M. MACKIE.

AXE.—This word occurs twice in the Gospels (Mt 3¹⁰, Lk 3⁹), each time in the report of the preaching of the Baptist. The old familiar tool of peace and weapon of war (1 K 6⁷, Ps 74⁵, Jer 51²⁰) has become a metaphor for the ministry of men with a mission of reform. This suits the spirit of one who, like John the Baptist, is filled with the teaching of the OT. For the axe gleams in its histories and flashes in its songs, while in prophetic mood the tool is changed to the person—the wielder is himself the weapon (Is 10³³ᶠ·, Dn 4¹⁴, Jer 51²⁰). All this is the forerunner's inherited world of ideas on this implement of industry and weapon of attack. He is a part of all that his race has been. He sees the men of old times 'as men that lifted up axes upon a thicket of trees' (Ps 74⁵). The

Messiah, the Coming One, is the last of the line. Nor are all in that line of the lineage of the house of David. 'As the Assyrian axe in the days of old, so now the Roman axe was laid at the root of Israel' (*Philochristus*, ch. 4). Thoroughly as these powers had done their part, yet more drastic was to be the work of the future ('every tree,' Mt 3¹⁰). Under this image of the axe, the road-maker (Mt 3³) has his vision of the wood-cutter and his effectual working (v.¹⁰).

But 'God fulfils Himself in many ways.' And when the Carpenter laid aside the axe of the workshop in Nazareth, the wood-cutter, 'thoroughly furnished unto every good work, a workman that needeth not to be ashamed,' was already prepared for going up against the trees. Jesus had been *tempered* by waiting, in solitude and temptation. And the stroke of His axe, when it fell, was deliberate, radical, universal (cf. He 4¹²ᶠ·). Men and institutions, the priests, the temple felt it. He would save the tree of humanity, even 'as a tree whose stock remaineth when they are felled' (Is 6¹³). Therefore He struck at the root of the evil in man and nature—sin. And because the strokes were meant to be regenerating and reforming, they were clean, swift, sharp, and stout (Jn 2¹⁷ 8¹ᶠᶠ·, Lk 13¹ᶠᶠ·).

Finally, the axe is not only the sign-manual of the mission of the forerunner and the Fulfiller, it is that of reformers in general. As the axe of the backwoodsman has been tempered in fire and water past the useless state of brittleness and beyond the extremity of hardness, so the tempering of the reformer is done, on the one hand, in a series of Divine and delicate processes in the personality of him who is being touched to fine issues by the Spirit, for the service of God and man, and, on the other hand, in a parallel series of providential dispensations in the mind and environment of the people, the race, or the institution with which he has to deal.

LITERATURE.—*Ecce Homo*, ch. 1 ; Reynolds, *John the Baptist*, Lecture 4 ; Tennyson, *Idylls of the King*, 'The Coming of Arthur,' *ap. fin.* ; Morley, *Life of Gladstone*, ii. 252.

JOHN R. LEGGE.

AZOR.—An ancestor of Jesus, according to the genealogy in the First Gospel (Mt 1¹³ᶠ·).

B

BABE.—**1.** βρέφος, lit. 'nourished'—by the mother, is used of an unborn infant (Lk 1⁴¹⁻⁴⁴), of an infant still in swaddling-bands (2¹². ¹⁶), and also of young children brought by their mothers to Jesus that He might touch them (18¹⁵). **2.** νήπιος, literally, 'one that cannot yet speak' (νη= 'not,' and ἔπος, 'word') ; cf. Lat. *in-fans*, 'infant,' which is a better rendering of νήπιος, though neither AV nor RV is consistent in the translation of the two Greek words. νήπιος is a child as contrasted with an older person, *e.g.* with 'the wise and prudent' in Lk 10²¹ and Mt 11²⁵ (cf. Gal 4³, Eph 4¹⁴). It is used also with θηλάζοντες, 'sucklings,' in Mt 21¹⁶, in which passage the root meaning of νήπιος is specially suggestive, 'Out of the mouth of speechless (babes) thou hast perfected praise.'

Jesus' fondness for these little ones was shown, both by His rebuke of the disciples who would have sent them and their mothers away when they came to Him for a blessing (Lk 18¹⁵ᶠ·, cf. Mt 19¹⁴), and by His frequent use of children to illustrate the Christian disposition (cf. Mt 18²⁻⁵,

Mk 10¹⁵, Lk 18¹⁶. ¹⁷). See, further, artt. INFANCY, CHILDREN.

The word 'babe' (βρίφος) is twice used of the infant Jesus Himself (Lk 2¹². ¹⁶). And it is worth noting that in v.¹² RV brings out a significance of meaning which is lost in AV. In the Gr. there is no art. prefixed to βρίφος in this verse ; the sign given to the shepherds was 'the sign of a babe.' Moreover, according to the reading which is most strongly supported, σημείον should have the art., so that what the shepherds were told was '*The* sign is a babe.' The meaning therefore is, not as AV suggests, ' you shall find the babe you are looking for in such and such a condition,' but rather this ' most extraordinary and suggestive one, You shall find the Saviour you are looking for, Christ the Lord, in the form of a babe, wrapped in swaddling-clothes, and lying in a manger.' See Dr. Monro Gibson in *Sunday Mag.*, Dec. 1891 ; and cf. Dr. Hastings in *Expos. Times*, iii. [1892] 196, and [1894] 147.

E. B. POLLARD.

BACK TO CHRIST.—The movement or tendency described in the phrase 'back to Christ' belongs mainly to the past half century, and both its wide extent and its far-reaching consequences for religious thought justify us in regarding it as the most important theological event of the period.

The phrase can be received as a correct description of the movement, only under the explanation that the return has not been to the Christ of dogma, but to the Christ of history. This distinction must be kept clearly in view. The Christ of dogma is Christ as exhibited in the creeds—the eternally begotten Son of God, the second Person in the Trinity, who, for our redemption, assumed our human nature and submitted to death as an atonement for our sins. He is the God-man, a Divine Person with two natūres and two wills. It is evident that these determinations move in a different region from that of empirical reality. They cannot be established on merely historical evidence; they have their ground in a judgment of faith. What we have in dogma is not a portrait of the historical Jesus in the religious and ethical traits of His character, but a speculative construction of His Person ; not an account of His historical ministry, but a doctrinal interpretation of it. The Christ of history is the concrete Person whose image meets us in the Gospels ; the Christ of dogma is the complex of metaphysical or doctrinal characters which the Church, on the ground of its faith, attributed to this Person. So far the distinction is clear enough, and meets with general acceptance. The difficulty begins when we raise the question whether such facts as the Virgin-birth, the Miracles (in the strict sense of the word), and the Resurrection are to be included in our conception of the historical Christ as resting upon historical evidence, or whether they are not rather to be transferred from the domain of history to that of faith. The question will come up again ; in the meantime it may be sufficient to call attention to the ambiguity which must attach to the term 'historical Christ' so long as it remains undecided.

When we speak of a return to the Christ of history, we imply that His image has been lost sight of, or at least obscured. It was not doubtless the intention of the Church that its doctrinal determinations should supplant the concrete reality in the thought and faith of the community. But this was what actually happened. More and more the historical Person was overshadowed by the speculative construction, the historical ministry by the formulas in which its significance was summed up. The figure of Jesus disappeared behind the pre-existent Logos, the earthly ministry behind the idea of the Incarnation, the cross behind the doctrine of the Atonement. This result is not to be explained by the fact that dogma, from its controversial character, attracted to itself an undue share of attention and interest as compared with matters that had never been in dispute. The cause lay deeper. It is to be found in the conception of Revelation and of Faith that has dominated the Catholic and also, to a large extent, the Protestant Church. Revelation has been understood as the supernatural communication of a system of doctrine ; Faith, as the submission of the mind to doctrine on the ground of its authority. The emphasis has thus been thrown, not on the historical life, but on the dogmatic construction. The historical life has occupied only a secondary place, its significance being found mainly in the basis it supplies for this construction or interpretation.

1. *Causes of the movement.* — What are the causes that have contributed to restore the figure of Jesus to its place in the centre of religious thought? We shall mention three as the chief.

(a) The first is the application of historical criticism to the Gospel narrative. In 1835, D. F. Strauss published his *Leben Jesu*, and this book proved the starting-point of a critical movement the end of which is not yet in sight. The results of Strauss' criticism were almost purely negative :

the Gospel story was resolved into a tissue of myths. There are still writers who find in that story only the most meagre basis of fact ; but their conclusions are far from representing the general results of the movement, which are much more positive than negative in their character, much more constructive than destructive. If doubt has been cast on some of the facts related about Jesus, and if the influence of subsequent ideas has been detected here and there in the presentation of His life and teaching, the substantial truth of the Gospel narrative has been amply vindicated. Moreover, the critical study of the NT has done for Christ what that of the OT has done for the prophets. It has reconstructed the contemporary background, given us a better understanding of His teaching, and enabled us to see the Man and His work in their human environment. To this enlarged historical knowledge and new feeling for the historical, we owe the recognition of the fact that the Christ of history is one thing and the conception of His Person that sprang up on the soil of the Church's faith another. As early as the Fourth Gospel the two images had been blended into one. Still further, criticism has contributed to the return to Christ by the mere fact that it has brought the problem of His historical reality and significance into the centre of attention and interest. Up to the appearance of the *Leben Jesu* the problems that occupied the theological field were almost purely speculative : when Christ was considered, it was as the vehicle or symbol of certain speculative ideas. The retirement of the speculative behind the historical is one of the signs of the times.

(b) A second and even more important factor in the movement 'back to Christ' is the widespread dissatisfaction with the traditional statements of Christianity. Since the rationalistic movement of the 18th cent. the history of dogma has been in the main a history of disintegration. Those who seek to go behind the creeds, back to the source of our religion, proceed on the ground that the creeds do not represent, with any sufficient correctness or adequacy, either the conceptions that Jesus taught or the significance that His Person has for faith. All we can do here is to indicate the main lines which the criticism of dogma has followed.

When we examine the formulas of Nicæa and Chalcedon, in which the Being of God and the Person of Christ are determined, we find one basal conception underlying them all. It is the conception of Substance. God is conceived primarily as the Absolute Substance ; that is to say, as the indeterminate, unchanging and permanent ground of the knowable world of variety, change, and transience. Christ is true God because He shares in the Divine Substance ; and because He has taken up human nature or substance into union with His Divine substance, He is also true man. The inner relations of the Godhead—Fatherhood, Sonship, the Procession of the Holy Spirit—are all expressed in terms of this category. It is true that the Church had other things to say about God and Christ than those of its formulas ; still the formulas were regarded as conveying the deepest and most vital truths, and their acceptance was made the criterion of orthodoxy and the condition of salvation. If the ethical was recognized, it occupied only a subordinate position in comparison with the metaphysical. Now, what is this idea of Substance which plays so great a rôle in the creeds? It was not derived from Christ or the New Testament. It was borrowed from Hellenistic philosophy ; and what it originally answered was not any religious need, but the purely intellectual demand that all the manifoldness of this time-world shall be reducible to the unity of a single principle. Even from a philosophical point of view the idea of Substance is open to fatal objections as a principle by which to explain personal or, indeed, any relations. To modern thought Substance is not a concrete reality; it is nothing more than the most abstract of all ideas. To hypostatize abstractions, equip them with causal power, and employ them as principles of explanation, was a peculiarity of Greek thought, and one that it is hopeless to revive. The use which the creeds make of this idea is even more objectionable when considered from the standpoint of religion. Absolute Substance has nothing in common with the holy, personal Will of the prophets, or with the gracious Father of our Lord Jesus Christ. One cannot, on such a foundation, build up a Christian conception of God. And to say that Christ is Divine in virtue of His participation in the Divine Substance, is not to present Him in any character that makes Him the object of our trust. What gives Christ His significance for faith is the fact that in His Person and ministry faith recognizes the revelation of God's gracious will towards sinful men. To substitute a divinity of Substance for a divinity of Revelation is to remove Christ from the realm of faith into that of speculation; and, further, since the category of substance is at bottom a physical category, it is to rank the physical above the personal and ethical.

In formulating these metaphysical doctrines, the Church no doubt believed that it was safeguarding vital religious interests. What seemed at stake was nothing less than the reality of the salvation mediated by Christ. But, it is contended, the conception of salvation that the Nicene and Chalcedon formulas were designed to safeguard is not an ethical, but a metaphysical, or, more correctly, physical, conception. The evil from which deliverance is sought is not primarily sin; it is the mortality that belongs to our fallen nature; and the good salvation brings is not ethical communion with God, but participation in eternal life, which is thought of as a natural quality of the Divine substance. Human substance is deified, invested with the quality of immortality, by being taken up into and penetrated by Divine substance. It is this metaphysical conception of salvation that requires a metaphysical Christ. Christ must be God and man in the substantial sense, since it was in His Person that the penetration (ἐπιχώρησις) of human substance by Divine took place. It is obvious that such a conception of Christ's Person can have little or no significance for those who regard religious relationships as being at their deepest and highest personal and ethical. An ethical conception of Redemption, as a change in our relation to God effected within our consciousness, requires us to seek the significance of Christ not in the metaphysical background of His nature, but in the ethical and religious traits of His character, which disclose to us the heart of God, and have the power to awaken within us the response of love and faith.

In the theology of the Greek Church the work of Christ was summed up in His Incarnation. In that act salvation was already achieved. A more practical and ethical conception entered the Church with the great figure of Augustine. The metaphysical antithesis of mortal, creaturely life and eternal, Divine life retired before the ethical antithesis of sin and grace. There was a transference of emphasis from the metaphysical Incarnation to the ethical Atonement. The change marked an important advance. Yet in the doctrine of the Atonement as formulated by Anselm, and even as subsequently modified, the ethical does not appear in its purity, but only under the form of the juristic. The work of Christ is interpreted by means of categories borrowed from the legal discipline of the Roman Church. But ethical relationships and ethical ends cannot be adequately expressed in terms of criminal law. The juristic no less than the metaphysical conceptions of the old theology have lost their hold on the modern mind. We interpret religious relations now in terms of ethics and psychology.

(c) The third cause that has operated in bringing the historical Person and work of Christ into the foreground, has been the new sense—reflected in the writings of men like Goethe, Emerson, and Carlyle—of the importance of great personalities as factors of historical change and progress. Neither Catholicism nor traditional Protestantism can be said to have shown much appreciation of the religious and ethical forces that radiate from Jesus as a historical personality. The saving activity of God in Christ has been conceived either in a mystical, semi-mechanical way, as affecting us through an operation in the substance or background of our being; or, again, rationalistically, as mediated through ideas or doctrines. The Rationalism of the 18th century and the speculative philosophy of the 19th, while rejecting the former of these views, only accentuated the latter. History was resolved into a dialectic of ideas : not personalities but ideas were regarded as the creative forces. In the speculative theology of the Hegelian period, the religious importance of Jesus was found almost solely in the fact that He was the introducer or the symbol of the supreme religious idea. This idea—the essential oneness of God and man, man as the eternal Son of God—is the active and creative thing. There is still a large and important school, represented by writers like Green, Edward Caird, Pfleiderer, A. Dorner, which continues the Hegelian tradition. But the past half century has witnessed a reaction from this exaggerated intellectualism. It is being more and more widely recognized that the elevation and enrichment of man's spiritual life have been effected far less by the movements and instincts of the mass, or by the introduction and development of ideas, than by the appearance on the stage of history of great creative personalities. Such personalities are fountains of life for many succeeding generations. In no province is their importance so marked as in that of religion. And Christ is the supreme personality. It was the impression produced by His Person, even more than the new ideas He taught, that created the Christian Church. 'The life was the light of men.' And in whatever way we account for it, it is certain that Christian ideas cannot be separated from Christ without being stripped of much of their power to maintain themselves in men's minds and hearts. The recognition of such facts has had no small share in bringing the Person of Christ into the centre of religious thought.

2. *Theological reconstruction.*—We pass from the causes that have brought about a return to the historical Christ, to consider some of the attempts at theological reconstruction or revision to which the movement has led. What is its dogmatic significance? The movement is not a uniform one; it has taken various directions; and while most of the thought of the day confesses its influence, this influence is much more marked in some cases than in others. We need not take into account a writer like Gore, who, though insisting on the importance of a knowledge of the historical Christ, yet derives his theology not from Christ, but from the Œcumenical Councils; or like Loisy, who, indeed, distinguishes between the Christ of history and the Christ of faith, but yet allows the former little significance except as the starting-point of the

movement known as Christianity. Our attention must be limited to the theologies in which the new feeling for the historical Christ has exerted some marked influence.

(1) We begin with that form of the movement which departs least from traditional orthodoxy, and to which the term 'Christo-centric' is usually applied. In this case the return to Christ has not led to anything like a reconstruction of doctrine; the most that has been undertaken is a revision. The traditional doctrines receive a reinterpretation and a fresh grounding in the light of the fuller knowledge of, and keener feeling for, the Christ of history. In the words of the most distinguished representative of the Christo-centric movement in this country, 'We cannot conceive and describe the supreme historical Person without coming face to face with the profoundest of all the problems in theology; but then we may come to them from an entirely changed point of view, through the Person that has to be interpreted rather than through the interpretations of His Person. When this change has been effected, theology ceases to be scholastic and becomes historical.' *

This claim to break with the scholastic method is partially, but only partially, justified. The doctrines of the Church are no longer treated as sacrosanct, and as the first principles of theological construction. Still further, it is recognized that even Scripture cannot be received as the ultimate source and norm of doctrine. The Apostolic conception of Christianity is not formally authoritative. We must not look at Christ merely through St. Paul's eyes; it is possible for us to see the Christ whom St. Paul saw, and to estimate St. Paul's thoughts from the vantage ground of this immediate knowledge. The idea of an external authority is not, however, surrendered; it is only carried back to the last possible resort, the consciousness of Christ. Whatever can be derived from the consciousness of Christ has an authoritative claim on our acceptance. And since His history is of a piece with His consciousness, the two must be taken together. The theological task is therefore to interpret God through the history and the consciousness of the historical Christ.

But here the question postponed at the beginning presses for an answer. The term 'historical Christ' is not unambiguous. What are the contents of His consciousness, what are the facts in His history, which give to Him His meaning for faith, and which must be regarded as constituting His historical personality? We know Jesus from the Synoptic Gospels as the teacher of an ethical ideal supreme in its depth and height, and of a religion of pure inwardness and spirituality. We obtain glimpses into an inner life of intimate and unbroken fellowship with God. He was conscious of a unique vocation, to bring men to the knowledge and service of the Father in heaven, and to introduce the Reign of God on earth. In His consciousness of this vocation and of His equipment for it, He accepted the title of Messiah. He carried out His vocation with an obedience to God that never wavered, with a trust in God that no storm could shake, with a love that shrank from no sacrifice, and that never grew cold. He accepted the cross in the confidence that God's purpose would not be overthrown by His death, but established. This at least criticism leaves untouched; and for some this human Jesus is the Jesus of history, and, at the same time, the Divine Christ, the Saviour of the world. The constitutive facts in His Person and history are the religious and ethical facts. But such is not the view of those whose position we are now describing. Accepting these facts, they do not regard them as supplying an adequate con-

ception of the Christ of history, or as disclosing the deepest meaning of His life. For Christo-centric as for traditional theology, the elements of cardinal importance in Christ's consciousness and history are the miraculous elements. The facts that give to His inner life its character are His moral perfection and consciousness of sinlessness, His assertion of a unique knowledge of God, and of a Sonship different in kind from that possible to His disciples, His assertion of His Messiahship and pre-existence, His demand for absolute devotion to His Person, His claim to a superhuman authority in forgiving sins and in dealing with OT institutions and laws, His claim to be the Saviour of the world, the arbiter of human destiny, the final Judge. Similarly His outer life receives its character from the Virgin-birth, the Miracles (interpreted in the strict sense), and, above all, from the bodily Resurrection. The historical Christ is the transcendent and miraculous Christ, the Christ who was conscious of a superhuman dignity, and who was declared by the resurrection from the dead to be the Son of God with power (Ro 1⁴).

This conception of Christ, with its subordination of the moral and religious in His consciousness and history to the miraculous, carries with it two momentous consequences. In the first place, it involves the view, is indeed founded upon it, that the Revelation of God is to be found not primarily in Christ's Person and ministry, but in the doctrines in which these are interpreted. Christ is brought before us as primarily a *problem* that demands solution. What constitute Him a problem are the above-mentioned facts in His consciousness and history, which cannot be accounted for except on the hypothesis that He was a superhuman, supernatural Being—a Being that stood in a relation to God beyond any that can be described in ethical terms. These facts are singled out as the essential ones, just because they set the problem and provide the basis for the transcendental hypothesis. The solution of the problem is given in the NT doctrines of Christ's Person and work. The Person and work constitute the facts; the doctrines supply their explanation or interpretation. Apart from the doctrinal interpretation the facts might still retain a certain ethico-religious significance, but they would lose their highest, their essential, meaning. It is the interpretation or construction that is the essential thing in Christianity. The gospel is not given with the character, teaching, and ministry of Christ, in their direct appeal to the heart and conscience; only the doctrinal interpretation of these facts — that the pre-existent Son of God assumed human nature, lived among men, and atoned by His death for their sin—has a right to the name. Christianity is given only when Christ is speculatively construed. *

Though the need for such a construction can be demonstrated, the construction itself is not to be regarded as a work of human freedom. We receive it as authoritatively given. To traditional theology the authority is inspired Scripture, the witness of the Apostolic writers no less than Christ's self-witness. It is characteristic of the Christo-centric school that, with a freer view of inspiration, it admits only the self-witness as the ultimate authority. Only Christ Himself could know and reveal the secret of His unique personality. The doctrine of the Apostolic writers is not to be regarded as the product of a religious experience created by Christ, but as the reproduction or development of ideas received from Christ's lips. These writers are only the channel by which the interpretation has reached us, not its source.

* Fairbairn, *Christ in Modern Theology*, p. 8.

* Fairbairn, *Philosophy of the Christian Religion*, p. 306.

A doctrinal conception of Revelation requires as its correlate a conception of Faith as primarily an intellectual act. Faith must be defined as the assent of the mind to a proposition on the ground of authority. This assent, however, though the primary element in faith, is not treated as the whole of it; it becomes effective only when reinforced by the practical elements of feeling and will.

More fruitful, perhaps, than its attempt at a fresh grounding of doctrine has been the contribution of the Christo-centric school to the revision of doctrine. It has sought to free the formulas that describe the Triune Being of God and the Person and work of Christ from their over-refinement, to translate them into the categories of modern thought, and to make them more ethical and less metaphysical.

(2) We pass to a second, and much more radical phase of the movement. To many, 'back to Christ' means back from historical Christianity, the religion founded upon Christ, to the religion which Christ taught, and which we see embodied in His life. More than a century ago the position was summed up by Lessing in his famous saying, 'The Christian religion has been tried for eighteen centuries; the religion of Christ remains to be tried.'

That the stream of religion flows purer at its fountainhead than at its lower reaches is a fact which the study of every historical religion confirms. As a religion advances through history, it loses something of its idealism and becomes more secular, takes up foreign elements, accumulates dogmas and ceremonies, parts with its simplicity and spontaneity, and becomes more and more a human construction. And every religious reform has signified a throwing off of foreign accretions, and a return to the simplicity and purity of the source. Did not Christ Himself represent a reaction from the elaborate legal and ceremonial system of Judaism to the simpler and more ethical faith of the prophets? The Reformation was a return to primitive Christianity, but less to Christ than to St. Paul. But we must, it is maintained, go behind even St. Paul and the early disciples. It is true, indeed, that, in the NT, Christianity is not the complex thing it afterwards became; still, the process of intellectual and ceremonial elaboration has begun. If we have not the fully-developed system of dogma and sacrament, we have at least the germs out of which it arose; and while much must be regarded as the legitimate development of principles implicit in Christ's gospel, there is also the introduction of a foreign element.

Let us contrast at one or two points the gospel as proclaimed by Jesus with the Church's rendering of it. Jesus' gospel contains no Christology. It is the glad tidings of a Father in heaven, whose love and care embrace all His creatures, in whose eyes every human soul is precious, and who is at once the righteous Judge and the pitiful, forgiving Saviour. Jesus was conscious of His unique position as the Mediator of salvation, but He never (according to the Synoptic tradition) required faith in Himself in the same sense as He required faith in God. God was the one object of faith; and if Jesus called men to Himself, it was only that He might lead them to God, and teach them to love, trust, and obey God. Turning to the gospel of the Church, we find a doctrine of Christ's Person at the heart of it. To believe the gospel is no longer, in the first place at least, to receive God's message of love and forgiveness, and to obey His summons to repentance, trust, and service; it is to believe that Jesus is Messiah, a pre-existent, heavenly Being, the second Person in the Trinity.

A doctrine of Jesus' Person is substituted for the Heavenly Father as the immediate object of faith.

Again, Jesus' gospel contains nothing like a developed doctrine of Redemption. The question as to the rationale of forgiveness is never raised, and there is no hint of the inability of God to forgive without a propitiation. Forgiveness is presented as flowing directly from God's fatherly love (Lk 15). And as little do we find the other propositions included in the Church's doctrine of Redemption. Jesus, indeed, teaches that none is good (Mt 19[17]), that even at the best we are unprofitable servants, who have done no more than our duty (Lk 17[10]); but He knows nothing of inherited guilt, radical corruption of human nature, human inability to do any good work. In the gospel of Jesus we are in the region of direct moral intuition; nothing is there merely because apologetic or system required it. We are also in the region of moral sanity. There is nothing of asceticism, and no attempt to cultivate a feeling of sinfulness. Men are bidden strive to be perfect as their Father in heaven is perfect (Mt 5[48]). Comparing the gospel of the Church with that of Christ, we find complication instead of simplicity, theological construction instead of intuition, and sometimes morbidness and exaggeration in place of sanity.

Finally, while the teaching of Jesus places the centre of gravity in the will, the Church transfers it to the intellect. 'This do and thou shalt live' (Lk 10[28]) is the command of Jesus: what the Church requires is belief rather than conduct.

The gospel of Jesus represents the crown of religion; it is the highest and, in its innermost nature, the final stage of religious development. No other historical religion can endure a moment's comparison with it. And the religions manufactured out of a few philosophical principles have still less claim to serious consideration, since they are wholly lacking in everything that gives a religion vitality. It can be said with literal truth that, for any civilized community, the choice is not between Christianity and some other religion, but between Christianity and no religion at all.

While the religion of Jesus is regarded as the one faith capable of meeting the need of this and of every age, it is not meant that it can be reproduced in every detail. We must distinguish between central and peripheral elements, and between the enduring spirit and the passing form of manifestation. We cannot, for example, revive the primitive expectation of the world's speedy end, or the ideas about angels, Satan, unclean spirits as the agents in disease, which Jesus shared with His contemporaries. The gospel must be translated into the language of to-day, and its spirit applied to the relations of our modern life.

How is Jesus Himself regarded by those who represent this type of thought? All speculative Christology, whether Biblical or ecclesiastical, is rejected, and it is asserted that such Christology has no basis in the language which Jesus used about Himself. Further, it is held that not Jesus, but the God whom Jesus revealed, is the immediate object of our faith. At the same time, the unique significance of Jesus, not only in the history of religion but also for the individual, is earnestly recognized. We quote the confession of Bousset: 'Thou art our leader, to whom there is none like, the leader in the highest things, the leader of our soul to God, the Way, the Truth, and the Life.' * The figure of Jesus is the grandest and most perfect that God has bestowed on humanity throughout the long course of its upward journey. Bousset can even adopt the confession of St. Paul, 'God

* Bousset, *Das Wesen der Religion*, p. 267.

was in Christ' (2 Co 5[19]). Harnack goes a step further. 'Jesus,' he says, 'is the way to the Father, and He is also the judge ordained by the Father. Not as a constituent does He belong to the Gospel, but He has been its personal *realization* and *power*, and will always be felt as such.'[*] But in thus insisting on the dependence of the gospel on the Person behind it for its power in awakening faith, Harnack is to be regarded as representing the type of thought to be described in the next section rather than that described here.

(3) The last type of theological thought which has to be considered, as bearing upon it the impress of the modern feeling for the historical Christ, is the most important of all. It is that represented by the great name of Ritschl. For Ritschlianism, even more than for traditional orthodoxy, Christ is the sum and substance of Christianity. In Him the living God reveals Himself to men ; He is the fact in history in which God meets us, to awaken our faith and lead us into the blessedness of His fellowship. What is it in Christ that gives Him His so momentous significance ? The answer which Ritschlianism gives to this question involves a new interpretation of the great Christian ideas,— Revelation, Gospel, Doctrine, Faith,—only it is claimed that this interpretation is nothing more than a carrying out of the fundamental principles of the Reformation.

In Catholic, and not less in traditional Protestant, theology the significance of Christ is concentrated in the doctrines in which His Person and work have received their interpretation. Christianity is summed up in the great speculative ideas of the eternal Sonship, the Incarnation, and the atoning Death. These ideas are regarded as constituting the content of Revelation and the object of faith ; into them the meaning and power of Jesus' life are gathered, and to believe them is to believe the gospel. Doctrine, Gospel, Revelation are treated as one and the same thing. For Ritschlianism, on the other hand, it is not the doctrinal interpretation that is the vital thing, but the Person and work interpreted. Doctrine has its own importance, but it must not be identified with Revelation or with the Gospel ; and consequently it is not the object of faith. The importance of doctrine lies in this, that it brings to expression what faith has found in Christ. The appropriation of the Revelation of God in Christ results in a new knowledge of God and of human life, and it is the task of dogmatics to exhibit this knowledge in its purity, free from any admixture of philosophical speculation, and in its connexion with the inner life. Doctrine is the explicitly formulated knowledge of faith. But the doctrines in which another's faith has expressed itself cannot be received by us as the ground of our faith. It is not by appropriating St. Paul's thoughts about Christ—that He was a propitiatory offering, a pre-existent heavenly Being, etc.—that we become Christians, but only by trusting Christ as St. Paul trusted Him. When there is this direct contact with Christ, St. Paul's thoughts will be reproduced as the fruit of our own experience, and only then will they have real meaning for us. To substitute for Christ as the object of faith a doctrine of His Person and work is to remove faith from its genetic ground. For the creative thing in Christianity is not the doctrines which, with more or less truth and fulness, describe Christ's significance ; it is the personal life in its inexhaustible wealth of meaning and power, and as it manifests itself to us in word and deed. Doctrine is a product of faith, not its causal ground. Moreover, the substitution of doctrine for Christ has this further result, that it carries with it a false view of faith. Faith is then

* Harnack, *Das Wesen des Christentums*, p. 91.

necessarily conceived in the Catholic manner as the submission of the mind to a proposition on the ground of its authority. But if the Reformation has taught us anything, it is that faith is not assent to a doctrine, but trust in the living God. Faith is no product of our own activity ; it is God-created—the result of the contact of the soul with Divine reality. In the Person of Christ, God so reveals Himself to us as to command our reverence, trust, and devotion.

Not a doctrine, therefore, but a life is for Ritschlian theology the medium of Revelation and the object of faith. But the further question arises, What are the facts in the life that clothe it with Divine meaning and power ? In traditional theology the main emphasis falls upon the element of the miraculous. This follows necessarily from the position assigned to doctrine. Doctrine is the object of faith, and it is the miraculous facts— Virgin-birth, Miracles, Sinlessness, unique Knowledge of God, bodily Resurrection—that supply the basis for the dogmatic structure. But in the Ritschlian system no importance is attached to the miraculous as such. The attempt to demonstrate the Divine significance of Jesus in a theoretical (or causal) way is abandoned as at once impossible and mistaken. It is not possible, it is maintained, by means of the facts to which traditional theology appeals, to prove scientifically that Jesus cannot be explained by the causes operative in history, and that the hypothesis of a transcendental origin and nature must be brought into the field. Only for faith is a miracle a proof of God's working ; for science it is either an unexplained fact or a deceptive appearance. Moreover, it is not through breaches in the continuity of nature or of history that God makes His presence and activity certain to us. The religious view of nature or history is no product of causal explanation. To faith alone does God reveal Himself, and the judgment that God is in Christ is a judgment of faith. To consider Jesus in the light of a problem that has to be explained is to abandon the religious attitude for the scientific.

The vital facts in Christ's life are, for Ritschlianism, those that exhibit the living Person, and His activity in His vocation. The Christ who knew God as Father, who never turned aside from doing the Father's will, who never in the darkest vicissitudes of His life lost His confidence in the Father's wisdom, power, and love, and who by His faith overcame the world and conquered death ; the Christ who, understanding and feeling the evil of sin as none else, in holy love and pity sought out the sinful, making them His companions and opening for them the door into the Kingdom of God, and who for their sakes surrendered His life as an offering, enduring the cross and despising the shame—this is at once the Christ of history and the Christ of faith. His unique consciousness of God and His sinlessness—or, as it is better described, His moral perfection—do not owe their religious importance to their serviceableness as proofs of a transcendental 'nature' ; their importance lies in their inherent worth and power as elements in His personality. That there is something inscrutable in Jesus' consciousness of God is strongly maintained ; only it is not our inability to account for Him that gives Him His religious significance. Similarly the miracles are not to be viewed as proofs, but as exhibiting His gracious activity in His vocation. What of the Resurrection ? Within the Ritschlian school there are some who include this as part of the historically given ground of faith. The view of the majority, however, and the one that seems most consistent with the general position, is that belief in Jesus' eternal existence is rather the final outcome of faith than its preliminary condition. Apart from the difficulties which the Resurrection narratives present, our belief that Jesus lives is not one that rests on human testimony. It depends on the impression produced on us by His Person, — He could not be holden of death (Ac 2²⁴), — and on our acceptance of His revelation of the Father-God.

The question has been raised whether it is the historical or the exalted Christ that is the object of faith. These alternatives are not, however, so opposed as they seem. Most would admit that our conception of the exalted Christ, if it is not to pass into the region of pure phantasy, must derive its content from the historical life ; and also, that the historical Christ must be thought of, not merely as a figure of the past, but as alive for evermore. The exalted Christ is the Christ of history, with the superadded thought that He is not dead but risen, and at the right hand of God.

The gospel, the glad message of God's Fatherly love and forgiveness, is, according to Ritschlian thought, already given in the simple proclamation of Jesus. To complicate this simple proclamation with doctrine is to pervert it. But this is not to say that Christ has no place in His gospel. In the first place, it is from Christ's Personality, and from His activity in His vocation, that the gospel derives its meaning. Apart from His ministry of love, our conception of the Fatherly love of God can have but little living content. That historical ministry in its inexhaustible richness stands as the enduring exhibition of what Divine love means. The dogmatic conception of the Father surrendering His eternal Son to death is much poorer as an exhibition of love than the historical reality. So also one can rise to the height of the gospel conception of God's righteousness and mercy only as one keeps in view the mind and character of Christ, and His treatment of sinners. The reconciliation of these two attributes is not a matter of jurisprudence, as the Atonement doctrine makes it ; it is the secret of a personal life. We see them reconciled in the mind and ministry of Jesus, who, undefiled and separate from sinners, yet received them into His fellowship.

But this is not all. In analyzing Christ's significance, Ritschlian theology attaches even greater importance to the idea of Power. Christ is that fact through which God enters as a force into history, to awaken and sustain faith. It is not natural for us to believe the gospel of God's forgiveness and Fatherly love and care. Rather does faith arise as a victory over nature. When we contemplate the iron system of mechanical forces and laws that beset us behind and before, and beyond which no theoretical knowledge can conduct us, it is a hard matter to persuade ourselves that these forces and laws are but the angels and ministers of a gracious personal will. It is supremely through Christ that we reach this assurance. He is the Divine fact that so masters us as to convince us that not mechanism, but the Good is the ultimate reality. The spiritual might of God becomes real to us as we contemplate the power of the Good in Jesus' life. Forgiveness becomes real and guilt becomes real when we feel behind them the throb of Jesus' holy love. The great redemptive forces—faith, love, self-sacrifice, moral fidelity—have their supreme seat and centre in the Person and life and cross of the man Christ Jesus. We may sum up the position by saying that in Him the will of God for man's salvation becomes effective.

Such are the three theological types in which the influence of the movement 'back to Christ' is most apparent. It would be premature to forecast the ultimate issue of the movement. But one thing is certain. So momentous an event as the recovery of the historical figure of Christ cannot leave theology exactly as it found it.

LITERATURE :—I. (1) Distinction between the historical and dogmatic Christ : Kähler, *Der sogenannte historische Jesus und der geschichtliche biblische Christus* ; Fairbairn, *Christ in Modern Theology*, p. 186 ; Loisy, *Autour d'un petit livre*, pp. 111, 90, 134 ; Sabatier, *Outlines of a Philosophy of Religion*, p. 141 f. (2) Criticism of dogma : *Histories of Dogma*, by Harnack [Eng. tr.], Loofs, and A. Dorner ; Kattenbusch, *Confessions-Kunde* ; Kaftan, *The Truth of the Christian Religion*, vol. i. ; Fairbairn, *op. cit.* (3) Religion and history : Harnack, *Das Christentum und die Geschichte* ; O. Kirn, *Glaube und Geschichte*.

II. (1) Christo-centric theology : Fairbairn, *Christ in Modern Theology*, and *The Philosophy of the Christian Religion* ; Denney, *Studies in Theology* ; Forrest, *The Christ of History and of Experience.*—(2) Religion of Jesus theology : Channing, *Sermons on Love to Christ* and on *Preaching Christ* ; Seeley, *Ecce Homo* ; A. B. Bruce, *With Open Face* ; *The Thinker*, 1893, p. 38 ; Hatch, *Hibbert Lectures*, 1888, pp. 333, 349, 351 ; Watson, *The Mind of the Master* ; Tolstoi, *My Religion* ; Harnack, *What is Christianity ?* ; J. Weiss, *Die Nachfolge Christi und die Predigt der Gegenwart* ; Bousset, *Wesen der Religion*, p. 192 ff.

III. Ritschlianism : Ritschl, *Justification and Reconciliation* ; Garvie, *Ritschlian Theology* ; Swing, *The Theology of Albrecht Ritschl* ; Herrmann, *The Communion of the Christian with God*, also *Ethik*, and *der Begriff der Offenbarung* ; Kaftan, *Dogmatik*.

W. MORGAN.

BAG (Jn 12⁶ 13²⁹ γλωσσόκομον ; in Lk 12³³ βαλάντια is tr. 'bags' in AV, but RV 'purses' ; see PURSE).

Γλωσσόκομον (in NT peculiar to St. John) meant originally a case for keeping the mouth-pieces of wind instruments (γλῶσσα, χομέω) ; so Phrynicus, who gives γλωσσοκομεῖον as the proper form, rejecting that of NT, which, however, is found in an old Doric inscription, in later Comic writers and in LXX (see Liddell and Scott). The RVm 'box' seems the better rendering. Field (*ON*) has a very full note, in which he concludes that γλ., both in its general and in its special sense, means not a bag, but a box or chest, always of wood or other hard material. Thus Hesychius defines it as a wooden receptacle of remnants (σορὸς ξυλίνη τῶν λειψάνων) ; Arrian mentions γλωσσόκομα made of tortoise-shell ; in the Anthology γλ. is apparently a coffin ('when I look at Nicanor the coffin-maker [σοροπηγόν], and consider for what purpose he makes these wooden boxes [γλωσσόκομα]') ; and in an inscription quoted by Hatch (*Essays in Biblical Greek*) γλ. means the strong box or muniment chest of an association. The LXX translates אָרוֹן in 2 Ch 24⁸ᶠ· by γλ. (the chest for the offerings, but κιβωτός in 2 K 12⁹ᶠ· as usually), which Cod. A also gives in 2 S 6¹¹ (the Ark). Aquila uses γλ. for אָרוֹן in all its significations, *e.g.* coffin (Gn 50²⁶), the Ark (Ex 37¹, 1 S 5¹, 2 S 6¹¹). Ancient Versions of Jn. agree with this view ; Vulg. gives *loculos*, the plural, says Field, 'indicating several partitions,' a small portable cash-box ; D lat. *loculum* ; Nonnus δουρατίην χηλόν, *lignean arculam*. In favour of EV it may be urged that something small and easily carried is required by the context, whereas the above instances are chiefly larger boxes (but note use of γλ. by Hesychius and Arrian above). Again, in 1 S 6⁸ᶠ· אַרְגָּז (EV 'coffer') is tr. γλωσσόκομον by Josephus, and is from a root 'to tremble, wag, move to and fro,' whence in Arabic there is a similar word meaning a bag filled with stones hung at the sides of camels to preserve equilibrium (see Gesenius, *Lex.*). In modern Greek also γλ. means purse or bag (Hatch).

The γλ. was the receptacle for the money of Jesus and the disciples ; it contained, no doubt, the proceeds of the sale of their goods, and gave the idea later of the common fund (Ac 4³²ᶠ·) ; it was replenished by the gifts of friends (Lk 8³) ; and from it the poor were helped (Jn 13²⁹). Judas may have been entrusted with it as being the best fitted for such work ; but what might have proved a blessing, as giving useful employment for his talents, became the means of his ruin. Other suggested explanations are : that Christ thought fit to call forth a manifestation of his sin as the only means of cure (Hengstenberg) ; or that it was simply a private arrangement between the disciples (Godet). The 'bag' could not have been taken from him, as Edersheim (*Life and Times*, ii. 472) remarks, without exposing him to the others, and precipitating his moral destruction. See JUDAS ISCARIOT.　　　　　　　　W. H. DUNDAS.

BAND.—A Roman legion, the full strength of which was about 6000 men, was divided into ten cohorts (600), and each cohort into three maniples (200). Greek writers use the word σπεῖρα, rendered 'band' in our versions, sometimes for *maniple* but usually for *cohort* ; hence RVm has regularly 'cohort.' The troops in Judæa, however, as in other provinces governed by a procurator, consisted simply of auxiliaries, not Roman citizens, but provincials; these were not formed into legions, but merely into cohorts, of strength varying from 500 to 1000, sometimes consisting purely of infantry, sometimes including cavalry also. The forces in Palestine seem to have been originally Herod's troops, taken over by the Romans; they were recruited in the Greek cities in or around the country, such as Cæsarea, Ascalon, Sebaste. One such cohort formed the garrison of Jerusalem, stationed in the fortress of Antonia, adjoining the Temple, under a chiliarch or tribune ('the chief captain of the band,' Ac 21³¹). From the account of the force at the disposal of Lysias (Ac 23²³), his cohort must have been a *cohors miliaria equestris*, consisting of 760 infantry and 240 cavalry; but this may not have been the case in our Lord's time, some 30 years earlier. This Roman force was probably granted by Pilate to effect our Lord's arrest (Jn 18³· ¹², where 'the band' under its 'chief captain' [RV] seems distinguished from 'the officers of the Jews,' *i.e.* the Temple police; see Westcott, *ad loc.*). Of course, only a portion of the whole cohort would be needed. In Mt 27²⁷ ‖ Mk 15¹⁶, the soldiers gather together 'the whole band' to mock our Lord; obviously all who were at hand and not on duty.

LITERATURE.—Grimm-Thayer, *s.v.* σπεῖρα; Schürer, *HJP* I. ii. 49–56; Marquardt, *Römische Staatsverwaltung* (1884), ii. 468 ff., 534 ff.   HAROLD SMITH.

BANK.—1. In the parable of the Pounds, Christ upbraids the slothful servant because he had not given his pound to the bank (ἐπὶ τράπεζαν), *i.e.* the office of the money-changers (Lk 19²³), who would have kept it safe, and also paid interest for it. 'Bankers' (τραπεζῖται) is used in RV of Mt 25²⁷ for 'money-changers' of the AV. In Greek cities the bankers sat at their tables (τράπεζα) in the market-place. They changed coins, but also took money on deposit, giving what would now seem very high interest (see articles 'Money-Changers' and 'Usury' in vols. iii. and iv. of Hastings' *DB*).

In this parable some suppose that Christ meant by 'the bank' to indicate the Synagogue, or the Christian Church as an organized body, which might use the gifts or powers of a disciple, when he could not, through timidity or lack of energy, exercise them himself. Others have supposed that He pointed to prayer as a substitute for good works, when the disciple was unable to do such. But all this is very precarious. (Cf. Bruce, *Parabolic Teaching of Christ*, p. 209 f.).

There is an apocryphal saying of Christ which may be connected with this parable. Origen (*in Joann.* xix. etc.) gives it thus: γίνεσθε τραπεζῖται δόκιμοι, 'Be ye tried money-changers.' This is explained in the Clementine *Homilies* (iii. 61) to mean that Christians should prove the words of Christ, as the bankers test and approve the gold and silver on their tables. But it may perhaps be looked at rather as connected with the stewardship of gifts and talents by the Lord's disciples, finding its parallel in such sayings as Lk 16¹² 'If ye have not been faithful in that which is another man's, who shall give you that which is your own?' The duty of a timid servant may be to use his gifts under the guidance and authority of others, but growing experience might advance him to be a τραπεζίτης himself, who is able to trade boldly with that which has been entrusted to him.

2. In Lk 19⁴³ 'bank,' AV 'trench' (Gr. χάραξ), probably stands for a palisade (so RVm) of stakes, strengthened with branches and earth, with a ditch behind, used by besiegers as a protection against arrows or attacking parties (Lat. *vallum*). Such a palisade was actually employed by the soldiers of Titus in the siege of Jerusalem, A.D. 70 (Jos. *BJ* v. vi. 2).   DAVID M. W. LAIRD.

BANQUET.—The people of Palestine in Christ's day—as, indeed, throughout the East generally—

were fond of social feasting. The word δοχή, rendered 'feast,' from δέχομαι, 'to receive' (cf. Eng. 'reception'), is used with ποιέω, 'to make' (cf. Heb. מִשְׁתֶּה עָשָׂה Job 1⁴). This is the social feast or banquet, as distinguished from the religious feast (ἑορτή). Levi made a great feast in his house (Lk 5²⁹); and Christ advised His followers, when they gave a banquet, to invite the poor and afflicted rather than the rich and influential (14¹³). Such banquets were usually given in the house of the host to invited guests (Lk 14¹³, Jn 2²), but there was more freedom accorded the uninvited than is common in Western social life (Lk 7³⁶⁻³⁸). Guests reclined on couches, leaning upon the left arm, and eating with the aid of the right hand, as in ordinary meals. Eating, and especially drinking of wine (cf. Heb. מִשְׁתֶּה 'drink,' and יַיִן 'wine,' used for 'banquet,' and Gr. συμπόσιον, 'drinking together'), music, dancing, joyous conversation, merriment, usually characterized such a festivity. Such a banquet was a part of wedding occasions. Jesus accepted an invitation to one of these at Cana in Galilee (Jn 2²ff·). Levi gave a banquet in His honour (Lk 5²⁹). There were often large numbers present (5²⁹), and gradations in the places (Mt 23⁶, Lk 14⁷ 20⁴⁶, Mk 12³⁹). One of the guests was usually appointed 'ruler of the feast,' or ἀρχιτρίκλινος (Jn 2⁸· ⁹), who superintended the drinking, etc. (cf. Lk 22²⁶).   E. B. POLLARD.

BAPTISM (βάπτισμα = 'the rite of Baptism,' always in NT distinguished from βαπτισμός, 'a washing,' Mk 7⁴, He 6² 9¹⁰ [but see Lightfoot, Com. on *Colossians*, p. 184]; but this distinction is not maintained in Josephus [cf. *Ant.* XVIII. v. 2]; and in the Latin versions and Fathers *baptisma* and *baptismus* and even *baptismum* are used indiscriminately, see Plummer's art. 'Baptism' in Hastings' *DB*).—A rite wherein by immersion in water the participant symbolizes and signalizes his transition from an impure to a pure life, his death to a past he abandons, and his new birth to a future he desires.

The points for consideration are (1) the Origin of Baptism, (2) its Mode, (3) John's Baptism of the people, (4) John's Baptism of Jesus, (5) Baptism by the disciples of Jesus.

1. The Origin of Baptism.—Baptism, as we find it in the Gospels, may be traced to a threefold source, natural symbolism, the lustrations of the Mosaic Law, and the baptism of proselytes. In many of the appointments of non-Christian religions the cleansing of the soul from sin is symbolized by the washing of the body (see the Vendidad, Fargard, ix. ; Williams, *Religious Thought in India*, 347 ; Vergil, *Æneid*, ii. 720 ; Ovid, *Fasti*, v. 680 ; and esp. MacCulloch, *Compar. Theol.*). As in other religions, so in Israel washings were the means appointed for restoring the person who had incurred ceremonial defilement to his place among the worshipping congregation. The Mosaic Law prescribed certain regulations for the removal of uncleanness by washing with water ; Lv 15⁵· ⁸· ¹³· ¹⁶ (λούσεται ὕδατι πᾶν τὸ σῶμα αὐτοῦ) 16²⁶· ²⁸· etc. But if the Jew himself needed almost daily washing ('Judæus quotidie lavat, quia quotidie inquinatur,' Tertull. *de Baptismo*, xv.), much more was the bath of purification necessary for the Gentile who desired to pass into Judaism. For the proselyte this baptism (מְבִילָה) seemed the appropriate initiation. 'Whensoever any heathen will betake himself and be joined to the covenant of Israel, and place himself under the wings of the Divine Majesty, and take the yoke of the Law upon him, voluntary circumcision, baptism, and oblation are required.' (See this and other passages in Lightfoot, *Horæ Heb.* on Mt 3⁶; Schürer, *HJP* § 31; and Edersheim's *Life and Times of*

Jesus, Appendix xii. on 'Baptism of Proselytes.' The question whether the baptism of proselytes was in vogue as early as the time of the Baptist has been laid to rest by Edersheim and Schürer). It may almost be said, then, that when John baptized the people, he meant to impress them with the idea that they must be re-born before they could enter the kingdom. He, as it were, excommunicated them, and by requiring them to submit to Baptism, declared that their natural birth as Jews was insufficient for participation in the Messianic blessings. No doubt also he believed himself to be fulfilling the predictions of Zec 13[1], Ezk 36[25], as well as the craving expressed in Ps 51[7].

2. *The Mode of Baptism.*—That the normal mode was by immersion of the whole body may be inferred (*a*) from the meaning of βαπτίζω, which is the intensive or frequentative form of βάπτω, 'I dip,' and denotes to *immerse* or *submerge*. In Polybius, iii. 72, it is used of soldiers wading through a flooded river, 'immersed' to their breast (ἕως τῶν μαστῶν οἱ πεζοὶ βαπτιζόμενοι). It is used also of sinking ships (in i. 51, the Carthaginians sank many of the Roman ships, πολλὰ τῶν σκαφῶν ἐβάπτιζον). [Many examples are given in Stephanus, and esp. in *Classic Baptism: An enquiry into the meaning of the word* βαπτίζω, by James W. Dale, 4th ed. Philadelphia, 1872]. The point is that 'dip' or 'immerse' is the primary, 'wash' the secondary meaning of βάπτω and βαπτίζω. (*b*) The same inference may be drawn from the law laid down regarding the baptism of proselytes: 'As soon as he grows whole of the wound of circumcision, they bring him to Baptism, and being placed in the water, they again instruct him in some weightier and in some lighter commands of the Law. Which being heard, he plunges himself and comes up, and behold, he is an Israelite in all things.' (See Lightfoot, *l.c.*). To use Pauline language, his old man is dead and buried in the water, and he rises from this cleansing grave a new man. The full significance of the rite would have been lost had immersion not been practised. Again, it was required in proselyte baptism that 'every person baptized must dip his whole body, now stripped and made naked, at one dipping. And wheresoever in the Law washing of the body or garments is mentioned, it means nothing else than the washing of the whole body.' (*c*) That immersion was the mode of Baptism adopted by John is the natural conclusion from his choosing the neighbourhood of the Jordan as the scene of his labours; and from the statement of Jn 3[23] that he was baptizing in Ænon 'because there was much water there.' (*d*) That this form was continued into the Christian Church appears from the expression λουτρὸν παλινγενεσίας (Tit 3[5]), and from the use made by St. Paul in Ro 6 of the symbolism. This is well put by Bingham (*Antiq.* xi. 11): 'The ancients thought that immersion, or burying under water, did more likely represent the death and burial and resurrection of Christ as well as our own death unto sin and rising again unto righteousness: and the divesting or unclothing the person to be baptized did also represent the putting off the body of sin in order to put on the new man, which is created in righteousness and true holiness. For which reason they observed the way of baptizing all persons naked and divested, by a total immersion under water, except in some particular cases of great exigence, wherein they allow of sprinkling, as in the case of clinic Baptism, or where there is a scarcity of water.' This statement exactly reflects the ideas of the Pauline Epistles and the *Didache*. This early document enjoins that Baptism be performed in running water; but if that is not to be had, then in other

water: 'And if thou canst not in cold, then in warm; but if thou hast neither, pour water thrice upon the head.' Here it is obvious that affusion is to be practised only where immersion is inconvenient or impossible. The Eastern Church has in the main adhered to the primitive form. But in the Western Church the exigencies of climate and the alteration of manners have favoured affusion and sprinkling. Judging from the representations of the performance of the rite collected by Mr. C. F. Rogers (*Studia Bibl. et Eccles.* vol. v. pt. iv.),—whose collection is more valuable than his inferences,—it would seem that at an early period a common form of administration required that the baptized person should stand in some kind of bath or tub, naked or nearly so, while the baptizer poured water three times over him. This restricted form gradually gave place to the still more meagre sprinkling of the head. But theoretically the form of Baptism by immersion was retained alike in the Roman, the Anglican, and the Presbyterian Churches. Thus Aquinas (*Summa*, III. lxvi. 7) determines: 'si totum corpus aqua non possit perfundi propter aquæ paucitatem, vel propter aliquam aliam causam, oportet caput perfundere, in quo manifestatur principium animalis vitæ.' The Anglican Church in her rubric for Baptism directs the ministrant to *dip* the child discreetly and warily, if the sponsors certify him that the child may well endure it; if not, 'it shall suffice to pour water upon it.' And the *Westminster Confession* guardedly says: 'Dipping of the person into water is *not necessary*; but Baptism is rightly administered by pouring or sprinkling water upon the person' (cf. Calvin, *Inst.* iv. 15, 19). This form of Baptism by sprinkling gives prominence to the 'pouring out' of the Spirit (cf. Tit 3[6]), but fails to indicate the dying to sin and rising to righteousness.

3. *John's Baptism of the people.*—The message of the Baptist as herald of the Messiah was, 'The kingdom of heaven is at hand.' The imminence of the kingdom produced in the people a sense of their unpreparedness for its enjoyment. A new sense of sin was created within them, answering to the forerunner's cry, 'Repent ye: *for* the kingdom of heaven is at hand' (Mt 3[2]). The hunger for cleanness of conscience thus awakened within them was responded to by John's Baptism of repentance 'for (εἰς) remission of sins' (Mk 1[4]). True repentance cleanses the soul, and Baptism represented and sealed this inward cleansing. The reality of the repentance, as John insisted, would be determined by its fruits. Many writers (cf. Reynolds, *John the Baptist*, pp. 288–289; and Lambert, *The Sacraments*, p. 60) hold that the preposition εἰς denotes that the remission of sins was not actually bestowed, but only guaranteed in John's Baptism. 'John proclaimed, with the voice of thunder, the need of repentance as a condition of the remission of sins; his Baptism was the external symbol of the frame of mind with which the penitent approached the great forerunner.' This seems, both exegetically and psychologically, untenable. The whole expression, 'Baptism of repentance for forgiveness of sins,' denotes a Baptism which the penitent submitted to that he might therein receive the pledge and assurance that he was forgiven. The Baptism meant the cleansing of the people from past sin that they might be fitted for entrance on the kingdom. But John's Baptism had a forward look also. It was the formal incorporation of the individual into the new community, his initiation into the kingdom. It was therefore in a very true sense Christian Baptism. That is, it pledged the recipient to the acceptance of Christ,—a feature of it which perhaps accounts for the Baptist continuing to baptize after Jesus had been proclaimed the Christ. In the same act, then, John excommunicated the whole people, putting them in the position of Gentiles who required to be re-born in Baptism, and gave them entrance to the coming kingdom.

The propriety of Baptism as the symbol of such initiation is obvious, and finds illustration in the forms of initiation commonly used in various races. The ceremonies which mark, among rude tribes, the transition from boyhood to manhood, frequently take the form of a pretended death and resurrection (Frazer, *The Golden Bough*[2], iii. 422 ff.). Among ourselves we have titles which preserve a memory of the old customs, though the customs themselves have died out. We still have 'Knights of the Bath.' Originally, the bath to purify from the past was first taken, and the novice then passed the night in a church with his armour beside him, as if he were dead, until in the morning he was raised to life by the touch of his sovereign, 'Rise, Sir M. or N.'

4. *John's Baptism of Jesus.*—When John began to baptize, Jesus was still an unknown artisan in Nazareth. But in this new movement He hears a call He cannot resist. He is conscious that He must attach Himself to it; possibly already conscious that He can guide, utilize, and prosper it. He appears, therefore, as a candidate for Baptism. But to the Baptist this presented a difficulty he had not foreseen: 'I have need to be baptized of thee, and comest thou to me?' (Mt 3[14]). Evidently what was in John's mind was not the initiatory, but the cleansing aspect of the rite. To this, therefore, the answer of Jesus must apply when He said, 'Thus it becometh us to fulfil all righteousness.' It would seem, therefore, that Jesus felt so keen a sympathy with His fellow-men that, as one with an unclean race, He judged Baptism to be appropriate. It is idle to tell the wife that she need not be ashamed though her husband is committed for fraud; idle to tell Jesus that He need not be baptized because He has no personal guilt. And it is to be noted that it is precisely at this point of truest union with men and of deepest humiliation that Jesus is recognized as King. It seems to have flashed upon John, 'Why, this is the very spirit of the Messiah. Here is the fulness of the Divine Spirit.'

The account given in the Fourth Gospel is different. The Baptist is there (Jn 1[33]) represented as saying, 'I knew him not (which, as the context shows, means, 'I did not know that he was the Messiah'), but he that sent me to baptize with water, the same said unto me, Upon whom thou shalt see the Spirit descending and abiding on him, the same is he that baptizeth with the Holy Spirit.' In this Gospel there is no mention of an actual dove being seen. John merely affirms that he saw the Spirit descending 'like a dove' (ὡς περιστεράν). He wishes to emphasize two things, that he saw the Spirit so clearly that it almost seemed a sensible presence, and that it was a Spirit of gentleness. Naturally, the Messianic Spirit might have been more appropriately symbolized by an eagle, but at the moment it was the overcoming humility and meekness of Jesus that convinced John that He was the Messiah.

The Baptism of Jesus thus became His anointing as King. Jesus becomes the Christ, the Anointed of God, not only nominated to the Messianic throne, but actually equipped with the fulness of the Divine Spirit. Here two points are to be noted: (1) Although Son of God, Jesus yet lived in human form and under human conditions, and therefore needed the indwelling of the Spirit. As His body was sustained by bread, as all human bodies are, so did His soul require the aids of the Divine Spirit, as all human souls do. ('Why callest thou me good? There is none good but one, that is, God,' Mk 10[18]). His human nature, by which He manifested God to men, was now endowed with the fulness of God's Spirit. (2) It was not a new thing that was conferred upon Jesus at His Baptism. From the first the Divine Spirit was His. But now, having reached the flower of manhood and being called to the greatest work, His human nature expands and girds itself to the most strenuous endeavour, and so gives scope to the fullest energy of the indwelling God.

5. *Baptism by the disciples of Jesus.*—Of Christian Baptism very little mention is made in the Gospels. That it was in use during the life of Jesus is apparent from the references to it in Jn 3 and 4. These references are interesting as showing that Baptism by the disciples of Jesus existed alongside of Baptism by John. The Baptist himself apparently never renounced his position as forerunner nor merged himself in the kingdom. The re-baptism of those mentioned in Ac 19[1-6], who had been baptized with John's Baptism, suggests the question whether all who had originally been baptized as disciples of John were re-baptized when they professed allegiance to Jesus. And although this can scarcely be considered likely, this case has been used as sanctioning re-baptism in certain circumstances. Calvin's answer is rather an evasion. He denies that the persons spoken of in Ac 19 were re-baptized. They only had the Apostle's hands laid upon them. The text no doubt says, 'They were baptized into the name of the Lord Jesus; and when Paul had laid his hands upon them,' etc. But 'hac posteriori locutione describitur, qualis ille fuerit Baptismus.' That is possible, but barely. It is more likely that those concerned, troubled by no questions as to the legitimacy of the renewal of Baptism, and accustomed to the many lustrations then in use, were re-baptized and were conscious of no inconsistency. Apparently they had only seen one half, and that the less important half, of the significance of John's Baptism, its relation to repentance, and not its efficacy as the ordinance of initiation into the kingdom of Jesus. This defect was now supplied.

Baptism could scarcely have gained so universal a currency as the initiatory rite of the Christian Church had it not been instituted by Christ Himself. No other initial ordinance seems ever to have been suggested. Yet it is expressly said (Jn 4[2]) that He Himself did not baptize; and it is doubted whether the explicit injunction of Mt 28[19] can be accepted as uttered by Jesus. Thus Harnack (*Hist. of Dogma*, i. 79 note) says: 'It cannot be directly proved that Jesus instituted Baptism, for Mt 28[19] is not a saying of the Lord. The reasons for this assertion are: (1) It is only a later stage of the tradition that represents the risen Christ as delivering speeches and giving commandments. Paul knows nothing of it. (2) The Trinitarian formula is foreign to the mouth of Jesus, and has not the authority in the Apostolic age which it must have had if it had descended from Jesus Himself.' (See the literature in Holtzmann's *NT Theol.* i. 379). That our Lord appeared to His disciples after the Resurrection and said nothing is inconceivable. Better deny the Resurrection altogether than think of a dumb, unsociable ghost floating before the eyes of the disciples. But the Trinitarian formula in the mouth of Jesus is certainly unexpected. For what may be said in its favour Lambert (*The Sacraments*, pp. 49–51) may be consulted. In any case the essential feature of Baptism was its marking the union of the soul to Christ, and therefore it sufficed to call it 'Baptism into the name of the Lord Jesus.' Further discussion of the genuineness of the ascription of these words to our Lord belongs rather to the Trinitarian than to the Baptismal problems.

LITERATURE.—MacCulloch, *Comparative Theology*, 235 ; Anrich, *Das antike Mysterienwesen* ; Lightfoot, *Horæ Hebraicæ* ; Schürer, *HJP* § 31 ; Suicer, *Lexicon, s.v.* ; Calvin, *Institutio*, iv. 15, 'de Baptismo' ; Reynolds, *John the Baptist* ; Feather, *John the Baptist* ; Lambert, *The Sacraments in the New Testament* ; Holtzmann's *NT Theol.* and the literature mentioned there, as above ; Edersheim's *Life and Times of Jesus the Messiah* ; C. F. Rogers, *Studia Bibl. et Eccles.* vol. v. pt. iv. 'Baptism and Christian Archæology' ; *Didaskaliæ fragmenta Veronensia Latina* (Lips. 1900) ; A. C. McGiffert, *The Apostles' Creed*, 1902, p. 175 ; J. F. Bethune-Baker, *Early Hist. of Christian Doctrine*, 1905, p. 376.   MARCUS DODS.

BARABBAS (Aramaic *Bar-Abba*, 'son of Abba' or 'son of father.' There is very slight documentary authority for the reading *Bar-Rabban*, 'son of a Rabbi,' which is adopted by Ewald and Renan. On the other hand, if *Bar-Abba* = 'son of father,' it would hardly differ in meaning from *Bar-Rabban* ; for in the time of Jesus 'Abba' was a common appellation of honour given to a Rabbi. But after all 'Abba' may have been a proper name ; for though it is sometimes affirmed [*e.g.* by Schmiedel in his article 'Barabbas' in *Encyc. Bibl.*] that it was not till after the time of our Lord that the word began to be used in this way, the authors of the corresponding article in the *Jewish Encyclopedia* assure us that 'Abba is found as a *prænomen* as early as Tannaitic times').

Only one Barabbas meets us in the Gospels, the criminal whom Pilate released instead of Jesus at the demand of the people. All the four Evangelists relate the incident (Mt 27¹⁵⁻²⁶, Mk 15⁶⁻¹⁵, Lk 23¹⁷⁻²⁵, Jn 18³⁹· ⁴⁰), which is again referred to in Acts in the account of St. Peter's sermon in the Temple portico (Ac 3¹⁴). From these narratives we gather that Barabbas was 'a notable prisoner,' 'a robber,' one who had taken part in 'a certain insurrection made in the city,' and who in this disturbance had 'committed murder.' It had probably been an old Jewish custom to release a prisoner at the Passover feast (Jn 18³⁹). According to the Roman habit in such matters, the procurators of Judæa had accommodated themselves to the Jewish practice. In his desire to save Jesus, Pilate bethought himself of this custom as offering a loophole of escape from the dilemma in which he found himself between his own sense of justice and his unwillingness to give offence to the multitude. So he offered them the choice between the life of Jesus and the life of Barabbas, probably never doubting that to Jesus the preference would be given. The fact that he seems to have expected this precludes the view which some have held that Barabbas was a pseudo-Messiah, and even the notion that he was no vulgar bandit, but the leader of a party of Zealots, since popular sympathy might have been anticipated on behalf of a bold Zealot or insurrectionary Messiah. The probability accordingly is that Barabbas was simply a criminal of the lowest type, a hater of the Romans it may be, but at the same time a pest to society at large. And unless we are to suppose, on the ground of the possible etymology, 'son of father' = 'son of teacher,' and the '*filius magistri eorum*' which Jerome quotes from the account of the incident in the *Gospel of the Hebrews*, that he was popular among the people because he was the son of a Rabbi, we have no reason to think that either the Jewish leaders or the multitude had any ground for preferring him to Jesus except their passionate hatred of the latter.

According to an old reading of Mt 27¹⁶· ¹⁷, the name 'Jesus' in both verses is prefixed to Barabbas, so that Pilate's question runs, 'Whom will ye that I release unto you? Jesus Barabbas, or Jesus which is called Christ?' If this reading were accepted, *Barabbas* would not have the force of a

proper name (like *Bartimæus*), but would be only a patronymic added for the sake of distinction (cf. 'Simon *Bar-jona*'). In his exposition of the passage, Origen refers to this reading, which is favoured by some cursive MSS and by the Armenian and Jerusalem Syriac Versions, and has been defended by Ewald, Lange, Meyer, and others, who have supposed that the accidental similarity of the name may have helped to suggest to Pilate the alternative which he presented to the Jews. Olshausen not only adopts this view, but finds a mournful significance in both of the (supposed) names of the condemned criminal—'Jesus' and 'son of the father,' and in the fact that the nation preferred this caricature of Jesus to the heavenly reality. Both dramatically and homiletically, no doubt, these ideas are tempting—the meeting of the two Jesuses, the irony of the popular choice, the sense of a Divine 'lusus' in human affairs. But the truth remains that the grounds on which this construction rests are very inadequate. There is ingenuity certainly in the suggestion, first made by Origen (who, however, prefers the ordinary reading), that 'Jesus' may have been dropped out of the early MSS of Matthew after the name had become a sacred one, because it appeared unseemly that it should be borne by a murderer ; but it is of too hypothetical a kind to counterbalance the immense weight of the documentary evidence against the presence of the name 'Jesus' at all. The fact that, even in the scanty MSS and VSS in which 'Jesus Barabbas' is found in vv.¹⁶ and ¹⁷, 'Barabbas' and 'Jesus' are set in direct antithesis in v.²⁰ tells strongly against the reading, as well as the circumstance that no trace of it is found in any MS of the other three Gospels. There is much to be said for the suggestion of Tregelles, by way of explaining the appearance of the 'Jesus' in some copies of Matthew, that at a very early date a careless transcriber repeated the last two letters of ὑμῖν (v.¹⁷), and that the IN was afterwards taken to be the familiar abbreviation of Ἰησοῦν.

LITERATURE.—The Commentaries of Meyer, Alford, and Olshausen ; Ewald, *History of Israel*, vol. vi. ; Lange's and Renan's *Life of Christ* ; art. 'Barabbas' in Hastings' *DB*, *Encyc. Bibl.*, and *Jewish Encycl.* ; Merkel, 'Die Begnadigung am Passahfeste' in *ZNTW*, 1905, p. 293 ff.   J. C. LAMBERT.

BARACHIAH.—Mt 23³⁵ (om. ℵ* and 4 cursives), Lk 11⁵¹ (ins. DS^c and 2 cursives). The name occurs in Mt. in a passage, recorded in substantial agreement by Mt. and Lk., in which the Lord declares that the blood of all the prophets (Lk.) or all the righteous blood (Mt.) will be sought from or come upon that generation, from the blood of Abel to the blood of Zachariah. In 2 Ch 24²⁰ᶠᶠ· is an account of the stoning of Zechariah the son of Jehoiada (LXX B has 'Azariah' for 'Zechariah,' but Lagarde prints 'Zechariah') in the court of the house of the Lord. This incident is repeatedly referred to in the later Jewish literature. In the Babylonian Talmud (*Sanh.* 96b ; *Gittin*, 57b), in the Jerusalem Talmud (*Taanith*, 69a), and in the Midrashim (*e.g. Echa Rabbati*, Introd. ׳ס ii. 2 ; *Koheleth* iii. 16 ; *Pesikta Rab. Kahana* xv.) it is recorded that Nebuzaradan slew many Jews in order to quiet 'the blood of Zechariah, who is called a prophet' (*Sanh.* 96b ; Midr. *Echa R.*, *Koheleth*) with reference to 2 Ch 24¹⁹. It seems natural, therefore, to suppose that the Zachariah of the Gospels is the Zechariah of 2 Chronicles. Abel's was the first murder of a righteous man recorded in the OT, Zechariah's the last (2 Chron. is the last book of the Hebrew Canon). Abel's blood cried from the ground (Gn 4¹⁰). Zechariah when dying said, 'The Lord look upon it and require it' (2 Ch 24²²).

But how are we to account for Mt.'s 'son of

Barachiah,' when we should expect son of Jehoiada'? In Is 8[2] we read of Zechariah 'son of Jeberechiah' (the LXX has υἱὸν Βαραχίου), in Zec 1[1] of Zechariah the son of Berechiah the son of Iddo (LXX, τὸν τοῦ Βαραχίου υἱὸν 'Αδδώ). The later Jewish tradition identified the two. So the Babylonian Talmud (Makkoth, 24b; cf. Pesiḳta Rab. Kahana xv., Targum of Is 8[2], Rashi on Is 8[2]). Further, there seems to have been a tendency to identify Zechariah son of Berechiah son of Iddo with Zechariah son of Jehoiada, for the Targum of La 3[20] calls the Zechariah of Chronicles 'son of Iddo.' We might therefore suppose that Christ spoke of Zechariah, who was really son of Jehoiada, as son of Barachiah, because the Jewish tradition of His age identified or confused the priest and the prophet; cf. the 'priest and prophet' applied to Zechariah son of Jehoiada in Sanh. 97b. In this case the omission of υἱοῦ Βαραχίου from Mt 23[35] in א* would be due to someone who wondered at the 'Barachiah' instead of 'Jehoiada.' Or the 'son of Barachiah' might be an insertion on the part of the editor of the Gospel, either on the ground of Jewish tradition, or in remembrance of the two LXX passages, Is 8[2], Zec 1[1]. The fact that this editor elsewhere employs LXX forms of proper names, as in 'Ασάφ, 'Αμώς (1[8. 10]), is in favour of the latter. Or 'son of Barachiah' may be a later insertion in the Gospel (so Merx). The insertion of the clause in Western texts in Lk. is due to assimilation to the text of Matthew.

The difficulty of the appearance of 'Barachiah' in Mt. has led to other and less probable identifications. Origen (de la Rue, iv. 845) supposed that Zacharias the father of John the Baptist was referred to, and quotes a tradition that this Zacharias was murdered in the temple. Cf. the Protev. Jacobi, 23, 24, which has a different account of the cause of the murder. Others refer to Jos. BJ IV. v. 4, where it is recorded that shortly before the last siege of Jerusalem one Zacharias the son of Baruch or Bariscaeus was murdered in the temple by the Zealots. It is therefore argued that the Evangelist has either blundered by writing 'of Barachiah' in reminiscence of this event, when he should have written 'of Jehoiada,' or that he is responsible for the whole of the clause in which this phrase occurs, and has put into Christ's mouth an anachronistic statement. But, apart from the difference between the Βαραχίου of the Gospels and the Βαρούχου or Βάρεις- or Βαρισχαίου of Josephus, the reference to 2 Chron. seems to satisfy the data better. The reckoning from Abel to Zechariah is Jewish in character, the 'of Barachiah' may be due to Jewish tradition, and the 'between the temple and the altar' is perhaps also due to current Jewish speculation or tradition. In the Jerusalem Talmud (Taanith 69a) the question is raised where Zechariah was killed, with the answer that it was in the court of the priests (cf. also the same tradition in Midr. Ḳoheleth iii. 16, Pesiḳta R. Kahana xv., Echa Rabbati, Introd. נ).

LITERATURE.—Lightfoot, Horæ Hebraicæ; Merx, Die vier Evangelien; Wellhausen and Zahn in their commentaries on Matthew.

W. C. ALLEN.

BAR-JONA(H).—See PETER.

BARLEY.—In the Gospels, barley is mentioned only in the account given by St. John (6[5-14]) of the miraculous feeding of the five thousand with five barley loaves and two fishes. The word occurs twice (vv.[9. 13]), and in both cases represents the adjectival form κρίθινος in the original. The noun κριθή (in ordinary Gr. usage almost invariably in the plur. κριθαί), which is employed in the LXX to render the Heb. שְׂעֹרָה, occurs only once in NT (Rev 6[6]). Barley was one of the most important of Biblical food - products. According to the elder

Pliny (HN xviii. 72), it was the most ancient nutriment of mankind. It certainly dates back to a very remote antiquity. It was cultivated by the Canaanites prior to the time of the Hebrew conquest (Dt 8[8]), and by the ancient Egyptians, as appears from Ex 9[31] and from the representations on the oldest Egyptian monuments. Among the Jews it was used for making bread (Ezk 4[9]), and it seems to have been the principal food of the poorer classes (Ru 2[17] 3[15], 1 K 4[22], Jn 6[9]). This is confirmed by Jg 7[13], where a cake of barley-bread is the symbol of an army of peasants, and is also in accordance with modern usage. Thus Dr. Thomson says: 'Barley bread is only eaten by the poor and the unfortunate. Nothing is more common than for these people, at this day, to complain that their oppressors have left them nothing but barley bread to eat' (Land and Book [1878 ed.], p. 449). He also mentions that the Bedawîn often ridicule their enemies by calling them 'eaters of barley bread' (l.c.). Barley was also grown as a forage crop. Its employment as provender for horses is mentioned in 1 K 4[28], and the chopped straw from the threshing-floor was likewise used as fodder. This practice continues to the present day, oats and hay being unknown.

In Palestine the normal time for sowing barley is about the beginning of October: when the winter is exceptionally cold and wet, sowing takes place early in February. In the Jordan Valley, the harvest begins in April, but it varies according to the elevation of the different regions. At the highest altitudes the crop is not ripe till July or even August.　　　　　　　　　HUGH DUNCAN.

BARN.—The same word (ἀποθήκη) is rendered 'barn' in Mt 6[26] 13[30], Lk 12[18. 24], and 'garner' in Mt 3[12], Lk 3[17]. In Græco-Roman times, buildings above ground were probably in use. καθαιρέω, 'to pull down' (Lk 12[18]) could apply only to such. But from ancient times until now Palestinian farmers have stored their grain in cistern-like pits. These are dug in dry places, often out of the solid rock, carefully cemented to keep out damp, with a circular opening at the top, through which a man may pass. When the mouth is plastered over and made air-tight, the corn will keep sound for several years. For security in a lawless country, the 'barn' is sometimes under the floor of the inmost part of the house, that of the women (cf. 2 S 4[6]). To escape the tax-gatherer, again, it is frequently made in a secluded spot, and so skilfully turfed over that discovery is almost impossible (cf. Jer 41[8]). Pits found near ruined sites, in districts that have lain desolate for ages, prove the antiquity of this method. Natural caves in the limestone rock, improved by art, with heavy stone doors blocking the entrance, have also served as 'barns,' and may be seen in use at Gadara to-day.　　　W. EWING.

BARTHOLOMEW (Βαρθολομαῖος) appears as an apostle in all four lists of the Twelve (Mt 10[3], Mk 3[18], Lk 6[14], Ac 1[13]), always in the second of three groups of four. In the Gospels he comes next after Philip (who in all four lists heads the second quaternion), and is followed by Matthew and Thomas: in Acts the order is 'Philip and Thomas, Bartholomew and Matthew.' The name, as the first syllable indicates, is a patronymic, and it is commonly interpreted 'son of Talmai.' In the LXX Talmai has many variants (Θολμί, Θολμεί, Θαλαμεί, Θολομεί, Θολμαίλημμ): and in Josephus (Ant. xx. i. 1) we have a bandit chief named Θολομαῖος. It is often assumed that 'Talmai' represents 'Ptolemy,' and that Bartholomew means 'son of Ptolemy'; but the Θ is against this. Edersheim (Messiah, i. p. 521) makes it mean 'son of Telamyon.' Bartholomew may be either a genuine patronymic used in addition to a proper name, like Simon Bar-jona ; or it may have become an independent proper name, like Barnabas. If the apostle Bartholomew had no other name, we know nothing about him from Scripture, and the later traditions about him are very untrustworthy (Lipsius, *Apokryphen Apostelgeschichten und Apostellegenden*, iii. pp. 54–108). These traditions begin with Eusebius (*HE* v. x. 3), and ascribe to him widely different fields of missionary labour, with different apostles as his companions, and different forms of martyrdom. He is often made to be one of the Seventy.*

But both by the early Church and by most modern writers Bartholomew is commonly identified with Nathanael. To treat this as almost certain (Schaff-Herzog) is to go beyond the evidence ; to call it 'the merest conjecture' (*Encyc. Bibl.*) is to err in the opposite direction.

In favour of the identification are the following points. (1) Bartholomew being a patronymic, the bearer may easily have had another name ; (2) the Synoptists never mention Nathanael, St. John never mentions Bartholomew ; (3) the Synoptists in their lists place Bartholomew next to Philip, as James next to his probable caller John, and Peter (in Mt. and Lk.) next to his caller Andrew ; (4) all the other disciples mentioned in Jn 1[38-52] became apostles, and none of them is so commended as Nathanael ; (5) all the companions of Nathanael who are named in Jn 21[2] are apostles. But all these reasons do not make the identification more than probable. St. John nowhere calls Nathanael an apostle, and we are not obliged to find room for him among the Twelve. The conjecture that he is Matthew or Matthias (Hilgenfeld) is supported by no reasonable evidence ; and that he is John himself under a symbolical name (Späth) is contradicted by Jn 21[2], where the sons of Zebedee are mentioned in addition to Nathanael.

On the other hand, there is nothing against the identification : it creates no difficulty. To say that a Galilæan would have remembered Is 9[1], and therefore would not have asked whether any good could come out of Nazareth, is unsound criticism. A person with Is 9[1] in his mind, and convinced that rich blessings would come from Galilee, might nevertheless think that Nazareth was not a likely place to be the dwelling-place of the Messiah. And who can tell whether a particular Galilæan would or would not remember a particular text?

LITERATURE.—In addition to the works cited above, reference may be made to artt. 'Bartholomew' and 'Nathanael' in Hastings' *DB* ; and to Garrett Horder, *The Poet's Bible*, NT, p. 102 ff.   A. PLUMMER.

BARTIMÆUS (Βαρτίμαιος).—Named only in Mk 10[46-52], where he is described as a blind beggar who was cured by Jesus as He left Jericho on His last journey to Jerusalem. But there can be little doubt that we have also accounts of the same miracle in the closely parallel narratives Mt 20[29-34], Lk 18[35-43]. There are, however, various divergences between the three narratives which have caused difficulty. Thus St. Matthew, while agreeing with St. Mark that the miracle took place on the Lord's *departure from* Jericho, speaks of *two* blind men as having been healed ; but St. Luke, reverting to the mention of a *single* sufferer, says his cure took place as the Lord *drew nigh to* the city. And again, while St. Mark is content to describe the healing as the result of a word of comfort, 'Go thy way, thy faith hath made thee whole,' St. Matthew tells us that it was effected by a touch, 'Jesus . . . touched their eyes' ; and St. Luke

* On the possibility that there was *another* Bartholomew, identical with the apostle Matthias, among the Seventy, see note by Dr. Nestle in *Expos. Times*, ix. [1898] p. 566 f.

assigns it to a direct command, 'Receive thy sight.' The divergences, no doubt, are very considerable, and have taxed the ingenuity of the harmonists both in ancient and modern times. Thus it has been supposed that St. Matthew combines the cure of one blind man at the entrance into Jericho (so St. Luke) with the cure of another at the departure from Jericho (so St. Mark), or that Bartimæus, begging at the gate, became aware of Jesus' entrance into the city, and, seeking out a blind companion, along with him intercepted the Saviour the next day as He was leaving Jericho, and was then healed. But it cannot be said that any such explanations are very satisfactory. And it is better simply to content ourselves with noting the divergences between the three accounts as an additional proof of the independence of the Evangelists in matters of detail, without, however, abandoning our belief in the general trustworthiness of their narratives. There are few miracles, indeed, in the Gospel story better vouched for than the one before us, authenticated as it is by the triple Synoptic tradition and by the preciseness of the details, while the very mention of the name of the healed man has been regarded as a proof that he must still have been known in the time of the Apostles ('valde notus Apostolorum tempore Bartimæus,' Bengel).

It has been conjectured, indeed, that *Bartimæus* is not really a proper name, but a designation derived from an Aramaic root *samya*, 'blind,' so that 'Bartimæus the son of Timæus' might mean no more than 'the blind son of a blind father' (see Lightfoot, *Hor. Heb.* on Mk 10[46] ; and for the various derivations that have been proposed, Keim, *Jesus of Nazara*, Eng. tr. v. p. 61 f.). But the word, as St. Mark interprets it for us, is clearly a patronymic (cf. Βαρθολομαῖος), and the defining clause ὁ υἱὸς Τιμαίου is quite in the style of the Second Evangelist, though it is placed before the patronymic and not after it as usually (cf., however, v.[48] ; and see Swete, *St. Mark*, p. 228).

It is unnecessary to recall further the details of the Gospel narrative ; but, from whatever point of view we regard it, it is full of instruction. Thus, in the case of Bartimæus himself, we have a notable instance of a *determination* that resolved to let no opportunity of being healed escape it ; of a *perseverance* that continued its efforts notwithstanding the difficulties placed in its path ; of an *eagerness* that cast off all that hindered its free approach ; of a *faith* that recognized in Jesus the Divinely-appointed Messiah ('Thou Son of David') before and not after the cure ; and of a *thankfulness* that showed itself in ready obedience and triumphant praise when the cure was complete ('followed him, glorifying God'). And if thus the narrative has much to tell us regarding Bartimæus, no less does it throw a vivid light on the character of our Lord Himself, when we remember the *sympathy* with which, notwithstanding His own approaching sufferings, He regarded the beggar's cry ; the *readiness* with which He placed Himself at his disposal ('What wilt thou . . . ?') ; and the saving *power* with which He bestowed on the sufferer even more than he asked.

LITERATURE.—In addition to the relative sections in the well-known works on our Lord's *Miracles* by Trench, Laidlaw, and W. M. Taylor, see, for the above and other homiletic details, S. Cox, *Biblical Expositions*, pp. 155–167, and *The Miracles of Jesus* by Various Authors (J. Robinson, Manchester). We may refer also to Longfellow's poem 'Blind Bartimæus.'
                GEORGE MILLIGAN.

BASKET.—All four Evangelists, in narrating the miracle of the feeding of the *five* thousand, describe the baskets in which the fragments were placed as κόφινοι (Mt 14[20] = Mk 6[43] = Lk 9[17] = Jn 6[13]) ; while the two who report the other miracle of feeding the *four* thousand, state that the fragments were placed in σπυρίδες (Mt 15[37] = Mk 8[8]). It is clear from Mt 16[9f.] (= Mk 8[19f.]) that the variation is intentional. The baskets used on the one occasion differed either in size, shape, or material from those used on the other (cf. RVm in Mt 16[9f.] and

Mk 8[19f.]). Our Lord preserved the distinction, and our present Gospels have also done so.

'Basket' occurs in the EV Gospels in the above passages only. The older English versions use the confusing rendering of 'baskets' for both words, except that Wyclif has 'coffyns' and 'leepis.' By 'coffyn' he evidently meant a small basket. Rheims renders σπυρίδων, 'maundes,' i.e. hand-baskets. Davidson (NT, 1875) at Mk 8[19. 20] has 'basketfuls' for κοφίνους and 'walletsful' for σπυρίδων, as if he had found σηρῶν.

The authors of such renderings as the above forgot that St. Paul (Ac 9[25]) made his escape in a σπυρίς. This fact at once excludes wallets or handbaskets. If the distinction was one of size at all, which is not certain, we should perhaps have to assume that the σπυρίς was the larger. Bevan (Smith's DB[1] i. 172) says that the κόφινος was the larger, quoting Etym. Mag., βαθὺ καὶ κοῖλον χώρημα, and the use of cophinus in Latin, e.g. Colum. xi. 3, p. 460, as containing manure enough to make a hotbed. Greswell (Diss. viii. pt. 4, vol. ii.) thought that the cophinus was big enough to sleep in. He probably misunderstood the passage in Juvenal quoted below; for though the hay may have been used as a bed, it is not said that it was in the cophinus. Nor is it clear that the Latin cophinus and the Greek κόφινος were at all times identical in meaning (so the French balle is not a cannonball but a musket bullet, while our cannon-ball is a boulet). Let us examine the two words more closely.

(1) κόφινος is said to be derived from κόπτω; but this appears to be more than doubtful, and the grammarians considered it less Attic than ἄρριχος, which was clearly a wicker or flag basket. In the Gr. OT it is used by LXX and Symm. for Heb. dúd in Ps 80 [81][6], and by Symm. only in Jer 24[1. 2] (where LXX has κάλαθος); and for sal by Aq. in Gn 40[16] (where LXX has κανᾶ). Certainly in the two latter passages a small basket, carried in the hand, or on the head, would suit the contexts. Suidas defines κ. as ἀγγεῖον πλεκτόν. In CIG 1625, lines 44–46, it is clearly a corn-basket of a recognized size; cf. also CIG 2347 k. In Xen. Anab. iii. 8. 6 it occurs as a dung-basket (see the Latin cophinus in Columella, as cited above). It is said that the Jews at Rome carried cophini about with them to avoid the chance of food contracting any Levitical pollution in heathen places. The reason given appears fanciful, and anyhow would hardly apply to the journeys of our Lord and His apostles. But the fact is vouched for by Juvenal (Sat. iii. 14 : 'Judæis, quorum cophinus fœnumque supellex'; vi. 542 : 'Cophino fœnoque relicto | Arcanam Judæa tremens mendicat in aurem') and Martial (Epig. v. 7).

(2) σπυρίς (or σφυρίς, as WH prefer) is not found in the LXX. It is generally connected with σπύρα = anything twisted (Vulg. sporta, of which the diminutives sportella and sportula occur, as small fruit- or provision-baskets). Hesychius explains σπυρίς as τὸ τῶν πυρῶν ἄγγος, as though from πυρός; cf. δεῖπνον ἀπὸ σπυρίδος (Athenæus, viii. 17). Hence Greswell thought that before Pentecost, the season of wheat harvest, when the second miracle took place, the disciples were able to use corn-baskets, while the first miracle happening before Passover time, they used another kind of basket! Besides the improbability of this, we may note that there is no proof that in either case the baskets belonged to or were carried about by the disciples, for they may have been borrowed when needed. Yet Trench (Miracles, p. 380 note 2) inquires why the apostles should have been provided with either kind, and mentions (a) that perhaps they carried their provisions with them while travelling through a polluted land, such as Samaria (yet cf. Jn 4[8] 4[31] 4[40], Lk 9[52]); and (b) he also mentions Greswell's theory, that the disciples carried these baskets in order to sleep in them sub dio. This all comes from applying to the Twelve in the Holy Land what Roman satirists said about Jewish beggars at Rome.

As σπυρίς in Ac 9[25] = σαργάνη in 2 Co 11[33], and as the Vulg. has sporta in both places (and also in the Gospels for σπυρίς but not for κόφινος), we are led to inquire as to the force of σαργάνη. It is used of anything twisted like a rope, or woven of rope (Æsch. Suppl. 791—πλέγμα τι ἐκ σχοινίων, Suid.). Fish-baskets were specially so made (ἀπὸ σχοινίων πλεγμάτων εἰς ὑποδοχὴν ἰχθύων, Etym. Mag.), as rush-baskets are called in London.

Meyer considered the difference between σπυρίς and κόφινος to lie not in size, but in κόφινος being a general term, and σπυρίς specially a food-basket. Perhaps the true force of the words we have discussed is to be discovered in the use made of them by Greek-speaking working people at the present day. The writer of this article has therefore consulted a Greek priest, the Rev. H. A. Teknopoulos. In his reply he says : 'In Asia Minor and in Constantinople our porters call κόφινος that big and deep basket in which they carry different things.

Σπυρίς is a smaller and round and shallow basket. Σαργάνη is a long bag, knitted by (i.e. of) rope, which is in one way very like the δίκτυον of fish, but is different from it in other way(s).'

One might ask whether the σπυρίς of Ac 9[25] is not an error of memory on the part of St. Luke. St. Paul in his own account of his escape would surely use the right word. If so, the supposed need for a σπυρίς being big enough to hold a person disappears, and we may accept the decision of those who consider it the smaller of the two kinds mentioned in the Gospels.

GEORGE FARMER.

BASON* (νιπτήρ only in Jn 13[5] εἶτα βάλλει ὕδωρ εἰς τὸν νιπτῆρα : Vulg. deinde mittit aquam in pelvim : AV 'after that he poureth water into a bason' : RV 'then he poureth water into the bason ').

The Gr. νιπτήρ is not found elsewhere in NT, nor in LXX, nor in Gr. profane literature (except in Eccl. writers dealing with this passage). Hence Liddell and Scott, s.v., refer only to this instance. The Vulg. pelvis, though found in Juvenal, etc., occurs in the Bible only in Jer 52[19].

The general sense of νιπτήρ is, of course, plain, both from the context and from the cognate verbs νίπτειν and νίζειν both in the Bible and in profane Greek. (The former is the Biblical form, 17 times in NT, including our passage (8 times), and 25 times in LXX). It is usually 'to wash a part of the body' —e.g. the face, Mt 6[17]; the hands, Mt 15[2] = Mk 7[5]; the feet, 1 Ti 5[10],—so Ex 30[18. 19] etc. Jn 9[7. 11. 15] seem to be exceptions, because the washing was in the Pool of Siloam ; but here it is only the eyes that are concerned, and therefore we need not assume that the man 'bathed.' A real exception is Lv 15[12], where the wooden vessel νιφήσεται ; but note contrasted use of νίπτειν, πλύνειν, and λούεσθαι in 15[11].

The noun νιπτήρ therefore denotes an article (not necessarily a vessel) specially suitable or intended for use in washing part of the body. We note the article τὸν νιπτῆρα, neglected by AV (a bason) but noticed by RV (the bason). Was it the ordinary νιπτήρ of the house? In that case the use of the article is like that in τὸν μόδιον, τὴν λυχνίαν in Mt 5[15] etc. Or was it a vessel set apart for ceremonial ablution, such as would be required by the religious feast in which they were engaged?

But, in spite of the Vulg. and modern versions, it is doubtful if the word 'bason' conveys to us a good idea of the article and of the scene.

The Eastern mode of washing either hands or feet, when performed by an attendant, seems to have been always by the attendant pouring water on the member, not by dipping the member in the water. Cf. 2 K 3[11] 'Elisha the son of Shaphat, which poured water on the hands of Elijah.' Kitto's note in Pictorial Bible[2], ii. 330, with two illustrations, is convincing on this point.

'The Hebrews were accustomed to wash their hands in the manner which is now universal in the East, and which, whatever may be thought of its convenience, is unquestionably more refreshing and cleanly than washing in the water as it stands in a basin—which is a process regarded by Orientals with great disgust. The hands are therefore held over a basin, the use of which is only to receive the water which has been poured upon the hands from the jug or ewer which is held above them. This cannot very conveniently be managed without the aid of a servant or some other person.'

Of course, this extract refers only to the washing of hands.

(1) The incident of the sinful woman who wept over our Lord's feet, and wiped them with the hairs of her head (Lk 7[37. 38]), is much better explained by comparing her action with that of the host or his servant pouring water on a guest's feet, than by supposing that the guest immersed his feet in a footbath (Lk 7[44]). (2) It is true that ποδανιπτήρ is found in Pollux, Onom. x. 78, but here

* In the appendix to Revised OT of 'Readings and Renderings preferred by the American Revisers,' § viii., we read : 'The modern spelling is preferred for the following words : "basin" for "bason,"' etc., but no such note appears in the appendix to Revised NT.

a definition of the νιπτήρ is contained in the word. 'Basins' are such common articles, that if St. John had meant to name one he need not have used an unique word. (3) The position of the Apostles and of the guests at the feast of Lk 7 was a reclining one. This would not be compatible with the use of a basin or footbath in the ordinary sense of even partially immersing the foot. (4) Dr. A. R. S. Kennedy (art. 'Bath, Bathing' in Hastings' DB i. 257ᵇ) shows that 'affusion, pouring on' of water, was probably meant in many cases where we read 'bathe' or 'wash.'

We therefore think that the νιπτήρ was a jug or ewer, with a dish, saucer or basin, under it to catch the drippings, but that the stress of the word is *not* on this under-basin. We also think that it was kept chiefly in the house, and used for the many 'hand-washings' which the Jews practised (Mt 15², Mk 7³ etc.), but also for any ceremonial ablution. Hence it was ready in the upper room, as part of the preparation made by the 'goodman of the house' (Mk 14¹⁵, Lk 22¹²), and therefore is distinguished by the article.

It may be asked whether the feet-washing in Jn 13 was ceremonial. As we understand the matter, the Galilæan disciples, either because they had never adopted the Pharisaic strictness about 'washings,' or (less probably) because our Lord had condemned them, were not in the habit of observing them (Mt 15², Mk 7¹·⁴). Our Lord defended His followers (Mk 7⁵·²³, Mt 15³·²⁰). In the upper room they found all things ready for the observance. Whether they did observe it before a meal which was not an ordinary one, we do not know. But there was another observance, not of ceremony but of courtesy and comfort (Lk 7⁴⁴), in which each might have acted as host or as servant the other if the spirit of love had ruled in their hearts. Christ would teach them this lesson (Jn 13¹²·¹⁶). Incidentally He taught them other lessons, which they could not fully understand at the time, about the cleansing of the soul, daily defilement, and the duty of preparation before receiving the Eucharist. In this Christian sense the feet-washing *was* ceremonial, or rather typical, but it was *not* a recognition of any validity in the 'traditions of the elders.' The main lessons for the time were those of humility, self-abasement, and love. Our Lord used the νιπτήρ standing by to teach these.

Kitto (*Pictorial Bible*², ii. 331) says : 'In the East, the basin, which, as well as the ewer, is usually of tinned copper, has commonly a sort of cover, rising in the middle, and sunk into the basin at the margin, which, being pierced with holes, allows the water to pass through, thus concealing it after being defiled by use. The ewer has a long spout, and a long narrow neck, with a cover, and is altogether not unlike our coffee-pots in general appearance : it is *the same which the Orientals use in all their ablutions.*'

We notice that the assistance of a servant or of a friend is necessary. This is sometimes mentioned, *e.g.* 1 Ti 5¹⁰, 1 S 25⁴¹, and is probably implied in Gn 18⁴ 19² 24³² etc. But in the cases where the English versions suggest nothing of the kind, the Heb. is the Ḳal of רחץ as in 1 S 25⁴¹ (cf. Dr. Kennedy's article cited above).

Lane's account (*Modern Egyptians*, ch. 5) is similar : 'A servant brings him a basin and ewer (called *tisht* and *ibreek*) of tinned copper or brass. The former of these has a cover pierced with holes, with a raised receptacle for the soap in the middle ; and the water being poured upon the hands, passes through this cover into the space below, so that when the basin is brought to a second person the water with which the former one has washed is not seen.'

Our conclusion therefore is that the νιπτήρ was most probably not a 'large basin,' but the set of ewer and basin combined, kept in every Jewish house for the purpose of cleansing either the hands or the feet by means of affusion.

Dr. Anton Tien,* in a full communication to the writer of this article, which we abridge, says *tesht* is the most correct render-

* Oriental Secretary to Lord Raglan during the Crimean War, translator of the Turkish Prayer-Book, and reviser of the Arabic Prayer-Book, author of Turkish, Arabic, and Modern Greek Grammars.

ing of νιπτήρ. The Bible Society's Arabic NT has *maghsal*, a noun of time and place = 'washing' and 'a place for washing,' not a correct rendering. The SPCK version has *mathar* (cf. Heb. מטהר)= 'purification,' 'place *or* time of purification,' also an incorrect rendering. The word *tesht* is the exact rendering of the Gr. word νιπτήρ. It comes from a root= 'to pour *or* rain slightly.'

The *tesht* and *ibreeq* are made of either metal or earthenware, with a strainer of the same material placed inside the *tesht* (or basin), never outside or under, and in the middle of the strainer there is a small raised place for the soap. The *ibreeq* (Syrian and Egyptian Arabic) is a water-jug, with a spout for the water to come through like a coffee-pot, from which the water is poured on the hands or feet, which are held over the basin. They are to be found in every Eastern house, especially in Mohammedan houses ; they are used continually in the mornings. There are no washstands in the houses. The servant holds the *tesht* on the palm of his left hand and the *ibreek* in his right hand, and a clean towel placed on his left shoulder for each person (Jn 13⁴), who washes his face and hands, taking the towel from off the servant's shoulder. The towel is thrown down, and the servant puts a fresh one for the next person to use.   GEORGE FARMER.

BATH, BATHING.—The immersing or washing of the whole person may be a matter of cleanliness, or of luxury, or of religious observance, or of health.

(1) Cleanliness *per se* may be set aside. It is possible to be cleanly with less elaborate apparatus ; and the majority in OT (or even NT) times would have 'neither privacy nor inclination' for bathing. (2) Luxury in the classical world (diffused even among the people, under Roman influence, at least subsequently to NT times) included plunge-baths and much besides. When Greek culture tried to invade Judæa under Antiochus Epiphanes (*c.* 168 B.C.), it doubtless brought Greek bathing establishments with it. And when Western culture came in resistlessly under Herod (B.C. 40–4), it must have introduced the practice in many places ; cf. an anecdote of Gamaliel II. in Schürer, *HJP* II. i. 18, 53. (3) Religious observance, under OT law, according to Professor Kennedy (art. 'Bath, Bathing' in Hastings' *DB* i. 257ᵇ), required a partial washing, or a washing *with* water rather than bathing. 'The Heb. of the OT does not distinguish' between bathing and a partial washing. 'Both are expressed by רחץ.' However, Schürer insists that Talmudic usage codifies the custom which had long been in vogue ; and Kennedy grants that 'the bath became,' even 'for the laity . . . an all-important factor in the religious life.' Nay, proselyte baptism must be earlier than the NT, and it requires a bath, *ṭĕbilāh* (*ṭābal* is used in one unambiguous OT passage, the miracle of Naaman's cleansing, 2 K 5¹⁴). We hear also of daily bathing among the Essenes (Jos. *BJ* II. viii. 5). And, finally, John's baptism was by immersion (as was that also of the early Christian Church, Ac 8³⁸, Ro 6³·⁴). (4) The use of mineral baths for health's sake is always popular. There are remains of such baths near Tiberias ; those at Gadara and at Callirrhoë were very celebrated in ancient times. Jn 5²·⁷ gives us an example of such bathing, though Christ's miracle dispensed with the waters of Bethesda. In another passage (Jn 9⁷) we have a partial washing (at the Pool of Siloam) as a stage towards completion of a miracle.

Thus bathing was well enough known in NT times. Our Lord's language in Jn 13¹⁰ turns on the distinction between *bathing* (the whole person) and *washing* (the feet). Quite conceivably a Christian sacrament might have grown out of this incident. Nothing is more impressive at Oberammergau than the threefold journey of the Christus round the company—so it is represented—ministering to the disciples (1) the feet-washing, (2) the bread, (3) the cup. See, further, artt. BASON, PURIFICATION.   ROBERT MACKINTOSH.

BATH ḲOL.—See VOICE.

BEACH.—The RV tr. of αἰγιαλός, which the AV

renders 'shore.' In the Gospels the word occurs only in Mt 13² ⁴⁸ and Jn 21⁴. In classical Greek αἰγιαλός usually, though not always, means that part of the seashore on which the tide ebbs and flows, and in the above passages in the Gospels it stands for the sandy or pebbly part of the shore of the Lake of Galilee washed by the waves. The derivation is doubtful, but is probably from ἄγνυμι and ἅλς, i.e. the place where the sea breaks. The greater part of the western margin of the Lake of Galilee is girdled with a belt of 'silver strand' composed of pebbles and sand mingled with delicate white shells. On such a beach, if the traditional scene be correct, the multitude was gathered listening as Jesus spoke from the boat; and on such a 'beach' He stood waiting for the disciples to come ashore in the morning, when for 'the third time he was manifested to them after that he was risen from the dead' (Jn 21¹⁴).   J. CROMARTY SMITH.

BEAM AND MOTE.—The proverb of the 'beam' and the 'mote' occurs in Mt 7³⁻⁵ and in the parallel passage Lk 6⁴¹˙ ⁴². It condemns the man who looks at the 'mote' in another's eye while a 'beam' unconsidered is in his own; and it points out the futility and hypocrisy of the attempt to cast out the mote from the eye of a brother while the beam remains in one's own eye. The proverb appears to have been current in various forms among Jews and Arabs. Tholuck, in his Commentary on the Sermon on the Mount, gives several illustrations; e.g. from the *Baba Bathra*: 'In the days when the judges were judged themselves, said the judge to one of them, Take the splinter out of thine eye; whereat he made reply, Take thou the beam out of thine eye'; and from Meidani (*ap.* Freytag): 'How seest thou the splinter in thy brother's eye and seest not the cross-beam in thine eye?'

There is no obscurity in the terms used. The word δοκός is common in classical writers for a beam of wood, and is used in the LXX (Gn 19⁸, 1 K 6², Ca 1¹⁷) to translate קוֹרָה, a beam used in the roof of a house. Grimm-Thayer derives from δέκομαι Ion. for δέχομαι with the idea of *bearing*, so that δοκός is that which supports a building. So Plummer ('St. Luke' in *Internat. Crit. Com.*) says: 'The δοκός is the bearing beam, the main beam, that which receives the other beams in a roof or floor.' A. B. Bruce ('St. Matthew' in *Expositor's Greek Test.*) says: 'δοκός, a wooden beam ('let in,' from δέχομαι) or joist.' Clearly a large piece of timber is suggested, such as could not literally be in the eye. The symbol has the touch of exaggeration familiar in Oriental proverbs, as, e.g., in the camel and the needle's eye.

The 'mote' (τὸ κάρφος, from κάρφω, 'to contract,' 'dry up,' 'wither') may be a dry stalk or twig, or any small dry body. The word is used in the LXX (Gn 8¹¹) to render עָלֶה, the adj. applied to the olive-leaf brought by the dove. Weymouth (*NT in Modern Speech*) renders 'speck.'

It is clear, therefore, that the point of the proverb lies in the contrast between a smaller fault in the person criticised and a greater one in the critic. The figures chosen express the contrast in a very emphatic way, pushing it, indeed, to the verge of absurdity, to suggest the essential folly of the unbrotherly and insincere faultfinder.

Various illustrations are given by commentators of the possibly greater defect of the man who is finding fault with his neighbour. Morison, e.g., quotes Augustine as comparing 'settled hatred' (the beam) with a passing burst of anger (the mote). A. B. Bruce (*l.c.*) says: 'The faults may be of the same kind: κάρφος a petty theft, δοκός commercial dishonesty on a large scale . . . ; or a

different sort: moral laxity in the publican, pride and inhumanity in the Pharisee who despised him.'

All such illustrations are to the point, for the proverb is capable of many applications; and it is very often true that men eager to correct others have great and obvious faults of their own which disqualify them for the office. It seems clear, however, that 'the beam' is very definitely the censorious spirit. Our passage, as it stands in St. Matthew, follows immediately upon the general exhortation 'judge not,' and the warning, 'with what measure ye mete it shall be measured unto you.' There is a spirit which sees and notes faults in others where true goodness would be blind. The 'beholding' is in the judgment of Jesus often a much greater evil than the fault it beholds. Such a spirit leads a man on to the officious attempt to correct others, and makes him doubly unfit for the task. To cast out the mote from another's eye is always difficult. It needs clear sight and wonderful delicacy of touch. To the censorious man, blind in his fancied superiority, it is of all tasks the most impossible. Moreover, the censorious spirit is closely akin to hypocrisy. It pretends to zeal for righteousness, but really cares only for personal superiority. A sincere man begins with that humble self-judgment which is fatal to uncharitable judgments of others. A zeal for righteousness which *begins* with correction of others stands convicted of dishonesty at the outset. If a man has once taken the true ground of lowly penitence, if he has cast out the proud, self-sufficient, censorious spirit, he will leave no other beam unnoticed in his own eye. He will be too much occupied with the task of self-discipline to be the quick and eager censor of others. Yet he will not be blind to moral distinctions. On the contrary, the single eye will be full of light; and while he will have no wish to 'behold' the mote in his brother's, he will see clearly to cast it out. Love and pride are both quick to observe; but with what different results!

In St. Luke's Gospel our passage stands in a slightly different connexion. There the command 'judge not' is separated from the proverb of the Mote and the Beam by the verses which speak of the reward of generous giving, of blind leaders of the blind, of the disciple not above his master. A. B. Bruce suggests that the parable comes in at this point, because censoriousness is a natural fault of young disciples. In any case the essential meaning of the passage remains unchanged.

LITERATURE.—Dykes, *Manifesto of the King*, 536 ff.; Dale, *Laws of Christ for Common Life*, 93 ff.

E. H. TITCHMARSH.

BEATITUDE.—

   i. Derivation and Meaning.
   ii. Significance of μακάριος.
   iii. The NT Beatitudes.
      1. Single Sayings.
      2. The Group of Sayings.
   iv. The 'Beatitudes' in Matthew and Luke.
      1. Their number in Matthew.
      2. The relation of the two versions.
      3. Order and connexion of thought.

i. DERIVATION AND MEANING.—The Latin word *beatitudo* is derived from *beātus*, the past participle of *beāre*, 'to make happy,' 'to bless' (cf. *bene* and *bonus*). Trench says that *beatitas* and *beatitudo* are both words of Cicero's coining; yet, 'as he owns himself, with something strange and unattractive about them.'* On this account they 'found almost no acceptance at all in the classical literature of Rome. *Beatitudo*, indeed, found a

* The only passage in which Cicero appears to use the two words is *de Natura Deorum*, i. 34: '*Ista sive beatitas, sive beatitudo dicenda sunt (utrumque omnino durum, sed usu mollienda nobis verba sunt).*'

home, as it deserved to do, in the Christian Church, but *beatitas* none' (*Study of Words*[18], p. 210).

The primary meaning of 'beatitude' is *blessedness*. In the earliest example of its use quoted in Murray's *Dictionary* (1491, Caxton), it signifies supreme blessedness ; hence it was frequently used to describe the bliss of heaven. Cf. Milton, *Par. Lost*, iii. 62—

> 'About Him all the Sanctities of Heaven
> Stood thick as stars, and from His sight received
> Beatitude past utterance.'

Trapp applies the word to 'such as are set out of the reach of evil in the most joyous condition, having just cause to be everlastingly merry as being *beati re et spe*, "blessed in hand and in hope."' But there is nothing in the connotation of the word itself to suggest whether the blessedness is enjoyed on earth or in heaven ; the context must show whether it refers to an experience in the present or to a hope for the future.

The secondary meaning of 'beatitude' is a *declaration of blessedness*. This declaration may be made of glorified saints in heaven, as in the Beatitudes of the Apocalypse ; or of disciples on earth, as in nearly all the Beatitudes of the Gospels. But the word is unduly restricted in its significance when it is used as a synonym for *beatification*,—a Roman Catholic ceremony wherein an inferior degree of canonization is conferred on a deceased person. The Pope considers his claims to beatitude ; and if these are approved, proclaims his admission to the Beatific Vision, and sanctions the ascription to him by the faithful of the title 'Blessed.'

ii. SIGNIFICANCE OF μακάριος. — In our Lord's declarations of blessedness He used a word (μακάριος) which has an instructive history, and passed by the pagan word for 'happiness' or 'well-being' (εὐδαιμονία) which is not found in the New Testament. In Homer the gods are the blessed (μάκαρες) ones, because they excel mortal men in power or in knowledge rather than in virtue. 'As compared with men, in conduct they are generally characterized by superior force and intellect, but by inferior morality' (Gladstone, *Homer and the Homeric Age*). The Greek despair of attaining blessedness on earth led to the frequent use of 'blessed' as synonymous with *dead*; Aristotle also distinguishes between μακαρισμός or Divine blessedness, and εὐδαιμονία or human blessedness (*Ethic. Nicom.* x. 8). It is therefore suggestive that the Christian conception of beatitude should find expression in a word closely associated with descriptions of the blessedness of the gods and 'originally stronger and more ideal than εὐδαίμων. . . . This is manifest in Aristotle, with whom the μακάριος as opposed to ἐνδεής is he who lacks no good' (Cremer, *Biblico-Theol. Lex. of NT Greek*, p. 776).

But the word which describes the blessedness of those who lack no good is ennobled by our Lord's use of it. He turns the thoughts of His disciples from outward to inward good ; He teaches that blessedness is determined not by fortune, but by goodness, and that it is attainable on earth by all who put themselves into right relation to God. In His Beatitudes, therefore, it is desirable to translate μακάριοι 'blessed' rather than 'happy.' (Cf. the saying of Carlyle that those who 'find blessedness' can 'do without happiness'). Since the word 'blessed' fell from the lips of Christ, His Beatitudes have worthily set forth an ideal of character loftier than the aristocratic virtue of the Platonists, a joy unknown to the most noble-minded of the pleasure-seeking Epicureans, a satisfaction of soul beyond the reach of the self-sufficient Stoic. Like the chiming of sweet bells,

the Beatitudes call men to enter the kingdom in which to be righteous is to be blessed ; they appeal to a universal longing of the human heart, and they promise a satisfaction of soul which can be found only in obedience to the law which the Son of Man proclaims in order that His brethren may be blessed. Beatitude is the final purpose of the most perfect law ; beatitude is the experience of the humble in whose heart there reigns the grace which came by Jesus Christ. The Beatitudes of our Lord bring the word 'blessed' down to earth and there set up the kingdom of heaven ; they portray no remote bliss, nor even a pleasure near at hand, but a fulness of joy within the soul. Henceforth blessedness is seen to be the privilege not only of those who are exalted above all earthly care and suffering, but also of those who still share the limitations of this mortal life ; it depends not on outward conditions such as wealth or education (cf. Plato, *Republic*, 354 A, 335 E), but on inward conditions such as meekness of spirit and purity of heart ; it is not the prerogative of the few who have been initiated into the secrets of a Divine philosophy, but the privilege of all who become loyal disciples of Him in whose life the perfect Law was perfectly fulfilled.

iii. THE NT BEATITUDES.—'Beatitude' is not a Biblical word, but it is properly applied to all the sayings of our Lord which contain a declaration of the conditions of human blessedness.

1. *Single Sayings.*—Isolated Beatitudes are recorded in Matthew, Luke, and John. They describe a blissful state which is the accompaniment of certain conditions of soul, or the reward of virtuous acts ; but the blissful state is almost always represented as attainable in this life. (The exceptions are Lk 14[14. 15]). The following is a list (omitting Lk [14. 15]) of the single sayings of Jesus in which He declares the blessedness of those who possess spiritual graces, or who exemplify some quality of virtue in their actions :—

'Blessed is he, whosoever shall find none occasion of stumbling in me.' (Mt 11[6], cf. Lk 7[23]).
'Blessed are your eyes, for they see ; and your ears, for they hear.' (Mt 13[16], cf. Lk 10[23]).
'Blessed art thou, Simon Bar-Jona : for flesh and blood hath not revealed it unto thee, but my Father which is in heaven.' (Mt 16[17]).
'Blessed are they that hear the word of God and keep it.' (Lk 11[28]).
'Blessed are those servants, whom the Lord when he cometh shall find watching.' (Lk 12[37], cf. vv. [38. 43], Mt 24[46]).
'If ye know these things, blessed are ye if ye do them.' (Jn 13[17]).
'Blessed are they that have not seen, and yet have believed.' (Jn 20[29]).

[In Mt 25[34] a different word (εὐλογημένοι) is used]. These scattered sayings suffice to indicate how often our Lord's teaching was expressed in words of blessing. With these Beatitudes in the canonical Gospels should be compared one preserved by St. Paul, and one found in the Codex Bezæ—

'It is more blessed to give than to receive.' (Ac 20[35]).
'If thou knowest what thou doest, thou art blessed ; but if thou knowest not, thou art under a curse, and a transgressor of the law.' (Lk 6[4] D).

The latter saying is addressed to a man who was working on the Sabbath ; probably it embodies a genuine tradition, but certainly it bears witness to the early recognition of the Beatitude as one of our Lord's favourite methods of imparting truth. In the fifth of the *New Sayings of Jesus* (see Grenfell and Hunt's ed. 1904) the word μακάριος can be restored, although the subject of the Beatitude has been lost. Prof. Adeney directs attention to the presence in the *Acts of Paul and Thekla* of a number of fresh Beatitudes. St. Paul is represented as giving utterance not only to some of the Beatitudes of Jesus, but also to such sayings as these—

'Blessed are they that keep themselves chaste, because they shall be called the temple of God.'

'Blessed be they who keep the baptism, for they shall rest in Father, Son, and Holy Spirit.'

The writer of this apocryphal book imitates our Lord's Beatitudes, and expresses in this form both Pauline teaching and his own ascetic doctrine (*Expositor*, 5th series [1895], vol. ii. p. 375).

2. *The Group of Sayings.* — When the word 'Beatitude' is used in the plural, it refers as a rule to those sayings of Jesus, grouped at the beginning of the Sermon on the Mount, in which He solemnly announces who are the blessed in the Kingdom of heaven. Early examples of its use in this significance are—'The eight beatitudes that . . . spryngeth of grace' (1531, *Pilgr. Perf.*); 'This quhilk S. Ambrose callis our Lord's beatitudes' (1588, H. King Canisius' *Catech.*). In his *de Offic.* (i. 6) Ambrose says: '*Hæ octo Christi Beatitudines sunt quasi Christi Paradoxa.*'

iv. THE BEATITUDES IN MATTHEW AND LUKE.

—1. *Their number in Matthew.*—The 'Beatitudes' are recorded in Mt 5[3-11] and Lk 6[20-22]. In regard to the number of Beatitudes in Matthew there have been diverse opinions; the decision depends upon the view taken of vv.[10-12]—

v.[10]. 'Blessed are they that have been persecuted for righteousness' sake : for theirs is the kingdom of heaven.'

v.[11]. 'Blessed are ye when men shall reproach you, and persecute you, and say all manner of evil against you falsely, for my sake.'

v.[12]. 'Rejoice, and be exceeding glad : for great is your reward in heaven : for so persecuted they the prophets which were before you.'

The seven Beatitudes in vv.[3-9] describe the graces of the Christian character ; these are followed in v.[10] by another Beatitude which assumes that those who possess these graces, and are, therefore, not of the world, will, so long as they are in the world, be exposed to its hatred. This general truth is first expressed ; it is immediately afterwards brought home to the disciples as our Lord, using 'ye' instead of 'they,' reaffirms (v.[11]) the blessedness of His hearers, should they endure reproach for His sake. If this interpretation be correct, there are eight Beatitudes in Matthew. In the first seven we behold the several rainbow hues of the light which reflects in human conduct the glory of the heavenly Father (v.[16]) ; in the eighth that light is seen in conflict with the darkness it is destined to overcome.

If Mt 5[10-12] is not counted as a Beatitude, the number of perfection—seven—is obtained. This course is followed by some because the eighth Beatitude is not a declaration of the blessedness of character, and by others because its promise of the Kingdom of heaven merely repeats what has already been said. Augustine speaks of a 'heptad of Beatitudes,' and regards the eighth as returning upon the first ('*octava tanquam ad caput redit*'). Bruce refers to the 'seven golden sentences' which sum up the felicity of the Kingdom, though he afterwards enumerates eight classes of the blessed (*The Training of the Twelve*, p. 42). Wordsworth (*in loc.*) prefers the mystical significance of eight to similar interpretations of seven ; for if seven is the number of rest after labour, 'eight is the number of blessedness and glory after rest' ; he also dwells on the annexing of the promise of the Kingdom of heaven to the eighth Beatitude as well as to the

first : 'This is the consummation of blessedness; the recurring note of the beatific octave ; also in the eighth Beatitude the word "blessed" is repeated for the sake of greater certainty and emphasis.'

This repetition of the word 'blessed' in what is here called the eighth Beatitude is the ground assigned by some for dividing it into two Beatitudes. Wright (*Synopsis of the Gospels in Greek*, p. 161) speaks of nine Beatitudes. In his judgment, however, the ninth, which is longer and in the second person, is an 'explanatory enlargement'; he is also disposed to regard the eighth short Beatitude as 'an editorial compilation, for the second half of it is repeated from the first Beatitude, and the commencement is an abbreviation of the ninth.' The so-called ninth Beatitude is best regarded as an enlargement of the eighth, but no sufficient reason is given for rejecting the eighth.

Delitzsch is alone in holding that there are ten Beatitudes in Matthew to correspond with the Decalogue. To obtain the number ten he not only counts vv.[10] and [11] as the eighth and ninth Beatitudes respectively, but also treats v.[12] as the tenth Beatitude. The words 'rejoice and be exceeding glad' (v.[12]) are regarded as equivalent to 'blessed.'

2. *The relation of the two versions.*—Only four Beatitudes are given in Lk 6[20-22] ; the relation of these to the eight Beatitudes in Matthew is one of the unsolved problems in NT criticism. The difference between Matthew and Luke is shown in the following table, the variations in Luke being printed in *italics* :—

'Blessed are

1. 'the poor in spirit : for theirs is the kingdom of heaven.'

(*1.*) '*ye poor* : for *yours* is the kingdom of *God.*'

2. 'they that mourn : for they shall be comforted.'

(*3.*) '*ye that weep now : for ye shall laugh.*'

3. 'the meek : for they shall inherit the earth.'

4. 'they that hunger and thirst after righteousness : for they shall be filled.'

(*2.*) '*ye that hunger now* : for *ye* shall be filled.'

5. 'the merciful : for they shall obtain mercy.'

6. 'the pure in heart : for they shall see God.'

7. 'the peacemakers : for they shall be called sons of God.'

8. 'they that have been persecuted for righteousness' sake : for theirs is the kingdom of heaven.

ye when men shall reproach you, and persecute you, and say all manner of evil against you falsely, for my sake.

Rejoice, and be exceeding glad : for great is your reward in heaven : for so persecuted they the prophets which were before you.'

(*4.*) '*ye when men shall hate you, and when they shall separate you from their company*, and reproach you, *and cast out your name as evil*, for *the Son of Man's* sake.

Rejoice *in that day, and leap for joy* : for *behold*, your reward is great in heaven : for *in the same manner did their fathers unto* the prophets.'

The chief elements in the problem to be solved are : the presence in Matthew alone of Beatitudes 3, 5, 6, 7 ; Luke's variations from Matthew's wording of Beatitudes 1, 2, 4, 8, especially (*a*) the absence from 1 and 4 of words which make blessedness depend upon spiritual conditions, and (*b*) the use of the second person throughout. This problem is part of a larger problem, viz., Do Matthew and Luke report the same discourse ? and if they do, which account is the more primitive ? (See art. SERMON ON THE MOUNT).

The view that Matthew and Luke narrate two different discourses is now generally abandoned. This theory accounts for all the variations, but it leaves unexplained the remarkable resemblances in the general purport of the teaching, the frequent identity of phraseology, and the close agreement of the introductory narratives and of the closing parables. Therefore, the question to be asked in regard to the two versions of the Beatitudes is part of the larger question : How is it that in two reports of the same discourse there are so many variations?

Some modern critics distinguish between *primary* and *secondary* Beatitudes, though different reasons are assigned in support of this distinction. (1) Wright (*op. cit.*) regards Beatitudes 1, 2, 4 as primary ; they belong to ' the proto-Matthæus,' because they are also found in Luke. The other Beatitudes have been ' added at different dates as recollections occurred.' But the non-occurrence of a saying in Luke is no proof that it is ' secondary,' unless it is certain that Luke is more primitive, and not a selection from the more original tradition in Matthew. (2) Weiss (in Meyer's *Com.*) describes the same three Beatitudes as authentic, because they point to the righteousness of the Kingdom as the *summum bonum* ; the first to righteousness as not yet possessed, the second to the want of righteousness as a cause of sorrow, and the fourth to righteousness as an object of desire The reasoning is entirely subjective. Weiss tests the authenticity of a Beatitude by its accord with his theory that the theme of the discourse is the nature of true and false righteousness ; on his own principles other Beatitudes might be proved authentic. The seventh might be said to point to the righteousness whose work is peace.

When the narratives in Matthew and Luke are taken as they stand, the question remains : Which version of the Beatitudes more correctly represents the actual words of Christ?

That the shorter form in Luke is more genuine is the opinion of many scholars. Dr. E A. Abbott thinks ' it is more probable that Luke represents the letter of the original words of Jesus more closely than Matthew, however much the latter may better represent the spirit of them' (*Enc. Brit* [9] x. 798[a]). But the words which better represent the spirit of the teaching may also rest on the authority of Jesus. Though the two versions represent the same discourse, the one discourse may not have been delivered with such formality as many theories imply. It is more than probable that the longer form in Matthew omits some of our Lord's comments on these sayings. The different versions of the eighth Beatitude in Matthew point to this conclusion. The declaration of blessedness having been made in its most general form, it is then reaffirmed and expounded in its special bearing upon the men to whom our Lord was speaking. The Apostles will have the privilege of bearing ' the reproach of Christ,' and as sharers in the experience of the prophets they shall receive the prophets' reward (cf. He 11[26]). Other Beatitudes may in like manner have been restated in a more specific form. For example, all who would enter the Kingdom of heaven need to be told that its blessings are bestowed on the poor in spirit ; but it is to His true disciples and not to the multitude that Jesus says, ' Ye, in your poverty, are blessed.' The argument for the primitive character of Luke is stated (*Expositor*, 5th series [1895], vol. ii.) succinctly and forcefully by Professor Adeney. The sayings of which Matthew gives a longer version than Luke are described as expositions of ' the hidden truth contained in the shorter utterances.' The Beatitudes peculiar to Matthew are not relegated to an

editor, but are held to be the true teaching of our Lord, though probably not in their original context. The literary problem is complicated by the absence from Matthew of the four Woes, which in Luke (6[24-26]) correspond to the four Beatitudes. The theory that Luke gives the more primitive form involves the assumption that Matthew omitted the Woes and inserted an equal number of Blessings. Yet Wright's conclusion, after a thorough study of the Synoptic problem, is that the Woes in Luke are either ' conflated from another source' or ' editorial inversions of the Blessings.'

The theory that Matthew gives the Beatitudes in their more primitive form has the support of Tholuck and Meyer among older writers, and more recently of H. Holtzmann and Beyschlag. On the authority of one who probably heard these words of Blessing, the Beatitudes peculiar to Matthew are regarded not only as authentic sayings of Jesus, but also as parts of the original discourse. Holtzmann also holds that Luke modified the language of Matthew in accordance with his own ascetic views (*Hand-Comm.*, ' Die Synop.,' p. 100) ; but this supposition is not essential to the theory. The shorter form of some Beatitudes in Luke may faithfully represent the words of Christ, perhaps His own special application of a general truth to His disciples. Dr. Bruce, who has no bias in favour of ' antiquated Harmonistic,' suggests that, as a critical description of Mt 5–7, ' The Teaching on the Hill' is probably more correct than ' The Sermon on the Mount' ; ' teaching' ($\delta\iota\delta\alpha\chi\eta$) as distinguished from ' preaching' ($\kappa\eta\rho\upsilon\gamma\mu\alpha$) implies both the announcement of a theme and its expansion. It follows that two forms of a Beatitude may be authentic, ' the one as theme, the other as comment.' According to this view, the theme of the first Beatitude is given in Luke, but in Matthew ' one of the expansions, not necessarily the only one.' It is of little moment whether the shorter form is primary, *i.e.* the enunciation of a theme afterwards expounded by our Lord ; or secondary, *i.e.* His own narrowing of a general assertion previously made. On either supposition, Luke, ' while faithfully reproducing at least a part of our Lord's teaching on the hill,' may state that teaching ' not in its original setting, but readapted so as to serve the practical purpose of Christian instruction' (*The Expositor's Greek Test.*, vol. i. pp. 94 ff., 509).

3. *Order and connexion of thought.*—The order of the second and third Beatitudes is reversed in Codex Bezæ and the Vulgate ; so also Clem. Alex., Aug., Orig., Eus., Greg. of Nyssa. Tholuck thinks that this change from the best authenticated order was made on mystical grounds ; either because the promise of the lower good should immediately follow that of heaven (Orig.), or because $\gamma\hat{\eta}$ represents mystically a higher stage of blessedness (Greg. of Nyssa).

In the generally accepted order of the Beatitudes a sequence of thought may be traced, though the ' scale of grace and glory' is perhaps not so carefully ' graduated' as some have supposed (cf. Amb. on Lk 6). The first grace—poverty of spirit—is the germ of all the rest ; the first and last Beatitude is the all-comprising word—' theirs is the kingdom of heaven.' The six Beatitudes that intervene unfold different aspects of Christian virtue and set forth its peculiar blessedness, for each blessing promised is the fitting reward of the inward grace, and each is included in the promise of the Kingdom. Dr. Fairbairn (*Studies in the Life of Christ*) divides the Beatitudes into two classes—' those of resignation and those of hope' ; the first four Beatitudes are placed in the former class, the last four in the latter class. This division is simple, and serves to emphasize the distinction between the passive and active graces of the Christian character. Yet it seems better to distinguish the eighth Beatitude from the other seven; it differs from them essentially, for it attaches blessedness to endurance of opposition and not to inward qualities, to conduct and not to character, to something a man does and not to what he is. In the seven Beatitudes on character, there are two triads. The first three, as Dr. Dykes points out (*The Manifesto of the King*, p. 101), are closely connected and refer to negative graces; in the last three, positive graces are intimately combined as elements of righteousness; the fourth or central Beatitude is the link between these first groups. 'As the first three, the trilogy of spiritual humiliation, lead up to and produce that blessed hunger after Divine righteousness; so the second three, a trilogy of characteristic Christian graces, are the fulfilment of the soul's hunger.'

With a 'proposal of the end—blessedness,' says Jeremy Taylor, 'our excellent and gracious Lawgiver begins His sermon' (*The Great Exemplar*, pt. 2, sec. xi.). Beatitude is the essence of Christianity, its beginning and end. The 'Beatitudes' reveal the nature of true blessedness and the conditions of its attainment; they reflect the light which shines from the Hebrew Scriptures that declare the blessedness of the righteous; but they are illumined not only by the Prophets and Psalmists who went before, but also by the Apostles and Teachers who come after. Wernle says with true insight: 'Jesus Himself made of Christianity a religion of hope. . . . If Paul in a later age preaches the religion of longing in words of enthralling eloquence, he is merely continuing in his own language the Beatitudes of Jesus' (*The Beginnings of Christianity*, i. 68).

LITERATURE.—In addition to the works already quoted, see art. SERMON ON THE MOUNT, below; Hastings' *DB*, Extra Vol. p. 14 ff.; Gore, *Sermon on the Mount*; Bruce, *Galilean Gospel*, 39–72; Leckie, *Life and Religion*, 209–270; Stanley, *Serm. to Children*, 95–131; Matheson, *Landmarks of NT Morality*, 143 ff.

J. G. TASKER.

BEAUTY.—This term is applied alike to the physical grace of men and animals, to external nature and works of art, and to moral character and action. In every relationship it is a quality capable of imparting exquisite pleasure, and a power that commands and captivates. The appreciation of beauty for its own intrinsic charm was a special characteristic of the Greeks, to whom the world was a wonder of order and adaptation, and who found an element of worship in the beauty that was a prerogative of the gods. With the Israelites, and in the East generally, beauty was esteemed rather as a sign of dignity and noble birth (Jg 8[18]), and beautiful things were valued as the accessories of official decoration. Much in the Gospels that we feel to be beautiful and describe by that name, is there specialized by such terms as 'grace,' 'glory,' 'excellency,' as indicating in each particular case the arresting feature of charm, sublimity, or pre-eminence that makes it beautiful. Thus in the appeal, 'If God so clothe the grass of the field' (Lk 12[28]), and in the declaration concerning the lilies of the field, that Solomon in all his glory was not arrayed like one of them (v.[27]), the beauty was due to external investiture rather than to any inherent fact of symmetry and proportion. So when the merchantman is described as seeking goodly pearls (Mt 13[45]), and the righteousness of Christ's disciples is expected to exceed that of the scribes and Pharisees (Mt 5[20]), the quality of beauty arises from the surprising rarity and recognized pre-eminence of the things referred to.

1. *Personal appearance of Christ.* — Much has been written about the face of Christ. Tradition, gathering its data from the apocryphal 'Letter of Lentulus,' the portrait which Jesus is said to have sent to king Abgar of Edessa, the story of Veronica's veil, the pictures and eikons of the early and mediæval Church, and accumulated literary traditions, has given to Art its typical presentation of Christ's countenance. The subject, however, is one about which there is no certain information. On the mount of Transfiguration the three disciples had a brief glimpse of the heavenly beauty that then shone out from the face of Christ. But those who were then eye-witnesses of His majesty (2 P 1[16]) tell us that the glorious vision surpassed all description. It remained with them as a restful and inspiring memory, like the 'unspeakable words' of St. Paul's ecstatic experience (2 Co 12[4]).

2. *Beauty in external nature.*—It is profoundly suggestive of the reality of the Incarnation that He by whom the worlds were made spoke so little about them. When He called Himself and His disciples 'the light of the world' (Jn 8[12], Mt 5[14]), the allusion to light was not in the spirit of Milton's sublime apostrophe (*Par. Lost*, iii. 1 ff.), but with reference to its conflict with darkness. When He pointed to the redness of the evening sky (Mt 16[2]), it was not to speak of a Presence immanent in the light of setting suns, but to express the feeling of wonder that those who could draw a practical lesson from something so remote could not hear the footsteps of moral destiny so close behind themselves. And so in the instances of the frail, beautiful grass and the lilies of the field (Mt 6[28ff.]), the allusion served as an argument for God's still greater care of things more precious.

3. *Ethical beauty.*—The life of Christ witnessed in every detail to His inspiring and impressive personality. It is surely a torso presentation of that life that would make 'sweet reasonableness' its prevailing characteristic. Rather it is marked by the absence of that philosophic detachment that would live and let live. In His mind truth took precedence even of the heavenly hope, and He assured His disciples that if that hope were a sweet but baseless imagination, He would have told them (Jn 14[2]). He had come as light into the world, and questionings not only of the defiant darkness (Jn 1[5]), but of the bewildering twilight (16[17ff.]), sprang up around His path. In His presence men were greater and less than they had been before. Even in the days of His flesh those who were Christ's were impelled to put on Christ, and were afterwards recognized as having been with Him (Ac 4[13]). He exemplified in His own life the principle by which His disciples were to live and extend His kingdom. His outward power was the measure of His inward submission. He came not to do His own will (Jn 6[38]). It was when He was lifted up that He would draw all men unto Himself (12[32]). Even so the life of the Christian has its condition of complete and continuous surrender, and in the service of the gospel it is found that men do not yield to the messenger, but to what they see that he yields to.

In the course of Christ's life on earth, along with the general impression of His teaching and ministry there were various incidents that showed in a special manner with what tender sympathy He took upon Him our nature and bore our infirmities. Among these may be mentioned the conversation with the Samaritan woman at Jacob's well (Jn 4), the blessing of the little children that were almost sent away (Mt 19[13ff.] ||), the touching of the leper in the act of healing (Mt 8[3]), and the words of hope concerning Nineveh (Mt 12[41]) and Tyre (Lk 10[13f.]), and those who should come into the Kingdom from the distant East and West (Mt 8[11]). On the cross we have the prayer for His persecutors (Lk 23[34]), His comradeship with the penitent thief (v.[42f.]), and the commending of His mother to the care of the disciple John (Jn 19[26f.]).

Also as in the lives of others, chiefly of women, He met with intuitions and actions which through His affinity of soul were noticed and commended by Him as bearing the stamp of moral and spiritual beauty. Such were the return of the Samaritan leper to give glory to God (Lk 17[16ff.]); the humble insistency of the Syro-Phœnician woman (Mk 7[26ff.]); the courage and consecration of the widow who gave her mites to the Lord (12[42ff.]); the act of the sinful woman who bathed His feet with her tears (Lk 7[44]), and of her also who unsealed, as for His burial, the alabaster vase of precious ointment (Jn 12[7]).

With regard to things physically and morally loathsome, on the other hand, the disease of leprosy (Mt 8[2], Lk 7[22] 17[12]) and the affliction of demoniac possession (Mt 9[32], Mk 7[26], Lk 8[39] etc.) could always claim His healing power; there was discriminating pity towards those who had sinned in ignorance (Lk 23[34]), or who had been overcome by some swift and overmastering temptation (Mt 26[41], Lk 7[47], Jn 4[16] 21[15]), or by the difficulties of outward circumstance (Mk 10[21f.], Lk 13[3]); while in sharp contrast with the above, there was His denunciation by descriptive parable and stern rebuke of the hopeless offensiveness of the Pharisaic type (Mt 21[19] 23, Lk 20[19] etc.).

LITERATURE.—Under (1) Hauck-Herzog, *PRE*, art. 'Christusbilder'; Schaff-Herzog, *Encyc. of Relig. Knowledge*, art. 'Christ, Pictures of'; Farrar, *Christ in Art*, pp. 67-95. Under (2) Wendt, *Teaching of Jesus*, i. 151 ff.; *Expositor*, 3rd ser. ii. [1885] 224 ff. Under (3) Liddon, *Bampton Lectures*[8], p. 192 ff.; Channing, *Complete Works* [1884], pp. 237-243.   G. M. MACKIE.

BED.—The word 'bed' (κλίνη, κράββατος, κοίτη) is found in the Gospels only in Mt 9[2. 6], Mk 2[4-12] 4[21] 7[30], Lk 5[18] 8[16] 11[7] 17[34], Jn 5[8-12]. There is little here to indicate the kind of bed, or beds, that were in use among the Hebrews in the time of Christ. Among the ancient Hebrews, however, as among other Oriental peoples of that day, the bed usually consisted of a wadded quilt, or thin mattress, to be used, according to the season, or the condition of the owner, with or without covering (cf. Ex 22[27] 'For that [the outer garment worn in the daytime] is his only covering: it is his garment for his skin: wherein shall he sleep?'). The very poor often made their bed of the skins of animals, old cloaks or rugs, or slept in their ordinary clothing on the bare ground floor, as they do to-day in the East.

The bedding ordinarily in use among Orientals now is, doubtless, much the same as it was in Christ's day: a mat made of rushes or straw to be laid down first; sheep or goat skins, or a quilt stuffed with hair or vegetable fibre, or both, to lie upon; and a covering consisting often only of the 'cloak,' or outer garment, of the poor man, but sometimes in summer of some light stuff in addition, or in winter of skins, or some heavier quilted stuff.

Various allusions are made in the Gospels to beds that could be carried: 'Arise, take up thy bed, and go unto thine house' (Mt 9[6]); 'Rise, take up thy bed, and walk'; 'And immediately the man . . . took up his bed, and walked' (Jn 5[8. 9]); 'Behold men bringing on a bed a man that was palsied' (Lk 5[18] RV). St. Luke and St. Mark tell us that on this occasion, when, because of the crowd in the house, the four men could not reach Jesus with the paralytic, they took him up on the house-top, broke through the roof, and 'let him down through the tiling with *the couch* (κλινίδιον; in v.[18], however, the word κλίνη, 'bed,' is used) into the midst before Jesus' (Lk 5[19]), or, as St. Mark puts it, 'let down *the bed* (κράββατος) wherein the sick of the palsy lay' (2[4]).

For ordinary use at night the bed was laid on the floor, generally on the mat, which served to

keep it off the ground, frequently on a light portable frame of wood which served a like purpose; but sometimes on a more elevated bedstead ('under the bed,' Mk 4[21] RV). In the morning the bedding was all rolled up, and, after being aired and sunned, was put aside on the raised platform, or packed away for the day in a chest or closet. A bedstead of any pretensions was rare among the Hebrews, and was looked upon as a luxury; the nearest approach to it being in general the raised platform on the side of the room. The richness of beds and of bedsteads among some of the Asiatic peoples, however, was at least equal to that of the Greeks and Romans (cf. Pr 7[16. 17], 1 S 28[23]). The degree of richness would depend, of course, upon the wealth of the family and the style of the house or tent, as it does to-day among the Bedawîn.

Usually a room was set apart as a bedroom, where the whole family slept. 'My children are with me in bed, I cannot rise and give thee' (Lk 11[5-8]). Among the poorest a portion of the single room occupied by the family was set apart for sleeping, and, generally, this was raised above the level of the floor. When the house was of two storeys, the beds were laid in one of the rooms of the upper storey, or, during the summer, preferably, on the flat roof. See, further, art. COUCH.   GEO. B. EAGER.

BEELZEBUB or BEELZEBUL.—It is strange that this name has never yet been satisfactorily explained; stranger still that no trace of it has been found as yet among the scores of Jewish names for angels and spirits. The first part of the name is clear enough; it is the Aramaic form of the Hebrew 'Baal'; nor is there anything strange in the dropping of λ before ζ in the MSS followed by modern editors like Westcott-Hort and Weiss [Cheyne in his art. 'Beelzebul' in the *Encyc. Bibl.* finds 'this scepticism as to λ in βεελ paradoxical,' 'the word βεεζεβουλ inexplicable and hardly pronounceable,' and urges against it 'the famous passage Mt 10[25], where the οἰκοδεσπότης implies the speaker's consciousness that בַּעַל is one element in the title,' but his objection completely misses the mark. The dropping of the λ is merely phonetical; cf. in Josephus βεζέδελ in codd. MVRC for βελζέδεκ (*BJ* iii. 25), Βάζωρος for Βαλέζωρος (*c. Apion*. i. 124), Βαζαφράνης for Βαρζαφρ. (*Ant.* xiv. 330); Ἀμεσάδ in Cod. Q of Dn 1[11] [Theod.] for Ἀμελσάδ; 'Philadephia' in the Syriac Version of Euseb.'s *HE*, etc.[*] More difficult is the change of β into λ at the end of the word, supposing the common explanation to be correct, that the name comes from 2 K 1[2]. It has been explained as an intentional cacophonic corruption (= 'god of the dung') or a dialectical or phonetic variation (cf. Beliar for Belial or Bab el-Mandel for Mandeb). The spelling with *b* was retained in the NT by Luther, whose Greek text had λ, and by RV in text; it was introduced by Jerome in the Vulgate, see the Index of Wordsworth-White, where 15 Latin spellings of the name are given, and cf. Jerome's remark in *OS* 66, 11: 'in fine ergo nominis b litera legenda est, non l; musca enim *zebub* vocatur.' λ is even found in Cod. 243 of the text of Symmachus in 2 K 1[2]; but see the Syriac Hexapla in v.[6], and note, what has generally been overlooked, that the Septuagint took זבוב not בעל for the name of the god of Ekron: ἐπιζητῆσαι ἐν τῇ Βάαλ (*dative*) Μυῖαν (*accusative*) θεὸν Ἀκκαρών; likewise Jos.: πρὸς τὴν Ἀκκαρὼν θεὸν Μυῖαν, τοῦτο γὰρ ἦν ὄνομα τῷ θεῷ.

On the *fly* in worship and legend see Plin. *HN* x. 28. 75; Pausan. *Descr. Gr.* v. xiv. 1; Ælian, *Nat. Anim.* v. 17, xi. 8; Usener, *Götternamen*, p. 260. There were Jewish legends about flies, such as that there were none in the temple (*A*both

* The best analogy is the Syr. name ברבעשמי, 'son of the Bel of heaven,' explained by Barheb. as 'he with four names.'

v. 8); Elisha was recognized as a prophet by the woman of Shunem, because no fly crept over his place at the table (*Berakh.* 10b); on the *yezer ha-ra* as a fly see *Berakh.* 61a, Targ. Jer. on Ec 10¹). The supposition that the name corresponds to Aramaic בעלרבב = 'enemy' is not very likely, nor the other that it is the Baal of the heavenly mansion who became the Baal of the nether world (*JAS*, 1878, pp. 220–221). Later Jews identified Baal-*zebub* with Baal-*berith*, and told that some would carry an image of him (in the shape of a fly) in their pockets, producing it and kissing it from time to time (*Shab.* 83b. 63b). Procopius states (*ad* 2 K 1): πλὴν ἔστι μαθεῖν ἐξ ὧν Εὐσέβιος ἐν ἀρχῇ τῆς Εὐαγγελικῆς Προπαρασκευῆς ἐκ τῶν Φίλωνος παρατίθεται, ὡς δαίμων ἦν, οὕτω λεγόμενος· μᾶλλον δὲ γυνὴ παλαιά τις, ἣν ἐθεοποίησαν. Zahn (on Mt 12³⁴) lays stress on the fact that the article is missing before ἄρχοντι τῶν δαιμόνων ('*a* prince of the devils, not *the* prince'); but the definite article is found in Mark and Luke, and in Mt 9³⁴ (if this verse be not a later addition) where several Latin documents have the name.

How scanty is our knowledge of NT times, when such a name, which appears quite popular in the NT, defies as yet all explanation, and is not found anywhere else! Origen on John xix. (p. 315, ed. Preuschen) remarks: πάντως γὰρ περὶ δαιμόνων τι μεμαθήκεισαν καὶ τοῦ ἄρχοντος αὐτῶν, ᾧ ὄνομα Βεελζεβούλ· ταῦτα δὲ οὐ πάνυ τι ἐν τοῖς φερομένοις κεῖται βιβλίοις.

LITERATURE.—In addition to works cited above, see A. Loisy, 'Beelzeboul' (*Rev. d'hist. et de lit. rel.* 1904, v. 434–466).

EB. NESTLE.

BEGETTING.—

The idea of begetting, as applied in the natural or in a metaphorical or spiritual sense, is expressed in the Gospels by the common words γεννάω, 'to beget' (which occurs in the LXX as the equivalent of the Heb. ילד, meaning either 'to beget' or 'to bear,' and is similarly used in the NT); γεννητός, properly 'begotten,' but which, like the verb, is also found in the sense of 'born'; μονογενής, 'only-begotten.' The common word γεννάω, with its derivatives, is, as might be expected, used to express natural begetting and natural birth. So μονογενών is, used in the Fourth Gospel only of the relation of Christ to God the Father, occurs in Lk 7¹² of the son of the widow of Nain, meaning simply 'only son' (cf. 8⁴² Jairus' daughter, and 9³⁸ the demoniac boy); and γεννητός in the sense of 'born' in Mt 11¹¹, Lk 7²⁸ ('among those that are born of women'). In Matthew and Luke again, τὸ γεννηθὲν and τὸ γεννώμενον are used to describe the miraculous conception of our Lord in the womb of the Virgin Mary; Mt 1²⁰ has 'that which is conceived in her (AVm 'begotten') is of the Holy Ghost,' and Lk 1³⁵ 'that which shall be born of thee (RVm 'is begotten') shall be called the Son of God.' In both cases obviously the expression will bear the rendering 'which is begotten' or 'which is conceived,' according to the ordinary sense in which the verb is known to occur.

The Messianic and the spiritual uses of the words for begetting are those which alone call for remark in connexion with the Gospels and the NT generally. In the Gospels, and there particularly in the Gospel of John, we find them applied to Christ and His relation to God the Father, and, in connexion with that reference, to the case of believers who, receiving Christ by faith, are, in virtue of the new principle of life thus imparted to them, born again, become children of God. This latter thought is suggested in the Gospels, and dwelt upon at length in the Epistles.

We may regard as the *locus classicus* of the theological or spiritual application of the idea of begetting, as we find it in the Gospels, the well-known passage in the Prologue to the Fourth Gospel : 'No man hath seen God at any time ; the only-begotten Son (ὁ μονογενὴς υἱός),* who is in the bosom of the Father, he hath declared him' (Jn 1¹⁸). Here the use of the term μονογενής in this connexion at once raises the question as to the precise sense in which it is applied to Christ, whether it refers to His being by Divine nature and essence Son of God, or merely to His manifestation in time as

* WH read μονογενὴς θεός, following א*BC*L.

Messiah, as one specially chosen to reveal to mankind the will of the invisible God. A little study of the history of the term 'only-begotten' shows that it is by no means peculiar to the Gospels, but is rather a familiar Messianic term, which depends, for a clear understanding of the thoughts denoted and connoted by it, upon what, we may gather from other sources, was the national belief as to God's self-revelation in the history of grace. We are reminded, for instance, that Israel (Ex 4²², Hos 1¹⁰), the kings of Israel (1 Ch 28⁶), and the Messiah (Ps 2⁷), of whom the latter were types, were successively called sons of God, or God's firstborn. Again, St. Paul (in Ac 13³³) and the Epistle to the Hebrews (1⁵ 5⁵) quote Ps 2⁷ as a Messianic prophecy which had been fulfilled in the mission of Jesus : 'Thou art my Son ; this day have I begotten thee' (σήμερον γεγέννηκά σε).

In view of this Messianic, spiritual application of the idea referred to, the words of Ps 2⁷ have been supposed to allude to some typical king like David or Solomon, and the expression, 'Thou art my Son, this day have I begotten thee,' to denote an act performed by God on the person addressed, as by constituting him king, He had moulded his life afresh and set him in a special relation to Himself. Applied to Christ, this might be taken as referring to such an event as the Resurrection, with reference to which St. Paul says in Ro 1⁴ that by it God 'declared him to be the Son of God with power.' This might be accepted as a fairly adequate account of the Messianic ideas held by the early disciples, and of the interpretation which they were likely to put upon the passage in the Second Psalm, when they studied it, as St. Paul did, by the light of the Resurrection of Jesus. They must have been largely influenced by traditional opinions on the subject of the Messiah, and would therefore interpret the words, 'This day have I begotten thee,' as referring not to any event in a past eternity or to any period prior to the Incarnation of the Son of God, but to some definite point in the history of His manifestation to the world, as, for example, to the period of the birth of Jesus, or of the Baptism, when the voice from heaven declared Him to be God's Beloved Son, or, as St. Paul appears to teach in his discourse in Acts (13³³) and in his Epistle to the Romans, to the period of the Resurrection.

Such an interpretation, however, of the passage referred to as we find in the teachings of St. Paul and of the Epistle to the Hebrews, does not adequately explain the language of the Fourth Gospel or the author's allusions to the pre-existence of Christ as Logos, and to His relation to the Father as the Only-begotten Son. The Evangelist speaks in such a way of the nature and mission of the Logos or the Son of God as plainly to assume the eternal pre-existence of that Logos or Son. When John, speaking for himself, says in the Prologue (1¹⁴), 'The Word was made flesh, and dwelt among us, and we beheld his glory, the glory as of the only-begotten of the Father,' the subject of the sentence is He of whom he has just spoken as having been in the beginning with God, and as having been God's agent in the work of Creation. Again, in v.¹⁸ 'No man hath seen God at any time ; the only-begotten Son, which is in the bosom of the Father, he hath declared him,' the expression 'which is in the bosom of the Father' is apparently meant for a further explanation or definition of the expression 'only-begotten Son,' the present participle ὁ ὤν signifying, as Alford puts it, '*essential truth* without any particular regard to time,' while the peculiar construction εἰς τὸν κόλπον, literally 'into' not 'in' 'the bosom' (as might have been expected —ἐν τῷ κόλπῳ), is, as that commentator again points out, 'a pregnant construction, involving the begetting of the Son and His being the λόγος of the Father,—His proceeding forth from God.' 'It is a similar expression on the side of His Unity with the Father to εἰμὶ παρὰ τοῦ θεοῦ on the side of His manifestation to men.' The meaning of the passage is that Christ, who is by nature the Son of God, begotten before all worlds, is He who alone could and did declare the nature and the will of that God whom no man hath seen or could have known apart from such a revelation. Here it is evident that the begetting referred to by the use of the word 'only-begotten' (μονογενής) is different from that which is spoken of in the Second Psalm.

Again, in His discourse to Nicodemus, Jesus Himself alludes clearly to His pre-existence and essential Sonship when He says that God 'gave his only-begotten Son, that whosoever believeth in him should not perish, but have everlasting life'; and in the next sentence it is added, 'For God sent not his Son into the world to condemn the world' (Jn 3[16. 17]). There the words 'gave' and 'sent' imply pre-existence on the part of the Son. Similar references occur elsewhere in the discourses of Jesus as recorded in the Fourth Gospel, for example, that of Jn 6[46] 'Not that any man hath seen the Father, save he which is of God (lit. 'from God,' παρὰ τοῦ θεοῦ), he hath seen the Father,' with which cf. v.[38] 'I came down from heaven,' and v.[62] 'What and if ye shall see the Son of Man ascend up where he was before?' passages which, as H. Holtzmann points out, 'connect the historic with the preter-historic being of the pre-existent Logos —the Son of God, that is, in the theological, not the Messianic sense.'

A comparison of these passages in the Fourth Gospel with Ps 2[7] shows that the thought of 'begetting,' as it affects the relations between the Father and the Son, has more than one meaning. Dorner notes even in the Synoptic Gospels three senses in which it is applied—the physical, the ethical, and the official. If we extend our view so as to include the Fourth Gospel, a similar division suggests itself: the theological, or, as it is sometimes called, the metaphysical; the official or Messianic; and the ethical or spiritual. Jesus as Logos is Son of God by nature. Essential Sonship, eternal generation, is predicated of Him. Then, in a special official sense, His setting apart to the Messianic office is, according to a familiar Scripture figure (cf. Ps 2[7]), regarded as 'a begetting,' that is, the inauguration of a new vocation or a new order of things. This notion of begetting is practically the idea conveyed by the word 'Messiah' or 'Christ' itself, and by what Jesus Himself says, according to Jn 10[36], 'Say ye of him, whom the Father hath sanctified, and sent into the world, Thou blasphemest; because I said, I am the Son of God?' Lastly, the thought of begetting is applied in the sense of a Divine communication of life, as when the Spirit of God descended and abode upon Christ. Thus when the Baptist saw the sign, the dove from heaven alighting upon Jesus, he tells us, 'And I saw, and bare record that this is the Son of God' (Jn 1[34]). This third aspect is important as illustrating the point of connexion between the Sonship of Christ and that of believers, the Divine Sonship based on a generation, that is, a Divine communication of life. Each of these aspects has its own significance.

1. The *theological* is associated with the apologetic aim of the Fourth Gospel. It was an important part of the object of the Evangelist to enable the Church to rid herself of the influence of the mischievous speculations of the time, of a humanitarian Ebionism on the one side, and of Gnosticism on the other. That Jesus is God from the beginning,—eternally God,—was his answer to those who would detract from the Divine dignity of

Jesus. Again, by his doctrine of Sonship, the application of the thought of generation to the relation of God the Father to Christ the Son, St. John gave a new meaning to the expression 'Logos,' which represented a well-known philosophical conception long current in the East and among the later Platonists and Stoics, while the speculations of Philo and the Alexandrian School had brought it into still greater prominence. According to the Fourth Gospel, Christ as Logos is the Revealer of the Father, not as Philo and others imagined, as being an 'emanation,' an outflow from the Inaccessible Deity, a shadowy existence to be described only by analogies and metaphors, or by mere negations, but as being the Son of God, who shared the Divine nature and glory, One who came at the Father's bidding to do the Father's will. What that mysterious 'begetting' meant, in virtue of which the Son of God was Son of God, John did not attempt to explain. To him it was a Divine mystery which none could penetrate. It was enough for him that God so loved the world as to send forth His Son, sharer of His Divine nature, for that world's salvation. Thus, according to the testimony of St. John, Jesus 'is μονογενής, the Only-begotten, as Logos; He *appears* as μονογενής through the Incarnation' (Beyschlag).

2. Again, in all four Gospels the idea of begetting is applied in an *official* or *Messianic* sense in connexion with Christ's actual appearing among men and with His redemptive mission. The three Synoptists record the Divine proclamation with which, at the Baptism, the first stage of Christ's ministry was solemnly inaugurated: 'This is my beloved Son, in whom I am well pleased' (Mt 3[17] ||). The same Evangelists testify to the events of the Transfiguration, when again the voice from heaven addressed the disciples in similar language, as if to inaugurate the final stage of Christ's ministry (Mt 17[5] ||). In the latter case the addition of the words 'hear ye him' to the original form of the Divine testimony would naturally suggest to persons familiar, as the disciples probably were, with the current Messianic interpretation of Ps 2[7], the thought of the Divine decree there spoken of, which constituted the subject of the prophecy King of God's people, having a Divine right to their loyalty and obedience. In the Fourth Gospel this official aspect of the idea of begetting in connexion with Christ is expressed in those passages in which Jesus speaks of Himself as One sent of God, and by that mission brought into a new relation to God and to mankind. That 'sanctification' and that 'sending' of which He speaks (10[36]) correspond to the begetting referred to by the Psalmist, though in this case they point to the Incarnation, and not, as in Ro 1[4], to the Resurrection. In illustration of this we may compare with the passages already quoted in another connexion (Jn 3[17] 6[38. 46. 62]) such utterances as these: 'I proceeded and came forth from God; neither came I of myself, but he sent me' (8[42]); 'Ye have believed that I came out from God . . . I came forth from the Father, and am come into the world' (16[27. 28]). 'Sending forth' and 'coming forth' appear, according to the Fourth Gospel, to have been favourite expressions in the mouth of Jesus with which to describe His Messianic commission, and that act of Divine grace which was, as it were, the genesis of the New Dispensation—the reign of 'grace and truth' inaugurated by Christ as Messiah; as St. John himself laid special stress upon the Incarnation of the Logos as an event which meant the manifestation of that 'life' (1[4]) which 'was the light of men.' The thought is the same. The idea—coming from heaven, being sent of God—is practically identical with that of 'became flesh.'

In this Messianic sense, then, the thought of 'begetting' may fitly apply to the beginning of Christ's manifestation in history.

3. The third aspect is the *spiritual* or *ethical.* In Christ, as the Only-begotten, the proofs of the Divine Sonship are found in His absolute sinlessness (Jn 8[46]), in that He did alway those things which pleased God (8[29]); that there was perfect harmony between Christ and the Father in all things, in willing and in working, and in the fact that Jesus was habitually conscious of the Father's presence, so that during the season of His sorest trial, when He was deserted by His disciples, He was 'not alone, for the Father was with him' (Jn 16[32]). This aspect of the doctrine of the Divine Sonship of Jesus is of great interest and importance in connexion with the idea of 'begetting,' being the point at which the doctrine of the sonship of believers is linked on to that of the Sonship of Christ Himself. It is in this connexion that St. John introduces at once the conception of Christ as the Word made flesh, and that of the regeneration of believers. The two thoughts are indeed, in the Prologue and elsewhere, so closely related that the one almost imperceptibly shades off into the other. Thus (1[12]) we read, 'As many as received him, to them gave he power to become the sons of God'; (v.[13]) 'which were born, not of blood, nor of the will of the flesh, nor of the will of man, but of God.' At this point the Evangelist proceeds at once to state the doctrine of the Incarnation of the Divine Logos. As has been remarked, 'the subject of the μονογενής is introduced only after we have learned what is involved in the thought of believers becoming children of God.' The same idea of the relation between the Divine descent of Christ, the Only-begotten of the Father, and the sonship of believers, is noted and emphasized in the First Epistle of John (in which the teaching of John's Gospel on this subject is worked out in greater detail), as when we read, 'If ye know that he is righteous, ye know that every one that doeth righteousness is born of him' (1 Jn 2[29]); and again, 'Whosoever is born of God doth not commit sin; for his seed remaineth in him: and he cannot sin, because he is born of God' (3[9]). The relation of the Son to the Father, His Divine setting apart for the accomplishment of the Father's will, the absolute oneness of Father and Son in respect of will and of work, and the mystery of Christ's miraculous entrance into the world, being conceived by the power of the Divine Spirit, are, throughout the Gospel of John, treated as analogues of the regeneration which must be wrought out in the heart and life of all who would enter the Kingdom of God. Thus those expressions which, in the case of Christ as the Incarnate Word, or in the case of believers who share the life and the grace of Christ, speak of a Divine begetting, of a birth from above, of regeneration by the Spirit, 'denote a new commencement of the personal life, traceable back to a (creative) operation of God.'

LITERATURE.—Cremer, *Bib.-Theol. Lexicon, s.vv.*; H. Holtzmann, *Lehrbuch der Neutest. Theologie,* i. p. 436; commentaries of Alford, Meyer, etc.; Beyschlag, *NT Theol.* i. pp. 68 ff., 242, ii. p. 46; Dorner, *Development of the Doctrine of the Person of Christ,* Div. I. vol. i. p. 53 ff.; Reuss, *Christian Theology in the Apostolic Age,* i. p. 162, ii. p. 416 ff.; Delitzsch, *Commentary on the Psalms, ad loc.* H. H. CURRIE.

BEGGAR.—Though beggars are seldom spoken of in the Gospel narratives (Mt 20[30-34]; cf. Mk 10[46-52], Lk 18[35-43], Jn 9[1-41], and Lk 16[19-31] parable of Rich Man and Lazarus), they undoubtedly formed a considerable class in the Gospel age.* This is

* As equivalents for 'beg,' 'beggar' of EV, we find two radically different words in the text of the Gospels—on the one hand, the verbs προσαιτέω (Mk 10[46], Lk 18[35]), ἐπαιτέω (Lk 16[3]), and

evident both from the references to almsgiving in the Sermon on the Mount and from the mention of beggars in connexion with places of a public character: the entrance to Jericho (Mt 20[30] and parallels), a city through which so many pilgrims went at festival seasons, the neighbourhood of rich men's houses (Lk 16[20]), and the gates of the temple (Ac 3[2]).

The prevalence of the beggar class was due to various causes besides indolence—to the want of any system of poor relief, to the ignorance of proper medical remedies for common diseases like ophthalmia, and to the impoverishment of Palestine under the Romans owing to cruel and excessive taxation. (For the last, see Hausrath, *History of NT Times,* vol. i. 188 [Eng. tr., Williams & Norgate]). Edersheim thinks that the beggar's appeal for alms may have been enforced by some such cry as 'Gain merit by me,' 'O tender-hearted, by me gain merit, to thine own benefit' (*Life and Times of Jesus,* vol. ii. 178). It is worthy of notice, however, that no beggar is recorded to have enforced his appeal to Christ by any reference to the merit to be gained by a favourable response to his appeal (though it must be remembered, on the other hand, that the appeal of a blind beggar to one who had power to restore his sight would naturally differ from his attitude to those from whom he merely sought an alms). It is also observable that the begging 'saint' of Mohammedan countries is not found in the Gospels.

The remark of the unjust steward in the parable (Lk 16[3])—'To beg I am ashamed'—favours the conclusion that begging, under any circumstances, was regarded as an unfortunate mode of existence, and, in the case of the indolent, was condemned as strongly by public opinion as it was in the days of Jesus the son of Sirach (Sir 40[28-30]).

LITERATURE.—The standard Lives of Christ; G. M. Mackie's *Bible Manners and Customs; The Jewish Encyclopedia, s.v.*; cf. Day's *Social Life of the Hebrews.*

MORISON BRYCE.

BELIEF.—Belief is the mental action, condition, or habit of trusting in or confiding in a person or a thing. Trust, confidence, reliance, dependence, faith are from this point of view aspects of belief. More narrowly considered, belief is the mental acceptance of a proposition, statement, or fact on the testimony of another, or on the ground of authority. The fact may be beyond our observation, or the statement beyond our powers of verification, yet we may believe that Britain is an island though we may never have sailed round it, and we may believe in the law of gravitation though we may not be able to follow the reasoning which proves it.

This is not the place to deal with all the phases or aspects of belief, or to trace the history of opinion on the question. It is an interesting chapter in the history of human thought, and it is of the highest importance in its practical reference. But we may only indicate the main outline of it in both respects. The contributions towards the right understanding of the province and character of belief in more recent years have been of great value. Recent psychology has become aware of the magnitude and complexity of the problem, and in the hands of such writers as Bain, James, Stout, Baldwin, and others it has received a treatment which may be described as adequate. Nor should we omit the name of Dr. James Ward, whose work in this relation is of the highest merit. These have endeavoured to mark

the noun προσαίτης (Jn 9[8] Revised Text); on the other, the adj. πτωχός (Lk 16[20. 22]). In the former case the root idea is that of asking (αἰτέω), while πτωχός suggests the cringing or crouching (πτώσσω) of a beggar. But πτωχός is the ordinary NT word for 'poor,' whether in the sense of needy (Mt 19[21]) or humble (Mt 5[3]).

off the field of belief, and to distinguish it from other mental states. Is it active or passive? Is it a state of mind which belongs to the sphere of feeling? or is it a state of mind which belongs to intelligence? or is it something which belongs to the sphere of action? and is it a result of the 'will to believe'? Weighty names may be adduced in favour of each of these views. But before the question is asked to what sphere of human nature belief is to be assigned, there is a previous question to be settled. Are we to give the name of belief to every mental state which relates to an object? Is every state of consciousness which arises in response to a stimulus and in relation to an object to be described as a state of belief? Can we say we believe in our sensations as we say we believe in our reasoned conclusions? The state of the question may be set forth most vividly in two characteristic descriptions of the nature of belief. Hume says: 'A belief may be most accurately described as a lively idea related to or associated with a present impression.' Professor Stout says: 'All belief involves objective control of subjective activity' (*Manual of Psychology*, ii. 544).

According to Hume, 'an opinion or belief is nothing but an idea that is different from a fiction, not in the nature or in the order of its parts, but in the manner of its being conceived. But when I would explain this manner, I scarce find any word that fully answers the case, but am obliged to have recourse to every one's feeling, in order to give him a perfect notion of this operation of the mind. An idea assented to feels different from a fictitious idea that the fancy presents to us; and this feeling I endeavour to explain by calling it a superior force, or vivacity, or solidity or firmness, or steadiness' (Hume's *Works*, i. 397 f., Green's ed.). The description of belief given by Hume is distinguished by the absence of that 'objective control of subjective activity' which, according to Professor Stout, is the mark of all belief. A closer examination of Hume's statement enables us to see that the superior force or vivacity of a belief is due not merely to the manner of conceiving it, but to a certain coerciveness which fact has and which a fancy has not. The feeling of belief is not a gratuitous addition made by the mind to the experience, it is dictated by the fact itself.

Without entering into the discussion in any detail, it is sufficient for the present purpose to say that all belief in the first place is teleological, that it is the tendency of the mind to make itself at home in the world in which it has to live. This general description includes the naïve uncritical belief of the child, and the reasoned critical belief of the mature man. In its simplicity it is a postulate. It may be almost called an instinct, an expectation that the world will afford to man a place in which to live and grow and work. Be the origin and character of instinct what they may, be they due to original endowment or to the accumulated and transmitted inheritance of the race, yet the instincts are there, and are of a kind to enable life to act before individual experience has had time to work. Our organic nature is related to its environment, and it postulates an environment with which it can interact. Thus all our organic instincts which find expression in appropriate acts, such as sucking, eating, moving our limbs in response to a stimulus, and so on, are called into action on the presentation of their appropriate objects. Action begets belief, and belief is again the mental situation which leads to further action. At the outset belief is dominated by our practical needs. In truth, the new school of Humanism holds that all activities whatsoever are in the interest of the practical needs of man, and by the emphasis it has laid on this aspect it has called attention to a factor of human experience which has been too much neglected. For there is no doubt that the character of belief is to be explained, in the first place at all events, from its function in relation to the practical needs of man. And all through the experience of man, belief is an expression of human need, and is the demand which a living creature makes on the Universe for a place to live in, to grow in, and to furnish itself with what shall satisfy its need. Thus the initial postulate of belief is that it is in a world in which it may make itself at home, and the final demand of belief in developed humanity is that it shall find itself in a rational, intelligible world, in which its ideals of unity, intelligibility, beauty, and worth may and will find their realization.

Our beliefs, then, in their generality are our postulates. They set forth our expectations, our desires, our wishes. They proceed on the assumption that our needs are related to reality, and that reality has a way of satisfying our needs. In all belief there is, of course, a certain risk. We may mistake our real needs, and we may make mistakes as to the nature of reality. But the postulate is there notwithstanding. In fact, to believe that a thing exists is to act as if it existed. To believe that the properties of a thing are so and so, is to act on that supposition. Thus, apart from any theory, we all postulate a kind of uniformity of nature.

From this point of view all axioms are postulates. They are unavoidable assumptions. Students of science are familiar with these. We do not at present raise the question whether the universal formulæ of science are more than postulates. They are postulates, and are demands which our nature makes on the Universe.

Our postulates, however, *may* mislead; they may be unwarrantable, and not unavoidable. Along, therefore, with the predisposition to believe in the reality and modes of being of the objects of experience, there goes the necessity of verification, criticism, and investigation. For postulates may be too readily made. Passing needs may be taken for permanent, and beliefs may be based on wrong impressions. Subjective hopes or fears may objectify their objects, and attribute reality to objects which have none. Thus we have beliefs which are irresistible and unavoidable. They are absolutely based in the constitution of the mind itself, and are the assumptions without which experience is impossible. Students of Kant will readily recognize them. They lie at the basis of our life and activity, they are acted on before we are conscious of them, and when they arise into clear consciousness we recognize that they are unavoidable and inevitable. In like manner there are other principles arising out of our intercourse with the external world which strike us as inevitable and unavoidable. To enumerate these would lead us too far afield.

Between the necessary and universal beliefs on the one hand, and the practical necessity which coerces our beliefs on the other hand, there lies a wide field of beliefs, the validity of which depends on our ability to sift, examine, and criticise them. The process of sifting and criticism is coextensive with experience. Man is ever sifting his beliefs, is ever criticising them, and is, more or less, successfully active in the endeavour to make them correspond with reality as he is able to apprehend and conceive reality. He ventures in the belief that there is a correspondence between his inward nature and the world in which he lives; he believes that there is a constancy in things, that the qualities of things will remain constant. He makes the venture, and the venture is justified, and his faith increases as his expectation is verified. Beginning with the need to live and to make himself at home in the world, going on to satisfy his dominant and controlling need to obtain some mastery of the world, he reaches the time when he pursues knowledge for its own sake, and, in a disinterested manner, seeks to obtain a consistent and complete view of the scheme of things. So the sciences, the philosophies, the poesies of the world arise, and all the manifold works of the human spirit.

The beliefs of man can, as we see, be looked at as movements of the human spirit arising out of his intercourse with the world in which he lives. Our account of the matter would be most imperfect were we to confine our attention to man considered only as an individual. Belief is largely a social product. The working beliefs of the civilized man are largely due to inheritance. Without entering on the mysterious question of heredity, and without inquiry into the amount or quality of our organic inheritance, there is no doubt that a large proportion of our working beliefs arise out of our social environment, and out of the intellectual, moral, and spiritual atmosphere of the society around us. The language we learn to speak is the registration of the beliefs of those who made and used it ; it tells the meaning which men found in the world and in their own life. It throbs with the life of all the past, is directive of the life of the present and the future. We learn the meanings as we learn to speak, and the meanings of those who speak to us become our meanings. Our beliefs and our meanings belong together. And ere we know it, we are furnished with a working body of beliefs which mainly represent the experience of our ancestors. As we speak with the accent of the family and the district, as our voices repeat the swing and cadence of the sentence, so we take over also the beliefs which sway the minds of those with whom we live. It is a mixed inheritance which we receive and actively appropriate. Beliefs unsifted, uncriticized, results of prejudice often, often of superstition, form part of the inheritance we receive. And the mind assents readily enough to the strange amalgam. For behind the beliefs are the trust which the young have in the old, and the natural homage which they yield to experience.

The persistence of beliefs from age to age is itself a proof that they have a certain correspondence with reality. As all belief is a venture and a risk, failure to realize an expectation is a questioning of its validity, and gives occasion for inquiry. Thus belief is always under the criticism of reality, and the stress of circumstance and the strain of living compel us to revise our beliefs and strive to make them correspond with the facts. It is a process that never ends ; and as experience widens and knowledge grows, the circle of our beliefs may contract in one direction and expand in another. Beliefs may take the rank of universal and necessary convictions, or they may be classed as merely probable, or may sink to the level of bare possibility. Our postulates may pass into the region of certainty, or may have to be abandoned as mere possibilities.

Looking at the matter from a historical point of view, perhaps the most striking factor in the genesis and growth of belief is that of *trust in a person*. Into this state of mind many elements enter. The earliest manifestation of belief among human beings is that which we call Animism, or the belief that all things have an inward life, and have their own nature and activity. A spirit dwells in all objects, whether it is in them originally, or has been put into them by some process or act. Crude as this belief is, it yet has in it the germs of growth, and by refinement of its terms and by the removal of its grosser elements it has

become the spirit and the meaning of the higher philosophy of to-day. What is the Hegelian conception of the final correspondence of thought and reality, but a higher form of the original belief of man that the world around him, and the objects with which he came into contact, had a thought and meaning in them akin to those which he found in himself? It were an easy task to extend this observation to other philosophies, but space forbids.

Animism itself was a form of belief which came to higher issues in the social intercourse of man with man. The belief which man came to hold as to the animistic character of all objects whatsoever attained to vividness and certainty when applied to his fellow-men. In this sphere there was certainty, for was there not the interchange of influence, of feeling and thought, between himself and his fellows? Mutual help, power of working together, concerted action with friends and against enemies, the need of increased adaptation to the conditions of life, all conspired to raise belief in one's fellow-men to a dominant height. Out of this social co-operation have arisen the sciences, the arts, the philosophies, and especially the institutions of civilized life. But in considering the rise and growth of these achievements of human life, we must always remember that they are the outcome of the striving of conscious beings. This has been so well put by Professor Villa that we quote his statement.

'The mainspring of the mental development of the individual and the species thus consists in two contrary forces, on whose equilibrium both individual and social progress depend. One—namely, "imitation"—is a conservative, the other—"invention"—is a progressive force. The former corresponds to biological heredity, and is responsible for social and individual habits and instincts ; the latter corresponds to the biological law of variations, and finds its highest expression in "genius." The naturalistic and positive schools of the nineteenth century were too much inclined to consider social development as a purely natural and unconscious evolution, and omitted accordingly to take these two forces into consideration. Instead of considering social institutions, ideas, and phenomena as spontaneous products of the nameless multitude, modern Psychology rightly considers them the outcome of individual genius, subsequently consolidated, diffused, and preserved for the whole species by imitation. This idea, admirably developed by Tarde, on which Baldwin founds his studies of social Psychology, has transformed the theories which were current with regard to the evolution of the collective mind, which is thus presented in the light of a conscious, and not of an unconscious evolution like that of geological phenomena. Genius, therefore, is not to be understood as a degeneration, a violation of the natural and conservative law of heredity, but as the integrating factor of the latter, expressive of variation, impulse, and motion, as a dynamic force, without which evolution itself would be impossible' (*Contemporary Psychology*, by Guido Villa, Eng. tr. p. 256).

Thus the whirligig of time brings about its revenges, and the uniform tradition of history as to the influence of great personalities on the race is being justified by modern Psychology. In this tradition every movement of advance was ascribed to great men. Advances in the practical control of nature, the making of tools, the use of fire, the sowing of grain, and so on, are in the tradition of the race ascribed to individual men. More particularly is this the case with regard to the founders of cities, the makers of laws, the founders or the reformers of religions, and the framers of institutions. The 19th cent. was celebrated for its endeavours to disintegrate great men, to minimize their influence, and to trace great historic movements to a process and not to a person. How much influence this predilection has had on historic criticism we shall not here inquire. But in the light of modern Psychology, perhaps, Romulus, Numa Pompilius, Solon, Lycurgus, and many others may be looked at as real persons, benefactors of the race, whose names represent real forces in the development of humanity. Perhaps modern Psychology may help men to have some real apprehension of Moses, as ancient

Psychology had so much to do with his disintegration.

In the sphere of religious belief we have clear and overwhelming evidence of the weight and influence of personality in the shaping of belief, and in the advance of men to clearer thought and purer embodiment of the religious ideals. It has been through the striving, the toil, the agony of great men that the ideals of religion have attained to form and reality. To them it was given to toil for the race, and the vision they saw and the moral and spiritual truth they won became the inheritance of other men, and through them were conserved for the good of the race. Nor is it the fact that the work and influence of great personalities on other persons have been of a narrow and cramping kind. On the contrary, all the religious truth we possess may be traced back to the moral, spiritual, and intellectual insight of great men, just as every great discovery of science is associated with some great historic name. This personal element in our belief is of universal validity. As a matter of fact, only those religions which have had a personal founder have become universal, or at least international. For, after all, personality is our highest category of thought and life.

Belief in great personalities may be historically and scientifically vindicated. They were needed to make the new departure, they were the first to see the vision, they made the discovery, or thought out the truth; but those unfitted to be pioneers may be quite able to think over again what is made plain to them by him who was the first to think out that truth. The insight of a great man may be verified by the experience of other men. In fact, we have daily illustrations of this in our own experience. We use telephones, we drive by means of steam or electricity, we command nature by using the means which others have placed at our disposal, though we may not have the power of making these discoveries. Plato, Aristotle, Kant opened out paths on which the feet of others may safely tread, and we may rise to the height of the vision of Dante, and rejoice in the universality of Shakespeare, though these would have remained undiscovered countries had not those great personalities opened the gates of entrance to us.

Yet the man in the street has something in common with the greatest and the highest. If he cannot initiate he may imitate, and if he cannot make the discovery he may appreciate and act on it when it has been made. For in the long-run the achievements of great men in any sphere, just in proportion to their truth and value, turn out to have elements of permanent value. Though the discoveries of a person, they have no mere personal value. They are objective, and because objective they may become the possession of every man. We have spoken up to this point of the work of great personalities only so far as that work was a help towards the discovery of truth and a help to life. Belief in them, trust in them, is thus far justified. But no great personality answers to the ideal of greatness in all the aspects of greatness. Great men have had their limitations, and greatness from one point of view has been accompanied with littleness in other respects. The leaders of men have had their limitations. Some have been great in action, some in thought, some in invention, some in power of poetic or prophetic vision, and some in other ways. Others have been great in gathering into a system the results of the work of former generations, and have thus marked out the stage to which humanity has come. But the limitations of great men have had their effect, and their achievements may come to hinder and not to help progress. In all spheres of human thought and action this has been true, and the imitative mind of man has striven to live in formulæ which have become outworn and effete. There has been also imitation of great men in those aspects of their activity in which they were not good or great. Illustrations of these facts abound, and need not be dwelt on at length.

But trust in personality as one of the greatest forces of human progress and one of the strongest elements in belief is justified notwithstanding. It alone can give the enthusiasm which confronts difficulties, the personal devotion and love which make men willing to live and die for a great cause. The great epochs of human life, the times which stand out in history as full of heroic endeavour, of far-reaching aspiration, and of substantial gain for other ages, have been pre-eminently periods of abounding trust in great ideals; and these ideals appear in all their grandeur as embodied in some great personality. The imitative mind found its ideal embodied in the great man of its time; and was touched as with a flame, and followed on and became greater than it knew. The great personality became for the lesser men the embodiment of the highest ideal they had ever known; and they, so far as they saw it, embodied it in their own action and character, and wrought it so far into the very constitution of humanity. So the vision grew; and as one personality after another revealed to men the possible synthesis of the ideal greatness of a perfect personality, men were educated to perceive what they ought to demand in the ideal of a perfect personality in whom they might completely and absolutely trust.

In the perfect personality in whom man may absolutely trust all kinds of ideals must meet, and be harmonized in a perfect unity. That is the postulate of the nature of man. And each part of man's complex nature makes its own demand and contributes its own share towards the realization of the ideal. Our intelligent nature demands unity and intelligibility in the Universe, and in Him in whom the Universe lives and moves and has its being. Our moral nature demands its ideal of perfect goodness, righteousness, and holiness in order to meet the needs of our moral nature, and to give us scope for the exercise of reverence towards that which is above us, love towards all that helps and sustains us, and benevolence towards all that needs our help. The æsthetic nature furnishes its ideal of perfect beauty and harmony, and demands that reality shall meet this as it meets every other demand. The heart demands goodness and love, and furnishes in its own action the type of what it demands. The Christian belief is that all these ideals meet and are realized in God. It is the business of Theism to show how these ideals are realized in God, and it is the business of the metaphysician, the ethicist, the æstheticist, and the poet to show how the various ideals converge to the one great ideal whom we reverently call God. Our intellectual, ethical, spiritual, artistic, and emotional ideals agree, must agree, if we are to attain to harmony of life and fulness of being. We repeat again that these are our needs, and our needs have their roots in reality, and reality does not disappoint us.

Is there a Personality who can be to all men what some personalities have been to some men, and to some nations? Is there one who can be to all nations what the national heroes have been to particular peoples, one who can embody their highest ideals, and who can so react on them as to make them work out these ideals in themselves? That is the claim which history makes for Christ, which Christians make for Him, and which they believe has been verified in human experience by all who have trusted and followed Him. He Himself makes the claim : ' I am the way, the truth, and the life' (Jn 14⁶). St. Paul makes it for Him : ' in whom are all the treasures of wisdom and knowledge hidden' (Col 2³). This is not the place to unfold the meaning of the claim of Christ to the reverence and trust of all men, nor to set forth His ability to meet all the needs of our nature and to satisfy all our ideals. It would take many treatises to do that work, instead of one brief article. But the scope of the proof may be indicated. First, as to the demands which our needs make on Christ ; and, second, as to His ability to meet them. The main demands of our nature may be summed up in the ideals we have noted above : the demand for unity, the demand for purity, the longing for beauty and harmony, the thirst for love and goodness and fulness of life. The demand for unity, and the belief that unity is there, have led men on towards the conquest of the world,—which conquest has embodied itself, so far as it has gone, in the sciences and their practical applications and in the philosophies of the world. The demand for beauty and harmony, and its result in the poetries, arts, and beautiful human constructions, and in increasing appreciations of the beauty of the Universe ; the demand for goodness, righteousness, love, which has embodied itself in the ethical and spiritual life of the world, are illustrations of the faith of man in the unity, beauty, goodness, and worth of reality, and his own achievements are tributes to the validity of his faith.

But the needs of man make this claim on the perfect human personality. We need One who can reveal to us what human life ought to be and what it may become. We need One who gathers into Himself all the types of greatness that have ever entered into the thoughts of men ; and One who has realized them in His own life and action. But we need to be educated and trained to appreciate the ideal, for it may be, nay, it is, the reversal of many human ideals. Man has often mistaken his real needs, and has also mistaken the ideals which alone can satisfy them. The first must become last and the last first. The intellectual, moral, æsthetic, and religious needs of man have sought satisfaction in the pursuit of false ideals, and have not found it. Yet the needs are real and the search was good, and the satisfaction is attainable. The perfect human Personality reveals to man how to show reverence to what is above man, love to all his equals, and benevolence to all that is subject to him. He has shown it in His own action, and inspires it in those who trust Him.

Belief in Christ is thus the outcome of the deepest needs of man's manifold nature, and the prophecy of their complete satisfaction. It means also that there is a revelation to man of what his real needs are. It means instruction, education, training into a true and adequate apprehension of his own nature and calling. He learns from Christ his own value and worth, and the sphere in which these may be realized. He learns how this supreme Personality has thought about him, cared for him, suffered for him, lives for him, and is ever working and striving in him and for him. Then, too, he learns, as he trusts Christ, what life and conduct ought to be, and he learns that it is possible through union with Christ to live that life and imitate that conduct. For the further development of this part of our theme we have to refer to Christian dogmatics, and specially to the NT documents. We may also refer to the practical experience of the Christian through the Christian centuries, and to what it has felt and accomplished.

As to the ability of Christ to satisfy our needs and meet our ideals, we have just to make the same

reference. We are beginning to understand the cosmical significance of Christ. As our knowledge of the primary revelation of God is widened by the patient and triumphant labours of scientific workers through the ages, we find increased validity in the process when we reflect that we are following in the footsteps of Him by whom every thing was made that was made. ' In Him all things consist,' and our faith in the Eternal Logos is confirmed as we trace out the logos of things. Then in the sphere of history we desire a meaning and a unity, we need the belief that a purpose runs through the ages, and we find that of Him, and through Him, and to Him are all things ; that ' God was in Christ reconciling the world to Himself,' and that there is a ministry of reconciliation in history. Then comes the personal knowledge of Him, in His perfect grace, love, wisdom, power ; and the union with Him, till He becomes the atmosphere we breathe, our outlook on life and its possibilities, the source of all our strivings, the goal of all our efforts ; and the only true description of it all is that we are ' in Christ Jesus.'

The correspondence is perfect between our needs and their satisfaction in Jesus Christ. Here the subjective is controlled by the objective, and the coercive power of Christ over the belief of those who trust Him is perfect. Much might be said on the educative power of Christ on man as to the true needs of man, and much might be said on the reasonableness of trust in this perfect Personality ; but enough has been said to indicate the congruity of this belief with the whole nature of belief in general, and to show that it is the outcome of all the factors which enter into and justify that attitude of the human mind which we call belief. See, further, art. FAITH.

LITERATURE.—The articles ' Belief' and ' Psychology' in the *Encyc. Brit*.9 ; James, *Principles of Psychology* ; Turner, *Knowledge, Belief, and Certitude* ; Flint, *Agnosticism* ; Royce, *The Religious Aspect of Modern Philosophy* ; Newman, *Grammar of Assent* ; Bain, *Emotions and the Will*, and *Mental and Moral Science* ; Villa, *Contemporary Psychology*. It may be well to refer to Kant in his three great Critiques, and specially to his treatment of ' Glaube' in the *Critique of the Practical Reason*. In the works of Sir William Hamilton, Mansel, and Herbert Spencer the reader will find discussions of some value. In truth, the literature which in one form or other deals with the nature and validity of belief is so enormous, that an exhaustive reference is out of the question. But reference ought to be made to Balfour's *Foundations of Belief* and to Kidd's *Social Evolution*, as these books present a somewhat peculiar view of the nature and validity of belief, specially in its relation to knowledge.
As to belief in Christ we need not give any reference, for all the literature of Christianity would be relevant here.

J. IVERACH.

BELOVED.—Wherever the word rendered ' beloved' (ἀγαπητός—in 9 places AV has ' dearly beloved' and in 3 places ' well-beloved' ; in every case RV has ' beloved' only) is used in the NT, it seems to imply a love deeper and more intimate than the common affections, and is therefore but sparingly employed. In the Epistles it is the indication of the inner brotherhood, and its very form ' beloved brethren' has passed into every liturgy. St. Paul uses it to distinguish, as with peculiar honour, those whom he has personally enlightened with the new faith, as Epænetus (Ro 16⁵), Timothy (1 Co 4¹⁷), or a whole community (1 Co 10¹⁴, Ph 2¹²). But in the Gospels the word is used solely concerning Christ, and marks out the Son's especial relationship to the Father. There is abundance of love throughout the Gospels : whether of Jesus for John and the rest, or of the disciples and others for Him : and there is no weakness or timidity in the expression of the love. But to none other save Himself is the word ' beloved' applied. He Himself uses it but once, and then in the parable of the Lord of the Vineyard, wherein the ' beloved son' is the evident picture of the Son of Man (Mk 12[6] [AV ' well-beloved '], Lk 20[13]). Elsewhere the Evangelists (Synoptists only), who give the word, report it as the utterance of God, the Divine recognition and approval of the Son. The influence of the OT is plainly visible in the words heard at the Baptism. Jesus hears the voice of God pronouncing a benediction in clearest remembrance of Ps 2[7], ' Thou art my son, this day have I begotten thee,' and of Is 42[1] ' My chosen, in whom my soul delighteth ' (quoted in Mt 12[18]; cf. Bruce, *Expos. Gr. Test.*, *in loc.*) ; for the Synoptists agree in the phrase ' My beloved son in $\binom{\text{thee}}{\text{whom}}$ I am well pleased ' (Mt 3[17], Mk 1[11], Lk 3[22]). And there is something beautifully fitting in this consecration of the opening of His ministry by a blended echo of psalm and prophecy. The other occasion of the word is that record of another great revealing moment of His life—the Transfiguration, when two of the three tell of ' a voice out of the cloud (saying), This is my beloved son, hear ye him ' (Mt 17[5], Mk 9[7] ; in the ‖ Lk 9[35] the true reading is ἐκλελεγμένος).

LITERATURE.—The *Lexicons* of Cremer and Grimm-Thayer, *s.v.* ἀγαπητός ; R. H. Charles, *Ascension of Isaiah* (1900), p. 3 and *passim* ; J. A. Robinson, *Epistle to Ephesians* (1904), 229 ; art. ' Beloved ' in Hastings' *DB*.   E. DAPLYN.

BENEDICTION.—Benedictions on the assembled people pronounced by an officiating priest or minister were a regular part of the liturgies of the temple and the synagogue, but no direct mention is made of these in the Gospel narratives. Quite similar in character, however, are the benedictions on persons, which are not a part of the ceremonial of Divine worship. Of these there are several examples in the Gospels (Lk 2[34] 6[28] 24[50] and Mk 10[16]). All such words of blessing are liable to have magical power attributed to them, but in form and origin they are simply a prayer addressed to God for the wellbeing of some person or persons in whose presence they are uttered. They may be exemplified from the benediction of the Jewish liturgy : ' The Lord bless thee, and keep thee ; the Lord make his face to shine upon thee, and be gracious unto thee ; the Lord lift up his countenance upon thee, and give thee peace ' (Nu 6[24-27]). In the NT the verbs εὐλογεῖν (Lk 2[34] 6[28] 24[50]) and κατευλογεῖν (Mk 10[16]) denote ' to utter a benediction ' in this sense.

εὐλογεῖν properly means to ascribe (to God) praise and honour (*benedicere*). In accordance with the usage of the OT and NT and of the Christian Church, this act also is termed ' benediction.' It is of the nature of thanksgiving and praise to God for His goodness, and differs essentially from that kind of benediction which is a prayer that Divine favour may be shown to those whom the speaker ' blesses.' In the NT this second kind of benediction is expressed by εὐχαριστεῖν, ' give thanks,' as well as by εὐλογεῖν. The Jewish custom of blessing God on every possible occasion (see below) supplies a probable explanation of the designation of God in Mk 14[61] ὁ εὐλογητός, ' the Blessed.' It does not, however, appear that this title was current in Jewish literature (Dalman, *Words of Jesus*, p. 200).* Elsewhere in the NT εὐλογητός is used as an *epithet* of God (*e.g.* Lk 1[68]). This is the Jewish usage of הַמְבֹרָךְ.

The double sense of εὐλογεῖν, just explained, is due to the meaning of בֵּרֵךְ and the LXX use of εὐλογεῖν. It has a third signification when God is the subject, namely ' bless,' *i.e.* prosper. This also is a meaning of בֵּרֵךְ (see BLESSING). In the Gospels the only instances of the third usage are cases where the participle εὐλογημένος, ' blessed,' is employed. εὐλογεῖν mean-

* Enoch 77[1] seems to supply a parallel. In *Berakhoth* vii. 3 (ed. Surenhusius) הַמְבֹרָךְ is an epithet qualifying אֲדֹנָי.

ing *to pronounce a benediction* never occurs in John, but εὐλογημένος appears in Jn 12[13].

1. *Benedictions on men.*—In Jewish life the occasions of pronouncing benedictions on men were numerous. Besides those of the temple and the synagogue, and perhaps even older than these, were the salutations customary at meeting and parting, entering a house and leaving it, which were all benedictions. The blessings of the aged and of parents were specially valued, and were often a part of the solemn farewell of the dying. In the temple a benediction was regularly pronounced at the conclusion of the morning and evening sacrifices. The statement in Lk 1[21] that the people waited for Zacharias may be an indirect reference to this custom. But the intercessory benedictions recorded in the Gospels are chiefly of the nature of greetings or salutations (Lk 1[28f.] 1[42] 13[35]=Mt 23[39]=Ps 118[26]). Our Lord commends to His disciples the practice of saluting a house when they enter it, *i.e.*, of pronouncing a benediction on those resident in it (Mt 10[12]=Lk 10[5]). The actual words of such a benediction are given in Lk 10[5] ' May peace rest on this house ' (cf. Lk 1[40]). Christ's farewell to His disciples before His ascension was expressed in words of blessing (Lk 24[50f.]). It is to be understood in the light of what has already been said regarding Jewish customs. Simeon's benediction (Lk 2[34]) was that of an old man and a priest. But in any circumstances benedictions were appropriate as expressions of goodwill (cf. Lk 6[28] and Mk 11[9f.]).

εὐλογημένος (=בָּרוּךְ) in formulas of blessing may be understood to express a wish, ' Blessed be thou.' This is clearly the meaning in Ps 118[26] (LXX), and consequently in Mk 11[9]=Mt 21[9]=Lk 19[38]=Jn 12[13] and Mt 23[39]=Lk 13[35], where the Psalm is quoted. In the Gospels RV makes the phrase a statement, and so does AV except in Lk 19[38] (cf. Mk 11[10]). There are similar phrases in Mk 11[10] and Lk 1[42]. μακάριος, although translated in the EV ' blessed,' is not used in benedictions, and has a different meaning (see BLESSING).

There is at least one clear reference to the *attitude* adopted in the act of benediction (Lk 24[50]). The uplifting of the hands there spoken of (cf. Lv 9[22]) is not peculiar to benedictions ; according to ancient custom, Babylonian and Egyptian as well as Hebrew, when prayer was offered in a standing posture the hands were uplifted or spread out (Ps 28[2], Is 1[15] etc.). It is not equally certain that the laying of hands upon the children who were blessed by Christ (Mk 10[16]) is directly connected with the act of benediction as such, although Gn 48[14] may be quoted in support of that view. The request made to Christ is that He should *touch* the children (Mk 10[13]=Lk 18[15] ; but cf. ‖ Mt 19[13]), and that is something different from a request that He should bless them (see Mk 5[28], and cf. possibly Lk 2[28]). Mt 19[13] may be regarded as an interpretation of Mk 10[16] ; benedictions of persons are intercessory prayers on their behalf.

2. *Benedictions of God.*—The practice of uttering benedictions on God is a highly characteristic expression of Jewish religious life. It is broadly formulated as a duty in the Talmud in the words, ' Whoever benefits from this world without (reciting) a benediction, acts as if he robbed God ' (*Berakhoth*, 35a). Any circumstance or event which recalls or exhibits God's goodness or power is an appropriate occasion for ' blessing ' God. At circumcisions, redemptions of the first-born, marriages, etc., benedictions of this class were employed along with others invoking blessings on men. Sometimes unusual experiences and special circumstances called them forth. But the ordinary routine of life, and particularly the daily meals of the family and the individual, equally fulfil the conditions which prompt their use. The Jewish 'grace' pronounced at meal-times was an act of thanksgiving to God, that and nothing more. The procedure is described in the Mishna (*Berakhoth*) and in other Jewish sources. When several sat down to a meal together, one usually gave thanks for all, although each in certain circumstances was expected to do so for himself. A company is said to be constituted by the presence of three persons. The meal commenced with a benediction and with the breaking of bread. Whoever broke the bread also spoke the benediction. This was the part of the master of the house, the giver of the feast, or the most important person in the company. There were differences in the words of blessing, according to the formality of the occasion and the character of the dishes that were served. During one meal several benedictions might be pronounced, referring to the various articles of food separately (for the ordinary formulas used in blessing bread and wine, see BLESSING). During the Passover meal benedictions were pronounced at several fixed points. Every meal was concluded with a benediction. In the Passover meal the last benediction was spoken before the actual conclusion ; a hymn was sung at the very end.

It is not easy to draw a line in principle between the thanksgiving of God which is benediction and that which is denoted by the word 'praise' (αἰνεῖν). But there is a practical distinction. The use of special formulas, and especially of the word בָּרוּךְ 'blessed' (εὐλογημένος), is characteristic of benedictions.

There are only three references in the Gospels to benedictions of God other than those pronounced at meal-times. In each case they are prompted by unusual manifestations of Divine favour to the speakers (Lk 1⁶⁴ RV, 2²⁸ 24⁵³). The actual words of benediction are not recorded in any case. Lk 2²⁹⁻³² is a prayer supplementing the benediction proper.

Four narratives in the Gospels allude to blessings pronounced at meal-times. The occasions are the miracles of the feeding of the 5000 and of the 4000, the institution of the Lord's Supper, and the evening meal at Emmaus. The reference in every case to the breaking of bread is noteworthy. It emphasizes the character of the act as one in accordance with Jewish custom. The Jewish formulas of blessing at meal-times make it perfectly certain that no blessing on the food is asked, but that God is thanked for the food. Illustrations of this meaning of the word 'bless' are found in the parallel narratives of the Gospels themselves. Lk 22¹⁹ has 'give thanks' (εὐχαριστήσας) in place of the 'bless' (εὐλογήσας) of Mk 14²² and Mt 26²⁶ ; Jn 6¹¹ has 'give thanks' where the Synoptists have 'bless' (cf. also the parallel expressions in 1 Co 14¹⁶). When the grammatical object of the verb is an article of food, 'bless' then signifies 'pronounce a benediction over,' *i.e.* 'give thanks to God for' the food in question (so Mk 8⁷ and Lk 9¹⁶). The same construction occurs in the OT (1 S 9¹³), (in the Mishna בָּרֵךְ עַל is generally used). Christ's blessing of the elements in the institution of the Lord's Supper should no doubt be understood in the light of these facts.

The only other passage in the NT where a material object is said to be blessed is 1 Co 10¹⁶, and it really belongs to the category just explained. The expression 'cup . . . which we bless' means simply 'cup for which we give thanks,' over which we pronounce our benediction. In Jewish phraseology material objects may be consecrated or hallowed, but they cannot be said in the same sense to be blessed.

Mk 6⁴¹ (and so the parallels) speaks of Christ looking up to the sky, and implies, no doubt, in accordance with the circumstances, that He stood while He offered His prayer of thanksgiving. But the ordinary Jewish practice seems to have been to sit while grace was being said. In Jn 6²³ it is not obvious at first sight why the words 'when the

Lord gave thanks' have been added. Perhaps they were intended to mean 'when the Lord was giver of the feast.' The statement in Lk 24³⁰ that the risen Christ was recognized in the breaking of bread seems to imply that the disciples were familiar with the manner in which He acted on such occasions, and that there was something peculiar or characteristic in the procedure which He followed. Doubtless the act as He performed it was always deliberate and impressive.

The application of the word εὐλογεῖν to meals is common to the Synoptists, but St. Matthew (15³⁶) and St. Luke (22¹⁹) both substitute on one occasion εὐχαριστεῖν for St. Mark's εὐλογεῖν (8⁷ 14²²). εὐλογεῖν with God as explicit object occurs in St. Luke only (1⁶⁴ 2²⁸ 24⁵³). St. John does not use the word at all in this sense (see 6¹¹ and cf. also 11⁴¹).

LITERATURE.—See the authorities cited at end of art. BLESSING.

W. B. STEVENSON.

BENEDICTUS.—The Song of Zacharias (wh. see), preserved in Lk 1⁶⁸⁻⁷⁹, is usually spoken of under the name familiar to us in the offices of the Church—a name derived from its opening word in the Latin version. St. Luke introduces it immediately after his narrative of the circumcision and naming of the future Baptist, with the copulative *and*, in these terms : 'And his father Zacharias was filled with the Holy Ghost, and prophesied, saying' (v.⁶⁷). But while he thus asserts the author's inspiration, and claims the Song as an outcome thereof, it does not follow either that the Holy Ghost came on Zacharias then and there,—He may have rested on him during the whole period of his miraculous dumbness, teaching him in that penitential silence, and bringing to his remembrance the dealings and promises of God;—or that the Song was extempore (it was while the old psalmist was musing, that the fire burned, Ps 39³). Zacharias may have had it ready for the long anticipated moment ; may have recited it then, and written it afterwards

Nor, again, does the fullest acceptance of its inspiration as a fact forbid that it should bear the marks of the time at which it was composed, and of the feelings of devout Israelites under the trials of their age. The Holy Spirit speaks through men, not through pipes. Their character, proved and purified by calamities,—public as well as private,— is of no small importance to Him. They were 'holy men of God,' who 'spake as they were moved by the Holy Ghost' (2 P 1²¹). Zacharias was an old man (Lk 1¹⁸) ; he might easily remember the capture of Jerusalem by Pompey (B.C. 63), and his pushing forward, like Antiochus Epiphanes, into the Holy of Holies. There were chief priests who 'opened the gates' to the heathen conqueror as 'sons to receive a father' (Ps-Sol 8¹⁸⁻²⁰); but among the ministering priesthood there then lived (as there still survived in Zacharias himself) a piety so genuine and fearless that, when the victorious Romans burst into the Temple courts, the officiating priests went on with the service as if nothing unusual were happening, and suffered themselves to be cut down at their posts. That awful day was the end of Jewish independence. Zacharias had lived through all the shame that followed, and the further Roman outrages of Crassus, who robbed the Temple (B.C. 54), and of Cassius, who sold 30,000 Jews into captivity (B.C. 51). The usurpations, the feuds, the subserviences to Herod and the Romans, the Sadducean unbelief of the high-priestly families, the immoralities which disgraced them,—must all have been fresh in his recollection, and may well have led him, as these things led the more quiet and religious Pharisees around him, to turn back for comfort to the Divine promise to David and his seed for evermore.

That such a terrible state of things should have

deeply affected Zacharias was as right as it was natural. That it wrought within him affections altogether good and holy is just a sign that it was the Spirit of Christ who taught him by them. The book already referred to, the Psalter (or Psalms) of Solomon, is the nearest Jewish work in point of time to the *Benedictus* and its fellows in the first two chapters of St. Luke : it is also the likest to them in style and character. Like these Songs, the Psalms of Solomon are a proof that sacred poetry, so far from being extinct among the Jews at this period, was living, and was being made the vehicle of intensest religious feeling. Nor are these Psalms deficient in merit. They are forceful, vivid, full of noble indignation against Roman oppression and Jewish secularity alike, of shame for 'the draggled purples' of the Hasmonæan princes, of acknowledgments that God is justified in His chastening of Israel. They look, like the *Benedictus*, for a Messiah of the House of David. They assign to Him the double work of 'thrusting' sinners out of the holy place, 'purging Jerusalem and making it holy as in the days of old,' and of avenging her upon the Romans. But with all this, they lack the characteristic elements of evangelical prophecy. They have little insight and less foresight. They emanated from the better sort of Pharisees, and they betray all the elements of Pharisaism as we see it in the Gospels. The Messiah they expect is purely human (cf. our Lord's contention on this point with the *Pharisees*, Mt 22⁴¹⁻⁴⁶, Mk 12³⁵⁻³⁷, Lk 20³⁹⁻⁴⁴). Their idea of God's salvation is political mainly : vengeance on their enemies rather than undisturbed devotion is the thing they long for. The whole tone of the book is fierce, narrow, separatist, self-righteous. The *Benedictus*, on the other hand, is in its closing notes very strikingly predictive : the father foretells, with proud exactness, the future ministry of his infant son. Even had this element been wanting, the Song is in the truest sense a prophecy, for it discerns the spiritual nature of Christ's kingdom with a clearness unknown even to the Apostles after Christ had been some time with them. It tells of 'salvation in the remission of sins' (v.⁷⁷ RV) through the mercy of God (v.⁷⁹, cf. Tit 3⁵) in Christ (v.⁶⁹), of human need and darkness, of reconciliation to life and peace, and of the worship of God without fear (cf. 1 Jn 4¹⁸) as its climax (v.⁷⁴). There is deliverance from every enemy, not from the Romans only, but no hint of revenge upon them. The tone of the Song is eminently gentle. The salvation is from God, according to His promise by the mouth of all His holy prophets from the beginning of the world ; it embraces in its range our fathers (v.⁷²) who are gone, as well as the living (cf. 1 P 2¹⁹, and Rev 6⁹) ; and is all given us through and in the Horn of Salvation, whom God has *raised* up 'in the house of his servant David' (v.⁶⁹), indeed, but who Himself is 'the Most High,' and 'the Lord' (v.⁷⁶), and 'the Dayspring from on High'—not rising gradually as does Nature's dawn, but bursting, as it were, upon our wondering eyes, full-orbed from the zenith (v.⁷⁸). It is very remarkable how subordinate to Him who is the subject of his Song is the position assigned by Zacharias to his own miraculously-born child. Even while he predicts John's office, it is in contrast with the greater dignity of the Redeemer. Alford justly remarks that the *Benedictus* 'shows the exact religious view under which John was educated by his father.' The fruit may be seen in all that is recorded of the Baptist (cf. Mt 3³· ¹¹· ¹² 11¹⁰, Mk 1¹⁻⁸, Lk 3⁴⁻¹⁷, Jn 1⁷· ⁸· ¹⁵· ¹⁹⁻³⁴ 3¹⁰). It is abundantly clear that the Song was composed in the light both of the Annunciation made to the Virgin Mary (Lk 1³⁵⁻³⁸) and of the inspired salutation wherewith she was greeted by Elisabeth (v.⁴³).

The *Benedictus* is thus emphatically a 'Hymn of the Incarnation'—'Canticum de Evangelio,' as the Antiphonary of Bangor styles it.

It differs from the other hymns in these two chapters of St. Luke mainly in this, that whereas the *Magnificat* (St. Mary's Song) is of Christ's kingship, whereby He casts down the proud and exalts the humble, and the *Nunc dimittis* (Simeon's) is of His prophetic or enlightening office, the *Benedictus*, as beseems the song of the blameless priest, is of Christ's priesthood. It is priestly throughout ; it begins with blessing and ends with peace. The work of the Deliverer is remission of sins and reconciliation with God, and its culmination is seen in a people of priests 'serving God (*i.e.* worshipping Him—λατρεύειν, same word as in Rev 22⁸) in holiness and righteousness before him all the days of their life.' It is evident that Zacharias has in his mind the history of Melchizedek (Gn 14) and the oracle, even then ascribed to the pen of David, which forms so important a commentary on that history (Ps 110).

The 'sources' of the Song, as of the two chapters of which it forms an integral part, will be discussed in art. LUKE (GOSPEL OF). It may be mentioned here that the text of the *Benedictus* varies little either in MSS or Versions. The one reading which exhibits an important difference from that of the *Textus Receptus* is in v.⁷⁸, where a future tense takes the place of a past. This has been adopted in the RV, but with a marginal note, 'Many ancient authorities read *hath visited us*.'

The structure of the *Benedictus* is simple. It consists of three stanzas—the first (vv.⁶⁸⁻⁷⁰) setting forth the fact of God's interposition in the approaching birth of the long-looked-for Saviour ; the second (vv.⁷¹⁻⁷⁵) telling the purpose of His incarnation ; and the third (vv.⁷⁶⁻⁷⁹) an apostrophe to Zacharias' babe, declaring his office as the forerunner of Christ.

The references in the hymn are marvellous alike in their number, range, and depth. The opening words remind us of the opening of Melchizedek's address to Abram (Gn 14) ; 'visited and redeemed,' of Israel's deliverance from Egypt (Ex 4³¹ 6⁶) ; the 'Horn of Salvation,' of Hannah's Song at the beginning of the story of the kings (1 S 2¹⁰) ; 'in the house of David' is from 1 Ch 17⁴ ; in 'from the beginning of the world,' ἀπ' αἰῶνος, we have possibly an allusion to the *Protevangelium* (Gn 3¹⁵) ; in 'in holiness' we may see reference to Ps 110³ ; while the Baptist's mission is described by quotation from Is 40³. Nor is the opinion of Bishop Wordsworth, accepted somewhat grudgingly by Alford, to be dismissed as fanciful, that in vv.⁷²· ⁷³ there is a paronomasia on the three names of the parties chiefly concerned with the Baptist's birth. The name of *John* had been fixed by the Angel (v.¹³) ; Zacharias knew that *it* must be significant, and it means 'the grace *or* mercy of God,' ἔλεος. He could hardly help reflecting that his own name *Zacharias* (from זָכַר *recordatus fuit*, and יָהּ *Jah* (Jehovah), means θεὸς ἐμνήσθη ; while *Elisabeth* (from אֵל *Deus*, and שָׁבַע *shāba' juravit*) is just ὅρκος θεοῦ. He puts all these together. '. . . The tender *mercy* of our GOD . . . in *remembrance* of his holy covenant . . . the *oath* which he sware.' If the paronomasia as a literary figure is out of fashion for the moment, we may remember that neither Dante nor Shakespeare thought it beneath their genius ; and Zacharias had sacred precedents for employing it in the histories of the births and blessings of the twelve patriarchs (Gn 30 and 49), and still more strikingly in Is 7 and 8, where, as Matthew Arnold has observed, the significant names are the keynote of the whole prophecy,

LITERATURE.—Plummer, 'St. Luke' (*Internat. Crit. Com.*), 38 ff. ; Godet, *Com. on St. Luke*, i. 110 ff. ; Wilkinson, *Johan. Document in Lk i.*, p. 17.   JAMES COOPER.

BENEFACTOR (εὐεργέτης).—A title conferred by a grateful sovereign or country for useful service rendered, often in time of difficulty or danger (Est 2²³ 6²). The names of royal benefactors were enrolled in a register (Herod. viii. 85, where see Rawlinson's note; Thuc. i. 129). In the Persian tongue the king's benefactors enjoyed a special title, possibly implying that their names were recorded. Besides the special appellation given to all who had done public service, the title 'benefactor' is occasionally mentioned as a perpetual epithet of kings, merely enhancing their dignity. So Antiochus VII. of Syria, Ptolemy III. of Egypt, and at a later period Ptolemy VII. (B.C. 145–117), were called benefactors. It is evidently this latter, complimentary or official, title to which our Lord chiefly alludes in Lk 22²⁵, and so RV rightly spells with a capital, 'Benefactors.' In worldly societies men reign in virtue of superior power, and Εὐεργέτης, 'Benefactor,' is a title of flattery which may be applied to the most cruel despot—as in the case of Ptolemy VII., otherwise known as Physcon ('Big-Belly'), and also called Κακεργέτης by a play upon his official designation. But in this new society which Jesus is instituting, the greatest is to be as the least, and he that is chief as he that doth serve. And this after the example of the Lord Himself, who, being the true Εὐεργέτης, 'came not to be ministered unto, but to minister, and to give his life a ransom for many' (see the parallel passage Mt 20²⁵⁻²⁸, and cf. the ὑπὲρ ὑμῶν διδόμενον, ὑπὲρ ὑμῶν ἐκχυννόμενον which Jesus had just spoken at the Last Supper [Lk 22¹⁹· ²⁰]).

LITERATURE.—Hastings' *DB*, art. 'Benefactor'; *Comm.* of Alford and Godet, *in loc.*; Smith, *Classical Dict.*, art. 'Ptolemæus.'   C. H. PRICHARD.

BENEVOLENCE. — The disposition which sets itself to desire steadfastly the welfare and happiness of others. Christian benevolence is this disposition of heart informed by the example and precept of Christ, this informing of the heart being the work of His Holy Spirit. Continual active benevolence is perhaps the most striking feature in the whole of the Gospel records. It is the keynote of the Sermon on the Mount, and merges into the harmony of love in the final discourses recorded in the Fourth Gospel. The *sons of the Most High* are to do good to their enemies as well as to their friends (Lk 6³⁵). The *sons of the Father which is in heaven* are to be kindly disposed and actively beneficent both to the just and to the unjust (Mt 5⁴⁵). And this benevolence, which is to reign in the hearts of His disciples, must have been included in that great last prayer (Jn 17²⁶) that 'the love wherewith thou lovedst me may be in them.' A simple rule is given to the follower of Christ for securing and testing this attitude of benevolence : ' All things whatsoever ye would that men should do unto you, even so do ye also unto them' (Mt 7¹²). The Divine image is not so marred in any man as to destroy the intention and desire to do good to relations and friends (Mt 5⁴⁶ 7¹¹, Lk 6³³ 11¹³), but the benevolence of the Christian heart is to be a kindly feeling towards all without exception (Mt 5⁴⁴, Lk 6²⁷· ³⁵). There is to be no single blot on the escutcheon ; Christians are to be *perfect, as their Heavenly Father is perfect* (Mt 5⁴⁸). Natural benevolence expresses itself in the exclamation of those who heard of the fate of the wicked husbandmen in the parable, 'God forbid' (Lk 20¹⁶). Christian benevolence meets us in the story of the arrest in Gethsemane, when the Lord addressed His betrayer as 'comrade' (ἑταῖρε, Mt 26⁵⁰).

Such being the intensive character, the extensive character of benevolence may be observed in Christ's compassion on the multitudes (Mk 8², Mt

14¹⁴), namely, on each individual ; and, again, in His healing *every one* of those around Him on a well-known occasion at Capernaum (Lk 4⁴⁰). By precept as well as by example benevolence is enjoined upon the ministry in the first commission to the Twelve : 'Freely ye have received, freely give' (Mt 10⁸). Not least beautiful and consoling is the assurance that it prevails in the angelic spheres, even towards poor sinners (Lk 15⁷· ¹⁰).

LITERATURE.—Hastings' *DB*, art. 'Love'; Butler, *Sermons* xi. xii. ; Newman, *Oxford Univ. Sermons*, p. 104 ff. ; Schulhof, *Law of Forgiveness* (1901), 121 ff.   W. B. FRANKLAND.

BETHABARA (בֵּית עֲבָרָה 'house of the ford *or* crossing').—The name is found in the New Testament only in Jn 1²⁸ (AV): 'These things were done in Bethabara beyond Jordan, where John was baptizing.' The place was, therefore, one suitable for the purposes of the Baptist in preaching and baptizing ; and it has been usually identified, though this is not precisely stated in the text, with the scene of the baptism of our Lord.

With the great majority of Gr. MSS (including א*ABC*) the RV has retained here the reading '**Bethany**,' with marginal alternatives 'Bethabarah' and 'Betharabah.' The latter (בֵּית עֲרָבָה 'house of the prairie,' cf. Is 40³ *et al.* ; or 'house of the Arabah *or* Jordan Valley,' cf. Dt 1⁷ ; or perhaps 'house of the poplar,' cf. נַחַל הָעֲרָבִים Is 15⁷) is possibly a reminiscence of the Beth-arabah of Jos 15⁶· ⁶¹ in the plain of Jericho, or it may be due merely to an accidental transposition of letters. The form 'Bethabara,' on the other hand, is found in a few extant manuscripts of the Greek text, both uncial and cursive, and in the Curetonian and Sinaitic Syriac. Origen adopted this reading, and it seems to have gained general currency mainly on his authority. He writes (*in Evang. Joannis*, vi. 24) that Bethany is found in almost all copies and in Heracleon, but after personal investigation of the district (γενόμενοι ἐν τοῖς τόποις ἐπὶ ἱστορίαν τῶν ἰχνῶν Ἰησοῦ καὶ τῶν μαθητῶν αὐτοῦ) he prefers 'Bethabara' on the twofold ground of the distance of Bethany, the country of Lazarus and Martha and Mary, from the Jordan, and of the non-existence of any place bearing the latter name within the Jordan Valley. He further reports (λέγουσι) a place Βηθαρά where he had been told (ἱστοροῦσι) that John baptized, and says that the word means οἶκος κατασκευῆς (possibly a confusion with עֲבָרָה, cf. LXX in Ex 35²⁴), Bethany being οἶκος ὑπακοῆς, adding a play upon the name as befitting the spot where the messenger sent to prepare (κατασκευάζειν, Mt 11¹⁰) the way of the Lord should baptize.

Origen's view, therefore, was mainly *a priori*, and it has seemed worth while to set it out at length, because later writers, as Epiphanius, Chrysostom, *et al.*, apparently adopt and repeat it with more or less amplification ; nor is it easy to decide how much weight is due to additional details they may give. According to Chrysostom, for instance, the more accurate copies read 'Bethabara,' a result that might readily be conceived to follow from Origen's criticism ; and he adds that Bethany was neither across the Jordan nor in the wilderness, but near Jerusalem.* The ancient writers do not seem to take into account the possibility of the names occurring more than once in Palestine. It is clear, however, that either 'Bethany' or 'Bethabara' would lend itself readily to duplication.

The only indication of position which the narrative itself gives is in the phrase πέραν τοῦ Ἰορδάνου, 'across (*i.e.* east of) the Jordan.' And if Bethabara or Bethany is the scene of the Baptism, then it

* Suidas, *s.v.* Βηθανία, says expressly that the right reading is Βηθαβαρά; and he also inserts ἐπί in the text before τοῦ Ἰορδάνου.

would seem that the site must be looked for in the northern part of the Jordan Valley, since Christ comes hither apparently direct from Galilee (Mt 3[13], Mk 1[9]). Conder finds all the necessary conditions satisfied by a ford '*Abârah* on the Jordan E.N.E. of *Beisân*, and at a distance of four or five miles from the latter place; and he explains the name 'Bethany' as equivalent to Batanea, Basanitis, or Bashan, the district immediately east of the Jordan, south and south-east of the Sea of Galilee (see C. R. Conder in *Pal. Expl. Fund Mem.* ii. p. 89 f., *Quart. Statement*, 1875, p. 72, *Handbook to the Bible*, p. 319 f.; Hastings' *DB*, art. 'Bethabara').

Bethabara has also been supposed to be the same as the Beth-barah (בֵּית בָּרָה, LXX Βαιθηρά, of Jg 7[24]) which lay on or near the Jordan. This is on the assumption that a guttural has been accidentally lost from the Hebrew text, and that we ought to read בֵּית עֲבָרָה. Dr. Sanday (*Sacred Sites of the Gospels*, p. 23) accepts the identification with '*Abârah*. But beyond the coincidence of the name, on which much stress cannot be laid, there is no direct evidence in its favour; and the indirect evidence is slight. The inference, moreover, which has been drawn from Jn 2[1], that Bethabara or Bethany lay not more than a day's journey from Cana of Galilee, is precarious. The marriage festivities at Cana would in all probability extend over several days, towards the close of which the supply of wine failed: and the language used is perhaps intended to convey that Christ and His disciples were not present at the beginning. (See on the prolongation of the ceremonies attendant on an Eastern wedding, P. Baldensperger, 'Woman in the East' in *PEFSt*, 1900 p. 181 ff., 1901 p. 173 ff.; H. B. Tristram, *Eastern Customs in Bible Lands*, ch. v.).

The traditional site of the baptism of Christ at *Makhâdet Hajlah* in the Jordan Valley near Jericho, though defended by Sir Charles Wilson and others, seems to be too far south. Others would read, by conjecture, in the text of St. John's Gospel, Βηθαναβρά, *i.e.* Beth-nimrah, on the *Wâdy Shaib*, five miles east of the Jordan, E.N.E. from Jericho (see T. K. Cheyne in *Encyc. Bibl. s.vv.*).

LITERATURE.—See above, and add Smith's *DB*[2] *s.v.*; G. A. Smith, *HGHL* (1894), p. 496; Stanley, *Sinai and Palestine*, p. 310; Farrar, *Life of Christ*, i. p. 140 n.; Weiss, *Life of Christ*, i. p. 361 f. and note; Edersheim, *Life and Times of Jesus the Messiah*, i. pp. 264, 278: Geikie, *Life and Words of Christ*, i. 388, and *Holy Land and the Bible*, ii. p. 257; Sanday, *Sacred Sites of the Gospels*, 11, 23, 35, 94; *PEFSt*, 1903, p. 161; and the Commentaries on Jn 1[28].   A. S. GEDEN.

BETHANY (Βηθανία). — **1.** A village whose interest arises mainly from its having been the residence of Lazarus, Martha and Mary. As to this it is well to note the following points. (1) None of the three Synoptists mentions Lazarus. (2) St. Matthew and St. Mark maintain the same silence as to Martha and Mary. (3) St. Luke (10[38-42]) records a sojourn of Jesus in 'a village' (κώμη τις), which he leaves unnamed. (4) St. John alone (11[1. 18] 12[ff.]) names Bethany as the place where the brother and the two sisters lived. (5) St. Matthew and St. Mark state that Bethany afforded hospitality to Jesus during the days that preceded His death (Mt 21[17ff.], Mk 11[11ff.]); but in connexion with His stay there they make mention only of the house of 'Simon the leper' (Mt 26[6ff.], Mk 14[3ff.]), and give no name to the woman who anoints the feet of the Lord. (6) St. Luke does not speak of this sojourn at Bethany, but simply says in a more general way that Jesus passed the night 'at the mount called the Mt. of Olives' (21[37]). (7) The data usually accepted regarding Bethany and the family that lived there and entertained Jesus in their house, are thus derived essentially from the Fourth Gospel.

Bethany is mentioned neither in the Canonical books nor in the Apocrypha of the OT; it makes its appearance for the first time in the NT, and is not named in Josephus. Its situation is relatively easy to determine. We know (Mk 10[46] 11[1], Lk 19[1. 29]) that it was on the road from Jericho to Jerusalem, at a distance of 15 furlongs from the latter (Jn 11[18]), lying thus on the E. or rather S.E. side of the Mt. of Olives. Origen asserts that in his time the position of Bethany was known. In the 4th cent. the Bordeaux Pilgrim (333) mentions a place where the 'crypta' of Lazarus was to be seen. Eusebius records that 'the place of Lazarus' was shown, and Jerome adds that it was 2 miles from Jerusalem (*OS*[2] 108. 3, 239. 10). According to Niceph. Callist. (*HE* viii. 30 [*Patr. Gr.* cxlvi. 113]), a church containing the tomb of Lazarus was built by the empress Helena. Another sanctuary marked the spot where Jesus met Mary (Jn 11[29ff.]). A number of ecclesiastical buildings have risen at Bethany; as many as three churches have been counted there. In its present condition it is a village without importance or interest, with a population of about 200. It bears the name *el-'Azariyeh*, derived from 'Lazarus' or from 'Lazarium' (Λαζαρίον), a form found as early as the Pilgrimage of Silvia (383); the initial L has been taken for the Arab. article. According to the Talmud, *Bethany* is = Aram. *Beth-Aineh* or *Beth-Hini*, 'place of dates' (?); but this etymology is uncertain. The same may be said of that which traces it to the root עני, and would yield the sense of 'place of affliction' or 'place of the afflicted one,' which may be simply a popular etymology (cf. Nestle, *Philologica Sacra*, 1896, p. 20).

The buildings which are shown at the present day as possessing a historical interest are—1. The 'castle' of Lazarus, a tower which dates from the time of the Crusades, and was probably built in 1147 by Queen Melissenda for the Benedictine nuns; according to others, its construction is still earlier. The name 'castle' is explained by the fact that the Vulgate renders the NT κώμη by *castellum*. 2. The tomb of Lazarus is shown to modern pilgrims, but its genuineness is so doubtful that it is questioned even by Roman Catholic writers, *e.g.* Mgr. Le Camus, bishop of La Rochelle (*Notre Voyage aux pays bibliques*, i. 245). 3. There are still shown—or there used to be shown—at *el-'Azariyeh* the house of Martha, that of Mary, and that of Simon the leper.

In Lk 24[50] the scene of the Ascension is placed, if not at Bethany, at least in its immediate vicinity: 'He led them ἕως πρὸς Βηθανίαν' (AV 'as far as to Bethany,' RV less satisfactorily, 'until they were over against Bethany'). On the other hand, Ac 1[12] relates that after the Ascension the Apostles 'returned unto Jerusalem from the mount called Olivet, which is nigh unto Jerusalem, a Sabbath day's journey off.' The statement in Luke's Gospel deserves the preference; it fixes the place of the Ascension itself near Bethany, while the text of Acts simply connects the return of the Apostles with the Mt. of Olives, on the slope of which Bethany lies, and does not speak necessarily of the summit of the mountain, as ecclesiastical tradition supposed (cf. Tobler, *Die Siloahquelle und der Oelberg*, p. 83).

LITERATURE.—Robinson, *BRP*[2] i. 431–433; Guérin, *Palestine*, 'Samarie,' i. 163–181; Buhl, *GAP* 155; Tobler, *Topogr.* ii. 422–464; *PEF Mem.* iii. 27 f.; Sanday, *Sacred Sites of the Gospels*, 24, 49.   LUCIEN GAUTIER.

BETHANY.—**2.** See BETHABARA.

BETHESDA.—Jn 5[2] 'Now there is in Jerusalem by the sheep-*gate* (ἐπὶ τῇ προβατικῇ) a pool, which is called in Hebrew Bethesda, having five porches'

(RV). Instead of Βηθεσδά (TR), the most ancient authorities have other spellings, as א Βηθζαθά, L and Eus. Βηζαθά (? for Βηθζαιθά = אתיﬠ נﬠ 'house of the olive'), B Βηθσαιδά, D Βελζεθά. As to the derivation, Delitzsch suggests בּﬠ חים אָסְפּﬠן 'house of pillars,' and Calvin בּﬠ חים אָשְׁדָּא 'house of outpouring'; but the most natural etymology is בּﬠ חים חָסְדָּא 'house of mercy,' possibly in allusion to the munificence of some charitable person who had these porches built to shelter the sick, or to the goodness of God in providing this healing spring.

As the adjective προβατικῇ, 'pertaining to sheep,' requires some substantive to be introduced, the AV supplies 'market,' the RV 'gate.' Since there is no reference to any sheep-market in the OT, while the sheep-gate is repeatedly referred to (Neh 3$^{1.32}$ 12^{39}), the latter method of supplying the sense is the more probable one. Now the sheep-gate is known to have been north of the Temple, and, as Bovet says, 'the small cattle which entered Jerusalem came there certainly by the east; for it is on this side that the immense pastures of the wilderness of Judæa lie.' The modern St. Stephen's Gate answers to these data. It is at the north-east angle of the Temple area, and is the gate through which the Bedawîn still lead their flocks to Jerusalem for sale. We must therefore look for the Pool of Bethesda in this vicinity, and may at once eliminate several proposed identifications elsewhere, such as the Hammâm esh-Shifâ, near the 'Gate of the Cotton Merchants,' about the middle of the west side of the Temple area, where there is a pool with pillars and masonry, some sixty feet below the present surface, the waters of which are still supposed to possess healing properties (Furrer); and the Pool of Siloam, where the remains of four columns in the east wall, with four others in the centre, 'show that a structure with five openings or porches might easily have been erected' (Alford); and the Fountain of the Virgin, the intermittent spring at the bottom of a deep cavern at the foot of the Ophel slope south-east of the Temple (Robinson). These are all too far from the sheep-gate as probably identified above.

Conder, who adopts the suggestion of Robinson that Bethesda was at the present Fountain of the Virgin, says, 'This answers the requirements that it still presents the phenomenon of intermittent "troubling of the water," which overflows from a natural syphon under the cave, and that it is still the custom of the Jews to bathe in the waters of the cave, when this overflow occurs, for the cure of rheumatism and of other disorders.' Against this view Grove (Smith's DB^2, art. 'Bethesda') and Barclay (City of the Great King, 325) urge the inaccessibility of the deep subterranean water to invalids, the confined size of the pool, and the difficulty of finding room for the five porches capable of accommodating 'a multitude'; and to the present writer, examining the cave in person, these objections seemed conclusive, apart from the difficulty of the locality.

Turning now to the neighbourhood of the sheep-gate, we find three proposed identifications. (1) Modern tradition identifies Bethesda with the Birket Israil, an empty reservoir, 360 feet long, 120 feet wide, and 80 feet deep, half filled with rubbish, which lies close to St. Stephen's Gate and under the north-east wall of the Haram area. (2) Warren and others would place Bethesda at the so-called Twin Pools, in the ditch at the north-west angle of Antonia, under the convent of the Sisters of Zion. Neither of these can be the true site, as both the Birket Israil and the Twin Pools were constructed after the events narrated in Jn 5. (3) In 1872 it was pointed out by M. Clermont-Ganneau that 'the Pool of Bethesda should be

sought near the Church of St. Anne, where an old tradition has placed the house of the mother of Mary, calling it Beit Hanna, "House of Anne." This expression is exactly identical with Bethesda, both expressions signifying "house of mercy, or compassion."' Sixteen years later this anticipation was verified by the discovery of what is now very generally conceded to be the ancient Pool of Bethesda, a short distance north-west of the present Church of St. Anne. In the autumn of 1888, 'certain works carried on by the Algerian monks laid bare a large tank or cistern cut in the rock to a depth of 30 feet, and Herr Schick recognized this as the Pool of Bethesda. It is 55 feet long from east to west, and measures 12½ feet in breadth. A flight of twenty-four steps leads down into the pool from the eastern scarp of rock. Herr Schick, who at once saw the great interest of this discovery, soon found a sister-pool, lying end to end, 60 feet long, and of the same breadth as the first. The first pool was arched in by five arches, while five corresponding porches ran along the side of the pool. At a later period a church was built over the pool by the Crusaders, and they seem to have been so far impressed by the fact of five arches below that they shaped their crypt into five arches in imitation. They left an opening for getting down to the water; and further, as the crowning proof that they regarded the pool as Bethesda, they painted on the wall of the crypt a fresco representing the angel troubling the water of the pool.' (Geo. St. Clair, Buried Cities and Bible Countries, 327–328. See also PEFSt, July 1888 and Jan. 1891).

This site is thus supported not only by the mediæval tradition, but by the early tradition as well. The Bordeaux pilgrim, who visited Jerusalem in A.D. 333, after mentioning two large fish-pools by the side of the temple, one at the right hand, the other at the left, says in another place (Itin. Hierosol. 589): 'But farther in the city are twin fish-pools having five porches which are called Bethsaida. There the sick of many years were wont to be healed. But these pools have water which, when agitated, is of a kind of red colour.' This is evidently the same place described by Eusebius (Onomasticon, 240. 15) in the same century and called by him Bezatha, though he gives no other clue to the situation—'a pool at Jerusalem, which is the Piscina Probatica, and had formerly five porches, and now is pointed out at the twin pools there, of which one is filled by the rains of the year, but the other exhibits its water tinged in an extraordinary manner with red, retaining a trace, they say, of the victims that were formerly cleansed in it.' Clearly, too, it is of the same place that Eucherius speaks in the 5th cent.: 'Bethsaida, peculiar for being a double lake, of which one pool is for the most part filled by winter rains, the other is discoloured by reddish waters.' It has been commonly assumed of late that the two tunnels under the convent of the Sisters of Zion are the twin pools mentioned by these writers; but the traditions of the 6th, 7th, and 8th centuries, to be presently quoted, place the pool with the five porches and the church called Probatica (cf. προβατικῇ, Jn 5^2) at or near the traditional birthplace of Mary, which is undoubtedly under the present Church of St. Anne. Thus Antoninus Martyr (A.D. 570) says: 'Returning into the city we come to the Piscina Natatoria, which has five porches; and in one of these is the basilica of St. Mary, in which many miraculous cures are wrought.' Sophronius, patriarch of Jerusalem (A.D. 632), says: 'I will enter the holy Probatica, where the illustrious Anna brought forth Mary.' John of Damascus (about A.D. 750) says: 'May all things be propitious to thee, O

Probatica, the most holy temple of the Mother of God! May all things be propitious to thee, O *Probatica*, ancestral domicile of a queen! May all things be propitious to thee, O *Probatica*, formerly the fold of Joachim's flocks, but now a church, heaven-resembling, of the rational flock of Christ!' Brocardus also speaks (A.D. 1283) of a large reservoir near St. Anne's Church, called *Piscina Interior*, just opposite *Birket Israil*.

Early tradition, therefore, as well as mediæval, seems to favour the site discovered in 1888. This is the site now generally accepted, though some recent writers are still unconvinced, such as Sanday (*Sacred Sites of the Gospels*, 55), who rejects Schick's identification but reaches no positive conclusion of his own, and Conder (Hastings' *DB*, article 'Bethesda'), who argues for the Virgin's Pool. The intermittent troubling of the water at the Fountain of the Virgin is, indeed, a point in its favour; but this phenomenon is not uncommon in the springs of Palestine (Thomson, *Land and Book*, iii. 288; Barclay, *City of Great King*, 560), and, while nothing of the kind is now seen at the pool under the Crusaders' church, it is not, perhaps, a too violent supposition that the same intermittence now observed in the Virgin's Fountain may have characterized this pool also in that early time of more copious 'rains of the year,' as Eusebius calls them, especially if, as some think, they both lie upon the same concealed watercourse.

The last clause of Jn 5³ and the whole of v.⁴, containing the account of the troubling of the water by an angel and the miraculous healing that followed, are relegated to the margin in RV, on the ground of their omission by the ancient manuscripts אBD, and the exceptional number of variants in the other MSS. Popular superstition seems to have attributed the periodic bubbling of the water to the action of an invisible angel. These passages were probably at first written on the margin as an expression of that opinion, and later were introduced into the body of the text.

W. W. MOORE.

BETHLEHEM.—Two towns of this name are mentioned in the Old Testament. **1.** Bethlehem (בֵּית לֶחֶם 'house of bread') of Zebulun, Jos 19¹⁵. The site is now occupied by a miserable village, 6 miles south-west of Sepphoris and about the same distance north-west of Nazareth, in a well-wooded district of country, planted with oaks (Robinson, *Biblical Researches*, iii. 113). That this Bethlehem cannot have been the scene of the Nativity, near as it is to Nazareth, is clear from the fact that both St. Matthew and St. Luke expressly place the birth of Christ at Bethlehem of Judæa. These narratives being independent of each other and derived from different sources, we have for the southern Bethlehem the convergence of two distinct traditions. These two Evangelists are joined in their testimony by the author of the Fourth Gospel, who assumes acquaintance on the part of his readers with the story of the birth of Christ at Bethlehem, the Bethlehem associated with David and his royal line. 'Some said, Shall Christ come out of Galilee? Hath not the Scripture said that Christ cometh of the seed of David, and out of the town of Bethlehem where David was?' (Jn 7⁴¹·⁴²). It is noteworthy that Bethlehem is never mentioned as having been visited by our Lord or in any way associated with His ministry But all Christian history and tradition maintain that the southern Bethlehem was the scene of the Nativity.

2. Bethlehem of Judah (בֵּית יְהוּדָה Jg 17⁷·⁹, Ru 1¹·² etc.) or Judæa (Mt 2¹, Lk 2⁴). This town (the modern *Beit Lahm*) is situated about 6 miles S.S.W. of Jerusalem, lying high up on a grey limestone ridge running from east to west, and

occupying the projecting summits at each end, with a sort of saddle between. The ridge rises to a height of 2550 ft. above sea-level, and falls away in terraced slopes on all sides, the descent to the north and east being specially steep. The terraces, as they sweep in graceful curves round the ridge from top to bottom, give to the little town the appearance of an amphitheatre, and serve to make to the approaching traveller a picture which closer acquaintance does not wholly disappoint. The names by which it has been known for millenniums, and is still known, are expressive of the fertility of the place — *Beth-lehem*, 'house of bread,' and *Beit Lahm*, 'house of flesh.' The hillsides around, merging into the hill country of Judæa, though they look bare to the eye at a distance, afford pastures for flocks of sheep and goats. The valleys below and the fields lying to the east produce crops of wheat and barley, as in the days when Ruth gleaned in the fields of Boaz; and the terraced slopes, under diligent cultivation, bear olives, almonds, pomegranates, figs, and vines. Wine and honey are named among the most notable of its natural products, and the wine of Bethlehem is said to be preferable to that of Jerusalem.

The modern town is highly picturesque. There is just one main street or thoroughfare, extending about half a mile, and largely occupied by workshops, which are little better than arches open to the street. The population is differently given as from 4000 to 8000 souls. Palmer ('Das jetzige Bethlehem' in *ZDPV* xvii. 90), writing in 1893, and founding upon personally ascertained figures, gives 8035 as the population, which he classifies in respect of religion as follows: Latins, 3827; Greeks, 3662; Moslems, 260; Armenians, 185; Protestants, 54; Copts and Syrians, 47. The small number of Moslems is said to be due to the severity of Ibrahim Pasha, who drove out the Moslem inhabitants and demolished their houses in the insurrection of 1834. It will be observed from the above enumeration that Bethlehem does not contain a single Jew. As in Nazareth so in Bethlehem, the associations with Jesus make residence repugnant to the Jews, and they have accordingly no desire to settle in the Christian Holy Places. They are, in fact, tolerated only as temporary visitors, but not as residents. 'In the cradle of his royal race,' says Canon Tristram (*Bible Places*, p. 72), 'the Jew is even more a stranger than in any other spot of his own land; and during the Middle Ages neither Crusader nor Saracen suffered him to settle there.' The inhabitants of Bethlehem are of superior physique and comeliness. The men have a character for energy and even turbulence; the women are noticeable for their graceful carriage and becoming attire. In the crowds which throng the Church of the Holy Sepulchre in Jerusalem at the Easter services, the women of Bethlehem, wearing a light veil descending on each side of the face, and closed across the bosom, with a low but handsome headdress composed of strings of silver coins plaited in among the hair and hanging down below the chin as a sort of necklace,—are easily recognizable, and make a favourable impression. The industries of Bethlehem, apart from the cultivation of the soil, are intimately associated with the Nativity, consisting of memorial relics and souvenirs manufactured for sale to the thousands of pilgrims and tourists who visit Jerusalem and Bethlehem every year. Models of the cave of the Nativity, figures of Christ and the Virgin, apostles and saints, are in great demand. Olive wood, and mother-of-pearl obtained from the Red Sea, with basaltic stone from the neighbourhood of the Dead Sea, are carved and wrought into useful and ornamental articles with no small degree of skill and taste.

Palmer mentions (*l.c.* p. 91) that an increasing number of the inhabitants go abroad with their products,—their mother-of-pearl carvings and other wares,—and, especially in America, find a good return for their enterprise.

Bethlehem, notwithstanding its royal associations and its renown as the birthplace of the world's Redeemer, has never been, and is never likely to be, more in the eye of the world than 'little among the thousands of Judah' (Mic 5[2]). 'In spite,' says Palmer, 'of the numerous visits of strangers and pilgrims, which are year by year on the increase, and in spite of the market-place which Bethlehem affords for the whole neighbourhood, and especially for the Bedawîn, who come from long distances from the southern end of the Dead Sea to make their purchases of clothing, tools, and weapons, and to leave the produce of their harvest and their pastures, Bethlehem appears likely to remain, unencumbered by trade and progress, what it has been for many years bygone—a shrunken, untidy village.' Even so, it can never be deprived of its associations with the Messianic King of Israel, 'whose goings forth have been from of old, from everlasting' (Mic 5[2]), associations which exalt it to the loftiest eminence, and surround it with a glory that cannot fade. These associations in their salient features are now to be set forth.

It is in the early patriarchal history that we meet first with Bethlehem, under its ancient name of Ephrath.[*] 'When I came from Padan,' said Jacob on his deathbed, recounting to Joseph in Egypt his chequered history, 'Rachel died by me in the land of Canaan in the way, when yet there was but a little way to come unto Ephrath : and I buried her there in the way of Ephrath ; the same is Bethlehem' (Gn 48[7], cf. 35[9ff.]). The sacred historian records that Jacob set a pillar upon her grave : 'that is the pillar of Rachel's grave unto this day' (Gn 35[20]). Rachel's grave is marked now by a Mohammedan wely, or monumental mosque, at the point where the Bethlehem road breaks off the road leading from Jerusalem to Hebron ; and though the monument has been repaired and renewed from generation to generation, it serves still to recall a real event, and to distinguish the spot where Rachel's 'strength failed her, and she sank, as did all the ancient saints, on the way to the birthplace of hope' (Dr. John Ker, *Sermons*, 8th ed. p. 153). Bethlehem becomes more definitely associated with the Messianic hope when it becomes the home of Ruth the Moabitess, the ancestress of David and of David's greater Son. From the heights near Bethlehem a glimpse is obtained of the Dead Sea—the sea of Lot—shimmering at the foot of the long blue wall of the mountains of Moab ; and the land of Moab seems to have had close relations with Bethlehem and its people in patriarchal as well as later times. With Ruth the Moabitess, through her marriage with Boaz, the 'mighty man of wealth' of Bethlehem-judah (Ru 2[1]), there entered a strain of Gentile blood,—although we remember that Lot, the ancestor of Moab, was the nephew of the great ancestor of Israel—into the pedigree of Christ according to the flesh (Mt 1[5]), as if in token that, in a day still far off, Jew and Gentile should be one in Him. With David, the great-grandson of Ruth, there entered the royal element into the genealogy of Jesus ; and Bethlehem has no associations more sacred and tender than its associations with the shepherd king of Israel, unless it be those that link it for ever with God manifest in the flesh. The stream of Messianic hope, as it flows onwards and broadens from age to age, is not unlike that river

of Spain which for a considerable part of its course flows underground, and only at intervals miles apart throws up pools to the surface, which the inhabitants call 'the eyes' of the Guadiana. The pools trace the onward progress of the river, till at length it bursts forth in a broad stream seeking the distant sea. So the hope of a great Deliverer from spiritual misery and death flows onward in the story of God's ancient people, throwing up its pools in the days of Abraham, Moses, David, Isaiah and the prophets ; and Micah indicates the direction of its flow with more explicitness than any who went before when he says : 'But thou, Bethlehem Ephratah, though thou be little among the thousands of Judah, yet out of thee shall he come forth unto me that is to be Ruler in Israel ; whose goings forth have been from of old, from everlasting' (Mic 5[2]). When the fulness of the time had come, the Messianic hope became the place of broad rivers and streams which we so happily know and enjoy, and the glad tidings was heard on the plains of Bethlehem, addressed to the watchful shepherds : 'Fear not : for, behold, I bring you glad tidings of great joy, which shall be to all people. For unto you is born this day in the city of David a Saviour, which is Christ the Lord' (Lk 2[10. 11]).

The story of the Nativity is told by St. Matthew and St. Luke with a simplicity and delicacy and beauty which are of themselves an evidence of its historical truth. Both narratives, as has been indicated, assign to Bethlehem the high honour of being the place of the Nativity and the scene of the stupendous fact of the Incarnation. The details are too familiar to require rehearsal here.

There is one particular handed down by early Christian tradition which may be regarded not as a variation from, but an addition to, the Evangelic narrative,—the statement made by Justin Martyr (A.D. 140–150), and repeated in the Apocryphal Gospels, that the birth of Jesus took place in a cave. Justin (*Dialogue with Trypho*, ch. 78) relates that, since Joseph had in that village no place where to lodge, he lodged in a cave near by. Justin relates other particulars which may have come to him—he was a native of Nablûs, not 40 miles from Bethlehem —by oral tradition or from apocryphal narratives : such as that the Magi came *from Arabia*, and that Herod slew *all* the children of Bethlehem. That the stable where the Infant Saviour was born may have been a cave is quite in keeping with the practice of utilizing the limestone caves of the hill country of Judæa as places of shelter for cattle and other beasts. Those Apocryphal Gospels which deal with the Infancy, notably the *Protevangelium Jacobi* and the *pseudo-Matthæus*, make mention of the cave. Pseudo-Matthæus (ch. 13) says, 'The angel commanded the beast to stop, for her time to bear had come ; and he directed the Blessed Mary to come down from the animal and to enter a cave below a cavern in which there was never any light, but always darkness, because it could not receive the light of day. And when the Blessed Mary had entered it, it began to become light with all lightness, as if it had been the sixth hour of the day. . . . And then she brought forth a male child, whom angels instantly surrounded at His birth, and whom, when born and standing at once upon His feet, they adored, saying, Glory to God on high, and on earth peace to men of good will.' The *Protevangelium* relates the story with curious imagery (ch. 18). 'And he [Joseph] found a cave there and took her in, and set his sons by her, and he went out and sought a midwife in the country of Bethlehem. And I Joseph walked and I walked not ; and I looked up into the sky and saw the sky violently agitated ; and I looked up at the pole of heaven, and I saw it standing still and the birds of the air still ; and I directed my gaze on the earth, and I saw a vessel lying and workmen reclining by it and their hands in the vessel, and those who handled did not handle it, and those who presented it to the mouth did not present it, but the faces of all were looking up ; and I saw the sheep scattered and the sheep stood, and the shepherd lifted up his hand to strike them and his hand remained up ; and I looked at the stream of the river, and I saw that the mouths of the kids were down and not drinking ; and everything which was being impelled forward was intercepted in its course.'

The *Protevangelium Jacobi* is generally recognized as belonging to the 2nd cent., and its testimony is a valuable confirmation of the early Christian tradition. Few scholars, if any, will agree in assigning it the place of importance attributed to it recently by the fantastic theory of Conrady (*Die Quelle der kanonischen Kindheitsgeschichten Jesu*, Göttingen, 1900), who regards the *Protevangelium* as the source of the Gospel narratives of the Infancy. The author of it, according to him, is an Egyptian, most likely of Alexandria, who introduces Bethlehem into the narrative not because of its place in Hebrew prophecy,

---

but because it was formerly a seat of the worship of Isis, and he wishes to incorporate this worship with Christianity. In concert with the priests of Isis and Serapis, he aided with his inventive pen the appropriation of this sacred site by the Church, and it was from the *Protevangelium* that the writers of the First and Third Gospels drew their separate narratives of the Infancy. Conrady returns to the subject with an article full of equally curious and perverted learning in *SK*, 1904, Heft 2, 'Die Flucht nach Ægypten.'

It is in the 4th century that Bethlehem begins to receive that veneration as a Christian Holy Place in which it is now equalled only by Jerusalem and Nazareth. As early as Justin Martyr attention is specially directed to Bethlehem as the birthplace of the world's Redeemer. In addition to the reference, already mentioned, to the cave, we find Justin quoting the well-known prophecy of Isaiah (33[16ff.]), 'He shall dwell in a lofty cave of a strong rock,' in the same connexion (*Dialogue with Trypho*, ch. 70). Even earlier than Justin's day it would appear that this particular cave was venerated by the followers of Christ ; for, as Jerome tells in one of his letters to Paulinus, the emperor Hadrian (A.D. 117–138), in his zeal to extirpate the very remembrance of Christ, caused a grove sacred to Adonis to be planted over the grotto of the Nativity, as he caused a temple to Venus to be erected over the site of the sepulchre of our Lord. Origen (*c. Celsum*, i. 51) says : 'If any one desires certainty as to the birth of Jesus at Bethlehem apart from the Gospels and Micah's prophecy, let him know that in conformity with the narrative in the Gospel regarding His birth there is shown at Bethlehem the cave where He was born and the manger in the cave where He was wrapped in swaddling clothes. And this sign is greatly talked of in surrounding places, even among the enemies of the faith, it being said that in this cave was born that Jesus who is worshipped and reverenced by the Christians.' The site is now marked by the oldest church in Christendom, the Church of St. Mary of the Nativity, built by order of the Emperor Constantine. It is a massive pile of buildings extending along the ridge from west to east, and comprising the church proper with the three convents, Latin, Greek, and Armenian, abutting respectively upon its north - eastern, south - eastern, and south - western extremities. The proportions of the church and its related structures are more commanding from its elevation and from the shabbiness of the town in comparison. The nave of the church is common to all the sects, and is shared by them together— Latins, Greeks, Armenians. From the double line of Corinthian pillars sustaining the basilica sixteen centuries look down upon the visitor, and the footsteps of nearly fifty generations of Christians have trodden the ground upon which he treads. Says Dean Stanley : 'The long double lines of Corinthian pillars, the faded mosaics, the rough ceiling of beams of cedar from Lebanon still preserve the outlines of the church, once blazing with gold and marble, in which Baldwin was crowned, and which received its latest repairs from our own English Edward IV.' (*Sinai and Palestine*, p. 433). It is the subterranean vault that continues to be of perennial interest. Descending the steps from the raised floor of the eastern end of the nave, and turning sharply to the left, the visitor finds a half-sunk arched doorway which leads down by thirteen steps to the Chapel of the Nativity—the rude cave now paved and walled with marble and lighted up by numerous lamps. This chamber is about 40 feet from east to west, 16 feet wide, and 10 feet high. The roof is covered with what had once been striped cloth of gold. At the east end there is a shrine where fifteen silver lamps burn night and day, and in the floor, let into the pavement, a silver star of Greek

pattern marks the very spot of the Nativity with the inscription : '*Hic de Virgine Mariâ Jesus Christus natus est.*' To the Christian the associations of the place make it full of impressiveness, and the visitor has no more sacred or tender recollections of holy ground than those which cluster round the Church and the Grotto of the Nativity. Not far off is a cave, cut out of the same limestone ridge, which was the abode of St. Jerome for over thirty years. Here, with the noble ladies whom he had won to the religious life, Paula and her daughter Eustochium, he laboured *totus in lectione, totus in libris*, preparing the Vulgate translation of the Holy Scriptures, which for more than a thousand years was the Bible of Western Christendom, and is a powerful tribute to his piety and learning. 'It is the touch of Christ that has made Bethlehem' (Kelman and Fulleylove, *The Holy Land*, p. 234). And the touch of Christ is making itself felt still in the works of Christian philanthropy and missionary zeal that are being performed there. There are schools and other missionary agencies maintained by Protestants and Roman Catholics to instruct in His truth and to enrich with His grace the community who occupy the place of His birth. Bethlehem appears among the stations of the Church Missionary Society, and the work done there among women and girls has borne good fruit. The Germans have built an Evangelical Church, which was dedicated in 1893. There is much superstition and error among the nominally Christian inhabitants of the place, but the efforts of the Protestant and Roman Catholic missionaries have stirred up the Greek Orthodox and Armenian Christians to activity for the moral and spiritual welfare of their people.

LITERATURE.—Andrews, *Life of our Lord* [2], p. 82 ; Cunningham Geikie, *The Holy Land and the Bible* ; Stanley, *Sinai and Palestine* ; Kelman, *The Holy Land* ; Sanday, *Sacred Sites of the Gospels* ; G. A. Smith, *Histor. Geog. of Holy Land* ; *The Survey of Western Palestine*, vol. iii.; Ramsay, *Was Christ born at Bethlehem ?* ; Palmer, 'Das jetzige Bethlehem' in *ZDPV* xvii.; articles in Kitto's *Cyclop.*, *PRE* [3], Vigouroux's *Dictionnaire de la Bible*, Smith's *DB*, Hastings' *DB*, and *Encyclopædia Biblica*.

T. NICOL.

BETHPHAGE (Βηθφαγή).—A place unknown to the OT, the Apocrypha, or Josephus, and mentioned in the NT only once—on the occasion of our Lord's triumphal entry into Jerusalem five days before His death. It was certainly situated upon the slope of the Mt. of Olives, on or near the road from Jericho to Jerusalem (Mk 10[46] 11[1], Lk 19[1. 29]), and in the immediate neighbourhood of Bethany. The site of the latter being accurately determined as the modern *el-'Azariyeh* (see art. BETHANY, 1), it might be expected that there would be little difficulty in locating Bethphage. Unfortunately, however, the texts of the three Synoptists [St. John does not mention Bethphage] are obscure on two points—

(1) As to the relation between Bethphage and Bethany, St. Luke (19[29]) alone mentions both places ('as he drew near to Bethphage and Bethany'). His language seems to imply that a traveller coming from Jericho would come first to Bethphage, then to Bethany, and finally to Jerusalem. St. Matthew (21[1]) mentions only Bethphage. As for St. Mark, his original text (11[1]) probably contained no reference to Bethphage, but this name has been inserted, and in the majority of MSS stands between Jerusalem and Bethany in such a way that, if this reading were accepted as the original one, we should have to place Bethphage in a different position in relation to Bethany from what is implied in the text of St. Luke.

To reconcile these divergent statements, a hypothesis has been started to the effect that Bethany may have lain a little off the direct route from Jericho to Jerusalem, upon a side road, and Bethphage at the point where this joined the main road. It would thus have been necessary to pass Bethphage both in going to Bethany and in returning from it. Support for this conjecture has been sought in the use of the word ἄμφοδον in Mk 11[4].

(2) In all three Synoptics, Jesus sends two of His disciples to a village (κώμη) to bring the ass on which He was to ride. Is this village, which is ' over against' (κιτέναντι), to be identified with Bethphage, or with Bethany, or with some third locality? Each of these views is capable of defence ; the traditional identification of the village of the ass's colt with Bethphage is at least questionable, especially in view of Mt 21[1] 'When they had reached Bethphage . . . then Jesus sent two disciples to the village over against.' A site for the village of the colt might be suggested at Siloë, or rather at Kefr et-Ṭur, on the top of the Mt. of Olives. [It is known that in the time of Jesus Christ there were houses on its summit]. In the circumstances of the case it would be hazardous to offer any opinion as to the probable situation of Bethphage.

Etymologically the name Bethphage appears to mean 'house (or place) of unripe fruits,' more especially 'of unripe figs' (cf. Ca 2[13], and see Dalman, Grammatik des jüd. pal.-Aramäisch, 1894, p. 152, and Arnold Meyer, Jesu Muttersprache, 1896, p. 166). Recently a connexion has been suggested by Nestle ('Etymologische Legenden?' in ZWTh xl. [1897], p. 148) between this etymology of the name Bethphage and the story of the barren fig-tree. But it may be noted that the latter is associated in the Gospels (Mt 21[17-22], Mk 11[11-14, 20-26]) with Bethany, not Bethphage. Formerly Nestle (SK, 1896, p. 323 ff., and in his Philologica Sacra, 1896, p. 16 f.) had pointed to the possibility of connecting, from the point of view of popular etymology, Bethphage (= בֵּית פַּגֵּי 'place of meeting') and the ἄμφοδον of Mk 11[4]. Finally, another explanation of Bethphage, viewed as a dwelling-place of priests (?), is furnished by Origen, and rests upon a curious combination of the Aramaic word פּוּם 'jaw,' with Dt 18[3], which assigns to the priests the jaws of sacrificial victims as part of their portion.

In the Middle Ages, Bethphage was shown to the north of Bethany, higher up the slope of the Mt. of Olives. The site of this mediæval Bethphage (which proves nothing for the Bethphage of Scripture) was recovered nearly thirty years ago, thanks to the discovery made by the Franciscan Fathers, controlled and described by Guillemot and Clermont-Ganneau, of a stone (the fragment of an altar?) bearing inscriptions and pictures relating to Christ's entry into Jerusalem.

LITERATURE.—PEFSt, 1874, p. 173 ; 1878, pp. 51–61, 146–149 ; PEF, 'Jerusalem,' pp. 331–340 ; Revue Archéologique, Dec. 1877, p. 366 ff.; Revue Biblique, 1892, p. 105 f. See also the discussion in Andrews, Life of our Lord [2], 429–432.

LUCIEN GAUTIER.

BETHSAIDA ('house of fishing').—The supposition that there were two places on the shore of the Sea of Galilee to which this name appropriately applies has been disputed or rejected by many writers (Buhl, G. A. Smith, Sanday, et al.) ; but the evidence in its favour, direct and indirect, has the support of a long list of authorities on Palestinian geography from the days of Reland to the present time. There are differences of opinion with respect to the precise location of both places, but there is a general agreement that one was on the east and the other on the west side of the Jordan or its expanse into the Galilæan Lake. Prominent on the list of those who advocate two Bethsaidas are the names of Ritter, Robinson, Caspari, Stanley, Edersheim, Wieseler, Weiss, Tristram, Thomson, van de Velde, Porter, Merrill, Macgregor, and Ewing. The facts and suggestions which bear

upon the supposition itself may be summed up as follows :—

1. Bethsaida of Gaulanitis.—The historic evidence for the existence and general location of this city is not disputed. Josephus describes it as a village 'situate at the Lake of Gennesaret which Philip the tetrarch advanced unto the dignity of a city, both by the number of inhabitants it contained, and its other grandeur, and called it by the name "Julias," the same name with Cæsar's daughter' (Ant. XVIII. ii. 1). In other passages he indicates its position as in 'Lower Gaulanitis' (Jaulân), 'in Peræa,' and as near the Jordan, which 'first passes by the city and then passes through the middle of the Lake' (BJ II. ix. 1, xiii. 2, also BJ III. x. 7, and Life, 72). In every instance, except the one above quoted, which gives a reason for the change of designation, Josephus drops the old name and calls it 'Julias.' Pliny and Jerome give it the same appellation, and locate it on the eastern side of the Jordan (Plin. HN v. 16 ; Jer. Com. on Mt 16[31]). The modern designation, 'Bethsaida-Julias,' is not to be found in ancient history, sacred or secular. The site of the city which thus became the successor, under another name, of Bethsaida of Gaulanitis, has not been identified with certainty. After careful research, Dr. Robinson came to the conclusion that a mound of ruins, known as et-Tell, was the most probable location of the long-lost city.

'The tell extends from the foot of the northern mountains southwards, near the point where the Jordan issues from them. The ruins cover a large portion of it, and are quite extensive ; but so far as could be observed, consist entirely of unhewn stones, without any distinct trace of ancient architecture' (BRP[2] ii. p. 413).

The site is over against one of the fording-places of the Jordan, and about 2 miles above its mouth. This tentative identification has been accepted by many recent explorers, but mainly for the reason that the location seems to be the most favourable, because of its commanding position, for such a city as Josephus describes. The objections to it are its distance from the Lake, and the absence of anything which would suggest its original name— 'the house (or place) of fishing.'

Another site, to which these objections do not apply, has been suggested by Dr. Thomson at el-Mas̱adiyeh, not far from the eastern bank of the river, and near the Lake, 'distinguished by a few palm trees, foundations of old walls, and fragments of basaltic columns' (Land and Book, ii. 422). This writer advocates the existence of a double city, lying on both sides of the Jordan, as the true solution of the Bethsaida problem, and indicates a site over against el-Mas̱adiyeh, where a few ruins have been found, as the probable location of the Galilæan portion of the city. The apparent objections to this site are the boggy and treacherous ground in the vicinity, and the absence of anything that would suggest the existence in former times of a fording-place or a connexion by means of bridges. Wilson accepts Thomson's views, and Schumacher, the noted explorer of the Jaulân region, agrees with him in locating the eastern city at el-Mas̱adiyeh. He suggests also that the royal residence of Philip may have been on the hill at et-Tell, and the fishing village at el-'Araj, near the mouth of the Jordan, where are ruins, and that both were connected by a good road still visible (see Jaulan Quarterly Statement, April 1888). Conder, who favours et-Tell, makes the plea on its behalf that local changes in the river delta may have increased the distance materially between this site and the head of the Lake.

Assuming this as a possibility, the place must always have been a considerable distance from the mouth of the Jordan. It is not unlikely, however, as Merrill suggests, that the landing-place of Julias was the original site of the town, and that among the local fishermen it retained the old name for some time after the building of the city of Philip, which would naturally be laid out on higher ground. In the only NT references which can with certainty be attributed to this place, the Evangelists make use of the older name (Lk 9[10], Mk 8[22]). In the first, the scene of the miracle of the five loaves, it is described as 'a desert,' or vacant place, 'belonging to the city called Bethsaida.' All the Evangelists concur in the statement that it was a place apart from the town, but evidently near it, where the native grass thickly covered the fallow ground and made a comfortable resting-place for the weary multitude. The location which fulfils all the conditions of the narrative is on the eastern ridge of the Baṭiḥa plain, in the immediate vicinity of the Lake.

In the second reference it appears that Jesus, after crossing to the other side from Dalmanutha on the west coast, came to Bethsaida *en route* to the towns of Cæsarea Philippi. While in the city a blind man was brought to Him. It is a significant fact, in keeping with His uniform attitude towards the Gentile cities of this region, that He took the blind man by the hand and led him out of the town, before He restored his sight. In this, says Farrar, 'all that we can dimly see is Christ's dislike and avoidance of these heathenish Herodian towns, with their borrowed Hellenic architecture, their careless customs, and even their very names commemorating, as was the case with Bethsaida-Julias, some of the most contemptible of the human race' (*Life of Christ*, ch. xxxv.).

2. Bethsaida of Galilee.—It has been alleged by some writers that the existence of a western Bethsaida was invented to meet a supposed difficulty in the narrative of the Evangelists. This is not a fair statement of the case. A Bethsaida belonging to the province of Galilee is designated by name as well as implied by incidental reference. Its claims are advocated mainly, if not solely, on the ground that it is in the Gospel record. The objection sometimes urged, that the existence of two towns of the same name in such close proximity is improbable, has little weight in view of the fact that these towns were in different provinces, under different rulers, and in many respects had little in common. The name itself suggests a place favourably situated for fishermen, and might be appropriately applied to more places than one by the Lake side. But see art. CAPERNAUM.

The main points of the argument in favour of a western Bethsaida are as follows :—

(1) *The direct testimony given in John's Gospel.*—In one passage it is affirmed that Philip, one of the Apostolic band, was of Bethsaida, the city of Andrew and Peter (1[44]); in another (12[21]), that Philip was of Bethsaida of Galilee. This is the testimony of one who is noted for his accuracy in geographical details, who knew every foot of this lake-side region, and who, in common with the other Evangelists, speaks of this trio of disciples as partners in a common industry, and as 'men of Galilee.' 'Cana of Galilee' is a similar expression in the same Gospel, and the fact that the writer mentions the province at all in this connexion, is a strong presumptive proof that he wished to distinguish it from the other Bethsaida on the eastern side. The mention of Galilee in John's Gospel determines this place on the *west* of the Jordan as decidedly as that of Gaulanitis does the other Bethsaida on the east. The assertion of G. A. Smith, that the province of Galilee included most of the level coastland east of the Lake,—if it applies to Galilee in the time of Christ,—is apparently in conflict with all the evidence which the history of that time has given us. It conflicts also with the positive testimony of Josephus, who places Julias—the city which Dr. Smith associates with Bethsaida—in Gaulanitis, and under the jurisdiction of Herod Philip.

(2) The well-attested fact that *all of the Apostles, except Judas Iscariot, were men of Galilee* (Ac 1[11]), furnishes another corroborative proof that the place of residence of the three above mentioned could not have been in the city of Philip (see also Mk 14[70]). They were typical Jews, and their place of employment and all their associations were with their brethren of the same faith on or near the plain of Gennesaret.

(3) In the narrative of the return journey from the place of

the feeding of the multitude, it is distinctly mentioned that the disciples embarked in a ship *to go before to the 'other side' unto Bethsaida* (Mk 6[45]). If the word 'unto' stood alone, there might be some ground for the supposition that the disciples aimed at sailing along the shore towards Julias, but in the description which follows, the Evangelist makes it plain that the 'other side,' as he uses the expression, meant the *west* shore of the Lake. 'And when they had passed over, they came into the land of Gennesaret.' The parallel accounts convey the same impression and are equally decisive on this point (Mt 14[22. 34], Jn 6[16]). It is true that John adds that 'they went over the sea towards Capernaum,' but there is no discrepancy between the several statements if Robinson is right in identifying Bethsaida with '*Ain eṭ-Ṭâbigha*. The general direction would be the same, and the distance between the two points does not exceed three-quarters of a mile. In keeping with these statements is the mention of the fact that the multitude on the east side, noting the direction taken by the vessel in which the disciples sailed, took shipping the next day and came to Capernaum, seeking for Jesus (Jn 6[22. 24]). These passages, interpreted in their natural and ordinary sense, show that the disciples aimed at going to the western side of the Lake in obedience to the command of Jesus. The contrary wind retarded their progress, but it did not take them far out of their course. The mention of Bethsaida, in this connexion, with Capernaum makes it highly probable also that its site was somewhere in the same neighbourhood.

(4) There is a manifest verification and corroboration of this testimony in the close *association of Bethsaida with Capernaum and Chorazin* in the judgment pronounced upon them by our Lord because of their peculiar privileges (Mt 11[21-23]). There is no uncertainty with respect to the import of this denunciation. It could not apply to a Gentile city like Julias, for it is here contrasted with the Gentile cities of Tyre and Sidon. It is evident, also, that its significance inheres in the peculiar privileges of Bethsaida through oft-repeated manifestations of supernatural power in connexion with the ministry of Jesus. In other words, it was in the very centre of that field of wonders in Galilee, honoured above all other places in the land as the residence of Jesus, to which multitudes flocked from every quarter. We have the record of three brief visits of Jesus to the semi-heathen population on the eastern side of the Lake, mainly for rest and retirement, but there is no record of 'many mighty works' in any of the towns or cities of this region. This of itself seems to be an unanswerable argument against the proposed identification of the city to which Jesus refers in this connexion with the Herodian city of Julias in the province of Gaulanitis.

The generally accepted site of Bethsaida of Galilee is '*Ain eṭ-Ṭâbigha*. It is situated at the head of a charming little bay on the northern side of the spur which runs out into the Lake at *Khân Minyeh*. Here, by the ruins of some old mills, is a copious stream of warm, brackish water, fed by several fountains, one of which is the largest spring-head in Galilee. Its course, which now winds and descends amid a tangled mass of rank vegetation to the Lake, was formerly diverted to the plain of Gennesaret by a strongly built reservoir, still standing, which raised the water to an elevation of twenty feet or more. Thence it was carried by an aqueduct and a rock-hewn trench to the northern end of the plain. There is little to indicate the site of the city, except an occasional pier of the aqueduct and the substructures of a few ancient buildings long since overthrown and forgotten.

The natural features of '*Ain eṭ-Ṭâbigha* are a safe harbour, a good anchorage, a lovely outlook over the entire lake, a shelving, shelly beach, admirably adapted to the landing of fishing boats, a coast free from débris and driftwood; and a warm bath of water, where shoals of fish ofttimes crowd together by myriads, 'their backs gleaming above the surface as they bask and tumble in the water' (Macgregor, *Rob Roy on the Jordan*, p. 337). Although surrounded by desolate wastes, this is still the chief 'Fishertown' on the Lake, where nets are dried and mended, and where fish are taken and sorted for the market, as in the days of Andrew, Simon, and Philip.

LITERATURE.—Andrews, *Life of our Lord*[2], pp. 230–236 ; Robinson, *BRP* [2] ii. 413, and iii. 358, 359 ; Tristram, *Land of Israel*, p. 418, also *Topog. of the Holy Land*, pp. 259–261 ; G. A. Smith, *HGHL* 457 f. ; Thomson, *Land and Book*, ii. 423 ; Stewart, *Mem. Places among the Holy Hills*, pp. 128–138 ; Reland, p. 653 ; Macgregor, *op. cit.* pp. 334–343 and 360–372 ; Merrill, *Pict. Pal.* i. 322 ; Ewing in Hastings' *DB* i. p. 282 ; Baedeker-Socin, *Pal.* 255 f. ; Buhl, *GAP* 241 ff. ; Sanday, *Sacred Sites of the Gospels*, 41 f., 45, 48, 91, 95.   R. L. STEWART.

BETRAYAL.—

The Gr. verb for 'betray' is παραδιδόναι. παράδοσις never occurs in the sense of 'betrayal' in the NT; in the Gospels it is used of 'the *tradition* of the elders' (Mt 15[2. 3. 6] = Mk 7[3. 5. 8. 9. 13]), by St. Paul also of the Christian tradition (1 Co 11[2], 2 Th 2[15] 3[6]). προδότης, 'traitor,' occurs in Lk 6[16]; cf. Ac 7[52], 2 Ti 3[4].

Had Jesus not been betrayed into the hands of His enemies, His death would hardly have been averted, but it would have been delayed. They would fain have seized Him and made short work of Him, but they dared not. He was the popular hero, and they perceived that His arrest would excite a dangerous tumult. The goodwill of the multitude was as a bulwark about Him and kept His enemies at bay, malignant but impotent. The crisis came on 13th Nisan, two days before the Passover (Mt 26[1-5] = Mk 14[1-2] = Lk 22[1-2]). He had met the rulers in a succession of dialectical encounters in the court of the Temple, and had completed their discomfiture by hurling at them in presence of the multitude a crushing indictment. Enraged beyond endurance, they met and debated what they should do. They were resolved upon His death, and they would fain have seized Him and slain Him out of hand; but they dared not, and they agreed to wait until the Feast was over and the throng of worshippers had quitted Jerusalem. 'They took counsel together to arrest Jesus by stealth and kill him; but they said: Not during the Feast, lest there arise a tumult among the people.'

Such was the situation when, all unexpectedly, an opportunity for immediate action presented itself. Judas, 'the man of Kerioth,' one of the Twelve, waited on the high priests, probably while Jesus was engaged with the Greeks (Jn 12[20-50]), and offered, for sufficient remuneration, to betray Him into their hands. Judas was a disappointed man. He had attached himself to Jesus, believing Him to be the Messiah, and expecting, in accordance with the current conception of the Messianic Kingdom, a rich recompense when the Master should ascend the throne of His father David, and confer offices and honours upon His faithful followers. The period of his discipleship had been a process of disillusionment, and latterly, when he perceived the inevitable issue, he had determined to abandon what he deemed a sinking cause, and save what he might from the wreck. It may be also that he desired to be avenged on the Master who, as he deemed, had fooled him with a false hope.* He therefore went to the high priests and asked what they would give him to betray Jesus into their hands. They leaped at the proposal, and offered him thirty shekels. It was the price of a slave,† and they named it in contempt not of Jesus but of Judas. Even while they trafficked with him, they despised the wretch. Impervious to contempt, he accepted their offer; and, as though in haste to be rid of Him, they paid him the money on the spot.

Such, at least, is St. Matthew's report. St. Mark and St. Luke represent them as merely promising money, the amount unspecified. It might be supposed that St. Matthew's account is

---

* It seems hardly necessary to refer to the theory popularized by De Quincey (*Works*, vi. 21 ff.), which has since his time found favour with not a few. This ingenious theory seeks to explain the conduct of Judas by attributing the betrayal not to covetousness or spite, but to an honest, if mistaken, determination to 'force the hand' of Jesus and compel Him to assert His Messianic dignity and hasten the establishment of His kingdom. It may suffice here to remark that this explanation, while psychologically possible, finds no support in the Gospel narratives, and appears to be quite irreconcilable with the stern words of condemnation spoken by our Lord with reference to the action of Judas (cf. *e.g.* Mt 26[24] 'Woe unto that man through whom the Son of man is betrayed! good were it for that man if he had not been born'). For a full discussion of the motives of the traitor see art. JUDAS ISCARIOT.

† Cf. Ex 21[32]; *Arakh.* xiv. 2: 'If anyone kills a slave, good or bad, he has to pay 30 shekels.'

assimilated to Zec 11[12. 13] (cf. Mt 27[9. 10]); but (1) Mt 27[3-5] proves that the money had been paid, at all events before the trial of Jesus by the Sanhedrin. (2) ἔστησαν, even if it be taken in its literal sense, 'weighed,' need not be an unhistorical embellishment borrowed from the prophecy. Cf. *PEFSt*, Apr. 1896, p. 152 : 'To this day it is usual in Jerusalem to examine and test carefully all coins received. Thus a Medjidie (silver) is examined not only by the eye, but also by noticing its ring on the stone pavement, and English sterling gold is carefully weighed, and returned when defaced.'

It remained that Judas should perform his part of the bargain, but he encountered a difficulty which he had hardly anticipated. Jesus was aware of his design, and, anxious to eat the Passover with His disciples ere He suffered (Lk 22[15]), He took pains to checkmate it. The next day was the Preparation, and, when His disciples asked where He would eat the Supper, He gave them a mysterious direction. 'Away into the city,' He said to Peter and John, 'and there shall meet you a man carrying a pitcher of water: follow him.' Some friend in Jerusalem had engaged to provide a room in his house, and Jesus had arranged this stratagem with him, in order that Judas might not know the place and bring in the rulers in the course of the Supper * (Mt 26[17-19] = Mk 14[12-16] = Lk 22[7-13]).

That evening, as they reclined at table, Jesus, desirous of being alone with His faithful followers, made the startling announcement: 'One of you shall betray me,' and, amid the consternation which ensued, secretly gave Judas his dismissal. The traitor left the room, and, hastening to the high priests, summoned them to action. See ARREST.

LITERATURE.—Hastings' *DB*, art. 'Judas Iscariot'; Fairbairn, *Studies in the Life of Christ*, p. 258 ff.; Stalker, *Trial and Death of Jesus Christ*, p. 110 ff.; Hanna, *Our Lord's Life on Earth* [ed. 1882], pp. 458–467; Bruce, *Training of the Twelve*[5], p. 362 ff.; *Expositor*, 3rd ser. [1889], p. 166 ff.; D. Smith, *The Days of His Flesh*, p. 436 ff.   DAVID SMITH.

BETROTHAL. —Betrothal among the Jews in the time of Jesus, like so many other social institutions, was in process of transition. Jewish marriage customs were in origin the same as those of other Semitic peoples, but Jewish civilization was far removed from its primitive stages. Unfortunately there is little positive information concerning the ceremony of betrothal in NT times proper. The Talmudic *seder* on marriage includes two tractates, *Kethuboth* and *Ḳiddushin*, dealing largely with the preliminaries of marriage, the latter especially with betrothal, but it is considerably later than the NT period. Accordingly, one cannot be sure that the elaborate laws therein set forth obtained in the time of Jesus. Yet it is possible by the study of betrothal customs in Hebrew and in Talmudic times to form a highly probable hypothesis as to such customs in the time of Jesus.

1. The OT betrothal ceremony perpetuated in a conventional fashion the recollection of the time when a woman was purchased from her family. This appears in the Heb. word אָרַשׂ (Dt 20[7], Hos 19[20]). Yet it would be a mistake to regard the use of this word as anything more than a conventional survival. In the days of the codes and the prophets the time was long past when a man's wife was strictly his property. At the same time it is clear that when a woman was designated (יָעַד, Ex 21[8. 9]) by the head of her family as the future wife of another man, there was paid over by the prospective bridegroom a certain sum of meney (or service, as in the case of Jacob), and a contract which was inviolable was then entered into (Gn 34[12], Ex 22[17]). Until the time of the marriage proper the bride-to-be remained in her own family. It was

---

* Euth. Zig. on Mt 26[18]: ὅπως μὴ μαθὼν τὴν οἰκίαν Ἰούδας ἐκδράμῃ πρὸς τοὺς ἐπιβούλους καὶ ἐπαγάγῃ τούτους αὐτῷ πρὸ τοῦ παραδοῦναι τὸ μυστικὸν δεῖπνον τοῖς μαθηταῖς.

not permissible to betroth her to any other man except by action amounting to divorce, and any violation of the rights established by the betrothal was as serious as if the two persons had been actually married (Dt 22²³⁻²⁴). In the OT period it is not possible to say with precision just how soon the betrothal was followed by the wedding. In later times, in the case of a virgin it was after the lapse of a year, and at least thirty days in the case of a widow; but it is impossible to establish more than a possibility of these periods in OT times. So, too, it is impossible to describe with any great precision the betrothal ceremony, but it certainly included the payment of some sum (*mōhar*; in addition to above references, see 1 S 18²⁵), and the making of a betrothal contract (either *viva voce*, Ezk 16⁸, or in writing) by the prospective bridegroom. We know nothing of any formal ceremony or of the use of a ring (unless [unlikely] it may be in Gn 24⁵⁸). The money payment belonged originally to the family of the woman, but gradually came to belong in part or wholly to the woman herself. The woman might bring wealth to her husband, as in the case of Rachel and Leah, but this was not obligatory in the Hebrew period, and cannot be said to belong to betrothal as such. The first advances might come from the family of either party. There is no clear evidence that the young woman had any right of appeal from the choice of her family. The bridegroom himself very probably did not conduct the negotiations, but the matter was in the hands of a third party, as his parents, or some trusted servant or friend.

After the Exile the custom of the earlier period seems to have continued, although with certain modifications. The payment to the bride's father on the part of the prospective groom had been increasingly regarded as the property, at least in part, of the bride. Such a payment during this period was often supplemented by a dowry in the true sense (To 8²¹, Sir 25²²). No consent of the girl was demanded, nor do we know of the recognition of any legal age of consent, unless, as in somewhat later times, it was not expected that boys would marry before the age of eighteen or girls before twelve (*Aboth* v. 21). Although families undoubtedly reached some sort of early arrangement, there is no clear reference to the betrothal of children.

2. In Talmudic times proper there was a distinct tendency to combine betrothal with the wedding. At present the wedding ceremony among orthodox Jews combines the two elements of the two older ceremonies. Possibly because of Western influences the Rabbis became more insistent upon the right of the girl (at least if she had reached her majority, whenever that may have been, *Ḳiddushin*, 41a) to give consent, Rab especially urging it. As the two ceremonies were united, in addition to the former betrothal there grew up a much less permanent form of engagement similar to that which obtains among Western peoples to-day. In Jerusalem, at least, there seem to have been certain opportunities (15 of Ab and *Kippurim*) for young people to become acquainted before the union was determined upon. All men were supposed to marry before the age of 20, and the age of women was a few years less. Other tendencies in Talmudic times were the fixing of the amount of the dowry at not less than 50 *zuz*, that of the *mōhar* at 200 *zuz*, and the use of a peculiarly shaped ring. It is interesting to note that the conventionalizing of the *mōhar* is evidenced in the words which are now used for the ceremony of betrothal: קדושין 'consecration,' אירוסין 'betrothal,' שדכין 'compact,' תנאים 'conditions.'

3. Thus the ceremony of betrothal in NT times probably involved the following acts: (1) A contract drawn up by the parents or by the 'friend of the bridegroom.' (2) The meeting of the two families concerned, with other witnesses, at which time the groom gave the bride a ring and declared his intention to observe the terms of the contract already arranged. (3) The payment of the *mōhar*. The act of betrothal gained in importance, and the two parties seem to have been seated under a canopy during the procedure, and the company to have joined in an increasingly jovial celebration. Strictly speaking, there was no religious ceremony connected with the act, but if a priest were present he doubtless pronounced some benediction which was subsequently elaborated into that used by later orthodox Judaism. The status of the man and woman was now, as in Hebrew times, practically the same as that of married persons, although it was now generally customary for the wedding ceremony proper to be celebrated at the expiration of a year in the case of a virgin, and in thirty days in the case of a widow. As in the older times, separation of betrothed persons demanded a divorce, and there seems to have been no reason why they should not live together as man and wife without a subsequent wedding ceremony. The children of such a union would be regarded as legitimate.

So far as the relations of Mary and Joseph are concerned, it would appear from the narrative in both Matthew and Luke that in their case the custom of the Jews was followed. The description of the betrothal in the *Gospel of Mary* is clearly unhistorical and born of pious imagination; but we are justified in believing that Joseph drew up the customary contract, paid a *mōhar* of approximately 200 *zuz*, and gave Mary a ring. After the formal betrothal (μνηστεύειν, Mt 1¹⁸, Lk 1²⁷ 2⁵) they are reported to have lived together without a second, or wedding, ceremony. As has already appeared, there would be no question as to the legitimacy of children born of such a union.

LITERATURE.—Complete details as to the Talmudic requirements regarding betrothal are given in *Ḳiddushin*; see also the article 'Betrothal' in the *Jewish Encyclopedia*, and Mielziner, *Jewish Law of Marriage and Divorce*. For the ancient Hebrew betrothal, see Benzinger, *Heb. Arch.* p. 133 ff.; and Nowack, *Heb. Arch.* i. 155 ff. Brief accounts are also to be found in Edersheim, *Sketches of Jewish Social Life*, and good articles in Hamburger, Herzog, Hastings' *DB*, and in the *Encyc. Biblica*.

SHAILER MATHEWS.

BIER.—The Gr. word σορός (Heb. מִטָּה, 2 S 3³¹), 'bier,' more strictly means 'a coffin.' Lk 7¹⁴ is the only place where the word appears in the NT. The bier was an open coffin, or simply a flat wooden frame on which the body of the dead was carried to the grave. Closed coffins were not used in the time of our Lord. According to the Levitical Law, contact with a dead body was forbidden as a source of defilement (Nu 19¹¹⁻¹⁴). In raising to life the widow's son at Nain, Jesus, by touching the bier only, avoided any infringement of the letter of the Law. But the miracle, prompted by that same intense sympathy with human sorrow which He so strikingly manifested on another occasion (Jn 11³⁵), pointed to a higher and more authoritative law—that Divine eternal law of compassion which received its freest and fullest expression for the first time in His own life, and which forms one of the most distinctive features of His Gospel.

DUGALD CLARK.

BILL.—1. Bill of divorcement: Mk 10⁴, Mt 19⁷ (RV): Gr. βιβλίον (a scroll or letter) ἀποστασίου; shorter equivalent, ἀποστάσιον Mt 5³¹. In all three passages the expression is used of the סֵפֶר כְּרִיתֻת demanded in Dt 24¹⁻⁴ of the husband who divorces his wife. In contrast with the older usage—still prevalent in the East—of divorce by a merely verbal process, the need of preparing a written document was calculated to be a bar against hasty or frivolous action, while the bill itself served the divorced wife as a certificate of her right to marry again. The Rabbis, who dwelt with special gusto ('non sine complacentia quadam'—Lightfoot) on the subject of divorce, had drawn up regulations as to the proper wording of the bill of divorcement, its sealing and witnessing, and the number of lines —neither less nor more than twelve—the writing must occupy. In the eyes of Jesus, no document, however formal, could prevent divorce from being a violation of God's purpose in instituting marriage. See Lightfoot, *Hor. Heb. in* Mt 5[31].

2. A bond (so RV) or written acknowledgment of debt, Lk 16[6. 7] : Gr. (Ti., Tr., WH) τὰ γράμματα, (TR) τὸ γράμμα. The word itself is indefinite (literally = 'the letters'), and throws no light upon a question much discussed by commentators on the parable of the Unjust Steward, viz. Was the bond merely an acknowledgment of a debt, or was it an undertaking to pay a fixed annual rental from the produce of a farm? Edersheim decides, though without giving his reasons, for the former alternative; Lightfoot inclines to the latter. Against the theory of a simple debt is the fact that the amount of the obligation is stated in kind—wheat and oil—and not in money; and the probability of the story is heightened if we are to understand that the remissions authorized by the steward— amounting in money value, according to Edersheim, to the not very considerable sums of £5 and £25 respectively—affected not a single but an annual payment. But, on the other hand, as van Koetsfeld, who argues strongly for the view that the document was of the nature of a lease, admits, there is no precedent for the word (χρεοφιλέται) rendered 'debtors' being used for tenants. Jülicher dismisses the whole controversy as irrelevant. Another point in dispute is whether the old bond was altered, or a new one substituted for it. Lightfoot and Edersheim again take different sides. The alteration of the old bond is suggested, though not absolutely demanded, by the language of the passage, and would be, according to Edersheim, in accordance with the probabilities of the case. Acknowledgments of debt were usually written on wax-covered tablets, and could easily be altered, the stylus in use being provided, not only with a sharp-pointed *kōthēbh* or writer, but with a flat thick *mōhēk* or eraser. In any case it is clear that the 'bill' was written by the person undertaking the obligation; that it was the only formal evidence of the obligation; and that its supervision belonged to the functions of the steward. Hence, should the steward conspire with the debtors against his master's interests, the latter had no check upon the fraud.

LITERATURE.—Edersheim, *Life and Times of Jesus the Messiah*, ii. 268–273 ; Lightfoot, *Hor. Heb., in loc.*; see also the various commentators on the Parables.   NORMAN FRASER.

BINDING AND LOOSING.—See CÆSAREA PHILIPPI, KEYS.

BIRD.—See ANIMALS, p. 65[a].

BIRTH OF CHRIST.—
  i. St. Luke's account.
    1. Jewish element and colouring.
    2. Objections taken to the contents of Lk 1. 2.
    3. Probable sources of St. Luke's information.
    4. Bethlehem as our Lord's birthplace.
    5. The census of Quirinius.
  ii. St. Matthew's account.
    1. Use of OT prophecy.
    2. Relation to Jewish legal requirements.
    3. Sobriety and delicacy of the narrative
    4. Objections taken to the contents of Mt 1. 2.
  iii. Apocryphal accounts.
  iv. Convergent traditions and the main facts.
      Literature.

i. ST. LUKE'S ACCOUNT.—**1.** *Jewish element and colouring.*—The two accounts of our Lord's birth in the Gospels carry us at once into the very heart of Jewish home life. In the fuller account of the two, that of St. Luke, the evidence of this Jewish element has been materially strengthened by recent literature and discussion. No one, *e.g.*, can read the early Canticles in St. Luke's Gospel without noticing their intensely Jewish character. This was amply shown by Ryle and James in their edition of the *Psalms of Solomon* (see esp. pp. xci, xcii), a work which may fairly be placed some half century or so before our Lord's Advent. In the same manner Chase has illustrated many points of contact between these Canticles and the language of the Eighteen Prayers of the synagogue.[*] More recently Sanday has emphasized the same argument, more especially in relation to the *Benedictus*, in which he finds quite a piling up of expressions characteristic of the old popular Messianic expectation ; the first five or six verses are quite sufficient to mark this essentially pre-Christian character (*Critical Questions*, p. 133 ; see also Nebe, *Die Kindheitsgeschichte unseres Herrn Jesu Christi nach Matthäus und Lukas ausgelegt*, 1893, p. 166 ff.; and even Gunkel, *Zum religionsgeschichtlichen Verständniss des NT*, 1903, p. 67).[†]

This question of the composition of the Canticles in St. Luke is a very important one, because it is constantly assumed that they were the invention of the author of the Third Gospel. But in this case we have to assume that the Greek Luke, or some unknown writer, was able to transfer himself in thought to a time when Jewish national hopes, which were shattered by the fate of the capital, were still vividly cherished in Jewish circles, and that he was able to express those hopes in the popular language current at the date of our Lord's birth with a marked absence of any later Christian conceptions.[‡]

And yet with all this Jewish colouring there is in these Canticles a depth and a charm which have appealed to men everywhere throughout the Christian centuries. No one recognized the Jewish element in these early chapters of St. Luke more frankly than M. Renan ; but he could also write of the *Magnificat, Gloria in Excelsis, Benedictus, Nunc Dimittis* : 'Never were sweeter songs invented to put to sleep the sorrows of poor humanity' (*Les Évangiles*, p. 278).

2. *Objections taken to the contents of Lk 1. 2.—* The extravagant assertion must, of course, not be forgotten, that we owe these opening chapters of St. Luke, or at least some of their details, to the influence of other great Eastern religions. A discussion of this assertion may more properly be referred to the art. VIRGIN BIRTH.[§] But a word

* 'The Lord's Prayer in the Early Church' (*TS* i. 3, p. 147 ff.).
† Harnack, in his *Reden und Aufsätze*, i. p. 307 ff. (1904), maintains that while St. Luke has undoubtedly used a Jewish-Christian document in chs. 1 and 2, he has also introduced touches acceptable to a Greek, and that one word, in common use to-day, was wanting in the original Christian phraseology, the word 'Saviour.' According to Harnack, we owe this word to St. Luke, a word so often used by the Greeks to designate their gods, and thus it found its way into Lk 2[11]. St. Paul scarcely knew it ; but shortly after his time, when we come to St. Luke, it is otherwise. It is further argued that we look for the word in vain in St. Mark or St. Matthew. But, to say nothing of its use by St. John, cf. Jn 4[42] and 1 Jn 4[14], St. Matthew (1[21]) emphasizes the meaning of the word *Jesus*, ' for it is he that shall save (σώσει) his people from their sins ' ; and St. Paul in his first recorded missionary address speaks of 'a Saviour Jesus' (σωτὴρ Ἰησοῦς), and connects His coming with the remission of sins (Ac 13[24. 38]). Cf. Ph 3[20] and Ac 5[31], an admittedly early source) ; also Ps-Sol 10[9] 16[5].

‡ Zahn well remarks : ' Passages like Lk 1–2, which in their narrative portions and the psalms introduced can be compared for poetical grace and genuinely Israelitish spirit only with the most beautiful portions of the Books of Samuel, could not have been composed by a Greek like St. Luke ' (*Einleitung*, ii. p. 404). The whole passage should be consulted. On the minute account of the ritual in the Temple (Lk 2[22ff.]), and its significance as pointing to an early date for the narrative, see Sanday (*l.c.* p. 135), and the *Church Quarterly Review*, Oct. 1904, p. 194, The whole point of St. Luke's full acquaintance with the legal ritual is well brought out by B. Weiss (*Leben Jesu*, i. p. 237).

§ See, however, amongst the most recent writers, A. Jeremias, *Babylonisches im NT*, pp. 48, 49, and his able criticism.

may here be said upon the most recent attempt to trace this alleged influence, in *Indische Einflüsse auf evangelische Erzählungen*, by G. A. van den Burgh van Eysinga, 1904. On p. 22 ff. a whole series of alleged parallels is quoted between the coming of the aged Simeon into the Temple and the coming of the sage Asita into the Palace to do homage to the infant Buddha. While the writer is constrained (p. 23) to admit that the whole of the story of Simeon is told in a strongly Hebraistic style, he maintains that it is not said that the original motive of the incident is also of Hebrew origin. But in this connexion it is very significant that, while a supposed parallel is alleged between every verse which tells of Simeon (Lk 2²⁵⁻³²) and the story of Asita, there is one verse (v.²⁶) for which no parallel is adduced; and it is difficult to see that any other than a motive of Hebrew origin could inspire such words as these: 'and it had been revealed unto him by the Holy Spirit that he should not see death before he had seen the Lord's Christ.' The contrast is rightly marked between the pious resignation of Simeon and the wail of Asita over his departure amid the ruins of old age and death. But what could be more absurd than to find a parallel (p. 22) between Asita taking his path across the sky by the way of *the wind,* and the statement of St. Luke that Simeon came ἐν τῷ πνεύματι into the Temple?

From a somewhat different point of view these Jewish conceptions are noteworthy. In Lk 1³² we read: 'He shall be great, and shall be called the Son of the Most High: and the Lord God shall give unto him the throne of his father David: and he shall reign over the house of Jacob for ever; and of his kingdom there shall be no end.' Here again we have language closely resembling that of the *Psalms of Solomon, e.g.* 17⁴·⁸·²³, full of Jewish thought and expectation, expressing the hopes of the times at which it purports to be written, but scarcely such as would have been invented by a Christian composer.* But we are asked to believe that into the midst of this Jewish language some Christian writer wished to introduce a statement of our Lord's virgin birth, and that he did so by the interpolation of the next two verses, Lk 1³⁴·³⁵. As a matter of fact, there is no valid ground for regarding these two verses as interpolated. They are retained by the most distinguished editors of the NT both in England and Germany, *e.g.* WH, Blass, Nestle; even Gunkel can see no reason for their excision (*Zum religionsgeschichtlichen Verständniss des NT*, 1903, p. 66).

There are one or two points connected with this alleged interpolation which we may notice without encroaching upon the art. VIRGIN BIRTH.

(*a*) We are struck with the extraordinary reserve and brevity of the statement, a reserve which characterizes the whole story in Lk 1. 2. These two verses (1³⁴·³⁵) contain, we are told, the only reference to the virgin birth. Let us suppose for a moment that this is so; and if so we cannot but contrast the language with that of the *Protevangelium Jacobi*, with its fantastic and prurient details, or even with that portion of the *Ascension of Isaiah*, viz. the Vision of Isaiah, which carries us back, according to Charles, within the lines of the first Christian century (*Ascen. Is.* p. xxii ff.).

(*b*) Let us suppose that these two verses are no longer to find a place in the story, what then? It has been urged with truth that *the whole of St. Luke's narrative* is impregnated with the underlying idea that when Christ was born His mother was a virgin, and that it is impossible to omit this element without destroying the whole (*Church Quarterly Review*, July 1904, p. 383).

* 'The phraseology of the suspected vv.³⁴·³⁵ is unmistakably Hebraistic' (G. H. Box in *ZNTW*, 1905, Heft 1, p. 92).

'The Christian belief,' writes Professor V. Rose of Fribourg, 'is manifest from the whole trend of the Gospel of the Infancy. Mary it is who, contrary to all Hebrew use, appears alone upon the scene. While Zacharias receives the celestial promise of the birth of a son, while he himself hymns the opening of the Messianic era and the destiny of John, Joseph plays not the smallest part in the mystery of Jesus. Mary is entirely in the foreground: to her the angel addresses himself; the prophecy of Zechariah has to do with her; she speaks to the child found in the Temple; Joseph says nothing; he keeps in the background. His position in the family is that of guardian, the supporter of Mary, the protector of Jesus' (*Studies in the Gospels*, 1903, p. 72).

(*c*) If the interpolator of these two verses in question had done his work so 'clearly and effectively' as Schmiedel maintains, it is surely surprising that he should have allowed any of those passages in the original document to stand which could refer in any way to Joseph's parentage. These references, *e.g.* 2²⁷⁻³³·⁴¹·⁴³·⁴⁸, would have seriously impaired both the clearness and effectiveness of his work. But suppose, on the other hand, that the whole story comes to us from one who was well acquainted with all the facts of the case, we can then understand why he could allow the passages about Joseph to stand; in common estimation our Lord passed for the son of Joseph; probably in the register of births He was thus described; and from a social point of view it was necessary, as we shall see, that this should be so.

3. *Probable sources of St. Luke's information.*—St. Luke's account gives us not only a picture of Jewish home life, but it also reveals the workings of a Jewish mother's heart; it gives us with unmistakable clearness, and yet with the utmost delicacy and reserve, information which could scarcely have come from any one in the first instance but a woman (this is admirably shown by Ramsay in the second chapter of *Was Christ born at Bethlehem?*). Whether this information reached St. Luke through a written document or whether it came to him orally, we cannot say, and from the present point of view it does not matter. For the impression which is derived from his account is twofold,—not only that it is of Palestinian origin, but also that it is derived from Mary the mother of the Lord, or from those who were closely acquainted with her.*

It has been lately suggested, with much force and learning, that the information derived in the first place from the Virgin herself may have reached St. Luke through Joanna (Sanday, *Critical Questions*, p. 157). Evidently St. Luke had some special source of information connected with the court of the Herods, and Joanna the wife of Chuza, Herod's steward, appears no fewer than four times upon the stage of the Gospel history. She accompanies our Lord amongst the other women in Galilee; she was one of the group of women who had witnessed the Crucifixion, and who afterwards went to the grave on the morning of the first Easter Day; and it may be safely inferred that she was one of the women in the upper room after the Ascension. We can scarcely doubt that she and the Virgin Mother were often in each other's company. It may, of course, be alleged that St. Luke's news about the Herods may have reached him through other channels, and that there is no proof that he was personally acquainted with Joanna.

If credit be allowed to the Acts of the Apostles, it would seem that St. Luke himself, as also St.

* See the remarks of Wright, *Synopsis of the Gospels in Greek*², p. 292; Dalman, *Die Worte Jesu*, i. 31. Recent attempts have been made to ascribe the *Magnificat* to Elisabeth, and the arguments for and against this view will be found in *PRE*³ vol. xii. [1903], p. 72 f. But in spite of all that has been urged by Harnack (*Sitzungsb. d. König. Preuss. Akad. der Wissensch. zu Berlin*, xxvii. 1900), it is difficult to believe that the words 'the lowliness of his handmaiden,' are not most naturally connected with the words of Mary to the angel, 'Behold, the handmaid of the Lord' (Lk 1⁴⁸), and that the words 'shall call me blessed' are not best referred to the words spoken by Elisabeth to Mary (vv.⁴²·⁴⁵). On the proposal to find in the words of Mary, 'all generations shall call me blessed,' an imitation of the words of Leah in Gn 30¹³, see Nebe, *Die Kindheitsgeschichte*, p. 136, Plummer, *St. Luke, ad loc.*, also Jacquier, *Histoire de NT*, ii. 504 (1905). The contrast far exceeds any comparison, as these writers show. The combination in Mary of the deepest humility with a firm consciousness of her own high calling and future renown is very striking. See, further, Burn, *Niceta of Remesiana*, 1205, p. cliii ff.

Paul, may well have come into personal contact with one or more members of the Holy Family. We read, for instance, in Ac 21[18], in one of the 'We' sections of that book: 'And the day following Paul went in with us unto James; and all the elders were present.' How much St. Luke may have learnt from St. James the Lord's brother, it is, of course, presumptuous to say; but he may at least have learnt something during his stay in Jerusalem as to the place and the circumstances connected with our Lord's birth. We cannot forget the Evangelist's claim to have traced the course of all things accurately from the first (Lk 1[2]), and he would scarcely have neglected the opportunities of information which were open to him in Jerusalem and afterwards in Cæsarea.

4. *Bethlehem as our Lord's birthplace.*—The intercourse just referred to would at least have saved St. Luke from the gross geographical blunder which he has been accused of making at the outset of his history, the blunder of confusing Bethlehem-Judah with another Bethlehem in Galilee (see, in relation to this alleged blunder, Knowling, *Our Lord's Virgin Birth and the Criticism of To-day*, pp. 6–13). But the recently published remarks of Sanday may well be remembered in this connexion (*Sacred Sites of the Gospels*, p. 25):—

'There are two Bethlehems, the second in Galilee, about seven miles west of Nazareth, and it has recently been suggested in the *Encyc. Biblica* that the Galilean Bethlehem was the true scene of the Nativity. There would be real advantages if Bethlehem could be thought of as near to Nazareth. But to obtain this result we have to go entirely behind our Gospels. Both St. Matthew and St. Luke are express in placing the birth of Christ at Bethlehem of *Judæa*. And as their narratives are wholly independent of each other, and differ in most other respects, it is clear that we have on this point a convergence of two distinct traditions.'

Professor Usener, indeed, fastens upon the passage Jn 7[41f.], and sees in it the hidden path by which Bethlehem found its way into the Gospel tradition (*Encyc. Bibl.* iii. 3347). But there is no reason for supposing that the writer of the Fourth Gospel was himself unaware of our Lord's birth at Bethlehem, because he expresses the popular expectation of the ignorant multitude. If the Gospel was written at the late date demanded by advanced critics, his ignorance of such a belief would be altogether unaccountable. Quite apart from our Gospels, Charles would refer the remarkable passage in the *Ascension of Isaiah* 11[2-22] to a very early date, deriving it from the archetype which he carries back to the close of the 1st cent. (*Introd.* pp. xxii–xlv); and from a comparison of v.[2] and v.[12] it can scarcely be doubted that Bethlehem-Judah was meant throughout the narrative as the scene of our Lord's birth. But if the writer of the Fourth Gospel was St. John, it is a most arbitrary procedure to see in this passage (7[41f.]) any proof that the place of the Nativity was unknown to him. Are we to suppose that St. John was also ignorant of our Lord's descent from David?[*] an inference which might equally seem to follow from the passage before us, unless we remember that the Evangelist is presupposing that his readers would be well aware of the true descent of Jesus and the actual place of His birth (see this point admirably put by Ramsay, *Was Christ born at Bethlehem?* p. 96).

Nor does the fact that our Lord was popularly known as Jesus of Nazareth in any way interfere with the truth that He was born at Bethlehem. It has, indeed, not unfrequently happened that a man has been associated with, or even named after, a town where his youth and early manhood have been passed, rather than after the actual place of

his birth, in which his parents may have sojourned for a while (B. Weiss, *Leben Jesu*[4], i. 227). It will, of course, be said that prophecy pointed to our Lord's birth at Bethlehem, and that St. Matthew (2[6]) distinctly quotes Micah's words in this connexion. But was the prophecy fulfilled? On the one hand, we are asked to believe that St. Luke starts his narrative not only with a geographical, but also with a grave historical blunder, and that he confuses an enrolment of Herod with the subsequent enrolment, some ten years later, of Ac 5[37]. On the other hand, it is urged that St. Luke's accuracy, so well attested in other respects, would have saved him from making an initial and needless error, and that the least consideration would have prevented him from connecting such an event as an enrolment of the people with the birth of the Messiah at Bethlehem, unless it was true. Undoubtedly both OT prediction and Rabbinic teaching pointed to Bethlehem, yet the prophecy was fulfilled according to the Gospel story by the introduction of a set of circumstances which were strangely alien to Jewish national thought and prestige: 'a counting of the people, or census, and that census taken at the bidding of a heathen emperor, and executed by one so universally hated as Herod, would represent the *ne plus ultra* of all that was most repugnant to Jewish feeling' (Edersheim, *Jesus the Messiah*, i. 181). At any rate, we know quite enough of Jewish susceptibilities and of Jewish fanaticism in the 1st cent. of our era to be sure that a ruler like Herod, and in his position, would naturally guard against any undue exasperation of Jewish national and religious feeling. If it is urged that the story of the Nativity was bound in any case to bring Joseph and Mary to Bethlehem, the city of David, it would have been easier and more significant to have adopted the theory of Strauss, to the effect that the parents were led to go to Bethlehem by the appearance of an angel, especially when we remember that the frequent introduction of angelic visitors is described as one of the special characteristics of the writings of St. Luke.

5. *The census of Quirinius.*—It is one of the great merits of Professor Ramsay's theory, that it not only claims credibility for the enrolment of Lk 2[2] as an historical event, but that it also combines with that claim a due recognition of Jewish national prejudices. The word for 'enrolment' (ἀπογραφή), or its plural, was the word for the periodic enrolments which beyond all doubt were made in Egypt, probably initiated by Augustus. These enrolments were numberings of the people according to households, and had nothing to do with the valuation for purposes of taxation. But H. Holtzmann urges in objection that Egypt is not Syria (*Hand-Commentar zum NT*, 1901, p. 316). On the other hand, however, it does not seem unreasonable to suppose that such enrolments would take place in other parts of the empire,[*] especially under a ruler so systematic as Augustus; and this probability Ramsay has not forgotten to illustrate. Moreover, as the same writer urges, we have to take into account the delicate and difficult position of Herod, who was obliged, on the one hand, to carry out the Imperial policy, whilst, on the other hand, he was called upon to rule over a fanatical people full of stubborn pride and inherent suspicions. What under such circumstances would be more likely than that Herod would endeavour to give a tribal and family character to the enrolment, in fact, to conduct it

---

[*] On the descent of Jesus from David see especially Dalman, *Die Worte Jesu*, i. 263; also Charles, *Ascension of Isaiah*, p. 95. For the meaning of Jn 7[41f.] see, further, Salmon, *Introduction to the NT*[5], p. 277.

[*] Percy Gardner (art. 'Quirinius' in *Encyc. Bibl.* iv. 3 ff.) admits that 'one or two definite, though not conclusive pieces of evidence seem to indicate that this periodical census was not confined to Egypt, but was, in some cases at all events, extended to Syria.'

on national lines which would harmonize as far as was possible with Jewish sentiment.* Here probably lies the true distinction between the first enrolment, which was one of a series, and *the* enrolment (Ac 5[37]) which was conducted after the Roman fashion, and became the cause not only of indignation, but of rebellion. Here, too, we have the probable explanation as to why Joseph and the Virgin Mother left their home at Nazareth for Bethlehem. If the enrolment had been taken on Roman lines, there would have been no motive for the journey, since in that case only a recognition of existing political and social facts would have been involved ; but in the present instance the Roman method was judiciously modified by the introduction of a numbering not only by households, but by tribes. There is, then, no confusion between this enrolment of Herod's and the subsequent enrolment of 6–7 A.D.,—a confusion that would involve a blunder of some ten years,—as Schmiedel and Pfleiderer maintain ; but, on the contrary, a careful distinction is drawn between them.

Moreover, since the publication of his first book on the subject, Ramsay has collected fresh details to support his thesis.† The year, for instance, which he claims for the first periodic census seems to demand an interval of some two years between it and the earliest date for the Birth of our Lord. This somewhat lengthy interval, which has been urged against the theory, may perhaps be accounted for by the situation of affairs in Palestine, which presented at the time considerable difficulty and anxiety. But a fair and contemporary analogy, so far as length of time is concerned, may be found in another part of the Roman Empire, and in a much simpler operation than that of a census. The kingdom of Paphlagonia was incorporated in the Roman province Galatia ; but although the taking of the oath of allegiance was, as compared with a census, a matter which required little preparation and instruction of officials, yet nearly, or perhaps more than, two years elapsed before the oath was actually administered (*Expositor*, Nov. 1901, p. 321 ff.).

One of the most acute and prominent opponents of St. Luke's accuracy in regard to the question before us is Professor Schürer, who in *GJV*[3] (vol. i. [1901] pp. 508–543) deals *seriatim* with the difficulties which, in his opinion, St. Luke's statement involves.

(1) Schürer, first of all, points out that history knows nothing of a general census of the empire in the time of Augustus But, as Ramsay rightly says, the contrary assertion stands on a very different level of probability from that which it occupied before the Egyptian discovery. And if there is evidence that the periods of the Egyptian enrolments were frequently coincident with the holding of a census in other parts of the empire, we come very near to St. Luke's statement, that Augustus laid down a general principle of taking a census of the whole Roman world.

(2) It is maintained by Schürer that if St. Luke describes Joseph as travelling to Bethlehem because he was of the house and lineage of David, this presupposes that the lists for the census were prepared according to descent and families, which was by no means the Roman method. But Ramsay's whole contention is that the 'enrolment' in question was conducted not according to Roman, but according to Jewish, methods.

'It is urged,' says Schürer, 'that in this census an accommodation was made to Jewish customs and prejudice.' But he argues that although this was often the case under the Em-

pire, yet in this instance such a method would have been too burdensome and inconvenient; and, further, that it is very questionable whether such an 'enrolment' according to tribes and families was practicable, since in many cases it was no longer possible to trace the link of connexion with some particular tribe or family. But with regard to the former of these points, it is quite consistent with Ramsay's theory that the 'enrolment' should have taken a considerable time, and with regard to the second point we are fortunately able to quote Dalman as to the accuracy with which family registers were kept among the Jews. He points out that the title 'Son of David' would not have been ascribed to Jesus if it had been believed that He did not satisfy the genealogical conditions implied by the name. The Book of Chronicles, which gives (1 Ch 17) the promise of 2 S 7, revived afresh the idea of the royal destiny of the family of David, and thereby contributed to the preservation of the household traditions of descendants of David. Dalman adds, 'Where, in addition to proud recollections, national hopes of the greatest moment were bound up with a particular lineage, those belonging to it would be as unlikely to forget their origin as, in our own day, for instance, the numerous descendants of Muhammad, or the peasant families of Norway who are descended from ancient kings.' And he adds, 'Hence it results that no serious doubts need be offered to the idea of a trustworthy tradition of Davidic descent in the family of Joseph' (*Die Worte Jesu*, i. p. 266).

(3) But Schürer has by no means come to the end of his argument. The decisive proof against a census in the time of Herod is this, that Josephus characterizes the census of Ac 5[37] as something entirely new and unheard of, and that it became on that account the cause of indignation and rebellion.* But admitting these statements of Josephus, what then? Simply this, that his language is amply justified with reference to the passage mentioned, viz. Ac 5[37]. The year A.D. 7, as Josephus has it, did mark a new departure ; the taxing then made was made after the Roman fashion ; it was wholly removed in its method and in its consequences from the earlier enrolment under Herod. It is therefore evident that whilst Josephus might well refer to the revolt under Judas of Galilee as the result of this taxation, there was no reason why he should refer to the enrolment of some ten to fourteen years earlier with which no rebellious excitement was connected.

(4) In his latest edition Schürer is very severe with regard to Ramsay's theory that Quirinius was associated with Quintilius Varus, the latter being the regular governor of Syria for its internal administration, while the former administered the military resources of the province. This, according to Ramsay, would bring Quirinius to Syria B.C. 7–6, and the 'enrolment' of Palestine took place at the same time. St. Luke does not say that Quirinius was *governor* ; he uses a vague word with regard to him, a word which might mean that the 'enrolment' was made while Quirinius was acting as leader (ἡγεμών) in Syria ; and it seems quite possible that St. Luke should speak of Quirinius in this way, since he was holding the delegated ἡγεμονία of the Emperor in his command of the armies of Syria. But Schürer presses this point, and makes much of the unlikelihood that St. Luke would date his census not from the ordinary governor, but from one who had nothing to do with the taking of the census. Yet it must be remembered that there are undoubtedly examples of frequent temporary associations of duties in Roman administration, and it is quite possible that Quirinius may have been concerned in the census, as Plummer suggests (art. 'Quirinius' in Hastings' *DB* iv. 183).† Moreover, it may be fairly urged, as it is in fact by Ramsay, that Quirinius ruled for a shorter time than Varus, and that as he controlled the foreign relations of the province he furnished the best means of dating (*Was Christ born at Bethlehem?* p. 246 ; see also p. 105). But if we once admit that St. Luke's words do not involve the belief that Quirinius was the actual governor of Syria, the view that Quirinius may have been sent as an extraordinary legate to Syria, and as such had undertaken the administration of the census, is well worthy of consideration. This view is mentioned by Schürer (*l.c.* p. 540), although only to be rejected. But Ramsay (p. 248) points out that if this supposition is accepted, it may be observed that Quirinius as the commissioner for Syria and Palestine would be a delegate exercising the emperor's authority, and might rightly be said ἡγεμονεύειν τῆς Συρίας. At all events this view offends against no method of Roman procedure (as Schürer apparently allows), and it may fairly be said to be quite compatible with the language which St. Luke employs.

When we consider the many difficulties which surround this *vexata quœstio*, it is somewhat surprising that Professor Schürer should affirm that all possible means of escape from the con-

---

* On this practical method of thus avoiding any outrage upon Jewish national feeling, see, further, B. Weiss, *Leben Jesu*[4], i. 231. Turner (art. 'Chronology' in Hastings' *DB* i. 404) also points out that Herod may well have been mindful of the susceptibilities of the Jews, and so, in avoiding the scandal caused by the later census (Ac 5[37]), avoided also the notice of history.

† Zöckler (art. 'Jesus Christus' in *PRE*[3]) speaks of Ramsay's theory in terms of approval ; Chase speaks of the same theory as having advanced many stages the probability that St. Luke's reference to the enrolment under Quirinius is historical (*Supernatural Element in our Lord's earthly Life*, p. 21) ; while Kenyon (art. 'Papyri' in Hastings' *DB*, Ext. Vol. 356) speaks of the light which the discovery of the census-records in Egypt has thrown upon the chronology of the NT, although, as he adds, Professor Ramsay's is the only attempt to work out the problem in detail.

* *BJ* II. viii. 1, VII. viii. 1.

† In this connexion Plummer points out that Justin Martyr refers to Quirinius at the time of the Nativity by a word equivalent to one holding the office of *procurator*, and not by a word signifying *legatus*, as Quirinius afterwards became in A.D. 6. The only other place in which St. Luke uses the word employed in the phrase 'when Quirinius was governor of Syria' refers to a *procurator* (Lk 3[1]), and this fact adds weight to the supposition that, while at the time of the enrolment Varus was actually *legatus*, Quirinius may have held some such command as that indicated above. H. Holtzmann (*Hdcom.*, 1901, i. p. 317) dismisses Ramsay's proposed explanation somewhat contemptuously ; but he has nothing to say with regard to the analogous cases of a temporary division of duties in Roman administration, or to those quoted by R. S. Bour, who is essentially in agreement with Ramsay in the proposed solution.

clusion are closed, the conclusion being that St. Luke's state-ment conflicts with the facts of history (*l.c.* p. 542). Having arrived at this very dogmatic result, he points out that anyone who cannot attribute such an error to Luke should bear in mind that the Evangelist is not free from the perpetration of other blunders. He confuses, *e.g.*, the Theudas in Ac 5[36], the Theudas who rises up before Judas of Galilee, with the Theudas who lived some forty years later. But Schürer must be well aware that many able critics do not accept this further summary assertion on his part of St. Luke's ignorance, and that his own learned countryman Dr. F. Blass passes the sensible judgment in his Commentary on Ac 5[37], that St. Luke's accuracy in other respects should prevent us from attributing to him here such a grave error as is sometimes alleged. Moreover, it should be remembered that it is precisely in points connected with the administration of the Roman provinces that St. Luke's accuracy has been so repeatedly proved. Consider as a single instance the manner in which in the Acts he is able not merely to dis-tinguish between Imperial and Senatorial provinces, but also to note accurately the particular period during which a certain province was under one or the other kind of rule. Or if we turn to the Gospel, we recall how a keen controversy has raged around the statement in Lk 3[1] with regard to Lysanias the tetrarch of Abilene. Here, too, St. Luke has been accused of manifest inaccuracy. But, to say nothing of the recent dis-covery of two inscriptions which have been fairly cited in support of St. Luke's correctness, it may be observed that Schmiedel reluctantly allows (art. 'Lysanias' in *Encyc. Bibl.* iii. 2842) that it cannot possibly be shown, or even assumed, that St. Luke is here mistaken, while Schürer entertains no such hesitation, and frankly states that 'the Evangelist Luke is thoroughly correct when he assumes that in the fifteenth year of Tiberius there was a Lysanias tetrarch of Abilene' (*l.c.* p. 719). And yet within a few lines of this evidence of correct-ness we are asked to believe that the same Evangelist was guilty of a gratuitous and stupid blunder in relation to the enrolment under Quirinius.

ii. St. Matthew's account. — 1. *Use of OT prophecy.* —

While St. Luke narrates the events which lead to the Birth at Bethlehem without making any definite reference to OT prophecy, it is noticeable that St. Matthew (2[6]) quotes definitely the prophecy of Micah (5[2]) with reference to the home of David : 'And thou Bethlehem, land of Judah, art in nowise least among the princes of Judah : for out of thee shall come forth a governor, which shall be shepherd of my people Israel.' The prophecy was undoubtedly regarded as Messianic (Zahn, *Das Evangelium des Matthäus*, 1903, p. 94 ; Schürer, *l.c.* ii. 527–530).

The difference in the wording of Mt 2[6] and Mic 5[2] is easily accounted for, if we bear in mind that the Evangelist repro-duces the prophecy in the manner popular at the time, *i.e.* he quotes some Targum on the passage, or, as Edersheim puts it, Mic 5[2] is rendered *targumically*, and this would fairly cover the variations in the two renderings (*Jesus the Messiah*, i. p. 206 ; cf. also Delitzsch, *Messianische Weissagungen*[2], p. 129). But if Schürer is correct in seeing in the prophecy of Micah words which might easily be understood to mean that the Messiah's goings forth had been from of old, from everlasting, *i.e.* to signify the Messiah's pre-existence, yet it cannot be said that Jewish theology pointed to a birth such as that recorded by St. Matthew.

It is no wonder that Zahn (*l.c.* p. 83) should characterize as altogether fantastic the attempt to derive the stories of St. Matthew and St. Luke from the Rabbinic exegesis of Is 7[14], when there is no reason to assume that the prophet's words were taken at the time of our Lord's birth to refer to the Messiah at all (see also Weber, *Jüdische Theologie*[2], pp. 354, 357 ; and von Orelli, art. 'Messias' in *PRE*[3], 1902, and esp. Dalman, *Die Worte Jesu*, i. 226). But this is a subject for which refer-ence may be made to art. Virgin Birth.

2. *Relation to Jewish legal requirements.* —

St. Matthew's account, which with every due con-cession may fairly be regarded as dating in its present form within the limits of the 1st cent., demands our attention for further reasons. It is remarkable, for example, how strictly it adheres to Jewish legality, and yet at the same time how delicately the feelings and thoughts of Joseph are portrayed (cf. G. H. Box, *l.c.* p. 82).

With regard to the first point, it may be noted that 'after the betrothal the bride was under the same restrictions as a wife. If unfaithful, she ranked and was punished as an adulteress (Dt 22[23f.]) ; and, on the other hand, the bridegroom, if he wished to break the contract, had the same privileges, and had also to observe the same for-malities, as in the case of divorce. The situation is illustrated in the history of Joseph and Mary,

who were on the footing of betrothal' (art. 'Mar-riage' in Hastings' *DB* iii. ; cf. also Nebe, *Kind-heitsgeschichte*, pp. 199, 200, and Zahn, *l.c.* p. 71). In this connexion one may also refer to another passage in Dalman with reference to the descent of Jesus : 'A case such as that of Jesus,' he writes. ' was, of course, not anticipated by the Law ; but if no other human fatherhood was alleged, then the child must have been regarded as bestowed by God upon the house of Joseph ; for a betrothed woman, according to Jewish law, already occupied the same status as a wife' (*Die Worte Jesu*, i. p. 263). See Betrothal.

If we bear this in mind, we can see how easy it is to interpret the reading of the Sinaitic-Syriac palimpsest, of which so much has been made, in Lk 2[5] 'he and Mary his wife, that they might be enrolled.' All that the words show, if we allow that they are the correct reading, is that Mary was under the full legal protection of Joseph : 'unless, indeed, our Lord had passed in common estimation as the son of Joseph,' it has been well pointed out that it is difficult to see how Joseph, according to Mt 1[19], could have gratified his wish 'not to expose' Mary. And so again 'Joseph was without doubt the foster-father of our Lord ; and if any register of births was kept in the Temple or elsewhere, he would probably be there described as the actual father. Such he was from a social point of view, and it was therefore no wilful suppression of the truth when the most blessed amongst women said to her Son, "Thy father and I have sought thee sorrow-ing"' (Mrs. Lewis in the *Expos. Times*, 1900, 1901, where illus-trations from Eastern social customs may be also found). Cf. W. C. Allen, *Interpreter*, Feb. 1905, p. 113.

3. *Sobriety and delicacy of the narrative.* —

If we turn again to what we may call the inwardness of St. Matthew's story, we can scarcely fail to be struck with its singular sobriety and reserve. We hear nothing of any anger or reproach on the part of Joseph against his betrothed, although as 'a righteous man' he feels that only one course is open to him. But with this decision other con-siderations were evidently still contending,—con-siderations the very existence of which bore testi-mony to the purity and fidelity of Mary. The words of the angel (Mt 1[20]) say nothing of the appeasement of indignation, they speak rather of the befitting conquest of hesitation and doubt : 'fear not to take unto thee Mary thy wife,' *i.e.* to take unto thee one who had and still has a claim to that honoured and cherished name. No wonder that Dean Plumptre could write that the glimpse given us into the character of Joseph is one of singular tenderness and beauty (see Ellicott's *Com-mentary, in loco*). If any one will read this delicate and beautiful description and place it side by side with that given us in the *Protevangelium Jacobi*, where, *e.g.*, both Joseph and the priest bitterly reproach Mary, and a whole series of prurient details is given, he will again become painfully aware of the gulf which separates the Canonical from the Apocryphal Gospels.

4. *Objections taken to the contents of Mt 1. 2.* —

St. Matthew's record, no less than that of St. Luke, has been the object of vehement and re-lentless attack. It is asserted, for instance, by Usener that in the whole Birth and Childhood story of St. Matthew a pagan substratum can be traced (art. 'Nativity' in *Encyc. Bibl.* iii. 3352, and also to the same effect *ZNTW*, 1903, p. 21). Thus we are asked to find the origin of the story of the Magi worshipping at the cradle of the infant Jesus in the visit paid by the Parthian king Tiridates with magi in his train to do hom-age in Rome to the emperor Nero. But the magi of the Parthian king were evidently, like many other magi of the East, claimants to the possession of secret and magical arts, and there is nothing strange in the fact that they are found among the retinue of a Parthian king. But what actual points of resemblance exist between this visit to Nero and the visit of the Magi to Bethlehem it is difficult to see. One crucial contrast, at any rate, has been rightly emphasized. Tiridates came to

Nero, not of his own accord, but because his only choice was to do homage to Nero or to lose his crown. Here there is no comparison with, but rather an obvious and essential contrast to, the Wise Men of St. Matthew, who came with joy and gladness to worship the Babe of Bethlehem.

Soltau, who also supports the same origin for St. Matthew's story, adduces the parallels which in his opinion may be fitly drawn between the visit of the Parthian king to Rome and the visit of the Magi to Bethlehem (*Die Geburtsgeschichte Jesu Christi*, 1902, p. 37). As might be expected, he makes much of the fact that Tiridates is said to have knelt and worshipped Nero just as the Wise Men fell down to worship Jesus. But the only other verbal parallel which he is able to adduce is this : Tiridates, according to Dio Cassius (lxiii. 2 ff.), did not return by the way which he came ; beneath the quotation of this statement Soltau writes as a parallel the words of St. Matthew : 'and they departed into their own country another way' (Mt 2¹²). A strong case scarcely stands in need of such parallels as these.*

But an attempt is often made to trace St. Matthew's story to Jewish sources, and reference is made to the words and expectations of the prophets. And no doubt it is easy to affirm that such a passage as Is 61¹ᶠᶠ· might have contributed to the formation of the legend of the adoration of the Magi. But the Evangelist, who loves to quote prophecies apposite in any degree to the events connected with our Lord's birth, makes no reference to this passage of Isaiah which Christian thought has so often associated with the Epiphany. As a matter of fact, it would seem that the prophecy referred primarily, not to the Messiah, but to the city of Jerusalem and to the day of its latter glory.

No doubt the Evangelist does definitely connect at least two Old Testament prophecies with the visit of the Magi and the events immediately subsequent to it. But the question may be fairly asked, Which is more probable, that the flight into Egypt actually took place, or that the Jewish Evangelist, or some later hand, introduced the incident as the fulfilment of an OT prophecy which had primarily no definite or obvious connexion, to say the least of it, with the Messiah ? †

Or, again, if some such event as the Massacre of the Innocents at Bethlehem actually occurred, we can understand that a Jewish Evangelist could find in that event, and in the mourning of the mothers of Israel, a further fulfilment of Jeremiah's words (31¹⁵). But there is no obvious reason why he should have hit upon and introduced such words unless some event had happened at Bethlehem which recalled to his mind the picture which the prophet had drawn, and the scene once enacted within a few miles of the city of David.

Other explanations are, of course, forthcoming. 'Why,' asks Usener, 'is Egypt selected as the place of refuge?' and one answer is that mythological ideas may have had their unconscious influence ; it is to Egypt that the Olympian gods take their flight when attacked by the giant Typhon ! (art 'Nativity' in *Ency. Bibl.* iii. 3351 ; and *ZNTW* p. 217).‡ In any consideration of such statements it is well to remember first of all that, whatever date we assign to St. Matthew,§ we are dealing with

* See also the recent criticisms of A. Jeremias, *Babylonisches im NT*, 1905, p. 55.

† On the exact words of Hos 11¹, quoted by St. Matthew from the Hebrew, see Zahn, *Evangelium des Matthäus*, p. 103 ; and also Delitzsch, *Messianische Weissagungen*², 1899, p. 105.

‡ Indications are not wanting that this constant and somewhat reckless appeal to supposed pagan analogies is being overdone ; see, *e.g.*, Farnell's remarks in the *Hibbert Journal*, July 1904, p. 827.

§ In art. 'Gospels' in *Encyc. Bibl.* ii. 1893, mention is made of the Syriac writing attributed to Eusebius, and it is maintained that, according to this document, the story of the Magi, committed to writing in the interior of Persia, was, in A.D. 119, in the episcopate of Xystus of Rome, made search for, dis-

an historic period of the world's history, and that the writer at least claims to place his events in relation to historical data. Nothing was more natural than that Egypt should be chosen as the place of refuge ; it was nigh at hand, the communication by caravan was very frequent ; in earlier days Jeroboam had fled thither from Solomon (1 K 11⁴⁰), and it was to Tahpanhes that Johanan, the son of Kareah, and his companions had gone to save themselves out of the hands of the Chaldeans (Jer 43⁷).

Nothing was more in accordance with the character of Herod than the deed of bloodshed ascribed to him, and modern days supply many proofs of the unscrupulous manner in which a jealous and suspicious potentate has not hesitated to rid himself of anyone likely to render his tenure of sovereignty insecure (see, *e.g.*, amongst recent writers Kreyher, *Die jungfräuliche Geburt des Herrn*, 1904, p. 83).* On the other hand, it is very improbable that the Evangelist would have invented a story in which the birth of the Messiah was made to bring bitter sorrow into so many Jewish homes.†

Nothing, again, was more likely than that Joseph should withdraw into Galilee after the return from Egypt, since we have evidence that Archelaus very soon after his accession gave proof of the same cruel and crafty behaviour as had characterized his father (Jos. *BJ* II. vi. 2).‡

In the next place, it is well to remember that there is at all events one instance of a prophecy cited in this part of the Gospel of St. Matthew the fulfilment of which is beyond doubt, if we can be said to know anything at all of the historical Jesus (2²³). And yet no one with any discernment could possibly maintain that our Lord's residence and bringing up in Nazareth were introduced for the sake of finding a fulfilment for a prophecy which it is so difficult to trace to any one source in OT literature. But if in this case it is certain that the prophecy could not have created the fact, why in the case of the other prophecies cited should their alleged fulfilment be credited to the extravagant imagination of the Evangelist, and to that alone ?§

iii. APOCRYPHAL ACCOUNTS.—It is of the greatest significance that just in that portion of our Lord's life concerning which the Gospels of St. Matthew and St. Luke are most silent, the Apocryphal

covered, and written in Greek. But Zahn (*Einleitung*, ii. p. 266) points out that this statement at least shows that by the date named the year of the coming of the Magi was discussed not only in Rome, but in various places. He further argues, with good reason, from the same statement of the pseudo-Eusebius, that the narrative of Mt 2 had already been incorporated in the Gospel before A.D. 119. See, further, *Ch. Quart. Rev.* July 1904, p. 389. In this connexion it may be noted that it is difficult to see why the statement of St. Ignatius, exaggerated as it is, should not be taken to refer to the star of the Magi (*Ephes.* xix. 2, 3). On the significance of this early reference to the Gospel narrative in St. Ignatius, see Headlam, *Criticism of the NT*, p. 166 (St. Margaret's Lectures). In his recent Commentary on St. Matthew's Gospel, Wellhausen begins with 3¹, which is certainly a short and easy method of dealing with the two earlier chapters.

* See, further, art. MAGI. It may, however, be here noted that Ramsay remarks on Macrobius, *Sat.* ii. 4, that it is not probable that Macrobius (a pagan, about A.D. 400) was indebted to a Christian writer for his information, and that therefore the story of the Massacre of the Infants was recorded in some pagan source (*Was Christ born at Bethlehem ?* pp. 219, 220). Zöckler also refers to Macrobius as affording a testimony from a non-biblical source to the truth of the Massacre at Bethlehem (art. 'Jesus Christus' in *PRE*³). On the silence of Josephus see, further, Zahn, *Evangelium des Matthäus*, p. 109 ; and Edersheim, *The Temple at the Time of Jesus Christ*, p. 35 f.

† Zahn, *Evangelium des Matthäus*, p. 109. See, too, the same reference for the improbability of supposing that the story in St. Matthew was derived from the rescue of Moses (Ex 1¹⁵ 2¹⁰ ; Jos. *Ant.* II. ix. 2) ; and cf. art. MAGI.

‡ 'There is a noticeable difference between St. Matthew's references to the political situation in Palestine and St. Luke's. St. Luke speaks with the air of painstaking investigation ; St. Matthew, with that of easy familiarity, all the more noteworthy that the frequent and somewhat complicated succession of rulers would have made error easy.' This important point is noted by Burton in his *Introduction to the Gospels* (Chicago), 1904, p. 4.

§ See some excellent remarks of Bruce in the *Expositor's Greek Testament*, i. p. 78.

Gospels are most effusive.* Here was an opportunity for them to occupy a vacant space, and they lost no endeavour in trying to fill it. Both in the details of the Nativity and in the events just referred to as subsequent to it, we find ample proofs of this. Thus Elisabeth is fearful that in accordance with the commands of Herod her son John may be slain. And when she can find no place of concealment, she begs a mountain to receive mother and child, and instantly the mountain is cleft to receive her; and a light shines round about, for an angel of the Lord is watching for her preservation. And upon this there follows a tragic scene of the murder of Zacharias, who is slain for his refusal to betray his son. As the Holy Family pass through Egypt, the marvellous accompanies them at every step. In these apocryphal stories, lions, dragons, and panthers adore the infant Jesus; a palm tree bends at His word that His Mother may eat the fruit; in one day the travellers accomplish a journey of thirty days; the idols prostrate themselves in the temples before the Mother and her Child. And we know how the long silence of our Lord's life in our Gospels, which is broken only by one incident in St. Luke, and by the brief summary of St. Matthew, 'He shall be called a Nazarene,' affords further opportunity for the introduction of the same insipid and fantastic tales.† Even in modern days there have not been wanting writers who have boldly essayed to occupy the same ground with an equal lack of historical data.‡ In all this and much else we mark again and again the reserve so characteristic of St. Matthew and St. Luke alike, a reserve and restraint often emphasized by earlier commentators, and again recently referred to by German writers so far apart in point of view as Gunkel and Hermann Cremer.§

iv. CONVERGENT TRADITIONS AND THE MAIN FACTS.—It is often said that the narratives in our two canonical Gospels contradict one another. But although, no doubt, it is difficult to harmonize them in their particulars and sequences, their independence is evident proof that there was no attempt on the part of one Evangelist to make his work the complement or corrector of the other.|| Antecedently we might have expected that St. Luke, the Gentile Evangelist, would have told us of the adoration of the Magi, and that the Hebrew Evangelist would have given us the picture of obedience on the part of Mother and Child to the details of the Law and the worship of the Temple. And it is justly urged as no small proof of the truth of the narratives that each Evangelist could

* For a useful classification of the most important of the Apocryphal Gospels, and a list of those which claim to fill up the gaps in our knowledge of the Infancy and Childhood of Jesus, see art. 'Apocryphal Gospels' in Hastings' *DB*, Ext. Vol. p. 422.
In the same volume (art. 'Papyri,' p. 352) it is of interest to note that Kenyon in commenting upon the later Egyptian papyri remarks that one document written about the end of the 1st cent. has been held to show certain resemblances to the narrative of the Nativity of our Lord, but that the resemblance is, in truth, very slight and unessential.
† It cannot be said that Conrady's attempt to derive our Gospel accounts of the Nativity from the Apocryphal Gospels, especially from the *Protevangelium Jacobi*, is likely to gain acceptance (*Die Quelle der kanonischen Kindheitsgeschichte Jesu*; see, further, his article in *SK*, 1904, Heft 2). Such a derivation might well be called a literary miracle. For a criticism of Conrady's attempt, see *Theol. Literaturblatt*, 1901, p. 283.
‡ See, *e.g.*, C. A. Witz, *Keine Lücke im Leben Jesu*, 1895, described as 'Antwort auf die Schrift von Nikolaus Notowitsch, *Die Lücke im Leben Jesu.*'
§ Cf. Gunkel, *l.c.* p. 66, and H. Cremer, *Reply to Harnack*, p. 163, Eng. tr. 1903.
|| See especially Swete, *The Apostles' Creed*, p. 50, for the distinctness of the two accounts and the almost entirely different ground covered. For a probable order of the events see Plummer, *St. Luke*, p. 64; Andrews, *Life of our Lord upon the Earth*, 1892, p. 92; Rose, *Studies in the Gospels*, p. 64 ff., also *Évangile selon S. Matthieu*, p. 17.

thus transcend his own special standpoint and purpose (Fairbairn, *Stud. in Life of Christ*, p. 36).*

It is indeed urged that this same contradiction may be found in those parts of the canonical narratives which relate most closely to our Lord's birth (Lobstein, *The Virgin Birth of Christ*, p. 42, Eng. tr.). But the details vouchsafed to us, it may be fairly said, present no essential incompatibility, and two convergent traditions coming from distinct sources may be rightly affirmed to corroborate and sustain each other as to the main facts which they describe (*Church Quarterly Review*, Oct. 1904, pp. 200, 201; W. C. Allen, *l.c.* p. 115).

The belief that St. Matthew gives us an account which comes primarily from Joseph, while St. Luke gives us an account that comes primarily from Mary, has long been maintained by many able critics, and it is a belief which still commends itself as the most satisfactory explanation of the two stories. It is the simplest thing to see how in the one case the frequent repetition of the name 'Joseph' points to him as the primary source of information, and how in the other case the twice repeated reference to Mary points to her as occupying the same position: 'Mary kept all these sayings, pondering them in her heart' (Lk 2¹⁹); 'and his mother kept all these sayings in her heart' (v.⁵¹). One thing may be safely asserted, that if these two accounts had come to us agreeing in every particular, we should have been asked to discredit them on account of this very agreement.

LITERATURE.—A considerable amount of the literature has been indicated above, and for further information art. VIRGIN BIRTH should be consulted. The following works may be added here: W. H. Mill, *Mythical Interpretation of the Gospels*, 1861; C. F. Schmid, *Biblical Theology of the NT*, 1870 [Eng. tr. p. 25 ff.]; F. L. Steinmeyer, *Die Gesch. der Geburt des Herrn*, 1873; Wace, *The Gospel and its Witnesses*, 1883; F. Godet, *Commentaire sur l'évangile de Luc*, 1888; Nösgen, *Geschichte Jesu*, 1891, p. 113 ff.; *Geboren von der Jungfrau*, Anonymous, Leipzig, 1896; Bishop Gore, *Dissertations on Subjects connected with the Incarnation*², Grenfell and Hunt, *Oxyrhynchus Papyri*, i. 1899; *AJTh*, July 1902; J. Grill, *Untersuchungen über die Entstehung des vierten Evangelium*, 1902, p. 330 ff.; Briggs, *New Light on the Life of Jesus*, 1903; Dean of Westminster, *Some Thoughts on the Incarnation*, 1903; Randolph, *The Virgin Birth of our Lord*, 1903; J. E. Carpenter, *Bible in the Nineteenth Century*, 1903, p. 491 ff.; Bishop Wordsworth, *The Baptismal Confession and the Creed*, 1904; Th. H. Wandel, *Die Wunderbare Zeugung*, 1903; E. Burton, *Introduction to the Gospels* (Chicago): Appended notes on 'Quirinius,' and 'The Old Testament Law in Luke ii. 22-24,' 1904; Lepin, *Jésus Messie et Fils de Dieu*, 1904, pp. 55-75; P. W. Schmidt, *Geschichte Jesu*, 1904, ii. 13, 14; Cheyne, *Bible Problems*, 1905; W. C. Allen, *Interpreter*, Feb. and Oct. 1905; G. H. Box, *ZNTW*, 1905, Heft I.   R. J. KNOWLING.

BIRTHDAY.—In Mt 14⁶ and Mk 6²¹ this word represents the Gr. τὰ γενέσια in the account of the king's (Herod Antipas) feast to his nobles, at which John the Baptist was condemned to death. It has been suggested, however, though without much acceptance, that the anniversary referred to was that of Herod's accession, not strictly that of his birth. Γενέσια, which in Attic Greek means 'the commemoration of the dead,' is in the later language interchangeable with γενέθλια (birthday celebrations), and there seems no reason why the translation of RV and AV should not be right (see Swete on Mk 6²¹, and Hastings' *DB, s.v.*). The custom of observing the birthday of a king was widely spread in ancient times (cf. Gn 40²⁰, 2 Mac 6⁷; Herod. ix. 110).

For the question of the date of our Lord's birth, and the authority for the traditional 25th December, see art. CALENDAR.   C. L. FELTOE.

BLASPHEMY (βλασφημία; for derivation of word see Hastings' *DB*, vol. i. p. 305ª).—This word is used in the Gospels, as in other parts of the NT, for abusive speech generally, as well as for language that is insulting to God. Thus we read of

* A careful study of Resch's attempt (1897) to reconstruct a *Kindheitsevangelium* from the first two chapters of St. Luke and St. Matthew with the help of some extra-canonical parallels, and to restore the Hebrew original of the narrative, can scarcely be said to carry conviction with it.

'an evil eye, blasphemy (RV railing), pride,' etc. (Mk 7²²), where the position of the word indicates human relations. The evil eye is followed by the evil tongue, the one by look and the other by speech expressing malignity towards a fellow-man. Two questions concerning blasphemy come up in the Gospels, viz. the teaching of Jesus Christ on the subject, and the charge of blasphemy brought against our Lord.

1. The teaching of Jesus Christ concerning blasphemy.—Using the term in the general sense, our Lord does not always formally distinguish between insulting speech with regard to God and abusive language towards men. βλασφημία in any application of it is sin. As railing against our fellow-men, it comes in a catalogue of sins together with the most heinous—'murders, adulteries,' etc. (Mk 7²²). In this connexion it is treated as one of the 'evil things' that 'proceed from within, and defile the man.' Thus it is taken to be the expression of a corrupt heart, and as such a defilement of the person who gives vent to it. Nevertheless it is not beyond the reach of pardon. With one exception all revilings may be forgiven (Mk 3²⁸·²⁹, Mt 12³¹). The comprehensive sentence must include blasphemy against God, although that is not expressly mentioned. In Mt 12³² there is a reference to blasphemy against the Son of Man, and in both cases the unpardonable sin of blasphemy against the Holy Ghost is mentioned; but in neither case is there any reference to blasphemy against the Father. Perhaps the safest thing is to say that this was not in mind at the time, so that no direct pronouncement was made concerning it; and, further, it is to be observed that Trinitarian distinctions do not appear in these teachings of Jesus. Jesus is here the 'Son of Man,' not 'the Son,' *i.e.* of God, and the Holy Spirit is God in His manifested activity. Still, it must be implicitly contained in St. Mark's emphatic sentence, '*All* their sins . . . and their blasphemies *wherewith soever they shall blaspheme* (ὅσα ἂν βλασφημήσωσιν).'

To 'speak a word against the Son of Man' is taken as one form of the blasphemy or reviling. Here, therefore, the word is not used in its relation to God. It does not stand for what we now understand by 'blasphemy' in our narrower sense of the word. Jesus is not here standing on the ground of His divinity, to insult which would be blasphemy in this modern sense. He is speaking of Himself as seen among men, and referring to personal insults. But, since the term 'the Son of Man' appears to be a veiled reference to His Messiahship, for Himself and for the enlightened among His followers He must have meant that those who insulted Him, even though He was the Christ, were not beyond pardon ; cf. 'Father, forgive them,' etc. (Lk 23³⁴, om. BD*, etc.). Some doubt, however, is thrown on this reference to 'the Son of Man' because (1) it does not occur in the Mk. parallel passage ; (2) in Mk. but not in Mt. the phrase 'the sons of men' occurs in an earlier part of the saying (3²⁸).

The nature of blasphemy against the Holy Ghost (Mt 12²²⁻³², Mk 3²⁹, Lk 12¹⁰) must be learnt from the context. This excludes such notions as rejection of the gospel (Iren.), denial of the divinity of Christ (Athan.), mortal sin after baptism (Origen), persistence in sin till death (August.). The form of the blasphemy is given in the words 'because they said, He hath an unclean spirit,' and the occasion of it was Jesus' casting out of demons. Jesus declares that this is done 'by the Spirit of God' (Mt 12²⁸), or 'by the finger of God' (Lk 11²⁰). To ascribe this action to Beelzebub is to be guilty of, or to approach the guilt of, blasphemy against the Holy Spirit, because it is treating the Holy Spirit

as Beelzebub. Jesus did not expressly say that the scribes who put forward this Beelzebub theory of His work had actually committed this sin. He judged by thought and intention, not by outward utterance. A prejudiced, ignorant, hasty, superficial utterance of the calumny would not contain the essence of the sin. This must be a conscious, intentional insult. If one mistakes a saint for a knave, and addresses him accordingly, he is not really guilty of insulting him, for it is not actually the saint but the knave whom he has in mind. If the presence of the Holy Spirit was not recognized, there could be no blasphemy against the Holy Spirit. But when it was perceived and yet deliberately treated as evil, the action would indicate a wilful reversal of the dictates of conscience. Our Lord warns His hearers that such a sin cannot be forgiven either in the present age—the pre-Messianic, or in the age to come—the Messianic, that is, as we should say, the Christian age. The condition of such a person will be that he is guilty (ἔνοχος) of an eternal (αἰωνίου) sin (so RV of Mk 3²⁹, following אBL, etc., ἁμαρτήματος ; not 'damnation,' as in AV, after the Syrian reading κρίσεως, A, etc.). This cannot well mean 'a sin that persists, a fixed disposition,' as Dr Salmond understands it, because (1) the Greek word ἁμάρτημα stands for an act, not a state ; (2) there is nothing in the context to indicate persistency in the blasphemy ; (3) the Jewish current conception was that a sin once committed remained on the sinner till it was atoned for or forgiven. He had to bear his sin. Therefore one who was never forgiven would have to bear his sin eternally, and so would be said to have an eternal sin. Wellhausen understands it to be equivalent to eternal punishment ('schuldig ewiger Sünde, d. i. ewiger Strafe,' *Evang. Marci,* 28).

At the same time, while this must be understood as the correct exegesis of the words, the saying should be interpreted in harmony with the spirit of Christ. Now it is characteristic of legalism and the letter to make a solitary exception, depending on one external act. The Spirit of Christ is concerned with character rather than with specific deeds, and it is contrary to His spirit that one specific deed should be singled out for exclusion from mercy. Then, elsewhere, the breadth of His gospel indicates that no genuine seeker would be rejected. Therefore we must understand Him to mean either (1) that to be guilty of such a sin a man must be so hardened that he never would repent, or (2) that such a sin cannot be overlooked, forgotten, and swallowed up in the general flood of mercy. It must come up for judgment. Against (1) and for (2) is the fact that our Lord says nothing of the offender's disposition, but only refers to the sin, its heinous character, and consequent never-to-be-denied or forgotten ill-desert. See, further, art. UNPARDONABLE SIN.

2. The charge of blasphemy brought against Jesus Christ.—This charge was brought against our Lord on three occasions—two recorded in the Synoptics and one in the Fourth Gospel. In all of these cases the alleged blasphemy is against God, actual blasphemy in our sense of the word. The first instance is at the cure of the paralytic who had been let down through the roof (Mt 9³, Mk 2⁷, Lk 5²¹). Jesus had just said to the sufferer, 'Thy sins are forgiven thee.' Upon this the scribes and Pharisees who were present complained that He was speaking blasphemies because only God could forgive sins, that is to say, that He was arrogating to Himself a Divine prerogative. In His answer He distinctly claimed this right on the ground of His enigmatic title of 'the Son of Man,' and held it to be confirmed by His cure of the paralytic. The second occasion is that recorded by St. John, where the Jews declare that their attempt to stone

Jesus was 'for blasphemy,' adding 'because that thou, being a man, makest thyself God' (Jn 10^{33}). This was just after He had said, 'I and the Father are one ($\tilde{\epsilon}\nu$).' The third occasion is at the trial of Jesus. According to Mt 26^{65} and Mk 14$^{63.\ 64}$ when Jesus, after being adjured by the high priest to declare if He were the Christ, declared that they would 'see the Son of Man sitting at the right hand of power and coming with the clouds of heaven,' the high priest treated this as blasphemy, rending his garments as a token of horror at the words. Yet the claim was not for more than the Book of Enoch assigned to the Messiah. But the Messiah in that Apocalyptic book is a heavenly being. Such a being Caiaphas would understand Jesus to claim to be, and he reckoned the profession of such a claim blasphemous. This was the formal ground of the condemnation of Jesus to death by the Sanhedrin. The first charge, that of threatening to destroy the Temple and rebuild it in three days, had broken down because of the inconsistency of the witnesses. The second charge is suddenly sprung upon Jesus by the high priest on the ground of His words at the council ; and, on this account, as guilty of blasphemy, He was condemned to death, although it was useless to cite the words before Pilate, who would have dismissed the case as Gallio at Corinth dismissed what he regarded as 'a question about words and names' (Ac 18^{15}). Therefore a third charge, never mentioned in the Jewish trial,—*læsæ majestatis*, treason against Cæsar,—was concocted for use at the Roman trial.

It is to be observed that there is one common character in all these accusations of blasphemy brought against Jesus. He is never accused of direct blasphemy, speaking insulting words about God. The alleged blasphemy is indirect, in each case claiming more or less Divine rights and powers for Himself.

Lastly, it may be noted that Lk 22^{65} AV has the word 'blasphemously' for the way in which the mockers spoke of Jesus; but RV has 'reviling,' which is the evident meaning. There is no reference to our narrower sense of blasphemy as insulting the Divine ; the word ($\beta\lambda\alpha\sigma\phi\eta\mu o\tilde{v}\nu\tau\epsilon s$) is used in the common wider sense.

LITERATURE. — S. J. Andrews, *Life of Our Lord*, 505–514 ; Hastings' *DB*, art. 'Blasphemy'; Cremer, *Bibl.-Theol. Lex. s.vv.* $\beta\lambda\alpha\sigma\phi\eta\mu i\alpha$, $\beta\lambda\alpha\sigma\phi\eta\mu i\omega$; and in particular on blasphemy against the Holy Ghost, Martensen, *Christian Ethics*, ii. p. 123 ff.; Gloag, *Exegetical Studies*, p. 1 ff.; *Expositor*, 2nd ser. iii. [1882] p. 321 ff. ; A. Maclaren, *Christ's Musts*, 44–54.

W. F. ADENEY.

BLESSEDNESS. — Though the word 'blessedness' itself is never found in the recorded utterances of our Lord nor in the pages of the Gospels, the idea conveyed by it is very frequent. The adjective 'blessed' occurs in many contexts, and may, indeed, be termed a characteristic epithet on Christ's lips. The thought expressed by it was inherited, like so many others, from the Old Testament. It is one of the dominant notes of the Psalter (Heb. אַשְׁרֵי 'O the happiness of '), and constitutes one of the clearest and most common terms whereby to denote the ideal of Israel's highest hopes. It was natural, therefore, that Jesus should take the word to set forth the great spiritual realities of His kingdom. It is in this sense that it meets us on the earliest pages of St. Matthew's Gospel. The famous form of the sayings there collected (see art. BEATITUDES) is one of the best-known sections of the narrative. So throughout the pages of the Gospels and elsewhere in the NT we find sayings cast in the same mould. All of them are expressive of the spiritual graces to be looked for in disciples of the kingdom (*e.g.* Mt 11^6, Lk 7^{23}, Mt 24^{46}, Ac 20^{35}), or are indicative of high privileges open to believers in its message (*e.g.* Mt 13^{16},

Lk 11^{28}, Jn 20^{29}). Spiritual gladness is not only a note of service in the kingdom, but is to accompany all its true and inalienable rewards.

When we set ourselves to discover the significance of these sayings we are struck (1) by their *spiritual character*. Twice (Lk 11^{27} and 14^{15}) beatitudes of a material character are uttered by our Lord's hearers, and He at once rebukes them, and shows the necessity of fixing the desires of the heart on the inward and unseen. The main qualities designated and praised are meekness, purity, tenderness of heart, peaceableness, faith, patience, contrition, qualities which have no sooner been named than we are reminded of such lists of the fruits of the Spirit as we find in Gal 5$^{22.\ 23}$ or Eph 4$^{30-32}$. Blessedness, as Christ presented it, was therefore a condition of the mind and heart that expressed an attitude of faith and love towards God and men, and obtained the reward with certainty even if the sowing were 'in tears' and the 'interest far off.'

(2) Several of these sayings are marked by the sense of the *futurity of their fulfilment*. It is noteworthy that in the list of Beatitudes in Mt 5, while the majority speak of futurity, 'shall be comforted,' 'shall inherit,' etc., one or two are written in the present tense, *e.g.* 'theirs *is* the kingdom of heaven.' In v.^{10} we have the unique form of expression, 'have been persecuted . . . theirs is.' In St. Luke also we find the same commingling of present and future. This reflects a state of opinion that prevails throughout the Gospels, and gives rise to some of the greatest problems of interpretation, viz. in what sense the kingdom of God is to be understood—as a present or as a future condition. The Beatitudes are not only closely related to this question—they constitute a special aspect of it. As Titius puts it, ' Over every saying of Jesus may be written the inscription, "Concerning the kingdom of God."' These sayings, then, reveal the nature of the kingdom in its twofold aspect as an inward, spiritual, present reality which exists, progresses, suffers, is in perpetual conflict ; and, as a great future fulfilment, when conflict shall turn to peace, failure to victory, suffering to reward, and the inward desire and the outward attainment be one in the presence of perfected power.

Blessedness may therefore be regarded as one of the forms under which our Lord presented the character of His kingdom, and so it becomes an illuminative idea whereby to read the whole Gospel narratives. They all illustrate it. They all serve to make up its content. The word and thought derived from the Old Testament receive richer significance, and may be taken as equivalent to those other great terms, such as 'eternal life' and 'the kingdom of heaven,' under which, in the pages of St. John and St. Matthew, the great purposes of God in Christ are set forth.

LITERATURE.—The articles 'Blessedness' and, in particular, 'Sermon on the Mount' in Hastings' *DB* ; the articles in this Dictionary on BEATITUDES, KINGDOM OF GOD, ETERNAL LIFE, PARABLES, etc. ; the Commentaries on Mt 5 and Lk 6, and on the other verses quoted, especially, for practical purposes, Morison, Bruce [in *Expos. Gr. Test.*] ; Trench, *The Sermon on the Mount*. The most recent full commentary on Matthew is that of Zahn (in German). Books on the Kingdom of God should also be consulted, and, in particular, A. Titius, *Die NT Lehre von der Seligkeit*, etc., erster Teil, 1895 ; and Bousset, *Jesu Predigt in ihrem Gegensatz zum Judentum*. See also N. Smyth, *Christian Ethics*, 118 ff.; J. B. Lightfoot, *Sermons in St. Paul's*, 178 ; T. G. Selby, *The Imperfect Angel*, 25.

G. CURRIE MARTIN.

BLESSING.—

1. Introductory.
2. Terms.
3. Jewish usage.
4. Usage in the Gospels.
　　　　Literature.

1. *Introductory.*—The main underlying idea of the characteristic New Testament word for 'blessing' (εὐλογεῖν) seems to be that of goodwill, which, on the part of man towards God, has its appropriate expression in praise and thanksgiving. The close connexion of these two last ideas is clearly seen in the New Testament in the interchange of the expressions for 'to bless' (εὐλογεῖν) and 'to give thanks,' namely to God (εὐχαριστεῖν, cf. e.g. Mk 6^41 and ‖ with Jn 6^11; and see, further, below, § 4), and is explained by the Jewish development of the term for 'blessing' (bĕrākhāh; cf. further, § 4 b). In Jewish religious terminology, under the influence of the high ethical views of God's character and uniqueness, and His relation to Israel and mankind, that had been developed, 'blessing' acquires a lofty spiritual connotation. God 'blesses' man and his world by His ever active, beneficent Providence; man 'blesses' God by thankful recognition of this, and by pure acts of praise; man 'blesses' man by invoking the Divine favour for his fellows' benefit (cf. e.g. Ps 129^8); and even when material things are the objects of blessing, this finds its proper expression in an act of thanksgiving to the Divine Giver.

The original sense of the Heb. verb bērakh (Piel, denominative from berekh, 'knee') is more probably 'to cause to make progress' (so Cheyne) than any notion of adoration ('to bend the knee'). The primitive conception of blessing and cursing, according to which they were regarded as possessing an objective existence, more or less independent of the speaker after utterance (cf. Gn 27^35), naturally became moralized with the progress of monotheistic religion (cf. Pr 26^2 for a denunciation of 'the causeless curse').

2. Terms.—The terms for 'blessing' used in the Gospels are—

(a) εὐλογεῖν, 'to bless,' and εὐλογητός, εὐλογημένος, 'blessed.' All these forms are common in the LXX, where, in the vast majority of instances, they correspond to some form of the Heb. word ברך or its derivatives.

εὐλογεῖν is used—
(A) of men: (1) as in Greek writings, in the sense of 'to praise,' 'celebrate with praises,' viz. God. So several times in the Gospels: e.g. Lk 1^64 2^28 24^53 [syn. αἰνεῖν, 'to praise,' and δοξάζειν, 'to glorify'; see under αἰνεῖν, below]. (2) 'To invoke blessings upon' (a sense peculiar to Biblical Greek): e.g. Lk 6^28. (3) 'To bless' material objects (i.e. to bless God for their bestowal): c.g. Lk 9^13.
(B) of God: (4) 'To bestow blessings, favour, upon men': e.g. Lk 1^42 (εὐλογημένος). [The compound κατευλογεῖν, 'to call down blessings upon' occurs, according to the best attested reading, in Mk 10^16].

(b) εὐχαριστεῖν,* 'to give thanks,' viz. to God, esp. for food: e.g. Mt 15^36 26^27. With this compare also—
(c) ἐξομολογεῖν, 'to celebrate,' 'give praise or thanks to' (τινί): Mt 11^25 and ‖, and—
(d) αἰνεῖν, 'to praise, extol' God: Lk 2^13. 20 19^37 24^53 (reading doubtful). [Cf. the use of the synonymous expression δοξάζειν, Lk 17^15, and διδόναι δόξαν τῷ θεῷ,† 'to give glory to God,' Lk 17^18—both of thanksgiving].
(e) μακαρίζειν, 'to pronounce blessed': once only in Gospels, Lk 1^48; and μακάριος, 'blessed,' 'happy' (esp. in a congratulatory sense): e.g. in the Beatitudes (Mt 5^3-11, Lk 6^20-22; cf. Jn 20^29). Both words are common in the LXX.

It is remarkable that the term εὐχαριστεῖν occurs very rarely (and only in the Apocryphal books) in the LXX. The common LXX equivalent for 'to give thanks' (Heb. hôdāh) is ἐξομολογεῖν. αἰνεῖν is also of frequent occurrence there. The Bishop of Salisbury (The Holy Communion^2, p. 135 n. 34) suggests that εὐλογεῖν in the NT was 'often purposely exchanged . . . for the more classical and intelligible εὐχαριστεῖν.'

3. Jewish usage.—The elements that entered into the Hebrew idea of 'blessing' ‡ sketched

above (§ 1) were elaborately developed in later Jewish usage. Here the most important points for the illustration of the Gospels may be briefly summarized.

(A) Blessing of persons.—According to Jewish ideas, God is the sole source of all blessing, both material and spiritual; and to Him alone, therefore, praise and thanksgiving are due (cf. Eph 1^3 for a beautiful Christian application of the idea). Thus, even in the great Priestly Blessing (Nu 6^22-27), which filled so large a place in Jewish liturgical worship both in the temple and (in a less degree) in the synagogue, it was not the priest per se who blessed, but God (Sifre, ad loc.).* The blessing of man by man finds one of its most prominent expressions in greeting and farewell, a custom of great antiquity, and not, of course, in itself specifically Jewish.† But the formulas connected with it naturally reflect Jewish religious sentiment in a marked degree. The fundamental idea of goodwill is worked out into an invocation of the Divine favour and providence, and consequent prosperity, on the recipient. These ideas find beautiful expression in the Priestly Blessing, and in the poetical amplification of it embodied in Ps 67.‡ The characteristic word employed in greeting and farewell is 'peace' (Heb. shālôm, Greek εἰρήνη), which has a wide connotation, embracing the notions of security, safety, prosperity, and felicity.§ Thus the regular formula of greeting is 'Peace be to thee' (Jg 6^23, Dn 10^19), and, for farewell, 'Go in peace' (cf. 1 S 1^17 etc.). 'To greet' is expressed in Hebrew by the phrase 'to ask of a person concerning peace (welfare)' (cf. Gn 43^27, Ex 18^7 etc.), and similar formulas.‖ The use of the word 'blessed' (Heb. bārûkh), both in solemn greeting (1 S 15^13 'Blessed be thou of J',' cf. Ps 118^26 'Blessed is he that cometh') and parting (1 K 10^9), should also be noted in this connexion.

The custom of imparting a solemn blessing at final departure (from life.¶) is attested in the Talmud (e.g. Ber. 28b—death of Johanan ben Zakkai, c. 75–80 A.D.).

Besides the salutation, other forms of blessing prevailed, notably the blessing of children by parents (and sometimes by others). This custom is well attested in the OT (cf. e.g. Gn 9^26 27^t. 48^9). Jacob's blessing of Ephraim and Manasseh is esp. notable, because it fixed the formula which has been used among the Jews in later times.** The earliest literary evidence for the existence of this particular custom is quite late (17th cent.); but that some form of parental blessing was well known by the NT period may be inferred from Sir 3^9 (cf. Mk 10^13-16 and ‖).

According to the minor Talmudical tractate Sopherim (xviii. 5), which contains valuable old traditional material: 'In Jerusalem there was the godly custom to initiate the children at the beginning of the thirteenth year by fasting the whole Day of Atonement. During this year they took the boy to the

---

* The derivatives εὐχαριστία ('giving of thanks') and εὐχάριστος ('thankful') do not occur in the Gospels.
† See, further, on this expression Grimm-Thayer, Lex. s.v. δόξα, ii.
‡ The wide variety of meaning attached to ברך in the OT (cf. Oxford Hebrew Lexicon, s.v.) well illustrates this.

* The special sanctity with which the Aaronic blessing was invested in the later period lay in the pronunciation of 'the ineffable name,' which was permitted to the priests only. Originally, however, this restriction was not in force. Thus the Mishna (Ber. x. 4) cites Ru 2^4 as proving that 'the name' was used in ordinary greetings; cf. also Ps 129^8.
† See the article 'Salutation' (with reff.) in Kitto's Biblical Cyclopædia^3, iii. p. 739 f.
‡ The whole Psalm gives a fine analysis of the contents of the Hebrew idea of blessing. Other echoes of the Priestly Blessing occur in the Psalter (Ps 46 3^116 80^3. 7. 19).
§ Note that this word forms the climax of the Priestly Blessing (Nu 6^26).
‖ For further details see the Hebrew Lexicons, s.v. שָׁלֹם.
¶ Cf. 2 K 29.
** For boys the formula runs: 'May God make thee like Ephraim and Manasseh'; for girls: 'May God make thee like Sarah, Rebekah, Rachel, and Leah' (cf. Ru 4^11). Any other blessing suggested by the occasion or special circumstances might be added. See, further, Jewish Encyc. (as cited below, § 4, end).

priests and learned men that they might bless him, and pray for him that God might think him worthy of a life devoted to the study of the Torah and pious works.'*

(B) *Blessing of things.*—The feeling of praise and thanksgiving, which is so striking and prominent a feature of Jewish devotional life and worship, has crystallized itself into a regular form of benediction known as *Bĕrākhāh* (lit. 'Blessing'). In its technical sense the term denotes a set form of prayer, which opens with the words, 'Blessed art Thou, O Lord our God, King of the Universe, who,' etc., and, in its fully developed form, closes with a repetition of the same words. This class† plays an important part in the Jewish Liturgy.

In its simplest and shortest form the *Bĕrākhāh* opens as described, but has no closing refrain. It contains a brief expression of thanks to God for some benefit conferred or privilege enjoyed.‡

Undoubtedly the most ancient kind of benediction is that recited at the meal. The Book of Samuel attests the antiquity of the custom, for in one passage (1 S 9[13]) we are told that the people refused to eat the sacrificial meal until it had been blessed.

The Biblical command on which the obligation of grace at meals (Heb. *birkath ha-māzôn*)—*i.e.* according to the Rabbis (*Ber.* 21*a*, 48*b*; Tos. *Ber.* vii. 1), grace both before and after eating—is founded, occurs in Dt 8[10] ('When thou hast eaten and art full, thou shalt bless the Lord thy God for the good land which he hath given thee').

The Benediction over bread, which is recited before the meal begins, and which may have been known to our Lord, runs: 'Blessed art Thou, O Lord our God, King of the Universe, who bringeth forth bread from the earth.' The corresponding one said before drinking wine is: 'Blessed art Thou, O Lord our God, King of the Universe, who createst the fruit of the vine' (cf. Lk 22[18]).

Note.—The Benediction (thanksgiving) over wine was especially associated with the hallowing of the Sabbath and festival days embodied in the ceremonies of *Ḳiddûsh* ('Sanctification') and *Habdālāh* ('Separation' or 'Distinction'). For a full description of these observances see the *Jewish Encyc. s.vv.* 'Kiddush' and 'Habdalah'; and for a possible connexion with the Gospels reference may be made to an article by the present writer in the *Journ. of Theol. Studies* (iii. [1902] p. 357 ff.) on 'The Jewish Antecedents of the Eucharist.' Though thanksgiving is an essential, and indeed the most prominent, element in consecration or sanctification, the ideas must be kept distinct. Cf. Bp. of Salisbury, *op. cit.* p. 135 f.

The more important Benedictions in this connexion are reserved for the recitation that follows the meal. Of these there are now four (see Singer's *Prayer-Book*, p. 286). The first ('Blessed art Thou, O Lord . . . who givest food unto all') is ascribed by the Talmud (*Ber.* 48*b*) to Moses; the second ('for the land and for the food') to Joshua, who led Israel into the land; the third ('Blessed art Thou, O Lord, who in Thy compassion rebuildest Jerusalem') to king Solomon; the fourth ('Blessed art Thou, O Lord our God . . . who art kind and dealest kindly with all') to the Rabbis of Jamnia in the 2nd cent. A.D.§

The act of thanksgiving *after* the meal is not explicitly alluded to in the Gospels. That the custom is an ancient one, however, appears from the fact that, by the time of the compilation of the Mishna, rules as to its ordering had been fully developed (cf. *Ber.* vii.). It constitutes a sort of service, with responses (which vary according to the number, etc., of those

* Quoted by Schechter, *Studies in Judaism*, p. 380.
† The most important example is the well-known group of the 'Eighteen Blessings' (*Shĕmônê 'Esrê*), the nucleus of which is undoubtedly pre-Christian. It is notable that here the element of petition accompanies that of praise and thanksgiving (for text of these in English see Singer's Heb.-Eng. *Prayer-Book*, pp. 44–54).
‡ A very large number of these short Benedictions, expressive of thankful recognition of God's goodness and providence as shown in various ways, has been developed. For a full enumeration see *Jewish Encyc. s.v.* 'Benedictions,' or the Prayer-Books.
§ Cf. *Jewish Encyc.* iii. 9.

present). Details and text of prayers can be read in Singer, pp. 278–285.

Another ancient form of Benediction (with responses), which, however, is not alluded to in the Gospels, is that offered before and after the reading of Scripture (for the modern forms cf. Singer, p. 147 ff.). This has a Biblical basis in the practice of Ezra mentioned in Neh 8[6], and was doubtless well known in the time of Jesus.

Enough has been said above to make it clear that the set form of Benediction, based as it is upon Biblical precedents, had been developed by the NT period. The first tractate of the Mishna (compiled in its present form, probably from earlier collections, at end of 2nd cent. A.D.) deals with the various forms of the *Bĕrākhāh* (hence its name *Bĕrākhôth* = 'Blessings'), and embodies the earliest Rabbinical tradition on the subject. According to the Talmud (*Ber.* 33*a*), the recognized Benedictions were formulated by the 'men of the Great Synagogue.' Later the rule was deduced that a Benediction, to be regular, must contain the name of God and the attribute of God's kingship (*Ber.* 40*b*).

4. Usage in the Gospels.—The Jewish conception of 'blessing' (cf. §§ **1** and **3**) is reflected in the Gospel narratives in its purest and most elevated form. The central thought of God as the sole object of praise, of God's favour as the highest form of felicity (cf. Lk 1[28]), the duty of rendering thanks to Him as the Great Giver and Father, are strikingly enforced, especially in some of the sayings of Jesus. The Gospel usage may best be illustrated by an analysis of the passages in which the terms enumerated above (§ **2**) respectively occur. These may be grouped as follows:—

(*a*) *Passages involving the use of* εὐλογεῖν, 'to bless,' *and its derivatives*:

(1) With a personal object expressed, viz. :—
(A) *God* : Lk 1[64] 2[28] 24[53].

With this division should be considered the use of εὐλογητός, 'Blessed,' which is always explicitly applied to God in the NT. The term occurs twice in the Gospels, once as a periphrasis for God, Mk 14[61] (cf. the regular Jewish periphrasis, 'The Holy One,' 'Blessed be He'), and once in a liturgical ascription of praise, Lk 1[68] (opening line of the *Benedictus*).

(B) *Man* : in the sense of 'to invoke blessings on,' Lk 6[28] ; esp. at solemn parting or farewell, Lk 2[34] 24[50f.] (cf. the Rabbinical parallel quoted above) ; of solemn blessing of children, Mk 10[16] (better reading κατευλόγει), cf. Mt 19[14], and the Jewish illustration already cited.

Note.—Here it may be remarked that the blessing was imparted either by the imposition of hands, in the case of one or a small number (cf. Gn 48[17-19], Mt 19[15], Mk 10[16]) ; or, in other cases, with uplifted hands (Lv 9[22], Lk 24[50] ; cf. Sir 50[20]).

Here naturally comes to be considered the use of εὐλογημένος = 'blessed' (viz. by God) : it occurs six times in the acclamation, borrowed from Ps 118 [117][26], of 'him that cometh' ; Mt 21[9] 23[39] and the ‖ passages, Mk 11[9], Lk 13[35] 19[38], Jn 12[13] (where D reads εὐλογητός) ; once of the mother of the Lord and her Son, Lk 1[42] (εὐλογημένη, κ.τ.λ., in 1[28] is not well attested) ; also of 'the nations on the King's right hand' (Mt 25[34]), and of 'the kingdom of David' (Mk 11[10]).

(2) With a material object : Mk 8[7], Lk 9[16] (both of food). 'In these cases blessing the bread must be understood as "blessing God the giver of the bread"' (Westcott), in accordance with the Jewish usage illustrated above (§ **3**).

(3) Absolutely, without any object expressed (always of food and sustenance) : Mk 6[41] ‖ Mt 14[19] (feeding of the five thousand), Mk 14[22] ‖ Mt 26[26] (in ref. to bread at Last Supper), and Lk 24[30].

In close connexion with the above we have to consider here—

(*b*) *The use of* εὐχαριστεῖν, 'to give thanks,' *in the Gospels.*

(1) Of food and wine. The word occurs eleven times, and in eight of these has reference either to

food or wine, viz. : Mk 8⁶ ‖ Mt 15³⁶ (of the feeding of the four thousand), Lk 22¹⁹ (in ref. to the bread at the Last Supper), Jn 6¹¹· ²³ (of feeding of the five thousand), of thanksgiving over the cup at the Last Supper, Mk 14²³ ‖ Mt 26²⁷ and Lk 22¹⁷.

It is clear from a comparison of the parallel passages noted above that εὐλογεῖν and εὐχαριστεῖν are freely interchanged (cf. Cremer, *Bib.-Theol. Lex. s.vv.*; Swete, *JThSt* iii. [1902] 163). It thus appears that the predominant idea in the Gospel usage of such expressions as 'blessing the bread' is not so much that of sanctification or consecration as of thanksgiving to God for the gift.*

(2) Of thanksgiving to God in other connexions : Lk 18¹¹, Jn 11⁴¹.

(3) Of thanksgiving to Christ : Lk 17¹⁶.

(Note here that the act of thanksgiving was accompanied by 'glorifying God' (v.¹⁵), and that it is on this feature that Jesus lays stress (v.¹⁸), 'Were there none found that returned to give glory [here = 'to render thanks'] to God save this stranger?')

(c) and (d) *The use of the terms* ἐξομολογεῖν, 'thank,' *and* αἰνεῖν, 'praise' (cf. δοξάζειν, 'glorify'), in a more or less synonymous sense (the sense of thanksgiving), has been sufficiently explained above (§ 2), and does not call for further remark here.

Note, however, that αἰνεῖν is never used of or by Jesus.

(e) *The use of* μακάριος, 'blessed,' is frequent in the sayings of Jesus (its employment in the 'Beatitudes' has already been noted above). It is used especially in a congratulatory sense, corresponding in the LXX to the Hebrew term 'ashrê = 'happy' (lit. 'O the happiness of'). In this way it is employed, especially in personal address (a good instance occurs in Mt 16¹⁷ 'Blessed art thou, Simon Bar-jona,' etc.). Especially notable are such sayings as that recorded in Lk 11²⁷· ²⁸ ('Blessed is the womb that bare thee' . . . 'Yea, rather, blessed are they that hear the word of God and keep it'), in which Jesus pointedly insists on the idea that true blessing and true blessedness are to be found in thought and action that are immediately related and directed to God and the Divine requirements. The Jewish conception of blessing and blessedness is thus set forth in its purest and most elevated phase.

LITERATURE.—The most important original authorities for the Jewish *data* are the recensions of the tractate *Bĕrākhôth* extant in the Mishna (various ed. of Heb. text; Eng. tr. in Barclay's *Talmud*, 1877, and De Sola and Raphall's *Mishnah*, 1845), and the Tosephta (Heb. text, ed. Zuckermandel). For a full account of these see *Jewish Encyclopedia, s.v.* 'Berakot.' For an account of the various Jewish forms of blessing see the articles 'Benedictions,' 'Blessing of Children,' and 'Blessing (Priestly),' with the literature cited, in the same work. Cf. also the art. 'Abschied' in Hamburger's *RE für Bibel und Talmud*, vol. ii. Some relevant data are also to be found in the article 'Benedictions' (by R. Sinker) in Smith's *Dictionary of Christian Antiquities*. There is a valuable 'Additional Note' in Westcott's *Hebrews* on 'The Biblical Idea of Blessing' (p. 209 ff.); and a careful synopsis of references in Harper (W. R.), *Priestly Element in OT²*, (1905) 136 ff. Reference may also be made to the works of Edersheim (esp. *The Temple: its Ministry*, etc., where the Jewish material is set forth fully) and those of the elder Lightfoot. Other references have been given in the body of the article.   G. H. BOX.

BLINDNESS.—Blindness is a very common disease in the East. It is mainly due to ophthalmia caused partly by the sun-glare and partly by lack of cleanliness. The word 'blindness' or 'blind' is used in the Bible, however, very frequently of a spiritual condition ; and the references in the Gospels are specially interesting as the physical and the spiritual states are sometimes intertwined, the former being used as emblematic of the latter.

* Cf. the valuable remarks of the Bp. of Salisbury on this point (*op. cit.* p. 135 f.). He notes the occurrence of the expressions εὐχαριστηθεῖσα τροφή, εὐχαριστηθεὶς ἄρτος, etc., 'thanksgiven food,' 'thanksgiven bread,' where we should say 'consecrated food or bread' (*ib.*). Cf. also *Didache* x. and xv.

In Mt 11⁵ the first evidence of His Messiahship, adduced by Jesus to the disciples of John the Baptist, is that the blind receive their sight. The first miracle of this nature in the life of Jesus is recorded by St. Matthew (9²⁷ff.) as occurring at Capernaum.

Two blind men followed Him, crying, 'Thou Son of David, have mercy on us.' Jesus seems unwilling at first to grant their request, as we are told that it was not till they had entered the house with Him that He turned a favourable ear to their entreaty. Satisfied of their faith, and of the spirit in which they approached Him, He pronounced the word of healing.

In St. Mark (8²²ff.) another miracle of restoring sight to the blind is recorded which has features of its own.

Jesus leads the blind man out of the village (Bethsaida), and, having spit upon his eyes, touches them. Sight is only gradually restored, as at first he sees men like trees walking. This is one of the many instances of the realism of St. Mark. Probably it is a reminiscence of the well-known difficulty experienced by the blind-born, to whom sight has been given through a surgical operation, of adjusting the knowledge acquired by the new faculty with that derived through the other avenues of sense-perception.

The story of the blind man or men at Jericho is recorded in all three Synoptics (Mt 20²⁹ff., Mk 10⁴⁶ff., Lk 18³⁵ff.). It has also features in common with the incident narrated in Mt 9²⁷.

St. Mark and St. Luke speak of only one blind man, St. Matthew has two. All three give the words of healing differently. There have been many attempts made to harmonize the various accounts,* but the necessity for making such attempts arises out of a mechanical theory of inspiration which is difficult to maintain. Is it not enough for all practical purposes to hold the substantial accuracy of the Evangelic narrative without troubling ourselves about those minute divergences which occur in different versions of the same event narrated by the most trustworthy witnesses?

The miracles recorded in Mt 12²² and Jn 9 stand by themselves as having a very close relation to the teaching of Jesus which follows. St. Matthew tells us that there was brought to Jesus one possessed with a devil, blind and dumb ; and He healed him, insomuch that the blind and dumb both saw and spake. This gave rise to the charge of the Pharisees, that the miraculous power of Jesus was not a God-given, but a devil-given power. 'This fellow doth not cast out devils, but by Beelzebub the prince of the devils.' To the clear moral vision of Jesus the attitude implied in this objection showed a radical depravity of nature, an inability to discriminate between fundamental ethical distinctions. 'A house divided against itself cannot stand.' If Satan inspires to deeds of beneficence, then he ceases to be Satan. He who does good is inspired of God, and the measure of the good he does is the measure of his conquest over Satan. It is in this connexion that Jesus utters the remarkable reference to blasphemy against the Holy Ghost as the unforgivable sin. See art. BLASPHEMY.

The other instance where the miraculous cure of blindness is made a text for the most characteristic teaching of Jesus is that recorded in Jn 9. Here it is a man blind from his birth that Jesus cures. And when the Pharisees seek to persuade him of their peculiar theological tenet that the power of Jesus is derived from Satan, the man has strength of mind enough to fall back on that primary moral instinct to which Jesus always appeals. 'Whereas I was blind, now I see. This man has done good to me, and for me, therefore, he is good. It is not the function of the prince of darkness to give sight to the blind.' He cannot, therefore, accept their theory of the source whence Jesus derives His power.

This leads us to a predominant feature of the teaching of Jesus—His presentation of the gospel as *vision*. Jesus claims to be the Light of the world. Light to those who see is its own evidence, and

* For a summary of these see Plummer, *Internat. Crit. Com.*, 'St. Luke,' *in loco*.

Jesus, therefore, in making this claim can desire no recognition other than that spontaneously made by the soul when purged from the sinful passions that obscure or deflect its vision. To secure effective vision there must be not only light, but also a healthy visual organ. Blindness may arise from the absence of light, from mere functional derangement of the organ of vision, or from some fatal organic defect in the organ. It is to those whose blindness comes from either of the first two causes that Jesus appeals. He comes as Light, strengthening the visual faculty, dispelling the darkness that envelops the soul, and revealing to it the spiritual realm. 'I am come into this world that they which see not might see' (Jn 9³⁹). This presentation of Jesus as Light appealing to the organ of spiritual vision and vindicating empirically His unique Divinity dominates the whole of the Fourth Gospel. But the principle is as clearly enunciated in the Synoptics. It is the pure in heart who see God (Mt 5⁸), because the pure heart is the organ of the God-consciousness. In the great confession of St. Peter the real point of our Lord's commendation lies not in the clear enunciation of the Messiahship and the Divine Sonship of Jesus, but in the manner in which the profoundest of all spiritual truths has been reached. 'Blessed art thou, Simon Bar-jona: for flesh and blood hath not revealed it unto thee, but my Father which is in heaven' (Mt 16¹⁷).

Jesus, the Light of the world, can appeal only to those who have the faculty of sight. Where the faculty of sight is impaired or destroyed, however clearly the light may shine, there is no vision. This obscuration of the spiritual orb is what is called 'judicial blindness.' The phrase implies that there never can be such radical defect of vision without personal guilt in the person so affected. It is a penalty of sin, the judgment that comes through neglecting the light (cf. Jn 9⁴¹). Inasmuch as Jesus is the true Light that lighteth every man that cometh into the world, there is in human nature, as such, the capacity of spiritual vision; but this capacity, either by disuse or perversity, may be so radically corrupted as to be impervious to the light. And when this is so, the sinner rushes to his doom heedless of the plainest warnings. This is a truth always recognized in the Gospels. St. John in his Prologue says that the Light shineth in darkness, but the darkness comprehended it not (cf. Mt 6²²ᶠ·). It is the meaning of the blasphemy against the Holy Ghost, a sin unforgivable, inasmuch as it does not recognize itself as sin, and thus renders impossible that repentance which is the condition of forgiveness (but see art. BLASPHEMY).   A. MILLER.

BLOOD (דָּם, Aram. אְמָא, Gr. αἷμα).—Underlying the use of the term 'blood' in the Gospels is its root conception, as contained in the OT. This root conception is clearly seen, e.g., in Lv 17¹¹·¹⁴ *'The life ('soul' נֶפֶשׁ) of the flesh is in the blood . . . it is the blood that maketh atonement by reason of the life. . . . For as to the life of all flesh, the blood thereof is all one with the life thereof . . . for the life of all flesh is the blood thereof.'* The close connexion between 'life' and 'blood'—amounting even to identification — was doubtless realized by man from very early times; for constant experience taught him that loss of blood entailed weakness, while great loss resulted in death, i.e. the departure of life. This would have been noticed again and again in everyday life, whether in hunting, or in slaughtering (both for food and sacrifice), or in battle.* This belief was by no means confined to the Hebrews, but

was universal in ancient times, just as it is now among primitive races.* The reiterated prohibition with regard to the eating of blood contained in the Hebrew Code was due, firstly, to the fact that God had made use of it as a means of atonement, and that therefore it ought not to be used for any other purpose; and, secondly, because it was believed to contain the soul or life. In the one case, the prohibition is due to the holy character of blood;† in the other, to its essential nature,‡ it being the centre from which animal life in all its various forms emanated. Blood was therefore holy from the Divine point of view, because God had sanctified it to holy uses; and it was holy from man's point of view, both because it had been ordained as a means of atonement in the sight of God, and because human life, of which blood was the essence, was sacred to Him.

In the Gospels one or other of these conceptions underlies the use of the word 'blood.' Its use may be briefly summarized thus:

1. *Blood in its material sense, e.g.,* the woman with the issue of blood (Mk 5²⁵, Lk 8⁴³). The power which went out from Christ stayed the flow of the woman's blood; it is implied (Mk 5²⁶ ἀλλὰ μᾶλλον εἰς τὸ χεῖρον ἐλθοῦσα) that this outflow was the ebbing-out of her life. The ancient conception is, therefore, plainly present here.

2. *Blood used in the sense of life (i.e.* poured out in death). It is interesting to observe that in all the Gospel passages in which blood is used as synonymous with life, the reference is either to an OT occurrence, or else to Christ as fulfilling OT types. The passages are the following: Mt 23³⁰ 'We should not have been partakers with them in the blood of the prophets'; 23³⁵ 'That upon you may come all the righteous blood shed on the earth, from the blood of Abel the righteous unto the blood of Zachariah son of Barachiah, whom ye slew between the sanctuary and the altar,' cf. Lk 11⁵¹; Mt 27⁴ 'I have betrayed innocent blood'; 27⁶ 'the price of blood'; 27⁸ 'the field of blood'; 27²⁴ 'I am innocent of the blood of this righteous man'; 27²⁵ 'His blood be upon us.' In each of these passages the meaning of blood as implying life is sufficiently clear.

3. In Lk 13¹ occurs a reference to 'the Galilæans whose blood Pilate mingled with their sacrifices.' There is no reference to this event either in Josephus (although there is mention of a similar occurrence in *Ant.* XVII. ix. 3) or elsewhere; but the meaning appears to be that they were offering up their usual sacrifice in the ordinary course, when they were fallen upon and butchered by the Roman soldiery, probably as a punishment for some act of revolt [the restlessness of the Galilæans was notorious, cf. Ac 5³⁷].

4. A further use of the word is seen in Mt 16¹⁷, where the expression 'flesh and blood' occurs.§ In this passage the use of 'blood' is somewhat modified from what has been found hitherto; the phrase σάρξ καὶ αἷμα denotes what is human, abstractly considered; 'the antithesis is between knowledge resulting from natural human develop-

---

* Cf. H. L. Strack, *Der Blutaberglaube in der Menschheit*⁴, p. 1 ff.

* Rob. Smith, *Rel. of the Semites*², p. 337 ff. ; Wellhausen, *Reste arabischen Heid.*² p. 226 ff. ; Strack, *op. cit.* p. 9 ff. ; J. G. Frazer, *Golden Bough*², i. 353, where other authorities are cited ; Bähr, *Symbolik des Mosaischen Cultus*², i. 44 ff. ; Trumbull, *Studies in Oriental Social Life*, p. 157 ff.

† See, further, with regard to this point, the many interesting details in Trumbull's *The Threshold Covenant*, and Doughty's *Arabia Deserta* (2 vols.) ; the references are too numerous to quote, but both works will well repay careful study.

‡ Cf. Strack, *op. cit.* p. 75 ff. ; Franz Delitzsch, *System der biblischen Psychologie*, pp. 196, 202.

§ The expression σάρξ καὶ αἷμα (also in the order αἷμα καὶ σάρξ) is frequent in Rabbinical writings (בָּשָׂר וָדָם) ; 'the Jewish writers use this form of speech infinite times, and by it oppose men to God' (Lightfoot, *Horæ Heb. et Talm.* [Gandell's ed.] ii. 234) ; see also Sir 14¹⁸, where 'flesh and blood' are compared to the leaves on a tree.

ment, or on the basis of natural birth, and knowledge proceeding from the revelation of the Father in heaven, or on the basis of regeneration' (Lange).* The expression therefore emphasizes the contrast between human and Divine knowledge (cf. Gal 1^{16} 'immediately I conferred not with flesh and blood'; cf. also He 2^{14}, 1 Co 15^{50}, Eph 6^{12}). The special meaning attaching to 'blood' here is that it belongs to human nature; and significant in this connexion is the passage Lk 24^{39} a 'spirit hath not flesh and bones as ye behold me having,' where 'flesh' is clearly intended to include blood; † the primary difference in bodily structure between a natural and a spiritual body being the absence of blood in the latter. If in the ordinary human body blood is conceived of as being the source of life, the body without blood receives its life in a manner utterly different,—it is the life which comes from Christ: 'I am come that they might have life, and that they might have it more abundantly' (Jn 10^{10}). Closely connected with this are the words in Jn 1^{13} '... which were born, not of blood ‡ ... but of God'; here, too, the contrast is between that which is born 'of blood,' i.e. according to a natural birth, and that which is born 'of God,' i.e. according to a spiritual birth.

5. A very mysterious use of 'blood' is that contained in the words 'bloody sweat' (Lk 22^{44}).§ 'It is probable that this strange disorder arises from a violent commotion of the nervous system, and forcing of the red particles into the cutaneous excretories.' ‖ 'The intensity of the struggle,' says Godet, 'becomes so great, that it issues in a sort of beginning of physical dissolution. The words, *as it were drops*, express more than a simple comparison between the density of the sweat and that of blood. The words denote that the sweat itself resembled blood. Phenomena of frequent occurrence demonstrate how immediately the blood, the seat of life, is under the empire of moral impressions. Does not a feeling of shame cause the blood to rise to the face? Cases are known in which the blood, violently agitated by grief, ends by penetrating through the vessels which enclose it, and, driven outwards, escapes with the sweat through the transpiratory glands (see Langen, pp. 212–214).' ¶ See SWEAT.

6. One other passage must be referred to before coming to the spiritual use of 'blood,' namely, Jn 19^{34} 'and straightway there came out blood and water.' On the phenomenon of the effusion of water together with the blood, see Godet's *Gospel of St. John,* iii. 274 f. With regard to the flowing of the blood, there seems to be a striking significance in the fact; it was a visible instance of the fulfilment of Christ's own words: 'Think not that I came to destroy the law or the prophets; I came not to destroy, but to fulfil . . .' ** (Mt 5$^{17. 18}$); for

---

* Commentary on Matt. in loc. Cf. the words of Tholuck: 'It designates humanity with reference to its character as endowed with the senses and passions' (*Com. on Matt.*); see also Olshausen, *Com. on the Gospels,* vol. ii. (T. & T. Clark).

† See, further, art. BODY.

‡ The use of the plur. here ἐξ αἱμάτων (Vulg. *ex sanguinibus*) appears, according to Westcott, 'to emphasize the idea of the elements out of which in various measures the body is framed' (*Com. on St. John, in loc.* ; cf. also Godet's *Com. on St. John,* vol. i. p. 357 ff. (T. & T. Clark).

§ Regarding the text here, see Westcott-Hort, and Godet, *in loc.*

‖ Stroud, *Physical Cause of the Death of Christ,* pp. 74, 380, quoted in Trumbull's *The Blood Covenant,* p. 279 note; cf. also the letters of Dr. Begbie and Sir James Y. Simpson, given in App. i. of Hanna's *Last Day of Our Lord's Passion.*

¶ *Com. on Luke,* ii. 306 (T. & T. Clark). There is certainly one other instance on record of a like mysterious flow of blood, that, namely, of Charles IX. of France. It is said of him that on his deathbed his bitterness of sorrow and qualms of conscience, on account of the massacre on St. Bartholomew's Eve, were so intense that in the anguish of his soul he literally sweated blood.

** Cf. the frequent occurrence of such phrases as 'that the Scripture might be fulfilled.'

---

it was of the essence of sacrifice under the Old Dispensation that blood should *flow,** and that it should flow from a vital part, usually from the throat, though the spirit of the Law would obviously be fulfilled when the blood flowed from such a vital part as the region of the heart, the central part of man; † the sacrifice was consummated when the life, *i.e.* the blood, had flowed out.‡ Kalisch points out that, guided by similar views, the Teutons pierced the heart of the sacrificial victims, whether animals or men, because the heart is the fountain of the blood, and the blood of the heart was pre-eminently regarded as the blood of sacrifice.§ See also the following article.

7. The passages which speak of the blood of Christ (Mt 26^{28}, Mk 14^{24}, Lk 22^{20}, Jn 6$^{53-56}$), *i.e.* of blood in its *spiritual* meaning, can be here only briefly referred to [see ATONEMENT, LAST SUPPER]. They must be taken in conjunction with such expressions elsewhere as 'the blood of Christ' (1 Co 10^{16}, Eph 2^{13}), 'the blood of the Lord' (1 Co 11^{27}), 'the blood of his cross' (Col 1^{20}), 'the blood of Jesus' (He 10^{19}, 1 Jn 1^{7}), 'the blood of Jesus Christ' (1 P 1^{2}), 'the blood of the Lamb' (Rev 12^{11}).

From the earliest times among the ancient Hebrews the various rites and ceremonies, indeed the whole sacrificial system, showed the yearning desire for a closer union with God; this union was to be effected only through life-containing and life-giving blood. The very existence of these sacrifices proved (and the offering up of their firstborn sons only emphasized the fact) that men deemed the relationship between God and themselves to be unsatisfactory. Useless as these sacrifices were in themselves, they were at any rate (when not unauthorized) *shadows of good things to come* (He 10$^{1. 4}$); and they served their purpose of witnessing to profound truths which God intended to reveal more fully as soon as man's capacity for apprehension should have become sufficiently developed. The shedding of Christ's blood effected a new relationship between God and man; it sealed a *New Covenant,*‖ and became the means of the *salvation of many* (Mt 26^{28}, Mk 14^{24}, cf. Lk 22^{20}). But the ancient conception, the God-revealed truth only dimly apprehended, was right: *the life was in the blood,* inasmuch as the shedding of blood brought life—'I lay down my life, that I may take it again' (Jn 10^{17})—only it was a life which it was impossible to conceive of before the Author of it brought it to man. 'Having in His own blood the life of God and the life of man, Jesus Christ could make men sharers of the Divine by making them sharers of His own nature; and this was the truth of truths which He declared to those whom He instructed.' ¶

LITERATURE.—There are many books which give information on this subject, but as regards the special relationship between 'blood' and Christ it is difficult to point to any particular work; many details are to be had, but they must be gathered from numerous sources; some of the more important of these are: Franz Delitzsch, *System der biblischen Psychologie,* Leipzig, 1855; P. Cassel, *Die Symbolik des Blutes,* Berlin, 1882; C. Bähr, *Symbolik des Mosaischen Cultus*^{2}, 1874; F. Godet, *Biblical*

---

* This was originally based on the conception of blood being the drink of gods (cf. Ps 50^{13}); see Rob. Smith, *op. cit.* p. 233 ff.; Curtiss, *Primitive Sem. Rel. To-day,* p. 223: 'The consummation of the sacrifice is in the outflow of blood.'

† Cf. the words of Philo, *de Concupisc.* x.: 'Some men prepare sacrifices which ought never to be offered, strangling the victim and stifling the essence of life, which they ought to let depart free and unrestrained' (quoted by Kalisch, *Leviticus,* i. 184).

‡ 'Under the symbolic sacrifices of the Old Covenant it was the *blood* which made atonement for the soul. It was not the death of the victim, nor yet its broken body; but it was the blood, the life, the soul, that was made the means of a soul's ransom, of its rescue, of its redemption' (Trumbull, *The Blood Covenant,* p. 286). 'Blood atones by virtue of the life that is in it' (Bähr, *op. cit.* ii. 207).

§ Kalisch, *op. cit.* i. 189.

‖ A covenant was always ratified by the shedding of blood.

¶ Trumbull, *op. cit.* p. 274.

Studies in the OT and NT (Eng. tr. by Lyttelton), London, 1876 ; L. J. Rückert, Das Abendmahl . . ., Leipzig, 1856 ; H. L. Strack, Der Blutaberglaube in der Menschheit[4], München, 1892 (a work of extreme interest). A great fund of information is to be found scattered in the three books of H. C. Trumbull, The Blood Covenant, London, 1887, The Threshold Covenant, Philadelphia, 1896, Studies in Oriental Social Life, London, 1895 ; and in C. M. Doughty's Travels in Arabia Deserta, 2 vols., Cambridge, 1888. Other works that should be consulted are : J. Lightfoot, Horæ Heb. et Talm., 4 vols. (ed. Gandell), Oxford, 1859 ; Rob. Smith, Rel. of the Semites[2], London, 1894, Kinship and Marriage (ed. S. A. Cook), London, 1903 ; S. I. Curtiss, Primitive Semitic Religion To-day, London, 1902. Various notices will also be found in the Commentaries of Lange, Tholuck, Olshausen, Godet, and Westcott. See also the art. on 'Blood' and kindred subjects in the Bible Dictionaries, such as Hamburger, Riehm, Hastings, Cheyne, and the Jewish Encyclopedia.　　　W. O. E. OESTERLEY.

BLOOD AND WATER (Jn 19³¹⁻³⁷).—When the soldier, whom tradition names Longinus,* to make sure that He was really dead, drove his spear into the side of Jesus on the cross (see CRUCIFIXION), a strange thing happened. On being withdrawn the spear was followed by a gush of blood and water. It was a singular phenomenon. The Fathers regarded it as a miracle,† but St. John does not venture on an opinion. He neither attempts to account for it nor pronounces it a miracle, but contents himself with solemnly asseverating that he had witnessed it, and could vouch for its actual occurrence. He felt the wonder of it to the last (cf. 1 Jn 5⁶⁻⁸).

Medical science has confirmed his testimony, and furnished an explanation which at once defines the phenomenon as a perfectly natural occurrence, and reveals somewhat of the awfulness of our Lord's Passion. During His dread and mysterious dereliction on the cross (see DERELICTION) His heart swelled until it burst, and the blood was 'effused into the distended sac of the pericardium, and afterwards separated, as is usual with extravasated blood, into these two parts, viz. (1) crassamentum or red clot, and (2) watery serum.' When the distended sac was pierced from beneath, it discharged 'its sanguineous contents in the form of red clots of blood and a stream of watery serum, exactly corresponding to the description given by the sacred narrative, "and forthwith came there out blood and water."'‡ Jesus died literally of a broken heart—of 'agony of mind, producing rupture of the heart.'

It was a favourite idea with the Fathers that the Water and the Blood were symbolic of the Sacraments. St. Augustine, following the v.l. ἤνοιξε for ἔνυξε in v.³⁴, comments (in Joan Ev. Tract. cxx. § 2) : 'Vigilanti verbo Evangelista usus est, ut non diceret, Latus ejus percussit, aut vulneravit, aut quid aliud ; sed, aperuit : ut illis quodammodo vitæ ostium panderetur, unde Sacramenta Ecclesiæ manaverunt, sine quibus ad vitam quæ vera vita est, non intratur.' Cf. Chrysost. in Joan. lxxxiv. : οὐχ ἁπλῶς οὐδὲ ὡς ἔτυχεν αὗται ἐξῆλθον αἱ πηγαί, ἀλλ' ἐπειδὴ ἐξ ἀμφοτέρων ἡ ἐκκλησία συνέστηκε. καὶ ἴσασιν οἱ μυσταγωγούμενοι, δι' ὕδατος μὲν ἀναγεννώμενοι δι' αἵματος δὲ καὶ σαρκὸς τρεφόμενοι. ἀρχὴν λαμβάνει τὰ μυστήρια, ἵν' ὅταν προσίῃς τῷ φρικτῷ ποτηρίῳ, ὡς ἀπ' αὐτῆς πίνων τῆς πλευρᾶς οὕτω προσίῃς.

LITERATURE.—Besides the Comm. consult S. J. Andrews, Life of Our Lord upon the Earth, 566–569.　　DAVID SMITH.

BOANERGES.—In Mk 3¹⁷ we read that Christ 'gave to James and John name(s) Boanerges, that is, sons of thunder' (καὶ ἐπέθηκεν αὐτοῖς ὄνομα [v.l.

---

* Ev. Nicod. x. (Lat.) [xvi. (Gr.)]. Cf. 'Aug.' Manual. xxiii : 'Longinus aperuit mihi latus Christi lancea, et ego intravi et ibi requiesco securus.' The name is probably derived from λόγχη, 'spear.'
† Orig. c. Cels. ii. 36 : 'Blood does not flow from dead bodies, τοῦ δὲ κατὰ τὸν Ἰησοῦν νεκροῦ σώματος τὸ παράδοξον.' Cf. Euth. Zigabenus.
‡ Stroud's Treatise on the Physical Cause of the Death of Christ ; J. Y. Simpson in Append. to Hanna's Last Day of Our Lord's Passion. Cf. Calvin.

ὀνόματα] Βοανηργές, ὅ ἐστιν υἱοὶ βροντῆς).*　The equation Boanerges = 'sons of thunder' presents two difficulties : (a) the Hebrew בְּנֵי does not naturally give rise to the two vowels oa ; (b) no known Hebrew or Aram. root rgs or rgsh has the meaning 'thunder.' A third difficulty might be added, that the title Boanerges, whatever its meaning, does not accurately correspond to ὀνόμα(τα), 'name(s).'† If the Evangelist be right in saying that the original title meant 'sons of thunder,' we must suppose that Βοανη or Βοανε is due to inaccurate transliteration of בְּנֵי, or to a conflation of two readings with a single vowel (see Dalm. Gram.² p. 144). But the difficulty as to ργες = βροντή remains. Jerome (on Dn 1⁷) thought that Boanerges should be emended into Benereem = בְּנֵי רָעַם. In that case the s is a mistake on the part of the Evangelist or his copyists for m. Others prefer to think that the original title was בְּנֵי רְגֵז = 'sons of wrath,' or בְּנֵי רְגַשׁ = 'sons of tumult,' and that υἱοὶ βροντῆς is an inaccurate translation on the part of the Evangelist. The Syriac Version (Sinaiticus) unfortunately gives us no assistance. It transliterates Bĕnai Ragsh or Ragshi, and omits the explanation ὅ ἐστιν υἱοὶ βροντῆς (see Burkitt, Evangelion Da-Mepharreshe, i. 181, ii. 280). It is possible, however, that the corruption lies deeper than this. Just as Dalmanutha (Mk 8¹⁰) is probably a corruption of an Aramaic proper name (see Burkitt, ii. 249), so Boanerges may be a fusion of two names answering to the ὀνόματα. In that case the Evangelist, misreading or mishearing his Aramaic original, has fused two names into one, and has tried to give a rough translation of the word thus formed. The first name might be בַּנִּי (Banni), בַּנַּי (Bannai), or בֻּנַּי (Bunnai). Curiously enough, the Babylonian Talmud gives Bani as the name of one of the disciples of Jesus (Bab. Sanh. 43a). For the second name we offer no conjecture. See, further, JOHN, JAMES.

LITERATURE.—Encyc. Bibl. art. 'Boanerges' ; Expositor, III. x. [1889] 332 ff.　　　W. C. ALLEN.

BOAT.—

πλοῖον : AV 'ship,' RV 'boat.' πλοιάριον : Mk 3⁹ AV 'a small ship,' RV 'a little boat' ; Jn 6²² AV and RV 'boat,' RVm 'little boat' ; v.²⁴ ἐνέβησαν εἰς τὰ πλοιάρια AV 'took shipping,' RV 'got into the boats,' marg. 'little boats' ; 21⁸ τῷ πλοιαρίῳ AV 'in a little ship,' RV 'in the little boat,' [Lk 5² Tisch., WH marg. πλοιάρια : WH,TR πλοῖα. Jn 6²³ Tisch., TR,RV πλοιαρία : WH πλοῖα].

The word 'ship' is rightly expelled from the Gospels by the Revisers. It corresponds to ναῦς, which occurs nowhere in the Gospels, and in the NT only in Ac 27⁴¹. Being a small lake, the Sea of Galilee had no 'ships' ; but it had numerous 'boats' mostly employed in fishing (termed πλοῖα in the Gospels, also [τὰ] σκάφη in Josephus). Some of these were biggish craft, and usually swung at anchor on the Lake (cf. Jos. Vit. 33), being attended by πλοιάρια, 'punts' (cf. Jn 21³˙ ⁸). In Ac 27¹⁶. ³⁰. ³² the small-boat of St. Paul's ship is called ἡ σκάφη. To quell the revolt in Tiberias, Josephus mustered all the boats on the Lake, and they numbered as many as 230 (Jos. BJ II. xxi. 8). A boat which could accommodate Jesus and the Twelve must have been of considerable dimensions ; and in the battle on the Lake, under Vespasian, the Romans fought on rafts and the pirates on boats. Though small and weak in comparison with the rafts, the boats must have been of considerable size (Jos. BJ III. x. 9).

Jesus had much to do with boats during His Galilæan ministry, and one use that He made of them is peculiarly noteworthy. In two recorded instances He employed a boat as His pulpit (Lk 5¹⁻³, Mt 13¹⁻² = Mk 4¹). Getting into it to escape

---

* The MSS give : βοανηργες ℵAB, etc., βοανεργης D, βοανεργες EF, etc.
† ὀνόματα is read by ℵAC, etc., ὀνομα is the reading of BD.

the pressure of the multitude, He pushed out a little way from the land and addressed the people ranged along the sloping beach, as St. Chrysostom puts it, 'fishing and netting those on the land (ἁλιεύων καὶ σαγηνεύων τοὺς ἐν τῇ γῇ).' Only two instances of His resorting to this device are recorded, but it seems to have been His practice. Early in His ministry, St. Mark says (3⁹), ' He spake to his disciples that a little boat should wait on him because of the crowd, lest they should throng him' ; and it is interesting to observe how the Evangelist subsequently alludes to 'the boat' (Mk 4³⁶ 6³²). Cf. Mt 8²³ τὸ πλοῖον TR, Tisch. ; πλοῖον WH), meaning the boat which had been put at His disposal.   DAVID SMITH.

BOAZ.—The husband of Ruth, named in the genealogies of our Lord (Mt 1⁵, Lk 3³²).

BODY.—i. THE HUMAN BODY GENERALLY.— 'Body' in the Gospels invariably represents σῶμα in the original. Always in Homer and frequently in Attic Greek σῶμα = a dead body ; and in this sense the word is occasionally used in the Gospels (Mt 27⁵².⁵⁸.⁵⁹ ‖ Lk 17³⁷). The usual meaning, however, here as in the rest of the NT and in ordinary Greek usage, is the living body, and in particular the body of a living man (Mt 6²² 26¹², Mk 5²⁹). In the records of our Lord's life, teaching, and whole revelation, we find the dignity and claims of the body as an integral part of human nature constantly recognized. This meets us in the very fact of the Incarnation (Jn 1¹⁴), in the most solemn utterances of Jesus (Mt 25³⁵.⁴²), in His tender regard for the bodily needs and pains of those around Him—His feeding of the hungry and healing of the sick ; but above all in the narratives of His Resurrection and Ascension, which show that the Incarnation was not a temporary expedient of His earthly mission, but a permanent enfolding of our human nature, body as well as soul, within the essential life of the Godhead.

The Gospels give no support to the philosophic tendency, so often reflected in certain types of religious teaching, to treat the body with disparagement. Jesus accords full rights to the corporeal side of our being. He was neither an ascetic nor a preacher of asceticism—'the Son of Man came eating and drinking' (Mt 11¹⁸. ¹⁹). At the same time, we find in His teaching a clear recognition of a duality in human nature—a distinction drawn between body and soul, flesh and spirit (Mt 6²⁵ 26⁴¹). Moreover, He lays strong emphasis on the antithesis between the body as the lower part of a man, and the soul as the higher. Though the body is a true part of our humanity, its value is not to be compared for a moment with that of the spiritual part (Mt 10²⁸). Those who follow Jesus must be prepared, if need be, to surrender their bodies to the sword and the cross (Mt 23³⁴) ; but ' What shall a man give in exchange for his soul ?' (Mt 16²⁶).

In the teaching of Jesus the doctrine of the resurrection of the body, which had gradually taken root in the Jewish mind, is everywhere presupposed (as in His references to the Future Judgment), and at times is expressly proclaimed (Lk 14¹⁴ 20³⁵, Jn 5²⁸·²⁹). And by the grave of His friend Lazarus our Lord gave utterance to that profound saying, ' I am the resurrection and the life' (Jn 11²⁵), which reveals the ultimate ground of Christian faith in the resurrection of the body, and at the same time invites us to find in the nature of the risen Christ Himself the type, as well as the pledge, of that new and higher corporeal life to which He is able to raise His people.

ii. THE BODY OF CHRIST.—(1) *Christ's natural body.*—As ' the man Christ Jesus,' our Lord was possessed of 'a true body' as well as of 'a reasonable soul.' When the time was come in the counsels of God for the redemption of mankind, the Second Person of the Holy Trinity took upon Him human flesh by the operation of the Holy Spirit in the womb of the Virgin Mary (Mt 1¹⁸, cf. Gal 4⁴). In due time, according to the laws of human life, He was born at Bethlehem (Lk 2⁵. ⁷). The child thus born was seen in His infancy by the shepherds and the wise men, and, when He was eight days old, by Simeon and Anna (2²⁵. ³⁶). From His conception and birth His body developed in the manner usual to human beings. 'The child grew,' we are told (Lk 2⁴⁰) ; arrived at 'twelve years old' ; and still 'increased in stature' (vv.⁴². ⁵²).

After He had arrived at man's estate, we find Him living under the conditions to which the bodies of men in ordinary life are subject. We learn that He suffered hunger (Mt 4²) ; that He was wearied with journeying (Jn 4⁶) ; that He experienced pain (Mt 27²⁶) ; and that He underwent death (v.⁵⁰). In healing sickness He frequently used common bodily action, and His power of motion, with one miraculous exception (Mt 14²⁵ ‖), was limited to that which men in general possess. After death, His body, nowise different from that of an ordinary man, was delivered by Pilate to Joseph of Arimathæa, who wrapped it in a clean linen cloth and laid it in his own new tomb (Mt 27⁵⁸ᶠ·), where it rested till the moment of the Resurrection. Down to that moment, then, the Lord's body had been a human body with the powers, qualities, and capacities of the body of an ordinary man.

(2) *Christ's body after the Resurrection.*—It was the same body as before His death. The grave was left empty, because the very body which Joseph of Arimathæa laid there had risen and departed. Moreover, it had in most respects the same appearance. His disciples might doubt and hesitate at first (Lk 24¹⁶. ³⁷, Jn 20¹⁴), but they did not fail to recognize Him (Lk 24³¹. ⁵², Jn 20¹⁶. ²⁰. ²⁸ 21⁷. ¹², Ac 1³ 2³²). We find Him eating and drinking as a man (Lk 24⁴²), making use of the natural process of breathing (Jn 20²²), declaring to His disciples that He had flesh and bones (Lk 24³⁹), showing them His hands and His feet (v.⁴⁰), and giving them the assurance that His body was the identical body which they had seen stretched upon the cross, by inviting the disciple who doubted, to put his finger into the print of the nails and thrust his hand into the wound in His side (Jn 20²⁷).

On the other hand, our Lord's resurrection body was freed from previous material conditions and possessed of altogether new capacities. It seems to be implied that it could pass at will through material objects (Jn 20²⁶) ; and it does not appear to have been subject as before to the laws of movement (Lk 24³⁶), or visibility (v.³¹), or gravitation (Mk 16¹⁹, Lk 24⁵¹). These new powers constituted the difference between His pre-resurrection and His glorified body. It was in His glorified body, thus differentiated, that He ascended into heaven ; and in that same glorified body He is to be expected at His final coming (Ac 1⁹. ¹¹).

There is little ground for the idea of Olshausen (*Gospels and Acts*, iv. 259–260) and others, revived by Dr. Newman Smyth (*Old Faiths in New Light*, ch. viii.), that the transformation of Christ's body from the natural to the glorified condition was a process which went on gradually during the Forty Days, and was not completed till the Ascension. Rather, it must be said that on the very day of His Resurrection the spirituality of His risen body was as clearly shown as in the case of that much later manifestation by the Sea of Tiberias (cf. Lk 24³¹. ³⁶, Jn 21⁴ᶠᶠ·). We are not to think of the body of Jesus during this period as in a transition state with regard to its substance—partly of earth and partly of heaven. It was with a spiritual body that He rose, that glorified body of which His Transfiguration had been both a prophecy and a foretaste ; and if we see Him moving for a time along the borders of two worlds, that was because, for the sake of His disciples and the future Church, He made use of the natural in order to the revelation of the spiritual. It is in this way that we must explain His asking and receiving food (Lk 24⁴¹ᶠᶠ·, Ac 10⁴¹). He cannot have depended upon this food for His bodily support. His purpose in taking it was to convince His disciples that He was still a living man, in body as well as in spirit, —that same Jesus who had so often in past days partaken with them of their simple meals.

In respect of His body the risen Jesus now belonged to the mysterious regions of the invisible world, and it was only when He chose to reveal Himself that His disciples were aware of His presence. It is to be noticed that St. John describes His appearances as 'manifestations': He 'manifested Himself,' 'was manifested,' to the disciples (Jn 21¹·¹⁴). His resurrection body was a spiritual body, but it had the power of materializing itself to the natural senses, and Jesus made use of this power from time to time in order to convince His disciples, by the actual evidence of sight and sound and touch, that the victory of His whole human personality over death and the grave was real and complete. And when this work was accomplished, He parted from them for the last time, and went up to the right hand of the Father in a kind of royal state which not only proclaimed His own lordship over both worlds, but became a prophecy of the truth regarding the divinely appointed destiny of those whom He is not ashamed to call His brethren. In the body of Christ's glory both St. Paul and St. John find the type after which the believer's body of humiliation is to be fashioned at last (Ph 3²¹, 1 Jn 3²). We are to be like our Lord in the possession of a human nature in which the corporeal has been so fully interpenetrated by the spiritual that the natural body has been transformed into a spiritual body (1 Co 15⁴²⁻⁴⁹).

There is no ground to suppose that our Lord's entrance upon the state of exaltation implies any further change in His bodily nature. Certainly no new quality could be developed which would be inconsistent with the essential characteristics of a body. One of these characteristics is the impossibility of being in two places at the same moment. As long as He was on earth His body could not be in heaven, though He was there by His Spirit; and as long as He is in heaven His body cannot be on earth, although He is present by His Spirit, according to His promise to be with His followers where they are gathered together in His name (Mt 18²⁰, cf. 28²⁰). St. Peter preached that the heavens must receive Him until the times of restoration of all things (Ac 3²¹) ; and Christ Himself taught the Apostles that it was expedient for them that in bodily form He should leave them, so that the Comforter might take His place in the midst of the Church (Jn 16⁷).

(3) *Christ's mystical body.*—In 1 Co 12¹²ᶠᶠ· (cf. Ro 12⁵) St. Paul uses the figure of a body and its members to describe the relations of Christian people to Christ and to one another, and then in v.²⁷ he definitely applies the expression 'a body of Christ' (σῶμα Χριστοῦ) to the Corinthian Church. With reference to the body politic the figure was a familiar one in both Greek and Latin literature, and the Apostle transfers it to the Church for the purpose of emphasizing his exhortations to Church unity and a sense of mutual dependence among the people of Christ. As yet, however, the figure is quite plastic, while the anarthrous σῶμα suggests that it is the local Church which is immediately in view. Here, accordingly, we have in their first draft the Apostle's grand conceptions on the subject of the Lord's mystical body. When we come to Ephesians (1²²·²³ 4¹²) and Colossians (1¹⁸·²⁴) we find that his ideas have been elaborated, and that 'the body of Christ' (τὸ σῶμα τοῦ Χριστοῦ) has become a fixed title of the Church not as local merely, but as universal, nor simply as empiric, but as an ideal magnitude. We notice this further distinction, that in the earlier Epistles Christ is conceived of as the whole body, of which individual Christians are the particular members; while in Ephesians and Colossians He becomes the head of the Church which is His body (Eph 5²³·²⁴, Col 2¹⁹)—the vital and organic centre of the whole. The idea of this striking figure is similar to that presented by our Lord Himself in the allegory of the Vine and the Branches (Jn 15¹⁻⁸). The lesson of the figure, as of the allegory, is not only that in Christ all believers are bound together into the unity of the Church, but that the spiritual vitality, indeed the very existence, of individual Christians and Christian communities depends upon the closeness of their relations with Jesus Christ who is their head.

(4) *Christ's symbolic body.*—On the night in which He was betrayed, Jesus, in instituting the sacrament of the Supper, said of the bread which He took and broke and gave to His disciples, 'This is my body' (τοῦτό ἐστι τὸ σῶμά μου: Mt 26²⁶, Mk 14²², Lk 22¹⁹, 1 Co 11²⁴). Similarly St. Paul, writing to the Corinthians, says of the bread which is broken at the Supper, 'Is it not the communion of the body of Christ?' (1 Co 10¹⁶) ; while in the same Epistle he describes the person who eats the sacramental bread unworthily as 'guilty of the body of the Lord' (11²⁷), and says that a man eats and drinks judgment unto himself 'if he discern not the body' (11²⁹). Opinions have differed greatly in the Church as to the full significance of this language, whether on the lips of Jesus or of St. Paul. But whatever its further meanings may be, there can be little doubt that primarily the broken bread of the Supper is a symbol of the crucified body of Christ. With this symbolic use of the word 'body' many have sought to identify the words of the Lord in the Fourth Gospel about 'eating the flesh' of the Son of Man (Jn 6⁵³⁻⁶³). But as the word σῶμα denotes the body as an organism, while 'flesh' (σάρξ) applies only to the substance of the body, and as σάρξ is never employed elsewhere in the NT to describe the sacramental bread, it is unlikely either that Jesus would use σάρξ with this intention, or that the author of the Gospel would have failed to use σῶμα, the ordinary sacramental term, if it had been his intention to represent our Lord as furnishing in the Capernaum discourse a prophetic announcement of the institution of the Supper. See art. LORD'S SUPPER.

LITERATURE.—Grimm-Thayer, *Lexicon, s.v.* ; Cremer, *Biblico-Theological Lexicon, s.v.* ; Laidlaw, *Bible Doctrine of Man, s.v.*; Salmond, *Christian Doctrine of Immortality, s.v.* 'Resurrection'; Lange, *Life of Christ,* vol. v. p. 126 ff. ; Forrest, *Christ of History,* pp. 150 ff., 411 ff. ; *Expositor's Greek Testament, passim* ; arts. 'Resurrection' and 'Ascension' in Hastings' *DB.*

F. MEYRICK AND J. C. LAMBERT.

BOOK. — The word 'book,' representing two Greek words, βίβλος and βιβλίον (with dim. βιβλαρίδιον, Rev 10²·⁹ᶠ·), is of fairly frequent occurrence in the NT, although it is found only nine times in the Gospels. Very probably a book in the form familiar to us did not exist in NT times. The book of Scripture was a roll, as we may gather from such a text as Rev 5¹, 'A book written within and on the back, sealed with seven seals.'

The Scriptures used in the synagogues up to the fall of Jerusalem were probably leather rolls, or at least rolls of skins tanned in some way; but papyrus rolls were in very general use. Parchment was in use also, as we see from 2 Ti 4[13], but probably also in the roll and not the codex form. The distinction between the books (τὰ βιβλία) and the parchments (τὰς μεμβράνας) in the passage just referred to was, in all probability, simply one relating to the material used and not to the form of the manuscript, although it is not absolutely certain at what date parchments began to be folded instead of rolled.

The word 'book' is not always used in a strictly technical sense. In Mt 1[1] 'The book of the generation of Jesus Christ' means simply the record of, or writing about, the genealogy of Jesus. There is no reason to think that St. Matthew meant it to be understood that the genealogy formed a little roll by itself. Again in such expressions as 'the book of life' (although that expression does not occur in the Gospels), it is evident that the writer is speaking figuratively. Our Lord said to His Apostles (Lk 10[20]), 'Rejoice because your names are written in heaven'; and in the OT (Ex 32[32]) there is express mention of a book which God had written: 'If not, blot me, I pray thee, out of thy book which thou hast written.' The connexion of the expression 'book of life' with the words of our Lord to His Apostles, and with the daring yet splendid utterance of Moses, is obvious enough. To say that names are in 'the book of life' and 'the Lamb's book of life,' is to say that those bearing these names are accepted and accounted as members of the heavenly kingdom here and hereafter.

The word 'book' is used in its technical sense of an actual roll or volume in Mk 12[26], Lk 3[4] 4[17. 20] 20[42], and Jn 20[30]. It is noteworthy that in Mk 12[26] the writings of Moses are called not 'the books,' but simply 'the book.'

The books mentioned in Ac 19[19] as having been brought by their possessors and burned, were probably, many of them at least, simply amulets, spells, *grammata Ephesia*, little strips of parchment with words professedly of magical value written on them.

LITERATURE.—Comm. on the NT; art. 'Writing' in Hastings' *DB* and in the *Encyc. Biblica*; Schürer, *HJP*, Index, *s.vv.* 'Books,' 'Scriptures'; Sanday, *Inspiration*, 157, 297; Kenyon, *Handbook to Textual Criticism of NT*, ch. ii.

GEO. C. WATT.

BORDER (Gr. κράσπεδον for Heb. צִיצִת).—This word plays a significant part in the Gospels (Mt 9[20] 14[36] 23[5], Mk 6[56], Lk 8[44]). When Jesus was on His way to heal Jairus' little daughter, a certain woman who had an issue of blood twelve years came behind Him and touched the 'border' ('hem') of His garment (τοῦ κρασπέδου τοῦ ἱματίου) and was healed (Mt 9[20-22], Lk 8[44], Mk 6[56]). In Mt 14[36] we read of many sick ones who sought healing in the same way. Again, in that remarkable denunciation of the scribes and Pharisees which constitutes the climax of one of our Lord's most striking discourses, He makes this charge among others: 'All their works they do to be seen of men: they make broad their phylacteries, and they enlarge *the borders of their garments*' (Mt 23[5]).

What is this 'border of the garment' that plays such a rôle? Clearly in our Lord's time the Jews had come to attach great importance to it. To them it was the chief of three 'sensible signs,' or material reminders, of their obligations under the Law, the other two being the PHYLACTERIES (*tĕphillîn*) and *mĕzūzôth*, oblong boxes fixed above the door-posts, on which Dt 6[4-9] and 11[12-21] were written, according to the directions there given. The Law first required (Dt 22[12]) that 'twisted

cords' (Heb. *gĕdhîlîm*, incorrectly rendered '**fringes**' by AV and RV) be formed upon the four corners ('four borders,' RV) of the mantle or 'outer garment.' This thing termed *gĕdhîlîm* acquired later the special name *ẓîẓîth*,—it is so rendered by the Targum in Dt 22[12]. The same law is found in the Priestly Code in expanded form: 'And the Lord spake unto Moses saying, Speak unto the children of Israel, and bid them that they make them fringes (*ẓîẓîth*, κράσπεδα) in the borders' (more correctly 'tassels in the corners,' RVm) 'of their garments throughout their generations, and that they put upon the fringe of each border (*i.e.* 'the tassel of each corner') a cord of blue' (Nu 15[37. 38]).

The 'twisted cords' of Dt 22[12] were clearly intended to be fastened to the four corners of the outer garment (usually called *simlāh*). The Priestly Code, however, further called for a 'tassel' to be attached to each corner by a cord of blue. Now, it is to these 'tassels' that the Gr. translators give the name κράσπεδα—the term exclusively used in the NT. The *simlāh* was worn like the Gr. ἱμάτιον (the NT equivalent), the loose end being thrown over the left shoulder. The 'tassel' attached to this corner, then, could be reached with ease from behind, as in the case of the woman with the issue of blood (Mt 9[20]).

Some think that behind this law was an ancient Semitic custom with superstitious and magical associations, which, however, was impressed with a new significance by the Hebrew legislation. At any rate, we see here, as elsewhere, that in NT times a special virtue was still thought to be attached to the 'tassels on the four corners' (cf. Mt 14[36], Mk 6[56] with Lk 4[7] and 1 K 1[50]).

In the Mosaic Law they were evidently intended to be, as to the more spiritually minded doubtless they were, simply reminders of the obligations resting upon Jehovah's people to walk in this law and to keep all His commandments (Nu 15[39. 40]). The ostentatious Pharisees, however, went beyond others in their use of these signs, by making them large and conspicuous.

Jewish hearers and readers would at once understand what Jesus meant by this charge against the scribes and Pharisees, 'who sit in Moses' seat.' Making their phylacteries unusually broad and enlarging the borders ('tassels') of their garments would both be understood as their way of calling every casual observer to witness that they were remarkably pious. It was this ostentatious display of an empty, outward piety which Jesus here and elsewhere denounces, and which has given such a sinister and forbidding significance to 'Pharisaism' the world over.

LITERATURE.—Schürer, *HJP* II. ii. 111 ff.; Edersheim, *Life and Times*, i. 624 ff.; Hastings' *DB* and Kitto's *Biblical Cyclopædia*[3], art. 'Fringes.'   GEO. B. EAGER.

BORROWING.—See LOANS.

BOSOM occurs 5 times in EV of the Gospels (Lk 6[38] 16[22. 23], Jn 1[18] 13[23]), representing in each case the Gr. κόλπος, the word which in LXX regularly corresponds to חֵיק of the Heb. text and 'bosom' of the EV. κόλπος is found only once more in NT, viz., in Ac 27[39], where it has the secondary sense of a bay or bight (a bosom-like hollow); cf. Eng. 'gulf,' which comes from this root.

In classical Greek, in the LXX, and in the NT κόλπος, like Lat. *sinus* (which Vulg. gives in all the above passages), is used in the two principal senses of (*a*) the human bosom, the front of the body between the arms; (*b*) the bosom of the garment, *i.e.* the hollow formed in front when the upper garment was bound round the waist with the girdle. In EV of the OT 'bosom' is to be understood.

according to the context, in one or other of these two senses. *E.g.* in expressions like 'the wife of thy bosom' (Dt 13⁶), 'Naomi took the child and laid it in her bosom' (Ru 4¹⁶), the first sense is evidently the proper one. On the other hand, when we read of putting one's hand into one's bosom (Ex 4⁶· ⁷), taking fire into the bosom (Pr 6²⁷), receiving a gift in the bosom (21¹⁴), it is the bosom of the garment of which we are to think. See art. DRESS.

1. In Lk 6³⁸, where our Lord says to willing givers, 'Good measure, pressed down, shaken together, running over . . . shall they give into your bosom,' it is clear that the word has the sense of (*b*). The overhanging front of the upper garment when confined by the girdle was used as a convenient receptacle, serving the purposes of the modern pocket. An adequate paraphrase would thus be, 'Your pockets shall be filled to overflowing.' In the remaining passages two distinct questions emerge. First, the more important one as to the general meaning in each case of the expression 'in the bosom' or 'on the bosom.' Next, in those cases in which the phrase is taken to refer to the position at table of one guest in relation to another, as to whether the 'bosom' is the bosom proper or the bosom of the garment.

2. To begin with the simplest passage, the general meaning of Jn 13²³, in the light of the table customs of the period, is perfectly plain. In the time of Christ it was customary at a set feast to recline on a divan or couch, with the feet stretched out behind, the left arm supported on a cushion, and the right hand free for eating. Moreover, the usual plan was that the guests reclined not at right angles to the table, but obliquely, this being manifestly much the more convenient way of reaching the viands (cf. Lightfoot, *Hor. Heb. et Talm.*, *ad loc.*). By this arrangement a second guest to the right hand lay with his head towards the bosom of the first, and so on. But what precisely is meant by 'bosom' in this connexion? Whether is the word used in the sense of (*a*) or of (*b*) as described above? Probably in the latter, the meaning being that the head of the second reached 'to the *sinus* of the girdle' of the first (see Meyer, *Com. in loc.*). It could not well have reached to the other's bosom in the strict sense of the word, for this would have interfered with his freedom and comfort in eating and drinking. This view is confirmed by the fact that when the Evangelist describes St. John as leaning back (ἀναπεσών) on Jesus' breast to ask Him a question, a different word (στῆθος) is employed (v.²¹, cf. 21²⁰, and see RV in both cases). See art. GUEST-CHAMBER.

3. The expression 'Abraham's bosom' (Lk 16²²· ²³) has already been dealt with in its general eschatological signification (see art. ABRAHAM). A question remains, however, as to the precise form of the figure which the words are meant to suggest (note that the plur. in v.²³ has no separate connotation from the sing. in v.²². Cf. Homer, *Il.* ix. 570, and see Winer-Moulton, *Gram. of NT Gr.* 219 f.). Is Abraham to be thought of, fatherlike, as enfolding Lazarus in his arms (cf. 'Father Abraham,' vv.²⁴· ²⁷· ³⁰), or rather as receiving him into the place of the honoured guest, the place nearest to himself at a heavenly banquet? 'Into Abraham's bosom' (εἰς τὸν κόλπον 'A., v.²²) might suggest the former, but 'in his bosom' (ἐν τοῖς κόλποις αὐτοῦ, v.²³) may very well be used with reference to the idea of a feast, after the analogy of Jn 13²³ (κόλπος is used in the plural form both of the human bosom and of the folds of the upper garment. See Liddell and Scott and Grimm-Thayer, *s.v.*). And this seems to be confirmed by that other passage (Mt 8¹¹, cf. Lk 13²⁸· ²⁹) in which Jesus says, 'Many shall come from the east and the

west, and shall sit down (RVm 'recline,' Gr. ἀνακλιθήσονται; cf. ἀνεκλίθη in TR reading of Lk 7³⁶, which AV renders 'sat down to meat') with Abraham and Isaac and Jacob in the kingdom of heaven.' Alike for the social outcast (Lazarus) and for the religious outcasts (the Gentiles), Jesus holds out as a joyful prospect the thought of sitting down with Abraham at a heavenly banqueting-table. The conception of Paradise, moreover, under the figure of a feast, is specially appropriate, because of the contrast it presents to the earthly condition of Lazarus as a starving beggar (v.²¹), just as it is in keeping with the great reversal in the positions of the two men that Dives, who on earth had 'fared sumptuously every day' (v.¹⁹), should now lack even a drop of water to cool his burning tongue (v.²⁴).

4. The only passage that remains is Jn 1¹⁸, where Jesus Christ is described as 'the only-begotten Son, which is in the bosom of the Father.' In this case the image of neighbours at a feast seems quite inappropriate, though some have suggested it; and it is in every way more suitable, in view of the whole purpose of the Prologue no less than the language of the immediate context, to take 'in the bosom of the Father' in that closer and more tender meaning in which in the OT the expression is used to describe, whether literally or figuratively, the relation of a wife to her husband (Dt 13⁶), or of a child to his father (Nu 11¹²) or mother (1 K 17¹⁹). This beautiful term of human affection is employed here to denote the intimate fellowship of perfect love which exists between God and His Son. Some difficulty is occasioned by the fact that the phrase in the original is εἰς τὸν κόλπον, literally, 'into the bosom.' Meyer insists on giving to εἰς its ordinary meaning of 'direction towards,' and so recognizes as the prominent element in the expression the idea of *having arrived at.* He admits that 'so far as the *thing* itself is concerned,' the εἰς τὸν κόλπον of v.¹⁸ does not differ from the πρὸς τὸν θεόν of v.¹, but maintains that in v.¹⁸, at all events, the Evangelist desires to express the fullest fellowship with God, not before the Incarnation, but after the Ascension into glory. In this case, however, the description of Jesus Christ as εἰς τὸν κόλπον of the Father would be inappropriate, for the Evangelist is in the act of explaining how it is that the Only-Begotten Son was made to 'declare' the Father while on earth (note the aorist ἐξηγήσατο). It seems proper, therefore, to take ὤν as a timeless present, and to understand the author to mean that Jesus had declared God on earth because His inherent relation to the Father, before the Incarnation as after the Exaltation, was one of being 'in his bosom' (cf. 16²⁸ 'I came out from the Father, and am come into the world'; 17⁵· ⁶ 'the glory which I had with thee before the world was . . . I manifested [ἐφανέρωσα, aor.] thy name'). The εἰς in this case may either simply be used for ἐν, after the fashion of the *constructio prægnans* (cf. Mk 13⁹· ¹⁶, Ac 7⁴ 8⁴⁰), or, as Godet and Westcott think (*Comm. in loc.*), may point to a relationship not of simple contiguity merely, but of perfect communion realized through active intercourse. The Father's bosom is not a place but a life. 'The Son *is* there, only because He plunges into it by His unceasing action; it is so with every state which consists in a moral relation' (Godet, *ib.*).

LITERATURE.—Grimm-Thayer, *Lex.*, *s.v.* κόλπος; the Comm. on the various passages; Hastings' *DB*, artt. 'Dress,' 'Abraham's Bosom.'   J. C. LAMBERT.

BOTTLE.—This is the AV rendering (RV 'wine-skin') of ἀσκός, which denotes the tanned skins of sheep and goats that are used in the East for holding water, oil, wine, and cheese (see art. 'Bottle' in Hastings' *DB* i. 311). In the Gospels the allusion to ' bottles ' occurs in connexion with a question that had been addressed to Christ with regard to an observed difference between His disciples and those of John the Baptist and the Pharisees (Mt 9¹⁴⁻¹⁷, Mk 2¹⁸⁻²², Lk 5³³⁻³⁸). A certain outward conformity was expected in religious teaching and example, and the absence of fasting among His disciples seemed to create a perplexing and objectionable departure. The interview takes place immediately after the incident of Levi's feast, when Christ's eating with publicans and sinners was objected to as lowering the standard of the religious life.

The simile reminds us that the life of institutions as of individuals has a limit. It is sufficient for the wine-skin to have once held and matured and preserved its new wine. The attempt to repeat the act of filling and distension involves the loss of both the wine and the vessel which holds it. The most venerated form was once an innovation on what preceded it, and by the operation of the same law a fresh expansive force will again alter external conditions and create new conformities. Christ claims the entire devotion of His disciples, and while the fasting that was largely a commemoration of the past was suspended during His presence, it would receive in days to come a fresh impulse from His absence.

The important truth taught by the simile of the wine-skin and its contents is emphasized by the twofold fact that religious forces are the most expansive of all, and that their receptive forms often attain to a degree of rigidity which preserves the outward shape after the contents have been withdrawn. With regard to the principle of fasting, the affinity of mind and body that connects sorrow with sighing (Is 35¹⁰) abundantly authorizes the observance under naturally suitable circumstances, but fasting by statute has usually been found to be linked, both as cause and effect, with ecclesiastical segregation and asceticism.

LITERATURE.—Bruce, *Parabolic Teaching*, p. 295 ff., *Galilean Gospel*, p. 180 ff. ; F. W. Robertson, *The Human Race*, p. 190 ff.

G. M. MACKIE.

BOY (the word).—In the AV this word does not occur in the Gospels, nor indeed in NT, and only three times in OT (Gn 25²⁷, Jl 3³, Zec 8⁵). We usually have ' male child ' for a very young boy, and ' lad ' for an older one, where ' boy ' would be used in modern English. And RV has retained the older use in most cases.

But there is in modern English an ambiguous use of ' boy.' It sometimes approximates to the sense of ' servant ' (cf. ' doctor's boy '), and in some of our colonies is used of a native male servant irrespective of age. A ' boy ' in this sense may be grey - headed. This force of the word made it suitable as a rendering of παῖς in certain cases. In Mt 8⁵⁻¹³ = Lk 7²⁻¹⁰, the centurion's servant is sometimes described as a δοῦλος (RVm, ' bond-servant ') and sometimes as a παῖς (RVm, ' boy '). RV text keeps the AV ' servant ' throughout for both words. A comparison of Mt 8¹³ with Lk 7¹⁰ shows that the two words apply to the same person. It is in the centurion's *own* speech (Mt 8⁶⁻⁸ = Lk 7⁷) that he refers to the slave who was ' precious unto him ' (Lk 7² RVm) by the milder word. The narrative (except Mt 8¹³) uses δοῦλος, as the centurion himself does in Mt 8⁹, Lk 7⁸. The variation is either a natural simple touch, proving the veracity of the narrative, or it is an instance of the highest art. See art. SERVANT.

As in the above instance παῖς = δοῦλος, so in the narrative of the healing of the epileptic child (Mt 17¹⁴⁻¹⁸, Mk 9¹⁴⁻²⁷, Lk 9³⁷⁻⁴³) we find in St. Matthew and St. Luke (not St. Mark) that παῖς can = υἱός. Here Mt 17¹⁸, Lk 9⁴² RV have ' boy ' in the text, for the AV ' child.' Similar is the use in Lk 8⁵¹⁻⁵⁴, where ἡ παῖς is ' maiden ' and ' maid ' in EV.

Except where the context requires a different rendering, παῖς is usually translated ' servant ' in both versions, and RV often points out occurrences of δοῦλος by putting ' *or* bond-servant ' in the margin. In Jn 4⁵¹ both versions have ' son ' (= παῖς) where RV had far better have put ' boy ' as in the above instance, keeping ' son ' strictly for υἱός.

GEORGE FARMER.

BOYHOOD (Jewish).—So little is recorded on this subject in the Gospels, or in the NT generally, that we are dependent on other sources for our facts. These sources are chiefly the OT, the OT Apocrypha, Josephus, the Talmud, and modern Eastern life. The first of these authorities is too early, and the last two too late, to justify us in basing on them any very positive statements as to Jewish boyhood in the time of Christ. With this caution they are used in the present article. And it will be remembered (1) that the Jewish life of our period was the result of the previous life of the nation ; (2) that Israel is a nation of great conservatism in matters of religion and the home, although receptive of new ideas ; (3) that some of the Apocryphal books were late enough to be products of an age in which Pharisaism, Hellenism, and other Jewish views met each other, much as they did in the early part of the 1st cent. A.D.

i. THE HOME.—Boys, until their fifth year, were under the charge of the women, afterwards they passed under the father's control. We therefore treat the period of boyhood as commencing at the age of five. Although no doubt many mothers retained their influence after the boy's childhood, it is surely a mistake to quote Pr 31¹ in this connexion, as Phillott does (Smith's *DB*¹ i. 305ᵇ).

The special influence implied here is surely that of the queen-mother over an adult reigning king, which, according to Eastern custom, exceeds that of a wife. For there may be many wives, but only one mother of the sovereign. The queen-mother (*gĕbirāh*) is mentioned 1 K 15¹³, 2 K 10¹³, Jer 13¹⁸, and the name of the king's mother is given with emphasis in the account of his accession (1 K 14²¹ 15² etc.). So, in David's lifetime, Bathsheba shows him great outward respect (1 K 1¹⁶), but is seated at Solomon's right hand (1 K 2¹⁹) when the latter is king. Phillott also refers to Herod. i. 136 ; Strabo, xv. 733 ; Niebuhr, *Descript.* p. 24.

More to the point is St. Paul's reference (2 Ti 1⁵ 3¹⁴·¹⁵) to the example and teaching of Lois and Eunice, which no doubt was only one instance out of many of good maternal influence. And the Mosaic law placed the mother on an equality with the father in her claim on the obedience and love of her son (Ex 21¹⁷, Lv 20⁹ etc.). The house-mother of such a family as our Lord's was neither so ignorant, so secluded, nor so debased as the woman sometimes described by travellers in the East. Judaism was not in this respect the same as Mohammedanism. Even now we are told that the home of the Syrian Christian is superior to that of his Mohammedan neighbours. And even among the latter the seclusion of the harem belongs chiefly to the life of the rich. In working and middle-class homes the wife and mother takes her part, as in the West, in the training of the children, and in necessary outdoor business. The OT and the Gospels show this. For instance, ' women's apartments ' are never referred to in the latter. And Christ apparently met the wife of Jairus, the wife of Chuza, Susanna, Martha and Mary, Peter's wife's mother, and others, without the obstructive conditions of zenana life. We lay stress on this, because we believe that views of one side of Eastern life are often applied too widely, and because from this freer, higher status of woman in Israel there followed her greater fitness for wifehood and motherhood. We believe that in Galilee, at least, an almost Western freedom of intercourse between the sexes must be considered in estimating the influences affecting Jewish boyhood.

The period of boyhood, as we understand it for

the purpose of this article, was from the 5th to the 13th year. The legal 'coming of age' was at 13 for boys, but 12 or even earlier for girls. But Schürer (*HJP* II. ii. 51 f.) thinks that the definite age was fixed in post-Talmudic times, and that nothing but 'the signs of approaching puberty' settled in earlier times whether a child was bound or not bound to the observance of the Law. We shall consider the ceremonies of this 'coming of age' later on. One thing connected with this date was the power of giving evidence. Schürer quotes the Mishna (*Nidda* v. 6): 'When a child is twelve years and one day old, his oaths are tested; when he is thirteen years and a day, they are valid without further ceremony.' Here, for our period, we may compare the commentators on Jn 9²¹ 'He is of age, ask him; he shall speak for himself.'

ii. PLAY.—The few allusions in the Bible to children's games do not allude specially to those of boys. Zec 8⁵ 'The streets of the city shall be full of boys and girls playing in the streets thereof,' is quite general, and is 500 years too early. The use of *yeled* ('boy') and *yaldāh* ('girl') even leaves a vagueness as to the ages of the children. But the prophet no doubt based his words on the customs and sights of his day, and thus a fairly early period of life is meant. It is *not* said that the sexes were playing together, they might be in different groups. Nature, even in England, soon leads to this, and the early ripening of the East must be remembered. Therefore, soon after the period of infantile games, comes that of sports practised by each sex alone, and in the case of boys 'manly' exercises soon follow, if practised at all. In many parts of the East the climate is often quite unsuited for the 'school-boy' games of Northern lands. The absence of these is noticed by the teachers of many Mission schools. But in this respect there must be great differences. That lassitude which is true of children in Bombay, for instance, cannot at all seasons apply to those of Nazareth, which is about 1500 feet above sea-level. A caution is necessary when such excellent books as Lane's *Modern Egyptians*, dealing chiefly with Cairo, or even works on Persia or India, are used not merely to illustrate the Bible, but to add to the descriptions in it.

There were, of course, in the 1st cent. A.D. athletic sports and physical exercises in some of the large towns of the Holy Land. But these were so connected with Hellenic immorality that they were offensive to every pious Jew. They were chiefly confined to the cities which had a large heathen population, and we cannot imagine a gymnasium at Nazareth or Hebron. At Jerusalem, during the high priesthood of Jason (B.C. 173), a gymnasium was set up, and 'the very priests forsook their service at the altar and took part in the games of the palæstra' (Schürer, I. i. 203; 2 Mac 4¹²⁻¹⁴). Tiberias, Jericho, Tarichæa had each a hippodrome or a stadium (Schürer, II. i. 33). Had the exercises for which these buildings were erected commended themselves to the Jews, the older boys would soon have emulated their adult countrymen as far as possible, just as English boys are cricketers and footballers because Englishmen are so. But Judaism completely condemned the exercises in which Greeks and Romans delighted. By their history as well as by their surroundings and details these exercises were connected with heathenism and apostate Judaism (Jos. *Ant.* xv. viii. 1). No son of pious Jewish parents could copy even the innocent side of these exercises (Brough, 76, 77). See art. GAMES.

An older boy in districts like Upper Galilee or the hill country of Judæa would find much physical exertion called for by the contour of the country. Almost every journey implied hill-climbing. Moreover, there were (and are) in many parts of Palestine many minor field-sports practised, such as the snaring of small birds, which would form a pastime for older lads. Skill in *slinging* (Jg 20¹⁶, 1 S 17⁴⁰, 2 K 3²⁵, 1 Ch 12², Job 41²⁸⁽²⁰⁾, Pr 26⁸ [AV, RVm], 1 Mac 6⁵¹) could be obtained only by early training and practice. The same remark applies to the *archery* so often mentioned in the OT. That both these accomplishments were maintained in NT times may be believed from the many references to bowmen and slingers in Josephus (*BJ, passim*). But specific references to these arts as boyish exercises are apparently wanting.

Young English children play at 'horses,' 'school,' 'work,' 'mothers,' etc., which we may call *games of imitation*. The Talmud alludes to these; and our Lord noticed the little children playing at marriages and funerals (Mt 11¹⁶· ¹⁷, Lk 7³²). These would be played by *young* children of both sexes.

It is curious that the Apocryphal Gospels have a legend about our Lord modelling birds out of moist clay (*Syr. Boyhood of the Lord Jesus* 1, pseudo-Matthew 27, Thomas 11, *Arabic Gospel of the Infancy* 36 etc., in B. H. Cowper's *Apocryphal Gospels*). Some of these accounts describe our Lord's playmates as also modelling objects. While we reject the miraculous statements that our Lord endued these figures with life, we may accept the narratives as based on actual childish games. It is indeed said that Judaism would have shrunk from any representation of animate beings (Schürer, II. i. p. 36), but there is no proof that all good Jews took a puritanical, Pharisaic view of the prohibitions of the Law; and even if the Judæo-Christian Apocryphal Gospels are absolutely wrong in describing this modelling as a specimen of our Lord's play in childhood, they may be right in using it as an element in a picture of Palestinian infancy. Are the children of orthodox Jews now forbidden the use of dolls or wooden horses?

In *PEFSt*, April 1899, p. 99, is an account, with illustrations, of three soft limestone slabs, resembling draught-boards, found in the excavations at Tell Zakarîya. One is complete, measuring 23 cm. × 20 cm. (about 4½ in. × 4 in.) and 7 cm. thick. It is ruled (incised) so as to form 144 squares of irregular size. The other two are fragments only. They belong to the Greek period. Such draught-boards have also been found at Gezer and at Tell-es-Sâfi. Some have fewer squares, and clearly there were various arrangements of the squares (*PEFSt*, Oct. 1900, p. 321; Oct. 1903, p. 300). A collection of small waterworn pebbles, each about the size of an ordinary ivory card counter and three times as thick, was found in the lower Jewish stratum at Gezer. These were either draught-men, or counters for calculation (*PEFSt*, Oct. 1903, p. 300).

Two small draughtsmen of green enamelled paste (possibly Egyptian), found at Gezer, are described *PEFSt*, Oct. 1903, p. 213, and pl. ii., figs. 25, 26). Others of pottery of local manufacture have also been discovered.

iii. SCHOOL.—The majority of Jewish boys were as unable to study in the *bêth ha-Midrāsh* as the majority of our population are to procure a University training (Ac 4¹³, Jn 7¹⁵· ⁴⁹, and, on the other hand, Ac 22³ etc.). In any case this higher education belonged to an age beyond boyhood. Elementary schools, however, existed at least wherever there was a synagogue. In them reading was certainly taught; and even if Scripture was the only text-book, the knowledge thus acquired would avail in other directions. Writing also was taught, probably as a help to the reading more than for its own sake (Jn 8⁶· ⁸ compared with 7¹⁵ show that it was an 'elementary subject'). Arithmetic, etc., is not mentioned in our authorities, but some acquaintance with it is, of course, a probable part of the course. It would be of more interest to know if Greek was ever taught in the synagogue schools of Palestine. It must have been so necessary in the many bilingual districts. It was the means of communication between the natives and the Roman authorities.

A training in a foreign or in a dead language is always a mental advantage. Even if Greek were not taught to most Jewish boys, Hebrew was; and the Hebrew of the OT which we know they studied was not the Hebrew (Aramaic) which they spoke in their homes (*e.g.* Mk 5⁴¹). If only the mother-tongue was used, then the Scriptures were read (or verbally taught) in a Targum.

According to the Jewish authorities, the elementary or synagogue school was called the *bêth ha-Sêpher*, 'house of the book' (*i.e.* the Scriptures), to distinguish it from the *bêth ha-Midrāsh* or *bêth ha-Talmūd*, theological colleges where the Rabbinical explanations and additions were taught. The teacher of the school was usually the *hazzān* or servant of the congregation (Lk 4²⁰; *Shabbath* i. 3).

An elementary native Mohammedan school at the present day, where the instruction is reading and writing Arabic, and the study of the Koran, will give us an idea of the probable methods. The scholars sit cross-legged at their teacher's feet, he being slightly above them (Lk 2⁴⁶, Ac 22³, cf. Mt 5¹). The letters are first taught by tracing with a stick in sand. All reading is aloud, and in a kind of rhythmical chant or drone. Even in after life the sacred Book is always read aloud, and so Philip (Ac 8³⁰) *heard* the eunuch reading his roll of Isaiah. The discipline is of the sternest kind, corporal punishment being freely used. Does a foundation of fact, or at least *vraisemblance*, lie beneath the legends of our Lord's treatment by His schoolmaster? (Gospel of pseudo-Matthew 31; Gospel of Thomas 14. 15; *ib.* (Latin) 12. 13 etc.). It is noticeable how the Lord and His Apostles silently ignore all such advice about the training of children as we find in Pr 13²⁴ 19¹⁸ 23¹⁰, Sir 30¹⁻¹³. We believe that Judaism, like some sections of Christendom, had read such OT passages too literally, or applied them too severely, and Eph 6⁴ is much more in the spirit of the Gospel.

How far was elementary education universal and compulsory? The Jewish tradition asserts that it was both (cf. Jerus. *Kethuboth* viii. 11, quoted in Schürer, II. ii. 49). Schürer concludes that schools were general in the time of Christ; and thinks that the tradition is by no means incredible that Joshua, the son of Gamaliel (1st cent.), enacted 'that teachers of boys should be appointed in every town, and that children of the age of six or seven should be brought to them.' At least it is possible that education was fairly universal in our Lord's day, within the limits indicated above. See, further, art. EDUCATION.

iv. RELIGIOUS INSTRUCTION AND PRACTICE.— Although the school education was on a religious basis, it does not appear to have clashed with or superseded the religious teaching of the home. The responsibility remained with the parents. This was in accordance with the OT and especially the Pentateuch, which gives no commands for formal religious instruction (schools, tutors, etc.) as in later Judaism. But it is clearly laid down in the Law and OT generally that children are to be taught (cf. Gn 18¹⁹ (J), Ps 44¹ 78³⁻⁶, Dt 4⁹ 6⁷ 11¹⁹ 32⁴⁶). The Wisdom books imply parental teaching only (Pr 1⁸ 2¹ 3¹ 4¹ 7¹ 10¹ 13¹ 15²⁰ 22⁶ 23²²⁻²⁵ 29¹⁷, Sir 3. 7²³ 30³ etc., also To 4 and 14, *passim*). We notice in Ex 12²⁶ff· 13⁸ the direction that the people were to join the instruction of the children in the history and meaning of the Passover with the feast itself. In Ex 13¹⁴⁻¹⁶ the presentation of the firstborn is made another opportunity for such instruction. It is the fathers who have the religious instruction of young Israel in their hands, for other rites, ceremonies, festivals would naturally be explained to the children in like manner. Not by catechisms, reading lessons, tasks learned, or dry instruction in a school, but by sharing in the ritual worship, with interest aroused for the coming explanations offered, which were based on the history, were the children taught.

Many occasions presented themselves for such teaching as arises from the child's own inquiries and interest. There were the suggestive little rolls of parchment hung up in the doorway (the *mězūzôth*) and the phylacteries (*těphillin*) worn on the forehead and wrist (Dt 6⁹ 11²⁰ and Ex 13⁹· ¹⁶, Dt 6⁸ 11¹⁸· ²⁰). See art. PHYLACTERIES. Another opportunity for religious instruction without set lessons was given by the wearing of the fringes (*zizith*), Nu 15³⁷⁻⁴¹. See art. BORDER. The feasts observed at home and in the synagogue, and the pilgrimages to Jerusalem also afforded opportunities for oral and interesting instruction on the part of the parents. Though Judaism is a ritualistic and ceremonial religion, teaching through the eye in a way well adapted to the capacities of children, the ritual and ceremonies are largely for the home. The master of the house, the boy's father, did and does much more than 'conduct family prayer.' Although the Passover was held at Jerusalem, the greater part of the service and all the sacred meal were celebrated in private houses and family circles. The outward forms of religion at least met the boy in his home more than they do with us. There were more opportunities for a pious parent to do the duty which we have seen was cast upon him by the Law and by the customs of Israel.

Moreover, the Biblical history occupied the place of national history, of ballad poetry, of folk-lore tales, and of all that, in ages before the invention of printing, took the place of our 'children's literature.'

In many cases, no doubt, perhaps in most, Haggadistic embellishments were made to the OT narratives, some of which have perhaps crept into one or both of our present Biblical recensions, that of Palestine and that of the Dispersion. Ruth as a scarcely altered love-tale; Judith and Jonah, allegorical fictions; Esther, especially in its Greek form, a greatly amplified history, are instances of books which we now have in written forms, but which were once the 'fireside stories' (to use a Western phrase) of many Jewish homes. Here, rather than in a purposeful foolishness of the Rabbis, was probably the source of much that is strange and *bizarre* in Jewish literature.

Who would listen so attentively to the father or old grandfather telling his evening story when work was done as the young boys and girls in the outer part of the family circle? The story-telling taste of the East is a well-known fact (witness the *Arabian Nights*); true history and the truth of God were probably taught orally in a somewhat analogous manner.

Religious instruction was aided in two other ways. No one can doubt that the historical Psalms (78. 81. 105. 106. 114) as well as the alphabetical ones (9–10. 25. 34. 37. 111. 112. 119. 145) were well adapted for use by young people, even if they were not composed expressly for the purpose of assisting those who were to learn them by heart. The 'Hymn of the Fathers' (Sir 44–50) has apparently a similar object. It is far too long for liturgical use, of which besides there is no record.

And, lastly, the synagogue services, with the lections from the Law (Ac 15²¹) and the Prophets (Lk 4¹⁷⁻²⁰, Ac 13¹⁵), filled their place in the training of a Jewish boy. It is in the highest degree unlikely that every household, even every pious household, possessed rolls of all the OT books. There was not perhaps a definite 'Canon' in our modern sense. More families would possess the 'Law,' but expense would prevent even this being universal. The oral teaching at home, the reading in school, and the hearing in the synagogue,—all had a share in producing that knowledge of the Jewish Bible which, as we see in the Gospels, was possessed even by working men like the fishers of Bethsaida (Lk 9⁵⁴ etc.). But the oral teaching, however and wherever it had been given, is clearly referred to in Mt 5²¹· ²⁷· ³³· ³⁸ (*heard* not *read*) 17¹⁰ (hearsay of Mal 4⁵· ⁶). Our Lord constantly referred to OT incidents (Mt 6²⁹ 8⁴ 12⁴⁰· ⁴¹· ⁴² etc.) as to facts well known by the multitudes. (Do all Mohammedan families possess a Koran? Yet they know their faith). But then He also referred to *haggādôth* (Mt 8¹¹) and to the OT Apocrypha (Lk 6⁹, cf. 1 Mac 2³²⁻⁴¹) in much the same way. The contrasted phrase, 'Have ye never *read*?' (Mt 21¹⁶· ⁴² 22³¹ etc.), was said to the religious leaders, who would have more advantages and opportunities than the bulk of the population, and who were supposed to study the *written* Revelation.

Up to the age of 12 or 13 a Jewish boy was called *ḳāṭān* ('little') or *tinōḳ* (cf. both words used of school children in passages quoted by Schürer, II. ii. 49 ff.).

The second word is a form of יוֹנֵק *yônēk*, suckling (יָנַק to suck), which however is used of schoolboys in the Talmud; and this meaning has clearly been reached by a language-change similar to that by which *infant* has come in English law to mean, in spite of its etymology, a person who may be twenty years old.

At the age mentioned above, the Jewish boy became bound to fulfil the Law. He was therefore called a 'son of the Law' (*bar-miẓvāh*), or a 'son of the Precept,' and the ceremony in which he was recognized as such by the community was naturally regarded as important and interesting.*

Opinions differ as to how much of the Law and the Precepts a boy was bound to observe before this ceremony. Probably there was no uniformity. The practice for sons of Pharisees is naturally the one recorded for us, rather than the popular one. And probably also the exact period when the fullest obligations fell on the boy was not fixed at first, but was settled individually (as Schürer suggests) by the appearance of signs of approaching manhood. We must remember that Orientals attain physical maturity at an earlier age than we do.

Later on, when the age of 13 was fixed, the Rabbis found support for it, or rather for that of 12. At that age Moses was said to have left the house of Pharaoh's daughter (but cf. Ex 2¹¹ with Ac 7²³). They taught that Samuel was 12 when he began to prophesy (1 S 1²⁴ is followed by 2¹⁹· ²¹, implying an interval of some years before 3⁴, at which time Samuel was old enough to open the doors of the house of the Lord, 3¹⁵. The age is also stated by Jos. *Ant.* v. x. 4). Solomon was (absurdly enough) said to have been 12 years old when he gave his judgment (1 K 3¹⁶⁻²⁷). The only instance which was not entirely founded on conjecture or tradition is that of Josiah's age when he carried out his reform, 2 Ch 34³ (not in 2 K 22³). These instances all look like attempts to date the origin of the Rabbinical rule further back into OT times.

According to modern rule, the boy must be 13 years old and a day. He is then presented in the synagogue on a Sabbath, called 'the Sabbath of Phylacteries' (*těphillîn*) because the boy is then invested with them, and wears them in prayer, and is bound to observe the feasts and fasts. In olden days the obligation to attend the feasts at Jerusalem perhaps became binding after this ceremony. Women and children were exempt by the Law ('all thy males,' Dt 16¹⁶). But Schürer (II. ii. 51) quotes a decision of the school of Shammai as to the meaning of 'child' (*ḳāṭān*): 'Every one who cannot yet ride on his father's shoulders from Jerusalem to the temple mount'; while the school of Hillel said: 'Every one who cannot yet go up from Jerusalem to the temple mount led by his father's hand.' We think that Lk 2⁴² neither affirms nor denies any previous visits of Christ to the temple, either annually or three times a year. The fact that His life had been in danger in Judæa (Mt 2¹³· ¹⁶· ²²) might lead Joseph and Mary to observe the rule less strictly than they otherwise would have done. Perhaps boys who lived at or near Jerusalem did more than the provincials. If Joseph went up alone annually he probably did as much as most of his Galilæan neighbours. The Jews of the Dispersion certainly only went up annually (usually at Pentecost), if they went more than once or twice in a lifetime. St. Paul had omitted many years (Ac 24¹⁷), although a strict observer himself of the Law.

In modern times the Jewish boy reads (or rather *sings*) the lesson, and gives the blessing for the first time at the *bar-miẓvāh* ceremony in the presence of his relatives and the congregation. It is to his parents a time of joy and honour, and as he intones the holy words, the prayers of his pious friends are offered. Was this reading by the boy a custom in the 1st century? If the ceremony existed at all, it probably was a part of it, and Lk 4¹⁶· ¹⁷ implies that the Carpenter had officiated many times before. The first occasion may well have been at the close of boyhood.

Nowadays also the presiding Rabbi usually gives an address garnished with personal allusions. Presents to the boy from his friends, and a feast at the parents' house follow the ceremony. Much in the whole service may well be ancient, and date from before the time of Christ; but the absolute silence of the NT, Philo. and Josephus on the subject prevents our being positive about it.

To those boys who lived far from the capital and temple the periodical visits must have been of great importance, apart from their religious purpose, and if their homes were in quiet villages,

* The expression *bar-miẓvāh* has been found in the Talmud, but does not seem to have become used generally for an adult till the Middle Ages (cf. Schürer, II. ii. 51, 52 note 38, and his authorities).

the crowds at the feasts would arouse their keenest interest. They would also see the luxury of the rich, the noisy bargaining of traders, and signs of that imperial power which, however it was hated, was the great *fact* of the time.

v. WORK.—Every well brought-up Jewish boy was taught an occupation. This may have arisen from the many warnings against idleness in the Wisdom books of the OT (Pr 6⁶· ¹¹ 10⁴· ²⁶ 12²⁴). 'Abundance of idleness' (RV 'prosperous ease') is noted in Ezk 16⁴⁹ as a cause and concomitant of sin, and the Rabbis appear to have realized the truth about the usefulness of manual labour to much the same extent as did the founders and leaders of Western monasticism. Rabban Gamaliel III., son of R. Judah ha-Nasi, said: 'For exertion in both (the study of the Law and labour) keeps from sin. The study of the Law without employment in business must at last be interrupted, and brings transgression after it' (*Aboth* ii. 2; Schürer, II. i. 318, § 25). Another said: 'He who teaches not his son a trade teaches him to be a thief.'

St. Paul's father was wealthy enough to give him a good Greek education at Tarsus (probably) and a Rabbinical one at Jerusalem. His wealth is also implied in Ph 3⁷· ⁸, if that passage refers, as some commentators think, to St. Paul's being disinherited for his Christianity. His private means somehow disappeared, so that he had to depend either on the contributions of others or on his labour. But he had a trade to fall back upon (Ac 18³, 1 Th 2⁹, 2 Th 3⁸). And the warnings about idleness in the NT were addressed by him to Gentile Churches, rather than by him or other Apostles to Jewish converts (Eph 4²⁸, 2 Th 3¹⁰⁻¹²). Our Lord was not only the carpenter's son, but the carpenter (Mk 6³); and Justin Martyr speaks of ploughs and yokes having been made by Him (*Trypho*, 88). But His earthly condition was not wealthy; and this may have been the case with Aquila (Ac 18³), as it probably was with the fisher-Apostles of Galilee. See, further, artt. TRADES, WORK.

LITERATURE. — J. Brough, *The Early Life of Our Lord*, London, Murray, 1897 (a full, well-arranged and useful compilation, but needing careful testing, as authorities divided by many centuries are used in the same paragraph without a word of caution); F. Delitzsch, *Artizan Life in Nazareth*; Schürer, *GJV*³ [Eng. tr. *HJP*] *passim*; Lightfoot, *Hor. Heb. et Talmud.*; Schwab, *Le Talmud de Jérusalem*; Joseph Simon, *L'Éducation, etc., chez les anciens Juifs*; the 'Lives of Christ' by Edersheim, Didon, Farrar, Keim, Geikie, etc. (the remark on Brough's work applies to some of these also); the relevant articles in the Bible Dictionaries and Encyclopædias; Keil, *Biblical Archæology*, ii. 175 ff. § 111; the *Heb. Archäol.* of Nowack and of Benzinger, *s.v.* 'Familie.'

Much 'local colour' is to be gained from the works of travellers in Palestine—Kitto, Tristram, Robinson, etc., and from the issues of the *PEFSt.*　　　　　　　GEORGE FARMER.

BOYHOOD OF JESUS.—1. *The Biblical data.*—The preceding article expresses the present writer's ideas as to religious training, education, and recreation in the time of Christ. The Gospels tell us nothing except by inference. The complete absence of *haggādôth, i.e.* such religious fiction as we find in the Talmud, from our Lord's teaching, implies either want of training in it, or positive rejection of it. But Christ acquired such a knowledge of the Old Testament, and perhaps of some books outside the Palestinian canon, that the teachers in the temple 'were astonished at his understanding and answers' (Lk 2⁴⁷). We do not doubt that Scribism and Rabbinism had begun, and had a considerable following. But we doubt if it had made such progress that a good Israelite in the provinces, living in private life, was bound to live and to order his household according to the rules laid down and enforced by the leaders of the nation in the next and following centuries after the great upheaval of the Jewish war with Rome. Then, by political necessity, the 'traditions' of a sect became the life of a nation. Perhaps, also, Christianity took out of Judaism those pious souls who were 'zealous of the law,' but not necessarily so of the 'traditions,' and there were left only those leaders and followers whose sayings supply us with the picture of 2nd century Judaism (cf. Schürer, *HJP* II. i. § 25, 'Scribism'—especially pp. 365–379). Yet it must be admitted, in favour of a contrary view, that Peter at least was guided by some rules which went beyond those of the OT, and which came from the scribes, Pharisees, and Rabbis (Ac 10²⁸; Gal 2¹²—eating with non-Jews). But if any pious persons and households were as yet free from the Rabbinical 'yoke of bondage' (Gal 5¹), surely that freedom was to be found in the household of Nazareth. A protest is needed, because some writers illustrate (?) Christ's early life entirely by Rabbinical rules. The many illustrations from Jewish books which are brought forward to prove that all Jewish boys learnt a trade are hardly needed to prove that Christ did so. Apart from Mk 6³ (the only passage in which He is called ὁ τέκτων, and not merely ὁ τοῦ τέκτονος υἱός), common sense would teach us that He who deigned to live in a carpenter's household, under real human conditions, in His youth, would help Joseph, and learn the art he practised. This is implied in His subjection to Joseph (Lk 2⁵¹). Perhaps the parable of the Mote (chip or splinter) and Beam (Mt 7³⁻⁵) derives its outward form from the work of His youth (cf. Justin Martyr, *c. Tryphon.* 88).

During the stay at Nazareth, where Joseph and Mary settled after their return from Egypt (Mt 2²³), the Babe (τὸ βρέφος, Lk 2¹⁶) passed into the stage of young boyhood. He grew in bodily height (ηὔξανε, Lk 2⁴⁰) and in bodily strength (ἐκραταιοῦτο, Lk 2⁴⁰). The omission of πνεύματι in this verse by אBDL Vulg. and most crit. edd. takes away any ground for discussing its meaning. The next words πληρούμενον σοφίας (or σοφίᾳ) imply a gradual, progressive filling.* What does 'wisdom' mean? Just as any manifestation of 'supernatural' power was out of place in this stage of our Lord's life, so would have been any such manifestation of knowledge, of adult acquirements, of power to instruct others, or of any other form of 'wisdom' which was clearly unsuitable to His age. He was the perfect child, with the perfection suited for each successive stage of childhood. And others recognized and valued this, no doubt (cf. 'in favour . . . with men,' Lk 2⁵²). But nothing occurred in His childhood (or later, up to the time of His beginning His ministry) to prevent His neighbours being astonished when His work began, and wondering at His words and works, which clearly were new to them and unexpected by them (Mk 1²⁷ 2¹² 6²⁻⁶ etc.).

Had it been found that He knew all human knowledge (*e.g.* reading, writing, arithmetic) without any instruction, there would have been a contradiction to the above facts. The σοφία then was (as we should expect in this Hebraistic passage) the opposite to 'folly' in the OT sense. As each fresh experience of life, each external difficulty (perhaps temptation) from His environment came on, *pari passu*, with His growth, there was heavenly wisdom to meet it. Tact, gentleness, veracity, the 'soft answer,' were the sort of things which distinguished Him from other lads, and not miraculous knowledge, or miraculous power such as is described in the Apocryphal Gospels.

'*And the grace of God was upon him.*' God's favour was clearly upon Him, as had been foretold in Is 11². ³. Men noticed (Jn 1¹⁴) that He was full of grace and truth. But we must remember that

---

* The reading is doubtful. Treg. and WH prefer σοφίᾳ, and Lachmann gave it in his margin, supported by אᶜBL pl; and this, as the more unusual construction, may be right.

it was a gift to His human nature, and therefore words are used which are used of His brethren (*e.g.* Ac 6⁸ Στέφανος δὲ πλήρης χάριτος). At the end of the next section St. Luke (2⁵²) tells how He progressed in favour (χάρις) also with men.

'*And his parents went every year to Jerusalem at the feast of the Passover*' (Lk 2⁴¹). From our Lord's own presence at other feasts, both of Divine and human appointment, and from the large crowds at them, we are led to reject the idea that pious Jews at this time went to Jerusalem only for the Passover. No doubt the greatest attendance was at that feast, and those who could attend only one probably chose it. Jews resident outside the Holy Land seem, probably on account of the more favourable season for travelling, to have preferred Pentecost (Ac 2¹⁻¹¹ 18²¹ 20¹⁶ 21²⁷ 24¹⁸, 1 Co 16⁸). We think it probable, therefore, that the emphatic words of the sentence are οἱ γονεῖς. Joseph *may* have gone at other seasons; at this season Mary usually (ἐπορεύοντο, imperfect of 'habit') accompanied him. Women were not *bound* to attend any feast (Dt 16¹⁶ 'all thy males'). Jn 7². ⁸⁻¹⁰ show that the 'brethren of the Lord' attended the feast of Tabernacles, which may be an indication of what Joseph's custom was. But if women went to any one feast, it would be, if possible, to the Passover, partly because it was the most esteemed, partly because the Supper (both sacrificial and social) was an essential element in it, and partly because of the examples of Peninnah and Hannah (1 S 1³. ⁷. ²¹).

In Lk 2⁴² we are told of Christ going with them, being twelve years old. Does this imply that He had never been with them before? We doubt it. The mention of His age may be made only in order to mark at what period of His life the incident which follows occurred. The commentators, etc., lay great stress on His having become a 'son of the Law' or a 'son of the Precept,' and represent this Passover visit to Jerusalem as a sort of 'First Communion' after a sort of 'Confirmation.' The whole of the legislation about the *bar-mizvah* dates *after* the destruction of the Jewish polity in A.D. 70 (cf. Schürer, *HJP* II. ii. 51 f.). There may have been earlier traces of it in Pharisaic Judæan circles. Besides, when a definite age for 'full membership' of the Jewish community was fixed, it was at thirteen, and not at twelve years of age. The current views would never have been brought forward, but for the assumption by the elder Lightfoot and others that in this Talmudic rule we find the explanation of the mention of our Lord's age.

Moreover, are there any Biblical grounds for supposing that a child of five, or ten, or any other age, might not be present at the Passover, and eat of the Paschal lamb? Ex 12³. ⁴ rather implies the contrary, for if all children under thirteen were excluded, few households would be large enough to consume a yearling lamb. If the custom of the present Samaritans is any guide, it is stated that even little girls eat of the lamb (cf. J. E. H. Thomson in *PEFSt*, 1902, p. 91).

But if it was our Lord's *first* Passover (which St. Luke does *not* say), we can find another reason than the age He had reached for the previous omission. Herod the Great had tried to kill the Child, Archelaus was considered by Joseph to be as dangerous, and therefore Jesus was kept out of his dominions. Now Archelaus was in exile; in 759 A.U.C. a Roman governor had been appointed over Judæa, and Roman law and justice, however defective at times, at least ensured safety for the Boy who had been sought for ten or eleven years before as an Infant. Of course, it is possible that the later Jewish rule prevailed in Christ's day, but it does not appear to us to be *proved*, either from St. Luke's words, or from any contemporary or earlier source.

What did our Lord do at Jerusalem? The Biblical accounts of the Passover ritual are mainly confined to the first or Egyptian Passover. This differed naturally from later ones in some respects, and in others a difference had been made by liturgical regulations. For instance, the eating of the lamb in a recumbent instead of a standing posture was a change (Ex 12[11], 1 S 1[9] 'rose up,' Lk 22[14, 15] etc.). So were the psalms, the prayers, the blessings, the four cups of wine, and other well-known customs. One of the best popular accounts of the Jewish ritual is in Bickell's *Messe und Pascha*, of which an English version by Dr. Skene has appeared. He rightly states that our *oldest* source is as late as the end of the 2nd cent. A.D., with large additions from the 11th to the 16th centuries (p. 112 f. Eng. tr.). Bickell also points out that 'the Paschal Lamb was an actual offering. It was slain in the Temple, its blood was sprinkled by the priest on the altar, its flesh was consumed as a sacrificial meal. Therefore, after the destruction of Jerusalem, when the Temple service . . . came to an end, it could no longer be eaten.

'The same thing is true of the Chagiga, the meat of a slain thank-offering, which was wont to be previously brought with the Passover Supper.' And we must remember that the ritual was probably not written down while it was a 'living rite.'[*] The earliest written sources are based on an oral tradition of what had been done a century before.

We may reverently conjecture our Lord's meditations as He saw the lamb sacrificed, and sat down to the Feast. The death of the lamb was a figure of His own death. The feast shadowed forth His feeding His people. Did He as yet know of His destiny? Perhaps it was beginning to unfold itself to His human consciousness (1) by His growing knowledge of His nation's religion, history, and sacred books; (2) by His mother's telling Him some of the incidents of His birth and infancy; (3) by the inner unveiling of His Divine nature to His human nature. We can only conjecture. But His answer to Joseph and Mary (Lk 2[49]) implies some self-knowledge, and perhaps a step in the acquisition of that self-knowledge and consciousness.

On another point we are on surer ground. At the Paschal feast it was customary for the youngest present to ask, 'Why is this night different from all other nights?' adding a mention of some of the ritual acts. 'What mean ye by this service?' (Ex 12[26] 13[7, 8], Dt 6[20]). And the head of the household or company replied by a recapitulation of the history of the Exodus, which in later times was called the Eastern *Haggādā*. No doubt our Lord followed this custom, and no doubt also Joseph gave the explanation, either in the traditional words as handed down to the modern Jews, or in a freer, perhaps a fuller manner (cf. Ex 12[27] 13[8], Dt 6[21-25] 26[5-9]; cf. Bickell, Eng. tr. pp. 118–120). Other details of the Passover ritual in the time of Christ, such as the sop, the cups of wine, and the singing of the Great (or third or final) Hallel, are vouched for by the accounts of the Last Supper given by the Evangelists and by St. Paul.[†] See art. PASSOVER.

* Compare the usual view of the earliest liturgies. We will not therefore dwell on the Jewish accounts of the ecclesiastical amplifications of the Scriptural order, and still less on modern Jewish use. But the present Samaritan customs (mode of dressing the lamb, the spit in form of a cross, the mode of roasting, etc.) are very probably similar to the Jewish rites before the destruction of the Temple. Cf. J. E. H. Thomson in *PEFSt*, 1902, Jan. pp. 82–92, and *Expos. Times*, xi. [1900] 375 (very interesting), and other accounts by Dean Stanley, Mills, Petermann, Vartan, in Baedeker's *Palestine and Syria*, etc.

† Many writers who mention the Great Hallel ignore the various accounts as to the Psalms which composed it; cf.

'*When they had fulfilled the days*' (τελειωσάντων τὰς ἡμέρας). Our first impression is undoubtedly that the whole *seven* days of the Feast (Ex 23[15] etc.) are meant. We should expect pious Jews, like Joseph and Mary, to remain the whole time, not because it was a precept, but out of devotion. 'It was more laudable to remain the whole seven days, especially on account of the last day, which was a Feast Day' (Lightfoot; cf. Ex 12[16]). Edersheim (*Life and Times of Jesus the Messiah*, i. 247) argues that Joseph and Mary set out for home *before* the close of the Feast, because the Talmud says that '*during* Feasts' (not *after* them) 'the members of the Temple Sanhedrin came out on to the terrace and taught the people, contrary to the usual custom of sitting as a court of appeal,' and he thinks that Christ was there. In dealing with this suggestion we have to notice the expression τελειωσάντων τὰς ἡμέρας instead of the ὡς (ὅτε) ἐπλήσθησαν αἱ ἡμέραι of Lk 1[23] 2[6] 2[21, 22], and ἐπλήσθη ὁ χρόνος of Lk 1[57]. The two words are sometimes synonymous in effect, but the distinction between them has been defined as follows: 'τελειοῦν is to complete so that nothing remains to be done, but the thing or work is τέλειον; it implies an end or object (τέλος) to be looked forward to and fully attained. πληροῦν looks at the *quantity* to be done, not at the *end* to be reached, and so is to fill a thing full, so that it lacks nothing.' St. Luke's words are therefore *perhaps* compatible with Joseph and Mary having left on the third day, the so-called *half-holiday*, when it was lawful to return home, but we prefer (in spite of Edersheim's Talmudical argument) to think that they 'stayed to the end' of the Feast. It might be said, however, by those who believe in the earlier return, that our Lord's staying behind was a tacit rebuke, especially if ἐν τοῖς τοῦ πατρός μου (Lk 2[49]) be taken in a *local* sense. St. Luke's use of the simple μένειν in the Gospel and Acts should be noted: the compound occurs only here and in Ac 17[14] in his writings: and in the latter case it is also used *in contrast* to Paul's departure. St. Luke, however, does *not* say that Jesus remained for any such reason, nor that Joseph and Mary lost sight of Him through any failure of duty. Popular books add much to the narrative.

All the pilgrims used to go to the Temple on the day of their departure, by a rule possibly based on 1 S 1[19]. There would be a great crowd, and the temporary separation of a family in the colonnades and on the steps would be (as in great public gatherings now) a natural occurrence, causing little alarm. Possibly Joseph and Mary joined their fellow-travellers from Galilee, in the belief that the Child, who would know the time and point of departure, was among the younger pilgrims. The little fear they felt on the first day (Lk 2[44]) rather supports the view mentioned above, that it was not Jesus' first Passover.

Our Lord's 'parents' (γονεῖς, Lk 2[43]—'Joseph and his mother' is a correction in the interests of orthodox dogma), being ignorant of His having stayed behind, went therefore a day's journey towards home. As we do not know the route they travelled by, it is impossible to say that they went as far as Beeroth (Farrar, *Life of Christ*, and others). Jericho is quite as probable a resting-place.

The search among the kinsfolk and acquaintances being in vain, they returned to Jerusalem, and found Him 'after three days' (probably from

Bickell, pp. 126, 127. They are not justified in saying which Psalm or Psalms our Lord used. Ps. 136 has the general support. The Babylonian Gemara mentions Ps 23. The 114th Psalm, which Christian tradition (cf. the name of its tune, 'Peregrinus') connects with the Passover, cannot have been the one mentioned (Mt 26[30]), as its use occurred *before* the actual supper (Bickell, p. 120). See art. HALLEL.

the time of separation). We need not inquire whether this expression means 'on the third day' (μετὰ ἡμέρας τρεῖς, cf. Mk 8³¹ μετὰ τρεῖς ἡμέρας).* The search on the road back to and in Jerusalem was a thorough one (ἀναζητοῦντες). There must have been many persons who could be inquired of with safety, persons in sympathy with the pious hopes of Simeon and Anna (Lk 2²⁵⁻³⁸), though these had probably passed away. It is St. Luke who tells us (2³⁸) that there was a group of pious persons, who looked for *the redemption of Jerusalem*.† As this refers to a period only twelve years previous, Joseph and Mary could easily find some of these residents of Jerusalem, even if the connexion had not been kept up in the yearly Passover visits (Lk 2⁴¹). We think that the reason for Joseph and Mary spending at least a day in Jerusalem before going up to the Temple, was that they *and our Lord* were well known to this group of persons, and that they thought of Him as possibly among friends at Jerusalem, just as they had thought it possible on the first day of the separation that He was among the pilgrims.

Christ in the Temple.—'And it came to pass, after three days they found him in the temple, sitting in the midst of the doctors (RVm ' or *teachers*'), both hearing them, and asking them questions' (Lk 2⁴⁶). By being present at the meeting of the Rabbis, Christ was obeying the counsel of Ben Sira (Sir 6³⁴⁻³⁶), which was possibly a commonplace piece of instruction in pious Israelite families.

'Stand thou in the multitude of the elders;
And whoso is wise, cleave thou unto him,
Be willing to listen to every godly discourse;
And let not the proverbs of understanding escape thee.
If thou seest a man of understanding, get thee betimes unto him,
And let thy foot wear out the steps of his doors.'

A discussion has been raised as to the meaning of 'in the midst' (ἐν μέσῳ). It is usually thought that Christ sat, as scholars did, on the floor, with the Rabbis on a raised bench or divan, arranged perhaps in a semicircle. ἐν τῷ μέσῳ occurs in Ac 4⁷, where it cannot mean more than 'present in a central position where others could see and hear,' yet apart from the members of the court. Kuinoel watered down the expression here to 'in the same room with the teachers.' It has, however, been suggested that the Rabbis, being struck by the searching power of the questions put by Christ, and the depth of knowledge of the Law which they displayed, invited Him to take a seat among themselves, as a mark of admiration, as well as for more convenience in the conversation. If this was so, their action would be somewhat similar to that in a British court of justice where a distinguished visitor, or even witness, is sometimes complimented by an invitation to 'take a seat on the Bench.' It is said that members of the Sanhedrin did sometimes, on extraordinary occasions, admit an inquirer to the same seat as themselves. It would be a probable thing to do, where the youth of the person made him, as in this case, liable to partial concealment among older and taller bystanders.

There is no ground for supposing that Christ *disputed* with the Rabbis. It is clear that He in nowise offended their prejudices on this occasion. All that He said, although remarkable for His age,

* The mystical school of interpreters have pointed out several parallels to this period: (a) Bengel says: 'For the same number of days, when He lay in the grave, He was considered as *lost* by His disciples (Lk 24²¹).'

(b) Another writer says beautifully: 'Seeing Mary sigh for three days for her Divine Son, I see again humanity during the 3000 years of paganism, wandering in search of God.'

† So RV with אB, etc., but cf. AV and AVm. The Vulgate has the more easy *redemptionem Israel*; Amiatinus: *Hierusalem*, and so Peshiṭṭa.

was suitable to it. The mode of higher religious teaching among the Jews seems to have been neither didactic nor catechetical, but by mutual interrogation between the teacher and the scholar. Hence the freedom used by the disciples and others in questioning *their* Teacher. Christ answered some questions and put others, no doubt with all marks of respect to those who 'sat in Moses' seat' (Mt 23²).

What led to Christ's desire to interview the Rabbis at all, and what was the subject of His questions? We can understand His intense interest in the recently celebrated Feast, its history and its meaning. Or, building on His previous knowledge of the Law and the Prophets, and on the current Messianic hopes, He might desire to learn from the Rabbis about the Messiah and the Messianic kingdom. Questions such as those discussed in Mt 2⁴·⁶, Mk 9¹¹, Jn 7⁴² would be raised and would interest Him. Lk 20²². ²⁸⁻³³, Mt 10² give us other authentic instances of the points discussed by the Jewish teachers of that age. It has, moreover, been suggested that on the journey up to Jerusalem, Mary for the first time told Him the story of His birth, of the messages of the angels, of the Magi, of Simeon, of Anna, of the flight into Egypt, and of the dreams of Joseph. It would be an overpowering revelation, for which, however, as an exceptional, though true child, He would be ready.

We are in the realm of pure conjecture, but certainly it might be God's way of revealing to the Divine Child a part of the truth about that Child's nature and mission. That to Him, as to the Church, to the world, and to each of us, the truth should come 'by divers portions and in divers manners' (He 1¹) is a conceivable, and perhaps the most probable theory. And such a revelation, falling on an unusually gifted soul (Lk 2⁴⁰), on a soul infinitely more receptive, because of its sinlessness (Wis 7²². ²³ etc.), than any other soul could be, would quicken into energy His whole life. If this were so, we have an adequate exposition of our Lord's desires, an adequate explanation of His action.

'*All that heard him were amazed* (AV *astonished*) *at his understanding and his answers*' (Lk 2⁴⁷). As, later on, 'never man so spake' (Jn 7⁴⁶), so now, never child so spake. Yet as in the later case there was nothing contrary to true manhood, so now we ought not to think of anything contrary to true boyhood. It is worth noting that while AV has 'astonished' for the feeling of the bystanders (2⁴⁷ ἐξίσταντο) and 'amazed' for that of Joseph and Mary (2⁴⁸ ἐξεπλάγησαν), RV simply reverses the terms. The former word is often rendered 'beside himself,' 'beside themselves,' but it is difficult to express in English the difference between the two verbs.* See artt. AMAZEMENT, ASTONISHMENT.

In spite of the assembly of 'grave and reverend signiors,' Mary's feelings were at once vented in audible address (εἶπε) to her Son: 'Child! why hast thou thus dealt with us? Behold, thy father and I have sought thee sorrowing!' Her trouble overpowered her amazement. No doubt they were proud of Him in their hearts, but Mary thought it necessary mildly to chide Him for having caused them so much anxiety. We say 'chide' as the nearest expression of our thought, but few parents in the East or anywhere else would speak of what

* For ἐξιστάναι, cf. Mt 12²³, Mk 2¹² 3²¹ 5⁴² 6⁵¹, Lk 8⁵⁶ 24²², Ac 27. 12 89.11.13 9²¹ 10⁴⁵ 12¹⁶, 2 Co 5¹³; and for ἐκπλήσσειν, Mt 7²⁸ 13⁵⁴ 19²⁵ 22²³, Mk 1²² 6² 7³⁷ 10²⁶ 11¹⁸, Lk 4³² 9⁴³, Ac 13¹². The context sometimes offers no reason for the choice of one word rather than the other. The latter one may be the weaker of the two; in Mt 19²⁵, Mk 10²⁶ 7³⁷ it needs an adverb to strengthen it. Etymological arguments cannot be pressed with regard to the popular Greek of the 1st century.

they deemed to be a child's error so courteously and with such an absence of 'temper.' We notice that it was Mary who spoke, and this may possibly be urged as a point in favour of the orthodox view of the 'Virgin Birth.' If Joseph had been the natural father of Christ, he would have spoken to a son of that age, at least in addition to the mother. His silence seems to us to balance such expressions as 'thy father and I,' or 'his parents.'* Mary joined Joseph with herself not only in her account of the continuous careful seeking (ἐζη-τοῦμεν), but also in her sorrow.†

We now come to our Lord's reply, which is a veritable *crux interpretum*. There is no variant in the Greek (Τί ὅτι ἐζητεῖτέ με ; οὐκ ᾔδειτε ὅτι ἐν τοῖς τοῦ πατρός μου δεῖ εἶναί με ;). Nor is there any doubt that the words were a reminder (with a slight touch of rebuke) that Joseph was not His father (cf. ὁ πατήρ σου κἀγώ, 2⁴⁸), and that in any case the claims of His Divine Father were paramount. The principal interpretations of ἐν τοῖς τοῦ πατρός μου are : (a) 'in my Father's house'; (b) 'about my Father's business'; (c) 'among my Father's servants and friends'; (d) combinations of (a) or (b) implying an intended vagueness. The Vulg. is *in his quæ patris mei sunt*; the Pesh. supports (a) 'in my Father's house,' having [Syriac text] [But does not *beth* support (c) as much?; cf. 1 S 2³⁰ etc., *i.e.* by Semitic idiom 'house' (as in English) *may* mean family, connexions].

In favour of (a) is the circumstance that τά τινος, which strictly means 'that which is a person's property,' came to be used specially of his house, the word 'house' being omitted. Field and Humphrey compare the colloquialism 'I am going to my father's.' In profane Greek cf. Herod. i. 111, ἐν Ἀρπάγου : Philostratus, *Vita Apollon.* ii. 28, ἐν τοῦ βασιλέως : Lucian, *Philop.* ἐν Γλαυκίου : and many other cases where οἶκος or rather οἰκήματα is to be understood. L. Bos, who collected many of these instances in his work on *Greek Ellipses*, held strongly that πράγμασιν ('business') was not the word to be supplied here. He gave (p. 193) the same explanation of Jn 1¹¹ (16³² 19²⁷) and Ac 21⁶, but in these we find τὰ ἴδια. In the LXX, cf. Est 7⁹ καὶ ὤρθωται ἐν τοῖς Ἀμὰν ξύλον, κ.τ.λ. : Gn 41⁵¹ where πάντων τῶν τοῦ πατρός μου represents the MT 'all my father's house,' and Job 18¹⁹. On the other hand, the supporters of (a) say that no example has been produced in Biblical or profane Greek for 'to be about a person's business' as a rendering of εἶναι ἐν τοῖς τινος, though it is admitted that ἐν τούτοις ἴσθι (1 Ti 4¹⁵) approaches it closely. Origen, Epiphanius, Theodoret, Theophylact, and Euthymius show a chain of commentators, explaining a passage *in their own language*, who take it in the sense of 'house.' Sir 42¹⁰ ἐν τοῖς πατρικοῖς αὐτῆς (Vulg. *in paternis suis*) also seems to support it.

Against this, and in favour of (b), it has been said that Christ did not mean to say 'I could not return, I was in the Temple of God,' but 'My Father's business is the most important thing for Me.' It is also said that 'the necessity of our

Lord's being in His Father's house could hardly be intended by Him as absolutely regulating all His movements, and determining where He should be found, seeing that He had scarcely uttered the words in question before He withdrew with Joseph and Mary from that house, and spent the next eighteen years substantially away from it. On the other hand, the claim to be engaged in His Father's concerns had doubtless both frequently been alleged explicitly in respect of the occupation of His previous home life, and continued to be so during the subsequent periods of His eighteen years' subjection to the parental rule ; His acknowledgment of that claim being in nowise intermitted by His withdrawal with His parents from His Father's house. Intimations of a more general kind seem 'easily capable of being read between the lines of the inspired narrative, which increase the probability that the AV, rather than the RV, expresses the meaning of the Evangelist' (Dr. R. E. Wallis). It should also be noted that the expression 'my Father's house' occurs in Jn 2¹⁶ in plain terms.

In favour of (c) we may quote the words of Jul. Döderlein (*Neues Jahrbuch für deutsche Theologie*, 1892, i. 204): '"In My Father's house" is not correct : Christ soon leaves the Temple. "Business" is little better. . . . Joseph and Mary could hardly have been expected to understand that their child had special work to do for God's kingdom' (*i.e.* at that age). . . . 'Had they sought Him among the good, they would not have needed to seek long. Instead of this, they sought Him ἐν τοῖς συγγενέσιν καὶ τοῖς γνωστοῖς, who afterwards tried to cast Him down from the hill (4²⁸·²⁹), and therefore even then would converse little about God's word : on the other hand, He was to be found ἐν τοῖς τοῦ πατρός μου, who held the office of the Word (Mt 23²), and as such gladly listened to His eager questions . . . the masculine, so to speak, has the first claim on the τοῖς, which is formed from οἱ, not from τά. There is no mention of *things* in the context. . . . In Ro 12¹⁶ Luther, AV and RVm give the masculine, "them of low estate." 1 Co 12⁶ 15²⁸, Col 3¹¹ πάντα ἐν πᾶσιν = "all things in all men," not "all things in all things." In Lk 2⁴⁴ no one would render ἐν τοῖς γνωστοῖς, "in the known places." Again the με at the end of the phrase seems to be antithetical and emphatic. "Among those of My Father must *I* not be?" . . . Not in what *place*, but in what *company* He must be, the anxious ones are able to learn once for all . . . "where men speak of God, I shall surely be found"' (cf. a review in *The Thinker*, 1893, iii. 171 ff.). We think this explanation deserves more consideration than it has received.

The syncretic combination of (a) and (b), as, *e.g.*, by Alford and others, does not commend itself to the present writer. Finally, we should not forget that this conversation is one of the most likely ones in the Gospels to have been held in Aramaic and not in Greek. It will therefore be wise not to lay too much stress on the analogies quoted above on various sides of the question. Even the Greek of these two chapters, as we have it, is noted as Semitic in style, not in St. Luke's classical manner (except, of course, 1¹⁻³). The Pesh., as we noticed above, supports (a). The Sinaitic palimpsest has 'Wist ye not that I must be with my Father ?' (*Expos. Times*, xii. [1901] p. 206).*

Joseph and Mary '*understood not the saying which he spake unto them*' (Lk 2⁵⁰). Therefore He

---

* Where did Alford find ground for saying, 'Up to this time Joseph had been so called ('father') by the holy Child Himself, but from this time never'? It may be so, but it is not recorded.

† ὀδυνᾶσθαι occurs four times in Luke (here, 16²⁴·²⁵, Ac 20³⁸) and nowhere else in NT. 'Sorrowing' (AV and RV) does not seem strong enough. 'With intense anguish' is rather the meaning. Farrar (*St. Luke*) suggests 'with aching hearts.' In Lk 16²⁴·²⁵ AV has 'to be tormented,' but RV 'to be in anguish,' of the sufferings of the rich man in Hades. In Ac 20³⁸ it expresses the grief of the Ephesian elders at parting with St. Paul. The word used in the Peshitta here, is used for στενοχωρία in Ro 2⁹. As ὀδυνᾶσθαι is frequent in Galen, Aretæus, and Hippocrates, it may be one of St. Luke's medical words. We are reminded by it of that later poignant sorrow, commemorated in the 'Stabat Mater.' She felt already the 'sharp and piercing sword.'

* Besides the works quoted above, the reader should consult Field's *Otium Norvicense*, Pars Tertia ; *Expository Times*, x. 484 ; Farrar, *St. Luke* in Cambridge Bible for Schools, 368, 369 (in which he abandons the view taken in *Life of Christ*, i. 78) ; and most reviews and criticisms on the Revised NT generally.

had not learned this from them, nor from other teachers, nor had He previously spoken much, if at all, of the Father. Their difficulty, of course, was not the literal question of grammar which troubles us. It was that they did not so realize the spiritual force of His saying (οὐ συνῆκαν τὸ ῥῆμα).

Although Joseph and Mary understood neither His words, nor His actions, nor Himself, and although His words and actions show that He now knew more than He had done of His Father, of Himself and of His mission, yet 'He went down with them, and came to Nazareth and was subject unto them.' As W. R. Nicoll says : 'He went their messages, did their work, humbled Himself, as if this episode at Jerusalem had never been' (*The Incarnate Saviour*, p. 41). The twelve years of hidden life were followed by another eighteen years of retirement. Even Nathanael, living at Cana, a few miles off, had not heard of Him (Jn 1⁴⁶·⁴⁷). We may be sure that He who would 'fulfil all righteousness' (Mt 3¹⁵) did not omit the yearly attendance at the Passover, and other feasts. He had at least to lead the life of example to His family and to His fellow-townsmen. Although we do not think that He or His were bound by all the rules of Pharisaic or of later Rabbinic Judaism, we may be sure that He did what was usual among pious Jews, partly because He would obey those who sat 'in Moses' seat' (Mt 23²·³), and partly because, like His future Apostle (Ro 14¹⁶, 1 Co 8¹³ etc.), He would put no stumbling-block in anyone's way (Mt 17²⁷).

We know that after Christ's ministry began, He spent much time in prayer, usually secret and for secrecy's sake, on the mountain (Mt 14²³, Mk 1³⁵ 6⁴⁶, Lk 3²¹ 5¹⁶ 9¹⁸·²⁸·²⁹ 11¹). We cannot believe that this communion with His Father began with His ministry. Yet it seems unlikely that Christ in His early childhood would have followed this custom. May we date it from His return to Nazareth in His twelfth year? Then, His claim for liberty to be ἐν τοῖς τοῦ πατρὸς (αὐτοῦ) would not seem to be a claim which either lay dormant for eighteen years ('my Father's business') or which was at once relinquished (by His return) and only taken up at intervals ('my Father's house'), in which case no claim for liberty was needed. Moreover, 'His Father's business' for the next eighteen years was, as the event proved, *preparation*. And this is just what Christ did, and the secret prayer and meditation were part of it. If this custom began, or at least took a larger part in His life then, we can reconcile His words in the Temple with His life in the following years. And if 'house' instead of 'business' be the word to be supplied, we can also believe that He knew that the whole Universe is the Father's house (Jn 14²), and not only the Temple 'made with hands.'

It must also be noted that His growth 'in wisdom' implies not only learning by prayer and meditation, and learning from the written word, but also learning from observation of human life. We learn by these three sources, and He was made like unto His brethren. But for this last source of learning, time and the attainment of greater age are required. Did He know when His active work was to begin? Moses sinned by beginning too soon, but ignorance, and the thought that the right time might be sooner than it was, would be no sin. Yet He who 'was in all points tempted like as we are, yet without sin' (He 4¹⁵), might conceivably be tempted as Moses was. We tread here on difficult ground, and our ignorance, our desire not to err from the Faith, and our reverence for our Lord, bid us say no more. Meanwhile He did His duty in retirement, passing from boyhood into manhood, and waiting for the call which came

later. Was the non-appearance of the forerunner (Mal 3¹) the sign that the time had not come, and his appearance the sign that the time was fulfilled (Mk 1¹⁵)?

'*And his mother kept all these sayings in her heart*' (διετήρει occurs in NT only here and Ac 15²⁹; cf. Gn 37¹¹ of Jacob concerning Joseph. ὁ δὲ πατὴρ αὐτοῦ διετήρησεν τὸ ῥῆμα, where E has the same tense as here διετήρει, perhaps by assimilation). But Jacob lost hope (Gn 37³⁵), while Mary kept these sayings in her heart. It was a close, persistent, faithful keeping, but a keeping in silence, even when it might have changed the attitude of His kinsmen towards Him, or indeed have saved His life. She spoke, no doubt, when the right time came. Stress is laid on her faithfulness and meditation also in Lk 2¹⁹. We may ask whether τὰ ῥήματα included other sayings than the ῥῆμα of Lk 2⁵⁰. The πάντα of some MSS in the place of the ταῦτα of others leads us to think either of other sayings of Christ, or of the remarks of the Rabbis and others about Him (as in Lk 2¹⁹). And though He 'was subject unto them,' the goodness of Joseph and Mary, His own wisdom and advancing years, and now the deepened thoughts Mary had about Him, would surely prevent their making His subjection an obstacle or a hindrance to His development.

Again we read of His progress (Lk 2⁵²), though this refers to a time beyond the Boyhood. The statement about *wisdom* is a continuation of that in 2⁴⁰. The next word ἡλικία is ambiguous. If we take the meaning 'stature' (AV and RV text), it applies only to a part of the time between twelve years of age and thirty. But the margin of AV and RV 'age' would seem to be preferable. Though increase in age is as inevitable as increase in stature, yet St. Luke, having spoken of Christ's twelfth year, goes on to speak of His thirtieth, and characterizes by his transitional passage the whole of those eighteen years as a period of development. He cannot mean our thoughts to stop at the period when adult height was reached. The advance in ἡλικία must grammatically have the same duration as the advance in wisdom, and in favour with God and man.*

2. *Dogmatic conclusions*.—The doctrines of the Incarnation, of the Union of the two Natures in one Person, and of the Kenosis are beyond the limits of this article, though it is impossible to avoid bearing them in mind in dealing with our subject. But an exegetical study of Lk 2⁴⁰⁻⁵² shows a genuine human development of Christ in His boyhood. Body, soul and spirit made regular progress. With other children it is often the irregularity which troubles their older friends. Childishness (in the bad sense), where we expect some measure of intelligence; stupidity, which is sometimes the result of imperfect mental growth, and sometimes the result of the childish sins of laziness and self-will, are the common faults of children. Later on, the desire *not to be subject* to parental, or other restraint, and the premature longing for freedom (not necessarily for evil) are marks of sinful imperfection which we all recognize. Christ was free from them. When He was a child He *lived*, *spake*, and no doubt *thought* as a child, but as a sinless one. The awakening of the human consciousness was gradual. As Oosterzee (on Lk 2) says : 'His recognition of Himself (we add 'and of His mission') formed part of His filling with wisdom. His public ministry did not begin with a sudden impulse, but was prepared for

---

* Mere comparisons with other passages, even in this Gospel, cannot outweigh the above considerations. In 19³ no doubt the *stature* of Zacchæus is referred to ; 12²⁵ and Mt 6²⁷ are doubtful. In Eph 4¹³ 'stature' is probably right. Jn 9²¹·²³ and certainly He 11¹¹ mean 'age.' In the LXX, Ezk 13¹⁸, 2 Mac 4⁴⁰, Job 29¹⁸ seem to bear the same meaning. But Symmachus in Ca 7⁷ must have meant 'stature.'

by His whole life. It was the forgetting or over-looking this which led some early heretics to date the Incarnation from the Baptism. But we see that at the age when childhood passes into youth, Christ was already aware (in part perhaps) of His mission.' 'The consciousness of His Divine Nature and power grew, and ripened, and strengthened, until the time of His showing unto Israel.'

Those who in times of controversy have most firmly held the Divinity of Christ have sometimes found a difficulty in admitting the ideas of growth and development in our Lord. This was specially so in the time before the careful statements of the Great Councils and the Fathers of that period. So Epiphanius (*Hær.* li. 20) states that 'some Catho-lics were inclined to admit the miracles of the Infancy (as in the Apocr. Gospels) as affording an argument against the Cerinthians, and a proof that it was not at His Baptism that Christ was first united to the man Jesus.' Jeremy Taylor (*Life of Christ*, pt. i. § 7) has a passage which is worth quoting : 'They that love to serve God in hard questions use to dispute whether Christ did truly, or in appearance only, increase in wisdom. For, being personally united to the Word, and being the Eternal Wisdom of the Father, it seemed to them that a plenitude of Wisdom was as natural to the whole Person as to the Divine Nature. But others, fixing their belief upon the words of the story, which equally affirm Christ as properly to have " increased in favour with God as with man, in favour as in stature," they apprehend no incon-venience in affirming it to belong to the verity of human nature, to have degrees of understanding as well as of other perfections ; and although the humanity of Christ made up the same Person with the Divinity, yet they think the Divinity still to be free, even in those communications which were imparted to the inferior Nature, and the Godhead might as well suspend the emanation of all the treasures of wisdom upon the humanity for a term, as He did the beatifical vision, which certainly was not imparted in the interval of His sad and dolorous passion.' * See art. CHILDHOOD.

LITERATURE.—The works named in the preceding article and those quoted above. On the *dogmatic* problem see Hooker, *Eccles. Polity*, v. lvi. 10, liv. 6 ; Thomas Aquinas, *Summa*, Pars Tertia, Quæstiones 7–12 ; Dorner, *History of the Development of the Doctrine of the Person of Christ*, on the true growth of the Humanity, Division II. vol. i. 45, 343 ; vol. ii. 89, 125, 139, 204, 213, 214, 281, 285, 287, 365, 368, 432 ; vol. iii. 18, 20, 30, 127, 140, 147, 256. On the Apocryphal stories of the Boyhood see Trench, *Miracles*, Introd. iv. 2 ; Nicolas, *Étude sur les Évan-giles Apocryphes*, Paris, 1865 ; also the 'Lives of Christ' and the Commentaries on St. Luke.

The fact that the passage Lk 24[1ff.] is the liturgical Gospel for the first Sunday after the Epiphany in the Anglican and Roman liturgies, has produced a mass of homiletical and devotional literature, which naturally deals more with the spiritual lessons of the Boyhood of Christ, but which often has other useful matter. We can name only a small portion of this literature : Goulburn, *Gospel of the Childhood, Thoughts upon the Liturgi-cal Gospels*, i. 132, ch. viii. ; Bourdaloue, Sermon for 1st Sunday after the Epiphany ; Duquesne, *L'évangile médité*, i., *Médita-tions* 18, 19, 20 ; Bossuet, *Élévations sur les Mystères*, 20th week, i. to xii. ; Rothe, *Sermons for the Christian Year*, p. 100 ; Gordon Calthrop, in *Quiver*, Dec. 1889 (on Lk 24[49]) ; Vallings, *Jesus Christ the Divine Man*, ch. vi. ; Samuel Cox, *Bird's Nest*, etc. p. 16 ; W. R. Nicoll, *The Incarnate Saviour*, chs. ii. and iii. ; Godet, 'Life of Jesus prior to His Public Ministry' in *Thinker*, vii. 390–404 ; F. W. Robertson, *Sermons*, 2nd ser. p. 175 ff. ; *Expositor*, 2nd ser. viii. [1884] p. 17 ff., 4th ser. iv. [1891] p. 1 ff., 5th ser. ii. [1895] p. 69 ff. ; Liddon, *Bampton Lect.*[8] p. 456 ff. ; Farrar, *Christ in Art*, pp. 271–291.

GEORGE FARMER.

BRASS.—Wherever we find the word 'brass' in the EV, we may be reasonably certain that copper or bronze is intended. Copper was universally used by the ancients, on account of its extreme ductility. In Bible lands it was mined in the region of Lebanon, in Edom, in the Sinaitic pen-insula, where the great Egyptian mines were

* The reference in the last sentence is, of course, to Mt 27[46], Mk 15[34].

located, and in the isle of Cyprus. *Brass* is a fictitious metal, an alloy of copper and zinc ; *bronze* is a mixture of copper and tin. But while in ancient vessels a combination of tin with copper is frequently found, analysis hardly ever reveals the presence of zinc.

1. The word χαλκία in Mk 7[4] (found here only in the NT), AV and RV 'brasen vessels,' may be tr. 'copper vessels,' and is actually so rendered in the German and Dutch versions.

2. The noun χαλκός, tr. 'brass,' is used by Christ in Mt 10[9] 'Get you no gold nor silver nor brass in your purses,' by metonymy for copper coin. χαλκός occurs also in Mk 6[8] 12[41], where it is tr. 'money,' marg. 'brass.'

3. The word χαλκολίβανον, white copper, tr. 'fine brass' (RV 'burnished brass') in Rev 1[15] 2[18] (cf. Dn 10[6]), is descriptively applied to the feet of Christ as He appeared in the vision of St. John in Patmos. There is quite a diversity of opinion as to its correct meaning. Some have supposed it to be that rare metal, more precious than gold, *Orichalcum*, whilst others have thought of frank-incense and even of amber. In this connexion it evidently refers to the strength and stable majesty of the glorified Christ, in the same way as the Heb. *nĕhôsheth* is used in the OT (Ps 107[16], Mic 4[13], Zec 6[1]).

LITERATURE.—Hastings' *DB*, art. ' Brass' ; Smith, *Dict. of Antiq. s.v.* 'Aes' ; Grimm-Thayer, *Lex. s.v.* χαλκολίβανον.

HENRY E. DOSKER.

BREAD.—In Syria and Palestine there are cer-tain shrines and groves that have been preserved undisturbed through times of political change, and are to-day venerated by all the religions of the country. Such also has been the unchanged history of bread in Bible lands. It is to-day practically what it has always been with regard to (1) the materials of which it is made, (2) the way in which it is pre-pared, (3) its importance and use as an article of food, and (4) the symbolism and sanctity suggested by its value.

1. *Materials.*—Bread is usually made of wheat flour, the wheat of the Syrian plains being remark-able for its nutritious quality. An inferior and cheaper kind of bread is also made from barley flour, and less frequently the meal of Indian corn is used.

2. *Modes of preparation.*—The most primitive way is that of making a hollow in the ground, burning twigs, thorn-bushes, thistles and dry grass upon it, and then laying the flat cakes of dough upon the hot ashes. These loaves are about seven inches in diameter and from half an inch to an inch in thickness. The upper surface is frequently studded with seeds of Indian corn, and they are generally turned in the process of baking (Hos 7[8]). They are 'cakes upon the hearth' (Gn 18[6]), 'baken upon the coals' (1 K 17[12. 13]). Such probably were the barley loaves brought to Christ at the feeding of the five thousand (Jn 6[9. 13]). Out of this custom, prevailing among the pastoral tribes and the poorest of the peasantry, were developed several improved methods made possible by more civilized conditions of life. (*a*) Large smooth pebbles were laid over the hollow in the ground, and when the fire had been kept up for a sufficient time, the ashes were removed and the loaves were laid upon the hot stones.—(*b*) Thinner cakes of both leavened and un-leavened bread were made upon a flat pan or convex griddle. These are now made especially at times of religious festival, and are coated on the upper surface with olive oil and sprinkled with aromatic seeds. They recall the 'oiled bread' of Lv 8[26], and the 'wafers anointed with oil' of Ex 29[2] and Lv 2[4].—(*c*) The cavity for the fire is deepened, and a cylindrical hole about the size of half a flour barrel is made of stone and lime with a facing of plaster.

The pebbles are still left at the bottom for the better preservation of the heat, and the same fuel is applied till the oven has been sufficiently heated. The dough is then rolled out into broad thin cakes, and each disc, after being still further distended by being passed with a quick rotatory motion between the hands of the female baker, is laid on a convex cushion or pad, and is thus transferred evenly to the hot wall of the cavity. In a moment it is fired, and as it begins to peel off it is lifted and laid above the others at her side.—(d) The most developed form is that of the public oven in the village or town. Here features of the more primitive types still survive, but the cavity now becomes a low vaulted recess about twelve feet in length, and the pebbles are changed into a pavement of smoothed and squared stones. On it wood and lighter fuel of thorns are burnt, and the glowing ashes are finally brushed to each side of the vault. When the oven has been thus prepared the discs of dough are laid in rows upon long thin boards like canoe paddles, and are inserted by these into the oven, and by a quick jerk of the arm slipped off and placed upon the hot pavement to be fired. These loaves, when fired, are about an inch in thickness and about eight inches in diameter, and when newly baked are soft and flexible.

3. *Use and importance of bread.*—In the West bread is eaten more or less along with the other articles of food that chiefly constitute the meal; but in the East those other articles are rather eaten along with bread, and are regarded as merely accessory to it. When the farmer, carpenter, blacksmith or mason leaves the house for the day's labour, or the messenger or muleteer sets out on his journey, he wraps his other articles of food in the thin loaves of home-made bread. In the case of loaves fired in the public oven, these, owing to the glutinous adhesiveness and elasticity of the dough, and the sudden formation within them of vapour on the hot pavement, puff out into air-tight balls. They can then be opened a little at one side, and the loaf thus forms a natural pouch enclosing the meat, cheese, raisins or olives to be eaten with it by the labourer. As the loaf thus literally includes everything, so bread represents generally the food of man. A great exclusion was expressed in 'Man shall not live by bread alone' (Lk 4⁴). In the miraculous feeding of the multitude (Mt 14¹⁵ff. ‖) it was enough to provide them with bread. It was three loaves of bread that the man asked from his neighbour to put before his guest (Lk 11⁵). Two would have been sufficient for his actual needs; but even in such an emergency a third loaf was required to represent that superabundant something which as a touch of grace, often passing into tyrannical imposition, so deeply affects Oriental social life.

In the act of eating, Oriental bread is broken or torn apart by the hand. This is easily done with the bread of the public oven, as it can be separated into two thin layers. The thin home-made bread is named both in Hebrew and Arabic from its thinness, and is translated 'wafer' in Ex 29²³, Lv 8²⁶, Nu 6¹⁹, 1 Ch 23²⁹ (RV). Such bread is called רָקִיק (*rāḳîḳ*; Arab. *marḳûḳ*, from *waraḳ*, 'foliage,' 'paper'). At a meal a small piece of such bread is torn off, and with the ease and skill of long habit is folded over at the end held in the hand. It thus makes a spoon, which is eaten along with whatever is lifted by it out of the common dish. This is the dipping in the dish (Mt 26²³), and is accomplished without allowing the contents of the dish to be touched by the fingers or by anything that has previously been in contact with the lips of those who sit at meat.

4. *Symbolism and sanctity of bread.*—In a land where communication with other sources of supply was difficult, everything depended upon the local wheat and barley harvest. As this in turn depended upon the rain in its season, which was beyond the control of the sower, a special sanctity attached itself to what was peculiarly a gift of God, and a reminder of His continual and often undeserved care (Mt 5⁴⁵). To the disciples of Jesus, 'Give us this day our daily bread' would seem a very natural petition. An Oriental seeing a scrap of bread on the road will usually lift it up and throw it to a street dog, or place it in a crevice of the wall or on a tree branch where the birds may find it. It should not be trodden under foot in the common dust. Thus the most familiar article of food, so constantly in the hands of all, both rich and poor, and used alike by the evil and the good, had in it an element of mystery and nobility as having been touched by the unseen Giver of all good. How deeply this feeling of reverence possessed the mind of the Lord Jesus is evidenced by the fact that He was recognized in the breaking of bread (Lk 24³⁵).

In the social customs of the East, the giving and receiving of bread has always been the principal factor in establishing a bond of peace between the host and the guest at his table. It was a gravely unnatural offence to violate that law of hospitality. Of this offence Judas Iscariot was guilty at the Last Supper.

In travelling through Palestine and partaking of the hospitality of the peasantry, one may notice in the bread the indentations of the pebbles, and small patches of grey ash, with here and there an inlaid attachment of singed grass or charred thorn, the result of the simple baking process. It is bread, however, the best that the poor can give, and it is given with gladness and the dignity of a high duty towards the guest. When Christ sent forth His disciples to tell of His approach, He charged them to take no bread with them (Mk 6⁸). It would have been a serious discourtesy to have set aside as unfit for their use that which was offered to them willingly by their own people, and would have hindered the reception of the good tidings of the Kingdom.

To the crowd that selfishly followed Christ the giving of bread as by Moses was the sordid summary of Messianic hope (Jn 6³¹). God's gift of natural food to His people enters into the praises of the Magnificat (Lk 1⁵³). When Christ called Himself 'the bread of life' (Jn 6³⁵), He could confidently appeal to all the endeared and sacred associations connected in the East with the meaning and use of bread. In the initiation of the Passover, and in its commemoration afterwards, bread was regarded by the Israelites as the most general and effective symbol of their life in Egypt. In the initiation of the new covenant also the same humble article of food was adopted at the Lord's Supper, to be, with wine, the token of fellowship between Himself and His Church, and the symbol among His disciples of the Communion of Saints. The use of a symbol so familiar and accessible to all, and so representative of common life, seems to suggest that to the mind of Christ some realized and visible communion among the members of His Church was possible and to be expected.

G. M. MACKIE.

BREAKFAST.—Lk 11³⁸ (RVm). See DINNER and MEALS.

BREAST.—See BOSOM.

BREATHING.—On the evening of the Resurrection, the Lord appeared to the disciples, gave them the commission 'As my Father, etc.,' 'and when he had said this, he breathed on them (ἐνεφύσησε), and saith unto them, Receive ye the Holy Ghost

(Λάβετε Πνεῦμα Ἅγιον). Whose soever sins . . . retained,' Jn 20²¹ᶠ. The word ἐμφυσάω is that employed by LXX to translate נפח in Gn 2⁷, Ezk 37⁹. As Westcott observes, ' the same image which was used to describe the communication of the natural life [at the Creation] is here used to express the communication of the new, spiritual life of re-created humanity.' The figure of human life depending on the breath of God is frequent in the Bible ; besides above passages, see Job 12¹⁰ 33⁴, Ps 33⁶, Is 42⁵, Dn 5²³, Ac 17²⁵. In the following the breath of God is synonymous with the manifestation of His power : 2 S 22¹⁶, Job 37¹⁰ 41²¹, Is 11⁴. Both ideas seem to underlie our Lord's action. The Church was now receiving its commission, and the efficacy and reality of the commission must depend upon the indwelling in the Church of the same Spirit as was in Christ Himself. ' Alike the mission of the Church and its authority to forgive or retain sins are connected with a personal qualification, "Take ye the Holy Ghost"' (Edersheim, ii. 644). The work was not new, but was that already received from the Father by the Son and now handed on to that Church which was to be Christ's body on earth. He had compared the action of the Spirit to breath (Jn 3⁸). ' By breathing on them He signified that the Holy Ghost was the Spirit not of the Father alone but likewise His own ' (Aug. St. John, tr. 121).

Considerable difference of opinion exists as to whether the act of breathing, with the authority to retain or forgive sin, was bestowed upon the Apostles only or on others besides. Those who limit it to the Apostles urge that ' disciples' is always in the later chapters of St. John used to signify Apostles ; and that, even if others were present, the analogy of Mt 28¹⁶ and Mk 16¹⁴⁻¹⁸ implies that the breathing and commission were limited to the Apostles. They would then see in the act a formal ministerial ordination.* On the other hand, Westcott and many others, comparing Lk 24²³, see no reason whatever for limiting the act and commission to Apostles. Even of the Eleven we know that Thomas at least was absent (Jn 20²⁴). The commission was one given to the Christian society as a body : in it in its corporate capacity would dwell the Holy Ghost, and the authority of retaining or forgiving sins.

LITERATURE. — The Commentaries on *St. John* ; Westcott, *Revelation of Risen Lord*, p. 81 ; Edersheim, *Life and Times of Jesus the Messiah*, ii. 644 ; Gore, *Christian Ministry*, p. 229 ; Stanley, *Christian Institutions*, p. 192.

J. B. BRISTOW.

BRETHREN OF THE LORD.—The only three theories about ' the brethren of the Lord' which are worthy of serious consideration are those which are called by Lightfoot (1) *the Hieronymian* (from its advocacy by Jerome [Hieronymus]), (2) *the Epiphanian* (from its advocacy by Epiphanius), and (3) *the Helvidian* (from its advocacy by Jerome's opponent, Helvidius).

According to the Hieronymian view, the ' brethren' of Jesus were His first cousins, being sons of the Virgin's sister, Mary the wife of Clopas. According to the Epiphanian view, they were sons of Joseph by a former wife. According to the Helvidian view, they were sons of Joseph and Mary born after Jesus. All these views claim to be Scriptural, and the Epiphanian claims in addition to be in accordance with the most ancient tradition.

i. POINTS THAT ARE CERTAIN.—In discussing a question of such intricacy as the present, it is well to begin by distinguishing what is reasonably certain from what is uncertain. A careful com-

* Stanley (*Christ. Inst.* p. 192) states that ' in the Abyssinian and Alexandrian Church ordination was, and still is, by breathing.'

parison of the relevant Scripture passages renders it certain—

(1) *That the brethren of the Lord, whatever their true relationship to Him was, lived under the same roof with Jesus and His mother, and were regarded as members of the Virgin's family.* The common household is implied in Jn 7³, and more distinctly still in 2¹², where we read that ' he went down to Capernaum, he, and his mother, and his brethren, and his disciples : and there they abode not many days.' That the brethren were members of the same family as Jesus, and stood in some definite filial relation to Joseph and Mary, is distinctly stated in Mt 13⁵⁵ ||, ' Is not this the carpenter's son ? is not his mother called Mary ? and his brethren, James, and Joseph,* and Simon, and Judas ? And his sisters, are they not all † with us ?' (cf. also Mt 12⁴⁷ ' Behold *thy mother and thy brethren* stand without, seeking to speak to thee'). In harmony with this the Gospels represent the brethren of Jesus as habitually going about in company with the Virgin (Mt 12⁴⁶ ||).

(2) *That the brethren of Jesus were jealous of Him, and up to the time of the Resurrection disbelieved His claims.* Thus the Gospels represent Jesus as lamenting the unbelief and want of sympathy of His near relatives : ' A prophet is not without honour, save in his own country, and *among his own kin, and in his own house*' (Mk 6⁴) ; and again, ' My time is not yet come, but your time is alway ready. The world cannot hate you, but me it hateth' (Jn 7⁶ᶠ.). There are, moreover, the still more definite statements, ' For even his brethren did not believe on him' (Jn 7⁵) ; and, ' his friends (οἱ παρ' αὐτοῦ) went out to lay hold on him, for they said, He is beside himself' (Mk 3²¹).

Some attempts have been made to attenuate the force of these passages. Cornelius a Lapide, for instance, commenting on Jn 7⁵, says : ' Licet enim viderent eum tot signa et miracula facere, illaque vera esse non dubitarent, tamen dubitabant an ipse esset Messias et Dei Filius : *licet enim hoc verum esse optarent, et ex parte ob tot ejus miracula crederent*—tamen alia ex parte videntes ejus paupertatem et neglectum, dubitabant. Ut ergo certi hac de re fiant, hortantur Christum ire secum in Jerusalem, etc.' But St. John asserts *disbelief* (οὐδὲ ἐπίστευον), not doubt, and implies *jealousy* and *hostility*. Other critics have maintained that *some only* of the brethren disbelieved. But St. John's language at the very least asserts that *the majority* (that is, three out of the four brethren) disbelieved, and almost certainly implies the disbelief of all.

From this there follows the necessary inference—

(3) *That none of the brethren were numbered among the Twelve Apostles.* This conclusion is confirmed by the manner in which they are distinguished from the Twelve in Ac 1¹⁴, ' [The eleven] all with one accord continued steadfastly in prayer with the women, and Mary the mother of Jesus, and *with his brethren*.' With this may be compared 1 Co 9⁵ (' Have we no right to lead about a wife that is a believer, even as the rest of the apostles, *and the brethren of the Lord*, and Cephas ?'), which, though less decisive than Ac 1¹⁴, because Cephas is first classed among the Twelve and then separately, points in the same direction. It is no sufficient reply to this to say that in Gal 1¹⁹ James is called an Apostle (' But other of the apostles saw I none, save [εἰ μή] James the Lord's brother'). Granting that this is the case, though it has been denied (*e.g.* by Grotius, Winer, Bleek ; cf. RVm), it may be fairly maintained that St. James is called an Apostle in that wider sense in which the term is applied to St. Paul himself, to St. Barnabas (Ac 14⁴· ¹⁴, 1 Co 9⁶), to Andronicus and Junias (Ro 16⁷), and perhaps also to Silvanus

* In Mt. the correct reading seems to be Ἰωσήφ (so WH and RV, with BC, etc.). In Mk 6³ Ἰωσῆτος (BDL, etc.) is certainly right.

† Epiphanius says that there were only *two* sisters, Mary and Salome, but the πᾶσαι shows that there were *three* at least. The present passage seems to indicate that they were married, and resided at Nazareth.

(1 Th 2^6, cf. 1^1). That James the Lord's brother was one of the Twelve is implied already in the Gospel according to the Hebrews (c. A.D. 100),[*] but the evidence of this dubious source cannot outweigh the strong negative presumption afforded by the canonical writings.[†]

ii. THE HIERONYMIAN VIEW.—With these three points established, we proceed to consider the Hieronymian view that the brethren of Jesus were really His first cousins. Jerome's theory, as stated by himself in his acrimonious but able treatise *adversus Helvidium*, involves the following positions:—

(a) That James the Lord's brother was an Apostle, being identical with James the Less, the son of Alphæus.

(b) That the mother of James and of the other 'brethren' was 'Mary of Clopas' (Jn 19^{25}).

(c) That this Mary was the Virgin's sister.

As developed by subsequent writers, the Hieronymian theory affirms in addition—

(d) That Simon the Zealot and Judas 'not Iscariot' were also brethren of the Lord.

(e) That Clopas is identical with Alphæus, and that consequently 'Mary of Clopas' is not to be regarded as the daughter of Clopas, but as his wife.[‡]

As these two additional points are maintained by all modern followers of Jerome, we shall regard them as integral parts of the Hieronymian theory. Jerome's theory has already been virtually disproved by the proof (i. 2, 3) that the Lord's brethren were not Apostles, but its great ingenuity and wide acceptance[§] render full discussion of it necessary.

A. *Arguments for the Hieronymian view.*—

(1) James the Lord's brother must have been of the Twelve, because he is called an Apostle, Gal 1^{19}. (For a reply to this see i. 2, 3).

(2) James the Lord's brother must have been of the Twelve, because he exercised great authority among, and even over Apostles. Thus at the Council of Jerusalem he presided and pronounced the decision, although St. Peter himself was present (Ac 15^{13}). St. Paul names him before St. Peter as one of the chief pillars of the Church (Gal 2^9). The Galatian heretics appealed to his authority as superior to that of St. Paul (Gal 2^{12}), and his importance is further shewn by such passages as Ac 12^{17} 21^{18}.

Reply.—St. James' prominent position is admitted, but it can be accounted for without supposing him to have been of the Twelve. For—

(a) His close relationship to Jesus (whatever the relationship was) would have sufficed of itself to gain him great consideration among the first Christians. He probably owed in part at least to this his election to the see of Jerusalem. Relationship to Jesus was clearly the main motive in the appointment of his successor, Symeon the son of Clopas,[‖] who was a cousin of Jesus (Eusebius,

[*] This Gospel represents him as present at the Last Supper, and therefore clearly as one of the Twelve.

[†] It is perhaps worth adding that St. James in his Epistle does not claim to be of the Twelve, and that his brother St. Jude seems even to exclude himself from the number of the Apostles (Jude 17).

[‡] Jerome himself says : ' Mariam Cleophæ Joannes Evangelista cognominat, sive a patre, sive a gentilitate familiæ, aut quaquumque alia caussa ei nomen imponens ' (xiii.).

[§] Jerome's treatise converted Augustine, who originally held the Epiphanian view, and the united influence of these two great doctors caused the Hieronymian view to prevail exclusively in the West. It is this view which is implied in the Liturgy, which, both in its Roman and in its Anglican form, regards James the Less, Simon Zelotes, and Judas not Iscariot as brethren of Jesus.

[‖] This Clopas was Joseph's brother, and is perhaps identical with the Clopas of Jn 19^{25}. If so, and if (as is supposed by many) ' Mary of Clopas ' was the *wife* of Clopas, and the *sister* of the Virgin, two brothers (Joseph and Clopas) must have married two sisters (the Virgin Mary and Mary of Clopas). For reasons to be presently given, we regard this combination as improbable.

HE iii. 11). Hegesippus speaks of the relations of Jesus as ' ruling the churches ' as such. Even as late as the reign of Domitian they were sufficiently important to incur the jealousy of the tyrant (*l.c.* iii. 20).

(b) James the Lord's brother possessed personal qualities which fully account for his elevation. Even the Jews, according to Hegesippus, reverenced him for his piety, his unceasing prayers, his life-long Nazirite vow, and above all for his justice (*l.c.* ii. 23). Josephus mentions the indignation which his execution excited among the Jews (*Ant.* xx. ix. 1), and in a passage not now extant ascribes the sufferings endured by the Jews during the siege of Jerusalem to Divine vengeance for his murder (Origen, c. *Celsum*, i. 47).

(3) James the Lord's brother must have been of the Twelve, because there were only two prominent Jameses in the Church, as the expression ' James the Less ' (Mk 15^{40}) indicates. He was therefore either James the Great, son of Zebedee, or James the Less, son of Alphæus. But he was not the former, who was martyred as early as A.D. 44 (Ac 12^2). Therefore he was the latter, the son of Alphæus.

Reply.—Jerome and his followers have been misled by the Latin translation *Jacobus minor*, ' James the Less.' The Greek is Ἰάκωβος ὁ μικρός, ' James the Little,' the allusion being to his short stature.

(4) The names of James, Simon, and Jude occur together, and in the same division, in all the Apostolic lists. This suggests—(a) that they were brothers, and (b) that they are identical with our Lord's brethren of the same name (see Mt $10^{2ff.}$, Mk $3^{16ff.}$, Lk $6^{14ff.}$, Ac 1^{13}).

Reply.—It has already been conclusively proved that our Lord's brethren were not Apostles (see i. 2, 3) ; but, waiving this point, we answer : (1) The occurrence of the three names together in the list of Apostles is no proof of fraternal relationship. (2) There is definite proof that the three were *not* brothers. For had they been so, it would naturally have been mentioned in some at least of the Gospels, as it is in the cases of the brothers Peter and Andrew, James and John. Moreover, the father of James is *Alphæus*, but the father of Jude is a certain *James*, of whom nothing definite is known. It is true that some propose to translate Ἰούδας Ἰακώβου (Lk 6^{16}, Ac 1^{13}) ' Jude the *brother* of James,' but so unusual, and probably unexampled, a meaning would require at least to be indicated by the context. We conclude, therefore, that James was certainly not the brother of Jude, and there is no evidence that he was the brother of Simon. If he was the brother of any Apostle, it was of Matthew (Levi), whose father was also called Alphæus (Mk 2^{14}). But even this, in the absence of any evidence of the identity of the two Alphæuses, must be pronounced doubtful.

Equally evident is it that these three Apostles were not brethren of Jesus. The coincidence of three such common names as James, Simon, and Jude in the list of brethren and in the list of Apostles proves nothing. So common are the names that they are duplicated in the Apostolic list itself. If it could be shown that James, Simon, and Jude, Apostles, were also *brothers*, the coincidence would be worth considering ; but since they were not, the coincidence is without significance. The very way in which these three Apostles are designated shows that they were not brethren of Jesus. It was necessary to distinguish them from three other Apostles of the same name, and yet they are not once called, for distinction, ' the Lord's brethren.' James is called ' of Alphæus,' perhaps also ' the Little ' ; Simon is called ' the Cananæan,' and ' the Zealot ' ; Jude receives no less than four distinguishing titles, ' not Iscariot,' 'of James,' 'Thaddæus,' and 'Lebbæus' (Mt 10³, Western Text). How strange, if he really was the Lord's brother, that he is not once so described !

(5) The last argument consists of three distinct steps. (a) James, the son of Alphæus, the Apostle, is identical with 'James the Little' of Mk 15⁴⁰ = Mt 27⁵⁶. But this James the Little had a brother Joses, clearly a well-known character, and therefore (since no other Joses is mentioned in the Gospels) the same as *Joses the brother of Jesus* (Mk 6³ ; and Mt 13⁵⁵, where the authorities are divided between the forms Joses and Joseph). (b) The mother of this James is called by the Synoptists Mary, and she is further described in Jn 19²⁵ as 'Mary of Clopas' (Μαρία ἡ τοῦ Κλωπᾶ). This might mean 'Mary *daughter* of Clopas,' but since Clopas and Alphæus are the same word, both being transliterations of the Aramaic חלפי (חלפּי), the correct translation is ' Mary *the wife* of Clopas.' (c) This Mary, wife of Clopas, is said by St. John to have been the Virgin's sister. Accordingly James and Joses (and consequently also Simon and Jude), the Lord's 'brethren,' were really His *first cousins on His mother's side.*

Reply.—This argument is ingenious rather than strong. For (a) the identification of James the Little (Mk 15⁴⁰) with the son of Alphæus, though generally accepted and not improbable, is only a guess. Indeed it may be argued that since St. Mark in his Gospel gives no hint that the son of Alphæus was called 'the Little,' he must mean by 'James the Little' another person. But conceding the identity (which, however, whether true or not, is too precarious to bear the weight of an important argument), we still cannot concede the identity of Joses, the brother of this James, with Joses the brother of Jesus. The identity of James of Alphæus with James the Little may be conceded, because, though it is weakly attested, nothing of weight can be urged against it. But if this Joses, the brother of James, was also the brother of Jesus, then three of our Lord's brethren were Apostles, a conclusion which is negatived by an overwhelming weight of evidence (see i. 2, 3). In such a case the mere coincidence of a name (and Joses or Joseph is, as Lightfoot shews, a particularly common name) is of no weight at all. (b) Jerome's assumption that 'Mary the mother of James and Joses' (Mt., Mk.) is identical with 'Mary of Clopas' is probably, though not certainly, correct. But there is no ground for supposing, as Jerome's supporters do, that this Mary was the *wife* of Clopas. There being no indication in the context to the contrary, the natural translation of Μαρία ἡ τοῦ Κλωπᾶ is 'Mary the *daughter* of Clopas.' * It is maintained, indeed, that since she was the' mother of James the Little (who was an Apostle), her husband must have been Alphæus, *i.e. Clopas.* But it is doubtful if James the Little really was an Apostle, and it is still more doubtful if Alphæus is the same person as Clopas. Κλωπᾶς, or, as it should probably be accented, Κλώπας, is a purely Greek name, being contracted from Κλεόπατρος (cf. Ἀντίπας from Ἀντίπατρος). Ἀλφαῖος (Ἀλφαῖος, WH), on the other hand, is the Aramaic חלפּי (Halpai), the initial guttural being, as is frequently the case, omitted. The names are therefore linguistically distinct. It is true that if there were strong independent reasons for identifying Alphæus and Clopas, the linguistic difficulties might possibly be surmounted, but there are no such reasons, or at least none are alleged.

Against the identification of Κλώπας and Alphæus it may be urged : (1) That inasmuch as initial sh'va is almost invariably

---

* So Jerome himself understood it. The Vulg. *Maria Cleophæ* preserves the ambiguity of the Greek.

---

represented by a full vowel in Greek (שְׁלֹמֹה = Σαλομών ; צְבָאוֹת = σαβαώθ ; etc.), there is a presumption against a word like Clopas, which begins with two consonants, representing a Semitic name. (2) Although ח is occasionally transliterated χ in the middle or at the end of a word, this never, or hardly ever, happens at the beginning. (3) חלף (חלף) is transliterated quite regularly Χαλφί in 1 Mac 11⁷⁰. (4) The ω of Κλώπας cannot be derived from חלף. The nearest Semitic equivalent of Κλώπας would be some such form as קלֹפָא. (5) The Semitic versions uniformly regard Ἀλφαῖος as a Semitic word, but Κλώπας as Greek, transliterating the χ by ק.

(c) There is more plausibility about Jerome's contention that Mary of Clopas is described in Jn 19²⁵ as the Virgin's sister. The words are ἱστήκεισαν δὲ παρὰ τῷ σταυρῷ τοῦ Ἰησοῦ ἡ μήτηρ αὐτοῦ καὶ ἡ ἀδελφὴ τῆς μητρὸς αὐτοῦ, Μαρία ἡ τοῦ Κλωπᾶ, καὶ Μαρία ἡ Μαγδαληνή. It must be candidly admitted that the *prima facie* impression which this passage makes upon the mind is that only three women are mentioned, and that the Virgin's sister is Mary of Clopas. There are, however, important considerations on the other side. (1) When persons or things are enumerated in pairs (cf. the list of Apostles, Mt 10²⁻⁴), the copula is not inserted between the pairs. If, therefore, St. John in this passage designs to speak of *two pairs of women*, καί is correctly omitted before Μαρία ἡ τοῦ Κλωπᾶ. (2) The Synoptic parallels show that *Salome, the mother of James and John*, was present at the Crucifixion, and since it is unlikely that St. John would omit to mention the presence of his own mother, ἡ ἀδελφὴ τῆς μητρὸς αὐτοῦ is probably not Mary of Clopas, but Salome. The suppression of her name is quite in the style of the Evangelist, who is very reticent in personal matters, and never even names himself. (3) If Mary of Clopas· was sister to the Virgin, then two sisters had the same name, a circumstance most improbable, unless they were only step-sisters. The point is undoubtedly a difficult one, and different opinions will continue to be held about it, but fortunately its decision does not affect the main point of our inquiry, because, whether Mary of Clopas was the Virgin's sister or not, *there is no reason for supposing that she was the mother of the brethren of Jesus.*

B. *Objections to the Hieronymian view.*—

The Hieronymian view is to be rejected, partly because the arguments in its favour, though ingenious, are inconclusive and often far-fetched ; partly because no trace of it is to be found before the time of Jerome, who apparently invented it ; * partly because it is obviously an attempt of an ardent champion of celibacy to maintain the perpetual virginity not only of Mary, but of *Joseph* ; † partly because it involves an unnatural use of the term 'brethren' ; ‡ but chiefly because it is incon-

---

* Papias of Hierapolis (A.D. 120) used to be quoted on Jerome's side, but Lightfoot has shown that the Papias in question lived in the 11th century. Hegesippus (A.D. 160) and Clement of Alexandria (A.D. 200) have been wrongly claimed on the same side. In reality they support the Epiphanian view.

† Jerome indeed admits this : 'Tu dicis (he is addressing Helvidius) Mariam virginem non permansisse : ego mihi plus vendico, etiam ipsum Joseph virginem fuisse per Mariam, ut ex virginali conjugio virgo filius nasceretur' (*adv. Helv.* xix.).

‡ It is true, as Jerome warmly urges (*adv. Helvidium,* xiv., xv.), that the OT usage of 'brother' is somewhat wide. In 1 Ch 23²¹. ²² first cousins are called brethren (אֲחֵיהֶם = ἀδελφοὶ αὐτῶν, LXX) : in Lv 10⁴, first cousins once removed (אֲחֵיכֶם : = τοὺς ἀδελφοὺς ὑμῶν, LXX). So also in Gn 14¹⁴ ¹⁶ Abraham's nephew is called his brother (אָחִיו) ; and in Gn 29¹⁵ Jacob is called Laban's brother. It cannot therefore be pronounced *impossible* that our Lord's cousins might occasionally be alluded to as His brethren, especially if it be true, as is generally alleged, that there is no word in Aramaic for cousin. At the same time it should be remembered that all Jerome's examples of an extended use of 'brother' are taken from the OT ; that the usage of ἀδελφός is much less elastic than that of אָח ; that no instances of ἀδελφός = ἀνεψιός are cited from profane writers ; and that even the OT does not sanction the *habitual* use of אָח to describe any other relationship than that of brother. The term ἀνεψιός is not avoided in the NT (see Col 4¹⁰), and Hegesippus

sistent with the three certainties, which, as we have shown, a true theory must necessarily presuppose, namely, the common household, the unbelief of the brethren, and their non-inclusion among the Twelve. Jerome's theory is inconsistent not only with the last two of these certainties, but even with the first, for though his supporters allege that the two sisters were both widows and kept house together, this does not explain the fact that the brethren of Jesus are regarded in Scripture as belonging to the *Virgin's* family, and are continually represented as being in her company, and never in the company of their alleged mother, Mary of Clopas.*

iii. THE HELVIDIAN AND EPIPHANIAN VIEWS.— The rejection of the Hieronymian view leaves the choice open between the Helvidian and the Epiphanian views, both of which have the immense advantage over the Hieronymian of not being inconsistent with the three certainties laid down in i. 1, 2, 3.

A. *Arguments for the Helvidian view.*†—

(1) The Helvidian view, which maintains that the brethren of Jesus were sons of Joseph *and Mary*, gives a fuller and more natural meaning to the term ἀδελφοί than the Epiphanian, which denies that they were blood-relations of Jesus at all.

Reply.—The advantage of the Helvidian view in this respect is but slight. Joseph was not a blood-relation of Jesus, and yet he is called, not only by friends and acquaintances (Mt 13⁵⁵ = Mk 6³, cf. also Jn 1⁴⁶ 6⁴²), but also by the Virgin herself (Lk 2⁴⁸), and by an Evangelist who lays great stress upon the supernatural birth (Lk 2⁴¹), the *father* of Jesus. Since, therefore, even in the Holy Family Joseph was called the father of Jesus, it is certain that if he had had sons, they would have been called the brethren of Jesus.

(2) In Lk 2⁷ Jesus is called Mary's *first-born son* (πρωτότοκον). This implies that she had other children.

Reply.—πρωτότοκος among the Jews was a technical term, meaning 'that which openeth the womb' (Ex 34¹⁹ff·), and does not imply the birth of other offspring. Indeed, the redemption-price of a first-born son, required by the Mosaic law, was due at the end of a month (Nu 8¹⁵ff·), before it could be known whether there was any likelihood of further offspring. Dr. Mayor objects that in a purely historical passage, like Lk 2⁷, this technical meaning is not to be thought of; but the subsequent statement 'they brought him up to Jerusalem to present him to the Lord, as it is written in the law of the Lord, *Every male that openeth the womb shall be called holy to the Lord*' (Lk 2²². ²³), renders it certain that it was precisely this which was in the Evangelist's mind when he called Jesus πρωτότοκον (so already Jerome, *l.c.* x.).

(3) Mt 1¹⁸, 'before they came together' (πρὶν ἢ συνελθεῖν), implies that the connubial relations of Joseph and Mary were of the ordinary kind.

Reply.—συνελθεῖν need not mean more than living together in the same house.

(4) Mt 1²⁵, 'and knew her not till she had brought forth a son' (καὶ οὐκ ἐγίνωσκεν αὐτὴν ἕως οὗ ἔτεκεν υἱόν),‡ implies that he knew her afterwards, especially as the Evangelist mentions brothers and sisters

(A.D. 160), in discussing the subject of our Lord's human relationships, keeps the two terms distinct, calling Symeon, the second bishop of Jerusalem, and our Lord's *cousin*, ἀνεψιός ; but James, the first bishop of Jerusalem, always ἀδελφός. Clearly, therefore, Hegesippus did not regard ἀδελφὸς τοῦ Κυρίου as equivalent to ἀνεψιός, and he is our oldest and best authority.

* In every passage of Scripture where the brethren are mentioned, except Jn 7³, it is expressly said that they were in the Virgin's company.

† The whole of these arguments were advanced by Helvidius himself, and the substance of most of the replies is to be found in Jerome.

‡ The πρωτότοκον of the TR here is certainly an interpolation from Lk 2⁷.

of Jesus, without any warning that they were not Mary's children.

Reply.—This is an argument of real weight, and is not adequately answered by Jerome, Cornelius a Lapide, Pearson, etc., who allege such passages as Mt 28²⁰, 'Lo, I am with you alway, even unto the end of the world,' and 2 S 6²³, 'Michal the daughter of Saul had no child until the day of her death,' as a proof that 'until' does not fix a limit or suggest a subsequent change. It is quite true that in such passages as those quoted, *where the circumstances of the case preclude the idea of change*, 'until' does not imply change. But 'until' *does* imply change when it introduces a state of things in which change is naturally to be expected. Thus, as Dr. Mayor justly remarks, if 2 S 6²³ be made to read 'Michal the daughter of Saul had no child, *until she left David and became the wife of Phaltiel*,' then 'until' *does* imply that she had a child afterwards, because child-bearing is a natural and usual sequel of marriage. So in the present case it may be fairly argued that inasmuch as connubial intercourse is the natural accompaniment of marriage, the Evangelist in asserting that it did not take place *until* a certain date, affirms that it took place afterwards. Still the argument, as applied to this particular case, is not convincing. The Evangelist is not (even by implication) comparing together the connubial relations of Joseph and Mary before and after the birth of Jesus (as, in the case supposed by Dr. Mayor, Michal's connubial relations with David and Phaltiel are compared), but simply affirming in the strongest possible way that Joseph had no share in the procreation of Jesus. Bengel's laconic comment is therefore, upon the whole, justified—'*donec*] Non sequitur, ergo *post*.' The subsequent mention of the brethren of Jesus (Mt 13⁵⁵) does not affect the question, because it was well known, when the Evangelist wrote, who the brethren were, and there was no need to guard against misconception.

(5) The fact that the brethren not only lived in the same house with the Virgin, but continually accompanied her wherever she went, is an indication that they were her children as well as Joseph's.

Reply.—The tie which unites a step-mother and her step-sons is often extremely close, and considering that Joseph was almost certainly dead before our Lord's ministry began, and that Jesus was fully occupied with public affairs, it cannot be regarded as surprising that her step-sons (if such they were) constituted themselves her guardians and protectors.

B. *Arguments for the Epiphanian view.*— We shall now state the arguments for the theory of Epiphanius, and subject them to criticism from the Helvidian point of view.

(1) *The Perpetual Virginity* of Mary is implied in the narrative of the Annunciation (Lk 1²⁶⁻³⁸). The angel Gabriel appeared to Mary, and after saluting her as 'highly-favoured' announced the manner of Christ's birth as follows: 'Behold, thou shalt conceive in the womb, and shalt bring forth a son, and shalt call his name Jesus.' The reply of Mary was, '*How shall this be, seeing that I know not a man?*' (Πῶς ἔσται τοῦτο, ἐπεὶ ἄνδρα οὐ γινώσκω ;). It is plain from this reply (1) that she understood the angel to mean that the child would be born in the natural way; and (2) that there was some obstacle which prevented her from having a child in the natural way ('I know not a man,' 'ἄνδρα οὐ γινώσκω'). These words cannot mean, 'I do not *yet* know a man.' That would have been no obstacle to the fulfilment of the promise. The angel's words related to *the future* (v.³¹), and inasmuch as Mary was already betrothed (v.²⁷), and might shortly expect to be taken into her

husband's house, there was every prospect, so far as Mary's *status* went, that the angel's words would shortly be fulfilled. The only meaning, therefore, which in such a context Mary's words can bear, is that she had devoted herself (with her betrothed's consent) to a life of virginity, and that she expected to preserve, even in marriage, her virginal integrity (so nearly all the older expositors, including Ambrose, Augustine, Gregory of Nyssa, Theophylact, Bernard, Bede, Anselm, Aquinas, Cornelius a Lapide, Maldonatus, Grotius; and in more recent times Bisping, Schegg, Schanz).*

Reply.—Such a vow or resolution is improbable in Mary's case, because the Jews regarded virginity as less honourable than marriage, and childlessness as a calamity. Moreover, it is improbable that, if she had formed such a resolution, Joseph would have consented to be betrothed to her.

These objections are undeniably weighty, but they do not fully meet the strong exegetical argument for the traditional view. Moreover, it must be remembered (1) that the case in question is a unique and peculiar one, and that it is doubtful how far the canons of ordinary probability ought to be applied to it; (2) that esteem for virginity among contemporary Jews is vouched for (though only to a limited extent) by the writings of Philo, and the existence of the sect of the Essenes; (3) that a high esteem for virginity characterized the Christian movement from the first (Ac 21[9], 1 Co 7), and formed part of the teaching of Christ (Mt 19[12]); and consequently it is not incredible that Joseph and Mary, by whom Jesus was brought up, shared the sentiment, and communicated it to Him.

(2) Virginity is regarded, not only by Christians, but by nearly all men, as, *ideally* at any rate, superior to marriage. It is therefore probable that the most privileged and holiest of women remained ever a virgin, as has been believed by most Christians from the first.†

Reply.—This argument has weight, but is not conclusive. For (1) though *ideally* virginity is superior to marriage, being the condition of the holy angels and of the saints in heaven (Mt 22[30]), yet *practically* marriage is in most cases to be preferred to celibacy, as a more useful means of serving God. And since the estate of marriage is altogether holy, and is a religious mystery or sacrament, symbolizing the union between Christ and His Church (Eph 5[32]), it is consistent with the *highest reverence* towards our Lord's mother to

believe that after the birth of Jesus she bore children to her husband.*

(3) Reverence for Mary as 'Mother of God' would have prevented Joseph from cohabiting with her as her husband.

Reply.—If we could be sure that Joseph and Mary regarded the infant Jesus as *God*, this argument would have great weight; but it is just this point which is doubtful. The angel described the infant as *the Messiah*, and *the Son of God*, but neither of these terms involved necessarily to Jewish ears the idea of *Divinity*. The term *Son of God* is used in the OT even of the Davidic king.

(4) The brethren of Jesus behave to Him as if they were elder brothers. Thus they are jealous of His popularity (Mk 6[4]), criticize and advise Him in no friendly spirit (Jn 7[1ff.]), attempt to control His actions, and even to place Him under restraint (Mk 3[20f.], cf. Mk 3[31] ||). But if they were older than Jesus, they were not Mary's children.

Reply.—It cannot be denied that their actions seem like those of elder brethren, but it is possible that they were only *slightly younger* than Jesus, and if so their conduct is perhaps intelligible.

(5) Jesus upon the Cross commended His mother not to His 'brethren,' but to St. John (Jn 19[26. 27]). He would have been very unlikely to do this, if His 'brethren' had really been the Virgin's sons.

Reply.—(*a*) The cause of this arrangement may have been the great poverty of the brethren of Jesus, and the comparative affluence of St. John, who, after all, was a near relation of Jesus (a first cousin). This is, of course, possible; but there is nothing to indicate that the brethren of Jesus were specially poor. They were living with St. Mary, and their united earnings would, under ordinary circumstances, have sufficed to maintain a single household in comfort. (*b*) Some allege as a cause the unbelief of the brethren. But this is unlikely, because Jesus must have known that within a few days their unbelief would pass into faith.

(6) The most ancient ecclesiastical tradition, especially that of Palestine, favours the Epiphanian view. The testimony of Hegesippus, a native of Palestine, and a man of learning, who wrote about A.D. 160, is definitely against the Hieronymian, and (as is almost certain) in favour of the Epiphanian view. His works are lost, but in the fragments which remain, he consistently speaks of the first Bishop of Jerusalem (James) as the Lord's brother; but of the second (Symeon) as His cousin (ἀνεψιός, which he more exactly defines as ὁ ἐκ θείου τοῦ Κυρίου, the θεῖος being Κλώπας, the brother of Joseph).† Clearly, therefore, Hegesippus did not regard the brethren of Jesus as His cousins. That he did not regard them as sons of Mary, is shown by his description of Jude, the Lord's brother, as τοῦ κατὰ σάρκα λεγομένου αὐτοῦ ἀδελφοῦ, and by the fact that Eusebius and Epiphanius, who draw their information mainly from him, regard the brethren as children of Joseph by a former wife.‡ This view is taken by Clement of Alexandria, Origen, Hilary of Poitiers, Ambrose, Ambrosiaster, Gregory of Nyssa; in fact, so far as we know, by all the Fathers before Jerome, with the exception of Tertullian, who probably, though his statements are not explicit, held the view of

---

* This important passage is not alluded to by Mayor and Lightfoot, and is very inadequately dealt with by most recent commentators. B. Weiss (Com. *in loc.*) says that it is 'a bewildered question how she, the unstained maiden, can possibly come into this position.' Considering that she was already *betrothed*, no such bewilderment was possible. If the angel had said that she would have a son *before marriage*, such bewilderment would have been natural enough, for the *concubitus* of betrothed persons, though not exactly forbidden, was not approved. But the angel had not hinted at this. Dr. Plummer reproduces Weiss. Godet simply says : 'Her question is the legitimate expression of the astonishment of a pure conscience.' Schmiedel (*Encyc. Bibl.* iii. 2956) regards the words as an interpolation. Only Schanz (Com. *in loc.*) gives anything like an adequate discussion of the passage. Of the older expositors Cornelius a Lapide and Maldonatus are full, but uncritical.

† The early Christians, however, while believing the Perpetual Virginity as a fact, did not regard it as an article of faith. As late as c. A.D. 370, St. Basil could write : 'The words, *He knew her not till she brought forth her first-born son*, do indeed afford a certain ground for thinking that Mary, after acting in all sanctity as the instrument of the Lord's birth, which was brought about by the Holy Ghost, did not refuse to her husband the customary privileges of marriage. But as for ourselves, even though this view does no violence to rational piety (εἰ καὶ μηδὲν τῷ τῆς εὐσεβείας παραλυμαίνεται λόγῳ), for her virginity was necessary until she had fulfilled her function in connexion with the economy, whereas what happened afterwards concerns us little as not being connected with the mystery, yet since lovers of Christ cannot bear to hear that the Mother of God ever ceased to be a virgin, we regard the testimonies (to her perpetual virginity) which we have produced as sufficient' (*Hom. in Sanct. Christ. Gen.* ii.).

* Quite unjust, therefore, is the customary Hieronymian abuse of Helvidius as 'spurcus hæresiarcha,' and the characterization of his theory as 'blasphemia.' Those who use such language virtually deny the sanctity of marriage. Helvidius' theory is perfectly reverent. Whether it is true or not is another question.

† It is possible, but not capable of proof, that this Clopas, the brother of Joseph, and the father of Symeon (not Symeon the Lord's brother), is identical with the Κλώπας of Jn 19[25], or the Κλεόπας of Lk 24[18]. Κλωπᾶς (Κλώπας) and Κλεόπας are etymologically the same word, both being contractions of Κλεόπατρος.

‡ The statements of Hegesippus about our Lord's brethren are noted by Eusebius, *HE* ii. 23, iii. 20, iii. 32, iv. 22.

Helvidius. Since Jerome the Western Church has adopted the Hieronymian theory, but the Eastern Church still maintains that of Epiphanius. The traditional evidence, therefore, is almost entirely on the side of the Epiphanian view.

Reply. — It is possible that the Apocryphal Gospels, especially the Gospel of Peter and the Protevangelium of James, and not any authentic tradition, are the source of the Epiphanian theory. This is Jerome's view, who taunts Epiphanians with following 'deliramenta apocryphorum.' This, however, is not likely. The statements of the best informed Fathers seem based on Hegesippus, who made an independent investigation, under specially favourable conditions. The Apocryphal Gospels probably adopted, rather than originated, the current view.

C. *The main objection to the Epiphanian view.* —There is one objection to the Epiphanian view so important that it deserves special notice. It is well known that a high—an even extravagant— estimate of virginity prevailed extensively in the early Church; and therefore there is some reason to suspect that, just as, at the close of the 4th cent., zeal for the virginity of Joseph produced the Hieronymian theory, so, three centuries earlier, zeal for the virginity of Mary produced the Epiphanian. That this may have been so, no cautious critic will deny; but it does not, upon the evidence, appear to be probable. For (1) if Mary bore to Joseph, as the Helvidian theory assumes, seven children, of whom one was Bishop of Jerusalem, and three others prominent members of the Church, the non-virginity of Mary after the birth of Jesus must have been so notorious a fact in the Apostolic Church, that the (practically) unanimous tradition of her perpetual virginity could never have arisen. (2) The tradition of the Perpetual Virginity was already prevalent early in the 2nd cent., that is, long before ascetic views were dominant or even aggressive in the Church. It prevailed, moreover, in Palestine, where, there is reason to believe, ascetic views had less influence than elsewhere. For these reasons we are inclined to think that the Epiphanian tradition has a real historical basis.

iv. PROBABLE CONCLUSIONS. — The scantiness and ambiguity of the only really trustworthy evidence, the Scriptural, obliges us to be content with merely probable conclusions. The only conclusion that seems to be certain is that Jerome's theory is false. The claims of the two other theories are nearly evenly balanced; nevertheless, it appears to us, after weighing the opposing arguments to the best of our power, that there is a slight but perceptible preponderance of Scriptural, and a much more decided preponderance of historical, evidence in favour of the Epiphanian theory.

LITERATURE. — Jerome, *adversus Helvidium*; Epiphanius, *adversus Antidicomarianitas* (*adversus Hæreses*, iii. 2) (both important); Pearson, *On the Creed*; Mill, *Accounts of our Lord's Brethren vindicated*; Schegg, *Jakobus, der Bruder des Herrn*; Schanz, *Comment. über Mt., Mc., Lc.*; Meyrick, art. 'James' in Smith's *DB*; Sieffert, art. 'Jakobus,' and Zöckler, art. 'Maria' in *PRE*[3]; Lightfoot, *Galatians*, pp. 252–291; Mayor, *Epistle of St. James* (v. ff.) and art. 'Brethren of the Lord' in Hastings' *DB*; art. 'Clopas' in *Encyc. Bibl.*; Farrar, *Early Days of Christianity*, ch. xix.; Patrick, *James the Lord's Brother*, 1906, p. 4 ff.   C. HARRIS.

BRIDE, BRIDE - CHAMBER, BRIDEGROOM, BRIDEGROOM'S FRIEND.—See MARRIAGE.

BRIMSTONE (burning stone or sulphur [θεῖον, commonly derived from θεῖος, 'divine,' either because sulphur was used for religious purification, or because lightning—the bolt of the gods—emits a sulphurous odour: others connect it with θύω, 'agitate,' cf. *fumus*, 'smoke']).—Its use in Scripture in the imagery of Divine judgment is founded on the story of the destruction of Sodom and the

cities of the Plain (Gn 19$^{24-28}$), a catastrophe to which the Gospels frequently refer (Lk 17^{29} 10^{12}, Mk 6^{11}, Mt 10^{15} 11$^{23, 24}$). The story of this tragedy of Divine judgment casts its lurid light all down Scripture history, and has coloured Christian belief in its presentation of the Divine wrath. The imagery of 'fire and brimstone' appears in the prophets and the Psalms as an impressive metaphor of heaven's most pitiless judgment, while the story itself is often recalled both in the OT and in the NT. In the Book of Revelation it is a notable feature in the description of the Apocalyptic riders (9$^{17, 18}$), that their breastplates are of fire and brimstone, and from the mouths of their horses proceed the same dread emblems of wrath; while no more impressive figure can be found to describe the final doom of the wicked in the end of the ages than that they shall be cast into the 'lake of fire and brimstone,' there to be 'tormented day and night for ever and ever' (Rev 19^{20} 20^{10} 21^{8}).

J. DICK FLEMING.

BROOK (Jn 18^1; RVm '*ravine*, Gr. *winter torrent*,' χείμαρρος) is the usual LXX equivalent of נַחַל, and seems to correspond in meaning with the Arab. *wādy* = 'valley,' but, more particularly, the watercourse in the bottom of the valley. The winter rains, rushing down from the mountain range, have hollowed out great channels westward, towards the Mediterranean. Much deeper are the gullies eastward, where the descent is steeper, towards the Jordan. Most of these are quite dry during the greater part of the year. Although some are called 'rivers,' *e.g. Nahr el-'Aujeh*, in the Plain of Sharon, and the Kishon, while others, such as *el-'Amûd*, which crosses the Plain of Gennesaret, and *el-Yarmuk*, which comes down from the eastern uplands, draw abundant supplies from perennial springs, yet 'brook' more accurately describes them.

The **Kidron** contains water only after heavy rains. It is the one 'brook' mentioned in the Gospels. Over it Jesus passed from the upper room to Gethsemane on the night of His betrayal.

The name קִדְרוֹן, from קדר, is usually referred to the dark colour of the stream or ravine. The various forms of the name in Gr. are τοῦ κίδρου, τοῦ κίδρων, and τῶν κίδρων. WH in 'Notes on Select Readings,' after reviewing the evidence, conclude in favour of τῶν κίδρων. 'It probably preserves the true etymology of קדרון, which seems to be an archaic (? Canaanite) plural of קדר "the Dark [trees]"; for, though no name from this root is applied to any tree in Bib. Heb., some tree resembling a cedar was called by a similar name in at least the later language (see exx. in Buxtorf, *Lex. Talm.* 1976); and the Gr. κέδρος is probably of Phœnician origin.' They suggest that isolated patches of cedar forests may have survived from prehistoric times. Lightfoot quotes (*Chorag. Cent.* 40) a Talmudic reference to two gigantic cedars standing on the Mt. of Olives even in the latest days of the Temple (Jerus. *Taanith*, fol. 69. 1), which may be taken as supporting this view.

The valley begins in the wide hollow between the city and Mt. Scopus on the north. Turning southward, and passing under the eastern battlements, by a deep ravine it cuts off Jerusalem from Olivet. It is joined by the Valley of Hinnom, and thence, as *Wady en-Nâr*, 'Valley of Fire,' it winds down an ever deepening gorge, through the Wilderness of Judæa, to the edge of the Dead Sea. The name *Wady er-Râhib*, 'Valley of the Monks,' attaching to part of it, comes from the convent of Mar Saba, built on the right-hand face of the gorge, a sort of reformatory for refractory monks, in the midst of the wilderness.

The modern name of the brook Kidron is *Wady Sitti Maryam*, 'Valley of the Lady Mary.' As early as Eusebius and Jerome it was known as the Valley of Jehoshaphat, Jl 3^2 [Heb. 4^2]. According to a tradition, common to Jews, Moslems, and Christians, this is to be the scene of the final Judgment. As against the Temple, which overlooked it, the valley ranked as an unclean district, and it seems to have afforded burying-ground for people of the humbler orders (2 K 23⁶). To this day the Jews greatly covet a grave in the Ķidron valley.

W. EWING.

BROTHERHOOD.—The word (ἀδελφότης) does not occur at all in the Gospels, and is found only twice in the NT (1 P 2¹⁷ and 5⁹). The idea, however, is common and of very great importance.

1. *The natural brotherhood of man* is assumed rather than asserted. It probably underlies Christ's argument about the Sabbath (Mk 2²⁷ and parallels), and also such language as is found in Lk 15¹¹⁻³² and 16²⁵. This is the more likely in view of such OT passages as Gn 1²⁶⁻²⁸ 9⁵⁻⁷, Job 31¹³⁻¹⁵, and Mal 2¹⁰ (which regard it as a corollary of our creation by the one God and Father), and Lv 19¹⁸. ³⁴ (which not only commands love of neighbour, but also explicitly enjoins like love for the stranger). Hillel and other Rabbis gave this law the broadest interpretation, and Philo declares that man must love the whole world as well as God (see Kohler, *Jewish Encyc.* art. 'Brotherly Love,' and Montefiore in the *JQR*, April 1895). This, however, does not represent the dominant feeling among the Jews in our Lord's time. They narrowed the term 'neighbour,' as His language in Mt 5⁴⁴ plainly implies. It was the scribe's suggestion of this narrow view that drew from Jesus the parable of the Good Samaritan, in which the term 'neighbour' is made the equivalent of brother-man (Lk 10²²ff.).

Into this brotherhood Christ entered when He 'became flesh.' That at least is implied in the title 'Son of Man' which He so frequently applies to Himself. He was 'the seed of the woman.' The Son of Mary, of David, of Abraham, was also Son of Adam (Lk 3³⁸) and one of the race.

Yet of natural brotherhood the NT has surprisingly little to say. Very little importance is attached to it. No hopes are built on it. The reason, doubtless, is that it had been destroyed by sin—a melancholy fact visible in the threshold tragedy of Cain and Abel. Such is St. Paul's summary of OT teaching (Ro 3⁹⁻¹⁸). So Jesus found it when He was in the world. Men were dead to brotherhood as to all else that was wholly good (Jn 6⁵³, cf. Eph 2¹). For thirty years He moved among men with a true Brother's heart, but met no equal response, even among those peculiarly His own (Jn 1¹⁰. ¹¹). 'Of the peoples there was no man with him' (Is 63³). He was sorrowfully alone (Is 53³), standing among sinful men like one unharmed temple amid a city's ruins.

2. *The new brotherhood.*—Under these circumstances nothing short of a new beginning would serve. Anything less radical must fail. A new creation is necessary (Gal 6¹⁵). This Jesus states explicitly. Men must be born again (Jn 3⁶; cf. Eph 2⁵). They must be redeemed from sin and given a new life. This was His appointed mission (Mt 1²², Jn 10¹⁰). To that work He formally dedicated Himself in His baptism, which also symbolized the means by which the redemption should be effected, namely, His own death (with Mt 3¹⁵, cf. Mt 20²⁸ 26²⁸ and Ro 3²⁴⁻²⁶, 1 Co 15³, Eph 1⁷, 1 P 1¹⁸. ¹⁹, Rev 1⁵). Tempted to swerve from it, He held to that stern, slow path. Meantime He begins to gather about Him a band of brothers on the new basis. They are such as believe or receive Him. In faith they follow Him and forsake all else (Mk 1¹⁸. ²⁰ 10²⁸, Lk 14³³). That it is no mere external following is manifest. A vital union is established between them and Him, the significance of which is indicated by the figure of the vine and the branches (Jn 15¹⁻⁸). The new birth is effected (Jn 1¹². ¹³), the new life received (Jn 6⁵⁷ 10²⁷. ²⁸), and their sins graciously forgiven (Mk 2⁵⁻¹¹, Lk 7⁴⁷. ⁴⁸; cf. Col 1¹⁴). Thus they become partakers of the

Divine nature (2 P 1⁴), children or sons of God τέκνα, υἱοί, 1 Jn 3¹⁶, Ro 8¹⁴. ¹⁶. ²¹, Gal 3²⁶ 4⁷), endowed with a deathless life (Gal 3²⁶, Jn 10²⁸), and Christ becomes the firstborn among many brethren (Ro 8²⁹). Elsewhere the change is called a new creation (2 Co 5¹⁷, Gal 6¹⁵, Eph 2¹⁰), of which Christ is the beginning (Rev 3¹⁴, Col 1¹⁸).

It is this profound experience which underlies and accounts for the remarkable statements of Jn 1³⁵⁻⁵¹. St. Peter's new name is a sign of it (v.⁴²); the 'Israelite indeed in whom is no guile' is a condensed description of the new man (v.⁴⁷; cf. Ps 32², the first half of which is the germ of Ro 3²¹⁻ 5²¹, and the second of Ro 6¹⁻8³⁹). These men are nearer to Jesus now than any other persons. Hence the appropriateness of the strong language of this early record in the most spiritual of the four Gospels. St. John had learned meantime the potency of the faith that began so simply, and in the light of that recalls those wonderful early utterances and the steady progress of their faith from strength to strength.

Equally appropriate is the Cana incident which immediately follows (Jn 2¹⁻¹¹). There Jesus breaks with the old order in the words, 'Woman, what have I to do with thee?' Addressed as they were to her who represented it in its fondest tie, they show the break to be of the most absolute sort. That is the negative side, the turning from the old; the positive, the turning to the new, is indicated by the place assigned to the disciples in the record. They are identified with Him as others are not, and especially in a growing faith, to which others—even His mother and His brethren—are as yet strangers. What was there taught in the veiled language of sign is taught plainly and explicitly in Mt 12⁴⁶⁻⁵⁰ and Mk 3³¹⁻³⁵. How far Mary and His brothers were from understanding Him, how wide the gulf was that separated Him from them, is shown by the fact recorded in Mk 3²¹ that they regarded Him as out of His mind. The disciples, on the other hand, are seated about Him drinking in His sayings. Them He declares to be His mother and His brethren (Mt 12⁴⁹). And looking upon the multitude also sitting around and listening to His words, He generalizes the teaching and declares that 'Whosoever shall do the will of God, the same is my brother, and sister, and mother' (Mk 3³². ³⁵). Such constitute the new brotherhood.

(1) So the first characteristic of the new brethren is that they do the will of God. They are in right relation to Him. When men are not so, they cannot be rightly related to one another. To be bound together by the tie of brotherhood, they must first be bound by the filial tie to God, their Heavenly Father. Loving obedience is the test and evidence of that (1 Jn 5³, Jn 14¹⁵⁻²¹).

It is worth noting that this is the first great law of the Kingdom of heaven (Mt 6, and summarized in v.³³). Really the brotherhood and the Kingdom (in one sense of the term) are different aspects of the same thing. As to membership the two are coextensive. God is at once Father and King; the brethren are both subjects and children, 'fellow-citizens with the saints and of the household of God' (Eph 2¹⁹). Both ideas run through the Sermon on the Mount, which is Christ's proclamation of the nature and principles of the Kingdom.

Doubtless the new brotherhood and the Church may be similarly equated. Their membership too should coincide. This is indicated not only by Christ's solemn recall of Peter's new name, and His assertion that His church should be built of such confessors as he (Mt 16¹⁸), but also by the uniform practice in the Acts and Epistles of referring to the members of the churches as 'brethren.'

(2) The second characteristic is· that they love one another. Loving God as their Father they instinctively love also His other children, their brothers (1 Th 4⁹, 1 Jn 4²⁰ and 5¹). This is Christ's new commandment and the badge of discipleship (Jn 13³⁴ff.). Though an old command, it has been made new in experience by Christ's death for them.

And they in turn make it new afresh when they lay down their life for one another (1 Jn 3¹⁶, 2⁷⁻¹¹). The love that makes the greatest sacrifice will make the lesser. In the OT the law of Israel's brotherhood enjoined kindness, and definitely forbade such sins as contempt, extortion, oppression, etc. (Dt 22¹⁻⁴ 23⁷· ¹⁹ᶠ· 24⁷· ¹⁴ 25³, and elsewhere). So in the ·NT special mention is made of charity (1 Jn 3¹⁷, Ja 2¹⁵· ¹⁶); hospitality (He 13¹, Ro 12¹³); forgiveness (Col 3¹³); truthfulness (Eph 4²⁵); mutual admonition (2 Th 3¹⁵); a humility that prefers others and renders even lowly service (Mt 18¹⁻¹⁸, Jn 13¹²⁻¹⁷, Ro 12¹⁰, Ph 2¹⁻¹¹, 1 P 5⁵ᶠ·); practical sympathy with the persecuted (He 12³), etc. Brotherly love insists on the essential equality of those who are of the same family. Natural affection exists among them (Ro 12¹⁰ φιλόστοργοι). There can be no caste among them (Col 3¹¹); all selfish ambition and striving after pre-eminence must be eschewed, and the way of service chosen (Mt 20²⁰⁻²⁸). Differences of gifts are recognized. But those who are one in Christ must regard them not as signs of inferiority and superiority, or grounds of pride and servility, but as means of mutual helpfulness, and as all necessary to the general well-being. Different gifts are different functions for the common good. For Christ and His brethren form a body, and each member is necessary to the perfect well-being of the rest. This is developed in Ro 12, 1 Co 12, and Eph 4.

The love the brethren bear each other is special. It is distinguished from that they feel toward those that are without (1 P 2¹⁷ and 2 P 1⁷). It is closer, more affectionate, complacent, satisfying. But they must love others—even their bitterest enemies. So do they become like their Father in heaven (Mt 5⁴³⁻⁴⁸; cf. St. Paul in Ro 9¹⁻⁵).

Christ calls them His brethren, and is not ashamed to do so (He 2¹¹). Still His position in the brotherhood is unique. He is one of them, yet He transcends them. He is Master and Lord (Jn 13¹³ᶠ·) as they are not nor should seek to be (Mt 23⁸⁻¹⁰). For He is Son of God in a unique sense (μονογενής, Jn 3¹⁶ and 1¹⁸, in which the reading θεός is probably correct and explains the uniqueness). That truth He ever guards in the expressions He employs. Examples are seen in Mt 11²⁷ and frequently in the Fourth Gospel; in Mt 6⁹, where the emphatic 'ye' and the character of the prayer exclude Him from the 'our,' and in Jn 20¹⁷, where distinction, not identity, of relation is intended.

When the law of brotherhood is lived out in sincerity and truth, in justice and righteousness, in courage and faith, in all wisdom and spiritual understanding, the solution of social problems will be hastened. These problems are not new. But they are seen to-day as never before. Conditions that once were accepted are accepted no longer as just or right or tolerable. And it is precisely because Christ's ideas of brotherhood have grown clearer to men's minds that they feel the inequalities and injustices of the present order. That is the cause of the present discontent. Christ foresaw that such conflicts would be occasioned by His gospel (Mt 10³⁴⁻³⁹). And nothing but the gospel that has caused the conflict can bring the proper issue. The cause must be the cure. Loyalty to the way of the Cross is the way of salvation. The age waits for Christians to embark in the honest, whole-hearted application of the great principle of brotherly love. It will not do to say with Wernle that Christ's demands are impractical for any society. They are impractical for any society that lacks the martyr spirit. They are not impractical for the society that is charged with it. Christ's way was the way of the Cross. That is the only way that leads to victory. Only in the spirit of Jesus can the world's need be met, and its problems

finally solved. For that the new brotherhood has been created. Only the fresh vision of the Father's love, the surrender to the Saviour's Cross, and the appropriation of the Spirit's power will inspire, fit, and equip it for the holy task to which God summons.

LITERATURE.—Material will be found in most Commentaries, Lives of Christ, and books on Biblical Theology and the Teaching of Jesus. But in addition to the references already made, special attention may be called to Seeley's *Ecce Homo*; Renan's *Life of Jesus*; Denney's art. 'Brotherly Love' in Hastings' *DB*; Westcott's *Social Aspects of Christianity*; and especially Peabody's *Jesus Christ and the Social Question*; Mathews' *The Social Teaching of Jesus*; and Tolstoi, *passim*.

J. H. FARMER.

BROTHERLY LOVE.—See BROTHERHOOD and LOVE.

BUFFETING.—In Mt 26⁶⁷ and Mk 14⁶⁵ this word (Gr. κολαφίζω) is used to describe the ill-treatment received by Christ in the house of the high priest after His condemnation was pronounced. The crowd present seems to have participated in inflicting this personal indignity. St. Mark, with his usual attention to details, notices that the officers received Him with blows of their hands. κολαφίζω carries the significance of a blow with the clenched fist (κόλαφος, 'a fist'). It vividly represents the brutal manual violence to which our Lord was subjected. The word also came to imply a meaning of general ill-usage or persecution, and, as such, occurs in 1 Co 4¹¹, 2 Co 12⁷ ('a thorn in the flesh, a messenger of Satan to buffet me'), 1 P 2²⁰; cf.—

'A man that fortune's buffets and rewards
Hath ta'en with equal thanks.'
—*Hamlet*, Act III. Sc. ii.

W. S. KERR.

BUILDING (οἰκοδομή, 3 times; οἰκοδομεῖν, 23 times in the Gospels).—**1.** *Literal.*—The lifetime of Jesus nearly coincides with the period which was undoubtedly the golden age of building in Palestine. The Herods, with their 'Napoleonic passion for architecture,' eclipsed in this respect even the fame of Solomon, and left their mark in all parts of the country in the shape of palaces, fortresses, theatres, and a variety of splendid structures, some serving a useful purpose (as the great harbour at Cæsarea), but many arising merely out of a love of pomp and display. Herod the Great had begun his extensive work of rebuilding the Temple at Jerusalem nineteen years before the Christian era, and the work was still in progress at the time of Christ's final visit to the city (Mt 24¹· ², Mk 13¹· ², Lk 21⁵· ⁶). Herod Antipas began the foundations of his ambitious new city of Tiberias shortly before Jesus emerged from the obscurity of Nazareth; and Pilate was engaged, during the public ministry of Jesus, in constructing an elaborate aqueduct for Jerusalem. It is certain that, wherever Jesus went, He would hear the sound of hammer and chisel; He would observe the frequent construction of a class of building hitherto little favoured in His country, such as hippodromes, baths and gymnasia (Jos. *Ant.* xv. viii. 1); and would notice the adoption of a style of architecture foreign to Jewish tradition.

It was not only Herodian princes, Roman magnates, and well-to-do proselytes (see Lk 7⁵) who lavished large sums on buildings. Wealthy Jews seem to have spent fortunes in erecting luxurious mansions in the Græco-Roman style. Jesus mentions this eagerness for building as one of the passions which preoccupied His generation, and led Him to compare it with the materialist and pleasure-seeking age in which Lot lived (Lk 17²⁸). He gives a vivid description of a prosperous farmer designing ampler store-houses on his estate (Lk 12¹⁸). In another passage He probably alludes to some actual instance of the building-mania over-reaching itself, when He describes the tower left half finished for lack of funds (Lk 14²⁸). In His denunciation of the Pharisees who ‘build the sepulchres of the prophets, and garnish the tombs (μνημεῖα) of the righteous’ (Mt 23²⁹), He refers perhaps to the growing practice, unknown in the pre-Grecian period, begun, it seems, in Maccabæan times, and now become a dilettante cult, of erecting monumental tombs ‘reared aloft to the sight’ (1 Mac 13²⁷), as distinguished from the simple rock-hewn tombs of former days.* See TOMB.

O. Holtzmann (*Life of Jesus*, p. 100 f.) suggests a special reason for the frequent references which Jesus makes to building operations. He calls attention to the fact that the handicraft in which He had been brought up was one of the building trades. It is usual, indeed, to describe Him as ‘the carpenter’ (Mk 6³), and the passage is often cited in which Justin Martyr (*Trypho*, 88) represents Him as ‘making ploughs and yokes.’ But Justin Martyr is quoting nothing more than a popular tradition, and there is no reason for limiting the term τέκτων to a worker in wood. There was hardly the division of labour at Nazareth that exists among our own mechanics. The epithet τέκτων has probably not less significance than the term ‘carpenter’ as used in *Hamlet*, v. i. 46—‘What is he that builds stronger than either the mason, the shipwright, or the carpenter?’, where it indicates one who has to do with the construction of buildings. We may say that there is good reason to conclude that Jesus was Himself a builder, and that He understood at least the art of ordinary house-construction, though it can hardly be admitted that the passages which Holtzmann quotes in support of this are sufficient to prove his point. By a similar method it is easy to prove that Shakspeare was a lawyer or a doctor, a Romanist or a Puritan.

On the other hand, it is not to be inferred, from the somewhat disparaging terms in which Jesus appears to have alluded to the building operations of His time, that He was insensible to the beauties of architecture, or that there was an iconoclastic strain in His nature. It would be easy to marshal passages from the Gospels with the object of showing that He was indifferent to, and even evinced contempt for, sacred places and edifices. But such a conclusion would be contrary to all that we know of His many-sided sympathy and genial tolerance. Rather was the case this—that, like St. Paul amid the temples of Athens, or like St. Francis of Assisi, careless of cathedrals in an age of cathedral-builders, He found His contemporaries so smitten with the love of outward magnificence, so absorbed in the thought of the material edifice, that He bent His whole effort to the task of emphasizing the inward and spiritual structure. It is therefore in this direction that all the great sayings of Christ about building look. On each occasion when He is led to speak of a temple, whether at Jerusalem or in Samaria, He takes the opportunity of insisting that the only true Temple is one not made with hands.

It may be suggested that some of His sayings of this kind are lost, but that the reminiscence or influence of them is to be traced in the remarkably frequent use by the NT writers of the term ‘building’ in a spiritual sense, whether applied to the individual believer or to the company of the faithful (see, *e.g.*, Ac 20³², 1 Co 3⁹, Col 2⁷, 1 P 2⁵ etc.). And just as Jesus said, ‘Ye are a city set on a hill,’ He may well have said, ‘Ye are the temple of God.’

2. *Figurative.*—The actual passages in which Jesus spiritualizes the term ‘building’ may be grouped under three heads.

(1) In two remarkable passages Christ speaks of Himself as a *Builder*. (*a*) The first of these (Mt 26⁶¹, Mk 14⁵⁸, Jn 2¹⁹), while it is certainly a genuine saying of Christ’s, has come down to us in a form which leaves us doubtful as to the exact connexion in which it was first uttered. The general sense, however, is clear enough. The buildings of the

* Furrer (*Wanderungen*, p. 77) and Fergusson (*The Temples of the Jews*, p. 142 f.) think that the Tomb of Zecharias in the Valley of Jehoshaphat, ‘a lovely little temple, with . . . pillars of the Ionic order,’ belongs to the first years of the 1st cent. of our era.

Temple might be razed to the ground, but Christ, by His presence among His people, would perpetuate the true sanctuary (cf. Mt 18²⁰, Jn 4²⁴). Had the author of the Epistle to the Hebrews this saying in his mind when he referred to Christ (He 3³) as the ‘builder of the house’? (*b*) The second passage is that in which Christ contemplates Himself as the Builder of His *Church* (Mt 16¹⁸). That with which He is concerned is not the material edifice reared on the rocky summit of Mount Moriah, but the spiritual building—the body of believers—founded on a common faith in Himself.

(2) In one passage, cited from the OT, Jesus varies the metaphor. In the ‘germ-parable’ of the Rejected Stone (Mt 21⁴², Mk 12¹⁰, Lk 20¹⁷) He is no longer the Builder, but the Foundation. In the original passage (Ps 118²²) the Rejected Stone is Israel, but Christ appropriates the image to Himself, and once more draws attention to the fact that the work of God proceeds on lines not to be anticipated by a type of mind which is governed by worldly considerations.

(3) In two minor parables Jesus uses the art of building to illustrate the principles which must animate His followers. (*a*) In Mt 7²⁴, Lk 6⁴⁸ He shows that, as the stability of a house depends on the nature of its foundation, so stability of character can be attained only when a man uniformly makes the word of truth which he has received the basis of his behaviour. *Doing* is the condition of progress. Christian attainment is broad-based upon obedience (cf. Jn 7¹⁷). (*b*) In Lk 14²⁸ He checks a shallow enthusiasm, apt quickly to evaporate, by reminding impulsive disciples that for great works great pains are required. The parable is the Gospel equivalent of our saying, ‘Rome was not built in a day,’ with special reference, however, to the necessity of the individual giving himself up, in absolute devotion, to his task (cf. Shakspeare, *2 Henry IV.* I. iii. 41).

The foregoing passages exhaust the sayings, as reported in the Evangelic tradition, in which our Lord employed the image of building. But, we may ask, whence did St. Paul derive his favourite expression, applied both to the Church and to the individual, of *edifying*? (see Ro 15², 1 Co 14⁵, Eph 4¹² etc.). It does not appear that οἰκοδομεῖν was ever used by classical writers in this sense. Fritzsche (*Ep. ad Rom.* iii. p. 205) thinks that St. Paul derived it from the OT usage, בָּנָה being sometimes used, with the accusative of the person, in the signification of blessing (see Ps 28⁵, Jer 24⁶). But is it not at least as likely that St. Paul derived the metaphorical use from the custom of Christ, who so often and with such emphasis applied building terms to the spiritual condition alike of the individual and of the company of believers? If Christ did not Himself use the expression ‘edify,’ all His teaching pointed that way.

LITERATURE.—Hausrath, *Hist. of NT Times*, §§ 5, 10, 11; articles ‘Baukunst’ in *PRE* ³ and ‘Architecture’ in Hastings’ *DB*; Josephus, *Ant.* xv. viii. 1, ix. 4–6, x. 3, xvi. v. 2, *BJ* I. xiii. 8, xxi. 1–11, VII. viii. 3; Schürer, *GJV* ³ ii. 176, 430, 446, etc.; O. Holtzmann, *Life of Jesus*, p. 100 f. etc.

J. ROSS MURRAY.

BURDEN.—Both in Christ’s discourse against the Pharisees (Mt 23⁴, Lk 11⁴⁶) and in His saying, ‘Come unto me,’ etc. (Mt 11²⁸·³⁰), the ‘burden’ (φορτίον) is that of the legal and Pharisaic ordinances of such a minute and exacting kind that they became intolerable and crushed out real heart-religion. ‘My burden,’ Christ says, ‘is light’ in comparison with these; for I put men under the law of love, which is a law of liberty. With loving, gracious hearts, My disciples become a law unto themselves. The new law is written on the fleshy tables of the heart. St. Peter, in Ac 15¹⁰, speaks of the traditional legal observances as a yoke which 'neither ye nor your fathers were able to bear,' while faith in Christ can purify the heart and make strict rules for outward conduct unnecessary. In Mt 11[30] Jesus gives utterance to the germ at least of the Pauline idea of a new spirit of life in Christ Jesus, setting free from condemnation. While, in the first instance, Christ meant by 'burden' the Pharisaic ordinances, the truth would become ever deeper to His disciples, till they understood the full contrast between the fulfilment of legal precepts through painful effort, and the joyous service of a living God and Father, growing into pervading holiness of character.

The 'burden ($\beta\acute{a}\rho os$)[*] of the day and the heat,' in the parable of the Labourers (Mt 20[12]) is a description of toil which strains and wearies. In the interpretation of the parable, if any stress were laid on this detail, it might be the long and conscientious fulfilment of duty in the Christian life, which, though it must receive recognition in the end, gives no claim on God as one who rewards of debt, nor allows the worker to glory over another who has been less richly furnished with opportunity.

LITERATURE.—On the 'burden' of Mt 11[28-30] ref. may be made to *Expos. Times*, iii. [1892] 512 ff.; *Expositor*, 1st ser. vii. [1878] p. 348 ff., xi. [1880] p. 101 ff.

DAVID M. W. LAIRD.

BURIAL.—In contrast to the Greek and the later Roman custom of cremation, the rites of burial were observed amongst the Jews with great reverence, and an account of their ordinary practice will help to illustrate several passages in the NT. Immediately after death the body was washed (Ac 9[37]), and wrapped in linen cloths in the folds of which spices and ointments were laid (Jn 19[39. 40]). The face was bound about with a napkin, and the hands and feet with grave-bands (Jn 11[44] 20[7]). Meanwhile the house had been given over to the hired mourners (Mt 9[23] ||; cf. 2 Ch. 35[25], Jer 9[17]), who lamented for the dead in some such strains as are preserved in Jer 22[18], and skilfully improvised verses in praise of his virtues. The actual interment took place as quickly as possible, mainly on sanitary grounds; very frequently, indeed, on the same day as the death (Ac 5[6. 10] 8[2]), though it might be delayed for special reasons (Ac 9[37f.]). In its passage to the grave the body was generally laid on a bier, or open bed of wicker work (Lk 7[14]; cf. 2 S 3[31], 2 K 13[21])—hence at Jesus' command the widow of Nain's son was able to sit up at once (Lk 7[15]). The bier was, as a rule, borne to the tomb by the immediate friends of the deceased, though we have also traces of a company of public 'buriers' (Ac 5[6. 10]; cf. Ezk 39[12-16]). In front of the bier came the women, and in Judæa the hired mourners, and immediately after it the relatives and friends, and 'much people of the city.' Attendance at funerals was, indeed, regarded as a pious act, and was consequently not always wholly disinterested. Among modern Orientals it is called 'attending the merit,' an act that will secure a reward from God (G. M. Mackie, *Bible Manners and Customs*, p. 127).

The place of burial in NT times was always outside the city (Lk 7[12], Jn 11[30], Mt 27[52. 53]), and frequently consisted of a natural cave, or an opening made in imitation of one. These rock-sepulchres were often of considerable size, and sometimes permitted of the interment of as many as thirteen bodies. Eight, however, was the usual number, three on each side of the entrance and two opposite. The doorway to the tomb was an aperture about 2 ft. broad and 4 ft. high, and was

* In Gal 6[2. 5] Lightfoot contends that $\beta\acute{a}\rho os$ and $\phi o\rho\tau\acute{\iota}o\nu$ mean, respectively, a burden that may and ought to be got rid of, and one that must be borne.

VOL. I.—16

closed either by a door, or by a great stone—the *golel*—that was rolled against it (Mt 27[66], Mk 15[46], Jn 11[38. 39]). It is sometimes thought that it was in some such rock-tomb that the demoniac of Gadara had taken up his abode; but more probably it was in one of the tombs 'built above ground,' which were 'much more common in Galilee than has been supposed' (Wilson, *Recovery of Jerusalem*, p. 369, *ap.* Swete, *St. Mark*, p. 88).

As a rule, sepulchres were whitened once a year, after the rains and before the Passover, that passersby might be warned of their presence, and thus escape defilement (Mt 23[27]; cf. Nu 19[16]). And though it was not customary to erect anything in the nature of our gravestones, in NT times it was regarded as a religious duty to restore or rebuild the tombs of the prophets (Mt 23[29]). In addition to family sepulchres of which we hear in the earliest Hebrew records (Gn 23[20], Jg 8[32], 2 S 2[32]), and such private tombs as the tomb of Joseph of Arimathæa (Mt 27[60]), special provision was made for the interment of strangers (Mt 27[7. 8]; cf. Jer 26[23], 2 Mac 9[4]). See art. TOMB.

It will have been observed how many of the foregoing particulars are illustrated in the Gospel narrative of the burial of Jesus; but it may be well to summarize briefly what then took place. No sooner had it been placed beyond doubt that Jesus was really dead, than Joseph of Arimathæa obtained permission to take possession of His body (Mt 27[57ff.]; cf. the merciful provision of the Jewish law, Dt 21[23]). Haste was required, as the Jews' Preparation was close at hand, and the body, after being, perhaps, bathed (so *Gospel of Peter*, 6), was at once wrapped 'in a clean linen cloth' (Mt 27[59]), the 'roll of myrrh and aloes,' of which Nicodemus had brought about a hundred pound weight (Jn 19[39]), being apparently crumbled between the folds of the linen ($\delta\theta\acute{o}\nu\iota a$). It was then borne to the 'new tomb wherein was never man yet laid,' and reverently laid on the rocky ledge prepared for the purpose, while the whole was secured by a 'great stone' placed across the entrance, which was afterwards at the desire of the Jews sealed and guarded (Mt 27[62ff.]; cf. *Gospel of Peter*, 8). There the body remained undisturbed over the Jewish Sabbath; but when on the morning of the first day of the week the women visited the tomb, bringing with them an additional supply of 'spices and ointments' to complete the anointing which want of time had previously prevented, it was only to find the tomb empty, and to receive the first assurance of their Lord's resurrection (Lk 24[1ff.]). In connexion with this visit, Edersheim has drawn attention to the interesting fact that the Law expressly allowed the opening of the grave on the third day to look after the dead (*Bible Educator*, iv. p. 332). In entire harmony, too, with what has already been said of the general structure of Jewish tombs, is the account which St. John has preserved for us of his own and St. Peter's visit to the tomb of Jesus (Jn 20[1ff.]). He himself, when he reached the doorway, was at first content with stooping down ($\pi a\rho a\kappa\acute{v}\psi as$) and looking in, and thus got only a general view ($\beta\lambda\acute{e}\pi\epsilon\iota$) of the linen cloths lying in their place. But St. Peter on his arrival entered into the tomb, and beheld—the word used ($\theta\epsilon\omega\rho\epsilon\hat{\iota}$) points to a careful searching gaze, the eye passing from point to point—not only the linen cloths, but the napkin that was about Christ's head 'rolled up in a place by itself.' These particulars have sometimes been used as evidence of the care and order with which the Risen Lord folded up and deposited in two separate places His grave-clothes before He left the tomb. But it has recently been shown with great cogency that what probably is meant is that the grave-clothes were found undisturbed on the very spot where Jesus had lain, the linen cloths on the lower ledge which had upheld the body, the napkin 'by itself' on the slightly raised part of the ledge which formed a kind of pillow for the head. The empty grave-clothes, out of which the Risen Lord had passed, became thus a sign not only that no violence had been offered to His body by human hands, but also a parable of the true meaning of His Resurrection: 'all that was of Jesus of Nazareth has suffered its change and is gone. We—grave-clothes, and spices, and napkin—belong to the earth and remain' (H. Latham, *The Risen Master*, p. 11 : see the whole interesting discussion in chapters i.–iii.).

Apart from these more special considerations, it is sufficient to notice that the very particularity of the description of the burial of Jesus is in itself of importance as emphasizing His true humanity and the reality of His death. From nothing in our lot, even the sad accompaniments of the grave, did He shrink. On the other hand, the empty grave on the morning of the third day has always been regarded as one of the most convincing proofs that 'the Lord is risen indeed.' Had it not been so, then His body must have been stolen either by friends or by foes. But if by the latter, why in the days that followed did they not produce it, and so silence the disciples' claims? If by the former, then we have no escape from the conclusion that the Church of Christ was founded 'not so much upon delusion as upon fraud—upon fraud springing from motives perfectly inexplicable, and leading to results totally different from any that could have been either intended or looked for' (W. Milligan, *The Resurrection of our Lord*[4], p. 73).

LITERATURE.—See artt. 'Burial' and 'Tombs' in Kitto's *Cycl.*, Smith's *DB*, Hastings' *DB*, *Encyc. Bibl.* ; 'Beerdigung' in Hamburger's *RE* ; 'Begräbnis bei den Hebräern' . *PRE*[3] ; Edersheim, *Sketches of Jewish Social Life*, p. 161 ff. ; Thomson, *Land and Book* ; Bender, 'Beliefs, Rites, and Customs of the Jews connected with Death, Burial, and Mourning,' in *JQR*, 1894 and 1895.   GEORGE MILLIGAN.

BURNT-OFFERING is a word of rare occurrence in NT (Mk 12[33], He 10[6. 8]). This is probably due to the fact that the more generic word for sacrifice (θυσία) is commonly used, since the distinctions of the Old Covenant, which was vanishing away, did not require to be perpetuated in the NT Canon. It is probable, however, from the train of thought, that in some instances the sacrifice which was prominently before the mind of the writer was the burnt-offering (Ro 12[1]). And though not named, it is latent in certain passages (see below). It is known in the OT as the עֹלָה 'ōlāh : more rarely and partly in poetical passages as the כָּלִיל kālîl ; in Ps 51[19] both terms are used. The most common LXX rendering is ὁλοκαύτωμα, and in this form it appears in the NT. The 'ōlāh is connected with a root meaning 'to ascend,' the idea being, probably, that the essence of the sacrifice ascended to heaven in the smoke ; kālîl, with a root meaning 'to be complete,' an idea reproduced in the LXX translation. Details of the rite may be found in Lv 1. 6[8-13] 8[18-21]. Unlike most sacrifices, it was to be wholly burnt (Lv 1[9]), the skin only falling to the priest as his perquisite.

The burnt-offering was the principal sacrifice of the Mosaic dispensation, and continued as such till the destruction of the Temple by Titus. It was offered, the victim being a male yearling sheep, every morning and evening (Ex 29[38-42]) ; hence its Mishnic name *tāmîd*, the perpetual offering. In addition, on Sabbaths, new moons, the first day of the seventh month, the three great feasts, and the Day of Atonement, other victims were offered (Nu 28 f.). Burnt-offering was associated with other sacrifices (Lv 9[3. 4] 15[15]), could be offered for individuals, even Gentiles, and even for the Roman

emperor (Jos. *Wars*, II. xvii. 2). The altar stood in the court of the priests in front of (eastward of) the Temple building. The offering was made publicly, in the presence not merely of the large group of ministering priests, but also of 'the men of station,' representatives of what may be called the Jewish laity.

Although the word is nowhere recorded as being spoken by Christ, and only once as spoken to Him, it must be remembered that His connexion with burnt-offering was, of necessity, more intimate than the mere occurrence of the word suggests. As a Jew, acquainted with the OT, He could not have been unacquainted with the Pentateuchal legislation on this point ; nor is it conceivable that as a visitor to the Temple He failed to be a witness of this rite. The altar on which burnt-offering was offered, from its great size, its frequent use, and its standing visibly in the court of the priests, was emphatically '*the* altar,' and it was before this that He directed the offending brother to leave his gift (Mt 5[23]). At the Presentation in the Temple (Lk 2[24], cf. Lv 12[6-8]) the second of the turtle doves was intended for a burnt-offering (the other bird forming the usual sin-offering at such a time) ; it was the offering of the poor, and the ritual is described in Lv 1[15-17]. The Temple tax to which He contributed was in part used for the provision of burnt-offerings (Mt 17[24]).

The two occasions on which, in NT, the burnt-offering is referred to, emphasize the imperfect and transitory character of the OT sacrificial system, and the spiritual, perfect, and abiding character of that which superseded it. In Mk 12[33] the scribe inferred from our Lord's teaching as to the first commandment, that to love God with all the heart and one's neighbour as oneself was 'much more than all whole burnt-offerings and sacrifices,' and was for this commended as 'not far from the kingdom of God.' In He 10[6. 8], where only besides the word occurs, while the writer dwells on many points of the Temple, its furniture, and its service, he fails to apply the burnt-offering very closely to the redeeming work of Christ. But he quotes Ps 40[6] as declaring that the Divine pleasure lies not in 'victim and Minhah' (Delitzsch, *in loc.*), and infers the superiority of Christ's obedience to any expiatory sacrifice (sin-offering) or dedicatory sacrifice (burnt-offering) presented by means of an animal victim. His obedience is the burnt-offering that has enduring value and needs no repetition.

LITERATURE.—Articles on 'Burnt-offering' and 'Sacrifice' in *Bible Dictionaries* of Hastings, Smith, and *Encyc. Bibl.*; *Bible Archæology* of Keil, Nowack ; Kurtz, *Sacrificial System of OT* ; *OT Theology* of Schultz, Oehler ; Cave, *Scriptural Doctrine of Sacrifice* ; Edersheim, *The Temple : its Ministry*, etc. ; Girdlestone, *Synonyms of OT* ; Schürer, *HJP* II. i. 278 ff.

J. T. L. MAGGS.

BUSH (βάτος).—Mk 12[26] ‖ Lk 20[37] * refers to the 'Burning Bush' (Ex 3[2. 3. 4], Dt 33[16] where LXX uses βάτος to tr. סְנֶה of the original). Before the [probably mediæval] division into chapters and verses it was not easy to cite Scripture with precision. 'In *or* at the Bush' (AV in Mark and Luke respectively) means not 'beside that memorable bush,' but 'in the passage in Scripture describing the theophany in the bush' (RV, '*in the place concerning* the Bush').

The derivation of סְנֶה is not known, and all attempts to identify it have failed. There is no justification for the suggestion of Gesenius (*Lexicon, s.v.*) that it is connected with the *senna* plant, nor for Stanley's assumption (*Hist. of the Jewish Church* [ed. 1883], i. 97) that it was the wild acacia. The fact that in the LXX it is translated by βάτος shows that it was believed to be a thorn bush. βάτος is specially used of the bramble (*Rubus*), but according to Post (Hastings' *DB*, *s.v.* 'Bush'), '*Rubus* has not been found wild in Sinai, which is south of its range, and climatically unsuited to it.'

* The parallel passage in Matthew (22[31]) omits the reference to 'the Bush.'

βάτος occurs once again in the Gospels : Lk 6⁴⁴ ;
AV and RV ‘bramble bush’ [Matthew’s parallel
(7¹⁶) has ‘thorns’]. It was thought necessary to
alter the translation ; the word which in the other
passage had such lofty associations is here used
by Christ almost with contempt. Moreover, a
vine might well enough be described as a ‘bush’
in the abstract ; it does not grow high, and has no
strength of wood (Ezk 15). ‘Bramble’ in older
English means ‘thorn bush,’ not necessarily ‘blackberry bush.’ Yet the translation seems apt enough,
even according to modern usage. Liddell and Scott
give βάτος as = ‘blackberry bush’ or ‘wild rasp-
berry,’ but the adjective βάτεις = ‘thorned.’
                                    ROBERT MACKINTOSH.

BUSHEL (ὁ μόδιος, Mt 5¹⁵, Mk 4²¹, Lk 11³³—a
Lat. word with a Gr. form).—The Roman *modius*,
equal to 16 *sextarii*, or approximately one English
peck, was not a measure in common use in Jewish
households. Although the definite article is probably generic (‘*the* bushel,’ so RV), the measure
which would lend itself naturally to our Lord’s
illustration, and that to which He actually referred, was the Hebrew *ṣeah* measure used by the
housewife in preparing the daily bread. While
the *ṣeah* measure varied in size according to
locality, it is generally regarded as being equal to
one *modius* and a quarter, though Josephus (*Ant.*
IX. iv. 5) states : ‘A *ṣeah* is equal to an Italian
modius and a half.’
    To the influence of Roman customs was no doubt
due the substitution of *modius* for *ṣeah* in the
report of the saying (Mt 5¹⁵ etc.) ; and in like
manner, since no importance was attached by our
Lord to exactness of measure, the familiar ‘bushel’
of earlier English versions has been retained by
the RV, although ‘peck’ would be a more accurate
rendering.
    The saying of our Lord is as picturesque as it is
forcible. It gives us a glimpse into a Galilæan
home, where the commonest articles of furniture
would be the lamp, the lampstand, the *ṣeah*
measure, and the couch. And who could fail to
apprehend the force of the metaphor? ‘When the
word has been proclaimed, its purpose is defeated
if it be concealed by the hearers ; when the lamp
comes in, who would put it under the *modius* or
the couch of the *triclinium*?’ (Swete on Mk 4²¹).

LITERATURE.—Art. ‘Weights and Measures’ in Hastings’ *DB*
iv. 911ᵃ, 913ᵇ, and the *Encyc. Bibl.* iv. col. 5294 f.
                                    ALEX. A. DUNCAN.

BUSINESS. — **1.** The first recorded words of
Jesus stand in the AV, ‘Wist ye not that I must
be about my Father’s business?’ (Lk 2⁴⁹). This is
the only passage in the Gospels where the word
‘business’ occurs, and it is not without some sort
of regret that we are obliged to acknowledge the
greater accuracy of the RV, ‘Wist ye not that I
must be in my Father’s house?’ The familiar
rendering, however, finds a place in the margin ;
and indeed in this case, as in so many others,
the AV well represents the inner meaning of the
original words. Translated quite literally, the
phrase (ἐν τοῖς τοῦ πατρός μου) means ‘in the things
of my Father’ : it denotes a person’s property or
estate, and is equivalent to our colloquialism ‘at
my father’s,’—the whole stress falling on the idea of
ownership,—and in this way it is fairly frequently
used in Greek authors. The closest parallel in
Biblical Greek occurs in the Septuagint translation of Est 7⁹, where ‘in the house of Haman’ of
the RV is represented by the phrase ἐν τοῖς Ἀμάν,
and it is clear that the gallows, fifty cubits high,
must have stood in the precincts of the house, or
on the estate, of Haman. (For other instances, see
Excursus I. in Farrar’s *St. Luke* in the Cambridge
Bible for Schools, where a summary is given of
the essential points from an important monograph

on the passage by Dr. Field of Norwich : this
monograph has been reprinted in *Notes on the
Translation of the NT, by the late Frederick Field*,
Cambridge, 1899).
    The Latin Versions render the Greek phrase as
literally as the language allows, and throw no
light on the interpretation. The Sinaitic Syriac
has the suggestive paraphrase, ‘Wist ye not that
I must be with my Father?’ The idea of a sympathetic relation with God is indeed of the essence
of the passage ; perhaps we can best render it by
borrowing from the symbolical language of the
parables, ‘Wist ye not that I must work in my
Father’s vineyard?’
    A passage of Clement of Alexandria (*Strom.* IV.
xxiii. 148) affords an interesting parallel to the
translation of the Sinaitic Syriac just quoted :
‘For the dispensation of creation indeed is good,
and all things are well arranged, nothing happens
without a reason ; *in the things that are Thine
must I be* (ἐν τοῖς σοῖς εἶναί με δεῖ), O Almighty, and
if I am there I am with Thee.’ In another passage
(*Strom.* VI. vi. 45) the phrase is used with an even
wider application ; of the souls in Hades, Clement
says that they are *in the things* (*i.e.* within the
domain) of God. With this compare the teaching
of the ‘Elders’ referred to by Irenæus (v. xxxvi. 1):
‘For this cause they say that the Lord said that
in the things of My Father are many mansions.
For all things are God’s, who gives to all men the
habitation that befits them.’ Thus what in Jn 14²
is called ‘the house of my Father,’ is by the substitution of the phrase τὰ τοῦ πατρός μου extended
to mean the whole Universe, including, as the
context shows, heaven, paradise, and the ‘city’
of the re-created earth. In *Protrepticus*, ix. 82,
Clement seems to have the incident of Lk 2⁴⁹ in
his mind as implying the complete consecration of
life : ‘But I suppose that when a man is enrolled
and lives as a citizen and receives the Father, then
he will be *in the things of the Father*.’
    Godet (in his Commentary on St. Luke, *ad loc.*)
points out that the phrase ‘I must be’ (δεῖ εἶναί με)
conveys the idea of an absolute and morally irresistible consecration to the service of God on earth.
To the awakening consciousness of the child Jesus
the Temple at Jerusalem was the symbol of the
Father’s dominion over all things ; He said in
effect to His parents, ‘Ye ought to have sought
me in the place where men are occupied with the
things of God.’
    These first recorded words of Jesus then set a
standard by which must be tested every manner
of life. How far is it possible for a life spent in
business, with which a linguistic accident connects
these words for English readers of the Bible, to be
lived *in the things of the Father*, according to the
teaching of His Son? As an aid towards reaching
an answer to this vital question, let us see what
we can learn, from our Lord’s acts and words, of
the attitude He adopted towards the business life
of the time of His Incarnation.
    2. At the next recorded visit of Jesus to the
Temple, we find Him in conflict with men who
conducted business improperly : those who bore
rule there did not understand that they were ἐν τοῖς
τοῦ πατρός. It is well known that St. John (2¹³ᶠᶠ·)
narrates a ‘Cleansing of the Temple’ as taking
place quite early in the Lord’s public ministry,
while the Synoptists (Mt 21¹²ᶠ·, Mk 11¹⁵ᶠᶠ·, Lk
19⁴⁵ᶠ·) describe a similar event as occurring in
Holy Week. It is at least possible that the holy
zeal of Jesus was twice displayed in this manner ;
but if a choice had to be made, there would be
strong reasons for preferring the chronological
arrangement of St. John. Without entering into
this question, however, we can simply study the
attitude of Jesus towards those who conducted

the Temple market. The traffic was of two sorts, the sale of sacrificial animals, and the exchange of money : in both cases it may well have been legitimate in itself, and even necessary : the sin was connected with its being carried on within the sacred precincts. It seems obvious that the Sadducean rulers of the Temple, whose cupidity was notorious, must have made money out of the business carried on there ; no doubt the sites for stalls within the Temple precincts would command a good rent ; and, further, if the animals sold there were certified officially as being unblemished and fit for sacrifice, while those bought outside were liable to a scrutiny on being brought into the Temple, it is easy to see how the privileged trades men may have gained an almost complete mono poly, for which they would willingly pay a high price. If the conjecture (see Edersheim, *Life and Times*[4], 1887, p. 367 ff.) that this Temple market was identical with the unpopular 'Bazaars of the Sons of Annas' is right, then the notorious Annas and his son-in-law Caiaphas had probably a direct interest in the trade carried on. It seems prob able that the 'changers of money' (κερματισταί, Jn 2[14] ; κολλυβισταί, Jn 2[15], Mt 21[12], Mk 11[15]) were the official *Shulhanim* (Lightfoot, *Horæ Heb.* on Mt 21[12] ; Edersheim, *The Temple*, p. 70 ff.) who sat to collect the half-shekel for a fortnight before the Passover : they were allowed to make a charge on each half-shekel whether change was given or not, and Edersheim places their probable annual gain from this source at £9000. Very likely the ordinary business of exchange of money was carried on, as obviously no coins bearing images or idolatrous symbols could be offered in the Temple. Moreover, the mention by Josephus (*BJ* VI. v. 2) of treasure-chambers in the Temple belonging to private individuals suggests that ordinary banking business, including the receipt of money on deposit, may have been made a source of profit, which would be enhanced by the security afforded by the sanctity of the place. These con siderations have been put forward to show that it is likely that the ruling priestly faction turned to financial account the consecrated character of the buildings committed to their charge. Probably it was this making money out of holy things, rather than the ceremonial violation of the sanctity of the Temple, that caused the severity of our Lord's condemnation of the whole system which made His Father's house into 'a house of merchandise,' according to St. John's account, or in the stronger words of the Synoptists, into 'a den of robbers.' It is clear that Jesus would not suffer business to be carried on in a manner that interfered with the honour due to God : doubtless He would have applied this principle to the Day, no less than to the House, of His Father. The same lesson is taught in the parable of the Royal Marriage Feast (Mt 22[1ff.] ; cf. Lk 14[16ff.]).

3. But the Son of Man, to whom nothing human was void of interest, in no way stood aloof from business. Himself a carpenter by trade (Mk 6[3]), He did not hesitate to tell the 'fishermen' Apostles that there was a likeness between their former worldly and their future spiritual vocation (Mt 4[19], Mk 1[17]) ; the would-be disciple, who wished first to bid farewell to those at his house, was told that he might have learned behind the plough the need of concentrating his whole interest and attention on the task he had in hand (Lk 9[62]). Both before and after the resurrection (Lk 5[4ff.], Jn 21[1ff.]) Jesus granted special revelations of Himself to the disciples while engaged in their usual occupations. In the command to render to Cæsar the things that are Cæsar's (Mt 22[21], and parallels), we are struck by the business-like recognition of actually existing circumstances. Several of the parables

prove how fully Jesus understood and entered into the business spirit, and show that, when conse crated by devotion to God, it is necessary to those who seek the kingdom of heaven. The merchant man who sold all that he had in order to buy one pearl of great price, gave proof of that confidence in his own judgment, joined with willingness to stake all upon it, which is indispensable to success in great mercantile ventures, and is said to be even now characteristic of the Jewish nation (Mt 13[45f.], cf. 13[44] 'the hidden treasure'). In the parable of the Labourers in the Vineyard the fulfilment of a contract is sharply opposed to the voluntary gift of money to those who had presumably been will ing but unable to earn it (Mt 20[1ff.]). A proper return is rightly expected from the ownership of land (Mk 12[7ff.], and parallels) and of money (Mt 25[27], Lk 19[23]). It is worthy of notice that the case just referred to of the 'unprofitable servant' follows in St. Matthew's Gospel directly after that parable which shows how unbusiness-like neglect to buy oil on the part of the foolish virgins led to their exclusion from the marriage-feast. The man who failed to make correct calculations as to the cost of building a tower is regarded as a fit object for mockery (Lk 14[28ff.]). On the other hand, the unjust steward, who took advantage of his position of authority to make friends of his master's debtors, showed a business-like shrewdness which would have been of value if employed honestly in a good cause (Lk 16[9ff.]).

4. A terrible warning of the danger of misusing business capacity is afforded, not in the imaginary story of a parable, but in the actual life of Judas Iscariot. St. Matthew (26[14f.]) and St. Mark (14[10f.]) connect the determination of Judas to betray Christ with the anointing of His feet at the feast in the house at Bethany. St. John, in narrat ing the same incident (12[4ff.]), tells us that it was Judas who gave expression to the false idea that the giving of money to the poor was of greater value than personal devotion : 'Now this he said, not because he cared for the poor ; but because he was a thief, and having the bag used to take away (ἐβάσταζεν, see Westcott in *Speaker's Commentary, ad loc.*) what was put therein.' Judas, no doubt on account of natural aptitude, had been made treasurer to Jesus and His disciples ; he was vexed that so large a sum of money as three hundred pence had been wasted in the pouring out of the ointment instead of passing through his hands for the supposed benefit of the poor. Comparing together these different passages, it seems clear that St. John traced the fall of Judas, culminating in the betrayal, to the misuse through covetous ness of his business faculties.

5. It can be, and often is, argued that the morality taught by Christ cannot be strictly and literally applied in the conduct of business. Probably the impossibility is no greater in the life of the business man than it is in the life of any one who tries to live as a consistent Christian. The main difference seems to be that in business practical morality is daily, and often many times a day, put to a test the extent of which can be estimated in money, and failure to conform to a high standard is easily detected. The business man is obliged to have a definite standard of practical morality, high or low according to his own character and the exigencies of his trade, and according to that standard he must act. Self deception in his case is practically limited to one particular form,—which, however, is extremely prevalent,—that of attempting to separate personal from business morality. The ordinary non-busi ness man, on the contrary, generally has a curiously vague and more or less ideal standard, and it is a very difficult thing even for a man of honest thought to settle how nearly he lives up to it. Business morality in a measure analyses itself, while the morality of ordinary life almost defies analysis : a comparison between the two is thus extremely dangerous, as they are practically incommensurable quantities.

Jesus Christ evidently believed that the moral and religious truths which He taught were capable of being applied in business. We have seen above that He severely condemned the Sadducean hierarchy, who may be taken to represent the capitalist class of those days at Jerusalem, because their business was conducted on wrong principles : they maintained merely ceremonial purity, and would not put the 'price of blood' in the treasury (Mt 27[6]), but they did not shrink from making gain of holy things. This shows the uncompromising attitude of Christ towards what was morally bad. But there was a great difference in His manner of dealing with another typical class of business men, the Publicans. He did not follow popular opinion in regarding their occupation as absolutely unjustifiable ; He looked on their calling as a legitimate one, while demanding honesty in carrying it out. The Baptist had taken the same line, 'Exact no more than that which is appointed you' (Lk 3[13]). Zacchæus, for his charity and earnest desire to avoid extortion, is declared to be truly a son of Abraham (Lk 19[9]).

It is worthy of note that St. Luke places the parable of the Pounds in close connexion with the Zacchæus incident, as if to teach us that lessons of eternal value can be learned in business. The slaves are rewarded with ten or five cities, according to the capacity which each had shown in trading with his pound.

This brings us to the centre of the whole matter : the life of business is a legitimate one for followers of Christ so far as it can be lived 'in the things of the Father' ; then it is a means of imparting training and of teaching lessons which can be used now and hereafter in the service of God. 'God has set you,' writes the Rev. Wilfrid Richmond (*Christian Economics*, 1888, p. 159), 'in the world with other men to learn, by mutual interchange of the means of life, the laws of love. Your wealth, whatever it may be, little or great,—the wealth you make, the wealth you spend,—is treasure, corruptible or incorruptible, treasure on earth or treasure in heaven, according as it is or is not, in the making and in the spending, the instrument of love.'

LITERATURE.—Besides the works referred to in the art., reference may be made to E. S. Talbot, *Some Aspects of Christian Truth*, 208 ; A. Whyte, *Walk, Conversation, and Character of Jesus Christ our Lord*, 59 ; C. R. D. Biggs, *The Diaconate of Jesus*, 19 ; S. Gregory, *Among the Roses*, 191 ; H. Bushnell, *Sermons on Living Subjects*, 243 ; *Expos.* 2nd ser. viii. [1884] p. 17.   P. M. BARNARD.

BUYING.—See TRADE AND COMMERCE.

C

CÆSAR (Καῖσαρ). — In the Gospel record this name occurs 18 times, in 16 of which it answers to 'reigning emperor,' who in each case was Tiberius Cæsar ; in the remaining two the more individual name is found,—in the one case Augustus (Lk 2[1]), and in the other Tiberius (3[1]).

The name 'Cæsar' was assumed by Augustus in 44 B.C., immediately after the tragic death of his grand-uncle, Julius Cæsar, being considered by him part of the inheritance left to him. We have Cicero's authority (*ad Att.* xiv. 5, 10, 11, 12) for saying that the friends of Octavius began to address him as 'Cæsar' within a week or two of the Dictator's assassination. Augustus himself soon gave evidence that he meant to gather up and concentrate on himself all the fame that was associated with 'Cæsar.' Not many years passed till he came to exercise a world-wide sway, such as the great Julius had never known. He handed on the title to his successors very much as we find it used by the writers of the NT, in the sense of the great ruler or Kaiser. His own name (Gr. Σεβαστός, Lat. *Augustus*) was quite familiar to them as applied to the reigning emperor (Ac 25[21, 25], Nero). The fame of the first Cæsar had come to be overshadowed by the remarkable career of the founder of the Empire. The way was thus prepared for the still later development, when the title of 'Cæsar' was given to the junior partner of the two joint-emperors, and 'Augustus' remained the distinguishing name of the supreme ruler. In the Gospel record there is clear confirmation of the first part of this historical development, and there is at the same time no contradiction of the second.

In the majority of the cases of the use of the title 'Cæsar' in the Gospel writings, the question of paying the tribute has come up. This reveals the great change that had taken place from the time of the 'census' under Augustus, when 'every one went to enrol himself in his own city' (Lk 2[3]), to that of the trial before Pilate, when the chief charge against Jesus was said to be 'the forbidding to give tribute to Cæsar' (23[2]). In those thirty-three years of interval the relation between the Roman power, as represented by 'Cæsar,' and the Jewish people, had undergone a radical change. Judæa had become a Roman province, and was under obligation to 'pay tribute' as well as submit to an enrolment of its heads of households. In perfect accord with this historical fact, St. Luke wrote (3[1]) : 'Pontius Pilate being governor of Judæa,' with the tetrarchs for Galilee, Ituræa, and Abilene, desiring to mark the period in the reign of Tiberius Cæsar when 'the word of God came to John in the wilderness.' The change came with the death of Herod the Great in 4 B.C. While Varus, the governor of Syria, was engaged in quelling serious outbreaks of rebellion in Jerusalem, the sons of Herod were in Rome waiting the decision of Augustus as to their conflicting claims. At length all parties were heard by the emperor in an assembly that met in the celebrated temple of Apollo, behind his own house on the Palatine. The imperial verdict, announced after a few days, upheld substantially the will of Herod. To Archelaus were assigned Judæa, Samaria, and Idumæa—not as king, but as ethnarch ; to Antipas, Galilee and Peræa as tetrarch ; Batanæa, Trachonitis, Auranitis, Gaulanitis, and Paneas to Philip, also as tetrarch (Jos. *Ant.* XVII. viii. 1, xi. 4). The kingdom of Herod was thus divided into three separate territories after his death. As it was in Jerusalem that the question as to the tribute money was raised, our subject in this article has to do only with Archelaus. After some nine years of rule over Judæa, Archelaus was summoned to Rome to answer charges brought against him by a deputation of leading men from Judæa and

Samaria. He was deposed and banished by Augustus to Vienne in Gaul in A.D. 6. His territory was put under direct Roman rule, becoming a part of the province of Syria, with a Roman of equestrian rank for its governor. An end was thus put to the uniform consideration for Jewish traditions and national prejudices shown by Herod and his sons. The first notable instance of this in history is met with in the rebellion of A.D. 6, on the occasion of the great census, while Quirinius was governor of Syria, which is referred to in Ac 5[37]. The tumult, with its accompanying bloodshed, must have been of no slight moment, when a quarter of a century thereafter Gamaliel could effectually use it in restraining the Council from slaying the Apostles. Between A.D. 6 and A.D. 30, whichever length of cycle for the imperial census be taken, there must have been at least another 'enrolment' for purposes of taxation. We do not read of a serious revolt having taken place then as in 6 A.D. The Roman authorities, no doubt, were better prepared for what might happen, and the Jewish people also had learned the fruitlessness of rebellion. As the time of Christ's public ministry approached, their spirit nevertheless became more and more embittered. It was inevitable that at some point or other in that ministry the question should be pressed upon Him, ' Is it lawful to give tribute to Cæsar or not?' (Mt 22[17] ||). It was one of the burning questions of His time. A distinction must here be drawn between the ' customs ' or duties upon goods and the land tax with poll tax. The latter only passed into the ' Fiscus ' or imperial treasury. With perfect accuracy, therefore, it could be described as ' tribute to Cæsar.' This tax was exacted annually, and as the Jews were not yet subject to military conscription, it formed the chief sign of their subjection to the Roman yoke. Officers of state collected it, the procurator for the tax in the case of Judæa being also the governor, Pilate. It was different with the ' customs,' which were farmed out to the highest bidder, thus creating that intense antipathy which is revealed in the phrase ' publicans and sinners.'

The tribute payment after all was based on the fact of the kingship of Cæsar. The combination of ' Cæsar ' with ' king ' sounds entirely unhistorical to one familiar with the rise and growth of the Roman Empire. ' King ' was a term which Augustus was most careful to avoid from the time that it may be said to have cost the first ' Cæsar ' his life. Among Eastern peoples, however, it was the most usual title for their ruler. During the long reign of Herod no name was more familiar to the Jews than ' king.' It was most natural for them to transfer it to ' Cæsar.' Any one claiming to be a ' king ' within the wide dominion of Cæsar was seeking to establish a rival authority. This was the charge which they found it so easy to frame against Jesus when He and they were in the presence of Pilate : ' forbidding to give tribute to Cæsar, and saying that he himself is Christ, a king ' (Lk 23[2]). No more powerful appeal could they have made to Pilate's fears, as they thought, than when they cried out, ' If thou let this man go, thou art not Cæsar's friend : whosoever maketh himself a king, speaketh against Cæsar ' (Jn 19[12]). The title on the cross, ' Jesus of Nazareth, the king of the Jews ' (Jn 19[19]), as Pilate actually wrote it, served him better than their proposed modification, ' He said, I am king of the Jews ' (v.[31]). Should he ever be called in question by Cæsar for giving Jesus up to death, that title, written out by his own hand, would form an ample justification. The greater probability lies in the supposition that Pilate so named Him to spite the Jews, in accordance with those other words, ' Shall I crucify your king ?' (v.[15]). The whole attitude of Jesus towards

Cæsar, not only in the question of the tribute, but throughout the trial before Pilate, must have entirely disarmed the Roman governor of any fear that He was, or ever had been, a rival of Cæsar's.

J. GORDON GRAY.

CÆSAREA PHILIPPI.—The town called Cæsarea Philippi in the Synoptic Gospels (Mt 16[13], Mk 8[27], cf. Jos. Ant. XX. ix. 4, BJ III. ix. 7, VII. ii. 1) bore at one time, certainly as early as B.C. 198 (Polybius, Hist. xvi. 18, xxviii. 1), the name Panias (Πανιάς or, Πανεάς), which is still preserved in the modern Banias. Situated to the north of the Sea of Galilee on a plateau at the southern foothills of Mount Hermon, it lay in the territory that Philip received from his father, Herod the Great. The place, as well as the surrounding country, received its original name from a cave or grotto in a hill near by, which was called τὸ Πάνειον, because sacred to Pan and the Nymphs. In the face of the cliff there are still several niches with inscriptions in which Pan is mentioned. From the cave (Mugharet Ras en-Neba'), now partly filled with fallen stone, issues a strong stream of water which has long been reckoned one of the chief sources of the Jordan (Jos. Ant. XV. x. 3). On the hill above, Herod built a white marble temple in honour of Augustus (Jos. Ant. XV. x. 3, BJ I. xxi. 3), and here the Crusaders built a castle, the ruins of which still stand some fifteen hundred feet above the town, and about a mile and a quarter to the east (Kula't Subeibeh). Philip enlarged and beautified Panias, and called it Cæsarea (Καισάρεια) in honour of Augustus. The statement of Eusebius (Chron. ed. Schoene, pp. 146–147) that Philip built Panias, and called it Cæsarea, in the reign of Tiberius, is rendered improbable by coins which show that Cæsarea had an era dating from B.C. 3 or 2. To distinguish it from Cæsarea on the seacoast (Καισάρεια Στράτωνος or Καισάρεια τῆς Παλαιστίνης), it was commonly called Cæsarea Philippi (Καισάρεια ἡ Φιλίππου). Under Agrippa II. it received and bore for a short time the name Neronias (Νερωνιάς, Jos. Ant. XX. ix. 4). The place has probably no part in OT history, since its identification with Dan (Smith, HGHL pp. 473, 480) is not certain (Buhl, GAP p. 238).

Into this region Jesus came with His disciples during one of His tours of retirement from the common scenes of His Galilæan activity ; but He does not seem to have entered Cæsarea itself. St. Matthew (16[13], cf. 15[21]) tells us that Jesus came into the region (εἰς τὰ μέρη) ; St. Mark (8[27]) mentions more specifically and vividly the villages of Cæsarea (εἰς τὰς κώμας). In the territory of which Cæsarea was the chief city there were smaller towns, and it was through these that Jesus moved with His disciples and others who followed Him. St. Luke alone (9[18ff.]) of the Synoptists seems to have lost the touch of local colour fixed so indelibly upon the narratives of Mt. and Mk.—an authenticating element whose force even those who question the Synoptic tradition at this point find it difficult to escape (cf. Wrede, Messiasgeheimnis, p. 239). The narrative in Lk. lends itself, however, to the setting of Mt. and Mk., both by the way in which it is introduced without definite localization (καὶ ἐγένετο ἐν τῷ εἶναι αὐτὸν προσευχόμενον), and by the fact that in Lk.'s order it follows the feeding of the five thousand in the neighbourhood of Bethsaida. According to Mk 8[22. 27], it was from Bethsaida that Jesus went into the villages of Cæsarea, and in Jn 6[68ff.] we read of a confession of Peter immediately after the discourse of Jesus in Capernaum, occasioned by the feeding of the five thousand. St. Luke's material may have come to him in the form of a group centring around a saying of Jesus, but without definite localization. By inserting it after the feeding of the five thousand he has preserved the historical order without, however, giving us the exact local setting. For this we must look to St. Matthew and St. Mark.

By our First and Second Evangelists the same group of events is not only connected with a place which lends peculiar significance to them, but set in a larger context which extends to the feeding of the five thousand. Mt. and Mk. alike represent Jesus' arrival in the region of Cæsarea Philippi as part of a course decided upon shortly after that event. The decision which led to the retirement into the region of Tyre and Sidon must have been confirmed by His experience on returning to Galilee. For Jesus withdrew again, this time going north into the region of Cæsarea Philippi. Located at Cæsarea and standing in the period of retirement, this group of events points back to the beginning of the period for the explanation of its characteristic features. The Gospels do not enumerate the causes which led to such a change in the scene of Jesus' activity, but their narratives do indicate a situation which will in a measure account for it.

But, besides change of scene, this group of events reveals, as do the earlier events of the period of retirement, a change in the method of Jesus' work. His retirement from Galilee is from the people and their religious leaders into more intimate companionship with His disciples, from His popular instruction of the multitudes and beneficent activity in their midst to teach His faithful followers in more secluded intercourse the significance of His own person for the Kingdom He had been proclaiming, and to prepare them for His Passion. The period has fittingly been called, from its chief characteristic, the Training of the Twelve, and in no incident does this characteristic more clearly appear than in the events of Cæsarea Philippi.

The immediate occasion of Jesus' retirement from Galilee and the change in His method of work are indicated in Mt. and Mk. by their account of His attitude towards the traditions of the elders (Mt 15$^{1-20}$, Mk 7$^{1-23}$). The fundamental opposition between Jesus and the legalism of the Pharisees which had appeared in His attitude towards the Sabbath customs, and in the Sermon on the Mount, came now to sharp expression in His attack on the whole system of external formalism in religion. The people, moreover, had shown themselves unprepared to receive and unable to appreciate His teaching, even after the work of John the Baptist and His own labours in their behalf. And so the form of His teaching had changed from the gnomic to the parabolic, causing a separation between the mass and those who had ears to hear. How utterly the people had failed to comprehend Him is revealed by their attempt after the feeding of the five thousand to take Him and make Him king (Jn 6^{15}). After His discourse in Capernaum (Jn 6$^{26ff.}$), St. John tells us that many of His disciples walked no more with Him (Jn 6^{66}). Finally, the mission of the Twelve had widely extended His work, and shortly thereafter we are told that Herod (Antipas) heard of Jesus (Mk 6^{14}, Mt 14^1, Lk 9$^{7ff.}$). Bitter hostility from the religious leaders, failure on the part of the people to understand the character of His work, interested attention from the murderer of John the Baptist,—in the midst of such conditions Jesus withdrew from Galilee, and from His popular preaching activity, to devote Himself to His disciples.

Jesus' first retirement is into the region of Tyre and Sidon, part of the Roman province of Syria. Returning to Galilee, He feeds the four thousand, refuses the request of the Pharisees and Sadducees for a sign from heaven, with its evident Messianic implication, warns His disciples against the leaven of the Pharisees and Sadducees (so Mt 16^6; Mk 8^{15} has 'Pharisees and Herod'), heals a blind man near Bethsaida (Mk 8$^{22ff.}$), and retires from Galilee for the second time, coming with His disciples into the region of Cæsarea Philippi.

The key to the situation at Cæsarea, its controlling idea, is to be sought neither in the confession of Peter nor in the promise to Peter, but in Jesus' announcement of His approaching Passion. To this Peter's confession leads up ; around it Jesus' instruction of the disciples regarding Himself and the conditions of discipleship centres. The theme, moreover, becomes characteristic of His subsequent teaching (Mk 9$^{12. 31}$ 10$^{33f.}$ 12^7 14^8 etc.).

St. Luke tells us that Jesus had been praying alone (9^{18}, cf. 3^{21}), and that His disciples were with Him. St. Mark vividly locates the question that Jesus put to His disciples, as 'in the way' (8^{27}). St. Mark and St. Luke agree in the form of the question, 'Who do men (Mk. οἱ ἄνθρωποι, Lk. οἱ ὄχλοι) say that I am ?' St. Matthew, however, gives it in the third person, and introduces the title 'Son of Man'—'Who do men say that the Son of man is ?' * In either form the question is a striking one, by reason of the prominence it gives to Jesus' person. Emphasis until now had been placed by Him on His message and on His works of mercy, though both had stood in intimate relation to His person. He desires to know now what men think of the messenger.

The form given to Jesus' question in Mt. has been regarded as secondary, on the ground that by calling Himself the Son of Man, Jesus suggested the answer to His question in asking it. As a matter of fact, however, the answer is not given in terms of this title. In the Synoptic Gospels the title 'Son of Man' is always a self-designation of Jesus. Even where it appears in the Fourth Gospel in the mouth of others, this is in evident dependence on its use by Jesus (Jn 12^{34}). St. Stephen's use of it also looks back to Jesus' words (Ac 7^{56}, cf. Lk 22^{69}), and the usage of the Apocalypse is probably to be explained by the influence of Dn 7^{13} (cf. Rev 1^{13} 14^{14}). There can, moreover, be no doubt that Jesus so designated Himself during the conversation with the disciples at Cæsarea Philippi. The phrase occurs in Mk 8^{31} and Lk 9^{22}, but it is neither more adequately motived than in Mt., nor is it explained. The disciples must have been familiar with it as a self-designation of Jesus, even if they did not understand its full significance. The way in which it is introduced both in Mt. and Mk.-Lk. makes it difficult for us to think that it was now used for the first time ; and the Synoptic Gospels do indeed give earlier instances of its use (Mk 2$^{10. 28}$, Mt 8^{20} 9^6 10^{23} 11^{19} 12^8· $^{32. 40}$ 13$^{37. 41}$, Lk 5^{24} 6$^{5. 22}$ 7^{34}). Dalman questions this order, regarding it as improbable that Jesus called Himself Son of Man at an earlier time (Worte Jesu, p. 216), and Holtzmann holds that if Jesus did so it was in a different sense (NT Theol. i. pp. 257, 263). The Synoptic representation is self-consistent, however, in presupposing its earlier use, and this we must accept even while admitting that the meaning of the term cannot be fully determined apart from its usage here and subsequently, where it is associated with Jesus' suffering, resurrection, exaltation, and coming again in judgment. See, further, art. SON OF MAN.

In answer to Jesus' question, the disciples report the opinions current among the people concerning Him. The report must have been discouraging. Not only was there variety of opinion, some thinking that He was John the Baptist (cf. Mk 6^{14}), others Elijah, and still others Jeremiah (Mt 16^{14}) or one of the prophets ; but in the midst of this variety there was general agreement that Jesus, whoever else He might be, was not the Messiah. A forerunner of the Messianic Kingdom He might be, but not the Messianic King. His activity in proclaiming the Kingdom, whatever Messianic expectations it may have aroused, had resulted only in the popular recognition of His prophetic character, and in His association with the Messianic Kingdom in some preparatory sense. Manifestly Jesus was not the popular Messiah. His

* In Mt 16^{13} με before λέγουσιν in the TR is to be omitted with א B c vg cop syr^{hr} (cf. also Mt 10^{32}, Lk 12$^{8f.}$, Mk 8^{38}, Lk 9^{26}, Mt 5^{11}, Lk 6^{22}, Mt 16^{21}, Mk 8^{31}, Lk 9^{22}).

work, directed as it was towards spiritual ends, did not accord with the popular conception of the Messianic Kingdom. Moreover, Jesus had not spoken plainly in Galilee of His Messiahship. He had not assumed a popular Messianic title, and when individuals had recognized in Him the Messiah, He had commanded silence. His work, however, like that of John the Baptist, had excited interest, and called forth opinions which associated Him with the coming Messianic Kingdom. The report of the disciples so accurately describes the situation and so faithfully represents the tenor of popular opinion, that it cannot be regarded merely as the background sketched by the Evangelists for the purpose of bringing into sharp relief the confession of Peter.

In the Synoptic narratives the question of Jesus about the opinion of the people leads up to a similar question addressed to the disciples about their own, and the answer in the one case stands in sharp contrast to the report given in the other,—a contrast which is vivid and real because true to the historical situation. To the question addressed to the disciples, 'But who say ye that I am?' Peter answers, 'Thou art the Christ' (so Mk.; Lk. gives simply 'the Christ of God,' and Mt. 'Thou art the Christ, the Son of the living God'). Unlike the people, the disciples had recognized in Jesus the Messiah, and to this conviction Peter gave brief expression. However inadequate may have been the content which Peter and his companions gave to their formal statement of their faith, it was a matter of great importance that they were able to affirm clearly, and in opposition to the opinion of the people, their belief that in Jesus the Messianic King had come. The readiness and decision with which Peter formulated the faith of the disciples are an indication that their faith, though now expressed in this form for the first time, did not originate here (cf. J. Weiss, *Das älteste Evang.* p. 51). Their very presence with Jesus at this time gave evidence of such a conviction (cf. Jn 6[68ff.]). In this faith they had answered His call to discipleship; in it they had associated with Him, heard His teaching, and seen His wonderful works; their appointment as Apostles implied it, as did their subsequent mission to Israel. They had seen opposition arise and develop into bitter hostility; but when Jesus withdrew into the region of Tyre and Sidon, and again into the region of Cæsarea Philippi, they still companied with Him. They knew the popular opinion, but they still adhered to their own conviction.

The significance of Peter's confession, however, lies not simply in the fact that it gave expression to a deep and long-cherished conviction, thus evidencing the permanent, unchanged character of his faith; it had reference also to the future. It was made in answer to a question of Jesus which had as its occasion His intention to reveal to the disciples the necessity of His suffering. The faith of the disciples had stood all the tests to which it had been subjected in the past. Jesus, however, clearly foresaw a still greater test in the near future. In order to prepare them for it, there was need that definite expression be given to their faith. The revelation which was to be made to them would thus serve the purpose of clarifying the content of their faith. In Mk. and Lk. the confession of Peter is accordingly brought into close connexion with the announcement of the Passion. Mt. alone gives the words of Jesus to Peter (16[17-19]), not only confirming what we may infer from Jesus' reception of the confession (Mk.-Lk.), its essential correspondence with His own consciousness, but going further and giving us positive knowledge of Jesus' estimate and appreciation of Peter's faith.

Addressing Peter as Simon Bar-Jona,* Jesus declares him to be blessed in the possession of a faith which, transcending the human sphere of flesh and blood, has its origin in the heavenly sphere and from His Father. In thus describing the revelation-character of Peter's faith, Jesus does not define more nearly the process or time of origin, the psychological moment, but treats his faith simply as a definite fact of the past. Continuing with the emphatic 'But I,' Jesus makes Peter's confession the occasion of revealing His plan for the future, and the part that Peter is to fulfil in it. With the words 'Thou art Peter,' Jesus recalls the name He had given to His disciple and apostle (cf. Jn 1[42], Mk 3[16], Mt 10[2], Lk 6[14]). The Greek Πέτρος, like the Aramaic *Kêphâ*, means a **rock,** and suggests the idea of firmness or strength. In giving such a name to Simon, Jesus had looked beneath the surface and read the character of Peter in terms of motive and underlying disposition. A man of decision, he was full of energy and strength, a man of action rather than of contemplation, a natural leader; and if at times impulsive, rebuking his Master and even denying Him, he was in the one case loyal to his faith, however unwisely so, and in the other was following Jesus to be near Him when he fell. In maintaining and confessing his faith in Jesus, Peter had shown himself true to the character which Jesus recognized when He named him Peter. Upon this rock Jesus now affirms His intention of founding His Church: not upon any rock, and therefore not simply upon a strong and firm foundation, but upon *this* rock indicated by the name Peter. In the Greek the word for Peter (Πέτρος) and the word for rock (πέτρα) differ in form, but in Aramaic the same form was probably used. The Pesh. has *kiphâ* in both instances (cf. also Mt 27[60]; in Mt. 7[24f.] *šū̆ â* is used). The rock intended by Jesus to be the future foundation of His Church is Peter, realizing the character indicated in his name. The function thus assigned to Peter is indeed not apart from his confession, nor is the fact that he evidently spoke in a representative capacity to be overlooked. The address of Jesus, however, is distinctly to Peter, and it is his name that is interpreted. The confession which precedes is indeed closely related to the words of Jesus, but it cannot be understood as the rock-foundation intended by Jesus. In itself it furnishes the occasion rather than the ground of Jesus' promise. It cannot therefore be treated abstractedly as something separate from Peter, but must be regarded as a manifestation and, in its measure, a realization of the character which Jesus saw in Peter when He gave him his name. The content of Peter's faith, moreover, was entirely inadequate when measured by Jesus' conception of what His Messiahship involved. Much had still to be learned in the school of experience (Mk 8[31ff.] 14[66ff.], Lk 22[31], Jn 21[15ff.], 1 Co 15[5]), but the character was fixed in principle. Jesus saw its strength, and chose the man for the work He had for him to do. The opening chapters of the Acts of the Apostles give some account of the way in which he accomplished his charge.

The figure of a rock-foundation, used to describe Peter's future function in the Church, suggests naturally a single rock underlying a whole struc-

* *Bar-Jona,* or 'son of Jonas,' probably means 'son of John' (cf. Jn 1[42] 21[15-17]). In Hebrew the words יוֹנָה and יוֹחָנָן differ, but the Greek rendering of יוֹחָנָן is sometimes the same as that of יוֹנָה (cf. 1 Ch 26[3], 1 Es 9[23], 2 K 25[23]). Zahn attributes the difference between Mt. and Jn. to a confusion by the Greek translator of Mt. of the two Hebrew words (*Kommentar*, p. 537). Wellhausen gives his verdict briefly: 'Jona ist Jona und keine Abkürzung von Johanan, und Mt wird nicht bloss gegen das Hebräerevangelium, ein spätes Machwerk, recht haben, sondern auch gegen das vierte Evangelium' (*Das Evang. Matt.* p. 83 f.).

ture, and not one stone among a number built together into a foundation (cf. Mt 7[24ff.]). Neither the figure nor the function thus assigned to Peter excludes the work of the other Apostles (Eph 2[20]), much less the work of Jesus (1 Co 3[10f.]), which is clearly indicated in οἰκοδομήσω. The figure describes simply what Peter, by reason of his strong, energetic character, and in view of Jesus' intention, is to be for the Church which Jesus will build. The idea of building a community or Church was familiar from the OT (cf. Ps 28[5], Jer 18[9] 31[4] 33[7]), and recurs in the NT (cf. Mt 21[42], Ac 4[11], 1 P 2[4ff.], Ro 15[20], 1 Co 3[9ff.], 2 Ti 2[19ff.], He 3[1ff.]). By the use of the future tense and the choice of the word meaning to build rather than to rebuild (ἀνοικοδομέω, cf. Ac 15[16]), Jesus not only points to the future for the origin of His Church, but declares that it will be His own creation. It was expected that the Messiah would have a people and would rule over them in an organized community. The idea of such a community cannot have been strange to the disciples who had just confessed their faith in Him. It would have been strange had Jesus made no reference to His Church. By speaking of it He made plain to them that the idea was included in His purpose, and thus formed an element in His Messianic consciousness. The future founding of the Church is set by Him in evident contrast to present conditions, but the fact that this is included in Jesus' present purpose and thus made part of His Messianic work brings it into vital and organic relation with the present. His work had, indeed, not yet taken on its Church-form, but this was not due to the fact that the idea of such a Messianic community was foreign to His purpose. He thus encourages His disciples in the midst of popular disaffection and unbelief, by giving them assurance with regard to His intention.

The disciples had confessed their faith in Him, and He now tells them that however little promise present conditions may give of such a future, He will found His Church. And He will do this in the face of conditions which may seem to them to make such a future impossible. Instead of improving, the conditions will become worse. With His conception of the spiritual nature of His work and the consequent character of His Church, Jesus saw the necessity of His completed work and final exaltation in order to the full realization of His Messianic functions in such a Messianic community, and hence speaks of its building as a future event (Ac 2[36], Ro 1[4]). It is not strange, therefore, that He speaks but seldom of His Church, and dwells on the ideas of the Kingdom, faith and discipleship, in which its spiritual character and principles are set forth.

The word ἐκκλησία, regularly used in the LXX to translate קָהָל (ḳahâl), occurs frequently in the writings of St. Paul, but only here and in Mt 18[19] in the words of Jesus. Its authenticity has been questioned (cf. Holtzmann, Hdcom.; but, on the other hand, Köstlin in PRE[3] x. 318), but its use has an adequate basis in the teaching of Jesus, and is naturally motived here not simply by the confession of Peter, but also by Jesus' thought of the future, controlled as it is by the revelation of His Passion which He is about to make to His disciples.

So permanent and strong will be the structure built by Jesus on Peter, the rock-foundation, that the gates of Hades—a figurative expression used to suggest the idea of the very greatest strength, since they withstand all effort to force them open (Is 38[10], Wis 16[13], 3 Mac 5[51])—shall not surpass (κατισχύσουσιν) it in strength.* Changing the figure

* Others understand κατισχύσουσιν in the sense that the attack going forth from the gates of Hades shall not overcome the Church (Zahn), or again that the gates of Hades shall not prove strong enough to withstand the attack made on them by the Church, Hades in the former interpretation being conceived as the kingdom of evil, in the latter as the kingdom of death (Meyer).

and having the superstructure in mind, Jesus declares that He will give to Peter the keys of the Kingdom of Heaven. What he binds upon earth shall be bound in Heaven; what he looses upon earth shall be loosed in Heaven. The phrase 'Kingdom of Heaven' frequently takes the place in Mt. of the corresponding phrase 'Kingdom of God' in Mk. and Lk. Here it is to be understood not of the Kingdom which is in Heaven, but of that Kingdom which has its origin and centre in the Heavenly sphere, whence it receives its character as the rule of God and its determinative principles as moral and spiritual. This is the Kingdom which Jesus preached, whose coming He declared to be at hand, whose character and principles He expounded, and whose blessings He mediated. But while having its centre in Heaven, this Kingdom was to be realized upon earth, and, in its future manifestation at least, is associated closely with the Church. The authority which Peter is to exercise has reference to the Church, but the reciprocal relation between the Kingdom and its Heavenly centre is to continue in its future manifestation as Jesus had known it in His own experience and had declared it in His teaching. What Peter does as His representative in the Church which Jesus will build shall be ratified in Heaven. The keys of the Kingdom of Heaven symbolize administrative authority (cf. Is 22[22], Rev 3[7f.]), and the phrase 'bind and loose' is another figurative expression in which the idea of regulating seems to be fundamental : in Aramaic the words 'aṣar and shěrā mean to allow and to disallow (cf. also Mt 18[18], Jn 20[23]). Both figures seem to have reference to the internal affairs of the Church, and are therefore not to be understood as descriptive of Peter's proclamation of the gospel, as if by means of it those who accepted the gospel message were to be received into the Church (keys) and loosed from their sins, and those who rejected it were to be excluded and so bound in their sins. The description of Peter's work in the proclamation of the gospel is given in the figure which represents him as the foundation-rock of the Church. The power of the keys and that of binding and loosing, however, are not only closely associated together, but they are separated from the figure of the rock, and together describe Peter's function in the Church and his relation to its internal management as that of an οἰκονόμος. See also art. KEYS below, and 'Power of the Keys' in Hastings' DB, vol. iv.

In the command of Jesus to His disciples that they should tell no one that He is the Christ, Mt. not only joins again the narrative of Mk.-Lk., but rightly interprets the briefer form, in which they gave the command, by the words ὅτι αὐτός ἐστιν ὁ Χριστός. The authenticity of this and similar commands, especially in the Gospel of Mk., has, indeed, been called in question (Wrede, Das Messiasgeheimnis); but the command is quite natural here, and cannot be regarded as having its origin solely in the general apologetic purpose of St. Mark. It has reference to the form in which Peter's confession was made, and to deny its authenticity would necessitate a complete reconstruction of the account which the Gospels give us of Jesus' life and work.

The climax of the scene at Cæsarea is reached in Jesus' announcement of His Passion. Both Mt. and Mk. signalize His words as the beginning of instruction on this subject (Mk. καὶ ἤρξατο. Mt. more specifically ἀπὸ τότε ἤρξατο, Lk. connecting the announcement directly with the command to silence, εἰπὼν ὅτι δεῖ τ. ὑ. τ. ἀ. πολλὰ παθεῖν). When Jesus became aware of the necessity of which He here for the first time speaks explicitly to His disciples does not appear clearly from the Synoptic

Gospels. The Fourth Gospel indicates that He was not unaware of it from the beginning of His public ministry (Jn 2[19], cf. 2[21], Mt 26[61]). The Synoptic Gospels, however, give evidence that Jesus looked forward at an early period in the Galilæan ministry to the time when He would be removed from His disciples (Mk 2[20]). Certainly the narrative here does not justify the inference that He now for the first time became conscious of the necessity of His suffering, any more than the question to Peter and Peter's confession justify the inference that Jesus or His disciples now for the first time became conscious of His Messiahship. The conditions of His ministry may well have influenced Jesus to speak of the subject to His disciples at this particular time. Foreseeing not merely the necessity of His suffering, but its near realization, He spoke to the disciples of it for the purpose of preparing them for the issue of His work and of clarifying the content of their faith. The necessity of which Jesus speaks is to be understood as moral rather than physical, since it sprang out of the nature of His Messianic work by which He was brought into conflict with existing conditions. But if faithfulness to His work involved suffering, the necessity of which He speaks becomes voluntarily conditioned by a willingness to suffer, and this finds its ultimate explanation only in the Messianic consciousness of Jesus. A necessity springing out of faithfulness to His work, and thus to Himself, is, however, not only moral, but falls within the Divine purpose; and Jesus evidently so conceived it, since in rebuking Peter He speaks of it as τὰ τοῦ θεοῦ. The idea of a suffering Messiah, if current at all at the time of Jesus, was certainly not a prominent feature of the popular Messianic hope. The traces of it which are found, moreover, do not explain the form in which it appears in the Synoptic Gospels. For here we find it closely associated with a resurrection and a glorious coming of the Son of Man in His kingdom.

However clearly Jesus may have foreseen His suffering, and however calmly He may have announced its necessity, the care with which He prepared for, as well as the actual result of, His statement, reveal plainly the fact that the idea was foreign and repugnant to the thought of the disciples. A Messiah, though in retirement, opposed by the leaders and unrecognized by the people, they could believe Him; but that He should suffer, and that in Jerusalem where as Messiah He should rather establish His kingdom, seemed to them incredible. Peter's action in rebuking Jesus sprang naturally and spontaneously from the limitation of his outlook into the Messianic future. The view which would exclude suffering from His future, Jesus, however, rejects not only as human in character and origin, but as opposed to the Divine purpose; so that Peter in urging it, however conscientiously, became for Jesus a tempter, a hindrance in His way.

In the words which follow Peter's rebuke, Jesus sets forth the conditions of discipleship, and points out that the way of the disciple in following Him, like His way in going to Jerusalem to suffer, involved not only suffering, but willingness to suffer for His sake—the voluntary taking up of the cross and following Him in the pathway of self-sacrifice. Emphasis is placed by Jesus on personal relationship to Him, revealing a consciousness on His part of His own supreme significance for the world of spiritual realities made accessible through Him and His message (cf. also Mt 10[32ff.]). The fate of the soul, with its possibilities of spiritual life, is made dependent not on a denial of the will to live, but on a denial of the will to live for self and earthly gain. He who would be Jesus' disciple must seek his true and highest life-principle in self-sacrifice for Jesus' sake (cf. Gal 2[20]). Self-surrender to Jesus is made the principle of spiritual life, and as such it must be absolute, superseding even the desire for life itself. In stating such conditions of discipleship, Jesus reveals a consciousness of His own significance for men which transcends the present and partakes of the character of the truth which He proclaimed. Discipleship is thus drawn into and made part of that future in which He Himself was conscious of holding a place of highest authority. His words set the present in closest relation with the future, since its true worth will then be revealed. The relation which men sustain to Him now will then have its intrinsic value made manifest by His attitude towards them. 'For the Son of man shall come in the glory of his Father, and with his angels; and then shall he render to every man according to his deeds.' This prophetic description of the future closes with these words: 'Verily I say unto you, There be some here of them that stand by, which shall in no wise taste of death, till they see the kingdom of God come with power' (so Mk.; Lk. has simply 'till they see the kingdom of God'; Mt. more fully, 'till they see the Son of man coming in his kingdom'). The words are prophetic, and describe an experience in which some of those then in Jesus' company shall share. The object of this experience is in Lk.-Mk. the Kingdom, or the Kingdom (having) come (Mk. uses the perf. part. ἐληλυθυῖαν) in power. It seems thus to be conceived as a future but actually existing state or fact rather than event. In Mt. the same experience is described, but the fact of the Kingdom's presence is associated with or described in terms of the Son of Man's coming (ἐρχόμενον) in His kingdom. In their context the words seem to refer to the Messianic kingdom, and to describe it in one of its eschatological aspects. The disciples had just confessed Jesus, who called Himself the Son of Man, to be the Messiah, and He had declared that the Son of Man would come in glory. He now declares that some of those present will live to witness the coming of the Son of Man, the Messiah, in His kingdom; by which we may understand the establishment of His kingdom in power. This, however, was to be realized in the Church; for Jesus, in speaking of His intention with reference to the future founding of His Church, had not only indicated the close relation of the Church to the Kingdom of Heaven, the one being the future manifestation-form of the other, but also stated that He Himself would build the Church, thus directly revealing His power in it. It is therefore not unnatural to understand the 'coming of the Son of Man in his kingdom' or 'the kingdom (having) come in power' as referring to the establishment of His Church, its equipment with power through the gift of the Spirit at Pentecost, and its activity in realizing the Kingdom under His direction. Others seek the fulfilment of Jesus' prophecy in the Transfiguration, His appearances to the disciples after the resurrection, or specifically in the gift of the Spirit at Pentecost, or in the fall of Jerusalem, or still more generally 'in some convincing proof that the Messiah's kingdom had been actually set up, as predicted by prophets and by Christ Himself' (Alexander, *Matthew*, p. 446).

LITERATURE.—Reland, *Palæstina*, ii. 918–922; Guérin, *Description de la Palestine*, 'Galilée,' ii. 308–323; *SWP* i. 95, 109–113; G. A. Smith, *HGHL*, 473–480; Buhl, *GAP* 238 ff.; Baedeker, *Palestine*[5], 291 f.; Schürer, *HJP* (Index); artt. 'Cæsarea' (Ewing) and 'Peter' (Chase) in Hastings' *DB*; 'Cæsarea' (G. A. Smith), 'Ministry,' 'Simon Peter' (Schmiedel) in *Encyc. Bibl.*; 'Gaulanitis' and 'Palästina' (Guthe), 'Kirche' (Köstlin), 'Petrus, der Apostel' (Sieffert) in Herzog's *PRE*[3]; Holtzmann, *Handkommentar*, i., *Neutest. Theologie*, i. p. 211 f.; Zahn, *Evangelium des Matthäus*; Dalman, *Words of Jesus*, p. 254 ff.; Vos, *The Teaching of Jesus concerning the Kingdom of God and the Church*, 140–168; Lowrie, *The Church and its Organization*, 102–123; Hort, *The Christian Ecclesia*; A. B. Bruce, *The Training of the Twelve*, ch. xi.

WILLIAM P. ARMSTRONG.

CAIAPHAS (Καιάφας; according to Josephus, 'Joseph Caiaphas') was appointed high priest of the Jews in or soon after A.D. 18, and held office until he was deposed by Vitellius about A.D. 36 (Jos. *Ant.* XVIII. ii. 2, iv. 3). He is referred to as the high priest in Lk 3[2] (with Annas), Mt 26[3. 57], and is mentioned along with Annas, John, and Alexander among the heads of the Sanhedrin in Ac 4[6]. The length of his rule, compared with the short periods allowed to his immediate predecessors, suggests that he proved a satisfactory and submissive agent of the Roman policy. By two of the Evangelists, St. Matthew and St. John, Caiaphas is specially connected by name with the procedure which led to the condemnation and death of Jesus. When, after the raising of Lazarus, the 'high priests and Pharisees' held a meeting of the Sanhedrin (informal, as Caiaphas does not appear to have presided), it was Caiaphas who gave the ironically prophetic advice that it was expedient that one man should die for the people (Jn 11[50]). 'St. John, contemplating that sentence years after, could not but feel that there was something in those words deeper than met the ear, a truth almost inspired, which he did not hesitate to call prophetic' (F. W. Robertson, *Sermons*, i. 134). In saying that 'being high priest that same year he prophesied,' the Evangelist does no more than claim for the theocratic head of the nation the function which might be supposed to be latent in his office (cf. the remark of Philo quoted by Westcott: 'the true priest is a prophet'; see also the remarks of Dale, *The Atonement*, p. 169 ff.), and had, as a matter of fact, been exercised by some of his predecessors in the office (Nu 27[21]). The threefold repetition by St. John of the statement that Caiaphas was high priest 'that same year' (AV; RV 'that year') has been made the ground of charging the Fourth Evangelist with ignorance of the fact that the high priest might hold office for more than one year. But this criticism rests on a misapprehension of the phrase (τοῦ ἐνιαυτοῦ ἐκείνου), which emphasizes not the date, but the character of the year = 'that fateful year' (cf. Jn 20[19] Mk 4[35]).

The resolution thus prompted took effect in the arrest of Jesus; but, as son-in-law to Annas, Caiaphas permitted the prisoner to be taken first before him (Jn 18[13]) for a private examination. Whether this took place in the 'palace' of Caiaphas, where Annas was living, or elsewhere, is not clear. It is also uncertain whether the Fourth Gospel contains any record of an examination of Jesus by Caiaphas. According to the reading and interpretation of Jn 18[24] in RV, it does not; but it is held by some (*e.g.* Meyer and Edersheim, against Westcott) that AV may be correct, and that the high priest referred to in vv.[15. 19] and [22] was Caiaphas. According to the narrative of the Synoptists, it was to Caiaphas the 'high priest,' or the 'house of Caiaphas,' that Jesus was led, and there, at the (irregular) meeting of the Sanhedrin at daybreak (Mt 26[59], Mk 14[55], Lk 22[66]), Caiaphas presided; and it was he who brought the trial to a conclusion by declaring Jesus guilty of blasphemy, and demanding sentence upon Him.

Caiaphas appears again in Ac 4[6] in company with Annas and others, as initiating the persecution of the Apostles, and in the later proceedings is probably the 'high priest' referred to in Ac 5[17. 21. 27] 7[1] and 9[1].

LITERATURE.—On the name, Nestle in *Expos. Times*, x. [1899] p. 185. On the historical circumstances, Schürer, *HJP* ii. i. 182 f., 199; Andrews, *Life of our Lord*, 137, 505. On the ethical significance of Caiaphas' attitude to Christ, F. W. Robertson,

Sermons, i. 132; J. B. Lightfoot, *Sermons in St. Paul's*, 75; A. Maclaren, *Christ in the Heart*, 255; E. H. Gifford, *Voices of the Prophets*, 73; W. H. Simcox, *Cessation of Prophecy*, 278; H. H. Henson, *Value of the Bible*, 294; *Expos. Times*, iv. [1892] p. 49.   C. A. SCOTT.

CAINAN.—The name occurs twice in St. Luke's genealogy of our Lord : (1) of the son of Arphaxad (Lk 3[36]); (2) of the son of Enos (v.[38]).

CALENDAR, THE CHRISTIAN.—

I. The Christian Week.
   1. The Lord's Day.
   2. Wednesday and Friday.
   3. Saturday.
II. The Christian Year.
   1. Easter.
     (*a*) The name.
     (*b*) Early observance of Easter.
     (*c*) The Quartodeciman Controversy.
     (*d*) Determination of Easter. Paschal cycles.
     (*e*) The fast before Easter.
     (*f*) Palm Sunday.
     (*g*) Maundy Thursday.
     (*h*) Easter Week.
   2. Pentecost and Ascension.
     (*a*) The name 'Pentecost.'
     (*b*) Connexion of Pentecost and Ascension.
   3. Christmas and Epiphany.
     (*a*) Their origin.
     (*b*) Advent.
   4. Presentation of Christ in the Temple.
   5. Commemoration of Saints, etc.
   Recapitulation of festal cycles.
   Literature.

The Christian Calendar in its origin appears to have been based mainly on the desire to commemorate, by festival or by fast, the events of our Lord's life upon earth. These commemorations were either weekly or annual. But while the weekly observances were developed early—almost, or in part quite, from Apostolic times—the annual celebrations were of very slow growth, and for some three hundred years were confined to the two seasons when the Jews and Christians in common observed a commemoration, Easter and Pentecost. It is noteworthy, as showing that the main desire was to commemorate the events in the life of Jesus, that one of the very earliest books which exhibit any considerable development of the festal cycle is the so-called *Pilgrimage of Silvia*, otherwise of *Etheria* (about A.D. 385), in which the customs at Jerusalem are described. It was natural that those who lived in the land where the events narrated by the sacred history took place, should wish to commemorate them on the spot by annual observances. But this development took place only in the 4th century.

I. THE CHRISTIAN WEEK.—**1. The Lord's Day.**—It is significant that the first meeting of the disciples after the evening when they saw their newly-risen Master was, as far as the Gospel tells us, on the immediately succeeding 'first day of the week' (Jn 20[26] μεθ' ἡμέρας ὀκτώ: note how emphatically the Evangelist says of the preceding week, τῇ μιᾷ τῶν σαββάτων, 20[1], and τῇ ἡμέρᾳ ἐκείνῃ τῇ μιᾷ σαββάτων, 20[19]). It was more than an accidental coincidence if, as is very generally assumed, the birthday of the Church (Ac 2[1]) was also on the first day of the week. At Troas the Christians met together, or held a *synaxis* (συνηγμένων ἡμῶν), on the first day of the week for worship and the Eucharist (Ac 20[7], where ἐν τῇ μιᾷ τῶν σαββάτων appears to be more than a mere chronological reference, and to indicate a custom), and also probably for the Agape (cf. 20[7] with 20[11]). In this and other passages it is necessary to remember that the 'first day of the week' began, from the point of view of a Jew, with what we should call Saturday night; and this consideration is against Prof. Ramsay's view that the service at Troas began on what *we* should call Sunday night (*St. Paul the Traveller*, ch. xiii. § 3). That it was the custom for Christians to meet together for worship on the first day of the week appears also from 1 Co 16[2] (κατὰ μίαν σαββάτου), where the Corinthians are bidden each to 'lay by him in store,' that there might be no collection when the Apostle came. This would point probably to a weekly assembly at which alms were collected. Otherwise there is no reason why any one day of the week should be specially mentioned.

The first mention of the 'Lord's Day' by name is Rev 1¹⁰, if indeed this is the right interpretation (ἐγενόμην ἐν πνεύματι ἐν τῇ κυριακῇ ἡμέρᾳ). This phrase has been variously interpreted of the first day of the week, or of the Day of Judgment, or of the Sabbath, or of Easter Day. The last two interpretations may be dismissed as having no support from the earliest ecclesiastical writings. The identification of ἡ κυριακὴ ἡμέρα with the Last Day has more probability; it would then be equivalent to ἡ ἡμέρα τοῦ Κυρίου (2 Th 2² ; cf. 1 Th 5² ἡμέρα Κυρίου, Ac 2²⁰ from Jl 2³¹, 2 P 3¹⁰, 1 Co 1⁸ ἐν τῇ ἡμέρᾳ τοῦ Κυρίου ἡμῶν Ἰησοῦ Χριστοῦ, and 1 Co 5⁵, 2 Co 1¹⁴, Ph 1⁶), and would mean that the Apocalyptist is carried forward in vision to the day of the end of the world. It is a valid objection to this view that it would practically make the Apocalypse deal only with the future, and that almost the earliest ecclesiastical authors after the canonical writers use κυριακή in the sense of the first day of the week (see below). The more probable interpretation of the phrase in question is therefore the first mentioned above.

The NT evidence does not compel the belief that the Lord's Day was of universal observance in the earliest ages of the Church, but it at least makes it probable (especially when we find it so generally established in the next age) that it was of Apostolic precept. And there is nothing to forbid the supposition that it was a following of the spirit of the teaching of the great Forty Days (Ac 1³). But we may gather, with the historian Socrates (HE v. 22), that the 'Saviour and His Apostles' did not make fixed rules as to the observance of days, and 'enjoined us by no law to keep this feast [he is speaking of Easter, but his argument applies equally to Sunday], nor do the Gospels and Apostles threaten us with any penalty, punishment, or curse for the neglect of it, as the Mosaic Law does the Jews. . . . The aim of the Apostles was not to appoint festival days, but to teach a righteous life and piety.'

To pass to the post-Apostolic age, Barnabas (xv. 9) says : 'We keep the eighth day for rejoicing, in the which also Jesus rose from the dead, and, having been manifested, ascended into the heavens,' a passage which throws some light on the occasional observance in later times of Ascension Day and Pentecost together. Barnabas purposely names the 'eighth day' rather than the first, as he has just spoken of it as following the Jewish Sabbath, the seventh day. 'I will make the beginning of the eighth day, which is the beginning of another world.' The Didache speaks of the synaxis on the Lord's Day, and uses the pleonastic phrase κατὰ κυριακὴν Κυρίου συναχθέντες ; the purpose of the synaxis was that the Christians might break bread and celebrate the Eucharist, having confessed their sins that their sacrifice might be pure (§ 14).—Ignatius (Magn. § 9) speaks of Christians no longer observing Sabbaths, but fashioning their lives after the Lord's Day (μηκέτι σαββατίζοντες, ἀλλὰ κατὰ κυριακὴν ζῶντες), which at least involves a general observance of the first day of the week.—Pliny (Ep. 96) says only that the Christians met on a fixed day, and does not say which ('soliti stato die ante lucem convenire carmenque Christo quasi deo dicere secum invicem . . .'). He apparently, as Lightfoot observes (Ignatius², i. p. 52), confuses Baptism and the Eucharist ; but we may probably gather from his account that the Christians of Bithynia met before dawn on a fixed day to celebrate the Eucharist, and later in the day met for the Agape. This inference is disputed by some.—Justin Martyr describes the assembling 'on the day called Sunday' (τῇ τοῦ ἡλίου λεγομένῃ ἡμέρᾳ) for the Eucharist by 'all who live in cities or in the country' (Apol. i. § 67). He also explicitly mentions the Sunday collection of alms, as in 1 Co 16². In the Dialogue also Justin extols the 'eighth day' (cf. Barnabas, l.c.) as possessing a 'mysterious import,' which the seventh day had not ; he is referring to the Jewish circumcision as a type of 'the true circumcision by which we are circumcised from deceit and iniquity, through Him who rose from the dead on the first day after the Sabbath' (Dial. 24, 41).

That κυριακή became a common name in the 2nd cent. for the first day of the week is further clear from the fact, which Eusebius tells us (HE iv. 26), that Melito, bishop of Sardis about A.D. 170, wrote a book περὶ κυριακῆς (ὁ π. κ. λόγος). Dionysius of Corinth (A.D. 171) in his Epistle to Soter calls Sunday 'the Lord's Day' (Eusebius, HE iv. 23 : τὴν σήμερον κυριακὴν ἁγίαν ἡμέραν διηγάγομεν). After this the name becomes very common, and we find it both in Greek (e.g. Clement of Alexandria, Strom. vii. 12) and in Latin, dies dominica (e.g. Tertullian, de Cor. 3).

There is little evidence as to the way in which the Lord's Day was observed in the earliest ages. The Eucharist and probably the Agape were celebrated ; but perhaps to a great extent other occupations went on much as usual. It would not be easy for Christian working men to absent themselves from their avocations on a day when everyone around them was working ; and this may have been the reason why the synaxis took place at night or before dawn, as in the examples in Acts and in Pliny. St. Paul apparently began his journey from Troas (Ac 20) on Sunday. There is no evidence in the earliest ages of any attempt to transfer the obligations of Sabbath observance to the Lord's Day. The Jewish Christians already had their day of rest on the Saturday. But, as Zahn observes (Skizzen aus dem Leben der Alten Kirche, p. 214), the Gentile Christians must have very quickly learnt all over the world to keep the Lord's Day ; they were never compelled to keep the Sabbath, which was not one of the four observances enjoined in Ac 15²⁹.

Tertullian, however, is the first to mention a Sunday rest (Apologet. 16, de Orat. 23), saying that the Christians postponed ordinary duties and business only on that day, the day of the Lord's resurrection, and that they gave up 'the day of the sun' to joy. He contrasts the Christian with the Jewish rest by implication. He says that Christians did not kneel on the Lord's Day (de Orat. 23, de Cor. 3). This custom we already find in Irenæus (Fragm. 7), who traces it to Apostolic times ; and it was afterwards laid down in the 20th canon of Nicæa.

For the 3rd and 4th cents., the Church Orders, some of which have only lately come to light, and the early Didascalia (i.e. the work as it was before it was incorporated in the Apostolic Constitutions, and as we have it, for example, in the Verona Latin Fragments, edited by Dr. Hauler) throw some light on the question of the Lord's Day. The Christians are bidden 'on the Lord's Day (die dominica), putting aside everything,' to assemble at church (Hauler, p. 44). The fragment breaks off in the middle of a sentence explaining the object of Sunday churchgoing ('audire salutare uerbum et nutriri ab . . .') ; but we can fill the gap from other forms of the Didascalia, such as the Syriac edited by Mrs. Gibson, from which we see that the Eucharist is being spoken of ('be nourished with the divine food which endureth for ever,' Gibson, ch. xiii.). This appears to come from the original *Didascalia*, and it is emphatically said that the Lord's Day is the great time for the Christian assembly, for prayer, Eucharist, and instruction ; and this emphasis is all the greater as it was not yet customary to have public daily prayers for all men. But about A.D. 375 the writer of the *Apostolic Constitutions*, in adapting the *Didascalia*, alters this direction for Sunday worship to a command to assemble twice daily, morning and evening (ii. 59). In the *Testament of our Lord* (c. 350 ?), the way is being felt towards public daily service by providing daily forms for the clergy and the presbyteresses, with whom the devout might be invited to join [see, further, on daily service, Wordsworth's *Ministry of Grace*, ch. vi. ; and Cooper and Maclean's *Testament of our Lord*, p. 189]. We may then say that until the latter part of the 4th cent. Sunday was the only regular and universal day for Christian assemblies. There is a possible local and temporary exception in the *Hippolytean Canons* (§ 217, ed. Achelis), which command daily service ; but some have concluded that this is an interpolation, as it is thought to be in contradiction to § 226. These *Canons* allow a bishop to celebrate the Eucharist when he pleases. And again, a daily celebration of the Eucharist is perhaps found in Cyprian (*de Orat. Dom.* 18). But no further trace of this is found till the latter part of the 4th century. The result arrived at does not mean, however, that the Christians were not bidden to pray daily ; from a very early period, certainly from about A.D. 200 onwards, regular daily hours of prayer were prescribed (*e.g. Can. Hippol.* § 223 ff.). But private prayers are here meant, even though sometimes they were said in church. For other *synaxes* in the week, see below (§§ 2, 3).

The Lord's Day was the usual day for the ordination or consecration of a bishop ; so the older *Didascalia* in Mrs. Gibson's form, § iii. [but this is an interpolation from one of the following books], the *Egyptian Church Order* (ed. Tattam, § 31), the *Apostolic Constitutions* (viii. 4), and the *Testament of our Lord* (i. 21) ; also in the *Ethiopic Church Order* (§ 21), according to Achelis, though Ludolf (*ad suam Hist. Æthiop. Comment.* p. 323) has 'in die sabbati.' The *Canons of Hippolytus* perhaps mention Saturday, though Achelis gives 'in ea . . . hebdomade' ; but the Arabic for 'Saturday' and 'week' are pronounced alike (see Rahmani, *Test. D. N. Jesu Christi*, p. xxxvi).

The rest on the Lord's day appears (especially until the time of Constantine) to have been mainly to allow of church-going. But in the edict of Constantine in 321, the magistrates and people in cities are bidden to rest, and all workshops are directed to be closed ' on the venerable day of the sun' ; while no such obligation is laid on those engaged in agricultural pursuits. Whatever the motive of the emperor in making this decree may have been (and this is disputed), it doubtless did much to bring about a weekly holiday on the Lord's Day.

2. Wednesday and Friday fasts.—Almost from the beginning we can trace an observance of these two days for the purpose of fasting. In this way the early Christians interpreted our Lord's words in Mt 9[15], that they should fast when the bridegroom should be taken away from them ; though, as we shall see, some found a more particular fulfilment of these words in the fast before Easter. The reason why Wednesday and Friday were chosen is not entirely obvious. The stricter Jews had made a practice of fasting ' twice in the week' (Lk 18[12]), and, as we learn from the *Didache* (§ 8), the Christians took over the practice, but changed the days. Probably ever since the Return from the Captivity, Monday and Thursday had been the Jewish fasts, though we read of Judith fasting daily save on Sabbaths and New Moons and the eves of both and 'the feasts and solemn days of the house of Israel' (Jth 8[6]). Monday and Thursday were chosen, or were afterwards accounted for, because there was a tradition that Moses went up into the Mount on the latter day and came down on the former. But these were not matters of law, for the Mosaic Code prescribes only the Day of Atonement as a fast ; and though occasional fasts were ordered in times of trouble, these were never permanent nor of universal obligation. Thus the Pharisee's boast in Lk 18[12] was that he did more than he was obliged by law to do (see, further, in Plummer's *St. Luke, in loc.*). In the sub-Apostolic age the Christians went a step further and seem to have tried to make the Wednesday and Friday fasts universal. The *Didache* (§ 8) says : ' Let not your fastings be with the hypocrites [the Jews], for they fast on the second and the fifth day of the week ; but do ye keep your fast on the fourth day and on the preparation' (there is a change of construction : νηστεύουσι . . . δευτέρα σαββάτων . . . ὑμεῖς δὲ νηστεύσατε τετράδα καὶ παρασκευήν. For the latter, νηστεύω with direct accusative, see the parallel *Apost. Const.* vii. 23 and v. 15 ; and *Oxyrhynchus Logia*, 2 : ἐὰν μὴ νηστεύσητε τὸν κόσμον, and *Testament of our Lord*, ii. 6 and 12 [apparently]). A reason was found for the choice of Wednesday and Friday in the fact that on the former day the Jews made a conspiracy against our Lord, and that He was crucified on the latter. But this first appears in Peter of Alexandria († 311), who gives this explanation in his *Canonical Epistle* (canon xv.). It reappears elsewhere, *e.g.* in *Apost. Const.* v. 15. Another explanation is given by Clement of Alexandria (*Strom.* vii. 12). He says that the fourth and sixth days are named from Hermes and Aphrodite respectively. The true Christian or 'Gnostic' fasts in his life in respect of covetousness and voluptuousness, from which all the vices grow. Considering, then, that the symbolical explanations differ, and that they are not found until a somewhat later date than the first mention of these days, it is reasonable to suppose that they are afterthoughts. Yet it is probable that, when the Jewish fast days had to be changed, Friday was not accidentally fixed upon, but that our Lord's death on that day would make it appropriate as a fast ; and when once Friday was chosen, Wednesday would follow from mere considerations of convenience.

Other early authorities for week-day fasts are Hermas, Tertullian, Hippolytus, the *Hippolytean Canons*, and Origen. Hermas (*Sim.* v. 1) does not mention the days on which it was usual to fast ; but he says that he was fasting and seated on a certain mountain, giving thanks to the Lord, when he met the Shepherd, who asked him why he was there. He replies that he is keeping a ' station' (στατίωνα ἔχω), which he explains as being a fast. Tertullian expressly mentions Wednesday and Friday (*de Jejun.* 2 and 14 : 'stationibus quartam et sextam sabbati dicamus, et jejuniis parasceuen'—a difficult phrase, since the sixth day and 'parasceue' are one ; perhaps the meaning is that Wednesday was a ' half-fast' [*de Jejun.* 13] in Tertullian's time, and Friday a whole one, or perhaps Tertullian means Good Friday here by ' parasceue'). He says that the Eucharist was celebrated on those days (*de Orat.* 19). For Hippolytus, see below (§ 3) on the Saturday fast. The *Hippolytean Canons*, which, whether they represent Roman usage or Alexandrian, probably date from the first half of the 3rd cent., prescribe fasts ' feria quarta et sexta [et quadraginta],' though it approves of individuals adding other fasts to these (§ 154; the bracketed words seem to be an interpolation). Origen speaks of Wednesday and Friday as days 'quibus solemniter jejunamus' (in Lev. Hom. x., but see II. 1 e, below).

But hereafter there is a break, except that Peter of Alexandria gives evidence for Egypt, and that in the Edessene Canons of the first half of the 4th cent. there are directions for the Eucharist on Sundays, for service 'on the fourth day,' and for service 'on the eve' [of the Sabbath] at the ninth hour (canons 2, 3). Apparently the observance of these two days was not universal, at any rate in the East, till towards the end of the 4th century. There is no mention of them in the Testament of our Lord (c. 350 A.D. ?), which alludes to the possibility of a fast day falling in the week (i. 22), but does not prescribe one. There is in this curious Church Order a regulation for bishops and presbyters to fast three days a week, perhaps only for one year from their ordination, but they are not tied down to any fixed days, and the rule is expressly said to be 'for the priests only.' The Arabic Didascalia (§ 38, c. 380 A.D. ?), which is probably based on the Testament, mentions explicitly Wednesday and Friday as the two fast days of the week, and says that when a festival falls on these days they shall pray and not receive the holy mysteries, and shall not interrupt the fasting till the ninth hour [see a German translation of these later chapters in Funk's Apostol. Konstitutionen; the rest is not published]. There is abundant evidence towards the end of the 4th cent. for these days: Apost. Const. v. 15, vii. 23; Apost. Can. 69 (68); pseudo-Ignat. ad Phil. 13; Epiphanius, Hær. lxv. 6 (ed. Dionysius Petavius, lib. iii. 6, p. 910), and Expos. Fid. 21. The Apostolic Constitutions are here (vii. 23) based on the Didache, and repeat its language about the change of day from those of the 'hypocrites.' The Apostolic Canon makes it incumbent on all, under penalty, to keep these days, unless in sickness. Pseudo-Ignatius, who is probably the same as the author of the Apost. Constitutions [so Harnack, Brightman; but Lightfoot (Ignatius², i. 265 f.) thinks otherwise] re-echoes their language. Epiphanius says that these two days were observed everywhere (ἐν πᾶσι κλίμασι τῆς οἰκουμένης); he calls them τετράς and προσάββατον. Bp. J. Wordsworth conjectures that the restoration of these days in the East was largely due to Epiphanius (Min. of Grace, ch. VI. ii.). Probably in Egypt and in many parts of the West their observance was continuous.

Usually the Eucharist was celebrated on Wednesdays and Fridays; perhaps often (as the Arabic Didascalia may suggest) at a late hour, so that the fast might be preserved, though Tertullian speaks (de Orat. 19) of the service being during the hours of fasting on these days, and of scrupulous communicants reserving the elements in private so as not to break the fast. In 'Silvia' (iv. 3, in Duchesne's Origines, Appendix) the observance of Wednesdays and Fridays in Lent is spoken of: 'Diebus vero quadragesimarum . . . quarta feria ad nona in Syon [the traditional scene of the descent of the Holy Spirit, possibly the site of St. Mark's house, called by Epiphanius and St. Cyril of Jerusalem the Church of the Apostles] proceditur juxta consuetudinem totius anni, et omnia aguntur quæ consuetudo est ad nonam agi præter oblatio. . . . Sexta feria autem similiter omnia aguntur sicut quarta feria,' which must mean that the Eucharist was usually celebrated on Mount Zion after none at 3 p.m. except in Lent, though Duchesne seems to invert this conclusion (p. 130 n. 4, Eng. ed.). 'Silvia' says that on these days, unless a festival of the martyrs fell on one

of them, even the catechumens fasted. In the 5th cent. an exception to the Wednesday and Friday Eucharist is mentioned by Socrates (HE v. 22) in the case of the Wednesday and Friday before Easter.

These days were called 'half-fasts,' semi-jejunia (Tertull. de Jejun. 13), because on them Christians broke their fast at 3 p.m. or even at noon; or more frequently 'station days' as in Hermas (l.c., though he does not specify the days) and in Tertullian (de Jejun. 14). This is a military metaphor. Tertullian (de Orat. 19) says: 'If the Station has received its name from the example of military life —for we are God's military [cf. 2 Co 10⁴, 1 Ti 1¹⁸]— certainly no gladness or sadness chancing to the camp abolishes the Stations of the soldiers; for gladness will carry out discipline more willingly, sadness more carefully.' And St. Ambrose says: 'Our fasts are our encampments which protect us from the devil's attack; in short, they are called Stations, because standing and staying in them we repel our plotting foes' (Serm. 25, ed. of 1549, p. 716c).

3. Saturday.—There was a considerable divergence of custom with regard to the observance of Saturday. In the East it was commonly regarded as a feast, while in many parts of the West it was a fast, that of Friday being continued to the Saturday, and the added fast being called a 'superposition' (superpositio, ὑπέρθεσις). Tertullian (de Jejun. 14) mentions and condemns the custom of fasting on Saturday: 'You [' psychic' Christians] sometimes continue your station even over the Sabbath, a day never to be kept as a fast except at the Passover season.' St. Jerome writing to Lucinius in A.D. 398 (Ep. 71) discusses the question, and says that it had been 'treated by the eloquent Hippolytus' and others; but he does not tell us what their opinions were. The Council of Elvira in Spain (c. 305 A.D.) ordered superpositions each month except in July and August (canon 23); and in canon 26 says that the error is to be corrected 'ut omni sabbati die superpositiones celebremus,' which may mean that superpositions were to be held every Saturday (Hefele), or that this weekly fast was henceforward forbidden (Bp. J. Wordsworth). The latter meaning would suit canon 23 better, but Hefele's construction suits canon 43. St. Augustine says that in his time they did not fast at Milan on Saturday (Ep. liv. ad Januar. § 3). Writing in the 5th cent., Socrates (HE v. 22) says that in his day almost all Churches celebrated the sacred mysteries on the Sabbath of every week [Saturday], yet the Christians of Alexandria and Rome, on account of some ancient tradition, had ceased to do this. This 'ancient tradition' may probably go back before the 4th century. Socrates goes on to say that the Egyptians near Alexandria and those of the Thebaid held synaxes on the Sabbath, but, unlike other Christians, 'after having eaten and satisfied themselves with food of all kinds [the Agape?], in the evening make the Offering (περὶ ἑσπέραν προσφέροντες) and partake of the mysteries.' Sozomen (HE vii. 19) repeats Socrates' statements.*

The Testament of our Lord (i. 23), according to our present Syriac text, prescribes Eucharists on Saturday or Sunday; but we must probably correct 'or' into 'and,' by the omission of one Syriac letter (ܘ into ܘ), and the rule will then agree

---

* Dom Leclercq (Dict. d'Archéol. Chrét. s.v. 'Agape,' col. 822) thinks that in Socrates and Sozomen there is no trace of an Agape, but only of a Eucharist. But it appears clear to the present writer that the words 'eating and satisfying themselves' point to the Agape, and that the whole purpose of the custom described is to keep up the example of the Last Supper. For a full discussion of the origin and date of introduction of the Agape, see Hastings' (forthcoming) Dict. of Religion, s.v.

with the *Arabic Didascalia*, § 38. In the *Apostolic Constitutions* (ii. 59) Saturday and Sunday are specially appointed for Divine service ; and we note that in this passage Saturday is the author's interpolation into his source, the old *Didascalia* mentioning only Sunday (Hauler, *Verona Fragments*, p. 44). Pseudo-Ignatius forbids a Christian to fast on Sunday, save on Easter Even [the reading of the last words is doubtful, but the sense is clear], lest he be a 'Christ-slayer' (χριστοκτόνος). And so the same author in *Apost. Const.* vii. 23 bids his hearers feast on the Sabbath and the Lord's Day, except on Easter Even ; and in v. 13, 15, he bids them leave off fasting on the seventh day, save on that Sabbath when the Creator was under the ground. The *Apostolic Canons* strongly make the same prohibition as to fasting on ordinary Saturdays (Canon 66 [65]).

As we saw above, Alexandria did not celebrate the Eucharist on Saturday for some time before Socrates. St. Athanasius (*Apol. con. Arian.* 11) implies that it was celebrated on Sunday only. He replies to a charge against Macarius of breaking a chalice, and shows that the place alleged was not a church, that there was no one there to perform the 'sacred office,' and that the day was not the Lord's Day, and did not require the use of it [the sacred office]. This at least shows that there was no fixed day except Sunday for the Eucharist. And Brightman (*Journ. of Theol. Stud.* i. 92) thinks that the same is implied in the Sacramentary of Serapion (*c.* 350 A.D.), which gives 'The first prayer of the Lord's day' (κυριακῆς), without arranging for any other day. But this is hardly conclusive, especially as Thmuis was not Alexandria, and Socrates says that the 'neighbours of Alexandria' *did* have a Saturday Eucharist. By A.D. 380 the latter was already established in Alexandria (Timothy of Alex. *Respons. Canon.* 13, see Brightman, *l.c.*). Cassian says that in his time there were no public services in the day among the Egyptians except on Saturday and Sunday, when they met at the third hour for Holy Communion (*Inst.* iii. 2). St. Augustine sums up the matter by saying that in some places no day passed without the sacrifice being offered ; in others it was only on Saturday and the Lord's Day, or, it may be, only on the Lord's Day (*Ep.* liv. *ad Januar.* § 2).

For Phrygia and Cappadocia we have no satisfactory evidence with regard to the observance of Saturday in the 4th century. The 49th canon of Laodicea in Phrygia (*c.* 380?) says that during Lent the bread shall not be offered except on Saturday and Sunday, from which it may perhaps be inferred that these two days were 'liturgical' all through the year. St. Basil in his 93rd Epistle, *ad Cæsariam* (*v.l.* Cæsarium ; in the Paris ed. of 1618, *Ep.* 289), says that he communicated four times a week, on the Lord's Day, Wednesday, Friday, and the Sabbath, and on other days if there were a commemoration of any saint (*v.l.* martyr) ; he refers to and defends the practice of private reservation, and says that in Egypt each layman kept the Eucharistic elements in his own house and partook when he liked. Thus the fact that Basil communicated on the days mentioned does not necessarily imply a Eucharist on those days.

It is noteworthy that Saturday and Sunday have remained in the Greek Church as the only 'liturgical' days in Lent, as provided in the Laodicean canon ; whereas the Nestorians provide Eucharistic lections for every day in certain selected weeks in Lent (called the 'weeks of the mysteries') with the one exception of Saturday.

II. THE CHRISTIAN YEAR.—In addition to the weekly observances, there were annual commemo-

rations of events in our Lord's life, although their development was slow. Two of these, Easter and Pentecost, passed to the Church from the Jews ; while others, such as Good Friday, Lent, Ascension, Christmas, Epiphany, Advent, are of purely Christian origin.

1. Easter. — (*a*) *The name.*—'Pascha' (πάσχα) was the common name for Easter at least from the 2nd cent. onwards in Greek and Latin Christianity ; and it is of some importance to gather from the earlier writers the reasons for its use, as they will show us the exact meaning of the commemoration. πάσχα is taken from the Aramaic אחספ (*pishā*), the equivalent of Heb. חספ (*pesaḥ*) 'the passover.' Syrian Christians, however, have

usually written the word in the form ܦܨܚܐ

(*peṣḥā*) as if from ܦܨܚ 'to rejoice' (see Payne - Smith, *Thesaurus Syriacus, in loc.*) ; though, in translating into Syriac from Greek, James of Edessa and others use the form ܦܣܟܐ (as in the *Testament of our Lord, passim*) ; and

the Lexicons give a verb ܦܨܚ 'to celebrate Easter.' The meaning in Syriac literature is usually 'Easter,' though the Nestorian writers, like their descendants to this day, use it in the sense of 'Maundy Thursday.' The older Greek and Latin writers commonly derive it from πάσχειν, 'to suffer,' and draw analogies from etymology between the paschal lamb and the suffering Christ. Thus, perhaps, Justin Martyr (*Dial.* 40 ; he is showing how the lamb sacrificed as the passover is a type of the Passion) ; and most probably Irenæus (*Hær.* IV. x. 1 : 'Moses foretold Him after a figurative manner by the name given to the passover, and at that very festival did our Lord suffer, thus fulfilling the passover'). And so perhaps Tertullian (*adv. Jud.* 19, Migne, vol. ii. col. 670): 'It is the Lord's passover, that is, the Passion of Christ.' Lactantius expressly adopts this etymology (*Div. Inst.* iv. 26, Migne, vol. i. col. 531): 'Pascha nominatur ἀπὸ τοῦ πάσχειν, quia passionis figura est.' Augustine, on the other hand (*Ep.* lv. 1, *ad Januar.*, A.D. 400) denies this interpretation, while he proposes a scarcely better one : 'The word Pascha itself is not, as is commonly thought, a Greek word ; those who are acquainted with both languages affirm it to be a Hebrew word. It is not derived, therefore, from the Passion because of the Greek word πάσχειν, signifying *to suffer*, but it takes its name from the transition of which I have spoken, from death to life ; the meaning of the Hebrew word Pascha being, as those who are acquainted with it assure us, a *passing over* or *transition*. To this the Lord Himself designed to allude when He said : "He that believeth in me is passed from death to life. . . ."'

The question then arises, What did these earlier writers mean by Pascha ? Was it the commemoration of the Passion, or of the Resurrection ? Irenæus wrote a work, περὶ τοῦ πάσχα (quoted by psendo-Justin, *Quæst. et resp. ad Orthodoxos*), which is probably the letter to Victor from which Eusebius gives extracts (*HE* v. 24). In this he speaks of a festival preceded by a fast of varying duration (see below, *e*) ; and he may use the word πάσχα of the festival or of the festival and fast combined. Bp. J. Wordsworth (*Ministry of Grace*, iii. § 1) says that the Christian πάσχα always in the first three centuries and often in the fourth means the celebration of the fast of Good Friday, extended no doubt by ὑπέρθεσις or superposition in most cases over Easter ; and he adduces

Tertullian, *adv. Jud.* 10, as above (but this hardly shows it), and *de Bapt.* 19 (' Pascha affords a more solemn day for baptism, when all the passion of the Lord, in which we are baptized [tinguimur], was completed '). We may add *de Orat.* 18, where he says that they did not give the kiss of peace ' die paschæ ' when there was a general fast. But in *de Cor.* 3 he seems to use the word of Easter Day; he says that the Christians did not kneel ' a die Paschæ in Pentecosten usque ' ; and in *de Jejun.* 14 he speaks of celebrating Pascha, and of the fifty ensuing (*exinde*) days being spent in exultation, which is suitable language if Pascha means Easter Day, but hardly if it means Good Friday. It may, however, in these passages, mean Easter *and* the preceding fast, and this would suit the remark which follows in *de Jejun.* 14, that Saturday was never a fast ' nisi in Pascha.' Origen (*c. Cels.* viii. 22) distinguishes παρασκευή from πάσχα, and doubtless means Easter by the latter. He mentions the observance of the Lord's Day, of the Preparation, of Pascha, and of Pentecost; and cannot here mean *every* Friday by the ' Preparation,' for then he would also have mentioned Wednesday, as in *Hom. in Lev.* x. (see above, I. § 2).

One may conjecture that there was some divergence in the first three centuries both as to the name and as to the actual observance of this commemoration. It seems likely that in many cases the Resurrection and the Passion were observed on the same day. This must usually have been the case with the Quartodecimans, who observed the fourteenth day of the lunar month ; but it was also apparently often the case with those who kept the Sunday, for, as we shall see below, the fast observed before the Sunday was often only of one day's duration, and did not always include the Friday. Even well on in the 4th cent. we find a relic of this in the *Testament of our Lord*, where the Friday before Easter is not mentioned as the day of commemorating the Passion but as a preparation for the festival, and the Passion and Resurrection are apparently commemorated together, just as the Ascension and Pentecost were often joined (see below, § 2 *b*). There is nothing *a priori* incongruous in commemorating and giving thanks for the Redemption of mankind on a day of rejoicing, especially when a severe fast of a day or two had just preceded. The probable conclusion, then, is that Pascha usually meant, before the 4th cent., the commemoration both of the Death and of the Resurrection of Christ, the festival with its preceding fast, and that the erroneous derivation from πάσχω favoured a certain indefiniteness in the use of the word. This derivation, it may be observed, as well as the equally false Syrian one, probably explains why a name with such a very Jewish association became so popular. When, somewhat later, a distinction had to be made between Good Friday and Easter Day, the names πάσχα σταυρώσιμον and πάσχα ἀναστάσιμον were invented (Ducange, *s.v.* ' Pascha ').

Another use of the name Pascha is to be noted. In the *Testament of our Lord* (i. 28, 42, ii. 8, 11, 12, 18) it means the forty days before Easter, though of these forty days only the last two were fasts. Holy Week is called ' the last week of Pascha.' The end of Pascha is to be after the Saturday at midnight. The ' forty days of Pascha ' are specially mentioned. Similarly in *Apost. Can.* 69 (68) we find τὴν ἁγίαν τεσσαρακοστὴν τοῦ πάσχα. But in the *Testament*, Pascha is used absolutely in this sense. In this work, however, we also read of ' the feast of Pascha ' (i. 42), when widows (presbyteresses) are to give alms and bathe. The bathing was on the Thursday before Easter. ' Pascha ' was sometimes used for Holy Week.

Thus in *Apost. Const.* v. 18 we read : ' Fast in the days of Pascha beginning from the second till the Preparation and the Sabbath, for they are days of sorrow, not of feasting.' And so perhaps *Can. Hipp.* § 195 ff. (below, *d*).

Other names for Easter were : among the Latins, ' Dominica gaudii ' (Bingham, *Ant.* XX. v. 5) ; among the Greeks, μεγάλη κυριακή ; while the common Syrian name was and is ܚܰܓ݁ܳܐ ܕ݁ܩ݂ܝܳܡܬ݁ܐ

' the feast of the Resurrection.'

(*b*) *Early observance of Easter.*—The Apostles, no doubt, continued to keep the Jewish Passover (Ac 20⁶) ; but it is uncertain if the first Gentile Christians observed it in any way, or whether they were content with the weekly commemoration. It is not even certain if the Jewish Christians kept it in any way as a *Christian* festival. Yet the phrases τὸ πάσχα ἡμῶν . . . Χριστός and ἑορτάζωμεν (1 Co 5⁷·) would be specially appropriate if the Christians at Corinth were at the time when St. Paul wrote from Ephesus, namely, before Pentecost (1 Co 16⁸), observing an Easter festival. But it is significant that there is no mention of Easter in the Apostolic Fathers or in Justin Martyr ; and its absence in the *Didache* is specially noteworthy, since that Church Order mentions the Lord's Day, the fast before baptism, and the Wednesday and Friday fasts. We can, however, trace the observance of Easter at Rome back to the time of Pope Xystus, *c.* 120 A.D., for Irenæus tells us (*ap.* Eusebius, *HE* v. 24) that Xystus and his immediate successors, while not observing the Quartodeciman practice themselves, yet were at peace with those who did ; and from what follows it is clear that Irenæus means that Xystus observed the Sunday as Easter Day. In Asia Minor the observance can be traced back still further ; for Polycarp, as Irenæus says (*ib.*), traced his custom of keeping Easter to St. John. The conclusion may probably be, either that Easter was not universally observed as an annual commemoration early in the 2nd cent., or, more probably, that it had not then the great importance which it acquired later in the century, from the disputes as to the day when it should be kept.

(*c*) *The Quartodeciman Controversy.* — A brief summary only of this question is necessary for the purposes of this Dictionary ; for more detailed accounts of it, reference may be made to the works mentioned at the end of this article. The controversy arose in the 2nd cent. and came to a head in the last decade of it ; it was concerned with the question whether the Paschal commemoration should follow the day of the week or the day of the lunar month on which the events commemorated originally occurred. Those who upheld the former practice no doubt laid chief stress on the Resurrection of our Lord, since they fixed on Sunday for their commemoration ; while the latter, who were called Quartodecimans or τεσσαρεσκαιδεκατίται (Socrates, *HE* v. 22, Sozomen, *HE* vii. 19), probably at first emphasized our Lord's death, as they adhered to 14th Nisan, the day on which He died, or was thought by them to have died ; whereas, on no calculation did He rise on that day. The theory has, indeed, been advanced by the Tübingen school that the Quartodecimans commemorated the Last Supper rather than the Passion or Resurrection. According to the Synoptists, the Last Supper appears to have taken place on the evening of 14th Nisan, and the Crucifixion to have been on the 15th ; while, according to the Fourth Gospel, the Death of our Lord would appear to have been at the time of the killing of the Paschal lambs, and the Last Supper therefore to have taken place at the end of 13th Nisan. We are not here concerned with the seeming contradiction between the Gospels except in so far as the Tübingen school deduced from the known facts that the Quartodecimans could not have accepted the Fourth Gospel, because their practice rather agreed with the Synoptists. Western readers need, however, to be reminded that in the ordinary Eastern reckoning, at any rate the ecclesiastical reckoning, then as now, the Last Supper and the Crucifixion fell on the same day; for the day began at sunset. Thus, if the Quartodecimans observed 14th Nisan, it must have been because they thought that our Lord both celebrated the Last Supper and also died on that day. It is a pure assumption that their Paschal commemoration began at the moment when the lambs were killed. In that case they would have been rather Quintodecimans. It is generally agreed that the lambs were killed, at any rate in ancient Jewish times, in the afternoon of 14th Nisan, *i.e.* when that day was drawing to a close. The inference, then, is that the Quartodecimans made their Paschal commemoration coincide with the day which began at the Last Supper and ended soon after our Lord's death, and that they thought that that occurred at the time of the killing of the lambs. The deduction is the exact opposite of that drawn by the Tübingen school, and is that the Quartodecimans followed the Fourth Gospel (as they, perhaps rightly, interpreted it) rather than the Synoptists. The supposition that they commemorated the Last Supper in particular has, moreover, no basis of fact. And the view given above is further supported by the fact that in the time of Melito (A.D. 170) the Quartodecimans clearly accepted the Fourth Gospel. Melito, in one of his fragments, speaks of our Lord's three years' ministry, which he could never have gathered from the Synoptists ('de Incarn. Christi,' in Routh's *Reliquiæ sacræ*, vol. i.).

It has been thought by some (as by Hefele) that the Quartodecimans kept their commemoration of the Resurrection on the third day after 14th Nisan, *i.e.* on 16th Nisan, or even on the Sunday after. But this is very improbable. If it were so, why should they have broken off their fast on 14th Nisan? It is much more likely that they commemorated the Passion and the Resurrection together.

The history of the controversy is given by Eusebius (*HE* v. 23, 24), who takes up the question at its third and most acute stage, namely, at the dispute between Victor and Polycrates at the very end of the 2nd century. He tells us that synods held in that century unanimously decided that 'the mystery of the resurrection of the Lord should be celebrated on no other but the Lord's day, and that we should observe the close of the paschal fast on this day only.' These synods were held in Palestine, Rome (under Victor), Pontus, Gaul (under Irenæus), and Osrhoëne in N.-W. Mesopotamia. Perhaps the last-named synod was held at the famous Edessa or Ur-hai, which is in that district. There were also personal (*i.e.* not synodical) letters of Bacchylus, bishop of Corinth, and many others, all of whom concurred in the decision mentioned above. On the other side 'Asia' (*i.e.* probably the Roman province, though the Quartodeciman practice extended to other provinces also—even to Antioch), led by Polycrates, bishop of Ephesus, maintained that the paschal commemoration should take place on 14th Nisan, on whatever day of the week it should fall. Polycrates, who is very highly praised by St. Jerome (*de Viris Illustr.* 45) and by implication by Eusebius, who preserves his letter (*l.c.*), alleges the example of 'Philip, one of the twelve Apostles, who fell asleep in Hierapolis, and his

VOL. I.—17

two aged virgin daughters, and another daughter who lived in the Holy Spirit and now rests at Ephesus'; also of John 'who was both a witness and a teacher, who reclined upon the bosom of the Lord, and being a priest wore the [sacerdotal] plate (τὸ πέταλον). He fell asleep at Ephesus.' He also adduces Polycarp, Melito, the martyr Sagaris, and others, who all agreed with his practice.

Victor *attempted* to excommunicate all 'Asia'; ἀποτέμνειν ὡς ἑτεροδοξούσας . . . πειρᾶται are Eusebius' exact words. But Socrates (*HE* v. 22) declares that he did actually excommunicate them. He probably issued a letter of excommunication, but it was not effective. For Eusebius goes on to say that Irenæus, bishop of 'Gaul,' intervened in the dispute in the interests of peace, and he who 'was truly well named became a peacemaker in the matter.' Part of Irenæus' letter is preserved by Eusebius, and it is specially interesting as mentioning that 'the presbyters before Soter who presided over the Church which thou [Victor] now rulest, Anicetus and Pius and Hyginus and Telesphorus and Xystus, neither themselves observed [the fourteenth day] nor permitted those after them to do so; and yet' they were at peace with those who did observe it; and also that when Polycarp went to Rome in the time of Anicetus (bishop of Rome), the two bishops 'disagreed a little about certain other things,' but immediately made peace, 'not caring to quarrel over this matter'; nor did it interfere with their remaining in communion with one another, or with Anicetus allowing Polycarp to celebrate the Eucharist in his church at Rome, 'manifestly as a mark of respect' (ἐν τῇ ἐκκλησίᾳ παρεχώρησεν ὁ Ἀνίκητος τὴν εὐχαριστίαν τῷ Πολυκάρπῳ κατ᾽ ἐντροπὴν δηλονότι). It has been suggested that these words mean only that the two bishops communicated together; but in that case they are mere repetitions of what had just been said, and there would be no special mark of respect.

Eusebius here does not mention the intervening dispute in which Melito, bishop of Sardis, figures. But in iv. 26 he speaks of him, and from the account we gather that he was a prolific writer; a list of his books is given. In the quotation from Polycrates in v. 24 we find the name of Melito appearing as a Quartodeciman, but it is not said that he was a writer. From the earlier passage we learn that he wrote a book περὶ τοῦ πάσχα, from which a quotation is given: 'While Servilius [Rufinus gives 'Sergius'] Paulus was proconsul of Asia, at the time when Sagaris suffered martyrdom, there arose in Laodicea [in Phrygia] a great strife concerning Pascha, which fell according to rule in those days (ἐμπεσόντος κατὰ καιρὸν ἐν ἐκείναις ταῖς ἡμέραις), and these things were written [*sc.* because of the dispute].' So McGiffert ['Eusebius' in *Nicene and Post-Nicene Fathers*] renders these words, though it is not obvious what they mean; for when did not Pascha fall according to rule? For other explanations see Salmon in Smith-Wace, *Dict. of Chr. Biog. s.v.* 'Melito.' Eusebius goes on to say that Clement of Alexandria refers to Melito's work, and himself wrote one with the same title, 'on occasion' (ἐξ αἰτίας) of Melito's treatise, *i.e.*, probably, in opposition to it, though Hefele thinks that Clement's book was meant to *supplement* Melito's.

The *Paschal Chronicle* mentions that Apolinarius, bishop of Hierapolis, of whom Serapion, bishop of Antioch (*c.* 200 A.D.), is the first to speak—but he was then dead—wrote a book περὶ τοῦ πάσχα, and preserves two fragments of it. It is disputed whether Apolinarius was a Quartodeciman. If so, he was not an extreme partisan; he certainly wrote before the discussion became acute, as in the time of Polycrates. He held (the *Paschal Chronicle* states) that our Lord, being the true Paschal Lamb, was slain on the day of the Passover feast. Some have asserted that there were two parties of Quartodecimans, the one Judaizing and the other not. But it is perhaps unnecessary to divide them, with Hefele, into ' Ebionites' and ' Johanneans.' Eusebius (iv. 27) mentions Apolinarius' writings, but not the work in question.

There were thus three stages in the controversy : (1) the discussion between Polycarp and Anicetus, c. 150 A.D., when they agreed to differ, and parted amicably ; (2) the dispute at Laodicea about A.D. 170 ; (3) the bitter contest between Victor and Polycrates about A.D. 190.

The other Churches, as a rule,—those outside ' Asia,'—agreed with Victor in his practice, but disapproved of his excommunicating the Quartodecimans. The Roman Pascha gradually prevailed, and was affirmed by the Council of Nicæa in 325, in whose decision the bishop of ' Asia' acquiesced. Thenceforward the Quartodeciman practice was confined to a few communities which were considered heretical. It lasted till the 5th cent., and Sozomen (*HE* vii. 19) speaks of it as still going on in his day, c. 443 A.D.

(*d*) *Determination of Easter: Paschal cycles.*— The defeat of the Quartodecimans did not ensure that all should keep Easter on the same day, for different calculations were in use for determining the paschal full moon. This had long been the case. For a time the Christians were dependent on the Jews for the date of their festival. The *Hippolytean Canons* (§ 195, ed. Achelis) say that the week when the Jews celebrate Pascha is to be observed by all with the utmost zeal as a fast. And the older *Didascalia*, according to Codex Sangermanensis (Gibson's *Didasc.* 1903, p. 97), bids the Christians ' keep your fast with all care, but commence when your brethren of the Nation keep Pascha' ; the Verona Fragments are wanting here. And in the 4th cent. pseudo-Pionius, in his *Life of Polycarp* (§ 2 ; for the date see Lightfoot's *Ignatius*, iii. 429), says that ' the Apostle [Paul] plainly teaches that we ought neither to keep it outside the season of unleavened bread, as the heretics do, especially the Phrygians, nor yet, on the other hand, of necessity on the fourteenth day ; for he said nothing about the fourteenth day, but named the days of unleavened bread, the Passover, and the Pentecost, thus ratifying the Gospel.'

On the other hand, the *Apostolic Constitutions* (v. 17) expressly say : ' Be no longer careful to keep the feast with the Jews, for we have now no communion with them' ; and the Jews are said to have erred in their calculations. [The passage inserted before this in Dr. Donaldson's translation in the *Ante-Nicene Christian Library*, taken from Epiphanius, belongs to the older *Didascalia*, and is not part of the *Apostolic Constitutions* at all].

And long before this Hippolytus had made an elaborate calculation, so that it might be no longer necessary for the Christians to follow the Jews, who had gone wrong in their computation through lax calculations of the lunar year. Hippolytus follows the system adopted by the Greek astronomers to harmonize the lunar and solar years. He makes the lunar year to be 354 days of twelve months, which alternately have 30 and 29 days. To supply the difference of $11\frac{1}{4}$ days between the lunar and solar years, he interpolates three months of 30 days each in every eight years ($8 \times 11\frac{1}{4} = 90$). He also puts two eight-year periods together, for convenience of determining the day of the week as well as the day of the year, and he thus makes a cycle of 16 years. But, as a matter of fact, the lunar year is longer by nearly nine hours than Hippolytus reckoned it, and this error made the cycle very soon to be obviously wrong. Calculating backwards on this cycle, he fixed on Friday 25th March A.D. 29 as the day of the Crucifixion, and this computation, though quite erroneous, has ever since been the basis of a large part of the Church Calendar (see on Christmas below, § 3). The same date, March 25, is also found in the *Acts of Pilate*, which probably was written after Hippolytus, and was indebted to him. Epiphanius (*Hær.* I. 1, *contra Quartodecimanos*, lib. ii. tom. 1) says that some, following the *Acts of Pilate*, always kept Pascha on March 25. These Christians, who thus anticipated a reform much desired in modern times, were not strictly Quartodecimans, for they abandoned 14th Nisan, although they observed Pascha on any day of the week, and so were separated from the Catholics. A slight modification on Hippolytus' system was made (c. 243) by pseudo-Cyprian in his *de Pascha Computus* (see Dr. Salmon's article, ' Chronicon Cyprianicum,' in Smith-Wace, *Dict. of Chr. Biography*).

The Alexandrian Church is thought by Dr. Salmon to have used the Metonic cycle of nineteen years, which, somewhat modified, is still in use. Anyhow, the Alexandrians and Romans frequently kept Easter on different days. Another source of error was the determining of the vernal equinox, which at Rome in the 3rd cent. was thought to fall on 18th March, at Alexandria from c. 277 A.D. onwards on 19th March (the calculation was made by Anatolius of Laodicea). The date was changed to 21st March (as it is now) in the reign of Diocletian.

The later disputes in Britain between the Columban and Augustinian missionaries were due to the former using a cycle which had been employed at Rome itself about A.D. 300, but had long been given up. The Columban missionaries were in no real sense Quartodecimans, though they professed to follow St. John.

(*e*) *The fast before Easter* —In the ancient literature we find two aspects of this fast. In the first it is a preparation, whether for the paschal commemoration itself or for baptism, whether (moreover) the former emphasized the Death or the Resurrection of our Lord. In the second it is designed to mark the sadness of Christians in the days when ' the Bridegroom is taken away' - namely, the days when our Lord's body was in the tomb. In this case it must be looked upon as a Good Friday fast, extended by ' superposition' to the Saturday. As the normal time for baptism was Easter, usually early on Easter morning,—a fact which the discovery of so many *Church Orders* has lately made abundantly clear,—it follows that the resultant fast would be the same, whichever account of its origin is the more primitive.

For the first aspect we have the *Didache*. This *Church Order*, as has been said, does not mention Easter. But it gives what seems to be an exhaustive list of the fasts known to the writer at the beginning of the 2nd cent., and says (§ 7) : ' Before the baptism let him that baptizeth and him that is baptized fast, and any others also who are able ; and thou shalt order him that is baptized to fast *a day or two before.*' It then prescribes the Wednesday and Friday fasts. We thus have the curious result that a fast of one or two days is mentioned earlier than the festival which at that time, or at any rate soon after, followed it ; and the fast is connected not with the death of our Lord, but with baptism. It is significant that in the *Didache* not only the baptized and the baptizer fast, but also ' any others who are able.' And the silence of the Apostolic Fathers and Justin Martyr about Easter makes it not impossible that early in the 2nd cent. the pre-baptismal fast was emphasized more than the paschal festival. Irenæus also speaks of the fast before Easter Sunday in a way which seems to exclude the idea of a Good Friday fast extended to Saturday. His words are thus given by Eusebius (*HE* v. 24): 'Some think that they ought to fast for one day, others for two days, others even for several, while others reckon forty hours both of day and night to their day. And this variety in its observance has not originated in our time but long before, in that of our ancestors' (. . . οἱ δὲ καὶ πλειόνας· οἱ δὲ τεσσαράκοντα ὥρας ἡμερινάς τε καὶ νυκτερινὰς συμμετροῦσι τὴν ἡμέραν αὐτῶν κ.τ.λ.). Some have put a stop after τεσσαράκοντα (among others Rufinus, who translated Irenæus into Latin), making the writer say that some fasted forty days. But a forty days' fast, as we shall see, was an invention of the 4th cent., and Rufinus is interpreting Irenæus by the practice of his own day. Moreover, this punctuation makes no sense of the words that follow, for no one can suppose that there was an absolute fast, night and day, for forty days, and, if not, the reference to 'night and day' has no point. Irenæus seems clearly to mean that the fast lasted, variously, for one day, for two days, for several days, while some made a continuous fast of forty hours. The words, especially 'several days,' seem definitely to determine his point of view, that the fast was a preparation for the festival rather than an extension of Good Friday. The *Church Orders* definitely speak in the same sense. Baptism is described as taking place before the Easter Eucharist, and the directions for the paschal fast and solemnities generally follow immediately after the directions for baptism. The arrangement suggests that in the mind of the author of the lost ancestor of so many of these manuals,— for most of them are of one family and follow the same outline,—the preparation for baptism was the original object of the Lenten fast. The *Canons of Hippolytus* (§§ 150–152; but these are bracketed by Achelis as probable interpolations) speak of a baptismal fast of the newly baptized, and those who fast with them. In § 106 a fast of the candidates on the Fridays is mentioned; on the Saturday they are exorcized (§ 108) and keep vigil all night, and are baptized at cock-crow (§ 112). The *Egyptian Church Order* (Sahidic Eccles. Canons, § 45) prescribes a Good Friday fast. The Verona Latin Fragments are wanting in the parallel passage, but make the fast a two days' one in a later chapter (Hauler, p. 116). The *Testament of our Lord* (ii. 6) says definitely: 'Let them fast both on the Friday and on the Saturday'; and this is not improbably also the meaning of both the *Hippolytean Canons* and the *Egyptian Church Order*. The latter, at least, in a later section (§ 55) speaks of the fast as a two days' one. Now the *Egyptian Church Order* and the Verona Fragments say that if a sick person cannot fast on the two days, he is to fast on the *Saturday*. The *Testament of our Lord* (ii. 20) implies the same thing. But this puts the idea of a Good Friday fast extended over the Saturday out of the question. Even the *Apostolic Constitutions*, which exhibit a later stage and a longer fast, speak of the two days' absolute fast, and say that if any one cannot fast on the two days he is at least to observe the Saturday (v. 18). It is a characteristic of this last named *Church Order* to retain ancient features even when somewhat inconsistent with its own later point of view.

The other aspect, namely, of a Good Friday fast extended, is found in Tertullian. He speaks of the 'Psychics,' — *i.e.* the Church at large, from which he had now separated,—thinking that those days were definitely appointed for fasts in which the Bridegroom was taken away. The same language is found in the chapter of *Apost. Const.* just quoted, which thus combines the two ideas. It may not improbably be gathered from the evidence that the former point of view is the original one, and that the Lenten fast originated in the preparation for baptism, and that the second point of view was an afterthought.

The length of the fast was originally, as we have seen, one day, or two days, or forty hours. But it was an absolute fast. Another custom grew up in some countries in the 3rd cent. of observing the whole week before Easter, not as an absolute fast, but as a time of severe abstinence from food. It was called 'the week of *xerophagy*' (for the name cf. Tertullian, *de Jejun.* 2, 9). This is mentioned in the *Hippolytean Canons* (§ 197), which allow bread and salt and water only, and by Dionysius of Alexandria in his *Epistle to Basilides* (can. 1). He says that 'all do not carry out the six days of fasting either equally or alike; but some pass even all the days as a fast, remaining without food through the whole; while others take but two, and others three, and others four, and others not even one.' It is possible, as many think, that Dionysius is the author of the *Hippolytean Canons*, and that they represent Alexandrian usage, not Roman. The Montanists observed a two weeks' fast, a custom which they kept up till the 5th cent., when, as Sozomen tells us (*HE* vii. 19), they were distinguished by fasting *less* than their neighbours; formerly they had fasted *longer*, when Holy Week had been the maximum (cf. Tertullian, *de Jejun.* 15, when he says that the Montanists offered to God two weeks of *xerophagies* in the year, Saturday and Sunday being excepted). Epiphanius says that the Catholic Church observed a whole week, as opposed to the Quartodecimans, who observed only one day (*Hær.* l. 3, lib. ii. tom. 1).

Fasting for forty days was unknown till the 4th century. To maintain this proposition we must, with Achelis, eliminate 'et quadraginta' from *Can. Hippol.* 154 (the canons having obviously suffered interpolations), unless these words could refer to the 'forty hours' absolute fast mentioned by Irenæus; and similarly we must, with almost all scholars, reject the words in Origen's tenth *Homily on Leviticus*: 'Habemus enim quadragesimæ dies jejuniis consecratos,' which come just before he speaks of the Wednesday and Friday fasts. We have the homily in Rufinus' translation only, and Rufinus was notoriously lax in interpolating and altering Origen's words. These eliminations will be generally agreed to, for we can see the forty days' fast growing before our eyes in the 4th century. We find τεσσαρακοστή mentioned in the fifth canon of Nicæa, A.D. 325, but as a season only (the holding of synods is the subject), doubtless as a solemn time, but without any reference to fasting. Duchesne seems to have overlooked this point, which adds to his argument (*Origines*, viii. § 4). In the *Testament of our Lord* (ii. 8) the 'forty days of Pascha' are spoken of as a time of vigil and prayer, specially used for the preparation of catechumens for baptism, but it is not a fast. On the other hand, in the *Apostolic Canons* (69 or 68), *c.* 400 A.D., we read of τὴν ἁγίαν τεσσαρακοστὴν τοῦ πάσχα as a compulsory fast. This is one of the indications of a comparatively early date for the *Testament*. Duchesne (*l.c.*) has traced in Athanasius' 'Festal Letters' the growth of the fast. At first we read of the *time* of Lent and of the *week* of the fast, but later on of the *fast* of Lent and the Holy Week of Pascha.

In the Edessene Canons (can. 7; see 'Syriac Documents' in the *Ante-Nicene Christ. Libr.* p. 39) a forty days' fast is prescribed; 'and then celebrate the day of the Passion and the day of the Resurrection: because our Lord . . . fasted forty days, and likewise Moses and Elijah.' . . . Can this be a relic of the observance of the Passion and the Resurrection on the same day?

In *Apost. Const.* v. 13 the forty days are exclusive of Holy Week, and so in pseudo-Ignatius (*Philipp.* 13), and in St. Chrysostom (*Hom.* 30 *in Gen.* § 1). In the *Testament of our Lord* they include Holy Week.

Socrates (*HE* v. 22) says that the fasts before Easter differed in his day. At Rome they fasted for three continuous (συνημμίνας) weeks, save on Saturday and Sunday; in Illyricum and Greece and Alexandria for six weeks, which they called τεσσαρακοστή; others, beginning their fast seven weeks before Easter, fasted three periods of five days only, but still called it τεσσαρακοστή. A difficulty is seen in this passage because Socrates had just said that every Saturday was a fast at Rome. Duchesne proposes to emend Socrates as far as the word 'continuous' is concerned, and supposes that the three weeks were the first, fourth, and sixth weeks of Lent. He justly remarks that the divergence of fasting, while the same name τεσσαρακοστή was kept, points to the fact that the 'forty days' were introduced for another purpose than that of fasting. In fact, the prevalence of forty days is due largely to the fact that catechumens were under instruction for that time. The catechumenate was indeed often longer, though St. Jerome (*Ep.* 61) says that in his time forty days was the usual period. We find two years at Elvira, three years in the *Egyptian Church Order* and the *Testament of our Lord*, though a good deal of discretion was allowed. But in any case, at the beginning of the forty days the selected candidates for baptism (*competentes*) were put apart and went through special instruction, with prayers, benedictions, and exorcisms, as is described at length in the *Church Orders.*

(*f*) *Palm Sunday* appears for the first time in the *Pilgrimage of 'Silvia.'* Formerly we had only known of it as being kept at the end of the 5th cent., a hundred years later; it is mentioned in the life of Euthymius († 472). The appearance of the festival at Jerusalem is significant. It was doubtless due to the desire to commemorate our Lord's entry into Jerusalem on the spot where it happened. 'Silvia' says: 'On this day, at the seventh hour (1 p.m.) all go to the church on the Mount of Olives, where service is held; and at 5 p.m. they read the Gospel story of the events of the day, and all proceed on foot to Jerusalem, the people crying, Blessed is he who cometh in the name of the Lord; some bearing palm branches, some olives; and so the bishop, after the type of our Lord, is conducted to the Holy City very slowly.' The palms and olives are an instructive comment on the Gospel account.

(*g*) *Maundy Thursday* is not in early times mentioned as being observed in commemoration of the Last Supper. Duchesne (*Orig.* viii. § 3) seems to think that it was so observed at Rome at least, in the primitive ages, but there is no evidence for it. The earliest authority for an Eucharist on this day is the *Testament of our Lord* (*c.* 350?), which in a very difficult and apparently corrupt passage prescribes it (ii. 11); probably, as a comparison of the Copto-Arabic tr. of the work with James of Edessa's Syriac shows, in the evening (see Cooper-Maclean's note, p. 226). On this day also the deacon offered 'a lamp in the temple' (*ib.*). 'Silvia,' at the end of the same century, describes the Eucharist in the church called 'The Martyrium' or Golgotha, in the afternoon; it was over by 4 p.m., and then there was—on this occasion alone in all the year—a celebration of the Eucharist in the little chapel of the Cross, to the east of Golgotha. The bishop celebrated, and all communicated. In Africa at the same time there was an evening Eucharist on this day, and the people were exempted from the customary fast before Holy Communion on this occasion by the Third Council of Carthage, A.D. 397 (can. 29: 'excepto uno die anniversario quo cœna domini celebratur,' Mansi-Labbé, iii. col. 885). It will be seen that, strictly speaking, these Eucharists, if celebrated after sunset, were at the beginning of Good Friday rather than on the Thursday. St. Augustine (*Ep.* liv., see below) says that there were in his time two Eucharists on the Thursday, one for the sake of those who could not fast till evening, and would not receive the Eucharist otherwise.

In the preparation for baptism this Thursday played an important part. The candidates were bidden to bathe on this day, apparently as a ceremonial washing (*Hippol. Can.* 106; *Egyptian Church Order,* 45 [so Lagarde rightly]; *Test. of our Lord,* ii. 6; Augustine, *Epp.* liv. 10, lv. 33 *ad Januarium*). Bathing at Pascha was not confined to the *competentes*; in the *Testament* the widows (presbyteresses) are bidden to bathe on that day (i. 42). There appears also to have been on that day the custom in some places of washing the feet of the *competentes* in memory of the *pedilauium* of Jn 13⁴ᵃ·—a custom which afterwards gave the name to Maundy Thursday (from the 'new command-

ment,' *mandatum,* Jn 13³⁴). Elsewhere the *pedilauium* took place after baptism. The council of Elvira (can. 48) forbade priests or clergy to wash the feet of the newly baptized. Pseudo-Ambrose (*de Sacramentis,* iii. 1) says that this was the custom at the place where he wrote (not Milan?), but that it did not obtain at Rome. In the Gallican Church also it was common (Hefele, *Councils,* i. 158, Eng. tr.).

(*h*) *Easter Week.*—The observance of the days after Easter is mentioned in the *Apostolic Constitutions* ('the great week [Holy Week] and that which follows it,' viii. 32). This fortnight was to be a time of rest for slaves, that they might be instructed. St. Chrysostom (*Hom.* 34 *de Res. Chr.*) also mentions Easter Week. In 'Silvia,' Easter, as well as Epiphany [Christmas] and the Dedication, has an octave during which 'stations' are held at the various churches in and near Jerusalem. But, with this exception, octaves outside Easter Week are Western and not Eastern.

2. Pentecost and Ascension. — (*a*) *The name 'Pentecost'* had in the first four centuries two meanings, the fiftieth day after Easter, and the whole season of fifty days after that festival.

(*a*) It is used as a *day* in NT: Ac 2¹ ('the day of Pentecost'), 20¹⁶ (*id.*), 1 Co 16⁸ ('until Pentecost'); the Jewish nomenclature was continued in the Apostolic age. We find the same sense in succeeding ages, though perhaps not so frequently as the other. A fragment of Irenæus, quoted by pseudo-Justin (*Quæst. et Respons. ad Orthodoxos,* 115) seems to speak of the *day*: 'Irenæus . . . in his treatise περὶ τοῦ πάσχα . . . makes mention of Pentecost also, on which (ἐν ᾗ) we do not bend the knee because it is of equal significance with the Lord's Day.' Pseudo-Justin in the corresponding question has ἀπὸ τοῦ πάσχα ἕως τῆς πεντηκοστῆς. The 43rd canon of Elvira (*c.* 305 A.D.) has: 'ut cuncti diem Pentecostes celebremus.' 'Silvia' (vi. § 1) has 'a Pascha usque ad Quinquagesima, id est Pentecosten,' and (§ 3) 'Quinquagesimarum die, id est dominica.'

(*β*) On the other hand, the use of the name for *the whole season* is also common. Tertullian (*de Bapt.* 19) says that 'after Pascha, Pentecost is a very extensive (*latissimum*; *v.l. lætissimum*) space for conferring baptisms, wherein, too, the Resurrection of the Lord was repeatedly proved among the disciples, and the hope of the Advent of the Lord indirectly pointed to, in that at that time, when He had been received back into the heavens, the angels told the Apostles that He would so come as He had withal ascended into the heavens, of course at Pentecost.' But he goes on to say that Jeremiah signified 'the day of the Passover and of Pentecost, which is properly a feast day.' In *de Cor.* 3 he has 'from Pascha to Pentecost.' In *de Idol.* 14 he says that the Jews would not have shared with Christians the Lord's Day, nor yet Pentecost. Thus he uses the word in both senses. Origen talks of 'living in the season of Pentecost' in the same passage (*c. Cels.* viii. 22) in which he talks of observing certain days, as, for example, the Lord's Day, the Preparation, the Passover, or Pentecost. He refers to the Descent of the Spirit. The 20th canon of Nicæa forbids kneeling in the 'days of Pentecost,' as on the Lord's day. This is unlike St. Paul's usage; he knelt at this season (Ac 20³⁶ 21⁵). The *Testament of our Lord* speaks of 'the days of Pentecost' (i. 28, 42, ii. 12); it forbids any one to fast or kneel then, for these are 'the days of rest and joy.' St. Basil speaks of the 'seven weeks of the holy Pentecost' (*On the Spirit,* ch. 27, *aliter* § 66).

The quotations given above show that Pentecost as a *Christian* festival goes back at least to Irenæus. It is rather curious that there is no reference to it between the NT and that Father; and with this fact we may compare the silence of the earlier writers about Easter; but, as Duchesne remarks (*Orig.* viii. § 4), Pentecost is implied rather than explicitly mentioned in early Christian writings.

(*b*) *The Ascension.*—The fortieth day after Easter was not, so far as we know, observed as a commemoration of our Lord's going up to heaven until at least the middle of the 4th century. In the *Edessene Canons* (can. 9) the Ascension is observed with Pentecost: 'At the completion of fifty (*v.l.* 'forty,' but this is clearly a later correction) days after His Resurrection, make ye a commemoration of His Ascension.' And so in 'Silvia' on the day of Pentecost there is a 'station' at the Mount of Olives, at the church called Imbomon, 'that is in that place whence the Lord ascended into heaven,' where the lection of the Ascension is read. This 'station' is held after another 'in Syon,' where the lection of the Descent of the Holy Ghost is read. Thus in this account both events are commemorated on the same day. The curious thing is that in 'Silvia' there is also an observance of the fortieth day after Easter; but then the 'station' is at Bethlehem, and there is no mention of the Ascension. The coupling together of the two events, which has its parallel in the joining together of Good Friday and Easter, as mentioned already, is illustrated by the passage from the Epistle of Barnabas cited above (I. § 1); the writer thought that the Ascension fell on a Sunday. Compare also Tertullian, *de Bapt.* 19 (see above, § 2 *a*).

Ascension Day is not found in the *Testament of our Lord* (c. 350 A.D.?) or in any of the earlier *Church Orders*, but it is found in the *Apostolic Constitutions*, the author of which made it his aim to increase the festal cycle (v. 19, viii. 32). Sermons preached on this occasion are found in the 4th cent., by Eusebius of Emesa (?) c. 350 A.D., Epiphanius, Gregory of Nyssa, and Chrysostom. The title of Gregory's sermon calls the festival ἐπισωζομένη, which apparently means 'an extra festival.' It does not appear certain, however, that these Fathers kept it on the fortieth day after Easter. St. Augustine (*Ep.* liv. § 1, *ad Januar.*) treats it as universal in A.D. 400: 'They are held as approved and instituted either by the Apostles themselves or by plenary councils ... for example, the annual commemoration by special solemnities of the Lord's Passion, Resurrection, and Ascension, and of the Descent of the Holy Spirit from heaven.'

3. Christmas and Epiphany.—(*a*) *Their origin.*

These festivals are of much later date than Easter and Pentecost, and were probably unknown till nearly A.D. 300. They were both, in their origin, one festival, and both were meant to commemorate the Nativity of our Lord; but the East fixed on one day and the West on another as the date of the birth of Christ, and so in course of time two separate festivals emerged.

Before we consider the evidence for the observance of 25th December and 6th January as festivals, it will be desirable to investigate the reason why these two days were chosen. The most probable solution of the matter, in the light of our present knowledge, is that of Duchesne (*Origines*, ch. viii. § 5), whose theory is followed here. The date 25th December was first arrived at apparently by Hippolytus. Other calculations had fixed on 18th or 19th April or 29th May (Clement of Alexandria, *Strom.* i. 147, ed. Potter, Oxford, 1715, p. 407: 'on the 25th day of the month Pachon'; see the whole passage); and about A.D. 243 the treatise *de Pascha Computus* of pseudo-Cyprian (see above, II. § 1 *d*) named 28th March. The calculations of Hippolytus, which were his mature results (for he had formerly fixed on 2nd January), prevailed all over the West. They are found in his Commentary on Daniel (iv. 23, p. 244, ed. Bonwetsch; *aliter* iv. 9). They depend on the assumption that the earthly life of our Lord, from His conception to His death, lasted an exact number of years. The upholders of symbolical systems of numbers treated all fractions as imperfections. Acting on this idea, Hippolytus fixed on 25th March for the Annunciation, because he had, as he thought, discovered that the Crucifixion took place on that day (see above, § 1 *d*); he reckoned the Saviour's life as thirty-two years, from B.C. 3 to A.D. 29. Adding nine months, he arrived at 25th December as the day of the Nativity.*

The other date, 6th January, is not so easily accounted for. But Duchesne mentions a coincidence which increases the probability of his theory as to 25th December being correct. Sozomen (*HE* vii. 18) says that 'the Montanists who are called Pepuzites and Phrygians' celebrated the Passover on 6th April. They reckoned that the world had been created on 'the ninth day before the kalends of April,' the vernal equinox, and that the sun was created 'on the fourteenth day of the moon occurring after the ninth day before the kalends of April'; and they always celebrated the Passover 'on this day, when it falls on the day of the Resurrection,' otherwise they celebrated it on the following Lord's day. They probably, then, thought that our Lord died on 6th April; and, as Duchesne remarks, that 'the Passover of Christ, being the true Passover, must fall due at typical maturity reckoned from the origin of all things.' But reckoning nine months from 6th April, on the same reasoning as that of Hippolytus, we arrive at 6th January.

We do not read of either of these days being observed *as festivals* in the 3rd century. The first mention of such a commemoration on 25th December is in the Philocalian Calendar (see below, § 5), which was copied in 354 A.D., but represents the official observances at Rome in A.D. 336. We find the entry: 'viij kal. Jan. Natus Christus in Bethleem Judæ.' It is not indeed absolutely certain that 25th December was at that date observed as a feast; but it is highly probable that this was so, as the other days, commemorations of bishops of Rome and martyrs, seem to be noted in order that they might be observed. This was more than a century after Hippolytus.

It will be observed that the theory given above of the choice of 25th December takes no account of the heathen festival of the sun held on the same day. But it is quite possible that when, in the 4th cent., the Christians began to observe the Nativity as a festival, they seized on the coincidence between the day as calculated by Hippolytus and the heathen feast-day, and Christianizing the latter as the Birth of the true Sun of Righteousness, showed a good example to the pagan world by making the day a true holy day.

The Eastern festival of 6th January may be traced to about A.D. 300 among the orthodox. Clement of Alexandria, indeed (*Strom. l.c.*), says that the followers of Basilides celebrated the day of Jesus' baptism, 'spending the whole preceding night in lections.' But the earliest orthodox mention of the day is in the *Passion of Philip of Heraclea*, in the Diocletian persecution, A.D. 304. Philip says: 'Epiphaniæ dies sanctus incumbit' (Ruinart, *Act. Mart. Sinc.* p. 410). That it was of recent introduction when the *Testament of our Lord* was written (c. 350?), appears from there being no regulations for it as there are for Pascha and Pentecost. It is only just mentioned in that work ('Epiphany,' Syr. ܐܦ݂ܝܦ݂ܢܝܐ). And during the greater

* Other Patristic assumptions were that the ministry of our Lord lasted one year only, the 'acceptable year of the Lord' (Lk 4¹⁹; see, *e.g.*, Clem. Alex. *l.c.*, 'It was right for Him to preach for one year only'), and that Jesus was baptized on His thirtieth birthday (Lk 3²³ ὡσεὶ ἐτῶν τριάκοντα). This last idea accounts for the baptism of Christ being commemorated on 6th January.

part of the 4th cent., and in some countries even later, 6th January was the only day observed in the East. The sixth Edessene canon prescribes 'the Epiphany of our Saviour, which is the chief of the festivals of the Church [this is significant], on the sixth day of the latter Kanun,' *i.e.* 6th January. Epiphanius knew of no other day. In *Hær.* li. ('the Alogi,' lib. ii. tom. 1) he speaks of 'A.D. vi Id. Nov.' as being 60 days before the feast 'of the Epiphanies,' when Christ was born according to the flesh (§ 16), and of 'the day in which He was born, that is, of the Epiphanies, which is the sixth of January.' Cassian, at the end of the 4th cent., speaks of 'Epiphany, which the priests of that province [Egypt] regard as the time both of our Lord's baptism and also of his birth in the flesh, and so celebrate the commemoration of either mystery not separately as in the Western provinces, but in the single festival of this day' (*Conferences*, x. 2). Even later, Gennadius (*de Vir. Illustr.* 59) says that 'Timothy the bishop wrote on the Nativity,' and that this work was thought to have been composed at Epiphany. Only 6th January was observed at Jerusalem in the time of 'Silvia,' when there was a 'station' at Bethlehem at night. As the manuscript is defective, we do not know whether there was a celebration of the Eucharist there, but it is probable that there was one, and this nocturnal 'station' may have been the origin of the Christmas midnight Eucharist of later days. The name of the Eastern festival was the 'Epiphanies' or 'Theophanies.' Traces of the older custom in the East of observing 6th January only are found in the 6th cent. at Jerusalem, where Cosmas Indicopleustes mentions it. He says that the Nativity and the Baptism were observed on the same day (Migne, *Patr. Gr.* vol. lxxxviii. 197). The Armenians still observe only that day.

The Easterns, however, even at the end of the 4th cent., began to adopt the Western day in addition to their own; and probably soon afterwards the Westerns adopted the Eastern day as a separate festival. And thereafter on 25th December the Church commemorated the Nativity, and on 6th January other manifestations of our Lord's Divinity and glory. In the East the Baptism, with its manifestations, was and is alone emphasized on 6th January. In the West, as St. Augustine says early in the 5th cent. (see below), the coming of the Wise Men was the great commemoration. The Calendar of Polemius Silvius (A.D. 448) combines it with our Lord's baptism and the miracle at Cana (Wordsworth, *Min. of Grace*, viii. § 1; Migne, *Patr. Lat.* xiii. 676). In the present day all three events are commemorated.

St. Chrysostom in A.D. 386 tells us that Christmas, as distinct from Epiphany, had been only lately introduced at Antioch, less than ten years before (*in Diem Natalem*, ed. Montfaucon, Paris, 1718, ii. 355 A). In *de Beato Philogonio* (i. 497 C) he speaks of Epiphany, Easter, and the other festivals taking their origin from Christmas; for, if Christ had not been born, He would in no wise have been baptized, for that is the feast of the Theophanies. In the *Apostolic Constitutions* both Christmas and Epiphany are mentioned (v. 13), and this is one of the chief factors in determining the date of that Syrian document. At Alexandria both festivals were observed before the year 432; for Paul, bishop of Emesa, preached there on his mission of peace after the Council of Ephesus on the Sunday before Christmas, on Christmas Day, and on the following Sunday, New Year's Day 433 (Smith-Wace, *Dict. Chr. Biog.* iv. 261, *s.v.* 'Paulus 30'),

In the West, St. Augustine tells us that both days were observed in his time; he says that the

Epiphany was kept 'per universum mundum,' but that the Donatists would not accept it. He implies that it had been introduced from the East, and says that the Donatists did not love unity, and did not communicate with the Eastern Church where that star [of the Magi] appeared (Sermon 202 in *Epiphania Domini*, iv.; see also Sermons 199–204. The six Sermons are almost entirely taken up with the coming of the Wise Men).

(*b*) *Advent.*—The first trace of this season is in the canons of Saragossa in Spain (*Concilium Cæsaraugustanum*), *c.* 380 A.D. (Mansi-Labbé, iii. 633), which provide that from xvi kal. Jan. to the 'day of Epiphany, which is viij Id. Jan.,' all are sedulously to attend church (can. 4). We notice here that 25th December is apparently unknown to this council, and that the preparatory season before 6th January is a solemn season of prayer and churchgoing, but not of fasting; much as the 'forty days of Pascha' are in the *Testament of our Lord*. The latter work speaks of the 'days of Epiphany,' which may mean the days after Epiphany, or possibly the days before it, just as the 'days of Pascha' mean in this work the forty days before Easter, and the 'days of Pentecost' mean the fifty days before Whitsunday. But the reference to Advent is too uncertain to be built on.

4. The Presentation of Christ in the Temple.—For this commemoration 'Silvia' is our earliest authority. On this day, she says, all the presbyters preached, and last the bishop himself, 'on the events of the day, when Joseph and Mary bore the Lord into the temple, and Simeon saw Him, and Anna the prophetess, the daughter of Samuel' (*sic*). Then the Eucharist was celebrated. 'Silvia' calls this day 'Quadragesima de Epiphania,' *i.e.* 14th February. The assembly was at the Church of the Anastasis. Here we have a clear indication of the way in which festivals at Jerusalem increased out of a desire to commemorate Gospel events in the holy places. From Jerusalem this festival spread elsewhere; but we do not hear of it, except in 'Silvia,' till the 6th century. Its name then was ὑπαπαντή or the Meeting [of our Lord and Simeon] —a name still retained by the Greeks.

Although Hippolytus had fixed 25th March as the date of the Annunciation, no trace of any observance of the day as a festival is found in the first four centuries, nor indeed for long after. Possibly its frequent concurrence with the Paschal solemnities or the Lenten fast prevented this. The Nestorians keep neither the Presentation nor the Annunciation.

5. Commemorations of Saints, etc.—These can be glanced at only briefly in a Dictionary of Christ and the Gospels. They were originally of local origin, and did not at once become popular except in the places where they began. The earliest known collection of local saints' days is the *Philocalian Calendar* of A.D. 354, which may be conveniently seen in Ruinart's *Acta Martyrum Sincera et selecta*, p. 617, and in Migne's *Patrologia Latina*, vol. xiii.; reference may also be made to Bishop Lightfoot's essay in his *Clement* (i. 246, on 'The Liberian Catalogue'). It is the only extant calendar which is certainly older than A.D. 400, though portions of a Gothic calendar remain which may be dated shortly before that year. The so-called *Hieronymian Martyrology* is much later than St. Jerome. The Christian section of the Philocalian Calendar (for it has also a heathen section) is a Roman list. It has two parts: the *Depositio* (burial) *episcoporum*, and the *Depositio martyrum*. Under the first head it contains twelve names: Dionysius, Felix, Sylvester, Miltiades, Marcellinus, Lucius, Caius, Stephen, Eusebius, Marcus, Eutichianus, Julius. Julius and Marcus come out of their calendrical order (not Marcus in

Ruinart), and are probably later additions (Lightfoot). The second part begins with Christmas (as above, § 3), and contains no other festival of Christ. It is, no doubt, the official list of martyrs commemorated at Rome at the time. Its names are all local, except Cyprian and Perpetua and Felicitas, which are African. In all there are 37 entries, as given by Ruinart; but some have more than one name. The first part begins at vi kal. Jan., and its latest date is vi Id. Dec. Of the second part viii kal. Jan. is the beginning and Id. Dec. is the end. The beginning of the year must therefore have been reckoned as Christmas Day (25th December), or at least some day between 13th and 25th December. It is interesting to note in this early calendar 'iii kal. Jul. [*i.e.* June 29] Petri in Catacumbas et Pauli Ostiense Tusco et Basso Coss.,' that is the translation of the bodies of these Apostles.

A Syriac Martyrology published in 1866 by Professor Wright must also be mentioned, as, though the copy in the British Museum dates from 411, it gives (if careful examination be applied to it) earlier lists still. It is an Eastern Martyrology translated into Syriac and abridged at Edessa about 400 A.D. from a collection made in Greek out of local calendars. It has two Roman entries, one African, and the rest are Eastern; it must have been originally Arian, as it does not contain the name of Athanasius, but has that of Arius ('at Alexandria, Arius the presbyter'). Analysis shows it to have been made up of the local lists of Nicomedia, Antioch, and Alexandria. The two latter appear to have contained, at about A.D. 350, 24 and 26 entries respectively. This shows the limited numbers of commemorations in the 4th century. The lists, however, speedily grew to large dimensions. For other early calendars reference may be made to the works mentioned below.

The observance of the death-days (*natales*) or burial days (*depositiones*) of martyrs may be traced back to the 2nd cent., c. 155 A.D.; the letter of the Smyrneans on the martyrdom of St. Polycarp speaks (§ 18) of his burial-place 'where the Lord will permit us to gather ourselves together . . . to celebrate the birthday of his martyrdom for the commemoration of those that have already fought in the contest, and for the training and preparation of those that shall do so hereafter.' This letter was written soon after the martyrdom (see Lightfoot's *Ignatius and Polycarp*, iii. 353 ff.). St. Cyprian says that the death-days of the martyrs were to be carefully noted, that they might observe such commemorations with Eucharist (*Ep.* 12, to his presbyters and deacons). The 18th Edessene Canon orders commemorations of the martyrs. And such commemorations are mentioned by St. Basil (*Ep.* 93, as above, I. § 3).

For the purposes of this Dictionary, the observances of the days following 25th December are of interest, as being closely connected with the Nativity of our Lord. These observances date from the 4th century. St. Gregory of Nyssa, preaching the funeral oration of his brother St. Basil (who died 1st January 379), says that they were then celebrating these saints' days, which were convenient (he remarks) because Apostles and Prophets were first constituted and ordained, and after that pastors and teachers. He first mentions the commemoration of the Apostles and Prophets after Christmas, namely, Stephen, Peter, James, John, Paul; and then Basil (*in Laudem Fratris Basilii, ad init.*, ed. Paris of 1638, p. 479). It does not necessarily follow that the saints mentioned were commemorated on different days. The *Apostolic Constitutions* mention a commemoration of the martyrs and 'blessed James the bishop' [the Lord's brother], and 'the holy Stephen our fellow-

servant' (v. 8; so viii. 32). The Syriac Martyrology mentioned above gives St. Stephen on 26th December, St. James and St. John on 27th December, St. Peter and St. Paul on 28th December. With this we may compare two later usages, the Armenian and the Nestorian (East Syrian), as these separated Christians have retained many early customs which others have dropped. The Armenians, who do not observe 25th December as Christmas, commemorate St. David and St. James the Lord's brother on that date, but follow the Syriac Martyrology for the other days, save that they transpose 27th and 28th December (Duchesne, *Orig.* viii. § 5. 2). The Nestorian usage is somewhat different. That Church keeps its saints' days according to the movable Christian year rather than according to the month, and most of them fall on Fridays. The Fridays after Christmas (25th December), if there are sufficient before Lent, are (1) St. James the Lord's brother, (2) St. Mary, (3) St. John Baptist, (4) St. Peter and St. Paul, (5) Four Evangelists, (6) St. Stephen; and other festivals of later origin follow (Maclean, *East Syrian Daily Offices*, p. 264 ff.). Duchesne conjectures that the 'Four Evangelists' is a transformation of St. James and St. John, the latter having attracted to him the three other Evangelists, and the former being omitted. The Orthodox Easterns now commemorate St. James the Lord's brother on the Sunday after Christmas.

'Silvia' has not, like the *Apostolic Constitutions*, a general martyrs' festival; nor yet have the other *Church Orders*. But considering the great development of festivals in 'Silvia,' it is not improbable that she did describe such a general commemoration; only the manuscript breaks off suddenly in the middle of the account of the Dedication festival, and we cannot be sure of what was in the *lacuna*.

Speaking generally, we note a difference between these commemorations and the festivals of our Lord. The former were at first local only, and of inferior importance. The Nestorians to this day keep up a sharp distinction between the two, calling

the former ܕܘܼܟ̈ܪܵܢܹܐ *commemorations*, the latter

ܥܹܐܕܹ̈ܐ *festivals*, or ܥܹܐܕܹ̈ܐ ܡܵܪܵܢܵܝܹ̈ܐ *festivals of our Lord*; and the distinction is ancient.

Dedication festivals were common in the 4th cent., though they are not mentioned in the *Church Orders*, even in those, like the *Testament of our Lord*, which describe the church buildings minutely. These festivals concern us here only as contributing to the calendar Holy Cross Day, which was the commemoration of the dedication in 335 of the churches built by Constantine on the site of the Holy Sepulchre and Calvary, and of the alleged discovery of the true cross by St. Helena, Constantine's mother. 'Silvia' says that the anniversary was observed with great ceremony in her time, many pilgrims from distant lands attending, and the churches being adorned as at Easter and Christmas. This day (14th September, but among the Nestorians 13th September) passed from Jerusalem to Constantinople; at Rome it was not introduced till the 7th century.

Of the other days of Apostles, Martyrs, or Confessors, most of which are of later introduction than the 4th cent., it may be observed that the majority, at least, are due to the local dedication of a church named after the saint at Rome, Constantinople, or elsewhere. See Duchesne, *Orig.* ch. viii. *passim.*

RECAPITULATION OF FESTAL CYCLES.—
Fathers of the first three centuries: Pascha and Pentecost.

Testament of our Lord: Pascha, Pentecost, and Epiphany.
Apostolic Constitutions: Ascension, Pentecost, Pascha, Christmas, Epiphany, Apostles' days (plural), St. Stephen and All Martyrs' day (singular)—viii. 32 Lagarde (*aliter* 33). Add St. James the Lord's brother, v. 8. [The sections of the *Apost. Const.* mentioned in this article are all Lagarde's].
Pilgrimage of 'Silvia': Epiphany with octave, Presentation, Palm Sunday, Easter with octave, Fortieth day after Easter, Pentecost (including Ascension), Dedication (Holy Cross Day).
Cappadocian Fathers and Syriac Martyrology: Add St. Stephen, St. Peter and St. Paul, St. James and St. John.

The account of the Christian calendar is thus brought down to about A.D. 400. For festivals introduced after that date reference may be made to the various works on Christian history and antiquities.

LITERATURE. — (1) General: Duchesne, *Origines du culte chrétien* (Eng. tr. from third ed. entitled *Christian Worship, its Origin and Evolution*); Bp. J. Wordsworth, *Ministry of Grace.* — (2) Calendars: Achelis, *Die Martyrologien*, 1900; Dom Butler, notice of Achelis' book in *Journ. of Theol. Studies*, ii. 147; and Duchesne and Wordsworth as above.— (3) On the Lord's day: Zahn, *Skizzen aus dem Leben der Alten Kirche*, 1894, ch. vi.; Hessey, *Bampton Lectures*, 1860; Trevelyan, *Sunday*, 1902. — (4) Christmas: Salmon, paper on Hippolytus' Commentary on Daniel in *Hermathena*, vol. iii. Dublin, 1893; and Duchesne and Wordsworth as above.— (5) The Quartodeciman Controversy: Salmon, *Introduction to NT*, Lect. xv.; McGiffert's note on Eusebius, *HE* v. 22, in *Nicene and Post-Nicene Fathers*; Schaff, *Church History*, ii. 209 f.; Hefele, *Conciliengeschichte*, i. 298 ff. (2nd Eng. ed.); Schürer, 'Die Paschastreitigkeiten' in *Zeitschrift für hist. Theol.* 1870, p. 182 ff.—(6) Paschal Cycles: Hefele, *Concilieng.* i. 317 ff.; Salmon, article in Smith-Wace, *Dict. Chr. Biog.* on 'Hippolytus.'

A. J. MACLEAN.

CALF.—See ANIMALS, p. 63[b].

CALL, CALLING.—
1. Terms.
  (*a*) OT.
  (*b*) Gospels.
  (*c*) Epistles.
2. Secular calling.
3. Spiritual calling.
  (*a*) Our Lord's Messianic vocation.
  (*b*) The Apostolic calling.
  (*c*) Other calls to service.
  (*d*) The Gospel call in Christ's own teaching.
    Literature.

1. THE TERMS.—(*a*) *The OT.*—The substantive 'call' is not found in the English Bible. If used of an animal's call, it tends to imply a *significant* note—e.g. a mother's call to her brood (Bunyan, *PP* ii. 62)—not a mere emotional cry. The English verb 'call' has for its primary meaning 'to speak *loudly*.' In Hebrew we note the same implication in קָרָא, e.g. Pr 8[1]; but in Hebrew the word still more strongly suggests articulate *human* speech, even perhaps in Ps 147[9] (although the partridge probably derives its name קֹרֵא from its *calling*). It is indeed the technical word for reading (e.g. Is 29[12]): the Hebrews read *aloud* and prayed aloud. Eli suspected Hannah (1 S 1[13]) not because her lips moved in private prayer—rather because in the intensity and modesty of her desire she prayed without sound. Loudness may express authority; or it may be a simple effort to attract notice. Anyway, a 'call,' Hebrew or English, is a loud and definite communication from one person to another. Either language may use the verb intransitively, but always with a sort of latent transitiveness. In Greek, on the other hand, καλέω is transitive. What is implied in the other languages is explicit in this one. Definiteness (and perhaps authority) receives reinforcement when the calling is *by name*. We are probably not to confuse this with the mere *giving* of a name; though, according to the ideas of the ancient world, so much power is wrapped up in names that there

may be a certain infiltration of that thought in the Biblical usage of calling *by name*. But, more simply, one's name arrests one's attention, and assures one that the call is addressed to him. In Deutero-Isaiah it is said that Jehovah has a name for every star (Is 40[26] [we need not discuss whether the stars are here conceived as alive], imitated in Ps 147[4]). That signifies His power; it is rather His condescension that is shown when He calls the prophetic servant, Israel, by name (Is 43[1]). Again, He calls Cyrus 'by name' to his historic functions (Is 45[3, 4], cf. also Ex 31[2] [P]). If our text is to be trusted, Jehovah even 'surnames' Cyrus (Is 45[4]). It is a mark of kindliness when a servant is not simply 'waiter' or 'guard' to his rich employer, but has a name and a recognized personality of his own. (Here cf. Ex 33[12, 17]). To 'surname,' at least in the strict sense, is a still stronger proof of friendly interest; surnames are a token of some new destiny, or else imply knowledge of idiosyncrasies. (Acc. to P, Jehovah renames 'Abram' and 'Sarai,' Gn 17[5, 15], while Moses renames 'Hoshea,' Nu 13[16]; cf. also the surnames given by our Lord to the three leading Apostles, Mk 3[16, 17]). It is also in Deutero-Isaiah that we find the emergence of 'call' in a sort of theological sense; the 'call' of Abraham (51[2] 'I called him').

Another important section of the OT for our terminology is the 'Praise of Wisdom,' Pr 1–9. Several things are noticeable here; the loud call —Divine Wisdom as a street preacher (8[1], cf. 1[20]); the solemn religious conception of the call rejected (1[24]); the call as an invitation to a feast (ch. 9). This last usage ('call'='invite'), while obsolete in modern English, is found in its literal sense both in OT and NT of our version; e.g. 1 K 1[9], Jn 2[2] AV.

Still another group of OT passages may seem to require notice—those describing the 'call' of various prophets. The term is *not so used* in OT (unless Is 51[2]?—see above—Abraham is a 'prophet' in Gn 20[7] [E]). But there is a passage which would lend itself excellently to this interpretation—the tale of the call of the young Samuel, where we have three interesting parallel usages: Jehovah 'called *to* Samuel' (1 S 3[4] literally), '*called* Samuel' (v.[8]), 'called . . . *Samuel, Samuel*' (v.[10]). There are therefore several usages of the word 'to call' in OT which we ought to keep in mind as we approach the Gospels. It means command, or it means invitation. It means a summons to special function, or it means (along with that) a peculiar mark of gracious condescension.

(*b*) In the *Gospels*, the verb may occur in the literal sense (Mt 20[8]). But in general a compound form is preferred for such sense; e.g. when Jesus calls (προσκαλεσάμενος) His disciples near Him for a short talk (Mk 10[42]). We have the simple form in one important passage when James and John are 'called' (Mk 1[20] || Mt 4[21] ἐκάλεσεν), though the compound (προσκαλεῖται) is found in Mark's record of the selection of the Twelve (3[13]), while in the parallel in Luke (6[13]) προσεφώνησεν is employed. It might be argued that, even here, the mere *word* 'called' means no more than 'called to Himself.' Still, in view of OT antecedents, that is questionable. Anyway, as a matter of fact, those 'calls' were commands and invitations, to 'leave all (Mk 10[28]) and follow Jesus—to take up solemn functions in His service. When compounds of καλέω are used, or when φωνέω is used, we need not suspect deep religious or theological significance in the *word*. Yet here again the fact has to be dealt with. Jesus may simply 'call to' (φωνεῖν) Bartimæus (Mk 10[49]); but the result of the conversation (and miracle) is that he who had been blind 'follows Jesus in the way' (10[52]). In two other passages the group of meanings associated with Pr 1-9—privilege rather than authority; invitation, rather than command—come to the front: 'I came not to call (καλέσαι) the righteous, but sinners' (Mk 2¹⁷, Mt 9¹³; Lk 5³² adds 'to repentance'), and 'many are called (κλητοί), but few chosen' (Mt 22¹⁴; in 20¹⁶ these words are rightly dropped by RV as not belonging to the original text).

(c) Though our concern is with the Gospels, we cannot refuse to consult the *Epistles* for the light they may throw on Gospel usage. They give us a cognate substantive; not 'call' but 'calling.' 'Call' as a substantive occurs in English much earlier than our AV, but presumably the purely physical idea—the audible call—was too strongly marked in it to allow of its standing for God's address to the conscience. 'Calling,' which was preferred, reproduces the form of the Greek substantive κλῆσις. This term is mainly Pauline (e.g. 1 Co 1²⁶), though it extends into Hebrews (3¹) and (at least so far as the verb is concerned) into 1 Peter (1¹⁵ 2²¹). As moulded by St. Paul, there is no doubt that the 'call' is primarily one to salvation (Ro 8²⁸⁻³⁰), though it may also signify special (Apostolic) function (Ro 1¹). The Epistle to the Hebrews preserves the same twofold reference. All believers 'partake of a heavenly calling' (3¹), but none may take high honour or office upon himself except when 'called' by God thereto (5⁴). Later in the history of English speech, the physical implications of the noun 'call' having been in some measure rubbed off, it came into religious use, so as generally to displace 'calling.' We say the 'call' not 'calling' of Abraham; but if Scripture had used a substantive, 'calling' would have been installed by our translators in this phrase. The NT 'calling' is a single definite act in the past, whether personal conversion [sometimes acceptance of Divinely imposed duty] or the historic mission of Christ. He who 'called' us is holy (1 P 1¹⁵). In our modern use of 'calling,' something seems borrowed from the idea of a *worldly* calling, viz. *habitualness*. Acc. to Murray's *Dictionary*, 1 Co 7²⁰ introduced—almost by an accident —the use of 'calling' for worldly rank, station, external surroundings. 'Hence,' it adds, ' "calling" came to be applied to the various means of bread-winning.' [The exegesis of the verse is disputed, but the view the *Dictionary* proceeds on seems to be right. It is not, of course, pretended that 'calling' in 1 Co 7²⁰ means *exactly* trade or profession. St. Paul would never make it matter of conscience that a Christian should refrain from changing his trade]. Both these senses—viz. (1) station, and (2) trade—are often (unwarrantably, the *Dictionary* seems to think, as far as etymology goes) regarded as Divine vocations. This is surely obscure. If 1 Co 7²⁰ taught so little, can we hold it responsible for a twofold set of meanings? May not professional 'calling' rather mean, in the first instance, 'what I am called'—William [the] Smith, John [the] Tailor? a still humbler etymology. However that may be, the idea of Divine vocation in daily concerns could not be ruled out from Christian thought. Thus inevitably Christians have been led to formulate the idea of a *lifelong Divine vocation*, covering all externals, but centring in the heart. It may be repeated that 'calling' (the substantive) is not found in the Gospels; of course the word is not found anywhere in the EV in the sense of 'trade.'

2. SECULAR CALLING.—It is unnecessary to pass under review the occupations followed by our Lord in youth and by His Apostles. See artt. TRADES, CARPENTER, FISHING, etc.

3. SPIRITUAL CALLING.—(a) *Our Lord Himself*, who calls all others, was 'called of God' (He 5⁴) to the Messiahship. It is an irrelevant sentimentality that dwells too much on the 'carpenter of Nazareth.' Jesus was full of the consciousness of His calling, its requirements, its limitations. Not to cite the Fourth Gospel—abundant signs of this, but in the usual golden haze blurring all sharp outlines—we have Mk 1³⁸(?) 2¹⁷ 10⁴⁵, Mt 5¹⁷ 15²⁴ etc. etc. It is one of the services of Ritschl to recent theology—with anticipations in von Hofmann—that he has made prominent the thought of Christ's *vocation*, displacing the less worthy and less ethical category of Christ's *merit*. In the Gospels this vocation is expressed by the word 'sent' or I 'came' (as above; or 'him that sent me,' Jn 4³⁴ etc.), not by 'call.' If there is any one point in our Lord's life where it may be held that the 'call' definitely reached Him,—where He became conscious of Messiahship,—we must seek it at His baptism (Mk 1⁹⁻¹¹; three parallels).

(b) In dealing with *the call addressed by Christ to His disciples*, we begin with the Apostles. Taking the different Gospels together, we seem to recognize three stages. (1) According to St. John, Christ's first disciples were Galilæans who, like Himself, had visited the Jordan in order to be baptized by John: Andrew, John, Simon Peter, Philip, Nathanael (presumably = Bartholomew; see art. BARTHOLOMEW, above), and presumably James the brother of John (Jn 1³⁵⁻⁵¹). The only one mentioned as called with a 'follow me' is Philip (1⁴³); and it is possible that this is rather an invitation to follow on the journey to Galilee than through life (and death). For the rest, we have acquaintanceships and attachments apparently forming themselves—elective affinities displayed, rather than the Master's will exercised *ad hoc*; but the result, according to St. John, is the formation of a small yet definite circle, who are disciples (2². ¹². ¹⁷ etc. etc.) of Jesus now, as others are (and as they themselves previously were) of John the Baptist. (2) The Synoptists tell us of the call in Galilee ('Come ye after me,' Mk 1¹⁷ || Mt 4¹⁹; 'He called them,' Mk 1²⁰ || Mt 4²¹) of Peter, Andrew, James, John. The first two are called with a sort of pleasantry; they are to be 'fishers of men,' in allusion to their former occupation. St. Luke has the same narrative (5¹⁻¹¹) in a more picturesque form; the borrowing of Peter's boat, in order to teach from it as a pulpit; payment after sermon in the form of a miraculous draught of fishes; Peter's fear as a sinner at the near presence of the supernatural; the same kindly *bon mot*; all four fishermen [? v.⁷] on the spot; all four becoming disciples. Here the call (see art. DISCIPLE below) involves leaving everything to follow Christ (Lk 5¹¹, Mk 10²⁸ cf. 1¹⁸. ²⁰, Mt 19²⁷ cf. 4²⁰·²²). Previous acquaintance with these men may have induced Jesus to begin His teaching by the Sea of Galilee [an 'undesigned coincidence'?]. Other members of the disciple circle in Galilee must have been added one by one; some by elective affinity! Not all volunteers might be repelled like the scribe of Mt 8¹⁹ || Lk 9⁵⁹. Matthew the publican, however (Mt 9⁹, Lk 5²⁷ Levi, Mk 2¹⁴ Levi the son of Alphæus), is called straight from his place of toll to 'follow,' and instantly obeys; a memorable incident. (3) The final 'call' in this series appears when Jesus 'calls to him whom he himself will,' and 'appoints twelve, that they may be with him, and that he may send them forth to preach and . . . cast out devils' (Mk 3¹³ etc.; so too, though less clearly, Lk 6¹³; not in Mt.; 10¹ 'his twelve disciples,' v.² 'the twelve apostles'). (4) Or, if there is another stage still, it is marked when they are 'sent out' for the first time (Mt 10⁵, Mk 6⁷, Lk 9¹), or when in consequence of this the name 'apostles' (see art. APOSTLE) is attached to them. Thus, in the case of at least twelve men, the call has issued in a very definite calling; permanent, and in a sense official.

(c) Another group possesses a varied interest. It includes volunteers; it relates 'calls' to service addressed to those who were *not destined to be Apostles*; it offers examples of the call *rejected*. There are four cases; the rich young ruler (Mk 10[17] etc. and parallels), and a group of three found together (Lk 9[57-62]; partial parallel Mt 8[19-22]). The scribe (see Mt.) who volunteers means, or professes to mean, discipleship in the intenser sense. He will follow 'wherever the Master goes'; he will 'leave all,' like the Twelve; the stumbling-block of property, which was too much for the young ruler, is no stumbling-block to him. This volunteer meets not with welcome but rebuff; and, so far as we know, there is an end of *his* gospel service. Again, the man whose father is just dead—that seems the inexorable sense of the words—is needed immediately as a herald of the 'kingdom of God' (so Luke). And the other volunteer, who, with less urgency (so far as we are told) is anxious 'first' to bid farewell to his home circle, is 'looking back' from the *plough*. St. Luke seems well justified in making these narratives introduce a wider mission (that of the 'Seventy'). And here we get important light on the demand that the rich young ruler should give away his property. This may have seemed to our Lord's discernment necessary for the man's own safety—does not the sequel point in that direction? But, even independently of that, though a Christian might be a man of means (see below), a wandering preacher could hardly be. These were calls to service, which met, temporarily or finally, with tragic refusal. Whatever else the refusal may have implied is God's secret.

(d) So far we have dealt chiefly with *authority*; when we consider the few cases in the Gospels where the call is generalized—'not the righteous but sinners' (Mk 2[17] ‖ Mt 9[13] ‖ Lk 5[32]); 'many called, few chosen' (Mt 22[14])—*invitation* comes to the front. The parable depicting the Kingdom of God as a feast (Mt 22[2ff.], Lk 14[16ff.]), while, of course, a parable and not to be pressed too far, emphasizes this. Its language recalls Pr 9. And it has been remarked that the well-known lovely 'gospel invitation' (Mt 11[28-30]) strongly suggests Divine Wisdom speaking. More questionable is the idea started by Bruce in the *Expos. Gk. Test.* that Jesus literally invited outcasts to a free meal at a public hall in the name of Levi (Matthew)—a sort of Free Breakfast or Midnight Supper. On the other hand, the very earliest form of the general call is pure authority; 'Repent' (Mt 4[17], Mk 1[15]).

In all these cases, language itself helps us to vindicate the great truth, that the call of Christ is not merely a call to some external form of service under rapidly vanishing conditions, but a call addressed to heart and conscience; in other words, that Christianity is essentially a religion. Of course, this truth becomes clearer in the Epistles, or in the Fourth Gospel, than in the earlier and less reflective Gospels; but, in regard to our 'calling,' as in all respects, the teaching of Christ Himself traces the plain outlines within which His Apostles afterwards work. Perhaps we ought to note here a difference at least in language between Christ and St. Paul. To the latter, the 'called' are *eo ipso* the 'elect' or 'predestinated' (Ro 8[29. 30. 33]); to Christ, 'calling' (inviting) comes first (Mt 22[14]), and *selection* follows; 'after trial,' as it has been expressed. Our Lord's words, therefore, mark our Christian calling as a calling to service and as a probation. Though we are admitted to His friendship and love, all is not assured. According to His language in the Fourth Gospel, one 'given'

to Christ may 'perish' (Jn 17[12]). The 'unfruitful' branch is 'taken away,' 'cast forth,' 'burned' (Jn 15[2. 6]). All must stand before His judgment-seat; a thought which the parables spoken in view of separation, parables addressed to His own, particularly emphasize (Mt 25; some parallels). All must 'take up the cross' and 'follow Christ' to the uttermost (Mk 8[34] etc. etc.). The last command addressed to a friend by Christ, like the first, is 'follow me' (Jn 21[19. 22]).

The question has been raised whether Jesus' call did not imply a sort of fanaticism based on a mistaken expectation of the near end of the world. This is at least suggested by the purely eschatological view of the Kingdom of God (see art. KINGDOM OF GOD, below) in the Gospels, as taught by Bousset, J. Weiss, and others. If the imputation of fanaticism were historically warranted, all Christians must have been required to live in a fashion possible only to the first few; the call to repent must have been swallowed up in the call to share the Master's wandering life; our 'high calling' (Ph 3[14]), as declared by Christ, must have been deeply tinged with delusion. It is enough to point in reply to women friends of Jesus; to homes whose hospitality He consented to share; to a convert under exceptional circumstances not called nor even permitted to be with Christ, but sent home to be a witness there (Mk 5[19] ‖ Lk 8[39]). The grain of truth in this heap of error has been indicated above. Our Christian calling is not merely to salvation, it is to service. One may add, that the principles of the Master's own teaching are likely to reveal lessons of severity for the Christian conscience which have been neglected in the past—to the great loss of both Church and world.

LITERATURE.—See further, for (a), the present writer's *Christ and the Jewish Law*; A. Ritschl, *Justification and Reconciliation*, vol. iii. (translation) p. 445; Baldensperger, *Selbstbewusstsein Jesu*, 1888 [2nd ed. 1892, 3rd ed. with altered title in progress]; artt. by present writer on 'Dawn of Messianic Self-consciousness' in *Expos. Times*, 1905; a different view, Forrest's *Christ of History and of Experience*, 1897, p. 93 ff. For (b) see Bruce, *Training of the Twelve*; Latham, *Pastor Pastorum*; for (c) and (d) compare *Ecce Homo*, ch. 6, 'Christ's Winnowing Fan' [characteristically dwelling rather on the *moral* aspects of the Divine message]; also Bruce's treatment of Mt 9[9-13] and parallels [notes on all three should be read in *Expos. Gr. Testament*]. The last paragraph of the above article refers to discussions begun by J. Weiss, *Die Predigt Jesu vom Reiche Gottes*, 1892; Bousset, *Jesu Predigt in ihrem Gegensatz zum Judentum*, 1892; cf. also especially J. Weiss, *Die Nachfolge Christi und die Predigt der Gegenwart*, 1895; good reply in Harnack's *Wesen des Christenthums*, 1900 (translation, 'What is Christianity?'); interesting reference to such views and to later developments in Lewis Muirhead's *Bruce Lecture* on 'The Eschatology of Jesus,' 1903.

ROBERT MACKINTOSH.

CALVARY.—See GOLGOTHA.

CAMEL, CAMEL'S HAIR.—The camel is by far the most useful of all animals in the East. There are two kinds of camels—the Turkish or Bactrian camel and the dromedary. The first is larger, has a double hump, and is capable of sustaining greater burdens; the latter is swifter, has a single hump, and is far less affected by extreme heat. The camel has been domesticated from time immemorial; it is now at least nowhere found in its aboriginal wild state, and nature has adapted it to its specific environment. Its nostrils are close and flat, to exclude the dust of the desert; its feet are heavily padded, and its anatomy shows provision for the enduring of great privation. It mocks hunger and thirst alike; it can go without water from sixteen to forty days.

The camel forms the staple wealth of the Arab of the desert, who utilizes every part of the animal, even to the dung, which is used as fuel. Its flesh was forbidden to the Jew (Lv 11[4], Dt 14[7]). Its milk is extremely nutritious, and on fermentation becomes an intoxicant. A thick mat of fine hair protects the animal against the extremes alike of heat and cold.

The camel is mentioned three times in the Gospels, on two occasions as a synonym for size or bulkiness; Mt 19²⁴ (= Mk 10²⁵, Lk 18²⁵), 'It is easier for a camel to go through a needle's eye, than for a rich man to enter into the kingdom of God'; and 23²⁴ 'Ye blind guides, which strain out the gnat, and swallow the camel.' In the former of these passages two attempts have been made to evade the Oriental hyperbole, firstly, by reading κάμιλος, 'a rope,' for κάμηλος; and, again, by explaining the 'eye of the needle' as the small door for foot-passengers which is generally made in the frame of the large entrance-door of an Eastern house. The expression 'eye of the needle,' however, is only the English equivalent of the Greek words denoting a 'hole.' The eye of a needle stands for something narrow and hard to pass, as in the Egyptian proverb, 'Straiter than the eye of a needle' (Burckhardt, 396). A similar proverb is given by Freytag (ii. p. 19), 'Narrower than the shadow of a lance and than the hole of a needle.' And in the Koran we have (vii. 38), 'As for those who declare our signs to be lies, and who scorn them, the doors of heaven will not be open to them, nor will they enter Paradise, until a camel shall penetrate into the eye of a needle'— that is, never.

In the second of the two passages above, the camel is contrasted with the gnat, 'Ye blind guides, which strain out a gnat, and drink down a camel.' The gnat stands for an emblem of smallness in the Koran (ii. 24, 'God is not ashamed to strike a proverb out of a gnat'). In Arabic the elephant rather than the camel is chosen to designate hugeness, as in the song of Kaab ibn Zuheir—

'If there stood in the place which I stand in an elephant,
Hearing and seeing what I see and hear,
His shoulder muscles with dread would be twitching';

and the camel is an emblem of patience and silent endurance, and goes by the name of 'the father of Job.' The elephant must have been a not unfamiliar object in Palestine in the first century, but would naturally be thought of in connexion with Hellenism and idolatry.

Camel's hair or wool, as it is called, is woven by the Arabs into tent-covers, and also into rough outer garments for the peasantry. In Israel this coarse mantle was the badge of the prophet (Zec 13⁴ 'The prophets shall be ashamed each one of his vision, when he prophesieth; and they will no more wear a hairy garment in order to deceive'); and in 2 K 1⁸ Elijah is described as being a 'owner of hair' (שֵׂעָר בַּעַל, that is, wearing this garment of the prophets; AV, 'an hairy man'), and girt with leather. As the successor of Elijah and of the prophets, John the Baptist adopted the same dress (Mt 3⁴, Mk 1⁶). It is generally supposed that the Oriental mystic or *sufi* is so named from his dress of wool (*suf*); cf. Rev 11³.

T. H. WEIR and HENRY E. DOSKER.

CANA (Κανὰ τῆς Γαλιλαίας) is mentioned four times in the Fourth Gospel. It was the scene of our Lord's first miracle (Jn 2¹· ¹¹); the place to which 'a certain king's officer (βασιλικός), whose son was sick at Capernaum,' came to find Jesus (4⁴⁶); and the native place of the disciple Nathanael (21²). After the miracle, Jesus 'went down' (κατέβη) to Capernaum; and the king's officer besought him to 'come down' (καταβῇ) to heal his son. Those references place Cana of Galilee on higher ground than Capernaum. There is no other direct evidence as to its position.

Josephus states (*Vita*, 16) that he resided for a time 'in a village of Galilee which is named Cana.' From this village he made a descent during the night upon Tiberias (17). Later (41) he speaks of residing in the great plain, the name of which was Asochis. If these residences are one and the same place, the Cana of Josephus may well be Khirbet Ḳāna or Ḳānat el-Jelīl, on the N. slopes of the plain of Buṭṭauf, and about 8 miles N. of Nazareth. This, however, would not decide the site of St. John's Cana. [The Κανὰ of *Ant*. xv. v. 1 should be, according to *BJ* I. xix. 1, Καναθά].

Etymology and tradition are divided between the above mentioned site on the plain of Buṭṭauf and *Kefr Kennā*, a hamlet on the direct road to the lake, and about 3½ miles N.E. of Nazareth, where there is a fine spring. Etymology certainly favours *Khirbet Ḳāna*, the doubling of the medial 'nun' being against *Kefr Kennā*. Tradition is indecisive. The references in Placentinus (*Itin*. 4), Phocas, John of Würzburg, Quaresmius (*Elucidationes*, ii. 852 f.), etc., favour *Kefr Kennā*, where the monks of the Greek and Latin Churches have considerable ecclesiastical properties. On the other hand, the notices of Theodosius (A.D. 530), Saewulf, Brocardus, Fetellus, Marinus Sanutus (p. 253), and others, suit the northern site. In later times, Robinson (*BRP*² ii. 348 f., iii. 108) supports the claims of *Khirbet Ḳāna*, and is followed by Ritter, Thomson, Ewald, Socin, Keim, and others. Eusebius and Jerome (*Onom. s.v.* Κανα) identify Cana with Kanah* in Asher (Jos 19²⁸). This could not be *Kefr Kennā*, which is not in Asher, but might be *Khirbet Ḳāna* (*Encyc. Bibl.* i. 638). Other recent writers contend for *Kefr Kennā*, among whom are Guérin, de Saulcy, Porter, Tristram, etc. The balance of evidence is perhaps on the side of the northern site (Hastings' *DB* i. 346ᵇ). Conder (*PEF Mem.* i. 288) suggests as a possible site a spot nearer to Nazareth than *Kefr Kennā*, called 'Ain Ḳāna, and not far from Reineh. Dr. Sanday appears to support this, and claims Guthe as agreeing (*Sacred Sites*, 24 n.).

LITERATURE. — Hastings' *DB* i. 346; *Encyc. Bibl.* i. 637; Robinson, *BRP*² ii. 348 f., iii. 108; Conder, *PEF Mem.* i. 288; Stanley, *SP* 368; Guérin, *Galilée*, i. 175 ff.; Thomson, *Land and Book*, 425 f.; Tristram, *Land of Israel*, 455; Socin, *Pal.* 358, 367; Murray, *Pal.* 366; Buhl, *GAP* 219 f.; Ewald, *Gesch.* vi. 180 n.; Keim, *Jesus of Nazara*, iv. 116 n.; Ritter, *Comp. Geogr.* iv. 378 f.   A. W. COOKE.

CANAANITE.—See CANANÆAN.

CANAANITISH.—The RV rendering of Χαναναία (AV 'of Canaan') in Mt 15²² (only here in NT). The word is used to describe the woman who came out of the borders of Tyre and Sidon, desiring to have her daughter healed who was grievously vexed with a devil. St. Mark (7²⁶) calls her a Greek ('Ελληνίς), a Syro-phœnician (Συροφοινίκισσα) by race. A Canaanite, signifying properly 'dweller in the lowland,' is used in a wider or a narrower meaning in the OT, Canaan being a name applied either to the strip of seacoast from Gaza to Sidon, or, more loosely, to the whole possession of Israel, or that part which lay west of Jordan (Gn 10¹⁹; cf. Jos 5¹, Nu 13²⁹, Gn 11³¹). The LXX renders Canaanite (כְּנַעֲנִי) indifferently by Φοίνιξ and Χαναναῖος (Ex 6¹⁵, Jos 5¹, Nu 13²⁹· ⁽³⁰⁾, Jg 1³⁰⁻³³, while in Ex 16³⁵ and Jos 5¹² we find אֶרֶץ כְּנַעַן tr. by μέρος τῆς Φοινίκης and χώρα τῶν Φοινίκων. These coast inhabitants being the great traders of the old world, 'Canaanite' or 'Phœnician' was often used simply to mean 'a merchant' (Is 23⁸ [LXX ἔμποροι], and cf. Hos 12⁷, Zeph 1¹¹).

The woman who came to our Lord was a 'Canaanite' in the sense that she belonged to the stock of the old Phœnicians of Syria termed 'Syro-phœnician' to distinguish them from those of Africa. These were heathen, and between them

* This *Kanah* is probably the modern village of *Ḳāna*, 7 miles S.E. of Tyre (*Encyc. Bibl.* ii. 2652; Hastings' *DB* ii. 831).

and the Jews existed the bitterest hostility ; see Jos. *c. Apion.* i. 13 (who mentions the Phœnicians, especially of Tyre, with the Egyptians as bearing the greatest ill-will towards the Jews). This fact makes instructive a comparison between our Lord's treatment of this woman and His dealing with the woman of Samaria ; cf. especially Jn 4⁹ with Mt 15²⁶. The Clementines (*Hom.* ii. 19, iii. 73) mention her by the name of Justa, and maintain that the Lord first won her from heathendom, and after that was able to heal her daughter, whose name is given as Bernice.*

LITERATURE.—The Commentaries on the Gospels, esp. Swete on Mk 7²⁶; the articles in Hastings' *DB* and the *Encyc. Bibl.*; Trench, *Miracles, ad loc.*; Edersheim, *Life and Times of Jesus the Messiah*, ii. 37 ff. ; *Expos. Times*, iv. [1892] p. 80 ff. ; W. Archer Butler, *Serm.* i. 155 ff. ; Lynch, *Serm. to my Curates*, p. 317 ff. ; Ker, *Serm.*, 2nd ser. p. 200 ff. ; Bruce, *Galilean Gospel*, p. 154 ff. **J. B. BRISTOW.**

CANANÆAN.—'Cananæan' (RV, following the reading Καναναῖος adopted by Lachmann, Tischendorf, Tregelles, WH, and modern scholars generally) or **Canaanite** (AV, following the TR reading Καναντης) is a description applied by St. Matthew (10⁴) and St. Mark (3¹⁸) in their lists of the Twelve to the second of the two Apostolic Simons, who is thus distinguished from Simon Peter. There can be no doubt that 'Canaanite,' which means an inhabitant of Canaan, is a false rendering. The Gr. for Canaan is Χαναάν (Ac 7¹¹ 13¹⁹), and for Canaanite, Χαναναῖος (Mt 15²²) not Καναντης. Transliterating the Καναντης of the TR, the AV should have spelled the word 'Cananite,' as indeed was done in the Geneva Version, and in some editions of the AV, though not in that of 1611. But it is practically certain that Καναναῖος (which in the text of Mk. especially is very strongly supported, *e.g.* by אBCDLΔ) is the correct reading. The word seems to be a construction from the plural form קַנְאָנַיָּא of the late Heb. קַנְאָן, corresponding to the Biblical קַנָּא, 'jealous' (see Schürer, *HJP*, I. ii. 80 f. ; and note that the noun קִנְאָה, which in the Heb. text of the OT is used in the sense of 'zeal' as well as of 'jealousy,' is sometimes rendered in the LXX by ζῆλος [Is 9⁶ 26¹¹]). This is borne out by the fact that St. Luke, on the two occasions on which he gives a list of the Apostles (Lk 6¹⁵, Ac 1¹³), employs ὁ Ζηλωτής, instead of ὁ Καναναῖος, to describe Simon—which seems to show that the two epithets are synonymous.

Jerome, who in the Vulg. adopts the form 'Cananæus,' in his *Com. in Matt.* interprets it 'de vico Chana Galilææ'; and he has been followed by many scholars in modern times, who have taken the name to be a corruption of Καναῖος, and to mean 'a man of Cana,' probably Cana in Galilee. This view, however, now obtains little support, though Cheyne (*Encyc. Bibl.* ii. col. 2624, iv. col. 4535) appears to favour it. Meyer (*Com. on Matt., in loc.*), while holding that the form of the word makes the derivation from Cana impossible, maintains that it is nevertheless 'derived from the name *place* or other'; and would explain its use in Mt. and Mk. from the fact that Simon, as a *quondam* zealot, 'bore the surname קַנְאָנִי, ζηλωτής, a name which was correctly interpreted by Luke; but, according to another tradition, was erroneously derived from the *name of a place*, and accordingly came to be rendered ὁ Καναναῖος.' This is ingenious, but seems needlessly far-fetched. It is quite arbitrary, too, to say that the form Καναναῖος must be derived from the name of a place. The termination -αῖος is common in the Grecized rendering of names of sects (*e.g.* Φαρισαῖος, Σαδδουκαῖος, Ἐσσαῖος ; see Grimm-Thayer,

* Χαναναῖος is to be distinguished from Καναντης, TR Καναναῖος (Mt 10⁴), which means a Zealot, and is the designation of the Apostle Simon. See CANANÆAN.

Lexicon, s.v. Καναναῖος). And Καναναῖος from קַנְאָנָא is as natural as Φαρισαῖος from פְּרִישָׁא, *stat. emphat.* of Aramaic פְּרִישִׁין for Heb. פְּרוּשִׁים (see Schürer, *HJP* II. ii. 19). **J. C. LAMBERT.**

CANDLE.—Candles were not much in use in an oil-bearing country like Palestine, and are not referred to in the Bible. But the word occurs in the AV 8 times as the translation of λύχνος ('lamp'); and λυχνία ('lampstand') is always translated 'candlestick.' [On the other hand, λαμπάς, which is generally translated by its derivative 'lamp,' should be rendered either 'torch' or 'lantern'; for it generally refers to a lamp which could be carried out of doors (Mt 25¹ᶠᶠ., Jn 18³, and even Ac 20⁸, where the λαμπάδες ἱκαναί may have been torches that had been brought in by those who had assembled by night), thus corresponding to Heb. לַפִּיד].

The λύχνος (Heb. נֵר, נִיר, the latter used only in a figurative sense) was, as a rule, an earthenware vessel, like a tiny flat teapot, with a flaxen wick (Mt 12²⁰) in the spout, and supplied with oil (mostly from olives, but also from sesame, nuts, radishes, or fish), through a hole in the centre, from an ἀγγεῖον (Mt 25⁴) or other vessel. It could either be carried about (Lk 15⁸) or set on a stand (Mk 4²¹ etc.). For illustrations of lamps see Hastings' *DB*, vol. iii. p. 34.

In the teaching of the Son of Man the illuminating sign of God's presence in the world is *human* example and *personal* witness, as, *e.g.*, in the ministry of John the Baptist (Jn 5³⁵). The Christian life is to be one that lightens and kindles others (Mk 4²¹), and points men to the 'Father of lights' (Mt 5¹⁶). It must, therefore, first be itself lit. That is the key to the difficult passage in Mt 6²²ᶠ., Lk 11³⁴ᶠ. Light may be everywhere, yet it is of no use unless received by the eye, which is the lamp of the body. Sin makes a man see dimly or double, and must be renounced with an undivided mind if the life is to be illumined with Divine truth and love (*Expos.*, 2nd ser. i. [1881] 252 ff. ; cf. 180 ff., 372 ff.).

But one other important quality Christ illustrated by the use of the lamp, viz. *watchfulness.* It was the custom in private houses, as well as in the temple, to keep lamps burning through the night (Pr 31¹⁸). So, in view of the subtlety and suddenness of temptation and trial, the disciple must have his loins girded and his lamp lit (Lk 12³⁵). The parable of the Ten Virgins with their λαμπάδες teaches a similar lesson. Of Christ as the Lamb it is said that He is Himself the lamp (λύχνος) of the Holy City (Rev 21²³). **A. NORMAN ROWLAND.**

CANDLESTICK.—In RV of the Gospels this word is without exception correctly changed into 'stand,' λυχνία being the stand which held the little oil-fed lamp. It might mean anything from a luxurious candelabrum, generally of wood covered with metal, to a bit of stonework projecting from a cottage wall. It was to the lampstand in lowly domestic use (cf. 2 K 4¹⁰) that Christ referred in Mk 4²¹ as being necessary to complete the value of the lamp for those in the house (Mt 5¹⁵) and those who enter it (Lk 8¹⁶ 11³³). And the lesson is that if we have received a truth or a joy through Christ, who is the Light of the World, it is common sense and common justice not to hide it in fear or selfishness, but to use it as a means of illustrating our Father God and illumining those around us (Mt 5¹⁶). Practical illustrations of this parable are found in Mk 5¹⁹. ²⁰, Mt 10²⁷. ³², Lk 10²¹ 17¹⁸ (cf. Lk 15⁶. ⁹. ³²).

LITERATURE.—Maclaren, *God of the Amen*, p. 292 ; *Expositor*, 2nd ser. i. [1881] pp. 180 ff., 252 ff., 372 ff., 6th ser. 271 ff. **A. NORMAN ROWLAND.**

CAPERNAUM.—

1. The name.
2. Description of the localities.
3. Identification.
4. Capernaum and Bethsaida.
5. References in NT.
6. History.
      Literature.

The question as to the position of Capernaum is of great importance for the Gospel story. It is the pivot on which hinges the determination of the scene of the greater part of our Lord's active ministry. The three places, Capernaum, Chorazin, and Bethsaida, must all be taken together, and they must in any case be not far from the Plain of Gennesaret. This plain is undoubtedly the modern *el-Ghuweir* (*i.e.* 'the little *Ghôr*' or 'hollow'); there is also no doubt that Chorazin is the modern *Kerâzeh*. The present article is written in the belief that Capernaum is *Tell Ḥûm* (which is the view of the majority of scholars), and that Bethsaida was the port (now called *el-ʿAraj*), on the Lake, of Bethsaida Julias (*et-Tell*).

1. *The Name.*—The correct form of the name is undoubtedly Καφαρναούμ. This is found in all the oldest authorities to the end of the 4th cent. (Evv. codd. opt. ; Verss. antiq. Latt. Syrr. Ægypt. Goth.; Jos. *BJ*, *Onomast.* Euseb. Hieron.). The spelling Καπερναούμ begins to appear in the 5th cent., but after that date rapidly covered the ground. In Josephus (*Vita*, § 72), mention is made of a village the name of which Niese prints as Κεφαρνωκόν, but there are many various readings, and the text is pretty certainly corrupt. The exact relation of the ancient name to the modern does not work out very clearly. It is easy to understand how *Caphar* (mod. *Kefr*='village'), as a habitation of living men, might become *Tell* in the sense of 'a heap of ruins' (strictly = 'mound,' but there is no mound on the site). But there are difficulties in the way of regarding *Ḥûm* as a contraction for 'Nahum'; and some good philologists (Buhl, *op. cit. inf.*, cf. Socin, Guthe, *ib.*) prefer to regard *Tell Ḥûm* as a corruption of *Tenḥûm* or *Tanḥûm*, which occurs in Jewish authorities.

2. *Description of the localities.*—The beautiful Plain of Gennesaret is closed on the north-east by a spur of the hills which slopes down gradually to the Lake. In the hollow formed by this, on the rising ground where the caravan-route begins to ascend the ridge, is the ruined *khân* of *Khân Minyeh*. On the low ground beneath, and also on the ridge above, there are a few more inconspicuous remains ; and between the *khân* and the Lake is a fountain (*ʿAin et-Tîn*). Rounding the little promontory, on which is a German hospice, we come to a bay, on the further side of which is a group of springs. One of these is described by Sir Charles Wilson as 'by far the largest spring in Galilee, and estimated to be more than half the size of the celebrated source of the Jordan at Banias' (*Recovery*, etc. ii. 348). The waters of this spring come to the surface with great force, and, after being collected in a strongly-built reservoir, they were carried by an aqueduct, in part cut through the rock, round the promontory and to the rear of *Khân Minyeh*; from thence they were used to irrigate the plain. The modern name of this fountain is *ʿAin eṭ-Ṭâbigha*. The ancient name was 'Seven Fountains' (*Itin. Hieros.* ed. Vindob. p. 138) or *Heptapegon* (of which *eṭ-Ṭâbigha* is an echo). A full mile and a half, or two Roman miles farther, are the ruins of *Tell Ḥûm*. These cover a considerable extent of ground, half a mile in length by a quarter in breadth. The houses generally were built of blocks of black basalt. A single public building of larger size (74 ft. 9 in. ×56 ft. 9 in.) was of white limestone. This is commonly identified with the synagogue.

'Seen alone there might have been some doubt as to its character, but compared with the number of ruins of the same character which have lately been brought to notice in Galilee, there can be none. Two of those buildings have inscriptions in Hebrew over their main entrances ; one in connexion with a seven-branched candlestick, the other with figures of the paschal lamb, and all without exception are constructed after a fixed plan, which is totally different from that of any church, temple, or mosque in Palestine' (Wilson, *Recovery*, etc. ii. 344).

Two Roman miles up the course of a stream which enters the Lake just beyond *Tell Ḥûm*, are ruins which bear the name of *Kerâzeh*; but between *Tell Ḥûm* and the mouth of the Jordan there are no more ruins and no special features. Across the Jordan a little way back from its mouth, is *et-Tell*, which is now generally held to mark the site of Bethsaida Julias. This was in ancient times connected by a paved causeway with a cluster of ruins on the shore of the Lake, now known as *el-ʿAraj*.

3. *Identification.*—It will be seen that there is really not very much choice. Chorazin is certainly *Kerâzeh*, and Bethsaida Julias, built by the tetrarch Philip, is pretty certainly *et-Tell*. The alternatives for Capernaum are thus practically reduced to *Khân Minyeh* and *Tell Ḥûm*. And the broad presumption must be in favour of the latter, as Capernaum was no doubt the most important place at this end of the Lake, and the ruins are here far more extensive than those at *Khân Minyeh*, as well as demonstrably ancient. The *khân* at *Khân Minyeh* appears to have been built in the 16th cent. (Sepp, *op. cit. inf.* p. 165), though the place name first occurs in the time of Saladin.

Is this broad presumption overruled by any decisive consideration? A few minor arguments have been adduced against it. Capernaum was a place where tolls were collected (Mk 2¹⁴ ||), and it is thought that this would be more natural on the main caravan road : but a place of the size of *Tell Ḥûm* must in any case have had its tolls, and there was certainly a road along the north end of the Lake leading to Bethsaida Julias (Guthe). The bay of *eṭ-Ṭâbigha* is much frequented by fish, and the beach is suitable for mooring boats. But there is little, if any, trace of ruins that are not quite modern. The ruins about *Khân Minyeh* are also inconsiderable, though further excavation is needed to bring out their real character.

The point that seemed for a time to outweigh all the rest turned upon the position of the fountain. Josephus, who is our earliest and best authority, expressly says that the Plain of Gennesaret was watered by the fountain of Capernaum (*BJ* III. x. 8). The only fountain to which this statement can apply is that of *eṭ-Ṭâbigha*. There are other fountains, but none of them could be said in any sense to irrigate the plain as in ancient times this fountain certainly did. This indication might seem *prima facie* to support the claims of *Khân Minyeh*. The fountain is a short mile from this site, and two short (Roman) miles from *Tell Ḥûm*. But it has to be remembered that these large villages or towns on the Sea of Galilee had each its 'territory.' Thus Josephus speaks of the 'territory' of Hippos (Ἱππηνή, *BJ* III. iii. 1) ; and the 'Gerasene' demoniac (in Mk 5¹⁻¹⁷ ||) is a case of the same kind—the swine were not feeding in the town itself but in its territory. In like manner the fountain was situated within the territory of Capernaum, whether it was at *Khân Minyeh* or at *Tell Ḥûm*.

This leaves room for the natural presumption to tell in favour of *Tell Ḥûm*. And the identification is confirmed by the fact that the pilgrim Theodosius (*c.* 530 A.D.), coming from the West, arrived at Heptapegon before he came to Capernaum : this he would have done if it were at *Tell Ḥûm*, but not if it had been at *Khân Minyeh* (*Itin.*

Hieros. p. 138; cf. *JThSt* v. 44). Other indications, whether Biblical or derived from the narratives of the pilgrims, are all indecisive.

Just for a time there was a certain swing of the pendulum (which may be said to have reached its height in the last decade of the last century) in favour of *Khân Minyeh*. But the balance of the criticism of the last fifty years is pretty clearly on the side of *Tell Ḥûm*. But absolutely decisive results can only be obtained, if at all, by thorough and systematic excavation.

4. *Capernaum and Bethsaida.*—The two questions of Capernaum and Bethsaida are so closely connected, that a word should be added upon the latter. The only Bethsaida in these parts known to general history is that of which we have just spoken as located at *et-Tell* to the east of the Jordan. It has often been thought necessary to postulate a second Bethsaida, which is most commonly placed at the bay of *eṭ-Ṭâbigha*. The main reasons for this are two. (*a*) In Jn 12²¹, the Bethsaida of the Gospels is described as 'Bethsaida of Galilee,' whereas Bethsaida Julias was, strictly speaking, in Gaulanitis (*BJ* II. ix. 1). (*b*) The phrase εἰς τὸ πέραν in Mk 6⁴⁵ seems to imply that Bethsaida was on the opposite side of the Lake to the scene of the Feeding of the Five Thousand. These reasons are, however, insufficient to warrant the invention of a second Bethsaida so near to the first, and itself so wholly hypothetical. In the bay of *eṭ-Ṭâbigha* there are no ruins to prove its existence. On the other hand, (*a*) there is evidence enough to show that 'Galilee' was often loosely used for the country east of Jordan and of the Lake (*BJ* II. xx. 4, III. iii. 1; *Ant.* XVIII. i. 1, 6); and the geographer Ptolemæus speaks of Bethsaida Julias as 'in Galilee,' just as St. John does (Buhl, *GAP* p. 242). Political boundaries were so shifting, and the adjustments of territory in these little principalities were so constantly changed, that a loose use of terms grew up, and the more familiar names were apt to displace the less familiar. (*b*) The phrase εἰς τὸ πέραν cannot be pressed; it might be used of an oblique course from any one point on the shore of the Lake to any other: Josephus (*Vita*, § 59) uses διεπεραιώθην of taking ship from Tiberias to Taricheæ, which are on the same side of the Lake, and very little farther from each other than Bethsaida from the scene of the miracle.

5. *References in the Gospels.*—So far as our Lord had any fixed headquarters during His Galilæan ministry, they were in Capernaum. It is called His 'own city' (ἰδία πόλις) in Mt 9¹. The same close connexion is implied by the special reproach addressed to the city in Mt 11²³ (=Lk 10¹⁵). The public ministry, in the more formal sense, was opened here by the call of the four leading Apostles (Mk 1¹⁶⁻²⁰); and here, too, were the labours of which we have a graphic and typical description on the Sabbath that followed (Mk 1²¹⁻³⁴ ‖). We have repeated mention of a particular house to which our Lord resorted, which was probably St. Peter's. During the early part of His ministry He must have spent much time here, but during the latter part His visits can have been only occasional.

Perhaps we should be right in inferring from the presence of the 'centurion' (Mt 8⁵ᶠᶠ·, Lk 7²ᶠᶠ·) that Herod Antipas had a small garrison here. St. Luke tells us that this centurion, though a Gentile, had built the synagogue of the place. Is it too sanguine to believe that this was the very building the remains of which are still most conspicuous among the ruins? There appears to be good reason for the view that they are really the remains of a synagogue. A comparison with similar buildings elsewhere in Galilee brings out the distinctive features of the ground plan, and the presence of religious emblems seems to render

this probable. The richness of the architecture (cf. pl. xvii. in the present writer's *Sacred Sites of the Gospels*) may seem to suggest that the ruins date from the palmy days of Galilæan Judaism (A.D. 140–300), and Schürer refers them to this period. But there is one argument that perhaps points in a different direction. There was a synagogue at Chorazin hardly less elaborate than that at Capernaum, though with its ornaments cut in the black basalt, and not in limestone (Wilson, *Recovery*, ii. 3, 4, 7). Now, we know that when Eusebius wrote his *Onomasticon*, the site of Chorazin was already 'deserted' (*Onomast.*, ed. Klostermann, p. 174). This desertion is not likely to have been very recent. And it is perhaps after all more probable that elaborate building took place at a time when Galilee had a prince of its own with architectural ambitions, who must have gathered around him a number of skilled artificers at Tiberias. The Herods were all builders; and the period of their rule was probably that in which Galilee enjoyed the greatest material prosperity.

6. *Later history.*—From A.D. 150 onwards the shores of the Sea of Galilee became a stronghold of Rabbinical Judaism. The fanaticism of this district would not tolerate the presence of Christians; it is expressly stated by Epiphanius (*Hær.* xxx. 11; cf. Harnack, *Expansion of Christianity*, ii. 261) that down to the time of Constantine no one had ever dared to erect a church either at Nazareth or Capernaum, or at other places mentioned in the neighbourhood. That means that there must have been a complete break in the Christian tradition; so that, when we read later that a church was built on the supposed site of Peter's house, it is not likely that the guess had any real authority (*Itin. Hieros.* pp. 112 f., 163, 197). Still Capernaum was one of the sacred places, and from the 4th cent. onwards it was frequented by Christian pilgrims. Eusebius (and Jerome after him) mentions the place as on the Sea of Gennesaret, but throws no further light upon it beyond fixing its distance as two Roman miles from Chorazin (*Onomast.* pp. 120, 174). We have seen that Theodosius came to it from Tiberias after passing through Magdala and Seven Fountains (*Itin. Hieros.* p. 137 f.). Arculfus (*c.* 670 A.D.) did not enter Capernaum, but saw it from a neighbouring height stretching along the Lake, and observed that it had no wall (*ib.* p. 273 f.). The nun who tells the story of St. Willibald (*c.* 723 A.D.) makes him first come to Capernaum, then to Bethsaida, then to *Corazaim, ubi Dominus dæmoniacos curavit*, where there is an evident confusion between Chorazin and Gerasa (mod. *Kersa*), the scene of the healing of the demoniac. The same blunder occurs in the anonymous *Life*, so that it probably goes back to St. Willibald himself (see Tobler, *Descript. Terr. Sanct.* pp. 26, 63). We have seen that the history of *Khân Minyeh*, so far as we can trace it, belongs to the Saracenic and Turkish periods. Saladin halted at *al-Munaja* in 1189, but the building of the *khân* is referred by Sepp to Sinan Pasha under Suleiman the Magnificent (1496–1566).

LITERATURE.—The most important descriptions and discussions are as follows:—On the side of those who would place Capernaum at *Khân Minyeh*: Robinson, *BRP* 2 ii. 403–408, iii. 344–360; Sepp, *Neue Entdeckungen* (München, 1896); G. A. Smith, *HGHL* 4 p. 456, and in *Encyc. Biblica*. On the side of those who identify Capernaum with *Tell Ḥûm*: W. M. Thomson, *LB* (ed. 1901) pp. 350–356, cf. also 359 f.; Sir Charles Wilson, *The Recovery of Jerusalem* (London, 1871), ii. 375–387; and a solid phalanx of the most judicious German writers, *e.g.* Furrer in Schenkel's *Bibel-Lexikon* (1871); Socin (in Baedeker's *Pal.*³ p. 291 f.); Schürer, *GJV* 3 ii. 445 f.; Guthe, *Kurzes Bibelwörterbuch*, and elsewhere; Buhl, *GAP* (1896) pp. 223–225, cf. 242. The writer of this article gave a hesitating adhesion to the former view in *Sacred Sites of the Gospels* (Oxford, 1903), but retracted that opinion in *JThSt* for Oct. 1093, vol. v. pp. 42–48.

W. SANDAY.

CAPTAIN.—I. This word is the AV rendering of two Greek terms in the Gospels :—(1) χιλίαρχος, properly 'leader of a thousand' (Jn 18[12], RV 'chief captain,' RVm 'military tribune'; see also Mk 6[21], Ac 21[31. 32. 33. 37] 22[24. 26. 27. 28. 29] 23[10. 15. 17. 18. 19. 22] 24[7. 22. 23], Rev 6[15] 19[18]). (2) στρατηγός, properly 'leader of an army,' 'general' (Lk 22[4. 52]; see also Ac 4[1] 5[24. 26]).

1. χιλίαρχος is used (*a*) in a vague general sense of a superior military officer, and (*b*) technically as the Greek equivalent of the Roman *præfectus* or *tribunus militum*. The Roman garrison in the citadel at Jerusalem, consisting of a cohort (τάγμα = NT σπεῖρα, 'band' [καθῆστο γὰρ ἀεὶ ἐπ' αὐτῆς τάγμα 'Ρωμαίων, Jos. *BJ* v. v. 8]) of provincial troops, Syrian Greeks, and Samaritans, whose commandant would be a *civis Romanus* (Ac 22[28]), while they would be presented with the Imperial franchise on their discharge, was reinforced during the Passover by additional troops which were stationed in one of the Temple buildings (Mommsen, *Prov. Rom. Emp.*, Eng. tr. ii. 186). The χιλίαρχος is also called φρούραρχος by Josephus (*Ant.* XV. xi. 4, XVIII. iv. 3); see Schürer, *HJP* I. ii. 55. The legion consisting normally of 6000 men, the six *tribuni* took command for two months in turn. Palestine, however, being a Roman province of the second rank, did not possess a full legionary garrison. Mommsen gives its strength, at a subsequent period, as consisting of a detachment (*ala*) of cavalry and five cohorts of infantry, or about 3000 men.

2. στρατηγὸς τοῦ ἱεροῦ, the commandant of the Temple Levites. Josephus mentions the 'captain' (στρατηγός) of the Levitical guard in the time of Claudius (*Ant.* XX. vi. 2), and in that of Trajan (*BJ* VI. v. 3). Possibly the officers (ὑπηρέται) who assisted in the arrest of Jesus (Jn 18[3], cf. 7[32. 45]) belonged to this body. This 'captain' of the Temple (2 Mac 3[4] ὁ προστάτης τοῦ ἱεροῦ) is mentioned in Jer 20[1] LXX as ἡγούμενος and in Neh 11[11] as ἀπέναντι τοῦ οἴκου τοῦ θεοῦ, 'the ruler of the house of God' (Vulg. *princeps domus Dei* = איש הר הבת Mishna, *Middoth* i. § 2). The duty of this 'captain of the mount of the Temple' was to keep order in the Temple, visit the stations of the guard during the night, and see that the sentries were duly posted and alert. He and his immediate subalterns are supposed to be intended by the 'rulers' (ἄρχοντες) mentioned in Ezr 9[2] and Neh. *passim* (στρατηγοὶ or ἄρχοντες). See Schürer, *HJP* II. i. 258. The chief constable of this priestly corps of Temple police was naturally himself a Levite.

LITERATURE.—Josephus, *Ant.* x. viii. 5, xv xi. 4, xviii. iv. 3, xx. vi. 2, *BJ* v. v. 8, vi. v. 3; Schürer, *HJP* i. ii. 55, ii. i. 258; Hastings' *DB*, article 'Captain.'

P. HENDERSON AITKEN.

II. Besides these two military or semi-military uses of 'captain' in the Gospels, we have to notice the employment of the term as a title for Christ in He 2[10] (AV and RVm) and 12[2] (RVm). In both cases the corresponding word in the Greek text is ἀρχηγός, a word which otherwise is found in the NT only in Ac 3[15] 5[31] (both times in Acts applied to Christ, and in each case rendered 'Prince,' with 'Author' as a marginal alternative in 3[15]).

In accordance with its derivation (ἀρχή and ἡγέομαι), ἀρχηγός originally meant a leader, and so naturally came to be applied to a prince or chief. From this the transition was easy to the further meaning of a first cause or author, which is not infrequent in the philosophical writers. For the 'Captain' of AV in He 2[10], RV substitutes 'author,' giving 'captain' in the margin; and in 12[2] both VSS have 'author,' though RV again gives 'captain' as a marginal rendering.

But when Jesus is called ἀρχηγὸς τῆς σωτηρίας (2[10]), the meaning is not merely that He is the Author of our salvation. The context suggests that the idea of a leader going before his saved ones (cf. 6[20]) ought to be adhered to (see Davidson, *Hebrews, ad loc.*). Similarly when He is called τῆς πίστεως ἀρχηγός (12[2]), the idea is that of one who has led the way along the path of faith. In both cases the term 'Captain' may be unsuitable, since it is apt to suggest military images which had no place in the writer's mind; but 'leader,' at all events, should be retained, since the idea of leadership and not of authorship seems best to express his purpose (see Bruce, *Expositor*, 3rd ser. viii. [1888] p. 451). For a full treatment of the subject in its apologetic and homiletic aspects, Bruce's chapter on 'The Captain of Salvation' (*op. cit.* pp. 447–461) should be read in whole.

LITERATURE.—The *Lexicons* of Grimm-Thayer and Cremer, *s.v.*; W. R. Smith in *Expos.* 2nd ser. [1881] ii. 422; D. Brown, *ib.* 5th ser. [1895] ii. 434 ff. See also C. J. Vaughan, F. Rendall, and B. F. Westcott on He 2[10]; J. A. Selbie in Hastings' *DB* iv. 102[a]; and F. H. Chase, *Credibility of the Acts*, 129 f.

J. C. LAMBERT.

CARE (μέριμνα, μεριμνάω, μέλω, ἐπιμελέομαι).—The teaching of Jesus on care has been slightly obscured for English readers of the NT through the change in meaning through which this word and the word 'thought' have passed. Properly meaning *trouble* or *sorrow*, 'care' was from an early period confounded with Lat. *cura*, and from the idea of *attention* thus obtained was held to express the particular trouble of the mind due to over-attention, viz. *anxiety* (see Hastings' *DB* i. 353), while in modern language care, and especially its compounds 'careful' and 'carefulness,' are often used in a sense which indicates no trouble, but the well-directed effort of the mind in relation to present affairs and future prospects. The AV rendering 'take no thought' (Mt 6[25. 31. 34]) is still more misleading. As used by the translators, it meant 'distressing anxiety' (see Trench *On the AV* p. 39; Hastings' *DB* iv. 754). That the phrase μὴ μεριμνᾶτε is not 'take no thought,' but 'be not anxious' (RV), seems clear by the derivation of μέριμνα from μερίς, with its sense of dividing and, as applied to the mind, of distraction; and is rendered certain by comparison with the word θορυβάζω or τυρβάζω coupled with it in Lk 10[41], and with the expressive phrase μὴ μετεωρίζεσθε used in Lk 12[29], which expresses the metaphor of a ship tossed and helpless on the waves (see Cox in *Expositor*, 1st ser. i. [1875] p. 249).

The warning of Jesus against care is therefore in no sense applicable to reasonable forethought (πρόνοια). Man cannot live his life like the birds and the flowers, without a sense of the present necessity and the impending future. He can and must think, plan, and toil. The forethought and work necessary to provide food and raiment for himself and for those dependent upon him, are part of the Divine discipline of character. A careless life would be essentially a godless life. But Christ's reproofs are directed against all feverishness and distraction of mind. Whatever is the exciting cause of the distress—how food is to be obtained (Mt 6[25. 26], Lk 12[23. 24]) or clothing (Mt 6[28-30], Lk 12[27. 28]), how the unknown future is to be met (Mt 6[34]) though there seems no obvious source of supply (Mt 10[9]; cf. Mk 6[8], Lk 9[3] 10[2. 4]), though the duties of life press hardly (Lk 10[41]), and though there is impending and certain peril (Mt 10[19] 12[11]), He says, 'Be not anxious.'

The argument of Jesus against care is clothed in language of rare geniality and felicitousness. 'Which of you by being anxious can add a cubit to his stature' [rather, 'a span to his age']? Worry does not help forward the great designs of life. It cannot even accomplish 'that which is least.' It may take a span from one's age; it cannot prolong life. It is futile, and it is needless as well. Nature reads to man the lesson of trust. The wild flowers, though their life is so brief, are decked with loveliness by the great God. God takes care for the flowers. And He is *your* Heavenly Father. The argument is *a minori ad majus.* God's care for the flowers is a constant rebuke of His children's feverish anxiety concerning their own wants. The Providence, unforgetful of 'that which to-day is, and to-morrow is cast into the oven,' is, in relation to His children, an all-wise and all-loving Fatherhood.

But the geniality of the argument does not disguise the seriousness with which Jesus regarded care. The context of the *locus classicus* (Mt 6²⁵⁻³⁴, Lk 12²²⁻³⁴) is not the same in the two Evangelists. St. Matthew attaches the warning against care to the saying, 'No man can serve two masters . . . ye cannot serve God and mammon.' In Lk. it follows as a deduction from the parable spoken against covetousness and the closing saying, 'So is every one that layeth up treasure for himself, and is not rich toward God.' There is no need to decide the question of the priority of the two accounts, for the moral context of both is practically the same. Care arises from a division at the very centre of life, an attempt to serve both God and mammon, to 'worship the Lord and serve other gods,' or it arises from the radically false idea that ' a man's life consisteth in the abundance of the things which he possesseth.' Such a false estimate of values, involving the desire for and the pursuit of material goods for their own sake, inevitably produces the fever and distraction of mind called care, and it is the moral condition out of which it arises, as well as the consequences which it engenders, that makes it so serious a fault in the eyes of Christ. 'The cares of this life' are part of the hostile influences which choke the good seed of the kingdom, so that it bringeth forth no fruit to perfection (Mt 13²²; cf. Lk 8¹⁴). In a mind so preoccupied by worldly interests and anxieties the word of Christ may survive, but it never comes to maturity, or produces its potential harvest in life and service. Hence the severity which underlies the gentleness of Christ's rebuke of Martha (Lk 10⁴¹·⁴²). She was distracted about much serving, anxious and troubled about many things, and her worry spoiled her temper, and the service of Christ to which her love for Him impelled her. So serious indeed may be the consequences of this distress of soul, that Jesus, in His warning against the evil things which may overcharge the heart, and make men utterly unprepared for the coming of the Son of Man, combined with surfeiting and drunkenness 'the cares of this life' (Lk 21³⁴).

In opposition to care Jesus sets trust in the Heavenly Father. The assurance of His intimate knowlege of life and all its needs, and of His loving care, ought to exclude all anxiety concerning the wants of the present, and all fear of the future. But trust in God's love must be continually subordinate to the doing of God's will. The assurance of His Fatherly love and providential care is mediated to loving obedience. Thus in sending forth the Twelve (Mt 10⁹; cf. Mk 6⁸, Lk 9³), and in the case of the Seventy (Lk 10³·⁴), Jesus bids them make no elaborate provision for their physical needs. God takes care of His servants when they are in the path of obedience to His will. And similarly, when He warns His disciples that they shall be brought before the ecclesiastical and civil authorities because of their allegiance to Him, He calls upon them to have no anxiety as to the reply they shall give (Mt 10¹⁹, Mk 13¹¹, Lk 12¹¹). Jesus would have them believe that the moral order and the providential order of the world are essentially one, and are both controlled by the love of the Heavenly Father, so that they who seek

His Kingdom and do His will shall not want any good thing.

Christ's own life is the supreme example of perfect peace, conditioned by absolute trust in the Heavenly Father, and loving obedience to His will. The pressing necessity gave Him no anxiety, and the impending peril no fear. 'Thou wilt keep him in perfect peace whose mind is stayed on thee, because he trusteth in thee' (Is 26³).

LITERATURE.—Hastings' *DB*, art. 'Care'; Maclaren, *Serm. pr. in Manchester*, 1st ser. p. 235; Dale, *Laws of Christ*, p. 157; Munger, *Appeal to Life*, p. 149; Alex. Macleod, *Serm.* p. 119; Fairbairn, *City of God*, p. 317; Drummond, *Nat. Law in the Spir. World*, p. 123; *Expositor*, I. xii. [1882] 104, III. ii. [1885] 224; Moore, *God is Love*, 82; Allon, *Indwelling Christ*, 110; Zahn, *Bread and Salt from the Word of God*, 287.

JOSEPH MUIR.

CARPENTER.—Mt 13⁵⁵ 'Is not this the carpenter's son?' The question of Christ's own countrymen, when they were offended at the lowly station of the Teacher at whose wisdom they marvelled, tells us the exact conditions under which Jesus passed His early years. The parallel Mk 6³ 'Is not this the carpenter?' is still more interesting, for it tells us how Jesus Himself was occupied in His youth and early manhood. This flashlight photograph of the artisan in the workshop is all we know of the eighteen years between the visit to Jerusalem in His boyhood and the baptism which marked the entry on public life. The passage Mt 13⁵³⁻⁵⁷ ‖ Mk 6¹⁻⁴ presents a curious and quite undesigned antithesis to Sir 38²⁵⁻³⁴, specially these words, ' How can he get wisdom that holdeth the plough? . . . so every *carpenter* [Heb. חָרָשׁ, Gr. τέκτων, RV 'artificer'] and workmaster that laboureth night and day. . . . They shall not sit high in the congregation . . . and they shall not be found where parables are spoken.' Possibly this reference explains why the people were specially offended at Jesus the carpenter for presuming to speak in the synagogue and in parables. The passage of Sirach quoted is from the chapter describing the honour of a physician, with which may be compared the proverb, 'Physician, heal thyself,' quoted by Christ in similar circumstances at Nazareth, when they said, 'Is not this Joseph's son?'

An attempt to make Mk 6³ conform to Mt 13⁵⁵ is seen in some old MSS (including the good cursives 33-69) as well as in Eth. and Arm. versions, where we find ' carpenter's son ' in place of 'carpenter.' This reading must represent a very old text, for Origen (*c. Cels.* vi. 36) says, 'Nowhere in the Gospels current in the Churches is Jesus Himself called a carpenter,' alluding apparently to other Gospels in which this trade was ascribed to Christ. It is also clear that the TR reading must be as old, for Celsus founded on it. One may gather that the change in MSS and versions was not merely accidental or harmonistic but deliberate, and due to those who considered that Jesus was dishonoured by being described as a carpenter. Justin Martyr (*Dial. c. Tryph.* 88) supports TR in an interesting manner when he says that Jesus, 'when amongst men, worked as a carpenter, making ploughs and yokes, thus teaching the marks of righteousness, and commending an active life.' Such making of ploughs and yokes is precisely the kind of work expected of a country carpenter like one at Nazareth, though possibly Justin's words are a rhetorical expansion of Mk 6³. A curious anecdote is recorded by Farrar, to the effect that Libanius, a pagan sophist and devoted admirer of Julian the Apostate, inquired of a Christian, 'What is the carpenter doing now?' The answer was, ' He is making a coffin.' Very soon afterwards came the news of Julian's death. [Strangely enough, in relating this anecdote, Farrar himself quotes in *Life of Christ* ' carpenter's son,' but in *Life of Lives* he has ' carpenter '].

Whichever of the above readings be adopted, however (and in Mk 6³ the TR is supported by all the chief MSS), the probability is that Joseph by this time was dead, and that Jesus as his reputed son had carried on the business. Nor are we to reckon this as anything derogatory to the Lord. On the contrary, it is another proof of His condescension, when, though He was rich, yet for our sakes He became poor (2 Co 8⁹). By His toil at the bench He has dignified and consecrated manual labour. We may derive the practical lesson expressed in Faber's hymn, 'Labour is sweet, for

Thou hast toiled.' Even more to us than St. Paul the tent-maker is Jesus the carpenter. He was not an Essene, holding Himself aloof from temporal affairs, but a true Son of Man, taking His part in the business of life. Before He preached the good tidings of the kingdom, He preached the gospel of work. The work that His Father had given Him to do was not the exceptional duty of the teacher, but the ordinary industry of the artisan. His first pulpit was the carpenter's bench, and His first sermons were the implements and utensils He made for the country folk of Galilee.

Attempts have been made to find in Christ's parables and other utterances some reference to the trade in which for so many years He was actively engaged. The metaphor of the green wood and the dry (Lk 23³¹), and the similitude of the splinter and the beam (Mt 7³⁻⁵), are the nearest approaches to such reminiscences (cf. also one of the recently discovered 'Sayings of Jesus': 'Cleave the wood, and there you will find me '), but are too slight to found on them any inference. Yet may He not have often sighed in the workshop of Nazareth as He handled the nails and the hammer, and thought of the day when the Son of Man must be lifted up? As in Holman Hunt's famous symbolical picture, the figure of the young carpenter with outstretched arms released from toil as the sun went down, would make the awful shadow of the Cross.

LITERATURE.—The various *Lives* of Christ; WH App. on Mk 6³. With Holman Hunt's *Shadow of Death,* referred to above, may be compared Millais' *The Carpenter's Shop* (otherwise known as *Christ in the House of His Parents*). See *The Gospels in Art,* pp. 110 and 112; Farrar, *Christ in Art,* p. 274 ff.
ARTHUR POLLOK SYM.

CAVE (מְעָרָה, חֹר, σπήλαιον).—Caves, both natural and artificial, abound in Palestine; the soft chalky soil of Syria readily lends itself to both. Caves were used in Palestine for a variety of purposes; originally as dwelling-places * (cf. the 'Horites' or 'cave-dwellers,' Gn 14⁶ 36²⁰ff., Dt 2²², see also Gn 19³⁰). In the Ḥaurân there must have been many of these; sometimes regular underground towns, such as the ancient Edrei, existed:† even at the present day there may be seen in Gilead (*Wâdy Ezrak*), a village, named Anab, of Troglodyte dwellers; in this village there are about a hundred families.‡ Caves were used, further, as places of refuge (Jg 6², 1 S 13⁶ 14¹¹, 1 K 18⁴, He 11³⁸, Rev 6¹⁵), as hiding-places for robbers (Jer 7¹¹, cf. Mt 21¹³, Mk 11¹⁷, Lk 19⁴⁶), as stables,§ as cisterns,‖ as folds for flocks,¶ and, above all, as burying-places (Gn 23¹⁹ 49²⁹ Jn 11³⁸); the accounts of the burial caves discovered in the lower strata of the site of ancient Gezer are of the highest interest.**

It is, however, in reference to the place of birth and the place of burial of Christ that the chief interest in caves centres here. Justin Martyr (*Dial. c. Tryph.* lxxviii.), in recounting the story of the birth of Christ, says that it took place in a cave (ἐν σπηλαίῳ τινι) near the village of Bethlehem.†† That cave-stables, both ancient and modern, are to be found in Palestine, admits of no doubt. Conder‡‡ says that there are 'innumerable instances of stables cut in rock, resem-

* Recent excavations in Palestine have thrown considerable light on Troglodyte dwellings, see *PEFSt,* 1903, pp. 20–23.
† Wetzstein, *Reisebericht über Hauran und die Trachonen,* p. 44 ff.
‡ Nowack, *Hebräische Archäologie,* i. 136.
§ Conder, *Tent Work in Palestine,* p. 145.
‖ *PEFSt,* 1903, p. 315.
¶ *Jewish Encycl.* iii. 634.
** See *PEFSt,* 1902, pp. 347–356; 1903, pp. 14–20; 1904, pp. 18–20, 113, 114.
†† Cf. also Tobler, *Bethlehem in Palästina,* pp. 145–159; Palmer, 'Das jetzige Bethlehem' in *ZDPV* xvii. p. 89 ff.
‡‡ *Op. cit.* p. 145.

bling the Bethlehem grotto. Such stables I have planned and measured at Tekoa, 'Aziz, and other places south of Bethlehem, and the mangers existing in them leave no doubt as to their use and character.' It seems, therefore, not unreasonable to accept the ancient tradition that Christ was born in a cave. See art. BETHLEHEM.

Rock-hewn tombs, or caves for burial, were of four distinct kinds: (1) tombs which were cut down into the rock, in the same way in which graves are dug at the present time in European countries; the body was let down into these; (2) tombs cut into the face of the rock, into which the bodies were pushed; (3) tombs, somewhat like the last class, excepting that within, against the wall, there was a kind of step, about two feet high, upon which the body was laid; (4) tombs which were little more than a shelf cut into the rock, just long enough and high enough to hold the body. The first three of these classes varied very much in size; in the case of the first, the top, which was level with the ground, was covered with a stone slab; the others were closed by means of a stone slab which could be pushed aside (Mt 27⁶⁰), or else a small door was fixed at the entrance. Tombs were not infrequently furnished with an antechamber, from which one entered into an inner space, the tomb proper, through a low doorway. As a rule, a raised shelf ran round the burial-chamber, and upon this the body was laid; that part on which the head rested was slightly higher.* See BURIAL, TOMB.

The data to be gathered from the Gospels are not numerous; see Mt 27⁶⁰, Mk 15⁴⁶, Lk 23⁵³, Jn 11³⁸ 20¹⁻¹².

LITERATURE.—Guthe in *ZDPV,* 'Zur Topographie der Grabeskirche in Jerusalem,' xiv. 35–40; Schick in *ZDPV,* 'Neu aufgedeckte Gräber,' xvi. 202–205, where a very interesting plate is given; T. Tobler, *Bethlehem in Palästina,* pp. 124–227, S. Gallen, 1849; Bädeker, *Palestine and Syria*³, p. cxi ff., Leipzig, 1898; the references, given above, in *PEFSt.* See also W. R. Smith, *RS* 197 f., and the '' Index of Subjects ' in Hastings' *DB,* Extra Volume.
W. O. E. OESTERLEY.

CELIBACY.—According to the ordinary Jewish view, marriage was of universal obligation (cf. for instance, *Yebamoth* vi. 6; *Kethuboth* v. 6, 7; *Giṭṭin* iv. 5). There does not appear to be evidence whether exceptions were recognized as possible because of some special vocation, as that to particular forms of the prophetic office. In the time of Christ the Essenes in general eschewed marriage, though one section of them practised it (Josephus, *Ant.* XVIII. i. 5; *BJ* II. viii. 2). The teaching of Christ does not contain any explicit reference to this difference between the Essene practice and the ordinary Jewish view. His teaching about divorce and His reassertion of the primitive law of marriage (Mt 5³¹· ³² 19³⁻⁹, Mk 10¹⁻¹², Lk 16¹⁸) imply not only that He was dealing with marriage as an existing Jewish institution, but also that He contemplated it as a permanent element in Christian life. It is not unnatural to draw a similar inference from His presence at the marriage at Cana (Jn 2¹⁻¹¹).

St. Matthew records a saying of Christ in which it is contemplated that by a special vocation some are called to celibacy. Christ's prohibition of divorce led the disciples to say that, without freedom to divorce, 'it is not expedient to marry.' Our Lord in His reply recognized that there are some for whom this 'saying' of the disciples is true, but only those 'to whom it is given.' He explained that there were three classes who might be regarded as having the vocation to celibacy: —(1) 'Eunuchs which were so born from their

* Nowack, *Heb. Arch.* i. 191; Benzinger, *Heb. Arch.* pp. 225–227; Latham, *The Risen Master,* pp. 32 ff., 87, 88, and see the two illustrations at the commencement of the work.

mother's womb,' *i.e.* those whose physical constitution unfitted them for marriage; (2) 'eunuchs which were made eunuchs by men,' *i.e.* those 'who by actual physical deprivation or compulsion from men are prevented from marrying' (Alford); (3) 'eunuchs which made themselves eunuchs for the kingdom of heaven's sake,' *i.e.* those who by voluntary self-sacrifice abstained from marriage in order that they might be (*a*) more faithful citizens of the kingdom of heaven in their own personal life, or (*b*) more effective instruments for the strengthening or expansion of the kingdom of heaven. He then repeated in a different form, 'He that is able to receive it, let him receive it' (Mt 19$^{10-12}$), the previous statement that the 'saying' of the disciples, to which He had thus given a higher and deeper meaning, was not a maxim for all His followers, but only for those who, having the Divine call to the celibate life, had with it the Divine gift of power to obey the call. This particular saying is not recorded by any of the Evangelists except St. Matthew. There is a connected line of thought, however, in words recorded by St. Luke; for in Lk 18$^{29.\ 30}$ (also in TR and RVm of Mt 19^{29} and in TR of Mk 10^{29}) a wife is mentioned among those relatives whom Christ contemplates His disciples as leaving for the sake of the kingdom of God (Lk.), or for His name's sake (Mt.), or for His sake and the sake of the gospel (Mk.); and it is promised that those who make such acts of self-sacrifice shall receive great rewards in the present time and shall hereafter inherit eternal life. In Mt 19^{30} and Mk 10^{31} the warning that 'many that are first shall be last; and the last first' is associated with this promise; and in Mt 20$^{1-16}$ the parable of the Labourers in the Vineyard is added to illustrate that maxim.

It is a mistake to interpret Mt 5^{28} ('Every one that looketh on a woman to lust after her hath committed adultery with her already in his heart') as a condemnation of marriage; the context shows the meaning to be that to cherish the desire for fornication or adultery is the same thing as committing those sins in the heart. Nor is there any disparagement of marriage in the words, 'They that are accounted worthy to attain to that world and the resurrection from the dead neither marry nor are given in marriage' (Lk 20^{35}); the meaning is shown by the context to be that the physical accompaniments of marriage belong to the present world, not to the future life, which, as it has not death, has not birth. Lk 14^{26} ('If any man cometh unto me, and hateth not his own . . . wife, . . . yea, and his own life also, he cannot be my disciple') refers not to celibacy, but to the general law that a Christian must be prepared to surrender everything human for the sake of Christ, if called by God to do so, or if such surrender be necessitated by faithfulness to the obligations of the Christian religion.

On the whole, then, the teaching of Christ may be summarized to the effect that (1) marriage is a good state, contemplated as the usual lot, in ordinary Christian life, of those who have not received some special call; (2) celibacy is the subject of a distinct vocation involving dangers and having attached to it high promises. It is probable that the regard paid to celibacy in the Christian Church was based partly on the references to it in the teaching of Christ, and partly on inferences connected with the fact of His birth from a virgin. Clement of Alexandria (*Strom.* III. xv. 97) quotes as a saying of Christ, with the introduction 'The Lord says,' the following: 'He who is married, let him not put away his wife; and he who is not married, let him not marry; he who with purpose of chastity has agreed not to marry, let him remain unmarried.' Some have thought

this saying to be a reminiscence of 1 Co 7$^{8-11.\ 27}$ ascribed to Christ because of the words 'not I, but the Lord' in 7^{10}; but Clement apparently has our Lord's words in Mt 19^{12} in view, for a little later in the same chapter he says, 'They who have made themselves eunuchs from all sin for the kingdom of heaven's sake, these are blessed, they who fast from the world.'

Clement of Alexandria also refers to a conversation between our Lord and Salome mentioned in the lost 'Gospel according to the Egyptians' (*Strom.* III. vi. 45, ix. 63, 64, 66, xiii. 92; *Exc. Theod.* 67). Our Lord is there reported to have said that death would have power 'as long as ye women bear children'; that He 'came to destroy the works of the female'; and that the kingdom of God would come 'when ye shall have trodden down the garment of shame, and when the two shall be one, and the male with the female, neither male nor female.' Part of this last quotation is also in pseudo-Clement of Rome, 12 : 'The Lord Himself, being asked by one when His kingdom should come, said, When the two shall be one, and the outside as the inside, and the male with the female, neither male nor female.' In interpreting these sayings, notice must be taken of Clement of Alexandria's comment that our Lord spoke in condemnation not of marriage, but of sins of the flesh and the mind, and to show the natural connexion between death and birth; and of the further words of Salome, 'Then I did well in not bearing children,' with our Lord's reply, 'Eat every herb, but that which hath bitterness do not eat.' It is possible that in these passages the 'Gospel according to the Egyptians' preserved an echo of Mt 19^{12}, or some saying of our Lord unrecorded in the NT. It is not likely that the actual words were spoken by Him, since, as Lightfoot (*Apostolic Fathers*, I. ii. 237) pointed out, they differ in character from the utterances recorded in the authentic Gospels, and the reference to Salome as childless contradicts facts, though, as regards this last point, 'Then I did well in not bearing' might easily be a copyist's mistake for 'Then I should have done well if I had not borne' (καλῶς οὖν ἐποίησα for καλῶς οὖν ἂν ἐποίησα).

LITERATURE.—Neander, *Life of Jesus Christ*, § 224; Lange, *Life of the Lord Jesus Christ*, ii. 473, 474; Stier, *Words of the Lord Jesus*, iii. 13–18; Edersheim, *Life and Times of Jesus the Messiah*, ii. 335, 336; Dalman, *Words of Jesus*, pp. 122, 123; Alford on Mt 19$^{11.\ 12}$; Knabenbauer on Mt 19^{12}; Dykes, *Manifesto of the King*, p. 245 ff.; Wendt, *Teaching of Jesus*, i. 352 ff., ii. 73 ff.; Martensen, *Christian Ethics*, iii. 7–46.

DARWELL STONE.

CELLAR.—Used only once in the Gospels, in Lk 11^{33}, where RV gives 'cellar' for AV 'secret place,' following the correct reading κρύπτη, 'a vault,' 'crypt,' or 'cellar,' not κρυπτόν, 'hidden.' Josephus uses the same word, κρύπτη, in a way to make its meaning very clear: 'They set a tower on fire, and leapt into the cellar beneath' (*BJ*, V. vii. 4).

Abundant proof is forthcoming from the examination of the ruins of many ancient Eastern houses, from allusions in the Bible (cf. 1 Ch 27$^{27.\ 28}$) and in other writings of the times, as well as from modern dwellings in the East which are typically Oriental, that many ancient houses were provided with 'cellars beneath,' and that ordinarily these 'cellars' were used as store-houses rather than as dwelling-places.

Looking at the passage Lk 11^{33} in the light of the connexion in which we find it in Mt 5$^{14-16}$ and Mk 4^{21}, the idea is that a course of concealment on the part of Christians is unreasonable, and contrary to the Divine design. Christians are 'the light of the world,' the light by which the mass of mankind may see the things of religion. As such they cannot escape observation if they would, and they should not wish to escape it if they could, for this would be contrary to the very purpose of God in making them sources of light. The unreasonableness of such a course, from cowardice or any other motive, is what is set forth in this and the other significant figures used by our Lord : 'No man, when he hath lighted a lamp, putteth it in a cellar, neither under a bushel, or a bed (Mk.), but on a lamp-stand, that they which come in may see the light.' The very purpose in lighting the lamp is that men may see it, or see by it. Is it, then, to be put in the cellar, where people do not live, or under a bushel or a bed, where it would be obscured? Is it not rather to be put on the lamp-stand, where all comers may see it, and see by it?

LITERATURE.—Meyer, *Com. in loc.*; *Expositor*, II. i. [1881] p. 252 ff.
                                                    GEO. B. EAGER.

CENSUS.—This English word does not occur in the NT, the Greek term ἀπογραφή being rendered **taxing** in AV and **enrolment** in RV both in Lk 2² and in Ac 5³⁷. In the former case, with which we are mainly concerned, 'enrolment' is certainly the better word; for the purpose of the enumeration was apparently not fiscal. That mentioned by Gamaliel, however, was a valuation as well as an enumeration, and it was called 'the taxing' with some reason. It was also better known than the other; *par excellence* it was '*the* census' because a great tumult arose under Judas of Galilee in connexion with it, which made the occasion famous. That which took place at the time stated by St. Luke was so little known by the period when his Gospel was written, that he thinks it needful to insert a note about its date, lest it should be mistaken for the other. 'This was the first enrolment made when Quirinius was governor of Syria.' This note, however, has been itself a matter of great perplexity, because the date thus indicated does not apparently tally with the ascertained facts of secular history. For the discussion of this intricate question see articles BIRTH OF CHRIST, DATES, and QUIRINIUS.

The nature of the census of Lk 2¹⁻³ is a topic of some interest, on which light has been shed by Ramsay in *Was Christ born at Bethlehem?* (1898). It seems to have been an enrolment by households, such as Kenyon (*Classical Review*, March 1893), Wilcken, and Viereck have shown was the practice in Egypt. Augustus had a great belief in the proper and systematic enumeration of his subjects, and the reckoning of them by households was a method which was carefully followed every fourteen years in Egypt. Many of the actual census papers have been found in that land in recent times, the earliest as yet discovered referring to the year 20 A.D. (Ramsay, *op. cit.*, Preface, p. x note). This was quite different from the fiscal statistics compiled annually under the direction of the provincial governors of the Roman Empire, papers dealing with which have also been found. The household enrolments took place in cycles of fourteen years, and were dated according to the emperor in whose reign they were carried out. No mention was made in them of the value of property and stock, as in the annual returns, and the only financial purpose they served was to determine who were liable for the poll-tax exacted from all subjects between the ages of fourteen and sixty. This poll-tax was the tribute (κῆνσος) referred to by the Pharisees in the question to Christ as to the lawfulness of payment (Mt 22¹⁷; see art. TRIBUTE). It would seem that in Syria women as well as men were required to pay this tax (Ramsay, *op. cit.* 147 note); and if that was the case also in Palestine, this fact may possibly explain why, on the first occasion when the enrolment that was the basis of the poll-tax was made, Mary accompanied Joseph to Bethlehem despite her critical condition.

The discovery of the household-enrolment papers in Egypt throws light on the statement of Lk 2¹ 'there went out a decree from Cæsar Augustus that all the world should be enrolled.' 'All the world' (πᾶσαν τὴν οἰκουμένην) was formerly supposed by some scholars, such as Kitto (*Cycl. of Bib. Lit.*, art. 'Cyrenius'), to mean merely the whole land of Palestine, so as to escape the difficulty that secular history, so far as then known, was silent as to any general census. The meaning of the phrase cannot be so restricted. It means certainly the whole of the Roman Empire, which in the days of Augustus meant for all practical purposes 'the inhabited earth.' Not only was Rome itself included, with all the provinces, whether in Italy or elsewhere, but also those lands which, though having kings of their own, were really under the Roman suzerainty. Such was that portion of Syria under the dominion of Herod the Great.

The silence of history as to such an enumeration as was now to be made is no proof that it did not take place; for of other enumerations to which casual allusion is made by historians, Augustus himself in his record of his achievements makes no mention, except in so far as Roman citizens were concerned. The counting of alien subjects was probably not deemed of sufficient importance to be chronicled. Moreover, the household enrolments which have been traced back in Egypt by extant papers to A.D. 20 suggest at least that there may have been earlier ones in A.D. 6 and B.C. 8, which brings us back to the approximate period to which St. Luke refers. It may here be observed that the Evangelist does not actually say (Lk 2¹), and very likely does not mean, that the intention of Augustus was that one single enumeration should be made of the whole Roman world. The tense of ἀπογράφεσθαι rather signifies that a census of this nature on the household-enrolment principle was to be the practice, this being the first occasion of its being ordered; which precisely tallies with the following verse when rightly rendered, 'This was the first enrolment made at the time when Quirinius was governor of Syria.' A fuller discussion of this latter statement is reserved for the article QUIRINIUS.

The enrolment with which we are particularly concerned, then, would be appointed for B.C. 8; but in the case of Herod's kingdom it was not achieved till about a couple of years later, apparently for reasons which Ramsay has indicated, but which need not here be reproduced. They refer to the strained relations which then existed between Augustus and Herod. When it was made, the usual Roman method of enrolment at the residence of those enumerated was not followed, but one more in consonance with Jewish ideas. The people had often before been numbered by their tribes, and Herod probably judged that, especially on this first occasion of such an enrolment, the use and wont would be more acceptable to his subjects than a method new to them, and would be less likely to arouse resentment or even tumult. The Roman practice was to interfere as little as possible with the usages of the nations which had been subjugated; and therefore we may reckon that the particular method of taking the census would be left to the decision of the ruler of the district. Accordingly it was arranged that the tribal method should be followed, and that in subordination thereto the enrolment should be by persons registering themselves at the place from which the head of the family had sprung. Hence we read that 'all went to enrol themselves, every one to his own city. And Joseph also went up from Galilee, out of the city of Nazareth, into Judæa, to the city of David, because he was of the house and family of David, to enrol himself with Mary who was betrothed to him' (Lk 2³⁻⁵). If, as Mt 1²⁵ leads us to believe, Mary was actually recognized at this period as Joseph's wife, she would be enumerated as one of his household, whatever her own lineage was; but if St. Luke's expression 'betrothed' is to be pressed, would indicate not merely that the marriage was not publicly known or officially recognized, but that she herself must also have been of the family of David, and as such was enrolled in her own right. It may also be observed that the great gathering of those who claimed to be of 'the stock of Jesse' would help to explain how, when Joseph and Mary arrived, 'there was no room for them in the inn' (Lk 2⁷).

LITERATURE.—*Lives* of Christ and Commentaries on St. Luke; articles in Bible Dictionaries, as Smith, Kitto, and Hastings; Ramsay, *Was Christ born at Bethlehem?* (1898); Zumpt, *Das Geburtsjahr Christi* (1869); Zahn, art. in *Neue kirchl. Ztsch.* (1893); Schürer, *HJP* I. ii. 105.

ARTHUR POLLOK SYM.

CENTURION (Lat. *centurio*; in Mark always κεντυρίων [15³⁹·⁴⁴·⁴⁵]; in Matt. and Luke and Acts ἑκατοντάρχης acc. to אֲ, or ἑκατόνταρχος in other uncials; the latter form being more Attic, the former more frequent in Hellenistic [cf. Blass, *Gram.*, Eng. tr. p. 28, on fluctuation between first and second declensions]; in Polybius the centurion is called ταξίαρχος).—As the name denotes, a centurion was an officer in the Roman army who had command of a *centuria* containing 100 men. The legion at its full strength consisted of about 6000 foot-soldiers, consequently it included 60 centurions. These were of different ranks or degrees of promotion and importance, according to the position occupied in battle by their special company or maniple. Though laughed at for their hob-nailed shoes and thick calves (Juv. *Sat.* xvi. 14. 24) and for their general unkempt roughness (*ib.* xiv. 194), these officers were the very 'backbone of the army.' Their badge of office was the vine-rod (*vitis*), which they freely used on the men, even without the authorization of the tribune (cf. Tacitus *Annal.* i. 23). Polybius describes the ideal centurion as 'not so much overventuresome and fond of danger as possessing the faculty for command, steady and serious (βαθεῖς ταῖς ψυχαῖς); not prone to rush into battle nor eager to strike the first blow, but ready to die in defence of their posts if their men are overborne by numbers and hard pressed' (vi. 24; cf. Vegetius, ii. 14).

The centurions mentioned in the NT are attractive specimens of the manly, serious-minded, generous Roman. In the Gospel narrative two centurions find a place. The one (Mt 8⁵⁻¹³ ‖ Lk 7¹⁻¹⁰) resident in Capernaum may probably have been in Herod's service; but in any case he was a Gentile, for in his humble faith Jesus sees the first-fruits of a world redeemed, and recognizes that even if 'the children of the kingdom' prefer the outer darkness to the light and joy within, the provided feast will still be furnished with guests. The distinctive characteristic of this centurion's faith was his persuasion that a word of command uttered by Jesus could set in motion forces sufficient for the emergency, even as the κέλευσμα of the Roman officer at once accomplished his will. The μόνον εἰπὲ λόγῳ is the key to the incident, and absolutely differentiates this centurion from the βασιλικός of Jn 4⁴⁶, who insisted that Jesus should 'go down' and heal his son.

The centurion charged with superintending the crucifixion of Jesus (Mk 15³⁹ ‖ Mt 27⁵⁴ ‖ Lk 23⁴⁷) paid so striking and unexpected a tribute to His greatness, that it finds a place in each of the Synoptic Gospels. The terms of the tribute are best understood from the account of St. Luke, who frequently preserves what is evidently the original form of a saying. Certainly 'son of God' in the mouth of a Roman could mean little more than St. Luke's 'just man.' But the expression 'son of God' might be suggested by the 'Father' in our Lord's last cry.

LITERATURE.—Ramsay's *Rom. Antiq. s.v.*; St. George Stock's *Cæsar de B. Gall.* pp. 208–215; J. E. B. Mayor's *Juvenal*, notes on passages cited above.
MARCUS DODS.

CEPHAS.—See PETER.

CEREMONIAL LAW.—See LAW.

CERTAINTY.—The ways in which 'certainty' is expressed in the Gospels are frequently indirect. So far, however, as certainty is expressed by direct terms, various phrases are employed for the purpose. Of these the most frequent are ἀσφαλής and its derivatives ἀσφαλίζω, ἀσφάλεια, ἀσφαλῶς. These always express objective security; the certainty which is or might be verified, and which consists in an accurate correspondence with facts.

Thus in his preface St. Luke (1⁴) says he has 'traced the course of all things accurately . . . that thou mightest know the certainty . . .' (ἀσφάλεια, cf. Ac 5²³, 1 Th 5³); the traitor says, 'Take him and lead him away safely' (Mk 14⁴⁴ ἀσφαλῶς, cf. Ac 2³⁶ 5²³ 16²³); Pilate says, 'Command that the sepulchre be made sure' (Mt 27⁶⁴·⁶⁵·⁶⁶ ἀσφαλίζω, cf. Ac 16²⁴). With these passages may be compared the use of ἀσφαλής elsewhere in NT, viz. Ac 21³⁴ 22³⁰ 25²⁶, Ph 3¹, He 6¹⁹. The derivatives of βέβαιος are also employed, but with a force more or less distinctly moral or subjective. Thus the disciples are said to have 'preached everywhere, the Lord working with them and confirming the word' (Mk 16²⁰ βεβαιόω, cf. Ro 15⁸, 1 Co 16⁶·⁸, 2 Co 1²¹, Col 2⁷, He 2³ 13⁹). Sometimes it is the disciples themselves who are 'confirmed' or 'stablished.' Outside the Gospels βέβαιος and βεβαίωσις occur with some frequency, being specially characteristic of the Ep. to Heb. (cf. 2 P 1¹⁰·¹⁹, Ro 4¹⁶, 2 Co 1⁷, He 2² 3⁶ 6¹⁶·¹⁹ 9¹⁷, Ph 1⁷). In Lk 23⁴⁷ ὄντως occurs, 'Certainly this was a righteous man'; and in Lk 4²³ πάντως, 'Doubtless ye will say to me . . .' (cf. Ac 21²² 28⁴, 1 Co 9¹⁰); but these are adverbial qualitatives of no great importance. [It is hardly necessary to remark that in the great majority of the passages in which the word 'certain' occurs in the English versions, it renders the indefinite pronoun τις, where it has nothing to do with certainty, but is merely an idiomatic phrase equivalent to 'some' in a quite indefinite sense].

With this use of language it is instructive to compare the opposite 'uncertainty' which is expressed by ἀπορία, ἀπορίομαι, commonly translated 'perplexed,' though the meaning is rather that of hesitancy than of perplexity, as one finds no way out of a difficulty, and so is brought to pause. These words occur in Lk 21²⁵ and Jn 13²² 'doubting of whom he spake' (cf. Ac 25²⁰, 2 Co 4⁸, Gal 4²⁰). It is also worth while to compare such occasional use of πίστις as 'given assurance unto all men' (Ac 17³¹); and that of πληροφορία, 'full assurance' (Col 2², 1 Th 1⁵, He 6¹¹).

But apart from special terms expressing certainty, the broad fact itself has, of course, a large place in the Gospels and in the mind of the Lord Jesus. This is usually represented by saying that a person or a thing is 'known,' where οἶδα is the verb employed. This verb is a 'perfect-present,' and by its very form indicates the possession of knowledge, not its acquirement. In a number of passages the sense is accordingly best rendered not by 'I know,' but by 'I am sure of.'

The following are instances from the Gospels of this way of expressing certainty :—'Fear ye not, for I am certain that ye are seeking Jesus who was crucified' (Mt 28⁵); 'Master, we are certain that thou speakest and teachest straightforwardly' (Lk 20²¹); 'We speak what we are certain of, and bear evidence of what we have seen' (Jn 3¹¹); 'No longer do we believe through thy report, for we ourselves have heard and are certain' (4⁴²); 'What sign doest thou that we may feel certainty, and may trust thee?' (6³⁰); 'This is Jesus the son of Joseph ; we are certain of his father and mother' (6⁴², cf. 7²⁷); 'Give glory to God ; we are certain this man is a sinner. He therefore answered, If he is a sinner I am not so certain ; of one thing I am certain, that, being blind, henceforth I see' (9²⁴·²⁵); 'Even now I am certain that whatsoever thou mayest ask of God, God will give thee' (11²²); 'He that hath seen beareth witness, and his witness is true (ἀληθινή), and he is certain that he speaketh true (ἀληθῆ), that ye also may believe' (19³⁵, cf. 21²⁴). Sometimes οἶδα is used of God's knowledge with its unerring certainty ; and at other times of man's knowledge of God which springs from personal trust and love.

It is characteristic that the grounds on which certainty is shown in the Gospels to rest are moral grounds rather than intellectual ; for commonly it is moral certitude, not scientific security, which is in view. On the one hand, the foundation of certainty is the faithfulness of God : this is well illustrated in the case of Zacharias (Lk 1¹⁸⁻²⁰), and in that of Mary (vv.³⁷·³⁸). On the other hand, certainty is won through men's trust (πίστις) in God or in Christ. So the Lord said, 'Whosoever shall say unto this mountain . . . and shall not doubt (διακρίνω) in his heart, but shall believe . . . he shall have it' (Mk 11²³ ‖ Mt 21²¹). To Peter as he began to fear and sink He said, 'O thou of little faith, wherefore didst thou doubt ?' (διστάζω,

Mt 14³¹). And when it is recorded of the disciples to whom the Lord appeared after His resurrection, that 'they saw him, and worshipped, but some doubted' (διστάζω, 28¹⁷), He met this mixed regard by a great personal affirmation, and a great charge laid on them, which formed in point of fact the strongest appeal to their most certain trust. See, further, art. ASSURANCE.

LITERATURE.—See the lit. at ASSURANCE, and add—E. White, *Certainty in Religion*; J. Clifford, *Christian Certainties*; W. R. Harper, *Religion and the Higher Life*, pp. 88–100; G. A. Coe, *Religion of a Mature Mind*, 109–132; A. E. Garvie, *The Gospel for To-day*, 34; *Princeton Theol. Rev.* i. 138 (Warfield); *Homiletic Rev.* xlvi 413 (Wright); *Expos. Times*, vii. 438, 533.

E. P. BOYS-SMITH.

CHAFF.—The term used in English to denote the protective coverings and appendages of the growing corn—the glumes, scales, and awns—after they have been dried in the ripening of the plant and in the wind and sun, and separated from the grain and straw. The Greek word is ἄχυρον (Lat. *palea*), 'mostly used in plural for chaff, bran, husks' (Liddell and Scott); perhaps derived from ἀχ, indicating its pointed nature. But the older authorities, and most writers on the Greek of the NT, incline to regard the ἄχυρον as including the cut or broken-up straw which mingles with the chaff proper.

Schleusner, controverting the opinion of previous lexicographers, says that the word for the outer integuments (*palea*) is ἄχνη, and that ἄχυρον includes *totum calamum frumenti inde a radice usque ad spicam quæ grana continet*, and that it is equivalent to the Heb. תֶּבֶן *tebhen*; and Post (art. 'Straw' in Hastings' *DB*) suggests the use of the Arab. word *tibn*, which denotes the mingled chaff and cut or broken straw.

In reaping it was often the practice to leave all the straw, except an inch or two cut off with the ear. The dust of the chaff is in the LXX χνοῦς (Ps 1⁴ 35⁵, Is 29⁵, Hos 13³), and once χνοῦς ἀχύρου (Is 17¹³), and once κονιορτός (Job 21¹⁸).

The combination of broken straw with the chaff is explained by the process of harvesting, threshing, and winnowing in Palestinian agriculture. The threshing-machine, or threshing-waggon (see art. 'Agriculture' in Hastings' *DB*), which, by repeatedly passing over the sheaves, broke up the short straw into fragments, separated the grain from its dried envelopes. The threshing-floor was so placed, usually in an elevated and breezy position, that the wind could be utilized to separate the lighter, heavier, and heaviest materials from one another, and the method of winnowing secured that the grain should fall in the centre, the heavier straw at a small distance from the grain heap, while the broken straw and chaff(ἄχυρον) were carried away by the wind, either out of the threshing-floor, or so that it could be swept together for burning. The complete separation of the chaff, which included fragments of the awns and straw, from the corn was effected by means of the winnowing-fan (πτύον), the broad shallow shovel with which corn after threshing was thrown up against the wind, and so finally cleansed of the chaff. See art. 'Shovel' in Hastings' *DB*. This final stage of the winnowing process is referred to by John the Baptist in the only occurrences of the word 'chaff' in the NT (Mt 3¹², Lk 3¹⁷).

The imagery of the threshing-floor was finely adapted to express the sweeping reform of the national life which the ardent soul of the Baptist expected to characterize the coming of the Jewish Messiah. The chaff well represented (1) the insincerity and hypocrisy of the national religious leaders, profession without substance, looking at a distance like grain, but proving on near inspection to be chaff; and (2) the light irresponsibility, the absence of true principle, in the people who accepted this formalism and pretence as genuine grain of godliness. And the winnowing represented the readiness with which such unsubstantial elements of national character would be carried away by the first wind of trial, or burnt up by the divinely authorized Messiah, whose coming John expected to be with swift discrimination and judgment. John looked for the immediate separation of the false from the true, the bad from the good. The Christ would come as Malachi (3¹⁻⁵) predicted, with searching and striking condemnation of all that was worthless and injurious; and the comparative slowness and indirectness of our Lord's method was the moving cause of his perplexed question, when he heard in the prison the works of Christ, and sent his disciples to ask, 'Art thou he that should come, or look we for another?' (Mt 11³, Lk 7¹⁹).

LITERATURE.—Mackie, *Bible Manners and Customs*, pp. 34–36; Tristram, *Eastern Customs in Bible Lands*, ch. 6; Jahn, *Biblical Archæology*, pp. 66–73; Thomson, *Land and the Book*, pp. 538–540; Nowack, *Heb. Arch.* i. 233 f.; artt. 'Agriculture,' 'Chaff,' 'Straw,' in Hastings' *DB*. T. H. WRIGHT.

CHAINS.—The usual NT word for 'chain' is ἅλυσις. πέδαι (Mk 5⁴ AV and RV **fetters**) are for binding the feet. δεσμός is a more general term, meaning anything to tie or fasten. AV renders δεσμοί, 'chains,' in Jude 6, but RV substitutes 'bonds.' For critical reasons 'chains' disappears from 2 P 2⁴.

In NT chains invariably denote instruments for binding, or restraining the liberty of the person, *e.g.* the demoniac (Mk 5³), St. Peter (Ac 12⁶), the dragon (Rev. 20¹). Imbeciles appear always to have received consideration, if not even reverence, in the East; but demoniacs, and persons suffering from certain forms of delirium, have been treated with horrible cruelty. Often they are loaded with chains and bound to a staple firmly fixed in the ground. The tortures applied are ostensibly for the purpose of driving out the evil spirit that possesses them.

Under the Roman law, *vincula* was a form of punishment, or of safe custody. The prisoner was chained to a soldier, who was responsible for his safe keeping. The chain was fastened round the right wrist of the prisoner and the left wrist of his guard. To this chain St. Paul refers (Ac 28²⁰, 2 Ti 1¹⁶). For greater safety two soldiers might be assigned as guards to one prisoner, a hand of each being chained to one of his. Thus St. Peter was confined in the stormy days of the persecution (Ac 12⁶); and St. Paul, when Lysias thought him a dangerous person (Ac 21³³). The use of πέδαι in their modern form may be seen to-day at Acre, in the groups of Turkish prisoners chained together by the ankles. W. EWING.

CHAMBER.—See CLOSET, and GUEST-CHAMBER.

CHANCE.—The word occurs only once in EV of the Gospels, viz. in Lk 10³¹, where in the parable of the Good Samaritan the priest is said to have been going down that way 'by chance.' In the original the phrase is κατὰ συγκυρίαν, Vulg. *accidit ut*. The word συγκυρία is found nowhere else in NT, and rarely in the Gr. authors. The idea of 'chance' is ordinarily expressed in Gr. by the nouns τύχη, συντυχία, or by the verb τυγχάνω. Neither of these nouns occurs in NT, and the verb, in its intransitive sense of 'chancing' or 'happening,' but rarely. Examples are 1 Co 15³⁷ εἰ τύχοι σίτου, which EV translates 'it may chance of wheat' (the only other occasion on which the word 'chance' is found in EV of NT), and 14¹⁰ εἰ τύχοι, EV 'it may be.'

In the Gospels τυγχάνω is used in its intransitive sense, with the idea, viz. of 'happening,' only once, and that is, curiously enough, in TR reading of Lk 10³⁰, the verse immediately preceding the one under consideration, where the robbers are said to have left their victim ἡμιθανῆ τυγχάνοντα. The τυγχάνοντα here, as Meyer and others have pointed out, is not simply equivalent to ὄντα, though the AV translators appear to have so regarded it. The expression properly means 'half dead as he chanced to be.' The shade of suggestion is that the robbers left him in complete indifference to his fate, to live or die just as it might happen. The fact, however, that τυγχάνοντα is lacking in אBDLΞ, *al.* justifies its omission from the text by WH and other critical editors.

Unlike τύχη and συντυχία, συγκυρία does not denote 'chance' in the proper sense of the word, *i.e.* something which 'falls out' independently of the ordinary laws of causation ('chance' comes from the Low Lat. *cadentia*, 'a falling,' and may have been suggested by the falling of the dice from a dice-box). Derived as it is from σύν and κυρέω ('fall in with'), it corresponds almost exactly to our word 'coincidence.' All that our Lord's use of the phrase κατὰ συγκυρίαν accordingly suggests is, that by a coincidence of events a certain priest came by just as the wounded traveller lay helpless on the road. And, as Godet remarks, He may even have used the expression with a kind of irony, since 'it is certainly not by accident that the narrator brings those two personages on the scene' (*Com. on Lk. in loc.*).

Apart from any further occurrence of the word 'chance' in EV of the Gospels, the idea of hap or chance may seem to be conveyed by the use of 'haply' in Mk 11[13], where Jesus is said to have come to the fig-tree, 'if haply he might find anything thereon,' and in Lk 14[29], where He Himself says of the builder who could not finish his tower, 'lest haply when he hath laid a foundation, and is not able to finish it.' But in both cases we have to do in the original simply with conjunctions and particles, εἰ ἄρα in the one passage and μή ποτε in the other.

As a matter of fact, the idea of chance was as foreign to the ancient Jewish as to the modern scientific mind; for while the scientist holds that the universal reign of law renders the operation of chance impossible, the Hebrew may be said to have believed (cf. Pr 16[33]) of every so-called chance that 'Eternal God that chance did guide.' In popular language the idea of things happening by chance appears to be admitted in both OT and NT (cf. 1 S 6[9], Ec 9[11], 1 Co 15[37]), as it constantly is among ourselves. But in the case of the Scripture writers, at all events, it denoted only human ignorance of proximate causes, not the occurrence of events independently of the Divine will (with 1 S 6[9] cf. v.[12], with Ec 9[11] cf. v.[1], with 1 Co 15[37] cf. 3[7], Gal 6[7f.]).

As bearing upon the subject of chance, reference may be made to the casting of lots by the Roman soldiers for the garments of Jesus. The incident is mentioned by every one of the Evangelists, and is explained by John as referring only to His seamless tunic (Mt 27[35], Mk 15[24], Lk 23[34], Jn 19[23. 24]). Among the Jews the casting of lots was regarded not as a reference of a question to the fickleness of chance, but as a solemn appeal to the Divine judgment (cf. Pr 16[33]). And though by the time of Christ such a game of chance as dice-playing (κυβεία) had been introduced into Palestine (cf. St. Paul's ἐν τῇ κυβείᾳ τῶν ἀνθρώπων, 'by the sleight of men,' lit. 'by the dice-playing,' because of the trickery and cheating which had come to be associated with the game), it was repudiated by those who adhered strictly to the Jewish law (see Schürer, *HJP* II. i. 36). With the Roman soldiers it was otherwise. Dice are thought by some to have been an invention of the Romans, and certainly dicing was very common among them. In his famous 'Crucifixion' in the Church of Sta. Maria degli Angioli at Lugano, Luini represents the four soldiers as rising from a game of dice to dispute with one another the possession of the seam-less robe. And more than one writer who has sought to describe the awful scene of Calvary has considered it natural to suppose that the soldiers would amuse themselves during the hours of waiting by playing their favourite game (see Farrar, *Life of Christ, ad loc.*). No information is given us by the Evangelists as to the manner in which the lots were cast. But it may be that a cast of the dice-box was the plan which suggested itself most readily to those rude men, and that they actually gambled for the Saviour's coat while He hung above them on the cross, dying for the sins of the world. See, further, art. LOTS (CASTING OF).

J. C. LAMBERT.

CHARACTER may be defined as the result of the interaction between a personality and its environment; or, if the word is used in its special and favourable sense, as the advantage gained by personality over its environment, especially by the exercise of the will. In the terms of Aristotle (*Nic. Eth.* I. vii. 15), it is 'an energy of the inner life on the lines of virtue.' The question to be answered is, How have the life and gospel of Christ made this more possible? First, He diminished the moral weight and dread of life's environment. Secondly, He enlarged the resources and opportunities of personality.

1. The following are some of the powers which the soul has to meet in conflict :—

(1) *Suffering.*—'If a perfectly good man foreknew what was going to happen to him, he would co-operate with nature in both falling sick and dying and being maimed, being conscious that this is the particular portion assigned to him in the arrangement of the Universe' (Epictetus). Christ inspired men to put their foot on disease as an evil (Mt 10[8], Mk 16[18]), and won His first fame by His own powers of healing (Mt 4[23-25] 11[4-6] etc.). Such deeds were good on the Sabbath day (Lk 6[6ff.]), for it was a breaking of Satan's tyranny (Lk 13[16]).

(2) *Death.*—He died to 'deliver them who through fear of death were all their lifetime subject to bondage' (He 2[15]). Jesus not only so faced death as to convince a Roman centurion and a dying criminal that He was more than man (Mt 27[54], Lk 23[40f.]), but did not in His teaching allow it to have a decisive place in life, except to the fool (Lk 12[20]). He spoke of it as a sleep (Jn 11[11ff.]), which the good man need not fear (Mt 10[28]), and as a going to the Father and His many abiding-places (Jn 14[1-3]).

(3) *The world.*—

'If but the Vine- and Love-abjuring band
Are in the Prophet's Paradise to stand,
Alack, I doubt the Prophet's Paradise
Were empty as the hollow of one's hand' (Omar).

Jesus was in complete independence of all that the world offers, accepting poverty (Lk 9[58]), repudiating popularity (Jn 6[15]), not expecting to be waited on (Mk 10[45]). 'Be of good courage,' He said, 'I have overcome the world' (Jn 16[33]); and on account of the promise of His presence His disciples were built up in the same αὐτάρκεια (Ph 4[11]).

(4) *Racial barriers.*—'It is an unlawful thing for a man that is a Jew to join himself or come unto one of another nation' (Ac 10[28]). Jesus struck at the limitations of race prejudice and enmity in the parables of the Good Samaritan (Lk 10[29ff.]) and the Last Judgment (Mt 25[31ff.]). Though He sought first the lost sheep of the house of Israel (Mt 10[5f.]), He 'opened the Kingdom of Heaven to *all believers*' (Mt 8[10-13], cf. Mk 7[29]), and thereby achieved on moral lines what the status of Roman citizenship created on legal lines. His short career was an encounter with the dead hand and narrowing force of nationalism (Mk 12[9], Mt 21[42-44]), and it was in the name of Son of Man that He lived and died.

(5) *Caste distinctions.*—'It was the hereditary disability the Aryans had succeeded in imposing

upon races they despised, which, reacting within their own circle and strengthened by the very intolerance that gave it birth, has borne such bitter fruit through so many centuries' (Rhys Davids, *Hibbert Lectures*). 'A workshop is incompatible with anything noble' (Cicero). Jesus kept the same way open to all without regard to social or religious status; did not reject the rich (Mt 8⁷ 9¹⁸ᶠ·, Lk 7³⁶), but counted their wealth a disadvantage (Mk 10²¹· ²³, Lk 6²⁰). He chose His companions from men who were mostly of no class (Mk 1¹⁶ 2¹⁴), was known as the friend of publicans and sinners (Mt 9¹¹, Lk 15¹· ²), and threw away His own triumph to give Zacchæus a moral chance, 'forasmuch as he also is a son of Abraham' (Lk 19¹⁻¹⁰).

(6) *Family control.*—'To every individual,' says Sir Henry Maine, referring to the Roman civilization, 'the rule of conduct is the law of his home, of which his parent is the legislator.' Though Jesus maintained the sanctity of the marriage tie (Mt 19⁴ᶠᶠ·), and illustrated as well as taught filial obedience and honour (Lk 2⁵¹, Jn 19²⁶· ²⁷, Mk 7¹¹ᶠᶠ·), He broke the decisive control of the family for the sake of the individual personality (Mt 10³⁵⁻³⁷ 12⁴⁸⁻⁵⁰, Lk 9⁵⁹⁻⁶² 11²⁷⁻²⁸, Mk 10²⁸⁻³⁰).

2. In the second place, Christ enlarged the resources and opportunities of personality, by making the soul conscious and confident of a new environment, in which it could find release and reinforcement. The secret of this spiritual environment which awakens and sustains the soul's faculties of faith, hope, and love is grace, in which alone they can move and have their being. The essential fact of grace is illustrated in the teaching of Christ chiefly in the following doctrines— the Divine Fatherhood, the Divine Forgiveness, the Divine Indwelling, and the Divine Reappearing. All that was dim or distorted in the human views of these truths, which mean so much to personality and character, He rectified and made authoritative.

(1) The clear revelation of the Divine *Fatherhood* had this immense bearing on character, that it brought out the worth of the individual soul. It is not necessary here to argue the question whether we are really God's sons, apart from faith in Christ. It is enough for the purpose that Christ undoubtedly used the truth of the Divine Fatherhood as the chief motive to the new ethic. The first and most important effect on character is that the starting-point is *trust*. Trust in God is illustrated in contentment with circumstances, courage in regard to human opposition. Whatever be the straitness of life and however menacing the future, there may well be trust in One who cares for the individual with more than the purpose and solicitude of an earthly father (Mt 6⁷· ⁸ 7¹¹, Lk 12⁶· ⁷· ²²⁻³⁰). And as for hostility, it is well worth standing firm for truth and righteousness, for thus the approval of the Father is gained (Mt 5¹¹· ¹² 16²⁴⁻²⁷, Lk 12⁴ᶠᶠ·, Jn 15²⁶ᶠ· 16¹⁻³). The natural vehicle of such trust is prayer, which Jesus Himself used for the solution of His perplexities and the bearing of His burdens (Lk 10²¹, Mk 14³⁵ etc.), and which the disciples were also to use freely and urgently (Lk 11⁵⁻¹³ 18¹).

This leads to the second characteristic of a life that acts on the teaching of the Divine Fatherhood—its religion will be in spirit and *truth* (Jn 4²³). Prayer is no mere performance, but secret and real (Mt 6⁵⁻⁸), in faith (Mk 11²²⁻²⁴), with a softened heart (Mk 11²⁵), and looking for the highest things (Jn 15¹⁶ 16²⁶). Religion is not a matter of external or traditional compulsion, but rests upon a gospel of Divine love (Mt 11²⁸ 23³⁷, Jn 6⁴⁴· ⁴⁵). The Father can care for nothing that is not spontaneous and sincere like childhood (Mk 10¹⁵· ⁵¹· ⁵² 14⁹ Mt 18²¹· ²²), and the fruit of real growth (Jn 15⁸). The consummation of life is to be so sanctified by

the truth as to enjoy God as Christ the Son Himself did (Jn 17²⁰⁻²⁶).

And the bearing of the Divine Fatherhood on our relations to our fellows produces a wise *tolerance*. The disciples of Christ are to imitate the character of Him who 'maketh his sun to rise on the evil and the good, and sendeth rain on the just and on the unjust,' and refuse to treat any man as an enemy (Mt 5⁴³⁻⁴⁸). Indeed, the truth of the Fatherhood is the great inspiration to kindness and charity. The positive character of the 'Golden Rule,' which is its Christian distinction, is directly drawn from the ways of the 'Father in heaven' (Mt 7¹¹· ¹²), and the blessedness of peacemakers is in being called sons of God (Mt 5⁹). The parable of the Good Samaritan (Lk 10²⁵⁻³⁷) illustrates in particular what the parable of the Great Assize (Mt 25³¹⁻⁴⁶) sets forth with ideal completeness, that there is no real love to God which is not expressed in spontaneous and appropriate help to every human being that requires it. Thus in the teaching of Christ went forth 'an edict of Universal Love'; 'humanity was changed from a restraint to a motive (*Ecce Homo*, ch. 16).' And that this was the secret of the Christian message, is indicated in the parting commission, 'Go ye and make disciples of all the nations, baptizing them into the name of the Father and of the Son and of the Holy Ghost' (Mt 28¹⁹).

(2) The gospel of Divine *Forgiveness* has had a distinctive and powerful effect upon the characters of those who have accepted it. Indeed, it has produced a new type of character, which can be described only as being born again (Jn 3³, 2 Co 5¹⁷· ¹⁸). Forgiveness was by no means a new idea, for it has never been set forth with more beauty and completeness than in the Prophets and the Psalmists of the Old Testament. But Jesus was the first to apply it to the individual soul with the view of producing the character of a child of the Kingdom; and it was this which made His teaching seem revolutionary and even blasphemous in the eyes of the guardians of the Old Covenant (Mk 2⁵⁻¹², Lk 7³⁹⁻⁵⁰). The average good person is now as much as ever inclined to resent the 'opening of the Kingdom of heaven to all believers' through the remission of sins. It contradicts the view accepted by all average moralists that it is by the maintenance of virtue that heaven must be won, and that any contradictory doctrine must loosen the bands of character. Their view is necessary as a caution, not only against the Antinomians, who treat the fact of forgiveness as a term of logic, and argue 'let us sin that grace may abound,' but also against all who preach faith as something apart from ethical enthusiasm. But St. Paul had learned the secret of his Master when he flung himself into the advanced position of 'justification by faith.' It was Jesus Himself who had the daring originality to base character on a new foundation without fearing to debase it (Lk 7⁴⁷⁻⁵⁰, Mt 26²⁷· ²⁸).

It must, however, be remembered that it was not so much the intention of Jesus to set up a rival type of character, as to restore the character of those who had lost it; to give a new chance to the personality that was overborne and fettered by its environment. He was essentially a physician of the sick (Lk 5²⁷⁻³²), a seeker of the lost (Lk 15. 19¹⁰, Mt 18¹²ᶠᶠ·), a giver of rest to the heavy laden (Mt 11²⁸ᶠᶠ·), fulfilling the words, 'He shall be called Jesus: for he shall save his people from their sins' (Mt 1²¹, cf. Jn 3¹⁷). The great contribution, then, to the forming of character in the gospel of Forgiveness is not that it adds anything to the ideal of virtue, but that it unseals the great motive of humble and adoring gratitude, and opens the way for that tide of love which is itself the fulfilling of the Law (Lk 7⁴⁷ 19⁸· ⁹). The business of Jesus was not the chiselling and polishing of character, but primarily its creation among the multitudes who would be shut out by the Pharisees from the kingdom of righteousness. The gospel does not so much teach how to be good as why to be good. Yet it must be admitted that in this teaching of grace as a redeeming power, Jesus did not simply profess to level sinners up to the virtuous. Rather He made the beatitude of the forgiven appear in comparison with the self-complacency of the virtuous as sunshine to moonlight (Lk 6$^{22-26}$ 18$^{9-14}$). The result of thus opening the fountains of a great deep was to be seen in a new humility and tenderness, an unexampled moral scrupulousness and solicitude, for the pride of the natural man is overwhelmed by the sense of what he owes (Mt 18$^{21-35}$, John 21$^{15-19}$, Gal 2^{20}, Col 3$^{12.\ 13}$).

(3) The third illustration of grace through which the scattered forces of character can be regathered is the Divine *Indwelling*, which, although not made conspicuous in the Synoptists, is essential to the Christian conception of character. The remarkable transformation which came over the chief Apostles after the events of Calvary and the Garden, was expressly attributed by them to the fulfilment of Christ's promise to return and dwell in them through the Spirit (Ac 19$^{1-6}$ 2$^{16f.\ 38}$, Jn 14$^{15-18}$). The character that has learned its worth from the Divine Fatherhood, and found its release in the Divine Forgiveness, gains its strength and means of independence from the Divine Indwelling. The real strength of character from the Christian point of view lies in the sense of weakness and the dependence on grace. Its ideal is not self-possession and self-complacency, but a possession by Christ (Gal 2^{20}), and a pleasing of Christ (Ph 1^{20}). And because its standard is so high, namely, the perfection of God Himself (Mt 5^{48}), the only chance of attaining it is to realize that the sufficient power comes from the imparted life (Jn 20$^{21-23}$), to take the yoke of Christ (Mt 11^{29}), or to abide in Him (Jn 15^4). If we can rely on God's Fatherhood, we can be sure He will give the best gift, the Holy Spirit (Lk 11^{13}), which is to enable the disciples to do greater things even than Jesus Himself (Jn 14^{12}), because thus His own power will be multiplied in and through them (1 Jn 4$^{12.\ 13}$).

From the Christian point of view, then, character depends for its final strength and beauty on the measure of its surrender and receptivity. Its turning-point is found in that decisive acceptance of Christ which is called 'conversion,' and which is not mere acquiescence, but allegiance as well, not only requiring an attitude of the soul, but also its adventure with and for the Lord it has recognized. When room has been made for the Divine indwelling in immediate sequence to the Divine forgiveness, there may be an assurance that through grace and with much patience the fruits of Christian character will come (Mk 4$^{8.\ 20.\ 26-29}$). Christian character depends on Christ's indwelling; for its virtues, which are more appropriately termed graces, are called 'fruits of the Spirit,' indicating that they are not the attainment of the old nature, but the growth of the new, according to the 'law of the Spirit of life which is in Christ Jesus our Lord.' In Gal 5$^{22.\ 23}$ they are thus given: 'love, joy, peace, long-suffering, kindness, goodness, faithfulness, meekness, temperance'; and in 2 P 1$^{5-8}$: 'faith, virtue, knowledge, temperance, patience, godliness, brotherly kindness, and love.' From which it will be seen that there is no ordered system of ethics in the New Testament; but the sum and substance of it is that life is primarily to be the gradual demonstration of the Divine indwelling, that the world may see that Christians are alike possessed

and controlled by a power and spirit not their own.

(4) There is one further contribution to the making of character in the name of grace which belongs to the Christian revelation, viz. the Divine *Reappearing*. However erroneously it was conceived, there can be no doubt that it exercised a powerful effect upon the moral qualities of the early Christian community (1 Th 1$^{9.\ 10}$), and its essential truth is still responsible for much that is unique in Christian ethics. It was sufficient to slay worldly ambitions outright, so that men sold their possessions (Ac 4^{34}), and at a later age secluded themselves in hermit or monastic dwellings. The journey of Israel to the Promised Land became the framework of the Christian conception of life—a pilgrimage through a wilderness. The result of this view has been the withdrawal of much imagination and energy from the problems of the present world in the name of an expected heaven—whereas the real watching is in right employment here and now (Lk 17$^{20.\ 21}$ 19$^{11-27}$). But it would be a mistake to miss the great contribution made by the doctrine of Christ's reappearing to the improvement of character (Lk 12$^{35-37}$, 1 Th 5^{23}). When it is understood in the light of the words and example of Jesus Himself rather than of Messianic expectations, which again and again He disappointed in favour of spiritual interests (Lk 9$^{54.\ 55}$, Jn 6$^{14.\ 15.\ 25.\ 26.\ 41.\ 65-68}$, Ac 1$^{6-8}$), its effect is purifying and searching to the last degree, and arms the personality with the weapon of a new hope in the conflict with its environment (Ph 3$^{13.\ 14}$). The reappearing of the Saviour, whether it be when physical disabilities fall from us at death, or in some other way, is essentially a final judgment (Mt 7$^{21-23}$ 13^{30} 25$^{31-33}$; cf. 2 Co 5^{10}) in which hidden things will be brought to light (Lk 8^{17} 12$^{2.\ 3}$, Mt 25$^{35-45}$).

Firstly, it gives a motive to *purity of life* which no other religion has been able to supply (1 Jn 3^3, 2 P 3$^{11-14}$), and to a consecrated use of every natural faculty (Ro 12^1). The promise of the resurrection rescues the body from the contempt with which philosophers were inclined to regard it, for as companion of the soul it is both sacred and serviceable (1 Co 6$^{19.\ 20}$). It is to be changed from a body of humiliation to the likeness of the body of His glory (Ph 3^{21}), and meantime its members are to be disciplined as instruments of righteousness (Ro 6^{13}), every ability being turned to good account (1 P 4$^{10.\ 11}$, Col 3$^{16.\ 17}$).

Next, it gives a deeper sanction to the *social relationships* of life. The spiritual side of marriage has been greatly developed by the revelation of the issues of life (Mt 19$^{4-9}$, Eph 5$^{22-33}$). The relations of parent and children, of master and servant, were likewise dignified by being seen *sub specie æternitatis* (Col 3$^{20-25}$ 4^1), and in the remembrance that for responsibility we must give account (Lk 12$^{45-48}$). It was this truth which gave its special meaning to Church membership, so that the Christian community was knit together with bonds unknown in any contemporary clubs or guilds (Mt 18$^{19.\ 20}$, Eph 1$^{18-23}$ 2$^{19-22}$, 1 Co 12$^{12-30}$). Though there was discontent and division in the Church, and even an occasional subsidence to the vicious levels of pagan society, the ideal could be steadily built up again in the sure hope of a radiant future, when the secret working of the absent Bridegroom in His own should be accomplished (Eph 5^{27}, Col 3$^{3.\ 4}$, 1 P 1$^{3-5}$). And this hope was a continual summons to every Christian to rise and be worthy of his calling (Ro 13^{11}, 1 Co 3$^{10-15}$ 9^{24}).

Finally, the hope of a Divine reappearing exercises its influence upon the common toil and *appointed duty* of every day. It is as if the owner of an estate went away entrusting to each man his work, and bidding the porter to watch (Mk 13³⁴). It is required that a steward be found faithful (1 Co 4¹⁻⁴) ; and it is well for the Christian if he has used to advantage the talents given (Mt 25¹⁹⁻²³), and the opportunities offered on every hand for the wider human service (Mt 25³⁴⁻⁴⁰), for there is an appropriate reward (1 Co 3¹²⁻¹⁴). Lowly service is the path to ennoblement and the seats of influence (Mk 10⁴³⁻⁴⁵, Lk 12⁴²⁻⁴⁴).

The promise of the Divine Reappearing thus supplements, as it were, the promise of the Divine Indwelling ; for whereas the latter brings out the need for the Christian's faith in a power not his own, the former requires that he be faithful with the powers that are his own. And taking all four aspects of the revelation of grace through Jesus Christ together, we see that they equip His followers for that conflict with environment out of which character emerges, by giving the soul a new *worth, freedom, power,* and *motive.*

This revelation is above all in the Cross, in which Christ was most fully manifested (Lk 9²², Jn 10¹¹ 12²³). There we see convincingly the love of the *Father* (Ro 8³², 1 Jn 4¹⁰), who counted men of such value (Mt 18²⁻¹⁴, Lk 15¹⁰) that He would have all to be saved though at infinite cost (Jn 3¹⁴⁻¹⁶). There is the place of the breaking forth of *forgiveness* (Mt 26²⁸), the supreme illustration of that redeeming love by which men's freedom is purchased (1 P 1¹⁸· ¹⁹, Ro 14⁷⁻⁹, Rev 1⁵· ⁶). There the life was surrendered to the Father (Jn 10¹⁷· ¹⁸), to be bestowed as an *enabling* power (Jn 14¹²⁻¹⁴, Ac 4¹⁰) by an indwelling Spirit (Jn 1¹², Ro 8⁹ff.), wherewith He might bring many sons to glory (He 2¹⁰). And there, finally, the eternal *future* was clasped to the tragic present (Jn 12²⁴⁻³²) as the ever-living Son submitted to taste of death (He 2⁹· ¹⁴), that neither earthly trouble nor spiritual principality might ever separate His people from Him (Ro 8³¹⁻³⁹, Ph 1²¹⁻²³).

In another summary, it may be said that the Christian ethic revolves between two poles which are discovered in the light of Christ's teaching, the inwardness of religion, and its practical nature. The first had been neglected by the Jew and the second by the Greek. And one-sidedness is still only too possible, when, for instance, in the name of Christianity the ascetic visionary holds to the first alone, or the social revolutionary to the second. But all ethical deductions can and must be rectified by reference to the work and word of Christ, who started from inward character and aimed at social regeneration.

And in a final analysis of what Christ has distinctively done for character, it may be said that (a) He treated the personality as a *whole.* All ethical systems are based on one or other element of our threefold nature. The pivot of the good life was, according to Socrates, *knowledge* ; according to Epicurus, *feeling* ; according to Zeno, *the will.* Christ gave a due and natural place to each of these ; for character with Him was not a system, as it was with Greek, Jew, or Roman, or as it is with Confucian or Mohammedan, but a growth from within, deeper even than our own nature, rooted in the ever-living grace of God. (b) He treated it as *free.* This also is crucial to Christian character, and depends on the truth that the ultimate fact of life is not Fate, but a God of grace, a Father. Jesus looked for repentance as the first consequence of His good tidings (Mk 1¹⁵). Whatever a man's past had been, he could be released and renewed, if out of the darkness and bondage he put forth the hand of faith. And so in the last resort life is self-determined. These two essential truths for the making of character, viz. the integrity and the freedom of personality, have been recognized and realized in the light of the four

great truths enumerated above. Thus Christ has enlarged the resources and opportunity of personality, and enabled it to be victorious over its material and moral environment.

Literature.—Sidgwick, *History of Ethics* ; Martineau, *Types of Ethical Theory* ; Seeley, *Ecce Homo* ; Illingworth, *Christian Character* ; Wilson Harper, *The Christian View of Human Life* ; Church, *Discipline of Christian Character* ; Knight, *The Christian Ethic* ; Martensen, *Christian Ethics* ; Garvie, *The Christian Personality* ; Kilpatrick, *Christian Character* and *Christian Conduct,* etc. ; Herrmann, *Protestant Ethics* ; Sermons by Butler, Newman, Martineau, Paget, Maclaren, Inge, etc.   A. NORMAN ROWLAND.

CHARACTER OF CHRIST.—

Introduction : (a) Aim. (b) Sources : (1) their trustworthiness ; (2) their sufficiency. (c) Theological value of a study of the character of Christ.
  i. Formative influences—
    1. Parentage.
    2. Home.
    3. Education.
    4. The years of silence.
  ii. The Vocation of Christ, the determining principle of His character—
    1. His Designation of His vocation.
    2. His Dedication to His vocation.
    3. His Confirmation in His vocation.
  iii. Characteristics of Christ—
    1. Spiritual-mindedness : (1) His knowledge ; (2) His teaching ; (3) effect of His presence.
    2. Love to God : (1) obedience, (2) trust.
    3. Love to men.
  iv. Social relations, and virtues manifested therein—
    1. Family.
    2. Friends : (1) His dependence upon them ; (2) His self-communications to them ; (3) their response to Him.
    3. Mankind : (1) lowliness ; (2) considerateness ; (3) compassion ; (4) forbearance and forgiveness.
  v. Virtues of His vocation—
    1. Faithfulness.
    2. Courage.
    3. Patience.
    4. Calmness.
    5. Self-sacrifice.
  Concluding Estimate—
    1. His absolute goodness.
    2. His sinlessness : (1) testimony of those who knew Him. ; (2) His own self-knowledge and self-witness.
    Literature.

Introduction.—(a) The aim of this article is to make a purely ethical study of the character of Christ. In such a study there must be no dogmatic presuppositions regarding the constitution of His person, whether favourable or hostile to the statements of Nicene orthodoxy. There must be no abstract separation of His humanity from His Divinity, and no attempt to relegate certain acts or phases to one side and others to the other side. We must proceed in the case of Jesus Christ as we do in that of the great men who have forced succeeding ages to the task of understanding them, though it may well be that in the end we shall be constrained to set Him, with reasoned conviction, in a class apart, high above the greatest of men.

(b) The sources for such a study are, of course, the four Gospels. It is obviously impossible to appeal to the Epistles, save for any reminiscences they may contain of the *historic* Christ. Their conceptions of the *risen* Christ cannot come here into view. In thus restricting ourselves to the earthly life of Christ, we are not excluding any view which faith might take of His present existence. If Christ be alive now, He must be the same, morally, as He was when on earth. There is no other Christ than the Christ of the Gospels.

As soon as we turn to the Gospels, we are met by various critical problems. The solution of these must be sought in the various works which are devoted to their discussion. For the study in which we are to be engaged two positions are essential, which may be stated here as *assumptions,* though they are in reality *conclusions* of the study itself. (1) The first is the *trustworthiness* of the Gospels as portraitures of Christ. Grant the ordinary critical results, that the Gospels were written late in the 1st cent., that contemporary ideas and experiences have influenced their authors or editors, that in some cases the Evangelists have misunderstood or misreported their Master; yet the fact remains, that the character of Christ, as presented in these documents, was not, and could not have been, an invention or a fiction, a product of progressive meditation, or a creation of enthusiastic feeling. Do justice to the portrait of Christ, let its harmony and its uniqueness, its profound naturalness and its transcendent loveliness, make their due impression, and the conclusion presses, that the Christ of the Gospels is not a construction but a memory, an actual Figure, once beheld by eyes of flesh, and now discerned through a medium upon which contemporary influences have had no distorting effect, and which, accordingly, permits Him to be known as He was.

It may be said that, while these remarks are true of the Synoptic Gospels, they cannot fairly be applied to the Fourth Gospel. A distinction, however, must be observed. The Synoptic Gospels are mainly ethical in their aim and method. Ontological and theological conclusions are certainly suggested; but they are not explicitly stated. In the Fourth Gospel these results are avowed in the Prologue, referred to again and again in the body of the work, and summarized in the conclusion. While thus frankly theological, however, it presents its doctrinal positions as the result of an ethical study, which it also gives. With the correctness of these doctrinal inferences we are not concerned. Our sole interest lies in the portrait of Christ; and with respect to it two things are certain: it is in complete harmony with that given by the Synoptists, it is another picture of the same person; and it can be regarded, as little as that of the Synoptists, as an invention or fiction. For our present purpose, accordingly, which is ethical and not theological, we shall use the materials presented in the Fourth Gospel, for a study of the character of Christ, with the same freedom and confidence with which we turn to the Synoptic narratives.

(2) The second assumption follows naturally upon the first, and maintains the *sufficiency* of the Gospels for knowledge of Christ. It is obvious that they do not aim at *extensive* completeness. They are not chronicles; nor are they biographies in the modern sense. A shorthand report of the sayings of Jesus, a minute record of His life, during even the short period covered by the narratives, would have swelled their brief outlines to portentous volumes. It is certain that they do aim at *intensive* or central completeness. We do not need to *know everything about* a man in order to *know him*. For the purpose of character study, much that is interesting, that affectionate curiosity would like to know, is needless and irrelevant. The materials of our study must be, and need only be, such words and deeds as express the whole man, and are the organic utterance and outcome of his very self. This is one aspect of the uniqueness of the Gospels, one element in the proof that they are memorials, not inventions, that the Christ they represent is a unity. There is not the faintest trace of artificiality, of an ingenious synthesis of heterogeneous elements. No portrait painter, no artist in words, ever invented a figure of such perfect harmony. There are many things about Christ which we should like to know; but such things have been told as enable us to know Christ. From the Gospels we learn enough to know what manner of man He was. And if He be alive now, and able to influence persons now living on this earth, it is certain that His communications will be simply the unfolding and the application of the character

which was expressed in such words and deeds as the Gospels record.

(c) The relation of a purely ethical study of the character of Christ to the theological consideration of His person is obvious. The one presents the problem with which the other deals. However high we may place Christ as a moral teacher, or even as the founder of a religion, nevertheless, if His moral type remain the same as that recognizable in other pure and lofty souls, if His moral achievement is generically the same as theirs, there can be no problem of His person. Christology is not merely an impossibility, it is a huge irrelevancy. Only if a study of the character of Christ raise from within the question of His relation to men on the one side and to God on the other, can there be a theological problem of the constitution of His person. Only in that case are the Christological elements in the NT warranted, and the long controversies of subsequent theological development justified. If the Divinity of Christ is not to be a dead dogma, soon to be abandoned by the minds which it perplexes and the religious instincts which it depresses; if it is to be a living conviction, sustaining faith and unifying thought, it must not be treated as though it hung, gaunt and naked, in a metaphysical vacuum; it must be regarded and expounded in its organic connexion with the character of which it is the necessary presupposition, and from which it derives its intellectual cogency. The only pathway to faith is that trodden by the first disciples. Belief in the Godhead of Christ, if it is to be more than a mere theologoumenon, must be rooted in acquaintance with Him; and that acquaintance is informed and enriched, made close, luminous, and full, through the medium of the portraiture in which the character of Christ is disclosed to our reverent gaze.

i. FORMATIVE INFLUENCES.—In the making of men, three factors are to be distinguished—influences operating from without, the reaction of personality, and the agency of the Divine Spirit. It would be a mistake, in the case of Christ, to concentrate attention wholly upon the second of these, as though He were a mere apparition in the moral universe, standing in no vital or intelligible relation to His visible or invisible surroundings. The other factors are amply recognized in the Gospel narrative. The first of them alone comes into view in our present study. The operations of the Spirit of God belong to the theological interpretation of the character of Christ, and can be understood only from the point of view of a definite conception of His person, to which our present effort is introductory. We approach our subject, accordingly, by briefly indicating the influences which operated on the youth of Jesus.

1. Parentage.—Pre-natal influence, whose mode of operation is beneath observation, is an undoubted fact. Parentage affords the conditions, physical and psychological, under which that recapitulation of the ancestral past, which gives to human character its richest and most interesting elements, takes place in the individual. If we conclude (anticipating our judgment) that in Jesus there is reproduced and perfected the highest type of OT spiritual life, the *conditio sine qua non* of this most lovely product is to be found in His parentage. This thought does not even suggest a supernatural birth. The question of the Virgin-birth is part of the wider and profounder problem, which we are not now facing, whether His person is to be regarded as an evolution from beneath or an incarnation from above, the entrance of God, at the crisis of human need, for the redemption and perfecting of men. It remains true, however, that whether we assume or deny the Virgin-birth, it is to His mother we are directed in our view of

His parentage. The idea of her sinlessness is certainly not even suggested in any record of her life ; it is merely the logical result of the blunder of making the sinlessness of Jesus depend on physical conditions. Yet it is beyond all doubt that she belonged to the inner circle of those who, in Israel, best preserved the spiritual heritage of the race ; and it is beyond cavil that of this deeply exercised generation of waiting souls she was herself a choice and lovely representative. With a fitness which suggests, in its tenderly human and deeply religious quality, a Divine selection, she filled the office of living personal medium, through which the stream of spiritual energy, which flows through the whole history of Israel, poured in upon her Son, to well up within His soul in the finest features and characteristics of the national religion. In part, at least, we understand Jesus through His mother. Most assuredly, He was more than a Hebrew ; but He was a Hebrew born. What He came to be is determined, in His case as in others, by the dark and mystic tabernacle wherein His physical frame was formed, by the bosom whereon He lay, and the life-force whereby His own was nourished. Preparation is thus made in birth for a character which shall be true to the national type, and, at the same time, deeply and broadly human.

2. Home.—Of all the characters who have risen to eminence from the lowliest surroundings, Jesus Christ is the most remarkable. What attracts attention to His home, however, is not the contrast between His early circumstances and His later attainments, but the harmony between the setting of His childhood's years and the noblest of His manhood's virtues and achievements. The chief quality of His home was its pure humanity. None but the simplest elements of human life are here. The home at Nazareth is as far removed from luxury and artificiality on the one hand, as it is from squalor or depravity on the other. The inward features of the home correspond with its outward conditions. The father and mother belong to what we know as 'the special seedplot of Christianity.' They were 'poor in spirit' ; they 'waited for the consolation of Israel.' Lofty aspirations, prayers and songs inspired and moulded by OT conceptions and forms, conversation enriched by the ideas of the profoundest thinkers on religion whom the world has ever known, lives instinct with pure and passionate devotion to God : amid such benign and holy influences the plastic soul of Jesus grew to its maturity. Such a home provides a perfect environment for One whose personal secret is His communion with God, whose message is God's fellowship with men.

Without mere fancifulness we can conceive what the childhood of Jesus really was — contented, happy, trustful. Certain features of His manhood, His freedom from extremes of feeling, His openness of mind, His wide and deep charity, find the conditions of their growth in His childhood's home, with its thorough naturalness and its nearness to central truth regarding God and man.

The words which record that 'Jesus advanced in wisdom and stature, and in favour with God and men' (Lk 2[52]), describe a perfectly normal human growth, a development without breach or strain or crisis, conducted by the Spirit of God, toward the realization of the Divine ideal of humanity. It is impossible to reconcile them with an abstract conception of His Godhead ; impossible also to reconcile them with an equally abstract conception of His ' *mere* humanity' (whatever that may be). But it is certain they present a unique fact, which must have full weight given to it in any estimate of the character and the person of Christ. It might be suggested, indeed, that the complete

normality of His growth may have been imperilled by communications made to Him by His mother regarding the mystery of His birth or the greatness of His vocation. Such communications, however, were not made before His twelfth year. Mary's words in the temple (Lk 2[48]) make that certain. Even on the supposition that certain communications were made at a later date, they may have aided Him in the discovery of His relation to God and His mission to men ; but the thoughts they may have awakened in His mind would not then act injuriously upon the growth of a perfectly proportioned human character. The greatness which was coming upon Him was leading Him nearer to men, not farther away from them. We must always look for what is unique in Christ *within* and not *beyond* His normal human character.

3. Education.—Hellenic or Roman culture might be brilliant, but it was narrow, limited to the conditions of life in a Greek city, or to the uses of a ruling race. Its faults are plain : intellectual pride, superficial cleverness, abundance of ideas together with dearth of ideals. Conceive now the training of a Hebrew boy. Ignorant of much that a Greek lad knew, he was thoroughly instructed in the books of the OT. These constituted a national literature, which, on any fair comparison, vastly excels the utmost that the Hellenic spirit could produce, in its power to quicken and direct the activities of the soul, to deepen it, and to enrich it with noblest conceptions of human life and destiny. Such a literature is the most splendid instrument of education the world has ever seen ; and such was the education even of a carpenter's son in an obscure village. No doubt even a system so excellent might be perverted ; but always in education the result is determined not by the perfection of the instrument, but by the reaction of the pupil. From school Jesus might have gone on to be a Rabbi of the common dogmatic and narrow type. If He did not, if His thought is wide, His insight deep, His spirit noble and gentle ; if He moves on the plane of the greatest prophets of the OT, and sees beyond their highest vision ; we must trace this result to His education, and to the response made to it by His quick and intelligent sympathy. It is because He is moulded by the influences of the OT that His character is at once more spiritual and more universal than it would have been, had He been steeped to the lips in Hellenic culture. The measure of His acquaintance with the apocalyptic literature which many of His contemporaries were studying, cannot accurately be determined. But we shall make a profound mistake, if we imagine that we can explain His teaching or understand Himself by any such reference. We can come within sight of Him only by retracing the steps of His own education, and approaching Him from the point of view of the OT. The groundwork of His character and the spring of His thinking are to be found in the OT. What He came to be or to reveal, beyond that stage of moral and religious attainment, stands in organic connexion with it. Other educational influences must be remembered and their power duly estimated : the historic scenes which were within His view, with the splendid and tragic memories they were fitted to awaken ; the highways of the world's business which were visible from the hills behind which Nazareth lay ; the pleasant country which was spread all around His home. Such aspects of His character as His intense patriotism, His wide humanitarian sympathies, and His feeling for nature, find their antecedents in the physical surroundings of His early years.

At this point we pause to note an incident which enables us, as efficiently as a score of haphazard reminiscences would have done, to discern the fruition of His life's preparation, so far as it had gone. Here it is well to remind ourselves of the reverence which is due to all childhood in our endeavour to analyse its utterances. 'How is it that ye sought me? Wist ye not that I must be about my Father's business?' (Lk 2⁴⁹).* No platitudes as to moral paternity, no pedantic references to the Trinity, help us to understand this wondering question. The words have no doctrinal meaning. They ought not to be used as proof of a dogma. Did Mary ask her Son what He meant? If she had asked, could He have made her understand? The words, however, while thus far removed from ontological problems, do reveal most surely what manner of child He must have been who uttered them. He must have lived till that hour in a fellowship with God which had known no interruption, which had been so deep and holy and tender, that Mary's word, applied to an earthly parent, provides its secret. 'Thy father and I,' said His mother; and He replied, surely not in any self-conscious, didactic mood, but in glad and confident adoption of her word, 'my Father's business.' It is certain that one who uttered this phrase out of the fulness of a child's unreflective experience, had never passed through the agonies of a violated conscience. His experience is not the abnormal type to be seen in St. Paul, Augustine, Luther, Bunyan, but the profoundly normal type of the human relation to God, as God designed it to be. Operating *upon* Him, through parentage and home and education, operating *within* Him in ways beneath consciousness and beyond observation, the Divine Spirit had led Him into, and enabled Him to abide within, a continuous, loving fellowship with God, of which the earthly relationship of father and son is the reflexion and the symbol. It is certain that Jesus never knew any inward dislocation of spirit, never passed through agonies of conviction, or emerged into the rapture of an experience which overwhelmed the judgment with surges of emotion. His character is not created by the healing of some deep breach of soul. It bears none of the marks of manufacture. It is a steadfast growth, the uninterrupted unfolding of the wealth of ethical meaning that lay, from the beginning, within His soul. From the village street He passes to the temple courts, to find Himself there at home, and to occupy Himself with His Father's concerns. From the temple He returns to His village home, without surprise and without disappointment, still to be in His Father's presence, and to be about His Father's business. 'He went down with them, and came to Nazareth; and he was subject unto them' (Lk 2⁵¹).

4. The years of silence.—For eighteen years we lose sight of Jesus. When they are past, not His physical frame only but His moral stature also has reached its fulness. The years themselves, apart from the incidents which must have filled them, are the most potent of the formative influences which are our guide to the understanding of Jesus. There are certain deeply marked features of His character, which are the imprint upon Him of the passage of these silent years.

(1) *Quietness and confidence.*—In His manhood there is no restlessness as of one who is uncertain of his goal, none of the strained eagerness of one who is still in pursuit of undiscovered truth. Plato's image of the aviary in no way resembles the mind of Jesus. No distinction is to be found in Him between possessing and having. He possesses, or rather is possessed by, fundamental and universal

principles. His life and teaching are their exposition and illustration. We may debate their validity, but we cannot dispute the absolute certainty with which He grasped them. Eighteen years of silence had breathed their restfulness into Him, and conferred on Him the precious gifts of a quiet mind and an assured heart.

(2) *Foresight.*—Jesus had no magical acquaintance with future events. Yet it is most noteworthy that He moved amid the circumstances of His life with no hesitating step. It is not merely that, as a religious man, He knows that God has a plan for Him, and will submit to it, whatever it brings Him, however grievous or disappointing; but also that *He knew what the plan was.* He was in the secret of His Father. In His speaking and acting there is no trace of hesitation or doubt. He never acts on a mere balance of judgment, never wastes a moment on conjecture, not one moment on regret. He acts with instant perception of what is wanted, and goes forward with confident step and calm foreseeing eye. He marvels (twice it is recorded of Him, Mt 8¹⁰, Mk 6⁶); but it is the wonder which is at once the parent and the child of knowledge, not the stupid astonishment of mere ignorance. Events which threatened destruction to Himself and His mission were met by Him with solemn recognition as the issue of a purpose which He served with full intelligence. Such calm wisdom, such quiet faithfulness, such undisturbed peace, had a history; and it lies in these eighteen years of silent waiting.

(3) *Serenity and self-possession.*—He was haunted by misconception, beset by malice, harassed by malignity. Yet He preserved an austere reserve, which permitted no rash action, no unguarded speech. He met His enemies with a silence which was no dumb resentment, but was on some occasions a most moving appeal, on others a most solemn judgment. No man can be thus silent who is driven ignorantly toward an unknown destiny. The silence of Jesus is proof that His life lay within both His purview and His command. Only in solitude and obscurity can such qualities be developed. Eighteen silent years are not too much to make a soul like that of Jesus Christ, strong, deep, calm, and wise. Not dogmatic prejudice, but respect for the unity of Christ's character, and for the self-evidencing truth of the portrait presented in the Gospels, condemns, as an outrage upon all psychological probability, the practice of packing into the three recorded years alternations of thought and purpose, and tracing supposed distinctions between the hopes with which He began His career and the convictions which were forced upon Him toward its close. Naturalism of this sort is simply unnatural and foolish. There is nothing too great to be the outcome of years so sublimely silent. What He is to be was then formed within His soul. What He has to say was then laid up for utterance. What He has to do and endure was then foreseen and then accepted.

ii. THE VOCATION OF CHRIST. — The unity of Christ's character stands out impressively in the Gospel portrait. The allowances we make, and the averages we strike, in estimating the conduct of other men, are not needed in His case. Woven of the strands of common life, it is yet 'without seam throughout.' When we seek to explain this unity, it is not enough to refer to the will of Christ, as though it were a power operating in an ethical vacuum. His is the normal human will, which realizes its freedom by identifying itself with some all-determining principle. When we ask, further, what this principle is, which thus determines His will and unifies His life, we shall be in error if we regard it as an absolutely new idea, to be ascribed to His inventive genius. He is not with complete

---

* ἐν τοῖς τοῦ πατρός μου. Our argument is not affected whether we adopt the above rendering (AV and RVm), or that of RV, 'in my Father's house.'

appropriateness to be designated a religious genius. He has nothing to reveal which is new, if by that epithet we mean to indicate a conception which has no organic relations with the past. Jesus, as believer, thinker, preacher, starts from the OT. His originality consists in perfectly understanding it, in carrying out into concrete reality its ruling conceptions. When, therefore, we seek for the determining principle of the life and character of Christ, we must turn to the OT. From childhood to manhood He lived the life of the ideal Israel, in communion with God and consecration to His service. What is unique in Him is not some idea, derived we know not whence, but His actual adoption of the purpose of God toward Israel as the purpose of His own life. When we endeavour to enter sympathetically into the experience of the Prophetic authors of the OT, and when we compare with their writings the character and career of Jesus, we are led to the conclusion : First, that the core of the OT religion is God's redeeming purpose toward Israel ; and, second, that the vocation of Christ, as understood and accepted by Himself, was to fulfil that purpose. In the nature of the case we cannot have from Jesus a narrative of the experiences which culminated in this great resolve, or an abstract statement of His ideas upon the topic of redemption. Yet, as we follow the occasions of His life, we overhear pregnant sayings, and we observe significant incidents, which corroborate and illustrate the impression which His whole career makes upon us. These we may thus arrange—

1. His Designation of His vocation.—When we inquire how Jesus designated His life's aim, we are met early in the narrative with one general, yet most definite statement. He is addressing an audience composed of His own disciples, together with a wider range of auditors for whom also His words are meant. We have, indeed, no verbatim report of what is usually called the Sermon on the Mount. Its theme, however, is unmistakable. It is the Kingdom of God as it exists at the stage which, in the person of the Speaker, it has now reached. Plainly, the Kingdom, as Jesus proclaims it, is a new thing. Its righteousness is new. Its blessings are new. At once the question arises, and was thrown at the Preacher with bitter controversial animus, How does this new Kingdom stand related to that which had endured through the centuries of Israel's history, which was now indeed obscured by political oppression, but which was destined one day to receive a glorious vindication? How do its new views of God and man and duty compare with the venerable system of law, of which the Scribes and Pharisees were the acknowledged defenders?

Then Jesus pronounces words which place Him in the central stream of the Divine purpose, and designate Him as its goal and its complete realization : 'I came not to destroy, but to fulfil' (Mt 5^{17}). It is noteworthy that to 'the Law' Jesus adds 'the Prophets,' thus emphasizing that element of the OT religion which the legalists of His day were most apt to neglect. He grasps the OT as a spiritual whole, and this totality of Divine meaning He declares it to be His vocation to fulfil. He has come into the world to carry forward all that had been signified by Law and Prophets to an end foreseen, or at least felt, by OT believers, but not attained in their experience. In Him the OT religion is at once perfected, and accomplished as an abiding reality.

Such a consciousness as this may well suggest thoughts as to the person of Him who thus asserts Himself. What is important for us now, however, is the fact that it *was* His consciousness, that the vocation thus announced was the end for which

Jesus lived, and constituted the organizing principle to which is due the perfect unity of His character.

The same impression of the loftiness and the definiteness of His vocation, as Jesus conceived it, is deepened by a consideration of other sayings in which He condensed the purpose of His life. While, of course, critical conclusions are manifold, it is not reasonably open to doubt (a) that Jesus claimed to possess authority to forgive sins, and so dispense the characteristic blessing of the New Covenant (Jer 31^{34}, Mt 9^6) ; (b) that He claimed to possess a knowledge of God which, in its immediacy and fulness, was generically distinct from that enjoyed by the most advanced OT saint, and to be empowered to reveal God, thus known, to men (Mt 11^{27}) ; (c) that He regarded His death as laying the basis of the New Covenant, and being, therefore, the medium of its blessings (Mt 26^{28} and parallels).

Again, we cannot fail to feel, in connexion with such words, the drawing on of a mystery in the person of Him who uttered them. Turning aside, however, from all such suggestions, and refraining from all doctrinal construction, we are, nevertheless, not merely permitted, but constrained, to observe that they described the commission under which He acted. They disclose the root of conviction from which His character grew. Take this away, and His character falls to pieces, and becomes no more an ethical unity, but a congeries of inconsistencies. The belief that He was commissioned of God to execute the Divine purpose towards Israel, and, through Israel, towards the world, moved Him from beginning to end of His career, and made Him the character which He was, which we come to know in the Gospels, and which has put its spell upon all subsequent generations.

2. His Dedication to His vocation. — The determining purpose of His life was not made known to Jesus for the first time in the experiences of His baptism. The consciousness which He then manifests had certainly a history. The experiences through which He then passed imply a perfectly prepared soul. In His whole bearing, from the moment of His approach to John, there is not a trace of hesitation or bewilderment. A new thing, no doubt, came to Him ; but it did not take Him by surprise or usher Him into a calling which He had not foreseen, or from which He had shrunk. By the discipline of the silent years in Nazareth, by the operation of the Divine Spirit, acting along with all external instrumentalities and beneath the conscious movements of His own spirit, His mind had been informed of the task which awaited Him, His faculties had been exercised in the appropriation of so great a destiny, His soul had been fed at sources of Divine strength, and thus enabled to accept in deep surrender the Divine appointment. His character, when first we see Him pass out of obscurity into the light of history, is not like an unfinished building, with scaffolding to be cleared away, and much still to be done before it be beautiful or habitable. It is like a living organism, rooted in the discipline of past years, perfected by adequate preparation, and now ready for its destined uses and its full fruition. His thirtieth year found Him well aware of His vocation, and waiting only for the summons to take it up. The cry of the Baptist reached Him in Nazareth, and He knew that His hour was come. 'Then cometh Jesus from Galilee to the Jordan, unto John, to be baptized of him' (Mt 3^{13}). His baptism is at once Christ's dedication of Himself to His vocation, and the first step in its accomplishment. His experiences at such an hour are too intimate and profound to be comprehended even by the most reverent study. But their meaning must gather round three points — (1) First, the word 'thus it becometh us to fulfil all righteousness' (v.[15]). In this pregnant saying we are conveyed back to the heart of the OT. God is righteous when He fulfils the obligations which He imposed on Himself when He instituted His covenant with Israel. It is still His righteousness which moves Him, when, after Israel has sinned itself out of the covenant relationship, He promises a New Covenant, and brings near a better salvation. This is the righteousness which Jesus has full in view on the verge of Baptism. If this righteousness is to be fulfilled, He who is the executor of the Divine purpose must not shrink from His task, whatever it may bring Him, and he who has a lesser function in the Kingdom must not withstand or hinder Him through any mistaken reverence.

(2) Second, the symbolic deed of baptism. Here also the only possible clue is to be found in the OT. There we see the godly in Israel, themselves right with God, bearing in their own souls the load of the people's transgressions. What is thus, through successive generations, done and suffered by exercised believers, is assigned in Deutero-Isaiah to the Servant of the Lord, who is in that writing the ideal Israel making atonement for the sins of the actual Israel. In descending to baptism, Jesus is certainly not acknowledging personal unworthiness. It is not even enough to say that He is vicariously confessing the sins of others. He is definitely assuming the place and office of the Servant of the Lord. Himself righteous, He assumes in His deepest soul the load of human sin, and thus at once fulfils the righteousness of God and 'makes many righteous.' The Baptism of Christ, accordingly, is at once the culmination of a life's experiences, the product of long years of thought and prayer, and the inauguration of a career whose movement and whose goal were already plainly before His inward eye.

(3) Third, the Divine response (v.[16f.]). A decision, whose issues we cannot calculate, was accompanied by a pain which we cannot fathom. The doctrine of the two natures, even supposing it to be proved, throws no light on the experiences of that hour. Jesus never found relief in His Divinity from His human suffering. He took refuge in prayer (Lk 3[21]). The Father answered with an endowment ample enough even for the task, an assurance strong enough to raise Him above all doubt. The terms in which the assurance is given form a synthesis of the two great figures through whom in the OT the consummation of the Kingdom is achieved, the Messianic King and the Servant of the Lord (Mk 1[11]), and afford additional proof of the consciousness with which Jesus began His ministry. What we observe in lesser men, we see in Jesus—a great purpose determining the life, creating the character. In His case, as in others, to miss the purpose leaves the character a hopeless enigma, the life a meaningless puzzle.

3. His Confirmation in His vocation. — Jesus does not sweep forward in emotional enthusiasm from Baptism to the announcement of His claims. The tide of His endowment 'drove' Him (St. Mark's phrase) not to cities and throngs, but into desert solitudes, there to win through conflict what was His by right. Jesus certainly did not describe to His disciples in full detail the strife by which He won His soul. Something He did tell, and told it, as alone it could be told, in symbols. The point at issue in the conflict is the vocation to which Jesus has just dedicated Himself. That vocation is the synthesis of all the lines of action by which, in the OT, God's purpose was being gradually fulfilled; and specially the synthesis of sovereignty and service. The strain of the Temptation is directed to the rending asunder of these

two. The effort to which Jesus is summoned is to hold them together in indissoluble connexion, and not, under whatever subtle seductive influences, to snatch at the one and renounce the other. Any breach between them will mean the defeat of the Divine righteousness. Failure here will make Jesus not the Servant of the Lord but His adversary, servant of His enemy. The stages of the Temptation, accordingly, turn upon the humiliations which the element of service will bring into His career, and their supposed incompatibility with the sovereignty, which is His goal. Surely hunger and toil and poverty are insuperable barriers in the way of reaching that supremacy which Jesus would exercise with such benignant grace! The alternative lay clear before Him, the pathway of supernatural power, leading away from normal human experience, or the pathway of service and suffering, leading nearer and nearer to the throbbing heart of humanity. Jesus made His choice, and in that great decision gained His vantage ground. As for Him, He would be man, and would stand so close to men that He could assume their responsibilities and bear their burdens. Thus Jesus won His victory, a solitary man, in death grips with evil, with no strength save the Spirit of God, no weapon save the Word of God. It was a complete victory. Within a character, thus welded by trial, there was no room hereafter for breach with God or with itself. Though other assaults will be made, though they be made by His dearest (Jn 2[3. 4]), His most loyal (Mt 16[22. 23]), though in one final onslaught they wring from the Victor sweat of blood, the certainty of their overwhelming defeat is already guaranteed. In studying the character of Christ, we are led from one surprise of loveliness to another ; but we are never in any uncertainty as to its permanence, never haunted by any dread of its failure. From the beginning there is the note of finality and absoluteness.

iii. CHARACTERISTICS OF CHRIST.—All character study is necessarily incomplete. A character which could be exhaustively analysed would not be worth the pains taken in making the necessary investigations. The quality of mystery certainly belongs to the character of Christ to a degree that suggests a source of power, deeper and less restricted than that which would suffice to explain shallower and more intelligible personalities. No biography has ever comprehended Him ; the intent meditation of nineteen centuries has not exhausted His fulness. It would, accordingly, be both pedantic and unreal to attempt a logical articulation of the elements of His character or a classified list of His virtues. It seems best, therefore, in this article to move from the more general to the more particular, without too great rigidity of treatment. We begin, then, with those impressions of His character which are at once the broadest and the deepest.

1. Spiritual-mindedness.—St. Paul's great phrase in Ro 8[6] φρόνημα τοῦ πνεύματος, 'the general bent of thought and motive' (Sanday-Headlam) directed toward Divine things, which is applied even to the best men we know, with reserves and limitations, exactly expresses the prevailing direction of Christ's life and character. He possesses the spiritual mind to a degree which stamps Him as being at once unique among men, and also true and normal man, realizing the ideal and fulfilling the duty of man as such. He moves habitually in the realm of heavenly realities. He does not visit it at intervals. He dwells there, even while He walks on earth, and is found amid the throngs and haunts of men. He carries with Him the aroma of its holiness and peace and blessedness. That His disciples were 'with him' (Mk 3[14]) was the secret of their preparation, the source of any wisdom they manifested, any success they achieved. The most mature experience of the power of Christ, and the most lofty conception of His person, find their ultimate warrant in this, that the unseen world becomes visible in His character. Apart from this, they are composed of things so unreal as feelings and opinions. Illustration and proof of the spiritual-mindedness of Christ are too abundant to be specified in detail. The following points will suffice to indicate its quality and significance.

(1) *His knowledge.*—He Himself, on one occasion, distinguished the objects of His knowledge as heavenly things (ἐπουράνια), and earthly things (ἐπίγεια, Jn 3[12]). The former are the mysteries of the Kingdom, the counsels of Jehovah, which in the OT He makes known by the medium of the prophets. The latter are the facts of human nature, as that is essentially related to the being and character of God, and is capable of receiving and experiencing the powers and truths belonging to the Kingdom of God. There is no doubt as to the kind of knowledge He evinced, and believed Himself to possess, regarding heavenly things. He is not inquiring like Socrates, nor reasoning like Plato, nor commenting like a scribe. He knows with absoluteness and fulness (Mt 11[27]). He beholds with immediate direct vision (Jn 1[18] 6[46]). He reports what He sees and hears (Jn 3[11] 8[38] 15[15]). ' He does not in any formal way teach the religion which lives in Him. . . . The thing itself He merely expresses, nay, still more presupposes than expresses ' (Beyschlag).

Christ's knowledge of earthly things, *i.e.* His insight into the subjective experiences of men and the moral condition of their souls, has the same note of absoluteness ; and His judgments upon them and His dealings with them have an authority and finality which would be unwarrantable did they not rest on perfect discernment (Mk 10[21], Lk 7[39], Jn 1[42. 47] 2[25]). Of this He Himself could not but be aware ; and, indeed, He expressly made it His claim (Jn 13[18]). Peter's heart-broken appeal (Jn 21[17]) belongs to the incidents of the Forty Days, and so cannot be used directly as proof ; but no doubt it reflects the impression which the historic Christ made upon those who knew Him, viz. that He saw into their inmost souls with a discernment as intimate and deep as God's, which, like God's, could neither be evaded nor hindered.

Whether Christ possessed supernatural knowledge of facts in the order of external nature has been much discussed, but does not now concern us. We are not even concerned at present with any explanation of His knowledge of Divine things. But we are bound to note, and to give full weight to the fact, that in the Gospel portraiture the world of heavenly realities, both in themselves and in their earthly manifestations and applications, is open to Jesus, that He is in complete spiritual affinity with it, and speaks upon all matters that belong to it with definite and self-conscious authority. Even if His Divinity be denied, it must be allowed that He is a man possessed of undimmed spiritual vision.

(2) *His teaching.*—Jesus is not a lecturer, making statements, however brilliant and luminous, of the results of investigation. He is a revealer, disclosing in ' the mother-speech of religion' the heavenly realities which were open to His inward eye. His teaching, therefore, is inexhaustible, begetting, in the process of studying it, the faculty of ethical insight, and continuously raising, in the effort to practise it, the standard of the moral judgment. Yet it retains the quality of spiritual delight which enchained its first listeners. It is *gracious* in its unfoldings of the Divine compassions ; in its disclosure not merely of the fatherli-

ness, but of the fatherhood of God ; in its invitations, pleadings, promises ; and, most of all, in its astounding declaration, which pride deemed blasphemous and humility never questioned, of the Divine forgiveness, deep, and free, and fearless. It is *holy* and *spiritual*, rejecting conventional piety, emphasizing, as even the OT had not done, the inward state of a man's heart Godward, describing the type of character required in citizens of the Kingdom in terms of such unearthly purity and loveliness, as would produce despair were any other than Himself the speaker. It is *universal*, perfecting the Law and the Prophets, in this respect also, that it declared the height of spiritual privilege to be attainable, not merely by Israel, but by man as such, irrespective of merit or privilege.

Such a voice had never been heard in Israel ; not Hosea's, with its tears of Divine compassion ; not Isaiah's, with its royal amplitude ; not his who in pure and lofty song heralded the return from Babylon ; not John's as it rang out from hill to hill his summons to repentance. Astonished by its novelty, wooed by its charm, bowed by its authority, the multitudes followed a little way as it called them heavenward ; and some elect souls rested not till they too entered the universe of truth whence Jesus uttered His voice. The greatest foe to faith is the haste which seeks to construct dogmas about Christ before Christ is known. To some souls the time for dogma comes late, or not at all. In any case, dogma, however accurate, must rest on the trustworthiness of Jesus in His disclosure of spiritual fact.

(3) *The effect of His presence.*—A spiritual mind produces upon those who come under its influence a twofold impression, that of remoteness and that of nearness and sympathy. This is conspicuously the case with Jesus. We have abundant evidence of His having a dignity of presence, which smote with awe those who had but occasional glimpses of Him, and filled at times His most familiar friends with fear, and also of His being the kindest, gentlest, and most sympathetic of souls. It could not be otherwise. To have discerned the end which created His career, to make choice of it with such full intelligence of all that it involved, to live for it in such entire consistency with its scope and requirements, means a moral grandeur unapproached by sage or prophet. Separated from the mass of men, removed from their pursuits, He must have been. Yet the very greatness of His vocation, the very depth of His insight both into the purpose of God and the need of man, produced in Him, along with that deep distinctiveness, the kindliest appreciation of the little things which make up the life of man, the most sympathetic interest in ordinary human concerns, and an entire approachableness to the humblest applicant for counsel or comfort. This combination of a majesty which smites to the ground the instruments of prostituted justice, with a manner so tender that babes smile in His arms and women tell Him the secret of their care, must have its source deep in the heavenly region which was His habitual abode.

2. Love to God.—The heavenly region which Jesus inhabited was not an abyss of being where the finite loses itself in the absolute. It was a realm of persons, Divine and human, who dwelt together in intelligent, spiritual fellowship. The doctrine of 'the One,' which is found in every climate and revives in every century, is not the clue to Jesus' thought of God. The key to His theology is the doctrine of the Father ; His love to the Father is the motive of His life. He proclaimed love to God, absorbing all energies, comprehending all activities, as the first, the great commandment, of which the second, love to man, is the direct corollary. But when we compare His own obedience to the first commandment with that of other men, a very significant distinction is to be observed. The most devout souls in their nearest approach to God are conscious that their love is not perfect. This defect is due in part to sin, and the chastened soul rebukes the coldness of its affection; and in part to finitude, and the adoring soul continually aspires after higher attainments. In the case of Jesus, the note, either of compunction or of aspiration, is never heard. The explanation of this is not that in later recensions of the tradition such notes were struck out, in deference to a mistaken sense of reverence, or to support a novel view of His person; but that the impression of complete spiritual attainment belongs to the very essence of the character as set forth in the Gospels. We may dispute whether such a character ever *existed*; but we cannot question the fact that such a character has been *portrayed*, with a verisimilitude which makes the portraiture a greater miracle than the actual reality of the character depicted would have been. Jesus loved God perfectly: this is the only fair interpretation of the record. There is no trace of moral disparity, no failure of mutual understanding, no sign of effort on the part of Jesus to cross a chasm, however inconsiderable, between Himself and God. He receives the communications of the Father's love without perturbation or amazement, as of one overwhelmed by the Divine condescension; and He responds without extravagance of emotion, in words which do not labour with overweight of meaning, but are easy, natural, simple, and glad, the very language of One who is the Son of such a Father. He and the Father are one. The Synoptic picture, as well as that of the Fourth Gospel, makes this feature plain. There can be no doubt that this fact raises the Christological problem in its profoundest form. What man is He who thus receives and returns the love of God?

Two of love's characteristic manifestations, moreover, are found in Christ in perfect exercise. (1) *Obedience.* We have seen that the character of Christ is created by the vocation to which He dedicated Himself. We now observe that this vocation is, in the view of Jesus, nothing impersonal, but is the personal will of the Father. This is the Father's 'business,' and to it He, as the Son, is entirely devoted. The will of the Father does not mean for Jesus a series of commands. It is rather to His deep conviction a purpose, moving throughout His whole life, and comprehending every detail of His activity. The obedience of the Son, accordingly, is not a series of events. It is the identification of His will with the will of the Father, and a complete reproduction of that will in the whole conduct of His life. Sayings in the Fourth Gospel, such as 4^{34} 6^{38} 8^{29}, bring into clear utterance the impression conveyed by the whole career of Jesus, and express an obedience which has lost the last trace of distance between the will of the Son and the will of the Father. Again, we must postpone all discussion of the possibility of such obedience, and must emphasize the actuality of the representation. Two things are plain: first, Jesus was conscious of being in complete and constant harmony with God, and profoundly unconscious of even the slightest failure to fulfil the whole will of God; and, second, those who knew Him best believed that in Him they had witnessed a unique moral achievement, viz., an obedience absolutely perfect, both in its extent and in its inward quality. (2) *Trust.* 'Perfect love casteth out fear' (1 Jn 4^{18}). Jesus' trust in God was, like His obedience, complete. It amounted to an entire and unfailing dependence upon God, so that whatever He did, God wrought in Him. In other servants of God

we observe, even in their deepest experiences, a certain dualism of self and God, a self assisted to a greater or less degree by God. This account would not be adequate to the experiences observable in the record regarding Christ. He is, without doubt, a person, not will-less, but acting in complete self-determination, and yet His deeds are the Father's. No process of analysis can distinguish in any word or deed of His an element which comes from Himself and another which comes from God. In Christ we find a perfect spiritual organism—a man so completely inhabited by God that His words and deeds are the words and deeds of God. Follow Him in His career, as it passes with unbroken steadfastness from stage to stage of an unfolding purpose, study Him in His dealing with men, and note the sureness of His touch, penetrate the secret of His consciousness as He from time to time lifts the veil (Jn $5^{20. \ 30}$ 7^{16} 12^{49} $14^{10. \ 24}$); and the result to which we are forced is, that here is a human life rooted in the Divine, filled and environed by it. This is, of course, no ontological explanation; but it states the ethical and spiritual phenomenon which demands an explanation; and this explanation must reach to the sphere of personal being.

Precisely at this point, however, when the facts we are describing seem to pass beyond the limits of normal human experience, we are summoned to observe that the trust and obedience of Jesus were not maintained without strenuous solicitude, or the use of those means which aid the human spirit in its adherence to God. His obedience was not easy. His will, in its ceaseless surrender, was subjected to increasing strain. He learned obedience by the things which He suffered (He 5^8). The 'disposition of obedience' was always present. 'But the disposition had to maintain itself in the face of greater and greater demands upon it. And as He had to meet these demands, rising with the rising tide of the things which He suffered, He entered ever more deeply into the experience of what obedience was' (A. B. Davidson on He 5^{7-10}). His ability to bear the strain to which He was thus subjected is due to a trust in God which was continually revived by His habit of prayer, to which there is such frequent and significant reference in the narrative (Lk $3^{21. \ 22}$, Mk 1^{35}, Lk 5^{16} $6^{12. \ 13}$, Mt 14^{23}, Lk $9^{18. 28}$, Mt 26^{36-44}, Lk 23^{46}). An increasing revelation of the Divine will, an unceasing advance in obedience, a continuous exercise of trust, are the strands woven together in the character of Christ. The product is that perfect thing, a life which is His own, and is entirely human, which is also, at the same time, the coming of God to man.

3. **Love to men.**—The source of this characteristic, which shines resplendent from every page of the narrative, is to be found in that which we have just been considering, Christ's love to God. Here we must do justice to the facts brought before us in the portrait. The noblest servants of God in the field of humanity have done their work out of a sense of obligation. They have received so much from God, that they have felt themselves bound, by constraint of the love of which they are recipients, to serve their fellow-men; and in this service their love for men has grown, till it has become no unworthy reflexion of the love of God. It would be, however, a miserably inadequate account of the facts of Christ's ministry among men to say that He loved them out of a sense of duty, and served them in discharge of a debt which He owed to God. The vocation which formed His character was not bare will. It was love, seeking the redemption of men. Jesus' acceptance of this vocation meant that His love to God entered into, and blended with, the love of God to men. He loved God, and the love of God to Him became in Him

the motive-power of His love to men. His love to God and His love to men constitute one energy of His soul. He turns toward the Father with the deep intelligence and the full sympathy of the Son ; and straightway He turns toward the world with the widest and tenderest charity (Mt 11[27. 28], cf. Jn 10[15]). Those, accordingly, upon whom Jesus poured His love, never sought to distinguish between it and the love of God. Enfolded by the love of Christ, they knew themselves to be received into the redeeming love of God ; and their grateful love to Jesus was the proof and seal of the Divine forgiveness. 'Her sins, which are many, are forgiven : for she loved much' (Lk 7[47]). Long before the doctrine of His Divinity was framed, the love of Christ was regarded by its recipients as the spiritual medium in which the Divine compassion reached them. Hebrew thought did not work with categories of being and substance. The human heart never works with categories at all. But it can identify love when it receives it ; and therefore it makes an experimental synthesis of the love of Christ and the love of God, and sets Christ in a relation toward God occupied by no other man.

The love of God to man being such as He extends to no lesser creature, implies that man has a value for God which no other creature possesses ; and to Jesus man has the same supreme value. Of this value there are no earthly measurements, not any created thing (Mt 10[31] 12[12]), not any institution, however sacred (Mk 2[27]), not even the whole world (Mk 8[36]). Even the moral ruin, in which sin has involved human nature, does not diminish its value, but rather accentuates its preciousness, and adds to the love of God, and therefore also of Jesus, a note of inexhaustible passion (Mt 18[10. 12-14]). Christ's doctrine of man does not breathe the spirit of 18th cent. individualism. Not for man as a spiritual atom, self-contained and all-exclusive, does Jesus have respect. But for man akin to God, capable of Divine sonship, He has deep and loving admiration. Not for man, harassed with passions for whose might he is not responsible, guilty of acts which to comprehend is to pardon, does Jesus have regard. But for man, meant for so much and missing so much, framed for perfection, destroyed by his own deed, He has love and pity, throbbing in every word, passing through action and through suffering to the ultimate agony, the final victory of the Cross.

iv. SOCIAL RELATIONS.—We have now to follow the character of Christ, which we have been studying in its origin, its development, and its leading features, as it manifests itself in the relations in which He stood to His fellow-men. The narratives attempt no enumeration of incidents. They present us with typical instances, in which the true self of Jesus is disclosed. From these we are able to conceive the figure of Christ as He moved amid the circles where human life is ordinarily spent.

1. **Family.**—It is difficult, from the very scanty materials before us, to trace the relations of Jesus towards the members of His family circle, and to distinguish clearly their attitude towards Him. Yet the following points may be regarded as certain : (1) The life of Jesus, prior to His baptism, was spent within the family circle, and was characterized by two features. First, a loyal and affectionate discharge of the duties of a son, presumably as breadwinner for His mother. The very astonishment of His fellow-villagers at His subsequent career is sufficient evidence that during the period prior to His public ministry He fulfilled the ordinary obligations of family life. Second, a deepening sense of His vocation, which, while it did not render Him less dutiful as a son and brother, could not fail to give Him a distinctiveness

which would inevitably excite adverse criticism on the part of His kindred, should they prove unsympathetic or unintelligent.

(2) The attitude of His mother towards Him, both before and after His baptism, was twofold. (a) Belief in His unique mission and extraordinary powers. Her words to Him in Cana of Galilee (Jn 2[3]) are pointless, unless they express a persuasion, born of long pondering, and revived by the recent events connected with His baptism, that He has a mission which could be nothing less than Messianic, and that the time has come for the display of powers with which necessarily He must be endowed for the fulfilment of His task. (b) A profound misconception of the nature of His mission, and of the means by which it should be inaugurated and carried on, together with a critical attitude towards Him, in regard to what she evidently considered an inexplicable, and even blameworthy, negligence on His part to seize the opportunity presented in the circumstances of the feast. For this misunderstanding we need not greatly blame her, for it was shared by His disciples even after the Resurrection ; unless, indeed, we conceive, what is most probable, communings between mother and son during those long silent years, which might lead us to marvel that she, who surely might have understood, failed as completely as others to discern His purpose.

(3) The attitude of His 'brethren' is still less intelligent. There is no suggestion in the narrative of any sympathy with Him whatsoever. After thirty years together, they could find no other explanation for His behaviour than temporary insanity, and could conceive no other plan than to put Him under temporary restraint. If His mother joined in this estimate and this proposal (Mk 3[21]), it must have been with the conviction that she had the right and duty of intervening to save Him from Himself, and rescuing Him from a course which would prove fatal to His mission as she conceived it. It is certain that she joined His 'brethren' in making an approach to Him, with the obvious intention of inducing Him to change His plan of action (Mk 3[31]). At a later stage His brethren offered Him a final challenge (Jn 7[3. 4]). They did not believe in Him (v.[5]), and therefore their suggestion to Him has not quite the sense of Mary's at Cana of Galilee. It expresses their demand to have this matter of His Messiahship (about which *they* had no doubts) settled once for all by open demonstration : 'Manifest thyself to the world.'

Here, then, is the situation of Jesus with respect to His family. He loves His kindred as son and brother ; but He knows that His vocation demands the sacrifice of family life, and this sacrifice, with its deep pain, He is prepared to make. He is called upon, however, to endure a yet deeper pain. Not only has He to leave the dear fellowship of the home, and face a world which will prove in the end bitterly hostile, but among the members of the home He can find no understanding hearts to cheer Him and comfort Him on His lonely way. Worse still, when His nearest and dearest withstand Him, or seek to divert Him from His appointed path, He has to repel them in words which He knows must keenly wound them. To be tempted by His very love for His mother and His brethren to deviate from the line of obedience to His mission, must have put a peculiar strain upon His spirit, and brought Him most exquisite pain. In each of the incidents alluded to above we feel this note of pain : when He declines the intervention of His mother (Jn 2[4]) ; when He turns from His mother and His brethren to His disciples (Mk 3[31-35]) ; and when He has, in plain words, to state to His brethren that they and He belong to two different worlds of thought and action (Jn 7[3-9], cf. 15[19]). That between Him and His mother there was a bond of love deeper than all misunderstanding, gains pathetic proof when from the cross He commends her to His beloved disciple : 'Woman (the very word, γύναι, He had used in Cana of Galilee, courteous and affectionate, and yet suggestive of a cessation of the old relationship of mother and child), behold thy son.' 'Behold thy mother' (Jn 19[26f.]).

2. Friends. — The vocation of Christ was one which could be executed by Himself alone. Necessarily He lived in a deep spiritual solitude, to which no human being could have access. Yet no sooner did He take up the burden of His mission than He proceeded to surround Himself with companions, and to cultivate human friendships. In the relations of Jesus to His friends three points are to be noted.

(1) *His dependence upon them.*—It will be a profound mistake if we conceive the end for which Jesus lived in any barely historical or formal manner. The end was the Kingdom of God, or the New Covenant ; but these titles do not, in the mind or language of Christ, stand for a political or ecclesiastical institution. They mean, fundamentally, an experience of God generically identical with that enjoyed in Israel, but perfected, and therefore also universalized. This experience is destined, in the counsels of God, for humanity. To secure it for mankind, so that under fit spiritual conditions all men may enter into it, is the task which Jesus in clear consciousness definitely assumed. Suppose Him, however, to have fulfilled His task as the Servant of the Lord, He will lose His labour, unless He secure representatives and witnesses, who shall declare to all whom it concerns the accomplishment of God's gracious purpose. This testimony, moreover, cannot be borne by mere officials. Suppose, for instance, that the Resurrection was a fact. Suppose, further, that it had been verified by the investigations of experts drawn from the chief seats of learning of the ancient world. Nothing is more certain than that this testimony, taken alone, would not have advanced by a hairbreadth the purpose to which Jesus devoted Himself. Testimony to certain facts, there is no doubt He required ; but this testimony would be valueless, did it not presuppose, and rest on, personal acquaintance with Himself, and participation in His own fellowship with God. His representatives must be His friends, bound to Him by personal ties of close and intelligent sympathy ; capable of bearing witness, not merely to a series of His acts, but to His character and to His influence ; having an understanding not merely of His doctrine, but of Himself. It was essential, therefore, that from the outset He should have friends about Him, to whom He should fulfil all the sacred obligations of a friend. When, accordingly, He comes to give them their commission, He makes it plain to them that His vocation is their vocation, having the same Divine origin, and carrying with it His own spiritual presence (Lk 4[18. 21. 43], Mt 15[24] 10[40-42], Jn 20[21], Mt 28[19. 20]).

How much the friendship of His disciples was to Jesus, the whole narrative bears witness. Their faith in Him was the greatest encouragement, apart from immediate Divine assurances, that He could receive as He faced the appalling difficulties of His task. There is an unmistakable note of pathos in His clinging to His disciples, when the natural support of family loyalty is denied Him. They were to Him brother, sister, mother. There can be no doubt that, had His three most intimate friends watched unto prayer, His last agony would have been alleviated. It is

the pathos of His position that His friends never knew how much He depended on them. To them He was the Strong One upon whom they leaned, from whom they took everything, to whom, in unconscious selfishness, they gave but little. Love must have been to Jesus a constant hunger. Never in all His life did He get it satisfied ; and yet it never failed, but remained the master passion of His soul. 'Having loved his own which were in the world, he loved them unto the end.'

(2) *His self-communications to them.*—The chief thing a friend can give to a friend is himself ; and Jesus poured out on His friends the wealth of His personality : His love (Jn 13[34]), His knowledge (15[15]), His example (13[15]) ; so that, when He reviews His life, He can plead with His Father His own perfect fulfilment of love's obligations (17[6. 8. 12]). The riches of Christ, thus bestowed upon them, vivified their imagination, quickened their emotion, enlightened their understanding, subdued and renewed their wills, till they came to be not wholly unfit representatives of Him on whose errand they went. This influence, which Jesus exerted, had none of the aspect of an impersonal force. It consisted in the touch of spirit upon spirit in the mystic depths of fellowship ; and this touch is not to be conceived as having the equal pressure of the atmosphere. Under certain conditions, which are necessarily too deep and delicate for analysis, the love of Christ gathered an intensity which made His friendship in these instances special and emphatic (Jn 11[3. 5] 13[23]). Yet so exquisite was His tact, so evident His goodwill, that those about Him, though they might quarrel among themselves for pre-eminence, never brought against Him the charge of favouritism. They knew He loved them according to the measure of their receptivity, and with a reserve of tenderness and power for ever at their disposal. They assented as in a dream to His own word, 'Greater love hath no man than this, that a man lay down his life for his friends' (Jn 15[13]). Afterwards they awoke, and remembered, and understood.

(3) *Their response to Him.*—It is impossible to miss the brighter aspect of their attitude towards Him. *They were glad in His company*, happier than the disciples of the Pharisees or of John, happy as sons of the bride-chamber (Mk 2[19]). This joy of theirs in His presence throws a very lovely light upon His character. He knew the goal toward which His steps were taking Him, and was standing within sight of the cross. Yet no shadow from His spirit clouded theirs. They rejoiced in Him, and in the new world of religious experience to which He introduced them. They knew themselves to be possessed of privileges, which from the point of view of the OT had been no more than an aspiration. In the fellowship of their Master and Friend they stood nearer to God than the ripest saint of the OT, immeasurably nearer than any legalist of their own day. This joy of theirs in Him is, besides, reflection and proof of His joy in them. It is strange, when we consider the spiritual elevation at which He lived, but it is certain, that He had a very real joy in their presence. He delighted to stimulate their minds by questioning, to enrich their conceptions by definite teaching. He welcomed every indication of their growing intelligence ; and when He discerned that they were awake to His meaning, 'He rejoiced in the Holy Spirit' (Lk 10[21]).

They trusted Him.—The result at which Jesus aimed in all His dealings with them was the production in them of faith ; and by faith He meant a trust in Himself as complete as that which men ought to repose in God. Without doubt, this raises far-reaching questions regarding His personal relation to God. But the fact itself remains.

as an element in the portrait of Christ, whether presented by the Synoptics or by the Fourth Gospel, that Jesus directed men to Himself as the source of all good, whether lower or higher (Mt 8[10. 13], and many instances connected with the healing of the body; Lk 7[50], and other instances where spiritual effects are secured by faith, which are to be found in the Synoptics, and more copiously in the Fourth Gospel). His 'training of the Twelve' was not wholly fruitless. They gave Him what He sought, though not with the largeness and simplicity for which He longed.

It is noteworthy that their faith in Him is not to be gauged by its verbal expression. That might be surprisingly full, while the faith might be most rudimentary; or the expression of faith might wellnigh be silent, while yet the trust itself remained, scarce distinguishable from despair, and yet a root whence life might come. From the beginning Jesus produced an impression upon those admitted to His company, for which they felt there was only one possible interpretation; and this, even at that early stage, they stated with great fulness (Jn 1[41. 45. 49]). Jesus, however, did not consider that His end was gained, but proceeded with His education of these men, and allowed all factors in the case, especially such as seemed to exclude the possibility of Messianic glory, to make their due impress. Then, at the proper psychological moment, He put the supreme question—'Who say ye that I am?' and received from Peter's lips the confession of His Messiahship (Mt 16[16f.]). Even then Jesus was under no illusion with respect to the faith which had received such emphatic expression. He made allowances for an eclipse of faith which might seem total; but still, in spite of all appearances, He believed in His disciples' faith in Him, not indeed in their intellectual or emotional utterances, but in the surrender of their wills to Him, and their personal loyalty.

We are thus recalled to the darker side of their relations with Him. Indeed, readers of the narrative are apt to be more severe in their judgment upon the disciples than was the Master Himself. Certainly their defects and shortcomings are patent enough, and the contrast between their Master and them can scarcely be exaggerated. He has not where to lay His head; their minds are occupied with the question of rewards (Mt 19[27]). He is meek and lowly in heart; they dispute about pre-eminence (Mt 18[1-3], Lk 22[24]). His kingdom is for the poor in spirit; they lay plans for private advantage (Mt 20[20]). It is not of this world; to the end they are thinking of physical force (Lk 22[49]). He invites all to His fellowship; they are narrow and exclusive (Mk 9[38-40]). Fury is not in Him; they would invoke judgment upon adversaries (Lk 9[54-56]). They boasted their courage; but in the hour of His uttermost peril 'they all forsook him, and fled' (Mt 26[56]). There can be no doubt that these things greatly moved Him, but the note of personal offence is entirely lacking. There is astonishment at their slowness, but no bitterness or petulance: 'Do ye not remember?' (Mk 8[18]); 'Are ye also even yet without understanding?' (15[16]); 'Have ye not yet faith?' (Mk 4[40]). Sometimes silence is His severest answer: 'Lord, here are two swords! It is enough!' (Lk 22[38]). He makes His very censures the occasion of further instruction: 'It is not so among you. . . . The Son of Man came to minister' (Mk 10[43-45]). Even when His spirit was most grieved, there was no flash of resentment, but only the most poignant tenderness: 'Simon, sleepest thou? couldest thou not watch one hour?' . . . (Mk 14[37]); 'The Lord turned, and looked upon Peter' (Lk 22[61]).

This ignorance and waywardness on the part of His disciples, combined with their genuine love

for Him and His abounding love for them, constituted a very severe trial of Jesus' fidelity to His vocation. 'The greatest temptation,' says a keen analyst of character, 'is the temptation to love evil in those we love, or to be lowered into the colder moral atmosphere of intense human affection, or to shrink from what is required of us that would pain it.' Jesus loved His friends. He knew that His course of conduct would inflict upon them unspeakable disappointment and distress; and this knowledge must have filled His own heart with keenest pain. When, accordingly, the disciple who most clearly confessed His Messiahship denounced the path He had chosen, the path of suffering, as inconsistent with the rank He had led His friends to believe was His, He felt Himself assailed in what the author above quoted ventures to call His 'weakest point.' It was the Temptation repeated; and as such He repelled it with hot anger.

In the case of one of the Twelve, it is to be noted that his criticism was not a temptation, because it was not the result of uncomprehending love, but of intelligent and bitter hate. Judas discerned the inevitable issue of Jesus' line of action; perceived that it involved all his own secret ambitions in utter ruin; and in revenge determined to be the instrument of the destruction which he foresaw. Again and again Jesus interposed to save him by warnings, which Judas alone could comprehend in their dreadful significance: 'One of you shall betray me' (Jn 13[21], cf. 6[70] 'One of you [the Twelve] is a devil'). In the end He had to let him go: 'That thou doest, do quickly' (v. [27]). The depth of Jesus' acquaintance with God, the honour He put on human nature, may be measured by His dealing with Judas. There are some things God cannot do. This Divine inability Jesus recognized, and made it the norm of His own dealing with souls. We need not apologize for Jesus' choice of Judas. He chose him for the very qualities which led Him to the others, and which were, perhaps, present in Judas in a conspicuous degree. He loved him as He loved the others, and with a yet deeper yearning. But there came a time when, in imitation of the Father, He felt bound to stand aside. To have saved Judas by force would have violated the conditions under which the redemption of man is possible.

Even the briefest review of Christ's relations to His friends constrains the inference that, in the essential qualities of friendship, He is perfect; and the supposition becomes altogether reasonable, that, if He were alive now and accessible, the possession of His friendship would be salvation, and the loss of it would be the worst fate that could befall any human being.

3. Mankind.—The attitude of Jesus toward His fellow-men is determined by the function which He had been led, through His deep sympathy with God, to assume on their behalf. He believes Himself called to 'fulfil,' i.e. to perfect, and so to accomplish as permanent spiritual fact, the religion of the OT. We must not raise premature questions, but we must not evade plain facts. Jesus springs from the OT. He transcended it in this, that He believed the privileges of the New Covenant were to be verified, consummated, and bestowed upon men, through His mission. This mission He accepted, in clear prevision of what it involved, and in deep love to God and to men. It is plain that such a position carries with it unique authority, and warrants claims of extraordinary magnitude. He who knows Himself to be the mediator of the highest good to men knows Himself to be supreme among men. This consciousness is clear and unmistakable in the utterances of

Jesus. He presents Himself to men as the object of a trust and a reverence that are nothing less than religious (Mk 2[17], Lk 19[10], Mt 10[32] 18[20]). He passes verdicts upon their inner state that are not less than Divine in their insight and their absoluteness (Lk 9[57-62], Mt 9[2. 6]). He makes demands which no one has a right to make who does not know Himself to be completely the organ of the Divine authority (Mt 4[19] 9[9] 19[21] 10[37]). He claims to be the arbiter of the final destinies of men (Mk 8[38], Mt 7[21-23] 13[41] 16[27], together with the undoubted teaching of the so-called eschatological discourses Mt 25[1ff.]), a function which in the OT belongs not even to Messiah, but to Jehovah alone (Jl 3[12], Mal 3[1] 4[3]). Such a consciousness, whose intensity suggests, if it does not prove, a unique constitution of the person of Christ, throws into high relief aspects of the character of Christ which seem at a cursory glance incongruous with it.

(1) *Lowliness.*—The self-assertion of Jesus is not the assertion of a self independent in its power and dignity, but of a self which has no interest save the cause of God, no glory that is not His. At the heart of the self-assertion of Jesus there is profound self-renunciation. It would be a mistake to describe Jesus as selfless. He has a self, which He might have made independent of God, which, however, in perfect freedom of act, He surrendered wholly to God. The lowliness of Christ, accordingly, is not mere modesty or diffidence. It is the quality of a self, at once asserted and denied. This paradox is carried out during His whole career. In youth, when the purpose of His life is being formed, there is no irritable self-consciousness. In manhood, when the knowledge of His mission is clear and full, and the spiritual distance which separated Him from other men is obvious to His inward eye, there is no outward separateness of manner. The life of the common people was His life, without any trace of condescension or hint of masquerade. His acceptance of the lowly conditions of His life is so complete, that there is no sense of incongruity on His part between what He was and the world He lived in. In His teaching He is able to attack pride without any risk of having imputed to Him a pride more subtle and more offensive. More remarkable still, He offers Himself as a pattern of the very humility He is inculcating, without raising any suspicion of unreality. The words, 'I am meek and lowly in heart' (Mt 11[29]), on the lips of any other man, would refute the claim they make. In His case it is not so. They mean that the self which lays its yoke on men is already crucified, and has no claim to make on its own behalf. Toward the close of His life its open secret is given, when, at the Last Supper, in full consciousness of His personal dignity, He washed the feet of those who, He knew, would fail Him in the end, and of one by whose impending treachery His own would soon be nailed to the cross.

(2) *Considerateness.*—With His idea of man and His conception of His vocation, it was impossible for Jesus to regard human personality as other than sacred. All the dues of humanity, accordingly, He paid with scrupulous exactitude. It would be superfluous to search in the narratives for instances of His justice, honesty, and truth. The distinctiveness of His calling kept Him apart from the ecclesiastical and political institutions of His country; but He was careful not to disturb them, even when He felt most critical of them (Mt 17[24-27], Mk 12[17]), and the charge of rebellion was readily seen by Pilate to be baseless. The same distinctiveness deprived Him of a business career, and, therefore, of the sphere wherein many virtues are most severely tried; but it is noteworthy that the disciple company had a treasurer,

whose duty it was to take care of the money intrusted to him, and whose dishonesty became a step toward Calvary (Jn 12[6]). Towards individuals His attitude was wholly without respect of persons. He paid men the honour of being perfectly frank and fearless in all His dealings with them. He did them the justice of letting them know the judgment He passed upon them. Herod, Pilate, the Pharisees, stood before His bar and heard their sentence. His fairness is never more conspicuous than in His dealing with Judas, whom He would not permit to suppose that he was undetected, Jesus fully recognizing that a man's probation can be carried on only in the light.

But there is due to human nature more than the strictest honesty or truth. Jesus' authority over men, instead of leading Him to be careless in the handling of a soul, impelled Him to an exquisite carefulness which extended from the needs of the body to the more delicate concerns of the mind. If He imposes heavy tasks, He remembers the frailty of the human frame: 'Come ye apart, and rest awhile' (Mk 6[31]). If the coming grief saddens His companions, He turns from His own far deeper sorrow to still their tumultuous distress: 'Let not your heart be troubled, neither let it be afraid' (Jn 14[1]). If He must rebuke, His reproaches pass into excuses: 'The spirit indeed is willing, but the flesh is weak' (Mt 26[41]). Most lovely of all is His treatment of those who might seem to have forfeited all claim to respect. He laboured by a more emphatic courtesy, a more tender chivalry, to bind up the broken self-respect, and to rebuke that insolent contempt of the sinful and degraded which so deeply dishonours God. Before the ideal in publican and harlot He bowed in reverence, and constituted Himself its resolute defender.

(3) *Compassion.*—The respect which Jesus has for human nature becomes, in presence of human need, a very passion for helping, healing, saving. The qualities which most deeply impressed the men and women of His day, and which shine most clearly in His portrait, are not His supernatural gifts, but His unwearied goodness, His sincere kindness, His great gentleness, His deep and tender pity. By these He has captivated the imagination, and won the reverence of humanity. The narratives have felt the throbbing compassion of Jesus' heart, and have used the very phrase with a sweet monotony (Mk 1[41], Mt 20[34] 9[36], Lk 7[13], Mt 14[14] 15[32]).

The compassion of Jesus is manifest in *the wonderful works* which are ascribed to Him. All of them, with the exception of 'the coin in the fish's mouth' and 'the withering of the fruitless fig-tree,' which have a special didactic aim, are works of mercy. They are, no doubt, proofs of power; but they are essentially instances of the sympathy of Jesus, in virtue of which He enters into the fulness of human need. The instinct of one Evangelist has no doubt directed subsequent thought toward the truth. When Jesus wrought His healing miracles, He was fulfilling a prophecy which had special reference to sin (Mt 8[17]). By no easy exercise of power did He relieve the distresses of men, but by a real assumption of their sorrow. Every such act stands in organic connexion with the deed of the Cross, in which He bare the sin which is the root of all human infirmities.

Yet more conspicuously the compassion of Jesus is to be seen in the *method of His ministry*, which led Him to seek the company of sinners, not because their sin was not abhorrent to His nature, but because He loved His vocation, and loved those who were its objects. The disinterestedness which Plato ascribes to the true physician deepens, in the case of this Healer of men, to a pure and burning passion. Twice His compassion found vent in tears: once in presence of man's mortality, once in sight of the city whose abuse of privilege had earned extremity of woe. There are depths here we cannot fathom, since there is mercifully denied us perfect knowledge of the evil which Jesus'. knowledge of God fully disclosed to His view. Knowing God, living in unbroken fellowship with Him, Jesus knew, as none other could, what sin and death were. He lived and died with the spectacle of their power ever before Him. His knowledge is the measure of His compassion, and both are immeasurable.

(4) *Forgiveness.*—Without doubt, Jesus believed Himself to be the agent of the Divine love, the mediator of the Divine forgiveness. He had power *on earth* to forgive sins (Mt 9⁶). This forgiveness He announced as the prerogative of His office; but the actual experience of forgiveness, as the redeeming act of God, came through the love which Jesus Himself manifested. His welcome of sinners was their reception into the fellowship of God. This is a fact which no prejudice against doctrine ought to invalidate, which, probably, no doctrine can adequately explain. Hence follow two features of the portrait of Christ, each most significant and suggestive. He accepted the gratitude of forgiven sinners as though He were God's own representative (Lk 7⁴⁰⁻⁵⁰); and He regarded sins committed against Himself as committed against God, who in His mission was seeking to save men. His forgiveness of such offences, accordingly, is not measurable in terms of quantity—unto seven times or seventy times seven; but has the very qualities of boundlessness and inexhaustibleness which He attributes to the forgiveness of God. There is only one limitation, and that does not belong to the character of God, but to the constitution of human nature. There is a sin which hath never forgiveness (Mt 12³¹·³², Mk 3²⁸·²⁹, Lk 12¹⁰). It does not consist, however, in a definite offence against God or His Christ, but in a frame of mind, an habitude of soul, which is psychologically beyond reach of forgiveness. Apart from this limit, which on God's side is none, forgiveness is infinite.

When, accordingly, we proceed to examine the sins committed against Jesus, we perceive that they form an ascending scale of guilt, according to the advancing measure of light and privilege against which they were committed, and so also of pain to Him and of peril to the transgressors. First, there is the sin of those who were directly responsible for His death. Dark and dreadful though this was, compounded of the vilest qualities of polluted human nature, it was, nevertheless, even in its deadliest guilt, not a sin against absolutely clear conviction. Hence the victim of so much wrong prays even while the nails rend His flesh: 'Father, forgive them; for they know not what they do' (Lk 23³⁴). It is impossible to narrow the scope of this petition to the unconscious instruments, the Roman soldiers; it must extend also to the Jews themselves, to the mob, and even to their more guilty rulers. Peter (Ac 3¹⁷) and Paul (1 Co 2⁸) cannot have been mistaken in their interpretation of the crime which slew their Lord.

Second, there is the sin of those who deserted Him in His need, and especially of him who denied his Master with oaths and curses. They were bound to Jesus by every tie of affection and of loyalty. He trusted them, and they failed Him. Yet it could not be said of them that they *knew* what they did. Their action was without premeditation, without real sense of its meaning. A spasm of overpowering fear confounded their intelligence and destroyed their resolution. Shameful it was, and must have wrung the heart of Jesus with anguish; yet at its worst it was committed against the Son of Man, not against the Holy Spirit. They knew not what they were about to do, but He knew (Mk 14²⁷), and broke their hearts with His free forgiveness (v.⁷²).

Third, the sin of Judas. Of all the crimes of which guilty man is capable, treachery is, in the judgment of all men, the most dreadful; and therefore Dante (*Inferno*, xxxi. 134) has placed Judas in the jaws of Lucifer. Did Judas, then, commit the sin against the Holy Spirit? It is profitless to discuss the question. No absolute verdict is possible. It is certain that Jesus dealt with Judas, in clear light of truth, with the utmost consideration, and with far-reaching forbearance. Appeal after appeal He made to him, seeking to reveal him to himself, while scrupulously shielding him from the suspicions of his fellows, and retaining him to the last possible moment within the sphere of loving influence. Finally, He gave him that permission to do wrong which human freedom wrings from Divine omnipotence, and which is, at the same time, God's severest judgment upon the sinner (Jn 13²⁷, Mt 26⁵⁰ RV). Who can tell if it be not also God's last offer of mercy? In the end (perhaps not too late), the goodness of Jesus smote with overwhelming force upon the conscience of Judas. He 'repented himself' (Mt 27³). Whatever value may be attached to such repentance, whatever destiny may have awaited Judas beyond the veil of flesh, which he so violently tore aside, there can be at least no more impressive testimony to the forbearance, the love, and the wisdom of Jesus, than this overwhelming remorse.

V. THE VIRTUES OF HIS VOCATION.—The end for which Jesus lived determined all His actions, and called into exercise all the virtues of His character, as well the more general characteristics of spiritual-mindedness, love to God, and love to men, as the specific virtues of His social relations. The vocation of Jesus, however, as Servant of the Lord was definite; and with respect to it He had a definite work to do. Questions as to the conceptions which it implies with respect to the constitution of Christ's person do not now concern us. But we are concerned to observe that, in His discharge of His duty, certain aspects of His character shine forth with special beauty. They are such as these—

1. Faithfulness.—There is an unmistakable note of compulsion in His life. He has received a precise charge, and He will carry it out with absolute precision and unswerving fidelity. This is the mind of the boy, when as yet the nature of His mission cannot have been fully before Him (Lk 2⁴⁹). This is the conviction of the man, who has come to know what office He holds, and what is the thing He has to do or endure (Mt 16²¹, Mk 8³¹). Many specific expressions (*e.g.* Jn 4³⁴ 9⁴·⁵ 11⁹·¹⁰) and the whole tenor of His life convey the same impression of a man looking forward to a goal, in itself most terrible, yet pressing toward it with unwavering determination. The imperative of duty, and the burden of inexorable necessity, are laid upon His conscience; and He responds with complete obedience.

The author of the Epistle to the Hebrews, who displays a singular insight into the ethical conditions of Christ's work, mentions the virtue of fidelity as being conspicuous in 'the Apostle and High Priest of our confession' (He 3²·⁶), and draws a far-reaching parallel and contrast between Him and Moses, as between a son and a servant. In filial faithfulness there are three aspects: (*a*) perfect identification with the Father's will, (*b*) entire absorption in the Father's concerns, (*c*) free access to the Father's resources; and these are plainly seen in Christ's discharge of His duty. There is not the slightest trace of servility. The will to which He yielded absolute devotion is that of One whom He perfectly loved and trusted, to whom He could freely come for everything He required. The absolute control of the Divine resources, which is attributed to Him in the Fourth Gospel (Jn 13³), is borne out by every trait of the Synoptic portrait. He was not toiling with inadequate resources at an uncomprehended task. Even when the strain upon His will is heaviest, and His whole soul shrinks from what lies before Him, there is one word which delivers His faithfulness from any suspicion of bondage : '*Father*, if it be possible' . . . (Mt 26³⁹. ⁴², Mk 14³⁶, Lk 22⁴²).

2. Courage.—The courage of Jesus Christ is the crown of His faithfulness. It was not tested by such occasions as the sinking ship or the stricken field, but by conditions yet more severe. Outraged prejudice, wounded pride of caste, threatened privilege, were banded together to destroy Him. They disguised themselves in zeal for the honour of God. They, no doubt, attracted to their side sincere, though unenlightened, loyalty to His cause ; and Jesus must have known the reformer's keenest pain, the sense of wounding good and true men. They sought alliances with powers most alien to their professed aims. They found support in the ignorant enthusiasm of the multitude, who mistook the aims of Jesus, and in the more culpable misunderstanding of His disciples and friends. The Fourth Gospel is surely historic in representing the breach between Jesus and the leaders of the religious world of His day as having taken place in the opening weeks of His ministry. It is inconceivable that the wide divergence of His views from those of the Pharisees and Sadducees should not have been manifest in the very first announcement of them. He certainly was not, and His adversaries could not have been, blind to the issues of the controversy. It had not proceeded far, when it became apparent to them that it could be terminated only by their defeat or by His destruction. With unscrupulous plans and bitter hate they laboured to compass His ruin. With sublime courage He persevered in His vocation, though He was well aware that every step He took only made the end more certain. When the end comes, it finds Him spiritually prepared. He moves with firm and equal tread. From the loving fellowship of the Supper He passes, without bewilderment, to the conflict of Gethsemane. From the shadow of the trees and the darker shade of His unknown agony, He goes to face the traitor, with no other tremor than that of amazement at such consummate wickedness (Lk 22⁴⁸) ; and surrenders Himself to the instruments of injustice, less their captive than their conqueror. Amid the worst tortures men can inflict, we hear no murmur. We do not merely observe, with what of admiration it might have deserved, a stoical fortitude, which proudly repels every assault on the self-sufficiency of the human spirit. We observe a more moving spectacle, the Servant of the Lord accepting unfathomed pain as the crown of His vocation, thus rendering to the Father a perfect obedience, and finishing the work given Him to do.

3. Patience.—It is an error to describe patience as a 'passive' virtue, if by that epithet is indicated the spirit which makes no resistance, because resistance is seen to be futile. Patience is rather the associate of courage, and springs from the same root, namely, identification of will with a great and enduring purpose. Jesus has made the eternal purpose of God for the redemption of man the controlling principle of His life ; and therefore He is enabled to be patient, in the widest and deepest meanings of the term. *He patiently waits for God.* This lesson He learned from the OT ;

this gift He acquired in that deep communion with God, which was the privilege of the OT believer, and is the heart of all true religion. Nothing is more remarkable in a man so intense, endowed, moreover, with supernatural powers, than His reserve. He is eager for the achievement of His task, straitened till His baptism be accomplished (Lk 12⁵⁰). Yet He is never betrayed into rashness of speech or action. He maintains His attitude of intent expectancy. The idea of an 'hour' for Himself, and for His work, and for His great victory, known to the Father, and made known at His discretion, lies deep in the heart of Jesus (Mk 13³² 14⁴¹, Lk 10²¹, Jn 2⁴ 4²¹. ²³ 5²⁵. ²⁸ 7³⁰ 8³⁰ 12²³. ²⁷ 13¹ 17¹). To Him time was the measure of God's purpose ; death, 'God's instant.' He μακρο-θυμεῖ, *suffers long with wayward or injurious persons.* God hides Him in His pavilion from the strife of tongues, and from that sense of personal injury which enkindles temper and provokes unadvised speech. So identified is He with God, that offences against Himself lose themselves in Divine forgiveness. His meekness is not weakness, but that amazing strength which can take up a personal wrong, and carry it into the Divine presence with vicarious suffering. He ὑπομένει, *endures in undying hope the severest trial* (He 12². ³). The idea that His death was unexpected by Jesus, and felt by Him to demand an explanation which He attempted to provide in obscure suggestions and laboured analogies, is most false to the profound unity of His character. The Cross is the key to His character. This was the climax of His mission, the introduction to the victory which lay beyond ; and this, when it came, He endured with a 'brave patience' which was rooted in His assurance that His vocation was from God and could not fail. This was His victory, even His patience (Rev 1⁹).

4. Calmness.—The patience of Jesus has for its inner correlative deep serenity of soul. He lived in God ; and, therefore, He was completely master of Himself. We observe in Him, as a matter of course, that control of the so-called lower desires of our nature which was the Greek conception of sober-mindedness or temperance. We see, beyond this, a more remarkable proof of self-possession in His control over the very motives and desires which impelled Him to devote His life to the service of God and man. There is no feeling of strain in the utterances of His soul as He speaks of or to His Father. The phenomena of excitement or rapture, which disfigure so many religious biographies, are wholly absent from the record of His deepest experiences. In His attitude toward men, whom He regarded it as His mission to save, there is perfect sanity. The harsh or strident note, which is scarcely ever absent in the speeches of reformers, is never audible in His words. His love for men is not a mountain torrent, but a deep, calm current, flowing through all His activities. We cannot, with verbal exactness, attribute to Him the 'enthusiasm of humanity,' which the author of *Ecce Homo* regards as the essential quality of a Christian in relation to his fellow-men, if, at least, the phrase suggest even the slightest want of balance, or any ignorance of the issues of action, or any carelessness with respect to them. He is the minister of the Divine purposes, never of His own emotions, however pure and lofty these may be. Yet we are not to impute to Him any unemotional callousness. He never lost His calmness ; but He was not always calm. He repelled temptation with deep indignation (Mk 8³³). Hypocrisy roused Him to a flame of judgment (Mk 3⁵ 11¹⁵⁻¹⁷, Mt 23¹⁻³⁶). Treachery shook Him to the very centre of His being (Jn 13²¹). The waves of human sorrow broke over Him with a greater grief than wrung the bereaved sisters (Jn 11³³⁻³⁵).

There were times when He bore an unknown agony, which could be shared by none, though He sought for human sympathy up to the very gates of the sanctuary of pain (Jn 12²⁷, Mk 14³²⁻³⁴). Yet, whatever His soul's discipline might be, He never lost His self-control, was never distracted or afraid, but remained true to His mission and to His Father. He feels anger, or sorrow, or trouble, but these emotions are under the control of a will that is one with the Divine will, and therefore are comprehended within the perfect peace of a mind stayed on God.

5. Self-sacrifice.—'Christ pleased not Himself' (Ro 15³). These words, brief though they be, sum up the character of Christ as St. Paul conceived it. They convey, without doubt, the impression made by the record of His life. If this estimate is just, if Christ was an absolutely unselfish man, if He made a full sacrifice of Himself, His character stands alone, unique in the moral universe. We cannot make this statement without raising problems of immense difficulty, which it is the business of theology to face. But no mystery beyond ought to restrict our acknowledgment of ethical fact. Christ had a self, like other men, and might have made it, in its intense individuality, His end, laying a tax upon the whole universe in order to satisfy it. The ideal of self-satisfaction was necessarily present to His mind, inasmuch as it is inevitably suggested in all self-consciousness. It was definitely presented to Him in His temptation in the wilderness. But once for all in that initial conflict, and again and again in life, He beat back the temptation, rejected that ideal, surrendered Himself to His vocation, and sought no other satisfaction than its fulfilment. His life is a sacrifice. He set the world behind His back, and had no place or portion in it (Lk 9⁵⁸). The way He went was the path of self-denial and cross-bearing (Mk 8³⁴, Jn 12²⁵·²⁶). His death was a sacrifice. The death of one whose life was a sacrifice must have had sacrificial significance for God and man. It could not be a fate to be explained by an after-thought. It must have been essentially an action, a voluntary offering made to God, laid on the altar of human need. The story of the Passion, read from the point where He steadfastly set His face to go to Jerusalem to the point where He went, *as He was wont*, to the Mount of Olives, and so through every detail of suffering, portrays, indeed, one led as a lamb to the slaughter, but as certainly one who, having power to keep His life, laid it down, in free surrender, in deep love to the Father (Jn 10¹⁷·¹⁸). He was endowed with powers which He might have exerted to deliver Himself from the hand of His enemies; He did not so exert them. He did not even employ them to win one slightest alleviation of His sufferings. He might have saved Himself; yet, with deeper truth, Himself He could not save. The self-sacrifice of Christ is the foundation of the Kingdom of God, the purchase of man's redemption, the basis of that morality which finds in Him its standard and its example.

Concluding estimate.—When we have studied the character of Christ from the points of view suggested in the foregoing scheme, we are conscious that we are only on the threshold of a great subject, to whose wealth of meaning no formal study can do justice. The character of Christ presents 'unsearchable riches' to every sympathetic student. Every generation, since His bodily presence was withdrawn, has been pursuing that investigation; none has comprehended His fulness, or been forced to look elsewhere for information and inspiration. He has laid upon us the necessity of continuously seeking to understand Him, and of applying, in the manifold occasions and circumstances of life, the fulness of the moral ideal presented in Himself.

1. When, however, we pause in our detailed study —to whatever length we may have carried it—or in our application of His precept and example— however successfully, or with whatever wistful consciousness of failure, we may have pursued it; when we lift our gaze afresh to the portrait presented in the Gospels, the impression deepens upon us with new and overwhelming conviction, that in Christ there is achieved, as a fact of the moral universe, **goodness**, not merely comparative, but absolute. It is not merely that among the choice spirits of our race He occupies the front rank, but that He stands alone. Jesus Christ is the Master of all who seek to know God, in the sense that His character is supreme and final in the moral progress of humanity. He is completely human. Like men, He pursued the pathway of development. Like men, He was assailed by temptation, and waged incessant warfare with evil suggestions. Yet He is absolutely unique. He is not merely better than other men. He is what all men ought to be. It is not merely that we see in Him an approximation to the moral ideal, nearer and more successful than is to be discerned in any other man; but that we find in Him the moral ideal, once for all realized and incarnated, so that no man can ever go beyond Him, while all men in all ages will find it their strength and joy to grow up toward the measure of His stature. Again and again we are made to feel, when we contemplate such virtues as have been adverted to in the preceding pages, *e.g.* love to God, love to men, consecration, unselfishness, and the like, that there is the note of absoluteness in His attainment. Between Him and the ideal there is no hairbreadth of disparity. His fulfilment of the will of God is complete. What God meant man to be is at once disclosed and finished.

2. The positive conception of the absolute goodness of Jesus carries with it the negative conception of His **sinlessness.** As we stand before the figure in the Gospels, our sense of His perfection reaches special solemnity and tenderness in the impression of His stainless and lovely purity. Attempts, no doubt, have been made to fasten some charge of sin on Jesus, *e.g.* that of a hasty or imperious temper; or even to extract from Himself some acknowledgment of imperfection (Mk 10¹⁸). These attempts have totally failed, and have exhibited nothing so clearly as the fact that they are afterthoughts, designed to establish the *a priori* dogma that sinlessness is an impossibility. Such procedure is, of course, wholly unscientific. If a record, otherwise trustworthy, presents us with the portrait of a sinless man, we are not entitled to reject its testimony because, if we accept it, we shall have to abandon a dogma or revise an induction. When, accordingly, we study the NT with unprejudiced mind, two great certainties are established beyond question.

(1) *The impression of His sinlessness made upon His disciples.* —Some of these men had been in close contact with Him, a fellowship so intimate that it was impossible that they could be mistaken in Him. Through this intimacy their moral ideas were enlarged and enriched; their spiritual insight was made delicate and true. The men who created the ethic of the NT are the spiritual leaders of the human race, and they owed their inspiration to their Master. They knew all the facts. They were spiritually competent to form a sound estimate. Without a tinge of hesitation they ascribe to Him complete separation from the very principle of evil (1 P 2²², 2 Co 5²¹, 1 Jn 3⁵, He 4¹⁵ 7²⁶). They assign to Him an office which required absolute sinlessness, knowing that any proof of deviation

from the holiness of God would have reduced the claim they made on behalf of their Master to utter confusion (Ac 3[14] 7[52] 22[14], 1 Jn 2[1]). A group of men, who knew Christ thoroughly, believed Him to be sinless. A generation, which had the facts fully before them, accepted this as the truth regarding Jesus of Nazareth. Add to this the mysterious effect the personality of Jesus had upon those whose contact with Him was brief, even momentary — Pilate (Lk 23[4]), Pilate's wife (Mt 27[19]), the centurion who superintended the judicial murder (Mk 15[39], Lk 23[47]), the malefactor who died beside Him (Lk 23[40ff.]). Among all the witnesses the traitor himself is the clearest and fullest (Mt 27[4]).

The knowledge which spirit has of spirit, the insight of our moral nature, the verdict of conscience, are all confounded if the taint of sin lay on the soul of Jesus.

(2) *His own self-knowledge and His own self-witness*, which establish the fact of a conscience at once perfectly true and absolutely void of any sense of sin.

(a) He taught His disciples to pray for forgiveness; but He never set them the example of asking it on His own behalf. He was their example in prayer as in all else; but that which is a constituent element in the prayers of all sinful men, the confession of sin and the supplication of forgiveness, does not appear in any prayer of His. There is even a scrupulous avoidance of any phrase which would seem to include Himself in the class of those whose prayers must contain this element, e.g. Mt 6[9. 14] 7[11], where 'ye' is emphatic and significant.

(b) He is absolutely intolerant of evil. He counsels the extreme of loss in preference to its presence (Mk 9[43-49]). He traces it to its source in heart and will, and demands cleansing and renewal there (Mk 7[15-23]). Yet nowhere does He bewail His own pollution, or seek for cleansing. He lives a life of strenuous devotion; but there is not a hint of any process of mortifying sin in His members. Such unconsciousness of sin is a psychological impossibility, if His was simply the goodness of an aspiring, struggling, human soul, striving after the ideal, and ever drawing nearer it. By the very height of His ideal He would be convicted of shortcoming. But nothing in His language or bearing suggests, even remotely, such a conviction. We know this Man, and we know that in His own consciousness there was no gulf between Him and perfection, and that to His own deepest feeling there was between Him and the Father perfect moral identity. If this Man be a sinner, the competence of the moral judgment is destroyed for ever.

(c) He required moral renewal on the part of all men (Mt 18[3], Jn 3[5]). But there is no record of the conversion of Jesus, and there is no hint of a belief on His part that He needed it. True, He accepted, or rather demanded, baptism of John; but His action, as interpreted by Himself, plainly implies that in uniting Himself with the sinful people, He was under constraint of love, and not under the compulsion of an alarmed and awakened conscience. That there was anything in His experience analogous to a death to sin of His own, and a rising into a life of new obedience, is contradicted by every line of the Gospel portrait.

(d) He loved and pitied sinners. His sympathetic treatment of them stands in lovely contrast with the cruelty of the Pharisaic method. Yet, in all His dealing with sinners, He preserves the note of ethical distinction. He unites Himself with sinners. His sin-bearing is a fact, even before Calvary. Yet at the point of closest and most sympathetic union with sinners there is complete inward aloofness from their sin. The contention that only a sinner can properly understand

a sinner and fully sympathize with him, is purely *a priori*, and absolutely refuted by the ministry of Jesus. Did any philanthropist, any lover of souls, ever sympathize as Jesus did with sinners? Long before Christ, Plato had noted and disposed of the fallacy that a man needs to be tainted with sin before he can effectively deal with it. 'Vice can never know both itself and virtue; but virtue in a well-instructed nature will in time acquire a knowledge at once of itself and of vice. The virtuous man, therefore, and not the vicious man, will make the wise judge' (*Republic*, 409). Let us add, not a wise judge merely, but a loving friend and helper. Sin is a hindrance, not a help, in loving. The crowning help which Jesus bestowed on sinners was the forgiveness of sins. This was beyond doubt a Divine prerogative, both in the minds of those who observed His conduct and in His own. If He exercised it, therefore, while aware of His own sinfulness, He was uttering blasphemy, and the worst verdict of His critics was justifiable. His forgiving sin is absolute proof that to His own consciousness He was sinless.

(e) He died for sinners. What has just been said of His forgiving sinners applies with yet mightier force to His deed in dying. He believed it to be of such unique value for God that, on the ground of it, He could forgive the sins of men. Without trenching on the discussions that gather round the death of Christ, and without attempting any dogmatic statement, we are safe in asserting that to Jesus His blood was covenant blood, ratifying the New Covenant which had been the profound anticipation of OT prophecy (Jer 31[31-34]). No man, conscious of being himself a sinner, could have supposed that his death would create the Covenant and procure the forgiveness of sins. Since Jesus certainly believed that His death would have this stupendous effect, it is certain also that He believed Himself to be utterly removed from the need of forgiveness.

What is thus to be traced, as the implication of our Lord's dealing with sinners, becomes in the Fourth Gospel His explicit self-assertion. It may be that, had these utterances stood alone, they might have been discounted as due to dogmatic preconceptions on the part of the writer. Since, however, they are in complete psychological harmony with the whole Synoptic portraiture, they cannot be thus explained away. They are, besides, precisely what might be looked for, and carry with them strong internal evidence of their genuineness. Innocence may be unconscious of itself, but not that sinlessness which is the correlate of perfection. Self-knowledge must accompany that goodness which grows toward maturity, and maintains its integrity against temptation. Jesus did not live in a golden mist. He may be trusted in His self-witness; and the occasions mentioned in the Fourth Gospel on which He bore such witness are precisely those of great trial or deep experience, when a man is permitted, nay required, to state the truth regarding Himself. He bears witness: (a) before His enemies, as part of His self-defence (Jn 8[46]), arguing from His purity of heart to His undimmed vision of things unseen; (β) to His own, as example and encouragement (Jn 15[10]), revealing the secret of a serene and joyful life, as part of His last charge and message; (γ) to His Father, in an hour of sacred communion (Jn 17[4]), as the review and estimate of His life; (δ) on the cross (Jn 19[30]), as the summary of His long warfare, the note of final achievement of the whole will of God.

If Jesus were in any degree sinful, He must have known it, and had He known it He would have told us. If He knew it and did not tell us, we should have just cause of complaint against

Him, since, in that case, He must have allowed a false impression to grow up regarding Him. If He was sinful and did not know it, He must fall out of the rank of the best men, because in that case He lacks the noblest and most moving element in the character of those who have agonized heavenward,—a deep sense of demerit and an adoring sense of the grace of God. But, in truth, the mere statement of these alternatives and inferences is intolerable. The conscience of the race has been created by Jesus Christ. His character is at once the rebuke and the inspiration of every age. He is the moral ideal realized once for all. There is no other, no higher goodness than that which is incarnated in Him; and, as has been said, 'the difference between the highest morality that exists and a perfect one is a difference not of degree, but of kind' (Davidson, *Theol. of O.T.*).

To this affirmation regarding Jesus we are constrained to come. Nothing less is a fair interpretation of the record. He stands alone. Man though He be, He is distinguished from all men by unique moral and spiritual excellence. Between Him and God there is a relationship to which there is no parallel in the case of any other man. The absolute distinctiveness of the character of Christ is not a dogma, constructed under philosophical or theological influences. It is a fact to which every line of the portrait bears unanswerable evidence. Stated as a fact, however, it becomes at once a problem which cannot be evaded. 'Whence hath this man these things?' How the answer shall be framed,—whether the Nicene formula is adequate, or, if not, how it is to be corrected and supplemented, is the task laid upon the intellect and conscience of the Church of to-day. It is certain that upon the earnestness and honesty with which she takes up that task will depend her vitality and her permanence. It is certain also that intellectual progress in apprehending the mystery of the Person of Christ will be conditioned by moral progress in apprehending, appropriating, and reproducing the perfection of His character.

LITERATURE.—The main source for any character study of Christ must be sought in the Gospels themselves. The *Lives* of Christ will, of course, give abundant information and help: Neander, Edersheim, Didon, Weiss, Beyschlag, Keim. Works dealing directly with the character of Christ as an ethical study seem to be rare. All Dr. Bruce's works are penetrated by the ethical spirit: *Training of the Twelve, Kingdom of God, Galilean Gospel, Apologetics, Humiliation of Christ.* Seeley's *Ecce Homo*, and Abbott's *Philochristus* are helpful. An anonymous work, *The Gospel for the Nineteenth Century* (Longmans, Green, & Co.) has a most valuable study of the character of Christ. Robinson's *Studies in the Character of Christ* (Longmans, Green, & Co., 1900), Ullmann's *Sinlessness of Jesus*, Forrest's *Christ of History and Experience*, and Prof. Garvie's recent papers in the *Expositor* on 'The Inner Life of Christ,' Godet's *Defence of the Christian Faith*, Mackintosh's *Primer of Apologetics*, Nicoll's *The Church's One Foundation*, all deal with aspects of the subject. References also are to be found in works on *Systematic Theology*, by such writers as Dorner, Martensen, Oosterzee, and in last-named author's *Image of Christ*, as well as in treatises on *Christian Ethics*; cf. also Stalker's *Imago Christi*; Fairbairn's *Studies in the Life of Christ*, ch. iii.; Herrmann's *Communion with God*, p. 70ff.; Liddon's *BL*, Lect. iv.

T. B. KILPATRICK.

CHARGER.—The utensil referred to (Mt 14[8.11], Mk 6[25.28]) was a flat tray or salver (Gr. πίναξ) with a narrow rim, and was usually made of brass, the surface being plain or ornamented with engraved or embossed designs, and varying in size from one to three feet in diameter. At an Oriental meal the tray is laid upon a low stool, the dishes being placed upon it, while those who partake sit or recline around it. The tray is also carried around by an attendant when presenting wine or drinks composed of water flavoured with lemon, rose, or violet essences.

In the two passages that describe Salome's request at Herod's birthday feast, the charger is mentioned as an essential part of the stipulation. In both narratives the demand is for the head of John the Baptist in a charger. In explanation of this it has to be noted that the daughter of Herodias had demeaned herself to play the part of a hired Oriental dancer, with the usual accompaniments of paint and jewellery, loose and showy costume, and gestures of indelicate suggestion. The appearance and dancing of the young princess had captivated the guests already exhilarated by the royal banquet, and prepared them to applaud anything clever and audacious from the same person. The king entered into the spirit of the occasion, and treating her as a paid performer, offered her for her services anything she might desire. And so when she requested that the head of John the Baptist might be served up to her on one of the trays from which the guests were being regaled, the unfeeling jest implied that this would be to her both her professional fee and her portion of the feast.

It was John the Baptist's last testimony against the artificial and insincere spirit of the age. When such a crime could be so lightly committed, the day of the Lord upon the nation could not be far off. Afterwards, when Herod addressed his questions to Christ, it was to find Him absolutely silent (Lk 23[9]). The atrophy of moral feeling may be gradual, and be relieved by intervals of wrestling and regret, but at last unwillingness to feel becomes inability to feel.

A touch of witty caricature or grotesque exaggeration has often since then given pass and plausibility to something essentially wrong and in itself repulsive. When society is made selfish and artificial by luxury and the love of pleasure, it will keep its oaths of personal vanity although the gratification should stifle the voice of sincerity and truth.   G. M. MACKIE.

CHICKENS.—See ANIMALS, p. 64[a].

CHIEF PRIESTS (ἀρχιερεῖς). — In the Gospels ἀρχιερεύς properly denotes the individual who for the time being held the office of Jewish high priest; and when the word occurs in its singular form, 'high priest' is the almost invariable rendering it receives throughout the NT, both in AV and RV (in Lk 3[2] ἐπὶ ἀρχιερέως Ἄννα καὶ Καιάφα is rendered in AV 'Annas and Caiaphas being the high priests,' and in RV 'in the high priesthood of Annas and Caiaphas.' In Ac 19[14] ἀρχιερεύς, as applied to 'one Sceva, a Jew,' is rendered 'chief of the priests' in AV, 'a chief priest' in RV). For a general treatment of the office of the ἀρχιερεύς in NT times, and also of the use of the word as a title of Christ by the author of Hebrews, reference must be made to art. HIGH PRIEST. But in the Gospels and Acts the word occurs very frequently in the plural form (cf. Jos. *Vita*, 38, *BJ* IV. iii. 7, 9, 10, and *passim*), and on all such occasions, both in AV and RV, it is translated 'chief priests.' It is these ἀρχιερεῖς, not the ἀρχιερεύς proper, with whom we are concerned in the present article.

The precise meaning of ἀρχιερεῖς, as we meet it in the Gospels and Josephus, is not easily determined. A common explanation used to be that these 'chief priests' were the heads or presidents of the twenty-four courses into which the Jewish priesthood was divided (1 Ch 24[4], 2 Ch 8[14], Lk 1[5.8]; Jos. *Ant.* VII. xiv. 7), or at least that these heads of the priestly courses were included under the term (see, *e.g.*, the Lexicons of Cremer and Grimm-Thayer, *s.v.* ἀρχιερεύς; Alford on Mt 2[4]). It is true that some support for this view may be found in the expressions 'all the chief (RV 'chiefs') of the priests' (2 Ch 36[14], Neh 12[7]), 'the chief priests' (RV 'the chiefs of the priests,' Ezr 10[5]). But it is noticeable, as Schürer pointed out ('Die ἀρχιερεῖς im NT' in *SK* for 1872), that in the LXX the word ἀρχιερεῖς is never used of the heads of the priestly courses, and that the nearest approximations to this term are such phrases as ἄρχοντες τῶν πατριῶν τῶν ἱερέων (1 Ch 24⁶), ἄρχοντες τῶν ἱερέων (Neh 12⁷). And most scholars now take the view that the ἀρχιερεῖς were high priests rather than 'chief priests,' not leading representatives from the general body of the priesthood, but members of an exclusive high priestly caste.*

As applied to this high priestly class, the word ἀρχιερεῖς would seem to denote primarily the official high priest together with a group of ex-high priests. For by NT times the high priestly office had sunk far from its former greatness. It was no longer hereditary, and no longer held for life. Both Herod and the Roman legates deposed and set up high priests at their pleasure (Jos. *Ant.* XX. x. 1), as the Seleucidæ appear to have done at an earlier period (2 Mac 4²⁴; Jos. *Ant.* XII. v. 1). Thus there were usually several ex-high priests alive at the same time, and these men, though deprived of office, still retained the title of ἀρχιερεῖς and still exercised considerable power in the Jewish State (cf. Jos. *Vita*, 38, *BJ* II. xii. 6, IV. iii. 7, 9, 10, IV. iv. 3). In the notable case of Annas, we even have an ex-high priest whose influence was plainly greater than that of the ἀρχιερεύς proper (cf. Lk 3², Jn 18¹³· ²⁴, Ac 4⁶).

But Schürer further maintains that, in addition to the ex-high priests, the title was applied to the members of those families from which the high priests were usually chosen—the γένος ἀρχιερατικόν of Ac 4⁶. It appears from a statement of Josephus that the dignity of the high priesthood was confined to a few select families (*BJ* IV. iii. 6); and that this was really the case becomes clear upon an examination of the list which Schürer has compiled, from the various references given by the Jewish historian, of the twenty-eight holders of the office during the Romano-Herodian period (*HJP* II. i. 196 ff., 204). Above all, in one passage (*BJ* VI. ii. 2) Josephus, after distinguishing the υἱοὶ τῶν ἀρχιερέων from the ἀρχιερεῖς themselves, apparently combines both classes under the general designation of ἀρχιερεῖς. Schürer accordingly comes to the conclusion, which has been widely adopted, that the ἀρχιερεῖς of the NT and Josephus 'consist, in the first instance, of the high priests properly so called, *i.e.* the one actually in office and those who had previously been so, and then of the members of those privileged families from which the high priests were taken' (*op. cit.* p. 206). These, then, were in all probability the 'chief priests' of the EV. They belonged to the party of the Sadducees (Ac 5¹⁷; Jos. *Ant.* XX. ix. 1), and were, formally at least, the leading personages in the Sanhedrin.† But in NT times their influence, even in the Sanhedrin, was inferior to that of the scribes and Pharisees, who commanded the popular sympathies as the high priestly party did not (Jos. *Ant.* XIII. x. 6, XVIII. i. 4 ; cf. Ac 5³⁴ff· 23⁶ff·).

LITERATURE.—Schürer, *HJP* II. i. pp. 174–184, 195–206, and 'Die ἀρχιερεῖς im NT' in *SK*, 1872, pp. 593–657 ; Edersheim, *Life and Times of Jesus the Messiah*, i. p. 322 f. ; Ewald, *HI* vii. p. 479 ff. ; Hastings' *DB*, artt. 'Priests and Levites' and 'Priest in NT'; Hauck-Herzog, *PRE*³, art. 'Hoher Priester'; *Jewish Encyc.*, art. 'High Priest.'   J. C. LAMBERT.

CHILDHOOD.‡—i. The Childhood of Jesus.— In the Lukan narratives of the Infancy and Childhood our Lord is described both as τὸ παιδίον Ἰησοῦς

---

* In accordance with this view, Dr. Moffatt, in his *Historical New Testament*, renders ἀρχιερεῖς 'high priests,' a plan which has also been adopted by the editor of *The Corrected English New Testament* (1905).

† When ἀρχιερεῖς are mentioned in the NT along with γραμματεῖς and πρεσβύτεροι, they almost invariably occupy the first place.

‡ For the Greek terms relating to the period of childhood, see following article.

---

in His earliest years (Lk 2²⁷· ⁴⁰ : so also in Mt 2 throughout), and as Ἰησοῦς ὁ παῖς when twelve years old. Beyond, however, the brief stories of Mt 2 and Lk 2 we seek in vain for any information having any authority whatever concerning the early years of Jesus, or, for that matter, any part of His life prior to the Ministry. And what small fragments these beautiful stories are! This dearth of information for which so great a craving has been felt has repeatedly been remarked on : yet, after all, need we wonder very much at the silence of the Evangelical narratives concerning these matters? The early life of Jesus appears not to have come within their scope ; for the purpose of the Evangelical compilation was not to furnish a 'Life' in the modern sense, but to set forth a gospel. Their interest in Jesus in this respect begins pre-eminently with His baptism, as the simple exordium of St. Mark's Gospel indicates—'The beginning of the gospel of Jesus Christ.' Even in the case of St. Luke's Gospel, with its peculiar stock of early narratives in chs. 1. 2, the preface to the Acts indicates that its great concern was with the things that Jesus *did* and *taught* (Ac 1¹). Whatever may be our views as to the source and authority of what is recorded in Mt 1. 2, and whether we care to use the term 'envelope' (see Bacon, *Introd.* p. 198) or not in speaking of this portion of the Gospel, it is clear that these two chapters are something superadded to the main body of the Synoptic tradition ; and it is the same with Lk 1. 2. The main narrative begins in the case of each of these Gospels at ch. 3, where parallels with St. Mark also begin to be furnished.

All that we have in the Canonical Gospels concerning the childhood of Jesus, strictly speaking, is found in Lk 2⁴⁰⁻⁵². The first twelve years are covered by v.⁴⁰, whilst v.⁵² has to suffice for all the remaining years up to the commencement of the Ministry. The writer has nothing to tell save the story of the Visit to the Temple, and contents himself for the rest with simple general statements in Hebraic phraseology that irresistibly reminds us of what is said of 'the child Samuel' (1 S 2²¹· ²⁶). He has used practically the same formula to cover years of John the Baptist's history (1⁸⁰). As for the story of the Visit to the Temple, there is that about it which carries conviction that we have here a genuine and delightful glimpse of our Lord in His childhood—one only glimpse, which, however, suffices to show us what manner of child He was, on the principle of *ex uno disce omnes*. It is to be noted that there is no hint that He was regarded as a prodigy by His parents and the neighbours with whom He travelled up to Jerusalem. The element of the merely marvellous is at a minimum. The wonder that does show itself is in the region of the spirit, and appears in the beautiful intelligence and rare spiritual gleams (vv.⁴⁷⁻⁵⁰) which the Boy displayed, astonishing alike to the Rabbis and to His bewildered parents.

The silence and restraint of the Canonical Gospels on this subject are best appreciated when viewed against the background which the Apocryphal Gospels supply. Perhaps the most valuable service that the latter writings render is that comparison with them so strongly brings out the intrinsic value and superiority of our Canonical Gospels. They show us conclusively what men with a free hand could and would do. This is conspicuously the case with reference to the early years of Jesus. The extravagant and miraculous stories told concerning His infancy and childhood, taken by themselves, would suffice to crush out the historicity of Jesus and consign Him to the region of the mythical. We seek in vain in these writings for anything like a sober account of our Lord's growth and general history during this period: we find nothing but a congeries of grotesque wonder-tales concerning the doings of the Boy. His miraculous powers prove to be of singular advantage to Joseph, for when a beam or plank has been cut too short Jesus rectifies the mistake by merely pulling it out to the required length. He changes boys into kids, and anon restores them to their former condition. He carries both fire and water quite easily in His cloak. When playing with other boys and making figures of various beasts and birds, Jesus makes those He had formed walk and fly, and eat and drink. Wonderful works of healing are also ascribed to the Child; and some of them take strange forms, in curious contrast to the stories of the works of Jesus found in our Gospels. E.g. Simon the Cananæan as a boy is nigh to death through having been bitten by a serpent. Jesus makes the serpent itself come and suck out all the poison from the wound; then He curses it, and immediately the creature bursts asunder. The cure of demoniacs, of lepers, of the blind and maimed and sick, and the raising of the dead, are all ascribed to the Child Jesus, and always with more or less grotesqueness of circumstance. Strangest thing of all, a whole series of vindictive and destructive miracles are given which offer the most flagrant contrast to all that we know of our Lord, and which, if true, would have made Him a veritable terror to all with whom He came into contact. Boys who thwart Him in play are immediately struck dead: others who take action against Him are blinded. It is true the mischief is usually repaired by Him in response to earnest entreaty; but the vengeful malevolence is conspicuous throughout. In the stories, again, relating to His early education, Jesus is represented as being un enfant terrible to more than one master to whom He was sent to learn His letters. But a comparison of the story of the Visit to the Temple, as told in the Arabic Gospel of the Infancy and other such writings, with the narrative as we have it in Lk 2, serves as well as possible to show the untrustworthy character of the Apocryphal Gospels, whatever curious interest may attach to them. For the simple and natural statement of St. Luke, that 'all that heard Him were amazed at His understanding and His answers,' we find Him represented as not only getting the upper hand of the great Rabbis in relation to the knowledge of the Torah, but as giving profound instruction to philosophers in astronomy, natural science, and medicine, explaining to them 'physics and metaphysics, hyperphysics and hypophysics,' and many other things.

The Apocryphal writings which, in particular, abound in these tales of the childhood of Jesus, are the *Gospel of pseudo-Matthew*, the *Protevangelium of James*, the *Arabic Gospel of the Infancy*, and the *Gospel of Thomas* in its various forms. The Thomas Gospel is mainly answerable for the stories of vindictive miracles referred to above. The Syriac form of this Gospel is entitled in the MS (6th cent.) the 'Boyhood of Our Lord Jesus.'

With every allowance for whatever scanty touches of beauty and elements of value may here and there be found, a survey of this Apocryphal literature gives fresh force to Edersheim's remark (*Jesus the Messiah*, bk. ii. ch. 10): 'We dread gathering around our thoughts of Him the artificial flowers of legend.' In default, however, of authentic records there remains one expedient for meeting the deep silence of our Gospels which modern writers who essay the construction of a 'Life of Christ' are full ready to make use of. All available knowledge regarding the times in which our Lord lived, the surroundings and conditions in which He grew up, and the manner in which Jewish boys were educated (see artt. BOYHOOD and EDUCATION), can be employed to help us to form a sober and reverent conception of Him in the days of His childhood. Perhaps, indeed, such matters in their general treatment enter into some Lives of Christ even to prolixity. It is a true instinct, however, which bids us set aside early and mediæval legends, with all their naiveté, and frame a conception of Him as living the life of a normal Jewish boy of His own time and station, distinguished only by a rare personal charm of goodness and grace. The unfolding of a human life in growing beauty and nobility of character more truly proclaims 'God with us' than could such miraculous accompaniments as would tend to make the Child an object of mingled wonder and fear. Painters who have represented the Holy Child in simple human grace, without the encircling nimbus, have not on that account fallen behind others in suggesting His true Divinity.

'He came to Nazareth, *where He had been brought up*' (Lk 4[16]) — how much that phrase covers! The great factors entering into His education were home training, the synagogue both as a place of worship and as a school, the many-coloured life of the district in which He spent His youth, the natural features of the locality, and all the scenery round about Nazareth, so full of beauty and stirring historical associations. Later on, after He had attained 'years of discretion,' in our phrase, becoming a *bar-mizvah* (בַּר מִצְוָה = son of commandment = one responsible for compliance with legal requirements), as the Jews express it, His repeated visits to Jerusalem to attend the feasts would also count for much. If we are to understand the visit mentioned in Lk 2 to be the first that Jesus paid to Jerusalem (though the narrative does not explicitly say it was), we may take it that at the age of twelve (Lk 2[42]) He was regarded as having reached that important stage in a boy's life, although the usual age for such recognition was somewhat later.

Jesus belonged to a people unsurpassed for the care bestowed upon the education of children. His earliest teacher would be His mother; and we cannot doubt that of all Jewish mothers none could excel Mary ('blessed among women') in all such work. Among other things He would probably learn from her the *Shema'* (Dt 6[4])—that sacred formula which attends the devout Jew from his earliest years to his latest moment. This is quite consistent with the fact that education was one of the things for which the father was held responsible as regards his son. At an early age Jesus would be sent to school at the synagogue, there to be taught by the *ḥazzan*, or schoolmaster, to read and recite the Jewish Scriptures. The instruction given did not go beyond this, with writing and possibly a little arithmetic as additional and subordinate subjects. It was in a supreme degree a religious education, designed to fit children for the practical duties of life. The education of Jesus was just that of the great mass of the people: unlike Saul of Tarsus, no *bêth ha-Midrâsh*, or college of Scribes, received Him as a student ('*Whence* hath this man these things?' Mk 6[2]; cf. Jn 7[15]). As a schoolboy, too, Jesus would have His recreations. School hours were not excessive, amounting to no more than four or five hours a day. Truly Jewish games, however, were but few. They had little or nothing corresponding to our school sports; and the cult of athletics was looked upon as something alien. Little children, like those of other times and races, found amusement in playing at doing as grown-up people did: and the words of our Lord in Mt 11[16. 17] very likely contain not merely the result of His observation, but a memory of His own childhood. For the rest, as a boy He would find abundant means of recreation in rambling round about Nazareth amidst the sights and sounds of nature. The open-air atmosphere of His preaching, with its abundant allusions to the life of the field and to the varied aspects of nature, betokens an early-formed and loving familiarity.

On His visit to Nazareth, described in Lk 4, 'He entered, *as His custom was*, into the synagogue on the Sabbath day' (v.[16]) : and that custom, we may be sure, was a growth from His earliest years. Children, in those days, were admitted to religious celebrations in the Temple at an early age. A boy's religious life was considered to begin at the age of four. Both boys and girls accompanied their mothers to the synagogue when very young. And Sabbath by Sabbath, throughout His early peaceful years, Jesus was found in the synagogue with His mother Mary ; and a benediction and a joy it must have been to all the frequenters of that synagogue at Nazareth to look upon the fair, winsome, earnest face of the Child. When we read, as we do, of boys playing in the synagogue during worship and causing annoyance to their elders, it interests us to recognize the counterpart of a familiar experience in modern times; but without taking anything from the naturalness of our Lord's boyhood, it is impossible to think of Him in any such association. We can only think of Him as showing forth a spirit of wondrous grace, a growing responsiveness towards the prayers and praises, becoming more and more familiar and dear, a deepening love of the noble words in which He heard the laws, the hopes and the faith of Israel set forth. The whole unfolding of His life in all the religious discipline and education of the home, the synagogue and the whole round of the Jewish year of feasts and fasts, must have been beautiful to those to whose care He was entrusted. When a boy became *bar-mizvah*, there was a lightening of the paternal responsibility regarding him, and a sense of relief surely found expression in the benediction pronounced by the father on that occasion—'Blessed be He for having freed me from this punishment.' There could have been no room for such an utterance when Jesus left His mother's side, henceforth to take His place among the men in the congregation.

Our most profitable reflections on the childhood of our Lord, however, are best summarized in the saying of Irenæus, to the effect that, in completely participating in the conditions of human life, He became a child for the sake of children, and by His own experience of childhood He has sanctified it (*adv. Haer.* II. xxii. 4).

ii. CHILDHOOD IN THE TEACHING OF JESUS.— It was only to be expected that Jesus would exhibit an unquestionable love for children ; and it is in complete accord with the whole tenor of His teaching that He should specially emphasize the importance and value of the child. The well-known words of Juvenal, 'Maxima debetur puero reverentia' (*Sat.* xiv. 47), gain their profoundest significance when the attitude assumed by our Lord towards children is considered. The story of Jairus' daughter (τὸ θυγάτριόν μου is the father's appealing expression in Mk 5[23]) suggests a special tenderness in Jesus towards children for whom His healing was sought ; He could not resist such an appeal as, 'Sir, come down ere my child (τὸ παιδίον μου) die' (Jn 4[49]) ; and it was anything but indifference to the woes of a little heathen girl (θυγάτριον, Mk 7[25]) which made Him apparently reluctant to yield to the entreaties of the Syrophœnician woman. Such cases, we may be sure, are only representative of many more. And that our Lord Himself had a singular attraction for children admits of no doubt. His triumphal Entry into Jerusalem and the Temple cannot have been the

only time when He had child-friends to greet and attend Him (Mt 21[15]). It was no new thing for parents to seek a Rabbi's blessing for their children, but it was a unique charm in Jesus which led mothers—surely mothers were at least among 'those that brought them'—to desire His blessing for their little ones (Mk 10[13-16] and parallels). St. Mark's special touch in describing how He welcomed them (ἐναγκαλισάμενος, v.[16]) is entirely true to the spirit of the Master. His benediction was as remote from the perfunctory as it could be.

The teaching of Jesus concerning children and childhood gathers round two occasions—when He blessed the little ones (as above), and when He rebuked the ambition of the disciples,—see Mk 9[33-37], Lk 9[46-48], and Mt 18[1-14], with notable amplifications.

(*a*) In the former instance the untimely interposition of the disciples leads to the saying, 'Of such is the kingdom of God.' In Mark and Luke this is followed by a further solemn saying— 'Whosoever shall not receive the kingdom of God as a little child, he shall in no wise enter therein.' Though Matthew lacks this in this connexion, he has a corresponding utterance in 18[3. 4]. Wendt (*Lehre Jesu*, Eng. tr. ii. pp. 49, 50) considers that all the stress of these words lies on the *receptivity* demanded by Jesus on the part of those who would enter the kingdom. 'Not the reception of the kingdom of God at a childlike *age* (*sic*), but in a childlike *character*, He declares to be the indispensable condition of entering the kingdom of God; and under this childlike character He does not understand any virtue of childlike blamelessness, but only the receptivity itself. . . .' And no doubt in the second of these sayings the manner in which men are to receive the kingdom is set forth with emphasis. Those who find themselves for one reason and another outside the kingdom, can obtain admission thereinto only when the offer of its gracious blessings is received, not with 'blamelessness' indeed (which is out of the question here), but, with the simple trust, the unpretentiousness, the earnest desire and the reality which are characteristic of a child. But there is something more than this in the words of Jesus. The first saying has hardly its due weight given to it if we stop here. 'Of such is the kingdom of God.' The kingdom *belongs* to such. And we cannot accept 'the childlike' as the complete equivalent of 'such.' Wendt, it is true, acknowledges children to be 'susceptible subjects for the preaching of the kingdom of God' (as above, p. 50); but are we to understand that they are to be invited to receive it as having been *outside from the first*? We verge here on controversies that have loomed large on the troubled way of the diversified development of Christian thought and opinion. But the saying of Jesus, as it stands, surely implies that the kingdom comprises not only the childlike, but little children *qua* children as well. They are its inheritors. They may forfeit its blessings subsequently by their own act, or others may be specially responsible for their failing to retain their inheritance (Mt 18[6]); but that is another matter. As Bengel says (on Mt 19[14]), 'τοιοῦτος notat substantiam cum qualitate.' And the relation of our Lord to humanity at large makes this but the natural interpretation of His words. 'If they who are like little children belong to the kingdom of heaven, why should we for a moment doubt that the little children themselves belong to the kingdom?' So Morison, who is altogether admirable on this point (see especially *Com.* on Mt 19[14]).

(*b*) The way in which Jesus dealt with the disciples' dispute concerning precedence (Mk 9[33-37] and parallels) further brings out the qualities of childhood which were most precious in His eyes, and the value and importance He attached to little children themselves. The little one He called to Him and so lovingly embraced (St. Mark's special touch again), was held up to the disciples as an example and guide to greatness. To be great in the kingdom of heaven (Mt 18[1, 4]) it was necessary to have a spirit of simplicity and humility such as was seen in the child in whom self-regard and self-seeking had as yet no place. It is one of our Lord's great paradoxes. To be childlike is to be truly great. The same truth is emphasized in a saying which in varying form is found twice over in each of the Synoptics—the man who wishes to be first shall be last; the man willing to be least shall be great. We here learn further how Jesus regards little children as in a real sense belonging to Him. To receive a little child *as belonging to Him*, bestowing loving care upon it, is a high service rendered to Him and to God by whom He was sent. In Mt 10[40-42] the importance attached to such service is strikingly expressed in the progressive series in which Jesus promises a reward to those who thus receive His messengers—a prophet, a good man, 'one of these little ones.' It is most natural to understand that in using such an expression as the last our Lord actually referred to some children who were hard by when He was speaking. And as here, so in the more extended sayings in Mt 18, whatever the reference to childlike and lowly-minded disciples in general, the words of Jesus must apply to children themselves. The terrible warning of Mt 18[6] applies to those who hinder such little ones in relation to the kingdom. Though it is not expressly so stated, what is said about receiving children suggests that such a wrong done to any child is as a wrong done to Christ Himself. The preciousness of a little child in the sight of 'our Father in heaven' is emphatically asserted by Jesus in Mt 18[10-14]. The children's angels, He says, are ever in the presence of God (v.[10]). Whether this remarkable saying be understood as referring to guardian angels or to representative angels (in some way corresponding to the Zoroastrian *fravashis* or 'spiritual counterparts'—see art. by Dr. J. H. Moulton in *Journal of Theol. Studies*, July 1902), it clearly declares that no little one is an object of indifference with God, no wrong inflicted upon a child can escape His notice. The closing saying of this group (vv.[12-14]) embodies the illustration of the one stray sheep, found in another connexion in Lk 15, and teaches that, whatever ruin may befall 'one of these little ones,' it is not a matter of the Divine pleasure and ordination that even one such should be 'cast as rubbish to the void.' See also art. CHILDREN, which is written from a different standpoint.

LITERATURE.—The various Lives of Christ (Edersheim, Keim, Didon, Farrar, Andrews, D. Smith, etc); artt. BOYHOOD, and EDUCATION; cf. art. 'Education' in Hastings' *DB* and the *Encyc. Biblica*; Brough, *Childhood and Youth of our Lord*; G. A. Coe, *Education in Religion and Morals*, 1904; S. B. Haslett, *Pedagogical Bible School*, 1905; R. Rainy, *Sojourning with God* (1902), p. 151; Donehoo, *Apocryphal and Legendary Life of Christ*; Ramsay, *Education of Christ*; Schürer, *HJP*; Wendt, *Teaching of Jesus*, ii. 48 ff.; G. B. Stevens, *Theology of the NT*, pp. 81, 93.　　　　J. S. CLEMENS.

CHILDREN.—In the regeneration of society which has been wrought by the forces brought into the world by Christianity, the family, of course, has had its part. Or rather, since to Jesus also the family was the social unit, this regeneration began with the family and spread outwards from it. The emphasis laid by our Lord on the institution of the family deserves even to be called extraordinary. Not only did He habitually exhibit sympathy with domestic life in all its phases, and particularly reverence for women and tenderness for children: and not only did He adopt the vocabulary of the family to express the relations

subsisting between Himself and His followers, and even as His choicest vehicle for conveying to them a vitalizing conception of their relations to God, 'from whom,' as that one of His servants who best represents His teaching in this aspect of it declares, 'every family in heaven and on earth is named' (Eph 3[15]); but, deserting His customary reserve in dealing with social institutions, in the case of this one alone did He advance beyond general principles to specific legislation. (Cf. F. G. Peabody, *Jesus Christ and the Social Question*, p. 145 ff.).

This specific legislation does not directly concern children. It is true that childhood owes as much to the gospel as womanhood itself (cf. *e.g.* Uhlhorn, *Conflict of Christianity with Heathenism*, p. 182). And the causes of the great revolution which was wrought by the gospel in the condition of children and the estimate placed on childhood, are undoubtedly rooted in the life and teaching of our Lord, and are spread on the pages of the Gospels. But we shall search in vain in the recorded teaching of Jesus for either direct legislation, or even enunciation of general principles regulating the relations of parents and children, or establishing the position of children in the social organism. He has left us no commandments, no declarations, not even exhortations on the subject. He simply moves onward in His course, touching in life, act, word on the domestic relations that were prevalent about Him, and elevating and glorifying everything that He touched. Thus He has handed down to us a new ideal of the family, and lifted to a new plane our whole conception of childhood. (Cf. Shailer Mathews, *The Social Teaching of Jesus*, p. 101 ff.).

The domestic economy which forms the background of Jesus' life, and is assumed in all His dealings with children and in all His allusions to them and their ways, is, of course, the wholesome home-life which had grown up in Israel under the moulding influence of the revelation of the Old Covenant. Its basis was the passionately affectionate Semitic nature, and no doubt certain modifications had come to it from contact with other civilizations; but its form was determined by the tutelage which Jehovah had granted His people. (Cf. Edersheim, *Sketches of Jewish Social Life in the Days of Christ*, chs. vi.-ix., and *The Life and Times of Jesus the Messiah*, bk. II. chs. ix. and x.; also Hastings' *DB*, articles 'Child,' 'Family.' For later Jewish child-life see Schechter, *Studies in Judaism*, xii.; and, above all, L. Löw, *Die Lebensalter*. Cf. also Ploss, *Das Kind in Brauch und Sitte der Völker*).

The tender love which the Hebrew parent bore to his child, and the absorbing interest with which he watched and guided its development, doubtless find partial expression in the multiplicity of designations by which the several stages of childhood are marked in that pictorial language. Besides the general terms for 'son' (*ben*) and 'daughter' (*bath*), eight of these have been noted tracing the child from its birth to its maturity: *yeled* (fem. *yaldāh*), the 'birthling'; *yónēk*, the 'suckling'; *ôlēl*, the suckling of a larger growth, perhaps the 'worrier'; *gāmûl*, the 'weanling'; *ṭaph*, the 'toddler'; *elem*, the 'fat one'; *na'ar*, the 'free one'; *bāḥūr*, the 'ripe one.' (So Hamburger, *RE* i. 642, after whom Edersheim, *Opp. citt.* p. 103 f. and i. p. 221, note 3).

This series of designations may, of course, be more than matched out of the richness of Greek speech. Here the general term of relation, 'child' (* τέκνον, dimin. * τεκνίον), parts into the more specific 'son' (* υἱός, dimin. υἱάφιον, υἱδιον) and 'daughter' (* θυγάτηρ, dimin. * θυγάτριον); while the multitude of terms describing stages of growth quite baffles discrimination. The grammarians have handed down to us each his several list, among which that of Alexion (*Eust.* 1788, 22), for instance, enumerates ten stages between the newborn infant and the mature young man: * βρέφος; * παιδίον; * παιδάριον; παιδίσκος; * παῖς; πάλλαξ, or βούπαις, or ἀντίπαις, or μελλίεφηβος; ἔφηβος; μειράκιον or μεῖραξ; * νεανίσκος; * νεανίας. Needless to say, the sequences of such lists cannot be taken too strictly. And equally needless to say, they by no means exhaust the synonymy.

* Those terms which occur in NT are marked by an asterisk.

Alexion's list, for example, does not contain even all the terms of this class that occur in the Gospel narratives. The series afforded by them would run something like this: βρέφος, νήπιος, θηλάζων, παιδίον, παιδάριον, παῖς, νεανίσκος, to which would need to be added the distinctively feminine θυγάτριον, κοράσιον [παιδίσκη], παρθένος.

It is not difficult to recognize the general distinctions between these terms. (For the detailed synonymy see especially Schmidt, *D. Synonymik d. griech. Sprache*, c. 69, for the terms belonging distinctively to childhood; c. 152 for those describing the stages between childhood and maturity; and c. 47 for some terms denoting youthfulness; cf. Thayer, *Lex. NT*, *s.v.* παῖς). Τέκνον (with its diminutive τεκνίον, Jn 13³³ only) is, like υἱός and θυγάτηρ, used in the Gospels only of relationship, literal or figurative, never of age (for the synonymy of τέκνον, υἱός, and παῖς, see an interesting discussion by Höhne in Luthardt's *ZKWL*, 1882, p. 57 ff. ; and cf. Cremer and Thayer, *s.vv.*). For the rest, βρέφος is here, as in post-Homeric Greek in general, distinctively the 'newborn baby' (1 P 2²), the 'child in the arms' (in Homer it is the unborn child, the embryo, as also often in later Greek, *e.g.* Lk 14¹· ⁴⁴): and νήπιος and θηλάζων (the NT substitute for θηλασμός, θηλαμινός) range with it as descriptive of early infancy. Παιδίον is equally distinctively the 'little child,' although its application is somewhat broad; now it is entirely synonymous with βρέφος (Lk 15⁹· ⁶⁶ etc., Mt 2⁸ etc., Lk 18¹⁵· ¹⁶), and again it designates a little maiden of twelve years of age (Mk 5⁴¹· ⁴²). Its companion diminutive παιδάριον is ordinarily employed of a somewhat older 'lad,' and may very well be so used in the only passage where it occurs in the Gospels (Jn 6⁹). The simple παῖς has a range sufficiently wide to cover all these stages, from infancy itself (*e.g.* Mt 2¹⁶) up to youthful maturity (Hippocrates says up to the age of 21). It designates, says Schmidt (p. 429), 'the child of all ages up to complete young manhood; παιδίον, the child up to his first school years; παιδίον, exclusively the little child.' Νεανίσκος is the appropriate designation of every stage of youthful maturity from so early an age that μειράκιον or παῖς might be interchanged with it up to so late a period—about 40—that it is on the point of giving way to old age. Of the distinctively feminine terms that occur in the Gospels, παρθένος is a term of condition rather than of age, and occurs only in connexion with Mary (Mt 1²³, Lk 1²⁷) and in the parable of the Ten Virgins (Mt 25¹· ⁷· ¹¹), and παιδίσκη is employed only in the secondary sense of 'maid-servant' (Mt 26⁶⁹ and parallels, Lk 12⁴⁵). The diminutives θυγάτριον and κοράσιον, though capable of employment with quite a wide range, yet naturally imply tenderness of years where tenderness of affection is not obviously conveyed by them (*e.g.* Mk 7²⁵, Mt 9²⁵ ‖). Thus it appears that in the narratives of the Gospels there is brought into contact with our Lord every stage of childhood and youth from the cradle to maturity—the baby on its mother's bosom (Lk 18¹⁵), the little child, boy (Mk 9²⁴) and girl (Mk 7²⁵) alike, children of a larger growth (Jn 4²⁷, Lk 8⁵¹), and the maturing youth (Lk 7¹⁴, Mt 19²⁰).

What Jesus did for children, we may perhaps sum up as follows. He illustrated the ideal of childhood in His own life as a child. He manifested the tenderness of His affection for children by conferring blessings upon them in every stage of their development as He was occasionally brought into contact with them. He asserted for children a recognized place in His kingdom, and dealt faithfully and lovingly with each age as it presented itself to Him in the course of His work. He chose the condition of childhood as a type of the fundamental character of the recipients of the kingdom of God. He adopted the relation of childhood as the most vivid earthly image of the relation of God's people to Him who was not ashamed to be called their Father which is in heaven, and thus reflected back upon this relation a glory by which it has been transfigured ever since. The history of the ideal childhood which Jesus Himself lived on the earth is set down for us in the opening chapters of Matthew and Luke, especially of Luke, whose distinction among the Evangelists is that he has given us a narrative founded on an investigation which 'traced the course of all things accurately from the first' (Lk 1³). Accordingly, not only does he with careful exactitude record the performance by our Lord's parents in His behalf, during His infancy, of 'all things that were according to the law of the Lord' (Lk 2³⁹); but he marks for us the stages of our Lord's growth in His progress to man's estate, and thus brings Him before us successively as 'baby' (2¹⁶ βρέφος), 'child' (2⁴⁰ παιδίον), and 'boy' (2⁴³ παῖς), until in His glorious young-manhood, when He was about 30 years of age, He at last manifested Himself to Israel (3²³). The second chapter of Luke is thus in

effect an express history of the development of Jesus ; and sums up in two comprehensive verses His entire growth from childhood to boyhood and from boyhood to manhood (2⁴⁰· ⁵²). The language of these succinct descriptions is charged with suggestions that this was an extraordinary child, whose development was an extraordinary development. Attention is called alike to His physical, intellectual, and spiritual progress ; and of each it is suggested that it was constant, rapid, and remarkable. Those who looked upon Him in the cradle would perceive that even beyond the infant Moses (Heb. 11²³) this was 'a goodly child'; and day by day as He grew and waxed strong, He became more and more filled not only with knowledge but with wisdom, and not only with wisdom but with grace, and so steadily advanced 'not alone in power and knowledge, but by year and hour in reverence and in charity.' Man and God alike looked upon His growing powers and developing character with ever increasing favour. The promise of the goodly child passed without jar or break into the fruitage of the perfect man : and those who gazed on the babe with admiration (2²⁰· ³⁰· ³⁸), could not but gaze on the boy with astonishment (2⁴⁷) and on the man with reverence.

It is therefore no ordinary human development which is here described for us. But it is none the less, or rather it is all the more, a normal human development, the only strictly normal human development the world has ever seen. This is the only child who has ever been born into the world without the fatal entail of sin, and the only child who has ever grown to manhood free from the deterioration of sin. This is how men ought to grow up : how, were they not sinners, men would grow up. It is a great thing for the world to have seen one such instance. As an example it is indeed set beyond our reach. As the ideal childhood realized in life, it has ever since stood before the world as an incitement and inspiration of quite incalculable power. In this perfect development of Jesus there has been given to the world a model for every age, whose allurement has revolutionized life. He did not, as Irenæus (*adv. Hær.* II. xxii. 4, cf. III. xviii. 4) reminds us, despise or evade the humanity He had assumed ; or set aside in His own person the law that governs it : on the contrary, He sanctified every age in turn by Himself living His perfect life in its conditions. 'He came to save all by means of Himself,' continues Irenæus, 'all, I say, who through Him are born again unto God,—infants and children, and boys, and youths. . . . He therefore passed through every age, becoming an infant for infants, thus sanctifying infants ; a child for children, thus sanctifying those who are of this age, being at the same time made to them an example of piety, righteousness, and submission ; a youth for youths, becoming an example to youths, and thus sanctifying them for the Lord.' . . . On the few details given us of the childhood of our Lord see artt. Boyhood of Jesus and Childhood.

During the course of His life begun with this ideal childhood, Jesus came into contact with every stage of youthful development, and manifested the tenderness of His feeling for each and His power and willingness to confer blessings upon all. A lurid light is thrown upon the nature of the world and the character of the times into which He was born by the slaughter of the Innocents, which marked His advent (Mt 2¹⁶⁻²⁰). But one function which the record of this incident performs is to serve as a black background upon which His own beneficence to childhood may be thrown up. Mothers instinctively brought their babies to Him for benediction ; and when they did so, He was not content until He had taken them in His arms (Mk 10¹⁶, cf. 9³⁶). His allusions to children in His teaching reflect the closeness of His observation of them. He celebrates the delight of the mother in her baby, obliterating even the pangs of birth (Jn 16²¹); the fostering love of the father who cuddles his children up with him in bed (Lk 11⁷); the parental affection which listens eagerly to the child's every request, and knows how to grant it only things that are good (Mt 7⁹, Lk 11¹¹⁻¹³). He notes the wayward impulses of children at play (Mt 11¹⁶, Lk 7³²). He feels the weight of woe that is added to calamities in which the children also are involved (Mt 18²⁵); and places among the supremest tests of loyalty to Him, the preference of Him even to one's children (Mt 19²⁹, Lk 14²⁶ 18²⁹; cf. Mk 10²⁹).

A number of His miracles, worked for the benefit of the young, illustrate His compassion for their sufferings and ills. The nobleman's son at Capernaum, whose healing Jesus wrought as a second sign when He came out of Judæa into Galilee (Jn 4⁴⁶⁻⁵⁴), was at least a 'child' (παῖς, 4⁵¹), for so the servants call him in cold sobriety; and probably was a 'little child' (4⁴⁹), although it is, of course, possible that on the lips of the father the diminutive expresses tenderness of affection rather than of age. The possessed 'boy' (παῖς, Mt 17¹⁸, Lk 9⁴²) —the only son of his father (Lk 9³⁸)—whom Jesus healed as He came down from the Mount of Transfiguration (Mt 17¹⁴⁻²¹, Mk 9¹⁴⁻²⁹, Lk 9³⁷⁻⁴³), and whose affliction had dated from his earliest infancy (ἐκ παιδιόθεν, Mk 9²¹), was more certainly distinctively a 'little child' (Mk 9²⁴). Jairus' 'little daughter' (θυγάτριον, Mk 5²³)—also an only one—whom Jesus raised from the dead in such dramatic circumstances (Mt 9¹⁸⁻²⁶, Mk 5²²⁻⁴³, Lk 8⁴¹⁻⁵⁶) and who is spoken of in the narratives indifferently as 'child' (παῖς, Lk 8⁵¹· ⁵⁴), 'little child' (παιδίον, Mk 5³⁹· ⁴⁰· ⁴¹) and 'maiden' or 'girl' (κοράσιον, Mt 9²⁴· ²⁵, Mk 5⁴¹; ταλιθά, Mk 5⁴¹), we know to have been about twelve years old (Lk 8⁴²). We are not told the exact age of the 'little daughter' (θυγάτριον, Mk 7²⁵—here probably the word is the diminutive of age, not of affection, as it occurs in the narrative, not the conversation) of the Syrophœnician woman; but we note that St. Mark calls her also distinctively a 'little child' (παιδίον, 7³⁰). The only son of the widow of Nain (Lk 7¹¹⁻¹⁸), the desolate state of whose bereft mother roused so deeply the pity of our Lord (7¹³), is addressed indeed as a 'young man' (νεανίσκε, 7¹⁴), a term so broad that it need imply no more than that he was in his prime; but the suggestion of the narrative certainly seems to be that he was in his youthful prime (7¹⁵). Thus is rounded out a series of miracles in which our Lord shows His pity to the growing youth of every stage of development.

When on that great day on the shores of Gennesaret Jesus appeared to His disciples and gave to His repentant Apostle His last exhortation, He commanded him not merely 'Feed my sheep,' but also 'Feed my lambs.' Though the language, doubtless, rather expresses His love for His flock than distributes it into constituent classes, we may be permitted to see in it also the richness of our Lord's sympathy for the literal lambs of His fold. Certainly He provided in His kingdom a place for every age, and met the spiritual needs of each. Touching illustrations of this are offered us at the two end stages of youthful development (Lk 18¹⁵ βρέφος; Mt 19²⁰ νεανίσκος), in the blessing of little children and the probing of the rich young ruler's heart, which are brought into immediate contiguity in all three of the Synoptics as if they were intended to be taken together as a picture of our Lord's dealing with youth as a whole, perhaps even as together illustrating the great truth that in the kingdom of God the question is not of the

hour of entrance,—first or eleventh,—but of the will of the Master, who doeth what He will with His own (Mt 20¹⁵).

What is particularly to be borne in mind with respect to the blessing of the little children (Mt 19¹³⁻¹⁵, Mk 10¹³⁻¹⁶, Lk 18¹⁵⁻¹⁷), is that these 'little children' (παιδία, Mt 19¹³· ¹⁴, Mk 10¹³· ¹⁴, Lk 18¹⁶) were distinctively 'babies' (βρέφη, Lk 18¹⁵). Therefore they needed to be received by Jesus 'in his arms' (Mk 10¹⁶); and only from this circumstance, indeed, can all the details of the narrative be understood. It is from this, for example, that the interference of the disciples, which called out the Master's rebuke, 'Let the little children come to me; forbid them not,' receives its explanation. The disciples, to speak briefly, had misapprehended the nature of the Lord's mission: they were regarding Him fundamentally as a teacher sent from God, who also healed the afflicted; and they conceived it to be their duty in the overstrain to which He was subjected to protect Him from needless drafts on His time and strength by the intrusion of those needing no healing and incapable of instruction. It seemed to them out of the question that 'even the babies' (Lk 18¹⁵) should be thrust upon His jaded attention. They should have known better; and Jesus was indignant that they did not know better (Mk 10¹⁴), and took this occasion to manifest Himself as the Saviour of infants also. Taking them in His arms and fervently invoking a blessing upon them (Mk 10¹⁶ κατευλόγει), He not only asserted for them a part in His mission, but even constituted them the type of the children of the kingdom. 'Let the little children come unto me,' He says; 'forbid them not: for of such is the kingdom of God.' And then proceeding with the solemn 'Verily'—'Verily I say unto you, Whosoever shall not receive the kingdom of God as a little child, shall in no wise enter therein' (Mk 10¹⁴· ¹⁵, Lk 18¹⁶· ¹⁷; cf. Mt 19¹⁴).

Wherein this childlikeness, in which alone the kingdom of God can be received, consists, lies on the face of the narrative. Certainly not in the innocence of childhood, as if the purpose were to announce that only the specially innocent can enter the kingdom of God. Our Lord was accustomed to declare, on the contrary, that He came to call not the righteous but sinners, to seek and save that which was lost; and the contradiction with the lesson of the publican and the Pharisee praying in the temple, which immediately precedes this narrative in Luke, would be too glaring. But neither can it consist in the humility of childhood, if, indeed, we can venture to speak of the most egoistic age of human life as characteristically humble; nor yet in its simplicity, its artlessness, ingenuousness, directness, as beautiful as these qualities are, and as highly esteemed as they certainly must be in the kingdom of God. We cannot even suppose it to consist in the trustfulness of childhood, although we assuredly come much nearer to it in this, and no image of the children of the kingdom could be truer than that afforded by the infant lying trustingly upon its mother's breast. But, in truth, it is in no disposition of mind, but rather in a condition of nature, that we must seek the characterizing peculiarity of these infants whom Jesus sets forth as types of the children of the kingdom. Infants of days (βρέφη, Lk 18¹⁵) have no characteristic disposition of mind; and we must accordingly leave the subjective sphere and find the childlikeness which Jesus presents as the condition of the reception (not acquisition) of the kingdom in an objective state; in a word, in the helplessness, or, if you will, the absolute dependence of infancy. What our Lord would seem to say, therefore, when He declares, 'Of such is the kingdom of God,' is, briefly, that those of whom the kingdom of God is made up are, relatively to it, as helplessly dependent as babies are in their mothers' arms. The children of the kingdom enter it as children enter the world, stripped and naked,—infants, for whom all must be done, not who are capable of doing.

There was another occasion on which even more formally Jesus proclaimed to His disciples childlikeness as the essential characteristic of the children of the kingdom (Mt 18$^{1-4}$, Mk 9$^{33-37}$, Lk 9$^{46-48}$). The disciples had been disputing among themselves who of them should be greatest. Jesus, calling to Him a little child, placed it in their midst and said, ' Verily I say unto you, Except ye turn and become as little children, ye shall in no wise enter into the kingdom of heaven.' There could not have been uttered a more pointed intimation that the kingdom of heaven is given, not acquired; that men receive it, not deserve it. As children enter the world, so men enter the kingdom, with no contributions in their hands. We are not, indeed, told in this narrative, in express words, that the child thus made the type of the children of God was a ' newborn baby ' ($\beta\rho\epsilon\phi$os) : it is called only a ' little child ' ($\pi\alpha\iota\deltaίον$). But its extreme infancy is implied : Jesus took it in His arms (Mk 9^{36}) when He presented it to the observation of His disciples ; and we must accordingly think of it as a baby in a baby's helplessness and dependence.

We do, to be sure, find in our Lord's further words a requisition of humility (Mt 18^4) : ' Whosoever then shall humble himself like this little child, the same is the greatest in the kingdom of heaven.' To become like a little child may certainly involve humility in one who is not a child ; and it is very comprehensible that our Lord should therefore tell those whom He was exhorting to approach the kingdom of heaven like little children, that they could do so only by humbling themselves. But this is not the same as declaring humility to be the characteristic virtue of childhood, or as intimating that humility may ground a claim upon the kingdom of heaven. What our Lord seems to tell His followers is that they cannot enter the kingdom He came to found except they turn and become like little children ; and that they can become like little children only by humbling themselves: and that therefore when they were quarrelling about their relative greatness, they were far from the disposition which belongs to children of the kingdom. Humility seems to be represented, in a word, not as the characterizing quality of childhood or of childlikeness, but rather as the attitude of heart in which alone we can realize in our consciousness that quality which characterizes childhood. That quality is conceived here also as helplessness, while childlikeness consists in the reproduction in the consciousness of the objective state of utter dependence on God which is the real condition of every sinner.

From the point of view thus revealed in objectlesson and discourse, it was natural for our Lord to speak of His disciples as ' babes.' ' I thank thee, O Father, Lord of heaven and earth,' He cries on one momentous occasion (Mt 11^{25}, Lk 10^{21}), ' that thou didst hide these things from the wise and understanding, and didst reveal them unto babes' ($\nu\eta\pi\iotaοιs$, the implication of which is precisely weakness and neediness). And then He proceeds with a great declaration the very point of which is to contrast His sovereign power with the neediness of those whom He calls to His service. Similarly as the end approached and the children ($\pi\alpha\hat{\imath}\deltaεs$) in the temple were greeting Him with hosannas, He met the indignant challenge of the Jews with the words of the Psalmist : ' Yea, did ye never read, Out of the mouth of babes and sucklings thou

hast ordained praise ? ' (Mt 21^{16}). The meaning is that these childish hosannas were typical of the praises rising from the hearts of those childlike ones from whose helplessness (because they owed much to Him) His true praise should spring.

From the more general view-point of affection our Lord derived the terms by which He expressed His personal relations to His followers, and a large part of the vocabulary of His proclamation of the kingdom of God is drawn from the relationships of the family. His disciples are His ' children ' ($\tau\epsilon\kappa\nu\alpha$, Mk 10^{24}), or with increasing tenderness of expression, His ' little children ' ($\tau\epsilon\kappa\nu\ί\alpha$, Jn 13^{33}), His ' babies' ($\pi\alpha\iota\delta\ί\alpha$, Jn 21^5), and perhaps with even more tenderness still, simply His ' little ones' ($οι$ $\mu\iota\kappa\rhoοί$, Mt 10^{42} etc., but see art. LITTLE ONES). Similarly the great King, whose kingdom He came to establish, is the Father of His people ; and they may therefore be free from all fear, because, naturally, it is the good pleasure of their Father to give the kingdom to them (Lk 12^{32}). Every turn of expression is freely employed to carry home to the hearts of His followers the sense of the Fatherly love for them by Him who is their King indeed, but also their Father which is in heaven (Mt 5$^{16.\ 45.\ 48}$ 6$^{1.\ 4.\ 6.\ 8.\ 9.\ 14.\ 15.\ 18}$ 6^{32} 7^{11} 10$^{20.\ 29}$ 13^{43} 23^9, Mk 11^{25}, Lk 6^{36} 11^{13} 12$^{30.\ 32}$, Jn 20^{17}) ; and they accordingly His sons (Mt 5$^{9.\ 45}$, Lk 20^{36}), His children (Jn 1^{12} 11^{52}), and therefore heirs of His kingdom. In this representation, which finds its most striking expression in such parables as that of the Prodigal Son (Lk 15$^{11f.}$), it is, to be sure, rather the relationship of father and child that is emphasized than the tenderness of the age of childhood. Neither is it a novelty introduced by our Lord ; it finds its root in Old Testament usage. But it is so characteristic of our Lord's teaching that it may fairly be said that the family was to His mind the nearest of human analogues to the order that obtains in the kingdom of God, and the picture which He draws of the relations that exist between God and His people is largely only a ' transfiguration of the family.'

Such an employment of the relationships in the family to figure forth those that exist between God and His people could not fail to react on the conceptions which men formed of the family relationships themselves. By His constant emphasis on the Fatherhood of God, and by His employment of the helplessness of infancy and the dependence of childhood as the most vivid emblems provided by human society to image the dependence of God's people on His loving protection and fostering care, our Lord has thrown a halo over the condition of childhood which has communicated to it an emotional value and a preciousness, in the strictest sense, new in the world. In the ancient world, children, though by their innocence eliciting the affection, and by their weakness appealing to the sympathy, of their elders, were thought of chiefly as types of immaturity and unripeness. The Christian world, taught by its Lord, reverences their very helplessness as the emblem of its own condition in the presence of God, and recognizes in their dependence an appeal to its unselfish devotion, that it may be an imitator of God. This salutary respect and consideration for childhood has no doubt been exaggerated at times to something very much like worship of the childlike ; and this tendency has been powerfully fostered by the prevalence in sections of Christendom, since the 14th cent., of an actual cult of the infant Saviour (cf. E. Martinengo-Carresco in *The Contemporary Review*, lxxvii. 117, etc.), and the early rise and immense development in the same quarters of a cult of the Madonna, to the tender sentiments underlying which all the resources of the most passionate devotion, the most elevated literature, and the most perfect art have been invoked to give widespread influence (see especially Zöckler, art. *Maria die Mutter des Herrn* in *PRE*³, xii. 309, etc., who gives an extensive classified bibliography. Cf. in general H. E. Scudder, *Childhood in Art*, also in *The Atlantic Monthly*, lv. and lvi.). Such exaggerations cannot, however, obscure the main fact that it is only from Jesus that the world has learned properly to appreciate and wholesomely to deal with childhood and all that childhood stands for. Cf. art. CHILDHOOD.

BENJAMIN B. WARFIELD.

CHILDREN OF GOD.—The teaching of Jesus Christ about the children of God cannot be understood apart from His teaching about the Fatherhood of God : indeed, it is from the latter standpoint that it must be approached. In such an approach the main positions seem to be as follows :—

(1) Jesus asserts absolutely the fatherly nature of God. His use of the name 'Father' implies that the fatherly nature is eternal in God. God does not become Father ; He is 'the Father.' All knowledge of God is deficient which does not 'know the Father' (Mt 11²⁷, Jn 14⁶⁻¹¹). This fatherly nature of God necessarily manifests itself in all God's dealings. He cannot be other than Father, and 'he maketh his sun to rise on the evil and the good, and sendeth rain on the just and the unjust' (Mt 5⁴⁵).

(2) This eternal Fatherhood in God is complemented by an eternal Sonship in God. Jesus used habitually the name 'My Father.' It implied a special relationship between the Father and Himself, which is summed up by John, 'The only begotten Son which is in the bosom of the Father' (Jn 1¹⁸).

(3) The fatherly heart of God does not rest satisfied in the eternal Sonship in God. He desires the response of filial love from all who are capable of giving it (cf. esp. Lk 15¹⁻³², Jn 4²³). Jesus assumed that the filial attitude is expected from all men. This is implied in His method of teaching. The Divine Fatherhood is woven into its texture. Therefore the picture of God the Father is offered to everybody, with its necessary appeal to the hearer to enjoy the filial relationship. Since the outlook of the gospel is universal, the sonship may be universal. Even 'publicans and sinners' may enjoy the filial feeling.

(4) But Jesus taught plainly that this filial attitude is not general amongst men. He told the Jews that they were of their father the devil (Jn 8⁴⁴), and distinguished 'the good seed, the sons of the kingdom,' from 'the tares, the sons of the evil one' (Mt 13³⁸) ; cf. also Mt 23¹³⁻³³.

(5) Certain conditions are laid down as essential to the enjoyment of the filial relationship to God. These conditions are usually described by Jesus in terms of character. The children of God are 'peacemakers,' are those who love their enemies, and who do the will of the Father (cf. Mt 5⁹· ⁴⁴ 12⁵⁰) : they 'do good and lend, never despairing,' and are 'merciful' (Lk 6³⁵· ³⁶). But in the discourses in John's Gospel, Jesus Himself is offered as a touchstone for the filial relationship (cf. Jn 8⁴²⁻⁴⁷). In this connexion the demand for the new birth must be noticed. Jesus connected entrance into that Kingdom which He came to found, with being 'born anew' (Jn 3³) ; He demanded that His disciples should be converted and become as little children if they would enter the Kingdom (Mt 18³ ‖). It may fairly be said that in the mind of Jesus there is an intimate connexion between these two modes of teaching. The moral character befitting the children of God is secured by the new birth 'of water and of the Spirit' (Jn 3⁵).

From these propositions we can gather the teaching of Jesus about the children of God. The relationship is apprehended by Jesus ethically, not physically. To identify Divine sonship with human birth brings the relationship down to the physical sphere. Jesus kept it in the religious sphere. The Fatherhood of God is an ethical attitude eternally present in the Godhead ; man's Divine sonship is his ethical response to this Divine Fatherhood. God is ever waiting to welcome men as sons, and to give them the position of sons at home (Lk 15). But their assumption of this filial position depends upon their adoption of the filial attitude, 'I will arise and go to my father.' As Wendt says, 'God does not *become* the Father, but *is* the heavenly Father, even of those who *become* His sons. . . . Man is a true son of God . . . from the fact of his comporting himself as a son of God' (*Teaching of Jesus*, i. p. 193).

This religious attitude which betokens Divine sonship, includes four elements. (*a*) Children of God love their heavenly Father. Love is the golden bond in all home relationships. Jesus declares it to be the sovereign law in the true relationship between man and God. For He taught that the greatest commandment is to love the Lord our God with all our heart and soul and mind and strength (Mt 22³⁷, Lk 10²¹). When claiming to have come forth from God, He said to the Jews : 'If God were your father ye would love me,' where love of Himself is identified with love of the Father whom He revealed.

(*b*) Children of God obey their heavenly Father. This is implied in all Jesus' exhortations to men to do the will of God. It is clearly stated in these sentences : 'Whosoever shall do the will of my Father which is in heaven, the same is my brother, and sister, and mother' (Mt 12⁵⁰) ; 'Not every one that saith unto me, Lord, Lord, shall enter into the kingdom of heaven ; but he that doeth the will of my Father which is in heaven' (Mt 7²¹) ; cf. also Mt 21³¹ 24⁴⁵ ‖.

(*c*) Children of God trust their heavenly Father. This mark of Divine sonship is emphasized in the Sermon on the Mount. Jesus exhorts His disciples not to be as the Gentiles, but to rely upon their heavenly Father's knowledge of their needs and His desire to help them. Anxiety must be banished from the hearts of God's children, who are fed and clothed by their Father (Mt 6²⁵⁻³⁴, Lk 6²²⁻³⁴).

(*d*) Children of God try to be like their heavenly Father. They are to be perfect, even as their heavenly Father is perfect (Mt 5⁴⁸). This must not be interpreted, as it often is, 'Be as perfect as your Father.' Its exhortation is to take the fatherly character of God as the standard of perfection. 'Be ye perfect, *even as* He is perfect.' The Father loves all men : let His children do likewise. By thus taking the fatherly character of God as the standard, His children will fulfil the second great law, 'Thou shalt love thy neighbour as thyself' (Mt 22³⁹). The natural man adopts other ideals of perfection ; but the children of God try to be like their Father.

Jesus gave immortal expression to the desires characteristic of the children of God, in 'the Lord's Prayer.' That prayer is put into the lips of those who can say 'Our Father which art in heaven.' It includes all the marks of God's children that have been found elsewhere in the teaching of Jesus. The hallowing of the Father's name implies the sanctification of His children after His likeness. The prayer 'Thy will be done' lifts us to the loftiest level of obedience. Only those who trust God can pray 'Give us our daily bread,' and can limit their desires for material good to such humble bounds. The prayer breathes throughout the spirit of love : that spirit is the warp into which the weft of the petition is woven.

The blessings enjoyed by the children of God are all the good that Jesus Christ came on earth to offer to men. This good is summed up in the phrase 'the kingdom of God' or 'the kingdom of heaven.' All the children of God are members of that Kingdom; cf. Mt 13³⁸ 18³⁻¹⁰. The Kingdom is God's proffered blessing: 'It is your Father's good pleasure to give you the kingdom' (Lk 12³²). The Kingdom includes the blessings of forgiveness (Mt 6¹⁴ ‖); of guardian care (Mt 6³³); of the Holy Spirit (Lk 11¹³); of eternal life (Jn 5²¹⁻²⁶ 17³); and finally, the enjoyment of the Father's house (Mt 25³⁴, Jn 14². ³).

This identification of the blessings enjoyed by the children of God with the good of the Kingdom, leads naturally to the statement that the ethical attitude characteristic of the children of God can be secured by faith in Jesus Christ. He not only spoke of Himself as the Son of God; He also declared that His revelation of Sonship made sonship possible to men. Considerable importance attaches to the solemn words in Mt 11²⁷ 'All things have been delivered unto me of my Father: and no one knoweth the Son, save the Father; neither doth any know the Father, save the Son and he to whomsoever the Son willeth to reveal him.' They declare that the knowledge of the Father must be experimental. Only one who has lived as a son can know the Father. Men do not know God primarily as Father. They think of Him as King, as Judge, as Law-Giver; and because they are sinners they cannot know Him purely as Father. The shadow of the broken Law falls across God's face, making it appear the face of a judge, and falls upon the attitude of men, chilling it into that of servants. But 'the Son' knows God as Father. He has no fear of Him as Judge; He claims to be Himself the King in the kingdom of God (Mt 25⁴⁰); He is conscious that He has never broken God's law. Therefore He can know God as the Father; and He is able to reveal God to men as Father. Jesus does this by ransoming captive spirits from the bondage of sin and death (Mt 20²⁸), by persuading them to trust the fatherly love of God, and by strengthening them to break away from the self-life in favour of the life of surrender (Mt 16²⁴⁻²⁷ ‖).

The close connexion between this great word and the gracious invitation which follows it (Mt 11²⁸⁻³⁰), must not be overlooked. That invitation shows the universality of Christ's outlook. The Son is willing to reveal the Father to all. But the connexion explains the personal note in the invitation. Jesus does not say 'Go to the Father'; He says 'Come unto me, and I will give you rest.' This is because He is the revealer of the Father; and the rest He offers is rest in the Fatherhood of God. The chapter describes the discouragements that darkened the noon of His ministry. He found rest to His own soul in the Father: 'I thank thee, O Father . . . Even so, Father' (vv.²⁵. ²⁶). This rest He desires to give to others. The only way in which men can come to the Father is by coming to Himself.

Two things are implied. One is that the Fatherhood of God is made accessible to men in Jesus Christ. He is the appointed trysting-place where men are sure to meet their heavenly Father. He was lifted up as an ensign (Is 11¹⁰. ¹²): when the nations see Him they know where to seek God. The children of God are scattered on the dark mountains of ignorance. Jesus is the trysting-place where they are gathered at the feet of their heavenly Father (Jn 11⁵²). If men come to Him, they see the Father. The other fact is that Jesus gives men knowledge of the Father by teaching them to live as God's children must live. They must be meek and lowly in heart (cf. Mt 5³⁻⁵); He

can make them so. They must also learn obedience to the Father's will. He offers to teach them this, saying with marvellous condescension, 'Take my yoke upon you, and learn of me.' He is wearing the yoke of obedience to the Father, and He finds it 'easy.' A yoke is made for two. Jesus invites each man desiring to be a son of God to put his shoulder under the other end of His own yoke. Then he will walk in step with the great Elder Brother. Thus learning from Jesus, he will become a worthy child of God.

This great word has special significance because it forms a link between the Synoptic teaching and the teaching of Jesus in John's Gospel. There the enjoyment of filial privileges is made to depend upon man's relation to the Son (see especially Jn 5¹⁹⁻⁴⁷ 6²⁸⁻⁴⁰ 8¹⁹. ²³⁻⁵⁶). The words declaratory of the love of God in sending the Son to save men are variously assigned to Jesus and to the Evangelist. But even if they are the Evangelist's reflexion upon the words of Jesus, they do no more than sum up the teaching of the Lord in the chapters quoted above.

In particular, it may be noted that Jesus claimed kinship with the Father because 'I do always the things that are pleasing to him' (Jn 8²⁹). This is in harmony with His reference to men who do the Father's will, as His 'brethren' (Mt 12⁵⁰). Men who accept His revelation of God and duty become His brethren; all these 'brethren' are related to God as His children. They comport themselves in a befitting manner, which is essentially different from the self-centred conduct of unregenerate men. This filial demeanour is gained by faith in Jesus as the Saviour. He offers Himself to men as the Redeemer, through whom they can break away from sin and adopt the filial attitude toward God (Mt 23⁸, Jn 10¹⁵. ²⁵⁻²⁹).

This conception of the teaching of Jesus on this subject is expressed by the Evangelist John in the striking sentence, 'As many as received him, to them gave he the right to become children of God, even to them that believe on his name: which were born not of blood, nor of the will of the flesh, nor of the will of man, but of God' (Jn 1¹². ¹³). Here men are described as becoming children of God by believing on the name of Jesus. They attain the dignity by a new birth that is from above. Their natural birth does not make them children of God. Before they stand in this relationship they must receive a Divine energy. This energy is brought to them by the Word made flesh, who offers Himself to the world. Moreover, this reception of Christ is a continuous exercise of faith (τοῖς πιστεύουσιν), implying an attitude Godward that is maintained from day to day.

If an illustration may be permitted, it would seem that Jesus represents men as like Robinson Crusoe's first canoe. It was designed to float in the water and was capable of doing so: but it could not get into the sea. So it lay on the shore like a log. Man is designed for fellowship with God, and is capable of living in filial relationship with Him. But before he can realize this destiny, he must be carried away from his native selfishness and be launched on the sea of Divine love. Jesus Christ is the mighty deliverer who can lift men out of death in sin and bring them to the Father. When men believe on Him, this purpose is fulfilled. They realize their destiny and become children of God. Then they spread their sails to the wind of heaven, and have 'life that is life indeed.'

The scope of this article does not include the general teaching of the Epistles on this topic. But a brief reference must be made to that teaching in so far as it involves a distinct reference to Jesus Christ. In general it may be said that the teaching of the Epistles reproduces all the main features of the teaching of Jesus. The children of God are possessors of a new life that has come to them by faith in Jesus Christ : Ro 8¹⁻¹⁴, Gal 2²⁰, 1 Jn 2²³ 5¹³. This new life manifests itself in a new moral state befitting God's children and due to the power of Christ : Gal 5¹⁶⁻²⁶, Eph 2¹⁻¹⁰, Col 3⁵⁻¹⁰. In this connexion it may be noted that Christians are called 'children of light,' who before becoming Christians were 'children of disobedience,' suffering 'the wrath of God' (Eph 2² 5⁶, Col 3⁶). Thus Christ is the Saviour through whom the children of God are re-born and morally renewed.

In particular, three descriptions of God's children are connected with aspects of Christ's work. (a) As Redeemer, He secures man's adoption into the family of God (Ro 8¹⁴⁻¹⁶, Gal 3²³⁻⁴⁶). This 'adoption' has been interpreted, in connexion with the antithesis between sonship and servitude, to denote the emancipation of sons enslaved by sin. This is the shade of meaning prominent in Galatians. In Romans the idea of adoption of those not previously sons is emphasized. In both cases, however, the adoption is due to the redeeming work of Jesus Christ, ministered to men by the Holy Spirit. The word 'adoption' is not used in Hebrews. But the idea is found there in the figure of the Author of salvation leading many sons to glory (2¹⁰). (β) As High Priest, Jesus secures access to the Father for all who come unto God by Him (Eph 2¹⁸, He 7²⁴·²⁵). This priesthood is exercised by Him as our 'Brother,' and was granted to Him in view of His experience of our temptations (He 2¹⁷ 4¹⁵). (γ) As King, Jesus Christ bestows a rich inheritance upon all His brethren. The children of God are 'joint-heirs with Christ' (Ro 8¹⁷).

In regard to this whole question, it should be remembered that in all probability our human speech cannot describe adequately relations that reach into the eternal, and concern God. The figure of 'children' is an analogy rather than an exact parallel. Therefore we should be misunderstanding the teaching of Jesus if we pressed the analogy too far and sought to discover the exact counterpart of each element of the human relation in that which we bear to God. Also it is important to recall that Jesus was not concerned with abstract relations. His purpose was practical and religious, and He used terms just so far as they served that purpose. His terminology was consistent ; it may not seem conclusive on all points that suggest themselves to abstract reasoning.

Literature.—Articles in Hastings' *DB* on 'God, Children of,' 'Jesus Christ,' 'Romans,' and 'Regeneration'; Commentaries on the NT, especially those of Sanday-Headlam, Westcott, and Lightfoot; Fairbairn, *Christ in Modern Theology*; Watson, *The Mind of the Master*; Bruce, *Kingdom of God*, and *St. Paul's Conception of Christianity*; Wendt, *Teaching of Jesus*; Beyschlag, *NT Theology*; Coe, *Religion of a Mature Mind*, 187-216, *Education in Religion and Morals*, 65 ff., 373 ff.; Dalman, *Words of Jesus*; Stevens, *Christian Doct. of Salvation*, and *Theol. of NT*.   J. Edward Roberts.

CHILIARCH (χιλίαρχος).—The title of this military officer is twice used in the Gospels : Jn 18¹² and Mk 6²¹ (AV 'captain,' 'high captains'; RV 'chief captain,' 'high captains'; RVm 'military tribune(s), *Gr.* chiliarch(s)'). It is the Greek equivalent for the Roman office of *tribunus militum*, an office of great historical antiquity, from the analogy of which the famous *tribuni plebis* took their name. The *tribunus militum* is called by Mommsen 'the pillar of the Roman military system'; he was an officer commanding a cohort. See, further, Legion.

A chiliarch with his 'band' (σπεῖρα) is represented by St. John as coming with Judas to take our Lord in the Garden of Gethsemane. If this is to be understood strictly as standing for a *tribunus militum* and his cohort, the use of so large a force

would point to a great (real or assumed) fear of popular disturbance on the part of the authorities. The words may, however, be used in a general sense for a body of troops under an officer (see Westcott, *ad loc.*).

In St. Mark's account of the martyrdom of John the Baptist, Herod the tetrarch of Galilee is represented as making a feast to his μεγιστᾶνες (highest civil officials), χιλίαρχοι (highest military officers), and πρῶτοι τῆς Γαλιλαίας (leading provincials). These 'chiliarchs' were officers of the army of the tetrarch, which would be organized on Roman models. For the association of μεγιστᾶνες and χιλίαρχοι cf. Rev 6¹⁵. (See Swete's *St Mark, ad loc.*).

M. R. Newbolt.

CHOICE.—In the Gospels, choice is always expressed by one small group of closely connected words, viz. ἐκλέγομαι, ἐκλεκτός, ἐκλογή. And these at once define the nature of the choice, which is not that of 'decision,' but that of 'selection.' Perhaps the English term which more precisely than any other answers to ἐκλέγειν is to 'cull,' to choose here and there one, that is to say, out of a larger number laid out in view. And this force of the word is rather emphasized by the fact that in the NT the active voice of the verb is not employed, but only the middle or passive, with derivatives which are passive in character. It is not, then, the action of choosing which is prominent, but its result ; or else the status or nature of that which is chosen. And this point is of some importance in view of the use to which some passages of the NT have been put by those who have attempted to elaborate from them doctrines of election or predestination. Stress is never laid chiefly on the election or predestination of the Almighty, but on the fact that such and such are actually found among those whom God has culled for Himself, and who constitute His own people. It would be an advantage to accurate Christian thought if the rendering 'elect' were eliminated from the NT, and were replaced by 'chosen' or 'select,' although it is a direct derivative of the original.

The central meaning of the terms employed is well shown in the following cases.—' He marked how they chose out the chief seats' (Lk 14⁷); 'Mary hath chosen the good part' (10⁴²); 'He called his disciples, and chose from them twelve, whom also he named apostles' (6¹³), with which other passages relating to the choice of the Twelve should be compared, viz. Jn 6⁷⁰ 15¹⁶·¹⁹ 13⁴⁸, Ac 1², and, as essentially the same, Ac 1²⁴; cf. also 1 Co 1²⁷·²⁸, Ja 2⁴. A further selection for some special service is indicated in such passages as—'God made choice among you that by my mouth . . .' (Ac 15⁷, cf. 6⁵ 15²²·²⁵); 'Many are called, but few chosen' (Mt 22¹⁴). And by an almost insensible gradation the use of the word passes on to such instances as the choice of Saul, 'a chosen vessel' (Ac 9¹⁵), 'the Christ of God, his chosen' (Lk 23³⁵, cf. 9³⁵), and the chosen people of God (Ac 13¹⁷, Eph 1⁴, 1 P 2⁴·⁶·⁹). The last named appear in a group of passages in the Gospels (on the lips of Christ Himself) which are of apocalyptic character, and in all which the English rendering is unfortunately 'elect'; *e.g.* 'Shall not God avenge his chosen?' (Lk 18⁷); 'For the sake of his chosen whom he chose, he shortened the days' (Mk 13²⁰·²²·²⁷ ‖ Mt 24²²·²⁴·³¹). To these there are many similar instances in the Epistles (Ro 8³³ 11⁵·⁷·²⁸, Col 3¹², 2 Ti 2¹⁰, Tit 1¹, 1 P 1¹; cf. Rev 17¹⁴). Individuals are spoken of as chosen (Ro 16³³, 1 P 5¹³, 2 Jn¹·¹³), and also angels (1 Ti 5²¹); while God's purpose of selection is mentioned (Ro 9¹¹), and the status of those selected (1 Th 1⁴, 2 P 1¹⁰).

From the foregoing it is clear that in the Gospels, and in the NT generally, 'choice' expresses a selection of some among other alternatives, and commonly selection for some special service ; God's people being selected that they may become His servants who serve Him and so serve all in the furtherance of His purposes of love, rather than on their own account alone. Moreover, God's choice is always viewed as an actual fact seen in its results, and never as an intention in advance ; except perhaps in reference to St. Paul's apostolate and Jacob's destiny, both of which are, however, so referred to only when seen in retrospect. See Elect, Freewill.

E. P. Boys-Smith.

CHORAZIN. — Mentioned once only in the Gospels, Mt 11²¹ = Lk 10¹³, along with Bethsaida, as one of the 'cities' (πόλεις) where most of Jesus' mighty deeds were done. The name is not found in the OT nor in Josephus; and it is not certain whether it be the same place as כרוב or כרויים mentioned once in the Talmud (*Menaḥoth*, 85a), where the superior quality of its wheat is praised. Jastrow's *Dictionary* gives '*Karzayim* near Jerusalem,' Dalman's 'כְּרוֹיִם name of place.' One MS has כרוב, two; see Rabbinowicz, *Variæ Lectiones*; Neubauer, *Géographie du Talmud*, p. 220. Most MSS of the NT spell Χοραζ(ε)ίν, others, especially in Luke, Χωραζίν; so Stephen in Luke, but not Elzevir, Mill; D both times Χοροζαίν, and the same form prevails in the Latin texts: C(h)orozain. Why the editions of the Peshiṭta, even Gwilliams', spell ܟܘܿܪܵܙܝܼܢ *Kōrāzīn*, we fail to see. Barhebræus gives expressly ܟܘܿܪܙܝܼܢ *Kurzīn* as the vocalization of the Peshiṭta, and *Chorazin* as that of the Greek.

Neither the grammatical form of the name (on which see Schwöbel, *ZDPV* xxvii. 134) nor its etymology is sufficiently clear. The place has been identified with *Khersa* on the eastern shore of the Lake of Galilee, but more probably with *Khirbet Kerāzeh*, 4 kilometres N. of Tell Ḥûm, first discovered by Thomson in 1857. Eusebius calls it a κώμη (*oppidum*), 12 Roman miles from Capernaum, in his time deserted; but 12 seems to be a misspelling of the MS for 2, as given by the Latin translation of Jerome (Eusebius, *Onomasticon*, ed. Klostermann, 174. 25, 175. 25).* On the ruins of Kerāzeh, especially its synagogue, see the literature quoted by Schürer, *GJV³* § 27, n. 59. Cheyne's list of Proper Names (in the Queen's Printers' *Aids to the Student of the Holy Bible*) recommends the pronunciation *Cho-ra'zin*; this is supported by the modern form *Kerāzeh*, if it be the same name; the accentuation of the first syllable, common in German, has the support of *Kurzin* in the Peshiṭta; in Latin *Chorozain*. The mediæval explanation of the name 'hoc mysterium meum' = הוא ראזי, goes back to Jerome (*OS* 61. 8). There was once a tradition that the Antichrist was to be born in Chorazin, and that its inhabitants were proud of this, and therefore the place was cursed by Jesus; see *Expos. Times*, xv. [1904] p. 524. The name Chorazin is, like that of Nazareth, an interesting illustration of the scantiness of our literary tradition.†　　Eb. Nestle.

CHOSEN ONE.—This, like 'Beloved' (wh. see), seems to have been a pre-Christian designation of the Messiah. ὁ ἐκλεκτός μου occurs in the LXX of Is 42¹, and is there defined as Ἰσραήλ. But in the Book of Enoch 'the Elect one' is a common title of the Messiah (cf. 40⁵ 49² 51³·⁵ 52⁶·⁹ 61⁵·⁸·¹⁰ 62¹). Traces of it still survive in the Gospels, but there seems to have been a tendency to avoid its use, perhaps on the ground that it might seem to favour so-called 'Adoptionist' views of the nature of Christ's relation to God. Lk 9³⁵ substitutes ὁ ἐκλελεγμένος (אBLΞ (1), 274 ᵐᵍ Syr Sin a ff. l. vg.

* In the Latin text (*OS²* 114. 7) the name is spelt 'Chorazin,' not '*Chorozain*,' as stated in *Encyc. Bibl.*, where also the modern name *Kerāzeh* is once spelt with Ḵ, as if it were ק.

† Among the mighty works done in Bethsaida the feeding of the 5000 is certainly to be reckoned (Lk 9¹⁰ff., where ἐπισιτισμός of v.¹² is to be explained from Βηθσαιδά = οἶκος ἐπισιτισμοῦ [*OS* 174. 7, 188. 75]). Hence it is tempting to find one of the mighty works done at Chorazin in the healing of the demoniac in the land of the Gerasenes or Gergesenes (8²⁶), and to combine this name with Chorazin. In his *Philologica Sacra* (1896, p. 21) the present writer suggested that the prominent part played by the swine in that story may be derived from a local name like *Ras el-chinzir* or *Tell abu-l-chinzir*. The plural of *chinzir* (swine) is *chanazir*, of which *Chorazin* might be a transposition.

codd. aeg. aeth.ᶜᵒᵈ· arm) for Mk.'s ὁ ἀγαπητός, and in Lk 23³⁵ we have 'the Messiah of God, the Elect.' Elsewhere the evidence is more doubtful. ὁ ἐκλεκτός τοῦ θεοῦ occurs in Jn 1³⁴ in א* 77, 218, Syr Sin Cur e, and is adopted by Burkitt, *Evangelion Da-Mepharreshe*, ii. 309. Lastly, 'approved Son' is given by Syr Sin in Jn 3¹⁸ for τοῦ μονογενοῦς υἱοῦ τοῦ θεοῦ. St. Mark and the editor of the First Gospel after him seem to have avoided the ὁ ἐκλεκτός μου of the LXX (Is 42¹) in their accounts of the Baptism and Transfiguration, and to have fallen back on a Christianized version of Is 42¹ preserved for us in Mt 12¹⁸⁻²¹, in which ὁ ἀγαπητός μου had taken the place of ὁ ἐκλεκτός μου of the LXX.

Connected with the use of this title of the Messiah in the Gospels is the question as to the meaning of the aorist εὐδόκησα in Mk 1¹¹ = Mt 3¹⁷ = Lk 3²². Bacon (*Journ. Theol. Lit.* xvi. 136–139) urges that this means '(on whom) I fixed my choice,' *i.e.* 'whom I elected,' and refers in the thought of the Evangelist to the Divine election of Christ by God (cf. *AJTh* ix. 451 ff.). So far as the First Gospel goes, there is much to be said for this. We might bring together the following passages 3¹⁷ 17⁵ ἐν ᾧ εὐδόκησα, 11²⁷ πάντα μοι παρεδόθη ὑπὸ τοῦ πατρός μου, 28¹⁸ ἐδόθη μοι πᾶσα ἐξουσία ἐν οὐρανῷ καὶ ἐπὶ γῆς, and possibly the ἦλθον of 5¹⁷ 9¹³ 10³⁴ and the 'sending' of 10⁴⁰ 15²⁴, as all in the mind of the Evangelist referring to the Divine choice, endowment, and mission of the eternally existing 'Son' (cf. 11²⁷) into the world. To these should be added the citation in 12¹⁸ 'Behold my son (servant?) whom I adopted, my beloved in whom my soul was well pleased,' where the aorists are most easily explained as expressing the Divine selection and appointment of the Messiah in a pre-temporal period. In the thought of the Evangelist, Jesus, born of the Virgin by the Holy Spirit, was the pre-existent Messiah (= Beloved) or Son (11²⁷) who had been forechosen by God (3¹⁷ 17⁵), and who, when born into the world as Jesus, was 'God-with-us' (1²³). In this respect the writer of the First Gospel shows himself to be under the influence of the same conception of the Person of Christ that dominates the Johannine theology, though this conception under the categories of the *Logos* and the Divine *Son* is worked out much more fully in the Fourth than in the First Gospel. On the other hand, terms such as 'choice,' 'adoption,' which at an early period seem to have been borrowed from the Jewish Messianic doctrine to express it, and which survive here and there in the Synoptic Gospels and in the Acts (cf. 9²² [Fl. Gig.] and 2 P 1¹⁷) are absent from St. John. Such terms were probably gradually dropped out of use because they could be used to support the view of the adoption of the man Jesus to be the Son of God, which they certainly did not originally express.　　W. C. Allen.

CHRIST. — See Atonement, Authority of Christ, Birth of Christ, Dates, Death of Christ, Messiah, Person of Christ, Preaching Christ, etc. etc.

CHRIST IN ART.—i. Symbols.—The representation of Christ by means of symbols is not earlier than that by means of pictures. There are found in the Catacombs at Rome at the commencement of Christian art not only the Fish symbol, but also pictures of the Good Shepherd, and of our Lord in certain Gospel scenes, all before the middle of the 2nd cent.; and of these the Good Shepherd carrying a sheep occurs in the Catacomb of Domitilla before the end of the 1st century. It will be, however, convenient to begin with the Symbols, proceeding thence through the Types to more direct representations of Christ.

1. The Fish was the most popular symbol of our

Lord in the middle of the 2nd cent., and continued so till the end of the 4th, when it suddenly went out of use. More than one cause made it so general. Originating as an acrostic (the Greek word for 'fish,' IXΘΥΣ, standing for Ἰησοῦς Χριστός, Θεοῦ Υἱός, Σωτήρ), it formed a most convenient secret sign among the Christians, being readily understood by the initiated as representing Christ in the fulness of His divinity. It carried with it also the thought of the sacramental feeding upon the Son of God, which is so prominent in early Christian art : e.g. the two paintings in the crypt of Lucina, which belong to the middle of the 2nd cent., and represent two baskets of bread, each containing a glass cup of wine and resting upon a fish. The earliest known representation of this symbol is even more significant : it occurs in the *Fractio Panis* fresco, recently discovered by Wilpert in the Catacomb of Priscilla, which belongs to the beginning of the 2nd cent., and is a picture of a primitive celebration of the Communion,—seven people are seated at a table on which lie five loaves, two fishes, and a two-handled mug, while the bishop or president at the end of the table is in the act of breaking a loaf. In this deeply interesting picture of the Eucharist we see a further reason why the Fish symbol was felt to be appropriate ; it carried the mind to the miracle of the loaves and fishes, which was an early type of the Eucharist because of Jn 6⁹⁻⁵⁹. The Fish symbolizes not only the Eucharist, but the sacrament of Baptism as well ; this is brought out by the common representation of a fish as swimming in the water (see below under 'Symbolic Scenes'). 'We little fishes,' says Tertullian (*de Bapt.* i.), 'after the example of our *Ichthus* Jesus Christ, are born in water.' Cf. St. Clement below, under 'Other Symbols.' This double symbolism is tersely expressed in the 2nd cent. inscription of Abercius recently discovered by Ramsay at Hierapolis :—'. . . everywhere was faith my guide, and gave me everywhere for food the *Ichthus* from the spring.'

2. Other Symbols.—The Fish was early combined with other symbols, such as the Dove, the Cross, the Ship, the Shepherd, and especially with the Anchor, the combination of the Fish and the Anchor (first found on the sarcophagus of Livia Primitiva about the middle of the 2nd cent.) being a hieroglyph for the common epitaph '*Spes in Christo.*'

There is an early mention of Christian symbols in St. Clement of Alexandria (*Pæd.* iii. 11) : ' Let the engraving upon the gem of your ring be either a dove, or a fish, or a ship running before the wind, or a musical lyre, the device used by Polycrates, or a ship's anchor, which Seleucus had carved upon his signet. And if the device represent a man fishing, it will remind us of an apostle, and of children drawn out of water.'

All these symbols, it will be noticed, are common ones, such as would not excite comment among pagans. However, the Dove (at first a symbol of peace) and the Ship (which represented the Church), the Lyre (a symbol of Orpheus, see below) and the Anchor of hope (see also under 'Cross') are not direct symbols of Christ ; nor, except by way of the Eucharist, are they representations of bread, wine, or the grape. The *Agnus Dei*, a post-Constantinian symbol, may more conveniently be considered under the head of 'NT types.'

In mediæval art a trace of the Fish symbol survived—as indeed it survives to-day—in the *vesica piscis*, a figure which is still customarily restricted to the seals of ecclesiastical persons and corporations. The Dove, at first used as an emblem of peace, sometimes with an olive branch in its mouth (though it occurs in pictures of the Baptism of Christ in the Catacombs), was the recognized symbol of the Holy Spirit in the apsidal mosaics of the 4th and 5th centuries, and thus has continued ever since : the Lamb, the Hand of God, and the Cross (see below), found in connexion with the Dove in these mosaics, also continued as common symbols in the Middle Ages, when interlaced triangles and circles further represented the Trinity.

Two emblems of immortality, the Peacock (from the fabled indestructibility of its flesh) and the Phœnix, rising from its ashes, were early used as types of Christ. The Star (Rev 22¹⁶) and the Sun (Mal 4²) were also used ; the Rose and Lily (Ca 2¹) were very favourite subjects of decorative art after the 13th cent., but they came to be used rather as emblems of Christ's Mother than of our Lord Himself, and often as badges of the royal houses in England and France : the Pomegranate, split open, originally a type of Divine grace, became similarly common as a Tudor badge. In the Middle Ages, when great emphasis was laid upon the Eucharistic sacrifice, symbols of the Passion were much in vogue, in addition to the Vine and Corn, the Chalice and the Host. Hence the use of the Pelican, the great prevalence of the *Agnus Dei* and the Crucifix, and the constant use of the Instruments of the Passion, in addition to the almost infinite varieties of the Cross. The Instruments of the Passion, so common still in decorative art, are the Crown of Thorns, the Nails, the Coat and Dice, the Scourges, Pillar, Ladder and Sponge, the Five Wounds, Hammer, Pincers ; to which are sometimes added the Sword and Staff, Lantern, Thirty Pieces and Cock, the Pierced Heart, and the Vernicle or Napkin of Veronica, and the Superscription INRI. The Passion-flower, a popular emblem at the present day, was introduced by the Jesuit missionaries from Mexico, as containing symbols of the Twelve Apostles, the Five Wounds, the Three Nails, and the Crown of Thorns.

3. Sacred Monograms.—The Alpha and Omega naturally appear early (though not in monogrammatic or interwoven form) because of Rev 1⁸ ; the first instance in the Catacomb of St. Priscilla, 2nd cent.—'Modestina AΩ,' which means 'Modestina live in Christ.' Some of the sacred monograms are really contractions ; for instance, the familiar IHC and XPC are the first two and the *last* letters of IHCOΥC and XPICTOC, just as MR stands for MARTYR, or DO for DOMINO ; contractions of this sort were extremely common in sepulchral inscriptions (*e.g.* 'Lucretia pax tecum in DO'), but there was no fixed method ; the abbreviations IH and XP alone are sometimes found, and also the initials IX, which, combined, formed the earliest or pre-Constantinian monogram ✕ (the first instance being in a 3rd cent. fresco in the Catacomb of SS. Peter and Marcellinus). None of these, however, are found by themselves, but only as abbreviations in the course of an inscription. The Constantinian monogram ☧ (for XP) is the first to stand alone, though it does also occur in inscriptions (*e.g.* 'Roges pro nobis quia scimus te in ☧') ; this monogram was considered a form of the Cross (see below) ; it is characteristic of the conversion of the Empire, and is rarely found subsequent to the Sack of Rome by Alaric in 410. It is often surrounded by a wreath, and often has the A and Ω on either side to mark the divinity of our Lord ; in a 4th cent. lead coffin from Saida in Phœnicia, the letters of the old symbol IXΘΥC lie between the arms of the monogram. Three main variations of it appear in which the Cross is made more apparent ⚛, ⟊, and ✳, but these are later and less common.

The contraction IHC, as subsequently Latinized into IHS, is now called the Sacred Monogram *par excellence*, and is as popular as it was in the Middle Ages and in the 17th and 18th centuries, when it was almost the only symbol of the kind ; this was owing mainly to its being misunderstood as the initials of ' Jesus Hominum Salvator' (or even of ' In Hoc Signo') ; in mediæval times the confusion may not have arisen, in spite of the ambiguity of the Greek H in Gothic character, for the letter J was often replaced by IH or HI, and 'Ihesus' was a common way of spelling the holy name. Meanwhile the contraction of the title XPS has been almost forgotten; its use in such an inscription as IHS XPS NIKA would seem strange to our eyes; but IHS XPS occur on a portrait of Christ in the Codex Egberti (*c.* 1000), and are not unknown in late mediæval art, *e.g.* both are found among the tiles of Malvern Abbey.

The initials of the Superscription INRI ('Iesus Nazarenus Rex Judæorum'), which now rank next to the IHS in popular estimation, do not seem to have appeared till the 13th cent., after which they became the favourite abbreviation of painters (cf. below under 'Crucifixion').

4. The symbol of the **Cross** eventually supplanted altogether that of the Fish. But in early Christian art representations of it are very rare, and at first only given in a disguised form, although the sign of the Cross was already so greatly reverenced towards the end of the 2nd cent. as to be used by Christians before almost every act of daily life,—dressing, eating, bathing, going to bed, etc.,—'quæcumque nos conversatio exercet, frontem crucis signaculo terimus,' etc. (Tert. *de Coron. Mil.* iii.). This great reserve was due partly to the natural shrinking from the portrayal of an instrument which was still in use for the most degraded form of execution, partly also to the fact that *all* Christian symbolism was necessarily of a hidden nature in the ages previous to the Peace of the Church. Thus the first representations of the Cross are very indirect; the cross-marks on the round Eucharistic loaves, which are found as early as the 2nd cent. (on a sarcophagus in the Catacomb of Priscilla), merely represent the folding up of the corners of the bread to make it round. The Anchor (a symbol which is rare after the 3rd cent.) often has a crossbar so marked as to be clearly symbolic; it was, in fact, according to Marucchi, a hidden form of the Cross, a symbolized hope in the Cross.

The earliest representation of the Cross by itself —the *swastica* or 'fylfot' 卍—which is found in the Catacombs in the 3rd cent., and is not uncommon in the earliest Christian textiles—was a form so 'dissimulated' as to pass unnoticed among pagans who were accustomed to its use as a conventional ornament. Only one undisguised Cross occurs in the Catacombs during the ages of sepulture (*i.e.* before the Sack of Rome in 410), and this is the so-called Greek or equilateral Cross +, which has no special connexion with the Eastern Church; a small 4th cent. example of this Cross has been found in the nameless *hypogeum* near St. Callistus. There is a Cross, still dissimulated, in a 4th cent. fresco in the Catacomb of Callistus, a green tree with two branches, under which are two doves; for the rest, in the Catacombs the earliest 'true and proper Cross,' as Wilpert calls it, the earliest, that is, which is not a bare symbol, is in the Catacomb of Ponziano—a gemmed *Latin* Cross of the end of the 5th cent.; another similar example in the same place is attributed to the 6th or 7th. In a late 4th cent. mosaic in the church of St. Pudenziana, Rome, is one of the few undisguised Crosses that have been discovered of an earlier date than the 5th cent.; it stands in the midst of the half dome of the apse, and is of the so-called Latin shape (*crux immissa*), and gemmed; but the use of the Latin Cross did not become common till the 6th century.

The *crux commissa*, or Tau Cross, appears earlier; for, though a more exact representation of the actual instrument of death, it would pass unnoticed as the letter T. Of this form Tertullian says (*adv. Marc.* iii. 22), 'Ipsa est enim littera Græcorum Tau, nostra autem T, species crucis.' The Cross was probably recognized as hidden in the pre-Constantinian form of the Monogram ✗; and though it is still

disguised in the 'Constantinian Monogram,' yet this symbol ☧ was considered as a Cross in the 4th cent., and it must have been the 'Cross' which Constantine saw in the sky, since the Cross is always represented by this Monogram in contemporary art. In the later varieties of the Monogram, as we have seen, the Cross was more plainly introduced, *e.g.* ⚰.

Later ages increased the number of forms till there were about fifty, not counting subdivisions, which are duly named by the mediæval heralds, *e.g.* the Cross Potent, Fleurie, Fleurettée, Patonce, Moline, Botonnée, Pommée, Urdée, Fourchée, Paternoster, Triparted, Crescented, Interlaced, etc., in addition to the familiar Maltese Cross worn by the Knights Templars and the Knights of St. John, the Cross of St. James borne by the Knights of St. Iago, the Saltire of Scotland and Ireland, etc. It may be added that the use of small Crosses carried about the person dates from the 5th cent., when also processional Crosses came into use (*e.g.* a Cross is carried, and candles, in a 5th cent. ivory, at Trèves); it was not till later that the processional Cross came to be taken from its staff and placed on the altar during service time; indeed, the use of an altar-Cross continued to be far from universal throughout the Middle Ages.

5. The Crucifix, which became the principal feature of mediæval churches, is naturally of still later date than the Cross, for the motives which caused the early Church to shrink from an open representation of the latter would apply still more to the realism of the Crucifix. In addition to this, the blithe spirit of Christian art in the first four centuries was certainly against the portrayal of scenes of suffering and sorrow; representations of scenes from the Passion are very rare (see below), and pictures of death or martyrdom do not occur.

That the death upon the Cross was 'foolishness' to pagans as well as a stumbling-block to the Jews (1 Co 1[18. 23]), is curiously illustrated by the caricature of the Crucifixion which was scratched on the wall of the pages' quarter at the Palatine in the latter part of the 2nd cent., and was discovered in 1856; the figure on the Cross has an ass's head, and by it stands a worshipper with the scrawled inscription ΑΛΕΞΑΜΕΝΟΣ ΣΕΒΕΤΕ ΘΕΟΝ ('Alexamenos adores his god'). This caricature is, as a matter of fact, the only picture of a crucifixion that has been found within the first four centuries.

The earliest Christian example of any kind is on a panel of the 5th cent. doors of St. Sabina at Rome, about a century and a half after Constantine had abolished the penalty of crucifixion. The next is in a 5th cent. ivory in the British Museum. The third is in a Syrian MS of the year 586, and is the earliest dated example. But all these three belong to the category of 'Scenes from the Gospels.' The earliest actual Crucifix that is extant is a small amulet at Monza, which was given by Gregory the Great to Adaluwald the son of Queen Theodolind, and belongs therefore to the end of the 6th century. Early Christian literature (the reliability of which is illustrated by every fresh discovery in the realm of archæology) is markedly silent on the subject, the first mention of a picture of the Crucifixion being in the middle of the 6th century. At the close of that century Gregory of Tours supplies the earliest mention of an actual Crucifix, when he tells us that there was one in a church at Narbonne, and that Christ appeared in a vision to rebuke this representation because of its nakedness. About the time of Charlemagne (800) the use of Crucifixes became very general, and they gradually ceased to be of the ideal type; but as this development belongs rather to the representation of Christ in 'Scenes from the Gospels,' the details are given below under that head.

ii. TYPES.—**1. Pagan.**—Early Christian art is classical not only in its reserve about the Cross, not only in its use of the ordinary classical decorative subjects, but also in its use of certain pagan myths as symbolizing aspects of the Christian faith. It is remarkable that the moral value of the better elements of mythology should have been thus recognized at the very tombs of martyrs who had suffered at the hands of paganism. The figure of *Orpheus* was familiar as a funereal symbol among the ancients because of his fabled rescue of Eurydice from Hades: in the Catacombs it was adopted by the Christians as a symbol of the attractive power of the Master. There are five instances of Orpheus with his lyre in the Catacombs, the earliest being of the 2nd century.

Sometimes Orpheus is represented in his conventional Phrygian costume playing upon the lyre, while various beasts, birds, and reptiles listen to him; sometimes it is sheep that gather round, for Orpheus was a shepherd, and thus his story was interwoven with the Good Shepherd theme; sometimes the figure of Orpheus is even painted in the centre of a vault—in the place usually reserved for the Good Shepherd.

The story of *Psyche* was similarly used, typifying here the love of God for the soul. *Ulysses and the Sirens* occurs several times on Christian sarcophagi, and *Hercules* feeding the dragon with poppy-seed is also found. The *peacock* and the *phœnix*, symbols of immortality, and thus of Christ triumphing over death, as well as the *dolphin*, carrier of souls to the Isles of the Blessed, were other pagan types that continued in use among the Christians. In this connexion may also be mentioned the ancient Egyptian symbol of the so-called Nile key ♀,* which was used in textiles by the Christians in Egypt for several centuries after the conversion of that country.

2. OT types.—OT subjects are common in the Catacombs, and in some the principal figure is identified with Christ. This is the case with *Moses striking the Rock*, where Moses becomes the type of Christ and the water a type of Baptism, the point being sometimes emphasized by the conjunction of Christ drawing a fish out of the water, or in the sarcophagi by the raising of Lazarus. The *Sacrifice of Isaac* was also a favourite subject as typical of the Sacrifice of Christ. The story of *Jonah* was the most popular of all (there are 57 examples), as a type of the Resurrection which had been established by Christ Himself (Mt 12[40]). In the story of *The Three Children* the figure of the Son of Man is sometimes introduced. Although such OT subjects as *Adam and Eve* do not readily admit of the same typical treatment, yet in some 4th cent. sarcophagi Christ is introduced as the Logos standing between them. Representations of *Noah* appear as early as the end of the 1st cent., but the ark is a symbol both of deliverance and of Baptism (1 P 3[21]), so that Noah represents the saved rather than the Saviour. From the 4th cent., when mosaics came into use, OT subjects were largely employed in the great apsidal decorations of the succeeding centuries; but all that need here be mentioned are the 6th cent. mosaic of St. Vitale at Ravenna, where Abel with a lamb and Melchizedek with a loaf stand as types of Christ on either side of the Christian altar,—which is draped and has on it a two-handled chalice and two loaves,—and the 7th cent. mosaic at St. Apollinare in Classe, where Abel, Melchizedek, and Abraham leading Isaac stand round a similar altar.

3. NT types.—The earliest manner of representing our Lord as a solitary figure was under the type which He Himself had given—that of the *Good Shepherd*. In its reserve, its tenderness, its gracious beauty, the figure of the Good Shepherd was characteristic of the first Christian art, and its subsequent disappearance was also characteristic of much.

This figure, which appears first in the Catacomb of Lucina in the early part of the 2nd cent. and became thereafter exceedingly common, is in no sense an attempt at portraiture. The Shepherd is always a typical shepherd of the Campagna, a

beardless youth, bareheaded, clad in the tunic of the peasant; the tunic is generally sleeveless, with sometimes a small cape over the shoulders, while leggings complete the realism of the attire. There are two distinct classes of Good Shepherd pictures in the Catacombs:—(a) 21 represent him feeding his flock (in one case he protects it against a pig and an ass); these belong to the 3rd and 4th cents.; (b) 88 pictures represent him carrying a sheep (very rarely a kid—there is probably no foundation for the beautiful idea in M. Arnold's famous sonnet); in these the sheep, according to Wilpert, represents the soul of the departed person. Class b begins very early, 3 examples of the end of the 1st cent. occurring in the Catacomb of St. Domitilla. In spite of the realism of the Good Shepherd pictures, there is a certain hieratic grace and dignity about the figure that marks it at once as a Christian subject, though the figure of a shepherd was common enough in pagan art (e.g. the Hermes Kriophoros bearing a ram, or the Apollo Nomios) to make it both a safe and an accessible model for Christians. The theme is varied in many ways: occasionally the Good Shepherd carries a kid, sometimes other sheep or goats stand near him; in a fresco in the Catacomb of St. Callistus he is surrounded by the Four Seasons; sometimes he sits and plays upon a syrinx; sometimes he carries a crook, sometimes a milk-pail, a symbol of the gift of life,—indeed, the sheep and the milk-pail are occasionally represented by themselves, e.g. in the crypt of St. Lucina two sheep stand by an altar on which lie a milk-pail and a crook. Tertullian (c. 200) mentions the painting of the Good Shepherd on chalices as a common custom (de Pudic. vii.). Statues were probably not introduced before the time of Constantine, but an exception was made in the case of the Good Shepherd; and the most lovely example of all is the statue of the 3rd cent. which was found in the Catacomb of St. Callistus, and now stands in the Lateran Museum. Pictures of the Good Shepherd have become popular again in our own time, but they are attempts at portraiture and very far from the idealistic type—it may almost be called a symbol—of the early ages, which represents a shepherd as Christ, and does not attempt to portray Christ as a shepherd.

The symbolism of the Good Shepherd, which had held so prominent a place in the affections of the Church, disappeared rapidly after the 4th cent., and was replaced by another NT type, very different in its meaning, the *Agnus Dei*, the mystic Lamb of St. John the Baptist and of St. John the Divine. Apparently it was not possible for men's minds to keep in view the two ideas at once of Christ the Shepherd and Christ the Lamb, though this is attempted in the Catacomb of St. Domitilla (2nd cent.), where the Lamb bears the crook and milk-pail of the pastor. The earliest known instance of the identification of Christ with the Lamb is on the spandrels of the sarcophagus of Junius Bassus, who died in 350: Christ is represented among the Three Children, striking water from the Rock, raising Lazarus, multiplying the Loaves, baptized by John, while another spandrel represents the giving of the Law; and in each case all the characters (with the exception of Lazarus) are represented as lambs. In the Catacomb of SS. Peter and Marcellinus there is a fresco (c. 400) of the Lamb, haloed but with no Cross, standing on a hillock from which four streams issue. Apocalyptic scenes were the favourite subject of the great apsidal mosaics of the 5th and 6th cents., and naturally the 'Lamb, standing as though it had been slain,' became more and more the favourite type of Christ. Often the Lamb was accompanied by twelve other lambs issuing from Bethlehem and Jerusalem, to represent the Apostles, as in the apse of SS. Cosmas and Damianus at Rome, A.D. 530.

There is something significant in this identification of the Lord with humanity, paralleled as it is by the earlier tendency to represent under the Fish symbol not only Christ Himself, but also the Christian convert. Established as the type was before the end of the 4th cent., it was not till the 5th that the Lamb was pictured with the nimbus and the cross. By 692 this method of representing Christ had so superseded all others, that the Council in Trullo (Quinisext) decreed 'that henceforth Christ shall be publicly exhibited in the figure of a Man and not of a Lamb,' in order that 'we may be led to remember Christ's conversation in the flesh, and His passion, and saving death, and the redemption which He wrought for the world.' None the less, although the positive object of the decree was attained, the representation of the *Agnus Dei* was one of the most common symbols of the Middle Ages, in sculpture, in glass, in metal work and embroidery, and sometimes in painting, as in the culminating example of the Van Eycks' great picture at Ghent (c. 1430), where the Lamb stands wounded

---

* See art. 'Cross' by Count Goblet d'Alviella in Hastings' forthcoming *Dict. of Religion and Ethics*.

upon an altar, the blood flowing into a chalice, surrounded by a great company of angels and saints. Thus, this type has proved a most enduring one, in spite of the growing use of actual representations of our Lord after the Quinisext Council.

iii. PORTRAITS OF CHRIST.—1. Scenes from the Gospels.

The earliest pictures of Christ are not attempts at portraiture, but represent His figure only as occurring in scenes from the Gospels : the figure is needed to explain the subject, but it is the figure of a man of varying type, and, as in all early Christian art, without attributes ; the character is determined only by its position and by the fact that Christ, like the Apostles and generally other Scripture characters, is always represented as wearing the pallium of the philosopher (not the toga), a convention which has survived down to our own time, though realists like Tissot have begun its destruction. It was not till after the Peace of the Church that the head of Christ was distinguished by a nimbus : this custom began in the Catacombs c. 340, and the nimbus was reserved for the figure of Christ till the end of the 5th cent., when it was given to the Saints as well, and the nimbus of Christ began to be distinguished by a cross within the circle. Among the earliest instances in which the figure of Christ appears are those which represent Him in the same guise as that which was so common in later ages, viz. as an *infant in His Mother's arms* ; but it was for a different reason, since the Mother and Child are but parts of a complete scene, such as that of the Visit of the Magi.

The earliest of all is in the Capella Greca in the Catacomb of St. Priscilla, and belongs to the beginning of the 2nd cent., where three Magi approach the Mother and Child with their offerings : this subject was a very common one, fifteen instances being mentioned by Wilpert in the Catacombs, and it continued so in the succeeding ages of sculpture and mosaic. In the Catacomb of St. Priscilla there is another fresco (of the first half of the 2nd cent.), representing the Virgin and Child sitting, while a figure (the prophet Isaiah) points to a star. The picture of the Virgin and Child in this well-known fresco is very beautiful, recalling in stateliness and grace as well as in design Raphael's treatment of the subject : nothing could be more unlike the hieratic stiffness of the intervening Byzantine and Gothic types. The figure of the Child is naked in this instance, though in some it is draped ; but in all, the treatment is that which we are accustomed to associate with the Renaissance. A fine 3rd cent. fresco in the same catacomb has the figure of a female *orans* (representing a consecrated virgin) in the midst, while a bishop on one side sits in his cathedra, accompanied by his deacon, and in the act of dedicating a virgin ; he points to the figure on the other side of the picture, which is that of the Virgin Mary holding the Child Christ in her lap. There is also one instance of the Child lying alone in a manger (now much decayed) given by de Rossi. To carry the subject a step further, the important 6th cent. mosaics of St. Apollinare Nuove at Ravenna must be mentioned : along one wall of the nave a procession of male martyrs approaches Christ enthroned between angels, and along the other a procession of female martyrs approach the Virgin and Child similarly enthroned between angels ; the Virgin has a plain nimbus and that of the Child contains the cross, while both figures are of the lofty hieratic type that endured for so many subsequent centuries ; but it is remarkable that (while the figure of the enthroned Christ on the other wall is approached directly) the procession of female martyrs is led by the Magi, and thus the common tradition is still preserved by which the Mother and Child appear as part of this Gospel scene. This may be taken as a transitional instance, leading on to the later manner of representing the Virgin and Child, which has been the chief theme of Christian art since that age, and the occasion of so many masterpieces, from Cimabue, Giotto, Filippino Lippi, Botticelli, Della Robbia, and the great company of Christian sculptors, Raphael, Michael Angelo, Murillo, and countless others down to our own time.

In the 2nd and 3rd cent. frescoes of the Catacombs the adult figure of Christ appears in many pictures of Gospel events ; and it is remarkable that there is in the Catacomb of St. Pretestato a scene from the Passion which is almost as early as the first Virgin and Child,—viz. of the first half of the 2nd cent., — and yet occurs once only : the *Crowning with Thorns* is the subject represented, and other scenes from the Passion may have occupied the now vacant spaces which form part of the scheme ; yet no other picture of any Holy

Week event occurs in the Catacombs. It is remarkable also that the subject most referred to by indirect type—the Resurrection of our Lord—is never once illustrated until the 4th cent. ; while the figure of *Christ raising Lazarus* appears as early as the beginning of the 2nd cent., and occurs in no less than 53 extant examples. It must always be borne in mind that the Catacombs were not, as is popularly supposed, the ordinary churches or hiding-places of the Christians, but were designed and used for burials and services in connexion with the departed, and their art is entirely confined to subjects within this purpose. Thus, the Gospel events are all chosen with reference to two themes—the deliverance and blessedness of the departed, and the sacraments of Baptism and Holy Communion, which were closely bound up with the thought of the faithful departed, as is shown by the reference to baptism in 1 Co 15^{29}, and by the many chapels for and pictures of the Eucharist in the Catacombs. Thus, the Raising of Lazarus, the scenes of Healing, the Conversation about the Living Water with the Samaritan woman (as well as the pictures in which our Lord does not appear, such as Jonah and Daniel), all refer to deliverance from the powers of death ; while the Baptism of Christ, the Multiplication of the Loaves and Fishes, and the Miracle at Cana, are chosen for their reference to the Sacraments. There is a good deal of convention in the treatment of these subjects—*e.g.* Lazarus is represented as a mummy erect in a classical doorway, while Christ—youthful and beardless—touches him with a rod. The same scenes are carried on in the sculptures of the sarcophagi—Lazarus, the Miracles of Healing, of the Loaves, of Cana, the Epiphany, as well as the Good Shepherd ; while in the 4th cent. sarcophagi are found the Entry into Jerusalem, and Christ before Pilate ; the limited funereal cycle of subjects is widened out, and in the 5th cent. ivories and the carved doors of St. Sabina there are added Christ Preaching, the Agony in the Garden, the Betrayal, Christ bearing His Cross, Christ and St. Thomas, the Resurrection, and the Ascension.

But the number of events illustrated did not increase rapidly ; even in modern times it has continued to be limited, as we are reminded by a comparison with Tissot's illustrated Life of our Lord. The following list of the subjects from the life of Christ which are illustrated in ancient and mediæval art is given by Detzel ; those which occur in the Catacombs we have italicized :—

Nativity, *Virgin and Child*, Circumcision, Presentation, *Visit of Magi* and Shepherds, Flight into Egypt, Christ among the Doctors ;—*Baptism*, Temptation, *Miracle at Cana*, *Samaritan Woman*, *Healing of the Palsied*, *of the Woman with the Issue*, *of the Blind*, *of the Man with Dropsy*, *Lepers*, *Raising of Lazarus*, *of the Man at Nain*, *of Jairus' Daughter*, *Feeding of the Multitude*, *Casting out Devils*, Stilling of the Storm, the Transfiguration ;—Entry into Jerusalem, [Jesus taking leave of His Mother, by Dürer], Washing the Disciples' Feet, Last Supper, Agony in the Garden, Betrayal, Trial, Scourging, *Crowning with Thorns*, Carrying the Cross, Crucifixion, Descent from Cross [' Pietà' pictures], Burial, [Idealizations of the Passion or ' Misericordienbilder,' as, *e.g.*, in the legend of the Mass of St. Gregory], Christ in Hades ; Resurrection, and the subsequent events—Christ greeting the Women, ' Noli me tangere'—Journey to Emmaus, Christ appearing to the Apostles, Christ and St. Thomas, *Draught of Fishes at the Sea of Tiberias*, Ascension, [*Last Judgment*].

The set of fourteen pictures found in Roman Catholic churches and called the ' Stations of the Cross,' some of which are legendary, are of post-Reformation origin. One scene from the Gospels, the Crucifixion, must be taken separately.

The Crucifixion as a scene from the Gospels (not in isolation) first appears in the 5th cent. on the wooden doors of St. Sabina at Rome. In this earliest example the primitive feeling is shown by the fact that no actual cross appears ; Christ and the two thieves stand, almost completely naked, with the elbows near the body and the hands stretched out and nailed to little blocks of wood; the Christ is bearded and with long hair, and his eyes are open; the sculptor has filled up the background with a suggestion of the walls of Jerusalem.—The second example is also of the 5th century. It occurs on an ivory box in the British Museum: the cross is shown, and the Christ is nailed to it with arms stretched out horizontally; His face is youthful and beardless, His eyes open, and His body naked but for the loin-cloth; on one side stands a reviling Jew, on the other Mary and John, while near them Judas hangs from a tree: in this sculpture the title appears REX IVD. It is on another panel of the same box that the earliest representation of Christ bearing the cross appears.—The third Crucifixion is a miniature in a Syrian book of the Gospels, now at Florence, by Rabulas, a monk of Mesopotamia, and is dated 586: the Christ is bearded, and wears a long tunic; as in the former example, the feet are separate and the arms horizontal; the two thieves, St. John and the women, and the two soldiers with the spear and sponge, are included in the picture.

The history of the development of the Crucifix may be thus summarized. Appearing first as a scene of Gospel history in the 5th cent., it continued infrequent for another century, after which, in the 6th cent., the Crucifix in isolation begins also to appear. During the 5th, 6th, and 7th centuries it has the following characteristics: the Christ wears either a loin-cloth or a long tunic reaching to the ankles, there are nails in the hands and generally in the feet also, the feet are always separate, either with or without the block or 'suppedaneum,' the Christ is always living, He wears neither the royal crown nor the crown of thorns, the title, when there is one, consists generally of the letters IC XC, the cross is either *commissa* (T) or *immissa* (†); certain adjuncts also appear, the sun and moon generally, the thieves often, Mary and John generally, the two soldiers sometimes, sometimes also the soldiers dicing, and sometimes Adam and Eve.

About the time of Charlemagne (800) there was a great increase in the use of the Crucifix; and in addition to the early or Ideal type, a second type, the Realistic, began to appear. The Ideal type continued till the end of the 13th cent. (*e.g.* in the Codex Egberti at Trèves, *c.*1000, where the Christ is represented with a youthful, almost girlish face, and living, though without the royal crown, which is often added at this period to emphasize the triumphant aspect of the Crucifixion). The Realistic type, in which the Christ is represented dying, as in modern crucifixes, had become in the 11th cent. a distinctive mark of the Eastern Church, and figures in the disputes which ended in the great schism of 1054: Cardinal Humbert accused the Greeks of putting a dying Christ upon their crosses, and thus setting up a kind of Antichrist; the Patriarch Michael Cerularius retorted, in the discussion at Constantinople, that the Western custom was against nature, while the East was according to nature. None the less, the Eastern type had already found its way into Italy itself through the influence of the Byzantine craftsmen who worked there, and it spread steadily throughout the West, till by the 13th cent. it was the dominant type all over Christendom. There was sometimes in the transitional period a mingling of the types, as, *e.g.*, in the Crucifix over the gate of St. John's Church at Gmünd, where the figure is youthful, with open eyes and in a tranquil posture, without the crown of thorns, but the wounds and blood are shown, and the arms are bent and the head drooping. The complete Real-

istic type is well illustrated in the altar-cross at the Klosternenburg, Vienna, A.D. 1181, where the body is collapsed, the knees bent, the arms wrung, and the head sunk. In the 13th cent. the Crown of Thorns appears, and the feet are laid one over the other, so that the figure is held by three nails instead of four. The Realistic tendency of the Middle Ages entirely ousted the earlier triumphant type, and in the 14th cent. only the dead Christ is found upon the Cross in art. The revival of painting at this period led to a further increase of Realism, and the artists who pioneered the Renaissance delighted in the display of their anatomical knowledge: none the less there is much majesty of quiet reserve in such Crucifixions as those of Angelico in the 15th or that of Luini at Lugano in the 16th century. Among the famous examples may be mentioned those of Giotto (at Padua), Mantegna, Perugino (at Florence), Antonello da Messina, Martin Schongauer, Hans Memling, Raphael, Tintoret, Veronese, Rubens, and Vandyke,—the later being the more painful. The great Crucifixion by Velasquez, in the 17th cent. at Madrid, illustrates the furthest point which was reached. Westcott truly says that it 'presents the thought of hopeless defeat. No early Christian would have dared to look upon it.' The same type—a tortured figure hanging low from the hands—continued in the Crucifixes of the 18th cent., though the mediæval type was revived in the 19th, and at the present day there is a tendency to revert to the earliest Ideal type which showed Christ 'reigning from the tree.' There can be little dispute as to the fact that the mediæval Crucifix did tend to over emphasize one aspect of our Lord's life, though its constant use in Lutheran churches forbids us to connect it specially with one set of opinions. There would perhaps have been less feeling on the subject among English people if the Ideal type had been used—the benedictory figure, draped and crowned, which embodies the idea but does not attempt to represent the appearance of our Lord's death.

2. Symbolical Scenes.—As we have seen, the earliest of any representations of Christ is under the form of the Good Shepherd, and occurs before the end of the 1st cent., while close upon this come pictures of Him in His Mother's arms, and a picture of His Baptism and of the Crowning with Thorns in the first half of the 2nd century. Before the close of the 2nd cent. there appear representations of Him in scenes that are symbolical of Christian doctrine; and the earliest of these are in connexion with the Sacraments, while in the 3rd and 4th centuries the pictures of Him surrounded by Saints in glory begin to appear.

(*a*) *Sacrament Pictures.*— In addition to the Gospel scenes of the Feeding of the Multitude, the Miracle of Cana, and the Baptism of Christ, in the Catacombs, there are Sacrament pictures that are purely symbolical.

In the Sacrament Chapels of St. Callistus, whose decorations belong to the second half of the 2nd cent., there is a figure of our Lord, beardless and wearing the pallium as usual, stretching out His hands in the gesture of consecration over a tripod on which lie loaves and the mystic fish, while an *orans*, typical figure of the soul of the person buried in the tomb, stands by. Among other pictures in the same place is one supposed to represent the Seven Disciples at the Sea of Tiberias after the Resurrection; Christ is giving them bread and fish, while further along in the same picture a fisherman is represented drawing a fish out of the water, to symbolize union with Christ in baptism, and further still is Moses striking the rock: thus Baptism and the Eucharist are symbolized together. This connexion of the two Sacraments is very common, and often it is done by the juxtaposition of the Feeding of the Multitude, of which there are in the Catacombs 28 examples in all, and Moses Striking the Rock, of which there are no less than 68 examples. In the same chamber is a picture of the baptism of a catechumen, and near it the Baptism of Christ in the river, out of which a fisherman is drawing a fish. In other places the idea is abbreviated into a mere hieroglyph of loaves or loaves and fishes.

In the Middle Ages there was a very popular form of Sacrament picture, which had reference, however, to the sacrifice and not to Communion, viz. the 'Mass of St. Gregory,' referred to above, where Christ appears upon the altar with the attributes of His Passion, wounded, and crowned with thorns. The modern Eucharistic pictures of our Lord, which are common among both Catholics and Protestants, need only the bare mention here.

(b) *Pictures of Christ in Majesty.*—There are no pictures of our Lord alone, or of Him as the central dominating figure of a formal group, till the 3rd century. Up till then—from as early a period as the end of the 1st cent.—the artists, when they wished to represent Him alone (as often in the centre of a decorated vault), were content to do so under the type of the Good Shepherd. At the beginning of the 3rd cent. there appears in the Catacomb of St. Pretestato the earliest picture of Christ as a solitary figure; He sits reading the Law; the face is young and beardless, and the hair is so ample as to give almost a feminine aspect. In the same century pictures occur of our Lord sitting in judgment, surrounded by saints, as, *e.g.*, in the Nunziatella cemetery, where the Christ, beardless as usual, but with hair falling over the forehead, holds a scroll of the Law, and in the panels round the vault are four saints alternating with four *orantes*. There are seven examples in the Catacombs of Christ seated in the midst of the Twelve Apostles, and one of Him with the Four Evangelists, and also nine busts, all painted in the 4th cent., *i.e.* the Constantinian era; besides one of Christ giving crowns to saints, which is not earlier than the beginning of the 4th century. There is a sculpture of Christ enthroned on the sarcophagus of Junius Bassus († 350); and the same subject is often beautifully carved on the ivories of the 4th, 5th, and 6th centuries. By the end of the 4th cent. the great mosaic pictures of Christ in glory begin, the earliest being in the church of St. Pudenziana in Rome, *c.* 390. These became thenceforward the leading feature of the apsidal decoration of the basilicas in the 5th and 6th centuries; and they are by far the greatest and the most imposing of the early pictures of our Lord. He is represented in these mosaics as enthroned in the glory of the Apocalypse, among the angels, the Apostles, and other saints and martyrs. The last great mosaic of our Lord occurs over the central door within the nave of St. Sofia, Constantinople: in this famous picture Christ sits upon a throne, while an emperor prostrates himself at His feet, and on either side are medallions of the Virgin and St. Michael.

Pictures and statues of our Lord in Majesty are common in the Middle Ages, when other symbolical representations occur. A favourite one (which is often found in the uppermost light of stained glass windows, and in other forms of art) is the Coronation of the Virgin by our Lord, which, like the Mass of St. Gregory, is characteristic of the change that had come over Christendom at that time. There should be mentioned also, as illustrating the lowest depths of materialism in religious art, the anthropomorphic representations of the Holy Trinity, which appear as early as the 9th cent.; in some the Son bears a cross, while the Father is distinguished by a tiara, and the Holy Spirit by a dove over His head; in others there are two human figures with a dove between them; in others the Father holds a Crucifix upon which a dove descends: there are even examples of a human figure with three faces.

A new type of symbolical Portrait—the 'Sacred Heart'—has been popular among Roman Catholics since Margaret Mary Alacoque started that cultus in 1674. As a symbol by itself the Heart is already to be found in the 16th cent.—often with the Crown of Thorns, or the Nails, and the monogram IHS. In the Sacred Heart pictures and statues which appeared after the new cultus had been started, the heart of the Saviour is, by a violent symbolism, disclosed within His breast; it is marked with a wound, surmounted by a Cross, and often surrounded by flames and the Crown of Thorns.

3. Types of Portraiture.—In the first five centuries three distinct types appear in the portraiture of Christ. They are thus classified by Detzel:

First type.—A youthful beardless figure of purely ideal character, such as is found in the usual classical subjects, thus representing the perfect and eternal humanity of our Lord. Kraus calculates that there are 104 examples of this type in the Catacombs, 97 in the sarcophagi, 14 in the mosaics, 45 in gold glasses, 50 in other arts, and 3 in MSS. Although the earliest representations are of this kind (indeed the 3rd and 4th cent. pictures of Christ in Majesty are as purely ideal as are the 1st and 2nd cent. pictures of the Good Shepherd), there are instances also of the beardless Christ in the mosaics (*e.g.* in the Raising of Lazarus at St. Apollinare Nuova, and the Throned Christ at St. Vitale, both of the 6th cent.), in the time of Charlemagne, and as late as the 13th cent., *e.g.* in the golden altar at Aix-la-Chapelle, where the Christ is of youthful aspect and enthroned.

Second type.—Christ is represented bearded, in the fulness of manly strength; thus there is still the conception of an ideal humanity, immortal and unmortified, without harshness and without sorrow. Examples occur frequently in the mosaics of the 4th to 6th cents., as at St. Pudenziana, St. Maria Maggiore at Rome, St. Apollinare in Classe, and St. Vitale at Ravenna; and also in the late 7th or 8th cent. fresco of the Catacombs of St. Generosa.

Third type.—The Byzantine type, which appears thrice in the Roman mosaics of the 5th and 6th cents. (*e.g.* at St. Paolo fuori le Mure), and embodies the growing monastic asceticism of the time. Christ in this type appears older and more severe, with longer hair and beard, deep-set eyes and hard features. This developed into the still harder and stiffer 'debased Byzantine' type.

To these may be added the *Modern type,* in which artists innumerable have striven to embody their highest conceptions of human perfection and Divine goodness. After the long sleep of pictorial art, the revival of sculpture and painting gave us such statues as the Beau Dieu of Amiens, and all the famous pictures of such artists as Orcagna, Fra Angelico, Masaccio, Perugino, Raphael, Leonardo, Luini, Michael Angelo, Titian, Dürer, Guido, Murillo, Rubens,—to mention only some typical instances,—and the many works of our own times. All have followed in the main the type which the mediæval and Renaissance artists obtained from the legendary descriptions which are mentioned below.

iv. THE QUESTION OF THE LIKENESS OF CHRIST.—It is obvious from what has been already stated, that no true portraits of Christ have come down to us, and that no attempt was made at reproducing His likeness in the first centuries. The earliest portraits varied much in type, and had only this in common—that they were all idealistic, representing the countenance of a man unmarred by faults or peculiarities; while, in particular, the art of the Catacombs and of the earliest sculpture, with entire disregard of historic actuality, represented the Lord under the type of a beautiful youth. The early controversy as to the appearance of Christ shows how entirely all tradition of His actual appearance was lost.

Influenced by certain OT passages (*e.g.* Is 53), Justin Martyr had already said, in the earliest extant references to the aspect of Jesus, that He appeared 'without beauty' (*Tryph.* 14, 36, 85, 88); later, Clement of Alexandria had also argued in favour of

Christ being 'unlovely in the flesh' (*Strom.* iii. 17); Tertullian went so far as to say, He was 'not even in His aspect comely' (*c. Jud.* 14). So we find that Celsus taunted the Christians for worshipping one of mean appearance, to which Origen replied (*c. Cels.* vi. 75, 76) that Christ's person must have had about it something noble and Divine, and quoted the Transfiguration to show that His aspect depended upon the capacity of the spectator. St. Jerome, on the other hand, appealed to Ps 44 as a proof of Christ's beauty; and thus there arose two schools—those who held that He was 'fairer than the children of men,' among whom were St. Augustine, St. Ambrose, and St. Chrysostom, and those who, in their ascetic reaction against the vices of pagan beauty-worship, declared that He had 'no form nor comeliness' and 'no beauty that we should desire him,' among whom were St. Basil and St. Cyril of Alexandria.

If we turn from these disputations to the Gospels, we find, indeed, no descriptions of our Lord, but we discover on every page One whose personality had a wonderfully attractive power, and whose dignity impressed friends and foes alike. And we may conclude that the instinct of the Church as a whole was right in attributing beauty to the Son of Man, since the Incarnation was the taking on of the perfection and fulness of humanity. At the time of the controversy, those on the extreme ascetic side went so far as to make hideous pictures of the Redeemer; but the idealism of early art had an easy triumph in the end, because Christ is indeed the Ideal of humanity, and the outward form of man is ultimately the expression of the soul within.

The fact that the early portraits of Christ are purely ideal is the more remarkable, because there are strongly characterized portraits of St. Peter and St. Paul of the 2nd and 3rd centuries. The representations of Christ in the Gospel scenes of the 2nd and 3rd cents. are, as has been stated above, merely figures of the classical type necessary for the determination of the incident depicted, and only to be distinguished by the situation in which He is represented, and partly by the pallium in which He and the Apostles are always portrayed.

It is hardly necessary to dwell on the portrait of Himself which Christ was fabled to have sent to Abgar, king of Edessa, by the hand of Thaddæus; or on the various legends of Veronica and her napkin. St. Peter's at Rome claims to possess the true handkerchief of Veronica; but of this relic Bartier de Montault, who saw it in 1854, says that 'the place of the impression exhibits only a blackish surface, not giving any evidence of human features,' and he adds that the supposed copies of it have no iconographical value whatever (*Ann. Archéol.* xxiii. 232).

The emperor Alexander Severus (*acc.* 222) placed in his *lararium* the image of Christ, as well as those of Abraham and Orpheus; a sect of Gnostics also venerated images of Christ, Pythagoras, Plato, and Aristotle; but in neither case is it claimed that actual portraits were used. Eusebius (*c.* 325) tells us that a bronze statue of Christ stretching out His hands to a kneeling woman had stood till the time of the emperor Maximin Daia (*acc.* 308) at Cæsarea Philippi, and that he himself had seen it at Paneas (*HE* vii. 18): in his time it was regarded as a representation of Christ, erected in gratitude by the woman whom He had healed of the issue (also called Veronica). Most historians hold with Gibbon, that it was really the statue of an emperor receiving the submission of a province, and that this accounts for the inscription, 'To the Saviour the Benefactor'; but, on the other hand, it is urged as improbable that Eusebius should have mistaken so familiar a subject, or that it should have been removed by Maximin from its public position and ultimately destroyed by Julian the Apostate (*acc.* 361) if a pagan character could have been proved for it. There is thus a chance that one supposed actual portrait of Christ did exist before the 4th century.

Eusebius himself, however, in his well-known letter to Constantia (Migne, *Patr. Gr.* xx. 1515), says plainly that images of Christ are 'nowhere to be found in churches, and it is notorious that with us alone they are forbidden,' and mentions that he took away from a woman two painted figures like philosophers which the owner took for representations of Paul and the Saviour, 'not thinking it right in any case that she should exhibit them further, that we may not seem like idolaters to carry our God about in an image.' Here both the dislike of anything like portraits of Christ and the reason for that dislike are plainly stated. However, the establishment of Christianity in the Empire rapidly caused a change of feeling, and images were soon common. With the half-pagan people this led to idolatry, and the Iconoclastic Controversy in the East (716–842) was the result: one of the earliest incidents in that long struggle was the removal by Leo the Isaurian of the statue of Christ which stood over the bronze gateway of his palace at Constantinople; in its place he set up a plain cross. The second Council of Nicæa (787) vindicated the use of images; but they were not finally restored till 842. The West was untouched by the controversy, and the use of all kinds of images went on unchecked; but in the East statues are not allowed within the churches—but only pictures—to this day. The pictures of the East have retained their rigidly conservative character; but in the West the greatest artists have striven from age to age to represent our Lord in the utmost majesty and beauty.

The type which they ultimately settled upon was doubtless influenced by the supposed descriptions of Christ's appearance, though none of these have any historical value.

The most famous is the letter of ' Lentulus, president of the people of Jerusalem,' to the Roman Senate, a forgery of about the 12th century. 'There has appeared in our times,' writes the supposed Lentulus, 'a man of tall stature, beautiful, with a venerable countenance, which they who look on it can both love and fear. His hair is waving and crisp, somewhat wine-coloured, and glittering as it flows down over his shoulders, with a parting in the middle, after the manner of the Nazarenes. His brow is smooth and most serene; his face is without any spot or wrinkle, and glows with a delicate flush. His nose and mouth are of faultless contour; the beard is abundant, and hazel coloured like his hair, not long but forked. His eyes are prominent, brilliant, and change their colour. In denunciation he is terrible; in admonition, calm and loving, cheerful, but with unimpaired dignity. He has never been seen to laugh, but oftentimes to weep. His hands and his limbs are beautiful to look upon. In speech he is grave, reserved, modest; and he' is fair among the children of men.' This beautiful description was doubtless influenced by earlier works of art and embodied earlier traditions, as that, for instance, of St. John Damascene, the champion of images against Leo the Isaurian (*c.* 730) and the last of the Greek Fathers; he described our Lord as beautiful and tall, with fair and slightly curling locks, dark eyebrows which met in the middle, an oval countenance, a pale complexion, olive-tinted, and of the colour of wheat, with eyes bright like His Mother's, a slightly stooping attitude, with a sweet and sonorous voice and a look expressive of patience nobleness, and wisdom (J. Dam. *Opp.* i. 340). In another place (*ib.* 630) he indignantly reproaches the Manichees with the view once held by earlier Fathers, that the Lord was lacking in beauty.

Thus we may safely conclude that there is no authentic portrait or description of Christ, while admitting that the type accepted for more than a thousand years is all that a Christian can desire, since it is that of a perfect humanity in which, so far as men could portray it, the fulness of God dwells bodily.

LITERATURE.—Wilpert's *Roma Sotterranea* (1903) gives for the first time accurate reproductions of the frescoes in the Catacombs, with an exhaustive study carrying on the work of de Rossi (*Roma Sotterranea*, 1864–1867, tr. by Northcote and Brownlow). Garrucci's *Storia dell' Arte cristiana* (1873–1881) is being supplanted by the accuracy of mechanical reproductions. Also by Wilpert are *Principienfragen der christlichen Archäologie* (1889), *Ein Cyclus christologischer Gemälde* (1891), *Die Gottgeweihten Jungfrauen in den ersten Jahrhunderten* (1892), *Fractio Panis* (1896), *Die Malereien der Sacraments-Kapellen* (1897). The Catacombs are also described by O. Marucchi, *Le Catacombe Romane* (1903). See also A. Venturi, *Storia dell' Arte Italiana* (1901), an exhaustive illustrated history, in progress; H. Detzel, *Christliche Ikonographie* (1896) V. Schultze, *Archäologie der altchristlichen Kunst* (1895)

F. X. Kraus, *Geschichte der christlichen Kunst* (1896); O. Marucchi, *Éléments d'Archéologie Chrétienne* (1900). Among earlier works are Rohault de Fleury, *L'Évangile* (1874), *La Messe* (1883–1889); Grimouard de Saint-Laurent, 'Iconographie de la Croix' in Didron's *Annales* (1869). W. Lowrie's admirable illustrated handbook on *Christian Art and Archæology* gives a bibliography of special works on early painting, sculpture, ivories, mosaics, etc. Westcott, in his *Epistles of St. John*, Appendix iii., cites the Patristic authorities. The dictionaries by Smith-Cheetham (*DCA*, 1875–1893), Kraus (*RE*, 1886), and Martigny (*Dict. des antiquités chrétiennes*, 1877 and 1889) are all somewhat out of date, but the first is the best. Slighter books are A. Pérard, *L'Archéologie chrétienne* (1892); F. W. Farrar, *The Life of Christ in Art* (1894), which is useful but not always accurate; E. L. Cutts' handbook on *Early Christian Art* (1893). Wyke Bayliss' *Rex Regum* (1898) is a quite uncritical attempt to prove the existence of authentic portraits, based partly on Heaphy, *Likeness of Christ* (1880). Mrs. Jameson's *History of Our Lord* (1864), *Legends of the Madonna* (1857), *Poetry of Sacred and Legendary Art* (1848), are naturally in need of some revision. Later works are J. Hoppenot, *Le Crucifix dans l'Histoire* (1899); M. Engels, *Die Kreuzigung Christi* (1899); J. Cartwright, *Christ and His Mother in Italian Art* (1897); J. L. French, *Christ in Sacred Art* (1900); A. Venturi, *La Madonna* (1900), and many general books on art and artists.

PERCY DEARMER.

CHRISTIAN (The Name).—The word 'Christian' occurs in the NT only in Ac 11²⁶ 26²⁸ (about 20 years later), and 1 P 4¹⁶. The author of Acts alludes to it once in his earlier treatise (Lk 6²²), however, putting into the mouth of Jesus a sentiment whose linguistic form, at least, is coloured by the experiences and terminology of the Apostolic age. In some other passages where it is apparently mentioned (*e.g.* Ac 5⁴¹, Ja 2⁷), the 'name' is not 'Christian' but 'Christ,' while the references in Josephus (*Ant.* XVIII. iii. 3) and the Pompeii inscription (*CIL* iv. 679), it may be noted in passing, are too uncertain to be used as evidence for the title. Other and later inscriptions, however, are accessible.

For the origin and primitive usage of the term we are thus thrown back upon the three first-named passages. Of these, the fontal reference in Ac 11²⁶ explains that the name by which the religion of Jesus has been known for nineteen centuries was coined by the pagan slang of Antioch on the Orontes, a city which, like Alexandria, was noted for its nicknames. Yet the title is not a rough *sobriquet*. It expresses a certain contempt, but not derision, though St. Luke does not inform us whether it was coined by the mob or by government officials. 'Christian' (Χριστιανός) simply means 'a follower of Christ,' just as *Pompeianus* or *Herodianus* denotes 'a follower or partisan of Pompey' or 'of Herod.' 'Christ' was thus taken as a proper name. It meant no more to these Syrian pagans than some leader of revolt or obscure religious fanatic in Palestine. His name was ever on the lips of a certain set of people, and it was but natural that these should, for the sake of convenience, be distinguished as 'Christ's adherents' or 'Christians.' Unconsciously, in giving the title — which there is no evidence to show was applied previously to Jews—these citizens of Antioch were emphasizing one deep truth of the new religion, viz. that it rested not on a dogma or upon an institution, but on a person; and that its simple and ultimate definition was to be found in a relationship to Jesus Christ, whether 'Christos' to these Syrian Antiochenes was some strange god (Ac 17¹⁸) or a Jewish agitator. An outstanding trait in the Christians whom Pliny found in Bithynia was that they 'sang a hymn to Christ as to a god' (Plin. *Ep.* x. 96, *ad Trajan.*) at worship. From the impression made by facts and features like this, it was but a step to designate the new sect as 'Christ's folk or party.'

It was neither the original nor the chosen name of believers in Jesus Christ. Their inner titles (see Weizsäcker's *Apost. Age*, i. p. 43 f.) were 'brethren,' 'disciples,' and 'saints,' all of which preceded, and for some time survived alongside of,

'Christians.' Nor could the title have been coined by the Jews, who would never have admitted that Jesus of Nazareth was the 'Christ.' To them believers in Jesus were 'Nazarenes' or 'Galilæans.' It was the pagan community of Antioch alone that would invent and apply this title. Now a name implies life. Titles are not required unless and until a definite, energetic fact emerges. And the need evidently felt for some such designation as 'Christian' arose from two causes: (*a*) from the conspicuous extension of the new movement throughout the country and the city, and (*b*) more particularly from the predominance of Gentile Christians, who could not be provisionally grouped, like most of their Jewish fellow-believers, with the community and worship of Judaism. There was a Jewish ghetto at Antioch. But the local, heterogeneous paganism yielded an incomparably richer harvest to the efforts of the Christian age ts, so that the general success of the movement produced, for the first time, a noticeable alteration in the proportions of Jewish and Gentile Christians—so noticeable, indeed, that, as the historian points out, it necessitated an attempt on the part of the outside public to verbally classify the adherents of the new faith. The significance of this step is patent to the historian. He signalizes the crisis. The Christianity he knew was overwhelmingly a Gentile Christianity, and in Ac 11²⁶ he is keen to mark its début, as well as to suggest that the name 'Christian' was primarily and principally applied to Gentile Christians. 'Truly,' as Renan observes, 'it is remarkable to think that, ten years after Jesus died, His religion already possessed, in the capital of Syria, a name in the Greek and Latin languages. Christianity speaks Greek, and is now finally launched into that great vortex of the Greek and Roman world which it will never leave.' Its weaning from the breast of Judaism had commenced. And this was due to that increasing sense of Christ's personal authority which has been already noted (cf. Amiel's *Journal Intime*, Eng. tr. p. 3 f.). The more the significance of this came to be grasped, as the new faith expanded beyond the precincts of Judaism, the more did the distinctive universalism of the Gospel assume its true place.

For, while the basal conception of 'Christian' is Semitic ('Christ'), the linguistic termination (*-iani*) is either Latin or (more probably) Greek. Even were it Latin, it would be hasty to attribute (with Baur) the origin of the term to Rome, where Tacitus is our first pagan witness for its currency about A.D. 110. Early designations in *-ιανός* (cf. Mk 3⁶, Justin's *Dial.* 35) were not infrequent among the Greeks of Asia Minor, and it is arbitrary scepticism to hold that St. Luke in Ac 11²⁶ must have antedated and misplaced the origin of the name, or that Tacitus has done the same. The latter (*Annal.* xv. 44) describes Nero's victims as 'men whom the common people loathed for their secret crimes, calling them Chrestians. The name was derived from Christ, who had been put to death by Pontius Pilate, the procurator, during the reign of Tiberius.' Long before that period it must have been the interest of the Jews and Christians alike to differentiate themselves to some degree, one from the other. And the circumstances of the Neronic *émeute*, which was probably instigated by the Jews, must have made the distinction plain, once and for all, to the local authorities. The inherent probabilities of the case, therefore, seem to preclude any reasonable suspicion of a *hysteron-proteron* upon the part of the Roman historian; nor is it unnatural, even for rigid historical criticism, to admit that the distinctive name of 'Christian' may have been coined and current nearly twenty years earlier upon the banks of the Orontes. In short, both passages in Acts give one the impression of being historically authentic reminiscences; had the author been more anxious to emphasize the new name, he would not have employed it so sparely and incidentally. It is curious to notice that, outside the Church, Epictetus, slightly later than Paul, used 'Galilæans,' while Marcus Aurelius employed ·Christians.'

In 1 P 4[16] (cf. Lk 6[22], Jn 16[2]), together with Pliny's letters (*Epp.* x. 96, 97) less than fifty years later, we catch one glimpse of the connexion between the name 'Christian' and the civil or social penalties in which it involved believers (cf. Mommsen and Ramsay in *Expositor*, 4th series [1893], vol. viii.). To 'suffer as a Christian' *i.e.* (for being a Christian) covers a wide range of experience, from molestation to official and even capital punishment. The latter extreme, however, is not prominent in this passage, although the term ἀπολογία certainly suggests it. But the vague outline of 1 P 4[14-17] is filled out and vividly coloured by the later evidence of Pliny and of the 2nd cent. martyrs' literature, which shows how Christianity was treated as a forbidden or illicit religion, hostile to the national cult, and therefore exposing any of its adherents, without further question, to the punishment of death.

How soon and how far the mere name of 'Christian' was thus a capital offence, it is not easy to determine, but by the 2nd cent. the ordinary formula of confession before a magistrate was, 'I am a Christian.' This was put forward as the natural and sufficient reason for refusing to swear by the genius of the Emperor, and it was usually accepted by the authorities as final. Polycarp's martyrdom at Smyrna is our earliest case in point. But the story of the martyr Sanctus in Gaul, not long afterwards, shows how widespread was this habit. When tortured by the authorities, he steeled himself so firmly against them, that he would not so much as tell his name or nation or city. All his answer to their inquiries was, "I am a Christian" (Eus. *HE* v. 1). Pliny's account of his own judicial proceedings is equally blunt and plain. When people were accused of Christianity, he writes, 'I asked them personally whether they were Christians; if they confessed it, I asked them a second and a third time, threatening them with punishment. Then, if they adhered to their confession, I ordered them off to execution.' The test applied to doubtful cases was that of offering worship to the Emperor's statue. 'No real Christian,' says the governor, 'can be made to do that.' Nor could the name of Christian be legally borne by any one who added sacrilege to high treason, in refusing to worship the ancestral gods of the State. Christianity, *ipso facto*, was a challenge to these deities. Hence to avow the name of 'Christian' was to expose oneself to pains and penalties, either voluntarily or involuntarily incurred.

Both 1 P 4[16] and Ac 26[28] denote the use of the title by outsiders (Ja 2[7] referring probably to 'Christ,' not 'Christian'), and this is corroborated by the evidence of Christian writings in the 2nd cent., where we find that its comparatively rare occurrence is confined mainly to the Christian apologists, *i.e.* to writers who were principally concerned with the outward relations of the faith to society and to the State. Traces of its use among Christians themselves are to be found, however, in Asia Minor during the first quarter of the 2nd cent. (Ignatius—himself a native of Antioch—and the *Didache*, cf. *Mart. Polyc.* 3, 'the God-beloved and God-fearing people of the Christians'), in Gaul by the middle of the 2nd cent. (Eus. *HE* v. 1), and elsewhere (cf. *Ep. ad Diogn.* 'Christians are in the world as the soul is in the body,' etc. etc.). Gradually, as time went on, the title came to assume the position of authority which it has occupied for centuries, though it does not seem to occur on a tomb till the close of the 3rd cent. (Asia Minor). And this process was marked, if not accelerated, by a double play upon the word. (i.) It was often pronounced or mispronounced *Chrestiani*, as if derived from the familar proper name *Chrestus* (cf. Suet. *Claud.* 25), the vernacular adjective χρηστός being equivalent to 'kindly,' 'excellent,' 'worthy' (cf.

1 P 2[3], perhaps a slight play on the word). Such is the reading of ℵ in the NT passages, of most of the inscriptions, of Tacitus (apparently), and of Suetonius (*Claud.* 25, 'Chresto') certainly. Writers like Justin, Tertullian, and Clement of Alexandria catch at this idea. On the principle of *nomen et omen*, they retort upon their critics and opponents, 'If our name has this meaning, why hold it up to opprobrium? Does it not suit our characters?' Perhaps, too, as Harnack conjectures, the very choice of the imperfect *appellabat*, instead of the present *appellat*, indicates that Tacitus seeks to draw a distinction between the popular mistake in A.D. 64 and the more correct usage of his own day (*c.* 110). 'The common people used to call them *Chrestians* (while nowadays, of course, we know that their proper name is Christians).' (ii.) The other play upon the word was more private, though it also may have originated in some popular etymology. It was connected with *Christos* as 'the anointed.' 'We are called Christians,' says Theophilus (*ad Autol.* i. 12), 'because we are anointed with the oil of God' (χριόμεθα ἔλαιον Θεοῦ, cf. Tert. *Apol.* 3, and Justin's *Dial.*).—These and other motives contributed to render the term so popular, that there are traces, as early as Tertullian (*loc. cit.*) and Eusebius (*HE* II. iii. 3), of a disposition to ignore or deny its pagan origin and to represent it as a creation of the Apostolic or early Christian consciousness. So holy and catholic a title, it was felt, must have arisen inside the Church. Ignatius twice employs it in order to plead for Christians who are Christians in deed as well as in name (*Magn.* 4, *Rom.* 3)—a significant allusion. And he usually employs 'Christianity' (which first occurs in his Epistles, cf. *Magn.* 10, *Phil.* 6) as the antithesis to Judaism.

Two and a half centuries later came Julian's reaction against the title. It was dictated, as Gibbon admits, partly from a superstitious fear of the sacred name, and partly from contempt for it and for its bearers. 'As he was sensible that the Christians gloried in the name of their Redeemer, he countenanced, and perhaps enjoined, the use of the less honourable appellation of Galilæans' (*Decline and Fall*, ii. 540, Bell's ed.). Naturally this restriction had but a limited and transient effect. 'Christian' became more and more the watchword of the Church, despite the rise of 'catholic' within and the use of 'Nazarene' (in the East) without.

In the modern usage of the term, three points are of especial interest. One is the frank denial, by Strauss and others, of any right, upon the part of modern Christians, to the title in question (see an uncompromising article in the *Fortnightly Review*, March 1873, entitled 'Are we yet Christians?'), presupposing that the Apostles' Creed is the norm of Christianity. The opposite view is well put by Rathbone Greg (*Creed of Christendom*, vol. i. p. xlix f.). The second point is the deliberate repudiation of the name, as savouring of sectarianism, by certain Unitarians (cf. the first volume of Dr. Martineau's *Life*, by Drummond and Upton). And, thirdly, it is interesting to notice that an American sect, dating from the revival of 1801, called themselves by the name of 'Christians' (pronouncing the first *i* long), in order to bring out their unsectarian principles.

Bunyan made 'Christian' the antithesis to 'graceless,' and various other definitions, practical and philosophical, have been essayed. For Mr. Samuel Laing's, see his *Problems of the Future* (ch. viii.), and cf. Mr. Le Gallienne's *Religion of a Literary Man* (ch. vii.), and Sir John Seeley's *Natural Religion* (pt. ii. ch. iii.). 'He who can pray the Lord's Prayer sincerely must surely be a

Christian,' says Rothe; while Martineau's definition, in reference to a church, runs thus: 'imbued with Christ's spirit, teaching His religion, worshipping His God and Father, and accepting His law of self-sacrifice.' Perhaps the data of the NT would be covered adequately by the declaration that the name 'Christian' belongs to any one who can call Jesus 'Lord' in the sense of 1 Co 12³. See, further, the following article.

LITERATURE.—Besides the articles in Hastings' *DB* i. pp. 384–386 (Gayford), and *Encyc. Bibl.* i. 752–763 (Schmiedel), the Commentaries on Ac 11²⁶, and Histories of the Apostolic age (*s.v.*), consult Lipsius, *Über d. Ursprung u. d. ältesten Gebrauch d. Christennamens* (1873); Keim, *Aus dem Urchrist.* (1878), pp. 1–78; Carr in *Expositor* (June 1898), pp. 456–463; Harnack, *Ausbreitung des Christenthums* (1902), pp. 37–38, 54, 57, 294–297 [Eng. tr., see Index, *s.v.*]; also Zahn, *Einleitung in d. NT*, ii. pp. 34, 39–42; Renan, *Les Apôtres*, p. 234 f.; Westcott's note in his *Epistles of St. John*; Farrar, *Paul* (ch. xvi.); Lightfoot, *Apostolic Fathers*, pt. ii. vol. i. 400 f., vol. ii. 134. On the later use and form of the word consult Blass, *Hermes* (1895), p. 465 f.; Kattenbusch, *Das apost. Symbolum*, ii. 557 f.; Watkins, *Christ. Quart. Review*, i. p. 47 f.; Ramsay, *Church in Roman Empire* (Index, *s.v.*); Sanday in *Church Times* (June 21), 1901; and Leslie Stephen, *An Agnostic's Apology* (pop. ed.), 130.

JAMES MOFFATT.

CHRISTIANITY is the name given to the religion founded by Jesus of Nazareth, which is professed by more than one-fourth of the human race, including the foremost nations of the world. As an abstract name for a fully developed religion, it was not, and could not be, in use from the beginning. Only gradually, as the Christian community reached self-consciousness, and more especially as need arose from without of distinguishing its adherents from those of other religions, was a distinctive name adopted.

It is not the object of this article to sketch in outline the history of Christianity, to rehearse its doctrines, describe its triumphs, or vindicate its claims. But in a Dictionary of this kind it seems desirable to inquire into (1) the history of the name itself; (2) the proper connotation of the name and the best mode of ascertaining it; hence (3) the significance of the changes which have passed over Christianity in the process of its development; and (4) the essential character of the religion named after Christ and portrayed in the Gospels.

i. HISTORY OF THE NAME.—This is fully discussed in the preceding article.

ii. CONNOTATION OF THE NAME. — The difficulties which arise when we attempt to mark out the correct connotation of the word are obvious, and the reason why some of them are insuperable is not far to seek. A definition should be simple, comprehensive, accurate; whereas Christianity is a complex multiform phenomenon, one which it is impossible to survey from all sides at the same time, and accuracy cannot be attained when a word is employed in many different senses, and when that which is to be defined is regarded from so many subjective, diversified, and sometimes incompatible points of view. The essence of a great historical religion—with a record extending over some two thousand years, taking different shapes in many diverse nationalities, itself developing and altering its hue and character, if not its substance, in successive generations—cannot easily be summed up in a sentence. Whilst, if an attempt be made to describe that element of permanent vitality and validity in the religion which has remained the same through ages of growth, unaltered amidst the widest external and internal modifications and changes, the character of such a description obviously depends upon the viewpoint of the observer.

A religion may be viewed from without or from within, and an estimate made accordingly either of its institutions and formularies and ceremonies, or of its dominant ideas and prevailing principles. To the Roman Catholic—who represents the most widely spread and influential of the sections of modern Christianity—its essence consists in submission to the authority of a supernaturally endowed Church, to which, with the Pope at its head, the power has been committed by Christ of infallibly determining the Christian creed, and of finally directing Christian life and worship in all its details. The Catholic Church, according to Möhler and the modern school, is a prolongation of the Incarnation. To the Orthodox Church of the East, the paramount claim of the community on the allegiance of the faithful depends on its having preserved with purity and precision the formal creed, fixed more than a thousand years ago, from which, it is alleged, all other Christians have more or less seriously departed. The Protestant regards his religion from an entirely different standpoint. He may be of the 'evangelical' type, in which case he will probably define Christianity as the religion of those who have accepted the authority of an inspired and infallible Bible, and who trust for salvation to the merits of the death of Christ as their atoning Saviour. If he claims to be a 'liberal' Protestant, he will describe Christianity as a life, not a creed, and declare that all attempts to define belief concerning the Person of Christ and other details of Christian doctrine are so many mischievous restrictions, which only fetter the free thought and action of the truly emancipated followers of Jesus.

Under such circumstances, can any considerable measure of agreement as to the real essence of Christianity be reached, or a truly scientific definition be attained? The acceptance of the supernatural authority of a single community would put an end to all discussion, but those who appeal to such authority are not agreed amongst themselves. As an alternative, it has been usual of late to fall back on history as the sole possible arbiter. The historian can only recount with as much impartiality as possible the sequence of events in a long and chequered career, and leave the warring sects and parties to settle their differences as to what true Christianity is, without making any attempt to judge between them.

Both these methods—the purely dogmatic and the purely historical—virtually give up the problem. A better course than either may be adopted. The historical method must be employed at the outset; a careful induction must lay the basis for subsequent deduction and generalization. Christianity is an organism possessing a long and complex history, not yet finished. That life-history is better known and understood now than ever, from the upspringing of the earliest germ onwards, and the laws which have regulated its growth and the principles operating in its development, can be determined in broad outline by the scientific historian without much fear of contradiction. But the analogy between the growth of the Christian religion and that of an animal or vegetable organism in physical nature, fails in certain important respects. On the one hand, the growth of Christianity is not yet complete, the great consummation is as yet invisible. On the other, the origin of the religion of Christ cannot be compared with the deposit of a tiny and indeterminate and almost invisible germ. Before the period covered by the NT writings had passed, what may be called the formative and normative stage of the religion was complete. Sufficient advance had been made to enable any critical student to arrive at a standard by which the true character of subsequent developments may be judged. Criticism, for the purpose of determining the facts of history, must not be excluded from any scientific inquiry, as it virtually is by those who invoke the infallible authority of a Church or a Book. But, on the other hand, criticism must not be merely subjective and arbitrary, else religious truth is simply that which every man troweth, and Christianity nothing more than what individual Christians choose to think it. By a candid and careful comparison of the religion in its simplicity and purity with the various forms it has assumed in the course of centuries amongst various nations and races, an answer may be obtained to the question, What is Christianity? which is neither purely dogmatic on the one hand, nor purely empirical on the other. As Dr. Hort said of the Church, 'The lesson-book of the Ecclesia is not a law-book but a history,' so the history of Christianity becomes a lesson-book for all who would understand its real essence.

The question thus opened up is emphatically modern. As the name 'Christian' was not given till those outside the pale of the Church found it necessary to differentiate the believer in Christ from the adherent of other religions, so the need of a scientific definition of Christianity was never felt by faith, nor could one be formed, till the standpoint was occupied from which the young science of Comparative Religion has taken its rise. We have therefore to ask, What was precisely the nature of the religion founded by Christ as recorded in the Gospels and Epistles? Has it remained in substance the same without fundamental change? If, as is obvious, it has markedly altered during a long period of growth and expansion, has its development been legitimate or illegitimate? That is, has the original type been steadfastly maintained, or has it been seriously perverted? Is a norm fairly ascertainable and a return to type from time to time possible?

iii. CHANGES IN CHRISTIANITY IN THE COURSE OF ITS DEVELOPMENT. — During the lifetime of Jesus, discipleship was largely of the nature of personal attachment; it implied confidence created by the teaching, the character, and the works of the Master. Even during this period, however, not only was there room for reflexion and inquiry to arise, but eager inquiry was inevitable. The appearance of a unique personality who spake as no other man spake and wrought works such as none other man did, irresistibly suggested the question, 'Who art thou, what sayest thou of thyself?' Jesus Himself occasionally prompted such inquiry, and was not satisfied with an undefined loyalty. Once, at least, He pointedly asked His disciples, 'Who say ye that I am?' (Mt 16^{15}). Again and again in the course of His ministry a sifting took place, as the Master made more exacting demands upon the allegiance of His followers, and showed that a cleavage must take place between those who really understood the drift of His teaching and were prepared at all costs to obey it, and those who did not. The tests which were applied were for the most part practical in their character, 'Whosoever doth not bear his own cross and come after me, cannot be my disciple' (Lk 14^{27}). But the 'offences' which caused many to forsake Him as a teacher were often occasioned by His departure from traditional and familiar teaching, His assertion of superiority to the highest Jewish law (Mt 5^{21-48}), and His claims to a unique knowledge of the Father (Mt 11^{27}) and such a relation to Him, that His disciples were called on to believe not only the words that He spoke, but in Himself. Christ's ministry ended, however,—and, considering its brief and tragic character, it was bound to end, —without any clearly formulated answer to the question as to what constituted true discipleship, and how His followers were to be permanently distinguished from the rest of their nation and the world.

The question now arises, whether the normative period of the religion ends with the death of Christ.

May it be said that when His life is over, the work of the prophet of Nazareth is complete, His words have all been spoken, His religion propounded—it remains that His followers obey His teaching? This position has often been taken, and is usually adopted by those who reject the supernatural element in Christianity. Lessing is the father of those who in modern times think it desirable to return from 'the Christian religion' to 'the religion of Jesus.' Harnack on the whole favours this view, as when he urges that 'the Gospel, as Jesus proclaimed it, has to do with the Father only, and not with the Son'; or again, that it is 'the Fatherhood of God applied to the whole of life—an inner union with God's will and God's kingdom, and a joyous certainty of the possession of eternal blessings and protection from evil.' But he elsewhere rightly admits that 'a complete answer to the question, What is Christianity? is impossible so long as we are restricted to Jesus Christ's teaching alone.' The more powerful a personality is, 'the less can the sum-total of what he is be known only by what he himself says and does'; we must therefore include in our estimate the effects produced in his followers and the views taken by men of his work. See art. BACK TO CHRIST.

Further, if the miracles of Christ, and especially the great miracle of His Resurrection, be accepted, the whole point of view is changed. The disciples, during the short period of His ministry, were slow and dull scholars; only after the outpouring of the Spirit were they able to understand who their Master was and what He had done. Hence the Church with a true instinct included the Acts and the Epistles in the Canon, as well as the Gospels, and to the whole of these documents we must turn if we would understand what 'Christianity' meant to the Apostles and the first generation or two of those who followed Christ. Without entering into controversy such as would arise over exact definitions, we may say broadly that Christ became in thought, as He had always been in practice, the centre of His own religion. It circled round the Person, not so much of the Father as of the Son, yet the Son as revealing the Father. Personal relation to Christ continued to be—what it had been in the days of His flesh, but more consciously and completely—the all-important feature in the new religion. Significance attached not so much to what Christ said—though the authority of His words was supreme and absolute—as to what He was and what He did. His death and resurrection were seen to possess a special significance for the religious life of the individual and the community, and thus from the time of St. Paul and the Apostles onwards, but not till then, the Christian religion was fairly complete in its outline and ready for promulgation in the world.

But it is clear that the real significance of some features in the new religion could be brought out only in the course of history. The first great crisis which tested the infant Church arose over the question whether Christianity was to be a reformed and spiritualized Judaism or a universal religion, for the whole world and for all time. The controversy recorded in Ac 15, aspects of which emerge so frequently in St. Paul's letters, was fundamental and vital; the very existence of Christianity was at stake. It was chiefly to the Apostle Paul that the Church owed her hardly won freedom from the bonds of Jewish ceremonial law and the national and religious limitations identified with it. Henceforward in Christ was to be neither Jew nor Greek, barbarian, Scythian, bond nor free, but He Himself was all and in all.

The next two changes are not so clearly definable, though they are hardly less important and far-reaching. They were never brought to a definite issue before a council or assembly, and they do not come within the limits of the NT period. None the less they were fundamental in their character. They concern respectively creed and practice, doctrine and organization. In the first flush of enthusiasm which belongs to the earliest stage of a religious movement, the emotional—which means very largely the motive or dynamical—element is both pure and powerful. Belief, worship, spontaneous fulfilment of a high ethical standard, religious assurance and confident triumph over the world—all seem to flow forth easily and naturally from the fresh springs of a new life. But, as man is now constituted, this happy condition cannot last very long. A stage succeeds in which the white-hot metal cools and must take hard and definite shape. Faith passes into a formulated creed, the spirit of free, spontaneous worship shrinks within the limits of reverently ordered forms, the general sense of brotherhood narrows down into the ordered relationships of a constituted society, charismatic gifts are exchanged for the privileges which belong to certain defined ranks and orders of clergy; and, when the whole process is over, whilst the religion may remain the same in appearance, and to a great extent in character, it is nevertheless seriously changed. In Christianity such processes of development were proceeding, gradually but on the whole rapidly, during the latter half of the 2nd and the opening of the 3rd century. By the middle of the 3rd century the transmutation was well-nigh complete.

If at this stage the question, What is Christianity? were asked, a twofold answer would be returned. So far as its intellectual aspects are concerned, the substance of the Christian faith is summed up in certain forms of words accepted and accounted orthodox by the Church. So far as external position and status are concerned, the test of a man's Christianity lies in his association with a definitely constituted community known as the Church, possessing an organization of its own, which, with every decade, becomes more fixed and formal, less elastic in its constitution, and more exacting in its demands upon those who claim to be regarded as true Christians.

Such changes as these are in themselves not to be regarded as marking either an essential advance or a necessary retrogression. All depends on the way in which they are carried out. In human life, as we know it, they are inevitable. The mollusc must secrete its own shell if it is to live in the midst of a given environment. At the same time, in the history of a religion, such a process is critical in the extreme. The loss of enthusiasm and elasticity may be counterbalanced by increased consolidation, by the gain of a greater power of resisting attacks and retaining adherents. If the complaint is made that the expression of belief has become stiff and formal, the reply is obvious that genuine faith cannot long remain vague and indeterminate. The Christian must know what is implied in worshipping Christ as Lord, must learn the meaning of the baptismal formula, and must belong to a specific community, which for the sake of self-preservation must impose conditions of membership and translate abstract principles into definite codes and prescriptions. If a community is to exist in the presence of a hostile world, or to do its own work well as its numbers multiply, it must organize; and thus ecclesiastical orders, rules, and formulæ inevitably arise.

But the mode in which such processes are carried out varies considerably. The formulation and consolidation may be inefficiently done, in which case the young community is in danger of falling to pieces like a rope of sand. Or the organization

may be excessive, in which case formalism and fossilization set in. One of the chief dangers arises from the influx of unworthy or half-hearted members, those with whom religion is a tradition, not a living personal energy. 'When those who have laid hold upon the faith as great spoil are joined by crowds of others who wrap it round them like an outer garment, a revolution always occurs.' And especially when at such an epoch it is sought to define the essentials of a religion, there is the utmost danger lest secondary elements should be confused with the primary, lest an orthodox creed should be substituted for a living faith, and outward conformity with human prescriptions take the place of personal allegiance to a Divine and living Lord.

Whatever be thought of the way in which this all-important change was effected in the first instance, — that is to say, the transition from Christianity viewed as a life to Christianity viewed as a system of dogmatic belief and ecclesiastical organization, — few will deny that before long the alteration was so great that it may be said the religion itself was transformed. By the orthodox Roman Catholic this transformation is considered to be Divinely ordered; the process is regarded as one of steady advance and improvement—as a perfect child might pass into an equally admirable youth and man. According to Newman's theory, the original germs of doctrine and worship were developed normally and legitimately as determined by the criteria he specifies—Preservation of type, Continuity of Principle, Power of assimilation, Logical sequence, and the rest. Loisy, who is severely critical of the documents of the NT, holds the same view of the development of an infallible Church. To the eyes of others the change effected between the 2nd and the 6th centuries appears to be one of gradual but steady degeneration. In their view a living religion has hardened into a technical theology, vital union with Christ has passed into submission to the ordinances of a fast deteriorating Church, and the happy fellowship of believers in a common salvation and the enjoyment of a new life has almost disappeared under the heavy bondage of ceremonial observances and ecclesiastical absolutism.

The substitution of the worship of the Virgin Mary as an intercessor with her Divine Son for reverent intercourse with Christ Himself; the offering of the sacrifice of the Mass by an officiating priest for the benefit of the living and the dead, instead of a simple observance of communion with Christ and fellow-disciples at the Lord's Table; the obtaining of absolution only after private confession to a priest Divinely appointed to dispense it, in place of free and direct forgiveness granted to the penitent believer in Christ,— changes like these made in a religion are not slight and superficial. To some they represent a transition from crude infancy to vigorous maturity; to others they indicate deep-seated degeneration and the utter perversion of a pure and spiritual religious faith. An organism in process of growth depends upon its environment without, as well as its own living energies within. The history of the Christian Church does not present a complete parallel to this. No true Christian can believe either that it was left to a chance current of events, or that it was simply determined from without by natural causes. But the external factors which largely influenced the development of Christianity—Jewish beliefs and precedents, Greek philosophy and intellectual habitudes, Roman polity and law, the superstitious ideas and observances of paganism—must be taken into account by those who are studying the nature of the change which came over Christianity in the first thousand years of its history.

The point at issue in the 16th cent. between Roman Catholics and Protestants, one which still divides Christendom, concerned the real nature of this development. Had the growth of fifteen hundred years in doctrine, worship, and organization simply made explicit what was implicit in the New Testament ; or were the accretions to the original faith excrescences, exaggerations, or more serious corruptions ; and how was a line to be drawn between false and true ? The Reformation was a protest against abuses which had become ingrained in Catholicism. The need of ' reform in head and members ' had been felt and acknowledged long before, and only when repeated efforts to secure it peaceably had proved futile was it seen that a violent cataclysm like that brought about by Luther was necessary before effectual improvement could be attained. The Reformers claimed to be returning to original principles—to the New Testament instead of the Church ; to justification by faith instead of salvation by baptism, absolution, and the Mass ; and to direct acknowledgment of the Headship of Christ instead of blind submission to the edicts of His vicar upon earth. Luther, who had intended only to remove some obvious abuses which disfigured the creed and practice of the Church he loved, found himself cutting at the very roots of ecclesiastical authority and institutional religion. But, consciously or unconsciously, the movement of which he was partly the originator, partly the organ and servant, meant a resolute effort to return to the faith and spirit of primitive Christianity.

This effort was not final, of course. It is easy now to condemn Luther's procedure as illogical and indefensible, to say that he should either have gone further or not so far. Doubtless the result of the conflict between Romanism and Protestantism in the 16th cent. was not ultimate : the issues raised by Luther went deeper than he intended, but they were not deep and far-reaching enough. To every generation and to every century its own task. But the whole Reformation movement showed that Christianity as a religion possessed remarkable recuperative power ; that the organism could throw off a considerable portion of what seemed its very substance, not only without injury to its life, but with marvellous increase to its vigour ; and that the essence of the religion did not lie where the Roman Catholic Church had sought to place it. Subsequent history has confirmed this. ' Evangelical revivals,' great missionary enterprises, remarkable extensions of the old religion in new lands and under new conditions, unexpected manifestations of new features and resuscitation of pristine energies, have during the last two or three centuries illustrated afresh the same power of recovery and spiritual reinforcement, and raised afresh the question as to what constitutes the essence of a religion which is so full of vitality and so capable of developing from within unanticipated and apparently inexhaustible energies. The Christianity of to-day embraces a multitude of systems and organizations, it includes most varied creeds and cults, it influences societies and civilizations that are worlds apart, and the question is perpetually recurring whether there be indeed one spirit and aim pervading the whole, and if so, where it lies and what it is. This question becomes the more pressing when the future is contemplated. Many are prepared for still more striking developments in the 20th century. The spectacle of two or three great historical Churches on the one hand preserving the kind of stability which is gained by outward conformity to one doctrinal creed and ecclesiastical

system, and, on the other, an almost endless diversity of sects and denominations, with a tendency to fissiparous multiplication—cannot represent the τέλος, the ideal, the goal of the Christian religion. Christianity cannot be identified with one Church, or with all the Churches. Whilst many of these are enfeebled by age, the religion itself is young with a perpetually renewed vigour, and not for centuries has it shown more certain signs of freshly budding energy. Each new age brings new problems. As they arise, the power and permanence of a religion are tested by its ability to grapple with and to solve them, and by its success or failure is it judged. The problems of the present and the near future are mainly social, and the complaint is freely made that Christianity has proved itself unable to cope with them. But the principles and capabilities of a religion cannot be gauged by those of its representatives and exponents at a particular epoch. The assailants of Christianity as it is are often the allies of Christianity as it should be and will be. History has too frequently suggested the question which the poet asks of the suffering Christ—' Say, was not this Thy passion, to foreknow | In death's worst hour the works of Christian men ?' What new regenerative influences, swaying the whole of society with wider and freer quickening power, will be developed in the 20th cent. none can tell. But the present state of Christendom, no less than a survey of two thousand years of history, is anew compelling men to inquire, What, then, is the essence of Christianity ?

iv. ESSENTIAL CHARACTER OF CHRISTIANITY.— The interpretation of the facts thus hastily sketched appears to be this. Christianity in the concrete has been far from perfect, that is obvious ; its serious and widespread corruptions have often proved a scandal and a stumbling-block. But neither has its history manifested a mere perversion of a great and noble ideal. Again and again in the darkest hour light has shone forth, and at the lowest ebb a new flood-tide of energy has arisen, making it possible to distinguish the real religion in its purity and power from its actual embodiment in decadent and unworthy representatives.

What we see in Christian history, as in the personal history of Christ upon earth, is the progressive development of a Divine Thought unfolding itself in spite of virulent opposition, under pressure of extreme difficulties, struggling against the misrepresentations of false friends and imprinting its likeness upon most unpromising and unsatisfactory material. When it first appeared on the earth, embodied in the Person and the Work, as well as the teaching, of Jesus Christ, the Divine Idea shone with the brightness of a new sun in the spiritual firmament. It was not developed out of Judaism, the Jews were its bitterest opponents ; it was not indebted to Greek philosophic thought or to Roman political science, though afterwards it made use of and powerfully influenced both ; it had nothing in common with the current superstitions of Oriental religions ; it did not owe its origin to some cunningly devised religious syncretism, such as was not uncommon at the time when Christianity began to infuse life into the declining Roman Empire. A new idea of God, of man, and of the true reconciliation of man to God, formed the core and nucleus of the new faith. In the earliest records this idea appears as the germ of a nascent religion, a sketch in outline which remains to be filled up. In the history of nineteen centuries its likeness is to be discerned only as an image reflected in a dimly burnished mirror, in a troubled and turbid pool. None the less the dominant idea remains ; as St. Paul expresses it, the light of the knowledge of the glory of God is seen in a face—the face of Jesus Christ (2 Co 4[6]). Lecky, writing simply as a historian of European morals, describes it thus (*Hist. Eur. Mor.*[11] (1894) ii. 8 f.)—

'It was reserved for Christianity to present to the world an ideal character, which through all the changes of eighteen centuries has inspired the hearts of men with an impassioned love ; has shown itself capable of acting on all ages, nations, temperaments, and conditions ; has been not only the highest pattern of virtue but the strongest incentive to its practice ; and has exercised so deep an influence that it may be truly said that the simple record of three short years of active life has done more to regenerate and to soften mankind than all the disquisitions of philosophers, and all the exhortations of moralists.'

Whether the spectacle of an ideal human character alone has done this remains to be seen, but it is possible with care to distinguish between the glory of the Divine Thought and the imperfect medium through which its light has filtered. We see truth manifested amidst crudities and insincerities, amidst falsehoods which are bad and half-truths which are often worse ; a pure and lofty character struggling, mostly in vain, for adequate expression ; a kingdom not come but coming, of which we cannot say 'Lo here' or 'Lo there,' for it floats only in the midst of men as they move, in their hearts as they ponder and feel and hope—not as an achievement, not as a possession, but as a magnificent conception, an earnest longing, and a never fully attained, but ever to be attained, ideal.

In what, then, lies the perennial and imperishable essence of the ever changing phenomenon called Christianity? The unknown writer of the *Epistle to Diognetus* wrote in the 2nd century—

'What the soul is in the body, this the Christians are in the world. The soul is spread through all the members of the body, and Christians through the divers cities of the world. The soul hath its abode in the body, and yet it is not of the body. So Christians have their abode in the world, and yet they are not of the world.'

If for 'Christians' we read 'Christianity,' where is the soul, or vital spark, of the religion to be found? Nearly all are agreed that the centre of the Christian religion is, in some sense, the Person of its Founder. De Pressensé closes an article on the subject by saying, 'Christianity is Jesus Christ.' But it is the sense in which such words are to be interpreted that is all-important. The relation of Christ to the religion called by His name is certainly not that of Moses to Judaism, or that of Confucius to Confucianism. But neither does He stand related to Christianity as do Buddha and Mohammed to the religions named after them. Not as a prophet of Nazareth, a religious and ethical teacher, however lofty and inspiring, does Christ stand at the centre of history. As Dr. Fairbairn has said, 'It is not Jesus of Nazareth who has so powerfully entered into history ; it is the deified Christ who has been believed, loved, and obeyed as the Saviour of the world. . . . If the doctrine of the Person of Christ were explicable as the mere mythical apotheosis of Jesus of Nazareth, it would become the most insolent and fateful anomaly in history.' And as the secret is not to be found in the ethics, neither does it lie in the 'religion of Jesus.' Harnack is the modern representative of those who take this view when he says :

'The Christian religion is something simple and sublime ; it means one thing and one thing only : eternal life in the midst of time, by the strength and under the eyes of God.'

That is a fine definition of Theism, not of the historical Christianity which has done so much to regenerate the world. Nor can the essence of any religion be said to lie in its life, if by that be meant temper and conduct. These are fruits, and by their healthiness and abundance we judge of the sound-

ness and vigour of the tree. But the life of a religion in the proper sense of the word lies far deeper. The chief modern definitions of Christianity have been ably summarized and reviewed by Professor Adams Brown, who, in his *Essence of Christianity*, has produced an illuminating study in the history of definition which goes far to solve the problem before us. Schleiermacher, Hegel, and Ritschl are epoch-marking names in the history of Christianity during the last century, and their attempts at definition probably meet better than most others the conditions demanded by modern inquirers. Schleiermacher's view is thus summed up by Professor Adams Brown—

'Christianity is that historic religion, founded by Jesus of Nazareth and having its bond of union in the redemption mediated by Him, in which the true relation between God and man has for the first time found complete and adequate expression, and which, throughout all the changes of intellectual and social environment which the centuries have brought, still continues to maintain itself as the religion best worthy of the allegiance of thoughtful and earnest men.'

Hegel represents Christianity as the absolute religion, because in it is to be seen worked out in history the eternal dialectic immanent in the Being of God Himself, the ultimate principle of the Godhead, the Father, being revealed in the Son, the principle of difference, returning again in the synthesis of redemption. Finally, in the Holy Spirit Father and Son recognize their unity, and God as Spirit comes to full consciousness of Himself in history. Christianity, he says, is essentially the religion of the Spirit. Ritschl lays more stress on the idea of the Kingdom of God, but he follows in the steps of Schleiermacher when he defines Christianity as—

'the monotheistic, completely spiritual, and ethical religion, which, based on the life of its author as Redeemer and as founder of the kingdom of God, consists in the freedom of the children of God, involves the impulse to conduct from the motive of love, aims at the moral organization of mankind, and grounds blessedness on the relation of sonship to God, as well as on the kingdom of God' (*Justif. and Reconc.*, Eng. tr. p. 13).

Dorner is one of the best representatives of the many who lay chief stress upon the Incarnation as the 'central idea and fundamental fact' of Christianity, and who find in mediation through incarnation its archetypal thought. Professor Adams Brown himself considers the chief difficulty in framing a definition of Christianity to lie in the attempt to reconcile its historical and its absolute character, its natural and its supernatural elements—the two contrasted tendencies which mark respectively (1) its resemblance to other faiths, and its realization of their imperfect ideals ; and (2) its difference from all other religions as the one direct and supreme revelation from God Himself. His own solution may be indicated in the following sentences :—

'Christianity, as modern Christian thought understands it, is the religion of Divine sonship and human brotherhood revealed and realized through Jesus Christ. As such it is the fulfilment and completion of all earlier forms of religion, and the appointed means for the redemption of mankind through the realization of the kingdom of God. Its central figure is Jesus Christ, who is not only the revelation of the divine ideal for man, but also, through the transforming influence which He exerts over His followers, the most powerful means of realizing that ideal among men. The possession in Christ of the supreme revelation of God's love and power constitutes the distinctive mark of Christianity, and justifies its claim to be the final religion' (*Essence of Christianity*, 309).

These definitions are cumbrous, and no one of them is fully satisfactory. It is, however, clear that Christianity can never be properly defined if it is regarded merely as a philosophy, a system of ideas ; or as a code of ethics, providing a standard of conduct ; or as an ecclesiastical system, embodying rites and ceremonies of worship and institutions which are understood to be channels of salvation for mankind. It is a religion, that is, its root or spring lies in the relations which it reveals and establishes between God and men. It was the interpretation of the Person of Christ, the significance found in Him and His work, that changed the whole view of God and of human history, first for the Apostles and afterwards for all who followed them. Christ was to them doubtless a Lawgiver, His command was final. He was also an Example, perfect and flawless, the imitation of whom formed the highest conceivable standard of life. But unless He had been much more than this, the Christianity of history would never have come into being; and if it had had no other gospel for men than the most sublime human prophet could bring, it would not have regenerated mankind as it has done.

A religion may be described objectively or subjectively, from without or from within. As an objective religion in the world, Christianity is an ethical and spiritual monotheism of a high type, the highest that has been known in history, when its character and effects are fully estimated. So far there is general agreement. But the logical *differentia* has yet to be specified, and here opinions vary. If the characteristic and distinguishing doctrinal teaching of Christianity be considered, it may be said that the Incarnation is its central idea. But this must never be interpreted apart from Christ's whole work, including His death and resurrection, and the main purpose of that work, the Redemption of mankind, that Salvation and Reconciliation which He has made possible and open to all. Opinions may differ as to the exact mode in which this has been effected, but the Cross of Christ is its central feature. Christianity without a Saviour is a face without an eye, a body without a soul.

If the Christian religion be regarded from within, as a subjective, personal experience, its essence lies in a new life, conceived in a new spirit and animated by a new power. This power is directly imparted by the Spirit of God, but on the human side it arises from the new conceptions of God given by Christ and the new relation to Him established through the redemption and mediation of His Son. If the religion be viewed on its racial and social side, it may be described as having for its object the establishment of a brotherhood of mankind based on the Fatherhood of God and the Elder Brotherhood of Christ; a view of man which implies the inestimable individual worth of each, and the ultimate union of all in a renewed Order of which Christ has laid the foundation, given the foretaste, and promised the complete consummation and fruition.

The secret of the power of Christianity lies in the conviction which it engenders that—granted the fundamental principles of Theism—God has Himself undertaken the cause of man; that He enters into man's weakness, feels with his sorrows, and, chiefly, that He bears the terrible burden of man's sins; all this being assured by the gift of His Son and the work which the Son Himself has accomplished and is still carrying on by His Spirit. The metaphysical nature of Christ's Person may not be capable of being adequately expressed in words; the full scope of His redeeming work may be variously understood and may be incapable of being condensed into a formula; while Christians may widely differ as to the way in which the benefits of that work are best appropriated and realized and distributed by His Church in the world. But the essence of the religion lies in its conception of the spiritual needs of man, the ends for which he exists, his sin and failure to realize those ends; in its proclamation of Christ, the once dying and now ever living Lord as Himself the Way, through whom sin may be forgiven and failure remedied;

and above all, in the moral and spiritual dynamic which is supplied by faith in the great Central Person of the whole religion, and the life in Him which is rendered possible for every believer by the indwelling of the Holy Spirit.

As to the claims of Christianity to be the only permanent, universal, and final religion for mankind, no vindication of them can amount to actual demonstration. But the argument would take the direction of inquiring whether history thus far confirms the high claim of Christianity to suffice for the needs of man as man. Is Tertullian's phrase *anima naturaliter Christiana* borne out by facts? Has Christianity, not in its miserably imperfect and often utterly misleading concrete forms, but in the idea of its Founder and the best attempts made to realize it, shown the 'promise and potency' of a universal religion for the race? Such an argument would have to take full account of criticisms like those of Nietzsche and his school, who complain that Christianity in its tenderness towards the weak and erring, in its hallowing of sorrow and its preoccupation with the evil of sin, profoundly misunderstands human nature and man's position in the Universe; that it amounts, in fact, to a worship of failure and decay. These criticisms have not been widely accepted as valid, and they can easily be met—they were, indeed, substantially anticipated by Celsus and refuted by Origen. But such objections are sure to recur, together with kindred difficulties arising from a naturalistic view of man which claims to be supported by physical science. They can be effectually repelled only by practical proof that the teaching of Christianity accords with the facts of human nature and meets the needs of human life more completely than any other system of philosophy or religion.

On the other hand, the triumphs which Christianity has already achieved; the power it has manifested of being able to satisfy new and unexpected claims; the excellence of its ideal of character, one which cannot be transcended so long as human nature continues to be what it is; the success with which it has brought the very highest type of character within reach of the lowest, as attested by the experience of millions; the power of recovery which it has exhibited, when its teaching has been traduced and its spirit and aims degraded by prominent professors and representatives;—these, with other similar characteristics, go far towards proving the Divine origin of Christianity, and its claim to be the perfect religion of humanity, sufficing for all men and for all time.

It is certain, however, that if the true spirit of the Christian religion is to be rightly displayed generation after generation, and its work rightly done in the world, there must be a constant 'return to Christ' on the part of His Church. The phrase, of course, must be adequately interpreted. Much has been said concerning the 'recovery of the historical Christ' as characteristic of our time, and the expression represents an important truth. Christ is seen more and more clearly to be 'the end of critical and historical inquiry' and 'the starting-place of constructive thought.' But it is the whole Christ of the NT who is the norm in Christian theology, the object of Christian worship, the guide of Christian practice. The Christ of the Epistles cannot be separated from the Christ of the Gospels. The modern attempt, fashionable in some quarters, to distinguish between the Synoptic Gospels on the one hand as historic, and the Fourth Gospel and the Epistles on the other as dogmatic, cannot be consistently maintained, and does not adequately cover the facts of the case. The Sermon on the Mount does not reveal to us the entire Christ, nor the first chapter of St. John, nor the Epistle to the Romans ; but there is no inconsistency between these representations of the Christians' Lord. There is no contradiction between the Christ of the Synoptic Gospels and the Christ of Apostolic experience and the Christ of historical Christianity, except for those who reject the element of the supernatural, which, as a matter of fact, pervades the whole. The Christ of the NT is the object of Christian faith, as well as the Founder of the Christian religion in its historical continuity. To Him it is necessary for His Church—compassed with ignorance and infirmity and not yet fully purged from its sins—continually to 'return,' generation after generation, if His religion is to be preserved in its purity and transmitted in its power. The vitality of Christianity in the individual heart and in the life of the community depends upon the closeness of personal communion with Christ maintained through His indwelling Spirit. 'To steep ourselves in Him is still the chief matter,' says Harnack in one place. 'Abide in me and I in you,' was His own word to His first disciples, and it must ever be obeyed, if the characteristic fruit of that Vine is to be seen in abundance on its dependent branches.

What the Christianity of the future might be and would be, if this command were adequately fulfilled, none can say ; the capacities of the religion have been as yet only partially tested. In Christ, as St. Paul taught, are 'all the treasures of wisdom and knowledge'—the treasures of all-subduing love, of assimilating and transmuting power, of uplifting and purifying grace for the nations—'hidden' (Col 2^3). And the treasure is still hidden, because His followers, its custodians and stewards, do not adequately make it known —have not, indeed, adequately discovered it for themselves. But if in every generation there be, as there should be, a renewal of the very springs of Christian life by fresh recourse to the Fountain-head, then new claims, new needs, new problems, will only afford occasion for new triumphs of Christ and His Cross—the message of Divine self-sacrifice to the uttermost in redemption, as the one means of salvation for a sinning and suffering world.

LITERATURE.—From amongst the vast number of books which bear on the subject of this article, a very few recent volumes and articles may be mentioned here :—R. S. Storrs, *The Divine Origin of Christianity*, 1885 ; A. Harnack, *Das Wesen des Christentums*, 1900 [tr. by T. B. Saunders, *What is Christianity?* 1901], and *Die Mission und Ausbreitung des Christentums in den ersten drei Jahrhunderten*, 1902 [tr. by J. Moffatt, *The Expansion of Christianity*, 1905] ; A. M. Fairbairn, *The Place of Christ in Modern Theology*, 1893, and *Philosophy of the Christian Religion*, 1902 ; W. Adams Brown, *The Essence of Christianity*, 1903 ; see also the article on 'Christian, The Name of,' by P. W. Schmiedel in the *Encyc. Bibl.* i. 752 ff., and that on 'Christianity' by T. M. Lindsay in the *Encyc. Brit.*[9]

W. T. DAVISON.

CHRISTMAS.—See CALENDAR, and DATES, § 1.

CHRISTOLOGY.—See PERSON OF CHRIST.

CHRONOLOGY.—See DATES.

CHURCH.—It is proposed in this article to deal with the references to the Church in the Gospels, particularly as they bear upon Christ's relation to the Church. The other books of the NT, and the beliefs and practices of the early ages of Christianity, will be referred to only as far as they appear to throw light upon the teaching and actions of Christ as recorded in the Gospels. It will be assumed that the accounts of the life and teaching of Christ contained in the four Gospels as well as the narrative of the Acts are substantially historical, and that the thirteen Epistles usually ascribed to St. Paul are genuine. Without this limitation the inquiry would be of quite a different character.

The historical society known as the Church has never claimed to have come into complete existence until the day of Pentecost, and its growth and organization were a gradual process. We shall not, therefore, on any theory, expect to find in the Gospels a complete and explicit account of the foundation and characteristics of the Church, and it will be a convenient method of procedure to take the chief elements of the conception of the Church which was generally accepted at a later date, when the community was fully constituted, and to inquire how far these can be traced back to the teaching of Christ Himself, and how far they may be regarded as later accretions, or the natural but not necessary development of ideas which existed before, if at all, only in germ. Now our knowledge of the first days of Christianity derived from the NT is but fragmentary, and the period immediately following is one of great obscurity ; but from the middle of the 2nd cent. there is no doubt about the prevalent and almost universal belief of Christians with regard to the Church. It was believed that the Church, as it then existed, was a society founded by Christ as an integral part of His work for mankind. It was further believed that the Church possessed characteristics which were summed up under the words, One, Holy, Catholic, and Apostolic. And while it was believed that the Church stood in the most intimate spiritual relation to Christ, it was also held that its outward unity and continuity were secured by a definite organization and form of government, the essential features of which had been imposed upon the Church by the Apostles, acting under a commission given them by Christ Himself. The Church was further regarded as the instrument appointed by Christ for the completion of His work for mankind. The fact that these beliefs were generally held, at all events from the middle of the 2nd cent. onwards, suggests the following division of the subject. First, it will be asked whether the belief that it was Christ's intention to found a visible society is borne out (1) by what we know of His own actions and teaching, and (2) by the records of the earliest days of Christian life. Secondly, the characteristics ascribed to the Church in the Christian creeds will be examined in the light of the NT writings.

  i. Indications of a visible Church.
    1. In the teaching and actions of Christ : (*a*) the Messianic claim and the Kingdom of God ; (*b*) the body of disciples ; (*c*) the institution of sacraments
    2. In the earliest period of Christian history
  ii. Characteristics of the Church.
    1. Unity : (*a*) essential and transcendental ; (*b*) taking outward expression ; (*c*) imperfect.
    2. Holiness.
    3. Catholicity.
    4. Apostolicity : (*a*) doctrine ; (*b*) worship ; (*c*) discipline.
    Note.—The words 'Church' and 'Ecclesia.'
        Literature.

i. INDICATIONS OF A VISIBLE CHURCH. — 1. In the Teaching and Actions of Christ.—(*a*) *Relation of Christ to the Messianic Hope and the Kingdom of God.*—The idea of a covenant relation between God and man is found in the earliest records of the Hebrew race. Covenants were at first made with individuals and families ; but with the beginning of Jewish nationality there is a consciousness of a peculiar relation between the nation and Jehovah. The idea of a national God was, of course, shared by the Jews with all the nations with which they came into contact ; but as their conception of the Deity advanced, and their religion developed through monolatry into a pure monotheism, the idea of Jehovah as a national God passed into the idea of the selection of Israel by the one God of all the earth for a special destiny and special privileges. Thus the Jewish religion was a religion of hope, and its Golden Age was in the future. This national hope became closely associated in thought with the kingdom,—at first the actual kingdom, and then the kingdom to be restored in the future. After the fall of the actual kingdom, the idea of the future kingdom became, to a great extent, idealized, and in close connexion with it there grew up the expectation of a personal Messiah. It is not necessary for the present purpose to inquire when this expectation first becomes apparent, or to trace the growth of the Messianic hope in detail. The important fact is that at the time of Christ's birth Israel as a nation was looking for a kingdom of God and a Messianic King. With many, perhaps with most, the expectation may have been mainly that of an independent and powerful earthly kingdom; but the remains of Jewish literature in the last century before Christ show that the more spiritually minded Jews undoubtedly looked for a kingdom which would indeed have Jerusalem for its centre, and of which the faithful Jews would be the nucleus, but which would also be world-wide and spiritual in character. It must also be noticed that the doctrine of a Remnant, which had taken strong hold of the Jewish mind since the time of Isaiah, had accustomed them to think of a community of the faithful, within and growing out of the existing nation, who should in a special sense be the heirs of the promises.

The most conspicuous feature in the teaching of Christ, as recorded in the Synoptic Gospels, is undoubtedly His claim to be the Messiah, and His announcement of the coming of the Kingdom of God. In using these terms, He must have intended to appeal to, and to a great extent to sanction, the ideas and hopes of those whom He addressed. And yet it very soon became plain that the kingdom which He preached was something very different from anything that the most spiritual of the Jews had conceived. The old Jewish kings had led the people in war, they had judged them in peace, they had levied tribute; but these functions Christ expressly disclaimed. He would not allow His followers to think of appealing to force (Mt 26^{52}), He repudiated the idea of being a ruler or a judge of ordinary contentions (Lk 12^{14}), He accepted the payment of tribute to an alien potentate as a thing indifferent (Mk 12^{17}). But, on the other hand, the great acts which Jehovah Himself had performed for the Jewish nation, in virtue of which He Himself had been regarded as their King, Christ performed for a new nation. Jehovah had called Abraham and the patriarchs, and had attached them to Himself by intimate ties and covenants, and out of their seed had formed a nation which He ruled; and, in the second place, He had given this nation His own law. So Christ called from among the Jews His own disciples, from whom He required an absolute personal devotion, and to them He delivered a new law to fulfil or supersede the old (Mt 5^{17}). See, further, art. KINGDOM OF GOD.

What is the relation of the Kingdom of God to the Church?—The two things are not simply identical, and the predominant sense of the Kingdom in the NT appears to be rather that of a reign than of a realm. But these two ideas are complementary, and the one implies the other. Sometimes it is hardly possible to distinguish between them. It may be true that 'by the words the Kingdom of God our Lord denotes not so much His disciples, whether individually or even as forming a collective body, as something which they receive—a state upon which they enter' (Robertson, *Regnum Dei*); but at the same time the whole history of the growth of the idea of the Kingdom led, naturally, to the belief that the Kingdom of God about which Christ taught would be expressed and realized in a society. The teaching of Christ about the King-

dom of Heaven does not perhaps, taken by itself, prove that He was the Founder of the Church; but if this is established by other evidence, it may at least be said that His Kingdom is visibly represented in His Church, and that 'the Church is the Kingdom of Heaven in so far as it has already come, and it prepares for the Kingdom as it is to come in glory.'

(*b*) *How far the line of action adopted by Christ during His ministry tended to the formation of a society.*—Christ began from the first to attach to Himself a number of disciples. Their numbers varied, and they did not all stand in equally close relations to Him; they were indeed still a vague and indeterminate body at the time of His death, but they tended to define themselves more and more. There was a process of sifting (Jn 6^{66}), and immediately after the Ascension an expression is used which suggests some sort of list (Ac 1^{15}). As much as this, indeed, might be said of most religious and philosophical leaders, but Christ did more than create an unorganized mass of disciples. From an early period He formed an inner circle 'that they might be with him, and that he might send them forth' (Mk 3^{14}). The name 'Apostles' may have been given to the Twelve in the first instance with reference to a temporary mission, but subsequent events showed that this temporary mission was itself only part of a system of training to which Christ devoted more and more of His time. The Twelve became in a special sense 'the disciples,' and this is what they are usually called in the Fourth Gospel. The larger body are also disciples, but the Twelve are their leaders and representatives. Their representative character culminates at the Last Supper, where the Eucharist is given to them alone, but, as the event showed, in trust for the whole body.

Certain sayings recorded of Christ in connexion with the Apostles and their functions will be noticed later. For the present it is enough to call attention to the fact that, apart from any special saying or commission, the general course of Christ's actions not only tended to produce a society, but provided what is a necessary condition of the effectiveness and permanence of a society—the nucleus of an organization; and that the greater part of His labours was directed towards the training of this inner circle for carrying on a work which He would not complete Himself.

(*c*) *The significance of the institution of the sacraments.*—A society, to be plainly visible and unmistakable, requires some outward act or sign of distinction by which all its members can be recognized. Circumcision had been such to the Jews. And in order to be both effective and permanent, a society further requires some definite corporate action, binding upon all its members, and relating to the object for which the society exists. The observance of the Law has been the corporate action of the Jews. No society has, as a matter of fact, succeeded in maintaining itself in existence for an indefinite period without such signs of distinction and corporate actions. Both requirements were supplied by Christ, if the Gospel narrative may be trusted, in the sacraments which He instituted. In Baptism He provided a definite means of incorporation, and in the Eucharist a corporate act and a visible bond of union. This is indeed only part of the significance of the sacraments, but when they are regarded from another point of view it becomes all the more striking that the means appointed to convey the grace of God to the individual should be necessarily social in their character. The general tendency of the teaching of Christ, in the Sermon on the Mount and elsewhere, with regard to the Jewish Law and to the relation of the inward and outward, gives great significance to the fact that He should have ordered any external acts of the nature of sacraments, and makes it still more remarkable that He should have laid emphasis on their necessity as a condition of entrance into the Kingdom and into the possession of life (Jn 3[5] 6[54]). And the fact that these are necessarily social ordinances is of primary importance in considering the relation of the Church to Christ.

It thus appears from a general view of Christ's ministry as recorded in the Gospels, without taking into consideration particular sayings ascribed to Him, that before the Ascension He had provided everything that was necessary for the existence of a society, for the development of an organization, and for its permanence and corporate action. The only thing wanting to the complete constitution of the Church was the fulfilment of the promise of the gift of the indwelling Spirit, for which the disciples were bidden to wait (Lk 24[49], Ac 1[4]).

2. In the earliest period of Church history.— The conclusions to which the Gospels appear to point will be corroborated if there is evidence that a society actually did exist immediately after the events recorded in the Gospels. Of this early period the only existing record is that which is contained in the Acts. There is also contemporary evidence of the ideas of a somewhat later period in St. Paul's Epistles. If the evidence of the Acts is accepted, there is no doubt of its general tendency. Immediately after the Ascension there appears a well defined body of disciples, led by the Apostles (Ac 1[13-15]). At the day of Pentecost this body is fully constituted for its mission, and receives a large accession of numbers. The mention of definite numbers (Ac 1[15] 2[41] 4[4]) shows that there was no doubt who the persons were who belonged to the society. Nor is there any doubt, from the constant mention of baptism throughout the book, that this was the invariable means of acquiring membership. It is expressly mentioned even in the exceptional case recorded in 10[47f.]. Throughout the whole narrative the Apostles appear as the leaders and teachers of the whole community. Membership implies adherence to their teaching and fellowship, with 'the breaking of bread' and common prayer as a bond of union (2[42]). The practice of community of goods is an evidence of the closeness of the bond, while the fact that this was voluntary shows that 'neither the community was lost in the individuals, nor the individuals in the community' (Hort, *Christian Ecclesia*, p. 48). The meetings of the Church must have been in houses, and none in Jerusalem can possibly have contained all the disciples; but no importance is attached to the place of meeting, nor are house congregations ever spoken of or alluded to as separate units of Church life. A theory has been formed that the Church as a society arose out of a federation of house assemblies, but there is absolutely no trace whatever of such a possibility in the Acts: the whole body of disciples is the only unit. The word *ecclesia* occurs for the first time in Ac 5[11], and there it is the whole body which is spoken of. In the course of time the increase in the number of adherents led to an advance in organization, the Apostles delegating some of their functions to a lower order of ministers, and soon afterwards persecution caused an extension of the Church to other parts of Palestine. But there is as yet no subdivision; questions which arise in Samaria and Joppa are dealt with at Jerusalem (Ac 8[14] 11[1f.]). This state of things, however, could not last. When the process of extension had gone further, it became impossible to administer all the affairs of the community from a single centre. And so when a body of Christians established themselves in Antioch, a

new use of the word *ecclesia* appears (12[26]). Hitherto it has meant the whole body of the brethren; now it is applied also to parts of the whole. Each centre is capable of separate action, and deals with local affairs, while remaining in close union with the whole. And so the step which was perhaps the most momentous of any that have been taken in Church history—the mission of Paul and Barnabas—was apparently the work of the Church in Antioch alone, without any reference to Jerusalem (13[1ff.]). This mission led to the foundation of a large number of local *ecclesiæ*, each of which was provided by the Apostle with a local ministry (14[23]), while he exercised a continual supervision over them, and visited them as often as circumstances would allow. The difficult questions which arise out of this great extension of the Church are referred to the 'Apostles and presbyters' at Jerusalem. The precise relations between the authority of the whole body and the legitimate independence of the local communities are undefined, but the recognition of the unity of the whole Church and of the Apostolic authority is unmistakable. In the Epistles of St. Paul the term *ecclesia* is constantly used of the local communities, of which he had frequent occasion to speak; the church in a city (1 Co 1[2]) or even in a house (Ro 16[5], Col 4[15]) is a familiar expression, and the churches of a region are spoken of (1 Co 16[1. 19]) in a way that possibly suggests the beginnings of a provincial organization. But 'the Church' is the one undivided Church of which these several churches are only local divisions. It is in the Epistle to the Ephesians that his doctrine of 'the Church' culminates. It is particularly with reference to this teaching that a distinction has been drawn between the *actual* and the *ideal* Church. This distinction is a real one, if it means that the ideal of the Church has never yet been realized in fact. But neither St. Paul nor any other NT writer draws any distinction, or appears to be conscious of the need of any. The Church, like the individual Christian, is regarded as being that which it is becoming. As the individual Christian, in spite of his imperfections, is a saint, so the existing body of Christians whom he is addressing is the Body of Christ, which is to be presented a glorious Church, holy and without blemish (1 Co 12[27], Eph 5[27]). See ORGANIZATION.

ii. THE CHARACTERISTICS OF THE CHURCH.— Assuming now that the Church is a society founded by Christ to carry on His work for the redemption of mankind, the characteristic notes of the Church, as they have been embodied in the Creeds, may be considered with reference to the teaching contained in the Gospels. It is convenient to state at the outset what the principal passages in the Gospels are which bear upon the subject. In the first place, all the teaching relative to the Kingdom of God bears more or less directly on the Church. Some points with regard to this have already been noticed. Then there are the two passages in which the word *ecclesia* is used, Mt 16[13-20] and 18[15-20]. In connexion with the former, the other two 'Petrine' texts, Lk 22[28-32] and Jn 21[15-17], may be considered. There are also the charges given to the Apostles in general, Mt 10, Mk 3[13-15] 6[7-13], Mt 28[16-20], Jn 20[21-23], and the accounts of the institution of the Eucharist. And there is the long passage Jn 14–17, which specially bears upon the relations of Christ to the Church. The authenticity or credibility of some of these passages has been disputed on various grounds, but it will be assumed for the present purpose that they contain a credible record of the teaching of Christ. It will be convenient to consider this teaching under the heads of those notes of the Church which have been commonly ascribed to it from early times, and have been embodied in the Creeds.

1. Unity. — If the conclusion already reached about the origin of the Church is true, it is clear that it must be one society. The teaching of Christ on this point, as recorded in the Fourth Gospel, is very emphatic (Jn 17²¹⁻²³), and He bases the unity of the Church on the unity of God (cf. Eph 4⁴⁻⁶). It is also to be a visible unity, for it is to be a sign to the world : 'that the world may believe.' It is, however, implied that it will be a progressive unity, not at once perfectly realized (Jn 17²³ 10¹⁰). This is illustrated by St. Paul, who speaks of unity as a thing to be gradually attained to (Eph 4¹³). These three points may be taken in order.

(*a*) If the unity of the Church is based upon the unity of God, it follows that it is an *essential and transcendental*, and not an accidental unity ; *i.e.* it is not a merely political or voluntary association of men combining together with a view to effect certain ends, nor is it merely occasioned by the social instincts of human nature. These lower kinds of unity are not, indeed, excluded by the higher, but they are by themselves an insufficient explanation. It has been maintained that the idea of the unity of the Church is an afterthought, caused by the strong tendency to religious associations which prevailed in the Empire in the early ages of Christianity. Abundant evidence already exists, and more is being accumulated, of the existence of this tendency ; but even if it should be shown that non-Christian associations influenced the manner in which the Christian community framed its external life and that they assisted its growth, this would not in the least disprove the essential unity of the Church. As far, however, as investigation has gone at present, it seems that the Church owed remarkably little to heathen precedents. The fact that from the earliest times there were some who more or less separated themselves and stood aloof, has been alleged as a proof that unity was not regarded as essential. But imperfection, as has already been noted, is a condition of the earthly state of the Church ; and the strong condemnation with which separation is invariably spoken of in the NT and by all early writers, is very strong evidence of the belief of the Church that unity is one of its essential marks. The existence from the first of the power of excommunication (1 Co 5, etc.), is further evidence to the same effect.

The unity of the Church is, then, a theological unity, arising from the unity of God, from the fact that all members of the Church are members of Christ and abide in Him as the branches abide in the vine, and from the indwelling of the Holy Spirit. From this flows a moral unity of thought and action among the members of the Church, who are bound together by the invisible bonds of faith, hope, and love.

(*b*) But this invisible unity will express itself, as far as regards that part of the Church which is on earth, in an *outward* form. There has not unnaturally been a good deal of conflict of opinion throughout the greater part of Church history as to the precise nature of the outward form which is necessary. Confining ourselves to the teaching of Christ upon the subject, the first thing to be noticed is that institution of the visible actions called sacraments which has been already spoken of. The necessity for performing certain outward actions at once distinguishes those persons who perform them, and these particular actions are social in their nature, and cannot be performed except in connexion with a visible society. In the next place, the administration of sacraments implies discipline, for a certain amount of organization is necessary in order to enable a society to act, and social actions cannot be performed in isolation. For this Christ provided by the institution of a ministry in the persons of the Apostles, to whom He expressly committed the sacraments. It follows that among the things which are necessary to their valid administration, the preservation of the order instituted by the Church under the direction of the Apostles must be reckoned. And while the Church has recognized all its members as valid ministers of Baptism in case of necessity, the administration of the Eucharist has been confined amongst most Christians to those who have received special Apostolic authority for the purpose.

It is further held by a very large number of Christians, that in addition to the external bonds of union formed by the sacraments and the Apostolic ministry, the Church on earth, being visible, must have a visible head, and that this headship was given by Christ to St. Peter, and by implication to his successors. Union with the earthly head of the Church is therefore necessary to avoid the guilt of schism. It is alleged that this is the natural sense of the passages which record the special charges given by Christ to St. Peter (Mt 16¹³⁻²⁰, Lk 22²⁸⁻³², and Jn 20²¹⁻²³), and that this interpretation of His words is borne out by the claims made from the earliest times by the bishops of Rome, and allowed or acquiesced in by the Church at large. It is argued, on the other side, that the passages in question were not interpreted in this sense by early Church writers, and that the testimony of the Acts and Epistles and of early Church history shows that such a position was not actually held by St. Peter. The controversy is of such enormous proportions that it can only be alluded to here, but a few of the innumerable books that deal with the subject are mentioned in the list of Literature at the end.

(*c*) These inward and outward bonds of union give a real numerical unity to the Church, so that it will be one in any one place, one throughout the world, and one in all time. Nothing less than this can satisfy the conception of unity put before us in the NT. But it must be noted, in the third place, that unity may be real while it is still *imperfect*. The perfection of the Church, in respect of unity as well as of all other characteristics, is possible only when all its members are perfect, and therefore it cannot be fully realized in this life. Any loosening of those bonds which have been mentioned, whether inward or outward, must necessarily impair unity. It is not necessary that there should be an outward breach. A lack of charity, leading to party spirit, such as existed at Corinth, was regarded by St. Paul as impairing the unity of the Church although no visible severance had taken place. A want of faith, or errors concerning the faith, must have the same effect. A departure from the faith of the Church on fundamental matters is called 'heresy,' and any great want of either charity or faith on the part of a section of the Church commonly leads to a breach of the external conditions of union, which is called 'schism.' This again admits of different degrees, and is of two principal kinds. A suspension or refusal of communion between two parts of the Church undoubtedly amounts to a schism, even though both parts retain the due administration of the sacraments and the Apostolic ministry. Such a schism has arisen between the Churches of the East and the West, and it was the work of centuries of gradual estrangement, so that it is impossible to say at what precise moment the want of intercommunion became such as to amount to a formal schism. There is a breach of a very similar character between the Anglican Churches and those which adhere to the Roman obedience. There is also another kind of schism, which is caused when bodies of baptized persons form new associations which do not claim to be connected with the Apostolic Church, or which reject the sacraments. There is no other cause for such breaches of outward communion than the imperfection of the faith and charity of the members of the Church. But if such imperfection does not in itself destroy the unity of the Church, the external consequences which naturally result from it do not necessarily do so. Heresy and schism impair unity, but do not altogether destroy it, just as the spiritual life of the individual is not altogether destroyed even by grievous sins.

The Invisible Church.—So far only the unity of that part of the Church which is on earth has been spoken of. But members of the Body of Christ do not cease to be united to Him, and therefore to each other after death. That part of the Church which has passed away from earth is called the Invisible Church, in contrast to the Visible Church upon earth, but they are essentially one. With regard to the state of the departed, very little direct teaching is recorded to have been given by Christ Himself, and we must not presume to speculate too much where knowledge has been withheld. Perhaps little more can be said than that in the parable of Dives and Lazarus (Lk 16¹⁹⁻³¹) Christ gave a general sanction to current Jewish beliefs as to the state of the departed, and that His words to the penitent thief (Lk 23⁴³) assure us that union with Himself is not impaired by death. If this is so, it is sufficient justification for the universal belief of early Christians, that the Invisible Church is united to the Visible by common worship.

2. Holiness.—The Church may be called holy because it is a Divine institution, of which Christ is the head, and the special sphere of the working of the Holy Spirit, or because its members, being united to Christ as the branches are to a vine or the limbs to a body, are called to a life of holiness, and have a real though imperfect holiness infused into them. Something has already been said on these first points, and it is hardly necessary to show at length that Christ required holiness from His followers (Jn 17¹⁶⁻¹⁹, Mt 5⁴⁸). It is no less evident that the holiness spoken of here and elsewhere is a progressive holiness.

One difficulty which has arisen with regard to this characteristic of the Church is that the want of holiness in many of those who have fulfilled the outward conditions of Church membership has often in Church history led to attempts to secure greater purity by a sacrifice of external unity. The Novatians, the Donatists, and many later bodies of separatists, have made such attempts. The persistency of this tendency in the face of such teaching of Christ as is contained in the parables of the Tares and the Draw-net is somewhat surprising, but at all events it testifies to a deep underlying conviction of the necessity of holiness. St. Paul emphasizes the holiness of any body of Christians which he addresses, by giving them the title of 'saints,' however imperfect many of the individuals might be (Ro 1⁷, 1 Co 1², 2 Co 1¹, Eph 1¹, Ph 1¹, Col 1² ; cf. Ac 9³²). They are both individually and collectively a holy temple, and the habitation of the Holy Spirit (1 Co 3¹⁰· ¹¹· ¹⁶ 6¹⁹, Eph 2¹⁶⁻²²). And, as has already been pointed out, he does not draw any sharp line of division between the imperfect society on earth and that which shall be perfected hereafter (Eph 5²⁵⁻²⁷) : he regards both the individual and the society as being already that which they are becoming.

'As a whole the Church is holy in that it retains faithfully those means of sanctification which Christ gave her, holy Sacraments, holy laws, holy teaching, so that, amid whatever imperfections, her whole aim is that the tendency of her acts and her teaching shall be to promote holiness and the inward spiritual life. . . . An university is learned, or a city rich, which abounds in learning or riches, although there may be many unlearned or poor, and although the learned or rich may yet be short of the ideal of learning or wealth.'—Forbes, *Nic. Creed*, p. 278.

3. Catholicity.—The earliest extant use of the word 'Catholic' as applied to the Church is in Ignatius (*ad Smyrn.* viii. 2) : 'Wherever the bishop appears, there must the multitude be ; just as wherever Christ Jesus is, there is the Catholic Church.' The natural sense of the word would appear to be that of the Church throughout all the world as opposed to that in one place ; but this is not the sense in which the term has been commonly used. The Church has been called 'Catholic' not because it has actually extended throughout the world, for this it has never yet done, nor even simply because it is destined to be so extended, but rather as possessing characteristics which make it capable of being a universal religion, adapted to all classes of men in all parts of the world, and throughout all time. Even apart from particular words of Christ, such as those recorded in Mt 28¹⁹, nothing is more apparent in His teaching than that the religion which He taught was intended to be a universal religion, in special contrast to Judaism, which, like the religions of the ancient world generally, was a strictly national religion, and appealed only to a part of mankind. In spite of the many anticipations of universalism which are to be found in Jewish prophecy, the controversy which took place in the early Church about the observance of the Jewish law shows with what difficulty the idea was accepted by those who had been Jews. This quality, again, of universal applicability to all men at all times can belong only to a Divine revelation sufficient for the needs of all mankind. Such a revelation Christ professed to give, and the Catholicity of the Church must depend upon its faithfulness to the fulness of the truth revealed in Christ. And so, in addition to the idea of universal extension, the word Catholic has been used to convey the idea of orthodoxy in the communion of the Church. The well-known definition of Cyril of Jerusalem (*Cat.* xviii. 23) co-ordinates these two ideas. 'The Church is called Catholic because it extends throughout the whole world . . . because it teaches completely all doctrines which men ought to know . . . because it brings into subjection to godliness the whole race of men . . . and because it treats and heals every sort of sins . . . and has in it every form of virtue.' In this sense the Church was called Catholic when it was very far from being extended even over a considerable part of the world, and the term can be applied even to the Church in a particular place, as being in communion with and possessing the characteristics of the whole. So in the *Martyrdom of Polycarp* he is spoken of as 'Bishop of the Catholic Church that is in Smyrna.' The Church or any part of it approaches the ideal of Catholicity in proportion as it possesses all the qualities which are necessary to make it literally universal ; and, on the other hand, 'everything which hinders or lessens the capacity of the Church to be universal, everything which deprives it of part of the full truth or inserts in its teaching anything which does not belong to the truth, everything which cramps its power of getting rid of sin and increasing godliness, has a tendency to draw the Church away from the ideal of its Catholic life. To become such that it could not appeal to the whole world or to all classes of men, to deny essential parts of the revealed faith, to become in its accepted principles a necessary instrument of some sins or a necessary opponent of some virtues, would be, in proportion as this was wilful and deliberate and fully carried out, a sinking below the minimum which the note of Catholicity requires' (Stone, *The Church*, p. 59).

4. Apostolicity.—It has already been pointed out that Christ selected twelve of His followers to stand in a specially close relation to Himself, and to be charged with a special mission. In what is probably the earliest account of their appointment (Mk 3¹⁴), it is said they were to 'be with him,' and that He would 'send them forth.' Hence they were called Apostles (Lk 6¹³). The nature of this relation and this mission must now be examined in order to ascertain the sense in which the

Church may be called Apostolic. It may first be noticed that a sharp distinction has sometimes been drawn between the position of the Twelve as representative disciples, that is, as standing in a specially close relationship to Christ, of the same kind, however, as that of other disciples, and their position as Apostles, that is, as men sent forth on a special mission. No such sharp distinction is drawn in the NT, nor does it appear to be necessary. The two things are spoken of in the passage of St. Mark just referred to as two sides of the same fact, not as two separable things. The close discipleship was necessary to fit the Apostles for their mission, and it therefore formed part of it.

The nature of this Apostolic mission is stated in the most comprehensive terms in Jn 20^{21} 'As the Father hath sent me, even so send I you'; that is to say, it was the task of carrying on upon earth the work of Christ Himself. It seems to be of little or no consequence to our estimate of the nature of the Apostolic functions whether others besides the Twelve were present upon the occasion when these particular words were spoken. The Twelve are frequently called 'the disciples,' especially in the Fourth Gospel. And the mission of the Apostles is not a separate thing from the mission of the Church. If, as St. Paul so constantly teaches, the Church is one body with many members, the acts of the organs of the body are the acts of the body itself. St. Paul insists equally strongly upon the unity of the whole and the differentiation of function within the whole. And so the point to be considered is not whether a separate mission was given to the Apostles apart from that of the whole Church, but rather what special functions of the Church were committed to the Apostles to be performed, by themselves or under their direction, on the Church's behalf.

(*a*) One principal object with which the Apostles were sent out in the first instance was undoubtedly that they might *teach* (Mk 3^{14}). And it is equally clear that this was not merely a temporary, but a permanent function. Even the special directions given to them on their first sending out (Mt 10) are not intelligible unless a continuance of the work of teaching be understood. And the Twelve were specially trained by close and continual intercourse with Christ for the work of being witnesses to Him (Ac 1^8), and it is clear that they considered this as one of their special functions (1^{22} 2^{32} 3^{15} 4^{33} etc.). And although this personal witness to the actions and words of Christ was necessarily confined to those who had been with Him, the transmission of the witness and the function of teaching in general are permanent. The commission given by Christ to the Twelve to make disciples of all the nations (Mt 28$^{19. 20}$) is one which was not, and could not be, accomplished by themselves in person, and it implies the continuance of the teaching office of the Church until this end is accomplished. So it is recognized as one of the special duties of those who were appointed by the Apostles to take part in their work (1 Ti 3$^{12. 13}$ 5^{17} 6^{20}, 2 Ti 1^{14} 2^2, Tit 2^{15} etc.). It is this teaching work of the Church which corresponds to the prophetical office of Christ Himself.

(*b*) *The worship of the Church.*—The Sacraments, which were especially committed to the Apostles, have been spoken of as social acts necessary to the existence and cohesion of the Church as a visible society. They are also means by which the relation of the Church to God is expressed, and channels by which the individual receives Divine grace. The worship of the Church centres and culminates in the Eucharist, the specially appointed action by which the Church takes part in the sacrifice offered by Christ. It makes a memorial of that part of His sacrificial work which has been accomplished in time (Lk 22^{19}, 1 Co 11^{26}), and it

unites itself with Him in His present mediatorial work of pleading that sacrifice in heaven (He 7$^{24. 25}$). So the whole Church, as the Body of Christ, takes part in His priestly work (1 P 2^9, Rev 5$^{9. 10}$), and this has always been emphasized by the language of all the liturgies. See artt. LORD'S SUPPER, SACRAMENTS.

(*c*) *Discipline.*—A visible society could hardly exist, or at least continue to exist, without some form of discipline. Christ sanctioned for His followers (Mt 18^{15}), not only individual remonstrance, which may be considered as the gentlest form in which discipline can be administered (cf. 1 Th 5^{14}), but also, in the case of the failure of this, the collective censure of the community (cf. 1 Ti 2^{20}, Gal 2^{11}), and in the last resort the exercise of the natural right of a society to expel one of its members (cf. 1 Co 5^5, 2 Co 2$^{5-10}$). These last passages alone would suffice to show, what is certain enough, that the power of excommunication was recognized and practised in the Church from the earliest times.

A still more emphatic commission was given by Christ to St. Peter (Mt 16^{19}), and to 'the disciples' (18^{18}). Whatever may be the exact meaning of these words, it is difficult to give them any interpretation which does not include the idea of jurisdiction. At all events the words in Jn 20$^{22. 23}$ relate directly to discipline, and are of the most unqualified character. If the historical character of these passages is admitted, there can be no doubt that a disciplinary commission was given. There have been, however, differences of opinion as to the persons to whom it was given. The chief views held on this point may be roughly classed under four heads.

(*α*) It has been held that the position of St. Peter was different in kind from that of the other Apostles, and that jurisdiction was given directly to him alone, and to the other Apostles through him, and that the same holds good of his successors. (*β*) That jurisdiction was given directly to all the Apostles, and is inherent in their office and in that of their successors, but that it can be legitimately exercised only by those who preserve the unity of the Church by being in union with St. Peter and his successors. (*γ*) That jurisdiction was given equally to all the Apostles and their successors as the Divinely appointed organs of the Church, and that only a primacy of honour belonged to St. Peter or is due to his successors. 'All the Apostles were equal in mission, equal in commission, equal in power, equal in honour, equal in all things, except priority of order, without which no society can well subsist' (Bramhall). (*δ*) That the Apostles received no gift of jurisdiction from Christ Himself, and that any powers which they or their successors exercised were gradually conferred upon them by the act of the Church or of parts of it.

Closely connected with directly disciplinary functions are those general powers of direction and administration which must be exercised in a society by some persons appointed for the purpose. That they were used by the Apostles, even with regard to secular matters, is plain from the Acts and Epistles. The Apostolic background is everywhere present in the former book, and St. Paul assumes such powers throughout (*e.g.* 1 Co 11^{34}). It is by the exercise of such powers of discipline and government that the Church participates in the kingly office of Christ.

We may therefore conclude that the Church may be called Apostolic in so far as it has held fast to the teaching, worship, and discipline of the Church as intrusted by Christ to the Apostles, and according to the order established by them.

NOTE.—*The words 'church' and* ἐκκλησία.—The word 'church' is found in a great variety of forms in the Teutonic and Slavonic languages as the exact equivalent of ἐκκλησία, which has passed into Latin and all the Romanic and Celtic languages. There has been much dispute about its ultimate derivation. Suggested derivations from the Latin *circus* and from the Gothic are now set aside by philologists as impossible. The only derivation that will bear examination is from the Greek κυριακόν. This is used in the *Apost. Const.* (*c.* A.D. 300 ?) and in the canons of several councils early in the 4th cent., and was afterwards fairly common in the East. It means 'of the Lord,' and is used of 'the house of the Lord,' δῶμα being understood. The derivation of 'church' from κυριακόν is not free from philological difficulties, and there is no sufficient historical explanation of the curious fact that a less common Greek word should have been adopted by the Teutonic languages in place of the usual ἐκκλησία. But there is no other even plausible explanation of the derivation of the word 'church.'

The word ἐκκλησία is common in classical Greek in the sense of an assembly of the people—literally, *the calling them out* (ἐκκαλέω) by the voice of a herald or otherwise. It is used in the LXX as the translation of the Hebrew word ḳāhāl, which has a similar derivation and meaning. Another word, 'ēdhāh, is commonly translated by συναγωγή, and means properly the congregation itself, whereas ḳāhāl means rather the assembly of the congregation ; but there is no sharp distinction between the words, and in the later books of the OT 'ēdhāh almost disappears, and ḳāhāl or ἐκκλησία combines both shades of meaning. There is little or no evidence as to the precise contemporary ideas which would have been conveyed to a Jew of our Lord's time by the use of these words, but they could not fail to recall the thought of Israel as the congregation of God, and to suggest the idea of a Divine society.

It has often been supposed that the word ἐκκλησία was intended to convey the idea of a people or a number of persons called out of the world for the special service of God. The idea of Israel as a chosen people and the idea of the special election and vocation of Christians occur constantly in the Scriptures, but they never appear to be connected with the words ἐκκλησία or ḳāhāl. In both these words the idea of the summons to the assembly, which is their original significance, practically disappears, and the words mean simply the assembly itself, or the people who meet in assembly. See artt. 'Congregation' and 'Church' in Hastings' *DB*.

The fact that the word ἐκκλησία is found in the Gospels only in the two passages of St. Matthew already discussed, has led some to suppose that these passages are later insertions into the original narrative, made at a time when the idea of the Christian society had been developed, and when it was desired to add authority to the idea by a reference to the teaching of Christ. If, however, the view taken above of the general tendency of Christ's work and teaching is correct, His connexion with the Church does not depend upon these two passages only, and there would be much difficulty in explaining the fact that this term and no other was universally applied to the Christian society from the time of the Apostles onwards, unless it were the natural equivalent of Aramaic terms used by Christ Himself.

LITERATURE.—The number of books which deal with the subject of the Church from exactly the point of view taken in this article may not be very large, but the literature which bears more or less upon the original constitution and characteristics of the Church is of stupendous extent ; and the most that can be done here is to mention a very few specimens of different classes of books which relate to different parts of the subject. In the first place, most commentaries on the NT deal with the exegesis of the passages which bear upon the Church, but it is not worth while to attempt a selection here. The writings of most of the early Fathers contain either contributions to the history of the growth of the Church, or information as to the opinions of the writers on the subject. A few specially important works are mentioned here. During the Middle Ages there was a great mass of literature dealing with the Papal authority and the relations of the Church to the State. From the time of Hildebrand onwards this aspect of the question was especially prominent. The Reformation period naturally produced abundant discussions in which the presuppositions of the Middle Ages were to a great extent laid aside. In modern times, and especially during the last fifty years, the early institutions of the Church have been investigated with great minuteness, especially by German writers, and there has been a great abundance of general Church Histories, which often contain discussions on the doctrine of the Church. This is also dealt with in all treatises on Christian doctrine to a greater or less extent, and from all points of view. The books mentioned below must be regarded merely as examples of the different kinds of works in which the subject may be studied.

EARLY WRITERS : *Patres Apostolici* (ed. Lightfoot); Irenæus, *c. Hæres.* iii. 1-9 ; Tertullian, *de Præscr. Hæret.* ; Cyprian, *de Unitate Eccles.*, *de Lapsis*; Augustine, *de Baptismo*, and *c. Donatistas.*

GENERAL CHURCH HISTORIES : Neander, *History of the Planting and Training of the Christian Church* (Eng. tr. (1851); Gieseler, *Compendium of Eccles. Hist.* (Eng. tr. 1846); Renan, *Origines du Christianisme* (1883); Schaff, *History of the Apostolic Age* (1886); Weizsäcker, *Apostolic Age* (Eng. tr. 1895); Ramsay, *The Church in the Roman Empire* (1893); Cheetham, *History of the Christian Church* (1894).

CHURCH ORGANIZATION : Ritschl, *Die Entstehung der Altkath. Kirche* (1857); Lightfoot, *The Christian Ministry* (1868); Hatch, *Organization of the Early Christian Churches* (1880); Sohm, *Kirchenrecht* (1892); Gore, *The Ministry of the Christian Church* (1888); Lindsay, *The Church and the Ministry* (1902).

DOCTRINAL BOOKS (GENERAL) : (Roman Catholic) Scheeben, *Handbuch der Kath. Dogmatik* (1878); Schouppe, *Elementa Theologiæ Dogmaticæ* (1861); Hunter, *Outlines of Dogmatic Theology* (1895); (Lutheran) Dorner, *System of Christian Doctrine* (Eng. tr. 1880); Martensen, *Christian Dogmatics* (Eng. tr. 1866); (non-Catholic) Harnack, *History of Dogma* (Eng. tr. 1894); Seeberg, *Dogmengesch.* (1886); (Anglican) Forbes, *Explanation of the Thirty-nine Articles* (1867), and *Explanation of the Nicene Creed* (1865); Mason, *The Faith of the Gospel*

(1888); Gibson, *The Thirty-nine Articles* (1896); Stone, *Outlines of Christian Dogma* (1900).

BOOKS BEARING MORE EXCLUSIVELY ON THE SUBJECT OF THIS ARTICLE : Lacordaire, *Conférences de l'Église* (1849); Seeley, *Ecce Homo* (1866); Gore, *Roman Catholic Claims* (1898); Hort, *The Christian Ecclesia* (1893); Moberly, *Ministerial Priesthood* (1897); Robertson, *Regnum Dei* (1902); Tyrrell Green, *The Church of Christ* (1902).

                                    J. H. MAUDE.

CHUZA (Χουζᾶς).—The ἐπίτροπος or house-steward of Herod the tetrarch, and husband of Joanna one of the women who, having been healed either of a sickness or of an evil spirit, attached themselves to Jesus and 'ministered unto him of their substance' (Lk 8³). Chuza is identified by Mr. Stanley Cook (*Glossary of Aramaic Inscriptions*, Cambr. 1898) with the father of one Ḥayyân whose family erected a rock-cut tomb at el-Ḥegr in Arabia, with the inscription : לחין בר כוזא אחרה ' *To Ḥayyân, son of Kûzâ, his posterity (have erected this tomb*).' The monument is probably of the 1st cent. B.C. or A.D. Blass (*Philology of the Gospels*), on the authority of *l*, a 7th cent. MS of the Vulgate, identifies the name with the Greek Κυδίας ; but this seems more than doubtful. Chuza may have been of a Nabatæan family, married to a Jewish wife. Joanna is also mentioned (Lk 24¹⁰) as one of the women who came early to the sepulchre to anoint the Lord's body (see JOANNA).

Chuzas is preferred by the American Committee of Revisers as the more proper spelling of Chuza.

LITERATURE.—EXPOSITOR, v. ix. [1899] 118 ff. ; Edersheim, *Life and Times*, i. 429, 572.   R. MACPHERSON.

CIRCUMCISION (מוּלָה, περιτομή). — With the origin * of this rite we are not here concerned ; as regards the three main theories—that it was a tribal mark, that it was of the nature of a sacrifice to the deity, and that it was practised from hygienic motives—see the Literature at the end of this article.

Circumcision was very far from being confined to the Hebrews ; it was practised by the ancient Arabs (Eusebius, *Præp. Evangelica*, vi. 11 ; W. R. Smith, *Rel. of the Semites*², p. 328 ; Wellhausen, *Reste Arab. Heident.*² pp. 174–176 ; H. H. Ploss, *Das Kind in Brauch und Sitte der Völker*, i. 295–300 ; Bertherand, *Médecine et Hygiène des Arabes*, pp. 306–314) as well as by the Mohammedans (Nöldeke, *Sketches from Eastern Hist.* p. 68), by the Ethiopians (Philostorgius, *Hist. Eccles.* iii. 4), by the Kaffirs (J. G. Frazer, *Golden Bough*², i. 327) and other African races (Hartmann, *Die Völker Afrikas*, i. 178 ; Ploss, *op. cit.* i. 295 f.), by many central Australian tribes (J. G. Frazer, *Totemism*, p. 47 ; Lagrange, *Études sur les religions sémitiques*, p. 239 ff.; Ploss, *op. cit.* ii. 250, 255, who says it is practised by the central, northern, and north-western tribes, but not by those in the east and south-west), by the Egyptians (Ebers, *Ægypten und die Bücher Mose's*, i. 278 ; Lagrange, *op. cit.* p. 241 ff.), and by the Aztecs and other Central American races (*Jewish Encyc.* iv. 97), etc.

The great difference between the *national* observance of the rite by the Hebrews (however one may seek to account for the somewhat conflicting statements in Gn 17¹², Ex 4²⁵· ²⁶, and Jos 5⁵ ; cf. Jn 7²²) † and that of other peoples was, firstly, that its significance was wholly *religious*,—the outward symbol of a covenant with God,—it was a religious act, whereas, among other nations, whatever the reason may have been for practising circumcision, it did not occupy a position like this ;‡ and secondly,

---

* Its very early origin is shown by the fact that the rite was originally performed with a stone implement, see Riehm, *HWB*, art. 'Beschneidung' ; cf. Jos 5².

† It is noteworthy that as a *physical* act circumcision is not considered in the book of Deuteronomy, though it is used in a figurative sense, 10¹⁶ 30¹⁶.

‡ A certain religious element, though in quite a subordinate

that the Hebrews performed circumcision on the eighth day after birth,* *i.e.* in infancy, whereas among other races it almost invariably took place at the age of puberty.† It is possible that this difference between the Mosaic Code and the usage of others was due to the more humane character of the former, which enjoined the rite at a time when least painful.‡

It was the custom among the Hebrews at all times, as it is among modern Jews,§ to give a boy ‖ a name at his circumcision ¶ (see Lk 2²¹). The rite had to be performed on the eighth day after birth, even though that day happened to be a Sabbath; technically this was a breaking of the Sabbath, but the law concerning circumcision took precedence here (see Christ's words in Jn 7²²ᶠ·). If, however, from one cause or another, *e.g.* sickness, a child's circumcision had to be postponed, the rite could under no circumstances be performed on the Sabbath.** In the time of Christ the ceremony was performed in the house; by the 7th cent. it had become customary to perform it in the synagogue; the modern Jews, however, have gone back to the earlier custom, and have their children circumcised at home.†† How fully the Law was fulfilled in the case of Christ is seen from Lk 1⁵⁹ 'On the eighth day they came to circumcise the child [John]' (cf. Ac 7⁸, Ph 3⁵), and Lk 2²¹ 'And when eight days were fulfilled for circumcising him, his name was called Jesus' (cf. Gal 4⁴).

Whatever may have been the original object and signification of circumcision,‡‡ it had lost its primary meaning long before the time of our Lord. By the time of the Babylonian exile it had become one of the distinguishing marks of Judaism; yet in spite of this, it is remarkable to find that in later days there arose a divergence of opinion among the Jews as to the need of circumcision for proselytes. Hellenistic Jews did not enforce circumcision in the case of proselytes, affirming that baptism was sufficient (see the *Jewish Encyc.* iv. 94, 95, where further details are given); the Palestinian Jews, on the other hand, would not admit proselytes without circumcision. The view of the latter ultimately won the day, but the episode testifies to the fact that, in the opinion of a very influential and important class of Jews, circumcision and baptism were analogous rites. Now there was one element in circumcision which may possibly have been of greater significance than is often supposed. It was an essential part of the rite that blood should be shed (cf. the 'Mezizah'-cup, an illustration of which can be seen in the *Jewish Encyc.* iv. 99); but blood represented life, was even identified with life (Lv 17¹¹· ¹⁴, see art. BLOOD); it is therefore difficult to get away from the conviction that when a child was circumcised he was consecrated to God by the fact that his life (*i.e.* under the symbol of blood) was offered to

God. The fact of circumcision being called 'the sign of the covenant' (Gn 17¹¹ אוֹת בְּרִית; cf. also the modern name בְּרִית מִילָה, and the words in the service at a circumcision: 'From this eighth day and henceforth may his blood be accepted, and may the Lord his God be with him')* supports this view, for no covenant was ratified without the shedding of blood,† *i.e.* the symbolic laying down of a life.

If circumcision, then, was in a certain sense a *death* (or at least a symbol of life laid down), there is a very striking analogy between it and baptism; cf. the words of St. Paul in Ro 6³ᶠ· 'Are ye ignorant that all we who were baptized into Christ were baptized into his death? We were buried therefore with him through baptism into death: that like as Christ was raised from the dead through the glory of the Father, so we also might walk in newness of life...' Both circumcision and baptism were a figurative death, by means of which a new spiritual life was reached. In the later Jewish literature this view was held with regard to circumcision, as the following quotation, for example, will show: 'According to Pirke R. El. ... Pharaoh prevented the Hebrew slaves from performing the rite; but when the Passover time came and brought them deliverance, they underwent circumcision, and mingled the blood of the Paschal lamb with that of the Abrahamic covenant, wherefore (Ezk 16⁶) God repeats the words: *In thy blood live.*'‡ The same thought is brought out in the modern 'service at a circumcision,' when the *Mohel* § says, in reference to the newly circumcised: 'Let thy father and thy mother rejoice, and let her that bare thee be glad; and it is said, And I passed by thee, and I saw thee weltering in thy blood, and I said unto thee, "In thy blood live."' ‖

Taking these facts together, we must regard the circumcision of Christ as of the highest significance; for it was not only a fulfilling of the Law, but inasmuch as it was symbolic of a life laid down, it must also be regarded as a 'parable' of the Crucifixion (cf. Milton, *Poetical Works*, 'Upon the Circumcision'; Keble, *Christian Year*, 'The Circumcision of Christ').

LITERATURE.—H. H. Ploss, *Das Kind in Brauch und Sitte der Völker*, i. 295–300, ii. 250 ff., Stuttgart, 1876, *Geschichtliches und Ethnologisches über Knaben-Beschneidung*, Leipzig, 1885; A. Asher, *The Jewish Rite of Circumcision, with the Prayers and Laws appertaining thereto* (Eng. tr.), 1873, very useful, but must be used with caution; Stade in *ZATW*, 1886, a most interesting and instructive article on the origin of the rite in the Hebrew nation; an article in *ZDPV* xvii. 89 ff. is also useful; Harper, *Priestly Element in OT²*, Chicago, 1905, 149 f., and the lit. there; Driver, *Genesis*, London, 1904, pp. 189–191; Bertherand, *Médecine et Hygiène des Arabes*, Paris, 1855, gives many interesting details concerning the modern rite among Arabs generally, though the work deals mainly with Algeria. There is also much information to be gathered here and there in J. H. Petermann's *Reisen im Orient*, 2 vols., Leipzig, 1860. The articles in the works on *Hebräische Archäologie* by Nowack and Benzinger, as well as that on 'Beschneidung' in Hamburger's *RE*, should be consulted; cf. also art. 'Circumcision' in Hastings' *DB* and in the *Encyc. Bibl.* and the *Jewish Encyclopedia*.   W. O. E. OESTERLEY.

CIRCUMSTANTIALITY IN THE PARABLES.— A parable consists of two members, viz. an illustration and a didactic part, which, according to the view we hold, may be called either the interpretation or the application. Both members are necessary to make the parable complete, though the didactic part need not be expressly stated, the circumstances in which the illustration is given making its purpose plain. Unfortunately the

---

sense, has been observed in the performance of the rite in some races, *e.g.* among the Polynesians (see Ploss, *op. cit.* i. 299 f.). In later Judaism, when sacrifices had ceased, circumcision and the keeping of the Sabbath were regarded as substitutes for sacrifices.

* This applies also to the Samaritans.

† An exception to this is found among the Persians, who circumcise their children at any age from eight days to ten years, though it is unusual to do so at the earliest age (see, further, Ploss, *op. cit.* p. 248 ff.).

‡ Cf. Bertherand, *Médecine des Arabes*, p. 306; Driver, *Genesis*, p. 190.

§ The so-called Reform Jews are an exception.

‖ Girls receive their name on the day of birth.

¶ With this may be compared the custom among some primitive races of *changing* the name at circumcision.

** Cf. A. Asher, *The Jewish Rite of Circumcision*, p. 41 f.

†† For an account of the ceremony as performed at the present day, see Singer, *Authorized Daily Prayer-Book*, pp. 304–307; Asher, *op. cit.* p. xix f. Some interesting details will also be found in *Jewish Encyc.*, art. 'Circumcision.'

‡‡ See a remarkable art. by J. G. Frazer in *The Independent Review*, Nov. 1904.

---

* Singer, *op. cit.* p. 307.

† See Trumbull, *The Blood Covenant, passim*; W. R. Smith, *op. cit.* p. 314 f., *Kinship and Marriage in Early Arabia²*, p. 57 ff.

‡ *Jewish Encyc.* iv. 93ᵇ.

§ An official specially qualified to perform the rite.

‖ Singer, *op. cit.* p. 305.

parables of Christ are mostly preserved only in fragmentary form. We have the illustrations, but not the lessons they were designed to enforce ; and as we are uncertain as to the connexion in which those illustrations were given, it is sometimes difficult to make sure what Christ intended to teach by them. But if the Evangelists give little, sometimes even a misleading, light as to the context in which the parables were spoken, they record the illustrative portions of them with much fulness of detail. Particularly is this the case with those parables in which the illustration is in the form of a narrative. The story is told with much circumstantiality. Many little touches are introduced to heighten the effect. We are almost inclined to forget, at times, that the story is told with a purpose, so fully and circumstantially are its details narrated. Among the Evangelists, St. Luke is the most pronounced in the circumstantiality with which he reproduces the stories which Christ introduced in His parables. He likes to linger over them. He elaborates with a fulness of detail that brings the scene vividly before the mind. But though St. Luke is pre-eminent in this respect, all the Synoptists present the illustrative portion of the parables with more or less circumstantiality. And this feature of the parables suggests some questions which we may consider under the following heads : — (1) In how far is the circumstantiality of the narratives authentic? (2) If we accept the traditional principle of parabolical 'interpretation,' can we fix a limit beyond which it is illegitimate to interpret the details? (3) If we reject this principle of parabolical 'interpretation,' can we meet the objection that the circumstantiality of the illustrations is empty ornament?

1. The question of the authenticity of the circumstantiality of the illustrations is in many cases forced upon us by the fact that details which are recorded by one Evangelist are omitted by another For instance, in the parable of the Sower, St. Matthew and St. Mark say of the seed that fell by the wayside, that the fowls came and devoured it up, but St. Luke adds that it was trodden down (8^5). Again, in the parable of the Patch on the Old Garment, St. Matthew and St. Mark describe the patch as a piece of undressed cloth, while St. Luke heightens the folly of the proceeding by making the patch first be cut out of a new garment (ἀπὸ ἱματίου καινοῦ σχίσας, 5^{36}). In many cases we find the explanation of such variations in the details of the parables in the desire of the Evangelists to emphasize the point and heighten the effect of the illustration. Such is possibly the case with the examples just given, and many other instances of the same tendency might be cited. To give a few more,—in the parable of the Supper (Mt 22^{1-14}, Lk 14^{15-24}), St. Matthew merely says that the guests made light of the invitation and went their ways, one to his farm, another to his merchandise (v.^{5}) ; while St. Luke puts various excuses into the mouth of the guests (vv.$^{18-20}$). In the parable of the Lost Sheep (Mt 18^{12-14}, Lk 15^{4-7}), St. Luke represents the owner as taking the lost sheep, when he has found it, upon his shoulders. In the parable of the Houses built upon the Rock and upon the Sand (Mt 7^{24-27}, Lk 6^{47-49}), St. Matthew says merely that the wise man built upon the rock and the foolish upon the sand ; but St. Luke represents the one as having to dig and go deep to find a foundation, while the other builds without a foundation, upon the earth. But in other cases we must assign a different motive for the variation in the details of the parables. Many seem due to an allegorizing tendency on the part of the Evangelists. They regarded the characters and events

of the narratives as the counterparts of like characters and events in the religious sphere, and introduced details from this latter sphere into the illustration. Thus, for instance, when we compare St. Matthew's version of the parable of the Supper with St. Luke's (Mt 22^{1-14}, Lk 14^{15-24}), many of the new features in St. Matthew appear to be due to this tendency. The Supper of St. Luke has become the marriage-feast of the king's son, i.e. the Messiah ; the king, in spite of the refusal of the guests, sends them a second invitation (vv.$^{3.\ 4}$) ; they ill-treat and slay the servants who bring the invitation, and the king sends forth his armies to destroy them and to burn their city (vv.$^{6.\ 7}$). Evidently these details are suggested by the thought of Israel's behaviour towards her God, and the fate that overtook her. Again, in the parable of the Wicked Husbandmen, St. Mark relates that they took the son and slew him and cast him out of the vineyard ; while St. Matthew and St. Luke reverse the order, and make them first cast him out and then slay him, with evident reference to the fate of Jesus (Mt 27^{31-33}, cf. He 13^{12}). Again, in the parable of the Watchful Servants (Mk 13^{33-37}, Lk 12^{35-38}), St. Luke represents the master as girding himself and making them sit down to meat and serving them, though he has himself borne witness ($17^{7ff.}$) to the unlikelihood of such conduct on the part of any ordinary master. Such extraordinary condescension is probably an allegorical feature introduced with reference to the Parousia.

2. If we accept the traditional principle of parabolical 'interpretation,' in how far are we justified in seeking to interpret the circumstantial details so largely present in the parables? There are some who insist that every little detail is significant, and who regard that as the true method of interpretation which seeks to find some spiritual truth to correspond to every item of the illustration. 'Quanto enim plus solidæ veritatis,' says Vitringa (quoted by Trench, ch. iii.) 'ex Verbo Dei eruerimus, si nihil obstet, tanto magis divinam commendabimus sapientiam.' Teelman (quoted by Jülicher, *Die Gleichnisreden Jesu*, i. p. 270) insists that in every parable every word must be significant. And Petersen (ib. p. 271) maintains that Christ never introduces the slightest detail into any parable which is not designed to correspond to something in the interpretation. On the other hand, it has been generally recognized that there are limits beyond which the details of the illustration must not be pressed. 'Sunt autem quæ et simpliciter posita sunt,' says Tert. (*de Pudic.* 9), 'ad struendam et disponendam et texendam parabolam.' Chrysostom (*in Mt. Hom.* lxiv. 3) lays down the rule: οὐδὲ χρὴ πάντα τὰ ἐν ταῖς παραβολαῖς κατὰ λέξιν περιεργάζεσθαι, ἀλλὰ τὸν σκοπὸν μαθόντας, δι' ὃν συνετέθη, τοῦτον δρέπεσθαι καὶ μηδὲν πολυπραγμονεῖν περαιτέρω. But great difference of opinion exists, even among those who profess to observe Chrysostom's canon, as to where the πολυπραγμονεῖν begins. Indeed, if the principle of 'interpretation' be admitted at all, if the parables, as such treatment of them involves, in spite of all protest to the contrary, are really allegories, it is difficult to see on what ground a line can be drawn beyond which it is illegitimate to interpret the details. The more perfect the allegory, the more will it admit of interpretation down to the minutest circumstance. And so long as the significance attached to these details is relevant to the tenor of the whole, the interpreter may well demand on what ground it may be objected that the details in question are not to be regarded as symbolical. The artificiality of the method and the unsatisfactoriness of the conclusions may be urged as an objection to the general principle of parabolical 'interpretation' underlying such method, but on that principle the method itself appears thoroughly defensible.

3. If we reject the principle of parabolical 'interpretation,' does not the circumstantiality of the illustrations become mere useless ornament? This is an objection raised against those who contend that the parables are not to be regarded as allegories of which we have to seek the interpretation, but as comparisons between the principle involved in some case taken from everyday life and a similar principle which it is desired to establish in the spiritual sphere. Those who maintain this view insist that it is only the principles or relations involved in the two different spheres that are compared, not the details on either side. There is only the one point of comparison between the two cases, only the one lesson enforced by the parable. In answer to the objection that this seems to reduce the fulness of detail with which the illustrations are elaborated to mere useless ornament, it is replied that though the details are not regarded as significant in the symbolical sense, they are yet full of significance as serving to bring out with force and clearness the thought which it is the purpose of the parable to enforce. Were the illustrations not presented with such circumstantiality, they would not be so convincing as they are. The scene is brought vividly before our eyes; our interest is awakened, our sympathy enlisted. Many of the details which cause such trouble to the allegorical interpreters, as, e.g., the injustice of the Judge (Lk 18$^{1-8}$) and the fraudulence of the Steward (Lk 16$^{1-12}$), may easily be explained from this point of view. The injustice of the Judge serves to bring out more forcibly that it was the importunity of the widow that overcame him; the fraud of the Steward emphasizes the fact that it was for his wisdom alone that he was commended. And so with all the details with which the parables are supplied. There is no useless ornament. Every little touch serves to bring out more clearly the central thought enforced by the illustration, and so contributes to the effect of the parable.

LITERATURE.—See the list at the end of article PARABLE.

G. WAUCHOPE STEWART.

CITY.—In the East the city developed from the necessity of protection from hostile invasion, and its characteristic was the wall or rampart. It was the wall that originally constituted the πόλις, though in later times its position amongst the Jews was determined by its ability to produce ten men qualified for office in the Synagogue (see Hastings' DB, art. 'City'). The κώμη was the village or hamlet, without walls, and was generally a dependency of some neighbouring city. In Mk 1^{38} the word κωμόπολις is used, apparently as a designation of a large unwalled village or town. Bethlehem and Bethsaida, though generally classed as cities, are spoken of as κῶμαι in Jn 7^{42}, Mk 8$^{23, 26}$, the natural inference from which is that the words 'city,' 'town,' and 'village,' though having, as with us, a technical signification, were occasionally used in a looser and less precise manner.

The government of the πόλις was modelled on that of Jerusalem, where the Sanhedrin (wh. see) was the supreme authority on all matters which, after the Roman domination, did not fall within the province of the Roman governor. According to the Talmud (Mish. Sanh. i. 6), in every Jewish city there was a Council of twenty-three which was responsible to the Sanhedrin (Mt 5^{22}). Josephus knows nothing of such a Council. The Court which he mentions (Ant. IV. viii. 14) consisted of seven judges, who had each two Levites as assessors. The College of Elders who presided over the Synagogue had also judicial functions, but what was

its relation to the Council is not easy to determine. The gates of the city were places of public resort; the money-changers facilitated trade; and the various guilds of artisans had special districts allotted to them.

In the time of our Lord, Palestine was a land of cities. Galilee, measuring fifty miles north and south, and from twenty-five to thirty-five east and west—about the average size of an English shire—is said by Josephus (BJ III. iii. 2) to have had a population of 3,000,000. Allowing for patriotic exaggeration, the fact that the soil was so fertile as to make it a veritable garden, and that it was traversed by the three main trade routes of the East, would account for an exceptional density of population. Round the Lake of Galilee there were nine cities with not less than 15,000 inhabitants, some of them with considerably more, so that there must have been along its margin an almost unbroken chain of buildings. The blending of the Jewish with the Greek civilization must have given to these cities a striking picturesqueness alike in manners, customs, attire, and architecture. Tiberias, built by Herod Antipas, was a stately city, whose ruins still indicate a wall three miles long. Its palace, citadel, and public buildings were of the most imposing description, but it was almost wholly Gentile, no Jew who had the pride of his race setting foot within the walls of a city polluted alike by the monuments of idolatry and by its site on an ancient burial-place. Cities like Bethsaida and Capernaum, again, were preponderantly Jewish. Taricheæ, not mentioned in the Gospels, is described by Pliny (HN v. xv. 11) as one of the chief centres of industry and commerce, and by Josephus (Ant. XIV. vii. 3) as a stronghold of Jewish patriotism. Everywhere in Galilee there was an intense civic vitality. The problems of a complex civilization were presented with peculiar force. The Gospel narrative stands out from a background of a richer and more varied life than probably ever existed elsewhere in an organized community, and it reflects in a wonderfully accurate manner all its various phases. This is, indeed, one reason of its universal applicability. It is the application of absolute principles of conduct to typical situations of the most complex character.

This density of population passed over the Lake of Galilee to the region eastward. The Decapolis (Mt 4^{25}) consisted of a group of ten or more cities east of the Jordan, united in a league for purposes of defence. These were Greek cities in the province of Syria, but possessing certain civil rights, such as coinage, etc., granted them by Rome. The cities constituting the Decapolis are variously named. Pliny (HN v. xviii. 74) enumerates them as follows: Scythopolis, Hippos, Gadara, Dion, Pella, Gerasa, Philadelphia, Canatha, and, with less probability, Damascus and Raphana. To the north of Galilee again lay the Phœnician cities of Tyre and Sidon (Mt 15^{21}). Tyre, even in its decline, was a noble city, with a teeming population. The circumference of its walls is given by Pliny as nineteen Roman miles. Inland, Cæsarea Philippi nestled at the base of Mt. Hermon, in a situation of remarkable beauty and fertility. This city received its name from Herod the Great, who built there a temple to Augustus. It was in its neighbourhood that Peter made his striking confession (Mt 16$^{13ff.}$). The cities of Samaria to the south occupy no large place in our Lord's mission. Though Jesus passed through Samaria (Jn 4^4), it is not recorded that He visited its capital, and the disciples were specially enjoined to refrain from preaching the gospel in any city of the Samaritans (Mt 10^5). Samaria was itself a beautiful city—one of the cities rebuilt on a magnificent scale by Herod the Great owing to its strategic situation—the population being mixed, half-Greek, half-Samaritan, wholly alien, therefore, in sympathy from the Jews, alike through the Samaritan hostility and the Greek culture. The city of Sychar (Jn 4⁵), the scene of our Lord's conversation with the Samaritan woman, is generally identified with the modern *'Ain 'Askar*, at the foot of Mt. Ebal, about a mile from Nâblus (Shechem). Judæa, with its desolate mountain ranges, was never rich in cities. Jericho lay on its borders, situated in an oasis of remarkable fertility, a city of palms, in striking contrast to the stony and barren region of which it was the gateway. Jericho was rich in the natural wealth of the East, but singularly poor in heroic memories.

But to the Jew the city of cities—the city that symbolized all that was highest alike in his political and religious aspirations — was Jerusalem. Twice in St. Matthew's Gospel is Jerusalem called 'the holy city' (Mt 4⁵ 27⁵³), and as such it was enshrined in every Jewish heart through the noble poetry of the Psalter. It was the city where God had His chosen seat, and round which clustered the heroic traditions of the Hebrew race—the city, indeed, with which was intertwined the very conception of Judaism as a national religion, for in the Temple of Jerusalem alone could God be worshipped with the rites He had Himself ordained. The cities of Galilee owed their greatness and importance to commercial or political causes. Though some were preponderantly Jewish, and others, such as Tiberias, almost exclusively Gentile, there was yet in them all a mingling of races and a tolerably free and humane intercourse. Samaria was a great Roman stronghold, dominating the main trade-route from Cæsarea on the coast to the East. But Jerusalem remained a city of the Jews, cherishing its own ecclesiastical traditions, and holding its patriotic exclusiveness with a narrowness all the greater from the pressure of the Roman subjection. It had almost complete autonomy under the Sanhedrin. Cæsarea was the seat of the Roman Procurator, except during the great Jewish feasts, when he found it necessary to reside at Jerusalem to restrain the turbulence of a fanatically patriotic people who were ready to court martyrdom for the national cause. It is perhaps significant, as showing the ecclesiastical character of the population of Jerusalem, that it was a priest and a Levite who first passed the man lying wounded and bleeding on the road to Jericho (Lk 10³¹ᶠ·).

In the time of our Lord, then, the Jews had made the transition from a life mainly pastoral and agricultural to the more advanced life of the city. The Twelve and the Seventy are sent to preach the gospel in cities, and when they are persecuted in one city they are to flee to another (Mt 10¹ᶠᶠ· ²³, Lk 10¹). Jesus, after He had given instructions to the Twelve, departs to preach and to teach in their cities (Mt 11¹). The conception of the city as the flower and fruit of the highest civilization is emerging, and the *civitas Dei* is taking the place of the *regnum Dei*, and thus bringing Hebrew into line with Greek ideals. This fact is very significant for the modern presentation of the gospel. It is sometimes assumed that Christianity is possible only for a primitive community, and many modern ideals of communal life are based on the supposition that the city is wholly an artificial product, and that the way of true progress lies in reverting to village communities. All through the Christian centuries there has been a tendency on the part of many who have felt with singular intensity the influence of Jesus, to seek the cultivation of the Christian life either in isolation or in withdrawing themselves from the strenuous civic activities. The Christian ideal of saintship has been largely that of the cloister. But it is becoming more and more realized that Jesus lived His life in a crowd, that He was so seldom alone that occasions when He sought solitude are specially noted, and that it was the sight of great masses of people that most powerfully touched His emotions (Mt 14¹⁴, Lk 19⁴¹). The gospel of Jesus is essentially a social gospel. Its ideal is a civic ideal. Its precepts have no meaning and no applicability except to those who are living in a community. Its ultimate goal is the 'holy city, new Jerusalem, descending from God out of heaven, prepared as a bride adorned for her husband' (Rev 21²). The fact is noteworthy as showing the place and influence of Christianity in the natural evolution of humanity. For the history of civilization is the history of cities. Babylon, Nineveh, Jerusalem, Athens, Rome, Alexandria, Venice, Florence, and the mediæval cities all mark stages in the development of the higher culture of the race. The modern city, indeed, still lacks its *raison d'être*. It is as yet a huge amorphous entity, presenting problems which, so far from finding solution, are only now beginning to be fully faced. And the supreme test of the Divine power of the religion of Jesus in our day will lie in its capability of giving to the city rational meaning, of transmuting the blind force of economic pressure into the law of reciprocal harmony, of so applying the principles of the gospel to the marvellous complexities of our civic life as to educe the noblest faculties of the individual while securing the unity of communal existence.

LITERATURE.—Schürer, *HJP* II. 1. 154 ff., 160 f. ; G. A. Smith, *HGHL* pp. 420-435 ; Fairbairn, *City of God*, pp. 349-370; Westcott, *Hebrews*, pp. 386-389.   A. MILLER.

CLAIM.—The term expresses a twofold relationship, either to a claim as advanced and enforced or as accepted and complied with. The assumption or imposition of a claim upon another is an act of authority, a relationship of established right and superior power; while the recognition and discharge of the same claim represent the corresponding social duty.

The narrative of the Gospels describes how Christ moved amid the social and religious relationships of the world into which He came. It tells how He knew all things in the heart of man (Jn 2²³⁻²⁵), and occasionally drew the attention of His disciples to the real importance of certain personalities and actions (Mt 16⁶ 11¹¹, Lk 21¹⁻⁴), where a wrong impression might have been produced ; but, as a rule, He does not take the initiative in criticising and condemning in detail the standards, methods, and institutions then prevailing in society. His kingdom is declared to be entirely distinct from that of the world, and it is only when challenged on a question of right conduct that He lays down the principle that whatever Cæsar has an undisputed claim upon ought to be regarded as his, and whatever belongs to God should be rendered to Him only. On the ground of previous and higher claims, He expels those who had obtained the privilege of traffic within the temple area, inasmuch as the place had been dedicated to its Owner as a house of prayer (Mt 21¹³). The victims of masterful temptation and difficult surroundings (Mt 11¹⁹, Lk 7³⁷ 18¹³ 22⁶¹, Jn 8¹¹) are regarded with pity and hopefulness. His direct and indignant exposure is reserved for the attempt to give religious sanction to evaded duty (Mk 7¹¹), or where the name of religion is made unlovely by the proud and harsh claims of those who profess it (Mt 6² 23⁴⁻⁷· ²³).

Otherwise Christ moves amid the relationships of common life and the claims of organized society, using them as the field of parable and the vehicle of His teaching concerning the kingdom that was at hand. Thus He refers to purchasers of property, money-lenders and interest, employers of labour and the rights of the labourer. Similarly, we have allusions to war, judicial punishment, parental authority, marriage and divorce, fasting and sumptuous living. With regard to all such relationships and connected claims Christ uses the vocabulary and valuation current in the world. The prodigal son declares that he has forfeited the right to which he had been born (Lk 15[19]); Zacchæus (19[9]) and the woman bowed down with infirmity (13[16]) have, as children of Abraham, a family claim that should shut out more distant considerations. This fact gives emphasis to the exceptional instances of Naaman and the widow of Sarepta (Lk 4[25-29]). The Syro-Phœnician woman quite understands that local opinion as to race privilege does not allow her to share on equal terms with Israel (Mt 15[27. 28]). The lineage of natural descent implies that of ethical resemblance (Mt 23[31], Jn 8[39]). Parental affection is the basis of the assurance that our Heavenly Father will act still more wisely and lovingly towards His children (Mt 7[11] || Lk 11[13]). It is after the fullest recognition of the beauty and power of family claims that Christ calls His disciples to an even more intense and constraining relationship (Mt 10[37], Lk 14[26]).

The claims of neighbourhood and hospitality are frequently alluded to. Lazarus, even in Abraham's bosom, must be willing to serve one who had been an earthly neighbour (Lk 16[24]). A neighbour can be put to any inconvenience on behalf of a stranger guest in their midst (11[5-8]). The action of the woman who anointed Christ and bathed His feet with tears is shown to be right, inasmuch as the claim of a passing guest was greater than that of those who were always present (Mk 14[3], Lk 7[37. 38], Jn 12[7. 8]).

By the same use of current language and thought, religion is a codification of things bound and free, prohibited and permitted (Mt 16[19] 18[18]). Its duties, as imposed by the scribes and Pharisees, are like the load on the submissive baggage animal (23[4]). John forbids those who taught in Christ's name without having the qualifying claim of discipleship (Mk 9[38]). With the formal appeal of a litigant, 'Legion' demands a proof of Christ's right to interfere (5[7]). Satan is another taskmaster with claims to be satisfied, and disease is the mark of his property and power (Lk 13[16]). Rabbinical rules so far supersede the commandments of God that Christ can be condemned as an enemy to religion (Mt 23[13-39], Mk 3[10] 7[5. 9] 10[5] 11[17], Lk 13[14]). Afterwards, to one who understood it all, it was evident that attention to their own claims had blinded the religious leaders of Israel to the presence of the Lord of Glory (1 Co 2[8]), just as the worship of nature, degraded and degrading, had darkened and alienated from God the heart of the Gentile world (Ro 1[21]).

It is thus evident from the Gospel narratives that the Hebrew-Roman world, into which Christ came as the Son of Man, had reached a high stage of development with regard to social authority and obedience. The areas of privilege and exemption were carefully marked off from those of servility and compulsion. Legislated right and wrong, like guarding cherubim, faced each other at all the gates of public life. The rich and noble confronted the poor and unclassed, the strong and conquering had their counterpart in the subject and enslaved, the wise and enlightened stood out in relief from the ignorant and barbarous, the male had defined authority and predominance over the female, and free-born citizens exercised a jealous censorship over the admission of strangers and foreigners. The universal pressure of such claims and obligations gave sedimentary stratification to all that was highest and lowest in social order, and only the infusion and uplift of a new volcanic force could invert its masses and confuse such established lines of cleavage.

It was largely due to this prevalence of legal relationship that the first presentation of the gospel to the world took the familiar form of forensic process and judicial pronouncement. A similar desire to present afresh to the present age the mind of Christ and the spirit of His kingdom would in the West draw upon the discoveries of physical science, the principles of commercial expansion, and the incentives of political empire. In the East it would measure the following of Christ with the self-denial of the devotee, likeness to Him with the claims of caste, and turn towards our Heavenly Father the venerated claims of ancestor-worship.

There were, however, two great relationships in the Hebrew-Roman world that were strangely marked by aloofness and disruption, namely, spiritual fellowship between God and man, and the racial status of Jew and Greek. Among the Jews the voice of prophecy and of direct communication with God had ceased. The word of Ezekiel (37[11]) had been fulfilled, 'Our bones are dried, and our hope is lost.' The message of religious teaching had dropt its preface, 'Thus saith the Lord,' and had come to express the contention of a sect, the presentation of a view, the quotation of hearer from hearer. On this account the teaching of Christ arrested the ear as sounding a note that had become unfamiliar, the voice of original authority. In the Roman world, the most sincere and eloquent teacher of the age (Lucretius) had shown that there was no Divine care for man as had been once supposed, for in his vision of the opened heavens he had seen the gods in a happy seclusion of their own, undisturbed by the sound of human pain and sorrow (de Rer. Nat. iii. 18 ff. ; cf. Homer, Il. vi. 41 ff.). In that jaded and disenchanted day the most popular and reasoned religion could only unite gods and men in the creed of avoided care.

With regard to the mutual recognition of Jew and Gentile, the antagonism was regarded on both sides as radical and permanent. The Jew despised the Gentile as 'flesh and blood,' humanity without religion ; the Gentile saw in the Jew the negation of all social instinct, the genius of unnatural hate, religion without humanity. It must have been indescribably wonderful in such an age to learn that 'God was in Christ reconciling the world unto himself' (2 Co 5[19]). It was a great task that was soon to confront the gospel, for the Jew had to be convinced that the alien had been divinely provided for in the promises (Eph 2[19]), and the Gentile had to learn that there was no place for pride where a wild branch had been grafted contrary to custom into a cultivated stem, and owed not only its sustenance but the higher quality of its new fruit to that incorporation (Ro 11[17-24]). And yet in a quarter of a century after Christ's death it could be stated as something that had passed beyond comment and controversy,—'There is neither Jew nor Greek, there is neither bond nor free, there is neither male nor female, for ye are all one in Christ Jesus' (Gal 3[28] ; see POWER). The Christian was thus a 'new creature,' and for him all things had become new (2 Co 5[17]); but this did not mean that he had any resident authority enabling him henceforth to please himself. Everything was in Christ Jesus. To come to Christ was to accept His yoke, and the spirit of bondage (Ro 8[15]) had only been exchanged for a nobler constraint (2 Co 5[14]). Wherever there was freedom from the law of sin and death, there was the law of the Spirit of life in Christ Jesus (Ro 8[2]).

GEORGE M. MACKIE.

CLAIMS (OF CHRIST). — In any attempt to arrive at the truth with regard to the person of Christ, it is with the self-consciousness of Jesus and His witness regarding Himself that we must begin. To answer the question, 'What think ye of Christ?' we need above all to know what Christ thought of Himself. It was the men who knew Jesus only in an external fashion that took Him to be John the Baptist, or Elijah, or Jeremiah, or one of the prophets (Mt 16[14]). It was one who had come into the closest contact with the mind of the Master, and had learned to judge Him, not by outward signs merely, but by His implicit and explicit claims, that broke into the great confession, 'Thou art the Christ, the Son of the living God' (v.[16]). Hence it becomes a matter of the highest importance to consider the testimony of the Gospels as to our Lord's personal claims.

1. The fundamental claim of Jesus was a claim to *moral authority*. And this authority was asserted in two ways. (*a*) He claimed the authority of a *master*, an authority over the will and the life, to which obedience was the only natural response. It was by this most probably that the earliest disciples were first impressed. 'Follow me,' Jesus said to men (Mt 4[19. 21] || 8[22] 9[9] || 19[21] ||, Jn 1[43]); and they either rose up straightway and followed Him (Mt 4[20. 22] || 9[9] ||), or, if they failed to do so, 'went away sorrowful,' feeling in their inmost hearts that they had made 'the grand refusal' (Mt 19[22] ||). (*b*) But, further, He claimed authority as a *teacher*. If His immediate followers were first impressed by His claim to be obeyed, it was the authority of His teaching that first struck the multitude and filled them with astonishment (Mt 7[28. 29] ||). It was not only that He constantly placed Himself in opposition to their acknowledged instructors, those scribes who sat in Moses' seat, and set His simple 'Verily I say unto you' against all the traditional learning of the synagogue. He did much more than this. He claimed the right either to abrogate altogether or to reinterpret in His own way laws which were regarded as clothed with Divine sanctions—the law of retaliation (Mt 5[38ff.]), the law of divorce (v.[31f.]), and even the thrice-holy law of the Sabbath (Mt 12[1ff. 10ff.] ||, Lk 13[14], Jn 7[23]). See art. AUTHORITY OF CHRIST.

2. But moral authority, like all other forms of authority, must rest upon a power that lies behind. *What right has Jesus to speak thus?* men would ask; What right to call upon us to leave our homes, our friends, our all, to follow Him? What right to bid us accept His teaching as a perfect revelation of the will of God, and His interpretation of the Law as its true fulfilling? Moral authority quickly disappears when there is no moral power at the back of it. But our Lord's claim to authority rested upon an underlying claim to *holiness*—a claim which His hearers and disciples were in a position to verify for themselves. There is nothing which gives a man such sway over the consciences of other men as the possession of true holiness; while there is nothing more certain to be found out than the lack of this quality in one who professes to have it. It was the holiness of Christ's character that made His words fall with such convincing weight upon the hearts of men and women. It was His holiness that gave Him the right to command, and made them willing to obey. According to the Fourth Gospel, it was the Baptist's testimony, 'Behold the Lamb of God!' (Jn 1[36]), that brought the first pair of disciples to Jesus. They came to see if this testimony was true (cf. v.[37ff.]), and what they saw bound them to Jesus for ever. Publicans and sinners drew near to Him (Mt 9[10], Lk 15[1]), not, as His enemies insinuated (Mt 11[19] ||), because He was a sinner like themselves, but because they saw in Him One who, with all His human sympathy, was so high above sin that He could stretch out a saving hand to those who were its slaves (Mt 9[12] ||, Lk 7[36-50] 19[2-10]). And this holiness, which others saw and felt in Him, Jesus claimed, and that in the most absolute fashion. He claimed to be without sin. He claimed this not only when He said to His foes, 'Which of you convicteth me of sin?' (Jn 8[46]), but by the attitude of His whole life to the facts of moral evil. He claimed it by calling Himself the Physician of the sinful (Mt 9[12] ||), by assuming the power to forgive sins (Mt 9[6] ||, Lk 7[47f.]), by never making confession of sin in His own prayers, though enjoining it upon His disciples (Mt 6[12] ||), by never even joining with His disciples in common prayers, of which confession would necessarily form an element (on this point see Forrest, *Christ of History and of Experience*, p. 22 ff.; *Expos. Times*, xi. [1900] 352 ff.). See, further, artt. HOLINESS, SINLESSNESS.

3. A very important aspect of Christ's claims is their point of connexion with the national hope regarding the *Messiah* (which see). There can hardly be any doubt that from the very beginning of His public ministry the Messianic consciousness was fully awake in the heart of Jesus. We see the presence of this consciousness in the Temptation narratives (Mt 4[1-11] ||), in the sermon in the synagogue of Nazareth (Lk 4[17ff.]), in the claim of the preacher on the Mount that He came to fulfil the Law and the Prophets (Mt 5[17]). At a later stage He welcomes and blesses Peter's express declaration, 'Thou art the Christ' (Mt 16[16f.]), and, finally, He accepts the homage of the multitude as the Son of David (wh. see), who came in the name of the Lord (Mt 21[9] ||), and dies upon the cross for claiming to be the King of the Jews (Mt 27[11], cf. v.[37]). And if until the end of His ministry He did not call Himself or allow Himself to be called the Messiah (Mt 16[20]), this was clearly because the false ideals of the Jews regarding the Messianic kingdom made it impossible for Him to do so without creating all kinds of misunderstandings, and so precipitating the inevitable crisis before His work on earth was accomplished. But by His constant use of the title 'Son of Man' (wh. see), Jesus was giving all along, as Beyschlag says (*NT Theology*, i. 63), 'a veiled indication of His Messianic calling'; for hardly any one now doubts that He used this title with precise reference to the well-known passage in the 7th chapter of Daniel (v.[13ff.]), and that by so describing Himself He was claiming to bring in personally and establish upon earth that very kingdom of God which formed the constant theme of His preaching (see Mt 26[64]).

4. But if Christ's use of the title 'Son of Man' shows how He claimed to fulfil the Messianic idea, His further claim to be the *Son of God* (wh. see) shows that He filled this idea with an altogether new content, which formed no part of the Messianic expectation of the Jews. No doubt in popular usage the title 'Son of God,' through the influence especially of Ps 2[7], had become an official name for the Messiah (Mt 8[29], Mk 14[61], Jn 1[49]). But Christ's claim to be the Son of God evidently meant much more than this. In asserting His Divine Sonship He was not merely affirming His right to an external title of honour, but was giving expression to a consciousness of relationship to God the Father which was absolutely unique, and in which the very essence of His Messiahship consisted. It is true that in the Synoptics He does not expressly designate Himself the Son of God, as He does in the Fourth Gospel (5[25] 9[35] [*var. lect.*] 10[36] 11[4]); but at all events He repeatedly calls God His Father, and refers to Himself as 'the Son' when speaking of God, and that in a sense manifestly distinct from the general idea of God's universal Fatherhood (*e.g.* Mt 11[27] 12[50] 18[10]). In the Fourth Gospel, quite apart from those passages in which Christ assumes the title 'Son of God,' the sense of this unique relation to God as bearing upon His saving relationship to men meets us everywhere, but especially in the farewell discourse and the intercessory prayer which followed (Jn 14–17). But in the Synoptics also this Divine consciousness appears repeatedly (e.g. Lk 2⁴⁹, Mt 7²¹ 10³² 16¹⁷ 22²ᶠ·, Mk 12⁶), and it finds full expression in that great saying, 'All things have been delivered unto me of my Father; and no one knoweth the Son save the Father; neither doth any know the Father save the Son, and he to whomsoever the Son willeth to reveal him' (Mt 11²⁷, Lk 10²²), which serves in St. Matthew's account as the ground of the Saviour's universal invitation and of His promise of rest for the soul (v.²⁸ᶠᶠ·). See PREACHING CHRIST, 5 (c).

5. In connexion with His eschatological teaching, and forming its central and most essential feature, is the claim made by Christ to be the *final and universal Judge* of men. Not only did He declare the fact of His own Return, an astonishing declaration in itself, but He affirmed as the purpose of His Second Coming the Judgment of the world. This claim to be the arbiter of human destinies is distinctly announced again and again (Mt 7²²· ²³ 16²⁷, Mk 8³⁸). It is further implied in the parables of the Wise and Foolish Virgins (Mt 25¹⁻¹³) and the Talents (vv.¹⁴⁻³⁰), and is set forth in detail in that solemn picture of the Last Judgment by which these parables are immediately followed (vv.³¹⁻⁴⁶). The testimony of the Synoptics with regard to this claim of our Lord is supported by the testimony of the Fourth Gospel to the same effect (Jn 5²⁷ᶠᶠ·, cf. v.²²), and is confirmed by the fact that throughout the rest of the NT the office of the final Judge is constantly assigned to Jesus (Ac 10⁴² 17³¹, Ro 2¹⁶ 14¹⁰, 2 Co 5¹⁰, 2 Ti 4¹· ⁸, 1 P 4⁵, Ja 5⁸· ⁹), an office, be it noted, which was never ascribed to the Messiah either in the OT revelation or in the popular Jewish belief (see Salmond, *Christian Doct. of Immortality*, p. 318). This is in some respects the most stupendous of Christ's claims. It was a great thing for Jesus of Nazareth to assume the titles and functions of the Hope of Israel, to declare Himself to be the Fulfiller of the Law and the Expected of the Prophets. But it was something greater still to claim that with His Return there would arrive the grand consummation of the world's history (Mt 25³¹), that before Him all nations should be gathered (v.³²) and all hearts laid bare (vv.³⁵· ³⁶· ⁴²· ⁴³), that the principle of the Judgment should be the attitude of men to Himself as He is spiritually present in the world (vv.⁴⁰· ⁴⁵), and that of this attitude Christ Himself should be the Supreme Judge (vv.³²· ³³). See art. JUDGMENT.

6. That the doctrine of Christ's *pre-existence* is specifically taught in the Prologue to the Fourth Gospel, is apparent to every reader (Jn 1¹ᶠᶠ· ¹⁰· ¹⁴· ¹⁸). But it is not less plain that, according to the author, this doctrine was not simply a solution forced upon the Christian mind by a consideration of Christ's other claims and of His whole history, but was the unfolding of an affirmation made by Christ's own lips (6² 8⁵⁸ 17⁵· ²⁴). In spite of all that has been said by writers like Beyschlag (*op. cit.* i. 254) and Wendt (*Teaching of Jesus*, ii. 169), the theory of an ideal pre-existence is quite inadequate as an explanation of such language. Only by maintaining that John's picture of Jesus and presentation of His words is no record of historical fact, but a theologically determined construction of his own, can we escape from the conclusion that, as Jesus claimed to be in an absolutely unique sense the Son of the Father, so also He claimed to be the personal object of the Father's love and the sharer of His glory before the world was. See art. PRE-EXISTENCE.

LITERATURE.—Hastings' *DB*, artt. 'Son of Man,' 'Son of God'; Denney, *Studies in Theology*, ch. ii.; Forrest, *Christ of History and of Experience*, Lect. ii.; Beyschlag, *NT Theol.* i. 56–79,

236–266; Wendt, *Teaching of Jesus*, ii. 122–183; Weiss, *Bib. Theol. of NT*, i. 73–92; Stalker, *Christology of Jesus*; Ullmann, *Sinlessness of Jesus*, 69–81; Salmond, *Christian Doct. of Immortality*, 313–325; Robbins, *A Christian Apologetic* (1902), 59–87; Forrest, *Authority of Christ* (1906).

J. C. LAMBERT.

CLEANNESS.—See LAW, PURIFICATION.

CLEANSING.—See TEMPLE.

CLEOPAS (Κλεόπας, Lk 24¹⁸).—One of the two disciples to whom the Lord appeared on the afternoon of the Resurrection day as they went to Emmaus, distant about two hours from Jerusalem (see EMMAUS). The omission of all reference to the story in 1 Co 15 is not a sufficient ground for questioning its truth. We have no guarantee that St. Paul's knowledge extended to all the actual events of the Passion and Resurrection period (cf. Chase, *Credibility of the Acts*, p. 184). The story may have been received by the Evangelist from Cleopas himself: it bears marks of its early origin in the primitive Messianic ideas it preserves, and in the use of the name Simon for St. Peter. By some (Theophylact, Lange, Carr) the unnamed companion of Cleopas is identified with St. Luke himself; but this is unlikely, as both appear to have been Jews (οἱ ἄρχοντες ἡμῶν, v.²⁰), though they do not speak in a tone of such personal nearness to Jesus that we can accept the conjecture that they were of the Eleven. The two were in high dispute about late events, Cleopas apparently taking the more optimistic view, as, in spite of all, he clings to the few facts which make for belief. The inability of both to recognize Jesus is explained in St. Luke to be due to spiritual dulness (οἱ ὀφθαλμοὶ αὐτῶν ἐκρατοῦντο, v.¹⁶). The pseudo-Mark (whose allusion does not depend on St. Luke, for he gives a different sequel in Jerusalem) says that the Lord appeared 'in another form' (ἐν ἑτέρᾳ μορφῇ, Mk 16¹²); an interpretation favoured by Augustine, who compares the effect of the Transfiguration (μετεμορφώθη, Mk 9²). Whatever the cause, the Lord treated them with tenderness (v.²⁵ ἀνόητοι, 'O foolish men,' RV, not 'fools,' as AV; cf. Ramsay on Gal 3¹).

The discourse in which they were enlightened furnishes from Christ's own lips what in fact became the kernel of the preaching of the Apostles, as seen in the sermons recorded in the Acts (e.g. Ac 2²²⁻³⁶ 17³) and in the Gospels. The two disciples had already given the summary of the earthly life of Jesus (Lk 24¹⁹⁻²⁴). He now shows that it was required by OT prophecy that all this should be the means by which He was to enter into His glory (24²⁷ should be read in the light of vv.⁴⁴⁻⁴⁷). It is this teaching that invests the narrative with its peculiar value for the Church, and was doubtless a prime cause of its preservation.

Many of the speculations about the phrase, 'He made as though He would go further' (Lk 24²⁸), would have been avoided if the real spiritual meaning of the incident had been discerned. Knowledge of the Lord's presence is vouchsafed only in answer to prayer, it is not forced on anyone. This is the NT Penuel (cf. Gn 32²⁶ with Lk 24³⁰). It is a too rigid interpretation which regards the breaking of the bread here as a celebration of the Eucharist; rather it was an ordinary meal at which the Stranger, who had so impressed them on the road, was put in the place of honour. Something in His manner suddenly confirmed the suspicion of His identity which was forming itself in their minds. The result which the Lord desired, the corroboration of their faith, having been reached, He vanished from sight. To carry the tidings to Jerusalem, 'they who had dissuaded their unknown Companion from making a night journey now have no fear of it themselves' (Bengel).

LITERATURE.—Aug. *Ep.* 149; Stier, *Words of the Lord Jesus*, Eng. tr., vol. viii.; Trench, *Studies in the Gospels*, p. 324 ff.; Latham, *The Risen Master*; Swete on Mk 16[12]; A. Carr in *Expositor*, Feb. 1904; Deissmann, *Bible Studies*, p. 315; Ker, *Sermons*, 2nd ser. p. 264 ff.; *Expos. Times*, xvii. [1906] 333 ff.

C. T. DIMONT.

CLEOPHAS.—This form appears in some Latin MSS, and is retained in the Vulgate (though against the evidence of Codex Amiatinus) in both Lk 24[18] and Jn 19[25]. It was adopted by the early English versions (Wyclifite, Tindale), and passed into the AV of 1611. It still stands there in Jn 19[25] for Clopas (wh. see), but in Lk 24[18] it was replaced in 1629 by Cleopas (wh. see).

C. T. DIMONT.

CLOKE (the spelling in both AV and RV of the modern 'cloak').—There was originally a marked distinction between Classical and Oriental costume, a distinction which was lessened under the cosmopolitanism of the Roman Empire; thus the Greek words used in the NT bear different meanings. The two normal Classical garments, the χιτών and ἱμάτιον of Mt 5[40] and Lk 6[29], translated 'coat' and 'cloke,' were usually of extreme simplicity.

The χιτών, *tunica*, tunic, or shirt (see art. COAT), was the under-garment worn indoors by men and women alike, an oblong strip of material doubled round the body and fastened at the shoulders, without any shaping or sewing, sometimes girt and sometimes ungirt. The *sādin* of the Jews differed from this in being longer and furnished with sleeves; over it was worn the *kĕthôneth*, a long sleeved tunic, open in front, but folded across and girt; this latter formed a second *tunica*, which is the χιτών, apparently, of Mt 5[40] and Lk 6[29]. Oriental influences led to the adoption of the long tunic in Rome under the name of *tunica talaris*, a garment which, in Cicero's time, was regarded as a mark of effeminacy; in later years it was known in its white form as the *tunica alba* or alb. The ἱμάτιον, over-garment or 'cloke,' was, with the Greeks and Romans, originally an oblong strip, thrown over the tunic (χιτών) when the wearer went out of doors; in its simplest form it was the *pallium*; more elaborately folded, it was the *toga*. Thus the χιτών and the ἱμάτιον are the under- and the over-garment, though what we call underclothing was often worn also. But the use of sleeves among the Orientals made a still greater distinction in their over-garment; the *mĕ·'îl* and *simlāh* of the Jews were sleeved garments rather like a modern overcoat, open in front, and reaching to the feet. The 'long robe' of the scribes and Pharisees (Lk 20[46]) was the *mĕ·'îl*, rendered by St. Luke as στολή, which merely means a long sleeved garment, a *tunica talaris*, in fact; for which reason the 'great multitude' of the Apocalypse (7[9.13]) are also described as wearing στολὰς λευκάς, that is, long white tunics, or *tunicæ albæ*, though in Rev 3[5] the more general word is used—ἐν ἱματίοις λευκοῖς, 'in white garments' (RV).

The classical over-garment appeared in many varieties besides the changing fashions of the *toga*. The *pallium*, Greek in its origin, had become international in its character at the time of the Roman Empire, and was regarded as the mark of a philosopher or teacher; so Justin Martyr preached in the 'philosopher's robe,' and was thus recognized by Trypho as a teacher (*Tryph.* 1). It was for this reason that the *pallium* was chosen by the artists of the Catacombs as the distinguishing dress of Christ, the Apostles, and the Prophets, and has continued so by an artistic convention that has lasted from the 2nd cent. to the present day. The chlamys, χλαμύς, *sagum* or *paludamentum*, was made of a smaller oblong strip, fastened by a buckle on the right shoulder (as in the Apollo Belvidere); it was a light military cloak, and was the 'scarlet robe,' χλαμύδα κοκκίνην, which the soldiers put upon our Lord in mockery (Mt 27[28]). The seamless 'coat,' for which the soldiers cast lots at the Crucifixion, is distinguished by St. John (19[23]) by the word used for a tunic or under-garment, χιτών, and not by any of the terms used for the various forms of outer garment, such as we should expect if the 'coat' were the Jewish *simlāh*.

Another common form of outer garment is the φαιλόνης, the 'cloke' which St. Paul left at Troas (2 Ti 4[13]). This was the *pœnula* (φαινόλης, φενόλης,

φαινόλιον), a heavy woollen garment, generally red or dark-yellow in colour, worn as a protection against cold and rain, at first especially by travellers and by artisans and slaves; hence on the one hand its use by St. Paul, and on the other its frequent occurrence in the Catacombs of Rome (where the *tunica*, the *tunica talaris*, dalmatic, chlamys, *pallium*, and the *lacerna*, a cope-shaped garment, are also found, while the toga occurs only once). The *pœnula* was the original of the Eucharistic chasuble, and resembles it exactly in shape (a circle or ellipse, with a hole in the centre), though not in material. As time went on, it was used by all classes, and after the Peace of the Church it became in course of time restricted to bishops and presbyters. It is worn by the ecclesiastics in the famous 6th cent. frescoes at Ravenna, where appear also the *tunica talaris*, still adorned with the orphrey-like strips of the *clavus*, the dalmatic, *lacerna*, and the *pallium*, which, by the process of *contabulatio* or folding, has come to resemble a long stole, and is distinctive of bishops. Thus, while the toga, chlamys, and the original *tunica* disappeared, and are to us typical of classical antiquity, the *pœnula*, *pallium*, *lacerna*, dalmatic, and *tunica talaris* were handed on as ecclesiastical vestments (chasuble, pall, cope, dalmatic, and alb), the last named forming a link not only with imperial Rome, but also with the East. See, further, art. DRESS.

LITERATURE.—A. Conze, *Die antike Gewändung*; Keil, Benzinger, and Nowack, *Heb. Arch.*; Hastings' *DB*, art. 'Dress'; Schurer, *HJP*, Index, *s.v.* 'Clothing'; Wilpert, *Die Gewändung der Christen in den ersten Jahrhunderten*, and *Un capitolo di storia del vestiaro*; Braun, *Die priesterlichen Gewänder des Abendlandes*, and *Die pontificalen Gewänder des Abendlandes*; Duchesne, *Origines du culte chrétien*.

PERCY DEARMER.

CLOPAS (Κλωπᾶς).—Mentioned in Jn 19[25] as a relative, probably the husband, of one of the women who stood by the cross (Μαρία ἡ τοῦ Κλωπᾶ). By Chrysostom he was identified with Alphæus; but this is improbable (see ALPHÆUS). For his connexion with Joseph and the family of Jesus, see art. BRETHREN OF THE LORD and Hastings' *DB*, vol. i. p. 322. According to certain apocryphal Acts of the Apostles, he is the same as the Cleopas of Lk 24[18]. In that case the devotion which kept Mary of Clopas near the cross till the end finds a counterpart in her husband's sorrow at the Crucifixion. But the identification rests on the derivation of both names from a common Greek original, Cleopatros, and is denied by those who regard Clopas as a Semitic name (see Deissmann, *Bible Studies*, Eng. tr. p. 315, n. 2).

C. T. DIMONT.

CLOSET (ταμεῖον).—Mt 6[6], Lk 12[3] AV.

The older form of the Gr. word was ταμιεῖον (found in some NT MSS), but the later language frequently shows the coalescence of two following ι sounds.* The etymology (cf. ταμίας, 'distributor,' 'treasurer,' 'steward,' etc., akin to τέμνω) shows that 'store-chamber' is the primitive meaning of the Gr. word (*i.e. not* small sitting-room or bedroom). In this sense it occurs in Lk 12[24], and even the RV, following Vulg. and Luther, have been *compelled* to break their rule of uniformity of rendering in this case. The four occurrences of the Gr. word are dealt with as follows in the versions :—

	AV	RV	Vulgate	Luther
Mt 6[6]	closet	inner chamber	cubiculum	Kämmerlein
Mt 24[26]	secret chambers	inner chambers	penetralibus	Kammer
Lk 12[3]	closets	inner chambers	cubiculis	Kammern
Lk 12[24]	storehouse	store-chamber	cellarium	Keller

The Peshiṭta has ܠܘܼܬܐ (*ta-wânâ*) in all four passages, and it seems a pity that 'store-closet' or 'store-chamber' was not used by RV in the same way throughout.

* Cf. J. H. Moulton in *Expositor*, 6th ser. ix. [1904] 361: 'ταμιεῖον, πίιν and ὑγιεα are overwhelmingly attested by the papyri, where there are only *rare* examples of a curious reversion, like that in Mt 20[22]' (where WH read πίειν, elsewhere πίιν,

Every Jewish house, except the very smallest huts, would have a small room opening out from the 'living-room,' as our workmen's cottages have small pantries, larders, etc., in many cases; but few houses would have a small room specially for private prayer. Yet, curiously, many writers have assumed that Jewish houses did have 'prayer closets'; usually, they say, in the upper part of the house,* and many identify it with the ὑπερῷον (עֲלִיָּה *ăliyyāh*). Is there any ground for this? The 'upper rooms' mentioned in NT were usable as guest-chambers (Mk 14[15], etc.), large enough to accommodate thirteen persons reclining round tables, and (perhaps) even 120 persons (Ac 1[15]). Would the individual worshipper be able to enter such an important room in a house, and 'shut the door' (Mt 6[6]) against the rest of his family? Others (*e.g.*, Keil, *Biblical Archæology*, § 95) think of the frail summer-house *on* the flat roof.

According to modern European ideas, the Vulgate *cubiculum*, 'bedroom,' would suit the context and circumstances well in Mt 6[6], perhaps in Mt 24[26] and Lk 12[3], but not at all in Lk 12[24]. Moreover, (*a*) this rendering loses the connexion with the etymology; (*b*) the use of separate bedrooms is not common in the East; (*c*) there are other Gr. and Syr. words to express the idea.

It must be noticed that Mt 6[6] is founded on Is 26[20], εἴσελθε εἰς τὰ ταμεῖά σου, ἀπόκλεισον τὴν θύραν σου. But the motive in Isaiah is fear, in Matthew desire of loving communion. ταμεῖον occurs 40 times in LXX. In most cases it retains the meaning 'store-closet' (Dt 28[8], Sir 29[12], etc.). In other cases it is a private chamber of some sort as in Mt 6[6]: *e.g.*, Gn 43[30], Dt 32[25], Jg 3[24]. The last case is noticeable. ταμεῖον is defined by τῷ θερινῷ, and represents חֶדֶר (*ḥeder*), while ὑπερῷον in the context is *ăliyyāh*, rather implying a distinction. The summer 'upper room' (EV 'parlour') had a summer 'closet' (EV 'chamber') attached to it. In the one Eglon was with his attendants till Ehud came, but they afterwards supposed that Eglon had retired into the other, and would not disturb him.

We now get a group of passages which explain ταμεῖον. In Ex 8[3] (7[28]), Jg 15[1], 2 (4) K 6[12] 11[2], 2 Ch 22[11], etc., it is the special 'store-closet' (leading or opening out from the larger room) in which the bedding required by night was stored during the day (τὰ ταμεῖα τῶν κοιτῶν or ταμεῖον κλινῶν).† In such a 'closet' the Philistines were hiding while Delilah practised her wiles on Samson (Jg 16[9. 12], LXX, also Ec 10[20]). In such a 'closet' for holding the bedding, the baby prince Joash was concealed when Athaliah murdered the rest of the royal family. Samson was possibly in the 'living-room' when his wife's father prevented him from entering the ταμεῖον (Jg 15[1] LXX, note the variant of A εἰς τὸν κοιτῶνα). Such small rooms or closets could be used as more private sleeping-rooms if required, and would also be available for private conference, concealment, or any similar purpose, as well as for the normal use of storing the bedding and other things which were not immediately required. Our Lord advised their use for private prayer. Thus storage was the *primary* purpose of the apartment. The other uses were secondary ones, or adaptations.

The AV 'closet' is therefore quite as correct as the RV 'inner chamber.' Of course we do not think of an European cupboard with shelves, in

which a person could hardly stand. But Dryden (*Fables*) possibly uses 'closet' in the sense of a 'store-closet,' as ταμεῖον in Lk 12[24], though he *may* have meant 'private chamber':

' He furnishes her *closet* first, and fills
The crowded shelves with rarities of shells.'

Shakespeare has the other use:

'The taper burneth in your closet' (*Jul. Cæs.* ii. 1).*

On the curious Latin renderings of *d* (*promptalibus*) *e* (*promptuariis*) in Lk 12[3], and *d* (*promptuarium*) in Lk 12[24], cf. Rönsch, *Itala und Vulgata*, pp. 32 and 48, and Plummer, 'St. Luke,' in *International Critical Commentary*.   GEORGE FARMER.

CLOTHES.—See DRESS.

CLOUD.—The cloud appears in the Gospels at our Lord's Transfiguration (Mt 17[5] ∥ Mk 9[7], Lk 9[34]) and (if we may treat the first verses of the Book of Acts as practically part of St. Luke's Gospel) at His Ascension (Ac 1[9]). Twice also it has a place in His own prediction of His coming again (Mt 24[30] ∥ Mk 13[26] ∥ Lk 21[27], Mt 26[64] ∥ Mk 14[62]).

The most interesting occurrence of this cloud is that in connexion with the Ascension; but it is its appearance above the Mount of Transfiguration that rules the interpretation of its significance. For there a voice comes out of it which is that of the Heavenly Father: it is seen to be the veil of the Divine Presence. Veiling the glory which no mortal might see and live, veiling yet revealing the Presence of God, the cloud has two aspects, of which the greater and more characteristic is not the negative one of veiling, but that positive aspect in which it attests and manifests the Divine Presence. To come under its shadow (a 'shadow,' it would seem, of light, since it was νεφέλη φωτεινή) awoke in the disciples the dread felt by Jacob at Bethel. And for the same reason—that this cloud is a 'gate of heaven,' at which a man may stand to hear the voice of God. Here, in this bright cloud, the two spheres, earthly and heavenly, open upon each other. The cloud is less a veil than a lifting of the veil. Here the invisible barrier becomes a portal of heaven, through which may come the voice of the Almighty, and entering by which Christ is passed into heaven. It is a 'cloud of heaven': with earth and human life upon this side of it, and on the other side (not sky and stars, but) the invisible things of God, the heavenly sphere, the other world.

Thus in our Lord's Ascension we do not conceive of Him as 'going up' farther than would symbolize and declare His departure from this world: 'He was taken up, and a cloud received Him out of their sight'—they saw Him go and they saw what door opened to receive Him. As identifying this cloud with 'heaven,' compare Ac 1[9], 'a cloud received him,' with 1[11] 'received up from you into heaven': with which agrees 2 P 1[17. 18], 'there came a voice to him out of the excellent glory . . . and this voice we (ourselves) heard brought out of heaven.' The voice out of the cloud was 'out of heaven'—the disciples in beholding Christ enter the cloud 'beheld him going into heaven.'

If for us the cloud is as a door which closes, a veil that hides (as God verily is a God that hideth Himself), this is of grace: 'thou canst not follow

κατακῦν; cf. Liddell and Scott *sub voce*, WH, *Notes on Orthography*, ii. 146–170. The *Textus Receptus*, according to Scrivener, has the older form in Mt 6[6], but the later one in the three other places.
* Carr, *Cambridge Bible for Schools*; Tholuck, *Sermon on the Mount*; Lange, *St. Matthew*; after Kuinoel, and Vitringa, *de Syn.* i. i. 6.
† Lane, *Modern Egyptians*, ch. v.; Purdoe, *City of the Sultan*, i. 22; Kitto, *Pictorial Bible* on Pr 6[16] and 2 K 11[2]; Hastings' *DB* ii. 434[a].

* A late member of the Abp. of Canterbury's 'Assyrian Mission' informs the writer of this article that the Peshiṭta word in the form *ta-wănă* 'is still retained in certain parts of the mountain districts, where many old (classical) Syriac words are still in use, but it is not used colloquially in the plains. *Ta-wănă* is always the little room leading from the large living room; it is that in which the *spare* bedding is stored. Its primary meaning is therefore "store-room." Bp. Maclean (*Dictionary of Vernacular Syriac*) gives the meanings "closet," "store-room," but if he had reversed these two words, *i.e.* putting "store-room" first, I think it would have been better.'

me now' (Jn 13³⁶)—'ye cannot bear it now' (16¹²). And the cloud is, for Christ's disciples, itself an excellent glory, since He is now passed within it (not behind as our earthly sun), filling it with brightness of light. He, our Redeemer and Advocate, the Lord who is our Brother, is now within the cloud that covers Sinai, that leads through the wilderness, that shines above the Mercy-seat; that is to say—in all that by which God draws near to man (in His law as in Sinai, in His providences as in the shepherding of Israel, in religious life and worship as in the Holiest of all), Christ is present, and the love which He has made known, bestowed and sealed. To His disciples the Law is no more a threat and fear, but is written upon the heart for honour and obedience; and God's providence is trusted—the sheep follow, for they know His voice; and for the deep things of the soul there is a great High priest passed into the heavens, and they that know His name come boldly to the throne of grace.

LITERATURE.—The Comm. in loc., esp. Swete on Mk 9⁷; Ruskin, Frondes Agrestes, p. 178; Huntingdon, Christian Believing and Living, p. 168; Westcott, Revelat. of the Risen Lord, p. 180; Milligan, Ascension and Heavenly Priesthood of our Lord, p. 21 ff.; Paget, Studies in the Christian Character, p. 246 ff.   ARTHUR W. WOTHERSPOON.

COAL.—This word occurs in the Gospels only in Jn 18¹⁸ and 21⁹ (Gr. in both ἀνθρακιά, meaning properly 'a brazier filled with lighted charcoal'). As a mineral, coal does not exist in Palestine except in the Wâdy Hummanâ in the Lebanon, and was mined there only during the rule of Muhammad Ali about 1834 (Thomson, The Land and the Book, 1886, iii. 193). The rendering 'coal' must be taken as='charcoal.' Both in ancient and in modern times, the latter substance, prepared from native timber, has been the common fuel of the East. The destruction of the forests of Palestine and Syria may be assigned as the main reason for the absence of timbered gables, and the universal prevalence, instead, of brickwork cupola roofs, and also for the wretched substitutes for fuel now employed by the natives, such as sun-dried cakes of chaff and dung, etc. The charred roots of the desert broom (rôthem, see Ps 120⁴) make an excellent fuel, and are much in demand in Cairo (Tristram, Nat. Hist. of Bible, 1889, p. 360).

The geological survey of Palestine reveals its uniformly cretaceous formation, extending from the Lebanon ranges to the plateau of Hebron. The earlier rocks of the carboniferous period, if they do exist there at all under the subsequent strata, are buried at quite inaccessible depths. Traces of carboniferous outcrop, but destitute of carbonaceous deposits, have been found in the sandstone of the southern desert and the limestone of the Wâdy Nasb.

LITERATURE.—W. M. Thomson, The Land and the Book, 1886, iii. 193; Tristram, Nat. Hist. of Bible, 1889, p. 360; Conder, Tent Work in Pal. ii. 326; Hull, Mount Seir, etc., 1889, p. 194; Gesenius, Thesaurus, p. 280; Hastings' DB, article 'Coal.'
                        P. HENDERSON AITKEN.

COAT.—This word in the Gospels usually represents the Gr. χιτών, i.e. the tunic or long close-fitting under garment worn in Palestine, as opposed to the ἱμάτιον or full and flowing outer garment (see Hastings' DB, art. 'Dress').

Our Lord's instructions to the Twelve included one which forbade their wearing or having in their possession more than one such garment (Mt 10¹⁰, Mk 6⁹, Lk 9³; cf. Lk 3¹¹). And in the Sermon on the Mount (Mt 5⁴⁰; cf. Lk 6²⁹) we are bidden to cultivate such a spirit of meekness as would be illustrated by a readiness to part even with one's cloak (ἱμάτιον) to him who took away one's coat.*

* In Luke the order is transposed, the cloak coming before the coat, this being the order in which these two garments would be torn off.

The soldiers at the Crucifixion (Jn 19²³· ²⁴) took possession of the Saviour's garments, according, we suppose, to the usual practice. The outer robes they divided into four parts, one for each of the quaternion, but for the coat (τὸν χιτῶνα), in close fulfilment of Ps 22¹⁸, they cast lots, not wishing to tear it up, because it was 'without seam, woven from the top throughout.' Josephus (Ant. III. vii. 4), quoted by Bp. Westcott, tells us that the long robe (χιτὼν ποδήρης) of the high priest was of this character: 'This vesture was not composed of two pieces, nor was it sewed together upon the shoulders and the sides, but it was one long vestment, so woven as to have an aperture for the neck' (Whiston's tr.). Bp. Westcott further quotes Chrysostom, who perhaps wrote from personal knowledge, as thinking 'that the detail is added to show "the poorness of the Lord's garments, and that in dress as in all other things He followed a simple fashion."' Others incline to the view that there is a parallel suggested between the Eternal High Priest's garment and that of the Aaronic high priest. In any case the seamless robe of Christ has often been taken as a type of the One (ideally) Undivided Church, e.g. by Cyprian in a famous passage (de Unit. Eccl. § 7), where he contrasts the 'incorrupta atque individua tunica' of Christ with the prophet Ahijah's robe, which he tore in duodecim scissuras in token of the disruption of the kingdom (1 K 11³⁰ff·), and concludes: 'sacramento vestis et signo declaravit ecclesiæ unitatem.' For the part which the Holy Coat has played in legend at Trèves and elsewhere, those who are curious in such matters may consult Gildenmeister and v. Sybel, Der Heilige Rock zu Trier und die 20 anderen heiligen ungenähten Röcke³, 1845.

We may note finally: (1) that the word 'coat' (so RV; AV 'fisher's coat') in Jn 21⁷ stands for the large loose garment (ἐπενδύτης) which St. Peter threw as a covering over his almost naked body when he left his fishing and came into the Master's presence; (2) that it was the under-garments (χιτῶνες) that the high priest rent when he 'heard the blasphemy' at our Lord's trial (Mk 14⁶³; see Swete's notes, in loc.). See also CLOKE, DRESS.
                        C. L. FELTOE.

COCK.—See ANIMALS, p. 64ᵃ, and following article.

COCK-CROWING (ἀλεκτοροφωνία). — The word occurs only in Mk 13³⁵, where it is evidently used to designate the third of four parts into which the night was divided—'at even, or at midnight, or at the cock-crowing, or in the morning.' In OT times there were only three watches in the night—the first, the middle, and the last; but by the time of Christ the Roman division into four watches had become common, though it had not altogether superseded the threefold division of the Jews. The night was reckoned, roughly speaking, from our 6 P.M. to 6 A.M., and these twelve hours were divided into four watches of three hours each. Jerome says: 'Nox in quatuor vigilias dividitur, quæ singulæ trium horarum spatio supputantur' (Ep. cxl. 8). The cock-crowing in Mk 13³⁵ thus refers to the third watch of the night, between the hours of 12 and 3.

Although the noun 'cock-crowing' occurs only once in the NT, each of the four Evangelists records the fact that on the night of the betrayal Jesus forewarned Peter that before the cock crew he should thrice deny his Lord, and each of them also records a crowing of the cock immediately after the denial (Mt 26³⁴ and ⁷⁴· ⁷⁵, Lk 22³⁴ and ⁶⁰· ⁶¹, Jn 13³⁸ 18²⁷). In St. Mark we have the variations —all the more significant because of the writer's commonly acknowledged dependence upon the Petrine tradition—that Jesus said to Peter, 'Before the cock crow *twice*, thou shalt deny me thrice'; and in correspondence with this a record of two distinct cock-crowings (Mk 14³⁰· ⁶⁸· ⁷²).

Attempts have been made to distinguish between these two cock-crowings in St. Mark as occurring at definite seasons of the night, the one about midnight and the other at the first approach of dawn, just before the commencement of the fourth or morning watch, and to define the second of the two as the *gallicinium* proper, and consequently the only one of which the other three Evangelists take notice. No doubt it is true that in the most distinctive sense of the word 'the cock-crowing,' as an indication of time, refers to the breaking of the dawn; thus in the Talmud it is prescribed that at cock-crow the benediction shall be used: 'Praised be Thou, O God, the Lord of the world, that givest understanding to the cock to distinguish between day and night.' But as a matter of fact cocks crow during the night, in the East as elsewhere, at irregular times from midnight onward; and the narrative of Mk 14⁶⁶⁻⁷² does not suggest that there was an interval of anything like three hours between the first cock-crowing and the second. The probability is that Jesus meant no more than this, that before Peter himself had twice heard the cock crow he should thrice have been guilty of his great denial. And if we accept St. Mark's narrative as embodying Peter's own account of the incident, it will seem natural that the disciple to whom the warning was directly addressed, and on whom it would make the deepest impression, should distinguish between two separate cock-crowings where others thought only of the last.

There is no mention of the cock in the Mosaic law, and the supposed allusion to the breed in 1 K 4²³ (בַּרְבֻּרִים, translated 'fatted fowls' both in AV and RV) is very doubtful. It may be that Solomon had imported these birds from the East; but, on the other hand, the fact that in the Talmudical literature the cock is always called by the name *tarnĕgôl* (תַּרְנְגוֹל), suggests rather that it was introduced into Palestine from Babylonia.* But while the domestic fowl was quite familiar to the Jews of our Lord's time, both the Mishna and the Midrash state that, so long as the Temple stood, the breeding or keeping of cocks in Jerusalem was forbidden, on the ground that by scratching in the earth they dug up unclean things, thus spreading the contagion of Levitical uncleanness, and even contaminating the sacrifices of the altar. On this ground exception has sometimes been taken, especially from Jewish sources, to the statements of the Evangelists as to the crowing of the cock in Jerusalem on the night before the crucifixion. But if such an ordinance existed, it is very unlikely that it could be strictly enforced in a city like Jerusalem, with a large and mixed population. In particular, we must remember that cock-fighting was one of the favourite sports of the Romans; and the Roman soldiers of the garrison would concern themselves very little about any Jewish prohibition of this kind.

LITERATURE. — Grimm-Thayer, *Lexicon, s.v.* ἀλεκτοροφωνία; Smith's *Lat.-Eng. Dict. s.v.* 'Vigilia'; Meyer's Commentary on *Matthew*; Lange's *Life of Christ*; Andrews, *Life of our Lord upon the Earth*, p. 521; *Encyc. Bibl.* and *Jewish Encyclopedia*, articles 'Cock' and 'Day'; Hastings' *DB*, articles 'Cock' and 'Time,' cf. Extra Vol. p. 477 f.

J. C. LAMBERT.

COINS.—See MONEY.

COLT.—See ANIMALS, p. 63ᵃ, and ENTRY INTO JERUSALEM.

* A reference to the cock is found by some scholars in Pr 30³¹ (EV 'greyhound'), where the זַרְזִיר (*zarzir*) of MT is rendered by the LXX ἀλέκτωρ; similarly Aquila and Theodotion, the Peshiṭta ('ăbhakhă) and the Vulgate (*gallus*).

COMFORT.—The English word 'comfort' means being made strong together. The idea seems to be that sorrow weakens or shatters the whole system of the afflicted man, and that the dispelling of his grief braces him up anew. The sore is not merely plastered over or covered with a surface skin, but healed, so that the sufferer becomes as vigorous as before. Such is, indeed, the comfort imparted by Christ. In connexion therewith the words παρακαλέω and θαρσέω, or θαρρέω, are both employed. In NT 'beseech,' 'entreat,' 'exhort' are all used as equivalents for παρακαλέω, while παράκλησις is most frequently rendered 'consolation' in AV, and θαρσέω or θαρρέω (the former in imperat. only) is commonly translated 'to be of good cheer.' But both παρακαλέω and παράκλησις are occasionally rendered 'comfort' in AV (*e.g.* Mt 5⁴, 2 Cor 1³), while in RV 'comfort' has usually been substituted for 'consolation' of AV in the rendering of the noun. In three places (Mt 9²², Mk 10⁴⁹, Lk 8⁴⁸) AV renders θάρσει 'Be of good comfort.' In the first two RV substitutes 'Be of good cheer,' and in the last drops θάρσει from the text. In Jn, παράκλητος, which occurs four times (14¹⁶· ²⁶ 15²⁶ 16⁷), always appears in EV as 'the Comforter.'

While the mission of Christ was mainly to save men from their sins, it was also His purpose to bring them true relief from their troubles. In His sermon at Nazareth (Lk 4¹⁶⁻²⁷) He applied to Himself the prophecy of Isaiah (61¹⁻³), which tells that the Messiah was 'to comfort all that mourn.' He would indeed have failed to fulfil the Messianic expectation if He had not set Himself, alike by His person, His gospel, and His work, to heal the broken in heart and to comfort the people of God's choice (cf. Is 40¹). Among pious Jews the phrase had become a holy oath, *Ita videam consolationem*, etc. (Alford on Lk 2²⁵). Thus Simeon is said to have been 'looking for the consolation of Israel' (*loc. cit.*), where παράκλησιν has almost a personal import as though equivalent to τὸν Χριστὸν Κυρίου. The whole gospel of Jesus Christ is therefore one of good tidings to the afflicted, the destitute, the oppressed. The removal of the cause of woe involves the furtherance of the cure of woe. In answer to the Baptist's question, Jesus named, as one of the signs that He was ὁ Ἐρχόμενος, 'the poor have good tidings preached to them' (εὐαγγελίζονται). Accordingly, in the very forefront of His programme as announced in the Sermon on the Mount, Christ gave the beatitude of comfort to the mourners (Mt 5⁴). As the Revealer of the Father, moreover, He was bound to make comfort one of the most prominent features of His ministry, not less in action than in word. The Fatherly pity (Ps 103¹³) and the Motherly tenderness (Is 66¹³) of the All-merciful must be set forth by the Son of God, if, looking on Him and listening to Him, men were to be able to see the image and to hearken to the voice of God.

Christ is well fitted to afford comfort not only by His Divine knowledge of our deepest needs and of what best meets these needs, but by His own human experience of affliction and woe. The Man of Sorrows, the One acquainted with grief, as well as the God of all comfort, He can appreciate the necessity of consolation as well as apply the consolation that is availing. Having suffered in temptation, He is able to succour them that are tempted (He 2¹⁸). The pangs of Him who 'himself bare our sicknesses' fitted Him for being the true Physician for the wounded in heart. Through His own weariness He has won multitudes of the heavy-laden to come to Him for rest.* The exceeding sorrow even unto death of His own soul as He took the cup from His

* In *Expos. Times*, viii. 239 and x. 48, Nestle shows that rest and comfort are 'almost identical for Semitic feeling.'

Father's hand that He might taste death for every man, has made Him able to give ease and peace to His people in the valley of the shadow. One of the occasions when comfort is most needed is bereavement : and perhaps the tears of Jesus at the tomb of Lazarus (Jn 11³⁵) have been as potent to solace the stricken as His word to the widow of Nain, 'Weep not' (Lk 7¹³). When upon the cross He commended to one another's care and sympathy the Virgin Mother and the beloved disciple: 'Woman, behold thy son!' 'Behold thy mother!' (Jn 19²⁶. ²⁷), we see how truly Christ entered into the heart of the afflicted children of men.

Christ's dealing with His own chosen followers was one of special tenderness in their hour of sorrow. He knew that while on the whole His departure was expedient for them, yet it would be a terrible wrench, and expose them to bitter persecution. He therefore consoled them when sorrow filled their heart by telling them that He would not leave them orphans (ὀρφανούς, AV 'comfortless,' RV 'desolate'). After His ascension He would be nearer to them in spiritual presence than when with them in the flesh (Jn 14¹⁸⁻²⁰, cf. Mt 28²⁰). By rising from the dead He would be Victor over the world in its direst and fiercest assault, and if they shared with Him the world's hate they would also share His triumph. The discourse (Jn 14–16) which began, 'Let not your heart be troubled : ye believe in God, believe also in me,' fitly ended, 'In the world ye shall have tribulation : but be of good cheer ; I have overcome the world.'

The idea of future compensation for present sufferings is not wanting in the 'consolation in Christ.' In His Father's House are many mansions, on entering which He goes to prepare a place for His disciples, where they shall both behold, and be partakers of, His glory (Jn 14² 17²²⁻²⁴). The same idea of a compensating 'weight of glory' for 'light affliction which is but for a moment' (2 Co 4¹⁷) is involved in the parable where Abraham says of Lazarus, 'Now he is comforted' (Lk 16²⁵). On the other hand, those who are now satisfied with their riches and have no hunger for righteousness, the men of the world who have their portion in this life, 'have received their consolation' (Lk 6²⁴. ²⁵).

See also following article.

ARTHUR POLLOK SYM.

COMFORTER (παράκλητος).—A term applied to Christ in RVm of 1 Jn 2¹, and four times (Jn 14¹⁶. ²⁶ 15²⁶ 16⁷) to the Holy Spirit. For the meaning of the original and the probable source from which St. John derived it, see art. 'Paraclete' in Hastings' *DB* iii. 665–668. The active sense is confined to ecclesiastical usage, and may have been emphasized by translators, from its appropriateness to the circumstances amidst which the word first occurs in Jn 14¹⁶ ; but the passive sense may still be traced in relation to the Father and the Son, the Spirit being called and sent by Them to the help of men, as well as for the purpose of witnessing for God at the tribunal of the human reason (Jn 15²⁶). The English term is, however, quite inadequate. Whilst there is a suggestion of actual consolation in Jn 14¹⁶, the principal points of St. John's teaching are that the mission of the Spirit is contingent upon the departure of Christ (Jn 16⁷), is thenceforward continuous and permanent (Jn 14¹⁶), and includes functions in regard to both classes of men, the disciples and 'the world.' The latter He will convict (Jn 16⁸⁻¹¹) in respect of the three decisive matters of sin, righteousness, and judgment. With still a significant preference for words of an intellectual bearing, He will continue and complete the instruction begun by Christ (Jn 14²⁶), and guide the disciples

'into all the truth' (Jn 16¹³). See art. HOLY SPIRIT. The predominant cast of these phrases, almost all pointing to mental processes, is in itself a sufficient evidence of the unfitness of the term 'Comforter,' for which 'Paraclete' (wh. see) might with advantage be substituted.

R. W. MOSS.

COMING AGAIN.—Though He had appeared in the world to found the kingdom of God and fulfil the Messianic hope in its true spiritual meaning [see ADVENT], Jesus repeatedly gave it to be understood that the object of His mission would not be perfectly attained in that first coming among men. There was to be a break in His visible connexion with earthly affairs (Mt 16²¹); He would depart for a time (Jn 14¹⁹ 16⁷) ; but He promised that He would come again to continue His work and carry it on to complete fulfilment. As the clouds of danger gathered, and a violent death loomed in view, He began to speak with growing frequency of a marvellous and triumphant return, in which His living presence and power would be gloriously revealed. His sayings on this subject, however, are not always easy to interpret ; they do not all refer to the same event ; we find in them traces of His having in His mind more than one coming, and, in several cases, it is only by a careful study of the context that we can discover to which coming His words were meant to point.

The comings of which Jesus spoke from time to time may be distinguished as follows :

1. His coming after His death to make patent to the disciples His continued and exalted life, and thereby to establish their faith in Him as their ever-living Lord. He predicted a meeting with them in Galilee (Mt 26³², Mk 14²⁸), and indicated that though for a little while they should not see Him, yet after a little while again they should see Him (Jn 14¹⁹ 16¹⁶).

2. His coming to enter into fellowship with the disciples in a closer spiritual reunion. As the Risen One, He was to return to them and abide with them continually (Jn 14⁸⁻²²), manifesting His presence through the Paraclete, the Spirit of truth, and guiding, teaching, sustaining them by His gracious working in their hearts (14¹⁶. ¹⁷ 15²⁶ 16¹⁴). It would appear that in this sense Jesus regarded His coming again as a vital experience, to be shared by all believers in all after generations, thus foreshadowing His abiding presence through the Spirit in the Christian Church.

3. His coming to remove the disciples from their toils and struggles on earth, and take them to the place He would prepare for them in His Father's house (Jn 14². ³), that where He was they might be also.

4. His coming at the great crises of history to bring to their disastrous issues the sins of societies, nations, and religious institutions, and to vindicate His power over all the corrupt agencies in the world that oppose His truth. In the solemn discourse on the future recorded in Mt 24 and Mk 13, there are certain passages which, as usually interpreted, convey the impression that the destruction of Jerusalem and the fall of the Jewish State was one such momentous crisis that Jesus had particularly in view (Mt 24¹⁵⁻²². ³²⁻³⁴, Mk 13¹⁴⁻²³. ²⁹. ³⁰ ; cf. Lk 19⁴¹⁻⁴⁴ 21²⁰⁻²³. ³². ³³ 23²⁸⁻³⁰), although His words may be recognized as covering also all other marked epochs in history, in which His triumphant glory and the impotence of all the world-powers that come into conflict with Him are made clear. The course of events which was to culminate in the ruin of Jerusalem was to be the first startling revelation of His victorious energy in asserting His supremacy in the affairs of men and nations ; and this is apparently suggested, in vivid figurative language, by the statement to the high priest, 'Henceforth'—from this time onward—'ye shall see the Son of Man sitting at the right hand of power, and coming in the clouds of heaven' (Mt 26⁶⁴), as if a process of judicial and retributive manifestations of His power in human history would then begin.

5. His final coming at the end of the dispensation He had inaugurated, to sit in judgment over all classes and nations of men, to apportion their merit and demerit, decide their destinies, overthrow all evil, and bring the kingdom of God to its supreme triumph and glory. This final and most decisive coming—which will be more fully discussed under PAROUSIA—is described in terms that betoken the appearance of Jesus in august splendour and irresistible authority. He is to come in the glory of His Father with His angels, and reward every man according to his works (Mt 16²⁷); seated on the throne of His glory, He is to gather before Him all nations, and separate them one from another as a shepherd divides His sheep from the goats (Mt 25³¹·³²). That is to be the Last Day, the termination of the existing order of things, when all pretences will be exposed, obstinate unbelief and ungodliness punished, and faithfulness crowned with its eternal reward.

That these several comings were present to the mind of Jesus, seems sufficiently evident when His recorded utterances are duly weighed. We may assume that they were regarded by Him as the forms of manifestation by which, in the future, He would give proof of His living presence and conquering power. They were the varying stages in the development, after His death, of His victorious work for the establishment of righteousness and the destruction of evil. Hence they could all be conceived and predicted under one name; but, as Beyschlag remarks, under the conditions of prophecy, each stage was not seen as something apart; they were felt and described as so many phases of the whole, according to the suggestion of the moment (*NT Theol.* i. 202). On that account there is discernible in the predictions of Jesus an occasional blending of one coming with another; at least in the reports furnished by the Evangelists it does not always distinctly appear to what precise form of His future manifestation His words apply. Probably in the consciousness of Jesus all His future comings were wrapped up, as in a seed, in the thought of His spiritual coming, His coming in the fulness of His spiritual life and power, as an effective and abiding force on the side of God, to act on the hearts and lives of His faithful followers, and also on the general life of the world. This view makes His several comings fall into line as phases or stages of a continuous process, in which, sometimes through the quickened vitality of His Church, sometimes through the catastrophic action of the moral laws and forces which lie behind the movements of human society, His invincible operation should be revealed, until the final consummation is reached in the sovereign manifestation of His authority and glory at the end of the age.

It has been suggestively shown by Wendt (*Teaching of Jesus*, vol. ii. 297, 305) that it is on the utterances of Jesus regarding His spiritual coming in the hearts of believers that the Fourth Gospel lays the principal and almost exclusive stress; and probably it is in the light of Jesus' predictions of this spiritual or dynamical coming that we are to find the clue to what He meant in His sayings respecting the historical coming or comings, and the great apocalyptic coming, which the Synoptics report with special fulness and detail. The coming again of Jesus may thus be conceived as a series of manifestations of His living presence and activity in the world, culminating in a glorious triumph at the Last Day, when He shall sit as Judge of all.

G. M'HARDY.

COMING TO CHRIST.—Under this heading we bring together a number of passages, all sayings of Jesus, most of them in the Fourth Gospel, which express at once His widest invitation to men and His strongest claims upon them. Outside these there is a much larger group of passages, occurring in all the Gospels, many of which are intimately connected with the inner group. The expression thus frequently occurring, and used in the few passages first mentioned to convey the deepest truths of the gospel, is based on the everyday events of our Lord's ministry and of ordinary life. In its literal meaning it occurs constantly throughout the Gospel narrative. We may here disregard this widest class of passages, which speak of the multitudes who, from very various motives, 'came to Christ' to see and to hear Him, and fix our attention on those which have a moral and spiritual significance. The latter, bearing directly on the proclamation of the Kingdom of God and on the conditions of membership in it, are of supreme importance.

The constructions used in these groups of passages may here be noticed. In nearly all of them we have the simple verb ἔρχομαι followed by πρός with the accusative. In Mt 11²⁸ we have the interjectional adverb δεῦτε with πρός and the accusative. In the kindred passage, He 7²⁵, the compound προσέρχομαι occurs with the dative. In a closely allied group of passages, which we shall have occasion to notice later, ἔρχομαι is followed by ὀπίσω and the genitive. The call to the earliest disciples is δεῦτε ὀπίσω μου (Mt 4¹⁹, Mk 1¹⁷). In some passages (Mt 16²⁴ 19¹⁴, Jn 5⁴⁰ 6⁴⁴; cf. 7³⁴·³⁶ 8²¹ᶠ· 13³³) the aorist of ἔρχομαι is used, the 'coming' being regarded as complete, while in others the use of the present indicates that the 'coming' is thought of as in progress (cf. Westcott on Jn 6⁴⁴). In Jn 6³⁷ᵃ ἥξει with πρός and the accusative signifies arrival, attainment. In many passages of the second group, some of which will be used in illustration of the subject, we have the fact of the coming without the use of any of the phrases here mentioned.

Among the crowds who flocked to Jesus were many who came, or who were brought by their friends, because of some special need. Blind and deaf and dumb came to have their lost senses restored (Mt 9³²ᶠ· 20²⁹ᶠ·, Mk 7³²ᶠ·, Jn 9¹ᶠ· *et al.*). Lepers cried to Him for cleansing (Mt 8²ᶠ· ‖ Lk 17¹²ᶠ·). The lame and the palsied came, or were brought, to Him for renewal of their powers (Mt 9²ᶠ· ‖ Jn 5²ᶠ·). More than once the friends of the dying or the dead came beseeching Him to give them back their loved ones from the grasp of death (Mt 9¹⁸ᶠ· ‖ Jn 11¹ᶠ·). Obviously this 'coming' was in most cases much more than a mere physical fact. The whole motive does not in all cases lie open to us, but in many we know, and in others there is no room for doubt, that there was behind the coming an attraction of His person, a perception of and faith in His power to bless, a confidence in His mercy and grace, apart from which even the most needy would not have been moved to come to Him. This is in some instances conspicuously clear, and is recognized by Jesus with joy. Thus the 'faith' of the centurion (Mt 8⁵ᶠ·) is declared to be greater than any He had found in Israel. For her 'great faith' the prayer of the Syro-Phœnician woman is granted (Mt 15²²ᶠ·). The latter is one of many cases in which the faith of those who came to Him was tested by Jesus before He complied with their request (cf. Mt 9²⁸, Jn 4⁴⁸, and many others). This testing of faith shows the spiritual significance of the incidents, even where the blessing craved and granted, looked at merely from the outside, is purely physical. This is still more the case where the need which brought men to Christ was not physical, but moral or spiritual, *e.g.* Nicodemus to some extent (Jn 3), Zacchæus the chief publican (Lk

19²ᶠᶠ·), the woman who was a sinner (Lk 7³⁶ᶠᶠ·), and many others.

From these cases we pass by an easy transition to the higher level of meaning of the phrase 'coming to Christ.' The passages in which this occurs are entirely words of Jesus. He calls men to come to Him. For the most part His call is that of gracious, loving invitation. But the condemnation of the Jews because they would not come to Him (Jn 5⁴⁰; cf. Mt 22³, Jn 16⁹) shows that under the graciousness of the invitation there lies the assertion of a paramount claim. These are two aspects of Christ's call which it may be well to consider to some extent apart. Experimentally they must always go together.

In Mt 11²⁸ᶠᶠ· we have the great call of Jesus to those who 'labour and are heavy laden,' with its promise of 'rest.' These verses bear a likeness to several passages of the OT, especially to Jer 6¹⁶ 'Thus saith the Lord, Stand ye in the ways and see, and ask for the old paths, where is the good way, and walk therein, and ye shall find rest for your souls.' But the Heb. word מַרְגּוֹעַ 'rest,' is rendered in the LXX not by ἀνάπαυσιν, the word used in Mt 11²⁹ (cf. ἀναπαύσω, v.²⁸), but by ἁγνισμόν (or ἁγιασμόν). Some have thought that there is here an echo of the words of Jesus ben Sira (Sir 6²⁴ᶠ· ²⁸ᶠ· 51²³⁻²⁷), with which our Lord was probably familiar (see *Expositor's Greek Testament, in loco*). But the words of Christ, in the greatness of the call and of the promise, and in the connexion of both with His own person, go far beyond those of Ben Sira or anything which we find in the canonical books of the OT. The call is probably addressed in the first instance to those who, groaning under 'the yoke of the law,' which generations of Rabbinic teaching and Pharisaic formalism had made intolerable, had no hope of rest for their souls. But it goes beyond that, as the whole ministry of Christ shows, to all those on whom the burdens of life press heavily, and especially to those who are being borne down by the weight of sin. To all Christ offers 'rest,' a ceasing from the crushing weight and from the hopeless toil, an inward, satisfying peace.

The words of Jesus in Jn 7³⁷ (cf. 6³⁵) are even greater than those just considered. Under the natural figure of 'thirst' and the companion figure of 'hunger,' He speaks of the deepest needs and longings of the soul of man—not those which are passing and accidental, but those which are essential and permanent, above all, the need of God—and promises to all who come to Him a perfect and abiding satisfaction. They should not only themselves be satisfied, but by the 'receiving' of the Holy Spirit should become sources of blessing to others.

To these two great promises we may add the words of Jesus in Jn 5⁴⁰, which imply, under the condemnation of those who would not come to Him, a promise of 'life' to those who do come. This evidently means a life other than that which they already had, a life in union with God as contrasted with their life apart from Him, a life in whose abundance man finds perfect satisfaction and the purpose of God is realized, a life which is eternal. Into the enjoyment of this life he who 'cometh to Christ' enters at once, but its full realization belongs to the future.

The supreme promise of Christ, embracing and transcending all others, is implied in Jn 14⁶ 'No man cometh to the Father but by me.' Access to God, fellowship with Him, are dependent on coming to Christ, and are promised to all who come to Him (cf. Jn 6³⁷ᵇ).

We infer from our study of the passages cited, that, on one side, 'coming to Christ' is practically synonymous with faith in Him. It is the active movement of the soul towards Christ. More than once 'cometh' and 'believeth' occur as parallel, if not virtually synonymous, expressions (cf. Jn 6³⁵ 7³⁷ᶠ·). 'The first word presents faith in deed as active and outward, the second presents faith in thought as resting and inward' (Westcott on Jn 6³⁵). The 'coming' is the response of the soul in its natural cravings, in its need, in its sin, to the call of Christ. It is its recognition in act, the act of trust, of His readiness to receive and His power to bless.

This, however, is only one side of the meaning of the phrase. There is another which is largely overlooked, perhaps because it does not immediately appeal to man's sense of need. Christ's condemnation of the unbelieving Jews (Jn 5⁴⁰) has already been mentioned. This implies that man's destiny depends on his attitude to Christ. In Lk 6⁴⁶ᶠᶠ· this is still more clearly stated. 'Coming,' the first movement of the soul to Christ, is associated with, and derives spiritual and permanent value from, hearing and doing the words of Christ. The mere lip acknowledgment of Him is nothing, or worse than nothing, for it brings disaster; the heart acknowledgment, issuing in obedience, is everything. This is stated even more strongly in Lk 14²⁶ 'If any man cometh unto me, and hateth not his own father, and mother, and wife, and children, and brethren, and sisters, yea, and his own life also, he cannot be my disciple.' The next verse carries us a step further, from the 'coming to' to the 'coming after,' from the negative 'hating' or renunciation to the positive 'bearing' or 'taking up' of the cross (cf. Mt 16²⁴, Mk 8³⁴, Lk 9²³). These are Christ's conditions of discipleship, stringent, at first sight even repulsive. Mt 10³⁷ may be compared with Lk 14²⁶, not as toning down the demands of Christ, but as helping us to understand them. He claims to be the first, and in a profound sense the only object of man's affection and devotion. None other shall stand before Him, none other beside Him. There is here no condemnation, no abrogation of the claims of human affection, which are Divine in their origin, and have been strengthened and beautified under the influence of Christ. But there is a demand that these shall stand aside, shall be put aside ruthlessly and with the heart's whole passion, so far as they come into conflict or rivalry with the claims of Christ. The 'great possessions' of the rich young ruler stood between him and Christ. Father and mother, wife and child, do the same with others. If so, 'he cannot be my disciple.' Further, Christ demands the taking up of the cross; that is, not the acceptance of trials, often trifling trials, as they come to us, to which in common use this great word has been reduced, but the readiness, for His sake, to follow Him to shame and to death.

While, then, 'coming to Christ' means, on the one hand, faith in Him, a movement of the soul to Him for the acceptance of the blessings He offers, it means, on the other hand, no less clearly an absolute surrender of the soul, of the whole man to Him. This aspect of the truth already emerges in Mt 11²⁸ᶠᶠ· 'Take my yoke upon you, and learn of me. . . . For my yoke is easy, and my burden is light.' This involves the recognition of Him as 'Lord,' a whole-hearted obedience, an absolute surrender in which nothing, not even the dearest object of earthly affection, shall weigh with us against Him, a readiness to suffer shame and death for His sake. This is to 'come to him' in the fullest sense, to come 'to' in order to coming 'after'; this is to become His disciple. It seems harsh and repellent: it is not really so. It is the detachment from the lower in order to attachment to the higher. It is the weaning, it may be the wrenching, of the soul from all else, that it may be united to God. There is no other way to the highest good.

The call of Christ, whether it be regarded as an invitation or as a claim, raises in an acute form the question of His Person. Its bearing on this can only be indicated, not fully discussed, in this article. Christ's call is, on the one hand, a universal call. The 'all ye' of Mt 11[28] has no limits of space or time within the limits of human personality and need. It is the gospel for all men of all times and of all lands. It is the keynote of the whole NT and of all evangelical thought and preaching. On the other hand, Christ's call is an exclusive call. It is 'Come *unto me*,' shutting out all other teachers or saviours. He professes to be able to satisfy all human need, even the deepest—that of the consciousness of sin. He claims to be the only object of affection and obedience. He declares Himself the only way to God. Either His professions and claims are false and absurd, or He is more than a man, more than the greatest among the great, than the best among the good. If we admit His claims—and they find the fullest justification in the history of faith—we must make our confession with St. Peter: 'Thou art the Christ, the Son of the living God' (Mt 16[16]).

Another question, the full discussion of which lies beyond the scope of this article, must be mentioned. The movement of the soul to Christ does not originate with itself. Jesus traces it to the 'drawing' of the Father (Jn 6[44f.]; cf. Jn 12[32]). In this we have a suggestion of the doctrine of the Holy Spirit. But it is obvious that this involves neither compulsion on the one hand nor lessening of human responsibility on the other. A man's coming to Christ, under the Divine influence, is a voluntary surrender. A man's refusal to come is and will be just ground of condemnation.

It remains only to point out the harmony of the rest of the NT with the teaching of Christ in the Gospels in respect of our subject. The phrase 'coming to Christ' belongs, it is true, almost exclusively to the Gospels, and is found in its highest meaning mainly in that of St. John (but see 1 P 2[4], Rev 22[17], and cf. He 7[25]). But all the NT is Christo-centric, and implies a call to men to come to Christ. 'In none other is there salvation: for neither is there any other name under heaven that is given among men wherein we must be saved' (Ac 4[12]), sums up the whole teaching of NT history and letters. But there is a difference between the Gospels and the other books which it is important to notice, not a difference in essential truth, but in the point of view from which it is presented. In the Gospels, 'Come unto me' is the personal call of Christ as teacher and Lord. In the rest of the NT the call is to the crucified and ascended Christ. This is indeed anticipated in the Gospels (*e.g.* Mt 20[28], Jn 12[32] *et al.*), but its full development before the death of Christ would have been premature, if not impossible. Immediately after the Crucifixion and Ascension, however, these two great historical facts are placed in the foreground of Apostolic preaching, *e.g.* in St. Peter's sermon on the day of Pentecost (Ac 2), in his remonstrance with the people after the healing of the lame man (ch. 3), in the declaration before the Council (5[29ff.]). They are the central truths of the Pauline and other letters: 'We preach Christ crucified' (1 Co 1[23]), 'Far be it from me to glory, save in the cross of our Lord Jesus Christ' (Gal 6[14]), 'He is able to save to the uttermost them that draw near to God through him, seeing he ever liveth to make intercession for them' (He 7[25], cf. Rev 5[9] etc.). We must interpret the invitation and the claim in the light of the Cross and of the Throne.

Literature.—Westcott's and Godet's Commentaries on John's Gospel; *Expositor's Greek Testament*; Commentaries on the Gospels; Edersheim's *Life and Times of Jesus the Messiah*; Hastings' *DB*, artt. 'Jesus Christ' (Sanday) and 'Kingdom of God' (Orr); Denney's *Studies in Theology*; Drummond's *Relation of Apostolic Teaching to the Teaching of Christ*; Hort's *The Way, The Truth, and The Life*; Stevens' *Theol. of the NT*; Wendt's *Teaching of Jesus*; Beyschlag's *NT Theology*.

CHARLES S. MACALPINE.

COMMANDMENTS.—As commandments (ἐντολαί) Jesus recognizes (1) the injunctions of the Decalogue, (2) certain other requirements of similar ethical character laid down in the Law. In one instance (Mk 10[5]) the Mosaic regulation for divorce is quoted as a 'commandment,' but its temporary provisional nature is clearly indicated. 'This commandment,' given for a time in view of special circumstances, is implicitly contrasted with the true and abiding ἐντολαί. In the case of a purely ritual ordinance the term προσέταξεν is used (Mt 8[4], Mk 1[44], Lk 5[14]).

The main passages in which our Lord defines His attitude to the commandments are : (1) the exposition in the Sermon on the Mount (Mt 5[17-48]); (2) the criticism of Pharisaic tradition (Mt 15[1-20], Mk 7[1-23]; cf. also Mt 23); (3) the reply to the rich young ruler (Mt 19[17-21], Mk 10[19-21], Lk 18[20-22]); (4) the dialogue with the lawyer (Mt 22[35-40], Mk 12[28-34], Lk 10[25-37]). The treatment of the Sabbath commandment (Mk 2[24-27], Lk 6[1-10] 13[10-16]) will have to be considered under Law and Sabbath.

It is assumed by Jesus that the commandments were given directly by God, and as such they are contrasted with the 'traditions of men' (Mt 15[6], Mk 7[8, 9]). This assumption of their Divine origin determines His whole attitude towards them. As ordained by God they are valid for all time and authoritative; the keeping of them is the necessary condition of eternal life (Mt 19[17], Mk 10[19]); men will take rank in the Kingdom of Heaven according to their obedience to the commandments (Mt 5[19]). It is objected to the Pharisees as their chief offence that they have perverted and overlaid with tradition the commandments of God (Mt 15[3], Mk 7[7]).

In view, then, of the Divine origin of the commandments, Jesus accepts them as the eternal basis of morality. His own ethic is presented not as something new, but as a truer and more inward interpretation of the existing Law. It has been maintained (most notably in recent times by Tolstoi) that Jesus in the Sermon on the Mount enacts an entirely new moral code,—five new laws in contrast to those ordained 'in old time.' This, however, is opposed to His own declaration, 'I came not to destroy but to fulfil.' The authority which He claims for Himself is not an authority to originate laws, but to explain more fully in their Divine intention those already laid down by God. 'It was said to them of old time,—I say unto you,' implies an opposition not of the Decalogue and the new Christian code, but of the ancient interpretation of the Decalogue and the Christian interpretation. Where the men of old time stopped short with the letter, Jesus unfolds the inward principle which must henceforth be accepted as the true aim of the commandment. 'Thou shalt not kill' prohibits anger, scorn, contention. 'Thou shalt not commit adultery' demands chastity of heart as well as of outward act. The law that forbids false swearing requires in the last resort abstinence from all oaths, and perfect simplicity and truthfulness. The case is somewhat different with the two remaining rules which are subjected to criticism ('an eye for an eye,' 'thou shalt love thy neighbour and hate thine enemy'). Here our Lord indeed appears to set new laws of His own over against the imperfect maxims of the ancient morality. But He is still emphasizing what He conceives to be the real drift of the Divine legislation, in contrast to the false and limited constructions which men had placed upon it.

The ethical teaching of Jesus is thus based on the

Divinely - given commandments. It claims to be nothing more than a 'fulfilment,' a reinterpretation of them in the light of their inward spirit and purpose. At the same time, they are so transformed by this unfolding of their ultimate intention, as to result in a code of morality which is radically new. This is recognized in the Fourth Gospel, where the originality of the Christian law is brought into clear prominence (see art. NEW COMMANDMENT). It remains to consider how Jesus, while accepting the commandments, replaced them in effect by a new ethic, different in character as well as wider in range. The process by which He thus transformed them can be traced, with sufficient distinctness, in the Synoptic teaching.

(1) The Moral Law is freed from its association with outward ritual. Jesus does not definitely abrogate the ritual ordinances ('ye ought not to leave the other undone,' Mt 23[23]), but He makes the distinction plain between these and the higher obligations, justice, mercy, and faith. He subordinates the law of the Sabbath to the requirements of duty and humanity (Mk 2[27], Lk 6[9] 13[15. 16]); He confronts the formal piety of His time with the Divine demand as stated by Hosea: 'I will have mercy and not sacrifice' (Mt 9[13] 12[7]); He challenges the whole system of rules concerning meat and drink by His great principle, 'that which cometh out, not that which goeth in, defileth a man' (Mt 15[11], Mk 7[15]). This principle, applied to its full extent, meant the abolition of the Levitical law.

(2) In a similar manner the 'traditions' which had gathered around the Law and obscured its genuine meaning are swept away. The ethical teaching of Jesus is directed, in the first place, to restoring the commandments to their original simplicity and purity. In the glosses and corollaries with which Pharisaic ingenuity had overlaid them, He sees an attempt to narrow the scope and weaken the full stringency of the Divine law. He instances the casuistry which made it possible to evade a strict obedience to the command, 'Honour thy father and mother' (Mt 15[5. 6], Mk 7[10-13]). As against such trifling with the law of God, He insists on an honest acceptance of it in its plain and literal meaning. The ten thousand commandments into which the Decalogue had been divided and subdivided are to give place again to the simple ten.

(3) Not only is the Moral Law restored to its original purity, but it is simplified still further. While accepting the commandments as all given by God, Jesus recognizes that they are of different grades of importance. When the young ruler asked Him which of them were life-giving, He singles out the more distinctively ethical: 'Do not commit adultery, do not kill, do not steal, do not bear false witness, defraud not, honour thy father and mother' (Mk 10[18. 19], Mt 19[18. 19], Lk 18[20]). So the question of the lawyer, 'Which is the great commandment?' is admitted by Jesus to be a just one. It is significant that in His answer to it He does not quote from the Decalogue itself, but from Dt 6[5] and Lv 19[18]. He thus indicates that it is not the formal enactments which are sacred and binding, but the grand principles that lie behind them. Those sayings extraneous to the Decalogue, which yet lay bare its essential meaning, are 'greater' than any of the set commandments.

(4) The two requirements thus singled out are declared to be not only the greatest, but the sum and substance of all the others. The Law in its multiplicity runs back to the two root-demands of love to God and love to men. Of these two, Jesus insists on the former as 'the first and great commandment.' The duty of love to God is at once the highest duty required of man, and that which determines the right performance of all the rest.

In this sense we must explain the words that follow: 'The second is like to it' (Mt 22[37-39], Mk 12[29-31]). Its 'likeness' does not consist merely in its similar largeness of scope or in its similar emphasis on love, but in its essential identity with the other commandment. The love to man which it demands is the outward expression, the evidence and effect of love to God (cf. Gal 5[6] 'Faith that worketh by love'; 1 Jn 4[20] 'He that loveth not his brother whom he hath seen, how can he love God whom he hath not seen?'). Thus in our Lord's summary of the Law we have more than a resolution of the Ten Commandments into two, corresponding broadly to the two divisions of the Decalogue. We have a clear indication that even those two are ultimately reducible to one.

(5) In this 'summary' the Moral Law, however simplified and purified, is still presented under the form of outward enactment. The early Catholic Church so accepted it, and set the *nova lex* imposed by Jesus on a similar footing with the Law of Moses. Jesus Himself, however, passed wholly beyond the idea of an outward statutory law. His demand is for an inward disposition so attempered to the will of God that it yields a spontaneous obedience. This demand is implicit in the 'summary,' couched though it is in the terms of formal enactment. It says nothing of particular moral actions, and insists solely on love, the inward frame of mind in which all right conduct has its source and motive: 'A good man out of the good treasure of his heart bringeth forth that which is good' (Lk 6[45]); 'Either make the tree good and his fruit good, or else make the tree corrupt and his fruit corrupt' (Mt 12[33]). The ultimate aim of our Lord's ethical teaching is to produce a morality which will be independent of outward ordinance, and arise spontaneously out of the pure heart.

Thus the Decalogue, which in appearance is only revised and expounded, is virtually superseded by Christ. He bases morality on a new principle of inward harmony with God's will, and discards the whole idea involved in the term 'commandment.' It follows that in three essential respects His ethic differs from that which found its highest expression in the Decalogue. (a) Its demands are positive as distinguished from the old system of prohibitory rule. The Rabbinical precept, 'Do not to another what would be painful to yourself,' is adopted with a simple change that alters its whole character (Mt 7[12]). Where there is an inward impulse to goodness, it will manifest itself in active love towards men, in positive obedience to the will of God. (b) The ethic of Jesus makes an absolute demand in contrast to the limited requirements of the ancient Law. The chief purpose of the exposition in the Sermon on the Mount is to illustrate and enforce this difference. 'I say unto you, Refrain not only from the forbidden act, but from evil looks and thoughts. Obey the Moral Law without condition or reservation. Be perfect as your Father in heaven is perfect' (cf. the 'seventy times seven' of Mt 18[22]). This absolute demand is likewise involved in the substitution of an inward spirit for a statutory law. The moral task is no longer outwardly prescribed for us, and makes an infinite claim on our willing obedience. (c) As opposed to the Decalogue with its hard and fast requirements, the teaching of Jesus imposes a 'law of liberty.' The moral life, springing from the inward disposition, is self-determined. It possesses in itself a power of right judgment which makes it independent of any outward direction. It originates its own rules of action, and adapts them with an endless flexibility to all changing circumstances and times.

Our Lord's 'fulfilment' of the ancient Law has thus its outcome in a new morality which cannot be separated from His gospel as a whole. What He demands in the last resort is a change of nature such as can be effected only by faith in Him and possession of His spirit. The ultimate bearing of His criticism of the commandments is well indicated in the words of Luther : ' Habito Christo facile condemus leges et omnia recte judicabimus. Immo novos decalogos faciemus, qui clariores erunt quam Mosis decalogus, sicut facies Christi clarior est quam facies Mosis.' See also ETHICS.

LITERATURE.—The various Commentaries (in their section on the Sermon on the Mount), e.g. Holtzmann (1901), J. Weiss in Meyer's *Com.* (1901); Loisy, *Le discours sur la montagne* (1903); also articles on same subject in Hastings' *DB*, Extra Vol. (1904) [cf. art. 'Decalogue' in vol. i.], and *Encyc. Bibl.* (1903); Weizsäcker, *Das Apost. Zeitalter* (Eng. tr. 1897), i. 35 ff. ; Pfleiderer, *Das Urchristenthum* (1887), 489–501 ; Wernle, *Die Anfänge unserer Religion* (1901), 23–69 ; Herrmann, *Ethik* (1901), 124–140 ; Harnack, *Das Wesen des Christenthums*, 45 ff. ; Bruce, *Apologetics* (1895), 346 ff. ; Holtzmann, *Neutest. Theologie* (1897), 130–160. To these may be added Tolstoi's *My Religion*, and *The Spirit of Christ's Teaching* ; also books of popular or homiletical character, such as Horton, *Commandments of Jesus* ; Gore, *Sermon on the Mount* ; Dykes, *Manifesto of the King.*

E. F. SCOTT.

COMMERCE.—See TRADE AND COMMERCE.

COMMISSION.—Christ's last recorded words to His disciples, as contained in Matthew's Gospel, are weighted with the impressiveness befitting such an occasion. They contain a commission, which focusses the duty of professed followers with regard to His own Person and Work. All four Evangelists give this Commission in one form or another (Mt 28[18ff.], Mk 16[15ff.], Lk 24[46-49], Jn 20[21.23]). Without discussing the critical questions raised by these passages, what follows is based on their historicity, as that has been held by the Christian Church.*

On two other occasions our Lord formally commissioned His Apostles. First, the Twelve were sent forth on a trial mission (Mt 10[5.6], Lk 9[1ff.]). That mission was limited, both as to area—the towns and villages of Galilee—and to objects—the lost sheep of the house of Israel. It aimed (1) at preparing the way of the kingdom of heaven, which our Lord came to found ; and (2) at training the Apostles themselves in faith and fortitude for the more responsible work afterwards to devolve upon them. Later, seventy disciples were chosen (Lk 10), and sent—also, apparently—to itinerate in Galilee. Their instructions were similar to those of the Twelve. But, as opposition had now become more pronounced, greater emphasis is laid on it ; and the brethren, like *carabinieri* patrols in modern Italy, travelled two and two. The instructions given to both the Twelve and the Seventy may be called lesser commissions in comparison with the great Commission of Mt 28. As these commissions were local, temporary, and provisional, it is unnecessary to do more than mention them, except for purposes of comparison and contrast. At one point, however, there is an interesting link between them and the great Commission. After giving His instructions to the Twelve, Christ fell into an audible soliloquy, and went on (vv. 16-42) to speak of the trials, the duties, and the supports of those who in subsequent ages were to carry on His missionary work.

That Christ should speak frequently to the disciples about their future work during the forty days between His resurrection and ascension, is what might be expected. This accounts for the various forms under which all four Evangelists record His Commission. Conditions of time, place, and circumstances call for fuller, or more con-

* It should be noted, however, that as Mk 16[9-20] is lacking in the best MSS, modern scholars are practically unanimous in holding that these verses did not form a part of the original Gospel, so that it is doubtful whether they possess any independent value.

densed, general, or particular statements. Processes of repetition, condensation, expansion, or omission in recording the subject of conversations which extended over nearly six weeks, were present to each writer's consciousness as he penned his narrative. Grotius, as quoted in Poli, *Syn.*, says : ' Uno compendio Matthæus complectitur præcipua capita sermonum quos Christus cum Apostolis non in monte tantum, sed et Hierosolymis, antea et post, in cœlum jamjam ascensurus, Bethaniæ habuit.' Notwithstanding these conditions, certain essential features of the Commission correspond in the Gospels, as the following table shows :

CONTENTS OF COMMISSION COMMON TO EVANGELISTS.			
Mt 28[18ff.].	Mk 16[15ff.].	Lk 24[46-49].	Jn 20[21-23].
Universal Mission	Universal Mission	Universal Mission	Mission of undefined range
Baptism	Baptism and Faith	Repentance and Remission of sins	Message whose substance is Forgiveness
Promise of spiritual Presence	—	Promise of Comforter	Gift of Holy Ghost.

' All power is given unto me in heaven and on earth. Go ye therefore, and make disciples of (μαθητεύσατε) all nations, baptizing them into (εἰς) the name of the Father, and of the Son, and of the Holy Ghost : teaching them to observe all things whatsoever I have commanded you : and, lo, I am with you alway, even unto the end of the world ' (Mt 28[18-20]). These words constitute the charter of the Christian Church. They define in a solemn, authoritative, formal manner, the Commission under which the Apostles and that Church of which they were representatives were to prosecute to its consummation the work begun at Christ's Incarnation. If our Lord gave this Commission in presence of the five hundred witnesses referred to by St. Paul in 1 Co 15[6], we can understand the remark of Mt 28[16] that ' some doubted,' for these doubters could scarcely at this stage be any of the Eleven. Should this be so, ' it follows that the Lord Himself here committed His formal institutions and commissions to the whole assembled Church, with the Apostles at her head, just as at a later day He poured out His Spirit upon the whole assembled Church. And from this, then, we argue that, according to the law of Christ, the Apostolic office and the Church are not two divided sections. In the commission to teach and to baptize, the Apostolical community is one, a united Apostolate involving the Church, or a united Church including the Apostles' (Lange, *Com. on Matt.*, Edinburgh ed. p. 560).

Peculiarities in two of the Synoptists' accounts are noticeable. St. Luke tells how Christ opened the understanding of His disciples that they might understand the Scripture testimony to His suffering and resurrection on the third day. This is the line which we should expect Christ to take, if, on any of the occasions when He discussed their future work with the Eleven, He referred to His own part. The Divine necessity for His death would most readily impress itself on their minds when associated with intimations thereof in the Law, the Prophets, and the Psalms.

Mk 16[17f.] [a passage that is very early, even if

not from the pen of St. Mark],* where the promise of miraculous gifts ($\sigma\eta\mu\epsilon\hat{\iota}\alpha$) is made, has occasioned difficulty, because it seems strange that any of the Evangelists should have omitted to mention so great an endowment. On the other hand, the historicity of these verses is strongly urged by Calvin on *a priori* grounds. He argues that the power of working miracles was essential to the establishment of the disciples themselves, as well as necessary for proving the doctrine of the gospel at its commencement, that the power was possessed by only a very few persons [but cf. v.[17], where the power is to belong to them *that believe*] for the confirmation of all, and (though not expressly stated by Christ) granted only for a time.

Turning now to St. Matthew's narrative, as fullest and most formal, the first noticeable thing is that the Commission proper is prefaced by our Lord's claim of universal *power*; and concluded with a promise of His abiding *presence*. The risen and glorified Christ speaks as Lord and King of heaven and earth, in 'the majesty of His exalted humanity and brightness of His divinity' (Lange). His disciples, having to undertake a superhuman task, required to be assured that they were backed by superhuman authority. Nothing but the assurance of such power at their disposal could nerve men to attack those strongholds of sin and Satan which must be overthrown before the kingdom of heaven can be established in human hearts. Meyer defines the power claimed by Christ as the '*munus regium Christi* without limitation.'

By the *promise* 'And, lo, I am with you alway, even unto the end of the world,' Christ assures His followers that the universal power possessed by Himself will be at their disposal when engaged in doing His work. The mystery of Christ's name 'Ἐμμανουήλ—God with us, is here fulfilled—*I* in the fullest sense, as if He, the risen, exalted, all-powerful head of the Church, 'stretched out His hand from heaven' (Calvin). He is present in the Person of the Holy Spirit (Jn 14[16, 26]) through His Word (14[25]) and Sacrament (Mt 26[28]). This promise is made to the whole Church in the widest sense, as well as to the Apostles and all who should take up their official work in propagating and preserving the Christian Church as missionaries and pastors. Alford says: 'To understand $\mu\epsilon\theta'$ $\dot{\upsilon}\mu\hat{\omega}\nu$ only of the Apostles and their (?) successors, is to destroy the whole force of these most weighty words. . . . The command is to the Universal Church, to be performed in the nature of things by her *ministers and teachers*, the manner of appointing whom is not here prescribed, but to be learnt in the unfoldings of Providence recorded in the Acts of the Apostles, who by His special ordinance were the founders and first builders of that Church, but whose office, *on that very account, precluded the idea of succession or renewal.*'

The Mediatorial Presence is to last unto the end of the world—whether that refer to the end of the material order here, or the end of the present moral and spiritual order, for Christ's return will make all things new. Schaff points out that 'unto' ($\dot{\epsilon}\omega s$) 'does not set a term to Christ's presence, but to His *invisible and temporal* presence, which will be exchanged for His *visible and eternal* presence at His last coming.' An important link between the power and promised presence—one which connects them also with the intervening Commission—is this: The power is placed at the disposal *of*, the presence granted *to*, those alone who obey the command, Go and disciple the nations.

The Commission itself is evangelistic, or mis-

sionary, and pastoral—the one merging into the other, with Baptism as the link connecting these two departments. Its order is threefold—*Discipling, Baptizing, Instructing*. All nations are to be brought to the obedience of the faith. Their standing is to be sealed and ratified by the sign of the gospel. Then their instruction is to go on, that so these baptized scholars in the school of Christ may reach up to the measure of the stature of the fulness of Christ.

(1) 'Go ye therefore and make disciples of ($\mu\alpha\theta\eta$-$\tau\epsilon\dot{\upsilon}\sigma\alpha\tau\epsilon$) all nations.' 'Demonstrably, this was not understood as spoken to the Apostles only, but to all the brethren' (Alford). Go forth—out of the bounds of Israel—and disciple the nations,—convert them, enrol them as scholars in the school of Christ. St. Mark specifies the means by which this discipling is to be accomplished—'Preach the gospel' ($\kappa\eta\rho\dot{\upsilon}\xi\alpha\tau\epsilon$ $\tau\dot{\delta}$ $\epsilon\dot{\upsilon}\alpha\gamma\gamma\dot{\epsilon}\lambda\iota o\nu$); herald the good news of a crucified, risen, and exalted Saviour. By the mention of 'all nations' the restriction of 10[5. 6] is now removed: for the middle wall of partition, that divided Jew from Gentile, was broken down by Christ's death. Christ's words give no hint of an answer to that question, soon to disturb the early Church, about the method of Gentile admission; but the principle of their admission is emphatically laid down. The corresponding words in Mk 16[15] 'Go ye into all the world, and preach the gospel to every creature' ($\pi\dot{\alpha}\sigma\eta$ $\tau\hat{\eta}$ $\kappa\tau\dot{\iota}\sigma\epsilon\iota$), emphasize the universality of the gospel message even more strongly than those of Matthew. All the world is the sphere, every creature the object, of evangelistic effort.

(2) 'Baptizing them.' The Church of Christ being a visible community, to be gathered out of the world until it become itself universal, has its peculiar rites, by which that visibility is manifested. Besides being channels of Divine grace, they are seals of Divine favour, and pledges, on the part of disciples, of obedience to Divine commands. Baptism is the initiatory rite. It signifies both the bestowal and the reception of that grace of God in Christ which brings salvation. It testifies to the adoption of believers by grafting into the body of Christ, the washing of regeneration, and the imputation of a new righteousness on God's part. The person baptized, on the other hand, ratifies by his signature the faith in Christ through which these blessings are appropriated. A profession of that faith has been required in all ages of the Church from those of mature years when seeking admission to her pale. This profession was manifestly intended by our Lord when He instituted the rite of Baptism. A minority of the Christian Church confine the rite to those who are capable of cherishing and professing such a personal faith. See art. BAPTISM.

Baptism is 'into' ($\epsilon\dot{\iota}s$) the name of the triune God—by the authority and unto the authority of Father, Son, and Holy Ghost. The unity in Trinity of the Godhead is distinctly marked by the use of the singular $\tau\dot{\delta}$ $\dot{\delta}\nu o\mu\alpha$ instead of $\tau\dot{\alpha}$ $\dot{\delta}\nu\dot{\delta}$-$\mu\alpha\tau\alpha$. These words, 'into the name of the Father, and of the Son, and of the Holy Ghost,' have been used for ages as our formula of Baptism when admitting candidates into the covenant of Redemption—'into the name,' 'as the expression, according to the common Scripture use, of the whole character of God, the sum of the whole Christian revelation. The knowledge of God as Father, the spiritual birthright of sonship, the power and advocacy of the Spirit—all these privileges belong to those who, in the divinely appointed rite, are incorporated into the Divine name' (G. Milligan in *Expository Times*, vol. viii. [1897] p. 172).

(3) 'Teaching them to observe all things whatso-

ever I have commanded you.' The process begun *before*, must be continued *after* Baptism. Admission into the Church—whether visible or invisible —is only the beginning of Christian discipleship. Eternity cannot complete the process of learning what has to be known of an infinite God, and the relation of His creatures to Him. It is part of the pastoral duty of the Christian ministry to inculcate the truth as it is in Jesus, that every member may be built up into the full manhood of the Author and Finisher of our faith. The subject-matter of teaching is the doctrines and precepts of Christ, which lie at the root of Christian faith and Christian practice. On all the members of His Church it is incumbent to be diligent scholars in the school of Christ, learning obedience to His commandments from those appointed as teachers On some of these learners the additional duty rests of being official expounders of His law—teachers in their turn—devoting their lives, as the Apostles did, to edify the body of Christ.

The place assigned to Word and Sacrament in the spiritual perspective of this Commission is well worthy of notice. It portrays the minister of the gospel in the character of a teaching prophet rather than in that of a sacrificing priest. The ministry is first a ministry of the Word, and then of the Sacraments. Thus Baptism—the Sacrament of regeneration—is closely associated with preaching and teaching; while the Lord's Supper— the Sacrament of sanctification—is not directly mentioned, although included among the 'all things whatsoever I have commanded you.' The Word must not be exalted at the expense of the Sacraments, nor the Sacraments at the expense of the Word. When each is assigned its true place as a means of grace, the work of evangelizing and edifying, committed to His Church by Christ, will most surely prosper.

LITERATURE.—Besides the Comm. *in loc.*, see Latham, *Risen Master*, 273 ff.; Denney, *Death of Christ*, 69 ff.; *Expos.* 6th Ser. v. 43, vi. 241; *Expos. Times* iv. 557, vi. 419. For a clear statement of the views of those who question the authenticity of the Commission, see Harnack, *Hist. of Dogma*, i. 79, *Expansion of Christianity*, i. 40 ff. For the Baptismal Formula see Resch and Marshall in *Expos. Times* vi. 395 ff.; and the discussion by Chase and Armitage Robinson, in *JThSt*, July 1905, Jan. 1906.

D. A. MACKINNON.

COMMON LIFE.—The teaching of our Lord upon this subject is no more restricted and definite than it is upon any other of life's relations. It was never His purpose to draw up anything like a code of laws for the regulation of human life. Indeed, it is just this indefiniteness, this liberty, this leaving all detail to the spiritual guidance which He promised, that has made the religion of Jesus so far transcend every other religion that has been given to men. Christ left His teaching unrestricted, that by its inner and spiritual power it might be able to adapt itself to the ever-changing needs and thoughts of men. That doctrine which makes itself particular, which binds itself up with the peculiar circumstances of a definite people, a definite clime, a definite era, must of necessity pass away with those circumstances to which it specially applied. Our Lord, in that He laid down principles, not rules, has given us that which will apply to all peoples and climes and eras. Christianity is the universal faith, because it is founded upon the universal needs of the human heart (Jn 8³¹. ³² 14¹². ¹³).

It is, of course, true that Christianity is particular to this extent, that its Founder faces and combats those particular evils which chanced to be most prevalent at the time when He lived on earth. Had renunciation of the world in the monastic sense been as widespread as it became two centuries after His death, we should certainly have had more definite teaching upon our subject. But

it was Pharisaism that He had to oppose, not asceticism. There were, indeed, the Essenes at the time of Christ, but that community was never a large one, nor were their tenets so opposed to the truths He taught as to demand His special attention. The Baptist, it is true, was an ascetic (Mt 3⁴ ‖ Mk 1⁶, Mt 11¹⁸ ‖ Lk 7³³); but we never find him commanding others to lead his life. John preached repentance, but a repentance that did not entail renunciation of the world. Even the publicans and the rough soldiery of Herod, when they came seeking his advice, were not required to give up professions so fraught with temptation. All that he asked of them was that they should perform the duties of their callings honestly and honourably (Lk 3¹⁰⁻¹⁴). It was therefore in opposition to the ritualism of the Pharisees alone that Christ had to develop His teaching as to common life. Purity and holiness in the eyes of the Pharisees were matters of ceremonial observance far more than of heart and life; and to such an extent had they elaborated the Mosaic ritual, that it was no longer possible for the poor man and the toiler to attain to holiness in the sense which they had rendered popular. Only the wealthy and the leisured could win their esoteric righteousness. It is for this reason that we so continually find our Lord in strenuous opposition to all externalism. It is ever the religion of heart and life, not that of ceremonial, that He demands of His followers. Consider, for example, His fulfilling of the Law in the Sermon on the Mount. Throughout it is the Law's moral requirements that He treats of; and the discourse is prefaced by the assertion that the righteousness of the new kingdom must start by exceeding that of the scribes and Pharisees (Mt 5²⁰). He speaks of least commandments, the breaking of which does not exclude from the kingdom (v.¹⁹); and which He accounts the greater and which the less is manifested by His saying—'First be reconciled to thy brother, and then come and offer thy gift' (v.²⁴). From a similar standpoint He treats the observance of the Sabbath, subordinating all external and ceremonial requirements to those spiritual commands of love to God and to our neighbour which He made all-important (Mk 2²³⁻²⁸, Lk 6¹⁻¹² 13¹⁰⁻¹⁷). In regard to the question of washing the hands before eating, He comes into open conflict with the Pharisees, upbraiding their hypocrisy, and contending that defilement comes not from external things, but from within the heart (Mt 15¹⁻²⁰, Mk 7¹⁻²³).

All this tends towards the placing of a higher value upon common life. He is thus clearing the way for the reception of the thought that God may be as truly served in the round of daily life and toil as in those observances distinctively called religious. We have the boldest assertion of this truth in the parable of the Pharisee and the Publican (Lk 18⁹⁻¹⁴), wherein He points out that the strictest—nay, the supererogatory—performance of ritual cannot win justification in the sight of God, while simple repentance, utterly without these things, is assured of pardon and peace. We are not told whether the repentance of this publican entailed the giving up of his profession; but in the case of Zacchæus there is evidence that it did not (Lk 19¹⁻¹⁰). Apparently, then, in the eyes of our Lord, even this, the most despised of callings, could be followed by a member of the kingdom. Levi, it is true, was called to leave all and follow (Lk 5²⁷ᶠ·); but his case we must regard as an exception. He showed a special aptitude, and was called to a special office.

But it is rather the whole tendency of the teaching and example of Jesus, than any explicit statement, that in Christianity assigns to common life a dignity which it receives in no other religion.

That Christianity so early developed monkish asceticism cannot be adduced as an argument against Christ's teaching. The life of Jesus is throughout a clear admission of the value of that probation which God the Father and Creator has allotted to mankind. Jesus as the universal Man, the Example for all the world, assumed for Himself the most universal experience. For thirty years He lived the common life of a labouring man, working like any one of His brethren in the carpenter's shop at Nazareth. We have Him described as a carpenter, as one well known to His fellow-townsmen, as one but little distinguished from His brothers and sisters (Mt 13$^{55f.}$, Mk 6^3). Commonplace daily toil and family intercourse, and that throughout a period of thirty years, were thus the training which the Heavenly Father accounted the best for His Son who was to be the Saviour of the world. In this lowly sphere the Son of God grew 'in wisdom and stature, and in favour with God and man' (Lk 2^{52}). Than this there could be no stronger argument for the value and the nobleness of common life in the eyes of the Father and the Son. It is impossible to conceive that He who thus honoured the common lot could desire any renunciation of it on the part of those who wished to be His followers. Those who were called to be His missionaries must of necessity give up all to do a higher work, but not to attain a higher life. It is to be noted that when for a time that work is in abeyance, His chief disciples return to their old calling (Jn 21^3).

The whole attitude of Jesus towards the world of nature and of man is in accordance with His claim to be the Son of the Creator. He clearly recognized the wisdom and the beauty and the love that shine forth in Creation and Providence. The lilies of the field and the fowls of the air, the sunshine and the rain, are used by Him as evidences of the goodness of the Father. His teaching is bound up in closest harmony with the things of earth and time. For Him the family ties are types of Heaven. His kingdom is far more a family than a nation. The names of father, mother, brother, sister, wife, are ennobled by His use of them. From all the callings of men He draws images of Divine things. The physician, the sower, the reaper, the fisherman, the vinedresser, the shepherd, the king at war, the housewife at her baking, the commonest incidents of daily life, the simplest phenomena of nature,—all have a place in His doctrine; all are used to illustrate the character and development of His kingdom. He did not, it is true, enlarge upon the relations of life. That was not His mission. His reformation was to proceed from within, not from without. But everywhere there is the manifest acceptance of the order, alike social and natural, which God has ordained. Even the civil order, with which He came into contact in no ideal form in the Roman domination, receives His sanction. 'Render unto Cæsar,' He says, 'the things which are Cæsar's; and unto God the things that are God's' (Mt 22$^{15-22}$, Mk 12$^{13-17}$, Lk 20$^{20-26}$). There is duty to God and duty to civil order, and these must not conflict in religion's rame: the former should include the latter. Marriage is recognized by Him as a holy tie, an indissoluble Divine institution, and thus obtains a position more honourable than it had ever held before (Mt 19$^{3-9}$, Mk 10$^{2-12}$). His presence and first miracle at the wedding at Cana of Galilee (Jn 2$^{1-11}$)—a miracle which shows His deep sympathy with even trivial human needs—is in itself a consecration of marriage. That episode strikes the keynote of His life,—a life lived amid His fellows, sharing their joys and sorrows, their trials and temptations, their feastings and their mournings. The Son of man came eating and drinking, with no ascetic gloom; came to live in, and thus to sanctify, the whole round of common life.

Yet in the view of our Lord all these things had but a transitory value. They were but means to something higher. They were the temporal and seen, from which the unseen and eternal was to be extracted. In so far, then, as they conflicted with that higher good, that eternal treasure, Christ demanded renunciation in regard to them. His treatment of the young ruler (Mt 19$^{16-22}$, Mk 10$^{17-27}$, Lk 18$^{18-27}$) illustrates well this attitude. Wealth is not in itself an evil, but it is a great danger, and in certain cases it may destroy the life of the soul. For some, therefore, it is wiser and safer to discard it. It has an engrossing power that deprives the soul of its proper nourishment (cf. the parable of the Rich Fool, Lk 12$^{16-21}$). It tends to harden the heart against compassion and charity, to make the man self-sufficient, to give a physical delight so great as to close the eyes to that which is spiritual (cf. the parable of the Rich Man and Lazarus, Lk 16$^{19-31}$). But there are other blessings far more innocent that possess a like danger. Things as precious and as natural as the hand and eye and foot may yet lead to sin and obstruct the passage to the higher life (Mt 5$^{29f.}$, Mk 9$^{43-48}$). In such cases, too, these must be renounced. Even the family ties, if they become so binding as to come between the soul and its true weal—the service of God in Christ—must be broken; for the kingdom of God is the one aim and purpose of the spiritual man, and nought must be permitted to interfere therewith (Mt 10^{37} || Lk 14^{26}, Mt 6^{33}). Even life itself must be laid down for the sake of Christ (Mt 10^{39}, Lk 17^{33}, Jn 12^{25}).

Christ's teaching as to worldly good is particularly revealed in the parable of the Unjust Steward (Lk 16$^{1-12}$). There He calls the command of wealth and natural advantage by the name of 'the unrighteous mammon,' thus pointing to its seductive power and contrasting it with the true spiritual good. He calls it also 'that which is another man's' in distinction to 'that which is your own.' Of earthly good we are but the stewards. Wealth is never really our own. We may use it or abuse it, but sooner or later we must resign its control. The spiritual gifts of God are of a nature totally different. They become truly ours, a part of our true self. Yet the unrighteous mammon can be so employed as to win us spiritual advantage. By its means we can make us friends who will receive us into everlasting habitations. As the unjust steward employed his power to his own worldly advantage, so must we with the wisdom of light use to our highest advantage the worldly power which is ours which is always one with the service of God.

There is a remarkable passage in Mk 10$^{29f.}$ (cf. Mt 19^{29} and Lk 18^{29}), which promises that earthly loss suffered for Christ's sake and the gospel's shall receive an hundredfold reward 'now in this time' in the same kind in which the loss was suffered. That the Christian in his profession and practice of love to all men must have the family ties strengthened and extended an hundredfold, is readily to be understood; but the promise of lands is not so simple. To the mind of the present writer it suggests the great truth, which Christ's own life exemplified, that only the child of God is capable of the pure and perfect enjoyment of all that God has made. Only to the eyes of him whose heart is filled with the Father's love, is all the beauty of the Creator's work displayed. As one with the Father through Christ, as sharing the purposes of God, as beholding the Divine plan and submitting to and working for it, the Christian possesses the world in a sense in which no other can. It is his to rejoice in and to use for God's glory. (Cf. *Expositor* 1st ser. iv. [1876] 256 ff.).

To sum up the whole, we may say that there are two great ideas which underlie all Christ's teaching :—(1) The inestimable value of the human soul (Mt 16[26], Mk 8[36f.], Lk 9[25]), to the salvation of which all must be subordinated, for the sake of which all things, if necessary, must be renounced : the Gospel, therefore, which gives this salvation is all-important, and its service must have no rival ; and (2) the recognition of common life and daily toil, with all that these terms include, as the ordinances of a loving Father by whose Providence they are designed to be the chiefest elements in fitting men for citizenship in the Kingdom of Heaven. He who uses well the talents which God gives, in the sphere in which his lot is cast, who is faithful in a little, shall have his reward hereafter in the obtaining of a larger sphere wherein to exercise for God's glory those very qualities, purified and ennobled, which his earthly diligence has made his own (Mt 25[14-30], Lk 19[11-27]). Work that is the expression of love to God and man is always noble ; and there is no work on earth that may not be performed to God's glory.

Literature.—Beyschlag, *New Testament Theology*, ii. 250 ff. ; Weiss, *New Testament Theology*, ii. 347 ff. ; the standard Commentaries on the Gospels, and works on the Parables ; Stopford Brooke, *Christ in Modern Life*, p. 1 ff. ; R. W. Dale, *Laws of Christ for Common Life*, esp. chs. i. xi. xii. xiv. ; J. T. Jacob, *Christ the Indweller*, ch. ix. ; R. Glaister, 'Christ's Sympathy in Life's Commonplace,' *Exp. Times*, x. 360 ff. ; J. W Diggle, *Short Studies in Holiness*, 197.   W. J. S. MILLER.

COMMUNION.—It is surprising that neither the substantive (κοινωνία) nor the verb (κοινωνεῖν), which represent the concept of 'communion' in NT, is to be found in any of our four Gospels. It would, however, be unsafe, and indeed untrue to fact, to assume on this account that the idea of communion is wanting. While there is an absence of the words concerned, there is no absence of the conception itself. A careful study of the Gospels, on the contrary, not only reveals a plain recognition of this vital aspect of the religious life, but also (and especially in the records of our Lord's teaching preserved by St. John) presents the conception to us with a certain clear, if unobtrusive, prominence.

The subject contains three distinct parts, which will naturally be considered separately : (1) The communion of Christ with the Father ; (2) our communion with God ; (3) our communion one with another.

1. *The communion of Christ with the Father.*— The more conspicuous aspect of our Lord's communion with the Father as reflected in the Gospels, is that which characterized His earthly ministry. But it is not the only aspect presented. Christ Himself clearly claimed to have enjoyed pre-existent communion with His Father (Jn 17[5. 24]), and the Prologue of the Fourth Gospel in three or four weighty clauses confirms the claim. This pre-existent communion included both unity of essence and life, and fellowship in work. (*a*) The Word was πρὸς τὸν θεόν (Jn 1[1]), realizing His very personality 'in active intercourse with and in perfect communion with God' (Westcott, *in loc.*). His nature was the nature of Deity (καὶ θεὸς ἦν ὁ λόγος, *ib.*). His Sonship is unique (v.[14] ; and for the uniqueness of the relationship cf. the important Synoptic passage, Mt 11[27]=Lk 10[22]). His is the πλήρωμα—the sum of the Divine attributes (Jn 1[16], cf. Col 1[19] 2[9] ; Eph 1[23]), and He is μονογενὴς θεός (Jn 1[18])—'One Who is God only-begotten' (Westcott). (*b*) The pre-existent communion not merely consisted in identity of essence, but was also expressed by fellowship in work. The Word was the Agent

in the work of Creation (Jn 1[3. 10], cf. also 1 Co 8[6], Col 1[16] : His work in sustaining the Universe so created is taught in Col 1[17], He 1[3]). See art. CREATOR.

Our Lord's realization of His Father's presence during His life upon earth was constant. That He Himself laid claim to such fellowship is beyond contention. He did so directly in His words (Mt 11[27]=Lk 10[22], Jn 12[49. 50] 14[6. 10. 11] 16[28. 32]), emphasizing especially His unity with the Father (Jn 10[30-38] 12[44] 14[7ff.]), and accepting with approval the title of 'God' (Jn 20[28. 29]). He did so even more impressively, if less directly, by assuming His Father's functions in the world (Mk 2[5-7]=Mt 9[2. 3]= Lk 5[20. 21] 7[48]) and representing Himself as controlling Divine forces and originating Divine missions (Mt 11[27a], Jn 15[26] 20[22. 23]). Moreover, any attempt to explain away that intimate knowledge of God which the Gospels consistently ascribe to Him, is compelled to disregard not merely the passages in which His own words and actions distinctly assume it, but also not a few in which, whether with approval or with disapproval, others recognize that He claimed to possess it (Jn 5[18] 10[33] 13[3] 19[7], cf. also 17[7. 8]). See CLAIMS OF CHRIST.

But apart altogether from His specific claim to the enjoyment of this Divine fellowship, we have abundant evidence of its existence in His earthly life itself. The sense of communion was an integral part of that life. It is one of those elements in His personality that could not be eliminated from it. A Christ unconscious of intercourse with God would not be the Christ of the Gospels. It was this sense of communion that moulded His first recorded conception of duty (Lk 2[49], AV or RV). The thirty years of quiet preparation for a three years' ministry (the proportions are suggestive ; for other examples of equipment in seclusion see Ex 3[1], Lk 1[80], Gal 1[15-17]) may without doubt be summed up as one long experience of fellowship with His Father. And the recognition of this union, which marks His first thoughts of His mission, and which must so largely have constituted His earthly preparation for it, is found to be His constant support amid the stress of the work itself. It is present in a special manner in the Baptism which signalized the beginning of His ministry among men (Mk 1[10. 11]=Mt 3[16. 17]=Lk 3[21. 22]). It is His stay alike before the labours of the day begin (Mk 1[35]), at the very moment of service (Mk 6[41] ἀναβλέψας εἰς τὸν οὐρανόν ; cf. also 7[34] 8[24], Jn 6[11] 11[41]), and when refreshment of soul is needed at the close of the long hours of toil (Mk 6[46]=Mt 14[23], Lk 5[16]). The Gospels, indeed, make it plain that He regarded such communion as a condition on which the accomplishment of certain work depended (Mk 9[29], cf. Jn 5[30]), and we cannot fail to observe the frequency with which both He and His biographers insist that the Divine Presence is with Him in all His words and works (Lk 4[14. 18], Jn 3[34] 5[19-21. 36] 8[16. 26. 29]). So constant is the communion, that even the most familiar objects of Nature convey to Him suggestions of the Father in heaven (Mt 6[26. 28]). It is noteworthy that retirement for intimate converse with unseen realities is especially recorded as preceding Christ's action or speech at certain great crises in the development of His life-mission (Luke is particularly careful to draw attention to this ; see 3[21] 6[12. 13] 9[18. 28ff.] 22[41] 23[46] ; cf. also Mk 9[2], Jn 12[28] 17[1ff.]), and that intercession for individual men had its place in this sacred experience (Lk 22[31. 32], cf. 23[34], Jn 17[6-26]).

Thus constantly, alike at critical junctures and in more normal moments, did the sense of His Father's presence uphold Him. In one mysterious moment, the full meaning of which baffles human explanation, His consciousness of it appears to have wavered (Mk 15[34]) ; yet even this cry of desolation must not be considered apart from the certain restoration of the communion revealed in the calm confidence of the last word of all (Lk 23⁴⁶). See art. DERELICTION.

One further point may be briefly suggested. Our Lord's communion with the Father was not inconsistent with His endurance of temptation. Nay, it was under the strong impulse of that Spirit whose presence with Him was at once the sign and the expression of His union with God (see Mk 1¹⁰), that He submitted to the assaults of evil (Mk 1¹². ¹³, note ἐκβάλλει, = Mt 4¹ = Lk 4¹). The protracted testing (ἦν πειραζόμενος, analytical tense, cf. the suggestion of other occasions of temptation in the plur. ἐν τοῖς πειρασμοῖς μου, Lk 22²⁸, and Jn 12²⁷), successfully endured, itself became to our Lord the means of a fresh assurance and (perhaps we may add) a fuller realization of fellowship with the spiritual world (Mk 1¹³ διηκόνουν—impf.). In this respect, as in others also, His life of communion, while in one sense unique (Lk 10²²), is seen to be the exemplar of our own.

2. Our communion with God.—The reality of the believer's communion with God is plainly revealed in the teaching of the Gospels. This communion is presented sometimes in terms of a relationship with the Father, sometimes in terms of a relationship with the Son, sometimes in terms of a relationship with the Spirit; but all three presentations alike are relevant to our study (1 Jn 2²³ᵇ, cf. 1³, Jn 14¹⁶. ¹⁷).* If our outline is to be at once clear and comprehensive, we must treat the passages concerned under two headings. The first (a) will include those that deal with the *state* of communion with God into which a man is brought when he becomes the servant of God; the second (b) those that relate to the *life* of conscious communion with God which it is his privilege to live from that time forward. The distinction, as will shortly appear, is by no means an unnecessary one, the second experience being at once more vivid and more profound than the first need necessarily be.

(a) It is clear that in the case of every believer the barrier raised between himself and God by his sin has been broken down. In other words, he has been restored to a *state* of communion with God. The means by which this state is brought about have both a Divine and a human significance. It is in considering their Divine aspect that we reach the point of closest connexion between the communion of believers with God and the communion of Christ with His Father. For these in a true sense stand to one another in the relation of effect and cause (cf. what is implied in such passages as Jn 1¹⁶ 14⁶. ¹² 17²¹⁻²³). It is in virtue of our Lord's perfect fellowship with God that through His life and death we too can gain unrestricted admission to the Divine Presence. This truth is all-important. It needs no detailed proof. The whole story of the Incarnation and of the Cross is one long exposition of it. Perhaps it is symbolically represented in Mk 15³⁸. The conditions required on the human side for restoration to the state of communion with God appear plainly in our Lord's teaching. This state is described in varied language and under different metaphors. Sometimes it is presented as citizenship in God's kingdom (Mk 10¹⁴. ¹⁵, Jn 3³); sometimes as discipleship (Lk 14²⁶, Jn 8³¹), friendship (Jn 15¹⁵), and even kinship (Mk 3³²⁻³⁵) with Christ Himself. In other places it is spoken of as a personal knowledge of Him (1 Jn 2³); in others, again, as a following in His footsteps (Mk 8³⁴, Jn 8¹²); and in yet others as the possession of a new type of life (Jn 3¹⁶: for the definition of eternal life as 'knowing God' see Jn 17³, 1 Jn 5²⁰). As one condition of finding this experience, which, in whatever terms it be described, places men in a

* It is scarcely necessary to point out that for purposes of doctrine, 1 Jn. ranks as practically a part of the Fourth Gospel.

new relationship with God, Christ mentions childlikeness of disposition (Mk 10¹⁵). As other conditions He emphasizes poverty of spirit (Mt 5³, Lk 18⁹ff.), and the performance of the Divine will in a life of righteousness and love (Mk 3³⁵, Lk 6³⁵. ³⁶ 8²¹, Jn 8³¹ 14²³, cf. 1 Jn 1⁶ 2³⁻⁶ 3⁶). In one very important passage, addressed both to the multitude and to His own band of disciples, He may perhaps be said to include all individual conditions. 'If any man willeth to come after me, let him renounce himself' (Mk 8³⁴ and ∥). This saying has a meaning far more profound than that suggested by our English versions. Taken with the explanation contained in the verse that follows, it really leads us to the basis of communion. All communion between two persons, whether human and human or human and Divine, is possible only in virtue of some element common to the natures of both (see Jn 4²⁴ 8⁴⁷; cf. the same principle differently applied in 5²⁷). Man's sole possibility of communion with God lies in his possession, potential or actual, of the Divine life (cf. Jn 1⁹). But joined to the 'self' (the second ψυχή of Mk 8³⁵) which is capable of union with God, he is conscious also of another 'self' (the first ψυχή of Mk 8³⁵) which is incongruous with that close relationship to Deity. The condition of realizing the one 'self,' and with it, in natural sequence, communion with God, is the renunciation of the other and lower 'self.'

So both vv.³⁴ and ³⁵: the ἑαυτόν of Mk 8³⁴ is thus equivalent to the first ψυχή of 8³⁵ The 'taking up his cross'—i.e. for his own crucifixion thereon—defines the 'renouncing himself' more closely. The teaching of the whole passage is the Evangelic representation of the Pauline doctrine of self-crucifixion, cf. Gal 2²⁰ 5²⁴.

To change the figure somewhat, the unity of life involved in the idea of communion between man and God can be attained only through man's rising to God's life. This, it is true, would have been outside his power had not God first stooped to *his* level. But in the Incarnation this step of infinite condescension has been taken, and by it the possibility of mankind's rising to the life of God—in other words, the possibility of its entering into a state of communion with God—has been once for all secured. In order to make this state of communion his own, Christ teaches, each individual man must now leave his lower life, with all that pertains to it, behind; must be content to 'renounce himself'; must be willing to 'lose' that 'life' which cannot consist with the Divine life. So complete, indeed, is to be the severance from the past, that the experience in which it is brought about is called a 'new birth' (Jn 3³), as real as, though of a type essentially different from, the physical birth (v.⁶). When with this self-renouncement is combined that faith in Christ which leads to union with Him and reliance upon Him (πιστεύειν εἰς—Jn 3¹⁶. ³⁶ 6²⁹ 11²⁶), we have the experience which sums up into one great whole the various individual conditions required on the human side for entering into the state of communion with God.

(b) Quite distinct in thought from the *state* of communion into which all believers are brought, is the *life* of communion which it is their privilege to enjoy. The one is always a fact, the other is also a consciously realized experience. Like so many of the blessings revealed in NT, such a life of communion is too rich an experience to be described in any one phrase or under a single metaphor. In different contexts it is presented in different ways. Sometimes, for example, it is set forth as an abiding in Christ who also abides in the believer (Jn 15⁴ff.). In other places it is represented as an indwelling of the Spirit (Jn 14¹⁶⁻²⁰ 16⁷. ¹³⁻¹⁵, 1 Jn 2²⁰. ²⁷ 3²⁴ 4¹³), whose presence, to believers (as in a deeper sense to their Lord) the sign and expression of union with God, is to be with them from the moment of their initiation into the new life (Mk 1[8] and ‖‖, 1 Jn 3[24] 4[13]). Yet another statement, emphasizing in a remarkable metaphor the inwardness and intimacy of the union that results, sets the experience before us as a mystical feeding upon Christ (Jn 6, esp. vv.[53-58], cf. also v.[35]). But while there is variation in the language in which this sense of the Divine Presence is set forth, there is no question as to the reality of the experience itself. It is the inspiration of this Unseen Presence that shall give to believers definite guidance in moments of crisis and perplexity (Mk 13[11] and ‖, Lk 12[11. 12]). It is in this communion with God that they will find their surest refuge against fears and dangers (Mk 13[18] = Mt 24[20]) and against the assaults of temptation (Mk 14[38] and ‖). Such fellowship, too, is their ground of certainty, alike in their teaching (Jn 3[11]—note the plurals; 1 Jn 1[1-3]) and in their belief (cf. Jn 4[42]). It is, moreover, the source of all their fitness for service (cf. Gabriel's suggestive speech, Lk 1[19]) and the means of all their fruit-bearing (Jn 15[1-10]). As would have been expected, the full significance of this converse with God is not understood, nor is its closest intimacy appropriated, in the earliest days of initiation. Knowledge of God, like knowledge of men, has to be realized progressively (cf. χάριν ἀντὶ χάριτος, Jn 1[16]). There are degrees of intimacy (cf. Jn 15[15] and the suggestive interchange of ἀγαπᾶν and φιλεῖν in 21[15ff.]), and the extent to which the believer is admitted into fellowship is proportionate to the progress he has made in the lessons previously taught (cf. the significant connexion between Mk 8[31] and 8[27-29], which is clearly brought out in the emphatic καὶ ἤρξατο διδάσκειν of v.[31]: cf. also Mk 4[33], Jn 16[12]). The reason for this basis of progress is plain. An important element in communion being self-adjustment to God's will (cf. our Lord's own illustration of this, Mk 14[36] and ‖), the degree of intimacy that ensues will naturally be conditioned by the extent to which this element is rendered prominent. Thus, while its neglect will open up the possibility of lapsing even to one who has been on intimate terms with Christ (Mk 14[18], Jn 13[18]), its constant and progressive practice may bring a man to a union with God so close as to constitute his complete possession by Divine influence (cf. the Baptist's magnificent description of himself as a 'Voice,' Jn 1[23], taken from Is 40[3]). And the fellowship so enjoyed and ever more intimately realized under the restricted conditions of earth, is to find its perfect consummation only in the hereafter (Jn 12[26] 14[2. 3] 17[24], cf. 1 Jn 3[2]). See art. ABIDING.

The means by which, according to the Gospel teaching, the believer will practise this life of communion with God, may be briefly indicated. Prominent among them is seclusion from the world for the purpose of definite prayer. The importance of this our Lord emphasized by His own example. He also enjoined it upon His followers by oft-repeated precepts (Mt 6[6] 7[7. 8] 26[41] and ‖, Lk 6[28] 18[1]). At the same time the Evangelic teaching does not aim at making recluses. There are active as well as passive means of enjoying intercourse with God, and our Lord's whole training of the Twelve indicates, even more clearly than any individual saying (cf. Jn 17[15]), His belief in the Divine communion that is found in the service of mankind. The sense of fellowship with God vivified in secret devotion is to be realized afresh *and tested* in contact with men (so 1 Jn 4[8. 12. 16]).

Two more points call for separate attention. (1) Before His death our Lord ordained a rite which not only symbolizes the union of His followers with Himself, but is also a means of its progressive realization. If an intimate connexion between the Lord's Supper (Mk 14[22ff.] and ‖) and the Jewish Passover may, as seems reasonable, be assumed, that conception of the Christian rite which represents it as a means of communion between the individual soul and its Saviour would appear to have a basis in the foundation principle on which all ancient worship, whether Jewish or heathen, rests—the belief that to partake of a sacrifice is to enter into some kind of fellowship with the Deity. This aspect of the Lord's Supper does not, of course, exhaust its meaning (see art. LORD'S SUPPER), but it is certainly prominent, and it is emphasized both by St. Paul (1 Co 10[16]) and by Christ Himself (Jn 6[56], where the eating would certainly include that of the Lord's Supper, even though, as is most probable, it does not refer to it exclusively).

(2) One more suggestion may be put forward. Our Lord seems to hint at a special means of communion with Himself which is really a particular extension of the self-renouncement considered above. This is a mysterious fellowship with Him in His own sufferings for mankind (Mk 10[38. 39] = Mt 20[22. 23a]; for a symbolical illustration see Mk 15[21]). It is only a hint, but the words are significant; and, taken in conjunction with St. Paul's ἀνταναπληρῶ τὰ ὑστερήματα τῶν θλίψεων τοῦ Χριστοῦ ἐν τῇ σαρκί μου (Col 1[24]), and his purpose τοῦ γνῶναι . . . κοινωνίαν παθημάτων αὐτοῦ (Ph 3[10]; cf. also 2 Co 1[5] 4[10], 1 P 4[13]), would certainly seem to imply that the believer's own sufferings for Christ's sake may become a medium through which he may enter into close communion with his Lord.

Even this brief study will have revealed that the Gospel conception of the Christian's communion with God is essentially different from that of the Quietist. Whether we have regard to our Lord's example or to His teaching, whether we are thinking of the status of fellowship or of its conscious practice, the means by which the Divine communion is realized are not exclusively periods of secluded contemplation. In Christ's own life upon earth the two elements of active and passive fellowship are signally combined. The sense of union with the Unseen Father, fostered in lonely retreat, is also intensified in moments of strenuous activity. In His thoughts for the lives of His followers, too, the consciousness of God's presence is secured not alone by solitary worship, but also by the doing of the Divine will, by the earnest struggle to subdue the lower self, and even by active participation in the very sufferings of Christ. So the servant, as his Lord, must practise the communion of service as well as the communion of retirement (cf., again, Jn 17[15]). The desire for the permanent consciousness of the more immediate Presence must be sunk in the mission of carrying to others the tidings of salvation (Mk 5[18-20] = Lk 8[38. 39]). It is but natural that in the moment of special revelation on the mountain the disciple should long to make it his abiding place (Mk 9[5] and ‖); but his Master can never forget the need of service on the ordinary levels of life (Mk 9[14ff.] and ‖). And the experience of the one is the source of power for the other (Mk 9[29], cf. Jn 15[4]).

3. *Our communion one with another.*—Just as our communion with God was seen to bear a close relation to our Lord's communion with the Father, so our spiritual fellowship one with another rests upon the fellowship of each with Christ. As we had occasion to point out above, communion between any two persons is possible only in virtue of some element common to the natures of both. This common possession in the case of believers is the life, the 'self,' which is called into being and ever progressively realized in their individual communion with Christ. The possibility of our spiritual fellowship with one another rests ultimately upon what He is and our relationship to what He is (see 1 Jn 1[1-3], and especially 1[7]; cf.

also 1 Co 10[16. 17]). His Presence is the bond of union in which we are one, and in which we realize the oneness that we possess (Mt 18[20]). Indeed, the two types of communion—the communion with God and the communion with our fellow-believers—react each upon the other. On the one hand, as we have just seen, our communion with men rests upon our communion with Christ; on the other hand, our Divine fellowship may be intensified (Mt 18[20] again and 25[40]) or impeded (Mt 5[23. 24] 6[15] 25[45], Mk 11[25]) by our relations with our fellow-men.

That our Lord looked for the unity of His followers is not open to question. He both prophesied it (Jn 10[16]) and prayed for it (17[11b. 21]). An intimate friend, clearly one of an inner circle of disciples and probably John himself, understood its attainment to be part of His purpose in dying for mankind (Jn 11[52]). Moreover, it is natural to suppose that the desire to ensure it would contribute to His decision to found an organized society (Mt 16[18]) and to institute an important rite (Mk 14[22ff.] and ‖) for those who should believe in Him. The unity of His followers was even to be one of the grounds on which He based His appeal for the world's faith (Jn 17[21b]). Of His wish for this unity, therefore, there can scarcely be reasonable doubt. But when we ask in what He meant the unity to consist, agreement is not so easily reached. The expression of His followers' unity certainly includes kind and unselfish relations with one another—mutual honour and service (Mk 10[35-45] = Mt 20[20-28]), mutual forgiveness (Mt 6[14], Lk 17[3. 4]), mutual love (Jn 13[34] 15[12]). It is exemplified further by participation in the common work (Jn 4[36-38]). Another very special means of its realization, the Lord's Supper, we have already indicated. Although this particular aspect of the rite is not actually revealed in the Gospel narrative itself, it will scarcely be questioned that one of the great truths which it both signifies and secures, is that of the fellowship of Christ's followers. The sacred service in which the believer may realize communion with His Lord (see § 2 above), is also a means by which he is to apprehend his oneness with all other believers (see 1 Co 10[17]).

While, however, it is plain that in Christ's teaching the communion of Christians is at once attested and secured by means like these, it is disputed whether He designed their unity to be simply a spiritual or also an external one. Three important passages may be very briefly considered. (1) Jn 10[16] affords no support to the upholders of an external unity. The true rendering is unquestionably, 'They shall become one *flock*' (RV; cf. Tindale and Coverdale), and not, 'There shall be one *fold*' (AV; cf. Vulgate). The unity mentioned here is one that is realized in the personal relation of each member of the flock to the Great Shepherd Himself. — (2) There is teaching a little more definite in Jn 17[11] and [21. 22]. In both these places our Lord makes His own unity with the Father the exemplar of the unity of believers. Reverence forbids any dogmatic statement as to the point to which this sacred analogy can be pressed. But Christ's own words in the immediate context contain suggestions as to His meaning in using the analogy. It is noticeable that here also, as in Jn 10[16], the underlying basis of unity is the believers' personal relation to Christ (and the Father). 'That they may be one, even as we are one,' in v. [22], is at once defined more closely in the words, 'I in them, and thou in me' (v. [23]). The resultant unity is gained through the medium not of an external, but of a purely spiritual, condition (ἵνα ὦσιν τετελειωμένοι εἰς ἕν, v. [23]). In the same way, in the statement of v. [11], it is a spiritual relationship to God that will yield the unity Christ craves for His

disciples. This unity will follow upon their being 'kept ἐν τῷ ὀνόματί σου.' It will be assured if their relationship to the Father is a counterpart of what had been their relationship to Christ (v. [12]), *i.e.* a personal relationship. Whatever, therefore, be the exact meaning which the analogy used by our Lord was intended to convey, His own language in the context appears to make it plain that it must be interpreted with a spiritual rather than with an external significance.—(3) This conclusion derives not a little support from the incident of Mk 9[38ff.]. When a definite test case arose, He declared the real fellowship of His followers to depend not upon any outward bond of union between them, but upon each bearing such a relationship to Himself as would be involved in His working ἐπὶ τῷ ὀνόματί μου. True, the man in question may not have been a nominal disciple of our Lord, but that in His view he was a *real* disciple is distinctly stated (v. [40]). This instance, therefore, may be regarded as a practical application on the part of Christ Himself of the teaching under consideration; and thus it strongly confirms the interpretation that we have put upon it. It would be outside the scope of the present article to consider arguments for or against the corporate unity of Christians drawn from other sources, some of which are very strong and all of which must, of course, be duly weighed before a fair judgment on the whole question can be reached. But so far as the subject-matter before us is concerned, we find it hard to resist the conclusion that such external unity formed no part of the teaching of Christ and the Gospels.

One word must be added. The 'communion of saints' joins the believer not merely to his fellow-Christians upon earth, but also to those who have passed within the veil (cf. He 12[1]). This aspect of communion is not emphasized in the Gospels, but there are indications that the fellowship of believers upon earth was linked in the thought of Christ to the yet closer fellowship of those beyond death. At any rate, it is worthy of notice that in instituting the sacred rite which, as we have seen, at once witnesses to and secures our communion one with another, our Lord carefully pointed forward to the reunion that will take place in the world to come (Mt 26[29]; note μεθ' ὑμῶν); and that in a few suggestive words He represented the earthly gathering as incomplete apart from its final consummation in the heavenly kingdom (Lk 22[16]). See further artt. FELLOWSHIP, UNITY.

LITERATURE.—*DB, s.v.*; Wendt, *Teaching of Jesus*, ii. 151 ff.; Weiss, *NT Theol.* ii. 367 ff.; Beyschlag, *NT Theol.* i. 247 ff.; Herrmann, *Com. of the Christian with God*; Maclaren, *Holy of Holies*, chs. xvi.-xix.; MacCulloch, *Comparative Theology*, 216, 254; Stearns, *Evidence of Chr. Experience*, 179; Strong, *Historical Christianity*, 11; Westcott, *Historic Faith*, 123, 247; McGiffert, *Apostles' Creed*, 32, 200; *Expos. Times*, iii. 197, v. 464 (R. F. Weymouth); Tasker, *Spiritual Communion*.

H. BISSEKER.

COMPASSION.—See PITY.

COMPLACENCY.—

Of Scripture words expressive of the idea of complacency as distinguished from benevolence, we find in the Heb. of the OT חָפֵץ, רָצָה, variously rendered in the LXX by θέλειν ἐν, or by some derivative of the verb δέχομαι. In the NT the expressions used are εὐδοκία, εὐδοκία, εὐαρεστέω, εὐάρεστος, ἀρέσκω. The words ἀγαπάω, ἀγάπη are also used in this sense. In the OT we find חָפֵץ 'take pleasure in,' in 1 S 18[22] tr. in the LXX by the phrase θέλω ἐν, where Saul's servants say to David, 'Behold the king taketh pleasure in thee,' meaning that he was willing to regard with satisfaction a matrimonial alliance between David and Saul's daughter. Similarly the word רָצָה 'delight,' is rendered by the same Gr. equivalent in 1 Ch 28[4], where David says of God, 'He liked me to make me king.' רָצָה is used of God's pleasure in the work of the Servant of Jehovah in Is 42[1], where the LXX reads προσεδέξατο αὐτὸν ἡ ψυχή μου, 'my soul has accepted him'; St. Matthew, on the other hand, translates the whole phrase בְּחִירִי רָצְתָה נַפְשִׁי by ὁ ἀγαπητός μου ὃν εὐδόκησεν ἡ ψυχή μου, rightly rendered in the AV 'my beloved, in whom my soul is well pleased.' Here, apparently, the thought of the LXX inclines more to the idea of the Divine act of will by which the Servant of God was appointed to his mission, while St. Matthew emphasizes the love with which, because of His redemptive work, the Father regards His Son, and so he prefers ' my beloved' to 'mine elect' as a rendering of בְּחִירִי (Mt 12[18]). In other passages also where the word חָפֵץ is used, as in Is 53[10], the LXX makes prominent the idea of the good pleasure of the Father's will.

Again רָצָה is used in Pr 16[7] of the favour with which God regards the ways of the righteous, where the LXX renders the passage, 'The ways of righteous men are acceptable (δεκταί) with the Lord'; and the AV, 'When a man's ways please the Lord, he maketh even his enemies to be at peace with him.'

In the NT, where εὐδοκέω, εὐδοκία, are used, it is not always apparent how far the thought of complacency and how far that of will or choice is predominant. Εὐδοκία evidently occurs in the latter sense in those passages which refer to election, the determinate counsel and foreknowledge of God. So Eph 1[5.9], Ph 2[13] etc. According to Cremer, εὐδοκέω '(1) relates to a determination when it is followed by an infinitive, Lk 12[32] . . . ; (2) Where the matter under consideration is the relation of the subject to an object, the latter is expressed in profane Greek by the dative, rarely by the addition of ἐπί τινι. . . . In the NT the accusative occurs only in He 10[6.8] (from Ps 40[7]),' and here εὐδόκησας is obviously parallel to ἠθέλησας. ' Elsewhere ἐν . . .' So in Mt 3[17] ∥ Mk 1[11] ∥ Lk 3[22], and again Mt 17[5]. ' This mode of indicating the object is justified by the circumstance that εὐδοκεῖν may be classed among the verbs which denote an emotion, a mood, a sentiment cherished towards any one = to take pleasure in something, to have an inclination towards it.'

'Complacency,' as the word is commonly used, means a state of being pleased or gratified, and is synonymous with 'pleasure,' 'gratification,' 'satisfaction.' The appropriateness of such a word in the department of Biblical theology is suggested by what we know to be its recognized use in the sphere of ethics. Complacency, as a mental state, arises when there is perceived in the object contemplated some quality or qualities which call forth a feeling of pleasure or satisfaction. The object may be something without, upon which the mind can rest with pleasure, or it may be in the mind itself, when, in seasons of reflexion, thought turned inwards upon itself is in a condition of perfect harmony, finding in itself no jarring element. The mind or soul is self-complacent when it is at peace with itself, satisfied that all is as it ought to be, no disturbing or self-accusing thoughts arising. Again, the mind is said to regard with complacency any outward object, animate or inanimate, which suggests thoughts of order and beauty, as when it is affected with pleasure or contentment by the contemplation of the beauty of nature, of a fair landscape, or of the harmony of earth and sky. The word applies also to relations between intelligent beings, as between friends, between husband and wife, parent and child, brothers and sisters, when one is satisfied with the character, or state of health, or conduct, or prosperity of the object of his affection or interest. Complacency arises in the mind when one's efforts in any direction are successful, and the object aimed at is attained. The artist, or the composer in prose, poetry, or music, regards his work with complacency when he has succeeded in giving adequate expression to his ideas, the workman when he is successful in his workmanship, the merchant or tradesman when his enterprise accomplishes the end at which he aims, the philanthropist when his efforts for the material or moral or spiritual wellbeing of the objects of his interest are rewarded, and he sees the fruits of his labours in the happiness and the gratitude of his fellows.

In ethics, complacency is considered as one of the forms of love, and as such is distinguished from benevolence. The distinction is well put by Edwards in his 'Dissertation concerning the Nature of True Virtue' (*Works*, ed. London, 1834, vol. i. pp. 123–125):

'Love is commonly distinguished into love of benevolence and love of complacence. Love of *benevolence* is that affection or propensity of the heart to any being which causes it to incline to its wellbeing, or disposes it to desire and take pleasure in its happiness. And if I mistake not, it is agreeable to the common opinion that beauty in the object is not always the ground of this propensity, but that there may be a disposition to the welfare of those that are not considered as beautiful, unless mere existence be accounted a beauty. And benevolence or goodness in the Divine Being is generally supposed, not only to be prior to the beauty of many of its objects, but to their existence ; so as to be the ground both of their existence and of their beauty, rather than the foundation of God's benevolence ; as it is supposed that it is God's goodness which moved Him to give them both being and beauty. So that, if all virtue primarily consists in that affection of heart to being which is exercised in benevolence, or an inclination to its good, then God's virtue is so extended as to include a propensity not only to being actually existing, and actually beautiful, but to possible being, so as to incline Him to give a being beauty and happiness.

'What is commonly called love of *complacence*, presupposes beauty. For it is no other than delight in beauty, or complacence in the person or being beloved for his beauty. . . . When any one under the influence of general benevolence sees another being possessed of the like general benevolence, this attaches his heart to him, and draws forth greater love to him than merely his having existence ; because so far as the being beloved has love to the being in general, so far his own being is, as it were, enlarged, extends to, and in some sort comprehends, being in general, and therefore he that is governed by love to being in general must of necessity have complacence in him, and the greater degree of benevolence to him, as it were out of gratitude to him for his love to general existence, that his own heart is extended and united to, and so looks on its interest as its own. It is because his heart is thus united to being in general that he looks on a benevolent propensity to being in general, wherever he sees it, as the beauty of the being in whom it is ; an excellency that renders him worthy of esteem, complacence, and the greater goodwill. . . . This spiritual beauty, which is but a *secondary* ground of virtuous benevolence, is the ground, not only of benevolence but *complacence*, and is the primary ground of the latter ; that is, when the complacence is truly virtuous. Love to us in particular, and kindness received, may be a secondary ground, but this is the primary objective foundation of it. . . . He that has true virtue, consisting in benevolence to *being* in general and in benevolence to *virtuous* being, must necessarily have a supreme love to God, both of benevolence and complacence.'

According to this exposition, complacency as a moral quality is the result, for the most part, of benevolence reacting upon itself, love making the object beloved become worthy of affection. What one loved at first out of mere benevolence becomes an object morally beautiful, worthy of love, and thus an object of complacency. Scripture illustrations of the Divine love as benevolence and as complacency naturally suggest themselves, and enable us to understand how the latter is often the fruit of the former. The work of Creation is a typical instance of the benevolence of God, the Almighty forming the world out of nothing, bringing light out of darkness, beauty out of chaos, life out of death. When, at the completion of His work, God beheld the product of His benevolence, and pronounced all very good, He showed complacency. So also with regard to the work of Redemption, God's love to the ruined world (Jn 3[16]) was the love of benevolence. His love to sinners as redeemed, made a new creation by that love, is the love of complacency (Mt 3[17]).

Keeping this distinction in view, we find in the Gospels not a few instances in which the expression 'complacency' may be fitly applied to describe that particular aspect of the love of God, or of the love of Jesus Christ, or even that feeling of grateful affection and devotion which the Divine love kindles in the hearts of true believers, to which the Evangelists direct our attention. If complacency means pleasure in the contemplation of beauty, or pleasure in the results of benevolence, (1) the expression may with all propriety be in these respects used to describe the love of God the Father to God the Son, or again the love with which the Father contemplates the fruits of the Divine work of redemption in the hearts and lives of the redeemed. (2) It may be applied also to the witness of Jesus to His own character, life, and work, and to His gracious acceptance of the faith and devotion of His disciples. (3) Lastly, it is appropriate as a description of the joy and peace with which believers realize the love of God and the grace of Christ, and of their satisfaction with the all-sufficiency of the Redeemer's work.

1. *The love of God the Father to God the Son, especially with regard to His life and ministry.*—The ineffable love, with which from all eternity the Father has regarded the Son, is referred to in those passages which speak of the glory which Christ had with the Father before the world was (Jn 17[5. 24]), or which describe Christ as 'the only-begotten Son which is in the bosom of the Father' (1[18]). But the Divine complacency, in the aspect of delight in the contemplation of the beauty of Christ's character and work, is that upon which special emphasis is laid in the Gospels, in which our attention is carefully directed to the Father's interest in the ministry of His Son, and to His sympathy and satisfaction with Christ's perfect submission to His will, in connexion with His voluntary humiliation and suffering for the sake of man. And, it is worthy of special note, it is in this connexion that we find the expression 'be well pleased,' 'take pleasure in' (εὐδοκεῖν ἐν), where text and context plainly indicate that the thought of complacency is intended, as distinguished from the other sense in which the words εὐδοκεῖν, εὐδοκία occur in the NT, that of the Divine election, the will or purpose of God, 'His mere good pleasure.' The Gospels mention two occasions on which the words, 'This is my beloved Son, in whom I am well pleased,' were uttered by the voice of God Himself.

At the Baptism, God spoke thus (Mt 3[17] ‖ Mk 1[11] ‖ Lk 3[22]). By these words He testified the peculiar pleasure with which He regarded His Son at the moment of His consecration to His mission; His satisfaction with the spirit of submission to the Father's will which had characterized Jesus throughout the years of obscurity during which He prepared Himself for His ministry, and the lowliness with which He submitted to the baptism of John—because thus it became Him 'to fulfil all righteousness'; and His gracious acceptance of the voluntary offering which the Son now made to the Father. It was the moment of consecration to that ministry of humiliation to fulfil which Christ had come into the world. Therefore, in token of His acceptance of that act of submission, which spoke thus, 'Lo, I come to do thy will, O God,' the Father spoke thus from heaven in the audience of men and angels, 'This is my beloved Son, in whom I am well pleased.' We may not, indeed, here or in the other case in which this voice from heaven was heard, leave out of sight the additional thought suggested by the tense of the last word, εὐδόκησα, the Greek aorist—the thought, that is, of the complacency with which from all eternity the Father had regarded the Son. But this is the central thought of the passage, the peculiar pleasure with which the Father contemplated the Son's voluntary humiliation, His submission to the Law, and His resolve to fulfil all righteousness by a life of lowliest service.

Again, with equal appropriateness these words were used in the parallel case of the Transfiguration (Mt 17[5], cf. Mk 9[7], Lk 9[29]), when Jesus entered upon the final stage of His ministry. Then, in full view of the cross, at the close of our Lord's conference with Moses and Elijah concerning 'his decease which he was about to accomplish at Jerusalem,' that Divine voice spoke in the audience of Jesus and the three disciples. Thus a second time God set the seal of His Divine approval to His Son's submission, and testified to the complacency with which He regarded His resolve by His death to make atonement for the sins of the world.

In this connexion may be noted also those passages in which Jesus speaks of the glory of God in the triumph of redeeming love. Such are: Jn 10[17] 'Therefore doth my Father love me, because I lay down my life that I might take it again'; 13[31. 32] 'Now is the Son of Man glorified, and God is glorified in him, and God shall glorify him in himself, and shall straightway glorify him'; to which may be added St. Matthew's tr. of Is 42[1] in Mt 12[18] 'My beloved, in whom my soul is well pleased.'

The thought of God's complacency in connexion with His contemplation of the fruits of Christ's redemptive work in the regeneration and reconciliation of the world is suggested by the closing words of the Angels' Song (Lk 2[14] RV), 'on earth peace among men in whom he is well pleased' (ἐπὶ γῆς εἰρήνη ἐν ἀνθρώποις εὐδοκίας), where again we find the technical word, if such it may be called, for this aspect of the Divine love.

It is now very generally admitted that this is the sense in which εὐδοκίας, *bonæ voluntatis*, ought to be rendered. That is to say, here we have the assurance of another voice from heaven, a message expressly sent at the time of our Lord's nativity, for the comfort of those who waited for the consolation of Israel, of the complacent regard with which the Father, contemplating the objects of His grace, looked upon them as identified with His well-beloved Son. 'The eye of God could again with complacency rest upon mankind,' regarding them as being represented by His Incarnate Son, and in view of that state of spiritual excellence to which His work was destined to raise them. The expression is thus used in an ideal or prophetic sense, not of mankind as they actually were, but of the objects of the Divine love as, through their Representative, they should yet become.

The same thought, that of the pleasure which God the Father takes in the spiritual welfare of His children, is suggested by passages which speak of God's joy over the return of penitent sinners. Such are: Jn 10[17], Lk 15[7. 10. 22. 24. 32] (in the parables of the Lost Sheep, the Lost Coin, and the Prodigal Son, in which vv.[22. 32] are especially notable, where Jesus mentions the joy of the father over the son's return, and the reason which the father gives for that joy: 'It was meet that we should make merry, and be glad: for this thy brother was dead, and is alive again; and was lost, and is found'); our Lord's assurance in another place that the prayer of the Publican was accepted of God (Lk 18[14]); and again His testimony that prayer and almsgiving, if prompted by the right spirit, are rewarded by the Father who seeth in secret (Mt 6[4. 6]).

2. (*a*) *Christ is represented as regarding with complacency His own character and work, and His perfect harmony with the Father.*—This appears in many passages, especially in the discourses recorded by St. John. In conversation with the Woman of Samaria, Jesus declares that He only can bestow the gift of living water which the soul of man requires; and, in connexion with the same incident, tells His disciples that it is His meat and drink to do the Father's will and to finish His work (Jn 4[10. 34]). Again He says to the Jews that He is in full accord with His Father in respect of will and of work (5[17. 19]), that 'the Father loveth the Son, and showeth him all things that himself doeth. . . . That all men should honour the Son, even as they honour the Father' (vv.[20–23]). In His discourse on the Bread of Life (ch. 6) we find expressions indicative of His conviction that His work is in all respects well pleasing to the Father (v.[37ff.]). He challenges His adversaries to convict Him of sin (8[46]). He enjoys perfect communion with the Father (7[28. 29]). He claims that the Father glorifies Him, and bears witness of Him (8[54], cf. vv.[16–18]). He declares that He only is the Good Shepherd, and all that came before Him were thieves and robbers (10[3. 5. 8], cf. vv.[11. 14]). He speaks of the excellence and thoroughness of His work, and of the satisfaction with which the Father regards it (10[17ff.]). He speaks of the success of His mission, and testifies the complacency with which He surveys His ministry. On the night of the betrayal He declares that hostility to Himself means hostility to the Father ($14^{21.\ 24}$ 15^{23}). A distinct note of triumph marks His closing utterances. So in $12^{23\text{ff.}}$, cf. $13^{31\text{ff.}}$; and again, when He bids His disciples be of good cheer, for that He has overcome the world (16^{33}). Addressing the Father Himself in His intercessory prayer, He says: 'I have glorified thee on the earth: I have finished the work which thou gavest me to do' (17^4); and again, speaking of the disciples: 'Those that thou gavest me I have kept, and none of them is lost, but the son of perdition' ($v.^{12}$). Lastly, one of His last words from the cross is the exclamation of triumph, 'It is finished' (19^{30}). The force of such passages cannot be mistaken. They show the Christ seeing 'of the travail of his soul,' and expressing Himself as 'satisfied,' His complacency, as He surveys the work of redemption, appearing as a true parallel to the judgment pronounced by God upon the work of creation, when 'God saw everything that he had made, and, behold, it was very good' (Gn 1^{31}).

With the instances cited above may be compared in this connexion such a passage as that where Jesus, confirming the joy of the seventy disciples in the success of their mission, says: 'I beheld Satan as lightning fall from heaven. . . . Notwithstanding in this rejoice not, that the spirits are subject unto you; but rather rejoice that your names are written in heaven' (Lk $10^{18.\ 20}$).

(b) Jesus further expressed complacency with respect to *the wisdom of the Divine counsels*, and as He contemplated *the fruits of His work in the hearts of believers*. With regard to the first point, we note that which St. Matthew and St. Luke record—Christ's ascription of praise to the Father who 'hid these things from the wise and prudent, and revealed them unto babes' (Mt $11^{25\text{ff.}}$. || Lk $10^{21\text{ff.}}$.). With regard to the second, instances abound in the Gospels. Thus Jesus testified the pleasure with which He regarded the faith of Peter, as when at the first He welcomed him, and showed him what he should yet become (Jn 1^{42}, cf. Lk 5^{10}); and when, towards the end of His ministry, He accepted Peter's confession (Mt 16^{17-18}). He showed gracious appreciation of the character and devoutness of Nathanael (Jn 1^{47-49}). Again He expressed satisfaction with the loyalty of His followers, whom He promised to reward at the time of the final consummation (Mt 19^{27-29} || Mk 10^{28-30} || Lk 18^{28-30}; cf. Lk 22^{28-30}, Jn 13^{1-10}). As He showed pleasure in the faith of His immediate disciples, so also He welcomed that of others, as when He spoke with signal approbation of the devotion of Mary of Bethany (Lk 10^{42}), who had 'chosen the good part,' and of whose offering of gratitude at the supper in the house of Simon the leper He said that she had wrought a good work upon Him which could not be forgotten (Mt 26^{12} || Mk 14^{6-9} || Jn 12^{3-8}). He said of the simple faith of the Roman centurion at Capernaum: 'I have not found so great faith, no, not in Israel' (Mt 8^{10} || Lk 7^9). Similarly, He expressed delight in that of the Woman of Canaan (Mt 15^{28}). He testified concerning the sinful woman in the Pharisee's house, that 'she loved much,' wherefore her sins, which were many, were all forgiven (Lk $7^{44\text{ff.}}$.).

Again, an illustration of complacency is found in the blessing pronounced by our Lord upon little children (Mt 19^{13} || Mk 10^{13} || Lk 18^{16} || cf. Mt $18^{2\text{ff.}}$ || Lk $9^{47.\ 48}$); while the value which He attached to their faith and devotion is clearly shown in the incident of the children in the Temple, when Jesus silenced the cavils of the Pharisees and priests, and demanded, 'Have ye never read, Out of the mouth of babes and sucklings thou hast perfected praise?'

(Mt 21^{16}). Again, Jesus commended the liberality of the widow's offering (Mk $12^{43.\ 44}$ || Lk $21^{3.\ 4}$). He noted with pleasure the gratitude of the Samaritan whom He had cured of leprosy (Lk $17^{18.\ 19}$), and regarded with complacency even the work of the exorcist who cast out devils in His name yet did not join the company of Jesus (Mk 9^{39} || Lk 9^{50}). Christ's delight in receiving sinners and acknowledging their faith is a conspicuous feature in the Gospels. The parables of the Lost Sheep, the Lost Coin, and the Prodigal Son (Lk $15^{5.\ 6}$ || Mt $18^{13.\ 14}$, Lk 15^9 etc.) are full of this lesson. Lastly, that at the Judgment of the Great Day, Jesus will, as Judge, not only justify, but reward with liberal commendation and distinguished honour all faithful disciples, according to the service rendered by them to their Master or to their Master's servants, is the central lesson of the parables of the Pounds and Talents (Lk 19^{17-19}, Mt $25^{21.\ 23}$) and of the discourse on the Last Judgment (Mt 25^{34-40}).

3. Of complacency *on the part of man*, considered as a virtue, i.e. *pleasure in the contemplation of moral and spiritual beauty*, we find one notable illustration in the Gospels, in the Baptist's testimony to Jesus in Jn $3^{29\text{ff.}}$, where John expresses his pleasure in the success of Christ's ministry, and compares Jesus to the bridegroom and himself to the friend of the bridegroom, who 'rejoiceth greatly because of the bridegroom's voice.' Such complacency as that, sympathetic interest in the Saviour and His scheme of salvation, and grateful acquiescence in the will of God for man's salvation, is alone legitimate on the part of fallen man. As to complacency in view of man's own knowledge and attainments, Jesus teaches that it is wholly inadmissible. No man, in the imperfect state of this present life, has a right to be satisfied with himself. Self-complacency is a sure sign of ignorance and spiritual blindness. The penitent publican, not the complacent Pharisee, is justified of God (Lk 18^{11-14}). The followers of Jesus must, when they have done all, confess that they are unprofitable servants (Lk $17^{10\text{f.}}$); and Jesus, while generously acknowledging the faithfulness of His disciples and assuring them that they shall in nowise lose their reward, expressly warns them that the last may be first and the first last (Mt 19^{30} || Mk 10^{31}, cf. Mt 20^{16}).

Literature.—Cremer, *Bib.-Theol. Lex. s.vv.* εὐδοκέω, εὐδοκία, etc.; the Comm. of Alford, Meyer, Lange, etc.; Bengel's *Gnomon*; Herzog, *PRE*, artt. 'Gott,' v. 262 ff., 'Liebe,' viii. 388 ff., 'Versöhnung,' xvii. 92, 124, etc.; Jonathan Edwards, ed. London, 1834, vol. i. pp. 123–125, cf. *ib.* cclxxii. f., pp. 237, 240; Sartorius, *Doctrine of the Divine Love*, p. 215; Martensen, *Christ. Dogmatics*, p. 303; Schleiermacher, 'Der christliche Glaube,' ii. 199 (*Theol. Werke*, Bd. 4).

HUGH H. CURRIE.

CONCEPTION.—See VIRGIN BIRTH.

CONDEMNATION. — The disappearance of the term 'damnation' in the RV of the Gospels is suggestive of more sober and reasonable thoughts about the Divine judgment against sin. Condemnation at the last may indeed fall like a thunderbolt upon the rejected (Mt 21^{19}). The fig-tree in the parable has a time of probation and then may be suddenly cut down (Lk 13^{6-9}). At the *Day of Judgment* the universal benevolence of God experienced here (Mt 5^{45}, Lk 6^{35}) will give place to His righteous wrath against the persistently rebellious. Condemnation is the irrevocable sentence then passed upon the abusers of this life (Mt 25^{41-46}). Especially will this sentence of rejection and punishment descend then upon the hypocrite (Mk 12^{40}). The state of the condemned is a veritable Gehenna (Mt 23^{33}). *Weeping* and *gnashing of teeth* picture the dreadful condition of condemned souls (Mt 22^{13} 24^{51} 25^{30}). Not only, we must suppose, punishment by pain for rebellion, but regret at past indifference, remorse at past folly, shame at past malice, will be the terrible feelings lacerating souls that have found not forgiveness but condemnation. The condemned will regret their indifference to Christ's demands, which they have ignored (Jn 3[36]). They will be tortured by the keen perception of their extreme folly in rejecting the knowledge they might have used (Lk 11[31. 32]). They will feel the shame of having their secret thoughts of evil exposed to a light broader than that of day (Mt 23[28]). This will be the condemnation to perpetual darkness for those who have loved darkness more than the light (Mt 8[12] 22[13] 25[30]).

But in this present life there is always at work a certain inevitable and automatic Divine condemnation. 'The earth beareth fruit of herself' ($αὐτομάτη$, Mk 4[28]), and yet the fact is due to the directing will of God. So, even in this life, the Divine condemnation of evil is being worked out, without that irrevocable sentence which constitutes the final condemnation. The guest may already feel the lack of a wedding-garment (Mt 22[11]), and so, warned by the present workings of condemnation, escape the last dread sentence. Nothing but what God approves can endure the stresses and storms that are imminent (Lk 6[46-49]). Without the sap of God's favour the vine must already begin to wither (Jn 15[6]).

But this present immanent condemnation is rather a most merciful conviction of sin and wrongfulness (Jn 16[8-11]). In this present age condemnation is not final for any; nay, God's purpose is the eternal security of men in true peace and true happiness (Jn 3[17] 12[47]). So far from condemnation being any man's sure fate, there is no need for any member of the human family to have to undergo such judgment as might result in condemnation (Jn 5[29]). The strong assertion in the present ending to the second Gospel, 'He that disbelieveth shall be condemned' (Mk 16[16]), is surely the expression of the true conviction that Christ is the only Way to avoid condemnation (cf. Jn 3[36]). Condemnation is God's prerogative, and not the privilege or duty of the individual Christian as such: 'Condemn not, and ye shall not be condemned' (Lk 6[37]).   W. B. FRANKLAND.

CONFESSION (of Christ).—The words 'confess' and 'confession' are employed in common usage to express not only an acknowledgment of sin, but an acknowledgment or profession of faith. The AV affords many illustrations of this use, and the examples are still more numerous in the RV, which in several passages has quite consistently substituted 'confess' and 'confession' for 'profess' and 'profession' of the AV in the rendering of $ὁμολογέω$, $ὁμολογία$ (2 Co 9[13], 1 Ti 6[12], He 3[1] 4[14] 10[23]). A corresponding twofold use of terms meets us in the original, the verbs $ὁμολογέω$ and $ἐξομολογέω$ being used to denote both confession of sin and confession of faith (e.g. for $ὁμολογέω$, Mt 10[32] and 1 Jn 1[9]; for $ἐξομολογέω$, Mt 3[6] and Ja 5[16]). The noun $ὁμολογία$, however, in NT Greek is employed only with reference to the confession of faith.

In the OT it is Jehovah who is the personal object of the confessions of faith which we find on the lips of psalmists and prophets (e.g. Ps 7[1] 48[14], Is 12[2] 61[10] and passim); but in the NT it is Jesus Christ whom men are constantly challenged to confess, and it is around His person that the confession of faith invariably gathers. This lies in the very nature of the case, since personal faith in Jesus Christ constitutes the essence of Christianity, and confession is the necessary utterance of faith (Ro 10[10], cf. Mt 12[34b]).

i. WHAT IS MEANT BY THE CONFESSION OF CHRIST.—In the earlier period of the ministry of Jesus the faith of His followers did not rise above the belief that He was the long-expected Messiah; and it was this conviction which was expressed in their confessions. Typical at this stage are the words of Andrew, 'We have found the Messiah' (Jn 1[41]). It is true that even in this earlier period Jesus is sometimes addressed or spoken of as the 'Son of God' (Jn 1[34. 50], Mt 8[29] || 14[33]); but it is not probable that in these cases we are to understand the expression otherwise than as a recognized Messianic term (cf. Ps 2[7]), so that it does not amount to more than a recognition that Jesus is the Christ. And yet even this was a great thing—to see in the man of Nazareth the Messiah of prophecy and hope. It marked the dividing line between those who believed in Jesus and those who believed Him not. St. John tells us that the Jews had agreed that if any man should confess Jesus to be Christ, he should be put out of the synagogue (Jn 9[22]); that they actually cast out, for making such a confession, the blind man whom Jesus had cured (9[34]); and that through fear of excommunication many of the chief rulers who believed in His Messiahship refrained from the confession of their faith (12[42]). It was no small thing to confess that Jesus was the Christ, crude and unspiritual in most cases as the notions of His Messiahship might still be.

But in the minds of the Apostles, though crude ideas were far from vanishing altogether (cf. Mt 20[20f.], Mk 10[28], Lk 22[24]), there had gradually grown up a larger and deeper conception of their Master's person and dignity; and St. Peter's grand utterance at Cæsarea Philippi, 'Thou art the Christ, the Son of the living God' (Mt 16[16] ||; cf. Jn 6[69]), shows a great extension of spiritual content in the confession of Christ, as our Lord's language on the occasion plainly implies. The Apostle's language seems to enfold, in germ at least, the doctrine of Christ's divinity; and it formed the high-water mark of Apostolic faith and profession in the pre-Resurrection days.

After the Resurrection had taken place, faith in that transcendent fact, and readiness to bear witness to it, were henceforth implied in the confession of Christ (Jn 20[28. 29], Ro 10[9]). But while any profession of faith would have as its implicate the acceptance of the great facts of the historical tradition, all that was actually demanded of converts at first may have been the confession, 'Jesus is Lord' (1 Co 12[3]; cf. Ph 2[11], 2 Ti 1[8]): a confession of which an echo perhaps meets us in their being baptized 'into (or in) the name of the Lord' ($εἰς τὸ ὄνομα τοῦ κυρίου Ἰησοῦ$, Ac 8[16] 19[5]; $ἐν τῷ ὀνόματι τοῦ κυρίου$, 10[48]). At a later time the growth of heretical opinions rendered it necessary to formulate the beliefs of the Church more exactly, and to demand a fuller and more precise confession on the part of those who professed to be Christ's disciples. In the Johannine Epistles a confession on the one hand that 'Jesus Christ is come in the flesh' (1 Jn 4[2. 3], 2 Jn 7), and on the other that 'Jesus is the Son of God' (1 Jn 4[15]), is represented as essential to the evidence of a true and saving Christian faith. With this developed Johannine type of confession may be compared the later gloss that has been attached to the narrative of the baptism of the Ethiopian eunuch (Ac 8[37], see RVm), which is not improbably the reproduction of a formula of question and answer which had come to be employed as a baptismal confession in the early Church.

It may be noticed here that it was out of the confession of personal faith which was demanded of the candidate for baptism that the formulated 'Confessions' of the Church appear to have sprung. There can be little doubt that the so-called Apostles' Creed was originally a baptismal confession. And Hort, Harnack, and others have shown that what is known as the Nicene Creed is in reality not the original creed of the bishops of

Nicæa, but a creed which gradually grew up in the East out of the struggles of the Church with varying shapes of heresy, and the nucleus of which is probably to be sought in the baptismal formula of the Jerusalem Church (Hort, *Two Dissertations*, ii. ; Harnack, *History of Dogma*, iii. 209 ; Herzog-Hauck, *Realencykl.*, art. 'Konstantinopolitanisches Symbol').

ii. THE IMPORTANCE ATTACHED TO THE CONFESSION OF CHRIST.—We see this (1) *in the teaching of Christ Himself*. He showed the value He set upon it not only by the deep solemnity of His affirmations upon the subject, but by expressing the truth in a double form, both positively and negatively, declaring that the highest conceivable honour awaits every one who confesses Him before men, and the doom of unspeakable shame all those who are guilty of denying Him (Mt 10[32. 33], Lk 12[8, 9] ; cf. Mk 8[38]). We see it in the pathos of the warning He gave St. Peter of the approaching denial (Mt 26[34] ; cf. Mk 14[30], Lk 22[34], Jn 13[38]), in the look He cast upon him when the crowing of the cock recalled that warning to his mind (Lk 22[61]), in the Apostle's bitter tears as he remembered and thought upon the word of the Lord (Mt 26[75], Mk 14[72], Lk 22[61. 62]), and in the thrice-repeated 'Lovest thou me?' (Jn 21[15-17]) recalling the threefold transgression. But, above all, we see it in the words addressed at Cæsarea Philippi to this same Apostle, who, though afterwards he fell so far in an hour of weakness, rose nevertheless on this occasion to the height of a glorious confession (Mt 16[17-19]). The evident emotion of Jesus at St. Peter's language, the thrill of glad surprise which seems to have shot through Him and which quivers through the benediction into which He burst, the great benediction itself,—these things show the supreme worth He attached to this confession of His strong Apostle. But especially we see the significance of St. Peter's utterance in the everlasting promise which Christ then gave not to him merely, but to all who should hereafter believe on His name and confess Him after a like fashion : 'Upon this rock I will build my Church, and the gates of Hades shall not prevail against it' (v.[18]). Whether the 'rock' is St. Peter's confession or St. Peter himself is a matter of little moment ; for if the latter is meant, it is undoubtedly as a type of believing confession that the Apostle receives the splendid promise, and it is on the firm foundation of such confession as his that Jesus declares that His Church shall be built.

The view of a certain class of critical scholars (*e.g.* Holtzmann, *Zeitschr. f. wiss. Theol.* xxi. p. 202 ; Harnack, *History of Dogma*, i. p. 79 n. 2 ; Wendt, *Teaching of Jesus*, ii. p. 351 n.) that Mt 16[18f.] are not authentic utterances of Jesus, but a subsequent addition intended to canonize the dogmatic and constitutional situation of a later age, is not one that commends itself to those who do not accept the views as to the composition of the First Gospel which are represented by these writers and by Holtzmann in particular. There is no textual ground for objecting to the authenticity of the words, while there are very strong psychological grounds for accepting such words as true. See the admirable remarks of Prof. Bruce, *Expos. Gr. Test.*, *in loc.*

(2) If Jesus laid great stress upon the confession of Himself, the importance of such confession is not less prominent *in the teaching of the Apostles*. Even if baptism 'into the name of the Lord Jesus' did not imply an explicit confession of Jesus as Lord (though this seems by no means improbable), at all events the Christian baptism which meets us constantly from the earliest days of the Church (Acts, *passim*) clearly involved, in the relations of Christianity whether to the Jewish or the Gentile world, a confessing of Christ before men. St. Paul makes very plain his conviction that, in order to salvation, believing with the heart must be accompanied by confession with the mouth (Ro 10[9. 10]), though he also enlarges our conception of the forms which confession may take when he finds a confession of the Christian gospel not only

in words spoken but in liberal gifts cheerfully bestowed for the service of the Church (2 Co 9[13]). In 1 Timothy he commends the young minister of the Church in Ephesus because he had 'confessed the good confession in the sight of many witnesses' (6[12]), and finds in this matter the perfect example for Christian imitation in the 'good confession' which Christ Jesus Himself witnessed before Pontius Pilate (v.[13]) ; while in 2 Timothy we have an evident re-echo of the Lord's own language in the warning, 'If we shall deny him, he also will deny us' (2[12]).

In the Epistle to the Hebrews Jesus is described as 'the Apostle and High Priest of our confession' (3[1]), and that confession the author exhorts his readers to hold fast (4[14] 10[23]). In the Johannine Epistles, as we have seen, confession begins to assume a more theological form than heretofore, but the writer is not less emphatic than those who have preceded him in insisting upon its spiritual value. In one place it is said to be the proof of the presence of the Spirit of God (1 Jn 4[2]), and in another it becomes not the proof merely, but the very condition of the abiding of man in God and God in man (v.[15]).

iii. THE REASON FOR THE IMPORTANCE ATTACHED TO CONFESSION.—When we ask why such supreme value is set upon confession by Christ and His Apostles and all through the NT, there are various considerations which suggest themselves. (1) *Confession is nothing else than the obverse side of faith*. The two necessarily go together, for they are really one and the same spiritual magnitude in its inward and outward aspects. The word of faith, as St. Paul says, is at once in the mouth and in the heart (Ro 10[8]), and whatever value belongs to faith as a vital and saving power necessarily belongs to confession also. (2) *It is the evidence of faith*. Like all living things, faith must give evidence of itself, and confession is one of its most certain and convincing signs. According to St. Paul, it belongs to the very spirit of faith to believe and therefore to speak (2 Co 4[13]) ; and if the readiness to confess Christ begins to fail, we may take it as a sure evidence that faith itself is failing. How significant here are the words of Jesus to St. Peter just before He warned him of the sifting trial which was near at hand, 'Simon, Simon, behold Satan asked to have you that he might sift you as wheat : but I made supplication for thee that thy faith fail not' (Lk 22[31. 32]). (3) *It is a test of courage and devotion*. A hard test it often is ; witness St. Peter's fall. But it is by hard trials that the soldier of Christ learns to endure hardness, and gains the unflinching strength which enables him to confess the good confession in the sight of many witnesses (1 Ti 6[12]), and not be ashamed of the testimony of our Lord (2 Ti 1[8]). (4) *It has a wonderful power to quicken faith*. It both begets faith and quickens faith in others, as we shall see presently ; but what we are speaking of now is its reactive influence upon the believer himself. It is a matter of common experience that nothing transforms pale belief into strong full-blooded conviction like the confession of belief in the presence of others. Something is due to the shaping power of speech upon thought, but even more to the definite committal of oneself before one's fellows, and the kindling influences which come from the contact of soul with soul. And it is not till men have publicly confessed their belief in Christ that faith rises to its highest power, so that 'belief unto righteousness' becomes 'confession unto salvation' (Ro 10[10]). It is to the psychological experiences that were naturally attendant on the public confession of Christ that we must attribute much of the language used in the NT with regard to the effect of baptism upon the soul (Ac 22[16], Ro 6[3ff.], Gal 3[27], 1 Co 12[13], 1 P 3[21]). And it is worth noting how the author of Hebrews connects in the same sentence holding fast 'the confession of our hope' and drawing near to God in 'fulness' or 'full assurance' of faith (He 10[22. 23], cf. 4[14. 16]).

(5) But, above all, the value attached to confession in the NT seems to lie in the fact that *it is the great Church-building power.* The grand typical case of confession of Christ is that of St. Peter at Cæsarea Philippi (Mt 16[15. 16]); and this was the occasion on which Jesus for the first time spoke of His Church, and declared that on the rock of Christian confession that Church was to be built (v.[18]). So it proved to be in after days. It was by St. Peter's powerful testimony to Jesus as the risen Lord and Christ (Ac 2[32-36]) that 3000 souls on the day of Pentecost were led gladly to receive the word, and in baptism to confess Christ for themselves (vv.[37-41]). St. Paul knew the mighty power that inheres in confession, and both in his preaching and writing made much of the story of his own conversion (Ac 22[6ff.] 26[12ff.], Gal 1[15ff.]), thereby confessing Jesus afresh as his Saviour and Lord. It was above all else by the personal confessions of humble individuals—a testimony often sealed with blood (Rev 2[13] 12[11])—that the pagan empire of Rome was cast down and the Church of Christ built upon its ruins. And it is still by personal confession, in one form or another, that the word of the Lord grows and multiplies, and His Church prevails against the gates of Hades. It is by testifying to Jesus Christ as Lord that men become the ambassadors of Christ to the souls of other men. The secret of the influence exerted by such confession lies not only in the appealing grace of the Lord whom we confess, but in the subtle and mysterious power of a believing and confessing heart over its fellow. 'Blessed influence of one true loving human soul on another! Not calculable by algebra, not deducible by logic, but mysterious, effectual, mighty as the hidden process by which the tiny seed is quickened, and bursts forth into tall stem and broad leaf, and glowing tasselled flower' (George Eliot, *Scenes of Clerical Life,* p. 287).   J. C. LAMBERT.

CONFESSION (of sin).—In the OT a large place is given to the confession of sin, as being the necessary expression of true penitence and the condition at the same time of the Divine forgiveness. Witness the provisions of the Mosaic ritual (Lv 5[3ff.]), the utterances of the penitential and other psalms (*e.g.* 32[5] 51[3ff.]), and prayers like those of Ezra (10[1]), Nehemiah (1[6. 7]), and Daniel (9[4ff. 20]). It may surprise us at first to find that in the Gospels the confession of sin is expressly named on only one occasion, and that in connexion with the ministry of John the Baptist (ἐξομολογούμενοι τὰς ἁμαρτίας αὐτῶν, Mt 3[6], Mk 1[5]). But apart from the use of the actual phrase, we shall see that the Gospel narratives take full account of the confession of sin, and that, as in the OT, confession is recognized both as the necessary accompaniment of repentance and as the indispensable condition of forgiveness and restoration to favour, whether human or Divine. There are three topics which call for notice: (1) confession of sin to God; (2) confession of sin to man; (3) Christ's personal attitude to the confession of sin.

1. *Confession of sin to God.*—It is to God that all confession of sin is primarily due, sin being in its essential nature a transgression of Divine law (cf. Ps 51[4]). And in the teaching and ministry of Jesus the duty of confession to God is fully recognized. Our Lord begins His ministry with a call to repentance (Mt 4[17], Mk 1[15]). In the midst of His public career He characterizes the generation

to which He appealed as an evil generation because of its unwillingness to repent (Lk 11[29. 32]). Among His last words on earth was His declaration that the universal gospel was to be a gospel of repentance and remission of sins (Lk 24[47]). And as confession is inseparable from true penitence, being the form which the latter instinctively and inevitably takes in its approaches to God, we may say that all through His public ministry, by insisting upon the need of repentance, Jesus taught the necessity of the confession of sin.

But besides this we have from His lips a good deal of direct teaching on the subject. The prayer which He gave His disciples as a pattern for all prayer includes a petition for forgiveness (Mt 6[12], Lk 11[4]); and such a petition is equivalent, of course, to a confession of sin. In the parable of the Prodigal Son the prodigal's first resolution 'when he came to himself' was to go to his father and acknowledge his sin (Lk 15[17. 18]); and his first words on meeting him were the frank and humble confession, 'Father, I have sinned' (v.[21]). The parable of the Pharisee and the Publican, again, hinges upon this very matter of the acknowledgment of sin and unworthiness. It was the total absence of the element of confession from the Pharisee's prayer, and the presence instead of a self-satisfied and self-exalting spirit, that made his prayer of no effect in the sight of God; while it was the publican's downcast eyes, his smitten breast, his cry, 'God be merciful to me a sinner!' that sent him down to his house 'justified rather than the other' (Lk 18[10-14]; cf. the words of Zacchæus, another publican, Lk 19[8]).

Under this head may be included one or two cases of confession of sin to Christ. When Peter cries, 'Depart from me; for I am a sinful man, O Lord' (Lk 5[8]), and when the sinful woman in the house of the Pharisee silently makes confession to Jesus as she washes His feet with her tears (Lk 7[37. 38]), it is too much to say of these confessions, in Pliny's language (*Ep.* x. 96) with regard to the hymn-singing of the early Christians, that they were offered 'to Christ as to God.' But they were certainly made to one who was felt to be raised above the life of sinful humanity, and to be the representative on earth of the purity and grace of the heavenly Father.[*]

2. *Confession of sin to man.*—According to the teaching of Christ and the Gospels, confession of sin should be made not only to God but to man, and, in particular, to any one whom we have wronged. In Mt 5[23. 24] confession to a justly offended brother is directly enjoined; and more than that, it is implied that the very gifts laid on God's altar are shorn of their value if such confession has not first been made. In Lk 17[4] again, our own forgiveness of an offender is made to depend on his coming and confessing, 'I repent.' But apart from this confession to the person wronged, a wider and more public confession of sin meets us in the Gospels. The necessity of such confession is implied, for instance, in our Lord's denunciations of hypocrisy—in His condemnation of the life of false pretence (Mt 23[14]); of the cup and platter outwardly clean, while inwardly full of extortion and excess (v.[25]); of the whited sepulchres fair to look at, though festering with rottenness within (v.[27]). It is implied similarly in His frequent commendation of simplicity and single-mindedness, and honest truth in the sight both of God and man (cf. Mt 6[22. 23] 7[3-5] 8[8] 9[13]).

---

[*] It is a point worth noticing, in the comparative study of the Gospels, that St. Luke, who is pre-eminently the Evangelist of salvation for the sinful, supplies us with the great bulk of the Gospel evidence that the Divine forgiveness is conditioned by the confession of sin.

It seems to be recognized in the Gospels that acknowledgment of sin to man as well as to God has a cleansing power upon the soul. There may, of course, be a confession that is spiritually fruitless, to which men are urged not by the godly sorrow of true repentance, but by the goads of sheer remorse and despair. Of this nature was the confession of Judas to the chief priests and elders (Mt 27⁴, cf. v.⁵). On the other hand, the confession of the penitent thief to all who heard him (Lk 23⁴¹) was the beginning of that swift work of grace which was accomplished in his heart through the influence of Jesus. It illustrates George Eliot's words, ' The purifying influence of public confession springs from the fact that by it the hope in lies is for ever swept away, and the soul- recovers the noble attitude of simplicity' (*Romola*, p. 87).

3. *Christ's personal attitude to the confession of sin.*—That our Lord never made confession to man, and never felt the need of doing so, is sufficiently shown by His challenge, ' Which of you convicteth me of sin?' (Jn 8⁴⁶). But did He make confession of sin to God? The fact that John's baptism was ' the baptism of repentance ' (Mk 1⁴ ǁ), and that the people ' were baptized of him in Jordan, confessing their sins ' (Mt 3⁶), together with the further fact that Jesus Himself came to the Jordan to be baptized (Mt 3¹³, Mk 1⁹, Lk 3²¹), might be so interpreted. But against such an interpretation must be set the attitude of John both when Jesus first came to him (Mt 3¹⁴) and afterwards (Jn 1²⁹), the language of Jesus to the Baptist (Mt 3¹⁵), the descent of the Spirit (v.¹⁶), and the voice from heaven (v.¹⁷). The baptism of John, we must remember, had more than one aspect : it was not only the baptism of repentance, but the baptism of preparation for the approaching kingdom of heaven (Mt 3²) and of consecration to its service (Lk 3¹⁰⁻¹⁴). It is not as an act of confession, but as one of self-consecration (including, it may be, an element of sympathetic self-humiliation, cf. Ph 2⁸), that the baptism of Jesus is to be regarded. He had no sins to confess, but He knew that John was the prophet divinely commissioned to inaugurate the kingdom of righteousness (cf. Mt 21³²), and to inaugurate it by the rite of baptism (Mt 21²⁵ ǁ). And by submitting Himself to John's baptism He was openly dedicating Himself to the work of that kingdom, and taking up His task of fulfilling all righteousness (Mt 3¹⁵). (See Sanday in Hastings' *DB* ii. 611 ; Lambert, *Sacraments in NT*, p. 62 f. ; *Expos. Times*, xi. [1900] 354).

But, above all, it is to be noted that while Jesus taught His disciples to pray for the forgiveness of sins, we never find Him humbling Himself before God on account of sin, and asking to be forgiven. And the complete silence of the Gospels upon this point acquires a fuller significance when we observe that there is not the slightest evidence that He ever engaged in common prayer with the Apostles. When Jesus prayed to the Father, He seems always to have prayed alone (Mt 14²³ 26³⁶ ǁ, Lk 9¹⁸ 11¹ ; cf. Jn 17, where He prays in the presence of the disciples, but not with them). The reason probably was that while the attitude of a sinful suppliant and the element of confession, whether uttered or unexpressed, are indispensable to the acceptableness of ordinary human prayer, these could find no place in the prayers of Jesus. (See Dale, *Christian Doctrine*, p. 105 f. ; Forrest, *Christ of History and of Experience*, pp. 22 ff., 385 f., *Expos. Times*, xi. [1900] 352 ff.).

LITERATURE.—Young's *Analyt. Concord. s.v.*; Hastings' *DB*, art. ' Confession ' ; Ullmann, *Sinlessness of Jesus*, p. 69 ff. ; and for special points the works quoted in the article.

J. C. LAMBERT.

CONSCIOUSNESS.—We have to consider, so far as the facts recorded in the Gospels permit, our Lord's consciousness of Himself and of His mission. The subject is difficult. It is beset by perplexing psychological and theological problems. It also demands very careful treatment, for it opens up discussions which may soon pass beyond the limits prescribed by reverence. We shall be guided by the following division :—

I. The data, as found in the Gospels.
  i. Certain narratives that reveal the consciousness of Jesus.
  ii. The implications involved in His teaching generally, and in the impression He produced upon His disciples.
II. Psychological problems.
  i. Growth.
  ii. The Divine consciousness and the human.
  iii. Knowledge and ignorance.
III. Theological results.
  i. Uniqueness of our Lord's personality.
  ii. His Divinity.

I. THE GOSPEL DATA.—i. *Narratives revealing the consciousness of Jesus.*—**1.** Among the narratives which, in a specially clear way, reveal our Lord's consciousness, one of the most remarkable refers to a very early period of His life. St. Luke tells us (2⁴¹⁻⁵²) of His visit to Jerusalem at the age of twelve years. When, after long searching, He is found in the Temple, and His mother questions Him, ' Why hast thou thus dealt with us?' His reply shows plainly that extraordinary realization of God which is the most outstanding characteristic of His consciousness : ' How is it that ye sought me? Wist ye not that I must be in my Father's house?' (or, ' about my Father's business,' ἐν τοῖς τοῦ πατρός μου). Here is evident the work of the child's imagination, in which the dominant idea controls absolutely everything else, and the most unlikely events appear perfectly natural : ' How is it that ye sought me?' What is extraordinary is the nature of this dominant idea. Already, at the age of twelve, our Lord knows God as His Father, and that in a manner so intimate and so peculiar that ordinary human relationships are as nothing in comparison with the relation to God. The doing of God's will is already the supreme motive. It is to be noted also how the ' *my* Father' of His reply contrasts with the ' *thy* father' of Mary's question. It is perhaps more natural to regard this as the inevitable reaction of His consciousness than as a deliberate correction of His mother. If so, it is all the more impressive. It shows how fundamental was the position in His mind of the filial relation in which He stood to God. How unlike this was to the Jewish mind of the time is shown by St. Luke's statement about Joseph and Mary : ' They understood not the saying which he spake unto them.'

2. The Baptism occupies an important place in the data of our subject. It is clear that all the Evangelists intend to point out that our Lord's baptism was unlike all others performed by John the Baptist. It was not a baptism of repentance. This is most clearly shown in St. Matthew's account. John felt the difficulty and ' would have hindered him, saying, I have need to be baptized of thee, and comest thou to me? But Jesus answering said unto him, Suffer it now ; for thus it becometh us to fulfil all righteousness. Then he suffered him.' John discerned the incongruity, and our Lord acknowledged it, but gave a reason which showed how distinctly He realized His unique position and calling. The baptism was part of God's will for Him. It had a necessary place in His life and work. It is also noteworthy that the descent of the Spirit and the voice from heaven are stated by St. Mark to have been manifested to our Lord Himself. With this St. Matthew and St. Luke agree. Only from St. John do we learn that the Baptist shared the experience. In view of what has gone before, we cannot look upon this event as the beginning of our Lord's knowledge of His unique Sonship. It was, rather, an objective Divine confirmation of the truths which He already knew from the testimony of His inner consciousness. It was manifested to Himself and to the Baptist when the time had come for the public proclamation of the gospel of the Kingdom. It was a witness to His Sonship, 'Thou art my beloved Son'; to His sinlessness, 'in thee I am well pleased'; and to His Messiahship, 'He saw the heavens rent asunder, and the Spirit as a dove descending upon him' (see Is 42[1]).

Careful study of the Gospels shows that these three elements in our Lord's consciousness are those which are disclosed most frequently in His life and teaching.

Some able students (*e.g.* Wendt, *Teaching of Jesus*, i. p. 96 ff., Eng. tr.) think that at the Baptism Jesus first attained to the consciousness of His Messiahship, though already aware of His Sonship. But, as has just been pointed out, the answer which He gave to John the Baptist reveals a fully developed sense, not merely of His sinlessness and relation to God, but of His mission. The testimony of even one Evangelist (St. Matthew) on a point like this is superior, as evidence, to any amount of psychological speculation.

3. The Temptation of our Lord, following immediately (Mk 1[12]) after His Baptism, shows the nature of the internal conflict which He had to face when He set about the work of His life. There was no struggle with doubt as regards God, or Himself, or the end which He sought. The force of every temptation depended indeed on the clearness with which these were realized. His victory was an overcoming of the tendency to escape from the limitation, the lowliness, and the self-sacrifice which, to human thought, seem so unbecoming the Son of God in His great work of establishing the Kingdom.

It is impossible in the short space available here to deal with all the definite instances of self-revelation which are given in the four Gospels. It must suffice to dwell briefly upon a few of the more remarkable, and to mention such of the rest as cannot be omitted. It may be added that, to those who have really considered the question, almost every incident in our Lord's life is, in some way or other, a manifestation of His superhuman consciousness.

4. One of the most noteworthy instances is that given by St. Matthew (11[25ff.]) and by St. Luke (10[21ff.]). St. Luke introduces the passage with the remarkable words, 'In that same hour he rejoiced in the Holy Spirit, and said.' It is a proof that the Apostles recognized our Lord's utterance on this occasion as the open expression of His communion with God. The insight into the heart of God, which was the secret of the inner life of Jesus, finds here such utterance as human language can give it. He addresses God as 'Father, Lord of heaven and earth,' a great expression which foreshadows the truth which follows: 'All things have been delivered unto me of my Father; and no one knoweth the Son, save the Father; neither doth any know the Father, save the Son, and he to whomsoever the Son willeth to reveal him' (Mt 11[27]). It is impossible to exaggerate the importance of these words. They contain four great assertions about our Lord and His work: (1) His universal authority; (2) the mystery of His person, known in its fulness to the Father only; (3) the unique relation of the Son to the Father, as involved in the Son's perfect knowledge of the Father; (4) the knowledge of the Father, so far as it is possible to man, is to be had only through the Son. This short passage contains the whole Christology of the Fourth Gospel. It records for us an occasion when our Lord permitted His hearers to gain some insight into His consciousness of God, of Himself, and of His mission.

Among the many important passages which agree with those which have been discussed, may be mentioned the following: (1) The account of our Lord's reception of the disciples of John the Baptist who brought their master's doubts to Him for solution (Mt 11[2-7] and Lk 7[19-24]). Here our Lord's perfect confidence in His mission is obviously based upon His consciousness. The contrast with the intensely human searchings of heart displayed by John in his time of trial is very striking. (2) The narrative which includes the confession of St. Peter and the teaching which followed it (Mt 16[13ff.], Mk 8[27ff.], Lk 9[18ff.]). The announcement of His approaching death and the tremendous terms in which He claims the utmost self-sacrifice from His disciples, give an extraordinary depth to the revelation of our Lord's self-knowledge contained in this narrative. (3) Every incident and every teaching belonging to the last period of the ministry reveals the overpowering intensity of His consciousness of the mission which He had to fulfil and of its dependence upon Himself. All the circumstances of His public entry into Jerusalem are notable in this respect (Mt 21[1-16], Mk 11[1-11], Lk 19[29-47], Jn 12[12-19]; see especially vv.[39. 40. 41-45] in St. Luke's account). (4) His answers to those who questioned His authority (Mt 21[23-end], Mk 11[27]–12[12], Lk 20[1-19]) are equally impressive. The parable of the Wicked Husbandmen, which is given in all the Synoptic Gospels, is very striking, as showing how our Lord made an essential distinction between Himself and all other messengers of God. (5) The description of the Future Judgment (Mt 25[31-46], cf. Mk 8[38], which shows the same conception, and proves that the idea is not peculiar to St. Matthew among the Synoptists), contains as lofty a conception of the dignity of the Son as any passage in the Fourth Gospel: 'Then shall the king say' (vv.[34. 40]). What a depth of consciousness is involved in the words, 'ye did it unto me' and 'ye did it not to me' (vv.[40. 45]).

It would be possible to give many more instances almost as impressive. The fact is important, as showing that here we are dealing with an essential element in the Gospel history. So far our instances have been taken from the Synoptic Gospels, and mainly from narratives which are common to them all. When we turn to St. John, we find the self-revelation of Christ on every page, almost in every paragraph. See, as examples, Jn 1[51] 2[19] 4[26] 5[17-29] 6[38-42. 61. 62] 8[14. 46]. (sinlessness) [55] 10[38] 12[49. 50] 13[3] 14[9. 10] etc. The climax is reached in ch. 17, in which we are admitted to the sanctuary in which the Son pours out His heart in the presence of His Father. Here are evident all the elements already noted as peculiar to our Lord's thought about Himself and His mission: His unique Sonship, His sinlessness, His Messiahship, His universal authority, the mystery of His relation to the Father.

. ii. *Implications of His teaching and the impression He produced.* — When we come to consider how this consciousness is implied in His teaching generally and in His effect upon mankind, we find ourselves face to face with a mass of materials so great that selection becomes very difficult. It must suffice to point out certain classes of facts—

1. His mode of thinking and speaking about God. God is, for Him, 'the Father.' Sometimes, with clear reference to His own unique relationship, our Lord calls God 'my Father' (Mt 7[21] 10[32. 33] 11[27] 16[17] 18[19. 35], Mk 8[38] 13[32], Lk 10[22] 22[29], Jn 5[17] 6[32] 8[19], and throughout chs. 14–17, etc.). But it is perhaps even more remarkable that when Christ is teaching His disciples to think about God as their Father in heaven, and speaking of Him as 'the Father' or 'your Father,' He always adopts the manner of one who knows this truth from within.

It is not a doctrine which He has learned from Scripture, or proved by reason, or even gained by vision or revelation. It is spontaneous, a truth welling up from the depths of His being, and as essential and natural to His thought as breathing to His bodily life. To Him God, His Father, was an ever-present reality, the greatest and most intimate of all realities. He knew God as none else knew Him (Mt 11[27]). He abode in His Father's love (Jn 15[10]). These expressions describe in the simplest possible way the spirit which is manifested in all our Lord's utterances. Take, as an example, the Sermon on the Mount, the most distinctively ethical part of His teaching. Here, if anywhere, we should expect this purely religious apprehension of God to become dormant. In the introduction (Mt 5[3-13]), the promises all reveal a deep insight into the purposes and nature of God: they view the world with its many kinds of people from the Divine point of view (see also 5[16. 20. 45. 48] 6[1. 4. 6. 8. 9. 14. 15. 18. 20. 24. 26ff.] 7[11. 21]). All through, human things are viewed in the light of God's character. Jesus knew all these things about human life because He first knew God. Instances of this underlying consciousness might be multiplied indefinitely.

2. His self-assertion. It has often been pointed out (especially by Liddon in his *Divinity of our Lord*, Lect. IV.) that qualities which are incompatible in any other character combine freely and harmoniously in the character of Jesus. The most remarkable instance is the union of self-assertion with the most perfect humility. To those who believe in the Deity of Christ, the reason, the 'why,' of this fact is not far to seek. But the 'how' remains a difficulty. How is it that all seems natural and inevitable in the portrait as we find it in the Gospels? The answer must surely be that the self-assertion is the necessary expression of a real consciousness. It is well to be reminded how tremendous the self-assertion is. The following passages are a selection : Mt 5[11. 22. 28. 34. 39. 44] 7[21. 22. 28. 29] (the former verses show this 'authority' which astonished the multitude) 8[9. 10. 22] 10[15. 32. 33. 37. 38. 39] 11[27. 28. 29] (in these passages we have the self-assertion and the humility side by side : 'I am meek and lowly in heart' follows the illimitable claim of vv.[27. 28]) 12[6-8. 41. 42] 16[24ff.] 22[45] 25[31ff.], Mk 2[28] 8[34ff.] 10[29] 12[6] 13[26], Lk 9[23-26] 14[26ff.] 21[12ff.], and throughout St. John's Gospel (see especially 5[17. 18ff.] 8[12ff.] 10[30] 14[6ff.] etc.). In these passages our Lord declares Himself greater than Abraham, David, Solomon ; greater than the Temple, the Sabbath, the Law ; He claims for Himself all the homage and devotion of which the hearts of men are capable ; He calls Himself 'the King,' and describes Himself as the Judge of all the nations ; He demands as His right that honour which belongs to God alone (Jn 5[17-24]). Yet He is among men ' as he that serveth ' (Lk 22[27]).

3. The effect of this consciousness upon those who were brought under His influence is very evident. The impression which Jesus produced upon the minds and hearts of men was quite unique. He not only preached Himself, He revealed Himself. This revelation carried conviction with it. It is plain that He designed His ministry to be such a revelation. It was not His usual method to say exactly who He was, but rather to lead His hearers on until they were able to make that discovery for themselves (Mt 16[13-20]). We speak of our Lord ' claiming ' such and such things ; but whenever He made an assertion about Himself, it was because it was necessary that His hearers should know the truth on account of its essential importance for themselves. His object was to lead them to give Him the whole faith and love of their hearts, because in so doing they attained their highest good. A notable instance of the effect of our Lord's self-revelation occurs in the case of St. Peter (Lk 5[8]), ' Depart from me : for I am a sinful man, O Lord.' Here the depth of the impression is shown by the moral effect (cf. Job 42[5. 6] and Is 6[5]). It is clear that St. Peter was impressed not merely by the miracle, but by the moral glory of Christ. The miracle was but the occasion when there came to him a sudden insight into the character of Jesus. The intense faith which our Lord awakened in the hearts of those who responded to Him testifies to His self-revelation. He looked for a faith which rested in Himself as its object. Such faith always called forth His highest approbation. Almost every page of the Gospels witnesses to the truth of this. The case of the Centurion (Mt 8[5-13], Lk 7[1-10]), though perhaps the most striking instance, is yet only typical. The principle involved in it may be found everywhere ; see Mt 8[2. 3. 22] 9[22. 28] 10[22] 12[30] 13[58] 15[22-28] 19[29], Mk 1[40. 41] 2[5-11] 5[34] 9[23. 24. 37] 10[29. 52] 13[9] 14[3-9], Lk 7[37-50] 9[23-26] 10[13-16. 42] 13[34] 14[25-33] 17[17-19] 18[22] 19[40], Jn 5[24] 6[29. 35] 7[37. 38] 8[12] etc. The extraordinary claim involved in these passages, and in many others, would strike us much more than it does were it not for the fact that the experience of the Christian centuries has amply justified it. Christianity, together with all the moral and spiritual benefits which it has bestowed upon mankind, is the effect produced not primarily by any doctrinal system or method of organization, but by a personality. It was the deliberate aim of our Lord, with full consciousness of the method He was adopting, to influence humanity by the revelation of Himself.

II. PSYCHOLOGICAL PROBLEMS.—These are many and difficult.

i. *Growth.*—In the case of a merely human intelligence, growth is a necessary element ; and a psychological examination would aim at tracing the course of development by showing how the mind reacted upon the circumstances of its history and environment. Our Lord was truly human ; but He was not merely human, and therefore it is unsafe to reason from ordinary experience apart from the facts of His life as given in the Gospels. Concerning His early years, we are distinctly told that there was development. 'The child grew and waxed strong, filled (becoming full, πληρούμενον) with wisdom' (Lk 2[40]). And again (v.[52]), 'Jesus advanced (προέκοπτεν) in wisdom and stature.' The language in both places implies growth in the true sense of the term. We are not, then, to imagine the infant Jesus looking out upon the world, from His mother's arms, with eyes already gleaming with the fulness of that superhuman knowledge which He afterwards possessed, as certain ancient pictures would suggest. In His consciousness, as in His bodily frame, He developed from helpless infancy to maturity. But there is unmistakable evidence that, as His consciousness unfolded, it attained, in ways which were to it perfectly normal and proper, experiences which are unique among the phenomena of human existence. It is clear from what has been already stated, that Jesus, from His childhood, possessed a consciousness of God as His Father which was utterly different from the faith to which others attain through teaching and the influence of religious surroundings. The incident of His childhood which reveals this fact must be viewed in the light of the self-revelation which fills all His teaching. Then its meaning is clear. We learn that His knowledge of His Father in heaven and of the loving harmony of will which subsisted between them was not a revelation imparted when the time of His public ministry drew near. It was an essential element in His earliest spiritual experiences. So far we are carried by the mere facts.

Every attempt at a theological, or even psychological, co-ordination of these facts will carry us much further, and show that this inexplicable knowledge of God and consciousness of harmony with Him form together the ruling and guiding principle of our Lord's whole life.

We have already passed in review the large classes of passages which show most distinctly our Lord's self-revelation of His consciousness of union with His Father. The force of these passages is greatly augmented when certain negative characteristics most clearly manifested in the Gospels are taken into consideration.

1. There is no trace in our Lord's teaching or life of any effort to arrive at truth by means of reasoning. Jesus was never a seeker for truth: it was not any task of His to discern God's will before He began to do it, or to satisfy His own intelligence before He taught others. In dealing with the things of God, He moves with the absolute certainty of One who knew the truth from within. His use of Holy Scripture is never an effort to fortify His own mind: He speaks and acts as One who knew Himself a superior authority. Just as He was greater than the temple and Lord of the Sabbath, so is He above the Law and able to take the position of One who has the right to modify it or deepen it on His sole authority (see Mt $5^{17. 21. 22. 28}$ etc. $7^{28. 29}$ 12^6, Mk 2^{28}). When, in His teaching, He reasons from Scripture or from nature, it is simply that He may convey to others, in a way which corresponds to their mental equipment, the truth which He Himself knows independently. In such cases there is always some degree of that 'fulfilling of the Law,' that drawing out of a deeper meaning, of which so many instances occur in the Sermon on the Mount. Perhaps the most remarkable example is His proof of the future life from the revelation at the Bush (Mt 22^{32}, Mk $12^{26. 27}$, Lk $20^{37. 38}$). Here the real proof is the manifestation of the character of God as it is involved in the declaration to Moses. See for other instances of argument of this kind from Scripture, from reason, or from nature, Mt 5^{45} $6^{8. 24. 26ff.}$ $7^{11. 16}$ $12^{3ff. 11. 12. 25ff.}$, Mk $2^{9. 17}$ 3^4 $7^{17ff.}$ $10^{3ff.}$ $12^{35ff.}$, Lk 13^{15} $14^{5. 28ff.}$, Jn 13^{14}. It is quite plain in these and all other instances that our Lord is reasoning, not in order to satisfy His own mind, but to carry conviction to the minds of His hearers. There is not the faintest trace of the struggle for truth.

2. There is no sign that progressive revelations were made to Him during the course of His ministry. Many efforts have been made to show that Jesus attained at certain turning-points to new views of His mission, and of the means by which His work was to be accomplished. It is certainly true that in His teaching it is possible to discern two stages, the first marked by a broad and more ethical treatment of the Gospel of the Kingdom, the second dealing with the means by which the Kingdom is to be established, His own Person, sufferings, and death. But it is quite impossible to show that these two stages are not essential parts of one organic whole. The truth is that they are perfectly consistent, and form together one great scheme of revelation. To suppose any change of purpose, or even fresh insight into the means by which our Lord's mission was to be accomplished, during His ministry, is to go beyond the evidence afforded by the Gospel history, in obedience to some *a priori* psychological or theological theory. It is supposed by some that He began with the belief that the Kingdom would be, somehow or other, introduced miraculously when the people as a whole were ready to receive it, but that, as time went on, and He found Himself rejected by the leaders, He became convinced that the Kingdom was already being realized in the

hearts of the faithful, and finally saw that it was necessary that He Himself should die for its advancement. But how is this consistent with such passages as these: Mk $1^{17. 25. 34. 37. 38. 43. 45}$ 2^{20} 3^{12}, and the corresponding passages in St. Luke; also the whole Sermon on the Mount in St. Matthew? Why should our Lord so sternly and so consistently forbid the spread of popular excitement if He thought the Kingdom would suddenly appear, supervening miraculously upon the old order? Here is clear proof that from the beginning He understood the spiritual nature of the Kingdom. Why again should He, from the beginning, foreshadow the days of mourning 'when the Bridegroom shall be taken away,' unless He had in view all along the great sacrifice which was to end His ministry? (See Mt 9^{15}, Mk $2^{19. 20}$, Lk $5^{34. 35}$. This saying obviously belongs to the earlier days, when the disciples of Jesus were marked by their joyous acceptance of all the good gifts of their Father in heaven). These conclusions are greatly strengthened by a consideration of the crisis which was brought about by the feeding of the five thousand. That there was a crisis is evident from Jn $6^{15. 24. 66}$ compared with Mt $14^{23. 24}$ and Mk 6^{45-47}. But it was not a crisis in the consciousness of Jesus. It concerned rather the response of the people. Now at last they are utterly disappointed of their hopes of a worldly Messiah, and the very manner of their disappointment shows our Lord's perfect consistency. His conduct throughout is that of one whose mind is made up and whose course is absolutely clear. At the very end, it may be thought, we have, in the Agony in the Garden, a crisis at which He became at last fully persuaded of the necessity of His death. But surely it is much more in accordance with the whole history to regard this as a moral crisis, when, for the last time, He was tempted to turn aside. There are indications that, all along, this temptation was presented to Him (see Mt $16^{22. 23}$, Mk $8^{32. 33}$, Jn 12^{27}). Our Lord's utterances before the Agony show the very fullest consciousness of His mission, and of how it was to be accomplished.

3. Repentance had no place in the consciousness of Jesus. As Harnack (*What is Christianity?*, p. 32 f.) puts it, ' No stormy crisis, no breach with His past, lies behind the period of Jesus' life that we know. In none of His sayings or discourses . . . can we discover the signs of inner revolutions overcome, or the scars of any terrible conflict. Everything seems to pour from Him naturally, as though it could not do otherwise, like a spring from the depths of the earth, clear and unchecked in its flow.' This is the strongest proof of our Lord's perfect sinlessness. It is incredible that the keenest spiritual insight ever possessed by man should have been blind to its own condition. In confirmation of this the following passages are important: Mt $5^{20ff.}$ 7^{11} $18^{24. 25. 35}$, Mk $9^{42ff.}$, Lk $13^{3. 5}$ 17^{10} etc. show our Lord's sensitiveness to the presence of sin in the hearts of men ; how He recognized its universality in the world, and how high was His standard. Mk 1^{11}, Lk 6^{40}, Jn 4^{34} $8^{29. 46}$, give a direct insight into His consciousness of His own moral condition. Lk 5^8, 1 P 2^{22} 3^{18}, 1 Jn 2^{29} $3^{5. 7}$, 2 Co 5^{21}, He 4^{15} etc. show the impression He produced, in regard to this matter, upon the minds of His disciples. Our Lord's consciousness of union with His Father was not marred by any sin within His own soul.

On the subject of growth, then, our data lead us to the conclusion that there was a real development in the consciousness of Jesus during His youth, but that this development was completed, certainly in all its essential elements, before He began His ministry.

ii. The most perplexing of all the psychological problems opened up by our subject is that which is presented by the endeavour *to distinguish the Divine and human elements in our Lord's consciousness, and to define the mode of their union.* What in general the contents of His Divine consciousness were, so far as they have been revealed to us, we have seen above. But it is extremely hazardous to draw negative conclusions from these positive results, and every attempt at definition of the two elements involves negative as well as positive statements. Psychologically, we are presented with an insoluble problem. There are no facts, and no laws, known to the science of mind which can help us to understand the consciousness of Jesus. That He knew as man knows there can be no question. All the evidence we possess points to mental growth during the years of His youth ; and though, as we have seen, the facts of His history during the period of His ministry do not warrant us in attributing to Him progressive attainments in the knowledge of Divine things, it is clear that ordinary human knowledge came to Him as it comes to us. It is often said of Him, that He 'came to know' ($\gamma\nu\tilde{\omega}\nu\alpha\iota$, Mt 12[15] 22[18] 26[10], Mk 2[8] 8[17], Jn 4[1] 5[6] 6[15] 16[19] ; see Mason, *Conditions of our Lord's Life on Earth*, p. 130 ff.). Again, we are told that He was guided by the evidence of His senses : 'When Jesus saw it, he was moved with indignation' (Mk 10[14]) ; 'He came forth and saw a great multitude, and he had compassion on them' (Mt 14[14]) ; 'When he drew nigh, he saw the city and wept over it' (Lk 19[41]). Such passages are convincing ; and others, which tell of a supernatural knowledge of the thoughts and motives of men or of events (*e.g.* Jn 1[48] 4[18], Mt 21[2], Mk 14[13], etc.), do not weaken their force. But side by side with this human consciousness we find unmistakable evidence of a consciousness which knows the heart of God from within, and which therefore sheds an unparalleled illumination over the whole realm of spiritual things. Jesus could say of Himself, ' No one knoweth the Son save the Father ; neither doth any know the Father save the Son, and he to whomsoever the Son willeth to reveal him.' Such an assertion would be folly or worse were it not justified by the contents of His teaching. But the truth is that what Jesus showed mankind about the Father and His Kingdom, His Love and His holiness, and the revelation which Jesus gave of human life as seen in the light of this Divine manifestation, have ever remained the highest heights of spiritual vision. And, more wonderful still, this revelation has proved itself, as He foretold, inseparable from the Person who gave it. The teaching, Divine though it is, has ever been subordinate to the Teacher. It is always Jesus Christ who reveals the Father. Here then are the two elements, a consciousness of God and of Himself in relation to God different in kind from anything known in our experience, and side by side with it ordinary human knowledge based on the evidence of the senses. Harnack puts the problem thus : 'How He came to this consciousness of the unique character of His relation to God as a Son, how He came to the consciousness of His power, and to the consciousness of the obligation and the mission which this power carries with it, is His secret, and no psychology will ever fathom it' (*What is Christianity?* p. 128).

iii. *Knowledge and ignorance.*—We cannot enter here upon a general discussion of this question. It must suffice to note that our Lord in one instance pointedly confessed ignorance (Mk 13[32]), that He asked questions, evidently to gain information (Mk 5[30] 6[38] 9[21], Jn 11[34]), that He showed surprise (Mt 8[10], Mk 6[6]), that He sought for what He could not find (Mt 21[19], Mk 11[13]), and that there is no

trace in the Gospels of His possessing supernatural knowledge of human and secular things beyond what was necessary for His work. These facts may be connected with the following statements made by our Lord Himself : 'The Son can do nothing of himself, but what he seeth the Father doing' (Jn 5[19]) ; 'I can of myself do nothing ; as I hear, I judge : and my judgment is righteous ; because I seek not mine own will, but the will of him that sent me' (v.[30]) ; 'My teaching is not mine, but his that sent me' (7[16]) ; 'He that sent me is true ; and the things which I heard from him, these speak I unto the world' (8[26]) ; 'I do nothing of myself, but as the Father taught me, I speak these things' (v.[28]) ; 'I speak the things which I have seen with my Father' (v.[38]) ; 'The Father which sent me, he hath given me a commandment, what I should say and what I should speak' ; 'The things therefore which I speak, even as the Father hath said unto me, so I speak' (12[49. 50]) ; 'The words that I say unto you I speak not from myself ; but the Father abiding in me doeth his works. Believe me that I am in the Father and the Father in me' (14[10. 11] ; see also 14[24. 31] 15[15] 17[7. 8]). From these statements it surely follows that our Lord's Divine knowledge was imparted to Him in His communion with His Father. Apart from this means of knowing, He depended simply upon His human faculties. 'This being the case, we must see that, if anything which could not be known naturally was not made known to Him by the Father, it would not be known by Him' (Bishop O'Brien of Ossory, quoted by Canon Mason, *op. cit.* p. 192). The psychology of this communion with the Father, as a means of knowledge, is doubtless beyond us ; but the facts given in all the Gospels agree with the statements of our Lord Himself as recorded by St. John. See, further, AUTHORITY OF CHRIST.

III. THEOLOGICAL RESULTS.—i. The first result is an extraordinary emphasis upon *the uniqueness of our Lord's personality.* In the psychological sphere the consciousness of Jesus Christ is as miraculous as His resurrection is in the physical. There is this difference, however, that His consciousness is a fact which comes in all its freshness before everyone who reads with clear eyes the story of His life. It is the most truly living element in the Gospels, and it is the same in them all. It is a concrete fact, not an abstract doctrine. To attribute its unity and concreteness to the sudden development of a dramatic instinct among certain religiously-minded Jews of the 1st cent., is as impossible as to derive its amazing spiritual elevation from an idealizing tendency among those who believed in God and His promises, and were looking for the Messiah and His Kingdom. Every attempt at explanation of this kind has proved, and must ever prove, a failure. The truth and vividness of the Gospels flow from the reality of the Christ whom they portray, and the consciousness of Jesus is the soul of that reality.

ii. The study of the consciousness of our Lord is *the most convincing proof of His Divinity.* When such passages as Jn 5[17-30] 8[12-58] 10[27-38] 14[1-10] are compared with such as these from the Synoptics—Mt 11[25-30] 25[31-46], Mk 8[34-38] 10[28-30] 12[35-37] 14[7], Lk 9[22-27. 57-62] 10[21-24. 42] 12[8-10] 19[40] 20[13-15]— and both series are discerned to be the inevitable and consistent utterances of the mind of Him who called Himself the Son of God and the Son of Man, the conclusion is irresistible, unless, indeed, preconceived views of the nature of the Universe forbid the inference, that the traditional doctrine of Christianity is the only adequate interpretation of the facts of the life of Jesus.

LITERATURE.—Weiss, *Leben Jesu* ; Wendt, *Lehre Jesu* ; Mason, *Conditions of Our Lord's Life on Earth* ; Gore, *Dissertations* and *Bampton Lectures* ; Liddon, *Divinity of Our Lord* ; Baldensperger, *Das Selbstbewusstsein Jesu* ; Beyschlag, *Leben Jesu* ; Adamson, *Studies of the Mind in Christ* ; Fairbairn, *Place of Christ in Modern Theology* ; Godet, *New Testament Studies* ; Row, *Jesus of the Evangelists* ; Keim, *Jesu von Nazara* ; Harnack, *Das Wesen des Christentums* [Eng. tr. *What is Christianity?*]; Seeley, *Ecce Homo* ; R. Mackintosh, articles on 'The Dawn of the Messianic Consciousness' in *Expos. Times*, 1905.

In some of these, and in many other works which might be named, will be found a great deal of rather free speculation based upon psychological considerations, and often but loosely connected with the statements of the Gospels. The present writer has endeavoured to keep as closely as possible to the historical evidence. On account of the peculiar nature of the problem, he is convinced that psychology affords but little assistance, and he regards even an isolated statement by one of the Evangelists as evidence of higher quality than *a priori* arguments of any description. Yet he has not forgotten the views of modern critics, and has been careful to show, by an array of references to texts, that the principal contents of our Lord's consciousness are witnessed to by all the original authorities.   CHARLES F. D'ARCY.

CONSECRATE, CONSECRATION.—In the AV of NT 'consecrated' occurs twice. In both places the reference is to the work of Christ, but to two different aspects of that work, neither of which is suggested by the rendering 'consecrated.' (1) In He 7²⁸ the word used is τετελειωμένον = RV 'perfected.' Our Lord, as 'a Son perfected for evermore,' is contrasted with human high priests 'having infirmity.' The connexion of thought, obscured in the AV, is with 2¹⁰ 5⁹ etc. The perfection of Him who 'abideth for ever,' and whose priesthood is inviolable, is the result of the human experience of the Divine Son. By His life in the flesh, His lowly obedience, and His sufferings, He has gained that abiding sympathy with men which fits Him to be 'the author of eternal salvation.' (2) In He 10²⁰ the word used is ἐνεκαίνισεν = RV 'dedicated,' lit. 'made new.' Jesus 'dedicated for us a new and living way' into the Holy Place. The thought is that by means of His own blood our High Priest passed into the Divine presence, inaugurating a way for us. Because He passed through our human life, and out of it by the rending of 'the veil, that is to say, his flesh,' He is not only our representative, but also our forerunner ; in full assurance of faith we also may draw near and follow Him into that heavenly sanctuary.

In the RVm 'consecrate' is found three times, viz., Jn 10³⁶ 17¹⁷. ¹⁹. ἁγιάζειν, of which 'consecrate' is an alternative rendering, is usually translated 'sanctify.' The exception in the EV is the first petition of the Lord's Prayer (Mt 6⁹ = Lk 11²)—'Hallowed be thy name.' Here the Rheims version has 'sanctified be thy name'; on the other hand, Wyclif has 'halowe,' 'halowid' in Jn 10³⁶ 17¹⁷. ¹⁹.

The distinction between 'consecrate' and 'sanctify' turns rather upon usage than upon etymology. Both words mean 'to make holy.' But a person or a thing may be made holy in two different ways : (1) By solemn setting apart for holy uses, as when in the LXX ἁγιάζειν designates the consecration of a prophet (Jer 1⁵, cf. Sir 45⁴ 49⁷); (2) by imparting fitness for holy uses, as when St. Paul speaks (Ro 15¹⁶, cf. 1 Th 5²³) of his offering as 'made acceptable' because it has been 'sanctified by the Holy Spirit.' On these lines it now seems possible and desirable to distinguish the two English words which mean 'to make holy.' Ideally, consecration implies sanctification. But in modern English 'consecrate' suggests the thought of setting apart for holy uses, whilst 'sanctify' has come rather to imply making fit for holy uses.

The rendering 'consecrated' better suits the context of Jn 10³⁶ 'Say ye of him, whom the Father consecrated and sent into the world, Thou blasphemest ; because I said, I am Son of God?' Jer 1⁵ supplies a suggestive OT analogy, for the

word of the Lord reminds the young prophet that, in the Divine counsel, he was set apart for holy uses before his birth. The thought would be more appropriately presented by 'consecrated' than by RV 'sanctified' (LXX ἡγίακα). Similarly, as our Lord declares in His argument with the Jews (Jn 10³⁶), the Father consecrated His Son to His redemptive mission before sending Him forth to His work. More is implied in this statement than that the Father 'chose' or 'set apart' His Son. All things were given into His hand (Jn 3³⁵), and amongst the all things were 'life in himself' (Jn 5²⁶), fulness of grace and truth (1¹⁴), and the Spirit 'without measure' (3³⁴). 'The fact belongs to the eternal order. The term expresses the Divine destination of the Lord for His work. This destination carries with it the further thought of the perfect endowment of the Incarnate Son' (Westcott, *Com. in loc.*). It is only in this sense of complete equipment that the Divine Son was made fit for His sacred mission ; the Holy One had no need of sanctification 'in a way of qualification,' as the Puritan divines used the word, when they meant inward cleansing from sin and the Holy Spirit's bestowal of purity of heart.

Our Lord's words, 'I consecrate myself' (Jn 17¹⁹), are best understood in the light of His earlier saying that 'the Father consecrated' Him (Jn 10³⁶). The two statements are complementary. His consecration of Himself was the proof of His perfect acquiescence in the Father's purpose concerning Himself, His disciples, and the world. The secret of His inner life was continually revealed 'in loveliness of perfect deeds' which constrained men to acknowledge the truth of His words, 'I seek not mine own will, but the will of him that sent me' (Jn 5³⁰); the law that ruled His every word and work He was soon to fulfil to the uttermost; His readiness to drink the cup which the Father was about to put into His hands was involved in His calm word, 'I consecrate myself'; its utterance in this solemn hour affords a glimpse of the spirit of absolute devotion to His Father's will in which Jesus is finishing His work and consummating in death the self-sacrifice of His life. And as for the sake of His disciples Jesus consecrates Himself, He prays for them, knowing that the future of His kingdom depends on their having the same spirit of complete consecration to the Divine will.

Commentators who follow Chrysostom in regarding ἁγιάζω as practically equivalent to προσφέρω σοι θυσίαν (cf. Euth. Zig. ἐγὼ ἐκουσίως θυσιάζω ἐμαυτόν), and as connoting the idea of expiatory sacrifice, support their interpretation by references to OT passages in which ἁγιάζειν (=שִׁפְּקָה) is a sacred word for sacrifices, as, *e.g.*, Ex 13², Dt 15¹⁹ff., 2 S 8¹¹ (cf. Meyer, *in loc.*). They are obliged to give the word ἁγιάζειν two different meanings in the same sentence, as does the RVm : 'And for their sakes I consecrate myself, that they themselves also may be sanctified in truth.' But it is not from the word ἁγιάζειν that the nature of Christ's death is to be learnt ; that which differentiates the consecration of Christ from the consecration of His disciples is brought out rather by the other words in this pregnant saying. The consecration of Jesus is His own act, but He does not pray that apart from Him the disciples may follow His example and consecrate themselves ; His consecration is the pattern of theirs, therefore the same word is used of the Master and of His disciples ; but without His consecration 'for their sakes' (ὑπὲρ αὐτῶν), their consecration would be impossible, therefore it is said of the Master alone that He consecrates Himself on behalf of others.

If ἁγιάζειν be uniformly rendered 'consecrate' in our Lord's intercessory prayer, it will be seen that He twice expresses His yearning desire for the consecration of the men whom His Father had given Him out of the world : (1) Jn 17¹⁷ 'Consecrate them in the truth'; as Jesus sends forth His disciples on the same mission which brought Him into the world at His Father's bidding, He asks that they also may be set apart for holy service, and may be divinely equipped for their task, even as He was, by the indwelling of the

Father's love (v.[26]). They possess the knowledge
and the faith that the world lacks, for they have
come to know and to believe that the Father sent
the Son (vv.[8, 25], cf. vv.[21, 23]). It is because Jesus
desires intensely that the world may know and
believe, that He so fervently prays for the consecration of the men whose faith and knowledge
qualify them to speak in the world the word which
He has given them. (2) V.[19] 'And for their sakes
I consecrate myself, that they also may be consecrated in truth.' Reasons for departing from
the rendering of the RV and the RVm have been
given above. No doubt it is important to remember that men 'having infirmity' need by
inward sanctifying to be made fit for the holy
service to which they have been consecrated; but
the emphatic words, 'they also' (καὶ αὐτοί), suggest
not a contrast, but a resemblance,—a consecration
common to the Master and His disciples. It is a
resemblance not in the letter, but in the spirit.
Between their work as witnesses and His as
Redeemer there was a contrast; but their lives
might be ruled by the 'inward thought' (1 P 4[1]
RVm) which constrained Him to suffer for their
sakes. For the disciples of Jesus real consecration
consists in having the mind which was in Him,
who 'humbled himself, becoming obedient even
unto death, yea, the death of the cross' (Ph 2[8]).
It should also be noted that the consecration
spoken of in Jn 17[19] is, alike in the case of Jesus
and of His disciples, 'not a process but an act
completed at once,—in His case, when gathering
together in one view all His labours and sufferings,
He presented them a living sacrifice to His Father;
in theirs, when they are in like manner enabled to
present themselves as living sacrifices in His one
perfect sacrifice' (W. F. Moulton, *Com. in loc.*).
See, further, art. SANCTIFICATION.

J. G. TASKER.

CONSIDERATENESS.—It was a saying of St.
Francis, 'Courtesy is own sister to Love'; but considerateness is more than courtesy (wh. see), for it
takes account not only of our neighbour's feelings, but of all his circumstances and all his
wants. Our Lord 'knew all men, and knew what
was in man' (Jn 2[25]); and in this knowledge we
find Him acting always with the most exquisite
care for all their needs. Their *bodily* needs He
anticipates and provides for, as in the case of the
hungering multitudes (Mt 15[32], Mk 8[1-3], Lk 9[13], Jn
6[5]), where, moreover, He takes care also that
nothing of the store He had provided should be
lost (Jn 6[12]), and in the case of His over-wrought
disciples ('Come ye apart and rest awhile,' Mk 6[31]).
To which may be added His directions regarding
Jairus' daughter, when He had raised her from the
dead ('He commanded that something should be
given her to eat,' Mk 5[43]). Still more beautiful is
Christ's delicate consideration of men's feelings.
Among the many rays of 'his own glory' (Jn 2[11])
manifested forth in His first miracle, we must not
omit His considerateness for the mortification
which the falling short of their wine would cause
to His peasant hosts, and His taking care that
none save His mother and the servants knew
whence the new and better supply was drawn (Jn
2[9]). As instances of His considerateness of men's
spiritual needs, we may cite His giving scope for
the strong faith of the good centurion by *not* going
to his house (Mt 8[5ff.], Lk 7[2ff.]), while by *going
with* Jairus He supports his weak faith, and is
beside him when the stunning message reaches
him, 'Thy daughter is dead: why troublest thou
the Master any further?' (Mk 5[35]); His whole
action in the case of the woman taken in adultery
(Jn 8[1-11]); and His attention to the still deeper
need of the woman with the issue of blood, whose
faith, great as it was, required to be adorned with

gratitude to, and confession of, her healer (Mk
5[29-34]). Extreme pain tends to make men forget
everything except their own suffering: it only
brought out the more the all-embracing considerateness of Christ. His words from the Cross to the
Virgin Mother and St. John (Jn 19[26, 27]) teach, no
doubt, the new relationships created for believers
by the gospel (Mk 10[30], cf. Ro 16[13]; but they exhibit
also His considerate care not needlessly to mention
a relationship which might so easily have exposed
St. Mary to hustling by the mob, or to syllable
names which would have been repeated by irreverent tongues. The post-resurrection sayings to
Mary Magdalene (Jn 20[15, 18]), to St. Thomas (Jn
20[27]), and to St. Peter, who, as he had thrice denied
his Lord, is thrice restored with delicate allusion
to, but not mention of, his threefold fall (Jn 21[15, 17]),
are examples no less shining and illustrative. (Cf.
Bishop Paget's sermon on 'Courtesy' in *Studies in
the Christian Character*, p. 209).

J. COOPER.

CONSOLATION. — **1.** The word 'consolation'
(παράκλησις) occurs only twice in the Gospels (Lk
2[25] 6[24], both AV and RV). παράκλησις, however, is
a word of common occurrence in the rest of the
NT, where in AV it is usually rendered 'consolation,' although not infrequently 'comfort.' In
RV 'comfort' has been substituted for 'consolation' except in Ac 4[36] ('exhortation,' marg. 'consolation') 15[31] ('consolation,'marg. 'exhortation'),
He 6[18] ('encouragement'). Besides meaning consolation or comfort, παράκλησις sometimes denotes
exhortation, and is so rendered both in AV and
RV. When it is said of Simeon that he was
'looking for the consolation of Israel' (Lk 2[25]),
the word is used by metonymy for the Messianic
salvation as bringing consolation to the Chosen
People. Similarly the Messiah Himself was known
to the Rabbins as נחם, 'the Consoler,' or 'Comforter,' of Israel (see Schöttgen, *Hor. Heb. et
Talm.* ii. 18). In Lk 6[24] the rich are said to have
received their consolation, *i.e.* the comfort which
comes from worldly prosperity, in contrast to those
spiritual blessings which Jesus had just promised
that His disciples should enjoy in spite of poverty,
hunger, and tears (vv.[20-23], cf. 2 Co 1[3-5]).

2. *Consolation in the teaching of Christ.*—First of
all, there will ever stand the words : 'Come unto me,
all ye that travail and are heavy laden' (Mt 11[28-30]).
Amid outward storm and inward fear the Lord
greets His disciples : 'Be of good cheer: it is I ; be
not afraid' (Mk 6[50]). The Physician of the ailing
body and sick soul addresses the weary sufferer :
'Son, be of good cheer; thy sins are forgiven' (Mt
9[2]). To us to-day His Holy Spirit breathes the
same blessings in the gospel of mercy and peace,
the Spirit by whom He is with us 'all the days,
even unto the completion of the age' (Mt 28[20]).
His words do not pass away (Mk 13[31]), and from
His Divine lips no word is void of power (Lk 1[37]).
'Peace be unto you' is the first message of the
ascended as of the risen Lord (Jn 20[21, 26]). Still He
loves 'to the uttermost' (Jn 13[1]); still He can bear
to lose not one of those whom His Father has
given Him (Jn 18[9]), and still no enemy shall snatch
them from His hand (Jn 10[28]). Even the hairs of
the head of the children of God are objects of His
watchfulness (Lk 12[7] 21[18]), to number them and to
preserve them. So, truly, His service should be
without fear (Lk 1[74]). Amid the storms of this
changeful life we cry : 'Carest thou not that we
perish?' (Mk 4[38]),—and nevertheless the very purpose of His mission was and is that we should have
life, and have it more abundantly (Jn 10[10]). There
is no uncertainty on His part,—eternal life is the
settled purpose of God for man (Jn 6[40]). The grace
He bestows is in its nature prolific, and its fruit is
eternal life (Jn 4[14, 36]). He *gives* the Kingdom of

God (Lk 12³²). His message is a *gospel* (Mt 4²³). His ears are never closed to our cry (Mt 21²²). All things are possible with Him (Mk 10²⁷).

To these higher thoughts may be added precious truths which have a like consoling power in the conflict with evil ever surging within and without. Our Lord knows our human nature through and through (Jn 2²⁵). His purpose is to avert judgment and not to condemn whilst there is time for salvation (12⁴⁷). His condemnations were against hypocrisy and hardness of heart and contempt of His gospel. He came bearing our infirmities and saving us from our sins (Mt 1²¹ 8¹⁷, Lk 19¹⁰). What is done to the poor, sick, bereaved, afflicted, is done to Him; and He will remember (Mt 25⁴⁰). His blessing abides with the poor, meek, sincere soul, faithful to the end (Mt 5³⁻¹² 10²²). In this life the disciple must be content to expect little of worldly success, and yet he shall not be unconsoled (Mt 10²⁵, Mk 10³⁰, Jn 16³³). To His disciple Christ promises: 'I will love thee' (Jn 14²¹). See also art. COMFORT.

LITERATURE.—Hastings' *DB*, artt. 'Paraclete,' 'Comfort.' Grimm-Thayer, *Lex. s.v.* παράκλησις.

W. B. FRANKLAND.

CORBAN is a Hebrew word (קָרְבָּן) which appears in the Greek of Mk 7¹¹, transliterated κορβᾶν or κορβάν, and in this form passes into the English Versions. The same word in a modified form occurs also in Mt 27⁶, εἰς τὸν κορβανᾶν, 'into the treasury.' The termination -*as* in κορβανᾶς is the Greek method of indicating the Aramaic determinative in קָרְבָּנָא. Codex B reads κορβᾶν for κορβανᾶν.

The word has three meanings: (1) An offering, both bloodless and otherwise. In this sense it occurs about 80 times in OT, always in Leviticus and Numbers, except twice in Ezekiel. In EV it is rendered 'offering' or 'oblation,' but in LXX it is rendered by δῶρον, 'a gift,' and this is the tr. given to κορβᾶν in Mk 7¹¹. (2) A vow-offering, something dedicated to God. In this sense it occurs in the Heb. and Aram. portions of the Talmud, and also in Josephus. In his *Antiquities*, IV. iv. 4, Josephus says of the Nazirites: 'They dedicate themselves to God as a *corban*, which in the language of the Greeks denotes "a gift."' So also in *c. Apion.* i. 22, he speaks of *corban* as a 'kind of oath, found only among Jews, which denotes "a thing devoted to God."' (3) The sacred treasury into which the gifts for the Temple service were cast by the pious; or, the treasure therein deposited. Thus, in *BJ*, II. ix. 4, Josephus says that Herod 'caused a disturbance by spending the sacred treasure, which is called *corban*, upon aqueducts.' So in Mt 27⁶ the high priests say to one another: 'It is not lawful to cast them (Judas' silver pieces) into the treasury (εἰς τὸν κορβανᾶν, B* κορβᾶν), for it is the price of blood.'

The passage in which *corban* occurs in our English Bible is Mk 7¹¹. Our Lord is there replying to the criticism of the Pharisees that the disciples ate food with hands ceremonially unclean. Christ's reply is a retort. He accuses the Pharisees of attaching too much value to the tradition of the elders, so as even in some cases to set aside in their favour the plain moral commandments of God. The words of Jesus are: 'Is it well for you to set aside the commandment of God, in order that ye may observe your tradition? For Moses said, Honour thy father and thy mother; and, He that speaketh evil of father or mother, let him die the death. But *ye* say, If a man has said to his father or mother, That wherewith thou mightest have been benefited from me is *corban*, that is, a gift, [he is absolved]. Ye no longer allow him to do anything for his father or mother.' The same incident is recorded, with slight variations, in Mt 15³⁻⁵.

Commentators are divided as to whether the

dedication was meant seriously, and the property actually given to God and put into the treasury; or whether the utterance of the word was a mere evasion, and when the magic word *corban* had been uttered over any possession, the unfilial son was able to 'square' matters with the Rabbis, so as to be free from obligation to support his aged parents (Bruce on Mt 15⁵). It must be admitted that the Jews were much addicted to making rash vows. One tractate in the Talmud, *Nedarim*, is specially devoted to the subject. We there find that the customary formula among the Jews for devoting anything to God was, 'Let it be *corban*'; though, to allow a loophole of possible escape from the vow if they regretted it afterwards, they were in the habit of using other words which sounded like *corban*. *Nedarim*, i. 2, says: 'When any one says "ḳonâm, or ḳonâḥ, or ḳonâṣ (be this object, or this food)," these are by-names for *ḳorbân*.' These words came to be used as a mere formula of interdiction, without any intention of making the thing interdicted 'a gift to God'; *e.g.*, a man seeing his house on fire, says, 'My tallith shall be *corban* if it is not burnt' (*Ned.* iii. 6). In making a vow of abstinence a man says: '*Ḳonâṣ* be the food (vi. 1) or the wine (viii. 1) which I taste.' When a man resolves not to plough a field, he says, '*Ḳonâṣ* be the field, if I plough it' (iv. 7), Repudiation of a wife is thus expressed, 'What my wife might be benefited by me is *ḳonâṣ* (קוֹנָם אִשָּׁתִי נֶהֱנֵת לִי), because she has stolen my cup' or 'struck my son' (iii. 2). In viii. 11 we have the very same formula as in Mk 7¹¹, except that we have the subterfuge or substitute, קוֹנָם for קָרְבָּן לִי נֶהֱנֶה שָׁאַתְּ קוֹנָם (Lowe's *Mishnâ*, p. 88).

It is not necessary to think that Jesus had such cases of recklessness in His mind. We prefer to believe that He was thinking of *bonâ fide* vows, made to the Temple, hastily, perhaps angrily, without sufficient regard to the claims of aged parents. The question was a very intricate one, What ought the Rabbis to advise the man to do? The Law was most emphatic in its insistence that all vows, when once made, must be kept (Dt 23²¹⁻²³). Which has the higher claim on a man's conscience? The service of God, promoted by the gift, and the Law obeyed by keeping the vow inviolate? or, the support of poor aged parents, the Law broken and the vow violated? It was a delicate matter, and we can scarcely wonder that the Rabbis of Christ's day adhered to the literal significance of Dt 23²¹⁻²³, and held that nothing could justify the retractation of a vow. In other words, they allowed the literal and the ceremonial to override the ethical. Jesus disclosed a different 'spirit,' as He ruled that duty to parents is a higher obligation than upholding religious worship, or than observance of a vow rashly or thoughtlessly made.

In *Nedarim*, ix. 1, we find Eliezer ben Hyrkanos (*c.* A.D. 90), who in many respects felt the influence of Christianity, give the same view as the Lord Jesus with regard to rash vows. We translate the passage thus—

'R. Eliezer said that when rash vows infringe at all on parental obligations, Rabbis should suggest a retractation (*lit.* open a door) by appealing to the honour due to parents. The sages dissented. R. Zadok said, instead of appealing to the honour due to parents, let them appeal to the honour due to God; then might rash vows cease to be made. The sages at length agreed with R. Eliezer that if the case be directly between a man and his parents [as in Mk 7¹¹], they might suggest retractation by appealing to the honour due to parents.'

The words of R. Meîr (*c.* A.D. 150) are also interesting in this connexion as given in *Nedarim*, ix. 4—

'One may effect a retractation of a rash vow by quoting what is written in the Law. One may say to him: If thou hadst known that thou wast transgressing such commandments as these, "Thou shalt not take vengeance nor bear a grudge";

"Thou shalt not hate thy brother in thy heart"; "Thou shalt love thy neighbour as thyself" [Lv 19¹⁷ᶠ·]; "Thy brother shall live with thee" [Lv 25³⁶],—wouldst thou have made the vow? Perhaps thy brother may become poor, and thou (because of thy rash vow) wilt not be able to support him. If he shall say, If I had known that it was so, I would not have made the vow,— he may be released from his vow.'

These quotations show that, in some directions, the spirit of humaneness was triumphing over the literalism which Jesus combated in His day.

LITERATURE. — The Mishnic treatise, *Nedarim*; artt. on 'Corban' in Hastings' *DB, Encyc. Bibl.*, and *Jewish Encyc.*; Edersheim, *Life and Times of Jesus*, ii. 17 ff. ; the Commentaries of Wetstein, Grotius, and Bruce on Mt 15⁵ and Mk 7¹¹; Lightfoot's *Hor. Heb.*, and Wünsche's *Erläuterung, in loco.*

J. T. MARSHALL.

CORN.—In AV of the Gospels 'corn' is used to translate four distinct words in the original :

(1) σπόριμα : 'Jesus went on the Sabbath day through the *corn*' (Mt 12¹). Here 'corn' should be 'cornfields,' the rendering of RV in this verse, and of both AV and RV in the parallel passages in Mk. (2²³) and Lk. (6¹). σπόριμα properly means *seed land* (σπείρω), and in classical Greek is not found in its NT sense of 'cornfields.'

(2) σῖτος, in Mk 4²⁸, where a contrast is drawn between the different stages in the growth of the cornstalk—'first the blade, then the ear, after that the full *corn* in the ear.' In LXX, as in classical Greek, σῖτος is a generic word for cereals, but refers especially to wheat as the staple grain food. Corresponding to this, we find that elsewhere in the NT, both in AV and RV, the word is always translated 'wheat' (Mt 3¹² 13²⁵· ²⁹· ³⁰, Lk 3¹⁷ 16⁷ 22³¹, Jn 12²⁴).

(3) στάχυς = 'an ear of *corn*' (Mt 12¹ ‖ Mk 4²⁸). So in LXX as an equivalent for שׁבֹּלֶת in Gn 41⁵ etc.

(4) κόκκος = a single grain or 'corn.' It is rendered 'corn' only in Jn 12²⁴ (AV): 'Except a *corn* of wheat [ὁ κόκκος τοῦ σίτου] fall into the ground and die . . .' (cf. the use of the words 'peppercorn,' 'barleycorn'). Elsewhere in AV (Mt 13³¹ ‖ 17²⁰ ‖), as always in RV, it is rendered 'a grain.'

'Corn' is thus used in AV in four distinguishable senses—as applying to a cornfield, to a ripe cornstalk, to an ear of wheat, and to a single grain. And it is noteworthy in each case how intimately the Gospel references to corn are associated with our Lord's revelation of the mysteries of the Kingdom and the truth regarding His own person and saving work. The parable of the Blade, the Ear, and the Full Corn was used to unfold the law of growth in the Kingdom of God. The incident of the plucking of the ears of corn in the cornfields on the Sabbath day served as the occasion for a notable declaration regarding both the dignity of the Son of Man and the graciousness of Him who loves mercy more than sacrifice. The death and fruitful resurrection of the grain of wheat became the prophecy and type of Christ's Passion and consequent power to draw all men unto Himself. And these lessons from the corn in the records of the Lord's ministry may be greatly extended as we recall what He said about the sowing of the corn (parable of the Sower) and its reaping (the Tares and the Wheat); how He saw in the white fields a vision of a great spiritual harvest only waiting to be gathered (Jn 4³⁵); how at Capernaum He turned the people's minds from the barley bread of the previous day's miracle to think of Himself as the Bread of Life (Jn 6); and said of the broken loaf at the Last Supper, 'Take, eat, this is my body.'

For further information the reader is referred to AGRICULTURE, BARLEY, SOWING, etc.

LITERATURE.—Candolle, *Origine des Plantes Cultivées*; Löw, *Aramäische Pflanzennamen*; Tristram, *Natural History of the Bible*; see also Bruder's *Concord. NT Græci*; Grimm-Thayer's *Lex. s.vv.*

J. C. LAMBERT.

CORNER-STONE (פִּנָּה רֹאשׁ, κεφαλὴ γωνίας).—The quotation from Ps 118²² occurs at the close of the

parable of the Wicked Vinedressers (Mt 21⁴², Mk 12¹⁰, Lk 20¹⁷). A question was asked about the punishment of such unfaithful servants and the transferring of the vineyard to the charge of others; and the quotation afforded Scripture proof that the necessity for such a transference, however surprising to those rejected, may actually arise in God's administration of His kingdom.

1. *Literal meaning of corner-stone.* — The term 'stone of the corner' is applied in Palestine not only to the stones at the extreme corners of a building, but to the stone inserted in any part of the outer wall to form the beginning of an interior room-wall at right angles to it. It applies especially, however, to the stone that is ἀκρογωνιαῖος, belonging to an extreme corner of the building. In the construction of a large edifice, the foundations are generally laid and brought up to the surface of the ground, and are then left for several months exposed to the rain, so that the surrounding earth may settle down as close as possible to the wall. When the first row of stones above the ground line is to be laid, the masons place a long, well-squared block of stone at the corner to be a sure rest for the terminus of the two walls. It is the most important corner-stone (Eph 2²⁰).

2. *Selection and treatment of the corner-stone.*— It is always carefully chosen, and is specially treated in view of the service expected of it. (*a*) It must be sound, in the case of sandstone being free from weakening cavities, and in the case of limestone being without any white streaks of spar that under pressure and strain might lead to cleavage.—(*b*) It must be carefully dressed so as to be quite a rectangular block, whereas the ordinary stones usually slope away at the back, and the empty spaces are filled in with stone chips and plaster. It is expected to be in close and solid contact with whatever is under it and above it.— (*c*) In preparing a place for it, the mason gives it a more liberal allowance of mortar so as to increase the power of adhesion. These qualifications are summarized in Is 28¹⁶. Thus the corner-stone is expected to be strong and sound in itself, and able to control the tier that belongs to it, and check any tendency to bulge either outwards or inwards.

The thought of Mt 21⁴⁴ and Lk 20¹⁸ passes beyond the idea of a corner-stone, which is required to remain in its place, and neither falls on any one nor is fallen upon. The transition is so abrupt that some have been inclined to attach importance to the fact that the addition is omitted in Mk 12¹·¹², and that certain ancient authorities (*e.g.* D 33) omit it even in St. Matthew. It is a similar conception that appears in 1 Co 1²³, 1 P 2⁶· ⁷, namely, that of a stumbling-block on the public highway. The 'way of life' was a familiar religious term, 'the Way' being a descriptive epithet which Christ applied to Himself (Jn 14⁶), and one of the first designations of the Christian Church (Ac 9²). The same situation of conflict is presented in Is 8¹⁴, where the fear of the Lord would be to some a sanctuary, a place of safety and rest by the way, but to others a stone of stumbling and a rock of offence. Those who marked out to their own liking the moral highway of the nation had obscured the truth that Israel existed for God, not God for Israel, and left no space for the sufferings of Christ. It was an error of blindness like that of the house-builders concerning the rejected corner-stone. They should have made allowance for the immovable object of bed-rock truth that had the right of priority. In the Syrian town of Beyrout one of the carriage roads has at one point a third of its width occupied by an ancient saint-shrine, with its small rough room and dome. It is a useless and inconvenient obstacle to the traffic, but any petition to have it removed would be

frowned down as an act of irreverence and infidelity. The shrine was there before the road.

3. *Oriental respect for the builders.*—In connexion
with the rejection of a particular stone, it has to
be remembered that the ancients had no explosive
by means of which to lighten their labours. The
work had to be done by hammer, chisel, and saw,
though they knew how to insert wooden wedges
in prepared sockets in the line of desired cleavage,
and make them expand by soaking with water.
They would naturally pass by a stone that required
a great deal of work and yielded only ordinary
results. They carried this principle to the length
of often taking prepared stones from one building
for the erection of another at a considerable distance, as when the carved stones of the Ephesian
temple of Diana were taken to build the church
of St. Sofia in Constantinople, and the ruined
edifices of Roman Cæsarea supplied the material
for the city wall of Acre. It would, however,
sometimes happen that a stone discarded by certain builders would be recognized by a wiser master
as that which he needed for an important place in
his building, and this gave rise to the proverbial
saying quoted in Ps 118^{22}, which is familiarly repeated and applied to-day in Syria.

The epigrammatic value of the saying is enhanced by the fact that in the East the master-
knowledge of the different trades has always been
carefully guarded, and a sharp distinction is drawn
between the man who thinks and plans and the
man who by his elementary manual labour merely
carries out the orders of another. In the art of
building, a familiar proverb says, ‘ One stroke from
the master, even though it be behind his back, is
better than the hammering of a thousand others.’
In explanation of this the story is told of a Lebanon
prince who engaged a master-mason to build à large
bridge of one arch over the river Adônis, and
agreed to defray all costs and give the master a
certain sum when the work was done. When the
bridge was constructed, and nothing remained but
to remove the scaffolding, the master claimed his
remuneration ; and as the prince argued for a reduction of the sum, the master declined to remove
the scaffolding. Other men were engaged to do
this, but they found it to be such a complicated
and dangerous task that they abandoned it, and
the original builder had to be called in on his own
terms. He stepped forward, and, standing with
his back to the network of supporting beams, gave
a single tap with his hammer to a particular wedge.
Its removal liberated the supports, and as he
hurriedly sprang back, the scaffolding collapsed,
and left the empty arch of the completed bridge.
He alone knew how to do it. Similar proverbs are
current with regard to the baker, tailor, carpenter,
blacksmith, teacher, doctor, and almost every form
of technical industry and specialized profession.
The master in his trade occupies a position of
respect similar to that of the father in the family
and the sheikh in the tribe. In no department is
this submission more thoroughgoing than in the
deference shown to the Rabbis and priests as the
trained masters of religious observance and ecclesiastical duty. In consequence of this the people
of the country find a keen though guarded enjoyment in any situation that seems to discredit the
wisdom of the wise.

4. *Figurative applications of the corner-stone.*—
In Jg 20^2 and 1 S 14^{38} the word *pinnôth* (‘corner-
stones’) is translated ‘ the chiefs’ of the people,
as being those whose opinions and actions gave
stability and direction to others. In Is 19^{13} it is
stated that the error of Egypt was through her
trust in the princes of Zoan and Noph, who were
the corner-stones of her tribes. In the East, the
mason in laying a row of stones begins with the

corner-stone, and some twelve feet farther down,
or at the other terminus of the wall, if it be short,
another stone of the same height is laid with lime,
and then the mason’s measuring-line is stretched
tightly over the outer top-corner of each. This
gives the line of frontage and elevation to all the
stones that fill in the space between them. Zoan
and Noph, the corner-stones, being themselves in
a false position, affected all between that took
measure from them. In Zeph 1^{16} 3^6 the same
word is translated ‘ towers,’ as the corners of the
wall were especially fortified ; and in 2 Ch 26^{15}
‘ bulwarks’ (RV in all three passages ‘ battlements ’). In Job 38^6 the act of laying the foundation corner-stone of a house is made to describe
that of the creation of the world. In Jer 51^{26} the
inability of Babylon to furnish any more a corner-
stone is made to figure its perpetual desolation. In
Zec 10^4, in the prophecy of the pre-eminence of
Judah, the corner-stone is a conspicuous emblem,
along with the tent-peg and the bow, as signifying
that that tribe was to excel in the peaceful industries of the city and the field, and in the art of
war.

Such were the meanings of the rejected corner-
stone that in their Messianic application were
hidden from those who crucified the Lord of glory
(1 Co 2^8), but were revealed to the Gentiles, the
‘ other husbandmen,’ when the word of acceptance
and service came to them (Eph 2$^{19-22}$).

It is a tragical error to suppose that the message
of the rejected corner-stone was exhausted in the
forfeiture and fate of Israel. The city of God is
still being built, and blindness with regard to the
corner-stone, the mystical presence and the missionary command of Christ, may again expose the
builders to scorn, and necessitate another transference of the service.

LITERATURE.—Hastings’ *DB*, art. ‘ Corner-stone ’; *Expositor*,
5th ser. ix. [1899] p. 35 ff. ; *Expos. Times*, vii. 372, xiv. 384 ;
Jonathan Edwards, *Works* [1840], ii. p. 61 ff. ; Maclaren, *Sermons
Preached in Manchester*, 1st ser. p. 1 ff.

G. M. MACKIE.

COSAM.—A name occurring in the Lukan genealogy of our Lord (Lk 3^{28}).

COSMOPOLITANISM.—That the Jews were of all
nations the most exclusive, was familiar to classic
writers (cf. Juv. *Sat.* xiv. 103 ‘ non monstrare vias
eadem nisi sacra colenti,’ and Mayor’s references
ad loc.) ; though both political and social conditions
in the 1st cent. had made cosmopolitanism more
possible than it had ever been before (cf. Juv. *ib.*
iii. 62 ‘ in Tiberim Syrius defluxit Orontes ’). Under
the Roman emperors the world was becoming more
and more one great State ; St. Paul’s Roman citizenship stood him in good stead in Philippi as in Jerusalem (Ac 16^{21} 22^{25}). Even in Palestine there were
distinctly cosmopolitan elements, as was inevitable
in the case of a country lying across the great
trade routes of the world. Decapolis was almost
entirely Greek ; in Galilee there had for long been
a large Gentile population ; and foreigners as well
as proselytes from all parts of the empire found
their way to Jerusalem (Ac 2^7 ; see Schürer, *HJP*,
Index, *s.* ‘ Hellenism ’ ; and Merrill, *Galilee in the
Time of Christ*). The presence of foreigners, however, is seldom mentioned in the Gospels, save for
a few references to centurions (Mt 8^5, Lk 7^2 23^{47}),
strangers from Tyre and Sidon (Mk 3^8), a short journey to Decapolis (Mk 7^{31}, where, strangely enough,
the Aramaic word ‘ Ephphatha ’ finds special place
in the text), and the notice of the Greeks who
sought for Jesus at the feast—though no account of
His interview with them is given (Jn 12^{20}). Traces
of a cosmopolitan atmosphere may be detected in
Mk 15^{21} (‘ Simon, father of Alexander and Rufus ’),
in the Greek names of two of the disciples (Andrew

and Philip), and the trilingual 'title' on the cross (Jn 19[20]).

Jewish exclusiveness was apparently endorsed by Christ Himself (Mt 5[47] (RV) 6[7. 32]); the Twelve are forbidden to go into any way of the Gentiles (Mt 10[5]); and the Syrophœnician woman is at first addressed in thoroughly Jewish language (Mt 15[21], Mk 7[24]). On the other hand, our Lord speaks the parable of the Good Samaritan (Lk 10[30ff.]); commends the faith of a Roman centurion as greater than any faith He had found in Israel (Mt 8[10], Lk 7[9]); and, notwithstanding His first words to the Syrophœnician woman, recognizes and rewards the greatness of her faith (Mt 15[21ff.], Mk 7[24ff.]). Simeon welcomes the infant Messiah as a light to lighten the Gentiles (Lk 2[32]), in spite of the markedly Jewish tone of Lk 1 and 2. St. Matthew is the narrator of the visit of Wise Men from the East (Mt 2[1]); and if he traces the genealogy of Christ to Abraham (Mt 1[2]), St. Luke takes it back to Adam and God (Lk 3[38]).

It is true that the Gospels are full of protests against Jewish exclusiveness (Mt 3[9] 'Think not to say within yourselves, We have Abraham to our father'; cf. Jn 8[37ff.], where the claim founded on descent from Abraham is contemptuously dismissed; also Mt 12[41f.], Lk 11[31f.] 'the men of Nineveh . . . the queen of Sheba shall rise up in the judgment with this generation and shall condemn it'; Mt 8[11f.], Lk 13[29] 'many shall come from the east and the west . . . but the sons of the kingdom shall be cast forth'; and Mt 11[21], Lk 10[13], where the unrepentant Bethsaida and Chorazin are contrasted with Tyre and Sidon). So far as this break with the Jews shows itself, it rests on (a) enthusiasm for humanity; cf. esp. the references to publicans and sinners, Mt 9[11] 11[19], Mk 2[15], Lk 5[30] 7[37] 15[1], and the fragment in Jn 7[53]–8[11]; (b) the universalism of the gospel, Mt 24[14], Mk 14[9] ('what she hath done shall be preached in all the world'), Mt 28[19], Mk 16[15], Lk 24[49] ('make disciples of all the nations'); so Jn 3[16] 12[33] ('I, if I be lifted up, will draw all men unto myself'); the same thing would result from Mt 20[28], Mk 10[45] ('to give his life a ransom for many'), if carried out to its logical conclusion; (c) antilegalism in regard to the Sabbath (Mt 12[1], Mk 2[23], Lk 6[1] 13[14]), ceremonial ablutions (Mt 15[1], Mk 7[19]), the provisions of the Law (Mt 5[21. 33. 38. 43]), and the inadequacy of the righteousness of the scribes and Pharisees (Mt 5[20]). It is noteworthy that the ground of marriage fidelity is carried back from Moses to the Creation (Mt 19[4], Mk 10[6]), and the Sadducees are referred, on the subject of the resurrection, to God's language to the pre-Mosaic patriarchs (Mk 12[18], Lk 20[37]); still Christ regards as final a combination of Dt 6[4] and Lv 19[18] (Mk 12[28ff.]), and He asserts that His purpose is not to destroy the Law but to fulfil it (Mt 5[17], cf. Mt 3[15]).

The real nature of Christ's teaching cannot be understood apart from the deductions from it in the Acts, where the recognition of the cosmopolitanism of the gospel is forced on the Apostles almost against their will (Ac 8[26] 10[11. 34] 11[20]), and even opposed by a powerful party in the Church when explicitly stated by St. Paul (Ac 15[5]); but it reaches its full statement in Ro 10[12], Gal 3[28], Col 3[11] ('neither Jew nor Greek, bond nor free'), and Ph 3[20] ('our citizenship is in heaven'). (Cf. J. R. Seeley, *Ecce Homo*, ch. xii. 'The Universality of the Christian Republic'). It will thus be seen that the recognition of cosmopolitanism in the sense of a universal mission of Christianity is, in the Synoptic Gospels, only slight (cf. Harnack, *Expansion of Christianity*, Eng. tr. vol. i. pp. 40–48, especially the statement that, omitting what is probably unauthentic, 'Mark and Matthew have almost consistently withstood the temptation to introduce the Gentile mission into the words and deeds of Jesus,' p. 40). St. Luke differs from them in a slight colouring of expression rather than in the narration of fresh facts. St. John had both watched and taken part in the expansion; but the universalism of the Fourth Gospel is chiefly confined to the striking use of the expression 'the world' (see above and 4[42] 6[51] 12[47] 17[23] etc.), which silently bears out the view—to a Christian, abundantly confirmed after 70 A.D.—that the Jews were a reprobate people. From the rejection of one race followed the acceptance of all (Ro 11[11. 12]). See also articles EXCLUSIVENESS, GRECIANS, and UNIVERSALISM.   W. F. LOFTHOUSE.

COUCH.—The word 'couch' is found in Lk 5[19. 24] (as tr. of κλινίδιον), where Mt 9[2. 6] and Mk 2[4. 11] have 'bed' (κλίνη and κράβαττος respectively; κλίνη also in Lk 5[18]). It is found also in RVm of Mk 7[4] as tr. of κλίνη. In Ac 5[15], where the AV and RV have 'beds and couches,' the correct text is ἐπὶ κλιναρίων καὶ κραβάττων, 'small beds and couches,' or, as some render, 'small couches and beds.' The fact is, the terms used for 'couch' and 'bed' are not always sharply distinguished—certainly not by translators. The distinction made by Bengel and Kuinoel between κλινῶν (TR of Ac 5[15]) and κραβάττων, that the former denotes 'soft and costly,' and the latter 'poor and humble,' beds is quite arbitrary (Meyer). In English usage the distinction between 'bed' and 'couch' is clear enough; a couch is a piece of furniture on which it is customary to repose or recline when dressed. A like distinction was made by the Romans, and in a measure by the Jews in the time of Christ, when 'couches' were often used for the purpose of reclining at meals. They were known among the Romans as *triclinia*, because they ran round *three* sides of a table. Such 'couches' were undoubtedly in common use among the Jews of Christ's day, though they are not mentioned in the Gospels in express terms, unless, against the best authorities, we accept καὶ κλινῶν in Mk 7[4]. They were provided with cushions, such as are now in vogue, on which the left elbow could rest, so as to leave the right arm free; and were often arranged around three sides of a table in the form of a parallelogram, the fourth side of which was left open for the convenience of those waiting on the guests.

This practice of reclining at table first appears in the Bible in the prophecy of Amos (6[4], cf. Ezk 23[41]), and is denounced by the prophet as of foreign origin and as savouring of sinful luxury. The 'couches' there coming into view were of costly cedar-wood inlaid with ivory (6[4]); the feet were plated with silver, and the backs covered with gold-leaf (cf. Ca 3[10]). They were usually furnished with pillows and bolsters, often of fine Egyptian linen or silk, and richly embroidered coverings, costly rugs, etc. (cf. Pr 7[16]). The Tel el-Amarna tablets show how early such luxury prevailed in Palestine, and state that even in those ancient times couches of rare and costly wood inlaid with gold were sent as presents from Palestine to Egypt.

Keeping this in mind will throw light on some otherwise obscure passages in the Gospels, *e.g.* where the woman is spoken of (Lk 7[36-38]) as washing and anointing the feet of Jesus while He was 'sitting (reclining) at meat in the Pharisee's house'; where our Lord washed the feet of His disciples while they were at supper (Jn 13[5]); and where it is said of the beloved disciple at the supper that he, 'leaning back, as he was, on Jesus' breast,' spoke to Him of His betrayer (v.[25]).

There is reason to believe, however, that among the Jewish people in general, in the most ancient times and later, the 'bed,' so far as use went, was 'bed' and 'couch' in one—a plain wooden frame with feet and a slightly raised end for the head (Gn 47[31]), differing very little, indeed, from the bed of the Egyptians represented on the monuments (Wilkinson, *Anc. Eg.* i. 416, fig. 191). In the daytime and at meals people sat on it, in the most ancient times, perhaps, with crossed legs; and then at night they placed it here or there, as the season or need suggested, and slept on it. In the East to-day the beds are often made by laying bolsters on the raised part of the floor, or on the low divans which run along the walls, and the sitting-room of the day becomes a bedroom at night. (See BED, CLOSET).   GEO. B. EAGER.

COUNCIL, COUNCILLOR.—See SANHEDRIN.

COUNSELS OF PERFECTION.—See PERFECTION (human).

COUNTENANCE.—See FACE.

COURAGE.—ἀνδρίζομαι, the Gr. equivalent for Heb. חָזַק and אָמֵץ, is not found in the Gospels, and, except in 1 Co 16¹³, not in the NT. The valour of the battlefield, so often commended in the OT, nowhere comes into view. Christ's kingdom is not of this world. It does not call for the prowess of the warrior. But there was no taint of cowardice in Jesus, and to be His disciple did not involve any slackening of moral fibre, or impairing of true manliness. He foresaw a situation bristling with menace to His followers, and courage was therefore a prime desideratum in His disciples, as it was an outstanding quality of His own nature. With unsparing hand He lifted the curtain of the future, and disclosed to all who would follow Him the hostility and peril which discipleship must involve (Mt 5¹¹ 10¹⁶⁻³⁹ 24⁹ᶠᶠ·, Mk 13⁹⁻¹³, Lk 21¹²ᶠᶠ·, Jn 15²⁰ 16²). He who would follow Christ must not be faint-hearted or double-minded (Lk 9⁶²), he must be prepared to surrender many interests that were formerly dear to him, brace himself even to the renunciation of the closest earthly relationships, and, recognizing that the disciple is not greater than his Master, be ready to tread the same rough path, and bear the same cross. The demand for courage is all the more severe that it is not the courage of resisting, but of enduring wrong. The disciple of Jesus is called to meekness, to the patient endurance of suffering wrongfully inflicted, to the heroism of a calm and trustful heart. But the meek temper is not the sign of weakness. It is restrained strength. It is the high courage of endurance, in the spirit and for the sake of Christ. It is of this sustained heroism that Jesus says, 'In your patience (ὑπομονή, 'patient endurance') ye shall win your souls' (Lk 21¹⁹), 'He that endureth to the end shall be saved' (Mt 10²² 24¹³) ; and those who, in spite of pain and persecution, confess Him before men, He declares He will confess before His Father and the holy angels (Lk 12⁸, cf. Mt 10³²). Of this high moral courage Jesus Himself is the supreme example. The emphasis which is so rightly laid upon His gentleness and compassion tends to obscure His strength and virility. But the remark in Ac 4¹³ 'When they saw the boldness of Peter and John . . . they took knowledge of them that they had been with Jesus,' is the record of the dominant impression made by Jesus upon His enemies. The depth and warmth of His sympathy had not deluded them into the thought that He was deficient in courage. They bore witness to His fearlessness and fidelity to truth (Jn 7²⁶, Mt 22¹⁶). His fearless exposure of hypocrisy (Mt 15¹⁻¹⁴, Mk 7¹⁻¹³, Mt 23¹⁻³⁹ et al.), His disregard of, or opposition to, religious practices which had been invested with the sanctity of Divine law, and the performance of which was the hall-mark of righteousness (Mt 9¹⁴ 12¹·⁹, Mk 2¹⁸⁻³³ 7¹, Lk 5³³ 6¹⁻⁶), His defiance of social and religious caste in receiving sinners and eating with them were the moral utterances of a courageous righteousness and love (Mt 9¹⁰, Lk 15²). In circumstances of danger He is calm and self-possessed (Mt 8²⁶). He does not rush into danger, and more than once retires from scenes where His life is threatened (Lk 4³⁰, Jn 8⁵⁹ 10³⁹). At those times He felt that His hour had not come. His courage was inspired by faith in God (Mt 8²⁶), and was controlled by obedience to the Divine will. When He knows that His hour has come, He presses to the cross with an eagerness which made those who saw Him afraid (Mk 10³²). But it is only as we enter into the consciousness of Jesus and see Him in His perfect purity of soul taking upon Him the sin of the world, that we feel the wonder of His heroism. We do not marvel that He shrank from the cup His Father gave Him to drink. We are amazed equally at the love and at the courage which bore Him through until He said, 'It is finished' (Jn 19³⁰). See, further, FEAR.

LITERATURE.—Hastings' *DB*, art. 'Courage' ; Aristotle, *Ethics*, iii. 6–9 ; Denney, *Gospel Questions and Answers*, p. 85 ff.

JOSEPH MUIR.

COURSE.—See ABIJAH, and PRIEST.

COURT (αὐλή, tr. 'court' in Rev 11², 'sheepfold' or 'fold' in Jn 10¹·¹⁶, and 'palace' [RV 'court'] in Mt 26³· ⁶⁹ etc.).*—The 'court' is an essential part of the typical Oriental house. The Eastern house represented on the monuments of Egypt and Assyria is much like that now found, and doubtless found in the time of Christ, in Palestine. It is built around an open square called 'the court,' into which each room opens, seldom one room into another. Sometimes the house has more than one 'court,' if the wealth or the official station of the owner warrants it.

In the richer private and public houses the 'court' is fitted up with great magnificence. In Damascus we find several courts connected with a single house, in some cases of rare richness and beauty. The houses of two or more storeys have chambers on each floor opening on to a common balcony running round the inside of the court, with a staircase in a corner of the court open to the sky. This type of 'court' is usually paved with marble or flagging, and has a well or fountain in the centre (2 S 17¹⁸), with orange and lemon trees and other shrubs around it. Some of them are planted with choice tropical trees, and the walls, verandahs, staircases, etc., are covered and adorned with creepers and vines of untold varieties.

In Mt 26⁶⁹ it is said that 'Peter sat without, ἐν τῇ αὐλῇ,' i.e. in the 'court' of the high priest's house (v.⁵⁸). It was during the trial of Jesus ; and 'without' is used in contrast with an implied 'within'—the interior of the audience-room in which Jesus was appearing before the authorities. Peter was not allowed into this room, but was out in the open air of the 'court' ; and this was 'beneath' (Mk 14⁶⁶), i.e. on a somewhat lower level than the audience-chamber.

The 'court of the Gentiles,' which was 'without the temple' (Rev 11²), was on the lowest level or terrace of the Holy Mountain, and separated from the 'Sanctuary' or 'Mountain of the House' by a stone wall four or five feet high, called 'the Ṣoreg.' All Gentiles were warned to remain outside of this sacred enclosure under penalty of death (cf. Ac 21²⁸· ²⁹ 24¹¹ 26²¹). See also artt. DOOR, HOUSE.   GEO. B. EAGER.

COURTESY.—The courtesies of life have always received more strict and formal recognition in the East than in the West. The people of Palestine in Christ's time were no exception to this rule. They were punctilious about those conventional forms which hedge in and govern social life, and were not slow to resent the breach or neglect of

* 'In kings' courts' of Lk 7²⁵ represents ἐν τοῖς βασιλείοις [only occurrence of this Gr. word in NT].

these forms when it affected them directly (Mt 22[2-7], Lk 14[16-21]). A remarkably complete picture of the ordinary forms of courtesy observed by them may be made up from the Gospel narratives. The incidents of Christ's life, together with His sayings and parables, show us the marked deference paid to authority, position, and learning (Mt 17[14] 22[16. 24] 23[6. 7] etc.), the elaborate and somewhat burdensome hospitality bestowed on friends and strangers when received as guests into a house (Lk 7[44-46]), the embracings and prolonged salutations practised (Mt 26[49], Mk 14[45]; cf. Lk 10[4f.] 15[20] 22[47], Mt 10[12]), the formalities observed in connexion with feasts in rich men's houses (Mt 22[12], Lk 14[17]).

These courteous habits must not be regarded as mere superficial forms. The fact that the neglect of them, especially if believed to be intentional, caused such serious offence to the suffering party, is a sufficient evidence that they were more than surface forms. At the same time the courtesies practised were not always sincere (note the kiss of Judas), and were, moreover, occasionally violated in a peculiarly flagrant manner, as we learn from the treatment Christ received once and again from those who opposed Him, especially the treatment He received immediately before His death. The warm Oriental temperament, indeed, which had so much to do with creating these courtesies, and which found so much satisfaction in observing them, was ready, under certain circumstances, to violate them to an extent that the colder Western temperament would never have done.

Christ's attitude towards the established rules of courtesy is a question of interest and importance. His relation towards these time-worn rules was the same as His relation towards the Law of Moses. He observed them in the spirit and not in the letter, and only in so far as they sincerely revealed His thoughts and feelings. They were never mere forms to Him, much less forms used to hide the real intents of His heart. That His attitude was not the conventional attitude of others, but was peculiar to Himself, like His attitude towards the Law (Mt 5[17]), is evident from the following considerations: (1) He recognized and followed the customary laws in so far as they served to express His real sentiments (Lk 7[44-46] 10[5], Jn 13[4ff.]); (2) He transgressed them boldly at times, as in His cleansing of the Temple, His injunction 'Salute no man by the way' (Lk 10[4]), and His intercourse with tax-gatherers and sinners; (3) He gave a larger and more humane interpretation to them by His generous and considerate treatment, not only of tax-gatherers and sinners, but of women, children, Samaritans, and others who were regarded as more or less outside the ordinary rules of courtesy.

There are two instances where Jesus seems to fail in the matter of courtesy—in His reply to His mother, 'Woman, what have I to do with thee?' (Jn 2[4]), and in His reply to the Syro-Phœnician woman, 'Let the children first be filled: for it is not meet to take the children's bread, and to cast it unto the dogs' (Mt 15[26] ‖ Mk 7[27]). It is only in appearance, however, that He offends against courtesy in these instances. The study of the passages with the aid of a good commentary will clear up any difficulty attaching to them.

Literature.—Van Lennep, *Bible Lands, their Modern Customs*; G. M. Mackie, *Bible Manners and Customs*; Geikie, *Holy Land and the Bible*; Robinson, *Biblical Researches in Palestine* [contains *passim* personal experiences which throw light on the tedious courtesies of the East]; Martensen, *Christian Ethics*, i. 202 ff.; T. Binney, *Sermons*, ii. 226; Paget, *Studies in the Christian Character*, p. 209 ff.; Dale, *Laws of Christ for Common Life*, p. 107 ff.; *Expositor*, 1st. ser. iv. [1876] p. 179 ff.

Morison Bryce.

COVENANT.—In order to a correct apprehension of the term 'covenant,' as it is used by our Lord in the Gospels, a brief survey of the OT usage is necessary.

The covenant conception is of frequent occurrence in the OT. Used at first in connexion with single transactions and partial aspects of the religious intercourse between God and man, it later becomes the formula designating the entire structure and content of the religion of Israel in its most comprehensive sense. This latter representation occurs as early as Gn 17[1-14], Ex 19[5] 24[7. 8], and often in Deuteronomy. The earlier covenants belonging to the time of Noah and Abraham (Gn 6[18] 9[8-17] 15[18]) do not yet possess this comprehensive character, but appear as solemn religious rites whereby some particular promise of God is made sure. Whether the word *bᵉrîth* (בְּרִית) originally meant 'enactment,' 'appointment,' 'law,' a meaning which it undoubtedly has in several instances, or did from the beginning signify a two-sided agreement, cannot be determined with certainty. It seems easier to conceive of the former sense as developed out of the latter than the reverse. At any rate, the comprehensive signification in which it stands for the whole religious relationship between God and Israel, rests on the idea of the covenant as a two-sided agreement. It should be remembered, however, that the two-sidedness never extends so far that God and Israel appear on an equal footing in the determination of the covenant. The planning and proposing of the covenant belong exclusively to God. Still the fact that Israel voluntarily accepts the covenant is as strongly emphasized (Ex 19[5] 24[3. 7], and elsewhere). Indeed, the covenant idea serves primarily to express the free, ethical, historically originated bond that exists between God and Israel. Its covenant character marks off the religion of Israel as a religion of real, conscious, spiritual fellowship between God and His people, in distinction from the religions of paganism, in which either the Deity and the creature are pantheistically fused, or the Godhead after a deistic fashion is so far removed from the creature as to render true communion impossible, and where the relation between a national god and his worshippers is not a matter of choice but of necessity on both sides.

In the early Prophets the conception of the covenant is not particularly prominent. With Hosea, the figure of marriage, probably not viewed as yet by the prophet as a species of covenant, serves the same purpose. There is no reason, however, for denying that Hosea knew the covenant conception in its comprehensive religious sense, and on this ground to call in question the genuineness of 8[1]. Greater prominence the covenant idea obtains from the age of Jeremiah onwards. Besides the emphasis thrown on the ethical-historical character of Israel's religion, two other important principles attach themselves to the term, partly developing out of the principle just stated. On the one hand, the covenant idea begins to express the continuity of God's dealings with His people; as it is a bond freely established, so it is the fruit of design and the fountain of further history, it has a prospective reference and makes Israel's religion a growing thing; in a word, the covenant idea gathers around itself the thoughts we have in mind when speaking of a history of redemption and revelation. On the other hand, inasmuch as God is the originator of the covenant and has solemnly bound Himself not merely to fulfil His promises to Israel, but also to carry out His own purposes contemplated in the covenant, the same bond which originally expresses the freedom of the relation between God and Israel can also become the pledge of the absolute certainty, that God will not finally break with His people, Israel's infidelity notwithstanding. In Isaiah 40-66, and especially in Jeremiah, the covenant thus stands to express the continuity and sureness of the accomplishment of the Divine purpose with reference to Israel. Out of the combination of these two ideas arises the Messianic and eschatological significance which the covenant idea obtains in both these prophets. In Isaiah 40-66 it is more than once introduced to emphasize the infallible character of the Divine promise given of old (Is 54[9. 10] 55[3] 59[21] 61[8]). In two passages (42[6] and 49[8]) the servant of Jehovah is designated as בְּרִית עָם, a somewhat obscure phrase, of which the two most plausible interpretations are, either that the servant will be the instrument of realizing the future covenant between God and Israel, or, placing the emphasis on עָם, that he will be the means of establishing a people-*bᵉrîth*, a *bᵉrîth* in which Israel, in contrast to its present scattered condition, will once more become a unified, organized nation. These two passages are of importance, because they bring the idea of the covenant into connexion with the figure of the Servant of Jehovah, which, assuming that the latter was Messianically interpreted by our Lord and applied to Himself, would explain that He represents Himself as the inaugurator of a new covenant.

In Jeremiah the covenant idea appears as a Messianic idea in two forms. In so far as the promise given to the house of David was a promise pledged in solemn covenant, the Messianic blessings are a covenant gift (33[20. 21]; cf. Ps 89[28], Is 55[3]). This is an instance of the old application of the idea to a concrete promise, which, however, in the present case, owing to the wide scope of the promise involved, would easily become identified in the mind of later generations with the expectation of an eschatological covenant in the comprehensive sense. The latter is the other form in which Jeremiah uses the covenant with reference to the future (31[31-34]). This is the only place where the notion of a new covenant occurs explicitly, although the thought itself is not foreign to the older prophets. Hosea has it in the form of the new marriage which Jehovah will contract with Israel. Jeremiah conceives of the new covenant as the outcome of the covenant character of the relation between God and Israel in general. To the prophet's mind religion and the covenant have become so identified that the covenant idea becomes the stable, permanent element in the historical development; if in its old form the covenant disappears, then in a new form it must reappear. The newness will consist in the twofold feature, that the sin of the people will be forgiven, *i.e.* the former sin, and that the law of Jehovah, instead of being an outward, objective covenant obligation, will become an inward, subjective covenant reality, written on the heart in consequence of the universal and perfect knowledge of Jehovah which will prevail. This passage in Jeremiah lies at the basis of the NT use of the phrase 'the new covenant.'

Two further passages in the prophets, to which a Messianic application of the covenant idea could easily attach itself, are Zec 9¹¹ and Mal 3¹. In the former passage the original reads: 'Because of the blood of thy covenant, *I* have sent forth thy prisoners out of the pit wherein is no water'; the LXX has, in the second person of address to Jehovah, 'Because of the blood of thy covenant, *thou* hast sent forth,' etc. On the former rendering the covenant is the covenant made with Israel, or, since this interpretation of the suffix 'thy' is deemed impossible by some, we may refer the suffix to the compound phrase 'covenant blood,' and understand the phrase 'thy covenant blood' of the sacrificial blood by means of which Israel continually upholds and renews the covenant with Jehovah. On the rendering of the LXX the covenant is represented as the covenant made and maintained by Jehovah. In the Malachi-passage the coming of the 'angel' or 'messenger of the covenant' is predicted. This 'angel of the covenant' is not identical with the Lord, but as a distinct person he accompanies the coming of the Lord to His temple. He is called 'the angel of the covenant,' either because he realizes the covenant, or because his coming is in virtue of the existing covenant. It is easy to see how on either view a significant connexion could be established between the Messiah and the covenant.

The LXX regularly renders *berîth* by διαθήκη, the later Greek versions prefer συνθήκη. The latter term better expresses the idea of a two-sided agreement; but probably this was precisely the reason why the LXX translators, desiring to emphasize the one-sided Divine origin and character of the covenant, avoided it. It should also be remembered that in not a few instances *berîth* in the original meant not a covenant but an authoritative disposition, which, as stated above, is according to some scholars even the primary meaning of the word. On the side of the Greek, also, there were considerations which explain the choice of διαθήκη, in preference to συνθήκη. It is true, in classical Greek the former meant usually a testamentary disposition, and might in so far have seemed unsuitable as a rendering for *berîth*. But occasionally at least διαθήκη could stand for a two-sided agreement (Aristoph. *Av.* 432). The verb διατίθεσθαι was not bound to the notion of '**testament**,' but signified authoritative arrangements generally. And above all things it should be noted that the testamentary διαθήκη among the Greeks before and at the time of the LXX translation differed in many respects from our modern Roman-law 'testament,' and possessed features which brought it into closer contact with the Hebrew *berîth*. The διαθήκη was a solemn and public transaction of a religious character, by which an irrevocable disposition of rights and property was made, and which for its effect was not dependent on the death of the διαθέμενος, but immediately set in operation certain of the duties and relationships established. Thus conceived, the διαθήκη could all the more easily become the equivalent of the *berîth* between God and Israel, because already in the OT the idea of 'the inheritance' had significantly attached itself to that of the covenant.

In the NT the noun used is always διαθήκη, but the cognate forms of συνθήκη appear in the verb (Lk 22⁵) and the adjective (Ro 1³¹). διαθήκη occurs in the NT 33 times. The word retains the one-sided associations of the LXX usage, yet in most cases the NT writers show themselves aware of the peculiar covenant-meaning descended with it from the OT. An additional possibility of interpreting it in the sense of testament was furnished by the fact that the blessings of the Messianic era were derived from the death of Christ. Hence in He 9¹⁶·¹⁷ the new covenant is represented as a testament bestowing upon believers the eternal inheritance, because the death of Christ had to intervene to make the bestowal effectual. As Ramsay has pointed out (*Expositor*, Nov. 1898, pp. 321–330), this representation is based on Roman law, according to which a testament has no force until the death of the testator. On the other hand, the Pauline representation of Gal 3¹⁷·¹⁸ is based on the Græco-Syrian law of the earlier period, under which the διαθήκη, once made, could not be subsequently modified, and took effect in certain directions immediately. No reflexion is here made on the death of the testator. Still, that διαθήκη does not here have the unmodified OT sense of 'covenant,' but means 'testamentary disposition,' is plain from the fact that 'sonship' and 'heirship' are connected with it in the course of the argument. These two passages in Hebrews and Galatians are the only NT passages which explicitly refer to the testamentary character of the διαθήκη. In how far in other instances the associations of the testament idea lay in the speaker's or writer's mind cannot be determined with certainty (cf. Ac 3²⁵ υἱοὶ τῆς διαθήκης; Gal 4²⁴ διαθήκαι γεννῶσα εἰς δουλείαν).

In the AV of the NT διαθήκη is in 14 instances rendered by 'testament' (Mt 26²⁸, Mk 14²⁴, Lk 22²⁰, 1 Co 11²⁵, 2 Co 36·¹⁴, He 7²², 9¹⁵ *bis.* ¹⁶·¹⁷·¹⁸·²⁰, Rev 11¹⁹). As a marginal alternative 'testament' is also offered in Ro 9⁴, Gal 3¹⁵ 4²⁴, He 8⁶ 12²⁴ 13²⁰. In all these cases, except in He 9¹⁶·¹⁷, the RV has replaced 'testament' by 'covenant,' offering, however, as the former as a

marginal alternative in Mt 26²⁸, Mk 14²⁴, Lk 22²⁰, 1 Co 11²⁵, 2 Co 36·¹⁴, Gal 3¹⁵·¹⁷, He 7²² 8⁶·⁷·⁸·⁹ *bis.*¹⁰·¹³ 9¹⁵ *bis.*²⁰, Rev 11¹⁹. In the American RV the marginal reading 'testament' has in all these cases been dropped, except in He 9¹⁵·²⁰. The principle by which the Revisers were guided is plain. The only question can be whether, in view of what was stated above, they were right in rendering 'covenant' and not 'testament' in Gal 3¹⁵·¹⁷. The point to be determined in each case is not whether the associations of 'testament' were present to the speaker's or writer's mind, but whether those of 'covenant' were absent: only where the latter is the case ought 'covenant' to be abandoned, and Gal 3¹⁵·¹⁷ seems to belong to this class. What motives in each case underlie the choice of 'testament' and 'covenant' in AV is not so plain. Possibly these motives were not always exegetical, but derived from the usage of earlier (English and other) versions. The following explanation is offered tentatively: wherever the contrast between the old and the new διαθήκη is expressed or implied, 'testament' was chosen, because 'testament' had long since, on the basis of the Latin Bible, become familiar as a designation of the two canons of Scripture, in the forms 'the Old Testament,' 'the New Testament.' This will explain Mt 26²⁸, Mk 14²⁴, Lk 22²⁰, 1 Co 11²⁵, 2 Co 36·¹⁴, He 7²². In He 9¹⁵·²⁰, of course, the import of the passage itself required 'testament.' He 8⁶· ('a better covenant') ⁷· ('that first covenant') ⁸· ('a new covenant') ⁹·¹⁰·¹³ ('a new *covenant*'), 9¹ ('the first *covenant*'), 12²⁴ ('the new *covenant*'), seem to run contrary to the explanation offered, but in each of these instances the context furnished a special reason for favouring 'covenant': in He 8⁶⁻¹³ the discourse revolves around the quotation from Jeremiah, which had 'covenant'; 9¹ is still continuous with this section, and in 12²⁴ the contrast between the mediatorship of Moses and that of Jesus, and the reference to the transaction of Ex 24, suggested 'covenant.' In 2 Co 36·¹⁴ 'testament' was especially suitable, because here the idea of διαθήκη might seem to approach that of a body of writings (v.¹⁴ 'the reading of the Old Testament'). Strange and unexplained is Rev 11¹⁹ ('the ark of his testament'), cf. He 9⁴ ('the ark of the covenant').

It seems strange at first sight that a conception so prominent in the OT is so little utilized in the NT. Perhaps the main reason for this was the intensity of the eschatological interest in that age, which made other terms appear more suitable to describe the new order of things felt to be approaching or to have already begun. On the whole, the covenant idea had not been intimately associated with eschatology in the OT. The consciousness that the work of Christ had ushered in a new state of things for the present life of the people of God, distinct and detached from the legal life of Judaism, for which latter the word 'covenant' had become the characteristic expression, dawned only gradually upon the early Church. The phrase 'Kingdom of God,' while emphasizing the newness of the Messianic order of things, leaves unexpressed the superseding of the Mosaic institutions by the introduction of something else.

With this agrees the fact that the conception of Christianity as a covenant is most familiar to precisely those two NT writers who with greatest clearness and emphasis draw the contrast between the Mosaic forms of life and those of the Christian era, viz. St. Paul and the author of Hebrews. Even with St. Paul, however, the contrast referred to finds only occasional expression in terms of the covenant: as a rule, it is expressed in other ways, such as the antithesis between law and grace, works and faith. The Epistle to the Hebrews is the only NT writing which gives to the covenant idea the same central dominating place as it has in the greater part of the OT.

In the Gospels the word 'covenant,' in a religious sense, occurs but twice, in Lk 1⁷² and in the words spoken by our Lord at the Supper. In the former passage the covenant with Abraham is referred to, and the Messianic salvation represented as a fulfilment of the promise of that covenant. The emergence of the idea here is in harmony with the best OT traditions: it expresses the consciousness of the sovereign grace and undeserved faithfulness of God which pervades the prophetic pieces preserved for us in the gospel of the incarnation according to St. Luke. Of course, in a broad sense the idea of the relation between God and Israel embodied in the word 'covenant' underlies and pervades all our Lord's teaching. Notwithstanding the so-called 'intensive universalism' and the recognition of religion as a natural bond between God and man, antedating all positive forms of intercourse, our Lord was a thoroughgoing supernaturalist, who viewed both the past relationship of God to Israel and the future relationship to be established in the Kingdom not as the outcome of the natural religion of man, but as the product of a special, historic, supernatural approach of God to man, such as the OT calls 'covenant.' While probably the legalistic shade of meaning which the word had obtained was less congenial to Him, He must have been in full accord with the genuine OT principle expressed in it. Mk 8[38] and Mt 12[39] speak of the Jews as an 'adulterous generation,' and probably the later prophetic representation of the covenant as a marriage-covenant lies at the basis of this mode of statement.

The words spoken at the Supper were, according to St. Matthew (26[28]) and St. Mark (14[24]), τοῦτό ἐστιν τὸ αἷμά μου τῆς διαθήκης (AD in Matthew and A in Mark τῆς καινῆς διαθήκης); according to St. Luke (22[20]) and St. Paul (1 Co 11[25]) τοῦτο τὸ ποτήριον ἡ καινὴ διαθήκη ἐν τῷ αἵματί μου [in 1 Cor. ἐμῷ αἵματι]. There is some doubt, however, about the genuineness of the context in St. Luke in which these words occur. In D and some other MSS, 22[19b] (beginning with τὸ ὑπὲρ ὑμῶν) and v.[20] are lacking. The textual-critical problem is a very complicated one (cf. Westcott and Hort, *Notes on Select Readings* in the Appendix, pp. 63–64; Haupt, *Ueber die ursprüngliche Form und Bedeutung der Abendmahlsworte*, pp. 6–10; Johannes Weiss, *Das älteste Evangelium*, pp. 294–299; Johannes Hoffmann, *Das Abendmahl im Urchristenthum*, pp. 7, 8 [all of whom adopt the shorter text]; Schultzen, *Das Abendmahl im Neuen Testament*, pp. 5–19; R. A. Hoffmann, *Die Abendmahlsgedanken Jesu Christi*, pp. 7–21 [who are in favour of the TR]. It ought to be remembered, though it is sometimes overlooked, that the rejection of vv.[19b. 20] as not originally belonging to the Gospel is by no means equivalent to declaring these words unhistorical, *i.e.* not spoken by Jesus. Wendt, *e.g.* (*Die Lehre Jesu*[2], p. 496), assumes the originality of the shorter text in St. Luke, and yet believes, on the basis of the other records, that Jesus spoke the words which St. Luke, for reasons arising out of his 'combination-method,' omitted. (Similarly Haupt, p. 10). Still, as a matter of fact, with some writers the adoption of the shorter text is accompanied by the belief that it represents an older and more accurate tradition of what actually took place. On the other hand, it remains possible, even in retaining the TR as originally Lukan, to believe that St. Luke's source supplied him with a highly peculiar version of the occurrence preserved in vv.[15-19a], and that he assimilated this to the other more current representation by borrowing vv.[19b. 20] from St. Paul. On the whole, however, the acceptance of the genuineness of the longer text naturally tends to strengthen the presumption that a statement in regard to which all the records agree must be historical. Contextual considerations also seem to speak in favour of the genuineness of the disputed words. If vv.[19b. 20] do not belong to the text, St. Luke must have looked upon the cup of v.[17] as the cup of the Sacrament, for it would have been impossible for him to relate an institution *sub una specie*. But this assumption, viz. that the cup of v.[17] meant for St. Luke the cup of the Sacrament, is impossible, because v.[18] comes between this cup and the bread of v.[19]. Further, v.[18] so closely corresponds to v.[16] as to set vv.[15-18] by themselves, a group of four verses with a carefully constructed parallelism between the first and the third, the second and the fourth of its mem-

bers respectively; and inasmuch as v.[17] belongs to this group, it cannot very well have been connected by the author with v.[19] in such a close manner as the co-ordination of the cup and the bread in the Sacrament would require. In general, the advocates of the shorter text do not succeed in explaining how the author of the Third Gospel, who must have been familiar with the other accounts, and can hardly have differed from them in his belief that the Supper was instituted as celebrated in the Church at that time, could have regarded vv.[15-19a] as an adequate institution of the rite with which he was acquainted. It is much easier to believe that a later copyist found the cup of the Sacrament in v.[17], and therefore omitted v.[20], than that a careful historian, such as St. Luke was, should have deliberately entertained this view, even if he had found a version to that effect in one of his sources.

Altogether apart from the textual problem in St. Luke, the historicity of the words relating to the covenant-blood has been called in question. Just as the saying about the λύτρον in Mk 10[45] and Mt 20[28], so this utterance has been suspected since the time of Baur on account of its alleged Paulinizing character. Recently this view has gained renewed advocacy by such writers as W. Brandt, *Die Evangelische Geschichte*, pp. 289 ff., 566; Bousset, *Die Evangeliencitate Justin des Märtyrers*, p. 112 ff.; Wrede, *ZNTW*, 1900, pp. 69–74; Hollmann, *Die Bedeutung des Todes Jesu*, p. 145 ff. The principal arguments on which these writers rest their contention are, that whilst to St. Paul the idea of the new covenant is familiar, no trace of it appears elsewhere in the teaching of Jesus; that it is expressive of an antithesis to the OT religion and its institutions out of harmony with Jesus' general attitude towards these; that in Justin Martyr's version of the institution the disputed words do not occur (so Bousset); that the structure of the sentence in Matthew and Mark still betrays the later addition of the genitive τῆς διαθήκης (so Wrede). The mere fact, however, that a certain conception occurs with a degree of doctrinal pointedness in Paul, does not warrant us in suspecting it when it occurs in the mouth of Jesus. With St. Paul himself the shade of meaning of the word is not in every passage the same. It cannot be proved that the Apostle read into what were to him the words of the institution an anti-Judaistic significance, such as belongs to the conception in Gal 4[24] and 2 Co 3[6]. Even the characterization of the διαθήκη as καινή does not require us to assume this. Even to St. Paul, we shall have to say, the phrase καινὴ διαθήκη has in the present instance the more general soteriological associations, in view of which the antithesis of the new to the old and the superseding of the old by the new recede into the background. The new covenant is the covenant which fulfils the OT promises, rather than the new covenant which abrogates the OT law. With still more assurance we may affirm this of the words as ascribed to Jesus in Mark and Matthew. Here (apart from the hardly original reading of A and D in Matthew and A in Mark) the explicit designation of the διαθήκη as καινή is not found. While the thought of the substitution of one covenant for another is undoubtedly the logical correlate of the statement even in this form, yet such an inference, if present at all, can have lain in the periphery only, not in the centre of the consciousness of Him who thus spoke.

It ought to be observed that the literal rendering of the words is not: 'This is *my* covenant-blood,' with the emphasis on the pronoun, but: 'This is my blood, covenant-blood.' The enclitic μου is too weak to bear the stress the former rendering would put upon it. Accordingly, μου belongs neither to διαθήκη nor to the compound idea 'covenant-blood,' but to the noun 'blood' only, as is also required by this, that τὸ αἱμά μου should be the exact correlate of τὸ σῶμά μου. The other construction, 'my covenant,' could only mean either 'the covenant concluded with me,' as in the original of Zec 9[11], or 'the covenant made by me as a contracting party,' as in the LXX rendering of that passage, hardly 'the covenant inaugurated by me between God and you.' And yet the last it would have to mean here, if μου went with διαθήκη. By these considerations we are led to adopt the rendering 'this is my blood, covenant-blood'; and this rendering makes it appear at once, that our Lord does not in the first place contrast *His* covenant-blood with the Mosaic covenant-blood, but simply speaks of His blood as partaking of the character of covenant-blood after the analogy of that used by Moses. But even if the comparison with the Mosaic covenant bore more of an antithetical character than it does, it would still be rash to assert that such an antithesis between the relation to God inaugurated by Himself and that prevailing under the Mosaic law could find no place in our Lord's consciousness, especially towards the close of His life. His attitude towards the Mosaic law, as reflected in the Gospels, presents a complicated problem. This much, however, is beyond doubt, that side by side with reverence for the Law there is, both in His teaching and conduct, a note of sovereign freedom with regard to it. From the position expressed in such sayings as Mk 2[21. 22] 7[15-23] to the conception of a new covenant superseding the old there is but one step.

We take for granted that the words were actually spoken by Jesus. In view of the fact that He uttered them in Aramaic, the question, whether the rendering of Matthew and Mark or that of Paul and Luke more nearly reproduces the original, becomes difficult to decide and also of minor importance. Zahn (*Evan. d. Matt.* p. 686, note 52) suggests that from the Aramaic form רמי דריתקא both renderings might, without material modification of the sense, have been derived. That the thought is in both forms essentially the same will appear later, after we have inquired into the content of Jesus' statement.

The intricate problems connected with the institution of the Supper can here be touched upon in so far only as they bear upon the meaning of the words relating to the covenant. We give a brief survey of the various interpretations placed upon those words.

First we may mention the interpretation according to which the covenant spoken of by Jesus stands in no real connexion with His death. Most modern writers who detach the original significance of the act of Jesus from His death, assume that the reference to the covenant is a later addition. Thus Johannes Hoffmann makes Jesus say no more than 'This is my body,' 'This is my blood,' and interprets this as meaning, that the disciples must be closely knit together as members of one body, Himself forming the centre. The meal is a meal of friendship. The Saviour even at this eleventh hour did not expect to die, but confidently looked forward to the immediate glorious appearance of the Kingdom of God. With this thought in mind He asked the disciples to unite themselves symbolically into the little flock for which the Kingdom was appointed.

Dismissing this and similar views, because they leave the covenant words out of consideration, we note that Spitta has developed a hypothesis which, while cutting loose the Supper from the death of Christ, nevertheless interprets its symbolism as a covenant symbolism (*Zur Geschichte und Literatur des Urchristenthums,* i. pp. 207–337). According to Spitta, the covenant is none other than the Davidic-Messianic covenant promised by the prophets, and inasmuch as this covenant had been frequently represented under the figure of a great feast, our Lord could by means of the Supper give to the disciples a symbolic anticipation of its approaching joys, the more so since the figure of a banquet to describe the eschatological Kingdom occurs also elsewhere in Jesus' teaching. The partaking of this Messianic feast could be represented as a partaking of the Messiah ('This is my body,' 'This is my blood'), because the Messiah was the Author and Centre of these future blessings. Jesus, while knowing that His death was at hand, yet in faith projected Himself beyond death into the time of the Kingdom:

the Supper was to Him a feast of joy, not a memorial of death. It was a single triumphant anticipation of the great feast of victory, not intended to be repeated as a rite. The present description of the covenant as a *new* covenant in the Pauline-Lukan record is, according to Spitta, a later modification of the conception in an anti-Judaistic direction. So far as its understanding of the term 'covenant' is concerned, this hypothesis has a certain OT basis to rest upon. To be sure, the Davidic covenant, to which Spitta makes Jesus refer, is in the OT a past covenant, a covenant made with David, the pledge and basis of future blessings, not a name for the blessings of the Messianic age themselves. But this might easily become blended with the prophetic prediction of a new covenant in the Messianic time, and then actually the covenant of David could become equivalent to the Messianic blessedness (cf. Is 55[3] 'the sure mercies of David'). There is, however, no prophetic passage which joins together the conceptions of the Messianic covenant and of a feast, so that no explanation is offered of the association of the one with the other in the mind of Jesus. The account of Ex 24 far more plausibly explains the combination of these two ideas, for here the covenant and the feast actually occur together. And if this be the more direct source of our Lord's reference to the covenant, then it follows that the blood and the covenant stand in a much more direct connexion with each other than Spitta assumes. According to Spitta, it is the blood which represents the personality of Jesus, who is the Author and Centre of the covenant. According to Ex 24[8] it is the blood directly inaugurating the covenant. Apart from every reference to Ex 24, when the blood is brought into connexion with the covenant ('this is my blood of the covenant'), it becomes entirely impossible to think of anything else than a covenant based on sacrificial blood : every other mode of joining these two terms is artificial. Spitta's further assumption, that the eating of the bread and the drinking of the wine stand for a partaking of the Messiah's body and blood, as a symbol of the eating of the Messiah, altogether apart from His death, is highly improbable. The feast as a whole might be the symbol of a participation in the Messiah, though even the examples quoted by Spitta of this mode of speaking are not sufficient to prove a current usage, if the sacrificial meal be left out of account. Assuming, however, that the general phrase 'eating the Messiah' was familiar to Jesus and the disciples outside of every connexion with the sacrificial meal, the distributive form in which the records present the thought, that of eating the Messiah's body and drinking His blood, could hardly have possessed such familiarity, and compels us, while not rejecting the idea of appropriating the Messiah, to think of Him as appropriated in His sacrificial capacity.

We turn next to the theories which recognize that the covenant stands through the blood in connexion with the death of Jesus. When the blood is called 'covenant-blood,' this undoubtedly implies that Jesus' death is instrumental in introducing the covenant. Justice is not done to this when merely in some indirect way the death is supposed to prepare the way for the covenant, viz., in so far as it forms the transition to a higher life which will enable Jesus to bestow upon His disciples the covenant-blessings. Thus the direct nexus between the blood and the covenant is severed. The view stated is that of Titius (*Die neutestamentliche Lehre von der Seligkeit,* i. p. 150 ff.). According to this writer, the Supper is to be explained not from the idea of the forgiveness of sin, but from that of the communication of life. Titius does not identify this covenant with the consummate eschatological state ; it is something intermediate between that and the communion with God into which Jesus introduced His disciples before His death. The new covenant is made possible by the death of Jesus, because through this death He will be raised into heaven, whence the powers of eternal life can descend upon His Church through the gift of the Holy Spirit. It may be justly objected to this construction, that in it the death of Jesus appears not as a source of blessing by itself, but as a more or less accidental entrance into the life of glory, from which the blessing flows. As Titius himself admits, in the abstract it would have been quite possible to procure the new covenant and the perfected communion with God without the intervention of Jesus' death, viz., if it had pleased God to exalt the Messiah in some other way. Thus it becomes difficult to understand how so much emphasis can be placed by Jesus upon the appropriation of His death, or how He can require the disciples to drink His blood. The appropriation symbolized certainly cannot relate to the accidental form in which the blessing is prepared, it must have reference to the substance of the blessing itself. If the death is the object of appropriation, then it must possess a direct and intrinsic significance for the covenant in which the disciples are to share.

This is recognized by Wendt (*Lehre Jesu*[2], p. 502 ff.), according to whom Jesus regarded His death as a covenant-sacrifice, standing in the same relation to the new covenant predicted by Jeremiah as the sacrifice brought by Moses sustained to the Sinaitic covenant. In his opinion, the record of Ex 24 shows that the Mosaic sacrifice had nothing to do with atonement, but consisted of burnt-offerings and peace-offerings, meant as a gift to God expressing the people's consent to His revealed law, and hence became a seal of covenant relation. The sacrifice pledged both God and the people. In analogy with this, Jesus represents His death as a gift dedicated to God, for the sake of which God will establish the new covenant, *i.e.* the state of salvation in the Kingdom of God, not, to be sure, on any strictly legal principle of recompense, but in harmony with His inexhaustible goodness and grace. Wendt's interpretation is wrong, not so much in what it affirms as in what it denies. That Jesus regarded the sacrifice of His life as a gift to God, and ascribed to it saving significance because it was an act of positive obedience, may be safely affirmed. The confidence, however, with which He appropriates the effects of this act to the disciples does not favour Wendt's assumption, that He made these effects dependent on a gracious will of God, imparting to the sacrifice a value which intrinsically it did not possess. But, apart from this, the analogy with the Mosaic sacrifice leads us to believe that Jesus did not confine Himself to viewing His death under the aspect of a gift. The prominence here given to the blood forbids us to interpret the sacrifice as exclusively, or even primarily, a symbol of gratitude or consecration to God. Even though the sacrifices brought were not specific sin-offerings, but burnt-offerings and peace-offerings, this does not eliminate from them the element of expiation. The Law itself speaks of expiation in connexion with the burnt-offerings (Lv 14), and the Passover-sacrifice, closely akin to the peace-offerings, certainly had expiatory significance. It may even be doubted whether the idea of a gift to God, except in the most general sense in which every sacrifice is a gift, was present to the mind of the author of Ex 24. When Moses calls the blood sprinkled on the people 'the blood of the covenant which Jehovah has made with you,' this can scarcely mean 'the blood by the dedication of which God is induced to make the covenant.' It must mean either 'the blood by whose expiatory power the covenant is inaugurated,' or 'the blood by which, as a bond of life between God and the people, the covenant is established and maintained.' Perhaps it may express both of the thoughts just mentioned, since the ideas of *expiatio* and *communio* were often united in the conception of sacrifice. Besides this, the association in the mind of Jesus between the new covenant and the forgiveness of sins is rendered highly probable by the joint-occurrence of the two ideas in the Jeremiah-passage, where the forgiveness of sins is named as the great blessing of the new covenant. Now, if Jesus had this thought in mind, and spoke at the same time of the sacrificial pouring forth of His blood, then it was almost impossible for Him not to unite the two thoughts, so as to conceive of the blood as a blood of expiation securing forgiveness. It is by no means necessary to rest this argument on the words in Matthew 'unto the forgiveness of sins.' Supposing that these words are a later interpretation of the thought, we shall still have to recognize them as an essentially correct interpretation, which merely resolves the ὑπέρ of Mark and Luke into περί + εἰς.

A further argument may be added to this from the part which the covenant conception plays in the second part of the Book of Isaiah in connexion with the figure of the Servant of Jehovah, who is called, as we have seen, the עָם בְּרִית. In our opinion, although this has been denied by Ritschl and others, there can be no doubt that the Servant-of-Jehovah-prophecy, and particularly Is 53, was an influential factor in determining the Messianic consciousness of Jesus. In this prophecy, however, the sacrificial rôle of the Servant, in an expiatory, vicarious sense, is so distinctly delineated, that, once finding Himself in the chapter, Jesus could not conceive thereafter of His death, or of the relation of His death to the covenant, on any other principle than is here set forth (cf. Denney, *The Death of Christ*, pp. 13–56).

As a matter of fact, the trend of recent investigation of the problem of the Supper is towards the acknowledgment, that the words, as they stand, not merely in Luke and Paul, nor merely in Matthew, but even in Mark, clearly express, and were intended by the writers of the Gospels to express, the expiatory interpretation of the death of Jesus. So far as the purely exegetical determination of the sense of the words *ex animo auctorum* (in distinction from the estimate put upon their historic credibility) is concerned, the traditional Church-doctrine is being more and more decisively vindicated. True, many modern writers, while granting this, emphatically deny that our Lord spoke, or could have spoken, the words which St. Paul and the Synoptists attribute to Him, or that what He spoke can have had the meaning which the words in their present setting and form convey. The two main reasons for this denial are, that, on the one hand, the teaching of Jesus about the sinner's relation to God is such as to leave no room for sacrificial expiation as a prerequisite of the sinner's acceptance, forgiveness flowing from God's free grace; and that, on the other hand, in the early Apostolic Church the expiatory interpretation of the death of Jesus is not present from the beginning, as it would have been if Jesus had taught it, but marks a subsequent doctrinal development. Neither of these contentions has sufficient force to discredit the unanimous witness of St. Paul and the Synoptists. In point of fact, Jesus nowhere represents the forgiveness of sins as

absolutely unconditioned. It is one of the gifts connected with the state of sonship in the Kingdom. Consequently, it is bound to His own person in the same sense and to the same degree as the general inheritance of the Kingdom is. Unless one is ready to assert with Harnack, that in the gospel, as preached by Jesus Himself, there is no place for His person, it will be necessary to believe that our Lord considered His own Messianic character and work of supreme importance, not merely for the preaching, but also for the actual establishment of the Kingdom of God. This being so, it became necessary for Him to combine with the specific form He gave to His Messiahship a specific conception of the manner in which the blessings of the Kingdom are obtained by the disciples. His views about the forgiveness of sins would be less apt to be determined by any abstract doctrine as to the nature of God, than by the concrete mode in which the developments of His life led Him, in dependence upon Scripture, to conceive of the character of His Messiahship and its relation to the coming of the Kingdom. If He anticipated death, as there is abundant evidence to show He did, from a comparatively early point in His ministry, then He could not fail to ascribe to this death a Messianic meaning; and this Messianic meaning, if there was to belong to it any definiteness at all, could hardly be other than that portrayed by the prophet Isaiah in the suffering Servant of Jehovah.

It is quite true that the silence observed by our Lord in regard to this important matter till very near the close of His ministry is calculated to awaken surprise. But this silence He likewise preserved till the same point with regard to His Messianic calling in general; the problem is not greater in the former respect than in the latter; the reasons which will explain the one will also explain the other. Nor should it be forgotten that, side by side with His high conception of the love of God, Jesus ascribed supreme importance to the Divine justice. He carefully preserved the valuable truth contained in the exaggerated Jewish ideas about the forensic relation between God and man (cf. Keim, v. 331, 'A continual oscillation between the standpoint of grace and that of Jewish satisfaction can be established'). Recognizing this element in His teaching as something He did not hold prefunctorily, but with great earnestness of conviction, we have no right to assert that every idea of expiation and satisfaction must have been on principle repudiated by Jesus as inconsistent with the love of God. Nor is there much force in the second contention, namely, that the absence of the expiatory interpretation of the death of Jesus from the early Apostolic preaching proves the impossibility of deriving this doctrine from Jesus. The doctrine is certainly older than St. Paul, who declares that he 'received' ἐν πρώτοις, as one of the fundamental tenets of the Apostolic faith, that Christ died for our sins according to the Scriptures (1 Co 15³). This 'receiving' on the part of St. Paul is separated by no more than seven years from the death of Jesus; according to recent schemes of chronology, by an even shorter interval. When in the discourses of the earlier chapters of Acts the emphasis is placed on the resurrection rather than on the death of Jesus, this must be explained from the apologetic purpose of these discourses. They were intended to prove that, notwithstanding His death, Jesus could still be the Messiah. Probably even upon the disciples themselves, at that early date, the full meaning of the teaching of Jesus concerning His death had not dawned; but if it had, to make this the burden of their preaching to the Jews would have been an ill-advised method. We know from these same discourses in Acts that the disciples looked upon the death of Jesus as foreordained. It is not likely that, holding this, they can have rested in it as sufficient for their faith, and entirely refrained from seeking the reasons for the Divine foreordination, which in this, as well as all other cases, must have appeared to them teleological. In the light of this, the references to Jesus as the Servant of God, which occur in these early discourses, sometimes in connexion with His suffering, become highly significant, partly because they sound like reminiscences of Jesus' own teaching, partly because they render it probable that our Lord's death was interpreted in dependence on Is 53. Finally, attention should be called to the central place which the forgiveness of sins occupies in the early Apostolic preaching. The prominence of this theme requires for its background a certain definite connexion between the Messiahship of Jesus and the forgiveness of sins, and this is precisely what is afforded by the expiatory interpretation of the Saviour's death (cf. Denney, *The Death of Christ*, pp. 65–85, where the preceding points are luminously discussed).

On the grounds stated we conclude that there is neither exegetical nor historical necessity for departing from the old view, that Jesus represented His death as the sacrificial, expiatory basis of a covenant with God. The next question arising is, Who are meant as the beneficiaries of this expiation on which the covenant is founded? At first sight it would seem as if only one answer were possible, viz. those to whom He gives the cup in which the wine, the symbol of the expiating blood, is contained. Nevertheless, the correctness of this view has been of late strenuously disputed. This has been done mainly on the ground before stated, that for the disciples the whole tenor of our Lord's teaching represents the forgiveness of sins as unconditioned, assured by the gracious love of God as such. Hence it is assumed that Jesus intended the covenant-sacrifice not for His disciples, but for the unbelieving mass of the people, who were so hardened in their unbelief as to render an atoning sacrifice necessary in order to their reacceptance into the favour of God (thus Johannes Weiss, *Predigt Jesu vom Reiche Gottes*, p. 28 ff.; and R. A. Hoffmann, *Die Abendmahlsgedanken Jesu Christi*, pp. 60–88). Weiss, while believing that the covenant-blood is primarily shed for the nation, would not exclude the disciples from its effects. Hoffmann, on the other hand, distinguishes sharply between those who are concerned in the covenant-sacrifice as its direct beneficiaries, *i.e.* the enemies of Jesus, and those whom He desires to appropriate the spirit of His self-sacrifice for others, and therefore invites to eat His body and drink His blood. The words spoken with the cup express on this view two distinct thoughts: (1) the blood is covenant-blood for the unbelieving Jews; (2) the blood as the exponent of the spirit of self-sacrifice of Jesus must pass over into the disciples, so that they too shall give their life for others. In other words, the disciples do not drink the blood in the sense in which it is defined by the phrase τῆς διαθήκης, but in the sense in which it symbolizes the subjective spirit on Jesus' part which led Him to offer His life for others. It will be readily perceived that this introduces an intolerable dualism into the significance of the blood: it must mean at the same time objectively the life poured forth in death as the principle of atonement, and subjectively the life pouring itself forth in death as the principle of self-sacrifice. There is no hint in the words themselves at any such double meaning. From the simple statement no one would guess that the blood is drunk by the disciples in any other capacity than that in which the Lord describes it, as 'blood of the covenant.' St. Paul

and St. Luke have not understood Jesus in the manner proposed; for, according to their version, the cup, that which the disciples drink, is the new covenant itself in the blood, not merely the blood which for others is the covenant-blood. Hoffmann has to assume that St. Paul and St. Luke misinterpreted the intent of Jesus, and regards Mark and Matthew as giving the correct version. But even into the words of St. Mark and St. Matthew his view will not fit readily. If our Lord invited the disciples to drink His blood, in the sense of receiving into themselves the spirit of His self-surrender to death, the description of this blood as covenant-blood becomes irrelevant to the expression of this thought. Whether the blood is covenant-blood or serves any other beneficent purpose, is of no direct consequence whatever for the main idea, viz., that it is the exponent of a spirit which the disciples must imitate, nay, the introduction of the former thought only tends to obscure the latter. Our Lord certainly did not expect the disciples to make the sacrifice of their own life a covenant-sacrifice in the sense His was for the nation. The ὑπὲρ πολλῶν in Mark and the περὶ πολλῶν in Matthew, to which Hoffmann appeals, cannot prove the exclusion of the disciples from the covenantal effect of the blood. The phrase is derived from Is 53[11.12], where it serves to affirm the fruitfulness, the efficacy of the self-sacrifice of the Servant of Jehovah. This simple thought suffices here as well as in Mk 10[45] to explain Jesus' statement that many will be benefited by His death. Who the many are, disciples or non-disciples, the ὑπὲρ πολλῶν alone does not enable us to determine.

The one question that still remains to be answered is, whether the covenant-blood appears in the words of Jesus, 'This is my blood of the covenant,' primarily as the blood which through expiation inaugurates the covenant, or primarily as the blood which by being sacramentally received will make those who receive it partakers of the covenant. Both meanings are equally well suited to the words themselves. In order to choose definitely between them, we should have to enter upon the extremely complicated discussion that has of recent years been carried on, and is still being carried on, concerning the origin of the Lord's Supper and the significance of the act performed and the words spoken by our Lord on the last evening of His earthly life. A few remarks must suffice to indicate the bearings of this problem on the question before us. The two views above distinguished coincide with the so-called parabolic or purely symbolic and the so-called institutional or sacramental interpretation of the transaction. According to the former, Jesus did not mean to institute a rite, did not intend the act to be repeated, but simply enacted before the eyes of His disciples, in a visible parable, the drama of His death, indicating by the parabolic form He gave it that His death would be for their good through the inauguration of a covenant. According to the latter, Jesus instituted, and for the first time caused His disciples to celebrate, a rite in which He made the partaking of bread and wine, as sacramental symbols of His body and blood, to stand for the appropriation of His expiatory sacrifice and of the covenant founded on it.

It ought to be observed that these views are not in themselves mutually exclusive. The parabolic significance of the body and blood, as symbolizing death, must on the second view be assumed to form the background, expressed or presupposed, of the sacramental transaction—expressed, if the breaking of the bread and the pouring of the wine be made significant; presupposed, if the broken bread and the poured wine be made the starting-point of the observance. That the so-called parabolic view is frequently advocated in a form which excludes the sacramental complexion of the act, is due not so much to the view itself, but largely to a general theory on the nature of the parables of Jesus.

Jülicher, the foremost representative of the parabolic interpretation of the Supper (cf. *Theologische Abhandlungen C. v. Weizsäcker gewidmet*, p. 207 ff.), is also the strenuous advocate of the theory that in every genuine parable of Jesus there can be but one point of comparison. Consequently it is insisted upon that, if the broken bread and the wine stand as figures for the death of Jesus, figures which involve the destruction of these elements, they cannot at the same time stand as figures for the appropriation of the benefits of His death, because this would involve the usefulness of the elements, the very opposite of their destruction. Jülicher was not at first disposed to carry this to an extreme, but admitted that as a secondary point of comparison the usefulness of the bread and wine as food and drink might have stood before the mind of Jesus. Others, however, demand that on the parabolic view every figurative significance of the eating and drinking must be rigorously excluded, and make this a ground of criticism of said view, because in the records the eating and drinking are undoubtedly made prominent (cf. Johannes Hoffmann, *Das Abendmahl im Urchristenthum*, pp. 61–65, and Jülicher's review of Hoffmann's book in *Theol. Literaturzeitung*, 1904, col. 282 ff.).

Jülicher's canon of interpretation, while on the whole representing a sound principle of exegesis, leads in single instances to the rejection of undoubtedly genuine material. It makes Jesus construct His parables with conscious regard to the unity and purity of their form, rather than with the practical end of their efficacy in view (cf. Bugge, *Die Haupt-Parabeln Jesu*). Where, as in the present case, the two points of comparison, that of the dissolution of the elements and that of their appropriation for nourishment, are so naturally combined into the one act of the meal, it were foolish to require the exclusion of either on the ground of a puristic insistence on the rules of formal rhetoric.

In all probability the combination of these two aspects of the symbolism was not first made by our Lord, but was antecedently given in the union of the OT sacrifice and the sacrificial meal. Schultzen (*Das Abendmahl im Neuen Testament*, p. 53 ff.) has shown, to our mind convincingly, that the eating of the bread and the drinking of the cup are placed by our Lord under the aspect of a sacrificial meal, for which His own death furnishes the sacrifice. As in the sacrificial meal the offerer appropriates the benefits of the expiation and the resulting benefits of covenant-fellowship with God (Ex $24^{10.\,11}$, Ps 50^5), so the disciples are invited to appropriate by eating and drinking all the benefits of expiation and covenant-fellowship that are secured by the sacrifice of the Saviour's death.

We may assume, therefore, that both the symbolism of sacrifice and the symbolism of the sacrificial meal are present in the transaction performed by Jesus. But the question still remains unanswered, whether the former is present in explicit form or merely as the unexpressed background of the latter. Those who emphasize the symbolical significance of the breaking of the bread, a feature named in all the records, hold that the death is not merely presupposed but formally enacted. On the whole, however, the trend of the discussion has of late been in the direction of the other view, which attributes no special significance to the breaking of the bread or the pouring forth of the wine, but makes the broken bread and the wine, as symbols of the death as an accomplished fact, the starting-point for the enacted symbolism of the sacrificial meal. It has been pointed out with a degree of force that the formula, 'This is my body,' 'This is my blood,' in the sense of 'This symbolizes what will happen to My body and to My blood,' is out of all analogy with Jesus' usual parabolic mode of statement, because elsewhere not the symbol, but the thing symbolized, always forms the subject of the sentence (so Zahn, *Das Evangelium des Matthäus*, p. 687, note 53). It may also be urged that the natural sequence, in case a parabolic enactment of the death of Jesus were intended, would have been as follows : 'He brake the bread and said : This is my body ; and he gave it to them and said, Take,' and similarly with the cup.

As the record stands, the pouring out of the wine is not mentioned at all. It seems that Jesus took a cup which had already been filled. If He had intended to give a parabolic representation of the event of His death, He would have taken pains to fill one before their eyes. The fact that with both elements the giving to eat and to drink precedes the declaration of what the bread and the wine stand for, favours the view that this declaration deals primarily with the symbolism of the sacrificial meal. The words, 'This is my body,' then obtain the meaning : To partake of this bread signifies the partaking of My sacrificed body in a sacrificial meal ; the words, 'This is my blood,' the meaning : To partake of this wine signifies the partaking of My sacrificial blood in a sacrificial meal. Thus we would reach the conclusion that the phrase 'blood of the covenant' has for its primary import : blood through the partaking of which participation in the covenant is assured. The Pauline-Lukan version, 'This cup is the new covenant in my blood,' cannot be quoted with conclusiveness in favour of either view. This version may either mean : this cup is by the blood it contains the new covenant, or : this cup is the new covenant, which new covenant consists in My blood. Each of these two renderings leaves open the two possibilities, that the shedding of the blood is represented as the source of the new covenant, or that the drinking of the blood is represented as the participation in the new covenant. To prevent misunderstanding, however, it should be stated once more, that the sacramental interpretation of the words has for its background the symbolic significance of bread and wine as exponents of the expiatory death of Jesus itself.

In conclusion, we must endeavour to define the place of the covenant conception thus interpreted within the teaching of Jesus as a whole, and its correlation with other important conceptions. Like the Kingdom of God, the Messiahship, and the Church, the Covenant idea is one of the great generalizing ideas of the OT, the use of which enables Jesus to gather up in Himself the main lines of the historic movement of OT redemption and revelation. From the Kingdom the Covenant is distinguished in several respects. The Kingdom conception is more comprehensive, since it embraces the eschatological realization of the OT promises as well as their provisional fulfilment in the present life, being on the whole, however, eschatologically conceived, the present Kingdom-powers and blessings appearing as so many anticipations of the final Kingdom. The Kingdom is also comprehensive in this other respect, that it covers indiscriminately the entire content of the consummate state, the external as well as the internal, the judgment- as well as the salvation-aspect. Over against this the Covenant idea, while by no means pointedly excluding the eschatological state (in Hebrews the idea is used eschatologically, the new covenant coinciding with the αἰὼν μέλλων), yet is more characteristic as a designation of the blessings of believers in the present intermediate period. And among the manifold contents of salvation it pre-eminently designates the internal ones of forgiveness of sin and fellowship with God, as is already the case in the passage of Jeremiah.

If the word rendered by διαθήκη had in our Lord's mind the associations of the word 'testament.' and if the statement found in the context of Luke ($22^{29.\,30}$), 'I appoint unto you (διατίθεμαι ὑμῖν), even as my Father appointed unto me a kingdom, that ye may eat and drink at my table in my kingdom,' may be understood as having been suggested to Him by this testamental sense of διαθήκη, then this would bring the Covenant idea much nearer to the Kingdom idea, inasmuch as in the latter saying the full content of the blessedness of the final state is the object of the διατίθεσθαι. It is not certain, however, that the sequence of the narrative here in Luke is chronological, and that, therefore, these words were uttered immediately after the reference to the covenant-blood in the Supper. In Mt 19[27-29] words in part identical occur in a different connexion. In the Supper, God is the διαθέμενος, whereas here it would be Jesus. It is better, therefore, not to introduce the testamentary idea into the words of the Supper, and to adhere to the distinction between the Kingdom and the Covenant from the point of view already indicated. According to the Pauline interpretation, the Supper, and with it the Covenant, belong to the pre-eschatological state, in which believers are during the present life, for the Supper is a proclamation of the death of Jesus 'until he come' (1 Co 11[26]). The sayings in Mk 14[25], Mt 26[29], Lk 22[16, 18] also mark the Supper and the participation in the Covenant as belonging to a state distinct from the final Kingdom of God. Our Lord, however, does not place this second stage of the covenant-life of the people of God in contrast with the former stage from the point of view that it involves the abrogation of the OT legal forms of life, as St. Paul does in 2 Co 3 and Gal 3. If it is a new covenant, it is new simply for the positive reason that it brings greater assurance of the forgiveness of sin and closer fellowship with God.

From the idea of the Kingdom that of the Covenant is still further distinguished, in that it appears in much closer dependence than the former on the Messianic person and work of Jesus. In our Lord's preaching of the Kingdom, His Messianic person and work remain almost entirely in the background, at least so far as the verbal disclosures on this subject are concerned, while the matter comes to stand somewhat differently if the self-revelation contained in Jesus' Messianic acts be considered. The Covenant is explicitly declared to be founded on His expiatory death, and to be received by the partaking of His body and blood. This importance of the person and work of Jesus, both for the inauguration and the reception of the Covenant, agrees with the view that the Covenant designates the present, provisional blessedness of believers, for this stage is specifically controlled and determined by the activity of Christ, so that St. Paul calls it the Kingdom of Christ in distinction from the Kingdom of God, which is the final state. The Covenant idea shares with the idea of the Church this reference to the present earthly form of possession of the Messianic blessings, and this dependence on the person and work of the Messiah (cf. Mt 16[18] 18[17]). The difference is that in the conception of the Church, the organization of believers into one body outwardly, as well as their spiritual union inwardly, and the communication of a higher life through the Spirit, stand in the foreground, neither of which is reflected upon in the idea of the Covenant. The Covenant stands for that central, Godward aspect of the state of salvation, in which it means the atonement of sin and the full enjoyment of fellowship with God through the appropriation of this atonement in Christ.

LITERATURE.—Rückert, *Das Abendmahl*, 1856; Baur, *Vorlesungen über neutest. Theologie*, 1864, pp. 102–105; Volkmar, *Die Evangelien*, 1870, p. 566 ff., *Jesus Nazarenus*, 1882, p. 112 ff.; Guthe, *de Fœderis Notione Jeremiana*, 1877; Keim, *Jesus of Nazara* (Eng. tr.), 1881, v. pp. 275–343; Wellhausen, *Skizzen und Vorarbeiten*, 1887, iii. p. 122; A. Brandt, *Zeitschrift f. wiss. Theol.* 1888, p. 30 ff.; W. R. Smith, *RS*[2], 1894; Lobstein, *La Doctrine de la Sainte Cène*, 1889, pp. 62, 258; Bousset, *Die Evangeliencitate Justins des Märtyrers*, 1890, p. 112 ff.; V. Zittwitz, *Das Christliche Abendmahl im Lichte der Religionsgeschichte*, 1892, p. 5 ff.; Jülicher in *Theol. Abhandlungen C. von Weizsäcker gewidmet*, 1892, p. 217 ff.; Joh. Weiss, *Jesu Predigt vom Reiche Gottes*, 1892 (2nd ed. 1900), p. 28 ff., *Das älteste Evangelium*, 1903, pp. 289–299; W. Brandt, *Die Evangelische Geschichte*, 1893, pp. 289 ff., 566; Spitta, *Zur Geschichte und Literatur des Urchristenthums*, 1893, i. p. 207 ff.; Mensinga in *Zeitschrift f. wiss. Theologie*, 1893, ii. p. 267 ff.; Gardner, *The Origin of the Lord's Supper*, 1893; Haupt, *Ueber die ursprüngliche Form und Bedeutung der Abendmahlsworte*, 1894, p. 22 ff.; Schultzen, *Das Abendmahl im NT*, 1895, pp. 33–37, 41, 53, 55, 96; Grafe in *Zeitschrift f. Theol. u. Kirche*, 1895, pp. 101–138; Titius, *Die Neutest. Lehre von der Seligkeit*, 1895, i. p. 150 ff.; Joachim, 'Die Ueberlieferung über Jesus letztes Mahl' in *Hermes' Zeitschrift f. Klassische Philologie*, 1895, p. 43; Zöckler, 'Moderne Abendmahlscontroversen' in *Evang. Kirchenzeitung*, 1895, p. 108 ff.; Kattenbusch, 'Das heilige Abendmahl' in *Christl. Welt*. 1895, Nos. 13–15; Kraetzschmar, *Die Bundesvorstellung im AT*, 1896; R. A. Hoffmann, *Die Abendmahlsgedanken Jesu Christi*, 1896, pp. 47–77; Schaefer, *Das Herrenmahl*, 1897, pp. 388–392; Ramsay in *Expositor*, Nov. 1898, pp. 321–330; Eichhorn, *Das Abendmahl im NT*, 1898; Smend, *Alttest. Religionsgeschichte*, 1899, p. 24 ff.; Giesebrecht, *Die Geschichtlichkeit des Sinaibundes*, 1900; Wrede in *Zeitschrift f. d. Neutest. Wissenschaft*, 1900, pp. 69–74; Wendt, *Die Lehre Jesu*[2], 1901, pp. 257–258, 502–509; Hollmann, *Die Bedeutung des Todes Jesu*, 1901, p. 145 ff.; Denney, *The Death of Christ*, 1902, pp. 46–60; Joh. Hoffmann, *Das Abendmahl im Urchristenthum*, 1903. The literature on the Lord's Supper is not given complete, but only in so far as it is of importance for the discussion of the Covenant idea. See, further, art. LORD'S SUPPER.

GEERHARDUS VOS.

COVETOUSNESS.—This word (Gr. πλεονεξία) has the root-idea of *greed*, shown in a strong desire to acquire, even more than in a keen wish to keep. In the Gospels, as elsewhere in Scripture [see, however, Eph 4[19]], the term is confined to a reference to property; the verb (πλεονεκτέω) is wider in sense. As the complexity of social life increases, so may the shapes the evil can assume. To ordinary avarice have to be added subtle temptations in the realm of rank and fashion, conventional ambition, cultured ease, or delight in successful activity unsubordinated to ethical aims. The tinge of covetousness comes in wherever men so absorb their life in the temporal that they impair its high instincts for the spiritual. 'What is a man profited, if he shall gain the whole world and lose his own soul?' (Mt 16[26]).

To the mind of Jesus what stands condemned is, characteristically, the possession of a certain spirit—the spirit of grasping selfishness. The forms assumed, the methods employed, are not minutely dealt with, and not matters for specific cure. Rather the one tap-root is to be cut, or a general atmosphere created in which the noxious weed must perish. And the almighty power to this end is the holy spirit of the gospel, which on the one hand is a spirit of loving trust towards God the Father in providence, and on the other a tender feeling towards fellow-mortals which prompts to ready sacrifice of all things to their good. The man with the great possessions (Mk 10[17]), who attracted Jesus, had yet one luxury to discover—that of doing good, giving to the poor, and so coveting wealth of the right kind. Not the coming to our hands of earthly good is condemned, but the absence of the one spirit which shall inform and vitalize its use. The triumph of religion is to turn it into 'treasure in heaven' (v. 21).

A classical passage is Mt 6[19-34], with which compare Lk 12[22-34] and 16[13-15]. The higher life being concerned with faith and goodness and the things of the spirit—the realm revealed in the Beatitudes, it is clear inversion to be absorbed for their own sake in the things of time and sense. 'Moth and rust' are the emblems of their corruptibility; and they are unstable, like property exposed to 'thieves.' It is the mark of a pagan mind to be full of anxious and self-centred concern for meat and drink and raiment (v. 32). Such persons reverse unconsciously Christ's principle that 'the life is more than meat' (Mt 6[25]); and the Pharisees, 'who were covetous' (Lk 16[14]), by their blindness to the true order of importance called forth essentially the same rebuke, 'that which is highly esteemed amongst men, is abomination in the sight of God' (v. 15). Though they had one eye for religion, they kept the other for the world, hence inevitably their truly distorted views. In the last resort of psychological analysis 'no man can serve two masters' (Mt 6[24]), and the Pharisees are pilloried for evermore as the awful example of hypocrisy in this respect. With Jesus, in these passages, the first postulate of religious worth is, that people must be single-minded and whole-hearted in service—'Where your treasure is, there will your heart be also' (Mt 6[21]). And to only one quarter can the enlightened heart turn— 'the kingdom of God and his righteousness' (v.[33]). Coincident with that, as humble faith feels, all needed things shall be added unto us. With exquisite insight Jesus points to the fowls of the air and the lilies of the field as eloquent at once of the minuteness of Divine Providence, and the trust we may place in a Heavenly Father's care. 'Are not ye,' He asks, 'much better than they?' (v.[26]). (Cf. as an enforcement of the lesson, Christ's own unworldliness of character, and trustfulness in earthly matters. And as a counter-illustration to the Pharisees, cf. the convert from their straitest sect, St. Paul, who having food and raiment learned therewith to be content, 1 Ti 6[8], cf. Ph 4[11]).

On a question arising of family inheritance (Lk 12[13-15]), Jesus warns against covetousness, and for impressive depth nothing excels the summary there—'A man's life consisteth not in the abundance of the things which he possesseth' (v.[15]). As one concerned with the spiritual domain, Jesus refuses to touch the civil matter of property. Wisdom lay in leaving questions of the law to lawyers, although the consideration is doubtless implied that even then there should be found a permeation of the Christian spirit. The point which Jesus presses is the falsity of the vulgar notion that it is 'possessions' which make life worth living. Devotion to the outward is, in His gospel, vanity; the loving and discerning soul has God for its possession, and from sheer sympathy of heart joys in His work amongst men.

A parable follows (Lk 12[16-21]), not necessarily associated originally with the foregoing incident, although in full affinity of theme. The Rich Fool is the personification of the successfully covetous man, and yet a revelation in almost the same breath of how little such success amounts to from the standpoint of eternity. He sowed only to the world; therefore he reaped inwardly no riches of the spirit. 'So is he,' saith Jesus, 'that layeth up treasure for himself, and is not rich towards God' (v.[21]). There is affinity of teaching in the parable of *Dives and Lazarus* (which see).

LITERATURE.—The standard works on the Sermon on the Mount and on the Parables. Among special discourses: F. W. Robertson, *Sermons*, 2nd series, Serm. I. (with which compare XVII. of 1st series); J Service on 'Profit and Loss' in *Salvation Here and Hereafter*; J. Oswald Dykes, *The Relations of the Kingdom to the World*, pt. i; A. Maclaren, *A Year's Ministry*, 1st series, No. 16; J. Martineau, *Hours of Thought* ii. and iii.; *Endeavours after the Christian Life*, pp. 76–86; Mozley, *University Sermons*, pp. 275–290.

GEORGE MURRAY.

COWARDICE.—Cowardice must be distinguished from a natural timidity in circumstances of danger, from the awe which, in the presence of the miraculous or the extraordinary, may so possess the mind as for the moment to paralyze its activities, and above all from the fear of God, His paternal love, power, and holy judgment, which may be the strongest antidote to all base and servile fear, and the source of the highest courage. The distinction is partly preserved in the words φόβος and δειλία. The latter word is 'always used in a bad sense' (Trench, *Synonyms of the NT*, p. 34). It expresses 'not the natural emotion of fear, but the cowardly yielding to it. It is the craven spirit which shrinks from duty, loses hope, abandons

what it should hold fast, surrenders to the enemy, or deserts to his side' (Bernard, *Central Teaching of Jesus Christ*, pp. 188, 189). δειλία occurs only in 2 Ti 1[7], but δειλιάω Jn 14[27], and δειλός (EV 'fearful') Mt 8[26], cf. Mk 4[40] and Rev 21[8]. But the line of distinction cannot be drawn hard and fast by the use of these words. In Mt 8[26] (cf. Mk 4[40]) the question τί δειλοί ἐστε, ὀλιγόπιστοι; is not so much a serious imputation of craven fear, as the expression of 'personal fearlessness, to gain ascendency over panic-stricken spirits' (Bruce, *Expos. Gr. Test., in loc.*). On the other hand, an ignoble fear in face of danger or difficulty, or the disapprobation and hostile sentiments of others, is sometimes in view when φόβος, φοβεῖσθαι are used (Mt 10[28], cf. Lk 12[4], Mt 25[25], Jn 7[13] 19[38] 20[19]). When fear of physical consequences impairs fidelity to Christ, causing men to be ashamed of Him (Mk 8[38], Lk 9[26]), or even to go the length of denying Him (Mt 10[33]), it incurs His severest disapprobation (Mt 10[33], cf. Rev 21[8]). But it is not cowardice to fly from the rage of the persecutor. Jesus not only counselled flight in circumstances of peril (Mk 13[14], Lk 21[21]), but Himself evaded the malice which would have brought His life to an end before His hour was come, and His mission completed (Lk 4[30], Jn 8[59] 10[39]). It is only when the fear of man tempts to the compromise of truth, and the disowning of allegiance to Christ, that it becomes a snare and a sin. Cowardice is not ultimately evinced in feeling, but in action. It is cowardice when a man declines the task he was meant to render: 'I was afraid, and went and hid thy talent in the earth' (Mt 25[25]); when he turns away, however sorrowfully, from the path of self-sacrifice which the call of Christ points out to him (Mt 19[22]). (See Paget, *Studies in the Christian Character*, p. 104).

The antidote to cowardice lies in the fear of God, in His power over the soul as well as the body (Mt 10[28]), the יִרְאַת יהוה which drives out all baser fear; in the spirit of watchfulness and prayer that, in circumstances of trial, we do not fall into the temptation to forsake Christ or deny Him (Mt 26[41]); but most of all in faith (Mt 8[26], Jn 14[1·27]). Faith in the Fatherhood of God—that the manifest duty, however difficult and dangerous, is His will; that from Him life has its appointed twelve hours, and in the path of obedience to Him there is no possible foreshortening of them (Jn 11[8-10]); that over all is His unsleeping and loving care—will save the soul from all base betrayals of itself and its Divine trust through fear. To this end was the Comforter promised and bestowed, that, co-operating with the spirit of men, He might brace them to consistent courage in action and endurance. And the effect of His presence and power is seen in the contrast between those who 'all forsook him and fled' (Mk 14[50]), denied Him (Mt 26[69-74]), 'gathered in an upper room for fear of the Jews' (Jn 20[19]), and the same men, not many months later, impressing the authorities by their boldness (Ac 4[13]), and displaying, in circumstances of severest trial, minds delivered from all craven fear, and inspired with the high and solemn courage of faith. See art. FEAR.

LITERATURE.—Aristotle, *Eth.* iii. 7; Strong, *Chr. Ethics*; Paget, *Studies in the Christian Character*, 100 ff.; Denney, *Gospel Questions and Answers*, 86 ff. JOSEPH MUIR.

CREATION.—The beginning of the world, as the earliest starting-point of time, is mentioned in Mt 24[21], Mk 13[19]. The other Gospel references to this subject include one by an Evangelist and two by our Lord Himself. The first (Jn 1[3]) teaches that the Divine Word, who afterwards became incarnate in Jesus (v.[14]), was the direct Agent in Creation (cf. Col 1[16], He 1[2]; and see following art.). The second (Jn 5[17]) occurs in a discussion on the

Sabbath. In the words 'my Father worketh hitherto,' Jesus shows that the Divine rest following the work of creation has been a period of continued Divine activity. His primary object is to justify His own works of healing on the Sabbath day, but He shows incidentally that the seventh 'day,' and therefore also the other 'days,' of Gn 1 need not be understood in a literal sense. In the third allusion (Mt 19[4ff.], Mk 10[6ff.]) the words of Gn 1[27] 2[24], describing the original creation of man and woman, are quoted in support of Christ's ideal of marriage (cf. Eph 5[31]).   JAMES PATRICK.

CREATOR (CHRIST AS).—The Synoptic Gospels do not bring forward any specific teaching of Christ as Creator. Whatever Jesus may have taught on this subject, the controlling purpose of the writers of these Gospels did not require the inclusion of it. Hence it is that only by implication is any doctrine of Christ's creatorship introduced into the Synoptic Gospels. The implication, however, is striking and worthy of notice.

1. *The assertion of original power*, e.g. the healing of the leper (Mk 1[41], Mt 8[3], Lk 5[13]); the lordship of the Sabbath (Mk 2[28], Lk 6[5], Mt 12[8]). The Sabbath is a Divine institution, and only the establisher of it could have power over it. The forgiveness of sins (Mk 2[5], Mt 9[2]) is a prerogative of Godhead.

2. *The note of authority.*—The people felt this in Jesus' teaching (Mk 1[22], Lk 4[36]). He claims authority for Himself (Mk 2[11], Mt 9[6], Lk 5[24]). He gives authority to His disciples (Mt 10[1]), and the unstated assumption is that it is by an original right inherent in Himself.

3. *Miracles.*—Jesus quiets the sea as one who has original power over it (Mk 4[39], Lk 8[24]). This is the right of the Creator of it. He restores life to the dead (Mk 5[41], Lk 8[54] 7[14]). To give life is the prerogative of Creatorship. It is an original right of the Creator. Jesus exercises this right in His own name. He creates directly in the miracle of the loaves and fishes (Mk 6[41-44], Mt 14[19] 15[36]).

4. *Ownership.*—Jesus calls the angels His own (Mt 24[31]). His lordship of the Sabbath implies ownership (Mk 2[28]).

All these are clear, and the more significant because undesigned, narrations which imply the Creatorship of Jesus. If St. Paul held a supervisory relation to the Gospel of Luke, and St. Peter to the Gospel of Mark, as many of the best modern scholars believe, then we shall feel the corroborative evidence which is so outstanding in their Epistles for the Creatorship of Jesus.

This evidence in the *Pauline Epistles* lies in (a) the pre-existence of Christ (Ro 8[3], 1 Co 10[4], 2 Co 8[9], Gal 4[4], Eph 1[4], Ph 2[6], Col 1[17], 2 Ti 1[9]). The self-impoverishment (*kenosis*) implies previous Divine fulness. If all things were created through (διά), in (ἐν), and for (εἰς) Him, He would necessarily be pre-existent. The Pauline Christ of the Epistles is not merely the historic Christ, but more especially the Creative Principle both in the world and in man. (b) Creation is through Christ (Col 1[16]). He is the causal agent, according to the eternal purpose. (c) Creation is in Him, i.e. in the sphere of Christ, 'the creative centre of all things, the causal element of their existence' (Ellicott). Hence all things are to be gathered up in Him (Eph 1[10]). (d) Creation is for Him. He is the goal as well as the explanation of all creation. 1 Co 8[6] expands this idea, and makes Him both the source and the goal of all created things. (e) He is the bond which holds the whole fabric of men and things together. This is the doctrine of the Divine immanence (Col 1[17]), and sets forth Christ as the eternally existent Creative Principle in all things. All this teaching is an amplification of the teaching of the Synoptics, and sets forth the cosmic relations of Christ in Creation in order to show more clearly His cosmic relation in Atonement and Salvation.

There are two passages in the *Petrine Epistles* which teach the pre-existence of Christ (the Spirit of Christ in the prophets, 1 P 1[11]; and Christ before the foundation of the world, v.[20]), but there is no direct teaching of Creatorship.

The Gospel of John opens at once into a circle of new and profounder conceptions of Jesus. He is the Eternal Logos who was in the beginning (1[1]). He is the eternal and immanent Reason manifesting creative activities. He mediates the creation of the universe (v.[3]). The Prologue sets forth Jesus Christ in His fourfold mediation. (a) As the Eternal Logos, who was 'in the beginning with God, and was God' (1[1]), He mediates the creation of all things (v.[3]). The whole process and product of creation lie inwrapped in the Logos. Neither angels nor other beings assisted. 'And without him was not anything made that hath been made' (v.[3], cf. 1 Co 8[6]). (b) As the Creative Logos, He mediates life for men. He is immanent in the Creation. 'In him was life' (v.[4]), and 'He was in the world, and the world was made by him, and the world knew him not' (v.[10]). He was the ground and source of life. St. Paul's saying, 'The world through its wisdom knew not God' (1 Co 1[21]), shows the amazing inability of the world to recognize its Creator who was the ground of its own life. Sin had indeed become darkness which was incapable of apprehending the light (Jn 1[5]). (c) As the Logos made flesh or incarnate, He mediates a revelation of God to man (vv.[14-18]). The whole measure of revelation lies in the incarnate Logos. 'God manifested' to men was manifested wholly in Jesus Christ. (d) As 'the only-begotten from the Father' (v.[14]), He mediates an atonement or reconciliation, through His death, between a holy God and alienated sinners. This is the climax of His wondrous mediatorship, and makes Him the perfected Mediator. The historic Christ is brought forward in this Gospel only enough to explicate or illustrate the eternal Christ, but it was in the historic Christ that the eternal and cosmic Christ was first recognized. The transactional phases of the historic incarnation lead, in St. John's view, straight to·the eternal Logos who mediated the whole creation. Christ, as Creator, is so wrought into the Cosmos which He made and sustains, that upon the entrance of sin into the world He becomes of necessity the mediator of new relations between the sinner and God. His mediatorship of redemption rests on the fact that He was 'in the beginning' the Logos who mediated the creation of all things. Christ, as Creator, is the fundamental idea of this Gospel. It is the starting-point of the whole history of the earth and the heavens, of man, his fall and his doom, of the redemption and the final glory. It is the interpretive key to the whole framework of the Fourth Gospel, whose author sees the designed correspondence between the Creator and the created, and that creation was primarily intended to be responsive to Him. 'He came unto his own, and they . . . received him not' (1[11]), expresses the failure of creation to fulfil the Divine purpose. St. John gathers up all that the Synoptists have taught, but adds new conceptions of Jesus in a profounder interpretation of Him. He teaches (a) the pre-existence of Christ (1[30] 3[13. 31] 6[62] 8[56-58] 14[11] 17[5]) more plainly and fully than the Synoptists; (b) His authority (17[2]); (c) His inherent power to work miracles (2[8] 6[11] 11[43]); (d) His ownership of all things (1[11]). But new conceptions are added. (a) He is the source of an abiding or eternal life. He has power to give this life to whom He will (3[36] 4[10. 14] 5[21-24. 40] 6[27. 51] 10[28] 11[25] 14[19]

17^2). (β) His life is the light of men. But the fact that as Creator He is the source of both life and light to men does not prevent their rejection of Him (1^4 8^{12} 9^5 $12^{35.\ 36.\ 46}$). (γ) He shows His identity with the Father: 'I and the Father are one' (10^{30}); 'He that hath seen me hath seen the Father' (14^9 12^{45}). (δ) He shows familiarity with the life and conditions of Heaven (14^2 17^{24}).

But these conceptions of Christ, as well as those which St. John and the Synoptists have in common, rest on the fact of His having mediated the creation of all things. His rights in the whole creation, as well as the obligations which He has toward it, grow out of the fact of His Creatorship. The eternal and universal characteristics of both incarnation and reconciliation are grounded in the creational character of Jesus Christ.

LITERATURE.—B. Weiss, *Religion of the NT*, 190–191, and *Bibl. Theol. of NT*, ii. 99; G. B. Stevens, *The Christian Doctrine of Salvation*, 438; G. A. Gordon, *The Christ of To-Day*, 81–93; A. M. Fairbairn, *The Place of Christ in Modern Theology*, 341; D. F. Estes, *Outline of New Testament Theology*; A. B. Bruce, *St. Paul's Conception of Christianity*, 335; H. R. Reynolds, 'St. John' (*Pulpit Commentary*), vol. i. 1–21. The literature on the subject is very scanty.   NATHAN E. WOOD.

CRITICISM. — 1. A little more than seventy years ago (1835–1905), a turning-point was reached in NT criticism, the importance of which is generally admitted.[*] In the year 1835 **David Strauss** published his *Leben Jesu* (to be followed exactly ten years later by **F. C. Baur's** *Paulus*). The mythical theory was remorselessly applied by Strauss to the whole of the Gospel history.

It must not be forgotten that from the middle of the preceding century Semler had applied the word 'myths' to some of the OT narratives, as, *e.g.*, to the exploits of Samson; and later on at the beginning of the 19th cent. de Wette had not hesitated to point out the important part which, in his judgment, was played both by myth and by legend in the writings of the OT.[†] At the same time he had not hesitated to accentuate, in language very similar to some of the utterances familiar to us to-day, the difference which lay between the application of the mythical and of the legendary theory to the OT and to the NT.[‡] There were, indeed, two parts of our Lord's *life*, the beginning and the end, which this earlier criticism did not scruple to regard as shrouded in darkness, and to relegate to the same domain of myth or legend. The supporters of this kind of criticism were content, as Strauss himself expressed it, to enter the Evangelical history by the splendid portal of myth and to leave it by the weary paths of a natural explanation. This method of so-called natural explanation, which in its most crude form was characteristic of Paulus and the school which bore the name of Rationalists, a method which Strauss remorselessly attacked, became discredited and gave place to the mythical theory, which at least laid claim to thoroughness. But it is not too much to say that an explanation of the miraculous which is often akin to the crude exegesis of Paulus, meets us not infrequently in Strauss himself and in much more recent attempts to prove that miracles did not happen.[§]

But by another path of inquiry the way was being prepared for Strauss. In 1750, J. D. Michaelis published his *Introduction to the NT*, and in the fourth edition of that work he examined with caution and candour the origin of all the NT books. Michaelis was followed by Semler in his *Treatise on the Free Investigation of the Canon*, the very title of which seemed to mark the new principle of inquiry which was abroad. Semler has been recently called 'the father of criticism'; and if that title is not always appropriate to him, we may, at all events, speak of his epoch-making influence, and of the break which he caused between the traditional views of inspiration and the free examination of the authority and origin of each sacred book.[‖] The new century was marked by Eichhorn's *Introduction*. This writer applied systematically the principle laid down by his forerunners, like Semler and Herder, and continued the attempt 'to read and examine the writings of the NT from a human

point of view.' His rule was that the NT writings are to be read as human books, and tested in human ways.[*]

But up to this time and even later, no systematic attempt, if any, was made, as by F. C. Baur, to place the NT in relation to the varying phases and circumstances of early Church history and life. Even de Wette, one of the best representative men of the period, who combined so remarkably deep evangelical piety with freedom from prejudice and with thoroughness of learning, was often undecided in his judgment, and his conclusions were vague and uncertain. The criticism characteristic of the time was carried on, as it were, piecemeal: one book was defended or attacked, or the alleged author was accepted or rejected, but there was no attempt to bring the books of the NT under one general conception.

There were henceforth two great critical movements proceeding side by side—the effort to interpret the Gospel narratives, and the effort to investigate the origin of the NT books.

To the former of these efforts Strauss stood in the closest relation, and he claimed to introduce a theory of interpretation which should be complete and final.[†] To the latter Baur stood in the closest relation, and he claimed to make good a theory which treated the books of the NT from the point of view not only of their origin, but of their purpose. Baur's book on the Pastoral Epistles, published in the same year as Strauss' *Life of Jesus* (1835), showed that his intention was to treat the NT books in connexion with their historical setting.

Some of the most successful attacks upon the first edition of Strauss' book were based upon the fact that he paid so little attention to the Gospel sources. A few pages are all that he devotes to the authorship of the Gospels, and it is no wonder that men like Tholuck rightly fastened on this weakness in their opponent's position, and that much of Strauss' own subsequent vacillation was due to the same cause.[‡]

But in 1864, apparently stirred by the reception given to Renan's *Vie de Jésus*, Strauss published his popular edition for the German people. And here he showed how thoroughly he was prepared to endorse Baur's view of the late dates of the Gospels, and to assimilate the methods and conclusions of the Tübingen school.[§] But, as Dr. Matheson and other writers have so forcibly pointed out, the two theories of Strauss and Baur are incompatible. The conscious tendencies and the dogmatic purpose discovered by Baur in the composition of the NT books cannot coexist with the purely unconscious working of myth.[‖]

That which is mythical grows up unconsciously. But if our Gospels were constructed to meet or to modify certain special historical circumstances, if they are to be regarded as artistic creations, or as 'tendency' writings, they cannot be mythical, as Strauss maintained, nor can they be regarded as the spontaneous and unconscious workings of

---

[*] See, *e.g.*, Schwarz, *Zur Gesch. der neutest. Theol.*; Pfleiderer, *Development of Theology*, p. 133; Nash, *History of the Higher Criticism*, p. 123: 'Altogether 1835 is something more than a date in the history of literature. It stands for a new turn and direction in the Higher Criticism.'

[†] For a discussion of the differences between myth and legend, reference may be made to Knowling, *Witness of the Epistles*, p. 16 ff.

[‡] See, *e.g.*, Dr. Driver's remarks, *LOT* p. xvii, and further below.

[§] Lichtenberger, *History of German Theology in the 19th Century*, p. 328.

[‖] Cf. B. Weiss, *Einleitung in das NT*[3], p. 5 ff.

---

[*] Nash, *op. cit.* p. 114.

[†] On the unsatisfactoriness of the attempt to apply the mythical theory to the rise of the primitive Christian tradition, see esp. Fairbairn, *Philosophy of the Christian Religion*, p. 467 ff.

[‡] Cf. O. Zöckler. *Die christliche Apologetik im neunzehnten Jahrhundert*, 1904, p. 16.

[§] See Lichtenberger, *op. cit.* p. 333; and J. E. Carpenter, *The Bible in the Nineteenth Century*, pp. 277, 278.

[‖] Baur saw in the NT literature the workings of a compromise between the two radically antagonistic parties of Judaism and Paulinism. In the exigencies of his theory he divided the period of literary development into three divisions—(1) Extending to A.D. 70, a period including the *Hauptbriefe* of St. Paul and the Apocalypse of St. John. Here the antagonism was at its height between the original Ebionitic Christianity and Paulinism. (2) Extending to about A.D. 140, in which period we have the Gospels of St. Matthew and St. Luke, the former being Petrine, the latter (with the Acts) Pauline, but bearing marks of conciliation with reference to the above antagonism, and later the Gospel of St. Mark (also of a conciliatory type), whilst Ephesians and Colossians were invented by the Pauline party for the same conciliatory purpose. (3) Extending to A.D. 170, when the controversy was finally settled, and the conflicting extremes rejected by the 'Catholic' Church, a period marked by the Gospel and Epistles which bear the name of St. John, as also by the Pastoral Epistles assigned to St. Paul.

the human mind in its efforts to impart reality to its hopes. One cannot, in short, have the 'mythical' Gospels of Strauss and the 'tendency' Gospels of Baur.[*]

But while Strauss thus attempted to adapt this later work to some of the results and methods of the Tübingen school, he also came nearer to Baur in that he gave in this popular edition of his famous book an account of Jesus utterly incommensurate with the greatness of His influence and of the position which He achieved. Baur had taken little or no account of Jesus Himself and His Person, and now Strauss, by withdrawing what he had conceded in the second edition of his *Leben Jesu* as to the greatness and moral perfection of Jesus, was in a position no less impracticable than Baur's, so far as any satisfactory explanation of the work and person of the Founder of Christianity was concerned. We cease to be so much surprised that Strauss should regard the history of the resurrection of our Lord as a piece of colossal humbug, when the Jesus whom he depicted was so insignificant; or that Baur should regard this same account of the resurrection as a fact outside the province of historical inquiry, when he made no serious attempt to answer the question who Jesus was, or to understand Him and His life.

This supreme importance of the Person of Jesus had been rightly emphasized by earlier writers of the century. Paulus, with all his faulty method, had at least recognized that the miraculous in Christianity was Christ Himself, His Person. Schleiermacher had seen in Christ 'the greatest fact in history, the one only sinless and perfect Man, in whom the Divinity dwelt in its fulness.' Herder, of whom it has been said that his *Christliche Schriften* gave the first impulse to the immense literature generally known under the name of the *Life of Christ*, did not forget even in his constant denunciations of the corruptions of Christianity to hold up to admiration the Person of Jesus as the Prophet of the truest humanity.

This primary importance of the fullest consideration of the Person of Christ is nowhere seen more strikingly than in one of the earliest and most effective replies to Strauss' work, by **C. Ullmann**, a reply which so influenced Strauss that he modified his position, at least for a time, so far as to concede to Christ a place historically unique as a religious genius. As Ullmann insisted, Strauss was by his own fundamental philosophical assumptions debarred from doing justice to the Person of Jesus.[†] But if Strauss' position is correct, then it is impossible to understand why the disciples of Jesus should have regarded Him as the Messiah; for they could scarcely have done so, and with such surprising success, unless there had been something extraordinary about Him. The dilemma, therefore, which Ullmann proposed was really this— *Did Christ create the Church, or did the Church invent Christ?* If the former, Jesus must have been no mere Jewish Rabbi, but a personality of extraordinary power; if the latter, we have an invention which would make the history of Christianity quite incomprehensible. It was, of course, open to Strauss to reply that whilst the powerful personality of Jesus had created the Church, yet subsequently mythical hopes and conceptions might have been at work, transforming and magnifying the idea of the Christ.[‡] But at all events for a time Strauss hesitated. He not only ac-

knowledged the supremacy of Jesus in the sphere of religion, but he maintained that He possessed such power over the souls of men, to which there may have been conjoined some physical force like magnetism, that He was able to perform cures which were regarded as miraculous. He even went so far as to consider the Fourth Gospel as a possible historical authority.[*]

In face of all this confusion, and of the number of replies to Strauss and the position which they took up, it is easy to understand that the question of the sources of the Gospel history and a criticism of them assumed a growing importance. This importance Strauss had practically ignored, and now Baur's theory of early Church history and of the origin of early Christian documents was to be worked in to supply the want, and to be adopted by Strauss as a remedy for his own indecision or indifference as to the Gospel sources. Strauss felt, it would seem, the justice of Baur's reproof, viz. that he had written a criticism of the Gospel history without a criticism of the Gospels.[†]

But just as it may be affirmed that Strauss had started with dogmatic philosophical assumptions, so the same judgment must be passed upon Baur's starting-point. No one has admitted this more fully than Pfleiderer, so far as the first three Gospels are concerned (*op. cit.* pp. 231, 232).

Wilke and Weisse had already proved, says Pfleiderer, the priority of Mark (and had thus, with Herder, anticipated much later criticism), and it could only have been the fact that Baur was wedded to his dogmatic method which prompted him to place Mark's Gospel at least as late as A.D. 130, and to see in it a Gospel consisting of extracts from Matthew and Luke.

The impossibility of separating any account of the *life* of Christ from its sources became more and more evident in the succeeding literature.

2. Closely related in point of time to Strauss' popular book is that of the Frenchman **Renan**. To attempt any examination of the defects of this famous work would be beyond our province. But just as Strauss was blamed for his indifference to any treatment of the sources, *i.e.* the Gospels, so Renan was blamed for his half-and-half treatment of the same Gospels. For this he is severely taken to task by Schwarz.[‡] He blames Renan for passing so lightly over the inquiries of a man like Baur as to the origin of our Gospels; and he points out that Renan's half-and-half treatment of these same Gospels, especially of the Gospel of John, avenges itself upon him, in that it leads him on from half-rationalistic explanations of the miracles to explanations which are adopted even at the cost of the moral perfection of Jesus. And in this connexion he refers, like other writers, to the explanation which Renan gives of the resurrection of Lazarus. Of course the earlier Renan placed the Gospels, the more difficult it was for him to account for the miracles which gathered around Jesus; and it is not too much to say that the earliest Gospel, St. Mark, the Gospel which Renan himself regarded as the earliest, is bound up with the miraculous. Renan's short and easy method was to declare dogmatically that there was no room in history for the supernatural. Like Strauss and Baur, Renan too had his assumption as to the historical worth of the Gospels; he too sets out with a general and comprehensive judgment as to their contents; for him the Gospels are not biographies, after the manner of those of Suetonius, nor are they legends invented after the manner of Philostratus; they are legendary biographies.

---

[*] Matheson, *Aids to the Study of German Theology*, p. 151; cf. also B. Weiss, *Leben Jesu*[4], i. p. 153.

[†] To the same effect Weinel, *Jesus im neunzehnten Jahrhundert*, 1904, p. 42.

[‡] See Pfleiderer, *op. cit.* p. 220. For Ullmann and his reply to Strauss, reference may be made to Knowling, *Witness of the Epistles*, pp. 20, 132.

[*] Lichtenberger, *op. cit.* p. 328.

[†] See Schwarz, *op. cit.* p. 545 f.

[‡] *Op. cit.* pp. 538–540; see also B. Weiss, *Life of Christ*, i. pp. 203, 205, Eng. tr.

'I would compare them with the Legends of the Saints, the Life of Plotinus, Proclus, Isidorus, and other similar writings, in which historic truth and the purpose of presenting models of virtue are combined in different degrees.' It is not, perhaps, surprising that B. Weiss should speak of Renan's *Vie de Jésus* as not a history but a romance, and should add that, as our sources in their actual form were in many respects out of sympathy with, indeed almost incomprehensible to him, he could not escape the danger of rearranging them according to his own taste, or in a merely eclectic way.[*]

3. If we turn to **Theodor Keim** (1867–1872), to whom has sometimes been attributed *the* 'Life of Jesus' from a rationalistic standpoint, we notice that he too is severely taken to task by Pfleiderer for his unsatisfactory and fluctuating criticism of the Gospels as sources, and for his too close adherence to the views of Baur, especially in regard to the relation of the Synoptics to each other. St. Mark, *e.g.*, is a compilation from St. Matthew and St. Luke, and St. Matthew's is regarded as the earliest Gospel. In comparing Keim's various works relating to the life of Jesus, we certainly find a strange fluctuation with regard to his statements as to the sources and their validity. Thus he actually places St. Matthew in its primitive form as early as A.D. 66, and supposes it to have been revised and edited some thirty years later ; St. Mark he places about 100 ; and St. Luke, in which he sees a Gospel written by a companion of St. Paul, about 90.

But in 1873 Keim issued a book of a more popular character, and in this we find that the revision of St. Matthew is placed about 100, St. Mark about 120, St. Luke also about 100, while it is no longer referred to a companion of St. Paul. Some years later (1878) Keim's position with regard to the Gospels was again differently expressed, and he seems to be prepared to make certain concessions to his opponents, and to attach more weight to the two-document theory as the result of a fresh study of Papias.[†] But it will be noticed that Pfleiderer has nothing but praise for Keim's treatment of the Fourth Gospel, which in 1867 he places between 100 and 117, and a few years after (1873) as late as A.D. 130. It must not, however, be forgotten that, as Dr. Drummond rightly points out, Keim's position with regard to St. John's Gospel marks a very long retreat in date from the position of Baur, whilst Pfleiderer himself is the sole critic of importance who still places the Gospel in question at the extravagant date, 170, demanded by the founder of the Tübingen school.

But with all these variations as to dates, and with the free concession of the presence of mythical elements in the accounts of the great events of our Lord's life, Keim takes up a very different position from Strauss and Baur, and at all events the early members of the Tübingen school, with regard to the importance of the Person of Jesus and of our knowledge of Him. Nowhere is this more plainly seen than in the remarkable stress which he lays upon St. Paul's references to the facts of our Lord's earthly life and upon his high Christology. Baur and his followers had fixed men's attention upon Paul, Keim insists upon the unique and supreme importance of Jesus, and he sees in Him the Sinless One, the Son of God.

But Keim's portraiture of Jesus is marred by many inconsistencies. Thus he is prepared to admit that the miracles of healing may have happened in response to the faith evoked by the personality of Jesus, or he is thrown back in his treatment of the miraculous upon the old rationalistic methods ; the story, *e.g.*, of Jesus walking upon the sea had its origin in the words, 'Ye know not at what hour of the night your Lord cometh.' In some respects it is not too much to say that even the moral sinlessness of Jesus is endangered, if not sacrificed. Keim rejects,

it is true, the visionary hypothesis, but he finds no alternative except the conviction that nothing irrefutable can be known concerning the issue of the life of Jesus, an assertion equally unsatisfactory with that of Baur. He speaks sometimes of the early and Apostolic testimony rendered to the appearances of the risen Jesus, while at times he seems unable to realize the full force of this early testimony and its marked reserve. In his chronology we note another instance of Keim's arbitrary method, for he knows of no going up to Jerusalem before the last Passover, and the public career of Jesus is comprised within a single year.

In spite of much that savours of subjectivity, Keim, however, stands out as the writer who, in the '*Life of Jesus* movement,' as Nippold has called it, has hitherto treated most fully of the Gospels as authorities, with the exception, perhaps, of Weizsäcker. We have seen how this need of a full treatment of the Gospels as sources had been felt since the days of Strauss' first edition of his *Leben Jesu*, and we shall see that this need is still further felt and emphasized.

4. Within a few years of the latest publication of Keim's work, two important Lives of Jesus, which are often mentioned together, issued from the press in Germany, viz. **B. Weiss'** *Leben Jesu* and **Beyschlag's** book bearing the same title. These books are of interest not only as important in the '*Life of Jesus* movement,' but as further and valuable attempts to deal with our Gospels and their sources. Here it must be sufficient to say that they testify to the new importance which had been given to the Synoptic problem by H. Holtzmann's book, *Die Synoptischen Evangelien*, 1863.

5. **Holtzmann's** book gains its value not only by its rejection of the 'tendency' theories with regard to the composition of the Gospels, but also because, in its advocacy of the two-document hypothesis, as we now call it, it marks a new departure, and lays down a foundation for future study.[*] Holtzmann's investigations had been published in the year before Strauss gave to the German people his popular *Life of Jesus*, in which, as we have seen, his account of the Gospels was still based upon the Tübingen researches ; but Holtzmann's theory has a permanent interest for us to-day, while the author's subsequent statements of his views may be found in his published commentaries. It has indeed been said of the two-document theory that it may almost be reckoned to have passed out of the rank and number of mere hypotheses ;[†] and at all events any account of the life and teaching of Jesus, or any investigation as to the historical character of the Gospels, will have to take note of it not only in itself, but in its many possible combinations with other sources.

This statement can be easily verified by a perusal of recent expositions of their views by representative writers. We turn, *e g.*, to Wendt's *Die Lehre Jesu*, and we see how he allows a connexion in all likelihood between the statement of Papias as to St. Mark being the interpreter of St. Peter, and the actual contents of our earliest Gospel, and how he finds in the *Logia* of St. Matthew an uncommonly rich and valuable material of Apostolic tradition, which may be placed by the side of St. Mark as a complementary source for a knowledge of the teaching of Jesus. Bousset, in his little but important book, *Was wissen wir von Jesus?*, is loud in his praises of the way in which modern research as to the original sources of the Synoptics harmonizes so strikingly with the famous statement of Papias. So, too, von Soden refers to the previous work of Weizsäcker and Holtzmann, and speaks of two *Urevangelien* (although he uses this term with some hesitation), which go back one to St. Peter and the other to St. Matthew, and he finds it possible to trace a connexion between the familiar statement of Papias and our Gospels of St. Mark and St. Matthew (*Die wichtigsten Fragen im Leben Jesu*, 1904, pp. 42, 62).[‡]

---

[*] See also J. Estlin Carpenter, *The Bible in the Nineteenth Century*, p. 301, and his remarks on the two-document hypothesis. He points out that the conclusion of Weizsäcker's investigations pointed in the same direction (cf. his *Untersuchungen über die Evangelische Geschichte*, 1869, 2nd ed. 1901).

[†] Moffatt, *Historical NT*[2], p. 264.

[‡] So, too, Deissmann, 'Evangelium und Urchristentum' in *Beiträge zur Weiterentwicklung der christlichen Religion*, p. 128. Deissmann seems inclined to attach some considerable weight to oral tradition and its trustworthiness, a very important consideration.

---

[*] B. Weiss, *op. cit.* pp. 184, 187.

[†] Sanday, art. 'Gospels' in Smith's *DB*[2] ii. p. 1218.

It must, of course, be remembered that, like H. Holtzmann, these other writers referred to did not regard the two-document theory as alone sufficient to explain the origin of the Gospels. Other material was no doubt present in the Synoptics in addition to the two documents, as we can see in the case of St. Luke (cf. art. LUKE).[*]

And it must also be remembered that Holtzmann did not start with a belief that the sources of the first two Gospels, St. Mark and St. Matthew, must correspond with the two documents referred to by Papias. On the contrary, the investigation of the Gospels showed him that there were two sources at the base of our Synoptic writings, which closely resembled the statements of Papias with regard to the documents which he referred to St. Mark and St. Matthew.

6. But some half dozen years before Holtzmann's book was published, another, and in many respects a more serious, opposition to the methods of the Tübingen School, had made itself felt in the breaking away of **Albrecht Ritschl** from his former standpoint. In 1857 this final break was made, and for more than thirty years Ritschl was destined to be a great and growing factor of interest in the German theological world. Ritschl was keenly alive to the importance to be attached to the Person of Christ. In his treatment of the books of the NT he was to a great extent conservative, inasmuch as he accepted the traditional authorship of so many of those books, as, *e.g.*, of the Gospel of St. John.

But, on the other hand, it is urged that Ritschl's own peculiar doctrine and the paramount stress which he laid on our experimental knowledge of Christ's power to confer spiritual freedom and deliverance, no doubt tended to make him independent of, if not indifferent to, the results of criticism. Ritschl and his distinguished follower **W. Herrmann** lay the greatest stress, and would have us lay the greatest stress, upon the impression made upon us by the 'historical' Christ. But it is not easy to ascertain what is meant by this 'historical' Christ, by loyalty to whom the true Christian is known, This is the favourite Ritschlian position, this insistence upon the impression which Christ makes upon the soul historically confronted with Him. But we naturally ask, From whence and from what is this impression derived? Not, surely, from the impression of the earthly life of Jesus alone, as Herrmann maintained, but from what Kähler has called the 'Biblical Christ'; the Christ of the NT is the Christ not only of the Gospels, but of the Epistles and of the Church.

It is urged, indeed, by the Ritschlians represented by Herrmann, that this faith in the historical Christ guarantees that, whatever criticism may effect, it cannot interfere with the truth and power of the position already won, and with the response made by the human soul to the perfection of Christ presented to us in the Gospels. But whatever may have been the case with Ritschl himself, it can scarcely be said that his method has prevented those who claim in some measure to be his followers from dealing very loosely with the Gospel miracles, or with such events as the Virgin-birth and the Resurrection of the Lord. And it is difficult to see how this process of solution can fail to weaken the impression made by the 'historical' Christ, and our confidence in the revelation which we owe to His life.

Many of those who are classed as Ritschlians dismiss in a somewhat arbitrary fashion sayings and deeds of our Lord which seem to them to admit of difficulty. The manner, *e.g.*, in which **J. Weiss** has dealt with the oldest Gospel, that of St. Mark, in his *Das älteste Evangelium*, cannot be said to inspire a conviction of the truthfulness of many of the most familiar Gospel narratives. Herrmann's own statements help us to see how subjective his method may become. He maintains, *e.g.*, that through the impression which Christ makes upon us and our experimental knowledge of His power to confer freedom and deliverance, all uncertainty as to whether the figure of Jesus, which works thus upon us, belongs to legend or to history is in the nature of the case impossible.[*]

But it seems a curious argument to maintain that the impression which Jesus makes upon us is the positive revelation made by God in Christ, while the Gospels from which we derive that impression may or may not consist in this instance or in that of legendary and untrustworthy matter. Herrmann himself says that, in face of the seriousness of a desire for a salvation which means forgiveness of sins and life in spiritual freedom, the miracles in the NT necessarily become of minor importance . . . he who has found Jesus Himself to be the ground of his salvation has no need of those miracles (*op. cit.* p. 180). But if Jesus is 'found' through the portrait of His life presented to us in the NT, it is not too much to say that that life is inextricably bound up, from its beginning to its close, with the miraculous, and that the impression which that life has made upon the world has been made by a record from which the miraculous cannot be eliminated. Conviction of sin, *e.g.*, must precede deliverance from it; and St. Peter's cry, 'Depart from me; for I am a sinful man, O Lord' (Lk 5[8]), resulted not only from Christ's teaching, but also from the proof of His miraculous power.

7. It is in this attitude towards the miraculous, and in this effort to lessen its scope, that we may find a point of contact between what we may call the 'scientific' and the Ritschlian school. In a large and growing number of German critics who might be described as 'scientific,' if not as radical, there is an acceptance of the miracles of healing as due to the power of the personality of Jesus and to the response of faith which He evoked. We may see this in more or less degree in the statements of O. Holtzmann (*Leben Jesu*, pp. 58, 149, 166), or in those of Furrer (*Das Leben Jesu Christi*, pp. 129, 130), or in Bousset (*Was wissen wir von Jesus?*, p. 56). So, too, statements of a similar kind meet us again and again in the account of the miracles of Jesus given us in the series of popular little books on the religious-historical aspects of Christianity, which is now in course of publication in Germany (cf. *Die Wunder im NT*, pp. 32 ff., 51 ff., by Traub).[†] And in our

---

[*] The two-document theory is sharply criticized by M. Lepin (*Jésus Messie et Fils de Dieu*, p. xxxvi, 1905), although he admits that it is adopted by a certain number of Romanist writers, *e.g.* Loisy, Batiffol, Minocchi, Lagrange. M Lepin's contention is that the theory in question is not in agreement with the most ancient testimony, which regards St. Matthew as the first of the Gospels, composed for the Jewish Christians of the first days, and as an authentic work of the Apostle. He admits at the same time (p. xxxvi) that some Protestant writers claim to make this two-document theory accord with the full authenticity of the First Gospel (*i.e.* St. Matthew), and that admission is at least made of the semi-authenticity of this Gospel by those who claim to recognize in the primitive document, the *Logia* of Papias, the actual work of St. Matthew. He also observes that even Schmiedel allows that if St. Matthew was not the author of the *Logia*, he may at all events have been the author of a writing, more ancient still, upon which the *Logia* depended (*Encyc. Bibl.* art. 'Gospels,' ii. 1891). See also Stanton, *The Gospels as Historical Documents*, pp. 17, 18, for the fact that the Gospel which bears the name of St. Matthew is the most often quoted of the Synoptics in early days; and it is difficult, as even Jülicher allows, to account for the attribution of a Gospel to an Apostle so little known as St. Matthew.

[*] See, *e.g.*, *Communion with God*, p. 177, and cf. p. 81 ff. Eng. tr., for other statements made above.
[†] See on the value of these little books the *Hibbert Journal*, January 1906.

own country we remember how decisively Dr. P. Gardner would discriminate between mere wonders of healing and 'miracles proper,' and how he describes Jesus as a healer of disease as historic.[*]

But at the same time it is evident how much there is which is arbitrary in this modern treatment of the miraculous. Thus Lepin justly criticises **Schmiedel's** attitude in this connexion.[†] Schmiedel distinctly affirms that it would be wrong in any investigation of the miracle-narratives of the Gospels to start from any such postulate or axiom as that miracles are impossible (*Encyc. Bibl.* art. 'Gospels,' col. 1876). But a few pages later in the same article (col. 1885) he writes that it is quite permissible for us to regard as historical only those cures of the class which even at the present day physicians are able to effect by psychical methods—as, more especially, cures of mental maladies (cf. also Harnack, *Das Wesen des Christentums*, p. 18). The same occasional power is ascribed to Jesus by Professor N. Schmidt, *The Prophet of Nazareth*, p. 264.

So, too, Schmiedel (*op. cit.* col. 1882) and Wendt (*Die Lehre Jesu*, p. 471) agree in interpreting the words in our Lord's message to the Baptist as referring to the spiritually dead, 'the dead are raised' (Mt 11[5], Lk 7[22]), just as in their opinion the preceding words are to be interpreted of the spiritually lame and blind. But, in the first place, there is no proof that the previous clauses are to be interpreted in any such spiritual sense, and the Evangelists evidently did not so interpret them. It is urged that we can find a precedent for this spiritual interpretation in the familiar passage Is 35[5]; but nothing is said in Isaiah of the raising of the dead, a fact entirely ignored by N. Schmidt, who is at one with Schmiedel and Wendt in their interpretation (*l.c.* p. 238). Moreover, it is very open to question if there was any Jewish expectation that the Messiah would raise the dead, so that St. Matthew and St. Luke had no ground of general belief upon which to base the raisings of the dead which they so evidently attributed to Jesus of Nazareth. Even if there are isolated statements in Jewish theology which attribute to the Messiah the power of raising the dead, it would seem to have been far more generally believed that God would Himself raise the dead. Further, even in those passages which do attribute this power to the Messiah, it is most important to remember that they refer to the resurrection of *all the dead*, and that there is no allusion of any kind in Jewish writings to the raising by the Messiah of single individuals (cf. Edersheim, *Life and Times of Jesus the Messiah*, i. p. 632).

But this attitude, maintained by some of Ritschl's followers and by the representative critics of the 'scientific' school, extends to a crucial question and a crucial miracle, viz. *the Resurrection of our Lord from the dead*. We may readily grant Ritschl's own acceptance of this fundamental historical fact of Christian belief.[‡] But what is to be said of a large number of his followers? Some of them would no doubt allow that Christ awoke to a heavenly life with God, or they would labour to draw a distinction between the Easter faith and the Easter message ; or they would allow that the Resurrection was a fact of religious faith, or that, whilst the traditional record is often doubtful, the essential contents of the record are, and mean, everything.[§] But it is upon this question of the Resurrection that Feine rightly takes his stand, and upon the inclusion or exclusion of this fact

in any satisfactory picture of the historical Christ.[*]

If we turn again to one of the most prominent critics who may be classed as Ritschlians, **A. Harnack,** we are not only met by his famous distinction between the Easter faith and the Easter message, but we also become aware that his classification of the Gospel miracles is not calculated to increase our belief and confidence in the character of the Gospel narrative. Harnack admits, indeed, that the spiritual power of Jesus was so great that we cannot dismiss offhand as an illusion the reports that He could make the blind to see or the deaf to hear. But, apart from these reports of surprising cures, Harnack would regard the stories of the miraculous which are connected with Jesus as arising from exaggerations of natural and impressive events, or from the projection of inner experiences on to the outer world, or from an interest in the fulfilment of OT records, or from various parables and sayings. In these and in similar ways the miraculous stories arose. And yet, after all is said, it will be noticed that there are narratives of miracles which do not fall under the above heads, and these Harnack comprises under one category as impenetrable stories, the secret of which we cannot solve.[†]

8. One other and important point in which the 'scientific' German theologians and the left wing of Ritschl's followers agree is in *the rejection of the Apostolic authorship of the Fourth Gospel*. And with this rejection there must needs be a serious weakening of the evidence as to our Lord's Deity, although no doubt this evidence may be substantiated from the Synoptists alone. The remarkable thing is that both Ritschlian and 'scientific' critics are alike impressed with the indications that in the Fourth Gospel we are dealing with a source or sources full of minute details and vivid recollections.

Thus Wendt, while he refers the Gospel to some Christian of Asia Minor, admits that this Evangelist, whoever he was, belonged to the same circle in which the old Apostle St. John had lived, and that he thus had access to written information and to oral tradition received from the beloved disciple (*Das Johannesevangelium*, p. 216 ff.). P. W. Schmidt, in his *Die Geschichte Jesu* (1904, p. 95), cannot help feeling the force of the exact and minute geographical references which the Fourth Gospel contains, although he rejects the Johannine authorship. Von Soden, although he refuses to rank the Fourth Gospel amongst the historical sources for a 'Life' of Jesus, admits on the same page that the writer of that Gospel had access to good traditions in his notices of place and time, in the small details which mark his recitals, and in his information as to various personalities (*Die wichtigsten Fragen im Leben Jesu*, 1904, p. 5).[‡] If we turn to English critics we find Dr. Percy Gardner inclined to follow Dr. Harnack's view that the Fourth Gospel was the work of John the Elder, who was a disciple of John the son of Zebedee. Dr. Gardner, too, is so impressed with the writer's precise local knowledge, that he thinks it may well have been derived from one of the Apostles, and very likely from John the son of Zebedee.[§]

So far as English criticism is concerned, it cannot be said that anything which has been urged has broken down the strong lines of defence which we

---

* *A Historic View of the NT*, p. 141 ff.
† *Jésus Messie et Fils de Dieu*, 1905, pp. lxvi, lxvii.
‡ See the remarks of Garvie, *The Ritschlian Theology*, p. 225.
§ Orr, *Ritschlian Theology*, p. 203.

* Thus, in dwelling upon the contending parties and their disputes as to the 'historical' and the 'biblical' Christ, Feine writes: 'Die Streitfrage lief also darauf hinaus, ob die Auferstehung Jesu mit in die Bild des geschichtlichen Christus einzubeziehen sei oder nicht'; cf. *Das Christentum Jesu und das Christentum der Apostel*, 1904, p. 54.
† See especially the reply of Prof. W. Walther of Rostock to Harnack's *Das Wesen des Christentums*[5], 1904, pp. 47, 48. Harnack's last category is expressed by the word 'Undurchdringliches.' Reference should also be made to T. H. Wright's *The Finger of God*, 1903, p. 194, and his valuable Appendix on the view taken by Dr. Percy Gardner and by Dr. Harnack of our Lord's miracles, and also on early Christian and mediæval miracles.
‡ See, further, Lepin, *op. cit.* p. 360. He rightly emphasizes the fact that Jülicher, in the last edition of his *Einleitung* (p. 324), dismisses the attribution of the Fourth Gospel to a presbyter John as without value, and regards the Gospel as composed by a Christian, dependent upon the Apostle John, at the opening of the 2nd century.
§ *A Historic View of the NT*, pp. 153, 184.

owe to Lightfoot, Westcott, Sanday, and more recently to Dr. Drummond. As Dr. Stanton has rightly urged, there must have been good grounds for believing that the Fourth Gospel was founded upon Apostolic testimony, in order to overcome the prejudice which would be created by the contrasts between it and accounts which had been more generally received.*

9. But whilst, in the respects which we have mentioned, the position of the Ritschlian School is so unsatisfactory, we may welcome, with those who are not at all in sympathy with Ritschl's views or with the views of his followers, the witness borne by so many Ritschlians to a living Lord and the unique place which they assign to the Person of Christ in any account of Christianity.†

Among those, *e.g.*, who are classed as Ritschlians we have on the one hand men like Troeltsch supporting strongly and ardently the value of the study of Comparative Religion for a right knowledge of Christianity, and maintaining that the religious-historical method should be applied to every department of theological thought; whilst Harnack, with Reischle, hesitates to follow, and is evidently alive to the fact that the method in question may be carried too far. Dr. Harnack's words on the subject are remarkable. He expresses his desire that the German theological Faculties may remain so for the pursuit of inquiry into the Christian religion, because Christianity is not a religion by the side of other religions, but *the* religion, and because Christ is not one Master by the side of other Masters, but *the* Master; the disciples were conscious that they possessed in Christ not merely a Master, but that they knew themselves to be men, new men, redeemed by Him, and that therefore they could preach Him as Saviour and Lord.‡ It is quite true that the American writer, Professor W. A. Brown, sees in some of Harnack's statements, and in his recognition of the gospel of Jesus as that which satisfies the deepest depths of humanity, the promise of a better understanding between the two parties in the Ritschlian ranks : ' With this recognition of the *anima naturaliter Christiana,* of a preparation for Christianity within the very nature of man, we find Harnack, even while insisting with Ritschl upon the originality of Christianity, admitting the complementary truth for which the speculative school contend.' §
Unfortunately, however, the advocates of the religious-historical method, at least in its extreme form, show no disposition to confine themselves to the comparison of Christianity with other religions in respect to its inward witness alone; they extend this comparison to the historical facts of the NT, and they do so in a manner which savours of recklessness and extravagance.‖ The need of caution seems to be admitted even by Pfleiderer when he writes, ' Before all things, we must guard against the constant practice of imagining that the inward affinity of religious conceptions implies a connexion in their external history.' ¶
And when we turn to the Ritschlians, it is evident that men like Reischle are well aware of the many safeguards with which the religious-historical method and its study should be guarded.** His criticism, *e.g.* that we should not not only points of likeness but points of unlikeness in any pursuit of the method in question, is endorsed by Heinrici and others, who have joined with Harnack in opposing the religious-historical study of

Christianity as if it were only one of many religions. Thus Heinrici insists with great force that if the resurrection of Jesus is considered from the religious-historical point of view it is unique; and in the same manner A. Jeremias, in answer to Gunkel, insists that the resurrection of Jesus, as it is described as taking place, is without analogy in any other religion.* In the same pamphlet Reischle warns us against the danger of attaching too great value to analogies, and transforming them into relations of dependence. He does not deny that analogies exist between Oriental religions and Christianity, but he is keenly alive to the fact that their right and correct appreciation is a very difficult matter. He allows, *e.g.*, the existence of a Jewish Gnosticism in the Apostolic Age, but he regards as a fantastic hypothesis Gunkel's attempt to attach to this Jewish Gnosticism an important rôle in establishing points of connexion between Christianity and other religions (*op. cit.* pp. 30, 31). So, too, he rightly draws attention to the danger of overvaluing the form of an expression to the neglect of the actual meaning of its contents, and he quotes the aphorism, ' Si duo dicunt idem, non est idem' (*op. cit.* pp. 31, 33). He further illustrates this position by the use of the familiar formula, ' In the Name of Jesus,' of which Heitmüller has made so much.† Such words might, no doubt, be employed as a magical or superstitious formula, but they might also be used as a confession of Christian faith in Jesus, or as an invocation to Him in prayer, or as an appeal to Him as the Mediator with God.
Once more, and above all, Reischle rightly insists upon the insurmountable limits which beset the religious-historical method in any endeavour to solve the problem of the personal religious life of great religious personalities. If this is difficult in the case of Paul, it is still more so, urges Reischle, in the case of Jesus (*op. cit.* pp. 42, 43).‡

10. But this acknowledgment of the marvellous personality of Jesus may not only be seen in the writings of the Ritschlian School and its various and variant members. We may recognize it—it is not too much to say—in German writers of every school and in German works which appeal to all sorts and conditions of men.

Amongst modern Church historians in Germany no name stands more deservedly high than that of von Dobschütz. ' The Apologist,' he tells us in the concluding words of his work on *Primitive Life in the Early Church,* ' could point triumphantly to the realization of the moral ideal among Christians of every standing. That was due to the power which issued from Jesus Christ, and actually transformed men. In the midst of an old and dying world this new world springs up with the note of victory running through it. " If God be for us, who can be against us ? " " And this is the victory which overcometh the world, even our faith." . . . Christianity possessed what the speculations of Neo-Platonism lacked, the sure historical basis of Jesus Christ's Person.' But the remarks of von Dobschütz are of further interest, because he again emphasizes the importance to be attached to the Person and work of Jesus, in his contribution to the ' Religionsgeschichtliche Volksbücher,' in the course of publication in Germany. Here, too, he dwells upon the Apostolic Age, and he points out that in it we do not only find Judaism with a strong addition of Messianic expectation ; Jesus had transformed the stiff monotheistic belief in God into a living trust in God, and a joyous spirit of adoption as God's children had taken the place of Pharisaic self-satisfaction and timorous fear.§ Or we turn to another series of books, of a somewhat larger and more expensive kind, entitled *Lebensfragen,* and here, too, we meet with the same emphatic testimony. Thus Weinel tells us that the Hegelian philosophy hindered Strauss from estimating or understanding the greatness of the personality of Jesus (*Jesus im neunzehnten Jahrhundert,* p. 42, 1904). Again, a little later on (p. 64), in summing up the significance of modern criticism, he declares that no century has striven so earnestly to discover the features of the true historical Jesus as the nineteenth ; and he points out that whilst almost all the witnesses whom he cites in proof of this occupy a critical standpoint in dealing with tradition, they show at least respect, and for the most part reverence, for Jesus of Nazareth, and have recognized the power of salvation in the gospel which He taught. And as this image of Jesus in its living reality and in its purity is placed before the eyes of men, he prophesies that it will win the heart of humanity until all men are more and more transformed into its likeness.

11. But then we have to face the remarkable fact that this picture of the wondrous personality of Jesus is most frequently derived by advanced critics from the Synoptics alone. The Fourth Gospel is ruled out of court, or at the best reduced to a testimony of secondary worth. The account,

---

* *The Gospels as Historical Documents,* i. p. 277 ; and cf. to the same effect, Sanday, *The Criticism of the Fourth Gospel,* 1905, pp. 15, 41 ; see also Dr. Chase, *Cambridge Theological Essays,* 1905, p. 383. Mr. Conybeare has the boldness to assure us that any modern scholar who upholds the hypothesis of the Apostolic authorship of the Fourth Gospel is at least as wanting in perspective and insight as the much derided upholders of the view that the Pauline Epistles were only concocted in the 2nd cent. (*Hibbert Journal,* July 1903, p. 620). But he takes no notice of Dr. Drummond's defence, and, whilst he is loud in his praises of the Abbé Loisy, it may be of interest to note that another liberal Romanist, Père Calmes, has now given us an admirable defence of the Johannine authorship, *l'Évangile selon Saint Jean,* 1906. For a sharp and decisive reply to the extraordinary attack by Kreyenbühl upon the authorship, see Gutjahr, *Die Glaubenswürdigkeit des Irenäischen Zeugnisses über die Abfassung des vierten kanonischen Evangeliums,* 1904, p. 4 ff.
† See Orr, *The Christian View of God and the World,* pp. 53, 79, on the central place of Christ's Person in His religion. ' Ritschlianism is perhaps nothing more nor less than a determined attempt to find the whole contents of Christianity in the Person of Christ ' (*Cambridge Theological Essays,* 1905, p. 517).
‡ *Die Aufgabe der theol. Facultäten und die allgemeine Religionsgeschichte,* pp. 16, 17.
§ *The Essence of Christianity,* 1903, pp. 286, 287.
‖ See, *e.g.,* Dr. Blass on Gunkel's extraordinary theory as to the resurrection of our Lord on the third day, *Expos. Times,* xvi. [1904] p. 14 ; and the present writer may refer to *The Testimony of St. Paul to Christ,* pp. 526, 527, or A. Meyer's *Die Auferstehung Christi,* 1905, p. 167.
¶ *Early Christian Conception of Christ,* pp. 153, 154.
** See his *Theologie und Religionsgeschichte,* 1904, p. 27 ff.

* Heinrici, *Urchristentum,* 1902, p. 38 ; A. Jeremias, *Babylonisches im NT,* p. 43 : ' Die Tatsache der Auferstehung Jesu Christi ist in der Religionsgeschichte analogielos.'
† *Im Namen Jesu,* 1903, p. 197 ff.
‡ See on this pre-eminence belonging to the Person of Christ in contrast to other religions, Fairbairn, *Philosophy of Religion,* pp. 532, 533 ; and Söderblom, *Die Religionen der Erde,* 1905, pp. 62–64.
§ *Das Apostolische Zeitalter,* p. 5.

e.g., of the raising of Lazarus, if it is no longer treated after the manner of Renan as a flagrant deception to which Jesus lent Himself, is regarded not as historical but as allegorical.* But even in what is allowed to us of the Synoptic record, doubt is thrown upon our Lord's claim to judge the world, or upon His declaration that He would give His life as a ransom for many, to say nothing of the refusal to admit, as we have already noted, a large proportion of His miracles as historical.

In like manner the significance of St. Paul's testimony to the facts and teaching of the Gospels, as also the significance of his claim to work miracles in the power which Christ bestowed, is minimized, if not disregarded.

We thus owe this wonderful picture of a great personality mainly, if not entirely, to documents bearing the names of three writers of whom we are assured that we know very little, and whose claims to be the authors of the books (in their present shape at all events) which bear their names must be very largely and seriously discounted. And yet these obscure writers have given us the picture of a life and of a teaching the beauty and the excellence of which mankind has never ceased to acknowledge.

'Here,' says a learned and cultured Jew, after allowing that the Synoptic Gospels do contain teaching which in comparison with average Judaism is both valuable and original, both new and true, 'we have religion and morality joined together at a white heat of intensity. The teaching often glows with light and fire. . . . The luminous juxtaposition of even familiar OT doctrines may be novel and stimulating. The combination of Dt 6⁴·⁵ with Lv 19¹⁸—the love of God with the love of man—in Mk 12²⁹⁻³¹ was surely a brilliant flash of the highest religious genius.'† Elsewhere he speaks of 'the first-classness' of the Synoptics, and points out that there are one or two facts which still tend to weaken the effect of the best Rabbinic teachings and sayings upon the average Jewish consciousness. The first fact is that 'these nobler sayings and teachings are buried in a mass of greatly inferior matter, so that they are difficult to unearth. They are not collected together in a lovely setting, united and illumined by the story of a noble life.' He further remarks that, suppose we make a selection of the great sayings and teachings of the Talmud and the Midrash, it must be admitted that the same 'powerful, driving, and emotional effect as the sayings and teachings of the Gospels' is not produced.‡

12. But we note that this picture is in many respects entirely opposed to current Jewish conceptions of the day. No one has emphasized this more strongly than Bousset in relation to the Jewish anticipations and expectations of the Kingdom of God. He insists, indeed, upon the Messianic consciousness of Jesus, without which he regards not only the whole work of Jesus, but the conduct of His disciples after His death, as unintelligible. But if Jesus regarded Himself as the Messiah, it is evident, continues Bousset, that He did so in a manner totally opposed to the predominant and current Jewish expectations. Spiritual conceptions of the Messiah were not altogether wanting, but political hopes always occupied the central place in the picture. In the sense of such hopes Jesus was not the Messiah, and would never have become so. He expected the sovereignty of God and not that of Israel, the victory of good and the judgment of evil, not the triumph of the Jew and the annihilation of the Roman; He preached a kingdom in which the vision of God was granted to the pure, and as the preparer for and the ruler in that kingdom He regarded Himself.§ But the Synoptists no less than St. John furnish us with another picture which was even more decisively

opposed to the current conceptions of the Jewish nation, the picture of a suffering Messiah. It is not too much to say that 'the idea of the Messianic sufferings and death is one that wakes no echo in the heart of any Jewish contemporary of our Lord, not excepting even His disciples.'* In short, the words of Dalman are amply justified, 'Suffering and death for the actual possessor of the Messianic dignity are in fact unimaginable according to the testimony of the Gospels' (*Words of Jesus*, p. 265, Eng. tr.).

'Nothing could mark more strongly the contrast between Jewish Messianic notions and the picture of the Messiah as realized in our Gospels, than the following passage from the *Jewish Encyclopedia*: "Jesus' word on the cross, "My God, my God, why hast thou forsaken me?" was in all its implications itself a disproof of the exaggerated claims made for Him after His death by His disciples. The very form of His punishment would disprove those claims in Jewish eyes. No Messiah that Jews could recognise could suffer such a death."'†

This representation of a suffering Messiah which the Gospels presented so uncompromisingly, pressed hard for a solution upon the famous founder of the Tübingen School:

'Never was that which bore the outward appearance of ruin and annihilation turned into such signal and decisive victory, and so glorious a passage into life, as in the death of Jesus. Up to this time there was always a possibility that He and the people might come to agree on the ground of the Messianic faith . . . but His death made a complete and irreparable breach between Him and Judaism. A death like His made it impossible for the Jew, as long as he remained a Jew, to believe in Him as the Messiah. To believe in Him as the Messiah after His dying such a death involved the removal from the conception of the Messiah of all the Jewish and carnal elements which were associated with it' (*Church History*, i. p. 42, Eng. tr.).

Baur's solution of the difficulty forms one of the most curious pages in the history of modern criticism. He allows that nothing but the miracle of the Resurrection could restore the faith of the disciples after such a death as that of the Cross, and yet he assures us in the same breath that the question as to the nature and the reality of the Resurrection lies outside the sphere of historical inquiry. What history requires is not so much the fact of the Resurrection of Jesus, as the belief that it was a fact.

In more recent utterances we seem to catch an echo of Baur's words, and his remarks anticipate Harnack's familiar distinction between the Easter faith and the Easter message. The Easter faith, according to Harnack, is a conviction which tells us that the Crucified has achieved an inward victory over death, and has entered into eternal life. But this so-called Easter faith appears, not unjustly, to many thoughtful minds to do away with the need of Easter altogether. The Crucified overcame death on Good Friday, so far, that is, as an inward triumph was concerned. On Good Friday, and not upon the third day, He entered upon eternal life. And if nothing special happened on Easter Day, there seems to be little sense or point in talking about 'Easter faith.'‡

But, further, this contrast between the current ideas of the Messiah and the Messiahship of Jesus in the Gospels may be illustrated from the succeeding history of the Jewish nation and from the cul-

---

* See, *e.g.*, the remarks of Loisy, *Autour d'un petit livre*, 1903, p. 97 ff.; and, on the other hand, Loisy's fellow-countryman and religionist Th. Calmes, *L'Évangile selon Saint Jean*, 1906, pp. 68, 75.
† C. G. Montefiore, 'The Synoptic Gospels and the Jewish Consciousness,' in the *Hibbert Journal*, July 1905, p. 658.
‡ *Ib.* p. 652.
§ See Bousset's remarks in his *Was wissen wir von Jesus?* p. 61.

* Muirhead, *Eschatology of Jesus*, 1904, p. 256. See, further, Fairbairn, *Studies in the Life of Christ*, p. 308 ff.; J. Drummond, *The Jewish Messiah*, 1877, pp. 356, 357; Row, *Jesus of the Evangelists*⁴, pp. 140, 213; Bishop Gore, *Bampton Lectures*, p. 192. The whole appendix in Schürer's *GJV*³ ii. p. 553 ff., entitled 'Der leidende Messias,' should be consulted.
† Professor Votaw (Chicago), 'The Modern Jewish View of Jesus,' in the *Biblical World*, xxvi. No. 2 [Aug. 1905], p. 110. The passage above is cited from the *Jewish Encyc.* vii. p. 166; and the present writer would venture to refer for further literature to the *Witness of the Epistles*, pp. 23, 360.
‡ See Dr. Walther's valuable criticism, *Ad. Harnack's Wesen des Christentums für die christliche Gemeinde geprüft*⁵, 1904, p. 134; and also Dr. F. Blass, 'Science and Sophistry' in *Expos. Times*, Oct. 1904.

mination of the Jewish hopes in the pretender Bar Cochba in the reign of Hadrian. The report was circulated that the Messiah had at last appeared, and fabulous numbers are said to have joined his standard in insurrection against the Romans. We know how the struggle ended in terrible disaster to the Jews, although for some few years they fought with all their characteristic stubbornness and desperation. But the chief actor in the drama, Bar Cochba, reveals to us only too plainly the kind of Messiah whom the majority of the Jews expected, and whom they were prepared to welcome: 'Jesus offered Himself unresistingly to death; the impostor died in arms . . . whatever Jesus Christ was not, this pretender was. Whatever this pretender was, Jesus Christ was not.'[*] One feature in the new Messiah's career may be specially noted, viz. the absence of any attempt on his part to work miracles, although no doubt all sorts of exaggerated stories of strength and power gathered round his name.[†] But if, as we are told, there was an irresistible tendency to attribute miraculous powers to the Messiah, if, as Professor Percy Gardner asserts, there was every probability that whether actual or not the miracles would be reported, how is it that no such miracles gathered around the name of Bar Cochba? Is not the only explanation to be found in the fact that Jesus of Nazareth actually worked miracles, while the pretender worked none?[‡] Nor must it be forgotten in this connexion that the Jews in early times never attempted to deny that our Lord wrought miracles; on the contrary, they admitted the miracles, whilst they referred them to Satanic arts or to a knowledge of the sorcery which Jesus had brought with Him from Egypt.[§] In the same manner the modern Jews admit that our Lord gained His notoriety not merely from His teaching but from His miracles, specially from those which He wrought as a healer of the sick. 'It was not,' writes Dr. Kohler in the *Jewish Encyc.* vii. p. 167, 'as the teacher of new religious principles nor as a new lawgiver, but as a new wonder-worker that Jesus won fame and influence among the simple inhabitants of Galilee in his lifetime.'[‖]

13. But there were other claims made by our Lord, in addition to the claim to work miracles, and of these great and supernatural claims it may be said that they cannot possibly be derived from the picture of the Messiah which meets us in the OT. Some words remarkable in their bearing upon this subject were uttered by Dr. Charles in speaking before the University of Oxford on 'The Messiah of the Old Testament and the Christ of the New Testament':

'As other claims which are without parallel in the Old Testament prophecy of the Messiah, we shall mention first His claim to judge the world; and next, to forgive sin; and, finally, to be the Lord of life and death. In the Old Testament these prerogatives belong to God alone as the essential Head of the kingdom, and appear in those prophetic descriptions of the kingdom which ignore the figure of the Messiah, and represent God as manifesting Himself among men. Here, then, we have the Christ of the Gospels claiming not only to fulfil the Old Testament prophecies of the various ideals of the Messiah, but also to discharge the functions of God Himself in relation to the kingdom.'[¶]

* Row, *Jesus of the Evangelists*, p. 147 ff.
† Edersheim, *History of the Jewish Nation*, p. 200 ff.
‡ See especially the *Church Quarterly Review*, Jan 1904.
§ *Jesus Christ in the Talmud* (Laible), p. 45 [Eng tr].
‖ *The Modern Jewish View of Jesus*, by Prof. Votaw, p. 109, Chicago University Press, 1905.
¶ *Expositor*, 6th series, v. [1902] p. 258. In Jewish apocalyptic literature, it should be added, the Messiah is in many cases the agent of God in the judgment which takes place at the beginning or close of the Messianic reign; even in the final judgment He is represented as God's agent, and only in the later section of the *Book of Enoch* does He appear as the judge at the last day. We may also contrast our Lord's own words as to His Parousia with the fantastic and grotesque descriptions of Jewish theology.

Nor can it be said with any justification that these Divine prerogatives are ascribed to our Lord late in time, or that they were simply Christian accretions. We need look no further than St. Paul's earliest Epistle, 1 Thess., to come across statements which can scarcely mean anything less than that our Lord was associated as Judge with God the Father; that He is the medium of salvation, and that we obtain life through His death; that the prayers of Christians are to be addressed to Him; that whether we wake or sleep our true life is in Him (cf. 1 Th 3^{13} $5^{9.10}$). Nor is there any reason to suppose that in such statements to the Thessalonians St. Paul is putting forward a conception of Christ which differed from that entertained by the rest of the Church:[*] 'The Son of God,' he writes to the Corinthians, 'who was preached among you by us (not by St. Paul himself alone), even by me and Silvanus and Timothy, was not yea and nay, but in him is yea,' 2 Co 1^{19} (cf. 1 Th 1^1). Moreover, in the expression 'the Son of God' St. Paul's teaching no less than that of the Gospels indicates a unique relationship between the Father and the Son; cf. *e.g.* Ro $8^{3.32}$. And if we ask whence St. Paul's conception was derived, it seems not unreasonable to maintain that it was derived from the statements and the teaching of our Lord Himself.

There is a famous passage contained in two of the Synoptic Gospels which so strongly resembles the phraseology of St. John that it has been called, and not unjustly, an aerolite from the Johannine heaven: 'All things have been delivered unto me of my Father, and none knoweth the Son save the Father, neither doth any know the Father save the Son, and he to whomsoever the Son willeth to reveal him' (Mt 11^{27}, Lk 10^{22}). Dr. Harnack, although he does not deny that Jesus spoke these words, weakens their force and meaning, and it is well to turn for a criticism of his statements to Dr. Swete's remarks on 'The Teaching of Christ,' *Expositor* (6th Series, vii. [1903] p. 407):

'The knowledge claimed is that of a son, and it rests upon sonship; it is a strange misreading of the words which reverses this order, as Professor Harnack seems to do—it is not knowledge which makes Christ "the Son," but sonship which enables Him to know. He declares that He knows God as only a son can know his father, and that this knowledge is not a possession which other sons of God naturally share with Him, but one which belongs of right to Him alone, and to others only so far as He is pleased to impart it. This is to claim not only unique knowledge, but a unique Sonship. It is difficult to discover any essential difference between this statement of St. Matthew and the closing words of St. John's prologue.'

The Abbé Loisy does not allow that our Lord ever spoke these words, but affirms that they are derived from some primitive Church tradition; and he goes so far as to suppose that they were derived, in part at all events, from Sir 51.[†] But it is difficult to believe that such words could have found the place which they occupy in two of our Gospels unless they were spoken by our Lord. It should be remembered that they are regarded, not merely by conservative but by 'scientific' critics, as forming part of that 'collection of discourses' which probably comes to us from the Apostle St. Matthew. Indeed, Keim long ago affirmed that there is no more violent criticism than that which Strauss had introduced, viz., the repudiation of a passage so strongly attested. Moreover, the alleged dependences upon Sir 51 are in reality very superficial; in some particulars the alleged likenesses are such as might be found in the utterances of any Jewish speakers. It may also be noted that while the

* See, further, Dr. Sanday, *Criticism of the Fourth Gospel*, p. 231; Bishop Gore, *The Permanent Creed and the Christian Idea of Sin*, p. 10 ff. If we compare 1 Co 2^8 and Ja 2^1, it is notable how both St. Paul and St. James can speak of Jesus as 'the Lord of the (*i.e.* the Divine) glory.'
† See for a recent criticism, *Cambridge Theological Essays*, 1905, p. 455 ff.

points of comparison are preserved, the points of contrast are entirely omitted. For example, Jesus the son of Sirach in his prayer thanks God because He has hearkened to him and delivered him from peril; our Lord in His prayer thanks the Father for revealing to babes that which had been concealed from the wise and prudent.*

But it should further be borne in mind that these statements in Mt. and Lk. do not stand alone; that the Gospel which is probably the earliest of the Synoptics speaks of 'the Father' and of 'the Son' absolutely, and that the words employed can only be fairly explained as assigning to our Lord a unique relationship to God: 'But of that day or that hour knoweth no one, not even the angels in heaven, neither the Son, but the Father' (Mk 13³²). If such words are suspected, we may fairly ask who would have been likely to introduce them? Dr. Schmiedel, who generously allows us to construct a 'scientific' 'Life of Christ' from five sayings and four incidents of the Gospels, does not attempt to deny that our Lord spoke these words; and although, of course, he uses them for his own purposes of exegesis, we may now take it that this representative of the most advanced criticism allows us to regard this verse in St. Mark's Gospel as an utterance of our Lord Himself.† Professor N. Schmidt refuses to accept even Mk 13³², and regards the words in question, 'neither the Son,' as probably an interpolation (*The Prophet of Nazareth*, pp. 147, 231). Such words presuppose, he thinks, such a doctrine of subordination as was cherished in the Church of the second century. But has he forgotten the doctrine of subordination in 1 Co 15²⁸, a passage which even he dares not refuse to St. Paul?

In addition to Dr. Swete's remarks, to which reference has been made above, we may cite the following passage, as bearing closely on our subject, from the Dean of Westminster's *Study of the Gospels*, p. 109: 'Observe that the titles "the Father" and "the Son" are used absolutely (*i.e.* in Mt. and Lk. *loc. cit.*). We are familiar with this use from St. John's Gospel. But it occurs but once again in the Synoptic Gospels, Mark xiii. 32. . . . It is an important fact to be borne in mind in connexion with the Christology of John's Gospel, that this special mode of speech is attested once for St. Mark and once also for the non-Markan document. We could hardly have stronger evidence, from the historical point of view, that our Lord Himself did thus speak of Himself absolutely as "the Son." It is not necessary to explain how unique is the claim which is put forward by this language.' ‡

Professor N. Schmidt, indeed, has boldly argued against this uniqueness in His relation to the Father which our Lord claims, by asserting that He always availed Himself of the general expression 'Abba, Father,' and that the variants 'my Father' and 'your Father' were introduced by the Greek Evangelists.§ But, as M. Lepin has pointed out in his valuable book, it is to be noted that a distinguished Aramaic scholar, Dr. Dalman, does not hesitate to affirm, in contradistinction to the

* Cf. Lepin, *op. cit.*, Appendix, on the Abbé Loisy's position, 1904.

† See art. 'Gospels,' *Encyc. Bibl.* ii. 1881. For a valuable criticism of Schmiedel's position, cf. Fairbairn, *The Philosophy of the Christian Religion*, p. 303.

‡ See, further, Sanday, *Criticism of the Fourth Gospel*, p. 211; Fairbairn, *op. cit.* p. 476; Headlam, *Critical Questions*, pp. 190, 191; *Cambridge Theological Essays*, 1905, p. 431.

§ *Encyc. Bibl.* art. 'Son of God,' iv. 4696. This is one of the most painful articles in the whole of the four volumes, and we cannot be surprised that Professor Schmidt throws doubt upon our Lord's exact words, when at this time of day he can throw doubt, as in this same article, upon St. Paul's authorship of 1 Thessalonians. More recently Professor Schmidt has repeated these arguments, and he appears to regard Mt 11²⁵, Lk 10²¹ as casting an undeserved reflexion upon the character of Jesus! (*The Prophet of Nazareth*, p. 152). On Schmidt's denial that our Lord ever called Himself the Son of Man see Stalker's *Christology of Jesus*, p. 72, and Muirhead's *Eschatology of Jesus*, p. 148). If the Gospels were written as late as Schmidt believes, it is certain that the introduction into all of them of such a title as 'the Son of Man' would have been regarded with the gravest suspicion, and would have failed to gain acceptance in Christian circles where our Lord's Godhead was fully recognized.

assertions of Dr. Schmidt, that the unique position assumed by Jesus follows from the invariable separation which He makes between 'my Father' and 'your Father' (*Words of Jesus*, p. 281 [Eng. tr.]); and a few pages later Dr. Dalman writes: 'Nowhere do we find that Jesus called Himself the Son of God in such a sense as to suggest a merely religious and ethical relation to God, a relation which others also actually possessed, or which they were capable of attaining or destined to acquire' (p. 287).*

14. We must remember, too, that not only do a great number of English and German writers of note acknowledge the closeness of St. Paul's acquaintance with our Lord's life and teaching,† but that this testimony of St. Paul is materially and increasingly strengthened by the large number of Epistles which are now almost universally acknowledged to have been from his pen. Some sixty years ago (1845), F. C. Baur, the founder of the Tübingen School, published his 'Life' of St. Paul, and accepted only four of the Apostle's letters, in which he believed that he could discover the notes of a fundamental difference between Paul and the Twelve; to-day at least double that number of the Epistles which bear St. Paul's name is accepted by nearly all critics alike. It would be easy to point in proof of this to Dr. C. Clemen's statements in his recent *Life and Work of St. Paul* (see i. pp. 6–162). We must not forget that Professor Schmidt is prepared to accept only the *Hauptbriefe* and Philippians, and that he regards even the former as having suffered insertions; thus, 1 Co 15⁵⁻¹¹ is a later insertion (*The Prophet of Nazareth*, pp. 193, 200, 397). Colossians and even Philemon are rejected; and we are told, in the only reference to Bishop Lightfoot in the volume, that his is the ablest defence of these two Epistles, but that it fails to do full justice to the counter arguments (p. 194). It is not surprising after this that Professor Schmidt, following on the lines of Van Manen, rejects all the Epistles of St. Ignatius, and that he makes no reference to their acceptance by Lightfoot, Harnack, Zahn.

If we turn for a moment to the little books of a popular kind which are in course of publication in Germany, at the price of a few pence each, we find that to Professor Vischer of Basle (known to us in England first of all through Dr. Harnack) is committed the volume which treats of the Epistles of St. Paul. Vischer accepts all the Epistles, nine in number, which are accepted by Dr. Clemen; and even when he comes to deal with Ephesians (which Clemen rejects), he frankly acknowledges, with Erich Haupt in the latest edition of Meyer's Commentary, that the alleged objections are by no means decisive, and that more is to be said for St. Paul's authorship than against it. In cases, moreover, in which the traditional structure of the Epistles is questioned, as in 2 Cor., it is frankly allowed that the separate letter alleged to be found in chs. 10–13 is, no less than the rest of the Epistle, the work of St. Paul; and even in the case of the Pastoral Epistles, the existence of genuine Pauline fragments is constantly maintained (see, further, von Soden's *Urchristliche Literaturgeschichte*, 1905, pp. 28, 162).

* See also Lepin, *Jésus Messie et Fils de Dieu*, pp. 297, 300, 2nd ed. 1905.

† See, *e.g.*, Zahn, *Einleitung*, ii. p. 166 ff., where references to (1) the history, (2) the words of Jesus, are drawn out at length; J. Weiss, *Das älteste Evangelium*, 1903, p. 33 ff.; Weinel, *Paulus*, 1904, p. 246 ff.; P. W. Schmidt, *Die Geschichte Jesu*, 1904, ii. pp. 67, 68; Bacon, *Story of St. Paul*, 1905, p. 53; Fairbairn, *The Philosophy of the Christian Religion*, p. 443 ff.; Chase, *Credibility of the Acts of the Apostles*, p. 252 ff.; H. A. A. Kennedy, *St. Paul's Conceptions of the Last Things*, p. 96 ff.; Headlam, *Critical Questions*, 1903, p. 161 ff.; and the present writer would venture to refer to the last lecture in *The Testimony of St. Paul to Christ*.

15. It has been recently said by Dr. Driver that 'the testimony to our blessed Lord's life and work is so much more nearly contemporary with the events recorded than can often be shown to be the case in the Old Testament, and also so much more varied and abundant, that by an elementary principle of historical criticism it is of proportionately higher value.' * This claim to be so nearly contemporary with the events of the Gospels may fairly be made for the testimony of St. Paul; and even if Dr. Zahn is right in refusing to follow the recent trend of criticism, which places the Apostle's conversion within a year or two of our Lord's death, it is certain that St. Paul must have been acquainted, at a very early date, with those who had known the Christ, and who had recognized and felt His power (Gal 1[18. 19], Ro 16[7]). Professor Schmidt has lately argued (*The Prophet of Nazareth*, p. 157) that as the distance of time increased between Jesus and the later Pauline literature, the term Son of God assumed more and more a metaphysical significance. But Professor Schmidt accepts Philippians as undoubtedly the work of St. Paul. How then does he deal with the great Christological passage, Ph 2[6ff.]? We are simply informed that this passage may easily be an interpolation (p. 195 f.).

It seems to the present writer quite beside the mark to maintain that,'in investigating the facts and beliefs which lie between A.D. 30–45, we have no contemporary documents, that, in fact, none exist, and that our only guide is inference based on later writings and developments.† We have already seen the inferences to be derived from the statements in one of St. Paul's earliest and practically undoubted Epistles, 1 Th., and that these inferences of necessity presuppose a preaching and teaching considerably anterior in time to the actual date of the Epistle mentioned.

Moreover, we may well ask, What is meant by the word 'contemporary'? General Gordon was murdered in the Sudan in 1884. If a man wrote an account to-day of the closing years of Gordon's life, we should scarcely refuse to give it the title of a contemporary record.‡ But we are separated from the death of Gordon by a longer period of time than that which elapsed between the conversion of St. Paul and his earliest written testimony to the belief and practice of the primitive Church.§

16. But, further, in any attempt to estimate, however briefly, the bearings of modern criticism, it must not be forgotten that the Gospels are now placed at a much earlier date than formerly.‖

Strauss long ago maintained that the Gospel story would be impregnable if it was certain that it was written by eye-witnesses, or at all events by men who lived close to the events. And this hypothesis of Strauss has at least been verified to this extent in our day, by the acknowledgment that all three of the Synoptics rest in no small degree upon genuinely Apostolic sources. Even Jülicher, who places our First Gospel at the year 100 or thereabouts, admits that the writer used our Second Gospel and a collection of *Logia* made by St. Matthew; and in this Second Gospel he sees the work of John Mark, founded on reminiscences of the Petrine circle. And if, as is generally admitted, the writer of our Third Gospel employed Mark and the Matthæan *Logia* among his chief means of information, he, too, must have based a great part of his work upon two Apostolic sources.*

The force of St. Paul's contemporary testimony we have already noted, and we are now able to point in addition to the Apostolic sources underlying our Gospels. And thus we have a twofold guarantee against the alleged process of idealization which magnified by degrees the deeds and sayings of Jesus, a theory which, as M. Lepin observes, is urged by writers in many respects so far removed from each other as Schmiedel and Loisy.†

17. And if modern criticism has strengthened the external evidence for the early date of our Gospels, may we not say that it has strengthened the internal evidence also? If we turn, for example, to the Gospel of St. John, we find a remarkable testimony in Furrer's well-known *Leben Jesu Christi* (1905), a testimony the force of which is increased when we remember the writer's close acquaintance with the geography of the Holy Land. Thus Furrer speaks of the definite and exact geographical notices which are scattered up and down the pages of the Fourth Gospel, many of which we know only through the author of the book, and which correspond so thoroughly to the actual conditions.‡ The narrator must thus have been a man who was acquainted with the home of Jesus by his own personal observation, so that we have the feeling that we are able to realize the scenes as it were with our own bodily eyes. If we consider the picture drawn by the Synoptists, we are again struck with its vivid reality, its truthful correspondence to the conditions, social and political, of the country, its acquaintance with the religious parties of the Jews and the Messianic hopes of the people, with its curious mixture of a foreign civilization and government with the hereditary customs and judicial procedure of the Jews. But the picture thus presented to us could not have been drawn except by the hands of men contemporary with the events which they purport

---

* *The Higher Criticism*, 1905, pp. ix and 32; cf. also and esp. Dr. Driver's remarks in his *LOT* [6] p. xi, where the same point is more fully elaborated: 'Viewed in the light of the unique personality of Christ, as depicted both in the common tradition embodied in the Synoptic Gospels and in the personal reminiscences underlying the Fourth Gospel, and also as presupposed by the united testimony of the Apostolic writers belonging almost to the same generation, the circumstances are such as to forbid the supposition that the facts of our Lord's life on which the fundamental truths of Christianity depend can have been the growth of mere tradition, or are anything else than strictly historical. The same canon of historical criticism which authorizes the assumption of tradition in the OT forbids it—except within the narrowest limits, as in some of the divergences apparent between the parallel narratives of the Gospels—in the case of the NT.'

† This is apparently maintained by Dr. Moffatt, *Historical NT* [2], p. 66.

‡ Prebendary Sadler (*The Lost Gospel*, p. 196), writing in 1876, well asks if we should refuse to describe an account of the Crimean War (1854–1855) as a contemporary history.

§ In this connexion we may recall Renan's words, 'Jesus is known to us by at least one contemporary piece of evidence, that of St. Paul' (*Histoire du Peuple d'Israel* [2], 1887, i. p. xviii).

‖ An excellent summary of data bearing out this in connexion with prominent critics is given by Lepin, *op. cit.* p. xxxi. Cf. also Deissmann, 'Evangelium und Urchristentùm,' in *Beiträge zur Weiterentwicklung der Christlichen Religion*, 1905; and also Harnack, *Chron.* i. pp. 654, 655. In this first volume Dr. Harnack (1897) places the Synoptic Gospels well within the 1st century, and A.D. 110 is assigned as the furthest limit for the Gospel of St. John with the Epistles of St. John and the Apocalypse. In this and in other respects great jubilation was raised

at Dr. Harnack's conservatism; but he soon made it clear that the acceptance of the date or the authorship of a book by no means involves the acceptance of its contents. Hühn's series of 'Helps to the Understanding of the Bible,' which has had a large circulation in Germany, is not very satisfactory in relation to the Gospels. Hühn, however, admits that the 'Logia' which were used by Matthew, if not composed by him, date before A.D. 70. Of the author of the Gospel of Mark he holds that nothing definite can be known; but at the same time he speaks of Matthew as composed after 70, and of Mark as being of an earlier date. Luke is the latest of the three, and, like so many advanced critics, Hühn places Luke after 70 on the ground of 21[21 24]. But it does not increase our confidence in Hühn's researches when he places St. John's Gospel at 135–140, and gives as one of his chief reasons the passage Jn 5[43], in which he sees a reference to Bar Cochba (A.D. 132), who came 'in his own name,' and was recognized as the Messiah of the Jews (*Das Neue Testament*, 1904, p. 13 ff.). In answer to Hühn's inference from Lk 21[21] see Blass, *Philology of the Gospels*, 1898, p. 41.

* See *Biblical World* (Chicago), December 1895, art. 'Sources of the Life of Christ,' by Professor Burton, and the *Church Quarterly Review*, January 1905, art. 'The Synoptic Gospels and Recent Literature,' pp. 416, 417.

† *Op. cit.* pp. xlviii–l.

‡ See, further, Sanday, *Criticism of the Fourth Gospel*, p. 113.

to describe. It would have been impossible after the fall of Jerusalem in A.D. 70 and the entire *bouleversement* which that catastrophe caused, to recreate, as it were, the conditions which prevailed socially, politically, religiously before that capital event.[*] This impression of truthfulness which the contents of our Gospels cannot fail to make, is witnessed to even in quarters in which we might not altogether expect it. Thus Jülicher speaks of our Gospels as of priceless value as authorities for the history of Jesus ; and even if much of their data may be uncertain, Jülicher nevertheless maintains that 'the impression of the Saviour which they leave on the reader's mind is a faithful one ; if the total picture of Jesus which we obtain from the Synoptics displays all the magic of reality, this . . . is owing to the fact that they . . . painted Jesus as they found Him already existing in the Christian communities, and that their model corresponded in all essentials to the original.'[†]

18. In concluding this article, it will not be unfitting, especially in a Dictionary devoted to the subject of 'Christ and the Gospels,' to emphasize once again the importance attached to the Person of Christ in the current literature of to-day. It would be easy to refer in this connexion to the statements made by representative writers in England and America. We turn, *e.g.*, to Professor Nash's *History of the Higher Criticism*, and we find him speaking (p. 25) of 'that Christ who is humanity's Amen to all the Divine promises' ; or to Dr. P. Gardner's *Historic View of the NT*, and we find him maintaining (pp. 88–91) that the founder of Christianity stands above all other religious teachers.[‡] Even Professor Schmidt can speak again and again of the wonderful personality of Jesus : 'While other teachers may and will do much for our modern world, the healing, purging, elevating influence of Jesus is of priceless value. No man can come into contact with him without feeling that life goes out of him' (*The Prophet of Nazareth*, p. 360).

At the Liverpool Church Congress, 1904, one of the speakers on NT criticism, Professor F. C. Burkitt, remarked at the close of his speech that the only time when Christians would have cause to be afraid was when the far off figure of Jesus Christ no longer attracted the critic and the student, but that there was no evidence that that day was within sight. The last statement finds ample corroboration in the English and German literature of to-day.[§] We may look again at the little series of popular books to which reference has been made as in progress of publication for the German people. One of them is entitled *Die Quellen des Lebens Jesu*, by Professor Wernle of Basle, whose name is widely known in England for his works on the Gospels and the Beginnings of the Christian Religion. Here again we find this same primary importance attached to the Life and Person of Jesus, in spite of so much which betrays impatience of any definite dogmatic teaching. What-

ever else, in Wernle's view, we may learn from St. Paul, we may at all events learn this, that in Jesus, notwithstanding the fact that He died a death of shame on the cross, St. Paul saw his own life and that of the world divided, as it were, into two parts—with Jesus, without Jesus. In Jesus we behold a man who helps us to understand aright ourselves, the world, and God ; who accompanies us as the truest friend and guide in the needs and struggles of the present, and to whom we can entrust ourselves with all confidence for the future. In the same series Professor Pfleiderer, who discusses the preparation for Christianity, finds in the sentence, 'The Word was made flesh,' the dividing line between the many and varied speculations of philosophy and the full and actual manifestation of the Divine Logos in the life of the Son of God (*Vorbereitung des Christentums in der Griechischen Philosophie*, p. 66). Another writer, Dr. Bousset, to whom reference has been made, and who is also well known to English readers, expresses himself in the little book *Was wissen wir von Jesus?*, which H. Holtzmann recommends as the best guide-book for the German laity, in almost rapturous language :

'Gradually there rises before us a Form in which the soul rejoices, the Form of the great liberator, the mighty opponent of all forms of Pharisaism, and at all times the great upholder of simplicity in religion. And more even than this : there stands before us the Form of Jesus the friend of sinners, the preacher of the forgiveness of sins, who in all the greatness of His own moral strength condescends with all the tenderness of a woman to the lost and the outcast, the Form of One who, conscious of victory, could unite His disciples to Himself by an everlasting bond when the last sad night of His earthly life had come and death stood before His eyes.'

In this Personality Bousset finds the true origin of Christianity. Other factors no doubt contributed, but there was one factor above and beyond them all, the Person of Jesus. Jewish Messianic hopes, Greek philosophy, the social conditions of the Roman Empire, the organization and the spirit of the religious social clubs and of the mysteries, all these contributed. One by one, in a few graphic pages, Bousset passes them in review, and shows how each of them was insufficient alone, because each of them wanted the distinctive power which made Christianity all-sufficient and all-victorious, the power of a life-giving Personality, the possessor and the bestower of new spiritual agencies, the bringer of life out of death. In words of almost evangelical fervour Bousset proclaims the presence in history of this unique personal power. None can doubt the power of personality in the religious life, and all religions which occupy the foremost place in the world testify to this in some measure more or less.[*]

In face of such acknowledgments, we cease to wonder that von Soden in his recent *Die wichtigsten Fragen im Leben Jesu*, 1904, devotes so much of his book to a consideration of the Personality of Jesus (p. 82 ff.). Amongst other matters of varied interest, he points out that there is no evidence that Jesus was influenced in any direct manner by Buddha or Plato, or by Philo and his predecessors (p. 108). He was the child of His people and country, He knew no foreign literature (p. 109), He was far removed from any association with the hard and gloomy character of Pharisaic piety, but at the same time His life was in harmony with all that was best in the Jewish and

---

* Swete, *Critical Questions*, pp. 47, 48 ; and Lepin, *op. cit.* pp. xxi–xxx.

† See *Church Quarterly Review*, *l.c.* p. 411 ; and also Jülicher, *Einleitung in das NT*[3], p. 294.

‡ In a noteworthy passage (*op. cit.* p. 100) the same writer says, after referring to the fact that Jesus does not use the phrase 'Our Father in heaven' as including both Himself and His disciples : 'It would not show a want of the critical spirit to go further than this, and to maintain with Professor Harnack that Jesus assigned a special significance to His death in relation to the forgiveness of sins, claimed an unique dignity as King and Lord, regarded His death as a passage to glory, and anticipated a speedy return to the earth as judge.' It is disappointing to read the next paragraph : 'Yet I cannot persuade myself that on strictly historical grounds these statements could be definitely established.'

§ See, *e.g.*, Fairbairn, *Christ in Modern Theology*, pp. 18, 21 ; and Sir Oliver Lodge in *Hibbert Journal*, Apr. 1906, p. 644, where he 'accepts the general consensus of Christendom as testifying to the essentially Divine character of Christ.'

* This insistence upon the importance of the personal influence is again notably marked in one of the most recent of popular 'Lives' of Jesus by Dr. Furrer of Zürich. See, *e.g.*, the closing page of his *Leben Jesu*, 1905, p. 261, in which, after insisting upon regarding Jesus as man, he ends, as he himself expresses it, with the confession of the centurion, 'This man was the Son of God.' Furrer's treatment of his theme is marked by reverence and sympathy, and he rightly points out that, until the heart is in sympathy, no justice can be done to the holiest portraiture of humanity (*Vorwort*, p. v).

Greek types of humanity, and von Soden concludes his book (p. 111) by saying that this Personality which was beyond the invention of the Evangelists, and which is presented to us in a picture which knows no flaw, is an irrefutable, integral fact, and *the* wonder of wonders in the world's history rich in wonders. (See, further, the same writer's *Urchristliche Literaturgeschichte*, p. 5).

Once more; we turn to H. Wendt, another German well known in England, not only by his works on the Teaching of Jesus and the Gospel of St. John, but by two lectures delivered in this country in 1904. He speaks of the significance of Jesus in revelation (*The Idea and Reality of Revelation*, p. 28 ff.). Jesus is for him the highest revelation of God, although not the only one.* At the foundation of all the forms of Christianity there is a reverence for Jesus Christ as Saviour and Mediator. And Wendt concludes by assuring us that a large number of the German theologians of to-day aspire to lead Christianity back to its original form, to the simplicity and sublimity of the primitive teaching of Jesus (p. 91). There is much in such acknowledgments which carries us back to the confession of A. Réville. For him 'Jesus is supremely great,' and he adds, 'Let us fear nothing as to the glory of the Son of Man. We owe it to Him, to the Divine ideal dwelling within Him, that we know ourselves to be the children of God ; it is in His pure heart that love between God and man has been realized, and in this He possesses a crown which none can ever take from Him' (*History of the Doctrine of the Deity of Jesus Christ*, Eng. tr. p. 164).

In such utterances as these, which might be easily multiplied, although they fall very far short of the language of the Church and the Creeds, we mark how the interest of thoughtful minds in Germany, America, France, England is centred in the Person of Christ, and how also many of these writers whom we have mentioned admit that there was a relationship between Jesus and the Father so intimate as to be, if not metaphysical, yet at all events unique, and that this is conceded by critics who would depreciate St. Luke's opening narrative of the Gospel history or St. Peter's confession at Cæsarea Philippi (Mt 16[16]).

And as we listen to such utterances, sometimes full of hope and confidence, sometimes full of pathos and tender religious feeling, we are conscious that the old question, 'Lord, to whom shall we go?' has not lost its interest for the world or for ourselves, and we thankfully recognize the acknowledgment rendered even by the spirit of criticism and inquiry, as it searches into the will and the teaching of Him who alone is the Revealer of the Father, 'Thou hast the words of eternal life.'

LITERATURE.—Lichtenberger, *Hist. of Germ. Theol. in 19th Cent.*, Eng. tr.; Mill, *Mythical Interpretation of the Gospels* ; Pfleiderer, *Development of Theology, Germany and Great Britain* ; J. E. Carpenter, *The Bible in the Nineteenth Century* ; Nash, *Hist. of the Higher Criticism* ; Matheson, *Aids to the Study of Germ. Theol.*; Fairbairn, *Place of Christ in Mod. Theol.*, and *Philos. of Christ. Rel.*; Schwarz, *Zur Gesch. der neuesten Theol.*; A. S. Farrar, *Crit. Hist. of Free Thought* (Bampt. Lect. 1862) ; Plumptre, *Christ and Christendom* (Boyle Lect.); Nippold, *Hdbch. der neuesten Kirchengesch.* vol. iii. pt. 2 ; C. L. Broun, 'Protest. Crit. of NT in Germany,' *Interpreter*, vol. ii. No. 1 ; W. Adams Brown, *The Essence of Christianity* ; Weinel, *Jesus im neunzehnten Jahrhundert* ; N. Schmidt,

* In this book (p. 88) Wendt speaks of the Gospel type of Christian piety which has no analogy in other religions, and the significance of salvation by Jesus Christ is found in His revelation, as perfect Son of God, of God's fatherly love, and in the powerful impulse which He has exerted on men to draw them into this blessed sonship. This Gospel type, he adds, has found its expression in Apostolic times in many great passages of the Pauline letters, and above all in the First Epistle of St. John, which Wendt regards as the genuine work of the disciple who stood nearest to Jesus, the most beautiful record of a mind directly inspired by His words and life.

The Prophet of Nazareth, p. 21 ff.; Harnack, *Chronol. der Altchrist. Litt.* i., and *Das Wesen des Christentums* ; Cremer, *A Reply to Harnack on the Essence of Christianity*, Eng. tr. ; Walther, *Ad. Harnack's Wesen des Christentums für die Christliche Gemeinde gepruft* ; Herrmann, *Communion with God*, Eng. tr.; Orr, *Christ. View of God and the World*, and *Ritschlianism: Expository and Critical Essays* ; Garvie, *Ritschlian Theology* ; Reischle, *Theol. und Religionsgesch.*; Söderblom, 'Religionen der Erde,' iii. Heft 3, in *Religionsgesch. Volksbücher* and other volumes in the same series, as, *e.g.*, 'Der Ursprung des Buddhismus' by Hackmann, and 'Welche Religion hatten die Juden als Jesus auftrat?' by Hollmann ; Bousset, 'Die Religionsgesch. und das NT' in *Theol. Rundschau*, July 1904 and following numbers ; Cumont, *Les mystères de Mithra* ; A. Jeremias, *Babylonisches im NT* ; Gunkel, *Zum religionsgesch. Verständniss des NT* ; 'Impressions of Christianity from the point of view of non-Christian Religions,' *Hibbert Journal*, July 1905 and following numbers ; Farnell, *Evolution of Religion* ; Jordan, *Comparative Religion* ; Cheyne, *Bible Problems* ; Westcott, *The Gospel of Life* ; Wace, *Christianity and Agnosticism* ; Illingworth, *Reason and Revelation* ; Swete, *The Teaching of Christ* ; Stalker, *The Christology of Jesus* ; Godet, *Defence of the Christian Faith*, Eng. tr. ; Row, *The Jesus of the Evangelists* ; Stanton, *The Jewish and the Christian Messiah* ; Dalman, *Die Worte Jesu*, i.; Hennecke, *Neutest. Apokryphen*, 1904 ; Baldensperger, *Die Messianisch-apokalyptischen Hoffnungen des Judenthums* ; Schürer, *GJV*[3] ; Muirhead, *The Eschatology of Jesus* ; Votaw, 'Modern Jewish View of Jesus,' *Biblical World*, xxvi. 2 [1905] ; Sanday, *Inspiration*, and *Criticism of the Fourth Gospel* ; J. A. Robinson, *Study of the Gospels* ; Gore, *The Permanent Creed and the Christian Idea of Sin*, *Contentio Veritatis*, 1902 ; Headlam, *Critical Questions*, 1903 ; *Cambr. Theol. Essays* (esp. those by Chase, Mason, Foakes-Jackson) ; *Criticism of the NT* (St. Margaret's Lectures), 1903 ; W. M. Ramsay, *The Education of Christ* ; P. Gardner, *A Historical View of the NT*, with Sanday's criticism in *JThSt*, Jan. 1902 ; Moffatt, *Historical NT* ; von Soden, *Urchristliche Literaturgeschichte* ; Gamble, *Christ and Criticism* ; Loisy, *L'Évangile et l'Église*, and *Autour d'un petit livre* ; Lepin (esp. in reply to Loisy), *Jésus Messie et Fils de Dieu*, 2nd and 3rd edd.; T. A. Lacey, *Harnack and Loisy* ; Hollmann, 'Leben und Lehre Jesu' in *Theol. Rundschau*, April 1904 and following numbers ; Luthardt, *Gesammelte Vorträge*, pp. 3–173 ; G. Uhlhorn, *Das Leben Jesu in seinen neueren Darstellungen* ; E. de Pressensé, *Jésus-Christ*, pp. 4–56 ; Annibale Fiori, *Il Christo della Storia e della Scrittura*, 1905 ; Vischer, 'Jesus und Paulus' in *Theol. Rundschau*, April, May, 1905 ; Feine, *Jesus und Paulus* ; Deissmann, 'Evangelium und Urchristentum' in *Beiträge zur Weiterentwicklung der Religion*, 1905 ; M. Dals, *The Bible*. See, further, books mentioned above, and in artt. BIRTH OF CHRIST, GOSPELS, etc.

R. J. KNOWLING.

CROSS, CROSS-BEARING.—For the historical aspects of the literal cross, see CRUCIFIXION.

The English word 'cross' is from the Latin *crux* through the French *croix*, Old French and Middle English *crois*. But σταυρός (from ἵστημι) is not synonymous with *crux*, but was originally a wider term, and, like σκόλοψ, meant a stake (Hom., Herod., Thuc., Xen.). In the NT, however (not present in LXX), it is used only in the sense of *crux*.

This article deals only with the figurative uses of the term in the Gospels or in relation to the death of Christ on the cross as interpreted in the Acts and Epistles. For the archæological and magical history of the sign of the cross outside as well as within the pale of Christianity, see Zöckler's *Das Kreuz Christi* (1875 [Eng. tr. 1878]), Goblet d'Alviella's *Migration of Symbols* (1894), and his art. 'Cross' in Hastings' forthcoming *Dictionary of Religion and Ethics*. The true mysticism in the cross of Christ as conceived by St. Paul comes properly before us.

1. The use of the word by Jesus in the sense of *cross-bearing*.—On three separate occasions Jesus spoke of cross-bearing as essential to discipleship. The first is in Mt 10[38], when He sent out the Twelve on a special preaching tour at the close of the Galilæan ministry, just a little over a year before His death. Meyer, *in loco*, considers this passage proleptically misplaced by St. Matthew, and thinks it should come after Mt 16[24]. But there is no need of this supposition, for the figure of bearing one's cross would be quite intelligible to Jews since the days of Antiochus Epiphanes, Alexander Jannæus, and Varus. Josephus (*BJ* v. xi. 1) even says that Titus crucified so many that there were not places for the crosses, or crosses for the victims. The Jews themselves had not favoured crucifixion, save Alexander Jannæus, the 'Thracian' in spirit. Broadus (on Mt 16[24]) rightly denies that this saying of Jesus about bearing one's cross is an anachronism before His own crucifixion. He did bear His own cross (Jn 19[17]), perhaps the crosspiece properly speaking; but so did the criminals usually who were crucified, for Plutarch says: ἕκαστος κακούργων ἐκφέρει τὸν αὑτοῦ σταυρόν (de Sera Num. Vind. 9). It is a general illustration that the disciples could have easily understood, though they were not yet able to see the evident prophetic allusion to Christ's own literal experience. It is not without special point that Jesus thus expressed the fundamental principle of self-sacrifice under the image of the cross. He did not plainly say that He would be crucified till shortly before His death (Mt 20[19]), but Jesus Himself is conscious of the death on the cross which 'He himself will be called upon to endure' (Meyer on Mt 16[24]).

The second time that Christ spoke of cross-bearing was when He rebuked Peter for playing the part of Satan (Mk 8[34], Mt 16[24], Lk 9[23]). On the first occasion the Master was giving directions to the disciples about their preaching, but here He addressed this vivid condition of discipleship 'unto all' (Lk 9[23]) as a 'deterrent in a high degree, suggesting a procession of furciferi headed by Jesus and consisting of His followers' (Swete on Mk 8[34]). Many of the followers of Judas and Simon in Galilee had been crucified (Jos. Ant. XVII. x. 10). St. Luke adds 'daily,' though the aorist term ἀράτω is used. The permanence of this cross-bearing is emphasized by the present tense of 'follow' (ἀκολουθείτω).

St. Luke alone gives the third use of the expression (14[27]), and it is in Peræa, not long before the raising of Lazarus from the dead. In this instance βαστάζω, not αἴρω, is used, the only NT example of the figurative, as Jn 19[17] is the only NT instance of the literal, use of the verb with σταυρός (Plummer, Internat. Crit. Com. in loco).

2. The term 'Crucified' comes to be a favourite one with the name of Jesus. The angels at the empty tomb speak of 'Jesus the Nazarene, the Crucified One' (Ἰησοῦν ζητεῖτε τὸν Ναζαρηνὸν τὸν ἐσταυρωμένον, Mk 16[6], Mt 28[5]). St. Peter in his great address on the day of Pentecost charges the Jews with having crucified Jesus (Ac 2[36]). He repeats the charge when brought before the Sanhedrin (4[10]). St. Peter elsewhere always (Ac 5[30] 10[39], 1 P 2[24]) speaks of Christ as hanging on a tree (ξύλον); but this non-classical use of ξύλον as equal to gibbet or cross (the stocks in Ac 16[24]) is found in the LXX as tr. for Heb. עֵץ (Gn 40[19] etc.). St. Paul so uses the term also in Ac 13[29] and Gal 3[13] (quotation here from Dt 21[23]). Each example in the NT is a quotation from the LXX. But in the LXX ξύλον does not refer to crucifixion, but rather to the prohibited nailing up of unburied bodies after the manner of the heathen nations (1 S 31[10]). But St. Paul speaks rather of 'Christ crucified,' more properly, 'Christ as crucified' (predicate), Χριστὸν ἐσταυρωμένον (1 Co 1[23]), and once he sharply accents the idea by saying Ἰησοῦν Χριστὸν καὶ τοῦτον ἐσταυρωμένον (1 Co 2[2]), in opposition to his Judaizing opponents. This was his method of openly setting forth (προεγράφη) Jesus as crucified (Gal 3[1]), like a public placard. The blindness of the enemies of Christ comes out in St. Paul's use of the term with the Lord of glory (1 Co 2[8]), and yet He was crucified in weakness (2 Co 13[4]). Rev 11[8] merely identifies Jerusalem as the city where Jesus was crucified.

3. The cross as *the epitome of the gospel.*—The disciples naturally passed to this idea when they came to understand the meaning of the death of Christ. The cross that had seemed the destruction of their hopes (Lk 24[21]) now became the symbol of the gospel of grace. 'But we preach Christ cruci-

fied' (1 Co 1[23]), says St. Paul, as opposed to Jewish spectacular apocalyptics and Greek philosophizing; and he preached nothing else, not simply at Corinth, for he had done so at Athens (Ac 17[31]), and this was the settled purpose of his ministry (1 Co 2[2]). It was not the example of Jesus that St. Paul preached, but Jesus as the crucified Saviour, who, and not Paul, was crucified 'in your behalf' (1 Co 1[13]). It was, in fact, by His death on the cross that Jesus made the sacrifice for our sins, in our behalf, and in our stead. We are under (ὑπό) a curse (Gal 3[10]), and Christ became a curse (κατάρα) for (ὑπέρ) us, and so redeemed us from (ἐκ) or out from under the curse of the Law (v.[13]). He became the curse, and came between us and the overhanging law of God.

This conception of the cross reappears in Col 1[20], where Jesus is said to have made peace and reconciliation with God possible according to the good pleasure of God 'through the blood of his cross.' The word 'blood' is probably used here to emphasize, against the early Docetic Gnostics, the reality of the human nature of Jesus. So in Col 2[14] by a vivid image the Law itself is represented as nailed to the cross with the body of Christ, and so taken out of the way and no longer binding on us as a means of salvation (cf. Ro 7[4]). In Eph 2[16] the cross is presented as the basis for a double reconciliation, both with God and so with each other, 'through the cross, having slain the enmity thereby.' So both Jew and Gentile have 'access in one Spirit unto the Father,' and the middle wall of partition is broken down. They form one body in Christ, the Church of all the elect of which Christ is head, one new man. 'The word of the cross' (1 Co 1[18]), then, is St. Paul's message to men. It was to proclaim this truth that Christ sent him forth (1 Co 1[17]); and this he will do by holding fast to the great essential fact rather than by fine-spun theories (1 Co 1[17] 2[5]), lest the gospel be emptied of all real power (κενωθῇ).

4. The *shame* of the cross.—It was a real shame that Jesus underwent when He suffered on the cross as a common malefactor. The Jews considered as accursed one whose dead body merely was hung upon a gibbet, and St. Paul recognized this shame as belonging to Jesus (Gal 3[13]). Jesus not only foresaw the fact and the character of His death, but was fully aware of the shame of the cross. This death, called by Cicero 'crudelissimum teterrimumque' (in Verr. v. 64), had its side of glory to Jesus, who saw the joy in store at the end (ἀντί) of the race, and so consciously despised the shame (He 12[2]). Here σταυρός is used without the article, as in Ph 2[8], 'in order to fix attention on the nature of the death' (Westcott). It is in Ph 2[8] that the cross is used to express 'the very lowest point of Christ's humiliation' (Vincent). Jesus became obedient μέχρι θανάτου, θανάτου δὲ σταυροῦ. It is the bottom rung in the ladder that led down from the throne of God. The cross was a real stumbling-block to the disciples themselves till they were convinced of the fact of the resurrection of Jesus from the dead. It remained to the unbelieving Jews an insuperable barrier. It was so when Jesus spoke of it before the event (Jn 12[32-34] 'Who is this Son of man?'). St. Paul found that Christ crucified was to the sign-seeking Jews a stumbling-block (1 Co 1[23]). The writer of Hebrews (13[13]) urges Christians to go outside the camp of Judaism, as Jesus suffered outside the gate, when it was clear that the two ways must part, 'bearing his reproach.' The follower of Jesus must not be ashamed of the shame of the cross. Some of the Judaizers, indeed, were not willing to 'be persecuted for the cross of Christ' (Gal 6[12]), but St. Paul did not seek to escape 'the stumbling-block of the cross' (Gal 5[11]). Indeed, some carried their dislike of the cross to the point of enmity (Ph 3[18]). These men would endure neither persecution nor self-denial. But the philosophical Greeks took the matter more lightly, and considered the preaching of the cross to be foolishness (1 Co 1[18. 23]), though in truth the cross reveals the hitherto hidden wisdom of God (1 Co 2[6f.]).

While the Christian is to share the shame of the cross, he is not to add to the suffering of Christ by crucifying Him afresh (ἀνασταυρόω, He 6[6]).

5. *The triumph of the cross over the flesh and the world.*—In a mystic, yet real, sense the Christian is crucified with Christ on the cross : Χριστῷ συνεσταύρωμαι, St. Paul said of himself (Gal 2[20]). It is 'a real crucifixion of heart and will' (Rendall). This spiritual crucifixion of the old man on the cross is the common experience of all genuine believers (Gal 5[24], Ro 6[6]) who have died to sin and have entered into the new life in Christ as symbolized by baptism. In a word, the power of the world over St. Paul's fleshly nature is broken by the cross of Christ. There is a double crucifixion between him and the world (Gal 6[14]). The world in its sinful aspects is dead to him and he to it. Hence not only is St. Paul not ashamed of the cross of Christ, as the Judaizers are who are seeking to enslave the Gentiles to the ceremonial law (Gal 6[12]), but he finds his only ground of glorying in the cross of our Lord Jesus Christ (Gal 6[14]). This sublime mysticism does not degenerate into magic and crucifixes. The true philosophy of the cross lies in the spiritual interpretation of man's victorious conflict with sin, which is made possible by the shameful death of the Son of God on the cross as the supreme expression of the love of the Father for sinful men, and as the propitiatory sacrifice on the basis of which the repentant soul can find access to the Father. The 'blood of the cross' lies at the root of redemptive grace as set forth by Jesus (Mt 26[28]), by St. Peter (1 P 1[2]), by St. Paul (Ro 3[24f.]), by the writer of Hebrews (9[14]), and by St. John (1 Jn 1[7]).

Mention should be made of the ingenious theory of Prof. C. C. Everett in his *Gospel of Paul*, which denies the penal character of the death of Christ on the cross, and sees in this supreme event only the ceremonial defilement which Christians share who take Christ as Lord and who thus likewise become accursed (Gal 3[13]), and so have the power of the Law over them removed. But this theory misses the deeper aspects of the whole problem, by overstraining an incidental truth connected with the death of Christ on the cross. See the matter well disposed of by Bruce, *St. Paul's Conception of Christianity*, p. 184 ff.

LITERATURE.—Zöckler, *Das Kreuz Christi* (1875) ; Brandt, *Die Evangelische Geschichte*, etc. (1893) ; Fulda, *Das Kreuz und die Kreuzigung* (1878) ; Lipsius, *de Cruce* (1595) ; Everett, *The Gospel of Paul* (1893) ; articles on 'Cross' in Hastings' *DB*, in Smith's *DB*, in Herzog's *PRE*, and in the *Encyc. Bibl.*; Cremer, *Bibl.-Theol. Lex. of NT Greek* (1892) ; the Lives of Christ and Paul ; the critical Commentaries ; the Biblical Theologies.

A. T. ROBERTSON.

CROWD.—In many passages of the Gospels we read of the rapid gathering of a crowd around Jesus. The healing of the man with the withered hand seems to have been the first occasion on which a great company was drawn to Him by curiosity or by the hope of healing. 'His fame went throughout all Syria.' The multitude was gathered from Galilee, Jerusalem, Judæa, Idumæa, and from the district round Tyre and Sidon ; the whole country was moved (Mt 4[25], Mk 3[7-9], Lk 6[17-19]). When Jesus retired for quiet to a desert place after receiving the news of the death of John the Baptist, He was followed by a crowd of five thousand people (Mt 14[14], Mk 6[34], Lk 9[11]). The words used for 'crowd' are ὄχλος and πλῆθος (both usually rendered 'multitude' in EV, but in

Mk 2[4] 5[27. 30], Lk 8[19] 19[3], ὄχλος is tr. '**press**' [RV 'crowd']). In classical Greek πλῆθος means the common people, the *plebs*, as opposed to ὄχλος, the inchoate throng that comes together on any special occasion, the *turba*. But in the NT the distinction is not uniformly maintained ; in Mk 3[7-9] the words are used interchangeably. St. Luke is more exact in his use of language, and in Ac 15[30] uses πλῆθος in a technical sense, common enough in the inscriptions, as meaning the membership of a political or religious association in its totality (Deissmann, *Bible Studies*, Eng. tr. 232). The question arises whether there were any special circumstances in those days that favoured the coming together of such masses of people upon very short notice.

1. The Messianic expectation was the motive of many such gatherings. The misgovernment under the Herods had cast the nation's thoughts back upon God, and the Messianic hope awakened with new power. The attention that John the Baptist attracted was due to the belief that he was the Messiah, a belief that he took pains to shatter. To John there flocked at the outset of his ministry the people in the neighbourhood, but afterwards the movement reached the north and the inflammable Galilee. Jos. (*Ant.* XVIII. v. 2) says that John was put to death because Herod feared lest the crowds he was gathering about him should 'put it into his power and inclination to raise a rebellion, for they seemed ready to do anything he should advise.' It was in consequence of a similar movement among the Samaritans that Pilate was recalled. The bloodshed with which the movement was checked led to an information being laid against him at Rome (Jos. *Ant.* XVIII. iv. 2). It is clear from these incidents that the Messianic hope was very present with the people ; and whenever the times raised up a man who seemed to have a distinctive message, the Jews were more than willing to flock to listen to him.

2. The splendid road system of Palestine facilitated the gathering of such crowds. The Romans made their roads partly on commercial grounds, and partly to permit of the passage of troops among the turbulent people. The commerce of the country must have been considerable in spite of the grinding taxation. Herod's annual income (Jos. *Ant.* XVII. xi. 4) was 900 talents, nearly £400,000 of our money. The regular raising of such a sum implies a settled trade, and much coming and going between different parts of the country. The excellence of the roads is borne witness to by the fact that the Roman procurator, who resided at Cæsarea, could reach Jerusalem with troops by way of Antipatris in less than twenty-four hours. The distance is about sixty miles. Along these splendid roads the crowd would stream on the first hint of the appearance of one who might be the Messiah.

3. The small size of the country must also be remembered. Palestine bulks so large in spiritual significance that one is apt to forget how small it is. And yet from the shore of the Dead Sea one may view the glittering snow of Hermon, while from the hill above Nazareth may be seen on the one hand the ships in the Mediterranean, and on the other the rolling hills of Gilead. This land, only about ⅕th the size of England, was densely populated. To-day its population is a little over 600,000, but in OT and Roman times must have been very much larger. 2 S 24[9] implies a population of 6,500,000 ; and, while it may be questioned whether the land ever could have carried so great a population as this, it is clear, both from the notices in history and from the existing ruins, that the desolations of to-day were formerly densely peopled. The population in the time of Christ is generally reckoned to have been about 2½ millions (Sanday, *Sacred Sites of the Gospels*, p. 16). See, further, art. MULTITUDE.   R. BRUCE TAYLOR.

CROWN OF THORNS (στέφανος ἐξ ἀκανθῶν or ἀκάνθινος στέφανος, Mt 27²⁹, Mk 15¹⁷, Jn 19²·⁵).—This was plaited by the soldiers and placed on Christ's head in mockery of His claim to Kingship, after Pilate had condemned Him to be scourged. It was a garland hastily twisted from the twigs of some thorny plant, which it is difficult now to identify. Tristram (*Nat. Hist. of the Bible*, p. 429) supposes it was the thorn-tree or *nubk* of the Arabs, which is very common in the warmer parts of Palestine. It abounds near Jerusalem, grows to a great size; its twigs are tough and pliant, and the spikes very sharp and numerous. Others incline to think it was the *Zizyphus Spina-christi*, a spiny plant covered with sharp prickles. The purpose of the soldiers was rather, perhaps, mockery of the Jews than cruelty to Christ. Pliny speaks (*HN*) of 'the meanest of crowns, a thorny one.'

In the writings of St. Paul a crown is promised to faithful followers of Christ, and in many parts of the NT Christ Himself is spoken of as wearing a crown. Sometimes the word for a victor's wreath is used (στέφανος), and sometimes that for a royal crown (διάδημα).* The emblematic significance, afterwards seen by the Church in the crown of thorns, is possibly hinted at in He 2⁹ 'crowned with glory and honour.' As a sacrificial victim, in being led out to death, often wore a garland of flowers, so Jesus, in the eyes of God and His own disciples, even in suffering the deepest humiliation, wears a crown of glory. In the death of Christ His Church sees mankind crowned with life, because the law of sin and death was thereby abrogated, and the Kingdom of heaven opened to all believers. The thorns with which a hostile world pierced the Saviour's brows are an emblem of the sin of man, the curse of thistles and thorns having been threatened after the Fall (see Dr. H. Macmillan's *Ministry of Nature*, ch. v., where this idea is finely worked out). But these wounds become the world's salvation. Through the sinful cruelty of man new life comes to a condemned world. God thus makes the wrath of man to praise Him. What was meant as derision is really a prediction of glory. See also art. THORN.

                        DAVID M. W. LAIRD.

CRUCIFIXION.—Crucifixion was originally an Oriental punishment. It was practised by the Persians (Herod. ix. 122), by the Phœnicians and their colonists the Carthaginians (Valer. ii. 7), and by the Egyptians (Thuc. iv. 110). It was practised also by the Greeks, probably in imitation of the Persians (Plut. *Alex.* 72. § 2), and by the Romans, who, though Cicero ascribes its introduction to Tarquinius Superbus, probably learned it from their enemies the Carthaginians. Regarding it, however, as an ignominious doom, the Romans reserved it for slaves (whence it was called *servile supplicium*), the worst sort of criminals such as robbers (Sen. *Ep.* vii.), and provincials. To inflict it on a Roman citizen was reckoned an impiety (Cic. *in Verr.* v. 66). It was a horrible punishment. Cicero designates it *crudelissimum teterrimumque supplicium.* The verb cognate to *crux*, 'cross,' was *cruciare*, 'to torture' (cf. 'excruciating').

There were two kinds of cross:
1. The *crux simplex*, which was a single stake. Sometimes the victim was fastened to it by his hands and feet, the former being extended above

his head. Usually, however, it was a sharpened stake (σκόλοψ), and the victim was impaled upon it. It passed through the length of his body, issuing from his mouth. Cf. Sen. *Ep.* xiv. : 'adactum per medium hominem qui per os emergat stipitem'; cf. *de Consol. ad Marc.* xx. The former method was called c̣ ̃xio, the latter *infixio*.

2. The *crux compacta*, which was composed of two pieces. It had three forms: (1) The *crux decussata* **X**, called also the *crux Andreana*, because it is said to be the cross on which St. Andrew suffered at Patræ. It was this form of cross that the Fathers had in view when in the crossing of Jacob's hands as he blessed Ephraim and Manasseh (Gn 48¹³⁻¹⁴) they saw a prophecy of the Crucifixion. Cf. Tert. *de Bapt.* § 8; Isid. Pel. *Epp.* i. 362. (2) The *crux commissa* or St. Anthony's cross, resembling the letter **T**. Cf. Barn. *Ep.* § 9; Luc. *Jud. Vocal.* § 12. The upright was called *stipes* or *staticulum*, and the transom *patibulum* or *antenna*. (3) The *crux immissa*, which had the top of the upright protruding above the transom, **†**. From the middle of the upright there projected a peg, the seat (*sedile*) or horn (*cornu*), on which, to support its weight, the body rested as on a saddle. Cf. Iren. *adv. Hær.* ii. 36. § 2 : 'Ipse habitus crucis fines et summitates habet quinque, duos in longitudine et duos in latitudine, et unum in medio in quo requiescat qui clavis affigitur'; Just. Mart. *Dial. c. Tryph.* p. 318 C (ed. Sylburg.) : τὸ ἐν τῷ μέσῳ πηγνύμενον ὡς κέρας καὶ αὐτὸ ἔξεχον ἐστίν, ἐφ' ᾧ ἐποχοῦνται οἱ σταυρούμενοι.

It was generally assumed in early times that the cross on which Jesus suffered was a *crux immissa*. Thus Augustine (*in Psalm.* ciii. § 14) finds in Eph 3¹⁸ a mystic allusion to the cross : 'breadth' being the transom on which His hands were outstretched; 'length,' the upright on which His body was fastened; 'height,' the head of the upright protruding above the transom; 'depth,' the lower end buried in the earth. And it is a confirmation of this opinion that the board inscribed with His name and accusation was put up over His head (Mt 27³⁷), apparently on the projection of the upright.

<small>The early Apologists fancifully defended the sacred symbol of the cross against the sneers of unbelievers by pointing to its appearance everywhere, as though nature and art alike did homage to it. It is seen in the quarters of the heaven, two transverse lines, as it were, running from N. to S. and from E. to W.; in a bird soaring upward with spread wings; in a man swimming or praying with outstretched hands; in the nose and eyebrows of the human face; in a ship's mast and yard; in a galley's oars projecting on either side; in the yoke of a plough and the handle of a spade; in the shape of trophies and *fasces*.* See TREE.</small>

The *cruciarius* was spared no circumstance of ignominy. He was required to carry the transom to the place of execution; † he was driven thither with goad and scourge along the most frequented streets, that the populace might profit by so signal an exhibition of the terrors of justice; and a herald went before, bearing a board whereon the victim's name and offence were inscribed.‡ Thus burdened and tormented, Jesus went His sorrowful way from the Prætorium till He reached the gate of the city (Mt 27³²); and there His strength failed, and He could go no farther. Tradition has it that He fell. The soldiers relieved Him of His burden, and, impressing Simon of Cyrene, laid it on his shoulders. Even then Jesus was unable to walk unsupported, and had to be borne along to the scene of His crucifixion. Cf. Mk 15²² φέρουσιν αὐτόν.

---

* The distinction between στέφανος, the badge of merit, and διάδημα, the badge of royalty, is not consistently observed in Hellenistic Greek (see *Encyc. Bibl.* i. 963).

* Just. Mart. *Apol.* ii., ed. Sylburg. p. 90 C–E; Tert. *Apol.* § 16; Jer. on Mk 15²¹. Cf. Lips. *de Cruc.* I. ix.
† Plut. *de Ser. Num. Vind.* § 9; Artemidor. *Oneir.* ii. 61; Wetstein on Mt 10³⁸.
‡ Eus. *HE* v. 1; Lightfoot on Mt 27³¹.

On arrival at the place of execution (see GOL-GOTHA), four soldiers were told off by the centurion in charge to do the work (cf. Jn 19²³). They proceeded in the customary way. First of all, the *cruciarius* was stripped naked, his garments being regarded as the rightful perquisites of his executioners.[*] Then he was laid on his back over the transom and his hands fastened to either end. Thereafter the transom was hoisted on the upright and his feet were fastened to the latter. Usually the hands were nailed through the palms and the feet were fixed either by two nails, one through each instep, or by a single nail transfixing both through the Achilles tendon ; sometimes, however, the hands and feet were simply tied.[†] Though less painful at the moment, the latter was the more terrible method, since it protracted the victim's sufferings. He hung till he died of hunger and exhaustion, or was devoured by birds and beasts of prey.[‡] The hands of Jesus were certainly nailed, but it seems that His feet were only tied (cf. Jn 20²⁰·²⁵·²⁷).[§] The sole Evangelic authority for supposing that they were nailed is Lk 24³⁹ [40], which is probably assimilated to Ps 22¹⁶. From two circumstances, (1) that a soldier could reach the lips of Jesus with a short reed (Mt 27⁴⁸ = Mk 15³⁶ = Jn 19²⁹), and (2) that wild beasts could tear out the entrails of the *cruciarius* as he hung,[‖] it appears that the cross was of no great height. It was enough if the feet cleared the ground.

There was a humane custom among the Jews, based on Pr 31⁶, that a potion of medicated wine should be administered to the *cruciarii* in order to deaden their sensibility. The merciful draught was provided by a society of charitable ladies in Jerusalem.[¶] It was offered to Jesus ere the nails were driven through His hands, and He raised it to His thirsty lips ; but on tasting what it was He would not drink it. What was His reason for rejecting it ? It was not that the endurance of physical pain was necessary to the efficacy of His sacrificial death ;[**] nor was it merely that He had a sentimental repugnance to the idea of dying in a state of stupefaction.[††] It was rather because He was bent on doing to the last the work which had been given Him to do. It was well for the penitent brigand that Jesus did not drink the potion.

It was usual for the victims of that frightful punishment, maddened by terror and pain, to shriek, entreat, curse, and spit at their executioners and the bystanders ;[‡‡] but Jesus endured the torture meekly. A cry broke from His lips as they were hammering the nails through His hands ; but it was a prayer—not an appeal to them for mercy on Himself, but an appeal to God for mercy on them : ' Father, forgive them : for they know not what they are doing.'[§§] The transom with its quivering load was hoisted on the upright, and there He hung, conscious of all that passed around Him. It is said that St. Andrew, as he hung upon his cross at Patræ, taught the people all the while ;[‖‖] and Jesus also in His anguish was mindful of others. Two brigands had been crucified with Him, two of

those outlaws who infested the steep road from Jericho to Jerusalem, and by their deeds of violence gave it the grim name of ' the Ascent of Blood ' (cf. Lk 10³⁰) ; and when one of them, recognizing the majesty of the meek Sufferer, turned to Him and prayed Him to remember him when He ' came in his kingdom,' He granted more than he sought, promising him a place that very day in Paradise. And He thought of His mother, as she stood by distracted with grief, and commended her to the care of the beloved disciple. While He hung, He was compassed with insults. The Jewish rulers, exulting in their seeming triumph, mocked Him, and the multitude joined in the poor sport. So did the soldiers who were charged with the duty of watching the crosses lest a rescue should be attempted.[*] Heated by their labour, they were refreshing themselves from their jar of *posca*, the vinegar which was the only drink allowed to soldiers on duty (see VINEGAR). Jesus was in their eyes a pretender to the Jewish throne, a rebel against the imperial government ; and, hearing the gibes of the rulers, they joined in, and, holding up their cups in mock homage, drank His Majesty's health (Lk 23³⁶).

Crucifixion was a lingering doom. The victims sometimes hung for days ere they died of hunger, exhaustion, loss of blood, and the fever of their wounds,[†] unless they were despatched either by a spear-thrust or by the *coup de grace* of the *crurifragium*, a brutality which the Romans practised usually on slaves, beating the life out of them by shattering blows with a heavy mallet.[‡] It was, however, contrary to the Jewish law (Dt 21²²·²³) that they should hang overnight ; and it was the more necessary that the requirement should be observed in this instance, since the next day was not only the Sabbath but the Sabbath of the Paschal week, a day of special solemnity (Jn 19³¹). Therefore the rulers waited on Pilate, and requested that Jesus and the brigands might be despatched by the *crurifragium*, and their bodies taken down from the crosses ere 6 o'clock that evening, when the Sabbath would begin. Pilate consented, and the soldiers set about the brutal work. They despatched the two brigands, but when they came to Jesus, He was already dead. There was no need to strike Him with the mallet ; but one of them, to ensure that He was really dead, drove his spear into His side. See BLOOD AND WATER.

The prominent characteristic of crucifixion was the ignominy of it (cf. Gal 3¹³, He 12²). This constituted ' the stumbling-block of the cross ' (Gal 5¹¹) in Jewish eyes. Since it was expected that the Messiah would be a glorious and victorious King, it seemed incredible that one who was slain, and not only slain but crucified, should be the Messiah. In the eyes of the NT writers, on the contrary, its very ignominy constituted its supreme suitability to the Messiah. It identified Him utterly with sinners, making Him a sharer in the worst extremity of their condition. St. John recognized a providential dispensation in the enslavement of the Jews to the Romans, inasmuch as it brought about the Crucifixion (18³¹·³²). Had they been free, Jesus would have been stoned as a blasphemer ; but since they were vassals of Rome, it was not lawful for them to put any one to death (Jn 18³¹). The Sanhedrin's sentence had to be referred to the procurator. It was invalid without his ratification, and it was executed by his authority after the Roman manner.

It is remarkable that, unlike the mediæval

[*] Cf. Wetstein on Mt 27³⁵.
[†] Cf. Lips. *de Cruc.* II. viii.
[‡] Cf. *ib.* xii.–xiii.
[§] Cf. *Ev. Petr.* § 6 : τότε ἀπέσπασαν τοὺς ἥλους ἀπὸ τῶν χειρῶν τοῦ Κυρίου.
[‖] Cf. Lips. *de Cruc.* II. xiii.
[¶] Cf. Lightfoot on Mt 27³⁴ ; Wetstein on Mk 15²³. See art. GALL.
[**] Cf. Calv.: ' Nam et hæc pars sacrificii et obedientiæ ejus erat, languoris moram ad extremum usque sufferre.'
[††] Cf. Dr. Johnson : ' I will take no more physic, not even my opiates ; for I have prayed that I may render up my soul to God unclouded.'
[‡‡] Cf. Cic. *in Verr.* i. 3, *pro Cluent.* 66 ; Jos. *BJ* IV. vi. 1, VII. vi. 4 ; Sen. *de Vit. Beat.* 19.
[§§] Lk 23³⁴, an interpolation, but unquestionably an authentic fragment of the Evangelic tradition. Cf. WH, *Notes.*
[‖‖] Abdiæ, *Hist. Apost.* iii. 41.

[*] Cf. Petron. *Sat.*: ' Cruciarii unius parentes ut viderunt noctu laxatam custodiam, detraxere pendentem ' ; Jos. *Vit.* 75 : three *cruciarii* taken down ; one recovered from his wounds.
[†] Cf. Lips. *de Cruc.* II. xii.
[‡] Cf. *ib.* xiv.

artists, who loved to depict the Man of Sorrows as He hung on the cross abused and bleeding, the Evangelists have drawn a veil over the scene, detailing none of the ghastly particulars, and saying merely : 'They crucified him.' They recognized in the Crucifixion not the triumph of human malice but the consummation of a Divine purpose—'the determinate counsel and foreknowledge of God' (Ac 2²³). At the moment all was dark to the disciples ; but when their minds were illumined by the Holy Spirit, they saw not only 'the sufferings that befell Messiah' but 'the glories that followed these' (1 P 1¹¹). Their Lord had never seemed so kingly in their eyes as when He 'reigned from the tree.'* In early days, according to some authorities, Lk 9³¹ ran : 'They were speaking of *the glory* which He was about to fulfil at Jerusalem.'† So Chrysostom quotes the passage ; and this is the constant conception of the NT. 'We look upon Jesus,' says the author of the Epistle to the Hebrews, 'because of the suffering of death crowned with glory and honour' (2⁹ ; cf. Ph 2⁸ᶠ.).

Throughout His ministry Jesus recognized the inevitable necessity of His Passion. He had come to die. Cf. Mt 9¹⁵=Mk 2²⁰=Lk 5³⁵ ; Mt 16²¹=Mk 8³¹=Lk 9²² ; Mt 17²².²³=Mk 9³¹=Lk 9⁴⁴ ; Mt 20¹⁸.¹⁹=Mk 10³³.³⁴=Lk 18³².³³. As early as the close of the 2nd cent. Celsus stumbled at the idea that Jesus foreknew and foretold all that happened to Him (Orig. *c. Cels.* ii. 13). Strauss pronounces those intimations mere *vaticinia ex eventu.* A crucified Messiah was 'to Jews a stumbling-block and to Gentiles foolishness' (1 Co 1²³) ; and the Apostles, eager to remove 'the stumbling-block of the Cross,' represented the Crucifixion as no ignominious catastrophe, but 'a link in a chain of higher knowledge, part of a Divine plan of salvation.' Keim, on the other hand, regards the announcement as 'the expression of a natural, reasonable, correct anticipation,' suggested by the fate of the Baptist and the difficulties wherewith Jesus was beset. The definite details, however, must be pruned away. In point of fact, the Lord's prescience of the end is inextricably interwoven with the Gospel history. The cross was His goal, and He knew it all along.

LITERATURE.—In addition to the works quoted in the art. and the standard *Lives* of Christ, reference may be made to Fairbairn, *Studies in the Life of Christ*, 'The Crucifixion' ; Newman, *Selected Sermons*, pp. 175-188 ; Liddon, *Bampton Lect.*⁸ p. 472 ff. ; Farrar, *Christ in Art*, pp. 389-423 ; Dale, *Atonement*⁷, p. 436 ff.   DAVID SMITH.

CRUSE.—The word occurs frequently in the OT (generally as rendering of Heb. צְלֹחִית), where it means a 'small earthen bottle or jar' in common use among the Hebrews chiefly for holding liquids, such as water (1 S 26¹¹) or oil (1 K 17¹²). 'Cruse' (marg. 'flask') is substituted by RV for 'box' of AV in Mt 26⁷ (‖ Mk 14³, Lk 7³⁷) as the designation of the ἀλάβαστρος used by the woman who anointed our Lord. See ALABASTER and ANOINTING.

                       DUGALD CLARK.

CRY.—The term 'cry' occurs in the NT with various shades of meaning corresponding to different Greek words, which express sometimes articulate, sometimes inarticulate utterances ; in some cases it connotes strong emotion, in others a more or less heightened emphasis is all that is expressed.

According to classical usage, the Gr. terms employed in the NT may be thus distinguished : χαλεῖν denotes "to cry out" for a purpose, *to call* ; βοᾶν, to cry out as a manifestation of feeling ; κράζειν, to cry out harshly, often of an inarticulate and brutish sound (Grimm-Thayer, *s.v.* βοάω). κραυγάζειν is the intensive of κράζειν. The corresponding nouns are βοή, 'a cry for help,' and κραυγή, 'outcry, clamour' (both rare in NT). To these should be added the use of φωνεῖν='to cry' (most freq. in Lk.).

In classifying the NT usage of the term, it will be convenient to group the instances in each case under the Greek equivalents.

* In the LXX version of Ps 96¹⁰ many codices add ἀπὸ τοῦ ξύλου after ὁ Κύριος ἐβασίλευσεν. So Old Lat. and Copt. versions, Just. Mart., Tert., Aug. ; cf. Venant. Fortunat. *Hymn. de Pass. Dom.*:
    ' Impleta sunt quæ concinit
        David fideli carmine,
      Dicens : In nationibus
        Regnavit a ligno Deus.'
† Chrysost. *in Matth.* lvii.: τὴν δόξαν ἣν ἔμελλε πληροῦν ἐν Ἱερουσαλήμ. τουτέστιν, τὸ πάθος καὶ τὸν σταυρόν. οὕτω γὰρ αὐτὸ καλοῦσιν ἀεί. Euth. Zig. on Mt 17³: τινὰ δὲ τῶν βιβλίων οὐκ ἔξοδον ἀλλὰ δόξαν γράφουσι. δόξα γὰρ καλεῖται καὶ ὁ σταυρός.

A. (1) 'To cry' or 'cry out' (=κράζειν, ἀνακράζειν) :
(a) of *articulate cries*, followed by words uttered (often with 'saying' or 'and said' added) : of *joy*, Mk 11⁹ and ‖ ; Mt 21¹⁵ (children crying in the temple, 'Hosanna') ; of *complaint* or *distress*, Mk 10⁴⁸ ‖ Lk 18³⁹, Mt 20³¹ (Bartimæus) ; Mt 14³⁰ (Peter crying out while walking on the water) ; * Mk 1²³ ‖ Lk 4³³ (ἀνέκραξεν ; Lk. adds 'with a loud voice') ; Mk 9²⁴ ; Lk 4⁴¹ (demons crying out and saying), cf. Mk 3¹¹ 5⁷ ; of the *angry cries* of the multitude, Mt 27²³, Mk 15¹³.¹⁴† (cf. Ac 21³⁶) ; *in ref. to Jesus*, of solemn and impressive utterance, Jn 7³⁷ (cf. 1¹⁵ 7²⁸ 12⁴⁴).
(b) *of inarticulate cries : with ref. to the possessed*, Mk 5⁵ (cf. Lk 8²⁸ ἀνακράξας) ; Mk 9²⁶ ‖ Lk 9³⁹ ; of *the disciples*, Mt 14²⁶ ('and they cried out for fear') ; *with ref. to Jesus*, of the cry on the cross (prob. inarticulate), Mt 27⁵⁰ ('cried ... *with a loud voice*, and yielded up his spirit').‡
(2) 'To cry' or 'cry out' (=κραυγάζειν) :
(a) *of articulate utterances* [cf. (1) (a)] : of *joy*, Jn 12¹³ ('Hosanna') ; of *distress*, Mt 15²² (Canaanitish woman . . . 'cried, saying' : cf. v.²³) ; *with ref. to Jesus*, of utterance under strong emotion, Jn 11⁴³ ('Lazarus, come forth !').
(b) *of undefined or inarticulate utterance* : in the quotation from Is 42², cited in Mt 12¹⁹ ('He shall not strive nor *cry*' [κραυγάσει], *i.e.* indulge in clamorous self-assertion).
(c) 'Cry'=κραυγή : 'the loud cry of deeply stirred feeling of joyful surprise' : Lk 1⁴² (Elisabeth's greeting of the Virgin-mother : 'she lifted up her voice with *a loud cry*) ; the midnight cry, Mt 25⁶ ('Behold the bridegroom cometh').

For He 5⁷ see below under B.

(3) 'To cry' or 'cry out' (=βοᾶν, ἀναβοᾶν, ἐπιβοᾶν) :
(a) *of articulate utterances* : of solemn and impressive *emphasis* (=to speak with a high, strong voice), Mt 3³ ‖ Mk 1³, Lk 3⁴, Jn 1²³ (all in the quotation from Is 40³ 'the voice of one crying,' etc.) ; of *distressful appeal*, Lk 9³⁸ ; esp. 'to cry for help to' (=אֶל זָעַק in OT), Lk 18⁷ (the elect who *cry* day and night) ; *in ref. to Jesus*, of the cry of agony on the cross ('My God, my God,' etc.), Mk 15³⁴ and ‖ Mt 27⁴⁶.

In this connexion the passage in Ja 5⁴ deserves notice : 'Behold the hire of your labourers . . . crieth out (κράζει) ; and the cries (βοαί) of them that reaped have entered into the ears of the Lord of Sabaoth.' Here the verb is used of crying for vengeance (cf. Hab 2¹¹) and the noun (βοαί) of cries for help. The latter sense is esp. frequent in the Psalms (*e.g.* 5² 18⁶. ⁴¹ etc.), corresponding to the Heb. שׁוע and derivatives. This word is 'used exclusively of crying for help' (Driver).§ Though frequent in the Psalms (LXX and Heb.), it occurs rarely in the NT.

(b) *of cries of joy, pain* (inarticulate) : of *joy*, Gal 4²⁷ (quotation from Is 54¹) ; cf. of *pain*, Ac 8⁷ (of unclean spirits crying with a loud voice).
(4) 'To cry,' 'cry out,' or 'cry aloud' (=φωνεῖν, ἐπιφωνεῖν) :
(a) *emphatic*, followed by words uttered, Lk 8⁸.⁵⁴ ; cf. 1⁴² (ἀνεφώνησεν, 'she spake out,' AV ; 'lifted up her voice,' RV) ; of *angry cries of multitude* (ἐπιφωνεῖν), Lk 23²¹.
(b) of the *inarticulate cries* of the possessed, Mk 1²³ ('and the unclean spirit . . . *crying with a loud voice* ').
(c) 'cry'=φωνή, esp. in the phrase φωνῇ μεγάλῃ, 'with a loud voice or cry,' added to verbs.
B. 'Crying' in He 5⁷.—This passage, which has direct reference to our Lord, calls for special notice here : 'Who, in his days of flesh, having offered up, with strong crying (μετὰ κραυγῆς ἰσχυρᾶς) and

* Probably here should be added Mt 15²³ ('she crieth after us '), where articulate cries seem to be meant, though the words uttered are not given.
† In ‖ passages Lk 23²¹ has ἐπεφώνουν λέγοντες, Jn 19⁶ ἐκραύγασαν λέγοντες.
‡ In the ‖ passages Mk 15³⁷ has ἀφεὶς φωνὴν μεγάλην, and Lk 23⁴⁶ φωνήσας φωνῇ μεγάλῃ.
§ *Parallel Psalter*, p. 441.

tears, prayers and supplications unto him that was able to save him out of death,' etc. The ref. is doubtless primarily to Gethsemane (so Delitzsch, Westcott), though 'a wider application of the words to other prayers and times of peculiar trial in our Lord's life' * is not excluded. Schoettgen (*ad loc.*) † quotes a Jewish saying which strikingly illustrates the phrase : 'There are three kinds of prayers, each loftier than the preceding : prayer, crying, and tears. Prayer is made in silence ; crying, with raised voice : but tears overcome all things.' The conjunction of the terms mentioned often occurs in OT, esp. in the Psalms, *e.g.* Ps 39[13] :

> 'Hear my *prayer*, O Lord,
> And give ear unto my *cry* (שַׁוְעָתִי);
> Hold not thy peace at my *tears*.'

Also Ps 61[2], and cf. Ps 80[5. 6].

The close association of the idea of prayer with that of 'crying' or 'cry' may be illustrated from the Gospels, esp. perhaps in the case of our Lord's cries on the cross (Mt 27[46. 50], Lk 23[46]). According to Jewish tradition, in the solemn prayer for forgiveness uttered by the high priest on the Day of Atonement in the Holy of Holies, the words אָנָּא הַשֵּׁם כַּפֵּר 'O Lord, forgive,' were spoken with heightened voice, so that they could be heard at a distance.

LITERATURE.—Art. 'Call' in Hastings' *DB* i. 343 f., and the *Gr. Lexicons* under the various Gr. terms (esp. Grimm-Thayer).

G. H. BOX.

CUBIT.—See AGE, and WEIGHTS AND MEASURES.

CUMMIN.—Cummin (or cumin) is the seed of the *Cuminum cyminum*, an annual herbaceous umbellifer. It has a slender, branching stem, and grows to the height of a foot. The seeds, which are ovoid in form, are strongly aromatic, and have a flavour not unlike that of caraway, but more pungent. Cummin was used by the Jews as a condiment, and also for flavouring bread. It has carminative and other medicinal properties, and was employed not only as a remedy for colic, but also to stanch excessive bleeding, and to allay swellings. It is indigenous to Upper Egypt and the Mediterranean countries, but it was also cultivated from early times in Western Asia, India, and China.

Cummin is mentioned twice in the Bible (Is 28[25-27] כַּמֹּן, and Mt 23[23] κύμινον). In the latter passage Jesus rebukes the Pharisees, because they paid tithe of mint, and anise, and *cummin*, and omitted the weightier matters of the Law.

LITERATURE.—*Encyc. Brit. s.v.* ; Tristram, *Nat. Hist. of the Bible.*

HUGH DUNCAN.

CUP (ποτήριον, in general significance corresponding to the Heb. כּוֹס and so used in the LXX ; Vulg. equivalent is *calix*).

1. *Literal.*—A few references to the cup as a vessel in common use occur in the Gospels : Mk 7[3. 4], Mt 10[42] (= Mk 9[41]) 23[25. 26] (= Lk 11[39]). The first of these passages is plainly an explanatory parenthesis furnished by the Evangelist for the information of readers unacquainted with Jewish customs. ποτήρια, he says, are amongst the things subject to ' washings ' (βαπτισμοί)—which washings were not such as simple cleanliness required, but were prescribed by the decrees 'intended to separate the Jew from all contact with the Gentiles.' The Talmudic tractate *Kelim* names seven kinds of things requiring such ceremonial purification, and amongst them are earthenware vessels and vessels of bone, metal, and wood. Resting on such Levitical prescriptions as are to be found in Lv 11 and Nu 31, the purification of vessels was carried to the furthest extreme of stringent requirement by ' the tradition of the elders.' Vessels that had in any way come into contact with the

* Westcott.   † Cited in Westcott, *ib.*

common people ('am hā'āreẓ) were on that account to be cleansed. (Maimonides, *Yad. Mishkab and Moshab*, 11. 11, 12, 18).

The words of Jesus in Mt 23[25. 26] are simply an instance of the use of a homely figure to express hypocrisy.

2. *Figurative.*—Our Lord uses the familiar Heb. figure of a ' cup ' to denote the experience of sorrow and anguish in two instances : (1) in His challenge to James and John, checking their ambition (Mk 10[36. 39] = Mt 20[22. 23], ' Are ye able to drink the cup which I drink ?') ; and (2) in connexion with His Passion, both in His cry of agony (Mk 14[36] ‖ in Mt. and Lk. ' this cup '), and in His calm rebuke of Peter's hasty attempt to defend Him against His captors (Jn 18[11] ' The cup which my Father hath given me, shall I not drink it ? '). In each case there is the same reference to His singular experience of bitter sorrow which was no mere ' bitterness of death.'

It is noticeable that in the Gospels the use of this figure occurs only in connexion with trouble and suffering. In the OT the use is much wider. Experiences of joy, blessing, and comfort are thus expressed (*e.g.* Ps 16[5] 23[5] 116[13], Jer 16[7]), as well as those of trembling, desolation, and the wrath of God (Is 51[17ff.], Jer 25[15ff.], Ezk 23[32ff.], Zec 12[2]). Rabbinic writers exhibit the figurative use of ' cup ' for trouble and anguish (Gesen. *Thes. s.v.* כּוֹס). The kindred expression, ' taste the taste of death,' is also to be met with (Buxtorf, *Lex. s.v.* טְעַם). The conception of death as a bitter cup for men to drink underlies it. (Note the *Etymologicon Magnum* gives ποτήριον . . . σημαίνει καὶ τὸν θάνατον). Instances of this phraseology in the Gospels are (in the words of Jesus) Mk 9[1] (= Mt 16[28]) and (in the words of the Jews) Jn 8[52]. Cf. also He 2[9].

3. *In the institution of the Lord's Supper.*— There are strong inducements to see in the cup in the Last Supper one of the cups which had a place in the later ceremonial of the Paschal feast. But was the supper the usual Passover ? This is a much-debated question ; but on the whole the weightier considerations seem to support the view presented in the Fourth Gospel, the account in which may be intended, as some suggest, to correct the impression given by the Synoptics. That is to say, the supper was not the Passover proper, and it took place on the day previous to that on which the Passover was eaten. It might still be held that it was an anticipatory Passover. St. Paul, it is true, speaks of the Eucharistic cup as ' the cup of blessing ' (1 Co 10[16]), and one is inclined to make a direct connexion with the third cup at the Paschal celebration, which was known as the Cup of Benediction (כּוֹס הַבְּרָכָה), and is often referred to in the Talmudic tractates (*e.g.* Berakhoth, 51*a*). If St. Luke's account of the Last Supper were to be received without question, it would be tempting to trace three out of the four Paschal cups, viz. the one mentioned in Lk 22[17], the one common to the Synoptics—the cup of blessing, and the fourth, or Hallel cup, suggested by ὑμνήσαντες (Mk 14[26] = Mt 26[30]), taking the hymn referred to as none other than the second part of the Hallel (Pss 115–118), with which the Passover was usually closed. Lk 22[19b. 20], however, is not above suspicion : and on other grounds we cannot definitely connect the cup of the institution with the ceremonial of the Paschal feast.

But the cup was an important feature in other Jewish festivals and solemn seasons besides the Passover. And even though the institution took place at the close of an ordinary meal, the bread and the cup were accompanied with the due Jewish graces (Mt 26[26f.], Mk 14[22f.], Lk 22[17. 19]), and in the after-view the cup thus used, and with such significance, might well stand out as *par excellence* the Cup of Blessing.

The words of Jesus regarding the cup are given with some noticeable variation. Mk. gives τοῦτό ἐστιν τὸ αἷμά μου τῆς διαθήκης τὸ ἐκχυννόμενον ὑπὲρ πολλῶν (14[24]) ; and Mt. reproduces this with but slight changes, possibly of a liturgical character

(26^{28}). The wording in Lk 22^{17} makes no reference to the 'blood,' whilst 22^{20} (referred to above) appears to be but an interpolation, clumsily ($ἐν τῷ αἵματι \ldots τὸ \ldots ἐκχυννόμενον$) combining the form in St. Paul with that in St. Mark. The solemn expression, 'my blood of the covenant,' or 'my covenant-blood,' can be explained only by reference to Ex 24^{6-8}. St. Paul's phrase, $ἡ καινὴ διαθήκη \ldots ἐν τῷ ἐμῷ αἵματι$ (1 Co 11^{25}), introduces no important difference of meaning as compared with the Markan formula. To lay stress on the idea of a '*new* covenant' is all in keeping with the Pauline standpoint. One other point as regards the words of the institution alone remains to be mentioned. As with the bread so with the cup, St. Paul alone represents our Lord as saying $τοῦτο ποιεῖτε εἰς τὴν ἐμὴν ἀνάμνησιν$ (1 Co $11^{24.\ 25}$). Is it possible, then, that no permanent sacramental rite was contemplated by Jesus in doing what He did at the Last Supper? Is the conception of a memorial celebration due rather to St. Paul as a prime factor in the development of Christianity? Obviously this is not the place to deal with this important question, and the attitude of historical criticism respecting it. We have assumed that what took place at the Last Supper was an 'institution.' See artt. COVENANT, LORD'S SUPPER.

4. *In the Eucharist.*—(1) From the first the common usage in administration no doubt gave the cup after the bread, in accordance with the order observed in Mark, Matthew, and Paul. St. Luke in his shorter (and better supported) account (22^{17-19}) exhibits a noticeable divergence in placing the cup first in order. This may be due, as Wright suggests (*Synopsis of the Gospels*, p. 140), to some 'local Eucharistic use.' The *Didache* (ch. 9) also puts the cup first; but the fact as to the general established usage remains unaffected.

(2) As to the cup used in the communion there would at first be no difference between it and such vessels as were in ordinary use, and the materials of which the Eucharistic vessels were made were by no means of one kind. Zephyrinus of Rome, a contemporary of Tertullian, speaks of 'patens of glass,' and Jerome (*c.* 398 A.D.) speaks of 'a wicker basket' and 'a glass' as in use for communion purposes. Cups of wood and of horn also appear to have been used in some cases. We find certain provincial councils in the 8th and 9th cents. prohibiting the use of such, and also of leaden vessels. Cups were sometimes made of pewter; and bronze, again, was commonly used by the Irish monks, St. Gall preferring vessels of this material to those of silver. At the same time the natural tendency to differentiate in regard to vessels devoted to such a special service must have begun soon to manifest itself. Where it was possible, at an early period the cup was made of rich materials, such as gold and silver. Similarly as regards form and ornamentation. Tertullian (*de Pudicitia*, 10) speaks of the cup as being adorned with the figure of the Good Shepherd. In the course of time we get chalices of great price and wonderful workmanship, corresponding to the rare and costly Passover and other festal cups which Jews similarly cherish as art treasures.

It is needless to mention particularly the several kinds of chalices which came to be distinguished as the Eucharistic rites were made more elaborate. Our own times, again, it may just be noticed, have given us the 'individual communion cup,' which, on hygienic grounds, finds favour in some quarters. Though in some respects a modern institution, perhaps it may claim a precedent in the most primitive usage. The use of separate cups might be inferred from 1 Co 11^{17-34}. Nor is the hygienic objection to the common chalice wholly new. The difficulty was felt in mediæval times when the plague was so rife. In the 14th cent. special 'pest-chalices' were in use for sick cases.

(3) The custom of mixing water with the wine in the chalice, to which Justin Martyr makes a well-known reference (*Apol.* i. 67), accords with Jewish precedent. Speaking of the Jewish use, Lightfoot (*Hor. Heb.* on Mt 26^{27}) says, 'Hence in the rubric of the feasts, when mention is made of the wine they always use the word *mizgu*, they *mix*

for him the cup.' Maimonides (*Ḥameẓ umaẓ.* 7, 8) assumes the use of water. If the cup our Lord gave to His disciples were one of the ceremonial Paschal cups, we may take it that it contained a mixture of water and wine. And if it were not, nothing is more likely than that the Apostles, in observing the rite, would follow the Jewish custom of mixture. A passage in the Talmud (Bab. *Berakhoth*, 50, 2) suggests that water was thus added to the wine for the sake of wholesomeness and in the interests of sobriety.

In the course of time various fanciful suggestions came to be made as to a symbolic purpose in connexion with the mixed chalice in the Eucharist, ignoring its simple origin in an earlier Jewish custom. Thus it was variously held that in this way the union of Christ and the faithful was signified; that the water from the rock was represented; that the water and the blood from the pierced side of the Crucified were commemorated. At last it was affirmed that the water was added to the cup 'solely for significance': and so the addition of a very small quantity of water (a small spoonful) came to be considered sufficient. 'One drop is as significant as a thousand' (Bona, *Rer. Liturg.* II. ix. note 3—'Cum vero aqua mysterii causa apponatur vel minima gutta sufficiens est').

(4) Was wine from the first invariably used and regarded as obligatory in the Eucharist? Harnack ('Brod u. Wasser,' *TU* vii. [1892]) holds that it was not so up to the 3rd cent., and traces the use of bread and water (but see, in reply, Zahn, 'Brod u. Wein,' *ib.*; Jülicher's essay in *Theol. Abhandlungen*; and Grafe, *ZThK* v. 2). It would be difficult to maintain that the genius of the sacrament vitally depended on the use of wine; but in its favour we have the great preponderance of custom and sentiment. In modern times there are those who, for one reason and another, feel a difficulty regarding communion wine, and are disposed to use substitutes of some kind. Such might be disposed to welcome a sort of precedent in the use permitted by Jewish regulations in certain cases as regards their festival cups. In northern countries, *e.g.*, where wine was not accessible as a daily beverage for the mass of the Jews, syrup, juice of fruits, beer or mead, etc., are named as instances of allowable substitutes. Such substitutes are curiously included under the common appellation 'the wine of the country.' (See *Shulḥan 'Arukh, Oraḥ Ḥaq.* 182. 1, 2)

(5) The withholding of the cup from the laity in the Communion, which came into vogue in the Western Church, and is still a Roman Catholic usage, may be briefly referred to. It is admitted by Romish authorities that communion in both kinds was the primitive custom for all communicants. Cardinal Bona, *e.g.*, says: 'It is certain, indeed, that in ancient times all without distinction, clergy and laity, men and women, received the sacred mysteries in both kinds' (*Rer. Liturg.* II. xviii. 1). The practice of withholding the cup does not come into view before the 12th century. The danger of effusion was offered as a reason for it. Short of this, as an expedient against effusion, we find slender tubes (*fistulæ*) or quills brought into use, the communicants drawing the wine from the chalice by suction. Another intermediate stage towards communion in one kind was the practice of intinction, *i.e.* administering to the people the bread dipped in the wine. This practice, however, was condemned in the West, but it remains as the custom of the Eastern Church still, the sacred elements in this form being administered to the laity with a spoon ($λαβίς$). Ultimately the rule of communion in one kind was ordained in the West by a decree of the Council of Constance in 1415; and the reason assigned for the decree was that it was 'to avoid certain perils, inconveniences, and scandals.' This momentous change, however, was not brought about without much demur and opposition. The decree of Constance itself did not immediately and universally take effect; for after this

time there were even in Rome cases where the cup was administered. The great Hussite movement in Bohemia, contemporaneous with the Council of Constance itself, offered determined opposition to the withdrawal of the cup ; and the kindred Utraquist Communion in that country continued for two centuries their protest as Catholics who claimed the celebration of the Lord's Supper in both kinds, after the primitive usage. The badge of the Utraquists, a large chalice together with a sword—significant conjunction !—bespoke the sternness of the conflict.

What really lay at the root of this prohibition of the cup was the tremendous dogma of transubstantiation, with all its implicates, together with a hardening of the distinction between the clergy and the people. The growth of this Eucharistic custom proceeded *pari passu* with the development of the dogma. Naturally, therefore, the restoration of the cup to the people was a necessary part of the Reformation claim. It is also worthy of remembrance that even in the Tridentine Council there were not wanting Romanist advocates of this as well as other reforms ; but 'no compromise' counsels prevailed, and the rule in its fullest rigidity was reaffirmed.

How strange to look back over the welter of controversy and the many saddening developments connected with but this one point of Eucharistic observance, away to that simple evening - meal which took place 'in the same night that he was betrayed' !   J. S. CLEMENS.

CURES.—The details of medical knowledge possessed by the Jews of our Lord's time and of current medical practice can only be gathered piecemeal from various sources, and relate largely to what is known of these in OT and in post-Biblical times. It is not unreasonable to believe that from these sources one can with fair accuracy gather what was the knowledge and practice of our Lord's own generation. In the NT references are made to physicians in Mt 5[26], Lk 8[43]. The value of diet and the use of oil and wine in cases of bodily injury are indirectly referred to in Lk 8[55] 10[34]. Visitation of the sick is a Christian virtue, and was warmly commended by Jesus (Mt 25[36, 43]), in terms implying that it was practised ; but the Talmud, which also recognizes the virtue, makes an exception in cases where visitation might aggravate the disorder. The balm of Gilead had an ancient reputation for healing virtue, and the Pools of Siloam and Bethesda and the springs at Tiberias and Callirrhoë were reputed to be curative. Medical theory among the Jews was almost entirely borrowed empirically, and no system of medical training and education existed in Palestine in Bible times. Prevention of disease by sanitary precautions was more emphasized, and it has even been suggested that the whole Levitical legislation was based upon hygienic considerations, so far as these were understood. The priestly class were the depositaries of such medical knowledge as was possessed, although Solomon is said to have known about the use of drugs, and various references in the Talmud attribute to him a book of cures which was said to have been withdrawn from the people by Hezekiah.

In the time of Jesus medical practitioners would be in possession of such medical lore as was held and practised in former generations, and would therefore be familiar with the art of midwifery, and possibly had attained to considerable skill in its practice, though there are few references to surgical operations. Probably an aversion existed to surgery, as to the practice of bleeding, on account of the national belief concerning the blood ; but later this aversion was overcome, and Jewish

physicians fell into line with the leading classical schools, which freely employed bleeding as a remedy. The Talmud (*e.g. Bekhoroth*, 45*a* ; *Nazir*, 32*b*) bears witness to some anatomical knowledge possessed by post-Biblical practitioners, and from this and other Rabbinical sources the common maxims of the physicians, and indications of their principles and methods, may be not obscurely learned. The Talmud mentions myrrh, aloes, cassia, frankincense, cinnamon, spikenard, and camphire as having medicinal properties. Dietetic rules and sanitary regulations were also carefully enjoined, and many bodily disorders were treated by homely remedies. Wunderbar (*l.c. infra*) gives examples of the application of drugs and the like to various ailments, but also plainly shows that occult methods, involving astrology, and the wearing of parchment amulets or charms, were with more confidence prescribed. Various incantations were in use to prevent miscarriage, and to ward off the machinations of evil spirits from the cradle of the newborn. Drugs and magic were, in fact, generally employed, the chief reliance being placed on the latter.

With these methods our Lord's action in the healing of disease had no affinity. Necromantic or superstitious observances were entirely foreign to His spirit. He never taught that sicknesses were the result of the action of evil spirits [on Lk 11[13ff.] see below, and art. IMPOTENCE]. And it is equally clear that He had no recourse to such medical knowledge as was familiar to the physicians of His time, and that He was not endowed with knowledge of disease and of the curative art in advance of His own generation. In the cures recorded in the Gospels He employs nothing beyond His word, addressed either to the patient or to a parent or friend, and sometimes a touch. For use of saliva, see art. SIGHT. The method of Jesus must be sought on an entirely different line.

In every process of healing, whether in the time of Jesus or in our own day, there are two elements : the physical, and the mental or psychical. On the one hand, the disturbing and enfeebling causes, functional or organic, in the bodily tissues and organs, are gradually removed by the action of drugs or other medical treatment. On the other, a new tone and vigour are restored to the unseen and intangible but essentially real 'life' of the patient. The two are most intimately and vitally connected with each other, and neither element can be ignored. Mind and body are mutually interpenetrative, and although the relations between them are in many respects still profoundly obscure, yet advancing knowledge only makes more certain what is already firmly established, that this interdependence and mutual influence are of the closest character. The uncertain and incalculable element in every sickness or feebleness, passing beyond all power to adequately diagnose, is the psychical. The physical condition may clearly point to a particular issue of the infirmity—recovery or death—and, so far as the physical goes, this might be determined with considerable accuracy ; but the action of the incalculable element remains, cannot be predicted, and may produce most surprising results. These are matters of common knowledge, and amount to commonplaces. But they must be steadily borne in mind when cases of restoration—those in process to-day, and those recorded in the Gospels—are considered.

The action of Jesus was upon the complex personality, body and spirit, but upon the body through the spirit. His power went directly to the central life, to the man, the living person, and this may be traced in all His dealing with disease and infirmity both of body and of mind (see LUNATIC). The Divine power was, through His life, at one with itself, brought to bear with living energy on the unseen springs of the being. Consideration of the actual phenomena of our Lord's working in the restoring of the sick will make these facts more manifest.

1. *Our Lord's own dependence upon the Divine power.*—Not only did He declare this close, trustful dependence (Jn 5[19. 30] 8[28] 10[25. 32. 37. 38] 14[10]), but it is evinced spontaneously in His action (Mk 7[34], Jn 11[41. 42]). The customary association of prayer with His works of healing was proof of His uttermost dependence upon God. The power of prayer, which He marked as the condition of all human victory, He indicates as vital also to His own action (Mk 9[29]). The prayer He desiderates is no slack and formal petitioning of a far-distant Deity, but a close absoiption of life in a very-present Helper. And this was the quality of our Lord's own dependence upon God. He cherished the largest expectations from the power of the Living God, of which He was so conscious. He felt the throbbing in His own life of that Mighty Will and Love which animated all being, and therefore He intimated that the true value of prayer, for Himself and for mankind, was that it established in man a close sympathy with, and an absolute dependence upon, the Source of all healing and life.

2. *His healings were an expression of intensest sympathy with suffering humanity.* Compassion was the moving cause of many of His beneficent actions (Mt 15[32] 20[34], Mk 8[2], Lk 7[13]). True sympathy is a mighty human energy in which the Divine power is at work, and even on the lower levels of our feeble personal force it has a continuous tendency towards healing. Experience multiplies the evidence of this fact as the years pass. And we are led to conceive in some measure the vast resources of power in the full compassion of Him who was morally one with the Source of all love and pity. His sympathy was never vitiated or weakened by personal imperfection, and so it possessed the power of self-identification with God and man. The healing of the Issue of Blood (see article) shows that this sympathy with distressed humanity worked even apart from His direct will.

3. His conviction that *disease and suffering were not part of the right and natural order of things.* This feature is seen in all His actions, but found its clearest expression in the case of the woman who could in no wise lift up herself (Lk 13[11-17]) (see IMPOTENCE). 'Ought not this woman, being a daughter of Abraham, whom Satan hath bound, lo these eighteen years, to have been loosed from this bond on the day of the Sabbath?' In addition to our Lord's antagonism to the pedantry and inhumanity of His critics, the underlying note is heard that humanity ought not to be held in bonds of sickness and infirmity. Disease and suffering and untimely death are not part of the natural, *i.e.* the right and Divine, order of things. And all the power of right is on the side of those who labour to set man free and to enable him to stand erect in body, mind, and soul before God and his fellows.

4. A clear feature in our Lord's healings was *His sense of the need of dealing with the sin which often lay at the root of the sickness and infirmity.* Jesus very carefully guards against the unwarranted assumption made by the friends of Job, and by the disciples (Jn 9[2]), that sin was the secret cause of all suffering and pain. Other and Diviner reasons might account for much of the deprivation and trouble of man (Jn 9[3]). But in two cases (Mk 2[5-10], Jn 5[14]) He not obscurely marks the sin as the deepest cause of the weakness (see artt. PARALYSIS and IMPOTENCE). Sin is the violation of the whole nature of man, body, mind, soul, as well as disobedience to the Holy Will of God. It

depresses the springs of personal vitality, and therefore continually makes for sickness and feebleness of body.

5. *Faith was required on the part of the one to be healed.* Faith must be clearly distinguished from mental assent and from credulity, which vainly arrogate to themselves that august word. Faith, as Jesus conceived it, was the noblest activity of man's being, the triumphant assertion of the essential and Divine part of his nature against all that dwarfs, disfigures, and oppresses it, and this faith our Lord most keenly desired to see. The absence of it, even the fear of its absence, chilled and dismayed His spirit (Jn 4[48], Mk 9[22. 23] RV). He marks faith as the truly favourable condition for His healing power to be efficacious (Mt 9[29], Mk 10[52], Lk 17[19] 18[42], Jn 5[6]). Apparent exceptions to this connexion between healing and faith may be traced in Mt 9[1-8] 12[9-13], Lk 13[11-17] 14[1-6] 22[50. 51], but in all these cases the details are not reported, the fact of the healing being in these instances less prominent than other features of the narrative, such as the controversy of Jesus with the cold critics in the synagogue, and the personal characteristics of the Saviour in His beneficent action with respect to Malchus. It has also been thought that demoniacs as such were incapacitated from the exercise of faith in Jesus. But while this is in part true, it is significant that our Lord does in these instances seek to gain access to the true personality and to set it free from the oppression of all alien powers (see LUNATIC).

6. *Jesus laboured to produce this faith.*—Not only does He ask for it as a condition of healing, but He spends Himself in the effort to evoke it. His careful treatment of the blind man (Mk 8[22-26]), the deaf and dumb (Mk 7[31-37]), the blind and impotent (Jn 9[1-7] and 5[6]) is best understood as the effort of our Lord to produce the essential conditions of receiving His healing virtue. In each case the means used, as well as the words spoken, are adapted to the particular case. We have not one set of means used indiscriminately. The ears and the tongue of the deaf-mute are touched, the blind man in one case is led out of the town, saliva is applied to his eyes, and the touch of the Lord's hand ; in the other the eyes are anointed and the patient is sent to a distant pool in the exercise of faith. The labour is to set free the patient from all unnatural conditions of mind and spirit and from hopelessness, which is the most unnatural of all to men to whom God is so near.

This effort in Jesus produced weariness. It involved a deep expenditure of nervous, physical, and spiritual energy, and often in the Gospels we read of the spent, tired worker seeking refreshment in rest and in solitude, and most of all in fellowship with God. 'He went out into the mountain to pray' (Mt 14[23], Mk 6[46], Lk 6[12]).

7. *Several of our Lord's cures were wrought while He was at a distance from the patient:* the Syro-Phœnician's daughter (Mt 15[21-28], Mk 7[24-30]), the nobleman's son (Jn 4[46-53]), and the centurion's servant (Mt 8[5-13], Lk 7[1-10]). Difficulty is felt by many on the ground that the power of a unique personality which they acknowledge in Jesus could not be active in these cases. Dr. Abbott discusses the third instance (*Kernel and Husk*, Letter 18), and, excluding any '*bonâ fide* miracle,' he inclines to regard the story as due to an exaggeration or to the influence of the knowledge of his friend's intercession with Jesus, 'with a sentimental reserve in favour of brain-wave sympathy.' Since the time Dr. Abbott wrote, telepathy has become a recognized fact in psychical research, and we have no need to deny its possible action in these cases. But the explanation given of all His works by our Lord goes beneath all such conjectures and hypotheses. He ascribed His healing to the Divine power with which He was able to bring men into living communication. That Divine all-pervading Life which informed His humanity was not at a distance from any human life. Space and Time are to the Infinite Power non-existent, and only our bondage to the limited human ideas can present any difficulty.

8. In the three above cases and in the case of the demoniac boy (Mt 17¹⁴⁻²¹, Mk 9¹⁴⁻²⁹, Lk 9³⁷⁻⁴³) our Lord significantly seeks *the co-operation of parent and friend in the work of healing* ; and the fact is most significant of the closeness of human sympathy, and most of all of that most vital and mysterious sympathy lying in the life-bond between parent and child, and the intimate dependence of these ties upon the life-giving power of the Almighty. These deep-lying sympathies that bind parents to their own offspring are essentially allied to the Divine power. They 'consist' by its indwelling, and Jesus desires this power to be informed by a living faith, and so be at once at its highest point of energy and also in living union with God.

9. In some of the cures effected by Jesus *a process* is observable in the recovery. The nobleman's son was first set free from the fever, and from that decisive time began 'to amend.' The crisis was safely passed, and the rest was left to nature's gentle action. The Syro-Phœnician's daughter was delivered from her besetment and left 'thrown upon the bed,' physically prostrate, and requiring rest and care. The daughter of Jairus was ordered rest and food, and the blind man at Bethsaida was only by degrees restored to perfect sight. These indications, casually given, and probably not understood by the narrators, lead us to think that a similar process would be manifest in the other cures were they fully and adequately reported, and it is always a salutary reminder that our Gospels are only most fragmentary. It was a principle of Jesus not to do anything by extraordinary which could be accomplished by ordinary means.

10. The healing power of Jesus went out *freely* among the suffering multitude (Mt 8¹⁶· ¹⁷ 14³⁴⁻³⁶ 15³⁰· ³¹, Mk 1³²⁻³⁴ 6⁵³⁻⁵⁶, Lk 4⁴⁰· ⁴¹ 9¹¹). The contagious influence of a multitude, in producing an atmosphere in which remarkable psychical phenomena are manifest and the result is seen in healing of the sick, is not uncommonly recognized in modern times. In this way are explained the miracles of which some genuine cases undoubtedly happened around the tomb of Becket, the healings that are associated with Lourdes, and many of the similar results that we may believe were gathered round famous saints like St. Francis of Assisi and St. Theresa. A contagion of expectation is initiated and spreads rapidly through a whole countryside, and this condition of expectation and hope is one which the most prosaic science recognizes as favourable to the production of real cures, especially of ailments a large element of which is nervous. We have seen that the working of Jesus did not disdain to utilize these and all other forces in human nature which make for healing ; and by reason of His unique and perfect alliance with the Divine Source of all life and health, He was able to bring instantaneous and permanent relief and restoration to whole companies of sufferers.

11. Our Lord's method has *considerable affinity with modern medical science.* The power of the mind over bodily ailments, in the maintenance and restoration of health, is being increasingly acknowledged. Dr. Schofield says truly that most remedies, if not all, are partly psychical in their operation. Not only such prescriptions as change of occupation, environment, and climate, physical and mental shocks and emotional incentives, ethical and religious influences, travel, study, ambition and social influences, but also drugs, changes of diet, baths and waters, minor operations, depend much for their efficacy on their psychical action ; while the personality of the doctor—in some cases the unintelligibility of his prescription and the magnitude of his fee—are valuable therapeutic agents. In this way full recognition is given to the influence of any power which can set free the mind from its hopeless condition, its lethargy and depression, as a most potent force in the work of healing. Schmiedel (art. 'Gospels' in *Encyc. Bibl.*) says of our Lord's miracles : 'It is only permissible to regard as historical that class of healings which present-day physicians are able to effect by psychical methods.' But he overlooks the influence of mental action in the cure of all kinds of disease, and not only of mental diseases to which the above observations point.

Psychical methods, intelligently and of set purpose applied to the cure of bodily ailments, are as yet in their preliminary stages. On the same line, if on no other, much greater possibilities remain for human knowledge and power to achieve. No limit can be laid down beyond which the occult forces of human life may not be taken advantage of for the healing not of nervous diseases only, but of purely physical. Dr. Osgood Mason gives abundant evidence, from his own knowledge and practice, of the influence of suggestion, with or without hypnosis, in the healing of many physical ailments. And the Christian faith, based upon the suggestions found in the Gospels as they describe, without at all understanding them, our Lord's methods, is that Jesus Christ, by His commanding action upon the human mind and spirit, and by the Divine power dwelling in Himself, was able to control physical and physiological processes in the human body so as to produce curative effects of a permanent character.

LITERATURE.—For ancient Jewish cures, see art. 'Medicine' (by Macalister) in Hastings' *DB* ; Wunderbar, *Biblisch-Talmudische Medicin*, 1850–60 ; art. 'Krankheiten und Heilkunde der Israeliten' in Herzog's *PRE* ³. For detailed accounts of individual cures wrought by Jesus, see the Lives of Christ and Comm. on Gospels, *e.g.* Gould on 'Mark,' Plummer on 'Luke' in *Internat. Crit. Commentary* ; Trench, *Miracles* ; Laidlaw, *Miracles of our Lord* ; Belcher, *Miracles*. For valuable information and suggestion respecting psycho-therapeutics, consult artt. by Dr. Tuke on 'Influence of the Mind over the Body' in *Dict. of Psychol. Medicine* ; Dr. Lloyd Tucker on 'Psychotherapeutics,' *ib.* ; Dr. Osgood Mason on 'Hypnotism and Suggestion,' *ib.* 1901 ; and recent popular medical works by Dr. A. T. Schofield on *The Force of Mind*, and *Unconscious Therapeutics* (Churchill, London).　　　　　T. H. WRIGHT.

CURSE.—Two widely different words are in AV translated 'curse.' It will be sufficient to trace their meaning, so far as the ideas represented by them are found in the Gospels.

1. חֵרֶם, ἀνάθεμα, 'an accursed (AV) *or* devoted (RV) thing.' (*a*) In its higher application this word signifies a thing devoted—wholly or in part, permanently or temporarily, voluntarily or by Divine decree—to a use (or an abstinence) exclusively sacred. This is not a curse at all in the modern sense of the word ; it corresponds more nearly to the nature of a vow. With this extension of meaning we may see a *genuine* instance in the special consecration of John the Baptist (Lk 1¹⁵ 7³³), and a *corrupt* instance in the system of Corban (Mk 7¹¹ff·). (*b*) In its darker application it denotes an extreme and punitive ban of extermination. This is of frequent occurrence in OT, but in the Gospels no clear case is found, unless, indeed, under this head we include all the death-penalties of the Jewish law (Jn [?] 8⁵), especially the punishment attempted (Jn 8⁵⁹ 10³¹ff·) and finally inflicted upon Christ Himself on the charge of blasphemy (Mk 14⁶³ᵗ·, Jn 19⁷). It is well to notice, in connexion with this kind of anathema, the strong expression used by Christ in addressing the Canaanitish woman, as one descended from a 'devoted' race (Mt 15²⁶). It may be added that profanity, in the special form of self-cursing, seems to have adopted language derived from this ban; see Mt 26⁷⁴, Mk 14⁷¹ (καταθεματίζειν and ἀναθεματίζειν. Ro 9³ naturally suggests itself as a verbal illustration; in other respects it is a complete contrast.* (c) The ban of extermination gave place, under certain conditions, to the remedial discipline of excommunication; that is to say, a temporary 'cutting off from the congregation'; referred to, as a Jewish institution, in Jn 9²² 12⁴² 16², and, as a Christian (apparently), in Mt 18¹⁷. (See also Westcott on 1 Jn 5¹⁶).

2. קְלָלָה, κατάρα, 'curse.'—(a) This is the word regularly used to denote a curse in the general sense, as the natural antithesis of a blessing; it is not charged (as 'anathema' essentially is) with sacred associations; its quality, which is capable of all degrees, from Divine to devilish, is to be decided by the context. (b) The disappearance of cursing in the NT marks very forcibly the contrast between the spirit of the New dispensation and that of the Old; for in the OT its presence is at times painfully prominent. See Lk 9⁵⁴ᵗ., where even the unauthorized additions of some MSS are undoubtedly a true comment. Such instances as are found or are alleged in the Epistles are judicial in tone, not irresponsible and malevolent. The exceptional case which occurs of a curse uttered by Christ (upon the fig-tree [see art.], Mt 21¹⁹ᶠᶠ., Mk 11¹²ᶠᶠ.) is probably to be taken as a sign given to impress His warning of impending judgments (Mt 21⁴¹. ⁴³ 23³⁷ᶠ. 24²¹ᶠᶠ. ³²ᶠᶠ. etc.). It is a reminder that we may not so exaggerate the goodness of God as to leave no place for His severity. Christ applies the words 'ye cursed' to those who shall be on His left hand at the Last Day (Mt 25⁴¹). (c) Christ became a 'curse' (Gal 3¹³, see Lightfoot, ad loc.). It belongs to the Epistles to unfold the bearing of this truth; but the fact is implied in the measures taken by the Jews, after the Crucifixion, to avert its consequences (Jn 19³¹, cf. Dt 21²²ᶠ.). In the Roman view the shame of crucifixion, in the Jewish view its accursed nature, formed the special sting of such a death. Hence in the matter of salvation, which 'is from the Jews' (Jn 4²²), the curse must necessarily be involved in the Death's redemptive efficacy. F. S. RANKEN.

CUSHION.—In NT only in Mk 4³⁸ RV [AV 'pillow'] for προσκεφάλαιον, a cushion for the head, but also for sitting or reclining upon (see references in Liddell and Scott, s.v.). By προσκεφάλαια LXX renders כָּסָתוֹת of Ezk 13¹⁸ where the Arabic equivalent is mekhaddât. Mekhaddeh (sing.) is just the word used by the Sea of Galilee fishermen for the cushion they place in the hinder part of their fishing-boats for the comfort of the passenger to-day. These boats are probably similar to those used by our Lord and His friends, and on just such a cushion the present writer has often rested in crossing the same waters.

The cushions universally used to support the head or the arm in reclining on the diwân are

in size about 24″ × 15″ × 5″. They are usually made of straw—less frequently of cotton or hair—sewn into strong canvas, and covered with coloured print or silk. The larger cushions for the seat of the diwân, and employed in the boats, are of the same material. See PILLOW. W. EWING.

CUSTOM.—See TRIBUTE.

CYRENE (Κυρήνη) was a Greek settlement on the north coast of Africa, in the district now called Benghazi or Barca, which forms the E. part of the modern province of Tripoli. It was founded B.C. 632. It was the chief member of a confederacy of five neighbouring cities; hence the district was called either Pentapolis or Cyrenaica. Under the first Ptolemy it became a dependency of Egypt; was left to Rome by the will of Ptolemy Apion, B.C. 96; was soon after formed into a province, and later, perhaps not till 27, united with Crete, with which under the Empire it formed a senatorial province, under an expraetor with the title of proconsul. It was noted for its fertility and for its commerce, which, however, declined after the foundation of Alexandria. It produced many distinguished men, such as the philosophers Aristippus and Carneades, the poet Callimachus, and the Christian orator and bishop Synesius.

Jews were very numerous and influential there. The first Ptolemy, 'wishing to secure the government of Cyrene and the other cities of Libya for himself, sent a party of Jews to inhabit them' (Josephus, c. Apion. ii. 4). Cyrenian Jews are mentioned in 1 Mac 15²³, 2 Mac 2²³ (Jason of Cyrene). According to Strabo (ap. Jos. Ant. XIV. vii. 2), the inhabitants of Cyrene were divided into four classes—citizens, husbandmen (i.e. native Libyans), sojourners (μέτοικοι), and Jews. The Jews enjoyed equality of civil rights (Ant. XVI. vi. 1, 5). An inscription at Berenice, one of the cities of Cyrenaica, of prob. B.C. 13, shows that the Jews there formed a civic community (πολίτευμα) of their own, under nine rulers (CIG iii. 5361). The Cyrenian Jews were very turbulent; Lucullus had to suppress a disturbance raised by them (Strabo, l.c.); there was a rising there at the close of the Jewish war, A.D. 70 (Jos. BJ VII. xi.; Vita, 76); and a terrible internecine war between them and their Gentile neighbours, under Trajan (Dio Cass. lxviii. 32; Euseb. HE iv. 2).

Simon of Cyrene (the father of Alexander and Rufus [wh. see]), who was impressed to bear our Lord's cross (Mt 27³², Mk 15²¹, Lk 23²⁶), was doubtless one of these Jewish settlers. Other NT references to Cyrenian Jews are: Ac 2¹⁰ (at Pentecost), 6⁹ (members of special synagogue at Jerusalem, opposing Stephen), 11²⁰ (preaching at Antioch to Greeks [or Hellenists]), 13¹ (Lucius of Cyrene, probably one of these preachers, a prophet or teacher at Antioch).

LITERATURE.—Rawlinson's Herodotus, iii. p. 130 ff.; Smith, Dict. of Greek and Roman Geography; Schürer, HJP I. ii. 283, II. ii. 230 f., 245 f.; Marquardt, Römische Staatsverwaltung (1881), i. 458 ff.; art. 'Diaspora' (by Schürer) in Hastings' DB, Extra Vol. p. 96ᵇ. HAROLD SMITH.

CYRENIUS.—See QUIRINIUS.

* In Mt 15⁴ ‖ Mk 7¹⁰ RV rightly substitutes 'he that speaketh evil of' for AV 'he that curseth': the Greek is ὁ κακολογῶν, quoted from Ex 21¹⁷.

D

DAILY BREAD.—See LORD'S PRAYER.

DALMANUTHA.—Mk 8¹⁰ only. The textual and geographical problems involved in this name have not found as yet a satisfactory explanation. After the feeding of the 4000, Jesus embarked with His disciples, and came, according to Mt 15³⁹, εἰς τὰ ὅρια Μαγδαλά (TR) or Μαγαδάν (all critical editions); according to Mk 8¹⁰ εἰς τὰ μέρη Δαλμανουθά.

In Mt. the variations are few and unimportant, except the difference between Magdala and Magadan. For ὅρια we find occasionally ὅρια, ὅρη (with following ἁμαγδαλά), ὅρη. Cod. D places τῆς before the proper name. Μαγαδάν is the reading of אBD (B³ -άν), Μαγεδάν of אᶜ; the Old Latin has Magadan, Mageda, -am, Magidam; Vulg. Magedan; syr ˢⁱⁿ מגדן, ᶜᵘʳ מגרין, ᵖᵃˡ מגרין, ᵖᵉˢʰ מגרו (Magdu; so also the Arabic Tatian). Most uncials and cursives Μαγδαλά; CM 33. 102, etc., Μαγδαλάν.
In Mk. τὰ μέρη is replaced by τὰ ὅρια in DΣ.
  ,,   ,,   ,,   τὰ ὅρη ,, N.
  ,,   ,,   ,,   τὸ ὅρος ,, 28, syr ˢⁱⁿ; but in the latter the addition of a dot makes the plural; syr ᶜᵘʳ is missing; B has the spelling Δαλμανουθά, 474 Δαμανουθά, 184 ᵉᵛ Δαλμουνουθά; Vulg. Dalmanutha (with unimportant variations); arm. Dalmanunca. But this is now replaced by:
Μελεγαδά (not Μαδεγαδά as read by Stephanus) in D*.
Μαγαιδά (not Μαγαδά as printed by Tischendorf) in D¹.
Μαγειδά in 28, 81.
Μαγδαλά in 1. 13. 61. 69, etc.
Syr ˢⁱⁿ מגדל, syr ᵖᵃˡ מגדל, Got. Magdalan, Old Lat. Mageda, -an, -am, Magidan. It is a natural supposition that in Mk. all readings differing from μέρη Δαλμανουθά are due to assimilation to Mt., perhaps under the influence of Tatian. The confusion of ὅρια and ὅρη (ὅρος) must be very early, and has its parallels in many passages of the OT, from Jos 11¹⁶ 15¹¹ to Ezk 11¹⁰, Mal 1³. On its occurrence in syr ˢⁱⁿ see especially Chase, *The Syro-Latin Text of the Gospels*, p. 97, esp. n. 2, where he justly remarks: 'This reading of the Sinaitic raises two questions: (a) Was there an early *Greek* Harmony of the Gospels? . . . (b) What is the relation of Sin. to Tatian?' On the Cod. 28 which supports the reading of syr ˢⁱⁿ, see WH ii. 242 ('which has many relics of a very ancient text').
That *Magadan*, not *Magdala*, is the true reading in Mt. is probable (independently of the witness of MSS) on internal grounds; for it is difficult to explain how a name like *Magdala*, which was well known through Mary Magdalene, should have become *Magadan*. The introduction of both forms into MSS of Mk. points to the fact that there were several stages in the revision of our MSS. Both the readings, *Magadan* and *Magdala*, may, however, go back to the same Heb. מגדל, as is shown by Jos 15³⁷, where B has Μαγαδὰ Γάδ for Μαγδὰλ Γάδ of A. Even for *Dalmanutha* such an explanation has been attempted by Dalman (*Gramm.* p. 133; change of γ into ʏ, and transposition of syllables Δαλμανουθά from Μαγδαλουθά = מגדלות. But in the 2nd ed. p. 168 he has left out this note and all references to this word).

That τὰ ὅρια in Mt. and τὰ μέρη in Mk. are almost identical expressions, is shown by Mt 15²¹ εἰς τὰ μέρη Σιδῶνος καὶ Τύρου compared with Mk 7²⁴ εἰς τὰ ὅρια (TR μεθόρια) Τύρου (καὶ Σιδῶνος), and by the fact that in the OT 4 of the 11 Heb. equivalents for ὅριον (יר, מול, פאה, קץ) reappear among the 22 Heb. equivalents of μέρος. The next supposition is therefore that *Magadan* (or Magdala) in Mt. = Dalmanutha in Mark. But how is this possible?
Many explanations have been started. The one proposed by Dalman may be dismissed at once, as it is given up by himself; cf. also Wellhausen's remarks on it (*Ev. Marci*). Lightfoot and Ewald derived *Dalmanutha* from צלמון by the supposition of an Aramaic or Galilæan pronunciation. Keim (*Jesus of Nazara*, Eng. tr. iv. 238) explained it similarly as 'Shady Place.' Schwarz (*Das heilige Land*, p. 189) derived it from the cave Teliman (טלימאן), which cave, however, according to Neubauer, was in the neighbourhood of Herod's Cæsarea. J. W. Donaldson (*Jashar: fragmenta archetypa carminum Hebraicorum*, editio secunda, 1849, p. 16) suggested: 'Δαλ- istud residuum esse veri nominis Μαγδαλά scil. מגדל-אל, μανουθά autem re-

præsentare pluralem vocis מָנֶה *pars, portio*, quam in Græco μέρη conversam habemus.' A similar idea was struck out independently by R. Harris (*Codex Bezæ*, p. 188) and the present writer (*Philologica Sacra*, p. 17; *ExpT* ix. 45), that *Dalmanutha* is the transliteration of the Aramaic equivalent of εἰς τὰ μέρη, which by some form of dittography took the place of the proper name. Against Harris see Chase, *Bezan Text of Acts*, p. 145, n. 2; and against the whole suggestion, Dalman, *Words of Jesus*, p. 66 f. Dalman doubts whether מְנָה in Aramaic meant anything else but 'portion.' But in the Syriac Bible at least it is frequently used for the allotted portions of land (Jos 14² 15¹, Is 57⁶). N. Herz saw in the word an Aramaized form of the Greek λιμήν 'harbour' (*ExpT* viii. 563, ix. 95, 426). Others, finally, give no explanation, and consider *Magadan* and *Dalmanutha* as the names of two different places near each other, neither being very well known. But this leads to the topographical problem.

Eusebius in his *Onomasticon* has but one paragraph on a name beginning with M immediately after names from the prophet Jeremiah (Mephaath, Maon, Molchom, 48²¹· ²³ 49¹). It runs (in Klostermann's edition, p. 134 [= Lagarde, *OS* p. 282]):

Μαγαιδάν (Mt 15³⁹). εἰς τὰ ὅρια Μαγαιδὰν ὁ Χριστὸς ἐπεδήμησεν, ὥς ὁ Ματθαῖος. καὶ ὁ Μάρκος δὲ τῆς Μαγειδὰν μνημονεύει, καὶ ἔστι νῦν ἡ Μαγειδανὴ περὶ τὴν Γερασάν.

In Jerome's translation:
'Magedan, ad cuius fines Matthæus evangelista scribit dominum pervenisse, sed et Marcus eiusdem nominis recordatur, nunc autem regio dicitur Magedena circa Gerasam.'

The unique MS, in which the work of Eusebius is preserved, writes Μαγαιδάν (as D*) and Μαγαιδανή. Eusebius may have been reminded of the name by the occurrence of Μαγδώλω beside Μέμφις in Jer 51 (44)¹, which he quotes a few lines before (ed. Klost. p. 134, l. 15). At all events it follows from the entry, that Eusebius did not find *Dalmanutha* in his text of Mark, and that he sought the place on the eastern side; but Gerasa seems too far from the Lake, unless we are to suppose that it had some sort of enclave on its shores.
A strange identification is that with the 'Phiala' Lake mentioned by Jos. *BJ* III. x. 7 as one of the sources of the Jordan. See the Maps published by Röhricht, i. (*ZDPV* xiv. 1891):
'Hunc fontem Josephus appelat *Phialam*, Marcus *Dalmanicha*, Matthæus *Magedan*, Saraceni *Modin*. Hinc est verus ortus Jordan; unde paleæ hic missæ recipiuntur in Dan subterraneo meatu ductæ.'

Furrer (*ZDPV* ii. 59) identified Dalmanutha with *Khân Minyeh*, which name he connected with *mensa* (the table where Jesus sat with the Twelve, first mentioned in the *Commemoratorium*, A.D. 808), and this with (Dal)manatha; but see against this Gildemeister (*ib.* iv. 197 ff.). Thomson (*LB* 393) suggests a ruined site up the Yarmūk half a mile from the Jordan called *Dalhamia* or *Dalmamia* (Robinson, *BRP* iii. 264, 'Delhemiyeh'); Tristram, a site one and a half miles from Migdel; Sir C. Wilson, a site not far from the same. The aged Prof. Sepp in a recent paper, 'Die endlich entdeckte Heimat der Magdalena' (*Völkerschau*, iii. 3, pp. 199–202, 1904), argued for *Miqdal Gedor* or *Magdala Gadara*, a Jewish suburb of Gadara (Jerus. *Erubin* v. 7). Wellhausen has no doubt that it must be sought on the eastern shore, in the neighbourhood of Bethsaida (Mk 8²²), if this town itself did not belong to it. For he holds 8⁹ᵇ· ¹⁰ to be identical with 8¹³, the object αὐτούς of ἀφείς in 8¹³ being the ὄχλοι, not the Pharisees, and πάλιν he regards as a harmonistic insertion. He believes that 8¹³ originally followed immediately upon 8²² καὶ ἔρχονται εἰς Βηθσαιδάν.

Thus not even the geographical problem is solved. If the suggestion on the origin of *Dalmanutha*, as put forward by Donaldson, Harris, and the present writer, were to turn out correct, it would have important consequences for the Synoptic Problem. For then this reading cannot well have had its origin in oral tradition, but presupposes a written (Aramaic) document as the basis of our Second Gospel.

LITERATURE.—A collection of Notes on 'Dalmanutha' left by Gildemeister (*ZDPV* xiv. 82); the monograph of Martin Schultze, *Dalmanutha: Geographisch-linguistische Untersuchungen zu Mk* 8¹⁰, Oldesloe, 1884; A. Wright, *NT Problems*, p. 71; Henderson in Hastings' *DB*; G. A. Smith in *Encyc. Bibl.*; Sanday, *Sacred Sites of the Gospels*, p. 22 f.; Merx, *Die vier kanonischen Evangelien*, ii. 2 (1905), p. 79 [warns against identification with *Eddelhemiye*, gives as reading of the Arm. *Dalmanoun*, and claims for the reading Dalmanutha, which is not recognized by the old texts (syr ˢⁱⁿ D, Old Lat. Ulf.), an Egyptian origin].   EB. NESTLE.

DANCING.—1. *Manner.*—The Oriental dance was performed either by an individual man or woman, or by crescent lines of men dancing together and holding each other's hands, or of women by themselves performing similar movements. The one at the end of the line waved a scarf and acted as *chorēgos*, or dance-leader. At times also a line of men and women, with hands joined, confronted another similar line, and the dance consisted in their alternate advance and retreat, accompanied by the hand-clapping of the onlookers beating time to the music, by the scarf-waving and occasional shout, and, at regulated intervals, the resounding tread of the dancers. In the case of the individual, the abrupt muscular actions were artistically relieved, as in the contrasting lines of male and female attire in the Western dance, by the soft and swaying undulations of the dancer's figure. The accompaniment of song, hand-clapping, and musical instruments served to control the energy and secure unity of movement.

2. *Place.*—On the occasion of a wedding in a peasant's house a space was kept clear near the door, and into it one after another stepped forward and danced, and retired among the shadows; the dancing of the bride receiving especial attention and applause. For dancing in companies, the flat roof, or any level space beside the house, was resorted to. In the cities and in the houses of the rich, the large reception room, or the open paved court, into which all the apartments opened, was available for the purpose. In festive processions the male or female performers, singly or in couples, stepped to the front and danced with sword and shield, and then gave place to others.

3. *Occasions.*—In the East, dancing has never been regarded as an end in itself and promoted as an entertainment chiefly for those actively taking part in it, but rather as a demonstration of feeling due to some special incident or situation. In family life this was principally the event of marriage (Mt 11¹⁷, Lk 7³²); and a similar expression of feeling often attended the birth of a son, recovery from sickness, return from a journey, or the reception of a guest whose presence called for such a manifestation of grateful rejoicing. Birthdays did not usually receive such notice, as they lacked the element of relief from danger, recompense and rest after hardship, or the introduction of something new into the family conditions. Herod's birthday feast (when Salome danced before the guests, Mt 14⁶, Mk 6²²) was an imitation of Gentile customs. More general occasions were the founding of a building, the ingathering of harvest, and the religious festivals of the year.

The prevalence of such a custom, embracing old and young, and including all classes, indicated a simple life, in which the feeling of the moment found hearty and uncritical expression. The view of life was one that recognized the easy and rapid interchange of joy and grief (Ps 30⁵·¹¹, La 5¹⁵, Ec 3⁴). Further, it implied a very close connexion between mental and physical states. As there was a union of mirth and dancing, so there was an equally natural correspondence between sorrow and sighing (Is 35¹⁰). Even in places dedicated to relaxation and delight, by the rivers of Babylon, it was impossible for captive exiles to sing the songs of the Lord's deliverance (Ps 137¹⁻⁴). The elder brother could take no part in mirth and dancing of which the occasion was so affronting and offensive to himself (Lk 15²⁵⁻²⁸). Hence among a people marked by mobility of temperament and prone to extremes of feeling, the children in the market-place might well reproach their companions who heard the wedding music without rising to the dance, and the wail of bereavement without being moved to pity (Mt 11¹⁷, Lk 7³²).

LITERATURE.—Hastings' *DB*, art. 'Dancing'; Delitzsch, *Iris*, 189 ff.; Thomson, *Land and Book*, 555 f.
        G. M. MACKIE.

DANIEL.—The influence of Daniel on the Apocalyptic conceptions of the Gospels is profound (see APOCALYPTIC LITERATURE). For the possible influence of Dn 7¹³ see SON OF MAN. The only passage in which the book is explicitly mentioned is Mt 24¹⁵, where the phrase τὸ βδέλυγμα τῆς ἐρημώσεως ('the abomination of desolation') is quoted. See art. ABOMINATION OF DESOLATION. It is to be noted that in the corresponding passage in Mark (13¹⁴), no mention is made of Daniel. In view of the accepted priority of Mark and his closer fidelity, and also of Matthew's fondness for OT references, the absence of the clause raises the suspicion that it is not part of the original utterance, but a comment added by the latter Evangelist. In that case it would not be necessary to assume that Jesus meant to use the phrase in the same sense as it is used in Daniel. He may have only adopted or borrowed it as a current popular expression to describe some minatory event which He foresaw portending the forthcoming calamity.
        A. MITCHELL HUNTER.

DARKNESS.—The word 'dark' is used in the sense of the absence of natural light in Jn 6¹⁷ 20¹. The darkness that lasted for the space of three hours at the crucifixion is referred to in Mt 27⁴⁵, Mk 15³³, Lk 23⁴⁴·⁴⁵. For a brief summary of the views held as to the nature of this darkness, see Hastings' *DB*, art. 'Darkness.' It may suffice to remark that, the Passover falling at full moon, there can be no question here of a solar **eclipse.**

Generally 'darkness' is used in a metaphorical sense, but with slightly different significations. Darkness is the state of spiritual ignorance and sin in which men are before the light of the revelation of Jesus comes to them (Mt 4¹⁶, Lk 1⁷⁹, Jn 8¹² 12⁴⁵·⁴⁶). This darkness the presence of Jesus dispels, except in the case of those who love the darkness and who therefore shrink back into the recesses of gloom, when the light shines, because their deeds are evil. Those who have a natural affinity to the light, when Jesus appears, follow Him and walk no longer in darkness.

But there is the deeper darkness that comes through incapacity of sight (Mt 6²³, Lk 11³⁵). This state results from long continuance in evil (Jn 3¹⁹). It is the judgment passed upon the impenitent sinner. To love the darkness rather than the light is to have the spiritual faculty atrophied, and this is the Divine penalty to which he is condemned. The light that is in him has become darkness. The gospel contemplates for the human soul no more dire calamity.

And the final fate of the impenitent sinner is to be cast into outer darkness (Mt 8^{12} 22^{13} 25^{30}). There is a kingdom of darkness which wars against the light, and which has power at times to prevail (Lk 22^{53}). This is the darkness of sin, chosen and loved as sin, the instinctive hatred, inwrought with what is radically evil, of the Divine purity and light. It is the negative of all good—outer darkness, the darkness that has ceased to be permeated or permeable by any ray of light.

Darkness is twice used of secrecy or privacy (Mt 10^{27}, Lk 12^3). In these cases, however, a metaphorical use of the word is also implied. In the former passage the reference is to the darkness of perplexity and sorrow ; in the latter, to the darkness of sin. See also LIGHT, UNPARDONABLE SIN.

In the later mystical theology there is a use of the term that may be here referred to. There is a 'Divine darkness' which is the consummation of the experience of the purified soul— the darkness that comes from excess of light. The pseudo-Dionysius speaks of the 'luminous gloom of the silence' which reveals the inner secrets of being, and in which the soul is raised to the absolute ecstasy. It is an attempt to express the infinitude of the susceptibility of the human soul to emotions of either joy or anguish. From the outer darkness to the light which is above light, and therefore inconceivable, the soul of man is capable of responding to every shade of experience.

LITERATURE.—Cremer, *Bib.-Theol. Lex. s.vv. σκότος, σκοτία* ; Martineau, *Endeavours after the Christian Life*[6], p. 463 ff. ; Phillips Brooks, *Candle of the Lord*, p. 74 ff.; *Expositor*, II. iii. [1882] 321 ff.   A. MILLER.

DATES.—The chronological sequence of the Gospels is quite as important as that of the Epistles to the student of the beginnings of Christianity, and forms an essential branch of the study of the development of our Lord's revelation and His Messianic consciousness. The difficulties in the way of forming an exact time-table of the dates in the Gospels are due (1) to the indifference of the early Christians, as citizens of the heavenly city, to the great events that were taking place in the world around them ; (2) to their lack of means of ascertaining these events, and their obliviousness of the important bearing they might have on the evidences of the faith ; (3) to the fact that, the early Christian traditions being recorded in the interest of religion and not of history, the writers confined their attention to a few events, which were arranged as much according to subject-matter as to time sequence. The result is that there are many gaps which can be only approximately filled up by strict inference from casual remarks. The author of the Third Gospel is the only one to give parallel dates of secular history in the manner of a true historian, and to profess to relate things 'in order' (καθεξῆς, Lk 1^3). There are many inferences as to time to be drawn from statements in Mt., but they are of an accidental character. St. John marks points of time of significance in his own and in his Master's life, but his purpose is to trace the development of the drama of the Master's passion, not to suggest its chronological relation to the history of the world.

The early Fathers, Irenæus, Tertullian, Clement of Alexandria, Africanus, and Hippolytus, were the first to attempt to arrange the events of the Gospel in chronological sequence. But these attempts are not always to be relied upon, owing to the difficulties of ascertaining many of the dates of secular history, to which reference has already been made, and which were still further increased in their case by the different ways of reckoning the years of reigning monarchs and of calculating time in the different eras. For example, Lk 3^1 'in the 15th year of the reign of Tiberius' may be reckoned from Augustus' death, Aug. 19 A.D. 14, or from the time when Tiberius was associated with Augustus in the empire by special law ; but that law, again, is variously dated, being identified

by some with the grant of the *tribunicia potestas* for life in A.D. 13, but assigned by Mommsen (after Velleius Paterculus, ii. 121) to A.D. 11. So that we have to choose between A.D. 29, 28, and 26. Furthermore, the Roman calendar began on Jan. 1, so that the imperial year might be adjusted to the civil year (1) by counting the fractional year as a whole, and by commencing a second imperial year on the first New Year's Day of each reign,—Lightfoot (*Ignatius*, ii. 398) mentions the practice of Trajan and his successors of beginning a second year of *tribunicia potestas* on the annual inauguration day of new tribunes next after their accession, —or (2) by omitting the fractional year altogether, and calculating the emperor's reign from a fixed date, like Eusebius, who seems to commence each emperor's reign from the September following his accession (see art. 'Chronology' in Hastings' *DB* i. 418). The Julian reform of the Roman calendar, by which the year B.C. 46 was made to contain 445 days, in order to bring the civil year into line with the solar year, adds to the complications.

Furthermore, the Jewish calendar bristles with problems. Originally the Paschal full moon was settled by observation, but that became impossible when the people were spread over distant lands, and was also hindered by atmospheric causes ; and, in any case, the beginning of the month was determined not by the astronomical new moon, but by the time when the crescent became visible, about 30 hours afterwards, the first sunset after that event marking the beginning of the new month. A fresh difficulty was created by the 13th month, Veadar, which was intercalated whenever the barley was not within a fortnight of being ripe at the end of the month Adar ; but this was forbidden in sabbatical years, and two intercalary years could not be successive. The lunar year was correlated with the solar by the rule that the Paschal full moon immediately followed the spring equinox. There were also various calculations of the equinox, Hippolytus placing it on March 18, Anatolius on March 19, the Alexandrians on March 21.

And with regard to chronology in general it is to be noted that in the East the year almost always began with September. The Jewish civil year began in Tishri (Sept.) ; the religious and regal in Nisan (April) (Jos. *Ant.* I. iii. 3), the order of months beginning with the latter, that of the years with the former. The Alexandrian year began on Aug. 29 ; the era of the Greeks started from Sept. B.C. 312, the Olympiads from July B.C. 776. In the Christian era, also called the Dionysian after Dionysius Exiguus of the 6th cent., 753 A.U.C. =1 B.C., and 754 A.U.C.=1 A.D.

The points of chronology in our Lord's life which have to be settled before any table of dates can be drawn up are (1) date of nativity, (2) age at baptism, (3) length of ministry, (4) date of crucifixion. While no one of these can be verified with anything like precision, it is certain that the accepted chronology, based on the calculations of Dionysius Exiguus in the 6th cent., is erroneous.

Dionysius started, seemingly, from Lk 3^1, the 15th year of Tiberius, placed the public ministry of our Lord one year later, and counted back 30 years, on the strength of Lk 3^{23}. This gave 754 A.U.C. for the year of Christ's birth. Following Hippolytus, he fixed on Dec. 25 in that year, and, according to the usual method for reckoning the years of monarchs, counted the whole year 754 as 1 A.D. (see Ideler, *Handbuch*, ii. 383 f.). That his views need correction will be proved in the course of this article.

1. Date of Nativity.—This may be fixed somewhat approximately by its relation to (*a*) the date of Herod's death (Mt 2^{1-22}), (*b*) the enrolment under Quirinius (Lk 2^1), and by (*c*) Patristic testimony.

(*a*) Herod's death, the *terminus ad quem* of the Nativity, is generally settled by the Jewish chronology in *Ant*. and *BJ*, in which are found indications of the dates of Herod's accession and death, and of the dates of his predecessor Antigonus, and of his immediate successors, Archelaus, Herod Philip, and Herod Antipas. For notice of Herod's death see *Ant*. XVII. viii. 1, 'having reigned, since he had procured the death of Antigonus, 34 years, but, since he had been declared king by the Romans, 37 years.' The death of Antigonus is noted in *Ant*. XIV. xvi. 4. 'This destruction befell the city of Jerusalem when Marcus Agrippa and Canidius Gallus were consuls at Rome, Olym. 185, in the 3rd month, on the solemnity of the fast, like a periodical return of the misfortunes which overtook the Jews under Pompey, by whom they were taken on the same day 27 years before.' The consuls mentioned held office B.C. 37, and 27 years from B.C. 63 (consulship of Cicero and Antonius), when Pompey took Jerusalem (*Ant*. XIV. iv. 3), allowing for the three intercalary months of B.C. 46, gives practically the same date, B.C. 37, for the confirmation of Herod in his kingdom. Herod's death might therefore be placed in the month Nisan (see below) B.C. 4 (Sivan 25 B.C. 37 to Nisan B.C. 4, according to the method of counting reigns, being 34 years).

Of Herod's successors (1) Archelaus, ethnarch of Judæa, was banished in the consulship of Lepidus and Arruntius (A.D. 6), in the 10th year of his reign (*Ant*. XVII. xiii. 2), or in the 9th (*BJ* II. vii. 3), and therefore would have come to the throne B.C. 4, being probably banished before he celebrated the 10th anniversary of his accession. (2) Herod Philip died in the 20th year of Tiberius, having been tetrarch of Trachonitis and Gaulanitis 37 years (*Ant*. XVIII. iv. 6), and would have commenced his reign B.C. 4–3.

There are two more data to help us to fix the year of Herod's death: the eclipse of the moon which preceded his last illness (*Ant*. XVII. vi. 4), and the Passover which followed soon after (XVII. ix. 3). The lunar eclipses visible in Palestine during B.C. 5–3 were those of March 23 B.C. 5, Sept. 15 B.C. 5, March 12 B.C. 4. As it is quite possible that the final scene of Herod's life and his obsequies did not cover more than one month, we might, with Ideler and Wurm, fix on the eclipse of March 12 B.C. 4 (Wieseler, *Chron. Syn.* p. 56), which is also indicated by the Passover that immediately followed. B.C. 4, Herod's death, would therefore be the *terminus ad quem* of the Nativity.

But how long before B.C. 4 Jesus was born cannot decisively be said. The age of the Innocents, ἀπὸ διετοῦς καὶ κατωτέρω (Mt 2¹⁶), would give B.C. 6 as the superior limit and B.C. 5 as the inferior, as this clause is qualified by the diligent investigation of Herod (κατὰ τὸν χρόνον ὃν ἠκρίβωσε παρὰ τῶν μάγων). This massacre, quite in keeping with the growing cruelty and suspicion of Herod, who had recently procured the murder of his two sons, Alexander and Aristobulus, was secretly carried out and seemingly of small extent, not being mentioned by Josephus, and being apparently limited to children to whom the star which the Magi saw in the east, at least six months before, might have reference. Although Mt 2¹¹ τὸ παιδίον does not suggest an infant babe, the stay of the Holy Family in Bethlehem, where the Magi found them, cannot have been long, the presentation in the Temple following 40 days after the Nativity. B.C. 6–5 would then be approximately the date of the Nativity.

Of the star in the east it cannot be said with truth that 'the star shines only in the legend' (von Soden in *Encyc. Bibl.* art. 'Chronology'), for the appearance of a striking sidereal phenomenon between the years B.C. 7 and B.C. 4 has been proved by Kepler and verified by Ideler and Pritchard. Kepler suggested that a conjunction of Saturn and Jupiter in the zodiacal sign of the Pisces, similar to that which took place in Dec. 1603, took place in B.C. 7. But this would be too early for the star that

stood over Bethlehem. Wieseler (*l.c.* p. 67) therefore, elaborating another suggestion of Kepler, held that a brilliant evanescent star, similar to that which appeared in Sept. 1604 between Jupiter and Saturn, and waned in March 1606, may have appeared then. The Chinese tables mention such an appearance in B.C. 4. Edersheim (*Life and Times of Jesus the Messiah*) suggests that the conjunction in B.C. 7 first aroused the attention of the Magi, and that the evanescent star of B.C. 4 stood over Bethlehem. Two Jewish traditions, one that the star of the Messiah should be seen two years before His birth, and the other that the conjunction of Saturn and Jupiter in Pisces portended something of importance for the Jewish nation, might be mentioned. The former is found in the Midrashim, the latter in Abarbanel's *Com. on Daniel* (15th cent.). While no theory could be established on such a basis as this appearance, yet it may support a theory founded on more certain data. If the coming of the Magi took place shortly after the death of Herod's sons Alexander and Aristobulus (B.C. 7) and the mission of Antipater, his heir, to Rome (B.C. 6), their question, 'Where is he that is born king of the Jews?' would, indeed, be startling to Herod.

(*b*) The enrolment under Quirinius (Lk 2² αὕτη ἡ ἀπογραφὴ πρώτη ἐγένετο ἡγεμονεύοντος τῆς Συρίας Κυρηνίου, 'this enrolment took place for the first time when Quirinius was governor of Syria'; cf. ὅτε πρῶτον ἐκέλευσαν ἀπογραφὰς γενέσθαι [*Strom.* i. 147]). A Roman census took place in A.D. 6, after the deposition of Archelaus, and caused the revolt of Judas of Gamala (*Ant*. XVIII. i. 1), who in consequence became the founder of the Zealot party, which resisted Gentile taxation and authority. This taxing (XVIII. ii. 1) was concluded in the 37th year of Cæsar's victory at Actium (A.D. 7). To this enrolment the author of Ac 5³⁶ refers. But it cannot be the enrolment of Lk 2². And Josephus should not be accused of having ascribed to A.D. 7 what took place in B.C. 6–5, as the census he mentions was made after and in consequence of the removal of Archelaus. Mommsen and Zumpt suggest that Quirinius held office *twice* in Syria. And his, indeed, might be the name wanting in a mutilated inscription, describing an official who was twice governor of Syria under Augustus. But Saturninus was governor B.C. 9–7, and Varus B.C. 7–4, being in power after Herod's death ; so that no place can be found for the rule of Quirinius before B.C. 4, the *terminus ad quem* of our Lord's birth. He may have come, B.C. 3–2, and completed a census begun by his predecessor. And there is also the possibility of his having received an extraordinary military command by the side of Varus. The *Annals* of Tacitus (ii. 30, iii. 22, 48) describe him as a keen and zealous soldier (*impiger militiæ et acribus ministeriis*), who had obtained a triumph for having stormed some fortresses of the Homonadenses in Cilicia, but who was distinctly unpopular on account of his friendship with Tiberius, his sordid life and 'dangerous old age.' Such an officer would have been a most useful agent for Augustus in preparing the document called by Suetonius (*Aug.* 28) the *rationarium imperii*, which contained a full description of the 'subject kingdoms, provinces, taxes direct and indirect' (*regna, provinciæ, tributa aut vectigalia*, Tac. *Ann.* i. 11), made out by the emperor himself, especially as Varus was slack, and inclined to favour Archelaus. Certain riots mentioned in Josephus (*Ant*. XVII. ii. 4), in which the Pharisees appear, may have been due to the census. Justin Martyr (*Apol.* i. 34, 46 ; *Dial. c. Tryph.* 78) appeals to the ἀπογραφαί made in the time of Quirinius, whom he styles 'the first ἐπίτροπος or procurator in Judæa.' For until Palestine became a Roman province in A.D. 6 there could be no procurator in the strict sense of the term. Previous to that, if Q. did hold office, it would be as a military officer of Syria, and so he might be well described by the vague ἡγεμονεύοντος, although the word is also applied (Lk 3¹) to Pilate, whom Tacitus styled procurator (*Ann.* xv. 44). With regard to the census, of which no mention is made in contemporary history, it is to be noted that there is evidence that periodic enrolments, ἀπογραφαί, were made in Egypt (*Class. Rev.*, Mar. 1893). Prof. Ramsay (*Was Christ born at Bethlehem?*) builds on these. It is quite possible that a series of periodical enrolments in a cycle of 14 years were initiated by Augustus, an indefatigable statistician, in other parts of the empire, and that the first of these may have taken place in the days of Herod, who would have carried it out according to Jewish tastes, and so without much disturbance (unless the riots of *Ant.* XVII. ii. 4, *BJ* I. xxxiii. 2 might be connected with it), whereas the later census was conducted according to Roman ideas, and provoked a rebellion. If this be true, the first census would occur B.C. 7–5, just where it would be required. Some hold that it is possible that St. Luke made a mistake in the name Quirinius (C. H. Turner), and also in the census (von Soden).

(*c*) Patristic testimony, as represented by Irenæus, Clement of Alexandria, and Hippolytus, and perhaps based upon Lk 2², favours a date between B.C. 3 and B.C. 2. Irenæus wrote, ‘Our Lord was born about the 41st year (B.C. 3, reckoning from the death of Julius Cæsar B.C. 44) of the empire of Augustus’ (*Hær.* iii. 21. 3). Clement stated, ‘Our Lord was born in the 28th year (B.C. 3, counting from battle of Actium, B.C. 31) of the reign of Augustus, when first they ordered the enrolments to be made’ (*Strom.* i. 147). Hippolytus said, in his *Com. on Daniel*, ‘Our Lord was born on Wednesday, Dec. 25, in the 42nd (B.C. 2) year of the reign of Augustus.’

With regard to *the month and day of the Nativity*, no data exist to enable us to determine them at all. Farrar (*Life of Christ*, p. 9) inferred from the presence of the shepherds in the fields that it was during winter, but Lewin (*Fasti Sacri*, pp. 23, 115) argues for August 1 as the approximate date. The date of the Annunciation is given in Lk 1²⁶ as ἐν δὲ τῷ μηνὶ τῷ ἕκτῳ—‘in the sixth month,’ which is generally referred to Lk 1³⁶ οὗτος μὴν ἕκτος ἐστὶν αὐτῇ, κ.τ.λ., ‘this month is sixth with her,’ but which may with equal probability refer to the sixth month of the Jewish calendar, Elul, or to both dates, both terms of six months running concurrently. The date of the service of the course of Abia, the eighth in order (1 Ch 24¹⁰), for the year 748 A.U.C. (B.C. 6) has been calculated from the fact that the course in waiting on Ab 9 A.D. 70, when Jerusalem was taken, was the first, Jehoiarib (*Taanith* on ‘Fasting,’ p. 29*a*; *BJ* VI. iv.). This would give courses of Abia for 748 A.U.C., B.C. 6, April 18–24, and (24 weeks later) October 3–9. Six months from the latter date would give a day in March as the date of the Annunciation and a date in December for the Nativity; but six months from the former date would give Elul, or the sixth month of the Jewish year, beginning about Sept. 19, for the Annunciation, and the third month, Sivan or June, for the Incarnation. Elul was the month of the constellation Virgo, who holds in her hand the *spica Virginis*, which may be ‘the offspring of a Virgin.’ The fourth month belongs to Cancer, among two stars of which is a group called ‘The Manger.’

Patristic tradition. — Hippolytus is the first to give Dec. 25 for the date of the Nativity. On his chair in the library of St. John Lateran in Rome his celebrated table is given. The second year of the cycle has April 2, γένεσις Χριστοῦ, evidently the conception, the calculation being made on the strength of Lk 1³⁶, which seems to imply an interval of 6 months between the conception of our Lord and that of the Baptist, and on the popular presumption that Gabriel appeared to Zacharias on the great Day of the Atonement, the 10th day of the seventh month. This would bring the conception of our Lord to the 14th day of the first month, or the Passover full moon. Hippolytus afterwards, in his

Com. on Daniel, in order to allow for two additional years in our Lord’s life, altered the date April 2 to March 25, on which the Church has always celebrated the conception, and consequently the Nativity was assigned to Dec. 25. Edersheim (*The Temple*, p. 293) suggests the influence of the feast of the Dedication of the Temple, held on the 25th of Chislev.

2. The Baptism of Jesus might be settled, but not very approximately, by (1) the statement (Lk 3²³) that He was ὡσεὶ ἐτῶν τριάκοντα ἀρχόμενος (at the beginning of His ministry); (2) the date of the Baptist’s preaching, Lk 3¹ ‘Now in the fifteenth year of the reign of Tiberius Cæsar . . . the word of God came unto John the son of Zacharias in the wilderness’; and (3) by the retort of the Jews in Jn 2²⁰ ‘Forty and six years was this temple in building.’

(1) This is an elastic expression, which gave the Valentinian Gnostics a basis for their belief that Jesus was in His 30th year when He came to His baptism (*Hær.* ii. 25. 5). But as Irenæus, in his reference to Jn 8⁵⁷ ‘Thou art not yet fifty years old,’ pointed out, 40, not 30, is the perfect age of a master (cf. Bab. *Aboda Zara*); and on the strength of this statement the presbyters in Asia Minor, who misled Irenæus, ascribed an age of 40 or 50 years to Jesus. Again, while the maximum age of a Levite was 50 years, the minimum varied between 20 (1 Ch 23²⁴· ²⁷, where the change is ascribed to David), 25 (Nu 4³· ⁴⁷ LXX), and 30 (Nu 4³· ⁴⁷ Heb.). This latitude, added to the general sense of ὡσεὶ (‘about’) and the vague ἀρχόμενος, which is omitted in Syr. Sin., makes this indication of our Lord’s age indefinite, and capable of meaning either two years over or under 30.

(2) The preaching of the Baptist is the *terminus a quo* of the baptism of Jesus, and is assigned to the 15th year of Tiberius. Dating that reign from the death of Augustus, Aug. 19 A.D. 14, the 15th year corresponds with A.D. 28–29. B. Weiss and Beyschlag, however, count from A.D. 12, when Tiberius was made co-regent with Augustus. W. M. Ramsay has pointed out that on July 1 A.D. 71, during the life of the Evangelist, Titus was similarly associated in the empire with Vespasian, which would give A.D. 26–27 as the first year of the Baptist’s work. This would agree with the office of Pilate, who could hardly have arrived much sooner than A.D. 27, as he held office for 10 years, and was on his way to Rome in A.D. 37, when Tiberius died (*Ant.* XVIII. iv. 2). We might, therefore, if it is permitted to follow Weiss and Beyschlag, fix on A.D. 27–28 for our Lord’s baptism.

(3) Jn 2²⁰ τεσσαράκοντα καὶ ἓξ ἔτεσιν ᾠκοδομήθη ὁ ναὸς οὗτος (cf. Ezr 5¹⁶ ᾠκοδομήθη καὶ οὐκ ἐτελέσθη). The Jews do not refer, therefore, to the completion of the restoration, which took place much later (*Ant.* XX. ix. 7). This work was begun in the 18th year of Herod (*Ant.* XV. xi. 1, reckoning from B.C. 37, death of Antigonus), in the 15th (*BJ* I. xxi. 1, reckoning from B.C. 40). This gives B.C. 19–18, from which to A.D. 28 is 46 years. The Passover of A.D. 28 would be a likely date for the events of Jn 2¹⁴⁻²⁵. The time of Jn 1¹⁹–2¹² has yet to be settled. Prof. Sanday (art. ‘Jesus Christ’ in Hastings’ *DB* ii. 609) gives the time as ‘Winter, A.D. 26.’ Now there are certain indications of the time of year in which our Lord was baptized which show that His visit to the Baptist may have syn-chronized with the preparations for the Passover in the month Adar (cf. Jn 11⁵⁵ ‘And the Jews’ passover was at hand, and many went out of the country up to Jerusalem before the passover to purify themselves’), while His sojourn and fast in the wilderness, of which St. Matthew and St. Luke give details, may have been due not only to a desire to be alone to reflect upon His mission, but

also to the feeling of the necessity of a great self-restraint in order to check the urgings of His Messianic consciousness to manifest Himself to the Passover crowds in His connexion with His country as its Redeemer, with the Temple as the Son of God and its Priest, and with the world as its King. It was on His return from the desert that He was pointed out by the Baptist, when the marks of the recent struggle and fasting on His brow would have given additional point to the Baptist's remark, 'Behold the Lamb of God, which taketh away the sin of the world' (Jn 1[29]), which has a true Passover ring (cf. 'Christ our passover [or Paschal lamb, τὸ πάσχα] was sacrificed for us,' 1 Co 5[7]). Passover time would also account for the presence of so many Galilæans in Judæa, while the atmosphere of the scenes of the baptism of Jesus and of His interviews with His first disciples in Jn 1 is spring, the budding life of the year, in the buoyant sunshine when men's hearts are most ready for a change of life. Nathanael, an Israelite without the guile of Jacob, at the feast exclusively for Israelites, is meditating under a fig tree, most likely on the story of Jacob. Passover seems a favourite time for baptism. It was after the Passover of Jn 2[13] that Jesus and His disciples baptized in Judæa, while John was baptizing in Ænon near to Salim (Jn 3[22f.]). And it is most improbable that Jesus would have stayed away from the Passover.

On the other side may be urged the fact that Bethabara, for which the best MSS, אABC, read 'Bethany,' has been identified by Conder with a ford called 'Abârah, N.E. of Beth-shean, 'a site as near to Cana as any point on the Jordan, and within a day's journey' (art. 'Bethabara' in Hastings' DB). On the other hand, Encyc. Bibl. art. 'Bethany' follows Sir G. Grove and Sir C. W. Wilson (Smith's DB[2], s.v. 'Bethnimrah') in holding that Beth-nimrah on the east of Jordan, opposite to Jericho, is the place meant. Beth-nimrah, now known as Nimrîn, is 'beyond Jordan,' πέραν τοῦ Ἰορδάνου (Jn 1[28] 3[26]); it is well supplied with water, and accessible both from Jericho and Jerusalem, and may have produced the variants 'Beth-abara' and 'Bethany.' Origen advocated Bethabara because he could find no Bethany beyond Jordan. But the variant Βηθαραβα for Βηθαβαρα is found in his text. That variant and the traditional site of our Lord's baptism, Makhadet Hajla, are strongly against Col. Conder's suggestion, while tradition connects our Lord's temptation with the district of Quarantania, named from His 40 days' fast; and something must be allowed for tradition in such matters. 'The third day' of Jn 2[1] may possibly be counted from Jn 1[43] 'On the day after.' But it is probable, in fact it is to be inferred from His mother's information of the exhausted wine, that our Lord was not present on the first day of the marriage festivities, which generally extended over a week, and were concluded with a supper (art. 'Marriage' in Hastings' DB), and it was quite possible for Him and His disciples to have accomplished the journey from the vicinity of Jericho to Nazareth (about 60 miles) in three or four days; so that there is no necessity to select a site for His baptism within one day's journey of Cana. Again, the favourite time for such marriages was March (Wetzstein in Ztschr. f. Ethnol. v. [1873]). So that we have another indication of the early season of the year, which supports the hypothesis of a baptism at the Passover preceding the Passover of Jn 2[13], a period of time required for the preparation and selection of the disciples, and for the nursing of their nascent faith by miracles, of which one, a typical sign, as are all the seven signs in the Fourth Gospel, is narrated in Jn 2[1-12]. To this faith reference is made in v.[11] 'And his disciples believed in him.' Nor does the Master's change of manner (v.[24] 'But Jesus would not trust himself to them') suggest the beginning of a mission.

The order in St. Mark's Gospel is of little service here. For Mk 1[14] ('Now after that John was put in prison Jesus came into Galilee preaching') refers to an event, the imprisonment of the Baptist, which was clearly later than Jn 4[1], and is, therefore, to be taken not as a note of time, but as a general introduction to the Galilæan ministry, which forms the subject of the Second Gospel. The selection of the disciples (Mk 1[16-19]), the missionary work of Mk 1[38] ἄγωμεν εἰς τὰς ἐχομένας κωμοπόλεις, a portion of Mk 1-3, and apparently Lk 5[1-11] (the scene with Peter on the lake), may belong to the Galilæan work previous to Jn 2[13]. On this hypothesis, which fills in the awkward gap between the 13th and 14th verses of Mk 1, the baptism of Jesus would fall on the Passover of A.D. 27.

3. Length of the Ministry.—If the date of the beginning of the ministry be approximately fixed, the year of its close will vary according to the estimate we form of its length. Prof. von Soden (Encyc. Bibl. art. 'Chronology') reduces it to a one year basis, while Prof. Sanday (art. 'Jesus Christ' in Hastings' DB ii. 610) requires nearly 2½ years for his scheme of our Lord's ministry. This difference is due to the fact that St. John seems to extend that ministry over three Passovers, while the Synoptists mention but one Passover.

(a) In the Second Gospel there seem to be three data for a chronology. (1) Mk 2[23] mentions ears of corn (τίλλοντες τοὺς στάχυας). As the earliest barley was in April, the latest in June, it is believed that the point of time we have here is Passover, which was of old associated with 'ears of corn'; the name of the month in which it was held being formerly 'Abib אָבִיב or 'ear of corn.' (2) Mk 6[39] describes the miracle of the feeding of the 5000, in the course of which we read that the people were arranged in companies, πρασιαὶ πρασιαί (a phrase suggestive of garden-plots), and seated ἐπὶ τῷ χλωρῷ χόρτῳ, an indication of early spring. (3) Mk 11, final Passover. In these data Turner ('Chronology of NT' in Hastings' DB) sees a suggestion of a two years' ministry. But it is evident that the arrangement of this Gospel is according to subject-matter, not to time. The time relation of the episode of the ears of corn cannot be satisfactorily settled with regard either to the events it precedes or those it follows in the narrative. It is, therefore, quite possible that it preceded the Passover of Jn 2[13]. In St. Luke's Gospel it occurs shortly after the scene with St. Peter on the Lake (Lk 5[1-11]), which must have preceded Jn 3[22], where Jesus and His disciples go into the land of Judæa and continue baptizing there; and in both the Second and Third Gospels it directly follows the question, 'Why do the disciples of John and of the Pharisees fast, and thy disciples fast not?,' which occasioned the Parable of the Bridegroom and the Children of the Bridechamber, which seemingly but not really corresponds with the discussion in Jn 3[26] between the disciples of John and a Jew about 'purifying,' which evoked from the Baptist the rhapsody on the bride and bridegroom. For the questions are quite different, and belong to distinctly different contexts; that in the Synoptists being caused by the feast of Levi and perhaps indirectly by the feast at Cana of Galilee, while that of the Fourth Gospel arose in connexion with the work in Judæa after the Passover of Jn 2[13].

No fresh light is thrown on the passage by the disputed point of time ἐν σαββάτῳ δευτεροπρώτῳ, which Wetstein explains as the first Sabbath of the second month, Scaliger as the first Sabbath after the Feast of Unleavened Bread, Godet as the first Sabbath of the ecclesiastical year. The ripeness of the wheat suggests the month of Iyyar or May. And it is quite possible to conceive our Lord in that month (called in the old style Ziv (זו) or the 'month of flowers,' and in the new style 'Iyyar (אִיר) or 'the bright and flowering month') teaching the people in the plain and on the hill to 'consider the lilies of the field, how they grow' (Mt 6[28]). It seems not impossible, therefore, to reconstruct the Second Gospel on the basis of a single year following the Passover of Jn 2[13], with a year or greater part of a year previous to that Passover.

(b) St. Luke's Gospel is divisible into two parts. The second (9[50]–19[28] containing matter peculiar to him), being devoted to the doings and teachings of the Master as the days of His assumption were being fulfilled (9[51]), seems to restrict the Lord's ministry to a single year, 'the acceptable year of the Lord' (4[19]; cf. Is 61[2]). The reference to 'three years' in the parable of the Fig-tree (13[7]), which suggested to many (Bengel among others) the beginning of a third year of ministry, is a vague expression to which 13[32] ('to-day and to-morrow, and on the third day') might be a parallel. In 4[14]-9[50] there is but one apparent reference to any work outside the Galilæan, Ἰουδαίας (אBCL) of 4[44] being a variant for Γαλιλαίας. But 'Judæa' in the days of St. Luke included all Palestine (cf. 23[5]).

(c) The Fourth Gospel has seven notes of time between the Baptism and the Crucifixion:

(1) 2[13. 23] 'And the Jews' passover was at hand, and Jesus went up to Jerusalem . . . And he was in Jerusalem at the passover during the feast.'
(2) 4[35] 'Say ye not, There are yet four months (τετράμηνος), and then cometh harvest? behold, I say unto you, Lift up your eyes, and consider (θεάσασθε) the fields that they are white already to harvest.'
(3) 5[1] 'After these things there was a [or the] feast of the Jews, and Jesus went up to Jerusalem.'
(4) 6[4] 'Now [the passover, τὸ πάσχα, uncertain] the feast of the Jews was nigh.'
(5) 7[2] 'Now the Jews' feast of tabernacles was at hand.'
(6) 10[22] 'Then the dedication took place in Jerusalem.'
(7) 12[1] 'Jesus then, six days before the passover, came to Bethany.'

Jn 4[35] (a) οὐχ ὑμεῖς λέγετε ὅτι ἔτι τετράμηνός ἐστιν καὶ ὁ θερισμὸς ἔρχεται; (β) ἰδού, λέγω ὑμῖν . . . ὅτι λευκαί εἰσιν πρὸς θερισμόν, is a difficult note of time. The simplest interpretation is to take a literally of a harvest still remote, and β spiritually of a harvest already ripening. Origen, however, held that it was already the middle or end of harvest when these things happened (in Joan. tom. xiii. 39. 41); but it is evident that our Lord made no long delay in Judæa after the unpleasantness that had occurred between His disciples and John's, and it would not be long before the popular Baptist, with his great following, would hear of his greater Rival (Jn 3[26]), or before the Pharisees would note the falling off of the Baptist's followers. The fact that the impression His works in Jerusalem had made on the Galilæans was still fresh (Jn 4[45]), and that He did not tarry more than two days, possibly only one (μετὰ δὲ τὰς δύο ἡμέρας, Jn 4[43]), among the kindly and believing Samaritans, and that He was wearied with the journey (4[6]), points to no long interval between 2[13] and 4[45] and to no leisurely mode of travelling. Again, the word ἔτι has a touch of reality, which suggests the natural interpretation of τετράμηνος against those who would read the passage proverbially : 'Is it not a saying that there are four months between sowing and reaping?' There is nothing, however, to prevent one taking the lateness of the Galilæan harvest into account, and reading the passage thus : 'Say ye not, ye men of Galilee, where the harvest is later than in Judæa, where Jeroboam held his feast of ingathering on the 15th day of the eighth month (1 K 12[32]) instead of on the 15th day of the seventh (Lv 23[34]), that harvest is yet four months off?' If these words were spoken towards the end of Nisan, the four months referred to would be Nisan (March–April, end), Iyyar (April–May), Sivan (May–June), and Thammuz (June–July, beginning). This would be in keeping with the fact that the harvest naturally varied not only with season, but also with elevation, etc., and that, while it commenced in the lowlands of the Jordan Valley in April, it ended on sub-alpine Lebanon in August (see art. 'Wheat' in Hastings' DB).

Jn 5[1] 'And there was a feast of the Jews, and Jesus went up to Jerusalem' (with alternative readings, ἑορτή and ἡ ἑορτή, the latter being supported by the Alexandrian type of text, doubtless through the influence of Eusebius, who maintained a three years' ministry with four Passovers). What this feast was cannot definitely be said. Irenæus regarded it as a Passover. The early Greek Church identified it with Pentecost. West-

cott (ad loc.) suggests Trumpets (September), as 'many of the main thoughts of the discourse—Creation, Judgment, and Law—find a remarkable illustration in the thoughts of the festival.' But Ex 19[1] states that it was in the third month (i.e. after Passover) that the Law was given on Sinai. This would correspond with Pentecost, which is described in the later Jewish liturgy as 'the day of the giving of the Law' (Saalschütz, Das Mos. Recht, p. 42a), and by Maimonides (Moreh neb. iii. 41) as 'dies ille quo lex data fuit.' Furthermore, the strict regulations and calculations of the Sabbaths of the harvest period between Nisan 16 and Pentecost, the Feast of Weeks, add point to the controversy concerning the Sabbath day (Jn 5[10-18]). The voluntary nature of the cure, a contrast with the signs of 2[11] and 4[54] performed by request, suggests that this act was in accordance with the Pentecostal regulations of Dt 16[10], a free-will offering of His own hand, and according to Lv 23[22] the gleaning of His harvest for the poor.

There is a useful indication of time in Jn 5[33-36], where the Baptist, whose popularity is waning in 4[1], and whose utterance in 3[28-36] seems to contain a presentiment of doom—'He must increase, but I must decrease'—is referred to as a lamp that no longer shines. 'He was the burning and shining lamp, and ye were willing for a time to rejoice in his light.' It is probable that Herod Antipas, who was jealous and suspicious of the Baptist's influence (Ant. XVIII. v. 1), seized the opportunity of his decreasing popularity to have him betrayed (παραδοθῆναι, Mk 1[14]) and arrested. The report of that arrest may have reached our Lord on His journey through Samaria to Galilee (Jn 4). If so, the Synoptic statements of Mk 1[14], Mt 4[12], regarding His work in Galilee as connected with the imprisonment of the Baptist would be suitably introduced by the healing of the nobleman's son at Capernaum (Jn 4[46-54]).

The interval allowed by the Synoptists between the arrest and the death of the Baptist, in which room is found for an extended work of Jesus in Galilee (Capernaum especially, Mt 11[1-30]), for the Baptist's mission to Jesus (11[3]), and for Herod's procrastination with the Baptist, whom he feared, tried to keep safe, and for whom he did many things (Mk 6[20]), is also allowed in the Fourth Gospel. In it Jesus is represented as walking in Galilee (7[1-10]) before the Feast of Tabernacles, nearly five months (Sivan 8–Tishri 15) after the Feast of Pentecost (5[1]), but not afterwards,—a fact which is in agreement with the Synoptic account (Lk 9[10], Mt 14[13], Mk 6[31]), which describes our Lord withdrawing from the jurisdiction of Herod Antipas to Bethsaida Julias, Cæsarea Philippi, and other districts of Herod Philip—the best of all the Herods—in consequence of the former's identification of Him with the Baptist, whom he had beheaded (Mk 6[14]).

With regard to the date of the Baptist's execution, Keim, Hausrath, Schenkel, and others, on the strength of Josephus' account of the defeat of Antipas by Aretas (A.D. 36), in connexion with his narrative of the Baptist's death, which the Jews regarded as divinely avenged in that battle, have held that the divorce of Herod Antipas' wife cannot have been long before A.D. 36. But Josephus notes also a dispute about boundaries in Gamalitis (Ant. XVIII. v. 1) as subsequent to the divorce of the daughter of Aretas, which he describes as 'the first occasion' of the bitterness between him and Herod. And there is nothing in the annals of the Herods to controvert the date A.D. 28 for the scene in the castle of Machærus as described in the Synoptics. In fact, A.D. 28 would be a more suitable date for the elopement of Herodias, and the description of her daughter

Salome as τὸ κοράσιον (Mk 6²². ²⁸), than A.D. 36. Herodias was the sister of Agrippa I., who (*Ant.* XIX. viii. 2) was 54 years old when he died in A.D. 44, and was, therefore, born B.C. 10. Herodias must have been born shortly before or after, as she was betrothed by Herod the Great (*Ant.* XVII. i. 2), after the death of her father Aristobulus (B.C. 7), when quite a child, to Philip his son by Mariamne II., daughter of Simon the high priest, whom he married in the 13th year of his reign, *c.* B.C. 24 (*Ant.* XV. ix. 3). Herodias would, therefore, be about 37 years old, and her husband 52 in A.D. 28, and her daughter Salome not more than 18, as Herodias was married 'when arrived at age of puberty' (*Ant.* XVIII. v. 4). In A.D. 36 she would be 45 years of age, and Salome 26. The former age is, therefore, more probable. The fact that retribution was connected with the defeat in A.D. 36 proves nothing, as retribution is proverbially long delayed.

The fourth point of time is Jn 6⁴. The difficulty in it is the reading τὸ πάσχα. By many it is retained; by others omitted. If it is retained, there are three Passovers mentioned in Jn. (2¹³ 6⁴ 12¹), making the ministry extend over two years. But if it is removed, this feast of the Jews becomes identified with the Feast of Tabernacles of 7². And the chronology of the ministry can be reckoned on the basis of a year and several months previous.

1²⁹–2¹². Work in Galilee.
2¹³. Passover in Jerusalem (Nisan).
5¹. Pentecost in Sivan (May–June 1).
6⁴. Tabernacles in Tishri (September–October).
7². Tabernacles in Tishri.
10²². Dedication in Chislev (November–December).
11⁵⁵. Passover in Nisan (March–April).

Hort urges the omission of τὸ πάσχα, which is supported (1) by documentary evidence; (2) by the fact that χόρτος πολύς of Jn 6¹⁰ apparently=χλωρῷ χόρτῳ of Mk 6³⁹; (3) by the note (Jn 7¹), 'After these things Jesus walked (περιπάτει) in Galilee,' which implies some interval between the events of chs. 6 and 7, but on the Tabernacles hypothesis sufficient time would not be allowed, as the same feast was 'near' in 6⁴ and in 7²; and (4) it is said that St. John, who was writing for Christians who had holy associations with Passover and Pentecost but not with Tabernacles, would hardly have spoken of that feast as 'the Feast' κατ' ἐξοχήν. On the other hand, it is more than probable (1) that Irenæus would have mentioned 6⁴ among the Passovers, if he knew of it, even though ostensibly he was merely recording the Passovers at which our Lord went up to Jerusalem, as his main object was to confute the Gnostics, who held that Jesus suffered a year after His baptism (*Hær.* ii. 22. 3); (2) that ἐγγύς is a vague term allowing for comparative nearness, and our Lord did not hurry Himself for the feast, arriving only in the middle of it (7¹⁴); (3) that Origen's *Com. on St. John* clearly postulates the omission of a Passover between 4³⁵ and 7²; (4) that St. John wrote as one familiar with Jewish fasts and feasts, and Josephus (*Ant.* VIII. iv. 1) calls the Feast of Tabernacles ἑορτὴ σφόδρα παρὰ τοῖς Ἑβραίοις ἁγιωτάτη καὶ μεγίστη, and it is in OT sometimes called '*the* Feast' (1 K 8². ⁶⁵, Ezk 45²⁵); (5) that the tradition of the Gnostics might have been more easily confuted by Irenæus by a reference to a Passover in Jn 6⁴ than by an attempt to identify the feast of 5¹ with a Passover; (6) that the Alogi, according to Epiphanius (*Hær.* 51. 22), found in Jn. only a Passover at the beginning and another at the end of His ministry; (7) that the words τὸ πάσχα might have easily been suggested by the discourse on the sacrificial feast and the 'barley' loaves (ἄρτους κριθίνους), which, however, has a nearer reference to the offerings (two leavened loaves of the best wheat, etc.) and customs of Pentecost, which was distinguished by thank-offerings (זֶבַח הַתּוֹדָה=εὐχαριστήσας) and festive gatherings for the poor (Lv 24²²); (8) that the insertion of a Passover here would break the unity of the plot and interfere with the development of the drama from Jn 2¹³ to 12¹, creating a gap between chs. 4 and 6 out of all proportion to the other intervals in the Gospel after Jn 2¹³. These reasons are not conclusive, but they are sufficient to prove the possibility of τὸ πάσχα being an early gloss on ἡ ἑορτή.

The interval between the Feast of Tabernacles (Tishri, A.D. 28) and the Passover (14 Nisan, A.D. 29) is sufficiently ample to allow for the work in the towns of Cæsarea Philippi (Mk 8²⁷), the preparation of the disciples for His death (Lk 9²²f.= Mk 8³¹), His Transfiguration six days after (Mt 17¹⁻¹³), His slow progress to 'Jerusalem, preceded by the Seventy' (Lk 10¹), 'when the days were

well-nigh come that He should be received up' (Lk 9⁵¹), the visit to Jerusalem at the Feast of Dedication (Jn 10²²), His work in the Peræa (Jn 10⁴⁰, Mk 10¹), and in the wilderness of Judæa (Jn 11⁵⁴). A ministry from Passover A.D. 27, when He was baptized, to Passover A.D. 29, is quite long enough to allow for the development of the life of the Master, and for the many journeys and missionary tours in a district as small as Wales, and where the festivals at the capital were so frequent. The details would be distinctly meagre for a longer mission.

4. Date of the Crucifixion.—The procuratorship of Pilate and the high priesthood of Caiaphas roughly indicate the date. Josephus (*Ant.* XVIII. ii. 2) notes the appointment of Valerius Gratus by Tiberius (*c.* A.D. 14–15), his return to Rome after 11 years (*c.* A.D. 25–26), and the appointment of Pilate in his place. In *Ant.* XVIII. iv. 2 we read that 'Pilate when he had tarried 10 years in Judæa made haste to Rome; but before he could reach Rome, Tiberius died' (A.D. 37). His office might be, therefore, dated A.D. 26–36. Pilate at the trial of Jesus seems to have already had trouble with the Jews and Galilæans and Herod. His yielding to them in the present instance through fear of their accusing him to Tiberius, and his release of 'a notable prisoner' (δέσμιον ἐπίσημον, Mt 27¹⁶), 'who for a certain insurrection made in the city and for murder' (Lk 23¹⁹) 'was lying bound with them that had made insurrection' (Mk 15⁷), imply at least part of the 10 years of cross purposes which marked Pilate's rule, but need not be ascribed to the censure received from Tiberius, *c.* A.D. 33, on account of the votive shields (Philo, *Legat. ad Gaium*, § 38), as he had in his very first year of office experienced the inflexibility of the Jews (*Ant.* XVIII. iii. 1). A Passover earlier than that of A.D. 28 would hardly suit.

The high priesthood of Annas, referred to in Jn 11⁴⁹ 18¹³. ²⁴, is a *terminus ad quem* of the Crucifixion, his deposition occurring about the same time as Herod Philip's death. It is assigned by Josephus (*Ant.* XVIII. iv. 3, 6) to the 20th year of Tiberius. The latest possible date of the Crucifixion would thus be A.D. 34, the earliest A.D. 26.

As it is hard to believe that such an event would not be exactly chronicled by the Church, it is quite possible to regard Lk 3¹—'in the fifteenth year of Tiberius'—as an indication of the 'acceptable year of the Lord' which terminated on the cross, whether with Bratke (*SK*, 1892) we regard that acceptable year as terminating in the 15th, or with von Soden (*Encyc. Bibl.* art. 'Chronology') in the 16th of Tiberius. A well-known tradition of the Church assigns the Crucifixion to the consulship of the Gemini, L. Rubellius and C. Rufius, A.D. 29, which year, according to the strict method of computation from Aug. A.D. 14, would correspond with Tiberius 15, but, counting as a year the semester Aug. A.D. 14–Jan. A.D. 15, when the consuls dated their term of office, would be Tiberius 16.

Among Patristic authorities for the year of the Crucifixion the following are chief:—Clement of Alexandria: 'With the 15th year of Tiberius and 15th of Augustus so are completed the 30 years to the Passion' (*Strom.* i. 147). Origen: 'If you examine the chronology of the Passion and of the fall of Jerusalem . . . from Tiberius 15 to the razing of the temple are 42 years' (*Hom. in Hierem.* xix. 13). Tertullian: 'In the 15th year of the reign Christ suffered . . . in the consulship of Rubellius Geminus and Rufius Geminus' (*adv. Jud.* 8, but authorship doubtful); and Hippolytus, who in his work on *Daniel* stated: 'Our Lord was born on Wednesday, Dec. 25, in the 42nd year of the reign of Augustus. . . . He suffered in the 33rd year, on Friday, March 25, in the 18th year of Tiberius, and the consulship of Rufus and Rubellio', evidently attempting to combine a three years' ministry with Lk 3¹. In his *Chronicle* the length of our Lord's life is estimated at 30 years. Dr. Salmon in *Hermathena*, No. xviii., suggests that Hippolytus altered the chronology of the latter work in A.D. 234, on discovering that St. John's chronology was incompatible with a one year's ministry. In the tables of Hippolytus the Passion is assigned to the 32nd year of the cycle, which, reckoning back by cycles of 112 years from A.D. 222, the first year of the cycle, is A.D. 29, which may have been suggested by the consulship of the Gemini, whose names he gives erroneously with or after the *Acts of Pilate* as Rufus and Rubellio. Other authorities who may be cited are Julius Africanus, who seems to hover between Tiberius 16 (in the Greek of Eusebius, *Dem. Evang.*) and Tiberius 15 (Latin of Jerome's *Com. in Dan. ix.*); Lactantius, who wrote : 'In the 15th year of Tiberius, that is, in the consulship of the Gemini' (*Div. Inst.* IV. x. 18); the *Liberian Chronicle*, which has, 'Under Tiberius, the two Gemini consuls, March 25'; and Augustine (*de Civ. Dei*, xviii. 54): 'Consuls the Gemini, March 25.' A.D. 29 is therefore well supported by Christian tradition. The note of the annalist Phlegon, referred to by Origen (*c. Cels.* ii. 33), and the *Chronicle* of Eusebius (under Ol. 202. 4 = A.D. 32-33), which mentions the earthquake in Bithynia and the darkness at the sixth hour of the day, obviously comes from some unreliable Christian source.

(a) *Day of week and month.*—Some indications of the day of the week are found in Scripture. The general belief that the Crucifixion took place on Friday is founded on inference from the fact that He rose 'on the third day,' τῇ τρίτῃ ἡμέρᾳ (1 Co 15[4]), the Jews counting their days inclusively. Westcott, however, held that it took place on a Thursday, on account of the 'three days and three nights' of Mt 12[40], a saying found there also, and evidently equivalent to 'on the third day' (Gn 42[17. 18], Est 4[16] and 5[1]).

(b) *Day of month.*—The question is, Did the Crucifixion take place on the Passover, Nisan 15, or on the day preceding, Nisan 14? This question also concerns the relation of the Passover to the Last Supper ; for while, strictly speaking, both events took place on the same day, on the Jewish reckoning from evening to evening, according to the ordinary Roman method the Crucifixion fell a day later than the Supper. Sanday (*Authorship and Historical Character of the Fourth Gospel*), Westcott (*Introduction to the Gospels*), and many others maintain that it took place on Nisan 14. The principal champion for Nisan 15 is Edersheim, who holds that the Last Supper synchronized with the Passover, and that the Pascha of which the Jews desired to partake was the *Chagigah* or festive offering of the first festive Paschal day. The Synoptists in some places identify the last meal with the Passover, but in others give indications of an opposite view ; while the Fourth Gospel gives unqualified support to the opinion that the feast of which our Lord partook had a quasi-Paschal significance, and preceded in order to supersede the Jewish Passover. A list of passages from the Gospels for both views makes this clear :

For Nisan 15, the Passover—
  Mt 26[17] 'The first day of the feast of unleavened bread the disciples came to Jesus, saying unto him, Where wilt thou that we prepare for thee to eat the Passover?'
  Lk 22[7] 'Then came the day of unleavened bread, when the Passover must be killed.'
  Mk 14[12] 'And the first day of unleavened bread, when they killed the Passover.'
  Lk 22[15] 'With desire I have desired to eat this Passover with you before I suffer.'
For Nisan 14—
  Jn 13[1] 'Now before the feast of the Passover.'
  Jn 18[28] 'And they themselves went not into the prætorium, lest they should be defiled, but that they might eat the Passover.'
  Jn 13[29] 'Buy that we have need of for the feast.'
  Jn 19[14] 'And it was the preparation of the Passover.'
  Jn 19[31] 'Since it was the preparation, and that Sabbath day was a high day.'
  Mt 26[3-5] 'Then assembled together the chief priests . . . and consulted that they might take Jesus by subtilty and kill him. But they said, *Not on the feast day*, lest there be an uproar among the people' (cf. Mk 14[2]).
  Mt 27[62] 'Now the next day, that followed the day of the preparation.'
  Lk 23[54] 'And that day was the preparation, and the Sabbath drew on.'

Other incidents in the Synoptics point to Nisan 14, such as the holding of the trial on the feast day, the purchase of linen and spices, the arming of Peter, the coming of Simon 'from the field' (Mk 15[21]), the unseemly hurry with the trial, the execution and the final dispatch of the victims, the

sword of Peter (14[47]), the armed multitude with Judas (14[43]), it being unlawful to carry arms on the feast day. It is to be noticed that Mt., Mk., and Jn. represent the Crucifixion as taking place on the *Paraskeue*, which is distinctly Friday in Jn 19[31], being mentioned in connexion with the Sabbath, and in Mk 15[42], where it is defined as προσάββατον. St. John in 19[14] describes it as 'the preparation of the passover,' but as the weekly *Paraskeue* in 19[31], and 19[42] referring to the removal from the cross and the hasty entombment says 'for it was the preparation' and 'because of (διά = because it was) the preparation of the Jews.'

Against all these passages there stands one expression common to all the Synoptists, 'the day of unleavened bread,' for Lk 22[15] may merely indicate the Paschal nature of the Last Supper. That expression is, therefore, to be reckoned with.

Chwolson (*Das letzte Passamahl Christi*, p. 3 f.) maintains that the Synoptists start with an error, for 'from the Mosaic writings down to the Book of Jubilees . . . indeed, down to the present day, the Jews have always understood by the phrase "the first day of the feast of unleavened bread" only the 15th and not the 14th, so that it would be a contradiction in terms to say with Mk 14[12], 'on the first day of unleavened bread when they sacrificed the Passover.' Ewald (*Antiquities of Israel*, p. 358 ff.) treats the Passover, which he shows from Ex 12[3-6] was originally fixed for the 10th of the month when the Paschal lamb was to be selected, as the preparatory expiatory festival of the Spring Feast of Unleavened Bread, just as the Day of Atonement, on the 10th day of the 7th month, preceded the great autumn festival of Tabernacles. 'Not till the 14th day, during the last three hours before and the first three hours after sunset, was the sacrificial animal slain and eaten. . . . It was always appointed for the 14th, and in the earliest times at least the view was strictly upheld that the Feast of Unleavened Bread did not begin till the following morning.' Philo distinguished the πάσχα of Nisan 14 from the τὰ ἄζυμα of Nisan 15-21. Mk 14[1] unites without confusing them. ἦν δὲ τὸ πάσχα καὶ τὰ ἄζυμα μετὰ δύο ἡμέρας.

It would seem that some technical error was committed by the Synoptists, which may have been due to (1) St. Peter's inexact knowledge of the Feast of Unleavened Bread, and probable identification of it with the removal of leaven before noon on Nisan 14 (Ex 12[15]) ; (2) the custom of the Galilæans, who, unlike the people of Judæa, who worked until the noon preceding, abstained from work the whole morning preceding the Passover, which was reckoned from evening to evening, and consequently would make their preparations after sunset on Nisan 13 (*Students' Com.* on Mt 26[17]) ; (3) some verbal confusion between the Syriac words for 'before' (*kedâm*, Mt 8[29]) and 'first' (*kadmâyâ*, Mt 26[17]) owing to Peter's broad Galilæan accent, which may have caused St. Mark's mistake ; (4) a comparative use of Gr. πρῶτος (cf. Jn 1[15] πρῶτός μου, 'before me'; 15[18] ἐμὲ πρῶτον ὑμῶν, 'before you'), in which case Mt 26[17] would mean 'on the day before the Feast of Unleavened Bread' ; (5) a difference in the mode of reckoning the days adopted by St. John, who, according to Westcott (Jn 19[14]), used the Western method of counting from midnight to noon, and by St. Mark, who adhered to the legal reckoning from evening to evening (Mk 15[42]) ; (6) a natural confusion of the preparation of the Passover (Jn 19[14]) on Nisan 13 with the weekly *Paraskeue* on Nisan 14 (Mk 15[42]), or of the day when leaven was removed from the houses (Ex 12[15] [LXX ἀπὸ τῆς ἡμέρας τῆς πρώτης]) with the Festival of *Mazzôth*, which commenced after the Passover day. The argument that the expression 'not on the feast' (μὴ ἐν τῇ ἑορτῇ, Mt 26[5]) cannot refer to Passover has to reckon with Ex 12[14], where the Passover is called 'feast' (ἑορτήν, LXX).

Support for Nisan 14 as day of Crucifixion in NT and tradition (Christian and Jewish).—(1) 1 Co 5[7] τὸ πάσχα ἡμῶν ἐτύθη Χριστός, identifies Christ with the Paschal lamb slain between 'the two evenings'; and 1 Co 15[20] identifies the Risen Christ with the First-fruits of the 2nd day of the Feast of *Mazzôth*, ἀπαρχὴ τῶν κεκοιμημένων. (2) The Quartodecimans, among whom was Polycarp, held a fast on Nisan 14 as the day of Crucifixion (letter of Irenæus to Victor). (3) Jewish tradition fixes the Crucifixion on the 'erebh Peṣaḥ or Passover eve, and the Greek Church always used leavened bread in the Eucharist. (4) Apollinaris of Hierapolis (c. A.D. 180) pointed out that the 14th is connected with the Crucifixion. (5) Clement of Alexandria said that Christ did not eat the Passover, but suffered on the 14th. (6) Hippolytus of Portus declared that Christ ate a supper before the Passover, 'for He was the Paschal lamb who had been promised and was sanctified on the appointed day.' (7) Tertullian (adv. Jud. 8—a doubtful work) suggests Nisan 14. (8) Irenæus (Hær. IV. x. 1), discussing Moses' prediction of Jesus, says, 'The day of whose Passion he did not ignore, but foretold it in a figure, calling it Pascha.' This is not very decisive, but suggests a memory of 1 Co 5[7]. This view of Nisan 14 may be said to be the best supported in the first two centuries.

Tradition in support of Nisan 15.—Origen, in his comment on Mt 26[17], follows the Synoptic tradition: 'Jesus celebravit more Judaico pascha corporaliter.' Chrysostom declares (*Hom. in Mt.* 82) that the new feast appointed by Jesus superseded the Passover. Ambrose, Proterius and others follow on the same side. This view seems more recently popular than the other. But the controversy of Apollinaris in περὶ τοῦ πάσχα λόγος shows that there were some in the 2nd cent. who connected Nisan 14 with the Supper, and therefore Nisan 15 (according to Roman reckoning) with the Crucifixion.

The cumulative evidence of St. John, St. Paul, and the early Fathers, joined with the incredibility of Jesus having been arrested, tried, and executed on the great Sabbath of the Jewish Year, and the statement of the Synoptists that that day was the *Paraskeue*, seem to turn the scale in favour of Nisan 14 as the day of the Crucifixion. See also LAST SUPPER. Nisan 14, A.D. 29, is the date to be now tested by other evidence.

Clement of Alexandria (*Strom.* i. 147) notes the various views of the Basilidians. 'With regard to the Passion, some, after precise calculations, say it took place in the 16th year of Tiberius on Phamenoth 25 (March 21); others on Pharmuthi 25 (April 20); others, again, on Pharmuthi 29 (April 24). March 18 and March 25, however, are the best supported. Epiphanius (*Hær.* i. 1) had seen copies of the *Acts of Pilate* which gave March 18 as the date, but the Quartodecimans kept March 25 on the strength of these *Acts*; this is evidence of some hesitation between these dates. Hippolytus (*Com. on Dan.*) gives March 25. With regard to this date, also given in the *Paschal Cycle*, Dr. Salmon says (*Hermathena*, No. xviii. p. 175): 'We can therefore regard the date March 25 as inseparably connected with the sixteen years' cycle of Hippolytus.' As the Easter full moon was on March 25 in A.D. 221, and, working on the principle that after 16 years full moons return to the same day, Hippolytus trusted his cycle that it must have been on the same day in A.D. 29. But, as Dr. Salmon shows, in that year the full moon really fell on March 18, a week previous. An interesting confirmation of the date March 18 is given by the Jewish calendar of Paschal moons, from which it would appear that Friday, which is generally accepted as the day of the Crucifixion, could not have fallen on Nisan 14 or 15 in the years A.D. 28, 31, 32, so that we are left to choose between 29, 30, 33, and of these A.D. 29 answers all the required conditions best, as the 14th day of the moon would fall in that year on Friday, March 18 (so C. H. Turner, 'Chronology' in Hastings' *DB*).

Dr. Salmon, in the article cited, said it was doubtful if Hippolytus had any historical authority for fixing on the year 29 over and above the reason 'that the day which his cycle exhibited as the Crucifixion Day should be a Friday,' and that 'the only years he would find fulfilling this condition were, 26, 29, 32, and of these 29 is chronologically the most probable.' Baron H. von Soden prefers A.D. 30, in which Nisan 15 would fall on Friday April 7, and opposes A.D. 29 on the ground that Nisan 15 fell on April 16 in that year. But the previous lunation, March 4-5, with 14th on March 18, would be more in keeping with the ripening of the barley harvest, and would have a prior claim.

The following table of dates is based on the arguments in the preceding pages, the years, months, and days especially, in each case, being offered as merely approximate.

TABLE OF DATES OF EVENTS IN THE GOSPELS.

Herod's reign	B.C. 37-4.
Restoration of temple commenced . .	B.C. 19-18.
Star in the east	B.C. 7-5.
Courses of Abia in temple . . .	B.C. 6, April 18–24, Oct. 3-9.
Conception of Elisabeth	B.C. 6, Oct. [or April (25)].
Annunciation (6 months after) . .	B.C. 5, March (25) [or Sept. (19)].
Birth of Baptist	B.C. 5, June (24) [or B.C. 5, Jan.].
Birth of the Christ at Bethlehem during an enrolment	B.C. 5, Dec. (25) [or B.C. 5, June].
Circumcision	B.C. 4, Jan. (1).
Visit of Magi	B.C. 4, Jan. (6 circa).
Presentation in temple 40 days after Nativity	B.C. 4, Feb. (2 circa).
Herod plans massacre	B.C. 4, Feb.
Flight into Egypt, apparently from Jerusalem	B.C. 4, Feb.
Death of Herod	B.C. 4, March (before Passover).
Archelaus ethnarch of Judæa . . .	B.C. 4-A.D. 6.
Herod Antipas tetrarch of Galilee . .	B.C. 4-A.D. 37.
Return of Holy Family to Nazareth . .	B.C. 3.
The child Jesus in temple (12 years old) .	A.D. 7.
Annas high priest	A.D. 7-15.
Caiaphas high priest	A.D. 24-34.
Pontius Pilate procurator of Judæa . .	A.D. 26-36.
Preaching of the Baptist (15th year of Tiberius), 'beyond Jordan,' in the Peræa, 'where John at first baptized' (Jn 10[40]), 'the country about Jordan' (Lk 3[3])	A.D. 26-27.
Baptism of Jesus in Bethabara, John's second sphere of work	A.D. 27 (Passover).
Selection and training of disciples, and work in Galilee, with Nazareth for a time as headquarters (Mt 4[13]) (early chapters of Mt. and Mk. and Jn 1[29]-2[12])	A.D. 27-28 (Passover).
Purification of the temple and work in the city during the Feast of Unleavened Bread (Jn 2[13-23])	A.D. 28, Passover, March 30–April 6.
Work in Judæa broken by conflict between His disciples and the Baptist's (Jn 3[22-36] and 4[1-4])	April 7–14 (circa).
Arrest of the Baptist by Herod (Mk 6[17], Mt 14[3]) (probably at Ænon near to Salim, his third sphere of work)	April.
Departure of Jesus into Galilee through Samaria (Jn 4[1-45])	April 14–18 (circa).
Work in Galilee, with Capernaum as centre (Jn 4[46], Mk 1[14], Mt 4[12. 13], where His departure from Nazareth is noted; see also Lk 4[16])	April 18–May 14
Jesus at Feast of Pentecost in Jerusalem (Jn 5)	May 20 (circa).
Miracles in Galilee (Nain), and consequent fame (Lk 7[11-17])	
Injunctions to the Twelve, and their mission (Mt 10, Mk 6, Lk 9)	
Deputation from the Baptist (Mt 11[2], Lk 7[18]).	
Jesus at Feast of Tabernacles (Jn 7) . .	October.
Execution of the Baptist (Mt 14, Lk 9, Mk 6)	
Herod hears the fame of Jesus (Mt 14[1])	
Return of the Twelve with this and other news (Mk 6[30])	
Jesus, in consequence, departs finally from Galilee (Mk 6[31], Mt 14[13], Lk 9[10])	
Work in Tyre and Sidon, Decapolis, and villages of Cæsarea Philippi (Mk 7[24. 31] 8[27], Mt 16[13])	
The confession of St. Peter (Mt 16[16], Mk 8[29], Lk 9[20], Jn 6[68. 69])	
The Transfiguration, 'six days after' (Mt 17[1], Mk 9[2]), 'about an eight days after' (Lk 9[28])	
Prediction of death (Mt 17[22])	
The great journey, which may be described as a tour, whose final objective was Jerusalem, commences 'when the days were well-nigh come that he should be received	

up' (Lk 9^51); given at great length (Lk 9^51–19^28)

Rejected by a village of Samaria (Lk 9^52)

Mission of the Seventy before His face (Lk 10^1-17) [in Samaria, where He was in Roman territory, safe from Herod, Samaria having been added to the Province of Syria after the banishment of Archelaus, Jos. *Ant.* XVII. xiii. 5]

Sentence on Galilee and Capernaum (Lk 10^13-16, Mt 11^20-24)

Journeys towards Jerusalem, teaching in the towns and villages (Lk 13^22), moving southwards between the borders of Samaria and Galilee (17^11), the Jordan on His left hand

At the Feast of Dedication in Jerusalem　.　A.D. 28, Dec. 10 (*circa*).

Escapes from city into the Peræa, πίραν τοῦ Ἰορδάνου (Jn 10^40, Mt 19^1, Mk 10^1)

Returns to Judæa for the raising of Lazarus at Bethany (Jn 11^7)

Withdraws to Ephraim (Jn 11^54) in wilderness of Judæa

Final journey towards city

Prediction of His death (Mk 10^32, Lk 18^31)

At Jericho: Zacchæus and blind Bartimæus (Lk 19^1-11, Mk 10^46-52)

Approaches city, at Bethany (Mt 21^1, Mk 11^1, Lk 19^29, Jn 12^1) six days before the Passover　　A.D. 29, Nisan 9 (March 12).

The chronology of the last six days is still further complicated by the difference between the Second and Fourth Gospels regarding the Anointing at Bethany. Mk 14^1-3 gives the account of the Anointing apparently in connexion with the date 'after two days was the feast of the Passover and the unleavened bread,' while Jn 12^1-3 gives the account of the Supper seemingly under the note of time, 'Then Jesus six days before the Passover came to Bethany.' Two ways of getting out of the difficulty are (1) by referring the note of time in Mk. to the events of vv.^1. 2. 10. 11 as giving the connexion of the conspiracy of the chief priests against Jesus, and the offer of Judas, and regarding the scene of the Anointing as an intrusion of strange matter similar to Mk 6^14-29 7^25-30; (2) by restricting the application of the note of time Jn 12^1 to the arrival at Bethany. The notice of the day of the entombment (τὴν ἡμέραν τοῦ ἐνταφιασμοῦ, v.^7) would come more appropriately on the date given in Mk 14^1, the reason of the mention of the feast in connexion with the date of Jn 12^1 'six days before,' etc., being, perhaps, the fact that Jesus and His disciples made the house of Lazarus and his sisters the headquarters of His last mission to the city. Against this it may be urged that it is equally probable that this feast, which was attended by many out of curiosity to see not only Jesus but Lazarus whom He had raised (v.^9), occasioned on the one hand the splendid reception given to Him by the multitude, and on the other the malignant opposition of the chief priests, who made plans to procure the death of Lazarus also (v.^10). And the anointing of Jesus' feet in so lavish a style would be in keeping with His entry as the Messiah, the Anointed, into the city, which follows in the Fourth Gospel. St. Mark's order of events, however, is quite different. Our Lord proceeds straight from Jericho to Jerusalem by way of Bethphage and Bethany (Mk 11^1), and when He entered the temple and looked round on all things, the hour being late (ὀψίας ἤδη οὔσης τῆς ὥρας, v.^11), He withdrew to Bethany with the Twelve. The cleansing of the temple, which immediately follows the entry in Mt 21 and Lk 19, is thus reserved for the next day, and the banquet for the last evening spent in Bethany. May it not be possible that there were two banquets, and two similar acts of homage paid by women to Jesus, one at the beginning of His last mission, when His feet were anointed, and the other at the close of His mission, when His head was anointed, the former being recorded by St. John (12^2-8), who marks the commencement of the year's work by the purification of the temple, the latter by the Synoptists, St.

Matthew and St. Mark, who signalize its closing scenes with a similar act?

In the week itself there are three difficult notes of time. (1) 'Then Jesus six days before the Passover came to Bethany' (Jn 12^1 πρὸ ἐξ ἡμέρων τοῦ πάσχα, cf. Am 1^1 LXX πρὸ δύο ἐτῶν τοῦ σεισμοῦ [שְׁנָתַיִם לִפְנֵי הָרָעַשׁ], 'two years before the earthquake'). Six days before Friday, Nisan 15, that is, according to Jewish reckoning, six evenings before the evening that followed the sunset of Nisan 14, would directly give the evening that directly followed the sunset of the Sabbath of Nisan 9, in which case the Supper would take place in the evening that was the close of the Sabbath. Or if, as Westcott held, the Passion fell on Thursday, the arrival at Bethany took place on a Friday, in which case the Sabbath would be kept as a day of rest, and would be followed by a feast on the next evening. (2) 'After two days is the Passover' (Mt 26^1), or 'After two days was the Passover and the unleavened bread' (Mk 14^1). This date, including the day on which the words were spoken, but excluding that of the Passover, points to Wednesday, Nisan 13, the Crucifixion falling on Friday, Nisan 15. Bengel allows an interval of one day only, 'biduum a feriâ quartâ ad quintam quæ Paschatos et azymorum dies erat'; cf. Mk 8^31, where μετὰ τρεῖς ἡμέρας = τῇ τρίτῃ ἡμέρᾳ. (3) 'On the first day of the unleavened bread the disciples of Jesus came to him, saying, Where wilt thou that we prepare for thee to eat the Passover?' (Mt 26^17). Strictly speaking, that day would be Nisan 16, this feast commencing on the evening after the close of Nisan 15, the Passover, and lasting seven days. But this note of time refers probably to the legal beginning of the 14th day, the evening following the sunset of Nisan 13, or may be due to a confusion with the day Nisan 14 on which leaven was removed.

With regard to the method our Lord followed in His mission, see Luke 21^37 'And during the days he was teaching in the temple; but during the nights going forth to the mount that is called the Mount of Olives, he used to abide (ηὐλίζετο) there: and all the people came to him at early dawn (ὤρθριζε) in the temple to hear him'; cf. Lk 22^39 'And he came out and went κατὰ τὸ ἔθος to the Mount of Olives; and his disciples followed. And when he was at the place' (ἐπὶ τοῦ τόπου, evidently some familiar locality [see Jn 18^1. 2 'Jesus went forth with his disciples beyond the brook Ḳidron, where was a garden, into the which he entered, and his disciples. And Judas also, which betrayed him, knew τὸν τόπον']). It would seem then that the night was generally spent in prayer on the mountain side during this mission. But the evening after the Triumphal Entry was spent in Bethany (Mk 11^11. 12); yet evidently the greater part of night and morn was spent in prayer in the open air ηὐλίσθη ἐκεῖ (Mt 21^17). This fact would explain His hunger on the morrow from missing the morning meal. For His practice of going out to pray 'a great while before day' see Mk 1^35.

The following is a provisional arrangement of the days and occurrences of the Last Mission:

Sabbath, Nisan 9, 6th Day before Passover.	Arrival in Bethany (Jn 12^1). Supper in the evening (12^2-8). The Anointing of His feet.
First Day of Week (Palm Sunday, ἡ κυριακὴ τῶν βαίων), Nisan 10, 5th Day before Passover	Triumphal entry into Jerusalem (Mk 11^1-11, Mt 21^1-11, Lk 19^29-44, Jn 12^14-19). Works of mercy in Temple (Mt 21^14. 15). Returns in the evening to Bethany (Mk 11^11, Mt 21^17).
Second Day of Week, Monday, Nisan 11; day of selection of Paschal lamb (Ex 12^3), 4th Day before Passover.	Returns on the morrow (τῇ ἐπαύριον) from Bethany (Mk 11^12); hungry after midnight vigil or early morning prayer (1^35). Blasting of the Fig-tree; sign of an unfruitful nature (11^12-14). Purification of the Temple, more drastic and thorough in Mk 11^15-18 than in Lk 19^45-48 or Mt 21^12. 13. Leaves the city in evening (Mk 11^19). Conspiracy of foes (Lk 19^47).

Third Day of Week, Tuesday, Nisan 12, 3rd Day before Passover.	Returns early (πρωΐ) past the withered fig-tree (Mk 11²⁰). Combination of foes, chief priests, Sadducees, Pharisees, Scribes, Herodians. Day of Questions and Answers touching the authority of Jesus, the baptism of John, the tribute money, the brother's wife, the first commandment of all. 'What think ye of Christ? Whose son is he?' (Mt 21. 22). 'From that day forth no man dared ask him any more questions' (22⁴⁶). Woes on Pharisees (23¹⁻³⁶). Jesus in Treasury, the widow's mite (Mk 12⁴¹⁻⁴⁴). The visit of Greeks, and parable of Seed-corn (Jn 12²⁰⁻³⁶). Final Rejection (12³⁷). Lament over Jerusalem (Mt 23³⁷⁻³⁹). Prediction of the destruction of the Temple, and final scenes of the coming of the Son of Man (24. 25). Counsel of Caiaphas (Mt 26³⁻⁵).
Fourth Day of Week, Wednesday, Nisan 13, 2nd Day before Passover.	'After two days is the Feast of Unleavened Bread' (Mt 26²). It is supposed that our Lord remained all this day in Bethany, not returning to the city openly after Jn 12³⁶. The Anointing of His head at the Supper in the evening. The Bargain of Judas.
	The morning was occupied by disciples with preparations for the Supper (Mt 26¹⁷⁻¹⁹), by Jesus in prayer.
	(*A*) The events of the evening may be arranged according to the four Roman (as distinguished from the three Jewish) watches, ὀψέ (6 p.m.–9 p.m.); μεσονύκτιον (9 p.m.–12); ἀλεκτοροφωνία (12–3 a.m.); πρωΐ (3 a.m.–6 a.m.), used in the Gospels (Mk 13³⁵, Mt 14²⁵, Mk 6⁴⁸).
ὀψία or ὀψέ. 6 p.m.– 9 p.m.	The Supper with the Twelve, ὀψίας δὲ γενομένης (Mt 26²⁰, Mk 14¹⁷). The washing of feet at Supper (δείπνου δὲ γενομένου) or during it, see *v.l.* γινομένου (Jn 13²). Departure of Judas. Institution of Lord's Supper. Upper Room Discourses (13³¹–14³¹). Departure from Upper Room (14³¹).
μεσονύκτιον (9 p.m.–12).	Parable of Vine (Jn 15). Promise of the Holy Spirit (16). Prayer for disciples (17). Gethsemane (18¹, Mt 26³⁷⁻⁴⁶, Mk 14³³⁻³⁸, Lk 22⁴¹⁻⁴⁶). Agony, 'one hour' (Mk 14³⁷).
The Day before the Passover, ἡ παρασκευὴ τοῦ πάσχα (Jn 19¹⁴), **Thursday, Nisan 14, Fifth Day of Week.** τῇ δὲ πρώτῃ τῶν ἀζύμων (Mt 26¹⁷), 'the first day of unleavened bread' evidently being identified with 'the first day' on which leaven was removed (Ex 12¹⁵), the bread of Passover being unleavened (Dt 16³).	
ἀλεκτοροφωνία 12–3 a.m. Cock-crow.	Arrival of Judas, Arrest of Jesus (Jn 18²⁻¹²). Preliminary trial before Annas (18¹³). Peter's denial; ἀλέκτωρ ἐφώνησε (18²⁷). Jesus sent to Caiaphas (18²⁴). Trial before Sanhedrin ὡς ἐγένετο ἡμέρα (Lk 22⁶⁶), πρωΐας δὲ γενομένης (Mt 27¹ loosely), ἐπὶ τὸ πρωΐ towards the morning watch (Mk 15¹ more precisely).
πρωΐα or πρωΐ 3 a.m.– 6 a.m.	Led to Pilate πρωΐ (Jn 18²⁸), from Pilate to Herod (Lk 23⁷), back to Pilate (23¹¹). 'Behold, the man!' (Jn 19⁵). 'And it was the preparation of the Passover, and about the sixth hour' (19¹⁴). Delivered to be crucified (19¹⁶).
	(*B*) The third, sixth, and ninth hours of the morning, which were wont to be proclaimed by an officer of the Prætor (Smith's *Dict. Ant. s.v.* 'dies'), marked similar divisions of the day which the Jews ended in the evening. Preparation for Crucifixion. 6 a.m.–9 a.m.—'And it was the third hour (*i.e.* 3rd after the last watch of the night [3–6 a.m.], or 9 a.m.); and they crucified him' (Mk 15²⁵). [There is no need to suggest a corruption of *F* for Γ or *vice versa* to explain the difference of Mk 15²⁵ and Jn 19¹⁴, as the former hour marks the crucifixion and the latter the hour of sentence, between which some interval must have elapsed.] 9 a.m.–12.—Jesus on the Cross. 12–3 p.m.—'And when the sixth hour (12) was come there was darkness over the whole land until the ninth hour (3 p.m.) . . . and at the ninth hour Jesus cried with a loud voice, saying, Eloi, Eloi, lama sabachthani?' (Mk 15³³. ³⁴).

Between the evenings [בֵּין הָעַרְבַּיִם Ex 12⁶], as the Paschal lambs were being sacrificed in the Temple, Jesus gave up the ghost. The Removal from the Cross ensues, Pilate marvelling if He were already dead (Mk 15⁴⁴), ἤδη ὀψίας γενομένης (after 3 p.m.), the women following to the sepulchre and returning to prepare spices and ointment (Lk 23⁵⁵. ⁵⁶).

Friday, Nisan 15 (March 18).	The Passover, also the Weekly Preparation, ἡ παρασκευή or τὸ προσάββατον (Mk 15⁴²).
Nisan 16, Saturday.	First Day of Unleavened Bread, coincided with weekly Sabbath. 'The day of that (ἐκείνου) Sabbath was an high day' (Jn 19³¹), or 'that (ἐκείνη) day of the week was a high day.' 'And (the women) rested the Sabbath day according to the commandment' (Lk 23⁵⁶). This was a day of holy convocation in which no servile work should be done. Visit of Sanhedrin to Pilate, τῇ δὲ ἐπαύριον ἥτις ἐστὶ μετὰ τὴν παρασκευήν (Mt 27⁶²). In the Grave.
Nisan 17, Sunday. The First Day of Week and Second of Feast of *Maẓẓôth*, on which sheaf of new corn was presented as first-fruits, πρώτη σαββάτου (Mk 16⁹), τῇ δὲ μιᾷ τῶν σαββάτων (Jn 20¹, Lk 24¹), τῆς μιᾶς σαββάτων (Mk 16²), εἰς μίαν σαββάτων (Mt 28¹).	After the Sabbath (διαγενομένου τοῦ σαββάτου), Mary Magdalene, Mary the mother of James, and Salome, brought spices for the anointing (Mk 16¹). It was still dark, σκοτίας οὔσης (Jn 20¹), in early dawn, ὄρθρου βαθέος (Lk 24¹, cf. Mt 28¹), very early after sunrise (Mk 16²), when they came to the sepulchre, bringing the spices they had prepared (Lk 24¹). *Jesus rose early,* ἀναστὰς πρωΐ (Mk 16⁹). The first-fruits of them that slept, ἀπαρχὴ τῶν κεκοιμημένων (1 Co 15²⁰). Vision of angels to the women (Mk 16⁵⁻⁷). Visit of Peter and John to the Sepulchre (Jn 20³⁻¹⁰). Appearance of Jesus to Mary Magdalene (20¹¹⁻¹⁸); appearance to St. Peter (Lk 24³⁴). 4–6 p.m.—Appearance to two disciples, who would not have left Jerusalem until after evening prayer (cf. Ac 3¹), on way to Emmaus (Lk 24¹³ff.). 8 p.m. (*circa*).—Appearance of Jesus to the Eleven and those with them (Lk 24³⁶). In the account of interview with disciples (Jn 20¹⁹ff.), Thomas absent.
Sunday Week, Nisan 24.	Jesus appeared to the disciples, Thomas being present (Jn 20²⁶ff.).

Further appearances recorded by Evangelists :—To seven Apostles on the shore of the Sea of Tiberias (Jn 21). To the Eleven Apostles on a mountain in Galilee (Mt 28¹⁶⁻²⁰). To the Apostles in Jerusalem (St. Luke in Ac 1⁴). Ascension from Bethany forty days after Passion and ten days before Pentecost (Lk 24⁵⁰, Ac 1⁶⁻¹²).

LITERATURE.—Josephus, *Ant.* and *BJ*; Irenæus, *adv. Hær.*; Clement of Alexandria, *Strom.*; Hippolytus, *Com. on Dan.*, and *Paschal Cycle*; Origen, *Com. on St. John*; Ideler, *Handb. der Chronol.*; Wieseler, *Chronol. Synops. der Evang.*; Salmon in *Hermathena*, No. 18; Farrar, *Life of Christ*; Westcott, 'Gospel of St. John' (*Speaker's Com.*), and *Introduction to the Gospels*; Sanday, *Authorship and Historical Character of the Fourth Gospel*, and art. 'Jesus Christ' in Hastings' *DB*; Hitchcock, *Studies in Our Lord's Last Mission*; Westcott and Hort, *Greek Testament*; artt. 'Chronology', 'Fasts and Feasts', 'Passover', 'Pentecost' in Hastings' *DB*.

F. R. MONTGOMERY HITCHCOCK.

DAUGHTER (θυγάτηρ).—The word 'daughter' is used in various senses in the Gospels: (1) in the literal sense, Mt 9¹⁸ 10³⁵, Mk 5³⁵ 6²² 7²⁹, Lk 8⁴²; (2) as a term of kind address, Mt 9²², Mk 5³⁴, Lk 8⁴⁸; (3) collectively for the inhabitants of a city, Mt 21⁵, Jn 12¹⁵ (cf. Zec 9⁹); (4) as a term of address to the female inhabitants of a city, Lk 23²⁸; (5) in the Hebrew sense of descendant, Lk 1⁵ 13¹⁶.

The diminutive θυγάτριον is found twice in the Gospel of Mark (5²³ 7²⁵). Like all diminutives, it is a term of endearment.

HENRY E. DOSKER.

DAUGHTER-IN-LAW (νύμφη).—The Greek word is presumably derived from the lost root νύβω, Lat. *nubo*, 'to cover,' inasmuch as the bride was brought veiled to her bridegroom. Although the word applies to married women in general, its associated idea is that of youth. Hence its antithesis with πενθερά, the mother-in-law (Mt 10³⁵, Lk 12⁵³). The son usually brought his bride to his father's house, where she was subject to the father's wife, as was the son to the father and the daughter to the mother (Mt 10³⁵, Lk 12⁵³).

HENRY E. DOSKER.

DAVID.—

For the student of the Gospels the most important OT passage concerning David is **2 S 7**. David expressed to Nathan a strong desire to build a temple for Jehovah in his new capital, a wish indicative of worldly wisdom as well as piety on the part of the king. Jehovah denies David's request, but promises to build for him an everlasting house, a dynasty without end. David's throne is to stand for ever. Pss 2 and 110 are founded on this notable promise, and the author of Ps 89 in a far later time, when David's throne had been overturned by the heathen, reminds Jehovah of His ancient promise, and pleads earnestly for the speedy passing of His wrath. The early prophets, Amos (9¹¹), Hosea (3⁵), Isaiah (9⁷ 16⁵ 37³⁵), unite with the author of Kings (1 K 2⁴⁵ 6¹² etc.) in the expectation that the promise made to David in 2 S 7 will not fail. The prophetic hopes for the future of Israel spring from Nathan's message as branches from the trunk that gives them life. Jeremiah (23⁵ᶠ· 33¹⁵ᶠᶠ·) carries forward the work of his predecessors of the 8th cent. B.C., asserting the perpetuity of David's dynasty in most emphatic terms. Ezekiel (34²³ᶠ· 37²⁴ᶠ·) cheers the discouraged exiles with the picture of a glorious restoration of the throne of David. The great ruler of the future will be a second David. In the period after the return from Babylon, the author of the last section of Zechariah (12⁷-13¹) describes the glories of the coming time in connexion with the Davidic dynasty : 'The house of David shall be as Gód, as the angel of Jehovah before them.' The Messianic hope in the inter-Biblical period, like that of the OT, attached itself to David. The author of Ecclesiasticus (47¹¹) reminds his readers that the Lord exalted David's horn for ever, entering into a covenant and promising him a throne of glory in Israel. About a century later the author of 1 Mac. (2⁵⁷) says, 'David for being merciful inherited the throne of a kingdom for ever and ever.' Most important for the student of the Gospel history is Ps 17 of the Psalms of Solomon, a collection of patriotic hymns belonging to the period immediately following Pompey's capture of Jerusalem (63–48 B.C.). Ps 17 is a notable Messianic prophecy, prayer and prediction being freely intermingled after the fashion of the OT prophets and poets. The Messianic King is to be David's son (17⁴· ²¹). Jehovah Himself is Israel's King for ever and ever (17¹· ⁴⁶); but the Son of David is His chosen to overthrow the heathen, and institute a righteous reign in Israel (17³⁰· ⁴²ᶠ·).

The four Evangelists unite in the view that the Messiah was to come from the seed of David (Mt 1¹, Mk 10⁴⁷, Lk 2⁴, Jn 7⁴²). 'The Son of David' was synonymous in the time of our Lord's earthly ministry with 'Messiah' or 'Christ.' Both the scribes and the common people held this view. When the children cried in the temple, 'Hosanna to the Son of David' (Mt 21¹⁵), both the rulers and the multitude looked upon the words as a distinct recognition of the Messiahship of Jesus. The Epistles (Ro 1³, 2 Ti 2⁸) and the Revelation (5⁵ 22¹⁶) concur in calling attention to the Davidic origin of Jesus. The interest of NT writers in David is confined almost exclusively to his relation to our Lord Jesus as His ancestor and type.

Jesus refers to one incident in the life of David in reply to the accusation of His enemies as to His observance of the Sabbath (Mk 2²⁵, cf. 1 S 21¹⁻⁶). This incident is said to have taken place 'when Abiathar was high priest.' [On the difficulties created by this statement see art. ABIATHAR.]

During the week preceding our Lord's crucifixion, perhaps on Tuesday, He asked the Pharisees a question which put them to silence and confusion. Having drawn from them a statement of their belief that the Christ would be the son of David, He at once quoted David's words in Ps 110¹ to show that the Messiah would also be David's Lord (Mt 22⁴¹ ‖). Jesus wished to show His foes and the multitude that the orthodox view of the time overlooked the exalted dignity of the Messiah. He was to be far greater than David, for He was his Lord. See, further, Broadus on *Mt. ad loc.*, and, for the meaning of 'David' and 'Moses' in our Lord's citations from the OT, art. MOSES.

LITERATURE.—Gore, *BL* 196ff.; Gould, 'St. Mark,' and Plummer, 'St. Luke,' in *Internat. Crit. Com. in loc.* ; *Expos. Times*, iii. [1892] 292ff., viii. [1897] 365ff.; *Expositor*, v. iii. [1896] 445ff.

JOHN R. SAMPEY.

DAY. — **1.** *Literal.* — The length of the 'day' among the ancients was reckoned in various ways : thus, from morning to morning (Babylonians), from sunset to sunset (Athenians), from noon to noon (Umbrians), from midnight to midnight (Egyptians), and from dawn to dark by the common people, ordinarily (see Plin. *HN* ii. 79). The early Israelites seem to have regarded the morning

as the beginning of the day (cf. Gn 1⁵· ⁸ᶠᶠ·), but they likewise (due to the influence of the new moon) reckoned it from 'even unto even' (Lv 23³²). In Lk 22³⁴ also the new day began after sunset (cf. 4⁴⁰). In the NT ἡμέρα was employed to express : (1) *the period of light in opposition to night* (Lk 6¹³ 'and when it was day,'—a frequent phrase in St. Luke's writings, cf. 4⁴² 22⁶⁶, Ac 12¹⁸ 16³⁵ 23¹² 27²⁹· ³³· ³⁹, also Jn 9⁴, 2 Co 11²⁵); (2) *the natural day*, including the periods both of light and darkness (Mt 28¹ ἐπιφωσκούσῃ, cf. Lk 22³⁴); (3) *an indefinite period of time* (Lk 1⁵· ³⁹ ἐν ταῖς ἡμέραις ταύταις, 'in those days'; St. Luke is fond of this expression, it is not found in Jn., and occurs but four times in Mt. and the same number of times in Mk. ; cf. Lk 2¹ 4², Ac 2¹⁸ 3²⁴ 7⁴¹ etc., also Mt 2¹ 3¹, Mk 1⁹ 8¹ 13¹⁷· ²⁴ in true Hebraistic style).

Except the Sabbath, the days of the week were *numbered* by the Israelites, not *named*. Nor had the Hebrews any precise subdivision of the day, for they had no word for 'hour'; even the Aramaic שָׁעָה, which occurs in Dn 4¹⁶ 5⁵, has no exact connotation. Like the Greeks, they seem to have learned from the Babylonians how to divide the day into 12 hours,—a division first met with in the NT : 'Are there not twelve hours in the day?' (Jn 11⁹, cf. Ac 2¹⁵, Mt 20³⁻⁶ 27⁴⁵· ⁴⁶ etc.). The length of the hour, however, was for a long time a variable quantity, depending, as it did, upon the season of the year, for it was always reckoned as the twelfth part of the light period. It therefore ranged from forty-nine to seventy-one minutes, according to the calendar. The more common divisions of the day among the Hebrews were morning, noonday, and evening (Ps 55¹⁷); but they frequently spoke of 'sunrise' and 'dawn' (Mk 16², Jn 20¹, Rev 22¹⁶), 'the heat of the day' (Mt 20¹²), 'noon' (Gn 43¹⁶, Dt 28²⁹), 'the cool of the day' (Gn 3⁸), and 'between the two evenings,' *i.e.* towards evening (Ex 12⁶ 16¹², cf. Ac 3¹ 10³· ³⁰). The time of incense, and of cock-crowing (wh. see) was in the morning (Mk 14³⁰· ⁷², Lk 1¹⁰); the time of the 'meal-offering' was in the middle of the afternoon (1 K 18²⁹· ³⁶); while 'the time that women go out to draw water' was towards evening (Gn 24¹¹).

2. *Figurative.*—Figurative and metaphorical uses of the word 'day' are also frequent in the NT : *e.g.* the day of Christ's appearance, *i.e.* of His apocalypse, or self-revelation (Lk 17³⁰ 'in the day that the Son of Man is revealed,' ἀποκαλύπτεται, a technical expression : cf. Lk 17²⁴, Jn 8⁵⁶ 14²⁰ 16²³· ²⁶, Ro 13¹², 1 Co 1⁷· ⁸, 2 Th 1⁷, 1 P 1⁷· ¹³ 4¹³); 'the day of his *Parousia*' (Mt 7²² 24³⁶, Mk 13³² 14²⁵, Lk 21³⁴, 2 Th 1¹⁰, 2 Ti 1¹⁸, He 10²⁵); the days of His death and departure (Lk 5³⁵ ἐλεύσονται δὲ ἡμέραι, 'But the days will come,' *i.e.* days very different from the joyous days of wedding festivity); the Last, or Judgment day (Jn 6³⁹· ¹¹²⁴ 12⁴⁸, Mt 11²², 1 Jn 4¹⁷, 1 Th 5², 2 Ti 3¹, Ja 5³, and by contrast 1 Co 4³ ὑπὸ ἀνθρωπίνης ἡμέρας, which describes human judgment as opposed to Christ's day of final account, ἡμέρα τοῦ κυρίου); His day of the offer of salvation (2 Co 6², Jn 9⁴ 11⁹); 'the day of Christ' (Ph 1¹⁰); 'the day of the Lord' (2 Th 2², Ro 2¹⁶, 2 Co 1¹⁴, Rev 6¹⁷); 'the day of God' (2 P 3¹²); 'the Lord's day,' ἡ κυριακὴ ἡμέρα (Rev 1¹⁰); the day of the gift of the Spirit (Jn 14²⁰); the day of completed salvation (Ro 13¹²); 'the evil day,' of trial and temptation (Eph 6¹³); 'as children of the day,' *i.e.* as sons who abstain from doing evil (1 Th 5⁵· ⁸, Ro 13¹³); a day of fuller knowledge (2 P 1¹⁹); and, lastly, the somewhat enigmatical passage, 'Give us this day (σήμερον) our daily (τὸν ἐπιούσιον) bread' (Mt 6¹¹, Lk 11³); the latter expression (see art. LORD'S PRAYER) is not found in classical Greek, and seems to have been specially coined by the Evangelists to convey in this single context the idea of 'needful' or 'the coming day's'; the Vulgate has *supersubstantialem* (cf. Amer. RVm). See, further, artt. DAY OF CHRIST, DAY (THAT), DAY OF JUDGMENT.

LITERATURE.—Art. 'Day,' by H. A. White in Hastings' *DB*, by Karl Marti in *Encyc. Bibl.*, and by F. W. Farrar in Smith's *DB*[2]; also 'Tag' in Riehm's *HWB*; esp. Swete's Com. on *St. Mark*, and Plummer's Com. on *St. Luke*, *ad loc.*; and cf. the artt. TIME, NIGHT, ESCHATOLOGY.

GEORGE L. ROBINSON.

DAY OF ATONEMENT (כִּפֻּרִים [יוֹם הַכִּפֻּרִים]‎ ["י], ἡμέρα [τοῦ] ἐξιλασμοῦ).—The chief OT passages bearing on it are Lv 16. 23[26-32], but some further details are given in Ex 30[10], Lv 25[9], Nu 29[7-11]. An earlier and simpler form of the ceremony is prescribed in Ezk 45[18-20]. The day is not mentioned in the Gospels, but it is referred to as ἡ νηστεία in Ac 27[9] (also Ep. Barn. 7[3. 4], Jos. *Ant.* XVII. vi. 4).

1. It is not necessary in the present article to describe fully the ritual and worship of the day; only the salient features are here touched upon which offer some analogy with the Christian Atonement. The more important parts of the ceremony were, briefly, as follows:—

(*a*) The high priest procured and brought before the Tent a bullock as a sin-offering for himself, and two goats upon which lots were cast, one being destined as a sin-offering for the people, and the other to be 'for Azazel.' He sacrificed the bullock, and carried its blood into the Holy of Holies, where, after enveloping the mercy-seat with a cloud of burning incense, he sprinkled the blood before it. He then came out and sacrificed the goat for the people, and, re-entering the Holy of Holies, sprinkled its blood before the mercy-seat. He next sprinkled the blood of each animal on the altar of incense in the Holy Place; and, lastly, he sprinkled the mingled blood of bullock and goat on the brazen altar in the outer court. Thus the blood (the life) of the animals, representing the life of priest and people, was offered before God; and they, and the three parts of the Tent polluted by their presence during the preceding year, were cleansed, and atonement was made for them.

(*b*) The goat for Azazel was then brought near. The sins of the people were confessed over it, and it was led into the wilderness. The two goats were intended figuratively to represent one and the same being, who, though sacrificed, was yet living, and able to carry away the sins of the people. In the Mishna (*Yômā* vi. 1, cf. Ep. Barn. 7[6]) this thought was afterwards emphasized by the regulation that the goats must resemble each other as closely as possible.

(*c*) The high priest offered two rams as a burnt-offering for himself and the people, signifying the complete offering up of the worshippers' lives and persons to God.

(*d*) The skin, flesh, and dung of the bullock and the goat, whose blood had made atonement, were burnt outside the camp.

2. The great spiritual truths typified by this ceremony are to a certain extent drawn out in He 9[7-14. 21-28] 10[19-22].

(*a*) The high priest entered 'into the second [part of the Tent] once a year' (ἅπαξ τοῦ ἐνιαυτοῦ, *i.e.* on one day in the year), 9[7]. But Christ entered into 'the Holies' once for all (ἐφάπαξ, v.[12]); and see v.[24f.] 10[11f.]. Thus His blood—*i.e.* His life freed for eternal uses by death—is perpetually presented before God.

(*b*) The earthly 'holies' are 'made with hands,' 'types corresponding to the real ones' (ἀντίτυπα τῶν ἀληθινῶν). But Christ entered into 'heaven itself,' 9[24].

(*c*) The high priest entered 'in the blood of another' (9[25])—'with the accompaniment of [by means of, διά] the blood of goats and calves': Christ, with His own blood, 9[12]. And the Tent, 'the copies (ὑποδείγματα) of the things in the heavens,' must be purified with the former: but the heavenly things with better sacrifices than these, 9[23]. With regard to the meaning of this, Westcott says: 'It may be said that even "heavenly things," so far as they embody the conditions of man's future life, contracted by the Fall something which required cleansing. Man is, according to the revelation in Scripture, so bound up with the whole finite order, that the consequences of his actions extend through creation in some way which we are unable to define.'

(*d*) The sacrifices of the Day of Atonement and other sacrifices—'the ashes of an heifer,' see Nu 19) can effect only the purifying of the flesh; *i.e.* outward ceremonial cleansing. But if they can effect that, *a fortiori* the blood of Christ can purify our consciences from the defiling contact of dead works, 9[13f.].

(*e*) The high priest entered alone; which fact signified that while the first Tent continued to have a standing among men (ἐχούσης στάσιν), the way for all men into 'the Holies' was not yet manifested, 9[7f.]. But now 'we have confidence which leads us to enter into the Holies in the blood of Jesus by a new and living way which He inaugurated for us, through the veil, that is to say [the way] of His flesh,' 10[19f.].

The main truths, then, at which the writer of the Epistle arrives by direct reference to the Day of Atonement are: that Christ is both Priest and Victim; that His sacrifice is eternally efficacious, and that it is being eternally presented by Him in Heaven; that its effects are not ceremonial but spiritual; and that we now have free access to the Father.

3. But other points of analogy and contrast suggest themselves, some of which are partially supplied by the Ep. to the Hebrews.

(*a*) The high priest offered a bullock for the atonement of his own sins. 'The law appoints as high priests men possessed of weakness,' He 7[28] 5[1-3]. But the Son was 'such an high priest as was fitting for us, holy, guileless, undefiled,' 7[26]. And the sinfulness of the high priest appears to have been the reason of his causing a cloud of burning incense to hide the mercy-seat from his sight. He was unfit, until atonement had been made for his sins, to look upon the place of God's Presence. But now that Christ has 'procured eternal salvation for us,' not only our High Priest but we ourselves may 'come boldly unto the throne of grace.'

(*b*) An obvious contrast between the Jewish and Christian Atonement is afforded by the fact that the former was possible only in the case of unwitting offences (ἀγνοήματα, He 9[7]), sins committed 'in ignorance' (Lv 4[2. 13. 22. 27], Nu 15[24-29], contrast Nu 15[30f.]). If Christ's Atonement were thus limited, our faith were vain, we should be yet in our sins.

(*c*) It is important to notice that the Jewish sacrifice was very different from those of the heathen. Its purpose was not to appease—to buy the good-will of—a cruel and capricious deity. The offerings did not originate with men; they are represented as commanded and appointed by God Himself. They were due to His own loving initiative; He showed the way by which men, who were hostile by reason of their sins, might be reconciled to Him. So likewise 'God so loved the world that *he* gave his only-begotten Son' (Jn 3[16]). Nay more; Christ the Victim voluntarily offered Himself (Jn 10[17], Mt 20[28] ‖ Mk 10[45]). Scripture nowhere speaks of God being reconciled to man; see Ro 5[10] 11[15], 2 Co 5[18-20]. God is not hostile to us, although by His very nature He must be angry with sin and punish it; but we are hostile to God (Lk 19[27], Ph 3[18], Col 1[21], Ja 4[4]).

(*d*) The ceremonies performed by the high priest were not a mere *opus operatum*, the magic of a medicine man. The whole congregation had morally to take an active part. The Day of Atonement was to be a day of cessation from work, like a Sabbath, and a day when every man must afflict (ענה) his soul—*i.e.* render his soul contrite and penitent by means of fasting, self-humiliation, and confession of sins. It is true that Is 58[4-7] denounces the outward expressions of this 'affliction of the soul' when they are unaccompanied by the necessary moral fruits, as Christ Himself does (Mt 6[16]); but Lv 23[26-32], Nu 29[7-11] clearly imply that real penitence is necessary for atonement. The Mishna also recognizes that, while the ceremonies of the day are effectual for Israel as a whole, individuals must appropriate the results by repentance. 'If a man says, "I will sin and (then) repent, I will sin and (then) repent," Heaven does not give him the means of practising repentance; and if he says, "I will sin, and the Day of Atonement will bring atonement," the Day of Atonement will bring no atonement' (*Yômā* viii. 8, 9). And similarly a Christian's faith in the atoning death of Christ is not merely an intellectual acceptance of the fact that He died for each and all. Faith, as the NT teaches it, involves a conscious co-operation with Christ's work. That work was not accomplished to free us from the necessity of doing anything. The atoning work of the God-Man is in living union with the longings and strivings of men for atonement, and thereby makes them effectual. But if a man does not repent,—does not wish to be free from sin,—for him the Atonement brings no atonement. The results of Christ's death are 'a power of God, leading to salvation' (Ro 1[16]); but the energy remains potential and useless until the human will renders it kinetic by deliberate appropriation.

(*e*) And this truth was foreshadowed in the Jewish atonement not only by the fasting of the people, but in the ceremony which formed the centre and kernel of it all. The killing of an animal and the shedding of its blood contained a meaning which far transcended that of mere death. The body is 'the expression of life in terms of its environment'; the blood represents the life set free from its limiting environment for higher uses (Lv 17[11]). When Christ, therefore, entered heaven 'with his own blood' (He 9[12]), 'to appear in the presence of God for us' (v.[24]), He began 'the eternal presentation of a life which eternally is "the life that died."' But 'we reckon that one died on behalf of all; in that case *all died*' (2 Co 5[14]); and as the high priest offered the blood of the goat which symbolized the life of the whole people, so 'the life that died' is our life, in complete union with Christ's (He 10[19]). The same truth is expressed in another form in He 10[1-10]. Christ's voluntary self-offering consisted in absolute obedience to the Father's will, an obedience having its seat in a body prepared for Him. 'In which will we have been sanctified through the body of Jesus Christ once for all.' But that is rendered possible only because of His living union with us which makes us part of His body. 'The Church is the extension of the Incarnation.' And this vital union is strengthened and perpetuated by the faithful appropriation of it in the Sacrament of His body and blood.

(*f*) It has been said above that the goat 'for Azazel' (AV 'scape-goat') was considered figuratively to be the same animal as the goat that was sacrificed. Its blood was shed for the atonement of the people, and, at the same time, it took upon itself the burden of their sins in order to carry it away. There is no distinct reference to the scapegoat in Hebrews, but a possible allusion occurs in 9[28], where the writer quotes Is 53[12 (6)]. Christ was 'once offered to bear (ἀνενεγκεῖν) the sins of many.'

The verb seems to contain the double thought of 'offering up' and 'taking up upon oneself' as a burden; cf. Jn 1[29].

(*g*) After the atonement was completed and the sins carried away, there followed the sacrifice of the rams as a burnt-offering. It is peculiarly significant that in Lv 16[24] the high priest is bidden to 'offer his burnt-offering and the burnt-offering of the people, and *make an atonement* for himself and for the people.' The great atonement in the sanctuary, though complete, was only an initial act which needed the continued burnt-offering to render its effects permanent. This symbolizes the sequel and corollary of the truth which formed the subject of (*d*) and (*e*). Our own life having been offered upon Calvary in union with Christ's, we 'died with him,' and we are 'alive unto God' through Him. That being so, we are bound to make an active appropriation of our part in His eternal presentation of the offering in heaven; we are bound to render permanent the effects of the great Atonement by yielding up our whole spirit and soul and body as a perpetual burnt-offering. See Ro 12[1], 1 P 2[5], He 13[15].

4. The above suggestions are those dealing with the more fundamental points, but they are, of course, far from being exhaustive of the analogies which may be drawn. The isolation of the high priest when he entered the sanctuary suggests a comparison of He 9[7] (μόνος) with 7[26] (κεχωρισμένος). His double entrance, first for himself and then for the people, seems to foreshadow the two entrances of Christ into the Unseen, once when He entered it at death, from which He returned victorious, and again when He entered it by His resurrection and ascension 'to appear before the face of God on our behalf' (He 9[24]). Again, the return of the high priest to the people in the outer court at the close of the ceremony recalls the words of He 9[28], 'a second time without sin shall he appear to them that wait for him.' And, finally, the burning of the sacrifice outside the gate is used as yet another type of Christ (He 13[11f.]).

LITERATURE.—1. On the ceremonies of the day: Comm. on Lv 16, esp. Dillmann; Mishna, *Yômā* (ed. Surenhusius, with Lat. tr. and notes, 1699); Maimonides' account of the ceremonies (tr. by Delitzsch at the end of his Com. on *Hebrews*); Jos. *Ant.* III. x. 3; art. in Hastings' *DB*, vol. i. p. 199 ff.
2. On the significance of the ceremonies: Sheringham's *Yômā* 2, to which is added (p. 105 ff.) an elaborate comparison by Rhenferd of the work of the high priest with that of Christ; Comm. on *Hebrews*, esp. Westcott, with the Add. Notes on chs. 8–10; Milligan, *Ascension and Heavenly Priesthood*.
3. On the doctrine of the Atonement: M'Leod Campbell, *On the Nature of the Atonement*; R. W. Dale, *The Doctrine of the Atonement*; H. N. Oxenham, *The Catholic Doctrine of the Atonement*; F. D. Maurice, *The Doctrine of Sacrifice*; B. F. Westcott, *The Victory of the Cross*; Dorner, *System of Christian Doctrine*; esp. iv. 1–124. Intimately connected with the subject are treatises on the Incarnation.   A. H. M'NEILE.

DAY OF CHRIST.—This is the general expression used by certain of the NT writers to indicate that moment in time in which Jesus the Christ shall reappear to establish His Messianic kingdom. It marks the beginning of that new age which Jews and Christians expected would follow the present evil one. The term thus lacks the precise reference of the Day of Judgment (wh. see), and is also more general than the term Parousia; but all three of these terms refer to the same point in time, and represent different phases of the same event. It is spoken of indiscriminately as the 'day of Christ' (Ph 1[10]), 'day of the Lord' (1 Th 5[2]), 'day of Jesus Christ' (Ph 1[6]), 'day of our Lord Jesus Christ' (1 Co 1[8]), and 'day of our Lord Jesus' (2 Co 1[14]). It is generally thought of in connexion with the great assize which is to be established by the reappearing Christ (1 Th 5[2], Ph 1[6. 10]). It was then that the process of sanctification was to reach its real completion (Ph 1[6]) and salvation be consummated (1 Co 5⁵). It was to come unexpectedly (1 Th 5², 2 P 3¹⁰), but was to be preceded by certain premonitory conditions which had not been fulfilled at the time of the writing of 2 Thessalonians (2 Th 2¹·²). There is no reference in the NT to an identification of the Fall of Jerusalem with this day, and all such interpretations must be read into it. In order to grasp its real significance, it is necessary to remember that the early Christians did not believe that Jesus had done strictly Messianic work during His earthly career, and that they looked forward to His return as the time when He would take up the work of the Messiah pictured in the apocalypses. This work was to be inaugurated with the resurrection of the dead, the establishing of judgment, and the conquest of His enemies. In the Apocalypse (Rev 6² 15¹⁴· ¹⁶ 19¹¹· ¹³) this period of conquest is prominent, but not in other portions of the NT. Here also there is to be noticed a distinction drawn between the 'day of Christ' and that 'great day of God' which follows the one thousand years' reign of Christ on earth. Such a view, however, is not clearly presented in other portions of the NT, the nearest approach being 1 Co 15²³· ²⁴, in which Jesus is spoken of as giving over the kingdom to God the Father. See, further, DAY OF JUDGMENT, PAROUSIA.

SHAILER MATHEWS.

DAY OF JUDGMENT.—i. IN THE TEACHING OF JESUS.—**1.** The Day of Judgment is one of the concepts inherited by Jesus. Its origin is to be sought in the religious belief, common to practically all primitive peoples, in a tribal deity who would punish the enemies of the tribe. This elemental concept gained varied forms in the development of different peoples. In some cases it was never carried over into the field of individual ethics, and in others it shared in the moral growth of its possessors. In the case of the Hebrews it is to be seen in the 'Day of Jahweh,' which formed so large and important an element of the prophetic message. In its earliest forms the expectation of this day involved simply the punishment of the enemies of Israel by Jahweh the God of the nation. As the moral content of prophetism developed, however, this punishment inflicted by Jahweh was foretold to include the punishment of the Hebrew nation. Amos and the great prophets who succeeded him warned a luxurious nation that it had grown guilty and degenerate, and would be destroyed as an indication of Jahweh's righteousness (Am 2⁶⁻⁸ 3⁹⁻¹⁵ 5¹⁰⁻¹³ 6⁴⁻⁸). After Amos the Day of Jahweh never lost its religious colouring, but its use was extended until it included in its scope not only wicked Israel but a wicked world (Zeph 1²⁻¹⁸ 2⁴⁻¹⁵ 3⁸· ¹⁴⁻²⁰). Ezekiel conceived of it as a day of battle in which Jahweh would conquer Israel's foes (Ezk 30²ᶠᶠ· 34¹² 39⁸ᶠᶠ·) ; but Malachi foretold the fearful punishment of all the wicked, Jews and Gentiles alike. It was this extension of punishment, and the increase in the number of the condemned, that gave particular force to the idea of the remnant which was to be saved.

Obviously the formal concept here is that of the Oriental monarch who establishes a court of justice, and decrees rewards and punishment. Jahweh was never conceived of by the prophets in terms of natural law, but always in terms of this analogy. In fact it would be probably truer to say that the monarchical concept of God was not an analogy but something more. It was this concept which conditioned teaching as to punishment throughout the entire Biblical period. Subsequent to the prophetic era, under the influence of Persian dualism, there was a marked tendency to extend the range of judgment to nature as well as to men, and the God who sat upon the throne was more than a mere national deity judging the enemy of a par-

ticular people. This extension of the idea is to be found in the apocalypses, which in so many ways lie behind the Judaism current in the time of Jesus. In these apocalypses the Day of Judgment became one of the most essential elements in the Messianic scheme. The Day of Judgment of Messianism is the prophet's Day of Jahweh given new content by the appropriation of certain elements from the cosmic myths of Babylon, and new colour because of the new literary vehicle, the apocalypse. As a part of the more highly developed Messianism, it sometimes ceased to represent a single judicial act on the part of the sovereign Deity, and with something like a recurrence to the picture of Ezekiel, came to stand for the period of struggle in which the Messiah was to overcome and punish the enemies of a righteous nation. In its new form the thought of the day became increasingly transcendental, and joined to itself the idea of hell newly derived from the older belief in Sheol. In fact it would be difficult to understand the full force of the Day of Judgment, as it appeared both in Jewish and Christian literature, without reference to the fate of the dead. In the place of a penalty consisting of national punishment, there grew up during the Greek period of Jewish history a tolerably elaborate belief as to punishment inflicted upon individuals after death. It is difficult to know just when this idea of hell as a place of punishment, as over against Sheol as the abode of the disembodied dead, was first brought into relation with the Day of Judgment, but by the time of the apocalyptists we find the correlation complete (Eth. Enoch 27²· ³ 48⁹ 54¹· ² 62¹²· ¹³ 90²⁶· ²⁷). In fact the punishment inflicted upon men is distinctly recognized as adjusted to the conditions of their life in Eth. Enoch 22¹⁻¹⁴.

Thus the Day of Judgment as a form of the Day of Jahweh became the central point in Messianic eschatology and the nomistic morality of Judaism. Different teachers elaborated its details in different ways, but, by the time Judaism was fairly developed, the Day of Judgment was conceived of as involving the examination of the records of each individual (Dn 7¹⁰). More or less literally, books were believed to be kept in heaven, generally by one of the seven angels, in which the deeds of men were recorded (Eth. Enoch 89⁶¹ 90¹⁴⁻²², Ascens. Isaiah 9²¹). In the final assize these books were opened and balanced, and the future of the individual was determined according to the preponderance of his good or evil deeds (Eth. Enoch 51⁵²· ¹⁵ 89⁶¹ᶠᶠ· 90¹⁷· ²⁰, *Pirḳe Aboth* 3²⁴, Ascens. Isaiah 9²² ; cf. Lk 10²⁰, Rev 3⁵ 13⁸ 17⁸ 20¹⁵ 21²⁷). The difficulty in such a mechanical basis of judgment was to some degree mitigated by the introduction of something approaching the later doctrine of supererogation, by which the merit of the patriarchs could be transferred to the Jews. This particular doctrine, however, it is difficult to trace distinctly in the days of Jesus, although later the transfer of merits from the patriarchs is distinctly recognized. From this idea of the assize, in which sentences were formally passed by the judge, arose the two opposing concepts of condemnation and acquittal. These two concepts are the two foci of much of the NT teaching concerning the outcome of conduct.

While Jesus opposed the mercantile conception of rewards and punishment, the Day of Judgment occupied a central position in His teaching. With Him as with all men of the prophetic type, the Judgment stretched across the horizon of human destiny. No action in life was morally neutral. A man would give account at the Judgment for the very words which he spoke (Mt 12³⁶). It was through the outcomes of life that Jesus estimated conduct, and these outcomes converged into what the Gospels designate the consummation of the age; that is, the great catastrophe in which the present evil age comes to a close and the new Messianic age begins.

2. The *terms* which the Gospels represent Jesus as using to indicate the Day of Judgment are various.

(*a*) Sometimes the great event which would determine the final destinies of men is called expressly 'the day of judgment' (Mt 10^{15} $11^{22. 24}$ 12^{36}), or more simply 'the judgment' (Mt $5^{21. 22}$ 12^{41-44}). These two terms are essentially the same.

(*b*) In one instance (Mt $11^{22. 23}$) the 'judgment of Gehenna' is mentioned, but this refers not so much to the Judgment-day itself as to the punishment inflicted upon hypocrites and sinners (cf. 5^{22}).

(*c*) Parallel with these terms is 'that day' (Mt 7^{22}, Mk 13^{32}, cf. Mt 24^{42} 26^{29}, Lk 10^{12}). It is in this term that the day is described in the apocalypse of Mark (cf. Mk 12^{40}), for the Second Gospel does not use the term 'the day of judgment.' Possibly the same reference is to be found in the sayings of Jesus recorded in Jn 16^{23-26}. See DAY (THAT).

(*d*) 'The day of the Son of Man' as a precise expression is found only in Lk 17^{24-30}, where the thought of Judgment is immediately related to the eschatological reappearance of Jesus as Christ. A similar, although not a precise, reference is to be found in other passages speaking of the Parousia, notably Mk 13^{26} 14^{62} and their parallels.

(*e*) 'The last day' is a favourite expression of the Fourth Gospel, to denote the day on which men were to be raised from the dead (Jn $6^{39. 44. 54}$ 11^{24}). That this day of resurrection is to be identified with the Day of Judgment appears not only from the entire drift of the Messianic expectation current in the time of Jesus, but also expressly in Jn 12^{48}.

3. The *time* of the Day of Judgment was not precisely fixed by Jesus, and in fact He is said to be ignorant concerning it (Mk 13^{32}); but the Gospels represent Him as announcing its coming before His contemporaries die (Mk 13^{30} 9^{1}||, Mt 10^{23}, cf. Jn 21^{20-23}), and this was the expectation of the Apostolic Church in general. Notwithstanding the indefiniteness of its coming, the day is one for which all should be watching (Mk $13^{33. 35. 37}$ 14^{38}, Lk 12^{38} 21^{36}), and its nearness can be argued from the signs of the times (Mt 16^3) as well as from various portents described in the phraseology of prophecy and apocalyptic.

Whether Jesus Himself regarded the Judgment-day as involving the fall of Jerusalem, or whether He regarded the inevitable destruction of the Jewish State as one of the forerunners of the Judgment, will remain a matter of dispute until the critical composition of Mk 13 is more precisely fixed. On the whole, however, in view of Jesus' forecast of the punishment to come upon the Jewish people both in Galilee and in Jerusalem, it seems probable that He did in some precise way correlate the fall of Jerusalem with the eschatological Judgment. But it would be a serious mistake to regard that destruction of Jerusalem as exhausting the content of His expectation of His Parousia. The punishment inflicted was to be universal, not Jewish. Had the disciples regarded the fall of Jerusalem as in any true sense the Judgment of the Parousia, it is inconceivable that the Fourth Gospel and the other portions of the NT written subsequent to A.D. 70 should have given no hint of such interpretation. In them as in the Synoptics the Judgment is not a process but a single event, future, eschatological. At the same time it is to be borne in mind that the Fourth Gospel appreciates the truth to which attention must be presently called, namely, that while the Judgment is eschatological (Jn $5^{22. 27. 29. 30}$ 16^8), a man does not need to wait until that event to fix his destiny. That is already determined by the acceptance or rejection of Jesus (Jn $3^{18. 19}$ 12^{31}). Such passages as contain the teaching are, however, not to be interpreted as indicating a loss of belief in the coming of the Judgment-day as a point in time, but rather as the Johannine equivalent and supplement of the Apostolic doctrine of justification by faith.

4. The *Judge* is apparently to be Jesus Himself in His Messianic capacity (Mt 13^{30} 24^{50} $25^{12. 19. 31}$). At the same time, in the Synoptics God is also referred to as Judge (Mt 18^{32} 20^8 22^{11}, Lk 18^7). This double conception is to be found also in the apocalyptic literature, and is easily understood by reference to the representative character of the Messiah. In Lk 22^{30} the Apostles are also regarded as judges in the case of the twelve tribes of Israel. This is a form of the belief in the judicial prerogatives of the saints which seems to have been current in the early Church (cf. 1 Co $6^{2. 3}$), and may be inferred also from the request of the sons of Zebedee to occupy seats on the right and left of Jesus when He came in His kingdom

(Mt 20^{21} || Mk 10^{37}). The Fourth Gospel represents Jesus as expressly denying (Jn 8^{15} 12^{47}), and also as affirming that He is the Judge (Jn $5^{22. 27. 30}$ 8^{16}). But such inconsistency can be resolved either by considering that Jesus at one time is thinking of His historical and at another of His eschatological duties, or by a reference to the general position of the Evangelist that the mission of the Christ in His historical ministry was for the purpose of salvation rather than for condemnation (Jn 3^{16}).

5. The *subjects* of the Judgment are men at large, with particular reference to those who have come in contact with the historical Jesus, including His disciples. The question as to whether those who never heard of Jesus are to be subject to this Judgment is not distinctly raised or settled in the Gospels, but the universality of the Judgment seems inevitable from Christ's warnings, notably in the parable of the Tares (Mt $13^{24-30. 36-43. 47-50}$). These passages further indicate that at the Day of Judgment mankind will be gathered together before the Judgment-throne by the angels —a further utilization by Jesus of a conventional Messianic expectation.

6. The *awards* of the Judgment-day are: (*a*) for those who have accepted Him as Christ, eternal life, including the resurrection (Mk 9^{47} 10^{17} 12^{25}, Mt $19^{23. 24}$ 25^{46}, Jn 5^{29} $6^{39. 40. 44. 54}$). (*b*) For the wicked the Judgment-day fixes the destiny of misery, which is described in a variety of figures, such as the Gehenna fire (Mk 9^{47}, Mt 5^{22}), destruction (Mt $10^{28. 29}$, Mk $8^{36. 37}$). The terror of the day is also forecast in the various portents with which it is to be ushered in, drawn from the figures of prophecy and apocalypse (Mt $24^{6. 8. 49}$, Mk 8^{11}).

7. There is a critical question as to whether many of these sayings concerning a Messianic Judgment-day may not be a reflexion of the Apostolic hope rather than the express teaching of Jesus. This is particularly true in the case of all passages quoted from Mt 25^{31-46}. It is not possible, however, so to explain all the teaching contained in the Gospels. Objective criticism must decide that many, if not a great majority, of these sayings come from Jesus Himself. The only ground upon which they can be rejected as genuine logia is the dogmatic presupposition that Jesus was superior to, and independent of, current Messianism. Such a position is difficult, however, in view of the relation of Jesus to His times, and His undoubted expectation that He would return with completed Messianic dignity. It is an unsafe method of criticism which determines first what Jesus could or could not have said, and then makes this determination the critical criterion by which to decide His relation to the current of developing Messianism. His superiority to the apocalyptic expectation of His contemporaries is no more marked than His use of certain elements of their hope for the coming of the eschatological Messianic era. Yet it is to be borne in mind constantly that here, as in so much of the teaching of Jesus, a new content is given by Him to current vocabularies and concepts. The standards of judgment are no longer those of the apocalyptic writers. Ethnic prerogatives are swept away. A man's destiny is to be settled not by his relation to Abraham, but by his relation to God. Not even those who called Him 'Lord,' but those who did God's will, were to enter the kingdom of heaven. Care bestowed upon a poor disciple was an assurance of the bliss of heaven. Such a change of moral values carries Jesus over into something other than a mechanical doctrine of rewards and punishments and of statutory merit. Instead of a balancing of good deeds and bad, it is evident from both the Synoptics and the Fourth Gospel that He recognized in eternal life the *summum bonum*, which is quite other than the sensuous joys of Enoch and some of the Rabbis. Eternal life with Jesus is not an artificial reward, but rather the consummation of personality which is determined by faith and relationship with God, and includes the resurrection of the body. The Day of Judgment, however else it may be used by Jesus, is primarily a pedagogical point of contact with morals and religion. It is an integral point of His teaching, not in the sense that it was an opportunity for God to wreak vengeance upon the enemies of the Jews, but in that it expressed the outcome of life, which is always to be lived in view of an impending eternity. The imagery with which He clothes this fundamental idea is Jewish, and must be treated in the same method as all prophetic imagery. But in such treatment it is impossible to deny that Jesus distinctly teaches that the final destiny of mankind is a matter that lies beyond death, and is conditioned by one's life before death. Any constructive use of the concept of the Day of Judgment, as it is described in the Gospels, is accordingly subject to the general considerations which must obtain in the constructive use of the entire Messianic scheme of Judaism as it appears in the NT. So far as Jesus Himself is concerned, this is one of the inevitable problems of His position as a revelation of God in terms of a historically conditioned individuality. The truth of Christianity in this, as in others of its phases, does not rise and fall with the finality of its expository and pedagogical concepts. Within the concept of the Day of Judgment lies the profound recognition on the part of Jesus of the fact that a man's ultimate destiny will be fixed in accordance with the immutable laws of God. To be saved is something more than to win the blessings of an acquittal at the Judgment-day of Judaism. It is rather to possess a quality of life due to the soul's relation with God through faith, which will eventuate in those blessed results which are pictured by the Gospels in terms of the apocalypse.

ii. IN THE TEACHING OF THE APOSTLES.—In the teaching of the Apostles the Day of Judgment has a position quite as central as in the teaching of Jesus. But even more important is it in what may be called their system of teaching. With them as with Jesus, the chief end of faith is the achievement of salvation, that is, eternal life; but their thought is more formally concentrated on the events of the great day. St. Paul draws out the logical relations of these elements more elaborately than any of the other NT writers, but it is easy to see that there is no radical difference at this point between him and them. All alike held that there was no escaping the Judgment of God (Ro 2³, cf. He 9²⁷, Gal 1⁶ᶠ. 2⁶⁻⁹. 15ᶠ.).

1. The term 'day of judgment' does not occur in the Pauline teaching, and in fact only in 2 Peter and 1 John. The day is commonly denominated 'the judgment,' and even more frequently is referred to in specific phrases as 'that day' or 'the day' (1 Co 3¹³). With this must be identified also the 'day of Christ,' although the term has a somewhat wider connotation (see DAY OF CHRIST) (1 Co 1⁸ 5⁵, 2 Co 1¹⁴, Ph 1⁶· ¹⁰ 2¹⁶), or 'day of the Lord' (1 Th 5²). In one or two instances also it is called 'the great day' (Jude⁶, Rev 6¹⁷). The belief in the same great assize is to be seen lying behind the idea of condemnation (κρίμα) which is so frequently met with in the NT.

2. It is around this Day of Judgment, as one of the elements in the establishing of the Messianic era, that the 'judgment' of the Apostles continually circles. All of them referred to it as one of the things to be assumed as believed in by all Christians (He 6², κρίμα). It might seem strange to the heathen (Ac 17³¹), but it was one of the elementary expectations of all Jews and proselytes.

It was to come within the lifetime of men living during the first age, and its awards would be final for the eternity which then began. Its subjects were to be all mankind, as St. Paul elaborately argues in the opening chapters of Romans. They were to be both the living and the dead. This, of course, implies the bringing of the dead from Sheol, and therefore accounts for the exceptional expressions which speak of the 'resurrection of judgment' (Jn 5²⁹, cf. Ac 10⁴², Rev 20¹². ¹³). Such a resurrection of the dead must be treated as something other than the acquisition of the body of the resurrection, which was to be a part of the great reward of the believer. In accordance with the apocalyptic literature, angels were also to be judged, and that, too, by the saints (1 Co 6². ³).

3. This universality of the Judgment lay at the bottom of much of the discussion concerning justification by faith. The Christians believed that they, as well as others, were to stand before the Judgment-seat of Christ to give an account of the deeds done in the body. The conditions of acquittal at the Judgment were conceived by the Jerusalem Church as including participation in the blessings promised exclusively to Jews as sons of Abraham. In the case of the party of the circumcision, at least, it was the belief of the Jerusalem Church that believing Jews and proselytes alone were to be acquitted in the Day of Judgment. The Pauline position, that any one who had accepted Jesus as Christ was to be acquitted, was exposed to certain misapprehensions. On the one hand, St. Paul insisted that it was not necessary for those who believed in Jesus as Christ to be subject to the Law as a statutory enactment; on the other hand, he was aware that the Christian life was far enough from being in absolute conformity with the will of God. How then could believers hope to be acquitted? His reply is that they *know* they are to be acquitted because they have the Holy Spirit, the first instalment of the heritage of salvation. His answer to the consequent question why a man who no longer feared condemnation at the Judgment of God should be good, constitutes one of the most vital of his ethical teachings It amounts to this: Realize in conduct the moral possibilities of the regenerate self. His answer to the more particular question as to what should happen to erring Christians at the Judgment is equally profound. In 1 Co 3¹⁰ he argues that the foundation of faith in Jesus Christ must always abide, but that the building which each believer erects upon this foundation may be worthless. His figure clearly teaches that the Christian is subject to the Judgment as truly as any one else, and that although he will be given the body of the resurrection and the other blessings of salvation, he will also suffer certain losses. At this point, therefore, there is to be seen the rudiments of a logical doctrine as to rewards and punishment which is far enough from the mechanical expectation of the apocalypses. And, further, it must be added that the early Church believed that it was possible even for those who, so far as could be judged by ordinary standards, had accepted Jesus as Christ, to fall away and be ultimately lost. Christians were always in danger of committing sins which at the Judgment would shut them out of the kingdom of God (Gal 5²¹, 1 Co 6⁹· ¹⁰· ¹¹, Ro 13² 14²³). It is clear, therefore, from such teaching, that St. Paul moved over into the moral as distinct from the purely formal field. The Judgment-day is something other than the time of registering the arbitrary decrees of God, and becomes the time when the ultimate destinies of men are determined by their actual moral conditions, these conditions including, rather than being supplanted by, faith in Jesus.

4. The details of the day are not clearly worked out by the Apostles. In their case, as in that of Jesus, there is the double expectation that both God and Jesus will be the Judge. In the Apostolic thought, however, the recognition of Jesus as Judge (assisted, as has already been pointed out, by the saints, 1 Co 6[2]) is very distinct. He is to sit upon the throne, and mankind is to stand before Him, and bow to Him, and be subject to Him. At the same time the correlation between His position and that of God is distinctly made (Ro 2[16]). He is to be God's agent, and at 'the end' is to give over the kingdom to the Father (1 Co 15[24]).

5. In the Apocalypse there are two Judgment-days spoken of. The first, which is established at the appearance of Jesus, is confined to the worldly powers, and Satan is then bound and shut up in the abyss (Rev 20[1-3]). Then follows the reign of Christ on earth for a thousand years, which is ushered in by the resurrection of the martyrs (20[4-6]). At the end of this period of one thousand years the great day of God (16[14]) comes, in which all those believers who survive and the members of the one thousand years' kingdom are carried up to heaven, and all the dead are raised to stand before the Judgment-seat of God (20[12. 13]). Here again there must be a distinction drawn between the idea of the ascension from Sheol and the acquisition of the body of the resurrection. At this final Judgment the evil are sent to the lake of fire (21[8]), where they continue in endless misery. In this last Judgment it may be noticed also that one's future is determined by the records in the books of the Judge (20[12. 13]).

6. As in the case of the teaching of Jesus, the award at the Day of Judgment for the wicked is eternal condemnation, which is described in a variety of ways, chief among which are 'destruction,' 'fire,' and 'death,' the general term for such misery being the anthropomorphic expression 'wrath of God.' For believers there is, on the other hand, salvation which, in the resurrection of the body, marks the completion of that eternal life already begun in the earthly life of the believer through the presence of the Spirit in the believer's heart.

7. It is improbable that the Church of the NT times ever ceased to think of the Day of Judgment as a distinct point in time, and of the coming of Christ as a definite event of the future (Ac 24[25], Ro 2[3]). See PAROUSIA. Such late books as Jude and 2 Peter are particularly emphatic as to His coming, although the writer of 2 Peter is obviously perplexed at the delay in the return of Jesus (2 P 3[4]).

8. It is at this point, however, that one realizes more clearly than ever the impossibility of treating any one of the particular elements of the Christian eschatological Messianic hope apart from the others. The reason for this lies in the origin of the hope. In so far as it is not the outcome of the historical facts of Jesus' life, death, and resurrection, it is the bequest of Judaism to the Christian Church. As such, its component elements are really phases of one hope, and are so inextricably combined as to make it almost impossible to separate them. The Parousia, the Day of Christ, the Day of Judgment, the resurrection of the dead, are all alike different aspects of the same great event toward which the whole creation moves. They all embody the fundamental expectation of early Christianity, that the Christ who had been crucified would shortly return to establish His Messianic kingdom. In such an establishment there was involved the punishment of all those who were the enemies of God and of His Christ, as well as the rewarding of those who were His loyal subjects. Its terrors were as far as possible from being figurative to the early Christians.

From the time of Pentecost onwards men were first warned of the approach of the Judgment which all Jews expected, and were then told how by faith in Jesus as Christ and Lord they might gain acquittal in that Judgment. It is further noteworthy that in all matters relating to the future condition of mankind and the method of escaping punishment and winning salvation at the Day of Judgment, all the Christian writers are essentially at one. Differences in emphasis and methods of presentation should not be permitted to obscure this identity in elementals.

Such an expectation embodies both permanent and transitory elements. Those are transitory which depend upon an impossible cosmology and a literal monarchical conception of God's relation to the world. Those are permanent which embody the immutable laws of the moral world and the facts of the historical Jesus (including His resurrection). To distinguish between these two groups of elements is not difficult for the historical student, and will result in a larger appreciation of the fundamental truth of an apocalyptically conceived Judgment-day. See also ESCHATOLOGY.

LITERATURE.—This is voluminous, but it is often dogmatic and apologetic in character. The unhistorical method of treatment will be found set forth in all the old treatises on theology. On the Day of Jahweh see J. M. P. Smith, 'The Day of Yahweh,' *AJTh*, 1901, p. 501 f. Views of Judaism may be found in Bousset, *Relig. des Judentums*, 245, 248; Weber, *Jüd. Theol.*[2] § 88; Charles, *Crit. Hist. of Eschatology*; Volz, *Jüd. Eschatologie*. For general treatment see Wendt, *Teaching of Jesus*, ii. 274 f., 360 f.; Mathews, *Messianic Hope in the NT*; Muirhead, *Eschatology of Jesus*; Haupt, *Eschatol. Aussagen*. J. Weiss (*Die Predigt Jesu vom Reiche Gottes*), Wernle (*Beginnings of Christianity*), Fiebig (*Der Menschensohn*, Lect. IV.), and Baldensperger (*Das Selbstbewusstsein Jesu*) treat the subject from the point of view of Judaism, and of Jesus' teaching concerning His relation to the Kingdom of God. Teichmann (*Die Paulin. Vorstellungen von Auferstehung und Gericht*), Kennedy (*St. Paul's Conceptions of the Last Things*), Kabisch (*Eschatol. des Paulus*) discuss the teaching of St. Paul on the subject. In general see Biblical Theologies, esp. those of Beyschlag and Weiss, and art. 'Parousia' in Hastings' *DB*.   SHAILER MATHEWS

DAY (THAT).—It was near the close of His ministry that the Lord began to speak especially of the Last Things. At an early stage we find a reference to 'that day' (Mt 7[22]). The hypocrites will plead in vain, *in that day*, how they had professed Christ. The day is the Day of Judgment, the day of the sealing of citizenship in the Kingdom of heaven. There is also a reference to 'that day' in the Commission to the Apostles. It will be more tolerable for Sodom *in that day* than for a city that will not receive them (Lk 10[12]). Here the parallel denunciation in the First Gospel gives 'in the day of judgment' (Mt 10[15]). Thus 'that day' is a phrase to denote the terrible day which is ever imminent, the day of Christ's coming to judge the world and inaugurate His universal reign. But among His last words the Lord included warnings of the fate of Jerusalem as well as of the doom of the world. These messages about the end of the city and the end of the world are intertwined in the Synoptic records of the close of His ministry. Reasonable care should not fail to disentangle the threads. The expression 'in that day' is used, for instance, to refer quite plainly to the fall of Jerusalem (Lk 17[31]; in Mk. and Mt. 'those days'). But then the phrase has its usual significant euphemistic use for the day of Christ's coming in judgment in all three Gospels where they recount the Lord's solemn warnings to be ready (Mt 24[36], Mk 13[32], Lk 21[34]). 'That day' is in the foreknowledge of God alone; it will come on the whole world *as a snare* to the unready. It may be immediate in its coming (Lk 12[40]), and it will be quick as lightning when it does come (Mt 24[27]). Evidently 'that day' is an epoch; not an era, but the beginning of one era and the end of another. 'That day' of the revelation of the Son of Man will be as sudden and final as the experiences of Noah and Lot appeared to each (Lk 17³⁰). As the end of this present age is the beginning of the reign in glory of Christ and His redeemed, the allusion to 'that day' at the Last Supper may be understood in the same sense as hitherto. In 'that day' the Kingdom shall be established, and all things shall be new, and the King will drink the new wine first again in 'that day' (Mk 14²⁵, Mt 26²⁹). On this pathetic promise of the Saviour on the eve of His crucifixion Irenæus comments: '*promisit . . . ostendens, et hæreditatem terræ in qua bibitur nova generatio vitis, et carnalem resurrectionem discipulorum Ejus*' (v. xxxiii. 1).

St. John's references to 'that day' are to an era, however, rather than to an epoch (Jn 14²⁰ 16²³·²⁶). 'In that day' the disciples shall recognize their Lord's Divinity, and pray to the Father in His name. In the Fourth Gospel, therefore, the phrase describes the era which had its beginning at Pentecost when the Holy Spirit was bestowed so fully upon the Church.

LITERATURE.—Cremer, *Bibl.-Theol. Lex. s.v. ἡμέρα*; Hastings' *DB*, art. 'Eschatology of the NT'; Beyschlag, *NT Theol.* i. 190 ff.
W. B. FRANKLAND.

DAYSPRING.—The dawn or beginning of the day; cf. for the word 1 S 9²⁶, Job 38¹²; in NT only Lk 1⁷⁸ (*ἀνατολή*), but cf. the prophecy quoted Mt 4¹⁶ (*φῶς ἀνέτειλεν αὐτοῖς*). Zacharias saw, in the remarkable events taking place, the coming of the new day and the dawning of hope for Israel: 'the Lord, the God of Israel, hath visited and wrought redemption for his people' (v.⁶⁸); 'the dayspring from on high shall visit us' (RV fut. אB). '*Ἀνα-τέλλειν* is often used for the rising of the sun (Mt 13⁶, Mk 16², Ja 1¹¹) and stars (Nu 24¹⁷, 2 P 1¹⁹), and *ἀνατολή*, either in sing. or plur. form, for the East (Mt 2¹·²etc.). In Rev 7² 16¹² *ἡλίου* is added, and there RV substitutes 'sunrising' for AV 'east.' In LXX *ἀνατολή* occurs for the rising of the moon (Is 60¹⁹). Light frequently stands for salvation and deliverance (Is 58¹⁰ 60¹, Mal 4², Lk 2³²), and was specially applied to the Messiah, cf. Jn 1⁹ etc., Eph 5¹⁴ (see Edersheim, *Life and Times*, ii. 166). For *ἀνατολὴ ἐξ ὕψους* in Lk 1⁷⁸ Vulg. has *oriens ex alto*.

'*Ἐξ ὕψους*, 'from on high,' presents some difficulty, as dawn does not come from on high; perhaps the ref. to a bright shining star is more in keeping (Meyer); 'He is the Daystar from on high, bringing a new morning to those who sit in the darkness and death-shadows of the world' (Liddon, *Bamp. Lect.*⁸ p. 248). Godet would connect these words with *ἐπισκέψεται* ('it is from the bosom of Divine mercy that this star comes down, and it does not rise upon humanity until after it has descended and has been made man'), but this seems hardly necessary; *ἐξ ὕψους* represents 'from God,' and *ἀνατολὴ ἐξ ὕψους* is simply 'God's Messiah' (Dalman, *The Words of Jesus*, pp. 223, 224).

A different translation is based on the fact that *ἀνατολή* in LXX stands several times for צֶמַח, a 'shoot' or 'branch,' one of the prophetic names of the Messiah (Jer 23⁵, Zec 3⁸ 6¹²; cf. Jer 40[33]¹⁵ Theod.). So Edersheim: 'Although almost all modern authorities are against me, I cannot persuade myself that the expression rendered "dayspring" is not here the equivalent of the Heb. צֶמַח Branch' (*op. cit.* i. 158 n.). But it seems a fatal objection that none of the other expressions in the passage correspond ('to shine upon' *ἐπιφᾶναι*, 'to guide' *κατευθῦναι*); and *ἐξ ὕψους* causes much greater difficulty (cf. Is 11¹). Bleek wishes to combine the two meanings by supposing a play of words on the sprouting branch and the rising star; no Hebrew word will bear the double meaning, but LXX comes near identifying this Messianic name with the appearance of light when it renders Is 4²('in that day shall the branch (צֶמַח) of the Lord be beautiful and glorious') by *ἐπιλάμψει ὁ θεὸς ἐν βουλῇ μετὰ δόξης*. If the source of Lk. be Aramaic, *ἀνατολή* may stand for some other word; cf. its use for נֹגַהּ 'brightness' (Is 60¹⁹), and in one MS, Qᵐˢ, for זָרַח 'rising' (Is 60³). See the *Comm.* of Godet and Plummer, *in loc.*
W. H. DUNDAS.

DEAD, THE (*οἱ νεκροί*).—**1.** The reverence and regard due from the living to the dead, according to the ideas which the Jews shared with other nations, are clearly illustrated in the Gospels. All honour is paid to the corpse in preparation for burial: it is anointed with spices and unguents (Mk 16¹, Lk 23⁵⁶, Jn 19³⁹; cf. what Jesus says in Mk 14⁸), and wrapped in fitting cerements (Mk 15⁴⁶ etc.). Reverent burial is given, the funeral train following the body borne uncoffined upon a bier (Lk 7¹¹⁻¹³). The omission of any mention of burial in the case of Lazarus in the parable (Lk 16²²), as contrasted with the case of the rich man, who 'had a funeral,' bespeaks a poor abject. The dead are bewailed by kinsfolk (Jn 11³¹·³³), by sympathetic neighbours, and by hired mourners (Mk 5³⁸, Mt 9²³). Jesus in the noteworthy saying in Lk 9⁶⁰ (=Mt 8²²), 'Let the dead bury their dead,' overrides a chief charge on filial affection, the burial of a father, as He emphasizes the paramount claims of discipleship. Such observances are not only the expression of natural grief; they involve belief in the continued existence of the dead, as is also the case with other forms of duty to the dead such as are insisted on in the Talmud. *E.g.* their wishes are to be respected and fulfilled (*Giṭ.* 14b), they are free from all obligation (*Shab.* 30a), it is unlawful to speak evil of them (*Berakh.* 19a)—cf. the familiar proverb, *De mortuis nil nisi bonum.*

2. *The teaching of Jesus concerning the dead.*—Whatever may be gathered from the words of Jesus touching the state of the dead is to be regarded in the light of the current Jewish beliefs of His day, to see how far He sanctions such beliefs, and in what respects He corrects and modifies them. The tenets of the Sadducees, denying the resurrection, future retribution, and indeed any continuance of personal being after death, constituted a sectarian opinion from the standpoint of later Judaism. The Sadducees, it is true, seemed to adhere to the older teaching of the OT, wherein for the most part nothing is allowed concerning the dead (*rĕphā'îm*) but a thin, shadowy existence in Sheol. They were, however, influenced in this respect by Hellenism and their affectation of culture rather than by zeal for the earlier Jewish faith (Schürer, *HJP* II. ii. 38 f.). The common belief, illustrated in the later literature of Judaism, was virtually that of the Pharisees, who held that the soul is imperishable, that rewards and punishments follow this life under the earth (cf. Lat. *inferi*), that for the wicked there is an eternal imprisonment, but for the righteous a resurrection to eternal life (Jos. *BJ* ii. 8; *Ant.* xviii. 1). This resurrection is connected with the glory of the Messianic kingdom.

Jesus definitely repudiates the Sadducean view (Mk 12²⁴·²⁷), and endorses, as to its substance, that of the Pharisees. (For a different view, cf. E. White, *Life in Christ*, ch. 16). In His dealing with the Sadducees and their catch-question on this subject (Mk 12¹⁸⁻²⁷ and parallels), He teaches that the dead are really alive and in a state of consciousness. So also in the parable of the Rich Man and Lazarus (Lk 16¹⁹ff.), with a sharp distinction between experiences of misery and bliss as entered upon by souls after death. This parable also favours the belief in the soul's direct and immediate entrance upon this new conscious state, as do our Lord's words in Lk 23⁴³ 'To-day shalt thou be with me in paradise.' We are not, however, to allow a literal interpretation of His language in this connexion to dominate our appreciation of what the Gospels afford as regards belief concerning the state of the dead. The expression 'Abraham's bosom,' *e.g.*, is of no dogmatic value to us, though suitable and significant to the men of our Lord's day. Similarly with the other pictorial elements; they are only of the same order as the imagery with which other faiths have invested ideas concerning the hereafter. The matter of abiding importance here is the teaching that at death a judgment already takes effect, the portion of the soul in the after life being determined with direct reference to the life lived in the present world, with results that may be in startling contrast to the estimates of a man and his condition formed by his fellow-men here. This conception seems to find expression in a symbol found on early Christian tombs in Phrygia, viz. an open book or set of *tabellæ*, which Ramsay explains as 'indicating death and the judgment of God after death; the tablets are open to indicate that the process of judgment has begun' (see art. in *Expositor*, March 1905, p. 223).

Such a representation of the condition of the dead in Hades is not, however, to be understood as excluding a remoter crisis in the soul's history, such as is suggested by the prominent NT conception of '*the* judgment' and 'the day of judgment.' As Weiss says, the retribution thus set forth as befalling a soul in Hades 'does not exclude an ultimate decision as to its final fate' (*Theol. of NT*, i. p. 156 note, Eng. tr.). 'Abraham's bosom' or 'Paradise,' moreover, does not denote a final and 'perfect consummation and bliss,' in the eschatological views of the Jews in the time of Christ. The resurrection lies beyond. Jesus in His encounter with the Sadducees uses the language of His time, and speaks of the resurrection as a transition and crisis awaiting the dead (Mk 12²⁵, Mt 22³⁰). The wording of the Lukan account (20³⁵) is particularly noticeable—οἱ δὲ καταξιωθέντες τοῦ αἰῶνος ἐκείνου τυχεῖν κ. τῆς ἀναστάσεως τῆς ἐκ νεκρῶν. There is an 'age to come' (rather than 'world,' see Dalman, *Worte Jesu*, Eng. tr. p. 153), which is to be attained by those that shall have been deemed worthy of it, an age evidently to be thought of as ushered in by the resurrection from among the dead. That age (='the kingdom' elsewhere), embodying the highest hopes of the Jews for the hereafter, answers to all the highest conceptions as to human destiny found amongst people of other faiths. And evidently it is not immediately attained at death, according to the language of Jesus. If, then, an accumulation of weighty considerations seems to some to support the doctrine of an **intermediate state** for those who have passed from this life—a doctrine already familiar to the Jews in our Lord's time (see Salmond, *Chr. Doct. of Immortality*, p. 345 f.)—the teaching of the Gospels offers no definite opposition. A state, *i.e.*, not simply of vague gloom or attenuated being, but of vivid consciousness; for the blessed dead 'a condition in fellowship with God, containing in itself the germ of an everlasting heavenly life towards which it tends' (Wendt, *Lehre Jesu*, Eng. tr. i. p. 223), with progress and growth from more to more; and in the case of others, a state affording room for the hope that there a solution is to be found for a multitude of otherwise inscrutable life problems in regard to man's salvation. Such comfortable words as Jn 14². ³ 17²⁴ do not conflict with this conception as regards the state of the blessed dead, and they are to be thought of as being 'with Christ' in a manner which is 'very far better' (Ph 1²³) than what may be known in the present life.

Salmond (*op. cit.* ch. 5), arguing on the whole against the doctrine of an intermediate state, relies mainly on the fact that no positive doctrine of this kind is found in Christ's words, and observes that towards this subject 'His attitude is one of significant reserve'; but this *argumentum e silentio* of itself tells just as much one way as the other. Those who maintain that death brings irrevocable doom to all and admits immediately to full and final destiny, are hard pressed by manifold difficulties. What expedients they are driven to in order to mitigate these are illustrated, *e.g.*, in Randles' *After Death*. The author eagerly urges how much is possible in the way of repentance and pardon even *in articulo mortis*. 'After all intercourse between the dying and their friends has ceased, a saving work of God proceeds'; 'repentance and faith, pardon and sanctification, may proceed with speed and power such as were never evinced in previous years' (p. 250 f.). Greatly to the credit of his heart, in anxiously maintaining his position he also advances considerations which lead, he thinks, to the conclusion that 'the proportion of the finally lost to the saved will be about as the proportion of the criminal part of England's population to all the rest' (p. 244 f.)! The consideration of the solemn subject of final destiny lies beyond the scope of this article.

3. *Christ's figurative use of the term 'dead.'*—The use of the term as descriptive of a certain spiritual condition, unperceiving, unresponsive, is illustrated in the saying of Lk 9⁶⁰, quoted above. In Lk 15²⁴ it occurs as tantamount to 'lost.' The dead spoken of in Jn 5²¹⁻²⁶, to whom the Son gives eternal life, are so described in virtue of their condition prior to their believing on Him.

LITERATURE.—Artt. 'Eschatology' and 'Resurrection' in Hastings' *DB*; 'Eschatology' and 'Dead' in *Encyc. Bibl.*; 'Duty to the Dead' in *Jewish Encyc.*; Schürer, *HJP* (as quoted); Weiss, *Bib. Theol. of NT*, Eng. tr. in the relative §§; Wendt, *Teaching of Jesus*, Eng. tr. in the relative §§; Stevens, *Theol. of NT*, p. 166; Salmond, *Christian Doctrine of Immortality*; Drummond, *The Jewish Messiah*; Stanton, *The Jewish and the Christian Messiah*; Luckock, *After Death*; Randles, *After Death*; Beet, *Last Things*; White, *Life in Christ*.

J. S. CLEMENS.

DEAF AND DUMB.—**1.** *Link between deafness and dumbness.*—(*a*) It appears impossible to separate these two maladies of deafness and dumbness, whether one approaches them from the standpoint either of the scientist or of the student. The consequence of the former disease is that the sense of hearing is diminished or abolished; the consequence of the latter is that the power of articulating sounds is defective or impossible. There is, indeed, no physiological connexion between the maladies; but the acute stage of either leaves the patient now with a correspondent incapacity of hearing, now with a correspondent incapacity for speaking. The acutest form of these maladies is seen when congenital; then the link is observed at its closest: the maladies, so to speak, draw into one, and the remedies which surgery or treatment, and the artificial aids of hand, or lip, or sign language can afford, are invariably applied as if these maladies had some common source and a unity of their own.

(*b*) This conception of an inherent unity between deafness and dumbness is curiously illustrated by the Greek adjective with which this article is chiefly concerned. κωφός is derived from the root κοπ, *i.e.* that which is smitten, crushed, or blunted, opposed to ὀξύς, 'sharp,' 'keen.' Thus κωφός is used in Homer of a blunt weapon,* of the dumb earth † [cp. Lat. *bruta tellus*], and, with a wonderful picturesqueness, of the noiselessness of a wave before it crashes upon the shingle. ‡ It is thus only by a slight metaphorical turn that the adjective stands to describe the impairment or loss of powers of the mind or body; and so of vision, of hearing, and articulating.

2. *References in the Gospels.*—In the Gospels κωφός (the word is not found outside them in the NT) is applied only to the two maladies under discussion, *i.e.* to describe the dwarfed and blunted powers of the deaf and dumb. Indeed, as it furnishes a common description of both maladies, a less careful student would be in danger, at least in the chief characteristic passage (Mk 7³¹⁻³⁷), of misrendering, or rather misapplying, the adjective, which plainly signifies 'deaf.' But later in the same Gospel (9²⁵) κωφός probably means 'dumb.' This free transference of the adjective by the same writer, as descriptive now of the one malady and now of the other, is clearly not due to any scientific

* *Il.* xi. 390.　　† *Il.* xxiv. 44.　　‡ *Il.* xiv. 16.

knowledge of the Second Evangelist; it was enough for him that it connoted the crushing, maiming character of both diseases. It is curious to note that even St. Luke the physician, in the three passages in which the word occurs, uses κωφός in this double application (1^{22} 11^{14} of dumbness, 7^{22} of deafness). St. Matthew again uses the expression indifferently as applicable to deafness (11^5) or dumbness (9^{33}).

It is, of course, mainly on our Lord's works of healing that the interest of the question turns. A glance will be sufficient at the striking passage in the opening of St. Luke's Gospel (1^{5-22}) in which the announcement of the birth of the Baptist was made to the aged Zacharias. It is significant to observe that Zacharias was on this occasion the victim not merely of lack of faith in the angel's message, but of real alarm at the vision. The penalty for this lack of faith was temporary speechlessness. Its infliction was indeed pronounced by Gabriel, but it may well be supposed that it was brought about by natural causes. There are many instances in which sudden emotion has brought on deafness or dumbness, and, strangely enough, there are instances on record in which a sudden emotion, like terror, has led to the restoration of lost powers of this character. The medical faculty always regard hopefully patients who have become suddenly deaf or dumb from these instantaneous causes, and it may be assumed that neither Zacharias himself nor his friends regarded the visitation as permanent, apart from Gabriel's consoling limitation of its consequences.

Two miracles recorded by St. Mark have suggestions about the deaf and dumb which are full of interest, and to which only inadequate commentary is possible within the space of this article. The former is that wrought by the Lord, on the edge of the Holy Land, upon an unnamed sufferer (Mk 7^{31-37}). He is described as deaf, and as having an impediment in his speech. The strange term * here employed (v.^{32}), which does not occur elsewhere in NT and is found only once in LXX (Is 35^6), indicates at once the closeness of link between the two maladies which has been already emphasized, and also declares that the man was not so dumb as he was deaf. He spoke, but only with difficulty; a trial, no doubt, to others as to himself. In this narrative, given by St. Mark with such extraordinary vividness of detail,† —the taking aside, the mysterious remedies applied, the sigh, the word spoken, not of magic but of power,‡—in all these we see the Divine figure of the Son of Man as traced by St. Mark, in His compassion for suffering humanity, in His teaching as significant by action as by word, in His sublime confidence that He had that to give, for which He looked not in vain from heaven. St. Mark puts in simple, unscientific terms the record of the cure. The sufferer's ears were opened, his tongue was no longer a prisoner, speech came back orderly and intelligible to those around.

The other miracle, also recorded by St. Mark (9^{14-29}), is upon one whose dumbness was linked with demoniacal possession. An examination of the passage shows how the case had baffled Christ's disciples. The father of the possessed felt that he had in the Great Teacher his final resort. Our Lord's question elicited the reply that the malady, aggravated by demoniacal suggestion, was congenital. The man's dumbness was of the acutest form. The narrative of the

* μογιλάλος; there is no English equivalent. The French word *balbutiant* approaches its meaning closely.
† See present writer's article in *Expositor* (v. iv. [1896] p. 380) on 'He took him aside.'
‡ The Aram. *Ephphatha* (v.^{34}) applies not only to the man's hearing but to his speech; to the open ear, but also as by a frequent Hebraism to the open lip.

miracle is not out of line with the experience of the medical faculty. It is not only that deafness and dumbness are allied, but the patient at his worst and unhappiest suffers some form of dementia or idiocy. With the former instance, which lacked the distressing epileptic symptoms, our Lord dealt directly. In the latter He faces an evil, hostile power, 'Thou speechless * and dumb spirit, come out of him, and enter no more into him.' The former cure was calmly, quietly brought about. This was accompanied by awful convulsions. But the issue in both was the same, neither physical defects nor demoniacal agency resisted the word of pity and of power.

It is to be observed that none of our Lord's miracles excited such interest or won such admiration as those wrought upon the deaf and dumb. This would answer to common experience. The restoration of sight to the blind, for it is none other than this which special treatment in Germany seems now and again to have brought about, and of which one marvellous instance is known to the present writer, would not cause such astonishment as the recovery of a deaf or dumb friend. Blindness does not interrupt personal relationship as deafness and dumbness do, and, the moment hearing and speech are recovered, the results and consequences are communicable to others. It is no wonder, therefore, that the astonishment of the multitude passed into praise. Its verdict was, 'He hath done all things well' (Mk 7^{37}).

3. *Spiritual applications of deafness and dumbness.*—The senses of which these human bodies of ours stand possessed are so wondrous in their character and operations, that one would expect to find in Holy Scripture lessons drawn from them of great spiritual import. And so it is. The open eye, clear, candid, trustful, is a figure of faith throughout both Testaments (Ps 119^{18} 121^1, Pr 20^{12}, Mk 8^{18}, Jn 12^{40}, Ro 11^8). With equal force the open ear is significant of obedience. Students of the Psalter and of the Prophets will bear in mind the denunciations poured, both for spiritual deafness and dumbness, upon a people which refused to listen to the voice of Jehovah, and which was silent when the Divine Name and His praise were concerned (Ps 81^{11} etc., Is 6^{10}). On the other hand, again, through both Testaments, from Samuel to St John the Divine, a commendation and blessing has ever attended the ear willing to receive, the lips open to prayer and to praise. It is in and through the combination of these that the message of the Gospel can be disseminated (Ro $10^{10.17}$). And so of all the spiritual gifts, most dear to Apostolic men was παρρησία (Eph 6^{20}), born of the courage of conviction, and marking a mind and temper capable of standing at the last before the Son of Man. B. WHITEFOORD.

DEATH.—It belongs to the profoundly spiritual character of our Lord's thinking that He says comparatively little on the subject of physical death. His attitude towards it is indicated in the words, 'She is not dead but sleepeth' (Mt 9^{26} = Mk 5^{35}, Lk 8^{52}). He recognized that man's true being was something apart from the mere bodily existence, and death thus resolved itself into a natural incident, analogous to sleep, which broke the continuity of life only in seeming. The idea is presented more definitely in the charge to the disciples, 'Fear not them that kill the body, and after that have no more that they can do,' etc. (Lk 12^4 = Mt 10^{28}), where it is expressly declared that life resides in the soul, over which God alone has power. The accident of death, of the separation of the soul from its material body, can make little difference to the essential man.

* The rarer word ἄλαλον is used in vv.$^{17.25}$.

The three recorded miracles of raising from the dead are, in the last resort, concrete illustrations of this side of our Lord's teaching. The Johannine account of the raising of Lazarus is indeed bound up with a more complex theological doctrine; but the Synoptic miracles, in so far as they are more than works of compassion or exhibitions of Divine power, are indicative of the transient nature of death. Jesus awakens the daughter of Jairus and the youth of Nain as if from ordinary sleep. The life which to outward appearance had ceased, had only been withdrawn from the body, and could be reunited with it at the Divine word.

Attempts have been made to connect these miracles and the whole conception of death as sleep, with the contemporary Jewish belief that for three days the soul still lingered in the neighbourhood of the dead body. The earliest stage of death might therefore be regarded as a condition of trance or slumber from which the spirit could yet be recalled. It is in view, probably, of this belief that St. John emphasizes the 'four days' that had elapsed since the death of Lazarus, whose soul must thus have finally departed from his body when Jesus revived him. But we have no indication that our Lord Himself took any account of the popular superstition, much less that He was influenced by it. His conception of death as a passing sleep was derived solely from His certainty that man, being a child of God, was destined to an immortal life. Abraham, Isaac, and Jacob cannot be permanently dead, for God is not the God of the dead but of the living (Mt 22^{31} = Mk 12^{26}). In virtue of their relation to God they must have passed into a more perfect life through apparent death.

The traditional view of death as something evil and unnatural had therefore no place in the thought of Jesus. He nowhere suggests the idea which St. Paul took over from the OT and elaborated in his theology, that death is the punishment of sin. This prevailing Jewish belief is indeed expressly contradicted in the words concerning the slaughtered Galilæans and the eighteen on whom the tower of Siloam fell (Lk 13$^{1-4}$). Jesus there insists that death, even when it comes prematurely and violently, is not to be regarded as a Divine judgment. Sin is punished, not by physical death in this world, but by a spiritual death hereafter. This is doubtless the true interpretation of the warning, 'Except ye repent, ye shall all likewise perish.' Destruction is in store for *all* sinners; and the punishment cannot therefore consist in death by violence, which falls on few. Much less can it consist in natural death, from which the good can escape no more than the wicked.

While thus regarding death as nothing but one of the incidents in man's earthly existence, our Lord anticipates a time when it will be done away. In the perfected Messianic kingdom 'they cannot die any more' (Lk 20^{36}). Those who survive until the Son of man returns in glory 'will not taste of death' (Mt 16^{28}), since they will have entered on the new age in which it is abolished. Even in such passages, however, it is not suggested that death is an evil. The idea is rather that it forms part of a lower, imperfect order of things, and that this will give place entirely to a higher. Those who inherit the kingdom cannot die, 'because they are equal unto the angels' (Lk 20^{36}), and have so entered on another condition, governed by different laws. The cessation of death is conjoined with that of marriage (vv.$^{35.\ 36}$). As the marriage relation is natural and necessary to man's earthly state, but has no place in the life of higher spirits, so with death.

Jesus, it is thus evident, has broken away from the Jewish conception, according to which the death of the body possessed a religious significance as the effect of sin. His own idea of its spiritual import is of an altogether different nature, and can be gathered with sufficient clearness from certain explicit sayings. (1) The willingness to endure death for His sake is the supreme test of faith (cf. 'Can ye drink of the cup that I shall drink of?' etc. [Mt 20^{22} = Mk 10^{38}]; 'If a man hate not . . . his own life also,' etc. [Lk 14^{26}]). (2) Death is the fixed limit appointed by God to all earthly pleasures and activities. The thought of it ought therefore to guard us against over-anxiety about the things of this world, and to keep us always watchful, and mindful of the true issues of life ('This night thy soul shall be required of thee' [Lk 12^{20}]; parable of Rich Man and Lazarus [Lk 16$^{20ff.}$]). (3) Above all, death marks the beginning of the true and eternal life with God. This higher life can be obtained only by sacrificing the lower, and surrendering it altogether, if need be, at the call of Christ ('He that loseth his life for my sake shall find it' [Mt 10^{39} = 16^{25}, Mk 8^{35}, Lk 9^{24}]).

In several Synoptic passages Jesus speaks of a death which is spiritual rather than physical. He recognizes that the mass of men are in a condition of moral apathy and estrangement from God, and out of this 'death' He seeks to deliver them. His message to John the Baptist, 'The dead are raised up' (Mt 11^{5} = Lk 7^{22}), would seem, in the light of the context, to bear this reference, as also the charge to the disciples, 'Raise the dead' (Mt 10^{8}). The same thought is expressed more unmistakably in the saying, 'Let the dead bury their dead' (Mt 8^{21} = Lk 9^{60}), and in the words of the parable, 'This my son was dead and is alive again' (Lk 15^{24}). Such allusions are not to be explained as simply figurative. As 'life,' to the mind of Jesus, consists in moral obedience and communion with God, so in the opposite condition He perceives the true death. It involves that 'destruction both of soul and body' which is far more to be feared than mere bodily death.

The view represented by the Fourth Gospel gives a further development to this aspect of our Lord's teaching. Death as conceived by St. John is something wholly spiritual. The idea is enforced in its full extent that physical death is only a 'taking rest in sleep,' and in no wise affects the real life (Jn 11$^{4.\ 11-14}$). Lazarus, although he has lain four days in the tomb, has never truly died; for 'he that believeth in me, when he is dead, continues to live' (11$^{25.\ 26}$). The miracle by which he is 'awakened out of sleep' is meant to show forth, under the forms of sense, the inward and spiritual work of Jesus. He is 'the resurrection and the life.' He has come to raise men out of the state of death in which they find themselves, and to make them inheritors, even now, of the life of God.

To understand the Evangelist's conception, we have to remember that here as elsewhere he converts into present reality what is future and apocalyptic in the Synoptic teaching. Jesus had spoken of life as a reward laid up in 'the world to come,' and had contrasted it with the 'casting out' or 'destruction' (ἀπώλεια) which is reserved for the wicked. These ideas reappear in the Fourth Gospel, divested of their pictorial, eschatological form. Life is a spiritual possession here and now, and has its counterpart in 'death,' which is likewise realized in the present world. St. John, indeed, contemplates a future in which the life, and by implication the death, will become complete and final (6$^{39.\ 44.\ 54}$); but they will continue the same in essence as they already are on earth.

Death is thus regarded not as a single incident but as a condition, in which the soul remains until, through the power of Christ, it passes into the opposite condition of life. It is not, however, a state of moral apathy and disobedience, or at least does not primarily bear this ethical character. Life, in the view of St. John, is the absolute, Divine life, in which man, as a creature of earth, does not participate (see LIFE). His natural state is one of 'death,' not because of his moral sinfulness, but because he belongs to a lower world, and the life he possesses is therefore relative and unreal. It is life only in a physical sense, and is more properly described as 'death.' The work of Christ is to deliver men from the state of privation in which they are involved by their earthly nature (3^6). As the Word made flesh, He communicates to them His own higher essence, and makes possible for them the mysterious transition 'from death unto life' (5^{24}).

In this Johannine doctrine Greek-philosophical ideas, transmitted through Philo, have blended with the original teaching of Jesus as recorded in the Synoptics. The simple ethical distinction has become a distinction of two kinds of being,—earthly and spiritual, phenomenal and real. Jesus 'raises the dead' in the sense that He effects a miraculous change in the very constitution of man's nature. At the same time the ethical idea, while not directly emphasized, is everywhere implied. It is assumed that the state of exclusion from the true life is also a state of moral darkness, into which men have fallen 'because their deeds are evil' (3^{19}). The 'freedom' which Jesus promises is described in one passage (in which, however, the borrowed Pauline ideas are imperfectly assimilated) as freedom from sin (5^{33-36}). In the great verse, 'God so loved the world,' etc. (3^{16}), the ethical conception almost completely overpowers the theological. Men were 'perishing' through their estrangement from God, and from this death God sought to deliver them by His love revealed in Christ.

For the teaching of Jesus in regard to the significance of His own death see the following article.

LITERATURE.—Cremer, *Lex. s.v. θάνατος*; Titius, *Die neutest. Lehre von der Seligkeit* (1895–1900), esp. i. 57–87, iii. 17–31; Fries, 'Jesu Vorstellungen von der Auferstehung der Toten,' *ZNTW* (Dec. 1900); Schrenck, *Die johanneische Ansch. vom Leben* (1898). See also the literature mentioned in art. LIFE.

E. F. SCOTT.

DEATH OF CHRIST.—I. IN THE GOSPELS.—The aim of the present article is to examine the place of the death of Christ in the moral order of the world. What is the moral order of the world? The question may be answered as follows:—The will and purpose of God are in the way of coming to realization in the individual and social life and destiny of humanity. They are still very far from having attained to universal realization, but they are destined to reach it in the perfected kingdom of God. This is what is here understood as the moral order of the world. It began to exist and to be evolved on the earth with man's appearance as a being with a moral nature and created for a moral destiny. Its evolution is still very incomplete, but it is certainly though slowly making for a predestined end in which all men in Christ shall be morally perfect as God is; and in the moral relations of God to men, and of men to God and to one another, an order of perfect moral unity and universality shall reign for ever.

In this order of things, then, and its evolution, the death of Christ occupies a place of the highest importance and value. It is only from the point of view of this moral order of things and its evolution that the essential merits of His death can be properly understood. A consideration of it from the same point of view is called for by the methods of modern thought and inquiry. And it is only

thus that the cultured Christian conscience can find true, adequate, abiding moral satisfaction. But it is necessary, in order to prevent confusion of ideas, to mark the important distinction that exists in the nature of things as they now are in man's moral history, between the moral *order* of the world and the moral *course* of the world. The moral order of the world as just defined is only one of the constituent factors of the world's moral course. Besides it there are two more. There is, on the one hand, the factor which consists of all those facts or phenomena in the individual and social life and history of mankind which fall under the designation of sin or moral evil; and, on the other, the moral government of God, which presides immanently, persistently, and universally over the relations between sin and the moral order of things or the order of righteousness. These three factors constitute that actual moral course that the world is ever following; and the predestined end of their relation to one another will be realized in the complete and eternal victory and triumph of righteousness over sin, through the unerring and all-sufficient administrative judgments of God's moral government of the world (Mt 13^{41-43}, 1 Co 15^{24-28}). It is the moral course of the world as so understood that explains the nature and methods of the historical revelation, contained in the Bible, of God's will and purpose in their relation to man's moral life and destiny. The course of the world as so understood occupied a determinative place in our Lord's conceptions of man's moral life and destiny (see PROGRESS). And it was from the point of view of Sin, Righteousness, and Judgment that He contemplated the fullest and profoundest significance of His obedience unto death. It was on the place of His death in the moral order of the world, and as therein related to man's sin and God's governmental judgment, that He depended for the victory and triumph of Righteousness over Sin in the dispensation of the Spirit (Jn 17^{7-11}). From the point of view here raised His death may be considered in various aspects.

1. He was *put* to death on the Cross. How did this happen? What were His leading thoughts about it as so viewed? He lived and died without sin. He fulfilled all righteousness in the course of His obedience unto death, freely and perfectly uniting Himself and all the activities of His will and life with the will and purpose of God, and with Him His Father was well-pleased. This means that although He appeared and lived and died in the moral course of the world, He was not of the world, had absolutely no fellowship with it in so far as it was under the domination of sin. He loved sinners in their character as moral beings with perfect love. But sin He hated with perfect hatred; and He lived and died to save men and the moral course of the world from it. His life of perfect union with His Father's will and purpose in all things implied not only that He lived entirely on the side and in the interests of the moral order of the world, but also that the latter found in Him, for the first time on earth, the One Individual moral Being in whom it had secured its perfect form of manifest realization, in so far as this was possible in one life in human form. It was this fact, on the one hand, and the hatred of the men over whom the world's sin had gained complete domination on the other, that determined His way to His destiny on Calvary. This conjunction of righteousness and sin, and their creative influence on His earthly history and experience, affected Him in three ways, each of which should have a regulative effect on every one's thoughts as to the meaning and value of His death.

(1) He regarded the existence of the sin that arose and developed in increasing antagonism

against Himself and His mission, in the course of His ministry, as a thing that *ought not to be*. Saying after saying of His, bearing on this point, seems almost to convey the impression that He must have regarded this sinful and guilty opposition, without which He would not have been put to death, as not required by the interests and objects of the moral task which He had come into the world to accomplish (Mt 23³³⁻³⁹, Lk 13³¹⁻³⁵ 23²³⁻²⁷, Jn 7¹⁹ 8²¹⁻⁵⁹ 15¹⁷⁻²⁷ 19¹⁰⁻¹¹). (2) Then, again, His own words show that the inward 'moral' struggles and agonies of His life arose out of the prospect and contemplation of the development of the manifestations of the world's sin and unbelief against Him and against His claim to be entirely identified with His Father's will and purpose in all His words and deeds. His experience of inward crushing sorrow, arising from the cause alluded to, reached its culmination in the Garden of Gethsemane. But before the hour which He spent there in anguish and bloody sweat, He had foretastes of the terrible bitterness of the Passion which He knew was awaiting Him as His destiny (Mt 20²² 26³⁶⁻⁴⁵, Jn 12²⁷). (3) In spite of these two facts as to our Lord's thought and experience in connexion with His death, He always cherished perfectly optimistic confidence and hope as to the issues of the latter. Through the discipline of experience and through prayer He became strong enough to be obedient even unto death. He had perfect faith in His Father as the Lord of heaven and earth. He knew that all the future interests and objects of His mission and work on earth were absolutely safe in His hands. He knew before He died that His death could not hinder, but would be made to further these objects and interests (Jn 12²⁴·³² 16⁷⁻¹¹), and the first word He spoke about His death after He had risen from the dead was, 'Ought not Christ to have suffered these things, and to enter into his glory?' (Lk 24²⁶).

2. The question now arises as to the *nature, meaning, and value* of our Lord's unique achievement on earth, which reached its perfect accomplishment in His death on the cross. This achievement from beginning to end was made by Him in His position as internally related to the moral order of the world, and through it to the world in its character, aspirations, and activities as under the domination of sin. His achievement, as so viewed, consisted in the perfect realization of His Father's will and purpose in His unique moral Individuality, and in all the manifestations of the latter in His relations with God and with men. It is to be observed, then, for one thing of highest importance, that this achievement of His, in its nature, meaning, and value, was purely, entirely, exclusively *moral*. There are two considerations which place this fact in the region of absolute certainty.

In the first place, the fact has its validity in the established nature of the moral order of the world and in Christ's own place in this order. This is an order of things which has its foundations in the moral nature of God; in the moral nature of man as made in the image of God as a Moral Being; in the fact and in the nature of the moral relations between God and men and between man and man; and also in the fact that Christ as the Son of God came into the world to qualify Himself for occupying His momentous position of mediation within the sphere of the moral relations of God to men and of men to God. These are all indisputable facts, and they make it certain that the essential nature and objects of our Lord's earthly achievement, which culminated in the manner in which He met His death on the cross, were absolutely and exclusively moral. That it was so in our Lord's own way of conceiving of the nature, mean-

ing, and value of His life of obedience unto death, is manifest from His own words, *e.g.*, in Jn 16⁷⁻¹¹.

But, secondly, the same conclusion follows from His attitude of resistance to the whole system of *legalism* which He found Judaism had developed and set up, as an order of fixed and unchangeable conditions, in the relations between God and men — between Him and them as individuals, and between Him and the Jewish nation at large as His own peculiar covenant people. The effect of this system, as being both theoretically and administratively legal, was conceived and opposed by our Lord as subversive of that moral order of things in which inward, direct, universal, and eternal relations are established between God and men (Mk 7¹⁻²³). And it is a fact written broadly and deeply in all the Gospels, that if there was anything that He ever attempted more manifestly, strenuously, uncompromisingly, and more persistently than another, it was this, viz.: to overthrow completely and for ever the entire order of ideas which rested upon the stupendous error that the direct relations between God and men are legal, that they are founded on legal conditions, that they are to be maintained, administered, and mediated by legal means, and that, therefore, they are not inward but external (Mt 5–7. 15¹⁻²⁰ 23, Lk 11³⁸⁻⁵⁴, Jn 5⁵⁻¹⁷ 7³⁷⁻⁵³ 8³¹⁻⁵⁹ 12³⁷⁻⁵⁰). What, then, does His attitude of unreserved and bold antagonism to the legal system of Judaism imply in the point of view here considered? (1) It implies that in His position in the moral order of the world He stood on the eternal fact and truth that the direct relations between God as a Moral Being and men as moral beings are inward and therefore essentially moral. (2) It implies, again, that He stood upon the predestined fact and truth that His position and work of mediation within the domain of these relations were also essentially moral and therefore anti-legal.

3. But, further, it follows from the nature of our Lord's earthly task that the achievement of it in the manner in which He lived and died was a moral *unity*. His personality or moral individuality was a unity. His will was a moral unity, and the entire series of the manifold inward and outward free moral activities of His life until His last moment on the cross, were related to one another as a perfectly consistent order of moral unity. He came into the world, as He Himself always represented, on one entirely homogeneous moral undertaking; and when this undertaking was fulfilled, He spoke of it in terms which show that He regarded the finished task as one homogeneous moral result (Jn 17⁴ 19²⁸). In other words, our Lord's obedience in His manner of living and dying followed the law of moral continuity. His obedience unto death was regulated, on His part, by *one* determinative moral principle; but there was diversity of incidental moral significance and value in the various positions in which His moral vocation summoned Him to act, and to be faithful and loyal to this principle.

(1) What was the principle which constituted the perfect moral unity of His obedience unto death? It was perfect love, manifesting itself in perfect self-sacrifice and service, and, in doing this, ever paying perfectly wise and loyal regard to the moral requirements of human life and destiny on the one hand, and to the moral requirements of God's holy will and purpose in relation to those human requirements on the other (Mt 20²⁸ 26³⁹, Mk 10⁴⁵, Jn 10¹⁷·¹⁸ 13¹⁻¹⁷ 3¹³⁻²¹ 4³⁴ 5¹⁷⁻⁴⁴ 8⁴⁹·⁵⁰·⁵⁴·⁵⁵ 17¹⁻⁷·²⁵·²⁶). From such sayings of our Lord's as are here referred to, it is obvious that the principle which regulated all the moral activities of His life was, in effect, of the nature and compass just defined. There are no words of His reported in any of the

Gospels which justify the making of any *essential* distinction between the nature of His obedience or moral achievement during the time of the Passion, and the nature of it prior to the hour when He allowed Himself to fall into the power of His enemies. The period of His Passion was indeed unique in two things as regards His own part in it. From the moment that He began to pray in Gethsemane till the moment when He said ' It is finished,' on the cross, He endured unspeakable suffering, physical and moral, altogether unparalleled in His antecedent experience. Again, it was precisely during this period of His extremest suffering that all His powers of moral activity were subjected to their severest strain, and that they, under this strain, reached the highest possible point of their morally victorious, triumphant achievement. But these two facts, so distinctive of His Passion, made no real breach in the moral continuity and unity of the moral achievement of His life as a whole. His moral suffering did not begin with the last tragic hours of His life. There was an element of moral suffering in the compassion with which He was so often moved. He had looked forward to His predestined 'hour'; and His words, ' I have a baptism to be baptized with ; and how am I straitened till it be accomplished !' (Lk 12^50), suggest that, in anticipation of His cross, He may have spent many an hour in painful moral wrestling, in view of His destiny, long before His anticipations began actually to be realized. In any case, it may be taken as certain that there was no form of inward moral activity called forth in Him during the hours of His Passion, which had not been evoked many times over in previous situations of His life. But on the cross these moral activities of His, in the superlative degree of their strenuousness and in the transcendent magnitude of their victory over sin and temptation, eclipsed all the moral achievements of His past life. And yet in reality He died, in the sense of all that was essentially moral, as He had lived. He lived and died determined by the same moral principle, in the same spirit of love and self-sacrifice and service, and in the same spirit of perfectly wise and loyal regard to all the demands of God's will and purpose on Him, and to all the demands on Him of the world's moral needs.

This view of the moral unity of the achievement of Christ's earthly activities is the truth as it was in His own thought. His thought was this : ' Therefore doth my Father love me, because I lay down my life ($\epsilon\gamma\grave{\omega}\ \tau\acute{\iota}\theta\eta\mu\iota\ \tau\grave{\eta}\nu\ \psi\upsilon\chi\acute{\eta}\nu\ \mu o\upsilon$), that I might take it again. No man taketh it from me, but I lay it down of myself. I have power to lay it down, and I have power to take it again. This commandment have I received of my Father' (Jn 10^17, 18). Now there is absolutely nothing in these words to justify any theologian in limiting the application of them to what our Lord did during the hours of His Passion. What He did then, in the exercise of His powers of moral activity, was to *submit*, in a way perfectly pleasing to God, to the sort of death predestined for Him. Again, for Him who was in God, and who had God in Him, ' it was not death to die.' He never was more alive, in the highest and deepest sense of the word as applied to a perfect moral being, than in the very moment on the cross when He cried with a loud voice, saying, ' Father, into thy hands I commend my *spirit*' (Lk 23^46). He did indeed lay down His life in submitting to His death, which He indisputably contemplated in the same way as St. Peter did in the words, ' Him . . . ye have taken, and by wicked hands have crucified and slain' (Ac 2^23, cf. Mt 16^21, Jn 7^19 8^37). But how did it come to pass that He was able to lay down His life in dying, doing so in such a manner that His Father loved Him in the doing of it and for the doing of it? It so came to pass because He had never done anything else but lay down His life ($\psi\upsilon\chi\acute{\eta}$) in *living*. All the moral powers of holy love, self-sacrifice, and service that were individualized in Him as the incarnate Son of God and man's Redeemer,—these powers, which were *His* life, He laid down, consecrated, employed, every moment and in every situation of His life of free activity, in order perfectly to fulfil His life's vocation as determined for Him by His Father's will and purpose, and by the moral necessities of the world which He had come to save. And it was because He did all this in living that He was able so successfully and triumphantly to do it all in dying. And the effect of this truth is neither to dim the moral splendour nor to detract from the moral value of our Lord's death, but rather to reveal how great was the moral splendour and value of all the activities, words, and deeds of His life.

(2) But if His life prepared Him for dying, His death on the cross raised the moral splendour and value of His whole life to its highest powers of revelation and effect in the human soul and in the moral history of the world. The supreme distinction of the cross, as our Lord Himself understood it and trusted and hoped in it, as related to man's redemption, was the unique, stupendous, tragic conjunction of sin and righteousness and judgment, a moral tragedy of which the cross was but the outward visible symbol. The complex event for which the cross stands is the most momentous and the most creative moral event in the history of the world's moral course. In the tragic moral truth of this event God and Christ and man, God's righteousness and love in Christ, man's sin and salvation, and eternal judgment, were and are all directly concerned in the highest degree. The fact of Christ's death is thus pregnant with all the inexhaustible powers necessary for the moral regeneration of the individual human soul and of the human race. Out of this fact springs the inspiration necessary to illuminate the human conscience with divinest moral ideas, and to make it live in the divinest power of moral sentiment. And it is in this internal moral renewal and its manifestations that the soul finds its true redemption and its highest life ; so Christ Himself evidently thought (Jn 16^7-11).

4. It now remains to note, from the standpoint of the moral order of the world, some features of our Lord's place and work therein, as *the Mediator between God and men.* His work of mediation in the flesh ended with His death on the cross, and it was preliminary to His mediation in the Spirit (Jn 14^12-26 16^7-11). His mediation in the Spirit, which will be continued until the Kingdom of God is perfected, is dependent for its existence and efficiency on the moral and historical conditions provided in His earthly life of obedience unto death, and in the revelation of sin, righteousness, and judgment in which the completion of His work in the flesh issued. What, then, are the nature, the objects, and the methods of our Lord's mediation?

(1) Its general object is to save individuals from their sin by reconciling them to God, to perfect them as individuals in their moral nature and life, and to unite all who are thus saved in a life of eternal oneness with God, and with one another in Him.—(2) The sphere within which the mediation of Christ is carried on with a view to that end is that of the inward and immediate moral relations of God as a moral Being to men, and of men as moral beings to God. It was so even during the time of His earthly life and ministry in so far as His mediation took real saving effect in the moral nature and life of any of His disciples. It is so still in

the current dispensation of the Spirit by whose agency His mediation is brought to saving effect in souls. All the methods of the Spirit's work and all the moral effects that result from it imply the existence of internal, direct, living, moral relations between the soul and God in Christ.—(3) The mediation of Christ, as brought to effect by the Spirit's work, is in every case a relation of His mediation to the *individual*. For the Spirit cannot work in any number of individuals as a body unless in so far as He works in the moral nature and life of each. — (4) The mediation of Christ operates through the Spirit's agency by means of moral illumination and power—and moral illumination is always moral power.—(5) The moral means in question consist in the revelation of the holy gracious love or righteousness of God as realized by Christ, and manifested in His life and death of perfect self-sacrifice for the world's salvation. The best name for all this is 'grace'—the grace of the Lord Jesus Christ, or the grace of God in Christ, which was and is no other thing than the sum of the living activities of God as holy love, evoked by men's need of salvation from sin—men as moral beings. And this grace of God in Christ is moral. It is the highest and grandest form of the self-manifestation of God as a perfect moral Being.— (6) Hence it is only by means of appropriate moral conditions, existing in the individual's own moral nature and inner life, that he can enter into and abide in a saving relation to the grace of God as mediated by Christ through the work of His Spirit. And these internal moral conditions are repentance, faith, and the spirit of free and loyal obedience to Christ or to God, all of which are essentially related to one another, in every one of which the whole of the individual's moral nature comes to forms of manifestation in harmony with the will of God, and all together have the effect of uniting the individual directly and inwardly with God in Christ.—(7) This internal, immediate union of the individual with Christ, and therefore with God, is the true way of salvation and life for man (Jn 14[6]). This secures not only forgiveness, but every moral or spiritual blessing that the individual needs for this world and the next, every blessing that God has to give or that it is possible for Him to bestow in Christ and through the work of His Spirit in the heart. The inward, direct union of the individual with Christ through repentance, faith, and the spirit of obedience, means that the law of the Spirit of life in Christ Jesus has made him free from the law of sin and death (Ro 8[1-4]). This law of the Spirit of life in Christ is the law of eternal righteousness. Thus the moral regeneration of the individual through his entrance into a state of union with Christ, and with God in Him, is a new life, which carries in it the whole principle of eternal righteousness; and his union with Christ, his dependence on Christ, his fellowship with Him in the love that is of God, are guarantees that the law of righteousness will eventually receive complete fulfilment through his walking not after the flesh, but after the Spirit. And what is the law of the Spirit of life and righteousness in Christ but the law of that moral order, through which Christ Jesus, by means of His mediation, first in the flesh and then in the Spirit, is establishing and perfecting all the moral relations of individual men to God and to one another in Him? This is the new creation that Christ is evolving in the moral course of the world by means of His mediation. And, having made peace by the blood of His cross, He will continue His mediation until He has reconciled all things in heaven and on earth unto Himself, and therefore to God (Col 1[20]).

Literature.—Dale, *Atonement*[7], *Christian Doctrine*, chs. x.-xii.; Bruce, *Training of the Twelve*, chs. xii., xvii., xviii.,

xxii., *Humiliation of Christ*, 317-400; *Lux Mundi*, ch. vii.; Denney, *Death of Christ, Atonement and Modern Mind*; Weiss, *Bib. Theol. of NT*, i. 419-452; Beyschlag, *NT Theol.* ii. 133-164; Kaftan, *Dogmatik*, p. 446 ff.   W. D. Thomson.

II. In the Epistles.—In keeping with the amount of space devoted in the Gospels to the story of Christ's Passion is the place assigned to our Lord's death in the Epistles, and the significance evidently attached to it. The material is so abundant that it is impossible to give it in full detail. All that can be attempted is a brief sketch covering the chief epistolary groups, in which, however, the Apocalypse may be included, as containing the 'Letters to the Seven Churches,' and forming an important part of the Johannine cycle. Two distinct features come before us: (1) the place given in the Epp. to the death of Christ; (2) the meaning assigned to it.

1. The place given to the death of Christ.— Beginning with *1 Peter*, we see the prominence which the subject occupied in the Apostle's mind when we find him in his very first sentence speaking of 'the sprinkling of the blood of Jesus Christ' (1[2]), and thereafter referring repeatedly to those sufferings of Christ on our behalf (1[18f.] 2[21ff.] 3[18] 4[1]) of which he himself had been a witness (5[1]).

Coming to *St. Paul*, we have not only the fact, apparent to every reader, that he set Christ's death in the forefront of all his teaching, but his testimony that in doing so he was following the example of the earlier Apostles and the primitive Church. 'I delivered unto you first of all,' he writes, 'that which also I received, how that Christ died for our sins according to the Scriptures' (1 Co 15[3]). And St. Paul's preoccupation with the death of Christ was not a passing phase of his religious experience. We find him speaking of it in the first and last chapters of his earliest Epistle (1 Th 1[10] 5[10]). In the great Epistles of his middle period it is his dominating thought. The Ep. to the Galatians is a passionate *apologia* for the gospel which he preached (1[8ff.]), a gospel whose substance he sums up in the words 'Jesus Christ . . . crucified' (3[1]), and with regard to which he exclaims, 'God forbid that I should glory save in the cross of our Lord Jesus Christ' (6[14]). In 1 Cor. he declares that when he came to Corinth he determined not to know anything there save Jesus Christ and Him crucified (2[2]); and further assures his converts, in a passage already referred to, that in proclaiming Christ's death 'first of all' he was only maintaining the Christian tradition as he had received it (15[3]). In this same Epistle he hands on (11[23]) the special tradition of the institution of the Lord's Supper, refers to that rite as the central purpose for which the members of the Church came together (cf. v.[18] with v.[20ff.]), and says that in the observance of this great solemnity of the Christian faith we 'proclaim the Lord's death till he come' (v.[26]). 2 Cor., besides many other references, contains the great classical passage in which Christ's death is set forth as the convincing proof of His love and the basis of the ministry of reconciliation (5[14ff.]). In Romans the expressions 'Christ died' and 'his death' occur more frequently than in all the rest of St. Paul's Epistles put together. 'Christ died for the ungodly,' we read (5[6]); 'while we were yet sinners, Christ died for us' (v.[8]); 'he died unto sins once' (6[10]); 'it is Christ Jesus that died, yea rather that was raised from the dead' (8[34]). Similarly, the Apostle writes, 'We were reconciled to God through the death of his Son' (5[10]); 'we were baptized into his death' . . . 'buried with him . . . into death,' 'united with him by the likeness of his death' (6[3. 4. 5]). And when we pass to the last group of the Pauline writings, although we find that in two of them, Colossians and Ephesians, the writer has a larger outlook than before, and thinks of Christ's work now as having a cosmic and not merely a human significance (Col 1[15ff.], Eph 1[10. 20ff.]), he still exalts Christ's death as the very core of the work He did. It is 'the firstborn from the dead' (Col 1[18]) who is 'the firstborn of every creature' (v.[15]). 'He is before all things, and by him all things consist' (v.[17]); but it is 'through death' (v.[22]), 'through his blood' (v.[14]), 'through the blood of his cross' (v.[20]), that He brings peace and redemption and reconciliation (cf., further, Eph 1[10. 20ff.] with 2[13. 16] 5[2. 25]).

Very different views have been taken of the relation in the mind of the author of *Hebrews* between the incarnation and the death of Christ. But in any case it is agreed that it is upon the latter subject that the writer's attention is especially fastened. It is in what he has to say about the death of Christ and its purpose that we find the real message of the work. It is to elucidate and illustrate this great theme that the author draws so freely upon his intimate acquaintance with the sacrificial rites and ministering priesthood of the OT Church (1[3] 2[9. 14] 7[27] 9[12ff. 26ff.] 10[10. 19f. 29] 12[2. 24] 13[12]).

With regard to *the Apocalypse*, it is noteworthy that at the very beginning of the book Jesus Christ is introduced to us as 'the firstborn of the dead,' and that the ascription immediately follows, 'Unto him that loveth us, and loosed us from our sins by his blood' (1[5]). And very significant surely is the constant recurrence, throughout the book, of the figure of the Lamb, a figure the meaning of which is made clear when the Lamb is described as 'the Lamb that was slain,' the Lamb by whose blood men of every nation have been 'purchased unto God' (see esp. 5[6. 9. 12] 7[14] 12[11]). 1 Jn. is a treatise not on the death of Christ but on the 'word of life' (1[1]). Jesus is conceived of as the manifested life (1[2]), and union with Him through faith as the source of eternal life to men (5[11-13]). And yet the condition of our transition from death to life is the fact that Christ 'laid down his life for us' (3[14. 16]), and a Christian life which can be described as a 'walk in the light' is secured only by the fact that Jesus Christ the righteous is 'the propitiation for our sins,' and that His blood 'cleanseth us from all sin' (1[7] 2[1. 2]).

2. The meaning assigned to the death of Christ. —Having established the place given in the Epp. to Christ's death, we must now consider the meaning which is assigned to it. (1) The fundamental thought in all the groups is that the death of Christ is *a manifestation of the love of God.* 'God commendeth his own love toward us,' says St. Paul, 'in that while we were yet sinners Christ died for us' (Ro 5[8]). This Pauline keynote is one that is constantly struck. In 1 Peter 'the sprinkling of the blood of Jesus Christ' is brought into immediate connexion with 'the foreknowledge of God the Father' (1[2])—a view of the Father's relation to the *death* of Jesus which must not be lost sight of when the Apostle exclaims in the next verse, 'Blessed be the God and Father of our Lord Jesus Christ, who according to his great mercy begat us again unto a living hope by the resurrection of Jesus Christ from the dead' (v.[3]). The author of Hebrews declares that it was *by the grace of God* that Jesus tasted death for every man (2[9]), and that it was *by the will of God* that we were 'sanctified through the offering of the body of Jesus Christ once for all' (10[9. 10]). In 1 Jn. we have the great utterance, 'Herein is love, not that we loved God, but that he loved us, and sent his Son to be the propitiation for our sins' (4[10]).

In all these writers, then, the grace of the Heavenly Father is the source of the redemption which is bound up with the death of Christ. In the case of St. Paul the attempt is frequently made

to show that his teaching on the subject of Christ's death as a necessary sacrifice for sin is inconsistent with the utterances of Jesus Himself (*e.g.* in the parable of the Prodigal Son, Lk 15[20ff.]) with regard to the Father's spontaneous love for sinners. But whatever St. Paul said as to the propitiatory character of the death of Christ, it is evident that he never felt that he was compromising the love of God in any way. On the contrary, he saw in God's love the original motive of Christ's sacrifice (2 Co 5[18]), and in that sacrifice the commendation of the Father's love (Ro 5[8]).

(2) Further, the death of Christ is uniformly represented as *the supreme expression of the love of Christ Himself.* With St. Paul this is a central and constantly recurring thought. 'The love of Christ constraineth us,' he exclaims in one of his greatest passages, 'because we thus judge, that one died for all' (2 Co 5[14]). 'Christ also,' says St. Peter, 'suffered for sins once, the righteous for the unrighteous, that he might bring us to God' (1 P 3[18]). In the view of the author of Hebrews, Jesus 'offered himself' (through His death, viz., as the preceding phrase, 'the blood of Christ,' shows) to purge the human conscience (9[14]). And St. John writes, 'He' (*i.e.* Christ) 'laid down his life for us' (1 Jn 3[16]).

The Father and the Son are thus represented as working together in Christ's death for man's salvation, and working together from motives of love. As St. Paul expresses it, 'God was in Christ reconciling the world unto himself' (2 Co 5[19]). But Christ is not the involuntary instrument of the Father's love for men; He is Himself a willing sacrifice. He is the 'Lamb of God,' indeed, as the Baptist said (Jn 1[29. 36]); but He is not 'brought as a lamb to the slaughter,' as in the dim figure of the OT prophet. Rather, as in the conception of the writer of Hebrews, He is the High Priest who makes the offering, even more than the Lamb that is laid on the altar (9[11-14]). St. Paul sums up the matter apart from the imagery of the Tabernacle and the Temple, and in the simple dialect of the heart, when he says, 'The Son of God loved me, and gave himself up for me' (Gal 2[20]).

(3) But while springing from the Divine love, the death of Christ is represented in the Epp. not less clearly as *a propitiation for sin.* According to St. Paul, as we have seen, it was the initial article of the primitive tradition that 'Christ died for our sins according to the Scriptures' (1 Co 15[3]). And this part of the primary deposit of Apostolic testimony reappears in the witness of all the different epistolary groups. It reappears so constantly that no reader of the NT will challenge the statement that Christ's death is invariably associated with the putting away of sin (cf. 1 P 1[18f.] 2[24] 3[18], Gal 1[4] 3[13] 6[14], 2 Co 5[14], Ro 3[21ff.] 5[8ff.], He 9[26. 28], 1 Jn 1[7] 2[2] 4[10]). The discussion of the precise nature of the relation between these two magnitudes—the death of Christ and the sin of man—belongs properly to the doctrine of the Atonement (see ATONEMENT, RANSOM, RECONCILIATION, REDEMPTION). But this at least may be said, that however the matter may appear to those who deal with it from the point of view of a philosophy of the Atonement, any interpretation of the mass of NT evidence seems difficult and forced which does not recognize that, in the view of these writers, Christ's death was really our death in a vicarious and propitiatory sense—that Jesus Christ died on our behalf that death which is the fruit of sin, taking upon Himself the Divine condemnation of sin, so that there might be no condemnation to those who are found in Him. That this is the Pauline teaching is generally admitted (see Ro 3[22ff.] 4[23ff.] 5[6ff.] 8[1] and *passim*). But it seems not less the teaching of the other Epistles, if we take the language of the writers in its general connexion and natural

sense. Is not this what St. Peter means when he says, 'Who his own self bare our sins in his body on the tree, that we, having died unto sins, might live unto righteousness' (1 P 2[24]) ; and when he says again, 'Because Christ also suffered for sins once, the righteous for the unrighteous, that he might bring us to God' (3[18])? Is it not the meaning of the author of Hebrews when he finds in the sacrifices of the Old Covenant types and shadows of the sacrifice of Christ, and speaks of Him as 'having been once offered to bear the sins of many' (9[28])? And is it not the Johannine view also, seeing that we find 'Jesus Christ the righteous' described as 'the propitiation for our sins, and not for ours only, but also for the whole world' (1 Jn 2[2], cf. 4[10] ; see also Rev 1[5] 5[6. 9. 12])?

(4) Once more, the death of Christ is set forth in the Epp. as *a death from which there springs a life of holiness*. These writers relate the death of Christ to the power as well as to the guilt of sin ; they conceive of it not only on the side of its propitiatory effect, but as bringing a mighty regenerating influence into the life of man. St. Peter connects the sprinkling of the blood of Jesus Christ with sanctification of the Spirit and obedience (1 P 1[2]), and His death upon the tree with our living unto righteousness (2[24]). The author of Hebrews, who says that Christ offered up sacrifice for sins 'once for all, when he offered up himself' (7[27]), also says that the blood of Christ, by cleansing the conscience from dead works, sets us free 'to serve the living God' (9[14]). St. John, writing of those who are already Christians, declares that the blood of Jesus Christ, God's Son, cleanseth them from all sin (1 Jn 1[7]). But it is above all in the Epistles of St. Paul that we find a full treatment of this idea of Christ's death as the secret spring of a new life in the Christian himself, of a crucifixion with Christ whereby the very life of the Son of God flows into the heart (Gal 2[20]) ; of a burial with Christ which leads to a walk in newness of life, and a union with Him by a likeness to His death which carries with it the promise and the potency of a likeness to His resurrection (Ro 6[4. 5]).

There are some modern writers who insist that there is a duality in St. Paul's view when he approaches the subject of Christ's death in its relation to sin, and who distinguish between what they call his juridical and his ethico-mystical doctrines of reconciliation. The former is sometimes represented as nothing more than the precipitate of the Jewish theology in which the Apostle had been trained, while the latter is accepted as the genuine and immediate product of his personal experience (Holtzmann, *NT Theologie*, ii. 117 f.). The common tendency among such writers is to hold that the Apostle had two quite distinct theories, which lay side by side in his mind in an entirely unrelated fashion. He set himself, it is supposed, to the high argument of showing how God and man could be reconciled, but never took the trouble to attempt to reconcile his own thoughts about the efficacy of Christ's death. This, however, seems less than just to St. Paul. His theology as a whole hardly warrants the conclusion that he had no gift of systematic thinking, or that he would be content to allow his ideas on justification and regeneration respectively to lie together in his mind without concerning himself as to any possible connexion between them. It seems in every way more reasonable to think, for example, that in Ro 6[1ff.] the Apostle is not suddenly introducing a set of entirely new conceptions, connected with the sacrament of baptism, about a mystical fellowship with Christ in His death, considered as an archetypal dying unto sin, which conceptions stand in no sort of relation to all that has been said in 3[25ff.] about justification through faith in the propitiating blood of

Christ. Rather it appears natural to hold, in Professor Denney's words, that the justifying faith of which St. Paul speaks in the earlier passage 'is a faith which has a *death* to sin in it' (*Expositor*, 6th ser. iv. [1901] p. 306), so that when by faith we make Christ's death our own, sin becomes to us what it is to the Sinless One Himself—we died to it as He died, and in dying to sin become alive unto God.

Literature.—Denney, *Death of Christ, Studies in Theol.* chs. v., vi., *Expositor*, VI. iv. [1901] 299 ff.; Stevens, *Chr. Doct. of Salvation*, pt. i. chs. iv.–vii.; Seeberg, *Der Tod Christi*; Weinel, *St. Paul*, ch. xx.; Weiss, *Bib. Theol. of NT*, i. 419–452; Kaftan, *Dogmatik*, p. 446 ff.; *Expos. Times*, xiv. [1903] 169.

J. C. LAMBERT.

DEBT, DEBTOR.—The Jews, being an inland people, and not directly interested in the world's trade, were slow to gain touch with the credit-systems of more commercial communities. But by Christ's day their business ideas, modified already in part by the Phœnicians, are seen overlaid and radically affected by Roman domination. The people, on the one hand, as they listened to the reading of the Law in public, had the OT ideal before them, which was one of notable mildness, backed by humanitarian ordinances. Debt in their old national life had been regarded as a passing misfortune, rather than a basal element in trading conditions. In the popular mind it was associated with poverty (Ex 22[25]), a thing that came upon the husbandman, for instance, in bad seasons (Neh 5[3]). Being thus exceptional, and a subject for pity, little or no interest was to be exacted (Ex 22[25]), and a strict tariff excluded many things from the list of articles to be taken in pledge (Dt 24[6. 17], Job 24[3], Am 2[8], etc.), while in the Seventh or Fallow year (Ex 23[10. 11ff.], Lv 25[1-7]), and again amid the joys of Jubilee (Lv 25[30ff.]), the poor debtor had ample reason to rejoice. There was harshness in the tone, on the other hand, of the Roman methods, which were developed more on the lines of modern commerce. Often the more impoverished the debtor, the greater the exaction, as Horace expressly puts it (*Sat.* I. 2. 14), 5 per cent. a month (60 per cent. per annum) being cited by him as a rate of interest not unknown.

In the Gospels we have suggestions of the money-customs of the day at Mt 21[12-13], Mk 11[15-18], Lk 19[45-48], and Jn 2[13-17]. There are pictures of indebtedness in the parables of the Two Debtors (Lk 7[41-42]), the Talents (Mt 25[14-30]), and the Pounds (Lk 19[11-27]). Lending and repaying are seen in practice at Lk 6[34] ; also a credit system at Lk 16[6-7], if the reference there be to merchants, and not simply to those who paid rents in kind. Imprisonment for debt appears in Mt 5[25-26] ; and in unmitigated form in the story of the Two Creditors (Mt 18[21-35]), with selling into slavery, accompanied by the horror of 'tormentors' (v.[34]), although the whole passage is to be interpreted with caution, because Jesus in the fancied features of His tale may be reflecting, not the manners of His own land, but the doings of some distant and barbaric potentate. Enough that in the time of Christ there was seizure of the debtor's person, and the general treatment of him was cruel.

But whatever the law and custom, it was not the manner of Jesus to attack it. The civil code was left to change to higher forms in days to come. The exhibition of a certain spirit in face of it was what His heart craved, a spirit which should do justice to the best instincts of a true humanity. We can transcend in loving ways the nether aims even of bad laws ; and it was the evasion of clear duty in this respect, by those in the high places of the religious world, which moved Jesus most. He was the champion of the merciful essence of the old enactments (Mt 5[17]), while others around Him, prating of orthodoxy the while, were harsh to those unfortunately in their power (Mt 23[14]), all in the name of an ancient law whose real inwardness they missed. The Sadducees, whose love of money was whetted by enjoyment of the Temple dues, were not the men to show mercy to a debtor, nor were the Pharisees behind them, more Puritanic in zeal, and rigidly enforcing the letter of their writs. 'An eye for an eye, and a tooth for a tooth' (Mt 5[38]), as an old catchword, would infect the spirit in which, in the name of 'righteousness,' they complacently sued. Jesus lays down no outward rules such as might bear upon the modern business world. There fair and square dealing must be a first postulate; but, in the light of His gospel, men should be keener than they are to note hardships, and their hearts warmer towards cases of distress. In the spirit of the Golden Rule (Mt 7[12], Lk 6[31-36]) merciful dealings will show themselves in undefined ways; and the love of brothermen should counteract the love of money which prompts to stern exactions in every case alike. The soul saved by Christian feeling from sordid views of life adds to its true treasure by making the circumstances of unfortunate ones an exercise-ground for tender, pitying grace. The metaphors of Jesus in Mt 5[39-42] are exceeding bold, and the generous treatment there inculcated may sound almost incredible, not to say subversive of social order; but the enlightened heart will recognize at once the kindly and sacrificing spirit meant to be strongly emphasized. The dynamic in the whole matter, with Jesus, is the remembrance of the pitiful nature of our own plight before God, to whom on the strict requirements of law we are indebted in countless ways. The more this inward situation is brought home to us, the more we shall outwardly be compassionate in turn. Here comes in the moral grandeur of the Beatitude on mercy (Mt 5[7]), a principle which melts into prayer when we connect it with the tender breathing of the Petition on forgiveness (Mt 6[12]). The humble and the contrite heart holds the key to magnanimity. See, further, art. 'Debt' in Hastings' *DB*.

Debtor.—There remains the question of debt as the emblem of moral short-coming (ὀφείλημα, Mt 6[12]. See LORD'S PRAYER), and the Supreme Creditor's way with men in this regard, especially as depicted in certain well-known parables. The image is natural which pictures the Deity sitting like a civil judge, to try men for defaults; and while some think more of the majesty of the law, and what must be exacted to satisfy the interests of order, others love to dwell on the prerogative of mercy, and favour judgments which are ameliorative as well as punitive. No reader of the Gospels can fail to see the latter characteristic strong in the teaching of the Master. Pardon befits the royal clemency, and God is known in the kingdom for sovereign displays of grace. Yet due weight is given to the other aspect of the image also—the satisfaction of the law; for Jesus teaches that it is only the pure in heart who see God (Mt 5[8]); the holiness that avails must be inward, not that of the legalist (v.[20]), and only they who are merciful obtain mercy (v.[7]). But what is characteristic in the Gospel treatment of the subject is not any dwelling upon absolute judgments — these are left to the Searcher of Hearts; rather we are taken by Jesus to the sphere of *proximate evidence*, and shown that in the individual life the presence or absence of the forgiving spirit is sure token of the presence or absence of the Divine condescension as regards the person himself. In other words, principles discovered in the relations of men with each other are *a fortiori* valid for their relationship to God (Mt 6[14-15]).

The elder brother of the Prodigal (Lk 15[25-32])

illustrates the point; representing as he does the Pharisaic type of mind—common in all ages and pronouncedly so in the time of Jesus—which complacently fancies itself well within the Kingdom, but shows by its harsh attitude to fellow-mortals that it is inwardly not right with God. The elder brother is pictured, not without point, as remaining outside the banquet-hall, so long as he continued in his implacable mood.

The story of the Two Debtors (Lk 7[36-50]) shows the vital contrast of the matter in the persons of the Woman who was a Sinner—truly gracious in her doings, because full now of penitence and faith and love—and Simon, hide-bound and censorious like his class, with no disciplined sense of having been humbled like her before God. The latter, like the debtor of the trivial fifty pence, had little reaction of wholesome feeling in his mind; the former had manifestly much, like the man overjoyed to find himself relieved from a financial peril ten times greater. This is a concrete instance of the method of the Master. Certain visible acts of the woman at the banquet bespoke the inward action of God's Spirit, and argued a state of reconciliation with Him. From the scanty graciousness of Simon, on the other hand, one inferred just as truly a heart imperfectly attuned to goodness, and knowing little of the joy of pardon. 'To whom little is forgiven, the same loveth little' (v.[47]). As to which is the root and which the fruit, rival systems of theology may battle; but the fact is, the two graces are eternal co-relatives, and either may be first in the order of thought when neither is entitled to absolute precedence in fact. See FORGIVENESS.

The parable of the Two Creditors (Mt 18[23-35]) shows the other side of the shield from the Woman's case, in a person of downright inhumanity concerning whom it is equally clear that he had no saving experience of God's mercy himself. The story, as a story, is remarkable for simple force; we feel the horror of the implacable attitude of the servant forgiven for a great indebtedness, who failed to show goodwill in turn to a subordinate for a default infinitely less. Nemesis descends (v.[34]) when he finds he is not forgiven after all—he loses that which he had seemed to have (v.[27]). 'So likewise shall my Heavenly Father do also unto you, if ye from your hearts forgive not every one his brother their trespasses' (v.[35]).

Jesus saw many around Him glorying in fancied privilege and very zealous for the Law, yet omitting its essential matters—justice, mercy, faith. To such especially this Gospel message was addressed; broadening out in what for Him was the supreme truth, that love to God is seen and tested in love to man. To be sympathetic, sacrificing, generous, is not only the pier from which the heavenward arch springs, but the pier to which it returns. The forgiving God cannot possibly be seen in those who hide themselves from their own flesh (Lk 6[36]).

LITERATURE.—Besides art. 'Debt' in Hastings' *DB*, the Comm. on the passages referred to, and the standard works on the Parables, the following may be consulted:—Edersheim, *Life and Times*, ii. p. 268 ff.; Schürer, *HJP* II. 1. 362 f.; *Expositor*, I. vi. [1877] p. 214 ff.; Ker, *Serm.* 1st ser. p. 16 ff.

GEORGE MURRAY.

DECAPOLIS.—A league of ten Greek cities (ἡ Δεκάπολις) in eastern Palestine, which was probably formed at the time of Pompey's invasion of Palestine, 64–63 B.C. By the Greek cities Pompey was hailed as a deliverer from the Jewish yoke, and many towns elevated Pompey's campaign to the dignity of an era. The coins of Gadara, Canatha, Pella, Dion, and Philadelphia use the Pompeian era. At first the league must have comprised just ten cities. According to Pliny

(*HN* v. 18), these were Scythopolis (*Beisân*), Hippos (*Susieh*), Gadara (*Umm Ḳeis*), Pella (*Fahil*), Philadelphia ('*Amman*), Gerasa (*Jerâsh*), Dion, Canatha (*Kanawât*), Damascus, and Raphana. The formation of a confederation of Greek cities in the midst of a Semitic population was necessary for the preservation of Hellenic civilization and culture. From the days of Alexander the Great, who sought to Hellenize the Orient by founding Greek cities throughout the conquered lands, there were Greek cities in Palestine. The Seleucid kings of Antioch and the Ptolemies encouraged the immigration of Greeks into this region. Among the cities occupied before 198 B.C. by the incoming Greeks were Pella, Dion, Philadelphia, Gadara, and Abila in the region east of the Jordan. Hippos and Gerasa are first named in the early part of the 1st cent. B.C. (Jos. *BJ* I. iv. 8). Among the cities liberated by Pompey from the Jewish yoke, Hippos, Scythopolis, and Pella are expressly named ; and Gadara, which had been destroyed by the Jews, was rebuilt (*BJ* I. vii. 7). Pompey annexed these cities to the province of Syria, but conferred upon them municipal freedom. All the cities of the Decapolis had in the Roman period the rights of coinage and asylum, and were allowed to maintain a league for defence against their common foes.

The first references in literature to the Decapolis are found in the Gospels. On our Lord's first journey through all Galilee, He was attended by crowds from all parts of Palestine, among whom were persons from Decapolis (Mt 4[25]). Most likely these were Jews, who formed a considerable part of the population even in Greek cities. The fierce Gerasene demoniac, whom our Lord healed, published in the Decapolis what things Jesus had done for him (Mk 5[20]). The presence of two thousand swine on the eastern shores of the Lake of Galilee would of itself suggest the presence of a Gentile population in that vicinity. When our Lord returned from Tyre and Sidon to the Sea of Galilee, He crossed the upper Jordan and passed south through the district governed by the tetrarch Philip to the eastern shore of the Lake. In order to reach the Sea of Galilee, He went 'through the midst of the borders of Decapolis' (Mk 7[31]). Hippos lay just east of the Lake, Gadara a few miles to the south-east, and in full view from the southern end ; Pella and Scythopolis were not far to the south ; while the other cities of the Decapolis lay to the north-east, east, and south-east of the Lake. Our Lord visited the Jewish population of Peræa in His later ministry, but He seems never to have made a tour to the great cities of the Decapolis. His rebuff in connexion with the destruction of the herd of swine was rather discouraging (Mk 5[17]).

Two famous writers of the latter part of the 1st cent. A.D. speak of the Decapolis. Pliny not only preserves the names of the ten cities (*HN* v. 18), but also praises the small olives of the region (15[4]). Josephus refers to Decapolis repeatedly. In the 2nd cent. A.D. Ptolemy (v. xv. 22) names eighteen towns as belonging to the league of Decapolis. He omits Raphana from Pliny's list, and adds nine, most of the new members of the confederation belonging to the district just south of Damascus. In his day Hellenic civilization and commerce in the region beyond the Jordan were at their zenith. The modern traveller, wandering over the ruins of temples, theatres, and baths at Gerasa, Philadelphia, and Gadara, is impressed with the glories of the Grecian life in Palestine during the period of our Lord's earthly ministry and for some centuries afterwards.

LITERATURE.—Schürer, *HJP* II. i. 94 ff. ; G. A. Smith, *HGHL* 593 ff.; G. Hölscher, *Palästina in der pers. u. hellen. Zeit* ; Schumacher, *Across the Jordan* ; Merrill, *East of the Jordan*.

JOHN R. SAMPEY.

DECEIT, DECEPTION, GUILE.—

1. *Words and references.*—Mk 7[22], Jn 1[47] (δόλος, 'bait,' 'stratagem,' 'guile,' 'craft,' 'treachery'; cf. Ro 1[29], 2 Co 11[13] 12[16], 1 Th 2[3], 1 P 2[1. 22], Rev 14[5]); Mt 13[22] (ἀπάτη, 'trick,' 'fraud,' 'deceit'; cf. Eph. 4[22], Col 2[8], He 3[13]); Mt 24[4], Jn 7[12] (πλανάω, 'lead astray,' 'deceive'; πλάνος, 'deceiver'; πλάνη, a 'leading astray,' 'cheating'; cf. 1 Th 2[3], 1 Jn 1[8]).

2. Pfleiderer in *Early Christian Conception of Christ* (1905) devotes a chapter to the subject of Christ as the Conqueror of Satan—'that old serpent, called the Devil, which *deceiveth* the whole world' (Rev 12[9]). His aim is to find parallels to Christ in various nature myths and heathen religions, and by so doing to explain the Gospel story as only a special embodiment of a universal tendency. While rejecting Pfleiderer's theory, we admit that one of the most suggestive aspects under which the life of our Lord may be considered is to regard it as a deadly conflict between the Divine Representative of the Truth, and the instruments and agents of the spirit of deception and guile. Such a conflict was inevitable. The coming of One who had the right to say, 'I am the light of the world,' 'I am the truth'; 'every one that is of the truth heareth my voice' (Jn 8[12] 14[6] 18[37]), was bound to stir into bitter hostility all the forces of untruth and craft. The antagonism is set forth in universal terms in Jn 3[19-21]. At every stage of the Divine drama we see that those 'who loved darkness rather than light'—the men of perverted mind and crooked ways—turned from Jesus with aversion and sought His destruction. The whole significance of the struggle may be said to have been summed up and symbolized in our Lord's conflict with the Pharisees. Their hostility to Him began in *self-deception*. Wedded to their own ideas and standard of character and duty, they resented His teaching. They could not conceive the possibility of a revision of life in the light of a larger and nobler ideal of righteousness. But the vision of moral beauty must either captivate or blind. Before long the Pharisees brought down on themselves the severest denunciations for their moral obtuseness, duplicity, and hypocrisy (Mt 23, Jn 8[12-59]). The estrangement was complete. To destroy Jesus they now 'plumed up their wills in double knavery' (Iago). In almost every glimpse we get of them they are moving in a murky atmosphere of craft, intrigue, and hate. They do not hesitate to resort to every artifice and stratagem which unscrupulous cunning could suggest. They endeavour, by subtle questions, to entangle Him in His talk (Mt 22[15]) ; they attempt to deceive the people as to His true character (Mk 3[22-30], Jn 9[24]) ; they plot together as to how He may be put to death (Jn 11[53]) ; they enter into a covenant with Judas to betray Him (Mt 26[14. 15]) ; they set up false witnesses, and pervert and misrepresent His teaching (Mt 26[59-62], Lk 23[1]). It was by deceit and guile that they obtained Pilate's permission to crucify Him (Jn 19[12]).

3. We gain a heightened impression of their character and conduct by contrast. While the men of deception and guile hated the Light, we see another class attracted by it. From the beginning of His ministry, Jesus drew to Himself the sincere, the childlike, the men of 'honest and good heart' (Lk 8[15]). The first Apostles of the Lord were by no means exempt from serious faults and frailties of character ; but, with the exception of Judas, they were singularly honest and upright men ; men with a genuine enthusiasm for goodness. One of them drew from Jesus on His first approach the suggestive exclamation, 'Behold an Israelite indeed, in whom is no guile' (Jn 1[47]). In the teaching and training of these first Apostles and disciples, our Lord especially emphasized the necessity of those virtues of character in which the

Pharisees were so singularly deficient (Mt 5[8] 7[1-4] 10[16] 11[25] 18[3], Lk 12[1-3]). In this connexion it is of vital importance to bear in mind Mt 6[22. 23]. There are various degrees and stages of deception and guile, beginning with over-intellectual refinement, and passing finally into deliberate fraud and treachery. But in every case it means the lack of the 'single eye,' of perfect sincerity, and simplicity of nature. And, therefore, if Christian men and women are to keep themselves free, not merely from 'fleshly lusts,' but also from the more subtle forms of 'spiritual wickedness,' they must be continually testing and reviewing their ideals and conceptions of character and conduct in the light of their Master's life and teaching. Unless they do this, the light that is in them will turn to darkness.

'There is, I believe,' says Bishop Gore, 'nothing to which in our time attention needs to be called more than to the fact that conscience is only a *faculty* for knowing God and His will. It is certain, unless it is educated, to give wrong information. *And the way to educate it is to put it to school with the " Light of the world."* Alas! there must be multitudes of respectable and self-enlightened people of whom it is true that the light which is in them is darkness' (*The Sermon on the Mount*, p. 147). The testimony of the late Dr. Dale is not less emphatic. 'I doubt whether most of those who have been formed by the faith and traditions of the Evangelical movement are sufficiently impressed by the necessity of educating the conscience. . . . This partly explains how it is that some Christian people are worse men—morally—than some who are not Christians. The faculty of conscience requires a great deal of education if we are to distinguish between the right and the wrong in all the details of life' (*The Evangelical Revival*, p. 98).

LITERATURE.—In addition to the books already referred to, the reader may consult Newman Smyth, *Christian Ethics*; Prof. Knight, *The Christian Ethic*; F. D. Maurice, *The Conscience and Social Morality*; J. R. Illingworth, *Christian Character*; H. Wace, *Christianity and Morality*; R. W. Church, *Discipline of the Christian Character*.

ARTHUR JENKINSON.

DECREE (Gr. δόγμα, Lk 2[1]).—In the Gospel of Luke, the birth of Jesus at Bethlehem is traced to the fact that a census of the people of Israel was being taken, which made it necessary that Joseph and Mary, who were both of Davidic descent, should go up from their home at Nazareth to the City of David. This census was brought about by the issue of a decree of Cæsar Augustus, that the Roman world should be taxed or registered. Historians find much to question here as to St. Luke's accuracy. Was it likely that Herod's independent kingdom would be included in such a decree? Is there any evidence that such an order on so great a scale was then issued? As to Cyrenius [Quirinius], in whose governorship of Syria this census is said to have taken place, can it be proved that he was twice governor of Syria? He was governor, some 10 years later, when the census took place, which caused the rebellion under Judas of Galilee, in 760 A.U.C. The researches of Wieseler, Zumpt, and W. M. Ramsay (*Was Christ born at Bethlehem?*) have shown, however, that St. Luke's statement is capable of a good defence, and may turn out to have full corroboration. Such a plain historical note, put in, with evident intention, by St. Luke, we should be slow to reject from one who is generally so well informed. See AUGUSTUS, BIRTH OF CHRIST, QUIRINIUS.
DAVID M. W. LAIRD.

DEDICATION, FEAST OF (τὰ ἐγκαίνια).—This Feast was kept by the Jews on 25 Chislev and throughout the week following. The dedication commemorated in it was the dedication of a new altar by Judas Maccabæus in B.C. 164 (1 Mac 4[36-59], 2 Mac 10[1-8], Jos. *Ant.* XII. vii. 6, 7). The old altar of Zerubbabel's temple had been defiled in B.C. 167, when 'an abomination of desolation' was erected upon it (1 Mac 1[54]), and the climax was reached on 25 Chislev, when sacrifices were offered upon this idol-altar standing on the altar of

God (v.[59]). For three years this state of profanation had continued, but when the third anniversary of the desecration came round, the heroic efforts of Judas Maccabæus and his companions had reached such success that they were able to cleanse the Holy Place and to set up a new altar in place of that which had been defiled, spending a week in special services for its dedication; and, in order to commemorate this, Judas Maccabæus ordained 'that the days of the dedication of the altar should be kept in their seasons from year to year by the space of eight days, from the five and twentieth day of the month Chislev, with gladness and joy' (1 Mac 4[59]).

The Feast is mentioned once in the Gospels (Jn 10[22]) as the occasion of a collision between our Lord and the Jews in the temple, when He made the claim, 'I and the Father are one,' and the Jews took up stones to stone Him. The occasion of the incident is full of significance. When the Holy Place was being cleansed in B.C. 164, the question had arisen as to how the old altar ought to be treated, seeing that it had suffered from heathen pollution, and the conclusion reached was that it should not be used any more, but a new one dedicated in its place, and that the old one should be pulled down and its stones stored in a convenient place 'until there should come a prophet to give an answer concerning them' (1 Mac 4[44-46]). On the anniversary of this event, some two centuries later, there stood Christ in the temple courts, and in effect, though not in so many words, the question was actually put to Him whether He was the prophet foretold. 'How long dost thou hold us in suspense?,' they asked, 'If thou art the Christ, tell us plainly' (Jn 10[24]). It was, indeed, a fitting occasion on which to raise the question, since the whole Festival breathed hopes connected with the national deliverance of Maccabæan times, looking forward to another deliverance in the future such as would come with the Messiah. Unhappily the questioners were not sincere, and would not receive the testimony of our Lord, not even when He referred them to His works as proving His claims; and so the matter ended where it began. Had they listened, they would have found the Deliverer whom they were expecting, and incidentally also they would have learned the solution of the old difficulty about the stones of the desecrated altar— that these might lie where they were, being needed no more, for there was being dedicated another Temple to supersede the old (cf. Jn 2[19]).

It is not quite clear how much of St. John's narrative belongs to Dedication, whether the incidents of Jn 9[1]-10[21] happened then, or whether they belong to the Feast of Tabernacles (7[2]). These two Feasts had much in common; in fact, it appears that Dedication was to some extent modelled on Tabernacles (2 Mac 10[6], cf. 1[9]). In particular, the ritual of both included a special illumination, which was so marked at Dedication that, according to Josephus (*Ant.* XII. vii. 7), the Festival was actually called 'Lights.' In either case, therefore, there is special point in our Lord's announcement in Jn 9[5] 'I am the light of the world,' in which He pointed to the brilliant illuminations of the Temple and Jerusalem generally, whether at Tabernacles or Dedication, and claimed that, while these lamps and candles made the city full of light, He Himself was giving light to the whole world.

LITERATURE. — Art. 'Dedication' in Hastings' *DB* and in Encyc. Bibl.; Schürer, *HJP* I. i. 217 f.; Edersheim, *Life and Times of Jesus the Messiah*, ii. 226, *The Temple*, 333 ff.
C. E. GARRAD.

DEFILEMENT.—See PURIFICATION.

DELIVERANCE (ἄφεσις).—The English word does not occur in the Gospels, except in a quotation from the OT (see below), but the Gr. word is found 8 times (in Mt 26²⁸, Mk 1⁴, Lk 3³ 1⁷⁷ 24⁴⁷ it is rendered 'remission' [of sins]; in Mk 3²⁹ 'forgiveness'; in Lk 4¹⁸ *bis* (*a*) 'deliverance' [AV], 'release' [RV], (*b*) [to set] 'at liberty'); while the fact of deliverance underlies all that is recorded of Jesus, and has coloured the entire thought of Christianity. To think of Christ is to think of Him as Saviour. In such utterances as 'The Son of Man is come to save that which was lost' (Mt 18¹¹), and 'the Son of Man is not come to destroy men's lives, but to save them' (Lk 9⁵⁶), we have the keynote of Christ's mission. He sounds it in the beginning when, preaching in the Nazareth synagogue (Lk 4¹⁸), He declares His work to be, in the words of Is 61¹, 'to preach deliverance to captives.' His days are passed in saving men from every slavery that binds them to the transient. This is at the root of all His acts of deliverance—even the healings. When He gives physical renewal to the lame, the diseased, the dumb, the blind, the paralyzed, it is always that they may the easier find spiritual perfection. Moral and spiritual deliverance are often associated with a bodily purification—greatly to the confusion of contemporary traditionalists. They are astonished that He should say to the one sick of the palsy, 'Thy sins are forgiven thee' (Mk 2⁵), or to the leper, 'Thy faith hath made thee whole' (Lk 17¹⁹). In the typical prayer taught to His disciples there is no word about-life's miseries, poverty, or pain : the petition is simply 'Deliver us from evil' (Mt 6¹³, Lk 11⁴) : the soul's need being eternal outweighs the need of mind and body. And we can hardly doubt that, as He looked upon that long and sad procession of the bodily wrecks that came to Him 'at even' (Mk 1³²), the heart of the Missioner in Christ was kindled by the vision of souls that would be set free to fulfil better their purpose of life when the numbed or tortured body was given rest and cure. Conscious of the necessities of daily life, He, better than all others, knows how temporary they are, and lifts His voice continually against the soul's voluntary bondage to things material. 'Seek ye first the kingdom of God' (Lk 12³¹); 'Lay up treasure in heaven' (Mt 6²⁰); 'Beware, and keep yourselves from covetousness' (Lk 12¹⁵); 'If thou wouldst be perfect, go, sell that thou hast, and give to the poor . . . and come, follow me' (Mt 19²¹)—such phrases indicate the deliverance from the world and its anxieties which culminates in the invitation of Jesus—'Come unto me . . . and I will give you rest' (Mt 11²⁸).

The highest of the self-chosen titles ring with deliverance. Jesus calls Himself the Good Shepherd, who will even give His life for the sheep (Jn 10¹¹); He is the Way, the Truth, and the Life (14⁶), leading from earth and time to heaven and eternity ; He is the Light of the World (8¹²), to bring all wanderers safely from darkness and danger to light and safety. The Christian Church has always read in His titles, His words, and His actions this moral and spiritual significance. Christ has been, and is, the Saviour of men from sin and evil rather than from pain and suffering. See FORGIVENESS.   E. DAPLYN.

DEMON, DEMONIACAL POSSESSION, DEMONIACS.—1.

The demonology of the Gospels is based upon beliefs which were current among the Jews previous to the time of Christ ; these beliefs arose gradually, and were ultimately stereotyped in the Talmud. For the proper understanding of Gospel demonology some insight into these Jewish beliefs is indispensable. But the demonology of the Jews was profoundly influenced and coloured, at different times, by Babylonian, Egyptian, Persian, and Greek teaching on the subject, while the beliefs of these highly cultured peoples were developments of

the much earlier conceptions of man in a very much lower stage of civilization, — conceptions which are practically universally prevalent among savage races at the present day. To deal with the subject, therefore, in all its bearings would be impossible here ; it must suffice to give references to a few of the many works which deal with the different branches of this vast subject. Details of Jewish demonology must, however, be given, for it will be seen that they are necessary for a proper understanding of Gospel demonology; added to these will be found some few references to the earlier beliefs upon which they are based.

For the beliefs of primitive man—
Maury, *La Magie et l'Astrologie dans l'antiquité et au moyen-âge*, Paris, 1857 ; Frazer, *The Golden Bough* ², ch. iii., *passim*. London, 1900 ; Lang, *The Making of Religion* ², ch. vii., London, 1900 ; Tylor, *Primitive Culture*, ch. xiv. etc., but the whole work should be studied. Cf. Réville's *Hist. of Religions*, chs. iii.–vi., London, 1884.*

For Assyro-Babylonian beliefs—
Budge, *Assyrian Incantations to Fire and Water*, London, 1883 ; Hommel, *Gesch. Bab. und Ass.* pp. 237–269, 388 ff., Berlin, 1885 ; Jastrow, *Die Rel. Bab. und Ass.* ch. xvi., Giessen, 1902 ff. [this is enlarged from the Eng. tr.] ; A. Jeremias, *Das AT im Lichte des alten Orients*, pp. 218 ff., 330, 340 ff., Leipzig, 1904 ; King, *Babylonian Magic and Sorcery*, London, 1896, *Babylonian Religion and Mythology*, p. 200 ff., London, 1899 ; Lenormant, *La Magie chez les Chaldéens et les origines accadiennes*, Paris, 1875 ; Sayce, *Hibbert Lectures*, v., London, 1887 ; Stübe, *Jüdisch-babylonische Zaubertexte*, Halle, 1895. Many indirect points of importance will be found in Ball's *Light from the East*, London, 1899 ; Morgenstern, 'Doctr. of Sin in the Bab. Rel.' in *Mittheil. der vorderasiat. Gesellsch.* iii., 1905 ; Weber, 'Dämonenbeschwörung bei den Bab. und Assyr.' in *Der Alte Orient*, vii. 4, Leipzig, 1906.

For Egyptian beliefs—
Budge, *Egyptian Magic*, ch. vii., London, 1899 ; Ed. Meyer, *Gesch. des alten Aegyptens*, ch. iii., Berlin, 1887 ; Wiedemann, 'Magie und Zauberei im alten Aegypten,' in *Der alte Orient*, vi. 4, Leipzig, 1905, cf. also, by same author, and in same series, iii. 4, 'Die Unterhaltungslit. der alten Aegypter.'

For Persian beliefs—
Darmesteter, *The Zend-Avesta* (Part i. 'The Vendîdâd '), Fargard xix., xxi. ; Geiger, *Ostiranische Kultur im Alterthum*, § 38, Erlangen, 1882 ; Haug, *Essays on the Sacred Language, Writings and Religion of the Parsis* ³ (tr. by E. H. West), London, 1884 ; Spiegel, *Eranische Alterthumskunde*, vol. ii., Leipzig, 1871–1878 ; Stave, *Ueber den Einfluss des Parsismus auf das Judenthum*, Haarlem, 1898 [see especially the third division, §§ 4, 5. A most helpful book on this particular branch of the subject] ; Windischmann, *Zoroastrische Studien*, pp. 138–148, Berlin, 1863.

For Greek beliefs—
Gruppe, *Die Griechischen Culte und Mythen . . .*, i. pp. 184–196, Leipzig, 1887 ; Maury, *Hist. des Religions de la Grèce antique*, i. pp. 565–581, ii. pp. 91–93, iii. pp. 419–443, Paris, 1857 ; Preller, *Griechische Mythologie* ⁴, under 'Daemonen,' Berlin, 1887 ; Roscher, *Lexikon der Gr. und Röm. Mythologie*, art. 'Daimon' [where full literature on the subject is given], Leipzig, 1884, etc. See also Lobeck, *Agloaphamus*, pp. 695, 696, 1092, Berlin, 1829.

For a *résumé* of Babylonian, Egyptian, Persian, and Greek influence on Jewish demonology, see the remarkably able series of articles by F. C. Conybeare in *JQR* viii. ix. (1896, 1897). See also *Encyc. Bibl.* art. 'Demons,' §§ 7, 11.

2. THE OLD TESTAMENT.—The demonology of the OT is probably somewhat more complex than is sometimes assumed.† The analogy of other races would *prima facie* support the inference that the Israelites also had their beliefs in demons (see Literature below). Much weight cannot be laid on the (not frequent) occurrence of δαίμων and δαιμόνιον in the LXX, as they stand for varying words in the original ; but there are a number of Hebrew expressions which must be connected with demons, at all events as far as the popular imagination was concerned ; these are : רוּחַ רָעָה 'evil spirit,' Jg 9²³, 1 S 16¹⁴ ; רוּחַ עִוְעִים 'spirit of perverseness,' Is 19¹⁴ ; שֵׁדִים 'demons,' Dt 32¹⁷, Ps 106³⁷ ; שְׂעִירִים 'satyrs,' Lv 17⁷, Is 13²¹ 34¹⁴ ; קֶטֶב 'destruction,' conceived of as due to demoniac power, see the whole verse, Ps 91⁶ ; עֲלוּקָה 'female blood-sucker,' Pr 30¹⁵ ; לִילִית 'night-hag,' Is 34¹³. ¹⁴ ; עֲזָאזֵל, Lv 16⁸ᶠᶠ. 'Azazel,' a desert spirit. This last instance clearly shows

---

* There are a number of works on Comparative Religion in which the beliefs in demons and the like are incidentally dealt with ; but a detailed list of these would be inappropriate here.

† 'It is singular that the OT is so free from demonology, hardly containing more than one or two examples thereof' (F. C. Conybeare, *loc. cit.* above).

how firmly embedded in popular imagination was this belief in evil powers of the solitude.* It is true that Babylonian influence during and after the Exile was responsible for much of this;† but that the Israelites from the earliest times, like every other race, peopled the world with innumerable unseen powers, cannot admit of doubt. According to OT conceptions, the evil spirits are not the subjects of some supreme ruler; in the earlier books they are represented as fulfilling the commands of Jehovah in doing harm to men, but later on they seem to enjoy complete independence, though even here the conceptions are not consistent (cf. Job 1⁶⁻¹²). When we come to the Apocrypha, we find that an immense development has taken place; see, e.g., To 3⁶. ⁸ 6⁷. ¹⁷ 8²ᶠ., Bar 4⁷. ³⁵, Wis 2²⁴, Sir 21²⁷; cf. as regards other late literature the Book of Enoch 15. 16. 19. 53. The more important literature bearing on this branch of the subject is as follows:—

W. R. Smith, RS², p. 120ff.; Wellhausen, Reste Arab. Heident.² p. 148 ff.; Doughty, Arabia Deserta, ii. p. 188 ff.; Curtiss, Primitive Semitic Religion To-day, pp. 68, 184, etc.; Nowack, Heb. Arch. ii. p. 186 ff.; Sayce, Hibbert Lectures, 1887, p. 146, etc.; Hastings' DB, the Encyc. Bibl., and the Jewish Encyc. under artt. 'Demons,' 'Lilith,' 'Azazel'; Hamburger's Real.-Encyc., Riehm's HWBA, Herzog's PRE³ under artt. 'Geister,' 'Feldgeister,' 'Dämonen,' etc. Other works that should be consulted are: Baudissin, Studien zur Sem. Volksrelig.; Lagrange, Études sur les rel. Semit.²; Frazer, Golden Bough², ii.

3. Later Judaism.‡— The following are the Talmudic words for demons: מַלְאֲכֵי הַשָּׁרֵת ,מַלְאֲכֵי חבלה, רוחות (πνεύματα), רוּחַ רָעָה (πνεῦμα ἀκάθαρτον), רוּחַ שֵׁד (πνεῦμα δαίμονος). See further below. While it is abundantly clear that external influences have left their marks on Jewish demonology, it is certain that much of the latter was of indigenous growth; the whole system, so immense, so intricate, and in many respects so puerile, is stamped too plainly with the Judaic genius for this to be questioned. Only a very brief summary of the main points can be here indicated.§

(a) Origin of demons.—As has not infrequently been found to be the case with Jewish tradition, there are varying accounts; in this case two distinct traditions exist. According to the one, it is said that the demons were created‖ by God before the world was made; Satan,¶ who is identical with the serpent, is the chief of the demons. They were of both sexes, and their species was propagated through cohabitation with Adam and Eve during a period of 130 years after the Creation. The other tradition is based on Gn 6¹⁻³ (cf. 2 P 2⁴. ⁵); two angels, Assael and Shemachsai, loved the daughters of men, and, forsaking their allegiance to God, descended from heaven to earth; one of these angels returned to heaven and did not sin, but the other accomplished his desire, and his offspring became demons.

(b) The nature of demons.—The general name for all demons is mazzîḳîn (מַזִּיקִין), and this indicates their nature, מַזִּיק = 'one who does harm.'** The head of

* Cf. Whitehouse in Hastings' DB i. 591ᵃ.
† 1b.
‡ By this is meant the period during which the Talmud was in process of formation; it was not completed until about A.D. 500, but the traditions concerning demons and the general teaching on the subject (even in the latest portions) embody conceptions of much earlier date.
§ The details here given have been gathered from a large number of sources which cannot be individually specified; see the Literature at the end of this article.
‖ It is their supposed creation on a Friday which makes this day one of ill-omen.
¶ Satan, according to another account, was created at the same time as Eve; Cain was their offspring (cf. Gn 4¹ where the Heb. קָנָה is not the usual word for begetting). 'Baal-zebul' is also regarded, in the Talmud, as a prince among demons, and is looked upon as the most evil of all evil spirits.
** This is illustrated in Jn 8³⁷. ⁴¹. ⁴⁴ ' Ye seek to kill me . . . ye do the works of your father . . . ye are of your father the devil.'

them is Satan (הַשָּׂטָן = 'the adversary'); it is his aim to mislead men into evil, and then to accuse them before God, hence the further name מקטנגר (κατήγορος) = 'accuser' (cf. Zec 3¹). He is at liberty to enter the Divine presence at all times (cf. Job 1⁶) and accuse men before God; only on the Day of Atonement is he refused admittance. As the angel of death, he is identical with Sammael, who is known also as 'the head of all the Satans.' The kingdom of Satan (cf. Mk 3²³ᶠᶠ.) consists of himself, as head, and an innumerable horde of angels or messengers (מַלְאָכִים) who do his will;* this is the exact antithesis of the kingdom of God † (see, further, Satan). These constitute the first grade of demons, those who were created before the world was made; these were originally in the service of God, but rebelled against Him (cf. Lk 10¹⁸).

There are also demons of a lower grade, those, namely, who came into being during the 130 years after the Creation, and who are semi-human; ‡ they occupied a position between God and man.§ They have the names (besides those given above) of shēdîm,‖ lîlîn ¶ and rûḥîn (Aramaic; Heb. rûḥôth **); the first of these is their commonest name. The head of these lower-grade demons is Asmedai †† (Asmodæus, To 3⁸, cf. 6¹⁴ 8³); they have the power of becoming visible or invisible at will; they have wings, and fly all over the world ‡‡ for the purpose of harming men; in three respects they resemble man, for they eat and drink, they are able to propagate their species, and are subject to death; they also have the power of assuming various forms, but they usually choose that of men, though with the difference that their feet are hens' feet, and they are without shadows; they are very numerous (cf. Mk 5⁹)—7½ millions is said to be the number of them, while elsewhere it is stated that every man has ten thousand on his right hand, and a thousand on his left (cf. Ps 91⁵⁻⁷). They live mostly in desert places (cf. Lk 8²⁹), where their yells can be heard (cf. Dt 32¹⁰ 'howling wilderness'); also in unclean places, where their power is great, e.g. in the בֵּית הכסא; in waterless places (cf. Lk 11²⁴), for water is the means of cleansing; §§ and among tombs‖‖ (cf. Mk 5²), dead bodies being unclean; ¶¶ they are most dangerous to the traveller, more especially if he travels alone; they tend to congregate together (cf. Lk 11²⁶ 8². ³⁰); at certain times they are more dangerous than at others, viz. at mid-day, when the heat is intense, and from sunset to cock-crowing (cf. Ps 91⁵. ⁶, Mk 14⁷², Jn 13²⁷. ³⁰), after which they return to their abode. Unlike angels, who understand only Hebrew (the

* The very term 'the angel of Satan' is used, cf. ἄγγελος Σατανᾶ, 2 Co 12⁷.
† Cf. the dualistic system of the Persians, which has influenced Judaism here.
‡ Among the Greeks the demons stand between men and gods, and all the elements of mythology that were derogatory to the character of the national deities were referred to the demons. Greek influence, therefore, stimulated the growth of Hebrew angelology and demonology (Hastings' DB, art. 'Demons').
§ According to another tradition, these semi-human demons originated thus: God had created their souls, but before He had time to create their bodies the Sabbath dawned; they were thus neither men nor angels, and became demons.
‖ A loan-word from Assyr.-Bab. šidu = 'good or evil genius.'
¶ The Assyr.-Bab. lilitu, 'Lilith.'
** They are also known under the general term רוּחִין בִּישִׁין (πνεύματα πονηρά); Blau holds that originally the רוחות were the spirits of the departed, see Das altjüdische Zauberwesen, p. 14.
†† This is one of the chief signs of Persian influence; Asmedai is borrowed from the Persian demon of lust, Aeshma daeva.
‡‡ Cf. 'the prince of the power of the air' (Eph 2² 6¹²). It was a Persian belief.
§§ Drinking water at night is especially dangerous, presumably because the wrath of the demon would be aroused by the use of water during his privileged period of activity, the night-time.
‖‖ 'Cemeteries were regarded with awe by the ancient Egyptians, because of the spirits of the dead who dwelt in them' (Budge, Egyptian Magic, p. 219).
¶¶ Even at the present day a cohen who looks upon a corpse is unclean.

'holy tongue' (לְשׁוֹן הַקֹּדֶשׁ), demons can understand all languages, for they are active among the Gentiles as well as among the Jews, whereas angels restrict their activity among men to the children of Abraham. The power for harm of the demons is greatest among the sick, among women in childbirth, among brides and bridegrooms, mourners, and those who are about to become teachers; further, those who travel by night, and children who are out after dark are specially subject to their attacks. There is one demon, Shabriri, who makes people blind (cf. Mt 12²²), and there is a special demon of leprosy, and a demon of heart-disease. As emissaries of the angel of death, Sammael (the 'full of eyes,' cf. the Greek *Argus*), men are in constant dread of them (cf. He 2¹⁴⁻¹⁶). It was also believed that demons were able to transfer some of their powers to men, and especially to women; so, for example, the secret of magic drinks, which could harm people in various ways (cf. Mk 16¹⁸), and change them into animals; they could also endow men with the faculty of exercising the 'evil eye' (cf. Mk 7²², see also Sir 31¹³, and cf. 14⁸· ¹⁰, To 4¹⁶), by means of which the good fortune of others could be turned to evil; there is a special formula for use against the 'evil eye.'* There are certain animals in league with the demons (cf. Lk 8³²), such as serpents (cf. Mk 16¹⁸, Ac 28³⁻⁶), bulls,† donkeys,‡ and mosquitoes. The *shēdîm* are male demons; female demons are called *lîlîn*, 'night-spirits,' from the queen of the demons, Lilith (cf. Is 34¹⁴); they have long flowing hair, and are the enemies of children, for which reason special angels have charge of children (cf. Mt 18¹⁰, He 1¹⁴).

(c) *Safeguards against demons.*§—God is the only ultimate protector against demons; but He sends His angels to counteract their deeds, and to help men to withstand their attacks (cf. Mt 18¹⁰, Mk 1¹³). At the same time, God has given to man various means whereby to nullify the machinations of demons. First among these is the saying of the *Shema'* (*i.e.* the Jewish profession of faith contained in Dt 6⁴ff·), because the holy name occurs in it; then, prayer to God (cf. Mk 9²⁹). There are also special formulas which are effective, either for warding off an attack or for throwing off the demoniacal influence, *e.g.* 'The Lord rebuke thee, Satan' (cf. Zec 3², Jude ⁹); Ps 91 is recommended for recitation before going to sleep; a demon may be chased away by repeatedly calling out his name, but uttering one syllable less each time; ‖ obedience to certain commands is also a safeguard, *e.g.* fixing the *mĕzûzāh*,¶ and wearing the

---

* The superstition of the 'evil eye,' the possession of which is regarded as being due to the indwelling of an evil spirit, both in animals and in human beings, is still universally prevalent among the peasantry of all European countries: the writer has personally met with some curious instances in the country districts of Lower Austria.

† This is due to Assyro-Bab. influence: Satan is believed to dance between the bull's horns.

‡ This is due to Egyptian (Typhon-worship) influence; according to Plutarch the ass was considered demoniac (δαιμόνιον) in Egypt, because of its resemblance to Typhon (*de Is. et Os.* 30).

§ In the Talmud there is no word for 'possession'; it is true that an 'evil spirit' is once spoken of as 'dwelling' in a person, but this is the same word as is used for the Shekinah 'taking up its abode with' someone; *Shekinah*, however, in the Talmud is not a personality, but rather an inspiration. A demon, or evil spirit, is said to take hold of a man, to injure him, or to speak to him; there may be one or two possible exceptions, but, generally speaking, demoniacal action is all external to those who are under its influence. This is in striking contrast to the Gospel accounts.

‖ See the use of a 'name' in Stübe, *Jüd.-bab. Zaubertexte*, p. 25, and many further details in Blau, *Das altjüd. Zauberwesen*, pp. 61 ff., 156 ff.; cf. To 6¹⁰ 8³. Exorcism of demons, to whom all sickness was ascribed, was very ancient in Egypt.

¶ A small glass or metal case, containing Dt 4⁶·⁹·¹³·²¹ written on parchment, which is fixed upon the right-hand post of the door of the house and of each room. It was done in obedience to the command in Dt 11²⁰·'

---

tĕphillin; * to eat salt (cf. 'salt of the covenant,' Lv 2¹³, see Mk 9⁴⁷⁻⁵⁰) at and after meals, and to drink water is also efficacious. Demons love the darkness and hate the light (cf. Lk 22⁵³, Eph 6¹², Col 1¹³), hence a lighted torch sends them away, but the light of the moon is most potent in scaring them. On Passover night the demons have no power.

4. THE GOSPELS.—Demons are designated by various names in the Gospels, viz. δαιμόνιον Mt 10⁸ (δαίμων is sometimes found, it would imply more definite personality), πνεῦμα Lk 9³⁹, πνεῦμα ἀκάθαρτον Mt 10¹ (τὸ ἀκάθαρτον πνεῦμα Mt 12⁴³), πνεῦμα πονηρόν Lk 7²¹, πνεῦμα δαιμονίου ἀκαθάρτου Lk 4³³, πνεῦμα ἄλαλον Mk 9¹⁷. In Matthew δαιμόνιον is almost always used; in Mark both δαιμόνιον and πνεῦμα ἀκάθαρτον occur frequently, though the latter predominates; in Luke there is a more varied use; in John the few references to a demon (the plural does not occur) are always in relation to Christ, and the word used is always δαιμόνιον. In the vast majority of cases these expressions are used in the plural form.

(a) *Origin of demons.*—The existence of demons is taken for granted in the Gospels, and nothing is said directly concerning their origin; however, as is shown below, Satan, Beelzebub, and the 'prince of the demons' are one and the same, and Christ speaks of His having seen Satan falling 'as lightning from heaven' (Lk 10¹⁸). This last passage would seem to imply that Satan was in existence before the world was made, which would agree with the one rational tradition on the subject preserved in the Talmud. There are, moreover, also one or two indications in other NT books which support this, *e.g.* 1 Jn 3⁸ 'the devil sinneth from the beginning,' Rev 20² 'the old serpent which is the Devil.'

(b) *The nature of demons.*—That possession often takes the form of a purely physical disorder is clear; yet from the expressions used to designate demons, given above, they were undoubtedly regarded as being morally evil. On the one hand, possession is frequently mentioned in the same category as ordinary sickness (*e.g.* Mt 10¹), dumbness is said to be due to possession (Mt 9³³, Lk 11¹⁴), so too epilepsy (Mt 17¹⁵) and blindness (Mt 12²²); demons are spoken of as taking up their abode in a man without his having, apparently, any choice in the matter (Mk 5¹ff·); it is, moreover, noteworthy, that the wicked (*i.e.* Pharisees, publicans, and sinners) are never spoken of as being possessed (*e.g.* Lk 11³⁹ff· 15¹), and the possessed are permitted to enter the synagogue (Mk 1²³, Lk 4³³), which would hardly have been the case had they been regarded as notoriously evil; another fact which should be taken into consideration in this connexion is our Lord's words to the demons (see below). On the other hand, the evidence is still stronger for possession having been regarded as a moral as well as a physical disorder. Demons are directly referred to as evil (Lk 7²¹ 8²); there are degrees of badness among them (Mt 12⁴⁵), some are merely malignant, some do more physical harm than others (Mt 15²², where κακῶς δαιμονίζεται implies some specially virulent form of possession), some are referred to as being morally as well as physically harmful (Lk 8² πνευμάτων πονηρῶν, 11²⁶); † in one case a demon is such that it can only be expelled by prayer (Mk 9²⁹),‡ which implies that in

---

* 'Head-ornaments': small leathern cases, containing Ex 13¹·¹⁰ 11¹·⁶, Dt 6⁴·⁹ 11¹³·¹⁴ written on parchment; these are bound round the head and left arm by means of long leather straps. This was done in obedience to the command in Dt 11¹⁸. The Greek name (φυλακτήρια) shows that they were regarded as safeguards, *i.e.* against demons (cf. Mt 23⁵). Both this and the custom just mentioned are observed by all orthodox Jews at the present day.

† Cf. also the distinction in Lk 13³² ἐκβάλλω δαιμόνια καὶ ἰάσεις ἀποτελῶ.

‡ The addition of καὶ νηστείᾳ is not well attested.

the generality of cases this was not necessary, and, indeed, we find this to be the case, since in every other recorded instance the *word* was sufficient. Then, again, Beelzebub, the prince of the demons, is identified with Satan (Mt 12[24-30], Mk 3[22-30], Lk 11[15-19], cf. Rev 16[14]), and Satan himself is by name reckoned among the demons in Lk 10[17-20]; and he is the originator of sin in man, as shown by the Temptation, the parable of the Tares (Mt 13[24ff.]), and the sin of Judas (see especially Lk 22[3]). The demons are intangible, incorporeal,* and (if one excepts those passages in which Satan is represented as having been seen, *e.g.* Lk 10[18] 45[ff.]) invisible; 'the NT writers believed that the physical constitution of a spirit, whether holy or impure, was akin to vapour.' The demon enters (εἰσέρχεται) a man at will, and he goes out (ἐξέρχεται) at will (Lk 11[24]), but in most cases he goes out only on compulsion (ἐκβάλλειν); he is also able to take possession of animals (Mk 5[13]); there are good grounds for the supposition that a storm-fiend was believed in, as will be seen by comparing the phraseology of the two following passages: Mk 4[39] ἐπετίμησεν τῷ ἀνέμῳ καὶ εἶπεν τῇ θαλάσσῃ Σιώπα, πεφίμωσο; Mk 1[25] ἐπετίμησεν αὐτῷ ὁ Ἰησοῦς λέγων Φιμώθητι. . . .† Desolate places, such as the desert (Lk 8[29]), or mountainous regions (Mk 5[5]), or among tombs‡ (Mk 5[2]), and waterless places (Lk 11[24]), *i.e.* places to which men come only in small numbers or singly, are those for which demons have a preference. They are represented as congregating together (Mk 5[9], Lk 8[30]), sometimes in sevens§ (Lk 8[2] 11[26], cf. Rev 1[4]); for this reason the plural form is usually employed. In Mk 5[10] the demons beseech Christ not to send them out of the country; they are thus able to speak, or, at all events, so to overmaster their victim as to make his faculties their own (Mk 1[26]). Nothing is said in the Gospels, directly, as to where the permanent home of the demons is,‖ but the 'abyss' is spoken of as, apparently, a place whence they could not return if once banished there; this would, at all events, account for their entreaty not to be banished thither in Lk 8[31]; ¶ they clearly realized that a time of torment was in store for them (Mt 8[29]), and that this torment might take place before the appointed time (Mk 5[7], Lk 8[28]), and so the sight of Christ filled them with dread.

There is nothing in the Gospels to show that demons were believed to be the unquiet spirits of the wicked departed, and the belief that they were heathen gods is equally absent (cf., on the other hand, 1 Co 10[14-22. 28]).

(*c*) *Demoniacal possession, demoniacs.*—The usual term for this is δαιμονιζόμενος (*e.g.* Mt 4[24]), but a number of other expressions for it are found in the Gospels, viz. δαιμονισθείς (Mk 5[18], Lk 8[36]), ἄνθρωπος ἐν πνεύματι ἀκαθάρτῳ (Mk 1[23] 5[2] ἐν = 'in the power of'), ἔχων δαιμόνια (Lk 8[27]), ἄνθρωπος ἔχων πνεῦμα δαιμονίου ἀκαθάρτου (Lk 4[33]), ἐνοχλούμενος ὑπὸ πνευμάτων ἀκαθάρτων (Lk 6[18]), ἐλαυνόμενος ἀπὸ τοῦ δαίμονος (Lk 8[29]), σεληνιάζεσθαι (Mt 4[24]). With but few exceptions those who are said to be possessed are grown-up men; the exceptions

* Cf. Ignatius (*ad Smyrn.* iii. 2), who tells us that Christ said to His disciples after His resurrection: οὐκ εἰμὶ δαιμόνιον ἀσώματον.

† Cf. Conybeare in *JQR* ix. 460; see also an example of a spell addressed to the storm-god in Sayce's *Hibbert Lectures*, p. 317.

‡ Cf. the highly interesting inscription, the text of which is given in Deissmann's *Bibelstudien*, p. 26 ff.

§ Companies of seven evil spirits are not infrequently mentioned in Assyr.-Bab. incantations, *e.g.* 'there are seven wicked sons of the abyss,' which occurs in an incantation to fire; see Budge's *Assyrian Incantations to Fire and Water*; cf. also the 'seven wicked spirits' in ancient Babylonian belief (Sayce, *op. cit.* iii.).

‖ The 'eternal fire' is, according to Mt 25[41], reserved for the devil and his angels; but there is no mention of these in Lk 16[23ff.], where the flame in Hades is spoken of.

¶ In the parallel passages there is no mention of the abyss (cf. Mt 8[31], Mk 5[10]).

are: certain women who had been healed of evil spirits, and Mary Magdalene (Lk 8[2]); the woman who had been bound by Satan for eighteen years (Lk 13[11. 16]); Peter's wife's mother (see below, Lk 4[39]); a boy (Lk 9[39]); and the little daughter of the Syro-Phœnician woman (Mk 7[25]). It is, however, probable that others, besides men, are included in such passages as Mk 1[32ff.], Lk 7[21]. The *signs* of possession may be thus summarized: dumbness (Mt 9[33], Mk 9[18]), dumbness and deafness (Mk 9[25]), blindness and dumbness (Mt 12[22]), savage fierceness (Mt 8[28], Mk 5[4], Lk 8[29]), abnormal strength (Mk 5[4], Lk 8[29]), falling into the fire and water (Mt 17[15]), convulsions (Mk 1[26] 9[20], Lk 4[35]), raving (Mk 5[5]), grinding the teeth (Mk 9[18]), foaming at the mouth (Lk 9[39. 42]). These are all signs of epilepsy (σεληνιάζεσθαι); in Mt 4[24] the σεληνιαζόμενοι are distinguished from the δαιμονιζόμενοι.* Fever would also appear to have been regarded as a sign of possession, for Christ is said to 'rebuke' (ἐπετίμησεν) the fever, the identical word which is frequently used by Him when addressing demons, *e.g.* in the next verse but one to the passage in question (Lk 4[41]). One other sign of possession must be noted, a man who is 'mad,' in the modern sense of being out of his mind, is said to have a demon; this is said of John the Baptist (Mt 11[18]), and of Christ (Jn 10[20]).

A demoniac is spoken of as the dwelling-place of a demon (Mt 12[45]), and a number of demons can dwell in one person (Mt 12[45], Mk 5[9], Lk 8[2]). Sometimes the demon is differentiated from the man possessed (Mk 1[24]), at other times the two are identified (Mk 3[11]); striking in this respect is the passage Mk 5[1-20]; † differentiation is strongly marked when an expression such as that in Lk 6[18] is used: οἱ ἐνοχλούμενοι ἀπὸ πνευμάτων ἀκαθάρτων. Lastly, the same outward signs are at one time spoken of as possession, at another as ordinary sickness (cf. Mt 4[25] 17[15] etc.).

(*d*) *Christ and the demons.*—One of Christ's chief works on earth was to annihilate the power of demons; the demons themselves realize this (Mk 1[24], Lk 4[34], and cf. 1 Jn 3[8]); the destruction of their kingdom was necessary for the establishment of the Kingdom of God. Christ's attitude towards demons may be briefly summed up as follows:— With two exceptions (viz. the case of the woman 'bound by Satan' for eighteen years, Lk 13[11. 16], and that of Peter's wife's mother, Lk 4[39]) no instance is recorded of His laying His hands upon, or in any way coming in direct contact with one who is possessed by a demon. On the other hand, His words are never severe when addressing the possessed; very remarkable, moreover, is the fact that even when He speaks to the demon itself, Christ's words are never angry; He 'rebukes' the demon (Mk 1[25], Lk 4[35]), but the words of rebuke are simply: 'Hold thy peace and come out of him,' or a command that He should not be made known ‡ (Mk 3[12], but cf. Lk 8[39]); on one occasion the request of demons is granted (Mt 8[31. 32] = Mk 5[12. 13] = Lk 8[32]). The power which Christ has over demons is absolute, they are wholly subject unto Him, and are compelled to yield Him obedience (Mk 1[27], Lk 4[41]); that it is an unwilling obedience is obvious, and this is graphically brought out, *e.g.* when it is said of a demon that before coming out of a man it threw him down in the midst (Lk 4[35]).§ The recognition of Christ by demons is of a kind which

* See, further, Delitzsch, *System der bibl. Psychologie*, § 16.

† 'What in the demoniac strikes us most is the strange confusion of the physical and the psychical, each intruding into the proper domain of the other' (Trench, *Miracles, ad loc.*).

‡ For the reason of Christ's not wishing to be made known see Sanday in *JThSt*, v. p. 321 ff., and Wrede, 'Zur Messiaserkenntnis der Dämonen bei Markus,' in *ZNTW* v. [1904] p. 169 ff.

§ Cf. also, in the preceding verse, the exclamation of displeasure, Ἔα (= הָאַח).

is very striking, for He is not only recognized as Jesus of Nazareth, *i.e.* as one born of men, but is also addressed as the 'Holy One of God' (Lk 4³⁴), and as the 'Son of God' (Lk 4⁴¹), *i.e.* as one of Divine nature, and this latter title is emphasized by their knowledge of His power to cast them into the abyss (Lk 8³¹), which also accounts for their fear of Him. The power of Christ over demons is regarded as something new * (διδαχὴ καινή, Mk 1²⁷); this was because the method of exorcism which was familiar to the Jews hitherto was the pronouncing of a magical formula over the possessed. In the Gospels, as a rule, the casting out of a demon is stated without specifying by what means it was done (Mk 1³⁴, Lk 7²¹ 8²), but we learn this from a number of other passages: λόγῳ (Mt 8⁶), ἐν πνεύματι θεοῦ (Mt 12²⁸), ἐν δακτύλῳ θεοῦ (Lk 11²⁰), ἐπετίμησεν (Mt 17¹⁸), ὑπάγετε (Mt 8³²), ἔξελθε (Mk 5⁸, Lk 4³⁵); on one occasion the words are addressed to the mother of a child who is possessed : γενηθήτω σοι ὡς θέλεις (Mt 15²⁸, Mk 7²⁹), the possessed child not being in His presence (Mk 7³⁰), so that His power did not depend on His visible personality.† Christ transfers this power of casting out demons (Mt 10¹, Mk 3¹⁴); when His disciples cast them out it is by virtue of His name ‡ (τῷ σῷ ὀνόματι δαιμόνια ἐξεβάλομεν, Mt 7²², Lk 10¹⁷), but they are not able to do this without faith (Mt 17²⁰); we read, however, in Mk 9³⁸·³⁹ of one who was not a follower of Christ, but who was, nevertheless, able to cast out demons in His name (cf. Mt 12·⁷, Lk 11⁹). In Mk 3²² the scribes say of Christ that 'he hath Beelzebub,' and in 3³⁰ occur the words, 'because they said, He hath an unclean spirit.' That Beelzebub the 'prince of the demons' and 'unclean spirit' are synonymous with 'demon' cannot be disputed. Christ is thus declared to be possessed ; § nevertheless, it is not this which calls forth His words, 'whosoever shall sin against the Holy Ghost hath never forgiveness' (v.²⁹), but the fact that He was accused of being in league with Beelzebub ; this is important, as it would seem to support the theory, which is elsewhere adumbrated in the Gospels, that possession was not necessarily, *per se*, a moral disorder ; there is also reason to believe that at least some forms of possession were regarded as mental derangement : Christ speaks of John the Baptist having been looked upon as possessed (Mt 11¹⁸, Lk 7³³); he was so regarded, because there seemed to be something eccentric about his behaviour ; in Jn 7²⁰ Christ is said to be possessed by a demon, because He said they sought to kill Him ; Jn 8⁴⁸·⁴⁹, where it is said : 'Thou art a Samaritan and hast a demon,' points to the fact that a man who was possessed was despised because he spoke what was deemed nonsense ; also, the supposed connexion between possession and mental derangement is pointedly brought out in Jn 10²⁰ 'He hath a demon and is mad.' While fully realizing that the Fourth Gospel stands by itself, it must be conceded that it contributes one very important consideration, especially as the idea of possession found there is not without parallel in the Synoptic Gospels, as shown above. The belief that possession was a species of mental derangement, wholly unconnected with the question of morality, is what the Fourth Gospel teaches ; but then it must be remembered that 'the devil' and 'Satan,' who are identified ‖ (as in the Synoptic

* The method was new ; cf., as regards Christ's general teaching, Mt 7²⁸·²⁹ 'They were astonished at his teaching ; for he taught them as one having authority, and not as the scribes.'
† Cf. the case of grievous bodily sickness also cured, though Christ was not present (Lk 7²ᶠᶠ.).
‡ Cf. Sayce, *Hibbert Lectures*, p. 302ff. ; Conybeare in *JQR* ix. 583 ff.
§ In the parallel passages (Mt 9³⁴ 12²⁴ᶠᶠ·, Lk 11¹⁴ᶠᶠ·) there is no mention of Christ being possessed, the accusation is that He cast out demons by Beelzebub.
‖ Cf. Jn 13² ὁ διάβολος with 13²⁷ ὁ Σατανᾶς.

Gospels), are differentiated from 'demon'; whereas, according to the Synoptics, all belong to the same category, Satan being the chief (Mt 12²⁴). The passage Jn 10²⁰ receives additional significance in the light of the Heb. equivalent, compared, *e.g.*, with Hos 9⁷ 'the man that hath the spirit is mad' (אִישׁ הָרוּחַ מְשֻׁגָּע). Delitzsch (*NT in Heb.* renders Jn 10²⁰ δαιμόνιον ἔχει καὶ μαίνεται, by שֵׁד לוֹ הוּא וּמְשֻׁגָּע, the last words of which should be compared with the rendering of the Pesh. ܡܫܰܢܰܝ

ܕܰܝܘ̈ܐ.*

Gospel demonology may, therefore, be briefly summed up thus :—
(1) Demons are under a head, Satan ; they form a kingdom. (2) They are incorporeal, and generally, though not necessarily, invisible. (3) They inhabit certain places which they prefer to others. (4) They tend to live in groups. (5) They have names, and are sometimes identified with their victims, at other times differentiated from them. (6) They are the cause of mental and physical disease to men, women, and children. (7) They can pass in and out of men, and even animals. (8) More than one can take possession of a man at the same time. (9) Christ made it one of His chief aims to overthrow this kingdom, and set up His own in its place. (10) He cast out demons through His own name, or by His word. (11) He could delegate this power, which was regarded as something new. (12) He never treats the possessed as wilful sinners, which is in strong contrast to His words to the scribes and Pharisees. (13) Only on the rarest occasions does He come into direct contact with the possessed. (14) His Divine and human natures are recognized by demons. (15) At His second coming the members of this kingdom are to be condemned to eternal fire.

5. In endeavouring to reach some definite conclusions on this difficult subject of Gospel demonology, it is well to place certain considerations in juxtaposition. On the one hand, the history of mankind shows that a superstitious belief in evil-disposed demons, to whom every imaginable untoward circumstance is attributed, is universal ; there is a remarkable similarity, in essence, in the demonology of all times ; it stretches, from the earliest times to the present day, like a great chain along the course of human history. The demonology of the Gospels shows itself, in many respects, unmistakably akin to this universal superstition. It is impossible to ignore the fact that, in its broad outlines, Gospel demonology is in accordance with the current Jewish beliefs of the time. It will, moreover, have been noticed, from the details given above, that the data in the Gospels themselves are inconsistent. Again, the way in which in the Gospels much is attributed to the action of demons (deafness, dumbness, etc.), looks naïve to modern eyes. There is also this further consideration which conspires in discrediting the Gospel accounts on the subject, viz. that those who at the present day believe in the continued activity of demons are almost invariably such as are on a low stage of civilization, or they are peasants in country districts who have but rare opportunities of coming into contact with cultured people. And, lastly, account must be taken of the fact that very few could be found nowadays who would claim to point to any instance in their experience of the existence of demoniacal possession ; thus the only parallels to Gospel demonology would have to be sought among the acknowledged super-

* The Syro-Hex., following the LXX, has a doublet, but the idea of madness is brought out in both.

stitions of the Middle Ages, and the like. These considerations tend to the conclusion that the Gospel accounts of demons cannot be regarded as essentially different from the innumerable accounts from other sources.

But there is a second set of considerations, and to ignore these would be most unscientific. When the whole chain of demonology, from primitive times to the present day, is considered, it is quite impossible for an unbiassed mind to be blind to the fact that, in spite of many points of similarity and even of essential identity, the demonology of the Gospels offers something *sui generis*; one becomes conscious of the fact that this link in the long chain is very different from all the other links. Another thing that strikes the student of the subject as very remarkable is, that Gospel demonology and the current Jewish belief are not more alike than is the case; they agree in so many respects, that one feels that only the existence of some extraordinary factor prevents their being wholly identical. But more than this, the dissimilarity between the two is just as striking as their points of similarity: in the one there is nothing eccentric, nothing done for effect, or for self-glorification,* there is no casting out of demons for the sake of exhibiting power, there is none of the 'wonder-working' which characterizes other systems; one object, and one only, runs through the whole of the accounts of the casting out of demons, namely, the alleviation of human suffering. To give in any detail the points of difference between the general subject of demonology and Gospel demonology would be impossible here, but, when the great mass of facts has been studied, the contrast between the two can be compared only to the contrast between folly and seriousness. Another conviction to which one is compelled in contemplating Gospel demonology in its broad outlines is that it is connected in the closest possible manner with the subject of sin; the *symptoms* of the 'possessed' in the Gospels are such as are common to humanity, and nobody doubts the accuracy with which these are described; the real *crux* arises when their cause has to be determined; this is ascribed by the compilers of the Gospels to the action of demons, *i.e.* to an evil agency; nowadays the same symptoms are ascribed to different causes—broadly speaking, to 'natural causes'; but may it not be that behind both theories there lies a deeper cause, the principle of Evil, occupying a vacant place in individuals which they themselves have provided by the abandonment of their self-control? There are cases in the Gospels to which this would not apply, but it is worth taking into consideration in contemplating the subject as a whole. It is well also to remember that the advance of Modern Science, especially in the domain of Psychology, has revealed problems whose most important result is to show how extremely little we know about such things as 'secondary personality,' the 'subliminal self,' 'change of control,' etc. etc.—in a word, how hidden still are the secrets of the region of the supersensuous.

Upon a subject that bristles with so many difficulties nobody would wish to dogmatize; no conclusion that has been reached is free from serious objections, and the same is the case with that here offered:—

Christ saw in the case of every 'possessed' victim a result of sin, not necessarily through the co-operation of the victims;† sin He saw embodied in 'Satan,' who is identified with 'demon' (see above); he was the personification of the principle of Evil, which was manifested in men in a variety of ways. When Christ 'exorcized' a 'demon,' He, by His Divine power, drove the evil out, and at the same time obliterated the visible results of sin. When the words and acts of Christ came to be written down, they were not always understood; * they were, no doubt, in their broad outlines, correctly reproduced; but what more natural than that they should be told in accordance with the ideas then current? Not the essence but the form differed from the actuality.

LITERATURE. — Blau, *Das altjüdische Zauberwesen*, Strassburg, 1898 [most interesting and useful]; Brecher, *Das Transcendentale, Magie und magische Heilarten im Talmud*, Vienna, 1850 [for gaining an insight into the connexion between demons and magic, according to Rabbinical notions, this book is indispensable]; Franz Delitzsch, *System der biblischen Psychologie*, Leipzig, 1855; Edersheim, *The Life and Times of Jesus the Messiah*[5], chs. xiv. xxv., London, 1890; Eisenmenger, *Entdecktes Judenthum*, Dresden, 1893; Kohut, in *Abhandlungen fur die Kunde des Morgenlandes*, vol. iv., issued by the *ZDMG*, Leipzig, 1859, etc.; Schubert, *Die Krankheiten und Storungen der menschlichen Seele*; Stube, *Jüdisch-babylonische Zaubertexte* Halle, 1895; Trench, *Notes on the Miracles*[14], pp. 161–175; Weber, *Jüdische Theologie auf Grund des Talmud und verwandter Schriften*[2] (esp. § 54), Leipzig, 1897 [this most important work is an improved edition of the earlier *System der altsynagogalen palästinischen Theologie*]; Wrede, 'Zur Messiaserkenntnis der Damonen bei Markus,' in *ZNTW*, July 1904; Winer, *Biblisches Realworterbuch*, Riehm, *HWBA*, Hastings' *DB*, the *Ency. Bibl.*, under 'Demon,' etc.

For the subsequent beliefs and superstitions about demons prevalent during the Middle Ages, and even up to the present day, a few references may be given out of a large number of works dealing with the subject :—

In the arts. in *JQR* by Mr. Conybeare, already referred to, there is an admirable survey of the beliefs of the Church Fathers (viii. pp. 594–608, ix. pp. 59–72). Another work of M. Maury, who is one of the chief authorities on the subject, is his *Croyances et légendes du moyen-âge*, Paris, 1896. Andrew Lang deals with the psychology of the subject in his *Making of Religion*, mentioned above; so too Delitzsch, *System* . . ., also referred to above. Two other books are, Nevins' *Demon Possession and allied Themes*, New York, 1895; and Wall's *Devils*, a popular sketch of demons in ecclesiastical art, with good illustrations (London, 1904).

W. O. E. OESTERLEY.

DEN (Mt 21^{13} = Mk 11^{17} = Lk 19^{46} σπήλαιον [λῃστῶν]; elsewhere in the Gospels only Jn 11^{38} to describe the tomb of Lazarus, ἦν δὲ σπήλαιον).—In estimating the meaning of our Lord's declaration that the Temple had been made a den *or* cave of robbers, the immediate occasion of the words must be kept in view. It was the feast of the Passover, and the Temple courts were crowded by those who sold sheep, oxen, and pigeons, while the money-changers also carried on their trade. As no trace is found in the OT of such a market existing, it may be supposed it sprang up some time after the Captivity. It would plead for justification the needs of the new condition of the nation. Foreign Jews would thus be able to obtain on the spot both the Temple half-shekel required by the Law (Ex 30^{13}), and also animals necessary for sacrifice, probably with the additional advantage that the latter would have an official guarantee of Levitical fitness for sacrifice, which must be obtained for any animal purchased elsewhere.

The profits from these sources were enormous. It has been calculated that the annual income derived from money-changing can hardly have been less than £8000–£9000, while the sale of pigeons is specially referred to as furnishing alone a large annual income. These profits appear to have been largely, if not entirely, appropriated by the priests. Certain booths are frequently mentioned as belonging to the 'sons of Ḥanan' (Annas), and appear to have existed until about three years before the destruction of Jerusalem, when they were destroyed. Besides the mere fact that the Temple was made a house of merchandise (Jn 2^{16}), many passages in the Rabbinical writings appear to indicate that the Temple market was notorious for dishonest dealings, upon which passages it has been

---

* Cf. Christ's rebuke to His disciples in Lk 10^{20}.
† It is necessary to read Ro $7^{7\cdot25}$ and 1 Co $10^{14\cdot22}$ $11^{17\cdot32}$, esp. vv.$^{30\cdot 32}$, in this connexion.

* This was often the case during Christ's lifetime (see Mk 8^{21} 9^{32}, Lk 9^{45}, Jn 3^{10} etc. etc.).

remarked (*Speaker's Com. in loc.*) that the spaces in the court were probably let out to traffickers at an exorbitant rate. The remembrance of this state of things gives new force to the quotation from Jer 7[11] here used by our Lord.

Josephus (*c. Apion.* ii. 24) writes: 'The Temple ought to be common to all men, because He is the common God of all'; but, far from its being thus, it had become the possession of a few. 'Ye gather together here money and animals, as robbers collect their booty in their den' (Fritzsche, quoted by Lange).

Those who ought to have been the first to teach others the sacredness of the place had seized upon it, as robbers would seize some den or cave in the mountains, in which they might maintain their unity for the purpose of spoil. See, further, art. TEMPLE in vol. ii.

LITERATURE. — Edersheim, *Life and Times of Jesus the Messiah*, also *The Temple*, etc.; Farrar, *Life of Christ*; Derenbourg, *Hist. de Pal.*; and the *Comm. ad loc.*

J. B. BRISTOW.

DENARIUS.—See MONEY.

DENIAL.—The verb ἀρνεῖσθαι, 'to deny,' is used in contrast with ὁμολογεῖν, 'to confess' (Mt 10[32f.] ‖ Lk 12[8f.], where ἀπαρνεῖσθαι is also employed; cf. 2 Ti 2[12], where ἀρνεῖσθαι is used specially of the verbal denial of Christ, due to fear of suffering). As confession of Christ (wh. see) is the outward expression of personal faith in Him, so denial of Him is (1) the withholding, (2) refusing, or (3) withdrawing such confession. In the first of these categories are included those who, like some members of the Sanhedrin (Jn 12[42]), believed on Christ, but did not confess Him; in the second, those who did not believe on Him, and as a natural result did not confess Him; and, in the third, those who have confessed Him, but, through fear of men, deny Him in times of persecution. It is the third class to which reference is made in Mt 10[33] 'Whosoever shall deny me before men, him will I also deny before my Father which is in heaven.' Open disavowal of faith in Christ ('before men') is taken as a clear indication of the offender's attitude towards Him, and eventuates in his exclusion from the blessings of the perfected kingdom in heaven. Such disavowal must be deliberate and persistent, and is to be distinguished from a momentary lapse of personal weakness, like that of Simon Peter, which by timely repentance became the means of strengthening his character, and enabling him to strengthen others (Lk 22[32]). In the narrower and stricter sense, therefore, denial means public apostasy from faith in Christ, the guilt of which is visited with a punishment in exact correspondence with it.

1. The discourse in which the great warning against denial is found (Mt 10[17-33]), and which was addressed to the Twelve in view of their Apostolic mission after the Resurrection, evidences its lateness by the serious situation depicted, in which exposure to the severest forms of persecution is contemplated, including punishment in the synagogues, arraignment before Gentile tribunals, and death itself. It must belong at earliest to the period of growing opposition, and has been assigned to as late a date as the close of the ministry. The Second Evangelist places a portion of it in the eschatological discourse spoken on Olivet to the four disciples on the Wednesday or Thursday of Passion-week (Mk 13[9-13]). Christ no doubt foretold almost from the outset of His ministry that His disciples would be exposed to reproach and obloquy (Mt 5[11f.]), but the first intimation of serious opposition synchronizes with the first plain intimation of His own death (Mk 8[34f.]). It was in prospect of the undisguised hostility awaiting them in connexion with their Apostolic mission that Christ cautioned His disciples against the danger of denial.

If He suffered death for claiming to be the Messiah (Mk 14[61-64]), it is evident that those who afterwards proclaimed Him as such must run the risk of sharing a fate like His.

2. Due stress must be laid on the fact that the object of denial is the *person* of Christ, not simply His message or His words, which in any case derive their ultimate authority from His person. It is admitted that 'His earlier demand that men should fulfil the condition of participation in the Kingdom of God by repentance and trust in the message of salvation, became narrowed down afterwards to the demand that men should unite themselves to Him as the Messiah, and cleave fast to Him in trust' (Wendt, *Teaching*, ii. 308). But the force of the concession is quite destroyed by the further representation that 'union to the person of the Messiah is nothing else than adherence to the message of the Kingdom of God brought by Him' (p. 310.) This is to reduce the person of the Messiah to a compendious formula for His teachings, and ignores the fact that, after the great confession at Cæsarea Philippi, Christ grounded on His Messiahship a claim to absolute self-surrender and self-sacrifice (Mk 8[34f.]). Devotion to Himself is henceforward made the supreme test of discipleship, and the withdrawal of such devotion seals the doom of the offender hereafter. We are in a region where personal relations and obligations are everything; where the injury done by denial is not measured by the rejection of a message merely, but by the wound inflicted on One who has rendered unparalleled services.

3. It is the rupture, though but for a moment, and without deliberate intention, of tender, intimate, personal ties by the act of the disciple, that renders the great denial of the chief Apostle so affecting an incident (Mt 26[69ff.], Mk 14[54. 66-72], Lk 22[54ff.], Jn 18[15-18. 25-27]). His fall is the more surprising by reason of Christ's clear announcement of it beforehand, and Peter's strong protestations of fidelity (Mt 26[34f.] ‖ Mk 14[30f.], Lk 22[33f. 61], cf. Jn 13[37f.]). · Deep as the fall was, however, care must be taken not to exaggerate its criminality. That the thrice-repeated denial was due to want of faith or devotion on the Apostle's part, there is nothing to show. It was indeed ardent attachment to Christ that led him, after his hasty retreat, to follow at a distance, and seek admission to the house of Annas, before whom the preliminary examination of Christ took place. He was determined to keep near his Master, and it was doubtless this very determination that betrayed him into sin. When challenged in the porch by the maid who kept the door, he gave an evasive reply (Jn 18[17], Mk 14[68]), fearing that to own his discipleship would lead to his exclusion from the premises. When taunted later on with being a disciple by the rough servants gathered round the fire in the courtyard (Jn 18[18. 25]), he denied it in more categorical fashion, hoping thereby to evade further remarks, and avoid the summary ejection which would have followed the detection of his previous falsehood. Having travelled so far on the downward path, it became well-nigh impossible to turn back, and on being charged by one of the kinsmen of Malchus with having been with Christ in the garden at the moment of the arrest, overcome by fear that he might be called to account for his rash act, he denied his Master for the third time, and backed up his denial with oaths and curses (Jn 18[26f.], cf. Mt 26[74]). It has been suggested that his falsehoods would sit lightly on his conscience, on the ground that he felt justified in giving no kind of information about himself or his Master which might compromise a movement which he imagined was but temporarily arrested. He probably experienced no scruples in deceiving his Master's enemies, especially as this seemed the only way of carrying out his purpose to keep as near to Christ as possible without risk of detection. But when all due allowance is made for the excellency of his motives, his conduct is utterly indefensible. When he affirmed so confidently that he was ready to go to death, what he thought of was a public testimony to Christ, for whom he counted no sacrifice too great. 'A great deed of heroism is often easier than loyalty in small things,' and Peter, who had courage enough to defend his Master at the cost of his life, displayed lamentable weakness in a minor emergency. The sound of cock-crow, announcing the approach of dawn, was a painful reminder that he had proved lacking in genuine fidelity, and false to the pledges so recently given. But that his love to Christ still remained the same, was abundantly evidenced by his subsequent act of sincere contrition.

W. S. MONTGOMERY.

DEPENDENCE.—1. The feeling which impels men to look up to, and depend upon, a Power higher and other than themselves is essentially human, universal, and, in the position which it occupies in their lives, most prominent. It supplies them with an intuitive hope, which is quickened by their sense of need and helplessness, that this Power will supply their wants, and fill the mysteriously void places of their being. This hope finds expression in the universal desire for communion with that Power by prayer, worship, sacrifice, and so on. Some of the most beautiful aspirations which breathe out of the Psalms of the Jewish Church are the outcome of men's longing after and dependence upon God (cf. Ps 42. 73²¹⁻²⁸ 108. 139, etc.); and when the Psalmist sings 'My soul cleaveth (דָּבְקָה, LXX ἐκολλήθη) after thee' (Ps 63⁸), he is putting into words, suited to his own individual experience, the same idea which St. Paul says, in his address to the assembled Athenians, is universally human (ζητεῖν τὸν θεόν, Ac 17²⁷). A direct relationship, which is personal, is everywhere in the OT postulated (cf. e.g. Gn 5²²· ²⁴ 6⁹, Mal 2⁶, Am 3³) as existing between Jehovah and His people. On the one side is the Supreme Personal Will which projects Itself into a world of created intelligences, either in the form of law objectively revealed (Dt 5², cf. the prophetic formula, 'Thus saith the Lord'), or in that form which, in the words of the writer of the Fourth Gospel, 'coming into the world lightens every man' (Jn 1⁹, cf. Ro 2¹⁵, Jer 31³³). On the other, there is the being made in 'His own image' (Gn 1²⁶ᶠ· 5¹ 9⁶, cf. 1 Co 11⁷, Ja 3⁹, Sir 17³, Wis 2²³), whose life, touching His life at all points, owes its existence to the continued exercise of His will (cf. Ac 17²⁸).

We have here, not the antithesis of eternal and temporal, finite and infinite, so much as an emphatic synthesis effected by a close personal relationship, in which we may say consists all that is essentially true in religion. The error into which Schleiermacher, for example, fell when he made religion consist in a feeling of dependence (Abhängigkeit) on a Higher Power is obviously an error of defect, as it leaves out of account the element of Personality just referred to (see his Christliche Glaube). At the same time it would be a mistake no less fatal to eliminate this feeling from the domain of man's spiritual life; for it is one of the ultimate realities of our being, finding expression in a variety of ways according to the individual life which is lived.

2. The sense of dependence upon God is seen most clearly and fully in the life of Jesus Christ. It is focussed, as it were, in the story of the Incarnation, and in the circumstances in which the Incarnate life was passed from childhood onwards. In this, as in other respects, that life is the epitome of all that is true in the life of man. The time when

the foreordained 'mystery of God' (1 Co 2¹, cf. Eph 3³⁻⁵ 6¹⁹, Col 1²⁶ᶠ·) should be revealed, depended on the wisdom and will of the Father (Gal 4⁴, cf. Mk 1¹⁵). The manner of its revelation was conditioned by the laws of motherhood ('made of a woman, made under law,' Gal 4⁴, cf. Lk 2⁶, where the natural law of parturition is referred to explicitly), and the safety of the Divine Child's life depended on the vigilance of Joseph (Mt 2¹³⁻¹⁵) no less than on the maternal tenderness and love of His mother. His education was that of a Jewish child in a pious Jewish home, where the language spoken was the current 'Hebrew' or Palestinian Aramaic (see a very useful article, 'The Dialects of Palestine in the time of Christ,' by Ad. Neubauer in Studia Biblica, vol. i. pp. 39–73 [Oxford]; with this we may compare a similar discussion by J. B. Mayor in his Epistle of St. James), which was Jesus' mother-tongue (cf. Mk 3¹⁷ 5⁴¹ 7³⁴ 14³⁶ 15³⁴, Jn 1⁴², Mt 5²²). In point of fact, it is not too much to say that He was governed in His earthly life, physical and intellectual, by the ordinary laws of nature. If He violated these laws, even in the interests of His work, He had to pay the penalty which nature inexorably demands (cf. Mt 4²=Lk 4², Mk 11¹²=Mt 21¹⁸, Jn 4⁶ 19²⁸, and Mt 8²⁴).

In the moral sphere we observe the same phenomenon, which finds a prominent place in the Christological teaching of the Epistle to the Hebrews. Even as we are, so is He, 'compassed with infirmity' (5²). Like ourselves in all things, 'apart from sin,' He suffered from the assaults of temptation (4¹⁵, cf. 2¹⁸). He had, as we have, to learn slowly and with pain the moral virtue of obedience, notwithstanding the unique character of His Sonship (5⁸). In Him also the law, by which alone progress is assured, exacted implicit submission, although the lesson was hard (2¹⁰, cf. 5⁹, 7²⁸). That Jesus was fully conscious of the necessity of this bitter experience is seen from His own saying, in which He defies the threatened persecution of Herod, and which contains the same verb as is used in Hebrews, to denote the final cause of His sufferings (τελειοῦμαι, Lk 13³²).

Even in the sphere of His mental life we find Him depending on the laws which govern intellectual growth universally. Side by side with His physical growth, as the Lukan narrative tells us, there was a corresponding expansion of His intellectual and spiritual faculties ('Ιησοῦς προέκοπτεν τῇ σοφίᾳ καὶ ἡλικίᾳ καὶ χάριτι κ.τ.λ., Lk 2⁵², with which we may compare the words in v.⁴⁰, where the participle πληρούμενον in conjunction with σοφία is a distinct assertion of continuous and gradual development). Nor have we any just reason to suppose that the operation of this law ceased at any given stage in His life. On the score of credibility it will be found as difficult to believe that gradual growth along these lines ever found a place in Jesus' life, as to believe that it entered so completely into the warp and woof of His experience that it accompanied Him all through His life, even to the very end (cf. art. 'The Baptism, Temptation, and Transfiguration: A Study,' in Ch. Quart. Rev., July 1901). There is no period in the life of Jesus when we can say, 'at this point He ceased to learn, or to advance towards perfection' (τελείωσις, cf. 'Additional Note' on He 2¹⁰ in Westcott's The Epistle to the Hebrews). His lesson was only finally 'learned' in its entirety when, yielding Himself unreservedly into His Father's hands, He became 'obedient unto death, yea, the death of the cross' (Ph 2⁸), and 'the author (αἴτιος) of eternal salvation' (He 5⁹) to all who are so far partakers of His Life that they too learn the meaning of perfect obedience (ὑπακοή). See art. ACCOMMODATION, p. 15.

In close connexion with what we have been saying is the repeated disavowal by Jesus of all intention to assert His own will (cf τὸ θέλημα τὸ ἐμον, Jn 5³⁰ 6³⁸, see also Mt 26³⁹. ⁴²=Mk 14³⁶ =Lk 22⁴²). His complete dependence on the will of His Father may, perhaps, suggest fewer difficulties to the student of Jesus' life than His continuous insistence in setting that will, as it were, over against and above His own. At the same time we must remember that by this differentiation He deliberately reminds us, again and again, how complete His subordination, in the sphere of His human existence, has become, not only in word and deed, but also in His inner life of thought and intention. He has laid aside the power of doing anything 'of himself' (Jn 5³⁰), because the will of His Father is for Him the object of thought and loving service (ὅτι . . . ζητῶ . . . τὸ θέλημα τοῦ πέμψαντός με). The accomplishing of the work (4³⁴) which that will has put before Him is the nourishing sustenance (ἐμὸν βρῶμα) which is necessary for the building up of His life. 'The will of God' (τὸ θέλημα τοῦ θεοῦ) is the sovereign objective of Jesus' life, and perfect conformity to it in every point is the goal of His life's work. Looking over the uses of the word θέλημα in the NT, we find that it is almost universally used of the carrying out *by others* of the purposes of God, the accomplishment in the world of that which the Divine will ordains for execution (for other usages of this word, see Jn 1¹³, Lk 23²⁵, etc.). It is in this sense pre-eminently that the word is used in connexion with Jesus' work (cf. Jn 6³⁹ᶠ., where the will of God, in the redemption of humanity, is the object of the Incarnation, and furnishes the work which Jesus avowedly sets Himself to accomplish). We are thus not surprised at the transference of the words of Ps 40 to the work of Christ by the writer of the Epistle to the Hebrews (Ἰδοὺ ἥκω τοῦ ποιῆσαι τὸ θέλημά σου, He 10⁹), who sees in this passage the aptest illustration of the object of Jesus' life.

3. This protracted and willing subordination on the part of Jesus had its final reward in that perfect harmony between His own and His Father's will, which left no room, in the sphere of His human activity, for anything but the most complete community of interests. Looking at this side of His life, we can appreciate the element in His teaching, so constantly emphasized, which insists on the lowliest and most complete self-surrender in others. He, the Man Jesus, succeeded in bringing His human will into absolute conformity with that of His Father, and so He teaches men to pray, 'May thy will be done . . . on earth' (Mt 6¹⁰, cf. 26⁴²=Lk 22⁴²). Our right to participate in the privileges of that family relationship which Jesus is not ashamed to own (He 2¹¹) depends on the fidelity with which we enter, by our actions, into the spirit guiding His own work (see Mt 12⁵⁰). This is the touchstone by which men shall be ultimately tested, and by which their right of entry into the Kingdom of heaven shall be decided (Mt 7²⁰).

4. Nor must we forget that this phenomenon is observable in Jesus' relation to His fellow-men. And here it is significant to note that, although always willing to exercise the prerogatives of His Divine Sonship in favour of the distressed, yet He never works a miracle on His own behalf. If He is hungry or thirsty, He trusts to the kindness and goodwill of others (Jn 4⁷ 19²⁸ᶠᶠ., Mt 21¹⁸ᶠ. 4²ᶠᶠ., Mk 1¹³. ³¹). The lack of sympathy has a marked effect on the power of His ministrations ('And he could there do no mighty work,' Mk 6⁵), and He recognizes that, in certain cases at least, the exercise of His power of miraculous healing may be marred or promoted by the absence or presence of a sympathetic trust on the part of those with whom He is dealing ('All things are possible to him that believeth,' Mk 9²³, see Mt 9²⁸ᶠ, with which we may also compare a remarkable extension, in the application of this rule to the sufferer whose friends stand sponsor, as it were, for his faith and trust [τὴν πίστιν αὐτῶν, Mt 9²]). Indeed, the presence of a captious spirit in His hearers moved Him, on more than one occasion, to indignation or grief (cf. μετ' ὀργῆς, Mk 3⁵ ; ἐμβριμώμενος, Jn 11³⁸), feelings which were also aroused in His breast by any action tending to stifle in others the expression of their trust in, and sympathy with, His work and Person (cf. the emphatic verb ἠγανάκτησεν, Mk 10¹⁴).

Closely allied to this is the impatience which Jesus shows with the spiritual dulness of His disciples (Mk 9¹⁹, Jn 14⁹ 20²⁹,

Mt 26¹⁰, Mk 8¹⁷. ²¹ etc.). It appears sometimes as if, in His eagerness to discover the smallest germs of spiritual reciprocity, He would gaze into their very hearts. In all the four Gospels the word βλέπειν (with compounds) is used to denote this anxiety on the part of Jesus (cf. e.g. ἐμβλέψας αὐτῷ. Mk 10²¹ ; ἐμβλέψας αὐτοῖς, Mk 10²⁷, Mt 19²⁶ ; see also Jn 14² and the pathetic use of the same verb Mk 22⁶¹ (ἐνέβλεψεν τῷ Πέτρῳ). For the use of the verb περιβλέπεσθαι, which is almost confined to St. Mark, compare Mk 3⁵=Lk 6¹⁰, Mk 3³⁴ 10²³. Even when dealing with the question of the profound, vital union of Himself with those who believe in Him, Jesus is fully conscious that His work is conditioned by their attitude to Him. The imperative clause 'abide in me' (Jn 15⁴) is supplemented by another clause, which may be interpreted as containing a contingent promise, 'I will on that condition abide in you,' or, more probably, as a complementary imperative, 'permit me to abide in you.' In either case it is true to say that Jesus here recognizes and teaches the doctrine that 'the freedom of man's will is such that on his action depends that of Christ' (see Plummer's 'St. John' in *Cambridge Greek Testament, in loc.*).

5. Not the least remarkable feature in the teaching of Jesus is that on which the writer of the Fourth Gospel lays particular stress. The union between Him and the Father is so complete, that He describes it as a mutual indwelling or coexistence (Jn 10³⁸ 14¹⁰ᶠ. ²⁰). He derives from the Father, as the ultimate source of each (Jn 16¹³), both the terms of the message He delivers (Jn 8²⁸ 7¹⁶ ἡ ἐμὴ διδαχή, 12⁴⁹) and the power which renders His work 'coincident and coexistent with that of the Father' (Jn 5¹⁹, see Westcott's *Gospel of St. John, in loc.*). Jesus refuses to claim the right or even the ability to act separately from the Father, and the character of His works is determined by the fact that it is not He Himself who is the author of them, but the Father dwelling in, speaking and acting through Him (cf. Jn 5³⁰ 14¹⁰). It is quite true, in a very real sense, to say with Westcott that 'Christ places His work as co-ordinate with that of the Father, and not as dependent on it'; at the same time it is true in a sense no less real that 'the very idea of Sonship involves . . . that of dependence,' as will be seen if we refer to such phrases as ἀπ' ἐμαυτοῦ (5³⁰), ἐξ ἐμαυτοῦ (12⁴⁹). What this phraseology implied, in the mind at least of the writer of the Fourth Gospel, will perhaps be better understood by observing his use of it in other connexions (cf. e.g. Jn 11⁵¹, where the 'prophecy' of Caiaphas is made to depend for its validity on the χάρισμα inherent in the high priestly office ; see also 15⁴ 16¹³, where the deeds done and the words spoken are relegated to a higher source than to the energy possessed by the actors).

6. Another side of Jesus' self-revelation as to the condition of dependence in which His spiritual life on earth was lived, is to be found in His doctrine of *our dependence upon Him*. Just as He can do nothing 'of himself,' but traces the source of His manifold activities to the mutual indwelling of the Father and Himself, so He tells His disciples they are powerless for good if they are 'apart from' Him (χωρὶς ἐμοῦ οὐ δύνασθε ποιεῖν οὐδέν, Jn 15⁵). He is the derived source of their vital energy in the same sense that the tree is the source of the fruit-bearing life of its branch. It is significant that this writer uses the same verb and preposition (μένειν ἐν) to express the nature of the union of the Father and Jesus, and that of Jesus and those who believe in Him (cf. 14¹⁰ 15⁴ etc.). The words of St. Paul to the Athenians, 'In him we live and move and have our being' (Ac 17²⁸), are as true of Jesus as they are of all the children of men, 'for both he that sanctifieth and they that are sanctified are all of one' (ἐξ ἑνός, He 2¹¹). It is this very likeness (ὁμοίωμα, Ph 2⁷, cf. He 2¹⁷) of nature which makes interdependence, in the sphere of active work, between Christ and believers a prominent feature in all sound Christologies (cf. Mk 16²⁰, 1 Co 3⁹, 2 Co 6¹). The well-known Pauline ἐν Χριστῷ (cf. 2 Co 5¹⁷, 1 Co 15²², Col 1²⁸ etc.) is balanced by the no less Pauline Χριστὸς ἐν ὑμῖν (Ro 8¹⁰, Co 1³⁰, cf. Eph 3¹⁷, Gal 2²⁰).

Life in Christ is the normal condition of redeemed humanity (1 Co 15²²). As the head is the seat of the vital functions in the human body, and without the head the body is helpless and lifeless, so Christ is the source of the Church's life and energy (Eph 4¹⁵ᶠ·, Col 1¹⁸ 2¹⁹ etc.). Her capacity for development springs directly from Him, considered in relation to His place in her constitution (Eph 2²⁰ᶠ·), and it is impossible even to conceive of the Church apart from this relationship (1 Co 3¹¹). 'The Head,' 'the chief corner-stone,' 'the foundation,' are the principal Pauline formulæ used by the Apostle to picture the mysterious nature of a union upon which the very existence of the Church depends. The symbol of the marriage relationship, with all the consequences involved, is not only found in the Johannine idealism (Rev 19⁷ 21². ⁹), but discovers itself underlying St. Paul's ideas as to the nature of the tie which binds the Church to Christ, in its aspect both of loving equality (Eph 5²⁸ᶠ·) and of dependent subordination (Eph 5²⁴. ³³).

Relative to what we have been saying, it may not be amiss to recall the difficult words of St. Paul, which emphasize this side of a mysterious truth—'Now I . . . fill up on my part that which is lacking of the afflictions of Christ in my flesh for His body's sake, which is the Church ' (Col 1²⁴, cf. the strange translation of this sentence in Moffatt's *The Historical New Testament*²). It is as if the Apostle said that Christ is still, in a certain sense, subject to His Father's disciplinary control (cf. Ac 9⁴, Jn 15¹ᶠ·), where the Father, as the husbandman, prunes the branches, and consequently the tree out of which the branches grow. The tribulations and disappointments which the Church experiences from age to age are manifestations of the same spirit of unbelief and opposition encountered by Jesus during His work on earth (Jn 15¹⁸⁻²¹ 17¹⁴⁻¹⁶) Nor ought we to be surprised if we observe this continued display of hostility in one form or another, because Jesus Himself knew that it would be so, and that He was the object of opposition. He said that the world would hate to accept the directing influence of that body which professes to derive its life directly from His Life (cf. Lk 6²² 21¹⁷, Mt 10²² 24⁹, 1 P 2²¹ 4¹³ᶠ·).

The other side of the same truth is not forgotten by Jesus, who taught that the conscious recognition of His claims over the lives of His followers, and the consequent acts of goodwill towards the latter, will not escape His notice (cf. ἐν ὀνόματι ὅτι Χριστοῦ ἐστε, Mk 9⁴¹, and εἰς ὄνομα μαθητοῦ, Mt 10⁴²). See also Mt 25⁴⁰. ⁴⁵, where, in His solemn portraiture of the Judgment Day, Jesus emphasizes the great truth of His self-identification with all who have their lives grounded in Him (cf. τούτων τῶν ἀδελφῶν μου τῶν ἐλαχίστων, v.⁴⁰).

7. We must not close our consideration of this subject without referring to a feature of the Christian life which is supplementary to and dependent upon the foregoing. The life of the believer is not bounded by his own immediate interests, although as an individual that life is immeasurably enriched and ennobled by its personal contact with, and share in, the Incarnate Life of Jesus Christ. In the parables of the Vine and the Good Shepherd He leads to the conclusion that all His disciples stand in a relationship to each other of the closest kind. There is an interdependence between them which springs out of their common relationship to Christ their Head. This truth is especially dwelt on by St. Paul in his reasoning on the variety of work but unity of purpose which characterizes the lives of professing Christians considered in their corporate capacity, and as constituent parts of a great whole. No individual life can be considered as self-centred in the sense of its being independent of the lives of its fellows. However unconscious one may be of the fact, it nevertheless remains true that no single member of 'the body of Christ' (σῶμα Χριστοῦ) is unaffected by the fortunes of its brethren. Various as are the functions of the parts, vital as is the dependence of each on Him in whom their common life has its roots, it is still the truth that the fulness of the life of every individual is affected by the joy or the sorrow, the strength or the weakness, of every other (cf. 1 Co 12¹²⁻³⁰, Gal 3²⁷ᶠ·, Col 3¹¹, Eph 3¹⁵ᶠ·). The recognition of this common share in the one higher life is necessary as affording scope for

the exercise of the greatest of all human virtues (ἡ ἀγάπη, 1 Co 13¹³).

The incapability of fully appreciating this feature of Jesus' teaching, which is ultimately bound up with His ideals and aspirations, will largely account for the signal failure of Christendom to realize that spiritual as well as visible unity of life and purpose to which He looked forward in the later stages of His ministry. Oneness is just the characteristic which cannot be predicated of the Christian community. More especially is this the case if we consider the nature of the oneness aspired after by Jesus for His followers—a oneness which has its roots in the Divine life, and 'in which each constituent being is a conscious element in the being of a vast whole' (ἵνα ὦσιν τετελειωμένοι εἰς ἕν, Jn 17²³, cf. vv.¹¹. ²¹. ²², Ro 12⁵, 1 Co 12²⁰; see also Westcott's *Gospel of St. John*, p. 246 f.).

The opening years of the twentieth century give promise of a profounder realization of this Divine idea; and the craving after unity, in some sense at least, may issue in a truer conception of the inter-relations of Christian people, in a real synthesis of the individual's freedom and his subordination and dependence as a member of that which is essentially one whole (cf. ὅτι εἷς ἄρτος, ἓν σῶμα οἱ πολλοί ἐσμεν, 1 Co 10¹⁷). Perhaps it is not without significance that, in recording the prayer of Jesus for His Church, St. John uses the present tense of the verbs πιστεύω and γινώσκω (Jn 17²¹. ²³), which points to the ultimate, albeit gradual, acquirement by 'the world' of that faith and knowledge which the spectacle of a union so vital and so profound is calculated to impart.

LITERATURE.—W. R. Harper's *Religion and the Higher Life* will be found very useful in connexion with this subject ; as will also A. Dorner's *Grundprobleme der Religionsphilosophie*, especially Lecture II. in that volume. Westcott's *Gospel of St. John* and *The Epistle to the Hebrews* will be found in places very helpful ; as also his *Christus Consummator*, *The Incarnation and Common Life*, and *Christian Aspects of Life* ; cf. G. B. Stevens, *The Theology of the New Testament* ; B. Weiss, *Biblical Theology of the NT* ; Liddon, *Some Elements of Religion* ; Wendt, *Lehre Jesu*, Eng. tr. (T. & T. Clark) ; Hall, *The Kenotic Theory* ; Bruce, *The Humiliation of Christ* ; Gore, *Dissertations on Subjects connected with the Incarnation*, *The Church and the Ministry*, *The Body of Christ* ; Seeley, *Ecce Homo*. See also articles in Hastings' *DB* : 'Communion' (J. Armitage Robinson), 'Church' (S. C. Gayford), 'Kingdom of God' (J. Orr; with which may be studied articles 'Messiah' and 'Eschatology' [especially §§ 82, 101] in the *Encyc. Bibl.*), 'Jesus Christ' (Sanday ; which might be studied in conjunction with Edersheim's *The Life and Times of Jesus the Messiah*, B. Weiss, *The Life of Christ*, O. Holtzmann, *The Life of Jesus*).

J. R. WILLIS.

DERELICTION.—Mt 27⁴⁶ = Mk 15³⁴. About three o'clock in the afternoon, when Jesus had hung for six hours on the cross, the bystanders were startled by a loud cry from the meek Sufferer : *Eli, Eli, lama 'azabhtāni*,* 'My God, my God, why hast thou forsaken me?' It was a sentence from that psalm which, says Tertullian,† 'contains the whole Passion of Christ.' What was it that wrung from His lips that exceeding bitter cry? The Evangelists have not drawn the veil aside and revealed what was passing in the Redeemer's soul, and it becomes us to refrain from curious speculation, and recognize that there is here an impenetrable mystery. Yet it is right that we should seek to enter into it so far as we may, if only that we may realize its greatness and be delivered from belittling thoughts.

An explanation has been sought mainly along two lines. (1) *Jesus was standing in the room of sinners and enduring vicariously the wrath of God.* This opinion is at once unscriptural and irrational. It was indeed possible for God to inflict

---

* Ps 22¹ אֵלִי אֵלִי לָמָה עֲזַבְתָּנִי. For עֲ Mt. gives Aram. שְׁבַקְתָּנִי (σαβαχθανει), D [ἀ]ζαφθανει, being a reminiscence of the original. Mk. further aramaicizes אֵלִי into אֱלָהִי. Cf. Dalman, *Words of Jesus*, p. 53 f.
† *adv. Marc.* iii. 19.

upon Jesus the punishment which is due to sinners ; but it is inconceivable that He should have transferred His wrath from them to Him— as it were saying, 'I will be angry with Him instead of them.' Jesus never endured the wrath of God. 'We do not suggest,' says Calvin,[*] 'that God was ever His adversary or angry with Him. For how should He be angry with His beloved Son in whom His mind rested?' At every step of His progress through the world He was the beloved Son, and He was never so well pleasing to the Father as in that hour when He hung a willing victim on the cross, 'obedient even unto death' (Ph 2[8]). His sacrifice for the sin of the world was not merely His death ; it was His entire life of unspotted holiness and vicarious love (cf. He 9[14]). His death was not the whole of His sacrifice, but the consummation of it. He bore the sin of the world from Nazareth to Calvary, and, if God was angry with Him at the last, He must have been angry with Him all along.

(2) *Jesus was not really forsaken by God, but His soul was clouded by the anguish of His flesh and spirit, and His faith, hitherto victorious, gave way.* 'We have here,' says Meyer, 'the purely human feeling that arises from a natural but momentary quailing before the agonies of death, in every respect similar to that which had been experienced by the author of the psalm.' It was a 'subjective feeling,' and there was no 'actual objective desertion on the part of God.' This explanation is very inadequate. At the ninth hour the worst was over, and the end was at hand. It is incredible that He should have faltered then after enduring the sharpest pangs with steadfast fortitude. Whatever His dereliction may have meant, it was no mere subjective feeling, but an objective reality, and it came from God.

According to the *Wolfenb. Fragm.*, the cry of Jesus was a despairing confession that His cause was lost : God had failed Him. But He had foreseen the cross all along. See CRUCIFIXION. According to Renan, it was wrung from His lips by the ingratitude of men : 'He repented suffering for a worthless race.' The *logion* is indubitably authentic ; it is one of Schmiedel's 'absolutely credible passages' (*Encyc. Bibl.* art. 'Gospels,' § 139).

If Jesus was indeed the eternal Son of God, 'bearing our sins in his body on the tree' (1 P 2[24]), it is in no wise strange that His experience at that awful crisis should lie beyond our ken ; but some light is shed upon the mystery by the profound truth, so often reiterated in the NT, that it was necessary for Him, in order that He might redeem the children of men, to be identified with them in every particular of their sorrowful condition. That He might 'redeem us from the curse of the law' it was necessary that He should be 'made a curse for us' (Gal 3[13]) ; 'it behoved him in every respect to be made like unto his brethren, that he might prove a merciful and faithful High Priest' ; and it is because 'he hath himself suffered, having been tempted,' that 'he is able to succour them that are being tempted' (He 2[17. 18]). The uttermost strait in human experience is the passage through the valley of the shadow of death, and nothing but the sense of God's presence can relieve its horror (cf. Ps 23[4]). Had Jesus enjoyed the consciousness that God was with Him in that dread extremity, He would have been exempted from the most awful experience of the children of men, and His sympathy would have failed us precisely where it is most needed. And therefore the sense of the Father's presence was withheld from Him in that awful hour.

It was not necessary to this end that the Father should be angry with Him. When the eternal Son of God became man, He was made in every respect like unto His brethren ; and what differentiated Him from them was the closeness of His

[* *Instit.* ii. 16. § 11.]

intimacy with God and the singular graces wherewith God endowed Him. He had a unique acquaintance with the Father's purposes, but He had this because the Father showed Him all things which He did (Jn 5[20]) ; He had marvellous wisdom, but it was the Father's gift (7[16. 17]) : 'the word which ye hear is not mine, but the Father's that sent me' (14[24]) ; He wrought miracles, but of Himself He could do nothing (5[30]) : 'the Father abiding in me doeth his works' (14[10]). 'God,' says St. Peter, 'anointed him with the Holy Spirit and with power,' and 'he went about doing good, and healing all that were under the tyranny of the devil ; *because God was with him*' (Ac 10[38]). Had the Father at any moment refrained from His ministration and left Him alone, Jesus would have been even as the rest of the children of men. And thus is revealed something of the mystery of the Dereliction. That He might be one with the children of men in their uttermost strait, the communion of God was withheld from His beloved Son, and He passed through the valley of the shadow of death alone, without that presence which had hitherto cheered and supported Him (cf. Jn 16[32]).

LITERATURE.—Bruce, *Humiliation of Christ*, Lect. vii. ; Dale, *Atonement*, Note G ; Wendt, *Lehre Jesu* [Eng. tr. ii. p. 249 f.] ; Meyer on Mt 27[46] ; *Expos. Times*, iv. [1893] 511 ff. ; Fairbairn, *Studies in the Life of Christ*, 'The Crucifixion' ; Mrs. Browning, *Cowper's Grave.*　　　DAVID SMITH.

DESERT.—See WILDERNESS.

DESIRE.—'Our nature corresponds to our external condition. Without this correspondence there would be no possibility of any such thing as human life and human happiness : which life and happiness are, therefore, a result from our nature and condition jointly : meaning by human life, not living in the literal sense, but the whole complex notion commonly understood by these words' (Butler's *Analogy*, pt. i. ch. 5, § 1). This is one of the observations of Bishop Butler in which he anticipates the conclusions of modern science. The nature of man corresponds to external nature ; organ and environment, faculty and its sphere of operation are in correspondence. Man is in relation to the world in which he lives, and his whole life is a process of adaptation to the life of the Universe. All the endowments of his nature, whether intellectual, emotional, or volitional, whether they are bodily or mental, may fruitfully be looked at as teleological, as a means towards the great end of living. The teleological relation begins in the individual ere consciousness awakens in him, and he is so constituted that he acts in relation to the environment ere he can consciously adapt himself to it. Even consciousness may be looked at as part of a process of adaptation. Bishop Butler also remarks that 'the several external objects of the appetites, passions, and affections, being present to the senses, or offering themselves to the mind, excite emotions suitable to their nature' (*l.c.* ch. 4, § 1). In his view there is not only a general correspondence between man and his environment, but a special adaptation between the several aspects of nature and the particular characteristics of man. Appetites have their objects, and these objects excite emotions in man suitable to their nature. Passions and affections have also their objects and their suitable emotions. Every external object makes its own appeal, and the inward nature of man makes a response in correspondence with the appeal. Nor does the Bishop limit the meaning of the word 'object' to those things which appeal to man directly through his senses, and which are presented to him, as it were, ready made. That there are such objects it is not necessary to affirm. But the objects which appeal to man are not limited to those which nature presents to him. Within the range of his interests are included not only the world as it is presented to perception, but the world as it has been transformed by human reflexion, as it is filled with the achievement of the ages, and pervaded by the life, the imagination, and the reflexion of man. Objects are not merely what is presented to the senses, but what is presented to man as constituted by the experience of the race, by the education of the individual, by the results of art, science, poetry, philosophy, and theology,—in short, by all the wide interest with which man has invested the world of his experience. Appetites have their respective objects, though even the appetite of a rational being has something which transcends sense, and even into appetite may enter that element of infinity with which a rational being invests all his objects.

Coming more closely to the subject, we take a description of Desire from Professor Mackenzie: 'In the case of what is strictly called desire, there is not merely the consciousness of an object, with an accompanying feeling of pleasure and pain, but also a recognition of the object as a good, or as an element in a more or less clearly defined end' (*Manual of Ethics*³, p. 46). Three elements appear in this description. There is, first, the consciousness of an object; there is, second, the feeling of pleasure and of pain ; and there is, third, the recognition of the object as a good, or as an element in a defined end. If all these elements are involved in Desire, then Desire can be experienced only by beings who live a reflective life. They must be conscious beings; they must have the consciousness of an object, and be able to associate that object with pleasure and pain ; and they must be able to reflect on the object, and judge it to be a good, or an element in a defined end. It may be well to have a term the meaning of which is such as has been defined by Professor Mackenzie ; but is Desire such a term? Is it so in the ordinary use of language, or is it so in the accepted use of psychological writers? What of those writers who define the good in terms of pleasure and of pain? If we were to accept the definition of the term Desire as it is set forth by Professor Mackenzie, we should be constrained to say that the presence of Desire always involves the action of reflective judgment, the presence of ideas or trains of ideas to consciousness, and a comparison of possible processes which might lead to the accomplishment of a wished-for end. As a consequence, we should be compelled to shut out from the region of Desire not only all the lower forms of life, but also all those people who do not live a reflective life. It seems, then, that the definition of Desire given by Professor Mackenzie is an ideal one. It describes Desire as it is felt by a fully developed, reflective consciousness, a consciousness in possession of trains of ideas, and of the world as built up of such mental attainments and experiences. Along the whole course of mental growth, from the first beginnings of conscious life up to the complete attainment of self-mastery, Desire may be considered to be present, and to afford a ground of action. As a definition of life must include all living things, so a definition of Desire must include every feeling which in common language can lay claim to be a desire. There is an element of desire in every case in which there is subjective selection, or rejection of one object and the preference of another. In the simplest mental experience, even in those in which the living being reacts against the environment, whether it means the avoidance of pain or the attainment of pleasure, there is the germ of desire. Movements that result in pleasure attract

attention. Movements which procure the removal of pain, and become inseparably associated with that result, are elements in the making of a world, and that world grows into the world of Desire. It may be that reactions against the environment correspond to stages in the growth of mind, so that we might properly ascribe Desire to movements for the attainment of objects of which the organism is aware through the senses ; but it is not necessary for us to enter into the discussion of that topic. As Dr. Ward says, 'Provided the cravings of appetite are felt, any signs of the presence of pleasurable objects prompt to movements for their enjoyment or appropriation. In these last cases we have action determined by perceptions. The cases in which the subject is incited to action by ideas as distinct from perceptions, require a more detailed consideration ; such are the facts mainly covered by the term "desire"' (art. 'Psychology,' *Encyc. Brit.*⁹ vol. xx. p. 73 f.).

Without entering on the question as to whether action can be determined by perceptions, or the further question as to whether there can be perceptions apart from something like ideation, we are disposed to contend that where there is awareness of an object, and a movement towards the appropriation of it, there must be the rudiments of Desire. It is not necessary, however, to discuss the matter, for it is not to be questioned that by ideas, and trains of ideas, and ideas, as Dr. Ward points out, 'sufficiently self-sustaining to form trains that are not wholly shaped by the circumstances of the present—entirely new possibilities of action are opened up' (p. 74). Ideas and trains of ideas form elements in shaping a world of desire. It is not possible to mark off the area where these properly begin, any more than we can delimit the sphere of intellection, and say where it begins. But for our purpose it is sufficient that the presence of reflective thought does mark a terminus ; on one side there is mental action of a simpler sort, and on the other side the fulness of a reflective life. But apparently there is desire on both sides.

Taking the definition of Professor Mackenzie as a goal and an ideal, we ask, In what ways have thinkers looked at Desire in the past, and what is the view they take of it in the present hour? To set this forth with fulness would be a great task. For Desire, the analysis of it, and the place assigned to it, mark off the schools of philosophy from each other, and, according as they view it, it gives the keynote to different systems of ethics. From the time of the beginnings of Greek thought down to the present time, the attempt to find a sufficient definition of Desire has ever been renewed, and at present the old controversy between Plato and the Sophists has its counterpart in the controversy between Green and his supporters on the one hand, and Sidgwick and the various supporters of Hedonism on the other. Both the theory of knowledge and the theory of conduct are involved in the discussion of the question.

One of the many debts which the world owes to Socrates is the introduction of the conception of a supreme end of life. That there is one end which all men seek, and that every action must be judged by reference to that end, brought unity into man's conception of human life. Up to the time of Socrates men had thought of conduct as obedience to certain practical rules, useful from the point of view of prudence. But Socrates showed that men's thoughts and actions must be guided by their desire for something which they regarded as desirable. Rules were simply the ways by which the desirable end could be obtained. Illustrations of this principle abound in the statements ascribed to Socrates. A religious man desires to win the approbation of the gods ; a just man is persuaded

that the practice of justice will bring satisfaction ;
a man seeks knowledge because it is a satisfaction
to know. Thus, in all departments of life there
is some desirable end, and the thought of a desirable end actually defines Desire as it appears to
Socrates.

While a great advance was made when the thought
of a supreme end of life dawned on the human
mind, yet the question arose as to the nature of
the end, and it received different answers. Is the
end pleasure, or a pleasurable state of feeling? Is
it the avoidance of pain, or is it indifference to,
or superiority over, both pleasure and pain? Is
pleasure—pain, or indifference to pleasure—pain, or
any other description of the end of life something
to be referred to and determined by the individual
man, or must we bring the thought of common life
to bear on the solution of the problem? If we
refer to the individual man the power of deciding
what is the end of life and what is desirable as a
means to that end, are we to think of the end in
terms of pleasure as it appears to the cultured
man, a man who is familiar with ideas and trains
of ideas, or are we to think of pleasure as it
appears to the natural man? All these questions
were keenly debated in the schools of Greece, and
all of them have a bearing on the definition of
Desire.

Nor is it easy to say what are the views of the
great masters of Greek thought on the question of
desire. It is perhaps comparatively easy to say
what were the views of Aristippus or of Epicurus,
but not so easy to say what were the views of Plato
or of Aristotle. Still a brief description may be
useful. We quote from Dr. Jowett. 'Plato, speaking in the person of Socrates, passes into a more
ideal point of view, and expressly repudiates the
notion that the exchange of a less pleasure for a
greater can be the exchange of virtue. Such virtue
is the virtue of ordinary men who live in the
world of appearance ; they are temperate only that
they may enjoy the pleasure of intemperance, and
courageous from fear of danger. Whereas the
philosopher is seeking after wisdom and not after
pleasure, whether near or distant : he is the mystic,
the initiated, who has learned to despise the body,
and is yearning all his life long for a truth which
will hereafter be revealed to him. In the *Republic*
(ix. 582) the pleasures of knowledge are affirmed to
be superior to other pleasures, because the philosopher so estimates them ; and he alone has had
experience of both kinds. In the *Philebus*, Plato,
although he regards the enemies of pleasure with
complacency, still further modifies the transcendent-
alism of the *Phœdo*. For he is compelled to confess,
rather reluctantly, perhaps, that some pleasures,
i.e. those which have no antecedent pains, 'claim a
place in the scale of goods' (Jowett's *Plato*, vol. iv.
p. 29 f.). Plato rejects the view that pleasure is
necessarily preceded by pain. 'True pleasures are
those which are given by beauty of colour and
form, and most of those which arise from smells;
those of sound, again, and in general those of
which the want is painless and unconscious, and
the gratification afforded by them palpable to
sense and unalloyed with pain' (*Philebus*, 51 A,
Jowett's tr.). He prepared the way for the fuller
analysis of pleasure and desire which we owe to
Aristotle, for he showed that pleasures which
accompany the active discharge of function are
pleasant in themselves ; the pleasures which are
truly desirable are the pleasures of the wise, all
others are a shadow only (*Rep.* 583 B). Thus Plato
rejects the earlier theories of movement and re-
plenishment, distinguishes pleasures that are preceded by pain and want as pleasant only by contrast, and as it were by accident, from those
pleasures which accompany active discharge of

function ; and he sets forth as the only true pleasure
the pleasure of the good man. Pleasure, according
to Plato, is always a process towards the normal
condition of a subject, and is never in itself an end.
The absence of finality from pleasure proves that
pleasure taken by itself could never be t e end of
life. The treatment of pleasure and pain is conducted by Plato always from a moral point of view.

While Aristotle builds so far on the results of
the analysis of Plato, yet he is dissatisfied with
the argument that pleasure cannot be the *summum
bonum* because it is a mere process towards an end.
Pleasure, he contends, is an ἐνέργεια ; it arises from
the unimpeded operation of our faculties ; it arises
when an organ which acts perfectly comes into
contact with its appropriate object, just as pain is
the outcome of thwarted action on the part of
either a sensitive or an intellectual faculty (*Eth.
Nic.* vii. 12, 1153. 13). The moral value of the
feelings of pleasure and pain arises, says Aristotle,
out of the fact that by means of them man passes
from a state of a merely cognitive and intellectual
being, and becomes a moral and active being. 'It
is when the sense perceives something as pleasant
or painful that the mind affirms or denies it, pursues or avoids it' (iii. 7. 2, 431. 8). Aristotle has
ever before him the unity and wholeness of human
nature. He is never merely intellectual, and is
never wholly practical. He always lays stress on
the correspondence between the speculative and the
practical sides of human nature. Truth and error
in the intellectual sphere become good and evil in
the moral sphere. What t e mind affirms as truth
and error in the intellectual sphere becomes pursuit
and avoidance in the practical sphere. In both
spheres the mind is active. Impressions in the
cognitive sphere become, through the activity of
the subject, objects of cognition ; feelings of pleasure
and pain, through a similar activity of the subject,
are translated into objects of desire or aversion ;
become motives to action.

Two main factors, according to Aristotle, enter
into the conative nature of man. It is difficult
within our limits to expound this fully. But, briefly,
it is that Desire and Reason must co-operate in
order that a moral conclusion may be carried into
effect. Moral choice or προαίρεσις may be described
as νοῦς ὀρεκτικός, reason stimulated by desire, or
ὄρεξις διανοητική, desire guided by understanding.
The significant part of the view is that both the
irrational and the rational elements must act together ; desire and reason are constant elements in
distinctive moral action. For the merely logical
understanding never leads to action. Reason, as
mere reasoning, is powerless to shape the will, and
mere appetite is quite as powerless. In order to
cause action, pleasure and pain must be translated
into the higher forms of Good and Evil. Desire
must always have an object (ὀρεκτικὸν δὲ οὐκ ἄνευ
φαντασίας (433b. 28)) ; but the object of desire determines conduct only when thought has marked it
out, defined it, and in a word constituted it (τὸ
ὀρεκτικὸν κινεῖ οὐ νοηθῆναι ἢ φαντασθῆναι (433b. 12)).

'The true object of consciousness in this union of desire and
reason is not two objects,—one of desire, another of reason,—it is
one single common force which finally becomes the principle of
action. And when we ask how this object of our final wish is
framed, the answer must be, that it is so through the agency of
reason. Ultimately, and transcendently in fact, there is no
difference between the object of thought and the object of wish ;
the βουλητόν and the νοητόν are merely different aspects of one and
the same great generality. Even in our own experience it is
thought which determines desire : and the principle and starting-
point of conduct turns out to be an exercise of reason. And when
Aristotle proceeds to state more definitely what is this object of
perfect wish which thus determines and regulates our natural
desires, he becomes still more of an idealist. For while the
object of wish to any individual is but the apparent and relative
good, still to a perfect man it is the absolute ideal good : and
the aim of life comes to be an attempt to make our practical
views in life elevate themselves to the full height of the absolute
ideal of goodness. . . . The same writer who reproduces Plato's

idea of good as the constructive reason which gives both knowledge and reality to things, now finds the determining aim of conduct in an absolute ideal which constitutes the pattern to which morality must raise itself' (*Aristotle's Psychology in Greek and English, with Introduction and Notes*, by Edwin Wallace, M.A., Introduction, p. cxxiii f.).

We quote from Mr. Wallace, whose work represents the high-water mark of Aristotelian exposition, as it sets forth in brief space an interpretation of Aristotle which deserves study. It may be that Mr. Wallace has read Hegel into Aristotle, but in the present case he is right in saying that for Aristotle the world of desire is a rational world, and that the ground of conduct is the union of desire and reason. In short, the view of Aristotle corresponds to the definition of desire set forth by Professor Mackenzie. 'It is then,' says Aristotle, 'on good grounds that people have viewed as springs of action these two faculties of desire and practical intellect: for the faculty of desire has itself a motive force, and the intellect excites to action just in so far as the object of desire supplies it with a starting-point: just as, similarly, imagination when it moves to action does not do so independently of desire. The spring of action thus resolves itself into one single thing, viz. the object of desire' (Wallace's tr. p. 179).

As to the question whether animals can have desires, Aristotle decides that 'no animal can have the faculty of desire unless it have imaginative power' (Wallace, p. 183); but then, as imaginative power is connected with the reason or the senses, so animals may have the imaginative power connected with the senses, and thus have what can be designated desires. But they do not possess the kind of desire which forms itself as the conclusion of syllogism, so that their desire is destitute of any faculty of deliberation. 'In the case of men, however, sometimes the images of sense overcome and move the rational volition; sometimes, as in incontinence, two things overcome and stir up one another, desire thus following on desire, much as a ball that players toss about; but the normal and natural course is always that in which the superior course of reason is the more supreme and stimulates to action' (pp. 184–185). Desire thus, according to Aristotle, implies deliberation, choice, the use of means towards an end. In a significant passage in the *Nicomachean Ethics* he says (we quote the paraphrase of Sir A. Grant): 'If the object of purpose is that which, being in our power, we desire after deliberation, purpose will be a desire of things in our power. After deliberating we decide, and form a desire in accordance with our deliberation' (Grant's *Aristotle's Ethics*, vol. ii. p. 23). Desire ranges, according to Aristotle, through all life. Wherever life is in presence of an object there is rudimentary desire. The animal world feels it in presence of an object present to its senses. A self-conscious being feels desire in proportion to its realization of self, and to its realization of the objects as existing in an ordered world. It is possible to regard the teaching of Aristotle as containing in itself the fuller analysis of desire as that analysis has been conducted by English Hedonists and by the English Neo-Hegelians.

Were there space, it would be instructive to trace the analysis of desire, or rather the description of desire, in subsequent philosophical speculation. But that would far exceed our limits. Nor is it necessary, for there is not much to be added to the result won by Aristotle until we come to the Utilitarian school of England. Some valuable remarks occur in Spinoza's *Ethics*, but the current of modern speculation on the topic was set agoing by Hobbes. For the history of the process, readers may be referred to Professor Watson's (Kingston, Canada) *Hedonistic Theories*, and to Dr. Albee's (Cornell University) *A History of English Utilitarianism*. In addition to the account of the main ethical theory known as Utilitarianism, and a criticism of it, there will be found in these able books a particular account of that doctrine we have immediately in hand. In the posthumous work of Professor Green, *Prolegomena to Ethics*, there is a lengthened and incisive analysis of Desire; and in the posthumous work of

Professor Sidgwick, *The Ethics of T. H. Green, Herbert Spencer, and J. Martineau*, as also in the various editions of the *Methods of Ethics*, we find a criticism of Green. These two works represent the most recent, as they also represent the most searching, accounts of Desire which can be found in the whole range of philosophical speculation.

In the analysis of Desire, as in the analysis of Knowledge, the work of Locke was epoch-making. He stated the problem in a form which occupied the thoughts of all his successors in England. Berkeley, Hume, Hartley, Tucker, Stuart Mill, and Spencer are in the succession, and all of them attack the problem of the will from the point of view of pleasure and desire. We take the statement of Locke's position from the admirable work of Professor Watson, *Hedonistic Theories* (p. 111 f.):

'Why does the same man will differently on different occasions? The reason is to be sought in the character of Desire as the imagination of pleasure. To different persons, or to the same person under different circumstances, one pleasure presents itself in his imagination as preferable to another. Under the impulse for knowledge one man will forget his bodily wants until hunger drives him to his meals; another man will neglect study, and live for the pleasures of sense, unless he is driven to change his course by the stronger impulse of shame. But as each man's desire is determined not by him but for him, and the desire determines the will, what he prefers in any case is that which alone he can prefer, and freedom is a word without meaning.'

This, then, is the problem which the majority of English ethical thinkers had before them. A man's desires are determined for him not by him, and the desire determines the will. Nor is much added to the solution of the problem from the time of Locke to that of Stuart Mill. Hume had tried to prove the utilitarian doctrine of the particular virtues, and Stuart Mill, using the same argument, sought to prove the general principle of Utility.

'The sole evidence, I apprehend, it is possible to produce that anything is desirable, is that people do actually desire it. If the end which the utilitarian doctrine proposes to itself were not, in theory and in practice, acknowledged to be an end, nothing could ever convince any person that it was so. No reason can be given why the general happiness is desirable, except that each person, so far as he believes it to be attainable, desires his own happiness' (*Utilitarianism*, ch. iv.). Farther on in the same chapter he identifies pleasure and desire. 'Desiring a thing and finding it pleasant, aversion to it and finding it painful, are phenomena entirely unseparable, or rather two parts of the same phenomena.' Thus Mill would find it necessary to show that people never do desire anything save pleasure or happiness. On this Sidgwick remarks: 'As a matter of fact, it appears to me that throughout the whole scale of my impulses, sensual, emotional, and intellectual alike, I can distinguish desires the object of which is something other than my own pleasure' (*Methods of Ethics*, p. 45).

In truth, the Hedonistic account of Desire, from Locke to Mill, and including Sidgwick in some measure, is inadequate, because it is too exclusively psychological. Psychology, as it is usually conceived, cannot give a full account of Desire. For psychology deliberately limits itself to a description of mental processes, events, and occurrences, taken in abstraction from the self whose the mental states are, and from the outer world. An analysis of mental states can never give a complete account of the system to which the self belongs, and of the interests and values which are such because they are referred to the self. Thus the psychological account of Desire, and its relation to will, set forth by English Hedonism, is defective, not psychologically, but in reality. It is the merit of Green, and specially of those who with him have so fruitfully worked at ethical problems under the inspiration of Kant and Hegel, to point out that mental and moral values cannot be appraised, and cannot be the objects of desire, if we look at them in abstraction from the self, and from the world-system. In the *Prolegomena to Ethics* and in the Introduction to Hume, Green has brought the self in its concrete reality within the vision of English thinkers. He has been ably helped by such writers as Professor Muirhead in his manual *The Elements of Ethics*, by Professor Watson in *Hedonistic Theories*, and Professor Mackenzie in the *Manual of Ethics*. Other writers might be mentioned, but these will suffice to show the significance of the new departure in Ethics, and of the introduction of the self into English philosophy. Desire, according to Green, involves consciousness of self and of an object, and is to be distinguished from instinctive impulse, which implies only the feeling of self. A consciousness of self is something beyond self-feeling, is really a transformation of self-feeling. Self-consciousness being also a consciousness of objects, is thus the basis of desire and of knowledge. Even in the desire for food, what is desired is really some ulterior object, not the mere pleasure of eating. But most of our desires are for objects which are not directly dependent on animal susceptibility at all, or which, even where so dependent, are transformed by the addition of new elements derived from self-consciousness itself. There is a real unity in all our desires, only it is the unity of the self, not the unity of desire.

'There is one subject or spirit, which desires in all a man's experiences of desire, understands in all operations of his intelligence, wills in all his acts of willing ; and the essential character of his desires depends on their all being desires of one and the same subject which also understands, the essential character of his intelligence on its being an activity of one and the same subject which also desires, the essential character of his acts of will on their proceeding from one and the same subject which also desires and understands' (*Prolegomena to Ethics*[4], p. 138).

It is well to have an emphatic statement of the unity of the thinking, willing, feeling subject placed on record ; for up to Green's advent we were allowed to see thinking, willing, feeling, but the self was altogether out of sight. At the same time, while Green lays stress on the unity of the self in all its activities, and rightly so, there seems to be a defect in his analysis. He seems to take for granted that the self-conscious self, in its conscious apprehension of objects as desirable, will always act wisely, prudently, and rightly. But does not the self-conscious being, in making a choice, sometimes choose unwisely and wrongly ? As Sidgwick points out, 'It seems to me to be fundamentally important to distinguish between choice (even deliberate choice) and judgment as to choice-worthiness, since they may diverge' (*The Ethics of T. H. Green*, etc. p. 30). Are we to hold that a man, following out what he thinks self-interest, clearly seeing the end in view and choosing appropriate means for its accomplishment, if he acts self-consciously, is always acting rightly ? For Green in his description of the self-conscious subject does not seem to contemplate the possibility of wrong or vicious action. He takes for granted that the process of the self-conscious being on his way towards the appropriate action, towards the satisfaction he will feel when the object is attained, will always be right. But may there not be all the characteristics of the action of the self-conscious being, as these are described by Green, present in the course of conduct of a man who wades through slaughter to a throne ? In truth, there is needed a further analysis, leading us beyond the mere processes of a self-conscious being, in order to find a justification for man's action. We need a better description of the desirable than any that can be found in Green. All that he sets forth with regard to Desire and the self-conscious subject and its action may be true, and truly realized in the case of the man who has an unworthy end in view. He may identify himself with his object, he may find satisfaction in the attainment of it, and yet the choice may not be worthy.

It is the experience of mankind that a man may make an unworthy choice, may form a wrong ideal, may be mistaken, and yet may all the time act as a self-conscious being. So a further criterion is needed in order to guide men in their choice, in order that it may be a worthy choice. True, the values of life lie in their relation to the self. And the realization of the self is one of the great ends of life. But the self has to grow in relation to the ideal, and the ideal has to grow as well. How shall a man learn to recognize the true ideal, and to desire it ? Here we ought to enter into the religious experience of man to realize the fact that man has formed wrong conceptions of life, has worshipped false ideals, and desired unworthy ends. One might pass into the sphere of that religious experience which has had its highest expression in the Scriptures. There, too, we are in a universe of desires, and the task of Scripture is to teach man what to desire. Scripture recognizes the possibility of wrong desire leading to wrong action, and it also recognizes that towards the making of desire all the faculties of man contribute. What it teaches is largely the reversal of human ideals : it puts last what men have put first, and it places in the front place, as the best and mightiest, what men have despised and forgotten. The self-conscious being has to be taught something which it would never have learnt through the mere exercise of self-conscious activity. It is not necessary to enter into an analysis of Scripture terms, or to trace the history of the term 'desire' through the Scriptures. For Scripture proceeds on the fact that men have had wrong desires, false ideals, and have pursued wrong objects ; so it proceeds to teach them what is the really good, the true ideal ; and, further, to give to men the power to recognize the good, the true, and the beautiful, and to desire them. We need this education, and the world of desire cannot be really described until we bring in the revolutionary power of religion, and learn to know that reversal of human judgments inaugurated by Christ.

Here, too, the strongest influence in this education is the commanding power of personality. It is not without significance that in the last resort Plato and Aristotle were driven back to the concrete standard of the 'good man.' Through the influence of personality men learn to recognize ideals and to love them. Around personalities cluster the thoughts, emotions, aspirations, tendencies which help to form the world of desire. It is so in the OT, where it is said of their devotion to the living God of Israel : 'Whom have I in heaven but thee ? and there is none upon earth that I desire beside thee' (Ps 73[25]) ; or, 'To thy name and to thy memorial is the desire of our soul' (Is 26[8]). It is recognized that there is a world of wrong desires, objects which the self-conscious man may desire, long for, strive after ; and the story of the Bible is the attempt to implant in these self-conscious beings the power to free themselves from that world of false desire. In the NT the first step towards that freedom is to bring men into contact with a living personality, in whom is sphered all perfection, whose service is perfect freedom, and through whom they may learn what to desire and what to long for, and what to attain. The laws of desire, as these are in human nature, and as they are disclosed to us through research and reflexion, rule in this sphere ; but then they have new material to illustrate their working.

Illustrations of the working of Desire abound in religious experience. To enter into them would occupy us too long. It need only be said that attachment to a pure and holy Personality, love to One who is the ideal of human life, purifies the world of desire and intensifies the power of action. Men who have felt the expulsive power of a new affection and the intensive power of a holy love are lifted into a new world, and those who love Christ learn that the world of their desires is formed by Him; they learn to love what He approves, and to hate what He hates. The world in which they live, the universe in which their desires terminate, are constituted by the Person and by the Love of Christ. See art. IDEAL.

LITERATURE.—Jowett's *Plato*; Aristotle's *Ethics* (Grant's ed.), and *Psychology* (ed. Edwin Wallace); Mackenzie, *A Manual of Ethics*; Muirhead, *Elements of Ethics*; Watson, *Hedonistic Theories*; Green, *Prolegomena to Ethics*; Sidgwick, *Methods of Ethics*, and *The Ethics of T. H. Green*, etc.; Shadworth Hodgson, *The Metaphysic of Experience*, esp. vol. iv.; Albee, *A History of English Utilitarianism*; Douglas, *Ethics of J. S. Mill*; Ward, art. 'Psychology' in *Encyc. Brit.*[9]; James, *Principles of Psychology*; Bowne, *Introduction to Psychological Theory*, and *Principles of Ethics*. JAMES IVERACH.

Use of the term 'desire' in the Gospels.—In AV of the Gospels the word 'desire' is of frequent occurrence. As a noun it is found only once (Lk 22[15]), as the equivalent of ἐπιθυμία, but in the verbal form it represents no fewer than 8 verbs in the original:—ἐπιθυμέω (Mt 13[17], Lk 16[21] 17[22] 22[15]), θέλω (Mk 9[35], Lk 5[39] 8[20] 10[24] 20[46]), αἰτέω (Mt 20[20], Mk 10[35] 11[24] 15[6. 8], Lk 23[25]), ἐξαιτέω (Lk 22[31]), ἐρωτάω (Lk 7[36] 14[32], Jn 12[21]), ἐπερωτάω (Mt 16[1]), ζητέω (Mt 12[46. 47], Lk 9[9]), παρακαλέω (Mt 18[32]). Twice we have the adj. 'desirous' (Lk 23[8], Jn 16[19]), but in both cases the vb. θέλω is used in the Greek. In RV, however, αἰτέω, ἐξαιτέω, ἐρωτάω (except in Lk 7[36]), and ἐπερωτάω are rendered by 'ask,' ζητέω by 'seek,' and παρακαλέω by 'beseech'; so that ἐπιθυμέω and θέλω are left as the two verbs which in a more exact use of language have the meaning of 'desire.' When we distinguish between them, ἐπιθυμέω may be regarded as denoting the desire of the feelings (θυμός), θέλω the desire of the will. In the latter the element of purpose and resolve is usually more strongly present (cf. Jn 8[44] τὰς ἐπιθυμίας τοῦ πατρὸς ὑμῶν θέλετε ποιεῖν). Sometimes, however, θέλω is used where a distinction from ἐπιθυμέω can hardly be pressed (see the parallel passages Mt 13[17], Lk 10[24]).

In the language of Christ and the Gospels, desire in itself is, properly speaking, neither good nor bad, its quality depending altogether upon the subject who experiences it or the object to which it is directed. The scribes 'desire' to walk in long robes (Lk 20[46]); while many prophets and righteous men have 'desired' to see Christ's day (Mt 13[17] ∥ Lk 10[24]). The Prodigal 'desired' (ἐπεθύμει, EV 'would fain') to fill his belly with the husks that fed the swine (Lk 15[16]); and Jesus said, 'With desire I have desired (ἐπιθυμίᾳ ἐπεθύμησα) to eat this passover with you before I suffer' (Lk 22[15]). But owing to the corruption of the human heart, 'desire' tends to have a predominantly bad meaning, and so ἐπιθυμία comes to denote the sinful 'lusting' of a sinful will. In Mk 4[19] ('the lusts of other things') the word is already passing over to this fixity of a dark connotation; the 'other things' may not be evil in themselves, but as they are allowed to choke the word and render it unfruitful, they have to be classed as 'thorns.' In Mt 5[28] ἐπιθυμῆσαι expresses 'lust' in the specific sense in which it has come to be used in modern speech, as unholy sexual desire. In Jn 8[44] ἐπιθυμίας denotes the very 'lusts' of the devil as they are seen reappearing in his children.

According to the teaching of Jesus, impure desire, apart altogether from overt acts of sin, is itself a transgression of the Divine law (Mt 5[28]). This is the point at which Christ's ethical teaching so immeasurably transcends that of all other masters, and specifically the 'righteousness' of the scribes and Pharisees of His day. He taught that goodness and badness essentially lie not in the outward conduct but in the will and the heart, and that it is by the evil thoughts and feelings which issue

from within that a man is defiled (Mt 15[19f.]). It is this same teaching with regard to ἐπιθυμία, now used definitely in the sense of 'lust' or sinful desire, that we meet again in characteristic forms in the writings of St. Paul and St. James. St. James (1[14f.]) in his powerful figure shows how a man, seduced by his own ἐπιθυμία, begets the sin which issues finally in death. St. Paul (Ro 7[8ff.]) tells how the commandment οΥκ ἐπιθΥμΗσεις stirred up in his heart πᾶσαν ἐπιθυμίαν, and so forced him at length to understand that nothing but the law of the Spirit of life could set him free.

LITERATURE.—Moulton and Geden's *Concordance to the Greek Testament*, and the Lexicons of Grimm-Thayer and Cremer, *s.vv.* ἐπιθυμία, ἐπιθυμέω, θέλω; Müller, *Christian Doct. of Sin*, i. 157 ff.; Martensen, *Christian Ethics*, ii. 85 ff.; Liddon, *Elements of Religion*, p. 148 ff.; Dykes, *Manifesto of the King* p. 245 ff.; *Expositor*, IV. iv. [1891] 42 ff.; Milton, *Paradise Lost*, ii. 681 ff. J. C. LAMBERT.

DESOLATION.—The history of Israel had given to this word in the time of Christ a peculiar and sinister significance. To nearly all the prophets the idea of a wasted and depopulated land, such as is given in the graphic description of Is 1[7-9], is familiar. When Jeremiah and Ezekiel, who most frequently use the words, mention חָרְבָּה or שַׁמָּה, they always have one thing in their mind—the vision of a once peaceful and flourishing place which by fire and sword has been laid waste, and is left uninhabited. Few countries have suffered so much as Palestine from the havoc wrought by civil war and foreign invasion. To understand the full force of the term 'desolation,' we have to add to the features of war, as known to us, something which was then the frequent accompaniment of conquest—the carrying away of a whole population captive. And to the bitter memory of bygone devastation we have to add the apprehension of what might at any time happen if the country were swept by the Romans, of whose methods their own historian wrote, 'they make a solitude and call it peace' (Tac. *Agricola*, 30). The word 'desolation,' then, understood in the sense in which it was used when the AV was made ('I desolate—I make a countrey unhabyted,' Palsgrave, A.D. 1530), gives the exact sense of both the Hebrew and the Greek (ἐρήμωσις). It is in this sense that the word is used in the passage when Jesus pronounces doom upon Jerusalem (Mt 23[38], Lk 13[35]). The words, 'Your house is left unto you desolate,' are a reminiscence of Jer 22[5] (LXX—εἰς ἐρήμωσιν ἔσται ὁ οἶκος οὗτος), and it makes little difference whether ἔρημος stand in the text or not; the general idea is that the house (i.e. the city, not the temple) is 'abandoned.' There is not necessarily in this passage any prediction of the fall of Jerusalem, though the context may seem to suggest this. The idea is rather that, the glory of Jerusalem consisting in her being the city of the great King, she loses all when He abandons her. If she rejects Him, and He departs, she is a forsaken city (cf. the passage in Bunyan's *Holy War* where Emmanuel leaves Mansoul; also Jos. *B.J.* VI. v. 3). Grimm-Thayer interprets 'desolate' here as 'bereft of Christ's presence, instruction, and aid.' Contrast with this the promise to the disciples in Jn 14[18], which the AV renders, 'I will not leave you desolate' (ὀρφανούς).

In another passage (Mt 12[25], Lk 11[17]), 'Every kingdom divided against itself is brought to desolation,' Jesus uses as a forcible illustration that fatal tendency to faction and internal discord which had so often brought His countrymen to ruin (cf. e.g. Jos. *Ant.* XIV. iv. 2). See also art. ABOMINATION OF DESOLATION.

J. ROSS MURRAY.

DESPISE.—1. ἀθετεῖν.—(1) The primary signification of the word is to *render* or *consider invalid* (ἄθετον), to *set aside something laid down* (θετόν τι), to *bear oneself toward a thing as if it were not*, to *ignore* : Mk 7[9] ἀθ. τ. ἐντολὴν τ. θεοῦ (AV and RV 'reject'), to set aside the command of God, replacing it by tradition, and thus to deprive it of its force, by teaching and practice (cf. Is 24[16], Jude [8]). Hence (2) to *thwart the efficacy of anything* : Lk 7[30] τ. βουλὴν τ. θεοῦ (AV and RV 'reject'), to *set at nought as superfluous and invalid* (cf. Gal 2[21] 3[15], He 10[28]). Hence (3) of persons, to *ignore, bear oneself towards them as if they were not.* or *as if they need not be regarded or honoured* : Mk 6[26] αὐτήν (AV and RV 'reject'), *break faith with*, and then *disappoint* (Field, *Ot. Norv. in loc.*; cf. Ps 14(15)[4]), Lk 10[18] (RV 'reject'), to *ignore*, to *treat with contempt as deserving no recognition* (cf. 1 Th 4[8]). To ignore the messenger is to ignore the Son whose message he bears, and this is to ignore the Father who has sent the Son (Jn 12[48], AV and RV 'reject'). To ignore Christ and refuse His word is not to escape responsibility, or to disprove His claims. Denial is not disproof. 'The word cannot be banished. It still clings to the hearer as his judge. Spiritual judgment is a consequence involved in the rejection of the revelation : it is self-fulfilled : it cannot but be carried out.' Though rejected now, 'the word of Christ must justify itself' (Westcott) ; cf. Is 33[1].

2. ἐξουθενεῖν (-δενεῖν, -δενοῦν [see WH, App. p. 106]), to *hold* or *treat as of no account, despise utterly, set at nought* : Lk 18[9] (RV 'set at nought'). The Pharisees 'invented the most high-flown designations for each other, such as "Light of Israel," "Glory of the Law," etc., but they described the vast mass of their fellow-countrymen as "accursed" for not knowing the Law (Jn 7[49]), and spoke of them as empty cisterns' (Farrar, *in loc.*, cf. Ro 14[3. 10], 1 Co 16[11], Gal 4[14] etc., Pr 1[7]). The same word tr. by both AV and RV 'set at nought,' is used of the contempt and mockery with which Jesus was treated by the rulers (Mk 9[12] ἵνα ἐξουδενηθῇ ; Lk 23[11] ἐξουθ. αὐτὸν ὁ Ἡρῴδης), where the special significance of the word is that He was treated not even as a criminal, deserving examination of his case and righteous judgment, but as a mere cypher, to. be utterly despised ; cf. Ac 4[11], Ps 21 (22)[6], Is 53[3] [Symm.], Ezk 22[8].

3. καταφρονεῖν, to *look down upon* from a position of superiority, whether assumed or real, to *think lightly of*, to *neglect*, to *disdain*, with more or less actively hostile design (cf. Herod. i. 5. 66, viii. 10). Mt 6[24] ‖ Lk 16[13] : two masters, with opposing interests, cannot be served by the same person, the esteem in which they are held will vary according to the reward offered ; one will be actively honoured and diligently served, the other will be thought lightly of and his interests will be neglected. Mt 18[10] : μικροί are not to be held in disdain. (1) They are under the special care of God. Adopting the current Jewish doctrine of angels as guardian spirits, our Lord tells His hearers that children have friends in the court of heaven, in close nearness to the King Himself, whose 'Face' they always see ; there they are not thought lightly of, here they must not be despised. (2) Accepting the order of the verses, there is a close connexion between 'despising' and 'offending.' No hostile action must be taken towards them, even unconsciously, no carelessness as to conduct or example which might hurt them ; 'hindrances' to the life of young disciples, 'despised' because of their weakness, are sins against His love to them. (3) If the connexion with vv.[1-4] is original, the young are not to be 'despised,' because the childlike disposition is the true way to eternal life ; the humility which is essential for entering into the Kingdom of heaven has its symbol in the consciousness of weakness and imperfection that belongs to children, who are

therefore not to be 'despised' but 'received' (cf. Pr 13[13], Gn 27[12]).

The active hostility implied in the word is seen in Ro 2[4] τ. μακροθυμίας καταφρονεῖς : God's longsuffering not only treated with contempt, but also opposed by being sinned against (cf. 1 Ti 4[12]). In He 12[2] αἰσχύνης καταφρ., the simply passive sense is given—enduring with the resignation that arises from the disdain of real superiority. 'What men count shame was seen by Christ in another light. From His position, raised infinitely above them, He could disregard their judgment' (Westcott, *in loc.*).

ἀθετεῖν and ἐξουθενεῖν are not used by classical writers. καταφρονεῖν is in constant use from Herodotus onwards.

R. MACPHERSON.

DESPONDENCY.—Despondency fills so frequent and serious a place in human life that we could hardly have felt that our Lord was 'tempted in all points like as we are' (He 4[15]), if He had not experienced it. But the profound depression in the garden of Gethsemane, even if it were alone, and the memorable word, 'My soul is exceeding sorrowful, even unto death' (Mt 26[38] ‖ Mk 14[34]), testify that He had such experience. What was the cause of this depression in Gethsemane ? Was it due to bodily exhaustion, the body affecting the mind and making it more sensitive to sad surroundings ? Was it due to the mental strain of publicity and opposition, or to loneliness and the pain of failure ? ('He came unto his own, and his own received him not,' Jn 1[11]). All these were elements in the despondency of Elijah when he sat under the juniper tree, and requested for himself that he might die (1 K 19[4]). And we may not say that such influences were wholly without effect on our Lord ; but in His case, as we learn from His own words, the great cause of despondency was the pressure on His spirit of what He saw near before Him, His cross—that death in which He was (in St. Peter's language) to bear our sins in His own body (1 P 2[24]), or (in St. Paul's) to be made sin for us (2 Co 5[21]), and in which He was to endure that sense of separation from God which was so new to the experience of the well-beloved Son. But why was the depression so great now in Gethsemane when He had looked forward to this from the beginning of His ministry, saying in an early stage of it, 'The Son of man must be lifted up' (Jn 3[14]) ? Part of the answer to this question must be that our Lord's mind, being truly human, was liable to those often mysterious alternations of feeling which, in common men, we call changes of mood. As He drew nearer the accomplishment of the great work of atonement, we find Him sometimes hastening eagerly towards it, full of great purpose, even of joy, and at other times foreseeing the darkness of the experience and shrinking from it. At one of the stages of His approach to that event, and of His own inward acceptance of it, namely after the dismissal of Judas, this joyful anticipation was expressed by Him in language even of exultation —'Now is the Son of man glorified, and God is glorified in him' (Jn 13[31]). At another stage He speaks in quite a different manner, 'Now is my soul troubled ; and what shall I say ? Father, save me from this hour' (Jn 12[27]).

Dr. Maclaren has finely illustrated this alternation of feeling. 'Like some great pillar elevated on a mountain, when the thunder-clouds fill the sky, it stands out grim and dark ; and then, in a moment, the strong wind sweeps these away, and the sunlight smites it, and it shines out white and lustrous. With such swift alternations . . . to Jesus Christ the Cross was dark and the Cross was radiant' (*Last Sheaves*, 27).

The Gethsemane experience was perhaps that in which our Lord felt most profoundly the dark and heavy pressure of the anticipation of the Cross. How dark and heavy that was appears in the 'sweat as it were great drops of blood falling down upon the ground' (Lk 22[44]), in the 'strong crying and tears' (He 5[7]), and perhaps as much in these words of His prayer, '*if it be possible*'—in His seeking a possibility of the cup passing from Him, although

He had said long before, 'The Son of man must be lifted up' (Jn 3¹⁴), and was to say soon after, 'For this cause came I unto this hour' (12²⁷). See, further, art. AGONY.   J. ROBERTSON.

DESTRUCTION.—The AV and RV tr. of ἀπώλεια in Mt 7¹³. In Mt 26⁸ and in the parallel passage in Mk 14⁴ ἀπώλεια is translated 'waste' in both Versions, and in Jn 17¹², the only other instance where the word is used in the Gospels, both render it '**perdition.**' In Mt 7¹³ our Lord speaks of 'destruction' as the opposite of life eternal. In profane authors ἀπώλεια invariably means, as its derivation from ἀπόλλυμι implies, *extinction, annihilation*; and this fact has been largely used by the advocates of the Conditional Immortality theory in support of their contention. Still the 'destruction' spoken of by our Lord in Mt 7¹³ has been held by expositors with practical unanimity from the first to mean a continued life, whether endless or not, of misery after death. All the same, it has been admitted generally, *e.g.* by Cremer, that eternal misery as a meaning of ἀπώλεια 'is a signification peculiar to the NT, and without analogy in classical Greek.' There appears, on the whole, to be general agreement that whether 'destruction' means a terminable or interminable life of misery after death, it does, at any rate, mean a prolongation of existence: it is exclusion from salvation, whether final or not. Whether or not there is a term to the duration of misery hereafter—presuming that there is a continuance of life after death for those who go in the way of destruction—does not enter into the scope of this note (see ETERNAL PUNISHMENT), but it may be remarked as significant that the 'lost sheep' are spoken of by our Lord as being found again, and that the word for 'lost' is the participle of ἀπόλλυμι. This is one of the considerations that have made many feel warranted in holding 'the larger hope' even for those who go meanwhile in 'the way that leadeth to destruction.'
        J. CROMARTY SMITH.

DEVIL.—See DEMON and SATAN.

DEVOTION.—The word does not occur in the Gospels, but the idea is present everywhere, as marking the attitude of the man Jesus towards God, and thus providing a standard for imitation by every other man. Intrinsically the word denotes the act of presenting solemnly some gift or service to a deity, or to any one invested in thought for a time with some of the qualities or claims of a deity; but its use has been extended to cover alike such service itself, and even the psychological condition from which the act springs. As such, a correct analysis must find blended in devotion each of the three elements—thought, emotion, and volition—which are the mutually dependent fragments of the unit of personality, expressing itself as a whole in the exercises often called devotions. The intellectual element is a recognition of the dignity and patient grace of God, the sensitive a feeling of gratitude and desire to please, the volitional a strong resolve to carry out that desire; and these three pass together quickly into appropriate action, the whole man in the harmony of all his powers indicating by praise or service the depth of his loving regard.

In some definitions, too much prominence is given to the will, and devotion is confused with religion generally, as in Aquinas, *Summa*, II.² lxxxii. 1: 'Devotio nihil aliud esse videtur, quam voluntas quædam prompte tradendi se ad ea, quæ pertinent ad Dei famulatum.' In certain phrases the word is used as a synonym for worship, or even for a form of worship, as when devotion to the Sacred Heart is spoken of; and in others, as 'feasts of devotion,' it acquires an entirely technical sense, implying the absence of express obligation, with an appeal only to the discretion and good feeling of the worshipper. But in the better use internal devotion is contrasted with external

worship (Atterbury, *Sermons*, iv. 213), and may be resolved into four principal constituents. The self-conscious determination of the will towards God is followed by the actual exaltation of the soul to God and its suffusion with the reverent sense of His nearness and mercy. This is exhibited in various loving acts and exercises, such as prayer and praise. And the whole is effected in the heart under the influence of the Holy Spirit.

1. In the case of *Christ* each of these phases of devotion is represented in the Gospels. (*a*) Though but a mere lad, He indicates already a habitual Godward set of His will (Lk 2⁴⁹, He 10⁷); and afterwards He speaks of His purpose, sometimes with quiet assurance (Jn 5³⁰ 6³⁸ 7¹⁸), sometimes with a certain glow of satisfaction (4³⁴ 17⁴). Hindrances and sore temptations, in which the play of a natural and useful instinct may be traced, did not divert Him (Lk 9⁵¹ 22⁴²). Glad, complete conformity with the will of God, such as is an integrant of every right conception of heaven, is set forth as on earth the aim of every disciple (Mt 6¹⁰), reached at once and maintained without defect, though not without effort (cf. Harnack, *What is Christianity?*³ 129 f.), by Him alone who could say, 'I and the Father are one' (Jn 10³⁰).

(*b*) Instances of the exaltation of His soul in the calm sense of security because of the accord of His will with that of the Father, occur in the impression His fearlessness made at the cleansing of the Temple (2¹⁶ᶠ·)—in His endowment with 'honour and glory' at the Transfiguration (2 P 1¹⁷)—in the strengthening ministry of angels after the Temptation (Mt 4¹¹), and the Agony (Lk 22⁴³ RVm). The joy of Mt 11²⁵ and Lk 10²¹ is another instance, as is also the outburst of triumphant relief at the retirement of Judas (Jn 13³¹ᶠ·). Nor should His perfect repose in the midst of peril (Mk 4³⁸ᶠ·), and in the presence of angry or eager mobs (Lk 4²⁹ᶠ·, Jn 8⁵⁹ 10³¹ᶠ· 6¹⁵), be overlooked. Partial and auxiliary explanations may be found in the exhaustion of fatigue or the mastery of His nerves; but the real cause was moral and not physical, and should be sought in the self-consciousness of Jesus, in the stable correlation of His will and God's. The two streams of volition, human and Divine, met and merged in Him; and thus He becomes for men at once an example of perfect devotion and a pledge of perfect grace.

(*c*) The exercises appropriate to devotion, which, however, so far from confining itself to them, enriches the entire nature and affects every relation of life, are praise and prayer (see sep. artt.), with the addition of meditation, and occasionally of fasting or some form of self-discipline. The prayer and praise are not exactly such as accompany public worship, but assume rather the character of communion or reverent conversation, the element of specific supplication being often, not always, absent. In the case of Christ the praise is illustrated in such passages as Lk 10²¹ᶠ·, the practice of meditation and prayer in the lonely night-watches and the desert in Mk 6⁴⁶, Lk 5¹⁶, whilst the supplication becomes more specific in Lk 6¹², in Gethsemane, and perhaps also on the Mount of Transfiguration. Of actual fasting by Jesus as a definite process of devotion, there is no certain case in the Gospels; but there is no reason to suppose that He did not follow the usage of His country on the Day of Atonement. Fasting, too, is associated with the Temptation (Mt 4²), of which one lesson is that a pure conscience and an ideal conformity with God can be attained or retained only by self-discipline and hard steadfastness under testing. And even in the Sermon on the Mount the practice is guarded from abuse, and implicitly commended in Mt 6¹⁶ᶠ·; and the supposition is warranted that our Lord was prepared to exemplify in His own person whatever He recommended to His disciples. His life, as well as His teaching, shows that fasting in itself has no devotional or any other religious value, but is serviceable only when and in so far as it promotes the closeness of communion with God. See FASTING.

(d) The plenary presence of the Holy Spirit with Christ is an implication of the NT, which, however, is comparatively reticent as to the Spirit's influence in the interval from the Temptation to the eve of the Passion. The action of the Spirit at the Temptation is referred to by all the Synoptists (Mt 4[1], Mk 1[12], Lk 4[1]), and His aid must be regarded as part of the explanation of Christ's sinlessness on this and all subsequent occasions. Not only were His miracles wrought in the power of the Spirit (Mt 12[28], Lk 4[14. 18]), but His oneness with the Spirit made His life uninterrupted devotion, and 'through the eternal Spirit' He 'offered himself without blemish unto God' (He 9[14]). The rapture of His soul is attributed to the influence of the Spirit in Lk 10[21], though this particular is omitted in the corresponding narrative of Mt 11[25]. And the devotion of Christ is an example for man, not only because it exhibits human triumph over temptation and human fellowship with God, but also because of the similarity of the means and aids. His complete unction is the promise and measure of the anointing available to every one.

2. In the case of *man*, devotion appears in the Gospels as an act or state of the entire personality, with all its powers harmoniously and intensely engaged. Prominence is given to the same elements as are traceable in the devotion of Christ Himself, whilst ample safeguards against error and fanaticism are provided. The great rule of Dt 6[5] is adopted by Christ, and applied in each of the Synoptics (Mt 22[37], Mk 12[30], Lk 10[27]) with little variations of phrase that add to the uncompromising vigour. In the Sermon on the Mount the exclusiveness of devotion, as admitting no rival claim and absorbing supreme affection, is recognized in Mt 6[21. 24]; so in another connexion in Lk 16[13]. And in the closing discourses Christ puts Himself forward as actually and solely central to the life of His disciples (Jn 14[6]), the source of all their strength, the right object of their trust and love (15[9-11] 16[22]), with the recurring refrain, emphasized by its modifications, 'Abide in me' (15[4. 5] *et al.*). Fruitfulness in the graces of personal character, and then secondarily in obedience and service, results from the deliberate regarding of Christ as 'all in all,' as so filling up the sphere of thought and desire as to control everything else therein. The last clause in Jn 15[5] means by implication that possibilities to the disciple are proportionate to the closeness of his devout union with his Lord; and that union may, and should, reach a stage of completeness, in which the indwelling Christ becomes the unquestioned ruler of all within the heart, and the whole life in the flesh is lived 'in faith, the faith which is in the Son of God' (Gal 2[20]). It is the crown of Christian devotion, not the joint sovereignty of Christ and the ego, but the loving and eager retirement of the ego that Christ may be substituted, appropriating its functions and reigning in its stead. Thus Christ Himself teaches in one of the most sacred parts of Scripture: 'I in them' (Jn 17[23. 26]) is the final and fullest blessing and privilege conceivable in that hour of vision for those whom He loved 'to the uttermost' (13[1] RVm).

(a) Specifically, as might be expected before Pentecost, the Gospels give more prominence to the action of the human will as a condition of discipleship than to its subsequent concentration as the condition of progress and perfecting. But the example of Christ Himself is, in this matter, a sufficient safeguard and sanction, and is enforced by teaching of at least two types. 'If any man willeth to do his will' (Jn 7[17]), supplies the key not only to the knowledge of the things of the Kingdom, but also to the fulfilment in personal character of God's purpose of sanctification, Bengel's *suavis harmonia* being both a cause and the effect of insatiable yearning. Again, glad consent, with persistency of will, is an important element in our Lord's frequent exhortations to His disciples to 'abide' in Him or in His word (Jn 15[4] 8[31] *et al.*). One of the characteristics of the Johannine setting of the Gospel, as of the prophecies of Jeremiah in the OT, is the emphasis laid on the sustained determination of the will towards God.

(b) The exaltation of spirit, accompanying and enriched by this firmness of purpose, receives more adequate expression in later times, but is far from being left entirely without illustration. Such passages as Jn 12[19. 32] speak of a magnetic influence on the part of Christ, to which the response was at the beginning more than that of admiration, and soon deepened into supreme and rapturous attachment. The *Magnificat* (Lk 1[46-55]) and the *Nunc Dimittis* (Lk 2[29-32]) anticipate the exultation of men, partly at the accomplished work of Christ, partly at the abundance and the effect of His grace to the individual; and the self-forgetfulness of grateful and passionate devotion is illustrated in Lk 7[37-48]. Mary's 'Rabboni' (Jn 20[16]) and Thomas' 'My Lord' (Jn 20[28]) express absorbed attachment as well as conviction. In the parables the joy is occasionally festal and general, but sometimes becomes that of personal and assured possession (Mt 13[44. 46]), or is even lifted up into likeness to the Saviour's own joy, incapable of dimness or of eclipse (Jn 15[11], Mt,25[21]). The disciple in his Lord's bosom (Jn 13[23. 25]) is a type and guarantee.

(c) The loving acts and exercises in which the devout spirit beneficially expresses itself are of almost infinite variety in their character, and, though their most ingenious exhibition is met with subsequently, they are not left without trace or starting-point in the Gospels. Beyond the example of the Saviour, an encouragement to quiet meditation may be found in Mk 6[31], a commendation of private prayer in Mt 6[6]. Self-discipline, as removing the occasions of sin and as aiding the communion of the human spirit with God, is enjoined in such passages as Mt 5[29. 30], though in others the object becomes the avoidance of conduct that might offend or imperil the souls of the weak.

That self-discipline is in itself and apart from its motives meritorious, is nowhere taught by Christ, and such a notion is quite contrary to the genius of Christianity. Christ's treatment of fasting is an illustration. He evidently looked forward to its practice by His disciples not only in their association and in times of general calamity and mourning (Mt 9[14. 15], Mk 2[18-20], Lk 5[34. 35]), but individually under the prompting of personal need and as a preparation for personal blessing. That an access of spiritual power might thereby be secured is a legitimate inference from Mt 17[21] and Mk 9[29], though textual evidence is against any specific reference to fasting in these verses, the corruption of which may well have been due to the incorporation of a devotional gloss. In Mt 6[16-18] it is assumed that disciples will fast; injunctions are given with a view to secure purity of intention, and the good effect is guaranteed in the 'recompense' of the Father. Hence private fasting as an observance is distinctly recognized by Christ. According to His rule, invariable except in the case of prayer (where, moreover, the prescription is that of a model rather than a form), He does not prescribe forms. He puts in its right place of control the object of pleasing the Father, who sees in secret, and knows the whole heart and way of a man. And with this implicit injunction of fasting, and protection against its misuse and perils, He leaves every disciple to determine for himself the best application of the principle in the interest of the well-being and enrichment of the soul.

(d) Before Pentecost the action of the Holy Spirit in human devotion is, for the most part, anticipatory and a matter of promise, but as such is none the less important. His presence is that which will prevent the disciples from becoming 'desolate' and without resource (Jn 14[18]) on the departure of their Master; and, being present, He will act in them as the Father's Paraclete (Jn 14[16] *et al.*), advocating the cause of God and promoting all Godward impulse and desire. Specifically, He will guide 'into all the truth' (Jn 16[13]), bringing the disciples into right relation, both intellectual and practical, with saving truth, and maintaining within them a condition of composure and serenity (Lk 1[79]). The power to do 'greater works' is associated with the return of Christ to His Father (Jn 14[12]), and therefore, by implication, with the mission of the Spirit; and if the complaint is sometimes just that those greater works are not being done, the cause is to be found not in the inadequacy of opportunity or resource, but in the defectiveness of personal devotion. Its degree is commensurate with that of right volition on the part of the disciple, and with that of possession on the part of the Spirit; and these two, again, are mutually dependent. 'In the Spirit' by fixed and abiding purpose, is the law on the one side; the Spirit in the disciple is the correlated privilege, with the absolute harmony between Christ and the Spirit as the only limit of possible human experience, and as its inspiration and pledge.

LITERATURE.—Dykes, *Manifesto of the King*, 333–437; Stalker, *Imago Christi*, ch. vii. R. W. Moss.

DIDRACHM.—See MONEY.

DIDYMUS.—The alternative name of the Apostle Thomas, given in three passages in the Fourth Gospel (Jn 11[16] 20[24] 21[2] Θωμᾶς ὁ λεγόμενος Δίδυμος). The adj. δίδυμος is regular Greek from Homer onwards, with the meaning 'twofold'; hence δίδυμος as subs. = 'a twin.' Δίδυμος is the translation, as Θωμᾶς is the transliteration, of אֲרָאָה = תֹּאם 'a twin.'

Why St. John calls special attention to this name is not clear. Westcott suggests that Thomas may have been familiarly known in Asia Minor among the Gentile Christians as *Didymus*. Jn 4[25] ('Messiah . . . which is called Christ') shows that Thomas was not called *Didymus* as an additional name. See THOMAS. E. H. TITCHMARSH.

DINNER (ἄριστον, Mt 22[4], Lk 11[38] [RVm 'breakfast'] 14[12]).—In the East there is no meal properly corresponding to our breakfast. Even the guest is allowed to depart in the morning without 'bite or sup.' Eating and drinking early in the day are held to be marks of effeminacy and self-indulgence, and are regarded as bad for the system. Many, especially when on a journey, are content with one meal in the twenty-four hours, taken after sunset. In general, however, a light meal is eaten about the middle of the day, consisting of bread, olives, fruit, *leben* (sour curded milk), cheese, etc.; but the principal meal is in the evening. Eating at other times is quite casual and informal. It is probably correct to say that in NT ἄριστον and δεῖπνον correspond respectively to our luncheon and dinner. See, further, art. MEALS.

W. EWING.

DISCIPLE.—1. In the NT 'disciple' (sing. and plur.) occurs very frequently in the Gospels and Acts, but not elsewhere in NT. In every case it represents the Gr. μαθητής = (1) 'learner,' 'pupil,' in contrast to 'teacher,' as Mt 10[24]; and (2) 'adherent,' one who is identified with a certain leader, or school, and adopts a corresponding line of conduct, as Mk 2[18] 'Why do John's disciples and the disciples of the Pharisees fast, but thy disciples fast not?' cf. Jn 9[28] 'Thou art his disciple; but we are disciples of Moses.' Our Lord Himself points to and discourages a loose use of the term 'disciple,' according to which it meant no more than 'hearer,' when He says, 'If ye abide in my word, then are ye truly my disciples' (Jn 8[31]; cf.

His statement of the conditions of discipleship, Lk 14[26. 27. 33] and Jn 15[8]). As used by the Evangelists, 'disciples' has sometimes a broader and sometimes a narrower significance. For the former, see Lk 6[13. 17] 'a great multitude of his disciples,' Ac 6[2] 'And the twelve called the multitude of the disciples unto them,' cf. 4[32]. It is evident that to St. Luke τῶν πιστευσάντων and τῶν μαθητῶν were equivalent expressions. Hence, when we read in Ac 19[1f.] of 'certain disciples,' who when they 'believed' heard nothing of the gift of the Holy Ghost and were baptized 'into John's baptism,' we must understand thereby *Christian* disciples, though in an 'immature stage of knowledge' (see Knowling's note on the passage, *Expos. Gr. Test.*). For 'disciples' in the narrower sense = the inner circle of the followers of Jesus, 'the Twelve,' see Mt 8[23] 11[1] 14[15] 26[18], and frequently. Thus, as applied to the followers of our Lord, 'disciples' is a term of varying content. It is of interest in passing to note the various appellations by which the disciples address the Saviour, expressing divers aspects of the relation which they held to subsist between themselves and Him. He was to them (1) Teacher (διδάσκαλος), Mk 4[38], Jn 13[13f.]; (2) Superintendent (ἐπιστάτης), only in Lk.: 5[5] 8[45] 9[35] 9[49]; (3) Lord (κύριος; from Lk 6[46] we should gather that this was the designation most usually adopted by the disciples); (4) My Teacher (ῥαββί), Mt 26[25], Mk 9[5], Jn 4[31] 11[8].

2. Restricting ourselves to the more limited sense in which 'disciples' is used of the followers of our Lord, we may note the *composition of the Twelve*. The Synoptics and Acts provide the following lists:—

Mt 10[2ff.].	Mk 3[16ff.].	Lk 6[14ff.].	Ac 1[13].
Simon.	Simon.	Simon.	Peter.
Andrew.	James.	Andrew.	John.
James.	John.	James.	James.
John.	Andrew.	John.	Andrew
Philip.	Philip.	Philip.	Philip.
Bartholomew.	Bartholomew.	Bartholomew.	Thomas.
Thomas.	Matthew.	Matthew.	Bartholomew.
Matthew.	Thomas.	Thomas.	Matthew.
James of Alphæus.	James of Alphæus.	James of Alphæus.	James of Alphæus.
Thaddæus (Lebbæus).	Thaddæus.	Simon the Zealot.	Simon the Zealot.
Simon the Cananæan.	Simon the Cananæan.	Judas of James.	Judas of James.
Judas Iscariot.	Judas Iscariot.	Judas Iscariot.	..

Comparing these lists, it is apparent that common to them all is the division of the Twelve into groups of four. The sequence of the groups is the same in each list. Within the groups the order of the names varies, save as regards the first name of each of the three groups, which in all the lists is same—the first, fifth, and ninth places being occupied in all by Simon (Peter), Philip, and James of Alphæus respectively. See, further, art. APOSTLES, p. 103[a] f., and the separate articles on the above names.

3. *The calling of the Twelve.*—If this phrase be taken quite strictly, there is no difficulty in determining when and under what circumstances the call to which it refers was given. The Synoptic accounts are in virtual accord. They show that it was not at the outset of His ministry that our Lord increased the company of His immediate followers until it numbered *twelve*. That increase took place when the fame of His teaching and words, as He went through the towns and villages of Galilee, 'preaching the gospel of the kingdom, healing all manner of disease and all manner of sickness' (Mt 9[35]), both attracted to Him the attention of the populace, and so excited the resentment of the scribes and Pharisees that they began to take counsel with the Herodians 'how they might destroy him' (Mk 3[6]). The need for more labourers was evident, and not less evident to Jesus the

signs that the time for training such labourers might be short. St. Matthew tells, immediately before he records the calling of the Twelve, that when Jesus 'saw the multitudes he was moved with compassion for them, because they were distressed and scattered, as sheep not having a shepherd. Then saith he unto his disciples, The harvest truly is plenteous, but the labourers are few. Pray ye therefore the Lord of the harvest, that he send forth labourers into his harvest' (Mt 9[36ff.]). That summons to prayer becomes more urgent and pressing in the light of St. Luke's record, that immediately prior to His choosing the Apostles our Lord 'went out into the mountain to pray; and he continued all night in prayer to God. And when it was day, he called his disciples, and he chose from them twelve' (Lk 6[12ff.]). The immediate purpose of the call is expressed by St. Mark thus: 'And he appointed twelve that they might be with him, and that he might send them forth to preach, and to have authority to cast out devils' (Mk 3[14f.]). On the question whether some of the Twelve had not received a previous call, or perhaps more than one previous call, to be followers of Jesus, and if so, in what relation these earlier callings stand to the appointment of the Twelve, see art. APOSTLES.

4. *The training of the Twelve.*—When St. Mark tells us (3[14]) that Jesus 'appointed twelve that they might be with him, and that he might send them forth to preach,' he discloses the characteristic and the all-important feature of the method of their training. They were to see the works of the Saviour and to hear His words, and in addition to that they were to be constantly in contact with His personality : they were to be *with Him* (see above, p. 107).

That 'course of instruction,' as Keim calls it, which contact with Jesus secured to His disciples, was maintained with very slight interruption from the calling of the Twelve until the Betrayal. The chief intermission, of which we have any word, of the intercourse of Jesus with His chosen followers, was occasioned by that mission on which the Twelve were sent quite soon after their call (Mt 10[5]). The interval occupied by the mission was probably not more than a few days—'at least a week' (Latham, *Pastor Pastorum*, p. 301). That mission was a testing of the Apostles themselves, not less than an act of service to those to whom they were sent; and the test was so endured that it needed not to be repeated. The Twelve went forth under the conditions which Jesus prescribed : they delivered the message He bade them, and they used freely the power to heal with which they were entrusted. No similar service separated them again from their Master,—unless, indeed, they had part in that mission of the Seventy of which St. Luke tells (10[1ff.]). The time would yet come for them to deliver their testimony and to fulfil their ministry. Meanwhile the Saviour jealously guards for them the precious opportunities which remain for free intercourse with Himself. He leads them away from the crowds, taking them now to 'a desert place' (Mk 6[31]), and again to the remote 'parts of Cæsarea Philippi' (Mt 16[13]). We gain the impression that as the brief spell of His own earthly ministry neared its term, our Lord concentrated Himself increasingly upon the inner band of His followers. Ewald is true to the indication of the Gospel narratives when he says that 'the community of His friends' was to our Lord 'during the last year and a half the main object of His earthly labours' (*HI*, vol. vi. 417). Should it be asked more particularly what was the *instruction* of which the Twelve were the recipients, a full answer would require a recapitulation of all the teaching of Jesus. This much

may be said here, that the Twelve shared the instruction given to 'the multitude,' with the added advantage of the explanations which they sought, and which our Lord freely accorded them, 'when he was alone,' 'privately.' See Mk 4[34], on which Swete (*Gospel according to St. Mark*, p. 84) comments : 'Exposition now regularly followed (ἐπέλυεν πάντα) the public teaching.' Furthermore, the Gospels contain records of discourses addressed only to the inner circle of the disciples. Among such discourses should be reckoned in all probability part at least of the group of addresses known as the 'Sermon on the Mount'—notably the part contained in Mt 5, which bears all the marks of a discourse to more immediate followers. Not, however, that the more immediate followers are in this particular connexion to be restricted to the Twelve, since the discourse in Mt 5 must—in spite of the position St. Luke gives to his version of it (6[12ff.])—be placed earlier than the calling of the Twelve ; it 'has throughout the character of an early and opening discourse.' None the less it is to be accounted among our Lord's less public utterances: it is 'Jesus' address of welcome to His band of disciples' (Keim, *op. cit.* 286–290). Again, in Mt 10[5-42] we have what appears at first sight to be a sustained address to the Twelve in reference to their mission. But on a comparison with Mk 6[8-11] and Lk 9[2-5] it seems likely that only vv.[5-14] were spoken with direct reference to the mission, and that vv.[15-42] are grouped with them, though coming from a later time, because they contained sayings of Jesus in reference to a kindred topic — the future missionary labours of the Apostles. Yet further must be added to the discourses delivered to the Twelve alone, the apocalyptic discourse Mt 24 (cf. Mk 13 and Lk 21), with its parabolic sequel in ch. 25 ; and the discourse in the upper room on the night of the Betrayal (Jn 14–16). And when we endeavour to tabulate the instruction imparted more privately to the Twelve, we may not omit the *signs*, each so full of teaching for them, of which they alone—and in one case but three of their number—were the spectators. The Walking on the Sea, the Transfiguration, the Cursing of the Barren Fig-tree, the Feet-washing in the Upper Room, the Miraculous Draught of Fishes (Jn 21[4ff.]),—these all surely formed part of the lessons most indelibly impressed on the Twelve.

Our Lord Himself has characterized for us the purpose and the content of the teaching He imparted to His followers. It was that to them might be given 'the mystery of the kingdom of God' (Mk 4[11]). 'As given to the Apostles it was still a secret, not yet to be divulged, nor even except in a small degree intelligible to themselves' (Swete, *op. cit.* p. 72). The Kingdom, the characteristics of its subjects, its laws, its service, and, finally, its Lord reigning through suffering—such in broad outline was the course of the instruction imparted by Jesus to the Twelve. It moved onward from the simpler to the more profound. 'At first, sayings are given them to remember; latterly, they receive mysteries on which to meditate. In the Sermon on the Mount men are told plainly what it is desirable for them to know ; afterwards, the teaching passes through parables and hard sayings up to the mysteries conveyed by the Last Supper' (Latham, *op. cit.* 120). But no teaching, not even the teaching of Jesus Himself, could overcome the reluctance to believe that it behoved that the Christ should suffer, or arouse anticipations of the glories that should follow. The crucifixion and death of our Lord found the Eleven unprepared, and ready to despair, though they still held together in the bonds of a love they had acquired in the school of Jesus. It needed the actual fact of the Resurrection, and converse with the risen Saviour, and the illumination of the Spirit, to bring them to a true understanding of all that reiterated teaching concerning His death and His rising from the dead which Jesus had given 'while He was yet with them.' But once that understanding was attained by the disciples, the truth against which their minds had been stubbornly closed became central in their proclamation. There is abundant evidence that the Apostles were slow learners—men with no special quickness of insight, and with the hindrance of strongly developed prejudice. It is also evident that their slowness and prejudice have for us an apologetic value (see esp. Bruce, *Training of the Twelve*, p. 482 : 'They were stupid, slow-minded persons ; very honest, but very unapt to take in new ideas. . . . Let us be thankful for the honest stupidity of these men, it gives great value to their testimony. We know that nothing but facts could make such men believe that which nowadays they get credit for inventing'). It concerns us yet more to recall the evidence which their training affords of the patience and transforming power of Him who now, not less truly than in the days of His flesh, calls weak men to Himself that they may be with Him, and that He may send them forth to bear witness on His behalf, enduing them with His Spirit, that their testimony, like that of the Apostles, may not be in vain. See also art. APOSTLES.

LITERATURE.—Bruce, *The Training of the Twelve* ; Latham, *Pastor Pastorum* ; Neander, *Life of Christ* ; Ewald, *History of Israel*, Eng. tr. vol. vi. ; Keim, *Jesus of Nazara*, Eng. tr. vol. iii. ; Weiss, *The Life of Christ* ; Sanday, *Outlines of the Life of Christ* [art. 'Jesus Christ' in Hastings' *DB*] ; Edersheim, *The Life and Times of Jesus the Messiah* ; Greenhough, *The Apostles of Our Lord.* GEORGE P. GOULD.

DISCIPLESHIP.—In the Gospels no word expressive of 'discipleship' occurs, although they are full of the living reality which it expresses. This is not surprising, for it is never God's way to teach abstract truth, but truth embodied in actual life. From the concrete and the living facts it is left to us, by the exercise of our natural faculties, to abstract the generalization or induction which presents the idea in its purity. Christ always followed the Divine method ; and, accordingly, while He made disciples, and trained them in discipleship, He hardly made any attempt to define or describe what this involves ; nor did He give much instruction which represented with any directness the ideal that He had in view. From these negative facts themselves the primary truth on this subject may be learnt : Discipleship, in the Christian sense, is essentially a matter for living realization rather than for psychological analysis or formal compliance.

If for His followers later the making of disciples began with preaching the gospel, for the Lord Himself it commonly began with the authoritative appeal, 'Follow me.' There were, of course, times when this summons called a man literally to arise and go with Jesus to some new place and duty ; as when the first among the Twelve 'left the nets and followed him' (Mk 1[18. 20]). But the same summons was still employed by the Lord after His resurrection, when it could have no such literal signification (Jn 21[19]). And there is a group of instances (Mt 10[38] 16[24], Jn 12[26]) in which 'bearing the cross' and 'disowning oneself' are conjoined with the call to follow Him, where it is clear that 'following' has wholly a spiritual sense. The fact that we speak of 'following an example' too often leads to the misinterpretation of this pregnant call to discipleship which was so characteristic of the Lord Jesus. It is no injunction to copy Him, though, of course, the imitation of Christ must enter into the aim of

every disciple. That, however, belongs to a rather later stage of discipleship, while the summons to 'follow' is its initiation. The choice of this word rests upon the ancient metaphor of a 'way of life' which Christ adopted for Himself when He affirmed 'I am the Way,' and which underlay and coloured not a little of His language. So the call, 'Follow me,' is an appeal to trust His guidance, and venture oneself along the track that He explores into the unknown regions of life, with the need of 'bearing the cross' and 'losing life to find it.' 'Come on ! Fear not to go through the valley of the shadow of death with me in the quest of life. "He that is near me is near the fire ; he that is far from me is far from the kingdom."' Thus at the threshold of discipleship lies the requirement which He always made of those to whom He rendered service,—the requirement of courageous trust or 'faith.' And for such as are ready to obey this first appeal to 'follow' He opens 'a new and living way through the veil' which hides so much of the realms of life from our eyes. And this way is 'human to the red-ripe of the heart,' and fit for human feet to travel, for the way is 'His flesh,' His mortal life, His human nature—what for us men and for our salvation He came down to make His own.

There are some few sayings in which the Lord delineates the features of discipleship under one or another of its aspects. *E.g.* 'A disciple is not above his master . . . it is enough for the disciple that he be as his master. . . . If they have called the master of the house Beelzebub, how much more them of his household?' (Mt 10[24f.]). And in close connexion with this stands the reiterated teaching, 'Whosoever he be of you that renounceth not all that he hath, he cannot be my disciple' (Lk 14[25-33]). Elsewhere He emphasizes not the outward lot, but the inner character of discipleship : *e.g.* 'Come unto me all ye that labour. . . . Take my yoke upon you, and learn of me ; for I am gentle and lowly in heart : and ye shall find rest unto your souls' (Mt 11[28f.]). The same gentleness and lowliness which are ever ready to render loving service are again taught as characteristics of discipleship in the action of washing the disciples' feet on the last evening, when, having sat down again, He said, 'Perceive ye what I have done to you? Ye call me Teacher and Lord : and ye say well ; for so I am. If I then, the Lord and the Teacher, washed your feet, ye also ought to wash one another's feet. For I gave you an example that ye also should do as I have done to you' (Jn 13[12ff.], cf. also Lk 22[24-26], Mk 9[33-37], Mt 23[10-12]). What the disciple must learn is not mainly 'teaching'; he must 'learn Christ.' 'Truth is in Jesus,'—'the Truth and the Life,'—and the disciple must grow 'in the knowledge and love of God and of His Son Jesus Christ our Lord.' So love is what must be learnt above all else, and affords the test of true discipleship. 'By this shall all men know that ye are my disciples, if ye have love one to another' (Jn 13[35]). And the Lord traces discipleship down to its roots when He declares, 'No man can come to me except the Father which sent me draw him. . . . It is written . . . They shall all be taught of God. Every one that hath heard from the Father, and hath learned, cometh unto me' (Jn 6[44f.]).

A large proportion of the Lord's teaching bears, of course, upon the nature of discipleship and the character of the disciple, even when it is not cast in the form of dealing with this directly. *E.g.* the Beatitudes (Mt 5[3ff.]) are, under one aspect, all so many facets of discipleship ; metaphors like 'the salt of the earth,' the 'light of the world' (Mt 5[13. 14]), 'a little flock' (Lk 12[32]), 'the branches of the vine' (Jn 15[5]), 'every plant which my heavenly Father hath not planted' (Mt 15[13]), and many another, including those developed into parables,—all sketch some features of discipleship, as do such sayings as that one must be reborn, and much of the teaching concerning the Kingdom.

The final charge which the Lord laid upon the disciples whom He had trained and tested Himself was, 'Going forth, make ye disciples of all the nations' (μαθητεύσατε πάντα τὰ ἔθνη, Mt 28¹⁹). Discipleship for all is thus set forth as His own ultimate aim. In reading the words one must carefully guard against the lamentable imperfection of rendering in the AV, and borrowed thence in some of the language of the Book of Common Prayer; also against the faulty punctuation of the sentence which is found alike in the AV and the RV. 'Teaching' is no translation of μαθητεύσατε, which means far more; while a colon ought to replace the comma after 'nations,' and only commas, or at the most semicolons, should separate the succeeding clauses. Without attention to this, the great importance of this passage must be missed. Rightly read, it gives the Lord's own interpretation of how discipleship is constituted. The whole commission is, 'Make disciples of all'; and three steps are then indicated in so doing, which answer to three essential factors in discipleship—(1) Baptizing into the Name; (2) teaching to observe all commands; (3) the constant spiritual presence of Christ. There is no complete discipleship without these three elements. The first is the portal of discipleship, the admission to a new destiny; at once the begetting of a new life on the part of God, and the profession of a new hope and purpose on the part of those whom He claims as His children. The second is the training needed to make the promise good; for only in the course of life's discipline can character be formed or resolutions realized,—it is 'in our endurance that we must win our souls.' The third is the pledge that none shall ever be left to face the stress of life's probation alone, but that for every disciple union with Christ is a support which may be securely trusted, the Divine Incarnation working itself out for ever till the goal shall be reached, when 'God shall be all, in all' (1 Co 15²⁸). The first disciples understood the charge which had been given them, and acted on the lines laid down from the earliest day on which they began to 'make disciples' for their Lord. So when, on the day of Pentecost, those who had been touched by Peter's preaching put the inquiry, 'Brethren, what shall we do?' the answer of the Apostle was explicit: 'Repent ye . . . be baptized . . . ye shall receive the gift of the Holy Spirit' (Ac 2³⁷⁻ ³⁸). Here are the same three elements of discipleship; for 'repentance' (μετάνοια) is the form which 'observing all things commanded' necessarily takes to start with in those who are passing from walking in their own ways to following the way of Christ; while the Holy Spirit is, of course, the Spirit of Christ present permanently with those whom He unites to Himself. See also preceding article.

LITERATURE.—Seeley, *Ecce Homo*, ch. vii.; Latham, *Pastor Pastorum*; *Expositor*, IV. iv.,[1891] 286 ff.

E. P. BOYS-SMITH.

DISCIPLINE. — The Gospels reveal a twofold discipline—that which Christ Himself experienced, and that to which He subjects His servants. It will be convenient to treat these separately.

1. *The discipline to which Christ submitted.*— The NT teaches clearly that even our Lord required to be 'perfected' (τελειωθῆναι) in order to ensure the consummation of the work for which He had become incarnate. Such a τελείωσις consisted in His being brought 'to the full moral perfection of His humanity, which carries with it the completeness of power and dignity' (Westcott); and its necessity is recognized, not by the writer of the

Epistle to the Hebrews alone (He 2¹⁰ 7²⁸ etc.), but also by Christ Himself (Lk 13³²).

It is taught with equal clearness that our Lord attained His 'perfection' through the discipline which He voluntarily endured. This included several elements. (1) Among the most important was the discipline of *temptation* (Mk 1¹². ¹³ ‖ He 2¹⁸); and in this connexion it is important to remember that His testing was not only searching in its strength, but repeated in its assaults (note plur. Lk 22²⁸, and cf. Mk 14³²ff. ‖, He 4¹⁵). (2) A second element in His discipline was that of *delay*. The incarnate Son, with His love eager for the completion of His saving work, must have exercised no ordinary self-restraint, as, amid the opposition of foes and the misconception of friends, the stages of its progress passed slowly by (Lk 12⁵⁰; cf. the probable force of the temptation in Mt 4⁸. ⁹ and of ἐνεβριμήσατο τῷ πνεύματι in Jn 11³³; cf. also 2 Th 3⁵). (3) The discipline of *sorrow* was also included in this 'perfecting' of Christ. His experience of sorrow was limited to no single kind. He felt the force of all the ills that vex our human life. In a most suggestive citation one sacred writer shows in how real and literal a sense He took our human sicknesses upon Him (Mt 8¹⁶. ¹⁷, cf. Mk 5³⁰). He knew no less the pang of regret with which a pure man views opportunities wasted by those for whom he has cherished high ideals (Lk 19⁴¹⁻⁴⁴—note ἔκλαυσεν). His, too, were the tears shed over a family bereaved and a 'loved one lost' (Jn 11³⁵). (4) The last aspect of Christ's discipline of which mention must be made was that of *pain and suffering*. Of this there is no occasion for offering detailed illustration. The story of His sufferings is the story of His life (for a few examples see Mk 8³¹ ‖ 14³²ff. ‖ 15¹⁶⁻³⁹ ‖, He 5⁸; note the use of παιδεύω in Lk 23¹⁶. ²²).

The experience of this discipline, revealing itself under different aspects and affecting His human nature at different points, was necessary to the fulfilment of our Lord's mission. It was in virtue of His 'perfection' through suffering that He reached His absolute sympathy with humanity, and in consequence His complete qualification to be its Saviour (He 2¹⁸ 4¹⁵. ¹⁶ 5²). See PERFECTION.

2. *The discipline which Christ imposes upon His followers.*—Discipline is an essential part of the Christian life, and the NT points out several forms under which it is to be experienced. In some of these it is restricted to a certain number of those who call themselves by the name of Christ. (1) There is, for example, a discipline to which Christians are rendered liable by *falling into error* (1 Co 11²⁹ff., esp. note παιδευόμεθα in v.³²; see also παιδεύω in Rev 3¹⁹). (2) The discipline of *persecution* also does not of necessity come to all Christians. At the same time, as both record and exhortation prove, it is no uncommon experience. It certainly befell our Lord's early followers (Mk 13⁹, Mt 10²². ²³, Jn 15²¹ 16³³; cf. the Epp. *passim*, and see esp. He 12⁴⁻¹³, where παιδεία is cited in this reference), and He Himself attributed a special blessedness to those who found a place in its honoured succession (Mt 5¹⁰⁻¹²). (3) In a third aspect, however, discipline falls to the lot of every Christian. No man can be a true follower of Christ who is not willing from the first to practise the discipline of *self-renunciation*. Such self-renunciation, indeed, is one of the conditions of entering His service (Mk 8³⁴ff. ‖ Mt 10³⁸). And there is to be no limit to the sacrifice required. It must be endured even to the severance of earth's closest ties (Mt 10³⁷) and the loss of life itself (24⁹, Jn 16²). Few things are more impressive than the manner in which, from the very beginning of His ministry (cf. Mk 1¹⁷. ¹⁸), our Lord assumed His right to claim from His followers that utter self-repudiation, and confidently expected on their part a willing response to His demand (Mt 9[9] 19[21]).

One particular aspect of this Christian self-denial calls for separate consideration. The Gospel teaching affords little support to those who have sought to express self-renunciation in the form of morbid asceticism. Christ's own example, in suggestive contrast with that of His forerunner, leads us to the very opposite conception of religious discipline (Mt 11[18f.]). Along the pathway of poverty (Mt 8[20]) and persecution (Jn 7[19] 8[37]) to which He called His disciples, He Himself walked; yet alike in His own life and in His thought for them (Mt 9[14], cf. 1 Ti 5[23]) ascetic discipline received no prominence. There appears to be just a hint of it in one of His sayings (Mt 19[12], cf. 1 Co 7[32ff.]), but even there it is distinctly stated less as a rule for the many than as an ideal for some few to whom a special call might come. In Christ's view the 'fasting' consequent upon real sorrow was so inevitable, that any merely formal anticipation of it was to be deprecated rather than approved (Mt 9[15]). See, further, art. ASCETICISM.

For ecclesiastical 'discipline' see art. CHURCH.

H. BISSEKER.

DISCOURSE.—No attempt is here made to discuss in all its bearings the general theme of the discourses of Jesus. His Teaching, Parables, Sermon on the Mount, etc., receive attention in special articles. All that is here undertaken is to mention in some sort of classification all the discourses, and to append a brief outline of their principal characteristics.

i. CLASSIFICATION AND MENTION. — The difficulties of any attempt at classifying the discourses of our Lord are apparent at a glance. They arise alike from the forms in which the discourses are recorded and from their character and contents. Considering the fact that our Lord did not write anything, or even cause His discourses to be exactly reported; considering, too, the great variety of occasions which called forth His utterances, and His own easy freedom and mastery of method in dealing with these occasions; considering, further, the differences in length, form, contents, and yet the cross-similarities and repetitions which the discourses exhibit, we see at once that a scientific and satisfactory classification is impossible. Yet there are obvious advantages for study in mentioning the discourses in some sort of orderly way. For our purpose it will not be necessary to take account of critical questions concerning the differences between the Fourth Gospel and the Synoptics, or between the Synoptics themselves, or to pay attention to matters of harmony and chronology, though under each grouping the commonly accepted order of events is followed. The classification proposed runs upon the general principle of audiences, and groups the discourses according as they were delivered to (1) individuals, (2) a select few, or (3) the public. Subdivisions will be apparent under these general heads.

1. *Interviews with individuals.* — Leaving out colloquies with particular persons in presence of others, there are to be mentioned under this head only (1) the discourse with Nicodemus on Regeneration (Jn 3[1-21]), and (2) the discourse with the woman of Samaria on Worship and Salvation (4[5-26]).

2. *Talks with a few.*—These may be subdivided as follows: (1) Discourses with others than the disciples. At these we cannot be sure of the absence of disciples, but their presence is not stated or certainly implied, and the words were not specially addressed to them. To this class belong: the discourse on Forgiveness, with the parable of the Two Debtors, given at the house of Simon the Pharisee (Lk 7[36-50]); the beginning of the discourse on Tradition (eating with unwashen hands), though

later 'he called the multitudes,' 'and the disciples came unto him' (Mt 15[1-20], Mk 7[1-20]); the Denunciation of the Pharisees and Lawyers at the house of a chief Pharisee (Lk 11[37-54]); the discourse at another Pharisee's house, where He discussed Modesty, Giving Feasts, and spoke the parable of the Great Feast and Excuses (Lk 14[1-24]); finally, the discourse at the house of Zacchæus, with the parable of the Pounds (Lk 19[1-27]).

(2) Discourses with the disciples and others. Here the audience consisted in part of the disciples and in part of others, the presence of both classes being either distinctly stated or clearly implied. As to the numbers present, the circumstances seem to restrict them somewhat, though it is difficult to say just to what extent, and therefore how far these should be regarded as properly public discourses. To this class belong: the discourse on Fasting (Mt 9[14-17], Mk 2[18-22], Lk 5[33-39]); the response to objectors on Sabbath Observance (Mt 12[1-8], Mk 2[23-28], Lk 6[1-5]); responses about Following Him (Mt 8[19-22], Lk 9[57-62]); response to the lawyer about Eternal Life, and parable of the Good Samaritan (Lk 10[25-37], cf. v.[23]); on Divorce (Mt 19[3-12], Mk 10[2-12]); response to the Rich Young Ruler, with discourse on the Perils of Wealth and on Forsaking All and Following Him (Mt 19[6-30], Mk 10[17-31], Lk 18[18-30]); the parable of the Labourers in the Vineyard (Mt 20[1-16]); response to the request of certain Greeks, with remarks on His Death and Glory (Jn 12[30-36]). Other discourses of the last Passover week seem to have been given in presence of the crowd, though directly addressed to smaller groups.

(3) Discourses with the disciples alone. These contain some of the most notable of our Lord's utterances. In some cases others than the Twelve were present, but usually the audience was all, or a portion of, the Apostles. It will not be necessary to observe this distinction in the enumeration. This group of discourses may be subdivided into two kinds. (a) Short occasional discourses: the explanation of the Parable of the Tares, with the short parables that follow (Mt 13[36-52]); the caution against Pharisaic Leaven (Mt 16[4-12], Mk 8[13-21]); remarks about His Church upon Peter's confession (Mt 16[13-20], Mk 8[27-30], Lk 9[18-21]); the immediately following discourse on His Death and on Self-Denial (Mt 16[21-28], Mk 8[31]-9[1], Lk 9[22-27]); talk after the Transfiguration (Mt 17[9-13], Mk 9[9-13]); a second foretelling of His Death and Resurrection (Mt 17[22, 23], Mk 9[30-32], Lk 9[43-45]); discourses at the Mission and Return of the Seventy (Lk 10[1-24]); teaching as to Prayer, with parable of the Friend at Midnight (Lk 11[1-13]); parable of the Unjust Steward (Lk 16[1-13]); teaching as to Offences, Faith, Service (Lk 17[1-10]); third prediction of His Death and Resurrection (Mt 20[17-19], Mk 10[32-34], Lk 18[31-34]); talk about Faith suggested by the Withered Fig-tree (Mt 21[20-22], Mk 11[20-26]); talk following the Washing of the Disciples' Feet (Jn 13[12-20]); institution of the Lord's Supper (Mt 26[26-29], Mk 14[22-25], Lk 22[19, 20]); after the resurrection, talk with the Two Disciples on the way to Emmaus (Lk 24[17-27]); with the Apostles, Thomas absent (Lk 24[36-49], Jn 20[19-25]); talk with some of the Apostles at the Sea of Galilee (Jn 21[4-23]); the Great Commission (Mt 28[16-19]).—(b) Extended discourses. Probably some of those mentioned in the preceding group were longer in reality than in report. But of the longer discourses with the chosen few we have the following: the Mission and Instruction of the Twelve (Mt 10[1-42], Mk 6[7-13], Lk 9[1-6]); on Humility, Offences, Forgiveness (Mt 18[1-35], Mk 9[33-50], Lk 9[46-50]); discourse on the Mount of Olives on His Second Coming and the Final Judgment (Mt 24. 25, Mk 13, Lk 21[7-36]); the Farewell Discourse and Prayer (Jn 14-17).

3. *Public addresses.*—Of these we may again in

a general way distinguish three groups, according to the extent either of the actual discourse or of the form in which we have it. (1) Discourses mentioned with some general description or remark, but with little or no detail of contents. Here we have: the beginning of His ministry (Mt 4[17], Mk 1[14.15], Lk 4[14.15]); the sermon at Nazareth (Lk 4[16-28]); the first preaching tour in Galilee (Mt 4[23.24], Mk 1[39], Lk 4[44]); at Capernaum (Mk 2[1.2.13], Lk 5[17]); the second preaching tour in Galilee (Lk 8[1-3]); at Nazareth again (Mt 13[54-58], Mk 6[1-6]); the third preaching tour in Galilee (Mt 9[35-38], Mk 6[6]); a tour alone after sending out the Twelve (Mt 11[1]); teaching and journeying (Lk 13[10.22], cf. Mt 19[1], Mk 10[1]); teaching in the Temple (Mk 11[17f.], Lk 19[47.48] 21[37.38]).

(2) Short occasional discourses. Of these there are a great number and variety, spoken sometimes to great multitudes, sometimes to groups, but publicly: on Blasphemy (Mt 12[22-37], Mk 3[19-30]); on Signs (Mt 12[38-45]); latter part of discourse on Eating with Unwashen Hands, and Traditions (Mt 15[1-20], Mk 7[1-23]); on Signs again (Mt 16[1-4], Mk 8[11.12]); on Demons and Signs again (Lk 11[14-36]); on Confession, Worldliness, Watchfulness (Lk 12); on Repentance, with parable of the Barren Fig-tree (Lk 13[1-9]); on the Good Shepherd (Jn 10[1-18]); on His Messiahship and Relations with the Father (Jn 10[22-38]); Sabbath Healing, parables of Mustard Seed and Leaven (Lk 13[10-21]); on the Salvation of the Elect (Lk 13[23-30]); Lament over Jerusalem (Lk 13[34.35]); on Counting the Cost of Following Him (Lk 14[25-35]); reproof of the Pharisees, with parable of the Rich Man and Lazarus (Lk 16[14-31]); on the Coming of the Kingdom (Lk 17[20-37]); on Prayer, with parables of the Importunate Widow, and of the Pharisee and Publican (Lk 18[1-14]); the colloquies with His critics in the Temple, on His Authority, on the Tribute to Cæsar, on the Resurrection, on the Great Commandment, on the Son of David (Mt 21[23-22[46]], Mk 11[27-12[37]], Lk 20); remarks on Belief and Unbelief (Jn 12[44-50]).

(3) Extended discourses. Only a few of the great discourses of our Lord are reported in extenso: the Sermon on the Mount (Mt 5–7, Lk 6[17-49])—in a sense public, though addressed primarily to the disciples; discourse at the feast in Jerusalem on His Relations with the Father (Jn 5[19-47]); on John the Baptist and suggested topics (Mt 11[7-30], Lk 7[24-35]); the first great group of parables, the Sower, etc. (Mt 13[1-53], Mk 4[1-34], Lk 8[4-18]); discourse in the synagogue at Capernaum on the Bread of Life (Jn 6[22-65]); colloquy in the Temple on His Mission (Jn 7.8); second great group of parables, the Lost Sheep, etc. (Lk 15[1-17[10]]); last public discourse, Denunciation of the Pharisees (Mt 23[1-39], Mk 12[38-40], Lk 20[45-47]).

ii. SOME CHARACTERISTICS.—A survey of the discourses of Jesus presents in a general way some of their characteristics, which may be summarily outlined as follows:

1. Their great variety. (1) Of occasion. (2) Of contents. (3) Of form.
2. Their wonderful charm. (1) Of personality —even in the report: how much more in His presence! (2) Of sympathy. (3) Of manner.
3. Their authority. (1) Consciousness of God. (2) Self-assertion.
4. Their power. (1) 'Magnetism'—personality, demeanour, tone. (2) Thought—then and ever-more.

LITERATURE.—Broadus, Harmony of the Gospels, and Lectures on Jesus of Nazareth; Clark, Harmony of the Gospels; Weiss, Life of Christ; Stier, The Words of Jesus; Wendt, The Teaching of Jesus; Swete, Studies in the Teaching of our Lord; Brown, Exposition of the Discourses and Sayings of our Lord; Bruce, The Training of the Twelve, The Galilean Gospel, With Open Face; Nicoll, Life of Christ; Stalker, Imago Christi.

E. C. DARGAN.

DISEASE.—

i. Current preconceptions prevalent in time of Christ.
ii. References to sickness and disease in the Gospels.
  1. Diseases resulting in physical defect or incapacity.
  2. Fever and allied diseases.
  3. Cutaneous affections.
  4. Dropsy.
  5. Nervous diseases.
  6. Nervous and psychical disorders.
    Literature.

i. CURRENT PRECONCEPTIONS IN TIME OF CHRIST.—Two ideas respecting disease had a powerful influence on conceptions current in our Lord's day: (1) The belief that all sickness and physical disease and pain were penalties imposed as the result of sin; (2) the idea that demonic agency was concerned with all human suffering. These kindred and allied ideas have been common among ancient peoples, and were strongly developed among the Babylonians, Persians, and Greeks.

Sayce, in his Hibbert Lectures (310, 334–5), gives evidence of the ancient Akkadian belief that disease and sickness were caused by specific malevolent spirits which possessed the person. The demons had been eaten with the food, drunk with the water, or inbreathed from the air; and until the evil power had been expelled the victim had no chance of recovery. Exorcism was effected by the sorcerer-priest, the intermediary between mankind and the spiritual world, using magic spells consisting of the names of deities, the name signifying the personality of the god, who was compelled by this use of the name to attend to the exorcist.

Among the Semites any mysterious natural object or occurrence appealing strongly to the imagination or exciting sentiments of awe and reverence was readily taken as a manifestation either of Divine or of demonic life (W. R. Smith, RS 119 ff.). The demons, if offended, avenged themselves by sending various forms of disease. Indications are found in the Gospels that such ideas were not extinct in the time of Christ. The old Semitic strain of conception was modified and quickened by contact with Babylonian, Persian, and Grecian peoples, and prevailed with considerable force in the later Judaism. The NT reflects the ideas of a time when the older conceptions were breaking up, but had not yet disappeared.

Our Lord gives no sanction to any such thought of disease, and when the disciples betrayed their mode of thought (Jn 9[2]) He took occasion to combat the ancient superstition. Although He did frequently mark sin as the cause of much physical weakness and disease (see art. IMPOTENCE), yet He denies that all sickness was penal in character. Other ends were in the Divine purview besides the punishment of personal sin (Jn 9[3]). In St. Luke's Gospel high fever seems to be attributed by implication to an evil agency, and Jesus is said to have rebuked (ἐπετίμησεν) the fever (Lk 4[38.39]); but probably this must be explained as a reflexion of the current preconceptions. In Lk 13[16] no reference is necessarily made to sin having given power to Satan to afflict the woman. Demons were associated with disordered conditions of human life, as disease and infirmity: with dumbness (Mk 9[17], Lk 9[39]), with deafness and dumbness (Mk 9[25]), with blindness and dumbness (Mt 12[22]), and with epilepsy (Mk 1[26] 9[20], Lk 9[39]). These physical defects are not necessarily manifestations of demonic influence, but are regarded as in close alliance with them. In St. Luke's Gospel, also, it is noteworthy that a distinction is recorded as made by Jesus between the exorcism of demons and ordinary cures (ἐκβάλλω δαιμόνια καὶ ἰάσεις ἀποτελῶ, Lk 13[32]).* See, further, art. DEMON.

* Hobart (Medical Language of St. Luke) and other writers claim to trace in the writings of the Third Evangelist the influence of a medical training. But the argument may be easily pressed beyond the truth. St. Luke's style and vocabulary have many affinities with classical Greek, and many of the medical expressions he uses occur in the LXX, and may have

ii. REFERENCES IN THE GOSPELS TO SICKNESS AND DISEASE.—

The terms employed by the Evangelists to denote bodily ailments are—

(1) ἀσθένεια, literally *want of strength* (α priv. and σθένος), primarily denoting weakness, and usually 'infirmity' or 'infirmities'; in Ac 28⁹ tr. 'diseases' (ἔχοντες ἀσθενείας); in Mt 8¹⁷ tr. 'infirmities,' and associated with νόσος; in Jn 11⁴ AV and RV 'sickness'; elsewhere [Lk 5¹⁵ 8² 13¹¹. ¹², Jn 5⁵] 'infirmity'; associated with νόσος in Lk 4⁴⁰.

(2) μαλακία (μαλάσσω, 'soften') denotes:
  (*a*) softness or effeminacy, as well as sickness; (*b*) periodic and chronic sickness and consequent languor of body. The word is used in Mt 4²³. ²⁴ 9³⁵ 10¹, where it is associated with νόσος. The first named passage is one in which the various ailments that our Lord healed are enumerated and apparently discriminated (cf. AV and RV).

(3) νόσος (from νη- 'not,' and σόος 'sound' [?]) is employed to indicate more acute and violent seizures than μαλακία; found in Mt 4²³. ²⁴ 8¹⁷ 9³⁵ 10¹, Mk 1³⁴ 3¹⁵, Lk 4⁴⁰ 6¹⁷ 7²¹ 9¹. In the Markan and Lukan (exc. Lk 4⁴⁰) passages the diseased are distinguished from the demonized.

(4) νόσημα, a disease or sickness, Jn 5⁴ (only).

(5) τοὺς κακῶς ἔχοντας is a frequent expression for those that were sick, and in Mk 1³⁴ we have the fuller expression πολλοὺς κακῶς ἔχοντας ποικίλαις νόσοις.

Of the presence of specific diseases much fuller indications are more or less distinctly given in the OT than in the NT. Instances of these may be understood as included in the miscellaneous cases of sickness and disease which our Lord repeatedly dealt with. Among them are various forms of skin disease, which were and are very common in the East; also of fever and allied disorders, extending to plague and pestilence; diseases of the digestive organs; infantile and senile diseases; affections of the brain or other parts of the nervous system; and disordered conditions of the psychical side of human nature. All of these are referred to in the OT with some amount of definiteness as to symptoms.

The diseases mentioned in the Gospels, and dealt with in direct and Divine fashion by Jesus (see art. CURES), include cases of physical defect; fevers and kindred diseases; skin diseases, notably that of leprosy; a solitary case of dropsy; ailments and infirmities that were nervous in character; and others which were a combination of nervous and psychical disorder. These various afflictions are not always to be certainly identified with particular forms of disease with which modern medical science is familiar. The description of the cases is, for the most part, far removed from being scientific, but yet enables us to broadly distinguish them from one another and to classify them with fair exactitude.

1. Diseases resulting in physical defect, or incapacity.—(1) *Defect in the organs of speech.*—The case of the dumb man recorded in Mt 9³². ³³ was associated with features of mental disturbance leading the people to attribute the dumbness to demonic possession. 'When the demon was cast out, the dumb spake,' as though no physical defect existed apart from the psychical disturbance. Interesting cases are known in which mental derangement has been manifested in an inhibition of one of the senses. Ray (*Factors of an Unsound Mind*) gives an instance in which the patient was unable to see the Column in the Place Vendôme in Paris, and believed it to have been removed. A similar inhibition, resulting from psychical rather than physical causes, might be applied to the organs of speech.

(2) *Defect in the organs of sense.*—Among defects notably common in the East is that of blindness (see art. SIGHT, B). Deafness is usually accom-

panied by dumbness, being indeed often the main cause of it—the term deaf-mute thus accurately describing the limitation. See DEAF AND DUMB.

(3) *Defects in the organs both of sense and speech.*—In Mt 12²² blindness and dumbness are combined, together with mental disturbance. In this case the restoration is not spoken of as a casting out of the demon, but as a healing (ἐθεράπευσεν), indicating that there was serious physical defect to be remedied. Mt 17¹⁴⁻²⁰ = Mk 9¹⁷ff. = Lk 9³⁷⁻⁴³ records a case in which both deafness and dumbness were found along with epilepsy and periodical mental derangement. Mt. and Lk. do not give the features of deafness and dumbness, but confine themselves to the mental features, which they do not describe so fully as Mark. Mk 7³²⁻³⁷ is a peculiarly interesting instance of deafness combined with incapacity of speech. The description is κωφὸν καὶ μογιλάλον. The deafness might give rise to the stammering, and the fact that total dumbness had not resulted rather points to a comparatively early stage of the affliction. The signs employed by Jesus in the healing are exactly adapted to reach the intelligence of such a defect-bound soul (see art. CURES).

2. Fever and allied diseases.—Various diseases of a kindred nature to fever were common in the East and from the earliest times, and were probably not very rigorously distinguished from each other: fever, ague, and a wasting disease resembling Mediterranean fever. The NT speaks of πυρετός, 'fever,' in Lk 4³⁸ and Jn 4⁵². The term in Mt 8¹⁴ and Mk 1³⁰ is πυρέσσουσα; while in Lk 4³⁸ the illness of Peter's wife's mother is spoken of (possibly with a reference to the division made by the Greeks into greater and lesser fevers) as one in which the patient was συνεχομένη πυρετῷ μεγάλῳ, indicating a continued and probably malignant fever, rather than an intermittent feverish attack such as characterizes ague. The supernormal feature of the healing consisted in the immediacy of the recovery without the regular debility following the disease. The ailment described in the Gospels was probably a form of malarial fever which prevailed in the valleys of Palestine and round the Sea of Galilee.

3. Skin diseases.—The OT bears witness to the prevalence in Palestine of many forms of cutaneous disease, and the writings of travellers and eye-witnesses testify to the fact that these are still fearfully common, being perhaps the most characteristic malady of the East. These varieties of skin disease are not referred to in the NT, the only one in evidence there being that most dreaded affection of the skin, which was also in the worse forms a serious constitutional malady affecting the whole organism, which bears the name *leprosy* (wh. see).

4. A solitary case of **dropsy** is recorded in Lk 14², described as ὑδρωπικός. No account is given of the trouble, the controversy with the Pharisees regarding the right use of the Sabbath being the main interest. No indication is given as to the seat of the disease which caused the dropsy, whether kidneys, heart, or liver.

5. Diseases of the nervous system.—Out of 22 cases of healing wrought by Jesus upon individuals, 8, and most probably 10, are to be classed among nervous disorders, either with or without the complication of psychical disturbance. The general exorcism which mark our Lord's career are of the same order, and among the general healings of sickness and infirmity which are recorded some may reasonably be supposed to be of the same character, and possibly many of them were purely nervous or hysterical afflictions. Disease of brain centres or of the nerve may also account for some of the cases of blindness

come to the Evangelist from that source. The varied terms applied to the lunatic (or epileptic) and the demonized, which give a plausibility to the suggestion that the Evangelist distinguished between these ailments, are found not in Luke, but in Matthew (see art. LUNATIC).

The attempt, however, to show (1) that our Lord's healings may be all reduced to cases of hysteria and of temporary nervous disorder, such as readily yield to treatment by known therapeutic remedies, and (2) that these are the best attested of the miracles, signally fails (see art. MIRACLES); and yet it may be freely recognized that many of the ailments cured by Jesus belonged to the nervous category. It still remains that those who desire to minimize to the fullest extent the super-normal powers of Jesus are not helped by these facts, for in order to deal effectively with these troubles He must not only have removed the disturbing cause in the psychical nature, but also brought a Divine power to bear on the whole nervous system, dispersing in some cases organic defect and disease.

Under this head are included—

(1) *Paralysis or Palsy* (see art. PARALYSIS).

(2) *Epilepsy.* The cases in the NT of this distressing nervous malady are complicated with forms of mental disturbance (see art. LUNATIC). But it may be supposed that among those who were regarded as possessed and whose restoration was included under the general exorcisms, some were cases of simple epilepsy (wh. see).

(3) Probably the two cases of *general impotence* must be included here—mentioned in Jn 5[2, 9] and Lk 13[11-17] (see art. IMPOTENCE).

(4) In all likelihood also the man with the *withered hand* was one nervously afflicted. The case is recorded in Mt 12[9-13], Mk 3[1-5], Lk 6[6-11]. The incapacity and wasting might be due to (*a*) infantile paralysis, the disease arresting the development and growth of tissue, leaving the limb shrunk and withered; or (*b*) it may have been congenital; or (*c*) it might be due to some direct injury to the main nerve of the limb, preventing its proper nutrition.

Among the halt and withered of Jn 5[3] probably there were cases of chronic rheumatism, joint diseases, and other wasting ailments, in many instances complicated with nervous exhaustion and weakness, if not with positive disease.

6. Nervous and psychical diseases. — Cases of lunacy, of epilepsy combined with insanity and perhaps those allied with idiocy, and others generally described as instances of demonic possession are given in the Gospels, and are to be recognized as having a twofold causation, on the one side physical, on the other psychical; and the problem as to which of these is primary in any particular case is not to be lightly determined. In this connexion arises the outstanding question as to the possibility of a genuine spiritual possession (see art. LUNATIC), a matter which may well remain with us for some time yet as a challenge both to medical and to theological investigation. The science of anthropology may throw much light upon it, and possibly in the course of further inquiry some of the conclusions of that science may be found in need of serious modification.

LITERATURE.—For facts relating to the nature and spread of disease in Oriental lands, and especially in Syria, consult Hirsch, *Handbook of Historical Pathology* (Sydenham Soc. Tr.); Macgowan in *Jewish Intelligence* and *Journal of Missionary Labours,* 1846; Thomson, *Land and Book,* pp. 146–149, 356, and, for leprosy, ch. 43; also consult generally ' Krankheiten' in Herzog's *PRE*[3]; Jahn, *Archæologia Biblica,* pt. I. ch. xii.; J. Risdon Bennett, *Diseases of Bible*; Hobart, *Medical Language of St. Luke*; Mason Good, *Study of Medicine*; art. by Macalister on ' Medicine' in Hastings' *DB.* For Talmudic conception of disease and medical treatment in vogue, see Wunderbar, *Biblisch-Talmudische Medicin.*

T. H. WRIGHT.

DISH.—1. The only place in the NT (EV) where this word is found is in the record of the betrayal of Jesus given by two of the Synoptists (Mt 26[23], Mk 14[20]).

The form of the Greek equivalent (τρύβλιον, Vulg. *catinum* [Mk 14[20]], but in Mt 26[23] Vulg. has *paropsis,* for which see

below) is that of a diminutive, although there is no example of a cognate or simpler form (see Liddell and Scott, *s.v.*). With it we may compare the diminutive ψωμίον (Jn 13[26ff.]) in the latest Apostolic account of the same period of Jesus' life. The use of this word, as well as of another (ἐμβάπτειν) occurring in the same context, by these two authors would seem to prove beyond doubt a close literary relationship between their writings—not, indeed, a relationship of direct inter-dependence (cf. Wright's *Synopsis of the Gospels in Greek,* p. 140), but rather one of common dependence upon the same or kindred sources, oral or written (cf. the 'anonymous fragment' μήτι ἐγώ εἰμι, ῥαββεί; Mt 26[25]).

A comparative study of the four records which tell of Jesus' reference to His impending betrayal brings to light some not unimportant minor differences, and at the same time reveals the agreement of all the writers in the belief that He knew of the intentions of Judas, and warned the latter against the dark deed. To the Markan account which makes Jesus answer the anxious question of His disciples (μήτι ἐγώ;) by the vague statement, '(it is) one of the twelve who is (now) dipping with me in the dish,' which is equivalent to the previous ὁ ἐσθίων μετ' ἐμοῦ (v.[18]; on this, however, cf. Gould's *St. Mark, ad loc.*), St. Matthew not only adds a more distinct note by employing the aorist (ἐμβάψας) instead of the present Middle (ἐμβαπτόμενος), by which he evidently intended to convey the idea of time, but he also informs us that Jesus gave a direct affirmative reply (σὺ εἶπας) to Judas' question. On the other hand, St. Luke agrees with St. Mark in leaving out all reference to an indication of the traitor beyond the statement that one of those present at the meal (ἐπὶ τῆς τραπέζης, Lk 22[21]) was guilty, while the author of the Fourth Gospel agrees with St. Matthew in making Jesus, by a sign (ἐκεῖνός ἐστιν ᾧ ἐγὼ βάψω τὸ ψωμίον καὶ δώσω αὐτῷ, Jn 13[26]), point him out to his fellow-disciples.

One thing seems to emerge clearly from the fourfold account, there was but one τρύβλιον on the table, and each one dipped his bread into it as he ate (see O. Holtzmann's *Leben Jesu,* Eng. tr. p. 458). This dish contained a sour-sweet sauce (חֲרוֹסֶת), which was composed of 'a cake of fruit beaten up and mingled with vinegar' (see *Encyc. Bibl.* art. ' Passover, § 17[n]; cf., however, B. Weiss' *The Life of Christ,* iii. p. 279). Into the sauce pieces of unleavened bread and bitter herbs were dipped and handed round by the chief person of the assembled party, which was evidently preliminary to the general partaking of the dish (cf. μετ' ἐμοῦ, Mt 26[23] = Mk 14[20]). It seems that this was a custom of late introduction into the Passover rite, and that it was intended to enrich the meaning of the feast by a symbolic reference to the brick-making period of Israel's Egyptian bondage (see art. ' Passover' in Hastings' *DB* iii. p. 691[b]).

Most scholars have sought to establish the relative positions of Jesus and Judas at this Passover feast from the incidents referred to by all four Evangelists (cf. Edersheim's *Life and Times of Jesus the Messiah,* ii. pp. 493–507; art. ' Apostle John' in Hastings' *DB* ii. p. 681[a]; Farrar's *Life of Christ,* ii. 284 ff. etc.). The variety of conclusions arrived at shows how impossible it is to settle a question of the kind. If, indeed, opposite each *triclinium* at the table there had been a τρύβλιον, then the answer of Jesus to His disciples' questions would show clearly that Judas reclined immediately on His left. This, however, as we have already intimated, is not probable; and the only data by which an approximately correct impression may be received lie in the words spoken by Jesus to Judas himself, and recorded partly by St. Matthew and partly by St. John (cf. Mt 26[25] and Jn 13[27ff.]). It seems more than probable that the traitor reclined somewhere in close proximity to Jesus, that their hands met as both dipped together into the dish (cf. the use of the Middle voice by St. Mark; see Bengel's *Gnomon of NT* on Mk 14[20]), and that in this way Jesus was able to convey privately to Judas the fact that He knew of the latter's intention.

2. A very good example of the way in which the didactic sayings of Jesus were caught up and handed down by His different hearers is afforded by the Matthæan and Lukan versions of the words by which He denounced the legal quibblings and Pharisaic hypocrisy of His day (Mt 23¹ff·, Lk 11³⁷ff·). There is just sufficient identity both in language and sense to guarantee the genuineness of the teaching. At the same time there is a marked variety in details as to locality, wording, and even as to the particular objective of Jesus' remarks. According to St. Luke, Jesus denounces the Pharisees, while a guest in the house of one of their number, for their punctiliousness in keeping the outside of their vessels clean, their own hearts all the time being full of uncleanness. The contrast is between the outside of their utensils (τὸ ἔξωθεν . . . τοῦ πίνακος) and their own inner lives or characters (τὸ δὲ ἔσωθεν ὑμῶν, Lk 11³⁹). Here we may notice that the word translated 'platter' is the word used to denote the flat dish (EV 'charger') on which (ἐπὶ πίνακι) the Baptist's head was sent to Herodias (Mt 14⁸· ¹¹ = Mk 6²⁵· ²⁸). On the other hand, St. Matthew makes Jesus utter this discourse to 'the multitudes and to his disciples' in the Temple (Mt 23¹, cf. 24¹). The denunciation is more sustained and rhetorical, as becomes the situation. When the writer comes to the contrast spoken of above, he makes Jesus institute one between the outside of the dish and its contents, looked on as the outcome of rapacity and gluttony (ἐξ ἁρπαγῆς καὶ ἀκρασίας). This is again more suitable to the word he employs, which is the only place in the NT where it is found (τὸ ἔξωθεν . . . τῆς παροψίδος stands opposite to ἔσωθεν =τὸ ἐντὸς . . . τῆς παροψίδος, see Mt 23²⁵f·; cf., however, WH's text in Mt 23²⁶).

The word παροψίς was originally, in Attic Greek, used of entrées or dainties (see Liddell and Scott, s.v.). It afterwards came to be applied to the four-cornered ('quadrangulum et quadrilaterum vas,' see art. 'Meals' in *Encyc. Bibl.* iii. 2998, n. 1) dish in which they were served; and, lastly, it became a name for dishes generally used at table.

In both these cases of variation it is possible to see the hand of the editor carefully compiling and arranging his materials before their publication in permanent form.   J. R. WILLIS.

DISPERSION (διασπορά).—The word (RV of Jn 7³⁵, Ja 1¹, 1 P 1¹) is a collective term denoting either the Jews resident outside their native country, or the lands in which they lived.

1. The Pharisees and chief priests sent officers to arrest our Lord, and He told them that in a little while He would go where they could not find Him or be able to come to Him. The Jews who were present asked where He could possibly go that they could not find Him. Would He go to the 'dispersion among the Greeks' (εἰς τὴν διασπορὰν τῶν Ἑλλήνων) * and teach the Greeks? i.e. would He make the dispersed Jews a starting-point for teaching the Greeks? Narrow-minded Jews, distinct from 'the people' (ὁ ὄχλος) of vv.³¹· ⁴⁰, they would not dream of defiling themselves by going out and mixing with Gentiles, and they sarcastically suggested that that was the only way in which Jesus could escape them.

2. It is unnecessary in this article to deal fully with the history and fortunes of the Dispersion; but a very brief sketch may be useful. In the time of Christ the Jews of the Dispersion were to be found in six main colonies: Babylonia, Egypt, Syria, Asia Minor, Greece, and Rome.

(a) *Babylonia.*—The Jews in the far East were

    * For the genitive, cf. 1 P 1¹.

the descendants of those who remained when small bodies returned under Zerubbabel and Ezra. And their numbers were afterwards increased by a transportation of Jews to Babylonia and Hyrcania under Artaxerxes III. Ochus (358–338). Many have thought that 1 P 5¹³ refers to a community of Christians among the Jews in Babylon; but this is improbable (see Hort, *1 Peter*, pp. 5 f., 167–170). From Babylon, Jews moved in many directions to Elam (cf. Is 11¹¹), Persia, Media, Armenia, and Cappadocia. The Babylonian Jews were the only portion of the Diaspora which maintained its Judaism more or less untouched by the Hellenism which permeated the West. Their remoteness, however, did not prevent the loyal payment of the annual Temple-tax, which was collected at Nehardea and Nisibis and sent to Jerusalem (see below).

(b) *Egypt.*—Jews had migrated to Egypt as early as 586, when Johanan son of Kareah conducted a small body of them, including Jeremiah, to Tahpanhes (Jer 42. 43). Jews also settled (Jer 44¹) in Migdol, Noph (Memphis), and Pathros (Upper Egypt). The great majority of the colonists in *Alexandria* must have settled there early in the period of the Ptolemies, in which case they may have been among the earliest inhabitants of Alexander's new city; and they undoubtedly received special privileges (Jos. *c. Apion.* ii. 4; *BJ* II. xviii. 7 f.). The kindness which they received in Palestine from Ptolemy I. Soter induced numbers of them to migrate to Egypt during his reign. And many more may have been transported as prisoners of war during the subsequent struggles between the Ptolemies and the Seleucids. Philo (*in Flacc.*, ed. Mangey, ii. 525) less than ten years after our Lord's death says that two entire quarters of Alexandria were known as 'the Jewish,' and many more Jews were sprinkled over the rest of the city. Another congregation of Jews was formed at *Leontopolis* in the nome of Heliopolis on the Eastern border of the Nile delta. The high priest Onias, son of Simon the Just, was granted permission by Ptolemy VI. Philometor to settle there when he fled with some adherents in 173 or 170 from his enemies Antiochus IV. Epiphanes and the sons of Tobias. He built a fortress, and within it a temple where the worship of Jehovah was carried on. This continued till A.D. 73, when the temple was destroyed by order of Vespasian (Jos. *Ant.* XIII. iii. 2, XIV. viii. 1; *BJ* I. ix. 4, VII. x. 2-4).

(c) *Syria.*—The Egyptian Diaspora had been formed largely owing to the increased facilities for travel and intercourse resulting from Alexander's conquests. And the same causes operated in Syria. Damascus had received Israelite colonists in very early times (1 K 20³⁴). In Nero's reign there were, according to Josephus (*BJ* II. xx. 2), no fewer than 10,000 Jews in the city. Antiochus IV. Epiphanes conceded to the Jews the right of free settlement in Antioch; and, owing to the successes and prestige of the Maccabees in Palestine, the neighbouring provinces of Syria received a larger admixture of Jews than any other country (*BJ* VII. iii. 3).

(d) *Asia Minor.**—Through Syria Jews passed to Asia Minor and the neighbouring islands, Cyprus, Crete, etc., where from B.C. 130 and onwards they flourished under Roman protection. See Hort, *1 Peter*, Add. note, pp. 157-184, and Ac 13-20.

(e) *Greece.*—It is related in 1 Mac 12²¹ that the Spartans sent a letter to the high priest Onias saying 'it hath been found in writing concerning

    * It is convenient to use the term, although its first known occurrence is in Orosius (*Hist.* i. 2. 26), A.D. 417. He speaks as though it were his own coinage: 'Asia regio vel, ut proprie dicam, *Asia minor.*'

the Spartans and the Jews that they are brethren, and that they are of the stock of Abraham.' This, though legendary, implies that there was at least an acquaintance between members of the two races. Jewish inscriptions, moreover, have been found in Greece ; and there were firmly established Jewish communities in Thessalonica, Berœa, and Corinth when St. Paul visited them (Ac 17. 18).

(*f*) *Rome.*—The first contact of the Jews with Rome was in the time of the Maccabees ; embassies were sent by Judas and Jonathan, and a formal alliance was concluded by Simon in B.C. 140 (1 Mac 14²⁴ 15¹⁵⁻²⁴). A few Jews probably reached Rome as traders ; but the first large settlement dates from the capture of Jerusalem by Pompey, B.C. 63. Julius and Augustus admitted them to a legal standing throughout the Empire (see the series of enactments in Jos. *Ant.* XIV. viii. 5, x. 1–8); the latter allowed them to form a colony on the further side of the Tiber ; but they soon gained a footing within the city, and had synagogues of their own. Tiberius in A.D. 19 banished 4000 to Sardinia. In the early days of Claudius the Jewish cause was upheld at court by the two Agrippas ; but before 52 'Claudius had commanded all Jews to depart from Rome' (Ac 18²)—'impulsore Chresto assidue tumultuantes' (Suet. *Claud.* 25). Under Nero the Jews in Rome once more gained ground.

3. The Jews dispersed in these various settlements did not entirely cut themselves off from their national centre, Jerusalem. Even the Jews at Leontopolis, though their worship was strictly speaking schismatical, did not allow their religious separateness to quench their national feeling. They embraced Cæsar's cause in Egypt, contrary to their first impulse, because of the injunctions of Hyrcanus the high priest at Jerusalem, and Antipater the Jewish general (Jos. *Ant.* XIV. viii. 1 ; *BJ* I. ix. 4).

There were two important links which bound the Diaspora in all parts of the world to their mother city.

(*a*) The annual payment of the Temple-tax (the half-shekel or didrachm), and of other offerings. One of the privileges which they enjoyed under the Diadochi and afterwards under the Romans was that of coining their own money for sacred purposes. [It was this sacred coinage that foreign Jews were obliged to get from the money-changers in exchange for the ordinary civil money, when they came to Jerusalem for the festivals, Mt 21¹², Mk 11¹⁵, Jn 2¹⁴ᶠ. And it was this variety of coinage that enabled our Lord to give His absolutely simple but unanswerable decision on what the Jews thought was a dilemma ; deep spiritual meaning, no doubt, underlay His words, but their surface meaning was sufficient to silence His opponents : 'Render to Cæsar the civil coin on which His image is stamped, and render to God the sacred coin which belongs to Him and His Temple worship,' Mt 22²¹, Mk 12¹⁷, Lk 20²⁵]. The sacred money was collected at different centres (cf. Mt 17²⁴ οἱ τὰ δίδραχμα λαμβάνοντες) and carried under safe escort to Jerusalem (Philo, *de Monarch.* ii. 3). Josephus relates (*Ant.* XVI. vi.) that the Jews in Asia and Cyrene were ill-treated, and that the Greeks took from them their sacred money ; but that decrees were issued by Augustus, Agrippa, and two proconsuls to the effect that the sacred money of the Jews was to be untouched, and that they were to be given full liberty to send it to Jerusalem. The Babylonian Jews made use of the two strong cities Nehardea and Nisibis to store their sacred money till the time came to send it to Palestine. 'The Jews, depending on the natural strength of these places, deposited in them the half-shekel which everyone, by the custom of our country, offers to God, and as many other dedi-

catory offerings (ἀναθήματα) as there were : for they made use of these cities as a treasury, whence at the proper time they were transmitted to Jerusalem' (*Ant.* XVIII. ix. 1). Such priestly dues as consisted of sacrificial flesh, which could not be sent to Jerusalem, were paid to any priest if there happened to be one at hand (*Challa*, iv. 7–9, 11 ; *Yadaim*, iv. 3 ; *Chullin*, x. 1 ; *Terumoth*, ii. 4).

(*b*) The pilgrimages made to Jerusalem by immense numbers of foreign Jews at the three annual festivals—Passover, Pentecost, and Tabernacles. Josephus says that Cestius Gallus had a census made during the Passover, and the priests reckoned 2,700,000 people (*BJ* VI. ix. 3), in round numbers three millions (*id.* II. xiv. 3).

In reading the Acts it is evident that, had there been no foreign dispersion of the Jews, the rapid progress of Christianity could not have been what it was. At the feast of Pentecost there were gathered Jews from the four quarters of the Diaspora—the far and near East, Europe, and Africa ; and soon afterwards Jews received Apostolic teaching at many centres, and when converted helped to spread it throughout the known world. But it is important to remember that before that time One greater than the Apostles came, more than once, into immediate contact with the masses of pilgrims who visited Jerusalem for the festivals. As a boy of twelve He first met them (Lk 2⁴²), and He probably attended many festivals in the 18 years which intervened before His ministry (see v.⁴¹). At a Passover He displayed to them His Divine indignation at the desecration of God's sanctuary (Jn 2¹³⁻¹⁷), and many believed on Him when they saw His miracles (v.²³). It would seem as though the longing seized Him to bring all these thousands of foreigners to His allegiance at one stroke, by revealing to them His true nature. If we may say it reverently, it must have been a temptation to Him to send them back over many countries to tell all men that God had become man. But His own Divine intuition restrained Him (vv.²⁴ᶠ·). Immediately before another Passover He saw the crowds moving along the road on their way to Jerusalem ; and they came to Him, and He fed them (Jn 6⁴⁻¹³). Here, again, the temptation offered itself in their wish to make Him king ; but He resisted it, and was able to persuade them to leave Him (6¹⁴ᶠ·). At a feast of Pentecost (so Westcott) He suddenly appeared in their midst at Jerusalem, and many believed Him to be the Messiah when they heard His preaching (Jn 7²· ¹⁰⁻³¹· ⁴⁰ᶠ·). Yet again at a Passover the crowds of pilgrims gave Him another opportunity of becoming king (Mt 21¹⁻⁹, Mk 11¹⁻¹⁰, Lk 19³⁵⁻³⁸, Jn 12¹²⁻¹⁵), but He chose rather to gain His kingdom through death. It was for their benefit that the inscription upon the cross was trilingual—Aramaic, Greek, and Latin (Jn 19²⁰). A Jew from Africa, on his way into the city, was forced to perform an office which few envied him at the time, but which has never been forgotten by the Christian Church (Mk 15²¹). Thus time after time the accounts of His miracles and preaching, and finally of His patient suffering and His death, and perhaps also reports of His resurrection, would be carried back by wandering Jews into 'every nation under heaven.'

4. One colony of the Diaspora possesses a special importance in connexion with Christianity. Among the Alexandrian Jews originated the Greek translation of the OT—the version used by our Lord, the Apostles, and the great majority of the early Church. It remained in almost complete supremacy among Christians until it was superseded by the Vulgate. See art. SEPTUAGINT. The importance of Alexandria in connexion with the Fourth Gospel would be enormous if the contention of some writers were true, that St. John derived his doctrine of the Logos from Alexandrian philosophy. The doctrine, however, has affinities rather with Jewish than with Alexandrian thought. The most that can be said is that St. John may have employed the term because it already had a wide currency among both Jews and Greeks (see Westcott, *Gospel of St. John*, pp. xv–xviii, and art. 'Logos' in Hastings' *DB*).

LITERATURE.—Besides the authorities cited in the article, see artt. 'Diaspora' in Hastings' *DB* (Extra Vol.), 'Dispersion' in *Encyc. Bibl.* (with the literature there), and in Smith's *DB*. Much illustrative matter may be gathered from Jewish histories, especially Schürer, *HJP*. See also E. R. Bevan, *The House of Seleucus*; J. P. Mahaffy, *The Empire of the Ptolemies*.

　　　　　　　　　　　　　　　　　A. H. M‘NEILE.

DITCH ($\beta\delta\theta\upsilon\nu o s$, Mt 15¹⁴, Lk 6³⁹; rendered ‘pit’ Mt 12¹¹).—The parabolic language of our Lord in the first two parallel passages is suggested by the frequency of danger from unguarded wells, quarries, and holes. Into these the blind easily fell; and the risk increased if the leader of the blind were himself blind. The metaphor has been interpreted as referring to Gehenna: more probably it refers simply to danger of hurt, or even ruin, from wilful or careless perversion of the truth leading to moral wandering and fall. For the idea, cf. Pr 19²⁷ ‘Cease, my son, to hear the instruction that causeth to err,’ and St. Paul's taunt of the Jew as ‘a guide of the blind’ (Ro 2¹⁹).　　　R. MACPHERSON.

DIVES.—The Latin adjective for ‘rich,’ commonly employed as a *quasi*-proper name for the rich man in our Lord's parable of the Rich Man and Lazarus (Lk 16¹⁹⁻³¹). This use of the word Dives, derived, no doubt, from the Vulgate, is common in English literature, and can be traced back at least to the time of Chaucer, who, in *The Somnour's Tale*, lines 169, 170, says:

> ‘Lazar and Dives liveden diversly,
> And divers guerdon hadden they ther-by.’

Compare also *Piers the Plowman*, passus xvi. lines 303, 304:

> ‘And Dives in his deyntes lyuede· and in douce uye;
> And now he buyeth hit ful bitere · he is a beggere of helle.’

Although we are not concerned in this article with the interpretation of the parable as a whole, we may yet appropriately refer to the various opinions which have been held as to who was intended by our Lord under the figure of the rich man.

The noticeable circumstances that in this alone of all His parables our Lord names one of the characters, *i.e.* Lazarus, while the other chief character, the rich man, is significantly nameless, and that the parable has no prefatory introduction, such as ‘He spake another parable,’ or the like, have given rise to the conjecture that this is not a parable pure and simple, but that it is either a narrative of facts, or that persons more or less known are alluded to in the story.

1. Some, as Tertullian and Schleiermacher, have supposed that in Dives allusion was made to Herod Antipas, and that Lazarus represents John the Baptist, who is referred to in v.¹⁶, cf. also v.¹⁸, where our Lord speaks about adultery. This, however, is surely an extravagant notion which scarcely needs refutation.

2. Another equally improbable suggestion, put forward by Michaelis, is that Dives represents Caiaphas, son-in-law of Annas, and that Lazarus is Christ; and so the five brethren of the rich man are explained as the five sons of Annas (Jos. *Ant.* XX. ix. 1).

3. Closely connected with this opinion is another which has the support of Ambrose, Augustine, Teelman (quoted by Trench, *Parables*), and others, according to which, while Lazarus is Christ, Dives is the Jewish people who despised and rejected

Him who for their sakes was poor and afflicted. This, however, is an allegorizing of the parable which, though attractive at first sight, will not bear close examination.

4. Another interpretation, supported by Aphraates, Augustine (as an alternative), Gregory the Great, and Theophylact, and widely held in all sections of the Universal Church, is, that Dives represents, as in the last case, the Jewish people, but that Lazarus represents the Gentiles. Bleek, Godet, and Alford reject this view, the two latter saying that the very name Lazarus (*i.e.* a Jewish name) is against it. Yet, though not the primary, this may be a true application of the parable, and is not lightly to be set aside.

5. According to a tradition alluded to by Theophylact and Euthymius Zigabenus, Dives and Lazarus were actual persons known at the time, and our Lord, while honouring the poor man by naming him, passes over the guilty rich man's name in merciful silence.

6. The interpretation which best suits all the facts of the case is that the rich man is a typical instance of the religious leaders of the people, Pharisees and Sadducees, and that Lazarus is a representative of the despised publicans, or of the neglected ‘common people.’ If this is the primary significance of Dives and Lazarus, then we can see, as stated above, that interpretation 4 is not lightly to be set aside; for if Pharisees and Sadducees despised and neglected those of their own nation, much more would they contemptuously overlook ‘sinners of the Gentiles.’ Under this head it has been debated whether Dives is a typical Pharisee or a Sadducee. Didon (*Life of Christ*), Mosheim, and Wetstein hold that he is a Sadducee, since the Pharisees were not characterized by luxurious living or by unbelief; but if, with the majority of expositors, who say that the connexion of the parable with what precedes requires it, we hold him to be a Pharisee, he is at least a Pharisee who, as Stier says, ‘lives as a Sadducee.’

As to the special sin of Dives, opinions have differed. All, however, concur in pointing out that he is not accused of any positive crime,—his sin is negative. It may be, indeed, that our Lord in the parable glances back at what is said in vv.¹³⁻¹⁶; yet Dives' chief sin most evidently was that he left undone the things which he ought to have done. He is an instance, in fact, of one who did not make to himself friends of the mammon of unrighteousness. Doubtless the cause of this was his virtual unbelief in a kingdom of God here implying a brotherhood of all men, and a kingdom of God hereafter implying a retribution.

Euthymius says that some asserted that, according to a tradition, the rich man was called Ninevis; and Tischendorf (*Gr. Test. in loc.*) quotes a scholion εὗρον δέ τινες καὶ τοῦ πλουσίου ἐν τισιν ἀντιγράφοις τοὔνομα Νινεύης λεγόμενον. Further, the Sahidic Version adds to the mention of the rich man: ‘whose name was Nineue.’ It has, however, been suggested (Rendel Harris, *Expositor*, March 1900) that this name may have been evolved from the words ‘hic dives,’ or ‘en dives,’ accompanying some ancient pictorial representation of the parable. Harnack (*ib.*), however, has thought that the word may be a corruption of Φινεέs (Finæus in pseudo-Cyprian, *de Pascha Computus*, c. 17), and ‘that since in Nu 25⁷ Phinehas is said to be the son of Eleazar, an attempt has been made to suggest that the poor man . . . was the rich man's own father.’ See art. LAZARUS.

　　　　　　　　　　　　　　　　　ALBERT BONUS.

DIVINITY OF CHRIST.—

I. Preliminary considerations.
　　1. The mystery of Christ.
　　2. The movement ‘Back to Christ.’
　　3. Certain results of the movement.
II. Bases of Christological belief.
　　1. Primarily a new experience.
　　2. Analysis of the experience.
　　　　(a) Christ's Messianic character.
　　　　(b) His self-consciousness: (α) His interior life,
　　　　　　(β) His method in teaching, (γ) His sinlessness, (δ) His oneness with God.

    (c) His appeal to deeper personality.
    (d) His teaching and works.
  3. Validity of the experience.
III. Beginnings of the doctrine of Christ's Person in the NT.
  1. General character of the doctrine.
  2. Divine names applied to Christ.
  3. Divine properties and acts attributed to Christ.
  4. Divine relations as to God, man, the world.
IV. Subsequent development of NT ideas.
  1. History of the doctrine.
    (a) Patristic.
    (b) Mediæval.
    (c) Modern.
  2. Denial of the doctrine.
    (a) Its history and motive.
    (b) Its failure.
          Literature.

I. Preliminary Considerations.—1. *The mystery of Christ.*—The historic question of Jesus to His disciples, 'Who do men say that I the Son of Man am?' (Mt 16¹³, Mk 8²⁷, Lk 9¹⁸), was put not to confound, but to reveal, by awakening the desire for knowledge. The intelligent answer to the question preserves the precious truth, which is nothing less than God's *age-long secret about Himself.* The disciples had been nurtured on a religious literature in which the whole national and individual future was seen blending in one anticipation, the coming of God to His people to deliver and save. One like the Son of Man comes, and there is given to Him dominion and glory and a kingdom which shall not pass away. This was the figure in which the Jewish imagination clothed the Jewish hope. Modern criticism dwells upon the factors in history which determined the form in which this hope took shape. The Hebrew religion, we are assured, was wrought out under constant pressure of disaster. It was the religion of a proud, brave people, who were constantly held in subjection to foreign conquerors. Hence came a quality of intense hostility to those tyrannous foes, and also a constant appeal to the Divine Power to declare itself. The hostility and the appeal inspire the Messianic Hope. Was there nothing more? Surely behind the history and the imagination lay elemental forces of the soul. What lend essential and abiding worth both to the Hebrew hostility to Gentile oppression and the Hebrew appeal to Jehovah's righteous right hand are a faith and a passion which, if quickened into power by the vicissitudes of history, were themselves underived from history, and native to the spirit of the nation. Nor in this high conviction do the Hebrews stand alone. Everywhere, wherever thought has advanced sufficiently near its Object, it has come to a yearning, at times poignant, for closer contact. The numerous idolatries of the lower religions are simply the objectivation of this desire. The no less numerous conceptions of Divinity in more cultured peoples are due to the same stress. There has been a ceaseless demand of the human race for an embodiment of Deity. The demand is a product of the hungry human heart for closer communion with God and larger loyalty to Him.

The existence of an instinct so universal is the guarantee of its fulfilment. The two considerations, that the Hebrew race had worked out the conception of the Messiah, and that the ethnic peoples were quite familiar with Divine incarnations, processes both present admittedly to the mind of the Early Church, furnish no evidence to the contrary. In themselves they prove nothing against a true Incarnation historically manifested, if it can be shown that its historical manifestation is not wholly traceable to naturalistic origins in the Hebrew and ethnic genius. The presence, in particular, of many myths parallel to the Christian story need not mean that the Christian story is itself a myth. As has been well said, 'If the Christian God really made the human race, would not the human race tend to rumours and perversions of the Christian God? If the centre of our life is a certain fact, would not people far from the centre have a muddled version of the fact? If we are so made that a Son of God must deliver us, is it odd that Patagonians (and others) should dream of a Son of God?' (Chesterton, *Religious Doubts of Democracy*, p. 18). False beliefs live by the true elements within them. A persistent belief occurring in many false forms is likely to be true, and may reasonably be expected to occur in a true form. Each redeemer of heathenism is a prophetic anticipation of the satisfying of human desires in Jesus Christ, precisely as the Messianic disclosures of the OT were to the people of whom according to the flesh He came. They are anticipations only: since neither the pagan foregleams nor the Hebrew forecasts offered sufficient data for a complete or consistent delineation of an actual Person.* The earlier experiences of men made the gospel intelligible, but they had no power to produce it. It satisfies and crowns them, but does not grow out of them. The Person, when He came, did more than satisfy the old instinct by which men had hope, He reinforced and extended it: His advent not only accomplished the past promise, it gave earnest of greater things to come: He thus represented human ideals indeed, but still more Divine ideas. The highest prophecies of His appearance reveal, amid the circumstantial details, the element of mystery; that mystery is not eliminated when the Life appears. It is the singular significance of Jesus Christ that both in the anticipations of Him and in His actual appearance the details always lead on to inquiry as to what is not detailed, the facts to something beyond themselves; the Man and His words and works to the question Who is He? and Whence is this Man?

2. *The movement 'Back to Christ.'*—The question is prominently before the present age. The modern mind asks it with revived interest. Modern knowledge in its several departments of philosophy, history, science, has developed along lines and in obedience to principles which appear able to dispense with the old theistic axioms. God and Conscience are not so vividly active. And yet, on the other hand, the ancient instinct of the race for communion with God is assertive as ever. It turns for comfort almost exclusively to the Christian tradition. The Christian tradition, however, it is convinced, needs revision; and here the central necessity is the treatment and true understanding of the Person of Christ. The cry is 'Back to Christ.' It is a cry dear to all who desire a simpler gospel than that set forth in the Creeds; all who are wearied with speculation on the elements of Christian truth, or are distraught with the variety of interpretation offered of it; all who are eager to embrace the ethics and as eager to abjure what they term the metaphysics of the Christian system. The movement referred to is natural; and its plea so plausible as to merit attention. The aim is nothing short of recovering the image of the original Founder of the Faith, expressed in His authentic words and acts; to bring back in all the distinct lineaments of a living Personality the great Teacher whom we now see in the Gospels 'as through a glass darkly.' It seeks by a study of the original records in the light of all the historical and critical aids now open to us, and guided by the modern idea of evolution, not only to bring us face to face with Jesus of Nazareth, to listen to His direct words of wisdom, but to trace all the steps of His spiritual advance, all the steps by which He grew into the Messiah of Israel and the Ideal of humanity, giving the deepest interpretation to the prophetic dream of His nation,

---

* Cf. Westcott, *Gospel of Life*, pp. 295–297.

and so lifting it into that higher region in which the freely accepted Cross became the necessary means to the deliverance of man. The 'Jesus of history,' it is argued, has been buried in the 'Christ of dogma'; the Church in handing down the Saviour has presented Him with adoring hands and in idealized form. The more we throw off her encrustments, the nearer we get to the original, the nearer we are getting to the real Jesus, and, in Him, to the truth of our religion.

However natural the hope of such minds, it is based on illusion. It proceeds on erroneous ideas as to what we may learn from the past. 'What has been done,' says the adage, 'even the gods themselves cannot make undone.' All that historical reversions can do is to suggest that in the onward movement something precious has been left behind which it were well to recover before going further. There is no such Christ, no such Christianity in the first century as is sought for: a Christ and a Christianity purely invariable and true for all time and in every place. That is a conception which, the more it is studied, the more it will be found to be a pure abstraction to which no concrete *in rerum natura* corresponds. The absolute value of the Christian Faith, the real stature of the Christ, cannot be established by merely dropping the historical surroundings or setting of the traditional truth. The old truth that lived spiritually in the minds of those who first livingly apprehended it, and which has pulsated all through the historical process, has to be caught up again, realized in its essential vitality, and formulated anew in harmony with the modern spirit. We have to ask, Was the Christian Idea given in itself apart, in isolation, abstractly, and may this, as the 'essence,' substance, or soul of the gospel, be rediscovered? Or, on the contrary, was the Christian Idea planted as a Life in a company of believers who manifested its power in their lives, so that it cannot be reduced to an invariable essence except by an unreal process of abstraction? Cf., further, art. BACK TO CHRIST.

3. *Certain results of the movement.*—The effort to 'rediscover Christ' (the phrase is Dr. Fairbairn's) is important less in its avowed aim than in its subsidiary results. Through them it yields a real contribution to theological progress. We proceed to indicate three such results: (1) a *new idea of the nature of Christian doctrine*; (2) the insistence on *the distinction between primary and variable elements in doctrines*; (3) the deepened consciousness of *the extent of variation.*

(1) The same divines who have busied themselves in the search for the Christ of history have been instrumental in exhibiting Christian thought on His Person as *a process.* In that sphere of thought they have rigorously applied the idea of development, not indeed for the first time (since John Henry Newman, fifteen years before Darwin's *Origin of Species* was published, had fascinated their fathers by his use of the idea), but with a more thorough insight than Newman, and with better tests, furnishing in consequence widely different results from his. They are enabled to distinguish between Creed and Doctrine, between articles of faith and the whole process of reflexion, even of a conflicting character, by which articles of faith are reached and defined. By them interest is transferred from the result to the process. The forces entering into the process are minutely analyzed. It is discovered that theology has a history; that its history is mixed up with general history; that it has been moulded by a vast deal external to the subject-matter of theology; and not only so, but even, as some (notably Harnack) contend, has been substantially and in its inner essence modified, if not perverted, in the process.

It is seen that Christian dogmas were once inchoate; passed through many stages under influences social, political, intellectual; and that they have a constant tendency so to do in adapting themselves to their environment—that, in short, they are not dead formulas, but a living organism.

(2) The emergence of so many factors merely accidental has brought into clearer perspective *the reality immanent in the process.* Besides the soil and the influences on growth, there is the seed, the Divine Truth on which human thought and earthly event exercised themselves. It is traceable to the teaching and life of Jesus and His Apostles. Only fragments of His utterances have been preserved to us, but the brief discourses and conversations that we read in the Gospels stand unique in spiritual power among the utterances of the world. They represent a large body of teaching, lost to us in form but preserved in its fruits; for out of His spiritual wealth there poured throughout His ministry an abundance of spoken truth that remained to perpetuate His influence and serve as the foundation of Christian doctrine. Together with His life they formed and still form Truth, not simply in a definite invariable quantity, but as a constant fountain and source of truth, ever open and flowing for them who believe. He gave a new light on all things to men; and by an inevitable necessity they proceeded to apply, and still must apply, what He has shown, to the interpretation of all they thought and knew. Thus Christian doctrine bases itself ultimately on two sources: (*a*) the Facts as to Christ's teaching and life; and (*b*) the Experience of believers in Him interpreting life and its problems in the light of those facts. Christian doctrine has grown up as a vital thing in the soil of actual life; in the experience of Christian living. Jesus appeared among men and lived and taught. He gave the Truth by what He was, by what He said, by what He did. Words, Works, Personality: all preached. This rich and various utterance fell into the hearing and the hearts of men and women who became His followers. Into their very being it entered with transforming power, making them 'new creatures.' By and by it filtered through their minds and life, and expressed itself in the form which their own experience gave to it. It is this reproduction of the truth Jesus brought that constitutes Christian doctrine. Its fundamental elements are to be kept clearly in view—viz. the Christian Facts and the Experience of Believers.

(3) The *origin of variation in doctrinal belief* immediately becomes manifest. Believing experience cannot be expected to be invariable. Still less the expression of experience. Variety of views enters. There are differences of mind, of education, of disposition and degrees of sympathy, of ability to apprehend and explain: differences all of them, when given free scope, likely to lead to mixed results. Present-day religious thought is profoundly impressed with the fact and with the necessity of it. And if in consequence the theological mind is infected with a certain sense of insecurity, there is compensation in the new breath of freedom. Obviously it is gain to be able to review the doctrinal process and results of the past, to disentangle the Divine Truth from its temporary formulation, and to elaborate it anew in such wise as will subserve the highest interests of men to-day, as well as do justice to its own ever fresh wealth of content. (Cf. the interesting exposition in Dr. Newton Clarke's *What shall we think of Christianity?* Lect. II.).

II. BASES OF CHRISTOLOGICAL BELIEF. — **1.** *Primarily a new experience.*—The new methods found early application to the doctrine of Christ's Person. That doctrine is central in the Christian system. It is by Christ, His Person and Work, that salvation is mediated. Historically and experimentally the Church learned it so. A study of the NT and of the two subsequent centuries is chiefly a study of one great fact or truth, to the understanding and interpreting of which the mind and life of the period were devoted, and devoted with absorbing interest—the Person of Christ. That problem soon became at once the impulse and the starting-point of an entire science of God, of man, and of the essential and final relation between God and man. But primarily the question at issue was simply that of His Person. It was provoked by Christ's own questions and by His claims. Its urgency was enhanced by the experience of believers. Their experience was unprecedentedly novel. Unlike that of Hebrew faith, its ground was individual and personal.

Its origin lay in the *revolutionary impression His presence created* in the heart, an impression which came as a thing incomparable, and remained as the most precious fact of life. It grew as a new power in the soul to resist and overcome sin, assuring not the promise only but the potency of real holiness, imparting to the latent faculties of the changing heart an increasing plenitude of spiritual force making for righteousness. Concurrently with this feature in the new experience went another, or two others. Awakened by the sense of power in the inner life imparted by Christ, men came to understand what the evil is from which God seeks to save them, and what the good is which He seeks to impart to them. In Christ moral goodness, the righteousness of God, laid its inexorable claims upon man's life, determining feelings and shaping resolutions as does the real entrance of God into our hearts. *The impression of Christ was thus seen to be the power of God.* A further step was won when reflexion forced forward the question how it could be so, in what mode the nature of Christ's Person must be regarded in the light of the above experiences. But the root of the matter was reached when the fact was realized that the more the strength of His character overwhelmed them, the more undeniable was made the reality of God to them. That was reached, however, at the very outset. It was *the primary conviction* which entitled to the name of believer, and confession of it meant salvation. It formed the fundamental basis of Christological belief. Jesus comes acting on human hearts with winsome gentleness, with a soul-moving sorrow for sin, and with a great enabling power. The high demands He brings raise no fear, for He who demands approaches with the means of fulfilling, which He is ready to impart. Herein rests the real originality of His message, by which His gospel differentiates itself from all other religions on the one hand, and from all merely philosophical or ethical Idealisms on the other; in virtue of which also all interpretations of His Person on humanitarian lines prove inadequate. On this point a clear understanding is indispensable. It is to be insisted that the 'Christ of History' and the 'Christ of Experience' were not separable to the mind of the disciples; they were one and indivisible. Their Christ is not the Teaching of Jesus alone, or His Works alone; or both together alone, but both together along with what they revealed regarding the inner life of Jesus, and what they created in the inner life of believers. It is impossible to separate the last from the first. It is illegitimate to seek to resolve it into a creation of the religious idealizing faculty of believers in Him. The thought of the Apostles consciously felt itself engaged not in evolving dreams and speculations of its own, but in striving to receive and appreciate a truth which was before, above, independent of them. By no single fact in His

biography does His message, in this view, stand or fall, but by Himself whom the facts reveal; the facts come embedded, and are vital because thus embedded, in one cardinal fact, Himself. He came to them not as a prophet, although He had much in common with the prophets; nor as a culture-hero, the offspring of spiritual imagination; but as an inner force of life absolutely unique; an inner experience in which God entered into their hearts in a manner heretofore unparalleled, being borne in on them rather than presented to their imitation, leavening them practically with Himself, and demonstratively in such a way that henceforth to their very existence in God, He, the Revealer, must belong. In the NT we move amid scenes where the common has been broken up by vast events. God from the Unseen has struck into history a fresh note, and a new era has opened. The whole suggestion is of possibilities and resources waiting to be disclosed. (Cf. Wernle, *Beginnings of Christianity*). The beginning of Christianity is neither a theological idea nor a moral precept; it is an experience of a Fact, the Fact of Christ, revealing and imparting the life of God.

The impression Christ made on those who saw and heard Him is a solid fact which no criticism can upset. Is it possible to get behind this fact? The effort is strenuously made by many. What was He who produced the impression reported in the Gospels? Better still, What was He who produced not this or that impression, but the resultant of actual and permanent impressions which He has made upon the world? In seeking an answer, historical and critical research has been lavished on every aspect of the question. Christ's teaching, career, personality, have been studied as never before. The result is that He is better known to us than to any previous age. It is at the same time being increasingly felt that a naturalistic reconstruction of His life is not possible. Candid students of the anti-supernaturalist camps (*e.g.*, in history, Keim [*Jesus of Nazara*]; in philosophy, Ed. Caird [*Evol. of Religion*]; in science, Sir Oliver Lodge [*Hibbert Journal*, III. i.] and Prof. James [*Varieties of Religious Experience*]) practically confess the failure of past attempts, and succeed in evading the postulate of Divinity only by attributing to the human life so ample a magnificence as to make it embrace all that Christian thought understands by Divinity. The new rationalism shows how decidedly the old materialism has spent its force. Of special interest is its frank recognition of the presence and vitality of experiences on which hitherto naturalism has set taboo. The more the new criticism endeavours to revivify the dead past and live over again the life of the disciples who enjoyed the personal communion of Christ, the more it sees it must combine in itself all the qualifications necessary for seeing and understanding all that He really was. This conviction, however, involves the finding of a place for criteria for the adjudging of Christ, specifically extra-naturalistic, but not extra-scientific, and spiritual; and where this happens without prepossession, the irresistible sense of Christ's transcendence impresses. His mystery remains (cf. *Contentio Veritatis*, Essay ii.; also Rashdall, *Doctrine and Development*, v. and vi.).

2. *Analysis of the experience.*—But if we cannot go behind the fact in the sense of reaching something more ultimate, we may analyze its elements. It will be found in content to comprise at least four constituents: His teaching and works; His growing consciousness of His own nature; His response to prophetic promise; His appeal to deeper personality.

(a) Of these the most obvious is the third, the contemporary *conviction of His Messianic dignity.* 'That Jesus is the Christ' is one of the dominating ideas of the Gospels and Epistles. More than one recent writer (Martineau, Meinhold, Wrede, etc.) have sought to show that Jesus did not accept the title of Messiah ; but not even these deny its attribution to Him by the disciples, and that as their main view of His Person. Careful analysis indicates that in whatever respects the Synoptics differ in their representations,—and they are not absolutely harmonious, — they yet represent a general agreement of view, and set forth what the primitive belief was. In that belief Jesus stands forth as Messiah, Himself accepting as appropriate what they attribute ; a sublime figure, not merely human, or exalted to Messiahship only by self-mastery and self-dedication, but by peculiar nature and special appointment. The endeavour to reduce the Evangelic description of Messiah to human dimensions is ludicrously inadequate to the facts. If it be the case that His disciples 'caressed Him in the most familiar manner as a fellow-human being' (Crooker, *NT Views of Jesus,* p. 25), the statement is crudely one-sided, since the familiar fellowship He vouchsafed, as is very evident, is but the framework of an intimate disillusionment on the part of His followers, and a growing revelation on His part. We can trace the stages by which the higher idea was unfolded to them. It came in a series of disappointments, intended, probably, to wean them from the popular ideas of what the Messiah should be. There is first the death of the Baptist, the prophet of Messiah. Then there is the refusal to commit Himself to the enthusiasm of those who would have made Him a king (Jn 2²⁴ 6¹⁵). Again, Christ avoids or evades the challenge to manifest Himself to the world (Jn 7⁴·⁶). Lastly came the crisis, as it were, the open challenge to prove His Messiahship by a sign and legitimate His claim, a challenge refused (Lk 22⁶⁷ 23³⁵). Hand in hand with this progressive disillusionment of all that was contrary to His thought in current Messianic ideas went the progressive revelation of the true Messiah,—a revelation which became at once a testing and a discipline of the character of the disciples, and an unfolding of undreamt of forces in His ; so that at last they fell at His feet and worshipped, while others acknowledged Him as 'Lord and God' (Jn 20²⁸) ; and still others plainly felt that He was 'ascending to the Father' (v.¹⁷). That Jesus claimed to be the Messiah, and gave His sanction to the belief on the part of His disciples is certain * (see next sect.) ; no less certain (and admitted) is it that the disciples believed Him to be the Messiah. The point of importance for the present is, how the belief originated with the latter. It is a practice among many scholars to reverse the actual facts. They argue as if the belief had been first formulated and officially offered, so to speak, for their acceptance, a formal external idea taken up because it had been put forth by Jesus as a scheme in which to frame His person ; in the light of which they are to regard His life and words ; exercising a prodigious influence on, and lending a force to, His words and a sanctity to His person beyond that

* The inquiry into the Messiah-consciousness of Christ has led so far to little agreement. Opinions multiply. The main points under consideration are : (1) Did the Messiah idea enter into His ministry at all ? (2) If it did, when ? From childhood ? at baptism ? at some later point in His ministry ? and from what causes ? (3) How did He conceive of His Messiahship ? Was His conception complete at first, or the subject of development ? (see art. MESSIAH). Probably it is true to say that the present popular study of Christ's self-consciousness is less fruitful for the interpretation of His Person than the older method of studying His God-consciousness. His life is not so much a self-witness as a revelation of the Father.

which, but for it, they could possibly have had (cf. such writers as Mackintosh, *Nat. Hist. of Christ. Relig.* ; Percy Gardner, *Historic View of NT*, ch. iv. ; Estlin Carpenter, *First Three Gospels,* chs. ii., iii.). The actual facts of Christ's career, *i.e.,* are conformed in the NT narratives to already existing Messianic traditions. And because of this the accumulated sanctities of the old religion were laid claim to by the new, whereby the latter maintained itself in face of the opposition which it encountered at the first and found a soil prepared for its reception. The contention cannot be sustained. It may receive some countenance from the circumstance that the writers of the NT never record any fact or incident merely as fact or incident, but as part of the substance of the gospel, illustrating and conveying spiritual principles. But the very ease with which the NT method of presenting historical circumstance might be turned to account under the influence of Messianic bias becomes valuable evidence against that hypothesis. For although the NT history is presented with a bias, *i.e.* as bearing and bodying forth a Person, the presentation, whether that of the Synoptics, or of the Fourth Gospel, or of St. Paul and the others, cannot with any measure of success be wholly identified with or wholly summed up in that of the Messiah. The Messianic claims of Jesus may be made (as they are made) to rest on the facts ; but the facts are not exhausted in those claims, even in the immensely enriched and original form in which Jesus made them. There are other portraitures of Jesus in the NT besides that of Him as Messiah ; and even those writers who set forth to portray Him solely as Messiah cannot be restrained from bursting through their self-imposed limits, in fidelity to the facts, and portraying Him as more than they meant. Moreover, the same writers convey to us the explicit assurance that they have not apprehended all the truth about His Person. Subsequent theology accepted the assurance, departed widely from the purely Messianic portraiture, yet claimed, and with perfect justice, that the new departures were in no sense new additions to the original Gospel, but fresh interpretations, designed to recover and vitalize truths discernible in the Gospels, but imperfectly understood by the Gospel writers.

(b) What has been adverted to finds illustration in another source of Christological idea, *the self-consciousness of Jesus.* In the most noteworthy discussion of this subject, that of Baldensperger (*Das Selbstbewusstsein Jesu*), only about one half of the work is taken up with determining the sense in which Jesus regarded Himself as Messiah ; the second part is devoted to other aspects arising out of His self-designations, His teaching as to the Kingdom, etc. Withal, much that cannot be excluded from Christ's self-revelation is not even touched upon. Any adequate exposition of Christ's idea of His own nature will include the following features : His interior life, His method in teaching, His moral perfection, His oneness with the Father.

(a) The *true secret of Christ's life* is not open. Who can ever know His intimate mind ? Could He have revealed it even if He would ? We know His words and deeds ; we distinguish the forces He set agoing in the world's history ; we venture on assertions of growth both of idea and of action in His life ; but where was the source of these ? or what the process ? or when the great choices and decisive operations of His marvellous soul ? What were the supremely triumphant and supremely terrible moments of His life ? What were the events in which He 'found Himself' ? His abounding energy implies a rich self-consciousness ; the completest self-consciousness rests on a plenitude of interior self-relationships. That these last existed in Him we are certain. But in what manner or in obedience to what impulses, who can discern? The records give results not processes, and just at those points where our curiosity is most eager, the limitations of our power to perceive are most urgent. We see but a few things. We observe the self-indulgence of His own consciousness again and again. We have glimpses of its exercise in solitary communings with God, in a life of intercourse with men, in the collision with incident and event. Above all, we know it in its great occasions,—Baptism, Temptation, Discussion with the Doctors, Transfiguration, Agony in the Garden, Resurrection, Ascension,— all of which are equally discoveries of His nature to Himself and revelations to His disciples. Because the meaning of these events seems to lie on the surface, we must be careful not to give them a superficial reception. They must be so received when regarded as parts of a religious idea, and not, as they are, experiences of a real Person. They constitute events which were no mere form gone through to proclaim a spiritual truth to men or to certify to them by wondrous signs a new relation opened for them with God. They were not dramatic: they were as personal to Him as they are instructive for us. He did what He did because He was what He was—from a deeper necessity than any deliberate persuasion that His disciples needed this or that teaching at this or that time. These events are far from summing up His inner life. They are but flashes out of a deep darkness. They reveal a life that is really human, in constant communion with a source of sustenance beyond the human, receiving the fulness of that source and translating it into earthly relations, yet with a self-possession and self-knowledge, i.e. a consciousness differentiated and personal. But the revelation does not uncover all the secrets of that life, leaving nothing to elude or bewilder. There are reservations in the knowledge given (cf. Dale, *Atonement*, pp. 45, 47). And these are not to be identified with the necessary inscrutabilities inherent in all finite personality. They are the intimations of a glory in His nature which separates it from all common natures, signs that in Him there are abysses of impenetrable splendour into which finite natures may not enter, however closely they may touch.

(β) Christ's *method in teaching* was characteristic. He taught neither as the scribes (Mt 7[29]), nor as a prophet (Mt 11[9]). And this because of His own nature and the nature of His message. He came not as a teacher; compelling assent by the complete answer to every difficulty, silencing dispute with arguments. He was more personal and spiritual. His teaching did not profess to offer an absolute intellectual proof of itself which must convince all sufficiently intelligent persons. It claimed the belief of all men, but not on the ground of its incontrovertible evidence; on the ground rather that all men were created to be good, and to know the truth, and would know it if their perceptions were not dulled and distorted by sin. It convinced only by a process which at the same time purified. He made His message not an argument but a force.

Hence His method was both declarative and suggestive; both thought and incentive to further thought. At times He is clear and authoritative; His words are such that men may refuse them but cannot mistake them. At other times He shrouds His doctrine in parables, and, pointing to principles, leaves them to work and unfold their purport as men are found ready to receive them. This was so, because the teaching was not simply of truths but Truth, infinite, inalienable, imperishable; the

fulfilment of all partial truths. His 'Verily I say' asserts His belief that it was so. The 'mind of Christ' which the teaching offers is not mere neutrality but soul, personality—back to which the teaching goes for justification. He appeals to no higher sanction than Himself. For Himself also He assumes a right to revise the law of Moses (Mt 5[21]), and claims authority over every individual soul (Mt 19[29]). For this reason it is futile to found an argument against the final and the revealed character of His message on its fragmentariness or its want of originality, futile also to limit His teaching to any detached portion of its recorded whole, *e.g.* the Sermon on the Mount. The fragments are numerous enough to enable us with ease to trace His mind. They form a unity which is not a new edition simply of anything preceding. That some of His thoughts and precepts were anticipated by Jewish and ethnic men of wisdom does not detract from His originality (see art. ORIGINALITY), because that consists, not in isolated truths, but in the remarkable sum of truth in which they take their appropriate and articulate place. That doctrine again explains the precepts of the Sermon on the Mount more fully than the Sermon sums up the doctrine. The method of Christ challenges reflexion and suggests as origin of His teaching His own statement 'from God' (Mt 11[27], Jn 7[16]).

(γ) What is meant by *the moral perfection* of Christ is at times misconceived, yet embodies a difference in His nature as compared with ordinary men that is perfectly realizable. Ullmann in a treatise of great power has made it familiar under the term 'sinlessness' (*Sinlessness of Jesus*, T. & T. Clark). The term has been objected to as a negative conception, the negative absence of evil, a negative difficult to prove from the limited induction available in a life of a few years. To give the conception a concrete expression may be impossible; but the term is of value as pointing to the stainless purity of Christ. His moral self-witness is in the highest degree positive.[*] It implies not simply the consciousness of flawless conduct, but the consciousness of perfect character as well as the assurance of power to create in others perfect character. Man may fail to meet his moral obligation in three ways: by falling short of his ideal of duty, by forming lower ideals than he ought, by direct transgression. And the witness of the ordinary conscience is that man has failed in all three, and has reason to fear God. The peculiarity of Christ's moral life is that all suspicion of this is wholly absent. He never confesses sin. He never fears any consequences of His acts either from God or from men. He seeks forgiveness, but only for others. He dreads sin, but not for Himself. He claims to be apart from it. He gives the impression of breathing an atmosphere in which sin cannot be. He is possessed with a holy energy, constant and powerful. Yet His moral life finds exercise not in abstracts but within conditions of earthly existence. He fought His way through those experiences which make goodness difficult. For this reason His goodness is both provable and imitable. The crux of the proof must rest less in special pleading for particulars of conduct than in a central view of His moral personality. Particulars have been contested. He has been charged with harshness to His mother (Jn 2[4]); with petulance

---

* The passage, 'Why callest thou me good? There is none good but one, that is God' (Mk 10[18] ‖), is still a difficult question of criticism and interpretation. That it is a self-depreciatory word is the least tenable explanation. That, as a self-depreciatory saying it is the only certainly authentic word of Christ with reference to His moral nature (Schmiedel, *Encyc. Bibl.* ii. 1881), is perverse (cf. Marcus Dods, *The Bible, its Origin and Nature*, p. 205).

(Lk 2[49]) ; with brusque contempt (Mt 7[6]) ; with discourtesy and personal bitterness (Lk 11[37ff.]) ; with violation of property rights (Mk 5[13] 11[2-6. 15]) ; with underrating family duty and affection (Mt 10[37], Lk 14[25. 26]) ; with defective and impracticable theories as to civic virtue, wealth, almsgiving, non-resistance, etc. (For these and others cf. such writers as Voysey, Dole, Philip Sidney, Goldwin Smith ; and the tendency of younger Unitarians). Charges on particulars cannot be met except in the light of character. The above are all defensible consistently with the character of Jesus as that character appears in the record. Nor need we resort to the plea (Martineau) that the blemishes are due to the fault of the delineators. Christ's moral nature is a unity. It is a unity in virtue of that principle by which He knew Himself to be always doing the will of God. He knew Himself to be in the activity of spirit and will what God in nature gave Him to become. In this respect He felt Himself solitary among men, and acted on the feeling. His perfection thus consists, first, not in any completeness of precepts given or concrete relations sustained in conduct—these flow from it ; but in the possession of that spirit and of those principles which not only supply all due regulation as occasion requires, but give unity, consistency, and purity to the moral life. In the light of this consideration we argue for His constant maintenance of moral supremacy in particular acts. His moral consciousness penetrated all His thought and feeling, and all expressions of both. It was the secret, further, of His power over sin, both in the world (cosmic) and in man : His power 'to overthrow sin' and 'to forgive sins.' He did not disregard sin. He inherited the teaching of His race as to sin, a teaching characteristically striking and comprehensive. He appropriates all its truth, and develops it in His own original spirit. He did this just because He was so pure. Sin was the haunting dread of His days. In meeting its malign force and subduing it, He broke His life. Against it He put forth all His strength, and in so doing rose to the fulness of stature we know, ' being raised up by God to his right hand.' More by what He did against sin than by what He declared of sin or of His own goodness did He prove His sinlessness. He did what He was. His presence raised the disciples, as His story raises us, to a level which, like Him, knows no sin (1 Jn 3[5. 6. 9]).

(δ) His *equality with God* [*] connects itself chiefly (in the Synoptics) with the thought of His sinlessness and His power to forgive sins (Mt 9[2-6], Mk 2[10], Lk 5[20. 23]. Less unquestioned is Mt 28[19], where He includes Himself in the unity of the Divine name). St. John's Gospel is full of the idea (5[22f.] 6[33-35] 8[42. 58] 9[25f.] 10[9] 11[25] 14[1. 6. 9] 15[5f. 23]), and to this point attacks have in consequence been directed with vigour (cf. in particular Martineau's *Seat of Authority* ; and for an effective rejoinder, Forrest's *Christ of History and Experience*, Lect. I.).

(c) As remarkable a factor as any in the spell Christ laid on man's spirit has been His *appeal to the deeper forces of personal being*. There have been those whose presence seemed to lower for the time being the vitality and intelligence of those who came into contact with them, and so acted as to destroy their self-possession. Some men overawe and paralyze others who come within the field of their influence. The power of Christ acted contrariwise. It empowered. He revealed men to themselves in revealing Himself to their inner sense. In receiving Him into their hearts new powers therein arose, reserve forces showed themselves ; His influence was that of reason begetting

* See below under 'Divine designations,' 'Son of Man,' 'Son of God.'

reason, love begetting love. In fellowship with Him men came to higher ideals. From Him, in fact, mankind has learned to know itself as it ought to be, and to estimate its own best possibilities. He has lifted up human aspiration more than any other. The reason of this may be found in the fact that He appealed persuasively to human instinct. To appeal to such instinct is often to create it. When a child is told a story of heroism, when rough untaught natures are softened by the beauty of tenderness seen or pictured, there is a creation of courage or gentleness where it was not before. When the instinct is quickened we know that it is native. The movement Christ initiated has proved of unrivalled creativeness in the history of human instinct and in every direction of human activity. 'The idea of Jesus is the illumination and inspiration of existence' (Phillips Brooks, whose *Bohlen Lectures*, 1879, are an eloquent exposition of Christ's creative influence, in moral, social, intellectual, emotional life). The first perception of this fact glows through the NT writings : not one of the writers fails to make us understand that the One he writes about is One who has opened new powers in, and disclosed new horizons to, his own soul. This is their witness—a witness corroborated by every succeeding age—that He called them, and in communion with Him, He made them 'a new creation,' disciplining and elevating character, calling out a higher faith, creating profounder emotions, inspiring with ever-increasing reverence, and bringing into play those higher and more creative faculties of the soul that see the things of God in a wide perspective impossible to the reason.

(d) The specialities of Christ's *teaching and works* may be briefly indicated. Their speciality has been challenged. The opinion of a recent Gifford lecturer is shared by many, that 'it is difficult, if not impossible, to select any special article of religious faith which is in its general aspect a doctrine peculiar to Christianity. Its uniqueness lies rather in what some would call the personality of the founder' (Wallace, *Lectures*, iii.). That is true ; but its suggestion is not true, that there is no uniqueness in the teaching of Christ. The uniqueness of the Teacher draws with it uniqueness in the teaching ; and that both in its method (see above) and in its substance. Similarly His works exhibit higher potency than the ordinary human. A strong feeling to this effect is resulting from the minute analysis which at the present time both the 'Words' and the 'Miracles' are undergoing (cf. Wendt, *Teaching of Jesus* ; Dalman, *Words of Jesus, et al.*). His dependence on others, His anticipations by others, are less confidently asserted. It is difficult, if not impossible, to discover any form of Gentile culture which is likely to have entered into the formative influences of His mind. From Greek philosophy He probably lived remote as much by natural temperament as by patriotic interest. He was not beyond its range, but then as now the Jew had a wonderful power of living in the fire without suffering the smell of it to pass upon his garments. Every Jew appeared in his own eyes to stand morally and intellectually on a higher level than the Gentile ; his system of education seemed less destitute of vivifying and invigorating ideals. He was nurtured on the history, the scenery, the religion of his land, all of them of exquisite interest, stimulating the fresh mind in the highest degree to habits of independent wisdom (cf. Ramsay, *Education of Christ*, ch. 3). Of Jewish sects and teachers three have been suggested as contributory forces : the Pharisees, the Baptist, the Essenes. The first proved His worst foes ; they had an influence, but it was solely negative. The second is remarkable for his consciousness of his own inferiority, of Christ's higher range in mission and higher rank in Person. Of the third let Hausrath judge : 'From the Essenes His whole conception of the world separated Him.' * There can be little question that the impulse to reflexion was fostered in Christ by study of the sacred books, the Law and the Prophets, under the usual Rabbinical direction. The master-words of His teaching are drawn thence. The substance of His teaching, in numerous details, is defined negatively by contrast with the comments of the scribes and positively by 'fulfilment' of the Law through a clearer discernment and profounder enrichment of the proper principles of the Law. The substance of His teaching in its main positions is intrinsically so separate from even its closest approximations in previous prophecy as to be justly entitled to the claim of originality. The source of its originality was in Himself. Christ's teaching is His own exposition of the Divine life which was revealed in Himself † (Mt 11²⁵⁻²⁷). 'Out of a perfect relation with God flows His teaching like a crystal stream.' Its form is drawn from the religious vocabulary of the time ; its matter from His own mind. In this connexion the following is admirably put, and meets a common objection :

'It is not enough to show that particular statements of our Lord may be found embedded in earlier writings which consist mainly of foolish superstitions and childish conceits. It would be strange indeed if, with the Scriptures in their hands, the great teachers of Israel never said, or never uttered in pregnant phrase, any of those lofty spiritual truths which shine forth from the pages of the prophets. But if we find, on referring to contemporary literature, that such references are only like rare jewels shining among vast heaps of error and superstition, that they are only like flashes of lightning in an all-embracing night, then their concurrence in nowise diminishes our wonder. The problem only takes another shape. How is it, we ask, that out of all this spiritual lumber the soul of Jesus only selected what was good and great, and rejected all the rest? How is it, e.g., that from the teaching of Hillel He took (if, indeed, He took anything directly thence) only what was eternally true, rejecting at the same time all the frivolous ritualism and puerile casuistry in the consideration of which Hillel spent his life? Remember again that it detracts in nowise from our Lord's claim to originality, that even His master thought had been partially or casually expressed by those who went before Him. The question to be decided in our Lord's day was this, Which of all the thoughts about God that have passed through the mind of saints and prophets should become the master-thought of religion, which should condition and determine all the rest? It would not be true to say that Jesus selected one, as though He had been passing all in review and comparing them. No, the truth is that Jesus laid hold of one by His Divine intuition, in virtue of His direct insight into the nature of God' (Moorhouse, Teaching of Christ, p. 66 f.).

When we add that Christ's teaching was given, so to speak, casually ; not systematically, in no ordered or finished statement ; that the whole is comparatively small, and yet that it is easy to draw up from the scattered sayings a sum of doctrine coherent, self-consistent, and completely satisfying to the needs of the soul, further cogency is lent to the witness, 'Never man so spake' (Jn 7⁴⁶), and point to the question, 'Whence hath this man this wisdom?' (Mt 13⁵⁴). See artt. ORIGINALITY and UNIQUENESS.

To His words have to be added His works. His ordinary doings were those of a good man (Ac 10³⁸). His miracles proved a special presence of God with Him (Jn 3²). There is a crude view of the Gospel wonders which has made many see in them an unimportant part of the Gospel story, and even feel it desirable to do without them. So long as they are looked upon as thaumaturgic signs or violations of Nature's sequence, so long will both religion and science reject them. If, however, they are considered as indications of laws which embrace and in a sense unite the seen and unseen worlds, it is of immense importance to Christianity

* It hardly comes within the scope of this article to consider the alleged influence of Buddhism or Mithraism.
† Cf. Perowne's *Hulsean Lects.* pp. 93, 94.

that they should occur in connexion with the foundation of that faith. As a matter of fact, in face of all attempts to explain them or explain them away, a certain robust sense of the general mind has refused to concur in any view that denies their reality or their essential place in the history. They reveal Christ no less than His doctrine. They constitute warrants of His Divine power : they also form part of the Gospel. They stand as a real item in the list of testimonies to His impression. They are one of the modes in which His life found utterance, an authentic element of the original gospel offered to faith ' (A. B. Bruce, *Apologetics*, p. 376 ; *Miraculous Elements in Gospels*, chs. vi. and viii.). In this respect they are on a different plane from the prodigies credited to pagan heroes. That men might see the will of God at work, Jesus did the works of His Father. A reckless historical scepticism evaporates the miracles partly into odd natural events, partly into nervous healings, partly into gradually growing legends. Sane criticism, however, admits their congruity with the record, their naturalness to His Person, and their value to faith. The supreme miracle of the Resurrection (wh. see) is of primary import.

3. *Validity of the experience.*—The lines thus traced converge in one picture. Their effect is striking, and of the cumulative kind. They may not produce infallible certainty of the truth of Christ's Divinity. But no infallible certainty can be given. The Christ they portray is not absolute in the sense of abstract ; He is absolute in the sense of the fullest concrete ; all the elements, therefore, which go to make up this impression of His Person contribute to the proof of its power : by exhibiting what He is they testify to Him : their witness is, 'This is the Son of God.' It was men's experience of Christ as Divine that gave them the right to affirm His Divinity. *Is the witness true ?* The contention here made is that what we know along many lines as the Christian experience is a new and distinctive development, and demands a new and unique factor introduced to the human consciousness. Is the contention verifiable ? The witness is an interpretation : can we trust it ? Has the impression an exact equivalent behind it of objective fact? What were the dimensions of the objective fact capable of producing this inner effect? The answer must be that the same law of rationality holds here as in other parts of knowledge. The effect must have an adequate cause. What the soul realizes as the highest in its inner feeling is proof of reality that the reason may recognize. If the soul attains the vision of a Reality whose authority over it is absolute and from whom it receives a power that masters all other powers, then it knows the meaning of God. The finality of such experience cannot be questioned, when its source is personality (personality being the only full reality of which we have knowledge), and its seat the moral disposition and not individual temperament. Now to those conditions the impression of Christ recorded in the Gospels conforms. Behind the records He stands, greater than themselves, and that by their own showing ; and because of this they furnish to their readers a vision which does not fade but grows, a power that is new and permanent, a command from which the conscience cannot dissent, a mastery that sets free. He Himself had this effect on men as they companied with Him ; the record of their intercourse with Him has the same effect. The effect is a fact of continuous experience fundamentally identical in kind throughout the Christian centuries. Both are the envelope that enwraps Truth transcending time and place. Only the universal and everlasting can transcend the limitations of our separateness and speak in the same manner to thousands of different souls. The phenomena of Christian history are so diverse in kind from those of other historic faiths as to require the supposition of a supernatural origin (cf. Illingworth, *Personality Human and Divine*, p. 200). The witness that God Himself is here stepping into the history of the race must be accounted true.

III. BEGINNINGS OF THE DOCTRINE OF CHRIST'S PERSON IN THE NT.—1. *General character of the doctrine.*—It has been necessary to make the above analysis of the bases of belief in Christ as presented in the Gospels and to justify it, because it is only by understanding them fully that we gain any test by which to determine the character and worth of the belief itself, or reach the point of view for appreciating aright its beginnings and its growth. It is a doctrine that *has no finality*. It is based on an experience which cannot rest, but must grow with the growth of all life, and pervade all other experience of life. It is a doctrine therefore that has a history down to the present, and which is destined to continue beyond the present. We are now in the midst of a new growth of its meaning. In moving on we can purchase security only by retracing our steps, unravelling the web of the past and weaving it over again. Recurrence to the original will reinvigorate like the touch of earth to the feet of Antæus. In the first expression there is a universality which is apt to be lost in the divisions of later opinion : there is an implicit fulness in the beginning which is not completely represented in any subsequent stage. To that beginning we now advert. In the conviction that 'in Christ' they were 'a new creation,' 'partakers of a Divine nature' (2 Co 5¹⁷, 2 P 1⁴), the Apostles must seek expression of their conviction. The expression runs over into every phase of their thought and life. It breeds in them a sense of new relation to Christ akin to that felt towards God, originating a new thought of His Person. We see it in the Names they give to Him, in the Properties and Attributes they ascribe to Him, in their acceptance of wonders attending His Origin and His passing from sight, in the relations they proceed to institute between Him and previous history as well as future ages. The NT idea of His Divinity is not to be built up as an induction from these particulars ; these, on the contrary, are the reflexions, inevitable and faint, of the experience of His Divinity ; they are the inward seeking utterance.

It is an utterance that is quite spontaneous. It is the outcome of religious faith not of philosophic interest. The speculative instinct is wholly secondary to the spiritual facts. But while this is so, the philosophic interest is there, and that of necessity. While the Person hidden behind the life of the NT is vaster than the NT record of Him, it remains true that if that Person were to survive and His impression, they must be shown to ring true to the intellect. What happens to the emotions suggests problems to the mind. Proved facts, even those 'deep-seated in our mystic frame,' have to formulate themselves in thought. And so the moral life created by Christ furnished material for new great convictions fitted to be at once its expression and its safeguard. The doctrine of His Person was the necessary correlate of the impression of His Personality.

In the facts thus noted is to be found the answer to two inquiries of rationalism. On the one hand, it is asked, Why is He never called God ? and on the other, Why such *diversity of view among the writers*? Take the latter first. The criticism here has been carefully made by Dr. Martineau (*Seat of Authority*, p. 361) and others, who urge that Jesus was construed successively into (1) the Jewish ideal or Messiah, (2) the Human ideal or Second Adam, (3) a Divine Incarnation. This construction of theories is asserted to be only a fanciful achievement of early Christian thought. 'The personal attendants of Jesus worked out the first ; the Apostle of the Gentiles, the second ; the school whence the Fourth Gospel proceeded, the third.' In reply it may be affirmed that such criticism holds its ground only by (*a*) doing violence to the facts on which it seeks to rest, by subjecting them to a narrowly subjective standard : the facts include those in which Christ is represented as accepting the name of Lord ; by (*b*) an arbitrary application of the idea of development to the narrative. It is possible to prove the alleged constructions to have been made successively only by a series of unwarranted eliminations. The Synoptists are not without knowledge of (2) and (3), nor is (1) unknown to St. Paul and the Fourth Gospel. The facts, when viewed without prepossession, point to no such clear-cut theories. They do, however, indicate both movement and diversity of belief, changes constantly going on in the opinions respecting Christ's nature, and very material differences in individual emphasis and interpretation, a movement and diversity only less remarkable than the unmistakable unity pervading them. It was natural that men of the character and training of St. James and St. Peter should discover in OT conceptions of the Messiah approximate lines of thought wherewith to describe their experience of Christ. Temperamental and other causes led St. Paul and St. John as naturally to give representations of their experience such as they have done, the former anthropological and practical, the latter contemplative and mystical. As types these three are distinguishable, but not exclusively of each other. There are others also, as, *e.g.*, that of the Ep. to the Hebrews, of Ephesians and Colossians, of the Apocalypse. These expressions differ among themselves, and differ in precisely the manner that is natural and desirable. The variety is that of life and reality. These all represent differences that are not separate developments of substance in the doctrine so much as precious elements constitutive of a richer fulness than any one of them or all of them ; a fulness of necessary mysteriousness. They represent no signs of a struggle to assert Divinity in opposition to a bare humanity : of such a struggle there is not a trace in the NT.

As to the second point of criticism, it is possible with some reason to maintain that the term θεός is never applied to Christ. The matter is still in dispute among scholars. The crucial passages are (not taking into account Jn 1¹ 20²⁸, 1 Jn 5²⁰, He 1⁸ᶠ·) Ro 9⁵, Tit 2¹³, Ac 20²⁸, 1 Ti 3¹⁶, Ph 2⁶, 2 P 1¹, Col 2⁹. In 2 P 1¹ the rendering, ' Our God and the Saviour Jesus Christ,' is not excluded ; similarly Tit 2¹³. In Ro 9⁵ the doxology may be regarded as referring to God. In 1 Ti 3¹⁶ the true text is ὅς not θεός. In Ac 20²⁸ the AV reading is probably correct (' God '). Col 2², Eph 5⁵, 2 Th 1¹², Tit 2¹³ have been adduced as proofs that St. Paul speaks of Christ as God ; but erroneously. The two strongest passages are Ph 2⁶⁻⁸, Col 2⁹. But if the texts are not unambiguous, *that does not affect the truth of the Divinity of Christ*. It was scarcely natural for a Jew to use the Divine Name in any connexion (cf. Dalman, *Words of Jesus*, § vii., also p. 233). If it were used, it applied to God in His absolute being. Cf. Westcott, *Ep. of St. John*, p. 172. God manifesting Himself in Christ was affirmed in a variety of other modes. The Apostles were not so much concerned to 'prove His Divinity' as to persuade men to accept Christ as their Saviour. The question whether He was God or not was in this view a subordinate question. They wrote about Him as they preached, in His human manifestation and in His Exalted Glory. From that point of view they neither missed the consciousness of His Godhood nor failed abundantly to declare it. The declarations they make are of One who, they were persuaded, was absolutely unique in position, in character, in work; One whose relationship to God was perfect, who was the Saviour, Light and Life of men. Are such declarations consistent with anything short of His Divinity?

2. *Divine designations applied to Christ.*—Of the names implying distinctiveness of nature assigned to Christ in the Gospels and Epistles, there are four of supreme import: (*a*) 'Son of Man,' which stands by itself; (*b*) 'Son of God,' with which may be set as allied in significance, 'Son of the Highest,' 'Only - begotten Son,' 'My beloved Son' (or 'My Son, my Chosen'), and 'The Son'; (*c*) 'Christ'; (*d*) 'Lord.' Others are the 'Word of God' and 'the Word'; 'Son of David,' with which may be placed 'Root and offspring of David,' and perhaps 'Prince of life' and 'Prince'; 'Saviour'; 'Image of God'; 'Second Adam'; 'First and Last'; 'The Holy, Just One.'

Son of Man. — To this title there attaches a peculiar interest, which is reflected in the amount of discussion it has excited. Controversy circles round its use, its source, its meaning. It occurs in all the four Gospels. It is the one name Christ is represented as reserving for His exclusive use. That He did so is plainly implied in the narratives.

His use of it has been denied (cf. Bruno Bauer, Volkmar, Oort, Lietzmann, etc.). One of the most capable of recent critics (Wellhausen, *Das Evang. Marci*) argues that the term, if used at all by Christ, was not made current by Him but by the Christian community, and came into use in the following manner. The early Christians believed that Jesus had prophesied His Parousia. They hesitated to make Him say so outright, and hence represented Him as saying only that the 'Man' of Daniel should appear with the clouds of heaven. He could say that without meaning Himself. But the Christian interpretation soon read Him into the announcement, then used the title in the prophecies of the Passion and Resurrection, and finally as a simple equivalent of the first person singular on the lips of Jesus. The position, in this and other forms, fails to account, *inter alia*, for two facts: (*a*) the term is not found in St. Paul or elsewhere in NT, but almost solely on the lips of Jesus (instances to the contrary are Jn 12³⁴, Ac 7⁵⁶); (*b*) if a coinage of the Early Church, how does it—a term denoting lowliness—harmonize with the evident endeavour to portray a glorified Christ?

The expression occurs in previous Hebrew and Aramaic literature. The references of importance are in Ezekiel, Daniel (7¹³), and Enoch, in all of which the Messianic significance is not indisputable (see Schmidt, art. 'Son of Man' in *Encyc. Bibl.*, who inclines to refer even Dn 7¹³ to Michael, not Messiah). In what sense is it to be understood? The commonly accepted view (*e.g.* Beyschlag-Wendt) may be thus stated: Christ was desirous of being recognized as the Messiah. He was not desirous of fulfilling the current expectations of what the Messiah should be and do. He therefore did not apply the current designations of Messiah to Himself, but, finding one term, 'Son of Man' (in Daniel), employed it as expressing (1) Messianic character, and (2) much more than the expected Messianic character, viz. the generically human character.

Dalman (*Words of Jesus*) has adduced grave considerations against this view. It is a view, he holds, started by the Greek divines, and has no basis in primitive Christian thought. He maintains that Christ adopted it from Dn 7¹³, and used it of Himself in its original sense, a sense which was not widely prevalent in His time as applicable to the Messiah. There 'the emphasis rather lies on the fact that in contrast with the winged lion, the devouring bear, the four-headed leopard, the fourth beast with ten horns terrible exceedingly beyond its predecessors, he appears unarmed and inoffensive, incapable though any power of his own of making himself master of the world; he is only as a son of man. If ever he is to be master of the world, *God* must make him so.' The 'Son of Man,' on this view, is not the son of man in the sense of being a man like other men, but as being a man distinct from other men, in the sense

that God has given him to be what he is. The expression intimates less his human nature than his Divine. 'Son of Man' denotes 'that member of the human race, in his own nature impotent, whom God will make Lord of the world.'

To indicate results, it may be taken that there is a fair consensus of agreement on the following points: (*a*) that the use of the title as applicable to Himself is due to Christ; (*b*) that a wider source than the passage in Daniel is probable; (*c*) that in meaning it embodies a composite conception, combining various OT suggestions, and these the most rich and salient; the seed of the woman, the one like a son of man, the suffering Servant of Jehovah, the ideal people, the recipient of special privilege, the apportioner of judgment, of celestial origin. In wealth of content the expression stands alone. It was thus peculiarly appropriate as a self-designation of Christ. In it there met the two divisions of Messianic reference, those pointing to the glory and those pointing to the humiliation of the Messiah, comprising elements seemingly incongruous and irreconcilable, yet in essentials capable of being unified in a single character. In the course of His ministry He was to manifest Himself as the conqueror of Satan, as perfect man, as concentrating His race in an intense personal life, as conscious of a special mission from God, of absolutely intimate relation to God, of perfect dependence upon God, and as sharing with God in the judgment of the world, characteristics all of them Messianic, and impossible to be included in any of the terms of Messianic intention more fully than in this, the 'Son of Man.' Its meaning on His lips goes further than even the fulness of Messianic intention; so that it is not at once intelligible ('mystifying title' of Weisse and others is not justified), a feature it shares with Him whom it designates and the hopes it unified. In it these features find place: much contemporary Messianic belief of a familiar kind; less prominent ideas that had before this time passed into the background; novel functions in Christ's conception, such as the life of the Son of Man as a life of service, and His death as necessary to redeem men; and the combination of all these in a new synthesis which was not simply a mosaic of old data or gathering up of the disparate details of earlier expectation, but which was reached by the entrance of a new thing that made the fulfilment infinitely more glorious than the promise might have seemed to warrant (cf. art. SON OF MAN).

Son of God ('the Son,' 'My Son'). This title, like the former, belongs to the OT writings, being found in Gn 6², Ex 4²², 2 S 7¹⁴, Ps 2⁷ 82⁶ 89²⁷, Job 1⁶ 38⁷, Hos 1¹⁰ 11¹, and there applied in various connexions: to offspring of the gods, to angels, to judges, to Israel as a people serving Jehovah, to individual Israelites, to the theocratic king, to the Messiah (Dalman and others object to 'Son of God' as a Messianic title). The expression 'Son of God' [or 'My Son'] occurs in the Synoptics 27 times, and 'the Son' 9 times. In St. John 'Son of God' occurs 10 times and 'the Son' 14 times. Both occur in St. John's First Epistle, in several of St. Paul's, in Hebrews, in Revelation. In the Gospels they are applied to Christ by the Father, angels, demoniacs, Himself (rarely, and only in St. John), disciples (*N.B.*—St. Peter's confession, Mt 16¹⁶), elders, high priest, centurion. In determining its meaning, we may exclude the idea of pagan influence. There is little probability that the cult of the Roman emperors suggested either the word or its idea. Its application to believers (Mt 5⁹·⁴⁵, Lk 6³⁵, Eph 1⁵, Jn 1¹², 1 Jn 3¹·², Ro 8¹⁴·¹⁹, Ph 2¹⁵) does not necessarily confine its import to the merely human sphere. Its previous usage in the OT could not fail to prepare the way for a connotation of special relationship to God.

That the term contains Messianic reference is contested by few. In line with it are to be explained the testimony of the demoniacs (Mt 8²⁹ ‖ Lk 4⁴¹), and the heavenly voices at the Baptism and the Transfiguration (Mt 3¹⁷ 17⁵). Here, too, possibly lies the reason for Christ's use of the term in debates with the Jewish leaders (Jn 3¹⁸ 5¹⁵ff. 8²⁵ff.). The Messianic sense is obvious in St. Peter's confession (Mt 16¹⁶); less so in that of the centurion (Mk 15³⁹). The answer to the high priest's question was treated as blasphemy (Mt 26⁶³ff.), because by it He claimed more than Messiahship. St. John's statements enhance the feeling of the Synoptists. He points clearly to Christ's use of the term and in the solitary sense. He is careful in his use of names, and would hardly put into Christ's mouth a self-designation without some warrant of sanction from His personal usage. But the Synoptists are not without traces of the same clearness. In Mt 22⁴¹⁻⁴⁶, Mk 12³⁵⁻³⁷, Lk 20⁴¹⁻⁴⁴, the inference is inevitable that the Messiah is the son of One more exalted than David.

What meaning did Christ attach to the term? The above passage is significant. He is not denying Davidic descent. He affirms it (see on the other side Wellhausen, *Evangel. Marci*). By His descent from David He satisfies one condition expected in the Messiah. That fact, however, does not preclude Him from satisfying further conditions not included in the Messianic prophecy, evincing a power in Him which points to another and higher origin. This further scope in His filial relation is intimated in such passages as Mt 11²⁷ 16¹⁷, Lk 10²², Mt 3¹¹, Mk 4¹¹, Lk 8¹⁰, Jn 8³⁵. ³⁶ 15¹⁰ 4³⁴ etc.). He taught the disciples to call God 'our Father,' and called God His own Father in a special sense. He asserts that He alone adequately reveals and knows God. He suggests a special sonship in the parable of the Wicked Husbandman (Mk 12⁶). The double strain is present in His consciousness. He is Son in the Messianic sense. He is also Son in a Divine sense: of absolute oneness with the Father. He has the mission of the former with its dignity: He has the infallible knowledge with perfect obedience of the latter. Both features emerge in the Synoptics as in the Fourth Gospel. Both are not justly interpreted in such a sense as suggests a merely ethical relation to God, a relation which others may actually possess or are destined to attain. In them there is the basis of the ethical but of the essential as well. The Sonship of Christ is human and historical yet solitary and transcendent.

St. Paul corroborates the Evangelic positions. The earlier Epistles contain a large amount of teaching as to the Person of Christ. We have lucid references to the Sonship: 1 Th 1¹⁰, Ro 8³. ³², 2 Co 4⁴, Ro 1⁴, 2 Co 1¹⁹ff., Gal 2²⁰, Eph 4¹³, Ro 1⁹, Gal 1¹⁶ 4⁴, where, through the position assigned to Him on the one hand, and on the other the special Spirit dwelling in Him, equality with God is asserted and Divine functions attributed. In one passage, 2 Th 2, Christ, while not named 'Son,' is regarded in His capacity as the opponent of Antichrist as a consubstantial representative of God. This idea in another context we have in Col 1¹³⁻¹⁵, He 1²⁻⁸ 3³ etc.

A survey of the texts reveals a complex conception, including (1) a Messianic predicate asserting the place of Christ as the complete antitype of the theocratic king; (2) an ethical identity in the realization of Divine holiness in a stainless life; (3) a spiritual unity revealing itself in a perfect harmony with the mind of God and a perfect obedience to His will, which were as much innate properties of His personality as achievements of His moral self. In addition, the conviction of His pre-existent glory*

* See art. PRE-EXISTENCE.

and of His cosmic agency necessitates (1) a physical descent from Deity by a creative act of the Divine Spirit (see ANNUNCIATION and VIRGIN-BIRTH); and (2) an equality of essence in virtue of which Divine acts and qualities are ascribed to Him. Cf., further, art. SON OF GOD.

Christ ('the Christ'), **King of the Jews, Lord,** may all be taken together. 'Christ' is the Greek equivalent of *Messiah*. Both words signify 'the Anointed.' While applied in the OT to prophets (Ps 105¹⁵, 1 K 19¹⁶) and high priests (Zec 4¹⁴), the name is specially identified with the kings, from the passage (Ps 2²) implying that they were under the special protection of Jehovah, and exercised righteous government. Later, when Israel had come under Gentile rule, the idea entered into the name that the Messiah would overthrow the secular might and liberate the people, i.e. be at once the Saviour of the faithful and the Prince or King of the saved. In the NT the name is accorded to Jesus everywhere. It is practically His surname, a circumstance remarkable when it is remembered that He forbade its use in His earthly life. He is greeted also as 'King' and as 'Son of David,' recognitions of Him as Messiah. That He Himself accepted the rôle appears from the following: (a) His sanction of the terms 'Son of Man' and 'Son of God' as applicable to Him; (b) His consciousness of being endowed with the Spirit of God (Lk 4¹⁸ff.), a mark of the Messianic King (Is 11²) and of the Servant of Jehovah (Is 42¹ 61¹); (c) His self-witness as to His being the Son and Heir of God (Ps 2²); (d) His assurance of the reference in Ps 110 to Himself, where the King in Zion is in His view the Messiah; (e) He spoke of the building of the Temple in the same sense in which the Messiah is the builder of the Temple (cf. Mt 26⁶¹, Mk 14⁵⁸ with Zec 6¹². ¹³); (f) He spoke of His kingdom and therefore Messianic rank; (g) He described Himself as Judge of the world — a Messianic function; (h) He commended St. Peter's confession (Mt 16¹⁷); (i) He acknowledged His Messiahship before His judges (both Sanhedrin and Pilate); (j) He was put to death as 'King of the Jews.' Messiahship, it has been said, is not Divinity (Ottley, art. 'Incarnation' in Hastings' *DB*). True, but Messiahship as enriched by Christ is. The new features with which He fulfilled the old conception, suffering and resurrection, brought it as near Divinity as was possible for the Hebrew mind. In them was concentrated the work of salvation, always assigned in OT to Jehovah Himself, in the NT always and in all its parts assigned to Christ. The step is but a short one from the unhesitating acknowledgment of the Divinity of Christ's work to that of the Divinity of His nature.

The step is taken when He is called **Lord.** Christ refers to Himself as 'your Lord' (Mt 24⁴²). There is evidence of growth in the meaning of Lordship in NT usage. Resch has shown that the name was interchangeable in instances with 'Master' and 'Rabbi.' Between that stage and the view of the Epistles that Christ is Lord over Nature, the Universe, the Church (Col 1¹⁶⁻¹⁸, Ph 2¹⁰ff. etc.), there is a wide gulf. The transition was probably effected in Hellenistic circles, and aided by the use of 'Lord' as a title of the Roman Emperor and associated with the divine honours paid to him.

The Second Adam (the Man from Heaven) is a designation peculiar to St. Paul. In idea it is more speculative than the foregoing. The impulse to its construction is to be found in the Apostle's conversion through the glorified appearance of the Risen Christ on the way to Damascus. On the ground of that experience he contrasts men, as he finds them, subject to sin and death, and this man exalted over both (1 Co 15⁴⁵⁻⁴⁹, Ro 5¹²⁻²¹). The religious and moral destinies of the human race are traced to the action of two typical men, the first Adam, 'a living soul,' and the second Adam, 'a quickening spirit.' In so thinking, he gives an original turn to his Messianic views. The ordinary Messianic hopes of his nation he shares. He is acquainted also with the tradition of the life and teachings of Christ. But neither his intellect nor his conscience, endued with fresh vision and power by Christ risen, could rest satisfied with those. He departs from them, but not to supersede, rather to develop. He regards Christ as the foretold of the prophets (Ro 1²), His ministry as a manifestation of the righteousness of God (3²¹), His death and resurrection as the fulfilment of foreshadowings in the OT Scriptures (1 Co 15³· ⁴). He shares with the Synoptists and Acts the position that Christ is the Saviour and bringer-in of the kingdom of righteousness; with them he applies to Christ the names 'Son of God,' 'Christ,' etc., in a sense of exceptional dignity. What they had reached by a gradually increasing insight he won by the vision (Gal 1¹⁶), and from the point of view of his spiritual intuition he reads the Person of Christ. What he had seen colours all his thought, which is essentially a Christology centring in the idea of 'the Lord of Glory.' The term signified, of Christ's work, relief from the oppression and burden of sin and the law and death, with hope of regeneration for himself and all men; it signified, of Christ's Person, that He was Spirit (2 Co 3¹⁷); man, 'in the likeness of sinful flesh' but 'the man from heaven' whom the heavenly principle made perfect (5²¹), pre-existent (Ro 8³, 1 Co 10⁴, Gal 4⁴) and 'head of every man' (1 Co 11³), human nature in its archetypal form, particularly in creation (8⁶ etc.). That He of whom all this was affirmed was not conceived to be an ordinary human personality in His intimate nature, goes without saying. Taken in conjunction with other terms used, the 'Lord of Glory' declares Divinity. In the later Epistles, Eph., Col., Ph., Ti., Tit., the Divinity is explained in the same directions with greater precision and fulness, and exemplified in fresh relations.

The fact that these writings contain a more developed Christology than that of the undisputed Epistles has been made a ground for discrediting them. But without good reason. The later thought is in organic line with the earlier; both fix attention on what Christ did and does, and not on what He taught; both rise to the thought of the glorified Christ through the work of Christ on earth. The later illustrates and emphasizes rather than increases the heavenly dignity of Christ, assigning an increment of function rather than of rank (cf. Lightfoot, Col. p. 120).

In the Ep. to the Hebrews there is a remarkable type of doctrine which has not yet been definitively located. It has very little in common with the NT writings generally, or even with the Pauline. Its conception of Christ's Person is characterized by significant differences in substance and expression. After a prologue (almost in the manner of the Fourth Gospel and the Apocalypse, which looks like a summary of previous thought) it proceeds to its main thesis, the superiority of the New Covenant over the Old. In the first seven chapters Christ is presented as the Son, the Revealer, and the King-Priest. As the Son, He has been prepared for in Israel (1¹), has participated in the creation and is its consummation (1²), is the manifestation of the Father's glory as its effulgence (ἀπαύγασμα), and the expression of the Divine essence (ὑπόστασις) as its embodiment χαρακτήρ) (1³), and is now at the Father's right hand. As the Revealer, He is superior to angels and Moses; while yet a 'partaker of flesh and blood' (2¹⁴), wherein He has done away with sin and death, establishing and vindicating His glory by His sufferings. As the King-Priest He realizes

in perfection the qualifications of the priesthood imperfectly met in the OT system. In his exegesis the author applies to Christ two series of OT texts, the one having in view in their original meaning the Messiah (1⁵, cf. Ps 2⁷; 1⁸· ⁹, cf. Ps 45⁷· ⁸), the other relating to God (1⁶, cf. Ps 97⁷; 1¹⁰⁻¹², cf. Ps 102²⁶⁻²⁸). All three aspects point to such pre-eminence of Christ as makes Him incomparable with men, to be equalled with God alone. It is at the same time a pre-eminence appropriated in His human experience, made His own by obedience—a point insisted on. These two form the idea of Christ: He is God who by a Divine Incarnation fulfils Himself in man; and He is man who by a human faith and endurance realizes himself in God. If the terminology is less Hebraic than in St. Paul or the Synoptists, the motive is the same, viz. to express in the terms available the new contrasts and special aspects of Christ's Person impressed on the author's mind by his independent experience of Christ.

The Logos ('the Word') is the term distinctive of St. John (Jn 1¹· ¹⁴, 1 Jn 1¹, Rev 19¹³). It is introduced in a way which indicates that it was familiar to the writer and his readers. As a term it is traceable in both Palestinian and Alexandrian thought. Its idea is Hebraic not Philonian, and to be taken in connexion with 'the *Only-begotten*.' It is no impersonal abstract Idea. The Logos is, as in the Targums, personal and active as the equivalent of God manifesting Himself (1 Jn 1²). He is an historical human life (Jn 1¹⁴, 1 Jn 1¹⁻³), a fact not to be minimized. Yet His coming within the conditions of humanity was the coming of One who had been pre-existent with God in and from the beginning (1¹ 3¹³· ³¹ 6⁶²), sharing in the life of God and in the Divine acts of creation and preservation, and operative in previous history as an illuminating and quickening potency in the hearts of the righteous (1³· ⁴· ⁹· ¹² 10¹⁶ 11⁵²). Complementary is the thought of the Apocalypse of His eternity or semi-eternity in nature, the *Alpha and Omega*, and in redemptive activity—'Lamb slain from the foundation of the world,' and of the perfect and perpetual adoration accorded to Him with God in heaven. The recital of the work of the Logos, so brief, covering the vastest realms, cosmic, historical, personal, in the most summary space, is majestic. The absence of any line of intermediate beings between God and man is notable. The identification of the Word with God (θεός) is deliberate. The description gives no plausibility to the view that here we have a category taken from philosophy and applied loosely to the facts. There is nothing in the Synoptic representation of the human character and consciousness of Christ which unfits it or renders it inadequate for the Logos conception; equally there is nothing in the Logos conceived as becoming incarnate in the man Jesus which contradicts or impairs the reality or the completeness of His humanity as portrayed in the Synoptics.

The two are adequate and congruous to each other. They are also necessary to each other, each being a torso without the other. The source of the doctrine was the actual experience of the author, but it is the experience of a mind of profound spirituality and devout idealism. He gives the impression of having been determined in the particular cast he gives his doctrine by contemporary circumstances. A specific method is apparent. It is not that he seeks to prove that 'Jesus is the Christ, the Son of God' (Jn 20³¹); it is the special manner of his proof that differentiates his record, and above all the specially intense feeling towards Christ that pervades it, characteristics that have led some to assert that he sees Christ as primarily Divine and less human than the Synoptists see Him. It is truer to say that he sees Christ both as more Divine and more human than the Synoptists; driven beyond them by deepened experience of Christ on the one hand, and that richer reflexion on the other hand to which he was incited by the increasing Gnostic licence of the age. Gnosticism was a subtler foe than current Messianism. Its sophisms could be met only by a simpler and profounder—simpler because profounder—truth. The Fourth Gospel gives that truth. It attempts a portrait of Christ corresponding to the most intimate and overwhelming sense of His power conceivable, at once wholly revealing God, and the Divine revelation of the whole nature, life, and destiny of man. Hence to the historian it is an enigma, to the devout a poem. Its outline is simple and free because so broad and high. Its structure is less of the historic than of the spiritual sense. The test of its genuineness, like that of art, is not in its technique but in the dim and powerful feeling of infinite meaning it throws upon the reader. It is in consequence the most fruitful of all the sources of subsequent thought.

3. *Divine properties attributed to Christ.*—We may note, to begin with, the ascription to Christ of what had been ascribed by OT prophets to Jehovah (cf. Ps 45$^{6.\ 8}$ with He 1$^{8.\ 9}$; Is 7^{14} 9^6 with Mt 1^{23}; Jer 23$^{5.\ 6}$ [where the 'Branch of David' is called the 'Lord our righteousness'] 33^{16} with the NT term 'Root of David' applied to Christ; Mal 3^1, where the messenger about to come to his own temple is called 'Lord,' with Mk 1^2, Lk 1^{76}). Again, the tempting of Jehovah (Nu 14^2 21$^{5.\ 6}$, Ps 95^9) is the tempting of Christ (1 Co 10^9). In He 1$^{10.\ 11}$ what is attributed to Jehovah in Ps 102^{26} is attributed to Christ. In Jn 12$^{40.\ 41}$ it is asserted that the language of Isaiah (6$^{9.\ 10}$) concerning Jehovah refers to Christ. Is 45^{23}, compared with Ro 14$^{10.\ 11}$, shows that the judgment-seat of God is that of Christ. From Jl 2^{32} and Ro 10^{13} the name of Jehovah is the name of Christ.

More impressive are the references to Christ's participation in Divine *attributes*. He has self-existence like the Father (Jn 5^{26}), and therefore His life is eternal (Jn 1^4 11^{25} 14^6, 1 Jn 1^2 5$^{11.\ 12}$). He has pre-existence; cf. the Apostolic testimony (He 7^3, Rev 1^8 22^{13}) with Christ's (Jn 8^{28} 17^7). He cannot yield to death or see corruption (Resurrection narratives, also Jn 10^{18}, Ro 1^4, He 7^{16}, Jn 11^{25}, Ac 13^{37} 2^{27}), He will come again (Jn 14$^{3.\ 28}$, Ac 1^{11}, 1 Co 11^{26} etc.), He gives life to others (Jn 5$^{25.\ 21}$ 6^{40}, Ph 3$^{10.\ 11}$), He has all power (Mt 18^{18}, Rev 1^8, Jn 5^{19}, He 1^3, Ph 2^9), including power over nature and man (miracles and healings, cf. Lk 6^{19} 8^{46}, Mt 9^{28}, also Ro 8$^{10-23}$), a power He can communicate to disciples (Ac 9^{34} 3^{16} 4^{10}). St. Paul attributes to Him the Divine plenitude (Col 2^9). He has superhuman knowledge of God and superhuman insight into man (Jn 16^{30} 2^{24}, Rev 2^{28}), He is unchangeable as Jehovah (cf. Ps 102^{26} with He 1$^{11.\ 12}$, also 13^8).

Of Divine *acts* asserted of Christ are the following:—Creation (Jn 1^3, Col 1$^{16.\ 17}$, He 1$^{2.\ 10}$); Providence (He 1^3, Jn 5^{17}, Col 1^{17}); Redemption (Ac 20^{28}, Jn 13$^{18.\ 10.\ 16}$, Mt 9^{13}, Eph 5^{26}, passages too numerous to be specified); Forgiveness of sins (Mt 9^6, Mk 2^{10}, Lk 5^{24} etc.); Judgment (Jn 5$^{22.\ 27}$, Ac 17^{31}, Ro 14^{10}, Mt 25$^{31-46}$); Restitution of all things (Ph 3^{21}, 1 Co 15$^{24-28}$). Finally, the whole atmosphere of feeling and disposition towards Christ in the NT is one of worship. He claims it, and His disciples accord it. The faith given to God is given to Him (Jn 14^1 etc.). Examples of doxologies are 1 P 4^{11}, 2 Ti 4^{18}, Rev 1^6, 2 P 3^{18}, Rev 5^{13}. The honour of the Son equals that of the Father (Jn 5^{23}, Ph 2$^{9.\ 10}$, He 1^6). The Blessing of God is invoked from Christ not less. Distinctively Christian worship is a calling upon the name of the Lord Jesus Christ (1 Co 1^2, Ac 9^{14}). Distinctively Christian belief is the confession that Jesus is the Messiah, or that He is the Son of God (Ro 10^9, 1 Jn 4^{15}). Baptism is into His name (Ac 2^{38} 8^{16}), the Lord's Supper is significant of His Death and its specific virtue, new life (1 Co 10^{16} 11^{26}).

A patient study of the texts cited in the two preceding sections will set in relief several facts as to Apostolic reflexion on Christ's Person. The beginnings lie unquestionably in the Messianic hope and in Christ's claim to be the Messiah. The first proclamation of the gospel we have in the discourses in Acts, the one burden of which is the Messiahship of the Master. The Apostles there speak out of an experience whose roots lie in the nation's past, and which are renewed into fresh growth by Christ. The proof they offer is the evidence of facts and of what the facts point to. They detail three distinct orders of facts: the life and works of Christ, the death on the Cross, the resurrection and exaltation. They emphasize the peculiar and wondrous power revealed in all three, and especially in the last, in which they find the key to the whole—the Risen Lord. Traces of transcendental interest are not absent (Ac 5^{31} 3$^{15.\ 26}$ 10^{42}, 1 P 1^{23} 4^5 1$^{11.\ 20}$, Ja 2^1 5$^{8.\ 9}$ 1$^{18.\ 21}$), the perception of dignity and powers beyond the Messianic attaching to Him. This type of thought is common to St. Peter, St. James, St. Jude. It is a simple, objective, practical presentation of Christ, yet with features of its own so specifically new as to make it impossible to identify it with the existing religious schools. The other writings base themselves upon those beginnings, the Synoptics most obviously. They give the facts with fulness which are given in the Acts discourses in sum. They show the process of the movement, of which Acts gives the results. There are, however, important differences. The conviction of the higher nature of Christ is more prominent; it in fact pervades them; it is not imposed on their substance as an after-thought or under the stress of polemical tendency; it is part and parcel of the whole. Their portraiture is the portraiture of One who is man yet stands apart from men in character, and takes the place of God in the heart. Of speculation there is no sign. The growth of conviction is gradual, indeed, but comes in natural course by contact with facts. With the Synoptics we place the Apocalypse. Speculative features appear in St. Paul (earlier and later Epistles), the Fourth Gospel, Epistle to Hebrews, in the doctrines of 'the Man from heaven,' 'the Second Adam,' the Logos, and the 'Revealer,' and 'High Priest of the New Covenant' respectively.

There is a wide cleavage of opinion on questions as to the source and worth of the aforementioned factors. Were they due to the influence of the Hellenistic schools, or did they descend in the Palestinian tradition? Are they alien accretions to be cast aside, or are they of the essence of the Christian message? Much ingenuity has been expended in trying to prove that the original facts have been largely worked over in the Synoptic and in the Pauline and Johannine doctrines.

In the former case, it is maintained, there was a twofold process of adapting prophecy to suit the facts of the life, and of adapting the facts of the life to suit prophecy; in the case of the latter the facts of the life are interpreted in the light of some of the fundamental ideas of the Greek cults and philosophy, taking on along with the forms much of the substance of Greek religion. Thus originated the scenery of hyper-physical events that surrounds the life in the one instance, and the Logos Christology in the other. Both, it is alleged, changed the true character of the gospel, and are entirely inappropriate to its inner spirit.

Such contentions have certainly not yet been made good. They have nevertheless served to discover deep affinities existing between Apostolic thought and the higher mind of that age, affinities not directly derived from each other. Considerations are constantly increasing to vindicate the real independence of the Apostolic mind, and its essential continuity with the fundamental religion of the Hebrew race and the religious consciousness of Jesus. It is not intrinsically different from them. Its novel constituents are not alien ; they do not arrive from without, they are perceived within, as the result of the life and teaching of the Founder of their faith and still more as the effect of His character. There is a freedom both in previous Jewish religious ideas and in the religious consciousness of Jesus which assured to them a vast future vitally and organically related to them, to which the above theory does scant justice, and which suggests the warrant of truth to the Apostolic developments.

IV. SUBSEQUENT DEVELOPMENT OF NT IDEAS.—
1. *History of the doctrine.*—The Logos idea became the centre of a remarkable theological growth which engrossed the intellectual energy of the first five centuries. During that period the subtle Greek mind left its mark so substantially on the current forms of Christian belief as to render it problematical how far the definitions of the great Councils really embody the essence of the original faith. The naturalness of the development is acknowledged. Its necessity was created by certain obvious causes due to the historic character of the Church, and its presence as a living organization in the world. The age which witnessed the dissolution of paganism and the triumph of new ideals of thought and duty was one of missionary zeal and mental anguish. The early propaganda was extensive and intense. It had to confront the corruption of pagan morals and the medley of heathen beliefs. It had to justify its own novel convictions. Its final purpose was practical : to make men like Christ. A faithful delineation of what He was and did became imperative ; still more a consistent conception of what made Him what He was. The Church offered a new life, whose experiences were of profound interest, created and sustained by Christ, to a world of almost feverish intellectual curiosity. The mystery of Christ which had revived Hebrew devotion began to fascinate and excite the Gentile mind. Speculation was stimulated, and increasing effort made to bring the potential elements of Christ's teaching within the scope of men's understanding. The new world was at its best in reflexion, it yielded to Christ only after understanding Him.

Something to be understood there was. The whole process is intelligible only on the assumption of the unhesitating acceptance of belief in Christ's higher nature. The problem to the Jews had been, Is this rabbi more than the Messiah ? The problem to the Hellenic world now was, Is this Word more than our λόγος ? and before the problem was solved to its satisfaction, Greek thought passed through an experience as recreative and revolutionary as Jewish aspiration had done in the Apostolic age. The answer, further, preserved the best ideal of classical culture, and translated it into a constituent treasure of the Christian consciousness. The result was the conquest of the older conceptions of deity, whether of prophets or philosophers, by a new conception, a monotheism identical with no previous form, the richest hitherto reached, and one which eventually proved capable of imparting a spiritual unity to men of vastly more educative value than any system of organized culture before or since.

(a) *Patristic age.*—At first (up to A.D. 300) the process is slow and uncongenial. There are parties of practical outlook only and others of conservative instinct which fail to comprehend the new situation. But in the better representatives of the Christian movement there is a readier courage and a more vigorous intellect. They manifest, indeed, no lapse from Apostolic attainments. The desire to keep to what is primitive is with them, as with the others, passionate, but in no narrow spirit They are eager to search into the implications of their doctrine. But they plainly exhibit a want of equipment for the task. They are always vague, often conflicting. A clear theory cannot be gained from their writings. Both facts, the existence of sects which refused to theorize and the uncertainties of those who did, are alleged by some historians as a ground for denying to that age any assured belief in Christ's Divinity. The material for judgment is not too abundant, but there are certain guiding facts. Christ is everywhere worshipped as God. Cf. Pliny's well-known letter to Trajan ; the Vesper hymn of the Eastern Church, the *Gloria in Excelsis*, the *Tersanctus*, all in use in the 2nd century. Lucian's satire betrays a series of characteristic traits of Christians, including the worship of 'the crucified sophist.' There is the witness of the martyrs who preferred death to replacing Christ by the Emperor in their adoration. The baptismal professions of the period, too, maintain unimpaired the NT practice of combining the Son with the Father and Spirit. We distinguish between the popular belief embodied in the foregoing, and explanations of the belief in face of the Greek mind. The former was general —the latter were but tentative. The efforts of the *First Fathers* and *Apologists* were neither profound nor precise. They were directed towards three aims, (1) to justify the worship of Christ, (2) to define aright the relation of the Son to the Father, and (3) to elucidate the operation of the Word in creation. Their discussions have in view three types of opposition, of which the first refused to recognize Christ as the equal of God (Ebionism) ; the second denied His perfect manhood (Docetism) ; while the third, prepared for by Docetism and embracing an embarrassing mixture of tendencies known as Gnosticism, conceived amiss the relation between God and the Universe. The Christian thinkers were profoundly moved by this threefold antagonism. They keep their faith firm, but their apologetics are uncertain and incautious. An adequate philosophy is beyond their power. Let it be remembered, however, that the views they repel are also chaotic and crude : moreover, all of them represent some sort of a faith in Christ as a Being of a higher order. By the controversy conducted by writers such as Barnabas, St. Ignatius, Hermas, in particular, Church doctrine attains at this stage a certain measure of self-consciousness, especially over against Judaism, and to a slighter extent over against the abstract notions of heathen speculation.

Around the problems raised by the latter, thought in the next period deepens immeasurably, the seeds of all future discussion are planted, both of orthodox and heretical opinion. A succession of writers, interesting and copious in suggestion, including such names as Justin Martyr, Irenæus, Tertullian, Clement of Alexandria, Origen, develop the Christian positions in various directions with dialectical skill and considerable spiritual insight : (1) the nature of our knowledge of God as relative and our knowledge of the nature of God as wholly separate from the created world, spiritual and immaterial ; (2) our knowledge of the nature of the Logos as immanent in the Divine nature and expressed in the world of created things, as eternal and manifest in time ; (3) our knowledge of the identity of the Son with the Father as one in essence as in will, related by generation, and of the identity of the Son with the human race as its 'recapitulation' or archetype, leading to affirmations of a real Fatherhood in the Godhead and the conception of the Divine Unity as a life of moral relationships. The stress of the argument came to concentrate itself in the third of these points, against the Adoptionists on the one hand, who secured the unity of God by confining Christ within the limits of humanity, and against the Sabellians on the other hand, who secured it by treating the distinctions of Father, Son, and Holy Spirit as simply modes of the one God. By the beginning of the 4th cent. this long interior process of conflicting reflexion was ready for a final issue.

It came in the Arian disputes, which for a century —to A.D. 451—filled the Christian world and passed through several phases. Arius was incited to action by the teaching of Alexander the bishop of Alexandria, who taught the eternal generation of the Son ('there never was a time when He was not'). He maintained that as a father must exist before his son, therefore the Son of God did not exist eternally with the Father; that not being eternal He was created, but before time began; that being created, He is in all things unlike the Father. The Council of Nicæa (A.D. 325), convened by the Emperor for the settlement of peace, decided against Arianism, and defined the authoritative doctrine to be that the Son is 'of one substance' (ousia) with the Father; that He was 'begotten, not made,' that 'there never was a time when He was not,' that 'He was not created.' The Nicene Creed was established largely by the brilliant advocacy of Athanasius, subsequently bishop of Alexandria. It was a signal triumph in favour of the *essential* Divinity of Christ as distinct from a merely moral likeness to God. There can be little doubt that Arian contentions propagated themselves over a wide area; and that partly through the ability of the Arian leaders to gather into association with themselves much floating dissatisfaction with the deeper currents discernible and now becoming dominant, and partly by the aid of political and secular methods. It is unquestionably the case, however, that the Arian position had a vitality of its own which the Athanasian dogmatics never wholly quenched, and which has burst out again and again in subsequent thought. It is the natural standpoint of all minds that, in seeking to appreciate Christ, start from the idea of God rather than the fact of Christ; its main interest is not religious but theistic, a theoretical deduction, not the statement of an inner experience. Athanasius met it on the basis of that Christian experience which initiated the problem, and from the beginning had determined its development. His instinct was justified; for although the Arian agitation protracted itself all through the 4th cent., it was gradually deserted by the more religious adherents, whom the Athanasian divines took pains to conciliate by removing false impressions, by deepening their thought, and by popularizing it with illustrations.

The second great Council, that of Constantinople (A.D. 381), saw practically the death of Arianism. It reaffirmed the Nicene dogmas against various novelties, and especially that offshoot of Arianism which denied the Divinity of the Holy Ghost (Macedonians). The third Council, at Ephesus (in 431), and the fourth, at Chalcedon (in 451), dealt with other three consequences of Arian doctrine, known as the Nestorian, Apollinarian, and Eutychian heresies. The three have reference to the *constitution of Christ's Divine-human Person.* Jesus Christ being Divine in the Nicene sense, in what sense could He also at the same time be

human? It had been determined that He was primarily Divine; not a man like other men, who became Divine, but the personal Logos of God manifesting Himself through the human person with whom He had entered into union. According to this view, He was necessarily two distinct natures, to one of which it seemed impossible to render all the significance of its proper functions, viz. the human nature. In particular, Was His knowledge limited? Had He a true body and a reasonable soul? Was His Person single?—problems which enlisted the most earnest interest of Athanasius, the Gregorys, Cyril of Alexandria, Leo of Rome, and, above all, Augustine of Hippo. Briefly the answers were: (1) as to Christ's human knowledge, that omniscience belongs to the Godhead of the Word, but that the human mind which the Word took was limited; (2) as to Christ's body, that it was a true body, really born of Mary, and passible in the experiences of life; (3) as to the union of the Divine and human natures, that these two were each perfect, without confusion, and united in one Person; 'although He be God and man, He is not two but one Christ.' In the words of Chalcedon, He is—

'One and the same Son, our Lord Jesus Christ, the same being perfect in Godhead and the same being perfect in manhood, truly God and truly man, the same having a rational soul and a body, of one substance with the Father according to the Godhead, and the same being of one substance with us according to the manhood, in all things like unto us except sin . . . one and the same Christ, Son, Lord, only-begotten, acknowledged in two natures, without fusion, without change, without division, without separation; the difference of the two natures having been in no wise taken away by the union, but rather the property of each nature being preserved, and combining to form one person and one hypostasis.'

Or, in the words of the last of the great Creeds, the so-called 'Athanasian,' which fairly represents the theology of the 5th century:

'He is not two, but one Christ; One; not by conversion of the Godhead into flesh, but by taking of the manhood into God; One altogether; not by confusion of substance, but by unity of Person.'

(b) *Mediæval period* (5th to 15th centuries).—The conciliar definitions remained undisturbed as the official formulas of the Church right through the Middle Ages up to the present; and without important modification or advance. To account for this prolonged acquiescence of the mediæval mind is not at once simple, for the Nicene system is both uncritical and incomplete. The Church had to address herself to new and arduous tasks, chiefly of organization. She had assumed the external equipment of the Roman empire for practical efficiency in educating the multitude of peoples brought within her pale. Her paramount requirements were unity and a working belief. All available spiritual forces were ranged in a practical order for a practical end. The effect on the doctrine of Christ's Person is observable in the following results: (1) the less speculative and more practical discussion of the older problems, especially those concerned with the effect of the Incarnation on Christ's knowledge and will; (2) the consideration of Christ's Person in association with the soteriological aspects of His Work; (3) the systematic co-ordination of the several parts of Christological science into a connected whole, and of the whole with other doctrines such as those of God and the Church; (4) the more lucid realization of the nature and principles of this doctrine in line with the elaboration of the doctrine of transubstantiation and the Mass; (5) the popular illustration of its truth, mainly in its place as part of the Trinitarian conception, by analogies drawn from outward nature, and still more from the human mind. Two subsidiary streams are not to be omitted, noteworthy because of their influence in helping to discredit the methods of the Schoolmen and in preparing for the Reformation; viz. (6) free and fruitless inquiry into '*quotlibeta*,' *i.e.* questions arbitrarily suggested and only remotely affecting religious interests or fundamental truth; and (7) the rise of mystical and pietist communities cherishing an emotional, sometimes sentimental, contemplation of the Saviour in His purely human qualities. Scholasticism has often been criticised; but it taught the thoughtful theologian at least one great lesson, that it is unsafe to develop the theological consequences of any doctrine without continual reference to the proportion of the whole. It effectually awakened also the more religious minds to return for that reference to the primitive sources in the Scriptures and the Fathers.

(*c*) *Modern* (from Reformation era, 16th cent., onward).—The new spiritual experiences in which the Reformation originated brought out into clearer relief the disparity between the matter and the method of the Scholastic disputations. A religious Reason began to assert itself independently of the Scholastic process. It gave the intellect a new freedom to question the authority and relevancy of the old; one of whose first utterances expressed dislike of further speculation as empty. It blessed only those energies which made religion inward and personal. As the previous centuries had deepened the mind sufficiently to speak for itself, so now the age was dawning which should so completely sanctify the moral nature as to make its instincts supreme. In Luther pre-eminently, but not less in Calvin, Zwingli, and others, the *ethical* interpretation of spiritual facts takes rise. Hence the immense importance ascribed to that act of faith by which the individual soul connects itself with Christ (justification by faith), in a union not of intellect but of heart. Out of the experiences of this inner union we reach the true knowledge of Christ (and also of God). 'The man now who so knows Christ that Christ has taken away from him all his sin, death and devil, freely through His suffering, he has truly recognized Christ as the Son of God' (Luther, *Werke*, xvii. 265). And when we thus know Christ, we 'let go utterly all thoughts and speculations concerning the Divine Majesty and Glory, and hang and cling to the humanity of Christ . . . and I learn thus through Him to know the Father. Thus arises such a light and knowledge within me that I know certainly what God is and what is His mind' (xx. i. 161). It is in the experience of redemption that we know the Redeemer. Modern religious theory has been one long endeavour to appropriate this position. It has sought to explicate its principles (1) by a more radical and penetrating criticism of the past; (2) by the application to the problems of Christian theism of other categories than that of the Nicene *ousia* or substance; (3) in particular by insistence on moral personality as the determining principle of theological construction.

When we look back at this great historical development, it is impossible not to be struck by the parallel between the age of early Christianity, the beginnings of the Middle Ages, and the Reformation. The bankruptcy of the pagan world was not its defect but its merit. It had generated a universal need and a universal mode of feeling which were incompatible with the highest culture which had generated them, but which were destined ultimately to combine that culture itself with something beyond, viz. the new Christian experience. The so-called Dark Ages were brought on by a new possibility and a new necessity, the necessity of disciplining the mass of believers to appreciate that combination and apprehend its elements of culture and faith,—a discipline which, when it had accomplished its ends, left its subjects with a deeper experience than ever, and a more

positive possession of its substance. The first Reformers were clear on the central fact of this new experience. Their successors were forced by the exigencies of their ecclesiastical situation to limit themselves to simple defence of the fact. Later thinkers, with more freedom, and under the impulse of vast movements of philosophy and science, have gone on to unfold and organize its content. There is much that is still obscure. But we may venture to state these convictions, that although (1) the analysis of the forces that have entered into the development of Christian doctrine in the past, popular at present, has by no means vindicated beyond appeal its own presuppositions; nor (2) has it yet been proved that the predominant impulses of the modern spirit are sufficient adequately to mould anew all the facts and truths of the inherited faith; yet (3) it is indubitable that broad and abiding foundations are being laid for a system of religious thought at once expressive of the religious ideals of the age, and consistent with its historical and scientific temper. In elaborating that system it is already clear that two of its fundamental postulates must be these: (*a*) the principle that Christian truth is not the creation of the human intellect, nor are the forces of human reason and emotion sufficient to explain it; and (*β*) the principle of the absolute value of Christ's Person as the norm of all religious experience. *The Christological impulse is central.* In the moral personality of Christ, men are seeking better answers to the old problems. The past answers are not wrong; it is that they are not relevant. And this because of the growth, not of science but of conscience. The type of religious experience and emotion has changed, the experience is deeper, the emotion richer. The modern mind stands less awe-struck, perhaps, before the Deity of Christ, but it is more conscience-struck before the perfection of His human character, within the sacred processes of which it wistfully looks for the mystery of His Divinity and the secret of God.

2. *Denial of the doctrine of Christ's Divinity.*—
(*a*) *History and motive.*—Christianity has in all the stages of its evolution been accompanied by rationalistic hesitation. Based on experience, it has never commended itself to the reason unenriched by that experience. A strong undercurrent of antagonism runs through the centuries. It is possible to indicate special periods when the antagonism becomes more pronounced. Such periods will be found, on the whole, coincident with the points of transition in the advance of the doctrine. It may well be, as modern Unitarians argue, that Christ was regarded at first as a man simply, 'a prophet mighty in deed and word' (Lk 24[19]); but their contention that this is the point of view of the NT cannot be sustained. The Epistles, even the earliest, start from the Risen Christ, and the Gospel narratives are not to be comprehended apart from the initial experience of His higher dignity. Both sets of books owe their origin to the new sense as to His Person created by the new sense of power with which He possessed them. Their ostensible design is to set Him forth as 'Christ,' or 'Lord,' or 'Saviour,' or 'Word,' etc., *i.e.* as something more than man, to whom, as such, worship is paid. They show their authors busied with problems as to the constitution of His Person. Those problems emerged from the first, and among Jewish Christians who had to make clear to themselves Christ's true position if, in His lordship over them, they were no longer required strictly to follow the law of Moses, and were now required to conceive of the transcendence of God permitting fellowship with Him. But those were problems which could never have emerged at all unless from the conviction of His

suprahuman rank. The opposition, *Ebionism*, was not so much concerned with denial of His superior dignity as directed to affirm the supremacy of the Father. Its protest was immensely strengthened when the conflict with Gnostic theories necessitated an alien apologetic with an unscriptural terminology, derived from Greek philosophy, both obnoxious (and probably bewildering) to the pious Jew.

The second serious outburst of hostility was occasioned by the Nicene theologians. In Ebionism the Jewish temper found vent. In *Arianism* it was the heathen intellect. Amid Gentile surroundings christological ideas had never ceased to grow. Tradition, Scripture, experience, combined to deepen the conviction of Christ's Divinity, and to enlarge the range of its problems. Hellenic rationalism confronted the Church at every point. It could not tolerate the thought of two Gods ; and it had not yet grasped the unity of God as embracing eternal distinctions facing inward on each other. It revolted from an Incarnation in time and human form. It therefore denied to the Son coequality with the Father. Yet everything short of the full deity it was ready to acknowledge. For the Arian Christ is no mere man : He is much more than man, only not God, but a kind of demi-god, the loftiest of all creatures, to be imitated and worshipped. The idea, from its wide acceptance in that age, must have embodied certain prevalent mental tendencies of the time. Its plausibility depends on the idea of God which it conceives, viz. that of an abstract, otiose Being, beyond interest in human things. It is an idea as far removed from modern modes as from the Gospel facts. It is more beset with difficulty than the conception it opposed. In later times it has been often revived, but never effectively, and mainly in individual opinion.

The sincere emphasis laid on the proper Divinity of Christ throughout the Middle Ages has been continued in the Churches of the Reformation. The opposition has been correspondingly sincere and continuous. Its course manifests remarkable variation. In the earlier stages it was determined chiefly by the common study of the Scriptures now distributed to the multitudes. Almost every phase of former heresy was reproduced, but without real advance in thought or real influence on orthodox opinion. Afterwards the special developments of Reformed theology, notably in the doctrine of the Atonement, created, both by natural evolution and by reaction, the powerful contrary movement of *Socinianism*. The Socinian argument, assuming that the Infinite and the finite are exclusive of each other, maintained the Incarnation to be impossible, rejected the pre-existence, resurrection, and ascension of Christ, asserted the essential moment of His person to be His human nature, rendered free from sin by the Virgin-birth, and free from ignorance by special endowments of knowledge. Socinians did good service by bringing into clear relief the Docetic elements in the traditional doctrine, and in preparing for a deeper appreciation of the humanity of Christ in the work of salvation. The reverent recognition of this last (*finitum capax infiniti*), that the human is capable of bodying forth the essence of the Divine nature as distinct from merely being the bearer of the Divine attributes, is the greatest step that has been taken since the Nicene definitions. It has incited to a speculative ardour, and secured a place for the application of scientific method, in dealing with the contents of Christian thought, that are rapidly working out its complete reorganization and reconstruction. To discern and describe the ideal unity of the higher spiritual life which will exhibit the Divine-human principle of Christ's Person in its fulness, is the task of the modern

Church. The spiritual potentialities of the human mind are earnestly and perseveringly investigated. It is a complex process, building as largely on religious induction as on religious insight, and sustained by a magnificent confidence in the native powers of reason and conscience. But the same forces which have impelled to new Christological affirmation have infused new vigour into Christological doubt. The representatives of *Unitarianism* have been active and influential. They stand for a much more humanitarian view of Christ than either Arians or Socinians. But their phrase, 'the pure humanity of Jesus,' covers much diversity of conviction. Some are almost Trinitarians, approaching Christ on the Divine side, and affirming, in a real if unorthodox sense, His pre-existence, uniqueness, sinlessness, and spiritual authority. Others contemplate the human side, believe that He was naturally born, and endowed with qualities and gifts differing in degree and not in kind from those which all men enjoy ; that His character was a growth, and that by degrees He rose out of temptation and error into the serene strength of a pure and noble manhood ; that He became a providential teacher and leader of men to a higher spiritual development. The Unitarian polemic killed popular Calvinism ; in its higher forms it is rich in ethical appeal.

(*b*) *Failure.* — Unitarianism has at all times failed to lead. It has uniformly won a certain measure of popularity by successfully representing the dominant forces pulsating in the spirit of the age. But it is by not being an average that a man becomes a guide. Deniers of the Divinity have flourished in times of utter confusion, when whoever would attain some coherence of life and thought must let drop much that is held in solution, and show the path of progress by manifesting the direction of change. By this law Catholic theology has stood ; to representative insight it has added prophetic foresight. The sense of its insufficiency, when brought home, has only driven it the deeper into the inner secrets of that experience which yielded its original impulse, and so it has escaped becoming a prey to the narrower reason and limited emotion of the Unitarian schools. See also art. INCARNATION.

LITERATURE.—Besides the works mentioned in the body of the article, (1) for the history of the doctrine the following are to be consulted : Dorner, *Doctrine of the Person of Christ* ; Harnack, *Hist. of Dogma* ; A. Réville, *Hist. of the Dogma of the Deity of Jesus Christ* ; Hagenbach, *Hist. of Doctrines* ; Macarius, *Théol. dogmatique orthodoxe* ; Hefele, *Hist. of the Councils.*
(2) For the dogmatic aspects of the subject the older manuals of Systematic Theology are still of value, *e.g.* Shedd, *Dogmatic Theology* ; Dorner, *System of Christian Doctrine* ; Martensen, *Christian Dogmatics* ; cf. also Wilberforce, *Doctrine of the Incarnation* ; Dale, *Christian Doctrine* ; Gore, *The Incarnation* ; Strong, *Manual of Theology* ; and, for a more popular treatment, Liddon, *Divinity of our Lord* ; Eck, *Incarnation.* Of recent standpoint are Nitzsch, *Evangel. Dogmatik* ; Clarke, *Outline of Christ. Theol.* ; Denney, *Studies in Theology* ; Hodgson, *Theologia Pectoris* ; Bovon, *Dogmatique Chrétienne*, and *Théol. du NT* ; Fairbairn, *Christ in Modern Theology* ; Powell, *Principle of the Incarnation* ; H. Holtzmann, *Lehrb. der NT Theologie.*
(3) For the historical data of Christ's ministry, works, teaching, etc., see the numerous Lives of Christ, *e.g.* by Weiss, Beyschlag, Keim, Renan, O. Holtzmann, H. von Soden, Sanday, Farrar, Stalker ; G. Matheson, *Studies in Portrait of Christ.* Shorter dissertations on particular points form a large literature. Of special interest are those which attempt to define the primitive conception of Christ, such as Wrede's *Das Messiasgeheimniss in den Evangelien* ; Stanton's *Messiah* ; H. von Soden's *Urchristl. Literaturgesch.* ; Pfleiderer's *The Early Christian Conception of Christ* : Schmiedel's *Hauptprobleme der Leben-Jesu Forschung* ; Estlin Carpenter's *First Three Gospels* ; Mackintosh's *Natural History of the Christian Religion.*
(4) On the problem of Christ's Person for modern thought consult such works as Fairbairn's *Studies in the Life of Christ, Christ in Modern Theology*, and *Philosophy of the Christian Religion* ; Adams Brown's *Essence of Christianity* ; Losinsky's *War Jesus Gott, Mensch, oder Übermensch?* ; Kalthoff's *Das Christusproblem*; Dykes in *ExpT*, Oct. 1905–Jan. 1906.   A. S. MARTIN.

DIVORCE.—The teaching of Christ on this subject in the earliest Gospel, that of St. Mark, is clear and decisive. It is given in 10¹⁻¹². The Pharisees came to Him with the question, Is it lawful for a husband to divorce a wife? The Pharisees themselves could have had no doubt upon the point thus broadly stated. Divorce was, as they believed, sanctioned and legalized by Dt 24¹·². But they debated about the scope and limits of divorce (cf. Bab. *Giṭṭin*, 90a, where the views of the Schools of Hillel and of Shammai are given. The former allowed divorce for trivial offences, the latter only for immoral conduct). In putting the question to Christ, the Pharisees therefore had an ulterior object. They came, says St. Mark, 'tempting him,' knowing probably from previous utterances of His that He would reply in words which would seem directly to challenge the Mosaic Law (cf. His criticism of the distinctions between 'clean' and 'unclean' meats, Mk 7¹⁴⁻²³). Christ answers with the expected reference to the Law, 'What did Moses command?' They state the OT position: Moses sanctioned divorce. Notice how nothing is said as to grounds or reasons for divorce. Christ at once makes His position clear. The law upon this point was an accommodation to a rude state of society. But a prior and higher law is to be found in the Creation narrative, 'Male and female he created them' (Gn 1²⁷ LXX), *i.e.* God created the first pair of human beings of different sexes that they might be united in the marriage bond. Further, it was afterwards said that a man should leave his father and mother and cleave to his wife, and that he and his wife should be one flesh. In other words, married couples were in respect of unity, as the first pair created by God, destined for one another. The marriage bond, therefore, which may be said to have been instituted by God Himself, must be from an ideal standpoint indissoluble. 'What God joined, let not man sunder.'

In answer to a further question of His disciples, the Lord enforces this solemn pronouncement. A man who puts away his wife and marries another commits adultery. A woman who puts away her husband and marries another commits adultery. Upon this point Christ's teaching passes beyond the ordinary conditions of Jewish society. No woman could divorce her husband by Jewish law. But that is no reason why the Lord should not have expressed Himself as Mk. records. There were exceptional cases of divorce by women in Palestine (cf. Salome, Jos. *Ant.* xv. vii. 10: 'She sent him [Costobar] a bill of divorce, and dissolved her marriage with him, though this was against the Jewish laws'). And there is no reason why He may not have been acquainted with the possibility of divorce by women in the West, or why, even if He had not this in view, He may not have wished to emphasize His point by stating the wrongfulness of divorce, on either side, of the marriage bond.

With this earliest record of Christ's teaching the fragment in the Third Gospel (Lk 16¹⁸) is in agreement: 'Every one who puts away his wife and marries another commits adultery, and he who marries a divorced woman commits adultery.' That is to say, the marriage bond is indissoluble. The husband who divorces his wife and remarries commits adultery. And the man who marries a divorced wife commits adultery, because she is ideally the wife of her still living (first) husband.

In the First Gospel, however, we find this plain and unambiguous teaching, that divorce is inconceivable from an ideal standpoint, modified in a very remarkable way. In Mt 5³² occurs a saying parallel in substance to Lk 16¹⁸, but with the notable addition of the words, 'except for the sake of unchastity' (παρεκτὸς λόγου πορνείας). Thus modified, the Lord's teaching becomes similar to that of

the stricter school of Jewish interpreters. The supposed sanction of divorce in Dt 24¹·² is practically reaffirmed, the clause עֶרְוַת דָּבָר, which formed the point at issue in the Jewish schools, being interpreted or paraphrased as παρεκτὸς λόγου πορνείας, by which is probably meant any act of illicit sexual intercourse. In other words, Christ here assumes that divorce must follow adultery, and what He is here prohibiting is not such divorce, which He assumes as necessary, but divorce and consequent remarriage on any other grounds. It might further be argued that the words παρεκτὸς λόγου πορνείας affect only the first clause, and that remarriage after divorce even on the ground of adultery is here prohibited. But if this were intended, it would surely have been explicitly expressed and not left to be inferred. And such teaching would seem to be illogical. Because, if adultery be held to have broken the marriage tie so effectually as to justify divorce, it must surely be held to leave the offended husband free to contract a new tie.

In view, therefore, of Mk 10¹⁻¹² and Lk 16¹⁸, it must appear that Mt 5³² places the teaching of Christ in a new light. So far as Lk. is concerned, we might, with some difficulty, suppose that the exception 'save for adultery' was assumed as a matter so obvious that it needed no explicit expression. But in view of the disputes in the Jewish Schools, this is very unlikely. And Mk 10¹⁻¹², with its criticism of the alleged Mosaic sanction of divorce, leaves no room for doubt that on that occasion at least Christ pronounced marriage to be a divinely instituted ordinance which should under no circumstances be broken by divorce. It would not, of course, be difficult to suppose that on other occasions the Lord Himself modified His teaching. We might suppose that He taught His disciples that, whilst from an ideal standpoint, marriage, for all who wished to discern and to obey the guidance of the Divine will in life, ought to be an indissoluble bond, yet, human nature and society being what they are, divorce was a necessary and expedient consequence of the sin of adultery. But a careful comparison of Mt 5³² with Mk 10 and Lk 16 irresistibly suggests the conclusion that the exception in Mt. is due not to Christ Himself, but to the Evangelist, or to the atmosphere of thought which he represents, modifying Christ's words to bring them into accordance with the necessities of life. This conclusion seems to be confirmed when we compare Mt 19¹⁻¹² with Mk 10¹ᶠ·. It is on many grounds clear that the editor of the First Gospel is here, as elsewhere, re-editing St. Mark (see *Expos. Times*, Oct. 1903, p. 45, and 'St. Matthew' in the *Internat. Crit. Com.*). Contrast with the logical and consistent argument of Mk. stated above, the account of the First Gospel. The Pharisees are represented as inquiring, 'Is it lawful for a man to put away a wife on any pretext?' Christ answers, as in Mk., that marriage from an ideal standpoint is indissoluble. The Pharisees appeal to the Law against this judgment. In reply we should expect the Lord, as in Mk., to state the accommodating and secondary character of the legal sanction of divorce, and to reaffirm the sanctity of marriage. But instead He is represented as affirming that πορνεία constitutes an exception. Thus He tacitly takes sides with the severer school of interpretation of Dt 24, and acknowledges the permanent validity of that Law thus interpreted in a strict sense, which immediately before He had criticised as an accommodation to a rude state of social life. This inconsistency shows that Mk. is here original, and that κατὰ πᾶσαν αἰτίαν and μὴ ἐπὶ πορνείᾳ are insertions by the editor of Mt. into Mk.'s narratives, and confirms the otherwise probable conclusion that παρεκτὸς λόγου πορνείας in 5³² is an insertion into the traditional saying more accurately preserved in Lk 16. The motive of these insertions can only be conjectured. But, in view of other features of the First Gospel, it is probable that the editor was a Jewish Christian who has here Judaized Christ's teaching. Just as he has so arranged 5¹⁶⁻²⁰ as to represent Christ's attitude to the Law to be that of the Rabbinical Jews, who regarded every letter of the Law as permanently valid, so here he has so shaped Christ's teaching about divorce as to make it consonant with the permanent authority of the Pentateuch, and harmonious with the stricter school of Jewish theologians. To the same strain in the editor's character, the same Jewish-Christian jealousy for the honour of the Law, and for the privileges of the Jewish people, may perhaps be ascribed the emphasis placed on the prominence of St. Peter (10² πρῶτος, 14²⁹⁻³¹ 15¹⁶ 16¹⁷⁻¹⁹ 17²⁴⁻²⁷ 18²¹), and the preservation of such sayings as 10⁵· ⁶· ²³. And to the same source may perhaps be attributed the Judaizing of the Lord's language in such expressions as 'the kingdom of the heavens,' and the 'Father who is in the heavens.' See, also, artt. ADULTERY and MARRIAGE.

LITERATURE.—Hastings' *DB*, art. 'Marriage'; Dykes, *Manifesto of the King*, 255 ff.; Newman Smyth, *Christian Ethics*, 410 ff.; *Expositor*, IV. vii. [1893] 294. W. C. ALLEN.

DOCTOR.—The English versions have been very inconsistent in the translation of διδάσκαλος, νομοδιδάσκαλος, ῥαββεί, νομικός. They have generally followed Wyclif, who used *maister* for διδάσκαλος, and *doctour* only once (Lk 2⁴⁶). In the American RV 'master' and 'doctor' disappear as tr. of διδάσκαλος, and 'teacher' is uniformly used. The AV has 'teacher' only once in the Gospels (Jn 3²) out of a very large number of instances of διδάσκαλος. The English RV advances to only four uses of 'teacher' (Mt 23⁸, Lk 2⁴⁶, Jn 3²· ¹⁰). νομοδιδάσκαλος occurs only three times in the NT (Lk 5¹⁷, Ac 5³⁴, 1 Ti 1⁷). In the last example AV has 'teacher' and in the other two 'doctor of the law.' Of course, 'doctor' is simply Latin for 'teacher,' but the American RV would have done better to adopt 'teacher of the law' for νομοδιδάσκαλος also (Lk 6¹⁷, Ac 5³⁴).

The chief English Versions translate the word διδάσκαλος in Lk 2⁴⁶ as follows: Wyclif, *doctours*; Tindale, *doctours*; Cranmer, *doctours*; Geneva, *doctours*; Rheims, *doctors*; AV, *doctors*; RV, *doctors*; Noyes, *teachers*; Bible Union Revision, *teachers*; American RV, *teachers*; Twentieth Century NT, *Teachers*. νομοδιδάσκαλος in Lk 5¹⁷ and Ac 5³⁴ is translated *doctour of the lawe* by Wyclif, who is followed with variations in spelling by Tindale, Geneva, Rheims, AV and RV, American RV. The American Bible Union Revision has *teacher of the law* in Lk 5¹⁷ and Ac 5³⁴ also. Twentieth Century NT has *Teacher of the Law*.

It would seem that νομοδιδάσκαλος should be translated 'teacher of the law,' and διδάσκαλος 'teacher' always. The Old English word 'doctor' now often signifies a title. Pope's phrase, 'when doctors disagree,' referred to teachers. νομικός is used once in Mt. (22³⁵) and eight times in Lk., and is practically equivalent to νομοδιδάσκαλος. See RABBI, MASTER, TEACHER, LAWYER.

A. T. ROBERTSON.

DOCTRINES.—On the subject of doctrines in connexion with the Gospels but little light is shed by etymology.

Two words occur which have been translated 'doctrine'—διδασκαλία and διδαχή. The former, which is by its form properly an adjective and denotes 'of or belonging to a teacher' (διδάσκαλος), is used of the subject-matter of his teaching, as the analogous word, which is found in the NT only in the neuter form εὐαγγέλιον, 'that which pertains to an εὐάγγελος,' is used in the sense of 'the good news,' 'the gospel.' The adjectival form διδασκάλιον, which in plur. in classical Greek means a teacher's pay, as εὐαγγέλιον means the reward given to a messenger of good news, does not occur in the NT. The word διδασκαλία, as meaning that which pertains to a διδάσκαλος, has in the NT special reference to the authority of the teacher. It is never used of our Lord's teaching, and only seldom of that

of the Apostles. Further, it occurs in the Gospels only in those passages (Mt 15⁹, Mk 7⁷) in which Jesus accuses the scribes of 'teaching for doctrines the commandments of men,' and quotes against them the Septuagint rendering of Is 29¹³.

Διδαχή, the common word for the act of teaching or that which is taught, occurs more frequently. It is used with reference to the teaching of Jesus in a general sense, as where the people contrast His methods with those of the scribes (Mt 7²⁸, Mk 1²²), and again of His preaching, as in connexion with the parable of the Sower, where St Mark says (4²), 'And he taught them many things in parables, and said unto them in his doctrine.' Here διδαχή, 'doctrine,' exactly corresponds to ἐδίδασκεν, 'he taught,' and the phrase evidently means 'in the course of his teaching,' or 'in the course of his remarks.'

In the same general sense the word occurs again in Jn 18¹⁹, according to which the high priest examined Jesus concerning His disciples and 'his doctrine.' With reference to the subject-matter of His teaching it occurs in the answer of Jesus to the question of the Pharisees (Jn 7¹⁵· ¹⁷), 'How knoweth this man letters (γράμματα), having never learned?' The question refers to learning as it was understood by the scribes, that is, as theological science, those methods of Biblical interpretation in virtue of which they themselves were called scribes (γραμματεῖς), i.e. professional theologians. The answer of Jesus is, 'My doctrine' (ἡ ἐμὴ διδαχή) is not mine, but his that sent me'; in connexion with which Alford observes, 'Here only does our Lord call His teaching διδαχή, as being now among the διδάσκαλοι, the Rabbis, in the temple.' Elsewhere it is applied to Christ's teaching by the Evangelists themselves, in whose case it is sufficiently explained by the general use of the word with reference to teaching of any kind, and by the fact that Jesus was regarded and addressed as Rabbi or Teacher, and accepted the title. It is, however, important to note that, except where it is used in its most general sense, the word 'teaching' (διδαχή) occurs in connexion with the marked contrast which all observed between the authoritative teaching of Jesus and the instructions of the scribes, who slavishly adhered to such doctrines and methods as were sanctioned only by Rabbinical tradition, and laid emphasis upon trivial questions to the neglect of the weightier matters of the Law (Mt 15⁹ ‖ Mk 7⁷).

As regards the doctrines which Jesus taught in His own unique and authoritative way, it must be carefully borne in mind that He did not formulate them in the manner of a systematic theologian. They cannot therefore be rightly described as 'doctrine' in the technical sense of the word, and still less as 'dogma,' as that was understood by theologians of a later period; but rather as 'apophthegms,' to use the expression by which the LXX rendered the words of Dt 32², where Moses says of his teaching, 'My doctrine shall drop as the rain.' There the Gr. word ἀπόφθεγμα, 'a sententious saying,' is made to represent the Heb. קֶלַח 'that which is received.' This word 'apophthegm,' indeed, corresponds very nearly to the expression τὰ λόγια, 'the sayings' or 'utterances' of which Papias speaks as forming the kernel of the Gospels, and which, according to that writer, were taken down by St. Mark as the amanuensis of St. Peter. Such a term, moreover, would aptly apply to the style of Christ's doctrine, which, as Beyschlag remarks (*NT Theol.* i. 31), 'is conditioned not merely by a necessity of teaching, but rather springs chiefly from the nature of the things to be communicated. These are just the eternal truths, the heavenly things in earthly speech, which can be brought home to the popular understanding only by pictorial forms. It is therefore the mother speech of religion which Jesus uses.' As has been well observed, Christ's teaching has to do with His own unique personality, with a Person much more than with doctrine properly so called. Again to quote the words of Beyschlag (*op. cit.* i. 29), 'His teaching is that in His appearance and active life which is necessary to make that life intelligible to us, and without which the Apostolic teaching about Him would be only a sum of dogmatic utterances which we could not comprehend and whose truth we could not prove,—a result not a little awkward for that view which contrasts "the teaching of Jesus" as Christianity proper with the Apostolic "teaching about Christ."' Taking due account of these considerations, we may yet gather from the sources at our disposal, the simple narratives of the Synoptic Gospels and the more elaborate narratives and discourses of the Gospel of

John, sufficient materials to enable us to piece together a scheme of the doctrine of Jesus as He taught it and as it was understood by His immediate followers.

It appears most convenient to start, as has been suggested by Weiss, with the doctrine of the *Kingdom of Heaven* or the *Kingdom of God*.

The former of these expressions is peculiar to the Gospel of Matthew. The latter is more usual in the NT. Beyschlag suggests that the former was that which was most favoured by our Lord Himself (*op. cit.* i. 42). However that may be, it has for us the special interest that, as Alford points out, it is common among Rabbinical writers, a fact which seems to indicate that it was admirably adapted to illustrate the connexion between the current expectations of the Jews and the message addressed to them first by John the Baptist and then by Jesus, to the effect that the promise whose fulfilment they expected was already in course of being fulfilled. It is the natural link between the two dispensations. On the other hand, the peculiarly OT stamp which, though only by association, it bore, suggestive of Jewish theocratic ideas, would sufficiently account for the fact that in the other Gospels, specially designed to meet the wants of the Gentiles, to whom those ideas were strange and unfamiliar, it gave place to the alternative expression, 'Kingdom of God.' Practically, however, the two expressions mean the same thing. The earlier form may possibly, as has been suggested, have been by association so closely connected with the national hope of the Jews, and with that selfish exclusiveness which led them to regard themselves as in a peculiar sense the elect people of God, as to seem to countenance the old narrow views of Messiah's kingdom, to the prejudice of the more spiritual and catholic teaching of Jesus Himself, which impressed itself the more strongly upon His followers the more successfully they sought to win the Gentiles to the faith of Christ. At the same time, they express at most only different aspects of the same truth—Kingdom of Heaven, as the phrase occurs in the Gospels, denoting a condition of things in which God's will is done on earth as it is done in heaven, while Kingdom of God refers more directly and specially to God as the Sovereign of that regenerated society which the expression is used to describe. See KINGDOM OF GOD.

This conception is the central point in Christ's teaching, by reference to which its most characteristic features may be most conveniently gathered into a connected system—as its relation to the OT, its revelation of the nature and will of God, its teaching as to the nature and person of Jesus Himself, its doctrine of man, and of God's scheme for man's salvation. This central theme attracts our notice in the beginning of the Gospels. It is the subject of the preaching of the Baptist and also of Jesus, whose message is briefly summed up in the words, 'The kingdom of God is at hand: repent ye, and believe the gospel' (Mk 1[15]). The Sermon on the Mount itself starts with the idea of the Kingdom of Heaven, and the same thought is the subject of two successive petitions in the Lord's Prayer, 'Thy kingdom come, Thy will be done on earth as it is in heaven' (Mt 5[3. 10] || Lk 6[20], Mt 6[10] || Lk 11[2]). The fundamental teachings of Jesus naturally group themselves round this central theme.

1. The Kingdom being the true Israel of God, the first point of doctrine that suggests itself concerns the King, the Supreme Ruler of the regenerated people. We have thus, as the words 'Kingdom of God' indicate, to deal first with *Jesus' doctrine of God the Father*. This, it is to be carefully noted, is not a new theology. The God whom Christ reveals is the God of Abraham, Isaac, and Jacob (Mk 12[26]). That 'God is Spirit,' and can be worshipped only 'in spirit and in truth,' was not first taught to the woman of Samaria (Jn 4[23]). That principle lies at the root of the teaching of the Law and the Prophets. Jesus accepted this fundamental doctrine, while at the same time He cleared it from those later speculations which tended to make of it a mere abstraction, or to accentuate the idea of the remoteness and incommunicableness of the Supreme Being. This He did by describing God, just as the Prophets and the Law had done, as infinitely holy, righteous, and loving. As Sovereign of the kingdom of righteousness and love, God makes holiness and

love the essential laws of His kingdom, and commands His subjects to be as Himself. In particular, Jesus laid emphasis upon the Fatherhood of God, and taught His disciples to trust implicitly in the Father's care (Mt 6[25-34] || Lk 12[22-31]), and to believe that that care extended to the very details of their daily life; while He exhorted them not only to rely upon and claim His compassion and His forgiving love, but to imitate Him in respect of these attributes, that they might 'be the children of' their 'Father which is in heaven : for he maketh his sun to rise on the evil and on the good, and sendeth rain on the just and on the unjust' (Mt 5[45]; cf. v.[48], Lk 6[35-38]).

2. But the Kingdom of God, as Jesus proclaims it, resembles the Old Testament theocracy in this, that *the Supreme Sovereign reveals His will and rules His kingdom by One whom He has sent and to whom He has delegated His authority.* This, the hope of Israel, is an ideal which is already realizing itself. The prophecy of the Messiah is fulfilled in the person and work of Him whom God has sent. This is therefore the keynote of the gospel, that the Christ is come 'to fulfil all righteousness' (Mt 3[15]), to give effect to every part of the constitution of the Kingdom. Thus Jesus appears as the Divine legislator. In this capacity He not only, as in His parables, explains and illustrates the principles of His government, but, as in the Sermon on the Mount, appears as the authoritative expositor of the Law of God. He announces that He is come not to destroy but to fulfil the Law and the Prophets (Mt 5[17]), and in this connexion shows that the Law is not satisfied with the literal and formal obedience of the Pharisees, but extends to thought and motive; He warns His disciples that, except their righteousness shall exceed that of the scribes and Pharisees, they cannot enter the Kingdom of Heaven (vv.[18-20]); and in other passages He says that in the Day of Judgment men shall be judged so strictly that they shall give account of every idle word, and even of any neglect on their part of the law of kindness and compassion towards their neighbours (Mt 12[36] 25[45]).

This aspect of Christ's teaching, which is specially prominent in the Synoptic Gospels, has been represented by some as constituting the essence of His doctrine. But apart from the thought that, according to this view, the ethical teaching of Jesus would mean the enactment of a new code of religion and morality infinitely more difficult than the old which He professed to explain, it is abundantly clear from the Synoptists themselves, no less than from the testimony of St. John, that Jesus lays far more stress upon the subject of His own Person than upon any ethical doctrine or set of doctrines. In the Gospels of Matthew, Mark, and Luke, as distinctly as in that of John, Jesus lays down as the first condition of membership of the Kingdom the duty of accepting His testimony concerning Himself, and of following Him. As we read in the Fourth Gospel that 'to as many as received him' Jesus 'gave the right to become children of God' (Jn 1[12]), so, according to the testimony of all four, the Kingdom of God is come in the person of the Messiah (Mt 12[28] || Lk 11[20]). The Person of Christ is the centre of the gospel.

A remarkable feature, indeed, of the Gospels is the fact that the essential Divinity of Christ, and even the express doctrine of His Messiahship, appear to have been made in His public teaching the subject of gradual development rather than of direct and explicit teaching. Jesus suffered not the confession of His Messiahship by the demons whom He cast out of those who were possessed. And although, when He received the first disciples, John and Andrew, Peter, Nathanael and Philip,

He accepted their confession that in Him they had found the Messiah (Jn 1⁴¹⁻⁵¹), it was in but few cases that He declared Himself in so many words to be the Christ of God; as, for example, in that of His conversation with the woman of Samaria (Jn 4²⁶); again when He declared to His townsmen in Nazareth that Isaiah's prophecy of the Messiah as the great preacher and healer was fulfilled in Himself (Lk 4²¹); and again when He answered the doubting question of the Baptist, 'Art thou he that should come, or do we look for another?', by pointing to the testimony of His teaching and of His works of mercy (Mt 11²⁻⁶ ‖ Lk 7¹⁹⁻²³). For the rest, Jesus allowed the thought of His Divine claims to grow in the minds of His disciples, and it was not until within a few months of His death that Peter in their name confessed His Messiahship, when Jesus, in welcoming their faith, expressly declared that it had come to them by revelation from God. Nevertheless, throughout His ministry the personal element was the most prominent feature of His teaching. From first to last He asked of those to whom He spoke, not faith in doctrines so much as trust in Himself as the Sent of God who alone could reveal the Father's will.

And, notwithstanding the fact that He left the full recognition of His claims to develop gradually in the minds of His disciples, His testimony concerning Himself contained implicitly all the elements of a complete revelation of His Divine claims. Thus He familiarized His disciples with the use of names and titles, as 'Son of Man,' 'He who should come,' 'Son of God,' 'the Sent of God,' 'the Holy One of God,' 'the Christ,' which they gradually came to recognize as indicative of those claims. (See also NAMES AND TITLES OF CHRIST).

3. With regard to the Kingdom itself, Jesus spoke of it *now as a present thing, again as that which should be realized in the future.* So He said at one time, 'Theirs is the kingdom of heaven' (Mt 5³·¹⁰), and again, 'Neither shall they say, Lo here! or, lo there! for,·behold, the kingdom of God is within you' (Lk 17²¹). Again He spoke of the Kingdom as future, and that in connexion with the final coming, the Parousia, of the Son of Man; so in the parables of the Great Supper (Lk 14¹⁵·²⁴), of the Marriage Feast (Mt 22¹⁻¹⁴), of the Ten Virgins (Mt 25¹⁻¹³). In this there was no real contradiction, for the central conception of the Kingdom is that of a gradual development, the future growing out of the present. We recognize this in several conspicuous parables, and no less in the practical means which Jesus adopted of founding and developing His Church, notably in His choice and training of the Twelve as the nucleus of that society of which the Kingdom should consist. Of the former, the most important in this connexion are the parables of the Sower (Mt 13³⁻²³ ‖ Mk 4¹⁻²⁰ ‖ Lk 8⁵⁻¹⁵), of the Seed growing secretly (Mk 4²⁶⁻²⁹), of the Mustard Seed and the Leaven (Mt 13³¹⁻²³ ‖ Mk 4³⁰⁻³²). In these the obvious thought is that the Kingdom is already here, but only in germ, a secret, but a present and a growing thing, the complete realization of which only the day of the Lord shall declare. The Kingdom is thus not such as the common acceptation of the Messianic hope had led Israel to expect, a thought of which even the disciples found it hard to disabuse their minds—an external condition of society into which they should one day be ushered as a matter of favouritism or of covenant right, and in which there were places of pre-eminence which could be the objects of earthly ambition, or a condition of temporal benefit which could be enjoyed in the future irrespective of spiritual fitness. Instead of this it is a spiritual blessing, the gift of God to receptive souls, for the individual and for the community of believers a condition of heart and life gradually developed in them by the power of Divine love. So closely is future blessedness, the inheriting of the Kingdom, dependent upon present faith and patient persevering effort, that our Lord is careful to warn His disciples that while 'it is' their 'Father's good pleasure to give' them 'the kingdom' (Lk 12³²), it is possible for the most highly favoured to come short of it, and 'there are last which shall be first, and there are first which shall be last' (Lk 13³⁰; cf. Mt 19³⁰ 20¹⁶ ‖ Mk 10³¹, Mt 21³¹·³²).

4. In this Kingdom *the conditions of membership* are manifestly of the first importance. These are (*a*) Repentance, and (*b*) Faith in God and in Jesus Christ whom He has sent.

Repentance (μετάνοια) means a complete and radical change of heart and life, a change so thoroughgoing that it can best be characterized by the word 'conversion,' a turning round. 'Except ye be converted (στραφῆτε, 'turn'), and become as little children, ye shall in no wise enter into the kingdom of heaven' (Mt 18³), is the teaching of Jesus according to the Synoptics, to which His words to Nicodemus in the Fourth Gospel almost exactly correspond: 'Except a man be born again (or 'from above,' ἄνωθεν), he cannot see the kingdom of God' (Jn 3³). Such a complete change as these words imply—'change of mind' (μετάνοια), 'convert,' 'turn round' (ἐπιστρέφειν, Mt 13¹⁵), 'new birth' or 'birth from above' (γεννηθῇ ἄνωθεν, Jn 3³), is necessary for all, as Jesus shows by addressing His teaching on this theme not only to Pharisees like Nicodemus, but to His own disciples —notably in the parable of the Unmerciful Servant (Mt 18²¹⁻³⁵), in which, in answer to a question of Peter, He likens the condition of all recipients of the Divine forgiveness to that of a man who owes a debt of ten thousand talents, clearly meaning by that the infinitude of man's obligation to God. So universal and so heinous is sin according to the teaching of Jesus. Sin springs from the heart (Mt 15¹⁸⁻²⁰ ‖ Mk 7²⁰⁻²³), from its natural alienation from God, from the infirmity of the flesh (Mt 26⁴¹ ‖ Mk 14³⁸). Man is, moreover, tempted to sin by Satan as the author of evil; though Jesus does not teach any special doctrine of sin, or explain how evil first came into existence, but deals only with sin itself as an awful and universal fact. Then, as all are tainted with the universal disease, and as the righteousness which God demands must extend to the whole nature, not merely to word and action but to the heart and motives, it follows that man is lost, unable to save himself, and therefore Jesus describes His mission as that of seeking and saving the lost (Mt 18¹¹, cf. Lk 19¹⁰). All are thus dependent upon the sovereign pardoning grace of God, and so Jesus says, 'No man can come unto me, except the Father which hath sent me draw him' (Jn 6⁴⁴). But that this grace is not restricted in its operation by any hard and fast decree of election, Jesus teaches by the manner in which He describes His mission, which is that of seeking the lost '*till he find*' them (Lk 15⁴), and by the universal call which He addresses to the weary and heavy-laden (Mt 11²⁸).

While we may for convenience' sake distinguish between Repentance and Faith, Jesus so presents them as to represent Faith as the source of Repentance, the one involving the other and leading to it. Thus, to take one illustration, the repentance which in His conversation with Nicodemus He describes as a new birth, is spoken of in the same discourse as the result of an act of faith in Himself, which He likens to the simple look directed by the dying Israelites to the Brazen Serpent which Moses lifted up in the wilderness (Jn 3¹⁴). As Weiss has well put it (*Bib. Theol. of the NT*, i. 97)—

'The new revelation of God which is brought in the message concerning the Kingdom of God spontaneously works the repentance which Jesus demands. God does not demand that man should meet Him; He Himself meets man with graciousness, and thereby does the utmost that lies in His power to make man capable of the repentance in which He has His greatest joy (Lk 15$^{4-10}$). He does not make His revelation of salvation dependent upon the conversion of the people, as in the preaching of the prophets; He will work this conversion by the revelation of His grace.'

Thus, in the Gospel of John, Jesus makes faith in Himself the condition of salvation: 'He that believeth hath everlasting life' (Jn $^{'}$48); and in line with such declarations is that doctrine, characteristic of the Johannine discourses, which seems to represent faith as knowledge, the acceptance of the testimony of the Son of God (Jn 3$^{18f.}$). All that this means is that to accept Christ's testimony, and to accept Christ Himself as the revelation of the Divine grace, is to become a child of God and a member of the Kingdom of God.

Again, Jesus demands not only faith and repentance, but insists as strongly as John the Baptist or the prophets of the OT upon the importance of living proofs of faith, and of fruits meet for repentance (Mt 3$^{8-10}$ ‖ Lk 3$^{8ff.}$, Mt 7$^{21-27}$ ‖ Lk 6$^{43ff.}$). Christ's disciples must prove their conversion and their right to the privileges of the Kingdom of God by their 'moral imitation of their Heavenly Father'; sonship must show itself by the family likeness. But as that ideal is far beyond the possibility of present attainment, the Christian life is described as a steep and narrow path, to press along which requires constant effort and unremitting watchfulness and prayer (Mt 7$^{13-21}$ ‖ Lk 13^{24} 6^{46}; Mt 7$^{24-27}$ ‖ Lk 6$^{47-49}$).

5. With regard to the significance of the Death and Resurrection of Jesus as *the ultimate conditions of the establishment of the Kingdom of God*, our Lord treated that doctrine as He did His Messianic claims in respect of His Divine nature. It is represented in the Gospels as the subject of gradual development, as a truth not at the beginning clearly made known even to the most favoured disciples, but taught first by suggestions and figures more or less veiled, then by warnings and predictions, which became clearer as the end drew near, to the effect that Jesus must die. Still it is present from the first, though only in germ, and though it is noted as that part of their Master's teaching which the disciples were most slow to apprehend. Thus it is represented as having been suggested so early as in the time of the Baptist, whose words, 'Behold the Lamb of God,' first led John and Andrew to follow Jesus (Jn 1$^{29. 35-37}$). At a later period Jesus declared in express terms that 'the Son of Man came not to be ministered unto, but to minister, and to give his life a ransom for many' (λύτρον ἀντὶ πολλῶν), where the death of Jesus as a sacrifice of substitution appears to be distinctly spoken of (Mt 20^{28} ‖ Mk 10^{45}). The doctrine that salvation can come only through the voluntary sufferings and death of Jesus is so clearly taught by our Lord's later utterances as recorded in all the Gospels, and particularly in the Fourth, as, for example, in the discourse on the Bread of Life ('the bread which I will give is my flesh, which I will give for the life of the world,' Jn 6^{51}), in the discourse on the Good Shepherd ('the good shepherd giveth his life for the sheep,' 10$^{11. 15}$, cf. vv.$^{17. 18}$), etc., that it is hardly necessary to enumerate them. One of the strongest proofs that the disciples understood Jesus to lay special emphasis upon the necessity of His death as an atoning sacrifice, lies in the fact that so large a portion of the Gospels is devoted to the narrative of the sufferings, death, and resurrection of Jesus; while the full account which all the Synoptists give of the institution of the Lord's Supper (Mt 26$^{26-29}$ ‖ Mk ·14$^{22-25}$ ‖ Lk 22$^{17. 20}$), and particularly the signi-

ficant words of Jesus recorded by St. Matthew (26^{28}), 'This is my blood of the [new] covenant, which is shed for many for the remission of sins,' show that by appointing this ordinance by which to 'show forth his death,' as St. Paul expresses it (1 Co 11^{26}), Jesus singled out this part of His work as constituting the central truth of His manifestation to men, and summing up and applying the whole.

Again, like the Apostles in the Acts and the Epistles, all four Evangelists represent the Resurrection as the necessary seal of Christ's atoning work, confirming His victory over death and him that had the power of death, and as a testimony to the Father's acceptance of the sacrifice. So Jesus, in foretelling His death, conjoined with the prediction the assurance that He should rise again the third day. The Resurrection is the necessary complement of the Atoning Death.

6. Closely connected with these fundamental teachings of the Kingdom of God and the conditions of its realization are those which relate (*a*) *to the growth and maintenance of the Kingdom after Christ's Ascension*, and (*b*) *to the final consummation and the judgment of the world*.

(*a*) According to all the Gospels, the specialty of Christ's mission, as that was revealed to John the Baptist, was that He should baptize with the Holy Ghost (Mt 3^{11} ‖ Mk 1^{8} ‖ Lk 3^{16}; cf. Jn 1^{33}). All relate the descent of the Holy Spirit at the Baptism of Jesus (Mt 3$^{13-17}$ ‖ Mk 1$^{9-11}$ ‖ Lk 3$^{21. 22}$). John the Baptist testifies (Jn 1$^{31. 34}$) that He upon whom the Spirit descended and abode is He who baptizeth with the Holy Ghost. Jesus attributed His power to cast out demons to the Spirit of God (Mt 12^{28}). That the Spirit thus spoken of is a Person, and as such to be distinguished from Christ, is to be inferred from the solemn warning which Jesus addressed to those who attributed His miracles of exorcism to Satanic agency, when He said that blasphemy against the Son of Man should be forgiven, but that to blaspheme against the Holy Ghost was an unpardonable sin (Mt 12$^{31. 32}$ ‖ Mk 3$^{28f.}$ ‖ Lk 12^{10}). Jesus taught, however, that the prediction of John was to be fulfilled only after the Son of Man was glorified. Thus we read, with reference to the promise that the Spirit should be in believers a perennial fountain of grace, 'This spake he of the Spirit which they that believe on him should receive: for the Holy Ghost was not yet given; because that Jesus was not yet glorified' (Jn 7$^{37-39}$). And Jesus Himself says (16^{7}) to the disciples, 'It is expedient for you that I go away: for if I go not away, the Comforter will not come unto you; but if I depart, I will send him unto you.' The office of the Spirit is to abide with the disciples as the source of grace (7^{39}), to bring to their remembrance the teaching of Jesus (14^{26} 15^{26}) and guide them into all truth (16^{13}), to give them power to discharge their spiritual functions (20$^{22. 23}$) as leaders and teachers of the Church, and, as the Spirit of wisdom and utterance, to inspire them to testify faithfully and courageously for Christ in presence of their persecutors (Mt 10^{20} ‖ Mk 13^{11} ‖ Lk 12$^{11. 12}$). Further, His function is to 'reprove the world of sin, of righteousness, and of judgment' (Jn 16$^{8-11}$). With Christ's teaching concerning the Spirit His revelation of God was complete, and accordingly, in one of His last discourses after the Resurrection, He commanded His Apostles to 'make disciples of all nations, baptizing them in the name of the Father, and of the Son, and of the Holy Ghost' (Mt 28^{19}).

(*b*) Our Lord's teaching concerning *the final consummation of the Kingdom of God* may be briefly summarized. The disciples were instructed to live in constant expectation of His Second Coming (Mt 24$^{42-51}$ ‖ Mk 13$^{33-37}$ ‖ Lk 12$^{35-46}$; cf. Mt 25^{13}).

That might occur at any time. His coming should, according to the prophecies of the OT, be heralded by certain signs in the world, by tumult and distress among the nations, and by portents in nature, earthquakes, storms, and the like (Mt 24²⁹ff. ‖ Mk 13²⁴ff. ‖ Lk 21²⁵ff.). Nevertheless He should come as a thief in the night, and surprise the worldly and the careless in the midst of their business or their pleasure (Mt 24⁴³ff.‖Lk 17²⁷). Then also Christ should by His angels 'gather together his elect from the four winds' (Mt 24³¹) for the purpose of taking them to Himself and saving them from destruction (Lk 17³⁴. ³⁵). In connexion with this, Jesus spoke also of a time of sifting, at which all unworthy members should be cast out (Mt 13³⁰. ⁴¹. ⁴⁸f. 22¹¹⁻¹³ 25¹⁰⁻¹², Lk 13²⁵). Finally, after the Kingdom had been thus purified should come the ultimate consummation. Jesus should appear as the Judge of all nations (Mt 25³¹⁻⁴⁶), coming in the clouds (Mt 26⁶⁴‖Mk 14⁶²‖Lk 22⁶⁹) to reward the righteous with eternal bliss in heaven and to sentence the wicked to eternal perdition (Mt 25³⁴⁻⁴⁶). See also LEADING IDEAS.

LITERATURE.—Cremer, *Bib.-Theol. Lex. s.vv.* διδασκαλία, διδαχή ; *Comm.* of Alford and Meyer ; Beyschlag, *NT Theol.* (2nd Eng. ed.) i. 28–156, ii. 267–472 ; Schmid, *Biblical Theology of the NT*, 63–90 ; Weiss, *Biblical Theology of the NT*, 63–90.

HUGH H. CURRIE.

DOG.—See ANIMALS, p. 64.

DOMINION.—The word 'dominion' occurs only once in the AV of the Gospels, as part of the phrase 'exercise dominion over' (κατακυριεύουσιν), in that passage in the Gospel of Matthew (20²⁵) which records our Lord's reply to the ambitious request of Salome on behalf of her sons, and the words which He addressed to the disciples at the time. The RV of this passage, as of the parallel text in Mark (10⁴²), is 'lord it over.' The same idea is expressed in a similar passage in Luke (22²⁵), which gives Christ's words at the Last Supper with reference to the dispute among His disciples as to precedence, by the simple verb κυριεύουσιν, 'exercise lordship over' (RV 'have lordship over').

Again, in all three passages the verbs which are so translated are followed in the parallel clause of the verse by the words 'exercise authority over' or 'upon' (Mt 20²⁵ AV and RV ‖ Mk 10⁴² AV and RV, Lk 22²⁵ AV), 'have authority over' (Lk 22²⁵ RV), representing the words of the original κατεξουσιάζουσιν, ἐξουσιάζοντες. The word 'authority' (ἐξουσία) and the verbs formed from it thus suggest themselves for consideration in connexion with the word rendered 'dominion' in the passage in Matthew.

1. The passages quoted from the Synoptics illustrate a characteristic feature of the Gospels, the manner in which they represent Jesus as postponing the assertion of His kingly rights, and, in connexion with this, the express teaching which they attribute to Him as to the nature of the dominion which He claimed. Thus, as He withstood the temptation of Satan (Lk 4⁶) to assume the royal sceptre which belonged to Him as Son of God, and to reign as the Divinely appointed king of a visible and temporal realm, so He resisted, as a repetition of that temptation, every suggestion or appeal that was made to Him, by the people or by His disciples, formally and publicly to appear as the Messiah. He would not suffer the people of Galilee to make Him a king (Jn 6¹⁵). He declared to Pilate that, although royal authority was His by right, His kingdom was not of this world, and was therefore not to be won or maintained and defended by temporal weapons (Jn 18³⁶. ³⁷).

Now the texts which have been quoted from the Synoptics may be regarded as the *loci classici* of the teaching of Jesus with reference to the nature of the sovereignty claimed by Him, and to the principle of that spiritual dominion of which He spoke. They occur in connexion with what the Gospels tell us regarding the Messianic expectations of the Twelve, who, like most of their countrymen, anticipated in the near, and even, at times, in the immediate, future, the visible establishment of the personal reign of Christ as Prince of the House of David. They were addressed to the disciples at the close of Christ's ministry, in the one case in the course of His last journey to Jerusalem, in the other in connexion with the dispute at the Last Supper as to who should be accounted the greatest. The answer of Jesus in both cases—to the ambitious request of Salome, and to the dispute among the disciples—was the same, and the principle which He laid down was to this effect. For Master and for disciple the question of dominion is totally different from that which is agitated by the ambition of the world. Among the princes of the Gentiles the way to power and authority is the path of worldly ambition and self-assertion. It is not so in the Kingdom of God. There not self-assertion but self-denial is the way to supremacy. The way to dominion is the way of service. Places of supremacy there certainly are in the Kingdom of God, and they are reserved 'for those for whom they are prepared' of the Father. But they are allotted upon a definite, intelligible principle, and that not of favouritism but of spiritual character. They who shall hold rank nearest to Christ in His Kingdom are they who shall most closely resemble Him in respect of lowliness, self-denial, and humble service. For disciple and for Master the law is the same in this respect, that 'he that humbleth himself shall be exalted.' So Christ is 'among you as he that serveth' (Lk 22²⁷). In laying down the principle, Jesus illustrated it by reference to His own mission. 'The Son of Man came not to be ministered unto, but to minister, and to give his life a ransom for many' (Mt 20²⁸ ‖ Mk 10⁴⁵). And here as elsewhere the disciple must be as his Master, attaining his place in the Kingdom only by the way of self humiliation, self-denial, self-sacrifice.

2. The use in these passages, in immediate connexion with the idea of dominion, of the words 'have authority over' (ἐξουσιάζουσιν, ἐξουσιάζοντες), calls for some reference to the power or authority (ἐξουσία) attributed to Christ in connexion with His humiliation as well as with His exaltation. That during His ministry He possessed and exercised very complete and far-reaching authority, dominion in the sense of ἐξουσία, the natural synonym of κυριότης, 'lordship,' 'dominion,' is distinctly testified by all the Gospels.

Lordship (κυριότης) was expressly claimed by Him even in connexion with His state of humiliation. Thus, in controversy with the Pharisees, He claimed to be Lord of the Sabbath, and, as such, to be entitled to interpret the Sabbath law (Mt 12⁸ ‖ Mk 2²⁸ ‖ Lk 6⁵). St. Luke tells us in his account of the healing of the paralytic, that 'the power of the Lord was present to heal' (5¹⁷). The message to the owners of the ass on which Jesus rode to Jerusalem was 'The Lord hath need of him' (Mt 21³ ‖ Mk 11³ ‖ Lk 19³¹. ³⁴). When Jesus had washed the disciples' feet, and was applying the lesson of that incident, He said, 'Ye call me Master and Lord : and ye say well ; for so I am' (Jn 13¹³).

As Son of Man, He was invested with special power (ἐξουσία) to work miracles. As such He is represented as exercising a delegated authority, acting according to His Father's will (Jn 5³⁰ff.), but that with a spontaneity and directness unknown before. Such was His power over unclean spirits that they trembled and cried out at His approach, and were compelled to yield instant though fearful and reluctant obedience to His command (Mk 1²⁷ ‖ Lk 4³⁶). With a word He controlled the winds and waves (Mt 8²⁶⁻³¹ ‖ Mk 4³⁹⁻⁴¹ Lk 8²⁴·²⁵). So wide and great was His authority over the powers of life and death, that His word, even though spoken at a distance, was sufficient to effect an instantaneous cure, as when His word of assurance spoken at Cana to the nobleman was followed immediately by the cure of his child who lay sick at Capernaum (Jn 4⁵⁰); and when He confirmed the faith of the centurion, who likened Christ's power over disease to his own authority over his soldiers, by speaking the word which healed his servant (Mt 8⁸⁻¹³ ‖ Lk 7⁶⁻¹⁰). Three times He raised the dead with a word : in the case of the widow's son (Lk 7¹¹⁻¹⁶), in that of Jairus' daughter (Mt 9¹⁸⁻²⁶ ‖ Mk 5²¹⁻⁴³ ‖ Lk 8⁴⁰⁻⁵⁶), and in that of Lazarus (Jn 11¹⁻⁴⁴). He could even delegate to others His power over unclean spirits and to heal disease, as He did in His mission, first of the Twelve, and again of the Seventy disciples (Mt 10⁵ff· ‖ Mk 6⁷ff· ‖ Lk 9¹⁻⁶ 10¹⁻¹⁶). Again, He claimed and exercised power on earth to forgive sins (Mt 9⁶ ‖ Mk 2¹⁰ ‖ Lk 5²⁴, cf. Lk 7⁴⁸).

3. According to the Johannine discourses, Jesus declared that the Father had committed to Him power to execute judgment 'because he is the Son of Man' (Jn 5²⁷). This function refers specially to His state of exaltation. He came not to judge, but to save the world (Jn 12⁴⁷); 'I judge no man,' He said to the Jews (8¹⁵). At the same time His work and teaching, even His very presence in the world, meant a judgment, inasmuch as they compelled men to declare themselves either for or against Christ, and so pass judgment upon themselves (cf. Jn 9³⁹); and as Jesus said Himself, 'The word that I have spoken, the same shall judge him in the last day' (12⁴⁸). To Jesus as Son of Man all judgment and authority and power have been committed. All things are given into His hands (Mt 11²⁷, Jn 3³⁵ ‖ 13²), that He may guide and strengthen His Church (Mt 28¹⁸), and at His second coming appear as the Judge of all nations (Mt 25³¹ff·). It is He who is to pass the final sentence upon the just and upon the unjust. On that day He will say to those who have falsely called Him 'Lord, Lord,' 'I know you not' (Mt 7²²·²³). He will open to His faithful ones the door to the eternal festival of joy, but will close the door of the heavenly marriage feast on 'the unfaithful' (Mt 7²²·²³ 25¹¹·¹², Lk 13²⁷⁻²⁹). 'He shall sit upon the throne of his glory, and before him shall be gathered all nations' (Mt 25³¹·³²). In connexion with these predictions of the events of the Day of Judgment, Jesus says : 'The Son of Man shall send forth his angels, and they shall gather out of his kingdom all things that offend, and them that do iniquity' (Mt 13⁴¹). The angels are thus represented as being subject to the dominion of Christ in His exaltation, as His servants, obeying His behests; as even during His life on earth they appeared as ministering spirits obedient to His command, and waiting upon Him as courtiers upon their Sovereign (Mt 4¹¹ 26⁵³, Lk 22⁴³).

Lastly, as the fruit of His work of redemption, and as part of the glory which He has won by His perfect submission to the Father's will, there is given to Him, in that time of waiting which must pass before the final completion of His kingdom, 'all power in heaven and on earth' (Mt 28¹⁸), as the Father has 'given him power over all flesh, that he should give eternal life to as many as he has given him' (Jn 17², cf. 10²⁸). See also POWER.

LITERATURE.—Cremer, *Bib.-Theol. Lex. s.vv.* ἐξουσία, κύριος, κυριότης; Grimm-Thayer, *Lex. NT, s.vv.* κατακυριεύω, ἐξουσία,

κύριος, κυριεύω; H. J. Holtzmann, *Lehrbuch der NT Theol.* i. 319 f., ii. 409 ff. ; Wendt, *The Teaching of Jesus*, ii. 276 ; Beyschlag, *NT Theology*, i. 59–191, 241 ; *Comm.* of Meyer and Alford.   HUGH H. CURRIE.

DOOR (θύρα, cf. θυρωρός, 'doorkeeper,' 'porter'). —The word 'door' is frequently found in the Gospels, sometimes in the literal, often in the figurative sense.

1. We need, first, to get clearly in mind the meaning of the term in Oriental usage. By 'door' is usually meant the outside or entrance 'doorway,' but often the 'door' in distinction from the 'doorway,' the frame of wood, stone, or metal that closes the doorway. The outside of the Oriental house has little ornament or architectural attractiveness of any kind. The 'door,' however, and the projecting 'window' above it, are exceptions to this rule. The doors, windows, and doorways are often highly ornamented (Is 54¹², Rev 21²¹), enriched with arabesques, and, if to-day it be the house of a Moslem, the door will have sentences from the Koran inscribed upon it (cf. Dt 6⁹). The 'doors' are usually of hard wood, studded with nails, or sometimes covered with sheet-iron. They are often very heavy. They invariably open inwards, and are furnished on the inside with strong bars and bolts. They have usually wooden locks, which are worked by wooden keys of such size that they could make formidable clubs (Is 22²², cf. *Land and Book*, i. 493). There is an opening in the door for the insertion of the hand and the introduction of the key from the outside, the lock being reached only from the inside. On entering the 'door' there is usually a vestibule, where, in daytime, the 'doorkeeper' is found, and where the master often receives the casual visitor (cf. Gn 19¹³ 23¹⁰ 34³⁰ and Job 29⁷).

The 'doors' leading into the 'rooms' or 'chambers' that open upon the court are not usually supplied with locks or bolts ; a curtain, as a rule, being all that separates one of these 'chambers' from the 'court,' the idea being that all is private and secure within the outer gate (cf. Dt 24¹⁰, Ac 10¹⁷ 12¹³).

The 'doorway' consists of three parts : the threshold or sill (sometimes used for 'door'), the two side-posts, and the lintel (Ex 12⁷f·). The doors of ancient Egypt, and probably of contemporary nations, swung upon vertical pintles which projected from the top and bottom of the door into sockets in the lintel and threshold respectively. The commonest form of door had the pintle in the middle of the width, so that, as it opened, a way was afforded on each side of it for ingress or egress.

Occasionally we find that the 'chamber,' or private room, had its own door and fastenings. In Mt 6⁶, 'When thou hast shut thy door,' the word used means not only closed, but fastened it—giving the idea of complete privacy. See art. CLOSET. In Mt 25¹⁰, 'the *door* was shut,' it is clearly the outside or entrance-door that is meant. When this one outer door was shut, all communication with the outside world was cut off. Then nothing but persistent knocking at this door, and loud entreaty, would succeed in securing even a hearing. In this case the appeal was made to the bridegroom himself, who, to this day, is considered in the East sovereign of the occasion.

2. When Jesus said, 'I am the door' (Jn 10⁹), He clearly meant to exclude every other form or means of mediation. But *through Him* there is an unhindered entering into and going out of the fold (cf. Nu 27¹⁷).

3. When it is said that Joseph, 'a rich man of Arimathæa,' begged the body of Jesus, laid it in his own new tomb, which he had hewn out in the rock, and rolled a great stone to the *door* of the tomb (Mt 27⁶⁰, Mk 16³), we have a reference to a unique kind of door. The great roll-stone is often mentioned in the Talmud, but only in describing interments of the dead (Keim). It was clearly designed to protect the dead bodies and the other contents of the tomb from robbers, petty thieves, and birds and beasts of prey. One large tomb is now shown half a mile north of Jerusalem, which has a huge circular stone, like a great millstone on edge, cut from the solid rock, together with the channel in which it revolves. There are signs that it was originally furnished with a secret fastening, doubtless to protect the contents—spices, costly linen, jewellery, etc., against plunder. The 'Tomb of Mariamne,' recently uncovered south of the city, and the so-called 'Tomb of Lazarus' at Bethany, likewise have doors with similar 'roll-stones' (cf. art. TOMB). See also artt. COURT, HOUSE.

GEO. B. EAGER.

DOUBT.—

In Lat. *dubitare*, from *duo* 'two' and *bito* 'go'; Germ. *Zweifeln, Zweifel*; from *zwei*, 'two'; Mid. Eng. *douten*, 'to doubt,' had the meaning of *to fear* ('I doubt some foul play' [Shakspeare], 'nor slack her threatful hand for danger's doubt' [Spenser]), and this meaning, perhaps, survives in such expressions as 'I doubt he will not come.' But, as commonly used, *to doubt* means *to be of two minds, to waver, to hesitate*. It suggests the idea of perplexity; of being at a loss, in a state of suspense. The questioning attitude is implied. The word has, in short, a variety of meanings.

References in the Gospels.—The word 'doubt' occurs several times in AV and RV. It is used, however, to translate several Greek terms; nor are these invariably rendered by the word in question. A study of the respective passages reveals differing circumstances and conditions, different types of character, a variety of subjects exercising the mind. Doubt in several phases is in illustration.

(*a*) The doubt of perplexity. Thus in Mk 6²⁰, Lk 24⁴, Jn 13²² —where the verb ἀπορέω occurs (the strengthened compound διαπορέω is found in Lk 9⁷). There is no question in these passages of the apprehension of religious truth; the idea suggested is rather that of being taken aback, disturbed, distracted, by the unintelligible and the unexpected. Herod is 'much perplexed' (Mk 6²⁰ RV, cf. Lk 9⁷) as he listens to the Baptist, as reports reach him concerning Jesus; he is puzzled, at a loss for explanations. And thus in Jn 13²² 'the disciples looked one upon the other, doubting of whom he spake'; the unexpected statement has bewildered them. Similar feelings may be recognized in the case of the women at the sepulchre (Lk 24⁴); they are 'much perplexed'; utterly unable, that is, to account for the empty tomb. A like meaning may, perhaps, be read into the 'how long dost thou hold us in suspense?' of Jn 10²⁴ (τὴν ψυχὴν ἡμῶν αἴρεις): the Jews being understood as professing an uncertainty which could be at once dispelled by some plain declaration on the part of Jesus.

(*b*) Wavering faith. A second group of passages, where the verbs μετεωρίζεσθαι and διστάζειν occur, has now to be considered. Again the word 'doubt' is found in AV and RV, but with reference to a mental condition other than that which has been noted in the preceding paragraph. A religious significance is now observable; the existence of faith is implied, but it is an imperfect, a wavering faith. Because of distractions of one kind or another, confidence is impaired. The doubters referred to are sometimes the ὀλιγόπιστοι: their faith not only wavering but small. Thus in Lk 12²⁹ 'neither be ye of doubtful mind' (καὶ μὴ μετεωρίζεσθε), the context supplies the explanation; anxiety about earthly things is incompatible with absolute trust in the Fatherhood of God. So also in Mt 14³¹ 'wherefore didst thou doubt?' (εἰς τί ἐδίστασας;), where St. Peter's confidence has given way before sudden panic. And thus, perhaps, in

Mt 28¹⁷ 'but some doubted' (ἐδίστασαν). What, precisely, the condition of these genuine disciples was is difficult to determine, but it was one which left them unreceptive while others were convinced of a manifestation of the living Lord. With this passage may be compared Lk 24³⁸; the διαλογισμοί (RV 'reasonings') being significant of fearsome hesitation on the part of those who could not at once realize that the mysterious visitor was none other than Jesus Himself.

(*c*) The critical attitude. This is implied by the verb διακρίνεσθαι; a term which, as used in NT, denotes the absence of faith, the paralysis of faith. It occurs but twice in the Gospels (Mt 21²¹, Mk 11²³); where the power of faith is, by implication, contrasted with the impotency which is involved in the want of faith. Thought seems to be directed to the inevitable consequence of regarding Divine things as a subject for curious investigation rather than as matter of personal concern. On the one hand, there is the emphatic declaration which may be expressed in the words of Bacon, 'Man, when he resteth and assureth himself upon divine Protection and Favour, gathereth a Force and Faith [in its sense of fidelity] which Human Nature, in its selfe, could not obtaine.' On the other hand, there is the implied warning that, as the vision of God darkens and vanishes, man's capacity for useful action becomes weaker, until at length it dies away.

[For discussion of 'the doubt of Thomas' see THOMAS and UNBELIEF].

LITERATURE.—Lyttelton, *Modern Poets of Faith, Doubt, and Paganism*; Illingworth, *Christian Character*; James, *The Will to Believe*; Carlyle, *Sartor Resartus*; Browning, *Christmas-Eve and Easter-Day*; Tennyson, *In Memoriam* (edited, with commentary, by A. W. Robinson); Jowett, *Sermons*.

H. L. JACKSON.

DOVE (περιστερά).—Its gentle nature makes the dove a frequent simile in ancient literature. Christ bids His disciples to be harmless as doves, and to unite with such gentleness a wisdom like the serpent's (Mt 10¹⁶). Meyer, *in loc.*, takes this to mean, 'Be prudent in regard to dangers in which you are placed, quick to see and avoid dangers; and always be full of uprightness, never taking any questionable way of escape.' As the serpent is the most cunning of the beasts of the field, so should the Lord's disciples have wisdom to understand the subtleties of Satan; but no evil is to mix with such wisdom. Along with it there must be found a purity and simplicity of heart of which the harmless, gentle dove is the symbol. The truest wisdom for the Christian is to keep always the simplicity of the dove. A nature purified by the Spirit of Christ will have wise penetration enough to defeat all the wiles of Satan.

The dove, the emblem of perfect innocence, is used (Mt 3¹⁶ and parallels) as a symbol of the Holy Spirit, who is the power and wisdom of God, acting on the spirits of men. When the dove appeared to sit on the Saviour's head, it denoted the Divine recognition of His holiness (v.¹⁷), and His official consecration to the Messianic ministry. As the author of the Epistle to the Hebrews says, 'He was holy, harmless, undefiled, and separate from sinners' (7²⁶).

It has been thought that the dove had a sacrosanct character among the Hebrews. Though it was a favourite food with some neighbouring peoples, it was not eaten in Palestine. Young pigeons and doves were offered in sacrifice, where no sacrificial meal was involved. So we find in the temple courts them that sold doves (Mt 21¹², Mk 11¹⁵, Jn 2¹⁴· ¹⁶),—no doubt for such sacrifices, —whom Christ drove out, along with the money-changers. In Palestine the dove was considered sacred by the Phœnicians and the Philistines, and the Samaritans were often accused of worshipping it. There were holy doves at Mecca ; and, according to Lucian (*Dea Syria*, 54), doves were taboo to the Syrians ; he who touched them being unclean a whole day.

In Christian Art in representations of the Lord's Baptism, the presence of the Holy Spirit is indicated by the dove. In churches in early times the figure of a dove appeared in the baptisteries, a golden or silver dove being suspended above the font. Lamps, too, were sometimes made in the form of doves. In later times pyxes were sometimes made of gold and silver in the shape of a dove, and used for the reservation of the host.

Exclusive of the turtle-dove, four species of dove are found in Palestine : *Columba palumbus*, the ring-dove, or wood-pigeon ; *Columba œnas*, the stock-dove, found in Gilead and Bashan and the Jordan Valley ; *Columba livia*, the rock-dove, abundant along the coast and in the uplands ; *Columba schimperi*, closely allied to the preceding, and found in the interior.

LITERATURE.—Hastings' *DB*, *s.v.* ; Thomson, *Land and Book* (1878), p. 268 ff. ; *Expositor*, 1st ser. ix. [1879] p. 81 ff.

DAVID M. W. LAIRD.

DOXOLOGY. — An ascription of praise to God in forms of words more or less fixed by usage. Though the term does not occur in the NT, it contains many doxologies, and they were an important element in the devotional life of the primitive Christians. This indeed was inevitable, because they carried with them what was best in the practice of Judaism, and were especially influenced in the expression of their worship by the language of the OT.

1. *The OT and Jewish usage.*—Doxologies are common in the OT, being found in germ even in its oldest portions. In the Song of Deborah praise is given to Jehovah for national deliverance (Jg 5[2. 9] ; cf. Ex 18[10]). In 1 K 1[48] 8[15] there is thankful recognition of Jehovah's power and control in national events. The Psalms are especially rich (28[6] 34[2. 3.] 135, 146), though one form, 'give thanks unto Jehovah, for His lovingkindness endureth for ever,' seems to be the most common both in the Psalms and all post-exilic literature (Ps 106[1] 107[1] 118[1. 2. 3], 1 Ch 16[34], 2 Ch 5[13] 7[3. 6], Ezr 3[11]). The regular liturgical conclusion of the services of the Temple, and afterwards of the Synagogue, came to be a doxology beginning 'blessed be (or 'is ') God.' By the time of our Lord the employment of doxological expressions had increased so largely, that they were in the mouth of the people for any event which stirred their gratitude or wonder, in fact as thanksgiving for almost everything in life. Though the fundamental religious idea of the doxology, that Jehovah is the Holy One whose sovereign power must be acknowledged at all times, was a noble one, its use had too often degenerated into the veriest formalism.

2. *NT usage.*—Traces of Jewish custom may be seen in the Gospels (Mt 15[31], Mk 2[12], Lk 1[46. 68] 2[20] 5[25. 26] 7[16]). The words and attendant conditions of the life of Jesus so impressed the people that a new hope was born in them, and they praised God for signs of His returning favour to Israel through this prophet. Jesus does not yet receive Divine homage. No doxology is offered to Him anywhere in the Gospels, for the Messianic acclaim (Mk 11[9. 10]) is not to be so interpreted (see Dalman, *Words of Jesus*, 220ff., and Swete, *in loc.*). God alone has the right to such ascription, for He is 'holy' ; He is ὁ εὐλογητός, the One to whom blessing is due (Mk 14[61]), הַקָּדוֹשׁ בָּרוּךְ הוּא being a well-known Jewish formula. See artt. BENEDICTION and BLESSING.

Immediately after the Resurrection, Jesus is associated with the Father in glory, and receives worship as Messiah and Son of God. This is the universal Apostolic view (Ac 2[33-36] 3[13. 15] 5[31], Ro 1[4],

Ph 2[6-11], He 1[3] 2[9], Ja 2[1], 1 P 1[21]). So the ascription of doxologies to the risen Christ naturally followed. But the doxology continued to be addressed most frequently to God the Father (Ro 11[36], Gal 1[5], Eph 3[20. 21], Ph 4[20], 1 Ti 1[17] 6[16], 1 P 5[11], Rev 7[12]). In several Jesus Christ is associated more or less directly with God the Father (Ro 16[27], 1 P 4[11], Jude [25], Rev 5[13]). Ro 9[5] and He 13[21] present baffling evidence as to the recipient ; but in 2 Ti 4[18], 2 P 3[18], Rev 1[6] glory is ascribed to Jesus Christ. Thus in conformity with Christian belief the OT usage was expanded, so that at a very early date there arose a Christian formula, which in the. public adoration of the worship of the Church would serve in a secondary sense as a creed, expressing the doctrine that the risen Christ shared in Divine honour with the Father.

3. *Structure.*—The doxologies of the NT consist of three main parts.

(*a*) The Person to whom praise is given. This is, as we have seen, most frequently God the Father, though Jesus Christ is associated with Him. Attributes are often added, usually to emphasize the Divine blessing which has occasioned the praise. In Eph 3[20. 21], *e.g.* a clause descriptive of the power of the Almighty serves to justify the Apostle's prayer for strength on behalf of his readers. See Ro 16[27], 1 Ti 1[17] 6[16], 2 P 3[18], Jude [24. 25], Rev 1[5. 6] 5[13].

(*b*) The second term is almost invariably δόξα ('glory'), either alone or with some significant addition (Ep 3[21]), the chief exceptions being 1 Ti 6[16] ('honour and power '), 1 P 5[11] ('the dominion '). The amplitude of the doxologies in the Apocalypse deserves attention, the praise being threefold (4[11] 19[1]), fourfold (5[13]), or sevenfold in its perfection (7[12]). This full-voiced glory offered to the Lamb (5[13]) in this book of Hebrew cast, shows how thoroughly it was the belief of the circle from which it issued that Jesus transcended every created being.

Except in 1 P 4[11] the copula is omitted, so that it must be determined from the context whether the doxology is affirmative or precatory (see Lightfoot on Gal 1[5] ; Chase, *Lord's Prayer*, p. 169 ; *Didache*, viii. 2 ; Clement of Rome, 58).

(*c*) The third integral part of the doxology in its simplest form is εἰς τοὺς αἰῶνας ('unto the ages '), which denotes the eternity of the sovereign rule of the Lord. Before the mind of the Apostolic writers, however, the future rolls out in a series of æons, so that the normal form is expanded very frequently into εἰς τοὺς αἰῶνας τῶν αἰώνων, in order to cover all possible periods of time (Gal 1[5], Ph 4[20], 1 Ti 1[17], 2 Ti 4[18], He 13[21], 1 P 4[11], Rev 5[13] 7[12]). See also Eph 3[21], 2 P 3[18], Jude [25]).

The conclusion of all doxologies except 2 P 3[18] is ἀμήν.

4. *The Doxology in the Lord's Prayer* (Mt 6[13]).—It can no longer be doubted that this was not a part of the prayer as it stood originally in Matthew. The uncial evidence is very weak (LΔΣ), and the variations in the early versions are numerous (Syr[cur] omits 'and the power' ; the Sinaitic is defective, and the old Latin (k) and the Sahidic differ from each other and from the Syriac). The form found in the *Didache* (viii. 2, x. 5) ultimately developed into the full expression ('the kingdom and the power and the glory '), which probably passed into the Syrian text from the liturgical usage of the Syrian Church. (See Hort's *Notes on Select Readings*, p. 9). Of this final doxology the original source may have been 1 Ch 29[11], which shaped the Synagogue usage and thereby that of the Christian Church. No Jewish benediction was complete without reference to 'the kingdom' of Jehovah. 'It calls attention to this that He to whom the kingdom belongs, also has the power to hear the prayer which primarily has in view the establishing of that kingdom, and that He is therefore to be praised for ever' (Weiss). See, further, art. LORD'S PRAYER.

5. The Angelic Hymn (Lk 2[14]), in its longer and less correct text, gave rise to the *Gloria in Excelsis* (*Apost. Const.* VII. 47). The *Doxologia Minor* ('Glory be to the Father,' etc.) may possibly be traced back to Mt 28[19], but there is no other sign of it in the NT. However, to follow the fortunes of these doxologies would carry us beyond our limits. (See Smith's *Dictionary of Christian Antiquities*).

LITERATURE.—*Jewish Ency.* vol. viii. art. 'Liturgy'; Herzog-Hauck's *PRE*[3] vol. xi. art. 'Liturgische Formeln'; Chase, *The Lord's Prayer in the Early Church*; Westcott, *Epistle to the Hebrews*, Add. Note 'Apostolic Doxologies'.

R. A. FALCONER.

DRAUGHT OF FISHES. — A twice repeated miracle : (1) at the beginning of the Lord's ministry, (2) after the Resurrection. The main points are similar, but differences in the details have always been considered important and significant.

1. Lk 5[1-11]. At the Lake of Gennesaret, Jesus, after teaching from Peter's boat, bids him put out and let down the nets for a draught. He and his companions have toiled all the night without success, but obey, and enclose a great multitude of fishes, so that the nets are in danger of breaking. With the aid of their partners they fill the boats, which begin to sink. Peter, who some time before had been brought to Jesus by his brother Andrew (Jn 1[41]) and had followed Him as His disciple (Mt 4[18], Mk 1[16]), now begs Jesus to depart from him for he is 'a sinful man' [the vision of the Divine is the revelation of man's sin], but on a repeated command leaves all and follows Jesus.

2. Jn 21[1-14]. Some days or weeks after the Resurrection, when the Apostles have returned to their work as Galilæan fishermen, after a night of fruitless labour, when they are drawing near the shore, an unrecognized voice hails them, asking if they have anything to sell for food. On their answering in the negative, they are advised to cast the net on the right side of the ship. Having done so, they are not able to draw the net for the multitude of fishes. Instinctively John recognizes the Lord, and tells Peter, who at once swims to land. On drawing the net, the number of 'great fishes' is found to be 153, yet the net is not broken. None of the disciples has any doubt that 'it is the Lord.'

The natural explanation of the miracle, that from a distance Jesus saw what those in the boat failed to observe, is possible, but is not necessary. The power is rather that of guiding to the required place. 'The miracle lies in the circumstances and not in the mere fact. The events came to men from the sphere of their daily labour, and were at once felt to be the manifestations of a present power of God' (Westcott, *Characteristics of the Gospel Miracles*),—in the second case the manifestation of the power of the presence of the risen Lord.

The significant differences between the details of the two incidents have been drawn out by St. Augustine (*in Joh.* cxxii. 7). 'The one miracle was the symbol of the Church at present, the other of the Church perfected ; in the one we have good and bad, in the other good only ; there Christ also is on the water, here He is on the land ; there the draught is left in the boats, here it is landed on the beach ; there the nets are let down as it might be, here in a special part ; there the nets are rending, here they are not broken ; there the boats are on the point of sinking with their load, here they are not laden ; there the fish are not numbered, here the number is exactly given' (Westcott, *St. John, in loc.*). For interpretations of the number of fish (Jn 21[11]), see Westcott and other commentators.

LITERATURE.—The *Comm.* and *Lives of Christ* on the two passages ; Trench and Taylor on *Miracles ; Expositor*, IV. vi. [1892] 18 ; F. W. Robertson, *The Human Race*, 125 ; Ruskin, *Frondes Agrestes*, 152.

R. MACPHERSON.

DRAW-NET (σαγήνη, *seine*).—For fuller description see art. NETS. This kind of net is mentioned

in the Gospels only in the parable of Mt 13[47-50], where it is very much in point. Being usually of great size and sweeping through an immense area, it collects many varieties of fish—worthless, undersized, even dead fish, as well as the choice and the living. The process of fishing with a seine gives the impression of comprehensiveness and completeness. To one who has watched it—the very gradual progress of the operation, the extended area slowly encircled, the final drawing up of the net on the beach, and the sorting of its varied contents, with the reservation of some and the rejection of others—the aptness of the parable becomes very apparent.

The parable closes the series of seven in Mt 13, in which various aspects of the Kingdom of Heaven are presented. It is parallel in meaning to the second of the series,—the Tares and the Wheat,—yet it has its distinct individuality. It points, like that parable, to the intermixture of good and evil in the Church in its present stage, and it is implicit in the figure used that no absolute separation is possible or to be thought of now. But the emphasis of the parable and of the explanation added by our Lord, lies not upon the fact of the intermixture, but upon the certainty that there will be a decisive end to it. A time of deliberate (καθίσαντες) and final severance is announced as a warning to the evil, as an assurance to the good. The parable is concerned with the future rather than with the present, hence its suitability at the end of the series. As must be expected, the figure is not quite adequate. The whole operation of fishing is carried out by the same individuals. But the separation of the good and the evil at the end of the world will be effected not by the men through whom the Kingdom was extended, but by the angels, to whom this ministry is always assigned (Mt 13[41] 24[31] 25[31], Rev 14[18. 19]).

This parable, like that of the Tares, was much appealed to in the Donatist controversy. The Donatists, emphasizing purity as a note of the Church, maintained that all must be excluded from its outward communion to whom that note could not be attached. Augustine showed that such attempted separation was forbidden by our Lord, apart from the case of open evil-doers, and that He had not contemplated a community in its present stage free from admixture of evil. The net must contain both good and bad fish till it is drawn to the beach. As against schism, he points out the folly of those who, like fish breaking through or leaping over the net to escape the company of worthless fish within, refuse to wait the final and thorough separation appointed by God, and in mistakenly pressing the purity of the Church lose its catholicity (Augustine, *Enarr. in Ps.* 64. 6 ; cf. also *Enarr. in Ps.* 126. 3 ; *Coll. Carth.* d. 3 ; *ad Don. Post. Coll.* 4, 8, 10).

What conception of the Kingdom of Heaven is indicated by the parable ? The parable may be said to be an expansion of the idea contained in 'fishers of men.' Taken by itself, it might seem to support the identification of the Kingdom of Heaven with the Church ; but in other contexts the Kingdom of Heaven (or of God) requires a much more comprehensive explanation. Harnack's assertion that our Lord meant by this term, so constantly recurring in His teaching, only an inward experience of the believer (*Das Wesen des Christentums*, p. 35 ff.), seems quite unsuited to this passage. So, too, does the Abbé Loisy's explanation of the Kingdom as being still entirely in the future, and existing in the present only as an expectation (*The Gospel and the Church*, § ii.). The parable, naturally interpreted, certainly suggests a visible community. The Kingdom is conceived of both as inward and outward, consisting in its present stage both of those who are animated by its true spirit, and those who belong to it only so far that they are included in its external organization. Again, the Kingdom is represented as belonging to the present, and yet as awaiting its consummation in a future crisis of judgment. And it is in idea universal ('gathered of every kind'), tending to include all men within its bounds.

'The Kingdom in its highest and most Christian sense is the working of "invisible laws" which penetrate below the surface, and are gradually progressive and expansive in their operation. But in this, as in other cases, spiritual forces take to themselves an outward form : they are enshrined in a vessel of clay, finer or coarser as the case may be, not only in men as individuals, but in men as a community or communities. The society then becomes at once a vehicle and an instrument of the force by which it is animated, not a perfect vehicle or a perfect instrument,—a field of wheat mingled with tares, a net containing bad fish as well as good,—but analogous to those other visible institutions by which God accomplishes His gracious purposes amongst men' (Sanday, Hastings' *DB*, art. 'Jesus Christ,' II. B. b. (2), (vi.)).　　　　　　　　　A. E. ROSS.

DREAM.—The interest of the student of the Gospels in dreams turns upon the occurrence in the opening chapters of Matthew of the record of no fewer than five supernatural dreams (1^{20} $2^{12.\ 13.}$ $^{19.\ 22}$). Later in the same Gospel mention is made of a remarkable dream which came to the wife of Pilate (27^{19}). There is no reference to dreams elsewhere in the NT except in a citation from the OT in Ac 2^{17} and in an obscure verse in Jude (v. [8]).

No allusion is made in the Gospels, or indeed in the whole NT, to dreams as phenomena forming part of the common experience of man. Any such allusions that may occur in Scripture are, of course, purely incidental ; they are therefore in the whole extent of Scripture very infrequent. Barely enough exist to assure us that dreams were thought of by the Hebrews very much as they are by men of average good sense in our own day. Men then, too, were visited with pleasant dreams which they knew were too good to be true (Ps 126^1), and afflicted with nightmares which drove rest from their beds (Job 7^{14}). To them, too, dreams were the type of the evanescent and shadowy, whatever suddenly flies away and cannot be found (Job 20^8, Ps 73^{20}). The vanity and deceptiveness of dreams were proverbial (Ec 5^7, Is 29^8). The hungry man may dream that he eats, but his soul continues empty ; the thirsty man may dream that he drinks, but he remains faint (Is 29^8). Their roots were set in the multitude of cares, and their issue was emptiness (Ec $5^{3.\ 7}$). When the Son of Sirach ($34^{1.\ 2}$) represents them as but reflexions of our waking experiences, to regard which is to catch at a shadow and to follow after the wind, he has in no respect passed beyond the Biblical view. (Cf. Delitzsch, *Biblical Psychology*, p. 328 ; Orelli, art. 'Träume' in *PRE*[2]).

The interest of the Bible in dreams is absorbed by the rare instances in which they are made the vehicles of supernatural revelation. That they were occasionally so employed is everywhere recognized, and they therefore find a place in the several enumerations of the modes of revelation (Nu 12^6, Dt 13^{1-5}, 1 S $28^{6.\ 15}$, Jl 2^{28}, Ac 2^{17}, Jer $23^{3.\ 25}$ $23^{28.\ 32}$ 27^9 29^8, Zec 10^2 : Job 4^{13} 33^{15} stand somewhat apart). In this matter, too, the Son of Sirach retains the Biblical view, explicitly recognizing that dreams may be sent by the Most High in the very passage in which he reproves the folly of looking upon dreams in general as sources of knowledge (34^6). The superstitious attitude characteristic of the whole heathen world, which regards all dreams as omens, and seeks to utilize them for purposes of divination, receives no support whatever from the Biblical writers. Therefore in Israel there arose no 'houses of dreams,' there was no place for a guild of 'dream-examiners' or 'dream-critics.' When on rare occasions God did vouchsafe symbolical dreams to men, the professed dream-interpreters of the most highly trained castes stood helpless before them (Gn 37. 40. 41, Dn 2. 4). The interpretation of really God-sent dreams belonged solely to God Himself, the sender, and only His messengers could read their purport. There could be no more striking indication of the gulf that divides the Biblical and the ethnic views

of dreams. If there is a hint of an overestimate of dreams among some Israelites (Jer $23^{25f.}$ 27^9), this is mentioned only to be condemned, and is obviously a trait not native to Israel, but, like all the soothsaying in vogue among the ill-instructed of the land, borrowed from the surrounding heathenism (cf. Lehmann, *Aberglaube und Zauberei*, p. 56). If there are possible suggestions that there were methods by which prophetic dreams were sought (Jer 29^8, 1 S $28^{6.\ 15}$), these suggestions are obscure, and involve no commendation of such usages as prevailed among the heathen. All the supernatural dreams mentioned in the Bible were the unsought gift of Jehovah ; and there is not the slightest recommendation in the Scriptural narrative of any of the superstitious practices of either seeking or interpreting dreams which constitute the very nerve of ethnic dream-lore (cf. F. B. Jevons in Hastings' *DB* i. 622).

Very exaggerated language is often met with regarding the place which supernatural dreams occupy in Scripture. The writer of the article 'Songes' in Lichtenberger's *Encyc. des Sciences Relig.* (xi. 641), for example, opens a treatment of the subject dominated by this idea with the statement that, 'as everywhere in antiquity, dreams play a preponderant rôle in the religion of the Hebrews.' Even M. Bouché-Leclercq, who usually studies precision, remarks that 'the Scriptures are filled with apparitions and prophetic dreams' (*Histoire de la divination dans l'antiquité*, i. 278). Nothing could be more contrary to the fact. The truth is the supernatural dream is a very uncommon phenomenon in Scripture. Although, as we have seen, dreams are a recognized mode of Divine communication, and dream-revelations may be presumed therefore to have occurred throughout the whole history of revelation ; yet very few are actually recorded, and they oddly clustered at two or three critical points in the development of Israel. Of each of the two well-marked types of supernatural dreams (cf. Baur, *Symbolik und Mythologie*, II. i. 142)—those in which direct Divine revelations are communicated (Gn 15^{12} $20^{3.\ 6}$ 28^{12} $31^{10.\ 11}$, 1 K 3^5, Mt 1^{20} $2^{12.\ 13.\ 19.\ 22}$ 27^{19}) and symbolical dreams which receive Divine interpretations (Gn $37^{5.\ 6.\ 10}$ 40^{5-16} $41^{1.\ 5}$, Jg 7^{13-15}, Dn $2^{1.\ 3.\ 26}$ 4^5 7^1)—only some half-score of clear instances are given. All the symbolical dreams, it will be observed further, with the exception of the one recorded in Jg 7^{13-15} (and this may have been only a 'providential' dream), occur in the histories of Joseph and Daniel ; and all the dreams of direct Divine communication, with the exception of the one to Solomon (1 K 3^5), in the histories of Israel or of the nativity of Israel's Redeemer. In effect, the patriarchal stories of the Book of Genesis, the story of Daniel at the palace of the king, and the story of the birth of Jesus, are the sole depositions of supernatural dreams in Scripture ; the apparent exceptions (Jg 7^{13-15}, 1 K 3^5, Mt 27^{19}) may be reduced to the single one of 1 K 3^5.

The significance of the marked clustering of recorded supernatural dreams at just these historical points it is not easy to be perfectly sure of. Perhaps it is only a part of the general tendency of the supernatural manifestations recorded in Scripture to gather to the great historical crises ; throughout Scripture the creative epochs are the supernaturalistic epochs. Perhaps, on the other hand, it may be connected with the circumstance that at just these particular periods God's people were brought into particularly close relations with the outside world. We have but to think of Abraham and Abimelech, of Jacob and Laban, of Joseph and Pharaoh, of Daniel and Nebuchadnezzar, of Joseph and the Magi, to observe how near at hand the suggestion lies that the choice of dreams in these instances as the medium of revelation has some connexion with the relation in which the recipient stood at the moment to influences arising from the outer world, or at least to some special interaction between Israel and that world.

In entertaining such a conjecture we must beware, however, of imagining that there was something heathenish in the recognition of dreams as vehicles of revelation ; or even of unduly depreciating dreams among the vehicles of revelation. It has become quite usual to speak of dreams as the lowest of the media of revelation, with the general implication either that the revelations given through them cannot rise very high in the scale of revelations, or at least that the choice of dreams as their vehicle implies something inferior in the qualification of the recipients for receiving revelations. There is very little Scriptural support for such representations. No doubt, there is a certain gradation in dignity indicated in the methods of revelation. Moses' pre-eminence was marked by Jehovah speaking with him 'mouth to mouth,' manifestly, while to others He made Himself known 'in a vision,' or 'in a dream' (Nu 12⁶). And it is possible that the order in which the various methods of revelation are enumerated in such passages as Dt 13¹, 1 S 28⁶· ¹⁵, Jl 2²⁸, Ac 2¹⁷ may imply a gradation in which revelation through dreams may stand at the foot. But these very passages establish dreams among the media statedly used by God for the revelation of His will, and drop no word depreciatory of them ; nor is there discoverable in Scripture any justification for conceiving the revelations made through them as less valuable than those made through other media (cf. König, *Offenbarungsbegriff*, i. 55, ii. 9 f., 63 f.).

It is very misleading to say, for example (Barry in Smith's *DB* i. 617 ; cf. Orelli, *op. cit.*), that 'the greater number' of the recorded supernatural dreams 'were granted, for prediction or for warning, to those who were aliens to the Jewish covenant' ; and when they were given to God's 'chosen servants, they were almost always referred to the periods of their earliest and most imperfect knowledge of Him'; and, 'moreover, they belong especially to the earliest age, and became less frequent as the revelations of prophecy increase.' As many of these dreams were granted to Israelites as to aliens ; they do not mark any particular stage of religious development in their recipients ; they do not gradually decrease with the progress of revelation ; they no more characterize the patriarchal age than that of the exile or the opening of the new dispensation. If no example is recorded during the whole period from Solomon to Daniel ; so none is recorded from the patriarchs to Solomon, or again from Daniel to our Lord. If the great writing-prophets assign none of their revelations to dreams, they yet refer to revelations by dreams in such a way as to manifest their recognition of them as an ordinary medium of revelation (Jer 23²⁵· ²⁸· ³² 27⁹ 29⁸, Zec 10²). These passages are often adduced, to be sure, as suggesting that appeal especially to dreams was a characteristic of the false prophets of the day ; and it is even sometimes represented that Jeremiah means to brand dream-revelations as such as lying revelations. Jeremiah's polemic, however, is not directed against any one particular method of revelation, but against false claims to revelation by any method. His zeal burns no more hot against the prophet that 'hath a dream' than against him that 'hath the Lord's word' (23²⁸) ; no more against those that cry, 'I have dreamed, I have dreamed,' than against those who 'take their tongue and say, He saith' (23²⁵· ³¹). Nor does Zechariah's careful definition of his visions as received waking, though coming to him at night (1⁸ 4¹), involve a depreciation of revelations through dreams ; it merely calls our attention to the fact, otherwise copiously illustrated, that all night-visions are not dreams (cf. Gn 15¹² 26²⁴ 46², Nu 22²⁰, 1 Ch 17³, 2 Ch 7¹², Job 4¹³ 20⁸ 33¹⁵, Dn 2¹⁹, Ac 16⁹, 18⁹ 23¹¹ 27²⁴).

The citation in Ac 2¹⁷ of the prediction of Jl 2⁸ suffices to show that there rested no shadow upon the 'dreaming of dreams' in the estimation of the writers of the NT. Rather this was in their view one of the tokens of the Messianic glory. Nevertheless, as we have seen, none of them except Matthew records instances of the supernatural dream. In the Gospel of Matthew, however, no fewer than five or six instances occur. Some doubt may attach, to be sure, to the nature of the dream of Pilate's wife (27¹⁹). The mention of it was certainly not introduced by Matthew idly, or for its own sake ; it forms rather one of the incidents which he accumulates to exhibit the atrocity of the judicial murder of Jesus. Is his meaning that thus God Himself intervened to render Pilate utterly without excuse in his terrible crime (so Keil, *in loc.*)? Even so the question would still remain open whether the Divine intervention was direct and immediate, in the mode of a special revelation, or indirect and mediate, in the mode of a providential determination. In the latter

contingency, this dream would take its place in a large class, naturally mediated, but induced by God for the guidance of the affairs of men—another instance of which, we have already suggested, may be discovered in the dream of the Midianitish man mentioned in Jg 7¹³⁻¹⁵ (so Nösgen, *in loc.*). In this case, the five instances of the directly supernatural dream which Matthew records in his 'Gospel of the infancy' stand alone in the NT.

In any event, this remarkable series of direct Divine revelations through dreams (Mt 1²⁰ 2¹²· ¹³· ¹⁹· ²²) forms a notable feature of this section of Matthew's Gospel, and contributes its share to marking it off as a section apart. On this account, as on others, accordingly, this section is sometimes contrasted unfavourably with the corresponding section of the Gospel of Luke. In that, remarks, for example, Reuss (*La Bible*, NT, i. 138), the angel visitants address waking hearers, the inspiration of the Spirit of God renews veritable prophecy, 'it is a living world, conscious of itself, that appears before us'; in this, on the contrary, 'the form of communication from on high is the dream,—the form the least perfect, the least elevated, the least reassuring.' Others, less preoccupied with literary problems, fancy that it is the recipients of these dream-revelations rather than the author of the narrative to whom they are derogatory. Thus, for example, we are told that, like the Magi of the East and the wife of Pilate, Joseph 'was thought worthy of communion with the unseen world and of communications from God's messenger only when in an unconscious state,' seeing that he was not ripe for the manifestation of the angel to him, as to Zacharias and Mary, when awake (Nebe, *Kindheitsgeschichte*, 212, cf. 368). Of course, there is nothing of all this in the narrative, as there is nothing to justify it in any Scripture reference to the significance of revelation through dreams. The narrative is notable chiefly for its simple dignity and directness. In three of the instances we are merely told that 'an angel of the Lord appeared to Joseph,' and in the other two that he or the Magi were 'warned of God' in a dream, *i.e.* either by way of, or during, a dream. The term employed for 'appearing' (φαίνω) marks the phenomenal objectivity of the object : Joseph did not see in his dream-image something which he merely interpreted to stand for an angel, but an angel in his proper phenomenal presentation (see Grimm-Thayer, *s.v.* δοκέω, *ad fin.* ; Trench, *Syn. NT*, § lxxx. ; Schmidt, *Griech. Syn.* c. 15). The term translated 'warned of God' (χρηματίζω) imports simply an authoritative communication of a declaration of the Divine will (so, *e.g.*, Weiss, Keil, Alexander, Broadus, Nebe), and does not presuppose a precedent inquiry (as is assumed, *e.g.*, by Bengel, Meyer, Fritzsche). The narratives confine themselves, therefore, purely to declaring, in the simplest and most direct manner, that the dream-communications recorded were from the Lord. Any hesitancy we may experience in reading them is not suggested by them, but is imported from our own personal estimate of the fitness of dreams to serve as media of Divine communications.

It is probable that the mere appearance of dreams among the media of revelation recognized by Scripture constitutes more or less of a stumbling-block to most readers of the Bible. The disordered phantasmagoria of dreams seems to render them peculiarly unfit for such a use. The superstitious employment of them by all nations in the lower stages of culture, including not only the nations of classical antiquity, but also those ancient peoples with whom Israel stood in closest relations, suggests further hesitancy. We naturally question whether we are not to look upon their presence in the Scripture narrative just as we look upon them in the Gilgames epic or the annals of Assurbanipal, on the stêle of Bentrest or the inscriptions of Karnak, in the verses of Homer or the histories of Herodotus. We are not without temptation to say shortly with Kant (*Anthropologie*, i. § 29), 'We must not accept dream-tales as revelations from the invisible world.' And we are pretty sure, if we begin, with Witsius, with a faithful recognition of the fact that 'God has seen fit to reveal Himself not only to the waking, but sometimes also to the sleeping,' to lapse, like him, at once into an apologetical vein, and to raise the question seriously, 'Why should God wish to manifest Himself in this singular way, by night, and to the sleeping, when the manifestation must appear obscure, uncertain, and little suited either to the dignity of the matters revealed or to the use of those to whom the revelation is made?' (*de Prophetis et Prophetia*, ch. v. in *Miscell. Sacra*, i. pp. 22–27; cf. also Spanheim, *Dubia Evangelica*, 2nd pt., Geneva, 1700, pp. 239–240, and Rivetus, *in Gen. Exercit.* cxxiv.).

We have already pointed out how little there is in common between the occasional employment of dreams for revelations, such as meets us in Scripture, and the superstitious view of dreams prevalent among the ancients. It is an under-statement when it is remarked that 'the Scriptures start from a spiritual height to which the religious consciousness of the heathen world attained only after a long course of evolution, and then only in the case of an isolated genius like Plato' (Jevons, *loc. cit.* 622). The difference is not a matter of degree, but of kind. No special sacredness or significance is ascribed by the Scriptures to dreams in general. No class or variety of dreams is recommended by them to our scrutiny that we may through this or that method of interpretation seek guidance from them for our life. The Scriptures merely affirm that God has on certain specific occasions, in making known His will to men, chosen to approach them through the medium of their night-visions; and has through these warned them of danger, awakened them to a sense of wrong-doing, communicated to them His will, or made known His purposes. The question that is raised by the affirmation of such an occasional Divine employment of dreams is obviously not whether dreams as such possess a supernatural quality and bear a supernatural message if only we could get at it, but rather whether there is anything inherent in their very nature which renders it impossible that God should have made such occasional use of them, or derogatory to Him to suppose that He has done so.

Surely we should bear in mind, in any consideration of such a question, the infinite condescension involved in God's speaking to man through any medium of communication. There is a sense in which it is derogatory to God to suppose Him to hold any commerce with man at all, particularly with sinful man. If we realized, as we should, the distance which separates the infinite and infinitely holy God from sin-stricken humanity, we should be little inclined to raise questions with respect to the relative condescension involved in His approaching us in these or those particular circumstances. In any revelation which God makes to man He stoops infinitely—and there are no degrees in the infinite. God's thoughts are not as our thoughts, and the clothing of His messages in the forms of human conception and language involves an infinite derogation. Looked at *sub specie æternitatis*, the difference between God's approaching man through the medium of a dream or through the medium of his waking apprehension, shrinks into practical nothingness. The cry of the heart which has really seen or heard God must in any

case be, 'What is man, that thou art mindful of him? or the son of man, that thou visitest him?'

It should also be kept clearly in view that the subject of dreams, too, is, after all, the human spirit. It is the same soul that is active in the waking consciousness which is active also in the dream-consciousness,—the same soul acting according to the same laws (cf. Lehmann, *op. cit.* p. 397). No doubt there are some dreams which we should find difficulty in believing were direct inspirations of God. Are there not some waking thoughts also of which the same may be said? This does not in the least suggest that the Divine Spirit may not on suitable occasion enter into the dream-consciousness, as into the waking, and impress upon it, with that force of conviction which He alone knows how to produce, the assurance of His presence and the terms of His message.

'The psychology of dreams and visions,' writes Dr. G. T. Ladd, 'so far as we can speak of such a psychology, furnishes us with neither sufficient motive nor sufficient means for denying the truth of the Biblical narratives. On the contrary, there are certain grounds for confirming the truth of some of these narratives. . . . Even in ordinary dreams, the dreamer is still the human soul. The soul acts, then, even in dreaming, as a unity, which involves within itself the functions and activities of the higher, even of the ethical and religious powers. . . . The possibility of even the highest forms of ethical and religious activities in dreams cannot be denied. . . . There is nothing in the physiological or psychical conditions of dream-life to prevent such psychical activity for the reception of revealed truth. . . . It remains in general true that the Bible does not transgress the safe limits of possible or even actual experience' (*The Doctr. of Sacred Scripture*, ii. 436).

So little, indeed, do emptiness and disorder enter into the very essence of dreaming, that common experience supplies innumerable examples of dreams thoroughly coherent and consequent. The literature of the subject is filled with instances in which even a heightened activity of human faculty is exhibited in dreams, and that throughout every department of mental endowment. Jurists have in their dreams prepared briefs of which they have been only too glad to avail themselves in their waking hours; statesmen have in their dreams obtained their best insight into policy; lecturers have elaborated their discourses; mathematicians solved their most puzzling problems; authors composed their most admired productions; artists worked out their most inspired motives. Dr. Franklin told Cabanis that the bearings and issues of political events which had baffled his inquisition when awake were not infrequently unfolded to him in his dreams. It was in a dream that Reinhold worked out his table of categories. Condorcet informs us that he often completed his imperfect calculations in his dreams; and the same experience has been shared by many other mathematicians, as, for example, by Maignan, Göns, Wähnert. Condillac, when engaged upon his *Cours d'Études*, repeatedly developed and finished in his dreams a subject which he had broken off on retiring to rest. The story of the origin of Coleridge's *Kubla Khan* in a dream is well known. Possibly no more instructive instance is on record, however, than the account given by Robert Louis Stevenson, in his delightful *Chapter on Dreams* ('Thistle' ed. of *Works*, xv. 250 ff.), of how 'the little people' of his brain, who had been wont to amuse him with absurd farragos, harnessed themselves to their task and dreamed for him consecutively and artistically when he became a craftsman in the art of story-telling. Now, they trimmed and pared their dream-stories, and set them on all fours, and made them run from a beginning to an end, and fitted them to the laws of life, and even filled them with dramatic situations of guileful art, making the conduct of the actors psychologically correct, and aptly graduating the emotion up to the climax. (See Abercrombie, *Inquiries Concerning the Intellectual Powers*, etc., part iii. § iv., esp. **pp.**

216–221 ; Carpenter, *Principles of Mental Physiology*, p. 524 f. ; Lehmann as cited, p. 411 ; Volkelt, *Die Traumphantasie*, No. 15 ; Myers, *Human Personality*, etc., Nos. 417 f., 430, with corresponding Appendixes).

Instances of this heightened mental action in dreams are so numerous and so striking in fact, that they have given rise to an hypothesis which provokes Wundt's scoff at those 'who are inclined to think that when we dream the mind has burst the fetters of the body, and that dream fancies transcend the activity of the waking consciousness, with its narrow confinement to the limitations of space and time' (*Vorlesungen über die Menschen- und Thierseele*, Lect. xxii. pp. 366–370, Eng. tr. pp. 323–324). The well-known essay of Lange 'On the Double Consciousness, especially on the Night-Consciousness and its polar relation to the Day-Consciousness of Man,' printed in the *Deutsche Zeitschrift für christliche Wissenschaft und christliches Leben* for 1851 (Nos. 30, 31, and 32), still provides one of the most readable and instructive statements of this theory. But English readers will be apt to turn for it first of all to the voluminous discussions of the late Mr. Frederic W. H. Myers, *Human Personality and its Survival of Bodily Death* (London, 1903), where it is given a new statement on a fresh and more empirical basis. In Mr. Myers' view, the sleeping state is more plastic than the waking, exhibiting some trace 'of the soul's less exclusive absorption in the activity of the organism,' by which is possibly increased 'the soul's power of operating in that spiritual world to which sleep has drawn it nearer' (vol. i. pp. 151–152 ; cf. p. 135). Accordingly, 'these subliminal uprushes' which we call dreams, these 'bubbles breaking on the surface from the deep below,' may be counted upon to bring us messages, now and again, from a spiritual environment to which our waking consciousness is closed. On hypotheses like these it is often argued that the sleeping state is the most favourable for the reception of spiritual communications. It is not necessary to commit ourselves to such speculations. But their existence among investigators who have given close study to the phenomena of dreams, strongly suggests to us that those phenomena, in the mass, are not such as to exclude the possibility or the propriety of the occasional employment by the Divine Spirit of dreams as vehicles of revelation.

That powerful influences should occasionally arise out of dreams, affecting the conduct and the destiny of men, is only natural, and is illustrated by numerous examples. Literature is crowded with instances of the effect of dreams upon life, for good and evil ; and the personal experience of each of us will add additional ones. There is no one of us who has not been conscious of the influence of night visions in deterring him from evil and leading him to good. The annals of religion are sown with instances in which the careers of men have been swayed and their outlook for time and eternity altered by a dream. We may recall the dream of Evagrius of Pontus, recorded by Socrates, for example, by which he was nerved to resist temptation, and his whole life determined. Or we may recall the dream of Patrick, given in his *Confession*, on which hung his whole work as apostle of the Irish. Or we may recall the dream of Elizabeth Fry, by which she was rescued from the indecision and doubt into which she fell after her conversion. The part played by dreams in the conversion of John Bunyan, John Newton, James Gardiner, Alexander Duff, are but well-known instances of a phenomenon illustrated copiously from every age of the Church's experience. 'Converting dreams' are indeed a recognized variety

(cf. Myers as cited, No. 409, i. pp. 126, 127), and are in nowise stranger than many of their fellows. They are the natural result of the action of the stirred conscience obtruding itself into the visions of the night, and, as psychological phenomena, are of precisely the same order as the completion of mathematical problems in dreams, or the familiar experience of the invasion of our dreams by our waking anxieties. In the providence of God, however, they have been used as instruments of Divine grace, and levers by which not only individual destiny has been determined, but the very world has been moved. (Cf. Delitzsch, as cited, and 'Dreams and the Moral Life,' in the *Homiletic Review*, Sept. 1890).

With such dreams and the issues which have flowed from them in mind, we surely can find no difficulty in recognizing the possibility and propriety of occasional Divine employment of dreams for the highest of ends. Obviously dreams have not been deemed by Providence too empty and bizarre to be used as instruments of the most far-reaching effects. Indeed, we must extend the control of Divine Providence to the whole world of dreams. Of course, no dream visits us in our sleep, any more than any occurrence takes place during our waking hours, apart from the appointment and direction of Him who Himself never either slumbers or sleeps, and in whose hands all things work together for the execution of His ends. We may, now and again, be able to trace with especial clearness the hand of the great Potter, moulding the vessel to its destined uses, in, say, an unusual dream, producing a profoundly arresting effect upon the consciousness. But in all the dreams that visit us, we must believe the guidance of the universal Governor to be present, working out His will. It will hardly be possible, however, to recognize this providential guidance of dreams, and especially the Divine employment of particularly moving dreams in the mode of what we commonly call 'special providences,' without removing all legitimate ground for hesitation in thinking of His employment of special dreams also as media of revelation. The God of providence and the God of revelation are one God ; and His providential and revelational actions flow together into one harmonious effect. It is not possible to believe that the instrumentalities employed by Him freely in the one sphere of His operation can be unworthy of use by Him in the other. Those whom He has brought by His providential dealings with them into such a state of mind that they are prepared to meet with Him in the night watches, and to receive on the prepared surface of their souls the impressions which He designs to convey to them, He surely may visit according to His will, not merely by the immediate operation of His grace, but also in revealing visions, whether these visions themselves are wrought through the media of their own experiences or by His own creative energy. It is difficult to perceive in what the one mode of action would be more unfitting than the other.

LITERATURE.—Some of the special literature has been suggested in the course of the article. A good general account of dreams in their relations to the supernatural may be found in Alf. Lehmann's *Aberglaube und Zauberei*, Ger. tr., Stuttgart, 1898, p. 389 f. At the foot of p. 548 is given an excellently selected list of books on the general subject. On the history of the estimate of dreams in the nations into contact with which the Biblical writers came, see Lehmann ('Index'), and also the following : Ebers, *Aegypten und die Bücher Mose's*, 321 ; Lenormant, *La divination et la science de présages chez les Chaldéens*, 126–149 ; Bouché-Leclercq, *Histoire de la divination dans l'antiquité*, i. 276–329 ; Vaschide and Piéron, 'Prophetic Dreams in Greek and Roman Antiquity' in *The Monist* for Jan. 1901, IX., ii. 161–194 ; Audenried's ed. of Nägelsbach's *Homerische Theologie*, §§ 25–29, pp. 172–176 ; Aust, *Die Relig. der Römer*, 79, 108, 139, 160 ; Granger, *The Worship of the Romans*, 28–52. For dreams among the later Jews, see Hamburger's *RE* i. 996–998 ; *Jewish Encyc.* iv. 655–657 ; and cf. Philo. *de Somniis*. For Patristic views : Tertullian's *On the*

Soul, cc. 42–50; Synesius' *On Dreams*; and the interesting correspondence between Evodius and Augustine (*Aug. Epp.* 158, 159) may be profitably read. For the anthropological view see Tylor's *Primitive Culture* ('Index').

BENJAMIN B. WARFIELD.

DRESS.—

The words used in the original for articles of dress have lost much of their force through great variation in translation in the AV. For clothes in general ἔνδυμα occurs; it is tr. 'clothing,' Mt 7[15]; 'raiment,' Mt 34 6[25. 28 28]3, Lk 12[23]; 'garment,' Mt 22[11. 12]. ἱμάτιον signifies an outer garment, a mantle or cloak; it is tr. 'garment,' Mt 9[16. 20. 21] 14[36] 21[8] 23[5] 27[35], Mk 22[1] 5[27] 6[56] 10[50] 11[7. 8] 13[16] 15[24], Lk 5[36] 8[44] 19[35] 22[36], Jn 13[4. 12] 19[23]; 'cloak,' Mt 5[40], Lk 6[29]; 'clothes,' Lk 8[27] (sing. in Greek); (plural) 'clothes,' Mt 21[7] 24[18] 26[65], Mk 5[28. 30] 15[20], Lk 19[36]; 'raiment,' Mt 11[8] 17[2] 27[31], Mk 9[3], Lk 7[25] 23[34], Jn 19[24]. The scarlet or purple robe of Jesus is called ἱμάτιον in Jn 19[2], χλαμύς in Mt 27[28. 31], ἐσθής in Lk 23[11], and in Mk 15[17. 20] simply 'the purple,' τὴν πορφύραν (cf. Lk 16[19]). ἱματισμός is tr. 'raiment,' Lk 9[29]; 'vesture,' Mt 27[35], Jn 19[24]—in both passages it stands in antithesis to ἱμάτιον—and 'apparel' (ἐν ἱματισμῷ ἐνδόξῳ), Lk 7[25]. στολή—the Lat. *stola*—is used for the long garments of the scribes, tr. 'long clothing' Mk 12[38], 'long robes' Lk 20[46]; for the 'best robe' of the Prodigal Son, Lk 15[22]; for the 'long garment' of the Resurrection angel, Mk 16[5]—in the parallel passage ἐσθησις, 'garment' is used, Lk 24[4]. χιτών signified an under-garment, and is tr. in EV 'coat' in Mt 5[40] 10[10], Mk 6[9], Lk 3[11] 6[29] 9[3], Jn 19[23]. The plural is in Mk 14[63] tr. 'clothes,' though in the parallel passage Mt 26[65] ἱμάτια is used. Closely connected with clothes we have λέντιον, the towel with which Christ girded Himself, Jn 13[4. 5]; σουδάριον, 'napkin,' of Lk 19[20], Jn 11[44] 20[7]; ὀθόνιον, 'linen cloth,' of Lk 24[12], Jn 19[40] 20[5. 6. 7]; σινδών, 'linen cloth,' of Mt 27[59], Mk 14[51. 52]; and βύσσος, 'fine linen,' Lk 16[19]; ὑπόδημα, 'shoe,' Mt 3[11] 10[10], Mk 17, Lk 3[16] 10[4] 15[22] 22[35], Jn 1[27]; σανδάλιον, 'sandals,' Mk 6[9]; ζώνη, 'girdle,' Mt 3[4], Mk 1[6], 'purse,' Mt 10[9], Mk 6[8]; πήρα, 'scrip,' Mt 10[10], Mk 6[8], Lk 9[3] 10[4] 22[35. 36].

All the references to clothes in the Gospels are to male costume. There are very few indications of the materials of which they were made or of their shape. John the Baptist had his raiment (ἔνδυμα) of camel's hair, and a girdle of leather about his loins (Mt 3[4] ‖)—like many a roughly clad man in Palestine to-day. The rich man of the parable was clothed in 'purple and fine linen' (βύσσος), Lk 16[19]. The three body-garments commonly mentioned are the cloak (ἱμάτιον),—a word used also in the plural for 'garments' in general,—the 'coat' (χιτών), and the girdle (ζώνη). The head-dress is never definitely mentioned, but we know that it was practically universal to cover the head.

These references indicate that the clothes worn by Christ, His disciples, and the great majority of His adherents, were of the simplest kind; but among the richer classes there are indications, as is seen in the references given above, of more sumptuous robes. Indeed, among the better class of townsfolk it is probable that Jewish costume was largely modified under Hellenic and Roman influence. In dealing with the former more important subject, the probable costume of the founders of Christianity, the most hopeful sources of information are (1) the costumes of Jews, and (2) the dresses worn to-day among people of simple life in modern Palestine.

1. The dress of orthodox Jews is as various as their language and lands of residence. Neither in the head-dress, nor in the long Sabbath robes of the Rabbis, nor in the ordinary under-garments, are there any uniform features. There are, however, two special garments which are worn by orthodox Jews the world over; these are the *tallīth* and the *arba' kanphôth*. The *tallīth*, or praying shawl, is a rectangular woollen shawl about 3 feet by 5,* usually white, with dark stripes across two of the sides. From each corner hangs a tassel or fringe; these are known as the *zizith*. Each consists of eight threads twisted together in five knots (see BORDER). The *tallīth* is always worn in the synagogue and at prayer time: it then covers the head and shoulders. Jews who affect special sanctity—especially those living in the Holy Land —often wear it all day, as was once the common custom. In the Middle Ages, in consequence of

* Much larger *tallīths* are also worn, reaching at times even to the ankles. See art. 'Tallith' in *Jewish Encyc.* vol. xi.

the persecution which the Jews then underwent on account of their religious customs, the habit of wearing the *tallīth* in public had to be given up; but as the Jews view the wearing of the fringes as a religious duty (Dt 22[12], Nu 15[38]), they made a special under-garment to carry them. This consists of a rectangular piece of woollen or even cotton material, about 3 feet long by a foot wide; it has a large hole in the centre through which the head is put, so that the garment comes to lie over the chest and back like a kind of double chest-protector. At the four corners are the *zizith*, and the garment is known as the 'four corners,' *arba' kanphôth*, or sometimes as the *tallīth katon*, or small *tallīth*. It is worn by small children, but the *tallīth* proper only by a boy after he has become *bar mizvah*, a 'son of the Law,' at thirteen. As the earliest mention of the *arba' kanphôth* is in 1350, it is manifest that it cannot have existed in NT times. With the *tallīth*, however, the case is different. It is certain that this is the altered form of an outer garment which existed in early times, and was known in Heb. as the *simlah* and in Gr. as *himation*. In the 'hem' or 'border' (κράσπεδον, Mt 9[20] 14[36], Mk 6[56], Lk 8[44]) we have reference to the fringed border of the cloak; and even more definite is the reference in Mt 23[5], when the scribes and Pharisees are reproved for unduly lengthening the fringes (τὰ κράσπεδα) of their garments.

2. The clothes of the ordinary *fellah*, or peasant in modern Palestine, are five in number,—shirt, cloak, girdle, shoes, and head-dress.

The **shirt** or *kamîs* is a simple straight garment, extending from the neck almost to the feet, with short, or sometimes long, loose, sleeves. It is usually of calico; it may be of linen. Among the *fellahîn* it is white, among the Bedawîn (who often go about in nothing else) it is dyed blue. It is usually open in front more than half-way to the waist, but is brought together at the neck by a button or knotted thread. It is worn night and day.

Over the shirt is fixed the *zunnâr* or **girdle**, a most necessary article of clothing. It may be of leather, with buckles, or woven of camel's hair, or of brightly-dyed silk or cotton. The woven belt is wound tightly two or three times round the waist, and is fixed by tucking the free end into the belt itself. In the girdle is carried, as in NT days (Mt 10[9], Mk 6[8]), the money, often knotted into a corner of a handkerchief, and also the pen and ink of the learned or the dagger of the fighter. When the man is 'girded' for work the *kamîs* is hitched up to the tightened belt, as high as the knees. The upper part of the shirt is commonly drawn up loose above the girdle, so that a considerable space is left between the chest and the shirt. This is known as the *u'bb* or 'bosom,' and in this are carried many things; for example, the bread and olives for the midday meal, the seed or corn for sowing (Lk 6[38]), or, in the case of a shepherd, a newborn lamb or kid (cf. Is 40[11]).

In order of importance next comes the **head-dress**, of which two distinct types are in daily use—the turban and the *kufîyeh*. Under both of these is worn the *tekkiyeh* or *'arakiyeh*, a small plain close-fitting cap of felt, wool, or even cotton; this is commonly not removed even at night. When one has worn thin, a new one is placed on the top, so that two or three layers are quite usual; and between the layers the *fellah* keeps small papers of value. When a turban is worn, the red fez or *tarbush* is placed over the skull-cap, and the *leffeh* or turban is wound round its sides. The *leffeh* among the *fellahîn* is usually of parti-coloured cotton or silk, red and white or yellow being common. In the towns it is often ornamented with yellow silk worked in patterns; while the *haj* who has made the Mecca pilgrimage, and the Druse, wear plain white; and the *sherîf* or 'descendant of the prophet' wears green. The other form of head-dress is more ancient and the more primitive: probably it is more like the peasant dress of NT times. It consists of a *kufîyeh* or large napkin of white or coloured cotton or silk, as much perhaps as a yard square, folded diagonally to make a triangular piece, and laid on the head with the apex backward; and the *'akâl*, a rope-like circle of camel's hair, laid double over the top of the head to keep the *kufîyeh* in position. The free ends of the *kufîyeh* are wound round the neck according to taste, being used on journeys in the hot sun to cover, at times, all the face below the eyes. It is a most efficient and practical head-dress, especially when worn over a felt *tekkîyeh*. The **napkin** referred to in Lk 19²⁰ may have been of the same nature, and the napkins of Jn 11⁴⁴ 20⁷, though used to cover the face of the dead, may have been made for the head of the living.

These three garments are the essentials; in such will a man work all day, and, if very poor, even go journeys; but in the latter event he would be an object of pity unless he had an *'abâ* or **cloak**. This is made of camel's or goat's hair or of wool, and among the *fellahîn* is usually of white and brown in stripes or of plain brown. The superior qualities are often white or black. The ordinary *'abâ* is made of a long rectangular piece of material, with the sides folded in and sewn along the top; it is thus very square, when new, across the shoulders. It has no sleeves, and though there are slits just below the upper corners through which the arms may be put, it is almost always worn resting over the shoulders and upper arms. It extends half-way between the knees and the feet. During sleep, especially on journeys when the traveller has no bed, it is made to cover the whole person, the man either wrapping it round him, or, if there is a sack or mat on which to lie, curling himself under it as under a blanket.

Shoes are to-day almost universally worn; but a *fellah* with a new pair of shoes will often, when outside the town, prefer to save his shoes from wear and tear by carrying them. **Sandals** are still worn, but not commonly as formerly, when the sandal seemed to make the simplest foot-gear (Mk 6⁹).

The costume of the Palestine peasant, above described, was probably, with no doubt differences in materials and in cut, the costume of the country folk of NT and pre-NT times. The *kamîs* is the equivalent of the χιτών, and that was the *këthôneth* of the OT. Now, as then, it is at times woven in one piece without seam (Jn 19²³). The *'abâ* is the modern equivalent of the ἱμάτιον, the *simlah* of the OT. It was the outer cloak which might not be retained as a pledge after sunset (Ex 22²⁶). It is quite possible that in Mt 5⁴⁰ there is a reference to this. The Rabbis stated that the reason the cloak might not be removed was because the *zîzîth* with their blue and white threads were a reminder of the Law. Christ teaches here that when a man does an injury, within legal limits, as in taking the shirt, His follower must be prepared to go a step farther, and give up even what the Law protects him in keeping. The reversal of the order in Lk., though more intelligible to Gentiles, misses the special reference to the Jewish Law. Like the modern *'abâ*, the *himation* was cast aside for quick movement (Mk 10⁵⁰, Jn 13⁴·¹²), left aside when working in the fields (Mk 13¹⁶); and being dispensed with in fighting, might profitably be exchanged for a sword when danger was near (Lk 22³⁶). It might be spread on the ground to form a carpet for an honoured person (Mt 21⁸), and might

be used in lieu of a saddle, folded across an ass's back (Mk 11⁷·⁸). In every one of these details the use of the modern *'abâ* in Palestine could furnish parallels.

With respect to the χιτών in two separate references (Mt 10¹⁰ etc. and Lk 3¹¹), two 'coats,' *i.e.* shirts, are spoken of rather as luxuries than necessities for the traveller—as is to-day the case with the *kamîs*. Two 'cloaks' would be such unlikely baggage as not to need mentioning.

The girdle or *zunnâr* is the equivalent of the ζώνη, as is specially shown in its use as a purse. There is, however, another girding referred to in some passages. John the Baptist's girdle may quite probably have been a broad 'loin cloth' extending from waist to knee,—a very ancient dress, —while over the shoulders hung a rough coarse-haired *'abâ*. It is not unreasonable to suppose that, like the modern *dervîsh*, he wore his long hair uncovered. It is evident that his costume was intentionally distinctive. When Peter was found by the risen Master engaged in his old business of fishing, he, like the modern Galilæan fishermen when fishing near shore, was probably girded only with a loin-cloth, and therefore described as 'naked' (Jn 21⁷). Christ girded Himself with a towel before washing the disciples' feet, to make Himself in outward form more like a slave (Jn 13⁴·⁵). It is evident that in the crucifixion, at least of Jews, who would not have tolerated absolute nudity, the victim, after the removal of his clothes, was girded round the waist; Peter must have understood the words 'another shall gird thee' as foretelling that event (Jn 21¹⁸).

The long garments of the scribes and Pharisees find their modern counterparts in the long cloak used by Moslem religious leaders, the *jibbeh*, and in the velvet, plush, and silk robes of gorgeous colours favoured by the leading Rabbis of the Ashkenazim Jews, on Sabbath and feast-days. In city life, garments additional to those described above are always worn. Over the *kamîs*, but included within the girdle, is a striped coloured robe reaching to near the feet, called the *kumbaz*, and, among the better dressed, over this is worn the *sudrîyeh* or ornamental waistcoat. *Lebâs* or drawers, though utterly despised by the true Arab, are in common use in towns. Many other varieties of garments might be mentioned. Those already named and doubtless others all had their counterparts in NT times, but there is no hint that any but the simplest forms of peasant dress were worn by Christ and His disciples. It has indeed been thought that the garments divided by the soldiers must necessarily have been five, of which four, the cloak (ἱμάτιον), the shoes or sandals, the girdle and the head-dress, were 'divided among them,' and the fifth, the χιτών or shirt of finer quality, woven perhaps by the hands of His mother herself, apportioned by lot.

The στολή was evidently considered among the circle of Jesus a robe of dignity; it is the 'best robe' brought forth for the returning prodigal; it is used to describe the clothing of the 'young man' at the tomb (Mk 16⁵), and the imposing garments of the scribes (Lk 20⁴⁶ etc.).

The unsatisfactoriness of patching with new cloth a much worn garment (Mt 9¹⁶, Mk 2²¹), and the ubiquitousness of that scourge, the clothes-moth (Mt 6¹⁹·²⁰, Lk 12³³), are daily to be seen illustrated in Palestine. The custom of providing guests with clean 'wedding garments' is still known, though unusual, in the modern East. But the entertainment of the very poor by the well-to-do at such feasts, evidently then far from uncommon, must have made such a precaution absolutely necessary. In the account of the 'rich man' (Lk 16¹⁹), we have reference to two of the expensive materials for dress—the purple dye obtained from the *murex* on the coasts of Tyre, and the βύσσος, or 'fine linen,' which was imported at great expense from Egypt.

Reference is made at the beginning to the various terms used to describe the robe put on Christ by the mocking soldiers. Of these the χλαμύς, or military mantle, fastened by a buckle on the right shoulder so as to hang in a curve across the body, would appear to have been the most distinctive and suitable for the purpose.

LITERATURE.—Tristram, *Eastern Customs in Bible Lands*; Edersheim, *Life and Times of Jesus the Messiah*; art. 'Dress and Personal Adornment in Modern Palestine,' by Masterman in *Biblical World*, 1902; Nowack's and Benzinger's *Heb. Arch.*; artt. 'Dress' or 'Costume' in Hastings' *DB* (by Mackie), in the *Encyc. Bibl.* (by Abrahams and Cook), and in the *Jewish Encyc.* (by Nöldeke).   E. W. G. MASTERMAN.

DRINK, DRINKING.—See EATING AND DRINKING, FOOD, LORD'S SUPPER, MEALS, WINE.

DROPSY. — As the name (Gr. ὕδρωψ)* would seem to imply, this disease is characterized by an accretion or accumulation of water in the cellular tissue or serous cavities. In the only place in the NT where a reference to it occurs, no mention is made as to whether the patient suffered from a general *anasarca* or a local dropsical swelling (Lk 14[2]). The writer simply uses the adjective ὑδρωπικός (*sc.* ἄνθρωπος) instead of the noun. This is, however, in strict accordance with the usage of Greek medical writers, as we have it in the works of Hippocrates, Dioscorides, and Galen. That the disease was not unknown to the authors of some of the OT writings appears from the description of the trial by ordeal of a wife suspected of infidelity to her husband (Nu 5[11-31]). In vv.[21. 22] part of the punishment inflicted on the guilty woman was a dropsical swelling (cf. Jos. *Ant.* III. xi. 6), which looks as if dropsy used to be considered as an affliction sent by God upon the wicked for continued wilful sin (cf. Ps 109[18], and see also the Mishnic tractate *Shabbath* xxxiii. 1), and especially for the sin of self-indulgence (cf. Horace, *Carm.* II. ii. 13, 'crescit indulgens sibi dirus hydrops').

The healing of the dropsical man is introduced by St. Luke as part of a narrative which is peculiar to his Gospel, if, indeed, the parable in Lk 14[16-24] be not identical with that in Mt 22[2-14]—a conjecture which does not seem likely (see, however, Wright's *Synopsis of the Gospels in Greek*, p. 273 f.).

St. Luke alone of the Evangelists tells of Jesus being invited to partake of the hospitality of the Pharisees and of His accepting their invitations on three different occasions : 'to eat' (7[36]), 'to breakfast' (11[37]), 'to eat bread' (14[1]). It was on one of these occasions, as He was sitting probably at breakfast or the midday meal (ἄριστον, v.[12]) on the Sabbath, that He healed the dropsical man.

Like the story of the healing of the woman with the crooked spine, told in the preceding section, it furnishes a vivid illustration of the way in which the protracted controversy about the Sabbath rest was conducted by Jesus against the Pharisaic sabbatarians of His time (cf. Mk 2[23-3[5]], Mt 12[1-13], Lk 6[1-11] 13[10-17], Jn 5[9-18]). It is not easy to determine whether the diseased man was specially introduced into the house for a malignant purpose, or whether he appeared there unbidden in order to claim the sympathy and the help of Jesus. The presence of ἰδού seems to imply that the latter was the case, and that the host was as much surprised as any one else at the turn of events. In any case he could not have been an invited *guest*, as Jesus could not in that event, with courtesy, have dismissed him when healed, as St. Luke says He did (ἀπέλυσεν, v.[4]). Whatever was the im-

* Not found in NT, only the adj. ὑδρωτικός occurring in Lk 14[2].

mediate cause of the man's presence, Jesus utilized the opportunity thus afforded to emphasize once again His teaching on the Sabbath question. Here was a man afflicted with a most inveterate and dangerous malady, indicative of deeply rooted organic disease, and, according to contemporary belief, springing from moral as well as from physical sources. It was, moreover, a disease well known to those present ; and it seems to have been more or less prevalent in that region down to recent times (see *Jewish Intelligence*, 1842, p. 319).

The persistent character of the espionage to which Jesus was subjected is well expressed by the periphrastic imperfect of παρατηρείσθαι (v.[1]), a verb which is almost confined, in NT usage, to St. Luke (cf. Lk 6[7] 20[20], Ac 9[24] ; see also Mk 3[2] and Gal 4[10]).

The question addressed by Jesus on this occasion to 'the lawyers and Pharisees' aptly illustrates His method of 'carrying the war into the enemy's camp' (cf. 13[15], Mt 12[11f.], and Lk 7[41f.]). The effect of the question, which placed them on the horns of an ugly dilemma, is vividly narrated. They were forced to be silent because they were completely nonplussed (οἱ δὲ ἡσύχασαν, v.[3]). This verb, which occurs in the NT only once outside of St. Luke's writings (see 1 Th 4[11]), is often used in the sense of a silence produced by superior or determined argument (cf. Ac 11[18] 21[14] ; see also Neh 5[8] LXX). The nature of the difficulty, in which Jesus placed His enemies, will be understood if we remember the almost incredible minuteness with which the law of the Sabbath was treated by the Jewish Rabbins, and the childish way in which they regulated whether a physician should perform a deed of mercy on that day (see Schürer, *HJP* II. ii. pp. 96–105 ; Edersheim, *Life and Times of Jesus the Messiah*, App. XVII., and ii. pp. 59–61 ; Farrar, *Life of Christ*, vol. i. pp. 431–441).

Whatever might be the differences between the schools of Shammai and Hillel as to the class of works forbidden on the Sabbath day, the general practice of the Jews themselves was based on the recognition that danger to life superseded the Sabbath law, and the question of Jesus points out this with force. If they allowed a man to save his son or his ox from a position of imminent danger, and yet considered the Sabbath rest unbroken, how much stronger claim had a man, suffering from an incurable malady, upon Him whose power to heal had again and again been manifested ?

It is possible, perhaps, to trace an element of scorn in Jesus' attitude on this occasion. The conjunction of the words υἱός and βοῦς is at least remarkable, and points to vehemence on His part in pressing the argument. The very feast at which He sat as guest was a proof of insincerity in their attitude. How prevalent the abuse of Sabbath feasting became amongst the Jews is noticed by St. Augustine (*Enarr. in Ps* 91[1] : 'Hodiernus dies sabbati est ; hunc in præsenti tempore otio quodam corporaliter languido et fluxo et luxurioso celebrant Judæi').

St. Luke does not tell us plainly whether Jesus used any visible means in performing the cure of the dropsical man. He, however, uses one word which may point to a treatment similar to what He employed on other occasions (cf. ἐπιτιθέναι τὰς χεῖρας, 4[40] 13[13], Mk 5[23] etc., and ἅπτεσθαι, 5[13] 22[51], Mk 1[41], Mt 20[34] etc.). It is, of course, possible that ἐπιλαβόμενος (v.[4]) may have been used by the writer of the narrative to correspond with the word ἀνασπάσει (v.[5]), in order to emphasize the force of Jesus' argument, and that Jesus, in actually laying hold of the dropsical patient, intended to convey objectively the lesson which each one of them ought to have learned from the toil involved in pulling a drowning animal out of a well.

The reference to the 'well' (εἰς φρέαρ, cf. εἰς βόθυνον, Mt 12[11]) is particularly appropriate when the nature of the disease is remembered, and shows how wonderfully every incident was used by Jesus to illustrate the lesson He meant to teach. A very similar instance is observed when He compared the woman with the diseased spine to the animal which, tied to his stall, required to be loosed therefrom even on the Sabbath day for his daily watering (Lk 13¹⁵; 'congruenter hydropicum animali quod cecidit in puteum comparavit; humore enim laborabat,' Augustine, *Quæst. Evang.* ii. 29).

Literature.—Plummer, 'St. Luke' in *Internat. Crit. Com. in loc.*; Hastings' *DB* iii. p. 328; Trench and Taylor on *Miracles*; *Encyc. Brit.* art. 'Dropsy.'   J. R. WILLIS.

DROWNING.—Drowning never was or could be a recognized form of capital punishment in so poorly watered a country as Palestine, as it was in Assyria and Babylonia. It is mentioned in Mt 18⁶ (‖ Mk 9⁴², Lk 17²) as a fitting reward for those who 'offend one of these little ones which believe in me.' The last expression may either be taken literally, or this utterance of Jesus may be directed against those who cause the simple believer to stumble in his faith. The Greek word καταποντίζειν is used by the LXX to translate the Hebrew טבע in Ex 15⁴, and the expression used by Jesus may be a reminiscence of the drowning of the Egyptians in the Red Sea, or of the adventure of Peter (Mt 14³⁰), where the same word is employed.

In the Code of Ḥammurabi, drowning is the penalty for selling beer too cheaply' (C. H. W. Johns' *Babylonian and Assyrian Laws, Contracts, and Letters*, p. 52 ff.), as well as for more serious offences. The keepers of the beer-shops appear to have been women, and it is curious that drowning seems to have been considered the form of execution proper to female criminals. In Moslem law as defined by Abu Hanifah (d. 767 A.D.), killing by means of drowning was not accounted murder, and no retaliation could be claimed.   T. H. WEIR.

DRUNKENNESS.—Only one explicit utterance of our Lord relating to drunkenness is recorded (Lk 21³⁴). Elsewhere He warns against it indirectly, as in the parables where He holds up drunken servants to reprobation (Mt 24⁴⁹=Lk 12⁴⁵). But His references to the vice are surprisingly meagre. That must not be regarded as a measure of the contemporary extent of the evil, nor as indicating any lack of concern on His part. Our Lord's attitude to the matter must be estimated in view of the sentiments and practices of His times.

The habit of drinking to excess was widespread. Hebrew literature provides ample proof of familiarity with its unvarying moral and social consequences. The scandals associated with the early Christian love-feasts (1 Co 11²¹, Jude ¹²) were doubtless partly a recrudescence of pre-Christian practices. While excess was unsparingly condemned by moralists, moderation was uniformly commended. Occasional maxims hint at the expediency of abstinence in the interests of moral integrity and personal security. But where that is actually practised, it is invariably the outcome of purely religious impulse. It would seem that the Nazirites, the Rechabites, and other ascetics realized that indulgence in wine was inimical to spiritual life (cf. Lk 1¹⁵), or inexpedient in situations demanding the highest possible personal purity, or inappropriate to persons of singular and abnormal holiness (cf. John the Baptist, with whom some seem to have compared Jesus unfavourably, Lk 7³⁴). To the ordinary Jew, however, habitual indulgence was a matter of course. Abstinence required strong reasons to justify it. The Babylonian Gemara would even seem to suggest that abstinence might be a positive sin. 'The Nazirite has sinned by denying himself wine.' It bases this opinion on an arbitrary and erroneous interpretation of Nu 6²⁰ (see *Jewish Encyc.* art. 'Drunkenness').

Jesus seems to have adopted the prevailing popular attitude. He instituted no campaign

against the use of strong drink. He made it no part of His mission to denounce indulgence. He Himself followed the ordinary practices of His day, both using wine and giving His countenance to festivities in which wine played an important part (cf. Jn 2¹⁰). His various references to the beverage indicate that He regarded it as a source of innocent enjoyment (cf. Lk 5³⁰. ³⁸. ³⁹ 7³⁴ 17⁸). Nevertheless, that He did not overlook the fact that excess was common, and that He had an open eye for the obtrusive evils of over-indulgence, is abundantly evident from other references, as in the parables. That He did not feel called upon to command or commend abstinence in spite of this is partly to be explained, perhaps, by the fact that drunkenness was the vice chiefly of the wealthy. That seems to be implicitly recognized in Lk 21³⁴, where it is bracketed with surfeiting and subjection to the cares of this life, faults peculiarly associated with the rich or well-to-do. In the parable of the Householder (Mt 24⁴⁵⁻⁵¹=Lk 12⁴²⁻⁴⁶), the drunken characters whom He holds up to contempt are servants of one in high position, forming the *ménage* of a luxurious household in which creature comforts would be plentiful. In the circles in which Jesus Himself principally moved, and to which He chiefly appealed, excess does not seem to have been so common as to call for urgent protest or the starting of a crusade against the use of alcoholic liquors.

Christ's attitude to the whole matter was determined by the fundamental purpose of His mission. Drunkenness in general He regards as the accompaniment and symptom of a carnal unregenerate state of heart, the outcome of wickedness that defies restraint. He implicitly recognizes it also as strongly contributory to spiritual demoralization, as inducing such blunting of the spiritual sensibilities and disabling of spiritual faculty as incapacitate the soul for the proper exercises of the devout life, and endanger its future by reducing it to a state of unpreparedness for the last Divine catastrophe (Lk 21³⁴ᶠᶠ·).   A. M. HUNTER.

DUMB.—See DEAF AND DUMB.

DUNG.—See AGRICULTURE, p. 39ᵇ.

DUST (κονιορτός, Mt 10¹⁴, Lk 9⁵ 10¹¹, Ac 13⁵¹ 22²³; χόος=χοῦς, Mk 6¹¹, Rev 18¹⁹. The former means properly dust stirred up or blown about, as 'a cloud of dust'; the latter simply earth or soil thrown down or raised in a heap. In NT the two words are plainly synonymous).—The long droughts and fierce heat of Palestine, together with the softness of the limestone rock—the prevailing formation—make for the production of dust in great quantities. In high winds it penetrates to almost every part of the houses. The pedestrian suffers much from fretting of the feet by the dust, which neither sandal nor shoe excludes. This renders necessary, as well as pleasant, the washing of the feet when the journey is done (Lk 7⁴⁴).

An immemorial token of grief in the East is the casting of dust upon the person, especially upon the head, or the laying of the face in the dust; while of one utterly humbled, it is said that he 'licks the dust.'

The throwing of dust in the air is still a not uncommon way of expressing rage, or emphasizing an appeal for justice. This is probably meant to show that Earth herself joins in the petition for redress of intolerable wrongs.

Our Lord's direction that 'the Twelve' should shake off the dust of the cities that rejected their message, derived special significance from Jewish teaching. The very dust of a heathen road was held to produce defilement. To shake off the dust of their feet, as a testimony against house or city, meant that it had passed under the ban of their Lord, and the symbolic act proclaimed that 'nought of the cursed thing' clave to them. 'In this sense anything that clave to a person was metaphorically called "the dust," as, *e.g.*, "the dust of an evil tongue," "the dust of usury"; as, on the other hand, to "dust to idolatry" meant to cleave to it' (Edersheim, *Life and Times of Jesus the Messiah*, vol. i. p. 644). The modern Oriental, if asked regarding any questionable business, will daintily grip the lapel of his robe or tunic and gently shake it, turning aside his head as if he should say, 'Not even the dust of that transaction has touched me.'

W. EWING.

DUTY.—In the widest sense of the word, 'duty' is the correlate of 'ought.' * What I ought to be, to do, to feel, that is my duty. So the word covers the whole content of the moral ideal. But both to the plain man and to the philosopher duty usually has a narrower significance; and this we must make clear before we can trace the relation of the teaching of Jesus to the conception of duty.

Our type of duty is the soldier who kept guard at his post when Herculaneum was overwhelmed by lava and ashes. His station in life prescribed an action; and he fulfilled it. What his motives were we do not ask; we do not inquire how he felt in the execution of his task, or what manner of man he was. He did what he was commanded; he did his duty. A man's duty, then, at any time is the action determined by his station in life. He stands under a rule, which he must obey and apply. Such obedience does not, however, cover the highest moral excellence. Two men both do their duty, say, to the poor; but the one is hard, unsympathetic, the other benevolent; the one is just, the other full of charity. Although in point of duty they do not differ, we feel that the latter is a better man than the former; for he stands nearer to the ideal of goodness. This is the popular view.

But among the ancients the Stoics, and in modern times Kant, have judged differently. They exclude the emotions, and measure moral worth by the degree to which duty, and duty alone, is the motive of action. No man is good unless he obeys the law, simply because it is the law. Duty for duty's sake is their watchword. 'The sage,' says Seneca,† 'will succour, will do good, for he is born to assist his fellow, to labour for the welfare of mankind; but he will feel no pity. . . . It is only diseased eyes that grow moist in beholding tears in other eyes, as it is no true sympathy, but only weakness of nerves, that leads some to laugh when others laugh, or to yawn when others yawn.' Kant‡ argues in a similar way, but with greater depth and sincerity, that philanthropic action has true moral worth only if done by a man whose temperament is cold and indifferent to the sufferings of others, not from inclination, but from duty, simply because he respects the law under which he stands. Further, the moral judgment is directed not to what is done, but to what the agent intended to do, to what he has willed and taken every means in his power to bring about. But even this needs qualification. Kant holds that we must leave out of account the content of what is willed, and simply inquire whether the law is

obeyed just because it is the law. And so we reach the bare conception of duty for duty's sake, and find the moral law reduced to the mere form of universality. The flesh and blood of goodness have vanished, and we are left with the spectre of a law characterized only by the admission of no exceptions.

But no one can rest satisfied with an abstraction. Kant, therefore, restores content to the idea of duty by throwing into the form of Law Universal the various kinds of action which Society enjoins or forbids. Thus we receive a code of moral laws, each demanding unconditional obedience. But this is not always possible. Conflicts of 'duties' will from time to time appear, not in the sense that Duty issues conflicting commands (for under any given circumstances only one action can be right), but in the sense that one of two *normal* lines of conduct must overcome and contradict the other. Thus arise the problems that have exercised casuists and made real tragedies. Am I to refuse either to kill my fellow-men or to defend my country? Am I to tell a lie, or to become the accomplice, however unwilling, in the murder of my friend? * Such problems are inevitable and insoluble, if we conceive duty as a group of co-ordinate and absolute laws of action. Conflicts must ensue in the application of such laws, once the ideal system of moral relations on which they are based fails to correspond point for point with the actual system in which they claim realization. But the world is full of imperfection and sin, and every man has sinned and is weak. Consequently the only possible choice may often lie between two lines of conduct, both of which are ideally wrong.

Moreover, if the moral ideal is expressed as a code of rules of action, morality tends to become no more than the rigid observance of ceremonies that characterized the Pharisee. Life hardens into conventionality, if the emphasis is laid on doing rather than on being. We do not deny that character must express itself in action; that charity without works is a contradiction; that the good will cannot be formed save by doing good. But deeds are particular, and relative to time and place; and an ethical code which prescribes or forbids particular acts not only loses touch with real life, but diverts the attention from the spirit to the letter. In the same way the institutions by which a man's station and duties are determined tend also to become rigid and conventional.

Now Jesus Christ did not promulgate a new code of morals; nor did He do more than lay the foundations of a new society. Had He instituted a definite social, political, or ecclesiastical order, or prescribed a scheme of duties for His followers, the gospel would have possessed for Ethics only an historical interest, instead of affording, as it does, principles by which we may criticise every action and reform every institution. The words and works of Jesus are a well of living water, from which all men of whatever time or nation may drink. We do not disparage organizations and codes of duty. They are essential to the realization of any human ideal; and it is the part of practical Christianity to work out the gospel in a moral, social, and religious order, appropriate to the needs of each generation. In order to use ideas we must crystallize them; but in the process they become half-truths. The life of Jesus alone abides as the truth, reflected and refracted on the broken surface of the river of time.

We must, however, qualify what has been said in two respects. Jesus guarded the sanctuary of the family by the most stringent regulation of divorce. This was natural; for the family is the foundation-stone of the fabric of society. Where it does not remain pure and undefiled, to nourish love and duty, the nation becomes corrupt at its source. Again, Jesus instituted the Holy Sacraments by which we may participate in His

---

* The word 'duty' occurs only once in the Gospels, when Jesus describes as unprofitable servants those who have only done what it was their duty to do (Lk 17¹⁰). The word in the orig. is ὀφείλω, a verb which is twice used in Jn (13¹⁴ 19⁷) to express the idea of oughtness or moral obligation (EV 'ought'), more commonly expressed by δεῖ. For examples of this use of δεῖ in the reported teaching of Jesus see Mt 23²³ 25²⁷, Lk 12¹³ 18¹ etc. For the distinction between δεῖ and ὀφείλω see Cremer and Grimm-Thayer (*s.vv.*).

† Seneca, *de Clem.* ii. 6; contrast Jn 11³⁵.

‡ Kant's *Theory of Ethics* (Abbott's tr. pp. 14–16); contrast 1 Co 13⁴.

* *Op. cit.* pp. 361–365.

living Body and Blood,'*i.e.* in His Life and Spirit, to cleanse our hearts, to renew our wills, and to illuminate our minds with the vision of Truth.

Nothing can be gained by attempting to summarize the Sermon on the Mount. It is enough to emphasize three points.

1. Jesus turns the judgment and attention from the outward act to the *inward motive*, to the thought and feeling from which the act springs. 'Ye have heard that it was said by them of old time, Thou shalt not commit adultery : but I say unto you, That whosoever looketh on a woman to lust after her hath committed adultery with her already in his heart' (Mt 5²⁷ᶠ·). A standard such as this must shatter the Pharisaic complacency that accompanies the outward observance of a code of duties.

2. In the same way Jesus lays stress on *being*, not doing, on *character*, not action. Blessed are the meek, the merciful, the pure in heart, the forgiving, they which hunger and thirst after righteousness. Not that deeds are unimportant or unnecessary. Far from it. But the vital thing is the *will*. So Jesus transcends the point of view of the casuist. In the Christian ideal there are no contradictions. In the Gospels there is no delicate balancing of considerations and consequences.

3. Jesus subordinates the love of our neighbour to the *love of God*. It is often said that the Second Commandment, 'Thou shalt love thy neighbour as thyself,' is an adequate expression of the ultimate principle of morality. But the self that we love may be an unworthy self, perhaps even a sensual self. If so, we shall carry this conception into the treatment of our neighbour. There is much good-natured vice in the world. And apart from this, fashionable philanthropy is too often dominated by an ideal of mere comfort. That is why well-meant efforts at social improvement not seldom end in vanity and vexation of spirit. To avoid this, *altruism must draw its inspiration from true religion*. It must seek illumination from God, and in His light interpret the duty towards other men. In other words, the love of God, as He is seen and known in Christ Jesus, creates a new ideal of duty both in relation to ourselves and our neighbour. Finally, the Christian motive is not the abstract conception of duty for duty's sake, but charity, the pure love of the full, concrete, and perfect ideal of humanity, realized for all time in the Person of Jesus Christ.

Literature.—Kant's *Theory of Ethics*, tr. by T. K. Abbott ; T. H. Green, *Prolegomena to Ethics* (esp. bk. iii.); F. H. Bradley, *Ethical Studies* (Essay iv.); H. Sidgwick, *Methods of Ethics*, bk. iii.; Newman Smyth, *Christian Ethics* ; Gore, *The Sermon on the Mount*, **A. J. JENKINSON.**

E

EAGLE.—See ANIMALS, p. 65ᵇ.

EAR.—Of the Greek words translated 'ear' in EV, two (ὠτάριον, ὠτίον) refer exclusively to the bodily organ, and occur only in connexion with the case of Malchus (Mk 14⁴⁷, Jn 18¹⁰· ²⁶, Mt 26⁵¹, Lk 22⁵¹). In Mt 28¹⁴ the rendering is simply a paraphrase. In Mk 7³⁵ (ἀκοαί) 'his hearing' would be more exact. In all other instances the word οὖς occurs, and is used : (1) *literally*, to denote 'the ear' (Mt 10²⁷, Mk 7³³ 8¹⁸, Lk 1⁴⁴ 12³ 22⁵⁰), or (by transference) 'the range of hearing' (Lk 4²¹); but more frequently (2) *figuratively*, to denote a spiritual faculty symbolized by the natural ear (Mt 11¹⁵ 13⁹· ¹⁵ (*bis*), ¹⁶· ⁴³, Mk 4⁹· ²³, Lk 8⁸ 9⁴⁴ 14³⁵). The definitive passages for this use are Mt 13³⁻²³, Mk 4²⁻²², Lk 8⁵⁻¹⁵, where it forms the underlying subject of Christ's first parable, 'the Sower,' a parable concluded in each account by the phrase, 'He that hath ears (to hear) let him hear.' Indeed, the general principle of speaking in parables is in these passages connected with 'ears dull of hearing' (Mt 13¹³⁻¹⁵). Christ is speaking in reference to 'mysteries' (Mt 13¹¹, Mk 4¹¹, Lk 8¹⁰), that is, Divine truths not necessarily puzzling in themselves, but undiscoverable by man apart from a revelation of them (see Moule on Eph 1⁹ 3³⁻⁶, cf. also 1 Co 2⁷⁻¹⁰). When these have been revealed to him, man has the power to recognize their truth, fitness, and necessity (see Westcott on He 2¹⁰ 7²⁶), in proportion as he is determined to do the Divine will (Jn 7¹⁷ 8⁴³⁻⁴⁷). This faculty of recognizing the voice of truth and (as it were) vibrating to its utterance is fitly referred to by Christ as a spiritual 'ear.'

Literature. — Grimm - Thayer, *s.v.* οὖς ; *Expositor*, I. ii. 472 ff. **F. S. RANKEN.**

EARTHLY AND HEAVENLY (ἐπίγειος, ἐπουράνιος). —The Gr. words are found in the Gospels only in Jn 3¹² [ἐπουράνιος, however, occurs as a variant reading (TR) in Mt 18³⁵, where some critical editors prefer οὐράνιος], in Christ's conversation with Nicodemus, and are best interpreted in the light of the context. The attempt made by some commentators to explain them by collating passages where the same or similar words occur, yields no satisfactory result, the meaning of the words in these passages being so different from their meaning in Jn 3¹².

It is evident from the conversation with Nicodemus that the contrast drawn by Christ between things earthly and things heavenly was not a contrast between things natural and things super natural, or things physical and things spiritual, o things easily understood and things unsearchable and profound, or things belonging to the present and things belonging to the future economy, or things moral in which faith is active and things heavenly where it is passive (de Wette). It was a contrast between truths which were within the range of religious experience, and which should therefore have been within the knowledge and understanding of Nicodemus—'a master of Israel,' and truths pertaining to the gospel which were, for the time being, beyond the reach of the religious consciousness. The earthly things were those of which Christ had been speaking,—the necessity and mystery and reality of the new birth,—and also, as Godet rightly infers from v.¹² (note use of plural instead of singular in addressing Nicodemus), the truths previously preached by Christ. These were all of a moral-religious character, and could be known and verified by the spiritually-minded. The heavenly things were those which were to be revealed to men through the completed redemptive work of Christ. Their nature may be gathered from v.¹³ᶠᶠ·. The Divinity and the atoning death of Christ, God's eternal love, and salvation by faith, are indicated there as being among the heavenly things.

Literature.—Besides the Comm. on St. John, esp. Whitelaw and Godet, see Cremer's and Grimm-Thayer's *Lex. s.vv.* ; E. H. Hall, *Discourses*, 92 ; D. Wright, *Power of an Endless Life*, 158 ;

J. H. Jowett, *Thirsting for the Springs*, 64 ; *Expos. Times*, xii. [1900] 50.   MORISON BRYCE.

EARTHQUAKE.—Palestine abounds in traces of seismic and volcanic action. From the region of the Dead Sea northward along the Jordan valley and as far as Damascus the whole country must have been visited by tremendous earthquakes in prehistoric ages. Mention of several is made in the OT, sometimes coupled with significant reference to serious disaster and widespread alarm caused by them (1 S 14[15], Am 1[1], Zec 14[5] etc.). Regarded as supernatural visitations, signs of the times, they produced a deep impression.

Five times in the Gospels the noun σεισμός (fr. σείω, 'to shake') is used of an earthquake (Mt 24[7] 27[54] 28[2], Mk 13[8],.Lk 21[11]), and once (Mt 27[51]) the idea is expressed by the phrase ἡ γῆ ἐσείσθη (EV 'the earth did quake'). In LXX σεισμός (or συνσεισμός) is employed to render רַעַשׁ of the original. Though specifically applied to an earthquake, σεισμός properly has a wider connotation ; thus in Mt 8[24] it is used of a tempest (σεισμὸς μέγας ἐγένετο ἐν τῇ θαλάσσῃ). Hence Alford thinks that in Mt 28[2] it denotes not an earthquake, but the 'shock' produced by the rolling away of the stone from the sepulchre.

1. *Recorded earthquakes.*—Of these there are two, namely, the earthquakes at the Crucifixion and the Resurrection (Mt 27[51. 54] 28[2]). The historicity of these earthquakes is disputed. St. Matthew alone mentions them ; St. Mark (15[33. 38]) and St. Luke (23[44f.]), in agreement with St. Matthew in regard to the darkness and the rending of the veil, apparently know nothing of an earthquake at the Crucifixion [the Fourth Gospel has no allusion to any of the portents], and they are equally silent in the case of the Resurrection. Plummer ('St. Luke' in *Internat. Crit. Com.*) quotes a statement in the Gemara that some forty years before the destruction of Jerusalem the heavy gates of the temple were mysteriously flung open about midnight at the Passover ; but it would seem that sufficient evidence of earthquake shocks being felt in or near Jerusalem at the date in question is wanting. Probably a legendary element must be recognized in the passages under consideration. At the same time it should be borne in mind that the circumstance narrated is 'not in itself incredible' (Cary, *Synop. Gospels*). Earthquakes are frequently accompanied by a 'strange, bewildering darkness' (Plumptre, *Bibl. Studies*), and if shocks did then take place they would naturally be interpreted of the 'sympathy of nature.' (Cf. Corn. a Lap. : 'The earth, which trembled with horror at the death of Christ, as it were leaped with joy at the Resurrection').

2. *Predicted earthquakes.*—Mt 24[7], Mk 13[8], Lk 21[11]. The question arises, Do the Synoptists here preserve *ipsissima verba* of our Lord ? It must be remembered that 'a generation and a half . . . had passed between the events and the telling of the tale' (F. C. Burkitt) ; hence a possibility that the eschatological discourses as reported are coloured by events which had already taken place when the narratives were compiled. On the assumption that the predictions were uttered by Jesus, account should be taken of the fact that they are clothed in the language of current Messianic expectation. The setting up of the Kingdom was at hand ; it would be consequent on that national disaster which, looming in the near future, would be presaged by phenomena in which men saw the dread precursors of catastrophe. And this actually came about : between the Crucifixion and the destruction of Jerusalem the earthquake was frequent ; the earth was a prey to the most violent convulsions (Godet, *St. Mat.* p. 149 ; Renan, *L'Antichrist*, ch. xiv.).

LITERATURE.—Gilbert, *Student's Life of Jesus* ; Schürer, *HJP*, see Index ; Gould, 'St. Mark' in *Internat. Crit. Com.* ; Cary, 'The Synoptic Gospels' in *Internat. Handbooks to NT.*
                         H. L. JACKSON.

EASTER.—See CALENDAR, THE CHRISTIAN, p. 255 ff.

EATING AND DRINKING.—Eating and drinking are occasionally referred to in the Gospels as acts expressive of men's ordinary life. The simple natural life of Jesus was thus contrasted with the austere ways of the Baptist (Mt 11[19], Lk 7[34]). The servant waits till the master has eaten and drunken, and afterwards he eats and drinks (Lk 17[8]) ; in the days of Noah men went on eating and drinking, heedless of the coming flood (Lk 17[27. 28]) ; and the rich fool still says to his soul, 'Take thine ease, eat, drink, be merry' (Lk 12[19]). The careless self-indulgence of the servant who, in his lord's absence, began to eat and drink with the drunken (Mt 24[49], Lk 12[45]) is condemned on the one hand ; and so, on the other hand, is that over anxiety which keeps saying, 'What shall we eat? or What shall we drink? or Wherewithal shall we be clothed?' (Mt 6[24-34], Lk 12[22-34]). The scribes and Pharisees complained that Jesus ate and drank with publicans and sinners (Lk 5[30]), which was His glory ; and it will be the glory of those who continue with Him in His temptations that they will eat and drink at His table in His Kingdom (Lk 22[30]). See BREAD, CUP, FASTING, FOOD, LORD'S SUPPER, MEALS, WINE.

EBER (AV **Heber**).—The eponymous ancestor of the Hebrews ; named in our Lord's genealogy as given in Lk. (3[35]).

EBIONISM.—It would be going beyond the scope of this Dictionary to enter with any fulness into a discussion of the obscure and elusive subject of Ebionism as it meets us in its varying forms in the history of the early Church. What immediately concerns us is its bearing upon certain questions connected with the origin of the Gospels and the history and person of Jesus Christ Himself. But as these questions cannot properly be handled till we have determined what we are to understand by Ebionism, a brief treatment of the general subject appears to be necessary.

i. WHO AND WHAT WERE THE EBIONITES ?—The name Ebionites ('Εβιωναῖοι), it is generally agreed, is derived from the Hebrew *'ebyōnîm* אֶבְיוֹנִים 'the poor.' * It seems most probable that originally this name, like Nazarenes (Ac 24[5]), was applied to all Christians ; but whether it was first adopted by the followers of Christ themselves or given them by others it is impossible to say. The comparative poverty of the great mass of Christians in the early days of the Church, especially in Jerusalem, where the name doubtless arose, might lead to its being used by outsiders as a term of contempt. On the other hand, the Christians of Jerusalem may themselves have adopted it because of the spiritual associations with which 'the poor' (אֶבְיוֹנִים, עֲנִיִּים, דַּלִּים) are referred to in the OT (*e.g.* Ps 34[6] 69[33] 72[13], Is 11[4] 14[32] 29[19] ; cf. S. R. Driver, art. 'Poor' in Hastings' *DB* ; G. A. Smith, *Isaiah*, vol. i. ch. xxix. 'God's Poor'), and the blessings pronounced upon them by Jesus Himself (Lk 6[20], Mt 5[3]). If it was first given as a name of reproach, it could very easily and naturally be accepted as a name of honour.†

* Certain of the Fathers attempt to derive the name from a supposed founder called Ebion, who is said to have spread his doctrines among the Christians who fled to Pella after the fall of Jerusalem (Tertullian, *de præscr. Hæret.* 33 ; Epiphanius, *Hær.* xxx. 1, 2). But though Hilgenfeld has laboured to give historical reality to the figure of Ebion (*Ketzergesch.* pp. 422-424), modern scholars have practically agreed that he has only a mythical existence (Harnack, *Hist. of Dogma*, i. 299 ; Uhlhorn in *PRE* [3] v. 126).

† It is a later idea, evidently suggested by antipathy to the low Christological ideas with which Ebionism had come to be identified, that leads Origen (*c. Cels.* ii. 1, *de Princip.* IV. i. 22)

After the name 'Christian' (cf. Ac 11²⁶) had become the general designation for the disciples of Christ, 'Ebionites' appears to have been reserved as a distinctive title for Jewish as distinguished from Gentile Christians ('Εβιωναῖοι χρηματίζουσιν οἱ ἀπὸ Ἰουδαίων τὸν Ἰησοῦν ὡς Χριστὸν παραδεξάμενοι, Origen, c. Cels. ii. 1), but specifically for those Jewish Christians who, in some degree more or less pronounced, sought to maintain as essential to Christianity the now obsolete forms of the OT religion (the Fathers from the 2nd to the 4th cent. passim). Thus Ebionism becomes a synonym for Jewish Christianity in its antithesis to the universalism of the Catholic Church ; and it is in this broad and yet pretty definite sense that the word is properly to be employed (Harnack, l.c. i. 289 ; Uhlhorn, l.c. ibid.). It is true that in the 4th cent. we find Jerome using the two names Nazarenes and Ebionites in speaking of the Jewish Christians, with whom he had become well acquainted in Palestine (Ep. ad August. cxxii. 13), and this has led some to suppose that he is making a distinction between two entirely different sects (so especially Zahn, Kanonsgesch. ii. 648 ff.) ; but it is now generally held that in this case he was really using two names for the same thing, and that 'Nazarenes' and 'Ebionites' are both general designations for Jewish Christians as such (Harnack, l.c. p. 301 ; cf. Uhlhorn's art. 'Ebionites' in Schaff-Herzog, Encycl. of Rel. Knowledge, with his later art. 'Ebioniten' in PRE³).

While, however, it seems impossible to distinguish between Nazarenes and Ebionites, and improper in this connexion to think of a separation into clear-cut sects, there were undoubtedly differences of tendency within the general sphere of Ebionism. From the first a stricter and a more liberal party is to be discerned (the οἱ διττοὶ Ἐβιωναῖοι of Origen, c. Cels. v. 61), corresponding in some measure to the cleavage which emerged in the Council of Jerusalem (Ac 15¹⁻²⁹)—a Pharisaic party which held the Law to be essential even for Gentile Christians, and a party of broader mind, which, while clinging to the Law for themselves, did not seek to impose it upon their Gentile brethren (Justin, Dial. c. Tryph. 47). Finally, with the rise of the Gnostic heresy, a Gnostic or syncretistic type of Jewish Christianity makes its appearance, to which the name of Ebionism is still applied (Epiphanius, Hær. xxx. 1). This Gnostic Ebionism itself assumes various forms. It already meets us within the NT in the false doctrine which St. Paul opposes in Colossians, and in the teaching of Cerinthus to which St. John replies in his First Epistle. At a later period it is represented in the doctrines of the Elkesaites, who combined their Ebionism with influences drawn from the Oriental heathen world (Epiphanius, Hær. xix. 2, xxx. 1 ; Hippolytus, Philos. ix. 13).

ii. THE EBIONITE GOSPELS. — As against the Tübingen school, which held that primitive Christianity was itself Ebionism, and which took, in consequence, a highly exaggerated view of the influence of Ebionitic thought upon the history and the literature of the early Church, it is now admitted by nearly all modern scholars that there are no writings within the Canon of the NT which come to us directly from this circle. On the other hand, two of the Apocryphal Gospels, the Gospel according to the Hebrews and the Gospel of the Twelve Apostles (otherwise known as the Gospel of the Ebionites), are immediate products of the Judæo-Christian spirit—the former representing Ebionism in its earlier and simpler type, and the

and Eusebius (HE iii. 27) to treat the name as derived from the 'poverty' of the Ebionites in intelligence and knowledge of Scripture, and especially from the 'beggarly' quality of their Christology.

latter that syncretistic form of Jewish Christianity which afterwards sprang up through contact with Gnosticism (see GOSPELS [APOCRYPHAL]; and artt. 'Gospel according to the Hebrews' and 'Apocryphal Gospels' in Hastings' DB, Extra Vol.). The extant fragments of the Gospel of the Twelve Apostles show that its value is quite secondary, and that the author has simply compiled it from the Canonical, and especially from the Synoptic Gospels, adapting it at the same time to the views and practices of Gnostic Ebionism. Much more interest and importance attach to the Gospel according to the Hebrews. We have references to it, for the most part respectful and sympathetic, in the writings of Clement, Origen, Eusebius, and, above all, Jerome ; while several valuable fragments of it have been preserved for us in the pages of Epiphanius. Eusebius (HE iii. 25, 27) and Jerome (Com. on Mt 12¹³) both testify that this was the Gospel used by the Ebionites, and it is the latter who gives it its name of the 'Gospel according to the Hebrews' (secundum Hebræos). The numerous references in the Fathers to this work, and the extant fragments themselves, if they do not justify Harnack's statement that Jewish-Christian (i.e. Ebionite) sources lie at the basis of our Synoptic Gospels (Hist. of Dogma, i. 295), lend some weight to the idea that the distinctive features of the document, so far from being altogether secondary, ought to be regarded as indications of an early Aramaic tradition, which still held its own among the 'Hebrews' after the growing universalism of the Church had left it behind (see Prof. Allan Menzies in Hastings' DB, Extra Vol. 343ª).

iii. EBIONISM AND THE CANONICAL GOSPELS.— Apart from the existence of special Ebionite Gospels, the idea has been common, both in ancient and modern times, that certain of the Canonical Gospels owe something of their substance or their form to the positive or negative influence of Ebionite sources or Ebionite surroundings. (1) The Gospel of St. Matthew.—Jerome, who testifies, as we have seen, to the fact that the Jewish Christians of Palestine had a Gospel of their own (secundum Hebræos), also tells us that this Gospel was regarded by many as Matthæi authenticum, i.e. the original of Matthew (Com. on Mt 12¹³) ; and on one occasion refers to a copy of it which he himself had seen and translated as though he believed it to be the original Hebrew (ipsum Hebraicum) of St. Matthew's Gospel (de Viris Illust. ii. 3). Irenæus, two centuries earlier, says that the Ebionites use only the Gospel of Matthew (I. xxvi. 2) ; a statement which points, at all events, to this, that even in his time the Jewish Christians of Syria attached themselves to a particular Gospel, and that between that Gospel and St. Matthew the Apostle a close connexion was believed to exist. Irenæus does not seem to have been aware of the existence of the Gospel according to the Hebrews, and apparently confounded that work with the Canonical Matthew. But when his statement is taken together with those of Jerome, very interesting questions are raised as to the origin and connexions of the Synoptical Gospels, and of the First Gospel in particular, with the result that in modern theories upon this subject the Gospel according to the Hebrews has played an important rôle. It would be out of place to enter here upon any discussion of the questions thus raised (see GOSPELS). But it may be said that while the whole trend of recent scholarship is unfavourable to the views of those who would make the Gospel according to the Hebrews either the 'Ur-Matthæus' itself or an expanded edition of it, some grounds can be alleged for thinking that it represents an early Aramaic tradition of the Gospel story which was in existence when the author of Canonical Matthew wrote his book, and upon which to some extent he may have drawn,—a tradition which would naturally be more Jewish and national in its outlook than that represented by the Greek written sources on which he placed his main dependence (see Hastings' *DB*, Extra Vol. 342 f.).

(2) *The Gospel of St. Luke.*—On the ground that much of the teaching which is peculiar to St. Luke béars specially upon wealth and poverty, it has frequently been alleged that the Evangelist made use of a distinctly Ebionitic source, or was himself in sympathy with Ebionism. It is true that the Ebionites, as we meet them later in Church history, resemble the Essenes in taking an ascetic view of life, and regarding voluntary poverty as a thing of merit and a means of preparing for the Messianic kingdom. But it is altogether a misrepresentation of the facts to say that this is the type of the ideal Christian life as it meets us in Luke, or that his references to riches and poverty 'rest on the idea that wealth is pernicious in itself and poverty salutary in itself' (Weiss, *Introd.* ii. 309). The form in which the first Beatitude of Matthew (5³) is given in Luke, 'Blessed are ye poor: for yours is the kingdom of God' (6²⁰), together with the closely following Woe pronounced upon the rich (v.²⁴), has especially been fastened on as a clear proof that these sayings proceed from an Ebionitic circle 'ascetic in spirit and believing poverty to be in itself a passport to the kingdom, and riches the way to perdition.' Similarly in the parable of Dives and Lazarus (16¹⁹⁻³¹), it is supposed that Dives goes to the place of torment because he is rich, while the beggar is carried into Abraham's bosom simply because he is a beggar. Such interpretations, however, spring from a very superficial exegesis (cf. Bruce, *Expos. Gr. Test.* on Lk 6²⁰, *Parabolic Teaching of Christ*, p. 376 ff.). And, while it is true that St. Luke dwells, more than the other Evangelists, on the consolations of the poor and the perils of rich men (see, besides the passages already quoted, 4¹⁸ 7²² 12¹⁶ff. 16¹ff. 19²ff. 21¹ff.), the fact is sufficiently accounted for, on the one hand, by that humane and philanthropic spirit which is so characteristic of the Third Evangelist and so natural in one who is called 'the beloved physician'; and, on the other, as Zahn has suggested (*Einleitung*, ii. 379), by his sense of the appropriateness for one in the position of Theophilus, to whom his Gospel is immediately addressed, of our Lord's frequent warnings of the spiritual dangers of wealth and the worldliness to which wealth is so prone to lead. It is to be noted, however, that our Lord's strongest utterance against wealth is found in Matthew (19²⁴) and Mark (10²⁵), as well as Luke (18²⁵); and that a comparison of the Third Synoptic with the other two reveals occasional touches, on the one side or the other (note, *e.g.*, the presence of ἀγρούς in Mt 19²⁹, Mk 10²⁹, and its absence from Lk 18²⁹), which an ingenious theorist might very well use to support the thesis that Luke is not so Ebionitic as Matthew and Mark (see Plummer, 'St. Luke' in *Internat. Crit. Com.* p. xxv f.).

(3) It is curious to notice how, from the 2nd cent. to the 19th, *the Fourth Gospel* has been associated in two quite different ways with Ebionism, and specifically with Cerinthus, an Ebionite of the Gnosticizing type who taught in Ephesus towards the close of the Apostolic age. On the one hand, we have the statements of Irenæus and others that the Apostle John wrote his Gospel to combat the errors of Cerinthus (Iren. III. xi. 1) and the Ebionites (Epiphanius, *Hær.* li. 12, lxix. 23); statements which should be taken in connexion with the well-known story, attributed to Polycarp, of the dramatic encounter between St.

John and Cerinthus in the baths of Ephesus (Iren. III. iii. 4; Epiphan. *l.c.* xxx. 24).* Even down to recent times these statements have been widely accepted as furnishing an adequate account of the origin of the Fourth Gospel. Thus Ebrard says: 'We are thus led to the conclusion that the Cerinthian *gnosis* was the principal cause which induced John to believe that the time had come for him to make known his peculiar gift, which he had hitherto kept concealed. . . . He emphasizes faith in Jesus the Son of God (xx. 31) over against a bare *gnosis*' (Schaff-Herzog, *Encyc. of Rel. Knowledge*, ii. 1189).

At the opposite extreme from the belief of Irenæus was the view of a sect referred to by Epiphanius (*l.c.* li. 3), and named by him the Alogi (because of their refusal to accept St. John's teaching regarding the Logos), who ascribed the Johannine writings to Cerinthus himself, and on that ground discarded them altogether. A parallel of a sort to this view was furnished by the Tübingen writers when they assigned the Gospel to some Gnosticizing dreamer of the 2nd century.

The residuum of truth that lies between these two contrary views may perhaps be found in the fact that the author was a contemporary of Cerinthus, and that he wrote his Gospel in full view of prevailing Cerinthian error. It is a mistake, however, to suppose that the work was intended as a direct polemic against Cerinthus and his followers.

'It is decisive,' says Meyer, 'against the assumption of any such polemical purpose that, in general, John nowhere in his Gospel allows any direct reference to the perverted tendencies of his day to appear; while to search for indirect and hidden allusions of the kind, as if they were intentional, would be as arbitrary as it would be repugnant to the decided character of the Apostolic standpoint which he took up when in conscious opposition to heresies. . . . We see from his [First] Epistle how John would have carried on a controversy, had he *wished* to do so in his Gospel' (*John*, i. 44 f.; cf. Westcott, *John*, p. xli).

The author doubtless has in view the heresies of Gnostic Ebionism, but in the Gospel he refutes them only by the full and positive exhibition of what he conceives to be the truth about Jesus Christ. He tells us himself that his purpose in writing is that those who read 'may believe that Jesus is the Christ, the Son of God' (20³¹). What he means by 'the Christ, the Son of God,' he lets us see in the prologue; and his method in the rest of the work is to show by selected examples how this conception of the truth about Jesus Christ has been historically realized.

iv. EBIONISM AND THE PERSON OF CHRIST.—The distinctive feature of Judaic Christianity, when we first meet it, lies in its continued adherence to the Law; but with the growth of more definite conceptions regarding the Person of Christ, the question of the keeping of the Law recedes into the background, and Christology becomes the matter of supreme importance to the Church. From the beginning it was the tendency of Jewish Christianity to shrink from the idea of the Incarnation, and to be content to regard Jesus as the last and greatest of the prophets. And when the Church defined its Christological position, the Jewish section was found to be lacking at this particular and crucial point, and so the term 'Ebionism' came to be almost synonymous with the denial of Christ's Divinity and Virgin-birth. Irenæus, after referring to the way in which the Ebionites clung to the Law of Moses and rejected Paul as an apostate, adds that, besides this, they teach *consimiliter ut Cerinthus et Carpocrates* (cf. Hippolytus, *Philos.* vii. 34, τὰ δὲ περὶ Χριστὸν ὁμοίως τῷ Κηρίνθῳ καὶ Καρποκράτει μυθεύουσιν), denying the birth from the Virgin and holding Christ as a mere man. Origen, more than half a century later,

---

* In one version of the story it is the mythical 'Ebion' whom St. John meets in the bath.

distinguishes between two classes of Ebionites (οἱ διττοὶ Ἐβιωναῖοι), one of which confesses, like the Church generally, that Jesus was born of a virgin, while the other affirms that He was born like the rest of men (c. Cels. v. 61). According to Jerome, it appears that by the 4th cent. the Ebionites of Palestine had made progress in their recognition of the Divinity of Christ and the Virgin-birth, for he says of them, qui credunt in Christum filium dei natum de Virgine Maria . . . in quem et nos credimus (Ep. ad August. cxxii. 13).

But while it may be true of the vulgar or non-Gnostic Ebionites, over whom, as Harnack says, 'the Church stalked with iron feet' (Hist. of Dogma, i. 301), that their distinction from the Church tended more and more to disappear, the case was different with the Gnostic or syncretistic variety, of whom Cerinthus may be taken as an early type. To Cerinthus, according to Irenæus (I. xxvi. 1; cf. Hippolytus, Philos. vii. 33), Jesus was nothing more than a naturally-begotten man —the son of Joseph and Mary—upon whom at His baptism the Christ came down from the absolute power (αὐθεντία) of God, thus making him the revealer of the Father and the miracle-working Messiah; but from whom this Christ-Spirit departed before the Passion, so that it was only the man Jesus who endured the cross, while the spiritual Christ remained untouched by suffering.

In the case of the Elkesaites of a later period, we find Jewish monotheism combining itself not only with Greek speculation, but with strange heathen elements taken over from the Asiatic religions. This syncretism was characteristic of the age, and in that fact the strength of Gnostic Ebionism lay. It was much more aggressive than Ebionism of the simpler type, and had a far more widely extended influence. Of its fantastic and fugitive forms this is not the place to speak. But its Christology appears in general to have been akin to that of Cerinthus; in other words it was essentially Docetic, and involved a denial of any real and abiding union of the Divine and human in the Person of our Lord.

LITERATURE.—On the general subject the following should be read: Neander, Church History, vol. ii. pp. 8–41 (Clark's ed.); Harnack, Hist. of Dogma, i. 287–317; PRE³, artt. 'Ebioniten,' 'Elkesaiten'; Jewish Encyc., art. 'Ebionites.' For particular points see the various references given in the article.

J. C. LAMBERT.

ECCE HOMO.—'Behold, the man!' (ἰδοὺ ὁ ἄνθρωπος or ἴδε ὁ ἄνθρωπος) (Jn 19⁵) was the utterance of Pilate when our Lord came forth wearing the crown of thorns and the purple robe. We may believe that the words were spoken to excite the pity of the Jews. Pilate had given over our Lord to be scourged, and had allowed his soldiers to robe and crown Him in mockery, but all the time he was anxious to save Him from death; and there was undoubtedly an appeal to the compassion of the bystanders in the words, 'Behold the man.' Probably it was to mock the Jews that the soldiers had robed and crowned Him who was said to have claimed to be their king; and Pilate himself, we can see, was not unwilling to deal somewhat scornfully with them. But he does not seem to have looked scornfully, he rather looked pitifully, on our Lord Himself. And when he said, 'Behold, the man!' he was, as it were, pointing out that Jesus had suffered enough. But although Pilate's words were those of a weak but not wholly unfeeling man who wanted to move to pity those whom he was afraid to send angry and revengeful from his judgment-seat, he was really, although all unconsciously, paying an act of homage to our Lord. 'Ecce Homo.' He was bidding men look to the perfect man, the incarnate Son of God, men's

perfect example, their Divine yet most truly human Redeemer.

The scene of our Lord's appearing in the crown of thorns and the purple robe is naturally one to appeal to artists; and many great pictures, notably one of the greatest and most striking of modern times (by Munkacsy), have borne the title 'Ecce Homo!'

Ecce Homo is also the title of a very notable book by the late Sir John Seeley. The book cannot be discussed here. It deals with the manhood of our Lord in an original and striking way, and does not deny, although it does not discuss, His Divinity.

LITERATURE.—Comm. on passage cited; Seeley, Ecce Homo; Knox Little, Perfect Life (1898), p. 140; R. J. Campbell, City Temple Sermons (1903), 50; Rosadi, Trial of Jesus; Farrar, Christ in Art, p. 384 ff.; art. 'Christusbilder' in PRE³.

GEO. C. WATT.

EDUCATION.—Among the Apocryphal Gospels' fables of what befell during the Silent Years, there are some that are concerned with the school-days of Jesus—mostly silly and sometimes blasphemous stories of the sort which St. Paul brands as 'profane and old-wifish myths' (1 Ti 4⁷). For instance, it is told in Arab. Evang. Inf. xlix. that the wondrous Child one day had a dispute with His teacher about the Hebrew alphabet; and when the latter would have chastised Him, his impious arm was withered, and he died. Such stories are, of course, absolutely unhistorical; but it is indubitable that during His early years at Nazareth Jesus had to do with school and teacher. It is mentioned incidentally by St. Luke that He could read (4¹⁶), and by St. John that He could write (8⁸); and it is impossible that He should have grown up without an education. It is not the least merit of the Jewish people that they recognized the value of education, and brought it within the reach of the poorest. 'Our ground,' says Josephus,* 'is good, and we work it to the utmost; but our chief ambition is for the education of our children.' A father, according to R. Salomo,† had as well bury his son as neglect his instruction; and it was a saying of R. Judah the Holy that 'the world exists by the breath of school-children.'

A child's first school was his home and his first teachers his parents, in accordance with Dt 6⁶·⁷; and his instruction began very early, since youth was recognized as the season of opportunity. 'He who learns as a lad,' said R. Abujah, 'to what is he like? To ink written on fresh paper. And he who learns when old, to what is he like? To ink written on used paper.' ‡ St. Paul testifies that Timothy had known sacred literature 'from his infancy' (ἀπὸ βρέφους), his teachers being—since his father was a Greek and apparently deceased— his grandmother Lois and his mother Eunice (2 Ti 3¹⁵ 1⁵); and Josephus says that 'from the very dawn of understanding' a Jewish child 'learned the Law by heart, and had it, as it were, engraved on his soul.'§ It may be assumed that Joseph and Mary would be no less zealous than others in the discharge of this sacred and imperative duty.

When he reached the age of six or seven years,‖ the boy was sent to the elementary school, which, since the subject of study was the Book of the Law, was styled the House of the Book (bêth ha-Sēpher). This admirable institution, comparable to John Knox's parish school, was attached to the synagogue; and since there was a synagogue in every village in the land, there was also an

* c. Apion. i. 12.   † Wetstein on 2 Ti 3¹⁵.
‡ Taylor, Sayings of Fathers, iv. 27.
§ Vita, 2.
‖ According to the ordinance of Joshua ben Gamla. Joshua was high priest from A.D. 63 to 65, but his ordinance was merely a reinforcement of existing requirements. Cf. Schürer, HJP II. ii. p. 49.

elementary school in every village.* The establishment of this system of education was ascribed to the celebrated Simon ben Shetach, brother of Salome Alexandra, the queen of Alexander Jannæus (B.C. 104–78), and his successor on the throne (B.C. 78–69). Schürer † summarily dismisses the tradition with the remark that 'this Simon ben Shetach is a meeting-place for all kinds of myths.' Whatever be the worth of the tradition, Josephus' reiterated ascription to Moses of the exceedingly thorough system of education which prevailed in his day,‡ proves it no recent institution.

From the House of the Book such as desired to prosecute their studies and become teachers themselves passed into the Scribal College, styled the House of the Midrash (bêth ha-Midrâsh),§ where the great Rabbis taught. There were several of these colleges in Palestine. Sometimes, like the Christian ἐκκλησία (cf. 1 Co 16¹⁹, Col 4¹⁵), they met in an upper room in a private house,‖ but generally in some special place. The college at Jabne, where R. Eleasar and R. Ishmael taught, met in a place called the Vineyard. The principal college was that of Jerusalem, and it met within the Temple - precincts (cf. Lk 2⁴⁶), probably in the Temple-synagogue. The Rabbi occupied a low platform, and his disciples sat round him on the floor, 'powdering themselves in the dust of the feet of the wise,'¶—an arrangement which explains St. Paul's expression, 'educated at the feet of Gamaliel' (Ac 22³).

The disciples were employed in the study of the Oral Law—the Tradition of the Elders (Mt 15²), which in those days was regarded with even greater veneration than the Written Law,** and which until, at the earliest, the 5th cent. of our era †† was preserved in the memories of the Rabbis and orally transmitted from generation to generation. The method of study was Mishna, i.e. 'repetition,' ‡‡ the lesson being repeated over and over again until it was fixed in the memory; and proficiency lay in faithful reproduction of the ipsissima verba of the Tradition. It was a high eulogy of Eliezer ben Hyrcanus, a disciple of R. Johanan ben Zakai, when he was likened to 'a plastered cistern which loses not a drop.' §§

This mnemonic drill was not the sole employment in the House of the Midrash. Whatever difficulties they felt, the disciples propounded to the Rabbis for elucidation.

Often their questions were ridiculous quibbles, like that put to R. Levi ben Susi in connexion with Dt 25⁹ 'If his brother's wife have lost her hands, how is she to loose his shoe?'‖‖ But they were not always quite so trivial. One much discussed quæstio theologicalis was, 'Are they few that are being saved?' Some Rabbis held that 'all Israel would have a portion in the world to come'; others, that as only two of all that came out of Egypt entered into the land of Canaan, so would it be in the days of the Messiah.¶¶ Another question was, 'May a man divorce his wife for any cause?' (cf. Mt 19³). The strict school of Shammai permitted divorce only on the ground of unfaithfulness; but that of Hillel granted greater facility, allowing a man to put away his wife if he hated her; if he was dissatisfied with her cooking; if she went deaf or insane; if he saw another woman whom he fancied more.***

Not being designed for a Rabbi, Jesus never studied at any of the Scribal Colleges; but once

---

* Lightfoot on Mt 4²³; cf. Lk 5¹⁷.   † HJP II. ii. p. 49.
‡ Ant. IV. viii. 12; c. Apion. ii. 25.
§ 'The Midrash may be defined as an imaginative development of a thought or theme suggested by Scripture, especially a didactic or homiletic exposition, or an edifying religious story' (Driver, LOT⁶ p. 529).
‖ Lightfoot on Ac 1¹³; Taylor, Sayings of Fathers, i. 4: 'Let thy house be a meeting-house for the wise.'
¶ Taylor, Sayings of Fathers, i. 4, n. 11.
** Lightfoot on Mt 15².
†† See Margoliouth in Expositor, Dec. 1904, p. 403.
‡‡ The Greek term δευτέρωσις (cf. Jer. Algas. Quæst. x) is a literal rendering of Mishna.
§§ Taylor, Sayings of Fathers, ii. 10.
‖‖ Lightfoot on Lk 2⁴⁶.   ¶¶ Ib. on Lk 13²³.
*** Ib. on Mt 5³¹.

He sat at the feet of the Rabbis in the House of the Midrash at Jerusalem—on that memorable occasion when, on attaining the age of twelve years and becoming 'a son of the Law,' He for the first time (?) accompanied Joseph and Mary on their annual pilgrimage to the sacred capital to celebrate the Feast of the Passover. He lingered in the city when His parents set forth on their return journey, and they found Him on the third day after in the school of the Rabbis. 'Raise up many disciples' was the Rabbinical maxim,* and the new recruit would be welcome when He took His place among the disciples. He was 'sitting in the midst of the Teachers, both listening to them and questioning them' (Lk 2⁴⁶), and evincing an intelligence which amazed them.

There prevailed in early times a singularly unhappy misconception, that the Holy Child was confounding the wise men by an exhibition of Divine wisdom. The Arab. Evang. Inf. (l.-lii.) declares that He was puzzling them with questions about theology, astronomy, physics, metaphysics, and anatomy, 'things which the mind of no creature could reach'; and Origen says: 'He was questioning the Teachers; and because they could not answer, He Himself was answering the questions which He asked.' 'He was questioning the Teachers, not that He might learn aught, but that by questioning He might instruct them.'† This is rank Docetism, and is refuted by the Evangelist's testimony that 'Jesus made progress in wisdom and age' (ἡλικίᾳ) (Lk 2⁵²), as it were, pari passu. He had a human education. His mind grew even as His body.

It made Jesus an object of disdain in the eyes of the rulers that He had never attended a Rabbinical College. They called Him 'a Samaritan,' which was a nickname that they had for one who had never sat at the feet of the Rabbis.‡ At the same time they could not deny that He had a knowledge of the things of God far transcending their theological lore. Again and again He encountered the wise men of Israel in debate, and worsted them on their own proper field (cf. Mk 12²⁸⁻³⁴ = Mt 22³⁴⁻⁴⁰; Mt 22⁴¹⁻⁴⁶ = Mk 12³⁵⁻³⁷ = Lk 20⁴¹⁻⁴⁴). And once, when they heard Him discoursing in the Temple-court, they marvelled whence He had derived His wisdom. 'How,' they asked, 'hath this man learning, though he hath not studied?' (Jn 7¹⁵). His wisdom flowed from a higher source. The lofty truths which they were blindly groping after and ignorantly reasoning about, the Father had revealed to Him (cf. Jn 5²⁰).

All the vaunted wisdom of the Rabbis Jesus held in very slight esteem. It was not indeed His manner to despise the searchings of earnest souls after the knowledge of God, but the theology of His day was the very arrogance of ignorance, and blinded its votaries to the truth. It is a pathetic fact that nothing so effectually prevented the recognition of Jesus by the men of Jerusalem as their fancied knowledge of the things of God. Bred in an atmosphere of disputation, they were all controversialists, and at every turn they would raise some theological objection to His claims. Once, when some wondered if He were the Messiah, others answered that His origin was known, and, according to the Rabbinical teaching, the Messiah would appear suddenly, none would know whence, like a serpent by the way or a treasure-trove (Jn 7²⁰⁻²⁷; cf. v.⁴¹ᶠ·). Again it was objected that He testified concerning Himself; and it was a Rabbinical maxim that a man's testimony concerning himself was invalid (Jn 8¹³).§ Thus it fared with the Messiah when He made His appeal to the men of Jerusalem. Their minds were fenced by an impenetrable barrier of theological prejudice. It was otherwise in Galilee. Among the unsophisticated folk of that despised province the gospel gained a fair hearing and a ready welcome. All the Apostles save Judas were Galilæans. 'I thank

---

* Taylor, Sayings of Fathers, i. 1.
† in Luc. Hom. xviii, xix.   ‡ Wetstein on Jn 8⁴⁸.
§ Cf. Wetstein on Jn 5³¹.

thee, Father, Lord of heaven and earth,' said Jesus, perhaps when He was leaving Jerusalem, rejected by her wise men (Jn 10[39. 40]),[*] 'that thou didst hide these things from wise and understanding, and didst reveal them to babes' (Mt 11[25]).

It is important to take account of this. Does it not explain a difficulty which has been felt in connexion with the Fourth Gospel? St. John represents Jesus as a controversialist absolutely unlike the gracious Teacher of the Synoptists; and it has been alleged that these representations are incompatible. If Jesus spoke as the Synoptists report, He cannot have spoken after the Johannine fashion. But the difference is really a mark of verisimilitude. Jesus had different audiences in Galilee and in Jerusalem. To the simple people of the north He spoke the language of the heart, and couched His teaching in parable and poetry; but in Jerusalem He had to do with men whose minds were steeped in theology, and He met them on their own ground, talked to them in their own language, and encountered them with their own weapons. He adapted His teaching to His audiences. See, further, art. BOYHOOD.

LITERATURE.—Schürer, *HJP* II. ii. p. 44 ff.; art. on 'Education' in Hastings' *DB* and in *Encyc. Biblica*.

DAVID SMITH.

EGG.—See ANIMALS, p. 66[b].

EGYPT.—The Gospel narrative comes into contact with the land of Egypt at one point alone, and then only incidentally, in a manner which seems to have exercised no influence and left no trace upon the course of sacred history. The record, moreover, is confined to the first of the Evangelists, and is by him associated with the fulfilment of prophecy, as one of the links which drew together the ancient Hebrew Scriptures and the life of our Lord. The narrative is simple and brief. St. Matthew relates that Joseph, in obedience to the command of God, conveyed by an angel in a dream, took refuge in Egypt with the child and his mother from the murderous intentions of Herod the king (Mt 2[13f.]). The return to Palestine, again at the bidding of an angel of the Lord in a dream, is described (v.[19ff.]). Joseph, however, feared to enter Judæa because of Archelaus, Herod's son and successor; and in obedience to a second vision directed his course to Galilee, and settled at Nazareth (v.[22f.]).

To St. Matthew it would appear that the chief interest of the history lies in its relation to OT prophecy. Both movements, the Flight and the Return to Nazareth, are described as fulfilments of the word spoken 'through the prophet' (v.[15]), or 'through the prophets' (v.[23]). In the first instance the passage quoted is Hos 11[1] 'When Israel was a child, then I loved him, and called my son out of Egypt' (מִמִּצְרַיִם קָרָאתִי לִבְנִי, LXX τὰ τέκνα αὐτοῦ, 'his, *i.e.* Israel's, children'). Hosea recalls the deliverance and mercies of the past (cf. G. A. Smith, *Twelve Prophets, in loc.*); the Evangelist sees history repeating itself in a new exodus, which, like the earlier departure from Egypt, signalizes the beginning of a new national life, and is the promise and pledge of Divine favour. Egypt, therefore, to the narrator is no mere 'geographical expression.' The name recalls the memories of a glorious past, when Israel's youth was guided and sustained by the miracles of Divine interposition. And to him it is significant of much that this land should thus be brought into connexion with the birth of a new era for the people, in the Person of

a greater Son, in whom he saw the fulfilment of the best hopes and brightest anticipations of Israel's ancient prophets.

The narrative of the Evangelist is absolutely simple and unadorned, and amounts to little more than a mention of the journey into Egypt made under Divine direction. No indication is given either of the locality or duration of the stay in the country. The impression conveyed, however, is that the visit was not prolonged.[*] Had the case been otherwise, it would hardly have failed to find mention in the other Synoptic Gospels, if not in St. John. The absence, therefore, of further record is hardly sufficient ground for throwing doubt upon the reality of the incident itself.

This brief statement is supplemented and expanded in the Apocryphal Gospels with a wealth of descriptive detail. The fullest accounts are found, as might be expected, in the *Gospel of the Infancy*, and the *Gospel of pseudo-Matthew* (see Hastings' *DB*, Extra Vol. p. 430 ff.).

In the *Gospel of the Infancy* (ch. ix. f.), Joseph and Mary with the Child set out for Egypt at cock-crow, and reach a great city and temple with an idol to whose shrine the other idols of Egypt send gifts. There they find accommodation in a hospital dedicated to the idol, and a great commotion is caused by their entrance. The people of the land send to the idol to inquire the reason of the commotion, and are told that an 'occult god' has come, who alone is worthy of worship, because he is truly Son of God. Thereupon the idol falls prostrate, and all the people run together at the sound. The following chapter narrates the healing of the three-year-old son of the priest of the idol, who is possessed by many demons, and whose sickness is described in terms similar to those used of the Gadarene demoniac (Lk 8[27], Mk 5[2-5]). Thereafter Joseph and Mary depart, being afraid lest the Egyptians should burn them to death because of the destruction of the idol. Passing on their way they twice meet with robbers in the desert. In the first instance the robbers flee on their approach, and a number of captives are liberated. At a considerably later stage of their journey (ch. xxiii.) two bandits are encountered, whose names are given as Titus and Dumachus, the former of whom bribes his companion not to molest Joseph and Mary; and the child Jesus foretells His crucifixion at Jerusalem thirty years later with these two robbers, and that Titus shall precede Him into Paradise. On the road the travellers have passed through many cities, at which a demoniac woman, a dumb bride, a leprous girl who accompanies them on their journey, and many others have been healed. Finally, they come to Memphis (ch. xxv.), where they see the Pharaoh, and remain three years, during which period Jesus works many miracles; returning at the end of the three years to Palestine, and by direction of an angel making their home at Nazareth.

In a similar strain the *Gospel of pseudo-Matthew* (ch. xvii. ff.) records the number of attendants, with riding animals, a waggon, pack-oxen and asses, sheep and rams, that set out with Joseph and Mary from Judæa. In a cave where they had stopped to rest they are terrified by dragons, which, however, worship the child Jesus; and lions and other wild beasts escort them on their way through the desert. A palm-tree bends down its boughs that Mary may pluck the fruit; and as a reward a branch of it is carried by an angel to Paradise. A spring also breaks forth from its roots for the refreshment of man and beast. And the long thirty days' journey into Egypt is miraculously shortened into one. The name of the Egyptian city to which they come is said to be Sotines within the borders of Hermopolis, and there, in default of any acquaintance from whom to seek hospitality, they take refuge in the temple, called the 'capitol.' The 355 idols of the temple, to which divine honours were daily paid, fall prostrate, and are broken in pieces; and Affrodosius, the governor of the town, coming with an army, at sight of the ruined idols worships the child Jesus, and all the people of the city believe in God through Jesus Christ. Afterwards Joseph is commanded to return into the land of Judah. Nothing, however, is said of the actual journey, but a narrative of events 'in Galilee' follows, beginning with the fourth year of Christ's age.

According to the *Gospel of Thomas*, ch. i. ff. (Latin, Tisch. *Evv. Apocr.* p. 156 ff.), Jesus was two years old on entering Egypt. He and His parents found hospitality in the house of a widow, where they remained for a year, at the close of which they were expelled because of a miracle wrought by Jesus in bringing a dry and salted fish to life. A similar fate overtakes them subsequently in being driven from the city. The angel directs *Mary* to return, and she goes with the child to Nazareth. The *History of Joseph*, ch. viii. f., states the duration of the stay in Egypt as a whole year, and names Nazareth as the city in which Jesus and His parents lived after their return into the land of Israel.

The Flight of the Holy Family into Egypt has been at all times a favourite subject for the exercise

---

[*] Mt. and Lk. give this *logion* in different connexions, neither suitable (Mt 11[25-27] = Lk 10[21. 22]). It is probably one of the fugitive fragments which the Synoptists have preserved of the Judæan ministry. It is remarkably Johannine. Cf. Jn. 3[35] 13[3] 11[8] 6[46. 65] 10[15].

[*] Herod's death (Mt 2[19]) would appear to have occurred not long after the 'Massacre of the Innocents' in Bethlehem.

of Christian art. William Blake, Charles Holroyd, Eugène Girardet, Anthony van Dyke, William Dobson, and many others have painted the scenes by the way with a circumstance and detail which are indebted, where not wholly imaginary, to the accounts of the Apocryphal Gospels. The reality would doubtless differ widely from the tranquil and easy conditions under which it has usually been depicted, and from which most readers have formed their mental conceptions of the event. The simple reticence of the Gospel narrative is in striking contrast to the luxuriance and prodigality of miracle of the Apocryphal story. All that can be affirmed with certainty is that the flight would be conducted in haste and with the utmost secrecy, and probably for the most part under cover of night. See also FLIGHT.

LITERATURE.—For notes on the Gospel narrative see the Commentaries on St. Matthew; and for the Apocryphal additions to the history, Tischendorf's *Evangelia Apocrypha*, Leipzig, 1853. Certain features in the latter appear to betray Buddhist relations or parentage. For some account of the treatment of the subject in art, see Farrar, *Christ in Art*, pp. 263-273.

A. S. GEDEN.

EIGHTH DAY.—On the eighth day after birth, as is well known, Jewish male infants received the rite of circumcision, and, at all events by the time of our Lord, their proper name also, in memory of the change in Abraham's name (see Hastings' *DB*, art. 'Circumcision'). Accordingly St. Luke records the fact that both Jesus Christ (2^{21}) and His forerunner John the Baptist ($1^{59\mathrm{ff.}}$) were circumcised and named on the eighth day (cf. Ph 3^5, Ac 7^8 etc.); for thus it became them ' to fulfil all righteousness' (*i.e.* to observe all the requirements of the ancient Law in the spirit as well as in the letter). See, further, art. CIRCUMCISION.   C. L. FELTOE.

ELDER.—In the Gospels the term 'elder' ($\pi\rho\epsilon\sigma$-$\beta\dot{\nu}\tau\epsilon\rho\sigma\varsigma$) does not occur in the later Christian sense, denoting an officer of the Church (as in Ac 14^{23} 20^{17}, Tit 1^5, Ja 5^{14}, 1 P 5^1). In the Gospel of St. John the word occurs only once, and that in the doubtful passage concerning the adulteress (Jn 8^9), where it has not any official sense, but simply means older in years. In the Synoptics there is more frequent use, mostly in the official sense. The few cases of unofficial meaning of the term are: Lk 15^{25}, where it describes the 'elder brother' in the parable of the Prodigal; and Mt 15^2, Mk $7^{3.\ 5}$, where it means 'the elders' of a former age, the men of old from whom customs and maxims are handed down. In all the other passages (Mt 16^{21} 21^{23} $26^{3.\ 47.\ 57.\ 59}$ $27^{1.3.\ 12.\ 20.\ 41}$, Mk 8^{31} 11^{27} $14^{43.\ 53}$, Lk 9^{22} 20^1 22^{52}) the term 'elders'—invariably plural—bears the official meaning current among the Jews of our Lord's time. What is that meaning?

In the OT and Apocr. there is frequent mention of 'elders' in the official sense (see, *e.g.*, Gn 50^7, Ex $3^{16.\ 18}$, Lv 4^{15}, Nu 11^{25}, Dt 31^{28}, Jos 20^4, Jg 8^{16}, 1 S 16^4, 2 S 5^3, 1 K 20^7, Ezr 5^5, Ezk 8^1, Jth 6^{21}, 1 Mac 7^{33} 11^{23}, Sus $^{8.\ 18}$ etc.). From a study of these and similar passages it appears that in all the history of Israel, from the Egyptian bondage down to the time of Christ, 'elders' appear as an official class; but the descriptions and statements are not explicit enough to give a definite idea of how they were appointed to office, or of their exact functions. It is not improbable that they were chosen as representatives of the people; and the duties of the office appear to have been threefold—advisory, executive, judicial. Further, there is a distinction between local 'elders' (those of a city) and 'the elders of Israel,' 'elders of the congregation,' 'elders of the people,' as they are variously called. We are now to inquire how far this OT use of the word is illustrated in that of the Gospels.

One passage only (Lk 7^3) seems to indicate the local 'elders'—those of Capernaum, the scene of the event described; and even here the turn of the expression, 'elders of the Jews,' might possibly point to national 'elders' present or resident at Capernaum. But on the whole it seems more natural to take the term here in its local sense. In all the remaining passages cited above, the reference is to the national 'elders.' From Vitringa (*de Synag. Vet.* III. i. 1) downwards, NT scholars have held with apparent unanimity that the term designates the members of the Sanhedrin (wh. see). This view is sustained by the connexion and association of the term,—usually with 'scribes' and 'chief priests,'—and by Lk 22^{66}, where the Sanhedrin is called 'the presbytery,' or assembly of 'elders' ($\pi\rho\epsilon\sigma\beta\upsilon\tau\dot{\epsilon}\rho\iota\sigma\nu$, cf. Ac 22^5). There are various forms of expression: sometimes 'elders' simply, and sometimes 'elders of the people,' commonly associated with 'chief priests and scribes.' This is held by some to indicate that there were three orders or grades in the Sanhedrin, the 'elders' being the lay element, or representatives of the people. This may be the case, but is at best only an inference, neither contradicted nor supported.

LITERATURE.—Hastings' *DB*, art. 'Elder,' and the lit. there mentioned; *Jewish Encyc.* and lit.; Grimm-Thayer, *Lexicon of the NT*; Cremer, *Biblico-Theol. Lex.*; Vitringa, *de Syn. Vet.*; Schürer, *HJP*; Morrison, *The Jews under Roman Rule*; Weiss, *Life of Christ*; Edersheim, *Life and Times*.

E. C. DARGAN.

ELEAZAR.—An ancestor of Jesus, Mt 1^{15}.

ELECT, ELECTION ($\dot{\epsilon}\kappa\lambda\dot{\epsilon}\gamma\epsilon\sigma\theta\alpha\iota$, $\dot{\epsilon}\kappa\lambda\epsilon\kappa\tau\dot{\sigma}\varsigma$, $\dot{\epsilon}\kappa\lambda\sigma\gamma\dot{\eta}$).—Though we have no reference in the Gospels to any conscious effort on the part of the writers to grasp the significance of the Divine action in choosing and rejecting the human objects of His favour and the instruments of His will, we have sufficiently explicit statements, incidentally valuable, to show clearly that they inherited the OT conceptions on this question. The self-identification of Jesus with the ideal Servant of Jehovah (Lk $4^{18\mathrm{f.}}$ = Is $61^{1\mathrm{f.}}$) at the outset of His public ministry at once widens the scope of the revelation of His Father's elective activity, and emphasizes the profound depths in human-Divine relationships to which this activity in the freedom of its manifestation has penetrated. Once again, in what may without exaggeration be called the most critical moment of Jesus' public life, when suffering and death (Lk 9^{31}) assumed large proportions in His sight, the revelation of His position as the elect of God ($\dot{\sigma}$ $\upsilon\dot{\iota}\dot{\sigma}\varsigma$ $\mu\sigma\upsilon$ $\dot{\sigma}$ $\dot{\epsilon}\kappa\lambda\epsilon\lambda\epsilon\gamma\mu\dot{\epsilon}\nu\sigma\varsigma$, v.^{35}) not only assured His fearful disciples, but strengthened Himself in His often-expressed conviction that the consciousness of His eternal Sonship was well founded.

The variant reading $\dot{\sigma}$ $\dot{\epsilon}\kappa\lambda\epsilon\lambda\epsilon\gamma\mu\dot{\epsilon}\nu\sigma\varsigma$ instead of $\dot{\sigma}$ $\dot{\alpha}\gamma\alpha\pi\eta\tau\dot{\sigma}\varsigma$ (Mk 9^7 = Mt 17^5) is generally recognized as the genuine one, not only on account of the high authority of ℵ and B, but also because, according to an obvious canon of textual criticism, it is the more likely reading of the two (see Scrivener's *Introd. to the Criticism of the NT*, ii. 247 f.; cf., however, Nestle's *Criticism of the Greek NT*[2], p. 52, and art. 'Ascension of Isaiah' in Hastings' *DB*, vol. ii. p. 501a). The Matthæan and Markan versions bear evident traces of assimilation to the voice at Jesus' baptism. In this connexion it is important to remember how fully Jesus recognized that His position as the elect Son involved the fulfilment ($\ddot{\epsilon}\mu\epsilon\lambda\lambda\epsilon\nu$ $\pi\lambda\eta\rho\sigma\ddot{\upsilon}\nu$, Lk 9^{31}) by Him of conditions foreordained as inseparable from His earthly life (cf. Lk 9^{22} 13^{33} 24^7, in each of which places is found St. Luke's favourite and emphatic $\delta\epsilon\ddot{\iota}$; see also Mk 8^{31}, Mt 17^{21}). The determining factor in the free choice (cf. $\dot{\epsilon}\xi\sigma\upsilon\sigma\dot{\iota}\alpha\nu$ $\ddot{\epsilon}\chi\omega$ $\theta\epsilon\ddot{\iota}\nu\alpha\dot{\iota}$ $\alpha\dot{\upsilon}\tau\dot{\eta}\nu$, $\kappa.\tau.\lambda.$, Jn 10^{18}) by Jesus of the cross as the crowning act of His self-abnegation was its absolute necessity ($\sigma\dot{\upsilon}\chi\dot{\iota}$ $\tau\alpha\ddot{\upsilon}\tau\alpha$ $\ddot{\epsilon}\delta\epsilon\iota$ $\pi\alpha\theta\epsilon\ddot{\iota}\nu$, Lk 24^{26}). The ultimate synthesis of these apparently irreconcilable hypotheses may elude the keenest observation, but the reflexion that, in acting as He did, Jesus was fulfilling conditions which lie at the root of all well-ordered moral and spiritual activity (cf. $\ddot{\epsilon}\pi\rho\epsilon\pi\epsilon\nu$ $\alpha\dot{\upsilon}\tau\ddot{\omega}$, He 2^{10}; $\ddot{\omega}\varphi\epsilon\iota\lambda\epsilon\nu$, 2^{17}) will serve to remind us of a sphere where these seeming contradictions are discovered to be profoundly at one, both in their origin and in the end at which they aim. It is noteworthy that St. Luke not only gives the burden of the conversation between Jesus and His heavenly visitants;

he also implies that Jesus was there informed in detail of the character of the death which He was about to suffer (συνελάλουν αὐτῷ . . . ἔλεγον τὴν ἔξοδον αὐτοῦ, 9³⁰f.).

How universally the title of 'the Elect' or 'the Elect One' had become identified with that of 'the Christ' is best seen in the contemptuous irony of the scoffing rulers who mocked on the day of the Crucifixion. The demonstrative οὗτος and the titular ὁ ἐκλεκτός combine to mark the emphasis with which they rejected the Messianic claims of Jesus; and not only the claims, but the foundation upon which those claims rested (cf. Lk 23³⁵). It is remarkable that St. Luke seems to be the only NT writer who has adopted the use of the word as a designation, strictly speaking, of the Messiah (cf., however, the variant reading ὁ ἐκλεκτός in the Baptist's testimony to Jesus, Jn 1³⁴ WH). This statement is not affected by St. Matthew's quotation from Isaiah (42¹), who may be regarded as the originator of the title. Here we have the idea in prominence, but by way of interpretation rather than by direct statement (cf. his use of the verb ᾑρέτισα, Mt 12¹⁸, instead of the merely descriptive ὁ ἐκλεκός μου of Is 42¹).

The only other writing of a late date in which 'the Elect One' appears as a Messianic title is the Book of Enoch, which seems to have been the chief means of popularizing its use. Indeed, it would be interesting to trace the influence of that work in this, as well as in other respects, upon the Gospels of the NT. Of the many names by which the coming Messiah is designated there, the favourite one seems to be 'the Elect One' (see 40⁵ 45³f. 49².⁴ 51³.⁵ 52⁶.⁹ 55⁴ 61⁵.⁸.¹⁰ 62¹), and on a couple of occasions this is joined with another word or words which are equivalent to a characterization of the conditions upon which His election to the Messiahship rests ('the righteous and elect one,' 53⁸; 'the elect one of righteousness and faith,' 39⁶ [see *The Book of Enoch*, R. H. Charles' ed. pp. 106–186]). A somewhat fantastic representation of the method by which the Divine election of Jesus was consummated occurs in Hermas, where the servant elected by his lord (ἐκλεξάμενος δοῦλόν τινα πιστόν, κ.τ.λ.), after having approved himself as a zealous guardian of his master's interests, is chosen by the latter (μετὰ τοῦ πνεύματος· ἅγιον εἵλατο κοινωνίον) to occupy the position of 'great power and lordship.' Whatever we may think of the orthodoxy of this teaching, it is at least interesting as showing how completely the habits of thought in the early Church were dominated by this aspect of the Incarnation, and how men strove by the aid of reason to harmonize the ideas underlying the titles of 'Servant' and 'Son' (see *Sim.* 5, i.–vi.).

As the Christological ideas of the early Church begin to emerge and to crystallize, we find this one holding a firm place, while at the same time another equally emphatic conception begins to assert itself. The election, by God, of Jesus was held to be a means to a wider end—the establishment of a chosen body which should exhibit on earth the graces and virtues of Him in and through whom their election was accomplished (cf. 1 P 2⁴f. ⁹f., where the writer's insistence on the profound oneness of Jesus and His people is fundamentally and essentially Pauline, though he elaborates no argument to prove what he states; cf. ἐξελέξατο ἡμᾶς ἐν αὐτῷ, Eph 1⁴).

'The fundamental conception of Jesus dominating everything was, according to the OT, that God had chosen Him and through Him the Church. God had chosen Him and made Him to be both Lord and Christ. He had made over to Him the work of setting up the Kingdom,' etc. (Harnack, *Dogmengeschichte*, Eng. tr. vol. i. p. 81). 'The Christian community must be conceived as a communion resting on a divine election' (*ib.* p. 148).

We must not forget, however, that this Divine election has its roots struck deep in the election which issued in the Incarnation, and that, apart from the latter, which is the *rationale* and guarantee of the former, we cannot believe in the existence of 'an elect race' (ὑμεῖς δὲ γένος ἐκλεκτόν, 1 P 2⁹). This was apprehended very soon by the Fathers of the Church, who never separate the idea of the election of Jesus from that of the community (ὁ ἐκλεξάμενος τὸν Κύριον Ἰησοῦν Χριστὸν καὶ ἡμᾶς δι' αὐτοῦ, κ.τ.λ., Clem. Rom. *Ep. ad Cor.* lxiv.; cf. also the Paulinism ὁ λαὸς ὃν ἡτοίμασεν ἐν τῷ ἠγαπημένῳ αὐτοῦ, Ep. of Barnabas iii. 6). While it is recognized that the ultimate Author of all elective purpose is God the Father, it is agreed that the active Agent in

giving expression to the Divine decree is the Son, apart from whom (εἰ μὴ δι' ἐμοῦ, Jn 14⁶) it is not only impossible for men to approach God, but even to hear the voice of that calling (κλήσεως ἐπουρανίου, He 3¹, cf. 12²⁵) which He addresses to them in Christ (ὁ καλέσας ὑμᾶς . . . ἐν Χριστῷ, 1 P 5¹⁰), and which, when heard, is the antecedent condition of their election (cf. 2 P 1¹⁰; see οἱ κλητοὶ καὶ ἐκλεκτοὶ καὶ πιστοί, Rev 17¹⁴).

It will scarcely be contended that there is any practical difference in the Christology of those who speak of an election διὰ Χριστοῦ, and of those who in the same connexion use the phrase ἐν Χριστῷ. We are able, perhaps, to see in the former expression an emphatic assertion of the delegated activity of Christ who prepares 'for Himself' a people (αὐτὸς ἑαυτῷ τὸν λαὸν τὸν καινὸν ἑτοιμάζων ἐπιδείξῃ, Barn. v. 7, cf. xiv. 6) whose prerogatives and position shall be in correspondence with His royal priesthood, and with the Sonship to which He was chosen (1 P 2⁴. ⁹, Rev 20⁶ 16; cf. He 7²⁴ ἀπαράβατον τὴν ἱερωσύνην, Ro 8¹⁴⁻¹⁷ οὗτοι υἱοὶ θεοῦ εἰσίν . . . συνκληρονόμοι δὲ Χριστοῦ, κ.τ.λ.).

Nor is the teaching of Jesus Himself devoid of references to those chosen by God out of mankind 'as vessels made to honour' (cf. 2 Ti 2²¹, Ro 9²¹). He indirectly tells us that 'the elect' have an influence in the Divine government of the world which makes for mercy and pity and salvation. The awful scenes accompanying the destruction of Jerusalem would result in the annihilation of its doomed inhabitants, were it not that, 'for the sake of his chosen,' the Lord (some of the old Latin versions read *Deus*) had determined to cut short the duration of that period (cf. Mk 13²⁰ = Mt 24²², in both of which passages occurs the verb κολοβοῦν, found nowhere else in the NT, showing the interdependence of the two authors, although the forms of the verb in both places are not the same). St. Luke does not make any mention in this part of his record of the elect, but curiously enough he makes a reference to the vengeance of God being wreaked (ἡμέραι ἐκδικήσεως, Lk 21²²) on the unfortunate city, which reminds us of the words of Jesus contained in another passage in the same Gospel. Jesus there is said to speak of God 'avenging his elect' (ὁ δὲ θεὸς οὐ μὴ ποιήσῃ τὴν ἐκδίκησιν τῶν ἐκλεκτῶν αὐτοῦ, Lk 18⁷). It may be permissible to conjecture that St. Luke omitted to mention Jesus' reference to the elect in the former context because of the promise implied in the interrogatory sentence just quoted. On the other hand, it is possible that a displacement has occurred in the text, with the result that we have a double reference to God's activity on behalf of His chosen, each being suitable to the textual position it occupies. The subject of the prayers of those who appeal (τῶν βοώντων αὐτῷ) 'day and night' is that, in the first place, they may be delivered from injustice; and, secondly, that they may soon see the vengeance of God active on their behalf against those who oppress them (cf. ἐκδίκησόν με ἀπὸ τοῦ ἀντιδίκου μου, Lk 18³, where the first idea is prominent; and ἐκδικεῖς . . . ἐκ τῶν, κ.τ.λ., Rev 6¹⁰, in which the second thought is emphasized; cf. also the reference to the cry of Abel's blood for vengeance, cf. He 12²⁴ = Gn 4¹⁰). It is possible that, by interpreting the cry of the elect in this twofold sense, we are able to obtain a clearer idea of the meaning of the 'longsuffering' of God with regard to them (μακροθυμεῖ ἐπ' αὐτοῖς). The ambiguity of the expression is mitigated if we remember that the patience of God is needed even by His elect, whose insistent (cf. φωνῇ μεγάλῃ, Rev 6¹⁰, and ἡμέρας καὶ νυκτός, Lk 18⁷) appeal for vengeance on their enemies and oppressors is not in harmony with the voice of that blood by which they were redeemed (αἷμα ῥαντισμοῦ, He 12²⁴). Much more, of course, does the patient waiting of God, sometimes amounting even to seeming tardiness, reveal His tenderness when exemplified in the case of those who torment His elect (ὥς τινες βραδυτῆτα ἡγοῦνται, 2 P 3⁹). Arising out of this thought we are not surprised to find on more than one occasion that not only is it insufficient for their final acceptance that men should be 'called' (cf. the contrast πολλοί κλητοί and ὀλίγοι ἐκλεκτοί, Mt 22¹⁴), for this is in harmony with much of Jesus' teaching elsewhere (cf. Mt 7²⁴· ²⁶ etc.), but that there is even a danger that the elect may lose that to and for which they were chosen (see . . . ἀποπλανᾶν . . . τοὺς ἐκλεκτούς, Mk 13²², cf. Mt 24²⁴; εἰ δυνατόν can hardly be an implied assertion of the impossibility of success attending the efforts of the false teachers to lead astray the elect; it rather refers to that object which they had in view). Another and a further condition must be fulfilled before the chosen of God may claim the salvation to which they were elected (. . . τὴν ἡτοιμασμένην ἡμῖν βασιλείαν ἀπὸ καταβολῆς κόσμου, Mt 25³⁴; cf. 20²³, He 11¹⁶). On more than one occasion Jesus insists on the necessity of endurance or perseverance up to the very end of their experiences (ὁ ὑπομείνας . . . σωθήσεται, Mk 13¹³ = Mt 24¹³; cf. Mt 10²², Eph 6¹⁸), and, on the other hand, we are justified in applying to this place His warning, which He gave to those whose joy in receiving the gospel message was but a transitory (πρόσκαιρος, Mt 13²¹ = Mk 4¹⁷) emotion. Of a like nature is the incidental remark of the seer of the Apocalypse, that Jesus' companions in His warfare with 'the beast' are those who not only were called and elected, but whose calling and election had been crowned by their enduring faithfulness (πιστοί, Rev 17¹⁴). We are thus able to appreciate the anxiety of later Christian writers, who emphasized this part of Jesus' teaching, and who reminded their readers that their entrance into the eternal kingdom of Jesus was conditioned by their enduring zeal; for in this way alone their 'calling' and 'election' were made stable and lasting and certain (βεβαίαν ὑμῶν τὴν κλῆσιν καὶ ἐκλογὴν ποιεῖσθαι, 2 P 1¹⁰, cf. He 3¹⁴).

That Jesus held firmly by the Jewish belief in the election of that race to spiritual privilege, is evidenced by many signs both in His teaching and His methods of work. It is true that His words are in perfect harmony with the Baptist's scornful warning against that foolish pride of birth which leaves out of sight the responsibility involved by privilege (cf. Mt 3⁸ᶠ· and Jn 8³⁹ᶠ·). At the same time, He is no less ready to assert the claims of His fellow-countrymen to the rights which were theirs as the Divinely chosen people (ἡ σωτηρία ἐκ τῶν Ἰουδαίων ἐστίν, Jn 4²²; cf. τὸν ἄρτον τῶν τέκνων, Mt 15²⁶). The sting of His bitter denunciation of contemporary religionists lay in His recognition of their spiritual position, and of the fact that they of right were the teachers of the people (ἐπὶ τῆς Μωσέως καθέδρας, Mt 23², cf. v.¹³ᶠᶠ·). In spite of many disappointing experiences, He was again and again amazed at the lack of faith and spiritual insight amongst 'Israelites' (Mt 8¹⁰ = Lk 7⁹; Jn 3¹⁰, cf. Mk 6⁶), and His pathetic lament over the decaying Jerusalem shows how eagerly He had hoped to make the Jewish nation realize its ancient place as the 'first-begotten' in the family of His Father (Ex 4²², Jer 31⁹, cf. He 12²³). His activity in this direction betrays itself both in His words which incidentally express His feelings (ἄφες πρῶτον χορτασθῆναι τὰ τέκνα, Mk 7²⁷, Mt 15²⁴), and in His deliberate instructions to His disciples to confine their missionary labours 'to the lost sheep of the house of Israel' (Mt 10⁶). We are, however, bound to remember that St. Matthew alone records this restriction, and that there are some evidences of the abandonment of its strict enforcement even by Jesus Himself (Jn 4³⁹⁻⁴², cf. Ac 1⁸ 8¹⁴ᶠᶠ·).

Though Jesus felt Himself forced to recognize, in the attitude of the Pharisees and lawyers of His day, the failure of God's people to realize the Divine purpose in them, He also recognizes no less distinctly that, according to that purpose, theirs was a high destiny (. . . τὴν βουλὴν τοῦ θεοῦ ἠθέτησαν εἰς ἑαυτούς, Lk 7³⁰ [cf. for the use of βουλή in this sense Ac 2²³ 4²⁸ 20²⁷, Eph 1¹¹, He 6¹⁷]), and it seems as if at times His realization of what this people might have become, and His keen disappointment at their actual achievement, led Him into speaking disparagingly of those who were outside the Jewish covenant (cf. the contrast ὑμεῖς . . . ἡμεῖς, Jn 4²², which is the verbal expression of a contrast running through the whole narrative [see Westcott, *Gospel of St. John, ad loc.*]; cf. also the privilege involved in the word πρῶτον as well as the harsh contrast τέκνα [παιδία] . . . κυνάρια, Mk 7²⁷ᶠ·).

We may here note that St. Matthew has preserved several fragments which deal with the claim of Israel as God's people to be the sole recipients of the gospel message (Mt 10⁵ᶠ· ²³ 15²⁴ 23²ᶠ·), though he also records sayings of Jesus which conflict with this (24¹⁴ 28¹⁹, cf. Mk 13¹⁰ 11¹⁷ 14⁹ 16¹⁵, Lk 24⁴⁷). Perhaps the most striking instance of these just referred to is that in which Jesus avers, as His reason for the evangelization of Israel alone, that His 'coming' is imminent, and that no time is to be lost, because, in any event, the work will not be completed before that occurrence (. . . ἕως ἔλθῃ ὁ υἱὸς τοῦ ἀνθρώπου, Mt 10²³). It is evident that whatever may have been the case with regard to Jesus' actual knowledge of the date of His *parousia*, those who heard His words understood Him to mean that it would take place soon (cf. καὶ τότε, Mk 13²⁶, Lk 21²⁷, Mt 24³⁰; οὐ μὴ παρέλθῃ ἡ γενεὰ αὕτη ἕως πάντα γένηται, Lk 21³², see 1 Th 4¹⁵ᶠ·). Moreover, the Evangelists seem to have established an intimate connexion in the consciousness of early Christianity between His second coming and the preaching of His gospel to 'the cities of Israel' (Ac 3²⁶, Ro 1¹⁶; see Edersheim, *Life and Times*, i. 644 ff.; cf. also O. Holtzmann, *Leben Jesu*, Eng. tr. pp. 160, 301, etc.). 'It might, of course, be objected, that the idea of the universality of the judgment leaves no sufficient reason for restricting the disciples' work to the Jewish people, and that the heathen were perhaps even in more urgent need of the disciples' preaching than the Jews, since to the latter had been given the Law and the Prophets. The justness of the objection may be granted. But against it we have set the belief in the election of Israel,' etc. (O. Holtzmann, *op. cit.* p. 279 n.¹). His own assertion with the limiting words εἰ μή (Mt 15²⁴) is strongly emphatic as to His conviction with regard to the Divine favour towards Israel. 'The saying of Jesus to His disciples at the last supper, that they, to whom He committed His kingdom which He had received from His Father, would be beside Him . . . sitting on thrones, judging the twelve tribes of Israel (Lk 22²⁹ᶠ·), indicates that He viewed the activity of His disciples, and therefore also their future judicial function, as primarily extending to the people of Israel. Also when Jesus spoke of a coming of the heathen from the east and west . . . He was thereby thinking of an ingathering . . . which, as a whole, consisted of native Israelites' (Wendt, *Lehre Jesu*, Eng. tr. ii. 349 f.).

Not only do we find Jesus recognizing and acting upon the OT conception of the national election of Israel—that preferential treatment which His fellow-countrymen claimed as of right—though He reminded them from time to time that in order to a genuine Abrahamic descent it was necessary to cultivate an ethical and spiritual likeness to their great forefather, which would alone complete their title to the promises made to them through him (cf. the implied contrast between physical and spiritual descent in the words σπέρμα and τέκνα, Jn 8³⁷· ³⁹; cf. Lk 3⁸ = Mt 3⁹). Jesus also Himself, in establishing His Kingdom amongst men, proceeds along lines exactly parallel to these. He assumes to Himself the right to select certain instruments whereby His designs may be furthered and ultimately accomplished. As He was the Chosen and Sent of His Father, so He is delegated to choose and send others, who were to be the few through whom God's work upon the many was to be accomplished (cf. Jn 17¹⁸ 20²¹ 13¹⁸ etc.). It is true that at times Jesus speaks of His disciples as His Father's choice and possession (σοὶ ἦσαν, Jn 17⁶), and that they are His by His Father's gift (μοὶ αὐτοὺς ἔδωκας, 17⁶· ⁹; cf. καὶ τὰ ἐμὰ πάντα σά ἐστιν καὶ τὰ σὰ ἐμά, v.¹⁰). At the same time He is no less emphatic in His declarations that they are His own elect, the result of His own discriminating choice (ἐγὼ ἐξελεξάμην ὑμᾶς ἐκ τοῦ κόσμου, Jn 15¹⁹; cf. ἐγὼ οἶδα τίνας ἐξελεξάμην, 13¹⁸). Our knowledge of Jesus' acquaintance with the characters of His disciples prior to their selection by Him, is too scanty to permit us to judge accurately of His methods ; but from the fact that they were for the most part natives of that part of Galilee where His earliest activity displayed itself, and that some of them were antecedently disciples of the Baptist, we are led to conclude that He possessed sufficient individual acquaintanceship to warrant His choice (cf. Mk 1[16ff.], Mt 4[18ff.], Lk 5[10f.] ; see Jn 1[40ff.]). He seems, moreover, to have felt a heavy weight of responsibility on their account, and in the review of His work towards the end of His life, He seems to congratulate Himself on being able to render a good account of His stewardship in this respect. As the result of His guardianship (ἐγὼ ἐτήρουν αὐτοὺς . . . καὶ ἐφύλαξα, Jn 17[12]), they all justified His choice with but one exception, and that exception had its mournful justification (ἵνα ἡ γραφὴ πληρωθῇ), and, in spite of the necessity of such failure (κατὰ τὸ ὡρισμένον, Lk 22[22] ; cf. Ac 2[23], see also Lk 17[1] = Mt 18[7]), its awful warning (οὐαὶ δὲ τῷ ἀνθρώπῳ ἐκείνῳ δι' οὗ, κ.τ.λ., Mk 14[21], Mt 26[24]). The work which this chosen nucleus was destined to achieve finds also a definite place in the consciousness of Jesus as He looks out on the world and down the future ages. He does not, in fact, hesitate to name those who are to be brought to share in the glory and in the power of His judgment-coming, though they are scattered in all directions over the world (ἐκ τῶν τεσσάρων ἀνέμων ἀπ' ἄκρου γῆς ἕως ἄκρου οὐρανοῦ, Mk 13[27] = Mt 24[31]), His elect (τοὺς ἐκλεκτοὺς αὐτοῦ).

The work wrought by the little band chosen by Christ, and continued by their successors from one generation to another during the period intervening between the initiation of His Kingdom and its consummation, can hardly be better delineated than in the words of the present Bishop of Birmingham : 'The Apostles were the first "elect" in Christ with a little Jewish company. "We,"—so St. Paul speaks of the Jewish Christians, —"we who had before hoped in Christ." But it was to show the way to all the Gentiles ("ye also, who have heard the word of the truth, the gospel of your salvation") who were also to constitute "God's own possession" and His "heritage." The purpose to be realized is a universal one : it is the reunion of man with man, as such, by being all together reunited to God in one body. . . . And the Church of the reconciliation is God's elect body to represent a Divine purpose of restoration far wider than itself—extending, in fact, to all creation. It is the Divine purpose, with a view to "a dispensation of the fulness of the times, to sum up" or "bring together again in unity" all things in Christ. . . . This great and rich idea of the election of the Church as a special body to fulfil a universal purpose of recovery,' etc. (Gore, The Epistle to the Ephesians, p. 71 f.).

Here, then, we have in its incipient stages a revelation of this Divine process of working in its new and wider aspect. There is fundamentally no change of method, but rather a consecration of what has always in the OT been recognized as God's plan of work (cf. e.g. Am 3[2], Dt 7[6] etc.). In the fresh start, so to speak, which He has made we find His choice not merely involved in the Incarnation as the mode of procedure, but in the election of the Man Jesus (Lk 9[35]), whom He deliberately ordained or appointed (ἐν ἀνδρὶ ᾧ ὥρισεν, Ac 17[31], cf. 10[38]) for His work. Jesus, acting on authority delegated to Him, chooses certain men and sends them to carry out what He has commenced. In the end He breaks down all national barriers and limitations (Mt 28[19], cf. Mk 16[15]), and people in every nation (ἐν παντὶ ἔθνει, Ac 10[35]) are accepted by Him so long as they 'fear God and work righteousness.'

Keeping these facts and considerations in mind, we are at liberty to ask ourselves the very difficult questions, On what basis does the Divine election stand ? Is there any antecedent condition in complying with which men are placed amongst the number of God's elect ? From whatever point of view we look at this mystery, one thought, at least, clearly emerges : in His choice of Israel as the guardian of the sacred deposit of religious truth, God exhibited His wisdom in a way we, as students of the Divine government of the world,

can discern and appreciate. Their genius for the work entrusted to them is universally recognized (cf., on the other hand, such passages as Dt 9[5f.] 10[15], Jer 31[1. 3], Mal 1[2f.], which, however, do not conflict with the general truth of our statement, though they emphasize the absolute freedom of God's choice). From them and from them solely have come into the world those truths which spring from a pure and spiritual monotheism ; and we are not forbidden to recognize, in the analogous lessons taught to the world by other nations, that 'the principle of selection' (ἡ κατ' ἐκλογὴν πρόθεσις, Ro 9[11]) finds its place in their history too (see Sanday-Headlam, 'Romans' in Internat. Crit. Com. pp. 248 ff., 342 ff. etc.). When we remember that to the consciousness of Jesus the full and final revelation of His unique Divine Sonship was only made at His Baptism (Mt 3[17] = Mk 1[11] = Lk 3[22]), and confirmed beyond doubt during the period of His Temptation, we are at liberty to believe that His previous life was a gradual preparation for His final election, as well as a proof that in selecting Him for His work His Father had chosen the fittest Instrument to reveal Himself to mankind. Remembering, too, the gradual gathering together by Jesus of His little band of chosen disciples and followers, and the care taken by Him in training and disciplining them for their position and work, we are able to apprehend in some dim way the necessity of a moral and spiritual correspondence between Him who chooses and His chosen. The fact that Jesus Himself included Judas Iscariot amongst the number of His 'elect' (Jn 6[70]) does not invalidate this contention, as we may well be allowed to believe that the unhappy traitor exhibited a character sufficiently endowed with spiritual possibilities to justify his election to the Apostleship. Perhaps he may be adequately described as one of those labourers who, having been hired (μισθώσασθαι ἐργάτας, Mt 20[1]) to work in the vineyard, were ultimately rejected because they failed to correspond with their new environment.

We may here note two different uses to which the word 'elect' or its equivalent idea is put in the Gospels. (α) It describes those who are chosen for a certain definite work, and are for this purpose endowed with suitable characteristics, and elected to certain special privileges and spiritual graces (see Mt 24[22. 24], Mk 13[20. 22]). For them endurance and active perseverance to the end alone ensure their final salvation (ἐν τῇ ὑπομονῇ ὑμῶν κτήσεσθε τὰς ψυχὰς ὑμῶν, Lk 21[19]), though they are always to remember that God's active sympathy is ever on their side (18[7]). (β) It is also used of those whose salvation is assured by their sharing in the power and glory of the returning Messiah (μετὰ δυνάμεως καὶ δόξης πολλῆς, Mt 24[31] = Mk 13[26] ; cf. ὀλίγοι ἐκλεκτοί, Mt 22[14]).

In conclusion, we may be permitted to point out that in acting on 'the principle according to election,' God has for ever vindicated His justice and righteousness by choosing us 'in Christ' (see ἐν Χριστῷ, ἐν αὐτῷ, Eph 1[3f.]). By and in the Incarnation the human race and the separate individuals of the race have received those capacities and endowments which fit them for their work and for their Divinely appointed destiny (ὃς πάντας ἀνθρώπους θέλει σωθῆναι, 1 Ti 2[4]). No one in the foreordaining counsels of God is contemplated as doomed to eternal exclusion from His presence (μὴ βουλόμενός τινας ἀπολέσθαι, 2 P 3[9]), and if they are thus shut out finally (ὅπου ὁ σκώληξ αὐτῶν οὐ τελευτᾷ, κ.τ.λ., Mk 9[48]), it is because of their own deliberate action in causing their bodies to be servants of unrighteousness, and thus in being stumbling-blocks in the way of the salvation of their fellow-men (cf. Mt 5[28ff.] 18[6ff.], Mk 9[42ff.] etc.). No excuse as to lack of opportunity or privilege will avail ; for although inequality will always here as elsewhere exist, none shall be judged apart from their capacities and opportunities (ἑκάστῳ κατὰ τὴν ἰδίαν δύναμιν, Mt 25[15]); and all shall be recompensed according to the knowledge they were able to acquire (Lk 12[47f.]). It is true that apart from Christ ($\chi\omega\rho\lambda s \,\dot{\epsilon}\mu o\hat{v}$, Jn 15[5]) we are powerless for good ; but as none, not even those who have never heard His name, are outside Him ($\tau\grave{a}\,\pi\acute{a}\nu\tau a\,\dot{\epsilon}\nu\,a\dot{\nu}\tau\wp\,\sigma\nu\nu\acute{\epsilon}\sigma\tau\eta\kappa\epsilon\nu$, Col 1[17]; cf. Eph 1[10f.]), so none need be apart from Him in that profounder sense whereby human life becomes Divinely active and abundantly fruitful. To all is given the opportunity of attaining the end to which they are called and chosen.   J. R. WILLIS.

ELI [ELOI], ELI [ELOI], etc.—See SEVEN WORDS.

ELIAKIM.—Two ancestors of Jesus bore this name, according to Mt 1[13] and Lk 3[30].

ELIEZER.—An ancestor of Jesus, Lk 3[29].

ELIJAH (AV Elias) is mentioned in the Gospels on 9 occasions, reported in 15 passages (rejecting Lk 9[54]). Of these passages only one, Lk 4[25f.], alludes to the story of Elijah as it is contained in the OT. Here Jesus justifies His performance of miracles in Capernaum, while refraining from working them in Nazareth, by citing the well-known story of Elijah's going away from Israel in time of famine to relieve the distress of a Sidonian widow (1 K 17[8, 9]). All the other passages refer to the present or future work of an Elijah who, according to common Jewish belief, still lived and would appear again upon earth.

The dominant note in the belief is that the prophet was to appear as the forerunner of the Messiah. This notion appears in its simplest form in the accounts of the avowal of the Messiahship of Jesus at Cæsarea Philippi (Mt 16[13ff.], Mk 8[27ff.], Lk 9[18ff.]). The answers then given by the disciples to Jesus' question as to the popular estimate of Himself were varied, and doubtless representative: He was John the Baptist, Elijah, Jeremiah, or one of the prophets (cf. Mk 6[15], Lk 9[8]). Only one, Simon, saw in the work of Jesus the consummation, rather than the postponement, of their Messianic hope. The period of Elijah the forerunner is past, and the Messiah is here.

The relation between the prophet Elijah, the lawgiver Moses, and the Messiah Jesus, is dramatically presented in the narrative of the Transfiguration (Mt 17, Mk 9[2ff.], Lk 9[28ff.]). Here, too, the logical proof is presented that Elijah has come already, and is John the Baptist. When once Jesus has been accepted as the Messiah, the work of John cannot fail to be known as the great preparatory work of Elijah. This w·rk finds expression in St. Matthew's report of ·fesus' characterization of John (11[14]; omitted from the parallel in Lk.).

The Baptist's denial that he was Elijah (Jn 1[21ff.]) is the natural expression of his lofty idea of the work of preparation for the Messiah contrasted with the insufficiency of the work he had actually been able to perform. The passage incidentally describes one of the functions of Elijah who was to come, viz., that he should baptize. Baptism was then one of the preliminaries of the salvation which the Messiah was to bring.

Elijah is mentioned again in connexion with the Crucifixion (Mt 27[46-49], Mk 15[34-36]). The bystanders professedly misunderstood Jesus' cry, 'Eli, Eli,' as a call to Elijah. They proposed to wait and see if he would come down to help Him. Bearing in mind that Elijah is the forerunner of the Messiah, their curiosity seems not simply whether Jesus would have supernatural relief, as a man might, but whether Elijah would, by coming to His aid, prove that Jesus was after all the Messiah.

There remains the striking picture of the Baptist in the character of Elijah, drawn in Lk 1[19ff.]. The passage clearly assumes the developed doctrine of the Messiahship of Jesus, and the career of John the Baptist is analyzed from this point of view. The high spiritual plane of the identification is obvious. John comes in the spirit and power of the great prophet, reconciling families, reducing the disobedient to obedience, preparing Israel for the coming of the Messiah. Only on this high plane could the identification be successful. The *work* of the forerunner here finds fullest expression. He not simply proclaims, he prepares. This is, however, the implication of the other passages ; otherwise the suggested identification of Jesus with Elijah would not have been possible, for it was the very works of Jesus that called up the suggestion. The same is true in the case of John.

The belief in the reappearance of Elijah, held by the Jews of NT times, is a later stage of the belief which is expressed in Mal 4[5][Eng.]: he would come before the great day of Jehovah to reconcile the hearts of parents and children. Sir 48[10ff.] describes the same work more elaborately, and forms an early interpretation of the passage in Malachi.

The Rabbinical writings abound in expressions of the same belief, with characteristic extravagances and specifications. These Jewish traditions know Elijah as zealous in the service of God, and as a helper in distress, as well as the forerunner of the Messiah. Naturally his work is in behalf of their own people, and is performed in connexion with their own institutions.

As the Jews elaborated the earlier doctrine of the Messiah, and as in their thought He became more and more exalted in holiness and majesty, the impossibility of His appearance in the midst of all the sin and shame of Israel was increasingly felt ; and the character of Elijah, the holy prophet, zealous in his earthly life for the political and religious integrity of the nation, and already enshrined in tradition as having been spared death, was a fitting one to be chosen to carry on the great work of preparing Israel for the blessings of the Messianic era. Indeed, in some passages the doctrine of Elijah has developed to such an extent as well nigh to usurp the functions of the Messiah.

LITERATURE.—Volz, *Jüdische Eschatologie*, 192 and *passim*; *Jewish Encyc. s.v.*; Gfrörer, *Jahrhundert des Heils*, ii. 227 f.; Bacher, *Agade d. Tannaiten*, *passim*; Weber, *Altsyn. pal. Theol.* 337–339 ; Schürer, *GJV*[3] ii. 524 f.

       O. H. GATES.

ELISABETH.—The NT notice of Elisabeth is confined to the Third Gospel, and its brief record concerning her may well be due to St. Luke's acquaintance with Mary the mother of our Lord. It is interesting to know that she was a kinswoman ($\sigma\nu\gamma\gamma\epsilon\nu\lambda s$, Lk 1[36]) of Mary, though it is unfortunately impossible to verify the exact relationship that existed between them. Elisabeth is described, with her husband Zacharias (wh. see), as a faithful adherent of the OT type of religion—strict and regular in observance of the Law (v.[6]). She enjoyed the double distinction, according to Jewish thought, of being both a priest's daughter and a priest's wife (v.[5]). The joy of such a twofold honour was, however, diminished by the fact that she was barren (v.[7]), to an Oriental woman little less than a calamity. But a single event in the Gospel narrative at once dispelled her sorrow and entitled her to a place of honour not among Jewish women alone, but in the eyes of the whole world. In her old age (v.[36]) she became the mother of John the Baptist.

Between the promise and the birth of this child she was visited by Mary (v.[39]), who remained with her for a period of three months (v.[56]), and to whom she was made a proof of the Almighty's power (vv.[36-38]). On Mary's appearance she received a special inspiration of the Holy Spirit, which even enabled her to recognize in her kinswoman the mother of her 'Lord' (v.⁴¹ᶠᶠ·), and in Mary's Child a fulfilment of the promise of Jehovah Himself (v.⁴⁵). Herein she unconsciously illustrated the meaning of her own name, which in its Hebrew form signifies 'God is an oath.'

On the theory (upheld by Burkitt, Harnack, *et al.*) that the *Magnificat* ought to be attributed to Elisabeth and not to Mary, see artt. BIRTH OF CHRIST, p. 203ᵇ note, and MAGNIFICAT.

H. BISSEKER.

ELISHA (AV Eliseus).—The famous disciple, companion, and successor of Elijah. In NT he is only once referred to, viz. in Lk 4²⁷. Jesus, preaching in the synagogue at Nazareth, reminds His fellow-townsmen, who were unwilling to receive His teaching because He was one of themselves, that Elisha, who was an Israelite, healed but one leper, and he was a Syrian. He leaves them to draw the obvious inference as to the probable consequence of their rejection of Him. It is clear, however, that in this warning our Lord was looking far beyond Nazareth, and that He had in view the casting away of the Jews through unbelief, and the call of the Gentiles.   J. CROMARTY SMITH.

ELIUD.—An ancestor of Jesus, Mt 1¹⁴ᵗ·.

ELMADAM (AV **Elmodam**). — An ancestor of Jesus, Lk 3²⁸; perh. = Heb. *Almodad* (cf. Gn 10²⁶).

EMMANUEL.—See IMMANUEL.

EMMAUS ('Εμμαούς).—The question of Emmaus would seem at first sight to be simple, and the identification of this place easy. Indeed, Emmaus not being mentioned more than once in the Gospels, there are no different texts to be harmonized. We read in Lk 24¹³ that Emmaus was a village 60 furlongs from Jerusalem, and that after having arrived there at the close of the day, and having sat with Jesus at a meal, the two disciples were able to return the same evening to Jerusalem and there find the Apostles still assembled together. The only parallel passage in Mk. (16¹²), part of the unauthentic close of the Second Gospel, does not mention the name of the locality, and speaks only of an appearance to two disciples 'as they walked on their way into the country' (δυσὶν . . . περιπατοῦσιν . . . πορευομένοις εἰς ἀγρόν). On the other hand, Josephus says (*BJ* VII. vi. 6) that Vespasian established a colony of 800 Roman veterans on the lands which he gave them at a distance of 60 (*v.l.* 30) furlongs from Jerusalem, at a place called Emmaus. Now, there still actually exists to the west of Jerusalem, on the road which leads to Jaffa, a place named *Ḳolonieh*. It is true that the distance is less than 60 furlongs : authors estimate it sometimes at 45, but more frequently at only 35, furlongs. It might be held, however, that the territory of the colony extended over an area of several miles, and that it might, according to circumstances, be thus considered as being distant either 30 or 60 furlongs from the capital. Under these conditions nothing would seem to oppose our placing, on the grounds indicated above, the Emmaus of St. Luke, identified with that of Josephus, at *Ḳolonieh*.

It must, however, be remarked that the different reading noted in the passage from Josephus (60 or 30) creates some uncertainty. It must also be noted that, according to some authors, the name *Ḳolonieh* is not to be explained by the Latin *colonia* at all, but by the name *Ḳulon* (Κουλόν), mentioned in Jos 15⁵⁹ (LXX) as that of a town of Judah situated in the hill country. These difficulties, however, would not be altogether insurmountable if they were the only ones ; a further

and graver complication arises from the following facts.

In 1 Mac. an Emmaus is spoken of more than once as the scene of various occurrences : Judas Maccabæus vanquished Gorgias there in B.C. 166–167 (1 Mac 3⁴⁰· ⁵⁷ 4³⁻²⁵ ; cf. Jos. *Ant.* XII. vii. 4); and in B.C. 160 Bacchides fortified it and placed a garrison in it (1 Mac 9⁵⁰ᵗ· ; cf. Jos. *Ant.* XIII. i. 3). The position of this place is easy to determine ; it must have been situated between Jerusalem and Jaffa, nearer the latter, at the spot where the slopes of the mountainous region descend towards the great maritime plain. In this quarter, indeed, is found a site which has left important ruins, and which is mentioned several times in the course of the first centuries of the Christian era under the name Emmaus. From the 3rd cent. onwards it was called Nicopolis, without the remembrance of the ancient Semitic name being lost ; and, as is the cáse with most of those places with two names, under the Arab domination it resumed its earlier name and was called '*Amwās*, the appellation it still bears. Now, from the earliest times of ecclesiastical history, the opinion gained ground that this Emmaus-Nicopolis was the Emmaus of St. Luke. Eusebius, no doubt reflecting the views of Origen, and after him Jerome, maintained this identity (*OS*² 257. 21, 121. 6) ; and after them this view of the case held sway for a long time in the Church. If it is asked how this conclusion could be formed, seeing that Emmaus-Nicopolis is situated at a distance from Jerusalem which is estimated (according to the particular route adopted) at 180, 175, 170, or 166 furlongs, almost thrice the 60 furlongs mentioned above, the reply is promptly given : א and some other MSS read '160' instead of '60.' The tendency to identify Emmaus-Nicopolis and the Emmaus of St. Luke became so strong, so irresistible, that it led to a curious result : in the Middle Ages, at the time of the Crusaders and afterwards, the memory of Emmaus-Nicopolis having been lost, the Emmaus of St. Luke was looked for nearer Jerusalem, and when it was believed that it had been found, not only the name of Emmaus, but also that of Nicopolis, was given to it.

From the 13th cent. (1280) or perhaps from the last years of the 11th (1099, see *ZDPV* xvi. p. 300), a tradition arose which for more clearness may be called the Franciscan tradition, and which places the Emmaus of St. Luke at *el-Ḳubeibeh*, to the N.W. of *Ḳolonieh*, at some distance to the north of the road from Jerusalem to Jaffa, and about 60 (more exactly 62–64) furlongs from the capital. Still, indeed, all the efforts of the champions of the Franciscan theory are directed towards establishing that the Emmaus of the Evangelist is *el-Ḳubeibeh*. Interesting ruins have been discovered there : those of a church dating from the time of the Crusades, and in the interior of its *enceinte* the remains of a more ancient structure, which might be those of a Byzantine church, but which the defenders of the Franciscan tradition consider to be the very house of Cleopas, around which the sanctuary had been built.

The first question to clear up is that of the text. Now several authors, and in particular P. Lagrange (*Rev. Bibl.* 1896, pp. 87–92), have, in the opinion of the present writer, shown irrefutably that the original reading must have been '60 furlongs,' and that '160' is a correction meant to enable the Emmaus of St. Luke to be identified with that of 1 Maccabees. 'The 160 furlongs,' Lagrange concludes admirably (p. 89), 'represent neither the ancient tradition, nor the universal tradition, nor the unconscious tradition. This reading is a critical one, imposed by the authority of a master, very probably Origen, and collides almost everywhere with the firmly assured tradition of the Churches. To judge from the manuscripts, the question is settled : we must read " 60 furlongs.' '

We must remark, further, that Emmaus-Nicopolis was a town before the Christian era and long beyond (πόλις, Jos. *BJ* II. xx. 4), whereas the Evangelist speaks of a village (κώμη). Even after Emmaus-Nicopolis had been destroyed by the Roman soldiers of Varus (A.D. 4), it was not on that account a village ; a ruined town is not a village. It was even the chief town of a toparchy (Jos. *BJ* III. iii. 5 ; Plin. *HN* v. 14). The remains of a church have been found there, which date not merely from the Crusades, but very probably from the Byzantine epoch ; it is in vain that a recent author (Barnabé), who favours *el-Ḳubeibeh*, has tried to prove that this church was really nothing but a hot-baths establishment. But it is also vain to seek to infer from the presence of a church, even an ancient one, that we have to do with the Emmaus of St. Luke.

Another very strong argument against Emmaus-Nicopolis is its excessive distance. It is worth noting what efforts its partisans make to show that the two disciples could have returned the same evening to Jerusalem, walking for this purpose five or six hours. One of the most convinced defenders of this theory, Schiffers, does not hesitate to affirm that they could have set out again from Emmaus as early as 3 o'clock in the afternoon and arrived at Jerusalem at 9 o'clock (*Rev. Bibl.* 1894, pp. 26–40 ; see also his book *Amwâs, das Emmaus des heil. Lukas*, 1890). In that case it must be held that the words 'it is toward evening, and the day is now far spent' (Lk 24²⁹), may have been spoken immediately after noon.

The failure of the identification of Emmaus-Nicopolis with the Emmaus of St. Luke proves nothing in favour of *el-Ḳubeibeh*, which can produce only a late tradition in its favour. The argument which has been sought to draw from the name *el-Ḳubeibeh* as an alleged corruption of Nicopolis (!) refutes itself. But the probabilities indicated at the opening of this article in favour of *Ḳolonieh* are greatly weakened by the undisputed fact that the ecclesiastical tradition of the first centuries pronounces in favour of 'Amwâs-Nicopolis ; this fact proves that all recollection of an Emmaus situated nearer to Jerusalem had become effaced in the 3rd century. Under these circumstances the most elementary duty is to declare the problem unsolved, and incapable of solution under the present conditions and with the data which we possess.

Nor does the etymology of the name furnish any precise indication. We do not know to what Hebrew or Aramaic term *Emmaus* [we find also the forms *Ammaus, Ammaum, Emmaum* ; 'Αμμαούς, 'Αμμαούμ, 'Εμμαούμ] corresponds. A vain attempt has been made to connect it with the root *ḥamam*, and to prove thereby that baths existed at this spot. An argument in favour of this has been based on the fact that the baths situated near Tiberias were called by the same name (cf. Jos 19³⁵ *Ḥammath*), but it is now known that the correct reading is *Ammathus* ('Αμμαθούς ; cf. *ZDPV* xiii. pp. 194–198). It is on the frail basis of this hypothetical derivation that Mrs. Finn grounds her theory that Emmaus = *Urtas*, to the south of Bethlehem, near Solomon's Pools, 60 furlongs from Jerusalem (see *PEFSt*, 1883, pp. 53–64). It is by an equally dubious etymological process that Colonel Conder has been led to seek for Emmaus in *Khamasa*, to the S.W. of Jerusalem, at a distance, moreover, not of 60, but of 80–90 furlongs. We may also note the attempt to place the Emmaus of St. Luke at *Abu-Ghosh* (Ḳiriet-el-'Enâb). From the point of view of distance this would be

sufficiently exact, but there is nothing to lead us to conclude in favour of this particular spot rather than any other within the same circuit.

Lastly, we recall the fact that the Talmud speaks of *Ḳolonieh* as being also called Moṣa or ham-Moṣa, a name which we may connect with the המצה of Jos 18²⁶ (LXX : 'Αμωσά, but also 'Αμωκή). Near *Ḳolonieh* there exists to-day a place called *Beit-Mizzeh*, which recalls Moṣa.

LITERATURE.—*PEFSt*, 1874, pp. 149, 160, 162–164, 1876, pp. 172–175, 1879, pp. 105–107, 1881, pp. 46, 237 f., 274, 1882, pp. 24–37, 1883, pp. 53–64, 1884, pp. 83–85, 1885, pp. 116–121, 1886, p. 17, 1901, pp. 165–167, 210 ; *PEF Memoirs*, iii. 36–42, 130 f. ; *ZDPV* xiii. 194–198, xvi. 298–300, xix. 222, xxv. 195–203 ; *MNDPV*, 1901, 14 f. ; *Rev. Bibl.* 1892, pp. 80–99, 101–105, 645–649, 1893, pp. 26–40, 223–227, 1894, p. 137, 1896, pp. 87–92, 1903, pp. 457–467, 571–599 ; Reland, *Pal.* 427, 758 ; Robinson, *BRP* iii. 146–151, 158 ; Tobler, *Top. von Jerusalem*, ii. 538–545, 752 f. ; Schwarz, *Das heil. Land*, 98 ; Guérin, *Judée*, i. 257–262, 293–308, 348–361 ; Thomson, *The Land and the Book*, i. 116, 123 ff., 132, ii. 59 ; Sepp, *Jerusalem und das heil. Land*², i. 54 ff., *Neue Entdeckungen*, ii. 228–253, 260–263 ; G. A. Smith, *HGHL*, 214 ; Buhl, *GAP* 186 ; Conder, *Tent Work*, 8, 13, 140 ; Furrer, *Wanderungen*², 161–169 ; Le Camus, *Pays Bibliques*, i. 185–194, 204–207 ; Sanday, *Sacred Sites*, 29–31, 92 ; Zschokke, *Das neutest. Emmaus*, 1865 ; Guillemot, *Emmaüs-Nicopolis*, 1886 ; Buselli, *L'Emmaus evangelico*, 1885–1886 ; Domenichelli, *L'Emmaus della Palestina*, 1889, *Ultime discussioni*, 1898 ; Schiffers, *Amwâs, das Emmaus des heil. Lukas*, 1890 ; Rückert, ' Amwâs, was es ist und was es nicht ist' in *Theol. Qschrift*, 1892 ; Barnabé, *Deux questions d'archéologie palestinienne*, 1892 ; A. Duc, *Die Emmaus-Frage*, 1905 ; Merx, *Die Evv. des Markus und Lukas*, 1905, p. 523 f. ; see also the Bible Dictionaries, *s.v.* ; the Comm. on St. Luke, *ad loc.*, and the Lives of Christ. LUCIEN GAUTIER.

ENDURANCE.—The active qualities of perseverance and persistence, never absent from the biblical notion of endurance, form, in effect, the substance of the art. ACTIVITY, and need not be considered here. The passive aspect suggests an inquiry as to—

1. The *causes* of those trials which Christ had to endure.—Of (*a*) *supernatural* causes (1) the first, an all-inclusive cause, was the Divine will (Jn 10¹⁸), recorded beforehand in OT Scriptures (Mt 26⁵⁴, Mk 14²¹, Lk 22³⁷ 24²⁵ᶠ·), and referred to constantly by Christ in words of resignation (Mt 26⁴², Lk 10²¹), often under the figure of a 'cup' (Mt 20²² 26³⁹, Jn 18¹¹). (2) A second supernatural cause (under Divine permission) appears in the agency of Satan, acting both directly, in temptation and opposition (Mt 4³ᶠᶠ· 13³⁹, Lk 10¹⁸), and also oftener indirectly, through the weakness (Mt 16²³, Lk 22³¹) and wickedness (Lk 22³· ⁵³, Jn 6⁷⁰ 8⁴⁴ 13²) of men. These two causes, whether expressly referred to or not, are undoubtedly to be regarded as factors never absent (see Jn 19¹¹ and also 12²¹ 14³⁰ 16¹¹, where the title ' prince of this world' is significant in this connexion).

(*b*) *Internal* causes (supernatural also, in a different sense) were not wanting. (1) The prophetic mission of Christ (Jn 12⁴⁶ 18³⁷) made suffering and death morally inevitable at the hand of man (Lk 4²⁴ 11⁴⁹ᶠ· 13³³ᶠ·, Jn 7⁷), light and darkness being essentially opposed (Jn 3¹⁹ᶠ·; cf., for illustration, a remarkable passage in Plato, *Rep.* vii. 517 B, where a similar inevitability is declared even in the case of Socrates). (2) The revelation of His Divine nature, implied in His relationship to the Father's Being (Jn 5¹⁸ 8⁵⁸ 10³⁰ᶠᶠ·) and prerogatives (Mt 9², Lk 7⁴⁸ᶠ·) was bound to provoke deadly hostility in unbelieving Jews (Mt 26⁶⁵, Jn 19⁷). It is at the same time clear, from Christ's anxiety to avoid publicity (Mt 12¹⁶, Mk 7³⁶ 8²⁶ etc.) and needless offence (Mt 17²⁷), that persecution and death were not courted by Him.

(*c*) The *external* causes were more complex. (1) Many trials arose from the imperfections of His disciples ; their dulness (Mk 8¹⁵ᶠᶠ· 9³², Lk 24²⁵), spiritual powerlessness (Mt 17¹⁶ᶠ·), false zeal (Mt 15²³ 16²³, Mk 9³⁸, Lk 9⁵⁴), mistaken aims (Mk 9⁵ 10³⁵ᶠ·, Lk 22²⁴), and discreditable falls (Mt 26⁵⁶, Mk 14⁶⁶ᶠᶠ·, Lk 22⁴⁷ᶠ·). But (2) most arose from Christ's rejection by 'His own' (Jn 1[11], Mt 23[37], Mk 12[6ff.], Jn 5[43] 19[15]) from motives (which He well perceived, Mt 9[4] 12[25], Mk 9[33f.], Lk 6[8], Jn 2[25]) of fear (Mt 8[34], Jn 12[42f.] 19[12]), policy (Jn 11[49f.], Mk 15[15]), gain (Mt 26[14f.], Mk 10[22], Lk 16[14]), envy (Mt 21[38] 27[18], Jn 12[19]), and hate (Lk 19[14], Jn 7[7] 15[18. 24]) ; a rejection characterized in its display by indifference (Lk 14[18ff.]), ingratitude (Lk 17[17f.], Jn 5[15]), contradiction (Jn 8[13]), insult (Mt 10[25] 12[24], Mk 15[32], Lk 7[34] 22[63] 23[11], Jn 8[48] 9[24]), treachery (Lk 11[53] 20[20] 22[48]), injustice (Mk 14[55f.], Jn 19[4. 10. 16]), violence (Lk 4[28f.], Jn 8[59] 10[31]), brutality (Lk 22[64], Jn 19[1-3] etc.), and death (Jn 19[18]).

2. Some *features* of Christ's endurance are vitally connected with fundamental doctrines of His person and work. (1) It was *voluntary*. Of this the emphatic statement in Jn 10[17f.] leaves no doubt. Such an utterance may be hard to parallel, but prudence would almost make it so ; and the expressions used in Lk 9[31], Jn 7[33f.] 8[21] 13[31] seem to speak of a course equally spontaneous ; indeed, in one case (8[22]) a voluntary (*i.e.* a suicide's) death is actually suggested as their meaning ! (2) It was *perfect*. (*a*) Under suffering : for His spirit, words, and demeanour were admittedly supreme examples of His own teaching, *e.g.* upon submission (Jn 18[22f.], Mt 5[39]), retaliation (Lk 6[35] 22[51]), and love to enemies (Mt 5[44f.], Lk 23[34]). (*b*) Under temptation : otherwise it would be inexplicable that Christ should have urged repentance as a first essential for others (Mt 4[17] 11[20f.] 21[38 ff.], Lk 5[32] 13[3] 15, etc.), whereas He afforded no example of it in His own case. On the contrary, He laid claim to sinlessness both negatively (Jn 14[30]) and positively (8[29]), as unchallengeable (8[46]). An intuitive perception of His sinlessness appears in the self-abasing awe of a few good men (Mt 3[14], Lk 5[8]) more convincingly than in the ambiguous testimony of many other observers (Mt 27[3. 19], Lk 23[47], Jn 19[4] etc.). (3) It was *human*. Christ's capability of human suffering is beyond question. No mention, indeed, is made of sickness in the ordinary sense ; perhaps it is excluded ; but all other bodily needs and infirmities were shared by Him (Mt 4[2] 8[20. 24] 21[18], Jn 4[6f.] 19[28]). The emotions of His mind (Mk 3[5] 7[34] 10[14], Lk 19[41], Jn 11[35]) and spirit (Lk 10[21], Jn 11[33] 13[21]) were evident from their outward traces, as well as from His own statements (Mt 15[32], Lk 22[15], Jn 11[15]). On two occasions He referred to those of His soul (Jn 12[27], Mk 14[34]). That this capability of suffering was not counteracted by the exercise of miraculous power is proved by His reference to His 'temptations' (Lk 22[28]), by His prediction of sufferings on the part of His disciples similar generally to His own (Mk 10[38f.]), by the shrinking of His human will (Mt 26[39. 42], Lk 12[50], Jn 12[27]), by His refusal to allay His own hunger miraculously (Mt 4[3f.]), or to lessen His torments even by ordinary means (Mk 15[23]), by His craving for the support of human sympathy (Mk 14[33ff.]), and by His reliance above all else upon the Father's presence (Jn 8[29] 16[32]) and the spiritual support of prayer (Lk 6[12] 9[18. 28] 11[1] 22[41] etc.). As man He met temptation (Mt 4[4]), and overcame by faith (see Jn 11[41f.], Mt 27[43], and also the important expression 'my God,' Mt 27[46], Jn 20[17]).

In some respects, however, His endurance differed essentially from that of believers. (1) It was free from the inherent tendencies of a sinful nature (Jn 14[30]) and from the enslaving influence of sins committed (8[34-36]). (2) It contained the additional elements of prescience and perfect consciousness. Predictions of suffering are numerous and detailed (Mt 17[22f.] 20[18f.] 26[2], Mk 14[18. 30], Lk 9[22. 44] 12[50] 13[33], 17[25] 22[37] etc.). The knowledge (Jn 18[4]) whereby He 'saw' and 'tasted' death (Jn 8[51f.] 10[12]) was complete. (3) Above all, the relation between the Passion of Christ and the sin of the world (Jn 1[29]), symbolized by the supernatural darkness, laid on Him that infinite woe, almost amounting to despair

(Mk 15[33f.]), the prospect of which was undoubtedly the main factor in the Agony and other forebodings.

3. There remain to be considered the *purposes* for the attainment of which Christ's endurance was a necessity (Lk 24[26]). In the trials and temptations of (*a*) *His life*, two such purposes are prominently visible : (1) the fulfilment of all righteousness (Mt 3[15] 5[17]), described as a progressive course through service and suffering (Lk 22[27f.], Jn 13[14] 19[30]), in which Christ met continually the Father's approval (Lk 2[40. 52], Mt 3[17] 17[5], Jn 12[28]), being declared to be the 'Son of God' ideally as well as actually. (2) The acquirement of sympathy ; through experimental acquaintance with the weakness of the flesh (Jn 1[14], Mt 26[41]). Numerous instances might be given of the sympathy of Christ with human nature in its aspirations (Mk 10[21. 38ff.], Jn 21[17]), weakness (Mt 12[15ff.]), weariness (Mt 11[28], Mk 6[31]), misery (Mt 8[3]), and shame (Mt 11[19], Lk 15[1f.]). To Him, therefore, as 'Son of Man,' ideally as well as actually, is given authority to exercise pardon (Mk 2[10]), legislation (2[28]), and judgment (Jn 5[27]). Lastly, the great purpose which involved the endurance of (*b*) *His death* is in the main so clear as to leave no room for doubt. It may be summed up in the words 'forgiveness' (Mt 26[28]), 'redemption' (Mk 10[45]), and 'removal of sin' (Jn 1[29]) ; to which, in Jn 11[50ff.], is added the gathering of all the children of God into one in Christ (cf. 17[21ff.]), benefits potentially world-wide (Jn 1[29] 6[51]), but limited, in their highest realization, to believers (Jn 3[16ff.]). It need be no cause of surprise that these purposes are not more frequently enlarged upon in the Gospels, for they were incomprehensible to the disciples (and are remarked as such, Mt 16[22], Lk 9[45] 18[34], Jn 13[7]) until after the Crucifixion had taken place.

4. It may be added that Christ warned *His disciples* in all ages to expect trials comparable in some measure to His own (Mt 5[11f.] 10[24f.], Jn 15[17ff.]), and accompanied in many cases by decline and apostasy (Mt 24[12. 48ff.]). Hence He marked endurance as a continual test of genuineness (Lk 8[13. 15]) and an indispensable requisite for final salvation (Mt 24[13]). At the same time He declared a complementary truth, namely, the Divine preservation of His 'own sheep' (Jn 10[28f.] 17[12] 18[9], Mk 13[22]), a privilege commonly described as the 'perseverance of the elect.' However stated, the antithesis of these two truths is plain. The assurance in Jn 10[28f.] is largely parallel to that in Mt 16[18], except that the latter, the indestructibility of the Church, is more clearly collective in form. There are 'branches' (so it appears, Jn 15[2]) even 'in Christ' that the Father takes away ; moreover, the remarkable use of the imperative in 15[4] suggests an element of conditionality in the abiding or perseverance referred to. The practical inference is intended to lie in a direction quite the opposite of false security and presumption (Mt 7[22f.], Lk 13[24ff.] 21[34f.]. 22[32ff.]). 'Perseverance is undoubtedly the privilege of the elect, but there is no infallible sign of the elect except their perseverance' (Vaughan on Ph 1[6]).

                          F. S. RANKEN.

ENEMIES (ἐχθρός).—**1.** Of public enemies : twice in the *Benedictus*, Lk 1[71. 74], where the word implies Gentile persecutors. In Lk 19[43] it is spoken of the Romans and their threatened siege of Jerusalem. In the quotation from Ps 110[1] which occurs in Mt 22[44], Mk 12[36], Lk 20[43], He 1[13] 10[13], the same word denotes all the world forces opposing Christ. **2.** Of private enemies, in the correction of the old maxim enjoining hatred, 'Love your enemies,' Mt 5[43. 44], Lk 6[27. 35]. **3.** Of the devil and the powers of evil, in the parable of the Wheat and the Tares, Mt 13[25. 39]. **4.** Of the spiritual forces acting in opposition to Christ, of which the strongest is death,

1 Co 15^{25. 26}. **5.** Of wicked persons hindering the spread of Christ's influence, the enemies of the cross, Ph 3¹⁸. The word used in NT for enemies is usually applied elsewhere to private or personal enemies, not to public foes. See, further, artt. FORGIVENESS, HATRED, LOVE.

C. H. PRICHARD.

ENERGY.—The Gr. ἐνέργεια (tr. 'working') is used only of supernatural spiritual working, and only in the Epistles ; in Eph. and Col. of God, in Ph 3²¹ of the exalted Christ, in 2 Th 2⁹ of Satan. In Eph 1¹⁹ we find in one sentence four terms expressive of power—ἐνέργεια, κράτος, ἰσχύς, and δύναμις. These Divine qualities were exercised in the resurrection and exaltation of Christ, and the Christian soldier is exhorted (Eph 6¹⁰) to obtain a portion of them in equipment for his spiritual warfare. Of these terms the chief is δύναμις, 'power,' of which the application is manifold. On three occasions (Lk 5¹⁷ 6¹⁹ 8⁴⁶ or Mk 5³⁰) it is specially used of a healing power (AV 'virtue') that issued or was drawn from Jesus as from a storehouse of spiritual energy. See artt. FORCE, POWER, and VIRTUE.

1. 'Energy' in the physical sense means power or capacity of work. It includes the active and the potential side, force of motion and energy of position : two interchanging factors of which the sum total is constant. In its moral application there is a similar duality. The man of energy is not only an active agent, but also one in whom we recognize a reserve of power. This energy of character is partly physical, partly mental. It is altogether different from the purely physical quality of strength or might (κράτος, ἰσχύς), the virtue of the warrior or athlete. A physical basis is necessary, yet dauntless energy may be found in a feeble frame. The quality is essentially moral, because it involves the constant exercise of a powerful will. The fundamental requirement is unhindered mental force. Two modern statesmen may be instanced. One wrote in his diary the cardinal principles of his life—benevolence, self-sacrifice, purity, energy. Another expounds and exhibits the 'strenuous life.' The duty of work and the heroism of energy constitute a large part of the teaching of Carlyle. Such lessons and lives are illustrations of the spirit of Christianity. On the other hand, indolence and idleness are natural to many men and even to many nations. The habit of inactivity is fostered by mental indifference or the lack of any propelling emotion such as religion or patriotism. The duty and honour of work are Christian conceptions. In 2 Th 3⁸⁻¹¹ we have an early indication of a long struggle, in the course of which sloth was enthroned as one of the seven mortal sins. (Cf. Paget, *Spirit of Discipline*, pp. 1-50).

2. The life of our Lord Himself furnishes the supreme type of Christian energy. Energy is measured by the amount of work it can accomplish within a given time. The ministry of Jesus was limited to a very brief period, but into that little space there was crowded a work that has no parallel in the history of the world. Energy is also measured by the vastness and continuance of its effects, and after nineteen centuries the quickening influence of Jesus is operating on the world with undiminished power. Jesus was never idle. For Him every hour had its appointed task (Jn 2⁴), and every day was governed by a steady and strenuous purpose (Jn 9⁴). He was sometimes weary in His toils (Mt 8²⁴, Jn 4⁶), yet was ever ready to meet fresh calls upon His time and strength, His pity or His help. The reason was that the springs of His energy never ran dry. It is right to say that the secret of Christ's energy lay in His Divinely unconquerable will, but it is none the less true that the strength of His spirit was fed by His love to man and His faith in God. His boundless love and compassion for human beings inspired Him to go about doing good. His perfect faith in God enabled Him to feel, as no other on earth has ever felt, that nothing was impossible (Mt 17²⁰). But beneath all conscious faith and love there sprang up in the soul of Jesus a fountain of life and power through His abiding union with His Father. 'My Father worketh hitherto,' He once said, 'and I work' (Jn 5¹⁷). 'He went about doing good,' St. Peter declared, 'for God was with him' (Ac 10³⁸).

3. The teaching of Jesus on this subject may be divided into two parts. (1) He enjoins many qualities that contribute to the life of strenuousness. Such are diligence (parables of Talents and Pounds, Mt 25, Lk 19), readiness (Lk 12³⁵), use of opportunities (Jn 9⁴), watchfulness (Mk 13³³), perseverance and importunity of prayer (Lk 11⁵ 18¹), constancy and continuance of service (Lk 12⁴² 17¹⁰). Such precepts receive double force from the example of His life of unresting labour (Jn 5¹⁷ 9⁴). In St. Paul the same lessons are illustrated and inculcated (1 Co 15^{10. 58}).—(2) Faith is set forth as the supreme source of active energy. Faith receives healing ; it can also bestow healing. Before its presence both bodily and mental diseases disappear. Sayings of Jesus to this effect are remembered as maxims and metaphors. 'All things are possible to him that believeth' (Mk 9²³ 11²⁴). By faith mountains disappear and trees may be uprooted (Mk 11²³, Lk 17⁶). Such sayings passed into ordinary speech (1 Co 13²), and the life of achievement was regarded as illustrative of the power of faith (He 11). The fact that men of faith are the possessors of boundless energy is indeed writ large in the history of the world. But the living faith enjoined by Jesus and practised in the planting of Christianity procured an immediate possession of surprising power. Exorcists and magicians were abashed ; and demonic possession, still a plague of the East, disappeared before the advancing standards of the new faith. This spiritual energy depended on immediate communication with God. The last words attributed to Christ are these : 'Ye shall receive power after that the Holy Ghost is come upon you' (Ac 1⁸).

R. SCOTT.

ENOCH.—There is no mention of the patriarch Enoch in the Gospels except as a link in our Lord's genealogy, Lk 3³⁷.

ENOS.—An ancestor of Jesus, Lk 3³⁸.

ENROLMENT.—See CENSUS and QUIRINIUS.

ENTHUSIASM.—*Enthusiasm* means etymologically a Divinely inspired interest or zeal (Gr. ἐνθουσιάζω, to be inspired by a god, from ἐν 'in,' and θεός 'god') ; and therefore affords an appropriate modern rendering for the phrase πνεῦμα ἅγιον, 'Holy Spirit,' in the NT (Lk 1^{15. 35. 41. 67} 4¹, Ac 2⁴ 4^{8. 31} 6^{3. 5} 7⁵⁵ 9¹⁷ 11²⁴ 13⁹ ; see Bartlet's *Acts*, p. 386). The author of *Ecce Homo* has called attention to the *enthusiasm* Jesus required of, and inspired in, His disciples (pp. 141, 152, 154, fifth edition). His own life was marked by enthusiasm, intense and exalted emotions in regard to His vocation. As a youth He was *enthusiastic* for His Father's house (Lk 2⁴⁹) ; at the Baptism He devoted Himself to His calling (Mt 3¹⁵), and was conscious of receiving the Spirit (3¹⁶), the spirit of zeal and power. His first enthusiasm to use the new energy afforded the occasion for the temptation in the wilderness (Mk 1¹² 'straightway the Spirit driveth him forth'). In His call to His disciples, His teaching and healing, His journeyings from place to place in the early Galilæan ministry (Mk 1^{17. 27. 38. 41}), this mood of enthusiasm is dominant (Lk 4¹). The same impression is conveyed in St. John's record : His answer to His mother in Cana, the casting out of the traders from the temple, the challenge to the priests, the confession of His Messiahship to the woman of Samaria, the forgetfulness of the needs of the body in His absorption in His work (2⁴·¹⁷·¹⁹ 4²⁶·³²·³⁴), have all the same characteristic of an intense, exalted emotion. His mood was mistaken for madness by His relatives (Mk 3²¹), and His answer regarding His spiritual relationships would not remove their doubt (3³⁴·³⁵). His demands on His disciples to abandon all, and to cleave to Him (Lk 9⁶⁰·⁶² 14²⁶), and the Beatitudes He pronounced on the spiritually aspiring, and on the persecuted (Mt 5⁶·¹²), spring from the same inward source. He was deeply moved by any evidence of faith which He met with (Mt 8¹⁰ 15²⁸, Lk 10²¹, Mt 16¹⁷, Jn 12²³, Lk 23⁴³). He even intensely desired to fulfil His vocation in His death (Lk 12⁵⁰). The Baptist contrasted his own baptism with water and the Messiah's baptism with the Holy Spirit and fire (Mt 3¹¹). His words have been thus interpreted : ' He baptizes with water, in the running stream of Jordan, to emblem the only way of escape, amendment. Messiah will baptize with wind and fire, sweeping away and consuming the impenitent, leaving behind only the righteous' (Bruce, 'St. Matthew' in *Expositor's Gr. Test.* p. 84). When Jesus presented the same contrast in His demand to Nicodemus (Jn 3⁵), it is not probable that He referred to judgment, but to the inspiration which He brought to men in His ministry, the enthusiasm for God and His kingdom which He imparted. We have abundant evidence that He so inspired men in Galilee by His healing, teaching, forgiveness of sins, companionship (Mk 1²⁷·³⁷ 2¹²·¹⁹), and attracted many (Mk 3⁷ 6⁵³⁻⁵⁶). The people believed Him to be John the Baptist, Elijah, Jeremiah, or one of the prophets (Mk 6¹⁴, Mt 16¹⁴). That this mood was temporary Jesus recognized in the parable of the Sower (Mk 4⁵·⁶). The flame blazed up again for a moment among the Galilæan pilgrims at the triumphal entry (Mk 11⁸·¹⁰). The early ministry in Judæa and in Samaria, as recorded by John, made the same impression (Jn 2²³ 3²⁶ 4³⁹⁻⁴²). After His Resurrection and Ascension the Christian Church received at Pentecost the permanent and communicable gift of *holy enthusiasm* (πνεῦμα ἅγιον, as explained above).*

It is a difficult problem whether in His early ministry Jesus was not led by His enthusiasm to show less reserve in the expression of His claims and less restraint in the exercise of His powers than was His practice afterwards, when He had learned from experience the peril this course involved of a premature close of His ministry. The solution of the problem depends on the answer given to the wider question, whether such a change of method, due to the teaching of experience, would be compatible with His unerring moral insight and

---

* In this view of the meaning of Christian enthusiasm, as a power which finds its true source in the indwelling of the Holy Spirit, we get an interesting glimpse into both the history of language and the philosophy of that history, from the disrepute which attached to the word 'enthusiasm' during the age of Rationalism and Deism. Those were days when leaders in the Church set themselves to 'put down enthusiasm,' and Christian apologists were anxious to prove that neither Jesus Christ nor His Apostles were 'enthusiasts.' Hartley defines enthusiasm as 'a mistaken persuasion in any person that he is a peculiar favourite with God ; and that he receives supernatural marks thereof' (*Observations on Man*, i. 490), a definition which entirely corresponds to the contemporary ideas on the subject (see J. E. Carpenter, *James Martineau*, p. 92). In the 18th cent. enthusiasm was a synonym for fanaticism ; an enthusiast was simply a fanatic. And the constant application of the terms to the Evangelical Revival and its leaders shows that this debasing of their value was due to the spiritual deadness of the critics rather than to the extravagances of the enthusiasts. Similarly, the Jewish leaders said of Jesus, 'He hath a devil, and is mad' (Jn 10²⁰) ; Festus said to Paul, 'Thou art beside thyself' (Ac 26²⁴) ; and some of the people of Jerusalem, when they witnessed the charismatic gifts bestowed upon Christ's followers on the Day of Pentecost, exclaimed, 'These men are full of new wine' (Ac 2¹³).

sinless moral character, and the Divine guidance He constantly sought and found in the fulfilment of His vocation. If not, we cannot assume any such change. The question is discussed in *The Expositor*, 6th series, vol. vi. 'The Early Self-Disclosure.'

LITERATURE.—Arthur, *Tongue of Fire* ; J. C. Shairp, *Studies*, 362 ff. ALFRED E. GARVIE.

ENTRY INTO JERUSALEM.—This was one of the acted parables of Jesus, in which some immortal lesson is concealed. The washing of the feet, the entry, and the cleansing of the Temple, stand together as dramatic representations of the principles and ideas of the Kingdom of God ; of the humility and self-denial required in the life of the Christian ; of the mixture of condescension and majesty in the manner of the King's coming ; and of the peace He gives and of the judgment that follows in His steps.

Of the Synoptic accounts Mk. seems the original. Mt. describes the entry in keeping with his representation of Jesus as the *Malkā Mĕshîḥā* of the Jews, and in consonance with the prophecy of Zec 9⁹. The RV rendering of 21⁴ τοῦτο δὲ γέγονεν, ' Now this is come to pass,' seems to put the reference to the fulfilment of that prophecy into the mouth of Jesus. But the inference from Jn 12¹⁵·¹⁶ is that the prophecy is an afterthought of the disciples, in the light of the Ascension ; and the ten texts of 'fulfilment' in Mt. are always comments of the writer. Mt. seems to represent Jesus as riding on the she-ass and the colt (ἐπάνω αὐτῶν). In Zec 9⁹ the Heb. ו, as Rosenmüller points out, is exegetical not copulative, and as ' ass ' (חֲמוֹר) is male, the proper rendering is ' sitting on an ass, even a colt, the foal of she-asses.' There is thus only one ass in Zechariah. The apparent duplication is due to Hebrew *parallelismus*. Mt. is accused of embroidering the historical statement by adding a second ass in order to show the exact literal fulfilment of prophecy (Kirsopp Lake, at Liverpool Church Congress). Robertson's attempt (*Christianity and Mythology*, p. 368) to explain the two asses mythologically as signifying that the 'Sun-god is at his highest pitch of glory and is coming to his doom,' is not to be taken seriously. Mt.'s penchant for 'doubles' being well known (cf. 8²⁸ 9²⁷ 20³⁰⁻³⁴), the passage must not be pressed. Bengel's comment is 'pullo vectus est, asinâ item usus, pulli comite.' Farrar suggested rendering ἐπάνω αὐτῶν = 'on one of them' ; cf. Ac 23²⁴. Justin Martyr (*Apol.* i. 32) speaks only of a colt, but, connecting the incident with Gn 49¹¹, describes it as ' tied to a vine.'

The prophecy Mt 21⁵, a compound of Is 62¹¹ and Zec 9⁹, is taken partly from Heb., partly from LXX. LXX suppresses ὄνον, which is recovered from Hebrew. Mt. suppresses δίκαιος καὶ σώζων [יְשֻׁעַ] Niph. ptcp.: *salvatus* not *salvator*, trans. active, through influence of יְשֻׁעֲךָ (' thy salvation ') Is 62¹¹], emphasizing πραΰς, 'meek' (עָנִי).

In Mt. there is a description of the commotion (ἐσείσθη) in the whole city ; the question, ' Who is this ?' ; the answer, ' This is the prophet Jesus, he who is from Nazareth of Galilee,' and the greeting, ' Hosanna to the Son of David.' Mk 11¹⁻¹⁰ adds some vivid details. The colt, never before used (so Lk.), was tied ' at the door without in the open street' (ἐπὶ τοῦ ἀμφόδου [not 'where two ways met,' *bivium*, Vulg.], Just. Mart. ἔν τινι εἰσόδῳ κώμης (*l.c.*) ; ἄμφοδα, αἱ ῥύμαι (Hesych.). The woven branches (στοιβάδες) cut from the gardens (ἀγρῶν, *v.l.* for δένδρων) are different from the κλάδοι (olive branches in classical Greek) cut from the trees, in Mt 21⁸. The cry of the people is ' Hosanna ; Blessed in the name of the Lord (acc. to Hebrew accents and idiom, *e.g.* Dt 21⁵), Blessed be *the kingdom that cometh*, even that of our father David.' Mk. treats the visit as one of inspection. Jesus retires, 'having looked round on all things,' for the hour was late,' whereas Mt. and Lk. give it as prelude to the cleansing of the Temple. Lk

19²⁹⁻⁴⁵ gives additional touches. They placed Jesus on the colt ἐπεβίβασαν (ἐπεκάθισαν of Mt 21⁷ being doubtful); the exact place of the exhibition of popular enthusiasm is given, 'even now at the descent of the Mt. of Olives' (ἤδη πρὸς τῇ καταβάσει), from which, Dean Stanley states, the first view is caught of the south-eastern corner of the city as the road from Bethany begins to descend. The lament over the city, the retort to the Pharisees' objection, 'If these should hold their peace,' etc., are peculiar to Luke. The song is, 'Peace in heaven and glory in the highest,' a seeming adaptation of the 'Hosanna,' etc., to suit Greek taste, perhaps through the influence of the angels' song (Lk 2¹⁴).

Jn 12¹²⁻¹⁹ describes the scene from the standpoint of the people in the city who went out to meet Him (εἰς ὑπάντησιν): the blending of the two streams of people, the οἱ προάγοντες, 'those going before' of the Synoptics being those who had gone out to meet Him and had turned back when they met Him at the head of the procession, and thus preceded Him to the city; the testimony of the people who were with Him to the new-comers that (reading ὅτι for ὅτε) He had summoned Lazarus from the tomb; and the fact that the people from the city took branches of palm trees (τὰ βαΐα τῶν φοινίκων [from class. βαΐς, 'palm-branch,' not from βαιός, 'small'; note the three different words for 'branch,' κλάδος, στιβάς, and βάτον]. The prophecy is given in a shorter form. Jesus is hailed 'King of Israel,' and the Pharisees comment on their own powerlessness and His popularity (v.¹⁹).

This entry was connected with Jesus' consciousness of His Messianic mission, gradually developing as His work assumed definite direction and His doctrine definite form; was conceived after the prophecies of the OT, and planned in order to satisfy the expectations of many who were waiting for the coming of the Kingdom of God, 'the consolation of Israel,' 'the redemption of Jerusalem' (Lk 2²⁵·³⁵). After the feeding of the 5000 (Jn 6¹⁴) the multitude recognized Jesus as the prophet that should come into the world, and would have seized Him and made Him a king, but He defeated their purpose; for He could not allow an emotional peasantry, ever ready to flock to the standard of a deliverer, to identify His Kingdom with this world, or His cause with that of a Judas of Galilee. Here He devises the entry on the lines of Jewish prophecy, which, though free from any hostile intention, was equivalent to a declaration that He was the Messiah, and implied that He was more. It was not directly urged against Him at His trial; but it supplied Pilate with his question, 'Art thou the King of the Jews?' and, accordingly, with the legal basis for his sentence. This and the cleansing were His two first and last actions as Messiah. They were followed by the Cross. We may infer in some measure from the song, the prophecy quoted, and His mode of entry, how far Jesus fulfilled and how far He transcended the Messianic expectations of His day.

1. The Kingdom of our father David.—The Kingdom of God or of heaven in the sense of the rule or Herrschaft of God, 'the power of God in its present or future manifestation,' the spiritual sway and 'sovereignty of God' (Dalman, Words of Jesus, p. 94), not in the sense of Home Rule for the Jews, had always been the text of Jesus' public addresses (Mt 4¹⁷). Shortly before this the Pharisees had asked when the Kingdom of God should come (Lk 17²⁰). And His answer was in keeping with His object of purifying the Messianic ideas and exalting the Messianic ideals of His age. It was the Kingdom of His Father (Mt 26²⁹) and of the Father of the righteous (Mt 13⁴³) that He proclaimed; it was

the kingdom of their father David of which the people thought. And His question, 'What think ye of Christ?' (Mt 22⁴²), shows that He did not consider Davidic origin sufficient status in itself for the Messiah. 'The kingdom of our father David' recalls the grand ideal of the theocratic ruler, the representative of J″, the ideal son to whose descendants that throne was ensured (2 S 7¹⁶), upon which the prophets of the OT continued to build their hopes—hopes which had become greatly modified and materialized during the struggle with Antiochus and Rome, and by contact with Grecian thought, and which made the ordinary Jew dream of a deliverer with all the heroic qualities of a Judas Maccabæus, and the more philosophic think of an earthly empire, cosmopolitan and world-ruling like the Roman. It was the idea in the prophets, chiefly in Dn 7¹³·¹⁴·¹⁷, of a kingdom, holy, supernatural, universal and eternal, that Jesus sought to recover from the lumber-room of tradition; and in this He was assisted by the gradual revival of more spiritual Messianic hopes among thoughtful and devout Jews like Simeon and Anna (cf. also the angelic prediction of Lk 1³² 'And the Lord God shall give unto him the throne of his father David'). The Gospels give an account of the general Messianic expectations. The Messiah was not to come from Galilee but from Bethlehem (Mt 2⁵), was king of the Jews (v.²), was to perform miracles (Jn 7³¹), to be a prophet (4²⁹), to appear mysteriously (7²⁷), to be a descendant of David (Mt 9²⁷), and to restore again the kingdom to Israel (Ac 1⁶).

2. The address 'Son of David.'—The Messiah is first designated υἱὸς Δαυίδ in Ps-Sol 17²³—a title founded on Scripture expressions such as 'son' (Is 9⁶), 'seed' (Targ. 2 S 7¹²), 'branch' (Jer 23⁵ and Zec 6¹², where the Aram. paraphrase for 'branch' is 'Messiah'). The Davidic descent of Jesus, never refuted by His opponents, was accepted by St. Paul (Ro 1³). But Jesus based His authority on something higher than this (Mt 22⁴⁵).

3. The song 'Hosanna . . . highest' (cf. Ps 118²⁵·²⁶, the festal cry amidst which the altar of burnt-offering was solemnly compassed on the first six days of the Feast of Tabernacles, and on the last day seven times).—'Hosanna,' which may be a contraction for Hôshî'āh nā (σῶσον δή, LXX), or shorter Hiph. imper. with enclitic, הושׁיעה־נא, is evidently a salutation = 'greeting to (cf. Lat. Io triumphe) the Son of David,' not supplication as in Ps.; cf. Didache, x. 6, ὡσαννὰ τῷ θεῷ Δαβίδ ('hail'). ὡσαννὰ ἐν τοῖς ὑψίστοις (Mt.) = δόξα ἐν ὑψίστοις (Lk.). In Ps 72⁴ 116⁶ the Heb. נָא (=dat.) is found after Hiph. of יָשַׁע; but the fact that the branches at the Feast of Tabernacles were called 'hosannas' and Mt.'s remarkable omission from Zec 9⁹ of נוֹשָׁע (σώζων, LXX), which would have thrown a new light on this cry, seem to denude the expression of any special significance. See HOSANNA.

Dalman suggests that the original cry of the people was 'Hosanna, Blessed in the name of J″ be he that cometh' (op. cit. p. 222). It is also to be remembered that in the OT, J″ Himself is generally represented as Saviour, while the Messiah was the prince of the redeemed people; the idea that the Messiah was the Redeemer being more recent. An interesting connexion between Ps 118²⁷ 'Bind the sacrifice with cords or woven branches' (עֲבֹתִים = στοιβάδις, Mk 11⁸) and the entry of Jesus is brought out in Symm. συνδήσαστε ἐν πανηγύρει πυκάσματα.

It is possible to make too much of the ceremonies of the Feast of Tabernacles in connexion with this entry, which took place just before the Feast of Passover in spring. But it is equally possible that the song, etc., may have been due to reminiscences of the preceding Feast of Tabernacles, when Jesus was pronounced the prophet and the Messiah (Jn 7⁴¹), and that the whole passage was sung, that which used to be supplication now passing into greeting. Our conclusion is, then, that though the song 'Hosanna,' etc., was used in salutation, it contains an allusion to the preceding Feast of Tabernacles, expresses the convictions of many of the people, and offers a remarkable parallel to Ps 118[25-27].

4. The mode of entry.—Some of the same Galilæan folk who wished to make Jesus a king before the time of Jn 6[15] have now, in their progress to the city, gathered around Him and escort Him, their national Prophet, with song. Others come from the city to meet Him, and receive Him with acts of homage which show that they regarded Him at the time as the prospective deliverer of the nation. In 2 Mac 10[6. 7] Judas Maccabæus is welcomed with similar acclamations and 'branches and fair boughs and palms,' and in 1 Mac 13[51] Simon. In 2 K 9[13] the followers of Jehu, the newly proclaimed king, threw down their cloaks (ἱμάτια, as here) before him. Stanley also (*SP* 191) mentions that in recent times the people of Bethlehem cast their cloaks before the horse of the consul of Damascus. Dalman agrees with Wellhausen that the procession did not acquire its Messianic colour until a later period, and that few at the time thought of the prophecy in Zec. (*op. cit.* p. 222). In the light of after events, Jesus entered the city as Messianic king, priest, and prophet. (1) The 'prince' had to provide the sacrifices 'to make reconciliation for or to atone for [לְכַפֵּר] the house of Israel' (Ezk 45[15], cf. 46[4-6] and 2 Ch 30[34]). So does 'the Lord's Anointed' here. (2) The priest presents the offering. So does 'the priest after the order of Melchizedek' (Ps 110[4]) proceed, metaphorically speaking, to 'bind the sacrifice with cords unto the horns of the altar' (118[27]). The harmony between the two offices of the Messiah as king and priest is well described in Zec 6[13] 'and the counsel of peace shall be between the two' (so Rosenm.). The growing predominance of the priestly office of the Messiah is also expressed in the choice of the colt 'whereon never man sat' (Mk. and Lk.), cf. Nu 19[3] 'a red heifer . . . upon which never came yoke.' (3) The prophetic character of the Messiah as the 'messenger of the covenant' (Mal 3[1]), coming to His temple, J″s prophet to the world and a light to the Gentiles (Is 49[6]), was suitably expressed by the proclamation of the people, 'This is Jesus the prophet,' etc., and by their testimony to His miracles, generally connected with a prophet. (4) There was another ideal of the OT realized in Jesus on this occasion. The meek and afflicted [עָנִי] saint of Ps 22[24], the Psalm appropriated by Jesus on the cross, was represented by Him who wept over the city and entered it 'meek [עָנִי Zec 9[9] = πραΰς, Mt 21[5]; also in Mt 5[5] = Ps 37[11]], and sitting upon an ass.' Other significations of this Heb. adj., such as 'poor,' 'oppressed,' and 'persecuted' (in Isaiah), were also realized in Jesus. But it is His meekness that Mt. emphasizes, doubtless because of His riding on an ass. At one time the ass was not a despised animal. Judges rode on white asses (Jg 5[10]). But through contact with Gentiles the ass had fallen into contempt. For ὄνος Josephus substitutes κτῆνος and ἵππος. LXX in Zec 9[9] preferred ὑπο-ζύγιον and πῶλος to the despised word. It was, however, the tradition that the Messiah should come riding on an ass (Sepp, § vi. c. 6). (5) The conception of Messiah as the suffering Servant of Deut.-Isaiah was, however, most of all exemplified by Him who on this occasion humbled Himself [נַעֲנָה] (Niph. of עָנָה in reflexive sense) Is 53[7] = ἑταπείνωσεν ἑαυτόν, Ph 2[8]] in a voluntary manner in His progress to a death for His people.

Matthew describes Jesus as armed with authority (ἐξουσία, cf. 8[9]), and on this occasion depicts Him as the *Malkā Mĕshihā* of the Jews. His

authority is over all flesh, to make them feel their want of God and Him. The sense of power was derived from the sense of His mission and the consciousness that He was the Son of God, which made Him soar beyond the Messianic rôle and see Himself the Lord of the whole earth, holding sway by peace, spiritual peace, and by power, spiritual power. 'He claimed for Himself,' as Dalman remarks (*op. cit.* p. 313), 'an exalted position such as had not been assigned even to the Messiah,' and, as Harnack (*What is Christianity?* p. 141) observes, 'He leaves the idea of the Messiah far behind Him, because He filled it with a content that burst it.' It was in the same spirit that He affirmed His Kingship before Pilate (Mt 27[11]).

The object of this entry was the inauguration of Jesus' last mission to His people. The attraction of the provincial crowds, the Jerusalem populace, the Greeks and proselytes, if not the impressing of the Jewish hierarchy, this was the end desired, and in a great measure attained. He never seems to move in solitary state in the Temple; crowds are always around Him; He is the topic of the people's conversation and the subject of the priests' conspiracy. This was a suitable prelude to a great missionary enterprise all too brief, but crowded perhaps with more real work and witness for the King and His Kingdom than the preceding portion of His ministry. It led to the cleansing of the Temple on the same or the following day, and these together culminated in the Cross.

LITERATURE.—Dalman, *Words of Jesus*; Harnack, *What is Christianity?*; Stanley, *SP*; Farrar, *Life of Christ*; Edersheim, *Life and Times*; Hitchcock, *Mystery of the Cross*; artt. 'Hosanna,' 'Messiah,' 'Prophets' in Hastings' *DB*.

F. R. MONTGOMERY HITCHCOCK.

ENVY.—The word φθόνος occurs in the Gospels only in the two parallel passages Mt 27[18] and Mk 15[10] in connexion with the trial of Jesus. When the members of the Jewish hierarchy sought the death of Jesus at the hands of Pilate, they attempted to veil their motives under the pretence of loyalty to Cæsar. Pilate was too astute a man to credit these professions for a single instant. He perceived (ἐγίνωσκε, Mk 15[10]) the underlying feeling to be envy. If the word ᾔδει ('he knew,' Mt 27[18]) is significant, it supports the opinion that Pilate had previously become acquainted with the attitude of the chief priests toward Jesus. The message that Pilate later received from his wife (Mt 27[19]) somewhat favours this opinion. In fact it was the business of Pilate to know of the person of Jesus and His relations to the leaders of the Jews, and nothing but the contemptuous indifference of a Gallio would have hindered him from the inquiries necessary for gaining this knowledge.

Perhaps it might seem at first as though the feeling which prompted the priests might more properly be termed jealousy. A comparison of the two feelings, jealousy and envy, readily shows the distinctive character of each: 'Jealousy is the malign feeling which is often had toward a rival, or possible rival, for the possession of that which we greatly desire, as in love or ambition. Envy is a similar feeling toward one, whether rival or not, who already possesses that which we greatly desire. Jealousy is enmity prompted by fear; envy is enmity prompted by covetousness' (*Century Dictionary*, *s.v.* 'Envy'). 'Envy is only a malignant, selfish hunger, casting its evil eye on the elevation or supposed happiness of others' (Bushnell, *ib.*). In Trench, *Synonyms of the New Testament*, xxvi., the comparison is less happily stated. Apparently jealousy (ζῆλος) 'may assume two shapes; either that of a desire to make war upon the good which it beholds in another, and thus to trouble that good, and make it less; or, where it has not vigour and energy enough to attempt the making of it less, there may be at least the wishing of it less. And here is the point of contact which ζῆλος has with φθόνος: thus Plato, *Menex.* 242 A, πρῶτον μὲν ζῆλος, ἀπὸ ζήλου δὲ φθόνος: the latter being essentially passive, the former is active and energetic.' This citation from Plato shows that there may be a genetic relation between jealousy and envy, but it does not show that envy is passive. Trench quotes from Aristotle, *Rhetoric*, ii. 11, omitting ὁ δὲ τὸν πλησίον [παρασκευάζει] μὴ ἔχειν διὰ τὸν φθόνον [τὰ ἀγαθά]: 'One that is moved by envy contrives that his neighbour shall not have the good that he has or seems to have.' A careful examination of the use of φθόνος in classic Greek authors justifies this statement of Aristotle, and reveals that it means the same active malignant feeling as is expressed in modern English by the word 'envy.' It was φθόνος which moved the gods to prevent men from attaining a great or uninterrupted experience of prosperity. Pindar, the tragic writers, and orators also are found using the word to designate the active impulse to destroy another's prosperity so far as one has the power to do it. The Septuagint, according to Hatch's *Concordance*, uses φθόνος only in the Apocryphal books. The most noteworthy instance is in Wis 2²⁴ 'on account of the envy of the devil, death entered into the world.'

Since envy is an ill-will or malice aroused by the success or good gifts of another, it is the fitting word to designate the motive of the priests who protested their loyalty to Cæsar. Envy is not a primary emotion. Other feelings prepare the way for, and may enter into, it. It is the result of a development in the life of selfishness (Jul. Müller, *Lehre von der Sünde*, i. 233 f. [Eng. tr. *Christian Doctrine of Sin*, i. 171]). In the Gospels this development is not difficult to trace. The deeds and words of Jesus were from the outset attended by suspicion on the part of scribes and Pharisees. His growing popularity aroused their jealousy. When they could charge Him with a compact with Beelzebub (Mt 12²²ff., Mk 3²⁰ff., Lk 11¹⁴ff.), they had begun to hate Him because of the popular confidence in Him, and especially because this confidence was of a degree and a quality which they never had received, and which they could not hope to receive. This occurrence was an attempt to discredit Him with the people, and it showed that envy had obtained full lodgment in their hearts. From that time onwards it had so large a share in their lives, that when they appeared before Pilate they were so mastered by this feeling to which they had given free rein for months, that they were unable to conceal it. See also artt. COVETOUSNESS and JEALOUSY.

F. B. DENIO.

EPHPHATHA.—An Aramaic word, found in the Greek text of Mk 7³⁴. We there read that Jesus said to a man who was 'deaf and had an impediment in his speech, *Ephphatha*' (ἐφφαθά). The Evangelist appends a Greek translation of the word: ὅ ἐστιν διανοίχθητι, 'that is, Be opened.'

There are two Aram. words of which ἐφφαθά may be a transliteration: (1) אֶתְפַּח; (2) אֶתְפַּח. The former is a contraction of אִתְפַּתַּח Imperative Ithpaal; and the latter is a contraction of אִתְפַּתַּח Imperative Ithpeal of the verb פְּתַח 'to open.' In Greek MSS, א³D present ἐφφιθά, which is certainly Ithpeal, whereas ἐφφαθά may be Ithpaal. Jerome gives *Ephphetha*, and some Latin MSS give *effetha*, *ephetha*, and even *effeta*. Wellhausen in his Com. on Mk 7³⁴ prints ἐφφατά, but apparently without MS authority.

The form ἐφφαθά, when compared with its Aram. equivalent אִתְפְּתַח, presents several interesting peculiarities bearing on the dialect spoken by our Lord. (1) We note the disappearance of the guttural ח. We know that in Galilee and Samaria the gutturals were much neglected, or even interchanged; and they are often ignored in transliterating Semitic words into Greek. Thus we find Μεσσίας from מְשִׁיחָא; Βηθεσδά from בֵּית חִסְדָּא; γέεννα from גֵּי הִנֹּם; Σίμων from שִׁמְעוֹן (side by side with Συμεών, where the ι does duty for ע). (2) We note the assimilation of ת to פ, giving ἐφφαθά for ἰθφαθά; or in Aram. אַתְפַּח for אִתְפַּח. This is quite in accordance with a rule in Palestinian Aramaic, that frequently, and especially with the labials ב, מ, and פ, the ת in the passive prefix את is assimilated to the first radical (Dalman's *Aramäische Grammatik*, p. 201). (3) It is noteworthy that we have the repetition of the aspirate letter φ. According to Hebrew analogy, אֶתְפַּח ought to give ἰππαθά, inasmuch as the *daghesh* always indicates the harder and not the aspirated form of the letter פ. We infer, therefore, that in the Semitic language, which lies behind our Greek Test., there was a deviation from Hebrew rule as to the *daghesh*. If Heb. had been the basal language of the Gospels, we could not have had such forms as Βαρθολομαῖος from בַּר תּוֹלְמַי and Βηθφαγή from בֵּית פֵּ אָגֵי. The aspirated forms ת and פ after a closed syllable would be intolerable. The *daghesh forte* is also singularly treated in Ματθαῖος from מַתְאָי and Ζακχαῖος from זַכַּי. (4) The appearance

of ι in ἐφφαθά may possibly indicate that the dialect spoken by our Lord used the *Syriac* prefix את *eth* with passive forms, and not את *ith*, as is found in Palestinian Aramaic; in other words, used Ethpaal for Ithpaal.

As to what is the *subject* of the verb διανοίχθητι, 'Be thou opened,' there is room for difference of opinion. It may be the *mouth*, as in Lk 1⁶⁴ (so Weiss, Morison), or the *ear*, as in Targ. on Is 50⁵ (so Bruce, Swete); or it may be the deaf *man* himself who is addressed. One door of knowledge being shut, the man is conceived of as a bolted chamber: 'Jesus said to *him*, Be thou opened.'

LITERATURE.—Zahn, *Einleitung in das NT* i. 1-24; Kautzsch, *Gramm. des Biblisch-Aramäisch*, § 5; Dalman, *Aram. Gramm.* 201 f., 222; A. Meyer, *Jesu Muttersprache*, 52; Meyer, Bruce, Swete, etc., on Mk 7³⁴.

J. T. MARSHALL.

EPHRAIM.—Jn 11⁵⁴ only. After the raising of Lazarus, Jesus departed, in consequence of the plots of the chief priests against Him, 'unto a country (RV 'into the country') near to the wilderness, into a city called Ephraim, and there continued with his disciples.'

There are scarcely any textual variations. TR spells 'Εφραΐμ; Lachmann, Tischendorf, Westcott-Hort spell 'Εφραΐμ; Stephanus, 1550, had on the margin the reading 'Εφρίμ, which is supported by אL and Latin witnesses, and the name Σαμφουρείμ as to be supplied after χώραν. This is the reading of D, *Sapfurim* in its Latin part, for which Chase (*Syro-Lat. Text of Gospels*, 108) and R. Harris (*A Study of Codex Bezæ*, p. 184) suggested that σαμ might be the Heb. שֵׁם 'the name'; but more probable is the identification with *Sepphoris*, which in Jos. *Ant.* xiv. 91 is spelt Σατφόροις (v.ll. Σαμφόροις and other forms); so Jerome (s.v. 'Araba' in *OS* 17. 13 f.): 'Diocæsareæ, quæ olim *Safforine* dicebatur.'

Eusebius in his *Onomasticon* says (ad Ephron, Jos. xv. 9): καὶ ἔστι νῦν κώμη 'Εφραΐμ μεγίστη περὶ τὰ βόρεια Αἰλίας ὡς ἀπὸ σημείων κ; in the Latin rendering of Jerome: 'est et villa pergrandis *Efræa* nomine contra septentrionem in vicesimo ab Ælia miliario' (ed. Klostermann, p. 86. 1, 90. 18). With this has been identified *Afra* [=עַפְרָה Jos. xviii. 23]: 'in tribu Beniamin; et est hodie vicus *Efraim* in quinto miliario Bethelis ad orientem respiciens' (p. 29. 4; the Greek text [28. 4: καὶ νῦν ἔστι κώμη Αἰφρηλ ἀπό] is here defective); further, 1 Mac 11³⁴ =Jos. *Ant.* xiii. 127 [ed. Niese]: τοὺς τρεῖς νομοὺς 'Αφαίρεμα (v.l. 'Αφέρεμα) καὶ Λύδδα καὶ 'Ραμαθεὶν; finally, the notice of Josephus (*BJ* iv. 551), that Vespasian took Βηθηγά τε (earlier reading Βαιθήλ or Βηθήλ) καὶ 'Εφραιμ πολίχνια. Since Robinson, the site has been sought at the modern *eṭ-Ṭaiyibeh*, 4 miles N.E. from Bethel. Schürer (*GJV*³ i. 233) quotes Robinson, ii. 332-338; Guérin, *Judée*, iii. 45-51; Buhl, *GAP* p. 177; Heidet, art. 'Ephrem' in Vigouroux's *Dict.* ii. 1885 ff.; cf., further, art. 'Ephraim' by J. H. Kennedy in Hastings' *DB*, and by T. K. Cheyne in *Encyc. Biblica.**

Origen compares, for the retirement of Jesus, Mt 4¹²f. and then allegorizes: Ephraim, according to Gn 41⁵¹f. 'καρποφορία'; ἀπῆλθεν ἐκεῖθεν εἰς τὴν χώραν 'τοῦ ὅλου κόσμου,' ἐγγὺς τῆς ἐρήμου 'ἐκκλησίας,' εἰς 'Εφραὶμ τὴν 'καρποφοροῦσαν' λεγομένην πόλιν, etc. (new Berlin edition, pp. 420, 551). About the site he says nothing.

EB. NESTLE.

EPILEPSY.—There is but one specific instance of this awful malady recorded for us in the Gospels.† This case is, however, common to all three Synoptists (cf. Mt 17¹⁵, Mk 9¹⁷f., Lk 9³⁹); and the three accounts, while not in verbal agreement, are sufficiently harmonious to leave no doubt in the mind of the reader as to the nature and malig-

* Schürer (*GJV*³ ii. 163, n. 435) is certainly right in rejecting the identification of *Sapfurim* with *Sepharvaim* (2 K 17²⁴) put forward by Resch (*TU* x. 4, pp. 141, 204) and approved by Blass (*Ev. sec. Joh.* 1902, p. xl), and in finding in *Sapfurim* the name of the town Sepphoris, which covered a very large area. But it is not yet certain whether Codex D has preserved here a correct tradition. Lk 9¹⁰ offers similar variations in the text (πόλιν καλουμένην, τόπον λεγόμενον, τόπον ἔρημον, etc.). 'Εφραΐμ might itself be derived from Sepphoris, the first letter being dropped after the ς of εἰς.
† 'Epileptic' is substituted by RV for 'lunatick' of AV in Mt 4²⁴ 17¹⁵ as tr. of σεληνιάζεσθαι.

nant character of the disease. It is noteworthy that the writers all attribute it to the active agency of demons; and this is the more remarkable as St. Matthew, in another place, appears to differentiate between demon possession and epilepsy (Mt 4²⁴ δαιμονιζομένους καὶ σεληνιαζομένους). Not only do the Evangelists record their own and the popular belief in the connexion of evil spirits with epilepsy; they also lead us to believe that Jesus exercised His power on the presupposition of the truth of this contemporary idea (cf. Mt 17¹⁸, Mk 9²⁵, Lk 9⁴²).

It is well to remember in this connexion that medical thought at this time and, indeed, for a long period subsequent to this, was distinctly on the side of the Synoptists. Aretæus (c. 70 A.D.) in writing of it (Sign. Morb. Diuturn. 37) attempts to explain the reason why epilepsy was called 'the sacred illness' (ἱερὴν κικλήσκουσι τὴν πάθην). The remedy, according to this writer, belonged not to human but to Divine agency. Hippocrates, on the other hand, writing some five centuries earlier, refuses to accept the belief that there was anything supernatural about this disease. In his opinion it is to be explained in the same way as any other disease to which people are liable (ὥστε μηδὲν διακρίνοντα τὸ νόσημα θειότερον τῶν λοιπῶν νοσημάτων, κ.τ.λ., Morb. Sac. 303 [see Hobart's The Medical Language of St. Luke, p. 20]). The important place held by the belief in the malevolent influence of demons and in the powers of the exorcist will be recognized if we turn, e.g., to Tertullian, Apol. 23 ; Origen, c. Cels. vii. 334 ; Apost. Constit. viii. 26, amongst the written products of early Christian thought.

The word employed by St. Matthew in his description of the epileptic boy (σεληνιάζεται), as well as in his catalogue of ailments (4²⁴), shows that in the opinion of the ancients the moon had a preponderating influence in bringing on this disease (cf. Ps 121⁶ for a reference to the baleful effect which the brilliant rays of the moon were supposed to exert, and which from the context seems to have been thought as deadly as sunstroke). This belief, too, descended far down into the Middle Ages ; and, indeed, it can hardly be said to have altogether vanished from the popular mind, though it is probably now confined to the remoter quarters of human habitation.

A comparative study of the particular case described by each of the Synoptists reveals the fact that St. Mark gives a much more graphic and detailed account of the symptoms than either of the other two. According to this writer, the boy was deaf and dumb, he was liable to be seized with convulsions at any time or place (ὅπου ἐάν, v.¹⁸), to fall violently to the ground, foaming at his mouth, gnashing with and grinding his teeth. Finally, he is said to be gradually wasting away as a result of the frequency of the seizures. He was, moreover, afflicted from his childhood with this awful malady, a by no means uncommon feature of such cases (see art. 'Medicine,' by A. Macalister, in Hastings' DB iii. 327ᵇ). St. Mark also gives a vivid account of a fit which seems to have been brought on by the presence of Jesus, or by the excitement consequent on his introduction to that presence (9²⁰). No sooner did he come before Jesus than a seizure with terrible convulsions took place, and falling on the ground he rolled about (ἐκυλίετο in EV) foaming.

Perhaps the most peculiar part of the Markan narrative is the account of the healing process. According to the Matthæan and Lukan versions, the cure was not only perfect, it was instantaneous (Mt 17¹⁸ = Lk 9⁴²). St. Mark, on the other hand, says it was gradual and difficult of accomplishment. Jesus, adopting a tone of peremptory authority (ἐγὼ ἐπιτάσσω σοι, v.²⁵), addressed the spirit as a person, and was answered by the latter, who caused his victim to utter loud cries and to writhe with violent convulsions before he obeyed the command. Nor was the completion of the cure yet reached, for an unconsciousness supervened so profound (ἐγένετο ὡσεὶ νεκρός, v.²⁶) as to deceive many of the bystanders into the belief that death had claimed the victim. It was not until Jesus took the boy by the hand to raise him from the ground that the miracle took its final shape, and the people were enabled to witness and to marvel at 'the majesty of God' (Lk 9⁴³).

It is to be noted that this feature in the healing acts of Jesus does not stand alone in this place. It is revealed in another case also recorded by St. Mark. In a preceding section he tells

of the healing by Jesus of a blind man at Bethsaida. The cure in this case, too, was effected gradually, and was completed only by the contact of His hands with the afflicted patient (see 8²²⁻²⁵).

That 'the scribes' seized the opportunity afforded by this case to carry on their controversy with Jesus and His disciples is implied in St. Mark, where the element of hostility is referred to (see v.¹⁴ 'and scribes disputing against them' [πρὸς αὐτούς]). The method of healing adopted by Jesus was in striking contrast to that to which they were accustomed to lend themselves (cf. Shabbath 61 and Tosefta Shabbath, in loc., where we learn of the employment of charms, such as amulets and winged insects of a certain kind, in the cure of epileptics). With Jesus it is the assertion of personal superiority. His words carry with them the weight of indisputable authority. The command is that of One who claims the lordship over disease and death. At the same time directness and simplicity are the essential characteristics of His attitude and bearing. Nor did Jesus permit this contrast to pass unnoticed (see Mt 12²⁷, where He refers to a practice recognized as legitimate by the religionists of His day).

Exorcism was practised in public by men who professed to wield authority over the demon world (cf. Ac 19¹³, which is the only place where the word 'exorcist' occurs in the NT). These exorcists seem to have relied upon the repetition of certain names to effect their purpose, and along with this the recitation of special incantations, of which Solomon particularly was considered to be the author (see Jos. Ant. VIII. ii. 5; Schürer, HJP II. iii. 151–155, and also To 6–8 for the lengths to which belief in the efficacy of charms and incantations had made its way among the Jews). We must not forget, moreover, that the followers of Jesus framed their methods of healing the sick upon this contemporary model. The utterance of the name of Jesus found its place in their cures (Ac 3⁶ 16¹⁸, Mk 9³⁸. ³⁹ 16¹⁷ etc., where ἐν τῷ ὀνόματι Ἰησοῦ Χριστοῦ seems to be an essential part of the formula employed). See also DEMON, LUNATIC.

J. R. WILLIS.

EPIPHANY.—See CALENDAR, p. 261 f.

EQUALITY.—Equality in capability, responsibility, and future destiny is by no means taught by Christ in the Gospels. Christians are not reduced to one uniform level of worth and dignity, either here or hereafter. In the parables of the Talents and the Pounds the servants are not in a condition of equality during their period of probation or afterwards (Mt 25¹⁴⁻³⁰, Lk 19¹¹⁻²⁷). The inequality of Dives and Lazarus here is an admitted fact, and their inequality beyond the grave is a sure consequence (Lk 16²⁵). Christ repeatedly admits without deprecation the inequality observable among men. 'There are last which shall be first, and there are first which shall be last' (Lk 13³⁰, cf. Mt 19³⁰). There is, indeed, no suggestion whatever that a certain level of equality, tried even by internal criteria, is to be aimed at. Growth in grace follows the law of life, an increasing increment following upon each further increment (Lk 19²⁶). 'He that is but little in the kingdom of heaven' is greater than John the Baptist (Mt 11¹¹, Lk 7²⁸). Pre-eminence is not at all directly discouraged or deprecated, only it must be the deepest and truest excellence, apart from the odiousness of comparison with others. The sons of Zebedee are too anxious for the position of pre-eminence hereafter, and too heedless of the call to self-sacrifice now (Mk 10³⁷, Mt 20²¹). All disciples are in danger of desiring to be honoured by titles here, instead of awaiting God's bestowal of dignity in the new life beyond (Mt 23⁸⁻¹²). But, to be greatest in the Kingdom of heaven it is necessary to be as a little child here (Mt 18[4], Lk 9[48]). Such lowly and meek Christians are called 'little children,' and the Lord identifies Himself with them (Mk 9[37]). The disciple must not lord it over his fellow-disciples wantonly and arrogantly (Mt 24[48 ff.]). Not only superiority, but even equality, is forbidden as the goal of effort. Mutual service is to be the aim of the Christian community—the first is to be *bond-servant* of all (Mk 10[44]). This precept of service, instead of insistence upon equality (Lk 22[26. 27]), was beautifully and touchingly practised by the Master-Servant on the night of His betrayal (Jn 13[5]). Every man is to descend below the level of equality and leave it to God to call him higher if it be good in His sight (Lk 14[10]). Especially in respect of penitence for sin is it good to sink all considerations of comparative merit (Lk 18[14]). Except in the ideal sense, equality is neither an established fact nor a correct principle in the Christian Society. We are sons of one Father, and so brothers ; but brothers are not equal, for some are older or wiser or richer or better. We are servants of one Master, and so fellows ; but in this service there are various offices and diverse stations. Unity rather than equality is the leading characteristic of the internal economy of the Kingdom of heaven (Jn 10[16] 11[52] 17[11] etc.).

LITERATURE.—Bruce, *Parabolic Teaching of Christ*, pp. 178–225 ; Mozley, *Univ. Sermons*, p. 72 ff. ; Newman, *Selected Sermons*, p. 260 ff.　　　　　　W. B. FRANKLAND.

ER.—An ancestor of Jesus, Lk 3[28].

ERROR.—As one who lived in the undimmed vision of holiness and truth, 'who saw life steadily and saw it whole,' Jesus must have felt with an intensity we cannot fathom how sin had distorted the reason of man as well as perverted his affections. All around Him He saw men walking 'in the vanity of their mind, being darkened in their understanding, alienated from the life of God because of the ignorance that is in them, because of the hardening of their heart' (Eph 4[18]). He saw, also, as no one else had ever seen, that the recovery of those who had become 'vain in their reasonings' (Ro 1[21]) was to be achieved less by attacking their godless errors than by aiming at the renewal of the moral and spiritual nature. *This is the fundamental and vital point to emphasize.* Underlying all Christ's dealings with error there was the recognition of the dependence of men's opinions and beliefs upon their character. We seldom realize how much we contribute to the judgments we form. We set out with the intention of being wholly governed by the object. We want to know what it really is, and not merely what it appears to be. So we approach it, examine it, and form our opinion of it. But the eye brings with it the power of seeing ; what we see depends not merely upon the object, but upon the organ of vision. This is true especially with respect to all judgments of value, all questions of right and wrong, of duty and religion. The possibilities of error increase not merely with the complexity of the subject-matter, but with the way in which our interests and convictions, our desires and predilections, are bound up with it. In the region of the moral and spiritual life not only must the intellect be clear,--free from false theory,—but still more necessary is it that the heart be pure and the practice sound. To appreciate goodness a man must love goodness ; must be, if not good, at any rate good in many ways. 'Every one,' said Jesus, 'that is of the truth heareth my voice' (Jn 18[37]). This does not, of course, mean that all moral and religious errors are due simply to a depraved heart. Violent upholders of orthodoxy have been only too ready to assume that such is the case, and to

silence the heretic by declaring him a bad man. But it does mean that there is a moral aptitude for Christian discipleship. It was inevitable that men who had no enthusiasm for goodness should misunderstand Christ and reject Him. It was equally certain that His 'sheep' would hear His voice and follow Him.

There are a few striking illustrations of these principles in the Gospels which demand our attention.

1. *The necessity for inward, moral clarity and simplicity* is strongly insisted on by Jesus (Mt 6[22. 23], Lk 11[34-36]). 'We so often talk as if we were only obliged to "follow our conscience" ; as if no one could lay anything to our charge unless we were acting against the present voice of conscience. But this is very perilous error. We are also obliged to enlighten our conscience and keep it enlightened. It is as much liable to error as our uninstructed intelligence, as much liable to failure as our sight' (Gore, *The Sermon on the Mount*, p. 146 f.). The thought is expressed in other forms equally suggestive. Thus the 'pure heart' is the condition of the vision of God (Mt 5[8]). It is the 'honest and good heart' which, having heard the word, keeps it (Lk 8[15]). Heavenly truth is hid from the wise and prudent, but revealed unto babes (Mt 11[25]). The disciples must be converted and become as little children (Mt 18[2-5], Mk 10[15]).

2. *Our Lord's method of dealing with the ignorant and erring* is full of instruction. Take the case of the woman suffering from an issue of blood (Mt 9[20-22], Mk 5[25-34], Lk 8[43-48]). It would be hard to exaggerate the poor woman's ignorance. Her mind was full of erroneous thoughts of Jesus. At best she looks upon Him as a worker of magic. She thinks that she may be able to steal a blessing from Him in the crowd. But there was working, even in that darkness, the precious element of faith. She trusted Jesus as far as she understood Him, and that was enough for the Master. He knew that faith in Himself, even though it were only as a grain of mustard seed, would break through the incumbent weight of error and ignorance, and offer a free way for His grace : 'Daughter, be of good comfort : thy faith hath made thee whole ; go in peace.' Jesus adopted essentially the same method in dealing with persons like Zacchæus, Mary Magdalene, the woman of Samaria, and the 'publicans and sinners' generally. These victims and slaves of passion and ignorance were certainly not good. Their lives were stained by error and sin. The religious classes looked upon them as moral outcasts. And yet there were those among them open to conviction. Their wilful and passionate lives had not destroyed in them a strange yearning for better things. And when purity drew near to them, adorned with such Divine graciousness as it was in the Person of Jesus, they became responsive to it and yearned after it. That was faith, and Jesus saw in it a power which would work for the redemption of the whole nature. His one endeavour was to call it forth into fullest exercise. Erroneous thoughts of God and life, of duty and religion, would all slowly disappear under the influence of this new devotion to Himself. But, after all, those who responded to His invitations (Mt 11[28-30]) were never numerous. The great mass of the people was untouched and uninfluenced. Sunk in stupid ignorance, vice, and worldliness, the masses, at the best, followed Him for a time in gaping wonder, thinking far more of 'the loaves and fishes' than of the new life and truth He placed before them. Hence the sad words with which Jesus upbraided 'the cities wherein most of his mighty works were done' (Mt 11[20-24]).

3. *The Pharisees and the other religious leaders.* —At first it seems a strange thing that these men, on the whole, fell into the appalling error of rejecting Jesus. 'The gospel did not place itself, directly and at the outset, in opposition to the errors of the Pharisees. . . . But the dividing gulf was none the less real, and would baffle every attempt to fathom or bridge it over' (Reuss, *Christian Theology in the Apostolic Age*, p. 227). A few reflexions on the lines of the previous remarks will make this clear. The whole life and thought of the typical Pharisee was a closed system. His religion was already fully organized. 'In the hands of the Pharisees, Judaism finally became petrified.' It was a body of rules and doctrines which laid the main stress on conduct and outward ceremonies,—a rigid mould without plasticity or capability of expansion. It could only react in antagonism towards one who offered a religion of the spirit, a worship of the Father in spirit and in truth. The Pharisee did not know what to make of a renovating and inspiring call which bade him begin afresh, and completely revise his life and religion in the light of a higher ideal. He was self-satisfied, and resented criticism as an intolerable impertinence. He was like one who says that he must follow his conscience, but who does not continually seek to enlighten his conscience by confronting it with higher aspects of truth. He had ears, but he heard not; eyes, yet he was blind. This was the most fatal kind of error, the most hopeless of all moral states; and it was inevitable that it should come into deadly collision with Jesus. 'While the Pharisaic spirit had changed religion into a narrow and barren formalism, the gospel carefully distinguished the form from the essence in things religious. Its estimate of man's true worth and the certainty of his hopes rested not upon the outward conduct of the life, but upon the inward direction of the heart and feelings' (Reuss, *The Gospel and Judaism*, vol. i. p. 227). The errors of the Pharisees and the bitter hostility to Jesus which they provoked may be studied in the following passages—they are a mere selection: Mt 6$^{1-8}$ 12$^{1-45}$ 21$^{23-46}$ 23$^{1-39}$, Mk 3$^{1-6}$, Lk 6$^{1-11}$ 11$^{37-54}$ 18$^{9-14}$, Jn 5$^{30-47}$ 7$^{14-52}$ 8$^{12-59}$ 9$^{1-41}$.

4. *The errors of the disciples.*—It is not necessary to go into details here. In responding to His call the disciples of Jesus had placed themselves in training for the higher life. They had passed into a school where the scholar's ignorance and error would be dealt with patiently and wisely. They had much to learn, but the essential thing was that they were in communion with the Light of Life.

LITERATURE.—Illingworth, *Christian Character*; Gore, *The Sermon on the Mount*; Reuss, *History of Christian Theology in the Apostolic Age*; A. J. Balfour, *Foundations of Belief*; *Personal Idealism*, Essay I. by Prof. G. F. Stout; Descartes, *Meditation* IV.   A. J. JENKINSON.

ESCHATOLOGY.—

I. Eschatology in the Synoptic Gospels.
  A. Current Jewish eschatological conceptions.
    1. The coming Kingdom.
    2. The Jewish supremacy.
    3. The Messiah.
    4. Various forms of the conception of the Messiah.
    5. The preliminaries of the coming Kingdom.
      (a) The heirs of the Kingdom.
      (b) The Resurrection.
      (c) Hades, Gehenna, Paradise.
      (d) The Final Judgment.
  B. The main features of our Lord's eschatological teaching.
    1. His conception of the Kingdom of God.
    2. His Messianic consciousness.
    3. His view of the time of the Consummation.
II. Eschatology in the Gospel of John.
    1. The idealizing style of the Gospel.
    2. Its conception of Eternal Life.
    3. Its attitude to Eschatology proper.
      Literature.

The design of this article is indicated particularly under the letter B in the above Table of Contents.

It is to set forth the main features of the teaching of our Lord regarding the Last Things. His doctrine is presumably discoverable from the Four Gospels, and is capable of being exhibited in a self-consistent form. Yet in view of the facts of the case and the present state of critical opinion, it will be necessary to keep certain distinctions steadily in mind.

We must distinguish between (I.) the Synoptic Gospels and (II.) the Gospel of John; and we must distinguish between (A) current Jewish conceptions and (B) the conceptions of Jesus. In proportion to our feeling of the real unity of our subject, it will be impossible to maintain these distinctions with rigidity; yet a total disregard of them is impossible to any one who would keep on terms with the criticism of the Gospels in our own day, or, what is more important, would appreciate in any just degree the holy originality of Jesus. The bearing, however, of what is called the *Synoptic Problem* upon any matter important to our purpose is so slight that we may safely ignore it, mentioning only that we assume as a good working hypothesis the prevailing critical theory, which gives precedence in point of time, and even, in certain aspects, of importance, to the Gospel of Mark.

I. ESCHATOLOGY IN THE SYNOPTIC GOSPELS.— A. *CURRENT JEWISH ESCHATOLOGICAL CONCEPTIONS AS WITNESSED TO BY THE GOSPELS.*—So far as these are concerned, it does not seem necessary to make any distinction between the Synoptics among themselves or between them and John. It may be generally postulated, moreover, that the fundamental conceptions are those of the OT, although it will be found that some of these have undergone modification since the time of the latest canonical books. Our principal witnesses are naturally the Synoptics. In them we have the most accurate reports accessible to us of the words actually used by Jesus; and where His sayings, as there recorded, employ the language of eschatology, apart from explanations which give it a turn peculiar to Himself, we may assume that the language in its natural implications represents current Jewish belief.

1. The coming Kingdom.—It is clear that Jesus addressed people who had a perfectly distinct, though not accurately defined, idea of an *age* or *kingdom* to come, which should follow on the consummation (συντέλεια, Mt 13$^{39f.}$) of the present age. He speaks, *e.g.*, of rewards to the faithful 'in this *time* (καιρός),' and of eternal life in the 'world (αἰών) to come' (Mk 10^{30}); and the phrase 'Kingdom of God,' which was constantly on His lips, while doubtless subjected to expositions which charged it with new meanings for His followers, yet rested on a view of things common to Him and to even irresponsive hearers. It meant the perfect form of the Theocracy of which all the prophets had spoken.

2. The Jewish supremacy. — It was generally believed that the Kingdom would come through an act of power, in which God would visit His people,—the Jews,—delivering them from all their enemies, so that they might serve Him without fear in holiness and righteousness for ever (Lk 1^{74}). Men of the type of Simeon, Zacharias, and Joseph of Arimathæa waited for the consolation of *Israel*. Such persons doubtless believed with the prophets (*e.g.* Is 11$^{1ff.}$ 9$^{4ff.}$, Zec 9^9) that the supremacy of God's people would be maintained, if not actually accomplished, by methods of peace, and even in the spirit of brotherly alliance among the nations (see esp. Is 19$^{24f.}$), who would receive the 'law' from Mount Zion (Is 2$^{2-4}$). Yet obviously both they and the general populace, and even the disciples after the Resurrection (Ac 1^6), thought of a state of things in which the position of God's ancient people would be central and supreme.

3. The Messiah.—Beyond the general belief that the Kingdom would come through an act or series of acts of Divine power, there is abundant evidence that in the time represented by the Gospels there was among the Jewish people, though not confined to them,* the definite expectation that the Kingdom would come through the advent of a personal Ruler—called by the Jews the *Messiah* or, in Greek, the *Christ* = 'the *Anointed*'—on whom God would pour forth His Spirit in extraordinary measure. This belief, so far as the Jews were concerned, goes back to the testimony of the earlier prophets (esp. Isaiah and Micah), but its history within the OT period shows that it sometimes either disappeared altogether or retired into the background, its place being taken by such a view as that expressed in Jer 31[31ff.]—of a reign of Jahweh Himself through His law written on the hearts of His people.† We need not here inquire into the causes of this fluctuation. It is enough to remark that for about a century before the time of Christ the belief that the Kingdom would be established through an individual worldwide Ruler, who would exercise practically Divine powers, had been current in larger or smaller circles among the Jews. Sufficient proof of this lies in the circumstance that in the time of our Lord passages in the Prophets (*e.g.* Deutero-Isaiah) or in the Apocalypse of Daniel, which had originally no reference to an individual Messiah,‡ had come to be so interpreted. The interpretation is *current*. No other is even thought of. In some cases, no doubt—as notably in the fulfilments of prophecy marked by the First Evangelist—it may be difficult to decide whether the exegesis of a passage cited from a prophet is not of purely Christian origin; but there are unquestionably some cases (notably Dn 7[13]) in which the importation of a reference to an individual Messiah into passages which really contain no such reference, is of pre-Christian date.

4. Various forms of the conception of the Messiah.—It is difficult to determine with any minuteness how the Messiah was conceived, as regarded either His Person or His work. In regard to the former, *e.g.*, it would be unwarrantable to infer from Mt 1[23] (cf. Is 7[14]) that it was generally believed that He would be born of a virgin, and perhaps equally so to infer from the fact that the disciples (16[16] ‖), and perhaps others also (14[33]), expressed their belief in the Messiahship of Jesus by calling Him the Son of God, the prevalence of a belief among Jewish theologians of the 1st cent. that the Messiah was of one metaphysical being with Jahweh. The utmost perhaps which we can affirm is that it was largely believed that the origin of the Messiah would be mysterious (Jn 7[27]), and that this belief rested in all probability directly on the Messianic interpretation of Dn 7[13ff.].§ It seems possible, however, to distinguish two general types of belief regarding the Messiah and His work. The one may be called the *Prophetic*, the other the *Apocalyptic* type. The former type, which was the more popular and held its ground even with the scholars of the time (Mk 12[35ff.] ‖), rested on the early Prophetic testimony that the Messiah would spring from the house of David,—a belief of whose persistence and

of whose correspondence with the actual fact the circumstance that Jesus is confidently affirmed or assumed by five of the NT writers (Matthew, Luke, Paul, author of Hebrews, author of Apocalypse *) to have been of the seed of David may be considered the most striking proof. According to this type, so far as purely Jewish belief is concerned, the work of the Messiah, while superhuman, was conceived on comparatively secular lines. He would destroy his persistent enemies and establish a reign of lasting righteousness and peace over obedient and contented subjects. This type, taken by itself, hardly possesses for us eschatological interest. It belongs to a mode of conception in which the problems of death and immortality, if realized at all, cannot be solved. The sphere offered for solving them is too mundane. It is otherwise with the apocalyptic type of view, which rested mainly on the Book of Daniel, esp. Dn 7[13ff.] and 12[2f.]. Whether or not the author of Daniel in the latter of these passages conceived of a resurrection from the dead available for all past generations of faithful Israelites, it seems certain that in the time of our Lord this sense was assigned to his words by those who, like the Pharisees, held the doctrine. According to Josephus,† the Pharisees held a fatalistic doctrine of the present life—but not of human conduct—which seems to have resembled that of the Stoics, and which made them for the most part averse to schemes of political revolution. Their participation, therefore, in the popular view of the 'Son of David' was more theoretical than real. Their tendency was to conceive the final Kingdom on strictly supernatural lines. It was a wonder that would not spring from earth, but would descend from heaven. The Messiah was the Man of Daniel's vision, the Man of the Clouds.‡

Two points have recently been much in dispute: (*a*) Whether in view of the grammatical possibilities of Aramaic, as used in the time of Jesus, He could have applied to Himself the phrase 'Son of Man' or 'Man' as a title, basing on Dn 7[13]; and (*b*) Whether He could have done this so habitually as our Gospels represent. Even those who, like Lietzmann § and Wellhausen,‖ have reached on these points the most negative conclusions, do not doubt that in the latter part of His career, and perhaps habitually, Jesus held the apocalyptic view of the final Kingdom and of the glorious advent of the Messiah; and, even if we exclude the title 'Son of Man' from those passages in the Gospels which have no eschatological reference, there remains a sufficient number (about a third of the entire number, exclusive of John) where the eschatological reference is distinct. Thus, *e.g.*, out of 32 instances of 'Son of Man' in Matthew's Gospel, 14 are apocalyptic.¶

It is indubitable that in the time of our Lord the Book of Daniel and other Apocalypses modelled on it were much read by a considerable portion of the Jewish people. Many of those whose views were influenced by this literature saw no inconsistency in combining with these views others derived from literature of the 'prophetic' type, *e.g.* The Psalter of Solomon,** embodying the ancient and still popular conception of the 'Son of David.' Yet, as this veneration for ancient prophecy was combined for the most part with political quiescence, it may perhaps be said that in the more reflective minds 'Son of David' and 'Son of Man' represented one heavenly ideal. Jesus Himself expressly repudiated the implications of 'Son of David' (Mk 12[35ff.] ‖); but it is remarkable that this did not hinder the prevalence in Christian circles of the belief that He was of the seed of David according to the flesh, and the Evangelists Matthew and Luke risked publishing pedigrees,

---

* On this cf. Tacitus, *Hist.* v. 3; Suetonius, *Vesp.* 4; Josephus, *BJ* vi. v. 4.

† On this fluctuation see esp. Riehm's *Messianic Prophecy*, T. & T. Clark, 1900.

‡ In the case of *Daniel* this is disputed by such competent scholars as Hilgenfeld and Riehm.

§ On the antiquity of the Danielic conception itself see the interesting work of H. Gressmann, *Der Ursprung der isr.-jüd. Eschatologie*, p. 334 ff., Göttingen, 1905.

* Mt 1[1], Lk 3[31], Ro 1[3], He 7[14], Rev 5[5].

† *Ant.* xviii. i. 3; *BJ* ii. viii. 4.

‡ Gressmann, *l.c.*, p. 336.

§ *Der Menschensohn, ein Beitrag zur neutest. Theol.* 1896.

‖ *Skizzen u. Vorarbeiten*, Heft vi., Berlin, 1899.

¶ Muirhead, *Eschatology of Jesus*, p. 218, London, 1904.

** *Psalms of the Pharisees, commonly called The Psalms of Solomon*, Ryle and James, Cambridge, 1891.

whose apparent mutual inconsistencies constitute the chief difficulty of the modern mind in accepting the fact they were designed to establish.

Instructive in this connexion is the phrase 'Kingdom of the heavens' in Matthew's Gospel. The phrase is, of course, equivalent in meaning to 'Kingdom of God' which the other Evangelists employ. It need not, however, be questioned that Jesus, occasionally at least, used 'Kingdom of the heavens,' and it seems certain that He did not invent the phrase. It was current, and it pointed to the apocalyptic construction of the Messianic hope. The Kingdom belonged to the heavens, and would come thence to earth. It was the unlikeness of Jesus to the altogether wonderful Personage of the apocalyptic Messiah that offended the Pharisees. If He were the Messiah, why should He refuse a sign from heaven? (Mt 16[1ff.]).

5. The preliminaries of the coming Kingdom.—Assuming this leading idea of a Kingdom to come, heavenly in its origin and nature, we must now ask how the various matters preliminary to or accompanying its advent were conceived.

(a) Who were *the heirs of the Kingdom*? There were people 'just and devout' (Lk 2[25]) who 'waited for the consolation of Israel,' the still surviving type of Jahweh's 'poor ones' who 'cried unto him and he heard them' (Ps 34[6]). Such persons, however, did not advertise themselves, nor did they as a rule sit in the seat of the learned. The prevailing teachers were the scribes and Pharisees, whose yoke, practically intolerable, was yet theoretically imperative. It has been questioned how far readers of the Gospels get from them a fair impression of the moral and religious influence exercised by the teachers of the Law, and it has been contended, with perhaps some justice, that the impression so derived is as one-sided as the impression of the Roman Church one naturally gathers from histories of the Protestant Reformation. Still, the good type of scribe or Catholic is not due to the tendency against which the Evangelic text or the Reformation is a protest. It cannot be doubted that in the time of our Lord it was authoritatively taught by the Pharisees that the title to inheritance of the heavenly kingdom was a punctilious observance of the Law after the manner of their own practice. Their doctrine, indeed, on this point is not explicitly stated in the Gospels or in any contemporary documents. But the impression we gather from the situation depicted in the Gospels and from the record regarding the Apostle Paul favours the supposition that the view of the Pharisees in the time of Jesus is that represented by the Rabbinism of the 2nd cent., viz. that *the Messiah would come when Jahweh's people, the Jews, were found generally and carefully observing the Law.*[*] And the 'Law' meant not simply the legal precepts of the Pentateuch (in particular the Priestly Code), it meant the 'tradition' of the elders. While the average man inevitably shook off the punctilios of obedience, and the Pharisees themselves took refuge from their own rigour in an elaborate casuistry, we cannot doubt that the generally accepted view was that the passport to the Kingdom was 'the righteousness of the law.'

(b) *The Resurrection.* But generations of faithful Israelites passed, and the Messiah did not come. Would they miss the glory when it came? At least since the time of the Syrian persecution (B.C. 168–165)—the time of the Apocalypse of Daniel—it was taught that death formed no insuperable barrier to the inheritance of the Kingdom. Probably the author of Daniel (12[2f.]) had in

view mainly (we cannot say exclusively) those Israelites who had sealed their fidelity to the law of Jahweh with their blood, but it may be taken for certain that, long before the time represented by the Gospels, all idea of the blessings of the Kingdom being restricted to members of the holy nation who had suffered death for their fidelity (if such an idea was ever entertained), had completely disappeared. It was taught that there would be a resurrection of the *righteous* (Lk 14[14]), *i.e.* of those who kept the 'Law' and the 'Tradition.'

(c) *Hades, Gehenna, Paradise.* There is nowhere in the Gospels an explicit statement of what was held regarding the state of the dead; but four times (Mt 11[23] 16[18], Lk 10[15] 16[23]) the word *Hades* (Ἅιδης) occurs. In the LXX this word is the almost invariable equivalent of שׁאול; and when Jesus used it without comment, it must be held to have conveyed to His hearers the associations proper to that word. The NT as well as the OT[*] is dominated by a view of things in which the modern idea that annihilation may be the fate of some men has no place. The dead are in a land of darkness and forgetfulness, cut off from knowledge of affairs human and Divine. Still, in this condition—at most the pale reflexion of full-blooded life—they *exist*. Two things, however, must be observed: (i.) There is in the OT itself a marked, if not systematized, protest against the idea that permanent detention in Sheol or Hades can be the fate of the righteous, who had found their portion in the living God (see esp. Ps 16 and 73 and Job 14 and 19). Historically, doubtless, the experience of suffering under the various oppressors of the nation (Assyrian, Chaldæan, Græco-Syrian) had much to do with the development of this protest; but it is probably a mistake to suppose that it was when they were actually suffering under the yoke of the world-powers that the people of Jahweh adopted from foreign sources much or anything that bore on the problem of what lay beyond death. This caution applies specially to the relation of Hebrew thought to the mythological ideas of Babylon or Egypt. The impregnation of the Hebrew spirit with ideas coming from these sources dates in all probability from a much earlier period than the 6th cent. B.C. All we can say for certain, perhaps, is that the experience of national humiliation quickened in a special degree the peculiar Hebrew genius, leading it at this time (say from the 6th cent. onwards) to place the peculiar stamp of the Jahweh faith on mythical ideas or pictures, which in some cases it had carried with it since the days of its infancy in Mesopotamia. (ii.) Although there is no hint in the OT itself of effect being given to moral distinctions between the wicked and the godly in Hades itself, yet the suggestion of a possible escape for the godly from the gloom of the underworld could not but raise, and ultimately decide, another question, viz. whether the distinction between the godly and the wicked was not observed from the moment of death. For perhaps about 100 years before Christ the idea of separate compartments in Hades, for the godly and the wicked respectively, had more or less prevailed (see APOCALYPTIC LITERATURE, esp. the part dealing with the Book of Enoch). Obviously our Lord could not have uttered the parable of the Rich Man and Lazarus (Lk 16[19ff.]), or said to the penitent malefactor (23[43]), 'To-day shalt thou be with me in *Paradise*,' had He not been addressing people accustomed to the idea that in the intermediate state, previous to the resurrection and the final judgment, moral distinctions were accorded a real, if incomplete, recognition. It is obvious

---

* The Jerusalem Talmud (*Taan.* 64a) remarks on Ex 16[25] that 'if Israel only kept one Sabbath according to the commandment, the Messiah would immediately come.' See Edersheim's *Life and Times of Jesus the Messiah*, vol. ii. p. 713.

* On this whole subject of the conception of Sheol, etc., cf. esp. A. B. Davidson, *Theol. of the OT*, p. 425 ff., T. & T. Clark, 1904

from the entire tenor of our Lord's references (see esp. the instructive passage Mt 5$^{21f.}$) to *Gehenna* that He spoke to those to whom this term represented the utmost condemnation and punishment. It represented the fate of those who should still be enemies of Jahweh in that day when Jerusalem should be renewed by righteousness, and all flesh (*i.e.* all living) should go out and behold the carcases of those who had transgressed, for 'their worm shall not die, neither shall their fire be quenched' (Is 66$^{23f.}$). See artt. GEHENNA and PARADISE.

(*d*) *The Final Judgment.* In our Christian minds, as with the NT writers, the idea of the *Resurrection* is inseparably associated with that of the *Judgment* which follows it. In the main track of OT thought, indeed, this association did not exist. The habit of conceiving the subject of the Divine favour or punishment rather as a *nation* than as a number of *individuals*, made it possible, or even natural, practically to ignore the individual side of the problem of life and death, and the distinction, natural to us, between this world and that which is to come is represented in the OT mainly by the distinction between this life *with* God and this life *without* Him. Under this view of things the prevailing conception of judgment in OT times is that of a manifestation of Jahweh's righteousness (whether it be through His 'messenger' [Mal 3^1] or through the Messianic 'Son of David' [Is 11$^{1ff.}$]), in which He effectually visits His people with His mercy, and breaks the arm of the unrighteous peoples, who forget God and oppress them. These heathen return to Sheol (Ps 9^{17}); but the covenant of Jahweh with His faithful people is established for ever. The history seems to show that it was possible for pious Israelites to rest in this view, merging individual hopes in hopes for the nation, until the actual disaster of the Exile shook their faith in the permanence of the collective unit of the Jewish State. From this time, however, as we see clearly from the writings of Jeremiah and Ezekiel (cf. esp. Ezk 18), the claims of the individual come into prominence. It was felt that in the righteousness of God one generation ought not to suffer for the sins of its predecessors. Each generation, even each unit of a generation, had its own rights. Yet, in fact, it seemed as though these rights were ignored. It is with the problem raised by this conflict between the prophetic conscience and the facts, that the apocalyptic literature from Daniel onwards is concerned. The solution obtained springs from the despair that lies on the border of hope. The mundane element in the old idea of a Prince of the house of David tends to disappear. The blessing, which could not spring from earth, was expected from heaven, and at the touch of the new power, coming thence, even the 'dust' of the earth (*i.e.* esp. dead Israelites who had kept the covenant) should awake (Is 26^{19}). While, doubtless, the adumbrations of the conception of immortality which we find scattered throughout the OT had their origin in the sentiment that it must be well with the righteous for ever, this positive aspect of the matter was inseparable from a negative. The righteous could hardly be vindicated unless punishment fell on the rebels and transgressors. Hence even in Dn 12^2, which cannot be said to teach a *universal* resurrection, among the 'many' who awake from the dust of the earth there are 'some' who arise to 'shame and everlasting contempt.' It was inevitable that these conceptions should be universalized. If, as even the former Prophets and Psalmists in their own fashion had taught, there was to be a *universal* judgment (*i.e.* a vengeance of Jahweh exercised upon all rebel Gentiles and upon the transgressors

of the covenant in Israel), and if the collective unit of the *nation* was practically displaced by the *individual*, it is clear that the idea of universal judgment must have come to have for its counterpart the idea of universal resurrection. No doubt the conception was held vaguely, and was as little effective for practical consolation as it is to this day (cf. Martha's attitude, Jn 11^{24})—still it was there. When Jesus spoke of the 'resurrection of the dead,' or even of the Messianic 'Son of Man' as executing judgment, He was using language whose general implications were either entirely or (as in the case of 'Son of Man') at least partially understood by His hearers.

B. *THE MAIN FEATURES OF OUR LORD'S ESCHATOLOGICAL TEACHING.*—Turning now to the subject of our Lord's eschatological teaching, and looking to the present condition of critical opinion, we may make a distinction, which has in most respects only a theoretical value, between the eschatological views of the early Church as reflected in the Gospels and those held and taught by Jesus Himself. The Gospels are as a whole too entirely dominated by the spirit of truth as it was in Jesus to make it possible, without arbitrariness, to vindicate this distinction in detail. Yet the investigation in which we are engaged seems to reveal problems arising out of portions of even the Synoptic Gospels, in connexion with which it may be well to remember that the Master must not be measured even by His best reporters. The distinction may seem *a priori* to have even more warrant in reference to the Fourth Gospel, whose representation both of the Person and the words of Jesus stands in such obvious contrast to that of the Synoptics as to justify our dealing with it in a separate section. We may do this even though in the end we may find ourselves to agree with Haupt [*] that the Johannine presentation of the eschatology of Jesus supplies just the kind of supplement to that of the Synoptics which a critical study of the latter led us to think necessary. We therefore consider at present only the eschatology of Jesus as presented in the Synoptic Gospels.

1. His conception of the Kingdom of God.—Both John the Baptist and Jesus preached, saying, 'Repent: for the Kingdom of God (in Mt. most frequently 'the Kingdom of the heavens') is at hand.' There seems no reason to doubt that in general Jesus thought of the Kingdom just as John did. Modern writers on the Gospels, like Johannes Weiss [†] and Titius, [‡] warn us with considerable justice against reading our own philosophical thoughts into the simple realism of the Bible. The Kingdom of God meant the perfect rule of God over all things in earth and heaven for the benefit of His people. It was eternal, it was universal in the sense of embracing people of all nations, though, of course, only those in each nation who did righteousness; and it embraced not earth only, but also heaven, whence it should come, and to whose type, as regarded at least the character of its subjects, it should be conformed. It may be postulated perhaps, further, that the Kingdom was conceived by Jesus, in at least its external features, on the closest possible analogy to an earthly kingdom. In two important respects, however, it differed from the latter. (*a*) It was not promoted by the weapons of flesh and blood. It was a Kingdom where rank—even that of the King Himself—was determined by the measure of service. The spirit of service was the spirit of

---

* Haupt, *Die Eschatol. Aussagen Jesu in den Synopt. Evangelien*, Berlin, 1895.
† Johannes Weiss, *Die Predigt Jesu vom Reiche Gottes*, Göttingen, 1900.
‡ Titius, *Die neutest. Lehre von der Seligkeit*, pt. i. 1895.

lowly love. (*b*) It was a Kingdom which, while coming ultimately from God and heaven, came through a Mediator, by whom it would be administered. Since His baptism Jesus had the witness within Himself that He was the Mediator. He was the Messianic King who was truly the 'Son of God' (Ps 2). To Him the whole trust of the Kingdom was given, even all power in heaven and earth. Barring the mystery revealed at His baptism, which concerned primarily Himself only, we must admit that such a view of things was inevitable to One who found the form and substance of His faith in the OT, and at the same time believed, in harmony with the earlier Prophets and the prevailing tendency of His own time, in a personal Messiah. We seem therefore warranted in assuming that such was the view of Jesus at the commencement of His ministry. The Kingdom was coming from heaven. He Himself was the Person appointed to establish it on earth. Beyond this, however, the witness of the OT and His own special experience previous to and at the time of His baptism would not necessarily carry Him. It is perhaps permissible to find in the story of the Temptation (Mt 4[1ff.], Lk 4[1ff.]) the record of a period when, not without a struggle with the prince of this evil world, He renounced the idea that the Kingdom was to come immediately through some dramatic catastrophic exercise of the heavenly power with which He felt Himself to be charged. It is more to our purpose at present to note that while He renounced this catastrophic ideal (if we may call it so) to the extent of refusing to allow it to deflect Him from obedience to the Divine word, He did not, according to the Synoptics, renounce it so far as His general view of the mode of the Kingdom's advent was concerned. To the last He spoke in apocalyptic fashion of the Son of Man coming on the clouds. The glorious Parousia would illuminate simultaneously all quarters of heaven like the lightning (Lk 17[24]). It would happen within that generation although He could not tell the day nor the hour, and it would be preceded by disasters on a great scale, affecting not simply the human world, but the cosmical system. How far it is true to the mind of Jesus, as He spoke on earth, to take the language of the so-called 'great eschatological discourse' (Mk 13, cf. Mt 24) with strict literalness, has been of late keenly debated, and some have been disposed to see in this discourse and matter harmonizing with it in the Gospels, an example of the way in which our Lord found it necessary to accommodate His language to conceptions which were inevitable for the hearers if not for Himself. Others may perhaps incline to a view which has been advocated by the present writer,[*] that the phenomena of this peculiarly apocalyptic discourse offer an occasion on which it is profitable to remember that the thoughts of Jesus far transcended those of even the most forward of His disciples. But, while we may well acknowledge a certain elusiveness in the language of Jesus in which He deals with the future, we cannot without violence to the Synoptic record refuse to admit that in His habitual view the Kingdom of God was not something that had already come with Himself, but was rather something that still lay in the future. Everyone sees that when Jesus said, 'The kingdom of God is at hand' (cf. ἤγγικεν = *has come near*), or bade the disciples pray, 'Thy kingdom come,' He must have thought of the Kingdom as being still in the future.

But what of the passages in which it seems to be implied that the Kingdom is already present? For instance Mt 11[11] (cf. Lk 7[28]), in which John the Baptist is declared less than the least in the King-

dom of God, or Mt 12[28] (cf. Lk 11[20]), in which the expelling of demons in the name of God is offered as proof that the Kingdom of God has come, or the parables (Mt 13[31ff.], Mk 4[30ff.]) in which the Kingdom of God is represented as actually in process of coming to its proper magnitude in the world, and therefore already rooted there? It is the *crux* of the student of eschatology in the Gospels to show how these two modes of conception, *presential* and *futuristic* (sometimes distinguished as *ethical* and *eschatological*), can be reconciled. Perhaps the most satisfactory recent treatment of the subject is to be found in a brief but brilliant essay of Professor Wernle.[*] Wernle lays probably excessive stress on what he considers the 'ecclesiastical' element in the construction of even the Synoptic Gospels (esp. Matthew). But his book, read in the light of the contributions of predecessors to the same discussion (esp. Haupt, Titius, and Joh. Weiss), shows very convincingly that we must, in fairness to our authorities the Synoptics, and in view of the entire historical situation reflected in these writings, start from the fact that our Lord habitually thought and spoke of the Kingdom—however much He might identify it with Himself—as, so to speak, an *objective wonder of the future*. It does not, indeed, follow that this was the sole or even the most important aspect of it present to His mind; but it seems right that we should accommodate to it, if possible, those passages in which the Kingdom seems to be spoken of as if it were already present, and that this accommodation should be made apart from the intrusion of distinctively modern thoughts. This Wernle has done with great plausibility in the case of the passages above referred to, pointing out that when regard is had to the context, literal or circumstantial, the difficulty disappears. Thus in the passage Mt 11[11] (Lk 7[28]) a main element in the situation is a certain rivalry between the circle of John the Baptist and the circle of Jesus. The former approach the latter in an attitude of aggressive doubt. If Jesus is the Messiah, where is the Kingdom that should come with Him? In what respect are those who have attached themselves to Jesus better than those who hold to their old master, John? To such aggressive questioning the answer is: 'The Kingdom has come already. Its powers are seen working among us (v.[5f.]). Those who keep apart from the sphere of these wonders, however truly they may fulfil otherwise the conditions of membership in the Kingdom, are yet actually standing on the outside.' On this reading, the passage, so far from being antagonistic to the eschatological view of the Kingdom, in reality strongly supports that view. For a main point of the argument is the assumption that, while a high ethical standard in practice may be expected of the children of the Kingdom or may be a condition of entrance into it, the Kingdom itself is something more than this. It is the product of a power altogether supernatural and apart from the will of men. Not righteousness, but the working of this power, is the criterion of the Kingdom. Else surely the Kingdom would be with the greatest of men born of women, and not (as it actually is) with men of even much less stature than his.

The same line of solution seems available in the case of the other passages. Thus in the passage Mt 12[22ff.], esp. v.[28] (cf. Lk 11[14ff.], esp. v.[20]), a main element in the situation is again the element of attack. The Pharisees insinuate that the demons may be subdued by the power of Beelzebub, their prince. Jesus answers that such a state of the case is inconceivable. Satan cannot wish to overthrow his own work. If, on the other hand, the power be the power of God, then the Kingdom of God has come in effect. The strong man armed (the prince of this world and author of all evil in it) has been conquered and bound. Again, obviously, the criterion of the Kingdom is not

* *Die Reichsgotteshoffnung in den ältesten christlichen Dokumenten und bei Jesus*, 1903.

simply the presence of the good, but the presence of the good in *power*. Finally, there are the parables in which the Kingdom is spoken of as something growing in the earth and therefore already planted. Note especially the parables of the Mustard-seed and the Leaven. Here, indeed, we are left to imagine the context in which the parables were uttered, as even Mark (4:36ff.) in this instance follows the topical method of Matthew, and relates the parables only as specimens of the didactic method of Jesus (cf. v.[33]). But may we not reasonably suppose, as in the other cases, the context of a certain antagonism? Timid followers come to Him with a difficulty born of vision and reflexion : 'If Thou art He with whom the Kingdom comes, why is the word of the Kingdom really received by so few who hear it, or how shall even the wonders of God done in one little land affect the whole world?' To which Jesus replies in effect : 'Have patience, and you shall see.' The greatest things of the world are not always those that give promise of greatness. They are often those whose beginnings are remarkably small, and yet connecting beginning and end is the one power. If this was the occasion of the utterance of the parables under discussion (and it seems difficult even to imagine another), it is obvious that both the question of the doubters and the answer of Jesus assume that the constituent of the Kingdom is the supernatural Divine power before which no opposition can stand. The question is, Can the power really be present when there is so little to show for it? And the answer is, Yes, it can. The same power that begins with little ends with much. We read our own thoughts into the simple intention of these parables, when we speak as if Jesus intended to teach that the manifestation of the Kingdom would not be catastrophic, but would be a matter of growth and development. Doubtless the parables, taken by themselves, are capable of bearing this meaning ; but just this isolation of them from the general context of the situation reflected in the Gospel history is that of which we must beware. But there remains still what is, apparently, the most important passage, Lk 17:20ff.. Whether we translate 'in you' or 'among you' (ἐντὸς ὑμῶν, v.[21]), Jesus seems to say very emphatically that the Kingdom is present. On a nearer view of the passage, however, and a more careful articulation of its sentences, this appearance vanishes. V.[21] must be understood in harmony with v.[23ff.] (cf. the 'lo, here' and the 'lo, there' of vv.[21.23]). The leading thought of the passage is the suddenness (in the special aspect of simultaneousness) of the manifestation of the Kingdom. The advent of the great day shall be like the lightning flash, of which you cannot say, 'here' or 'there,' for it is everywhere and all at once.

It thus appears that there is nothing in the Synoptics really antagonistic to the 'eschatological' view of the Kingdom. The Kingdom is not *present* in any sense not reconcilable with the fact that it is also and mainly future. No one may understand the Gospels who cannot accept the fact that in a perfectly distinct sense the teaching of Jesus was not modern. It was in the highest degree sane and authoritative, yet it remained true to the traditional view that the Kingdom would come by miracle and catastrophe. The unmistakable indications of this are the facts that the references to the Kingdom in the Synoptics are prevailingly of futuristic implication (on this see Wernle, *op. cit.*), and that even in the Fourth Gospel there are numerous passages to show that Jesus never thought of the Consummation apart from the transcendent wonders of the Resurrection and the Judgment.

There was, however, one important modification of the traditional view. The Consummation and all that accompanied it were to be mediated and, indeed, effected by Himself. Prophecy, it is true, contained the promise of a Messiah. But the correspondences of fulfilment to prophecy are largely contrasts, and the impressiveness of history is perhaps mainly due to these contrasts. The efforts of the Evangelist Matthew to show—sometimes in strangely far-fetched ways—that Jesus fulfilled the prophecies, are an instructive index of the difficulties felt by even the most spiritually minded Jews in reconciling the Messiahship of Jesus with the testimony of prophecy. It becomes important to inquire how in an eschatological aspect Jesus conceived His own Messiahship.

2. His Messianic consciousness.—Of great significance in this connexion is the Temptation. The record of this cannot rest on other testimony than His own, and the key to the juxtaposition of the narratives of the Baptism and the Temptation must be sought in His Messianic consciousness. The latter, therefore, we must try reverently to conceive. It seems true to say that the Temptation represents a contrast or conflict of faith that pervades our Lord's entire ministry on earth. In general it is the contrast between God and man, between what is omnipotent and what is humanly possible ; in particular, it is the contrast between a measureless gift and the definite responsibility of using it aright. Jesus had received a practically limitless endowment. He was in the world as God, for He was the 'Son' of God accredited to His own consciousness by His Father. Yet He was flesh and blood, a genuine Brother of men. Each term of this contrast had its own place in the will of God. It was the task of the Messiah to reconcile them. Thus He would do the will of God. An unrestrained use of this gift would remove Him from the brotherhood of men ; a refusal to use it meant the failure of His mission. How was a superhuman task to be done by One who should yet remain a man? The key to this problem was grasped in the victorious experience of the Temptation. What the solution meant in detail we learn from the subsequent history. Reading that history in the light of the Temptation-narrative, we seem to discern in it two principles : (*a*) the one is the principle of *faith* ; (*b*) the other is the principle of *self-sacrifice*. These two principles have, of course, a common root in the one Messianic life ; but it is useful to view them apart. The principle of *faith* covers the strictly supernatural side of the work of consummating the Kingdom. It is the *hope of what GOD will do through His Messianic Son in bringing the promised Kingdom from heaven to earth*. We cannot do justice to the consciousness of our Lord reflected in the Gospels if we fail to note the supremacy of this principle. If we may make for the moment the distinction between *faith* and *duty*, we must find what is at once deepest and loftiest in the consciousness of Jesus—not in the thought of what He Himself is to do in the fulfilment of the Messianic career but—in what God is to do in Him and through Him. He never loses sight of the 'one like unto a son of man' who is to come with the clouds and receive a dominion universal and everlasting. The Messiahship is not simply His present *task*. It is His *hope* for Himself and for the world. The eschatology of Jesus is mainly His hope of the accomplishment of an act of omnipotence, in which God will finally constitute the Messianic Person and functions. This hope was necessarily shadowy in circumstantial outline, but it rested on an absolutely substantial foundation. Its foundation was the presence of the Spirit that fell to Him as the Son of God. The gift of the Spirit, moreover, was not simply the ground of a hope that related primarily only to Himself. It was a leading of duty and a power of benefit in relation to others. He could give to others helps that were not permissible to Himself. Hence there is a miraculous element in the Messianic ministry even on earth. The miracles are the premonitory signs of the final Messianic glory. They are the pledge that the Power which will be manifested in that glory is not far away. While these σημεῖα and δυνάμεις abound in the earthly ministry, they are always under the control of the principle of faith. No one is suffered to experience the extraordinary helps who does not believe.

The *other* principle, resting equally in the depths of our Lord's filial consciousness, is the principle of *self-sacrifice*. It is in the practical dominance of this principle that we may discern at once the originality of Jesus and the difference between His eschatology and that of contemporary Jewish faith. While He retains the traditional view that the Consummation will be effected in transcendent catastrophic fashion,—collapse of the present world, appearance of the 'Son of Man,' resurrection, judgment,—He reaches the conviction, possibly as early as the time of His baptism, that this Consummation will not be attained previous to His own death and resurrection. How entirely this conviction, once attained, dominated His conception of the Divine purpose and His teaching of His disciples, may be seen in the facts not only that in the Fourth Gospel the sacrificial death of the Messiah is prophesied by the Baptist, and is a matter of our Lord's consciousness from the very beginning of His ministry (Jn 2$^{19ff.}$), but also that (as regards the latter point) there is little if anything in the Synoptic Gospels opposed to the Johannine view. This may not decide the comparatively unimportant question as to *when* our Lord attained the conviction that He must as the Messiah submit to a violent death, but taken along with the testimony of the rest of the NT (say, especially, the Pauline and Petrine Epp.) it shows conclusively the practically predominant importance of this *event*—or rather *signal service*—in the mind and faith of the Christian Church. For every *one* text in the Epistles that calls attention to the glory of the Kingdom that is to come in the incomprehensible power of God, there are probably at least *two* in which the emphasis rests not on the *power* of God the Father, but on the *love* of the Son of God. Indeed, it may be questioned whether there is a single reference to the Consummation in the Epistles or the Apocalypse of the NT which does not in its immediate context suggest that the centre of the coming glory is the Person of Him who was delivered for the offences of His people, but raised for their justification. Even in the Epp. to the Thessalonians, which are commonly supposed to represent the most primitive type of Pauline doctrine, it is not the 'Kingdom of God,' but 'His Son from heaven,' that is to believers the object of waiting (1 Th 1^{10}).

This indissoluble connexion between the 'sufferings of the Christ' and the 'glory that should follow' (1 P 1^{11}) could not have been fixed so securely in the mind of the first believers had it not been first in the mind of Jesus Himself. The Synoptics bear witness to the importance of the connexion for Jesus not only by reporting the profoundly significant but isolated sayings, Mt 20^{28} 26$^{28f.}$ ||, but by the very distinct way in which they connect the critical incident of the disciples confessing their Master's Messiahship with the institution of a new order of lessons, the theme of which is the necessity and the near prospect of the Messiah's sufferings (16$^{21ff.}$ ||). This representation rests on a sure basis of reminiscence, and it seems to have a special guarantee in the fact that the teaching does not contain an articulated doctrine of atonement like that which is expressed in the Epp. (esp. Romans), but aims rather at expressing the necessity of the Master's sufferings in terms that apply equally to the disciple. Admitting the distinctiveness of the two sayings, Mt 20^{28} 26$^{28f.}$ ||, we seem warranted in saying that, according to the Synoptics, the view of things that practically determined the career of Jesus was that the good of which He possessed the pledge in His unique filial consciousness would not come during the period of His own life on earth. The spirit that brought help and healing to others was, as regarded Himself, a spirit of self-sacrifice. The sacrifice would culminate in His death. But the death would be momentary. In two or three days (cf. Hos 6^2) He would rise again. Yet the momentary death would not be in vain. The death and resurrection of the Messiah meant a conquest of death for a new believing Israel. The death would be the ransom price (λύτρον, Mt 20^{28}) which

neither man nor angel could pay for the soul of a brother man. It would be the institution and support of the true and abiding temple of the Divine presence (Ex 30$^{11ff.}$, Job 33$^{18-24}$, Ps 49$^{6-9}$. See on this A. B. Bruce's *Kingdom of God*: T. & T. Clark, 1889). The thought of the redemptive value of the sufferings of Jesus as the Christ dominates the Fourth Gospel, most of the Epistles, and the Apocalypse of the NT. If it is not prominent, it is certainly present, in the Synoptic Gospels. The lack of prominence finds its explanation in the reserve that naturally characterized the utterance of Jesus regarding His own death. The presence of frequent or elaborate references to the matter in these Gospels would have taken from our estimate of their 'objective' character. Jesus may well have felt that the work of the Messiah was to die, not to explain the consequences or power of that death. Of this there would be *another* Witness. He who sacrifices himself commits his case to God and to posterity. This brings us to another matter.

3. His view of the time of the Consummation.—We have seen that Jesus did not dissociate Himself from the traditional view that the end would come in the form of a catastrophic transformation, culminating in the advent of the Messiah Himself, who would come from heaven. He seems rather everywhere, both by the assumptions and by the direct references of His language, to set His seal to this view. When we consider how widely His consciousness of personal concern in the accomplishing of the Kingdom must have caused His view of things to differ from all views that were by comparison tentative and theoretical, and reflect how much there is in the ethical quality of His teaching, particularly in the parables which conceive the Kingdom under the analogy of natural growth, to suggest an openness of His mind to all that may be of abiding worth in the modern idea of evolution, the tenacity with which He adhered to the catastrophic view of the final event cannot but profoundly impress us. Reverent investigators will pause before accepting the conclusion that He was in this matter under some kind of delusion. They will strive rather to see in the attitude of One who was conscious of being not simply the herald but also the bearer of the Kingdom of God, a model for the attitude of all who would turn serious thoughts to the last things. Whatever else we bring to a study where there is room for all knowledge and all thought, we must give a final as well as a supreme and pervasive place to the wonder-working power of the living God. We have sure ground in the Synoptics for saying that, while Jesus regarded the work of His Father in heaven, even in what we call *nature* and *ordinary providence*, as wonderful (Mt 6$^{25ff.}$ etc.), this did not prevent Him from steadfastly contemplating a final wonder of destruction and reconstruction which should be the consummation of the Kingdom or its perfect establishment on earth. While so much is clear, there is very great difficulty involved in the question whether He predicted, so definitely and unmistakably as the Synoptics lead us to suppose, that the final wonder would be accomplished within the term of the generation then living. The problem is not to be solved either by the *quantitative* method of counting heads (whether Gospel texts or modern authorities), or by the *alternative* method of saying, Either He was mistaken, or such texts as Mk 9^1 13^{30} || are false reports. It can hardly be doubted that Jesus uttered words which were naturally understood, by those who heard them and by others to whom they were reported, to mean that the final wonder —the Parousia of the 'Man' of Daniel's vision and of age-long expectation—would happen within their own generation. It is inconceivable that an expectation so confident and definite could have rested on anything but a definite reminiscence of words used by Jesus which seemed capable of only one interpretation.

Is it, then, possible to justify such sayings as Mk 9¹ 13³⁰ ‖ apart from the blunt avowal that Jesus laboured under an illusion, and that He transmitted the illusion to His immediate followers not only *before* but *after* His death and resurrection? This has been felt to be among the most difficult questions of historical Christology, and various types of solution of the problem are still represented by leading authorities. These may be roughly classified under the heads: (*a*) *prophetic*, (*b*) *pictorial*, (*c*) *realistic*. Under (*a*) would be included all theories, such as that of Beyschlag, which emphasize the fact that in this instance at least Jesus spoke in the manner of an OT prophet, and that His utterance kept within the limitation common to all the prophets. This limitation required Him to see and announce the final salvation of Jehovah as about to happen within a measurable interval after the judgment (in this case the fall of Jerusalem) impending over the nation. Under (*b*) would be included theories of the type of Haupt's, which emphasize the necessarily pictorial character of language, which must express extra-mundane realities in mundane forms. Might not the assertion that the Son of Man would come on the clouds within their own generation be the most effective way of leading persons familiar with the apocalyptic style of language to the perfectly confident but also essentially spiritual type of faith represented in the NT literature? (*c*) The term *realistic*, finally, might describe all theories whose tendency is to insist on what has been called the 'biblical realism,' and to require us to put upon the language of Jesus the most literal or *natural* construction possible. The most distinguished representative of this type in its bearing on the present problem is perhaps Titius. Titius thinks that Jesus must be considered to have held in a *bonâ fide* sense the view which His words naturally express, viz. that His own generation would see the end of the present wicked world and the establishment on earth of the perfect heavenly Kingdom. But His confession of ignorance as to the day and the hour of the Consummation (Mk 13³²) shows that He held His own conviction in an attitude of reverent submission to His Father's will, which must have made the transition to acceptance of the differing reality easy and natural.

It is possible to incline to any one of the above types consistently with a reverential appreciation of the unique mental and spiritual equipment of Jesus; and valuable elements of truth may be found in them all. The opinion of English-speaking students of the Gospels has perhaps till recently inclined most to the *pictorial* type (*b*). For some time, however, this has been undergoing modifications from the increasing attention paid to the apocalyptic writings. This has fostered the belief that more regard than has been given is due to the realistic character of our Lord's mode of thought and utterance. On the whole, the variety and vacillation of opinion suggest the likelihood that we are not yet in a position to offer a solution of the problem that shall possess demonstrable certainty. Our information about Jesus, while adequate for spiritual and practical purposes, is insufficient for the purposes, or at least for the appetite, of biographical science. To a great extent we do not know, or are only slowly learning, either the exact occasions of His utterances or the amount of meaning they may have conveyed or failed to convey to those to whom they were delivered. Greater than the limitation arising

from defective information, because more intimate to ourselves, is that connected with the inability of even the modern mind to find within itself a measure for the words of eternal life. To those to whom Jesus was and is the unique bearer of the Kingdom of God both to themselves and to the world, it must seem pertinent to ask whether those who can never stand in the centre of such responsibilities can properly estimate the things falling within the vision of the one Person, bearing our nature, who did and does so stand?

Without presuming to offer a key that fits the lock of all the critical difficulties, the present writer ventures to call attention to the view of the whole matter expressed in his *Eschatology of Jesus* (Melrose, 1904). While it does not meet the difficulties of those whose view of the Person of Jesus is frankly naturalistic, it has some claim upon the attention of those to whom the historical Jesus was the unique manifestation in the flesh of the Power that is directing human history to its goal. To those for whom this conviction is fixed, the two following considerations may perhaps appear of paramount importance. The *one* is that many of the sayings of Jesus must have had a certain elusiveness. The mere fact that they were so habitually aphoristic and pictorial is itself almost a proof of this. Besides the meaning which immediately strikes us, there is a reserve of possible meaning which lies along the line of our vision, yet goes beyond what we actually see. There is a measure of this elusiveness in the language of all genuine seers. Must there not have been an extraordinary measure of it in the language of Jesus?

The *other* is that the elusive language of the seer is not *delusive*. Jesus does not set Himself to utter dark sayings; but His practical instinct keeps Him from dazzling His hearers with an excess of light. He gives them all the light they can take; but it does not follow either that this is all that fills the recesses of His own spirit, or, on the other hand, that in His utterance He is consciously keeping anything back. We must conceive the seer to deliver the truth in the form in which it holds his mind. But the *form* in this case is not the particular word or image. It is not even so impressive an image as that of the Son of Man coming with the clouds (Dn 7¹³, cf. Mk 13²⁶ 14⁶² ‖). The form concerns rather what may be called *spiritual emphasis*. It is the exact poise of the spiritual mind at the point of self-surrendering trust in the goodwill and immediate action of the good God. For such a mind the employment of definite words and images in relation to the secrets of the future may mean no more than a definite certainty of new and immediate manifestations of the Divine power and love. They do not necessarily mean a definite realization of the precise form in which the manifestation will be made. It is the definite certainty, not the indefinite form, which the words are calculated to convey. If they convey even to His most susceptible hearers something that is in one aspect more and in another less than this, this is due to the fact that their spiritual poise is inferior to His. The poise in their case is rectified by the subsequent teaching of the Spirit in the light of events.

Those who are able to accept this view will probably do so mainly for two reasons : (*a*) Because it explains the desire of Jesus to assure His faithful followers that they would live to see the manifestation of the Kingdom in power (Mk 9¹ 13³⁰ ‖, Mt 10²³). (*b*) Because it explains the ability of the Apostles and Apostolic writers to accept apparently without any great travail of mind the disappointment of first hopes, or even to regard the disappointment as part-fulfilment (see, *e.g.*, Jn 16¹²ff· and 2 P 3⁸ff·). To these may perhaps be added : (*c*) That this view has no necessary connexion with the idea that Jesus in this matter *accommodated* His expressions to the limitations of the disciples. The idea of accommodation is no doubt suggested by Jn 16¹²ff·;

but even if we suppose that the words of this passage are a literal reminiscence of what the Master said, we must observe that one who *professes* to be accommodating his words to the limitations of his hearers takes thereby all sting from the charge that he has compromised the truth. Many reverent students of the Gospels will probably, however, prefer to regard the words of Jn 16¹²ᶠᶠ. not as a literal utterance of the Master, but rather as a devout recognition proceeding from the inner circle of disciples of an element or quality in their Master which, in spite of all the simplicity of His utterance and His impressive veracity, had eluded and mystified them. They thought they had understood, yet how much they had misunderstood! On this view Jesus did not 'accommodate.' He spoke as the word was given Him, in the style that is most faithfully reflected in the Synoptics. Whatever may be the truth about Jn 16¹²ᶠᶠ., we seem warranted in saying that Jesus had but one way of speaking of the Consummation. During all His ministry, and up to the end of it, He spoke of it as imminent. It was something for the generation then living. Ac 1⁶ and the other books of the NT outside the Gospels may be taken as proof that He spoke of it in the same way after His resurrection. If in this regard He was 'limited' in the days of His flesh, He was limited also when He wore the body that was from heaven : if He 'accommodated' in the one sphere, He 'accommodated' in the other also.

The NT as a whole is filled with an expectation, which in the form in which it was entertained was not fulfilled ; and yet faith in Jesus and belief in the still coming Consummation lived on and live still. Our conclusion is, then, briefly as follows :—As a protest to His own people, Jesus predicted the downfall of the Jewish nation within a measurable period (see esp. Mt 23 and 24). While in all probability He depicted this catastrophe in colours that closely matched those of the event itself, the very intensity of His concentration upon a vision that might seem to concern only the Jewish nation serves to show that through the telescope of Jewish particularity He was looking out upon the whole human world. His vision was that of One uniquely alive to the purpose of God, of which He, the Messianic Son of Man, was the supreme executor. It was the vision of a prophet, seeing all things in relation to the Divine purpose, not the vision of a mere politician or patriot. The Jewish nation was chosen to bless the world with the knowledge of God. Failure to fulfil this vocation brought on it the destructive wrath of God ; and the condemnation of the chosen people involved in an obvious sense the doom of the world. That ignorance of God and hostility, of which the Jewish obduracy was the signal example, would reach a climax in the murderous death of the Son of God. From that moment the forces of final reconstruction would set in. *When* the Consummation would be attained, *when* the Son of Man should come in His glory, and all evil and evil-doers be put away, no man or angel knew. Not even the Son, only the Father. But this much was certain. The power of the Prince of this world—the Prince whose power was manifest in sin, disease, and death—was broken. The proofs of that victory could not be long delayed. Some would live to see signs of which they had not dreamt, that the Kingdom had come in power.

This covers in brief probably as much as we are able to report of the unique eschatological consciousness of Jesus. The account, however, would not be complete without a fresh reference to the blank space of our ignorance. This space we shall enlarge or diminish according to our estimate of the difference between the area of our knowledge, and that not merely of the general purpose of God, but of the consciousness of Jesus, the Son of God. All men are agnostics in the sense of admitting that they have not been made privy to the counsels of Creation and Providence ; but besides this common agnosticism there is a kind peculiar to Christians, which breathes the spirit of faith and reverence. Christians believe that 'all things,' including especially human destiny, have been committed to the hands of Jesus Christ. In that faith they can anticipate with calmness

the worst tragedies of personal or social history. They believe that there is no terror of the kingdom of darkness which the Son of God has not overcome with the armour of His holy light ; but, *because* they believe this, they do not presume to possess, even in the measure of His Spirit to which they have attained, a key that will open every secret that was stored in the depths of His personality, even while He was on earth. The last mystery to Christians is no longer the mystery of death, judgment, and the hereafter. It is rather the mystery—which is also the *fact*—of Jesus Christ, the mystery of the relation of these things to Him, or rather, perhaps, of His relation to them.

II. ESCHATOLOGY IN THE GOSPEL OF JOHN.— We pass by questions as to the date or authorship of this Gospel. The writing may be placed with confidence near the border dividing the 1st and 2nd centuries. It does not matter for our purpose on which side of the border it is placed. To the eyes of most Anglo-Saxon critics the Gospel reveals still the marks of an intimate of Jesus, and with them we assume that, even in the form in which we read the Gospel, it proceeded from the circle of a 'disciple whom Jesus loved.' We assume also —what probably no one denies—that there is but one mind between the author of the *Gospel* and the author of the *Epistles* that bear the name of John. Whoever was its author, the Gospel could not have reached so soon the position of authority it has held in the Christian Church since the 2nd cent., had it not been considered to express the living and profound belief of Christendom regarding what was most essential in the Person and History of Jesus. *This* is the matter of importance to our present inquiry. If we find that the view of our Lord's eschatological consciousness, which has seemed to us to be most reasonably deducible from the Synoptic Gospels, agrees on the whole with what is presented here, that view may be considered to have behind it a weight of authority that could not well be greater. For the authority is not simply the consciousness of an inspired Apostle or Apostolic man ; it is that of the consciousness of the Church as a whole at the critical period of the close of the Apostolic age. We may fix attention on three matters : (1) the idealizing style of the Gospel ; (2) its conception of Eternal Life ; (3) its attitude to Eschatology proper.

1. *The idealizing style of the Fourth Gospel.*— From the first it has been admitted that, as compared with the Synoptics, this Gospel is one rather of the mind than of the external actions of Jesus. Even the most remarkable external actions, the miracles, are but 'signs' of the mystery that is really important to us—that, viz., of the Person of the 'Son of God.' The 'signs' are recorded that we may believe that Jesus is the Son of God, and may have life through His name (20³⁰ᶠ.). The Logos that was 'towards God (πρὸς τὸν θεόν) and was God' (1¹), was made flesh, and the writer and his companions beheld His glory, and reported the vision, not so much from literal reminiscence of the acts and words done and spoken by Jesus on earth, as under the inspiration of the Spirit that came according to promise from the presence of the Father and the Risen Ascended Son. The author is concerned rather with the discourses of Jesus than with His actions, and the discourses are, we believe, not so much *reported* as *interpreted*. They are the words of an eternal life in which the ¡writer and his fellow-believers share (1 Jn 1¹ᶠ.). Jesus is Himself the Word, the Truth, the Life. What is told of Him represents but a few out of many instances of His self-manifestation. They are like the sparks that witness to

a hidden, mighty, and·continuous electric stream. One consequence of this mode of treatment is that there is little in this Gospel to indicate that Jesus experienced anything of the sinless infirmity of flesh and blood. There is, *e.g.*, no suggestion that He grew in knowledge of the path He had to tread as the Saviour of the world. There is no temptation, no agony in Gethsemane, no ignorance or doubt as to the times and seasons of the Consummation. The author does not, perhaps, consciously ignore these things, but to mention them is no part of his purpose to manifest the eternal life that was in the Son of God.

If such a view of the Person of Jesus were carried out with rigorous abstract logic, we should reach a result that would not only be glaringly at variance with the picture presented by the Synoptists, but would be indistinguishable from the heresy against which, at least in its germinal form, the author himself protests (1 Jn 2²², 5⁸), viz. that the incarnation of the Logos was mere appearance. The point to be observed is that the view is *not* carried out rigorously. The reason is that the author combines a sense of history with a sense of spiritual fact. But what mainly concerns him is the spiritual fact: what Jesus, who rose and ascended, is now to His Church, *that* in deep reality He has always been. No doubt He was truly human, and, because He was so, there was during His earthly sojourn real limitation, but the limitation was free because self-imposed (see, *e.g.*, 10¹⁸), and behind it there was always the Divine reality. He was never other than the Logos, the eternal and only-begotten Son of God.

Even though it be conceded, as we think it must be, that neither as regards incidents nor discourses is the Johannine picture of Jesus so strictly historical as that of the Synoptists, it does not follow that it is not, in another than the literally historical sense, a deeply true picture. The guarantee of its truth is the fact that the Christian Church has accepted it, and in doing so has conquered both its own feeling of disappointment in the delayed *Parousia* and the unbelief of the world. The Church discovered, that is to say, the presence in the mind and utterances of Jesus of a quality of which it had not at first grasped the significance. His words were 'spirit and life' (6⁶³). They could be interpreted only by His own perpetual teaching through the Spirit of truth (16¹³ff.).

We may call this, if we choose, the *idealism* of the Johannine Gospel and of the early Church ; but the question is worth pondering whether anything less than an idealism which rested on a sure, if profound, basis of truth, could have held the Church to its loyalty to the unseen Jesus in face of the disappointment of hopes which the Synoptic testimony, taken in its natural sense, had encouraged. In any case, the Johannine picture of Jesus may be considered to supply a striking confirmation of the opinion, already partly expressed in this article, that no amount of fragmentary sentences of Jesus, however accurately reported, and however definite their meaning may be when they are taken by themselves, can be a perfect index of a mind like His.

2. *Its conception of Eternal Life.*—Every reader of John notices the prominence of the words 'life,' or 'eternal life,' or 'spirit.' The phrase 'Kingdom of God' has practically disappeared, and 'life' or 'eternal life' takes its place. The fact is of importance to us in our present study, because it is the index of John's way of conceiving what in the Synoptic mode of speech might be called the *present* aspect of the Kingdom. Jesus appears as the possessor and even the direct dispenser of the Divine life. It is given to the Son to have life in Himself even as the Father (5²⁶), and no one can come to Him except it be given him from the Father (6⁶⁵). Yet neither the Father nor the Son dispenses life in its fulness till the Son is glorified through death, or returns to the glory which He had from the first with the Father (7³⁹). But once the life is imparted it is a new birth which carries

its own promise. It is, in a proper sense, sufficient for itself. If a man is born of God, the Divine seed remains in him. Its product is righteousness, and its perfect fruition is likeness to the only-begotten Son Himself (3⁵ 9⁴²·⁴⁷, 1 Jn 3²·⁹ etc.). It is clear that this mode of view brings the Divine boon nearer to the individual heart, and necessarily alters, at least for the individual, the perspective of the eschatology.

Not simply the great event itself,—the glorious Parousia of the Christ,—but the events of resurrection and judgment that accompany it, are regarded from within rather than from without. Those whose hope is set on Jesus do not lift to the heavens faces sick with deferred hope. They look within and behold Him with the vision of the pure in heart. For them Jesus has come already and keeps coming. The supreme matter is to abide in Him or in His love by keeping His words. Let a man thus live and believe in Him, and he shall never die. Nothing, that is, not even what we call death, will break the continuity of his life (11²⁵ff.) The water of life that Jesus gives shall be in him a well of water springing up unto everlasting life (4¹⁴). The *Judgment* similarly is, or tends to be, withdrawn from futurity. He who believes does not come to judgment ; he has passed already from death to life (5²⁴, 1 Jn 3¹⁴). On the other hand, he who disbelieves is condemned already. Life has come to him, but he chooses death ; light, but he chooses darkness. In turning from the only-begotten Son of God he puts from him his chance of being saved from a Divine wrath already present (3¹⁸ff·³⁶) Until he seeks the Father through Him who is the Way, the wrath of God abideth on him. Every thoughtful reader of Jn. perceives that such are the main ideas both of the Gospel and of the Epistles. He will hardly fail to reflect also that these are, and have remained ever since the time of these writings or earlier, the vital ideas of the Christian Church in its cultivation of individual and social life, both on its practical and its meditative side.—Comparing the Johannine testimony with the utterances in the Synoptic Gospels—few, it may be, but important— which reveal a consciousness in Jesus of a Kingdom of God that is present and not simply future, and considering especially the fact that in spite of their testimony to Jesus' sense of the imminence of a Kingdom yet to come, there is not in the Synoptic Gospels the slightest indication that this tremendous prospect at all diminished His appreciation of the worth of those ethical precepts (*e.g.* those relating to marriage and the parental relation (Mk 10²ff· 7⁹ff·) that have to do with the secular order, we shall hesitate before accepting the idea suggested by Joh. Weiss (*op. cit.*), that the precise meaning of the *ethical* utterances of Jesus is to be determined by our knowledge (?) of His eschatology, and that Jesus would not have spoken as He does, *e.g.*, in Lk 14²⁶, had He not believed that within a generation the institutions of marriage and the family would cease, and that those who should survive this end of the world, being 'sons of the resurrection' (Lk 20³⁶), should be thenceforward as the angels (*ib.*). In this reference also the Johannine Gospel confirms our sense of an element in the equipment and outlook of Jesus to which justice can hardly be done by those who lay unqualified stress on the distinctively eschatological portions of the Synoptic Gospels.

3. *Its attitude to Eschatology proper.*—Yet it has to be observed, finally, that, while the futuristic element is not prominent in the Johannine Gospel, it is by no means eliminated. It may be felt, indeed, that the terms in which it is expressed involve a departure from (or, at any rate, a transformation of) the *objective* standpoint of the Syn-

optics. The last three words of the phrase, 'the hour cometh *and now is*' ($5^{25ff.}$), suggest a state of mind in which the thought of a future radically or incalculably different from that which is already present to the vision of faith, is no longer keenly operative. The same is still more obvious in the Supper discourse (chs. 14–16), in reading which one feels that the line of distinction between the Lord's final coming to receive the disciples to Himself, and His continuous abiding with them or visitation of them through the comforting Spirit, tends to be a vanishing one.

Yet it does not follow that the distinctively eschatological utterances or references contained in the Johannine Gospel (*e.g.* $5^{28f.}$ $21^{22f.}$) are of the nature of a formally dutiful acknowledgment of an earlier mode of speech and a still lingering form of popular Christian expectation corresponding to it. Such a view, at least, is not an exhaustive description of the state of the case. It seems true rather to say that the futuristic outlook, while it lost, even within the time covered by the NT writings, its first aspect of keen expectation, was yet to the last of that period felt to be—what it is still—an indispensable element of Christian faith. That the matter is looked at from within, and attention fastened not on what is to *come to us*, but rather on what *we are to become* (1 Jn 3^2), does not alter the fact that the total on which we are looking belongs to the future as well as to the present, and that that future is in the wonder-working power of the Conqueror of death. It is *never* possible to neglect the aspect of futurity, and it is sometimes imperative to emphasize it. Such a passage as 1 Jn 2^{18} compared with Mk $13^{5f.}$ shows significantly how much the Fourth Evangelist, in spite of the depth of his insight into the Master's mind (or, shall we say, *because* of that insight), was to the last influenced by the eschatological utterances of the Synoptic testimony. He recognizes the antichrists of his own day, and is confident that it is the 'last time.' The 21st chapter of the Gospel speaks similarly for the attitude of the Evangelist's circle. The chapter is an appendix, and v.$^{22f.}$ show what is probably its main motive. The aged Apostle has passed away, and the question is raised, Did not the Master say that this disciple should not see death till He should come in glory? The expectation implied in the question connected itself in all likelihood with the utterance in Mk 9^1 ||. There was a general impression throughout the Churches of Asia that John was the person mainly intended, and a story was current to the effect that in predicting Peter's mode of death the Master had told that disciple of the survival of John. The author of the appendix claims to be in a position to tell the readers of the Gospel what the Master had really said. It was far from being a definite promise. It was only the hint of a possibility. The apology would hardly have been deemed necessary if the tendency to insist on a literalistic interpretation of the Synoptic testimony, placing the glorious final advent within 'this generation,' had not still been prevalent at the close of the 1st cent., *i.e.* at the time when John died.

Neither the author of the Gospel and the Epistles nor the author of the appendix to the Gospel has anything to object to the probability of an immediate Parousia of Jesus in glory; but the impression which their utterances leave upon our minds, and which from the first they were fitted to convey to the Church, is that the contrast important to the authors is no longer that between present and future, but rather that between God and the world, between the love of the Father and the love of this present evil world. The matter of absorbing interest is not that the Son

of God will come *again*, but that He *has come*. Life is not movement towards a point on a straight line: it is expansion from a centre, and because the centre is living he who is at the centre is also implicitly at the goal of the moving circumference.

The Evangelist has expressed this in very characteristic fashion in the closing words of his principal Epistle: 'We know that we are of God, and the whole world lieth in wickedness. And we know that the Son of God is come, and hath given us an understanding, that we may know him that is true, and we are in him that is true, even in his Son Jesus Christ. This is the true God, and eternal life' (1 Jn $5^{19f.}$).

Those who find their own consciousness expressed in such words, and feel impelled to trace that consciousness to its historical source, will not readily suppose that they have found the source anywhere nearer than the consciousness of Jesus Himself. Who but He could have been the first either to possess eternal life or to know that He possessed it?

LITERATURE.—For the literature on Eschatology in *general* or on *Scriptural* Eschatology see the art. 'Eschatology' in Hastings' *DB* and in *Encyc. Biblica*. It is indispensable for the student of the Gospels to understand the genesis and scope of Jewish apocalyptic literature, and for this purpose the Introductions in Driver's *Daniel* (in the 'Cambridge Bible for Schools and Colleges') and Scott's *Revelation* (in the 'Century Bible') will be found sufficient by most English readers. Of German works there may be mentioned, in this connexion, Hilgenfeld, *Jüdische Apokalyptik*, 1857 (still a standard work); Gunkel, *Schöpfung u. Chaos*, and his *Zum religionsgeschichtlichen Verständniss des NT*, 1895 and 1903; Bousset, *Der Antichrist*, etc., 1895, and his *Die jüd. Apokalyptik*, 1903; to which must now be added Gressmann, *Der Ursprung der isr.-jüd. Eschatologie*, 1905. On OT Eschatology see very specially A. B. Davidson's *Theology of the Old Testament* (T. & T. Clark, 1904), §§ xi. and xii. In regard to the Eschatology of the Gospels a good list of books will be found in Moffatt's *Historical New Testament* (T. & T. Clark), p. 639 f., bearing especially on the theory of the 'Little Apocalypse,' which many scholars, following Colani and Weiffenbach, suppose to be incorporated in Mk 13, Mt 24. Beyond the works of Haupt, Titius, Joh. Weiss, etc., mentioned in this article, the most comprehensive work, strictly *ad rem*, is probably Baldensperger's *Das Selbstbewusstsein Jesu*, of which only the First Part of the 3rd 'völlig umgearbeitete' edition, entitled 'Die Messianisch-Apok. Hoffnungen des Judenthums' (Strassburg, 1903), has as yet (1906) been published. A discussion of the matters specially emphasized by Joh. Weiss and Baldensperger will be found in a volume of the 'Decennial Publications of the University of Chicago,' entitled *The Messianic Hope in the NT*, by Professor Shailer Mathews, Chicago, 1905. See also Porter's *Messages of the Apocalypses*, and his art. 'Revelation' in Hastings' *DB*. For illustrations of Rabbinical views and interpretations, current more or less in the time of our Lord, see very specially the latest edition of Edersheim's *Life and Times of Jesus the Messiah* (London, 1900), vol. ii., Appendixes 5, 8, 9, 13, 14, 17, 19; also Weber's *Jüd. Theologie*[2], Leipzig, 1897. In P. W. Schmidt's *Die Geschichte Jesu* (Tüb. and Leipz. 1900), there is a section entitled 'Zukunftsprüche,' the views of which are defended in vol. ii. of the same work (1904), pp. 354–360. Of older works the following may be mentioned: I. A. Dorner, *de Oratione Christi Eschatologica, Mtth.* 24^{1-36}, Stuttgart, 1844; Herm. Cremer, *Die eschat. Rede Jesu Christi, Mtth.* 24 and 25, Stuttgart, 1860; E. J. Mayer, *Krit. Com. zu der eschat. Rede, Mtth.* 24 and 25, 1 Theil 'Die Einleitung,' Frankfurt-a-O. 1857; Rud. Hofmann, *Die Wiederkunft Christi u. das Zeichen des Menschensohns am Himmel* (Mtth. 24^{30}), gekrönte Preisschrift, Leipzig, 1849; Wilh. Weiffenbach, *Der Wiederkunftsgedanke Jesu*, Leipzig, 1873 (424 pp.), also his 'Die Frage der Wiederkunft Jesu' in *Denkschrift des evangel. Predigerseminars*, Friedberg, 1901. Of pamphlets and magazine articles, in addition to the last named, may be mentioned Tholuck, *Die Consequenzen der Reden Christi über seine Wiederkunft u. sein Gericht* in 'Programm der Universität Halle,' 1871; C. Bruston, 'L'enseignement de Jésus sur son Retour' in *Revue de Théol. et de Philosoph.* 1890 (pp. 421–452, see also some earlier articles in the same Review); Kingman's art. in *Biblical World*, 1897, i. pp. 167–178; Pfleiderer, 'Composition der eschat. Rede, Mtth. $244^{ff.}$' in *JDTh*, 1868, pp. 134–149; Kienlen, 'Die eschat. Rede Jesu, Mtth. 24,' *ib.* 1869, pp. 706–709; Joh. Weiss, 'Die Composition der Synop. Wiederkunftsrede' in *SK*, 1892, pp. 246–270.

In regard to the Jewish Apocalypses, it would be ungrateful not to mention the invaluable editions of *Enoch, Baruch*, etc., published by Professor R. H. Charles, Oxford, Clarendon Press, since 1893, when his *Book of Enoch, translated from Professor Dillmann's Ethiopic Text*, appeared. See in this the discussion on 'Son of Man' as at Enoch 46^2, pp. 127–129, and 'The Son of Man: Its Origin and Meaning' (Appendix B), pp. 212–317. Since the publication of Charles' *Enoch* the philological question regarding 'Son of Man' has been keenly discussed by Lietzmann, Wellhausen, Schmiedel, Dalman, Fiebig, and others.

See Muirhead's *Eschatology of Jesus* (Melrose, 1904), Lecture iv., and Riehm's *Messianic Prophecy*, 2nd Eng. ed. (T. & T. Clark, 1900) pp. 354–356.　　　LEWIS A. MUIRHEAD.

ESLI.—An ancestor of Jesus, Lk 3[25].

ESSENES.—The Essenes were an ascetic community among the Jews, the existence of which can be traced for over two centuries, from about B.C. 150 to the Fall of Jerusalem. For original information regarding them we are dependent on Josephus (*BJ* II. viii.; *Ant.* XVIII. i. 5, XV. x. 4, 5, XIII. v. 9) and Philo (*Quod omnis probus liber*, chs. 12, 13, ed. Mangey, pp. 457–459). Josephus has also scattered references to individual Essenes, and the elder Pliny (*HN* v. 17) an appreciative notice of them, for which he was probably indebted to Alexander Polyhistor and his work 'On the Jews.' Other ancient authorities are either secondary or untrustworthy.

Josephus introduces the Essenes as one of the three 'sects of philosophy' which were influential amongst the Jews, the others being the Sadducees and the Pharisees; but from the descriptions given of their practices and organization, they seem to have corresponded more closely to a monastic order than to a sect or a religious party. Their name is probably, though not certainly, derived from the Aramaic form of the Hebrew word *ḥâsîdîm* ('pious ones'), and this already suggests a close relation, especially in their origin, between the Essenes and the Pharisees. Their numbers are estimated by Jos. (*Ant.* XVIII. i. 5) and Philo at 4000; and while there is no evidence of their existence as an order outside Palestine, within its area they were widely distributed, being found in a great many of the villages and small towns, as well as in Jerusalem, where there was a 'Gate of the Essenes.' The members of the order were celibates, living in community houses and owning nothing as individuals, but having everything in common. They are extolled for their piety, their industry, which was confined to agricultural pursuits, the simplicity of their food, and their scrupulous cleanliness. Further characteristics of their life were that they had no slaves, used no oil for the purpose of anointing, dressed in white, and rigidly prohibited the use of oaths except on the admission of a new member to the order.

The order was held together by the strictest discipline. Full membership was granted only after a novitiate of two years, and then upon an oath to reveal everything to the members and nothing to the outside world. Offenders against the rules of the order were punished by exclusion; and as they were still held bound by their vows, they were unable to return to ordinary life.

What makes the Essenes 'the great enigma of Hebrew history' (Lightfoot, *Col.*[7] p. 82) is that, while they are distinguished by exaggerated adherence to the Jewish Law and by special reverence for Moses as lawgiver, they betray at the same time certain ideas and practices which are foreign to Judaism, and seem incompatible with its spirit. The indications of incipient dualism which may be found in their abstinence from marriage and in other ascetic practices, find a parallel in their doctrine of immortality, wherein they agreed with the Pharisees against the Sadducees as to the immortality of the soul, but differed from the Pharisees in denying the resurrection of the body. And they deviated still further from orthodox Judaism in the practice of making a daily prayer to the sun 'as if entreating him to rise,' and in refraining altogether from animal sacrifice. It followed that they were excluded from the services of the Temple. On the other hand, they were rigid beyond all others in their observance of the Sabbath; and they went beyond the Pharisees in their absolute determinism, affirming 'that fate governs all things, and that nothing befalls men but what is according to its determination' (Jos. *Ant.* XIII. v. 9).

It is in this apparent eclecticism that the problem of the origin of Essenism consists. While it is impossible to deny the Jewish foundation on which it rests, it is equally impossible to overlook the presence of foreign elements. The source of these has formed the subject of endless discussion, and has been found by various writers in Parsism and Buddhism (Hilgenfeld), Parsism (Lightfoot), Syro-Palestinian heathenism (Lipsius), and Pythagoreanism (Zeller, Keim). But all attempts to demonstrate any necessary connexion or indubitable channel between any one of these and Essenism have failed. And it remains either to assume that foreign influences had percolated unobserved, or to suppose that the characteristic phenomena emerged independently in Persia, Greece, and Palestine.

The Essenes are not directly referred to in the NT; but some have without sufficient reason claimed John the Baptist, and even Jesus, as Essenes. It has also been alleged that their influence may be traced within the circle of Christian ideas and practices. The possible relation of Essenism to the heresy controverted by St. Paul in his Epistle to the Colossians has been discussed at length by Bishop Lightfoot in his edition of the Epistle (cf. his *Galatians*[8], p. 322 ff.), and also by Klöpper, *Brief an die Kolosser*, pp. 76–95.

LITERATURE.—Schurer, *HJP* II. ii. 188 ff. (with full Bibliography); Bousset, *Die Religion des Judentums*, pp. 431–443; artt. 'Essenes' in Hastings' *DB* (by Conybeare) and in *Encyc. Bibl.* (by A. Jülicher), and 'Essener' in *PRE*[3] (by Uhlhorn).

　　　　　　　　　　　　　　　C. ANDERSON SCOTT.

ETERNAL FIRE.—An expression twice used by Christ in reference to the future punishment of the wicked. In Mt 18[8] βληθῆναι εἰς τὸ πῦρ τὸ αἰώνιον stands in contrast to εἰσελθεῖν εἰς τὴν ζωήν; and from Mt 25[41] we learn that this eternal fire, into which the wicked are to be cast, was prepared not for them but for the devil and his angels. These are the only passages in which the expression is found in the Gospels; but equivalent terms occur. In Mt 18[9] the eternal fire is identified with the fire of Gehenna; and in 25[46] we have κόλασις αἰώνιος. In Mt 3[12] and Mk 9[43] it is the unquenchable fire (ἄσβεστον), and in Mk 9[48] Gehenna is the place of punishment where their worm dieth not, καὶ τὸ πῦρ οὐ σβέννυται. The wicked after their separation from the righteous (Mt 13[42. 50]) are to be cast into a furnace (κάμινος) of fire.

A brief account of the origin of this phraseology will throw light on its meaning. The idea of punishment by fire comes from the OT. The destruction by fire of Sodom and Gomorrah supplied the typical example, and it is frequently referred to as such (Dt 29[23], Is 1[9] 13[19], Jer 49[18], Am 4[11], Wis 10[7], 3 Mac 2[5]; cf. such well-known NT passages as Jude 7). A similar judgment is spoken against Edom (Is 34[9. 10], where it is said that the fire is eternal and will not be quenched). In Am 1. 2, Damascus, Gaza, etc., are threatened with the fire penalty. See for other examples of the unquenchable fire, 2 K 22[17], Is 1[31], Jer 4[4] 21[12], Ezk 20[47. 48], Am 5[6]. The 'everlasting burnings' of Is 33[14] refer, like the preceding, to temporal judgments. But there are passages which at least suggest the extension of the idea and its imagery to the future world. According to Dt 32[22] the fire of Jehovah's anger reaches down to Sheol. Cheyne finds in Is 50[11] and 66[24] a reference to the punishment of souls in the underworld: but Salmond and A. B. Davidson see in the latter passage only the description of a present-world penalty: and this seems the more natural interpretation. This passage seems to have suggested the later Jewish belief regarding eternal punishment, for certain expressions in it are used in this sense in the Apocryphal writings (*e.g.* Jth 16[17], Sir 7[17]) and by Christ (Mk 9[47]). The scene of this judgment is, in all probability, the Valley of Hinnom, regarded by the Jews as a place accursed on account of its Molech sacrifices; and the fires which were kept burning, through which the victims passed, would readily suggest the idea of Gehenna and its eternal fire.[*]

――――――――――

[*] Kimchi's statement, that a fire was kept constantly burning in Hinnom to consume the offal and the dead bodies which were thrown into it, comes too late (A.D. 1200) to be accepted without evidence.

In the Apocryphal writings the fire penalty is extended without reserve to the future world, and in a greatly intensified form. Most of the writers have ceased to expect an equitable distribution of rewards and penalties in this life : their hopes are fixed on the future ; and they, therefore, transfer the OT imagery of retribution to the life after death. The Book of Enoch is the great storehouse of teaching on this subject. For the impure angels and the faithless angelic rulers an abyss of fire is prepared, in which, after the judgment, they will be tortured for ever (10⁶·¹³ 18¹¹ 21⁷·¹⁰ 54⁶ 90²⁴·²⁵). For human offenders, a fiery abyss is opened on the right hand of the Temple (90²⁶·²⁷); this is Gehenna. They descend into 'the flame of the pain of Sheol' (63¹⁰), or into the 'burning fire of Sheol' (103⁷·⁸). Thus it appears that the NT 'eternal fire' of Gehenna is anticipated in this book : the only difference being that, while in the NT the fire prepared for the devil and his angels is identified with that into which wicked men are cast, in the Book of Enoch they are always distinguished.

Two questions arise regarding the nature of the eternal fire. Is it material ? And in what sense is it eternal ?

(1) In many OT passages, even where it is said that the fire is unquenchable, and will burn for ever, *material fire* is undoubtedly meant, for fire is one of the physical agents which God commonly employs in His temporal judgments, and its burning for ever must refer to the lasting destruction which it effects. Sodom, Gomorrah, and Edom are given as examples of places on which the doom of eternal fire fell, and they still bear its proof-marks. But in other passages the literal sense cannot be maintained, as, *e.g.*, where God's anger or jealousy and man's wickedness are said to burn *like* fire. Nor can it be allowed in passages like Is 66²⁴ if Cheyne's interpretation is accepted ; since undying worms, preying on souls or bodies that are being consumed by unquenchable fire, is an impossible idea. In the NT, as we have seen, Christ drew largely on OT imagery in speaking of the 'last things.' But the whole drift of His interpretation of prophetic language is at variance with the literal sense of the fire penalty. What He gives in His eschatological teaching is not a dogmatic but an imaginative presentation of the truth ; and the imagery He employs belongs, not to the substance, but to the form of His thought. The prophet, like the poet and the artist, must present the future in terms and forms borrowed from present experience, and the underlying truth must be spiritually discerned. If, as Christ tells us, the eternal fire was prepared for the devil and his angels, it cannot be material fire ; for spirits cannot undergo physical torture.*

Death by fire was the severest penalty under the Jewish law, and as it was inflicted only for the most shameful sins (Lv 20¹⁴ 21⁹, Jos 7²⁵), a peculiar infamy was associated with it. Christ, therefore, when He employed this imagery in speaking of the doom of the wicked, intended to warn men that God has attached a terrible retribution to sin. At the very least it signifies an ordeal of suffering analogous to that which fire causes in the living tissues. To the question, How will the suffering be caused? Scripture gives only the figurative answer, 'as by fire.' Bp. Butler (*Anal.* pt. ii. ch. v.) thought that it might come in the way of natural consequence, without any direct infliction on the part of God. Sin, which yields pleasure *here*, becomes misery there without changing its nature, through the natural working of moral law. The agony of remorse, which sometimes overwhelms the sinner in this life, has been

* Yet the contrary has been maintained on high authority. Augustine held that the fire was material, and that spirits may be tortured by it, since it is always the mind and not the body that suffers, even when the pain originates in the body. He also suggests that devils may have bodies made of air, 'like what strikes us when the wind blows, and thus be liable to suffering from fire' (*de Civit.* xxi. 3, 9, 10). Th. Aquinas held that the fire is material (*Summa Theol.* pt. iii. supplmt. lxx. 3). And in our own day Ed. White inclines to the view that the wicked before extinction will be punished by material fire (*Life in Christ*, p. 352).

regarded as a foretaste of the eternal fire. The *pœna damni*, or the consciousness of being for ever cut off from the sight of God, the only satisfying good, will be, it has been said, intense suffering as by fire, when the distractions of the world have ceased to dazzle. And these will, doubtless, be elements in the retribution. But if this were all, a possible consequence would be that the penalty would fall most lightly on the most degraded. A soul that can be made miserable through remorse, or the conscious loss of God's presence, has not reached the lowest stage of hardening ; while experience tells us that those who have reached this stage are least liable to suffering from such a source. In them remorse can be awakened, not by the *pœna damni*, but by suffering externally caused. And the language of the NT suggests that in the future world an environment is prepared, with its appropriate agencies and influences, for the punishment of those who are morally and spiritually dead. Such expressions as 'Depart into the eternal fire,' 'shall be cast into the lake of fire,' etc., clearly presuppose such an environment, one in which the least worthy shall suffer the most, 'be beaten with many stripes.'

(2) *Why is the fire called eternal?*—In Mt 25⁴¹⁻⁴⁶ the adjective αἰώνιος is used with reference to 'the fire,' 'punishment,' and 'the life,' and no satisfying reason has been given for saying that, as regards the first two, it means 'time limited,' and, as regards the last, 'time unlimited.' If Christ's purpose had been to call attention to the duration of each, then 'endlessness' is the idea emphasized. But, except where this word or its Hebrew equivalent is applied to objects that, for the nonce, are invested with a *quasi*-eternity (Lv 3¹⁷, Gn 17⁸ 49²⁶), it takes us into a sphere of being to which time measurements are inapplicable, and in which objects are presented in their relation to some eternal aspect of the Divine nature. Thus eternal life does not mean natural life prolonged to infinity ; such a life might be lived without any experience of the eternal life, which signifies life in fellowship with, or that partakes in, the eternal life of God. God's relation to believers is such that between them and Him there is a community of life. Eternal fire, on the other hand, figuratively expresses the truth that, God's nature being what it is, there must be, under any economy over which He presides, a provision for the adequate punishment of sin. The eternal fire is such a provision, and, being eternal, it can be no mere temporary contrivance for tiding over an emergency, but must be the retributive aspect of the Divine holiness. God is, was, and ever shall be a consuming fire in relation to sin unrepented of ; this is His unchanging and unchangeable attitude. Some of the OT saints were all their lifetime subject to bondage through fear of death, for to them Sheol (Is 38) was a place where all life in fellowship with God was lost. But suppose that their worst fears had been realized, it would still have been true that they had had a passing experience of the life eternal. And similarly if, after ages of suffering, the wicked were to cease to be, it would, none the less, be true of them that they had been cast into the eternal fire. In Sodom, Gomorrah, Edom, etc., we have examples of what is meant by 'suffering the doom of eternal fire'; but this does not mean that ever since the fire destroyed the cities their inhabitants have been enduring its pains. Eternal fire may or may not mean everlasting suffering in it (see artt. ETERNAL PUNISHMENT and RETRIBUTION).

LITERATURE.—Origen, *de Princip.* II. x. 4–8, *c. Cels.* iv. 13, v. 15 ; Lactantius, *Inst.* vii. 21, 26 ; Augustine, *de Civ.* bk. xxi., *Ench.* cxi.-cxiv., *de Gest. Pelag.* 10, 11 ; T. Burnet, *Concerning the State of Departed Souls*, 1798 ; Matt. Horbery, *Duration of*

Future Punishment, 1744 ; J. Agar Beet, *The Last Things*[2] ;
R. H. Charles, *The Book of Enoch*, also *Critical History of the
Doctrine of a Future Life* ; J. L. Clarke, *The Eternal Saviour
Judge* ; H. Constable, *Duration of Future Punishment* ; J. Fyfe,
The Hereafter ; F. W. Farrar, *Eternal Hope*, and *Mercy and
Judgment* ; Salmond, *Christian Doctrine of Immortality* ; H. N.
Oxenham, *Catholic Eschatology* ; E. B. Pusey, *What is of Faith
as to Everlasting Punishment?* ; Ed. White, *Life in Christ*.
See also Literature at end of art. RETRIBUTION.

A. BISSET.

ETERNAL LIFE.—This phrase occurs more than
forty times in the New Testament. In many passages it denotes primarily a present possession or
actual experience of the Christian believer, while
in others it clearly contemplates a blessed life to
come, conceived as a promised inheritance. The
Greek expressions are ζωὴ αἰώνιος, ἡ αἰώνιος ζωή (Jn
17³, 1 Ti 6¹²), ἡ ζωὴ ἡ αἰώνιος (1 Jn 1²). The word
'life,' or 'the life' (ζωή, ἡ ζωή), without the qualifying adjective 'eternal,' is often employed in the
same general meaning.

There are passages in the Synoptic Gospels in
which the phrase 'eternal life' is used synony-
mously and interchangeably with 'the kingdom
of God' (Mk 9⁴⁵· ⁴⁷, Mt 7¹⁴· ²¹). The Kingdom of
heaven and the life eternal are very closely related
in the teaching of Jesus. Compare also the suggestive language of Ro 5¹⁷ 'shall reign in life
through Jesus Christ.' But it is especially in the
writings of St. John that we find 'eternal life'
presented as a heavenly boon which may become
the actual possession of believers in the present
life. God Himself is the source of all life, and 'as
the Father hath life in himself, even so gave he to
the Son also to have life in himself' (Jn 5²⁶). In
the Word 'which became flesh and dwelt among
us' there was a visible manifestation of the life
eternal : 'In him was life ; and the life was the
light of men' (1⁴) ; so that He Himself declares, 'I
am the way, and the truth, and the life' (14⁶). In
accord with these statements the very life of God
is conceived as begotten in the believer by the
Holy Spirit, so that he is 'born anew,' 'born from
above' (3³⁻⁷). Thus begotten of God, the children
of God become distinctly manifest, and God's
'seed abideth in them' (1 Jn 3⁹· ¹⁰). That is, in
these Divinely begotten children of God there
abides the imperishable germ (σπέρμα) of life from
above, the eternal kind of life which the twice
born possess in common with the Father and the
Son. Hence it is that the believer 'hath eternal
life' as an actual possession (Jn 3³⁶). He 'hath
passed out of death into life' (Jn 5²⁴, 1 Jn 3¹⁴).

In Jn 17³ we read what has to some extent the
manner of a definition : 'This is life eternal, that
(ἵνα) they should know thee the only true God, and
him whom thou didst send, even Jesus Christ.'
So far as this text furnishes a definition, it seems
clearly to imply that 'eternal life' consists in such
a knowledge of God and of Christ as involves a
personal experience of vital fellowship. It carries
with it the love and obedience which, according
to Jn 14²³, bring the Father and the Son into the
believer's inmost life, so that they 'make their
abode with him.' In view of the use of ἵνα in 4³⁴
15¹² 18³⁹ we need not refine so far as (with Westcott
on this passage) to maintain that the connective
here retains its telic force and indicates an aim
and an end, a struggle after increasing knowledge
rather than the attainment of a knowledge already
in possession. But it should not be supposed that
any present knowledge of God and of Christ is
inconsistent with incalculable future increase.
While the essence of this Divine life consists in
the knowledge of the only true God and His
anointed Son, such knowledge is not the whole
of eternal life, for other ideals with their additional content are also set before us in the teaching
of Christ and of His Apostles. Whatever else is
true touching this saving knowledge of the true

God, its present possession is one of the great
realities in the personal experience of the believer.
In 1 Jn 5¹¹⁻¹³ the gift and actual possession of this
eternal kind of heavenly life are made emphatic :
'God gave unto us eternal life, and this life is in
his Son. He that hath the Son hath the life ; he
that hath not the Son of God hath not the life.'
This language is incompatible with the thought
that the 'eternal life' spoken of is merely a promise, a hope or an expectation of such life in a
future state, as some of the older expositors maintained.

This heavenly kind of life in Christ, conceived as
a present experience of salvation, is further confirmed and illustrated by what Jesus said of Himself as 'the bread of life' and the giver of the
water that springs up into eternal life. We have,
no doubt, the enigmatical words of profound mysticism in Jn 6³⁵⁻⁵⁸. Jesus declares that He is 'the
bread of life,' which 'giveth life unto the world.'
'I am the living bread which came down out of
heaven : if any man eat of this bread, he shall live
for ever : yea, and the bread which I will give is
my flesh, for the life of the world.' 'Except ye
eat the flesh of the Son of man and drink his blood,
ye have not life in yourselves. He that eateth my
flesh and drinketh my blood hath eternal life : and
I will raise him up at the last day.' 'He that
eateth my flesh and drinketh my blood abideth in
me, and I in him.' 'He that eateth me shall live
because of me.' 'He that eateth this bread shall
live for ever.' These emphatic repetitions of statement would seem to put it beyond all question
that their author meant to teach that the Son of
God, sent by the living Father, 'lives because of
the Father,' and imparts the eternal life of the
Father to every one who believes in Him. Of this
living bread the believer now partakes, and 'hath
eternal life' (vv.⁴⁷· ⁵⁴). This life also is conceived
as attaining a certain goal, or receiving a definite
consummation 'at the last day.' For it is a permanent possession, and of a nature to advance
from strength to strength and from glory to glory.
The eating the flesh and drinking the blood of the
Son of Man have been thought by some expositors
to refer to the partaking of the body and blood of
Christ in the sacrament of the Lord's Supper ; but
such a reference to an institution not yet established, and utterly unknown to His Jewish opponents, would have been strangely irrelevant. The
life eternal into which the believer enters involves,
as matter of course, all due allowance for Divinely
appointed conditions, aids, provisions and means of
nourishing the life itself ; but to exalt these unduly
is to divert the thought from the more central and
profound mystic conception of Christ Himself as
the life of the world. So the remarkable sayings
of Jesus in the synagogue at Capernaum, recorded
in Jn 6³²⁻⁵⁹, are but another form and a mystic
expression of His emphatic declaration in 5²⁴ 'He
that heareth my word, and believeth him that sent
me, hath eternal life, and cometh not into judgment, but hath passed out of death into life.'

The exact meaning of the word 'eternal,' when
used to qualify 'the life,' is best understood when
the life is conceived as issuing from the eternal
Father, and so partaking of His Divine nature (cf.
2 P 1⁴). Having life in Himself, and giving to His
Son to have life in Himself (Jn 5²⁶), He imparts the
same life to all who believe in the Son ; and that
life is in its nature eternal as God Himself. It is
an eternal kind of life which belongs to the unseen
and imperishable things (cf. 2 Co 4¹⁸). In the
Johannine writings the word 'life' or 'the life,'
and the phrase 'eternal life,' are used interchangeably. The latter is the more frequent form of
expression, but it is evident that the writer often
employs 'the life' in the same sense. This life is

spoken of in contrast with 'death' and 'perishing.' The believer 'shall not perish, but have eternal life' (3^{16}), 'hath passed out of *the* death into *the* life' (5^{24}), 'shall never see death,' nor 'taste of death' ($8^{51.\ 52}$), 'shall never perish' (10^{28}). He who has not the life is in a condition of spiritual death, and must perish unless he receive the life of God, the eternal kind of life, which has been manifested in Christ. In these and other similar passages life and death are not to be understood as identical in meaning with existence and non-existence. The person who has passed out of death into life had existence before the new life came, and such existence, in estrangement from God and in disobedience of the gospel, may be perpetuated in 'eternal destruction from the face of the Lord' (2 Th 1^9). So the 'death,' which those who 'perish' taste, need not be understood as annihilation, or utter extinction of being. As 'the death' is a condition of moral and spiritual destitution in which one has no fellowship with God, so 'the life' is the blessed experience of fellowship and union with Christ as vital as that of the branch and the vine. And this participation in the very nature of the Eternal God is the essence of the 'life eternal.'

In the writings of St. Paul we also find a mystic element in which we note the concept of eternal life as a present possession. The exhortation to 'lay hold on the life eternal,' and the designation of it as 'the life which is life indeed' ($\dot{\eta}$ $\delta\nu\tau\omega s$ $\zeta\omega\dot{\eta}$, 1 Ti $6^{12.\ 19}$), may refer either to the present or the future; but when the Apostle speaks of believers as made alive and risen with Christ, and sitting with Him in the heavenlies (Eph $2^{5.\ 6}$), he implies a fruition that was already realized. It involved a positive experience like that in which 'the law of the Spirit of life in Christ Jesus made him free from the law of sin and of death' (Ro 8^2). He also has a wonderful appreciation of the heavenly illumination which 'shined in our hearts to give the light of the knowledge of the glory of God in the face of Jesus Christ' (2 Co 4^6). This surpassing light is conceived by the Apostle as a product of the Spirit of the Lord, and a reflexion of the glory of Christ as seen in the mirror of His gospel. In that mirror the believer beholds the glory of his Lord reflected, and by the power of the heavenly vision he is 'transformed into the same image' (2 Co $3^{17.\ 18}$). The Johannine doctrine of 'passing out of death into life' is conceived by St. Paul as a dying unto sin and being made alive unto God in Christ Jesus. The believer is 'alive from the dead' and 'walks in newness of life' (Ro 6^{1-13}). He has been 'crucified with Christ: and it is no longer I that live, but Christ liveth in me; and that life which I now live in the flesh I live in faith, which is in the Son of God' (Gal 2^{20}). And so in Pauline thought the spiritual life of faith, enjoyed in fellowship with God and Christ, is a 'life hid with Christ in God' (Col 3^3), and 'the free gift of God' (Ro 6^{23}). This conception is in essential harmony with the doctrine of St. John. Eternal life is in its inmost nature the free, pure, permanent spiritual life of Christlikeness. It is a present possession, a glorious reality, a steadfastness of conscious living fellowship with the Eternal Father, and with His Son, Jesus Christ.

But in all the Gospels and in the Epistles we also find eternal life contemplated as a future glorious inheritance of the saints. In St. John's Gospel the 'eternal life' which the believer now 'hath' is destined to attain a glorious consummation in the resurrection 'at the last day' ($5^{40.\ 54}$). For Jesus is Himself the resurrection as well as the life, and declares: 'He that believeth on me, though he die, yet shall he live; and whosoever liveth and believeth on me shall never die' ($11^{25.\ 26}$). Such a life must needs abide in eternal permanence.

Jesus spoke of 'the water of life' which becomes in him who drinks it 'a fountain of water springing up into eternal life' (4^{14}). He spoke of food 'which abideth unto life eternal,' and of 'gathering fruit unto life eternal' (4^{36} 6^{27}). In all the Gospels He is represented as teaching that 'he that loveth [or findeth, so Synopt.] his soul loseth it; and he that hateth [or loseth] his soul in this world shall keep it unto life eternal.' We read in Mk $10^{29.\ 30}$ 'There is no man that hath left house, or brethren, . . . or lands, for my sake and for the gospel's sake, but he shall receive a hundredfold now in this time, . . . and in the age to come life eternal' (cf. Mt 19^{29} and Lk $18^{29.\ 30}$). These Gospels also speak of eternal life as an inheritance to be received at a future day (Mt 19^{16}, Mk 10^{17}, Lk 10^{25} 18^{18}). Such contrast of 'this time,' 'this world,' 'on the earth' with 'the age to come,' and 'in heaven,' implies possessions in some other age or world beyond the present. In the picture of the Judgment (Mt 25^{31-46}), the righteous who go 'into eternal life' are said to 'inherit the kingdom prepared for them from the foundation of the world,' and to enter into the joy and glory of the King Himself.

This idea of eternal life as a glorious future inheritance finds also frequent expression in the Epistles. Those who 'by patience in well-doing seek for glory and honour and immortality' shall receive eternal life as a reward of the righteous judgment of God (Ro 2^7). All who are made free from sin and become servants of God 'have their fruit unto sanctification, and the end life eternal' (Ro 5^{21} 6^{22}). In the Epistle to the Hebrews (1^{14} 9^{15}) we read of 'them that shall inherit salvation,' and of them that 'receive the promise of the eternal inheritance.' In 1 P 1^4 the writer tells his readers that God has begotten them unto a living hope, 'unto an inheritance incorruptible, and undefiled, and that fadeth not away, reserved for them in heaven.' According to all these scriptures, eternal life is begotten in the Christian believer by the Holy Spirit of God, and is to be perpetuated through the ages of ages. It is eternal in quality as being a participation in the Divine nature of the Eternal One, and eternal in duration as continuing for ever and ever. It is a possession of manifold fulness, and is conditioned in a character of godlikeness, which 'has the promise of the life that now is, and of that which is to come' (1 Ti 4^8). There can be no living this life apart from God, for it is begotten in the soul by a heavenly birth, and must be continually nourished by the Spirit of God. Such vital union with the eternal Spirit brings unspeakable blessedness in this life and in this world; but it is as permanent and abiding as the nature of God, and is therefore appropriately called an incorruptible inheritance. Each individual life, whose 'fellowship is with the Father, and with His Son Jesus Christ' (1 Jn 1^3), is conceived as continuing eternally in that heavenly fellowship. In this age and that which is to come, in this world and in any other, on the earth or in the heavens, the child of God abides in eternal life.

See art. Eschatology ii. 2, and so far as this subject relates to the Future State, artt. HEAVEN, IMMORTALITY, RESURRECTION.

LITERATURE. — Gueder in Herzog, *Real - Encyclopädie* (ed. Plitt, 1881), vol. viii. pp. 509–517, also Kähler in same *Encyc.* (ed. Hauck, 1902), vol. xi. pp. 330–334; M'Clintock and Strong's *Cyclopædia*, vol. iii. pp. 313–317; Charles, *Crit. Hist. of Doctrine of Future Life*, pp. 368–370; Dalman, *Words of Jesus*, pp. 156–162; Drummond, *Relation of Apostolic Teaching to Teaching of Christ*, pp. 193–198; Hort, *The Way, the Truth, the Life* (Hulsean Lectures for 1871), Lect. iii.; Titius, *Jesu Lehre vom Reiche Gottes*, pp. 29–39; Wendt, *The Teaching of Jesus*, vol. i. pp. 242–255; Westcott, *The Epistles of John*, pp. 214–218; Beyschlag, *New Test. Theology*, vol. i. pp. 266–268, vol. ii. pp. 429–430; Holtzmann, *Neutest. Theologie*, vol. ii. pp. 516–518; Immer, *Theol. des NT*, pp. 512–515; Stevens, *Johannine*

Theology, pp. 312–327, also *Theology of the NT*, pp. 224–233; Weiss, *Bibl. Theol. of the NT*, vol. ii. pp. 347–352.

M. S. TERRY.

ETERNAL PUNISHMENT.—RV of Mt 25⁴⁶ (εἰς κόλασιν αἰώνιον). The AV here and in 26 other passages has 'everlasting.' The adjective αἰώνιος occurs 70 times in the NT (1 Ti 6¹⁹ omitted in RV), and in the RV, with one exception (Philem ¹⁵), is uniformly rendered 'eternal.' This is a distinct gain, as it leaves the exact significance to be determined by use. Three passages should be examined: 'Through times eternal' (Ro 16²⁵); 'before times eternal' (2 Ti 1⁹, Tit 1²); in these uses it is clear that 'eternal' and 'everlasting' are not interchangeable. This agrees with the LXX, in which αἰώνιος is used of the rites and ceremonies of Judaism which are done away in Christianity (Ex 12²⁴ 29⁹ 40¹⁵, Nu 18¹⁹ and others). The suggested use of 'æonian' has failed to find approval notwithstanding its advantages, and 'age-long' is inept.

For NT thought the use of the term in the Fourth Gospel should be studied. Excluding parallel passages, 'eternal life' is found 21 times in the Gospels, and of these 17 are in John. In this Gospel, as also in 1 Jn., the notions of succession and duration are eliminated, and 'eternal' becomes almost synonymous with 'Divine.' 'It is not an endless duration of being in time, but being of which time is not a measure' (Westcott, see Additional note on 1 Jn 5²⁰). See ETERNAL LIFE. In the Synoptic Gospels, to 'enter into life' and to 'enter into the kingdom' are used interchangeably (cf. Mt 19¹⁶· ¹⁷ with ²³, Mk 9⁴⁵ with ⁴⁷, Mt 25³⁴ 'inherit *the* kingdom,' and v.⁴⁶ 'unto eternal life'). In the Fourth Gospel 'eternal life' is the equivalent of 'the kingdom of heaven' of the Synoptic Gospels (cf. Jn 3³· ⁵, where 'the kingdom of God' occurs, with v.¹⁵). This suggests a very comprehensive and definite idea. 'Eternal life' is the life of the Kingdom of God, forgiveness, righteousness, salvation, blessing, whatever that life is declared to be in the teaching of Jesus. 'Eternal punishment' is the antithesis of 'eternal life,' the penalties upon all unrighteousness inseparably bound up with the Kingdom, and which, in His new teaching of the Kingdom, Jesus plainly sets forth. As a working principle, then, 'eternal' may be accepted as descriptive of things belonging to, essentially bound up with, the Kingdom, and is almost the equivalent of 'Messianic,' in the Christian, as opposed to the merely Jewish significance of the term, 'that ye may believe that Jesus is the Christ, the Son of God; and that believing ye may have life in his name' (Jn 20³¹). These deeper meanings of αἰώνιος in the NT should serve to remove the question of the time element in future punishment from the unsatisfactory basis of mere verbal interpretations.

In collating the teaching of the Gospels, full emphasis must be given to the following postulates: 1. *The certainty of retribution is inseparably bound up with the revelation of Jesus as to the will and character of God.* The Father who 'seeth in secret' and rewards unobtrusive righteousness (Mt 6¹ff.) will render to the unrighteous the due reward of their deeds (Mt 7¹⁹ 10²⁸ 12³⁶ 15¹³ 18⁶· ³⁵, Lk 18⁷ [*parallel passages omitted throughout*]). Hence the urgency of the call to repentance (Mt 4¹⁷), and to the obedience of righteousness as in the Sermon on the Mount, and, at any cost, to 'crucify the flesh' which prompts to sin (Mt 5²⁹· ³⁰ 18⁸· ⁹). In this Jesus takes His stand with the prophets of old and with the last of their order, John the Baptist (cf. Lk 3⁷⁻¹⁴). The revelation of the all-perfect Father never weakens, but ever adds new emphasis to the call to a life of righteousness, and to the certainty of penalty for all unrighteousness.

2. *The characteristic teaching of Jesus as to the penalties of sin is bound up with His gospel of the Kingdom.*—The incomparable worth of the Kingdom, as the richest 'treasure,' and 'pearl of great price' (Mt 13⁴⁴· ⁴⁵), and the supreme quest of it as the first duty and sovereign wisdom of life (Mt 6³³), have, as their converse, the incomparable loss which the rejection of the gospel must inevitably entail. This is the supreme penalty—exclusion from the Kingdom, to be cast into the 'outer darkness' (Mt 8¹² 22¹³ 25³⁰), denied by the Lord (Mt 7²³ 10³³ 25¹², Lk 13²⁵⁻²⁷), shut out from the glad presence of the King (Mt 25⁴¹). The use of the figures 'weeping and wailing and gnashing of teeth' in the sentence of exclusion clearly indicates that *remorse* is one element in future retribution (cf. Lk 16²⁵ 'Son, remember').

3. *The hearing of the gospel adds to human responsibility, and increases the severity of the inevitable penalty of disobedience.*—This is the burden of much of the teaching of Jesus. Light is come into the world, and with the light a more solemn duty (Jn 3¹⁹ 9⁴¹ 15²²· ²⁴ 16⁹, Lk 12⁴⁷· ⁴⁸). It is the apostate disciple who, as salt which has lost its savour, is cast out (Mt 5¹³). To His disciples Jesus gives the warnings of God's searching judgment (Mt 5²²ff.). To those who call Him 'Lord, Lord,' and in His name have done 'many mighty works,' He utters the dread 'Depart' (Mt 7²¹⁻²³, cf. Lk 13²⁵⁻²⁷). It is the disobedient hearers of His word who are compared to a foolish builder whose house, built upon sand, is ruined by the storm (Mt 7²⁶· ²⁷). Those who deny Him, He also will deny (Mt 10³³); those who are ashamed of Him, of them will He be ashamed (Mk 8³⁸). It is the unfaithful servant (Mt 24⁴⁸⁻⁵¹), the unwatchful (Mt 25¹⁻¹³), the unprofitable (Mt 25³⁰), who are cast out of the Kingdom. It is the unfruitful branch of the vine that is cast forth, withered, gathered, cast into the fire, burned (Jn 15⁶). The final condition of hopeless doom, the state of 'eternal sin,' is the direct result of self-willed, deliberate resistance to the Divine grace (Mk 3²⁹; see ETERNAL SIN). And in the larger issues the severity of judgment falls upon cities and generations 'exalted to heaven' in privilege and opportunity, but doomed because of neglect (Mt 11²⁰⁻²⁴ 12⁴¹· ⁴²).

In all this there is no reference to those to whom the gospel has not been made known. The mention of the Cities of the Plain (Mt 10¹⁵) and that of the men of Nineveh (Mt 12⁴¹) are too incidental and indirect to yield any determining principle. Even the great Judgment passage (Mt 25³¹ff.), if indeed it is to be interpreted universally as including all the nations of the earth, may be interpreted also as assuming a corresponding universality of knowledge, the gospel preached throughout the whole world. The judgments Jesus announces are vitally bound up with the message He brings. The problem of those to whom the offers of grace have not been made is not considered, and we are not justified in applying to *them* the severities of penalty and dread doom which, in the teaching of Jesus, fall only upon those who deny Him and reject His gospel.

4. *The final triumph of the Kingdom, and consequent final separation of the righteous and the wicked.*—This is again and again solemnly asserted and described. In the parables of the Tares (Mt 13²⁴ff.) and the Drag-net (Mt 13⁴⁷ff.), the ultimate overthrow, and, as the terms used would seem to imply, the final *destruction* of evil are decisively declared. From the explanation of the parable it is clear that the wheat and the tares represent *persons*—'the sons of the kingdom' and 'the sons of the evil one.' This sharp division of men into two classes entirely distinct to human vision impossible. The facts of life show the presence of 'wheat and tares,' good and evil in every man. The difficulty is unresolved. The end is declared, but not the stages by which it is reached. The Kingdom is to be all righteousness, out of it is to be gathered 'all things that cause stumbling, and them that do iniquity' (Mt 13⁴¹). Every plant not planted by the Father is to be uprooted (Mt 15¹³), and every tree which beareth not good fruit is to be cut down and destroyed (Mt 7¹⁹).

So far there can be little hesitation in setting forth the teaching of Jesus. The difficulties arise when we seek to determine exactly the nature and duration of the penalties and of the doom. The difficulty is accentuated by the fact that Jesus uses freely the religious symbolism current at the time. Gehenna, the worm that dies not and the fire that is not quenched, the outer darkness, the weeping and the wailing and the gnashing of teeth, were familiar figures, and are clearly used because familiar (see ETERNAL FIRE). If, then, we ask how far Jesus gave His sanction to the popular notions behind the symbols, we are confronted with the difficulty of determining what those notions were. The use of these figures to describe the place of punishment in the world of spirits is admitted, but it is not so clear which of the three doctrines which have divided Christian thought—endless punishment, annihilation, restoration—was held. Support has been found for each opinion, and from the words of Jesus Himself quite opposite conclusions have been reached. In what has been said above, *finality* would seem to be taught, but other opinions are held.

(1) Especially the great sayings in which the note of the universality of grace rings so clear (Jn 3¹⁶· ¹⁷), and the persistent search of the lost (Lk 15⁴⁻⁸) and the all-embracing work of Jesus are so absolutely declared (Jn 1²⁹ 12³¹· ³²), have been dwelt upon as justifying 'the larger hope.' The exact award of penalty, the few and many stripes according to the measure of disobedience (Lk 12⁴⁷· ⁴⁸), the completed sentence implied in 'till thou have paid the last farthing' (Mt 5²⁶, cf. 18³⁴· ³⁵), the startling symbolism of the phrase 'salted with fire' (Mk 9⁴⁹), which is said to teach 'that the destructive element performs a purifying part' (see *Internat. Crit. Com.* 'Mark' *in loco*), the use of κόλασις, *pruning,* 'suggestive of corrective rather than of vindictive punishment' (*Expos. Gr. Test.* on Mt 25⁴⁶), and the use of αἰώνιος as suggesting 'age-long,' have all been singled out as leaving room for the hope of final salvation through the fires of judgment.

The exact balance of the awards 'eternal life' and 'eternal punishment' (Mt 25⁴⁶) has often been insisted upon as teaching finality. As the life is certainly endless, so, it is urged, must the punishment be. But even this is not conclusive. The terms 'life' and 'punishment' point to an essential difference. Life is of God, essentially Divine; punishment is from God, a Divine act. It is well also to bear in mind that 'if good ever should come to an end, that would come to an end which Christ died to bring in; but if evil comes to an end, that comes to an end which He died to destroy' (Clemance, *Future Punishment,* p. 65).

But more than upon single texts, reliance is placed upon the revealed character and purpose of God in Jesus Christ.

(2) On the other hand, the strong terms, *destruction, perdition, unquenchable fire,* and the analogies of consumption of tares and chaff and withered branches by fire, are instanced as indicating annihilation. Two sayings of Jesus are indeed terrible in their severity, and ought not to be minimized: 'Be not afraid of them which kill the body, but are not able to kill the soul; but rather fear him which is able to destroy both soul and body in hell' (Mt 10²⁸). Whether the reference be to God as the object of fear (so Wendt, *Teaching of Jesus,* i. 201, and most commentators) or 'the tempter' and 'the devil whose agent he is' (so Bruce, *Expos. Gr. Test. in loco*), the statement as to the destruction of the soul itself remains. The same thought is suggested by the figure used in the saying, 'He that falleth on this stone shall be broken to pieces; but on whomsoever it shall fall, it will scatter him as dust' (Mt 21⁴⁴). Were utter extinction of being to be taught, it could hardly be in plainer terms.

(3) In close association, and lending support to the theory of annihilation, is the doctrine of 'conditional immortality' or 'life in Christ.' According to this theory the object of revelation is 'to change man's nature, not only from sin to holiness, but from mortality to immortality.' Many sayings in the Fourth Gospel are pressed to support this theory, especially those where the gift of life is declared to be only through the Son, and to those only who abide in Him by faith (Jn 3¹⁵· ¹⁶ 6³⁵· ⁵⁰⁻⁵⁸).

It is this evident and apparently 'insoluble antinomy' which has led many to conclude 'that we have not the elements of a complete solution, and we ought not to attempt it. What visions beyond there may be, what larger hopes, what ultimate harmonies, if such there are in store, will come in God's good time; it is not ours to anticipate them, or lift the veil where God has left it drawn' (Orr, *The Christian View of God and the World,* 397). This conclusion, so far at least as the Gospels are concerned, may be accepted. In the teaching of Jesus the emphasis is always upon *present* opportunity, duty, responsibility. 'One said unto him, Lord, are they few that be saved? And he said unto them, Strive to enter in by the narrow door' (Lk 13²³). 'Walk while ye have the light, that darkness overtake you not. While ye have the light, believe on the light, that ye may become sons of light' (Jn 12³⁵· ³⁶). God's eternal grace and man's 'boundless power of resistance' stand over against each other. Jesus honours both, but nowhere in His reported sayings does He disclose the final issue.

The teaching of the Epistles does not come within the scope of this article, but this brief reference is necessary. To the present writer, at least, it does appear that St. Paul's faith reaches a final issue. By him an endless dualism is decisively rejected. 'That God may be all in all' (1 Co 15²⁰⁻²⁸) is the final goal; but what that includes, or how accomplished, is not declared; only of Christ it is said, and we may hold this faith confidently, 'He must reign till he hath put all his enemies under his feet.'

LITERATURE.—This is very voluminous, and no attempt is made to include even all modern works. The following may be consulted:—(*A*) In favour of endlessness of punishment: Pusey, *What is of Faith as to Everlasting Punishment?*; S. Davidson, *The Doctrine of Last Things*; Salmond, *The Christian Doctrine of Immortality.*—(*B*) Treating the answer as unrevealed: Barrett, *The Intermediate State*; Beet, *The Last Things*; Clemance, *Future Punishment*; Orr, *The Christian View of God and the World,* Lect. ix.—(*C*) In support of annihilation: Row, *Future Retribution*; Stokes, *Conditional Immortality*; E. White, *Life in Christ.*—(*D*) Maintaining the 'larger hope': Cox, *Salvator Mundi*; Farrar, *Eternal Hope,* and *Mercy and Judgment*; Plumptre, *Spirits in Prison,* includes art. 'Eschatology' from Smith's *Dict. of Christian Biog.*; Jukes, *The Restitution of all Things.*—(*E*) On the general question: see Hastings' *DB,* art. 'Eschatology'; Alger, *Doctrine of a Future Life*; also Greg's *Enigmas of Life,* ch. vii., for a striking presentation of retribution as determined by the nature of sin; Stephen, *Essays in Ecclesiastical Biography,* the Epilogue.

W. H. DYSON.

ETERNAL SIN.—The RV of Mk 3²⁹ (αἰωνίου ἁμαρτήματος, so אBL; C* ᵛⁱᵈ D read ἁμαρτίας); AV 'eternal damnation' (κρίσεως, so AC²), 'a strong translation of an incorrect text' (Morison). It is not surprising that the latter explanation of a difficult word (ἁμάρτημα) should have found its way into the text of some later MSS. As an explanation of the correct text, 'eternal judgment'—or, as the judgment is clearly adverse, 'eternal condemnation'—is not without force. It has the merit of emphasizing the essential matter, which any interpretation, to be adequate, must take into account, that an 'eternal sin' is a sin which 'hath never forgiveness.' But this early gloss is inadequate. There is more than the emphasis of repetition. It is not the *penalty* of the sin, but its *nature,* which is declared; not the mere *duration* of the sin or of the sinning, but the *guilt*; not eternally sinning, but an eternal sin.

That sin tends to propagate itself is witnessed to by experience, and that continuance in sinning must exclude forgiveness is an essential principle of all moral judgment. Sin and penalty are of necessity coterminous. But *unforgiven* because *unrepented of* is true of *all* sin, and is no adequate explanation of an 'eternal sin' which carries the judgment 'unforgivable.' The absoluteness of the sentence is already declared in the words 'hath never forgiveness;' it is the ultimate ground of this judgment which is further declared.

'Eternal sin' finds its contrast and opposite in 'eternal life,' which is not simply or characteristically *endless* life, but essential, perfect life, 'the life which is life indeed' (1 Ti 6¹⁹ RV), the life of the Kingdom of God (cf. Mk 9⁴³. ⁴⁵. ⁴⁷ and Jn 3³. ⁵. ¹⁵), the life of God (1 Jn 1² RV). So 'eternal sin' is more than 'sin eternally repeating itself,' it is a fixed state of sin, sin which has become character, nature, moral death, which is death indeed. But see art. BLASPHEMY, p. 209ᵇ. This is the final revolt of man, free will carried to its ultimate in the defiance of God, a final condition, hopeless and beyond recovery, beyond the reach even of Divine illumination and influence. The writer of the Epistle to the Hebrews certainly contemplates in 6¹⁻⁸ the possibility of such fatal apostasy, cf. also 1 Jn 5¹⁶ 'sin unto death' (see Westcott, *ad loc.*); but neither of these passages appears to the present writer to afford help here.

Two questions must be distinguished — the *actuality* and the *possibility* of this state of moral depravity. That the grace of God should prove unavailing is indeed hard to believe, and by many the thought is rejected utterly. Yet there is much in the teaching of Jesus and in human life to justify the fear that this possibility may become an actual fact. The hardening of the heart which follows all unfaithfulness is the witness in human life to what must inevitably result if unfaithfulness is persisted in, a fixed state of spiritual blindness and insensibility. There is a law of degeneration in the moral world as in the natural. But it is in the Scripture doctrine of sin that the full ground of this fear is seen. According to the teaching of Jesus, the measure of responsibility is 'the light that is in thee' (Mt 6²³), and sin is wilful disregard of the light of truth. To be blind is to be without sin; but to those who say 'we see,' and yet walk in darkness, 'sin remaineth' (Jn 9⁴¹). So every increase of light brings increased responsibility (Jn 3¹⁹ 15²²); and for self-willed deliberate refusal of the Divine grace, refusal not in ignorance or misunderstanding but with full consciousness and choice of will so that the will itself becomes identified with evil, there can only be judgment, not because the Divine compassions fail, but because the redemption, as the Redeemer, is despised and rejected of men. In the final issue the free will of man is valid even against the beseechings of God (Jn 5⁴⁰, Mt 23³⁷).

The doom of the finally impenitent is here negatively told: 'hath never forgiveness'; but that includes the uttermost penalty, exclusion from the Kingdom of the Father, loss of the 'eternal life.' This is sin's last stage and uttermost working; it cuts the soul off from God, its source and life. 'Sin, when it is full grown, bringeth forth death' (Ja 1¹⁵). See, further, art. SIN.

LITERATURE.—The Commentaries on St. Mark; Salmond, *Christian Doctrine of Immortality*, pp. 306, 493; Row, *Future Retribution*, p. 254; Bruce, *Kingdom of God*, p. 319; Wendt, *Teaching of Jesus*, Eng. tr. ii. 87; Stevens, *Theology of the NT*, p. 102; *Expos.* II. iii. [1882] p. 321 ff.

W. H. DYSON.

ETERNITY.—There is no word either in OT Hebrew or in NT Greek corresponding to the abstract idea of eternity.

In Is 57¹⁵ both AV and RV have the phrase 'the high and lofty One *that inhabiteth eternity*.' MT has שֹׁכֵן עַד, lit. 'dwelling for ever'—the thought of the writer being evidently the *unchangeableness* of God. עַד probably comes nearest of all Hebrew words to express permanence. Originally it was a substantive connected with Assyr. *adû*, meaning 'time,' 'passing time,' 'the present.' But in OT it is used adverbially to express indefinite duration of time generally in the future. Its use is mainly poetical: of God (Is 57¹⁵), His law (Ps 19⁹), His attributes (111³. ¹⁰). But it is found also in connexion with things whose existence in Hebrew thought would be limited, *e.g.* a king's life (Ps 21⁶, Pr 29¹⁴), the lip of truth (Pr 12¹⁹).

A word of wider meaning and more general application is עוֹלָם, connected with Assyr. *ullânu*, meaning '*remote time*.' עוֹלָם is frequently used of the fast-days (Is 63⁹. ¹¹, Mic 5¹ 7¹⁴ etc.), people (Is 44⁷, Jer 5¹⁵), hills (Gn 49²⁶, Hab 3⁶). It is also used, like עַד, of God or His attributes as existing from the remote past (Ps 93² 119⁵², Is 63¹⁶. ¹⁹) to the remote future (Ps 138⁸, Jer 31³, 1 K 10⁹), specially in the phrase מֵהָעוֹלָם וְעַד הָעוֹלָם 'from everlasting to everlasting' (Ps 90² 103¹⁷, Neh 9⁵ etc.). But in the case of עוֹלָם also there are many places in OT where its meaning is obviously limited to the affairs and lives of human beings, *e.g.* of a slave (Dt 15⁷, 1 S 27¹²), of careless dwellers (Ps 73¹²), and in the familiar phrase, 'May the king live for ever' (1 K 13¹, Neh 2³). Often, however, the word is used to indicate the writer's hope or belief that a certain state of good [*e.g.* God's covenant (Gn 9¹⁶), or His promises (Is 40⁸), or His relations to His people (Ps 45¹⁸ 85⁶, etc.)], may continue indefinitely. Particularly is this true of the Messianic hope (Is 9⁶, Ps 110⁴ 45⁵). Sometimes this thought of permanence is emphasized by the use of the plural (Is 26⁴ 45¹⁷, Dn 9²⁴). In Ec 3¹¹, a very difficult passage, RVm gives as an alternative rendering of הָעֹלָם 'eternity.'

The other Hebrew phrases worthy of note are נֶצַח 'perpetuity' in the frequent phrase לָנֶצַח 'for ever' (Is 13²⁰ 25⁸, Am 8⁷, Hab 1⁴ etc.), and אֹרֶךְ יָמִים 'length of days,' Dt 30²⁰, Job 12¹², Ps 21⁴, and in the well-known passage Ps 23⁶ 'I shall dwell in the house of the Lord *for ever*.' Here the meaning is disputed, but the probability is that the highest anticipation of the Psalmist was to have the joy of spending an indefinite period in the Temple in prayer and meditation. Similar to לְעוֹלָם is the phrase לְדֹר וָדֹר, lit. 'to age and age,' *i.e.* to future ages (Ex 3¹⁵, Ps 10⁶ 33¹¹ 49¹¹). It is mainly poetical.

The idea of eternity, like the idea of immortality, was probably beyond the range of early Jewish thought. It arose after the Exile, partly through a natural development of the Hebrew conception of God, and partly through the force of circumstances. (1) The pious Jew, turning away more and more from the anthropomorphism of cruder religions, strove to differentiate the infinite God from finite man. God is transcendent—above the limitations of earthly existence. Hence He is eternal, from everlasting to everlasting. A thousand years in His sight are but as yesterday. (2) With the Exile came a decay of *national* ideals, and the Jew began to consider more his own personality and its relation to this eternal God. This thought developed slowly, and was mixed with various elements. The Jew found himself in an evil world. His own nation was oppressed, almost blotted out. Good men suffered; wicked men seemed to prosper. If the eternal, omnipotent God ruled the world, then all this must surely end. The Day of the Lord would come for oppressed Israel, for the oppressors, for the whole world, and (in Apocalyptic literature, Ps-Sol 3¹⁶ 13⁹ etc.) for the Jew himself. Then the present evil world (עוֹלָם הַזֶּה) would give place to a new and glorious era (עוֹלָם הַבָּא, see GENERATION). Whether this עוֹלָם הַבָּא would be *endless* the Jew did not at first stop to inquire. Sufficient for him that it *would* come with countless blessings in 'the end of the days' (קֵץ הַיָּמִים, cf. Mt 13³⁹ 24³). In the Book of Enoch, however, 'Time' is followed by 'Eternity' in the עוֹלָם הַבָּא. Later Judaism developed the idea, probably borrowed from the Zend religion, of a series of world epochs (cf. the world empires of Daniel's vision), followed by the Messianic age.

In the time of Christ, Jewish thought on the future had developed very much, and had assumed many forms (see ESCHATOLOGY). Jesus must have sifted the various elements. He retained and perhaps developed the view of a new age (עוֹלָם הַבָּא) about to dawn on the world as opposed to the present (עוֹלָם הַזֶּה ; Mt 12³², cf. 13³⁹ 28²⁰). *Then* 'the kingdom of heaven' (מַלְכוּת שָׁמַיִם) would be established. Jesus endeavoured to concentrate the thoughts of His hearers on their *personal* relation to this kingdom, and the desirability of sharing it (see LIFE, ETERNAL LIFE). Doubtless this kingdom would be for ever and its members live for ever (cf. Dn 12² חַיֵּי עוֹלָם 'eternal life'). The vexed question of the absolute endlessness of this kingdom, with its rewards and punishments, would probably never be raised in the minds of Jesus' hearers. At the same time, there is no evidence in the teaching of Jesus of any limit to the עוֹלָם הַבָּא, and while the frequent adjective αἰώνιος, 'eternal,' must be taken in the Gospels as referring in the first place to this coming kingdom, it may, so far as we know, be taken as implying also that quality of absolute permanence with which that kingdom has always been associated in the minds of men.

LITERATURE.—The subject is practically part of the larger topic Eschatology, and all books dealing with this latter subject refer more or less to Eternity. On the OT and Apocalyptic views see Stade, *Die Alttest. Vorstellungen vom Zustand nach dem Tode* ; Schwally, *Das Leben nach dem Tode* ; Schultz, *OT Theology*, vol. ii. pp. 364-398 ; Salmond, *The Christian Doctrine of Immortality* ; Orelli, *Die hebr. Synonyma der Zeit und Ewigkeit* ; Marti, *Geschichte der Israel. Religion*, pp. 270-310. On the NT see the various NT theologies, especially those of Beyschlag and H. Holtzmann. Cf. also Samuel Davidson, *Doctrine of the Last Things* ; Toy, *Judaism and Christianity* ; A. Beet, *Last Things* ² ; Dalman, *The Words of Jesus*.

G. GORDON STOTT.

ETHICS.—A very little reflexion will reveal the unusual difficulties that lurk in a subject like the present—the Ethics of Jesus, or, of the Gospels. Even the uninitiated is aware that we cannot in strictness speak of the 'Ethics' of Jesus at all—in the sense, that is, of a doctrine systematically developed according to principles, and exhaustively applied to the facts of life. For His was no scientific or methodical spirit ; His significance lies rather in the realm of personality, in the unique quality of His moral feeling and judgment, in the peculiar way in which men and things moved Him, and in which He reacted upon them. Hence we need not look for either an orderly arrangement of, or even an approximate completeness in, His ethical ideas. From the drama of His life we are unable to compile a system of morals, but we may see how a great Personality creates a moral standard by what He does and suffers, and how He elucidates it in His words.

But are we justified in connecting with Him the term 'ethical' at all? We speak accurately of Ethics or Moral Science only when we regard the conduct of men in their mutual relations as something by itself, abstracted from religious feeling and action, and when ethical ends and maxims are disengaged from religion, in virtue of their inherent worth ; and such an independent position of Ethics, whether it appear worth attaining or not, is simply beside the mark in the case of Jesus. His moral and His religious principles are so closely interwoven, His moral feeling, *e.g.* His love for man, is so inseverable from the religious basis of His belief in the Fatherhood of God, that it would seem to be impossible to delineate His 'Ethics' without at the same time treating of, say, the Kingdom of God, the Divine grace, or the final judgment. And if, nevertheless, we venture upon the task, we must never lose sight of the connecting lines that run between His ethical teaching and His religious principles.

Then there is the question whether our *sources* are at all sufficient for the full and accurate representation of the moral personality of Jesus. In restricting ourselves to the Synoptic Gospels, we are doing nothing more than recognizing the claims of historical science. But now, to what extent can we regard the three older Gospels as adequate sources for our theme? If we investigate the oldest of all, viz. Mark, we find that it nowhere makes any attempt to portray the Ethics of Jesus as such. In reporting His conflict and controversy with the Judaism of His time, it casts but an indirect light upon this side of His character, and that, moreover, in a series of isolated scenes. Of these the most outstanding are the Rabbinical disputations regarding the Sabbath (2²³-3⁶), purity (7¹⁻²³), divorce (10¹⁻¹²) ; then come the important passages narrating the conversation with the rich man (10¹⁷⁻²⁷) and regarding the 'first commandment' (12²⁸⁻³⁴). Various other aspects of His conception of life are vividly illustrated by such utterances as that to the paralytic (2⁵ᶠ·), about the physician and the sick (2¹⁷), the true kinship (3³⁵), children (10¹⁵ᶠ·), and tribute-money (12¹³⁻¹⁷). In the section dominated by the three predictions of His death (8²⁷-10⁴⁵) we have a mass of admonitions to the disciples—concerning readiness to suffer, loyalty, courage, humility, reverence for childhood, etc. We have here something of the nature of a primitive Christian catechism ; not instructions (as in the *Didache*, let us say) for tranquil seasons and everyday life, but rather articles of war for the *ecclesia militans* of the persecutions, a *manuale crucis*.[*]

An entirely different kind of appeal is made by the Sermon on the Mount in Mt 5-7. In its extant form the Sermon is the promulgation of a great programme, in which the Evangelist seeks to give a definitive and approximately complete statement of *Jesus' relation to the Law*, with a reference, moreover, to the representatives of the anti-legalistic standpoint, who think that He is come 'to destroy the law.' It is the purpose of the writer to convince these that Jesus, being in a general way the Fulfiller of Prophecy, is, as a lawgiver, the fulfiller of the prophecy regarding the second Moses, whom God was to raise up in the last days (Dt 18¹⁵), and who, so far from abrogating the Law, will rather consummate and even transcend it.[†] In our reading of the Sermon we cannot afford to ignore this design of the writer ; we must draw a distinction between what its words purported to him, and what they meant in the tradition he utilized. Similarly, in reading St. Luke's version of the Sermon on the Mount, we must bear in mind that he has materially abridged his material, not alone by discarding the Jewish and preserving only the typically human elements, but by considerably transforming it under the influence of his pronounced ascetic view.[‡] Both Mt. and Lk. thus throw us back upon the *source* of our Lord's words, in which the primitive Jewish-Christian community had grouped the Logia of Jesus for its own instruction. Hence we are forced to distinguish between the Ethics of the Evangelists and the Ethics of their source. Further, we must make a searching examination of the characteristically Lukan tradition as it appears in the parables of the Rich Man and Lazarus, the Good Samaritan, etc. ;[§] only so shall we be justified in attempting to answer the question, What was the ethical position of Jesus? An extremely complicated critical process must thus be gone through before we use our present authorities as documents for the solution of our problem. But as it is impossible to reproduce here the details of such investigation, only the results can be stated, with references to other works of the present writer.

[*] Cf. J. Weiss, *Das älteste Evangelium* (1903).
[†] Cf. J. Weiss, *Die Schriften des NT, neu übersetzt und für die Gegenwart erklärt* (1905), i i. p. 236 ff.
[‡] *Ib.* p. 413 ff.   [§] *Ib.* p. 380.

In an account of the Ethics of Jesus, the reader also looks for a comparison and contrast between Him and His Jewish, perhaps also His Græco-Roman, contemporaries. The fresh and original elements in His moral thought and feeling must be set over against traditional views. The favourite procedure in this connexion, that, namely, of placing His luminous figure on a background as sombre as possible, is one we cannot follow. Above all, the task of describing the ethical conditions of contemporary Judaism would take us beyond our allotted space, and is, moreover, beyond our capacity. Often as it has been tried, in more or less ingenious sketches, to reproduce some cross-section through the moral conditions of later Judaism, it has never been accomplished without subjective caprice and violent tendency-interpretations. Nor is this result to be wondered at; for it is quite impossible to describe faithfully, or estimate justly, the characteristic ethical complexion of a period so extensive as the two and a half centuries from B.C. 180 to A.D. 70, of the inner history of which we still know so little, which is represented by a literature so multiform, and of which the dominant currents veered so much—a period, moreover, meagrely equipped with first-rate or distinctly recognizable personalities. True, we can observe the behaviour of the circles from which sprang the Psalms of Solomon, we can lay our hand upon the devout breast of the pseudo-Ezra, we can enter into the spirit of the author of 1 Maccabees or Sirach; but how diverse are even these few casual types, and how impossible is it to make them fit into one harmonious picture! What, again, do we know of the Ethics of the Greek or Sadducean party? What vogue had the Essenes among the people? Are the Pharisees of the Psalms of Solomon identical with those of the time of Jesus? And, above all, what significance for our problem has the Talmud, so often named, so little known? Here, in sober truth, so many unsolved enigmas await the historian, that one cannot but marvel at the assurance of those who, in face of them all, are ready to sketch the Ethics of later Judaism as a foil for the Ethics of Jesus. We for our part renounce any such design. We have not the daring to institute a comparison between the Ethics of Jesus and the complicated historical phenomena of the period, and then, as impartial judges, to proceed to measure out the light and shade. We content ourselves with the question, *How did Jesus regard and estimate the Judaism of His time?* It is beyond doubt that His moral sense was chafed by many things, and in particular by Pharisaism, and that a material part of His teaching was formulated in antagonism to the Rabbis. We too must feel this antagonism, if we are ever to understand Him.

If, again, we are required to answer the question as to wherein consists the new and original element in the Ethics of Jesus, we are brought to a complete standstill. In His conflict with Rabbinism He is in close alliance with the Prophets, and is certainly not outside their influence. But to assume that a great gulf is fixed between the religion of the Prophets and Psalmists and that of later Judaism, is to forget that a goodly part of both the Prophets and the Psalms was a contribution of the post-exilic period, and, above all, to overlook the fact that these writings form the background, or, we might even say, the native soil of Judaism. However profoundly they were misunderstood, still it was not possible to prevent the intermittent welling up, from the soil, of many a copious spring; and many a document of the later period bears clear testimony to their influence. Thus we can do full justice to the moral creed of Jesus only by giving adequate consideration to the circumstance that He lived in intimate sympathy and steadfast accord with the noblest and devoutest thoughts of His people's Bible. Hence, if in view of these facts we inquire concerning the originality of Jesus, the result will be a surprise. For we shall find that of almost all His ethical ideas there are anticipations, precedents, and even parallels in the OT, as also in contemporary Judaism. A mere glance at any collection of parallels, such as that of Wetstein, will be sufficient to purge us of the notion that the uniqueness or greatness of Jesus consists in the novelty of His ethical teaching. Theology is still tainted with the propensity, inherited from Rationalism, to see in the production of ideas the all but exclusive factor in the making of history or the progress of man. It often fails to realize how plentiful ideas are in times that are spiritually alive, or how in all ages humanity has been enabled to take a step in advance only by the emergence of a personality who, with unwonted energy, sincerity, and enthusiasm, absorbed, elaborated, and formed anew from his individual experience the choicest products of his age. So with Jesus; His ideas as such are neither so novel nor so revolutionary as to create a new world; they derive their procreative virtue solely from the fact that He made them *His own, lived* them, and *died* for them.

From these preliminaries we turn to the exposition proper, premising that we shall on principle forego any systematic or exhaustive development of the material from a fundamental idea. Our purpose is to survey the figure of Jesus in its specific operation, and what better situation for this can we find than the actual scene of His conflict with His environment? It was the friction with that environment which kindled the fire within Him; it was His unconformity with it that gave Him the conviction of His peculiar heritage. Just as His anger at the profanation of the Temple moved Him to an involuntary display of a religious feeling superior to, and more delicate than, that of His fellows, so His collision with the leading representatives of Judaism evokes from Him not merely an indignant criticism, but also a manifestation of His own inherent character. In this connexion the great discourse against the Scribes and Pharisees in Mt 23 (cf. Lk 11[39-52]) furnishes invaluable testimony. Even if its artificial form (cf. the seven Woes) be derivative, still the majority of the sayings grouped in it, so expressive of individual feeling, so original in form, unmistakably show the characteristic touch of Jesus. In any case the discourse clearly reveals the distinction He drew between Himself and the Rabbis, and the traits in the latter by which the disciples, filled with His spirit, felt themselves repelled. It is, above all things, the *insincerity* of their practice, the contrast between the reality and the appearance, which is so vividly brought out in the metaphor of 'whited sepulchres' (23[27]). The supreme business of the scribes,—to which they apparently devoted themselves with surpassing zeal,—viz. the instruction of the people in the law of God (23[4]), they discharged in such a way as to superinduce the very reverse of what was intended: instead of bringing men into the Kingdom (23[13]) they keep them out by imposing intolerable burdens, in the bearing of which they render not the slightest help. It is, in fact, evident that the work of leading men to God was for them a matter of no consequence whatever. A glaring light is thrown likewise upon the propaganda of the Pharisees (23[15]): under their tutelage a proselyte becomes a child of hell, twice as wicked as themselves (or, as it was probably spoken at first, twice as wicked as he was before). These severe verdicts show at a glance how highly Jesus estimated the sacred and responsible office of the leaders of the people, which they so direly abused. With keen moral indignation He passes sentence upon the complacent and self-seeking father-confessors, who, on the pretext of pastoral zeal, with 'long prayers' devour widows' houses (Mk 12[40]). He shows inimitably the unscrupulousness of their over-scrupulosity : straining out gnats and swallowing camels, they are squeamish and strait-laced in regard to trifles, in the great moral matters lax for themselves and lenient to others, even to the point of apathy—and such has ever since been the practice of a hierarchy clothed with authority (23[24]). In these utterances Jesus reproves chiefly the scribes' insensibility to the primary moral sanctions ; they keep cup and platter clean, but are indifferent to the nature of the contents ; *non olet*, even though it has been accumulated by selfishness and greed, and is gorged with unbridled self-indulgence (23[25]). While with painful precision they attend to the tithing of the meanest garden produce, they neglect the weightiest matters of the Law—justice, mercy, and faithfulness (23[23]). In harmony with Mic 6[8] He enunciates the principle that the primary imperatives of morality surpass all ceremonial pre-scriptions in importance and urgency — a truth which, though ancient, needs ever to be emphasized anew. There can be no dubiety as to the purport of 'justice' or 'mercy' in this passage ; they are meant to cover the great social obligations of the ruling to the dependent classes—the non-perversion of the Law, the succour of widows and orphans, the relief of the poor. As to the third injunction, the Evangelists do not seem to have been sure of its meaning ; for 'faithfulness' St. Luke (11[42]) substitutes the 'love of God,' probably interpret-ing πίστις as 'faith' (as EV). Without doubt, however, Jesus intends this word also to connote a social and moral duty, viz. trustworthiness and candour in human relationships.

Mt. has in this verse inserted a clause (23[23b]) which should almost certainly be deleted from Lk. (11[42]), as a gloss involving a certain modification of the command. The preceding verses might lead us to infer that Jesus did not only set less store by the ceremonial law, but was willing to do away with it altogether. This, however, says St. Matthew, is not His meaning : 'These (moral duties) ought ye to have done, and not to leave the other undone.' The Evangelist is, in fact, keenly solicitous lest Jesus be regarded as hostile to the Mosaic law, as he shows also in 5[17] and the prefatory words 23[2f.] (neither passage in Lk.), implying that the teaching of the scribes is good, but that their works are evil, since they do not practise what they preach. Taking into consideration the writer's date and point of view, we can quite well understand the words ; but we naturally ask whether this con-ciliatory and conservative attitude towards the ceremonial law truly represents the mind of Jesus ?

The words about the cleansing of cups and platters, and about the tithing of mint, anise, and cummin, certainly sound so contemptuous as to compel us to ask whether Jesus set any value what-ever upon the ceremonial side of the Law, and, in particular, upon the special casuistical precepts of the scribes. The question may be answered pro-visionally and generally : Jesus was not a Pharisee, and this means that His attitude towards many of the scribal maxims was a dissentient one ; He was not a Judæan, but a son of the Galilæan peasantry, who knew how to evade the authority of Pharisaic doctors and lawyers, and who were, in consequence, liable to the curse merited by those who 'know not the law' (Jn 7[49]) ; and, accordingly, He regards Him-self and His followers likewise as above the Phari-sees' rules about purifying. But we also find ex-plicit remonstrances against the 'traditions of the elders' so dear to the scribes (Mk 7[5, 9, 13]) ; He char-

acterizes them summarily as the 'prescriptions' (EV 'tradition') of men (7[8]), thus contrasting them with the commandments of God. In this He evinces His independent attitude, for a genuine Pharisee could live only by the belief that the additions to and amplifications of the Law, even if devised by human teachers, were yet expressive of God's will. But Jesus goes still further, affirming positively that in their concern for these traditions the scribes reject, pervert, and even make void the commandment of God (7[8, 13]). He gives as an ex-ample the gross case of one who evades the plain human duty of supporting his parents by the manœuvre of dedicating to the Temple the money he might have spared for them : once the fateful word 'Corban' is spoken, then every penny so consecrated belongs to God, and is, as sacred pro-perty, interdicted from all secular uses, and so from that of the parents. It is bad enough that a son should so act ; but that jurists and theologians should *permit* him henceforward to turn his back upon father and mother, should declare his pledge to be inviolable, and refuse to 'release' him from it, is neither more nor less than the disannulling of the Fifth Commandment. [*]

Now the assertion that the great moral de-mands of God's law are of more importance than any ceremonial obligations, is primarily directed only against the traditions and prescriptions of the Rabbis ; in reality, however, it is a principle which threatens the very foundations of the Mosaic system. Already in the OT we see the strained relations between prophetic piety and priestly legality—brothers again and again at variance. In the personality and preaching of Jesus the pro-phetic religion reappears with unparalleled force and clearness, and braces itself to the work of overthrowing the fabric of Levitical ceremonialism. To treat the ethical and the ritual law as of equal validity belongs to the very nature of the priestly theocracy : the moment the former is placed on a higher level the whole edifice becomes insecure. In this reference St. Mark preserves a short but pregnant saying of Jesus (7[15]), viz. 'There is nothing from without the man that going into him can defile him, but the things which proceed out of the man are those which defile him.' As He is here speaking of clean and unclean meats, He says, 'Nothing going *into* the man,' but He might equally well say, and certainly means, 'Nothing from without the man coming *to* him,' *i.e.* coming into contact with him. But this is the reverse of what stands in the Law. For the whole complex of the Mosaic-Levitical legislation rests upon the postulate that a man *is* defiled by outer contact and contamination, or by partaking of certain foods, *i.e.* that he thereby becomes separated from God, is excluded from the sanctuary and segregated from the sacred community. Now the principle enunciated by Jesus cuts the ground from under all the particular commandments of the ceremonial law. It carries, indeed, a dissolving and explosive force. But His standpoint differs from mere rationalistic 'illuminism' by having a profoundly religious basis. Jesus had so intense a conception of man's relation to God as an ethical one, that He could not tolerate the thought that God would exclude any one from His presence merely because he had touched a corpse or eaten swine's flesh. It is the evil will, the impure heart, the false nature, that separate men from God.

All this, of course, is self-evident to us ; but when Jesus uttered it, and acted upon it, He found Himself at cross purposes with the most ex-emplary personages of His generation, and com-pelled to resist the drift of an age-long tradition. He raised His voice not only against the scribes,

[*] Cf. J. Weiss, *op. cit.* i. 1, p. 124

but against the very spirit of the Law they expounded. Moreover, in actual practice, His bearing towards the Law is quite unconstrained. He adds to the exceptions already conceded by the Rabbis (e.g. works of necessity on the Sabbath), and allows both Himself and His disciples a certain freedom, without taking counsel of the specialists. When challenged, He appeals to the example of David (Mk 2²³⁻²⁶). It is manifestly gratifying to the narrator that Jesus was able to justify His action so adroitly by the methods of Rabbinical exposition. But this is only an *ex post facto* justification, of which the disciples certainly were not thinking as they plucked the corn; they had acted without deliberation, simply availing themselves of the freedom which their fellowship with Jesus had made a matter of course. We learn the true meaning of Jesus from the twofold declaration subjoined by St. Mark (2²⁷ᵗ.). Doubtless what the *writer* means is that the 'Son of man,' *i.e.* the Messiah, is Lord of the Sabbath, and can absolve His disciples from its observance; but originally the saying must have run thus: 'Man has full power also over the Sabbath,' which, again, is of essentially the same tenor as the other, viz. 'the Sabbath was made for man, not man for the Sabbath.'* This saying, too, is more than an article in a confession; it is really a declaration of war against Mosaism. Scribe and doctor regard the Law as an end in itself, and obedience to it as the final purpose of human life, even if such obedience involve sacrifice, and indeed the surrender of life itself. But the assertion of Jesus that the Law is given for man's sake, as something designed for his benefit, and the inference that he is free from it whenever its observance conflicts with his welfare, proceed from an entirely different point of view, and have far-reaching implications. The rigid and *doctrinaire* aspect of the Law is thus cancelled; its behests are viewed as means for the realization of God's purposes of love towards men. All this, however, shows but the birth-struggle of an entirely new religious conception, destined in its further growth to do away altogether with the Law *as law*. A similar instance is the declaration (Mk 10¹ff.) that the Mosaic regulation regarding divorce was a concession to the Israelites' hardness of heart, and that it stands in antithesis to the statute originally promulgated in Paradise, which alone is the will of God and the precedent for man. Here the Mosaic ordinance is represented as something adventitious, as merely marking a stage meant to be left behind.

The boldness of Jesus in thus essaying to make a distinction within Scripture itself, and to discriminate between the law of God and human accretions, is of great moment for us. He has recourse to a mode of criticism which might be called subjective, but which really merits the attribute *prophetic*. This 'Prophet,' filled with Deity, this great religious Personality, ever directly conscious of His nearness to God, does not shrink from giving judgment as to what is the actual purpose of the Most High. Just as He fervidly announces the royal benignity of God towards both the evil and the good, just as He confidently speaks to the contrite of the Divine forgiveness, and without misgiving assures the wretched of the Divine succour, so He also undertakes, in face of the law of Moses, 'that which was spoken to the fathers,' to set forth a new law, in the glad conviction that He is thus expressing the will of God. Hence it is a misapprehension of the tenor and scope of the 'antitheses' in the Sermon on the Mount to imagine that in these Jesus is merely impugning the prevailing exegesis of the Law, or merely endeavouring to

* See J. Weiss, *op. cit.* i. 1, p. 87.

bring to light the real design of its promulgator. No; the rhythmical repetition of the phrase, 'But I say unto you,' makes it abundantly clear that Jesus is here reaching beyond Moses. And this undoubtedly corresponds to the historical situation. Take, for instance, the first two enactments, viz. regarding murder and adultery; it is clear that what Jesus means is that God asks more than mere abstention from these crimes: He demands perfect self-control and integrity of heart. The unheeded moments when the animal nature starts up in a fit of anger or of impure desire are grievously sinful in the eyes of God, as well as the actual misdeeds.

The religious-historical situation is as follows. The Jewish people were under a theocracy, and for them the Law of Moses was by no means restricted to religious or moral matters; it was at once a civil and a penal code, an order of legal procedure and a manual for the priesthood. Now it is the bane of a theocratic constitution that the Divine law, ingrafted as it is upon common life, tends to lose its majesty and inviolability. It has to adapt itself to the varied facts of existence by means of saving clauses and casuistical methods; and such a *régime* fosters above all the notion that the will and judgment of God reach no further than the arm of the civil magistrate, and that it is only the completed act, and not the intention, that God brings to judgment. Thus the moral relation of man to God sinks to the level of a legal one. Such a deterioration and externalizing of the religious life must all but inevitably ensue when its regulation and guardianship are committed to priests and jurists. It is the 'Prophet,' however, who now takes up the word. With incisive force He makes it clear that God looks upon the heart, the thought, the secret motions of the soul, and brings these things before His judgment-seat, and that the sin of intention passes with Him for no less than the overt act. To assert such equivalence of thought and deed may seem to us almost to overshoot the mark; for we rightly place a high value upon the self-command which keeps desire from passing into action. But the apparently partial view is to be regarded as the natural reaction of the heart and the conscience against the legalistic ossification and externalization of religion.

The verdict of Jesus upon *divorce* points in the same direction. The argument upon which He bases His prohibition of the separation permitted by Moses merits our attention. The statute laid down in Paradise is to be preferred, as the law of God, not merely in virtue of its great antiquity, but also on intrinsic grounds. When a husband puts away his wife, he places her in a position of moral jeopardy; for, should she associate herself with another man, whether in a second marriage or in a passing act of immorality, she thereby completes the dissolution of the first marriage, which hitherto was legally binding. The noteworthy element in this utterance is not that the ruptured matrimonial union is still binding, but in particular that the man is morally responsible for his wife, even after his dismissal of her; he must bear the guilt of her sin. Such is the only judgment possible, if marriage is to be regarded not merely as a legal bond, under the control of the civil magistrate, but as a moral covenant, for whose inviolability men are responsible, not to one another, but to God. See DIVORCE.

The profoundly irreligious subtlety of the lawyers is also exposed in Jesus' prohibition of oaths. First of all He shows that the evasions and periphrases by which those who swear hope to escape the danger of profaning God's holy name, are of no avail; every oath is and remains an adjuration of God.

But more : to the finer religious feelings, every oath is a gratuitous and irreverent bringing down of the Most High into the sordid and trivial concerns of the hour—the grossest case being that of the impulsive Oriental who puts his head in pledge, as if he had power over life and death, forgetting his complete dependence upon God, and that life and death proceed from Him alone. Thus Jesus supersedes the scrupulous anxiety and the petty evasions of the Rabbis by a much deeper religious motive : the oath, in truth, is but an element in a world under the domination of sin and Satan (Mt 5[37]), and he who feels God's majesty and purity in his inmost soul will have a sacred fear of bringing God upon such a scene, and will honour Him best by the plain and simple word of truth.

Of an entirely different character are the two final antitheses, viz. those relating to *non-resistance* and *love of enemies*, as given in Mt 5[38-42. 43-48]. In the foregoing precepts we have simply the utterances of a more earnest moral sensibility ; here we have the language of exultant and heroic enthusiasm, not meant to be judged by commonplace standards. In lieu of the typically Jewish principle of retaliation, which was applied both in legal and in personal affairs, viz. 'eye for eye, tooth for tooth,' Jesus demands the entire renunciation of self-defence or self-vindication. Nay more ; it is not mere tranquil endurance that He enjoins, but a readiness to present to the assailant the other cheek, to give more than what is asked, to surrender the cloak as well as the coat. These injunctions differ from those of St. Paul in Ro 12[19-21] in that they involve no thought of shaming or overcoming the adversary by pliancy and patience. St. Paul would seem, in fact, to have interpreted the words of Jesus in the practical didactic sense of certain Stoic admonitions. But the distinctive feature of the passage in the Sermon on the Mount is that the demands are made without any reason being assigned or any subordinate aim proposed, precisely, indeed, as if their authority must have been perfectly self-evident to the disciples. A theological exegesis has barred the way towards a right understanding of them by always starting from the question what these words mean *for us*, and how *we* shall obey them. And as a literal obedience to them seems to us impossible, recourse is had to new interpretations and modifications, by which the strength of their tremendous claims is sapped. Instead of putting such questions, we would rather ask how the words are to be understood in their original setting, and how Jesus came to utter them in that form. Now it is evident that their essential feature is a thorough aversion to the principle of retaliation by which the ignobler instincts of the Jewish national spirit were sustained and intensified. This aversion on the part of Jesus is so strong that the most emphatic utterance of the opposite quality is for Him precisely the right thing ; a consummate zeal for forbearance and renunciation whets His demands to their sharpest point. But what is the source of this enthusiasm ? It is no mere reformer of Jewish morals that speaks here, no legislator for centuries yet unborn, but the herald and apostle of the imminent dissolution of the world and of the Kingdom of God already at the door ! Hence a man can prepare himself for that day in no more worthy or more earnest way than by the surrender of all the present life is based upon — earthly repute, business capacity, personal property ; all these are but obstacles and fetters. Whoso renounces willingly, whoso suffers gladly—he is truly free, and ready for the great day that is at hand. We can appreciate and vindicate the words only if we interpret them by the mood appropriate to the twelfth hour.

' If so, they take our life,
Goods, honour, children, wife—
Let these things vanish all !
Their profit is but small :
The Kingdom still remaineth.'

The same enthusiasm pulsates through the words about love to enemies. It is unnecessary to paint the background of Judaism too black, to cavil at the Jewish 'love to one's neighbour' as narrow and partial, or even to lay too great a stress upon the 'hatred of one's enemies,' in order to feel that the demand of Jesus is not only something 'new,' but also a puissant, transcendent, superhuman ideal. He says, indeed, that the man who so acts will be perfect even as God is perfect, a worthy child of the all-loving Father. Now it cannot be sufficiently urged that this obligation to love one's enemies neither issues from nor can be fulfilled amidst the normal emotions of everyday life. If it is to be real to us, *i.e.* truly realized and not merely assumed, then it demands an enthusiasm which, if not 'contrary to the nature,' is certainly 'beyond the power' of the natural man. None but the possessor of a spirit profoundly religious and animated by the love of God, could possibly love his enemies, at all events according to the special sense which Jesus gave to the universal command, viz. 'Love them which hate you, pray for them which despitefully use you.'

Our view of this supreme command of Jesus thus brings us to the twofold law of love (Mk 12[29ff.], Lk 10[25ff.]). It is beyond question that neither this conjoining of love to God and love to one's neighbour, nor the focusing of the whole Divine law in that 'summa' is a specifically original thought of Jesus. According to the oldest form of the narrative (Lk 10[25f.]),[*] He elicits it from a scribe. Possibly enough there were earnest and pious Rabbis who, amid the jungle of thousands upon thousands of precepts, sought for some leading idea, and found in the requirement of love to God and man the nucleus of God's primal revelation : but none of them was ever able to carry such unification and simplification into full effect. Here again it is not the mere thought which matters, nor the fact that Jesus gave it utterance. The great thing is that, over and above, He furnished in His own life such an embodiment of the Law as carries conviction to all. In His personification of the ideal He welded the love of God and the love of man in an indissoluble union, in which they might foster and strengthen each other. He expressed the ideal in a perfect form, and stamped it upon the soul of the race. Since His day it has become obvious that the highest form of *religion* is that from which there radiates the soothing, genial, meek, and helpful *love of mankind* ; obvious also, that that *love of man* is the deepest, the truest, the most enduring, the most exacting, which has its roots in the depths of a soul pledged to the Most High, a soul which is permeated by His truth, and has been apprehended by His holy and gracious will.

LITERATURE.—J. Weiss, *Die Predigt Jesu vom Reiche Gottes* ; Bousset, *Jesu Predigt in ihrem Gegensatz zum Judentum* ; Jacoby, *NT Ethik*, bk. i. ; R. Mackintosh, *Christ and the Jewish Law.*   JOHANNES WEISS.

EUNUCH (εὐνοῦχος ; σπάδων occurs sometimes in LXX [see Gn 37[36] and Is 39[7], with which, however, cf. the corresponding passage 2 K 20[18]]).—From the single reference in the Gospels (Mt 19[12]) to the barbarous Oriental practice of mutilating individuals for certain purposes, we gather that the existence and purpose of eunuchs as a class were not unknown to the Jews of the time of Jesus. The religious disabilities under which men, deformed in this way, laboured, had the effect of

* Cf. J. Weiss, *op. cit.* i. 1, p. 172 ff.

making the practice (. . . εὐνουχίσθησαν ὑπὸ τῶν ἀνθρώπων) abominable to the Jews (Dt 23[1]; cf. Lv 22[23-25]). On the other hand, Josephus informs us that eunuchs were a normal feature of the courts of the Herods; and from him we also learn what share they were at that time supposed to have taken in the family intrigues (*Ant.* xv. vii. 4), and what base purposes they often subserved (*Ant.* XVI. viii. 1).

The passage containing the reference to eunuchs is peculiar to St. Matthew, and seems to be added to the Markan section, which deals with the question of divorce (Mk 10[2-12]=Mt 19[3-9]), from a source unknown to the author of the latter (see Tischendorf's *Synopsis Evangelica*[7], § 113, 'Interrogantibus de Repudio respondet'; and Wright's *Synopsis of the Gospels in Greek*, 'Anonymous Fragments,' p. 267). The remark made by the disciples touching the difficulties arising out of Jesus' interpretation of the law of marriage, shows the widespread influence of the lax teaching on this subject characteristic of the school of Hillel (see art. ADULTERY, p. 30[a]).

It matters not for our purpose whether in the reply of Jesus τὸν λόγον (v.[11]) be connected with οὐ συμφέρει γαμῆσαι (v.[10]), or, which is more intelligible to the present writer in the light of what follows, with the primal law quoted in v.[5] (ἕνεκα τούτου . . . οἱ δύο εἰς σάρκα μίαν). All men are not in a position to accept a hard and fast rule. Men are constituted differently by nature, or adventitious circumstances produce artificial dissimilarities. There is no question as to the law of nature. The married life is the norm of man's condition; and the union effected thereby transcends every other natural bond, even that of filial affection. At the same time, Jesus would have His hearers understand that there are cases, and these numerous enough to be taken seriously into account, where the rule does not hold. It is not granted * to every man to be in a position to fulfil the functions of the married state. Here it is of interest to note that Jesus, in speaking of three classes of 'eunuchs,' was making a distinction well known to those He was addressing. Moreover, the metaphorical use of the word in speaking of the third class finds also its place in the language of the Jewish Rabbins סְרִיס חַמָּה, סְרִיס אָדָם, סְרִים בִּידֵי שָׁמַיִם, cf. Lightfoot's *Horæ Heb. et Talmud.*, and Schöttgen's *Horæ Heb., in loc.*).

The well-known case of Origen, who literally emasculated himself 'for the kingdom of heaven's sake,' to which he afterwards seems to make pathetic, though incidental, reference in his commentary (*in Matt.* tom. xv. 1 ff.), was not the only example of a perverted interpretation of these words of Jesus. The Talmudic tractate *Shabbath* (152a) contains a reference to a eunuch of this class (cf. Midrash on Ec 10[7]), and the Council of Nicæa (c. 1) felt called on to deal with the danger, as did also the *Apostolical Canons* (c. 21), and the Second Council of Arles (c. 7). The common sense which thus prevailed amongst the guiding spirits of the Church is enhanced when we remember that the disabilities attaching to self-mutilation had no reference to those who were eunuchs from their mother's womb, or who 'were made eunuchs by men' (see for examples of both, Eusebius, *HE* vii. 32; Socrates, *HE* vi. 15; Sozomen, *HE* viii. 24; cf. Bingham's *Ant.* iv. 9).

It is not without significance that in the conversation of Jesus with His disciples no mention is made of any word of condemnation by Him of the horrible practice of emasculation. The complete lack of the sense of the dignity of human life, so characteristic of the ancient world, and the absence of the feeling of human brotherhood, found expression in no more terrible way than in this consequence of the laws of slavery. Yet Jesus refers directly neither to the institution of slavery nor to this, its result. He prefers the plan of instilling principles which lead by the processes of thought and application to the recognition that God hath 'made of one (ἐξ ἑνός) every nation of men for to dwell on all the face of the earth' (Ac 17[26]; cf. Lk 10[29ff.] 4[25ff.], Mt 8[11]=Lk 13[29]). It is as if He had an unconquerable belief in the power of the human mind ultimately to accept the truth, and to reject, finally and for ever, what has been false, in its provisional solutions of life's problems.

And as it was with His treatment of this form of cruelty practised by the strong upon the helpless, so it was with the mutilation of the body self-inflicted for so-called religious purposes. To the present writer it seems probable that Jesus made a conscious and deliberate reference to this practice (see Driver's 'Deuteronomy' in *Internat. Crit. Com.* on Dt 23[1]). Here, too, there is no condemnation expressed of an inadequate and artificial method which was the outcome of a legalistic conception of moral purity. It is rather by His positive teaching on the subject of purity that we are led to understand (ὁ δυνάμενος χωρεῖν χωρείτω) what are the lines along which we must move in order to reach the goal of perfect self-renunciation. There is another and a more excellent way of obtaining the mastery of the sexual passion than by literally 'cutting off' the offending fleshly member (cf. Mt 5[28f.] where the words βλέπων and ὀφθαλμός point to the radical character of the treatment insisted on by Jesus). The peculiarity about His method of treating this particular question is its loving cautiousness. It is not possible for all, but it is possible for some, to obtain as complete an ascendency over this strong instinct as if they were physically sexless; while, of course, the resultant moral victory is of infinitely more value than the merely negative, unmoral condition produced by self-emasculation. Those who adopt His method 'make themselves eunuchs' with a definite purpose in view (διὰ τὴν βασιλείαν τῶν οὐρανῶν), and the interests which are created by that purpose are so absorbing that neither time nor opportunity is given to the 'fleshly lusts which war against the soul' (1 P 2[11]).

The clear and definite teaching of Jesus on the subject of marriage will help to elucidate the words under review. The Divine idea (ὥστε οὐκέτι εἰσὶν δύο ἀλλὰ μία σάρξ, Mk 10[8]), on which He laid special stress, involves mutual effort and restraint. It is not possible but that even under the most favourable circumstances duties will arise which will prove irksome, and not less so because they are peculiar to the married state. Indeed, the Hebraistic ἔσονται εἰς (Heb. לְ הָיָה) emphasizes the truth that perfect union does not follow at once on the consummation of marriage. It is a gradual process, and, because it is so, it involves some amount of mutual self-abnegation. The cares and responsibilities which follow in the wake of those who are married necessarily mean absorption both of time and attention which may clash with the work given to some to do (cf. 1 Co 7[33f.]). It is for this reason that these find themselves debarred from ever undertaking the duties attaching to marriage. They voluntarily undertake eunuchism because they are completely immersed in, and engrossed by, the work of 'the kingdom of heaven.' There is no need to suppose, as Keim does, that Jesus is here deliberately referring to Himself and to the Baptist. At the same time, we are able to see in His life the highest expression of that 'blessed eunuchism' (Bengel, *Gnomon of the NT, in loc.*) which renounced all earthly ties for the sake of the work He was given to do * (cf. Jn 17[4]);

* The Lewis-Gibson Syriac Palimpsest adds 'by God.'

* See Clem. Alex. *Strom.* iii. § 1 ff.

and if St. Paul, in view of a stern emergency, felt justified in enjoining upon even the married the necessity of adopting this condition (see 1 Co 7²⁹), we know that he was speaking from the plane on which he himself stood (cf. 1 Co 9⁵ 7⁷ᶠ·). At the same time, the apparent harshness of his asceticism is softened by his repeated expressions of regard for the gift peculiar to each (ἴδιον χάρισμα). See, further, art. MARRIAGE.

LITERATURE. — *Ency. Brit.*⁹ art. 'Eunuch'; Neander, *Ch. Hist.* [Clark's ed.] ii. 493; Morison, *Com. on Mt. in loc.*; Wendt, *Teaching of Jesus*, ii. 72 ff.; *Expositor*, IV. vii. [1893] 294 ff.

J. R. WILLIS.

EVANGELIST.—Although the word 'evangelist' (εὐαγγελιστής) does not occur in the Gospels, it justly finds a place in this work because it is the name commonly given to the authors of the four Gospels. The verb εὐαγγελίζεσθαι, from which the substantive 'evangelist' is derived, signifies *to proclaim good tidings.* The corresponding verbs in Hebrew and Aramaic (Dalman, *NHWB, s.v.* בשׂר, *Words of Jesus*, 103) sometimes bear only the meaning 'announce,' but their prevailing import is to announce *good tidings.* There is no reason to doubt that the Aramaic word or words used by our Lord concerning His message to mankind described it as the proclamation of good news. Hence in Christian circles the term acquired the specific sense of announcing the gospel. The word 'evangelist' is not found in classical Greek or in the LXX, nor has it as yet been found in any papyri. So far as our present knowledge goes, it belongs only to the NT and to ecclesiastical Greek. It is used thrice in the NT, and in none of the instances is its meaning doubtful. It is applied to Philip (Ac 21⁸), either because of the labours described in Ac 8, or because he belonged to a class or order of Christian labourers whose function was to go abroad proclaiming the gospel to those who had not heard it. In the Epistle to the Ephesians, 'evangelists' are mentioned (4¹¹) as an order or class, after the Apostles and prophets, and before pastors and teachers. Here, too, the most probable view is that those spoken of were missionary preachers. Again, Timothy is charged by St. Paul (2 Ti 4⁵) to 'do the work of an evangelist.' Whether Timothy is here called an evangelist is open to discussion, but the nature of the work he is bidden to perform is clear: he is to visit new communities in order to preach the gospel to them. The force of the word suggested by its etymology is, therefore, the meaning attaching to it in the three passages of the NT where it is found. This is the view of all modern scholars of any note. Some of the Greek expositors, misled by the usage of their own time, assigned, at least to the passage in Ephesians, the sense which it came to bear subsequent to NT times, that of author or writer of a Gospel; but this interpretation has no supporters to-day.

How did this second sense arise? Can any links of connexion be traced between the earlier and the later signification? Is it possible to ascertain the time at which the later usage began? These questions are best answered by studying the references to the term in the *Church History* of Eusebius. It is obvious at once that Eusebius had two senses of the word before him; that he knew that its original import was a preacher of the gospel, but that this meaning had been largely displaced by another, that of a writer of a Gospel. Speaking generally, the Church in the age of Eusebius understood by the word 'evangelist' the writer of a Gospel, though scholars like Eusebius himself were aware that in earlier times it had borne another meaning. Accordingly the references of Eusebius to the original force of the term are all associated with the earlier history of the Church. Thus he relates that the Apostle Thomas sent Thaddæus to Edessa

as a preacher and evangelist of the teaching of Christ (*HE* I. xiii. 4). Again he speaks of those who in the age of Trajan started out on long journeys and performed the office of an evangelist, filled with the desire to preach Christ to those who had not heard the word of faith, and to deliver to them the Divine Gospels (III. xxxvii. 2). Once more, he tells that Pantænus was a herald of the gospel of Christ to the nations of the East, and that he was sent as far as India. For, he adds, there were still many evangelists of the word who sought earnestly to use their inspired zeal, after the example of the Apostles, for the building up of the Divine word (V. x. 2). In all these passages 'evangelist' evidently denotes an itinerant preacher of the gospel. On the other hand, when Eusebius names John the evangelist (III. xxxix. 5), he is speaking of him as the author of the Gospel, and the reference to the voice of the inspired evangelists and Apostles (II. iii. 1) is probably to be explained in the same sense. How then was the transition effected from the one of these significations to the other? How was the title transferred from a preacher to a writer? There are those who think that even from the first the term denoted not so much a travelling preacher in general as a preacher who set himself to relate the life and words of Jesus. Teaching and specific teaching regarding the addresses delivered by Jesus and the miracles He performed was a characteristic of the evangelist from the first, hence there is little difficulty in realizing how the title passed from those who related to those who wrote our Lord's life, the latter meaning being only the natural development of the former. Even a scholar like Meyer (in Ac 21⁸) affirms that the chief duty of the evangelist was to communicate to his hearers historical incidents from the ministry of Jesus, and some later writers of all schools have embraced the same view. It is believed to be corroborated by the language just quoted from Eusebius regarding the distribution of the written Gospels by evangelists. But there is nothing to show that the first evangelists of the Church made special use of the facts of our Lord's life, and that their teaching or preaching differed in this respect from that of the Apostles. The wide acceptation in which the words 'evangel' and 'evangelize' are used in the NT is adverse to this conclusion. The earliest gospel was not the life of Jesus, but the message of salvation. To preach the gospel was necessarily to preach Jesus, but not to give any sketch of the life of Jesus such as is found in our four Gospels. Nor is the view probable in itself. A modern missionary relates the life of Jesus as he sees it expedient, but he does not make the communication of the details of that life to his hearers one of his chief duties. The same freedom was doubtless exercised in the earliest ages of the Church. One evangelist would tell less and another more of the life of Jesus as he preached. Even the same evangelist would vary the amount of detail he gave regarding the life and words of Jesus according to the varying needs of his hearers. Beyond all doubt most of the addresses delivered by the evangelists *were* largely occupied by an account of the career of Jesus, and especially of His sayings and His miracles; but this was true of every person who sought to propagate Christianity, and not distinctive of the evangelist as such. Further, it is difficult on this hypothesis to explain the fact that the original signification of 'evangelist' as a preacher was current long after the Gospels had obtained the fullest recognition within the Church. The evangelists carried the Gospels with them if they were fortunate enough to possess copies; they referred to the Gospels as the authorities for the life of Jesus, yet they retained their title. There is no evidence that the later meaning drove out the earlier so long as the Church possessed evangelists or called them by this name. Undoubtedly the two meanings flourished side by side for a time.

If this argument is sound, the origin of the later import of the term must be sought in another quarter. That quarter is not remote. The Church possessed from early days four narratives of our Lord's life, and to these first the term 'Gospel' and subsequently its plural 'Gospels' was applied. It was necessary to refer to these writings individually, hence there arose the practice of speaking of the Gospel according to Matthew and the like: Matthew being regarded as the author of the Gospel bearing his name. Very soon it became necessary to find a term to serve as a common designation of the writers of the Gospels. No more suitable word for this purpose could be found than 'evangelist.' It was already in use in the Church; it stood in the closest affinity to the word 'evangel' or 'gospel,' which had acquired by this time its new sense of a written work, and the term once applied proved so useful that it immediately became popular. Just as the term 'gospel,' which denoted a spoken message, an announcement of good news, the Christian good news, was current long before the written books called Gospels existed, and nevertheless gave its name to them, so also was it with the term 'evangelist.' By a similar transition it became the designation of the writers of the Gospels. After the word 'Gospel' was used to denote a written narrative of the life of Jesus, the extension of the meaning of the word 'evangelist' to designate the author of such a work was only a question of time.

Is it possible to ascertain the date at which the term was first used in this specific sense? The evidence at present available shows that it was thus employed by Hippolytus and by Tertullian. The first occurrence of the word is in the *de Antichr.* of Hippolytus (56), where St. Luke is spoken of as 'the Evangelist.' The generally accepted date of this treatise is about the year 201 (Harnack, *Chronol.* ii. 214; Bardenhewer, *Altkirch. Lit.* ii. 521). Tertullian in his *adv. Prax.*, which has been assigned to the years 213–218 (Bardenhewer, ii. 368; Harnack, ii. 286), speaks of 'the preface of John the Evangelist' (21, cf. 23). This evidence shows that towards the beginning of the 3rd cent. the term was used to denote the authors of the Gospels. The incidental manner in which both writers employ the word suggests that its use was not new. But this inference is precarious, and it is possible that Hippolytus was the first to employ it, and that Tertullian imitated his example and gave it a Latin form. The absence of the word from the opening chapters of the third Book of Irenæus will appear to some to confirm the opinion that the use of the term is later than his time, but the proper conclusion is that a decisive verdict is impossible. All that can be affirmed with confidence is that, as the term 'Gospels' was admittedly used in the plural in the time of Justin Martyr (*Ap.* i. 66), the employment of the term 'evangelist' to describe the author of a Gospel could have begun in his age, but that the first occurrence of the word is half a century later.

In dealing with the topic 'Evangelist,' it is desirable to add a brief notice of the animal symbols by which the Gospels are designated. This symbolism makes no appeal to us to-day, but it enters so largely into early Christian art and poetry that some acquaintance with it is necessary. The symbolism is founded on the description of the four living creatures in the Apocalypse (4[7]). The first creature is stated to have been like a lion, the second like a calf, the third had the face of a man, the fourth was like a flying eagle. It occurred to Irenæus to compare, if not identify, these with the four Gospels, and it was therefore necessary for him to ascribe a particular symbol to each of the Evangelists. To him John is the lion, Luke the calf, Matthew the man, and Mark the eagle (*Hær.* III. xi. 11). The mode of illustration pursued by Irenæus strikes us to-day as forced and profitless, but the example he set was followed by Hippolytus (*Hipp.* I. ii. 183, Berlin ed.; cf. Bardenhewer, *Altkirch. Lit.* ii. 532). In a Syriac fragment he repeats the comparison, but advances an interpretation of his own. Now the lion is Matthew, the calf Luke, the man Mark, and the eagle John. The symbolism spread throughout the Church, but there was no agreement as to the connexion between the different living creatures and the separate Evangelists. However, the authority of Jerome (*Preface to Matthew*), despite the divergent opinion of Augustine (*Cons. Ev.* i. 6), prevailed throughout the West, and furnished the interpretation which is best known, as most largely represented in Christian art, and as embodied in the noble hymn of Adam of St. Victor, 'Psallat chorus corde mundo' (Trench, *Sacred Latin Poetry*, 67). According to this view, St. Matthew is the man, St. Mark the lion, St. Luke the calf, and St. John the eagle.

LITERATURE.—Commentaries on the NT passages; art. 'Evangelist' in Hastings' *DB*; works on the organization and history of the Early Church; Suicer, *s.v.*; Zahn, 'Die Tiersymbole der Evangelisten' in *Forschungen*, ii.; art. 'Evangelists' in *Dict. of Christian Antiquities*; Farrar, *Messages of the Books*, 13.

W. PATRICK.

EVENING (ἡ ὀψία [*sc.* ὥρα], ἑσπέρα).—The Babylonians divided the day into equal parts by sun-watches. The 'sixty system' of minutes and seconds was in vogue among them. Among Syrian peoples also, it is likely, the same system prevailed. No trace of this is found among the Israelites, however, in the pre-exilic period. Another marked difference between the Babylonians and the Israelites is noteworthy. With the Israelites the day began at sunset, with the Babylonians at sunrise. It is at least certain that the reckoning from eve to eve became the exclusive method in Israel with the triumph of the Law. A kindred system prevailed among Arabs, Athenians, and Gauls (Pliny, *HN* ii. 79). It was customary, too, in ancient Israel to distinguish between the 'first evening' and the 'second evening.' It is not certain just where they drew the line (Edersheim). The phrase 'between the two evenings' (bên hā'arbayim), Ex 16[12] 29[39], as a designation of the time of the daily evening offerings, clearly meant some period in the late afternoon. The 'first evening,' it is generally thought, began about 3 p.m. and extended to sunset; the second began at sunset and continued into the night.

In Mt 14[15. 23] we have the word 'evening' used in both senses. 'When it was evening' (v.[15]) clearly refers to the first evening (cf. Lk 9[12] 'and the day began to decline,' Bible Union Ver.). For when the disciples suggested that Jesus send the multitude away, that they might go into the villages and buy themselves food, Jesus said they need not depart; and the feeding of the five thousand and the sending away of the multitude followed before 'he went up into the mountain apart to pray.' Then a second evening is spoken of in the words: 'And when the evening was come, he was there alone' (v.[23]). In the latter case, Jesus, after seeing His disciples off (Jn 6[15]), evidently sought the mountain solitude, as He did on other occasions, to spend much of the night in prayer (v.[25]). This second evening, then, was evidently verging on the night.   GEO. B. EAGER.

EVIL.—It is customary to distinguish three

kinds of evil: (1) what Leibnitz called *metaphysical evil*, *i.e.* the incompleteness and imperfection which belong more or less to all created things ; (2) *physical evil*, *i.e.* pain, suffering, and death ; and (3) *moral evil*, which is a vicious choice of a morally responsible being.

1. METAPHYSICAL EVIL.—The writers of the OT were, for the most part, deeply impressed with the doctrine of God's transcendence ; *i.e.* His unique and unapproachable majesty, power, and holiness. Hence the nothingness and transitoriness of all earthly and visible things are a constant theme with them : 'Behold, heaven and the heaven of heavens cannot contain thee,' etc. (1 K 8²⁷) ; 'What is man that thou art mindful of him?' etc. (Ps 8⁴) ; 'All flesh is grass,' etc. (Is 40⁶) ; 'The inhabitants of the earth are as grasshoppers' (v.²²). Compared with God's ineffable holiness, the holiest of created beings are, as it were, unclean. In heaven the holy angels veil their faces in God's presence (Is 6²). The holy sanctuary of Israel required to be purged every year from its pollutions by the blood of sacrifices (Lv 16¹⁶). All human righteousnesses are as a polluted garment (Is 64⁶).

In the NT there is naturally less stress laid upon the Divine transcendence. The theme of the NT writers is the love of God shown in the Incarnation. The eternal Son of God has taken upon Him human nature, to raise it into fellowship with God, to clothe it with the garment of the Divine righteousness, and to cause it to partake of the Divine immortality. Yet the awful and unapproachable character of God, and the infinite abyss which separates the Creator from the highest creature, are never lost sight of. He alone is the Absolute Good (Mk 10¹⁸) ; He alone may lawfully be worshipped (Mk 12²⁹· ³², Rev 19¹⁰).

2. PHYSICAL EVIL.—(1) *Optimism and pessimism.*—Christianity may be classed philosophically as a moderate optimism. It is not an extravagant optimism, like that of Leibnitz, who maintained that this is the best of all possible worlds, or of Malebranche, who regarded it as the best conceivable. Christ would certainly not have endorsed the hyperboles of Pope, that all discord is harmony not understood, and all partial evil universal good ; yet He must certainly be classed among the most pronounced teachers of optimism. As against all forms of Gnosticism and Dualism, He maintained that the Universe, in all its parts, is the work of a perfectly good Creator, and that, in spite of all appearances to the contrary, it is under the guidance of His fatherly Providence : 'Behold the fowls of the air,' etc. (Mt 6²⁶) ; 'Are not two sparrows sold for a farthing?' etc. (Mt 10²⁹) ; 'He maketh his sun to rise on the evil and on the good,' etc. (Mt 5⁴⁵). The optimism of Jesus is particularly evident in His eschatology. He taught that in the end good will triumph over evil, and evil be absolutely excluded from the Universe : 'In the end of the world the Son of man shall send forth his angels,' etc. (Mt 13⁴¹, cf. 24³¹ 25³⁰· ⁴¹). He believed that there is a glorious goal to which the whole creation is moving. In one passage He calls it Creation's *new birth* (παλινγενεσία, Mt 19²⁸) ; but His usual term for it is the 'Kingdom of God' (or of Heaven) : 'Then shall the righteous shine forth as the sun in the kingdom of their Father' (Mt 13⁴³). For the coming of this Kingdom every Christian is directed to pray (Mt 6¹⁰) and to watch (24⁴² 25¹³). That the material Universe will be glorified along with the spiritual is not distinctly stated by Jesus, but is a necessary inference from the doctrine of the resurrection of *the body*, which was undoubtedly held by Him (Mt 5²⁹ 10²⁸ etc.), though in a more spiritual form than was generally current (22³⁰).

(2) *Pain, sorrow, disease, and death.* — The Gospels lend no countenance to the view that moral evil is the only genuine evil, and that physical evil is not evil in the strict and proper sense. Pain, sorrow, disease, and death were regarded by Jesus as things which ought not to be, and He spent much of the time of His public ministry in combating them : 'He went about doing good, and healing all that were oppressed with the devil : for God was with him' (Ac 10³⁸). He committed the ministry of healing to the Apostles and other believers : 'Preach, saying, The kingdom of heaven is at hand. Heal the sick, raise the dead, cleanse the lepers, cast out devils ; freely ye have received, freely give' (Mt 10⁷). Death was regarded by Jesus as in an especial sense 'the enemy.' Its ravages affected Him with acute distress (ἐνεβριμήσατο τῷ πνεύματι καὶ ἐτάραξεν ἑαυτόν . . . ἐδάκρυσεν, Jn 11³³ff·, where consult the commentators). Three of His most striking recorded miracles were victories over death (Mk 5⁴¹, Lk 7¹⁴, Jn 11⁴³) ; and His own resurrection, according to the energetic expression of the Apostle, 'abolished death, and brought life and incorruption to light' (2 Ti 1¹⁰).

As to the causation of physical evil, there is a great difference of point of view between the OT and the NT. The OT upon the whole (Job 1. 2. is an exception) regards physical evil as inflicted directly by God. According to the NT, however, physical evil is mainly the work of the devil. God tolerates, permits, and overrules, rather than directly inflicts it. Pain and disease and death belong to the devil's kingdom, not to God's ; and their universal prevalence is a sign of the usurped authority over the human race of 'the prince of this world.' The preaching of the Kingdom of God and the emancipation of mankind from the devil's thraldom were consequently accompanied by an extensive ministry of healing, and Christ appealed to His miracles as evidence that 'the kingdom of God is come upon you' (Lk 11²⁰). The NT does not, however, deny that physical evil is often inflicted by God for disciplinary or retributive purposes. He 12⁶ lays especial stress upon the wholesome chastening of affliction which all the sons of God receive. Examples of penal or retributive affliction are Mt 9² (palsy), Mt 23³⁵ (war and massacre), Jn 5¹⁴ (constitutional infirmity), Ac 5⁵ (death), Ac 13¹¹ (blindness). Jesus, however, strongly protested against the idea that every calamity is to be regarded as a punishment for individual sin. This specially Jewish idea, which Eliphaz, Bildad, and Zophar develop at length in the Book of Job, is definitely condemned (Lk 13⁴, Jn 9³).

3. MORAL EVIL.—(1) *Its nature and origin.*—The only possible way of accounting for moral evil without making God the author of it, is to attribute it to the abuse of free will on the part of created beings, angelic, or human, or both. The doctrine of free will has been severely criticised in all ages by the advocates of philosophical and theological necessity ; but it has, notwithstanding, held its ground, and is at the present time the faith of all the most progressive races of mankind. That it was held by Jesus does not admit of reasonable doubt. Thus He habitually spoke of the power which men possess to resist God and to frustrate His benevolent intentions : 'O Jerusalem, Jerusalem, . . . how often would I (ἠθέλησα) . . . and ye would not' (καὶ οὐκ ἠθελήσατε, Lk 13³⁴ ; cf. Jn 5⁴⁰, Mt 11²⁰ff·). His general invitations to *all men* to be saved imply the same doctrine : 'Come unto me, *all* ye that labour and are heavy laden, and I will give you rest' (Mt 11²⁸) ; 'And I, if I be lifted up from the earth, will draw *all men* unto myself' (Jn 12³²).

The reality of Christ's Libertarianism is not disproved by certain passages in the Gospels which seem at first sight to speak the language of Predestination, or even of Determinism

(Jn 6³⁷·³⁹, Mt 26²⁴ etc.). Predestination was not so held in Christ's time as to exclude free will. Josephus says of the Pharisees : ' When they say that all things happen by fate, they do not take away from men the freedom of acting as they think fit ; since their notion is that it hath pleased God to mix up the decrees of fate and man's will, so that man can act virtuously and viciously' (*Ant.* xviii. i. 3).

Jesus accordingly attributed the origin of evil not to the will of God, but to the perversity of God's creatures. Mankind, according to Him, is in rebellion against God ; but the whole guilt of rebellion is not his. Before man existed, there were myriads of finite spirits, higher in the order of creation than he, and of these some fell from their original innocence and became devils. The chief of these, Satan, is ever seeking to seduce the human race from its allegiance to its Creator, and is therefore emphatically called ' the tempter' (ὁ πειράζων, Mt 4³, 1 Th 3⁵), and the slayer of men (ἀνθρωποκτόνος, Jn 8⁴⁴). This last is the one certain allusion to the fall of Satan to be found in the Gospels (Lk 10¹⁸ is doubtful). From it we learn that he once existed in a state of innocence (ἐν τῇ ἀληθείᾳ), but did not persist in it (reading οὐκ ἔστηκεν with WH).

The position of Satan in the Universe is so exalted, and the power ascribed to him in the NT so great (cf. esp. Mt 4⁸, Jn 14³⁰), that some have regarded Jesus as a *Dualist.* But the authority attributed to Satan in the NT, though great, is subordinate. The devils recognize the power of Jesus, and come out at His word (Mk 1²⁴·³⁴ 3¹¹ etc.). If Satan is ' the strong man,' there is a Stronger, who can bind him and spoil his goods (Mt 12²⁹). At the Temptation the devil acknowledged that his power is a delegated one (ἐμοὶ παραδίδοται, Lk 4⁶). His kingdom will surely come to an end ; in fact its fall has already been virtually secured by the Passion and Resurrection of Jesus (Jn 12³¹). His final punishment has been determined, and it will be fully adequate to his delinquency (Mt 25⁴¹).

(2) *Original sin.*—There is no recorded teaching of Jesus about original sin. He recognized the fall of man (Jn 8⁴⁴), and the general sinfulness of the human race (Mt 7¹¹) ; but how He connected these two facts does not appear. It may, perhaps, be argued from Jn 9¹⁻³, that He would not have approved of any theory of original sin which regarded men as obnoxious to punishment from God merely because of an ancestral taint that they could not help inheriting. See, further, artt. SIN and ETERNAL PUNISHMENT.

LITERATURE.—Athanasius, *contra Gentes* ; Augustine, *Antipelagian Treatises*, etc. ; Origen, *de Principiis* (esp. i. 5, 6) ; J. Müller, *The Christian Doctrine of Sin* (tr.) ; Momerie, *The Origin of Evil* ; Naville, *The Problem of Evil* (tr.) ; Butler, *Analogy* ; Le Conte, *Evolution*, ix. ; Fairbairn, *The Philosophy of the Christian Religion*, i. 3, 4 : Tennant, *The Origin and Propagation of Sin*, and *The Fall and Original Sin* ; Bull, *The State of Man before the Fall* ; Paley, *Natural Theology*, xxvi. ; Harris, *pro Fide*, xiv ; A. Moore, *Science and the Faith*, and *Essays*, i., iii., and *Oxford House Papers*, vol. ii. ; artt. 'Sin' and 'Fall' in Hastings' *DB* ; Dixie, 'The Necessity of Pain' in *Oxford House Papers* ; E. A. Abbott, *The Kernel and the Husk*, ix. ; S. Laing, *A Modern Zoroastrian.* The subject is discussed in most systematic treatises on theology, ethics, and metaphysics.

C. HARRIS.

EVIL ONE. — See preced. art. and LORD'S PRAYER and SATAN.

EVIL SPIRIT.—See DEMON.

EVOLUTION (CHRIST AND).—The widespread acceptance of the Evolutionary philosophy, and the endeavours of its leading exponents to include the phenomena of religion within the sweep of its categories, have greatly accentuated the problem of the place of the Incarnation in the cosmic order, and of Jesus Christ, His Person, His work, and His redemptive function, in human history.

1. *The basis of discussion.*—At the outset we must distinguish sharply between the Materialistic type of the Evolutionary philosophy on the one hand, and the Theistic type on the other. The former may be described as including all efforts to explain the highest phenomena of the cosmos—in-cluding those of life, consciousness, and all forms of spiritual activity—in terms of mechanical motion and force. Such a philosophy rules out all recognition of the Divine Personality, of the possible independence of mind over matter, of the ethical responsibility and free spiritual activity of man, and of his capacity for immortal life. This disposes of the problem of the Incarnation as irrelevant, and throws us back on a purely 'naturalistic' explanation of the Person and life of Jesus Christ. The Theistic type of the Evolutionary philosophy, however—the central idea of which is that the goal of Evolution and not its beginnings provides us with the principle of cosmic interpretation, and that spirit and not matter furnishes the key to the riddle of the Universe—leaves us free to deal with the Supreme Person and Fact of history with open minds. Theism presents us with a conception of God as immanent in the Universe, but not as imprisoned within its material or psychical manifestations ; as transcendent, living a free, self-determined life in virtue of His own eternal Being, yet not separated from the forces and phenomena of the cosmos, which are manifestations of His creative activity and expanding purpose. It also presents us with a conception of man as a created but free spiritual person, physically a part of nature, but ethically above it, and capable of coming into conscious personal relations with his Creator.

2. *Theistic theory of Evolution compatible with a process of Incarnation.*—It is manifest that the idea of Incarnation is not *a priori* incompatible with such a philosophy of God and man. It represents the Universe as God realizing His creative purpose ; impersonally in Nature, personally in Man. Creation awakes in man to the sense of its own origin and the possibility of its own consummation in a life of free spiritual communion with God. Incarnation means that this fellowship is actually sought after and objectively consummated by an act of self-realization on the part of God. It implies the special compatibility of the Divine nature and the human personality. ' God is, as it were, the eternal possibility of being incarnated, man the permanent capability of incarnation.' ' The nature that is in all men akin to Deity becomes in Christ a nature in personal union with the Deity, and the *unio personalis*, which is peculiar to Him, is the basis of the *unio mystica*, which is possible to all ' (Fairbairn, *Christ in Modern Theology*, pp. 473, 475 ; see also Clarke's *Outline of Christian Theology*, p. 275).

3. *The Person and work of Christ in such a theory.*—The historical realization of this possibility of Incarnation in Jesus of Nazareth raises the further question of His place in a philosophy of history, and in Christian theology. The Christian contention is that in Him the Evolutionary process finds its consummation on the one side— He was the Ideal Man made actual ; and that a fresh Evolutionary start was made by the fusion of the Divine and human natures in Him on the other—He was the Son of God Incarnate, 'manifested to take away sin' (1 Jn 3⁵), and to project the race on the lines of its true development and life, which had been interrupted and swerved aside by the intrusion of sin into the world. This conception of the Person and work of Christ, while it falls into line with the Evolutionary idea in one direction, appears to fall foul of it in another, because of the claim it makes that there was in the nature of Christ an incommensurable factor, incapable of being explained by the laws of organic life, or by human psychology,—manifesting itself in a-life of unique goodness and power, begun by a free special act of God in the Virgin-birth, and consummated by the objective Resurrection of our Lord from the dead.

This difficulty, however, on deeper consideration is not incompatible with a wider view of the Evolutionary process. There were several stages in the known pathway of the upward movement from the star mist, in which the process began, to man, in whom terrestrial evolution finds its consummation, when fresh phenomena appeared which cannot be explained in terms of those that preceded ; *e.g.* at the emergence of organic life, of sentiency, and of ethical self-consciousness. So far, no rational bridge of theory has been found to span the gap between these diverse facts. It is, therefore, not unthinkable that there was in the Person of our Lord a superhuman element, which in Him mingled with the stream of human life, and started a fresh and higher line of evolution for the race. The question whether this was so in point of actual fact is thus purely one of evidence, and, if historically substantiated, must be accepted, whether we are able ultimately to 'account' for it theoretically or not. Our canons of Evolution must make room for all the facts of life and history, or be finally discredited as inadequate and obscurantist.

4. *Jesus Christ not explicable on naturalistic grounds.*—It is certain also that, so far, the innumerable efforts which have been put forth during the past century, from almost every conceivable point of view, to give a naturalistic explanation of the life and Person of Jesus Christ, have not, in whole or in part, disposed of this problem. There is no single theory or combination of theories which meets with general acceptance, even among those who take up a purely critical attitude ; and when we confront them with the Christian consciousness which is the historical outcome of faith in the Divine nature and mission and work of Christ, they fail utterly to carry conviction. (This last fact has so far not had its true place in the settlement of the problem). The Personality of Jesus Christ is thus still the unsolved problem of history, and it is more than doubtful if any fresh treatment of the question will succeed in bringing Him within the categories of an Agnostic Evolutionary Philosophy.

5. *Cur Deus Homo ?*—The Theistic Evolutionist has next to face the old question of the purpose and aim of the Incarnation in the cosmic order. 'Cur Deus Homo?' becomes a more burning question than ever in a scheme of Evolutionary thought. Two hypotheses present themselves, according as we take an *a priori* or *a posteriori* standpoint, which may be called the *Evolutionary* and the *Redemptive*. The first makes the Christ the consummation and crown of the process of cosmic Evolution, and postulates the Incarnation as its necessary climax ; the second occupies the old standpoint of Christian theology from the beginning, that, whether the Incarnation lay implicit or not in the process, it was historically conditioned by the fact of the sinful and 'fallen' state of humanity. The two views are not incompatible with one another, and both in combination are quite consistent with the teaching of Scripture. The upward striving of humanity for union with its Creator as personal finds its historical witness in (1) the universal function of worship, prayer, and sacrifice, and (2) the Hebrew prophetic vision of the Ideal Servant of Jehovah, and the Messianic hope ; and it suggests, as God is personal, a corresponding act of self-revelation in a historical Person who would unite in himself the human aspiration and the Divine manifestation ; while the gradual revelation consummated in the coming of Christ, and recorded in the Old and New Testaments; is in line with all the known laws of God's evolutionary methods. On the other hand, it is unquestionable that the Scripture doctrine of the Incarnation is indissolubly associated with the

redemptive purpose of God. This is its historical aim and character : 'He was manifested to take away sin' (1 Jn 3⁵, cf. 1 Co 5¹⁸· ¹⁹ etc.). While, therefore, we are justified on *a priori* grounds in believing that 'the Incarnation was no afterthought' (Dale, *Fellowship with Christ, and Other Sermons*, pp. 10, 252 f.), but that it would have taken place even if sin had not entered the world, the *form* which it took was historically conditioned by the actual condition of humanity ; *i.e.* it was soteriological in its manifestation.

6. *Three pregnant aspects of the historical Incarnation.*—More particularly, the significance of the historical Incarnation as a redemptive and perfective process may be described under three pregnant headings. It was (1) the realization of the perfect type of humanity—Christ as the Ideal Man ; (2) the achievement of a great restorative or saving work—Christ as the sufficient Saviour ; (3) the beginning of a fresh departure in the upward Life of the Race—Christ as the Founder and Head of His Church, and the source of the higher spiritual movements of history. These three aspects of His work are specially related to His human life as our great Exemplar ; to His Cross and Passion as our Sacrifice and Reconciler ; to His Resurrection and Ascension into the unseen world, and His influence through His Spirit on the individual and wider life of mankind.

(1) As the Ideal Man, Jesus revealed the possibilities and determined the type of perfect manhood for the race. This was done under special conditions, and at a given moment of time and place, race and environment. He was born in Palestine, during the reign of Herod, 'of the seed of David' (Ro 1³) ; *i.e.* He was a Jew, conforming to the special conditions and demands of His own times, and limited by the intellectual and social horizon of His day. There was much, therefore, in the outward life of Jesus which was temporary and local in its manifestations. Yet beneath all this we see a true revelation of the Perfect Man, universal in its scope, yet appealing to each individual man as his exemplar ; Ideal in its purity and holiness, yet throbbing with contagious life ; beyond the reach of literal imitation, yet quickening each of His followers to the realization of his own individual life and personality. Looked at from within, His life is depicted in the NT as one of perfect and joyous obedience to the Father's revealed will (Jn 5¹⁹), unbroken communion with Him (10³⁰), and supreme self-forgetfulness in the service of His brethren (2 Co 8⁹). Whatever transcendent elements may have been hidden (and sometimes patent) in the spiritual consciousness of Jesus, He is represented as truly temptable (Mt 4¹ etc.), as depending entirely on Divine help and grace for conquest over temptation (Jn 5¹⁹ etc.), and as having triumphed absolutely over evil, so that He was 'without sin' (He 4¹⁵). The impression left on those who knew Him best by this life of filial obedience and service was that it was of unique beauty and attractiveness (Jn 1¹⁴), and yet capable of emulation by all, under their own individual conditions of life and service (1 P 2²¹). And this NT picture of Jesus as the Ideal Man is one that the noblest minds of Christendom throughout the centuries have accepted. There is no historical character that has ever threatened to divide the sovereignty of Jesus in the spiritual homage of men ; and such 'detached' thinkers as Goethe and Carlyle, Strauss and Renan, Richter and Lecky have borne unqualified testimony to the solitary and unapproachable grandeur of the moral ideal incarnated in Him.

'*In the fulness of the time.*'—From the Evolutionary standpoint the question is often asked, whether such an ideal life must not necessarily have appeared as the consummation of the spiritual development of the race,—as the last link in the series. This *a priori* objection is of doubtful application, however, even in the lower ranges of organic life ; and as regards the self-conscious aspiring life of men, it is demonstrably lacking in cogency. Jesus, according to Scripture, appeared in the 'fulness' of the time, and at that precise moment in the order of history which enabled Him best to fulfil His mission (Gal 4⁴, He 1¹⁻⁴). The best minds of previous ages had been eagerly looking forward to a manifestation of the saving power of God (Mt 13¹⁷, Lk 24²⁵, Ac 3¹⁸, 1 P 1¹⁰ etc.), and, if the actual historical manifestation of the Messiah for whom they waited was not in accordance with their literal expectations, it was the true fulfilment of the spiritual movement of which their ideals and prophecies were a part. In Evolutionary language, the 'embryonic' Christ of prophecy became in due course the actual Christ of history, or, less figuratively, the dimly outlined Ideal Life of aspiration took objective form in the manifested life of the Son of God. Or, we may say that the right time for an ideal to be actualized in the life of humanity would be, at that precise moment when the capacity for conceiving and recognizing an ideal had been sufficiently developed to appreciate it. Before this, it would be wasted ; later, it would have been belated ; and Jesus came and embodied the Ideal Life just when humanity was capable of profiting by it, and of being stirred by it into higher aspiration and endeavour.

(2) The Redemptive work of Christ finds its place in an Evolutionary scheme of thought on cognate lines. It presupposes that a lapse, or at least a fatal halt, had occurred in the upward spiritual development of the race, and that all further progress was barred by the poisoning of the wells of progress by sin (see FALL). Before humanity could be released from this disability, which had interfered with the free interflow of the Divine and human fellowship, in the unrestricted action of which alone the spiritual life of man can develop, a process of reconciliation and at-one-ment with the source of the spiritual Life must be initiated. Apart from this, the presentation of an Ideal Life would be a mockery, for its realization would be impossible. Thus, as already stated, the historical Incarnation took a redemptive form, and it was consummated by an act of supreme sacrifice.

The process of 'progress by sacrifice' (see Bruce's *Providential Order*, ch. xii. p. 345 ff.) is deeply embedded in the organic world. The so-called cruel Law of *Natural Selection* is but another name for a rudimentary fact which finds its finest and most perfect realization in the Cross of Christ. In nature we find three grades or stages of this process. (1) The sacrifice of the weak for the strong, as when those creatures in every species which are ill-adapted for the propagation of their kind are elbowed out of existence by the vitally strong and efficient, and made 'subservient to another's good' in the way of food. (2) The sacrifice of the strong for the weak, exemplified in the action of the imperious parental instinct which is manifested by every living species above the very lowest, and which gradually increases in its range and its delicacy till it arrives through the higher mammals at man. Here there is more or less conscious self-denial on the part of the vigorous and capable organism on behalf of the helpless and the weak. (3) The sacrifice of the good for the bad, a fact manifested (in the necessity of things) only among ethical persons, and exemplified throughout history as one of the most potent forces for the uplifting and perfecting of humanity. These various stages of the sacrificial element in Nature do not exhaust the meaning of the Redemption wrought through the Cross of Christ, which has a unique character of its own as an 'atonement'; but they serve to link it with the world-process, and to make it more or less evolutionally intelligible. (See further on this subject Griffith-Jones, *The Ascent through Christ*, bk. ii. ch. iii. pp. 283-306).

(3) The Risen Life of our Lord initiates the final stage in the spiritual evolution of the race, and completes the range of forces that work for the perfecting of the human soul in its upward march. The Resurrection and the Ascension indicate a fresh epoch in the history of mankind, both in the development of the individual soul and in the progress of society. A new type of character emerges, and a new community is born ; each marking a higher achievement and indicating a further advance in spiritual life. Historical Christianity rests on the faith that Jesus rose again and passed into the unseen world, whence He continues to send forth His personal influence and saving grace by His Spirit among believers, and through them into the world at large. This He does first by quickening individual men in the New Life,

enabling them to conquer sin, and to put forth the distinctive Christian virtues ; and, secondly, by the perpetual renewal and invigoration of the Christian society or Church, which is composed of those believers who join in brotherly love in the active service of mankind in the name of their spiritual Head. This new force has leavened and in a measure created modern Western civilization, and though it has so far not succeeded in permeating it through and through with the Christian spirit, it is demonstrable that its finest and most potent elements are those derived from the Christian Ideal and ennobled by the Christian graces. The slowness of the world's spiritual development along Christian lines is undeniable, it is marked by ages of stagnation and by periods of unmistakable reaction ; this, however, is entirely consistent with the laws of evolution through all its upward stages, and is inevitable when we remember the potent forces of spiritual degeneracy and inertia which oppose its march. It is clear that there is no rival directive or inspiring ideal among mankind that could take the place of Christianity without crying halt to all that is noblest in the life of the race. The future of the world lies with Christ, unless it is to fall back on a lower stage of ethical and spiritual development on its way to utter disintegration and decadence. Since the lines of cosmic development have so far been on the whole in an upward direction, and since there is no indication that the Christian ideal has lost its hold on the best minds of the race, or is less potent than formerly in regenerating individual souls and in inspiring the Church to ever fresh activity and influence, there is reason for confident belief that at last the race as a whole will be raised to the Christian level, and that the future is with Him of whom it is prophesied that He shall reign in undisputed sway over the affections and command the obedience of all mankind (Ph 2⁹⁻¹¹, Rev 11¹⁵ etc.). See, further, art. INCARNATION.

LITERATURE.—Griffith-Jones, *Ascent through Christ*; Gore, Bampton Lectures on *The Incarnation*; H. Drummond, *Ascent of Man*.

E. GRIFFITH-JONES.

EXALTATION.—1. The general sentiment that the lowly in heart alone receive the true exaltation, is exceedingly prominent in both the Old and New Testaments. The life of Christ was throughout one of self-humbling, but He knew prophetically that it would end in the highest exaltation. In the Song of Mary at the Annunciation this principle of Divine procedure is stated : 'He hath put down the mighty from their seats, and exalted them of low degree' (Lk 1⁵²). In Christ's parable of the Wedding Feast He insists on this principle, as against the self-seeking and pride of the scribes and Pharisees, who love the chief seats in the synagogue, and the foremost places at feasts. It is better to take the lowest room, and wait till the host shall give their proper place to one's virtue and dignity, by saying, 'Friend, come up higher' (Lk 14¹⁰). The behaviour of a Christian among his fellows should have regard to this principle. He is not to be forward to lay claim to that which may even be his right (cf. Mt 23¹² ‖ Lk 14¹¹ 18¹⁴).

2. One of the clearest words of Jesus in regard to His own exaltation is Jn 12³². Some Greeks came desiring to see Him. Our Lord seeing in this desire of theirs something prophetic of the future ingathering of the Gentiles into His kingdom, opened up His heart to His disciples as to the way in which He hoped to conquer the hearts of men. He made somewhat enigmatic reference to His death. He knew that the hour had almost come for the suffering of the lowly Son of Man. But it is necessary that the seed which is to produce a great harvest must first die. So it is a law of the Kingdom of God that life in this world must be sacrificed, if need be, that life eternal may be gained as a permanent possession. After the Saviour's life of service, the due reward will be honour from God. When the heavenly voice spoke, the Saviour was consoled and uplifted by the thought that He would cast out the prince of this world, and be lifted up ($ὑψωθῶ$) as a victorious conqueror. It was a prediction of His final triumph over evil, and His eternal reign over all men. The outwardly shameful death of the cross would be His true exaltation as the world's Saviour. By the identification of outward events with their inward meaning, He advances men's thoughts to the idea of His exaltation to heaven as the victorious One. This anticipation of Jesus is the starting-point for the Church's fully developed doctrine of the Exaltation. 'He rose again from the dead on the third day, He ascended up into heaven, He sitteth on the right hand of God the Father, He shall come to judge the world at the last day.' See artt. ASCENSION, JUDGMENT, SESSION.

After the predictions of His suffering, He always spoke of His future glory. He would rise again from the dead (Mt 16²¹). 'In the regeneration the Son of man shall sit on the throne of His glory' (19²⁸). 'The Son of man shall come in the glory of his Father with his angels, and then shall he render unto every man according to his deeds' (16²⁷). In the sayings in the Gospel of John there are many lofty statements as to His heavenly glory (cf. 14³ 17²⁴ etc.).   DAVID M. W. LAIRD.

EXAMPLE.—

A. LINGUISTIC USAGE.—The word 'example' (or 'ensample') occurs 15 times in the AV and 17 times in the RV of the NT. In the two versions it stands 7 times (1 Co 10⁶, Ph 3¹⁷, 1 Th 1⁷, 2 Th 3⁹, 1 Ti 4¹², Tit 2⁷ RV, 1 P 5³) for $τύπος$, once (1 Ti 1¹⁶ RV) for $ὑποτύπωσις$, once (1 Co 10¹¹) in adverbial phrase for $τυπικῶς$, 5 times (Ja 13¹⁵, He 4¹¹ 8⁵, Ja 5¹⁰, 2 P 2⁶) for $ὑπόδειγμα$, once (Ac 20³⁵) as partial rendering of $ὑποδείκνυμι$, once (Jude 7) for $δεῖγμα$, once (Mt 11⁹) as partial rendering of $δειγματίζω$, and once (1 P 2²¹) for $ὑπογραμμός$. For our present purpose Mt 1¹⁹ falls quite out of account. $δεῖγμα$ (Jude 7) is a 'specimen,' 'an (illustrative) exhibit'—in this instance set forth as a warning, though of itself this simple form hardly suggests either imitation or shunning, as $ὑπόδειγμα$ does. The other passages all more or less illustrate the topic in hand. Besides these, there are, of course, many other passages which, though not employing the term 'example,' are no less relevant and significant than these.

$Τύπος$, whether tr. 'example' or 'pattern,' 'type,' has generally an important bearing upon our topic. Primarily the 'mark,' 'impression' of a stroke or blow (Jn 20²⁵ 'print'), hence 'figure,' 'image' (Ac 7⁴³), $τύπος$ is generally 'pattern,' 'type,' 'example.' Sometimes the example is by way of warning, as 1 Co 10⁶·¹¹. Generally, however, it is an example to be imitated. A corresponding sense is to be ascribed to $ὑποτύπωσις$ (1 Ti 1¹⁶, 2 Ti 1¹³). [In the latter passage Hofmann's and Cremer's interpretation 'Abbild' seems hardly warranted. Timothy is to hold fast the 'type' of doctrine which he had received from Paul, and this 'type' is not regarded as Timothy's copy of Paul's, but as something which had now become common to both].—$ὑπόδειγμα$ is a concrete illustration or exhibition, designed for imitation or for warning—generally the former. In one instance in the NT $ὑπόδειγμα$ is used for after-representation (Ger. *Abbild*).—$ὑπογραμμός$ is a 'writing-copy' (model), to be imitated by the pupil. Hence an example set before one for close imitation. This is perhaps the most vivid of the NT terms indicative of Christ's exampleship. The term itself implies the strictest imitation; though both the context and the general teaching of the NT will save us from the error of conceiving Christ's example as something formal and external.

Among the other terms which give expression to the idea of Christian example, the most prominent are $μιμέομαι$ and $μιμητής$ (AV 'follow' and 'follower,' RV 'imitate' and 'imitator'). The verb occurs 4 times in the NT (2 Th 3⁷·⁹, He 13⁷, 3 Jn 1¹), in one of these instances in connexion with $τύπος$. The noun occurs 6 times (1 Co 4¹⁶ 11¹, Eph 5¹, 1 Th 1⁶ 2¹⁴, He 6¹²—at 1 P 3¹³ the reading $μιμηταί$ is to be rejected), in every instance signifying 'imitator' in the ethico-religious sense. In Eph 5¹ we find $μιμηταὶ τοῦ θεοῦ$, in He 6¹² the exemplary saints who are to be imitated, in 1 Co 4¹⁶ St. Paul exhorts to the imitation of himself, rather than to turn away from him, inasmuch as he was their father in the faith. In 1 Co 11¹ he bids his readers imitate him as he imitates Christ. In 1 Th 1⁶ it is 'imitators of us and of the Lord,' while in 1 Th 2¹⁴ it is 'the

churches of God in Judæa,' of whom the Thessalonians had become imitators.

Jesus in gathering His disciples about Him generally bade men 'follow' Him ($ἀκολουθέω$; in one instance, Mt 4¹⁹, $δεῦτε ὀπίσω$). Primarily the expression means no more than 'to accompany' as a disciple, and yet manifestly it became, in our Lord's use of it, one of the most characteristic and intensely significant expressions of the idea of discipleship in all its deepest import. So where Christ bids the rich young ruler sell all that he has and 'come, follow me,' or in the words on 'taking up the cross and following,' and elsewhere (see esp. Mt 19²¹ 10³⁸ 16²⁴, Jn 12²⁶ 21²²). The verb is not found in the Epistles, except at 1 Co 10⁴.

Christ is represented as the 'image'—$εἰκών$—which Christians are to resemble (Ro 8²⁹, 1 Co 15⁴⁹, 2 Co 3¹⁸, Col 3¹⁰). But those passages also which represent Christ as the image of God must be taken no less into account; for Christ's claim to an unconditional personal authority is expressly based upon the fact that He *is* the image—the apprehensible representation—of the invisible God (Jn 1¹⁸ 14⁶ᶠᶠ·, 2 Co 4⁴, Col 1¹⁵, He 1³—in the last passage the word is $χαρακτήρ$). In this connexion mention must be made also of the expressions 'children of God,' 'of your Father,' 'of the Highest' (Mt 5⁹·⁴⁵, Lk 6³⁵ 20³⁶). Also in the Epistles the filial relation is made to imply the following of the example of God in Christ (*e.g.* Eph 5¹·⁸, 1 P 1¹⁴, 1 Jn 5²¹).

Besides the terms already considered, which give more or less formal expression to the Christian idea of exampleship, there are many more, which—some of them in the most elementary and untechnical terms—no less definitely express the same thought. The very idea of discipleship in our Lord's teaching involved the idea of the personal exampleship of the Master (see esp. Mt 10²⁴·²⁵, Lk 14²⁶·²⁷·³³, Jn 13³⁵ 15⁸). The same thought is expressed in Eph 4²⁰ 'Ye have not so learned Christ.' In He 6²⁰ Jesus is called our 'Forerunner.' His temptations are typical (He 2⁹·¹⁸ 4¹⁵), and He is our example in the enduring of temptation (He 3¹ᶠᶠ· 12³ᶠᶠ·). True believers have the 'mind of Christ' (1 Co 2¹⁶, Ph 2⁵, cf. Ro 8⁶·²⁷ 12²). Christ is the 'life,' and as such is the 'light' of men (Jn 14·⁹·¹⁴·¹⁸, cf. 3¹⁹ 8¹² 9⁵ 12³⁵·³⁶·⁴⁶, 1 Jn 1¹·³). He is Himself 'the way,' etc. (Jn 14⁶). Believers are to 'put on' Christ (Ro 13¹⁴, Gal 3²⁷, Eph 4²⁴, Col 3¹⁰). The Christian's 'walk' is to be according to Christ (see esp. Jn 12³⁵, 1 Jn 1⁷ 2⁶, Eph 5²·⁸, Col 2⁶). Finally,—for an exhaustive study of the linguistic usage is not intended,—many of the most characteristic expressions of the thought of exampleship in Christianity are effected without the use of any peculiar terms. The word 'as,' or something else equally simple and direct, often best serves the purpose (*e.g.* Mt 5⁴⁸, 1 P 1¹⁵, Eph 4³² 5², 1 Jn 3² 4⁷·²¹).

B. THE DOCTRINE. — i. *THE EXAMPLE OF CHRIST.*—**1.** In the *teaching of Jesus* no truth is more essential than that God the Father Himself is the original and absolute example for all personal life. The Law is holy, for it is the expression of the will of God. But the letter apart from God's immediate personal will is dead. As Jesus expounds the Law, the disciples learn to look through the particular commandment to the personal will of the living God. It is not enough to keep the commandment in the most scrupulous fashion, as if it were something standing apart and complete in itself (Mt 5²⁰). We have to do directly with God Himself. His will and personal nature are our sole and absolute standard (Mt 5⁴⁴⁻⁴⁸). In answer to the young ruler who asked what good thing he should do in order to have eternal life, Jesus refuses to be regarded as one who might propose some novel good—some good other than that which is already known from God. Apart from God there is no good (Mt 19¹⁶·¹⁷). To love God is the first commandment; and the coming of His kingdom and the doing of His will should be man's first concern (Mt 22³⁸ 6¹⁰·³³).

But Jesus does more than point to God as the absolute standard for personal life. He comes·to make God known. It is not enough to know that God is the standard, so long as God's nature is unknown. So Jesus was sent as the perfect revelation of the Father (Jn 14⁹·¹⁰). Not that God was hitherto unknown: what the Jews worshipped they knew (Jn 4²²). Jesus came to complete the revelation of God. He gives a perfect interpretation of the mind and will of God, and in His own Person perfectly exemplifies that mind and will. He is conscious of perfect accord with the will of the Father (Mt 12⁵⁰ 5¹⁰·¹¹, Jn 5¹⁹ 4³⁴ 6³⁸ 8²⁹ 14³¹). His words and acts He has learned from the Father, even from the Father's example (Jn 8²⁸ 5¹⁷·¹⁹). This principle determines His whole treat-

ment of the Mosaic Law. The inevitable limitations of mere statutes He overcomes by an appeal
to the Divine example and order (as in the case of
the law of the Sabbath and the law of marriage,
Jn 5[17], Mt 19[4-9], in the latter case appealing also
to Scripture as well as to fact). And because He
knows God as the Son knows the Father—immediately and perfectly (Jn 7[29] 8[55] 10[15], Mt 11[27]), and
because He perfectly fulfils the will of God, Jesus
demands an unconditional following, which shall
consist, not in copying the outward form, but in
the most inward appropriation of the ruling
principle of His life (Mt 7[21-27] 28[20] 10[32-39] 11[28. 29] 20[24-28]
16[24. 25] 20[22] 26[39] 8[19-22] 19[21], Jn 15[8-10] 8[12] 12[35. 36. 44-50]
13[12-17] 15[4-7] 17[21-23] 21[22]). He does not set Himself
forth as a substitute for the Father, but as the
One who knows God and teaches us to know Him.
He is the Light of Life, the Way, the Truth, the
Life, the visible manifestation of God (Jn 8[12] 14[6. 9]).
Christ's claim to absolute authority (which expressly included the judgment of the world, *e.g.*
Jn 5[22]) is based not upon His prophetic office alone,
but upon that unity of word and deed which constituted the perfect revelation of the will of God.
Jesus' own Person was not left out of His gospel
(cf. Harnack's statement, *Wesen des Christentums*,
p. 91 : 'Nicht der Sohn, sondern allein der Vater
gehört in das Evangelium, wie es Jesus verkündigt
hat, hinein'). Not, indeed, as one doctrine among
many, nor as an addition to the doctrine of the
Father, did Jesus present the truth concerning
Himself. But He claimed to be the perfect and
unique embodiment and exemplification of the
Father's will. Yet He is more than mere example.
He does not merely *show* the way ; He *is* the Way.
At the same time He is the Truth and the Life.
He gives not only the perfect example but also
life-power. In this sense, therefore, Jesus, even
according to His own teaching, is more than an
element in the gospel : He is the very essence of
the gospel.

2. Christ's demand of an unconditional personal
following is reproduced in the *Apostolic preaching*.
But after Christ's passion, resurrection, and exaltation, the thought of His exampleship is expanded
and heightened. The Christ who died for the sin
of the world is the perfect revelation of God's holy
love (*e.g.* 1 Jn 4[9. 10]), while His exaltation, coupled
with the gift of His Spirit, affords assurance that
the coveted likeness to Christ and the promised
sharing of His glory shall be realized (*e.g.* Ro
8[2. 3. 26-39]). The thought of Christ as our example
is so variously and abundantly applied by the NT
writers, that it will suffice here to notice particularly only the more characteristic passages. The
concreteness of the revelation in a personal life is
most frequently and most strikingly set forth by
St. John (Jn 1[4. 14. 18], 1 Jn 1[3] 4[2. 3]). Jesus is the
perfect example of the life of faith, even its Author
and Perfecter (He 12[2]). He was tempted like as
we are (2[9-18] 4[15]), and is the perfect pattern of
patient endurance of all temptation, even unto
death (3[1ff.] 12[3ff.], 1 P 1[11] 2[21-23] 3[18] 4[1] ; cf. Gethsemane
and Calvary in the Gospels). He is our example
of mercy and forgiveness (Eph 4[32], Col 3[13], 2 Co 2[10]) ;
in self-denial and humble service (Ph 2[5ff.], 2 Co 8[9],
Ro 15[2. 3. 7]) ; in meekness, gentleness, and forbearance (2 Co 10[1], Col 3[13], Eph 4[2], 1 P 2[23]) ; in the love
that su ers, labours, and dies for others (1 Jn 3[16],
2 Co 4[10] 5[14. 15], Eph 5[2. 25], Gal 6[2], Ph 2[5ff.]) ; in holiness and purity (Eph 4[20ff.], 1 P 1[15], 1 Jn 3[1ff.] 4[17]).
And then, more broadly, believers are exhorted to
'put on Christ,' or 'the new man,' renewed after
Christ's image (Ro 13[14], Eph 4[13-15. 24], Col 3[10. 11], Gal
3[27]) ; and to 'walk' in, or according to, Christ
(Eph 5[8], Col 2[6], 1 Jn 1[7] 2[6]). The highest destiny
of believers is to be made like Christ (Ro 8[29], 1 Jn
3[2]). In this connexion the significance of those

passages in which Christ is called the image of
God (Col 1[15], He 1[3], cf. Jn 1[14]) should not be overlooked ; for God has given us this perfect revelation *in a Person* just in order that we might find in
Him our true example and archetype.

In addition to these and all other specific expressions of the thought of Christ's exampleship,
there stands the great fact that the whole picture
which the Evangelists drew of Jesus was made
under the powerful influence of the twofold conviction that He was the image of the Father, so
that by Him we know the 'Christ-like God,' and
that He was the Ideal Man—not an ideal creation
of human fancy, but the Ideal-Real come from God
Himself.

3. It has already been briefly noted that Christ
Himself as well as His disciples bore witness that
He was to His own *much more than mere example*.
The relation of His followers to Jesus is something
more than that of those who are striving to copy
a model. Christ is example in a deeper sense. He
is not only 'type,' but also 'archetype' (*e.g.* 1 Co
15[20ff. 45-49], Ro 8[29], He 2[11. 12. 17]). An example for
personal life must in any case be something better
than a mould for the multiplication of its own
form. Personality is interested in inward traits
and principles, which are to be independently developed in the greatest variety of forms. But
Jesus' relation to us lies even deeper than this. He is
the 'archetype,' the 'original,' of our personal life.
Now an original is not passively there to be copied ;
it sustains some sort of active causal relation to
the copy. So Christ is our example in this more
vital sense : He is at once example and original
(admirably expressed in Ger. *Vorbild* and *Urbild*).
As our 'original,' Christ not only (as in the case
of mere examples in personal life) mysteriously impresses us, but also imparts life and power through
His Spirit (Jn 1[16. 17] 5[24-26], Ro 8[2], Gal 2[20], Col 3[3. 4],
1 Jn 5[11ff.], and many more passages). He who,
having fulfilled the Law, is henceforth Himself the
Law (Ro 10[4], Gal 3[24], 1 Co 9[21]), has engaged to work
likeness unto Himself in all who believe. So we
may say with Augustine : 'Give what Thou com-
mandest, and command what Thou wilt.' If Christ
is to us mere example, without renewing power,
we are, after all, 'under law,' and *not* 'under
grace.' 'But the Word became not only flesh, but
also spirit' (Kähler, *Wissensch. d. chr. Lehre*[3], p.
510. See Jn 20[21. 22] 6[63] 7[39], 2 Co 3[17. 18]). Yet the
inward operation of the Spirit in producing likeness
to Christ has constant and express reference to the
historic Christ (Jn 16[14], 1 Jn 3[1ff.]).

4. The actual *validity* of the picture of Christ as
example implies the genuine humanness of the
life and the adequate fulness and clearness of the
picture. Furthermore, the example must be capable of universal application. As to the humanness of the life of Jesus, it is sufficient in this connexion to point out that the Biblical witness is
without a trace of questioning as to its reality.
Even the highest confessions of Jesus as the Son
of God are never at the expense of the patent
fact that He is truly man. As to the pictures of
Christ in the Gospels, while these are not biographies, as that term is commonly understood,
they do give a wonderfully luminous and vivid
portrait of the personal life of our Lord. Using
the historical material for the sake of its content
of truth, they show us Jesus the Witness, in word
and deed, of the holy love of God, and as the
Bearer of love and truth and life to the world.
Affirming love to God and man as the supreme
law, He Himself fulfilled that law, gladly laying
down His life that He might glorify the Father
and bring salvation to the world. And this life
of unimagined self-sacrifice He led to the end, in
spite of manifold and tremendous temptations, with-

out once deviating from the path appointed by the Father. And with it all there was no ascetical denial of the values that are primarily temporal ; nor did He lose either joy or repose of soul through His sufferings and conflicts. A marvellous openness in word and deed was ever characteristic of Him who came a Light into the world. Besides all this, here is a life that manifestly reached its goal. The course of that life had been one continual renunciation of proffered worldly advantage and success ; nevertheless its end was a unique triumph. For the real end was not Calvary, but the exaltation to the right hand of God. However hidden this end may be from the unbelieving world, Christian faith sees in the resurrection and exaltation of Christ the one supreme proof that righteousness cannot fail. This is the 'conviction of righteousness,' because Jesus has gone to the Father (Jn 16[10]). Without such a revelation of the appointed end of faith and righteousness the example would be incomplete, and Christian ethics could not maintain its ideal.

This picture of Jesus is capable of universal application. It is true the vocation of Jesus was unique. And yet the principles which controlled that life—perfect trust in the Father, and perfect love to God and man—are manifestly applicable under all possible circumstances. Such love as Christ's is the fulfilling of the Law. In one respect only is there a seeming limitation—for it is only seeming—to the universality of Christ's example : He is without the struggle with inward sin—He can be no model for the transformation of a sinful life. Inasmuch, however, as the processes of renewal are not our affair—we need only to be joined to our Lord in faith and to follow Him—this is no lack. Although 'a Jew of the first century,' Jesus is the Son of Man, in everything essential to personality free from the limitations of His own time and people. He is not less the kinsman of all peoples ; He is 'the contemporary of every age.'

5. We have further to consider the *practical relation of the disciple to the example of Christ.* We are commanded to 'follow,' to 'imitate,' to 'put on Christ,' to 'follow in his steps.' But how are we to conceive the problem of discipleship? For, while the Church has never failed to hear the call of Jesus, 'Follow me !' the conception of discipleship has sometimes been much distorted. In the Middle Ages the dominant thought was asceticism. The ascetic imitation of Christ, of which St. Francis is the most noteworthy example, selects certain traits in His life, and by undue emphasis upon these, together with a neglect of others, produces a distorted image. Then there have been enthusiasts who thought to be able to follow Christ in sharing His redemptorial work— exaggerating and perverting such passages as Ph 3[10], Gal 6[2], 1 Jn 3[16]. Again, rationalism has made of Christ simply a model of virtues to be copied. These three are perhaps the most important types of perversion of the NT idea of Christ's exampleship ; but the three appear in various modifications and combinations. The only safeguard against such errors seems to lie in a consistent emphasis upon the *integrity* of the Biblical picture of Christ.

Among evangelical theologians the term 'imitation' of Christ is very commonly objected to as implying merely a formal copying of the Lord's example. The word, of course, *can* be so understood ; but so also may the word 'following.' In any event it must be insisted upon that the words 'imitate' and 'imitator' in the NT (RV) have no such unevangelical meaning.

The believer's practical attitude to the example of Christ may be profitably studied in the light

of a few characteristic passages : (*a*) Answering to the frequent declaration of the absoluteness of Christ's authority (*e.g.* Mt 23[8. 10], Eph 1[22], Ph 2[9-11]), there are many passages which emphasize the obligation of *exclusive loyalty* to Him (*e.g.*, 2 Co 10[5] 11[3], Col 3[17], Eph 4[5]). (*b*) We are to have the *mind of Christ*, and to set the mind on the things above, where Christ is (Col 3[1ff.], Ro 12[2], Eph 4[23]). (*c*) We shall be transformed into the image of Christ *by beholding Him*, though the energy that produces the result comes from 'the Lord the Spirit' (2 Co 3[18]—see also Drummond, *The Changed Life*). (*d*) Complementing the thought of meditation as a means to Christ-likeness, there are various passages which set forth the *more strenuous elements* in the following of Christ (*e.g.* Ph 3[10-16]). (*e*) Several passages bid us '*put on Christ*' or the 'new man' (Ro 13[14], Eph 4[24], Col 3[10ff.]). This relates to the *formation of a Christian character*. (*f*) Jesus left us an example, that we should 'follow in his steps' (1 P 2[21]). Just as 'the mind of Christ' means *inward renewal*, and 'putting on Christ' means *character-building*, so 'to walk in his steps' may fairly serve as a motto for *the exercise of Christian love in all social relations*. (*g*) The example of Christ in His personal consummation is the believer's most glorious *hope* (Ro 8[29], 1 Jn 3[2. 3], cf. Eph 3[19]). And the hope set within us is guaranteed by the earnest of the Spirit. We *already* have a measure of Christ-likeness—we are *now* sons of God, and His power is working in us to finish the work begun (Ro 8[23], 1 Jn 3[1. 2] 4[17], Eph 3[14-20], Col 3[10], Ph 1[6]).

But all these various aspects of our relation to our Example presuppose the vital fellowship of a personal faith. No 'imitation' of Christ is according to the gospel if it is anything else than an essential aspect of the life of faith. With all its rare beauty and power, the *Imitation of Christ* by Thomas à Kempis (?) is hardly conceived in the plane of the perfect law of liberty. And yet, over against the widespread questioning of the universal applicability of Christ's example, as well as the ethical shallowness and indefiniteness of a religion of mere feeling, too much stress cannot be laid upon the vocation of the Christian to take up the cross daily and follow the Lord. 'This is the love of God, that we keep his commandments' (1 Jn 5[3]). The full gospel principle of the freedom of the Spirit being presupposed, the question, 'What would Jesus do?' (see Sheldon, *In His Steps*), is not unwarranted. But to walk in the Spirit implies that we are not seeking merit or virtue for our own satisfaction, but are seeking to glorify God. To do all 'in the name of the Lord Jesus'—no more comprehensive or profound expression of the fundamental law of Christian living could be conceived ; and just this, after all, is what is meant by following Christ. Our task is not in the narrower sense to copy Him, but to receive His Spirit, to understand His mind, to let Him be formed within us. So we shall also 'walk' in Him.

ii. *THE EXAMPLE OF THE FOLLOWERS OF CHRIST.*—'One is your Teacher—one is your Master, even the Christ' (Mt 23[8. 10]). 'Other foundation can no man lay than that which is laid, which is Jesus Christ' (1 Co 3[11]). This relation of our Lord to us is unique and exclusive. He is our life. We have been renewed after His image. But just because this is so—just because He does beget in His followers a likeness to Himself—those who bear His image are fitted to be examples ; only, of course, their exampleship is relative and mediate. He who said concerning Himself, 'I am the light of the world' (Jn 8[12] 9[5]), said also to His disciples, 'Ye are the salt of the earth, ye are the light of the world' (Mt 5[13-16]). But they are this just because they are His followers, and in virtue of what they have from Him. In various ways our Lord recognizes the value of good example; for instance, where He warns against the *bad* example of the scribes and Pharisees (Mt 23[1-3]). He prays for His disciples: 'As thou didst send me into the world, even so sent I them into the world' (Jn 17[18]). They were to be His witnesses; they were to do nothing in their own name. And yet, in order that they might be true witnesses, they must be sanctified in the truth. Their ministry for Christ must be, like Christ's own ministry, an intensely *personal* one. And when the Lord gives to His disciples that 'example' of humble service in washing their feet (Jn 13[5ff.]), and elsewhere (17[21] 13[35]) shows that they shall preach Him through a life of love as well as by word, it cannot be doubted that He places a very high value on the example of His followers.

The NT writers generally, especially St. Paul and St. Peter, lay great stress upon the salutary effect of Christian example (1 P 2[11ff.]. 3[1. 2. 15. 16], Ph 2[15], 1 Th 1[7. 8], 1 Co 7[16], 1 Ti 6[1]), with special emphasis upon the example of those who are in authority in the Church (1 Ti 4[12], Tit 2[7. 8], He 13[7], 1 P 5[3]). On the other hand, the danger of an example not positively evil but only doubtful is clearly set forth (*e.g.* 1 Co 8[7ff.], Ro 14[13ff.]). St. Paul shows the peculiarity of repeated reference to his own example. Reckoning the passage Ac 20[35] as an authentic report, and including all the Epistles that bear his name, there are not fewer than eight passages (Ac 20[35], 1 Co 4[16] 7[7. 8] 11[1], Ph 3[17] 4[9], 2 Th 3[7·10], 2 Ti 1[13]) which distinctly commend to the Churches his own example, and a ninth (1 Ti 1[16]) in which the element of specific commendation is lacking. This fact is all the more striking because St. Paul is pre-eminent in the energy with which he repudiates all human merit. 'Christ is all in all.' It is St. Paul, moreover, who declares: 'We preach not ourselves, but Christ Jesus as Lord, and ourselves as your servants for Jesus' sake' (2 Co 4[5]). There is, however, no real incongruity here. An examination of the passages in question will show that St. Paul nowise assumes authority in his own person. 'Be ye followers of me, even as I also am of Christ' (1 Co 11[1]). This is thoroughly characteristic. It is but another way of affirming that his sole purpose is to lead them to purest, simplest devotion to Christ. 'What then is Apollos? and what is Paul? Ministers through whom ye believed; and each as the Lord gave to him' (1 Co 3[5]). St. Paul does not refuse to be judged as a minister of Christ and steward of the mysteries of God (1 Co 4[1]). He is but a servant and a witness. And if there is anything exemplary in him, it is only the faithfulness and sincerity of his own discipleship and service. 'By the grace of God I am what I am' (1 Co 15[10]). Glorying is excluded. And neither St. Paul nor any other NT writer ever makes the virtuous life of believers a *principal* proof of the doctrine; it is, however, powerfully confirmatory. The Apostolic doctrine thus outlined is of such simplicity, that its universal acceptance in the Church is hindered only by the same carnal mind that caused many even in St. Paul's day to 'walk according to man' (1 Co 3[3]).

LITERATURE.—The leading recent treatises on Christian ethics, especially Martensen, Frank, Smyth, Kähler (*Wissenschaft der christlichen Lehre*[3], 3 Teil, 1905), Herrmann[3], 1904, and Häring, 1902; Luthardt, *Gesch. der christl. Ethik*, 1888, 1893 (Eng. tr. of vol. i. 1889); Bosse, *Prolegomena zu einer Gesch. des Begriffs* '*Nachfolge Christi*,' 1895; Kähler, *Der sogenannte historische Jesus*,[2] etc., 1896, and *Dogmatische Zeitfragen*, 1898 (2 Heft, pp. 75–155); Herrmann, *Der Verkehr des Christen mit Gott*[4], 1903 (Eng. tr. of an earlier ed.); J. Weiss, *Die Nachfolge Christi*, etc., 1894; Schlatter, *Der Glaube im NT*[3]; Lütgert, *Die Liebe im NT*, 1905; Feine, *Jesus Christus und Paulus*, 1902; Scholz, '*Das persönliche Verhältnis zu Christus und die religiöse Unterweisung*' in *ZThK*, 1893; Ullmann, *The Sinlessness of Jesus*; Fairbairn, *Philosophy of the Chr. Religion*, 1902, and *The Place of Christ in Modern Theology*, 1893; Laidlaw, art. 'Image' in Hastings' *DB*, vol. ii.; J. R. Seeley, *Ecce Homo*, 1865; Hughes, *The Manliness of Christ*, 1879; Stalker, *Imago Christi*, 1889; Drummond, *Natural Law in the Spiritual World*, and *The Changed Life*; Sheldon, *In His Steps*, 1897; F. G. Peabody, *Jesus Christ and the Christian Character*, 1905; Thomas à Kempis(?), *The Imitation of Christ*.

J. R. VAN PELT.

EXCLUSIVENESS.—The term is here employed to denote that Christ's earthly ministry was confined to the people of Israel. The passages bearing on the subject leave no doubt that Christ regarded the Messianic mission entrusted to Him by the Father as limited to the Jewish nation, and in practice He kept within the limits imposed by the Divine decree. Only on one occasion do we find Him crossing the borders of the Holy Land into heathen territory (Mk 7[24]), and on that occasion His object was not to extend the sphere of His work, but to secure an interval of rest and leisure for the private instruction of His disciples. When the Syrophœnician woman, seizing the opportunity presented by His presence in the neighbourhood, appealed to Him to heal her demoniac daughter, He justified Himself at first for refusing by the statement, 'I am not sent but unto the lost sheep of the house of Israel' (Mt 15[24]). At an earlier date, in His instructions to the Twelve in view of their missionary journey, the area of their work was sharply defined in the words, 'Go not into any way of the Gentiles, and enter not into any city of the Samaritans: but go rather to the lost sheep of the house of Israel' (Mt 10[5. 6]). It has been alleged that this restriction of His work was occasioned by want of sympathy with those outside the Jewish pale, in proof of which appeal is made to some of His sayings, such as those in which He characterizes Gentiles as 'dogs' (Mt 15[26] ||), directs His disciples to treat an impenitent offender as 'an heathen man and a publican' (Mt 18[17]), and enjoins them to 'use not vain repetitions, as the heathen do' (Mt 6[7]).

The fact of Christ's attitude of aloofness toward the Gentile world throughout His earthly ministry is quite evident. In explanation of it various considerations have to be taken into account. (1) His vocation as 'a minister of the circumcision' (Ro 15[8]) led Him to avoid as far as possible work among Samaritans and Gentiles. As the Messianic King, who came in fulfilment of OT prophecies, His appeal would naturally be, in the first instance, to 'His own' (Jn 1[11]). (2) The whole history of the Jewish people having been a preparation for the Kingdom of God, He recognized in its members 'the children of the kingdom' (Mt 8[12]). By virtue of possessing the oracles of God, Israel alone was fitted to appreciate the message of the Kingdom, which could not be presented to the world at large without a preparatory training, involving more or less delay. (3) To secure a favourable reception for His message it was necessary to avoid, as far as possible, arousing the prejudice and alienating the sympathy of His Jewish hearers, who would have resented any teaching or practice tending to place Gentile communities on a level of privilege with themselves (Lk 4[25-29]). (4) The shortness of His earthly ministry made it imperative that He should restrict the field to be evangelized, and not be diverted from His immediate purpose of establishing the Kingdom among the chosen people by the claims of those outside, however urgent and undeniable. (5) Assuming that the Kingdom was destined ultimately to be universal, its triumph among the Jews would evidently be the most successful method of securing its extension to other nations. As a matter of fact, it was Jewish adherents who afterwards became the agents of spreading it among the Gentiles.

Among the reasons why Gentiles were excluded from the scope of Christ's personal ministry, want of sympathy cannot be included. The evidence, instead of proving want of sympathy, is all the other way. He granted the request of the Roman centurion who sought the healing of his servant, eulogizing at the same time his faith as something without a parallel even in Israel (Mt 8[10]). The apparent coldness of His demeanour toward the Syrophœnician woman was due to the embarrassing nature of her petition, which required Him to violate the principle by which His conduct had been governed hitherto. He was anxious to help, if He could do so without sacrificing the interests of those who had the first claim upon His services. The term 'dogs' has been objected to on the ground that it is insulting. The woman herself did not view it in this light, and her quick wit turned it into an argument in her own favour.

The term (κυνάρια), moreover, does not denote the ownerless dogs which act as scavengers in the East, but the household pets which serve as the children's playmates. The scruples which led Christ to withhold for a moment the help sought, were in the end overcome by the woman's faith, which won His cordial approval.

There is no trace of racial or religious bias in Christ's references to the heathen. Any repugnance implied in His language is toward what is evil in their system or in their conduct. It is their method of prayer with which He has no sympathy, and which He stigmatizes as unworthy of imitation. Their lives were often such as to make close association with them unadvisable, and the impenitent offender is regarded as on a par with them in this respect. Christ's attitude toward publicans, who are bracketed with heathen, was anything but unsympathetic ; and if He felt toward heathen in the same way, they were objects not of dislike, but of the deepest compassion. See also artt. GENTILES, MISSIONS.   W. S. MONTGOMERY.

EXCOMMUNICATION denotes the exclusion, either temporary or permanent, and specifically on moral or religious grounds, of a member of a religious body from the privileges which membership in that body ordinarily carries with it. The word does not occur in EV, but we have in the Gospels several references to the practice as it existed among the Jews in the time of Christ, while certain words of Christ Himself supply the germs of the usage of the Christian Church as it meets us in the Apostolic age and was subsequently developed in the ecclesiastical discipline of later times.

i. JEWISH EXCOMMUNICATION. — Passing over the segregation of lepers, though this generally implied exclusion from the synagogue (Mt 8[4] ‖ Lk 17[14]),* and coming to excommunication of the more specific kind, we find that it is certainly referred to four times in the Gospels, viz. Lk 6[22] (' blessed are ye . . . when they shall separate you from their company'—ἀφορίσωσιν ὑμᾶς), Jn 9[22] (' for the Jews had agreed already that if any man should confess him to be Christ, he should be put out of the synagogue'—ἀποσυνάγωγος γένηται), Jn 12[42] ('they did not confess him, lest they should be put out of the synagogue'—ἵνα μὴ ἀποσυνάγωγοι γένωνται), Jn 16[2] (' they shall put you out of the synagogues'—ἀποσυναγώγους ποιήσουσιν ὑμᾶς). It is not unlikely, however, that a fifth reference should be found in the ἐξέβαλον αὐτὸν ἔξω of Jn 9[34. 35] (so AVm and many commentators). Meyer and Westcott (*Gospel of St. John*) object to this that no sitting of the Sanhedrin had taken place, and that the persons who cross-questioned the formerly blind man were not competent to pronounce the sentence of excommunication. It is true, no doubt, that excommunication properly denotes a formal sentence passed by the officials of the congregation (Schürer, *HJP* II. ii. 60),—though in Talmudic times a minor form of excommunication by an individual, and especially by a rabbi, was also recognized (*Jewish Encyc.* vol. v. p. 286 f.),—but as it was 'the Jews,' *i.e.* in the language of the Fourth Gospel the Jewish authorities, who expelled the man, it seems quite possible that the examination described in Jn 9 was of a formal nature. This is confirmed by the expressions, 'they bring to the Pharisees him that aforetime was blind' (v.[13]), 'they called the parents' (v.[18]), 'they called a second time the man that was blind'

*Being forbidden to enter a walled town, they could not worship in the synagogue in such places; but in unwalled towns a corner was frequently reserved for them in the synagogue, on condition that they were the first to enter and the last to depart (see Hastings' *DB* III. 97[a]).

(v.[24]), which suggests an authoritative summons before an official body. And when we read in v.[25] 'Jesus heard that they had cast him out,' this seems to imply that some grave act of formal censure had been passed upon the man.

Of the fact that excommunication was practised in the Jewish synagogue in the time of Christ, these passages leave us in no doubt. But now comes the question whether at that time there were different kinds of excommunication. In the Talmud two degrees are recognized, a minor, *niddûi* (נִדּוּי), and a major, *ḥērem* (חֵרֶם) ; the former being a temporary exclusion from the synagogue together with a restriction upon social intercourse with others, while the latter amounted to a ban of indefinite or permanent duration.* It must be remembered, however, that as an authority upon Jewish usages the Talmud does not carry us back to the earliest Christian age, and that for the practice of Jewish courts in the time of our Lord the NT itself is our only real source of information. And while it has sometimes been fancied that in the Gospels we have an indication of two kinds or degrees of excommunication—the ἀποσυνάγωγος of Jn 9[22] 12[42] 16[2] being distinguished either, as something more severe, from the ἀφορίζειν of Lk 6[22], or, as something more mild, from the ἐκβάλλειν of Jn 9[34. 35]—the truth is that there are no adequate grounds for such discriminations. It is, of course, quite possible, and even likely, that in the time of Christ there were distinct grades of exclusion from the privileges of the Jewish community, corresponding to the later *niddûi* and *ḥērem*,† but the NT cannot be said to testify to anything more than the fact of excommunication itself.

For the immediate origin of the practice of excommunication as it meets us in the Gospels, we have only to go back to Ezra and the days after the Exile, when the strictest discipline was absolutely essential to the solidarity, indeed to the very existence, of the Jewish Church and nation. Ezra insisted that those Jews who had married foreign wives should either put away both their wives and the children born of them, or forfeit their whole substance and be separated from the congregation of Israel (Ezr 10[8]). But the ultimate roots of the practice are to be sought in the Pentateuchal legislation, with its exclusion of the ceremonially unclean from the camp of the congregation (Lv 13[45. 46], Nu 5[2. 3]), and its devotion to destruction (חָרַם, whence חֵרֶם) of whole cities or tribes as enemies of Israel (Dt 2[34] 3[6] 7[2] ; cf. Jg 21[11], where the men of Jabesh-gilead themselves fall under the ban of extermination for not coming up to Mizpeh along with their brethren).

With regard to the grounds on which, in our Lord's time, sentence of excommunication was passed, the Talmud speaks of twenty-four offences as being thus punishable—a round number which is not to be taken too literally (*Jewish Encyc.*, art. 'Excommunication')—though later Rabbinical authorities have carried out the list into its particulars. When we read that the rulers decreed that any one

*The attempt has sometimes been made to discover in the language of the Talmud a third and more awful kind of excommunication named *shammattâ* (שַׁמָּתָּא) ; and in accordance with this it has been supposed that there may be a reference to the three presumed degrees of Jewish excommunication in Lk 6[22]— 'they shall separate you from their company (*niddûi*), and reproach you (*ḥērem*), and cast out your name as evil' (*shammattâ*). But it is now generally acknowledged that the idea of this threefold distinction is due to a mistake, and that, as used in the Talmud, *shammattâ* is simply a general designation for both the *niddûi* and the *ḥērem* (see Buxtorf, *Lexicon, s.v.* שַׁמָּתָּא ; Schürer, *HJP* II. ii. 60).

† It is perhaps suggestive that ἀνάθεμα is the constant LXX rendering of the OT חֵרֶם (Jos 6[17. 18] 7 *passim* 22[20], 1 Ch 27), and that ἀνάθεμα and ἀναθεματίζειν meet us frequently in the NT as expressive of a curse or strong form of banning (Mk 14[71], Ac 23[12. 14. 21], Ro 9[3], 1 Co 12[3] 16[22], Gal 1[8. 9]).

who confessed Jesus to be Christ should be put out of the synagogue (Jn 9²² 12⁴²), this may show that they possessed a large discretionary power of fixing the grounds of ecclesiastical censure. But if the later lists of Talmudical writers rest on traditions that go back to the time of Christ, there were certain recognized categories of offence, such as 'dealing lightly with any of the Rabbinic or Mosaic precepts,' under which it would be easy for the Jewish casuists to arraign any one who called Jesus Master or acknowledged Him to be the Messiah.

ii. CHRISTIAN EXCOMMUNICATION.—It lies beyond the scope of this Dictionary to deal with excommunication as practised in the Apostolic Church, and as it meets us especially in the Pauline writings. But in the teaching of our Lord Himself we find the principles at least of the rules which St. Paul lays down in 1 Co 5, 2 Co 2⁶⁻¹¹, 1 Ti 1²⁰, Tit 3¹⁰. In Mt 16¹⁹ Jesus promises to St. Peter the keys of the Kingdom of heaven, so that whatsoever he shall bind on earth shall be bound in heaven, and whatsoever he shall loose on earth shall be loosed in heaven. In Mt 18¹⁷⁻¹⁹ He makes a similar promise to the Church generally, or to the Twelve as representing the *ecclesia*—not '*qua* apostles with ecclesiastical authority, but *qua* disciples with the ethical power of morally disciplined men' (Bruce, *Expositor's Gr. Test., in loc.*; cf. further Jn 2.¹²³). And in the immediately preceding context (vv.¹⁵⁻¹⁷) He gives directions as to the way in which an offending brother is to be dealt with in the Church. The injured person is first to go to him privately and endeavour to show him his fault. If he will not listen, one or two other Christian brethren are to accompany the first as witnesses—not in any legal sense, we must suppose, but because 'consensus in moral judgment carries weight with the conscience' (Bruce, *op. cit., in loc.*). If he is still obdurate, the Church is now to be appealed to: 'and if he refuse to hear the Church (ἐκκλησία) also, let him be unto thee as the Gentile and the publican.' That ἐκκλησία in this passage means the community of Christian believers, and not, as Hort, for example, thinks (*Christian Ecclesia*, p. 10), the Jewish local community, seems in every way probable. Jesus had already spoken at Cæsarea of the ἐκκλησία that is built on Christian faith and confession (Mt 16¹⁸), and it was altogether natural that on this later occasion He should refer to it again in speaking of the relations between Christian brethren. But it would be a mistake to find in this passage any reference to a formal process of excommunication on the part of the Church. The offender of whom Christ speaks excommunicates himself from the Christian community by refusing to listen to its united voice, and the members of the community have no option but to regard him as an outsider so long as he maintains that attitude. That Jesus meant nothing harsh by the expression 'as the Gentile and the publican,' and certainly did not mean a permanent exclusion from the Christian society, may be judged from the way in which He treated a Roman centurion and a Syrophœnician woman, and from the name given Him by His enemies—'the friend of publicans and sinners.' No doubt in an organized society a solemn and formal act such as St. Paul prescribes in 1 Co 5⁴· ⁵ is a natural deduction from the words of Christ in this passage; but it cannot be said that such an act is definitely enjoined by the Lord Himself. It is the attempt to find here the authoritative institution of excommunication as a formal act of ecclesiastical discipline that gives a colour of justification to the contention of some critics (*e.g.* Holtzmann, *Hand-Commentar zum NT, in loc.*) that what we have in this passage is not an actual saying of Jesus, but

a reflexion of the ecclesiastical practice in the Jewish-Christian circles for which the Gospel of Matthew was written.

From our Lord's teaching in this passage it seems legitimate to infer that, though excommunication may become necessary in the interests of the Christian society, it should never be resorted to until every other means has been tried, and in particular should be preceded by private dealing in a brotherly and loving spirit. From the two parables of the Tares and the Wheat (Mt 13²⁴⁻³⁰· ³⁶⁻⁴³) and the Draw-net (Mt 13⁴⁷⁻⁵⁰) we may further gather that Christ would have His people to exercise a wise patience and caution in the use even of a necessary instrument. Mt 18¹⁵⁻¹⁷ shows that there are offences which are patent and serious, and are not to be passed over. But from the two parables referred to we learn the impossibility of the Donatist dream of an absolutely pure Church. Not even those who have the enlightenment of the Spirit are infallible judges of character. The absolute discrimination between 'the good' and 'the bad' (Mt 13⁴⁸) must be postponed till 'the end of the age' (v.⁴⁹). Only under the personal rule of the Son of Man Himself shall all things that offend (πάντα τὰ σκάνδαλα) be gathered out of His Kingdom (v.⁴¹).

LITERATURE.—Artt. on 'Excommunication' in Hastings' *DB*, *Encyc. Bibl.*, and *Jewish Encyc.*; Schürer, *HJP* II. ii. p. 59 ff.; Weber, *Jüd. Theol.*², Index, *s.v.* 'Bann'; Martensen, *Christian Ethics*, iii. p. 330 ff.; the Commentaries of Meyer, Alford, Westcott (*Gospel of St. John*), and Bruce (*Expositor's Gr. Test.*) on the passages referred to; Bruce. *Parabolic Teaching of Christ*, p. 42 ff.   J. C. LAMBERT.

EXCUSE.—'To make excuse' (παραιτεῖσθαι, Lk 14¹⁸, means to avert displeasure by entreaty, to crave indulgence, to seek to be freed from an obligation or duty. (Cf. the use of 'excuse' in Dampier, *Voyages*, ii. 1. 99: 'In the evening he sent me out of the palace, desiring to be excused that he could not entertain me all night'). παραιτεῖσθαι is used by Josephus exactly as here of declining an invitation (*Ant.* VII. viii. 2). ἔχε με παρῃτημένον (vv.¹⁸· ¹⁹) may be a Latinism for *habe me excusatum*, but see Meyer and Weiss *contra*.

These guests had evidently received a previous invitation, as is customary in the East, which they had accepted (vv.¹⁶· ¹⁷). Their unanimity, the absence of an adversative ἀλλά or δέ, and the order of the words, combine to make παραιτεῖσθαι a surprise when it comes (contrast v.¹⁵). They did not give a direct refusal, they were detained by certain hindrances which were not wrong in themselves, but they all showed the same spirit in rejecting the invitation because they preferred to follow their own inclinations. The first had bought a field, he was elated by his already acquired possessions (Trench, *Parables*), and alleged a necessity (ἔχω ἀνάγκην); 'sæpe concurrunt tempora gratiæ acceptissima et mundana negotia urgentissima' (Bengel). The second may illustrate the anxiety of getting; he alleges rather his plan and purpose (πορεύομαι). The third was detained by pleasure; his marriage seemed a sufficient reason, and he simply said οὐ δύναμαι. Gerhard sums up the hindrances as 'dignitates, opes, voluptates,' cf. Lk 8¹⁴. 'His omnibus mederi poterat sanctum illud odium v. 26' (Bengel).

'Excuse' is also used in RV for πρόφασις (Jn 15²²), so Wyc., Vulg. (*excusatio*); AV follows Tindale 'cloke.' Cf. Ps 140 (141)⁴ τοῦ προφασίζεσθαι προφάσεις ἐν ἁμαρτίαις; Vulg. 'ad excusandas excusationes in peccatis.' The Jews had no longer anything to plead in their own defence, as was possible in times of ignorance.

LITERATURE.—Comm. of Meyer and Plummer, *in loc.*; works of Trench, Bruce, and Dods on *Parables*; Thomson, *LB* p. 125.
                                          W. H. DUNDAS.

EXORCISM.—See DEMON.

EXPIATION. — See ATONEMENT, DEATH OF CHRIST, RANSOM, RECONCILIATION, REDEMPTION.

EXTORTION (ἁρπαγή).—The word is used by Christ in His terrible arraignment of the scribes and Pharisees, on account of the way in which, by their methods of plunder, they openly violated the Scriptures they knew so well (Mt 23²⁵, Lk 11³⁹). Isaiah (16⁴) had predicted the cessation of the extortioner as one of the signs of the Messianic reign. Ezekiel (22¹²) had inveighed against this sin as one of the transgressions of Israel which called forth the Divine wrath. Yet they, who claimed to keep the Law to the letter, and who professed to be the teachers of the Law, fattened themselves on extortion and filled their cups by it. For the methods of extortion practised by the publicans see art. PUBLICAN.

HENRY E. DOSKER.

EYE.—The OT usage of 'eye' (עַיִן), with its material and figurative senses, is found to be faithfully continued in the Gospels.

The almost invariable word used in the Gospels is ὀφθαλμός; in two passages (Mt 20³⁴, Mk 8²³) ὄμμα is found, but used only in the plural. The difference in meaning between the two would appear to be that ὄμμα refers to the material organ as distinct from its function, while ὀφθαλμός is not only the vehicle of vision but that which sees.* The most usual verb used in connexion with the eyes is βλέπω (e.g. Mt 7³, Lk 6⁴¹), with its compounds διαβλέπω (Mk 8²⁵) and ἀναβλέπω (Mt 20³⁴, Jn 9¹²); more rarely we find ὁράω (Mt 13¹⁵, Lk 2³⁰ 16²³, Jn 12⁴⁰) and θεάομαι (Jn 4³⁵ 6⁵). A fairly frequent phrase is that of 'lifting up (ἐπαίρω) the eyes,' † e.g. Mt 17⁸, Lk 16²³ 18¹³, Jn 4³⁵; in every case in which the eyes of Christ are mentioned this word is used (Lk 6²⁰, Jn 6⁵ 11⁴¹ 17¹).

The word 'eye' is used—**1.** In the ordinary, *literal* sense : as illustrating the *lex talionis*, Mt 5³⁸ ; ‡ of the eyes being heavy with sleep, Mk 14⁴⁰ ; of the multitude fixing their eyes on Christ, Lk 4²⁰ ; especially of Christ giving sight to the eyes of the blind, § e.g. Mt 9²⁹· ³⁰ 20³³· ³⁴, Mk 8²³, Jn 9⁶. **2.** In a *literal* sense, but with a *figurative* sense implied : e.g. the words of Simeon, 'Mine eyes have seen thy salvation' (Lk 2³⁰), where there is primarily the literal looking down upon the babe before him, but also, by implication, the mental vision of God's salvation of which the visible child was the pledge ; again, in the words, 'Blessed are your eyes, for they see . . .' (Mt 13¹⁶, see also Lk 10²³), where we have both the literal seeing of Christ and the seeing, in the sense of understanding, His teaching ; further, a striking instance is contained in Lk 24³¹,

---

* Perhaps somewhat in the same way that one can differentiate between a musical instrument and the music it gives forth.

† It occurs very rarely outside the Code of Lk., Jn., and Acts.

‡ Cf. in this connexion the Code of Hammurabi, § 196, 'If a man has caused the loss of a gentleman's eye, his eye one shall cause to be lost' (see Johns' *The Oldest Code of Laws*, p. 43).

§ Regarding methods of curing blindness see *Encyc. Bibl.* col. 1455 f.

---

where it is said of the two disciples to whom Christ, after His resurrection, became known by the breaking of bread, that 'their eyes were opened, and they knew him.' There appears here (however it may be accounted for) an extraordinarily close connexion or correspondence between weakness in the bodily and the mental vision, for it is certain that their eyes were open, in the ordinary sense, before they recognized Christ. Another example is that in Jn 4³⁵ 'Lift up your eyes and look on the fields, that they are white already unto harvest.' What the bodily eye saw here was evidently intended by Christ to be a symbol of the great work of evangelization which He desired the mental vision of the disciples to discern. Under this head would come also Mt 5²⁹ 'If thy right eye causeth thee to stumble, cut it out and cast it from thee.' From the context the 'eye' is clearly used here in a material sense, while the 'cut it out' is equally clearly used in a figurative sense (cf. Mt 19¹²).

3. In a purely *figurative* sense it is found in Mt 7³⁻⁶ and Lk 6⁴¹· ⁴² (the mote in the brother's eye) ; also in Mt 6²²· ²³, Lk 11³⁴ ('The lamp of the body is the eye'), where the eye is spoken of as reflecting the spiritual condition of the heart, though even here it is possible that the thought of the expression of the material eyes may also have been in Christ's mind. Again, in Mt 20¹⁵ 'Is thine eye evil because I am good?' the eye is used figuratively to express an attitude of envy (see below). Lastly, it must obviously have been used in a purely figurative sense in Lk 16²³ 'In Hades he lifted up his eyes . . .'

4. There remains the strange expression 'evil eye' (ὀφθαλμὸς πονηρός, Mk 7²²). The meaning of this no doubt approximates to that of the similar expression in Mt 6²³ 20¹⁵, and, generally speaking, denotes envy ; * but it also implied demoniacal possession [see DEMON, iii. (b)],† and the 'evil' referred not only to the possessed himself, but also to the harm which might be done to others who came under the influence of the 'evil eye.' ‡

W. O. E. OESTERLEY.

EYE-WITNESSES (αὐτόπται, Lk 1² ; cf. ἐπόπται in 2 P 1¹⁶).—We have the assurance of the Third Evangelist that the Gospels are founded not upon second-hand reports, but upon the direct testimony of those who were present. Similarly in Jn 19³⁵ 21²⁴ (where the words μαρτυρεῖν and μαρτυρία are used), the record of the Fourth Gospel is certified to be reliable. (See Lightfoot on 'The Internal Evidence for the Genuineness of the Gospel of John,' in the *Expositor* for Jan.-Mar. 1890, pp. 1, 81, 176 ; and cf. art. GOSPELS).

T. GREGORY.

---

* Cf. the expression עַיִן רָע Pr 23⁶ ; see also Dt 15⁹, 1 S 18⁹.

† Among the Jews there was a special formula for use against the 'evil eye.'

‡ For examples of the belief in, and effect of, the 'evil eye' in Syria at the present day, see *PEFSt*, 1904, pp. 148-150.

F

FABLE.—See PARABLE.

FACE.—Of the words tr. 'face,' 'countenance,' the Heb. *pānîm* indicates *the front*, that which is presented to view, while *mar'eh* and the NT terms πρόσωπον, ὄψις, and ἐνώπιον correspond to *view*, *visage*, that which can be seen.

1. *Physical appearance.* — Beauty of face is frequently alluded to in the Bible in connexion with both men and women as a distinguishing per-

sonal charm, and a powerful influence for good or evil. The underlying thought is that a noble and beautiful face should be the index of a noble and beautiful spirit. There is a resemblance among the children of a king (Jg 8¹⁸). Along with this recognition there are intimations that the Lord seeth not as man seeth (1 S 16⁷), and that beauty is vain (Pr 31³⁰). In the mysterious personality outlined in Is 53 one of the arresting features is the absence of such beauty in a face singularly marred, and according to common standards confessedly unattractive. While there is a dark type of comeliness (Ca 1[5]), yet, as might be expected among a people accustomed to olive and sunburnt tones of complexion, it is the exceptional characteristic of a fair and lustrous face that marks the highest form of beauty. In the poetry of the Arabs, when beauty of face is referred to, the usual and ever-sufficient simile is that of the full moon (6[10]), and in the descriptions of Paradise in the Koran the female attendants of the 'faithful' are called *houris,* 'the white-faced ones.' The illumination on the face of Moses is still recalled in the Jewish synagogue when the officiating Levite, in pronouncing the benediction (Nu 6[24]) at the close of the service, veils his face with the *ṭallith,* or prayer-cloth. Similarly in the sacred art of the Church, the Transfiguration light on the face of Christ was perpetuated in the halo around the faces of the saints who suffered as His witnesses. In 2 Co 4[6] the consummation of the gospel is described as the hope of beholding and sharing the manifestation of God's glory as it had been seen in the face of Jesus Christ.

2. *In the expression of character and feeling.*—Although the face was understood to be only a medium or channel for the manifestation of inward thought and emotion, a more vivid impression was often gained by alluding to it as having the essentials of personality. Thus it has its own health (Ps 42[11]), it produces gladness in others (21[6], Ac 2[28]), and pronounces rebuke (Ps 80[16]), it falls (Gn 4[6]), is lifted up (Ps 4[6]), emits light (44[3]). All emotions are marked upon it : it is impudent (Pr 7[13]). harder than a rock (Jer 5[3]), and may be a face of fury (Ezk 38[18]). In Lk 12[56] the face of the sky is referred to as conveying to those who could read it a sign of its intentions. The face being thus closely identified with the person, any violence offered to the face was in the highest degree affronting (1 S 11[2], 2 S 10[4], Mt 26[67]). As the expression of the face was regarded as a trustworthy indication of the life within, the Pharisees cultivated an aspect of religious absorption ; and Christ showed that the thought behind this device was essentially blind and irreligious, inasmuch as the true service of the Kingdom required the spirit of the Beatitudes (6[17]). As the emblem of perfected sainthood and ordered harmony, the Church in its final form is represented as having the beauty of a face without spot or wrinkle or any such thing (Eph 5[27]).

The figure of the averted or hidden face (Dt 31[17], Is 53[3]) that declines to meet the look of supplication, owes its origin to the fact that Orientals are largely swayed by the strongest feeling of the moment, and can be moved from their previous purpose by well directed emotional appeals. When one man is seeking to appease or persuade another, it is customary, when the right moment has been reached, to put the hand quietly and tentatively under the chin, and thus turn the face so that eye may meet eye, and more kindly feelings prevail. Not to see the face at all is to intercept such emotional persuasion of prostration, pleading, and tears, and means that all hope must be abandoned.

G. M. MACKIE.

FACT AND THEORY.—Christianity is a religion which comes to man from God. It has to do with man's relation to God, and with God's will for man. Any knowledge, therefore, of the nature of Christianity depends upon revelation. This would still be true apart from the fact of sin and the fact that Christianity is a religion of redemption. For God is a personal Spirit; and the only way by which we can know even the finite persons about us is through their revealing themselves to us. When, further, we bear in mind the truth that God is an infinite Spirit, and that we men are finite, it at once becomes obvious that all knowledge of God as well as of His plan or purpose must rest upon a revelation by God. This revelation may be general. Thus the creation of the Universe and of man, with God's image in his heart and able to see God in the work of His hands, is to be regarded as an act of self-revelation on the part of God. But sin is a reality in this universe, and the noetic effects of sin have rendered necessary a special revelation of the holy God to sinful man. Sin has not only made man blind to spiritual realities, it has distorted the purity of the Divine image in man's heart and in nature. Accordingly special revelation must be external, consisting in supernatural acts of God to restore the image of God, and must also consist in a supernatural word-revelation or communication of knowledge to explain the meaning of these acts. Special revelation, then, being soteriological, accompanies the redemptive activity of God. This Divine redemptive activity is historical, and has entered this world of time and space. This was necessary, because sin, the effects of which the redemptive activity was to counteract, is a historical force at work in the world. Since, therefore, special revelation accompanies God's redemptive acts, it too is historical, taking place under the category of time. Hence we have, first of all, God's redeeming acts, culminating in the Incarnation, Death, and Resurrection of Jesus Christ. These redemptive acts are also revealing acts. Thus God's Son came into this world in the flesh in order to save sinners, as St. Paul tells us (1 Ti 1[15]). But His incarnation is also a revelation of God, as we learn from the prologue to St. John's Gospel. But we have also a word-revelation accompanying the Divine redemptive facts or acts, and giving us their meaning. Indeed, that which rendered necessary the fact-revelation, viz. the noetic effects of sin, also makes necessary an authoritative word-revelation to explain to us the meaning of those acts. Christianity, therefore, consists in facts which have a meaning, or in the meaning of the facts, whichever way we choose to put it. Take away either the facts or their authoritative interpretation, and we have no Christianity left. The mere external facts apart from their meaning are, of course, meaningless, and therefore do not constitute Christianity; while the abandonment of the facts no less destroys the Christian religion, reducing it to a mere natural religion, or religious philosophy. Neither can the abandonment of the facts be justified because of the co-ordination of revelation and redemption, and of the historical character of the latter, to which we have already alluded.

This is the conception of revelation which the Scripture writers themselves give us. They claim that they were spoken to by God, and not merely that they had their religious intuition aroused by the facts of God's revelation. Hence their interpretation of the meaning of the great facts of Christianity, according to their own account of the matter, is not mere human reflexion upon the facts. If, therefore, we reject their interpretation of the facts as itself immediately from God, and therefore authoritative, we shall not be able to trust them for the occurrence of the supernatural facts, and shall be driven logically to deny the immediacy and supernatural character of the Divine activity in the facts themselves. The meaning of the term ' revelation ' will have been changed. It will no longer signify the communication of truth by God's acts and words,* it will designate a product

---

* In speaking of word-revelation, we are not confounding revelation and inspiration; the former denoting the Divine supernatural communication of truth to the Scripture writer, the latter the Divine influence accompanying its record. The term 'word-revelation' is meant to denote especially the com-

of the religious life of man. This does away with the absoluteness of Christianity, and is in direct contradiction to the account given by the Scripture writers themselves of the way in which Divine truth came to them. The question, therefore, really resolves itself into that of the trustworthiness of Christ and His Apostles as teachers of doctrine. The evidence for their trustworthiness is just the evidence for Christianity as a supernatural religion, which, of course, takes us far beyond the limits of this article (cf. Warfield, art. 'The Real Problem of Inspiration' in *Pres. and Ref. Rev.* iv. p. 177 f.). But if we accept their authority (as we do, resting it on the above mentioned evidence), then Christianity consists in certain great facts, and in the true meaning of those facts. The meaning of a fact is its meaning for a mind. By their true meaning, of course, is meant their meaning for God. This meaning, therefore, He must authoritatively make known to us if we are to have any Christianity.

In the first place, then, to attempt to hold to the great supernatural facts of Christianity and to give up their meaning, is not only impossible, but, were it possible, would result in taking from the facts just that which makes them Christian facts, and which makes them constitutive of the essence of Christianity. There has been an attempt to distinguish between the facts of Christ's life as the permanent Divine element in Christianity and 'theories' as relative, human, and changing. This general tendency to separate between fact and theory in Christianity has assumed two forms: on the one hand, it is said that the Bible contains no explanation of the great facts of Christianity; on the other hand, it is admitted that the Bible does contain an explanation of the facts; but, while a special revelation in a series of supernatural acts of God is recognized, a special word-revelation is denied, and the whole doctrinal content of Christianity as contained in the Bible is reduced practically to human reflexion upon the acts of God.

In the former position, it is said that Christianity consists in facts, not in doctrines. We have in the Bible the fact of Christ, but no theory as to His person. We have the fact of the Atonement, but no theory or doctrine of its meaning.

This position has been held by R. J. Campbell and F. W. Farrar in their essays on the Atonement in a volume entitled *The Atonement and Modern Religious Thought*, 1900. For example, Farrar maintains that any attempt to explain the nature of the Atonement is a 'futile endeavour to be wise above what is written, and to translate the language of emotion into that of rigid scholasticism.' So also R. F. Horton, in his essay on the Atonement in a volume entitled *Faith and Criticism*, 1893, says that the NT contains no theory of the Atonement. (Horton has given up this position in his essay on the same subject in the same volume with Farrar's essay). A similar position seems to have been maintained by Astié, who is quoted by H. Bois in *De la Connaissance Religieuse*, p. 342; cf. Warfield, *The Right of Systematic Theology*, p. 30.

In regard to this position we should note, first of all, that 'bare facts,' *i.e.* meaningless facts, are impossible, for every fact has a meaning whether we know it or not. And still further, a 'bare fact' being a meaningless thing, there is no atonement in the 'bare fact' of Christ's death, and no Christianity in the events of His life regarded as 'bare facts.' If we clearly understand that a 'bare fact' is simply an event in the external world apprehended by the senses, or a subjective fact of some self-consciousness, then it may be the statement of a 'bare fact' to say that a man called Jesus was born some 1900 years ago, but we are not to say that He was God's Son made flesh for our salvation; we can say that He died on the cross without going beyond 'bare fact,' or even that He expressed

munication of truth to the Scripture writer in a supernatural manner. Of course, it should not be forgotten that inspiration is also necessary in order to render the truth infallible to us.

certain feelings, but we cannot say so much as that He died for our sin. It is not necessary to salvation that we should know the full and true meaning of Christ's death; we are not speaking, however, of the conditions of salvation, but of the essence of Christianity. And this lies in the meaning of the great redemptive facts of the Christian religion, or in the facts because of their meaning. We may conceive some false meaning of these facts, but like all facts they must have some meaning, and their true meaning is their meaning for God. Hence, as was said, if we are to know their true meaning, God must tell it to us. If, therefore, we were simply to hold to the facts of Christ's life considered as 'bare facts,' we should have taken away from them that which makes them Christian facts and redemptive facts. In short, this method of treating the facts of Christianity takes from them all that makes them constitutive of the essence of Christianity.*

We should observe, next, that the modes of statement of all those who hold this position suggest the impossibility of holding to 'bare facts.' They speak constantly of the 'fact of the Atonement.' But this is quite ambiguous. If it means that the atonement is real, then it is a true statement, but a statement which involves a theory or interpretation of the fact of Christ's death as atoning for sin. But, taken as they appear to mean it, the statement involves an error. We may speak of the fact of Christ's death, but in this as a 'bare fact' there is no atonement. As soon as we call it an atonement we have interpreted it by a theory. So, when Farrar says it is a 'landmark of the death of Christ,' that it is 'not only the declaration, but the ground of pardon,' he has gone a long way toward understanding its meaning, and, according to his position, has made the mistake of 'translating the language of emotion into the rigidity of syllogisms.' And this same ambiguity often attaches to the language of those who do not hold this position. Thus the late Dr. Dale, in his book on the Atonement, first seeks to establish its fact and secondly its theory. In reality, however, the first part of his book contains more general, and the latter part more specific, statements of the doctrine or theory. Precisely the same ambiguity is seen in the article 'The Fact of the Atonement,' by R. Mackintosh (*Expos. Times*, May 1903), who speaks of the 'fact of Christ's death' and the 'fact of the Atonement' as equivalent terms, and again of the 'fact that Christ died for our sins,' which statement, of course, contains a doctrine.

But we must observe, finally, that it is not sufficient to show the necessity of an interpretation of the facts of Christianity. The question of an external authority in religious knowledge cannot be evaded by saying that the Bible contains no explanation of these great facts. Whatever may be said as to the authority of Scripture, it is evident that the Bible does contain an interpretation of the great facts of Christ's life. And whatever interpretation be put upon the language of Christ and His Apostles, it is plain that they had definite ideas as to who Christ was, why and how He came into this world, why He died, and what His death means. To take only a few instances, and those only in regard to one fact, viz. Christ's death, it is scarcely a matter for dispute that, when He speaks of giving His life 'a ransom in the place of many' (Mk 10[45], Mt 20[28]), or of His blood as Covenant-blood 'shed for many unto the remission of sins' (Mt 26[28]), He intended to convey

* The necessity for an interpretation of the facts of Christianity has been shown by Denney, *Studies in Theol.* p. 106, and *The Death of Christ*, Introd.; cf. also J. Orr, *The Christian View of God and the World*, p. 25; H. Bois, *Le Dogme Grec*, pp. 110–117; Warfield, *The Right of Syst. Theol.* pp. 29–46.

a definite view as to the meaning of His death.*
The same thing could be shown in regard to all our
Lord's statements as to His Person and Work.
The whole of the Pauline letters are occupied to a
large extent with the interpretation of the facts of
our Lord's Incarnation, Death, and Resurrection.
It is not possible, then, to assert that the NT contains no interpretation of the facts which lie at
the basis of Christianity.

We must therefore face the question of the
authority of this interpretation. If we are unwilling to yield to its authority, and still insist
upon the distinction between the facts as Divine
and the theory as merely human, we shall be in the
second position mentioned, that of those who recognize a supernatural revelation in a series of facts,
but who reduce the whole doctrinal content of
Christianity, as contained in the Bible, to human
reflexion upon these facts (see Rothe, *Zur Dogmatik*, pp. 54–120; Weiss, *Bibl. Theol. des NT*[7],
§ 1 *c*, also note 3 on p. 4. For other instances of this
see Warfield, art. 'Revelation' in Johnson's *Encycl.*
vol. vii. p. 79). But this position is not a logical
one. For it is not the account which the Scripture
writers give of their interpretation of the facts of
Christianity. They claim a direct supernaturalism
in the communication to them of truth. Hence, if
by reason of an anti-supernaturalistic philosophy
we reject this claim, and regard their interpretation of the facts as relative and conditioned by the
conceptions of the time, we shall also be led logically to reject their statements as to the occurrence
of supernatural facts. The consequence of this
will be to regard the facts of Christianity, *i.e.* its
whole historical basis, no less than the Scripture
doctrine, as the mere 'husk' which contains the
'kernel' either of rational truth or of Christian
life; and thus Christianity will have been reduced
to a mere religious philosophy or a mystical life.
For, we are asked, can a history long past be the
object of religious faith any more than a doctrine
of a bygone age? Is not the whole of the historical and dogmatic element of the Scripture relative
and temporally conditioned? Accordingly the logic
of this position of recognizing a revelation only in
fact, is to drive us to Rationalism or Mysticism.
This is the result of abandoning the principle of
external authority in religion. But rational truth
and religious sentiment are not Christianity. If
we are to have any Christian religion, we must
have the great supernatural facts of Christianity
and an authoritative interpretation of them.
Whereas on this view revelation is only a product
of the religious life of man.

Accordingly we are brought to a position opposite
to that which we have been discussing, *i.e.* to the
position which does not do justice to the facts
of Christianity, subordinating them to a purely
human theory. This tendency reduces Christianity to a philosophy of religion; the historical
element being regarded as the 'husk' which contains the 'kernel' of eternal truths of reason.

This question of the importance of the historical element in
Christianity was prominent in the 18th cent. (cf. Lipsius, 'Die
Bedeutung des Historischen im Christentume' in his *Glauben
u. Wissen*). The difficulty which was felt with historic facts
was not, as more recently, that of attaining historic certitude.
The clearest, most undisputed fact, it was held, could not
support or be the content of religious belief. The objection
was therefore a metaphysical, not a historical one. Hence all
positive religions were regarded as but outward expressions of
the pure religion of reason. This was the position of the
Leibnitz-Wolffian philosophy (cf. Windelband, *Gesch. der Phil.*

* It is often asserted that the words first quoted show Pauline
influence on the Evangelist. But the unwillingness to admit
that Jesus uttered them rests on dogmatic grounds. There is
no external evidence against them, and, as Denney has shown,
they are perfectly in keeping with the context. So also Spitta's
idea that the words Mt 26[28] have no reference to Christ's death,
is admitted by him to be quite different from the view of the
Evangelist (see Denney, *The Death of Christ*, pp. 38 and 40).

p. 30 ff.). Lessing also gave utterance to his famous saying that
'accidental historical truths' can never be the ground of
'eternal rational truths.' And he seemed to regard all of the
historical element in Christianity as 'accidental,' for the ideal
kernel of Christianity was just rational religious truth. In the
same way Kant (*Die Relig. innerhalb d. Grenzen d. blossen
Vernunft*) considered pure moral truth as the abiding kernel of
all religions. Historical Christianity, he held, had clothed this
with accretions which are symbolical representations of eternal
truth. Fichte held practically the same position (see *Anwei-
sung zum seligen Leben*) Thus by distinguishing between the
'kernel' and the 'husk,' and by finding the former in the
truths of reason, the whole of Christianity was relegated to the
category of husk. Christianity, accordingly, was reduced to a
religious philosophy and destroyed, for it is not the product of
human reflexion. An attempt at a more adequate view of
history is seen in Schelling and Hegel, but with much the same
result so far as historical Christianity is concerned, because of
their adherence to the distinction between kernel and husk.
History is regarded by them not as an 'outer' 'empirical'
history, but as the history of God's life in the finite spirit.
Thus the history of Christ is not important as the history of an
individual, but in these symbols faith sees the eternal course
of the Divine life. Christ's death is simply a symbol of something which must be repeated in every man's inner life, and His
bodily Resurrection a symbol of the return of the finite spirit to
the Infinite. Thus historic Christianity is but one of the forms,
albeit the highest, of bare natural religion, in this case construed upon a pantheizing basis.

In England, T. H. Green has given a Neo-Hegelian construction of Christianity which subordinates its facts and the
Scripture interpretation of them to a philosophical theory
(*Miscell. Wks.*[2] vol. iii. pp. 160–185, 230–276). God and man are
identified. God is the ideal self of each man. Sin is self-assertion, and salvation consists in 'dying to live,' *i.e.* giving up
this individualistic self-assertion. This is held to be the revelation of Christianity, but no value is attached to the historic
Christ apart from the idea which He exemplified. This, it goes
without saying, is Neo-Hegelianism and not Christianity. The
claim, also, that faith which has a historic element in its content is therefore psychologically a 'historic faith' in the sense
of a dead faith, is specious. Faith may have a historical element
in its content without being changed as to its psychological
character as trust in God. (For a critique of Green's religious
philosophy see Kilpatrick in *The Thinker* for 1895; Rainy in
the *Theol. Review* for 1899; Forrest, *The Christ of Hist. and of
Experience*, Lect. 8).

From the standpoint of NT criticism, the art. by Schmiedel on
'The Resurrection and Ascension Narratives' in *Encyc. Bibl.*
vol. iv. p. 4040 f., illustrates the same distinction between
kernel and husk, and the giving up of the fact of the bodily Resurrection of Christ. Here an anti-supernaturalistic bias governs
the whole discussion, though Schmiedel asserts that he does
not presuppose the impossibility of a miracle.

The extreme result of this tendency to give up the authority
of Scripture, and the consequent subordination of the facts of
Christianity to a theory, is seen in an art. in the *Hibbert Journal*,
Jan. 1905, entitled 'The Christ of Dogma and of Experience,'
by W. A. Pickard-Cambridge. According to the author, the
fundamental error in Scripture is its identification of Jesus
Christ with the Spirit of God, communion with whom is the
essence of religion. The Apostles were confronted with a personality of 'overwhelming attractiveness,' and so made this
mistake. This, indeed, is Christianity without Christ. The
author's Christ is a mere man idealized by emotion.

In doing away with the historical element in
Christianity, these thinkers have done away with
Christianity itself. This is only to say that the
great facts of Christ's life are a part of the essence
of Christianity. The Christian religion is not a product of human ideas, but of a direct revelation of
God to men, accompanying God's direct interference in the downward course of the world caused
by sin, which is a historic force. Thus, having
abandoned all external authority, we lose the fact-
basis as well as its Scripture interpretation, and
are left with a philosophy of religion. But these
so-called eternal truths are either purely human,
in which case they cannot be eternally valid truth;
or else man's thoughts about God must be held to
be God's thoughts about Himself, in which case
even natural religion vanishes in Pantheism. This
type of religious philosophy may not admit the
authority of the Scripture, but it should frankly
admit that what it leaves us is not Christianity.
It is, however, simply the logical result of the
entire abandonment of the principle of external
authority in religious knowledge.

When we turn from the philosophers to the
'liberal theology' represented by Biedermann,
Lipsius, and Pfleiderer, we find that, notwithstanding the greater emphasis which they lay

upon the historic Christ, their difference from the philosophers is not so much one of principle as of degree, *i.e.* of how much of Christianity they will retain as kernel and how much they will throw away as husk. This is determined largely by their philosophical standpoint. Hence in their case also there is a subjection of Christian fact and doctrine to an unauthoritative theory. That they do not differ so much in principle from the preceding philosophical solvent of Christianity can be seen from the following considerations. Wherever the principle of external authority is given up, we are sure to meet with the same distinction between kernel and husk in reference to Scripture fact and doctrine. And whenever this takes place, the Scripture idea of revelation has been changed, revelation being simply the product of religious thoughts and feelings in the mind of man. This makes it the product of natural development, and subjects it to the laws of psychic life. Accordingly we find that, while these theologians differ from the preceding construction of Christianity in laying greater emphasis upon Christ and in insisting that the essence of Christianity lies not in eternal truth so much as in Christ Himself (see esp. Lipsius, *op. cit.*), they nevertheless regard the Scripture facts as Scripturally interpreted, *i.e.* both fact and dogma, as but the 'sensuous representation' of rational religious truth.

Christ is probably of least significance in the theology of Biedermann, who held that Jesus is simply the first realization of the idea of Divine Sonship (*Dogmatik*, ii. § 815). Whereas Lipsius, though an opponent of the Ritschlian school, resembles it in the emphasis laid upon Christ. Thus in the essay already cited he says that the Christian religion is historical, and that the eternal good which it offers is bound up with the person of Christ. Christianity, he says, consists not in ideas which Christ illustrated, but in Christ Himself. But Lipsius distinguishes between kernel and husk, and between some facts and others. Thus he says that 'faith has to do not with single historical facts as such, but with their religious value,' and that 'there are facts about whose historicity there is little doubt, and which are of no importance for our religious life, and there are others about which there may be much doubt, and yet, as sensuous representations of religious truths, they are of the greatest value.' Obviously, if facts about whose occurrence there is doubt are of such importance as 'sensuous representations' of religious truth, the really essential thing is the rational truth which they are supposed to represent. And this is actually the case with Lipsius' treatment of the great Christian facts. Thus the Cross is 'the symbol of the eternal truth that the old man in us must die, in order that man be born of God' (p. 138), though Lipsius does recognize in Christ's death more than a mere symbol (p. 139). At the same time the all-important thing is the idea symbolized. So also the Resurrection of Christ need not be true in its literal Scriptural form, but at the same time it symbolizes the truth of the entrance of Christ into the heavenly world. The 'form' in which we conceive it is expressly said to be of no importance. This is sufficient to show the complete subordination of Christian fact to philosophic theory in this movement. But not only are the great facts of Christianity put into the category of 'husk.' The dogmatic interpretation of them in the Scripture is also regarded as the external hull or symbol of rational truth. For, unlike the Ritschlian school, who hold that the Greek influence is largely later than the NT writings, the liberal theology carries this influence, and consequently the critical process of separating the kernel of truth from its husk, back into the NT. Thus Pfleiderer (*Glaubens- u. Sittenlehre*, p. 4) says that it is the business of Dogmatics to 'work over critically' the Scripture as well as the Church dogma in order to reach its abiding truth. The Scripture doctrine is said to contain a 'sensuous' element which is not rational and which must be rationalized.

It is evident that the principle of external authority in religious knowledge having been abandoned by this school also, the historic facts of Christianity as well as the Scripture interpretation are given up. Again, facts are subordinated to a human theory, and we have left a religious philosophy.

The subjection of the Scripture facts and doctrines to a subjective norm has taken also a more mystical form. This, indeed, is a natural consequence of the attempt to find a permanent basis for religious knowledge after the principle of external authority has been given up. For this kernel of rational truth seems to differ with each

theologian, and does not afford that permanency which should characterize the essence of Christianity. These so-called eternal truths are temporally conditioned just as are the Scripture dogmas. To hold to them, therefore, is a species of dogmatism. Accordingly it is natural that a demand for a truly undogmatic Christianity should arise, seeking to be rid not only of Scripture doctrine, but also of the rational element into which it had been distilled.

This demand was made by Dreyer in his *Undogmatisches Christentum*, the first edition of which appeared in 1888. Coming from the camp of the liberals, Dreyer directed his polemic against 'liberalism' and 'orthodoxy' alike. The liberal theology fails to satisfy the demands of the 'pious heart,' while orthodox dogma is in conflict with modern culture. We are therefore bidden to turn from dogma to the life of faith. Christianity is a life, not a series of facts or doctrines. Dogma is religious experience put into the form of concepts (p. 77). It is therefore put into a form of relative validity, and one that is continually changing. When these concepts are no longer valid, they no longer serve to express religious life, and must be rejected. The facts of Christianity fare no better at Dreyer's hands. He will not allow our idea of history to be governed by any dogmatic supernaturalism, and consequently, at the demand of an equally dogmatic anti-supernaturalism, he tells us the 'myth-forming process' is seen in the Gospel record of the life of Christ. Although something of external fact may remain, we can find no religious certitude in any historic fact, and are told to fall back on Christ's holy character, which is exalted above all the changes of theological science and historical criticism. This arouses life in us, and this life is the essence of Christianity, which is a life, not fact or doctrine.* A somewhat similar position has been taken in France by A. Sabatier.† His idea is that religion is life, not doctrine. External authority, whether of Scripture or the Church, kills religion. The essential thing in religion is life. But this life must express itself outwardly in institutions and symbols. Christian doctrines are but symbols of Christian life. They are higher than those of other religions because the life is higher. The essence of Christianity, therefore, is neither a series of facts nor a sum of dogmas, but a spiritual life.

We have not space to show the inconsistency of Dreyer's supposed escape from historical criticism, when he falls back on the inner life of Jesus as the ground of the life which constitutes the essence of Christianity; or to discuss the philosophy which underlies Sabatier's books. We can only stop to indicate briefly that when we have separated Christianity from all external facts and have made its doctrinal content entirely the product of the religious life, we have done away with Christianity, because we have done away with all that distinguishes it from natural religion. Of course it is true that Christianity is a life hid with Christ in God. It is also true that Christian doctrine can never produce Christian life. St. Paul has taught us this. Man is dead in sin, and the revelation of Divine truth in the Bible will fail to produce spiritual apprehension or life; for 'the natural man receiveth not the things of the Spirit' (1 Co 2¹⁴). These great truths are emphasized in the Reformed Theology. But the type of thought we are discussing means that the essence of Christianity consists in a life which precedes and is independent of facts and doctrines, and that doctrine

---

* In some respects Dreyer's position resembles that of the Ritschlians. Thus, *e.g.*, Kaftan in his *Glaube u. Dogma* replied to Dreyer that instead of an undogmatic Christianity we need a 'new dogma' which grows out of Christian faith. Dreyer rejoined, in a later edition of his book, that he admitted a 'science of faith' (*Glaubenslehre*), and so did not differ from Kaftan. Kaftan again replied, saying that Dreyer held that this science of faith contained a symbolic element, and was only of relative validity. This seems to be the most essential point of difference between Dreyer and Kaftan, viz., the latter claims absolute validity for dogmatics as 'the science of faith,' while the former admits a relative element in this 'science of faith' which he refuses to call a dogma. Dreyer's view of the inner life of Christ, as independent of historical criticism, and as the source of Christian life, resembles that of Herrmann in his *Verkehr des Christen mit Gott*. But Dreyer is a mystic, while Herrmann is not. See also, Dreyer, *Zur undogm. Glaubensl.* [posthum.], 1901.
† *Esquisse d'une Phil. de la Relig. d'après la Psych. et l'Histoire*, 1897 [also Eng. tr. 1897]. This book includes a lecture, 'The Vitality of Christian Dogmas,' published separately [also Eng. tr.]; also *Les Religions d'Autorité et la Religion de l'Esprit*, 1900 [also Eng. tr.].

is the product of life. Thus to eliminate fact and doctrine from Christianity is to leave nothing but bare natural religious sentiment. And it is a mistake to suppose that Christianity is the product of the religious sentiment (see Warfield, *The Right of Syst. Theol.*). It is no more the product of this than it is of rational reflexion.

Furthermore, there is now left no basis for the affirmation that Christianity is the final religion, and its doctrine absolute truth. For we can never be sure that Christian life may not reach higher levels and embody itself in more elevated doctrinal symbols. Writers of this type might and do reply to this, that, even apart from fact and doctrine, the Christian life is not the bare religious sentiment, but the product of God's Spirit, and that it is therefore the true life, and its doctrinal product final truth. But when they affirm this, they abandon their position. For it cannot be proved that this life is the true life if the norm of truth be drawn from the life itself. We believe that Christian life is the true life because of a fact and a doctrine independent of this life, viz. that it proceeds from the regenerating activity of the Holy Spirit. But in affirming this we have asserted a great fact as well as a doctrine, each independent of, as well as at the basis of, Christian life. In short, if Christianity is separated from the great supernatural facts of Christ's life and from the great supernatural facts of the action of God's Spirit on men's hearts, as well as from its authoritative doctrinal content, then that which differentiates it from mere religious sentiment is gone. What, then, to sum up, is the attitude of this type of religious thinking to the question of 'fact and theory' in relation, especially, to Christ? This question may be answered by saying that the facts and doctrines of Christianity have been subordinated to a psychological theory that feeling and sensation precede and condition thought. And as a consequence, we are left with a human Christ whose portrait is the product of the religious sentiment.

At this point we are met with a reaction from the neglect of the historical element in Christianity, and also from the demand for an undogmatic Christianity. This has come from members of the Ritschlian school. Thus, *e.g.*, Harnack (cf. his address, *Das Christentum u. die Geschichte*, 1896) and Herrmann (besides his *Verkehr* and *Begriff der Offenbarung*, see esp. his *Warum bedarf unser Glaube geschichtlicher Thatsachen?* 1884) have attempted to defend the importance of the historical basis of Christianity against Lessing and Kant; and Kaftan (*Glaube u. Dogma* [2], 1889) has written a reply to Dreyer, showing that the dogmatic element is essential to Christianity, and that what we need is a 'new dogma.' But this demand must be judged in the light of the motive, principles, and results of this theological movement. The fundamental motive of Ritschlianism is an apologetic one, viz., to find a ground of certitude in Christianity which shall be independent of the results of historical criticism and of metaphysics, and so to state the content of the Christian faith that it too shall be independent in both these respects. In order to accomplish this, it is common with theologians of this school to lay stress on the revelation of God in the 'historic Christ,' and to seek to find in Him the ground, as well as an essential element in the content, of the Christian faith. This ground of certitude and this dogmatic content are held to be independent of historical criticism and metaphysics, by means of their sharp distinction between religious and theoretic knowledge, the latter dealing with facts and their explanation, the former with religious values. In regard, then, to the historical element in Chris-

tianity or the Christian facts, this school emphasizes its importance as part of the essence of Christianity; but in order to maintain its independence of the results of historical criticism, falls back upon one fact, viz.—the so-called 'historic Christ.' It is not meant that Christianity is independent of the results of historical criticism in such a sense that, if there were no basis for their historic Christ in the Gospels, Christianity could still survive. Their idea is that the 'historic Christ' stands fast after historical criticism has done its work. But since this criticism is largely determined by an anti-supernaturalistic bias, it is evident that the historic Christ of the Ritschlians is not a Christ who is independent of historical criticism, but the Christ which a naturalistic criticism has left us. This shows that independence of the results of criticism is impossible, since Christianity is a historical religion. The supposed independence of its results turns out to be a surrender of all that is difficult to defend against a criticism which is determined by naturalism. Accordingly Harnack says (*Das Christentum u. die Geschichte*) that 'the tradition as to the incidents attending the birth and early life of Jesus Christ has been shattered.' This makes necessary the old rationalistic distinction between 'kernel' and 'husk,' and so in his lectures on the *Essence of Christianity* we are told that we must distinguish between the Easter message of the empty tomb, which is not essential to Christianity, and the Easter faith that Jesus gained a victory over death and still lives. Of course, if we follow this method, not only will all the external supernatural events of Christ's life have to be surrendered, but also those elements in His inner life which involve the supernatural must go. And so we find Herrmann in the *Verkehr* falling back upon the inner life of Jesus reduced to a merely ethical content.*

Thus the Ritschlian attempt at independence of historical criticism results really in a surrender to a criticism determined by naturalism. The virgin-birth and the bodily resurrection of Christ are given up, and we have no longer the Christ of the Gospels, but the Christ of a Gospel reconstructed by the critics. It is the subordination of Christian facts to a human theory.

When we turn to the demand for a 'new dogma,' which we saw was emphasized by Kaftan (*Glaube u. Dogma*), we find the other principle of the school at work, viz.—the separation of theology from metaphysics, and the distinction between religious and theoretic knowledge. The watchword 'theology without metaphysics,' however, does not mean simply theology which shall be free from a speculative reconstruction as in the Hegelian school. It means a theology without any metaphysical elements, *i.e.* with nothing that transcends experience. Hence we must not only distinguish the 'historical Christ' from the Christ of an uncritical tradition; we must also distinguish Him from the Christ of a metaphysical dogma of Greek origin. Accordingly the doctrines of the Trinity and of the two natures in one person in our Lord are to be abandoned as metaphysical. The new dogma expresses itself in

---

* It is true that both Herrmann and Reischle ('Der Streit über die Begründung des Glaubens auf dem gesch. Christus,' *Zeitsch. f. Theol. u Kirche*, 1897) make a sharp distinction between the 'ground' and the 'content' of faith; and what they seek is an independent ground of faith. But it is also true that the ground of faith once determined becomes in their hands a norm for distinguishing between kernel and husk in its 'content.' Accordingly their idea of the 'content' of faith is one that fits in with their idea of its ground. Kähler (*Der sogenannte historische Jesus u. d. gesch., biblische Christus* [2], 1896) has criticised this distinction between the ground and the content of faith. But it is more important to note that the idea which these writers have of Christ as the ground of faith determines absolutely its content by acting as a principle by which to distinguish the abiding content of faith from its historical form, and thus makes room for endless subjectivity.

religious knowledge which springs from faith, and not in metaphysical propositions. Christ, therefore, is not Divine in a metaphysical sense as in the doctrine of the two natures, but simply in the religious sense that in the man Jesus we have the perfect revelation of God, or else that the term 'Divinity' expresses His value for the believer. This latter is Ritschl's position, and members of the school who have taken a more positive attitude than Ritschl have fallen short of asserting Christ's Divinity in any metaphysical sense (cf. Kaftan, *Dogmatik*; Lobstein, *Lehre v. d. übernat. Geburt Christi*. Harnack, *op. cit.*, and H. Schultz, *Lehre v. d. Gottheit Christi*, occupy much the same position as Ritschl).

We must conclude that in the Ritschlian theology we have again the subordination of the great Christian facts and dogmas to a phenomenalistic philosophy and a historical criticism subject to a naturalistic bias. This amounts to their subjection to a human theory. For the fundamental question is—Upon what does this theology rest? Has it a more objective basis than rationalism and mysticism? It seeks to base revelation on Christ. The source of its dogma is not the individual Christian consciousness but the Christian life, or the revelation of God portrayed in the Bible. But its Christ is a human Christ who can give no absolute revelation of God; and the Scripture is not regarded as authoritative in any objective sense as containing a supernatural revelation, but simply as the record of the revelation by the human Christ. The Scripture is subjected to the Christian consciousness to such an extent that the Christian doctrines are not to be taken directly from Scripture as 'external revelations,' but only as 'appropriated' and 'authenticated' by Christian faith (cf. Kaftan, *Dogmatik*, § on the Scripture, p. 48). Thus the idea of revelation has changed its biblical sense of a supernatural communication of truth, and becomes the product of the religious life of those who stood nearest Christ. But the Christian life does not remove the noetic effects of sin all at once, and consequently this idea of special revelation does not meet the demand which made a special revelation necessary. In short, if we abandon the principle of external authority, we cannot escape the subjection of the facts and doctrines of Christianity to a philosophical theory.

The logical results of the abandonment of an external authority in religious knowledge have been recently exhibited in the new theological school which follows the method of Comparative Religion. For if Christ is only human, and the Christian revelation not supernatural, it will be impossible to maintain the absoluteness of Christianity as the Ritschlians sought to do. It will be impossible to maintain that Christianity consists in Christ and not merely in a principle of which He is the illustration. We thus have the distinction between the 'Christian principle' and the person of Christ. It is the distinction of the old rationalism, only now in quite a different form, since this school insists that principles can never be separated from their historical embodiment. Therefore the distinction between the 'kernel' and the 'husk' must be given up, since the kernel is always inseparable from its historical manifestation. All history is relative, yet not at all unimportant, for we cannot have religious truth except in a historically conditioned form. Thus, while a greater significance attaches to Christ than in the old rationalism, the great facts and the dogmatic content of Christianity have only a relative value, and are frankly given up at the demands of an avowedly naturalistic philosophy. This can be seen in Troeltsch, the dogmatician of the school (cf. his art. 'Geschichte u. Metaphysik' in *Zeitschr. f.*

Theol. u. Kirche, 1898, pp. 55-67. Cf. also *Die Absolutheit des Christentums u. die Religionsgeschichte*, 1902). Troeltsch admits the significance of personality in the religious sphere, and that Christ is the source of our communion with God; but in view of the power of development in Christianity, he holds that it is not possible to limit God's revelation to one person at the beginning of Christian history. Therefore the first form of Christianity, as connected with Jesus, is to be regarded along with later forms simply as illustrations of the Christian principle. Thus we have again the entire subordination of the facts and doctrines of Christianity to the theory of the naturalistic evolution of religious ideas.

We conclude, then, that Christianity consists in a series of supernatural facts together with their meaning; that their true meaning is their meaning for God, and that therefore He must tell it to us; that the noetic effects of sin make it necessary that this be in a special and supernatural manner. The abandonment of the authority of Scripture for the interpretation of the facts leads logically to the abandonment of the facts themselves, *i.e.* to their subordination to a theory which distinguishes their accidental Scriptural form from their abiding philosophical content. The Ritschlian endeavour to stem the tide of this logic is unsuccessful, and the newest development in theology has cast aside the Ritschlian claim as to the absoluteness of Christianity and the Divinity of Christ, and has subjected Scripture fact and doctrine to an avowedly naturalistic philosophy. If, therefore, we are not to lose the supernatural facts and their authoritative interpretation, *i.e.* if we are not to lose Christianity, we must abide by the Scripture as an external authority.

LITERATURE. — R. W. Dale, *The Atonement*, Introd. Lect.; *Faith and Criticism*, Essay on the Atonement by Horton; *The Atonement in Modern Religious Thought*, Essays by Campbell, Farrar, Adeney, Horton; Forrest, *The Christ of History and of Experience*, Lect. viii.; H. Bois, *Le Dogme Grec*; Warfield, *The Right of Systematic Theology*; Denney, *The Death of Christ*, Introd.; Griffin, 'Facts, Doctrines, and Ideals' in *Pres. and Ref. Rev.*, July 1901; R. A. Lipsius, 'Die Bedeutung des Historischen im Christentume,' pub. in *Glauben u. Wissen*. p. 111; A. Sabatier, *The Vitality of Christian Dogmas and their Power of Evolution*, cf. also Part 3 of his *Outlines of the Phil. of Relig.*; Dreyer, *Undogmatisches Christentum*; Harnack, *Das Christentum u. die Geschichte*; Herrmann, *Warum bedarf unser Glaube geschichtlicher Thatsachen*?; Kaftan, *Glaube u. Dogma*; Kirn, *Glaube u. Geschichte*; Kähler, *Der sogenannte historische Jesus u. der gesch. biblische Christus*; Troeltsch, 'Geschichte u. Metaphysik' in *Zeitschr. f. Theol. u. Kirche*, 1898, esp. pp. 55-67; E. Cremer, 'Der Glaube u. die Thatsachen' in *Greifswalder Stud*. p. 261; Munchmeyer, 'Die Bedeutung d. gesch. Thatsachen f. den Glauben' in *Neue kirchl. Zeitschr.* 1895, p. 349; Seeberg, 'Brauchen wir ein neues Dogma?' *ib.* 1891; W. A. Pickard-Cambridge, 'The Christ of Dogma and the Christ of Experience' in *Hibbert Journal*, Jan. 1905; 'Romanus,' art. 'The Historical Jesus and the Christ of Experience,' *ib.* Apr. 1905; Schanz, 'Geschichte u. Dogma' in *Theol. Quartalschr.*, 1 Quartalheft 1905.

Compare also — Kant, *Die Relig. innerhalb d. Grenzen d. blossen Vernunft*; Fichte, *Anweis. zum seligen Leben*; Hegel, *Lectt. on Phil. of Relig.*; T. H. Green, *Miscell. Works*, iii. pp. 160-185, 230-276; Pfleiderer, *Glaubens- u. Sittenlehre*, §§ on Christ; Biedermann, *Chr. Dogmatik*, ii. § 815; A. Sabatier, *Esquisse d'une Phil. de la Relig.* etc., also *Les Religions d'Autorité et la Relig. de l'Esprit*; Harnack, *Wesen des Christentums*, Lectt. i.-iii.; Herrmann, *Verkehr des Christen mit Gott.*, also *Der Begriff d. Offenbarung*; Kaftan, *Das Wesen d. Chr. Relig.*, Absch. 2, Kap. 3; Reischle, 'Der Streit uber die Begründung des Glaubens auf dem gesch. Christus' in *Zeitsch. f. Theol. u. Kirche*, 1897; Troeltsch, *Die Absolutheit des Christentums u. die Religionsgesch*.

C. W. HODGE.

FAITH (Heb. אֱמוּנָה, Gr. πίστις). —

1. Introductory.
2. The idea of 'faith' in the OT.
3. Later Jewish idea of 'faith.'
4. 'Faith' in the Gospels: (1) in the Synoptics; (2) in the Fourth Gospel.
5. Some characteristics of the Johannine conception of 'faith.'
6. The Johannine and Pauline conceptions of 'faith' contrasted.
7. The place of 'faith' in the teaching of Jesus.
Literature.

1. *Introductory.*—In the NT the term 'faith' has two main meanings, which may be distinguished as active and passive senses, viz. : (1) *belief,* 'the frame of mind which relies on another,' and (2) *fidelity,* 'the frame of mind which can be relied on.' Of these the former is the predominant use, and is marked by a rich, copious, and distinctively Christian development.

The two senses—the active and passive—both logically and grammatically pass by an easy transition from one to the other, and are not always clearly distinguishable, or are actually combined (as, *e.g.*, in οἱ πιστοί, 'the faithful,' applied to the Christian fellowship). In the OT the *quasi*-active sense of 'trust,' with the meaning 'exhibit faithfulness *or* confidence,' is expressed by the Hiphil הֶאֱמִין (constr. with בְּ = 'to believe in reliance on *or* in,' followed by the object or ground of the belief ; with לְ in a weaker sense, 'to believe,' the object here denoted by לְ being not so much that in which the confidence is reposed, as that on the (attesting) strength of which it is reposed in the absolute object). No noun-derivative from the Hiphil occurs in the OT (denoting 'faith' as an active principle). The substantive אֱמוּנָה 'firmness,' 'steadfastness,' 'fidelity' (notice the passive form) is the nearest equivalent for 'faith' ; but it always occurs with the passive sense, with the possible exception of Hab 2⁴ ('the just shall live *by his faith*').* In this passage the active principle of trust in God seems to be contrasted sharply with arrogant self-sufficiency. The Gr. πίστις (πιστεύω), seems to have followed the reverse order of development (from active to passive). Here the predominant meaning is active 'faith,' 'trust,' 'belief' (in Classical usage, however, with the slightest possible association with religious ideas). The LXX use of the word (πίστις = אֱמוּנָה usually ; sometimes אֱמֶת and אֲמָנָה) probably reacted upon the Hebrew, and on this supposition is it possible to explain the active sense which is certainly present in Rabbinical Hebrew, and which may be seen in the late Hebrew of Sirach (*e.g.* 46¹⁵).† In the Aramaic of the Targums the active sense is fixed in a substantive derived from the Aphel, הֵימָנוּתָא (used in Gn 15⁶ of Abraham's *faith*). Cf. the Syriac equivalent of πίστις in the NT

ܗܝܡܢܘܬܐ.

2. The idea of faith in the OT.—Faith as an active religious principle is relatively far less prominent in the OT than in the NT. The solitary instance in which the active meaning certainly emerges in the Heb. substantive אֱמוּנָה has already been referred to. But even the verb (הֶאֱמִין) is by no means common with a religious connotation. Trust or confidence in God and the unseen are, of course, essential to spiritual religion, and receive manifold expression, especially in the Psalms (note the use in this connexion of (בְּ, עַל\אֶל), בָּטַח with God as object). But, as Lightfoot ‡ has remarked, 'it is indeed a characteristic token of the difference between the two covenants, that under the Law the "*fear* of the Lord" holds very much the same place as "*faith* in God," "*faith* in Christ," under the Gospel. *Awe* is the prominent idea in the earlier dispensation, *trust* in the later.'

The object of 'faith,' as expressed (with a religious connotation) by the verb (הֶאֱמִין) in the OT, is sometimes the words or commandments of God, or a particular word or work of God, or the Divine revelation, or the Divine messengers the prophets, or God Himself in His own Person. Of this last usage the examples are the most important (Gn 15⁶, Ex 14³¹, Nu 14¹¹ 20¹², Dt 1³², 2 K 17¹⁴, 2 Ch 20²⁰, Ps 78²², Jon 3⁵).§ Here the verb is construed with בְּ. The classical instance is, of course, Abraham's faith (Gn 15⁶), which, with a true instinct, has been recognized, both by Jewish and Christian religious exegesis, as the supreme example of faith in its active exercise as a religious principle.

3. Later Jewish idea of 'faith.'—In early Rab-

* Targ., however, עַל קוּשְׁטְּהוֹן יְתְקַיְּמוּן. Perhaps, as Lightfoot (*Galatians*, p. 148) suggests, the 'transitional or double sense' should be recognized in the passage.

† ἐν πίστει αὐτοῦ ἠκριβάσθη προφήτης ; Heb. ש חזה נדר(אמונתו (Strack).

‡ *Op. cit.* p. 151.

§ Add to these the cases where it is construed absolutely : Ex 4³¹, Is 7⁹ 28¹⁶, Ps 116¹⁰ ; and cf. Ps 27¹³.

binical and other Jewish literature the term for 'faith,' besides its Biblical meaning of 'faithfulness,' also denotes active trust in God. This as a religious principle is emphatically praised by the Rabbis, and regarded by them as highly meritorious. The classical example is, as has already been stated, the faith of Abraham (Gn 15⁶), which became one of the commonplaces of theological discussion not only in Rabbinical circles but also in the Hellenistic school of Alexandria,* while its occurrence in the NT is, of course, a familiar fact. The most instructive example in Rabbinical literature is to be found in the early Midrashic work the *Mekhilta* (on Ex 14³⁰).† The passage runs as follows :

'*The people feared the Lord.* So long as they were in Egypt they did not fear God, but now : *the people feared the Lord, and they believed in the Lord and His servant Moses.* If they believed in Moses, much more did they believe in the Lord. From this thou mayest learn that whoever believes in the faithful Shepherd is (regarded) as if he believed in the word of Him who spake and the world was. . . . Great is faith whereby Israel believed in Him who spake and the world was ; for because Israel believed in the Lord, the Holy Spirit abode upon them, and they sang the song : for immediately after the words : *they believed in the Lord and in Moses His servant,* follow the words (Ex 15¹) : *Then sang Moses and the children of Israel this song to the Lord.* In like manner thou findest that Abraham our Father inherited this world and the world to come only by the merit of faith (אֲמָנָה) whereby he believed in the Lord, as it is said (Gn 15⁶) : *And he believed in the Lord, and He counted it to him for righteousness.* . . . R. Nehemiah says : Whoever receives unto himself one precept (of the Law) in true faith (בֶּאֱמָנָה) is worthy for the Holy Spirit to abide upon him ; for so we find in the case of our fathers that because they believed in the Lord they were deemed worthy that the Holy Spirit should abide upon them, and they uttered the song. For it is said : *they believed in God and in Moses His servant* ; and (immediately afterwards) it is said : *then sang Moses and the children of Israel,* etc. And so thou findest in the case of Abraham that he inherited this world and the world to come solely by merit of faith (בִּזְכוּת אֲמָנָה), whereby he believed in the Lord, as it is said (15⁶) : *Abraham believed,* etc. And in the same way we find in the case of Moses, David, and Deborah that they (by reason of faith) sang a song, and the Holy Spirit abode upon them. And in like manner thou findest that solely by merit of faith was Israel redeemed from Egypt, as it is said : *And the people believed,* etc. And so it is said (Ps 31²³) : *The Lord preserveth the faithful,* making mention of the faith of the fathers. . . . Of the righteous it is said (Is 26²) : *Open ye the gates that the righteous nation, which keepeth the faith, may enter in.* Into this gate all the faithful (בַּעֲלֵי אמונה) enter. David sings (Ps 92¹) : *It is a good thing to give thanks unto the Lord, and to sing praises unto Thy name, O Most High : to show forth Thy loving-kindness in the morning and Thy faithfulness in the nights, with an instrument of ten strings and with the psaltery, with a solemn sound upon the harp. For Thou, O Lord, hast made me glad through Thy works, and in the operation of Thy hand will I exult.* What is the cause of his joy here ? It is the reward of faith which our fathers showed in this world, wherewith they trusted by day and night. For thus is it said : to show forth thy loving-kindness in the morning and thy faithfulness in the nights.* And in like manner is it said of Jehoshaphat (2 Ch 20²⁰) : *And they rose early in the morning and went forth into the wilderness of Tekoa ; and when they went forth Jehoshaphat stood up and said : Hear ye me, O Judah, and ye inhabitants of Jerusalem ! Have faith in the Lord your God, and so shall ye be established ; and have faith in His prophets, and so shall ye prosper.* And (so) it is written (Jer 5³) : *O Lord, do not Thine eyes look upon faith ?* And (Hab 2⁴) : *The righteous liveth of his faith.* Also (La 3²³) : *They are new every morning, Thy faithfulness is great.* Also thou findest that the (Divine) intercourse is only accorded as the reward of faith, as it is said (Ca 4⁸) : *Come with me from Lebanon, my bride* ('Bride' = Holy Spirit), *come with me ; of faith shalt Thou be the familiar companion altogether* (lit. 'from the head').‡ In like manner it is said (Hos 2¹⁹. ²⁰) : *I will*

* In Philo the career of Abraham is made the subject of elaborate and frequent comment and allegory. Lightfoot (*op. cit.*) remarks : 'If we look only to the individual man, faith with Philo is substantially the same as faith with St. Paul. The lessons drawn from the history of Abraham by the Alexandrian Jew and the Christian Apostle differ very slightly.'

† The original can be seen in Weiss' ed. of the *Mekhilta*, 25*b*, 26. The *Mekhilta* is a halakhic midrash on part of Exodus, dating in its present form from the first part of the second Christian century, but containing much earlier material. It is invaluable for illustrating early Jewish ideas and religious thoughts of the Apostolic age.

‡ So the words of the original (תָּשׁוּרִי מֵרֹאשׁ אֲמָנָה) are understood here. 'Bride' (כַּלָּה) is a mystical designation of the Holy Spirit or Shekinah.

betroth thee unto me for ever ; yea, I will betroth thee unto me with faith (בֶּאֱמוּנָה). Great is faith before God, for on account of faith it is that the Holy Spirit abides (upon Israel),' etc.

In the early Rabbinical literature 'faith' wavers in meaning between 'belief' and 'fidelity' (to the Law).' The former is prominent in the *Apocalypse of Baruch* (1st cent. A.D.) But the latter is characteristic of the later period, 'faith' and 'works' being co-ordinated or combined.* 'Faith' (אֱמוּנָה) in the sense of fixed dogmatic belief is quite late in Hebrew literature (mediæval times).

In Rabbinical Hebrew, besides the nouns אֱמוּנָה, אֱמָנָה, a Hiphil-substantival form הַאֲמָנָה (= Aram. הֵימָנוּתָא) occurs (Tosefta *Baba bathra* v. 8). For the Gospel-expression ὀλιγό-πιστοι a Heb. parallel occurs in *Mekhilta* (on Ex 15¹) מחוסרי אמנה 'those lacking faith.' So in the Pal. Targ. (on Nu 11³²) מחוסרי הימנותא ('Then rose up those who had lacked faith and gathered the quails,' etc.); and *Gen. Rab.* § 32, קְטַנֵּי אֱמוּנָה 'men of little faith' (an exact parallel). In the Mishna, *Ṣota* ix. 12, the decline of the world is ascribed to the disappearance of 'men of faith' (אַנְשֵׁי אֱמָנָה).

4. 'Faith' in the Gospels. — The terms for 'faith' and 'believe' in contrast with those of the OT are characteristic of the whole NT language, and occur almost entirely with a directly religious connotation. In Philo the religious content of the terms had decidedly been heightened, but suffered from a certain vagueness in the conception of the object of faith, due to his transcendental philosophy. Faith, in Philo's conception, rests rather upon the abstract Divinity than upon the personal God of grace and salvation, and is rather the fruit and crown of righteousness than its antecedent. In the NT it is all-important to distinguish the different connotations of the terms according as the object is (*a*) God ; (*b*) the promises of God ; (*c*) Christ ; (*d*) some particular utterance, claim, or promise of God or Christ. 'The last of these senses is the one most common in the Synoptic Gospels.'†

(1) *In the Synoptics.* — In its active sense of 'faith,' πίστις usually means here belief or trust in God or God's power as manifested in Christ (the so-called 'miracle-faith').‡ The response of faith conditions the granting of relief to those in bodily distress (Mk 5³⁴ ||, 10⁵² ||), the effect being proportionate to the degree of faith exercised (Mt 9²⁹ 'According to your faith [κατὰ τὴν πίστιν ὑμῶν] be it done unto you' ; cf. 15²⁸, Lk 7⁹ ˙ ⁵⁰ ; and for degrees of faith see Mt 8¹⁰ ||, Lk 17⁵ etc.). In this connexion Mt 13⁵⁸ is instructive. We are told that 'He did not many mighty works there [' in his own country,' Nazareth] because of their unbelief' ('lack of faith,' ἀπιστίαν) ; cf. Mk 6⁶. The term 'faith' is also applied to the *confidence of the disciple that the power conferred upon him will be effective* (in the performance of miraculous works), Mk 11²²⁻²⁴, defined by Christ as 'faith in God' (v.²²). Possibly, however, this passage (as has been suggested by Menzies §) is intended simply to bring home to the disciples the power of faith in accomplishing the seemingly impossible. 'Jesus summons those who look to Him to have faith in God when they are in great danger, or when they are seeking with all their heart some boon which outward appearances declare to be all but hopeless' ; the special and (apparently insurmountable) difficulty here being the insensibility of the Jewish people as a whole to the message of the gospel

(symbolized by the withered fig-tree). Cf. the words of Christ to Jairus (Mk 5³⁶ 'Fear not, only believe'), to the father of the epileptic (9²³ 'If it be possible ! All things are possible to him that believeth'), to the disciples in the storm (4⁴⁰ 'Why are ye fearful ? Have ye not faith ?').

The words about the power to remove mountains (Mk 11²³ᶠ· || Mt 21²¹ᶠ·) occur also in a different connexion in Mt 17²⁰ in the rebuke administered to the disciples for their 'lack of faith' in dealing with the epileptic—a case of special difficulty). They have a proverbial ring,* and may easily have been used by our Lord more than once (cf. Lk 17⁶ 'If ye have faith as a grain of mustard seed, ye would say to this sycamine tree, Be thou rooted up,' etc.).

In one instance 'faith' is used in the Synoptic Gospels in a way that suggests the technical sense so frequent in the Epistles, viz. Lk 18⁸ (' When the Son of man comes, shall he find faith on the earth' ?) Here 'faith' = faith in Himself as Messiah and Redeemer.

In the Acts and Epp. πίστις, used absolutely, constantly occurs in a soteriological sense = 'saving faith.' It rapidly became a Christian technical term, and practically stood as a synonym for Christianity, marking out the new religion as essentially characterized by faith or belief in Jesus as Redeemer. 'Believers' becomes the designation of Christians ; 'to believe' = to become a Christian. As contrasted with this usage, the term in the Synoptics is, to some extent, undeveloped in meaning. Yet how near the soteriological lies to the 'miracle-faith' comes out clearly in such a passage as Ac 3¹⁶ (the healing of the lame man at the Gate Beautiful) 'By faith in his name hath his name made this man strong, whom ye behold and know ; yea, the faith that is through him hath given him this perfect soundness in the presence of you all' ; here 'faith in the Name' (of Jesus) is described as 'faith brought into being by Him' (ἡ πίστις ἡ δι' αὐτοῦ),† and the same conclusion results from a comparison of the language of Mt 9², Mk 2⁵, Lk 5²⁰ ('Thy sins are forgiven thee '), as well as from the language of Lk 7⁵⁰, Mt 9²², Mk 5²⁴.‡

(2) *In the Fourth Gospel* the absence of the substantive (πίστις)—which does not occur at all—is made up for by the frequent use of the verb (πιστεύειν).

πιστεύειν rarely occurs in the NT in the weakened sense 'to credit,' 'give credence to' ; only once apparently of a non-religious act (Mt 24²³· ²⁶, Mk 13²¹—in the warning about false Christs, 'believe it not') ; elsewhere of assent given to some definite act, event, or fact in the religious sphere : of believing prayer (Mt 21²² 'Whatsoever ye shall ask in prayer, believing ye shall receive) ; of belief in the fact of the resurrection of Christ (Jn 20⁸· ²⁵· ²⁹ *bis*) ; in God's word of promise (Lk 14⁵ ; cf. Ac 26²⁷), in the declarations of Jesus whether regarding earthly or heavenly things (Jn 3¹² ¹⁵⁰, Lk 22⁶⁷) ; of faith generally in the word of salvation (Lk 8¹² 'that they may not believe and be saved,' cf. Jn 17).

The usual sense of the verb in the Fourth Gospel is a soteriological one. It expresses saving faith directed to the Person of Christ. In some instances, it is true, the immediate object of the faith is the wonder-working power of Jesus (the 'miracle-faith') : Jn 4⁴⁸ (' Except ye see signs and wonders, ye will in no wise believe'), 11⁴⁰.§ But here also the same remark applies as to the similar cases in the Synoptics, that the soteriological meaning lies very close to, and is sometimes almost indistinguishable from, the other (cf. Jn 4⁴⁸ with v.⁵³ and 9³⁸, and 11⁴⁰ with v.¹⁵ and 12³⁹). In the following instances, however, the direct soteriological significance is clear and unmistakable : 3¹⁵· ¹⁸ 4⁴¹· ⁴²· ⁵³ 5⁴⁴ 6³⁶· ⁴⁷· ⁶⁴ 9³⁸ 10²⁵· ²⁶ 11¹⁵ 12³⁹ 14²⁹ 16³¹ 19³⁵ 20³¹. Of these passages the two last are particularly instructive : 'That ye may believe' (19³⁵), and 'These are written that ye may believe that Jesus is the Christ, the Son of God ; and that believing ye may have life in his name' (20³¹). Here faith occupies

---

* Cf. Charles' note on *Apoc. Bar.* liv. 21 : 'Faith in the Talmud is in one of its aspects regarded as a work which, as the fulfilment of the Law, produces merit.'

† Sanday-Headlam, *Romans*, p. 31 f. The passive sense of πίστις ('faithfulness,' 'fidelity') is very rare in the NT. The only instance in the Gospels seems to be Mt 23²³ (' the weightier matters of the Law, judgment and mercy and faithfulness' [καὶ τὴν πίστιν]).

‡ Nowhere in the NT is it used of man's faith in man.

§ *The Earliest Gospel*, p. 211.

* For the possible interpretation of the words בְּהַר יְהוָה יֵרָאֶה (Gn 22¹⁴) as a proverb = ' In the mountain (*i.e.* when perplexity is at its height) Jahweh will provide,' see C. J. Ball in *SBOT* note, *ad loc.* Cf. Zec 47.

† Cf. also Ac 14⁹.

‡ Cf. also the use of πιστεύειν for saving faith in Christ, in Mk 9⁴² 15³².

§ Cf. Mt 8¹³, Mk 5³⁶ 9²³· ²⁴, Lk 8⁵⁰.

a fundamental place. Its essential object is defined to be the belief that Jesus is 'the Christ, the Son of God.'

Once again the conclusion is reinforced that the undefined 'to believe' is practically a synonym for 'to be a Christian.' Indeed, it may be inferred from the NT usage generally of πιστεύειν that before the disciples were called 'Christians' (Ac 11²⁶), they were designated 'believers' * (οἱ πιστεύοντες is used as a participle in Mk 9⁴², but as a subst. perhaps in Ac 5¹⁴ᵇ 'And believers were the more added to the Lord'). Sometimes οἱ πιστοί is used in an equivalent sense (e.g. Ac 10⁴⁵, 1 P 1²¹, Rev 17¹⁴; cf. the use of πιστός in Jn 1²⁷), and ἄπιστοι occurs in the opposite sense of 'unbelievers' (e.g. 2 Co 4⁶ 6¹⁴ᶠ·; cf. Jn 20²⁷, Mt 17¹⁷, Mk 9¹⁹, Lk 9⁴¹). Cf. the cognate use of ἀπιστία, 'unbelief' (Mk 9²⁴ 16¹⁴, Mt 13⁵⁸, Mk 6⁶; also in the Epp.); ἀπιστέω, 'disbelieve' (Mk 16¹¹· ¹⁶, Lk 24¹¹· ⁴¹, Ac 28²⁴, 1 P 2⁷); and ὀλιγόπιστος, 'of little faith' (Mt 6³⁰ 8²⁶ 14³¹ 16⁸, Lk 12²⁸); ὀλιγοπιστία, 'little faith,' occurs Mt 17²⁰.

5. Some characteristics of the Johannine conception of 'faith.'

—The fundamental conception of 'faith' in the Fourth Gospel coincides with that of the other NT writers; it consists essentially in trustful self-committal to Christ and His salvation. Only it is concerned less than in the Synoptics with the appropriation of directly physical relief; it moves rather in the sphere of spiritual and eternal facts, and directs itself more exclusively to the Person of Christ. Trust in God and in Christ are equated (14¹); faith characterizes those who recognize His Divine mission (cf. also 16³⁰), and they are described as those 'who believe in his name.' The result of faith is an acknowledgment of Christ's unity with the Father (10³⁸ 14¹⁰).

Faith (πιστεύειν) and knowledge (γιγνώσκειν) are interchangeable ideas in the Fourth Gospel (cf. 6⁶⁹ 10³⁸ 17⁸), or rather they express the same truth looked at from different sides. 'To know' (γιγνώσκειν) in the Johannine language expresses the perception of eternal truth; 'to believe,' its temporal discovery and appropriation. The former is therefore the fruit of the latter (cf. esp. 10³⁸ 'believe . . . that ye may know'). The intellectual element is thus the product of a moral act, and is conditioned by it. Faith is not the result of logical operations, but is due to the Divine working (6⁴⁴ 'No man can come to me, except the Father which sent me draw him'). Where faith is not attained, this is due to the distraction exercised by lower and earthly ambitions or ideals ('glory one of another,' 5⁴⁴), or the deliberate choice of darkness rather than light (3¹⁹, cf. v.²¹). Trust is also shown to be characteristic of a real faith, which does not need 'signs,' and has risen above the necessities of 'sight' (20²⁹). The boon which faith appropriates is eternal life (5²⁴).

There is evident in the treatment of faith characteristic of the Fourth Gospel a spirit of protest against the false and exaggerated views of knowledge that were beginning to affect the Church. The subtle and pervasive danger of Gnosticism, with its dangerous glorification of a merely intellectual knowledge, and its contempt for simple faith, had to be met. This was effected in the Fourth Gospel, 'on the one hand by deepening the idea of knowledge to the knowledge of experience' (which is the fruit of simple faith), 'and on the other by insisting upon the immediate entrance of every believer into the possession of salvation.'† The writer of the Fourth Gospel 'would indeed have believers know what they believe, and who He is in whom they put their trust, and what He has done for them, and is doing, and will do in and through them; but this is not that they may know these things simply as intellectual propositions, but that they may rest on them in faith, and know them in personal experience.'‡ Nothing is more

* οἱ πιστεύσαντες (= those who had turned to Christ in trustful reliance) is perhaps used as a subst. in such passages as Ac 2⁴⁴ 4³², 2 Th 1¹⁰, He 4³.
† B. B. Warfield in Hastings' DB i. 836 (art. 'Faith').
‡ Warfield, ib.

characteristic of the Johannine conception than the insistence on the present experience and participation in eternal life of believers. 'He that believeth hath eternal life' (3³⁶ 5²⁴ 6⁴⁷· ⁵⁴; cf. 1 Jn 3¹⁴· ¹⁵ 5¹¹⁻¹³). The inheritance of the true Christian was not merely a future boon,—though the future had in store for him a greater glory than that of the present,—but the simple believer, by the mere act of faith, was already placed on a plane of life to which no knowledge could attain.'

It is worth noting in this connexion that ἀλήθεια (which like πίστις is employed in the LXX to translate אֱמוּנָה) seems to be used in the Fourth Gospel in the sense of faithfulness, rightness, rectitude, rather than with the meaning of intellectual truth. In 1¹⁴· ¹⁶ χάρις καὶ ἀλήθεια = חֶסֶד וֶאֱמֶת or אֱמוּנָה חֶסֶד, and by ἀλήθεια is to be understood 'faithfulness corresponding to certain obligatory relations or to certain promises' (Wendt *). Cf. also the phrase ποιεῖν τὴν ἀλήθειαν = 'to do the right,' i.e. to act conscientiously; also 8³². ⁴⁰. ⁴⁵. ⁴⁶ 17¹⁷. ¹⁹, and possibly also in 14⁶· ¹⁷ 15²⁶ 16¹³ 18³⁷ᶠ·—in all which passages the connotation seems to be a moral one ('faithfulness,' 'rectitude') rather than a purely intellectual one ('truth').

6. The Johannine and Pauline conceptions of 'faith' contrasted.

—This is not the place for an extended review of the Pauline view of faith, but one or two salient points of contrast with the Johannine may be briefly indicated. The different method of presentation in each case is explained by the different circumstances under which each was formulated. In the interests of spiritual religion the Apostle of the Gentiles was forced to wage uncompromising war with Jewish legalistic conceptions of religion, and prejudices in favour of their own privileged religious position, which (naturally enough) were ingrained in the Jewish consciousness, and threatened to pass over into the Christian Church.† As against Jewish privilege and advantages, St. Paul vindicated and maintained the great principle that in the domain of salvation there is no distinction between Jew and Gentile, and that the Jew has no other righteousness than that which comes through faith in Jesus Christ (Gal 3⁷ᶠ·), being in this respect in exactly the same position as the Gentile (cf. Ro 3³⁰). From this certain important results follow: (1) That 'no man is justified by the law' (Gal 2¹⁶ 3¹¹, Ro 3²⁰), and (2) that 'a man is justified by faith alone, apart from works of law.' This thesis was splendidly developed by St. Paul in his great dialectic. The absolute sufficiency of this saving faith is above all shown in the contemplation of its object. 'It is because faith lays hold of Jesus Christ, who was delivered up for our trespasses and was raised for our justification (Ro 4²⁵), and makes us the possessors of the righteousness of God through Him, that there is no room for any righteousness of our own in the ground of our salvation (Ro 10³, Eph 2⁸)' (Warfield). See, further, JUSTIFICATION.

On the other hand, the Johannine presentation is determined by an environment of different circumstances. The false emphasis laid on a merely intellectual knowledge had to be met. Hence the insistence in the Fourth Gospel on the true knowledge of Christian experience which is the fruit of a simple faith. It is regarded as a precious and permanent present possession. Briefly, it may be said that 'faith with St. John is rather contemplative and philosophic, where with St. Paul it is active and enthusiastic.'‡

7. The place of 'faith' in the teaching of Jesus.

—Christ no less than St. Paul combated the prevailing tendency among the Jews to rest in a

* Teaching of Jesus, i. p. 259 (Eng. tr.). God's faithfulness to His promises, as shown esp. in blessing His people, is an attribute constantly insisted on in the OT.
† As has already been pointed out above, 'faith' was regarded in Jewish circles as of the highest religious significance and value; only, in the background of the Jewish mind there always lurked the consciousness of privilege and superiority.
‡ Sanday-Headlam, Romans, p. 32.

position of privilege (cf. Mt 3[9], Ro 2[17]). But the dominant characteristic of His teaching, as reported both in the Synoptics and in the Fourth Gospel, is the consistent way in which He strives to draw all faith to Himself. Even when His language is general in character (Mk 11[22], Mt 21[22], Mk 9[24], Lk 18[8]), He speaks in a way that necessarily fixes attention upon His own Person as God's unique representative on earth. The soteriological significance of the so-called ' miracle-faith' has already been pointed out above. This comes out especially in such a passage as Mt 9[2], where healing of the body is conjoined with the claim to forgive sins. That Christ is the proper object of this soteriological faith is sufficiently attested even in the Synoptic account (Lk 8[12. 13] 22[32], Mt 18[6] [|| Mk 9[42]], Lk 7[50]; cf. Lk 24[25. 45]). It is in the Fourth Gospel, however, in the intimate discourses of Jesus which are there preserved, that the fullest account is given of the teaching of our Lord on this subject. Here, as is natural, faith in its higher aspects is consistently and abundantly set forth, as reflected and mirrored in the recollection of the ' disciple whom Jesus loved.' In the Fourth Gospel we are confronted with the personal testimony of the disciple who was uniquely fitted both by temperament and by character to receive and assimilate the deepest thoughts of his Master.

The testimony of the Fourth Gospel on this subject cannot be more adequately summed up than in the words of Warfield : *—

' In these discourses, too, Jesus' primary task is to bind men to Him by faith. The chief difference is that here, consonantly with the nature of the discourses recorded, much more prevailing stress is laid upon the higher aspects of faith, and we see Jesus striving specially to attract to Himself a faith consciously set upon eternal good. In a number of instances we find ourselves in much the same atmosphere as in the Synoptics (4[21f. 48f] 9[35]); and the method of Jesus is the same throughout. Everywhere He offers Himself as the object of faith, and claims faith in Himself for the highest concerns of the soul. But everywhere He begins at the level at which He finds His hearers, and leads them upward to these higher things. It is so that He deals with Nathanael (1[51]) and Nicodemus (3[12]); and it is so that He deals constantly with the Jews, everywhere requiring faith in Himself for eternal life (5[24. 25. 28] 6[35. 40. 47] 7[38] 8[24] 10[25. 38] 12[44. 46]), declaring that faith in Him is the certain outcome of faith in their own Scriptures (5[46. 47]), is demanded by the witness borne Him by God in His mighty works (10[25. 36. 37]), is involved in and is indeed identical with faith in God (5[25. 38] 6[40. 45] 8[47] 12[44]), and is the one thing which God requires of them (6[29]), and the failure of which will bring them eternal ruin (3[18] 5[38] 6[64] 8[24]). When dealing with His followers, His primary care was to build up their faith in Him. Witness especially His solicitude for their faith in the last hours of His intercourse with them. For the faith they had reposed in Him He returns thanks to God (17[8]), but He is still nursing their faith (16[31]), preparing for its increase through the events to come (13[19] 16[29]), and with almost passionate eagerness claiming it at their hands (14[1. 10. 11. 12]). Even after His resurrection we find Him restoring the faith of the waverer (20[29]) with words which pronounce a special blessing on those who should hereafter believe on less compelling evidence—words whose point is not fully caught until we realize that they contain an intimation of the work of the Apostles as, like His own, bringing men to faith in Him (17[20. 21]).'

The fundamental position of faith in the Christian religion, which is so strikingly expressed and implied throughout the whole NT literature, justifies the distinction of the old and new covenants as the ages before and after the ' coming of faith' (Gal 3[23. 25]). At the same time the way had been prepared for this historically by the circumstances of the time. The more the fulfilment of Israel's national hopes by special Divine interposition seemed to recede, the more stress was laid upon the necessity of trust and faith in the Divine ordering as a religious duty.

LITERATURE.—A comprehensive treatment of the whole subject will be found in B. B. Warfield's art. ' Faith' in Hastings' DB. To the literature there cited add R. J. Knowling, Ep. of St. James (1904), p. xlii ff., 53 ff.; R. St. J. Parry, Discussion of the Ep. of St. James (1903), p. 43 ff.; J. R. Illingworth, Reason and Revelation (1902), p. 204 ff., Christian Character (1904), p. 63 ff.; G. Ferries, Growth of Christian Faith (1905); W. Herrmann, Faith and Morals (1904), p. 7 ff. See also artt. BELIEF, DOUBT, JUSTIFICATION, RIGHTEOUSNESS.   G. H. BOX.

*Op. cit. ib.

FAITHFULNESS.—The quality of being faithful. ' Fidelity,' in the sense of trustworthiness, is a synonym ; so also ' loyalty,' ' constancy.' The thought is not primarily of belief entertained (although that is latent); rather of right conduct which, emanating from right motive, demands and receives confidence and approval. Thus George Eliot (Span. Gipsy, v.)—

' The deepest hunger of a faithful heart
Is faithfulness.'

The noun does not occur in the Gospels. There is, however, allusion to those in whom the quality (πιστότης) is conspicuous ; they are the ' faithful' (πιστοί) of Mt 24[45] 25[21. 23], Lk 12[42] 16[10-12]—where the word πιστός has the meaning of being trustworthy in the discharge of duty. It is their conduct, not their creed, to which attention is specially directed. At the same time it should be remarked that the πιστότης implied (certainly in Mt 24[45] 25[21. 23], Lk 12[42]) is closely bound up with an allegiance owned and recognized. It is suggestive of faith which, because genuine, compels to loyal obedience, and cannot but issue in works (' La foi qui n'agit point, est-ce une foi sincère ?' Racine). The trusty are the trustful (cf. Lightfoot, Gal. p. 155) ; and it is precisely those who feel themselves able to cling to something external to themselves who are most solicitous that their lives should be spent in useful service. See FAITH.   H. L. JACKSON.

FALL.—The various questions suggested in regard to the relation of the Fall to Jesus Christ may be treated under the following heads :

i. The Messianic element in the story of the Fall.
ii. The Fall in its bearing on the work of Christ in (1) the Incarnation, (2) its redemptive aspects.
iii. The Fall in its bearing on the Person of Christ.
iv. Our Lord's own teaching (or that of the Gospels) on the Fall.

i. THE MESSIANIC ELEMENT IN THE STORY OF THE FALL.—It is not within the scope of this Dictionary to discuss the general character of the OT narrative of the Fall. We may here simply assume as accepted the view that in Gn 3 we have an account, cast in the pictorial form characteristic of the period to which it belongs, of the beginning of human sin, with its attendant evils of suffering and death. Whatever opinion may be held as to the literary materials and composition of the narrative, it commends itself as in all essential features a unique and authoritative record of great fundamental facts of human life and history ; and its Divine inspiration is sufficiently attested by the profound truthfulness and significance of its moral and religious teaching.

In the midst of this story of sin and judgment we find the first promise of restoration, and thus the Divine purpose of redemption is brought into association with the very beginnings of human evil. ' I will put enmity between thee and the woman, and between thy seed and her seed : it shall bruise thy head, and thou shalt bruise his heel' (Gn 3[15]). That this utterance contains the germ of Messianic prophecy cannot be doubted ; but care must be taken to make neither too much nor too little of this element in it, and to interpret the passage in accordance with sound principles of historical exegesis, with due reference to the context, and to the general characteristics of OT prophecy. The embodiment of this Protevangelium in the primitive religious tradition, and in the inspired record of it, is a testimony to the fact that the Divine purpose of redemption is coeval with the existence of human sin. From the time when the consciousness of guilt and corruption first dawned in the human heart, there was also present the hope of restoration, and of man's ultimate triumph over those powers of evil by which he had been temporarily vanquished. This is the germ of which all the redemptive promise and prophecy of the OT are the development. Three progressive ideas may be traced in the teaching of the passage. (1) Under the symbolism of the repulsion with which the serpent species is regarded, there is conveyed the truth that there would be continual and deadly conflict between the human race and the powers of evil, each seeking to destroy the other. (2) The hopeful element in the struggle is indicated, and man's final victory suggested, by the specific way in which the conflict is described—'It shall bruise thy head, and thou shalt bruise his heel.' (3) There underlies the statement with regard to mankind in general the remoter and deeper significance applicable to the representative Man, in and through whom the warfare was to be brought to a crisis and a victorious issue.

The order of these points may also be taken as indicating the line along which the full meaning of the saying would unfold itself. It is one of those pregnant utterances of revelation whose content is gradually realized and defined by the progress of events. The Messianic ideas contained in it are as yet vague and general, yet real; rudimentary, but fundamental; implicit rather than explicit; yet enough to keep a spark of hope alive, and to inspire faith and effort till clearer light came in the providential unfolding of God's redemptive plan.

ii. THE FALL IN RELATION TO THE WORK OF CHRIST.—The fact of man's fallen condition, of which the narrative of Gn 3 is the historical explanation, is the *raison d'être* of redemption, and thus the Fall is very closely related to the whole work of Christ at every point. But it is with the *effects* rather than with the manner or history of the Fall that the gospel is supremely concerned, and after the story has once for all been given at the beginning of revelation, it is thereafter but little referred to in Scripture, and is scarcely ever brought into direct relation with redemption, except in two classical passages in the writings of St. Paul, viz. in Ro 5 and 1 Co 15. Our attention will here be confined to those points in which the Fall comes into more direct relation with the work of Christ, or in which the fall of man in Adam and his restoration in Christ serve to illuminate each other.

1. The relation of the Fall to the Incarnation.—The question here raised is between the two views expressed respectively by the words of Augustine, '*Si homo non pecasset, filius Dei non esset incarnatus,*' and of Andreas Osiander, '*Etiamsi homo non pecasset, Deus tamen incarnatus esset licet non crucifixus.*' The common belief has hitherto been that the whole mission and work of Christ were solely conditioned by the Fall. But the other view with regard to the Incarnation, maintained by the Scotists in the Middle Ages and by other distinguished thinkers, has of late gained fresh currency, especially in connexion with modern evolutionary philosophy. The relation of the Fall to the Incarnation determines the place of the latter in the plan of redemption, and opens up the question whether the Incarnation was subsidiary to the Atonement, or the Atonement a development and modification of the Incarnation.

(i.) The view that an Incarnation was, independently of sin, the consummation of God's purpose in relation to mankind, has been supported by arguments which can here only be briefly mentioned.

(a) The metaphysical argument that a possibility of becoming man must have existed eternally in the being of God, otherwise no Incarnation could have taken place. In other words, there was in God a 'self-disposition' for incarnation, a necessity (ethical, not metaphysical) for God, who is love, to make a perfect self-communication to His moral and spiritual creatures.

(b) The very conception of the *Mediator* in redemption implies a necessary and eternal relation both to God and to man, which,

even apart from sin, would have found its issue in incarnation. The Mediator is necessary for the *perfecting* of the world no less than for its redemption, and has a cosmical significance wider and deeper than His work as Redeemer.

(c) As Christ is necessary for the world's perfection, the Incarnation may be held to be involved in the 'eternal idea of the world.' This is the counterpart of the preceding arguments, and is as old as Irenæus. It means that man has in his very nature a need and a capacity for Christ, corresponding to God's self-communicating love, and this quite apart from sin.

(d) To base the Incarnation solely on the need of redemption, is to make Christ a means and not an end in Himself, or, in more modern language, to reduce the most glorious manifestation of God for the perfecting of humanity to an expedient contingent upon the untoward incident of sin. In Christ alone, as the centre and end, is the highest possible for man realized; if this were dependent on the Fall, then sin would be a '*felix culpa*' in the most emphatic sense.

(e) These somewhat speculative lines of reasoning are not without Scripture warrant. In such passages as Col 1[15ff.] and Eph 1[9. 10f.] we have at least a suggestion of a grand Christocentric plan for the universe, antecedent to, and occupying a plane quite above, the contingency of human sin. Christ is here presented in relation to the Universe as 'the firstborn of all creation,' *in* whom and *unto* whom all things were created, in whom all things hold together, and who becomes also 'the head of the body, the Church,' and 'the firstborn from the dead.' It was God's eternal purpose 'to sum up all things in Christ,' 'in whom also we were made a heritage' (cf. also Jn 1[3], He 1[2], 1 Co 8[6], Rev 3[14] etc.). Redemption is here presented as something which forms a harmonious part of a larger plan. Christ is at once the Alpha and the Omega, the medium and the end of creation, the beginning and the consummation of God's eternal purpose.

(ii.) The commonly received view that the Incarnation is simply a necessary part of the work of redemption, is supported by the *prima facie* teaching of Scripture. 'The Son of man came to seek and to save' (Lk 19[10]); 'God sent forth his Son . . . that he might redeem' (Gal 4[4f.]). These are examples of innumerable passages which represent the mission of Christ in this light. But to this it may be answered that, though historically and actually the Incarnation has taken this redemptive aspect, and is naturally and properly so presented in the Gospel, another view of it, under different conditions, is not excluded, of which, as we have seen, we are in fact permitted brief glimpses in a wider field of vision.

(iii.) Both the foregoing views may be united and harmonized in what is really the truest and deepest conception, viz. that God's purpose is an eternal and unchangeable unity, and every part of it, as wrought out in history, must be regarded as having its proper place in relation to the *whole*. It is by a misunderstanding of the absolute being and counsels of God that we discuss at all questions as to what might have been done under other conditions. The view of the question before us which is most worthy of a true conception of God, and which at the same time agrees with the broad teaching of Scripture, is that in the infinite counsels of Him who sees the end from the beginning, Redemption is wrought into the very fabric of God's eternal purpose, all parts of which—Creation, Redemption, Incarnation, Atonement, the Final Consummation,—hang together harmoniously as integral and correlated elements in one homogeneous, perfect, and unchangeable unity. The question as to the relation of the Fall to the Incarnation thus resolves itself into that of the place of the Fall in God's plan of the world; and we need not hold with hyper-Calvinists that sin was foreordained, in order to believe that the Fall, foreseen and permitted, enters into an intimate and essential relation to the whole of the Divine plan. In this plan Incarnation holds a central place, and its redemptive significance is one aspect of a wider relation to the world, as the means for *perfecting* as well as for *redeeming* the human race. This view preserves the place of Redemption in the foreground of God's revealed plan, avoids the necessity of conceiving any change in the Divine purpose contingent upon sin, and at the same time gives the Incarnation that cosmical significance worthy of its transcendent character. Thus Christ is central and supreme, and the whole scheme of Redemption is presented in a true perspective, more in harmony with the requirements of modern thought.

2. The relation of the Fall to the redemptive work of Christ.—In the distinctively soteriological aspects of Christ's work, we are brought at once into close relation to the Fall. We have here to consider (i.) the reality and general nature of the Fall, as seen in the light of Redemption ; and (ii.) the main points of detail in which the Fall and the redeeming work of Christ explain and illustrate each other.

(i.) The doctrine of the Fall is vital to the Christian system ; the reality and general nature of the Fall, as a great downward and retrograde step in the history of mankind, are confirmed and illustrated by the redemptive work of Christ. This aspect of Christ's work, which occupies in Scripture the foremost place, is everywhere represented as rendered necessary by something grievously abnormal in the condition of the human race. The Scripture doctrine of sin as absolute evil ; man's universal sinfulness, helplessness, and state of spiritual death, which form the very basis of Redemption ; the representation of mankind as 'lost,' 'alienated' from God, and yet capable and worthy of being redeemed and restored ;—all this, as so abundantly presented and emphasized in connexion with the atoning work of Christ, affords the strongest confirmation of the doctrine that man has fallen from a higher condition. Whatever may be said as to the Incarnation (see **1**, above), it is clear that the great outstanding fact of the Atonement, with all the suffering and sacrifice which it involved, can only be accounted for at once by the dignity and the degradation of man,—in other words, by the Fall.

(ii.) This is borne out by the more specific teaching in regard to the Fall in its relation to the work of Christ in Ro 5^{12-21} and 1 Co $15^{21.\ 22.\ 45-49}$. The general and clear line of argument in the former passage brings out the following points :
Adam's act of *disobedience* involved all men in (*a*) Sin, and (*b*) Death. By *sin* is here meant both actual sinfulness ('for that all sinned,' v.^{12}), and a condition of liability to penalty even apart from personal transgression (v.^{14}). This latter, however, is not to be held in any sense as personal participation in or responsibility for Adam's offence, though it is the transmitted effect of it (see below). *Death* here apparently means physical death in the first place (as in v.^{14}), but most probably includes also spiritual death. On the other hand, though the analogy is not fully expressed, it is clearly implied that in the same way Christ's act of *obedience* brings (*a*) Justification and (*b*) Life ; and in view of the emphatic reiteration, in various forms, of the surpassing fulness of Redemption in vv.$^{15-17}$, we may include under these terms : negatively, deliverance from *guilt*, from *sin itself*, and from *death* ; and positively, *the bestowment of judicial and actual righteousness, and of spiritual and eternal life.*

Another question raised in this connexion is concerned with the precise moral relationship between Adam and his posterity on the one hand, and between Christ and His people on the other. Adam and Christ ('the second Adam') are represented as standing in an analogous relation to mankind, forming the basis in the one case of universal sin and death, and in the other of restoration for believers. In regard to Adam it has been variously held (1) that the relation between him and his posterity was virtually one of *identity* ; mankind sinned in him and therefore share his guilt ; (2) that the relation is *representative* or

federal, Adam acting on behalf of his descendants ; and (3) that the relation is *natural*, the evil effects of Adam's fall being communicated to the race through the ordinary channels of heredity. The third view preserves any elements of truth in the other two, while it best explains the facts in harmony with true ethical principles. The transmitted effect of Adam's sin consists mainly of the loss of moral balance, an inborn tendency of heart and will towards evil, a *disability*, though not a total inability, for goodness. Though men are not personally implicated in the guilt of Adam's transgression, their condition involves demerit and necessitates redemption.* Turning to the other side, though we are not warranted in carrying the analogy too far, we find on the part of Christ (1) a relation of *identity with the race* through the Incarnation ; (2) a *representative* or covenant relation with His people (see 2 Co 5^{21} etc.), based on the one side on God's free grace, and on the other on believers' voluntary acceptance of it (Ro 5^{17}) ; and (3) a *vital union* between Christ and believers by which new life is imparted and the evil effects of the Fall counteracted (Jn 15^{1-6} etc.).

Christ is thus a new beginning for the fallen race, a fountain of life and righteousness, as Adam was of death and sin. Adam was a true 'figure of him that was to come,' a type based not on mere analogy, but on deep and real correspondences between his relation as 'psychical' parent to his natural descendants, and Christ's relation to His people as the 'second Adam,' the 'spiritual' originator of a regenerated race.†

iii. THE FALL IN RELATION TO THE PERSON OF CHRIST.—The Fall of Adam, as we have seen, introduced into the nature of all descended from him a fatal taint of sin, an insuperable moral disability. The question now before us is, How did Jesus Christ, the new Adam, as a true member of the fallen race, escape this evil influence? That Christ in His nature and Person was absolutely free from sin, is one of the clearest and most generally admitted as well as most vital facts of the gospel. Born into the world in the line of human descent, sharing human nature otherwise in its fulness, how was Jesus alone unaffected by the common heritage of sin?

The full answer to this question lies hidden in the mystery of the Incarnation ; but an indication of the line in which the solution lies is given in the great fact of the Virgin Birth of our Lord. The historical reality of this part of the Gospel narrative has been assailed by modern criticism, but the doctrine still retains its place in the best philosophy of the Incarnation, and the truth has been rather confirmed than otherwise by impartial study of the records. As a fact, the birth of Jesus in a supernatural manner commends itself as peculiarly in keeping with the whole scheme of redemption. (1) It indicates a new departure, a fresh beginning, the introduction into the human race of a new element, and marks a break in the normal and fatal continuity of spiritual helplessness and decay. (2) It suggests, though it does not fully explain, means by which Christ could become true man and yet be preserved from the hereditary effects of the Fall. 'The Holy Ghost shall come upon thee, and the power of the Most High shall overshadow thee : wherefore also that which is to be born shall be called holy, the Son of God' (Lk 1^{35}). Those who deny the Virgin Birth have still to explain the equally miraculous fact of the appearance of this single exception to the universal sinfulness of mankind. The manner of Christ's birth, as re-

* Note ἁμαρτωλοί in Ro 5^{19} and παράπτωμα, παράβασις in vv.$^{14.\ 15.\ 18}$; see Fairbairn, *Christ in Modern Theology*, p. 312.
† See full and suggestive drawing out of the analogy in Fairbairn's *Christ in Modern Theology*, pp. 311–313.

corded in the Gospels of Mt. and Lk., is so fully in harmony with His unique personality and character, that, though we cannot fully understand, we may at least be satisfied that all form parts of one Divine plan, and thus the moral miracle and the physical mutually support one another. See art. VIRGIN BIRTH.

iv. THE TEACHING OF CHRIST AND OF THE GOSPELS ON THE FALL.—Our Lord makes no reference to the story of the Fall in all His recorded teaching, His only allusion to our first parents at all being the general statement in connexion with marriage (Mt 19[4], Mk 10[6]). But the doctrine of the Fall underlies the whole teaching of Christ on sin and redemption, and is particularly confirmed and illustrated in the following points :
(1) *The universal sinfulness of man.* This is taken for granted. 'If ye then, *being evil*, know,' etc. (Mt 7[11], Lk 11[13]). This truth is involved in the whole character of our Lord's mission and teaching. See also Jn 1[29] 8[7]. (2) *The inwardness of sin.* 'Out of the heart come forth evil thoughts,' etc. '. . . These are the things which defile the man' (Mt 15[19. 20] and ||). Cf. also Mt 5[21-28], Mk 10[5], Lk 6[45]. (3) *The deep radical character of human evil.* 'Ye must be born anew' (Jn 3[7] and v.[3]). (4) *The hereditary disability of human nature.* 'That which is born of the flesh is flesh,' etc. (Jn 3[6] ; cf. 1[13]). (5) Jesus everywhere indicates clearly His view as to *the original dignity and value of man.* 'What shall a man be profited, if he shall gain the whole world, and forfeit his life ?' (Mt 16[26]). Cf. Lk 15[10], Mt 12[12], etc. ; and the general teaching of Jesus as to the Fatherhood of God. (6) The Fall may be said to be pictured for us more specifically in *the parable of the Prodigal Son* (Lk 15[11ff.]), and the corresponding parables of the Lost Sheep and the Lost Piece of Money in the same chapter. (7) Generally the whole mission of Christ to *ransom* men (Mk 10[45]), to *save* (Mt 1[21], Lk 19[10] etc.), and to *restore* to Divine Sonship (Jn 1[12]), is founded upon the doctrine of the Fall and the state of ruin resulting from it, combined with splendid possibilities of restoration through grace.

LITERATURE.—On OT narrative and Messianic elements : Ryle's *Early Narratives of Genesis* ; all good Commentaries, such as those of Dillmann, Gunkel, and Driver.
On Fall and Incarnation : Dorner, *Person of Christ*, vol. iii. pp. 361-369, vol. v. pp. 236-248, also the same author's *Christian Doctrine*, vol. iii. pp. 283-299 ; Martensen, *Christian Dogmatics*, pp. 258-263 ; Orr, *Christian View of God*, etc., pp. 319-327 ; Westcott, *The Gospel of Creation.*
On Adam and Christ : Relative sections of treatises on Systematic Theology, such as Dorner, Hodge ; Orr's *Christian View* ; Fairbairn, *Christ in Modern Theology* ; also Sanday-Headlam, *Romans* (on 5[12-21]), and other good Commentaries ; Beyschlag, *NT Theology*, vol. ii.
On Virgin Birth and Sinlessness of Christ : Sanday, *Bampton Lectures* ; Gore, *Bampton Lectures* ; all critical Lives of Christ ; Griffith-Jones, *Ascent through Christ* ; and for trustworthiness of Luke's narrative, Ramsay, *Was Christ born at Bethlehem ?*
On Christ's teaching : all good treatises, such as Wendt's ; and works on NT Theology, as those of Weiss and Beyschlag.

           J. E. M'OUAT.

FALSE CHRISTS. — The term ψευδόχριστοι or pseudo-Christs occurs only in Mk 13[22] (cf. 13[6]) = Mt 24[24] (cf. 24[5]). Despite its omission in Mk. by D, etc., it probably belongs to the original text of the eschatological discourse. But this discourse forms one of the sections in the Synoptic narrative which are specially permeated by reflexions of the Apostolic Church ; and even after a small Jewish or Jewish-Christian apocalypse has been disentangled from the discourse, the remaining *logia*, of which this forms one, require to be carefully scrutinized. They do not belong to the primitive tradition of Christ's sayings. Over them lie traces of the experiences of the early Christians during the latter half of the seventh decade in Palestine, when the political convulsion of the country was accompanied by religious agitation and moral crises of a strange nature. The 1st cent. of our era

was full of unrest for the Jews of Palestine. As the pages of Josephus testify, one rival Messiah followed another, each and all succeeding more or less in kindling the passions of the people against the Roman authorities. These popular leaders of revolt worked on the religious feeling of the nation. Messianic fanaticism became uncontrollable, and enthusiasts seduced the ardent by semi-political hopes (cf. Schürer, *HJP* I. ii. § 20, and Volz, *Jüd. Eschatologie*, 209-210).

If the words '*in my name*' (Mk 13[6] = Mt 24[5]) mean 'in the name of Jesus,' it is difficult to understand them. For it is hard to think of any Christians claiming to be Jesus. Christian false prophets there might be, and were, but we have no evidence during the 1st cent. of pretenders to the name of Jesus. False Christs in this sense of the term are scarcely credible, though later ages have furnished specimens of the type, as, *e.g.*, among some of the followers of George Fox the Quaker, who was himself accused of claiming to be Christ. Either, then, we must suppose that the phrase 'in my name' has been inserted by the Evangelists in order to stamp as Christian what was originally a Jewish prediction, or the phrase must be taken as equivalent to 'in the name of Messiah,' as is implied in 'I am he.' False Christs would thus be equivalent to false Messiahs (so Mk 13[21], Mt 24[23]), and the *logion* would be a warning against the claims and pretensions of the numerous impostors who swarmed in Palestine down to the days of Bar Cochba (131-135 A.D.), their last representative. It is in the light of this retrospect that Justin Martyr (about 155 A.D.) quotes this saying in his *Dialogue* (82. 308 C) thus : 'Our Lord said many false prophets and false Christs would come in His name and deceive many ; which is the case.' The false prophets, of course, are the heralds of the false Messiahs ; they guarantee the movement in question by means of miracles. But occasionally a false Messiah may have been, as Theudas was, a false prophet as well. The *Didache*, curiously enough, omits all mention of false Messiahs, though it notices the danger of false prophets (xvi. 3 ; cf., however, what is said in xvi. 4 about the appearing of the world-deceiver as Son of God).

The locale of the false Messiahs (Mt 24[26]) is either the wilderness (cf. Ac 21[38]), as in the case of Simon son of Gioras, or the inner chambers, as in the case of John of Giscala (cf. 1 K 20[30])— alluding possibly to the current idea that the Messiah was to remain hidden for some time previous to His appearance in public. But whether the one or the other happened to be chosen, the salient point is that in either case the elect are to be kept right by a wholesome scepticism. 'Christians, at Israel's great crisis, were to be *saved by unbelief* in pseudo-Messiahs and pseudo-prophets' (*Expos. Gr. Test.* i. 294). The situation would also manifest the difference between credulity and faith. Desperate situations foster an avid appetite for deliverance, which is too often indifferent to the particular quality of the aid offered. But faith keeps its head. Belief in Christ imparts a sanity of judgment which makes men cool even in emergencies. Finally, there is the thought that miracles of themselves are no guarantee of Divine authority.

The allusion in Jn 5[43] may be, but is not necessarily, to a single anti-Christ or pseudo-Christ, who, however, comes *in his own name* (cf. Loisy, *Le Quatrième Évangile*, p. 416). Neither here nor in Rev 13[11] 20[10] have we to do with an epitome or individual incarnation of the deceivers foretold in the Synoptic narrative. The plane of thought is at once later and different.

LITERATURE.—In addition to the literature cited above, consult the critical editors on the passages in question ; and see

V. H. Stanton, *The Gospels as Historical Documents*, i. 125 ;
Keim, *Jesus of Nazara*, v. 238 f. ; and Bousset, *The Antichrist
Legend*, p. 103 f.   J. MOFFATT.

FALSE PROPHETS.—**1.** For the understanding
of this expression in the NT, we must correctly
apprehend the character of *the false prophets of the
OT.* To earlier writers these men were essentially
and consciously false, either prophets of false gods,
holders of opinions which did not agree with the
revealed character of Jehovah the God of Israel,
or men who knowingly spoke falsehoods in the
name of Jehovah. Modern biblical science takes
a more lenient view. It does not deny the existence of such as either possible or actual (Jer 2[8],
Ezk 13[1-9]), though in the matter of creed many of
them were probably 'syncretistic' rather than
simply 'anti-Jehovistic' (A. B. Davidson). The
majority may be regarded rather as men accustomed to the outward signs of the prophetic office,
the hairy mantle (Zec 13[4], cf. 1 K 19[19]), the
methods of prophetic instruction (Jer 28[10]), and the
use of the prophetic formula, 'Thus saith Jehovah'
(Jer 23[25. 31], Ezk 13[6]), but who had never come
under the influence of, or had failed to remain in
personal contact with, the revealing Spirit 'who
spake by the prophets.' Hence the message they
gave was merely one that was agreeable to the
common thought of the people, whether it concerned the internal condition and life of the nation
or its relation to surrounding States. It was principally in the later prophetic period of Micah,
Jeremiah, and Zechariah that these prophets of
smooth things, subject to no true and Divine
revelation, came to be regarded as professional
tricksters, making a living out of their false predictions (Mic 3[5], Zec 13[4. 5]). But whether from the
desire of gain or of public favour, these false
prophets expressed the optimistic, what would be
regarded as the patriotic, view of the state and
future of their country, and have been described
as 'nationalistic rather than false.' It is this optimistic, nationalist outlook that particularly explains
the reference in Lk 6[26], 'in the same manner did
their fathers (speak well) to the false prophets.'
The false prophets, as declaring the things the
nation wished to hear, naturally succeeded in
gaining general approval and credence. This is
particularly shown in Jer 6[13-15] and Mic 2[11], and is
confirmed by instances, not a few, in which the
apparently unpatriotic attitude of the true prophet,
compared with that assumed by the false, resulted
in disfavour and even in persecution (1 K 22[27], 2 Ch
16[10], Jer 20[2]). It was the false prophet, representing the national 'wish that is father to the
thought,' of whom 'all men spoke well.' Our
Lord therefore takes such as types of that ill-
deserved general approval which may be won by
flattery, by concealment of the truth, by the
denying or minimizing of danger and of retribution : methods denied to those who 'are of the
truth.' This view of false prophecy as the saying
of things men wish to hear 'for the hire of wrong-
doing,' is to be discerned in 2 P 2[2f.], where the false
prophet is the analogue of the false teacher, himself guilty of 'lascivious doings' (cf. vv. [13-19] for the
character of this teaching).

2. *The false prophets in the Christian Church.*—
In the NT as in the OT, the prophetic ministry
must be regarded in its two branches as interpretative of God's mind and as predictive. False
prophets of both these classes were to be expected
in the Christian community. To grasp the significance of the warnings against these men, the
importance of prophecy in NT times must be
borne in mind. Prophecy was a more important
gift than tongues (1 Co 14), and the prophet is
in the list of officers associated with the Apostles,

taking, with this one exception, precedence of all
other ranks. The prominence of the prophet may
be seen in the *Didache* (c. 11), and in the part
played by him in the Montanist movement.
Hence their truth or falseness, their faithful use,
or their abuse of the spiritual gift, was an important factor for the infant Church. Hence our
Lord warns against them as 'wolves in sheep's
clothing' (Mt 7[15]), and St. John at the end of the
Apostolic age repeats the warning (1 Jn 4[1]). In
the former case the reference is apparently to
their unethical teaching ; in the latter to their
denial or misinterpretation of the fact of the Incarnation. Without using the name, our Lord
warns also against such men, as falsely predicting
or announcing the Parousia (Mt 24[5-7]). In 2 P 2[1]
stress is laid upon false teaching of an antinomian
character, the authors of which are called 'false
teachers,' but find their analogy in the 'false
prophets' of the OT.

LITERATURE.—Hastings' *DB*, art. 'Prophecy and Prophets'
(p. 111) ; Bonwetsch, *Die Prophetie in apost. und nach-apost.
Zeitalter* ; Harnack, *Lehre der Zwölf, ad* xi. 5 ; *Expositor*, v. ii.
[1895] 1 ; *Expos. Times*, v. [1893] 122.

                   J. T. L. MAGGS.

FALSE WITNESS.—The prohibition in the Decalogue of bearing false witness was endorsed by
Christ (οὐ ψευδομαρτυρήσεις, Mt 19[18] ∥). Originally
it dealt, not with lying in general, but with lying
against one's neighbour, perhaps because this is the
most frequent form of falsehood (see Dale, *Ten
Commandments*, p. 208) : Was it merely for brevity
that the limiting clause was dropped by Christ ?
or did it not rather imply a broadening and
deepening of the commandment ? Like other sins,
ψευδομαρτυρίαι come from the heart (Mt 15[19]).

At the preliminary investigation before Caiaphas,
the chief priests and the whole council *sought*
(ἐζήτουν) false witness on which such a capital
charge might be based as would demand Pilate's
attention (Mt 26[59], Mk 14[55]) ; ὡς μὲν ἐκείνοις ἐδόκει
μαρτυρίαν, ὡς δὲ τῇ ἀληθείᾳ ψευδομαρτυρίαν (Euthym.
Zig.); the Evangelists seem to mean more than
this. 'Hîc (ἐζήτουν) illa falsorum testium exorta
copia' (Bengel). While nominally judges, they were
really prosecutors, as they showed by disregarding
the rule that witnesses for the defence should first
be called (see Westcott on Jn 18[21]). Though many
false witnesses came (Mt 26[60]) and bore false witness (Mk 14[56]), yet their witness agreed not together
(ἴσαι αἱ μαρτυρίαι οὐκ ἦσαν, *ib.*), *i.e.* they were not consistent with each other, since it was necessary that
two at least should agree (Dt 17[6]), and witnesses
were examined separately, not in the presence of
each other (see Edersheim, *Jesus the Messiah*, ii.
560). Some (Erasmus, Grot. etc.) take ἴσαι in the
sense of 'sufficient for the purpose, equal to the
demand for weighty evidence, and justifying condemnation.' The parallel words in Mt 26[59. 60] lend
some support ('sought false witness against Jesus
that they might put him to death ; and they found
it not, though many false witnesses came') ; but it
is a strong objection that οὐδὲ οὕτως ἴση is used
of the witness of those who perverted His words
concerning the temple (Mk 14[59]), which constituted
a very grave charge ; cf. Ac 6[13. 14] (cf. *Expositor's
Greek Testament* on Mk 14[56]).

Even the spies who constantly laid wait for Him
had caught up nothing to serve their purpose ; but
at last two false witnesses (Mt 26[60] ; τινες, Mk 14[57])
came, who perverted certain words spoken at the
beginning of His ministry (Jn 2[19]) ; but their testimony also was not ἴση. Taking the meaning as
'did not agree together,' the difference may perhaps be traced in Mt. (δύναμαι καταλῦσαι) and Mk.
(ἐγὼ καταλύσω) ; certainly the perversion is evident,
since they ascribed to Him that destruction which
He ascribed to the Jews. It has been inferred

from Mt 27⁶³ that the rulers knew the true meaning ; but perhaps this is better referred to a knowledge of Christ's words in Mk 8³¹ etc. This false witness might have sufficed ; no other charge could be so effective before the Roman Procurator as that of being a fanatical seducer of the ignorant populace, who might lead them on to wild tumultuous acts ; while the claim that He would, or was able to, rebuild the temple within three days might be made to imply Divine or magical pretensions (see Edersheim, *op. cit.* ii. 559); but it also broke down (οὐδὲ οὕτως ἴση ἦν ἡ μαρτυρία αὐτῶν), cf. Ps 27¹² 35¹¹.

On the law concerning false witness see Hastings' *DB* iv. 351ᵃ ; Edersheim, *op. cit.* ii. 558. Witnesses who contradicted each other were not considered in Rabbinic law as false witnesses in the sense of being punishable. The Sadducees were less severe than the Pharisees in the interpretation of Dt 19¹⁶ᶠ·; they held that the punishment should be inflicted only if the falsely accused had been punished, whereas the Pharisees demanded punishment if the sentence had been pronounced, whether it was executed or not.

LITERATURE.—Besides the works cited above, ref. may be made to Taylor Innes, *Trial of Jesus Christ* ; and Rosadi, *Trial of Jesus, ad loc.* ; Schürer, *HJP* II. i. 194 ; *Expositor,* I. xii. [1880] 276 f.   W. H. DUNDAS.

FAME.—This term has had three meanings,—rumour, reputation, and posthumous renown. The last is modern ; the Elizabethan usage lies between, or may include, the other two. Bacon, who left a Fragment on the subject, and who loved to quote the mythological idea of Fame as the daughter of the angry Earth and the sister of the warring Giants, understood by the term disturbing Rumour —a thing dangerous to governments. Milton, who in an early poem (*Lycidas,* 70 ff.) described 'the last infirmity of noble minds,' in a late poem analyzed the temptation to seek fame or glory, and poured scorn on human judgments (*Par. Reg.* iii. 21-151). In the Gospels the meaning is simpler. The term describes the spreading talk of the admiring multitudes. It is a thing unsought, but unrestrainable, and in no small degree disquieting to the authorities.

We are told that early in the ministry of Jesus a fame of Him went through Galilee and the surrounding country, including Syria (Mt 4²⁴, Lk 4¹⁴). Special occasions were the restoration of a demoniac (Mk 1²⁸, Lk 4³⁷) and the cleansing of a leper (Lk 5¹⁵, cf. Mk 1⁴⁵). The First Gospel uses the term also in connexion with the restoring of Jairus' daughter and the giving of sight to two blind men (Mt 9²⁶· ³¹). And, finally, this Gospel tells us that the fame of Jesus affected Herod (Mt 14¹ RV 'report,' cf. Mk 6¹⁴, Lk 9⁷).

An examination of the Greek text shows that in no two parallel passages is the same term used. The term of the first two Gospels (except in Mt 9²⁶) is ἀκοή (lit. 'hearing' ; RV 'report'), used also for 'rumours' in the eschatological discourse (Mt 24⁶, Mk 13⁷). St. Luke, however, eschews this word, and in his three passages uses three others : φήμη (lit. 'speech' ; RV 'fame,' Lk 4¹⁴, so Mt 9) ; ἦχος (lit. 'sound' ; RV 'report,' Lk 4³⁷) ; and λόγος (lit. 'discourse' ; RV 'report,' Lk 5¹⁵). And elsewhere each Evangelist uses periphrasis. Thus we may conclude that the idea expressed by these terms was of an indefinite character. It included, in varying degrees, such elements as curiosity, attraction, wonder, faith, worship.

These passages, taken along with others that more directly express admiration or astonishment (Mt 7²⁸ 12²³ 15³¹), or that relate the concourse and following of multitudes (Mk 3⁷⁻⁹ 6³⁴· ⁵⁵ 10⁴⁶), show that during His whole public ministry the acts of Jesus

arrested the gaze of men. Not only in Galilee, but in all the provinces of Palestine, and in cities of Syria, men talked and speculated regarding a new Figure that was in their midst. A few who cherished sacred tradition believed that the Messiah had come (Jn 1⁴¹· ⁴⁹ 7⁴⁰, Mt 16⁴ 21⁹). Others less instructed talked wildly as if Elijah had descended, or the Baptist had risen (Mk 6¹⁴· ¹⁵, Mt 16¹³· ¹⁴), or some prophet of local tradition or expectation had appeared (Jn 7⁴⁰, Mt 21¹¹). Doubtless the multitudes that hung around Him were very mixed crowds. Vanity and selfishness mingled with their motives. They loved display. They desired a succession of palpable benefits. Some had political aims or ambitions. The majority failed to appreciate the renunciation and pure spirituality of the Teacher. And few were able to sustain the devotion of their higher moments. To Jesus it was often a relief to find a place of solitude for meditation and prayer. Yet He acknowledged the true instinct of the untutored worshipper (Mt 21¹⁶). And it is to the honour of human nature to remember that the common people heard Him gladly (Mk 12³⁷), and that not the nation at large, but the constituted authorities and their tools—a suspicious officialism, a proud and jealous priesthood—rejected the true Leader and Lord of men, the Shepherd and Bishop of souls. See, further, artt. AMBITION and GLORY.

R. SCOTT.

FAMILY.—1. *Membership.*—Jewish family life, while having many points in common with that of the Gentiles, was marked by a higher standard of purity, the avoidance of infanticide, and the condemnation of the selfish cruelty that in human sacrifice gave the fruit of the body for the sin of the soul (Mic 6⁷). The father was the head of the house, exercising restrictive authority over the wife, having complete disposal of the children, and giving his name to the family inheritance. Although living for years in another locality, he was regarded and registered as belonging to the place of his ancestral origin (Lk 2⁴).

The wife, as being legally the purchased possession of her husband, was under his law,—the bĕʿûlāh to her baʿal, or rightful possessor. Hence the land of Israel could be called the bĕʿûlāh of Jehovah (Is 62⁴). Betrothal (Mt 1¹⁸), as a covenant, was equivalent to marriage ; it prevented the woman from being married to any other man until she had received a writing of divorce. Among the duties of the wife, apart from the maternal charge of the family, was the daily preparation of the bread (Mt 24⁴¹), and the carrying of water from the village fountain (Jn 4⁷). The desire for male children was universal (Jn 16²¹), as these preserved the name and upheld the interests and rights of the family, and in due time enlarged its circle by bringing in daughters from other households. The pre-eminence of the father carried with it a corresponding responsibility of watching over the life and honour, the rights and welfare of his family. See artt. DIVORCE, MARRIAGE.

2. *References to the family.*—It was out of such relationships that Christ drew examples that were familiar to all, when He spoke of fathers who knew how to give good gifts to their children (Lk 11¹³), of sons who obeyed or disobeyed the father's command (Mt 21²⁸); and when, beyond the attachments of unselfish devotion fostered by the sacred institutions of the family, He set the higher claim of what was due to Himself from His disciples (Mt 10³⁷). The Lord's Prayer was a transfiguration of the family relationships.

3. *Religion in the family.*—It was especially in the superiority of its religious training that the Jewish home differed from the family life of the Gentiles. See artt. BOYHOOD, CHILDHOOD.

G. M. MACKIE.

FAMILY.—

1. Jesus as the member of a family.
2. Teaching of Jesus on the family.
   (a) Marriage.
   (b) Position of women.
   (c) Filial obedience.
   (d) The family and the Kingdom of God.

1. Whatever be the force of the phrase 'the brethren of the Lord' (see article *s.v.*), it is evident that Jesus took His place as a member of a human family in the fullest sense of the word. Such was the impression of His fellow-townsmen who saw Him in His daily life. The reticence of the Gospels about the childhood of Christ is in itself an indication that there was nothing which so differed from the ordinary family life of a Jewish household as to create a special tradition about His early years. It was not till a later age had forgotten the completeness with which the Lord identified Himself with human conditions that there appeared the painful attempts of the Apocryphal Gospels to break the silence of their Canonical prototypes. In the one authentic account of any event in the boyhood of Jesus (Lk 2^{41-51}), received perhaps from the Virgin herself (see Ramsay, *Was Christ born at Bethlehem?* ch. iv.), He is seen to be as others 'among their kinsfolk and acquaintance.' For the rest we only know that 'the moral perfections of God were being translated into those unostentatious virtues which constitute the dignity and the happiness of a human home' (Dale, *Laws of Christ for Common Life*, xi.).

When we come to the history of the Ministry, two stages can be discerned in the change which came over the relations between Jesus and His earthly kinsfolk. (1) The calling of the first disciples, narrated in Jn 1, did not lead at once to the withdrawal of the Lord from His family. His mother was present with Him at the marriage at Cana, and after that event He went down with her and His brethren to Capernaum and made a short stay there (Jn 2^{12}, cf. Mt 4^{13-16}). (2) But when the Apostolic band was complete and the work of training them began in earnest, then He subordinated the claims of His family to the higher claims of His mission, and no longer lived continually in the home of His youth. Immediately after the final choice of the Twelve occurred the incident near Capernaum, when those from His house (οἱ παρ' αὐτοῦ) went out to stop Him from preaching, under the impression that He was mad; shortly afterwards His mother and His brethren try to call Him away, apparently for a similar reason (Mk 3^{21}). From this it may be gathered that they were now living at Capernaum. From Mk 6^3 it has been mistakenly concluded that they were still living at Nazareth, but the verse plainly draws a distinction between them and His sisters (named, acc. to Epiphan. *Hær.* lxxviii. 9, Salome and Mary), who, either because they were married, or for some other reason, had settled down in their native town. Some have supposed that when the Lord left His family He dwelt in a house of His own in Capernaum. The Gospel of St. Matthew, it is true, speaks in a vague way of 'the house' ($9^{10.28}$ $13^{1.36}$ 17^{25}), but a comparison of, *e.g.*, 9^{10} with the corresponding passage in Lk 5^{29} shows that it is not a house of Jesus which is meant. After leaving the family home, when He entered into a city, He depended on the hospitality of His friends. It was this literal homelessness which drew from Him the saying recorded in Mt 8^{20} ‖ Lk 9^{58}; for it is unnecessary to give these words, with Augustine and others, a figurative sense. It is not possible to discover the precise moment at which they were uttered, as the two Evangelists give them in different connexions, but they must belong to the period when the total failure of His kindred to understand His mission had made it impossible

for Him to dwell with them any longer. The position given to them by St. Luke is the more probable. According to him, they were pronounced as the Ministry was entering upon its last stage (cf. Lk 9^{51}). Now in Jn 7^{1-7} the Lord's 'brethren' are found arguing with Him as if He still lived with them. The incident there alluded to took place just before the Feast of Tabernacles in the second year of the Ministry. From this we may accept the conclusion suggested by St. Luke's order, that the Lord's home was closed against Him towards the end of the Ministry, rather than near its beginning, as the position given to the saying in St. Matthew might imply. Perhaps it is not without significance that in the next chapter of St. Luke is introduced another home, that of Lazarus and his sisters at Bethany, in which the Lord was an honoured guest.

The reconciliation which the Lord's Passion won for all mankind was first reflected among His own kinsmen after the flesh. We cannot suppose that His mother had ever been parted from Him in any absolute sense, and after His resurrection His brethren also cast in their lot with those who believed in Him. According to the tradition which St. Paul received, the Lord Himself appeared to James (1 Co 15^7). This moment was probably but the last in a series during which the surrender to the claims of Jesus had been steadily replacing previous unbelief. Such at least was the interpretation of later days, when the story was told that beneath the Cross (or even at the Last Supper, acc. to the version of Jerome, *de Vir. Illus.*, quoting the Gospel of the Hebrews) James swore that he would neither eat bread nor drink wine till the Lord rose from the dead. With his conversion came that of the other brethren, and they with the Virgin are found at the opening of the Acts (1^{14}) among those who were waiting for the fulfilment of the promise of the Spirit. Thus the earthly family of Christ fittingly finds its place in the foundations of His spiritual family.

2. In the teaching of Christ, although the word 'family' does not occur, yet the institution is everywhere presupposed and its laws emphasized, as it is also connected with the first miracle recorded in the Fourth Gospel. (a) The pivot on which family life turns is *marriage*, and this subject holds a unique place in the teaching of Christ. On all other social topics He left no particular detailed instructions, but only general rules. On marriage His words are distinct and afford specific guidance about details. He lays it down that monogamy is not the result of any code of law, but a primal fact instituted 'in the beginning' (Mt 19^8). True marriage rests ultimately upon a spiritual basis, the physical aspect is but an accident. This is implied in the answer to the Sadducees (Mk 12^{18-27}). No human law, not even though it have the sanction of the name of Moses, can alter this. The possibility of ground for divorce is confined to the case of one offence (or even abolished altogether, if we regard the exceptive clauses in Mt 19^9 and 5^{32} as later glosses on the Lord's words; see Wright, *Synopsis of Gospels*, on Mk 10^{10}, and cf. artt. ADULTERY, DIVORCE, and MARRIAGE).

(b) The attitude of Jesus towards marriage was necessarily reflected in His *treatment of women*. In spite of all that can be urged to the contrary, it is clear that contemporary Judaism assigned to women a position far inferior to that of men. The tendency was rather to fall away from than to advance upon the standpoint of the OT. There woman is often found in a prominent and honourable place (*e.g.* Miriam, Nu 12^2; Deborah, Jg 4^4; Bathsheba, 1 K 1), but the days were now approaching when it could be said that he who talked with a woman was qualifying for Gehenna (*Pirḳe Aboth*, ed. Taylor, p. 29), an expression in which Judaism contrasted unfavourably even with the low estimate of women current among the Greeks (cf. Aristotle, *Poetics*, 15 ; *Nic. Eth.* vii. 7). In the treatment which Christ accorded to women is found the very antithesis of this harshness. This is sometimes (*e.g.* Jn 2[4]) obscured in the EV by the employment of 'woman' as a rendering of γύναι, a translation which is far from reproducing the respectful tone of the Greek. Jesus readily accepted the help of women, an aspect of the Ministry on which St. Luke seems to desire to lay special stress (cf. Plummer, *Internat. Crit. Com.* on 'St. Luke,' Introd. p. xlii). He gave them equal rights with their husbands, implying that as far as divorce was lawful at all, a wife might put away a husband as much as a husband a wife, a doctrine tolerated rather than accepted by His countrymen. A like care to secure justice for women appears in the narrative preserved in Jn 8[1-11]. This story, whether Apostolic or not, certainly reflects the teaching of Jesus by inferring that in such moral downfalls the crime is not always to be imputed to the woman alone.

(*c*) In another region of family ethics—the sphere of *filial duty*—our Lord again attacked contemporary Jewish conventions. Nominally, filial obedience was exalted to a high place by the teachers of the day, but in practice it might be reduced to a mere shadow by such vows as those alluded to in Mk 7[11]. By sweeping away the sophistries with which these vows were defended, Jesus made parental claims absolute and inviolable.

(*d*) *The family and the Kingdom of God.*—Not only is life in a family the normal life of a disciple, as pictured in the Gospels, but the family supplies the analogy by which men are led to the better understanding of the Kingdom of God. In the First Gospel especially we constantly see on the throne of the Kingdom the 'Father who is in the heavens,' while the ideal of the citizens is to be His true 'sons.' This aspect of the Kingdom is made familiar to all Christians by the Lord's Prayer. In its clauses are represented successively all the integral elements in the relations of a father to his children, the reverence and obedience which he expects from them, the support, forbearance, and protection which he extends to them (cf. Robinson, *Church Catechism Explained*, ch. ii.). The exclusion from the Kingdom, which results when they are lost, is exhibited in the parable of the Prodigal Son.

This fundamental conception erects an insuperable barrier between the teaching of Jesus and those varieties of Socialism which aim at the abolition of the traditional form of the family, which rests on the assumption that marriage is a life-long obligation. 'An association terminable at the will of either party' (Morris and Bax, *Socialism*) is diametrically opposed to the Gospel doctrine. Christian Socialism, if it is to be true to the will of Christ, must work for the removal, not of the family, but of those forces which are injurious to its perfect development. But this does not make it impossible for circumstances to arise in the lives of particular individuals which demand the postponement of family claims to those of the Kingdom of God. It is implied in Mk 10[28ff.] that the Twelve had put the following of Christ before the claims of home, and the reply which the reminder of this drew from Jesus makes it clear that the Christian must not draw back even from this if his own special call requires it. It is noteworthy that the First and Second Gospels seem to shrink from including the wife among the objects which are to be renounced, but both in the parallel passage here and elsewhere St. Luke inserts this also (cf. Mt 10[37] with Lk 14[26]). The disciple is to 'hate' domestic claims if there is any danger that they may lessen the reality of his service, as comes to pass when 'not only have we family and friendship, but also these have us' (Martensen). But such a conflict of claims can arise in the eyes of Christ only when devotion to home ties is ἰστο τοῦ. If a man cannot combine surrender to the bidding of the Gospel with the love of a wife, then he is right to remain unmarried (Mt 19[12]). This is far from the exaggeration which sets up an irreconcilable difference between the love of God and the love of home. In the life of Christ Himself the two appear in their right proportions. For the correct view is not that of Tertullian, who saw in such passages as Lk 8[19-21] a censure of the mother and brethren of Jesus for their anxiety

about Him (*adv. Marc.* iv. 19 ; *de Carne Christi*, vii.), but rather that of Bengel: 'Non spernit matrem, sed anteponit Patrem.'

Literature.—Westcott, *Social Aspects of Christianity* ; Peabody, *Jesus Christ and the Social Problem*, ch. iii. ; Shailer Mathews, *The Social Teaching of Jesus*, ch. iv. ; Gore, *The Sermon on the Mount*, pp. 68–73 (for the teaching on marriage) ; Harnack, *What is Christianity?* Lect. v. (Eng. tr.) ; Stalker, *Imago Christi*, ch. ii.   C. T. DIMONT.

FAMINE.—Though the general fertility of Palestine is frequently alluded to in the Bible, yet the country was, as we know, by no means free from the danger of famine, whether brought about by drought or by the devastations of locusts and other pests, or by the destructive hand of man. Our Lord refers to the familiar instance of famine in the days of Elijah (Lk 4[25f.]). In order to illustrate the truth that no prophet is best received in his own country, He reminds His hearers that Elijah was at that time sent not to one of the many widows in Israel, but to the widow of Sarepta in the territory of Sidon.

In the parable of the Prodigal Son, it was 'a mighty famine' (λιμὸς ἰσχυρά) in the land of his distant exile that helped to bring the wanderer to his senses (Lk 15[14]). He had squandered all his patrimony by the time it arose, and in his distress he had to seek a living by feeding swine. Even thus, food was so scarce with him that 'he would fain have been filled with the husks that the swine did eat.'

Lastly, in the eschatological discourses of our Lord recorded by the Synoptists (Mt 24[7], Mk 13[8], Lk 21[11]), 'famines in divers places' are included among the signs of the end. In St. Luke's account they are joined with pestilences, and in all three accounts with earthquakes. This portion of the prophecy at all events seems clearly to refer in the first instance to the approaching destruction of Jerusalem by Titus (A.D. 70), and only in a secondary sense, if at all, to the final end of all things. Josephus (*BJ* v. and vi.) again and again tells us that famine and pestilence were the terrible accompaniments of the city being taken by the Roman army ; and these were no doubt in great measure due to its crowded state on account of the many pilgrims who had come up to keep the Passover.   C. L. FELTOE.

FAN.—The fan (מִזְרֶה *mizreh*, the πτύον of Mt 3[12] and Lk 3[17]) was an implement used in the winnowing of grain (Is 30[24] [where it is mentioned along with the רַחַת *rahath*, EV 'shovel']). It was either a wooden shovel (Hastings' *DB* i. 51[a] ; Smith, *DB* i. 31 ; van Lennep, *Bible Lands*, p. 83) or a pitchfork (Hastings' *DB* iv. 509[a] ; *Encyc. Bibl.* i. 84 ; Mackie, *Bible Manners and Customs*, p. 42). The balance of probability is in favour of the latter.

We get no help from LXX and Vulgate. LXX omits the word ; the Vulg. renders by *ventilabrum*, which was, according to some, a shovel (Ramsay, *Roman Antiquities*, p. 482), and, according to others, a fork (Smith, *Lat.-Eng. Dict. s.v.*). Pesh. has *raphsho'*, which means 'shovel.' There is, however, the significant fact that down to the present day two winnowing implements are used in Palestine which bear practically the same names as those which occur in Is 30[24]. These are the *midrā* and the *raht*, and there is no substantial reason for doubting that they correspond respectively to the *mizreh* and the *rahath*. The *midrā*, which we accordingly identify with the 'fan' of Scripture, is a simple wooden fork about six feet long. It has from five to seven prongs, which are set in separately and bound together with a wrapping of fresh hide. The natural shrinkage of the hide renders it a very effective ligature. The *raht* is a wooden shovel about five feet in length.

The winnowing of the mixed mass of grain, chaff, and short straw produced by threshing is begun by tossing it into the air with the *midrā*. This process frees most of the chaff and straw, which are carried away by the wind (see AGRICULTURE, p. 40), but a good deal still remains mingled with the pile of grain. A second winnowing is therefore needed, and for this the *raḥt* is used. See also CHAFF.

LITERATURE.—On the meaning of Christ's winnowing-fan see Seeley, *Ecce Homo*, ch. vi.   HUGH DUNCAN.

FARM.—See AGRICULTURE, and HUSBANDMAN.

FARTHING.—See MONEY.

FASTING.—In the time of Christ, fasting appears to have been a prominent characteristic of Jewish piety. The fasts were both public and private. Of public fasts only one in the year was ordained by the law of Moses, the Day of Atonement; in Ac 27⁹ it is called simply 'the fast' (cf. Jos. *Ant.* XIV. iv. 3; Philo, *Vit. Mos.* ii. 4; Schürer, *HJP* I. i. 322). The four annual fasts, established in memory of national calamities and referred to by Zechariah (8¹⁹), had fallen into desuetude, and were not revived until after the destruction of Jerusalem by the Romans. The late 'fast of Esther,' on the 13th of Adar (Est 9³¹, cf. 4³ ¹⁶), was not at this time observed. But occasional public fasts were ordered from time to time during seasons of drought and public calamity. They were held on the second and fifth days of the week, — Monday and Thursday, — because Moses was believed to have gone up Mt. Sinai on a Thursday and to have returned on a Monday. They always began on the second day, so that a three days' fast would fall on the second, fifth, and second —Monday, Thursday, Monday (see *Didache*, viii.; *Const. Apost.* vii. 23; Epiphan. *Hær.* xvi. 1). Apart from these public occasions, however, many individuals were in the habit of imposing extra fasts upon themselves (Lk 2³⁷, cf. Jth 8⁶); and some, particularly among the Pharisees, fasted on Mondays and Thursdays all the year round (Lk 18¹²; Lightfoot and Wetstein, *ad loc.*). Religious teachers, moreover, were apparently accustomed to lay down rules about fasting for the guidance of their disciples (Mk 2¹⁸, Mt 9¹⁴, Lk 5³³). The 'frequent fasts' of the Jews are alluded to by Tacitus (*Hist.* v. 4); and Josephus, speaking of the spread of Jewish customs among the Gentile cities, mentions fasting (c. *Apion.* ii. 40; cf. Tert. *ad Nat.* i. 13). Among the Romans a mistaken idea seems to have been current that the Jews fasted on the Sabbath (Sueton. *Aug.* 76).

The manner of fasting differed according to the degree of strictness of the fast. Thus, on less strict fasts, while abstinence from food and drink from sunrise to sunset was enjoined, washing and anointing were still permitted. The strictest fast, however, lasted from one sunset till after the next, when the stars appeared; and during these hours not only food and drink, but washing, anointing, and every kind of agreeable transaction, even salutations, were prohibited (Schürer, II. ii. 119; Edersheim, *Life and Times*, i. p. 663, *Temple*, pp. 297–300). Fasting was generally practised in an ostentatious manner; on this point the testimony of Mt 6¹⁶ is confirmed by the Mishna.

Passing on to consider the attitude of Jesus towards fasting, we remark that, while on the one hand there is no reason to doubt that He observed the prescribed public fasts, and while He may even have undertaken a voluntary fast of forty days at the commencement of His ministry (Mt 4²; but see art. ASCETICISM), yet, on the other hand, it is evident that neither by practice

nor by precept did He lay any stress on this form of devotion. His ordinary mode of life was so unascetic as to bring on Him the reproach of being a 'gluttonous man and a wine-bibber' (Mt 11¹⁹, Lk 7³⁴). In His teaching He directly alluded to fasting only twice. The passages are as follow :

(*a*) Mt 6¹⁶⁻¹⁸. Here voluntary fasting is presupposed as a religious exercise, but the disciples are warned against making it an occasion for a parade of piety. 'Thou, when thou fastest, anoint thy head, and wash thy face; that thou appear not unto men to fast, but unto thy Father which is in secret.' Jesus thus sanctions fasting, but only as the genuine expression of a devout and contrite frame of mind. Its whole value depends on the purity and sincerity of the motive with which it is undertaken. As for the pretentious externalism of the Pharisees, that has its own reward.

(*b*) Mk 2¹⁸⁻²², Mt 9¹⁴⁻¹⁷, Lk 5³³⁻³⁹. In reply to the question of the disciples of John and of the Pharisees, Jesus deliberately refuses to enjoin fasting on His followers. Alluding to a Rabbinic ordinance that all mourning be suspended during the marriage-week, He says that fasting, which is a sign of mourning, would be inconsistent with the joy which 'the children of the bride-chamber' experience 'while the bridegroom is with them.' But He adds that the days of bereavement are coming, and then the outward expression of sorrow will be appropriate enough. Here, as in the Sermon on the Mount, Jesus certainly sanctions fasting as a form through which emotion spontaneously seeks expression. But to the form itself He attaches very slight importance. This is brought out clearly in the succeeding parables of the Old Garment and the Old Wineskins. It is futile to graft the new liberty of the gospel on to the body of old observances and practices, and yet more futile to attempt to force the whole new system within the ancient moulds. The new piety must manifest itself in new forms of its own. Nevertheless, while Jesus seems to suggest that the Jewish regulations are not in harmony with the Christian spirit, He can sympathize with the prejudice of conservatives who still cling tenaciously to the custom of their fathers. 'No man also having drunk old wine straightway desireth new: for he saith, The old is good.'

The allusions to fasting in Mk 9²⁹ and Mt 17²¹ are corruptions of the text; for similar combinations of prayer and fasting see To 12⁸, Sir 34²⁶, Lk 2³⁷. The second Logion of the Oxyrhynchus fragment discovered in 1897 commences with the words, Λέγει Ἰησοῦς, ἐὰν μὴ νηστεύσητε τὸν κόσμον, οὐ μὴ εὕρητε τὴν βασιλείαν τοῦ θεοῦ. Here, however, the fasting spoken of is obviously metaphorical. Another reference to fasting occurs in the fifth of the *New Sayings of Jesus*, published by Grenfell and Hunt in 1904, but the Logion is 'broken beyond hope of recovery' (*op. cit.* p. 18 f.).

On the general bearings of this subject see art. ASCETICISM.   F. HOMES DUDDEN.

FATHER, FATHERHOOD.—The one subject on which Jesus claimed to have unique and absolute knowledge was the Father (Mt 11²⁷). Yet, in saying this, He evidently did not mean that He knew all that God knows. He confessed or implied that His knowledge was limited (*e.g.* Mk 13³², Mt 9²¹·²²); and the very fact that He looked up to God as His God is sufficient evidence that, by knowledge of the Father, He did not mean comprehension of the Infinite. The record of His life and teaching makes it plain that His unique knowledge of God was knowledge of the Divine character and purpose. This was the sphere in which He lived and moved and had His conscious being. This was the sphere of His revelation.

In setting forth Jesus' conception of the Father-hood of God, we shall consider (1) the use of the name 'Father'; (2) the meaning of Fatherhood; (3) the Fatherhood of God in the Fourth Gospel; (4) the place of Fatherhood in the teaching of Jesus; and (5) Jesus' conception of God compared with that of the OT and of His contemporaries.

1. *Use of the name 'Father' by Jesus.*—The first recorded sentence of Jesus (Lk 2⁴⁹), and that which was probably the last (Lk 23⁴⁶), both contain the name 'Father.' The boy of twelve felt an inward constraint to be engaged in the things of His Father, and twenty years later, expiring on the cross, it was into the hands of His Father that He commended His spirit. Throughout His ministry His use of this name is what we might expect from the scene which St. Luke records from His boyhood. 'The child is father of the man.' When-ever the personal relation between Him and God is involved, Jesus employs no name but 'Father,' if we except a single passage where He quotes from the 22nd Psalm (Mk 15³⁴). In each of the five prayers where the words of Jesus are given, He addresses God as 'Father' (Mt 11²⁵⁻²⁷ 26³⁹· ⁴², Lk 23³⁴· ⁴⁶); and in the longest of these, which includes only three verses, the name is repeated five times (Mt 11²⁵⁻²⁷). When speaking of God in the third person, Jesus refers to Him once as 'the Great King' (Mt 5³⁵), and once as 'Lord of the harvest' (Mt 9³⁸); but in almost every case He uses the name 'God' or the name 'Father.' He never employs such circumlocutions as 'the Blessed One' and 'Holy One,' and never uses abstract designations such as 'Place,' all of which were common in the synagogue. It is significant to compare with this usage that of Philo, whose commonest titles of God are abstract (*e.g.* τὸ ὄν, τὸ ὄντως ὄν, τὸ πρὸς ἀληθινὸν ὄν, ὁ ὤν—Drummond, *Philo Judæus*, ii. 20). The name by which Jesus Him-self addressed God was also the name which He put on the lips of His disciples. It was their privilege to share His communion with God (Mt 6⁹ 23⁹).

2. *The Meaning of Fatherhood.*—What Jesus meant by the term 'Father' is to be learned both from His words and from His life. From His words we infer that He chose this term to describe the character of God. Thus He teaches that, as it is the very nature of a father to give good gifts to his children, so it is the very nature of God to give His good things to those who ask Him (Mt 7¹¹, Lk 11¹³). Earthly fathers, though evil, give to their children; much more will God give, who is absolutely and unchangeably good (Mk 10¹⁸). He is ready to bestow the Kingdom of heaven upon the poor in spirit, and to give the vision of Himself to the pure in heart (Mt 5³· ⁸); that is to say, He gives the best He has to any who will receive it. And even upon those who will not receive the best, He bestows much; for He maketh His sun to rise on the evil, and sendeth rain on the unjust (Mt 5⁴⁵). Jesus exhorts His hearers to have this spirit in order that they may become sons of the heavenly Father and share His perfection (Mt 5⁴⁵· ⁴⁸). Accordingly the term 'Fatherhood' de-scribes what God is in Himself. It does not concern merely or chiefly His relation to men, but it declares His very spirit, that which lies behind all relationships.

The story of the Lost Son perfectly interprets Jesus' conception of Fatherhood (Lk 15¹¹⁻³²). The lost son does not stand for a lost Israelite merely, a fallen member of the theocratic people, but repre-sents the *sinner*, whether Jew or Gentile. For, in the first place, the parable was spoken to justify Jesus' reception of publicans (Lk 15¹· ²), and pub-licans were rated as no better than Gentiles (Mt 18¹⁷); and, in the second place, the conclusion of

Jesus in the parables of the Lost Sheep and the Lost Coin, which are manifestly parallel to that of the Lost Son, is perfectly general. He there declares that there is joy in heaven over one *sinner* who repents (Lk 15⁷· ¹⁰). Therefore, when Jesus, in the story of the Lost Son, says that the father watched and longed for his son's return, and welcomed him at last with kisses and a joyful feast, He teaches that the Fatherhood of God is essential, and there-fore a fact of universal significance. It is in keep-ing with this when Jesus, addressing the *multi-tudes* as well as His disciples, said to all who heard Him, 'Call no man your father on earth: for one is your Father, who is in heaven' (Mt 23¹· ⁹). If we had more of the addresses of Jesus to the multi-tudes, we should probably have more instances of this same usage.

Again, the very life of Jesus shows what He meant by the Fatherhood of God, for He surely felt that the spirit of this Fatherhood was mani-fested through Him. He portrayed His own atti-tude towards the lost when He drew the picture of the father and his lost son. His brotherhood in-terpreted the spirit of the Divine Fatherhood. But the brotherhood of Jesus describes what He was. He did not simulate brotherliness. It was by the very necessity of His holy and loving will that He was the friend of sinners. It is impossible, there-fore, to suppose that, in His thought, the Father-hood of God was something less than essential, a figure setting forth His gracious relationship to certain favoured people. As His own love flowed out to men irrespective of all merely outward cir-cumstances, and as He believed that He knew the Father and was in harmony with His will, He must have believed that God loves men irrespective of all outward circumstances; in other words, that His Fatherhood is essential, and hence of universal significance.

It is true that Jesus considered Himself sent to the lost sheep of the house of Israel, and that He confined His labours chiefly to them; but it is equally true that this was solely a matter of *order*. He told the Canaanitish woman that the children should be fed *first* (Mk 7²⁷) which plainly suggests that the gospel was for all, but that for some reason it was to be offered first to the Jews. Moreover, He granted the woman's request, though He thus spoke; and in no case did He turn a Gentile away empty who came to Him for help. He healed a Samaritan leper (Lk 17¹⁸), and the servant of a Gentile centurion (Mt 8¹³). There is no indication that they were less dear to Him than were the Jews.

We conclude, therefore, both from the words and the life of Jesus, that He called God our Father, not because God created us,—a view common in Philo,—or because He rules over us, or because of the covenant which He made with Abraham, but simply and only because He loves us. The abstract statement that 'God is love' (1 Jn 4⁸) is a true interpretation of the word 'Father' as used by Jesus.

3. *The Fatherhood of God in the Fourth Gospel.*—The Fatherhood of God is more conspicuous in John than in the Synoptics, the word 'Father' occurring about 90 times as against 5 in Mark, 17 in Luke, and 45 in Matthew. Here also, as in the Synoptics, the word is found only on the lips of Jesus, with the exception of three passages where the author speaks from his own Christian point of view (Jn 1¹⁸ 8²⁷ 13³), and one passage in which he attributes his Christian usage to the Baptist (3³⁵).

The new feature of the subject in the Fourth Gospel is the emphasis laid on the universality of Fatherhood. Thus it is the *world* (κόσμος) which God is represented as loving up to the point of the highest sacrifice (Jn 3¹⁶). It is *all men* whom Jesus will draw unto Himself (12³²). In offering life to a *Samaritan*, Jesus feels that He is accom-plishing the Father's will (4¹⁰· ³⁴), and a visit of certain *Greeks* brought before His soul the vision of a great harvest for the Kingdom of God (12²⁰⁻²⁴).

Still more noticeable, and more divergent from the earlier usage, is the employment of ' Father ' in an absolute sense. The extent of this usage in John is not altogether clear. In the conversation with the Samaritan woman, Fatherhood is plainly universal : ' The hour cometh and now is when the true worshippers shall worship the Father in spirit and truth : for such doth the Father seek to be his worshippers ' ; ' Believe me, the hour cometh when neither in this mountain nor in Jerusalem shall ye worship the Father ' (Jn 4²¹· ²³). Another passage which admits of no doubt is Jn 20¹⁷ ' I am not yet ascended to the Father. But go to my brethren and say to them, I ascend to my Father and your Father, and my God and your God.' It is quite clear that the word ' Father ' in the first clause is unlimited ; for, in the later clauses, He who is here called ' the Father ' is called by Jesus ' my Father and your Father.' Two other cases of what appears to be the same use of the word are Jn 6²⁷· ⁴⁶.

In about one quarter of the passages where God is called ' Father,' He is so called in reference to Jesus, and the language is ' my Father ' (e.g. Jn 2¹⁶ 5¹⁷ 6³²). Since, now, there are some passages in which the absolute sense of ' Father ' is required, and since in the majority of the other passages, where the expression ' the Father ' is used, there is nothing which requires us to adopt a limited idea of Fatherhood, it must be regarded as probable that the author always employed the word in an unlimited sense when he did not associate a personal pronoun with it. Thus the Fourth Gospel would place a very striking emphasis on the thought that the Fatherhood of God is essential and universal. Such emphasis on this point in the teaching of John, of course, made natural by the missionary activity of the early Church, which had gone forward many years before the Fourth Gospel was composed.

The meaning of Fatherhood in the Fourth Gospel is the same as in the primitive tradition. It describes the character of God, and is expressed in love. It is perhaps probable that the author of the Fourth Gospel occasionally used the term ' Father ' in a metaphysical sense (1¹⁴· ¹⁸), but he has put no words on the lips of Jesus which require to be taken metaphysically. He often represents Jesus as saying ' my Father,' but it is unquestionable that Jesus would have every man address God in just this way. He taught His disciples to say ' our Father,' which, of course, implies that each individual may say ' my Father.' When Jesus, to comfort His disciples, is represented as sending them the message, ' I ascend unto my Father and your Father, and my God and your God ' (Jn 20¹⁷), He does not separate Himself from them by claiming a unique relationship to the Father, even God, but rather joins Himself closely with them by the thought that one and the same Father is theirs and His alike, one God the God of both. The Fatherhood of God according to Jesus, even in the Fourth Gospel, is one and ethical. but His appreciation and appropriation of that Fatherhood are unique.

4. *The Place of Fatherhood in the teaching of Jesus.*—In accordance with the fact that the sole subject on which Jesus claimed to possess unique knowledge was the character of God, or, as we may now say, the *Fatherhood* of God, we find that this truth is central and determinative in all His teaching. His conception of the Kingdom of heaven was dependent on His conception of the character of God. The Kingdom which He wished to see come on earth was the Kingdom of the *Father* (Mt 6⁹), a Kingdom in which the will of the Father should be done. Therefore the conception of the Kingdom of heaven is not the fundamental thought of Jesus. Nor was His teaching determined by

His sense of the imperfections of the Law. These imperfections He saw clearly, but not because of a critical analysis of the Law such as a philosophical student of history might make. He considered the Law from above, as one who possessed in Himself a higher standard, a more perfect knowledge of the Divine will. His work was, indeed, to fulfil the Law, and to establish the Kingdom of God on earth ; but the inspiring and ruling thought in all His work was the truth of God's Fatherhood. What He teaches of man's relation to God is determined by this truth. It is gathered up in the thought of sonship. The lost son is to return to the Father. His life is to be one of filial service in the Father's presence. And it is the goodness of the Father that draws him back.

The Fatherhood of God requires that the spirit of the religious life shall be love, out of which will be born perfect trust. It invites and draws man to communion with God, and determines the character of his devotion. What Jesus teaches of man's relation to man is also determined by His consciousness of the character of God. His morality is purely religious. The ethical life of His disciples is to be controlled by the fact of their sonship to God. The standard of that life is the very quality which constitutes the perfection of God (Mt 5⁴⁸). It is one and the same quality that makes Him the *Father* and makes man His *son*. Thus the entire teaching of Jesus is but the interpretation of the fact of God's Fatherhood. This is the sun in His heaven which lights and warms the broad field of human life.

5. *Jesus' conception of God compared with that of the OT, and with views of His contemporaries.*— The new revelation which Jesus gave of the character of God was put into a term which had long been applied to Him in Israel. The first of the great prerogatives of the Jewish people which are enumerated by St. Paul is the adoption (Ro 9⁴), that is, the appointment of Israel to be in a peculiar sense God's son. This thought was derived from the OT. God's message to Pharaoh by Moses involved a paternal relation to Israel, for Moses was to say in God's name, ' Israel is my son, my firstborn ' (Ex 4²²). Again, Deuteronomy represents Moses as saying to the people, ' As a man chasteneth his son, so the Lord thy God chasteneth thee ' (Dt 8⁵ 32⁶) ; and the Lord says in Hosea that when Israel was a child He loved him and called His son out of Egypt (Hos 11¹ 1¹⁰). In these passages, and in a few more, God is thought of as a Father to the people of Israel as a whole ; and He is the Father of Israel because He made them a nation and established them by His mighty power (Dt 32⁶). So far His Fatherhood is wholly national. There are, however, other passages in which we have an individualizing of the thought of Fatherhood. Thus the Lord says of the theocratic descendant of David, ' I will be his father, and he shall be my son ' (2 S 7¹⁴) ; and the Messianic king puts the decree of Jehovah concerning himself in these words, ' Thou art my son ; this day have I begotten thee ' (Ps 2⁷). There is also an individualizing of God's Fatherhood with reference to other persons, for the Psalter calls Him the Father of the fatherless ; and His pity for those who fear Him is like the pity of a father for his children (Ps 68⁵ 103¹³). Yet in all these passages we see only the relation of God to His chosen people, or to a particular class among them, or to His chosen king. ' Father ' is a word of relation, not yet a description of God's very character. It marks an advance upon that conception of Fatherhood which is derived from the fact of creation, but it is still far removed from the view of Jesus. The OT gave to Jesus the name ' Father ' for God, but He filled it with a new content.

When we come down from the OT to the time of Jesus, we find among the Jews a conception of God that is far more widely unlike that of the gospel, and which by contrast serves to bring out the thought of Jesus into strong relief. This Jewish conception of God was based on the traditional interpretation of the Law, not on the spiritual teaching of the Prophets. God was put further and further away; the conception of Him became increasingly abstract and transcendental.

Even as early as the translation of the OT into Greek (3rd cent. B.C.) this tendency towards a more abstract conception of God is manifest. The translators sought to remove the thought that God had come into actual contact with men. They do not, with Ex 15³, call God a 'man of war,' but render the passage by 'the Lord who makes war.' Moses no longer goes up 'to God in the mount,' as the original reads (Ex 19³), but he goes up 'to the *mount* of God.' Moses and those with him did not see the *God of Israel* (Ex 24⁹·¹⁰), but they saw the *place* where He stood.

As in the Greek translation of the OT, so in the Targums of Onkelos and Jonathan (1st cent. B.C.) appears the tendency to safeguard the holiness of God by removing Him far from men. An illustration may be cited from Gn 18⁸. It is said there that the heavenly visitants ate of the repast which Abraham had provided, but Onkelos changes it to 'it *seemed* to him as though they ate.' Such was the method of the Targumists. With the removal of God far from men there came to be associated in the course of time an elaborate doctrine of angels—a natural if not necessary correlate of the transcendental conception of God.

But though the scribes removed God far from contact with man and the world, their conception of Him was unspiritual.

He is pictured in the Talmud of Jerusalem as a great Rabbi. He studies the Law three hours each day, and observes all its ordinances. He keeps the Sabbath. He makes vows, and on their accomplishment He is released by the heavenly Sanhedrin. He also fulfils the injunction to rise up before the hoary head (see Gfrörer, *Das Jahrhundert des Heils*, i. 276; Weber, *Jüd. Theol.*² pp. 17, 18). Thus the external, ceremonial conception of religion at last took complete possession of the future world, and threw the mesh of its enslavement to the letter even around God Himself. The prophet's spiritual conception of Jehovah was lost; the glow of lovingkindness which they beheld in His face faded out utterly, and there remained a Being who was called 'the Holy One,' interesting perhaps to the scribe, but whom no one could really love.

To this conception of God the revelation of His Fatherhood by Jesus formed an absolute contrast. The scribes put God in the seventh heaven; Jesus taught that He is near. The scribes held that He is intensely concerned with outward ordinances; Jesus taught that He is full of love, and cares only for the heart of man. To the scribal mind God was the God of scribes; to Jesus He was the Father of all men. The religious teachers of Jesus' time fell very far below the prophetic conception of God; Jesus rose still further above it.

For the application of the term 'father' to Joseph, see artt. BIRTH OF CHRIST and JOSEPH.

LITERATURE. — The works on NT Theology by Holtzmann (H. J.), Beyschlag, Stevens, and Gould; Wendt, *Die Lehre Jesu*; Gilbert, *The Revelation of Jesus*; Bousset, *Die Religion des Judenthums*; B. Weiss, *Die Religion des NT*; Fairbairn, *Christ in Mod. Theol.* 440 ff.; Dale in *Expositor*, v. vii. [1898] 56, 150.

GEORGE H. GILBERT.

FATHERS.—The plural of 'father' is found in 14 passages in the Gospels, once (in the Greek) with no determining word (Lk 1¹⁷), twice with the article only, 'the fathers' (Jn 6⁵⁸ RV 7²²), and 11 times with a pronoun: 'our' (Mt 23³⁰, Lk 1⁵⁵·⁷², Jn 4²⁰ 6³¹); 'your' (Mt 23³², Lk 11⁴⁷·⁴⁸, Jn 6⁴⁹); 'their' (Lk 6²³·²⁶). With one exception (Lk 1¹⁷) where it means 'parents,' as contrasted with 'children,' it is always employed in the sense of 'ancestors,' as in innumerable passages in the OT (Gn 47⁹, 1 K 11⁴³ 14³¹ 15⁸ etc.), the Apocrypha and the Pseudepigrapha (2 Es 7³⁶, Ps-Sol 8²⁵ 9¹⁹ etc.), and the historical Assyrian texts (*šarrani abi-ia=* 'the kings my fathers,' *KIB* ii. 170, 172, etc.).

As early as about B.C. 200 the Heb. word '*ăbôth* came to have the narrower meaning of 'distinguished ancestors.' The long historical review in Sir 44–49 opens (Heb.):

Let me now praise godly men,
Our *fathers* in their generations.

The fathers praised are Enoch, Noah, Abraham, Isaac, Israel, Moses, Aaron, Phinehas, Joshua, Caleb, the Judges, Samuel, Nathan, David, Solomon, Elijah, Elisha, Hezekiah, Isaiah, Josiah, Jeremiah, Ezekiel, Job, the Twelve, Zerubbabel, Joshua the priest, Nehemiah. In a sort of appendix (49¹⁴⁻¹⁶) are given Enoch (again), Joseph, Shem, Seth, Enos, Adam. The Hebrew heading of these chapters, 'Praise of the fathers of the world,' or, as Cowley and Neubauer render, 'Praise of the patriarchs,' cannot be urged, as it may be of much later date. The Greek heading πατέρων ὕμνος is of more value, as it may be pre-Christian. Among these distinguished ancestors or 'fathers' a group of three was early singled out for special notice—Abraham, Isaac and Jacob. God is several times described in the OT as 'the God of Abraham, Isaac and Jacob' or 'Israel' (Ex 3⁶·¹⁶, 1 K 18³⁶, 1 Ch 29¹⁸, 2 Ch 30⁶). In a tradition preserved in the Babylonian Talmud (*Berak.* 16*b*) it is said: 'Only three are called fathers.' It is assumed that Abraham, Isaac and Jacob were 'the fathers' *par excellence*. The group is referred to 5 times in the Gospels (Mt 8¹¹ 22³², Mk 12²⁶, Lk 13²⁸ 20³⁷), and probably, without the names, in one of the passages cited above (Jn 7²² 'not that it [circumcision] is of Moses but of the fathers'). The 'fathers,' then, in the language of our Lord and His contemporaries, could mean ancestors in general, or the ancestors of some particular period, as, for example, the wandering in the wilderness (Jn 6³¹·⁴⁹·⁵⁸), or ancestors of notable piety or renown, more especially the three patriarchs who were regarded as the founders of the people.

The thought that the great goodness of some of the fathers, especially of Abraham, was helpful to their sinful descendants, which found expression in the phrase *zakkûth 'ābôth* 'merit of the fathers' so often met with in the Talmud, can be traced as far back as the time of Christ and the Apostles. It probably underlies the words of St. Paul: 'they are beloved for the fathers' sakes' (Ro 11²⁸); and evidently lurks in the proud boast of being the seed of Abraham or children of Abraham (Mt 3⁹, Lk 3⁸, Jn 8³³·³⁹ etc.). The phrase, however, is never met with in the Gospels. The allied belief that the holy fathers could effectually intercede for their wicked descendants, which is distinctly attested in some of the Pseudepigrapha (Syr. Apoc. of Bar. 85¹², Sib. Oracles ii. 330–333), is implied in the parable of the Rich Man and Lazarus. The rich man in Hades appeals, not to God, but to one of the fathers (Lk 16²⁴). Still there is no direct mention of their intercession in the Gospels.

The use of the term 'fathers' in the sense of 'distinguished teachers of the Law, who prolonged the line of tradition' which has become so widely known through the famous Talmudic tractate *Pirke Abôth* or *Masseketh Abôth*, is unrepresented in the Gospels, unless it is alluded to or echoed in the title 'father' applied to a living rabbi (Mt 23⁹).

LITERATURE.—R. H. Charles, *Book of the Secrets of Enoch*, pp. 69-70, note; Weber, *Jüd. Theol. auf Grund des Talmud*,² etc. 292 ff.; Schürer, *GJV*³ ii. 317.

W. TAYLOR SMITH.

FATHER'S HOUSE (οἰκία τοῦ πατρός μου).—The name applied by Jesus in Jn 14² to the eternal home, whither He goes to prepare a place for His disciples. To their fear lest they might never rejoin Him after the impending separation, He answers that in His Father's house there are many abodes (μοναί)—a place, therefore, for every one who believes in Him. See art. MANSION.

The expression occurs twice elsewhere in the Gospels, with reference to the Temple, and in both cases bears an emphatic meaning: (a) In Lk 2⁴⁹ the words ἐν τοῖς τοῦ πατρός μου, although capable of the translation 'about my Father's business' (as in AV), are more properly rendered 'in my Father's house' (RV). This rendering is supported by the context. See BUSINESS. The first recorded utterance of Jesus has an all-important bearing on the question of the development of His Messianic consciousness., His visit to the Temple, in the dawn of manhood, awakened in Him the sense of a peculiarly close relation to God, whom He recognized henceforth as His Father. (b) In Jn 2¹⁶ the words which appear in the Synoptic narrative as a quotation from the OT ('It is written, My house shall be called,' etc.) are given as a direct saying of Jesus, 'Make not my Father's house a house of merchandise.' The Speaker thus declares by what authority He cleanses the Temple. As Son of God He has the right of ordering His Father's house and casting out the intruders who have dishonoured it.

The 'Father's house' of John 14² has been explained (on the analogy of the above passages) as the heavenly Temple, of which the Temple at Jerusalem was the earthly type (cf. Is 6¹, He 9). Apart, however, from the particular difficulty that a temple could hardly be described as a place of μοναί, the whole tone of the passage demands a simpler explanation. Jesus thinks of the 'house' as a home, to which He is Himself returning, and in which He will be reunited at last with His disciples. The expression 'Father's house' has already been used implicitly with this larger meaning in Jn 8³⁵ 'The servant abideth not in the house for ever, but the Son abideth for ever.'

Theologically, the passage Jn 14²ᶠ· marks a departure from the prevailing type of Johannine thought. It withdraws into the future that communion with Christ and participation in His eternal life which elsewhere regarded as present realities. It further identifies the παρουσία with the coming of Christ to the believer in the hour of death (v.³), not (as in the sequel of the discourse) with His abiding spiritual presence. The divergence, however, does not necessarily involve a contradiction. While maintaining that Life is given in the present, St. John looks to a future in which it will become fully manifest (cf. 5²⁸· ²⁹ 6³⁹ etc.). For the believer, as for Christ Himself, death is the transition to a larger 'glory.' The allusion to the 'Father's house' is obviously figurative, and we cannot even infer from it that St. John conceives of the future world under forms of space. Such a conception seems, indeed, to be debarred by the great declaration (4²⁴) of the spiritual nature of God. The essential thought in the saying is simply that the believer will enter after death into that perfect communion with God which is impossible under the conditions of this world. In more than one Synoptic passage this communion is described by Jesus under the imagery of a feast (Mt 26²⁹ 8¹¹, Lk 14¹⁵ᶠᶠ·). This image is replaced in the Fourth Gospel by the less vivid but more adequate one of a perpetual sojourn with the Father in His house. But in both cases the image is only the vehicle, necessarily imperfect, of the spiritual idea, that the crowning blessedness of the believer will consist in nearness to God and perfect fellowship with Him.

This main idea is combined, in the Johannine passage, with several others which serve to render it more complete and definite: (1) The communion with God is mediated by Christ, who is Himself the Son, and therefore has the right to bring His chosen friends into His Father's house (cf. 8³⁵· ³⁶ 17²⁴). (2) It will be a lasting communion, not fitful and interrupted like that which is granted to us in the present. Those who were formerly servants will 'abide in the house for ever,' like the Son Himself. They will not be strangers, tarrying for an hour, but will have μοναί appointed to them—fixed places which they can call their own. (3) The emphasis on the 'many mansions' would seem to suggest that the perfect communion with God does not involve a mere absorption in Him. Each life will maintain its own identity and receive its

separate fulfilment. Jesus will be the same in the higher world as He was in this, and the disciples likewise will find themselves again, and resume their fellowship with each other and with Him. A certain resemblance can thus be traced between the thought of this passage and that of St. Paul in 2 Co 5¹⁻⁴. The Apostle anticipates for each believer 'a house not made with hands, eternal in the heavens,' which will take the place of the 'earthly house of this tabernacle.' The saying in the Gospel declares that there will be room for all these separate mansions within the one 'Father's house.'

LITERATURE.—The various commentaries on St. John's Gospel, *in loco, e.g.* Holtzmann, Loisy, Weiss, Bugge, Calmes, Godet; Schrenck, *Die johann. Anschauung vom Leben* (1898), p. 157 f.; Grill, *Entstehung des vierten Evangeliums* (1902), p. 360, etc.; Titius, *Die johann. Anschauung der Seligkeit* (1900), ch. vi.; Ker, *Sermons*, ii. 247; Maclaren, *Holy of Holies*, 12.

E. F. SCOTT.

FATLINGS.—See ANIMALS, p. 63ᵇ.

FAVOUR.—See GRACE and GRACIOUSNESS.

FEAR (φόβος, φοβοῦμαι ; in Mt 8²⁴ and Mk 4⁴⁰ 'fearful'=δειλός).—**1.** In many passages in the Gospels fear is a motive restraining or compelling action in the ordinary course of human relationships. Men fear others, and shape their conduct, at least in part, by their fears: *e.g.* Mt 2²² (Joseph is afraid to return to Judæa) ; 14⁵ (Herod would not put John to death because 'he feared the people') 21²⁶· ⁴⁶ ; Mk 11³², Lk 22² (where the Pharisees 'fear the multitude') ; Mk 9³², Lk 9⁴⁵ (the disciples are 'afraid to ask' the meaning of a saying) ; Mk 11¹⁸ (scribes and Pharisees wished to destroy Jesus, 'for they feared him') ; Jn 7¹³ 9²² 19³⁸ 20¹⁹ (men are silent or secret 'for fear of the Jews'). Similar passages are Mt 25²⁵, Mk 6²⁰ 12¹², Lk 19²¹ 20¹⁹ etc. This fear sometimes restrains bad men from carrying out their evil purposes ; but quite as often turns others aside from the straight path of right.

2. The Gospels also mention frequently the fear which men feel in the presence of what they believe to be supernatural or superhuman. This is often an accompaniment of the miracles of Jesus. It is mentioned of the disciples, at the stilling of the tempest (Mk 4⁴¹, Lk 8²⁵), when Jesus walked on the sea (Mt 14²⁶, Mk 6⁵⁰, Jn 6¹⁹· ²⁰), at the Transfiguration (Mt 17⁶· ⁷ and parallels). So the people of Judæa were afraid when they saw the demoniac healed (Mk 5¹⁵) ; so 'fear took hold on all' when the widow's son was raised (Lk 7¹⁶) ; and in the same way the centurion at the cross (Mt 27⁵⁴) and the witnesses of the Resurrection (Mt 28⁴· ⁸) were afraid ; cf. also Lk 1¹²· ⁶⁵ 2⁹ 5²⁶ etc.

3. Especially worthy of notice are those passages in which Jesus exhorts His hearers *not to fear.* He reassures Jairus when word comes that his daughter is dead (Mk 5³⁶, Lk 8⁵⁰) ; and Peter when the miraculous draught of fishes fills him with a sense of sin (Lk 5¹⁰) ; He meets the terror of the disciples on the sea with, 'It is I, be not afraid' (Mt 14²⁷) ; and touches them at the Transfiguration, with similar words (Mt 17⁷). When He sends the disciples out to preach, it is with reiterated injunctions against fear. The servants will meet with hostility from the enemies of their Lord ; but they must face such opposition without fear, 'for there is nothing covered that shall not be revealed' (Mt 10²⁴⁻²⁷). They are to be fearless preachers of the gospel, because no hostility of men can prevent the triumph of truth. They are not to fear even those who can kill the body, for their power is strictly limited to the body (Mt 10²⁸, Lk ·12⁴) ; they are to remember God's thought for the sparrows, and to be assured of the greater value of the servants of His Kingdom, and so to escape from fear (Mt 10³¹). If they are few in number facing a hostile world—a little flock surrounded by wolves

—they are to remember the sure purpose of the Father and not to be afraid (Lk 12³²).

Moral courage is a vital necessity of Christian discipleship. The Master is keenly conscious of moral paralysis which comes from the fear of man. Rev 21⁸ reflects His judgment when it groups 'the fearful' with 'the unbelieving' and 'the abominable' who are cast into the lake of fire which is the second death. And in our Lord's teaching faith is the antidote of fear. A true knowledge of the Father is the unfailing source of moral courage. 'Acquaint thyself with the Father and be delivered from fear' is the burden of His teaching. See COURAGE, COWARDICE.

4. The almost complete absence of direct exhortation to fear God is a very noticeable feature of the Gospels. The fear of God is, indeed, mentioned in the *Magnificat* (Lk 1⁵⁰), in the parable of the Unjust Judge (Lk 18²⁻⁴), and by the penitent thief on the cross (Lk 23⁴⁰); but in a direct injunction of Jesus only—if at all—in Mt 10²⁸ and the parallel passage Lk 12⁵. Here, as already mentioned, Jesus is sending out the disciples with the exhortation not to fear—even those who kill the body. But He adds to the negative a positive injunction, 'Rather fear him who is able to destroy both soul and body in hell'; or, as Lk. puts it, 'But I will warn you whom ye shall fear: fear him which after he hath killed hath power to cast into hell; yea, I say unto you, fear him.' It is most natural to think with the majority of commentators that God is the object of fear in this exhortation; but there are some who urge, on the contrary, that the devil is intended.

A. B. Bruce ('St. Matthew,' in *Expositor's Gr. Test.*) says: 'Would Christ present God under this aspect in such close connexion with the Father who cares even for the sparrows? What is to be greatly feared is not the final condemnation, but that which leads to it—temptation to forsake the cause of God out of regard to self-interest or self-preservation. Shortly, the counsel is: fear not the persecutor but the tempter, not the man who kills you for your fidelity but the man who wants to buy you off, and the devil whose agent he is.' Weymouth (*The NT in Modern Speech*) urges against the reference to God that ἐξουσία (Lk 12⁵) usually denotes 'delegated authority,' 'power enjoyed on sufferance'; and refers to Lk 22⁵³, Jn 19¹¹, Ac 26¹⁸, Col 1¹³, and Rev 13⁷ for illustrations of the ascription of power to Satan. On the other side Plummer ('St. Luke' in *Internat. Crit. Com.*) says: 'There is little doubt that this refers to God, and not to the devil. The change of construction points to this. It is no longer φοβήθητε ἀπὸ τούτου but τοῦτον φοβήθητε, "fear without trying to shun," which is the usual construction of fearing God. Moreover, we are not in Scripture told to fear Satan, but to resist him courageously.'

It may also be urged that the extreme punishment of the wicked is nowhere described as an exercise of Satan's authority. Gehenna is 'the eternal fire prepared for the devil and his angels' into which in Mt 25⁴⁰·⁴¹ those on the left hand are sent by the King. The ultimate 'destruction' of wicked men, whatever that may actually mean, must be conceived as an act of God and as the exercise of His authority; cf. Mt 21⁴⁰·⁴¹ 'The Lord of the vineyard . . . will miserably destroy those wicked men.'

5. Looking at the teaching of Jesus as a whole, we notice that, while He constantly urges men to faith rather than to fear, and to a trust in God's fatherly goodness, such as makes filial love the ruling motive of religious life, He does not altogether discard the appeal to fear as a motive for right conduct. There is a severity of God which cannot be ignored. Such parables as the Rich Man and Lazarus, the Unmerciful Servant, the Wheat and the Tares, and others, whatever interpretation we may put upon their details, at least suggest a Divine and holy sternness in regard to which men should keep a wholesome fear. Nor is it only in parables that we find this element of our Lord's teaching. We have in the Sermon on the Mount such passages as Mt 5²¹⁻³⁰ 7¹³·¹⁴ and ²¹⁻²⁷; and with these we may compare Mt 11²⁰⁻²⁴ 12³² 16²⁵·²⁶ 21⁴⁴ 26²⁴ and many others. The normal relation of the children of God to the Heavenly Father should be one of glad confidence and loving obedience. It should be ever approaching that perfect love which

casts out fear; but men who are trifling with great moral issues have no right, according to the teaching of Jesus, to this happy emancipation. For them fear is wholesome and necessary; for God is the Holy Father, and persistent defiance of His will must be visited with stern and righteous doom.

LITERATURE.—Cremer and Grimm-Thayer, *s.vv.* φόβος, φοβέω; Hastings' *DB*, art. 'Fear'; Maclaren, *Serm. pr. in Manchester*, i. 194; Bunyan, *Pilgrim's Progress*, Christian's talk with Hopeful after Ignorance was left behind.

E. H. TITCHMARSH.

FEASTS.—The religious Feasts of the Jews in our Lord's time were not so many as the religious Feasts of the Christian Church of to-day as enumerated in the English Book of Common Prayer, but they meant very much more in the way of outward observance. In the first rank—like Christmas, Easter, Ascensiontide, and Whitsuntide—there stood out the three great Feasts of Passover, Pentecost, and Tabernacles. Not unlike the Holy Days of the Church's Calendar, commemorating as they do various victories of the past, there were the annual Feasts of Dedication and of Purim, to which must be added the Feast of Trumpets together with its smaller counterpart in the monthly Feast of the New Moon. Corresponding to the Christian Sunday there was the weekly Feast of the Sabbath. Of these, Passover, Tabernacles, and Dedication are all specially mentioned in the Gospels, as well as the Sabbath, to which there are very many references, some merely incidental and some meant to show that it was our Lord's purpose to free the observance of that day from the artificial rules that had grown up about it in tradition. The Feasts are most prominent in the Fourth Gospel, where they are so mentioned as to form a framework into which the events of our Lord's Ministry fall. Three Passovers are there recorded: (1) Jn 2¹³, when our Lord cleansed the Temple almost at the beginning of His Ministry; (2) 6⁴, just after the feeding of the 5000; (3) 13¹ (cf. Mt 26², Mk 14¹, Lk 22¹), at the time of the Crucifixion and Resurrection.

It has indeed been contended that the reference to Passover in Jn 6⁴ is a mistake, and that really there were only two Passovers in our Lord's Ministry, the one at the beginning and the other at the end; it has also been contended that there may have been other Passovers, which are not mentioned, and that our Lord's Ministry may have included so many as ten or twelve, lasting over 10 or 12 years; but neither of these contentions can be made good, and it seems more likely that the record as it stands is both accurate and complete (see Turner in Hastings' *DB*, art. 'Chronology of NT').

Besides these three Passovers, mention is made of the Feast of Tabernacles in Jn 7², of the Feast of Dedication in Jn 10²², and of some Feast not particularized by name in Jn 5¹. To these St. Luke adds mention of an earlier Passover, when our Lord was 12 years old and was for the first time (?) allowed to accompany Joseph and Mary as they went up to Jerusalem year after year for the Feast (Lk 2⁴¹ᶠ·).

The Feasts of Passover, Pentecost, and Tabernacles were all of them Pilgrimage Feasts, that is to say, Feasts at which all male Jews above the age of 12 years were required to appear before the Lord in Jerusalem. It is noticed in Lk 2⁴¹ᶠ· that Joseph and Mary were both in the habit of going up to Jerusalem for the Passover every year. There was no requirement that women should thus attend at the Feasts, but Hillel seems to have encouraged the practice, and it was adopted by other religious women besides Mary (Edersheim, *Life and Times*, vol. i. p. 236). St. Luke in the same passage speaks of our Lord as going up at the age of twelve; that, too, was in excess of what was required by law, but was apparently in accordance with custom (so Edersheim, *op. cit.* p. 235; but cf. Schürer, *HJP* II. ii. p. 51, who represents that, strictly speaking, every boy who could walk ought to have attended, and that it was only by custom that boys who lived at a distance were allowed to wait till their twelfth year before going). Attendance at the Feasts was not confined to those who lived within easy reach, but Jews came as well from great distances, although naturally they could not attend so often as three times a year.

• Schürer writes (*op. cit.* p. 290 f.): 'There was nothing that contributed so much to cement the bond of union between the dispersion and the mother country as the regular pilgrimages which Jews from all quarters of the world were in the habit of making to Jerusalem on festival occasions.' He quotes Philo (*de Monarchia*, ii. 1) as saying: 'Many thousands of people from many thousands of towns made pilgrimages to the Temple at every festival, some by land, some by sea, and coming from the east and the west, from the north and the south,' and refers to Josephus' estimate of the number of Jews in Jerusalem at the time of the Feasts as being so many as 2,700,000 (*BJ* VI. ix. 3).

In accordance with this it is definitely stated in the Gospels that four times during His Ministry our Lord went up to Jerusalem to keep the Feasts, twice for Passover, once for Tabernacles, and once for an unnamed Feast. Possibly He went up quite regularly three times a year, for the notice that He was in Galilee shortly before the second Passover (Jn 6⁴) does not preclude the possibility of His having gone up a little later. At the first Passover mention is made of His disciples being with Him in Jerusalem (Jn 2¹⁷. ²²), evidently having journeyed from Galilee with the same purpose as Himself, to keep the Feast. Similarly at Tabernacles it is stated that His brethren went up from Galilee to keep the Feast (Jn 7¹⁰). In all the Gospel references to Passover and Tabernacles the impression is given of large crowds of Jews in Jerusalem. At the Feast of Dedication also our Lord was in Jerusalem, but that was simply because His work at that time lay close by. He did not go up to Jerusalem on purpose for it, since no pilgrimages were made except at the three great Feasts; but being close at hand He liked to mark the occasion by a visit to the Temple, and there found a considerable number of Jews resident in the neighbourhood who had been attracted thither like Himself. See, further, the sep. artt. on DEDICATION, PASSOVER, etc.

As regards the unnamed Feast of Jn 5¹, it is impossible to reach any certainty as to what Feast is intended. If the correct reading were ἡ ἑορτή, it would most naturally be the Feast of Tabernacles, which was above all *the* Feast of the Jews (Cheyne on Is 30¹⁹); but if the article be omitted, as almost certainly it should be, the expression is quite indefinite, and might refer to either Tabernacles or Passover or Pentecost, or to any of the smaller Feasts.

In attempting to decide between these, guidance may first be sought from the general sequence of events, so far as it is indicated by the following notes of time:
(1) Passover, *i.e.* March or April, Jn 2¹³.
(2) A reference to harvest, Jn 4³⁵.
(3) This unnamed Feast, Jn 5¹.
(4) A second Passover, Jn 6⁴.
Thus it appears that the unnamed Feast fell between the incident connected with the harvest in Jn 4³⁵ and Passover. This does not, however, give very much help, because Jn 4³⁵ may mean either that that was the actual time of harvest or that it was four months before harvest, so that it is impossible to tell whether the incident there described happened in the month of April or in midwinter. If that happened in midwinter, then Dedication (Dec.) and Purim (Feb.) are the only Feasts possible chronologically; but if, as is equally likely, that incident happened at harvest, then the chronology would admit almost any of the Feasts, either Pentecost (May), or Trumpets (Sept.), or Tabernacles (Sept.), or Dedication (Dec.), or Purim (Feb.). Thus the setting of the incident is quite indeterminate. In the description of the incident itself there are two points that need to be noticed. The one is that the introductory words are such as to suggest that the only reason for mentioning the Feast at all is to explain our Lord's presence in Jerusalem,—'After these things there was a Feast of the Jews, and Jesus went up to Jerusalem.' Since there were only three Feasts at which even the strictest Jews went up to Jerusalem, it appears that this must be one of these three, *i.e.* must be either Passover, Pentecost, or Tabernacles. At the smaller Feasts many of those Jews who were in or near Jerusalem would naturally congregate in the Temple courts (cf. Jn 10²²ff.), but none were in the habit of going up on these occasions from other parts of the country. Accordingly, though Purim may seem suitable in other ways, it quite fails to explain the one fundamental fact, our Lord's visit

to Jerusalem, and the same objection lies against all the smaller Feasts. The second point to be noticed is that St. John's use of so vague a phrase in reference to one of the three great Feasts can mean only that he was himself unable to recall the exact occasion. The events recorded were quite clear in his mind, and he remembered that they had happened on one of the occasions when our Lord went to Jerusalem to keep the Feasts, but at which particular one he could not recall. This being so, it is useless to try now to discover the secret from his writings, but there is no need to feel disappointment at the absence of information on this point, as if some part of the significance of the incident were lost through ignorance of its occasion, for the circumstances would not have dropped out of St. John's memory as they did, if they had been essential to the understanding of our Lord's words or actions. See also art. MINISTRY.

C. E. GARRAD.

FEEDING THE MULTITUDES.—The Gospels give us two accounts of multitudes miraculously fed by our Lord. In the first instance (reported in Mt 14¹⁵⁻²¹, Mk 6³⁵⁻⁴⁴, Lk 9¹²⁻¹⁷, Jn 6⁵⁻¹³) the number is given as 5000, exclusive (so Mt.) of women and children. In the second instance (reported in Mt 15³²⁻³⁹, Mk 8¹⁻⁹) the number is given as 4000, Mt. again adding women and children.

1. It will be better to consider these instances separately, and to treat the feeding of the 5000 in the light of the first three Gospels. The Synoptics agree that the place was a desert one on the east side of the Sea of Galilee; and Lk. fixes it at Bethsaida Julias (see CAPERNAUM). Mk. and Lk. connect the withdrawal to this place with the return of the Twelve and their report, Mt. with the execution of John the Baptist. Mk. seems to be correct, since he gives the specific reason that they needed rest, which they could not otherwise secure. All agree that a vast multitude followed them to their place of resort, thus defeating their purpose, and that it was the disciples who called the attention of Jesus to the needs of the people. Jesus then commanded His disciples to provide food for the multitude. One feels that He was preparing their minds for what He was about to do. Their astonishment at His command led them to point out the impossibility, if not absurdity, of the requirement, since they had but five loaves and two fishes. Then follows the astounding order to seat the people in groups easily accessible to the disciples, the blessing of the loaves and fishes, the distribution of the meagre supply, the satisfaction of the hunger of all, and the gathering up of the fragments.

Attempts have been made to rob this account of its miraculous character, the favourite method being to assume that the evident determination of Jesus to assuage their hunger induced those in the vast company who had supplies of food, to share, in the spirit of Jesus, with those who had none. The difficulty with this explanation is that the disciples, who had every opportunity of seeing what was done, thought that the multitude was fed with the five loaves and two fishes only. Against this, neither Mk 6⁵² nor Jn 6²⁶ is evidence, as Beyschlag will have it (*Leben Jesu*, i. 330). The immediate context in both passages shows that both Jesus and the Twelve thought of the transaction as miraculous. Admitting the miracle, some have thought to explain it as a miraculous satisfaction of hunger with a little, rather than as a multiplication of the loaves and fishes. This is contrary to the text in all four of the Gospels, which unite in saying that twelve baskets of fragments were taken up. This would be more than there was at the beginning (see art. BASKET), thus virtually affirming the multiplication. We are shut up, then, to the alternative of regarding the account as legendary, or else as a miraculous multiplication of their food supply. There are some difficulties in the way of believing it miraculous. (1) The question of Jesus, 'How many loaves have ye?' reminds one of the question of Elisha (2 K 4²), 'What hast thou in the house?'

and so suggests an imitation of Elisha's miracle, as in fact the whole process of multiplication suggests the miracle of the meal in the jar and the cruse of oil of 1 K 17$^{11-16}$. (2) The record is a trifle obscure. The whole stress is on the loaves, both in the gathered fragments, especially in Jn., and in the subsequent references of Jesus (see Mk 8^{19}), while the fish are ignored. (3) Usually, also, when such a miracle was performed, the observers are said to have been profoundly impressed (see Mk 4^{41} 5^{42} 7^{37}), but here no comment follows. (4) Besides, it seems to be in contradiction of His avowed purpose not to give the Jews what would be to them a convincing sign. As to all but the last of these difficulties, it may be said that they are, in themselves, not serious. The fourth assumes that the miracles of healing would not, but that a miracle such as the feeding would convince the Jews, and so be just the kind of sign the Jews demanded. But, in fact, the sign the Jews required and Jesus refused to grant was some miracle performed to order, and regardless of human need. Such a miracle as the feeding lacked these two characteristics. It was spontaneous, and it met a human want. In favour of the historicity of the miracle is the further fact that it is recorded in all the Gospels. The tradition was not open to question in the mind of any one of the Evangelists.

2. With regard to the second recorded instance, the feeding of the 4000, the case is quite different. It is found in but two of the Gospels. Lk. and Jn. evidently thought of but a single feeding. It is easy to see how the second account might have grown out of the first, and the similarities are so great as to suggest that it did have its origin there. The question of Jesus concerning the number of loaves, the remarkable circumstance that a second time the disciples had so little food with them, the seating of the people on the ground, the distribution to the Twelve for redistribution among the multitude, the eating until they were filled, the gathering of the broken pieces into baskets, are suspiciously like the feeding of the 5000. It is difficult to see how the disciples, with the memory of the feeding of the 5000 fresh in their minds, could have questioned Jesus as to the source of supply for this second company. And here it is that the narrative as given by Jn. sheds light on the question under consideration. Jn. betrays the fact that the same narrative was differently told, since he combines elements of both narratives as related by Mt. and Mark. Mt. places the second feeding on a mountain ; Jn. locates the feeding on a mountain. Jn. and Mt. and Mk. (second instance) agree that Jesus proposed the feeding. Mk., according to his usual custom of emphasizing the teaching as primary, and of making the miracles secondary, makes Jesus teach the shepherdless sheep out of sympathy, while Mt. makes this sympathy prompt Him to heal them, and Lk. combines the two ; this in the first feeding. In the second this sympathy was elicited by their hunger. In the second the point of difficulty with the disciples (according to Mt. and Mk.), or with Jesus (according to Jn.), was not the expense, as in the first, but that securing so much food in a desert place. This certainly looks as though Jn. had heard both accounts and deliberately undertook to combine them into one, or else as though the differences in the account of the same story led Mt. and Mk. to believe that there were two feedings. In any case Lk., by implication, and Jn., almost directly, favour the single feeding— that of the 5000. The only serious difficulty in this elimination of the second feeding is the record in Mk 8$^{19. 20}$ (cf. Mt 16$^{9. 10}$), according to which Jesus is made to refer to the two feedings as separate events. The denial of the second would

make it necessary to affirm that the words of Jesus are incorrectly reported. But here Mt. is evidently dependent upon the collection of narratives by Mk., not Mk. upon the collection of sayings made by Matthew. Mt. and Mk. are not two independent witnesses. We may not be able to account satisfactorily for the misunderstanding of Mk. in this case, but his testimony could hardly offset that of Jn., unless we were obliged, which we are not, to suppose that Mk. got his information on this point directly from Peter. Even if this were so, we should have to make our choice between Peter and Jn., which, in view of all the facts, would turn out in favour of the latter.

The significance of the feeding of the multitude for the humaneness of Jesus is not less great than that of the healings. The power was His, and He used it for the good of His fellow-men in whatever way was needful for their immediate welfare, and for setting an example of helpfulness in the everyday affairs of life to His disciples in all the centuries to follow.

LITERATURE.—Trench and Taylor on *Miracles*; Edersheim, *Life and Times*, i. 675 ff., ii. 63 ff.; Andrews, *Life of our Lord* [1893 ed.], 320 ff., 333 ff.; Bruce, *Training of the Twelve*, 118; Westcott, *Gosp. of St. John, in loc.*

C. W. RISHELL.

FEET. — The word occurs frequently in the Gospels. Figuratively it has a wide range of meaning. It is employed in phrases which express worthlessness ('to be trodden under foot,' Mt 5^{13}), supplication ('fell at his feet,' Mk 5^{22} 7^{25}), great honour or reverence (Lk 7$^{38-46}$ the woman who kissed Jesus' feet ; Jn 11^2 Mary ; Mt 28^9 'held him by the feet'), ignorant or blasphemous contempt (Mt 7^6 'trample under foot'), righteous condemnation or rejection (Mt 10^{14} 'shake dust off feet'), salvation through sacrifice (Mt 18^8 || Mk 9^{45} cutting off hand or foot), discipleship (Lk 8^{35} cured demoniac sitting at Jesus' feet ; 10^{39} Mary), helplessness (Mt 22^{13} 'bind hand and foot'), complete triumph (Mt 22^{44} || Mk 12^{36} || Lk 20^{43} enemies of Messianic King put under His feet), absolute safety (Mt 4^6 || Lk 4^{11} 'lest thou dash thy foot against a stone'), subjection (Mt 5^{35} earth the footstool of God's feet). In washing the feet of the disciples Jesus inculcates lessons of humility, mutual service, and the need of daily cleansing from sin (Jn 13$^{5-14}$). See artt. BASON, FOOT.

Of the feet of Jesus Himself mention is made in the NT very frequently. Before His feet suppliants fell down (Mk 5^{22} 7^{25}, Lk 8^{41}), and also a Samaritan who returned to give thanks (Lk 17^{16}). At His feet sufferers were laid to be healed (Mt 15^{30}). Neglectful of the courtesies of a host, Simon the Pharisee gave Him no water to refresh His feet (Lk 7^{44}) ; but a sinful woman on the same occasion wet His feet with her tears, wiped them with the hair of her head, kissed them, and anointed them with ointment (7$^{38. 44ff.}$) ; and Mary of Bethany showed her great love and gratitude in a similar fashion, when she lavished the contents of her alabaster cruse of precious spikenard (Jn 11^2 12^3 ; cf. Mt 26^7, Mk 14^3) upon the feet which had brought the Lord from beyond Jordan (Jn 10^{40} 11^7) to speak the life-giving word at her brother's grave (11$^{43f.}$) At Jesus' feet the restored demoniac sat (Lk 8^{35}), like Mary afterwards when she 'heard his word' (10^{39}). The two angels who guarded the sepulchre were seen sitting 'the one at the head, and the other at the feet, where the body of Jesus had lain' (Jn 20^{12}). It was His feet that the two Marys clung to when they first met Jesus on the Resurrection morning. [Though love prompted them to lay hold of Him, did reverence forbid them to touch more than His feet ?]. When Jesus in the upper room showed His hands and His feet to His disciples (Lk 24$^{39f.}$), it was doubtless to prove to them that He who now stood before them was the same Jesus who by hands and feet had been nailed to the cross (cf. Jn 20²⁰· ²⁵· ²⁷). St. Paul says of the ascended Christ that all things are put under His feet (Eph 1²²), and that beneath His feet death itself shall be destroyed (1 Co 15²⁵ff·). And in the Book of Revelation, when the heavenly Jesus appears to the seer of Patmos, the place of His feet has been made glorious (cf. Is 60¹³). Those feet which were dust-stained in the house of Simon the Pharisee, and weary by the well of Sychar (Jn 4⁶), and pierced with nails on the cross of Calvary, are now 'like unto fine brass, as if they burned in a furnace' (Rev 1¹⁵, cf. 2¹⁸).

It has been questioned whether the feet of Jesus were nailed to the cross. The doubt is based on the facts that in the Fourth Gospel Jesus mentions only His hands and side (Jn 20²⁰), and that sometimes in crucifixion the feet were simply tied to the cross. The nailing of the feet of Jesus would not have been disputed were it not part of an argument to prove that He did not really die on the cross. 'That the feet were usually nailed (in crucifixion), and that the case of Jesus was no exception to the general rule, may be regarded as beyond doubt' (Meyer on Mt 27³⁵). There is a difference of opinion as to whether the feet of Jesus were nailed to the cross separately, with two nails, or the one over the other with the same nail. In early art the feet are more frequently represented as separately nailed, but in later art as nailed together, the one over the other. Tradition favours the opinion that the feet were nailed separately. See art. CRUCIFIXION.

LITERATURE.—Meyer's *Com. on St. Matthew*; Ellicott, *Historical Lectures on the Life of Our Lord*, p. 353; Andrews, *Bible Student's Life of Our Lord*², p. 462 f.

JOHN REID.

FELLOWSHIP.—

Neither the word 'fellowship' (κοινωνία) nor any equivalent term occurs in the Synoptic Gospels, but the reality in faith, love, and joy is diffused like the fragrance of the flowers of Galilee through that bright spring of the world's life. As we pass to the Acts and Epistles, especially the Pauline, the word is found in a variety of meanings. Most frequently it is translated 'fellowship' (Ac 2⁴², 1 Co 1⁹, 2 Co 6¹⁴ ⁸⁴, Gal 2⁹, Ph 1⁵ 2¹ 3¹⁰). It is rendered 'communion' in 1 Co 10¹⁶ (RVm 'participation in') and 2 Co 13¹⁴; 'contribution' (AV 'distribution') in 2 Co 9¹³, cf. Ro 15²⁶; 'communication' (RV 'fellowship') in Philem 6, cf. He 13¹⁶. Though κοινωνία occurs only three times in the Johannine writings (1 Jn 1³· ⁶· ⁷), they are peculiarly rich in the religious ideas which give the term its content. The conception of fellowship in the NT is not exhausted by the varied significations of any one word; it becomes plain only as we comprehend the meaning of the life of the Early Church.

i. INHERITED FORECASTS. — Like most of the great religious conceptions of the NT, this idea has its roots deep in the OT. Isaiah proclaims that the religion of Israel can find its truest expression only in a spiritual fellowship of faith, independent of a national framework. In Israel there is an imperishable remnant, a stock from which new life will spring forth after desolation has swept over Jerusalem (Is 8¹³⁻¹⁸ 37³¹· ³²). By the time of Jeremiah the disaster of the nation had become so irretrievable that the prophet hardly dares to hope for more than the salvage of individuals from the wreck; but these rescued ones will form the true Israel under a new covenant (Jer 23³⁻⁸ 31³¹ff·). The Messianic blessedness which those prophets foresaw consisted of an intimate fellowship which, in the coming days, the redeemed company of Israel would enjoy with Jehovah (Is 49⁶⁻¹³, Jer 31³¹ff·). It was to be a fellowship of Israelites because it was primarily a fellowship with Israel's God (Is 52⁶⁻¹² 60). This thought of fellowship finds nowhere more vivid expression than in the Psalter. That storehouse of religious devotion is filled with prayers of communion with Jehovah, the supremely moral Person, righteous, faithful, holy, yet full of loving-kindness, who

satisfies the needs of man by bringing him into fellowship with Himself (Pss 16. 34. 40. 63). Though many of the psalms seem to be the utterance of individual yearning for God's presence, others express the religious desires of corporate Israel, a fellowship of saints with a common thirst for the springs of its life.

A special term had been coined for Israel in her religious rather than her national function—*kāhāl*, which was rendered in the LXX by ἐκκλησία ('church'). It signified the religious assembly of God's chosen people; but as this could never be completely realized, even in the great temple gatherings, the conception remained largely ideal. A rich spiritual legacy was transmitted from the OT in the words Israel, *ecclesia*, Kingdom of God; and though the Jewish heirs were unable to appreciate their inheritance, these two truths of the prophets and psalmists could never have quite perished—that there is an eternal commonwealth of saints, and that this fellowship of Israel is based upon fellowship with Jehovah.

ii. THE SYNOPTIC GOSPELS. — Jesus not only claimed to fulfil prophecy; by His words of grace He did much more than the most spiritually minded Israelite could have hoped. The spirit of the Lord which was upon Him awoke prophetic thoughts that had long lain in the hearts of those who were waiting for the consolation of Israel. He brought spring and quickened the seed sown in the past. He calls men to Himself and forms them into a new society, within which are to be enjoyed the blessings foretold by the prophets. In this company is found religious fellowship, based upon forgiveness of sins and eternal life through the knowledge of God revealed by Jesus as Father, of which the OT saints had but partial enjoyment or glad anticipation. He places Himself at the head of this society, claiming that He alone can impart the knowledge of God which will give rest to the souls of men (Mt 11²⁷⁻³⁰). Thus His followers, constituted into the society of the Messiah, become a Divinely ordered fellowship not dependent on outward organization, but united by a common faith in Jesus as the Revealer of God to them. They are the New Israel, the imperishable *ecclesia* (Mt 16¹⁶⁻¹⁹).

This society is no closed circle. Associating Himself more or less intimately with groups of disciples, Jesus sends them forth with the knowledge they have gained concerning Him, to proclaim to the people that the new epoch of Divine rule is about to be inaugurated, and that they should prepare for its advent. The condition of membership in this brotherhood is to follow Jesus, even though this may seem to the man of the world to be nothing less than to lose one's life. Fellowship with Jesus costs much. Family ties may be severed, the hatred of the world may be vented upon His disciples, billows of persecution may sweep over them, but in this society is life indeed (Mk 8³⁴⁻³⁸, Lk 14²⁵⁻³⁵). Jesus offers His followers a fellowship in this new brotherhood, which more than compensates for any worldly friendship that they may have to renounce (Mk 10²⁶⁻³¹). Their true kindred, even like that of Jesus Himself, will be found among those united by spiritual affinities in this new circle. New virtues abound in this brotherhood. Love working in helpful ministries for others is of the essence of fellowship in Messiah's company. Rank is assigned, not as in worldly kingdoms, but by the degree of service rendered by each to all (Mk 10³⁵⁻⁴⁵).

In time Jesus announces to His followers that His society, as the true Israel, is to take the place of the Jewish nation, which as such is becoming a *massa perdita*. Out of this perishing world His disciples are saved into the eternal Kingdom, and as heirs of salvation they are in reality, as they were afterwards called, 'the saints of the New Covenant' (Mk 12[1-12]). Before His death the Messiah gave concreteness to this fellowship by a solemn communion with His disciples in the Last Supper, which became the means of making real to them the blessings of the New Covenant. The connexion of the Supper with the Paschal meal, which may here be assumed as having existed, either by anticipation or directly, would suggest to the minds of the participants that in this New Covenant they were entering into fellowship with Jehovah, and that they were also binding themselves together as brothers in a new covenant with God (Mk 14[22-25]). A promise of enlarging fellowship fitly closes the Gospel of Matthew in the words, 'Lo, I am with you to the end of the ages' (28[20]), and gives us a glimpse of the transition from the earthly to the heavenly life of Jesus.

To sum up, the Synoptic Gospels show us the conception of an eternal Divine Commonwealth, made actual by Jesus in a society welded together by fervent loyalty to Himself as the Christ of God, and pervaded by a life of mutual service to the members. He brings His followers into true fellowship with Jehovah by revealing Him and pardoning their sins. They enjoy the life of a brotherhood, which is true life, in His company.

iii. THE PRIMITIVE JEWISH-CHRISTIAN CHURCH. —Fellowship is the most real definition of the unity which was a constituent quality of the Early Church. Intercourse, intimate and universal, among brethren, whose life was consecrated by a gracious Divine presence, and thus free from everything secular, constituted the Church as distinctively one. This unity was not expressed by any rigid cohesive organization, not even primarily by the leadership of the Apostles. Indeed, the disciples had been warned by their Lord not to allow themselves to be called 'Master' (Mt 23[10]). A company of baptized brethren, they had received the Holy Spirit from their risen Lord, who had welded them into one. His personal gifts were manifest in each brother passionately devoted to his unseen Lord, and so on terms of friendship with all who loved Him.

The Church appears on the stage of the public world as a new sect, holding to the belief that Jesus is Messiah. Outwardly the brethren were probably indistinguishable from good Jews, and such organization as they had would follow the lines of their former life. But it would seem that they did not think of themselves as a new organization. They were slow to cast loose their hawsers and swing out into the stream as an independent Church. Led by powerful personalities, Peter, John, and James, who had been either intimate or of close kinship with Jesus, they regarded themselves as the true Israel, and for a while hoped that the nation would repent. Before St. Paul's time, however, there was a change, for we find that the brethren throughout Judæa were organized into distinctive communities, not as 'synagogues,' but as 'churches' (Gal. 1[22]). But in these churches the utmost freedom of the individual, which is essential for true fellowship, prevailed; for the Church grew not by official initiative, but by the prophetic power of the Holy Spirit impelling the brethren to spread far and wide the good news of their gospel.

Little as the primitive Christians differed outwardly from the Jewish world, their inner world was a new creation. It was a brotherhood of Divine origin; for not only were they baptized into the name of Jesus the Lord of life, but they had received the Holy Spirit. How sacred this fellowship was is manifest from the terrible punishment meted out to Ananias and Sapphira for violating the mutual trust that made the brotherhood possible (Ac 5).

There were various manifestations of this fellowship. (a) It was a house-church. Brethren met as sons round the common board in the homes of those who could best provide accommodation, and partook of a daily meal consecrated to the memory of their unseen but present Lord. They held communion with one another because they held communion with the risen Jesus. Common prayers, songs, and thanksgivings rose to Jehovah from these family groups (Ac 2[42] 4[23-32]).

(b) This fellowship (κοινωνία) found further expression in a life of mutual service,—the rich for the poor, the strong for the weak. They rejoiced with those who rejoiced; they wept with those who wept. In fact, true κοινωνία could not be better defined than in the words of the Golden Rule—'Whatsoever ye would that men should do to you, do ye even so to them' (Mt 7[12]). No formal ordinance, such as the community of goods, was enjoined on the brethren; their love welled forth in such a pure and powerful stream that it made its own channels. All blessings, earthly and spiritual, were spontaneously shared with those who were in need (Ac 2[44-47] 4[32-35]).

So we have in the earliest days a true fellowship, a brotherhood united by love to a risen Lord, whom many of them had known on earth, and led without rivalry by favourite disciples of Jesus, enjoying gifts and graces from the ever present Spirit of their Lord. But that brotherhood gathered in the earthly Zion was nationalistic in sentiment. It was provincial in spirit, especially, it would seem, throughout Judæa, where the churches were in villages remote from the world of men.

iv. THE GENTILE CHURCHES OF THE PAULINE WORLD. — With the rise of Antioch a peril threatened the prestige of Jerusalem. Could the fruit of the Spirit thrive equally well in the valleys and on the plains of Syria and Asia as on the isolated plateau of Judæa? If so, it was bound to be very much more abundant. Fortunately, Paul the Apostle to the Gentiles was a man of varied culture. While his world was in cities and he thought imperially, he never treated the Jewish mind lightly, and he knew what that mind was. He understood its worth and its rights. He could discern every wave of feeling, every gust that shivered duskily across it. So St. Paul was himself the greatest power of his day making for the unity of the Church. It was a passion with him to avert a breach which would be fatal; and he was successful, for the other Apostles responded nobly as brethren, and gave him the right hand of fellowship (Gal 2[2, 9]). But the sections thus united had to be cemented; so he devotes much energy to effecting a durable κοινωνία by organizing the collection for the poor saints at Jerusalem. In 2 Co 8[4] 9[13] and Ro 15[26] the word κοινωνία is translated (RV) 'contribution'; but 'there is always at the root of κοινωνία, in the NT, the idea of Christian communion in one form or another. Those who bestow make common cause with one another and with the recipients' (Waite). The collection is a religious act, because it is a mark of Christian fellowship. Indeed, the Macedonians regard it as a signal token of Divine favour to be allowed thus to help those from whom they had received the gospel; and the poor Jewish Christians, who had made experience of the liberal Christian kindliness of the Gentiles, could hardly refuse to call them brethren (2 Co 8[1-5] 9[11-14]).

The Christian fellowship was world-wide. This brotherhood was one everywhere (1 P 5[9]), and in writing to the Corinthians St. Paul assumes that what he says will be of interest not only to them, but 'to all that in every place call upon the name of Jesus Christ our Lord, both theirs and ours' (1 Co 1[2]). The Church of God which is in Corinth is a visible but partial manifestation of the larger whole. This idea persisted after the Apostolic age; for 'Brotherhood alternates with Ecclesia in the oldest sets of ecclesiastical canons, while omnis fraternitas and πᾶσα ἡ ἀδελφότης are used to denote the whole of Christendom' (Lindsay). This world-wide brotherhood was not held together by any outward organization, though the Apostle Paul does group his churches by provinces. But organization is local: it does not follow the lines of provincial units. Of course, Christian life had to be expressed in outward fellowship wherever it was possible, so that all the brethren within a convenient radius, such as a city, would be grouped together to form the Church of God in that place. And the Spirit of God supplied these local churches with leaders who had the necessary gifts for the conduct of their life. This became the basis of a permanent ministry.

From the world they became outwardly separate, 'saints' chosen out of it and consecrated to God (Ro 1[7], 1 Co 1[2], Gal 1[4]), and so forming one family, 'the household' of faith (Gal 6[10], Eph 2[19]), throughout the empire of this world. Hence great stress is laid upon the grace of hospitality (He 13[1. 2]). In that busy world with its thronged highways, the Christian was always sure of a warm welcome wherever there was a church or a group of brethren (see per contra 3 Jn [9f.]), and the sufferings of the saints were made the occasion of active sympathy (He 6[10] 10[33. 34] 13[3]). St. Paul experienced many such marked tokens of fellowship, especially at the hands of the Philippians, for whom he cherished the deepest affection. They were unremittingly active in co-operation with him for the spread of the gospel; and whatever his needs, bodily or spiritual, might be, they were ready to do their best by gifts or sympathy to supply the lack. This was true fellowship (Ph 1[5. 7] 2[18] 4[14. 15]). Philemon also was a real Christian, whose faith in, and love to, the Lord Jesus was manifested in his kindly offices towards all the saints; and the Apostle delicately suggests that he should not stop till his benevolence becomes complete and embraces even the slave Onesimus (Philem [6. 15. 16]).

This religious idea of brotherhood issues in a new grace, 'love of the brethren' (φιλαδελφία), which is to be cherished as an especial sign of Divine life (1 Th 4[9], Ro 12[10], He 13[1], 1 P 1[22]). A fine word, ἁπλότης ('singleness'), is used by St. Paul to denote the quality of the man in whom fellowship (κοινωνία) is a ruling motive. He is ἁπλοῦς, 'single-minded,' 'liberal.' He does not serve God and Mammon. His eye is single. Looking only at the needs of his brother, he realizes the truth of the Lord's words that it is more blessed to give than to receive (Ac 20[35]). Among the brethren there is no almsgiving. All that is sordid in almsgiving is removed, and generosity becomes a choice token of fellowship (2 Co 8[2] 9[11. 13]). 'When men thankfully receive God's gifts, and in imitation of His bounty use them for the good of others, so that the recipients also thank God for the benefaction, it is as far as it goes the re-establishment of the right relation between God and men, and men and men.' The slave is not only made partaker of such bounty, but as he possesses this spirit he pays an ungrudging service to his master (Eph 6[5]).

The fellowship of church with church was further increased by the visits of Apostles and teachers, as well as by the interchange of correspondence. What was of interest to one was of interest to all in so far as it touched their common gospel. While we do not find any uniform creed or liturgy in these Epistles, there was almost certainly a substantially similar form of worship, and in their prayers and hymns the brethren gave utterance to the same faith in Jesus Christ, and in their teaching they adhered to the common truths which the Apostles taught (Ro 6[17], Gal 1[8]). We cannot fail to be impressed by the combination of a sense of unity with great individual freedom. The Spirit took the life of believer or church, and produced in it some distinctive grace or function, which brought diversity without disharmony, enrichment without lack of proportion. Manifold, however, as these gifts were, the greatest of all and that which lay at the root of their fellowship was love; for not only was it the best because the commonest, but it tempered and restrained the more individualistic endowments, which might easily destroy the harmony of the Christian company (1 Co 12[31] 13). True fellowship demands variety in unity, individual freedom working at the impulse of a common spirit.

The noblest exposition of Christian fellowship, outside the Gospel of John, is contained in the Epistle to the Ephesians. In that prose poem in praise of unity, the Church is described as one body of which each Christian is, or should be, a perfect member. A Divine creation purposed from all eternity by the Father's love, it was made actual in history through Jesus Christ. The Church is one because of the unities on which it is based. Its members are baptized into the name of the one Lord whom they confess. They are inspired by the same Spirit, and there is one God and Father of all, who is above all and through all and in all (Eph 4[4-6]). Historically the Church became one when, in Christ, Jew and Gentile were both reconciled unto God in one body by the cross (2[14-18]); and in the ages to come each individual with variety of function will reach his perfection in this perfect organism, and contribute to the completeness of the whole (4[7-13]). A fellowship so sublime in its ideal must be undisturbed by selfish desires. Only where love, patience, long-suffering and humility reign will there be on earth 'a communion of the saints.' 'In the Apostle's eyes all true life in an Ecclesia is a life of community, of the harmonious and mutually helpful action of different elements, so that he is giving instruction on the very essence of membership when in each of the nine Epistles addressed to Ecclesiæ he makes the peace of God to be the supreme standard for them to aim at, and the perpetual self-surrender of love the comprehensive means of attaining it' (Hort, Christ. Ecclesia, 123).

All the manifestation of fellowship among the brethren, the very brotherhood itself, is possible only because the individual members of the communion of the saints are in personal fellowship with Jesus Christ. He indeed is the fountain and source of communion. All human fellowship is derivative. The word κοινωνία is used by St. Paul only in 1 Co 10[16] to express this personal fellowship with Christ, the thought being that in the Lord's Supper believers are united in close communion, because through the cup and the bread they are enabled to participate in the life of Christ Himself. But the idea is central in St. Paul's religion—'I no longer live, but Christ liveth in me' (Gal 2[20]); 'For me to live is Christ' (Ph 1[21]). However, this fellowship of the individual is no selfish enjoyment. Only those who are 'rooted and grounded in love' are 'able to comprehend with all saints what is the breadth and length and depth and height; and to know the love of Christ which passeth knowledge,' that they may be filled with all the fulness of God (Eph 3[17-19]). Now the Apostle expects that even in his own imperfect churches there should be some real enjoyment of this fellowship with Christ. He reminds the Church of Corinth that they 'were called into the fellowship of his Son Jesus Christ our Lord' (1 Co 1⁹), *i.e.* the fellowship of which He is the soul. Fractured though the Church is by schism and marred by impurity, it is a society of redeemed sons, whose destiny is to be conformed to the image of Him who is the firstborn among many brethren (Ro 8²⁹. ³⁰), and even now it must reflect with real truth some of the glory of that future fellowship. The same conception is conveyed in 2 Co 13¹⁴ in the words, 'the communion of the Holy Ghost'; for the Spirit who unifies the Christian society into a body of redeemed men who have experienced the unmerited favour of Christ and the love of the Father, is the Spirit of Christ (2 Co 3¹⁷. ¹⁸). The Philippian Church also, pervaded by love and comforted by reciprocal compassion, has enjoyed fellowship because of the presence of this Spirit who brings the consolation of Christ Himself (Ph 2¹).

v. THE JOHANNINE WRITINGS.—Assuming that the books which bear the name of John came from the Apostle, we may consider them together, for they bring before us the conditions of a later period. The Gospel and the Epistles at least are the mature work of one who seeks to set before his readers the mind of Christ, after the attempt had been made for half a century to work His teaching into actual life. Much must be taken for granted. The visible Church is one; the old problem of Jewish and Gentile sections is a dead issue. Now the Church is face to face with the world. Two spiritual forces are opposed — the realm of light over which the Son of God rules, and the world of darkness organized and directed by the Prince of Evil. Error concerning the Person of Christ, and lack of love of the brethren, are disintegrating the Christian society. So the author takes his readers to the fountain of Christian fellowship, and allows them to taste its quality as it was enjoyed by the disciples of Jesus, whom having loved He loved unto the end (Jn 13–17). These discourses illuminate the Lord's Supper, and the feet-washing serves as a noble approach to it. There are two prominent aspects of the Eucharist as interpreted by John : (*a*) that it is a feast for the spiritual nurture of the faithful (6⁴⁸⁻⁵⁸); (*b*) that it sets forth the love of the Lord, and so becomes a love-feast of brethren. Love is the note of the conversations. Only through the clear atmosphere of love can they see their absent Master. If they obey Him and love one another, He will come to them bringing the peace and the joy which He alone can impart (14²¹. ²³. ²⁷). So will there be, as Loisy says, 'a hierarchy of love,' the disciples loving one another with the new love which springs from their Master, and their Master loving them as the Father loves Him (13³⁴ 17²⁶). These chapters teach respecting Christian fellowship that (i.) its source is God as revealed in Jesus Christ, (ii.) its agent is the Holy Spirit, (iii.) its condition in the believer is faith in and obedience to Jesus Christ, and (iv.) its fruit is a life of love, joy, and peace among brethren here, and perfect sonship hereafter.

Similar conceptions dominate the First Epistle of John. Fellowship with God is the goal of the Christian life (1 Jn 1³. ⁴). Such fellowship comes through knowledge, which is only another aspect of the love of God (4⁷. ⁸). But sin is a barrier to this fellowship, which would therefore be impossible were it not that it has been removed by the propitiatory sacrifice of Christ (2¹. ²). No sin is greater than hate; and since all love comes from God (4¹⁹), he who hates his brother cannot love God. If he love God, that love must first have come from God, and stream forth through the heart of the believer upon his brother. To live in loving fellowship with the brethren is at once the proof of fellowship with the Father and the ethical condition for receiving it, for only to hearts broadened and deepened by love can God reveal Himself and bring fellowship (4¹². ¹³. ²⁰. ²¹).

This mystic, whose spirit was more responsive than any other to the mind of the Master, opens up the profound depth of that fellowship which the early Christian Church enjoyed, as we have seen, in no inconsiderable measure. Since Christ is the soul of Christian fellowship, it is impaired by lack of truth concerning Him. But truth and love are inseparable. Therefore when we seek for the true unity of the Church of Christ, we must begin by keeping our Lord's great command to love the brethren, and thereby advance with all saints to a true knowledge of Christ.

Looking back through the dim distance we discover the foreshadowings of prophet and psalmist growing clearer, till in these latest books of the NT we can almost touch the reality on earth in this ideal of the Apostle whom Jesus loved. The supreme poetic description of that fellowship is the city of the King of Love in Revelation, whose citizens see the face of the Lord (Rev 22¹⁻⁵), the beatific vision for which the psalmists strained their eyes.

The Christian fellowship as it existed on earth in the 1st century was a stupendous creation. Philosophers had dreamed of Utopias. Humane Stoics had taught the brotherhood of man. But all attempts to realize these ideals had been comparatively ineffective. In the Christian Church, however, aliens and the disfranchised found fellowship with those who inherited religious promises and social privilege. Roman and Greek stooped to love the hateful Jew, and the Jew was willing to transfer the sacred name of Israel to Gentiles whose past was unclean. Well-born and slave greeted one another as brethren, without thereby disturbing social order. A love so compelling as to reverse the national and social values, must have been derived from a Presence altogether transcending the measurements of ordinary human life. Christian fellowship is not to be defined as intercourse glowing with human love at its highest. It is primarily a spiritual communion with the Supreme Person, whose love recreates life and makes it a complete expression of love. So the goal must be, as the writer to the Hebrews says, in the world to come, when Jesus shall have introduced His many brethren into the Holy of Holies, where they will, as a company of the redeemed, hold fellowship with the Father (He 2⁵. ¹⁰. ¹¹ 7²⁵ 12²²⁻²⁴). See, further, art. COMMUNION.

LITERATURE.—Hort, *The Christian Ecclesia*; Weizsäcker, *The Apostolic Age*; Lindsay, *The Christian Ministry in the Early Church*; v. Dobschütz, *The Early Christian Churches*; art. 'Communion' in Hastings' *DB*; Herrmann, *Communion with God*, pp. 49–133; Dale, *Fellowship with Christ*, Serm. i., also *The Living Christ and the Four Gospels*, Lects. I.–IV.; Harnack, *Expansion of Christianity in the First Three Centuries*.

R. A. FALCONER.

FETTERS.—See CHAIN.

FEVER (ὁ πυρετός, and in Ac 28⁸ οἱ πυρετοί, with corresponding participle in Mt. and Mk. πυρέσσουσα). There are only five passages in the NT in which fever is spoken of, and three of these, viz. Mt 8¹⁴ᶠ·, Mk 1³⁰ᶠ·, and Lk 4³⁸ᶠ· are parallel passages. One cannot say with certainty what specific fever is alluded to in these passages, or in Jn 4⁵², where the healing of the nobleman's son is spoken of. It may be, indeed, that St. Luke, whose training as a physician naturally led him to speak with exactness about medical matters, does specify the fever from which Peter's wife's mother was suffering (συνεχομένη πυρετῷ μεγάλῳ). It has been contended that there was a specific fever known as 'the great fever,' and that it was this, whatever it may have been, from which the sick woman in Capernaum suffered. This, however, has been questioned, and perhaps it is rather the intensity of the fever than its specific character that is indicated by the word 'great.' Probably both Peter's wife's mother and the nobleman's son suffered from malarial fever. Professor G. A. Smith tells us that the region about Tiberias is a very feverish region, and Dr. Cunningham Geikie says that malarial fever was common at Capernaum. It is very likely that there has always been a good deal of malarial fever about the shores of the Sea of Galilee, and especially about the more northerly portion of these shores. The fever from which the father of Publius suffered (Ac 28[8]) was fever accompanying or accompanied by acute dysentery. See also artt. CURES, p. 403[b], and DISEASE, p. 463[b].

LITERATURE.—NT Commentaries; artt. 'Medicine' in Hastings' *DB* and 'Diseases,' *Encyc. Biblica*; G. A. Smith, *HGHL*[1], p. 449; Cunningham Geikie, *Life and Words of Christ*, ii. 5 f.

GEORGE C. WATT.

FIELD.—

The three Greek words (ἀγρός, χώρα, χωρίον) rendered 'field' in the Gospels are distinguishable in meaning, and sometimes require more specific renderings. ἀγρός in general means 'field' in the sense of cultivated land, or open country thought of as subject to cultivation: *e.g.* 'sowed good seed in his field' (Mt 13[24]), 'lilies of the *field*,' 'grass of the field' (6[28. 30]), etc. χώρα denotes generally a region, or district of country, as 'the region of Trachonitis' (Lk 3[1]), 'the country of the Gadarenes' (Mk 5[1]). χωρίον is more distinctly locative, as 'a *place* called Gethsemane' (Mt 26[36]), 'the *parcel of ground* that Jacob gave to Joseph' (Jn 4[5]), etc. But, on the other hand, we find ἀγρός used also of the country in distinction from the city (Mk 5[14] 6[56], Lk 8[34] 9[12] 23[26]), χώρα used of fields of ripened grain, as in Jn 4[35] 'Look on the fields, for they are white' (cf. Ja 5[4] 'who have reaped down your fields'); and where St. Matthew uses ἀγρός of 'the field of blood' (27[8]), St. Luke uses χωρίον (Ac 1[19]).

A knowledge of certain peculiarities of the fields of Palestine is helpful to the full understanding of several of the parables of our Lord and some other passages in the Gospels. There are now, as there were of old, numerous fields in Palestine where 'the lilies' and many other flowers grow in gorgeous profusion without human care or culture, and where 'the grass of the field,' including fibrous weeds as well as shortlived flowers, when dried by the tropical sun, are still gathered as fuel, and used to heat ovens for baking bread (cf. Mt 6[28. 30]). The argument of the Master, drawn from 'the grass of the field which to-day is and to-morrow is cast into the oven,' still holds good, and still finds abundant illustration. It is true occasionally now, also, that after the owner of the land has 'sowed good seed in his field,' an enemy will in sheer spite creep in secretly and 'sow tares,' the noxious darnel (*Lolium temulentum*); but see TARES.

In Palestine, as in all unsettled countries, it was common, and in parts of the land it is still common, to resort to the field (the cultivated land or the open country) as a fit place in which to hide treasure (cf. Mt 13[44]) In ancient times the land was peculiarly subject to revolutions, exposed to raids from wandering tribes, and, in some districts, liable to plunder from robbers at home. So, in the absence of safety vaults and the like, owners of treasure who feared robbery or thievery (Mt 25[25]), or who were setting off on a journey to a distant country, would bury their money, jewellery, etc., in the field. Then, if the owner were killed in battle, or died in a far country, no one might know where his treasures were hid; and, according to usage, such valuables when found, if no owner appeared to claim them, belonged to the owner of the land—a fact which gives point to the parable of the Hid Treasure (Mt 13[44], cf. Job 3[21], Pr 2[4]). Many persons are found digging for hid treasure in Egypt and Palestine to-day, and not a few

spend their last farthing in the effort (cf. Thomson, *LB* ii. p. 640).

In the parable of the Sower (Mt 13[4], Mk 4[4], Lk 8[5]), where the AV has 'some (seeds) fell by the wayside,' the picture is really of grains of wheat or barley which fell *on the trodden pathway* leading across the field, and so were left exposed where the birds could see and devour them (cf. Lk 8[5] 'trodden under foot'). It is still common in Palestine to see flocks of birds following the peasant as he sows his seed, eagerly picking up every grain that is not covered by the quick-following harrow. And where it is said 'some fell upon *stony* places' (AV), the real allusion is to the underlying *rock* of limestone. The traveller finds numberless places where a broad, flat, limestone rock lies just beneath the surface of the field, with only a thin layer of earth upon it (cf. Lk 8[6. 13] 'the rock'). 'Stony ground' (AV, following early English versions) suggests a soil abounding in loose stones, such as is often found there producing good wheat; but the picture is rather of a soil into which the seeds could not sink deep, and, the film of earth being readily heated because of the underlying rock, they would come up sooner than elsewhere, and at first would look uncommonly flourishing; but, not being able to send roots deep into the moist earth (cf. Lk 8[6]), when the hot, dry weather came the stalks would wither, and thus show that the fair promise of a crop there had been deceptive (cf. Ps 129[6] 'grass upon the house-tops').

In the fields of Palestine, too, there are still found spots that are rich, but are peculiarly infested with briars and thorn-bushes, where one may see the wheat in scattered and spindling stalks struggling for life (cf. Mt 13[7]). In Mk 2[23] and Lk 6[1] (AV) we have 'corn-fields' where the Gr. word (σπόριμα) is the same as in Mt 12[1], where it is rendered simply 'corn,'—'through the corn' (after Tindale). It is literally 'through the *sown* (places),' *i.e.* the grain-fields, as Noyes and Bib. Un. Vers. render it, fields of wheat or barley, not of maize or Indian corn, of course. The picture is of Jesus and His disciples *going along*, either through the standing grain, or by a footpath which bounded the fields, the grain in either case being within easy reach. It was customary then, as it is now, in Palestine, for the lands of different owners to be separated, not by fences or walls, but usually only by crude individual stones set up at intervals on the surface of the ground as landmarks (cf. Dt 19[14]); and the roads, mere footpaths as a rule, were not distinct from the fields, as they are with us, but ran through them, so that the grain grew right up to the edge of the path. We are not meant to think of Jesus and His disciples as going ruthlessly through the fields and trampling down the grain, but as following one of these paths over or between the fields. But neither plucking the ears of wheat to eat, nor even walking across a pathless field, was, according to Jewish ideas (cf. Dt 23[25]), a violation of the rights of property any more than it is to-day among the Arabs. It was not of this, but of Sabbath-breaking, that the Pharisees complained.

GEO. B. EAGER.

FIERCENESS.—

The word 'fierce' occurs twice in AV (Mt 8[28] of the two demoniacs [χαλεποί], Lk 23[5] of our Lord's accusers [ἐπίσχυον RV 'urgent']). But the purpose of the present article is to examine in what sense and to what extent this attribute may be attributed to Christ. The popular conception of Him is perhaps too much that of a speaker of smooth things. It is forgotten that He could utter on occasion words of fierce energy. The beauty of the unanswering innocence of the Passion, that type of silent suffering and enduring, has made His outbursts of fierce reproach or condemnation fade from the memory. His 'judge not' (Mt 7[1]), or His parable of patience that has its part in the 'wheat and tares' being allowed to grow together (13[30]), or His doctrine of unlimited forgiveness (Lk 17[1-4]),—these are thought to be entirely representative. Yet, while they undoubtedly indicate the prevailing elements, something would be lost in our understanding of Jesus if we overlooked the impassioned fierceness with which He sometimes acted and spoke.

Of recorded deeds the incident of the driving out of the vendors and money-changers from the temple precincts (Mt 21[12], Mk 11[15], Jn 2[15]) is the most notable: but it is in the vigour of His language that the possibilities of fierceness in Him are most revealed. He has small patience with certain failings, such as the lack of an apprehensive faith, or worldliness, or hypocrisy, or vanity. There is a denunciatory strain in Him much resembling the force of the Baptist's 'offspring of vipers' of Lk 3[7]. It is present in the Nazareth sermon in His OT illustrations of prophets not honoured in their own country (Lk 4); in His declaration of war with evil, — 'I am come to send fire on the earth' (12[49]), and 'I came not to send peace but a sword' (Mt 10[34]); it even finds expression in the very phrase γεννήματα ἐχιδνῶν used by the Baptist (Mt 12[34]). None of the mildness of diplomacy is in the message to Herod—'Go ye, and tell that fox' (Lk 13[32]). When He encounters men or communities incapable of the heavenly vision, His words are swords. To trouble about them is to 'throw pearls before swine' (Mt 7[6]). They are a 'faithless and perverse generation,' or 'a wicked and adulterous generation' seeking after a visible and tangible sign of spiritual things (16[4]); they shall lose the Kingdom of God (21[43]); the heathen of Nineveh shall show themselves better judges of eternal realities (Lk 11[32]); there is more hope for Tyre and Sidon (10[14]) or for Sodom and Gomorrah than for the spiritually blind (Mt 10[15]); 'Ye are of your father the devil' (Jn 8[44]). The fierceness which marks His rejection of the third temptation (Mt 4[10]) is paralleled in the 'Get thee behind me, Satan' with which Peter's proffered intervention is repelled (Mk 8[33]). The perverter of the simplicity of childhood is told that he had better have been drowned with a millstone about his neck (Mt 18[6]). But the white heat of fierceness in the utterance of Christ comes when He meets with Pharisees, scribes, and teachers of the Law, who are unworthy of their high professions. They are 'false prophets . . . ravening wolves' (Mt 7[15]); 'hypocrites' is hurled at them in every phrase of Mt 23, in the close of Lk 11, and in Mk 7[6], where Isaiah's bitterest words against lip - service are quoted against them. They are 'whited sepulchres,' 'blind guides,' 'sons of them that slew the prophets,' 'serpents.' They 'say, and do not,' so that 'the publicans and the harlots go into the kingdom' before them (Mt 21[31]).

Thus to His Divine tenderness did Jesus add a strange fierceness, as though to teach that in faith's war with darkness lightning has its place. See art. ANGER.

LITERATURE.—Seeley, *Ecce Homo*, ch. xxi.; Butler, *Serm.* viii.; Dale, *Atonement*[7], p. 338 ff. E. DAPLYN.

FIG-TREE (in NT συκῆ, in OT תְּאֵנָה *tĕʾēnāh*; the *Ficus Carica*, L.).—**1.** The fig is the principal shade- and fruit-tree of Palestine, growing in all parts, in many places spontaneously. It seldom surpasses 20 ft. [Post, in Hastings' *DB*, *s.v.* 'Figs,' says 15 ft.] in height, but has a spread of from 25 to 30 ft. Its welcome shade and refreshing fruit make it the emblem of peace and prosperity (Dt 8[8], Jg 9[10. 11], 1 K 4[25], Mic 4[4], Zec 3[10], 1 Mac 14[12]). Besides this general symbolism, two characteristics of the tree,

appealing respectively to the eye and to the palate, have led to further comparisons.

(*a*) The fig-tree is conspicuous in early spring by the expanding of the tips of its twigs into little green knobs called פַּגִּים *paggîm* (Gr. ὄλυνθοι, Ca 2[13] RV 'green figs') which are the flower-fruit buds, and together with the leaf-bud, which expands shortly after and soon overshadows the *pag*, or fruit rudiment, serve as the herald of the coming summer (Mt 24[32] and ‖). This phenomenon of 'all the trees' (Lk 21[29]) is particularly noticeable in the fig-tree because of its early and conspicuous verdure. The ripening of the *pag* follows the 'appearance of the flowers on the fig-tree,' and accompanies the 'blossoming of the vine' as the feature of the advancing season and the time of mating (Ca 2[13]). In the same connexion may be mentioned the phenomenon of the dropping of great quantities of the immature fruit in consequence of imperfect fertilization, so that the scattered *paggim* covering the ground under the fig-trees become to the author of Rev 6[13] a symbol of the stars fallen to earth from the firmament, 'as a fig-tree casteth her unripe figs when she is shaken of a great wind.'

(*b*) The fig-tree has *two* (not three) successive crops of fruit each year. The *first-ripe* fig (Heb. בִּכּוּרָה *bikkûrāh*, Is 28[4], Jer 24[2], Hos 9[10], Mic 7[1]) is produced upon the old wood of the preceding year, the buds which remained undeveloped through the winter swelling into the little green *paggim* already described, towards the end of the season of spring rains (March–April), and coming to maturity in June. The תְּאֵנָה *tĕʾēnāh*, or autumn fig, is the fig of commerce, and is produced on the new wood of the same year. The leaf-bud, which expanded shortly after the *pag* and soon distanced it in growth, puts out in its turn a flower-fruit bud which matures in August, or later, according to the variety, the fruit hanging on the boughs until winter, when the branches are again left naked, grey, and straggling.

This phenomenon of successive fruitage in the fig-tree is doubtless the source of the description of the fruit-trees of the New Jerusalem (Ezk 47[12], Rev 22[2] 'the tree of life') as 'bearing fruit every month.' In the Talmud it is a symbol for the acquisition of learning, which, to be permanent, must come by little and little (Hamburger, *RE* i. 3, *s.v.* 'Feige,' p. 360 with references). Hence the saying, 'Whoso sees a fig-tree in his dreams, his learning shall be safe from forgetfulness' (*Berakhoth*, 57). The capacity of the tree for prolongation of its bearing season leads in fact to certain representations which easily pass over into exaggerations and misunderstandings important to avoid.

Edersheim (*Life and Times*, bk. iv. ch. xvi. p. 246) refers to 'a species (the *Benoth Shuach*) mentioned in *Shebh.* v. 1, of which the fruit required three years for ripening,' but which may more reasonably be understood as simply a late-bearing variety whose fruit reached maturity only in exceptionally favourable seasons, not oftener than once in three years. So with the rhetorical passage of Josephus (*BJ* III. x. 8) celebrating the delightful climate of the plain of Gennesaret. His statement that 'it supplies the principal fruits, as grapes and figs, uninterruptedly during ten months of the year,' cannot reasonably be made to prove more than the fact that in that semi-tropical depression, 600 ft. below sea-level, fresh fruit, *including* figs, could be obtained almost to the end of winter.

To explain the narrative of Mk 11[13] two other facts have been advanced of doubtful value and trust-worthiness. It is asserted that neglected relics of the autumn crop sometimes cling to the branches of the fig-tree throughout the winter; but Post (*l.c.* p. 6) was unable during a residence of 33 years in Syria to find, or hear of, such. The statement of Edersheim (*l.c.* v. ii. p. 374) that such left-over fruit about April 1 'would of course be edible' becomes admissible only by inserting a 'not' after 'of course.' It is also asserted that the *pag*, or green fruit, was eaten, even Benzinger (*PRE³ s.v.* 'Fruchtbäume,' p. 304) declaring that 'Jesus might expect to find such winter figs (the *paggîm*) on a tree already in leaf at the season of Passover, that is before the time of the ripening of figs.' In the sense that the rudimentary fruit-buds would be discoverable under the leaves, upon examination (unless the tree had become sterile by reversion to the wild type, as sometimes occurs), this statement is true; the present writer has found such dry tasteless 'figs' at *'Ain Far'a* near Jerusalem, on March 1, the size of an olive, though the tree was leafless. Boys sometimes nibble these buds, but to speak of the *paggîm* at this season as 'winter figs' is misleading. The evidence for the edible quality of the *pag*, drawn by Edersheim from the Talmud (Bk. v. ii. p. 375, referring to *Shebh.* iv. 7 and Jerus. *Shebh.* 35*b*, last lines) suggests only that *at a later season* the unripe fruit was sometimes used as a condiment 'with bread.' This, however, was after the *paggîm* 'began to assume a red colour,' and not when the foliage had only just begun to cover the setting fruit-bud. Apart from the question whether a tree could be properly rebuked for the absence of a quite exceptional product, the alleged phenomena, whether of neglected relics of the autumn harvest, or use of the unripe fruit, have neither of them any real bearing on the difficulty that Jesus should approach a wayside fig-tree, *with the intention of staying His hunger*, when, as so frankly stated in the record itself, 'it was not the season of figs.'

2. The Gospel references to the fig-tree include both parables and incidents, and make allusion to phenomena both of its leafage and its fruitage. As questions arise as to how great an extent the incidents may not be symbolic, parables becoming concrete in process of repetition, or even pure symbols, it is best to consider first the two instances in which the fig-tree is made the subject of undoubted parable by our Lord.

(*a*) *The parable of the Fig-Tree* (Mk 13²⁸·²⁹ = Mt 24³²·³³, paraphrased and interpreted Lk 21²⁹⁻³¹) is based on the early verdure of the tree. Its general sense is clear from Lk 12⁵⁴ff· (= Mt 16²·³ β text), a passage which leads to the insertion in Lk 21²⁹ of βλέποντες ἀφ' ἑαυτῶν (cf. 12⁵⁷). The meaning is: As you judge by the softening, burgeoning twigs of the fig-tree that the harvest season is approaching, so read the signs of the times. These (ταῦτα; Mk 13²⁹) treats the preceding context as if only *premonitions* of the Day had been spoken of, overlooking vv.²⁴⁻²⁷; but cf. Lk 12⁵¹⁻⁵³·⁵⁶ with Mk 13¹²·¹³·²⁹; πάντα ταῦτα, Mt 24³³ is more specific but less correct) signs prove that the judgment, the gleaning of God (cf. Mk 4²⁹, not 'the kingdom of God,' Lk 21³¹) is close at hand. As regards closer exegesis and criticism, we must say, with E. Schwartz ('Der verfluchte Feigenbaum' in *ZNTW* i. p. 81): 'Whoever would interpret with exactitude will meet with more than one difficulty.' Besides Schwartz, the reader may consult Gould, Swete, and Wellhausen, *ad loc.* The paraphrase of Lk. is the earliest attempt to interpret, but smooths over difficulties (note, *e.g.*, the additions 'and all the trees,' 'the kingdom of God,' and other changes).

(*b*) *The parable of the Barren Fig-Tree* (Lk 13⁶⁻⁹) stands in the same eschatological context as the warning to read the signs of the times (Lk 12³⁵⁻¹³⁹ paralleled by Mk 13³³⁻³⁶·¹²·¹³), and forms its climax. One is tempted to conjecture that the problematic 'parable' referred to in Mk 13²⁸, Mt

24³² (ἀπὸ δὲ τῆς συκῆς μάθετε τὴν παραβολήν, cf. Mk 7¹⁷ as against Lk 21²⁹ καὶ εἶπεν παραβολήν) was once no other than this. At all events it simply applies, in fuller form, the figure credited in Mt 3¹⁰ = Lk 3⁹ to the Baptist.

This is the common prophetic doctrine of the Divine ἀνοχή, the present a time of suspension of the Divine sentence to leave opportunity for repentance.

The once favourite allegorizing method of interpretation (*e.g.* the gardener = the Messiah, the three years = the three (?) Passovers of Christ's public ministry) is now fortunately discredited. Yet it is incorrect, with Wellhausen (*Ev. Lucæ, ad loc.*) to say that the fig-tree stands for the individual. Not merely is the girdled fig-tree an OT emblem of the punishment of Israel (Jl 1⁷, cf. Lk 23³¹), but the parable concludes a context wherein the men of Jerusalem, overwhelmed by the fall of the tower in Siloam, and the Galilæans, cut down by the sword of Pilate, are brought forward as 'signs of the times.' The warning, accordingly, is certainly against 'the overthrow of the Jewish people' (T. K. Cheyne, *Encyc. Bibl. s.v.* 'Fig-tree,' col. 1521). 'Except ye repent ye shall all likewise perish' is not spoken of the fate of individuals, but of the common overthrow, however this may be avoided by individual repentance; cf. Mt 12³⁸⁻⁴⁵ = Lk 11²⁹⁻³².

3. *The cursing of the fig-tree* (Mk 11¹²⁻¹⁴·²⁰⁻²⁵ = Mt 21¹⁸⁻²²).—Parabolic symbolism is so slightly concealed under the narrative features of this story that the majority of critics are disposed to regard it as a mere endowment of the Lukan parable of the Barren Fig-tree with concrete form, just as the parable of the Good Samaritan, and others, were long treated as instances of historical fact.

In favour of this explanation are several features of the narrative and its setting.

(*a*) The generally admitted incorporation of Mk. by Lk. implies that the omission of Mk 11¹²⁻¹⁴·²⁰⁻²⁵ was deliberate. The most natural explanation of it is that St. Luke regarded the story as a double of his parable, Lk 13⁶⁻⁹. Conversely the parable does not appear in Mt. or Mark.

(*b*) The withering of the tree (Mk 11²⁰⁻²⁵), a sequel of the next day after the cursing (11¹²⁻¹⁴), occupies a different position in Mt 21¹⁹ᵇ⁻²², taking place 'on the spot.' In both Gospels this appended sequel proves itself a secondary attachment, both by its material and its language. The contents of Mk 11²⁰⁻²⁵ consist in the main of two *logia*, torn from their proper context (cf. Mt 17²⁰, Lk 17⁶, and Mt 6¹⁴·¹⁵) and characterized by non-Markan expressions (cf. 'your Father in heaven,' Mk 11²⁵). Such loose agglomerations of stray *logia* are frequent in our Second Gospel (Mk 3²²⁻³⁰ 4¹¹·¹²·²¹·²⁵ 8¹⁵·³⁴⁻³⁶ 9⁴²⁻⁵⁰ 10¹⁰⁻¹² etc.). In Mt 21¹⁹ᵇ⁻²² the language is alien (παραχρῆμα, 'on the spot,' vv.¹⁹ᵇ·²⁰, occurs 17 times in Lk. and Acts, whereas Mt. and Mk. have invariably elsewhere εὐθύς or εὐθέως), and the *logia* taken from Mk. produce duplication of Mt 17²⁰ and almost of 6¹⁴·¹⁵. By transposing the sequel into immediate juxtaposition with the cursing, and abridging Mk 11²⁰⁻²⁵, Mt. avoids one of the two interruptions of the principal narrative of the purging of the temple and its consequences (Mk 11¹⁻¹⁰·¹⁵⁻¹⁸·²⁷ff.), and heightens the marvel, but fails to remove the evidence of his own dependence afforded by the duplication of 17²⁰, and only brings into stronger relief the supplementary and supererogatory character of the sequel.

This superfluousness of Mk 11²⁰⁻²⁵ is most apparent in the light of such attempted explanations as that of B. Weiss, who says: The cursing of the fig-tree was 'of course' meant by Jesus symbolically, the concrete fulfilment given it by God being without intention on Jesus' part. On this statement Wellhausen (*ad loc.*) comments sarcastically: 'Weiss understands him. God misunderstood him.' Nevertheless Weiss is clearly right in maintaining that the purpose of Jesus would be just as completely met if the story stopped with 11¹⁴ᵃ.

But even more fatal than the superfluousness of the sequel is its perversion of the real symbolism of the incident. Nothing is said of that which analogy (Mt 3¹⁰ 7¹⁶⁻¹⁹, Lk 13⁶⁻⁹) proves to be the real moral lesson; but the appended sayings are adapted to find in it more evidence of the wonder-working power of belief. The disciples are to learn that the prayer, or even the fiat, of faith—here taken as equivalent to undoubting assurance—can set at defiance the order of nature. This, the writer understands, was the purpose of the cursing. As part of the rebuke of the disciples' half-heartedness (διψυχία) in the case of the epileptic boy (Mt 17[19. 20]; cf. Lk 17[5. 6], 1 Co 13[2]), the hyperbolic saying on mountain-moving faith is justified. Adapted along with Mt 6[14. 15] to give the moral lesson of the withering of the fig-tree, both fall to a lower plane, scarcely above that of mere thaumaturgy. The symbolism of the cursing is lost in the mere wonder of withering a tree, a needless miracle of display.

(c) Even after recognition of the unhistorical character of the addition Mk 11[20-25], the incident of the cursing is still encumbered with inherent improbabilities, of which the most formidable is the imputation of hunger as the motive of Jesus' approach to the tree. It is not enough to admit that the curse must be explained, if at all, by the discovery, made upon close inspection, that the tree was empty, not only of those supposititious edible products which could not be reasonably expected, but of even the rudiments of a crop in the season, and to suggest that when Jesus arrived 'immediately the disappointment of unsatisfied hunger was lost in the moral lesson which flashed across His mind' (Post, l.c.). Change of motive is inconceivable, because hunger cannot have caused the approach. Relics of the last season's crop, if sought at all, would be sought on a tree whose still leafless branches left them in plain sight, not where they would be concealed by the foliage, if not thrust off by the new growth. So, too, of paggîm; but the degree of starvation necessary to suggest appeasing the stomach by paggîm at the season in question is improbable.

There remains as a historical basis for the story only the possibility that Jesus' footsteps might be attracted by the suggestion of a possible moral lesson in the precocious leafage of a wayside tree, the discovery that it covered no promise of fruit leading Him thereupon to an utterance in the vein of prophetic symbolism. Gould (Internat. Crit. Com. 'Mark,' 212) finds evidence in Hos 1[1-3], Jn 4[6-11], Mt 13[10-15] that 'such acted parables were not without precedent among the Jews.' More apposite might be the reference of Διδ. xi. 10 to prophets in the early Church who might 'do something as an outward mystery typical of the Church (Eph 5[32]) because in like manner did the prophets of old time'; cf. Ac 21[11]. But the only real parallel in the story of Jesus is the parable (unaccompanied by any narrative of fact) of the Stater in the Fish's Mouth, Mt 17[24-27]. The propensity of the reader, if not of the Evangelist himself, to take this symbolic direction to Peter as implying the real execution of a miracle, shows how easily a symbolic sentence of death, directed against the fig-tree as the representative of unrepentant Israel, might be taken to imply its literal withering away.

Due consideration for all three objections leaves the question still open whether the story of Mk 11[12-14a] records a specific utterance of this symbolic kind directed against a particular tree, on a particular occasion; or whether tradition and the Evangelist together have not simply localized between Bethphage ('Fig-town') and Jerusalem, on occasion of the supreme visitation of the latter, a visualized version of the parable Lk 13[6-9].

In favour of the former view may be cited critics no less radical than H. J. Holtzmann (Hdkom. ad loc.) and J. Weiss (Das Aelteste Evangelium, p. 268). Still more pronounced is Schwartz in favour of connecting the fig-tree of Mk 11[12-14], and even that of Mk 13[28] as well, with some sun-bleached skeleton from the orchards of Bethphage, a lone relic of the siege of Titus, pointed to by Jerusalem Christians as the memorial of Jesus' warning and promise; but Schwartz would not admit a

basis of fact for this early identification by tradition of 'the' fig-tree, but rather such as Cheyne instances in 'the inn' of the Good Samaritan.

The phenomena of the text indicate, however, that the process must at least precede our text of Mark. For our Evangelist the symbolic sense has already disappeared, leaving only the work of power. Before this stage of the process could be reached the parable of the Barren Fig-tree must already have been transformed by local tradition into symbolic cursing of some given tree, and the moral lesson have been subsequently eclipsed by the purely thaumaturgic interest.

More conservative criticism, while recognizing the secondary character of Mk 11[20-25], and perhaps admitting the fundamental identity of the symbolic cursing with the parable whose lesson is so obviously the same, may still demand more evidence before it surrenders the possibility that our Second Evangelist retains a substantially trustworthy tradition of the actual site and occasion of the utterance.

4. The fig-tree of Nathanael (Jn 1[48]). Symbolism admittedly enters to so large a degree into the narrative of the Fourth Gospel (cf. e.g. Jn 9[7] 12[33]), that it is not surprising if the more radical school of interpreters, looking upon it as the uniform product of an allegorizing fancy, should find in the unexplained reference of Jn 1[48] the suggestion of an allegorical sense, the fig-tree having the symbolic meaning of religious instruction applied in the Talmud, or even playing the part of the sacred Bo-tree (Ficus religiosa) in Buddhist legend. The fact that commentators from Schoettgen and Lightfoot (Hor. Heb. ad loc.) downwards have inferred that Nathanael was 'aut orans, aut legens, aut meditans, aut aliquid religiosum praestans' is proof that this mental association is natural; but it cannot be truly said that the Evangelist allegorizes. The words 'when thou wast under the fig-tree' are obscure, not because we fail to apply the key, but because the Evangelist has left something lacking. He utters an enigma, but gives no other clue than the recognition by Nathanael of Jesus' supernatural knowledge. He wishes the reader to guess that Jesus had here proved Himself the καρδιογνώστης λόγος (cf. Wis 1[6-8]), as in the case of the Samaritan Woman later (4[17-19. 29]); but he either does not trouble himself, or was unable, to relate the facts.

Cheyne indeed (Encyc. Bibl. s.v. 'Nathanael') considers the usual explanation 'hardly adequate. If it simply means, "when thou hadst retired under the shade of the fig-tree for meditation or prayer," we ask why the Evangelist did not express the Master's meaning more distinctly (contrast Jn 4[18]).' His answer is a conjectural emendation of the Hebrew (!) in a supposititious source of the Gospel, וְאַתָּה מְתַחֲנֵן 'when thou wast making supplication,' for וְאַתָּה תַּחַת הַתְּאֵנָה 'when thou wast under the fig-tree.' But conjecture of this sort discredits itself. To every reader it is manifest that an element of the narrative is intentionally or unintentionally suppressed. If it be granted that 'the Fourth Gospel is a composite work,' it is not unreasonable to suppose its compiler to have left untranscribed that portion of his source which would have explained the allusion to the fig-tree, just as he has omitted in his story of the feeding of the multitude (61ff.) Jesus' motive for the miracle [logical lacunæ of this character form indeed a distinctive feature of this Gospel].

If the traditional view be maintained, the Evangelist's reserve will be accounted for as reflecting the enigmatic nature of the actual dialogue, which, so far as bystanders were able to perceive, had no further explanation.

LITERATURE.—Besides the works referred to in the art. the following may be consulted: Thomson, LB, pt. ii. ch. xxiv.; Tristram, Nat. Hist. of the Bible, p. 352; Trench, Parables 12, p. 346 ff.; Bruce, Parabol. Teaching, p. 427 ff.; Trench, Miracles 10, p. 466 ff.; W. M. Taylor, Mir. of Our Saviour, p. 413 ff.; Liddon, Sermons on Some Words of Christ, p. 100; Godet and Westcott, Comm. in loc.; cf. Augustine, Conf. VIII. xii. 28.

B. W. Bacon.

FIRE ($\pi\hat{v}\rho$ except in Mk $14^{54}=$ Lk 22^{56} where $\phi\hat{\omega}\varsigma$ occurs) is referred to in the Gospels much more frequently in a figurative than in a literal sense.

1. The allusions to *literal* fire are the following. (*a*) Those concerned with the domestic use of fire for heating and cooking. In the better houses in Palestine the rooms were warmed by charcoal fires in portable braziers; in poorer houses the wood or other fuel was burned in a hollow in the earthen floor. The fire into which the epileptic boy fell (Mt $17^{15}=$ Mk 9^{22}) would be of the latter description. The fire of coals kindled for warmth in the middle of the court of the high priest's house (Mk $14^{54}=$ Lk $22^{55.\ 56}$, Jn 18^{18}),* and that employed for cooking on the shore of the Lake of Galilee (Jn 21^9), would be charcoal fires on the ground. (*b*) Fire from heaven (lightning, or something of the same kind, natural or miraculous) was a frequent form of Divine judgment in OT. One instance of this (the destruction of Sodom) is recalled in Lk 17^{29}, and another (in the life of Elijah) prompted the feeling and suggested the question of James and John in Lk 9^{54}.

2. The *figurative* references to fire are of various kinds. Since wood which was worthless for any other purpose was used as fuel, fire became an emblem of the judgment awaiting spiritual unfruitfulness (Mt $3^{10}=$ Lk 3^9, Mt 7^{19}, Jn 15^6). A similar idea was suggested by the burning of other worthless things, such as chaff (Mt $3^{12}=$ Lk 3^{17}) and tares (Mt $13^{30.\ 40.\ 42}$). The '**furnace of fire**,' which is part of the natural imagery of the parable of the Tares, becomes, in the parable of the Drag-net, a standing expression for the destiny of the wicked (Mt 13^{50}). Similarly we have 'eternal' (RV) or 'everlasting' (AV) fire (Mt $18^8\ 25^{41}$), 'unquenchable' fire (Mt $3^{12}=$ Lk 3^{17}, Mk $9^{43.\ 48}$), and (RVm) 'the Gehenna of fire' (RV 'the hell of fire,' AV 'hell fire') in Mt 5^{22}, Mt 18^9 ($=$ Mk $9^{43.\ 45.\ 47}$). The last of these expressions is found in the same context as the other two, and gives the key to their meaning. From the OT associations of the valley of Hinnom the name *Gehenna* had in Christ's time been appropriated in Jewish thought for the place of the final punishment of the wicked—a place of burning and corruption, in which body as well as spirit would be tortured. In the passages above mentioned our Lord must be understood to use the popular religious language of His time, though it may have been in a less literal and more parabolic sense than usual. To the group of sayings in Mk 9^{43-48} is attached another (Mk 9^{49}), in which fire is the emblem of the self-discipline in this world, by which the destruction of Gehenna in the next world is to be avoided. The destructiveness of fire made the phrase 'I will send fire' a common form of prophetic Divine threatening in OT, and this phrase is taken up by Christ (Lk 12^{49}) as expressing, in one aspect, the result of His earthly mission. Fire is used by John the Baptist as an emblem of the purity and intensity of the influence accompanying the baptism of the Holy Spirit which he foretold that Christ should bestow (Mt $3^{11}=$ Lk 3^{16}).

The eyes of the glorified Christ, as seen in the vision of the Apocalypse, are compared to a flame of fire (Rev $1^{14}\ 2^{18}\ 19^{12}$).

Origen (*Hom. in Jer.* xx. 3) has preserved the following *agraphon* of Jesus: 'He who is near me is near the fire; he who is far from me is far from the kingdom.'

JAMES PATRICK.

* In Mk $14^{54}=$ Lk 22^{56} $\phi\hat{\omega}\varsigma$ is used instead of $\pi\hat{v}\rho$ (cf. Lk 22^{55}). In classical Gr. a similar use of the word is found in cases where a fire is thought of as the source of light as well as heat (so also 1 Mac 12^{29}, cf. v.^{28} where $\pi\hat{v}\rho$ is employed). Its appropriateness in both the Synoptic passages is due to the fact that it was night, and, in the Lk. passage, to the further fact that it was the blaze of the fire which revealed Peter to the maid. In both cases RV brings out the meaning by rendering $\pi\rho\delta\varsigma$ $\tau\delta$ $\phi\hat{\omega}\varsigma$ 'in the light of the fire.'

FIRKIN ($\mu\epsilon\tau\rho\eta\tau\eta\varsigma$, Jn 2^6 only).—An Attic liquid measure, which is generally regarded as the equivalent of the Hebrew *bath* (cf. LXX 2 Ch 4^5), and is therefore 'able to contain seventy-two sextaries' (Jos. *Ant.* VIII. ii. 9), accurately 71·28 pints, or approximately 9 English gallons. 'Firkin' (AV and RV)—the *fourth* part of a barrel containing from 32 to 36 gallons—as a translation is sufficiently exact for ordinary purposes.

Previously emptied for the ablutions of the guests, the water-pots are filled afresh. Their character and contents prove the reality of the miracle. Very effective is the touch added by the expression $\tilde{\epsilon}\omega\varsigma$ $\check{\alpha}\nu\omega$, 'up to the brim,' if only in presenting a sure basis for calculating the quantity of this wedding gift. The lowest estimate of the quantity of wine must be over 12 firkins or 108 gallons; yet, had the vessels been larger they had been filled; had there been more vessels, more wine. To such lavishness there need not be imputed indiscretion. Our Lord did not give simply to meet a pressing need, or even for future use, but rather to exemplify the illimitable power of the Giver. 'It is His first miraculous sign . . . it must become the type of the fulness of grace and joy and strength which the only-begotten Son brings to the earth' (Godet on Jn 2^6).

LITERATURE.—Art. 'Weights and Measures' in Hastings' *DB*, iv. 911–913; *Encyc. Bibl.* iv. col. 5294 f.

ALEX. A. DUNCAN.

FIRST AND LAST ($\dot{o}$ $\pi\rho\hat{\omega}\tau o\varsigma$ $\kappa\alpha\grave{\iota}$ $\dot{o}$ $\check{\epsilon}\sigma\chi\alpha\tau o\varsigma$).—This title occurs three times in Rev. ($1^{17}\ 2^8\ 22^{13}$). In the first two passages it is clearly Christ who claims the title for Himself, as appears from the references to the Resurrection in the immediate contexts. In all probability the same is the case in the third passage (22^{13}), else there is an abrupt change of the speaker three verses later (v.^{16} 'I, Jesus, have sent mine angel,' etc.). However, Alford and some others hold that God the Father is the speaker in 22^{13}.

'The First and the Last' is claimed by Jehovah as a description of Himself, with slight variations in the form, in Is $41^4\ 44^6\ 48^{12}$ (cf. also 43^{10}). The Greek form of the title in Rev. is not identical with that given by the LXX in any of these passages, in all of which the LXX has differences representing differences in the Hebrew (41^4 $\dot{\epsilon}\gamma\grave{\omega}$ $\theta\epsilon\grave{o}\varsigma$ $\pi\rho\hat{\omega}\tau o\varsigma$, $\kappa\alpha\grave{\iota}$ $\epsilon\grave{\iota}\varsigma$ $\tau\grave{\alpha}$ $\dot{\epsilon}\pi\epsilon\rho\chi\acute{o}\mu\epsilon\nu\alpha$ $\dot{\epsilon}\gamma\grave{\omega}$ $\epsilon\grave{\iota}\mu\iota$; 44^6 $\dot{\epsilon}\gamma\grave{\omega}$ $\pi\rho\hat{\omega}\tau o\varsigma$ $\kappa\alpha\grave{\iota}$ $\dot{\epsilon}\gamma\grave{\omega}$ $\mu\epsilon\tau\grave{\alpha}$ $\tau\alpha\hat{v}\tau\alpha$; 48^{12} $\dot{\epsilon}\gamma\grave{\omega}$ $\epsilon\grave{\iota}\mu\iota$ $\pi\rho\hat{\omega}\tau o\varsigma$, $\kappa\alpha\grave{\iota}$ $\dot{\epsilon}\gamma\grave{\omega}$ $\epsilon\grave{\iota}\mu\iota$ $\epsilon\grave{\iota}\varsigma$ $\tau\grave{o}\nu$ $\alpha\grave{\iota}\hat{\omega}\nu\alpha$). It is plain, however, that a supreme description of Jehovah in the OT is applied in Rev. to Christ, and the significance of the transference as regards the Christology of the book is unmistakable. Besides this, in 22^{13}, where, as has been said, it is natural to regard Christ as the speaker, the title 'the First and the Last' stands between two others, 'the Alpha and the Omega,' 'the Beginning and the End,' the first of which is found also in 1^8 and 21^6, and the second in 21^6, in which passages the speaker may be either Christ or, as is maintained by some (Hastings' *DB*, vol. iv. p. 263^a), God the Father, or 'God in the Undivided Unity of His Being.' It may be, therefore, that in Rev. itself we have the same supreme titles given to God the Father and to Christ. But whether this be so or not, once it is admitted that 22^{13} is spoken by Christ, the accumulation in that verse of descriptions which could only belong to the infinite being of God emphatically marks the belief of the author of Rev. as to the nature of Christ (see Hastings' *DB*, vol. ii. pp. 690^b, 691^b, vol. iv. p. 263^a).

Of the 'Thirteen Principles of the Faith,' formulated by Moses Maimonides (12th cent. A.D.), the fourth is: 'I believe with perfect faith that the Creator, blessed be His name, is the first and the last' (*Authorized Daily Prayer-Book of the United Hebrew Congregations of the British Empire*², p. 89). Schoettgen says that the title was also given by the ancient Jews to the Messiah (*Hor. Heb.* tom. ii. lib. i. ['Nominum Messiæ, quæ divinam illius naturam indigitant '] : רֵאשׁוֹן Primus. Ipse Deus. Jesa. xliv. 6. *Ego*, inquit, *primus, et ego novissimus* ; quibus verbis æternitatem designatam voluit. Judæi vero antiqui etiam Messiam sic vocant ').

The nature of God necessarily transcends definition, but ' the First and the Last ' and the parallel titles are endeavours to suggest such conceptions of God as men can comprehend. It would not be enough to say that ' the First and the Last ' is the equivalent of ' the Eternal.' The title recalls the old covenant name of God, Jehovah (Jahweh), and its interpretation in Ex 3[14]. It seems plainly to be an expansion of that name, of which ' the Eternal ' is not a satisfactory rendering. Ex 3[14] ('I am what I am,' or, more accurately, ' I will be what I will be ') does not give to יהוה an abstract meaning. היה is γίγνομαι, not εἰμί. It does not mean *to be* essentially, but phenomenally. The idea of יהוה is not of abstract existence, but of active being ; manifestation in history. Jehovah is not a God who barely exists, but One who asserts His being, and enters into an historical relation with humanity. Not being determined by anything external to (before or after) Himself, He is consistent with Himself, true to His promises, and unchangeable in His purposes. He will not fail or disappoint His servants. He will approve Himself. What He will be is left undefined, or defined only in terms of Himself, for the very reason that His providential dealings with His people in their ever-varying needs are inexhaustible—are more than can be numbered or expressed (see Driver on ' The Tetragrammaton,' *Studia Biblica*, Oxf. 1885 ; and A. B. Davidson in Hastings' *DB*, vol. ii. pp. 199[b], 845[a]).

This interpretation of the Divine name is amplified in the prophets. Delitzsch on Is 41[4] says : 'It is the meaning of the Divine name Jehovah which is thus unfolded ('I the Lord, the first, and with the last, I am he'), for Jehovah is God as the absolute, eternally existing, and absolutely free Ego'; and, on 43[10] ('I am he : before me there was no God formed, neither shall there be after me') : 'He is the sole realization of the idea of God inherent in human consciousness, and He is this eternally. His being has no beginning and no end, so that no other being with Divine claims and character could precede or follow Him' (cf. also 45[5. 21. 22] 46[9. 10] 48[12]). These chapters again and again insist on the 'fundamental truth that God is eternally the same (as He is the only) Self-existent Personal Being. To Him the whole range of creaturely existence in all its cycles must be visible,—and to Him only can it be so' (*Speaker's Com.*). The prophets emphasize the expression of the moral unchangeableness of God in the name Jehovah (see esp. Is 26[4. 8] 41[4], Hos 12[5. 6], Mal 3[6]).

It may be said, then, that the title ' the First and the Last,' as applied to Christ in Rev., recalls, and attaches to Him, all that the OT writers had realized of the nature of God. How much more it contains for a writer who uses it in the light of the Incarnation may be gathered from Col 1[15-20], a passage related as resting upon the same Christological basis of faith, and which is indeed the ὁ πρῶτος καὶ ὁ ἔσχατος of Rev. written out at full length. Both authors alike claim for Christ absolute supremacy in relation to the Universe, the natural Creation, and in relation to the Church, the new Moral Creation, ἵνα γένηται ἐν πᾶσιν αὐτὸς πρωτεύων. For both Christ is πρωτότοκος πάσης κτίσεως,—prior to all creation and sovereign over all creation. He is the source of life to the Universe, the centre of all its developments, the mainspring of all its motions—ἐν αὐτῷ ἐκτίσθη τὰ πάντα (cf. Jn 1[4] ὃ γέγονεν ἐν αὐτῷ ζωὴ ἦν). And as all things had their origin in Him (the First), so all things return to Him as their goal and consummation (the Last) —τὰ πάντα δι᾽ αὐτοῦ καὶ εἰς αὐτὸν ἔκτισται (cf. Ro 11[36], He 2[10], where the reference is to God). All things have their sphere within the sphere of the life of Him who is ' the First and the Last.' In Him they originate and in Him they cohere—αὐτός ἐστι πρὸ πάντων, καὶ τὰ πάντα ἐν αὐτῷ συνέστηκεν (cf. Ac 17[28], in reference to God). He is the δεσμός of the Universe. And such also is His position in relation to

the Church, the new spiritual creation—He is absolutely prior and sovereign, because there too He is the source of life. His Resurrection is the ground of His headship of the Church (Rev 1[17]. See Lightfoot and Meyer on Col 1[15-20] ; cf. Eph 1[10], Ph 2[9. 10. 11]).

It is interesting to trace the same underlying thought about the nature of God in Rev. and in the Fourth Gospel. A connexion has been pointed out between ἐγώ εἰμι ὁ πρῶτος καὶ ὁ ἔσχατος of Rev. and the similar phrases of Is 41[4] 48[12] and the explanation of the Divine name Jehovah in Ex 3[14]. There seems to be a correspondence between the ἐγώ εἰμι of the LXX in these and other passages (Is 43[10. 13], Dt 32[39]) and the ἐγώ εἰμι of Jn 8[24. 28. 58] (cf. also 13[19]). In all these passages the words have a pregnant meaning. In Jn 8, Christ presents Himself to the Jews not simply as the Messiah, but as One who has ' life in Himself ' as being the spring of life. He *is* infinitely, as God is. He shares the being of God. Therefore He claims supreme control not only of the seen and the finite, but of the unseen and the infinite (see Westcott, *ad loc.*).

Cheyne (on Is 41[4]) thinks that the ἐγώ εἰμι of Jn 18[5] is intended in the same sense, and finds this view confirmed by the supernatural effect of the sounds described in v.[6].

All existence is necessarily relative to Him who is ' the First and the Last.' Nothing can enter into the final summing up of all things, or partake of eternity, which does not receive life from Him and is not conformed to His purpose. When Christ claims this title for Himself, it is plainly announced that the revelation of God in Christ, in what He was and what He did, is the key to the issues of human life. Christianity is final. See also art. ALPHA AND OMEGA.   A. E. ROSS.

FIRSTBORN.—

One of the fundamental ideas with regard to Jehovah in early Israel was that of His being owner of the land, and consequently lord also of all that the land brought forth and of all that lived upon it (Lv 25[23], Ps 50[10-12]). Closely connected with this idea was a further one to the effect that the land was held in tenure ; Jehovah was the landowner, His people the tenants ; but their tenancy depended solely on the will of Jehovah (Dt 30[20] etc.).* As lord of the land and giver of all that it produced, tribute was due to Him ; this tribute took the form of the offering of first-fruits.† Not only, however, was the land Jehovah's possession, but the people who lived upon it, and upon its produce, were likewise His ; this would follow naturally by virtue of Jehovah's overlordship. Therefore, just as Jehovah, being owner of the land, received the first-fruits of its produce as tribute due to Him, so, being also owner of the people, did He receive the firstborn as, in the same way, a tribute due to Him. This is not definitely stated in the Bible, but the notices of child-sacrifice lead us to infer that at some early period the rite of the sacrifice of the firstborn was performed, and the analogy of the offering up of the firstlings of the flock points to a similar usage with regard to man (Ex 13[2] 22[29] 34[20]) ; moreover, the prevalence of the practice among ethnologically allied races ‡ makes it in a high degree probable that originally the descendants of Abram sacrificed their firstborn as a tribute to the Deity (see below, ' Redemption of the firstborn '). As the firstborn are spoken of as being particularly the possession of Jehovah, one would expect to find them occupying the position of His special ministers ; it is possible that this was the case originally (cf. Hannah's vow, 1 S 1[11]),§ especially as in Nu 3[12] it is said : 'Behold, I have taken the Levites from among the children of Israel instead of all the firstborn that openeth the womb among the children of Israel ; and the Levites shall be mine' (cf. 3[45]) ; as a matter of fact, however, the earliest Code

---

* This OT conception is illustrated in the Gospels by the parable of the Wicked Husbandmen, Mt 21[33ff]. and parallel passages ; cf. also Mk 13[34].

† It will, of course, be understood that this was adapted to agricultural life from the earlier nomadic life with its flocks and herds (cf. Nowack, *Heb. Arch.* ii. p. 147 ff.).

‡ *e.g.* the Moabites, 2 K 3[27] ; the early Arabs (Wellhausen, *Reste* [2], pp. 115, 116) ; the Canaanites (*PEFSt*, 1903, *passim*) ; the Phœnicians (Rawlinson, *Hist. of Phœnicia*, ch. xi.) ; cf. the story of the attempted sacrifice of Isaac ; see *PSBA* xxiv. p. 253 ff.

§ There is a Talmudic tradition (*Zeb.* 112[b]), according to which the firstborn acted as officiating priests in the wilderness until the erection of the tabernacle, when the office was given to the tribe of Levi (*Jewish Encyc.* v. 396).

commands the redemption of the firstborn : ' All the firstborn of man among thy sons shalt thou redeem' (Ex 13¹³, cf. 13¹⁵ 34²⁰).

From the foregoing one can understand that the term 'firstborn,' πρωτότοκος (that which, as the most precious, belonged, in the first instance, to Jehovah), came to be one of particular honour (cf. Ex 4²², Jer 31⁹), and it is used as such in reference to Christ (Ro 8²⁹, Col 1¹⁵. ¹⁸).

The only occurrence of the term in the Gospels is in Lk 2⁷ καὶ ἔτεκεν τὸν υἱὸν τὸν πρωτότοκον,* and apart from its significance to the Jewish mind as outlined above, its importance lies in its bearing upon the question of the perpetual virginity of the mother of Christ. The term does not necessarily suggest the subsequent birth of other children ; for, in the first place, as a title of honour it would naturally be mentioned in connexion with Christ by the Evangelist ; and secondly, to Jews the significance of 'firstborn' lay in the special sanctity which attached to such ; † this is clear from what has been said in the previous section ; indeed, St. Luke directly implies as much when he quotes, in substance, from Ex 13². ¹² ' Every male that openeth the womb shall be called *holy* to the Lord' (Lk 2²³).

Redemption of the firstborn.—In the passage Lk 2²²ff. two distinct ceremonies are referred to : the presentation to the Lord, and the redemption ; the former of these implies the actual dedication of the child to God (cf. 1 S 1²⁸) ; from what has been said above, this ceremony must be regarded as the fulfilling in spirit of the primitive act of literally devoting (sacrificing) the firstborn son to the Deity. The distinction between the two ceremonies may be illustrated by the practice of modern orthodox Jews. The father of the child first presents his firstborn to the *cohen*, and makes a declaration ending with the words : ' It is said, Sanctify unto me all the firstborn, whatsoever openeth the womb among the children of Israel, both of man and of beast ; it is mine.' This is a definite act of presentation to God, of renunciation on the part of the father,—the child is no longer his. This part of the ceremony corresponds to Lk 2²². ²³. ²⁷. ²⁸. Then the father places fifteen shillings (five *selaim* or shekels) before the *cohen*, who thereupon asks : ' Which wouldst thou rather, give me thy firstborn son, the firstborn of his mother, ‡ or redeem him for five *selaim*, which thou art bound to give according to the Law ?' The father replies : ' I desire rather to redeem my son, and here thou hast the value of his redemption, which I am bound to give according to the Law.' § This ceremony corresponds to Lk 2²⁴. ‖ This redemption of the firstborn ¶ (פִּדְיוֹן הַבֵּן) took place thirty days after birth (Lk 2²² ; cf. Lv 12⁴, Nu 18¹⁶),** and the price of redemption was, according to Nu 3⁴⁷ 18¹⁶, five shekels ; in Ex 13¹³ the command to redeem the firstborn is given, though the price of redemption is not mentioned, while in Lv 12 there is no mention at all regarding the redemption of the firstborn, reference being made only to an atone-

* In Mt 1²⁵ τὸν πρωτότοκον is read by DC and the OL version only ; it must therefore be rejected in this passage.

† Cf. He 1⁶, where τον πρωτοτοκον means ' only-begotten.'

‡ The law of the redemption of the firstborn ' applies to the firstborn of the mother and not of the father. Hence the husband of several wives would have to redeem the firstborn of each one of them, while the husband of a woman who had had children by a previous marriage need not redeem her child although it was his firstborn ' (*Jewish Encyc.* v. 396). Moreover, the first male child of a woman need not be redeemed if a female child has been born before him.

§ The money is sometimes returned, but the Jewish authorities do not look upon this with favour.

‖ See *The Authorized Daily Prayer-Book*⁶ (ed. S. Singer), pp. 308, 309.

¶ According to Ex 13¹³⁻¹⁵ the redemption of the firstborn was instituted as an abiding act of thanksgiving to Jehovah for having spared the firstborn males of the children of Israel in Egypt. Concerning the connexion between the offering of the firstborn and the Passover, see Nowack, *op. cit.* § 99.

** The same custom is kept up by modern orthodox Jews ; if the day falls on a Sabbath or a Holy Day, the ceremony is performed on the following day.

ment which has to be made for the purification of the mother ; it may be owing to Lv 12 that in Lk 2²² ' their' purification is spoken of, *i.e.* of the child as well as of the mother ; at any rate v.²⁴ seems to point to an amalgamation of the offerings due from the mother for purification, and on behalf of the child for redemption ; * in the modern service of prayer of thanksgiving for women after recovery from childbirth no provision is made for any offering.

LITERATURE.—See the authorities referred to in the footnotes.
                                    W. O. E. OESTERLEY.

FIRST-FRUITS.—On the offering of first-fruits as a Jewish institution see Hastings' *DB*, vol. ii. p. 10 f.

The word rendered first-fruits (ἀπαρχή) occurs 8 times in the NT, and only in 1 Co 15²⁰. ²³ is it applied directly to our Lord : ' Now hath Christ been raised from the dead, the first-fruits of them that are asleep' ; ' Christ the first-fruits ; then they that are Christ's.' It is possible, as some have suggested, that there is a reference in v.²⁰ to the specific offering of the sheaf of the first ripe corn on the second day of the Passover feast (Lv 23¹⁰. ¹¹). The coincidence of our Lord's resurrection on the 16th Nisan—the day on which the sheaf was offered before the Lord—would no doubt suggest the idea of the first-fruits to the Apostle's mind. But, even apart from this specific reference, the figure of the risen Christ as the first-fruits from the dead is perfectly natural. And there is more here than might be at first supposed. Christ's resurrection is the pledge of His people's resurrection, just as the first-fruits were the pledge of the harvest to come. Christ is the first to be raised from the dead, and so stands in the front rank alone, as the first-fruits were plucked before the rest of the produce was ripe ; but, just as certainly as the harvest in due time followed the first-fruits, so shall those who sleep in Christ be raised up in due time, and stand in the second rank after Him. But, further, it is clearly implied here, and explicitly taught in other passages, that as is Christ the first-fruits, so shall be the rest of the harvest. There is implied here a community of nature and character between Christ, the first-fruits, and His people. It is only the *time* of their manifestation that is different. The portion gathered as first-fruits is of the same nature as the rest, and the rest is of the same nature and character and standing as the first-fruits. This is indicated specially in v.²¹, where it is said that, as death came by man, so it is only by man that the resurrection can come, *i.e.* resurrection and triumph over death can be man's possession only when given him by one who is man like himself. Man, therefore, must be of the same nature and character and standing as Christ, the first-fruits. What is suggested here is plainly taught elsewhere (Col 3⁴, Ro 8²⁹, 1 Jn 3²). Christ, according to these passages, is the first-fruits, the firstborn among many brethren, not only as the pledge that, as He rose, so His people shall rise from the dead, but also that *as* He is, in nature and character, so shall His people be. That is, perhaps, the most glorious promise of the resurrection first-fruits.

In Ro 8²³ the first-fruits of the Spirit received by Christ's people are referred to. That they have received the Spirit in some measure and have been sanctified inwardly, is the pledge that they shall receive it in yet greater abundance, that there shall be a final outpouring of the Spirit by which the body of man shall be redeemed even as the spirit has been sanctified—the psychical body being

* Among modern orthodox Jews, priests and Levites are exempt from the law of redeeming their firstborn ; this applies also to those whose wives are daughters of priests or Levites.

changed into a spiritual. In Ro 11[16] 16[5], 1 Co 16[15], Ja 1[18], Rev 14[4] the reference is to the future redemption of mankind, of which those already gathered in are the first-fruits and pledge. Those already redeemed and presented to God as holy are the first-fruits, the pledge of the coming harvest of a holy redeemed humanity.

LITERATURE.—Schürer, *HJP* II. i. 237 ; Edersheim, *The Temple : its Ministry, etc.*, xix. ; Stapfer, *Palestine in Time of Christ*, bk. ii. ch. 13 ; Josephs, *Judaism as Creed and Life*, bk. ii. ch. 5 ; art. 'First-Fruits' in *Jew. Encyc.* vol. v.

J. SOUTAR.

FISH, FISHER, FISHING.—The present article is not concerned with the fish of the Mediterranean, nor with those which inhabit various watercourses in the Holy Land, nor even with those that belong to the lower course of the Jordan or of its southern tributaries, or of the other streams that flow into the Dead Sea. The only fish mentioned in the Gospels, the only ones, consequently, which come within the scope of this Dictionary, are those of the Lake of Gennesaret, to which we naturally add those that are found in the upper course of the Jordan or in the springs in the neighbourhood of the Lake.

Fish (OT דָּג, דָּגָה) are designated in the NT only by the general term ἰχθύς, alternating occasionally with its diminutive ἰχθύδιον, without the employment of the latter term necessarily marking any intended distinction ; cf. for an instance in point, Mt 15[34] with v.[36]. Nowhere in the whole Bible do we find a special name for a definite species of fish.

Fish formed a large part of the food of the Lakeside population. This may be inferred from the threefold question of Jesus (Lk 11[11], cf. Mt 7[10]), in which the commonest foods are enumerated : bread, fish, eggs. The same conclusion is implied in what is related with reference to the two multiplications of the loaves. On the occasion of the first (Mt 14[13-21], Mk]30-44, Lk 9[10-17], Jn 6[1-15]) it is said that there was present a lad with five loaves and two fishes ; in the account of the second (Mt 15[32-39], Mk 8[1-10]) it is mentioned that, in addition to the seven loaves, there were also 'a few small fishes.' We may cite, further, Lk 24[42].

It is interesting to note that for the 'small fishes' of the other narratives the Fourth Gospel employs the term ὀψάριον, which properly signifies simply 'nourishment,' 'food.' Bochart (*Hieroz.* i. p. 41) has already shown that this word was employed in the same way by the best Greek writers, *e.g.* Plato, Menander, etc., and that ὀψοφάγοι is met with as synonymous with 'fish-eaters.'

It is legitimate to suppose that a trade in fish was carried on between the Lake of Tiberias and the rest of the country. The name of the town of Tari.cheæ (Ταριχεῖαι), situated on the shore of the Lake, implies a business connected with salted provisions (τάριχοι). It may be that this traffic extended as far as Jerusalem ; some have supposed that it was in this way that one of Jesus' disciples, the companion of Simon Peter, was known to the high priest (Jn 18[15f.]) ; but this is nothing more than an ingenious conjecture.

'Fisher'* or 'fisherman' (Heb. דַּיָּג) is expressed in the NT by ἁλεεύς or ἁλιεύς ; the verb 'to fish' by ἁλιεύειν. Several of the first and principal disciples followed the calling of fishermen. The Synoptics describe the scene when Jesus called them to follow Him (Mt 4[18-22], Mk 1[16-20], Lk 5[1-11]). These three narratives contain the promise, 'I will make you fishers of men.' Lk. connects the story with the miraculous draught ; cf. in this respect also Jn 21[6-11]. In one of the parables of the Kingdom (Mt 13[47-50]) Jesus compares the latter to a net ; and the separation which the fishermen make, in their catch, between what is good and what is bad, is used to symbolize the

* So AV and RV in Mt 4[18f.] and Mk 1[16f.], but 'fishermen' in Lk 5[2]. See Hastings' *DB* ii. 12[a].

separation of the righteous from the wicked at the Final Judgment. The criterion by which good and bad fish are distinguished is not expressly indicated. The point in view might be the difference between clean and unclean foods as defined by the Law (cf. Dt 14[9f.], Lv 11[9f.]) ; but there might be other motives, such as those which Lortet indicates in the case of modern fishermen, who reject certain fish on account of their inferior size (*Poissons et Reptiles du lac de Tibériade*, p. 52), their disagreeable aspect (*ib.* pp. 32, 82), or their unpleasant muddy flavour (*ib.* pp. 35, 58, 64).

The fishermen sometimes carried on their trade in partnership, as is still the case at the present day, when the fishermen of Tiberias form a kind of corporation with fixed rules. The number of fishing vessels on the Lake at the beginning of the Christian era must have been very considerable. Josephus (*BJ* II. xxi. 8) speaks of 330 (*v.l.* 230) ; see also Mk 4[36], Jn 6[23]. Forty years ago Furrer found only a single boat ; Lortet saw three in 1875 and six in 1880 ; Frei counted nine in 1886, and the present writer saw the same number in 1894, while in 1899 he noted fourteen ; and no doubt the number has increased since then.

The fishermen made use of **nets.** One of the Greek terms employed (Mt 13[47]) is σαγήνη, *seine*, 'drag-net,' a large net which two or more boats arrange in a circle in the lake, in such a way as to enclose a vast space with a kind of vertical wall. It is kept stretched by means of weights and floats. Then the two extremities are brought together, and the whole with its contents is dragged ashore. The other species of net mentioned in the Gospels (Mt 4[18]) is the *casting net* (ἀμφίβληστρον), which a single man throws with a skilful turn of the hand, and which is of circular form, like an umbrella. Once it has been plunged in the water it is drawn out with the captured fish. This is still the method most frequently pursued in our own time. The other passages where nets are spoken of (Mt 4[20f.], Mk 1[18f.], Lk 5[2-6], Jn 21[6-11]) use the general term δίκτυον, which might be applied to any kind of net. Some texts speak of washing and of mending nets (Lk 5[2], Mt 4[21], Mk 1[19]). See also NETS.

The Gospels only once mention line-fishing, namely in Mt 17[27], where we read of Peter casting the **hook** (ἄγκιστρον), which was certainly placed at the end of a cord or line, but we cannot say whether the latter was attached to a rod or long reed or was simply held in the hand. In the NT there is no mention of harpooning fish (contrast Job 41[7] [He 40[31]]). At the present day we still meet with examples of this practice.

The waters of the Lake of Tiberias are exceptionally rich in fish, especially by the shore of el-Baṭiḥa (to the east of the mouth of the Jordan), and in the bay of eṭ-Ṭabigha. These were in former times the favourite grounds of fishermen, and these spots are still preferred by them in our own day. There, on the shore of el-Baṭiḥa lay Bethsaida-Julias ; and, if there were two Bethsaidas (a much controverted question ; see artt. BETHSAIDA and CAPERNAUM), the second was at eṭ-Ṭabigha or in its vicinity. Now *Bethsaida* means 'house of fish,' 'fishery.' It was the native town of Peter and Andrew, of James and John,—all four fishermen,—as well as of Philip, whose occupation is unknown to us. According to Jn 21[2] Thomas and Nathanael (of Cana) appear also to have been fishermen, at least occasionally. The dress of the fishermen was more than simple ; according to Jn 21[7] Peter was γυμνός, 'naked' ; it is not quite easy to see why so many exegetes maintain that this term does not imply complete nudity. It is certainly most natural to suppose that Peter had discarded all his clothes ; the fact that he afterwards hastily girds on his ἐπενδύτης, lit. his 'upper garment,' does not necessarily prove that he was wearing another under it.

The fish of the Lake of Tiberias have been minutely studied and described by two experts, Dr. Lortet, dean of the Faculty of Medicine at Lyons, and Dr. Tristram. Out of 39 (Lortet) or 43 (Tristram) species known in Palestine, from 22 to 24 are found in the Lake of Tiberias and its immediate vicinity. They belong to a number of different genera. The genus *Chromis* has the richest representation of species: *Niloticus, Tiberiadis, Andreæ, Simonis, Microstomus, Flavii Josephi, Magdalenæ*; belonging to a genus near of kin is *Hemichromis Sacra*. These fish are the most abundant and make the best eating. The genus *Barbus* is also extremely prolific; three species belonging to it are found: *Canis*, which swarms, but is little appreciated; *Longiceps*, esteemed; and *Beddomii*, rare. Then, in the family of the *Cyprinides* come *Discognathus Lamta*; four species of *Capœta*: *Syriaca, Damascina, Socialis, Sauvagei*; *Leuciscus* (or *Phoxinellus*) *Zeregi*; *Alburnus Sellal*; *Acanthobrama Centisquama*; three species of *Nemachilus*: *Tigris, Galilæus, Leontinæ*. In the family of the *Blennides*: *Blennius Varus* and *Blennius Lupulus*. Finally, in the family of the *Silurides* we have the strange *Clarias Macracanthus*, already noted by Josephus (*BJ* III. x. 8) under the name κορακῖνος, which, in spite of its forbidding aspect, supplies an article of food not to be disdained. This fish has the strange peculiarity that, when it is withdrawn from its natural element, it utters cries like the mewings of a cat, and that it can live for several days out of the water.

A considerable number of the above species belong properly to Palestine, but the *fauna* of Palestinian fish shows, nevertheless, a close connexion with that of Africa and not with that of the Mediterranean basin. The ancients, *e.g.* Josephus, had already noted this fact, and they raised the question of the possibility of a subterranean communication between the waters of Egypt and those of Palestine. See also ANIMALS, p. 66[b].

LITERATURE. — Bochart, *Hierozoicon*, i. pp. 36–44; Lortet, *Poissons et Reptiles du lac de Tibériade*, 1883, and the same author's *La Syrie d'aujourd'hui*, 1884, pp. 506–510; Tristram, 'Fauna and Flora' (*PEF, SWP*), 1888, pp. 162–177, also *Natural History of the Bible*[8], 1889, pp. 282–294; J. G. Wood, *Bible Animals*, 1869, pp. 561–582; Ad. Frei in *ZDPV*, 1886, pp. 101–103; Libbey and Hoskins, *Jordan Valley and Petra*, 1905, vol. i. p. 130 f.; G. R. Lees, *Village Life in Palestine*, 1905, p. 5 [with photograph of two fishermen of the Lake of Tiberias casting their nets]. LUCIEN GAUTIER.

FLAX.—See SMOKING FLAX.

FLESH (σάρξ).—In every instance where this word is used by the Evangelists we observe that it is confined in its reference to the human race. The same remark, it may be noticed, holds good of the NT writers as a whole (cf., however, 1 Co 15[39], and the plural σάρκας of Rev 19[18]). The particular conception attaching to it varies in different contexts to a slight extent, though in almost every case a distinction or contrast is either stated or implied which has its roots in OT thought. It is interesting to remark that this is a word employed very rarely by St. Luke in either of his writings; and even when he does use it, we find that, for the most part, he is quoting from the OT (see Lk 3[6] = Is 40[5] [LXX], where in conjunction with πᾶσα it is simply a synonym for all mankind; cf. Mt 24[22], Mk 13[20], Jn 17[2], and Ac 2[17]). The reference, of course, is to the human race in its present condition of weakness and need of help, as contrasted with the power and the active love of God (cf. Dt 5[26], Ps 56[4] [55[5] LXX]).

In the only other place where the word is found in St. Luke's Gospel (24[39]) we have it used simply to denote the substance flesh considered as a constituent of the human body. The risen Jesus is represented as inviting His disciples to assure themselves by touching Him that He had risen not merely in a spiritual, but in a corporeal sense. The antithesis is that of 'spirit' and 'body' (πνεῦμα and σῶμα), the latter consisting of 'flesh' and 'bones' (σάρξ and ὀστέα). See art. BODY.

A still more emphatic expression signifying the distinction between man and God is found in St. Matthew's Gospel (16[17]), where σάρξ is joined with αἷμα to denote man in his present condition of spiritual limitation and of defective knowledge. A somewhat similar antithesis is incidentally, albeit elaborately, pointed out by St. John (1[13]), who, in his reference to the new life communicated through Christ to believers, lays stress on the fact that this higher life is not the result of human birth, whether the latter be considered as the outcome of a long line of descent (ἐξ αἱμάτων), or as springing from natural instinct inherent in the flesh (ἐκ θελήματος σαρκός), or even as the resultant of the will power resident in the entire man (ἐκ θελήματος ἀνδρός). Their infused life has its roots in Him who is the source of all life (. . . ἀλλ' ἐκ θεοῦ ἐγεννήθησαν), and is conditioned in every instance by their reception of the Word made flesh (ὅσοι δὲ ἔλαβον αὐτόν, see Westcott, *Gospel of St. John, ad loc.*, who notices a very early variant reading which would make 'the Word' the subject of the whole verse).

Another form of this antithetic relationship occurs in the same writing. In His conversation with Nicodemus Jesus draws attention to the limitations which surround the functions of man's nature considered on its sensuous side (ἐκ τῆς σαρκός), and those of the Spirit which finds scope for activity within another sphere of human life (ἐκ τοῦ πνεύματος). It is not the antithesis of evil and good that is here referred to. It is simply that within the realm of man's being there are two principles of energy which take their origin from two orders of existence. The law of nature which compels like to produce like holds good in man's complex life, and so 'What is born of the flesh is flesh, and what is born of the Spirit is spirit' (Jn 3[6]). With this we may compare another passage in the same Gospel where this idea is expressed in language more explicit still and as emphatic (Jn 6[63]). The contrast here between spirit, which not only has life in itself but can communicate that life as it wills (τὸ ζωοποιοῦν), and flesh, which 'is of no avail' above its own sphere (ἡ σάρξ οὐκ ὠφελεῖ οὐδέν), is categorically asserted.

So, too, on another occasion when engaged in controversy with the Pharisees, Jesus contrasts their method of judging with His own patience in that respect, and in so doing implies a further contrast —their imperfect and therefore incorrect judgment (κατὰ τὴν σάρκα) which is based on a superficial knowledge, and His just judgment which comes from His 'knowledge of all the circumstances, and aspects, and issues of life' (ἡ κρίσις ἡ ἐμὴ ἀληθινή ἐστιν, Jn 8[15f.]; see Westcott, *Gospel of St. John, ad loc.*).

Arising out of this conception we have the word employed to mark a psychological distinction between man's flesh and spirit. So real was this distinction to the mind of Jesus that we can almost hear in His words (Mt 26[41] = Mk 14[38]) the echo of personal experience (. . . γρηγορῆσαι μετ' ἐμοῦ . . . τὸ μὲν πνεῦμα πρόθυμον ἡ δὲ σάρξ ἀσθενής). In this place we may also notice that there was something present in the struggle engaged in by the disciples which was absent in the case of Jesus. They were unsuccessful in their efforts to 'watch,' because not only was their flesh 'weak,' but it had also to contend with an element of discord which further distracted their power for unremitting watchfulness. With Him was also present the flesh of weakness (see 2 Co 13⁴ ἐξ ἀσθενείας), but the relationship between His σάρξ and πνεῦμα was not perverted by the indwelling presence of sin, or by the downward tendency inherited as the result of sin.

On one occasion Jesus quotes with approval the translation of the LXX (Gn 2²⁴) where the word σάρξ occurs meaning the entire man (Mt 19⁵ᶠ· =Mk 10⁸), and that without any qualifying word. It would be a colourless interpretation of Jesus' words which would limit His teaching on the marriage relationship to a physical oneness following on and produced by the sexual union. The Hebraistic ἔσονται εἰς (Heb. ‏וְהָיוּ לְ‎) implies a gradual movement from a physical union to a higher and more complex unity, so that where two separate beings formerly existed there is now but one (ὥστε οὐκέτι εἰσὶν δύο, ἀλλὰ σὰρξ μία, which is Jesus' inference from the Heb. ‏בָשָׂר אֶחָד‎; see art. EUNUCH). It is because of the ultimately complete and spiritual character of this union that the sin which dissolves it and the human legislation which seeks to render it nugatory assume their dark proportions (cf. Gould, 'St. Mark' in *Internat. Crit. Com.* on Mk 10⁸ᶠ·).

Passing from the Synoptic to the Johannine use of this word, we find it clothing conceptions which are fuller and richer. In the simple but majestic sentence in which he announces the profound mystery of the Incarnation, St. John employs the word 'flesh' to express the totality of human nature, looked at on the side of its manifold limitations, that is to say, as it touches and is connected with the world of matter and of time (ὁ λόγος σὰρξ ἐγένετο, Jn 1¹⁴, with which we may compare the positive references to 'the soul' and 'the spirit' of Jesus in the same writing, *e.g.* 12²⁷ ἡ ψυχή μου, 13²¹ τῷ πνεύματι, etc.). The phrase 'the Word became flesh' implies the existence of an antithesis which has been reduced in its elements to a final and permanent synthesis. The Johannine conception leaves no room for doubt as to the perfection of the human nature of Jesus, which is universal both as regards time and race.

Keeping in mind this usage, we shall be enabled to apprehend more fully the thought underlying the language of Jesus about His power of imparting Himself in His perfect humanity (cf. Jn 6⁵¹⁻⁵⁶). His 'flesh,' by virtue of its union with His Divine Personality, is 'living' (ὁ ζῶν) food, and therefore possesses the power of communicating its life to all who will eat thereof (ἐὰν μὴ φάγητε τὴν σάρκα, κ.τ.λ.). Without this participation and consequent assimilation on the part of His followers, there can be no such thing as 'life' within them, for they deliberately reject what contains for them the germinal principle of that 'life' (οὐκ ἔχετε ζωὴν ἐν ἑαυτοῖς).

The question may be asked whether it is possible to trace any likeness or fundamental connexion between the Gospel and the Pauline uses of σάρξ. In St. Paul's writings very marked emphasis is laid upon this word, and for him it clothes a conception rich with ethical significance. The 'flesh' is the present abode of sin, which requires an obedient subject to execute its behests. So closely does he connect the power of sin with the existing weakness of the flesh that he does not hesitate to say from his own experience 'I know that in . . . my flesh dwelleth no good thing' (Ro 7¹⁸). At the same time, he is careful to point out that this is not the state appointed for man by God. The 'crucifixion' of the flesh is possible for every man who wills to walk not 'according to the flesh' but 'according to the Spirit' (οἱ . . . τὴν σάρκα ἐσταύρωσαν, κ.τ.λ., Gal 5²⁴·, cf. Ro 8⁴ᶠ·), and those who have the indwelling presence of the Spirit are no longer in the flesh (ἐν σαρκί) but in the Spirit (ἐν πνεύματι, Ro 8⁹). With these we may compare such expres-

sions as 'the mind of the flesh' (φρόνημα τῆς σαρκός) and 'the mind of the Spirit' (φρόνημα τοῦ πνεύματος, Ro 8⁶; ὑπὸ τοῦ νοὸς τῆς σαρκός, Col 2¹⁸), from which we can gather how present to St. Paul's mind was the connexion between sin and the flesh, and at the same time how strong within him was the glorious hope that such connexion in the ultimate result was abnormal and destined for destruction. There is no sign in the Pauline terminology that he was influenced in his theological conceptions by the spirit of that Greek dualism which wormed its way into subsequent Christian thought with lasting and for the most part evil consequences (see Müller, *Christian Doct. of Sin*, i. 320 ff.).

The redemption and the quickening of the body (. . . τὴν ἀπολύτρωσιν τοῦ σώματος, Ro 8²³ ; . . . ζωοποιήσει τὰ θνητὰ σώματα, Ro 8¹¹ ; cf. 6¹², 2 Co 4¹¹) are features essential to the scheme of salvation as outlined and systematized by St. Paul. The condemnation of sin 'in the flesh' by God, who for this purpose sent His Son 'in the likeness of the flesh of sin' (Ro 8³), is evidence that there is, for him, no naturally essential connexion between the flesh and evil.

We are not without signs that this is just the point of view from which the Evangelists looked at this question (cf. Jn 1¹⁴ 17², Lk 3⁶ 11³⁴ = Mt 6²²), and that neither they nor the Apostle of the Gentiles were touched by that false belief which identified sin with matter, and, therefore, with 'the body of the flesh' (cf. Col 1²² 2¹¹). The anthropology of the Gospels, as well as the psychological conceptions which emerge but rarely and incidentally from their pages, are essentially Hebrew, and are never stained by the potential immoralities which characterized the later Alexandrian and Hellenistic theology.

LITERATURE.—Stevens, *The Theology of the NT*, pp. 189 f., 338 ff ; Harnack, *Hist. of Dogma*, i. 53–224, iii. 183, 255 ff., etc.; H. H. Wendt, *Die Begriffe Fleisch und Geist* ; Laidlaw, *The Bible Doctrine of Man*, and his artt. 'Psychology' and 'Flesh' in Hastings' *DB* ; Weiss, *Biblical Theology of the NT*, § 27 ; Cremer, *Bibl.-Theol. Lex. of NT Greek*, *s.v.* σάρξ.

J. R. WILLIS.

FLIGHT.—The story of the flight of the Holy Family into Egypt is peculiar to the First Gospel (Mt 2¹³ᶠᶠ·). The omission of it, and also of the manifestation to the Gentiles (Mt 2¹⁻¹²), from the Third Gospel is surprising, since there rather than in Mt. we should have expected to find any story that brought Jesus into contact with the Gentile world. The surprise would deepen into suspicion were it not that the records of the Evangelists are so fragmentary ; but that fact instantly relieves the strain.

O. Holtzmann, who cites the well-known omission in Ac 9¹⁹⁻²⁶ of any reference to St. Paul's journey to Arabia (Gal 1¹⁷), frankly states that 'the author who left out this journey of Paul to Arabia might well pass over, in his other account, the journey of the Holy Family into Egypt,' and that 'if we had in Matthew an account absolutely above criticism, it would not be difficult to get over the gap in the narrative of Luke' (*Life of Jesus*, p. 85).

The silence of St. Luke does not, then, discredit the narrative of St. Matthew. But their records might prove to be mutually exclusive, so that acceptance of the one would involve rejection of the other. How stand the facts ? According to the Third Gospel, Nazareth was, prior to their marriage, the home both of Joseph and of Mary (Lk 2⁴ 1²⁶), whereas St. Matthew (2²³) first associates them with Nazareth after their return from Egypt, and gives no hint of any previous residence there. Further, St. Matthew, having told the story of the Nativity (1¹⁸⁻²⁵), goes on to record the visit of the Magi (2¹⁻¹²), the hurried flight from Bethlehem and the sojourn in Egypt (2¹³ᶠᶠ·), whereas St. Luke records merely the circumcision of the child (2²¹) and His presentation to the Lord (2²²ᶠᶠ·), and then adds that 'when they had performed all things according to the law of the Lord, they returned into Galilee, to their own city Nazareth' (2³⁹). From those words one would naturally infer that the return took place immediately after the events thus recorded, and that no room was left for the episodes of the First Gospel. Is that inference necessary, or even well founded? If the narrative of Acts must be so adjusted as to take in the sojourn of St. Paul in Arabia, he would be a bold critic who would maintain that the terms of the other narrative inevitably exclude the sojourn in Egypt. It is to be noted also that the time-table of the First Gospel is sufficiently elastic to embrace easily the events recorded in the Third. For we find there that, 'according to the time which he had carefully learned of the wise men,' Herod's inhuman edict included all the children in Bethlehem 'from *two years old* and under' (Mt 2¹⁶).

The difficulty, therefore, is not one of chronology. Even if it were, such an objection would lose both point and edge in the hands of those who used it, except on the theory that Jesus was, after all, born in Bethlehem. For, even granting that the immediate return to Nazareth is the natural inference from St. Luke's account, yet the force of any argument based upon it fails the very moment that Nazareth and not Bethlehem is made the scene of the Nativity. On that showing, St. Luke's story is itself untrustworthy, and so cannot be used to discredit another story which is inconsistent with it.

The real difficulty is of quite a different sort: it is that we have not in St. Matthew 'an account absolutely above criticism.' It might very pertinently be asked if we have any right to expect such an account. Stories of the childhood of a great man are never written while he is still a child, but only after he has achieved greatness; and even then they are written, not necessarily because of their own intrinsic importance, but because they have caught some of the glory of the afterglow. Now, it was not until Jesus had already won His place in the hearts of men that our Gospels were written. In the circumstances of the case, therefore, these records could not be other than fragmentary, and a fragmentary account can never be 'absolutely above criticism.'

But presumably the special criticism to which these incidents of the Infancy lie open, is that they are no more entitled to belief than, say, those recorded in the Apocryphal Gospels. The *Gospel of the Infancy*, e.g., weaves around the Flight into Egypt a fantastic garland of miracle and wonder. This wreath of fairy tales is by common consent stripped off and laid aside as unhistorical embellishment. Should not the Flight itself be laid with them as equally unworthy of credence? The question opens up a subject much too large to be discussed here. But one may at least ask if it is not too drastic a measure to destroy the ship because one has had to remove the barnacles, or to remove the peg because a worthless coat has been hung on it. Are these narratives so much of a piece that, if we reject some of them, we must reject all? Surely the fact is not without significance that the Evangelist preserves the story of the Flight, but records none of the marvels that have clustered round it. For if these other stories were extant when he wrote, he must have been cognizant of them, and his rejection of them must have been deliberate. On the other hand, if they were of a later growth, his tradition is thereby marked as older and, to that extent, more trustworthy.

But, says Keim (*Life of Jesus*, ii. 94), 'it bears all the marks of a poetic picture.' Is there, then, no poetry in real life? If a story is poetic, is it thereby branded as unhistorical? 'Intertwined with the narrative is a no less than threefold revelation by an angel, almost too much for the thrift of heaven.' The objection would be valid in the case of a story written in modern times by a man of the West, but is shorn of its force when one remembers that this story was written by an Oriental some eighteen centuries ago.

Much more apposite is the contention that 'the enormous toil of such a journey with a little child, was such as only legend, aided or not by miracles, could easily get over.' The toilsomeness of the journey is not denied; no one imagines that it was 'easily got over.' May not our Lord's own words (Mt 24²⁰, Mk 13¹⁸) be an echo of the hardships Joseph and Mary had to endure in bearing Him to a place of refuge? But the cogency of Keim's argument vanishes when we remember that this was a flight for life (see INNOCENTS). In such circumstances, hardships are little accounted. But 'they might have found a nearer refuge among the Arabs of the south or west.' Surely this criticism is singularly inept. A temporary and brief refuge might thus have been found, but no one knew how long it would be ere the wanderers could safely return to their own land. What was needed was an asylum in which they could quietly abide till all danger was past, and where Joseph could find employment which would enable him to provide for his household.

Equally beside the mark is the attempt to explain the story as in some way parallel to the sojourn of Moses in Egypt. The two stories are rich, not in resemblance, but in contrast: they have absolutely nothing in common save the word 'Egypt.' The attempt to derive the one from the other is a triumph of misdirected ingenuity.

Quite as little avails the expedient of deducing the narrative from the prophecy of Hosea (11¹), as O. Holtzmann would evidently do. 'For the story about the Lord's childhood the Gospel of Matthew seems to have drawn principally upon certain indications in the Old Testament' (*Life of Jesus*, p. 86). One can readily enough understand how a Jewish Christian might see in the narrative of the Flight a richer fulfilment of the prophet's words, but it is almost incredible that the incident should be invented as a commentary on the words, and all the more so when the words in question are not a prophecy, but a historical reference. Still less credible does the suggestion become when we find that we should require to believe not merely that the Flight was invented to explain the prophecy, but further that the Massacre of the Innocents had next to be invented to explain the Flight, and the visit of the Magi to explain the Massacre. Acceptance of such a theory involves a much larger draft on one's credulity than does acceptance of the incident itself as historical.

The question may still arise, What motive led the Evangelist to record this event? Need we seek for any motive? He wanted to tell about Jesus: would it not be enough for him that this was a story of the childhood of the loved Master, and that he believed it to be authentic?

'Egypt has, in all ages, been the natural place of refuge for all who were driven from Palestine by distress, persecution, or discontent' (Farrar, *Life of Christ*, ch. iv.). It need create no surprise, therefore, that it was towards Egypt the fugitives bent their steps. There they would be without Herod's jurisdiction and beyond the reach of his vengeance; the road was a well-known one, and some three days would suffice to bring them to the frontier. Of the incidents of the journey we have no reliable information, nor are we told in what part of Egypt the wanderers at length found rest and refuge. Tradition has assigned this distinction to Matarieh (the ancient Heliopolis), which lies a few miles north-east from Cairo ; and there is no good reason why the tradition may not be correct. It is known that in that neighbourhood there was a considerable Jewish population. That fact would have undoubted weight with Joseph, as it held out to him the prospect of obtaining suitable employment. The duration of the sojourn in Egypt has been very variously stated, some reckoning it as having extended over one, two, three, or even seven years. But we may take it as certain that it was in reality very brief, seeing the death of Herod occurred very shortly after the period at which the Flight must have taken place. See also art. EGYPT.

LITERATURE.—W. G. Elmslie in *Expositor*, i. vi. [1877] 401–411 ; Farrar, *Christ in Art*, 263–273. For a vivid conception of the circumstances of the Flight into Egypt, no less than of the relations between the Child Jesus and the slain infants of Bethlehem, see Holman Hunt's 'Triumph of the Innocents.'

HUGH DUNCAN.

FLOCK, FOLD.—For a general treatment of these words see SHEEP, SHEPHERD. But it may be noted here that, whereas in Jn 10[1. 16] we find in AV 'fold' three times ('he that entereth not by the door into the sheep-*fold*' ; and 'other sheep I have which are not of this *fold* ; them also I must bring, and . . . there shall be one *fold* and one shepherd'), there is in the original a marked distinction. Two words, absolutely unconnected with each other, are employed. In v.[1], and in the first clause of v.[16], the Greek word is αὐλή = 'enclosure,' 'court,' 'fold,' in the strict sense. It is the word used of the enclosed *court* of the high priest's palace (Mt 26[3], Mk 14[54], Lk 22[55], Jn 18[15]), of the strong man's palace (Lk 11[21]), and of the outer court of the Temple (Rev 11[2]). In using this word our Lord seems to refer to those 'walls of partition' (cf. Eph 2[14]) which separated the Jews from the Gentiles and made them a nation by themselves. Within this Jewish *fold* (αὐλή), our Lord tells us that, at the time when He spoke, He had a number of sheep who were His own ; and also that, outside of it, among the Gentiles, dark and miserable as their condition was, He had other sheep, who were His already, and were known to Him, even if they knew it not themselves. These, too, He announces, He must bring, and put them along with His Jewish-born sheep ; 'and,' He adds, 'there shall be one *flock* (He uses here the other word ποίμνη), one shepherd.' He does not say there will be 'one *fold*' (αὐλή), or, indeed, any fold at all. He has unity in view for His sheep—union ; but not such as is to be secured by the erection round His flock of such outwardly-enclosing, or constraining 'walls of partition'—geographical or racial—as had hitherto divided nation from nation and Jew from Gentile. The union whereof He speaks is to be the union of a flock, which is kept together on the one hand by its own instinct of gregariousness, or the mutual affection of the members, and on the other hand by its common subjection to its 'one Shepherd,' who loves it, died for it, and whom through all its members it knows. It does not, however, follow that this unity is not a visible unity. The unity of the *flock*, as it moves along the road under its shepherd's guidance, is just as visible to the beholder as the unity of the *fold* whose white walls gleam from the hillside. The difference is not in regard to the visibility of the effect, but the nature of the unifying bond. The distinction is brought out in RV.

JAMES COOPER.

FLOOD.—The Flood is referred to only in Mt 24[38. 39] and its parallel Lk 17[27]. Jesus is speaking of the concealment of the day and hour of the coming of the Son of Man, and He uses the Flood as an illustration which would be well known to His hearers. Men and women were eating and drinking, marrying and giving in marriage, until the day that Noah entered the ark ; and did not know until the Flood came and took them all away. So it would be at the time of the coming of the Son of Man. Jesus was, at the time of speaking, warning men of His coming, and the warning was intended, doubtless, to be sufficient to turn them, if they would be turned, from their evil. The emphasis in the use of the illustration is upon the indifference and wickedness of the antediluvians, as paralleled by that of men in the future who would not receive and act upon the warnings now given. The Gospel use, then, of the Flood is, like the meaning of the word used (κατακλυσμός), neutral as to the important questions raised by the OT story of the Deluge. See art. 'Flood' in Hastings' *DB*, vol. ii.

O. H. GATES.

FLOWERS.—Palestine has a flora of wonderful wealth and variety. The known species exceed three thousand, and even this large list is probably far from complete. But numbers alone convey no adequate idea of its varied nature. This little land contains within its narrow limits the most remarkable diversities of soil, surface, and climate. As is the land so is its flora, which at the one extreme, amid the heights of Lebanon, is Alpine in its character, and at the other extreme, in the gorge of the Dead Sea, tropical.

In the NT there are very few references to flowers, and these are of the most general character (Ja 1[10. 11], 1 P 1[24]). In the Gospels the only mention of them is in the words of our Lord, 'Consider the lilies of the field' (Mt 6[23], Lk 12[27]). It is noteworthy that it is to their beauty that Christ appeals ; elsewhere in the NT flowers are the emblem of frailty and evanescence. But in spite of the comparative infrequency of Scripture allusions to them or praise of their beauty, the Jews were lovers of flowers. This is attested by the floral ornamentation on the woodwork of the oracle (1 K 6[18]), the folding-doors (6[35]), and the pillars of the temple (7[22]), the brim of the molten sea (7[26]), and the golden candlestick (Ex 25[31. 33]). From the Mishna we learn that at the Feast of Harvest (Ex 23[16]) the first crop of fruit offered at the altar was decked with flowers (*Bikkurim*, ii. 3).

Among the beautiful flowers of Palestine may be mentioned anemones, crocuses, cyclamens, gladioli, hyacinths, irises, poppies, roses, and tulips.

HUGH DUNCAN.

FLUTE - PLAYERS.—Flute-playing is referred to twice in the Gospels : once in the narrative as an expression of sorrow (Mt 9[23] αὐλητάς, AV 'minstrels,' RV 'flute-players') ; and once in the Lord's teaching as an expression of gladness (ηὐλήσαμεν Mt 11[17] with the parallel passage Lk 7[32] 'we [have] piped'). The latter use, which is referred to several times in the OT and the Apocrypha (1 K 1[40], Is 5[12] 30[29], Sir 40[21], 1 Mac 3[45]), is attested for the later Jews by the mention in the Mishna of 'flutes for a bride' (*Baba Mezia* vi. 1). The other use, the employment of flutes for mourning, seems to have been widely diffused and of great antiquity, for it is clearly alluded to by Jeremiah (48[36]) ; and can be traced over a large part of the Gentile world— Phœnicians, Carians, Greeks, Romans, and probably Assyrians. In Greek society (or at least some sections of it) the custom was so general that the flute player at funerals was described by a special term (τυμβαύλης Ælian. *Var. Hist.* xii. 43). For the Jewish life of the 1st and 2nd cents. A.D. there is ample evidence in the Mishna and elsewhere. 'Flutes for a corpse' are mentioned in *Baba Mezia* vi. 1, and in *Kethuboth* iv. 4 is the often cited rule that a man who had lost his wife must engage, no matter how poor he might be, not fewer than two flute-players and one wailing woman. A remarkable historical illustration is supplied by Josephus (*BJ* III. ix. 5). When the news of the capture of Jotapata by the Romans in the summer of 67 A.D. reached Jerusalem, 'most people engaged flute-players to lead their lamentations.' Another illustration comes from Roman history. At the funeral of the Emperor Claudius in 54 A.D. there were flute-players in the procession. These funeral musicians seem to have been generally, if not always, professionals, and to have been held in very low esteem. The class seems to be unknown to modern Syrian society. The wailing woman remains, but the funeral flautist has gone (Bauer, *Volksleben im Lande der Bibel*, 1903, p. 213).

LITERATURE.—Note of Wetstein on Mt 9[23]; Wünsche, *Neue Beiträge zur Erläuterung der Evangelien aus Talmud und Midrasch*, p. 125; Levy, *Chaldäisches Wörterbuch*, 2ó1a; art. 'Music' in Hastings' *DB* iii. 461.   W. TAYLOR SMITH.

FOAMING.—See EPILEPSY.

FOLD.—See FLOCK.

FOLLOWING.—'Follow' represents several Gr. words which it is desirable to distinguish as far as possible.

1. Most frequently, ἀκολουθέω with dative (but μεθ' ἡμῶν, Lk 9[49]; ὀπίσω μου, Mt 10[38]), in nearly every instance used of *following Christ*, except Mt 9[19], Mk 9[38] 14[13] 16[17] (Tr. WH), Jn 10[4] 11[31]. 2. ἐπακολουθέω, *to follow close upon* (Mk 16[20], 1 P 2[21]). 3. κατακολουθέω *to follow after* (Lk 23[55]). 4. παρακολουθέω, *to follow so as to be always beside, accompany* (metaphor. in Mk 16[17] where Tr. WH give ἀκολ.; but 'there is a meaning of closeness of attendance which makes παρακολουθέω more individual and probable,' Gould). The same word in Lk 1[3] is tr. in AV 'having had understanding of,' and RV 'having traced the course of,' where Eusebius and Epiphanius curiously took τᾶσιν as masc. 'having followed the eye-witnesses and ministers of the word' (see Blass, *Philology of the Gospels*, p. 17). 5. συνακολουθέω, *to follow with*, so RV (Mk 5[37] 14[51], Lk 23[49] with *var. lect.* ἀκολ. in the two former, probably a correction to the more usual form). 6. διώκω, *follow after* (Lk 17[23]), often in LXX in a good sense of those in search of one. 7. καταδιώκω (Mk 1[36]), *to pursue closely*, 'the κατα gives the idea of hard persistent search, as in our 'hunt down' (Gould). 8. δεῦτε ὀπίσω μου, 'come ye after me,' Mt 4[19] (AV 'follow'); cf. Mk 1[17].

That great multitudes followed Jesus during His ministry is repeatedly noted; cf. Mt 4[25] 8[1] 20[29] 21[9], Mk 5[24], Lk 23[27] (see CROWD, MULTITUDE); publicans and sinners also (ἠκολούθουν, אB, Vulg. Mk 2[15], cf. Lk 15[1]). 'Follow me' (ἀκολούθει μοι) was His call to discipleship, Mt 9[9] ‖ Lk 9[59], Jn 1[43]; δεῦρο ἀκολούθει μοι (Lk 18[22] ‖) and δεῦτε ὀπίσω μου (Mt 4[19] ‖) also occur. The command would be at once understood in this sense, for 'it was not only the practice of the Rabbis, but regarded as one of the most sacred duties for a Master to gather around him a circle of disciples' (Edersheim, *Life and Times*, i. 474). Hence 'following' was a mark of belonging to the band of disciples (Mk 9[38] ‖). At first it might seem to imply only 'come with me on this journey' (cf. Jn 1[37. 43]), but gradually they learned that it meant abandonment of previous occupations (Mt 4[20] 9[9]) and duties (Mt 8[22]), and possibly the dearest ties (Lk 14[26]), as well as a participation in dangers and even death (Mt 10[28. 38f.], Jn 16[2]). Such an intensified meaning of following is seen in the case of Peter (Jn 1[40f.], Mt 4[19], Jn 21[19]). The call of Jesus differed from that of other teachers in that He did not simply invite, but *commanded* obedience as One who had the right, and as if they literally belonged to Himself; the most peremptory claims to rule over the affections and wills of men are found in Mt. and Lk. rather than in Jn., and can be explained only by His being the supreme Lord of life (Liddon). Further, the disciples followed Him not merely to learn more doctrine, but to be prepared for future work (Mt 4[19]; and of the Apostles, Mk 3[14]). Mk 10[32] is especially noteworthy, describing vividly

the manner of following on the last journey to Jerusalem.

The literal meaning tends to merge partly or wholly into the metaphorical sense of conforming to the example of Jesus in living, and also, if need be, in dying; cf. Mt 10[38] ‖ 16[24], Jn 8[12] 12[26] 13[36], 1 P 2[21] ('follow his steps'), Rev 14[4]. The two meanings seem combined in Jn 21[19. 20]. V.[20] implies that Jesus moved away, inviting Peter to follow along the rough shore perhaps for private conversation; and John though uninvited also followed. But there is probably a reference also to Jn 13[36]; and the action of Peter was symbolical of that obedient following in the rugged path of Christian duty, in the work of the Apostolic ministry (Chrys.), in the way of martyrdom (Meyer), which would lead to participation in His Master's glory (see Godet's note). This command differed from the similar command given before the Resurrection, says Westcott, because 'it now required further the perception of His course; the spiritual discernment by which His movements can still be discovered; and yet, further, the readiness to accept martyrdom as the end.'

Lk 9[57f.] = Mt 8[19f.] is important. All three aspirants for admission into the inner circle seem to have been already disciples, cf. Mt 8[21], the use of 'Master' and 'Lord,' and the work contemplated (Lk 9[60. 62]). Probably the appointment of the Seventy was in view (Lk 10[1]), or less likely, of the Twelve (so Trench, comparing Mt 10[1], which, however, does not apply to the *choosing*, but to the *sending out* of the Apostles). These were (1) a scribe (εἷς γραμματεύς, Mt.), who came saying, 'Master, I will follow thee whithersoever thou goest.' He meant, perhaps, 'to the end of the journey, wherever it might be, not aware of the continual wandering life led by Jesus' (Wendt, *Teaching of Jesus*, ii. 69); but he was warned of the utter homelessness of the Son of Man, and was shown the necessity of counting the cost (cf. Lk 14[25f.]). (2) Another was called to follow, and professed readiness to obey but alleged a hindrance: 'Lord, suffer me first to go and bury my father.' The words 'go and bury' (ἀπελθόντι θάψαι), and 'leave the dead,' RV (ἄφες τοὺς νεκρούς), naturally imply, and are usually taken to mean, that his father was then lying dead (so early Fathers, Alford, Trench, Godet, Edersheim, etc.). It was a son's most sacred duty to perform the last offices, but this was one of the cases where the Call must take precedence of all else. His going might involve a delay of seven days (the period of pollution, Nu 19[11f.]), during which good impressions might be dulled; and Jesus would have left the district whither, taking Lk.'s order, He was not to return. This man, too, was being called to active work for God; cf. regulations in Lv 21[11], Nu 6[7]. But some later commentators, as Theophylact, suppose that the father was still alive though weak and frail, and that the son wished to remain with him until his death. Thus the seeming harshness of Christ's reply would be mitigated; and it is pointed out that as the burial usually took place on the day of death, it was unlikely that the man would leave his home during the interval between these two events. Wendt (*op. cit.* p. 70) quotes a striking illustration in support. A young Turk was advised by a missionary in Syria to make a tour of Europe, and answered, 'I must first of all bury my father.' The missionary expressed surprise at the news of his death, as he had hitherto been in good health; but the young man explained that he only meant that one must before all things devote himself to the duties owed to relatives. Jesus did not recognize such duties as sufficient to justify delay in preaching the gospel. Clem. Alex. adopted a tradition that this man was Philip (τοῦ Κυρίου λέγοντος τῷ Φιλίππῳ, ἄφες τοὺς νεκρούς, κ.τ.λ., Strom. iii. 4. 50, 51, Migne); if true, it may be taken as an admonition occasioned by some slackness or symptom of decadence on the part of the Apostle (Alf.). (3) A third offered to follow, but wished first to say farewell to his relatives: he showed a divided affection; apparently, therefore, his request involved special danger. A saying of farewell (ἀποτάσσεσθαι) in quite a different sense was necessary (Lk 14³³). Augustine says of these three: 'obtulit se unus ut eum sequeretur et reprobatus est, alius non audebat et excitatus est, tertius differebat et culpatus est.' Edersheim sums up the three vital conditions of following as here illustrated: (a) absolute self-denial and homelessness in the world; (b) immediate and entire self-surrender to Christ and His work; (c) a heart and affections simple, undivided, and set on Christ and His work, to which there is no other trial of parting like that which would involve parting from Him, no other or higher joy than that of following Him (Life and Times, ii. 134).

For the result and rewards of following see Jn 8¹², Mt 19²⁷ᶠ. ‖.

LITERATURE.—Cremer, Bib.-Theol. Lex. s.v. ἀκολουθέω; art. 'Follow' in Hastings' DB; Trench, Studies in the Gospels (No. 6); Wendt, The Teaching of Jesus, ii. p. 70; Liddon, The Divinity of our Lord, Lect. iv.; Edersheim, Life and Times of Jesus the Messiah; Commentaries of Godet, Westcott, etc.; Bruce, Kingdom of God, p. 222 f.; Expositor, iv. iv. [1891] 286 ff.　　　W. H. DUNDAS.

FOOD.—While this word does not occur in AV in the Gospels, the Greek words βρῶμα (Mt 14¹⁵, Mk 7¹⁹, Lk 3¹¹ 9¹³, and Jn 4³⁴) and βρῶσις (Jn 4³² and 6²⁷·⁵⁵), rendered 'meat,' would be in each case better rendered 'food.' The first word, βρῶμα, means anything eaten; while the second, βρῶσις, is used elsewhere in NT for 'the act of eating'; but in the Gospels three times (in John) for that which is eaten; twice as a general term for food (Jn 4³² 6²⁷), and once as contrasted with drink (6⁵⁵). In these passages in John's Gospel, Jesus uses the term figuratively, of spiritual nourishment, which He Himself could give, describing His own body as 'food indeed.'

The ordinary food in Christ's day consisted chiefly of flesh, cereals, fruits, and herbs. Of flesh, that of sheep, oxen, kids, birds (Mt 12¹² 25³², Lk 13¹⁵, Mt 10²⁹), as well as fish (Mt 7¹⁰, Lk 24⁴², Jn 6⁹ 21¹³) was in common use. Of cereals, wheat and barley were favourite food-stuffs (Mt 3¹², Mk 2²³⁻²⁵, Lk 3¹⁷, Jn 6⁹ 21¹³); of herbs there is mention of mint, anise, and cummin (Mt 23²³, Lk 11⁴²); of fruits, we hear of figs (Lk 13⁷, Mt 21¹⁸·¹⁹) and grapes (Mt 7¹⁶, Mk 12²). The cereals were prepared by grinding in crude mills, and the flour was made into loaves or cakes baked in ovens. Food was seasoned with salt (Mk 9⁵⁰); mustard leaves and cummin were used as condiments. See art. MEALS.

John the Baptist, like some others of his day, lived nearer to nature, as a rebuke of prevalent luxury, and chose the native food of the wilderness, 'locusts and wild-honey' (Mt 3⁴, Mk 1⁶). Jesus came 'eating and drinking' the ordinary food of His time, rebuking the artificial abstemiousness of the Pharisees (Mt 11¹⁸ᶠ·, Lk 7³³ᶠ·), as well as the too great anxiety of many as to what they should eat or drink (Mt 6²⁵ᶠ·, Lk 12²²⁻²⁶).

　　　　　E. B. POLLARD.

FOOL.—This word occurs 6 times in the AV of the Gospels as the translation of ἀνόητος (Lk 24²⁵), ἄφρων (11⁴⁰ 12²⁰), and μωρός (Mt 5²² 23¹⁷·¹⁹). In the RV it occurs only twice (Mt 5²² 23¹⁷), being in Mt 23¹⁹ omitted from the text, and in the three remaining places the rendering given is 'foolish.' Further, μωρός occurs in Mt 7²⁶ 25²·³·⁸, and in these

places, both in AV and RV, it is translated 'foolish.'

These three Greek words, confused more or less by the principal versions,—the Harklean Syriac and Coptic are exceptions,—are not synonyms. Ἀνόητος implies a lack of comprehension or understanding, and so is very fittingly used in Lk 24²⁵. Ἄφρων, signifying 'mindless' or 'senseless,' frequently carries with it, in Biblical usage (cf. its constant employment in the LXX of Proverbs), an underlying meaning of moral defect, impiety, or unbelief; while in μωρός (cf. μωραίνεσθαι, Mt 5¹³ 'to become insipid') the predominant meaning is 'dull,' 'witless,' 'stupid.'

The meaning of μωρέ in Mt 5²² has been much discussed. Alford mentions three interpretations: (1) that it is to be understood as the ordinary Greek word for 'fool'; (2) that it is a transliteration of the Heb. מֹרֶה (môreh), meaning 'rebel' or 'perverse' (cf. Nu 20¹⁰), a word which is put in RVm as an alternative to 'fool'; (3) that it bears the sense of ἄθεος according to the Heb. usage of נָבָל (nābāl, and cf. 1 S 25²⁵). However, there seems to be no real reason for supposing the word to be other than the Greek μωρός used in its ordinary Biblical sense.

Our Lord wished to emphasize the enormity of murder. He said, 'Ye have heard that it was said to them of old time, Thou shalt not kill, and Whosoever shall kill shall be in danger of the judgment. But I say unto you that whosoever is angry [the inward feeling] with his brother, is in danger of the judgment; and whosoever shall say to his brother, Raca [a contemptuous utterance arising from the inward anger, and probably no definite word; see RACA], shall be liable to a more solemn judgment; but whosoever shall say, Thou fool [the angry feeling formulated in a definite word of contemptuous depreciation], shall be worthy of a more dreadful doom.' This is, in the main, Augustine's explanation (de Serm. Dom. in Mont. I. ix.); and thus our Lord leaves it to be inferred how heinous actual murder is in His eyes.

Every use of the word 'fool' is not, of course, condemned. Our Lord Himself (see above) and St. Paul (Gal 3¹) employed it in needful rebuke; but that use of it is condemned which springs from angry feelings, and which is one step on the way to violence or even to murder.

LITERATURE.—Grimm-Thayer, Lex., under the Greek terms; Expos. Times, iv. [1893] 495, 514, xi. [1900] 381; Law, Serious Call, ch. xxi.; Dykes, Manifesto of the King, 232.
　　　　　ALBERT BONUS.

FOOLISHNESS.—In the Sermon on the Mount, Jesus points out the grave sin of saying to our brother, 'Thou fool' (μωρέ, Mt 5²²). When He likened His critics to children in the market-place who would play at neither a sad nor a merry game (Mt 11¹⁶⁻¹⁹), was He not saying in His heart, 'Ye fools'? But anger and contempt are the sources of the former; wonder and pity, mingled with indignation, shape the latter.* He who knew what was in man had occasion to marvel at the foolishness of men. That foolishness is a ruinous self-deception in spiritual things. He points out this folly in these classes:

1. *The foolishness of worldly men.*—God said to the rich man, 'Thou fool' (ἄφρων, Lk 12²⁰). The parable (vv.¹⁶⁻²¹) was inspired by a request which showed to Christ a heart so absorbed in thought of material good that it could not listen to His message. That fact gives us the point of view from which to consider the parable. The good of life cannot be in earth's riches which pass from owner to owner, and whose possession is at the mercy of death, which is only an accident to the immortal

---

* Cf. Lk 24²⁵ Σ ἀνόητοι, 'O foolish men' [AV 'O fools' is too harsh]. See preceding article.

soul (v. [20]). Covetousness, a man's absorption in heaping up and enjoying things, is folly in so far as it hinders him from attaining to the true riches, treasure of the soul laid up with God (vv. [15. 21]).

2. *The foolishness of the formalist,* who shuts his eyes (μωροὶ καὶ τυφλοί) to the spiritual side, the inward consecration which gives meaning and value to conduct or to things (Lk 11[40], Mt 23[17]).

3. *The foolishness of the religious.*—This thought occurs more frequently. It is a mark of our Lord's teaching that it is concerned rather with the subtler forms of evil which beset the religious class. He assumes that those sins of sense and temper which all the world condemns, need no condemnation from Him. This foolishness consists generally in a lack of seriousness, a lack of whole-heartedness and simplicity in faith and conduct. There are those who hear His words and do them·not (Mt 7[26. 27]). These are believers whose whole spirit is a contradiction, children of faith in mind, children of unfaith in conduct. This foolishness of believers is the formative thought of the parables of the Unjust Steward (Lk 16[3-9]) and of the Ten Virgins (Mt 25[1-13]). The meaning of the former parable is said by Jesus to be, that the children of this world are wiser in their generation than the children of light. That wisdom consists in greater singleness of vision both as regards ends and means. The steward sees his end clearly : he apportions his means to that end, uses as best he may what resources he has. The inference is left as to the wavering vision, both of end and of means, on the part of the children of light. The same thought is in the subsidiary and incidental lesson as to making friends by means of the mammon of unrighteousness. Selfishness, not brotherliness, rules this fraudulent steward, but he sees clearly those facts of our human life, gratitude and kindliness, which make brotherhood possible, and he turns them to his ends. On the other hand, brotherhood is the faith of the children of light, and yet they greatly neglect this rich field. The parable of the Ten Virgins completes this teaching of the foolishness of a half-hearted faith. It hints the irrevocable loss believers bring upon themselves thereby. Life's opportunities come unexpectedly —calls to service, possibilities of honour and spiritual enriching — and the half-hearted miss these. Their heart-culture, their spirits' discipline have been sleeping ; and the chances of life pass them by.

The seat of all these follies is the heart (Mk 7[22]). It is not any mere action of the intellect which here comes into condemnation. All these forms of foolishness are a ruining self-deception. The mind is there the servant of the heart whose desires have confused and led it astray.

RICHARD GLAISTER.

FOOT.—The references in this connexion arise chiefly from the fact that the foot in relationship to the head is the inferior part of the body.

1. *Humility and defilement.*—A still lower level was reached by the shoes or sandals, which were in direct contact with the common earth. John the Baptist indicated his inferiority to Christ by saying that he was unworthy to unfasten His shoelatchet (Mk 1[7]). To walk barefoot was the sign of a captive prisoner (Is 20[4]), and as a voluntary act of self-infliction often forms part of a personal vow. To be trodden under foot was the symbol of utter degradation (Mt 5[13], Lk 21[24], He 10[29]). At the entrance to an Oriental house the shoes are removed, not merely for the sake of cleanliness as a preliminary to sitting down with the feet drawn under the dress, but also out of regard to the sanctity of family life, so that no defilement may touch the rugs and mats that have been hallowed by prayer and the Divine presence. He who stood

on holy ground had to put off his shoes (Ex 3[5], Jos 5[15]).

Orientals are not accustomed to wear stockings with their open shoes, and it was an act not only of ceremonial duty, but of personal comfort, to bathe the feet after a journey over the hot and dusty ground. It was a courtesy due to a guest to see that this ministry was not omitted. Christ drew attention to the fact that in the house of one who prided himself upon his precise fulfilment of the Law this service had been more than rendered to Him by a woman whom the Pharisee despised as a sinner (Lk 7[44. 46]). The charge to His disciples to shake the dust from their feet wherever the message of the Kingdom was not received (Mt 10[14], Mk 6[11], Lk 9[5] 10[11]), was a demonstration to both parties of the unfitness of such people for its membership. When Christ washed the disciples' feet, the cleansing meant not only that the feet under which His sacred hands had been placed could never turn aside to paths of evil, but that they could never be set down with harsh and proud authority over the lives and rights of others. His service could never lay upon those disciples any greater humiliation than had been rendered to them. It became a law of the Kingdom to 'wash one another's feet' (Jn 13[5. 14]).

2. *Authority and subjection.*—To approach the feet of the great was the conceded right of the weak in seeking the presence and help of the powerful. To kneel down and clasp the feet and even to kiss them is still the Oriental preliminary to an important request. When inferiors salute those of higher rank, the first act of gesture is to lower the hand towards the ground as if to imply that the whole body should be there. Sometimes the word is allowed to do service for the deed, as when the supplicant says, 'Allow me to kiss your feet.' The impression meant to be produced is that the party addressed has the power to do what is asked, and that the only unsettled point is the question of his willingness (Mt 18[29] 20[20], Mk 1[40] 10[17]).

The foot on the neck as a symbol of conquest seems to have been borrowed from the primitive pastoral life. When an Oriental shepherd wishes to punish a straying and inattentive sheep, he casts it on its side, and with all his weight presses and rubs the iron-studded sole of his shoe against its neck (1 Co 15[25. 27]). In killing a serpent, the Syrian peasant, even with a stick in his hand, usually, after a blow or two, jumps upon the serpent, and by a quick succession of stamps bruises it to death (Ps 91[13], Ro 16[20]). To sit at the feet of his teacher was the attitude of the disciple (Mt 10[24], Lk 10[39], Ac 22[3]). The Pharisees thus sat in Moses' seat (Mt 23[2]).

The risen Lord was recognized by the marks in His hands and His feet (Lk 24[40]) ; see PRINT. On Mt 18[8] ‖ see ASCETICISM, p. 129.

G. M. MACKIE.

FOOTSTOOL (ὑποπόδιον).—With the single exception of Ja 2[3] the word is used figuratively in the NT, to express the idea of 'subjection' or 'complete control.' In this sense it occurs frequently in the Gospels : *e.g.* Mt 22[44], Mk 12[36], Lk 20[43], where the Synoptists record Christ's quotation from Ps 110—a psalm always regarded by the Jews as distinctly Messianic. In Mt 22[44] RV, on the authority of some of the most ancient MSS and versions, accepts ὑποκάτω instead of ὑποπόδιον, and translates, 'till I put thine enemies under thy feet.' Similarly in Mk 12[36] ὑποκάτω is read by many ancient authorities, and is adopted by WH. Here, however, RV retains ὑποπόδιον (with marg. note) ; but (as also in Lk 20[43] and Mt 5[35]) translates more correctly 'footstool of thy (or his) feet' instead of AV 'thy (or his) footstool.'

In its application to Christ the word shows Him in His Kingly office triumphing over His enemies, and bringing all men into captivity to His obedience ; cf. 1 Co 15²⁵ 'For he must reign till he hath put all enemies under his feet.'

DUGALD CLARK.

FORCE.—**1.** Force, as defined by modern science, is inherent in matter and inseparable from it. It is defined also as the power of doing work. The modes and the effects of its activities are mechanical. It can neither exist nor act, therefore, within the moral sphere of the universe. And from this fact it follows that force and its activities are entirely foreign to the essential facts and truths of Christianity. This truth is recognized by the four Gospels, for in their records of Christ's life and mission, the entire import of which was moral, no word is employed capable of being construed into the meaning of force as just explained. The word 'force' occurs only twice in these records (Mt 11¹², Jn 6¹⁵ EV); and in both cases it is used as the translation of ἁρπάζω, which signifies *to seize* or *carry off* (an object by physical force or compulsion). It is the use of physical force or compulsion that is denoted by St. John's statement that the people wanted to take Jesus by force to make Him a king ; and it is probable that our Lord had the employment of force of the same kind in His mind when He said, as St. Matthew reports : ' From the days of John the Baptist until now the kingdom of heaven suffereth violence (βιάζεται = 'is carried by force *or* assault'), and the violent (or assailants) take it by force' (ἁρπάζουσιν). The order of ideas here expressed is exactly in terms of the principle of domination by force, which was universal in antiquity ; a principle which was entirely antagonistic to His essential ideas as to the moral nature of the kingdom of heaven, and the moral conditions by means of which alone entrance to it could be gained. And as He fully realized that the principle alluded to was hostile to the nature, interests, and laws of the heavenly kingdom, and warned His disciples against it (Mk 10⁴²⁻⁴⁵), it may be concluded that He did not express Himself in the language of the force which the dominating powers of the ancient world employed, meaning thereby that places in the kingdom of heaven, as He understood and wished His hearers to understand the latter, were in great demand, and that men were eagerly doing their utmost to secure them. His real meaning is not quite apparent. He Himself represented the kingdom of God. He had come to found it. In His life and activities its principles came to perfect realization. To subject Him in any way to the abusive treatment of the force of dominating powers or authorities, was to do ' violence ' in His Person to the kingdom of heaven ; and it was also ' to take' the kingdom, in the sense of making it in His Person an object of violent abuse. When He spoke the words in question His ministry in Galilee was closing in disappointing circumstances. John the Baptist had been already made a victim of violent abuse ; and He knew that His 'hour,' a more terrible destiny than John's, would not be long delayed. Might it not be His cross, then, that was in His mind when He spoke the words in question ? [For the more usual view that the violence which takes the kingdom by force is the friendly violence of those who seek to enter it, see A. B. Bruce, *Expositor's Gr. Test. in loc.*, *Expositor*, I. v. [1877] p. 197 ff.].

2. 'Force,' however, is a term which is not always used in its strictly scientific sense. In ordinary use it is synonymous with *strength* or *power*. '**Power**' is a word of frequent occurrence in the Gospels, and in many instances where it is employed it possesses moral significance of very high value. The word ' power ' in the EV of the Gospels is represented by two Greek terms in the original, viz. ἐξουσία and δύναμις, the former of which is sometimes translated by the word ' authority.'

'Εξουσία may be taken first. Power in the sense of this word is not always spoken of as *Christ's* power ; but it is as His power that it has its chief interest here. The power (ἐξουσία) that Christ possessed was a power in which might was combined with right ; and this is why it is sometimes called authority in the Gospels and sometimes power. He was able to do things because He had the right to do them ; and no one had any right to hinder Him or to call Him in question. And the things that He had the right and the power to do were all of a nature purely moral ; and things, moreover, which He alone could do, and which were of transcendent importance. What were they ? (1) He, as the Son of man, had power on earth to forgive sins (Mt 9⁶, Mk 2¹⁰). (2) He has power to give eternal life to those whom the Father has given to Him (Jn 17²). (3) He has power, or authority, also to execute judgment, because He is the Son of man (Jn 5²⁷). (4) He is invested with all power in heaven and in earth (Mt 28¹⁸). (5) Lastly, He had power to lay down His life on earth, and power to take it again (Jn 10¹⁸). The explanation of the various forms of power (ἐξουσία) possessed by Christ, and of the grounds on which His claim to the possession of them rests, lies in a domain of essential Christian truth.

It needs to be strongly emphasized that all the forms of the power in question are moral. The power to forgive sins, to judge men as moral beings, to give eternal life to men as moral beings, to lay down one's life in perfect self-sacrificing love and service for others' good, to exercise the moral government of heaven and earth,—to do all these things, to have the right and the power to do them, manifestly means the possession and the exercise of moral power of the highest possible order. Again, it is evident that this power in its nature and in all its forms of manifestation belongs to the supernatural order of things. But in the sphere of things into which the order of ideas considered here introduces one, the supernatural and the natural are one. It is within the sphere of the moral order of things that Christ, in His moral position as Mediator between God and men, exercised, or exercises, the forms of His power alluded to. And within this moral sphere there is no absolute distinction between the natural and the supernatural. Here all that is in harmony with God's will and purpose is in Him, and He is in it. This is the real truth ; and whether it be called natural or supernatural is only a difference in name.

Once more, all the forms of power that Christ claimed for Himself were His by delegation from God. But this does not mean that He had the right and the power to exercise them in a *merely official* capacity, without their having any relation to and dependence on what He was as a moral Being. He was invested with them by God, as all but one of the passages referred to above indicate. But one of the passages tells us that He had power on earth to forgive sins *as the Son of man* ; and another, that God had given Him authority to execute Judgment *because He was the Son of man*. He was both the Son of God and the Son of man in all that He was as a moral Being when on the earth, exercising the high moral powers that He claimed to possess. And it is as the same moral Being, now glorified, that He exercises every moral power that He claimed as His own by Divine gift and prerogative. In other words, the power to do all the things that have been specified is His because of what He *is as a moral Being*. To forgive sins, to judge men, etc., are all acts of moral power which belong to the administration of the moral order of the world as it now is *with Christ in it* as the one only Mediator between God and men. And the reason why the administration of all things belonging to the moral relations between God and men is in His hands, is—that in His life and death on earth He earned the moral right to occupy this momentous position of mediation and power. For He fills this position and administers its powers as one who has proved Himself all that God can be to men, and all that every man ought to become and be to God. He is thus, because of what He is, the Divinely human and the humanly Divine, true way of forgiveness, of judgment, of life, and of moral government for men. From His Father's own commandment He had the power to lay down His life, in living and in dying to qualify Himself for this destiny of absolute pre-eminence in the moral universe. And as the Father commanded Him, so He did. Therefore His name is now above every name (Ph 2⁵⁻¹¹, Jn 17²⁰⁻²⁶).

Δύναμις is the other word which is translated 'power' in the EV of the Gospels. It is noteworthy that none of the Evangelists includes the word 'energy' (ἐνέργεια) in his terminology; a word which St. Paul employed to denote the effectual working of God's redeeming power as manifested in (1) the raising of Christ from the dead, and in the setting of Him at God's right hand in the heavenly places, *i.e.* in the moral order of things (Eph 1¹⁹⁻²³); (2) the Divine grace that was bestowed on St. Paul himself by the working in him of Divine power (Eph 3⁷); (3) the working of the same Divine power in the creation or evolution of an order of moral unity in the relations of *all* men to one another in Christ; (4) the working of the same power as in Christ as destined to fashion the resurrection body of believers into the glorious likeness of His own, 'according to the working whereby he is able even to subject all things unto himself' (Ph 3²¹). But the absence from the Gospels of the term 'energy,' which occupies a place of such extensive and high importance in St. Paul's general conception of essential Christianity, does not imply the absence from them of that order of Divine working for which the word stands in the Apostle's writings. The entire body of moral phenomena, reproduced by the Evangelists in their several records, and in which the power of God in Christ was manifested, was a revelation of the Divine energy in St. Paul's sense of the word. But, further, the meaning of the word ἐνέργεια is included in that of the word δύναμις as the latter is used in the Gospels; for in them it signifies, on the one hand, the possession of power capable of action; and, on the other, power manifesting itself in a state of activity, in which case it appears in the form of energy. Power, then, as δύναμις, holds a fundamental place in the Gospels as records of how Christ conceived it and manifested it in His activities.

(1) Christ regarded the power with which He associated Himself and His activities and their effects as moral, and as having its ultimate source in God. He conceived God as a moral Being, and to Him as such He ascribed the power alluded to (Mt 22²⁹ 26⁶⁴, Mk 9¹ 14⁶², Lk 22⁶⁹).—(2) But, again, such being Christ's view, He never conceived of Himself as possessing and exercising power independently of God. His feeling of absolute dependence on God for power had a deep and controlling place in His consciousness. It was the feeling He gave unreserved and clear expression to when He said, for instance, 'The Son can do nothing of himself, but what he seeth the Father do'; 'I can of mine own self do nothing'; and, again, 'The Father that dwelleth in me, he doeth

the works' (Jn 5¹⁹· ³⁰ 14¹⁰).—(3) It was, therefore, through His dependence on God that our Lord obtained the power by means of which He was enabled to attain to His perfect moral self-realization, and by means of which He was enabled to finish the work His Father had given Him to do. And the question thus arises as to how He was kept in possession of a continuous supply of power for the great moral task and service of His life. The answer to this question is to be found in the Gospels. The secret of His strength lay in His inner life of perfect, never-broken union and fellowship with His Father in all things. But this life of union and fellowship with His Father needed itself to be continually maintained; and the Gospels also show how this was done by Him. He did it by paying perfect loyalty to His dependence on His Father; by striving in every situation of His life freely and perfectly to identify Himself with His Father's will and purpose for His life and His mission; by means of habits of self-discipline and prayer (Lk 3²¹· ²² 4¹⁻¹⁴ 6¹² 9²⁸⁻³⁵ 22³⁹⁻⁴⁶, Jn 3³⁴ 8²⁸· ²⁹).

(4) Christ, moreover, believed that His disciples needed the same Divine power that was His strength, in order to be able to fulfil the moral task in life to which He called them; and He believed that this power would be available for them as it had been for Himself during His life on earth. His Spirit in them would be the very power (δύναμις) that had been His own. And in their task of overcoming temptation, of moral self-realization, of achieving good in service for the kingdom of God, they would find His Spirit's power all-sufficient for them. But they would need to remember that the servant was not greater than his Lord. They would need to depend on Him as He depended on God. They would need to abide in union and fellowship with Him. They must keep His words as being the Father's words. And they must also follow Him in the path of humility, self-discipline, prayer, and self-denial (Mt 10³⁸ 17¹⁹⁻²¹ 26⁴¹, Lk 11⁹⁻¹³ 22³¹· ³² 24⁴⁹, Jn 12²⁴⁻²⁶ 13¹³⁻¹⁷ 14¹⁰⁻¹⁸ 15⁴ 17¹¹⁻¹⁹, Ac 1⁴· ⁵).

(5) It was, finally, in the exercise of the Divine power here referred to that our Lord performed those extraordinary works of His to which the name 'miracle' has been given. In some of the Gospels they are called 'mighty works' (*e.g.* Mt 11²⁰, Mk 6⁵, Lk 19³⁷). These works of power (δυνάμεις) were only special forms in which was manifested the same power that was revealed in so many other ways in the moral activities of Christ's life. He wrought His miracles by the same power that enabled Him perfectly to overcome all the temptations of His life, and to accomplish all those other things in which He fulfilled His Father's will and purpose.

Again, it never occurred to Him that in the doing of His mighty works He contravened or suspended any of those uniformities of nature to which the term 'law' is applied by modern science; though with many of those uniformities He was quite familiar, and, besides, attached to them great importance. The question raised for science by His mighty works is in reality not a question of natural *law*; it is a question of natural *force* or *energy*. Are the forces inherent and operative in the physical or moral order of the world of such a nature as to render it impossible for the miracles ascribed to Christ's power to have happened? That is the real point at issue as between the testimony of the Gospels and Science. And the man of science who has the most extensive and the deepest knowledge of the energy or forces of the Universe, and who has therefore entered furthest into the presence of the marvels and the mysteries of these forces and their modes of manifestation, would be the last person to answer the question in the affirmative.

Once more, the mighty works ascribed to Christ in the Gospels are not the most wonderful of His achievements. It is often pointed out in defence of these mighty works, and rightly, that they were wrought to serve beneficent ends, that they were manifestations of power and love ministering in various ways to human well-being ; and that as so viewed, they were originally and homogeneously related to all the other beneficent activities of our Lord's ministry. It is also argued in favour of the possibility and the historical truth of the miracles in question, that His perfect personal sinlessness and holiness was a moral miracle as great as, if not greater than, any of the mighty works reported by the Evangelists as performed by Him. There is justice in this argument. It was by the power of God immanent and operative in Him, and by His own free co-operation therewith, that He achieved His perfect moral self-realization in which He was morally as perfect as God. That was a miracle indeed ; and, to say the least, there is no mightier work on record in the Gospels and represented there as wrought by Him in the exercise of the Divine power of which He was a personal organ. See, further, MIRACLE.

But that was only the beginning of the mightiest work of all with which the power of God in Christ is associated, and which is only coming slowly to manifestation in the moral progress of humanity. Christ in the power of His Spirit is in the moral life of mankind. He is morally re-creating the life of the human race. The moral order of the world is being evolved by means of His moral power as the Mediator between God and men. By means of His moral power in man's life and history, He is conducting humanity onwards in the path that will bring it to a perfect moral destiny in the kingdom of God. This is the greatest, mightiest of all His miracles ; and whosoever understands the momentousness of the moral task it implies will not stumble at any of the mighty works on record in the Gospels.

LITERATURE.—On ἐξουσία and δύναμις see the *Lexicons* of Cremer and Grimm-Thayer, *s.vv.* On Christ's miraculous power see art. 'Miracles' in Hastings' *DB* ; Mozley, *Bampton Lectures*, esp. Lect. VI. 　　　　　　W. D. THOMSON.

FORERUNNER.—See JOHN THE BAPTIST.

FORESIGHT.—The interest of the student of the Gospels, and of the life of Jesus which forms their substance, in the topic of this article, is two-fold. Jesus is represented in the Gospels as at once the object and the subject of the most detailed foresight. The work which He came to do was a work ordained in the counsels of eternity, and in all its items prepared for beforehand with the most perfect prevision. In addressing Himself to the accomplishment of this work Jesus proceeded from the beginning in the fullest knowledge of the end, and with the most absolute adjustment of every step to its attainment. It is from this double view - point that each of the Evangelists depicts the course of our Lord's life on earth. They consentiently represent Him as having come to perform a specific task, all the elements of which were not only determined beforehand in the plan of God, but adumbrated, if somewhat sporadically, yet with sufficient fulness for the end in view, in the prophecies of the OT. And they represent Him as coming to perform this task with a clear consciousness of its nature and a competent control of all the means for its discharge, so that His whole life was a conscientious fulfilment of a programme, and moved straight to its mark. The conception

of foresight thus dominates the whole Evangelical narrative.

It is not necessary to dwell at length upon the Evangelists' conception of our Lord's life and work as *the fulfilment of a plan Divinely predetermined for Him.* It lies on the face of their narratives that the authors of the Gospels had no reservation with respect to the all-embracing predestination of God (cf. Hastings' *DB* iv. 54–56) ; and least of all could they exclude from it this life and work which was to them the hinge upon which all history turns. To them accordingly our Lord is by way of eminence 'the man of destiny,' and His whole life (Lk 2⁴⁹ 4⁴³) was governed by 'the δεῖ of the Divine counsel.' Every step of His pathway was a 'necessity' to Him, in the fulfilment of the mission for which He had 'come forth' (Mk 1³⁸, cf. Swete), or as St. Luke (4⁴³) in quite Johannine wise (5²³· ²⁴· ³⁰· ³⁶· ³⁸ 6²⁹· ³⁸· ³⁹· ⁴⁰ *et passim*) expresses it, 'was sent' (cf. Mt 10⁴⁰, Mk 9³⁷, Lk 9⁴⁸ 10¹⁶ ; Mt 15²⁴ 21³⁷, Mk 12⁶, Lk 20¹³, cf. Swete on Mk 9³⁷). Especially was all that concerned His departure, the accomplishment of which (Lk 9³¹, cf. v.⁵¹) was His particular task, under the government of this 'Divine necessity' (Mt 16²¹ 26⁵⁴, Mk 8³¹, Lk 9²² 17²⁵ 22²²· ³⁷ 24⁷· ⁴⁴, Jn 3¹⁴ 20⁹, cf. Ac 2²³ 3¹⁸ 4²⁸, and Westcott on Jn 20⁹). His final journey to Jerusalem (Mt 16²¹), His rejection by the rulers (Mk 8³¹, Lk 9²² 17²⁵), His betrayal (Lk 24⁷), arrest (Mt 26⁵⁴), sufferings (Mt 26⁵⁴, Mk 8³¹, Lk 9²² 17²⁵), and death (Mt 16²¹, Mk 8³¹, Lk 9²²) by crucifixion (Lk 24⁷, Jn 3¹⁴), His rising again (Jn 20⁹) on the third day (Mt 16²¹, Mk 8³¹, Lk 9²² 24⁷· ⁴⁴)—each item alike is declared to have been 'a matter of necessity in pursuance of the Divine purpose' (Meyer, Mt 24⁶), 'a necessary part of the destiny assigned our Lord' (Meyer, Mt 26⁵⁶). 'The death of our Lord' thus appears 'not as the accidental work of hostile caprice, but (cf. Ac 2²³ 3¹⁸) the necessary result of the Divine predestination (Lk 22²²), to which Divine δεῖ (Lk 24²⁶) the personal free action of man had to serve as an instrument' (Meyer, Ac 4²⁸).

How far the several events which entered into this life had been prophetically announced is obviously, in this view of it, a mere matter of detail. All of them lay open before the eyes of God ; and the only limit to pre-announcement was the extent to which God had chosen to reveal what was to come to pass, through His servants the prophets. In some instances, however, the prophetic announcement is particularly adduced as the ground on which recognition of the necessity of occurrence rests. The fulfilment of Scripture thus becomes regulative for the life of Jesus. Whatever stood written of Him in the Law or the Prophets or the Psalms (Lk 24⁴⁴) must needs (δεῖ) be accomplished (Mt 26⁵⁴, Lk 22³⁷ 24²⁶, Jn 20⁹). Or, in another form of statement, particularly frequent in Mt. (1²² 2¹⁵· ²³ 4¹⁴ 8¹⁷ 12¹⁷ 13³⁵ 21⁴ 26⁵⁶) and Jn. (12³⁸ 13¹⁸ 15²⁵ 17¹² 19²⁴· ³⁶), but found also in the other Evangelists (Mk 14⁴⁹, Lk 4²¹), the several occurrences of His life fell out as they did, 'in order that what was spoken by the Lord' through the prophets or in Scripture, 'might be fulfilled' (cf. Mt 2¹⁷ 26⁵⁴ 27⁹, Lk 24⁴⁴ ; in Jn 18⁹· ³², Lk 24⁴⁴ declarations of Jesus are treated precisely similarly). That is to say, 'what was done stood . . . in the connexion of the Divine necessity, as an actual fact, by which prophecy was destined to be fulfilled. The Divine decree expressed in the latter *must* be accomplished, and *to that end this . . . came to pass*, and that, *according to the whole of its contents*' (Meyer, Mt 1²²). The meaning is, not that there lies in the OT Scriptures a complete predictive account of all the details of the life of Jesus, which those skilled in the interpretation of Scripture might read off from its pages at will. This programme in its detailed completeness lies only in the Divine purpose ; and in Scripture only so far forth as God has chosen to place it there for the guidance or the assurance of His people. The meaning is rather that all that stands written of Jesus in the OT Scriptures has its certain fulfilment in Him ; and that enough stands written of Him there to assure His followers that in the course of His life, and in its, to them, strange and unexpected ending, He was not the prey of chance or the victim of the hatred of men, to the marring of His work or perhaps even the defeat of His mission, but was following step by step, straight to its goal, the predestined pathway marked out for Him in the counsels of eternity, and sufficiently revealed from of old in the Scriptures to enable all who were not 'foolish and slow of heart to believe in all that the prophets have spoken,' to perceive that the Christ must needs have lived just this life and fulfilled just this destiny.

That the whole course of the life of Jesus, and especially its culmination in the death which He died, was foreseen and afore-prepared by God, enters, thus, into the very substance of the Evangelical narrative. It enters equally into its very substance that *this life was from the beginning lived out by Jesus Himself in full view of its drift and its issue.* The Evangelists are as far from representing Jesus as driven blindly onwards by a Divine destiny unknown to Himself, along courses not of His own choosing, to an unanticipated end, as they are from representing Him as thwarted in His purposes, or limited in His achievement, or determined or modified in His aims or methods, by the conditions which from time to time emerged in His way. The very essence of their representation is that Jesus came into the world with a definite mission to execute, of the nature of which He was perfectly aware, and according to which He ordered the whole course of His life as it advanced under His competent control unswervingly to its preconceived mark. In their view His life was lived out, not in ignorance of its issues, or in the form of a series of trials and corrections, least of all in a more or less unavailing effort to wring success out of failure; but in complete knowledge of the counsels of God for Him, in perfect acquiescence in them, and in careful and voluntary fulfilment of them. The 'Divine δεῖ' which governed His life is represented as fully recognized by Himself (Mt 16²¹, Mk 8³¹, Lk 4⁴³ 9²² 17²⁵ 24⁷, Jn 3¹⁴ 12³⁴), and the fulfilment of the intimations of prophecy in His life as accepted by Him as a rule for His voluntary action (Mt 26⁵⁴, Lk 22³⁷ 24²⁶. ⁴⁴, Jn 2⁰⁹, Mk 14⁴⁹, Lk 4²¹, Jn 13¹⁸ 15²⁵ 17¹²; cf. Mt 13¹⁴ 15⁷ 24¹⁵ 26⁵⁶, Mk 7⁶). Determining all things, determined by none, the life He actually lived, leading up to the death He actually died, is in their view precisely the life which from the beginning He intended to live, ending in precisely the death in which, from the beginning, He intended this life to issue, undeflected by so much as a hair's-breadth from the straight path He had from the start marked out for Himself in the fullest prevision and provision of all the so-called chances and changes which might befall Him. Not only were there no surprises in life for Jesus (cf. art. AMAZEMENT, p. 48), and no compulsions ; there were not even 'influences,' as we speak of 'influences' in a merely human career. The mark of this life, as the Evangelists depict it, is its calm and quiet superiority to all circumstance and condition, and to all the varied forces which sway other lives ; its prime characteristics are voluntariness and independence. Neither His mother, nor His brethren, nor His disciples, nor the people He came to serve, nor His enemies bent upon His destruction, nor Satan himself with his tempta-

tions, could move Him one step from His chosen path. When men seemed to prevail over Him they were but working His will ; the great 'No one has taken my life away from me ; I have power to lay it down, and I have power to take it again' (Jn 10¹⁸), is but the enunciation for the supreme act, of the principle that governs all His movements. His own chosen pathway ever lay fully displayed before His feet ; on it His feet fell quietly, but they found the way always unblocked. What He did, He came to do ; and He carried out His programme with unwavering purpose and indefectible certitude. So at least the Evangelists represent Him. (Cf. the first half of a striking article on ' Die Selbständigkeit Jesu,' by Trott, in Luthardt's *ZKWL*, 1883, iv. 233–241 ; in its latter half the art. falls away from its idea, and ends by making Jesus absolutely dependent on Scripture for His knowledge of God and Divine things : 'We have no right whatever to maintain that Jesus received revelations from the Father otherwise than through the medium of the sacred Scriptures ; that is a part of His complete humanity' (p. 238)).

The signature of this supernatural life which the Evangelists depict Jesus as living, lies thus in the perfection of the foresight by which it was governed. Of the reality of this foresight they leave their readers in no doubt, nor yet of its completeness. They suggest it by the general picture they draw of the self-directed life which Jesus lived in view of His mission. They record repeated instances in which He mentions beforehand events yet to occur, or foreshadows the end from the beginning. They connect these manifestations of foresight with the possession by Him of knowledge in general, in comprehension and penetration alike far beyond what is native to man. It may perhaps be natural to surmise in the first instance that they intend to convey merely the conviction that in Jesus was manifested a prophet of supreme greatness, in whom, as the culminating example of prophecy (cf. Ac 3²². ²³), resided beyond precedent the gifts proper to prophets. There can be no question that to the writers of the Gospels Jesus was 'the incarnate ideal of the prophet, who, as such, forms a class by Himself, and is more than a prophet' (this is what Schwartzkopff thinks Him, *The Prophecies of Jesus Christ*, p. 7). They record with evident sympathy the impression made by Him at the outset of His ministry, that God had at last in Him visited His people (Mk 6¹⁵, Lk 7¹⁶, Jn 4¹⁹ 9¹⁷) ; they trace the ripening of this impression into a well-settled belief in His prophetic character (Mt 21¹¹, Lk 24¹⁹, Mt 21⁴⁶, Lk 7³⁹, Jn 7⁴⁰) ; and they remark upon the widespread suspicion which accompanied this belief, that He was something more than *a* prophet—possibly one of the old prophets returned, certainly a very special prophet charged with a very special mission for the introduction of the Messianic times (Mt 16¹⁴, Mk 6·⁵ 8²⁸, Lk 9⁸· ¹⁹, Jn 6¹⁴ 7⁴⁰). They represent Jesus as not only calling out and accepting this estimate of Him, but frankly assuming a prophet's place and title (Mt 13⁵⁷, Mk 6⁴, Lk 4²⁴, Jn 4⁴⁴, Lk 13³³), exercising a prophet's functions, and delivering prophetic discourses, in which He unveils the future (Mt 24²¹, Mk 13²³, Jn 14²⁹ ; cf. Mt 28⁶, Lk 24⁴⁴, and such passages as Mt 26³². ³⁴, Mk 16⁷). Nevertheless it is very clear that in their allusions to the supernatural knowledge of Jesus, the Evangelists suppose themselves to be illustrating something very much greater than merely prophetic inspiration. The specific difference between Jesus and a prophet, in their view, was that while a prophet's human knowledge is increased by many things revealed to him by God (Am 3⁷), Jesus participated in all the fulness of the Divine knowledge (Mt 11²⁷, Lk 10²², Jn 16¹⁵ 18⁴ 16³⁰ 21¹⁷), so that all that is knowable lay open before Him (Jn 17¹⁰). The Evangelists, in a word, obviously intend to attribute Divine omniscience to Jesus, and in their adduction of instances of His supernatural knowledge, whether with respect to hidden things or to those yet buried in the future, are illustrating His possession of this Divine omniscience (cf. Muirhead, *The Eschatology of Jesus*, p. 119, where, in partial correction of the more inadequate statement of p. 48, there is recognized in the Evangelists at least a 'tendency' to attribute to our Lord ' Divine dignity ' and 'literal omniscience ').

That this is the case with St. John's Gospel is very commonly recognized (for a plain statement of the evidence see Karl Müller, *Göttliches Wissen und göttliche Macht des johann. Christus*, 1882, § 4, pp. 29–47 : ' Zeugnisse des vierten Evangeliums für Jesu göttliches Wissen '). It is not too much to say, indeed, that one of the chief objects which the author of that Gospel set before himself was to make clear to its readers the superhuman knowledge of Jesus, with especial reference, of course, to His own career. It therefore records direct ascriptions of omniscience to Jesus, and represents them as favourably received by Him (Jn 16³⁰ 21¹⁷ ; cf. Liddon, *Bampton Lectures*, ed. 4, 1869, p. 466). It makes it almost the business of its opening chapters to exhibit this omniscience at work in the especially Divine form (Lk 16¹⁵, Ac 1²⁴, He 4¹², Ps 138 (139) ², Jer 17¹⁶ 20¹² ; cf. Swete on Mk 2⁸) of immediate, universal, and complete knowledge of the thoughts and intents of the human heart (cf. Westcott on Jn 2²⁵), laying down the general thesis in 2²⁴· ²⁵ (cf. 6⁶⁴· ⁷⁰ 21¹⁷), and illustrating it in detail in the cases of all with whom Jesus came into contact in the opening days of His ministry (cf. Westcott on Jn 1⁴⁷), Peter (1⁴²), Philip (1⁴³), Nathanael (1⁴⁷), Mary (2⁴), Nicodemus (3), the woman of Samaria (4). In the especially striking case of the choice of Judas Iscariot as one of the Apostles, it expressly explains that this was due to no ignorance of Judas' character or of his future action (6⁶⁴· ⁷⁰ 13¹¹), but was done as part of our Lord's voluntary execution of His own well-laid plans. It pictures Jesus with great explicitness as prosecuting His whole work in full knowledge of all the things that were coming upon Him (Jn 18⁴, cf. Westcott), and with a view to subjecting them all to His governing hand, so that His life from the beginning should run steadily onward on the lines of a thoroughly wrought-out plan (Jn 1⁴⁷ 2¹⁹· ²⁴ 3¹⁴ 6⁵¹· ⁶⁴· ⁷⁰ 7⁶ 8²⁸ 10¹⁵· ¹⁸ 12⁷· ²³ 13¹· ¹¹· ²¹· ³⁸ 14²⁹ 16⁵· ³² 18⁴· ⁹).

It is difficult to see, however, why St. John's Gospel should be separated from its companions in this matter (Schenkel says frankly that it is only because there is no such passage in St. John's Gospel as Mk 13³², on which see below. Whatever else must be said of W. Wrede's *Das Messiasgeheimnis*, etc., 1901, it must be admitted that it has broken down this artificial distinction between the Gospel of John and the Synoptics). If they do not, like St. John (16³⁰ 21¹⁷), record direct ascriptions of precise omniscience to Jesus by His followers, they do, like St. John, represent Him as Himself claiming to be the depository and distributer of the Father's knowledge (Mt 11²¹⁻³⁰, Lk 10²²⁻²⁴). Nor do they lag behind St. John in attributing to Jesus the Divine prerogative of reading the heart (Mt 9⁴, Meyer ; Mk 2⁵· ⁸ 8¹⁷ 12¹⁵· ⁴⁴, Swete, p. lxxxviii ; Lk 5²² 7³⁹) or the manifestation, in other forms, of God-like omniscience (Mt 17²⁷ 21², Mk 11² 14¹³, Lk 5⁴ 19³⁰ 22¹⁰ ; cf. O. Holtzmann, *War Jesus Ekstatiker?* p. 14 and p. 15, note). Least of all do they fall behind St. John in insisting upon the perfection of the foresight of Jesus in all

matters connected with His own life and death (Mt 9¹⁵ 12⁴⁰ 16²¹ 20¹⁸· ²²· ²⁸ 26²· ²¹· ³⁴· ⁵⁰, Mk 2¹⁹ 8³¹ 9³¹ 10³³· ³⁹· ⁴⁵ 11² 14⁸· ¹³· ¹⁸· ³⁰, Lk 8³⁴ 9²²· ⁴⁴· ⁵¹ 12⁵⁰ 13³⁵ 17²⁵ 18³¹ 19³⁰ 22¹⁰· ²¹· ³⁴· ³⁷ 24⁴⁴). Nothing could exceed the detailed precision of these announcements,—a characteristic which has been turned, of course, to their discredit as genuine utterances of Jesus by writers who find difficulty with detailed prediction. 'The form and contents of these texts,' remarks Wrede (*Messiasgeheimnis*, etc. p. 88), 'speak a language which cannot be misunderstood. They are nothing but a short summary of the Passion history—" cast, of course, in the future tense."' '"The Passion-history,"' he proceeds, quoting Eichhorn, '"could certainly not be more exactly related in few words."' In very fact, it is perfectly clear—whether they did it by placing upon His lips predictions He never uttered and never could have uttered, is another question—that the Evangelists designed to represent Jesus as endowed with the absolute and unlimited foresight consonant with His Divine nature (see Liddon, *Bampton Lectures*, ed. 4, p. 464 ff. ; and cf. A. J. Mason, *The Conditions of our Lord's Life on Earth*, pp. 155–194).

The force of this representation cannot be broken, of course, by raising the question afresh whether the supernatural knowledge attributed by the Evangelists to our Lord may not, in many of its items at least, if not in its whole extent, find its analogues, after all, in human powers, or be explained as not different in kind from that of the prophets (cf. *e.g.* Westcott, 'Additional Note on Jn 2²⁴; A. J. Mason, *Conditions*, etc. pp. 162–163). The question more immediately before us does not concern our own view of the nature and origin of this knowledge, but that of the Evangelists. If we will keep these two questions separate we shall scarcely be able to doubt that the Evangelists mean to present this knowledge as one of the marks of our Lord's Divine dignity. In interpreting them we are not entitled to parcel out the mass of the illustrations of His supernormal knowledge which they record to differing sources, as may fall in with our own conceptions of the inherent possibilities of each case ; finding indications in some instances merely of His fine human instinct, in others of His prophetic inspiration, while reserving others—if such others are left to us in our analysis—as products of His Divine intuition. The Evangelists suggest no such lines of cleavage in the mass ; and they must be interpreted from their own standpoint. This finds its centre in their expressed conviction that in Jesus Christ dwelt the fulness of the knowledge of God (Mt 11²⁷, Lk 10²², Jn 8³⁸ 16¹⁵ 17¹⁰). To them His knowledge of God and of Divine things, of Himself in His Person and mission, of the course of His life and the events which would befall Him in the prosecution of the work whereunto He had been sent, of the men around Him,—His followers and friends, the people and their rulers,—down to the most hidden depths of their natures and the most intimate processes of their secret thoughts, and of all the things forming the environment in which the drama He was enacting was cast, however widely that environment be conceived, or however minutely it be contemplated,—was but the manifestation, in the ever-widening circles of our human modes of conception, of the perfect apprehension and understanding that dwelt changelessly in His Divine intelligence. He who knew God perfectly,—it were little that He should know man and the world perfectly too ; all that affected His own work and career, of course, and with it, equally of course, all that lay outside of this (cf. Mason, *Conditions*, etc. p. 168) ; in a word, unlimitedly, all things. Even if nothing but the Law of Parsimony stood in the way, it might well be understood that the Evangelists would be deterred from seeking, in the case of such a Being, other sources of information besides His Divine intelligence to account for all His far-reaching and varied knowledge. At all events, it is clearly their conviction that all He knew—the scope of which was unbounded and its depth unfathomed, though their record suggests rather than fully illustrates it—found its explanation in the dignity of His person as God manifest in the flesh.

Nor can the effect of their representation of Jesus as the subject of this all-embracing Divine knowledge be destroyed by the discovery in their narratives of another line of representation in which our Lord is set forth as living His life out under the conditions which belong naturally to the humanity He had assumed. These representations are certainly to be neglected as little as those others in which His Divine omniscience is suggested. They bring to our observation another side of the complex personality that is depicted, which, if it cannot be said to be as emphatically insisted upon by the Evangelists, is nevertheless, perhaps, equally pervasively illustrated. This is the true humanity of our Lord, within the scope of which He willed to live out His life upon earth, that He might accomplish the mission for which He had been sent. The suggestion that He might break over the bounds of His mission, in order that He might escape from the ruggedness of His chosen path, by the exercise whether of His almighty power (Mt 4[3f.], Lk 4[3f.]) or of His unerring foresight (Mt 16[22] ||), He treated first and last as a temptation of the Evil One—for 'how then should the Scriptures be fulfilled that thus it must be' (Mt 26[54] ||)? It is very easy, to be sure, to exaggerate the indications in the Evangelists of the confinement of our Lord's activities within the limits of human powers. It is an exaggeration, for example, to speak as if the Evangelists represent Him as frequently surprised by the events which befell Him : they never predicate surprise of Him, and it is only by a very precarious inference from the events recorded that they can ever be supposed even to suggest or allow place for such an emotion in our Lord (cf. art. AMAZEMENT, p. 48). It is an exaggeration again to adduce our Lord's questions as attempts to elicit information for His own guidance : His questions are often plainly dialectical or rhetorical, or, like some of His actions, solely for the benefit of those 'that stood around.' It is once more an exaggeration to adduce the employment in many cases of the term γινώσκω, when the Evangelists speak of our Lord's knowledge, as if it were thereby implied that this knowledge was freshly born in His mind : the assumed distinction, but faintly marked in Greek literature, cannot be traced in the usage of the terms γνῶναι and εἰδέναι in their application to our Lord's knowledge; these terms even replace one another in parallel accounts of the same instance (Mt 22[18] || Mk 12[15] ; [Mt 9[4]] || Mk 2[8], Lk 5[22] ; cf. Mt 12[25], Lk 6[8] 9[47] 11[17], Jn 6[61]); γνῶναι is used of the undoubted Divine knowledge of our Lord ([Mt 11[25]] Lk 10[22], Jn 10[15] 17[25], Mt 7[23] ; cf. Jn 2[24. 25] 5[42] 10[14. 27]) ; and indeed of the knowledge of God Himself (Lk 10[22] 16[15], Jn 10[15] [Mt 11[27]]) : and, in any event, there is a distinction which in such nice inquiries should not be neglected, between saying that the occurrence of an event, being perceived, was the occasion of an action, and saying that knowledge of the event, perceived as occurring, waited on its occurrence. Gravely vitiated by such exaggerations as most discussions of the subject are, enough remains, however, after all exaggeration is pruned away, to assure us, not indeed that our Lord's life on earth was, in the view of the Evangelists, an exclusively human one ; or that,

apart from the constant exercise of His will to make it such, it was controlled by the limitations of humanity ; but certainly that it was, in their view, lived out, so far as was consistent with the fulfilment of the mission for which He came—and as an indispensable condition of the fulfilment of that mission—under the limitations belonging to a purely human life. The classical passages in this reference are those striking statements in the second chapter of Luke (2[40. 52]) in which is summed up our Lord's growth from infancy to manhood, including, of course, His intellectual development (cf. art. CHILDREN, p. 302), and His own remarkable declaration recorded in Mt 24[36], Mk 13[32], in which He affirms His ignorance of the day and hour of His return to earth. Supplemented by their general dramatization of His life within the range of the purely human, these passages are enough to assure us that in the view of the Evangelists there was in our Lord a purely human soul, which bore its own proper part in His life, and which, as human souls do, grew in knowledge as it grew in wisdom and grace, and remained to the end, as human souls must, ignorant of many things,—nay, which, because human souls are finite, must ever be ignorant of much embraced in the universal vision of the Divine Spirit. We may wonder why the 'day and hour' of His own return should remain among the things of which our Lord's human soul continued ignorant throughout His earthly life. But this is a matter about which surely we need not much concern ourselves. We can never do more than vaguely guess at the law which governs the inclusions and exclusions which characterize the knowledge-contents of any human mind, limited as human minds are not only qualitatively but quantitatively ; and least of all could we hope to penetrate the principle of selection in the case of the perfect human intelligence of our Lord ; nor have the Evangelists hinted their view of the matter. We must just be content to recognize that we are face to face here with the mystery of the Two Natures, which, although they do not, of course, formally enunciate the doctrine in so many words, the Evangelists yet effectively teach, since by it alone can consistency be induced between the two classes of facts which they present unhesitatingly in their narratives. Only, if we would do justice to their presentation, we must take clear note of two of its characteristics. They do not simply, in separated portions of their narratives, adduce the facts which manifest our Lord's Divine powers and His human characteristics, but interlace them inextricably in the same sections of the narratives. And they do not subject the Divine that is in Christ to the limitations of the human, but quite decisively present the Divine as dominating all, and as giving play to the human only by a constant, voluntary withholding of its full manifestation in the interests of the task undertaken. Observe the story, for example, in Jn 11, which Dr. Mason (Conditions, etc. p. 143) justly speaks of as 'indeed a marvellous weaving together of that which is natural and that which is above nature.' 'Jesus learns from others that Lazarus is sick, but knows without any further message that Lazarus is dead ; He weeps and groans at the sight of the sorrow which surrounds Him, yet calmly gives thanks for the accomplishment of the miracle before it has been accomplished.' This conjunction of the two elements is typical of the whole Evangelical narrative. As portrayed in it our Lord's life is distinctly duplex ; and can be consistently construed only by the help of the conception of the Two Natures. And just as distinctly is this life portrayed in these narratives as receiving its determination not from the human, but from the Divine side. If what

John undertakes to depict is what was said and done by the incarnated Word, no less what the Synoptics essay is to present the Gospel (as Mark puts it) of Jesus Christ the Son of God. It is distinctly a supernatural life that He is represented by them all as living; and the human aspect of it is treated by each alike as an incident in something more exalted, by which it is permitted, rather than on which it imposes itself. Though passed as far as was befitting within the limits of humanity, this life remains at all times the life of God manifest in the flesh, and, as depicted by the Evangelists, never escapes beyond the boundaries set by what was suitable to it as such.

The actual instances of our Lord's foresight which are recorded by the Evangelists are not very numerous outside of those which concern the establishment of the Kingdom of God, with which alone, of course, their narratives are particularly engaged. Even the few instances of specific exhibitions of foreknowledge of what we may call trivial events owe their record to some connexion with this great work. Examples are afforded by the foresight that the casting of the nets at the exact time and place indicated by our Lord would secure a draught of fishes (Lk 5⁴, cf. Jn 21⁶); that the first fish that Peter would take when he threw his hook into the sea would be one which had swallowed a stater (Mt 17²⁷); that on entering a given village the disciples should find an ass tied, and a colt with it, whose owners would be obedient to our Lord's request (Mt 21² ‖); and that on entering Jerusalem to make ready for the final passover-feast they should meet a man bearing a pitcher, prepared to serve the Master's needs (Mk 14¹³). In instances like these the interlacing of prevision and provision is very intimate, and doubt arises whether they illustrate most distinctly our Lord's Divine foresight or His control of events. In other instances the element of foresight comes, perhaps, more purely forward: such are possibly the predictions of the offence of the disciples (Mt 26³¹ ‖), the denial of Peter (26³⁴ ‖), and the treachery of Judas (26²¹ ‖). There may be added the whole series of utterances in which our Lord shows a comprehensive foresight of the career of those whom He called to His service (Mt 4¹⁹ 10¹⁷· ²¹ 20²² 24⁹ᶠ·, Jn 16¹ᶠ·); and also that other series in which He exhibits a like full foreknowledge of the entire history of the Kingdom of God in the world (cf. esp. the parables of the Kingdom, and such passages as Mt 16¹⁸ 24⁵· ²⁴ 21⁴³ 24¹⁴ 26¹³, Lk 19¹¹, Jn 14¹⁸· ¹⁹). It is, however, particularly with reference to His own work in establishing the Kingdom, and in regard to the nature of that work, that stress is particularly laid upon the completeness of His foreknowledge. His entire career, as we have seen, is represented by all the Evangelists as lying plainly before Him from the beginning, with every detail clearly marked and provided for. It is especially, however, with reference to the three great events in which His work in establishing His Kingdom is summed up—His death, His resurrection, His return—that the predictions become numerous, if we may not even say constant. Each of the Evangelists represents Him, for example, as foreseeing His death from the start (Jn 2¹⁹ 3¹⁴, Mt 12⁴⁰ 9¹⁵, Mk 2¹⁹, Lk 12⁴⁹ 5³⁴; cf. Meyer on Mt 9¹⁵ 16²¹; Weiss on Mk 8³¹; Denney, *Death of Christ*, p. 18; Wrede, *Messiasgeheimnis*, p. 19, etc.), and as so ordering His life as to march steadfastly forward to it as its chosen climax (cf. *e.g.* Wrede, p. 84: 'It is accordingly the meaning of Mark that Jesus journeys to Jerusalem because it is His will to die there'). He is represented, therefore, as avoiding all that could lead up to it for a time, and then, when He was ready for it, as setting Himself steadfastly to bring it about as He would; as speaking of it only guardedly at first, and afterwards, when the

time was ripe for it, as setting about assiduously to prepare His disciples for it. Similarly with respect to His resurrection, He is reported as having it in mind, indeed, from the earliest days of His ministry (Jn 2¹⁹, Mt 12⁴⁰ 16²¹, Mk 8³¹, Lk 9²²), but adverting to it with pædagogical care, so as to prepare rather than confuse the minds of His disciples. The same in substance may be said with reference to His return (Mt 10²³ 16²⁷, Mk 8³⁸ 9¹, Lk 9²⁶· ²⁷).

A survey in chronological order of the passages in which He is reported as speaking of these three great events of the future, cannot fail to leave a distinct impression on the mind not only of the large space they occupy in the Evangelical narrative, but of the great place they take as foreseen, according to that narrative, in the life and work of our Lord. In the following list the passages in which He adverts to His death stand in the order given them in Robinson's *Harmony of the Gospels*:

Jn 2¹⁹ 3¹⁴, Mt 12⁴⁰ (cf. 16⁴, Lk 11³²), Lk 12⁴⁹· ⁵⁰, Mt 9¹⁵ (Mk 2¹⁹, Lk 5³⁴), Jn 6⁵¹ 7⁶·⁸, Mt 16²¹ (Mk 8³¹, Lk 9²²), Lk 9³¹, Mt 17¹⁷ (Mk 9¹²), Mt 17²²· ²³ (Mk 9³¹, Lk 9⁴⁴), Lk 9⁵¹, Jn 7³⁴ 8²¹· ²⁵ 9⁵ 10¹¹· ¹⁵, Lk 13³² 17²⁵, Mt 20¹⁸· ¹⁹ (Mk 10³³, Lk 18³¹), Jn 12²⁸, Mt 20²⁶ (Mk 10³⁸), Mt 20²⁸ (Mk 10⁴⁵), Mt 21³⁹ (Mk 12⁸, Lk 20¹⁴), Jn 12²³, Mt 26², Jn 13¹ 13³³, Mt 26·⁸ (Mk 14²⁴, Lk 22²⁰), Mt 26³¹ (Mk 14²⁷, Jn 14²·), Jn 15¹³ 16⁵ 16¹⁶ 18¹¹, Mt 26⁵⁴ (Jn 18¹¹), Lk 24²⁶· ⁴⁶.

The following allusions to His resurrection are in the same order:

Jn 2¹⁹, Mt 12⁴⁰ (Lk 11³⁰), Mt 16²¹ (Mk 8³¹, Lk 9²²), Mk 17⁹ (Mk 9⁹), Mt 17²³ (Mk 9³¹), Jn 10¹⁸ [16¹⁶], Mt 20¹⁷ (Mk 10³⁴, Lk 18³³), Mt 26³² (Mk 14²⁸) [Mt 28⁶ ‖ Lk 24⁸], Lk 24⁴⁶.

The following are, in like order, the allusions to His return:

Mt 10²³ 16²⁷ (Mk 8³⁸ 9¹, Lk 9²⁶· ²⁷), Lk 10⁴⁰ 17²², Mt 19²⁸ 23³⁹ 24³ (Mk 13⁴, Lk 21⁶), 24³⁴·³⁷ (Mk 13³⁰, Lk 21³²), Mt 24⁴⁴ 25³¹ 26⁶⁴ (Mk 14⁶², Lk 22⁶⁹).

The most cursory examination of these series of passages in their setting, and especially in their distribution through the Evangelical narrative, will evince the cardinal place which the eschatological element takes in the life of the Lord as depicted in the Gospels. In particular, it will be impossible to escape the conviction that it is distinctly the teaching of the Evangelists that Jesus came into the world specifically to die, and ordered His whole life wittingly to that end. As Dr. Denney puts it (expounding Jn 10¹⁷, on which see also Westcott's note), 'Christ's death is not an incident of His life, it is the aim of it. The laying down of His life is not an accident in His career, it is His vocation; it is that in which the Divine purpose of His life is revealed.' 'If there was a period in His life during which He had other thoughts, it is antecedent to that at which we have any knowledge of Him' (*Death of Christ*, pp. 259 and 18). Nothing could therefore be more at odds with the consentient and constant representations of the Evangelists than to speak of the 'shadow of the cross' as only somewhat late in His history beginning to fall athwart our Lord's pathway; of the idea that His earthly career should close in gloom as 'distinctly emerging in the teaching of Jesus only at a comparatively late period,' and as therefore presumably not earlier 'clear in His mind': unless, indeed, it be the accompanying more general judgment that 'there was nothing extraordinary or supernatural in Jesus' foreknowledge of His death,' and that 'His prophecy was but the expression of a mind which knew that it could not cease to be obedient while His enemies would not cease to be hostile' (A. M. Fairbairn, *The Expositor*, 1897, i.; v. iv. [1896] 283, 285). It is not less unwarranted to speak of Him as bowing to His fate only 'as the will of God, to which He yielded Himself up to the very end only with difficulty, and at best against His will' (Wernle, *Synopt. Frage*, 200).

Such expressions as these, however, advise us that a very different conception from that presented by the Evangelists has found widespread acceptance among a class of modern scholars, whose efforts have been devoted to giving to our Lord's life on earth a character more normally human than it seems to possess as it lies on the pages of the Evangelists. The negative principle of the new constructions offered of the course and springs of our Lord's career being rejection of the account given by the Evangelists, these scholars are thrown back for guidance very much upon their own subjective estimate of probabilities. The Gospels are, however, the sole sources of information for the events of our Lord's life, and it is impossible to decline their aid altogether. Few, accordingly, have been able to discard entirely the general framework of the life of Christ they present (for those who are inclined to represent Jesus as making no claim even to be the Messiah, see H. Holtzmann, *NT Theol.* i. 280, note; Meinhold as there referred to; and Wrede, *Das Messiasgeheimnis*, especially Appendix vii.). Most have derived enough from the Gospels to assume that a crisis of some sort occurred at Cæsarea Philippi, where the Evangelists represent our Lord as beginning formally and frankly to prepare His disciples for His death (Mt 16^{21} ||).

Great differences arise at once, however, over what this crisis was. Schenkel supposes that it was only at this point in His ministry that Jesus began to think Himself the Messiah; Strauss is willing to believe He suspected Himself to be the Messiah earlier, and supposes that He now first began to proclaim Himself such; P. W. Schmidt and Lobstein imagine that on this day He both put the Messianic crown upon His head and faced death looming in His path; Weizsäcker and Keim allow that He thought and proclaimed Himself the Messiah from the beginning, and suppose that what is new here is that only now did He come to see with clearness that His ministry would end in His death,—and as death for the Messiah means return, they add that here He begins His proclamation of His return in glory. To this Schenkel and Hase find difficulty in assenting, feeling it impossible that the Founder of a spiritual kingdom should look forward to its consummation in a physical one, and insisting, therefore, that though Jesus may well have predicted the destruction of His enemies, He can scarcely have foretold His own coming in glory. On the other hand, Strauss and Baur judge that a prediction of the destruction of Jerusalem too closely resembles what actually occurred not to be *post eventum*, but see no reason why Jesus should not have dreamed of coming back on the clouds of heaven. As to His death, Strauss thinks He began to anticipate it only shortly before His last journey to Jerusalem; while Holsten cannot believe that He realized what was before Him until He actually arrived at Jerusalem, and even then did not acquiesce in it (so Spitta). That He went to Jerusalem for the purpose of dying, neither Weizsäcker, nor Brandt, nor H. Holtzmann, nor Schultzen will admit, though the two last named allow that He foresaw that the journey would end in His death; or at least that it possibly would, adds Pünjer, since, of course, a possibility of success lay open to Him (cf. H. Holtzmann, *NT Theol.* i. 285–286, note). As many men, so many opinions. As the positive principle of construction in all these schemes of life for Jesus is desupernaturalization, they differ, so far as the prophetic element in His teaching as reported by the Evangelists is concerned, chiefly in the measure in which they explain it as due more or less entirely to the Evangelists carrying their own ideas, or the ideas of the community in which they lived, back into Jesus' mouth; or allow it more or less fully to Jesus, indeed, but only in a form which can be thought of as not rising above the natural prognostications of a man in His position. A few deny to Jesus the entire series of predictions reported in the Gospels, and assign them in mass to the thought of the later community (*e.g.* Eichhorn, Wrede). A few, on the other hand, allow the whole, or nearly the whole, series to Jesus, and explain them all naturalistically. Most take an intermediate position, determined by the principle that all which seems to each critic incapable of naturalistic explanation as utterances of Jesus shall be assigned to later origin. Accordingly, the concrete details in the alleged predictions are quite generally denied to Jesus, and represented as easily explicable modifications, in accordance with the actual course of events, of what Jesus really said. The prediction of resurrection on the third day, for example, is held by many (*e.g.* Schwartzkopff) to be too precise a determination, and is therefore excluded from the prophecy, or explained as only a periphrasis for an indefinite short time, after the analogy of Hos 6^2 (so even B. Weiss). To others a prediction of a resurrection at all seems incredible (Strauss, Schenkel, Weizsäcker, Keim, Brandt), and it is transmuted into, at most, a premonition of future victory. By yet others (as Holsten) even the anticipation of death is doubted, and nothing of forecast is left to Jesus except, possibly, a vague anticipation of difficulty and suffering; while with others even this gives way, and Jesus is represented as passing either the greater part of His life (Fairbairn), or the whole of it, in joyful expectation of more or less unbroken success, or at least, however

thickly the clouds gathered over His head, in inextinguishable hope in God and His interposition in His behalf (cf. the brief general sketch of opinions in Wrede, *Messiasgeheimnis*, p. 85).

Thus, over-against the 'dogmatic' view of the life of Christ, set forth in the Evangelists, according to which Jesus came into the world to die, and which is dominated, therefore, by foresight, is set, in polar opposition to it, a new view, calling itself 'historical,' the principle of which is the denial to Jesus of any foresight whatever beyond the most limited human forecast. No pretence is ordinarily made that this new view is given support by the Evangelical records; it is put forward on *a priori* or general grounds—as, for example, the only psychologically possible view (*e.g.* Schwartzkopff, *Prophecies of Christ*, p. 28; cf. Denney, *Death of Christ*, p. 11, and especially the just strictures of Wrede, *Messiasgeheimnis*, pp. 2, 3). It professes to find it incredible that Jesus entered upon His ministry with any other expectation than success. Contact with men, however, it allows, brought gradually the discovery of the hopelessness of drawing them to His spiritual ideals; the growing enmity of the rulers opened before Him the prospect of disaster; and thus there came to Him the slow recognition, first of the possibility, and then of the certainty, of failure; or, at least, since failure was impossible for the mission He had come to perform, of the necessity of passing through suffering to the ultimate success. So slowly was the readjustment to this new point of view made, that even at the end—as the prayer at Gethsemane shows—there remained a lingering hope that the extremity of death might be avoided. So far as a general sketch can be made of a view presented by its several adherents with great variety of detail, this is the essential fabric of the new view (cf. the general statements of Kähler, *Zur Lehre von der Versöhnung*, 159; Denney, *Death of Christ*, 11; Wrede, *Messiasgeheimnis*, 86). Only such parts of the predictive element of the teaching attributed to Jesus in the Gospels as are thought capable of naturalistic interpretation are incorporated into this new construction. By those who wish to bring in as much as possible, it is said, for example, that our Lord was too firmly persuaded of His Messianic appointment and function, and was too clear that this function centred in the establishment of the Kingdom, to accept death itself as failure. When He perceived death impending, that meant to Him, therefore, return; and return to bring in the Messianic glory meant resurrection. When He thought and spoke of death, therefore, He necessarily thought and spoke also of resurrection and return; the three went inevitably together; and if He anticipated the one, He must have anticipated the others also. Under this general scheme all sorts of opinions are held as to when, how, and under what impulses Jesus formed and taught this eschatological programme. As notable a construction as any holds that He first became certain of His Messiahship in an ecstatic vision which accompanied His baptism; that the Messiah must suffer was already borne in upon His conviction in the course of His temptation; but it was not until the scene at Cæsarea Philippi that He attained the happy assurance that the Messianic glory lay behind the dreadful death impending over Him. This great conviction, attained in principle in the ecstasy of that moment, was, nevertheless, only gradually assimilated. When Jesus was labouring with His disciples, He was labouring also with Himself. In this particular construction (it is O. Holtzmann's) an element of 'ecstasy' is introduced; more commonly the advances Jesus is supposed to make in His anticipations are thought to rest on processes of formal reasoning. In either case, He is pictured as only slowly, under the stress of compelling circumstances, reaching convictions of what awaited Him in the future ; and thus He is conceived distinctly as the victim rather than as the Lord of His destiny.   So far from entering the world to die, and by His death to save the world, and in His own good time and way accomplishing this great mission, He enters life set upon living, and only yields step by step reluctantly to the hard fate which inexorably closes upon Him. That He clings through all to His conviction of His Messiahship, and adjusts His hope of accomplishing His Messianic mission to the overmastering pressure of circumstances,—is that not a pathetic trait of human nature ?   Do not all enthusiasts the like ?   Is it not precisely the mark of their fanaticism ?   The plain fact is, if we may express it in the brutal frankness of common speech, in this view of Jesus' career He miscalculated and failed ; and then naturally sought (or His followers sought for Him) to save the failure (or the appearance of failure) by inventing a new *dénouement* for the career He had hoped for in vain, a new denouement which—has it failed too ?   Most of our modern theorizers are impelled to recognize that it too has failed.   When Jesus so painfully adjusted Himself to the hard destiny which more and more obtruded itself upon His recognition, He taught that death was but an incident in His career, and after death would come the victory.   Can we believe that He foresaw that thousands of years would intervene between what He represented as but an apparent catastrophe and the glorious reversal to which He directed His own and His followers' eyes ?   On the contrary, He expected and He taught that He would come back soon—certainly before the generation which had witnessed His apparent defeat had passed away ; and that He would then establish that Messianic Kingdom which from the beginning of His ministry He had unvaryingly taught was at hand.   He did not do so.   Is there any reason to believe that He ever will return ?   Can the 'foresight' which has repeatedly failed so miserably be trusted still,—for what we choose to separate out from the mass of His expectations as the core of the matter ?   On what grounds shall we adjust the discredited 'foresight' to the course of events, obviously unforeseen by Him, since His death ? Where is the end of these 'adjustments' ?   Have we not already with 'adjustment' after 'adjustment' transformed beyond recognition the expectations of Jesus, even the latest and fullest to which He attained, and transmuted them into something fundamentally different,—passed, in a word, so far beyond Him, that we retain only an artificial connexion with Him and His real teaching, a connexion mediated by little more than a word ?

That in this modern construction we have the precise contradictory of the conception of Jesus and of the course of His life on earth given us by the Evangelists, it needs no argument to establish. In the Gospel presentation, foresight is made the principle of our Lord's career.   In the modern view He is credited with no foresight whatever. At best, He was possessed by a fixed conviction of His Messianic mission, whether gained in ecstatic vision (as, *e.g.*, O. Holtzmann) or acquired in deep religious experiences (as, *e.g.*, Schwartzkopff) ; and He felt an assurance, based on this ineradicable conviction, that in His own good time and way God would work that mission out for Him ; and in this assurance He went faithfully onward fulfilling His daily task, bungling meanwhile egregiously in His reading of the scroll of destiny which was unrolling for Him.   It is an intensely, even an exaggeratedly, human Christ which is here offered us : and He stands, therefore, in the strongest contrast with the frankly Divine Christ which the

Gospels present to us.   On what grounds can we be expected to substitute this for that ?   Certainly not on grounds of historical record.   We have no historical record of the self-consciousness of Jesus except that embodied in the Gospel dramatization of His life and the Gospel report of His teaching ; and that record expressly contradicts at every step this modern reconstruction of its contents and development.   The very principle of the modern construction is reversal of the Gospel delineation. Its peculiarity is that, though it calls itself the 'historical' view, it has behind it no single scrap of historical testimony ; the entirety of historical evidence contradicts it flatly.   Are we to accept it, then, on the general grounds of inherent probability and rational construction ?   It is historically impossible that the great religious movement which we call Christianity could have taken its origin and derived its inspiration—an inspiration far from spent after two thousand years—from such a figure as this Jesus.   The plain fact is that in these modern reconstructions we have nothing but a sustained attempt to construct a naturalistic Jesus ; and their chief interest is that they bring before us with unwonted clearness the kind of being the man must have been who at that time and in those circumstances could have come forward making the claims which Jesus made without supernatural nature, endowment, or aid to sustain Him.   The value of the speculation is that it makes superabundantly clear that no such being could have occupied the place which the historical Jesus occupied ; could have made the impression on His followers which the historical Jesus made ; could have become the source of the stream of religious influence which we call Christianity, as the historical Jesus became.   The clear formulation of the naturalistic hypothesis, in the construction of a naturalistic Jesus, in other words, throws us violently back upon the Divine Jesus of the Evangelists as the only Jesus that is historically possible.   From this point of view, the labours of the scholars who have with infinite pains built up this construction of Jesus' life and development have not been in vain.

What, then, is to be said of the predictions of Jesus, and especially of the three great series of prophecies of His death, resurrection, and return, with respect to their contents and fulfilment ? This is not the place to discuss the eschatology of Jesus.   But a few general remarks seem not uncalled for.   The topic has received of late much renewed attention with very varied results, the number and variety of constructions proposed having been greatly increased above what the inherent difficulty of the subject will account for, by the freedom with which the Scripture data have been modified or set aside on so-called critical grounds by the several investigators.   Nevertheless, most of the new interpretations also may be classified under the old categories of futuristic, preteristic, and spiritualistic.

The spiritualistic interpretation—whose method of dealing with our Lord's predictions readily falls in with a widespread theory that it is 'contrary to the spirit and manner of genuine prophecy to predict actual circumstances like a soothsayer' (Muirhead, *Eschatology of Jesus*, p. 10 ; Schwartzkopff, *Prophecies of Jesus Christ*, 78, 250, 258, 275, 312, etc.)—has received a new impulse through its attractive presentation by Erich Haupt (*Eschatolog. Aussagen Jesu*, etc., 1895).   Christ's eschatology, says Haupt, is infinitely simple, and all that He predicts is to be accomplished in a heavenly way which passes our comprehension ; there is no soothsaying in His utterances—'nowhere any predictions of external occurrences, everywhere only great moral religious laws which must operate everywhere and always, while nothing is said of the form in which they must act ' (p. 157).   A considerable stir has been created also by the revival (Schleiermacher, Weisse) by Weiffenbach (*Der Wiederkunftsgedanke Jesu*, 1873, *Die Frage der Wiederkunft Jesu*, 1901) of the identification of the return of Christ with His resurrection, although this view has retained few adherents since its refutation by Schwartzkopff (*The Prophecies of Jesus*

Christ, 1895), whose own view is its exact contradictory, viz. that by His resurrection Jesus meant just His return. The general conception, however, that ' for Jesus the hope of resurrection and the thought of return fell together,' so that ' when Jesus spoke of His resurrection He was thinking of His return, and *vice versa*' (O. Holtzmann, *War Jesus Ekstatiker?* 67, note), is very widely held. The subsidiary hypothesis (first suggested by Colani) of the inclusion in the great eschatological discourse attributed by the Evangelists to our Lord of a ' little Apocalypse ' of Jewish or Jewish Christian origin, by which Weiffenbach eased his task, has in more or less modified form received the widest acceptance (cf. H. Holtzmann, *NT Theol.* i. 327, note), but rests on no solid grounds (cf. Weiss, Beyschlag, Haupt, Clemen). Most adherents of the modern school are clear that Jesus expected and asserted that He would return in Messianic glory for the consummation of the Kingdom ; and most of them are equally clear that in this expectation and assertion, Jesus was mistaken (cf. H. Holtzmann, *NT Theol.* i. 312 f.). ' In the expectation that the kingdom was soon to come,' says Oscar Holtzmann in a passage typical enough of this whole school of exposition (*War Jesus Ekstatiker?* p. 133), ' Jesus erred in a human way ' ; and in such passages as Mk 9¹ 13³⁰, Mt 10²³ he considers that the error is obvious. He adds, 'That such an error on the part of Jesus concerning not a side-issue but a fundamental point of His faith,—His first proclamation began, according to Mk 1¹⁵, with the πεπλήρωται ὁ καιρὸς καὶ ἤγγικεν ἡ βασιλεία τοῦ θεοῦ,—does not facilitate faith in Jesus is self-evident ; but this error of Jesus is for His Church a highly instructive and therefore highly valuable warning to distinguish between the temporary and the permanent in the work of Jesus.' Not every one even of this school can go, however, quite this length. Even Schwartzkopff, while allowing that Jesus erred in this matter, wishes on that very account to think of the mere definition of times and seasons as belonging to the form rather than to the essence of His teaching (*The Prophecies of Jesus Christ*, 1895, Eng. tr. 1897, p. 319 ; *Konnte Jesus irren?* 1896, p. 3) ; and in that Baldensperger is in substantial agreement with him (*Selbstbewusstsein Jesu* ¹, p. 148, ² p. 205). From the other side, E. Haupt (*Eschatolog. Aussagen Jesu*, 1895, p. 138 f.) urges that Jesus must be supposed to have been able to avoid all errors, at least in the religious sphere, even if they concern nothing but the form ; while Weiffenbach (*Die Frage*, etc. p. 9) thinks we should hesitate to suppose Jesus could have erred in too close a definition of the time of His advent, when He expressly confesses that He was ignorant of its time (cf. Muirhead, *Eschat. of Jesus*, 48–50, and esp. 117). Probably Fritz Barth (*Die Hauptprobleme des Lebens Jesu*, 1899, pp. 167–170) stands alone in cutting the knot by appealing to the conditionality of all prophecy. According to him, Jesus did, indeed, predict His return as coincident with the destruction of Jerusalem ; but all genuine prophecy is conditioned upon the conduct of the human agents involved—' between prediction and fulfilment the conduct of man intrudes as a codetermining factor on which the fulfilment depends.' Thus this prediction has not failed, but its fulfilment has only been postponed—in accordance, it must be confessed, not with the will of God, but with that of man. It is difficult to see how Jesus is thus shielded from the imputation of defective foresight ; but at least Barth is able on this view still to look for a return of the Lord.

The difficulty which the passages in our Saviour's teaching under discussion present to the reverent expositor is, of course, not to be denied or minimized. But surely this difficulty would need to be much more hopeless than it is before it could compel or justify the assumption of error ' in One who has never been convicted of error in anything else ' (Sanday in Hastings' *DB* ii. 635—the whole passage should be read). The problem that faces us in this matter, it is apparent, in the meantime, is not one which can find its solution as a corollary to a speculative general view of our Lord's self-consciousness, its contents, and development. It is distinctly a problem of exegesis. We should be very sure that we know fully and precisely all that our Lord has declared about His return—its what and how and when—before we venture to suggest, even to our most intimate thought, that He has committed so gross an error as to its what and how and when as is so often assumed ; especially as He has in the most solemn manner declared concerning precisely the words under consideration that heaven and earth shall pass away, but not His words. It would be sad if the passage of time has shown this declaration also to be mistaken. Meanwhile, the perfect foresight of our Lord, asserted and illustrated by all the Evangelists, certainly cannot be set aside by the facile assumption of an error on His part in a matter in which it is so difficult to demonstrate an error, and in which assumptions of all sorts are so little justified. For the detailed discussion of our Lord's eschatology, including the determination of His meaning in these utterances, reference must, however, be made to works treating expressly of this subject.

BENJAMIN B. WARFIELD.

FORGIVENESS.—

Three words are used in the Gospels which are rendered in English by the word ' forgive ' :—ἀπολύειν, *to set free*, once only, in Lk 6³⁷ ; χαρίζεσθαι, *to show oneself gracious*, or *forgive frankly*, in Lk 7⁴² ⁴³ ; and ἀφιέναι, *to remit*, or *let off*, 37 times in the Synoptic Gospels. The noun ἄφεσις, ' remission ' or ' forgiveness,' is found 8 times in the Synoptics, the words ' of sins ' or ' of trespasses ' being either added or closely implied.

In the treatment of the subject in this article three things must be borne in mind. *First*, that the words employed by Christ and the ideas they represent are not entirely new as they come from His lips. Our Lord presupposes and then puts His own characteristic impress upon a doctrine of forgiveness with which His hearers were for the most part familiar, and which for us is embodied in the OT. *Secondly*, that no complete study of Christ's teaching concerning forgiveness can be made, unless other words, such as ' save,' ' justify,' and ' cleanse,' are taken into account, and the whole subject of release from the guilt and bondage of sin, as promised by Him, is kept in view. And, *thirdly*, that to stop short with the recorded words of Christ Himself on the matter is—speakingly reverently—not to know His whole mind upon it. It was impossible for Him in the course of His earthly ministry to set forth the full significance of His work for men, before it was accomplished. Hence for a complete account of the significance of His death we turn to the teaching of the Apostles, enlightened as they were by the Holy Spirit whom He had promised. In due course were revealed those ' many things ' concerning His cross and passion which His disciples could not ' bear ' during His lifetime. Down even to the very close of His short ministry on earth the rudimentary spiritual intelligence of the Apostles was unequal to carrying the full burden of the gospel as they afterwards understood it. The way in which that gospel was to be emphatically one of forgiveness, that ' through this man is proclaimed remission of sins, and by him every one that believeth is justified from all things from which ye could not be justified by the law of Moses,' was only made clear afterwards. It being therefore carefully borne in mind that the OT prepared the way for Christ's teaching on forgiveness, and that the Epistles developed and completed it, this article will deal only with that stage in the biblical doctrine of the subject which is represented by Christ and the Gospels. The consideration of it will be divided into four sections : (1) the Divine forgiveness of man, (2) Christ's own power to forgive sins, (3) the duty of men to forgive one another, (4) the extent to which authority to forgive is vested in the Christian community.

1. *God the Father as forgiving the sins of men.*— The first reference chronologically to this subject in the Gospels is found in the *Benedictus*, or Psalm of Zacharias (Lk 1⁷⁷). The prophecy concerning John the Baptist announces that he is to give ' knowledge of salvation unto his people, in the remission of their sins, according to the tender mercy of our God,' etc. The whole tenor of the canticle goes to show that God's ancient promises were about to be fulfilled in the coming of a Saviour through whom the great boon of remission of sins was to be secured in a fuller sense than had hitherto obtained. When the time came, John the Baptist is declared to have preached the baptism of repentance ' unto remission of sins ' (Mk 1⁴, Lk 3³). In the same connexion may be taken the interpretation of the name Jesus in Mt 1²¹ ' he shall save his people from their sins,' and the ' Saviour, Christ

the Lord,' of Lk 2[11], though the word 'forgiveness' does not occur. It was indeed implicit throughout our Lord's ministry, all His declarations concerning His coming 'not to call the righteous, but sinners' (Mt 9[13] ǁ), 'to seek and to save that which was lost' (Lk 19[10]), and His promise of 'rest to the souls' of men (Mt 11[29]), showing that the object of His ministry was to reclaim from sin, by bringing men to that forgiveness and cleansing which God had promised through repentance and faith in Him.

The explicit references to forgiveness of sin are comparatively few, but they are clear and definite in character, and quite sufficient to establish doctrine on the subject. They are : (a) the petition in the Lord's Prayer, 'Forgive us our debts,' Mt 6[12] ('our sins,' Lk 11[3]), combined with Mt 6[14. 15], Mk 11[25], which assert God's willingness to forgive under certain conditions. With these join Lk 6[37], a parallel passage with a different turn of expression, 'Release and ye shall be released,' the reference clearly being to sin. (b) The parables of Lk 15, especially that of the Prodigal Son, and of the Pharisee and the Publican in Lk 18[9-14]. (c) Our Saviour's prayer on the cross, 'Father, forgive them,' etc., Lk 23[34]. (d) Statements concerning God's willingness to forgive all sins, including those 'against the Son of man,' but excluding the unpardonable sin against the Holy Ghost, Mt 12[32], Mk 3[29], Lk 12[10]; add also Mk 4[12], in which Isaiah's prophecy is represented as being fulfilled, 'lest they should repent and be forgiven (healed).'

Putting these passages together, we are warranted in concluding that Christ taught the readiness of the Father always to hear the prayer of the truly penitent and in His mercy to pardon their sins, the chief questions being, What is the exact nature of forgiveness? Is it free to all mankind, or to those only who are in covenant relation with Him? Is any condition besides that of repentance laid down?

The meaning of the word 'forgiveness,' and the relation between God and man implied in it, must be gathered largely from the OT. Doubtless under the old covenant a progressive revelation is to be recognized, an advance in spirituality of teaching being discernible in its later stages. Doubtless also it is necessary to bear in mind the distinction between the ceremonial standpoint of the Law with its elaborate ritual and appointed sacrifices on the one hand, and the more purely spiritual view of the prophet and psalmist on the other. But, broadly speaking, Christ, like the more 'Evangelical' OT prophets, represents forgiveness as a pure act of grace on the part of God, who on the repentance of the sinner receives him graciously and pardons his transgression in the sense of replacing the offender in his former relation of acceptance and favour. Forgiveness is not mere remission of penalty, the forbearing to inflict deserved punishment, though such release is for the most part included. Punishment may still be exacted, but it has lost its penal character and becomes Divine chastisement inflicted for the improvement of the offender, or for the sake of others. Neither does forgiveness imply any false or arbitrary dealing with the past, any condoning of sin—which is essentially immoral—or ignoring of the transgression, as if it had not been committed—which would imply a weak and false attempt to secure the impossible. Nor, again, can any kind of remission of sins be predicated of God which implies unrighteousness in any form, the solemn sanctions of the eternal law of righteousness being secured by the conditions upon which forgiveness is granted.

But the essence of forgiveness lies in the establishment, or restoration, of a personal relation between sinful man and a grieved and righteously angry God. Omnipotence itself cannot erase the event from the history of the past, and holiness will not permit any concealment or pretence as to the heinousness of the offence committed. But the sin may be 'covered,' the guilt cancelled, in the sense that on certain conditions it shall be as if it had never been, so far as the relation between God and the sinner is concerned. Hence sin when forgiven is said to be 'cast into the depth of the sea' (Mic 7[19]), 'cast behind thy back' (Is 38[17]), removed 'as far as the east is from the west' (Ps 103[12]), 'remembered no more' (Jer 31[34]) against the sinner.

Ritschl says : 'God, in forgiving or pardoning sins, exercises His will in the direction of not permitting the contradiction—expressed in guilt—in which sinners stand to Him to hinder that fellowship of men with Him which He intends on higher grounds.' It does not, he adds, 'free them altogether from the consciousness of guilt, but from that mistrust which, as an affection of the consciousness of guilt, naturally separates the injured man from the offender.' And again, it is 'a reconciliation of such a nature that while memory, indeed, preserves the pain felt at the sin which has been committed, yet at the same time the place of mistrust towards God is taken by the positive assent of the will to God and His saving purpose.'

Forgiveness can never be adequately understood by means of any figure of speech, commercial or other. It represents a relation of persons, and its essence lies in the restoration of impaired confidence, affection, and favourable regard. It has to do not only with the past, but the present and the future, and it is exercised by God towards men just in proportion as they are capable of receiving it.

Repentance is the one condition clearly laid down and repeatedly insisted on in the Gospels. It is necessary as between man and man, much more between man and God. When John the Baptist comes to prepare the way of the Saviour, nothing can be done without that thoroughgoing repentance which implies reformation so far as man can effect it. Repentance is indeed a necessary ingredient of forgiveness if the two terms are rightly understood. Sorrow for sin and complete renunciation of it are not arbitrary conditions which the Sovereign chooses to exact before bestowing a boon; they belong to the very essence of the personal relation between Father and son which has been impaired or broken by error and disobedience, and which is to be restored in forgiveness. For an impenitent sinner not to be punished is conceivable, but for such a one to be forgiven is a contradiction in terms. The necessity for a forgiving spirit in one who hopes himself to be forgiven is dealt with below.

God is then 'good and ready to forgive' (Ps 86[5]), a God 'keeping mercy for thousands, forgiving iniquity, transgression, and sin' (Ex 34[7]). It would, however, be misleading to generalize and say that this attribute of mercy obviates all necessity for an atonement, or vindication of the law of righteousness, and that throughout the whole history of the world nothing more is needed to obtain Divine forgiveness of sin than confession and repentance on the part of man. The promises of the OT were given to those who stood in a covenant relation with God, in which His righteousness was effectually safeguarded. Christ's ministry was exercised amongst Jews in the first instance, and the presuppositions of OT Scripture must be taken into account.

The same may be said of the two gracious parables of our Lord which chiefly deal with this subject. It is impossible to found accurate doctrine on a parable only, and it is always a mistake to suppose that one parable can cover the whole range of doctrine. The three recorded in Lk 15 were uttered to show the nature of Christ's mission and His desire to seek and save the worst sinners, as well as the willingness of God to receive such, and the joy of heaven and earth when the penitent returns and is pardoned. The moral basis on which this becomes possible in the Divine government is another matter. The cosmic conditions of forgiveness are described in their proper place in Scripture. But in the parable of the Prodigal Son the lesson is impressed that the utmost failure in filial duty will be readily forgiven, if the wanderer will but repent and return. In the parable of the Pharisee and the Publican the essential teaching is the same—the danger lest those who comply with rules of ordinary morality should so plume themselves on their obedience as to lose the sense of their own deep need and ill-desert, and the fact that grave offenders against the fundamental laws of righteousness, like the publican and the harlot, may find their way into the kingdom of grace before the self-righteous Pharisee. But it would be utterly misleading, even to the subversion of the very foundations of ethics, if the inference were drawn that it matters nothing how deeply a man sins, provided that when his evil course is over he regrets his errors and asks for pardon, and that there is no reason in the moral government of the Universe why such a man should not be at once forgiven without infraction of the eternal law of righteousness.

This general conclusion is borne out by Christ's strong language concerning sin, and especially that sin which cannot be forgiven (see Mt 12^{32}, Mk 3^{29}, Lk 12^{10}). In spite of the long controversy which has taken place as to the mysterious sin against the Holy Ghost and the misunderstandings concerning it which have caused unspeakable spiritual anguish to thousands, there seems little question that the only sin thus pronounced unpardonable is that of wilful and persistent sinning against light till light itself is turned into darkness,—the perverting of truth at its very source, where the Holy Spirit Himself instructs the conscience, and thus poisoning the wells of the soul. Therefore, not in virtue of an arbitrary fiat of the Almighty, but by the necessity of the case, such sin cannot be forgiven. 'A lamp's death when, replete with oil, it chokes; a stomach's when, surcharged with food, it starves.' With this explanation harmonizes the Saviour's prayer in Lk 23^{34} 'Father, forgive them; for they know not what they do.' The sin of Christ's murderers, heinous indeed beyond expression, was a sin against the Son of man, and—at least in the case of most of those implicated and so far as the full gravity of the offence was concerned —it was not such a deliberate and complete perversion of conscience as to amount to a sin against the Holy Spirit. The reason why the unforgiving cannot be forgiven is to be similarly understood. Hence the general doctrine is laid down in the Gospels in unmistakable terms, that God the Father is ready to receive and pardon all sinners except those who shut themselves out from its possibility by wilfully cherishing a spirit known to be evil, and deliberately hardening their own hearts against the grace which was ready to receive and renew them. See UNPARDONABLE SIN.

2. It is clear that Christ's teaching concerning forgiveness was not exhausted by the proclamation of the Father's willingness to receive the penitent. *He Himself claimed the power to forgive*, which was recognized by all to be a Divine prerogative. In Mt 9, Mk 2, and Lk 5 is recorded the narrative of the healing of the paralytic, which had evidently impressed itself strongly upon tradition, since it is given by all three Synoptists at greater length than usual and almost in the same words. It was one of the grounds of offence which ultimately caused the death of Jesus, that, whilst lowly in demeanour, He put forth claims for Himself so lofty that to a reverent Jew He appeared often to

blaspheme. Jesus does not deny the fundamental assumption that none can forgive sins but God only. To a true believer in one God this is an axiom; there is but one Governor and there can be but one Fount of pardon. Jesus did not thereupon disclaim the possession of a Divine prerogative. He put His own claims to an easily applied test, Whether is it easier to tell a sufferer that his sins are forgiven, or to heal him of an incurable malady? In other words, any prophet may speak words of comfort or absolution, but one who shows the power of healing in order to establish his claim to pronounce forgiveness is no ordinary messenger, but proves Himself to be the Son of God with power. The whole incident evidently made a deep impression, for we are told that the people wondered, praised God, and acknowledged that unprecedented and superhuman power had been entrusted to a son of man.

The close connexion between the work that Christ did for the bodies of men and the power that He claimed over their souls in the forgiveness of sin, is suggested in other narratives, though somewhat less clearly. The inference has been drawn from Jn 5^{14} and the early tradition recorded in 8^{11}, that Jesus habitually pronounced remission of sin and gave power to amend the life in future, but the brief records in these cases hardly warrant such a conclusion.

The narrative of the woman who was a sinner, recorded in Lk 7^{36-50}, is full of instruction on the subject of forgiveness. The mission of Christ to save the outcast and the abandoned is here delicately and beautifully shown. The only doubtful point of interpretation relates to the ground of forgiveness as described in v.^{47}. Many commentators, including the chief Roman Catholic authorities, make the forgiveness extended to the woman to depend upon the love she showed, and at first reading this might seem warranted by the phrase 'for she loved much.' But on examination this is seen to be impossible. For (1) the whole scope of the parable of the two debtors shows that forgiveness precedes love; (2) the latter part of v.^{47} enforces the same lesson; and so (3) does the absolution pronounced in v.^{48}. The only ambiguity lies in the pregnant use of ὅτι in v.^{47}, and the meaning of the clause may be expressed by the paraphrase, 'This is the reason why I tell you that her many sins are forgiven—for (see) she has shown much love; but he who is forgiven little, loves little.' Her repentance and acceptance had taken place before, her grateful love was manifested in return by the outpouring of the ointment; and in v.^{48} Christ authoritatively confirms the assurance of her free and full pardon as One who had an absolute right to do so.

The doctrine of the forgiveness of sins on the basis of atonement through the death of Christ is not, properly speaking, revealed by Christ Himself. The Fourth Gospel contains passages like 1^{29} and a reference in 19^{36} to the Paschal lamb (?), but neither of these comes from the lips of the Master. The nearest approach to such teaching is found in the institution of the Lord's Supper and the reference to His blood as shed for the remission of sins in Mt 26^{28}, also perhaps in the directions given to the Apostles in Lk 24^{47}. By the time of St. Paul's earliest Epistles the doctrine of the atoning death of Christ as the ground of the forgiveness of sins was fairly developed, and the question is, How far had progress been made in this direction before the death of Christ took place? The answer appears to be that—as with the doctrines of the Incarnation and a Future Life in the OT—foreshadowings only had been given, hints and indications of a revelation which could not be clearly and definitely made until Christ's work was complete and the full gift of the Spirit bestowed. A reference is found in Mt 20[28] to the giving up of life by the Son of man ' as a ransom for many,' but the Apostles could not in Christ's lifetime understand at all the need for His death and the full meaning of the shedding of His blood upon the cross; and its connexion with the forgiveness of sins dawned upon them only gradually under the illumination of the promised Spirit.

3. One of the most noteworthy features in Christ's ethical teaching was His inculcation of *the duty of almost unlimited forgiveness of man by man.* The standard thus set up was practically new. In Pagan ethics to revenge an injury and punish an enemy to the utmost was manly, to forgive was mean-spirited. Some affronts might be passed over by the magnanimous man, simply because it was beneath his dignity, or disturbing to his equanimity, to notice them. But the idea of not only abstaining from vengeance, but actually restoring an offender to a relation of kindly regard, on the ground of human brotherhood and for the sake of helping an erring one to regain his forfeited position, was quite alien to the spirit of ancient morals.

Christ taught not only the duty of forgiveness on repentance, but that it was to be unlimited both in quality and in quantity. No offence was so serious, no repetition of offences so excessive, that forgiveness might be withheld, provided only that penitence were shown. The former of these points is not enlarged on by Christ, but it is involved in the proverbial completeness of the phrase ' unto seventy times seven ' (Mt 18[22]). Such forgiveness of injuries was based upon two fundamental principles of Christian ethics : (*a*) the duty of repressing all personal resentment, closely connected with the virtues of meekness and humility ; and (*b*) that love to all men, including enemies, which—paradoxical as it might appear—Christ enjoined as fundamentally incumbent on all His disciples (Mt 5[44]). The ' love ' and forgiveness thus inculcated do not depend upon personal merits, for they are to be exercised even towards the unthankful and the evil. But the one necessary condition—repentance—is insisted on, else the moral character of forgiveness is lost. For, as already explained, forgiveness is a relation between persons, and if it be included as a duty in a moral code, it must imply an ethical relation, such as is altogether lacking if evil is condoned, or its seriousness slighted. Hence the offender must, so far as in him lies, put away the evil thing, if it is to be no longer a barrier between him and one whose course is determined by the law of righteousness. The truly moral nature of Christian forgiveness is brought out in Lk 17[3], where it is closely joined with the duty of reproving sin—' If thy brother sin, rebuke him ; and if he repent, forgive him.' With this may be compared Lv 19[17], where the reproof of an evil-doer is spoken of as a mark of love. Just as in the Law the righteous man is bidden to rebuke his neighbour and not ' bear sin because of him,' so under the gospel he is bidden to forgive the penitent wrong-doer, that he may help him to a better life.

The close connexion between God's forgiveness of man and man's forgiveness of injuries against himself is brought out in Mt 6[12. 15], Lk 11[4] ; see also Lk 6[37] and Mk 11[25. 26]. In the last passage, as well as in Mt 5[23. 24], the duty of being ' in love and charity with our neighbours,' and ' in perfect charity with all men,' is laid down as a condition of acceptable prayer to God. The reason is akin to that described above. There are some states of mind in which a worshipper is not fit to pray, in which he asks for blessings that he is not capable of receiving. The principle is not to be understood

as a kind of Divine *lex talionis*, as in the parable of the Unmerciful Debtor (Mt 18[35])—that a man does not deserve mercy himself, if he will not show it to others, though this is true and appeals to a natural sense of justice. Rather is it to be understood that the unforgiving man shows essential impenitence, or at best an uneducated conscience in respect of his relations with his fellows. A man who cherishes hardness of heart towards those who have injured him so offends against the law of love that he cannot be received by the God of love, and cannot enjoy the restored relationship which he asks for in the Divine forgiveness, the whole significance of which is due to the supremacy of love. Or, as Beyschlag expresses it, ' he who would belong to the kingdom of love as a recipient must belong to it as an agent.' The merciful alone can obtain mercy, or rightly use it when it is granted to them.

4. Similar principles to those which regulate the relation of individuals are to be applied *where Christian communities are concerned.* The two are closely connected, as is shown by the passage Mt 18[15-18]. Christ deals first with the offending individual ; if it can be avoided, recourse must not be had to the authority of the Christian society. It may be that personal remonstrance will suffice to set right the offender, or at least the moral influence of the brotherhood exercised in private by the presence of two or three witnesses. If the whole community is compelled to act, the utmost penalty inflicted is expulsion from the brotherhood, the only rights then remaining to the excommunicated person being the inalienable ones of a fellow-man.

The question of forgiveness or condemnation as exercised by the community arises from the phraseology concerning binding and loosing contained in v.[18], with which should be compared the words addressed to St. Peter in Mt 16[18], and those addressed to a company which seems certainly to have included more than the Apostles, in Jn 20[23]. The power granted to the Christian community in the words, ' Whosesoever sins ye remit, they are remitted unto them ; and whosesoever sins ye retain, they are retained,' is not to be confused with Divine forgiveness of sins on the one hand, or with individual forgiveness on the other. Whilst more significant than the latter, it stops far short of the former. Individual Christians are to do their best privately to stop the progress of ill-feeling and enmity, but ' offences' will still arise. A power of checking them is therefore lodged with the community for the maintenance of purity and the avoidance of scandal. This is described as the power of ' binding and loosing.' Acting in the name of Christ, and presumably in the spirit of Christ, His Church will, He says, in a sense exercise His authority, and their action, whether of permission or prohibition, of condemnation or acquittal, will be ratified in heaven. This power, while great and important, is clearly not comparable to the Divine forgiveness of the individual sinner. This involves a full knowledge of circumstances and of the disposition of the inmost heart which no man can possess in relation to his fellow-man. No authority is given by Christ to a community—still less to a ' priest,' of whom it is needless to say that the Gospels know absolutely nothing—to exercise or to pronounce ' forgiveness' in the case of any individual. But just as an offender belonging to a Christian community needs to be rebuked by the Church in order that the Divine condemnation of wrongdoing may be echoed on earth, and earthly penalties may be inflicted which may arrest further evil and so prevent the terrible danger of worse punishment to come ; so the penitent needs assurance from an earthly authority to help him in his upward course of reformation, though the real and ultimate transaction of forgiveness must rest between himself and God alone. The high authority thus conferred upon the Christian society and the responsible character attached to its judgments depend entirely upon its possession of that spiritual discernment which the Holy Spirit alone can bestow, and its acting always in the name of Christ and under the direction and control of the Spirit of Christ.

LITERATURE.—From amongst the numberless books bearing directly or indirectly on the subject may be mentioned: Beyschlag, *NT Theology*, bk. i. ch. iv. § 11, and ch. vii. §§ 3 and 4; Stevens, *NT Theology*, pt. i. ch. viii.; Moberly, *Atonement and Personality*, chs. 2 and 3; Seeley, *Ecce Homo*, chs. 22 and 23; Knight, *Christian Ethic*, ch. 11; and especially Ritschl, *Christian Doctrine of Justification and Reconciliation*, 1874, vol. iii. [Eng. tr. under the above title, 1900]; see also Bethune-Baker, art. 'Forgiveness' in Hastings' *DB*.

W. T. DAVISON

FORSAKEN.—Mt 27[46] ‖. See DERELICTION.

FORSAKING ALL.—

ἀφιέναι, Mt 4[20. 22] = Mk 1[18. 20]; Lk 5[11]; Mt 19[27. 29] = Mk 10[28. 29] = Lk 18[28. 29]; ἀποτάσσεσθαι, 'renounce,' Lk 14[33]. In Lk 9[61] ἀποτάξασθαι τοῖς εἰς τὸν οἶκον μου may mean either 'bid farewell to those in my house' (cf. Mk 6[46], Ac 18[18], 2 Co 2[13]), or 'renounce the things in my house,' *renunciare negociis domesticis* (Erasm.).

Jesus had two classès of disciples. First there was the multitude of those who believed on Him; and, while He required that they should give Him the chief place in their affection and shrink from no sacrifice for His sake, He allowed them to remain where He had found them, prosecuting their old avocations, yet rendering no small service to the Kingdom of Heaven by testifying to His grace and confessing what He had done for their souls. Then there were the Twelve, whom He required to be always with Him, following Him wherever He went, sharing His lot, and entering by daily intercourse and discipline into the mysteries of the Kingdom of Heaven, that they might be fitted for the task of carrying on His work when He was gone. Some of the former, like the Gerasene demoniac, would fain have attached themselves to Him and joined the fellowship of His comrades; but He refused their offer. He had other work for them to do. 'Away to thine house unto thy people, and proclaim to them what great things the Lord hath done to thee, and how he had pity on thee' (Mk 5[19] = Lk 8[39]).

In every instance He laid it down as the inexorable condition of admission to His inner circle that the man should forsake all—home, kindred, and possessions. 'Come after me,' He said to Simon and Andrew when He called them on the shore of the Lake of Galilee, 'and I will make you fishers of men.' And it is written that 'they immediately left their nets and followed him.' Then He called James and John, and they also 'left their father Zebedee in the boat with the hired men, and went away after him' (Mk 1[16-20] = Mt 4[18-22]). And in His commission to the Twelve, when He sent them forth two by two to preach and heal, He reiterated this condition of Apostleship. He laid His hand on the tenderest of human affections and claimed for Himself a prior devotion: 'He that loveth father or mother above me is not worthy of me; and he that loveth son or daughter above me is not worthy of me. And one who doth not take his cross, and follow after me, is not worthy of me' (Mt 10[33. 38]).

Of course it was inevitable that those who followed Jesus wherever He went should share His homeless and desolate lot; but He had a special reason for His emphatic insistence on this condition. The men of His generation cherished a secular ideal of the Messiah. They looked for a king of David's lineage who should appear in might and majesty and, driving out the heathen, set up the fallen throne in more than its ancient splendour. Even the Twelve shared this ideal, and they clung to it to the last, reconciling themselves to the lowliness of their Master by the theory that it was only a temporary veiling of His glory, and that He would presently fling off His disguise and flash forth in His proper majesty. They had left all that they might follow Him, but they consoled themselves with the anticipation of a speedy and overflowing recompense. 'Behold,' said St. Peter after the young ruler's refusal to make the sacrifice which Jesus demanded, '*we* have left all and followed thee: what then shall *we* have?' It was towards the close, and the Twelve were beginning to fear that they had been hugging a false hope, and would have no such recompense as they dreamed . of. 'Verily I tell you,' answered Jesus, pitying their discomfiture yet resolute to correct their error, 'that ye that have followed me, in the regeneration when the Son of man shall sit upon the throne of his glory, shall yourselves also sit upon twelve thrones judging the twelve tribes of Israel. And every one who hath left brethren, or sisters, or father, or mother, or children, or lands, or houses, for my name's sake, shall receive manifold more, and shall inherit eternal life. But,' He added significantly, hinting at a reversal of their expectation, 'many last shall be first, and first last' (Mt 19[27-30] = Mk 10[28-31] = Lk 18[28-30]). They were right in expecting a recompense, but their recompense would be other than they conceived.

As time passed and He still trod the path of humiliation, they fretted at His inexplicable procrastination; and, as the darkness deepened, and the toils closed about Him, they reasoned that the inevitable *dénouement* could be no longer deferred. During His last progress to Jerusalem, with His intimation of the Passion in their ears, they were dreaming their worldly dream. He was going up to the sacred capital, and, they assured themselves, it could be for naught else than the claiming of His crown; and James and John, conspiring with their mother Salome, approached Him and essayed to extort from Him a promise that they should be awarded the chief places beside His throne (Mt 20[20-28] = Mk 10[35-45]).

Such was the Messianic ideal which dominated the minds of our Lord's contemporaries; and it was fraught with mischief, hindering more than aught else the recognition of His claims. In truth the marvel is not that so few accepted Him, but that with such an expectation any accepted Him. They were looking for a glorious Messiah, a king with a crown on his head and an army at his back; and Jesus presented Himself, the Son of man, meek and lowly, the very antithesis of what they believed, the Messiah should be. He lost no opportunity of protesting against the unspiritual ideal, and not the least striking of His protests is this condition which He constantly and emphatically placed before those who desired to attach themselves to Him. A scribe once came to Him and said: 'Teacher, I will follow thee wherever thou goest.' What was his notion? He had been convinced of the Messiahship of Jesus, and, sharing the prevailing expectation, thought to reap a rich harvest of honour and emolument in the new era which would presently be inaugurated. Certainly, he argued, when Jesus won His own and rewarded His faithful followers, He would award the foremost place to one so distinguished by rank and learning.[*] And how did Jesus answer? 'You are expecting,' He said, 'office and honour in an earthly kingdom. Realize the fact. If you follow me wherever I go, you must forsake all and share

[*] So Chrysost., Jerome.

my lowly and painful lot. The foxes have holes, and the birds of the heaven nests ; but the Son of man hath not where to lay down his head' * (Lk 9[57. 58] = Mt 8[19. 20]).

Again, when He was travelling through Galilee on His last journey up to Jerusalem, He was followed by an enthusiastic throng. Knowing whither He was bound, they concluded that He was going to declare Himself king of Israel, and they were for following Him all the way and sharing in His triumph. Suddenly He wheeled round (στραφείς) and addressed them : 'If any man cometh after me, and doth not hate his father, and mother, and wife, and children, and brethren, and sisters, yea, moreover, even his own life, he cannot be my disciple. Whosoever doth not bear his cross, and come after me, cannot be my disciple.' Then He added two parables, — the Unfinished Tower and the Two Kings,—warning against the folly of embarking upon an enterprise which one is incapable of carrying through. 'So, therefore,' He concluded, 'if ye would follow me, understand the condition. Count the cost, and determine whether you are prepared to meet it. Every one of you who doth not renounce all that he hath cannot be my disciple' (Lk 14[25-33]).   DAVID SMITH.

FORTY.—See NUMBERS.

FOUNDATION OF THE WORLD.—The phrase καταβολή κόσμου occurs in Mt 25[34], Lk 11[50], Jn 17[24] (κόσμου is doubtful in Mt 13[35], see RVm). It is a common expression in the NT, e.g. Eph 1[4], He 4[3] 9[26], 1 P 1[20], Rev 13[8] 17[8]. In general it denotes a time sense, implying a strong declaration of priority. It always occurs with the prepositions ἀπό or πρό. καταβολή primarily means the laying down or founding of anything, hence the absolute beginning. κόσμος is a word of much more varied meaning, into the different phases of which we need not here enter. Its present use as applied to the Universe is well established. The whole expression is equivalent to the phrase found in Mk 10[6] 13[19] 'from the beginning of the creation' (ἀπὸ ἀρχῆς κτίσεως). 'Old Testament Hebrew has no term which would quite correspond to the Greek ὁ κόσμος' (Dalman, Words of Jesus, p. 162). Mt 13[35] is an unliteral rendering of Ps 78[2] מִנִּי־קֶדֶם, which the LXX translates ἀπ' ἀρχῆς. 'The foundation of the world' stands for the definite epoch when this present Universe was originated.
          W. S. KERR.

FOUR.—See NUMBERS.

FOWL.—The word 'fowl' is now almost restricted to poultry, and especially to that familiar bird in a farmyard, the 'barn-door fowl' ; but it is used in the NT in a wider sense. The Gr. word πετεινά (lit. 'flying things') does not indeed signify, as its derivation might imply, all winged creatures —a meaning sometimes attached to 'fowls' in Old English (Hastings' DB, art. 'Fowl'). It denotes 'birds,' of which there are many species in Palestine, including some which are only birds of passage with us. Quite arbitrarily AV renders πετεινά by 'birds' in Mt 8[20] 13[32], Lk 9[58] ; and by 'fowls' in Mt 6[26] 13[4], Mk 4[4. 32], Lk 8[5] 12[24] 13[19]. In every case in which πετεινά occurs in the Gospels RV gives 'birds.'

Borrowing so much as He did from outward nature, our Lord often employed birds to illustrate His teaching. Their nests are contrasted with His own pillowless couch (Mt 8[20]). In the parable of the Sower they devour the seed that falls by the wayside (Mt 13[4]) ; in that of the Mustard Seed

they lodge under the shadow of the huge plant which grew out of such a tiny germ (Mk 4[32]). Their free undistracted lives play an important part in that cumulative argument which Christ builds up in the Sermon on the Mount against the tyranny of care. They neither sow, reap, nor gather into barns, yet the heavenly Father feeds them (Mt 6[26]), i.e. they are inferior to man in two respects. For (1) they cannot anticipate and influence the future as man can by the exercise of his reason or the labour of his hands ; (2) God is only their Creator, but He is man's Father, and will not forget His child. Though the 'fowls' cannot foresee, or work, or trust, they have no care. Yet they are fed. How foolish of man, who can do all these things, to fall so far beneath the 'fowls,' and worry over food and drink, when his first duty is to seek the kingdom of God and His righteousness !
          D. A. MACKINNON.

FOX (ἀλώπηξ).—Foxes and jackals are referred to indiscriminately in Scripture, although the fox is somewhat smaller in size, and is generally found singly, whereas jackals prowl around villages in small packs. Both animals are of a timid nature, and exhibit similar cunning and stealth in securing their prey, and live in deserted ruins and among the rocks of the mountain gorges. Christ's allusion to them (Mt 8[20], Lk 9[58]) takes its meaning from the fact that while places of refuge and rest were definitely allotted to such outcast creatures, the Son of Man had not where to lay His head. His reference to Herod as a fox (Lk 13[32]) is not only expressive of contempt, but may allude to the cause of the king's hostility : he was the invader of vineyards who had taken his brother's wife. The verses that follow also indicate that Christ's death must be otherwise brought about. The petty and furtive intentions of Herod must give way to the grander rapacity of Jerusalem as the historical destroyer of the prophets.   G. M. MACKIE.

FRAGMENTS (κλάσματα, pieces broken for distribution ; cf. κλασμάτων ἄρτων of LXX Ezk 13[19]).— All the Synoptists record that, when the miraculous feeding of the multitude ended, the broken pieces remaining over from the meal were gathered up and deposited in twelve baskets (Mt 14[20], Mk 6[43], Lk 9[17]). St. John adds that this was done in obedience to Christ's command, addressed to the disciples, by whom apparently the work was performed (Jn 6[12]). The surplus thus collected far exceeded the amount of the original stock, and bore witness to the abundance of the meal partaken of. The carefulness shown in collecting the remnants of food was intended to avoid any appearance of waste, and served to correct any tendency to undervalue what had come to the recipients so cheaply. The miracle was one of the very exceptional cases in which Christ provided for men's ordinary wants, was wrought only in view of the urgent necessity that had arisen (Mt 14[15]), and, while it raised expectations of similar benefits in the future (Jn 6[26]), was not designed to produce this result. The storing of the fragments for future use would tend to indicate that such miracles were not to be everyday occurrences. As in all Christ's miracles, there is strict economy of supernatural resources, which are resorted to only when natural resources fail.
          W. S. MONTGOMERY.

FRANKINCENSE (לְבֹנָה, λίβανος).—One of the ingredients of incense (קְטֹרָה), Ex 30[34], and one of the gifts brought by the Magi to the infant Saviour (Mt 2[11]). The name is derived from לבן 'to be white,' akin to which is lubân, the name by which frankincense is known in Arabia. It is a fragrant gum or resin, the produce of the tree Boswellia Serrata, of the natural order Amyridaceæ, from which it is obtained by slitting the bark. The

---

* τοῦ τὴν κεφαλὴν κλίνη, cf. Jn 19[30] κλίνας τὴν κεφαλήν. Jesus never rested till, His work being finished, He rested on the cross.

tree itself is a native of Central and Southern India, whence the gum, which requires no further preparation than being allowed to harden, is exported to Europe, the yellowish or inferior quality in larger quantities than the white. Some uncertainty has existed as to the source of the supply. It seems clear that no such tree existed in Palestine, but that the frankincense used there was imported through Arabia (cf. Is 60[6], Jer 6[20], where 'incense' in AV ought to be 'frankincense,' and is so rendered in RV). The opening up of India by Britain made it plain that the source of the supply, which had previously come through Persia, was to be found there.

The ritual use of frankincense, in the OT as among the heathen, denotes direct adoration. It is burned as an appendage to the *minḥāh* (Lv 2[2]). According to old allegorizing traditions, the frankincense offered by the Magi signified the Divinity of the Holy Child, the gold representing His royalty, the myrrh either His healing powers or His prospect of suffering.

LITERATURE.—Birdwood, *The Genus Boswellia*, London, 1870, also in *Trans. Linn. Society*, xxvii., 1871; *Encyc. Brit.*[9] art. 'Frankincense.'   S. J. RAMSAY SIBBALD.

FREEDOM.—See FREE WILL and LIBERTY.

FREE WILL.—It is not easy to give a definition of Free Will that is not tautological,—indeed, strictly speaking, it cannot be defined. It may, however, be described as the ability to determine within oneself as to one's acts or courses of action. We have not anywhere in the Gospels or, indeed, in the NT mention made in specific terms of Free Will, or any statement made in so many words that either the Divine will or the will of man is free. We have little, in fact, of philosophical or philosophico-theological discussion of any kind in the NT. The nearest approach to such a thing is in Ro 9[18-24], where the question of human freedom is approached, and even there such discussion is rather deprecated, as verging on impiety, than entered upon. But while the question of the freedom of the will, whether the will of God or the will of man, is not formally dealt with in the NT, it is quite plain that God is regarded as acting freely, and that man is recognized as a free agent.

1. That God is not bound by any necessity external to Himself, that He acts according to the counsel of His will, is rather to be gathered from the general spirit of Scripture teaching than to be deduced from particular passages. The freedom of the Divine will is, indeed, plainly implied, although not explicitly mentioned, in such words as (Ro 11[34-36]), 'For who hath known the mind of the Lord? or who hath been his counsellor? or who hath first given to him, and it shall be recompensed unto him again? For of him, and through him, and to him are all things: to whom be glory for ever. Amen.' But Scripture simply accepts the freedom of the Divine will rather than formally states it. We cannot, however, think of God as acting other than freely, if we are to accept Him as a living God at all. Did we suppose that there was any necessity outside of Himself constraining Him to act in a certain way, we should be making an impersonal force the true Deity. We are constrained to believe that God acts freely. Yet to say that the Most High acts freely does not mean that He acts capriciously. He acts in accordance with His own nature. We can conceive that He might have made the material universe other than He has made it, but we cannot conceive Him as acting otherwise than in love and holiness and justice. Still, the necessity by which, in a sense, He may be said to act where His moral government is concerned is simply the necessity of being true to His own nature.

2. That man is a free agent is not stated in so many words in the NT, but is assumed everywhere. Surely when our Lord said (Mt 11[28]) 'Come unto me all ye that labour,' and (Jn 5[40]) 'Ye will not come to me that ye might have life,' He accepted the freedom of man as a reality. No doubt He also said (Jn 6[44]), 'No man can come unto me except the Father which hath sent me draw him.' But in saying so He did not mean that men were mere passive instruments, but simply that all that appealed to the heart in favour of spiritual living was from on high, whence also all spiritual aids came. Those who hold that the will is not free, or, as we should rather put it, that men are not free to will, do not as a rule argue so much from Scripture, although they may do that in part, as from philosophical grounds, and what they regard as experience. No doubt those who regard liberty as incompatible with predestination may argue that predestination is the plain doctrine of Scripture, but the conclusion that because predestination is the doctrine of Scripture man cannot be free is their own, and is not taught in Scripture. Whether man is free or not is to a large extent a question of merely academic interest, although not wholly so. We all act upon the hypothesis that we are free. Certainly the conclusion that men are not free operates against contrition for sin and repentance,—hinders one from feeling that he is guilty before God,—and perhaps it is partly with the desire to get rid of the sense of sin that some men argue against our possession of freedom. But in a general way we proceed on the assumption that men are free agents, hence the discussion of freedom is mainly one, as we have said, of academic interest. Scripture, as before remarked, accepts man's freedom as a fact, and we all have the consciousness of being free. It is argued, however, on various grounds that the sense of freedom which we have is illusive. In his *Outline of Christian Theology* Dr. W. N. Clarke mentions four grounds on which the doctrine of human freedom is challenged: viz. (*a*) Fatalism, (*b*) Predestinarianism, (*c*) Necessitarianism, (*d*) Determinism.

(*a*) There is perhaps no need of seriously discussing *Fatalism*, which seems to be a mere philosophy of despair. We all at times feel the strange inevitableness of things, but fatalism cannot commend itself to us as a reasoned philosophy.

(*b*) *Predestinarianism* in some form or other we can hardly avoid accepting, if we believe in an ordered universe; and to resolve predestination, in so far as rational and moral beings are concerned, into simple foreknowledge, does not materially, or at least very materially, help us. Of course it may be argued that the knowledge that a thing is to occur does not necessarily imply that the doer of it must do it. From the antecedents of a man we may judge tolerably well what his course of action in given circumstances will be, but our knowledge as to how he is likely to act does not affect his freedom,—does not compel him to act in the way foreseen. And so, it may be argued, the Divine foreknowledge of an action does not make the action inevitable, does not make it one that must be done. And this is perhaps formally true, but it is only formally so. What God foresees will be done has a material inevitableness about it, and will just as surely be done as if it had been predestinated. And if an action is predestinated, or even Divinely foreseen as being sure to occur, how can it be said that a man does it freely? Freedom seems incompatible with foreordination,—even with Divine foreknowledge. Yet no reasoning, however logical it may appear, can ever make us lose the sense of freedom. We may try to persuade ourselves that we are not free, but the sense of freedom will remain with us notwithstanding, and we shall go on acting as if we were free.

(c) We may say about *Necessitarianism*, or the doctrine that every volition is caused by its antecedents, that it is in a way true, but that, as urged against the freedom of the will, it neglects consideration of the fact that we ourselves are contributing all along to the antecedents which so far determine every volition.

(d) And with regard to *Determinism*, or the doctrine that all volitions are determined by motives acting on the will, it may be said that it also is true, but that motives acting on the will are not like forces acting on a body and producing a resultant which may be mathematically calculated. Our motives are our own feelings and desires, however these may be affected by objects without us, and our decisions to act depend upon what we are, though that is not simply what, as we might say, nature has made us, but what to a large extent we have made ourselves. To suppose that we can act without motive of some kind would be to suppose what is contrary to all experience, for we are always more or less conscious of being influenced by motives, but the action of motives is no mere mechanical action. Our freedom, indeed, as Martensen (*Christian Ethics*, § 31, pp. 109, 110) well points out, is conditioned, not absolute. We are not free save within certain limits, and many things—our native tendency to sin, heredity, environment, above all the force of habit—operate against our acting freely in accordance with our consciousness of what is best. But the sense of freedom which we possess is not illusive. We need, doubtless, the Divine aid in order to true religious living. But we are bound by no iron chain of necessity. We are, save in so far as we may have ourselves enslaved our wills, bound by no outward or inward constraint to will other than the good. And even the enslaved will can be made free by Divine grace.

3. The notion of moral freedom which is presented in the NT differs from all merely philosophical ideas on the subject. Here freedom means the being set free from the bondage of sin, and thus enabled to realize the ideal of human nature as created in the image of God (Ro 6[20ff.]). The freedom of the Christian will lies not in the power to do whatsoever we please, but in the power to choose and follow that for which God made us. God Himself is absolutely free, precisely because He is the absolutely perfect moral Being ; and Christ's power to make others free springs from His own Divine freedom—that moral oneness with the Father in the strength of which He did always the things that were pleasing to Him (Jn 8[29]). In Christ's gospel a freedom after His own pattern is offered to all. The Son can make us free so that we shall be free indeed (Jn 8[36]). This freedom comes from union with Christ, for apart from Him we can do nothing (Jn 15[5]). The doctrine of the indwelling of Christ through the Holy Spirit, and the consequent endowment of His disciples with freedom and power, was taught, according to the Fourth Gospel, by Jesus Himself (see esp. 14–17). It is constantly enforced by St. Paul as the testimony of his own experience. Apart from the law of the Spirit of life in Christ Jesus, the will is powerless to realize its own ideals (Ro 7[19ff.] 8[2ff.]). But in accepting Christ as our Master, and yielding to His law as supreme, we pass into 'the glorious liberty of the children of God.' See, further, LIBERTY.

LITERATURE.—Art. 'Will' in Hastings' *DB* ; Martensen, *Christian Ethics* ; T. H. Green, *Prolegomena to Ethics* ; Sir W. Hamilton, *Discussions* (appendix, Philosophical) ; A. M. Fairbairn, *The Philosophy of the Christian Religion* ; Albrecht Ritschl, *Justification and Reconciliation* ; J. R. Illingworth, *Reason and Revelation* ; W. N. Clarke, *Outline of Christian Theology* ; R. Anchor Thompson, *Christian Theism* ; and Philosophical and Theological works in general.

GEORGE C. WATT and J. C. LAMBERT.

FRIENDSHIP.—1. PRE-CHRISTIAN AND CHRISTIAN FRIENDSHIP. — Friendship was esteemed among the pagans and received memorable treatment at the hands of Aristotle (*Ethics*, Bks. viii. and ix.) and Cicero (*de Amicitia*). The latter said, 'There is nothing in the world more valuable than friendship.' Jewish literature treated the same subject, as, for example, in Sirach (6[15]), 'There is nothing that can be taken in exchange for a faithful friend.' This appreciation of friendship as one of the chief means of happiness throws light upon the ancient attitude. The mutual kindness of friends, considered necessary to complete the happiness even of the philosopher, but which was confined to those of the same school or character, makes more prominent the absence of benevolence from the ancient system of virtue. Christianity has also a high regard for friendship, has ennobled it, but has at the same time placed limitations upon it.

(1) The *enlargement* of Christian friendship is twofold. (a) The area within which the grace may be displayed is much extended by the teaching of Christianity upon the dignity of woman, whereby marriage loses any trace of the offence with which even many enlightened Jews regarded it,[*] and becomes a lofty friendship. (b) This is further enlarged by the new ideal of benevolence, which is to penetrate all the relations of life. Humanity has been dignified by the Incarnation. Christian Ethics is not the successor to the virtues of paganism, but the new spirit that turned patriotism into brotherhood, elevated friendship into universal love ; φιλία becomes φιλαδελφία. The exceptional exhibitions of goodwill and charity displayed by heathen, remarkable because of their contrast with the prevalent selfishness, are taken for granted among the members of the Kingdom of God. Friendship ceases to be a luxury and becomes a responsibility. Love, the root of all Christian virtues, must pervade all the performances of life.

(2) The *limitation* placed upon friendship in the new religion follows from the doctrine of the Divine friendship, which causes a complete readjustment of human thought. The pagans found little spiritual rest or inspiration in their religion, and human friendship was neither a reflexion nor a suggestion of a Divine fellowship. With Christ, however, the love for God is paramount, and receives an importance far beyond any other relationship. 'Ye, my friends, shall leave me alone : and yet I am not alone, for the Father is with me' (Jn 16[32]). To furnish this higher friendship is the mission of Christ. He has come that we may have the power to become sons of God (Jn 1[12]). Religion takes precedence over friendship : man may not usurp God's place. The gospel which teaches that man attains his exaltation according as he bows down in humble submission to the will of God, necessarily modifies the view that human companionship is the most valuable thing in the world. The Christian doctrine of God recasts everything in a new mould. Theology reacts upon anthropology. 'God is the beginning and foundation of all true and lasting friendship' (Zwingli).

2. THE TEACHING OF JESUS ON FRIENDSHIP.— This is suggestive and incidental rather than formal and detailed. In parables and conversations Christ indirectly drops sentences which show how general was His observation of all the relations into which people might enter. (1) In the parables

[*] But cf. Pr 31[10ff.], and Sir 40[23] 'A friend and companion never meet amiss, but above both is a wife with her husband.'

of the Lost Sheep and the Lost Piece of Silver, He touches upon the much debated *basis* of friendship. The joyous discovery of lost possession leads to social communion. 'He (she) calleth together his (her) friends and neighbours, saying, Rejoice with me' (Lk 15⁶·⁹). This act is the natural result of the instinct for association. The consciousness of joy breaks through the bounds of individualism and runs over into the sphere of human companionship; for the feeling that life's great emotions are too strong for narrow limits constrains men to seek this expansion among others. The soul delights in self-revelation. 'But no receipt openeth the heart but a true friend : To whom you may impart, Griefes, Joyes, Fears, Hopes, Suspicions, Counsels, and whatsoever lieth upon the Heart' (Bacon). This spontaneous overflow, due to the instinct of association, has been implanted by God; and friendship is thus one of the good gifts of Heaven. Cicero also assigned a similar spontaneity to this virtue.

(2) Several types of *false friendship* are suggested by Jesus. (*a*) The parable of the Unjust Steward (Lk 16¹⁻⁹), 'who made friends out of the mammon of unrighteousness,' illustrates the *commercial* type. The material comforts of fellowship are gained by a clever distribution of money favours apart from all sympathy of heart or mind; and though Christ neither commends nor condemns, He indirectly reveals His mind in the remark, 'The children of this world are in their generation wiser than the children of light' (v.⁸). But true friendship is disinterested, and seeks the welfare of another rather than its own. 'Friendship is the wishing a person what we think good for his sake and not for our own, and, as far as is in our power, the exerting ourselves to procure it' (Aristotle, *Rhet.* ii. 4).—(*b*) The *exclusive* type of friendship is displayed in the parable of the Prodigal Son (Lk 15). The outwardly proper behaviour of the elder brother is marred by the lack of filial love; and his complaint, 'Thou never gavest me a kid that I might make merry with my friends,' shows how blind he was to the lavish affection of a father who bestowed his all upon him,—'Son, thou art ever with me, and all that I have is thine.' The son looked for a friendship apart from the nobler companionship of a loving father. His heart was not really in the home, for his secret longing was for the frivolous joys of the world, the merrymaking with friends, which he will have in isolation from the love of home. The unpleasant impression left by the picture of the elder brother is Christ's way of giving His opinion of a friendship which shuts itself up within the circle of favourite comrades, and is careless of the higher claims of love and benevolence. It then becomes a refined selfishness.—(*c*) The *irresponsible* type is described in Lk 11⁵⁻⁸, where the householder is so comfortably settled in bed that he refuses to rise and give bread to a friend, who is unexpectedly called upon to show a greater service to his friend. 'Friend, lend me three loaves, for a friend of mine in his journey is come to me.' Friendship here recognizes no responsibilities, and will not discommode itself to the extent of getting out of bed. Are we mistaken in seeing a touch of irony in this portrayal of a bond which lasted only with the enjoyment of benefits, but could not stand the strain of any personal inconvenience? Friendship is mutual assistance. 'A friend loveth at all times, and a brother is born for adversity' (Pr 17¹⁷).

(3) *The claim of old friends* was recognized by Jesus when He cast out the devils from 'Legion' (Mk 5¹⁹). The evil spirit, always an isolating influence, had excluded this unhappy man from the comforts of home and companionship. But when he is healed and the craving for intercourse is awakened, Jesus directs it to old channels : 'Jesus saith unto him, Go home to thy friends and tell them how great things the Lord hath done for thee.' These associates and guardians of his youth had borne with him through the evil days, and Jesus will not be a partner to any indifference to those obligations contracted by former benefits. He knew how keen was the sting of 'friend remembered not.'

(4) Jesus placed *restrictions* upon friendship at the feast given by the rich Pharisee, and condemned the selfish narrowing of the acts of hospitality. 'When thou makest a dinner or a feast do not call thy friends . . . but call the poor' (Lk 14¹². ¹³). The force of the verb is not prohibitive, but restrictive : 'Do not habitually call' (μὴ φώνει). Friendship must have open doors, and recognize the larger hospitality. Thus Jesus broadened the stream of friendship by bringing neighbours within the same flow of feeling, as is set forth in the parable of the Good Samaritan (Lk 10³⁰ff·). 'Thou shalt love thy neighbour as thyself.' Nor did Jesus stop at neighbour. He included enemy also. The Christian must have no foes. 'I say unto you, Love your enemies' (Mt 5⁴⁴). The sentiment of love must pervade every motive, filling the soul with gentle kindliness. Cicero had said that 'Sweetness both in language and manner is a very profitable attraction in the formation of friendship'; but what is with him an accident becomes an essential in the Kingdom of Jesus. The distinctive word with Christ is love and not friendship, and, by reason of this, Christianity excels the pagan ideals. The new commandment, 'that ye love one another' (Jn 13³⁴), decides all matters of conduct. True friends will not sanction any imperfection, or acquiesce in any weak neglect of talents in those whom they love; while at the same time the charity of the gospel will bear all things, will hope all things.

(5) Jesus also taught that the life of love was *endless*. The old friendships flourished under dark skies. Fears of an awful end haunted them, and when death came, 'They dreamed there would be spring no more.' But Christ has brought life and immortality to light through His gospel. He has spoken with certainty of the future, and has made the darkness beautiful. The Christian poet can rise out of the calamity of interrupted friendship into the repose of faith and self-control.

'Far off thou art but ever nigh,
I have thee still and I rejoice :
I prosper, circled with thy voice :
I shall not lose thee tho' I die' (*In Memoriam*, cxxx.).

Human affection will pass through the cleansing stream of death, and purified of all selfishness and evil will be made perfect in the presence of God.

3. The friendship of Jesus.—Christianity is a life as well as a system of teaching; and as each virtue or quality is best interpreted in the light of the highest example of its kind, so also human friendship becomes transfigured by the friendship which Jesus offers to all who will receive Him.

(1) *The friendship of Jesus as revealed in the Gospels.*—These narratives show how approachable Jesus was. His readiness to accept social invitations, to befriend all classes, to reveal His gracious message, testifies to His genius for friendship, and accounts in part for the contemptuous title, 'Friend of publicans and sinners.' He chose twelve 'that they might be with him' (Mk 3¹⁴), and to these He revealed what was dearest to His heart. On the Mount of Transfiguration He admitted three of them to the vision of His glory (Mt 17¹⁻¹³ ‖): in Gethsemane He opened to the same three the door of His grief (26³⁶⁻⁴⁶): He told His disciples of the stern struggle with temptation in

the wilderness of Judæa. The house at Bethany was a second home to Him, and His love for 'our friend Lazarus' was manifested in His visit to the sisters, and in the grief that overwhelmed Him at the grave (Jn 11).

In the second part of the Fourth Gospel the affection of Jesus is seen to lack the slightest 'grain of depreciation,' which Schopenhauer recommends among friends. The constancy of the perfect Friend is the first theme of this intimate writing (Jn 13–17), a constancy unimpaired by sorrow or joy. The foreboding of death ('knowing that he would depart out of this world') threatened to draw away His mind, as also the vision of a transcendent glory ('that he would depart unto the Father') imperilled His attachment; but neither the excess of grief nor the ecstasy of gladness availed to weaken His fidelity to those whom He had chosen; 'having loved his own, he loved them unto the end' (Jn 13[1]). In the following chapters the love of Jesus is unfolded with the eloquence peculiar to St. John's Gospel. Christ breathes about them the atmosphere of God's glory, lifts up their thoughts to the heavenly home, filling them with the fragrant truth of the endless love of God, all of which is summed up in terms of friendship in Jn 15[13-15]. (a) Jesus is a perfect friend because of His personal sacrifice : 'Greater love hath no man than this, that a man lay down his life for his friend' (v.[13]). Sacrifice is the most convincing evidence in the world, and the surrender of personal advancement for the sake of others is proof of the noble emotion of love. As there is nothing that a man can give in exchange for his life, the death of Jesus for us is the highest evidence of His perfect friendship. Sacrifice is also the food of love, and friendship is growth in self-sacrificing love. Each self-denial strengthens the bond of attachment, and when sacrifice is allowed its perfect work it forms a deathless union. Jesus experienced every stage of self-denial, suppressing His own desires, until His love, perfected through suffering, received its crown and goal on the Mount of Crucifixion. The sacrifice which was the evidence of His perfect friendship was also the only sustenance by which perfect friendship could be nourished. (b) Christ's friendship is an ethical constraint : 'Ye are my friends if ye do whatsoever I command you' (v.[14]). He is our kindest friend who makes us do our best, and who helps us to do what we thought we could not do. The consciousness of expanding power is purest joy. Christ arouses enthusiasm for the holy life, imparts new resolves to master temptation, and is the most effectual aid in the attainment of the ethical life. His friendship is our better self, our conscience. (c) There is intimate communion in the friendship of Jesus : 'Henceforth I call you not servants, but I have called you friends : for all things that I have heard of my Father, I have made known unto you' (v.[15]). Friendship is fellowship in which undue reserve is cast off. When Christ spoke out on the most sacred matters of religion, and shared with others His knowledge of the Father, He did the friendliest of acts. Christ's love was the most intimate relation into which any man could enter, and His constancy, devotion, communion, and inspiration gave Him the first place among friends.

(2) The friendship of Jesus as revealed in Christian experience.—The limits of human friendship are many, and suggest the blessings which all believers in Christ have enjoyed by their union with the living Saviour. In our human relationships no words are adequate to express the subtler, and more refined emotions and convictions of the soul, so that when we strive to reveal our true self we stammer. Besides, we often cannot define these things to ourselves, and we require one who will

first tell us our dream and then interpret it. Inhospitality of soul and our native bashfulness impede communion, while the sense of defect or unworthiness restricts our fellowship. Differences of experience separate us, so that we cannot match each other's moods. Distance and change of occupation place physical barriers, while too often the faults of temper and vexing cares drive apart those who once were knit together in sympathy. How precarious is our hold upon a friendship which 'death, a few light words, a piece of stamped paper,' can destroy. But Jesus transcends all these limits of human friendship. His spirit can commune with our spirits apart from language. He knows us altogether, and needs not that any should tell Him. He is master of large experience, having been tempted in all points like as we are, yet without sin. Physical barriers are all removed, since He will never go away from us or forsake us. He is the same yesterday, to-day, and for ever. The universal testimony of the Christian Church is that as we abide in the presence of Jesus by prayer, self-denial, and meditation, we are uplifted in soul, encouraged in our holy endeavours, and made partakers of spiritual joy. The believer finds that Christ is the way to the Father, that Jesus leads us to that communion with God which is the greatest fact of all the world. Religion is friendship between the believer and the living Christ.

LITERATURE.—Aristotle, Ethics ; Cicero, de Amicitia ; PRE3, art. 'Freundschaft' ; Lemme, Die Freundschaft, Heilbronn, 1897 ; Bacon, Essays, Golden Treasury Series, 1892, p. 106 ; Hugh Black, Friendship, 1900 ; Hilty, Briefe, Leipzig, 1903 ; Tennyson, In Memoriam ; Martensen, Christian Ethics, iii. 72 ff. ; Stalker, Imago Christi, 93 ff.

JAMES W. FALCONER.

FRINGES.—See BORDER.

FRUIT.—The consideration of this term as it is used in the Gospels divides itself into three parts : (1) The natural application of the word 'fruit' ($\kappa\alpha\rho\pi\delta s$) to the products of the field and the orchard ; (2) other references to fruit under their specific names ; (3) the spiritual lessons derived from these allusions.

1. In its natural sense the word 'fruit' is used : (a) in reference to grain-crops (Mt 13[8], Mk 4[7], Lk 8[8] 12[17]) ; (b) physiologically, of the fruit of the womb (Lk 1[42]) ; (c) of the fruit of (a) trees generally (Mt 3[10], Lk 3[9]) ; (β) the fig-tree (Mt 21[19], Mk 11[14], Lk 13[6]) ; (γ) the vine (Mt 21[41], Mk 12[2], Lk 20[10]).

2. Other references to fruits under their specific names, without the use of the word 'fruit' : (a) grapes (Mt 7[16], Lk 6[44]) ; (b) figs (Mt 7[16], Mk 11[13], Lk 6[44]) ; (c) husks (Lk 15[16], probably the fruit of the carob or locust-tree) ; (d) mulberry (Lk 17[6]) ; (e) olives (Mt 21[1]). Probably the 'thorns' ($\check{\alpha}\kappa\alpha\nu\theta\alpha\iota$) alluded to in Mt 7[16] are not the so-called 'Apple of Sodom,' but a generic term covering all sorts of prickly plants. The parallel use with 'thistles' ($\tau\rho\dot{\iota}\beta o\lambda o\iota$) suggests that the fruit was inconsiderable.

3. Spiritual lessons. — Christ Himself is intimately associated with (a) the Divine quest of fruit ; (b) the Divine creation of fruit ; (c) the Divine suffering and sacrifice of fruit-production. The processes of agriculture and horticulture are also, in many ways, utilized as symbols of the Christian's culture of the soul.

(a) Jesus describes Himself (Mt 21, Lk 20) under the figure of the Son whom the Master of the Vineyard sends to ask fruit of the husbandman. Our life is a rich gift to us from God ; it is a garden which God has designed with lavish care, endowed with unlimited possibilities, and handed over to our complete control. He has a right to expect that we should use our opportunities well.

(b) Jesus uses the figure of the Vine (Jn 15) and

the Branches to express the vital and mysterious connexion that exists between Himself and His disciples, and the necessity for our dependence upon Him and His continuous inspiration, if we are to bring forth fruit. It is our responsibility to 'abide in Him' by keeping His commandments. But it is His obligation to create the fruit. We who cannot so much as make a blade of grass grow without His co-operation, are not expected to accomplish the impossible and bring forth fruit of ourselves.

(c) Jesus manifestly alludes to His own death and sacrifice (Jn 12²⁴) under the allegory of the grain of wheat which falls into the ground and dies, and afterwards rises in the new life of the fruit. This figure betokens the utter consecration and determination of the holiness of God to our redemption. We are apt to shudder and tremble before the holiness of God, as a thing of terrible and inaccessible majesty associated with the Great White Throne. That is because we have not taken full views, but have isolated one part from the rest. God is glorious in His holiness (Ps 145); it is such holiness as man praises when he sees it; it is hospitable, friendly, and devoted to our welfare. It is determined even unto death to share its joy and health and purity with us (Jn 12²⁴ 17¹⁹).

In the Museum of the Vatican there is a little glass relic, taken from the Catacombs; it was made as an ornament to be worn round the neck of a woman, and was found in her grave; it represents Christ bringing again the fruit of the Tree of Life.* That relic summarizes the Divine aspects of the question of fruit as it is presented in the Gospels. It is Christ who loves fruit, and who desires to find it in us; and it is He who, in the inspiration and creation of the fruit, virtually gives Himself to us.

But, as in agriculture and horticulture the farmer and the gardener are co-operators with God in the production of the fruits of the earth and the fruit of the trees, so, in many ways, the Gospels lay upon us the injunctions of our duty.

(1) We are the ground which brings forth fruit, according as we receive the Word (Mt 13¹⁹ff., Mk 4¹⁵ff., Lk 8¹²ff.). If our hearts be like the wayside, trampled over and hardened by the interests and engagements of the world, or if they be readily affected by the opinions of men, or if they be choked by the cares of this life and the deceitfulness of riches, there can be no fruitfulness. It is our duty to prepare the ground by thought and prayer and a regulated life for the reception of God's truth. The harvest will correspond with the tillage.

(2) We are the branches which bear fruit according as we abide in the Vine (Jn 15). Just as the gardener prunes and purges a tree so that it may bring forth more fruit, so there are afflictions in this life which are only God's way of increasing our fruitfulness. The branches which draw most sustenance from the vine are the most productive, so the soul which keeps most faithfully the Lord's commandments abides the most in His love and is most fruitful.

(3) We are the grain of wheat which comes to fruit, if it dies (Jn 12²⁴·²⁵). In the first place, the Master alludes to His own death. But the second reference of the figure is to the essential principle of ethical life—'Die to live.'

To Hegel, 'the great aphorism (of Jn 12²⁵), in which the Christian ethics and theology may be said to be summed up, is no mere epigrammatic saying, whose self-contradiction is not to be regarded too closely; it is rather the first distinct, though as yet undeveloped, expression of the exact truth as to the nature of spirit. The true interpretation of the maxim—"Die to live,"—is, that the individual must die to an isolated life,— i.e. a life for and in himself, a life in which the immediate satisfaction of desire as his desire is an end in itself,—in order that he may live the spiritual life, the universal life which really belongs to him as a spiritual or self-conscious being' (Edward Caird, Hegel, p. 213).

* See Rex Regum by Sir Wyke Bayliss.

(4) We are the husbandmen, who are expected to tend the Vineyard (Lk 20), and to make it fruitful, and to yield up a proportion of the fruit at rightful times to the Lord of the vineyard. The original application of the parable is, doubtless, to the scribes and the chief priests who rejected Jesus, but it is equally applicable to any who think they can do as they please with their life and ignore all obligations to the Giver and Lord.

(5) We are the trees which are known by their fruit (Mt 7²⁰). Men do not gather grapes from thorns, or figs from thistles. A tree which is true to its nature and to its destiny brings forth its appropriate fruit. Man, who is by nature a child of God and by destiny an heir of Heaven, should produce the fruit of the Spirit of God.

LITERATURE.—For 1 and 2 see Hastings' DB and Encyc. Bibl. art. 'Fruit.' For 3, Expos. Times viii. [1897] 403 f., ix. [1898] 211 ff.; Expositor II. vii. [1884] 121 ff.; Maclaren, Holy of Holies, 168–189; Hull, Sermons, i. 51 ff.; A. Murray, Abide in Christ, 30 ff., 140 ff.; Macmillan, Bible Teachings in Nature, 174 ff.

H. HERBERT SNELL.

FULFILMENT.—The primary meaning of the English word 'fulfil' is simply to fill—by a pleonasm, to fill (until) full. We find this use in literature—

'Is not thy brain's rich hive
Fulfilled with honey?' (Donne).

Sometimes it is imitated even in modern English, though only by a deliberate archaism. For with us 'fulfil' is specialized to mean not literal material filling, but the carrying out into act of some word—some promise, threat, hope, command, etc. When the AV was made, 'fulfil,' according to the great Oxford Dictionary, meant 'fill,' and began to be used by the translators in its remoter sense on the pattern of the Vulgate, which wrote (unclassically) implere and adimplere for Heb. מָלֵא. Thus the transition from one sense to the other, or the metaphor of filling for fulfilling, is Hebrew. But in Greek, too, it is possible that the same metaphor sprang up independently of Hebrew influence; cf. classical references (under πληροῦν) in Cremer, also in Liddell and Scott (πληροῦν, ii. 5). In OT the usage is not very common. Possibly the earliest instance, chronologically, is Jer 44²⁵. What the Jews in Egypt have said, they do. Their threat to practise idolatry is not left an empty word; it is filled out, or filled up, in action. At Ps 20⁵ we have the word used of answers to prayer: 'Jehovah fulfil all thy petitions'; the empty vessel, as it were, standing to receive the Divine supplies. For 'fulfilling law' or 'fulfilling a command' there is no proper authority in OT, though EV at times introduces the term (Ps 148⁸; literally, the forces of nature 'do' God's word). In 1 K 2²⁷ 8¹⁵·²⁴ we have the most important usage of all, the 'fulfilling' of the prophetic word or prediction. The passages referred to are marked by modern scholarship as Deuteronomic. We may therefore probably conclude that the theological conception of 'fulfilling' is part of the religious language of that great forward movement in OT history, the Deuteronomic reform. Along with these theological applications מָלֵא may mean 'fill' anywhere in the OT. And so in NT (πληροῦν chiefly): in the parable of the Drag-net (Mt 13⁴⁸), the net is 'filled' with all kinds of fish; Mt 23³², 'Fill ye up then the measure of your fathers.' More generally, however, the word bears its derivative sense, and has a theological application. Though rare in OT, the usage is quite common in NT, very noticeably, of fulfilled prophecy, in the First Gospel. A beginning of differentiation or specification is made in the NT in this respect, that while πληροῦν may mean 'fill,' the simpler but kindred form πιμπλάναι [others assume πλήθω as root form] never means 'fulfil.'

A second metaphor underlies קִיֵּם. This is probably still later theological language. It means specially the fulfilling of prediction. We find it in Ezr 1[1]=2 Ch 36[22]. According to Bertholet (on Ezr *l.c.*; he refers to Dn 12[7] also), 'Fulfilment ranks simply as the *end* of the prophetic word, which, once spoken, enters among the powers of the real world and gradually works itself out.' This word and metaphor are also common in NT. Sometimes we have τελεῖν and cognates; though here again there is a tendency (less marked, however, than with πληροῦν in contrast to πιμπλάναι) to prefer a more specialized or technical term—τελειοῦν, τελείωσις. God's work is *begun* by the prophetic word, but *incomplete* till the fact matches the promise.

A third term and metaphor are of some moment in OT, but scarcely enter into NT—קוּם, βεβαιοῦν. (God's promise may seem to be tottering to its fall, —He will buttress it; support it). See Jer 29[10], Is 44[26], Ro 15[8]; but in the Gospels only Mk 16[20] 'confirming . . . with signs following.' (How fully this is a synonym for מָלֵא we see when we note the usage of מָלֵא at 1 K 1[14]). שָׁלֵם, lit. 'return' or 'reward,' occurs by an extension of meaning at Is 44[26. 28] for 'fulfil'; not imitated in NT. Also, as already implied, EV sometimes introduces 'fulfil' or 'be fulfilled' where the original has merely 'do' or 'be.' And we cannot say that this is illegitimate. A very important passage is the last clause of Mt 5[18] AV; but RV 'till all things be accomplished' [to mark the contrast with πληρῶσαι, v.[17]. See below—4.—on both verses.]

We have then to look chiefly to מָלֵא, πληροῦν, while not forgetting other forms. And the question may be raised, whether the NT writers were alive to the implication of steady quantitative growth towards fulfilment? Or had the original suggestions of quantity and of continuousness passed away,—was there assumed a mere *correspondence between* the word and its fulfilment? (If one pours water into a vessel, it fills *by degrees*. But if one is fitting together a ball-and-socket joint, the socket is empty at one moment, full at the next. The two correspond, but their correspondence is not reached by gradual growth). We shall have to distinguish in this as in other respects between different senses of πληροῦν (or its synonyms).

1. *Fulfilment of time.* Here, if anywhere, we may expect to find the ideas of continuity and gradualness. Now 'fulfil' is constantly used in the OT of the elapsing of a given time—alike in Hebrew, Greek, and English; or, in NT, alike in Greek and English. It is used of the period of a woman's gestation (*e.g.* Gn 25[24]; πληρόω, LXX; Lk 1[57] 2[6]—πιμπλάναι; RV 'fulfilled' in all 3 cases). There is no more striking or more frequently noted parable of

> The slow sweet hours that bring us all things good,
> The slow sad hours that bring us all things ill;

or sometimes, as George Eliot has expressed it in *Adam Bede*, of 'swift hurrying shame,' 'the bitterest of life's bitterness.' But the word is also used of other measured times—of periods fixed by OT law (*e.g.* Lk 2[21. 22], πιμπλάναι, RV 'fulfilled'; cf. Lv 12[4], מָלֵא (Qal); LXX πληρόω). From such usages as these, we pass on to times of Divine fulfilment. 'The fulness of the time came' (τὸ πλήρωμα τοῦ χρόνου), Gal 4[4]. And our Lord's own message is summed up in Mk 1[15]: 'The time is fulfilled (πεπλήρωται ὁ καιρὸς) and the kingdom of God is at hand; repent ye and believe in the gospel.' (Probably secondary in comparison with Mt 4[17], 'Repent ye, for the kingdom of heaven is at hand'; yet thoroughly significant of Biblical and primitive Christian beliefs, cf. Is 61[2], Lk 4[19]). The idea is, that God has fixed a time, 'His own good time,' as our pious phrase runs. (Is that a misquotation of Is 60[22]? RV 'in *its* time'; AV [same sense; archaic

English] 'in his time'). The number seventy (70 years of exile, Jer 25[11] [29[10]], cf. Dn 9[2. 24]) was specially important for this conception of a fixed period Divinely appointed. Yet we have signs that the 'time' or its 'fulness' is not, for the Bible writers, mechanically predetermined. The eschatological discourse (Mt 24[22]=Mk 13[20]) tells us that the time of trouble, at the world's end, shall be *cut short* out of mercy to God's people. [Lk. omits, and inserts a reference to 'times of the Gentiles' which must be 'fulfilled,' 21[24].] And it is possible that another popular religious phrase—the 'hastening' of God's kingdom—may have Biblical warrant. It appears at Is 60[22] [quoted above]. But when (as Marti advises) we refer back to Is 5[19], we find that the word 'hasten' was introduced originally to express the temper of a sneerer—'Let God hurry up, if He is really going to act [and not simply talk].' So that 'hasten,' when used at 60[22], may have come to mean no more than 'fulfil.' Cf. also Hab 2[3] and 2 P 3[4-9]. Still, when the fulness of a Divinely appointed time is spoken of, all these qualifications drop out of sight. In some sense a period of time is Divinely ordained; and efflux of time brings the day when God acts. Fulfilment of *time* is not indeed identical with fulfilment of God's *promise* [or threat]. The first is a *condition* of the second. In regard to the first, at least, the quantitative sense of 'fulfil' is maintained in clear consciousness. ('My time is not yet fulfilled,' Jn 7[8] = 'mine hour is not yet come,' 2[4]).

2. *Fulfilment of joy* (πληρόω). Here again there is an ambiguity. When St. Paul says (Ph 2[2]) 'Fulfil ye my joy,' what does he mean? Is it (1) 'Complete my happiness; unless I hear of your being thoroughly at one, I cannot be perfectly happy'? or (2) does he mean, 'I have sacrificed many ordinary sources of happiness; give me this my chosen joy'? Authorities seem to prefer the first; perhaps, 'complete the joy I already have in you.' That is, 'fulfilment' of 'joy' is taken as a quantitative and continuous idea. Elsewhere the phrase is peculiarly Johannine (Jn 3[29] 15[11] 16[24] 17[13], with 1 Jn 1[4], 2 Jn[12]). The Baptist, *e.g.* (3[29]), has *his* joy *in full*. He has *all* the joy he *can* expect. Yet there is more than this in the words: He has full joy—'rejoiceth greatly.' In the Johannine passages the *two* thoughts seem included: the joy (Christ's joy, *e.g.*) is given; and what is given is a full joy. So prominent is the latter thought—the more quantitative—that one is tempted to regard AV 'full' as a better rendering, in regard to *joy*, than the more literal 'fulfilled' of RV.

3. *Fulfilment of prophecy* or *of Scripture* or *of Christ's words* (usually πληρόω, Mt 1[22] and very often; Mk 15[28] [doubtful text]; Lk 1[20], Jn 12[38] and elsewhere. In Christ's death, Mt 26[54. 56] [a 'doublet']=Mk 14[49] [Lk 22[53] has not the *word*]; Lk 4[21] 21[22] 24[44], cf. 9[31] 'his decease'; 21[24] 'times of the Gentiles'; 22[16] the Passover 'fulfilled in the kingdom of God'; Jn 13[18] 15[25] and elsewhere. But τελειόω, Jn 19[28]. There is perhaps a slight difference in meaning—not the *word* of Scripture verified, but the terrible *things* spoken of in Scripture made actual—when we have τελέω at Lk 18[31] 22[37]. Purely in the sense of 'fulfilment,' perhaps, at Jn 19[28. 30]. συντελέω occurs Mk 13[4]; the noun συντέλεια [τοῦ αἰῶνος 'end of the world,' RVm 'consummation of the age'] in Mt.'s ‖, 24[3], and also at 13[39. 40] 28[20]. [He 9[26], συντέλεια τῶν αἰώνων 'end of the ages,' RV; marg. 'consummation']. τελειόω [AV 'finish,' RV 'accomplish'] is used in the Johannine discourses of Christ's work [ἔργον, 4[34] 17[4]] or works [5[36], cf. again 19[30]]). As far as the words rendered 'fulfil' are concerned, they are used in the same sense throughout; whether the fulfilment is of the past (the OT) in the present (Christ), or of the present (Christ's words) in the (eschatological) future. And several Greek words are fairly represented by the same English meaning. Moreover, for a full index of the Scripture teaching we should need to include passages like Lk 24²⁵⁻²⁷, where no *word* 'fulfil' occurs. (But we have it in Lk 24⁴⁴). This holds especially of the fulfilment of Christ's own words. It is true, the word as well as the thought occurs in the Fourth Gospel (18⁹⁻³²), but in the Synoptics the phrasing is different. The nearest approach is Mk 13³⁰ ‖, 'until all [these] things be accomplished (γένηται)—a difficult passage, discussed below (under 'Fulfilment of law'). We must lay down, in general, that the NT thinks of fulfilment as occurring in detailed mechanical correspondence with the letter of prediction. God has said so-and-so, therefore it must happen exactly as was said. In Jn 19⁻⁸ it is difficult to take any other view of the Evangelist's meaning than that Jesus exclaimed 'I thirst,' because the Passion psalms had spoken of the cruel thirst of the Sufferer. We must not, of course, exaggerate the simplicity of the Bible writers. A few verses earlier, where Jn 18⁹ interprets Jesus' protection of His disciples, at the moment of His own arrest, as the fulfilment of the word which He spake, 'Of those whom thou hast given me I lost not one,' the Evangelist knows perfectly, and trusts his readers to remember, that the true sense of Christ's words belongs to a different region. In that one instance, at least, he is consciously accommodating, as we might do in quoting a line of Shakspeare. And there is more. The Evangelist discerns in Christ's care for the disciples a type of the supreme spiritual transaction. Even outwardly, Christ saves others, while not saving but sacrificing Himself. Still, in general, the letter of the NT takes the letter of the OT as a magic book, foreshowing what must happen to Christ. Deeper views are no doubt latent in the NT, but they are nowhere formulated by it. They do not rise to the surface of consciousness in Evangelist or Apostle.

4. Fulfilment of law [and prophets ?]. [*Fulfilment generally ?*] The interpretation here raises very difficult questions, hardly to be settled without some critical surgery. First let us take what is simple ; to 'fulfil' the Law is to obey it—τελεῖν—at Ro 2²⁷, Ja 2⁸ ; or πληροῦν, Gal 5¹⁴, Ro 13⁸·¹⁰. (On these last, see below). Unambiguous, too, is 'to fulfil all righteousness' (πληρῶσαι, Mt 3¹⁵) ; and the saying may well be historical, though unsupported in the parallels. It fits the circumstances (see present writer's paper on 'Dawn of Messianic Consciousness' in *Expos. Times*, 1905, p. 215), if perhaps tinged in expression with the Evangelist's phraseology. But what of Mt 5¹⁷ ('Think not that I came to destroy the law or the prophets ; I came not to destroy but to fulfil'—πληρῶσαι)? (*a*) Much has been written on this subject since the present writer discussed the passage in *Christ and the Jewish Law*, 1886. Even more decidedly than then, he must insist that if v.¹⁸—and especially if v.¹⁹—is a genuine part of Christ's discourse, we are shut up to understand 'fulfil' in the sense of 'obey' (so Cremer's *Lexicon*, bracketing 5¹⁷ with 3¹⁵). But (*b*) the case for omitting v.¹⁸—with its Pharisaic aspect, its at least seemingly exaggerated canonization of the whole letter of the Pentateuch — is being very strongly pressed to-day (*e.g.* Votaw, art. 'Sermon on the Mount' in Hastings' *DB*, Ext. Vol.). If v.¹⁸ [some would say vv.¹⁸·¹⁹] be a gloss [or belong properly to a different context in a somewhat different form], we may render 'not to destroy but to *perfect* the law,'—raising it to its ideal height of purity, and carrying it to its ideal depth of inwardness. This view probably holds the field at present. It goes well with vv.²¹, etc., where our Lord, in a series of brilliant paradoxes, sweeps away the mere letter of the OT [? or the legal glosses added to it

by 'scribes and Pharisees' (v.²⁰)]. But there are difficulties. It is 'hard' to think that our Lord ever exercised the supposed conscious detailed intellectual criticism of the OT as such (so the late A. B. Davidson, in conversation with the present writer's informant). And would He have called His paradoxes a 'perfected' law ? They are at least as like a 'destruction' of the *régime* of law ! Moreover, we have the reference to the 'prophets.' (*c*) When 'fulfil' is predicated of 'prophecy,' the sense is well known ; the 'prophets' become the predominant partner in such a juxtaposition as 'to fulfil *law and prophets*' ; and we have to think of the OT's moral lawgiving as a sort of type, fulfilled, when the word of the prophets is fulfilled, in Christ's person. [*Christ and the Jewish Law* tried in a particular way to carry through this meaning of 'fulfil']. 'Law and prophets' repeatedly occur together in Christ's words, esp. in Mt. (also at 7¹² 22⁴⁰ 11¹³=Lk 16¹⁶, cf. Lk 24⁴⁴). We can hardly doubt that our Lord Himself used the expression ; and it is probable, too, that He used it as a general designation for the OT. Still, it is conceivable that *the Evangelist* has brought in the phrase here. A further measure of critical surgery would then dismiss (*c*), and leave the field so far to (*a*) and (*b*). But (*d*) we might raise a new possibility, either by exegesis, or if necessary by a minor form of critical excision. We might take Mt 5¹⁷ᵇ either as spoken here in pure abstraction—'I am not a destroyer but a fulfiller'—or as originally a separate *logion* worked into this context by the Evangelist.

In view of these rival interpretations one might turn for help to the Epistles. For, especially on ethical points, the teaching of Christ visibly moulds St. Paul's inculcation again and again. And in this way we might learn how the earliest Church understood its Lord's words. Gal 5¹⁴ and Ro 13⁸⁻¹⁰ [see above], while their use of πληρόω suggests Mt 5¹⁷, refer in substance rather to Mt 22³⁵⁻⁴⁰ [Mark's ‖, (12³¹) omits the very element which lives in the Epistles—love to God and man not only the chief duty but *the whole of duty*. In this case the Epistles decidedly support Mt.'s tradition. In Luke (10²⁷) we have an unwarranted suggestion that *the scribes* had already woven together Dt 6⁵ with Lv 19¹⁸. Thus Luke's tradition here seems still less exact. On Christ's originality in this matter, comp. Montefiore in *Hibbert Journal*, Apr. 1905]. Commentators seem to take Gal 5¹⁴—'all the law is fulfilled (πληροῦται) in one word, Thou shalt love thy neighbour as thyself'—as parallel not to Ro 13⁹ ('all the law is summed up—ἀνακεφαλαιοῦται—in Thou shalt love thy neighbour,' etc.), but rather to vv.⁸·¹⁰, 'Love πεπλήρωκε—is the πλήρωμα of the law.' St. Paul then takes fulfil=obey, as in (*a*), above. But does St. Paul's language really support (*a*)? Is there not something more than *obeying law* in the Pauline thought of 'fulfilment' (Ro 8⁴)? The requirement—δικαίωμα—of the Law is fulfilled in those who walk not after the flesh but after the spirit. The utmost we can say is that πληρόω, in the sense of 'fulfil,' had been given such currency in the Greek version of our Lord's words that St. Paul instinctively weaves it in when he is quoting another passage. Thus, after all, the evidence of the Epistles as to the original meaning of Mt 5¹⁷ is neutral, or at any rate not decisive.

Summary.—In Mt 5¹⁷, then, Christ claims either (*a*) to render a perfect obedience to law, or (*b*) to perfect the moral lawgiving of the OT, or (*c*) to fulfil absolutely the ideals of the OT generally, or (*d*) to be in general a fulfiller rather than a destroyer. (*a*) is not without evidence in its support. (*b*) is perhaps most generally popular. (*c*) we are inclined to regard as due to the mistaken intrusion in Mt 5¹⁷ of ['law] *and prophets*,'—words doubtless used by Christ (of the OT as a whole ?) in other connexions. (d) was on the whole supported in the above discussion—if necessary, at the cost of regarding v.[17b] as by rights an independent *logion*. (We have not discussed the extravagant suggestion that there was no Sermon on the Mount in Christ's ministry at all).

Mt 5[18]. We have quoted with sympathy a suggestion that this verse ought to be struck out of the context of Mt 5. But there is no ground for denying that it represents one of the sayings of Jesus. We have Luke's ‖, 16[17]; and, besides that, all three Synoptics have a similar phrase in the eschatological chapter. There they coincide almost to a word—'This generation shall not pass away till all [these] things be accomplished [γίνηται]. Heaven and earth shall pass away, but my words shall not pass away' (Mt 24[34. 35] = Mk 13[30. 31] = Lk 21[32. 33]). This (as nas often been pointed out) must surely be an alternative version of the *logion* Mt 5[18]. According to Mt 5, Christ spoke of the perpetuity of the Law; according to Mt 24, of the assured truth of His own words. We must note the presence of 3 corresponding clauses in each of the two passages: heaven and earth passing away — all things being accomplished—a Divine word not ‘passing away.’ In Mt 5[18] the first two elements jar against each other. The same sentence contains two limits—two clauses each beginning ἕως ἄν. In that respect 24[34. 35] shows to better advantage, and can advance the stronger claim to rank as the original. On the other hand, the verses in ch. 24 are themselves exceedingly difficult. It is no mere blind conservatism which hesitates to believe that our Lord pledged His supernatural knowledge for the conclusion of the world's story within a generation. The words, as we have them, mean that and nothing else; and it is surely incredible that Jesus should have so erred. We do not deny that He may have expected the end shortly; there is at least a strong NT tradition, direct and indirect, that He did. We do say that He could not stake everything, with the very greatest emphasis, upon—a date! which besides was a *mistaken* date. B. W. Bacon's solution is attractive—that the original *logion* referred to the *word of God*, but not specifically *either* to the OT law *or* to the Master's own words, though different lines of tradition insisted on one or the other identification.

5. ‘*Fulfilment*’ *in general.* — Some *individual passages.* (a) Lk 1[1] speaks of the things ‘fulfilled’ among us (πεπληροφορημένων; perf. particip. from a derivative of πληρόω, or at least of πλήρης). The connexion with v.[4]—‘the certainty of those things wherein,’ etc.—makes AV's rendering tempting; ‘things . . . most surely believed.’ But authority favours the rendering ‘fulfilled.’ Not, however, in the sense of ‘Divinely fulfilled.’ In these, the most classical verses from St. Luke's pen, we must look rather to classical models; and we should probably take ‘fulfilled’ as meaning ‘fully accomplished.’ So Holtzmann; or Adeney—‘Luke will record complete transactions, a finished story.’ Probably, therefore, there is nothing to be made of this passage. (b) In Lk 22[37] we read (RV), ‘This which is written must be fulfilled (τελεσθῆναι) in me, And he was reckoned with transgressors; for that which concerneth me hath fulfilment’ (τέλος ἔχει). Here there is room for difference of opinion. Holtzmann is respectful to the passage—a ‘valuable separate tradition of Luke's,’—but doubts whether the individual verse is a genuine saying of the Lord's. And he takes it as *meaning* merely that death, or *the end*, is hurrying near; on the analogy of Mk 3[26]—Satan if divided against himself ‘hath an end.’ On the other hand, Adeney, like the Revisers (apparently), thinks that Divine fulfilment is pointed to here. It is an interesting possibility. We can hardly say more. (c) If the suggestion offered above—(d)—regarding Mt 5[17b] should be adopted— if that were originally a separate *logion*, or if, at any rate, it was spoken quite *in general*—then the central Gospel passage on ‘fulfilment’ gives us a general point of view, in the Master's own words.

Any of these individual passages, if such an interpretation as we have discussed is warrantable, centres round the idea of the fulfilment of prophecy; though Mt 5[17b] would mean something broader or something profounder than what the letter of the NT generally attains to. It will be interesting if we can regard such broader and profounder teaching as coming directly from our Master.

Different senses of ‘fulfilment’ reviewed again. These do not to any great extent correspond to different Greek words. To *fulfil* joy is πληρόω (usually in the passive), to *complete* joy, but (sometimes at least, we thought) to *give* joy in its *fulness*. To *fulfil time* (again usually a passive) is also πληρόω, but might be the kindred πιμπλάναι, which is used even in NT in the less theological applications. The appointed time—whatever authority enacted it—is now *full*. To *fulfil Scripture*—or *prophets' words*, etc.—is indifferently πληρόω (or cognates, possibly once πιμπλάναι, Lk 21[22] *v.l.*; and possibly, but not probably, once πληροφορέω, Lk 1[1]; see above, **5**), or τελέω (or cognate τελειόω; once τέλος ἔχειν); nor should we forget γίνομαι in construction. To *fulfil law* in the Epistles is τελέω or πληρόω. In the Gospels we have πληρόω in kindred applications—once, ‘to fulfil righteousness’; and once, in the great passage, as we were inclined to think, in a purely general sense, ‘to *fulfil*.’ But see above, **4**. Cf. further in Epistles πληροφορέω, ‘to fulfil one's ministry,’ 2 Ti 4[5]; ‘fully to proclaim the message,’ τὸ κήρυγμα, 2 Ti 4[17].

Can we unify these leading senses? Probably not; probably not any two. They are, of course, connected, especially the first three. It is God who gives joy in fulness, God who ordains times, God who keeps His promise. At His own time His keeping of promise fills His people with joy. Nay more; the fourth sense is also near of kin. Christ, the fulfiller of all promises, is also, on any view of particular passages, the supreme pattern of obedience, and the author of new obedience in others. But the *word* ‘fulfil’ probably does not occur *on the same ground* in any two of the senses discriminated above. There is, in some cases, an idea of fulness as against half fulness (of time, or of joy); two different fulnesses, therefore. In others (prophecy, or law) there is a mere idea of correspondence— fulness against emptiness, so to speak—the act answering to the word (but answering it in two different ways).

Fulfilment : modern theological study. The central subject is fulfilment of prophecy. (It has also the most passages). Modern study of ‘Prophecy and Fulfilment’—title of a book by von Hofmann— brings out a truth which (unless possibly adumbrated in our Lord's words, Mt 5[17b]) is nowhere formulated in Scripture. Fulfilment is not only *like* what prediction expected, but is also in some ways *different*, because the prophets' partial wisdom was not adequate to the *full* splendour of the *fulfilment*. Christ, in so far as He differs from the Messianic portrait of the OT, is not lesser but greater spiritually; He *necessarily* differs. It is true, some elements of the fulfilment are transferred to Christian eschatology. As yet they are unfinished things. But if the First Advent differed (for the better) from the letter of expectation, we may infer that there are symbolical or metaphorical elements in the prophetic pictures of the Second Advent and eschatology. All this, while not formulated in the NT, is learned by believing study of the phenomena of Scripture, and is our age's proper contribution to the conception of fulfilment. The main lines of expectation fulfilled in Christ are perhaps three : (1) The hope of the Messianic King (Is 9 is the great passage)—most important, not because of its intrinsic spiritual depth (in that respect it did not stand very high), but from what we may call its dogmatic sharpness, and its emphasis in the NT age. It lent the Christian Church its first creed—viz. that ‘Jesus is Christ.’ It was fulfilled only through the transference of Christ's royalty from temporal to exalted, or from present to future conditions. (2) There is the hope of God's own coming to His people in person, Is 40[10] — and throughout Is 40-55. This pointed strongly to

Christ's Godhead. (3) There is the type or ideal of the Suffering Servant, included in Is 40–55 (also in Ps 22 and others), chiefly at Is 52¹³–53¹². This teaching furnished Christian theology with its deepest elements. We can also now explain what amount of truth is conveyed by the idea of 'double fulfilments.' When the historical reference of a prophecy is to some lesser or earlier personage than Christ Jesus, yet if that person is important in the history of God's purpose, the *same principle* may be fulfilled partially in him which is (ultimately) more perfectly fulfilled in Christ. Thus we may have a multiple, a repeated fulfilment of great principles; yet all pointing on to Christ as the grand or absolute Fulfiller. We *do not* affirm a great cryptogram, with designed artful ambiguity. The prophetic human speaker did not mean two (and just two) sets of events. He meant one event. But his words were capable of meaning many. And something in his spiritual messages corresponds to Christ more than to Christ's forerunner. Again, individual or detailed fulfilments have their own subordinate place. Some indeed may be rather a play of pious fancy than a serious argument. The OT is full of plays upon words; and the NT citations of 'I called my son out of Egypt,' and of 'He shall be called a Nazarene' (Mt 2¹⁵. ²³), are probably of this sort—things that carried more weight in Judæa long ago than they can possibly carry now. At times the resemblance to the OT is—innocently and unconsciously—filled out. The exact reproduction of Ps 22⁸, which we find at Mt 27⁴³, is unknown to the earlier narrative of Mark. Where the matter is of some weight (*e.g.* probably the birth at Bethlehem), its chief importance is that it emphasizes or advertises the deeper analogies and correspondences in virtue of which Christ fulfils—and, may we say, transcends—the spirit or the religion of the OT; alike *in Himself* and *in His gospel*.

LITERATURE. — See the Lexicons; also the following two articles, and the Commentaries. On Mt 5¹⁷, etc., see further the present writer's *Christ and the Jewish Law*, 1886; works on the Sermon on the Mount (B. W. Bacon; Votaw, in Hastings' *DB*, Ext. Vol., and literature there quoted). On the fulfilment of *prophecy*, modern works by von Hofmann, Riehm (Muirhead's tr.), A. B. Davidson, Woods (*The Hope of Israel*), etc. On the eschatological discourse, Schwartzkopff's *Prophecies of Jesus Christ* (Eng. tr.).   R. MACKINTOSH.

FULNESS (πλήρωμα).—The Gr. word is used in the Gospels in its natural, physical sense in Mt 9¹⁶, Mk 2²¹ 6⁴³ 8²⁰. It has a definite theological meaning in Jn 1¹⁶ [the only place in the Gospels where it is tr. 'fulness']. In the Epistles it is used: of time, to denote the period that fills up a certain epoch (Eph 1¹⁰, Gal 4⁴; see FULNESS OF TIME); of persons, the full number required to make up a definite figure (Ro 11¹². ²⁵); of measure, to indicate the full capacity, the entire content (1 Co 10²⁶. ²⁸, Ro 15²⁹), also this may be said to be its meaning in Ro 13¹⁰ where love is spoken of as the πλήρωμα νόμου. The word has also a definite theological meaning in Col 1¹⁹ 2⁹, Eph 1²³ 3¹⁹ 4¹³. The central conception of the word, wherever used, seems to be *completeness*, the totality of the things spoken of, that which binds them into a symmetrical whole. Even when it is the latest addition that is indicated as the πλήρωμα, the word refers back to the beginning, and signifies the completeness effected by the addition. Thus in the passages in St. Matthew and St. Mark which refer to the sewing of the new patch on the old garment, it is not the patch that is the πλήρωμα, it is the completeness that results from the patch; and, as Lightfoot correctly points out, the idea meant to be conveyed is the paradox that it is this very completeness which makes the garment incomplete. A false show of wholeness is worse than an open

rent,—an idea entirely in accordance with the method of the teaching of Jesus.

The theological meaning of πλήρωμα in St. John's Gospel must be taken in connexion with its use in St. Paul's Epistles. Granted the authenticity of the Epistles and the Gospel, St. John must have written more than a quarter of a century later, and must have addressed practically the same circle as that which St. Paul had in view in writing to the Colossians and the Ephesians. It is clear that St. Paul is dealing with the word in a technical sense as a word which is familiar to his opponents, but is used by him in a sense different from theirs; and St. John's use of the term is exactly similar. The πλήρωμα represented a leading thought in the Gnostic heresy, of which we find the first germs referred to in the vigorous polemic of St. Paul. Gnosticism was further developed by Cerinthus, a contemporary of St. John, and reached its culmination in the fully elaborated system of Valentinus. The problem with which these Gnostic heresiarchs were continually wrestling was one that is as old as human thought—how to pass from the infinite to the finite, and reconcile absolute good with the existence of evil. The details of the earlier systems with which the Apostles had to deal are unknown to us, but in the speculations of Valentinus, as preserved in the writings of the early Fathers, especially the *Philosophoumena* of Hippolytus, we have a system in which philosophical conceptions are clothed in Oriental imagery, and an attempt is made to give a consistent explanation of the mysteries of Creation, Sin, and Redemption.

From the Absolute Being or the Abysmal Depth, there issued twin emanations, having each a relative being in itself, but each pair, as they receded from the primal source of existence, had fainter traces of the pure Divine spirit. These emanations are personifications of the Divine attributes, and in their totality constitute the realm of pure spirit—the πλήρωμα of the Godhead. Opposed to the πλήρωμα is the κένωμα, the *emptiness*, the realm of matter and material things, the shadow-world as against the world of reality. It is the philosophical distinction between the noumenal and the phenomenal, the realm of archetypal ideas and the objects of sense perception, with a moral significance imparted into it. In the κένωμα, the thirty Æons of the πλήρωμα have their material counterpart, presided over by the Demiurge or Creator, who has no organic relation to the spiritual realm. This world of chaos and ancient night receives from the πλήρωμα a spiritual principle, reducing it to a semblance of order, in the person of Sophia Achamoth, an emanation from the Sophia of the spiritual realm. The higher Sophia, the latest of the Æons, and the furthest removed from the Absolute, had been consumed with a desire to reach upwards to the Primal Glory, and to emulate the Uncreated by giving birth to another Æon. The result was an abortion,—a being spiritual in essence but out of harmony with the πλήρωμα,—which was cast forth from the spiritual realm and found a place of exile in the κένωμα. Here Sophia Achamoth imparted of her essence to the Æons of the void, and thus introduced a spiritual principle which was capable of redemption. To those who had in them this spiritual essence Christ was sent, each of the Æons contributing something of its own perfection to fit Him for His errand. The Æon Christ entered into the man Jesus, and through Him effected the redemption of those spiritual beings who were involved in the lower realm of matter, but who had received quickening through the infusion of the spiritual principle into the κένωμα.

What degree of elaboration this fantastic theory had reached in the age of St. Paul, and still later in that of St. John, there is not now material to decide; but there are distinct traces of it in the Epistle to the Colossians in the reference to principalities, dominions, and powers (Col 1¹⁶); and we know that Cerinthus, a contemporary of St. John, thought out the religious problem on very similar lines, and used the word *pleroma* in a similar sense. We are to regard the use of the term, then, by the two Apostles as an assertion of the true doctrine of the *pleroma* as against a false doctrine which had wide currency. In the Logos, who became incarnate in Jesus Christ, the whole *pleroma* of the Godhead is contained. Jesus was not the last of the Æons, created as an afterthought. He is the image of the invisible God, the firstborn of all created beings (Col 1¹⁵). The long chain of mediators between God and man is relegated to the realm of myth, and the one Mediator, μονογενής, full of grace and truth (Jn 1¹⁴), through whom alone God effects His purposes in Creation and Redemption, is held up for the adoration of all men. And this fulness of the Divine, which is in Him through the closeness of His contact with God, is imparted to His disciples (Jn 1¹⁶) and to the Church which is His Body, and which in its ideality is the fulness of Him who filleth all in all (Eph 1²³). The Church is here regarded as the complement of Jesus. The Head and the Body make one whole —the *pleroma* of the Godhead, the full realization of the Divine purpose which centres in the redemption of man. For through this Church, which on earth possesses the potentiality of the *pleroma*, by means of its varied ministries, the fulness which is in Christ the Head passes to the individual, whose destiny it is to attain to the perfect man, to the possession, in his degree, of the entire *pleroma* of the Godhead.

It is scarcely sufficiently recognized that the NT doctrine of the Church is a philosophy of the Social Organism which embraces all essential human activities (Eph 4¹⁵. ¹⁶). Our difficulty in apprehending it lies mainly in this, that the Apostles, seeing the temporal in the light of eternity, are constantly confusing the boundary lines which separate the actual from the ideal, the process from the consummation.

LITERATURE.—Lightfoot on *Colossians*; Pressensé, *Heresy and Christian Doctrine*; Neander, *Church History*; Hippolytus, *Philosophoumena*; see also Hastings' *DB*, art. ' Pleronia,' with Literature there quoted.   A. MILLER.

FULNESS OF THE TIME (τὸ πλήρωμα τοῦ χρόνου). —An expression used by St. Paul (Gal 4⁴) to mark the opportuneness of the coming of Christ into the world, and the ripeness of the age for the great religious revolution He was to effect. It emphasizes the unique significance of the period as the culmination of a long course of events, by which the way had been providentially prepared for Christ's appearance, and His introduction of a purer type of religion. The evidences of such a providential preparation are indeed remarkable. Along different lines of historical development a situation had been created at the very centre of the world's life, that was singularly favourable to the planting and spread of a loftier faith. The main factors usually recognized as contributing to this result were: (1) the peculiar condition which the Jewish people had reached; (2) the dissemination of the Greek language, culture, and commercial activity; and (3) the unifying influence of Rome.

1. *The peculiar condition of the Jewish people.*— Centuries of chequered discipline had fixed in the Jewish mind the belief in one true and perfectly righteous God, and subsequently to the return from the Exile there had been no relapse into idolatry. Latterly, indeed, through the influence of the scribes and Pharisees, legalism and formality had crept in, and the externalization of religion had been carried far; yet in many classes of society there was a wistful straining after inner purity and a more living fellowship with God; and in spite of the soulless bondage of ceremonial observances, there was an amount of deep and reverent piety that kept the nation's heart sounder than might appear on the surface. At all events, nowhere else in the world did there exist so vivid a conception of the Divine holiness or so high a recognized standard of morality; nowhere else, therefore, were there so many devout minds ready to receive a new spiritual revelation, or so well fitted to furnish heralds and apostles for its propagation. Then there was the revival of the Messianic

hope, which, kept alive by the pressure of repeated misfortunes, had, under the tightening grip of Roman domination, sprung up with passionate intensity. The political situation was galling, and the Jewish people, pining to be free from the foreign yoke, consoled themselves with the thought of a glorious future. It was a time of high-strung unrest and expectancy; yet although the prospect of political emancipation was to a large extent entertained, there were multitudes of earnest souls yearning for a higher form of deliverance, the dawn of a reign of righteousness and peace, in the benefits of which not Israel only, but the whole world, should share.

Outside Palestine, again, the influence of Jewish religious ideas had been widely extended by means of the Dispersion. Conscious of being raised above the manifold forms of heathen superstition around them, the colonies of Jews settled in the trading cities of foreign lands felt themselves impelled to aspire after a certain elevation of life; while the loftier moral teaching they maintained in their synagogues attracted considerable numbers of proselytes from paganism. Thus the conception of the Divine unity and righteousness was being spread over a large section of the heathen world. So far, therefore, both at home and abroad the Jewish people had fulfilled their mission in the moral and religious preparation of the world for the entrance of Christianity.

2. *The dissemination of the Greek language, culture, and commercial activity.* — Ever since the conquests of Alexander the Great, the Greek tongue had attained supremacy among the civilized nations, and had become the current medium for the exchange of thought. Even the OT had to be rendered into Greek, in the translation known as the Septuagint. Moreover, Greek learning, literature, and speculation exercised a pervasive influence far and near. A significant indication of this is to be found in the rise among the Jews of the Dispersion of a school of thinkers who had imbibed the Greek culture, and who, quickened by the intellectual alertness of the Greek mind, were drawn to take part in the literary productivity of the age. The aim of this Græco-Jewish school was to make the purer religious faith and knowledge of Israel accessible to the world. With its chief seat at Alexandria, its leading representatives, such as Aristobulus and Philo, endeavoured to show that the Mosaic law, correctly understood, contained all that the best Greek philosophers had taught. Thus was brought about a mutual action and reaction of Jewish and Greek ideas, and a soil was being made ready for a more elevated spiritual teaching, based on the unity of the Godhead and the eternal obligation of righteousness.

At the same time the commercial enterprise of the Greeks was rapidly overcoming national exclusiveness, and producing a freer intercourse between men of different races. They were the cosmopolitans of the period—inquisitive, openminded, eager to enter into all vivid interests; and in the great trading cities in Asia Minor and along the Mediterranean shore they fostered the spirit of toleration and helped to secure full scope for the advocacy of all forms of belief.

But while thus stimulating intellectual receptiveness everywhere, the most important contribution of the Greeks in the preparation for Christianity was the universal prevalence they gained for their rich and expressive language, inasmuch as by this they supplied a common vehicle of intercourse, calculated to be of immense advantage in the announcement and promulgation of the Christian Evangel.

3. *The unifying influence of Rome.*—That the entire known world was then embraced within

Rome's imperial sway was a momentous factor in the situation which had been reached. As the barriers of language had been demolished through the influence of the Greeks, so through the influence of the Romans the barriers of nationality had been broken down. The whole world was but one country; and from the Euphrates to the Atlantic there was settled government, order, and the rule of law under one sovereign sceptre. In the lull of national strifes which had thus come— the *pax Romana*—merchant and traveller moved safely from land to land, and by the splendid system of roads for which the Roman Empire was famed, the lines of communication were opened in all directions. In this way Rome had performed its distinctive part by bringing about a political condition of the world hitherto unexampled in history. Thus the three great races of antiquity had contributed their share towards the fulfilment of a manifestly providential design, and the period had now arrived when their several lines of historical development converged to a meeting-point, producing a combination of circumstances which rendered issues of vast moment possible. As it has been aptly put, 'the City of God is built at the confluence of three civilizations' (Conybeare and Howson's *St. Paul*, i. 2).

It is worthy of note also that the little country of Palestine, where the Founder of Christianity was to appear, lay at the very centre of the then known world; and in view of the fact that through the provision of a common language and free means of movement and intercourse the avenues of access were opened to every land, it becomes clear that the most signal facilities were afforded for the dissemination of a faith that was destined to wield a world-wide power.

In addition to this, account has to be taken of the decay of the old pagan religions, and the simultaneous influx of Oriental ideas. There was a strange intermingling of races and also of religious beliefs, with the result that men's minds were unsettled, and a spirit of inquiry was awakened among those who had grown dissatisfied with the popular heathen cults.

Manifestly the age was ripe for a new revelation that would meet the deepest needs of the human soul; and in the situation created by the course of Jewish, Greek, and Roman history, the way for it had at length been prepared. Then Jesus Christ appeared. The 'fulness of the time' had come for the advent of the promised Saviour with His Gospel of life and grace for the regeneration of mankind.

LITERATURE.—Ewald, *Hist. of Israel* (Eng. tr.), vols. v. and vi.; Hausrath, *The Times of Jesus* (Eng. tr. 1888), i.; Schürer, *HJP* II. iii.; Pressensé, *Religions before Christ* (1862); Conybeare and Howson, *St. Paul* (1858), i. 4–14; *Lux Mundi*, 129–178; Edersheim, *Life and Times*, i. 3–108; Farrar, *St. Paul*, i. 115 ff.; Gwatkin, art. 'Roman Empire' in Hastings' *DB*; Wernle, *Beginnings of Christianity* (Eng. tr. 1903), i. 1–36.

G. M'HARDY.

FUNERAL.—See BURIAL, and TOMB.

FURLONG.—See WEIGHTS AND MEASURES.

FURNACE OF FIRE.—See FIRE, p. 595ᵃ.

FUTURE.—See ESCHATOLOGY.

G

GABBATHA (Γαββαθᾶ) occurs only in Jn 19¹³, as the 'Hebrew' or, more correctly, Aramaic equivalent of Λιθόστρωτος. For the etymology of the word see E. Nestle in Hastings' *DB* ii. 74 f., with the literature there cited. The word is apparently connected with a root נבב, of which the fundamental idea is that of *something curved or convex*. Hence it cannot be taken as identical in meaning with λιθόστρωτος, which implies a level tesselated surface. A surface of that kind on the summit of a hill, or with a rounded porch or an open cupola over it, beneath which might permanently stand, or be placed occasionally, the βῆμα or 'judgment-seat,' would best meet the conditions of the case. Such a spot might well be known amongst one class of the people (the Romans and their associates) as the Pavement, and amongst another as Gabbatha. The latter name has not yet been found elsewhere than in the NT. For the attempts to identify the locality, and for the usages involved in the reference, see PAVEMENT.

R. W. MOSS.

GABRIEL is mentioned in Lk 1 as appearing to Zacharias to announce the future pregnancy of Elisabeth and the birth of John, and to Mary with a similar announcement of the birth of Jesus. To Zacharias he declares that he is wont to stand in the presence of God, and that he is sent by Him on the mission stated. When he is asked for a sign, he is competent to impose the severe sign of dumbness until the fulfilment of the prediction that has been made. The Gospel mention of Gabriel, then, is as a messenger of the signal favour of God, at least in connexion with the Messiah and His forerunner.

He has a somewhat similar function in the only OT passage in which he is mentioned, Dn 8–10. Daniel was perplexed at the strange vision which he had seen. Pondering over it, he sees one 'standing before him like the appearance of a man,' and a voice is heard bidding Gabriel, for it is he, explain the vision. Daniel falls in a faint as the messenger approaches, and Gabriel lifts him up and explains the mysterious vision. Again he appears to the prophet under similar circumstances, and is now called 'the man' Gabriel. Still again Daniel has a similar experience (10⁵ᶠᶠ·). The details are identical or in harmony with the account in previous chapters, but the name of the messenger is not given. It is, however, generally assumed that the author had Gabriel in mind. He asserts that he is a prince who presides over the interests of Israel, as other supernatural beings preside over other nations.

Gabriel belongs to the creations of the imagination of the Jews in post-exilic times. When God had to them become universal and correspondingly great and glorious, but without parallel spiritualization of His attributes, He was thought to require agents whom He might send as messengers, 'angels' to transmit His messages. These angels were at first nameless, later they received names. Gabriel was one of the most important of them— one of four, of seven, of seventy, according to different enumerations in Jewish writings. See *Jewish Encyc. s.v.*   O. H. GATES.

GADARA, GADARENES.—In the AV in Mk 5¹ and Lk 8²⁶ Jesus is said to have come into the 'country of the Gadarenes.' In the RV this is corrected to 'Gerasenes.' On the other hand, the AV in Mt 8²⁸ has 'country of the Gergesenes,' while the RV has 'Gadarenes.' These are the only passages—all referring to the cure of the demoniac and the destruction of the herd of swine —where Gadara is mentioned in Scripture. How the reading Γαδαρηνῶν crept in, or, if original, what exactly it meant, we may not be able to explain satisfactorily, but one thing is certain, — the miracle cannot have taken place at the city of Gadara, the modern *Umm Keis*. For that town stands on a high plateau on the further side of the wide and extremely steep gorge of the Hieromax river, and is about a 3 hours' ride distant from the Lake. As Thomson says (*LB* ii. p. 354), 'If the miracle was performed at Gadara, then the swine must have run down the mountain for an hour, forded the deep Jarmuk (Hieromax), ascended its northern bank, and raced across the level plain several miles before they could reach the nearest margin of the lake—a feat which no herd of swine would be likely to achieve even though they were "possessed."' In short, no one who has *seen* the position of Gadara would ever dream of locating the miracle there. See GERA- SENES.   J. SOUTAR.

GAIN.—The word 'gain' occurs ten times in the AV of the Gospels, and on every occasion in one of the sayings of our Lord. These passages fall into three groups : (1) The parallel records of a saying repeated by all the Synoptists (Mt 16²⁶, Lk 9²⁵, Mk 8³⁶) ; (2) the parables of the Talents and the Pounds (Mt 25¹⁷. ²⁰. ²², Lk 19¹⁵. ¹⁶. ¹⁸) ; (3) the single record of the saying in Mt 18¹⁵. It is (with the exception of St. Luke's use of διαπραγματεύομαι, προσεργάζομαι, and ποιέω in the parable of the Pounds) always a translation of κερδαίνω. This verb and its cognate substantive κέρδος are used elsewhere in the NT by St. Paul (1 Co 9¹⁹. ²⁰. ²¹. ²², Ph 1²¹ 3⁷. ⁸, Tit 1¹¹), St. Peter (1 P 3¹), and St. Luke (Ac 27²¹, a peculiar use, but not without classical parallels).

1. Mt 16²⁶ (∥ ; cf. Ph 3⁷ and 1²¹) contrasts gain and loss as they touch the direct personal relation of the soul to God. A man may count the world a thing to be gained, and give his soul as the price of it ; or, with the wiser Apostle, may reckon communion with Christ a gain worth the sacrifice of everything else ; or, rising to the vision of the great beatitude, may look for the supreme gain, something better even than living here in Christ, to the life beyond the grave. This is the mystic's conception of religion—'I and God are alone in the world.' All gain apart from union with the Divine is really loss ; and loss, or what seems loss, incurred in achieving that union is gain. 'Qui invenit Jesum,' says Thomas à Kempis, 'invenit thesaurum bonum ; immo bonum, super omne bonum.' The thought finds its simplest and at the same time its fullest expression in the parables of the Hidden Treasure and the Pearl of Great Price, whose finder sells 'with joy' all that he has, to buy what he has discovered.

2. The parables of the Talents and the Pounds express the gain to character which comes of faithful use of powers and abilities. The thought is of the realization of the possibilities that are in man and the subsequent fitness for higher work. Here the gain depends less on sacrifice than on diligence and faithfulness. This is a common con- ception of the meaning of the Christian religion. In it life is not a period of aspiration for an unutterable beatitude, but a time of training, in expectation of the gain of the Master's praise and ultimate ability to do more and greater work for Him.

3. Mt 18¹⁵, with which must be connected 1 Co 9¹⁹ff., speaks of the gain of winning other souls for Christ. Here there is the need of sacrifice, the sacrifice of pride, of social and racial prejudice ; and there is also the need of faithfulness and diligence. This is the missionary's conception of Christianity. We find it in St. Paul and in all those after him who have felt the necessity laid on

them, 'Woe is me if I preach not the gospel.' The joy of this gain is anticipated in Dn 12³ (cf. Ja 5¹⁹. ²⁰). Its greatness is most fully known when we realize that we share it with God Himself and His angels (Lk 15⁶. ⁹. ²²ff.).

In all three classes of passages the language is that of the market-place where men get gain by bargaining or labouring ; but it is immensely sublimated and purified of all selfishness and greed.

LITERATURE.—Augustine, *Confessions* ; Francis de Sales, *The Spirit* ; Thomas à Kempis, *The Imitation of Christ* ; *Theologia Germanica* (tr. by S. Winkworth) ; Jeremy Taylor, *Holy Living* ; Goulburn, *Thoughts on Personal Religion* ; H. J. Coleridge, S.J., *Life and Letters of St. Francis Xavier* : R. Southey, *Life of John Wesley* ; Lives of eminent modern missionaries.
          J. O. HANNAY.

GALILÆAN (Γαλιλαῖος).—Twice Jesus is men- tioned as a Galilæan : once by a maid-servant (Mt 26⁶⁹) ; once when Pilate was anxious to transfer the trial of Jesus from his own to Herod's court (Lk 23⁶). It was during the trial of Jesus also that Peter was recognized as a Galilæan by the bystanders (Mt 26⁷³, Mk 14⁷⁰, Lk 22⁵⁹ ; see GALILEE, § 7). In Jn 4⁴⁵ we read that Galilæans, who had been at Jerusalem and had seen the works of Jesus there, received Him on that account in their own land. In Lk 13¹ we are told of Pilate's (evidently recent) punishment of some Galilæans, whom he had slain even while they were sacrificing. This event can- not be identified with any revolt mentioned in history. Some suppose Barabbas to have been arrested in connexion therewith ; some would asso- ciate it with the revolt of Judas of Galilee (Jos. *BJ* II. viii. 1), but this took place, according to Ac 5³⁷, more than twenty years before. Probably it refers to some small outbreak, summarily punished by Pilate as usual (cf. Philo, *Leg. ad Gaium*, 37).

For characteristics of Galilæans see GALILEE, § 7, 'People.'   G. W. THATCHER.

GALILEE.—**1.** *Name.*—The English form of the name 'Galilee' is derived from the Hebrew גָּלִיל (*Gālīl*), Aram. גְּלִילָא (*Gālīla* or *Gᵉlīla*), through Gr. Γαλιλαία and Lat. *Galilæa*. The Heb. word denotes simply a 'circuit' or 'district', and in Is 9¹ Galilee is called 'Galilee (RVm 'the district') of the nations,' and in 1 Mac 5¹⁵ Γαλιλαία ἀλλοφύλων ('Galilee of the strangers'). In other passages of the OT it is simply called 'the district.'

2. *History.*—When the Hebrew invasion of Pales- tine took place, the main part of Galilee was allotted to Zebulun, Asher, and Naphtali. Accord- ing to Jg 1³⁰⁻³³, Zebulun was not altogether success- ful in driving out the inhabitants of their portion, while Asher and Naphtali had to be content to settle as best they could among the inhabitants, 'for they did not drive them out.' These inhabit- ants seem to have been Amorites and Hivites from the Lebanon. An account of one (or two) of the battles fought in this country is found in Jg 4–5. In the days of the Monarchy, Galilee always suffered in the Syrian wars. It was ravaged by Ben-hadad (1 K 15²⁰), probably won back by Ahab, taken again by the Aramæans under Hazael (2 K 12¹⁸ 13²²), and recovered by Jeroboam II. It was also on the high-road of the Assyrian invasion, and was won for Assyria by Tiglath-pileser III. in 734 (2 K 15²⁹), many of its inhabitants being carried into captivity. From this time up to the end of the 2nd cent. B.C. the population was heathen, with a small number of Jewish settlers, who attached themselves to Jerusalem after the return from the Exile. About the year 164, Simon the brother of Judas Maccabæus pursued the Syrians to Ptole- mais, and on his way back brought the Galilæan Jews and their property to Judæa (1 Mac 5²¹⁻²³). Some 60 years later the whole state of affairs in Galilee was changed. According to Strabo, on the authority of Timagenes (Jos. *Ant.* XIII. xi. 3),

Aristobulus (B.C. 104–103) conquered much of Galilee, and compelled the inhabitants to be circumcised and live according to Jewish laws. This work had probably been already begun by John Hyrcanus (B.C. 135–105). Herod at his death bequeathed Galilee to Herod Antipas, who succeeded after much opposition in having his legacy confirmed at Rome.

3. *Extent*.—The amount of territory covered by the name 'Galilee' varied in different times. Originally it comprised the hilly and mountainous country to the north of the Plain of Esdraelon or the smaller plain of *el-Buṭṭauf*. The boundaries were probably not well defined, but on the north it included Ḳedesh (Jos 20⁷ 21³²). It was later spoken of in two divisions—Upper and Lower Galilee (cf. Jth 1⁸, 1 Mac 12⁴⁹), and in the Mishna is divided into three parts, these corresponding to the natural divisions of plain, hill-country, and mountain.

The boundaries of Galilee at the time of Christ are thus given by Josephus:

'Now Phœnice and Syria surround the two Galilees, which are called Upper and Lower Galilee. They are bounded on the W. by the borders of the territory belonging to Ptolemais, and by Carmel, which mountain of old belonged to the Galilæans, but now to the Tyrians; and next it is Gaba (*Jebâta**), which is called "the city of horsemen," because those horsemen that were dismissed by Herod the king dwelt therein; they are bounded on the S. by Samaria and Scythopolis, as far as the streams of the Jordan; on the E. by Hippene (the district of Hippos, *Sūsiyeh*) and Gadaris (the district of Gadara, *Umm Keis*), and also by Gaulanitis (*Jaulân*) and the borders of the kingdom of Agrippa; and their N. parts are bounded by Tyre, and the country of the Tyrians. As for what is called Lower Galilee, it extends in length from Tiberias to Chabulon (*Kâbûl*), and Ptolemais is its neighbour on the coast; and its breadth is from the village called Xaloth (*Iksâl*), which lies in the great plain, to Bersabe, from which beginning the breadth of Upper Galilee is also taken to the village Baca, which divides the land of the Tyrians from Galilee; its length is also from Meloth (*Meiron*) to Thella (probably *Tell Thala*), a village near the Jordan' (*BJ* III. iii. 1).

4. *Geography*.—The southernmost division of Galilee was Esdraelon (G. A. Smith, *HGHL* p. 379). It consists of (1) the triangular plain about 200 feet above sea-level, 29 miles long from the foot of Carmel to Jenîn, 15 from Jenîn to Tabor, and 15 from Tabor to the foot of Carmel; (2) the valley of Jezreel (*Nahr Jalûd*), running down for 12 miles from Jezreel to Bethshean, some 400 feet below sea-level. The Plain of Esdraelon is watered by the Kishon flowing to the Mediterranean; but, as the edges are somewhat higher than the centre, it is often marshy. It played a great part in the history of Palestine (cf. *HGHL* p. 391 ff.), but has no mention in the story of the Gospels.

On the other hand, the middle division of Galilee, known as Lower Galilee, contains nearly all the important sites of the Gospel record. Nazareth, Capernaum, Shunem, Nain, Cana, etc., are within its borders. It is bounded on the W. by the Plain of Ptolemais, on the S. by the Plains of Esdraelon and Jezreel, on the E. by the Sea of Galilee (though sometimes a part of the country east of the sea was considered Galilæan), and on the N. by a line passing from the N. end of the Sea of Galilee through Ramah to the coast. It consists of four chains of hills running east and west, intercepted by valleys and plains. The hills reach a height of about 1200 feet. The southern chain consists of the Nazareth hills, with Mt. Tabor; the next range contains the *Ḳarn Ḥaṭṭin* of Crusading fame; the third, the city of Jotapâta; while the fourth consists of the southern slopes of the mountains of Upper Galilee. The central plain of *el-Buṭṭauf* is about 500 feet above sea-level, while the coast of the Sea of Galilee is nearly 700 feet below sea-level. The whole country is well watered by streams flowing east or west, and was extremely fertile. The grass of the plains was green, and

* The identifications in brackets are those of Sir C. W. Wilson in Shilleto's translation of Josephus.

evergreen oaks grew on the hills. The corn-fields gave a plenteous harvest, and pomegranates abounded.

Upper Galilee ranged from the N. boundary of Lower Galilee to the Tyrian boundary, which seems to have been at the time of Christ just south of Ḳedesh, which according to Josephus was a Tyrian fortress on the borders of Galilee (*Ant.* XIII. v. 6; *BJ* II. xviii. 1, IV. ii. 3). It is a land of mountains, where the hills run from 2000 to 4000 feet in height. It too was a fertile land, with thick woods, sycamores, olives, vines, and green pastures by its waters.

5. *Roads*.—'Judæa was on the road to nowhere; Galilee is covered with roads to everywhere' (G. A. Smith, *HGHL* p. 425). Roads in the East even now are often mere tracks, scarcely recognizable by the Western. They are repaired for great occasions, and soon allowed to fall again into their natural condition. Remains of pavements, however, show that at the time of Christ the Roman genius for road-making had been at work in the district of Galilee. Especially was this the case on the great high-road, the 'Way of the Sea,' as it was called in the Middle Ages (from an interpretation of Is 9¹), which crossed the middle of Lower Galilee. The eastern termini of the main roads were the two bridges which crossed the Jordan. These were (1) the bridge about half-way between Merom and the Sea of Galilee, now called the 'Bridge of Jacob's Daughters.' To this came the road from Damascus and the intervening country. Westward from the river the road ran by Safed and Ramah to Ptolemais. From this a branch struck off a few miles west of the river, passed by Arbela (*Irbid*), and rejoined the high-road near Ramah. Another branch went southwards to the west coast of the Sea of Galilee at *Khân Minyeh*, and proceeded to Bethshean, where it joined the road from (2) the bridge a few miles south of the Sea of Galilee, now called the *Jisr el-Mujâmia*. Over this bridge came the traffic from Arabia and Gilead. From it one road passed through Bethshean, the Valley of Jezreel, and the Plain of Esdraelon, to the coast of the Mediterranean, and so on to Egypt; another by Cana and Sepphoris to Ptolemais. The main road from the shore of the Sea of Galilee to the highlands went by the *Wady el-Ḥammâm* past Arbela, then between Tabor and the Nazareth hills to Esdraelon. Along these and many other roads flowed a ceaseless stream of traffic, and the fulness of their life is reflected in the parables of Christ (cf. *Encyc. Bibl.* iv. 5191; *HGHL* p. 430 f.).

6. *Government*.—Galilee was a part of the Roman Empire; that is, in the days of Christ it was under the emperors Augustus and Tiberius. Roman garrisons were in towns all round the country. Roman influence was felt everywhere. But the mass of the people had little or nothing to do with the Roman Empire directly. The direct government of the land was in the hands of Herod Antipas, to whom, with the title of 'tetrarch,' it was assigned by Augustus after the death of Herod. Antipas was 17 years old at his accession to power, and established his capital at Sepphoris. About the year 22, however, he built a new city on the shore of the Sea of Galilee, named it Tiberias in honour of the emperor, and made it his capital. This city was governed after the Greek model by a council of 600, with an Archon and other officers. In these two cities was centred the chief legal administration of affairs in Galilee during the life of Christ. But in Galilee, as elsewhere, the chief details of life were regulated by the Jews' own religious laws rather than by ordinary civil enactments. The chief authority was the Sanhedrin (see SANHEDRIN) at Jerusalem, to which appeals could be made when local doctors differed. The chief local difficulties were usually satisfied by the decisions of local councils (cf. Mt 10[17]), probably associated more or less closely with the local synagogues (see SYNAGOGUE).

7. People. — Galilee was a populous country. 'The cities lie very thick, and the very many villages are everywhere so populous from the richness of the soil, that the very least of them contains more than fifteen thousand inhabitants' (Jos. BJ III. iii. 2). In another place Josephus says there were 240 cities and villages in Galilee (Life, 45), and that many of these had strong walls. From each of these to the others must have been a network of tracks and roads in addition to the main roads (see above), and the land was a scene of constant activity. The bracing air of the hills and the activity of everyday life formed a people of energy and vigour. 'The Galilæans are inured to war from their infancy, and have been always very numerous; nor has their country ever been destitute of men of courage' (Jos. BJ III. iii. 2). Regarded with a certain amount of patronizing contempt by the pure-blooded and more strictly theologically-minded Jews of Jerusalem and its neighbourhood, they still had the religious zeal of country-folk. This zeal was quickened by their pilgrimages to Jerusalem, which made a greater impression on their active minds than on those who were more familiar with the life of the Holy City. At any apparent insult to their religion they were ready to break out in revolt. Before, during, and after the life of Jesus, Galilæan leaders arose and flew to arms in the vain attempt to secure religious autonomy. Yet they differed in many respects from their Judæan brothers. The very technical terms of the market and the details of their religious customs varied from those of the South (cf. Schürer, HJP II. i. 4). Their pronunciation of the Aramaic language had peculiarities of its own (Mt 26[73]), one of these being the confusion of the guttural sounds. Besides, however, the natural bodily vigour and mental freshness of these highlanders, the most important difference between them and the people of Judæa lay in the different attitude in daily life towards the larger world of the Roman Empire and Hellenistic influence. Knowledge of, at any rate spoken, Greek was to them a necessity of business, and no attempt could be made, as in Jerusalem, to avoid the study of it (cf. Moulton, Prolegomena to Gram. of NT Greek, 1906, p. 8). Many must have been, like Matthew, in Government employ. All were brought into daily contact with Greek and Roman modes of life and thought. It was to this people of larger experience of life and broader ways of thinking that Jesus appealed in the greater part of His earthly ministry, and from it that He chose the men who were first to make His message known to the world. See also art. SEA OF GALILEE.

LITERATURE. — Artt. 'Galilee' in Hastings' DB, and 'Galiläa' in PRE[3]; Neubauer, Géog. du Talmud; Guérin, Galilée; Merrill, Galilee in the Time of Christ; G. A. Smith, HGHL, chs. xx, xxi.

G. W. THATCHER.

GALL (χολή, fel).—

In LXX χολή represents (1) רֹאשׁ (Dt 32[32], Ps 69[21]); and (2) לַעֲנָה wormwood (Pr 5[4], La 3[15]). רֹאשׁ and לַעֲנָה are sometimes combined, e.g. Dt 29[18] רֹאשׁ וְלַעֲנָה, LXX ἐν χολῇ καὶ πικρίᾳ, Vulg. fel et amaritudinem; La 3[19] לַעֲנָה וָרֹאשׁ, LXX πικρία καὶ χολή, Vulg. absynthii et fellis.

It thus appears that χολή was used of any bitter drug, and there is therefore no discrepancy between Mt 27[34] οἶνον [ὄξος is a copyist's assimilation to Ps 69[21]] μετὰ χολῆς μεμιγμένον, and Mk 15[23] ἐσμυρνισμένον οἶνον. The potion administered to the cruciarius (see CRUCIFIXION) was composed of wine

and a variety of drugs—frankincense, laudanum, myrrh, resin, saffron, mastich.* Thus 'wine mixed with gall' and 'myrrhed wine' are equivalent phrases, signifying generally medicated wine (cf. Swete, St. Mark, ad loc.). Mt 27[34] and Ac 8[23] are the only places in the NT where χολή occurs.

DAVID SMITH.

GAMES.—In the Gospels there are none of the analogies from athletic contests which are frequently drawn in the Acts and the Epistles. This variety in the range of illustration is traced without difficulty to the different interests of the readers or hearers. The Hebrews, unlike the Greeks and Romans, gave little attention to games. The climate of their land may help to account for this, but the chief reason must be found in their view of life, which made it impossible for them to look upon games with the eye of the Greek. Where the Greek had his Isthmian games, the Hebrew had his Passover, or other solemn festival. The introduction of a gymnasium by Jason (2 Mac 4[7-19]) was accounted an act of disloyalty to the faith of his fathers, and a surrender to Hellenic influences. He was accused of neglecting the altar for the palæstra. Herod is said by Josephus (Ant. XV. viii. 1) to have instituted solemn games in honour of Cæsar; but such practices never won the approval of the Rabbis, or of the nation as a whole. Jesus preached to a people who knew little of the games of the Greeks, and who had been taught to hate what they knew. But in Galilee the children played their immemorial games:

> 'A wedding or a festival,
> A mourning or a funeral,
> · · · · ·
> As if his whole vocation
> Were endless imitation.'
> (WORDSWORTH, Ode on Immortality).

From such play Jesus drew a description of the generation which had listened to John the Baptist and Himself (Mt 11[17], Lk 7[32]). Two groups are playing in the market-place; the musicians are divided from the others. They pipe, but the children will not play; they suggest 'funerals,' but their comrades sulkily refuse to join. The parable is a vivid picture of the fickleness, sulkiness, and self-will of the contemporaries of Jesus. It is not necessary to read into the parable a condemnation of those who should have outgrown childish things but are still playing at life. The 'musicians' have been likened by some to Jesus and John the Baptist, by others to the people (see a discussion by Stalker in Expositor, 4th series, vol. vii. p. 29).

The soldiers probably played with dice when they cast lots for the garments of Jesus (Mt 27[35]); and they may have been playing a game when they said to Jesus, 'Prophesy unto us, thou Christ; who is he that struck thee?' (26[68]).

Jesus did not deal with the problems which arise in modern society from the growing importance of games in the scheme of life. As far as we know, He did not discuss the Rabbinical attitude to the Hellenic games; nor do the Apostolic writers hint of dangers to Christian converts from the contests. The ethical questions must be decided by an appeal to the interpretation of life in the Gospels, and especially to the estimate given by Jesus of the true relations between body and spirit. It is clear that to Him the body was not an end in itself (Mt 10[28]), but must become the docile servant of the soul (18[8]), even at the cost of severe discipline. Games will be approved where they give bodily effectiveness, that it may be the 'earthly support' of the endurance of the spirit. They will be condemned if they lead to a neglect of the serious interests of life (6[33]), or of the duty

* Cf. Wetstein on Mk 15[23].

owed to others. The Christian ideal of a life temperate and just does not include a life whose first interest is amusement, or one in which ' distraction ' is necessary to prevent ennui (see Dorner, *Christian Ethics*, Eng. tr. p. 458).

LITERATURE.—Hastings' *DB*, art. 'Games'; Schürer, *HJP*, Index, *s.* 'Games'; *Expositor*, I. v. [1877] 257.

EDWARD SHILLITO.

GARDEN (κῆπος).—In its most precise application the term refers to a level piece of ground enclosed by a wall or hedge, in which plants, shrubs, and trees are cultivated by irrigation. Its area, ranging from a small vegetable plot beside the house to the dimensions of a farm, is limited only by the supply of water. While not excluding the idea of garden familiar in the West, its meaning in general is often nearer to that of our *nursery-garden* and *orchard*. In the irrigated garden, vines, fig, walnut, pomegranate, lemon, and other trees are grown for the sake of ornament, shade, and fruit. In the Gospels mention is made of mint, anise, and cummin (Mt 23²³) as the cheap and common garden produce that occupied the laboured scrupulosity of the scribes and Pharisees, to the neglect of more important matters.

The fact of its being artificially and continually watered, distinguishes the garden proper from the ordinary grain field, the vineyard, and the plantation of olive or fig trees. The necessity, however, of having a protecting wall for fruit trees gives also to such an enclosure in a more general sense the name and character of a garden. These may be resorted to and passed through without objection except during summer and autumn, when the fruit is ripening. Such may have been the garden of Gethsemane, to which Christ retired with His disciples (Jn 18¹· ²). In the garden containing the tomb in which Christ's body was laid, Mary's expectation of meeting with the gardener or caretaker (Jn 20¹⁵) at the time of Easter would rather point to the more careful cultivation of the irrigated garden.

To the Oriental the garden is a place of retirement and rest. Its sound of falling or running water is one of the luxuries of life. Its shade affords escape from the glare of the sun, and its recognized privacy forbids the introduction at the close of the day of disturbing news, exacting claims, or perplexing decisions. The voice of nature seems to say, ' I will give you rest.' It has thus become a symbol of Heaven, and supplies a common term of immortal hope to the three great monotheistic religions, inasmuch as the Christian ' Paradise ' is the equivalent of the Jewish *Gan-'Eden*, 'Garden of Eden,' and the Moslem *il-Gannat*, ' the Garden.'

G. M. MACKIE.

GARNER.—See BARN.

GATE.—The gate of a city, like the entrance to a tent and the door of a house, was a place of special importance, and its original use gave rise to various associated meanings.

1. *Military and protective.* — As the weakest place in a walled city, it was the chief point of attack and defence. Its strength was the strength of the city (Gn 22¹⁷, Jg 5⁸, Ps 24⁷ 127⁵, Is 26², Jer 14²). It had a place of outlook over the entrance, from which those approaching could be seen, and intimation given as to their admittance. This was evidently a development of the watch kept at the door of the sheepfold (Jn 10¹⁻³). The gates of the city were closed at night, hence in the vision of the city where there is no night they remain unclosed (Rev 21²⁵). In the charge to Peter, where the gates of Hades are said to be unable to prevail against the Church of Christ, the original meaning

of defensive strength seems to pass into that of aggressive force (Mt 16¹⁸).

2. *Judicial and commercial.*—The settlement of matters affecting contested right, transfer of property and internal administration, were attended to at the open space or covered recess behind the gate (Gn 23¹⁰, Dt 25⁷, Am 5¹²). The litigant was urged to come to terms with the adversary ' in the way ' before the gate was reached, for there the judge sat, and behind him were the officer, the prison, and the official exactors (Mt 5²⁵· ²⁶). In times of industrial peace, the protective challenge became a fiscal inspection, and there the tax-collector sat at the receipt of custom (Mt 9⁹).

3. *Figurative and religious.*—While the gates or doors of public buildings within the city might be lavishly ornamented (Is 54¹², Rev 21²¹ ; Jos. *BJ* v. v. 3, VI. v. 3), the gate of brass was the standard of external protection. The larger and more important the city, the more imposing would be its public gate. The Oriental name for the Ottoman Empire is the High Gate, or Sublime Porte. Christ's allusion to the broad gate that led only to darkness and destruction, and the gate that, though narrow, conducted into a broad place capable of accommodating visitors from all lands (Mt 7¹³· ¹⁴, Lk 13²⁴· ²⁹), was in keeping with His other statements as to the startling difference between *His* Kingdom and the Empire conception of the world.

City gates, as well as those at the entrance to gardens and to the open courts around houses, frequently have a small inserted door from two to three feet square by which an individual may be admitted. It has sometimes been thought that this was referred to when Christ spoke of a camel passing through the eye of a needle (Mt 19²⁴) ; but there is nothing either in the sense of the original words or in Eastern custom to support such a supposition. See CAMEL.

Gates had distinguishing names, indicating the localities to which they belonged or into which they led (Gn 28¹⁷, Neh 3, Ps 9¹³, Is 38¹⁰, Mt 16¹⁸), or describing some characteristic of the door itself (Ac 3²). In the prophetic picture of Zion restored and comforted, the gates were to be called ' Praise,' and those which John saw in the New Jerusalem bore on their fronts the names of the 'twelve tribes of the children of Israel' (Rev 21¹²).

For meanings connected more especially with the entrance to tents and houses see DOOR.

G. M. MACKIE.

GEHENNA.—The Heb. name *Hinnom* is generally preceded in the OT by the word *Gē-*, ' valley ' (Jos 15⁸ff.), thus *Gē-hinnôm*, or ' Valley of Hinnom,' whence the NT word γέεννα, which is translated in both the AV and RV 'hell' (Mt 5²²· ²⁹· ³⁰ 10²⁸ 18⁹ 23¹⁵· ³³, Mk 9⁴³· ⁴⁵· ⁴⁷, Lk 12⁵, Ja 3⁶) ; from which also we obtain the English word *Gehenna*. Historically, this valley is the traditional site of the worship paid to Molech, first by Ahaz (2 Ch 28³), and later by Manasseh (33⁶), who made their children pass through the fire ; but which was later defiled by Josiah (2 K 23¹⁰), and thereafter seems to have been made the receptacle of the city's offal ; and in later Jewish thought became a symbol of the supposed place of future punishments (cf. *Enoch* xxvii. 1). The NT use of γέεννα is exclusively in this figurative sense. Milton also employs it thus in his familiar lines :

' The pleasant vale of Hinnom, Tophet thence,
And black Gehenna called, the type of hell' (*Par. Lost*, i. 404).

Opinions differ as to the identification of the valley ; but most authorities, including Robinson, Stanley, Buhl, and many others, as well as modern Arab tradition, identify it with the valley on the W. and S. side of the Holy City, the upper portion of which is called in Arabic *Wādy er-Rabābi* ; the lower, *Wādy Gehennam*, or ' Valley of Hell.' It is a ' deep and yawning gorge ' (Wilson), and ' never contains water ' (Socin), its descent from its original source to *Bir Eyyub* being approximately 670 ft.

At the lower extremity are found numerous rock-tombs, for here seems to have been the potter's field for the burial of pilgrims, which was purchased with the '30 pieces of silver,' and known as Akeldama, or field of blood (Mt 27³⁻⁸, Ac 1¹⁸⁻¹⁹). On the other hand, the Arab writer Edrisi of the 12th cent. A.D., followed by Sir C. Warren in an extended and somewhat convincing article on 'Hinnom (Valley of)' in Hastings' DB, identifies it with the Ḳidron on the E. of Jerusalem, including also its continuation below the junction of the Eastern and Western valleys at Bir Eyyub; the whole of the valley in its descent toward the Dead Sea being known to the Arabs as Wâdy en-Nâr, 'Valley of Fire.' Still another identification is that advocated by Sayce, R. Smith, Birch, and others, who locate it between the Temple area and the City of David, identifying it with the valley known since Josephus' day as the Tyropœon; but the first identification is, on the whole, the most probable.

LITERATURE.—Robinson, BRP i. 353, 402 ff.; Stanley, SP 239, 571; Barclay, City of the Great King, 89, 90; Wilson, Recovery of Jerusalem, 6, 19, 307, Lands of the Bible, i. 403 ff.; Tristram, Bible Places, 152, 162; Conder, Handbook to the Bible, 329 f.; Baedeker-Socin, Pal. 99; Barrows, Sacred Geog. and Antiquity, 94–96; Ritter, Geog. of Pal. iv. 164 ff.; artt. 'Gehenna' and 'Hinnom (Valley of)' in Hastings' DB; 'Hinnom (Valley of)' in Encyc. Bibl.; Swete, Com. on St. Mark, ad 9⁴⁵; Riehm, HWB; Rosenmüller, Biblisch. Geog. ii. 156, 164; Smith's DB, art. 'Hinnom (Valley of).'

GEORGE L. ROBINSON.

GENEALOGIES OF JESUS CHRIST.—1. There is no evidence that any special stress was laid upon the Davidic descent of Jesus, either by Himself or in the preaching of the Apostles. It was assumed that He was 'Son of David,' and the title was given to Him as the Messiah; nor does it appear that His claim was ever seriously contested on the ground that His Davidic descent was doubtful. St. Paul in Ro 1³ speaks of Christ as 'born of the seed of David according to the flesh,' and in 2 Ti 2⁸ he names this descent, along with the Resurrection, as one of the salient points of the gospel he preached: 'Remember Jesus Christ, risen from the dead, of the seed of David, according to my gospel.' Similarly in his speech at the Pisidian Antioch, as recorded in Ac 13²³, he says: 'Of this man's (i.e. David's) seed hath God according to promise brought unto Israel a Saviour, Jesus.' St. Peter in his speech on the Day of Pentecost (Ac 2³⁰) mentions God's promise to David, 'that of the fruit of his loins he would set one upon his throne,' and points to its fulfilment in Christ; but in addressing Cornelius (10³⁸) he speaks of Christ as 'Jesus of Nazareth'; and this would seem to imply that the birth at Bethlehem, which brought into prominence the claim to Davidic descent, did not form part of his ordinary missionary preaching. The author of the Epistle to the Hebrews (7¹⁴) says: 'It is evident that our Lord hath sprung out of Judah.' In the Second Gospel blind Bartimæus (Mk 10⁴⁷ᶠ·, cf. parallels) uses the title 'Son of David' in addressing Christ, and the crowds at the Triumphal Entry into Jerusalem (11¹⁰, cf. Mt 21⁹ 'Hosanna to the Son of David') speak of the 'kingdom that cometh' as the 'kingdom of our father David'; but in a difficult passage (12³⁵⁻³⁷, cf. parallels) Jesus appears to raise difficulties as to the appropriateness of the current application of the title to the Messiah (see Holtzmann, Hdcom.² ad loc.). In the Apocalypse the Davidic descent is apparently assumed (Rev 22¹⁶) as well as the birth from the tribe of Judah (5⁵); but the use of the phrase 'the root of David' in both passages shows that the essential and spiritual priority to David was more prominent in the writer's mind than the physical descent from him. The evidence to be derived from the Fourth Gospel is of a doubtful character; in Jn 7²⁷ we find traces of the phase

of Jewish thought according to which the Messiah would appear suddenly and his origin would be secret: the answer of Jesus implies that the people did indeed know His human, but not His spiritual, origin. It is clear from 7⁴¹ᶠ· ⁵² that He was regarded by both the crowd and the rulers at Jerusalem as being of Galilæan, and therefore presumably not Davidic, parentage; it is by no means certain, and to many it may seem in no way probable, that the writer, in the interest of a 'tragic irony' (see Westcott, Speaker's Commentary on 7⁴²), refrained from noting the fact of the birth at Bethlehem, and the Davidic lineage of Joseph or Mary. Jesus' words in 7²⁸ᶠ· show clearly that He did not choose to support His claim by an appeal to fleshly parentage; while the words of Philip (1⁴⁵ 'We have found him, of whom Moses in the law, and the prophets, did write, Jesus of Nazareth, the son of Joseph'), and of the crowd at Capernaum (6⁴² 'Is not this Jesus, the son of Joseph, whose father and mother we know?'), left, as they are, without comment by the Evangelist, suggest that he was unacquainted with the story of the birth at Bethlehem, and laid no stress on the Davidic descent.

In all the books thus far mentioned no intimation is given whether the descent of Jesus is traced through Mary or Joseph: this fact must be recognized, however it is explained. In the Catholic Epistles there is no reference, direct or indirect, to the tribe or family of the Lord. The First and Third Gospels, which (at all events in their present form) teach the doctrine of the birth from a virgin, also contain formal pedigrees of Joseph, with the evident intention of proving that Jesus was the heir of David. In this lies the most important problem which the genealogies of Jesus present for solution.

2. The general facts in regard to the divergences of the two pedigrees of Joseph are well known. St. Matthew (1²⁻¹⁷) begins with Abraham, and traces the line in fourteen generations to David; then through Solomon in fourteen generations to Jechoniah at the time of the carrying away to Babylon: then in fourteen (or thirteen according to our present text) generations through Shealtiel and Zerubbabel to Matthan, Jacob, Joseph, and Jesus. Thus he brings the Messiah into relation with all who, whether in a literal or a spiritual sense, could call Abraham their Father.

St. Luke (3²³⁻³⁸) makes Joseph the son of Heli, and grandson of Matthat (by some identified without any proof with Matthan of Mt 1¹⁵), and traces his descent through Zerubbabel and Shealtiel to Nathan the son of David; then (with only slight or textually doubtful divergences from Mt.) back to Abraham; but, not stopping there, he carries the pedigree back to 'Adam the son of God,' thus bringing the Son of man into relation with all men whom God has created. A more detailed examination of the main characteristics of the two genealogies will show the fundamental differences of conception and treatment that exist between them, and prepare us for extracting whatever may be of value from the attempts that have been made to harmonize them.

3. St. Matthew's genealogy. — The heading is translated in the RV 'The book of the generation (βίβλος γενέσεως) of Jesus Christ, the son of David, the son of Abraham': in the margin the alternative rendering is given 'the genealogy of Jesus Christ.' If, as seems probable, the latter rendering is right, this heading will refer only to the pedigree which follows; the phrase βίβλος γενέσεως is most likely taken from Gn 5¹ (αὕτη ἡ βίβλος γενέσεως ἀνθρώπων: cf. 6⁹ αὗται δὲ αἱ γενέσεις Νῶε, and 10¹), where it introduces a list of Adam's descendants, and thus practically forms the title of a genealogical table. Zahn (*Einleitung in d. NT*[2], ii. pp. 270 f. and 290) argues without much cogency that the phrase could not be applied to a table of *ancestors*, and takes it as a title of the whole book ; he is, however, no doubt right in rejecting the view that it refers to the narrative of the birth, or of the birth and infancy. Taken as the title of the pedigree, it indicates clearly the intention of the writer—to show that in Jesus, as the heir of David and of Abraham, were fulfilled the promises made to them : the pedigree itself is intended to illustrate this, rather than to prove it, and it is not easy to avoid the conclusion that it is quite artificial, as is indeed implied by the more or less arbitrary division into 3 sections containing twice seven names apiece.

Confining our attention for the moment to the direct male line, we note that in the first section the names are taken from 1 Ch 2[1-15], and that if Salmon was the younger contemporary of Joshua (as is implied by his marriage with Rahab), there are only four generations to cover the 300 or 400 years between that time and David's reign. In the second section the names are from 1 Ch 3[1-16], but Joash, Amaziah, and Azariah are omitted before Jotham, and Jehoiakim before Jechoniah (=Jehoiachin). In the third section only Shealtiel and Zerubbabel are mentioned in the OT [the latter in 1 Ch 3[19] is called son of Pedaiah, the brother of Shealtiel, but in Hag 1[1] and numerous other passages, he is called son of Shealtiel, or Shaltiel, but without any intimation that he was of Davidic descent ; it is often assumed that Shealtiel adopted his nephew]. We have no hint as to the source from whence the remaining names are drawn. For about 460 years, from David to the Captivity, we have 14 names, and know there should be 18 ; for about 590 years, from the Captivity to Christ, we have, against all reasonable probability, only 13 (perhaps originally 14) names.

We now turn to the notes inserted at different points in the pedigree. A very small point may perhaps guide us to a true conclusion in regard to these. Holtzmann (*op. cit.* on Mt 1[6]) points out that the articles before Δαυείδ τὸν βασιλέα in v.[6], and before Ἰωσὴφ τὸν ἄνδρα Μαρίας in v.[16], are incorrect : it seems probable that the compiler of the Gospel had a pedigree before him in which each step was given in the simple form ' Abraham begat Isaac ' (Ἀβραὰμ ἐγέννησεν τὸν Ἰσαάκ), and that he added notes to this at certain points ; in vv.[6] and [16] he did not notice that the use of the article became incorrect when the notes were added. This original document may or may not have ended ' Joseph begat Jesus ' (Ἰωσὴφ δὲ ἐγέννησεν τὸν Ἰησοῦν) : it is perhaps the easiest solution of the difficulties of this verse to suppose that, if it did so end, the compiler omitted the last step, as in conflict with his belief in the Virgin-birth, and added a note to the previous step to explain the relation in which Jesus stood to Joseph. If in Westcott and Hort's edition of the NT the notes be struck out, it will be seen that a perfectly symmetrical pedigree of Joseph is left.

Mr. F. C. Burkitt, in a very important note on vv.[16-25] (*Evangelion da - Mepharreshe*, Cambridge, 1904, vol. ii. pp. 258–266), argues with great force that the genealogy is an integral part of St. Matthew's Gospel, and that the compiler himself drew it up ; but really his arguments apply only to the notes inserted in the genealogy. He discusses fully the reading in v.[16], and concludes that we cannot look on the reading of the Sinaitic Syriac (' Jacob begat Joseph ; Joseph, to whom was betrothed Mary the Virgin, begat Jesus, who is called the Christ ') as containing traces of an original text. Zahn (*op. cit.* ii. p. 292 f.) thinks that the Curetonian Syriac (' Jacob begat Joseph,

to whom was betrothed Mary the Virgin, who bore Jesus Christ ') represents the Greek from which the Syriac version was made more closely than does the Sinaitic. If, therefore, the compiler followed a pedigree ready to hand, he did so only as far as the step ' Jacob begat Joseph ' ; and textual criticism will not help us to reconstruct the presumed original document beyond that point. In the usual text stress is laid on Joseph being the *husband* of Mary, probably to show that, as he recognized his wife's son as in a *legal* sense his own, Jesus was legally the heir of David. In the reading that probably underlies the Ferrar group of MSS (' Jacob begat Joseph, to whom being betrothed the Virgin Mary begat Jesus that is called Christ '), and also the Old Latin and Syriac versions, this point is missed, and there is little doubt that the Received Text is right.

Added to vv.[6] and [11] are notes which mark important turning-points in the history of the family : with David it attained to royal standing, which it lost under Jechoniah at the Captivity. In v.[2] the addition of ' and his brethren ' to the name Judah marks the beginning of the tribe, in that Judah is chosen from among his brethren as founder of the royal tribe. The addition of Zerah to Perez in v.[3] marks the division of the tribe, and it is interesting to notice that we find an allusion to the house of Perez in Ru 4[12] ; perhaps, too, the compiler may have had in mind the strange story of Gn 38[28ff.], around which some Rabbinic lore may have clustered. The addition of ' and his brethren ' to the name Jechoniah is more puzzling. Zahn (*op. cit.* p. 273) thinks it is meant to mark the fact that till then the fortunes of the Davidic house centred in the reigning monarch, who was heir of all the promises, but that from that time onward a number of Davidic families existed, any one of which might be destined to receive the inheritance. Thus it would mark the change from *the* reigning family of the second section to *a* family of royal descent in the third section. But it is not clear from the OT that Jechoniah (=Jehoiachin) had any brothers, for the text of 1 Ch 3[16] seems suspicious. According to 2 Ch 36[10] his successor Zedekiah was his brother, according to 2 K 24[17] his father's brother. Possibly there has been some confusion with Jehoiakim, who had three brothers (including a Zedekiah) according to 1 Ch 3[15] ; more probably the compiler has added the note, for the purpose indicated by Zahn, without regard for strict genealogical data.

The four notes not yet referred to are of special interest, naming four of the ancestresses of Solomon. The selection of these names was evidently made with a purpose ; it seems as if the compiler wished to show that in the pedigree of the greatest of Jewish kings could be found instances of the breach of laws usually considered most binding. Tamar became a mother through incestuous intercourse with her father-in-law ; Rahab was a harlot ; Ruth was a Moabitess, and according to the Deuteronomic law (Dt 23[3], cf. Neh 13[1]) no Moabite was ever to enter into the congregation ; Bathsheba was an adulteress. Some have thought that these references to acknowledged breaches of morality in the pedigree of David's first great son form some kind of answer to the charges of immorality brought by the Jews against the Virgin : the argument would be that, if they did not reject Solomon in spite of acknowledged moral blots in his ancestry, they ought not to reject Jesus because of unfounded scandal. But this explanation is obviously unsatisfactory ; there is no real force in such an argument, even supposing it to be worked out and not merely vaguely indicated ; and all must feel that the compiler would have shrunk from drawing a parallel between the

Mother of Jesus and notoriously sinful women; also the reference to Ruth remains unexplained, as she was guilty of no immorality. Burkitt (*op. cit.* vol. ii. p. 260) suggests a different explanation, that these four women are thrust upon our notice 'as if to prepare us for still greater irregularity in the last stage.' But again a comparison between the Virgin-birth and incestuous or adulterous intercourse can hardly have been possible for the compiler.

The simplest explanation is probably the right one : the God about whom Jesus taught had shown Himself ready, in the history of the royal family, to accept strangers and sinners. In the case of Ruth this is fully satisfactory; and the conduct of the other three women is represented in Scripture as justified or pardoned. Judah was obliged to say of Tamar, 'She is more righteous than I' (Gn 38[26]); the remembrance of Rahab's former life was blotted out by her subsequent faith (Ja 2[25], He 11[31]); there is no intimation in Scripture that Bathsheba was morally responsible for the sin into which she was forced by a powerful king, and certainly the birth of Solomon is not represented as in any way displeasing to God, but rather the contrary (see 2 S 12[25], where Nathan named the child 'Jedidiah ['Beloved of Jah'] for the Lord's sake'; cf. the prophecy of 7[13f.]). Probably the thought uppermost in the mind of the compiler would be God's acceptance of these women, and not their sin.

In regard to Rahab, there is no evidence for her marriage with Salmon, nor is anything known that would be likely to have suggested the idea: it would seem that the compiler was determined to introduce the name, and therefore, without evidence and against all chronological probability, made her the wife of the father of Boaz.

This examination compels us to conclude that the genealogy is essentially and intentionally artificial; the word 'begat' ($\dot{\epsilon}\gamma\dot{\epsilon}\nu\nu\eta\sigma\epsilon\nu$) is not intended necessarily to imply physical birth, but merely marks the descent; the compiler was more interested in the throne-succession than the actual lineage, and used his material to illustrate and enforce his main proposition that Jesus Christ was the son of David and of Abraham, and he joined to the bare pedigree a sort of running commentary of notes.

Codex Bezæ in Lk 3 gives a pedigree in the Lukan form, but the names from Joseph to David are taken from Mt.; the names Jehoiakim and Eliakim are inserted between Jechoniah and Josiah as if they referred to two different persons, instead of being two names for the same man ; and also Amariah, Joash, and Ahaziah between Uzziah and Joram (see Resch, *TU* x. 5, pp. 182-201, and Græfe in *SK*, 1898, 1).

4. *St. Luke's genealogy.*—The descent of Joseph is traced through Nathan the son of David. It is possible that the family is referred to in Zec 12[12], where 'the family of the house of Nathan' is distinguished from 'the family of the house of David,' the latter phrase perhaps meaning the royal line. The rejection of the descent through Jechoniah may have been due to the influence of the prophecy of Jeremiah (22[30]) : 'Thus saith the Lord, Write ye this man childless, a man that shall not prosper in his days : for no man of his seed shall prosper, sitting upon the throne of David, and ruling any more in Judah'; but there is no apparent reason why the line of Nathan should be selected, unless St. Luke had evidence of the fact before him; and, in the case of a writer who so evidently based his work upon the results of careful research, it is only fair, and therefore scientific, to assume that he had such evidence. The agreement with St. Matthew's genealogy in the names Zerubbabel and Shealtiel has not been satisfactorily explained ; it is, of course, open to any one to assume, without the possibility of either proof or

refutation, that Jechoniah was actually childless, and adopted Shealtiel, a descendant of Nathan; but even so the further divergence in the descent from Zerubbabel remains as difficult as ever, for the pedigrees disagree with each other, and with the names given in 1 Ch 3[19ff.]. The number of derivatives of the name Nathan, and the repetition of the names Melchi, Joseph, and Jesus in the Lukan pedigree, can be taken equally well to prove its genuineness or the ingenuity of its compiler. Apart from small variations of little interest, there is nothing to notice in the names from David to Adam, except the insertion in v.[36] of a second Canaan in agreement with the LXX of Gn 10[24].

5. *Historical value of the two genealogies.*— From what has been said above, it appears that St. Matthew (or the compiler of the First Gospel in its present form) did not aim at historical accuracy ; but from what we know of St. Luke's methods it may be assumed that he would not have inserted matter in his Gospel unless he had had satisfactory evidence of its genuineness and historical accuracy, and we have seen that the character of the list of names he gives, from David to Joseph, agrees well with this view. Attempts to harmonize the two genealogies have not been successful, and it is only necessary to indicate the general lines they have followed, and to collect such pieces of evidence as may throw light on the possible transmission of the pedigree.

The question was first discussed by Julius Africanus, who flourished early in the 3rd cent. after Christ, in a letter addressed to an unknown correspondent Aristides, of which a considerable portion has been preserved by Euseb. *HE* i. 7 (cf. Routh, *Reliq. Sacræ*, vol. ii. p. 228 ff.). In his text of St. Luke the names Matthat and Levi were evidently left out, so that he regarded Melchi as grandfather of Joseph. He supposed that Matthan, a descendant of Solomon, married a woman named, according to tradition, Estha, by whom he had a son Jacob. On Matthan's death, Melchi, a descendant of Nathan, married his widow, who bore him a son Heli. Heli died without children, and Jacob, in accordance with the levirate law, raised up seed to his brother, and begat Joseph. Thus Joseph was physically son of Jacob, legally of Heli. The difficulties of this theory are sufficiently discussed by Dr. B. W. Bacon in Hastings' *DB*, art. 'Genealogy of Jesus Christ.' The various modifications of this theory that have been proposed (see, *e.g.*, Farrar's *St. Luke* in the Cambridge Bible for Schools, Excursus II.) in no way increase its probability, and practically no evidence can be adduced in support of it. Eusebius does indeed speak of a narrative ($\dot{\iota}\sigma\tau o\rho\dot{\iota}a$) which Africanus had received by tradition (*HE* i. 7; cf. vi. 31); Africanus, however, does not assert this in the fragments preserved, and himself admits that the conjecture is unsupported by evidence ($\epsilon\dot{\iota}$ $\kappa a\dot{\iota}$ $\mu\dot{\eta}$ $\dot{\epsilon}\mu\mu\dot{a}\rho\tau\upsilon\rho\dot{o}s$ $\dot{\epsilon}\sigma\tau\iota$), but claims that it is worthy of acceptance till a better or truer one is proposed.

Africanus does, however, mention people called 'Desposyni' on account of their kinship with the Saviour, and applies to them the epithet 'the before-mentioned,' so that in those parts of the letter that are now lost he may have specified more exactly how far his conjecture rested on evidence traditionally derived from them. After giving a very improbable story about the destruction of the public genealogical records of the Jews by Herod Antipas, he says that many people reconstructed their genealogies from memory or private sources, among whom were the Desposyni of Nazareth and Cochaba; probably, therefore, he derived from them the information that Joseph's grandmother was called Estha. The main interest of this statement is that, in spite of its being somewhat discredited by its context, it suggests a source from which St. Luke might possibly have obtained the pedigree he gives; we may well suppose that he pursued his investigations in Palestine during St. Paul's imprisonment at Cæsarea.

Hegesippus (quoted by Euseb. *HE* iii. 19, 20, and 32; see Routh, *Reliq. Sacræ*, vol. i. p. 212 ff.) supports the statement of Africanus in reference to the Desposyni, though that term is not found in the fragments of his writings that are preserved: he states that when Domitian gave orders to kill those who were of David's race, certain heretics gave information against two grandsons of Judas the Lord's brother according to the flesh, as being of David's race and akin to Christ; Domitian, on finding out that they were ordinary peasants, and that the kingdom they expected was not of this world, released them, and issued an edict stopping the persecution of the Church; they took leading positions in the Church, and lived till the time of Trajan. He also relates that a similar accusation was brought against Symeon son of Clopas, 'the Lord's uncle,' who, in consequence, suffered martyrdom at the age of one hundred and twenty. It would appear, therefore, that nothing was known of any who claimed kinship with Jesus after the time of Trajan, so that the statement of Africanus probably rests, at the best, on mere tradition, and it is not wise to build much on it. The statement of Africanus about the destruction of genealogical records by Herod is most improbable, and tends to discredit his whole story; Josephus (*c. Ap.* i. 7 and *Vita*, 1) speaks of the preservation of the genealogies of priestly families in public records in the Temple, but there is no certain evidence that those of other families were similarly preserved.

The expedient of supposing levirate marriages and adoptions is not only improbable, but fails to explain why the descent of Jesus is traced through Joseph. Burkitt (*l.c.*) is probably quite justified in saying that the compiler of the First Gospel was perfectly aware that the word 'begat' (ἐγέννησεν) was not literally true in the pedigree he gives, and that he would have felt no incongruity between the physical reality of the Virgin-birth and the legal descent from David through Joseph. But this reasoning can hardly be applied to the Third Gospel; the Virgin-birth is certainly not insisted on in it in the same way as in the First; the phrase 'thy father and I' in 2⁴⁸ (cf. 2³³· ⁴¹) seems almost incompatible with the belief, and there is some reason for thinking, on textual grounds, that the original text has in places been altered; the words 'as was supposed' might easily have been inserted in 3²³, although the variations of reading afford little or no evidence in favour of this supposition; above all, there is no reason to suppose that the writer had, or was likely to have, in mind the legal relation to Jesus in which Joseph, as husband of Mary, might be considered to stand. If, therefore, the suggestion first made by Annius of Viterbo in the 15th cent., and since adopted by many eminent theologians, that St. Luke gives the genealogy of Mary, could be accepted, it would have important results. It is a matter on which argument is hardly possible, the only point being whether any unprejudiced person could understand the words in 3²³ to mean 'being (as was supposed, son of Joseph, but really) grandson of Heli'—Heli being taken, without a shred of evidence, to have been the father of Mary. A passage has, indeed, been quoted from the Talmud (Jerus. *Chag.* 77*b*) to prove that Mary was called 'daughter of Eli'; but this has been shown to be a mistake by G. A. Cooke, *Expos.*, Oct. 1895, pp. 316 ff. In the *Protevangelium Jacobi* her parents are called Joachim and Anna. The early Fathers generally assumed that Mary was of the same family as Joseph, and

that her descent was involved in his; see, for instance, Euseb. *HE* i. 7 *ad fin.* and *Qu. ad Steph.* iii. 2 (Migne, iv. col. 881 f.), where reasons are suggested why Mary's genealogy was not given; this view is based on a mistaken interpretation of Nu 36⁸, as if all women were commanded to marry in their own families, whereas the regulation applied only to heiresses. Proof of the Davidic descent of Mary can be obtained from the NT only by assuming the truth of the doctrine of the Virgin-birth; it was no doubt on this ground that Justin Martyr (*Apol.* i. 32¹⁴) inferred that Mary was of the tribe of Judah (cf. *Protev. Jacobi*, 10, where she is said to be of the tribe of David). St. Matthew (1²⁰) and St. Luke (1²⁷ 2⁴) assert the Davidic descent of Joseph, but not that of Mary; contrast Lk 1⁵, where Elisabeth is said to be of the daughters of Aaron. Sanday-Headlam on Ro 1³ point out that in *Test. XII Patriarch.* we find the theory of a double descent from Levi and from Judah (*Sym.* 7 and *Gad* 8), and they remark that this is no doubt an inference from the relationship of Mary to Elisabeth (Lk 1³⁶).

We must conclude, therefore, that we have two independent attempts to establish the Davidic descent of Joseph, and that they can be harmonized only by suppositions which are incapable of proof and hardly probable.

LITERATURE.—This is sufficiently indicated in the body of the article.   P. M. BARNARD.

GENERATION.—A word of several meanings employed to render two different words in OT and four in NT. All are, however, related in thought, and all have a close connexion with the Gospels and Jewish thought in the time of Christ.

1. In OT 'generation' is used to render (1) the Heb. דּוֹר or דֹּר, connected with Assyr. *dârú*, 'to endure,' means primarily *a period of time*. This meaning has survived in OT chiefly in poetry, and in the phrases לְדֹר דֹּר Ps 45¹⁸ 617, דֹּר וָדֹר Ps 45¹⁸ Is 51⁹, Ps 72⁵, and such like, to indicate time stretching away into the past (Is 51⁹), or (more generally) into the future (Ps 33¹¹ 49¹²). It may refer both to past and future (145¹³), and is thus parallel to עוֹלָם (see ETERNITY).

Originally דֹּר must have meant the period defined by the life of a man or of a family (Job 42¹⁶). Hence by a loose usage it comes to mean the *people* living in that period (Gn 7¹, Ex 16, Dt 2¹⁴, Ec 1⁴, Is 53⁸ etc. etc.; cf. the modern use of the word 'age'). So also it may be used of a *class* of men living contemporaneously and possessing certain characteristics (Dt 32⁵, Pr 30¹¹· ¹²· ¹³· ¹⁴).

(2) The other word in OT (rendered always plural 'generations') is תּוֹלְדוֹת. Here the root-idea is 'birth,' 'descent,' 'offspring,' from ילד 'to bring forth.' Hence it is used of genealogies (Gn 5¹ 6⁹ 10¹ 11¹⁰· ²⁷, Ru 4¹⁸ etc.), of divisions by families, etc. (Nu 1²⁰· ²²· ²⁴ etc.). It is even used of the creation of the world (Gn 2⁴ lit. 'the begettings of the heaven and the earth').

2. Of the four words rendered 'generation' in NT two are unimportant so far as the Gospels are concerned. (1) In 1 P 2⁹ 'a chosen generation,' γένος ἐκλεκτόν, should be rendered as in RV, 'an elect race.' (2) In Mt 1¹ the rendering should be 'the book of the *origin* of Jesus Christ,' using the word γένεσις in its widest sense. The meaning in Mt 1⁸, Lk 1¹⁴ is slightly different, and is best expressed by 'birth' (EV). (3) The most important word used in the Gospels is γενεά, meaning (*a*) 'race,' 'offspring,' 'descent'; (*b*) the people of any given period; (*c*) a period loosely defined by the life of a man or of a family; (*d*) in such phrases as εἰς γενεὰς γενεῶν (Lk 1⁵⁰) it is used, apparently as the equivalent of דֹּר וָדֹר, to express indefinite time, generally in the future. Cf. the expression in Eph 3²¹ εἰς πάσας τὰς γενεὰς τοῦ αἰῶνος τῶν αἰώνων, which, however, is considered by Dalman (*Words of Jesus*, p. 165, Eng. tr.) as referring to all the generations of 'the current age' of 'the world period.' But the phrase seems rather to be the strongest possible way of expressing 'for ever.' That γενεά (rendered 'generation') does express 'the current age' of 'the world period' is obvious in the Gospels (Lk 16⁸, Mt 24³⁴, and less clearly Mt 23³⁶); also the *people* of that age (Mt 12³⁹ 16⁴, Mk 8¹², Lk 11²⁹). In the sense of (*c*) it is found only in Mt 1¹⁷ and apparently never in its original sense (*a*). (4) This last is expressed by quite a different word, viz. γέννημα. In Mt 3⁷ 12³⁴ 23³³, Lk 3⁷, AV has the phrase 'generation of vipers.' The Greek is γεννήματα ἐχιδνῶν, which RV renders 'offspring of vipers.' The rendering of AV is due to Tindale (see Hastings' *DB* ii. 142ᵇ). Elsewhere the word occurs as γένημα (Mt 26²⁹, Lk 22¹⁸, 2 Co 9¹⁰), rendered 'fruit.'   G. GORDON STOTT.

GENNESARET, LAKE OF.—See SEA OF GALI-LEE.

GENNESARET, LAND OF.—Thither Jesus and His disciples repaired after the feeding of the 5000 (Mt 14²², Mk 6⁴⁵). This miracle probably took place on the N.E. shore of the Sea of Galilee. When evening came, the Synoptists tell us, His disciples entered into a boat, and crossing over the sea, came to the land, unto Gennesaret, ἐπὶ τὴν γῆν εἰς Γεννησαρέτ (Mt 14³⁴, Mk 6⁵³).

1. *Name.*—The 'Land of Gennesar, *or* Gennesa-ret,' is mentioned but twice in the Bible (Mt 14³⁴, Mk 6⁵³). The name 'Gennesaret,' however, occurs elsewhere: once as the name of the Lake, παρὰ τὴν λίμνην Γεννησαρέτ (Lk 5¹), once in 1 Mac 11⁶⁷ τὸ ὕδωρ τοῦ Γεννησάρ, and is frequently found in Josephus, who uses both λίμνη Γεννησαρῖτις (*Ant.* XVIII. ii. 1) and λίμνη Γεννησάρ (*BJ* III. x. 7); in the Targums, גִּנּוֹסַר, גִּנֵּיסַר, and ; and in Pliny's writings, *Gennesara* (v. 15). The name of the Lake was derived from that of the Plain, and that in turn from the name of a city supposed by the Jews to have been situated on the W. shore of the Sea of Galilee; that portion of the plain bordering on Mejdel being called *Ard el-Mejdel.* On the derivation of the word *Gennesaret,* see art. SEA OF GALILEE.

2. *Situation.*—It is usually identified with the little plain situated on the western coast of the Sea of Galilee, and known to the Arabs as *el-Ghuweir,* 'little Ghor *or* hollow.' This identifica-tion is as good as certain. The description of it as given by Josephus can apply to no other. Several years ago an attempt was made by Thrupp and Tregelles (in the *Journal of Classical and Sacred Philology,* ii. 290–308) to identify it with the plain of *el-Baṭihah,* on the N.E. shore of the Lake, but without success (cf. Stanley's 'Note' in refutation, *SP* 455).

3. *Size.*—Shut in by the hilly promontory of *Khân Minyeh* on the N. and the still more promi-nent hills by Magdala on the S., and extending westward from the Lake only to the base of the rugged uplands of Galilee, its total area is exceed-ingly small. Its approximate measurements are about 3 miles long from N. to S. by 1¼ broad from E. to W. Stanley's measurements are wide of the mark when he says that the plain is 6 or 7 miles long by 5 miles broad (*SP* 442); and even G. A. Smith exaggerates when he describes it as 'four miles broad' (*HGHL* 443). Josephus' measure-ments are more nearly correct, viz. 30 × 20 stadia; though in fact it is a little longer than 30 and not quite so broad as 20. In form it is somewhat crescent-shaped or semi-elliptical. Its surface is comparatively level. Its altitude, like that of the Sea of Galilee, is over 650 feet below the level of the Mediterranean.

4. *Josephus' description of the Land of Gennes-aret.*—

'Its nature is wonderful as well as its beauty: its soil is so fruitful that all sorts of trees can grow upon it, and the inhabit-

ants accordingly plant all sorts of trees there; for the temper of the air is so well mixed that it agrees very well with these several sorts; particularly walnuts, which require the coldest air, flourish there in vast plenty; there are palm trees also, which grow best in hot air; fig trees also and olives grow near them, which yet require an air that is more temperate. One may call the place the ambition of nature, where it forces those plants that are naturally enemies to one another to agree to-gether. It is a happy contention of the seasons, as if every one of them laid claim to this country; for it not only nourishes different sorts of autumnal fruit beyond men's expectation, but preserves them a great while; it supplies men with the prin-cipal fruits, with grapes and figs continually, during ten months of the year, and with other fruits as they become ripe through the whole year; for besides the good temperature of the air, it is also watered from a most copious fountain. The people of the country call it Capharnaum. Some have thought it to be a vein of the Nile, because it produces the *coracin* fish as well as that lake does which is near to Alexandria. The length of this country extends itself along the banks of this lake that bears the same name for thirty furlongs, and is in breadth twenty. And this is the nature of that place' (*BJ* III. x. 8).

This classical passage from Josephus, though probably coloured to some extent, gives substanti-ally the truth about the Plain as it must have been in the time of Christ, and for this reason it is of the utmost importance. Jewish Rabbins of early times corroborate his description. They describe it as possessing both 'gardens and paradises'; as one of the garden spots of the world; as irrigated and cultivated so that no portion of it was barren; and as being dotted over thickly with towns and villages. Indeed, ruins of villages have been found at three or four different localities in the Plain, viz. at the opening of *Wady el-Ḥamam,* at 'Ain el-Mudauwarah,* south of 'Ain eṭ-Ṭin,* and on the N. side of *Wady er-Rubudiyeh.*

5. *Its condition to-day.*—Josephus' account is especially interesting because of the contrast be-tween its condition then and now. Then, it was a most charming spot—'the unparalleled garden of God,' as a certain Rabbi calls it; and 'the gem of Palestine,' as Merrill speaks of it (*Galilee in the Time of Christ,* 33): now, it is, as Thomson says, 'pre-eminently fruitful in thorns,' a veritable thicket of oleanders and nubk trees, of gigantic thistles and brambles. And yet even now one finds proofs of its former luxuriance in the wealth of its wild flowers, the heavy-headed wheat and barley growing here and there, and in the stout-ness of the thorns and thistles almost everywhere.

(1) The *soil* is wonderfully rich, like that of the Delta in Egypt. It consists of basaltic loam formed by the mingling of decomposed basalt with the alluvium of the lake. All travellers—Seetzen, von Schubert, Ritter, Burckhardt, Robinson, Wilson, and Thomson—praise the fertility of this Plain, and all except Stanley (cf. *SP* 451) lament its present desolate and uncultivated condition. The latter erroneously describes it as 'cultivated everywhere.' Only near Magdala are there signs of marsh.

(2) *Fountains and streams* supply it with water in copious abundance. Three winter torrents rush down from the hill country lying to the west, and bring with them abundance of water for the greater portion of the year. (*a*) One is known as the *Wady el-Ḥamam,* or the 'Valley of Pigeons,' a deep gorge bounded by almost perpendicular cliffs over one thousand feet in height, which enters the Plain from the S.W. This is a tremendous ravine, and from Josephus' day has been known as the ravine of the 'Robber Caves'—the chosen resort of brigands in former days. Thomson describes it in two connexions, as 'a great chasm' and as a 'profound gorge' (*Land and the Book,* ii. 395–397), and as leading up to a fort or castle known as *Kal'at ibn Ma'an,* and still on to the village of *Ḥaṭṭin.* Down this valley are poured large volumes of water, and down through this same ravine, as through a funnel, rush sudden blasts of wind, which break upon the Lake. The ruins of

Irbid, the Arbela of Josephus and 1 Mac 9[2], are not far to the south. (*b*) Another torrent, entering the Plain from the W., is that known as *Wady er-Rubudiyeh*. This is the largest, and yields the most plentiful supply of water furnished to the Plain. It is used to irrigate the Plain both N. and S., furnishing nearly three times the volume of water supplied by '*Ain el-Mudauwarah*. (*c*) A third torrent enters the Plain from the N.W. It is called *Wady el-'Amud*. Like *Wady el-Ḥamam*, it is a deep ravine, and scarcely less striking because of its narrowness. Its waters take their rise in the Jarmuk, the highest mountain in Galilee. For the greater part of its course it is called *Wady el-Leimum*. It is only a winter torrent. According to Thomson, all of these streams which enter the Plain disappear in summer before they reach the Lake.

Besides these waters which drain the region of Galilee immediately west of the Plain of Gennesaret, there are certain fountains in the Plain itself whose waters were used for irrigation : (*a*) '*Ain el-Mudauwarah*, or 'Round Fountain,' situated a little over a mile N.W. of Magdala, is the largest and most important. It is enclosed by a circular wall of hewn stones, 32 yards in diameter, surrounded by thick trees and brushwood, so that access is difficult ; but it yields a copious stream of clear water, which flows across the Plain to the Lake, irrigating right and left. The pool itself contains two to three feet of water and certain fish. Ebrard (*SK*, 1867, pp. 723–747) identified it with the fountain of Capharnaum mentioned by Josephus, but this has been shown to be highly improbable. Two other fountains assist in watering the southern end of the Plain : '*Ain el-Bareideh*, or 'Cold Spring,' also known as '*Ain el-Fuliyeh*, or 'Fountain of the Bean' ; and '*Ain es-Serar*, somewhat further to the S.W. (*β*) '*Ain eṭ-Ṭin*, or 'Fountain of the Fig Tree,' is another large and important spring. It is situated on the northern edge of the Plain, and bursts forth from under the cliffs of *Khān Minyeh*. Unfortunately, it is too close to the shore of the Lake to be used extensively for irrigating purposes. The stream which issues from it is choked with a jungle of oleanders and papyrus. Robinson identifies this fountain with the spring of Capharnaum of Josephus. (*γ*) '*Ain eṭ-Ṭabigha*, or 'Fountain of the Ruined Mill,' formerly supposed to be the scene of the miracle of the feeding of the 5000 (Mk 6[30-44]), is another large spring of water—according to Tristram, the largest in Galilee, and about one-half as large as the fountain at Cæsarea Philippi. It is not situated in the Plain, but considerably N.E., about half-way between *Khān Minyeh* and *Tell Ḥum*, the two rival sites of Capernaum ; but its waters were formerly conducted by a channel cut in the rock around the promontory on which *Khan Minyeh* is situated, and made to irrigate the N. end of the Plain of Gennesaret. This aqueduct was discovered first by Sir Chas. Wilson, and since then the fountain has been generally considered to be the spring of Capharnaum of Josephus (cf. Thomson, *Land and Book*, ii. 429).

(3) *Products.*—With all these resources of irrigation, it is not surprising that the Plain of Gennesaret should be described by the Rabbins as the 'Garden of God,' or that its superior and delicious fruits 'were not allowed at the feasts in Jerusalem lest some might attend primarily to enjoy these fruits' (Bab. *Pesachim*, 8 *b* ; Neubauer, *Géog. du Talmud*, 45 f.). But to-day, though its grapes, figs, olives, and walnuts have vanished, there are to be seen wild figs, oleanders, nubk trees, dwarf palms, papyrus plants, tall prickly centaureas ; in summer, magnificent lilac-coloured convolvuli hanging in long festoons of blossom from

the prickly shrubs ; wild flowers of countless variety —tulips, anemones, irises ; rice, wheat, the best and earliest melons and cucumbers in Palestine, sedges and rushes by the Lake ; also thorns and thistles, especially in the central portion ; in short, a tangle of luxuriant vegetation—a lovely floral carpet in February, a wilderness of thorns in summer. For here, indeed, Nature has lavished her glory in tropical profusion.

(4) *Roads.*—Two paths cross the Plain from S. to N.—the chief one leading from Magdala to *Khān Minyeh* in a direct course, and skirting the Lake shore within a few hundred feet ; the other following the base of the hills along its western side, and striking over the hills northwards. One of the best views obtainable of the Plain is from the top of the ridge above Magdala.

(5) *Inhabitants.* — The Plain is without settled inhabitants to-day. The *Ghawarineh* Arabs, more especially a certain tribe named *es-Senekiyeh*, roam over it, using it as winter pasture land. Wilson recounts that gipsies from India have been known to sojourn there with their tents and flocks (p. 138). As a rule, solitude reigns except near the village of Magdala and at *Khān Minyeh*.

(6) *Health.*—Fevers are still prevalent in this region as in the days of our Lord, when, not far distant, at least, Peter's wife's mother lay sick (Lk 4[38]). Thomson speaks of 'the heat and malarial influences of the Plain.' This probably accounts in part for its present desolation, though under the Turk it has fared but little worse than other portions of the Empire.

Such is the land of Gennesaret, on the immediate edge of which lay Capernaum, and over whose 'Eden-like landscape' the feet of our blessed Lord so often trod as He went about preaching from village to village, healing the sick and raising to life the dead. One can almost see Him, in fancy, pushing out in a little boat along the embayed and shell-covered shore, followed to the water's edge by the multitudes who pressed upon Him daily from populous Gennesaret, and hear Him speaking to them, as they sit upon the shore, concerning the gospel of the Kingdom, drawing illustrations from the sower, who, going forth to sow, allows some seeds to fall by the wayside, others on stony places, still others where they are choked by thorns ; and then, when He became weary, retiring to the mountains for rest and spiritual refreshment in prayer, only to return again and repeat His message of goodwill and comfort ; until, finally, when the great tragedy on Calvary is ended and He is risen from the tomb, He reappears to those same disciples, who meanwhile have returned to their nets. Surely no other spot of like size can possibly be of equal interest, to the Christian who loves to trace the footprints of His Master's earthly career, with what has justly been called 'the most sacred region of the Lake,' 'the gem of Palestine.'

LITERATURE.—Sanday, *Sacred Sites of the Gospels*, 39 f. ; Tristram, *Bible Places*, 311–315, *The Land of Israel*, 565 ; Thomson, *The Land and the Book*, i. 86, ii. 293 f., 298, 408, iii. 166 ; G. A. Smith, *HGHL* 443 ff. ; Merrill, *Galilee in the Time of Christ*, 33, 34, art. 'Gennesaret, Land of,' in Hastings' *DB* ; Robinson, *BR* iii. 277 ff , *Physical Geog. of the Holy Land*, 199 ; Cheyne, art. 'Gennesar' in *Encyc. Bibl.* ; Wright and Hackett, art. 'Gennesaret, Land of,' in Smith's *DB* ; Socin in Baedeker's *Palestine and Syria*, 291 ; Stewart, *Land of Israel*, 264 ; Conder, *Primer of Bible Geog.* 150 f. ; Stanley, *SP* 444–454 ; Wilson, *Lands of the Bible*, 137 ; Geikie, *The Holy Land and the Bible*, ii. 331 ; Ritter, *Geog. of Palestine*, ii. 265 ; Buhl, *GAP* 113 ; Neubauer, *Géog. du Talm.* 45 f. ; Josephus, *BJ* iii. x. 8 ; Ruetsche in *PRE*[3] v. 6 f. ; Furrer in Schenkel, ii. 322 ; Swete, *Com. on St. Mark*, ad 6[53] ; Plummer, *Com. on St. Luke*, ad 5[1].   GEORGE L. ROBINSON.

GENTILES.—In AV of the Gospels, 'Gentiles' and 'nations' are the translations of ἔθνη, RV agreeing with the rendering of AV in every place of the word's occurrence. In Mt 6[7] (ἐθνικοί) and

18¹⁷ (ἐθνικός) AV has 'heathen' and 'a heathen man' respectively; RV 'Gentiles' and 'the Gentile.' In Mt 5⁴⁷, where AV has τελῶναι, 'publicans,' RV with the reading ἐθνικοί has 'Gentiles.' Ἕλληνες, occurring in John only, is rendered 'Greeks' in 12²⁰ RV and AV; in 7³⁵ RV has 'Greeks,' AV 'Gentiles,' with, however, 'Greeks' in the margin. Ἑλληνίς (Mk 7²⁶) is translated 'a Greek' in both versions, but AV has 'Gentile' in the margin. The very wide diffusion of the Greek language after the conquests of Alexander the Great was the reason that in our Lord's day 'Greek' was often used as an equivalent for 'Gentile.' See GREEKS. The word 'Gentiles,' from the Lat. gentilis (adjective of gens, pl. gentes, 'a race,' 'people,' or 'nation'), is used in the Vulgate to render the Heb. גּוֹיִם and the Gr. ἔθνη, and has thus passed into English.

For a full discussion of the term 'Gentiles,' reference must be made to the Bible Dictionaries. It is only necessary here to allude to the origin and use of the expression in the OT. Just as ἔθνος in the Gospels, as a rule (for an exception see Mt 21⁴³), means the Jewish nation, and ἔθνη the nations other than Jewish, so in the OT גּוֹי (goï), as a rule (for an exception see Lv 20²³), stands for the former and the pl. גּוֹיִם (goïim) for the latter; and whilst often used in its purely ethnographical and geographical sense, with the meaning 'foreigner,' it is also constantly employed, especially in the Psalms, as a term of aversion and contempt, as connoting the practice of false religions and of immoral customs. The material and moral evils which the goïim had brought upon Israel in its later history tended to intensify the feelings of hostility with which the Jews looked out upon them from their own religious exclusiveness; and accordingly, in our Lord's day and in the generations following (see Acts and the Epistles passim), they were regarded by the Jews generally as aliens, having no claim whatever to the Divine recognition. This must be borne in mind when estimating our Lord's teaching on the subject.

A full consideration of the attitude of early Christianity towards the Gentiles requires a study of the Acts and Epistles at least, and is beyond the scope of this article: our Lord's teaching, however, afterwards developed by His followers, is quite plainly indicated in the Gospels, and must form the basis of any adequate discussion of the subject.

The fact that Jesus did not pass His youth in the religiously exclusive atmosphere of Jerusalem, but in the freer and more liberal surroundings of semi-Gentile Galilee, fits in with the prophetic word of Simeon at the Presentation, and the declarations of His forerunner: He was to be 'a light to lighten the Gentiles' (Lk 2³²); and, God was able to raise up to Abraham children (3⁸) who could not boast any natural descent from the patriarch. St. Matthew, although according to the usual account of his standpoint he had no especially Gentile proclivities, records two important prophetic utterances regarding the Gentiles as being illustrated and fulfilled in his Master's work: 'Galilee of the Gentiles; the people which sat in darkness saw great light; and to them which sat in the region and shadow of death light is sprung up' (4¹⁵· ¹⁶), and, 'In his name shall the Gentiles trust' (12²¹). At the beginning of His ministry, if we accept St. Luke's chronology (see NAAMAN), Jesus defied the Jewish prejudices of His hearers in the synagogue at Nazareth by citing cases of Gentiles blessed through the agency of Israel's prophets (Lk 4²⁵ff·); and, when driven from His native town, He took up His abode in a city of despised Galilee which belonged to that less Jewish portion of it known as 'Galilee of the Gentiles' (Mt 4¹⁵). Moreover, it was in the same Gentile-infected Galilee that the most important part of His ministry was carried on, and He even went into the borders of Tyre and Sidon (Mk 7²⁴), and also taught and healed those who came to Him from thence, together with those who sought Him from Decapolis (Mt 4²⁵), and from Idumæa, and from beyond Jordan (Mk 3⁸); nor did He disdain to remain on one occasion for two days among the Samaritans at their request (Jn 4⁴⁰). In His public teaching He showed no prejudice in favour of the Jews in His assignment of praise and blame: the grateful leper whom He blessed was a Samaritan (Lk 17¹⁶ff·); it was a good Samaritan who was set forth as an example in one of His most famous parables (10³⁰ff·); and He commended the faith of the centurion as being greater than any He had found in Israel (Mt 8¹⁰). On the other hand, the evil generation of whom the Pharisees were representatives, He declared should be condemned in the judgment by Gentiles, the men of Nineveh and the queen of Sheba (12⁴¹f·); and, setting the seal to the teaching of His forerunner, He asserted in effect that the true children of Abraham were those who did the deeds of Abraham, and were not necessarily those who were naturally descended from him (Jn 8³⁹ff·). In the Sermon on the Mount the same broad and world-wide outlook is manifested: there is hardly anything of importance in that great discourse which is local or temporary—it is obviously for all men and for all time. With this, too, coincides the teaching of His many parables about the Kingdom of heaven and that recorded in the Fourth Gospel—in this Gospel particularly all His utterances are in accord with His declaration to the Samaritan woman concerning the true worshippers (4²³), and with the impression produced on the Samaritans that He was the Saviour of the world (v.⁴²); for in this Gospel especially His words of warning, of encouragement, and of hope embrace all mankind: 'God so loved the world . . . that whosoever believeth . . . shall have eternal life' (3¹⁶). And, finally, at the end of His ministry, in the allegory of the sheep and the goats, spoken exclusively with reference to Gentiles, He applies to those on the right hand the word 'righteous,' which in the Jewish language was so often the technical term to designate only the chosen people (Mt 25³⁷).

There are two passages in the Gospels which demand a passing notice, as they might seem at first sight to be in opposition to our Lord's usual attitude towards the Gentiles. One is His saying to the Syrophœnician woman, 'I am not sent but unto the lost sheep of the house of Israel' (Mt 15²⁴); and the other is His injunction to the Twelve, 'Go not into the way of the Gentiles, and into any city of the Samaritans enter ye not; but go rather to the lost sheep of the house of Israel' (10⁵· ⁶). In the first case there is little doubt that our Lord's words were intended to test or to call forth the woman's faith, and are not to be understood as implying any unwillingness on His part to assist her (see SYROPHŒNICIAN WOMAN). And in the second case we are to notice that the prohibition was laid upon the Twelve only, and had no application to His own conduct; and, further, that the prohibition was distinctly removed by Him after the Resurrection in the great commission recorded in Mt 28¹⁹ 'Go ye therefore and teach all nations' [in Mk 16¹⁵ 'Go ye into all the world, and preach the gospel to every creature'], and in Ac 1⁸ 'Ye shall be witnesses unto me both in Jerusalem, and in all Judæa, and in Samaria, and unto the uttermost part of the earth.' And there are other passages, such as Mt 24¹⁴ 26¹³, from which it is plain that our Lord contemplated the world-wide preaching of the gospel by His followers, the fulfilment, in fact, of the ancient prediction to the father of the faithful : ' In thy seed shall all the nations (goïim) of the earth be blessed ' (Gn 22¹⁸). See MISSIONS.

LITERATURE.—Grimm-Thayer and Cremer, Lexx. s.v. ἔθνος ; art. ' Gentiles ' in Hastings' DB and Encyc. Bibl.; Schürer, HJP II. i. 51–56, 299–305, ii. 291–327 ; Edersheim, Life and Times of Jesus the Messiah, Index, s. ' Gentiles.'

ALBERT BONUS.

GENTLENESS.—St. Paul in 2 Co 10¹ appeals to the meekness and gentleness (πραΰτης καὶ ἐπιείκεια) of Christ. These qualities would be readily admitted to be so characteristic of Jesus as to require no specific illustration. Yet such is the objective character of the Gospels, that with the exception of His own claim to be 'meek and lowly in heart' (Mt 11²⁹) and the Evangelist's application of the prophecy, 'Behold, thy king cometh unto thee, meek . . .' (21⁵), neither quality is directly attributed to Him, nor, with the exception of Mt 5⁵, does either word occur in His recorded teaching.

These characteristics of Jesus are not easily defined in themselves, or distinguished from one another. (See art. 'Gentleness' in Hastings' DB, vol. ii. p. 150). Πραΰτης is rather an inward disposition of the mind, the quietness of soul which is the result of faith and self-restraint ; ἐπιείκεια is an active grace, exhibited in human relations, 'it expresses the quality of considerateness, of readiness to look humanely and reasonably at the facts of a case' ; it denotes in Jesus the tenderness of His dealings with the moral and social outcasts, the burdened and heavy laden, the weak and ignorant ; His gracious courtesy, geniality of address, thoughtfulness, and delicacy of touch. It is not the expression of a nature of such softness as to be always on the verge of tears, or of a sentimentalism which has little strength of conscience, and no power of moral indignation and repulsion. The gentleness of Christ can be appreciated only when it is related to certain other elements in His personality. (1) His consciousness of His Divine origin, and His royal vocation as founder of the Kingdom of God (cf. Jn 13³⁻⁵). (2) His moral consciousness. His is not the gentleness towards the sinful which arises from moral indifference, or the desire of a sin-marred nature to be judged of leniently. He is conscious of sinlessness ; He looks upon sin as the great tragedy of human life, but His passion for righteousness does not make Him harsh in judgment or unmerciful in dealing (cf. Mt 5⁶·⁷). (3) His consciousness of Divine power. It is the gentleness not of weakness, but of might. The Lamb of God answering Pilate so mildly was conscious that twelve legions of angels stood at His disposal (Mt 26⁵³).

The Baptist, himself stern of soul, foresaw the coming of one greater than he—greater, but not more gentle. The axe, fan, and fire of judgment were at His command, and He would wield these instruments of wrath to the destruction of wickedness (Mt 3¹⁰⁻¹²). But, to John's intense disappointment, Jesus found His ideal and method not in these symbols of violence, but in the conception of the Servant of Jehovah, who did not strive or cry or lift up his voice in the streets, who did not break the bruised reed or quench the smoking flax (Mt 12¹⁹·²⁰ ; cf. Lk 4¹⁸·¹⁹ and Mt 11⁴⁻⁶, and see Is 42¹⁻³).

The Gospels abound in illustrations of the winsome manner of Jesus. His reception of the little children (Mt 18² 19¹³), His thoughtfulness for the multitude lest they should faint by the way (15³²), the brotherly touch of His hand upon the leper (Mk 1⁴¹), the delicacy of His approach to the sorrowing (Lk 7¹³, Jn 11³⁵), His tender tones to His perplexed disciples—'little children,' 'I will not leave you orphans' (Jn 13³³ 14¹⁸), and His sense of their frailty in the words, 'Sleep on now and take your rest' (Mt 26⁴⁵), His consideration, even in the agony of death, for His mother (Jn 19²⁶·²⁷),—are but examples of that gracious gentleness which consisted with, and was the expression of, a Divine dignity of love. His attitude to the sinful is distinguished by the same tenderness. His intense love of holiness, quick moral sensitiveness, and stainless purity, made Him uncompromisingly stern in His rebuke of a self-righteousness which had little capacity of repentance ; but He combined with that a deep insight into the possibilities of sin-marred natures ; and by His disclosure to them of dormant powers of being, and the tenderness of His dealing with them, He won them to repentance and a new life (Lk 7³⁶⁻⁵⁰ 19¹⁻¹⁰). And, similarly, His rebukes, touched by His gentleness, become appeals, and are charged with the inspiration of a renewed trust. His 'O ye of little faith' (Mt 8²⁶), 'Can ye drink the cup that I drink of ?' (Mk 10³⁸), 'Martha, Martha, thou art careful and troubled about many things' (Lk 10⁴¹), 'Could ye not watch with me one hour?' (Mt 26⁴⁰), 'Simon, son of Jonas, lovest thou me?' (Jn 21¹⁵ff.),—were rebukes whose gentleness could leave no bitterness or despair, but recalled the soul to its loyalty to Him. So, although Jesus never formally held forth ἐπιείκεια as an ideal of Christian life, He left us an example that we should follow His steps (1 P 2²¹).

LITERATURE.—Trench, Synonyms, § xlii. ; M. Arnold, Literature and Dogma, vii. 3 ; A. L. Moore, God is Love (1894), 134 ; G. Jackson, Memoranda Paulina (1901), 61 ; J. Watson, The Inspiration of our Faith (1905), 190 ; J. W. Jack, After His Likeness (1906), 88.

JOSEPH MUIR.

GERASENES, GERGESENES.—The ' country of the Gerasenes' (Γερασηνῶν) or 'Gergesenes' (Γεργεσηνῶν) is mentioned in Scripture only in connexion with the healing of the demoniac. The AV reads 'Gergesenes' in Mt 8²⁸, and 'Gadarenes' in Mk 5¹ and Lk 8²⁶, while the RV reads 'Gadarenes' in Mt. and 'Gerasenes' in Mk. and Luke. There is preponderating evidence in favour of the changes (the reading Γαζαρηνῶν in ℵ in Mt. is undoubtedly for Γαδαρηνῶν. Many natives in the district surrounding the Sea of Galilee pronounce the Arabic ﺩ d and ﺫ dh like z—thus 'Gadarenes' they would pronounce 'Gazarenes'). The neighbourhood of the town of Gadara must be pronounced absolutely impossible for the miracle (see GADARA). How then account for the reading 'Gadarenes'? Perhaps, as Thomson suggests, the place where the miracle took place, 'over against Galilee,' was included within the district of Gadara. But as this would not be officially correct, Gadara having been the capital of the country to the *south* of the town, it might be better to say that popular usage gave to the whole district on the eastern shore of the Lake the name of the principal town. In the same way the reading Γερασηνῶν *might* be explained—being derived from the large and important city of the Decapolis, Gerasa—the modern *Jerash*. (It need scarcely be said that this latter town is out of the question as the scene of the miracle, being some 30 miles from the Lake). The derivation of the reading from the Decapolitan city, while not perhaps impossible, is very improbable. A more likely explanation is at hand. According to Origen, the majority of the MSS he had access to had the reading 'Gerasenes.' But this reading he objected to, inasmuch as he knew of only one *Gerasa*, the town of the Decapolis, which he rightly conceived could not have been the scene of the miracle. He suggested that 'Gergesenes' must be the true reading, as he knew of a town on the eastern shore of the Lake bearing the name *Gergesa*. Hence, on his authority, the reading 'Gergesenes' may have originated. But how then account for the, presumably, true reading which Origen found in the MSS? There can be here no certainty, but the probability is that Origen was right, and that the true name of the village or town where the miracle occurred, 'over against Galilee,' was Gergesa. It is extremely rare to find a soft changing into a harsh sound, such as *Gerasa* into *Gergesa*. But any one who has lived long in Palestine knows how common it is, among the uneducated natives, to find a hard sound like the second *g* in 'Gergesa' not only changing into a softer sound, but dropping out altogether. The pronunciation of 'Gergesa' among the common people would almost certainly be 'Ger'sa' (*Gerasa*). Hence from the common speech it would find its way into the text. The modern name of the village which has been identified as the scene of the miracle is *Khersa* or *Chersa*, which is nearer to 'Gerasa' than to 'Gergesa.'

The identification of the ruins of Khersa with the Gerasa of the Synoptists is due to Thomson, (*LB* ii. 355). The identification might have been made much earlier had not men's minds been set on selecting some place near *Gadara*. Had the eastern shore of the Lake been carefully scrutinized in the light of the three passages, Mt 8^{32}, Mk 5^{13}, Lk 8^{33}, the identification of Khersa with the place described must have taken place. There is *one spot only* on the eastern shore which answers completely to the description of the Synoptists. On the eastern side 'over against Galilee' Jesus landed from the boat, and 'straightway there met him out of the tombs a man with an unclean spirit.' The encounter, then, must have been close to the shore. Were that all we had to guide us, identification of the spot would be impossible, for there are caves, which may have been used as tombs, all along the mountain side. But it would appear from all three Synoptists that the place where the swine were destroyed ran down somewhat steeply to the water's edge. Now, as we have said, there is *only one place* on the eastern side where the mountain comes at all near to the beach, and just there the incline is such that one rushing down would be precipitated at once by the impetus into the water. Everywhere else along the coast there is a broad belt—half a mile or more at most parts—between the foot of the hills and the Lake. This spot is at Khersa just below *Wâdy es-Semak*. Sailing up the Lake from *Wâdy Fik*, which is almost exactly opposite Tiberias, the next valley, about a mile north, is *Wâdy es-Semak*. Close to the seashore directly below the Wâdy are the ruins of Khersa, the walls of which can yet be distinctly traced. Directly below Khersa the hills approach close to the Lake, leaving only a narrow pebbly strand, and here the slope of the mountain side is so steep and near to the water that a herd of animals would be likely in a headlong rush to be precipitated into the sea. In the mountains above, where in all probability the swine were feeding, there are numbers of caves and also rock-cut tombs where the demoniacs may have lived. See art. DEMON.

LITERATURE.—Thomson, *LB* ii. ch. 10; Wilson, *Recovery of Jerus.* p. 368 f.; Schumacher, *Jaulan*, 179; Macgregor, *The Rob Roy on the Jordan*, p. 422 ff.; artt. 'Gadara' and 'Gerasenes' in Hastings' *DB* and in *Encyc. Biblica*.   J. SOUTAR.

GERIZIM.—In relation to the life and teaching of Jesus, the interest of Mt. Gerizim lies in its being the mountain to which the woman of Samaria referred on the occasion when Jesus uttered His memorable words, 'Woman, believe me, the hour cometh, when ye shall neither in this mountain, nor yet at Jerusalem, worship the Father' (Jn 4^{21}).

The establishment of Mt. Gerizim and its temple as the sacred place of the Samaritans in rivalry to Jerusalem, is bound up with the growth of the jealousy and hatred between Jews and Samaritans, which had attained such magnitude in the days of our Lord. The story given by Josephus of the founding of the temple on Mt. Gerizim (*Ant.* XI. viii. 2–4) is that Manasseh, brother of Jaddua, high priest at Jerusalem, married the daughter of Sanballat (Neh 4). For this marriage he was threatened with expulsion unless he divorced his wife. He thereupon appealed to Sanballat, who built for him the temple on Mt. Gerizim, and made him its first high priest. This story 'seems to be derived from some apocryphal Jewish account of the origin of the Samaritan temple' (Sayce, art. 'Sanballat' in Hastings' *DB*). According to Neh 13^{28}, a grandson of Eliashib the high priest was son-in-law to Sanballat, and was expelled for this 'mixed marriage.' More reliable, if less definite, ground is to be found in 2 K 17$^{24-28}$, from which we learn that the king of Assyria sent back one of the priests whom he had carried away from the Northern Kingdom, to teach the heathen peoples whom he had settled there 'the manner of the God of the land.' Thus the worship of Jehovah was preserved in Samaria, and gradually asserted itself over the 'gods of their own' which every nation made. In the days of Ezra, when the temple at Jerusalem was being rebuilt, the Samaritans, who are called 'the adversaries of Judah and Benjamin,' desired to assist in the task, for they said, 'We seek your God as ye do.' This request was refused (Ezr 4$^{1-3}$), and thus the founding of a rival shrine became inevitable. See also art. SAMARITANS.

The claim of the Samaritans, that Mt. Gerizim was the true centre of the worship of Jehovah, rested upon a statement in their version of the Pentateuch (Dt 27$^{4f.}$ where 'Gerizim' is substituted for 'Ebal' of MT) definitely prescribing that an altar should be built there. They also supported the claim of their shrine by traditions in which it was represented as the mountain on which Abraham prepared to sacrifice Isaac (cf. G. A. Smith, *HGHL* 334, note), the place where Abraham was met by Melchizedek, and also the scene of Jacob's dream.

Apart from such traditions, the position of Mt. Gerizim and its *vis-à-vis* Mt. Ebal, at the head of the pass leading right through from the river Jordan to the sea, and also at the point where the great north road from Jerusalem to Galilee intersects this pass, has given them a commanding place in the topography of the Holy Land, and has led to their association with important events in the history of Israel. Shechem, which lay between Mt. Ebal and Mt. Gerizim, is associated with the entrance of both Abraham and Jacob into the promised land (Gn 12^6 33^{18}). It was near Shechem that Jacob purchased the parcel of land from the children of Hamor, on which he erected an altar, and sank a well for his family and flocks. It was in this parcel of land that Joseph was buried (Jos 24^{32}). Mt. Ebal and Mt. Gerizim, again, were the scenes of the great inaugural service of all Israel on taking possession of the promised land (Dt 11$^{29. 32}$ 27$^{11. 12}$, Jos 8$^{33. 34}$). And it was at Shechem that Joshua gathered together the people for the renewal of the covenant, 'and took a great stone and set it up there under an oak that was by the sanctuary of the Lord' (Jos 24$^{1. 28}$). It was on Mt. Gerizim that Abimelech, Gideon's son, spoke his parable of the trees (Jg 8^{31} 9$^{1. 7. 20}$). It was at Shechem also that all Israel gathered to make Rehoboam king (1 K 12^1), and this was the original capital of the Northern Kingdom.

In order to understand the significance of the question which the woman put to Jesus at the well (Jn 4^{20}), it is necessary to remember that she must have been well instructed in the notable history of Mt. Gerizim, and would accept all the traditions of her people without question. At the same time her own religious faith was probably bankrupt. She had not found God on Mt. Gerizim. There is a vein of scepticism in her words, as of one who, having lost personal faith, points with scorn to the differences of those who worship the same God. Yet even in her scepticism there is a faint hope apparent that this 'prophet' may have a living message for her. On the historical question involved Jesus pronounces quite definitely in v.^{22}, but not before He has lifted the whole subject out of this barren controversy and set it in relation to the fundamental principles of His teaching. There is embedded in the very beginning of the Samaritan worship of Jehovah the idea that Jehovah is the 'God of the land' (2 K 17²⁷), and throughout the whole controversy between Jerusalem and Mt. Gerizim there is to be found the assumption that His worship must have a local centre. To this Jesus makes answer, 'God is Spirit.' It follows at once from this fundamental idea of the true nature of God that the essential quality in worship which is acceptable to Him is not the place where it is offered, but the disposition of the worshipper. Wendt points out that our Lord's teaching in this passage as to the true nature of worship is a corollary of His teaching in the Sermon on the Mount, that the heart (the whole inward nature) is the true seat of the righteousness of the people of God. So that for the ethical expansion of Jn 4²³. ²⁴ we naturally turn to Mt 5–7, even as in Jn 4²⁴ we find the great doctrinal foundation alike of right conduct and right worship.

LITERATURE.—Stanley, *SP* v. ; G. A. Smith, *HGHL* 120, 332 ; Schürer, *HJP* ii. i. 5 ; Muirhead, *Times of Christ*, 108 ; Dods, 'St. John' in *Expos. Bible*, ix. and x. ; Wendt, *Teaching of Jesus*, i. 320 ; artt. 'Gerizim' and 'Shechem' in Hastings' *DB* ; Commentaries.   ANDREW N. BOGLE.

GESTURES.—Dr. Johnson defines 'gesture' as (1) 'action or posture expressive of sentiment' ; (2) 'movement of the body.' Adopting these definitions, we may consider the significance of the gestures recorded or implied in the Gospels.

1. Christ heals or blesses with an outward gesture.—In most of these cases the gesture is probably intended to confirm faith ; a visible sign accompanies the action. Thus (*a*) we read of our Lord *taking* the sick person *by the hand*, as in the case of Simon's wife's mother (Mk 1³¹ and ‖ Mt.), Jairus' daughter (Mk 5⁴¹ and ‖ Mt. Lk.), and the child with the dumb spirit (Mk 9²⁷). Similarly St. Peter takes by the hand the man at the gate of the temple and Tabitha (Ac 3⁷ 9⁴¹). Dr. Swete (on Mk 9²⁷) suggests that this gesture was used when great exhaustion had preceded. (*b*) Jesus *lifted up His hands* to bless (Lk 24⁵⁰). (*c*) Jesus *stretched forth His hand* to heal, and *touched* or *laid hands on* the sick, as in the case of the leper in Mk 1⁴¹ (and ‖ Mt. Lk.). In Ac 4³⁰ the Apostles speak of God the Father stretching forth His hand to heal. Other instances of Jesus' touching the patients, doubtless, as a rule, to confirm their faith, are : the blind men in Mt 9²⁹ 20³⁴ (the parallels to the latter in Mk.-Lk. mention no touching), the bier on which the widow's son at Nain lay (Lk 7¹⁴), the woman with the spirit of infirmity (Lk 13¹³), perhaps the dropsical man (Lk 14⁴, see Plummer, *in loc.*), Malchus (Lk 22⁵¹, the only account of this healing). Further, St. Luke speaks of a large number of sick folk brought to our Lord at sunset, when He 'laid his hands on every one of them and healed them' (Lk 4⁴⁰, not ‖ Mt. Mk.). The healings by anointing would also involve a touch, as by the Twelve (Mk 6¹³), or in the case of the blind man anointed with clay (Jn 9⁶) ; cf. Ja 5¹⁴ for the custom in the Apostolic Church. Similarly we read of the sick touching Jesus,—the woman with the issue of blood (Mk 5²⁷ and ‖ Mt. Lk.), the sick at Gennesaret and the neighbourhood (Mk 6⁵⁶ and ‖ Mt.) ; and St. Luke (6¹⁹) says that 'all the multitude sought to touch Him, for power came forth from him and healed them all.' This 'touch' of the Lord is recalled by the cures that are recorded to have been worked by handkerchiefs or aprons carried away from the body of St. Paul (Ac 19¹²), and by the shadow of St. Peter (Ac 5¹⁵, where it is implied that many tried to touch him). And inas-

much as the Apostles would follow the example of Jesus in lesser and greater things alike (cf. Ac 4¹³), we find that they adopted His gestures, whether for healings or for invocations of the Holy Spirit, or even in speaking. For the touching by laying on of hands, see Ac 6⁶ 8¹⁷ᶠ· 13³ 19⁶ and 9¹² 28⁸ ; the last two are cases of healing. (*d*) Jesus *laid on hands* to bless, as in the case of the little children (Mk 10¹⁶ and ‖ Mt.). We read twice in Mk. of our Lord's taking children in His arms (Mk 9³⁶ 10¹⁶ ἐναγκαλισάμενος), a gesture ascribed to Him in Mk. only, though a similar phrase is used of Simeon in Lk 2²⁸ ἐδέξατο αὐτὸ εἰς τὰς ἀγκάλας [αὐτοῦ]. In another way we read of Jesus' blessing with a gesture of the hand, as at the Last Supper (λαβών—εὐλογήσας, Mk 14²²) and at the meal at Emmaus (Lk 24³⁰· ³⁵). (*e*) Jesus *breathed* on His disciples when 'sending' them after the Resurrection, saying, 'Receive ye the Holy Spirit ·. whosesoever sins ye forgive,' etc. (Jn 20²²ᶠ·). Here the gesture is of a different nature ; our Lord, still using an outward sign, makes it signify that which is bestowed—the gift of the Spirit (πνεῦμα ἅγιον, without the article). Breath is the emblem of the Spirit, and by this gesture Jesus shows that the Holy Ghost is the 'Spirit of Christ' as well as of the Father (see Westcott, *in loc.*).

On the other hand, in some cases Jesus healed with a mere word. One cannot, indeed, always conclude that He did not use any outward gesture, such as touching, merely because an Evangelist is silent on the matter (*e.g.* cf. Mk 10⁵² with Mt 20³⁴) ; but in some cases, at least, Jesus healed *in absence*. The following are examples of cases where apparently no gesture was used : the paralytic (Mk 2¹⁰ and ‖ Mt. Lk.), the man with the withered hand (Mk 3⁵ and ‖ Mt. Lk.), the centurion's servant (Lk 7¹⁰), the ten lepers (Lk 17¹⁴), the nobleman's son at Capernaum (Jn 4⁵⁰ᶠ·). We find the same difference in the healings in Acts ; thus, in 9³⁴ 14¹⁰ no gesture seems to have been used.

The use by our Lord of an outward gesture or sign in His ministerial acts was only in accordance with Jewish thought. We may recall Moses stretching forth his hand over the Red Sea (Ex 14¹⁶· ²¹· ²⁶, cf. 17¹¹), and, by way of contrast, the stretching out of the hand in OT as an act of punishment (Ex 7⁵ ; see other instances collected by Plummer in his note on Lk 5¹³). It may be thought that this usage of Jesus in His ministry paved the way for His afterwards appointing outward signs in Baptism and the Eucharist, and for the Apostles' employing them for other Christian rites, such as ordination.

2. Christ uses gestures to emphasize His words, or as an expression of emotion.—(*a*) We read of the *stretching forth of the hand* toward the disciples when Jesus claimed them as His mother and His brethren (Mt 12⁴⁹) ; cf. St. Paul's gesture when addressing Agrippa (Ac 26¹). We cannot put under this head the hand outstretched in Mt 14³¹ 26²³, as there it does not express emotion ; but we may compare with the above gesture the hands outstretched in prayer (1 K 8²², Ps 28² 134², 1 Ti 2⁸). A 4th cent. writer has interpreted our Lord's 'stretching forth his hands' (cf. St. Peter, Jn 21¹⁸) of His accepting suffering voluntarily (*Testament of our Lord*, i. 23). (*b*) We read of many *gestures with the eyes*. Jesus looked up to heaven at the miracle of the feeding of the five thousand (Mk 6⁴¹ and ‖ Mt. Lk.), in His last prayer before going to Gethsemane (Jn 17¹), at the healing of the deaf man with an impediment (Mk 7³⁴), and the raising of Lazarus (Jn 11⁴¹). It is doubtless due to the first two of these passages that we find in many ancient Liturgies, from the *Apostolic Constitutions* onwards, this gesture ascribed to our Lord when He consecrated the Eucharist—as in the Greek St.

James (in the Syriac St. James it is only implied),
St. Mark both Greek and Coptic, Abyssinian (or
Ethiopic), St. Basil, Roman and Ambrosian. The
gesture is one of prayer, and implies that prayer
accompanied the actions described (see Job 22^{26};
cf. the publican, Lk 18^{13}). Again, the references to the 'glance' or 'look' of our Lord are
very frequent. In Mk 3^5 it conveys His righteous
anger (‖ Lk. does not mention the anger). In Mk
3^{34} 10^{27} (and ‖ Mt.) and Lk 6^{20} 20^{17}, it apparently
emphasizes the truth taught. In Lk 22^{61} it brings
conviction of sin to St. Peter after his denials.
In Mk 10^{21} it is a mark of love; here, as so often,
St. Mark alone relates the feelings of our Lord's
human soul. The glance to emphasize truth must
also be understood where we expressly read of
Jesus' 'turning' to those whom He is addressing
(Mk 8^{33}, Lk 7^9 9^{55} etc.). On the other hand, no
special significance must be attached to passages
where our Lord's 'look' is mentioned, but where
it was merely that He might see, as Mk 5^{32} (and ‖
Mt.), Lk 19^5 21^1. Corresponding with this gesture
of Jesus is the keen 'gaze' or 'fastening of the
eyes' which we read of in the case of the people of
Nazareth (Lk 4^{20}), the maidservant (Lk 22^{56}), St.
Peter (Ac 3^4, cf. 3^{12}), the Sanhedrin (Ac 6^{15}), St.
Stephen (Ac 7^{55}), Cornelius (Ac 10^4), St. Paul (Ac
13^9 14^9 23^1)—all having ἀτενίζειν, one of St. Luke's
favourite words; in the case of St. Paul it is difficult to reconcile with the idea that the 'stake in
the flesh' was ophthalmia.   (c) The gesture of
kneeling or prostration is mentioned only once of
our Lord, in Gethsemane (Mk 14^{35} and ‖ Mt. Lk.),
the first two Evangelists speaking of prostration,
the third of kneeling. As standing was the usual
attitude for prayer * (Mk 11^{25}, where see Swete's
note, Lk $18^{11.\ 13}$), we must interpret this kneeling
or prostration as specially signifying deep distress,
as in the early Church it signified special penitence, being forbidden by the 20th canon of Nicæa
on festival occasions like Sundays and Eastertide
(so Tertullian, de Cor. Mil. 3). And so it was
significant of deep distress in the case of St.
Stephen (Ac 7^{60}), and probably of St. Peter when
he raised Tabitha (Ac 9^{40}); in the case of St. Paul's
farewells it would be due to the great solemnity of
the occasion (Ac 20^{36} 21^5, cf. also 1 K 8^{54}, Ezr 9^5,
Dn 6^{10}, Eph 3^{14}). Nevertheless, the usual standing
to pray would not preclude the gesture of prostration at intervals to express special devotion, as is
the case to this day among all Eastern Christians.
To signify reverence the gesture of kneeling or
prostration is frequently thus practised in the Gospels.
We read of many thus kneeling to Jesus—the
leper (Mk 1^{40} and ‖ Mt. Lk.), demoniacs (Mk 3^{11} 5^6),
Jairus (Mk 5^{22} and ‖ Mt. Lk.), the Syrophœnician
woman (Mk 7^{25} and ‖ Mt.), the rich young man (Mk
10^{17}), the blind man (Jn 9^{38}), Mary of Bethany (Jn
11^{32}), the lunatic's father (Mt 17^{14}, not ‖ Mk. Lk.),
Salome (Mt 20^{20}, not ‖ Mk.), the Magi (Mt 2^{11}), St.
Peter at the miraculous draught of fishes (Lk 5^8),
and so the soldiers in derision (Mk 15^{19} and ‖ Mt.).
The devil tempts our Lord to kneel to him (Mt 4^9
and ‖ Lk.). The women prostrate themselves at the
tomb (Lk 24^5). Cornelius attempts to do so before
St. Peter (Ac 10^{25}), and St. John before the angel (Rev
19^{10} 22^8). (d) A gesture to emphasize speech may
probably be understood in Mk 12^{29} where it may
be that Jesus pointed to the scribe's phylactery,
which contained the words, 'Hear, O Israel,' etc.
(e) An isolated gesture is the stooping to write on
the ground in the 'Pericope adulteræ' (Jn $8^{6.\ 8}$),
apparently signifying 'intentional inattention.'
Westcott (in loc.) remarks that the very strangeness of the action marks the authenticity of the
detail.   (f) We read of gestures expressing grief.

* Our Lord sat to teach, the usual custom (Mt 5^1, Mk 4^1, Lk
4^{20} 5^3, Jn 8^2, cf. Ac 16^{13}).

Jesus sighed at weakness of faith (Mk 7^{34} 8^{12}), and
groaned (or was moved with indignation, ἐνεβριμήσατο), shuddered (ἐτάραξεν ἑαυτόν), and wept at
Lazarus' grave (Jn $11^{33.\ 35.\ 38}$); He shuddered at the
thought of the betrayal (Jn 13^{21}), and wept over
Jerusalem (Lk $19^{41ff.}$).
To speak generally, it may be noted that the
Fourth Evangelist is more chary of chronicling
our Lord's gestures than the Synoptists. He
dwells rather on Jesus' words than on the actions
with which He accompanied them.
3. Various gestures by others.—To an Oriental
people, gesture is almost as natural a method of
expressing the meaning as speech. We find in the
Gospels frequent references to such a method of
communication. This is not only when no other
is possible, as when dumb Zacharias makes signs
(Lk 1^{22}) and the people make signs to him (v.^{62}:
perhaps he was also deaf); just as in Acts, St.
Peter has to make signs to procure silence in
Ac 12^{17}, and St. Paul in Ac 21^{40} and perhaps 13^{16}.
But we find such expressive gestures as shaking
off the dust (Mk 6^{11} and ‖ Mt. Lk.; this is our
Lord's command to the Twelve), to signify the
dissociating of oneself from an offender. So Paul
and Barnabas did at Pisidian Antioch (Ac 13^{51}),
and so Paul 'shook out his raiment' against the
unbelieving Jews at Corinth (18^6). Again, rending
the garments was a common Jewish gesture of consternation or grief, often mentioned in OT (e.g.
Gn $37^{29.\ 34}$, Jl 2^{13}); in the Gospels we find it mentioned only of Caiaphas (Mk 14^{63} and ‖ Mt.); in
Acts (14^{14}) only of Paul and Barnabas at Lystra.
Smiting the breast as a sign of grief we find in Lk
23^{48} (where D adds τὰ μέτωπα), and in Mt 11^{17}
(ἐκόψασθε) and Lk 18^{13}. Wagging the head was the
derisive gesture of the passers-by at the Crucifixion
(Mk 15^{29} and ‖ Mt.; cf. 2 K 19^{21}, Job 16^4, La 2^{15},
Sir 12^{18} 13^7). Pilate's gesture of washing his hands
(Mt 27^{24}) has furnished a proverbial saying, but it
was familiar to the Jews (Dt 21^6). The kindred
idea of washing the hands to express innocency (i.e.
ridding oneself of evil) is found in Ex $30^{19f.}$ and Ps
26^6 73^{13}, and is a great feature of the Church
Orders and the great Liturgies. Lastly, we notice
the kiss as the sign of love, real or feigned, as in
the case of the sinful woman (Lk 7^{45}), of Judas
(Mk 14^{45} and ‖ Mt. Lk.), and of the Ephesian elders
(Ac 20^{37}). It is true that the kiss was the ordinary
way of greeting a Rabbi (see Swete on Mk 14^{45}),
but in all these cases much more than ordinary
courtesy is intended by the gesture, and probably
καταφιλεῖν in these passages means 'to kiss fervently,' or (in the case of Judas) 'ostentatiously.'
For the kiss in OT, cf. Gn 29^{11} 33^4 45^{15}, Ex 18^7, 1 S
20^{41}, 2 S 15^5 19^{39} 20^9, many of which passages speak
of kisses of greeting like that of Judas, to which
Joab's is indeed strangely similar.

A. J. MACLEAN.

GETHSEMANE (Γεθσημανεί, perhaps for גַּת שְׁמָנִי [ם]
'oil press').—Gethsemane is usually described as a
'place' with a garden attached to it; but, so far as
the words of Scripture show, it may have been
simply a garden. St. Matthew (26^{36}) and St. Mark
(14^{32}) use the word χωρίον, St. Luke (22^{40}) uses
τόπος, and St. John (18^1), describing it as ὅπου ἦν
κῆπος, refers to it again (18^2) as τόπος. It lay east
of Jerusalem, across the Kidron (Jn 18^1), at the
foot of or upon the Mount of Olives (Mt 26^{30}, Mk
14^{26}, Lk 22^{39}: cf. Euseb. OS^2 248. 18, and Jerome,
ib. 130. 22). The traditional site is in the Kidron
ravine, at a point about equidistant, as the crow
flies, from the Golden Gate and St. Stephen's Gate.
It is easily reached by the road passing through
the latter and crossing the Kidron bridge, just
beyond which it lies, a square plot of ground
with eight very ancient olive-trees. If the statement of Josephus (BJ VI. i. 1), that Titus cut down

all the trees upon that side of the city, be correct, the tradition that those trees are as old as the Christian era, or the tradition as to the site, must be abandoned. Both probably are unfounded, and, according to the general consensus of opinion, this site was fixed upon at the time of the Empress Helena's visit to Jerusalem (A.D. 326).

The scene of Christ's agonizing prayers immediately before the betrayal, and of His betrayal and capture (Mt 26³⁶⁻⁵⁷, Mk 14³²⁻⁵³, Lk 22³⁹⁻⁵⁴, Jn 18¹⁻¹³), it had long been a favourite resort with the Master and His disciples (Lk 21³⁷, Jn 18²). See, further, art. AGONY.

LITERATURE.—Robinson, *BRP* 2 i. 234 f., 270 ; *PEFSt* (1887) pp. 151, 159, (1889) p. 176 ; Conder, *Bible Places*, 204 ; Le Camus, *Voyage aux Pays Bibliques*, i. 252 ff.; art. 'Gethsemane' in Hastings' *DB* (by Conder) and in *Encyc. Bibl.* (by L. Gautier); art. 'The House of Gethsemane' in *Expositor*, iv. iii. [1891] 220–232 (by E. Petavel). On the form of the name see Dalman, *Gram.* 152.   JOHN MUIR.

GHOST.—Used in the Gospels only in the phrases 'giving up the ghost' and 'Holy Ghost': a survival of the meaning commonly associated with it in the times of the translators, when it was used as equivalent to 'spirit' (Germ. *Geist*). The usage of the word 'ghost' as equivalent to 'spirit' has become archaic. The meaning now uniformly given to it makes its continued use in our RV inexpedient. This was recognized by the American Revisers, who substituted 'Holy Spirit' in every instance for 'Holy Ghost.' See, further, artt. HOLY SPIRIT, SPIRIT.

         A. MITCHELL HUNTER.

GIFT.—Christ continually reminds His disciples that the Father is the source of all gifts. To Him we must trustfully turn. 'Ask, and it shall be given' (Mt 7⁷) ; 'Everyone that asketh receiveth' (Lk 11¹⁰), and not only 'daily bread' (Mt 6¹¹, Lk 11³), but 'whatsoever' is asked (Jn 15¹⁶ 16²³). He will never refuse the gift of the Holy Spirit to them that ask (Lk 11¹¹⁻¹³, Mt 7¹¹), for it is His 'good pleasure' to give them 'the kingdom' (Lk 12³²). When Christ has ascended, it is the Father who will send 'another Comforter' (Jn 14¹⁶) ; and when trials and persecution shall arise, it is the Father by whom, Christ says, 'it shall be given you in that hour what ye shall say' (Mt 10¹⁹). We see this confidence inspiring the multitude to glorify God 'which had given such power unto men' in the healing of the palsied man (Mt 9⁸), and making the practical Martha say, 'I know that whatsoever thou shalt ask of God, God will give unto thee' (Jn 11²²).

It is notable that Christ's only recorded request for a personal favour should have been the occasion of that deep saying concerning 'the gift of God' (Jn 4¹⁰). The word used (τὴν δωρεάν) implies a peculiar freedom in the giving; something of bounty not to be purchased. It is used nowhere else in the Gospels (save in the OT quotation in Jn 15²⁵) ; but in the Acts and Epistles it usually occurs as the distinguishing word for God's highest gifts, as of grace itself (Eph 3⁷), of the 'heavenly gift' (He 6⁴), of the 'unspeakable gift' (2 Co 9¹⁵), of the saving power of Christ's life and death (Ro 5¹⁵), of Christ in us (Eph 4⁷), or of the Holy Spirit (Ac 2³⁸ 8²⁰ 10⁴⁵ 11¹⁷). In Jn 4¹⁰ some hold that our Lord spoke of Himself as 'the gift of God' (cf. Jn 3¹⁶), others that He meant the unique opportunity the woman now had of gaining religious enlightenment from Him ; and the two ideas blend in His words. But the uppermost thought would be the parabolic suggestion of the water for which Jesus had asked, and 'the gift of God' would most naturally be that 'living water' which He Himself could give her, and which would solve her dimly discerned problems of conduct and worship. The Jews had long connected the precious gift of 'living water' with that ever-new and quickening power of the Spirit which, coming from God, can alone satisfy the soul's thirst for Him (Zec 14⁸, Jer 2¹³ 17¹³). So Christ seems to use it here. If the woman but knew 'the gift of God,' that fount of the living Spirit which, springing up within, and independent of the Law, is the assurance of eternal life (v.¹⁴), and if she could but recognize the supremacy of love and spiritual power in Him who was speaking, then she would not hesitate to ask an infinitely greater gift than He had asked of her. Thus Christ would be the agency ; the Eternal Spirit would be 'the gift.'

The greatest of all gifts would be one's life. This Christ gave. All other gifts of His are included in this. They are the fruit of this complete self-surrender, which could yield up all things for love of men. True, He gave, and gives His disciples, the unfathomable gift of a Peace which the world could not give (Jn 14²⁷), a Rest for all weary spirits (Mt 11²⁸). To His own He is the Living Water (Jn 4¹⁴), the Bread of Life (6⁵¹). He gives the keys of the Kingdom of Heaven (Mt 16¹⁹), the new commandment of Love (Jn 13³⁴), and Life Eternal (10²⁸). But the highest gift included these and more. It was the gift of His life, 'a ransom for many' (Mt 20²⁸, Mk 10⁴⁵). This He offered to the Eternal Father, to that Righteousness whose final decision was beyond the Son of man's bestowal : 'To sit on my right hand, and on my left, is not mine to give' (Mt 20²³, Mk 10⁴⁰). For the gift of the Holy Spirit see art. HOLY SPIRIT. See also art. GIVING.

         EDGAR DAPLYN.

GIRDLE.—See DRESS, p. 498ᵇ.

GIVING.—The duty of giving springs naturally out of the gospel fact. Jesus Christ is God's gift (Jn 3¹⁶), and when St. Paul associates the liberality of the Christians of Corinth and this grace of God (2 Co 9¹⁵), he is true to the mind of Christ. Giving and receiving are correlatives : 'freely ye received, freely give' (Mt 10⁸ ; the endowment is of Divine power and authority, and the service is to be as wide as human need ; cf. Ac 3⁶). Throughout the Gospel narrative the welcome of Christ awakens generous impulses. The new resolve of Zacchæus (Lk 19⁸) is the free expression of his new life. The grace of Christ had come near to him, and he, in that high fellowship, could not but be gracious. So, generally, giving is the necessary expression of Christian faith and love, the spontaneous outcome of Christian life.

Almsgiving is recognized by Jesus as a part of 'righteousness' (Mt 6¹ᶠ· RV), and the duty of practising it is often enforced (see ALMSGIVING). But the care of the poor by no means exhausts the activities of the generous spirit. Treasury gifts for the temple service were recognized by Jesus (Mk 12⁴¹ = Lk 21¹), and gifts for the upholding of public worship are an essential part of worship. So, too, Jesus accepted and honoured gifts directly bestowed upon Himself. 'Certain women which had been healed of evil spirits and infirmities . . . ministered unto him of their substance' (Lk 8²ᶠ·). In the same spirit were Matthew's feast after his call (Lk 5²⁹), the anointing by the woman of the city (Lk 7³⁷ᶠ·), and the supper at Bethany (Jn 12²). These were acts of grateful love, and they were welcomed by Jesus. The incident of the outpouring of the spikenard (Jn 12³ᶠ· = Mt 26⁶ᶠ·, Mk 14³ᶠ·) is the more significant because of the criticism it provoked, and the reply of Jesus, 'Ye have the poor always with you, and whensoever ye will ye can do them good' (Mk 14⁷). Is there here a hidden rebuke for neglect of opportunities ever present, on the part of those who here professed disapproval of waste? Certainly the reply suggests the thought 'that expenditure in one direction does not disqualify for beneficent acts in another. The willing-minded will always have enough for all purposes' (Expositor's *Gr. Test., in loco*). By accepting and honouring this costly act of thankful love Jesus sanctions the utmost that love prompts. It is in such giving that the joy of sacrifice is known and the secret of Jesus realized —'It is more blessed to give than to receive' (Ac 20^{35}).

But all service is included in Christ's law of giving, not alms to the poor alone, but all the manifold expressions of love, the helpfulness which springs out of the new family bond of brotherhood. How this spirit works practically is illustrated in the ministry of Jesus. Once and again before His gracious acts of healing or of bounty, it is said, 'he was moved with compassion' (Mt 9^{36} 15^{32}, Mk 6^{34}); and His fellow-feeling found expression in the sending forth of the Twelve, the feeding of the multitude, and in teaching.

So is it with His disciples. All tender ministries are the expression of a Divine compassion, 'the exceeding grace of God in you' (2 Co 9^{14}).

But the law of Christian service goes beyond this. It is founded in justice, the recognition of the true relations which men hold one to another in Christ. The second commandment of love to our neighbour (Mt 19^{19} 22^{39}) and the parable of the Good Samaritan (Lk 10$^{30ff.}$) teach the true inwardness of generosity.

True helpfulness is that which is due from one man to another because of the ties of humanity. Hence the personal equation in beneficence. All true giving resolves itself into self-giving, the expression of sympathy, reverence, affection, the charity of personal care and thought (Lk 6$^{27-38}$). It is this service of man as man, and because of the ties of a Divine humanity, which is the service of Christ. 'Ye did it unto me' (Mt 25^{40}) covers the whole ground.

But while it is ever true that 'money values are not the standard of gifts in the Kingdom of God,' this must not be pressed so as to minimize gifts of money. These must often measure 'the moral value of the giver.' Indeed, this is the lesson of the Treasury (Lk 21^4), they 'of their superfluity,' she 'of her want.' The frequent references to money in the Gospels show the importance which Jesus attached to this factor in life. The stewardship of all possessions is taught in the parable of the Rich Fool (Lk 12$^{16ff.}$; for 'rich towards God' cf. 1 Ti 6$^{17f.}$). Judgment is pronounced upon the selfish use of wealth in the parable of the Rich Man and Lazarus (Lk 16$^{19ff.}$). Hence the warnings against covetousness (Lk 12^{15}). Giving, thus exercised, becomes a 'means of grace,' by which the heart is cleansed (Lk 11^{41}; a suggestive rendering of this saying is given in *Expositor*, II. v. [1883], 318, 'but as to what is within, give alms, and behold all things are clean unto you').

The test of the young ruler (Lk 18^{22}) is not so much 'a counsel of perfection' for all, as the word in season for the individual. The general lesson on wealth and its uses is in the parable of the Unjust Steward (Lk 16$^{1f.}$). Confessedly difficult of interpretation as this parable is in detail, its main lesson can hardly be overlooked—Heaven, which cannot be bought by gold, may yet be prepared for by the best uses of wealth. The giving of money by men who know its value, and whose keenest activities are directed to get it, is a searching test of their self-denial and devotion. True liberality is the Divinely appointed safeguard against covetousness, with this caution, 'to whomsoever much is given, of him shall much be required' (Lk 12^{48}).

The question of definite 'proportionate giving' may be briefly dismissed. It has been sought to press the law of a tenth as binding upon all, and the words of Jesus (Mt 23^{23}) are quoted in support. But the ground is insufficient. An incidental reference cannot set aside the whole spirit of the Gospel. Any rule imposed from without is alien to the free spirit of love. Rules which the individual may lay down for his own guidance are for the individual conscience to determine, but 'the Christian law is the spirit of Christ, that Enthusiasm of Humanity which He declared to be the source from which all right action flows' (*Ecce Homo*). 'Charity has no other limit than charity itself' (Godet). Cf. Lk 6^{30}.

LITERATURE.—*Ecce Homo*, ch. xvii. : Bruce, *Parabolic Teaching*, p. 371 f.; Westcott, *Incarnation and Common Life*, p. 195 f.; Gladden, *The Christian Pastor*, p. 371 f.; Ruskin, *Seven Lamps* ['Lamp of Sacrifice'], also *Architecture and Painting*, §§ 44–45, and *Arrows*, ii. 191 ; Butler, *Sermons*, ii., vi.

W. H. DYSON.

GLAD TIDINGS.—See GOSPEL.

GLORY.—There are few commoner words in the English Bible than 'glory,' and few more difficult of definition. The word appears on the surface to be used in a strange variety of meanings and applications, and with both good and bad connotation. Reputation, praise, honour (true and false), splendour, light, perfection, rewards (temporal and eternal)—all these varying conceptions seem covered by the same word.

Nevertheless the underlying thought is simpler than would appear. In the OT a large number of words are translated in English by 'glory,' but by far the most common is כָּבוֹד, of which the root idea is 'heaviness,' and so in a metaphorical sense, 'weight,' 'worthiness.' The LXX frequently employs δόξα to translate this, as well as a great number of other Hebrew words ; and δόξα (with its connected verb δοξάζω) is the usual NT word rendered 'glory.' This word is derived, of course, from the root of δοκέω, 'to think *or* suppose,' and the primary meaning of δόξα is, no doubt, 'thought *or* opinion,' especially, favourable human opinion, and thus in a secondary sense 'reputation,' 'honour,' etc.

But an important new shade of meaning comes into the word when it is used in religious language. The δόξα of man, human opinion, etc., is shifting, uncertain, often based on error, and its pursuit for its own sake is unworthy. But there is a δόξα of God which must be absolutely true and changeless. God's 'opinion' marks the true value of things, as they appear to the eternal mind ; and God's 'favourable opinion' is true 'glory.' This contrast is well seen in Jn 5^{44} 12^{43}. Hence 'glory,' whether applied to God Himself or to His works as seen by Him, must imply the absolute truth which underlies all phenomena. This gives us the connecting link between 'the glory that cometh from God' and the 'glory' which man conceives of as belonging to God Himself. The 'glory of God,' therefore, must mean His essential and unchanging Godhead as revealed to man. And the familiar ascription 'Glory to God' would imply not only a right human praise, but the assigning to God of what He truly *is*, for nothing higher can be given Him. Similarly the true 'glory' of man or nature must be that ideal condition, that final perfection, which exists as a real fact in the Divine mind. The glory of God is what He is essentially ; the glory of created things is what they are meant by God to be, though not yet perfectly attained (He 2^{10}, Ro 8$^{18-21}$).

Passing on to that which this article is specially concerned with,—What is meant by the 'glory' and the 'glorifying' of Jesus Christ ? It must mean (a) the revelation of His essential Deity, that which He *is* in the mind of the Father, though veiled from man by the limitation of the Incarnation. See Jn 17[5], He 1[3], 1 Co 2[8], Ja 2[1]. (b) The revelation of the ideal and perfect condition of human nature, as elevated by its union with God in the Incarnation to that which God means it to be by the law of its creation, that which already in the mind of God it essentially *is*. Then the glory of Christ is the explanation and justification of Gn 1[27] (cf. 2 Co 3[18]).

But besides this fundamental conception of 'glory' which springs out of the primary meaning of the Greek word, it is to be noticed that 'glory' in Scripture usually carries with it ideas of 'light,' 'splendour,' and 'beauty.' Thus pre - eminently 'the glory of the Lord' in the OT is the visible shining forth of light, by which the Divine Presence is recognized by man, the שְׁכִינָה of the later Jews. So the 'glory' appeared to Israel at Sinai (Ex 24[16. 17]), at the door of the Tent (Lv 9[23], Nu 14[10] 16[19]), at the dedication of Solomon's Temple (1 K 8[10. 11]), in the visions of Isaiah (6[1-3]) and Ezekiel (1[28] 3[23] 8[4]). Similarly the Messianic hopes of Israel are expressed under the figure of 'glory dwelling in the land' (Ps 85[9]). See artt. 'Glory (in OT)' and 'Shekinah' in Hastings' *DB*. Passing to the NT, the same conception of 'glory' is seen in St. Luke's account of the Nativity (2[9]). And this is brought into direct connexion with the Person of Christ in the narratives of the Transfiguration, especially in St. Luke's (9[28ff.]). There the 'glory' of Christ shines forth visibly in the dazzling brightness of His countenance. It encompasses the forms of Moses and Elijah (v.[31]); it even transfigures material objects like Christ's clothing (v.[29]). With this passage should be compared the visions of Stephen in Ac 7[55]; of Saul of Tarsus (Ac 9[3] 22[6-11] 26[13]), and of St. John in Patmos (Rev 1[13-16]).

A more metaphysical conception of the 'glory' of Christ is seen in St. John's Gospel. The Evangelist may indeed be alluding to the Transfiguration in 1[14], and to the visible glory of Isaiah's vision in 12[41]. But in 2[11] and 11[40] he is evidently describing some revelation to the inward eye of what Christ essentially *is*, some intuition of His Divine power (only suggested by a visible 'sign') borne in upon the soul of the believer. In Christ's words and works His true nature, as the 'effulgence' of the Father's glory, flashes upon and illuminates not the intellectual faculties merely, but the whole being of man, filling it with the sense of light and beauty and satisfaction.

Thus we seem to arrive at a conception of 'glory' which combines both the ideas of δόξα, as 'splendour' and as the manifestation of eternal truth as it is in the Divine mind. In this sense Christ looks forward to and prays for the 'glorifying' of Himself by the Father (Jn 13[31. 32] 17[1. 5. 24]). This glorifying is in a true sense accomplished in the Passion, as issuing in the Resurrection, whereby the true nature of Christ and His redemptive work were recognized and rejoiced in by the faithful. There is a 'glory' which is yet to come, but the present revelation to the Church of Christ's glory is of the same order as the future one which will complete it (17[24]). The Christian community, already ideally perfected by the separation of Judas (Jn 13[31]), is henceforth to recognize permanently what individual intuition had already perceived and confessed at different points of the ministry. And this 'glorifying' of Christ is to be the 'glorifying' of the Father (Jn 17[1]), for the completion of Christ's work will reveal the Divine mind and purpose to the Church; and it is also the 'glorifying' of the believer and of the Church as a whole (v.[22]), for

the Church will be the permanent witness of God to the world (v.[23]), and man in union with Christ is on the way to attain the Divine ideal (v.[26]).

The same profound conceptions of 'glory' appear in the writings of St. Paul and St. Peter. The object of the Christian calling is 'the obtaining of the glory of our Lord Jesus Christ' (2 Th 2[14]). The invisible 'glory' of the Christian Church through its union with Christ by the Spirit is greater than the visible 'glory' of the Old Covenant (2 Co 3[7-11]). The 'glory' of God recognized in Christ by the believer is a new creation of light (4[6]). Present limitations and sufferings will be abundantly compensated in the full future revelation of 'glory' (v.[17], cf. Ro 8[18ff.]). Indeed, the 'glorifying' of the believer is already ideally complete (Ro 8[30]); it will be visibly completed in the Resurrection of the body (Ph 3[21], cf. 1 P 5[1. 4]).

In the Resurrection life, therefore, Christ will be seen and known by all the faculties, the whole being of man redeemed, as sharing fully and essentially in the 'glory' of the Godhead. His Divinity will be recognized in the 'glory' which was ever inseparable from it; His humanity will be seen filled full, illuminated by its union with His Divinity, 'taken up into God' (*Quicunque vult*), and so constituting the perfect expression and vehicle of His Divinity (1 Jn 3[2]). Hence in the ideal and perfected Church, as described in the Apocalypse, both humanity and its material setting are illuminated with 'the glory of the Lamb,' whose glorified humanity is, as it were, the 'Lamp' (Rev 21[23]) in which shines the 'glory' of the Godhead.

It will be seen that this one word 'glory' is really a summary of the Divine purpose for creation as revealed in Scripture—

'From Eden's loss unto the end of years.'

The 'glory of God' is revealed in the 'glory of Christ,' and both nature and man are in Christ progressing towards 'the liberty of the glory of the children of God' (Ro 8[21]).

LITERATURE. — Grimm - Thayer, *Bibl.-Theol. Lex. s.v.* δόξα; R. St. J. Parry, *Discussion of the Gen. Ep. of James* (1903), 36; and the Commentaries on the NT passages above cited, especially Westcott's *St. John*, 1890.

A. R. WHITHAM.

GLUTTONOUS.—In Mt 11[19] = Lk 7[34] we are informed that our Lord was reproached as a gluttonous man and a wine-bibber. The Greek is alike in both passages—ἄνθρωπος φάγος καὶ οἰνοπότης. The English versions are probably right in their rendering of φάγος and οἰνοπότης as implying intemperate excess. But this hardly lies in the words themselves. φάγος (Liddell and Scott, *s.v.*) is found only in these passages and in later ecclesiastical writers. οἰνοπότης does by usage (not by etymology) imply excess (Anacreon, 98; Call. *Ep.* 37; Polyb. xx. 8. 2). In Pr 23[20] it answers to סֹבֵא יַיִן 'one who is drunken with wine' (cf. Dt 21[20], Ezk 23[42], Hos 4[18] for use of the Heb. root); and it is parallel with μέθυσος in 23[21]. In Pr 31[4] (24[72] Swete) the verb οἰνοποτέω occurs in the bad sense. But it is possible that the real force of the insult to our Lord is shown by Dt 21[20]. The rebellious son is to be brought by his parents to the elders, to whom the parents are to say, 'This our son is stubborn and rebellious, he will not obey our voice, he is a riotous liver and a drunkard.' He is then to be executed by stoning. It is true that the LXX here συμβολοκοπῶν οἰνοφλυγεῖ has no resemblance to the phrase in the Gospels, but Pr 23[20] has μηδὲ ἐκτείνου συμβολαῖς as one half of the doublet, 'among gluttonous eaters of flesh' (בְּזֹלֲלֵי בָשָׂר); and in Pr 23[21] Aq., Sym., Theod. agree in using the Deuteronomic word συμβολοκόπος for זֹלֵל. Delitzsch in his *Heb. NT* uses the words found in Dt 21[20].

We need not wonder at the non-agreement with the LXX. For the discourse has several indications of having been spoken in Aramaic, such as the paronomasia probably to be found in the cry of the children (Mt 11¹⁷, Lk 7³² 'danced' and 'wept'; cf. Farrar, *Life of Christ*, i. 92; and the Peshiṭta), and the variation ἐργων—τέκνων (Mt 11¹⁹, Lk 7³⁵) which is best explained by supposing some error in reading an Aramaic document.

GEORGE FARMER.

GNASHING OF TEETH (ὁ βρυγμὸς τῶν ὀδόντων, Mt 8¹² 13⁴², ⁵⁰ 22¹³ 24⁵¹ 25³⁰, Lk 13²⁸). — A phrase describing a gesture which expresses mainly fury or baffled rage : Job 16⁹, Ps 35¹⁶ 37¹², Ac 7⁵⁴ ; cf. Ps 112¹⁰ 'The wicked shall gnash with his teeth, and melt away'; but these OT parallels * seem hardly sufficient to account for the set form which the phrase has in the Gospels.† The expression occurs in every case but one in parables of the Last Judgment, and even that exception (Mt 8¹²) may be called a parabolic representation. This does not detract from the force of the warning, but rather the pictorial element is added because of the Speaker's passionate desire to make the terrific consequences of sin vivid and memorable in order to the salvation of those that heard Him, and to deter them and us from the course that would lead to such a fearful end.   T. GREGORY.

GNAT.—See ANIMALS, p. 67ᵃ.

GOAT.—See ANIMALS, p. 63ᵇ.

GOD.—*Introduction.*—The sphere of the revelation of Jesus was limited to the Fatherhood of God (see FATHER), and all His other references to the Divine Being are more or less incidental. They involve conceptions which He shared with OT prophets, and to some extent also with contemporary Judaism ; but the form which some of these conceptions take in His teaching, and the relative emphasis which He laid upon them, are modified by that truth which was central and fundamental in His own experience and thought of God. Jesus, in all His references to God, spoke after the manner of a prophet, and not after the manner of the Rabbis or the Christian theologian. He never sought to prove the existence or the personality of God. These were invariably assumed. He never communicated any speculative views regarding the nature or the attributes of God. All that He said stood in direct relation to right conduct.

The aim of the present article is to set forth briefly those views of God, expressed or implied in the words of Jesus, which may properly be considered apart from the Divine Fatherhood, and which are, to some extent, characteristic of Jesus.

1. *God is one.* — To Jesus, as to His people through many centuries, God was one. He did not modify this ancient belief. To the scribe who asked which commandment was greatest, Jesus quoted the familiar confession from Deut. (6⁴ᶠᶠ·) which begins with the words, 'Jehovah our God is one Jehovah' (Mk 12²⁹); and the author of the Fourth Gospel represents Jesus as addressing these words of prayer to the Father—'This is life eternal, that they should know thee, the *only* true God ' (τὸν μόνον ἀληθινὸν θεόν, Jn 17³).

Jesus spoke of the Holy Spirit ; and if there is any place at which He suggests a personal distinction in the Divine Being, it is here. It is necessary, therefore, to consider His words on this subject. His references to the Spirit in the oldest Gospels are extremely rare ; and in only one instance do all the Synoptics agree in reporting the use of this term. This is the passage concerning blasphemy

against the Spirit (Mk 3²⁹, Mt 12³¹, Lk 12¹⁰). There are three other * occasions on which, according to one or two of the Synoptics, Jesus spoke of the Spirit. (*a*) The first of these occasions was when He spoke words of encouragement to His disciples in anticipation of their future need of support when called before governors and kings. According to Matthew (10²⁰), He said to them, ' It is not ye that speak, but the Spirit of your Father which speaketh in you.' In Luke we have two passages referring to the same, or at least very similar occasions ; one of these speaks of the Holy Spirit (τὸ ἅγιον πνεῦμα), while in the other Jesus is represented as saying, '*I* will give you a mouth and wisdom, which all your adversaries shall not be able to withstand ' (Lk 12¹² 21¹⁵). Mark has a similar word of Jesus, but puts it on a different occasion. The situation of the disciples is the same, and Jesus says, ' It is not ye that speak, but the Holy Spirit ' (Mk 13¹¹). The thought which all the accounts have in common is that of Divine assistance. The agent who assists is either the ' Holy Spirit,' the ' Spirit of your Father,' or Jesus Himself.

(*b*) Another reference by Jesus to the Spirit is found in His reply to those who accused Him of working in league with Beelzebul. Here He said, ' If I by the Spirit of God cast out demons ' (Mt 12²⁸) ; or, according to Luke, ' If I by the *finger* of God cast out demons ' (11²⁰).

(*c*) Finally, according to Mark (12³⁶), Jesus referred to the 110th Psalm as spoken in the Holy Spirit. Mt. has simply ἐν πνεύματι, and Lk. no reference to the Spirit.

Now the language of these passages does not appear to suggest a different view of the Spirit from that of the old prophets. If Jesus as a rule represented His disciples as dependent on the Father, and the Father as caring for them, and then in a single instance, when speaking still of the Divine aid, said, ' the Spirit of your Father ' or the ' Holy Spirit,' we cannot suppose that He made any personal distinction between them. His word is an echo of such a passage as Is 61¹ 'The Spirit of the Lord Jehovah is upon me,' and is in part a fulfilment of the promise in Joel (2²⁸) that the Spirit shall be poured out upon all flesh. The statement of Jesus regarding the 110th Psalm, that it was spoken in the Holy Spirit, is quite parallel to this word concerning His disciples. It shall be with them as it was with the author of this psalm. The Spirit of their Father will speak in them.

Again, when Jesus said, ' If I by the Spirit of God [or the *finger* of God] cast out demons,' it is manifest that His thought is that of God's presence and aid. It is like the language of Micah when he said, ' I am full of power by the Spirit of Jehovah ' (3⁸). The Fourth Gospel expresses the same thought when it represents Jesus as saying, ' The Father abiding in me doeth his works ' (Jn 14¹⁰).

Finally, when Jesus warned the scribes and Pharisees concerning the irremissible sin of blasphemy against the Holy Spirit, it is obvious that we cannot draw any personal distinction between this Spirit and God. These men had attributed the manifestly good work of Jesus to the prince of bad spirits. Thus they had wilfully called good evil (cf. Is 5²⁰). They had violated conscience ; they had quenched, at least for the moment, this inner and fundamental voice of God. This manifestation of God within them is called the Spirit of God in accordance with OT usage, which ascribes a spirit to Jehovah, in and through which He

---

* βρυγμός is used in Pr 19¹² of the roaring of a lion, and in Sir 51³ of beasts 'ready to devour.'

† The notion of some, that the phrase in the Gospels is based upon a conception of Gehenna as a place of extreme cold, and that 'gnashing'='chattering of teeth,' is very precarious.

* The Baptismal formula of Mt 28¹⁹ is not included, for the evidence against its genuineness is regarded by the present writer as conclusive ; and Lk 4¹⁸ is a quotation.

reveals Himself to the spirit of man (*e.g.* Is 42¹
63¹¹). See UNPARDONABLE SIN.

The teaching of the Fourth Gospel (Jn 14–16)
regarding the Spirit marks an advance on that of
the Synoptics, both in quantity and in character ;
but this teaching, as it now stands, like the other
discourses of John, cannot be attributed directly
to Jesus. It appears to represent a stage of
thought fully as late as that which we find in
Mt 28¹⁹. We need not, therefore, discuss it in
this connexion, where we are concerned with the
teaching of Jesus. And we conclude this paragraph with the statement that there is nothing in
the narrative of the genuine teaching of Jesus
which suggests a modification of the old prophetic
conception of a pure monotheism.*

2. *God is holy.*—The conception which Jesus had
of the holiness of God is implied rather than expressed in His teaching ; yet though not directly
stated, it is fundamental, and marks an advance
on the teaching of the OT. How fundamental
this conception was in the teaching of Jesus may
be illustrated from the Sermon on the Mount.
According to this, the standard of the Kingdom of
God called for a righteousness that exceeded the
righteousness of the scribes and Pharisees (Mt 5²⁰).
The Law declared that a man should not kill, but
Jesus taught that anger exposed one to the same
danger of judgment (v.²¹ᶠ·). The Law declared
against adultery, but He declared against the lustful desire (v.²⁷ᶠ·). Now this profounder conception
of sin, this attaching of the gravest penalties to the
secret feeling of anger and to the unclean desire,
implies a clearer and more ethical conception of
the holiness of God.

Again, Jesus' sense of the holiness of God is
reflected when He says that it is the aim of His
mission to call sinners (Mt 9¹³, Mk 2¹⁸ [Lk 5³² adds,
'to repentance']) ; and His feeling is still more
significantly seen in the Beatitude for the pure in
heart (Mt 5⁸). Finally, the intensity of His appreciation of God's holiness may be measured by
the severity of His judgment on impenitent sinners.
One of such tenderness of heart as Jesus showed
in all His relations to others—a tenderness which
He believed was an attribute of God—could not
have uttered such words of judgment as Mk 3²⁹
12⁹ and Mt 25⁴⁶, unless He had had an open vision
of the Divine purity.

It is obvious from this brief survey that, to the
thought of Jesus, the holiness of God was a fundamental fact, and it is equally plain that His conception of this Divine attribute was profoundly
ethical. Its demands could not be satisfied, as
the scribes taught, by the performance of any
number of statutes. Nothing but a righteous
state of the heart could satisfy them. Jesus
taught His disciples to ask for the pardon of their
sins, not on the ground of any fulfilment of the
Law, any good works of any sort, but simply on
the ground, as far as the human side of the pardon
is concerned, that they themselves have a forgiving spirit (Mt 6¹², Mk 11²⁵). The ethical character
of Jesus' conception of the holiness of God is seen
also in His own relation to sinners ; for it is clear
that His thought of God's relation to sinners was
illustrated by His own attitude toward them.
Now we are told that He came into personal contact even with the worst of men. He ate with
publicans and received harlots, having no fear of
defilement from them. He represented God under
the figure of a father embracing a son who had
wasted his substance in riotous living (Lk 15).

In the thought of Jesus, therefore, the holiness

of God did not imply, as with the scribes, that He
was far removed from sinful men, being Himself
subject to defilement. His holiness is not ritual,
but purely ethical. It is that quality or side of
His being which makes it incumbent on all men
to 'hallow' His name (Mt 6⁹). It is that which
defines His character with reference to sin. It is
that attribute of God which renders it impossible
to trace the origin of evil up to Him. Jesus everywhere assumes that evil originates either in the
freewill of man (Mk 3²⁸· ²⁹), or with a power called
the 'devil' (Mt 13³⁹) or 'Satan' (Lk 13¹⁶). It cannot
come from God, for He is the one absolutely good
Being (Mk 10¹⁸).

The conception of the holiness of God involved
in the teaching of Jesus, and perfectly illustrated
in His character, is thus seen to have been fundamental in importance and ethical in nature. It
has parallels in the OT, as, for example, in Ps 51⁶
and Hab 1¹³ ; but the clearness and intensity with
which it is expressed in the Gospels are unique.

3. *God is near.*—There is a third feature of Jesus'
thought of God which, though wholly incidental
and subordinate when compared with His revelation of the Divine character, is nevertheless so
conspicuous that it helps to mark off the Gospel
from the writings of the Old Covenant, and far
more noticeably from the views of contemporary
Judaism. This is the conception of the nearness
or presence of God. To a certain extent Jesus
shared the thought of His countrymen, and used
the current phraseology regarding God's habitation. Thus He spoke of heaven as the throne of
God, and the earth as His footstool (Mt 5³⁴ 23²²).
The idea of a Divine revelation clothed itself to
His mind in the imagery of an open sky, the
descent of the Spirit, and a voice out of heaven
(Mk 1¹⁰· ¹¹). But there is no special emphasis in
the teaching of Jesus on the thought that heaven
is the dwelling-place of God in a peculiar sense.
The emphasis is laid on another point, viz. the
practical thought of God's nearness. Though His
throne is said to be in heaven, He is no 'absentee'
God. On the contrary, He is personally present
with men. One may meet Him in the inner
chamber (Mt 6⁶). He reveals the mysteries of the
Kingdom of heaven unto 'babes' (11²⁵). He
worked in and through Jesus (12²⁸), and Jesus said
that God would speak in His disciples (10²⁰). This
statement may well be taken as suggesting the
way in which Jesus generally conceived of God's
presence with men. It is an inner spiritual nearness, a fact of which the soul takes cognizance,
and which is manifested to the world only through
the life of the man who realizes it.

But God is present not only with those beings
who are capable of communion with Him : He is
present also in Nature. He arrays the lily in
beauty (Mt 6²⁹), He cares for the birds (v. ²⁶), notes
the fall of a sparrow (10²⁹), and is unceasingly
active in works of mercy and kindness (Jn 5¹⁷).
How Jesus pictured to His mind this presence of
God in the material world we cannot learn from
the Gospels. His belief in this particular, as also
in regard to God's presence with men, was probably
like that of the Psalmists and Prophets (see, *e.g.*,
Ps 23⁴ 139⁷⁻¹², Is 40¹¹ 66¹³), though a more constant
and marked element of His teaching. It was,
doubtless, a consequence of His religious consciousness of God rather than a product of philosophic
thought.

LITERATURE.—See under art. FATHER.

GEORGE HOLLEY GILBERT.

GODS.—The single passage in the Gospels where
the word θεοί occurs (Jn 10³⁴ᶠ·) affords an excellent
example both of the style of Jesus' arguments with
His Jewish adversaries and of His attitude to the
OT. The phrase, 'I said, Ye are gods,' is a literal

---

* The story of the experience of Jesus at His baptism is probably to be traced back to Himself. This speaks of a descent
of the Spirit and a voice from God. It recalls Is 61¹, and presupposes the same conception of the Spirit.

quotation of Ps 82 (LXX 81)[6], and is introduced as such by the word invariably employed for that purpose (ἔστιν γεγραμμένον, cf. γέγραπται of Mt 4³· ⁶· ⁷· ¹⁰). It is plain that in quoting these words Jesus is arguing after the manner of the well-known *argumentum ad hominem*, from His use of the personal pronoun 'your,' as well as from His application of the title 'law' to the Psalms (ἐν τῷ νόμῳ ὑμῶν, cf. τῷ ὑμετέρῳ in 8¹⁷; and for a similar use of the term 'law,' cf. Jn 12³⁴ 15²⁵). It is an appeal to authority, the validity of which His hearers would be the first to recognize. It was impossible for them to escape a conclusion so immediately the outcome of premises universally accepted as true. At the same time it is an argument *a fortiori*. If their beloved Law, to which they were constantly appealing, hesitated not to designate as 'gods' (אֱלֹהִים) the judges whose partiality and injustice provoked their arraignment by God, and the solemn warning to 'judge the weak and fatherless, do justice to the afflicted and destitute' (Ps 82³), surely the charge of blasphemy came badly from those men who recognized in this Law their final court of appeal. His claim to be 'the Son of God,' whom the Father, in a unique sense, both 'sanctified and sent,' could be judged by His works, and it was sufficient to contrast those works which they could daily witness with the works of men whom God designated 'sons of the Most High' (בְּנֵי עֶלְיוֹן, Ps 82⁶).

Jesus in this place seems to adopt the interpretation of this Psalm which is given by the Targum, and which applies the title 'gods' to the earthly judges acting in their capacity as representatives of God. He, moreover, countenances the extension of the term 'Law' to other portions of the OT besides the Pentateuch. This was a common practice in the writings of the Jewish Rabbins, who spoke of 'the threefold Law'— Pentateuch, Prophets, and Hagiographa (*Shabbath*, 88a). Compare also the Talmudic tractate *Sanhedrin*, fol. 91, 92, for the question of R. Joshua, 'In what manner is the Resurrection of the dead proved from the Law?' with the answer that it is said in Ps 84⁴ 'They shall praise thee'; not 'they have praised thee.' To the same question propounded by R. Chaia the answer is that the Resurrection is proved from Is 52⁸ (see Wünsche, *Neue Beiträge zur Erläuterung der Evangelien aus Talmud und Midrash*).

There is another explanation current among the Jews which applied the term '*elōhîm* in this place to the Israelites who stood before Mt. Sinai and received the law (πρὸς οὓς ὁ λόγος τοῦ θεοῦ ἐγένετο, Jn 10³⁵). If, said they, their fathers had not sinned in the matter of the golden calf, they would have been as the angels; they would neither have begotten children nor been subject to death. For this reason it was, according to this interpretation, that the Psalm says, 'they shall die like men' (כְּאָדָם v.⁷), in spite of the fact that they were so marvellously privileged (see the Talmudic tractate *Abodah Zarah*, fol. 5. 1, quoted in J. Lightfoot's *Hor. Heb. et Talm.*, vol. iii. p. 359).

The evidential value of the whole passage with respect to Jesus' attitude to the OT Scriptures will, to some extent at least, be measured by the nature of the clause, 'the Scripture * cannot be broken.' If it is parenthetical, we have a direct assertion by Jesus that He regarded the OT as containing elements of abiding significance, and, moreover, that its meaning found its final and true explanation in His person and life (cf. Jn 13¹⁸ and Mt 5¹⁸ etc.). On the other hand, it is by no means certain that the clause is of the nature of a parenthesis, and not dependent upon the preceding conditional particle (εἰ). In this case the sense would be 'if the Scripture cannot be broken,' which would have the effect of presenting the *argumentum ad hominem* in a still stronger and more merciless form. This is again made more forcible by His use of the emphatic pronoun (ὑμεῖς), as if He intended to say, 'How is it possible for you, of all people, in face of the fact that you assert the inviolability of this passage, to find fault with the claims which I have put forward, and to say that I am a blasphemer?' (see Plummer in *Cambridge*

* It is to be noted here that ἡ γραφή does not mean the OT in general, for which the word would be αἱ γραφαί, but refers to the particular passage quoted (cf. Jn 20⁹ 2²² etc.).

Greek Test., and Westcott's *Gospel of St. John, ad loc.*).

It might be possible for an objector to urge that the whole argument was unworthy of the dignity of its alleged Author, and was too like what His hearers would themselves employ. On the other hand, we know that He did not shrink, at times, from meeting the Jews on their own ground (see art. ACCOMMODATION, p. 19 ff.), and indeed it would seem that He had no option but to do so, if His teaching was ever to penetrate their understandings. Nor did He at any time avoid confounding His adversaries out of their own mouth (cf. Mt 22⁴⁵, Lk 10³⁶ᶠ· etc.). At the same time it is evident that there is a profounder significance attaching to the quotation than at first sight appears, and it is in this fact that we have a more certain guide to the estimation in which the OT writings were held by Jesus. Whatever may have been the personal character of those who were designated '*elōhîm* in the Psalm, they were men unto whom the word of God had come, and who derived their title to be in a sense Divine from the fact that God delegated to them an authority which was His to give, and that He communicated His will through them to the people over whom they were placed.

The phrase ὁ λόγος τοῦ θεοῦ, occurring as it does in this passage, can hardly have been recorded by the author of the Fourth Gospel without a conscious reference to that Personal Word, about whom he speaks in his Prologue. The Logos, pre-existent and active, was the means by which God was effecting the eternal movement of man towards Himself and of Himself towards man. This movement became finally complete in the union of the Incarnation, when God and man met in an everlasting unity (ὁ λόγος σὰρξ ἐγένετο, Jn 1¹⁴). Nor was this marvellous synthesis 'sprung upon,' so to speak, the human race. It was being foreshadowed continually in the OT. The prophetic 'Thus saith the Lord' (cf. *e.g.* Is 38¹, Jer 19¹, Hos 4¹ etc.) was the outcome of a consciousness which felt its power to speak and act as God's earthly representative, and the fitness of this claim is vindicated by the oft-repeated assertion, 'The word of the Lord came unto [me]' (cf. Jer 16¹ 10¹ 9¹⁷, Is 8¹, Jl 1¹ etc.; see the emphatic הָיָה הָיֹה in Ezk 1³, where the prophet lays stress on the reality of his experience).

The union of God and man accomplished in the 'Word made flesh' was indirectly suggested in the bold words of the Psalmist, 'I said, Ye are '*elōhîm*,' and it is not difficult to believe that in repeating this expression Jesus had in His mind the realization of this profound idea, and that He desired to disclose it as an accomplished fact to those who had ears to hear and hearts to understand (Mt 13¹⁵).

J. R. WILLIS.

GOLD.—1. *Value.*—The Bible references to gold are in terms of use and abuse, in accordance with the great fundamental truth, 'The gold is mine, saith the Lord of hosts' (Hag 2⁸). Being the most precious of metals, it represents the possession and influence of wealth. It has a central place in the trilogy of life—length of days, riches, and honour (1 Ch 29²⁸). It seems to have a purchasing power over the other two—on the one hand in securing the conditions that tend to prolong life (Ps 17¹⁴ 73⁷· ¹²), and on the other by influencing opinion in favour of its possessors (Mt 19²⁵, Ja 2²). As the highest quotation of earthly values, it supplies a standard for estimating what surpasses it (Job 28¹⁷, Ps 119⁷²· ¹²⁷, Pr 3¹⁴ 8¹⁰ 16¹⁶, 1 P 1⁷· ¹⁸). It is only when, as the most beautiful and precious material available, it is used to give visible form to the Divine glory that gold becomes a thing of worthlessness (Ps 115⁴, Is 31⁷ 46⁶). The blindness that led to such idolatrous perversion among the Gentiles (Ac 17[29]) is also found among the Jews (Mt 23[16. 17]).

2. *Associated evil.*—As the emblem of wealth, gold is closely connected with that covetousness in the will and heart of man which is described as the motive and meeting-place of all idolatries (Col 3[5]). Job can plead that he has not made gold his hope (31[24]). Solomon is commended because he did not make request for riches (1 K 3[11]). The deceitfulness of riches is given as one of the explanations of the unfruitful life (Mt 13[22]). The self-centred ambitions and gratifications of wealth are all against the perception and service of a Kingdom in which even the poor seek the enrichment of other lives (Mk 10[24], 2 Co 6[10]). The order given to the disciples forbidding them to take gold or silver with them on their journey of proclamation (Mt 10[9]), was not meant as a commendation of poverty for its own sake. Indeed, it was just because money, clothing, and the wayfarer's staff were the often-proved necessaries of ordinary travel, that the omission of them in their case would impart to their message about the Kingdom a meaning of instantaneousness and urgency. The guest-law of the land would provide food and shelter for the passing stranger; and where they were asked to prolong their stay, those who were thus interested in their words would attend to their wants.

After playing many parts, such as being a medium of decorative art, a standard of value, and a means of good and evil in society, along with higher uses in the coinage of empires and the representation of the Godhead, gold renders its last symbolic service in providing a pavement for the feet of the saints (Rev 21[21]).

G. M. MACKIE.

GOLDEN RULE.—This name is given to a saying of Jesus recorded in the Sermon on the Mount. In Mt 7[12] its form is fuller and probably more original than in Lk 6[31]. The omission of the sentence, 'for this is the law and the prophets,' by the Gentile Evangelist, is in accord with the purpose of his Gospel; other variations may be due either to changes made in the course of oral transmission, or to divergences in two translations into Greek from the Aramaic. The two versions of the saying are as follows:

Mt 7[12] 'All things therefore whatsoever ye would that men should do unto you, even so do ye also unto them: for this is the law and the prophets.'
Lk 6[31] 'And as ye would that men should do to you, do ye also to them likewise.'

The saying is rightly called a *rule*, for it lays down a general principle for moral guidance, and furnishes a ready test of the social value of words and deeds. But it presupposes an ideal of social well-being which determines the end of conduct; its function is to prescribe means for the attainment of that end. To the disciples of Christ the coming of the Kingdom of God is the supreme end; for them this saying is, therefore, the *golden* rule, furnishing a standard of excellence whose practical value consists in its universal applicability. Interpreted in the spirit of Christ, the rule, 'Do as you would be done by,' implies the embodiment in action of the prayer, 'Thy will be done, as in heaven, so on earth'; they who walk by this rule are doing all that in them lies to bring in the Golden Age. Disparagement of the saying is the result either of failure to fathom the depths of its meaning, or of the rejection of Christ's teaching in regard to the blessedness in which all men's good consists.

The interpretation of the Golden Rule is little, if at all, affected by the connexion of thought. In the two Gospels the context varies. Wendt follows Luke's order, though this necessitates the reference of 'therefore' in Mt 7[12] to Mt 5[42]—the verse which corresponds to Lk 6[30]. On this supposition the word 'therefore' is made to appear superfluous; Zahn

rejects it on slight MS authority, because it seems to introduce a summary, which he regards as out of place here (א* L minn. Syr[pesh] om. οὖν). Yet Bengel's pithy comment, 'Imitate the Divine goodness,' suggests a natural link with the previous verse: as the Father gives 'good things' to His children in response to the prayer which expresses desire to receive them, so the motive of His children's actions should be a wish that others may share in the enjoyment of those good things from above. Another interpretation which preserves the unity of the Sermon on the Mount is that our Lord followed His encouragement to prayer by the reminder that if prayer is to be heard there must be a good life (Chrysostom). It is equally true, however, that the good life is impossible without prayer; the Father hears us when we ask His help, '*therefore* the most difficult duties of unselfish brotherly love to men become possible to us' (Dykes, *Manifesto of the King*, p. 572). The two views are complementary and not mutually exclusive. If we are doing unto others as Christ would have us do, He assures us that His Father will hear our prayers; on the other hand, if we will pray, He assures us that His Father will bestow the gifts of grace which will enable us to walk in love. In our Lord's farewell discourse there is a similar interdependence of thought. Communion with the Father in Christ's name is a means to an end, even the bearing of much fruit (Jn 15[7f.]); on the other hand, it is to disciples whose lives are fruitful that the promise of receiving what they ask is given (v.[16]).

The Golden Rule is not, as some philosophers have held, a mere *law of nature*. Nevertheless, at the basis of this contention there lies a truth, well expressed by Wesley: 'It commends itself, as soon as heard, to every man's conscience and understanding; insomuch that no man can knowingly offend against it, without carrying his own condemnation in his own breast' (*Sermon* xxx. § 22). Hobbes declares that moral regulations, which he calls 'immutable and eternal laws of nature,' may all be summarized in the simple formula, 'Do not that to another which thou wouldest not have done to thyself.' 'It is clear,' as Sidgwick points out (*Hist. of Ethics*[3], p. 167 n.), 'that Hobbes does not distinguish this formula from the well-known "golden rule" of the Gospel,—cf. *Leviathan*, ch. xv. p. 79, and ch. xvii. p. 85,—whereas the formula above quoted is, of course, the golden rule taken only in its negative application, as prescribing abstinences, not positive services.'

In its *negative* form the saying is found in both Jewish and pagan sources before the Christian era. Tobias is admonished by his father Tobit to love his brethren, 'and what is displeasing to thyself, that do not unto any other' (To 4[15]). Hillel's concise reply to a Gentile inquirer who asked to be taught the whole Law while standing on one foot, was, 'What is hateful to thee, do not unto thy fellow-man; this is the whole law, the rest is mere commentary' (Bab. *Shab.* 31a). A saying of Confucius is, 'Do not to others what you would not wish done to yourself' (Legge, *Chinese Classics*, i. 191 f.). Gibbon (*Decline and Fall*, liv n.) quotes from a moral treatise of Isocrates, ἃ πάσχοντες ὑφ' ἑτέρων ὀργίζεσθε, ταῦτα τοῖς ἄλλοις μὴ ποιεῖτε. The passage occurs in an address (written by Isocrates, a professional writer) of Nicocles, king of Cyprian Salamis (c. 374 B.C.), to his subjects, dealing with their duties as such (Isocrates, *Nicocles*, 61b).

The unique value of the Golden Rule of Jesus does not depend upon its never having been uttered by any earlier teacher in its *positive* form, but upon its connexion with His revelation of man's chief good, His perfect example of devotion to that good, and His power to inspire and sustain those who, at His bidding, become followers of that which is good. It remains true, however, that there is little evidence of the existence of any pre-Christian parallel to the positive rule. Diogenes Laertius (v. 21) tells us that Aristotle was asked how we should act towards our friends, and replied: 'as we would they should act to us.' The saying is quoted with no context, but a comparison with *Nicom. Ethics*, ix. 8 *fin.*, is in favour of its genuineness. Prof. Legge, commenting on the assertion that Confucius gave the rule only in a negative form, says: 'but he understood it also in its positive and most comprehensive force, and deplored, on one occasion at least, that he had not himself always attained to taking the initiative in doing to others as he would have them do to him' (*Encyc. Brit.*[9] vi. 264[b]).

In the Apostolic and post-Apostolic ages the negative form of the rule is more frequent, both in Christian and non-Christian writers. The oldest Christian authority is probably *Didache*, 1[2]. It is also inserted in the Western text of Ac 15[20. 29], but the source of the variant is uncertain. Zahn refers the addition to the *Didache* ; but, as Rendel Harris says, 'the negative precept turns up everywhere in the early Church, having been absorbed in the first instance from Jewish ethics.' (Cf. Knowling's succinct note on Ac 15[20] in *Expos. Gr. Test.*). Other examples are *Const. Apost.* vii. 1 ; Clem. Alex. *Strom.* ii. 23, 139 ; Tertullian, *c. Marc.* iv. 16. In non-Christian authors the negative form of the rule is found in Philo (Eusebius, *Præp.* viii. 7. 6). One of the best of the Roman emperors, Alexander Severus, had it inscribed in his palace and on public buildings (Lamprid. c. 51). Westermarck (*Origin and Development of the Moral Ideas*, i. 693) directs attention to an interesting passage in Epictetus (*Fragm.* 42) : the keeping of slaves is condemned in these words, 'What you avoid suffering yourself, seek not to impose on others.' The rule in its positive form is loosely quoted in Clem. Rom. *ad Cor.* c. xiii., 'As ye do, so shall it be done unto you . . . as ye are kind, so shall kindness be shown unto you.' Harless (*Christian Ethics*, p 110) ascribes to Seneca the saying, 'ab altero expectes alteri quod feceris,'—a suggestive and rare contrast to the Stoic maxim, 'Quod tibi fieri non vis, alteri ne feceris.'

A fair inference from these facts is that the positive form of the Golden Rule has been generally regarded as marking a distinct advance upon the negative form, its ideal of social duty being higher and therefore more difficult to realize. But Professor Hirsch takes the opposite view ; in the *Jewish Encyclopedia* (vi. 22[b]) he says : ' "What you would have others do unto you," makes self and possible advantages to self the central motive ; "what is hateful to you do not unto another" makes the effect upon others the regulating principle.' But how can self-interest be the motive for doing good to thankful and unthankful alike ? The positive precept puts 'doing' first, and bids us take thought in doing good ; we are to give what would please us, if we were in the place of those whom we are trying to benefit, though it may be quite certain that we shall receive nothing in return. The command of Christ accords with His teaching that they are 'blessed' who do not invite to their feasts those who will probably return the invitation, but those who cannot make such recompense (Lk 14[12ff.]). It is still more difficult to understand how 'doing nothing' to another ensures that our conduct will be regulated by altruistic principles. To do no harm is consistent with extreme selfishness. 'The negative confines us to the region of *justice* ; the positive takes us into the region of *generosity* or *grace*, and so embraces both law and prophets' (Bruce, *Expos. Gr. Test. in loc.*).

A subtle way of obtaining a negative result from the positive precept is mentioned by Schleiermacher (*Predigten*, iii. 84 ff.). One may say in haughty independence, 'What I wish is that others would let me go my own way ; therefore, I let them go theirs.' It is rightly said, in reply, that such pride is incompatible with obedience to the command of Jesus. His words, 'whatsoever ye would that men should do unto you,' are a recognition of the fact of men's mutual dependence. 'We are members one of another, and our chief danger is not that we should forget our claims on others, but that we should neglect our duties to others ; nevertheless there are occasions when our possibilities of doing good to others will be lessened by unwillingness to be served by others.

A practical difficulty presents itself to the minds of many who desire to walk in accordance with Christ's rule. A king cannot do to his subject what he desires his subject to do to him, nor can a father to his child, nor a master to his servant. But our Lord's command is '*even so* do ye unto them.' The narrow interpretation is not only false to the spirit, but also to the letter. The saying of Christ leaves abundant room for good actions which the recipient may be known to be altogether unable to return,—another reason for refusing to see in the positive form of the Golden Rule an appeal to self-interest. The Gr. word used is οὕτως, not ταῦτα ; its meaning is rightly given by Alford (*Com. in loc.*), 'After the pattern of ὅσα ἄν . . . Because what might suit us might not suit others. We are to think what we should like done to *us*, and then apply that rule to our dealings with others.' A baldly literal interpretation would miss the beauty of St. Paul's words, when, after enumerating the duties of servants to their masters, he says, 'And, ye masters, do the same things unto them' (Eph 6[9]). The rule for masters and servants alike is 'unto the Lord' ; on each side of this and of every human relationship there is opportunity for 'goodwill' and for 'doing the will of God from the heart' (v.[6f.]).

Many modern writers regard the Golden Rule as identical with the ethical maxim of Kant : 'So act as to treat humanity, whether in thine own person or in that of any other, in every case as an end withal, never as a means only' (cf. Votaw in Hastings' *DB*, Extra Vol. p. 42[a] ; Gore, *Sermon on the Mount*, 170 f.; Loofs, *Predigten*, ii. 227). In the language of philosophy, Kant forcefully expresses what is implied in the simpler words of Jesus. Doubtless it is inconsistent with the Golden Rule to exploit men for gain or for pleasure ; in a word, to have one ideal for ourselves and another for our neighbours. Loofs shows clearly how the *universality* of the ethical imperative on which Kant so strongly insists is a distinct note in the command of Jesus. He also makes an instructive application of this principle to a concrete case, and shows how vainly partners in guilt try to shelter themselves behind their own parody of this rule. As though mutual agreement could ever be any excuse for collusion in dishonest actions, deceitful evasions, or even immoral pleasures. His reply to those who act on the principle of the German proverb, 'The left hand washes the right, and the right hand washes the left,' is in substance as follows : Jesus does not say, 'Whatsoever one of you would that another should do to him, let him do the same to that other.' The rule is universal. There must be no arbitrary limiting of the extension of the term 'men' in the saying, 'Whatsoever ye would that *men* should do unto you, even so do ye also unto *them*.' A thief and his accomplice may, for the sake of dividing the spoil, wink at each other's crimes ; that is what is called honour among thieves. But neither of the accomplices can wish to make the rule of action universal ; they cannot desire to be deceived by all men as they have agreed to combine in deceiving others.

In the Golden Rule, John Stuart Mill found a fitting expression of the essential principle of his ethical system. 'To do as you would be done by, and to love your neighbour as yourself, constitute the ideal perfection of utilitarian morality' (*Utilitarianism*, p. 323). But when the crucial question is asked : How is the ideal perfection to be attained ? the reply is that utility enjoins, 'as the means of making the nearest approach to this ideal,' that (1) 'laws of social arrangements,' and (2) 'education and opinion' should strive to 'establish in the mind of every individual an indissoluble association between his own happiness and the good of the whole' (*op. cit.* p. 323). But no external force, such as law or education, can supply either the motive for doing as we would be done by, or the power to fulfil the precept we approve. It is true that on the lips of Christ the Golden Rule has its perfect expression ; but its superiority as an ethical maxim rests upon a broader basis. It is more to exemplify a rule than to formulate it ; it is still more to furnish the inward inspiration which constrains men to obey it. The disciples of Christ have another Golden Rule for their actions one toward another ; it is expressed in His words, 'as I have done to you' ; and their all-powerful motive is the assurance that 'ye did it unto me' (Mt 25[40]) will be their abundant reward, if whatsoever they would have done to Christ Himself, even so they do unto men, serving them lowlily and lovingly in His name and for His sake.

LITERATURE.—In addition to the works mentioned in this article, see SERMON ON THE MOUNT and the excellent Bibliography of Votaw in Hastings' *DB*, Extra Vol. p. 44 f.

J. G. TASKER.

GOLGOTHA (Γολγοθᾶ, Aram. גָּלְגָּלְתָּא, Heb. גֻּלְגֹּלֶת [2 K 9³⁵], 'skull'),—The name of the place where Jesus was crucified. This name is mentioned by three of the Evangelists (Mt 27³³ 'a place called Golgotha, that is to say, The place of a skull'; Mk 15²² 'the place Golgotha, which is, being interpreted, The place of a skull'; Jn 19¹⁷ 'the place called The place of a skull, which is called in the Hebrew, Golgotha'). The Greek equivalent (Κρανίον) is used by St. Luke (23³³ 'the place which is called The skull,' RV). Vulg. uses here the Latin equivalent *Calvaria*, whence 'Calvary' in AV.

Three explanations of this name have been suggested: (1) Jerome (*Com. in Eph* 5¹⁴) mentions a tradition that Adam was buried at Golgotha, and that at the Crucifixion the drops of Christ's blood fell on his skull and restored him to life. The skull often seen in early pictures of the Crucifixion refers to this. (2) It is supposed by some to have been the place of public execution, where bodies were left unburied (Jerome, *Com. in Mt* 27³³), but (a) it is most unlikely that dead men's bones would have been left lying about so near the city, when, according to the Mosaic law, they made any one unclean who touched them; (b) there was no reason why the place should have been named from the skulls rather than from any other parts of skeletons; (c) the expression is κρανίου τόπος, not κρανίων τόπος, as we should expect it to be if this derivation were correct. (3) The most probable view of the origin of the name is suggested by the form of the expression in St. Luke, 'the place which is called The skull.' It was probably so called because of its skull-like contour. The use of the article by the Evangelists seems to indicate that the place was well known, but they never call it a mountain. The Bordeaux Pilgrim (A.D. 333) speaks of it as *monticulus Golgotha*, and the expression 'Mount Calvary' appears to have come into use after the 5th century.

The site cannot be identified with certainty. All that we know from the Bible is that it was outside the walls of the city (He 13¹², Mt 27³¹. ³², Jn 19¹⁶. ¹⁷), that it was nigh to the city (Jn 19²⁰), that it was in a conspicuous position (Mk 15⁴⁰, Lk 23⁴⁹), that it was close to some thoroughfare leading from the country (Mt 27³⁹, Mk 15²¹. ²⁹, Lk 23²⁶), and that it was near a garden and a new tomb hewn out of the rock, belonging to Joseph, a rich man of Arimathæa (Jn 19⁴¹, Mt 27⁵⁷. ⁶⁰, Mk 15⁴³. ⁴⁶, Lk 23⁵³). These particulars are not sufficient to justify a positive decision in favour of any one of the proposed identifications of Golgotha, but they seem to be decisive against the first of the four conjectures mentioned below, to bear against the second slightly, but against the third more heavily, and to be most nearly satisfied by the fourth.

1. The peculiar theory of Fergusson (*Essay on the Anc. Topog. of Jerus.*, and art. 'Jerusalem' in Smith's *DB*), that Golgotha was on Mount Moriah, and that the mosque of Omar is the church erected by Constantine over the Holy Sepulchre, was quickly shown to be untenable (*e.g.* by Bonar, art. 'Jerusalem' in Fairbairn's *DB*).

2. Barclay (*City of the Great King*, p. 79) and Porter (Kitto's *Cycl. of Bib. Lit.* art 'Golgotha') maintained that the site of the Crucifixion was east of the city, between the then existing wall and the Kidron Valley. This place could have been quickly and easily reached from the palace of

Pilate and the judgment-hall, which probably stood at the N.W. corner of the Ḥaram area. According to this view, the soldiers, instead of taking their prisoner across the city towards the west, or out in the direction of the Roman road, hurried Him through the nearest gate and crucified Him near the road leading to Bethany. Two objections are urged against this: (a) that the Gospel narratives imply that the road passing Golgotha was a more frequented thoroughfare than this road to Bethany, and that the great highways of Jerusalem are all on the north and west of the city; and (b) that there is no skull-shaped site in this region.

3. That Golgotha was where the Church of the Holy Sepulchre now stands, seems to have been almost universally believed from the age of Constantine down to the 18th century. It is now agreed on all hands that the present Church of the Holy Sepulchre occupies the site of the one erected by Constantine in A.D. 335. On what grounds did he select this as the true site of the Crucifixion? Those who still believe it to be the true site generally assume not only that the early Christians at Jerusalem had a knowledge of the places where the Lord was crucified and buried, but also that this knowledge was handed down as a reliable tradition through three hundred years, notwithstanding the utter demolition of Jerusalem by Titus and again by Hadrian, and the altering of the whole aspect of the city by the latter when he rebuilt it as a Roman colony and changed its name to Aelia Capitolina. But Eusebius, in describing the discovery of the site by Constantine, says it had been 'given over to forgetfulness and oblivion,' and that the Emperor, 'not without a Divine intimation, but moved in spirit by the Saviour Himself,' ordered it to be purified and adorned with splendid buildings.

'Such language, certainly, would hardly be appropriate in speaking of a spot well known and definitely marked by long tradition. The Emperor, too, in his letter to Macarius, regards the discovery of "the token of the Saviour's most sacred passion, which for so long a time had been hidden under ground," as "a miracle beyond the capacity of man sufficiently to celebrate or even to comprehend." The mere removal of obstructions from a well-known spot could hardly have been described as a miracle so stupendous. Indeed, the whole tenor of the language both of Eusebius and Constantine goes to show that the discovery of the Holy Sepulchre was held to be the result, not of a previous knowledge derived from tradition, but of a supernatural interposition and revelation' (Robinson, *BRP*, Boston, 1841, ii. 75).

The same impression is made by the accounts of the writers of the 5th century, who, however, unanimously attribute the discovery not to Constantine, but to his mother Helena. Their story is that, guided by a 'Divine intimation' as to the place, she came to Jerusalem, inquired diligently of the inhabitants, and, after a difficult search, found the sepulchre and beside it three crosses, and also the tablet bearing the inscription of Pilate. At the suggestion of Bishop Macarius, the cross to which the inscription belonged was ascertained by a miracle of healing. The three crosses were presented in succession to a noble lady of Jerusalem who lay sick of an incurable disease. Two of them produced no effect, but the third worked an immediate and perfect cure. Eusebius, though contemporary with the alleged events, makes no mention of the discovery of the cross nor of the agency of Helena. But whether we accept the account of Eusebius or that of the writers of the 5th century, the traditional site of Calvary rests on a miracle, and, in the case of the latter, on a double miracle.

Those who now favour this site (*e.g.* Sanday, *Sac. Sites of the Gospels*, pp. 72–77) labour to show that there was a previous tradition which determined Constantine's selection of the spot, but the only proofs they adduce are : (*a*) vague allusions to visits made by early pilgrims to the 'Holy Places' of Palestine, an expression which is used of the Holy Land at large, and not of the Holy City only ; and (*b*) the alleged regular succession of bishops from the Apostle James to the time of Hadrian, through whom a knowledge of the place might have been handed down. This regular succession of bishops is more than doubtful. The only authority on the subject is Eusebius, who lived two centuries afterwards, and he says expressly that he had been able to find no document respecting them, and wrote only from hearsay. Moreover, even if it were possible to prove the existence of an earlier tradition, its value would be open to serious question, as is shown by the falsity of other traditions which did actually exist in the age of Constantine. For instance, Eusebius in A.D. 315 speaks of pilgrims coming from all parts of the world to behold the fulfilment of prophecy and to pay their adorations on the *summit* of the Mount of Olives, where Jesus gave His last charge to His disciples and then ascended into heaven. This is hardly consistent with the explicit statement of St. Luke (24[50. 51]) that ' he led them out until they were over against Bethany, and . . . he parted from them and was carried up into heaven.' Other sites shown to pilgrims in that uncritical age were impossible, such as that of Rephidim in Moab. The Bordeaux Pilgrim places the Transfiguration on Olivet, and the combat of David and Goliath near Jezreel. The fact that no pilgrimages were made to the site of the Holy Sepulchre before the visit of Helena, though they were made in plenty to the summit of Olivet, goes to show that there was no tradition concerning the Holy Sepulchre.

In the present Church of the Holy Sepulchre are shown not only the site of the Sepulchre and the rock of the Crucifixion, with the cleft made by the earthquake and the three holes, five feet apart, in which the three crosses were inserted, but also a great number of other traditional sites. Almost every incident of the Passion and Resurrection is definitely located. The very spots are pointed out where Christ was bound, where He was scourged, where His friends stood afar off during the Crucifixion, where His garments were parted, where His body was anointed, where He appeared to His mother after the Resurrection, and to Mary Magdalene ; the rock tombs also of Nicodemus and Joseph of Arimathæa ; the place where Helena's throne stood during the 'Invention of the Cross,' —and many others. The number of these identifications, all under one roof, does not increase our confidence in ecclesiastical tradition.

Not less damaging to the claims of the traditional site is the topographical evidence. Our Lord suffered 'without the gate' (He 13[12]). The Church of the Holy Sepulchre lies far within the walls of the present city, and, as Jerusalem at the time of the Crucifixion was much larger than it is now, the fair presumption is that it included the site of that church rather than excluded it. If we place Golgotha at the traditional site, we make Jerusalem at the time of its greatest prosperity no larger than the poverty-stricken town of the present day, ' containing not far from 200 acres, from which 36 acres must be deducted for the Ḥaram area' (Merrill). This difficulty arising from the present location in the heart of the city seems to have been felt as early as the 8th cent., and also in the 12th and 14th, but the first to reject the tradition openly was Korte, who visited Jerusalem in 1738, and who urged that the traditional site could not have been outside the ancient city, because of its nearness to the former area of the Jewish temple. The argument against this site has been greatly strengthened by the determination of the rock levels of

Jerusalem and the probable course of the ' second wall ' of the three mentioned by Josephus. The first wall, that of David and Solomon, encompassed the Upper City (Zion), and its north line ran eastward from the tower of Hippicus to the wall bounding the temple area. ' The second wall had its beginning from the gate called Gennath, which belonged to the first wall, and, encircling only the northern quarter of the city, it extended as far as the Tower Antonia.' (*BJ* v. iv. 2). This wall, which was probably built by Hezekiah, running in a circle or curve, seems to have had no angles like the first and third, and therefore to have required no extended description. If this curve included the Pool of Hezekiah (which must surely have been within the walls), it would naturally have included also the traditional site of the Sepulchre. If, in spite of the statement of Josephus, the wall be drawn with a re-entering angle so as to exclude the traditional site, there still remain apparently insuperable difficulties in the nature of the ground, since in this case the wall must have been built in a deep valley (Tyropœon), and must have been dominated from without by the adjacent knoll on which the Church of the Holy Sepulchre now stands (Acra). But 'fortresses stand on hills, not in deep ravines,' 'the wall must have stood *on the high ground*' (Conder). Immediately east of the Tower of David (at or near which Hippicus must have stood) a narrow ridge runs north and south, connecting the two hills Zion and Acra and separating the head of the Tyropœon Valley from the valley west of the Jaffa gate. As this is the only place where the wall could have protected the valley on the east and commanded the valley on the west, the natural course for the engineers would have been to build the wall along this ridge. Exactly along this ridge the remains of an ancient wall were found in 1885 by Dr. Merrill. One hundred and twenty feet of it were exposed in a line running north-west and south-east, at a depth of 10 or 12 ft. below the present surface of the ground. At some points but one course of stone remained, at others two, at others three. The stones correspond in size and work to those in the base of the Tower of David, a few yards farther south. This is probably a portion of the second wall. Later, another section, 26 ft. long, of similar work, was found farther north, besides traces at several other points. In explanation of the fact that entire sections are found towards the south and only débris of walls towards the north, Dr. Merrill cites the statement of Josephus, that Titus ' threw down the entire northern portion,' but left the southern standing and placed garrisons in its towers. From the statement that Titus made his attack ' against the central tower of the north wall ' he argues further, that if the wall ran from near Hippicus to Antonia in such a way as to exclude the traditional site of the Sepulchre, the two parts of the wall after it was broken in the middle should have been designated the ' eastern ' and ' western ' ; but Josephus calls them the ' northern ' and ' southern,' a description which is obviously more appropriate to a wall which ran well to the west and north of the traditional site (*Presb. and Ref. Rev.* iii. p. 646).

Parts of an ancient ditch and remains of walls have been recently discovered east of the Church of the Holy Sepulchre, and Schick regards these as remains of the second wall and of the city moat. But, as Benzinger says (Hilprecht's *Explorations in Bible Lands in the 19th Cent.*), his explanation ' is not convincing in itself, and there stand opposed to it important considerations of a general nature,' such as have been cited above, *e.g.* the military objection to locating a wall in a valley dominated from without by higher ground, and the fact that, had this been the course of the wall, Jerusalem could not have accommodated its great population at the time of Christ.

The existence of an undoubted Jewish tomb at the Church of the Holy Sepulchre, the one now called the Tomb of Joseph of Arimathæa, has been cited as evidence that the place was outside the old city wall, 'but we know from the Talmud that ancient half-forgotten tombs were allowed by the Jews to exist within Jerusalem, and any writer will admit that, in the time of Agrippa at least, this particular tomb was within the circuit of the town.' The third wall, which ran far to the north-west and north of the present city wall, was built by Agrippa only ten or eleven years after the Crucifixion, to enclose a large suburb that had gradually extended beyond the second wall. So that, even if it could be shown that the Sepulchre was outside the second wall, it certainly lay far within the line of the third, and in the midst of this new town which at the time of the Crucifixion must have been already growing north of the second wall. The words 'without the gate' and 'nigh to the city' could scarcely mean 'within the suburbs' (Schaff).

The genuineness of the traditional site has been defended by Chateaubriand (*Itinéraire de Paris à Jerusalem*), Williams (*The Holy City*), Krafft (*Die Topographie Jerusalems*), Tischendorf (*Reise in den Orient*), de Vogüé (*Les Églises de la Terre-Sainte*), Sepp (*Jerusalem*), Clermont-Ganneau (*L'Authenticité du Saint-Sepulcre*), Sanday (*Sacred Sites of the Gospels*), and others. It has been attacked by Korte (*Reise nach dem gelobten Lande*), Robinson (*BRP*, and *Bibliotheca Sacra* for August and November 1847), Tobler (*Golgotha*), Wilson (*The Lands of the Bible*), Barclay (*The City of the Great King*), Schaff (*Through Bible Lands*), Conder (*Tent Work in Palestine*), and others.

4. The theory that Golgotha is the skull-shaped knoll above Jeremiah's grotto, outside the present north wall, near the Damascus gate, was first suggested by Otto Thenius in 1849. A similar view was put forward independently by Fisher Howe (*The True Site of Calvary*) in 1871. Since that time the theory has come rapidly into favour, and has been accepted by Gen. C. E. Gordon, Sir J. W. Dawson, Dr. Merrill, Dr. Schaff, Col. Conder, and others. It answers all the requirements of the Gospel narratives, being outside the walls, nigh to the city, in a conspicuous position, near a frequented thoroughfare—the main north road, and near to ancient Jewish rock-hewn tombs, one of which was discovered by Conder about 700 ft. west of the knoll. The so-called 'Gordon's Tomb,' about 230 ft. from the summit of the knoll, is thought by Conder to be a Christian tomb of the Byzantine age; but Schick says it 'was originally a rather small rock-cut Jewish tomb, but became afterwards a Christian tomb.' The great cemetery of Jewish times lay north of the city.

Moreover, Jewish tradition regards this hill as the place of public execution, and the Jews still call it 'the Place of Stoning.' Christian tradition also, as old as the 5th cent., fixes this as the place of the stoning of Stephen. The fact that Christ was put to death by the Roman method of crucifixion and not by the Jewish method of stoning does not break the force of this argument, for there is no reason to suppose that Jerusalem had two places of public execution. No other place would have been so convenient to the Romans for this purpose, starting, as they probably did, from Antonia. The castle seems to have been itself a part of the outer ramparts on the north-east, with the north wall of the temple area stretching from it to the east and the second city wall to the north-west. There must have been some feasible route for the soldiers of the garrison, who were constantly going back and forth between this fortress and Cæsarea. There was no such route to the east or south. To go west would have taken them through the heart of the crowded city, with its

narrow streets and its perils from the mob. What more natural than that there should have been a road leading directly from Antonia to the open country northwards? Here, accordingly, only a short distance north of the city, we find the remains of a Roman road.

'If executions were to take place near the city, I think they must have been carried out on the line of such a road, where the soldiers would have free ground to act upon in case of an emergency, without being hampered by crowded streets, and where only one gate would be between them and their stronghold, and that one entirely under their own control' (Merrill).

LITERATURE.—Artt. 'Golgotha' in Hastings' *DB* and *Encyc. Bibl.*, 'Sepulchre, The Holy,' in *Encyc. Brit.*[9], 'Grab, das heilige,' in *PRE*[3]; Conder, *Tent Work in Palestine*, i. 372 ff.; *SWP* 'Jerusalem,' 429 ff.; Merrill in *Andover Rev.*, 1885, p. 483 ff.; *PEFSt*, 1892, pp. 120 ff., 177, 188, 205; Wilson, *Golgotha and the Holy Sepulchre*, 1906; and works cited in the article.   W. W. MOORE.

GOMORRAH (עֲמֹרָה, Γομόρρα [fem.] or Γόμορρα [neut.]).—

The word should be fem. in Greek as in Hebrew, but the final α led to its being treated as neut. plural. In the LXX it is fem. 9 times, neut. 5 times, and in 5 passages the gender is indeterminate. In the NT it is fem. in 2 P 2⁶ and Mt 10¹⁵ [CD], but neut. in *id.* [אAB].

The name occurs in the NT in Mt 10¹⁵, Ro 9²⁹, 2 P 2⁶, Jude⁷. (In Mk 6¹¹ it occurs in a sentence wrongly inserted in A and some Lat. MSS, whence it found its way through the TR into the AV). In every case it is coupled with Sodom, as it is invariably in the OT. It is to be noticed, however, that Sodom is mentioned alone in Mt 11²³ᶠ, Lk 17²⁹, Rev 11⁸. Not only so, but in Lk 10¹², the parallel passage to Mt 10¹⁵, Gomorrah is omitted. It seems probable, therefore, that in St. Matthew the insertion of the name is editorial and not original; and, moreover, the text is uncertain; אAB Γομόρρων, C Γομόρρας, D Γομόρας; again אC insert γῇ before Γομ., while ABD omit it. Our Lord, then, used 'Sodom' (or 'the land of Sodom') alone; in Ro 9²⁹ the passage is a direct quotation from Is 1⁹; while the OT expression 'Sodom and Gomorrah' is found only in the two late, and closely connected, writings, Jude and 2 Peter.

For the lessons drawn by our Lord from the wickedness and the destruction of Sodom, see art. SODOM.   A. H. M'NEILE.

GOOD (ἀγαθός, καλός).—It is not easy to define Christ's idea of what is good. His expressions vary from a conception of the Good as one with the infinitely and inimitably Perfect to the most commonplace uses of the word. He speaks of old wine as 'good' (Lk 5³⁹), of the wedding-guests as 'both bad and good' (Mt 22¹⁰), of salt as 'good' (Mk 9⁵⁰ ‖ Lk 14³⁴), of certain ground as being 'good' (Mk 4⁸ ‖ Lk 8⁸), of God making 'his sun to rise on the evil and on the good' (Mt 5⁴⁵), and He says of Judas, 'Good (καλόν) were it for that man if he had not been born' (26²⁴ ‖ Mk 14²¹). Yet when the young ruler comes to Him with the same conventional usage of the word, 'Good Master (διδάσκαλε ἀγαθέ), what good thing shall I do to inherit eternal life?' (Mk 10¹⁷ ‖ Lk 18¹⁸; cf. Mt 19¹⁶ᶠ and WH's 'Notes on Select Readings' *ad loc.*), Jesus rejects the title as applied to Himself, and asserts that 'none is good save one, even God.' Whether this be read as 'not denying that He is good, but insisting that none should call Him so who did not believe Him to be God' (Liddon, *Bampt. Lect.* i. 23), or as 'the self-judgment which felt hurt by the epithet good' (Martineau, *Seat of Authority*, 651), there can be little doubt that Jesus purposely made use of the young man's phrase to point him to the ideal Good. Behind the things to be done, which were in the questioner's mind,— greater than matters of law or ritual, or even charity,—was the necessity that he should recognize the Supreme Good, the Eternal Spirit of all goodness. This did not imply that man should be hopeless of attaining a certain measure of the good, that it was something beyond the reach of the race, but that the fundamental idea of the good is God, and that to define or limit it is as impossible as to define or limit the Eternal Himself. Only on this occasion does Jesus so suddenly soar beyond the intention of any questioner who approaches Him. Elsewhere He tells a parable, and puts into the mouth of the master of the vineyard (a most human representative of the Heavenly Master) the question, 'Is thine eye evil because I am good?' (Mt 20[15]); and He speaks of 'the good man,' who 'out of his good treasure bringeth forth good things' (12[35] ‖ Lk 6[45]. So we may look upon the story of the Rich Young Man as a unique expression of Christ's highest thought of the Good, but not as thereby ruling out all lesser conceptions. A man may begin to do good or to live a good life before he learns that the foundation of all the good he accomplishes or attains to is God Himself; that no ethical aims are good which lack a Divine sanction. It is better for a man when this inward recognition of the Eternal Goodness precedes the active goodness of his life, for then he finds the peculiar secret of St. Paul's dogma (Ro 8[28]), 'All things work together for good to them that love God.' But the doing of good for its own sake may be a man's first step towards the Kingdom of God, and later he will be prepared for any self-denial or self-sacrifice that may bring him nearer the heavenly perfection (Mt 18[8] ‖ Mk 9[43. 45. 47]), when he has learned that it is God's Kingdom he approaches and not the invention of his own sympathetic impulses alone.

In line with this thought of Christ's is the liberty in the modes of doing good which He frequently asserted. With Him the present was always the fitting opportunity of the good, though He might occasionally ask the opinion of the Pharisees and scribes as to whether it was 'lawful to do good on the Sabbath' (Mt 12[12] ‖ Mk 3[4], Lk 6[9]).

Some element of altruism enters into all His conceptions of good. The Greek masters (especially Plato and Aristotle) assert the good of a man to lie in his 'well-being' (Sidgwick's constant rendering of εὐδαιμονία), a condition which depends on certain visible 'goods' that are his own personal possession, and in no way bring him into contact with less fortunate men, such 'good things' as wealth, health, beauty, and intellect. But Christ regards that alone as good which lessens the distance between man and man, and man and God. The good a man should seek is that of each and all men, even 'them that hate you' (Lk 6[27]), for the doing of good to others is the final test of the practical value of religion, and became the distinctive note of the character of Christ in the Apostolic days when He was described as one who 'went about doing good and healing' (Ac 10[38]). This is indicative of all the visible elements of the good in His teachings. Love, His supreme dogma, finds its essence in self-surrender. The parables of conduct, such as the Good Samaritan, are insistent upon the actual doing of some good. When Jesus sends the Baptist His own record, the good things that will bear witness to Him, it is a tale of deeds of brotherly kindness, of help for the blind, lame, lepers, deaf, the poor, and even the dead (Mt 11[5]). Zacchæus is assured of his salvation when he has learned to share with his poorer brethren (Lk 19[8. 9]). The fact of giving is accepted by Christ as the evidence of a desire to do good (Mk 14[7]). The good man is not only devout; his personal piety may be the surest basis for the true spirit of goodness in him; but the good must take form in some actual warring with the world's evils, some earnest attempt to remedy the miseries, sufferings, diseases, afflictions, sorrows, or poverty of men. This is the vital test applied in the great parable of the Judgment (Mt 25[31ff.]). The Son of Man there asks no question as to spiritual apprehension, or intellectual convictions, or ecclesiastical obedience. 'The kingdom prepared from the foundation of the world'—from the moment of the birth of mankind—is for those who saw and served the King in brethren who were hungry, thirsty, outcasts, naked, sick, or in prison. Christ sanctions the popular judgment of what constitutes a good man,—that effectiveness in well-doing which moves steadily and lovingly towards the ultimate conquest of the world, that social message of the gospel which is the enthusiasm of true goodness, and is able to 'overcome evil with good' (Ro 12[21]). But all such doing rests on being. It is intimately connected with each man's own spiritual vision and condition, for it is the rudimentary realization of the Kingdom of heaven; it issues from that Kingdom which is 'within' (Lk 17[21]), where 'glory, honour, and peace' are the blessings which come 'to every one that worketh good' (Ro 2[10])—a Kingdom which a man may never have explored, but which is the ground from which grows all the practical good he does (Mt 12[35]). If the tree is good, the fruit is good (v.[33]), and when the whole being of a man is awake to the inflowing of the Divine Goodness, he becomes the more keenly sensitive to Righteousness, Truth, Love, and the Brotherhood, and finds increasingly St. Peter's utterance at the Transfiguration to be his own: 'Lord, it is good for us to be here' (Mt 17[4] ‖ Mk 9[5] ‖ Lk 9[33]). The Good enters imperceptibly; it is not born of the law, nor of any ethical analysis; and in the unexpectedness of its joy the disciple is conscious of having reached the highest heaven, of having found that delight in whatever is good which helps him to understand the true end of life, 'to glorify God and to *enjoy* Him for ever.'

EDGAR DAPLYN.

GOODNESS.—As resignation is the ideal of the Buddhist, and valour of the Mohammedan, so the essence of Christianity is goodness. Its Founder was the absolute personification of this characteristic quality. Nothing short of this could have so inspired the Apostles and Evangelists. Veiled within the few imperishable pages of the Gospels, and perhaps seen only by the meditating mind, is the figure of a perfect goodness once realized upon earth. It is not the novelty of His teaching that has attracted men, nor His deep sympathy with humanity, nor any spiritual utterances to the Father (which are all too rarely recorded). Behind the words and deeds of the four biographies stands a shining personality, a living type of goodness— One of whom they could speak as being 'without sin.' The Evangelists knew nothing of the dogmatic spirit, and could probably have given no clear definition and explanation of the sinlessness of Christ. To them He was the human expression of the Divine Goodness, and it mattered little whether a man should say that the Goodness was from eternity, so that by its nature sin had never been a moment's possibility, or that at birth Christ had been uniquely endowed with a passion for goodness that turned naturally from everything selfish, injurious to others, or sinful either to God or man; or that at His baptism He had been set aside to that brief ministry (which is nearly all men know of His earthly life), when the voice from heaven was heard saying, 'This is my beloved Son, in whom I am well pleased' (Mt 3[17]). However its genesis might be spoken of, the 'sinlessness' of Christ is the utterance of the measure of His goodness as it affected the disciples.

Throughout the Sermon on the Mount they would hear that note of human tenderness blended with unhesitating virtue which constitutes goodness. This alone could be the source of that merciful utterance which is perhaps His only new doctrine —'Love your enemies.'

In His message of the Divine Fatherhood they would behold that goodness sending 'rain upon the just and the unjust' (Mt 5[45]), forgiving the penitent as the father forgives the prodigal son (Lk 15[11ff.]), and even forgiving those whose repentance is yet to come (23[34]). Such conceptions would be born of the goodness within Himself, that breathed out in the intense sympathy of the story of the woman taken in sin (Jn 7[53]–8[11]), or the defence of Mary Magdalene in the house of Simon the Pharisee (Lk 7[36ff.]), or in the parable of the Good Samaritan (10[25ff.]). The same spirit marks the greater number of the miracles. None could be considered as entirely separated from human interest and influence, and the great majority (thirty-one out of thirty-seven recorded) were wrought openly and intentionally for the good of others. The blind, the deaf, the palsied, the lame, the lepers, the lunatic, the hungry crowd, the timid fishermen, the mourners for the dead,—all shared in the effective power of the innate goodness of our Lord. It was as though, in His purity and sinlessness, the very forces of nature became obedient to His transparent will,—the one will that sin has never overcome, the one luminous purity in which sin has found no vitalizing atmosphere. He had been tried at the beginning of His mission, but the temptations of the desert had ended in triumph. The goodness that was the breath of His being rose instinctively above the low promptings of a selfish wonder-working, or the presumption of pride, or the vanity of power, even though over 'all the kingdoms of the earth' (Mt 4[1] ǁ Lk 4[1], Mk 1[12]). He spoke harshly to the Tempter, for goodness does not always win by mild passivity against evil. He who knows that God is the beginning and the end of all goodness will waste little time in diplomatic parley with the powers of darkness. Victory will often lie in swift attack. So the goodness of Christ is not lessened by His fierce handling of the money-changers and traders within the Temple (Mt 21[12ff.], Jn 2[13ff.]), for He knows that lower ideas of God and goodness will unconsciously prevail if the house of God becomes a place for barter and bargain. It is part of the same zeal that had kept Him about His 'Father's business' in the days of His boyhood (Lk 2[49]), though it takes the more vigorous form we might expect in manhood. The inward knowledge of the simplicity and holiness of His motives makes fear not only impossible, but non-existent; and this is the spirit that inspires every true missionary. He also, as his Master, would show the winning charm of the visibly good — the goodness embodied in a life rather than in doctrines only—that which in Christ could say to the world, 'I am the bread of life' (Jn 6[35. 48]), 'I am the way, the truth, and the life' (14[6]), and 'I am the light of the world' (8[12] 9[5]), the witness of which is described by St. Paul, when he says that the fruit of the light is in all goodness and righteousness and truth' (Eph 5[9]).

The goodness of Christ brought a new force into Jewish religion, one that changed the nature of it. Judaism was formal, ceremonial, mainly an external worship. Its prophets had striven to kindle it into a moral and spiritual faith. But prophet and priest had stood apart. In Christ the middle wall was broken down, and into the old religion was poured the new spirit. Henceforth religion could not be separate from the moral life. A man could not be unrighteous, an evil-doer, and yet be religious. Goodness became a synonym for true

and undefiled religion. For man, having once seen the perfect manhood of the Christ, and felt His power to overcome sin and death, had gained a vision of religion that might perpetuate such a type, and the vision would not lightly fade. Through failures from within and tyrannies from without the Christian would bear witness to his Lord and to his faith, by a life of goodness modelled on that of his Master. This was the highest evidence he could offer of the Divine Incarnation.

EDGAR DAPLYN.

GOODWILL.—See COMPLACENCY, p. 356[b].

GOSPEL.—'Gospel' is the modern form of the Anglo-Saxon word 'godspell,' representing the Greek word εὐαγγέλιον. Formerly it was thought to be the literal translation, meaning 'good-story.' But now it is generally accepted as meaning 'God-story.' εὐαγγέλιον was originally used for 'the reward of good tidings,' and traces of this usage are found in LXX; cf. 2 S 4[10]. But the word came to denote the 'good tidings' themselves; and this is the Christian usage. It may be noted here that Dalman (*The Words of Jesus*, p. 103) says: 'In the verb בִּשֵּׂר, which must be assumed to be the original Aramaic expression, the idea of glad tidings is not so inherent as in the Greek εὐαγγελίζεσθαι. Even in the OT (1 S 4[17]) בִּשַּׂר is used of mournful tidings. . . . It thus appears that the sovereignty of God is the content of a "message" or "tidings," and not without further qualification of "a message of glad tidings."' It would seem, however, that the choice of the Greek verb εὐαγγελίζεσθαι, as well as the contexts of the word in the Gospels, provide that 'further qualification.'

1. The source for the Christian usage is found in Isaiah. In 61[1] the prophet describes the function of the servant of Jahweh (or perhaps his own function) in these words: 'The Spirit of the Lord God is upon me; because the Lord hath anointed me to preach good tidings unto the meek. . . .' The word is εὐαγγελίσασθαι. The meek are the exiles in Babylon. Good tidings are announced to them. God is coming to save them, and He is near. It is the acceptable year of the Lord, when He shall deliver His people from their enemies and restore them to their native land. A similar reference occurs in 52[7]. A messenger hastens to Jerusalem, and she sits in the dust of her ruins, bringing 'good tidings.' The exiles are to return to her, and she shall be inhabited again by her long-lost children. These instances exhibit clearly the meaning 'good tidings'; and both are claimed in NT to describe the Christian message. St. Paul quotes Is 52[7] in Ro 10[15]; and Jesus makes Is 61[1] the text for His sermon at Nazareth (Lk 4[18]).

This use of the word by Jesus stamps it at once with its Christian significance. 'He began to say, To-day hath this scripture been fulfilled in your ears.' He claimed to be a preacher of good tidings to the poor. The poor, the captives, the blind, the bruised, are no longer political exiles. They are the bond-servants of sin, those who waited for the consolation of Israel, the poor and outcast to whom Judaism had no message of hope. He is Jahweh's Anointed sent to bring good tidings of great joy to all the people (Lk 2[10]). This description of His mission seems to have endeared itself to the heart of Jesus. He made frequent use of the word, and soon after the rejection in Nazareth He described His Messianic function by it: 'I must preach the good tidings of the kingdom of God to the other cities also; for therefore was I sent' (Lk 4[43]). In particular, Jesus appropriated the name 'gospel' for the contents of His message. This was His description of it from the beginning of His ministry. St. Mark sums up that beginning thus: 'Jesus came into Galilee preaching the gospel of God, and saying, The time is fulfilled and the kingdom of God is at hand ; repent ye and believe in the gospel.' There are many proofs that Jesus used this word 'gospel' to describe His message ; cf. Mt 24^{14} 26^{13}, Mk 1^{15} 8^{35} 10^{29} 13^{10}, Lk 7^{22} ‖. It is not surprising, therefore, that the word came into general Christian use to describe the contents of the preaching of Jesus. All the Synoptics reflect this usage. In Acts and the Epistles it is an established custom. 'The gospel' became the normal Christian title for the message which Jesus came to proclaim, and which He sent forth the Apostles to preach to every creature.

2. But closer examination shows that the term was not used by the Evangelists to describe all that Jesus said ; nor was the verb 'preach good tidings' descriptive of all His work. In Mt. this sentence occurs twice : 'Jesus went about in all Galilee, teaching in their synagogues, and preaching the gospel of the kingdom, and healing all manner of disease and all manner of sickness among the people' (4^{23} 9^{35}). It seems to be an accepted formula summarizing the work of Jesus. It contains three main words—'teaching,' 'preaching,' 'healing.' The same distinctions are noticed elsewhere. St. Luke distinguishes 'teaching' and 'preaching the gospel' (20^1) ; and in 9^2 he tells that the Twelve were sent forth 'to preach the kingdom and to heal the sick.' St. Mark does not contrast the two words 'teach' and 'preach the gospel' in the same verse ; but in $1^{14.\ 21}$, he ascribes to Jesus 'preaching the gospel' and 'teaching.' In the latter case the effect produced by His 'teaching' is different from that due to His 'preaching.'

It would seem, therefore, that the work of Jesus was threefold : He preached the gospel, He taught, and He healed. If this distinction is valid, the term 'gospel' did not apply to all that Jesus said and did. It was reserved for the 'good tidings' that He preached. In addition to these 'good tidings,' there was 'teaching' that belonged to another category. Listeners would hardly describe such teaching as Mt 5^{19-48} by the title 'good tidings,' nor could the word apply naturally to Mt 10^{34-39} 12^{31-37} 19^{9-12} 21^{33-44} 23. 24 ‖. It seems clear that Jesus distinguished the gospel that He preached from the teaching that accompanied it.

3. What then was implied by the term 'gospel'? It was essentially 'news' or 'tidings.' It was the proclamation of a fact rather than instruction in the art of living well. It was offered to belief, and its acceptance must be preceded by repentance (Mk 1^{15}). It is called 'the gospel of God' (in Mk 1^{14} RV) ; the 'gospel of the kingdom' (in Mt 4^{23} 9^{35} 24^{14}). St. Luke uses the compound phrase, 'the gospel of the kingdom of God' (Lk 4^{43} 16^{16}). These phrases must be studied, and in addition it must be noted that Jesus connected the gospel with His own person.

(a) The phrase 'the gospel of God' indicates a message from God and about God that is good news to men. It is certain that Jesus gave the world a new idea of God ; and this gospel of Jesus was the revelation of God as 'our Father in heaven.' He did not discover the category of Fatherhood in its relation to God. This had been done under the Old Covenant. But He invested the idea with such radiance as to make it a new revelation. More specifically, He illumined the Fatherhood of God by teaching 'the infinite value of the human soul.' God is not merely the Father of a people. He is the Father of each individual soul (cf. 'thy Father,' Mt 6^{4-18}). His Fatherhood extends to all sorts and conditions of men (Mt 12^{50}). In particular, the Father seeks each sinner (Lk 15^{1-10}), and welcomes even the prodigal to His home (vv.$^{11-32}$). This 'gospel of God' includes,

further, the good news to the heavily laden Jew that 'the Father seeketh true worshippers to worship in spirit and in truth' (Jn 4^{23} ; cf. Mt 11^{28}), and that the Father is willing to forgive sins without sacrificial offerings (Mt 9^2 ‖). And when the child of God has entered into this blessed relationship with his Father in heaven, that Father may be trusted implicitly (Mt 6^{25-34}). Prayer must be offered to this Father continually (Lk 18^1). The Lord's Prayer (Mt 6^9) 'shows the gospel to be the Fatherhood of God applied to the whole of life ; to be an inner union with God's will and God's kingdom, and a joyous certainty of eternal blessings and protection from evil' (Harnack).

The Johannine tradition lays special emphasis upon this Divine Fatherhood in its relation to Jesus ; the relation between the Father and His children is referred to in terms of love. Indeed, St. John sums up this aspect of the gospel in the immortal words, 'God is love' (1 Jn 4^8). Jesus Himself spoke chiefly of love as the duty of man. To love God and to love one's neighbour are the supreme laws for human conduct (Mt 22^{37-39} ‖). But by His constant speech about the Father, Jesus taught also God's love to men. This relation of love between God and man has been pointed to as the distinguishing feature of the gospel. Thus Réville writes :

'The Christian gospel is essentially characterized by its declaration that the bond between God and man is one of love. God is the Heavenly Father ; man is the son of God ; God loves man ; man ought to love God ; the relation between the principle of the universe and the individual is one of love, in which the two terms subsist. God and man—man not losing himself in God, God not remaining aloof from man—meet in a living communion, so that man's dependence on God should no longer be one of compulsion, but of free and joyful self-consecration, and that the sovereignty of God over man should no more appear a tyranny, but a rule which we love and bless. Such is the distinctive mark of the Christianity of Jesus, differentiating it from the other great religions.' *

(b) The phrase 'the gospel of the kingdom' describes the good news brought by Jesus in its relation to that Kingdom of God or of heaven which He proclaimed. It implies that the Kingdom has 'a gospel.' The gospel and the Kingdom are not co-extensive any more than the gospel and God are. But there is good news concerning the Kingdom, and this good news is an essential part of the message of the Kingdom. In brief, this gospel was that the Kingdom of heaven is opened to all believers. The message of Jesus was that the Kingdom was not for select classes or nations, but for all. All Jews were summoned to share it ; even the publicans and sinners may come (Mt 21^{31}, Mk 2^{15} ‖). Nor are Jews alone to walk in its light. All nations must be invited to sit at its hospitable table (Mt 8^{11} 26^{13}, Mk 13^{10}). The conditions of entrance make it accessible to all. It is offered not to the rich or to the wise, but to all who will become as little children (Mt 11^{25} 18^3 ‖, Jn 3^3). Moreover, this Kingdom, which is offered to all, is a far higher good than men dreamed (cf. Mt $13^{31.\ 44-46}$). It is a spiritual blessedness, infinitely transcending the ceremonial righteousness secured by legalism, and the political supremacy envied by the patriots. The Kingdom, as Jesus preached it, offered the highest conceivable good to all men. It satisfied the religious instincts of the race ; and because these are the deepest and most universal instincts, the message that they can be satisfied is indeed 'good news' (cf. Mt 13 ‖). Men had never found true satisfaction in the material forms of a ritualistic religion. These were the husks that contained no nourishment for the soul. Jesus preached 'the gospel of the kingdom' when He offered the highest spiritual good to all penitent and humble souls.

(c) But these two forms of the gospel do not

* *Liberal Christianity*, pp. 69–70.

exhaust its fulness. The presence of Jesus in the world was itself a gospel. He connected the good tidings with His own person. As the good news Rhoda brought to the praying Church was that Peter himself was at the door (Ac 12[14]), so the presence of Jesus in the world was 'glad tidings of great joy to all people' (Lk 2[10]). This was due to the significance attached by Jesus to Himself. He was the Messiah (Mt 16[16]). His use of the title 'Son of man' implies His special significance for the race. In several of His parables He referred to Himself as the Son of God (Lk 20[13]), as the Judge and King of men (Mt 25[31]), as the bridegroom (Mt 9[15] 25[6]); these and other titles indicate the peculiar value of His person. The interest was not metaphysical but religious. His presence in the world manifested the love of God (Jn 3[16]). It proved that God had not forgotten men, but had come to their help.

In this connexion the significance of Jesus' offer of pardon must be noted. He raised much opposition by claiming 'power on earth to forgive sins' (Mk 2[10] ‖). Nevertheless He exercised the power (Lk 7[47], Jn 5[14. 22]). There is a close connexion between this 'good news' and the good news about God and about the Kingdom. The barrier between God and the soul is sin. It is sin that hinders enjoyment of the Kingdom. Therefore the best news that men can have is a message of full and free forgiveness for all repentant, trustful souls. And this was the message preached by Jesus. He removed pardon out of the sphere of material sacrifices in the temple, which limited the scope of forgiveness to a few, and He made forgiveness a possible boon for everybody. Thus He opened the way into the Kingdom even to the publicans and sinners.

(d) But the core of this aspect of the gospel is reached only when it is connected definitely with the redeeming work of Jesus. He was conscious of a profounder mission than *preaching* the gospel. More than once He gave utterance to words that touch the deepest mysteries of redemption. He came to give His life a ransom (Mt 20[28]). He was the Good Shepherd giving His life for the sheep (Jn 10[11]). He foretold His death and resurrection, directly He had brought His disciples to confess His Messiahship (Mt 16[21]). On the betrayal night in the upper room, He gave the cup, saying, 'This is my blood of the covenant which is shed for many' (Mk 14[24]). It was impossible for Jesus to connect the gospel chiefly with His death, before He was crucified. But it seems unquestionable that He referred to His death as achieving a wonderful deliverance for men in respect of sin. The sacrificial element was not introduced into His life for the first time when He offered Himself to die. 'The Son of man came to minister'; and all through His ministry He was giving Himself up for others. Nevertheless, He looked upon His own death as having a peculiar significance, awful for Himself (cf. Mk 14[32-39] ‖), but blessed for men (Jn 14[3]). It is certain that His followers accepted this interpretation of the cross. At once the death of Jesus, followed as it was by His resurrection, was made the main theme of Apostolic preaching (Ac 2[23] 3[14] 4[10] etc.). So central was this preaching about the death of Christ, that St. Paul identifies 'the gospel' with the message about 'Christ crucified' (1 Co 1[17]).

The meaning of the term 'gospel' as used by Jesus may now be summed up. It seems to describe the message He taught concerning—(a) the fatherly nature of God; (b) the inclusiveness and spirituality of the Kingdom; and (c) God's provision for men's deliverance from sin through His own mediation. This gospel was not only the theme of His preaching, but was exemplified continually in His manner of life. He revealed the Father by His own attitude to men. He illustrated the spirit of the Kingdom by seeking the lost. He mediated the grace of God by His unsparing self-surrender. In particular, He accepted death upon the cross in obedience to the Father's will, in order that thereby the scattered sons of God might be gathered again to their Father (Jn 11[52]).

4. We must return now to the distinction between 'preaching the gospel' and 'teaching.' Much of the teaching of Jesus could not be directly classed under the 'gospel' as sketched above. It was ethical teaching. It rested upon the gospel as its foundation. It appealed ultimately to the nature of God for its sanctions. It was connected with the Kingdom, being the legislation that befitted such a Kingdom of grace. Nevertheless it was an ethical code, intended to guide those who have previously accepted the gospel. The teaching of Jesus is the law-book of the Kingdom. The gospel of Jesus is the manifesto of the Kingdom, explaining its nature and inviting all to become its citizens.

This probably explains the subsequent use of the term 'gospel.' Wonderful as the teaching of Jesus was, the gospel seemed still more marvellous. At any rate, that gospel seemed of first importance. It had to be preached before the teaching of Jesus could follow; and whilst points of contact could be found between the teaching of Jesus and other ethical systems, there was nothing in the world like the gospel of Jesus. And thus the term 'gospel' was most frequently on the lips of the Apostles; and by a natural process it was extended to cover the entire contents of their report of Jesus, including His teaching. All that the Apostles had to tell about Jesus was called 'the gospel.' This usage is reflected in Mk 1[1], where the word refers to the whole story of Jesus Christ.

5. Two points need a further reference. The gospel brought by Jesus was not entirely new. It had its roots in the past. The preaching of Jesus was in historic continuity with the preaching of the prophets and of the Mosaic law (Mt 5[17]). But that earlier preaching was the faint light of dawn: His words are the strong light of noonday (Jn 8[12]). Hitherto men had only heard rumours of varying trustworthiness; He brought official news that was full and final. Some keen-eyed spirits had caught sight of the Fatherhood of God, as the Alps may be seen from the terrace at Berne on a fine evening. But Jesus led men into the heart of the mountains. The hopes of the nation had hovered for centuries round a kingdom. But only Jesus disclosed the true nature of the shining city of God. Prophets had encouraged lonely exiles with the cry, 'Behold your God cometh!' But it was not until Jesus appeared that one who waited for the consolation of Israel could say, 'Mine eyes have seen thy salvation' (Lk 2[30]). The gospel preached by Jesus gave full substance and final form to the faint and tremulous hopes of centuries. For this reason the gospel must be the unchanging element in the Church's message. Being 'news' about God and the Kingdom, it cannot change until they change.

A distinction has been drawn between the gospel which Jesus preached and His ethical teaching. The Church's teaching of the Christian ethics must be a changing message. It is the application of the principles of Christ's teaching to present circumstances. The Christian ethic of the last generation is out of date in presence of to-day's problems. The Church must study the ethical principles enunciated by Jesus, in order to apply them to modern needs. But whilst the Christian ethic develops and is modified by circumstances, the Christian gospel cannot change. It is good news about facts. It must be stated in modern phraseology, that men may hear it in their own tongue and understand it. But it remains an 'Old, old Story' through all time. If this distinction is remembered, it will explain the confusion that is felt in modern times as to the Church's true function. All are agreed that this is to preach the gospel. But very different views are held as to what is included under the term. In particular, there is an increasing demand for a social gospel, whilst some maintain that the gospel cannot be concerned with social conditions. Probably the term 'gospel' is being used in two senses. As Jesus used it, 'the gospel' is a definite message, distinct from the Christian ethic, and also distinct from the work of healing practised by the Lord. But from Apostolic days onward the term 'gospel' has been used to cover the threefold function — preaching the gospel, teaching the ethic, and healing the sick. In its original and more limited sense, 'gospel' is simply the 'news' brought by Jesus. In its historical and broader sense, 'gospel' is the whole 'God-story': it includes the entire record of Jesus Christ's life and work. Thus used, the term covers the ethic that Jesus Christ taught, and the social service that He practised. In this sense 'gospel' includes all ethical teaching and social service that are in accordance with the mind of the Master. It is open to question, however, whether the Church has not suffered loss by broadening the reference of this word. Jesus used it to describe the 'good news' He brought to the poor and the meek of the earth; and this 'gospel' must ever be the foundation upon which the Church builds, though the foundation is not to be confused with the fabric erected upon it.

6. A brief space must be given to the consideration of the gospel in the rest of NT in so far as it is connected with Christ. In one sense this would involve an exposition of many chapters of Acts and of all the Epistles, for He is 'the head-stone of the corner,' and the gospel is only 'complete in Him.' But all that can be attempted is an indication of the place occupied by Christ in the gospel as preached by the Apostolic Church.

When we pass from the Gospels to the Acts and the Epistles, we are conscious at once of a change of standpoint. In the Gospels, Christ's disciples are a group of learners. They stand beside their Master at the very centre of truth, and they try to follow His gaze as it sweeps the horizon of the love and the kingdom of God. In the Epistles the relative positions are altered. The disciples have become teachers; but they do not stand by their Master's side at the centre. Christ alone is at the centre; the disciples are on the circumference of the circle and are gazing at Him. Their efforts are directed towards the Lord, whom they would persuade everybody to know (Ac 2^{38}, 1 Co 2^2). The Lamb is in the midst of the throne, and those who have been gathered into the Kingdom of God worship Him (Rev 5^6). The Apostles are seeking to obey their Lord's injunction to preach the gospel to every creature (Mk 16^{15}). But their interpretation of this command was to urge their hearers to believe on the Lord Jesus Christ (Ac 16^{31}).

This identification of 'the gospel' with Christ Himself may be accounted for partly by the experience of the Apostles. They went forth as witnesses (Lk 24^{48}), not as philosophers. They had to tell what great things God had done for their souls. They could do this only by talking of Jesus. For He had become to them the mediator of God's redeeming love (Mk 8^{29}, Jn 14^1). They could not be witnesses concerning repentance and remission of sins without filling their lips with the one 'name given among men wherein we must be saved' (Ac 4^{12}).

But another point must be considered. The Apostles were commanded to 'preach the gospel.' The instruction had a definite meaning because of their Master's use of the words. Jesus Christ preached the gospel of the fatherly love of God, establishing a Kingdom into which all men might be admitted, and He offered Himself as the authoritative proof of that love (cf. Mk 12^6 ǁ Jn 8^{42}). The presence in the world of the Son of man, the Messiah of prophecy, demonstrated God's love in providing for men's deepest needs. Now it is evident that the crucifixion of Jesus shook such a gospel to its foundations. If the life of the Messianic Son of man ended with the cross, His speech about God's fatherly love and a heavenly Kingdom seemed worse than idle talk. How could the gospel preached by Jesus survive His death? Only if He Himself survived His death. To rehabilitate

His gospel, His authority must be rehabilitated. This result was secured by the resurrection of Jesus and by His ascension. When they had seen Him 'alive after his passion,' His disciples were prepared to go and 'preach the gospel to every creature' (Ac 1^3).

But it is evident also that these events themselves had profound importance. They did more than rehabilitate the authority of Jesus: they brought His own significance for the gospel into clear relief. Such unique events set the personality of Jesus in the heart of the gospel, investing Him with peculiar importance (Ac 2$^{22-36}$ 3$^{13-26}$ 5^{31}, 1 Jn 1$^{1-3}$, Ro 1^4, 1 P 1$^{3-8}$). Although they could not realize at once all that was involved in such events, the Apostles were compelled to take a new attitude to Jesus, and to adopt a fresh theory of His person. He had been their Master : now He becomes 'the Lord.' The primitive Christian community used the term before it was able to construct an adequate Christology. But it 'called Jesus "the Lord" because He had sacrificed His life for it, and because its members were convinced that He had been raised from the dead and was then sitting on the right hand of God' (Harnack). The significance of Jesus was decided religiously, though not metaphysically, at once. From the first, Jesus Christ had the religious value of God. Men were exhorted to believe in Him (Ac 2^{38}). The final expression of the Apostolic meditation upon the person of the Lord was given by John (Jn 1$^{1-18}$). But in Apostolic thought the gospel could never be preached apart from Jesus Christ, nor could the significance of Jesus Christ be understood apart from the gospel. In Him God's redemptive purposes and the sinner's acceptance of them may meet. Thus He is the central figure in history (Col 1$^{15-19}$). He is at once the Saviour appointed by the Father (Ac 2$^{23ff.}$, Ro 1^3 3^{25}, Gal 4^4) and the Head of the redeemed race (1 Co 15$^{22-45}$, Gal 3^{26}, Eph 1^{22}).

But this conception of the person of Jesus gave a deeper meaning to the great events in His experience which had so affected His disciples. It may be said that the events and the person reacted upon one another. Such events glorified the person; the glorified person deepened the significance of the events. At the first the Crucifixion of Jesus was looked upon as the wicked act of the Jews, which God had frustrated and even turned to His own glory by raising Jesus from the dead (Ac 2$^{23.\ 24}$ 3$^{14.\ 15}$ 4^{10} 5^{30}). The Resurrection was accepted at once as a proof of Divine Sonship (l.c.). The Ascension not only sealed this proof of Jesus Christ's Messianic dignity, but also exalted Him to a place of sovereignty over the world (Ac 2^{33} 3$^{16.\ 21}$ 4^{12} 5^{31}). But further reflexion upon them invested these unique events with profounder significance. His Death is the means whereby all men may be forgiven and may be reconciled to God—a sacrifice for the sins of the world (Ro 3^{25}, 2 Co 5$^{20.\ 21}$, 1 P 1^{19}, 1 Jn 1^7 2^2). His Resurrection is the earnest of the new life into which all those are introduced who are born anew by faith in Him (Ro 6^4, 1 Jn 3$^{2.\ 3}$). He is the first-fruits of them that sleep : His Resurrection involves the resurrection to eternal life of all in whom He lives (1 Th 4^{13}–5^{10}, 1 Co 15). His Ascension is the pledge of the glorification of all who are united to Him (Ro 8$^{29.\ 30}$, Ph 3$^{20.\ 21}$).

This aspect of the gospel is reflected in the Apostolic preaching. The Apostles 'preached Christ' (1 Co 1^{23}). All the sermons in the early chapters of Acts are full of Christ. The Epistles identify the gospel with Him (Ro 1^{16}). In particular, the preaching dwelt upon His Crucifixion, His Resurrection, and His Ascension, though the same 'mind' was discerned in the whole story of the

Incarnation (Ph 2⁵). It should be remembered that all this reference to 'Christ and him crucified' as 'the gospel,' is shot through and through with Jesus Christ's own message of the love of God in establishing the kingdom. Although the gospel as it was presented by the Apostles assumed a new aspect, becoming a message about Christ who died and rose and ascended to the Father's right hand, this was not intended to divert attention from the fatherly love of God and the Kingdom into which He invited men. But it was only through this message about Christ that such a gospel could be offered authoritatively to the world. Moreover, the gospel was seen in its true glory only when viewed through the medium of Christ's Death and Resurrection and Ascension. Without the interpretation of these events, God's fatherly love was a vague dream, and the heavenly Kingdom was an impossible ideal (1 Jn 4⁹· ¹⁰, Eph 2¹²⁻¹⁸, 1 P 2⁴⁻¹⁰). Thus Wellhausen, *IJG³*, p. 386, declares that St. Paul's especial work was to transform the gospel of the Kingdom into the gospel of Jesus Christ, so that the gospel is no longer the prophecy of the coming of the Kingdom, but its actual fulfilment by Jesus Christ. In his view, accordingly, redemption from something in the future has become something which has already happened and is now present. He lays far more emphasis on faith than on hope ; he anticipates the sense of future bliss in the present feeling of being God's son ; he vanquishes death and already leads the new life on earth. The presence of Christ among men is unceasingly emphasized as the supreme proof of the love of the heavenly Father (Gal 1³⁻⁵ 4⁶· ⁷, 1 Co 1⁹, Ro 3²⁴ 11³³⁻³⁶, 1 Jn 4⁹, 1 P 1³ etc.). 'The kingdom' is mentioned frequently as the objective of Christian effort (Ac 8¹² 14²² 19⁸ 20²⁵ 28²³· ³¹, Ro 14¹⁷, 1 Co 4²⁰ 6⁹ 15²⁴· ⁵⁰, Gal 5²¹, Eph 5⁵, Col 1¹³ 4¹¹, 1 Th 2¹², 2 Th 1⁵, 2 Ti 4¹· ¹⁸, Heb 12²⁸, Ja 2⁵, 2 P 1¹¹, Rev 1⁹ 12¹⁰) ; and the ideas of Jesus about the Kingdom are woven into the texture of Apostolic preaching. But the primary interest of the Apostles was to preach the gospel of the Kingdom ; and that meant the proclamation of Jesus Christ as the Divinely appointed Saviour, through whom all men may share the privileges of sonship with God.

Finally, it may be pointed out that although the term 'gospel' already in Apostolic times was used in the broader sense with which we are familiar, yet the NT does distinguish the gospel, as a glad message of life and peace that everybody is urged to accept at once, from the ethical teaching that the converts must obey. The 'gospel' is news about God and the Kingdom, which is maintained as true against the older conceptions enshrined in Judaism. The writer to the Hebrews emphasizes the Christian gospel as the fulfilment of the types of the Old Covenant. St. Paul, who was dogged by Judaizers, fought to keep the Christian gospel free from the trammels of Judaic sacramentarianism. The NT writers preach the gospel as a message of transcendent importance and of great joy to all people. But they do not rest content with preaching the good news. St. Paul spoke of a 'wisdom of God' which could be taught only to the spiritual (1 Co 2). And most of the Epistles are attempts to explain that 'wisdom,' and to enforce obedience to it, on those who had already become Christians by accepting the gospel.

LITERATURE.—Hastings' *DB*, artt. 'Gospel,' 'Jesus Christ,' and on Gospels of Matthew, Mark, Luke, and John, and Epistles to Romans and Corinthians ; Commentaries on the Gospels by Godet, Swete, Gould, Plummer, Westcott, and in *Expositor's Gr. Test.* For exposition of Christ's teaching : Bruce, *Kingdom of God*, and *The Training of the Twelve* ; Wendt, *Teaching of Jesus* ; Beyschlag, *NT Theology* ; Denney, *Death of Christ* ; Dalman, *The Words of Jesus* ; Harnack, *What is Christianity ?* ; Mackintosh, *Essays Toward a New Theology* ; Réville, *Liberal Christianity* ; Watson, *The Mind of the Master*. For transition to Apostolic teaching : Harnack and Beyschlag, *opp. citt.* :
Weizsäcker, *The Apostolic Age* ; Bruce, *Paul's Conception of Christianity* ; Commentaries on Acts and Epistles. For general reference : Forrest, *The Christ of History and of Experience* ; Newman Smyth, *Christian Ethics* ; Briggs, *New Light on the Life of Jesus.*
                        J. EDWARD ROBERTS.

GOSPELS. — The canonical Gospels (including the Synoptic Problem) are fully discussed in separate articles, so that the scope of this article does not necessarily include more than the subjects indicated in the following outline :

1. Definition of the term 'Gospels.'
2. What brought Gospels, oral or written, into being.
3. Transition from oral to written Gospels.
4. Literary use of the term 'Gospel' in the Pauline Epistles.
5. Source of St. Paul's knowledge of the Gospel story.
6. Evidence of the existence of Gospels, oral or written, when St. Paul wrote.
7. A Gospel is not a *Life of Christ*.
8. NT use of the term 'Gospel' in the sense of a written document.
9. Principle which guided the Church in her selection of Gospel material.
10. Relation between the canonical Gospels and recent literary discoveries.
11. Discussion of the evidence from Papias as to an original Hebrew Gospel.
12. Other considerations bearing on an original Hebrew Gospel.
13. A possible theory of the Synoptic Gospels.

1. The word 'Gospels' in Christian terminology, and as employed in this article, signifies accounts of the earthly life of our Lord Jesus Christ, of His manifestation in the historical sphere, narratives of His words and works, it being unimportant whether such narratives were delivered by word of mouth or committed to writing.

The term εὐαγγέλια occurs for the first time, in extant Christian literature, in the well-known passage in Justin Martyr's *First Apology*, c. 66, where he refers to it as being the usual designation of the Memoirs of the Apostles, οἱ γὰρ ἀπόστολοι ἐν τοῖς γενομένοις ὑπ' αὐτῶν ἀπομνημονεύμασιν ἃ καλεῖται εὐαγγέλια, κ.τ.λ. Justin's language here certainly implies that, when he wrote, the term 'Gospels' was in common use in the Christian Church. The phrase τὰ ἀπομνημονεύματα τῶν ἀποστόλων (c. 67) is intended only as a description, intelligible to heathen readers, of the nature and authority of the εὐαγγέλια.

2. The first question that presents itself is, *What was it that called Gospels into being?* The answer is to be found in that characteristic of Christianity by which it is distinguished from all other religions, viz., that it concerns the relation of mankind to a Person, not the relation of mankind to a new system of morals or philosophy. Jesus Christ was, of course, a great—we would say the greatest—moral teacher of mankind ; yet the Christian consciousness has always felt that what Jesus was, and did, and suffered, has an importance and significance far transcending that which He taught. Christian ethics is derived from and dependent upon the Person of Jesus the Son of God manifested in time. If it be permissible to use in this connexion the metaphor in which the Nicene Creed endeavours to set forth the relation of the Second Person of the Trinity to the First, the ethical teaching of Christ is light generated from light. It is not that Jesus Christ is important and significant to the historian as the originator and promulgator of a singularly lofty code of morals, but rather that in the days of 'Cæsar Augustus, 'the eternal life which was with the Father was manifested unto us' (1 Jn 1²) ; and from that life so manifested certain new commandments of love resulted as a necessary consequence, and 'old commandments which we had from the beginning' (2⁷) awoke into new life, and put on a strength which they had not had before.

Nothing, perhaps, more clearly proves the truth of what has been just said as to the importance in the Christian system of the personal history of Jesus, than the fact that His human origin and His death are treated in the Gospel narrative as having a significance outweighing all else. In the case of all other great men, birth and death, which are universal and inevitable, have for the most part only a chronological importance. But in Apostolic references to the life of Jesus Christ His human ancestry is co-ordinated with His resurrection, *e.g.* Ro 1¹⁻⁴ 'the gospel of God . . . concerning his Son, who was born of the seed of David . . ., who was declared to be the Son of God . . . by the resurrection of the dead'; and 2 Ti 2⁸ 'Remember Jesus Christ, risen from the dead, of the seed of David, according to my gospel.' Acknowledgment of the Lordship of Jesus, and belief in the historical fact of His resurrection, are declared to have saving efficacy (Ro 10⁹). It is evident, therefore, that a narrative of the main facts in the history of Jesus must have been from the very first the foundation or framework of the preaching of those who propagated His religion. These preachers met inquirers for the way of salvation, not with a recitation of the Saviour's gracious words, but with 'truth embodied in a tale': 'Believe on the Lord Jesus and thou shalt be saved' (Ac 16³¹). A little consideration will make it clear that a proclaiming of the resurrection of One who had been slain entails of necessity an account of who and what manner of man He was, and why He was put to death.

From indications scattered through the Book of the Acts, we gather that an evangelic narrative described Jesus as fulfilling in His lineage, character, and actions the various foreshadowings of Messianic prophecy as hitherto accepted; while the fact that He had suffered, and died, and been raised the third day, was shown to reveal the Messianic character of passages of the OT which had not been hitherto clearly understood. The Resurrection, again, was declared to constitute an authentication by God Himself of the prediction of Jesus that He would come again to judge the living and the dead; and salvation from the terrors of the judgment to come was offered on the conditions of repentance, followed by baptism into the name of Jesus. This is the barest outline of the main features in the first Christian preaching: the accomplishment in Jesus of all that was hoped for in the Christ; His death and resurrection illuminating the dark places of prophecy, and proving the truth of His own claims; judgment; repentance; baptism.

It is scarcely necessary to add that these facts or requirements would be 'commended to every man's conscience' (2 Co 4²) by examples of the wisdom, sublimity, and beauty of the Saviour's moral and spiritual teaching. Of this we have an example in St. Paul's speech at Miletus (Ac 20³⁵). In this case the audience was composed of Christian elders; and it may be that a true instinct led the early preachers, in addressing the unconverted, to dwell on the Woes rather than on the Beatitudes. However this may be, the meagre sermon sketches contained in the Book of the Acts do not enable us to make a positive statement as to what the preachers said, beyond what is indicated in the outline given above.

3. We may say, then, that it was the needs of the Christian Church in her natural expansion that first called Gospels into existence. The language of St. Luke (1¹⁻²) confirms what we might have otherwise guessed as to the history of *the transition from oral to written narratives.* Those who had been privileged to be 'eye-witnesses and ministers of the word' 'delivered' (παρέδοσαν) to others what they deemed essential in what they had seen and heard in the course of their attendance on their Master, and 'many' of their hearers 'took in hand to draw up narratives' (ἀνατάξασθαι διήγησιν). It may be remarked in passing that St. Paul, who always claimed an authoritative knowledge of the capital events of the Evangelic history, uses the

word παραδιδόναι of his own communications to his converts (1 Co 11². ²³ 15³, 2 Th 2¹⁵ 3⁶).

It is impossible to say how early the necessity for written Gospels arose. The expansion of the Church beyond Judæa began possibly immediately after the Pentecostal outpouring of the Holy Spirit; it certainly was in operation after the martyrdom of Stephen (Ac 11¹⁹). The number of those who could be reckoned as 'eye-witnesses and ministers of the word' cannot have been very great. Even if we make the large assumption that every one of the 120 persons who were gathered together for the election of Matthias (Ac 1¹⁵), or of the 500 brethren to whom the Lord appeared (1 Co 15⁶), could be so described, and that they were all subsequently engaged in active evangelistic work, yet the labour of spreading the new faith, even within the limits of Palestine, would have soon outgrown their power to cope with it. As far as the original witnesses were concerned, their memory would enable them to tell all that was necessary of the Saviour's life, even as much as is contained in the longest of our present Gospels. Indeed, there can be no doubt that from constant, perhaps daily, repetition of some portion of the story, the recollection of the whole would soon assume a stereotyped form. But as the number of evangelists who had not 'known Christ after the flesh' multiplied in every direction, it would very soon become impossible for the original witnesses even to instruct all those who were to teach others. To meet this imperative and growing need — the instruction of preachers—was, we may well believe, one of the objects with which the narratives alluded to by St. Luke in his preface were first drawn up. It is natural to suppose that at first such narratives were used to refresh the memory of the evangelists; afterwards, when the first generation of believers had quite passed away, the written Gospels would be openly read, as being the most authentic account of what the original witnesses had seen and heard.

Dr. Salmon is of opinion that even before the Crucifixion some of our Lord's discourses, or portions of them, had been committed to writing. Without going so far as this, it is scarcely open to reasonable doubt that written Gospels of some sort were in circulation well within the period covered by the Acts of the Apostles. In order the better to see this, we shall examine the evidence supplied by the Epistles of St. Paul. His writings, from their extent and the comparative certainty with which they can be dated, afford the most satisfactory grounds on which to base a conclusion.

4. It is obvious that the question when the word εὐαγγέλιον was first used in the sense in which we use it when we speak of the 'Gospel according to St. Matthew,' is quite distinct from the question as to when such written narratives first appeared and received any degree of public recognition. The first step towards what may be called the literary use of the term εὐαγγέλιον is to be found in passages where the word is used, not of the 'good news' itself, but in the sense of someone's presentation of it.

1 Th 1⁵ 'Our gospel came not unto you in word only.'
2 Th 2¹⁴ 'God called you [unto salvation] through our gospel.'
Gal 1¹¹ 'The gospel which was preached by me . . . is not after man.'
Gal 2² 'I laid before them the gospel which I preach among the Gentiles.'
Ro 2¹⁶ 'God shall judge the secrets of men, according to my gospel, by Jesus Christ.'
1 Co 15¹ᶠ· 'I make known unto you . . . the gospel which I preached unto you . . . in what words I preached it unto you.'
2 Ti 2⁸ 'Remember Jesus Christ, risen from the dead, of the seed of David, according to my gospel.'

In these instances, certainly in most of them, the word 'gospel' means not so much St. Paul's manner or method of presenting the good news of salvation to his hearers, as the actual substance of what he said. It is true that the substance of what any preacher of the gospel would say would include more than a narrative without comment, such as is one of the Synoptic Gospels; yet St. Paul's gospel evidently did contain some merely historical matter. This point will come up for consideration later. Here it is sufficient to say that the above instances of St. Paul's use of the word 'gospel' as meaning the substance of his evangelic preaching, would naturally suggest the application of the term to a narrative embodying all that it was necessary to know of the life of Jesus Christ as a means of salvation. So much was, no doubt, claimed by their compilers for the short narratives which St. Luke's Gospel was intended to supersede; much more may it be claimed for any one of the four Gospels which have come down to us.

5. An interesting question now arises, *What was the content of the Gospel presented by St. Paul to the Churches which he evangelized? and what was its relation to our existing Gospels, or any of them?* It ought to be unnecessary to remark that in an examination of the Pauline Epistles for the purpose of this question, any inference drawn from silence is peculiarly precarious. It is as unreasonable to expect to find Gospel material in St. Paul's letters as it would be to find it in the letters of a pastor or bishop of our own day. Paradoxical as it may at first seem, it is probably none the less true that the Churches to which St. Paul wrote had a more intimate and living acquaintance with the facts of the Gospel history than is usual with Christians in our own day. Every member of those Churches had been recently converted from either heathenism or Judaism. Consequently the interest they felt in their newly-acquired faith was fresh and absorbing; and the Apostle writes as though the main facts of the Gospel history were familiar to his readers. He is able to appeal in the most natural way to their knowledge of the character of Jesus, *e.g.* Ro 15³ 'Christ pleased not himself'; 2 Co 8⁹ 'Though he was rich, yet for your sakes he became poor'; and 2 Co 10¹ 'I . . . intreat you by the meekness (διὰ τῆς πραΰτητος) and gentleness of Christ.' It would doubtless be impossible to prove that St. Paul had in mind recorded sentiments of Christ similar to, or identical with, 'The Son of Man came not to be ministered unto, but to minister' (Mt 20²⁸); 'The Son of Man hath not where to lay his head' (Mt 8²⁰, Lk 9⁵⁸); 'I am meek (πραΰς) and lowly in heart' (Mt 11²⁹). But it may be safely affirmed that there was in those to whom St. Paul wrote a knowledge of deeds and words of Christ that made the Apostle's appeal intelligible.

What then was the source of St. Paul's knowledge of the Gospel narrative? To many, perhaps most, Christians this question may appear superfluous, in view of the Apostle's own explicit statements: Gal 1¹¹ 'The gospel which was preached by me . . . came to me through revelation of Jesus Christ,' and 1 Co 11²³ 'I received of the Lord that which also I delivered unto you.' Even if we grant, what is likely enough, that the passage from Galatians refers to St. Paul's favourite doctrines, yet his language to the Corinthians seems to imply that his knowledge of an objective historical circumstance came to him in a miraculous manner. The present writer has no desire to minimize the miraculous element in the NT narrative, or to call in question the reality of St. Paul's visions; but in this case an explanation can be given of the expression 'I received of the Lord' which will both satisfy the requirements of St. Paul's language and also take the matter out of the region of subjective visions, and so render the statement historically intelligible and verifi-

able. The question is, What would one of St. Paul's contemporary fellow-Christians have understood by 'I received of the Lord'? The answer is supplied by parallel phrases in the Book of the Acts, and by what we learn from that book and other sources as to the ministry of prophets in the Apostolic Church. When we read (Ac 13²), 'The Holy Ghost said, Separate me Barnabas and Saul,' etc., and again, (16⁷) 'The Spirit of Jesus suffered them not,' it is natural to ask, How did the Holy Ghost speak? and how did the Spirit of Jesus control the movements of St. Paul and his company? It was through the utterance of an accredited prophet, or number of prophets, in either case. This is placed beyond doubt by an instance given later (21¹¹), where a prophet, Agabus, begins his prediction with, 'Thus saith the Holy Ghost' (cf. 20²³ 'The Holy Ghost testifieth unto me in every city'). We see, then, that Ac 13² means that the separation of Paul and Barnabas was in consequence of an utterance of the prophets, or one of them, who are mentioned in the previous verse; while in 16⁷ it was an utterance of Silas (see 15³²), if not of Paul himself (see Ac 13¹, 1 Co 14³⁷), that forbade the missionaries to cross the frontier of Bithynia.

We are now enabled to understand 'I received of the Lord' (1 Co 11²³) in the same sense as we interpret 'The Spirit of Jesus suffered them not.' St. Paul did not really mean that his knowledge of the Gospel history had been acquired without human intervention, nor can he have intended his readers so to understand him. What he meant to convey was that he was convinced that the evangelist, or the source whence he derived his information, was indeed inspired by the Spirit of Jesus.

The alternative—evangelist, or source—has been purposely suggested, in order to leave it an open question, as, indeed, with our scanty information it must remain, whether St. Paul derived his knowledge of our Lord's life from oral teaching or from a written document. At the time of his conversion there was a Christian community of some importance at Damascus; and it is probable in the highest degree that the Church there had the advantage of hearing the story of Jesus from one of those who had companied with Him during His ministry. On the other hand, St. Paul's own statement (Gal 1¹⁶.¹⁷), 'I conferred not with flesh and blood . . . I went away into Arabia,' suggests a retirement for solitary study, meditation, and prayer. There does not seem any extreme improbability in supposing that even at that early date there was in circulation a Gospel narrative in Aramaic, or even in Greek. In any case, it is unreasonable to question that Saul the persecutor needed some instruction or study before he could 'proclaim Jesus, that he is the Son of God.'

It cannot be denied, however, that the language of the heavenly vision (Ac 26¹⁴), 'It is hard for thee to kick against the goad,' points most naturally to a long previous struggle between prejudices inborn and trained and the strange attractiveness of Jesus of Nazareth, whose glorious deeds and gracious words may have become known to the young Pharisee when he first arrived in Jerusalem from Tarsus. For him the gospel was a thing to which he could not be indifferent. It was either that he had learnt from man urged him to 'crush it, like a vice of blood, upon the threshold of the mind' (*In Memoriam*, iii.); the preventing grace of God bade him 'embrace it as his natural good.'

All that we can certainly state with regard to the Gospel story known to St. Paul, however he acquired his knowledge, is that his allusions to it, direct and indirect, 'proceed,' to use Paley's phrase (*Evidences*, i. 7), 'upon the general story which our Scriptures contain'; while it certainly was not identical with any of the four we now possess. This latter point is proved by the enumeration in 1 Co 15 of the appearances of the risen Lord. Of the five appearances there mentioned, two, namely that to James and that to 500 brethren, are not mentioned in the canonical Gospels. It is to be noted, as possibly significant, that the appearance to James was recorded in the Gospel according to the Hebrews (Jerome, *de Vir. illustr.* c. 2).

6. It would be irrelevant to the purposes of this article to call attention to any correspondences between the Pauline Epistles and our present Gospels other than those that are historical or literary. It would lead us too far afield to discuss St. Paul's Christology, and to inquire how far it was based on extant recorded statements of Jesus about Himself, how far on OT and subsequent Messianic conceptions, and how far on what we may for convenience call the Johannine theology, which, as distinct from its Johannine expression, seems to have existed in the Church from the beginning.

The faithfulness of God to His promise that the Christ should be not only of the seed of Abraham, but also of the lineage of David, is as markedly emphasized by St. Paul as it is in the Gospels : Ro 15[8] 'Christ hath been made a minister of the circumcision for the truth of God, that he might confirm the promises given unto the fathers'; words which echo those of Zacharias (Lk 1[72. 73]) ; Ro 1[3] 'Born of the seed of David according to the flesh' ; 2 Ti 2[8] 'Of the seed of David, according to my gospel.'

There is no explicit reference to the Virgin-birth in the Pauline Epistles. The expressions 'born of a woman' (Gal 4[4]) and 'the childbearing' (1 Ti 2[15]) refer, the former probably, the latter possibly, to 'the seed of the woman' (Gn 3[15]).

The account of the institution of the Lord's Supper, which St. Paul 'received of the Lord' (1 Co 11[23-25]), alludes to the betrayal of the Lord Jesus, and otherwise approximates most closely to that given by St. Luke, who possibly in a second edition of his Gospel revised his account in accordance with information received from St. Paul. In the previous chapter (1 Co 10[16]) and in 14[16] we have allusions to the words of institution which have always been used in the blessing of the bread and wine.

St. Paul's references to the death of Christ are for the most part doctrinal, not historical. He insists on its voluntary character : 'He gave himself for our sins' (Gal 1[4], cf. 2[20], Eph 5[2. 25], Tit 2[14]). The words of Jesus, extant only in Mt 20[28] 'The Son of man came . . . to give his life a ransom for many,' seem to underlie these passages, as well as those in which the death of Jesus is spoken of as an atonement or ransom (Gal 3[13], Ro 3[25], 1 Co 15[3], 1 Ti 2[6], Tit 2[14]). Of course the sacrificial aspect of Christ's death is also strongly emphasized in His own words when instituting the Supper.

It cannot perhaps be certainly affirmed that Col 3[13] 'Even as the Lord forgave you, so also do ye' (cf. Eph 4[32]), was suggested by the sentiment of 'Father, forgive them' (Lk 23[34]), for the verb is different, Lk. having ἀφίημι, Col. and Eph. χαρίζομαι. Nor can we base any argument on the statement in 1 Th 2[15], that 'the Jews killed the Lord Jesus' (see Ac 3[15]). There remains one definite historical allusion, 1 Ti 6[13] 'Christ Jesus, who before Pontius Pilate witnessed the good confession.' Our Lord's answer, 'Thou sayest' [i.e. 'yes'], to Pilate's question, 'Art thou the king of the Jews?' which is the only confession before Pontius Pilate reported in the Synoptic Gospels, hardly satisfies, important though it is, the requirements of St. Paul's solemn adjuration.

The proclamation by Jesus before Pilate of the nature of His Kingdom, and that He had come for the sole purpose of bearing witness unto the truth, which is recorded in the Fourth Gospel, is indeed a 'good confession'; and we must remember that although St. John did not commit his Gospel to writing until long after the death of St. Paul, yet, unless we are prepared to assert that it is a work of fiction, it seems unreasonable to question that the circumstances recorded in it, or some of them, were known to St. Paul. The omission in the Synoptic Gospels of the substance of 'the good confession' of which we are speaking is not more remarkable than their silence as to the appearances of the risen Lord to James and to '500 brethren at once.'

Passing on now to allusions by St. Paul to the moral and spiritual teaching of Jesus, there are only two explicit references to sayings found in our present Gospels. These are : (1) 1 Co 7[10] 'But unto the married I give charge, yea not I, but the Lord, That the wife depart not from her husband (but and if she depart, let her remain unmarried, or else be reconciled to her husband); and that the husband leave not his wife.' Our Lord's general prohibition of divorce is found in all three Synoptics ; but the prohibition of divorce of her husband by a wife, of which, or its equivalent, St. Paul here chiefly speaks, is found only in Mk 10[12]. It is conceivable that the prohibition was omitted by Mt. and Lk. either as unnecessary, such divorce being almost unheard of, or as implied in our Lord's declaration that marriage, generally speaking, is indissoluble. (2) 1 Co 9[14] 'The Lord ordained that they which proclaim the gospel should live of the gospel.' The reference is to 'The labourer is worthy of his food' (Mt 10[10]), or, more probably, to the form preserved by St. Luke (10[7]), in which 'hire' is substituted for 'food.' That the reference is to the latter form is almost certain from the fact that the saying is given in 1 Ti 5[18] exactly as in Lk 10[7]. The natural sense of 1 Ti 5[18] is that the saying in question was already 'Scripture,' in the same sense as was the quotation from Dt. with which it is coupled. This view does not involve the assumption that St. Luke's Gospel was then not only in circulation but also received as authoritative by the Church; it merely affirms that the saying was contained in some authoritative narrative of the life of Jesus, or some collection of His sayings.

The passages which speak of Christ as Judge at the Last Day

(Ro 2[16], 1 Co 4[5], 2 Co 5[10]), accompanied by angels (1 Th 4[16], 2 Th 1[7]), and executing His will with fire (1 Co 3[13. 15], 2 Th 1[8]); and that which states, as matter of common knowledge, that 'the saints shall judge the world' (1 Co 6[2]), can none of them be necessarily referred to the words and parables of Christ in the Gospels, which affirm the same things, inasmuch as these eschatological conceptions were part of the current Messianic ideas, and may all of them be derived from Dn 7. There are, however, two details which cannot be referred to that source : (1) that the coming of Christ to judge would be heralded by the sound of a trumpet (1 Th 4[16], 1 Co 15[52]), and (2) that it would be sudden and unlooked for (1 Th 5[2]). The wording of this latter passage is remarkable : 'Yourselves know perfectly that the day of the Lord so cometh as a thief in the night.' The only place in our present Gospels where the judgment trumpet is mentioned is Mt 24[31], and in v. 43 of the same chapter we have the illustration of the thief's unexpected and unsuspected attack.

There are, in conclusion, a number of passages in which it is difficult not to see references to recorded sayings of Christ.

Ro 13[7] 'Render (ἀπόδοτε) to all their dues,' etc. See Mt 22[21], Mk 12[17], Lk 20[25] 'Render unto Cæsar,' etc. (ἀπόδοτε).

Gal 5[14], Ro 13[9] 'Thou shalt love thy neighbour as thyself,' quoted as a summary of the second table of the Law. See Mt 22[40].

Ro 14[14] 'I know, and am persuaded in the Lord Jesus, that nothing is unclean of itself,' based on our Lord's teaching in Mt 15[11], more distinctly brought out in Mk 7[15. 19].

Ro 16[19] 'I would have you wise (σοφούς) unto that which is good, and simple (ἀκεραίους) unto that which is evil.' See Mt 10[16] 'Be ye therefore wise (φρόνιμοι) as serpents, and harmless (ἀκέραιοι) as doves.'

1 Co 6[7]. When deprecating litigiousness, 'Why not rather take wrong, be defrauded?' See Mt 5[39. 40], Lk 6[29. 30].

1 Co 7[1] 'It is good for a man not to touch a woman.' This private opinion, or preferred sentiment, of St. Paul's, is in agreement with that remarkable saying preserved only by St. Matthew (19[12]), 'There are eunuchs, which made themselves eunuchs for the kingdom of heaven's sake. He that is able to receive it, let him receive it.' The caution with which our Lord prefaces this saying, 'All men cannot receive this saying, but they to whom it is given,' finds also an echo in St. Paul's conclusion : 'Howbeit each man hath his own gift from God,' etc.

1 Co 9[17] 'I have a stewardship intrusted to me.' See Lk 12[42] 'Who then is the faithful and wise steward?' etc.

1 Co 13[2] 'If I have all faith, so as to remove mountains.' See Mt 17[20] 21[21] = Mk 11[23].

Col 1[23] 'The gospel . . . which was preached in all creation' (ἐν πάσῃ κτίσει). See Mk 16[15] 'Preach the gospel to the whole creation' (πάσῃ τῇ κτίσει).

The meagreness of historical material contained in these references to Jesus, His acts and sayings, which are to be found in the Epistles of St. Paul, will cease to surprise us when we compare them with the baldness of the Creeds of the Church, even of the Constantinopolitan.

7. The truth is that we have been hitherto misled by the 'Lives of Christ' which have from time to time appeared. The assumption that underlies an attempt to write the *Life* of any one is that it is possible to give an account not only of his birth and death, but to arrange in some orderly chronological sequence the movements of his life, using the term 'movement' in its most comprehensive signification. This it is well nigh impossible to do in the case of our Lord's earthly ministry. Between the age of twelve years and His death the only events which really mark intervals are, His baptism by John, the Temptation, and the Transfiguration. It is true that the Fourth Gospel notes the Passovers which took place during our Lord's ministry; but it cannot be said that any of the attempts to arrange the circumstances and discourses recorded in the Synoptics so as to fit in with St. John's notes of time have been such as to compel belief. Moreover, although conclusions based on internal evidence must always be more or less precarious, yet there are instances of sayings of Jesus which have an early place in the Synoptic record, but which from their tone it is difficult to assign to an early stage of our Lord's ministry.

A Gospel, in fact, is not a biography. What are of saving efficacy in the events of our Lord's life are His birth, death, and resurrection. The fact that 'He went about doing good, and healing all that were oppressed of the devil' (Ac 10[38]), and that His example and His moral and spiritual discourses threw a new light on the relations of men to God and to one another, this too is of great importance; but there is not any practical significance whatever in the order in which this or that miracle was performed, or this or that discourse spoken. It is not likely that the Apostolic preachers dwelt more on the historical sequence of the works and words of Jesus than do those in modern times ; and in consequence, speaking generally, such sequence would be disregarded, even by original witnesses. The events of any one memorable day might be remembered and repeated exactly in the order in which they had occurred ; and thus we have, no doubt, in Mk 1 an account of the incidents that were indelibly impressed on Peter's mind in connexion with the day on which he finally left all and followed Jesus.

8. We are now ready to discuss the question, *Is there any instance in the NT of the term 'Gospel' applied to a written document?* There are perhaps two such cases.

Before citing them, it may be well to premise, (1) that they were written at a time when there must have been written accounts of some sort of our Lord's works and words, and when the term 'Gospel' was unquestionably applied to oral narratives of the life of Jesus ; and also (2) that in Ignatius (*Phil.* 5) 'the Gospel' is quite naturally applied to the Evangelic story, and, being co-ordinated with 'the Apostles' and 'the Prophets,' implies that the story was written.

The passages are: Mk 1[1] 'The beginning of the gospel of Jesus Christ, the Son of God'; and Rev 14[6] 'I saw another angel flying in mid heaven, having an eternal gospel to proclaim unto them that dwell on the earth.' However visions are to be explained, they are essentially pictures, seen by the eye before they are interpreted by the mind. This picture of the angel 'having an eternal gospel' plausibly suggests a figure with a scroll or roll in his hand.

The opening clause of St. Mark's Gospel has indeed been explained as parallel to Ph 4[15], where *'the beginning of the gospel* is relative to the person apprehending it' (Grimm-Thayer), as though it referred to the preaching of John the Baptist. This interpretation seems to the present writer far-fetched. It is surely more natural to take it as the title of the book, and, as Dr. Salmon thinks, modelled on Hos 1[2] Ἀρχὴ λόγου Κυρίου ἐν Ὡσῆε. It is not easy to give reasons why a considerable interval should elapse between the application of the term 'Gospel' to an oral narrative, and to the same narrative when committed to writing. It may be fairly asked, How would the writer of the Second Gospel have been likely to describe his work? It is not probable that St. Mark's Gospel, as we have it, was actually the first narrative drawn up. Nor can it be fairly said that the language of St. Luke, in his preface, proves that he was unacquainted with the term 'Gospel' in the sense of a document. The use of a Christian technical term would have seemed to St. Luke out of place in a section in which he was carefully using what he deemed his best literary style.

9. What has been said in explanation of St. Paul's statement that his knowledge of Gospel facts had been received from the Lord, *i.e.* from a man inspired by the Lord, a prophet-evangelist, suggests the answer to the question, *How did the Church recognize the inspiration of the narratives which she finally, and at a very early date, acquiesced in as authoritative Gospels?* It was through the double and almost simultaneous action of the original Evangelist or Evangelists, and the judgment of the Church on the sections of the Gospel story delivered on successive Lord's Days, both directed and suggested and controlled by the Holy Spirit, the Spirit of Jesus.

It is the intention of the writer of the present article to deal with this subject from the standpoint of the Christian Church to a greater degree than is usual now among critical writers. The

indignant remonstrance of St. Paul to the individualistic Corinthians has a certain relevance to some modern exponents of early Christian literature: 'What? was it from you that the word of God went forth? or came it unto you alone?' (1 Co 14[36]). One sometimes hears or reads discussions on Christian literature which indicate that for the speaker or writer the Christian Church has no existence. The collection of writings which we call the NT is treated as though it were a fortuitous collection, the selection of which was determined arbitrarily, or at least on principles which have now no claim to respect ; as though Christianity were merely a matter of literary or antiquarian interest, so that some new discovery might change our whole conception of Christ's work and words, or alter the value of the Gospels already received. Now the existence of the Christian Church during the first centuries of our era is a fact ; a fact the recognition of which has no connexion with any special views we may hold as to what ought to be the constitution or organization of the Church in our own times. It is surely unphilosophical to ignore a fact which was admittedly one of transcendent importance to the first Christians. The Gospels, as we have them now, are a product of the Church of Apostolic and sub-Apostolic times. It is, to say the least, conceivable that some principle determined the Church in her final selection of Gospels ; and any suggestion as to what that principle was cannot be without interest, even if it fails to compel assent.

It may be proper to remark, by way of caution, that an inquiry into the principle or principles by which the Church was guided in her selection of authoritative Gospels is not precluded by any theory of inspiration. Even if we hold that the sacred books only are inspired, and that the Church was not inspired, or guided by the Holy Spirit, in her choice of them, the question must arise, How did the Church recognize the inspiration of the books?

'As the Father hath sent me, even so send I you' (Jn 20[21]). These words of the risen Lord express the idea that the Church is the representative of Christ on earth, and that, as 'in him dwelleth all the fulness of the Godhead bodily' (Col 2[9]), so is the Church His body, a body not only quickened by His life, but indwelt by His mind: 'We have the mind of Christ' (1 Co 2[16]). In the context immediately preceding this quotation, St. Paul claims for those who have this mind the possession of a special critical sense, a faculty of discernment in spiritual matters ; and other passages exhibit the practical operation of this critical sense, as it may be termed, *e.g.* 1 Co 14[29] 'Let the prophets speak by two or three, and let the others discern,' and v.[37] 'If any man thinketh himself to be a prophet, or spiritual, let him take knowledge of the things which I write unto you, that they are the commandments of the Lord.' This special sense was formed by those who had been 'from the beginning eye-witnesses and ministers of the word.' Their reports of what their Master had done and said, the conditions in which He worked, the tone and temper of His utterances, formed a standard by which it was possible to decide the claims to genuineness of stories told about Him. There is really nothing fanciful in this : it only supposes the Apostolic Church, or at least the leading members of it, to have had the same sort of sense of discernment which is undoubtedly possessed by good critics in other departments of literature. The very best attempts to imitate the style of a great poet or prose writer ring false in the ear of one who knows.

But not only did the Church, thinking through the accredited teachers 'who had the spirit,' or if it be preferred, the sanctified 'common sense of most,' determine which were the Gospels inspired by God; but also their form—at least so far as the Synoptics are concerned—was in all probability determined by the use made of them in the weekly Church assemblies. This use must have obtained from the very earliest times at which meetings were held for distinctively Christian worship. We cannot otherwise account for the familiarity on the part of his readers with the general tenor of the Evangelic story which is assumed by St. Paul in his Epistles.

In Justin Martyr's time (*Apol.* i. 67) the established custom was that two lessons were read, one from the Prophets, another from the Gospels. We cannot press Justin's language too closely, so as to exclude from public reading the non-Prophetical parts of the OT, or the Apostolic Epistles. We must remember that his intention was to give heathens a general idea as to the nature of the Christian worship; he was not composing rubrical directions for the clergy. It is more likely than not that more use was made of the Prophetical books than of any other portion of the OT: and in any case, it is to them that Justin most constantly refers his Gentile readers. That the Apostolic Epistles were also read in the Christian assemblies we know from other sources; but it is not likely that a Lord's Day ever passed without a recitation of some portion of the narratives of the works and words of Jesus.

When we examine the canonical Gospels with this consideration in our mind, we are struck by the fact that it is easy to imagine that the first three were compiled from sections read with a view to practical instruction, and that it is not so easy to think of the Fourth Gospel as having had this origin. The stories and discourses in the Synoptics have the effect of pictures reproduced in the words of the original witness, while the impression was still fresh in his memory, and before he had time to place them in any systematized doctrinal setting. St. John's Gospel, on the other hand, has the air of being an attempt to write a history, a spiritual history if you will, still a history, an orderly statement of words and deeds meditated on in the study, and recorded as they emerged from the writer's inner consciousness after the lapse of many years. To say this is not to undervalue the historical truth, much less the inspiration, of the Fourth Gospel. The difference between it and the Synoptics is similar to that between a diarist and a historian: a diary chronicles facts, a history interprets them.

It is possible that St. John's Gospel was known as a history for private reading only, for some considerable time before it was read in the congregation. This supposition would partly explain why so few of Justin's quotations of Christ's words are taken from it, although we have sufficient proof of his acquaintance with it. Even in our own day it is doubtful whether any judicious apologist for Christianity, in citing examples of our Lord's discourses to a non-Christian public, would make much use of the Fourth Gospel, though he might regard it as of inestimable value in his own devotional reading. He would feel instinctively that its wisdom is for those whom St. Paul calls 'the perfect,' or 'full grown,' not for 'babes' in Christ, much less for 'them that are without.' Moreover, apart from this difference in quality between St. John's Gospel and the Synoptics, the difference in literary style must have, even from the first, delayed its adoption in general public use. Those who think, as they read or listen, soon become aware that its simplicity of vocabulary and grammatical structure conceal great subtlety of thought: we are out of our depth after the first step.

10. A word is necessary as to *the relation between the canonical Gospels and the fragments of early Gospel material* which have already repaid the patient toil of scholarly excavation in Egypt. In 1892 a fragment of the lost *Gospel of Peter*, discovered at Akhmîm in 1886–7, was published by U. Bouriant; and in 1897, Messrs. Grenfell and Hunt published a papyrus containing eight *Sayings of Jesus* in a more or less fragmentary condition; and another fragment of five *Sayings* has since appeared. We are not at all concerned here with the so-called Gospel of Peter. It is confessedly the production of a sect of Docetæ not earlier than the latter half of the 2nd century. It

is undoubtedly interesting and valuable, as illustrating the beliefs of Gnostics; but it has no claim whatever to be an original source of information. It is instructive as a harmonistic narrative based chiefly on the canonical Gospels.

To the student of the Gospels, the recovery of the lost Gospel of Peter, or of a portion of it, has the same kind, but not the same degree, of interest as the recovery of a lost work by Justin Martyr would have: it serves as an illustration of the way in which the canonical Gospels were employed in the 2nd century. But the case is different with the newly discovered *Sayings of Jesus*. These seem to claim to be Gospel material. The question is, Are they *bona fide* Gospel material which has been practically rejected by the responsible thinkers of the Church, or are they only pseudo-Gospel material?

We have seen that a complete 'Gospel' must have contained a narrative of those facts of our Lord's life which have a redemptive significance; but besides Gospels, it is very probable, indeed almost certain, that there were current in Apostolic times sayings of our Lord, without any note of the occasion when they were spoken. We have one such saying in Ac 20^{35}, and in the extant Gospels there are many passages which it is difficult to believe are not based on collections of Sayings. An almost certain case is Lk 16^{14-18}, where we have a group of four Sayings, none of which has any connexion with the others, or with the parable that follows.

This example proves that the disconnected nature of the Sayings in the recently discovered papyri affords no presumption against their being genuine Gospel material. Moreover, the record by St. Luke of St. Paul's quotation (Ac 20^{35}) of a saying of Jesus which is not found in any canonical Gospel, proves that while St. Luke was no doubt desirous to make his Gospel as full as possible, he was yet aware that there were accessible to him sayings besides those of which he made use. So that we cannot reject the papyri Sayings on the ground that the canonical Gospels must necessarily contain all the sayings of Jesus that were known in Apostolic times.

On the other hand, on the principles we have adopted, we must decide that St. Luke, in his selection of sayings and discourses, was guided by the Spirit of Jesus; and it may be remarked that the fact that he did *select* is a presumptive proof that he wrote at a time sufficiently early for it to be possible for a Christian to consider any authenticated saying of Jesus to be not worth preserving. Contrast the eager anxiety of Papias to gather up every crumb from the recollections of early disciples. At best, the papyri Sayings belong to the same class as the interpolations in Codex D, that is to say, they are rejected Gospel material, rejected because the mind of the Church in the 1st cent. thought it to be unsuitable for preservation. The present conclusion to St. Mark's Gospel, on the other hand, and the *Pericope adulteræ*, are instances of floating Gospel material which have been stamped with the approval of the mind of the Church.

It may happen, however, that further discoveries and mature consideration will suggest that these papyri Sayings have only a relative value and significance, as being fragments of the very extensive religious literature of the 2nd century. If more of this literature had survived to our own day, we should be able to view them in a juster proportion. We know that, even in the lifetime of the Apostles, Christianity had developed so rapidly that there was an exuberant growth of 'divers and strange teachings' (He 13^9). Each of these sects, or schools of thought and speculation, must have had both its authorized expositions and its literary propaganda. We are apt to forget that the business of book production in the first centuries of the Christian era was enormous in volume.

We know from the lists given by Eusebius, and allusions in other authors, that our extant ante-Nicene Fathers represent a very small fraction of the literature of the Church before his time. We may judge from this fact how unlikely it would be that much of the writings of heretics would survive. Such literature did not belong to a body with a continuous organized life, as is the Christian Church, a life continuous in doctrine as well as by personal links. The doctrine of the Christian Church, being a living thing, grows and develops from one generation to another; but the new always has to reconcile itself with the old; they are connected. And so even uninspired Christian writings would continue to be preserved and respected long after they had ceased to be generally read. Whereas heresy, as it was called, is essentially transitory; its literature, even when not merely the expression of the thoughts of an individual, reflects the conception of only one generation. Those who inherit it have no reason for retaining interest in it after it has ceased to represent precisely their thoughts. On the whole, it seems to the present writer that these papyri Sayings of Jesus must be regarded as not an expression of the main line of Church thought of any century. They are, of course, profoundly interesting, as casting light on the religious conceptions of some, we cannot tell how many, in the 2nd cent., but they do not exhibit the general mind of the Church.

11. In any discussion as to *the language in which the first Gospel narrative was composed*, it is impossible to leave out of account the evidence preserved in the fragments of Papias that are cited in Eusebius, *HE* iii. 39.

It is not intended here to give a résumé of the controversy that has raged over these few lines; but merely to state what seems to the present writer their most probable sense and value. The title of Papias' book was Λογίων Κυριακῶν Ἐξήγησις. Besides Eusebius, Irenæus seems to be the only writer, of those whose works have come down to us, who exhibits a first-hand acquaintance with the book of Papias. The other writers who allude to him evidently knew no more about him than what they found in Eusebius or Irenæus. The nature of the work may be guessed from what Papias himself states in one of the fragments: ' I shall not hesitate also to put down for you, along with my interpretations, whatsoever things I have at any time learned carefully from the elders.' The book, then, had a twofold character: *interpretations*, and also *oral traditions*. It is these latter to which Eusebius refers when he says that the book contained ' certain strange parables and teachings of the Saviour, and some other more mythical things'; and from the fact that Eusebius quotes from Papias two statements concerning the Gospels of Matthew and Mark respectively, it is at least probable that the *interpretations* dealt with our Gospels. Eusebius does not conceal his contempt for Papias' literary capacity: ' He appears to have been of very limited understanding (σφόδρα σμικρὸς τὸν νοῦν), as one can see from his discourses.' This adverse verdict is certainly borne out by the puerile extracts preserved by Irenæus; and it does not seem reasonable to attribute Eusebius' hostile criticism to his want of sympathy with Papias' millenarian opinions. Eusebius speaks in unqualified praise of Irenæus, who shared those opinions.

We may now discuss the term λόγια κυριακά, as it occurs in the title of Papias' book. The word

λόγια may certainly be rendered ' oracular utterances,' as Professor Stanton points out (*The Gospels as Historical Documents*, p. 53); but λόγια κυριακά is not naturally rendered ' oracular utterances of the Lord,' in the sense uttered by the Lord,—which would be λόγια Κυρίου,—but oracular utterances relating to the Lord, just as κυριακὸν δεῖπνον does not mean the supper eaten by, or given by, the Lord, but the supper ordained as an institution by Him. κυριακός has the same force in the phrase ἡ κυριακὴ ἡμέρα.

As regards λόγια, it would, of course, be absurd to question the possibility that Papias was familiar with the word in the sense ' oracular utterances'; but it is more likely that his use of λόγια was intentionally analogous to that found in the NT (Ac 7³⁸, Ro 3², He 5¹², 1 P 4¹¹), where the term, variously qualified, is used of the Scriptures of the OT. λόγια κυριακά, then, would mean Holy Scriptures connected with the Lord, *i.e.* the Gospels. This meaning harmonizes with what we have otherwise inferred as to the nature of the book written by Papias. It dealt primarily with interpretations of the Gospels, and secondarily with oral traditions, of which he was evidently a very uncritical collector.

Papias distinctly tells us, as Eusebius points out, that among his informants were persons old enough to have had personal intercourse with the Apostles. He distinguishes two classes of authorities: (1) Persons who could tell him what Andrew, Peter, etc., *said* (εἶπεν), ' and (2) what Aristion and the presbyter John, the disciples of the Lord, *say* ' (λέγουσιν). Eusebius, who had read the book, states that the language of Papias implies that he was himself a hearer of Aristion and the presbyter John. We are certainly entitled to infer that they were his elder contemporaries; very much elder, if they really were ' disciples of the Lord' in the strict sense of the phrase. See, further, art. ARISTION.

' The order of the list' of elders given by Papias is, as Professor Stanton remarks (*op. cit.* p. 168), ' a somewhat strange one.' He gives the true explanation as to why John and Matthew are mentioned last, *i.e.* ' For the very reason that they had embodied their testimony in writing, they were less important than the rest for the particular purpose of which he is speaking here—the illustration of the written " oracles" by matter orally handed down.' It may be added that the omission in this list of Mark and Luke was most probably due to the consideration that these Evangelists could not be supposed to be able, from personal knowledge, to add anything to what they had embodied in their Gospels. One cannot help noting that the other names, ' Andrew, Peter, Philip, Thomas, James,' are those of the Apostles who are introduced in the Gospels as making observations, and that the first three names occur in that order in the first chapter of St. John's Gospel. We do not know which James Papias meant. Moreover, while Eusebius expressly states that Papias ' mentions Aristion and the presbyter John frequently by name, and gives their traditions in his writings,' he does not quote from Papias any tradition whatever based on the authority of an Apostle. We are forced to the conclusion that in point of fact Papias had none to record; and that when ' he questioned those who had been followers of the elders in regard to their words,' he learnt nothing of permanent interest. It is impossible to imagine that if Eusebius had found in the book of Papias any statement whatever as from an Apostle, he would not have preserved it in his *History*.

Of the two celebrated remarks cited from Papias about the Gospels of Mark and Matthew respectively, the first is given expressly as the statement of the presbyter John, and it is natural to suppose that the second came from the same source. Papias was credulous and unintelligent; but he does not seem to have made any statement on his own authority; so that it would be unreasonable to discount the statements of the presbyter John because of the stupidity of the person who recorded them. On the other hand, it is unreasonable to assume that the nearness of the presbyter John to the times of the Apostles is a guarantee that his assertions as to the composition of the

Gospels are altogether to be depended on. We need have no hesitation in rejecting any, or all, of them, if more convincing arguments oblige us to do so ; but the demonstrated falsity of one statement would not of necessity throw discredit on the others.

Thus, that Mark was 'the interpreter of Peter' is so probable a tradition that it has met with general acceptance ; it is, moreover, an assertion as to which it is quite impossible now to produce any rebutting evidence. But the assertion that Mark did not compose his narrative 'in order' is, at the present day, as generally rejected by those who have carefully studied the Synoptic Problem. Dr. Salmon, in particular, has pointed out that if we desire to follow the growth of our Lord's reputation as a teacher and healer, and the corresponding development of hostility against Him, we must consult the Gospel according to St. Mark in preference to the others.

Passing on to the statement of the presbyter John about St. Matthew, and judging it in the light of all the evidence at present available, we seem to find the same mixture in it of truth and error. The testimony of St. Jerome does not leave us room to question that there was an orthodox Hebrew Gospel which, as extant in his time, contained matters not found in any of the four canonical Gospels. This work had such a very limited circulation that it is impossible for us now to affirm with any confidence as to whether its peculiar features were in the original, or were later interpolations ; but we have no rebutting evidence that in its original form it was not the work of St. Matthew. On the other hand, nothing is more certain than that the Greek First Gospel, which has always been known in the Church as the Gospel according to St. Matthew, is not in its present form, which there is no reason to think was ever different—a translation from one Hebrew original. How then are we to explain 'Everyone interpreted them,' i.e. Matthew's Hebrew λόγια, 'as he was able'? Dr. Salmon's solution seems to give the most likely explanation of this ambiguous phrase. John the presbyter meant that the Greek St. Matthew was a translation of the Hebrew St. Matthew, and not by the author himself. The assertion is of the same kind as that about St. Mark, that he did not write 'in order' ; and both statements were suggested by an extreme theory of biblical inspiration, a theory which was very generally held until quite recent times—the absolute inerrancy of Holy Scripture in every detail.

One has sometimes heard discrepancies between different historical statements in the OT explained by the assertion that the errors which cause the discrepancies were not in the original, as it left the hand of the Divinely inspired writer, but were due to the slips of uninspired copyists ; and thus it is thought possible to reconcile belief in the inerrancy of the Word of God with the actual state of the case. The statements of the presbyter John about the Gospels of Mark and Matthew are best explained by supposing that he held some such theory of inspiration.

'When he finds what seems a disagreement between the Gospels, he is satisfied there can be no real disagreement. Mark's order may be different from Luke's (who declares in his preface that it was his intention to write in order—γράψαι καθεξῆς) ; but, then, that was because it was not Mark's design to recount the facts in their proper order. . . . If in Matthew's Gospel, as he read it, there seemed any inaccuracy, this must be imputed to the translators ; the Gospel as Matthew himself wrote it was free from fault' (Salmon, Introd. to NT, p. 93).

The conclusion, then, to which we are driven is that if the existence of an original Hebrew Gospel depended on the testimony of the presbyter John, we could not safely make any positive affirmation on the subject. The only other witness to

Matthew's Hebrew Gospel who seems to be independent, i.e. Irenæus, may not really be so. It has been generally believed that he adds to what Eusebius quotes from Papias a note of time, 'while Peter and Paul were preaching and founding the Church at Rome' ; but the Rev. J. Chapman has proved (JThSt vi. 563)· that this clause is neither derived from Papias nor is it a note of time.

12. However, whether St. Matthew wrote a Gospel in Hebrew or not, there can be no doubt, both from a priori considerations and also from the internal evidence of the extant Greek Gospels, that there was current in the infancy of the Church a Gospel in the Hebrew language as then commonly spoken in Judæa. The last command of our Lord, as recorded by St. Luke (24⁴⁷), that the gospel should be preached, 'beginning at Jerusalem,' is in itself a sufficient proof that one of the first Gospels, in the sense in which we have used that word, must have been in the Aramaic tongue. Even if our Lord sometimes, and in some places, taught in Greek, yet Aramaic was His mother tongue, and that of His Apostles, and of the vast majority of His hearers. In the early Jerusalem Church it is plain that the Hebrews outnumbered the Hellenists (Ac 6¹). These considerations make it certain that one of the forms which the Evangelic narrative assumed from the very first was in Aramaic. The facts that such a Gospel is not now extant, and that the external evidence for its existence at any time is so scanty, are fully accounted for by the destruction of Jerusalem in the year A.D. 70. That world-shaking event, among its other immediate consequences, was followed by the disappearance of the Hebrew-speaking Church of Jerusalem. Then, after not many years, the Hebrew-speaking Christian community in Palestine lost touch with the main current of Christian thought, and, in consequence, sank to the position of an obscure sect with an out-of-date theology.

It has been stated above that the internal evidence of the extant Greek Gospels suggests an Aramaic original. It must be confessed that the presence in a Greek document of Aramaic turns of phrase does not necessarily prove that it is a translation from the Aramaic. Dean Armitage Robinson has given good reasons for his theory that the Aramaisms in the first two chapters of St. Luke's Gospel are due to a deliberate imitation of the LXX of 1 Samuel. But there does not seem any likelihood that the author, or authors, of the common Synoptic narrative were, like St. Luke, conscious literary artists ; and even if we cannot follow Weiss in every application of his conclusions, there remains proof enough to render the theory of an original Aramaic Gospel, as underlying the Synoptics, probable to a high degree. This supposition is even more plausible in the case of the portions of St. Matthew's Gospel which are peculiar to that Evangelist. Bishop Westcott long ago pointed out, with regard to the quotations from the OT found in the Synoptic Gospels, that, while the cyclic quotations, as he calls them, agree with the LXX, those that are peculiar to St. Matthew seem to be independent translations from the Hebrew.

13. This is not a discussion of the Synoptic Problem ; but it may not be out of place to conclude this article with a suggestion as to the relations of the three Synoptic Gospels to each other. It is generally held now that the First and Third Gospels are altogether independent of each other, but that Mt. and Lk. derived the matter which they have in common with Mk. either from St. Mark's Gospel, or from an earlier source from which St. Mark selected the incidents and discourses which he relates. On the hypothesis that Mt. and Lk. copied our St. Mark, we have to assume the existence of another early Gospel, from which they derived the non-Markan matter which they have in common. In this case we conclude that the details peculiar to St. Mark were an original feature of that Gospel, and that Mt. and Lk. for various reasons omitted them. On the other hand, if the common Synoptic matter and the matter common to Mt. and Lk. be both assigned to one original, it will then be natural to think of St. Mark's peculiar details as additions made by him, probably on the authority of St. Peter.

The problem has been rendered unnecessarily complicated by an assumption that it is impossible that an Evangelist should have omitted anything from his work which he had reason to believe was true. The fallacy of this assumption will be evident, whichever hypothesis we adopt. The simplest method to account for all the facts is to suppose a Greek translation of an Aramaic original as the source of all the common Synoptic matter, and also of the matter common to Mt. and Lk. In this document the OT quotations would have been given in a LXX form. At least two other sources must be postulated for the matter found only in Mt. and Lk. respectively. We have already found reason to hold that the matter peculiar to Mt. was a translation from an Aramaic original.

Whatever solution of the Synoptic problem be ultimately adopted by the general consensus of critics, it does not seem likely that the complicated hypotheses of the German school of a generation ago will again commend themselves to scholars of sober judgment. It is a sound canon of criticism that sources are not to be multiplied beyond the necessity of the case.

LITERATURE.—The art. 'Gospels' in Hastings' *DB* and in *Encyc. Bibl.*, where a full Bibliography will be found. Of the more recent literature the following select list may be offered: Westcott, *Introd. to Study of Gospels*[8], 1895 ; A. Wright, *Compos. of Four Gospels*, 1890, with the same author's Preface to *Synopsis*, 1896, and *Some NT Problems*, 1898 ; Sir J. Hawkins, *Horæ Synopticæ*, 1899 ; Salmon, *Introd. to NT*, 1885 ; Rushbrooke, *Synopticon*, 1880 ; Abbott-Rushbrooke, *Common Tradition of the Synoptic Gospels*, 1884 ; Badham, *The Formation of the Gospels*[2], 1892 ; H. Holtzmann, *Die Synopt. Evangelien*, 1863, *Einleit. in d NT*[3], 1892 ; B. Weiss, *Life of Christ*, Bk. i. 'The Sources,' 1882, *Manual of Introd to NT*, 1886 ; C. Weizsäcker, *Untersuch. üb. die evangel. Gesch.* 1864 ; Wendt, *Lehre Jesu*, 1886 ; P. Ewald, *Hauptproblem d. Evangelienfrage*, 1890 ; Sanday, 'Survey of the Synoptic Question' in *Expos.* 1891. A posthumous work on the Synoptic Problem by Dr. Salmon, entitled *Eclipse Observations of the Human Element in the Gospels*, will, it is hoped, be published this year (1906).

N. J. D. WHITE.

GOSPELS (APOCRYPHAL).—i. TITLE.—In the sense in which the term is popularly understood, 'apocryphal' is synonymous with 'spurious' or 'false'; when, however, it is applied as a title to writings of the early Christian centuries, it bears the significance of 'extra-canonical.' By Apocryphal Gospels are, accordingly, meant all writings claiming to be Gospels which are not included in the Canon of the NT, without any implication that their contents are necessarily false or of questionable origin. (See, further, for the meaning of the term, art. 'Apocrypha' in Hastings' *DB* i. 112 ff. ; also Hennecke, *NT Apokr.* 3* ff., *Handb.* vii ff. ; and Zahn, *Gesch. d. NT Kan.* i. 127 ff.).

ii. ORIGIN.—For a generation after the death of Jesus, His teaching and the facts about His life were preserved by oral tradition in the circle of believers. With the rise of a second generation, however, the need was felt for reducing the oral reminiscences to written form. The reason for this was twofold. For one thing, the number of those who could give personal testimony of what Jesus did and said was rapidly becoming smaller ; and for another, the Christian faith was spreading far beyond the limits of its original home in Palestine. Both these facts made it imperative that, if trustworthy accounts of the teaching and life of

Jesus were to be preserved for the guidance of the scattered communities of Christians, the tradition should be committed to something more permanent and less liable to disturbing influences than oral reminiscence. The impulse of this necessity gave rise to our written Gospels, and to many other Evangelic records which have disappeared. Of the many attempts to write the story of Jesus, to which St. Luke in his prologue refers, none (with the exception of Mt. and Mk.) can be said with any certainty to have survived ;* although it is possible that the *Gospel Fragment of Fayûm* may be the wreckage of one of them. In any case, some of the earlier non-canonical Gospels, which are extant in more or less fragmentary condition, are probably the products of the general desire, that was everywhere felt, to have a more certain knowledge of Jesus and His teaching than was possible from the oral instruction of wandering evangelists. The *Gospel according to the Hebrews*, which is but little later than the Synoptics, belongs almost certainly to this class ; and the same may be true also of the *Gospel according to the Egyptians.*

The majority of extra-canonical Gospels are due, however, to other causes. Written at a time when the present Four Gospels were gaining, or had already gained, a place of exceptional authority,† they came into existence in answer to two desires, urgently felt in certain circles of Christians. (1) The first was the desire, popularly entertained, for fuller information about the life of Christ than that given by the four Gospels. This intelligible and not unnatural curiosity was directed chiefly to the facts antecedent to Christ's advent, and to those periods of His life which the older Gospels left in shadow—His parentage, His birth and childhood, and the period after the Resurrection. It is noteworthy that the writers who endeavoured to satisfy this desire for fuller knowledge made no attempt to fill up the silent years between Christ's childhood and His entrance on His public ministry, the reason in part probably being that 'it seemed too daring for them to illumine a darkness, for which there was not the slightest historical suggestion in the New Testament' (Hofmann, *PRE*[3] i. 655). With greater probability, however, it may be said that the reason was, not so much any self-restraint through loyalty to the data of history, as the absence of any clear dogmatic motive ; and dogmatic motives, as will appear, were almost invariably associated with the desire to satisfy curiosity. It may be safely assumed that, had any doctrinal interest called for the history of the silent years, no scruples about historical truthfulness would have prevented writers from enlivening them with the products of their fancy. In the main it is certain that the details furnished by the apocryphal writings regarding matters about which the canonical Gospels are silent, have little or no historical basis. They are in reality Christian *haggadoth*, popular stories similar to those in Jewish literature which were framed for purposes of pious entertainment and instruction. The *Gospels of the Infancy* and *Childhood*, for example, are full of legendary matter drawn from various sources, or freely invented by the fancy of the writers. Where the details are not entirely imaginative, they have their origin in the transformation of utterances of Christ into deeds, or in the literal interpretation of OT prophecies and Jewish expectations about the Messiah, or in the ascription to Jesus of miracles similar to those recorded in the OT (Hofmann, *PRE*[3] i. 655).

* The probability is that most of them disappeared early, being unable to maintain their position alongside of the Gospels which are now in the Canon.
† The authoritative position of the canonical Gospels, which was beginning to be recognized before the middle of the 2nd century, was assured by the end of the century.

As an example of the way in which the Christian haggadist worked, it may suffice to mention his treatment of OT texts. Ps 148⁷ reads : 'Praise the Lord from the earth, ye dragons'; accordingly, in pseudo-Matthew dragons are represented as coming out of a cave and worshipping the child Christ. The picture of Paradise regained in Is 11⁶ᶠᶠ· suggested the legend that all kinds of wild beasts accompanied the Holy Family on the way to Egypt (Cowper, *Apocr. Gosp.* lix f.).

But although the Apocryphal Gospels abound in legendary accretions of this kind, the mistake should not be made of assuming that there is no authentic material in the additions to the narratives in the four Gospels. Oral tradition maintained itself for a time after our present Gospels were reduced to writing, and it is not improbable that genuine sayings of Christ and authentic details about His life have been preserved in uncanonical books. On this point see further in § iii.

(2) A much more powerful motive than the desire to satisfy curiosity, leading to the production of Gospel writings, was the dogmatic interest, the desire to find support for beliefs which were held in various sections of the Church. This was especially marked in Gnostic circles, where numerous Evangelic writings (running into thousands, Epiphanius says [*Hær.* 26]) were produced, claiming the authority of a secret tradition for their peculiar doctrines.

Even in the earlier Apocryphal Gospels, which are of the Synoptic type, it is clear that theological prepossessions played a considerable part, as indeed they did to some extent in the canonical Gospels. Thus, in the *Gospel according to the Hebrews* the conception of Christ has an Ebionitic tinge, and in the *Gospel of Peter* there are expressions which betray Docetic sympathies on the part of the writer. The dogmatic motive is prominent as well in those writings which fill up with fictitious details the empty spaces of the Gospel narrative, and thus have generally been regarded as due to the desire to gratify the irrepressible longing for fuller knowledge. It is doubtful if this latter motive, although it was certainly operative, would have led to the invention of such a mass of fictitious matter, had it not been powerfully stimulated by dogmatic considerations. In the *Protevangelium of James* the legendary history of Mary's antecedents and of the circumstances of Christ's birth was due not merely to any *horror vacui*, but to the imperative dogmatic necessity, as the writer conceived it, of safeguarding in this way alike the true Divinity and the true humanity of Jesus Christ. Similarly, the *Childhood Gospel of Thomas*, with its repulsive stories of the child Christ's miraculous power and knowledge, would never have found acceptance in Christian circles had it not been for the witness which the miracles were supposed to bear to Christ's supernatural origin.

iii. RELATION TO CANONICAL GOSPELS. — The fragmentary condition and the uncertain text of many of the Apocryphal Gospels render a confident judgment as to their relation to the canonical Gospels exceedingly difficult. Where the question of affinity is raised, the problem to be solved is whether the uncanonical Gospels are dependent on the canonical, or draw from a common oral source. The latter possibility is one not to be dismissed without careful consideration ; but, on the whole, the evidence points in almost every case to the use of some or all of the four Gospels by the authors of the apocryphal writings. Only in the case of one Gospel, the *Gospel according to the Hebrews*, is there a strong consensus of opinion in favour of independence (see, however, vii. A. 1). Where there is an appearance of independence, this is frequently to be accounted for by a free manipulation and embellishment of old material, to bring it into line with the writer's peculiar point of view, or to suit it to the character of his surroundings.

While a large degree of dependence on the canonical Gospels must in general be maintained in regard to the Apocryphal Gospels, this must not be pressed so far as to exclude the possibility of their embodying details drawn from reliable oral sources. The fact must steadily be borne in mind that the stream of living oral tradition continued to flow for several generations, though in ever decreasing volume, alongside of the written Gospels ; * accord-

* Traces of the influence of oral tradition on the canonical Gospels, *after they were reduced to writing*, are to be found in the well-known additions to John (8¹⁻¹¹) and Mark (16⁹⁻²⁰).

ingly, where the uncanonical Gospels deviate from the canonical record, either by slight interpolations into common matter or by additions peculiarly their own, the possibility is always open that in these additions we have early and reliable traditions, either unknown to the four Evangelists or passed over by them as unsuitable for their purpose.

Two important considerations must, however, be kept in mind in estimating the trustworthiness of all such additions. In the first place, the authoritative position which the canonical Gospels early reached as authentic sources of the life and teaching of Jesus entitles them to be used as a touchstone of the probable authenticity of the additional matter contained in the Apocryphal Gospels. No saying of Christ or detail about His life has any title to be regarded as genuine if it does not fit into the conception which the four Evangelists have given us of the teaching and personality of Jesus. Secondly, when we keep in view the undoubted fact that fictitious writings were common in which the life and teaching of Christ were freely handled in the interest of heretical sects, it is clear that extreme caution must be observed in receiving as authentic any addition to the canonical record. If it would be less than just to say that all the Apocryphal Gospels stand in the position of suspect witnesses, with a presumption of unreliability against them in respect of their peculiar matter, it is nevertheless true that their exclusion from the Canon, as well as the notoriously tainted origin of some of them, render it imperative that their claim to embody a genuine tradition must be carefully sifted, and allowed only after the clearest proof.

iv. VALUE.—The question of greatest moment which arises in estimating the value of the Apocryphal Gospels naturally has reference to their worth as additional sources for the life and teaching of Jesus. From what has been already said about their origin and their relation to the canonical Gospels, their value in this respect will appear to be extremely slight. A comparison of the Apocryphal Gospels with those in the Canon makes the pre-eminence of the latter incontestably clear, and shows that as sources of Christ's life the former, for all practical purposes, may be neglected. The simple beauty and verisimilitude of the picture of Jesus in the four Gospels stand out in strong relief when viewed in the light of the artificial and legendary stories which characterize most of the Apocryphal Gospels. The proverbial simplicity of truth receives a striking commentary when (for example) the miracles of the Canonical Gospels are compared with those of the Apocryphal writings. The former, for the most part, are instinct with ethical purpose and significance, and are felt to be the natural and unforced expression of the sublime personality of Jesus ; the latter are largely theatrical exhibitions without ethical content. In them 'we find no worthy conception of the laws of providential interference ; they are wrought to supply personal wants, or to gratify private feelings, and often are positively immoral' (Westcott). In a few of the Gospels which show signs of independence, there may be here and there a trace of primitive and trustworthy tradition ; but all such details, which have a reasonable claim to be considered authentic, do not sensibly increase the sum of our knowledge about Christ. The conclusion, based on the comparison of the Apocryphal with the Canonical Gospels, is amply warranted, that in rejecting the former and choosing the latter as authoritative Scriptures the Church showed a true feeling for what was original and authentic.

Though the Apocryphal Gospels afford us little additional knowledge about Christ, they are invaluable as enabling us to realize more clearly the conditions under which the four Gospels were received in the Church, until they were finally established as authoritative in the Gospel Canon. The existence of so many Evangelic writings shows that for some time after the Canonical Gospels appeared, they had no position of commanding influence. The high place which oral tradition— 'the living and abiding voice'—still retained in the estimation of the Church (cf. Euseb. *HE* iii. 39. 4) militated against the acceptance of any written Gospel as authoritative beyond the communities in which it was current. In the early part of the 2nd cent. we have, accordingly, to think of the four Gospels as having merely a local and circumscribed authority, while in different sections of the Church the production of Evangelic literature still proceeded, in which the tradition was handled more or less freely to suit the dominant conceptions and needs. But by the middle of the century there were indications that the four Gospels, already widely known through the constant intercourse that united Christian communities together, were being elevated above their competitors to a place of exceptional authority. This was due, not to mere good fortune or to any arbitrary dealing on the part of the Church, but to the superior claims of the writings themselves, which were recognized when the necessity arose of counteracting, by trustworthy and authentic records, the rapid growth of a pseudo-tradition in Gnostic circles. This rise of our four Gospels to a commanding and unchallengeable position bears witness not only to their inherent value,—which the Church, with a fine spiritual sensitiveness, perceived,—but to the conviction that, as opposed to fictitious writings which appeared under the names of Apostles, they embodied the testimony of Apostolic writers. By the time of Irenæus (*c.* 180) the Gospel canon may be regarded as definitely fixed; and although Apocryphal Gospels continued to circulate, the authoritative position of the four Gospels was finally assured.

Perhaps the chief value of the Apocryphal Gospels is to be found in the light which they cast on the conditions of life and thought in early Christian times. They are of service in the difficult work of reconstructing the complex environment in which Christianity grew up.

When, for example, one reads in the *Childhood Gospel of Thomas* the account of the miracles wrought by the child Christ, and marks the spirit of *diablerie* so frequently exhibited, one is conscious of nothing but a painful feeling of wonder, that fables so bizarre and so revolting could ever have been tolerated in a community of Christians. Of any ethical sympathy with the spirit of Christ, of any recognition of the beauty and simplicity of Christ's childhood, as He grew in grace and wisdom, in favour with God and man, there is in this Gospel hardly the faintest trace. Though worthless as an account of Christ's childhood, the *Gospel of Thomas* is yet a mirror in which we see reflected the curious condition of the society which accepted it. We see here, in a typical instance, how strong were the external influences which played on the development of Christianity in early times. In the process of permeating the heathen world with its great thought of Redemption and its lofty ethical sentiment, Christianity, as was inevitable, was itself coloured, and in certain circles distorted, by the foreign elements of its environment. Oriental mythology and Greek philosophy had met, and given rise to syncretistic systems which exerted a deep influence on men's conceptions of the Christian faith and life. Traces of this are clearly discernible in the Apocryphal Gospels, most plainly in the Gnostic Gospels. Buddhist influences are possibly responsible for the childhood stories in the *Gospel of Thomas*.

The confusion and vagueness of the Christological views in the different Apocryphal Gospels also bear witness to the great variety of influences which were at work in the early Church, and enable us to realize with what trouble the conception of the Divine manhood of Jesus was eventually established. The indecision and one-sidedness which are revealed in doctrinal matters are also traceable in the interpretation of the ethical content of Christ's teaching and life. Ascetic and Encratite views are found in several Gospels, and no doubt

were characteristic of all the Gnostic Gospels. A close sympathy with the true ethical spirit of Christianity is, however, noticeable in the *Gospel according to the Hebrews*, in which stress is laid on acts of mercy and brotherly kindness ; and in the 'Traditions of Matthias' mentioned by Clement of Alexandria, and possibly identical with the Gnostic *Gospel of Matthias*, the doctrine of Christian responsibility for others' welfare, in its most stringent form, is very forcibly put : ' If the neighbour of an elect person sins, the elect has sinned ; for if he had lived according to the counsels of the Word, his neighbour would have so esteemed his manner of life that he would have kept free from sin.'

The *apologetic* interest which is so characteristic of 2nd cent. writers (witness the *Apologies* of Aristides, Justin, Tertullian, etc.) is reflected in several of the Apocryphal Gospels.

Traces are to be found in the *Gospel according to the Hebrews*, in which the servant of the high priest is a witness to the Resurrection. A later stage of the apologetic movement may be observed in the *Gospel of Peter*, where Pilate is practically exonerated from blame for Christ's condemnation, and is made to bear witness to Christ's Divinity. In the *Acts of Pilate* (*Gospel of Nicodemus*) the movement has reached its climax in the reverence which the Romans pay to Jesus at His trial, in the miraculous homage of the Roman standards, and in the irrefutable evidence given of Christ's resurrection, to the conviction of His enemies.

A subsidiary element in estimating the value of the Apocryphal Gospels is their antiquarian interest. A passage in the *Protevangelium of James* (ch. 18) affords an interesting parallel to the scene in the fairy tale, 'The Sleeping Beauty,' when by a magic spell the whole of nature suddenly stands still, and all living beings are immovably rooted where they are. The *Childhood Gospel of Thomas*, useless as it is as a source of information about Christ's youth, gives a remarkably vivid and convincing picture of Jewish village life. Caution must be observed in trusting the details of Jewish life in the *Protevangelium* ; many of them are entirely unhistorical.

v. DOCTRINAL CHARACTERISTICS. — As stated above in § ii., one of the main impulses which led to the production of Apocryphal Gospels was the desire to establish peculiar tenets held in certain Christian circles. Gospels of this type, although professedly narratives of our Lord's life and teaching, were in reality *Tendenzschriften*, doctrinal treatises conceived and written in the interests of a definite system of thought. Such were the numerous Gnostic Gospels, of which the smallest fragments remain. But even those Gospels in the production of which there was no deliberate dogmatic purpose, are doctrinally significant. It is true of them, equally with the canonical Gospels, that they were written in the interests of faith, ἐκ πίστεως εἰς πίστιν ; the writers were not mere chroniclers of past events, giving information about One in whose life and personality they had no vital concern ; they were believers, for whom Christ was Lord. The religious value which Jesus had for them, and the manner in which they conceived of His person, were reflected in their narrative of His life. However small the value of the writings may be as authentic sources of information regarding Jesus, they are interesting as showing by a side light what men thought about Him. How far the early Church as a whole was from any clear and uniform conception of Christ, is apparent from the Apocryphal Gospels. In them we have not only the reflexion of views representing the main stream of Christian thought, but also the foreshadowings of doctrines which later, in their developed form, were rejected as heretical.

The majority of the Apocryphal Gospels betray a heretical tendency, which varies broadly according as the Divine or the human nature of Christ is denied. On the one hand, there is the *Ebionitic* conception of Jesus, with its rejection of His heavenly origin ; on the other, the *Docetic*, with its obscuration or denial of His true humanity. Both these opposing views find expression in the Apocryphal Gospels. The former is found in the *Gospel according to the Hebrews* and in the *Gospel of the Twelve Apostles* ; the latter, somewhat veiled, in the *Gospel of Peter*, but fully developed in the Gnostic Gospels, in which the Saviour—the heavenly Christ—freed from the association with the phantasmal earthly Christ, and made the possessor of His full powers through the death and resurrection, declares the true wisdom to His disciples.

The *Childhood* Gospels stand in the main current of ecclesiastical doctrine in their view of the person of Christ. The *Gospel of Thomas* shows that the circles in which it found acceptance held to the doctrine of Christ's human and Divine natures. There are traces that point to a Gnostic origin, and to a conception of Christ in which His true humanity was obscured ; but in the later form in which it was current in the Church, the humanity and Divinity of our Lord are alike emphasized. The child Jesus is a boy among boys, taking His part in the usual games and occupations of childhood ; and yet the belief in His supernatural dignity is evidenced by the extraordinary miracles attributed to Him, and by His astonishing knowledge, which drew the confession from His teacher: 'This child is not earth-born ; assuredly he was born before the creation of the world' (ch. 7). The *Protevangelium of James*, too, it is clear, was written in the interests of orthodoxy, which were imperilled, alike by the belief current in Jewish-Christian circles that Joseph was the father of Jesus, and by the Gnostic doctrine that, in being born of Mary, Jesus did not partake of her human nature, but passed through her like water through a pipe (Epiphan. *Hær.* 31. 7). In opposition to this double attack on the generally accepted doctrine, the writer of the *Protevangelium*, while not leaving it in doubt that Jesus was born as a human child (the infant took the breast from His mother), sought to make His Divinity secure by depicting Mary as holy from her birth, as fed only on angels' food, as conceiving by the word of the Lord, as bringing forth her child in virginity, and as remaining a virgin to the end. It is noteworthy that, although the primary object of the *Protevangelium* was to safeguard the orthodox conception of Christ's person against hostile attacks, the method adopted had the result of elevating Mary above the ordinary levels of humanity, and of initiating a movement which, deriving strength from other sources, terminated in the worship of Mary, the All-Holy mother of God.

vi. INFLUENCE.—Although after the 2nd cent. no Gospels were reckoned as authoritative except those now in the Canon, the Apocryphal Gospels continued to be read for purposes of edification, both in public and in private. Those which were distinctly heretical gradually disappeared as the power of the Church grew, while those which were of a type similar to the canonical Gospels were unable for any lengthened period to maintain their position alongside their authoritative rivals. Still we find that the *Gospel according to the Hebrews* was read in some quarters in Jerome's day (end of 4th cent.), and was highly esteemed by that Father himself ; while the vitality of the *Gospel of Peter* is evidenced by the fact that a large portion of it was placed in the grave of a monk in the early Middle Ages (8th–12th cent.). The popularity of the *Childhood* Gospels was remarkable, especially in the Churches of the East. There the *Protevangelium* was so highly prized as a book of devotion that it was used for reading in public worship, and furnished material for the homilies of preachers. Translations of it circulated in Syriac, Coptic, and Arabic, and, along with other childhood legends, its stories, often greatly embellished and exaggerated, found a place in a comprehensive *Gospel of the Infancy and Childhood*, the so-called 'Arabic Gospel,' which had a wide circulation not only in the Churches in the East, but in Mohammedan circles. Passages from the *Protevangelium* stand in the lectionaries of the orthodox Church, for use at the festivals held in honour of Mary and of her reputed parents, Joachim and Anna.

In the Western Church the Apocryphal Gospels were regarded with more suspicion. Towards the close of the 4th cent. their authority was repudiated in the plainest terms by Jerome and Augustine, the former characterizing certain stories as *ex deliramentis apocryphorum petita* (Tappehorn, *Ausserbiblische Nachrichten*, 15). On the other hand, their contemporaries, Zeno of Verona, and Prudentius, the greatest poet of early Christian times, drew from the *Protevangelium* in their works in praise of Mary. The combined influence of Jerome and Augustine, however, determined the ecclesiastical attitude to the Apocryphal Gospels, and the ban of the Church fell upon them under Damasus (382), Innocent I. (405), and Gelasius (496). In the long run this condemnation by ecclesiastical authority proved unavailing to check the popular appetite for the apocryphal legends ; and by various devices the writings, which had incurred the censure of the Church, were brought back again into public circulation.

Harnack truly remarks that 'the history of apocryphal literature is a proof that the prohibition of books is powerless against a pressing need. In all sections and in all languages of the Church this literature is perhaps the most strongly represented alongside of the canonical writings, in a form, as one would expect, that is always changing to suit the taste of the age. It was really *apocryphal*, that is to say, it had what may be termed a subterranean existence ; but, suppressed and persecuted though it was, it always forced its way back to the surface, and at last the public tradition of the Church was defenceless against it' (*Gesch. d. altchr. Litt.* I. lx. note 5).

Within a century after the *Decretum Gelasii*, Gregory of Tours in his book *de Gloria Martyrum* (i. ch. 4) had no scruples in using the extravagant legends contained in the 'Transitus Mariæ'; indeed, so little store was apparently set by ecclesiastical condemnation, that about 435, thirty years after the decree of Innocent I., a mosaic of the Annunciation in S. Maria Maggiore in Rome, prepared under the direction of Sixtus III., embodied apocryphal details. Apocryphal writings are used by pseudo-Chrysostom (*c.* 600); and in the epic poem of the nun Hroswitha († 968), entitled *Historia nativitatis laudabilisque conversationis intactæ Dei genitricis*, the material is in part drawn from the later Gospels of the Childhood. From the 12th cent. onwards, the Apocryphal Gospels afforded an inexhaustible mine for poets and minstrels in Germany, France, and England ; and numerous miracle-plays represented incidents drawn from the same source. A powerful impulse was given to the spread of these legends by the Dominican Vincent de Beauvais, who in his work entitled *Speculum Majus*, published about the middle of the 13th cent., and translated in the following century into many languages, transcribed large portions of *pseudo-Matthew* and the *Gospel of Nicodemus*, etc. The latter half of the 13th cent. also saw the appearance of a collection of legendary Lives of the Saints, the *Speculum Sanctorum*, better known as the *Golden Legend*, written by another member of the Dominican order, Jacobus de Voragine, Archbishop of Genoa. This work, in which many of the apocryphal legends find a place, had an immense influence, there being manuscript translations extant in English, German, French, Italian, and Spanish. With the invention of the printing-press this influence was largely extended, the *Legenda Aurea* and Vincent's *Speculum* being among the earliest books to be set up in type. From that time onwards, the stories of the Apocryphal Gospels have had an influence on popular Christianity in Catholic countries far exceeding that of the Biblical narrative.

Roman Catholic writers have denied their claim to be in any sense authoritative sources of Evangelic history, and have uttered warnings against their incautious use ; an unfavourable judgment was passed upon them by the Papal Congregation of Rites as recently as 1884, in connexion with the proposal to celebrate in the following year the nineteen hundredth anniversary of the birth of Mary ; but, all this notwithstanding, these apocryphal stories, likened by Harnack to twining plants which, when cut down, spring up again from beneath and choke much that is healthy, have securely rooted themselves in the popular imagination, and have been the fruitful source of many superstitious beliefs. Even Tappehorn, a Roman Catholic writer, who, in his scholarly treatise on *The Apocryphal Gospels of the Childhood*, etc., speaks with deep regret of the tendency to accept these writings as trustworthy historical sources, cannot resist the temptation to retain as much of their contents as has been taken up into ecclesiastical tradition. He accepts, for instance, as reliable, the names of Mary's parents, the circumstances relating to her birth, her dedication to the Temple service, the marvellous story of her death, resurrection, and ascension, and declares that use of these apocryphal data may be made with an easy conscience for the purpose of religious edification (*op. cit.* 88).

The narratives of the Apocryphal Gospels have had an extraordinary influence on Christian art. Reference has already been made to the attraction which the legends had for poets from the earliest times, and especially since the date of the publication of the *Legenda Aurea*. (For details of the earlier poetry see von Lehner, *Die Marienverehrung*, 256 ff.). Sculpture and painting also owed many of their subjects to apocryphal sources, or were influenced in their treatment by apocryphal details. The history of Mary's reputed parents, her service in the Temple, her betrothal to Joseph, the Annunciation, the Birth of Jesus in a cave, the Flight into Egypt, the Assumption of Mary—these and other incidents described in the Apocryphal Gospels were favourite themes of painters and sculptors, especially during the Renaissance.

A marble tablet of the 4th or 5th cent. in the crypt of St. Maximin in Provence, represents Mary in the attitude of prayer, with the inscription in barbarous Latin, MARIA VIRGO MINESTER DE TEMPUIO GEROSALE—'The Virgin Mary, servant of the temple at Jerusalem' (von Lehner, *op. cit.* 327). The events in the life of the Virgin, arranged in a series, were depicted by different painters of the Renaissance, one of the best known series being that by Taddeo Gaddi in the Baroncelli Chapel at Florence (Mrs. Jameson, *Legends of the Madonna*, Introd. iii). Mary's presentation at the Temple, and her marvellous ascent of the Temple steps (narrated in *pseudo-Matthew*, ch. 4 and the *Nativity*, ch. 6), supply a subject for one of Titian's masterpieces (in the Academy, Venice), while her marriage to Joseph is represented in many fine pictures, notably in Raphael's beautiful early work (in the Pinacoteca, Milan). The Annunciation is a favourite theme in Christian art; in accordance with the narrative in the *Protevangelium*, Mary is represented either at the well with a pitcher of water or spinning wool for the veil of the temple (as in the mosaic, already referred to, in S. Maria Maggiore in Rome). Pictures of the Nativity betray the influence of the apocryphal stories; they show the mother and child and Joseph in a cave, where, according to the *Protevangelium*, Jesus was born; a dazzling light radiates from the face of the child; an ox and an ass (first mentioned in *pseudo-Matthew*) bow in adoration before Him—a frequent representation in early reliefs (von Lehner, *op. cit.* 314 ff.)—or in later pictures are introduced as mere picturesque details. An incident in the Flight to Egypt, the bending down of a palm-tree to yield its fruit to Mary, affords a subject for many beautiful works (*e.g.* by Pinturicchio, William Blake). The Assumption of Mary was frequently represented in paintings from the 10th cent. onward (*e.g.* Titian's in the Academy, Venice; Botticelli's in the National Gallery), while the consummation of her life is depicted in her coronation as Queen of Heaven (among others by Raphael, Fra Angelico, and Taddeo Gaddi). The second part of the *Gospel of Nicodemus*—The Descent into Hell —gives a subject to Fra Angelico (San Marco, Venice) and to Dürer (in his series of woodcuts composing 'The Little Passion').

The narratives in the Koran about Jesus, who is regarded as a forerunner of Mohammed, are drawn largely from apocryphal sources, either directly from the so-called *Arabic Gospel of the Infancy*, or indirectly from the popular tales which had an apocryphal origin. An account is given, for instance, of Mary's nativity,—in the Koran her parents are named Imran and Hanna,—of her dedication to the Temple, of the miraculous choice of Joseph to be her protector, etc. Jesus is represented as working miracles in His childhood; His making of birds out of clay (*Gospel of Thomas*) is mentioned. The Koran represents strongly Docetic views in its denial that Jesus died upon the Cross. In Sura 4. 156 the Jews are reported as saying: 'We have killed the Messiah, Jesus, the Son of Mary, the Messenger of God'; to which the answer is immediately given: 'Yet they did not kill and crucify Him, but a phantasm appeared to them. . . . In truth they did not kill Him, but God raised Him to Himself; for God is strong and wise.' Other legends about Jesus, not mentioned in the Koran, were collected by Moslem commentators, notably by Kessæus. See art. CHRIST IN MOHAMMEDAN LITERATURE in Appendix to vol. ii.

vii. CLASSIFICATION. — The classification here adopted follows that given by Harnack (*Gesch. d. altchr. Litt.* i. 4 f.) and by Tasker (Hastings' *DB*, Extra Vol. 422 f.).

A. Gospels of the Synoptic type, with some title to be regarded as embodying an early tradition.
 1. Gospel according to the Hebrews.
 2. Gospel according to the Egyptians.
 3. Gospel of Peter.
 4. Fayûm Gospel Fragment.
 5. Oxyrhyncus Gospel Fragment.
B. Heretical and Gnostic Gospels, written to establish peculiar conceptions of the person and life of Jesus.
 1. Gospel of Marcion.

 2. Gospel of the Twelve Apostles.
 3. Gospel of Thomas.
 4. Gospel of Philip.
C. Supplemental Gospels, written to throw light on the dark parts of Christ's history.
 (a) Gospels of the Childhood, together with those dealing with the parents of Jesus.
  1. Protevangelium of James with the recensions—
   (1) Gospel of pseudo-Matthew.
   (2) Gospel of the Nativity of Mary.
  2. Childhood Gospel of Thomas.
  3. Arabic Gospel of the Childhood.
  4. History of Joseph the Carpenter.
  5. The Departure of Mary.
 (b) Gospels dealing with the Passion and the post-Resurrection life of Jesus.
  1. Gospel of Nicodemus.
  2. Legend of Abgar.
D. Gospel Harmonies, in which several Gospels are worked together into one.
 Gospel of Tatian (*Diatessaron*).

A. 1. **Gospel according to the Hebrews.**—The earliest mention of this Gospel occurs in the Ὑπομνήματα of Hegesippus about the year 180 (Euseb. *HE* iv. 22. 8). The name 'according to the Hebrews' is not original; in the circles in which the Gospel was current, it apparently had no distinctive name, that which it now bears having been given to it by outsiders, to indicate that it was the Gospel in use among Hebrew Christians, the descendants of the original Church in Judæa. There is some probability in the view, which is strongly advocated by Harnack (*Chron.* i. 637 f.), that the Gospel was in use in the Jewish-Christian community in Alexandria, and that the title was given to it to distinguish it from the Gospel used by the native Christian community, the *Gospel according to the Egyptians*. The language in which the Gospel was written (as we learn from Jerome, *contra Pelag.* iii. 2) was West Aramaic, the language of Christ and His Apostles,—a circumstance which betrays its influence on the narrative in the fact that the Holy Spirit is represented as female ('My Mother the Holy Spirit,' the Aramaic *ruha* being feminine). The Gospel was translated into Latin and Greek by Jerome, who had a very high opinion of it, and was inclined to regard it as the original Matthew; but it is more than probable that it had already circulated in a Greek version in different parts of the Church, and found considerable recognition. It was wrongly identified by Jerome with the Ebionitic Gospel—*the Gospel of the Twelve Apostles*, also attributed to Matthew— which was written originally in Greek, and was in use among the Gnostic Ebionites.

As the fragments which have been preserved to us show, the *Gospel according to the Hebrews* was of the Synoptic type. Whether it contained a story of the Nativity is uncertain, but (considering the Jewish-Christian standpoint of the book) highly improbable. Included, however, were the Baptism, the Temptation, the Lord's Prayer, the Healing of the man with the withered hand, the *pericope adulteræ* (or something similar), the injunction to forgive unto seventy times seven, the conversation with the Rich Young Ruler, the entrance into Jerusalem, the parable of the Pounds, the Trial, the denial of Peter, appearances after the Resurrection, and sayings of Jesus not elsewhere recorded. As a rule, the fragments show a somewhat closer resemblance to Mt. than to the other Synoptics, but there are also details which have their nearer parallels in Luke.

The divergences from the Synoptics are in several cases remarkable in character, and point, in the opinion of many scholars, to an earlier and more reliable tradition. In the narrative of the Baptism, Jesus, in answer to the proposal of His mother and brethren that they should go and be baptized by John for the remission of sins, says: '*In what have I sinned, that I should go and be baptized by him? Unless perhaps this which I have said be ignorance,*'—an utterance which is generally interpreted as meaning that Jesus, though conscious of no sin, was humble enough not to make the claim of sinlessness. (This passage, regarded by some as primitive and authentic, is better understood as the product of reflexion at a time when Christ's baptism was felt to be a problem requiring solution. In the earliest days the presence of the problem was not felt. The writer of the Gospel, who holds to the sinlessness of Jesus, solves the difficulty by pointing to His deep humility).

After the Baptism, the descent of the Spirit is described with greater fulness than in the Synoptics; the dove is awanting, but the voice from heaven is put into the form of an utterance by the Spirit: '*It came to pass, when the Lord was come up out of the water, that the whole fountain of the Holy Spirit came down and rested on Him and said unto Him, My Son, in all the prophets I awaited Thy coming, that I might rest on Thee. For Thou art my rest; Thou art my firstborn Son, who reignest for-ever.*'

A passage, which probably belongs to the narrative of the Temptation, reads: '*The Lord said, Just now My mother, the Holy Spirit, seized Me by one of My hairs and bore Me away to the high mountain Tabor,*'—a fantastic description on the model of Ezk 8[3] and Bel and the Dragon [36].

In the Lord's Prayer the fourth petition runs: '*Give us to-day our bread FOR TO-MORROW.*' In the Aramaic *mahar* ('to-morrow') we may have the word used by Jesus Himself; in which case ἐπιούσιος, translated 'daily' in Mt 6[11], Lk 11[3], would be an adjectival form derived from ἡ ἐπιούσα (the following day). On the other hand, there are scholars who believe that the converse is the case, and that *mahar* is an attempt to give the meaning of ἐπιούσιος (Meyer in Henn. 18, *Handb.* 28 f.). The former alternative is the more probable.

The narrative of the healing on the Sabbath of the man with a withered hand represents the man as appealing to Jesus on the ground that he was a mason who earned his bread by working with his hands,—a detail which may well be authentic.

In the longest fragment of the Gospel we have a version of Christ's interview with the Rich Young Ruler, which shows notable differences from the Synoptic account. Where the Synoptists speak of the rich man's *sorrow* because of his inability to accept Christ's terms, the *Gospel according to the Hebrews*, in vivid and homely language, represents him as showing astonishment and a touch of resentment: '*(He) began to scratch his head, and it did not please him.*' Whereupon Jesus rebuked him for claiming to have fulfilled the law, when he had neglected offices of mercy and brotherly kindness: '*How sayest thou, I have done the law and the prophets? Since it is written in the law, Thou shalt love thy neighbour as thyself; and behold, many of thy brethren, the sons of Abraham, are covered with filth and are dying with hunger, while thy house is full of many good things, and nothing at all goes out of it to them.*' If this account is to be taken as genuine, it is clear that our estimate of the Rich Young Ruler's character, based on the Synoptic tradition, will have to be considerably revised. It is, however, more probable that in this passage we have a mistaken combination of the story of the Rich Young Ruler with the parable of Dives and Lazarus related by Luke.

After the Resurrection, Jesus is represented as appearing *first* to James, to release him from a vow which he had taken at the Last Supper: '*James had sworn that he would not eat bread from that hour, when he had drunk the Lord's cup, until He should see Him risen from those that are asleep.*' This is an obviously later form of the tradition of Christ's appearing to James, due most likely to the desire of Jewish Christians to exalt their head above the Apostles of Christ. It should be noted that James is here portrayed as one of Christ's followers who partook of the Last Supper,—an unhistorical detail. There is probably a confusion between James the Just and James the brother of John, an inference borne out by the reference to drinking the Lord's cup (cf. Mt 20[22]).

Into the difficult question of the relation of the *Gospel according to the Hebrews* to the Synoptics, it is impossible in this article to enter with any fulness. That it is closely allied to them, especially to Mt., is clear from the character of the fragments. Three different solutions of the problem have been suggested, all of them supported by competent authorities. (1) *Hebrews* is held to be the original Aramaic Matthew (Hilgenfeld), or an elaboration of it (Zahn), and as such, the groundwork of our canonical Matthew. This view is now almost universally rejected. (2) *Hebrews* is held to be independent of the Synoptics, the affinity being explained by a common reliance on oral tradition. This view, which is the one at present most widely held, is strongly supported by Harnack, who goes so far as to express the hope (*Chron.* i. 645) that, after Zahn's penetrating discussion of the question, no one will have the hardihood to repeat the statement that the *Gospel according to the Hebrews* is based on one or more canonical Gospels. That hope has not been realized. For (3) the view has recently been confidently advocated by Wernle (*Synop. Frage*, 248 ff.) that *Hebrews* is dependent on all the Synoptics, making use of Matthew, and in some cases combining the accounts of Matthew and Luke. Meyer (in Henn. 18) supports

this view, and strongly emphasizes the secondary character of the Gospel. In this judgment the present writer is disposed to concur. It appears to him that all the facts of the case are satisfactorily explained, if we hold that the *Gospel according to the Hebrews* was written by one who used canonical Matthew (and Luke), and built up his Gospel on the basis of a separate tradition, under the influence of his own doctrinal prepossessions.

But even should the view of the Gospel's independence be accepted, this does not necessarily imply that in it we are face to face with an earlier, or an equally early, stage of the primitive tradition. The realistic presentation, the fondness for little details, the quaint and, in some particulars, undignified language, which are characteristic of the Gospel, may possibly be indications that in some narratives we have the tradition in its original form; on the other hand, these features may with as much probability be due to later manipulation by popular evangelists. Details, such as Christ's words before His baptism, which are by some regarded as primitive on the ground that they are of such a character that they could not have been added later, are believed by others (in our opinion more justly), to be products of an age of reflexion. Traces of a later age than that of the Synoptics are found in the Resurrection fragment: there is the unhistorical detail in reference to the appearing of Christ to James, and the later apologetic interest is shown in securing witness for the resurrection from the enemies of Christ. (After rising from the dead, Jesus handed the linen cloth to the servant of the high priest). The judgment is warranted that, while the *Gospel according to the Hebrews* probably retains in some points the freshness of the original tradition, it contains many elements that are secondary, and that, as a whole, it represents not an earlier, but a somewhat later stage of the Gospel tradition than the Synoptics. A date towards the end of the 1st cent. is probable.

On the view here taken of the *Gospel according to the Hebrews*, the value of its fragments as a source of the life of Jesus is inconsiderable. It cannot justly lay claim to be an authority, as Oscar Holtzmann regards it, on the same level as the Synoptics. Some sayings, however, ascribed to Christ and not elsewhere recorded, have a genuine ring, giving us, if not the *ipsissima verba* of Jesus, at least true echoes of His voice. Christ is represented as saying to His disciples: '*Never be glad, except when ye look upon your brother in love,*'—a singularly beautiful precept condemning *Schadenfreude*, the disposition to rejoice in another's misfortune. The Gospel also reported a saying in which it was reckoned among the greatest offences that one should sadden the spirit of one's brother. Another striking saying, quoted from this Gospel by Clement of Alexandria (*Strom.* ii. 9. 45) and accepted by many as substantially a genuine utterance of Jesus, runs as follows: '*He that wonders shall reach the kingdom, and having reached the kingdom shall rest.*' In another passage (*Strom.* v. 14. 96) Clement records the saying in a longer form, which agrees almost verbally with one of the Oxyrhynchus sayings: '*He who seeks shall not cease until he finds; and when he finds, he shall be astonished, and being astonished he shall reach the kingdom, and having reached the kingdom he shall rest.*'

The ethical teaching of the Gospel, from all that we can gather, was in sympathy with the mind of Christ, stress being laid on brotherly love and forgiveness. Doctrinally, the Gospel occupies the position of the old Jewish Church. It exhibits Jesus as 'the Messiah sent from God, not as the Son of God conceived of the Holy Ghost in a special sense, but as the long expected Messiah of David's race, in whom prophecy finds its fulfilment' (Handmann, *TU* v. 3, p. 125).

LITERATURE.—Hilgenfeld, *NT extra can. receptum*, iv. p. 5 ff. ; Nicholson, *Gospel according to the Hebrews* ; Handmann, ' Das Hebräer-evangelium' (*TU* v. 3) ; Zahn, *Gesch. d. NT Kanons*, ii. 642 ff. ; Harnack, *Gesch. d. altchr. Litt.* i. 6 ff., *Chronologie*, i. 631 ff. ; Hennecke, *NT Apokr.* 11 ff., *Handb.* 21 ff. ; Menzies in Hastings' *DB*, Ext. Vol. 338 ff. ; Adeney in *Hibbert Journal*, Oct. 1904.

A. 2. Gospel according to the Egyptians.—This Gospel, whose ancient date may be inferred from the fact that, like the *Gospel according to the Hebrews*, it bears no author's name, was current in native Christian circles in Egypt. Our information regarding it is very slight : it is mentioned by Origen in his discussion of the prologue in Luke's Gospel, and characterized by him, apparently on the ground of his own knowledge of it, as a heretical writing (' Ecclesia quattuor evangelia habet, hæreses plurima, e quibus quoddam scribitur "secundum Ægyptios"' — tr. by Jerome). All that can with certainty be said to remain of the Gospel is a small group of sayings, recorded by Clement of Alexandria in treating of the attitude of different Christian communities to marriage. References to the Gospel are also found in Hippolytus (*Philos.* v. 7), who states that it was used by the sect of the Naassenes to support their peculiar views about the nature of the soul, and in Epiphanius (*Hær.* 62. 2), who mentions its use by the Sabellians.

The fragments which remain are part of a conversation between Jesus and Salome, and are all of the same character, dealing with the transient (if not sinful) nature of the sex relations. They read as follows :

1. 'Salome asked, "*How long shall death reign ?*" The Lord answered, "*So long as ye women give birth.*" When Salome had said, "*Then should I have done well, if I had not given birth ?*" the Lord answered, "*Eat every plant, but that which is bitter, eat not*"' (Clem. Alex. *Strom.* iii. 6. 45).
2. ' When Salome inquired when those things [the coming of the Kingdom] should be, the Lord said, "*When ye trample on the garment of shame, and when the two become one, and the male with the female, neither male nor female*"' (Clem. Alex. *Strom.* iii. 13. 92).
3. ' The Saviour said, "*I came to destroy the works of the female*"' (Clem. Alex. *Strom.* iii. 9. 63).

The Encratite tendency of these sayings is recognized by the majority of scholars, but is energetically denied by Zahn, who, however, rejects No. 3 as not having stood in the *Gospel according to the Egyptians*. If the third saying be put aside, it is certainly arguable that the first two do not go much farther in an ascetic direction than Mt 22³⁰ (' In the resurrection they neither marry nor are given in marriage, but are as the angels in heaven '). This view finds some support in the fragment of a Gospel discovered at Oxyrhyncus in 1903 (Grenfell and Hunt, *New Sayings*, 44). That Cassian, the Gnostic leader of the Encratites, from whom Clement quoted the sayings, used them to support his ascetic condemnation of marriage, is not decisive. It is noteworthy that Clement rejected Cassian's interpretation, and understood the sayings in a mystical sense. If, however, the Encratite sense of the words be maintained, Harnack is certainly justified by Clement's attitude in concluding that ' Encratism cannot have been the aim of the Gospel, in fact cannot have been stamped upon it as its characteristic feature, but that probably only this one passage occurred in it which could be adduced in favour of the extreme ascetic practice' (*Chron.* i. 616). That the Gospel contained much else that was entirely free from suspicion of heresy is probable ; and this natural inference becomes a certainty, if we accept the widely received opinion, that the *Gospel according to the Egyptians* was used as a principal authority by the writer of the so-called Second Epistle of Clement of Rome (*c.* 170). In this writing, besides a passage closely reminiscent of the *Gospel according to the Egyptians*,* there are several, containing sayings of Jesus, of which some show verbal agreement with the Synoptics, while others, with considerable divergences, are similar in character. On the assumption, which is possible though incapable of proof, that 2nd Clement drew the sayings of Jesus recorded by him from one main source, and this was the *Gospel according to the Egyptians*, Harnack based the conclusion that the Gospel ' contained nothing heretical, else the Roman Church about 170 would certainly not have read it ' ; and, further, that it was an independent Gospel, having affinities with Matthew and Luke,

and containing in some instances sayings in a form even more original than they (*Chron.* i. 619 f.). One must confess that so extremely favourable a judgment, reared on a somewhat uncertain basis, does not inspire entire confidence when over against it one places Origen's view of the Gospel as heretical and its use by the Naassenes and Sabellians. While it may be allowed that there were probably passages in the Gospel which ranked it with the Synoptics, it seems clear that it showed affinities with the speculative teaching of Gnostic schools. It contained references to ' manifold changes' of the soul which were relied on by the Naassene sect in building up their system of thought ; and Epiphanius in refuting the heresy of the Sabellians, who made use of the *Gospel according to the Egyptians*, declared that ' there were in it many things put into the mouth of the Saviour, and said as in a corner mystically, such as His declaration to the disciples that the Father, the Son, and the Holy Spirit were one and the same' (*Hær.* 62. 2).

With so little to rest a confident judgment on, it is extremely difficult to characterize this Gospel, but it may be near the truth to say that it was a Gospel of the Synoptic type with a slight Gnostic colouring.*

The disposition to refer to this Gospel isolated fragments and utterances of Jesus, such as the *Fayûm Fragment* and the *Oxyrhyncus Sayings*, is extremely hazardous. All that can with certainty be said is that some of the recently discovered sayings ' belong to the same sphere of thought ' as the Gospel. Further than that it is impossible to go (see Grenfell and Hunt, *New Sayings*, 27 ff.).

The date of the Gospel is about the middle of the 2nd cent., probably between 130 and 150.

LITERATURE.—Hilgenfeld, *NT extra can.* iv. 42 ff.; Harnack, *Gesch. d. altchr. Litt.* i 12 ff., *Chron.* i. 612 ff.; Zahn, *NT Kan.* ii. 628 ff.; Völter, *Petrusevangelium oder Aegypterevangelium*, 1893 ; Schneckenburger, *Ueber das Evangelium der Aegypter*, 1834 ; Hennecke, *NT Apokr.* 21 ff., *Handb.* 38 ff.; Tasker, *l.c.* 423 ff.

A. 3. Gospel of Peter. — In his enumeration of Petrine writings, Eusebius mentions (*HE* iii. 3) a Gospel which, along with the *Acts*, *Preaching* and *Apocalypse of Peter*, he declares to be spurious, and not considered authoritative by any ecclesiastical writer. Until fourteen years ago, our knowledge of the contents of the Gospel was of the scantiest description, being based on a slight reference by Origen, on a letter by Serapion, bishop of Antioch (end of 2nd cent.), and on a passage in Theodoret, now generally discredited, which states that the Nazarenes, who honoured Christ as a just man, used the *Gospel according to Peter* (*Hær. Fabb.* ii. 2). Origen's reference (*Com. in Matt.* bk. x. 17) tells us nothing more than that those who believed the brethren of Jesus to be the sons of Joseph by a former wife relied on the *Gospel of Peter* and the *Book of James* ; from which we infer that the Gospel contained the narrative of the Virgin - birth. From Serapion's letter (part of it preserved in Euseb. *HE* vi. 12), which was written to the Church in Rhossus in the diocese of Antioch, we gather the following facts about the Gospel. When on a visit to Rhossus, Serapion had the Gospel brought under his notice, as being the occasion of some ill-feeling in the Church. Not suspecting any heretical leanings on the part of those who were favourable to the Gospel, the bishop, without any careful examination of its contents, sought to establish peace by authorizing it to be read. Having learned afterwards that the Gospel had originated among the Docetæ, he procured a copy from some members of that party, and found that, while it contained much true teaching, there were additions of a questionable character, to which he proceeded to call attention. Until recently this was all that was known of the *Gospel of Peter* ; not a single fragment had been handed down ; one could only gather that it was a

---

* ' The Lord Himself having been asked by some one, When will the kingdom come? said, When the two shall be one, and the outside as the inside, and the male with the female, neither male nor female' (2 Clem. xii. 2).

* Von Dobschütz (*Die urchr. Gemeinden*, 190) finds in the Gospel a trace of the Gnostic idea of the subversion of all ordinary standards of value, from which ' it is only a short step to the perversion of all ethical conceptions.' This view is justly opposed by Zahn (*NT Kan.* ii. 640).

Gospel with a slight Docetic colouring, but for the most part entirely orthodox.

Of this long lost Gospel we have now a fragment of considerable length dealing with the Passion and Resurrection of Christ. The fragment was found in the winter of 1886–1887 at Akhmîm, in Upper Egypt, by the French Archæological Mission, and was published by M. Bouriant in 1892. The narrative claims to be the personal witness of the Apostle Peter, and reveals the Docetic tendency referred to by Serapion. The fragment begins at the end of the judgment-scene, after Pilate had washed his hands, and ends in the middle of a sentence, which introduces the narrative describing the appearance of Christ to His disciples at the Sea of Galilee. The nature of the contents can here only be indicated.

Herod is regarded as the real judge of Christ; throughout, there is the evident intention to exculpate Pilate, who washed his hands, while Herod refused. It is Herod who gives the order for the crucifixion, and his permission is required for the disposal of the body of Jesus. When Jesus was handed over to the people, it is stated that '*they clothed Him with purple and set Him on the seat of judgment, saying, Judge righteously, O King of Israel.*' * On the cross we learn that Jesus '*held His peace, as in no wise having pain.*' One of the malefactors reproached the Jews standing round the cross (not his fellow-sufferer, as in Lk 23⁴⁰), and '*they, being angered with him, commanded that his legs should not be broken, that he might die in torment.*' After referring to the darkness which came over the land, the narrative runs: '*And the Lord cried out, saying, My power, My power, thou hast forsaken Me. And when He had said this, He was taken up.*' After the death of Christ the Jews began to feel compunction for what they had done; they '*began to lament and to say, Woe for our sins; the judgment and the end of Jerusalem are nigh. . . . All the people murmured and beat their breasts, saying, If by His death those most mighty signs have happened, behold, how righteous He is.*' The Jewish authorities, having received soldiers from Pilate to guard the tomb '*for three days,*' themselves took part in the watch. The Resurrection is described with many miraculous details; there is a voice from heaven; two men, encircled by a great light, descend and enter the tomb, from which the stone rolls away of itself. Then the watchers '*see three men coming out of the tomb, the two supporting the one, and a cross following them; and the heads of the two reached as far as heaven, but that of Him that was led overtopped the heavens. And they heard a voice from heaven saying, Hast thou preached to them that sleep? And a response was heard from the cross, Yea.*' When Pilate was informed of all that had happened, he said, '*I am pure from the blood of the Son of God.*' He was entreated by the Jewish authorities to command the centurion and the soldiers to tell nothing of what they had seen, '*for it is better (say they) for us to be guilty of the greatest sin before God than to fall into the hands of the people of the Jews and be stoned.*' The rest of the fragment deals with the visit of Mary Magdalene and other women to the sepulchre, and with the grief of the disciples. The fragment closes as follows: '*But we, the twelve disciples of the Lord, wept and were grieved; and each one, being grieved for that which was come to pass, departed to his home. But I, Simon Peter, and Andrew my brother, took our nets and went to the sea; and there was with us Levi, the son of Alphaeus, whom the Lord . . .*'

The writer's peculiar point of view is clear from the quotations which have been given. (1) The most noticeable feature of the Gospel is its pronounced apologetic interest, shown in its friendliness to Pilate and its antipathy to the Jews. Pilate is freed from all blame in the death of Christ, Herod being the responsible judge; Joseph, who cared for the body of Jesus, is 'the friend of Pilate.' Pilate, too, is represented as acknowledging the Divine dignity of Jesus. On the other hand, the Jews acknowledge their sin in putting Jesus to death, and confess Him to have been a just man. The writer's fierce hatred of the Jews is betrayed in the utterance ascribed to the Jewish authorities, that they would rather be guilty of the greatest

* Justin Martyr (*Apol.* i. 35) has a similar statement. 'They mocked Him and set Him on the judgment‑seat, and said, Judge for us.' The corresponding passage in St. John's Gospel (19¹³) reads: 'When Pilate, therefore, heard these words, he brought Jesus out and *sat upon the judgment-seat*' (*καὶ ἐκάθισεν ἐπὶ βήματος*). It is, however, legitimate to translate *ἐκάθισεν* in the transitive sense, so that the verse would run: 'He brought Jesus out and set Him on the judgment-seat.' The passage in St. John, understood in this sense, is probably the source from which the statements in Justin and the *Gospel of Peter* are derived.

sin than fall into the hands of men. (2) The Docetic sympathies of the writer, which are somewhat guarded, are revealed in the statement that Jesus kept silence on the cross, '*as in no wise feeling pain*'; in the cry of dereliction, which points to a distinction between the impassible Divine Power residing in Jesus and His passible human nature; in the representation of Christ's death as a being taken up. That the Docetism was not of an extreme type is shown by the fact that the dead Christ is referred to as 'the Lord.' Gnostic influences are discernible in the speaking of the cross, and in the supernatural height of Jesus and the angels.

The Gospel is of the Synoptic type. It has close linguistic and material relations with the Synoptics, although there are many deviations in order and detail. There is a considerable probability that the author knew and made use of *all* our canonical Gospels, which he treated with great freedom, embellishing the narrative in the interest of his own point of view, and making additions of a legendary and highly miraculous character. That he had an independent tradition at his command is possible, and even probable (? ancient *Acts of Pilate*); but whether that be so or not, his Gospel adds nothing to our knowledge of the life of Christ. 'It appears to be a fair example of what may be called the second generation of non-canonical narratives, which are based upon the earlier and authentic records, and do not yet depart very widely from them, though they may have special tendencies in various doctrinal directions' (Kenyon, *Gospels in the Early Church*, 34).

The date of the Gospel is about the middle of the 2nd cent., although some critics put it considerably earlier. Its place of origin was almost certainly Syria.

LITERATURE.—Bouriant, *Mémoires publiés par les membres de la mission archéologique française au Caire*, ix. i. 137 ff.; Harnack, *TU* ix. 2; Zahn, *Das Evangelium des Petrus*; von Schubert, *Die Komposition des pseudopetr. Evangeliumfragment*, (tr. by Macpherson); Lods, *L'évangile et l'apocalypse de Pierre*; Robinson and James, *Gospel and Revelation of Peter*; Swete, *Gospel of St. Peter*; also editions by Rendel Harris, the author of *Supernatural Religion*, Rutherford (extra volume of Ante Nicene Library); Stülcken in Hennecke, *NT Apokr.* 27 ff.; *Handb.* 72 ff.; and numerous magazine articles.

A. 4. Fayûm Gospel Fragment.—A number of papyri were, in the year 1882, brought from Fayûm, a province in Central Egypt, to Vienna, by the Archduke Rainer. Among these, Dr. Bickell of Innsbrück discovered a small Gospel fragment, dealing with the incident in which Jesus foretold the denial of Peter. The fragment, which is badly mutilated, was published in 1885 by Bickell, who confidently maintained that it was a part of a very ancient lost Gospel, of the class referred to in Lk 1¹. The contents of the fragment closely resemble the Synoptic narrative (Mk 14²⁷. ²⁹. ³⁰, Mt 26³¹. ³³. ³⁴), with the omission of the verse containing Christ's promise to go before His disciples into Galilee after rising from the dead. Owing to the condition of the papyrus, the text, especially at the beginning of the fragment, is very uncertain; but, according to the reconstruction of Zahn (*NT Kan.* ii. 785), the translation is as follows:

'[*When they had sung a hymn, after*] *supper, according to their custom, He said again, This night ye shall be offended, according to the Scripture, I will smite the shepherd, and the sheep shall be scattered. But when Peter said, Even if all (shall be offended), I will not, He said, To-day before the cock crow twice, thou shalt deny Me thrice.*'

The nature of the document to which the fragment originally belonged is altogether uncertain. Bickell's opinion, that it is a part of a Gospel of high antiquity, has received the support of Harnack, who inclines to regard it as an excerpt from either the *Gospel according to the Hebrews* or the *Gospel according to the Egyptians* (*TU* v. 4. 493 ff., *Chron.* i. 590). On the other hand, Zahn believes it to be an extract from a Patristic writing, a free quotation from Mark made by a preacher or by the writer of a book for edification. This would satisfactorily account for the omission of Mk 14²⁸ (Mt 26³²). That the fragment probably belonged to a writing of this kind is further borne out by two striking deviations from the Synoptic phraseology. Instead of ἀλέκτωρ (cock) the fragment has the more classical ἀλεκτρυών; instead of the colourless φωνεῖν (crow) it has the more descriptive word κοκκύζειν. 'The probability is that the canonical expression is the original, which a preacher replaced in the one case by a more elegant word, in the other by one more significant' (Zahn, *NT Kan.* ii. 788). Hennecke (*NT Apokr.* 9) thinks it possible that the fragment may have been a part of a collection of sayings, but subscribes to Krüger's judgment, that 'the possibility is not excluded that the fragment merely represents an extract from one of our Gospels, or belonged to a Gospel harmony, perhaps even is drawn from a homily, and that one is not justified in drawing far-reaching conclusions from it.'

LITERATURE. — Bickell in *Zeitschrift für Kathol. Theologie*, 1885, iii. 498 ff. ; Harnack, Zahn, Hennecke (in *opp. cit.*).

A. 5. Oxyrhyncus Gospel Fragment.—In the year 1903 Messrs. Grenfell and Hunt discovered at Behnesa, the ancient Oxyrhyncus, in Central Egypt, a small portion of a Gospel containing the conclusion of a discourse by Jesus similar to a part of the Sermon on the Mount. This they published, along with a second collection of 'Sayings,' in the following year. The papyrus is in a very broken state, only a small part of that which it originally contained being decipherable. From the handwriting the discoverers adjudge the fragment to have been written not later than A.D. 250, although the original composition was much earlier.

The translation of the fragment, slightly altered from that given by Grenfell and Hunt (*New Sayings*, 40), is as follows :

'*[Take no thought] from morning until even, nor from evening until morning, either for your food what ye shall eat or for your raiment what ye shall put on. Ye are far better than the lilies which grow but spin not. Having one garment, what do ye [lack?] . . . Who could add to your stature? He Himself will give you your garment. His disciples say unto Him, When wilt Thou be manifest to us, and when shall we see Thee? He saith, When ye shall be stripped and not be ashamed. . . . He said, The key of knowledge they hid : they entered not in themselves, and to them that were entering in they opened not; but ye, be ye wise as serpents and harmless as doves.*'

The sayings here given are, for the most part, parallel to passages found in Matthew and Luke, in a form generally somewhat shorter than the canonical version. Christ's answer to the question of the disciples as to when He should manifest Himself, 'When ye shall be stripped and not be ashamed . . .,' recalls the saying reported in the *Gospel according to the Egyptians* : 'When ye trample upon the garment of shame,' etc., and suggests the conclusion that the fragment stood in intimate relation with that Gospel. The simpler form of the saying in the fragment, and the more direct allusion to Gn 3⁷, point to an earlier date than that of the version in the *Gospel according to the Egyptians*. Though it is possible that the fragment represents a tradition independent of the Synoptics, it is more probable that the Gospel to which it belonged worked up the material found in Matthew and Luke into new combinations, and added matter drawn from other sources. The date of the Gospel was probably somewhat earlier than the middle of the 2nd century.

**B. *HERETICAL AND GNOSTIC GOSPELS.*—Only a few of the more important Gnostic Gospels are referred to in this article. Many are known to us by name merely, or by some indication of the circles in which they were current. Although the

Gnostics repudiated the canonical Apostolic writings, they sought in many instances to secure authority for their Gospels by attributing them to Apostles or to others well known in Apostolic times. Besides those mentioned below, there were *Gospels of Matthias*, of *Bartholomew*, of *Andrew*, of *Barnabas*; and even the name of *Judas Iscariot* was associated with the authorship of the Gospel. Gnostic Gospels sometimes bore the name of the founder of the school (Valentinus, Basilides, Cerinthus), but in these cases the writer of the Gospel claimed to have received his information from some Apostle or follower of an Apostle. OT names were also attached to some Gospels ; Epiphanius (*Hær.* 26. 2) refers to a *Gospel of Eve*. For whatever knowledge we have of these Gospels, readers are referred to Hofmann's article (*PRE*³ i. 661 ff.) or to Tasker's article (*l.c.* 437 f.).

B. 1. Gospel of Marcion.—Shortly before the middle of the 2nd cent., Marcion, a native of Pontus, settled in Rome, where he devoted himself to the work of purifying the Church from all Jewish influences. The underlying principle of his system was the conception of the absolute antagonism between the God of the OT and the God of the NT. Only in Christ was the true God made known. He, accordingly, rejected the OT, and prepared for the Churches which he founded a canon of NT writings, divided into 'the Gospel' and 'the Apostle.' The original Apostles, he maintained, had misunderstood the teaching of Christ; only Paul had grasped the true significance of the gospel. Into his canon he admitted ten Epistles of Paul, largely expurgated, and one Gospel, which he claimed to be the Pauline Gospel (τὸ εὐαγγέλιόν μου, Ro 2¹⁶). This Gospel, according to the testimony of early Church writers, was the Gospel of Luke, from which great omissions had been made to free it from all Jewish colouring. All citations from the OT were cut out, and everything else which looked with favour on the Jews. From the quotations given by Tertullian, Epiphanius, and others, it is possible to reconstruct Marcion's Gospel. The whole of the Infancy narrative, the Baptism, and the Temptation were omitted, nothing of the first three chapters in Luke being retained but the chronological notice in 3¹. The history of Jesus commences with 4¹⁴, and from that point to the end of the Gospel larger or smaller portions are excised, amounting in all to over 120 verses. Among the passages excluded are the parables of the Prodigal Son and of the wicked Husbandmen. In all, including the omissions of the first three chapters and part of the fourth, we find that Marcion's Gospel was shorter than Luke's by fully 300 verses.

Against all Patristic testimony some critics (Semler and Eichhorn in the 18th cent., Baur, Ritschl, and Schwegler in the 19th) maintained the priority of Marcion's Gospel to that of Luke. The traditional view was, however, so completely vindicated by Hilgenfeld and Volkmar, that Ritschl retracted. In our own country, somewhat later, the battle was refought, with the same result. The author of *Supernatural Religion* revived the theory of Marcion's originality, and called forth a reply by Dr. Sanday (*Gospels in the Second Century*, ch. viii.), in which he conclusively proved, to the satisfaction of his opponent, that Luke's Gospel was from *one* hand, the same characteristics of style being evident in Marcion's Gospel and in the sections of Luke not found in it.

Where the text of Marcion differs from Luke, there is evidence in some cases to show that the variance is due, not to any arbitrary change made by Marcion in the interest of his peculiar views, but to the copy of the Third Gospel which lay before him. The readings of Marcion thus deserve consideration in the study of Textual Criticism.

LITERATURE.—Zahn, *NT Kan.* i. 674 ff., ii. 409 ff. ; Sanday, *Gospels in the Second Century*, ch. viii., art. 'Luke, Gospel of' (Hastings' *DB* iii. 168 f.); Salmon, *Introd. to NT*, 186 ff. ; Westcott, *Canon of NT*, 314 ff.

B. 2. Gospel of the Twelve Apostles.

—Among the heretical attempts to write the history of Jesus, Origen in his *Homily* on Lk 1[ff.] mentions 'the Gospel of the Twelve Apostles' (τὸ ἐπιγεγραμμένον τῶν δώδεκα εὐαγγέλιον). That this Gospel is the same as one which Epiphanius (*Hær.* 30. 3) describes as 'The Gospel according to Matthew' in use among the Gnostic Ebionites, is clear from the fact that in the opening passage quoted by Epiphanius we have the call of the twelve Apostles, of whom Matthew is specially addressed ('and thee, Matthew, I called, while thou wast sitting at the seat of custom'). Epiphanius further states that the Ebionites called their Gospel 'The Gospel according to the Hebrews,' a reference which may rest on a confusion on the part of Epiphanius (as Harnack thinks), but more probably is quite accurate. Nothing seems more likely than that the Gnostic Jewish-Christian sect, acquainted with the tradition that Matthew wrote his Gospel in Hebrew, should have claimed that their Gospel was the genuine Gospel of Matthew, and, accordingly, the true Hebrew Gospel (Hennecke, *NT Apokr.* 24). If this be so, we have an explanation of the error into which Jerome fell when he identified the *Gospel according to the Hebrews* with the *Gospel 'according to the Apostles'* in use among the Nazarenes (c. *Pelag.* iii. 2). That these two Gospels were entirely different is apparent from the widely divergent accounts of the Baptism,—the one incident, common to both, described in their extant fragments.

All that remains of the Gospel of the Ebionites is found in Epiphanius (*Hær.* 30. 13, 14, 16, 22). The Gospel opens with the ministry of the Baptist : '*It came to pass in the days of Herod, the king of Judæa, that John came baptizing with the baptism of repentance in the river Jordan.*' Then somewhat abruptly, after the manner of the Fourth Gospel, Jesus is introduced in the midst of the narrative dealing with the Baptist. '*There was a certain man named Jesus (and He was about thirty years old), who chose us.*' An account of the calling of the Apostles follows, special emphasis being laid on the call of Matthew. Then the broken thread of the narrative is again taken up. '*And John was baptizing, and Pharisees came out to him and were baptized, and all Jerusalem. . . . His food was wild honey, the taste of which was the taste of manna, like a honey-cake in oil.*' In the narrative of Christ's baptism which follows, *three* voices come from heaven ; the first, '*Thou art My beloved Son, in Thee I am well pleased,*' being repeated for the benefit of the Baptist, '*This is My beloved Son,*' etc. ; the second is addressed to Christ, '*I have this day begotten Thee.*' Another fragment describes the incident recorded in Mt 12[47-50] in words which vary only very slightly from the canonical version. Characteristic of the teaching of the Gospel are the two remaining fragments : '*I am come to destroy sacrifices, and except ye cease from sacrificing, wrath will not cease from you*' ; and '*Surely I have in no wise desired to eat flesh at this passover with you.*'

The tendency of the Gospel is characteristically Ebionitic. All that is reported of Jesus is in harmony with the views of the Gnostic Ebionites (Elkesaites), who combined the old Jewish-Christian belief in Jesus as a mere man, anointed to be Messiah through the descent of the Spirit at baptism, with the doctrine of a heavenly Christ, 'who wanders over the common earth among men, like a strange guest from heaven, in order that He may lead into His eternal kingdom all that is spiritual and pure in this impure material world' (Hennecke, 25). The matter-of-fact way in which Jesus is introduced in the Gospel ('there was a certain man named Jesus') points to the view that of Himself Jesus was nothing to the members of this sect, but only became significant as the object of faith through the descent of the heavenly Christ. The ascetic (vegetarian) views of the Ebionites and their hatred of sacrifices of blood are manifest in the fragments. In accordance with his vegetarian sympathies, the author removes locusts (ἀκρίδας) from the Baptist's diet, and by way of compensation states that the honey which he ate tasted like honey-cake (ἐγκρίς) in oil. The play on the words ἀκρίς and ἐγκρίς shows that our Greek Gospels, and not a Hebrew original, lay before the writer. The author in the composition of his work made use of the canonical Gospels in a free and clumsy manner. The narrative of the Baptism, in particular, is extremely awkward and badly told. No scruples deterred the writer from changing the words of Christ to the directly opposite sense by the simple insertion of a negative ('I have in no wise desired to eat this passover-flesh with you' ; cf. Lk 22[15]). The date of the Gospel is late in the 2nd cent. ; Zahn puts it at 170 ; Harnack not earlier than 180, and perhaps as late as the beginning of the 3rd cent.

LITERATURE.—Credner, *Beiträge*, i. 332 ff. ; Hilgenfeld, *NT extra can.* iv. 33 ff. ; Zahn, *NT Kan.* ii. 724 ff. ; Harnack, *Gesch. d. altchr. Litt.* i. 205 ff., *Chron.* i. 625 ff. ; Meyer in Hennecke, *NT Apokr.* 24 ff., *Handb.* 42 ff.

B. 3. Gospel of Thomas.

—A single citation from a Gnostic Gospel of Thomas is given by Hippolytus (*Philos.* v. 7), who states that he found it in a writing in use among the Naassenes : '*He who seeks me shall find me in children from seven years old ; for there concealed in the fourteenth æon I shall be made manifest.*' Origen (*Hom. in Luc.* i. 1) speaks of a *Gospel of Thomas* ; and a Gospel bearing that name is placed by Eusebius (*HE* iii. 25. 6) among heretical writings. Cyril of Jerusalem (*Cat.* iv. 36), referring to 'spurious and noxious Gospels,' mentions a *Gospel according to Thomas* written by the Manichæans ; and in another passage (*Cat.* vi. 31) he warns all against reading it, as it is written not by an Apostle, but by 'one of the three evil disciples of Manes.' The *Decretum Gelasii* condemns a *Gospel of Thomas* which was used by the Manichæans. In what relation (if any) the Manichæan Gospel stood to the Gnostic Gospel, referred to by Hippolytus, is indiscoverable, as no fragment of the former is known. That the Gnostic Gospel bears some relation to the *Childhood Gospel of Thomas* is practically certain from what we know of the latter, and from the character of the passage cited by Hippolytus. There are indications in the *Childhood Gospel* which point to a Gnostic origin ; and this being the case, if the two Gospels were entirely independent, it would be nothing less than marvellous that, while the one is composed of narratives of Christ's childhood, the only fragment preserved of the other should contain a cryptic utterance of Christ about children. (See below, C. (a) 2, where also literature will be found).

B. 4. Gospel of Philip.

—A solitary fragment of this Gospel is preserved in Epiphanius (*Hær.* 26. 13), who states : 'The Gnostics cite a Gospel, forged in the name of Philip the holy Apostle, as saying :

'*The Lord revealed to me what the soul must say in ascending to heaven, and how she must answer each of the upper powers: "I have known myself and gathered myself from all quarters, and I have borne no children to the Archon [the ruler of this world], but I have rooted up his roots and gathered the scattered members, and I know who thou art. For I am one of those who are from above." And so she is released. But if one be found who has borne a son, she is kept below until she is able to recover her own children and to educate them for herself.*'

The Coptic Gnostic writing, the *Pistis Sophia*, bears witness to the existence in the 3rd cent. of the *Gospel of Philip* in Gnostic circles in Egypt. It is there stated : 'And when Jesus had made an end of speaking these words, Philip leaped up and stood, and laid down the book which was in his hand, for he it is who writes all things which Jesus said and did' (Harnack, *Gesch. d. altchr. Litt.*

i. 14). It is clear from this notice, as well as from the passage quoted by Epiphanius, that the contents of the *Gospel of Philip* were not of the same character as those of the canonical Gospels, but were of an esoteric nature, revelations of hidden truth purporting to have been communicated by the Risen Lord. The extreme Encratite views of the Gnostic writer are apparent; the assertion of the soul that on earth it has abstained from marriage, is the only passport into heaven.

The *Gospel of Philip* belongs to the large class of Gnostic writings well described as Gospel-Apocalypses, which owed their origin to the peculiar conception which the Gnostics entertained regarding the person of Christ. The true Saviour was not the earthly Jesus, but the heavenly Christ who sojourned in Him, and who was fully liberated for the work of salvation by the Resurrection. Salvation consisted in freeing the souls of men from the dominion of the God of this world, by the communication of the heavenly knowledge (Gnosis); and this knowledge was revealed by Christ as a mystery to His Apostles, partly in parables whose meaning was hid from the common crowd, partly in a secret tradition given after the Resurrection. The true gnosis was reserved for the small number of πνευματικοί, whose spirit was derived from the upper world, and who, when purified from their connexion with the earth, returned into the kingdom of light. These views are clearly reflected in the fragment of the Gospel of Philip.

The date of the Gospel is towards the end of the 2nd century.

LITERATURE.—Harnack, *Altchr. Litt.* i. 14 f., *Chron.* i. 592 f.; Zahn, *NT Kan.* ii. 761 ff.; Hennecke, *NT Apokr.* 40, *Handb.* 91.

C. (*a*) **1. Protevangelium of James.**—This writing, dealing with the history of Mary and the Infancy of Jesus, was first published in the West in a Latin translation by the French humanist Postellus about the middle of the 16th century. Some years later the Greek text was issued by Michael Neander. The title 'Protevangelium' (Earliest Gospel) occurs for the first time, so far as we know, in the edition of Postellus; the writing itself claims to be, not a Gospel, but a *history*. ('The History of James concerning the birth of the All-Holy Mother of God,' or something similar, is the title in the MSS. See Tischendorf's *Evang. Apocr.* 1). It is not improbable that the name 'Protevangelium' was given by Postellus himself, who had an extremely high opinion of the book. In earlier times it is never referred to as a *Gospel*, save in the lists of spurious writings condemned by ecclesiastical authority in the 4th and 5th cents. : 'cetera autem (evangelia), quæ vel sub nomine Matthiæ sive *Jacobi minoris* . . . non solum repudianda, verum etiam noveris esse damnanda' (Decree of Innocent I., A.D. 405). The person referred to as the author ('I, James, wrote this history') was in early times universally believed to be the Lord's brother, the head of the Church at Jerusalem. The true author is unknown.

The earliest certain reference to the *Protevangelium* occurs in Origen (middle of 3rd cent.), who states that many, on the authority of the 'Book of James' (and the Gospel of Peter), believed the brothers of Jesus to have been the sons of Joseph by a former marriage. Allusions to details mentioned in the Gospel are found (*c.* 200) in Clement of Alexandria (*Strom.* vii. 16. 93), and (*c.* 140) in Justin Martyr (*Dial.* 78; 100, *Apol.* 33); these, however, do not necessarily point to dependence on the *Protevangelium*, but may have been, and in Justin's case probably were, drawn from floating tradition. Zahn dates the writing in the early decades of the 2nd cent. ; but most scholars place it later, in the second half of the century.

In its present form the *Protevangelium* narrates the childlessness of Joachim and Anna, the shame and reproach that fell upon them on that account, and the birth of Mary in answer to their prayer (chs. 1–5). When Mary is three years old, she is taken to the temple, where she lives until her twelfth year, being fed by the hand of an angel (chs. 7. 8). The priests then consult as to what they should do with her, and are instructed by an angel, in answer to prayer, to summon the widowers of the people, each with a rod in his hand, that God may give a sign whose wife she should be (ch. 8). Joseph attends in obedience to the summons, and is marked out for the charge of 'the virgin of the Lord' by a dove coming out of his rod and alighting on his head. Joseph would fain refuse, because he has children and is an old man ; but, being solemnly charged by the priest, he takes Mary to his house and immediately leaves home on business (ch. 9). Thereafter, the priests, desirous of having a veil made for the temple, summon 'the undefiled virgins of the family of David,' and among them Mary, who is chosen by lot to spin the true purple and the scarlet. With these she returns home (ch. 10). While drawing water at the well, she hears a voice pronouncing her blessed. When she returns, trembling, to the house, an angel appears to her as she sits spinning, and announces that she will conceive by the power of the Lord (ch. 11). Then follows the narrative of the visit to Elisabeth, at the close of which it is stated that 'she was *sixteen* years old when these mysteries happened' (ch. 12). Joseph now returns from his work of building, and, on seeing her state, reproaches her (ch. 13). An angel of the Lord appears to him and informs him of the mystery (ch. 14). Joseph is accused of defiling the virgin of the Lord ; and when both he and Mary proclaim their innocence, they are compelled to drink the water of ordeal, and are unhurt (chs. 15. 16). When the imperial decree of enrolment is issued, Joseph sets out to Bethlehem with Mary. On the way, near to Bethlehem, her days are fulfilled ; Joseph leads her into a cave, and, leaving his two sons with her, goes to seek a woman to attend her (ch. 17). [At this point the narrative changes suddenly from the third person to the first : ' And I, Joseph, was walking, and was not walking']. Joseph sees the whole of Nature standing still ; birds and sheep and men are motionless, a sudden arrest having been put upon their movements (ch. 18). A woman is found, who enters the cave, which is illumined by a dazzling light ; the light gradually decreases, and the infant is seen, who takes the breast from his mother. Another woman, Salome, appears, and is incredulous when she is told of the virgin-birth ; she seeks a proof, and her hand burns as with fire, but is restored when she touches the infant (chs. 19. 20). [The impersonal narrative is now resumed]. The visit of the Magi is next described in language very similar to that in Matthew (ch. 21). Herod, learning that he has been mocked by the Magi, orders the massacre of children under two years. Mary hides her child in an ox-stall (ch. 22). The rest of the narrative deals with John the Baptist and Zacharias. Zacharias, because he will not reveal where his son is concealed, is murdered in the temple. His body miraculously disappears, but his blood is found turned into stone (chs. 22–24). The narrative ends with a thanksgiving of James for having received the gift and wisdom to write the history (ch. 25).

There is a general agreement that the *Protevangelium*, as it has come down to us, is not in its original shape. The group of incidents dealing with Zacharias and John the Baptist are in no way essential to the author's purpose ; they are indeed irrelevant and disturbing. An ancient apocryphal writing, of which Zacharias was the subject, is known to have existed ; and it seems highly probable that part of this was awkwardly appended to the original Book of James. This happened, there is ground for believing, in the 5th century. That it did not form a part of the original writing finds some support in the fact that Origen, who refers to the *Protevangelium*, gives a different account of the death of Zacharias. There is considerable difference of opinion as to whether the rest of the book is the work of one author. The abrupt introduction of Joseph, speaking in the first person (chs. 18–20), gives convincing evidence that that section is not from the hand of the writer of the Gospel, although that by no means implies that it was introduced into his history by another. Harnack believes that the original Book of James did not contain this narrative by Joseph ; but if so, it was a singularly aimless piece of writing, stopping short of the consummation which gives the whole early history of Mary significance, and to which that history manifestly looks, namely, her giving birth to Jesus in virginity. We conclude that the *Apocryphum Josephi* (as Harnack calls it) was incorporated in his work by the author himself, and that not unskilfully, reference being found in it to details which had been already related. In the section dealing with Mary's connexion with the Temple, there are also signs of different sources. It is noticeable that, when Mary leaves the Temple under the care of Joseph, she is represented as being twelve years old ; on the other hand, it is said that at the time of her pregnancy she was sixteen years old, although it is clear, from the main scheme of the narrative, that the conception took place soon after her departure from the Temple, during Joseph's absence from home on business. It is more than probable that we have a combination of two accounts telling of Mary's association with the Temple, one narrating her residence there until she was twelve years of age, the other representing her as being brought, when she was sixteen, to spin material for the temple veil, because she was of the family of David. There is no reason, however, for supposing that these different traditions were combined by any one else than the author of the history.

With the exception of the Zacharias group of incidents, the *Protevangelium* is a well-designed unity, a skilfully constructed romance, in which the author, with the help of material lying ready to his hand, achieved to his own satisfaction the definite purpose which he had in view. What this purpose was it is not difficult to divine. It was to defend the orthodox conception of Christ's person against a double attack, and to give an answer to those who taunted Christians with the lowly if not shameful birth of Jesus. Accordingly, Mary was represented as of royal descent, the daughter of a wealthy man, brought up in the pure atmosphere of the Temple; that was a sufficient answer to every calumny about her character, and to every sneer about her humble rank. Against the Gnostic view that Jesus, in being born of Mary, did not partake of her human nature, it was enough to mention that the infant took the breast from His mother. The whole strength of the author was, however, devoted to safeguarding the Divinity of Jesus against Jewish-Christian misconceptions. That end, he conceived, could be best attained by exalting the person of Mary, by revealing her as one who, from birth to womanhood, had retained an absolute purity and virginity. She was born, in answer to prayer, to parents who had long been childless; she was brought up in the Temple, and fed on heavenly food; in virginity she conceived by the power of the Lord; in virginity she gave birth; in virginity she remained to the end. At every stage her virginity is raised above suspicion; the drinking of the water of the ordeal guarded her virginity in conception; the witness of Salome established it in the birth; while the statement, given under the authority of James, that the brethren of Jesus were sons of Joseph by a former wife, was sufficient to remove any doubts of her virginity to the last.

The author of the *Protevangelium*, it is clear, was no Jewish Christian. His ignorance of Jewish usages is notably betrayed in the representation of Mary as a temple-virgin (an unheard of thing among the Jews), and in the water of the ordeal being administered to Joseph (see Nu 5). The Hebraistic colouring is due to the sources which the writer used. In certain of the incidents he is influenced by OT narratives (birth and dedication of Samuel, Aaron's rod, etc.), which he doubtless read in the Greek version. The canonical accounts of the Annunciation and Nativity have been largely drawn upon. Conrady's views, that the *Protevangelium* was the source of Matthew and Luke (*Die Quelle d. kan. Kindheitsgeschichten*), and that it was originally written in Hebrew (*SK*, 1889, p. 728 ff.), have received no support. The former view Hennecke characterizes as 'kritische Geschmacklosigkeit.'

The *Protevangelium* was condemned by the Western Church in the decrees of Damasus (382), Innocent I. (405), and Gelasius (496). Popular Christianity, however, demanded something in the place of that which had been forbidden, and letters were forged, one to Jerome from the bishops Chromatius of Aquileia and Heliodorus of Altinum, the other the answer of Jerome, from which it appeared that the learned Father had acceded to the bishops' request to translate into Latin the original Hebrew Matthew. This explains the appearance of *The Gospel of pseudo-Matthew*, which freely worked over the contents of the *Protevangelium*, gave an account of the Flight to Egypt and the miracles wrought on the way, and added narratives drawn from the *Childhood Gospel of Thomas*. A detail, which is frequently represented

in Christian art,—the ox and the ass at the manger, —appears for the first time in this Gospel. The veneration of Mary, which received an impulse in the *Protevangelium*, has now grown to greater proportions; she is glorified as 'the Queen of the Virgins,' and her holy, nun-like manner of life is dwelt upon at considerable length. The date of *ps.-Matt.* is 6th century.

The Gospel of the Nativity of Mary, also connected with Jerome by another forged letter, covers the same ground as the *Protevangelium* (with the exception of the Zacharias legend). The aim of the book is to exalt Mary as the spotless virgin; after her betrothal to Joseph she does not go home with him, but returns to her parents' house. There she receives the angel's message. The Gospel closes with the bare mention of the birth of Jesus. This new recension of the *Protevangelium* was doubtless due to an orthodox revulsion of feeling against the somewhat coarse and extravagant nature of *pseudo-Matthew*. The date is probably late in the 6th century.

LITERATURE.—Hilgenfeld, *Einleitung*, 152; Tischendorf, *Evangelia Apocr.* xii–xxii; Zahn, *NT Kan.* i. 914 f., ii. 774 ff.; Harnack, *Altchr. Litt.* i. 19 ff., *Chron.* i. 598 ff.; von Lehner, *Die Marienverehrung*, 223 ff.; Conrady (works cited above); Mrs. Lewis, 'Apocrypha: Protevang. Jacobi' (*Studia Sinaitica*, xi); Meyer in Hennecke, *NT Apokr.* 47 ff., *Handb.* 106 ff.; Tasker, *l.c.*; tr. in Ante-Nicene Library, vol. xvi., Cowper, Orr (*NT Apocr. Writings*), etc.

C. (a) 2. Childhood Gospel of Thomas.—This Gospel, which deals with the marvellous events of Christ's childhood, was widely read in early times in all branches of the Christian Church. In its present form it does not claim to be a *Gospel*; it is generally referred to as Παιδικὰ τοῦ Κυρίου—Incidents in the Lord's Childhood. There is everything, however, in favour of the view that the original form of the writing was a Gospel in use in Gnostic circles, referred to by Origen and Hippolytus (see B. 3). Besides the appropriateness of the citation of Hippolytus to a *Childhood Gospel*, the relation between the two writings is supported by a statement in Irenæus (i. 20. 1) that the followers of the Gnostic Marcus had in their apocryphal books a story of Jesus as a boy putting His schoolmaster to confusion. This incident is found described twice over in the *Childhood Gospel of Thomas*. If the *Gospel of Thomas*, mentioned by Nicephorus in his *Stichometry* (date uncertain, 6th–8th cent.) as containing 1300 *stichoi*, had any relation with that known to us, the copy which lay before him was more than twice as long as the longest now extant.

The external evidence, then, converges on the view that our present Gospel was a compilation of stories drawn from a longer Gospel, which originated in Gnostic circles, the parts which were undisguisedly Gnostic in tone being omitted. This conclusion is confirmed by the character of the Gospel itself. A few Gnostic traces still remain, notably in the mysterious symbolism of the letters of the alphabet. The extraordinary miracles attributed to the child Christ, and His astonishing knowledge, were no doubt interpreted by Gnostics in a way to lend support to their own views. For them 'the worth of these miracles lay in the proof, which could be drawn from them, that Christ did not belong to this world, that even as a child He was raised beyond human development and limitation, so that as a child He could teach every human teacher' (Meyer in Henn. 64). The fragment in Hippolytus (quoted in B. 3) may have been a Gnostic utterance of the child Christ.

The figure of Jesus in this Gospel is a melancholy and hateful caricature of the grace, simplicity, and obedience of the Holy Childhood. The miracles which the child Christ is described as working are, for the most part, deeds of malevolence, or marvels without any ethical meaning. To the latter class belong His making birds of clay and causing them to fly; His carrying water from the well in His cloak after breaking the pitcher; to the former, His passionate vengeance on a boy who accidentally ran against Him, and was laid dead on the spot; the cursing of His teacher, who fell down in a swoon. The painful impression made by His petulant and vengeful spirit is not sensibly relieved by an occasional miracle of healing. His bearing and conduct are those of a spoilt and impudent child; in two instances He takes Joseph to task for venturing to correct Him. A single extract will enable the reader to form some idea of the youthful Gnostic at school. A teacher, Zacchæus by name, approaches Joseph, offering to teach Jesus letters, and how to greet His elders respectfully, and how to love those of His own age—much needed lessons! This is how Jesus profits by His attendance at school. 'He looked upon His teacher Zacchæus, and said to him: Thou, who knowest not the nature of the A, how canst thou teach others the B? Thou hypocrite! first teach the A if thou canst, and then we shall believe thee about the B. Then He began to question the teacher about the first letter, and he was unable to answer Him. In the hearing of many the child says to Zacchæus: Hear, O teacher, the disposition of the first letter, and observe how it has straight lines and a middle stroke which crosses those which thou seest to belong to one another; (lines) which go together, raise themselves, wind round in a dance, move themselves, and go round again, which are composed of three signs, are of similar nature, of the same weight, of the same size. Thou hast the lines of the A.' How vast is the gulf separating this absurd and pretentious display from the simple story of Christ among the doctors in the Temple! Here a forward and unbearably conceited boy, who is ready to teach his elders; there a child with the fresh wonder of life's greatness in his heart, eager to learn, ready to obey.

Many of the stories here narrated of Christ have their origin in folk-lore and mythology. Similar stories are told of Krishna and Buddha. But in all countries the popular imagination has borne unconscious witness to man's greatness by its delight in tales of wonder-children. Legends of this nature were laid hold of by the Gnostics, and used in the interest of their peculiar speculations about Christ. 'The wonder-child becomes a Gnostic, who looks down on the unspiritual world, and, in particular, heartily despises the religion of the Jews' (Meyer in Henn. 65). Apart from the speculations with which they were burdened, these stories took hold of the popular imagination in orthodox circles. The craving for the marvellous proved stronger than the sense of what was fitting in Jesus; and the silence of Christ's childhood, which had been regarded as an evidence of His true humanity, became thronged with silly and repulsive exhibitions of power and knowledge, which were believed to be signs of His Divine dignity.

In its present form the *Childhood Gospel of Thomas* cannot be older than the 3rd century. The Gospel exists in several recensions, which vary considerably in length.

LITERATURE. — Tischendorf, *Evang. Apocr.* xxxvi ff.; Zahn, *NT Kan.* i. 515, 539, 802, ii. 768 ff.; Harnack, *Altchr. Litt.* i. 15 ff., *Chron.* i. 593 ff.; Bost, *Les évang. apocr. de l'enfance de Jésus Christ*; Conrady, 'Das Thomasevangelium,' *SK*, 1903, p. 377 ff.; Meyer in Hennecke, *NT Apokr.* 63 ff., *Handb.* 132 ff.; Wright, *Contributions to the Apocr. Literature of the NT*; Cowper, Orr (*opp. citt.*).

C. (a) 3. Arabic Gospel of the Childhood.—This is a late composition, in which are worked up the materials of the earlier *Childhood Gospels*. The compiler has also added many legends of a wildly fantastic and highly miraculous nature. One or two examples may suffice to show the character of the greater portion of the book. The Magi receive from 'the Lady Mary,' as a souvenir of their visit to Bethlehem, one of the swaddling bands in which the infant Jesus was wrapped. On their return home they show their trophy to the assembled kings and princes. A feast is held, and a fire is lighted, which the company worships. The swaddling band is thrown into the fire, and, when the fire had burned itself out, it is found unharmed. Whereupon the cloth is laid up with great honour in the treasure house. Again, the water in which the infant Jesus is washed has a marvellous virtue, and children whose bodies are white with leprosy are cleansed by bathing in it. A young man who by witchcraft had been changed into a mule, is restored to human form by Mary's placing Jesus on the mule's back.

This Gospel was the main source of the knowledge of Jesus among the Mohammedans. For their edification, Kessæus incorporated its stories, with much embellishment, in his history of patriarchs and prophets.

LITERATURE. — Tischendorf, *Evang. Apocr.*; Thilo, *Codex Apocr. NT*; Walker, (Ante-Nicene Library, vol. xvi.); Tasker (*l.c.*); Meyer in Hennecke, *Handb.* 102.

C. (a) 4. History of Joseph the Carpenter.—In Egypt, where feast-days were multiplied to celebrate events or to commemorate persons held in high esteem by the Church, the History of Joseph was written for the purpose of being read on 20th July, the alleged day of Joseph's death. The narrative is placed in the mouth of Jesus, who discourses to His disciples on the Mount of Olives. After an introductory address, which has passages reminiscent of the Psalms, the Gospels, and St. Paul's Epistles, the life of Joseph is shortly described, in which evident use is made of the *Protevangelium* or one of its sources (*Apocryphum Josephi*). The circumstances attending the death of Joseph are described at great length. We are told of his dread of death; we listen to a bitter lament for his sins (among them his venturing to correct Jesus as a child), and to a prayer to be delivered from the demons of darkness who lie in wait for his soul. When Death approaches with his dread retinue, Jesus drives them back. In answer to His prayer, Michael and Gabriel carry off the spirit of Joseph to 'the dwelling place of the pious.' Thereafter Christ comforts the mourners, and Himself bewails the death of Joseph. It is plain, from this survey of the contents of the book, that its purpose was less to give the history of Joseph than ' to recommend Christianity as the deliverer in the extremity of death, and to teach the true Christian art of dying' (Meyer in Henn. *Handb.* 103).

The history, in all probability, was written in Coptic. Recensions of it in the Bohairic and Sahidic dialects exist, the latter fragmentary (Forbes Robinson, *Coptic Apocryphal Gospels*, 130 ff.). There is also an Arabic text, first printed in 1722.

Tischendorf puts the date of the history in the 4th century.

LITERATURE.—Tischendorf, Meyer, Forbes Robinson (*opp. citt.*).

C. (a) 5. The Departure of Mary.—The growing veneration of Mary in the Church led to the invention of incidents in her life parallel to those in the life of Christ. This was the motive that gave rise to the Departure of Mary (*Transitus Mariæ*), otherwise known as the κοίμησις (the Falling Asleep), *Dormitio, Assumptio*. As Christ had risen from the dead and ascended into heaven, so must Mary have risen and ascended. The story runs as follows:

One day, when Mary, according to her custom, had gone to 'the holy tomb of our Lord' to burn incense and pray, the archangel Gabriel announces her approaching death, and informs her that, in answer to her request, she shall ' go to the heavenly places to her Son, into the true and everlasting life.' On her return home she prays, and all the Apostles—those who are already dead and those still alive—are gathered to her bedside at Bethlehem. The Apostles narrate how they were engaged when the summons came to them. The heavens are filled with hosts of angels; miracles of healing happen, and the sick crowd to the house. The Jews endeavour to seize Mary; but the Apostles, carrying the couch on which 'the Lady, the mother of God,' lay, are borne on a cloud to Jerusalem. Here Christ appears to her, and in answer to her request declares: 'Rejoice and be glad, for all grace is given to thee by My Father in heaven, and by Me, and by the Holy Ghost; whoever calls on thy name shall not be put to shame, but shall find comfort and support both in this world and in that which is to come, in the presence of My heavenly Father.' Then, while the Apostles sing a hymn, Mary falls asleep. She is laid in a tomb in Gethsemane; for three days an angel-choir is heard glorifying God, and when they are silent all know that 'her spotless and precious body has been transferred to Paradise.'

In this story, which has had a remarkable influence in the Roman Catholic Church, we have the clear signs of an advanced stage of the worship of the Virgin. Prayer to her is here enjoined; and the tendency disclosed, to find parallels between her life and the life of Christ, marks a definite stage of the movement which eventually made her a sharer in the work of redemption. The epithet θεοτόκος (mother of God), which was first applied to

Mary by Cyril of Jerusalem (beginning of 4th cent.), and played so large a part in the Nestorian controversy (from A.D. 428), occurs in this writing.

The *Transitus* was written at the close of the 4th cent. In the Gelasian Decree (496) it was included among those apocryphal writings which are 'non solum repudiata, verum etiam ab omni Romana catholica et apostolica ecclesia eliminata atque cum suis auctoribus auctorumque sequacibus sub anathematis indissolubili vinculo in æternum damnata.' In spite of this the writing maintained its place, and by the 6th cent. it was held in the highest honour. It was in later days ascribed to Melito of Sardis (*c.* 170), and even to the Apostle John. Versions of it, in longer and shorter forms, are extant in Greek, Latin, Arabic, Coptic, and Syriac.

LITERATURE. — Tischendorf, Wright, Forbes Robinson, Orr (*opp. citt.*); Mrs. Lewis, 'Apocrypha' (*Stud. Sinaitica*, xi.).

C. (*b*) 1. The Gospel of Nicodemus.—This Gospel, dealing with the Trial, Death, and Resurrection of Jesus, and with His Descent into Hades, is a combination of two earlier writings—(1) *Acta Pilati*, and (2) *Descensus Christi ad inferos.* The older Greek MSS contain only (1) with an independent conclusion, while there are clear signs that the compiler had not thoroughly mastered all his material. The earliest form is found in a Latin version, probably of the 5th or 6th cent.; but it was not until the 13th cent. that the name of Nicodemus was associated with it. The writing claimed to have been written in Hebrew by Nicodemus, and to have been translated into Greek by Ananias or Æneas Protector.

The contents of the Gospel are as follows :

(1) Jesus is accused by the Jews. Pilate orders Jesus to be brought before him. The messenger, by Pilate's instructions, shows Jesus great respect. As Jesus enters the judgment-hall, the tops of the Roman standards bow down before Him (ch. 1). The charge that Jesus was 'born of fornication' is disproved (ch. 2). Pilate privately examines Him,—the passage is based on John 18$^{30-38}$,—and declares Him not worthy of death (chs. 3. 4). Various witnesses, among them Nicodemus and some who had been healed by Jesus, come forward and speak on His behalf (chs. 5–8). The Jews choose Barabbas instead of Jesus, and are reproached for their ingratitude by Pilate. Pilate washes his hands, and suffers Jesus to be led forth to crucifixion (ch. 9). Then follows an account of the crucifixion and burial, based on Lk 23 (chs. 10. 11). Joseph of Arimathæa is put into prison by the Jews for burying Jesus, but is miraculously delivered (ch. 12). The guards at the sepulchre report the resurrection to the Sanhedrin, and are bribed to say that the disciples stole the body (ch. 13). A priest, a scribe, a Levite from Galilee bear witness to Christ's ascension ; they are charged to keep silent, and are sent back to Galilee (ch. 14). On the proposal of Nicodemus, search is made for Jesus, but conclusive evidence is once more given of His ascension (chs. 15. 16).

(2) This purports to have been written down by Carinus and Leucius, sons of the aged Simeon, who had been raised from the dead by Jesus (ch. 17). 'A purple royal light' appears in Hades ; John the Baptist announces the near approach of Christ to visit those 'sitting in darkness and the shadow of death' (ch. 18). Seth tells of his prayer for oil from the tree of mercy to heal his father, and of Michael's promise that he should receive it when the Son of God came to earth (ch. 19). A conversation takes place between Satan and Tartarus, who dread Christ's coming (ch. 20). The summons is made (Ps 24[7]) in a voice of thunder to grant Jesus admission : Satan and Tartarus are powerless to exclude Him (ch. 21). Satan is delivered into the power of Hades, who reviles him vehemently, and consigns him to everlasting torment (chs. 22. 23). All the saints are gathered to Christ, and with them He comes up 'from the powers below' (ch. 24). The archangel Michael leads all the saints to Paradise, where they converse with Enoch and Elias and the penitent thief (chs. 25. 26). Having finished their writing, Carinus and Leucius are transfigured and vanish. Joseph and Nicodemus report everything to Pilate, who draws up an account of 'all that had been done and said concerning Jesus by the Jews,' and places it 'in the public records of his prætorium' (ch. 27). [In some MSS two other chapters are added : ch. 28 incorporates a Jewish chronology from Adam to Christ, which Annas and Caiaphas acknowledge, in Pilate's presence, to be a proof that Jesus was the long-promised Saviour ; ch. 29 gives a letter from Pilate to Claudius, dealing with the 'cruel condemnation,' crucifixion, and resurrection of Christ].

The first part of the *Gospel of Nicodemus*—the *Acts of Pilate*—exists in various recensions, the earliest of which cannot be much older than

the beginning of the 5th century. The question, however, is raised by references in Justin and Tertullian, whether these *Acts* are not based on much older documents. In his first *Apology* (ch. 35) Justin, after describing the crucifixion of Jesus, declares : 'And that these things happened, one may learn from the Acts drawn up under Pontius Pilate'; and again (ch. 48), when speaking of miracles which Jesus wrought, he adds a like testimony. Moreover, Tertullian in two passages (*Apol.* 5 and 21) speaks of a report sent to Tiberius by Pilate dealing with Christ ; and in the latter passage, after giving a brief account of Christ's life and a detailed description of His death, resurrection, and ascension, he states : 'Pilate, who in his heart was already a Christian, reported all these things about Christ to Tiberius, who was emperor at that time.' Many scholars believe that the report referred to by Tertullian is preserved in the Letter of Pilate to Claudius (ch. 29 of the *Gospel of Nicodemus*). On the other hand, Harnack holds the Letter to be later than Tertullian (*Chron.* i. 607 ff.). On the ground of Justin's references, Tischendorf (*Evang. Apocr.* lxiv), followed by Hofmann (*PRE*[3] i. 659), dates our extant *Acts of Pilate* in the 2nd century. Lipsius (*Die Pilatusakten*, 14 ff.), however, Harnack (*Chron.* i. 610 ff.), and others believe that Justin had no knowledge of any *Acts of Pilate*, and simply assumed their existence ; while von Schubert, followed by Stülcken (Henn. *Handb.* 146 f.), maintains that Justin was acquainted with *Acts of Pilate* which probably formed the basis of the present *Acts*. The question is an intricate one, and cannot be fully discussed here. Tischendorf's conclusion may, however, safely be set aside. Harnack bases his judgment mainly on the ground that, if Justin had had any real knowledge of *Acts of Pilate* dealing with the facts which he narrates, he would have quoted from them, while, as a matter of fact, his quotations are from the Prophets and the Gospels. Against this it must, however, be urged that, if Justin had not had some definite knowledge to go upon, he would never have dared in an address to the Emperor to ground his case on documents which presumably were in the public archives. The present writer inclines to the view that *Acts of Pilate*, at least believed to be genuine, were in existence in the 2nd cent., and that our present *Acts* were influenced by them. Whether the 2nd cent. *Acts* were based on any authentic report by Pilate, it is impossible to say.

It is clear that the *Acta Pilati* in their present form are largely dependent on the canonical Gospels, and that many of the additions are fabrications put forward for apologetic reasons. The aim of the writer is to furnish convincing proof of the truths of Christianity ; what could better serve his purpose than to show Pilate on the side of Christ, and to narrate incidents touching Christ's resurrection which not even His enemies could challenge ? Heathen aspersions on the birth of Jesus are also disposed of by evidence given at His trial.

The second part of the Gospel—*The Descent into Hades*—represents in a developed form the tradition, early and widely accepted, which was based on 1 P 3^{19} ('He went and preached unto the spirits in prison'). Earlier traces of the same tradition are found in the *Gospel of Peter* ('And they heard a voice from heaven, saying, Hast Thou preached to them that sleep? And a response was heard from the Cross, Yea'), and in the *Legend of Abgar*.

The *Gospel of Nicodemus* was taken up by Vincent de Beauvais in his *Speculum Majus* and by Jacobus de Voragine in his *Aurea Legenda*, and through these works it exerted a far-reaching influence.

LITERATURE.—Tischendorf, *Evang. Apocr.* liv ff.; Lipsius, *Die Pilatusakten, Apokr. Apostelgeschichten*; von Schubert, *Die Composition des ps. - petr. Evangeliumfragment*; Harnack, *Altchr. Litt.* i. 21 ff., *Chron.* i. 603 ff.; von Dobschütz, *Zeitschr. f. NT Wissenschaft* (1902), 89 ff., Hastings' *DB* iii. 544 ff.; Mommsen, *Zeitschr. f. NT Wiss.* (1902) 198 ff.; Krüger, *Gesch. d. altchr. Litt.* 36; Stülcken in Hennecke, *NT Apokr.* 74 ff., *Handb.* 143 ff.

C. (*b*) 2. The Legend of Abgar.

In Eusebius (*HE* i. 13. 6 ff.) we find letters purporting to have passed between Abgar v. king of Edessa, and Jesus. Eusebius states that the letters were preserved in the royal archives, and gives a literal translation of them from the Syriac. Abgar, who was suffering from an incurable disease, having heard of Christ's wonderful power of healing, wrote, entreating Christ to come and cure him, and offering Him a residence in Edessa, where He would be safe from the malice of the Jews. Jesus replied that He must accomplish His mission and ascend to Him who had sent Him, but that after His ascension He would send one of His disciples, who would cure the king and bring life to him and all who were with him. Then follows an account, also translated from the Syriac, of the fulfilment of Christ's promise in the sending by the Apostle Thomas of Thaddæus, one of the Seventy, to Edessa.

The legendary character of the correspondence is beyond all doubt, although its genuineness was accepted by Eusebius, and has been defended by several scholars, among them Cureton and Phillips in England (see Phillips, *Addai the Apostle*, ix ff.). It had its origin some time after the introduction of Christianity into Edessa (*c.* 170), owing to a desire to have an Apostolic foundation for the Church. The date of it is probably the second half of the 3rd century.

The correspondence and the narrative of Addai's mission found a place, with many additions, in the Syriac *Teaching of Addai*, which dates from about 400. The legend had a wide influence, and found credence in all sections of the Church, notwithstanding the doubts expressed regarding it in the Gelasian Decree; a Greek recension of it—the Acts of Thaddæus—contains in addition the story of the portrait of Jesus miraculously stamped on a napkin. See also art. ABGAR.

The legendary letter of Christ was in widespread favour as a talisman to guard against dangers of all kinds. For this purpose it was placed at the city gate of Edessa and at the doors of private houses. Up to quite recent times copies of the letter were to be found framed in the houses of the peasantry in England (see Donehoo, *Apocryphal and Legendary Life of Christ*, 223).

LITERATURE.—Lipsius, *Die edessenische Abgarsage*, 1880, *Die apokr. Apostelgeschichten*, ii. 2. 178 ff.; Zahn, *Forschungen*, i. 350 ff., *NT Kan.* i. 369 ff.; Tixéront, *Les origines de l'église d'Édesse*, 1888; Harnack, *Altchr. Litt.* i. 533 ff.; Krüger, *Altchr. Litt.* 228 f.; Phillips, *Doctrine of Addai the Apostle*, 1876; Stülcken in Hennecke, *NT Apokr.* 76 ff., *Handb.* 153 ff.

D. Gospel of Tatian.

The Gospel of Tatian, better known as the *Diatessaron*,* was a Harmony of the four Gospels, in all likelihood written originally in Syriac for the use of the Church at Edessa. The author of the Harmony was a disciple of Justin Martyr in Rome; but, being condemned for heretical views, he returned to his native land in the valley of the Euphrates about the year 172. Between that date and the close of the 2nd cent. his 'patchwork Gospel' was written, in which, using the chronological scheme of the Fourth Gospel, he wove into a connected narrative the four different accounts of our Lord's life. It is doubtful whether, before the appearance of the *Diatessaron*, the four Gospels circulated separately in the Syrian Church; but however that may be, it was clearly Tatian's intention to provide a Gospel for popular use which should obviate the disadvantages of having the narrative of Christ's life in different forms.* The evidence goes to show that the *Diatessaron* was in general use in the Syrian Church up to the beginning of the 5th cent. In the *Teaching of Addai* (*c.* 400) we read that 'a large multitude of people assembled day by day and came to the prayer of the service, and to the reading of the Old and New Testament, of the Diatessaron,' etc. (Phillips, *Addai the Apostle*, 34). In the middle of the 4th cent. Ephraem used the *Diatessaron* as the basis of his famous commentary on the Gospels. But from the 5th cent. onwards Tatian's Gospel was displaced from public worship by the new translation of the separate Gospels made under Rabbūla,—the Peshiṭta, the Syriac Vulgate,—although, largely owing to the commentary of Ephraem, it continued to be read and to exert an influence for many centuries later.

Neither the *Diatessaron* nor the commentary of Ephraem has been preserved to us in the original Syriac. There are, however, Latin and Arabic versions of the *Diatessaron*, and two distinct Armenian versions of Ephraem's commentary. For the reconstruction of the text of the *Diatessaron*, Ephraem's commentary is of the highest value, and the work has been brilliantly executed by Zahn (*Forschungen*, i.). Unfortunately, while the Latin and Arabic versions keep Tatian's arrangement of the narrative, they are of no value for the restoration of the text. The Latin Harmony (Codex Fuldensis), which belongs to about the beginning of the 6th cent., gives throughout the text of the Vulgate; while the Arabic version, which was originally made in the 11th cent., is evidently a translation from a text of the *Diatessaron* which had been accommodated to the Peshiṭta. In the 9th cent. an epic poem entitled *Héliand* was written, based on a translation of the Codex Fuldensis. It became widely known, and to it our Anglo-Saxon forefathers were largely indebted for their knowledge of the life of Christ (Hamlyn Hill, *op. cit.* 20, 38).

In accordance with Tatian's peculiar views, the *Diatessaron* reveals a slight Encratite tendency. According to Theodoret (*Hær. Fab.* i. 20), it omitted the genealogies of Christ and everything dealing with Christ's birth ('all things that show our Lord to have been born of the seed of David according to the flesh'). The Birth-narratives of Luke and Matthew are, however, found in the Arabic and Latin recensions, as well as in Ephraem's commentary.

LITERATURE.—Zahn, *Forschungen*, i. ii. iv. vii.; Ciasca, *Tatiani Evangeliorum Harmoniæ, Arabice*; Harnack, *Altchr. Litt.* i. 485 ff., *Chron.* i. 284 ff.; *TU* i. i. 196 ff., art. in *Encyc. Brit.*[9]; Burkitt, *S. Ephraim's Quotations from the Gospel* (cf. also his *Evangelion da-Mepharreshe*); Rendel Harris, *The Diatessaron of Tatian*; Hamlyn Hill, *Earliest Life of Christ*; Hemphill, *The Diatessaron*, etc.; Stenning in Hastings' *DB*, Ext. Vol. 451 ff.

A. F. FINDLAY.

GOVERNOR.

The word 'governor' (ἡγεμών, Lat. *praeses, dux*) is a comprehensive term, being the only Greek word which includes every class of provincial governor under the Roman empire. The following officials, for instance, are included under this title:—(1) Governors of Senatorial Provinces, namely, *pro consulibus* who are ex-consuls, and *pro consulibus* who are ex-prætors. The former class ruled the governmental spheres of

---

* Diatessaron (διὰ τεσσάρων) is variously interpreted. The expression is generally regarded as signifying a compilation in which only the *four* Gospels were used; but as the word was in use as a musical *terminus technicus* to denote a harmony, Tatian might have employed it as a description of his work, no matter how many Gospels he had drawn upon (Hamlyn Hill, *Earliest Life*, 21; Jülicher, *Einleitung*, 391 f.).

* To distinguish it from the fourfold form of the Gospel (*Evangelion da-Mepharreshe*, 'the Gospel of the Separated'), the *Diatessaron* received the name of *Evangelion da-Mehallete*, 'the Gospel of the Mixed').

duty, Asia and Africa; the latter all other provinces which by the arrangement between Augustus and the Senate in 27 B.C. were put under the authority of that body, such as Sicily, Macedonia, Achaia. (2) Governors of Imperial Provinces, namely, *legati Augusti pro praetoribus* who are ex-consuls; *legati Augusti pro praetoribus* who are ex-prætors; *procuratores*; *praefecti Aegypti*, etc. Examples of Imperial provinces are Syria, the Gauls (except Narbonensis), Judæa, and Egypt. These governors were all accountable to the Emperor, being put in charge of his provinces, but were by no means of equal rank. The *legati* were always members of the Senate, but the others were of the lower rank of *equites*. It was to this class that Pilate belonged (Mt 27. 28; see under PROCURATOR, PILATE). Every senator, being a member of the same class as the Emperor himself, was a possible rival to him; those of inferior rank were practically in the position of his servants.

Governors of provinces had certain powers of jurisdiction delegated to them, which it is now impossible accurately to define. These were embodied in *mandata* given to them before setting out. They were also, of course, influenced by the traditions of the province to which they were going. They administered the law with a competence and a justice which have never been surpassed. As the provinces had an appeal from their decisions to the Senate in the case of Senatorial provinces, and to the Emperor in the case of Imperial, it was dangerous for a governor to go against the strongly expressed wish of the subjects of Rome. A procurator, for example, could be cast aside by the Emperor and ruined for life, without the slightest chance of redress.

Governors were commonly changed annually. The emperor Tiberius, however, retained many governors for a number of years in one position, and he also instituted the custom of payment of definite salaries to such, thus doing away with the necessity for plunder in order to recoup themselves. The Roman system was sufficiently elastic to permit the appointment of officers for special service and the suspension of the regular order of things. It was probably under an arrangement of this kind that P. Sulpicius Quirinius was 'governor of Syria' (Lk 2²) in A.D. 6-9 (Ramsay, *Was Christ Born at Bethlehem?* ch. xi.), in order to carry on a campaign against the Homonadenses, and leave the ordinary governor free for civil duties. See art. BIRTH OF CHRIST.

In Mt 10¹⁸, Mk 13⁹, and Lk 21¹² 'kings' are coupled with 'governors.' The reference here is to 'client-kings' of the Roman empire (such as Herod) as well as the ordinary governors. The territory ruled by such kings was part of the *imperium Romanum* in the fullest sense of that term. In other words, the Romans had suzerainty over these kingdoms; but they left them under the rule of their kings until they were sufficiently civilized to become ordinary provinces under ordinary governors. Then they were taken over. In Lk 21¹² the 'kings' are mentioned before the 'governors.' If this change is not accidental, it would appear that St. Luke wished βασιλεῖς to be understood in the sense of 'emperors,' a sense quite in accordance with the Greek. The plural need be no difficulty, as it was the common practice for emperors to have their successors invested with the imperatorial powers, while they themselves were still alive and active.

LITERATURE. — H. F. Pelham, *Outlines of Roman History*, bk. v. ch. iii.; J. B. Bury, *A History of the Roman Empire*, ch. vi.; A. H. J. Greenidge, *Roman Public Life*, ch. xi.; for the regular course of an administrative career, see R. Cagnat, *Cours d'Épigraphie Latine* ³ (1898, with Supplement 1904), pp. 86–155; Schürer, *HJP* I. ii. 43-48.

ALEX. SOUTER.

GRACE (χάρις). — The Gr. χάρις, with which 'grace' in Eng. fully corresponds, is one of those words (cf. ἀγαπάω, ἀγάπη, 'love') which have been raised to a higher power and filled with a profounder content by the revelation of Jesus Christ. In accordance with its derivation from χαίρω, it originally signified in classical Gr. something that gives joy or delight, hence *charm* or *winsomeness*. From this it came to be used in a subjective sense of a courteous, kindly, or, as we say, a 'gracious' disposition; and so became equivalent to *goodwill* or *favour*. From the sense of favour as an attitude of will and feeling, the transition was natural to 'a favour,' a concrete token of kindness and goodwill. Finally, as grace implies not only a giver but a receiver, it was employed to denote the *gratitude* felt by the latter for the favour bestowed, and the *thanks* by which gratitude is expressed (cf. the Eng. phrase 'grace before meat'). In nearly all these senses the word is found both in the LXX and the NT. But, while the LXX does not carry us beyond the point reached in the classical authors, when we pass to the NT the old meanings of χάρις are wonderfully enlarged, until, as Cremer says (*Lex. s.v.*), 'it has become quite a different word in NT Greek, so that we may say it depended upon Christianity to realize its full meaning and to elevate it to its rightful sphere.'

1. Grace in the Gospels. — In AV of the Gospels, 'grace' occurs only 4 times, once in Lk. (2⁴⁰) and thrice in Jn. (1¹⁴. ¹⁶. ¹⁷). When we turn to the RV, however, and include the marginal readings, we find the word in 4 other Lukan passages. Thrice it is used as a marginal alternative for 'favour' or 'favoured' (Lk 1²⁸. ³⁰ 2⁵²), while in one important passage (4²²) 'words of grace' is substituted for 'gracious words.' In every case, both in Lk. and Jn., the corresponding Gr. word is χάρις, with the exception of Lk 1²⁸ where the derivative vb. χαριτόω is used. Besides these passages in which either in AV or RV it is rendered 'grace,' χάρις occurs 4 times in Lk. (6³². ³³. ³⁴ 17⁹) in the sense of 'thanks.'

(1) We observe that grace is not a word or idea that is used by the *Synoptists* generally, St. Luke being the only one who employs it. It is also worthy of notice that the term is not one which the Evangelist ever attributes to Jesus Himself. It is true that he represents Jesus as using χάρις 4 times, but only in the ordinary colloquial sense of thanks. Thus, although χάρις or 'grace' was to undergo something like a transfiguration through the influence of Christianity, and indeed was to become not only a specifically Christian word, but a word of which we might say that it shines like a jewel on the brow of Christ Himself, whose life and death and teaching gave birth to the ideas which it has come to express, it is not a term which we find in any of our Lord's recorded utterances.

In 4 out of the 5 Lukan passages in which 'grace' occurs, it has the ordinary sense of '**favour.**' Twice the Virgin Mary is declared to have been the object of the Divine favour (Lk 1²⁸. ³⁰). Of Jesus it is said in one passage that the grace (or favour) of God was upon Him (2⁴⁰), and in another that He advanced in favour (or grace) with both God and men (2⁵²). The remaining passage (4²²) is the only Synoptic one which may possibly carry us on to the peculiar Christian significance of the word. When Jesus preached His first sermon in the synagogue at Nazareth, His fellow-townsmen are said to have wondered ἐπὶ τοῖς λόγοις τῆς χάριτος. AV renders 'at the gracious words'; RV, more literally, 'at the words of grace.' But what does the expression mean? Does it point merely, as has commonly been supposed, to our Lord's winsomeness and charm as a speaker, His grace of manner, His possession of one of the most effective of the gifts of an orator? Or is χάριτος to be taken not as a Hebraistic gen. of quality, but as an objective gen., so that 'words of grace' = 'words about grace'? It is not impossible that by this phrase, which is thus capable of a double interpretation, St. Luke intended to convey a twofold meaning, and to let his readers understand that the words of Christ, as Dr. Bruce puts it, were 'words of grace about grace' (*Exp. Gr. Test. in loc.*). In any case, however, it seems probable that the objective meaning was the one immediately before the Evangelist's mind. The fact that genitives of quality are frequent in writings influenced by Heb., and that parallels to the use of χάρις to denote the quality of charm in a speaker can be adduced not only from the LXX (Ec 10[12], Ps 44[3], Sir 21[16]), but from the classical authors (Hom. *Od.* viii. 175; Dem. *Orat.* li. 9), weighs little in comparison with the analogies offered by the usage of St. Luke himself in Acts. It is admitted that λόγος τῆς χάριτος αὐτοῦ (Ac 14[3] 20[32]) means the message of salvation, and that τὸ εὐαγγέλιον τῆς χάριτος τοῦ θεοῦ (20[24]) means the gospel of the grace of God in the full Pauline and Christian sense of the expression. Moreover, the text from which our Lord preached His Nazareth sermon (Lk 4[18. 19], cf. Is 61[1. 2]) lends itself most readily to this larger interpretation, and so do the opening words of the sermon itself, 'This day hath this Scripture been fulfilled in your ears' (v.[21]). Noteworthy, too, in this connexion is the fact that in quoting the glowing words of the Evangelical prophet regarding 'the acceptable year of the Lord,' Jesus made the utterance still more gracious by omitting any reference to a coming day of Divine vengeance (cf. v.[19] with Is 61[2]). But, above all, we must bear in mind that whether the Third Gospel was written or not by Luke the companion of St. Paul, it is matter of common consent that strong Pauline influences run through it, and that more than any other it gives prominence to those aspects of our Lord's life and teaching which present His gospel as a message of Divine grace. This is the Gospel of the publican (18[10ff.] 19[2ff.]), of the 'woman which was in the city, a sinner' (7[36ff.]), of the malefactor forgiven even as he hung upon his cross (23[39ff.]). Above all, it is the gospel of the great 'Parables of Grace'—the Lost Coin, the Lost Sheep, the Prodigal Son (15). It seems natural, therefore, to conclude that the Evangelist, on whom Christ's grace to the sinful had made so deep an impression, intended in this 'frontispiece' to his story of our Lord's public ministry, when he described the listeners in the synagogue as wondering at 'the words of grace which proceeded out of his mouth,' to set Jesus before us not merely as a winning speaker, but as the anointed herald of the grace of God. See also art. GRACIOUSNESS.

(2) When we come to the *Fourth Gospel*, we find that in the Prologue the word 'grace,' no doubt through the Pauline teaching and its consequences, has blossomed fully into those greater meanings with which the Church had become familiar.* In 1[14] the author describes the Incarnate Logos as 'full of grace and truth' in His revelation of the Father's glory. The phrase recalls the frequent OT combination of 'mercy and truth' (חֶסֶד וָאֱמֶת, LXX ἔλεος καὶ ἀλήθεια) as a summary description of

* It is worthy of remark that while in the Prologue χάρις appears as a fundamental note of the revelation of Jesus Christ, the word is not used elsewhere in the work. In the rest of his Gospel, as in his Epistles, the author prefers the idea of love (3[16] 13[1], 1 Jn 3[16] and constantly). Like the Synoptists, he never once puts χάρις into the mouth of Jesus, not even in a passage like 7[19-23] (cf. 5[10-18]), where Jesus is speaking of His relation to the law of Moses. Does this not go to support the essential historicity of Christ's teaching as reported in the Fourth Gospel?

Jehovah's character (Ex 34[6], Ps 25[10] 85[10] 89[14] etc.). But the grace of Christ in the NT is something more than the mercy of God in the OT. It is remarkable that in the LXX χάρις is not considered a rich enough word to render the Heb. חֶסֶד. There χάρις signifies the Divine kindness or favour (corresponding to Heb. חֵן, cf. Gn 18[3] and *passim*), but is not used of those energies which belong properly to the sphere of redemption. For the חֶסֶד or mercy of God the word ἔλεος is employed; so that in the LXX ἔλεος may be said to be a stronger and richer word than χάρις. When we come to the NT, however, the case is reversed. χάρις, as applied to the Christian conception of grace, has become a grander word than ἔλεος; for while ἔλεος denotes the Divine compassion in the presence of man's pain and misery, χάρις is used to express God's attitude to man's sin. It is more than a Divine attribute, although it is that. It is the sum of those Divine forces from which our salvation flows.

In v.[16] the Evangelist says that out of Christ's fulness we all received, 'and grace for grace' (χάριν ἀντὶ χάριτος). In its general use, as we have seen, χάρις passes from a disposition of goodwill to be applied to the blessings which goodwill bestows. Here the reference is to the blessings of the Christian salvation. Christ's fulness is inexhaustible, and His grace is constantly bestowing itself upon His followers. But 'grace for grace' does not mean merely 'grace upon grace'—one grace added to another. The force of the ἀντί is not to be neglected. In the next verse the author is going to contrast the NT system of grace with the legal system of the OT. And here, by a bold use of language, he applies to the economy of grace the very formula of the opposite dispensation, so as the better to bring out its 'complete gratuitousness' (Godet, *Com. on Jn. in loc.*). Under the Law, with its system of exchanges, a blessing was received as the reward of (ἀντί) merit, but under the gospel it is Christ's free grace itself, received and appropriated, which becomes our title to fresh and larger bestowals.

'For the law was given by Moses,' adds the Evangelist; 'grace and truth came by Jesus Christ' (v.[17]). Here we have the justification of what we said above as to the χάρις καὶ ἀλήθεια of the NT being much more than the ἔλεος καὶ ἀλήθεια of the OT. The Divine mercy (ἔλεος) was an essential part of the OT revelation. It was on Sinai itself, and in connexion with the giving of the tables of the Law, that God revealed Himself to Moses as 'a God full of compassion and gracious, slow to anger, and plenteous in mercy and truth' (Ex 34[6]). But in comparison with the glory of the Christian revelation, the revelation to Moses was legal and hard. It lacked that element of spontaneous favour towards the sinful, and apart from every thought of merit gained by obedience, which belongs to the very essence of grace as we know it in Jesus Christ.

2. The grace of Christ in the Pauline Epistles. —In discussing the meaning of grace in the Third and Fourth Gospels, we have been obliged to anticipate in part what has now to be said about the Pauline teaching. For there can be no doubt that in the minds of both Evangelists that teaching was subsumed. It was the use which St. Paul had made of the word that determined its significance for Christianity ever afterwards.

(1) And first we notice that when the Apostle speaks of grace, he is invariably thinking of Jesus Christ in connexion with it. Most frequently it is the grace of God that he names; for God the Father is always recognized as the primal fountain of all the blessings of the Christian salvation, and no greater misrepresentation can be made of St. Paul's gospel than to describe him as bringing the

grace that is in Christ into some kind of opposition to the justice that is in God. Sometimes again ἡ χάρις stands alone ; for the Apostle treats it at times not merely as a Divine attribute, but as the operative principle of the whole economy of redemption. But as it is Christ who embodies this great principle in His own person, as it is in Him that the Father's grace is revealed, and by Him that it is mediated to men ; as, to use his own words, ' the grace of God was given you in Christ Jesus ' (1 Co 1⁴), and ' grace reigns through Jesus Christ our Lord ' (Ro 5²¹), he does not hesitate to speak of it again and again, and especially in the benedictions with which he concludes his Epp., as ' the grace of our Lord Jesus Christ ' (Ro 16²⁰, 1 Co 16²³, 2 Co 13¹⁴, Gal 6¹⁸ etc.; cf. the opening salutations, Ro 1⁷, 1 Co 1³, 2 Co 1², Gal 1³ etc.).

(2) When we ask how St. Paul arrived at this distinctive conception of the Christian gospel as an economy of grace, and of Jesus Christ as the dispenser of grace, the answer undoubtedly is that he owed it to that revelation of the Lord Jesus Himself near the gates of Damascus by which his whole life was suddenly transformed. As a Pharisee he had sought to earn salvation by his zeal for the Law. But everything he had done had proved ineffectual. The commandment which was unto life he found to be unto death (Ro 7¹⁰). Nay, in his endeavours to be exceedingly zealous according to the Law he had been led into the greatest sin of his career — his furious opposition to Jesus Christ, his savage persecution of the saints. Then came the great, astonishing act of spontaneous grace. Christ appeared in person to this bitter enemy, convincing him beyond the possibility of doubt that that Jesus whom he persecuted was no other than the Lord of glory, and at the same time addressing him in those tender and gracious and yet heart-shaking words of reproach and appeal by which Saul the persecutor was turned into the slave of Christ. From that day Christ was to Paul the Lord of grace no less than the Lord of glory. It was the grace of God in Christ, and that grace alone, which had called him and saved and made him what he was (Gal 1¹⁵, 1 Co 15¹⁰). And that same grace which had redeemed Paul at the first was with him all along. It guided him in the path of wisdom (1 Co 3¹⁰). It enabled him to be more abundant in labours than all others (15¹⁰). It taught him how to behave himself in the world (2 Co 1¹²). And when the messenger of Satan came to buffet him, and he thrice besought the Lord that this thing might depart, it was the Lord Himself who said to His servant, ' My grace is sufficient for thee ' (12⁷⁻⁹).

(3) What did St. Paul understand by the grace of Christ, as he used that term in his fully developed teaching? What distinctive contents did he put into this great Christian idea, which he knew in his own experience to be a great Christian fact ? (a) We shall perhaps find our best starting-point in a passage in which he sets a certain view of that grace before the Corinthians as one with which his teaching had made them familiar. He regards it as an act of *astonishing self-sacrifice.* ' For ye know,' he writes, ' the grace of our Lord Jesus Christ, that though he was rich, yet for your sakes he became poor, that ye through his poverty might become rich ' (2 Co 8⁹). How much was involved in this self-sacrifice he shows more fully in another Epistle, where he describes it as a self-emptying, on Christ's part, of His Divine form, the assumption of a lowly human nature, and the rendering of a lifelong obedience even unto the death of the cross (Ph 2⁵ff.). It is in this quality of self-sacrifice most of all that the grace of Christ in the NT differs from the mercy of God as revealed in the earlier dispensation. Christ's grace is not

merely the compassion which a great and strong and blessed nature feels for one which is sinful and sorrowful and weak. It is the self-renouncing love which so yearns to save that it surrenders all the wealth that is its own, and welcomes all the poverty that is another's. It is that love which finds its crowning symbol, as it found its absolute expression, in the cross of our Lord Jesus Christ. ' I am poor and needy,' said a saint of the OT, '*yet the Lord thinketh upon me* ' (Ps 40¹⁷). ' The Son of God,' exclaims St. Paul, ' *loved me, and gave himself up for me* ' (Gal 2²⁰).

(b) The *absolute freeness* of Christ's grace was another element in the Apostle's conception. This brings us to his characteristic antithesis between grace and law. We noticed this antithesis already in the Prologue to the Fourth Gospel, but it was St. Paul who first formulated it when he wrote, ' Ye are not under law, but under grace ' (Ro 6¹⁴). Formerly the Divine blessings were secured by obedience to the Law. Righteousness was the fruit of works, and rewards were reckoned not as of grace, but as of debt (Ro 4⁴). But now we are ' justified freely (δωρεάν) by his grace through the redemption that is in Christ Jesus ' (Ro 3²⁴). The grace that saves us has nothing to do with works (Ro 11⁶) ; it is the ' free gift ' of God by ' the one man, Jesus Christ ' (Ro 5¹⁵, cf. Eph 2⁸).

(c) Again, Christ's grace, in St. Paul's view of it, was marked by its *sin-conquering power.* Besides the great antithesis between grace with its free gifts on the one hand, and the Law with its works and debts on the other, we have in the Apostle's teaching a further antithesis between grace and sin. This antithesis follows of necessity from the former one, for it is the fact of the Law that leads to the imputation of sin (Ro 5¹³), and it is the coming in of the Law that causes trespasses to abound (v.²⁰). But that same grace of Christ which rises superior to the Law shows its power to master the sin which is the transgression of the Law. ' Where sin abounded, grace did abound more exceedingly ' (ib.). And this superabundance of grace over sin is manifested in two distinct ways : (a) It removes the guilt of sin and the dread consequences which flow from guiltiness. This it does by not only forgiving the sinner (Eph 1⁷), but justifying him freely (Ro 3²⁴), bestowing upon him the gift of righteousness (Gal 2²¹), and giving him the assurance that as sin reigned unto death, even so shall grace reign through righteousness unto eternal life (Ro 5²¹). (β) It breaks the dominion of sin over the sinner's heart. The antinomian indeed may say, ' Let us continue in sin, that grace may abound.' But St. Paul's answer is, ' God forbid ! ' (Ro 6², cf. v.¹). The free gift bestowed by the grace of the One Man (5¹⁵) carries within it an ' abundance of grace ' (v.¹⁷). And among the things included in this abundance of grace are a death to sin and a life unto God (6²ff.). The fact that we are not under the Law, but under grace, implies that sin's tyranny over us is broken (v.¹⁴), and that we have been set free from it (v.¹⁸) for a life of righteousness and holiness in the service of God (vv.¹⁸·²²).

(d) Finally, we may say that in the Pauline teaching the grace of Christ, the ' riches of his grace ' as we have it in Eph. (1⁷), stood for *the sum-total of all Christian blessings.* There is an abundance and superabundance in grace (Ro 5¹⁷·²⁰, 2 Co 4¹⁵), which makes it a stream of endless benefaction flowing from an inexhaustible fountain. Christ's riches are unsearchable (Eph 3⁸), but all that Christ is His grace is, for grace is the most essential quality of His being, while He Himself is the very incarnation of everything we mean by grace. We are called by grace (Gal 1¹⁵), and justified by grace (Ro 3²⁴), and sanctified by grace (6¹⁴). Through grace also we obtain eternal comfort and good hope (2 Th 2[16]), and strength (2 Ti 2[1]), and liberality (2 Co 8[1]), and happy songs (Col 3[16]). And so it was the great Apostle's custom, when he would gather up into a single word all his wishes and hopes and prayers for the Churches, to say, 'The grace of our Lord Jesus Christ be with you all' (2 Th 3[18], Ro 16[24]; cf. 1 Co 16[23] etc.).*

3. The grace of Christ in the rest of the NT.— The material here is very much scantier than in the Pauline writings, but it is quite sufficient to show how deeply the great Pauline word had lodged itself in the general Christian mind. It is true that we do not find grace defined as to its nature by those antitheses of law and works and sin which give the Pauline conception its peculiar colouring, but the word is still used to express the Divine favour as revealed in Christ, and those saving blessings of which He is the Mediator. The chief relevant passages in Acts have been referred to already in connexion with the usage of the Third Evangelist. In 1 Peter we find the grace of salvation made to depend on the revelation of Jesus Christ, and associated in particular with the Saviour's sufferings and the glories that followed them (1[9-13]). The author of 2 Peter exhorts his readers to 'grow in the grace and knowledge of our Lord and Saviour Jesus Christ' (3[18]). In Hebrews the fact that Jesus is our great High Priest is urged as the reason why we should draw near with boldness unto the 'throne of grace' (4[14-16]); and the treading under foot of the Son of God is regarded as equivalent to doing despite to 'the Spirit of grace' (10[29]). As in the Fourth Gospel apart from the Prologue, so in the other Johannine writings, love takes the place held by the idea of grace in the Pauline teaching. But the familiarity of the thought of Christ's grace is shown by its appearance in the forms of salutation (2 Jn 3, Rev 1[4. 5]). And what could be more fitting than that the NT as a whole, of which grace is the distinctive watchword, and over every page of which we might inscribe the words 'Grace reigns,' should conclude, in the last sentence of the Apocalypse, with the benediction, 'The grace of the Lord Jesus be with the saints' (Rev 22[21])?

LITERATURE.—The *Lexx.* of Liddell and Scott, Grimm-Thayer, and Cremer, *s.v.* χάρις; Hastings' *DB*, art. 'Grace'; *PRE*[3], art. 'Gnade'; Weiss, *Bibl. Theol. of NT*, Index, *s.v.*, but esp. i. 385 ff.; Dieckmann, *Die christliche Lehre von der Gnade* (Berlin, 1901); Wells, artt. on 'Grace' in *ExpT*, viii. ix. [1897]; Bruce, *Expos. Gr. Test. ad* Lk 4[22], *Galilean Gosp.* ch. ii.; Dale, *Ephesians*, ch. x.; *Expositor*, I. xii. [1880] p. 86 ff., v. ix. [1899] p. 161 ff.
                     J. C. LAMBERT.

GRACIOUSNESS. — The word 'graciousness' does not occur in the EV of the Gospels. The adjective 'gracious' occurs only once (Lk 4[22]) in the AV and not at all in the RV. The idea, however, covered by the noun is of very frequent occurrence, and may truly be said to be one of the leading characteristics of Jesus Himself, and of the gospel He came to proclaim.

1. The passage Lk 4[22] is rendered in the AV, 'And all bare him witness, and wondered at the gracious words which proceeded out of his mouth.' The RV keeps more closely to the form of the Gr. expression, and renders 'wondered at the words of grace.' In so doing it departs from the general practice of the older English versions, which from Tindale onwards adopted the form of the AV. Wyclif and the Rhemish version support the rendering of the RV, following in all probability the example of the Vulg. *in verbis gratiæ* which

they rendered literally. The best modern version (Weymouth's) paraphrases and expands the expression thus, 'wondering at the sweet words of kindness which fell from his lips'; while Weizsäcker's admirable German version translates simply *die lieblichen Worte*. The best rendering, where the phrase is thus understood, is probably that of Plummer, 'winning words.' The words of the original, ἐπὶ τοῖς λόγοις τῆς χάριτος, suggest such a rendering, since the original meaning of χάρις, as it is found in Gr. literature, is that of 'comeliness' or 'winsomeness' (see the *Lexicons* for examples). But general, popular, and attractive as such an interpretation is, another is probably the correct one. See preceding article.

2. The Gr. word χάρις occurs on several other occasions in the Gospels, and is variously rendered in the English versions. In order to gain a clearer idea of its meaning, it is necessary to examine these. Of the youthful John we read in Lk 2[40] 'the grace of God was upon him,' and of the child Jesus (2[52]) that He 'advanced in favour (RVm 'grace') with God and men.' Weymouth uses 'favour' in both passages. On three occasions, in Lk 6[32. 33. 34], we have the expression, 'What thank have ye?' representing the Gr. ποία ὑμῖν χάρις ἐστίν; and the same sense of the word is found in Lk 17[9]. The only other passage in the Gospels where the word occurs is in the prologue to the Fourth Gospel, where it is found three times (Jn 1[14. 16. 17]), and is rendered in each case 'grace.' See GRACE.

3. There remains for us to see how the quality of 'graciousness' is manifested in Jesus during His earthly ministry. Many who take the word 'gracious' of Lk 4[22] in the narrower sense noted above, look only for the 'graciousness' of our Lord to be revealed in His manner of dealing with men, in His outward conduct and speech. This view is, of course, true. His readiness to take part in all the festivities and social functions of everyday life marked Him off clearly to His contemporaries from the ascetic attitude of John the Baptist. His playful, gentle winsomeness that won the children to His knee was a scandal to His disciples. His brotherly attitude towards the diseased and stricken, His generous help, His readiness of sympathy, emboldened leprous, blind, and ashamed humanity to dare the publicity it shrank from, or the menace and rebuke of the crowd, to cast itself at His feet, and throw itself upon His gracious consideration. This same characteristic is revealed in His intimate association with the household at Bethany, and His special affection for John and Lazarus, as well as in such exquisitely human touches as His longing look of love given to the young questioner (Mk 10[21]).

'Men could approach near to Him, could eat and drink with Him, could listen to His talk, and ask Him questions, and they found Him not accessible only, but warm-hearted, and not occupied so much with His own plans that He could not attend to a case of distress or mental perplexity' (*Ecce Homo*, ch. 5).

This peculiar graciousness was displayed in such acts as washing the feet of His disciples, and in His patient tolerance of the scepticism of Thomas. But when we go deeper than form of speech or nature of deed, we find this quality still more clearly manifested. If 'graciousness' is to bear the richer meaning we have seen it may carry, then its significance in the words and works of Jesus is all the greater. His parables (*e.g.* the Lost Sheep, the Prodigal Son, the Good Samaritan), how full they are of this peculiar quality of the Divine revelation! His conduct to sinful men and women, how sharply did it contrast with the attitude of His contemporaries (Lk 7[36-50], Mk 10[35. 45])! His prayer for His enemies shows with wonderful tenderness how this spirit did not desert Him at the moment of greatest trial, how inherent

---

* Besides the use of the word 'grace' in the Pauline Epp. to designate the spontaneous favour of God to sinners as revealed and mediated by Jesus Christ, it is employed in various derivative senses, such as (Ro 5[2]) the state of grace (*status gratiæ*), a particular gift of grace (Eph 4[7]), the special grace required for the Apostolic office (Gal 2[8. 9], Eph 3[2. 7]). The discussion of these, however, lies somewhat beyond the scope of this Dictionary.

it was, therefore, in His very nature (Lk 23³⁴). In His thought the gracious method of His treatment of men was to become a general standard of conduct (Jn 13¹⁵), and would even constitute the basis of final judgment (Mt 25⁴⁵). It should not be overlooked that, while St. Luke is the Evangelist who most frequently and clearly reveals this characteristic of Jesus, and dwells most distinctly upon it, each of the others supplies sufficient evidence to prove that St. Luke's picture is no imaginary one, nor even his emphasis exaggerated. See GRACE.

LITERATURE.—The various Commentaries on the passages cited, in particular on Lk 4²²: Plummer, B. and J. Weiss (8th ed.), and B. Weiss (9th ed.); Adeney, Introduction in *Century Bible*, pp. 6–13; The *Lexicons* of Grimm-Thayer and Cremer, *s.v.* χάρις; Ross, *The Teaching of Jesus*, chs. 7, 8; Phillips Brooks, *The Influence of Jesus*, pp. 17–25; Wendt, *The Teaching of Jesus* (Eng. tr.), vol. i. pp. 148–151; Bruce, *Galilean Gospel*, 30 ff.; artt. 'Grace' and 'Gracious' in Hastings' *DB*.

G. CURRIE MARTIN.

GRAPES.—See WINE.

GRASS.—In the OT there are several Heb. words which are translated 'grass,' but they are all very general terms; in the NT the only word so translated is χόρτος. Strictly speaking, no plant should be called a grass unless it belongs to the botanical order *Gramineæ*, but this is a comparatively modern distinction. The Biblical writers do not, of course, employ the term with scientific precision. The modern Arab includes, under the common designation *hashish* (grass), field-flowers such as anemones, poppies, and tulips. If, as is probable, it was in this wider sense that Christ and His contemporaries used the word, it lends new point and charm to His appeal, 'If God so clothe the grass of the field' (Mt 6³⁰), and invests with fresh beauty the familiar words, 'All flesh is grass, and all the glory thereof as the flower of grass' (1 P 1²⁴ RV; cf. Ja 1¹⁰·¹¹).

The true grasses of Palestine are very numerous; Dr. Post gives the figures for Palestine and Syria as 90 genera and 243 species (Hastings' *DB* ii. 258). Pasture grasses vary greatly in quality and profusion according to climate, soil, and elevation. Turf is rare. Grass is much used as fuel (Mt 6³⁰), especially in districts where wood is scarce (see OVEN).

HUGH DUNCAN.

GRAVE.—See TOMB.

GRAVE-CLOTHES.—The account in the Gospels of the circumstances attending the burial of our Lord illustrates fully the general practice of the time with regard to grave-clothes. The body of Jesus, doubtless after being bathed, after the manner of the Jews as well as of the Greeks (Ac 9³⁷, cf. *Gospel of Peter*, 6), was 'wrapped' (ἐνετύλιξεν, Mt 27⁵⁹, Lk 23⁵³) or 'swathed' (ἐνείλησεν, Mk 15⁴⁶) in the shroud of linen cloth (σινδόνι) which Joseph of Arimathæa had procured on his way back to Golgotha, and which is described as 'fresh' or 'unused' (καθαρᾳ, Mt 27⁵⁹), in accordance with the sacred use to which it was put (cf. Mk 11²). Spices were next crumbled between the folds of the linen (μετὰ τῶν ἀρωμάτων, Jn 19⁴⁰), and the whole was then bound together with strips of cloth (ὀθονίοις, Jn 19⁴⁰; cf. κειρίαις, Jn 11⁴⁴). The face was covered with a separate face-cloth or 'napkin' (τὸ σουδάριον, Jn 20⁷).

In later Judaism it was held that the resemblance of the future to the present body was so close that men would rise in the same clothes in which they were buried, on the analogy of the grain of corn which comes up from the earth not naked, but clothed (cf. 1 Co 15³⁷). And accordingly the Rabbis were in the habit of giving careful directions as to their grave-clothes (Weber, *Jüd. Theol.*² p. 370). This frequently led, however,

to such unnecessary expense in the way of luxurious wrappings, that by way of protest Rabbi Gamaliel left directions that he was to be buried in simple linen garments, while his grandson limited the number of grave-clothes to *one* dress (see Edersheim, *Sketches of Jewish Social Life*, p. 168 f.). At the present day, among Jews as well as Mohammedans, the corpse is attired in the ordinary holiday attire of life.

LITERATURE.—See under art. BURIAL, also art. 'Begräbnis bei den Hebräern' in Herzog, *PRE*³, with the literature there cited.

GEORGE MILLIGAN.

GREATNESS. — **1.** *The greatness of Christ.* — Greatness is an attribute which more than once in the Scriptures is applied to Jesus Christ. It is used both relatively, in passages which suggest a comparison between His powers and those of such OT heroes as Jacob (Jn 4¹²), Jonah and Solomon (Mt 12⁴¹·⁴²), and Abraham or the prophets (Jn 8⁵³); and in an absolute sense, with reference to the esteem in which He was to be held in the eyes of Jehovah (Lk 1³²). In the teaching of Jesus Himself, however, greatness is less a status than a quality. In the few words in which He alludes to His own human greatness, He makes it to consist in capacity for service and for sacrifice (Mk 10⁴⁵ ‖), and it is significant that in the Epistles also the attribute is ascribed to Him only where the idea of service and sacrifice is prominent in the context (He 4¹⁴ 10²¹ 13²⁰).

In one passage the greatness of the Son is compared with that of the Father (Jn 14²⁸). This is admittedly a difficult saying. The important point to be borne in mind is that the statement must not be interpreted apart from the rest of Christ's teaching concerning His relationship to the First Person in the Trinity. A careful study of His whole attitude seems to show that, whether He is here referring to such inferiority as is involved in His possessing the Divine essence by communication or to that which belonged to His subordination as being incarnate upon the earth, the words 'are perfectly consistent with the belief in the unity of the Divine nature, and therefore with the belief in the equality of the Godhead of the Son with the Godhead of the Father' (Westcott, *ad loc.*; cf. Godet, *ad loc.*).

2. *The greatness of Christ's followers.*—Christ has less to say about His own greatness than about that of His followers. For there is a greatness that belongs to His Kingdom, and this He covets for each one of them. So exalted is it that it surpasses the highest conception of greatness hitherto received (Mt 11¹¹ = Lk 7²⁸). But this greatness of the Kingdom differs essentially from that in which the world delights. The world has confused greatness itself with certain caricatures of it known as 'fame' and 'power.' The teaching of Jesus draws clear lines of distinction.

(*a*) Greatness is *not fame*. Men's fame consists in what others say about them; Christians' greatness consists in what they themselves are. Of the former consideration Christ bids His followers to be exultingly independent (Mt 5¹¹·¹², note the strong word ἀγαλλιᾶσθε). Indeed, to share in their Lord's greatness will involve not praise but persecution (Jn 15²⁰). But upon the second consideration, that is to say, upon their character, their claim to greatness wholly depends. And the character demanded includes, not the assertive qualities of notoriety, but the milder attributes of childlike humility (Mk 9³⁴, Mt 18¹·⁴, Lk 9⁴⁸), and obedience to the Divine law (Mt 5¹⁹—a passage which has an important bearing on the relationship of the new dispensation to the old).

(*b*) Greatness is *not power*. This, it is true, is the current conception of it. In the world's view, to be great is to be able to exact from others as much as is possible of respect and service. The more servants a man has at his disposal, the wider the sphere in which he can command obedience, the greater he is held to be (Mk 10⁴²∥). Such was also the disciples' conception. Two of them were ambitious of sitting the one on Christ's right hand and the other on His left in His Kingdom; the others were jealous, because they coveted these seats of authority for themselves (Mk 10³⁵ff. = Mt 20²⁰ff.). In striking contrast with this view Jesus places His own pronouncement on greatness. According to His teaching as well as His example (see above), to be great is not to exact, but to give, as much service as possible. A man's greatness is measured less by the service he commands than by the service he renders (Mk 10⁴³⁻⁴⁵∥). In a glorious paradox the highest in the Kingdom is he who assumes the lowest place (Mt 23¹¹, Jn 13¹⁴⁻¹⁶, and, for the supreme example, Ph 2⁵⁻¹¹).

The practical importance of such teaching can scarcely be over-emphasized. Until the time of the Incarnation the position of a servant was the lowest of all; but when the Son of God appeared, He, in St. Paul's words, 'took the form of a servant' (μορφὴν δούλου, Ph 2⁷), and from that day the whole status of honourable service, in whatever capacity, has been consecrated and raised. The position it occupies is no longer menial; it is the most exalted of all. The servant's life, indeed, may be a life of *greatness*, inasmuch as Christ has placed the very essence of greatness no longer in power to command, but in willingness to minister. The very title which our Lord uses of Himself in appealing to His own example (Mk 10⁴⁵∥), suggests that the nearer a man's life approaches to the ideal of humanity, the more completely will he realize his greatness in the service of others.

The exact significance of the title 'Son of Man' (wh. see) has been much discussed. To the present writer the truest explanation appears to be that which makes it point to Christ as the ideal of humanity. That is to say, He was not only *a* man, but also the perfect representation of mankind. There was nothing in Him that is foreign to ideal human nature, nor anything lacking that belongs to it. He was, if we may so express it, the perfect specimen of what man was intended to be. It will be seen that, if this view is correct, the application of the title made above is justifiable.

One more saying of Jesus must be included in our study. To His followers, as we have shown, greatness does not mean power in any earthly sense. And yet the very men who refuse to exert such power shall be possessed by a power superior to all earthly might—the power of the Father's protection (Jn 10²⁹ — according to the probable reading).   H. BISSEKER.

GRECIANS, GREEKS.—i. DISTINCTION OF THE WORDS.—**1. Greek.**—The name Ἕλλην, derived from a small tribe living in Thessaly, was extended to include all of Greek race, whether natives of Greece or of the Greek islands or colonies. This is the use in classical Greek, and it also appears in the NT, *e.g.* Ac 18¹⁷ (TR), 'All the Greeks took Sosthenes,' etc.; Ro 1¹⁴ (the Greek division of mankind into Greeks and non-Greeks or Barbarians); perhaps also 1 Co 1²². ²³ (Schleusner). This meaning was widened by the Jews to include all non-Jews who lived as the Greeks, using their language and manners. Where Ἕλληνες are opposed to Jews, the primary reference is to a difference of religious worship (Grimm). So in LXX of Is 9¹⁰ where Ἕλληνες appears for 'Philistines'; cf. also 2 Mac 4¹³ and 6⁹. Thus the Jews divided mankind into Jews and Greeks, which corresponds to the division of Jews and Gentiles; cf. Ac 14¹ 19¹⁰, Ro 1¹⁶ 2⁹. ¹⁰ 3⁹ 10¹², 1 Co 10³², Gal 3²⁸, Col 3¹¹. In this sense Titus was a Greek (Gal 2³), and also the father of Timothy (Ac 16³). This use of the word was continued by the

Christian Fathers, such as Justin Martyr, Tatian, and Athanasius.

2. Grecian. — Ἑλληνιστής (from Ἑλληνίζω), AV 'Grecian,' one who copies the customs and uses the language of the Greeks, received among the Jews the technical meaning of a Jew of the Dispersion, born outside Palestine and living among the Gentiles. These remained faithful to Judaism, but spoke Hellenistic Greek, the vernacular of daily life in the Gentile world. In the NT Ἑλληνιστής is opposed to Ἑβραῖος, a Palestinian Jew (see Trench, *NT Synonyms*); cf. Ac 6¹. See J. H. Moulton, *Gram. of N.T. Greek*, ch. i.

ii. GREEK INFLUENCE IN PALESTINE.—**1. Historical.**—The conquests of Alexander the Great (B.C. 331) opened the East to Greek settlers. Numbers of his veterans settled in Syria, and Greek colonists were welcomed by his successors. Old towns (as Gaza, Askalon, Ashdod, and Samaria) were Hellenized, and new Greek towns (as Scythopolis, Pella, and Gerasa) were built. Alexander's policy of Hellenizing his conquests was to a great extent successful, and a large section of the inhabitants of Palestine favoured Greek culture. It appeared likely that Hellenism would slowly conquer Judaism, and that the zealous adherents of the Mosaic law would become a minority in the nation. Had this happened, the blending of Greek culture with Judaism might have taken place on Palestinian soil as it did in Alexandria. Judaism, however, was saved through the injudicious action of Antiochus Epiphanes, who ruled Syria B.C. 175–164. In B.C. 168, Antiochus endeavoured to thoroughly Hellenize Judæa. He forbade the Jewish worship, and ordered sacrifices to be offered to heathen deities in the cities of Judæa. The penalty of disobedience was death (1 Mac 1⁴¹⁻⁵⁷). This led to the rebellion of the Maccabees. During the troubled years which followed, the Jewish national party regained much of their lost ground. Hellenism was discouraged, and even persecuted. Subsequently Jewish patriotism took the form of zealous observance of the Law, and there resulted the strongly marked division between Jew and Greek which we find in the Gospels.

2. Extent of Greek influence in Palestine in the time of Christ.—(1) *Greek districts.*—The districts of Palestine which in the time of Christ were chiefly Jewish were Judæa, Galilee, and Peræa (Jos. *BJ* iii. 3; Schürer, *HJP* II. i. 3 ff.). Close to these were districts predominantly Greek. The towns of Philistia had heathen temples. The whole seaboard of the Mediterranean was Greek except Joppa and Jamnia. On the north, heathen territory was reached in Cæsarea Philippi, where there was a celebrated temple to Pan. On the east we find the Greek league of Decapolis (G. A. Smith, *HGHL* p. 593). Even in central Palestine heathen temples existed at Samaria and Scythopolis. In the Greek cities athletic contests took place, and the usual amusements of the theatre and gymnasium were provided. Thus within a few miles of the scenes of the Saviour's ministry there were Gentile cities with temples, society, and culture, fully Greek. But although Jesus went into the country districts of the Gentile portions of Palestine, we have no record of His entering any Greek cities. For instance, we do not know that He ever entered Tiberias, although frequently in that neighbourhood.

(2) *Jewish districts.*—Even in the Jewish districts of Palestine, Greek influence was distinctly felt. Foreign as the theatre and amphitheatre were to Jewish notions, they were built at Jerusalem by Herod the Great (Jos. *Ant.* xv. viii. 1), and they also existed at Jericho. Greek architecture found its way even into Herod's Temple. Even in the

most Jewish localities there must have been a considerable number of Gentiles. Commerce and civilization bear witness to strong Greek influence. The Greek language must have been understood by many, although Aramaic was the usual tongue. This linguistic influence is evident in several ways: (a) the Greek words which are transliterated into Hebrew in the Mishna; (b) the three languages in which the inscription on the cross was written; (c) the Greek names of some of the Apostles, as Philip and Andrew; (d) the NT writers' use of the colloquial Greek as found on papyri; (e) the quotations from the LXX in the NT. Hence Christ lived among a people which, although strongly Jewish, was greatly influenced by Gentile thought and civilization. (See Schürer, *HJP* II. i. § 22; Edersheim, *Life and Times*, i. 84–92).

iii. CHRIST'S CONTACT WITH THE GREEKS.—In two cases only do we find it explicitly stated that Greeks came to the Saviour. These are:

(1) *The Syro-Phœnician woman* (Mk 7[26]).—The Saviour was either on Gentile ground (note the strongly supported reading διὰ Σιδῶνος, Mk 7[37]) or very near it (so Edersheim). The woman was a native of the country, and is called a Greek, in the sense of not being a Jew, and she was a heathen. Legends of the woman's life are to be found in *Clem. Homilies*, ii. 19.

(2) *The Greeks who asked to see Jesus* (Jn 12[20]).—Some have considered that these Greeks were really Grecian Jews (properly Ἑλληνισταί) (so Calvin, Ewald, and others). But there seems no reason for thinking that the word 'Greek' is not used here, as commonly, as equivalent to 'Gentile.' Evidently they were also proselytes (Jn 12[20] 'to worship').

There are other cases in which Christ apparently came in contact with 'Greeks,' but without the term being used—(a) *The healing of the demoniac* (Mt 8[28-34], Mk 5[1-20], Lk 8[26-39]). Notwithstanding the uncertainty in the name of the place, it was evidently on the eastern shore of the Sea of Galilee, where the inhabitants were mainly Gentile (note Decapolis, Mk 5[20]). The keeping of so large a herd of swine betokens the presence of a Gentile population. (b) *The centurion whose servant was healed* (Mt 8[5-13], Lk 7[1-10]). That the centurion was not a Jew appears from Lk 7[5]. (c) *The healing of one deaf and dumb* (Mk 7[31-37]). This was in the Greek region of Decapolis.

iv. CHRIST AND THE GRECIANS.—The Dispersion of the Jews had compulsory and voluntary causes. Large numbers of Israelites had been carried away captive by the Assyrians and Babylonians; and Pompey had taken many Jewish captives to Rome. But a much larger dispersion was due to voluntary emigration. From the time of Alexander the Great, Jewish colonies were gradually formed in the great commercial centres. Thus large numbers of Jews were to be found in Alexandria, in Antioch, in all the important cities on the Mediterranean, and even in Bithynia and Pontus. These Grecian Jews were active representatives of Judaism among the Gentiles, and won large numbers of proselytes from heathenism. The word 'Grecian' (Ἑλληνιστής) does not occur in the Gospels, although, owing to the attendance of non-Palestinian Jews at the feasts and the residence of many in Palestine, our Saviour must often have met with Grecians. One reference only occurs, Jn 7[35]. The Jews wondered whether Christ would go to 'the dispersed among the Gentiles' (ἡ διασπορὰ τῶν Ἑλλήνων), and, from working among these Hellenistic Jews, proceed to teach even the Greeks (Ἕλληνες). In this surmise they really anticipated the way in which Christianity found in the Grecian Jews a bridge by which it passed to the conquest of the Gentile world.

For the Greek language see LANGUAGE OF CHRIST.

LITERATURE.—Grimm-Thayer, *s.vv.*; Schürer, *HJP*, Index, *s.vv.* 'Greek influences,' 'Hellenism'; Edersheim, *Life and Times*, i. 17–30, 84–92; artt. 'Grecians,' 'Greece,' in vol. ii. of Hastings' *DB*, and 'Diaspora' in Ext. Vol.; art. 'Hellenism' in *Encyc. Biblica*; M'Fadyen, art. 'Hellenism' in *AJTh* x. 30.

F. E. ROBINSON.

GREETINGS.—'To greet' and 'to salute' stand in NT for the same Gr. verb, ἀσπάζεσθαι: AV renders indifferently 'greet' and 'salute'; RV almost uniformly 'salute.' The exceptions are Ac 20[1] AV 'embraced,' RV 'took leave of'; Ac 21[6] AV 'took leave of,' RV 'bade farewell'; He 11[13] AV 'embraced,' RV 'greeted.' χαίρειν is used for 'greeting,' and in imper. in the sense of 'hail' or 'farewell'; *i.e.* χαίρειν *is* the greeting, while ἀσπάζεσθαι is general, circumstances determining in each case what the greeting is. Thus in Mk 15[18] ἤρξαντο ἀσπάζεσθαι αὐτὸν Χαῖρε, 'they began to salute him, Hail.'

The Oriental has always attached great importance to the formal courtesies of life. However easy in demeanour and free in conversation he may be, the laws regulating social customs, sanctioned only by immemorial usage, are punctiliously observed. Any breach of these is regarded as a grave offence. His honour (*sharaf*), in all matters of ceremony, is very delicate and brittle, but strangely tough in things of greater moment. He will bear lightly an exposure that would cover us with perpetual shame; treat him with less formal respect than he desires, and he will fall into a paroxysm of rage over his 'broken honour.'

Greetings vary with the rank of parties, from the abject prostration of the subject before his sovereign, to the familiar kiss of friendly equals. One of humbler station salutes in silence, showing respect by bending his hand to the ground, then touching his lips and forehead. He will, at times, kiss the hand of his superior, and raise it to his brow. One interceding for another (Mk 7[25]), or begging a favour (Mt 18[26. 29]), will fall down flat; while in token of utter submission one may kiss a benefactor's feet (Lk 7[38. 45]). Slaves or servants kiss the sleeve or skirt of their lord's clothing. To touch (Mt 9[20]) or kiss the hem of the garment indicates great reverence. Dervishes and other 'holy men' are thus saluted. In the Greek Church worshippers often kiss the skirt of the priest's robe. To kiss upon the cheek is a sign of warm affection (Lk 15[20]), of the love and esteem of friends. This stains with a darker infamy the treachery of Judas (Mt 26[49] etc.).

Usually the rider salutes the footman, the traveller those whom he passes on the wayside, the smaller party the larger (one speaking for the rest in each case), and the young the aged. In a crowded street it is, of course, impossible to greet everyone. Only venerable sheikhs, or men distinguished by rank, wealth, or sacred learning, are saluted. The Jews freed the Rabbis from all obligation to salute. To be saluted 'Rabbi' was a coveted honour (Mt 23[7], Mk 12[38]). They merely acknowledged the salutation and passed on. The Moslem salutes both on entering (Mt 10[12]) and on leaving a house.

To every form of salutation custom prescribes an answer. To use any other is regarded as proof of ignorance or vulgarity. The common salutation is *salâm 'aleik*, 'peace be upon you' (Lk 24[36]), to which the answer is, 'And upon you be peace.' It is a Moslem's duty to give this salutation to another; but it may be omitted without sin. When, however, the salutation is given, the Moslem is bound to return it. The Moslems claim this as 'the salutation of Islâm, and not for the mouths of the heathen, with whom is no peace nor fellowship, neither in this world nor in the next' (Doughty, *Arabia Deserta*, i. 503). Once Mr. Doughty was gravely imperilled because he 'had greeted with *Salaam Aleyk*, which they [the Arabs] will have to be a salutation of God's people only—the Moslemîn' (*ib.* ii. 369). If a Moslem by mistake give it to a non-Moslem, it should not be returned. On discovery the former may revoke it, as he does should a Moslem fail to return it, saying, 'Peace be on *us* and on the righteous worshippers of God' (Lk 10⁶). The insecure life of Hebrew and Arab, ever exposed to alarm of war or robber raid, no doubt gave special meaning to the greeting 'Peace.'

At meeting of friends, greetings are lengthy and wearisome. Of the Arabs, Doughty observes, 'The long nomad greetings . . . are for the most, to say over a dozen times with bashful solemnity the same *cheyf ent, cheyf ent*, "How dost thou? and how heartily again?"' (*ib.* i. 433). Dr. Mackie gives a good example of the more elaborate trifling of the Syrians (*Bible Manners and Customs*, p. 150). The phrases are set and conventional, the maximum of words conveying the minimum of meaning.

The Rabbis forbade one mourning for the dead to salute. Interruption of prayer was forbidden, even to salute a king, nay, to uncoil a serpent from the foot. The Rabbis all agreed that, to avoid distraction, no one should be saluted immediately before prayer (Edersheim, *Life and Times of Jesus*, ii. 137). The nature of the salutations indicated above sufficiently explains these restrictions, and also enables us to understand the prohibition of Jesus, 'Salute no man by the way' (Lk 10⁴). The urgency of that mission could brook no such delays.   W. EWING.

GRIEF.—See SORROW.

GRINDING.—See MILL.

GROANING.—See SIGHING ; and ANGER, p. 62ᵇ.

GROWING.—

Under this term students of the Greek Testament have to do with only one word—and that a verb, αὐξάνω. The consideration of the corresponding substantive does not properly form the subject of inquiry in this Dictionary. Rare in classical literature, αὔξησις is used only twice in the NT, viz. in Eph 4¹⁶ and Col 2¹⁹. The verb is, however, employed some twelve times within the four Gospels. It is a verb of exceedingly doubtful derivation, but probably is etymologically linked with the German *wachsen* and our own *wax* ; less certainly with the Latin *augeo*. Its underlying meaning is that of additional size, bulk, or power. The normal usage of the verb in the Classics implies that such access comes from without, it is superimposed by some external agency. This significance lies both in the transitive and intransitive use of the verb, and affords, as will be seen, a striking contrast with its use in the Greek Testament. Quotations are not needful. The verb is employed by classical writers from Homer downwards to mark efforts to increase the power of the State or of a country, of special honour paid to parents, of the exaggerations of orators, of the waxing of the moon, of the noontide heat of the sun, of the height of the waves of the sea. Enough to say that in classical literature the verb marks an increase or addition to a person or thing brought about by external agency.

The Hebrew language is very rich in terms which signify 'growth.' There are some 16 words, verbs and nouns substantive, which bear this general meaning. It is enough to say here that they are capable of a single classification. One set of expressions corresponds to αὐξάνω in the sense already indicated ; the other, which is preponderant, marks 'growth' of the physical order, seminal growth ; and is applied with a great wealth of illustration to the life of plants, trees, the brute creation, and of man himself. Every student of the Psalter or of the Prophetical books is aware of the word-pictures here in which the writers take delight, a delight which is spiritual more than intellectual, of the heart rather than the mind. The natural laws of physical development are by these writers boldly made to apply to the spiritual world. Jehovah, supreme in the one sphere, is supreme in the other. Growth is from within, but yet it is 'God who giveth the increase.'

When the student turns to the NT, and to the idea of growth which finds expression there, he finds that there is a greater affinity of conception between the inspired writers of both Testaments than there is between the writers of the NT and classical Greek writers. The affinity simply lies in the com-

mon conception, with its spiritual applications, of a germinal growth, expanding and blossoming unto fruitage whether in nature or in grace.

1. *References in the Gospels.*—With the above preliminaries, the issue may now be considered in relation to the four Gospels. And first, the less careful student must be warned that the quotation which records the pathetic plea of the disciples to their Lord, 'Increase our faith,' * stands out as an exception. The translation [AV and RV] may serve, but it is doubtful whether 'our' is admissible. Despite the verb, it is questionable whether the disciples then asked for a growth of that spirit of which they were consciously possessed. Were they not rather asking for some gift new and strange to their experience ? In any case growth of the physical order is not in place here ; for this we must look, as has been shown, almost exclusively to the verb αὐξάνω. This verb is of frequent occurrence in the Gospels, although only once employed by the Fourth Evangelist,† when the Baptist's language is rendered as expressing the growing authority of the new Teacher, and the increasing number of His adherents. It is interesting to observe that with regard to all other instances of the occurrence of this word, they either apply, as here, to the Lord Himself, or else form a part of His own utterances ; nor is the interest of the point largely affected by the admission that our Lord would normally use Aramaic. The Evangelists doubtless discovered in the verb αὐξάνω what they wished to convey about His childhood, and what they understood Him to teach in lessons drawn from the natural world.

In his unique account of our Lord's childhood the Second Evangelist declares of Him (Lk 2⁴⁰) that which he had in precisely the same terms declared of the Baptist (1⁸⁰), that 'the child grew and waxed strong, filled with wisdom' [of the Baptist, 'in spirit'] ; that is, the development of Christ, both spiritually and physically, was normal and equable in its character. The phraseology of St. Luke suggests a contrast with the Apocryphal Gospels, whose account of Christ's infancy makes Him appear a wonder-working prodigy, a phenomenal child, anxious for the display of supernatural powers. St. Luke will have none of this. He is not content with a single protest, for later (2⁵²) he solemnly declares that as the child Jesus advanced in years so He developed in wisdom and in favour with God and men. Here, however, the 'growth' is not explicitly stated, the rare verb (προέκοπτεν) used marking rather advancement, or progress triumphing over difficulties in the way.

The remaining instances of the verb αὐξάνω appear for the most part in our Lord's parabolic discourses. Thus it is seen to be the characteristic feature of the seed sown.‡ There is a process of secret assimilation between it and the good ground ; and growth, not sterility or a rash prematurity, is the consequence.§ In the immortal contrast (Mt 6²⁸, cf. Lk 12²⁷) between the lilies of the field and the garish splendour of Solomon's court dress, it is less upon the beauty of the flowers that Christ lays stress than upon their growth, gradual and all unconscious, spontaneous, effortless. In the parable of the Tares and Wheat this characteristic verb appears in the permission, at once generous and awful, of the master to his servants to let both grow together until the harvest (Mt 13³⁰). In the same parabolic discourse it is the growth of the mustard-seed, the development of the surprisingly little, which furnishes an analogue of the

---

* Lk 17⁵ πρόσθες ἡμῖν πίστιν.
† Jn 3³⁰ opposed to ἐλαττοῦσθαι.
‡ Mk 4⁸, cf. v.²⁷ where growth is expressed by μηκύνηται.
§ The lessons as to hindrances to growth taught in the Parable of the Sower would need a separate study.

spread of the Church universal (Mt 13³¹). Lastly, although we have not here the verb αὐξάνω, we find the mysterious condemnation passed upon the barren fig-tree (Mt 21¹⁹), a condemnation of that which is purely physical, sterility in fruit, which fruit in the world of men as in the life of plants and trees is the consequence of all true growth.

2. *The underlying idea.*—It seems somewhat strange, since the OT is so full of religious teaching drawn from physical growth, that only in the one instance, quoted above, of our Lord's childhood is a spiritual application of the idea directly made in the Gospel narrative. Christ, we may reverently say it, was content to lay the conception which was ever before Him, in garden, harvest field, and orchard, also before His own. If they had eyes to see these things, and ears to hear them,—if they would only 'consider' (Lk 12²⁴. ²⁷) them, — heart and conscience would do the rest. Then they, as we, would perceive this natural law in the spiritual world — a growing within, secret, beautiful, fertile, in men, and yet not of man, yielding the increase and harvest of the Spirit, His fruit rather than their works.

3. *Application of the idea.*—But if it is thought even by devout and careful students that such ideas are more than may be gathered from our Lord's actual utterances, those who treasured His sayings in the Apostolic age did not think so. St. Peter and St. Paul no longer use the idea of growing as a metaphor. It is a gracious fact both for the Church and the individual believer. Thus the Apostle of the Gentiles uses the conception of inward Christian growth (Eph 4¹⁵), and so as to form a shrine wherein the Divine presence may be manifest (2²¹); his prayer for his Colossian converts is that they may grow in further knowledge of God (Col 1¹⁰); his promise to them if they 'hold the Head' (2¹⁹), is that they shall grow with a Divine increase. Twice he assures the Corinthians (1 Co 3⁶) that this growth, although in them, has a Divine origin. St. Peter (1 P 2², cf. [2 P 3¹⁸]) shows that the Holy Scriptures have their own function in the growth of grace. It is enough; the conception is carried through from one Testament to the other, and its teaching is consecrated, its consolation is secured in and through Him whom the great Evangelical prophet (Is 11¹) prefigured as the very symbol of growing: 'There shall come forth a shoot out of the stock of Jesse, and a branch out of his roots shall bear fruit.' That fruit is still seen in every plant planted by the Divine Husbandman (Mt 15¹³).

LITERATURE.—Reference may be made to Drummond, *Nat. Law in the Spir. World*, p. 123 ff.; Bruce, *Parabolic Teaching*, pp. 90–143; Marcus Dods, *Parables of our Lord*, 1st Ser. p. 47 ff.

B. WHITEFOORD.

GUARD.—**1.** RV rendering of κουστωδία (Lat. *custodia*), Mt 27⁶⁵. ⁶⁶ 28¹¹, AV 'watch'; obtained by the chief priests and Pharisees from Pilate to guard the sepulchre. The need of Pilate's authorization and the risk of punishment from him (Mt 28¹⁴) show that this guard must have consisted, not of the Jewish Temple police, but of soldiers from the Roman cohort at Jerusalem; possibly, though not probably, the same as had guarded the cross (ἔχετε, 27⁶⁵, is probably imperative, 'have (take) a guard'). A watch usually consisted of four men (Polyb. vi. 33), each of whom watched in turn, while the others rested beside him so as to be roused by the least alarm; but in this case the guards may have been more numerous.

2. 'A soldier of his [Herod's] guard' (RV tr. of σπεκουλάτωρ, Lat. *speculator*, AV 'executioner') beheaded John the Baptist, Mk 6²⁷. *Speculatores* were originally spies or scouts (from *specula*, 'a look-out'); but we find them chiefly employed (*a*)

as messengers or couriers, carrying official despatches; (*b*) as military executioners. A certain number were attached to each legion, besides others belonging to the Prætorian guard, who were closely attached to the Emperor's person and ready for any special service. There are many examples in classical writers (*e.g.* Seneca, *de Ira*, I. ii. 4), Acts of Martyrs, and Rabbinic writings, of their employment as executioners; for reff. see Schürer, Wetstein, etc. The Herods had bodyguards (δορυφόροι, σωματοφύλακες, Jos. *BJ* I. xxxiii. 7–9, II. xv. 1, etc.), and may have given them the Roman title of *speculatores*; or the word may here be used generally for an executioner. Herod sent some of his guards (δορυφόροι) to kill his son Antipater (*Ant.* XVII. vii. 1, *BJ* I. xxxiii. 7).

LITERATURE.—Schürer, *HJP* I. ii. 62f.; Benson, *Cyprian*, 505 n.; Golling in Hase and Iken's *Thes. Nov.* ii. 405; Marquardt, *Römische Staatsverwaltung*, ii. pp. 420, 547.

HAROLD SMITH.

GUEST.—Hospitality was, and to a large extent still is, one of the chief virtues of Oriental life. This was due in large measure to the nomadic character of Eastern peoples, among whom there was no provision for the traveller apart from private entertainment. The casual passer-by, the unknown stranger, even the enemy, were welcomed to tent or house, provided with food and lodging, waited on often by the host himself, and dismissed without being expected or even allowed to pay for their entertainment. Even yet, where the influence of travellers and tourists from the West has not corrupted the ancient manners, the offer of payment is regarded as an insult. The practice of ages has invested the guest with a peculiar sacredness: a breach of hospitality is an almost unheard of disgrace. Underlying this ready hospitality of the East is the idea that every stranger is *daif Ullah*, 'the guest of God.' The host himself is a sojourner (Heb. *gēr*, Arab. *jar*) with God; the stranger is a fellow-guest, and loyalty to God demands that he should be hospitably entertained. Not unlike this, though on a higher plane, is the teaching of Jesus as to God's knowledge of and provision for our needs, which frees the trustful, childlike heart from all undue anxiety (Mt 6²⁵⁻³⁴, Lk 12²²⁻³¹).

In the Gospels, however, it is not the free hospitality of the nomad desert life that meets us, but the more restricted hospitality of the town, of meals and banquets.

The word 'guest' occurs in AV of the Gospels only in Mt 22¹⁰f. (in the parable of the Wedding Feast), where 'guests'=ἀνακείμενοι; and in Lk 19⁷, where 'to be guest' (RV 'to lodge')=καταλῦσαι. The Gr. word ἀνάκειμαι, which indicates the reclining posture then generally adopted, occurs frequently in reference to meals or banquets, and is usually translated 'sit at meat' (*e.g.* Mt 9¹⁰ 26⁷). In Jn 13²³ ἀνακείμενος is rendered in RV 'at the table reclining.' The same word is used in Jn 6¹¹ in the narrative of the feeding of the 5000, though they, of course, had neither couch nor table. In a few passages κατάκλινω occurs, with the same reference to reclining at table; *e.g.* Lk 7³⁶ (of a meal at which Jesus was present as a guest) 14⁸ (in Christ's warning against seeking the chief places); cf. art. GUEST-CHAMBER. The cognate verb ἀνακλίνω is similarly used several times, *e.g.* Mt 8¹¹ 14¹⁹ etc.

During His ministry Jesus was frequently invited to be guest in private houses. Thus Matthew (Levi) entertained Him when He had called him from the 'place of toll' (Lk 5²⁷ff. ||); Martha 'received him into her house' (Lk 10³⁸ff.); Zacchæus 'received him joyfully' (Lk 19¹ff.). He was one of the guests at the marriage in Cana of Galilee (Jn 2¹ff.), and after His resurrection He 'sat down to meat' in the house of the two disciples at Emmaus (Lk 24³⁰). The Pharisees complained bitterly of His eating with publicans and sinners, yet several of them invited Him to be their guest (Lk 7³⁶ff. 11³⁷ff. 14¹ff.), not, as it seems, with the purest motives of hospitality. The words of Jesus to His host on one of these occasions (Lk 7³⁶ff.)

introduce us to the courtesies which, if not necessarily shown to a guest, were marks of honour and regard, the giving of water to wash the feet, the kiss of welcome, the anointing of the head with oil.

It should be noted here that the request of Jesus to the Samaritan woman, 'Give me to drink' (Jn 4⁷), was virtually, according to Eastern ideas, a claim on her hospitality, and in ordinary circumstances it would have been recognized and responded to at once. Her astonishment at the request reminds us that between Jew and Samaritan there was no recognition of the law of hospitality (cf. Lk 9⁵³ 17¹⁸).

Some of the parables of Jesus reflect this aspect of Oriental life. The man to whom a friend has come unexpectedly at midnight is distressed because he has nothing in the house to offer him (Lk 11⁵ᶠᶠ·). In the parable of the Wedding Feast (Mt 22¹ᶠ·) we note the early invitation of the guests, the calling of them by servants on the appointed day (with καλέσαι τοὺς κεκλημένους, cf. Heb. הַקְּרֻאִים 1 S 9¹³· ²²), the provision of the wedding garment.

In some passages in the Gospels we have what seem to be traces of Oriental ideas as to the reception of guests, e.g. the instructions to the Twelve (Mt 10¹¹· ¹⁴ ; see also vv.⁴⁰⁻⁴²), to the Seventy (Lk 10⁵ᶠᶠ·). There is an Eastern saying that 'the guest while in the house is its lord'; the host often ministers to his needs with his own hands. With this we may perhaps compare such sayings as Mt 23¹¹. In Mt 8¹¹, Lk 13²⁹ the final blessedness of the Kingdom of Heaven is spoken of under the figure of a feast, at which guests from the east and the west shall sit down with Abraham and Isaac and Jacob. Most striking of all is the great prophecy of final judgment (Mt 25³¹ᶠᶠ·), where the destiny of men is made to turn on their granting or refusing to Christ, in the person of 'one of these my brethren, even the least,' the position and provision of a guest.

LITERATURE. — *Expositor's Gr. Test.*; Hastings' *DB*, artt. 'Guest,' 'Hospitality,' 'Host'; *Encyc. Bibl.*, artt. 'Meals,' 'Stranger'; *Jewish Encyc.*, art. 'Hospitality'; Vigouroux, *Dict. de la Bible*, art. 'Hospitalité'; Hamburger, *RE*, art. 'Gast'; Schenkel, *Bibel-Lex.*, art. 'Gast'; Robinson, *BRP*; Trumbull, *Studies in Oriental Social Life*, pp. 73–142; W. R. Smith, *RS²*; Van Lennep, *Manners and Customs in Bible Lands*; Burckhardt, *Notes on the Bedouins and Wahâbys*; Doughty, *Travels in Arabia Deserta* (passim); Wilkinson, *Manners and Customs of Ancient Egyptians*.

CHARLES S. MACALPINE.

GUEST-CHAMBER. — This word occurs in EV only in the parallel passages Mk 14¹⁴, Lk 22¹¹. Peter and John, sent by Jesus to prepare His last Passover, are told to ask the master of the house to which they would be guided, 'Where is the (Mk. 'my') guest-chamber, where I shall eat the passover with my disciples?' The Greek word here used (κατάλυμα) occurs elsewhere in NT only in the narrative of the Nativity (Lk 2⁷), 'There was no room for them *in the inn*' (ἐν τῷ καταλύματι). It is used by LXX as the rendering of כְּלִי (Ex 4²⁴, RV 'lodging place') and of לִשְׁכָּה (1 S 9²², RV 'guest-chamber'). [It may here be noted that the cognate verb καταλύω, rendered in RV 'lodge,' occurs in Lk 9¹² 19⁷]. The guest-chamber of the last Passover is also spoken of by Jesus as 'a large upper room' (ἀνάγαιον, Mk 14¹⁵, Lk 22¹²). With this may be compared the ὑπερῷον of Ac 1¹³ 9³⁷· ³⁹ 20⁸. It has been conjectured by some that the ἀνάγαιον of Mk. and Lk. and the ὑπερῷον of Ac 1¹³ are identical, but there is no evidence in support of this.

We must associate several incidents in the life of our Lord besides the last Passover with the guest-chambers of the houses in which they took place, e.g. the anointing, in the house of Simon the Pharisee, by the woman who was a sinner (Lk 7³⁶ᶠ·); the later anointing by Mary of Bethany in the house of Simon the Leper (Jn 12¹ᶠ·); Levi's

feast (Lk 5²⁷ᶠᶠ·); the dinner, or rather breakfast (ἀριστήσῃ), of Lk 11³⁷ᶠᶠ·; and the miracle and sayings of Jesus recorded in Lk 14¹ᶠ·.

The guest-chamber occupied in our Lord's time, as it does at the present day, an important place in the arrangement and economy of Oriental houses. In it all festivities took place; it was set apart also for the entertainment of guests during their stay. It varied in position and character with the size of the house. The smaller houses (see HOUSE) had only one court; in these the guest-chamber was on the ground-floor, the women's apartments being above. But in the larger houses of the wealthier classes, which had two or three courts, the women's apartments were hidden away in an inner court, and the guest-chamber occupied the first floor of the outer court (hence ἀνάγαιον, ὑπερῷον). In either case it was open to the court, so that all that took place in the one could be seen from the other. On the opposite side of the court was another chamber, equal in size to the first, but fronted with lattice-work filled in with coloured glass; this served as a winter guest-chamber. In some cases a room on the flat roof, the most pleasant and most retired part of the house, was used as a guest-chamber. This is the עֲלִיָּה of the OT (cf. 1 K 17¹⁹).

The guest-chamber was, of course, furnished according to the means of the owner of the house. Many no doubt were, as indeed they are still, like the prophet's chamber of 2 K 4¹⁰, furnished with 'a bed, and a table, and a stool, and a candlestick.' But those of the wealthy were furnished with the greatest luxury. In our Lord's time the custom of reclining at meals was common. The couches and tables, which in the larger houses were placed on a raised part of the guest-chamber called the *liwan*, occupied three sides of a square, and the guests reclined with their heads toward the table, the feet outward toward the wall, and the left arm resting on a cushion. This must be borne in mind in reading such narratives as those of the two anointings and of the last Passover. The places at table were allotted to the guests according to a strict etiquette, as to the details of which there is considerable uncertainty. The eagerness of the Pharisees to secure for themselves the 'chief seats' (πρωτοκλισίαι) at feasts brought on them the rebuke of Jesus (Lk 14⁷ᶠᶠ·), and gave occasion to His warnings to the disciples to avoid such unseemly eagerness for personal honour (Mt 23⁶, Mk 12³⁸ᶠᶠ·, Lk 20⁴⁵ᶠᶠ·).

Besides the guest-chambers of private houses, there were, as there are now, in most villages one or more guest-chambers, provided and maintained at the public expense, for the accommodation of travellers who arrived in larger numbers than could be privately entertained. They were shelters for man and beast of a very simple kind. Some think that the 'inn' of Bethlehem (Lk 2⁷) was of this character, but others are of opinion that it was rather an inn under the care of a host, like the πανδοχεῖον of Lk 10³⁴.

LITERATURE. — Hastings' *DB*, artt. 'House,' 'Hospitality'; *Encyc. Bibl.*, art. 'House'; *Jewish Encyclopedia*, art. 'House'; Trumbull, *Studies in Oriental Social Life*, pp. 73–142; Van Lennep, *Manners and Customs in Bible Lands*, pp. 442, 589 ff.; Robinson, *BRP²* i. p. 80 f., ii. p. 18 ff.; Lane, *Modern Egyptians*, i. p. 5 ff.; *Expositor's Greek Testament, ad loc.*; Swete, *Com. on Mark*; Edersheim, *Life and Times of Jesus the Messiah*, i. 564, ii. 206, 483, 493.

CHARLES S. MACALPINE.

GUIDE.—1. *The word 'guide.'*—In AV of Gospels the noun 'guide' is found only in Mt 23¹⁶· ²⁴, where it represents ὁδηγός (lit. 'a leader of the way'). ὁδηγός occurs also, however, in Mt 15¹⁴, where RV has consistently substituted 'blind guides' for 'blind leaders' of AV (cf. Ac 1¹⁶, Ro 2¹⁹). As a verb, 'guide' in AV of Gospels represents **two**

different words in the original. (*a*) ὁδηγέω (from ὁδηγός) in Jn 16¹³. ὁδηγέω is found also in Mt 15¹⁴, Lk 6³⁹ (cf. Ac 8³¹, Rev 7¹⁷), but is there rendered 'lead' in AV, which RV again properly changes to 'guide.' (*b*) κατευθύνω (lit. 'to make straight'), which occurs only once in Gospels (Lk 1⁷⁹; but cf. 1 Th 3¹¹, 2 Th 3⁵). An interesting contrast might be drawn between the false ὁδηγοί, the 'blind leaders of the blind' (Mt 15¹⁴ 23¹⁶, Lk 6³⁹), and the true ὁδηγός (who is also Himself ἡ ὁδός, Jn 14⁶), who came into the world to 'set our feet straight' into the way of peace (Lk 1⁷⁹), who promised before His departure that He would send the Spirit of truth to guide His people into all the truth (Jn 16¹³), and who will Himself hereafter 'guide them to life-giving springs of water' (Rev 7¹⁷). With Christ as ὁδηγός of His people cf. the ἀρχηγός of Ac 3¹⁵ 5³¹, He 2¹⁰ 12².

2. *Christ as our Guide.*—To communities and to individuals, otherwise walking in darkness, Christ is their Guide, the Shepherd leading His sheep, the Light preceding His people. There can be only one Guide,—a man cannot follow the lode-star and also make for every flickering will-o'-the-wisp that allures and entices him. Christ has deliberately and finally claimed the guidance of mankind. He bade sincere aspirants after life follow, not the Law as such, nor even God as unincarnate, but *Himself*, the Law-in-character and the God-in-man (Lk 18²², Mt 16²⁴, Jn 12²⁶). His guidance is to be universal in its scope (Jn 1⁴· ⁹), and will be sufficient in its nature (Jn 21²²). Without Him the mass of men are as sheep without a shepherd (Mt 9³⁶). He alone reveals God to man (Mt 11²⁷), and so displays the goal of man's being. He taught, therefore, as one having unique authority (Mt 7²⁹), and rightly draws all men to Himself (Jn 12³²). He Himself, and no other conceivably or possibly, is the Way as well as the Truth and the Life (Jn 14⁶). Hence the warning: 'Take heed that no man lead you astray' (Mk 13⁵). And so, on the other hand, the impossibility of the Christian's seeking any other guidance, expressed in St. Peter's exclamation: 'Lord, to whom shall we go?' (Jn 6⁶⁸). Of this sole claim and unique authority the three chosen disciples heard the ratification in the bewildering glory of the Transfiguration: 'This is my beloved Son: hear ye him' (Mk 9⁷). This guidance Christ gives to His follower by His Holy Spirit, guiding into all the truth (Jn 16¹³); and very especially through the Holy Scriptures, which tell of Him (Jn 5³⁹), and whose meaning He can make plain (Lk 24²⁷· ⁴⁵). Christ Himself ratified the guidance afforded by Scripture at crises of His life, in which example and precept were wedded together in indissoluble union, as in the Temptation, the Cleansing of the Temple, and on the Cross (Lk 4. 19⁴⁶ 23⁴⁶).

To put it in another way, the Father's will was Christ's will, even to the uttermost: 'Not what I will, but what thou wilt' (Mk 14³⁶). So Christ guides us to union with God, our true destiny; through Him we come to the Father (Jn 14⁶). Hence His guidance is into peace (Lk 1⁷⁹), as the aged Zacharias felt and declared. It is the steady, unvarying guidance of the heart towards its Divine home, the love of God, as the name *Immanuel* suggests (Mt 1²³). It is an absolute guidance, or no guidance (Lk 9⁵⁷⁻⁶²).

W. B. FRANKLAND.

GUILE.—See DECEIT.

GUILT is the state of the sinner before God, whereby, becoming the object of God's wrath, he incurs the debt and punishment of death. So closely are Sin, Guilt, and Death connected, both in the OT and NT, that the terms are almost interchangeable, and can be adequately discussed only in relation to one another (see art. SIN). It will suffice in the present article to show that the removal of guilt was the object of Christ's death, and that the recognition of sin as guilt is in consequence a prominent, if not the primary feature of the teaching of the NT concerning sin.

1. The gospel, as first preached by the Baptist (Mt 3²) and Jesus Himself (Mk 1¹⁵, Mt 4²³ 10⁷), was the Kingdom of God. Even the Fourth Evangelist, who usually presents it as Eternal Life, witnesses to this fact (Jn 3³· ⁵). The message, therefore, as coupled with the summons to repentance, involves a restoration of personal relations, God reigning in the midst of a reconciled people. Baptism, though the symbolism of cleansing is employed, is 'unto remission' (Mk 1⁴, Lk 3³) rather than to the washing away of sins; remission being not a vital act by which sinners are made just, but a personal favour (Mt 6¹², cf. 1 Jn 1⁹) by which they are accounted righteous. The risen Lord expressly carries on this view of His atoning work into the proclamation of the completed Christian gospel. Remission of sins was to be preached in His name among all the nations (Lk 24⁴⁷, cf. Mt 28¹⁹). To this message the primitive preaching shows an exact fidelity (Ac 2³⁸ 5³¹ 10⁴³ 13³⁸ 26¹⁸). The expression 'blotted out' in Ac 3¹⁹ emphasizes forgiveness as the cancelling of an account. And the statement of St. Paul in Ac 17³⁰ (cf. Ro 3²⁵), that God had 'overlooked' the times of ignorance, again gives prominence to the personal relation.

It is the guilt rather than the infection of sin which appears in *the teaching of Jesus*. The analogy between disease and sin, which the miracles of healing suggest, might appear to show the contrary. But it is doubtful whether the transition from the sickness of the body to that of the soul would have presented itself to the Hebrew in this form, and not rather through the conception of suffering as the punishment of sin. It is this, for example, that makes the problem of the 'marred visage' of Jehovah's Servant (Is 52¹³⁻¹⁵ 53) And the interpretation given by our Lord Himself in the case of the paralytic seems to be decisive. His power to cure the body is the evidence, not of His power to heal the soul, but of His authority (ἐξουσία) to forgive sins (Mk 2¹⁰). It is the 'debts' which remain as the permanent result of past 'trespasses,' for which we ask forgiveness in the Lord's Prayer (Mt 6¹², Lk 11⁴); and when we crave deliverance, it is not from the sick will, but from the 'Evil One' (Mt 6¹³), the personal enemy of God who has received a guilty allegiance. The importance of this aspect of sin is further marked by the requirement of human forgiveness as the condition because the pattern of Divine remission (Mt 6¹⁴· ¹⁵ 18²¹⁻³⁵). What, therefore, is removed is not, in the first instance, the subjective consequences, but an objective result of sin. If it be urged that Christ discharges the latter only in virtue of the fact that He destroys the former, as expressed in the words 'it is he that shall save his people from their sins' (Mt 1²¹, but cf. Ro 5⁹), the reply is that Jesus is here represented as Saviour in the sense in which Messiah was to save, and that this is determined by the meaning of 'salvation' as developed in the theology of the OT. The root idea of the Messianic salvation is liberation not remedy (Ex 14¹³ 15², Is 45¹⁷ 46¹³ 52¹⁰, Lk 1⁶⁹· ⁷¹· ⁷⁷).

Again, attention must be paid to the prominence given to judgment, especially the Day of Judgment, in the Synoptic narrative (Mt 5²¹· ²² 7¹· ² 10¹⁵ 11²⁰⁻²⁴ 12³⁶· ³⁷· ⁴¹· ⁴² 16²⁷· ²⁸ 19²⁸ 24 *passim* 25 *passim* 26⁶⁴, Lk 12⁵⁸· ⁵⁹). The unquenchable fire is not merely the automatic result of sin bringing forth death, but punishment inflicted by judicial sentence (Mk 9⁴³· ⁴⁸, Mt 25⁴¹). The wicked are workers of iniquity giving account for idle words and deeds (Mt 12[36] 16[27]). Blasphemy against the Holy Spirit, however it be interpreted, incurs condemnation as the unpardonable sin (Mk 3[28. 29], Mt 12[31. 32]). It is the personal relation, and therefore the guilt of sin, which appears in the parables of the Lost Sheep, etc. (Lk 15). The joy of the angels is represented as arising out of the reconciliation between the Father and the penitent (Lk 15[10]). The expiatory character of the Cross is not so fully evident. But Jesus gives His life a ransom (Mk 10[45] ||); the Agony was a cup given by His Father (Mk 14[36] ||); the sorrow of death was the forsaking by God (Mk 15[34] ||); the peace of Calvary the self-committal to the Father (Lk 23[46]).

2. *The Gospel of St. John*, dwelling, as it does, upon the gift of God as life, truth, and light, might seem on a superficial reading to obscure, if not to ignore, the view of sin as guilt. But even the Prologue couples grace, or God's free favour, with truth as that which came by Jesus Christ, and that in antithesis to the Law given by Moses (Jn 1[17]). The witness of the Baptist is to the Lamb of God (1[29. 36]), a sacrificial term involving expiation (19[36]; cf. Ex 12[46], Nu 9[12], 1 Co 5[7], Jn 6[52] with Westcott's note). To believe on the name of the Son of God is to escape judgment (Jn 3[18] 5[24]). It is 'accusation to the Father' which the Jews have to fear (5[45]). Through Christ we come to the Father (14[6]). The commission of the risen Christ to His disciples is to forgive and retain sins (20[23]; cf. Mt 16[19] 18[18]). It is the confession and forgiveness of sins which the First Epistle represents as effecting the cleansing from sin and unrighteousness through the sacrificial blood and heavenly intercession of our Advocate with the Father (1 Jn 2[1. 2]). The use of ἀνομία, 'lawlessness,' as a synonym for ἁμαρτία, 'sin,' implies the guilt of a broken law (3[4]). The condemnation or acquittal of the heart reflects the judgment of God (3[20]). In the Apocalypse, sin is set in relation to Him that sitteth on the throne (Rev 4[2]), incurring His wrath (6[16]), noted in His books (20[12]), and receiving His plagues (15[1]).

3. It is difficult to set forth *St. Paul's theory of guilt* without entering upon the whole question of his view of sin. But a few considerations will make it clear that he looks at sin, in the first instance, as incurring guilt. It is represented as an act committed against God (Ro 1[21]). All its essential features are recapitulated in each individual sin or transgression. It is only through the Law that it can appear as what it is (3[20] 7[7]). It can only be separated from its actual manifestations by being represented, not as a predisposing cause of these, but as itself an act of disobedience on the part of Adam (5[19]). Death is not so much its consequence as its punishment or wages (5[12] 6[23]), not following automatically, but inflicted by the sentence of an offended God (1[18], Eph 5[6], Col 3[6]). It involves responsibility (Ro 1[20]), desert (1[32]), condemnation (5[16. 18]). The work of Christ is primarily an act of righteous obedience (5[18. 19], Ph 2[8]), undoing the act of disobedience in which all sin is included; an offering for sin condemning sin in the flesh (Ro 8[3]), and wiping off the score of trespasses (Col 2[14]). Its effect in the broadest view is a reversal of the sentence of condemnation (Ro 8[1]) and reconciliation with God (5[10], 2 Co 5[18-20]). St. Paul's view of the function of law must here be remembered. The analogy of a therapeutic drug, administered in order that the disease may declare itself, is apt to mislead. This is not in the Apostle's thought. For trespasses or transgressions are themselves sin, not merely its symptoms (Eph 2[1. 5]). It is the removal of these, not of a cause distinguishable from them, which is the purpose of the Cross (Ro 4[25]; cf. 5[8] 8[32]). Death, which passed upon all men in consequence

of transgression (5[12]), reigned from Adam to Moses (5[14]). The figure is that of a ruler to whose sway all men have as a penalty been judicially consigned, and from whose custody the free favour of God in Christ releases them. 'All have sinned' (5[12]), whether with or without an explicit publication of law. St. Paul would not have allowed that through an involuntary taint of heredity men had at any time suffered without personal guilt. The Gentiles have the Law, being enlightened by conscience (2[14. 15]; cf. Mt 25[31-46]). Though the Law is not explicitly revealed, they are in effect transgressors. If in Ro 4[15] St. Paul declares that 'the law worketh wrath,' because 'where there is no law, neither is there transgression,' in Gal 3[19] he says rather that the Law was added (προσετέθη), came in between the promise and its fulfilment, because of transgressions; i.e. to bring home unmistakably to those who were already guilty the conviction of their offences.

So we are brought to the evidence of the doctrine of justification. Without pressing the forensic metaphor to a point inconsistent with St. Paul's thought, which would relegate the whole theology of guilt to a region of formal conceptions unchecked by experience, we are bound to remember that the Apostle is concerned with the probation of guilt assumed to exist, which is necessary before the sinner can throw himself upon the offer of free salvation secured to him through the gospel. Justification is not in itself a change of character, a transformation of life, but an alteration of status (Ro 5[1. 2], Eph 2[13]), a reversal of relations whereby the 'servants of sin' (Ro 6[17]), 'the children of wrath' (Eph 2[3]) become 'children of grace,' 'sons of God' (Gal 3[26]). It is the antithesis of trespasses (Ro 4[25]), no more to be confused with sanctification, which is its fruit (6[22]), than is transgression with uncleanness, which is its issue (1[24]). To be justified from sin is to have escaped—either by paying the penalty of death (6[7]) or by believing in Christ Jesus (3[24. 25])—from what in a figure is regarded as its claim or dominion over the life (6[12-14]), involving an obedience or yielding of the members. This is entirely in harmony with the conception of sin, from which St. Paul starts, as a voluntary withdrawal of allegiance admitting of no excuse.

We shall be saved from confusion with regard to the Pauline view of guilt, and the necessity of conforming the whole doctrine of sin to this primary idea, by considering what he means by 'adoption' and 'grace.' There is no clear instance in any Epistle of the use of the word χάρις in its later ecclesiastical sense of an infusion of spiritual strength (see Sanday-Headlam, *Romans*, note on 15 χάρις). In some passages, apart from other considerations, the term admits of this interpretation (e.g. Eph 4[7]). But the root idea is the free favour of God through Christ (Ro 4[4] 5[15]). It is not, therefore, an imparted gift, but an attitude of the Divine Mind. Again, the conception of sonship, as applied to the relation of the believer to God, while not excluding community of nature, gives prominence rather to the elective purpose of the Father (Eph 1[5]). It is not reached as a deduction from membership in Christ, as though the highest action of Divine grace were nothing more than the operation of a natural law. Modern theology, with its leading idea of solidarity, has tended to obscure the personal action of the Father in admitting mankind to fellowship. St. Paul's thought, on the other hand, is guided by the Hebraic conception of the son and heir, with its notion of privilege rather than primogeniture (Ex 4[22], Jer 31[9], Ps 89[27], Col 1[15], He 12[23]; cf. Job 18[13], Is 14[30]). Thus the Christian attains his rank in the family of God by 'adoption' (Gal 4[5], Eph 1[5]; cf. Gal 3[26], where sonship is presented as a privilege granted διὰ τῆς πίστεως). The Spirit which makes him a member of Christ is the 'Spirit of adoption' (Ro 8[15]), freely given by God to those whom He takes for His children (Gal 4[6], Ro 5[5] 8[9-11], 1 Co 12[13]). Membership in Christ is thus rather the result than the cause of the filial relation. The Christian life depends, not upon the eradication of evil, but upon the forgiveness of sins (Eph 1[7]), the clearing of the guilty on the part of a personal God in consequence of the personal satisfaction offered by Christ (Ro 3[21-28] 5[8], cf. Ex 34[6. 7]). This view of sonship, as involving God's elective purpose and man's free response, frequently underlies St. Paul's argument. Isaac is the child of promise (Gal 3[18] 4[23. 28], Ro 4[20] 9[8. 9]), Abraham the father of the faithful (Gal 3[7], Ro 4[12]). The redemption of the body is itself an 'adoption' (Ro 8[23]).

4. *The Epistle to the Hebrews* brings out the various elements in the conception of human guilt with conspicuous clearness. We have to do with the living God (He 3^{12} 4^{12} 10^{31}), who is a consuming fire (12^{29}), self-existent and separate from creation (12^{18-21}), the supreme lawgiver and judge (10^{30} 12^{23}), whom to see, therefore, demands a purifying separation on the part of His suppliant worshipper (9^{14} 10^{22}). What men need is boldness to approach His throne (4^{16} 10^{19}), and so to enter into His rest ($4^{1ff.}$). But there is an obstacle, typified by propitiatory rites and attested by universal experience (9^{6-10} $10^{3.11}$). The comers thereunto need a τελείωσις ($2^{10.11}$), the accomplishment of a preliminary act of satisfaction (2^{17} 5^9) which shall render them competent. The experience, which justifies the fulfilment of rites felt to be inadequate, is the fear of death (2^{15}), the spirit of bondage (*ib.*), the evil conscience (10^{22}). This is not the same thing as ignorance, error, or infirmity (5^2), all of which are recognized as present in human character and requiring to be dealt with. It is the consciousness that the offerer has a past which repentance cannot separate from him in respect of his relation to the Everliving ($10^{2.3.26.27}$), a record of offences for which none but One who Himself 'ever liveth' can atone by an abiding intercession (7^{25}, cf. 10^{12}). The conscience must be purged from dead works (9^{14} 10^{22}), which are to be distinguished from their present results in character. The 'redemption of transgressions' (9^{15}; cf. Ac 17^{30}, Ro $3^{24.25}$), the removal of a burden (2^{15} ἔνοχοι δουλείας, cf. Ja 2^{10}), is the method whereby consecration to God's service and boldness of access are secured. Even sanctification itself in Hebrews (12^{14}, cf. 2^{9-11} $10^{10.14}$ 13^{12}) is, not indeed the formal consecration of the sinner, but the removal of the 'weight' of guilt (12^1), of which the fulness of faith (10^{22}) is the counterpart in spiritual experience.

5. That *guilt is original*, *i.e.* attaches to all mankind, and may be predicated of each individual before particular evidence of transgression, is implied in the facts of redemption (see art. SIN), and explicitly taught in the NT. In the famous passage Ro 5^{12-21} nothing is said of a transmitted tendency to sin, though it has been often supposed that this is implied. But St. Paul does say that death 'passed unto all men' through Adam's transgression. The context shows that death is here regarded as a punishment inflicted by God. And guilt is implied in the remarkable sentence 'all have sinned,' which interprets the statement that 'through one man sin entered.' How St. Paul reached this apparent paradox seems clear from a consideration of Jewish theology. The OT bears abundant witness to the belief that the sins (plural) of the fathers are 'visited' upon the children (Ex 20^5 34^7), while at the same time the teaching of Ezekiel balances it by an emphatic vindication of the separate responsibility of each soul (Ezk $18^{4.20}$). Apart from the narrative of the Fall, which indicates a penalty involving the seed of the woman (Gn $3^{15.16}$), this is, perhaps, as far as the OT carries us. But the Book of Wisdom (2^{24}) represents death as entering the world through the envy of the devil, and Sirach (25^{24}) declares that sin originated from a woman, and 'because of her we all die.' The teaching of the Rabbis, however, differentiating the actual transgression of Adam from the potentiality of sin involved in his creation, expressly asserts that death was decreed against the generations of Adam. Elsewhere death is spoken of as incurred by the personal guilt of each

individual, and the statement of the Apocalypse of Baruch ($54^{15.19}$), that 'each of us is the Adam of his own soul,' looks like an attempt to express a mystery which alone can reconcile these divergent views. According to Weber (*Altsynag. Theol.* p. 216), the nett result of Talmudic teaching appears to be that 'by the Fall man came under a curse, is guilty of death, and his right relation to God is rendered difficult.' It is probably only in the sense of transmitted taint that Edersheim (*Life and Times*, etc. i. p. 165 ff.) disallows original sin as part of the doctrine of the older Rabbis; for, in common with other writers, he acknowledges the frequent assertion of inherited guilt. That St. Paul was familiar with this prevalent view hardly admits of doubt, or that he availed himself of it to interpret the relation of Jesus the Messiah to the whole human race, as giving the victory over sin, the wages of which is death (Ro 6^{23}), and the power of which is the outraged law (1 Co 15^{56}).

LITERATURE.—See art. SIN.   J. G. SIMPSON.

GULF (χάσμα, from χαίνω, *to yawn, gape, open wide*, Lk 16^{26} only. *Chasma* (shortened, *chasm*) is the exact transliteration of the Greek, but this word, in general use, is later than the AV. Tindale has 'a great space,' and the Geneva VS 'a great gulfe,' with 'swallowing pit' in the margin).—It is interesting to compare with this other representations of the division between the worlds of the unseen. In Plato's vision in the *Republic* there is an intermediate space where judges are seated, who divide to the right hand or to the left according as men are found just or unjust. Return to the upper world is possible; but when any incurable or unpunished sinners tried to ascend, 'the opening, instead of receiving them, gave forth a sound, and then wild men of fiery aspect, who were standing by and knew what the sound meant,' seized and carried them to be cast into hell (Jowett's *Plato*, iii. 512 f.). Virgil's vision is of 'a cavern, deep and huge, with its vast mouth, craggy, sheltered by its black lake and forest gloom, o'er which no birds might speed along unharmed; such an exhalation, pouring from its black jaws, rose to the vault of heaven; wherefore the Greeks named the spot Avernus.' The 'dreadful prison-house' is guarded by a 'gate of ponderous size, with pillars of solid adamant; so that no mortal might, nay, nor the dwellers in the sky, are strong enough to throw it down in war' (*Æneid*, vi. 236 f., 553 f.). Coming to Jewish representations, the Book of Enoch speaks of three separations between the spirits of the dead,—'by a chasm, by water, and by light above it' (ch. 22). In Rabbinical teaching (cf. Weber, *Jüd. Theol.*[2] 341) the separation between Paradise and Ge-hinnom is minimized; it is but 'a wall,' 'a palm-breadth,' a 'finger-breadth,' 'a thread.' With this representation the 'great gulf' of the parable is in striking contrast. It would be obviously wrong to interpret literally, or even to insist upon some spiritual counterpart of the detail of the parable, as it would be wrong to base upon the parable as a whole any doctrine of the future over and above its clear moral lesson and warning. But the solemn words of Jesus as to the possibility and danger of the fixity of character in evil must not be lightly set aside (see ETERNAL SIN).

LITERATURE. — Bruce, *Parabolic Teaching*, p. 393; Salmond, *Christian Doctrine of Immortality*, p. 277.

W. H. DYSON.

H

HADES.—See DEAD, ESCHATOLOGY, and HELL (DESCENT INTO).

HAIR.—The Jews seem to have shared with other peoples the belief that the hair is really 'a living and important part of the body' (W. R. Smith, RS^2 324; Frazer, *Golden Bough*[2], iii. 390). This lent importance to the oath by the head which was common among them (Mt 5^{36}), and it accounts for the attention given to the hair in connexion with vows (Ac 18^{18}; Jos. *BJ* II. xv. 1; on hair as offering and in vows see W. R. Smith, *l.c.* 323 ff.; Frazer, *l.c.* i. 370 ff.). In NT times long hair was regarded as a glory of women, but a disgrace to men (1 Co $11^{14. 15}$). Opinion had changed since the days of Absalom.

Among the Arabs the ancient sentiment survives. Many stalwart men, not merely 'immature lads' (RS^2 326), take pride in their long glossy locks. It is interesting also to note a change from the NT attitude to women's hair. The Jews in Poland permit no married woman to wear her own hair; it must be cropped close before the wedding, and replaced by a high head-dress of wool or silk. It is a terrible sin to neglect this rule (Hosmer, 'The Jews,' p. 363, in *Story of the Nations*).

It was customary to dress the hair with ointment (Mt 6^{17}), and women bestowed much care upon the *coiffure* (1 Ti 2^9, 1 P 3^3). It was a shame for a woman to appear with locks unbound and hair dishevelled.

Lightfoot (*Works*, ed. 1823, xii. 361) gives two Rabbinic quotations in point. 'Kamitha had seven sons who all performed the office of high priests; they asked of her how she came to this honour? She answered, "The rafters of my house never saw the hair of my head"' (*Vayyikra Rabba*, fol. 188. 2). 'The priest unloosed the hair' of the suspected woman, about to be tried by the bitter water, 'for greater disgrace' (*Soṭa*, fol. 5. 1).

When Mary (Jn 12^3) wiped the feet of Jesus with her hair, she thus 'testified that, as no sacrifice was too costly for her purse, so no service was too mean for her person' (Godet, *in loc.*).

Abundant hair on head and chin has always been regarded by Easterns as lending dignity to manhood, and the beard is an object of special reverence. 'I smooth my beard,' says Doughty, 'toward one to admonish him in his wrongful dealing with me, and have put him in mind of his honour. If I touch his beard, I put him in remembrance of our common humanity, and of the witness of God above us. The beard is taken in Arabia for human honour, and to pluck it is the highest indignity. Of an honest man they say, "His is a good beard"; of a vile, covetous heart, "He has no beard"' (*Arabia Deserta*, i. 268). What indignity then He suffered of whom the prophet wrote, 'I gave . . . my cheeks to them that plucked off the hair'! (Is 50^6).

Single hairs are taken to illustrate the minuteness of God's care (Mt 10^{30}, Lk 12^7 21^{18}). White hairs are a symbol of reverend and glorious majesty (Rev 1^{14}). The long hair, as of women, adds to the grotesque and terrible appearance of the locust monsters (Rev 9^8).

The Baptist's garment of camel's hair ($\theta\rho\iota\xi\ \kappa\alpha\mu\dot\eta\lambda\sigma\nu$, Mt 3^4) is probably identical with אַדֶּרֶת שֵׂעָר of Zec 13^4, and that of his great prototype (2 K 1^8, where we should read with RVm 'a man with a garment of hair'). The rough outer cloak generally worn is of goats' hair. *Wabar al-ibil*, the hair, or wool, ($\theta\rho\iota\xi$ can also mean 'wool,' *Il.* iii. 273, Hes. *Op.* 515) of the camel is softer, and of this an inner cloak is often worn, *e.g.* in winter by the fishermen on the Sea of Galilee.

Goats' hair is not named in NT, but most likely this was the material in which the Apostle Paul wrought at his trade (Ac 18^3), his native province supplying it in great quantities.

W. EWING.

HALL.—'Hall' appears in the AV in a way to cause not a little confusion, as tr. sometimes of $\alpha\dot\nu\lambda\dot\eta$ and sometimes of $\pi\rho\alpha\iota\tau\dot\omega\rho\iota\sigma\nu$. In Mt 27^{27} AV has 'the soldiers of the governor took Jesus into *the common hall*' (a circumlocution for $\pi\rho\alpha\iota\tau\dot\omega\rho\iota\sigma\nu$). In Mk 15^{16} AV has 'into *the hall called Prætorium*,' as tr. of $\dot\epsilon\sigma\omega\ \tau\hat\eta\varsigma\ \alpha\dot\nu\lambda\hat\eta\varsigma\ \ddot\sigma\ \dot\epsilon\sigma\tau\iota\nu\ \pi\rho\alpha\iota\tau\dot\omega\rho\iota\sigma\nu$. RV has not entirely relieved this confusion. The English Revisers render $\pi\rho\alpha\iota\tau\dot\omega\rho\iota\sigma\nu$ by 'palace,' following Rhem.; while the American Revisers, more literally, give *prætorium*, the Latin word which was carried over, transliterated, into the Greek, and which denoted originally the prætor's tent or abode, or the general's headquarters. Tindale introduced 'judgement-hall' for $\pi\rho\alpha\iota\tau\dot\omega\rho\iota\sigma\nu$, and is followed by AV in Jn $18^{28. 33}$ 19^9 etc. The AV renders $\alpha\dot\nu\lambda\dot\eta$ by 'palace' in Mt $26^{3. 58. 69}$, Mk $14^{54. 66}$, Lk 11^{21}, Jn 18^{15}, when the reference is to the place where the governor dispensed justice; by 'fold' in Jn $10^{1. 16}$ of the place where the sheep were kept at night; and by 'court' in Rev 11^2, as designating the court of the temple. RV more consistently renders $\alpha\dot\nu\lambda\dot\eta$ by 'court' instead of 'palace,' everywhere except in Jn 10^1 $\dot\eta\ \alpha\dot\nu\lambda\dot\eta\ \tau\hat\omega\nu\ \pi\rho\sigma\beta\dot\alpha\tau\omega\nu$, where it has 'the fold of the sheep' (cf. AV 'sheepfold'), and in v.[16], where it has simply 'fold.' Cf. Mt $26^{3. 58. 69}$, where the inner court of the high priest's official residence seems to be meant; in v.[69] 'Peter sat without in the palace' (AV); 'without' stands in contrast with the audience-room in which Jesus was appearing before the authorities, *i.e.* Peter was not in the room of the official residence where the trial was going on, but out in the open court, around which the house was built; and this was 'beneath,' or on a lower level than the audience-room. See also COURT, PRÆTORIUM.

GEO. B. EAGER.

HALLEL ('praise').—A technical Hebrew liturgical term, applied in Rabbinical literature to certain Psalms and psalm-pieces of praise, which characteristically have as their keynote the expression *Hallelujah* ('Praise ye Jah'). It is more particularly applied to one group of Psalms (113–118) regarded as a liturgical unit (so always in the Synagogue-liturgy).

Pss 113–118 form 'the Hallel' $\kappa\alpha\tau'\ \dot\epsilon\xi\sigma\chi\dot\eta\nu$, as distinguished from the 'Hallel of Egypt'* (Pss 113–114) and the 'great Hallel' (הלל הגדול) which is usually understood to mean Ps 136. In the Talmud and Midrash, however, the Psalms included in the 'great Hallel' are variously given, *viz.*: (1) Ps 136, (2) Pss 135[4]–136, and (3) Pss 120–136. The question is discussed in Jerus. *Pes.* v. 7. See further, Joel Müller, note to *Sopherim* xviii. 2 (p. 253). In one passage of the Mishna (*Pes.* x. 5) the Hallel (Pss 113–118) is designated 'Hallelujah.' For 'half-Hallel' see below.

1. *Origin.*—In its present form the Psalm-group (113–118) seems clearly to have been compiled for liturgical purposes at a comparatively late date. The most probable view is that the collection was formed in Maccabæan times for recitation on the Feast of *Ḥănukkā* (Dedication), on the eight days of which it is still chanted in the synagogue.

Ps 118^{24} ('This is the day which the Lord hath made; we will rejoice and be glad in it') points to some day of public

---
* הללא המצרי *Ber.* 56a. See J. Müller, *op. cit.* p. 288. In a *baraitha* (Bab. *Shabb.* 118b) Pss 145–148 are apparently called a 'Hallel.'

thanksgiving ; vv.4-24 suggest the Syrian war, and recovery of and entrance into the Temple. At the same time, the collection embodies other elements. Thus Ps 118²⁵⁻²⁹ seems to be an old song of praise for the Feast of Tabernacles. With this agrees the fact that, according to an old tradition preserved in the Jerusalem Talmud (Ṣukka iv. 5),* the Hallel was recited on 'eighteen days and one night of the year—the eight days of Tabernacles ; the eight of Ḥanukkā ; Pentecost (one day); and the first day of Passover with its (preceding) night.' It is noticeable that Tabernacles and Ḥanukkā are placed first in this list ; and it should be remembered that the latter feast seems originally to have been regarded as a sort of extension or reduplication of the former (cf. 2 Mac 1⁹) ; Cheyne (OP p. 33, note n) remarks : 'that the recitation of the Hallel on these occasions [Dedication and Tabernacles] goes back to Simon can hardly be doubted.' † A curious indication of its liturgical use may perhaps be seen in the fact that the Midrash on the Psalms counts only five psalms in the Hallel, Ps 115 not being regarded. The LXX and many Hebrew MSS treat the latter psalm as part of Ps 114. The reason assigned in one of the smaller Midrāshim is as follows : 'The Torā consists of five-fifths ; the Psalter of five-fifths ; and the Hallel of five-fifths.'

2. *Jewish liturgical usage.*—As already stated, the Hallel, according to tradition, was regularly recited at the Feasts of Tabernacles, Dedication, Pentecost, and Passover (first day and preceding night).‡

On certain other days of the year it became customary to recite the Hallel, viz. : on the last 6 days of Passover, and on new moons other than the new moon of Tishri (which introduces the solemn penitential period). But this usage was apparently late and unauthorized. This is shown (a) by the omission on these days of two sections of the complete Hallel, viz. : Ps 115¹⁻¹¹ and 116¹⁻¹¹ ; § and (b) that both Rashi and Maimonides protested against the use of the regular benediction before 'half-Hallel,' on the ground that its employment on these days was merely a pious custom without authority.

The recitation of the Hallel is preceded and followed by special blessings.‖ Certain parts are also recited with a responsive refrain :

(a) The first four verses of Ps 118 are said by the Reader, the people responding after each : 'O give thanks unto the Lord ; for He is good : for His mercy endureth for ever.' (b) The last nine verses of the same Psalm are also repeated, in part alternately, in part together, by Reader and congregation.

According to the Mishna (Pes. v. 7), which embodies old and (there is every reason to believe) trustworthy traditions as to the Temple-ritual, the complete Hallel was recited by the Levites during the slaughter of the Paschal lambs in the Temple-courts.¶ The use of Hallel in the Paschal meal at home, when the lamb was eaten, must be carefully distinguished from the above. Here the data are somewhat conflicting.

According to the Mishna (Pes. x. 6 and 7), the Hallel was here recited in two parts, and this is still the custom at the Jewish Paschal meal. The first part (Pss 113-114) immediately follows the Haggādā proper (the narrative of redemption) and precedes the drinking of the second cup of wine. It is appropriately closed by a special benediction for redemption. The second part (Pss 115-118, followed by 136 and the 'Blessing of Song') follows after the mixing of the fourth cup, when the banquet and grace after meat have been completed. And this arrangement is attested in the Mishna (ib.). The contents of the first part were, however, a subject in dispute between the schools of Shammai and Hillel, the former concluding it at Ps 113, the latter at Ps 114. The wording of the benediction for redemption was also not fully determined (ib.). It looks as though the recitation of the Hallel in the home-service were a reminiscence of the Temple-ritual, the family meal being partaken of between the two parts as a family sacrifice, just as the Passover lamb was sacrificed in the Temple during the singing of the Hallel. The custom, as the Mishna suggests, may quite well have arisen before the destruction of the Temple.

3. *Usage in the Gospels.*—It is usually assumed that the hymn referred to in Mt 26³⁰ ‖ Mk 14²⁶

---

* Cf. also Bab. Arakhin, 12a.

† Peritz (Encyc. Bibl. s.v. 'Hallel') connects the liturgical recitation of the Hallel with the Passover-meal (he denies that it was sung in the Temple-service), and thinks that it attained its present compass only 'during the first half of the second century.' But this is to ignore the data given above, which connect it primarily with Tabernacles and Ḥanukkā.

‡ With the doubling of the initial days of Festivals that takes place 'in exile,' the 18 days originally comprised in the above now amount to 21, and 1 night to 2.

§ Hence the designation 'half-Hallel' for this form.

‖ For these cf. Singer's Heb.-Eng. Prayer-Book, pp. 219, 224.

¶ For a graphic description of this see Edersheim, The Temple : its Ministry and Services, p. 191 f.

('when they had sung a hymn' [ὑμνήσαντες]) was the second part of the Hallel (Pss 115-118) * sung at the conclusion of the Paschal supper (see above). This is quite possible, in view of the probability that the custom had been established in connexion with the Paschal meal in the time of Christ.

In Delitzsch's Heb. NT the expression is well paraphrased : 'After they had completed the Hallel' (גמר את־ההלל). But there are some indications that the usage was subject to variation in the earlier period. Thus, according to one authority, for the 'completion' of the Hallel at the Paschal meal Ps 25 might suffice (Pes. 118a). The expression ὑμνήσαντες certainly suggests a Paschal meal. It is significant, however, that it is absent from the Lukan account.

LITERATURE.—Besides the works cited in the body of the article, the following are important : art. 'Hallel' in the Jewish Encyc., with the authorities there enumerated ; Delitzsch on Ps 113 ; Büchler, ZATW xx. [1900] 114-135 ; Buxtorf, Rabb. Lex. (ed. Fischer) s.v. הלל ; Hamburger, RE ii. 353 ff.

G. H. Box.

HALLOWED.—Used of the name of our Father —first petition in the Lord's Prayer (Mt 6⁹ ‖ Lk 11²), = 'revered' or 'counted holy.' It is, says Godet (Com. in loco), a prayer that 'unworthy conceptions of God and of His character may no longer prevail among men. The child of God beseeches Him to manifest with effect His holy character, in the conscience of men, so that all impure idolatry, gross or refined, as well as all formal Pharisaism, may be completely removed, and that every human being may unite with the seraphim in the anthem of adoration, "Holy, Holy, Holy."'

The verb ἁγιάζειν is in constant usage in LXX to render the different forms of Heb. קדשׁ (see Concord. s.v.). Isaiah (8¹³ 29²³) and Ezekiel (passim, e.g. 20⁴¹ 36²³) employ the word (rendered 'sanctify' AV and RV) of the Lord and His name, in exactly the same sense as the Lord's Prayer, of causing to be revered, whether by judgment or by deliverance. OT usage with reference to Sabbath, firstborn, etc., ought to be compared. Our Lord uses ἁγ. (1) of Himself (Jn 10³⁶ 17¹⁹) in the sense of consecration ('sanctify' AV and RV, cf. marg.) to the office of Messiah by His submitting to death ; and (2) of His disciples (Jn 17¹⁷·¹⁹) as consecrated by the truth. The root idea is setting apart for holy purposes, with the consequent development of a holy character. This ethical sense is derived from Lv 11⁴⁴ ἁγιασθήσεσθε καὶ ἅγιοι ἔσεσθε, ὅτι ἅγιός εἰμι ἐγώ (see Lightfoot on Ph 1¹). See, further, artt. CONSECRATE and SANCTIFY.

For usage of the English word see Hastings' DB (s.v.).   R. MACPHERSON.

HALTING.—A deficiency in gait, when one is not able to walk without limping. The word refers to the imperfection in the art of walking, rather than to the deficiency, injury, or weakness of the limb or limbs which is the cause. This differentiation is illustrated by a passage from Brand (1789) : 'He hath a halt in walking occasioned by a lameness in one of his legs' ; also Tennyson (Guinevere) : 'If a man were halt or hunch'd' ; Bunyan (Pilg. Prog. pt. ii.) : 'Mr. Ready to Halt,' cf. Ps 38¹⁷ ; Shaks., Timon, Ac. IV. Sc. i. : 'Thou cold sciatica, cripple our senators, that their limbes may halt as lamely as their manners' (an illustration also of the metaphorical use of the word 'halt' similar to that of 'lame') ; so Richard III., Ac. I. Sc. i.—

'Sent before my time
Into this breathing world, scarce half made up,
And that so lamely and unfashionable
That dogs bark at me as I halt by them.'

'Halt' is the tr. of χωλός in Mt 18⁸, Mk 9⁴⁵, Lk 14²¹, Jn 5³ ; but the translators of neither AV nor RV maintain a close distinction between the lame and the halt. The halting are included in the general healings wrought by Jesus among the multitude, and many of them would doubtless be of a character to yield readily to the method of our Lord, acting as He did on the line of existing therapeutic forces, even while going far beyond our present knowledge and experience of these forces.

T. H. WRIGHT.

* According to the school of Shammai, Pss 114-118.

HAND (יָד, כַּף 'palm or hollow of the hand'; χείρ; δεξιά 'right-hand,' ἀριστερά 'left-hand').—

OT usage.—In the OT there is a very large variety of meanings attaching to the word 'hand' and to expressions and phrases in which it occurs; a detailed consideration of these is not necessary here,* but a brief reference seems appropriate in view of the fact that NT usage is to some extent based, through the LXX, on that of the OT. In its origin the Hebrew word probably meant 'strength' (cf. Assyr. *idu*='strength'),† and it is used in this figurative sense in Jos 8²⁰ ('there was not in them strength [lit. *hands*] to flee'), Ps 76⁵ ('none of the mighty men have found their hands,' *i.e.* they are powerless). The word is used in a number of other figurative senses, see the *Oxford Heb. Lexicon* under יָד. Instructive is the passage Ex 14⁸ 'the children of Israel went out with a high hand' (cf. Ex 15⁶·¹², Nu 11²³ 33³); the reference is to the hand of Jehovah ('with a high hand'=with the *help* of the high hand, a meaning which the preposition בְּ frequently has); the 'hand,' strictly speaking, the 'right hand' (יָמִין), of God is the planet Venus;‡ this antique conception is much softened down, though a literal, anthropomorphic sense is still implied in the use of 'hand' in Ps 102²⁵ 'The heavens are the work of thy hands.'

In reference to man the word is used (just as is the case in the NT) in a variety of senses, according to the phrase in which it is found : 'to put one's life into one's hand' (Jg 12³), means to be ready to jeopardize one's life ; 'to clap the hands' is a sign of joy (2 K 11¹²) ; 'to fill the hand' (RV 'consecrate') is to instal in office (Jg 17⁵·¹²);§ 'to lift up the hand' (whether towards heaven or towards the altar is not always certain, see Nowack, *Heb. Arch.* ii. 260) was a symbolic action which accompanied an oath, it implied the calling of the Deity to witness‖ (Dt 32⁴⁰); the same action, with both hands, was the attitude adopted when blessing (Ps 134²); 'to open the hand' is to show generosity (Dt 15¹¹); to place the hands upon the head was a sign of grief (2 S 13¹⁹); to kiss the hand towards was a sign of homage (to a heathen deity in Job 31²⁷); 'to lay the hand upon the mouth' was done in token of humility (Pr 30³², cf. Is 52¹⁵); 'to strike hands' meant to go surety for someone (Pr 6¹). All these symbolic actions with the hand were common in the time of Christ, as they are at the present day also in Syria, Arabia, etc.

There is one other use of the word in the OT which demands a passing notice ; it means a sign or monument (1 S 15¹², 2 S 18¹⁸, cf. Gn 35¹⁴); according to Schwally,¶ it was originally so called because a hand was depicted upon the monument or pillar, this hand being a token of that wherewith the vow had been made (the uplifted hand), or perhaps wherewith an offering had been brought ; in view, however, of what has been said above, it is more likely that this hand was a representation of the hand of the Deity.

Usage in the Gospels.—In a very large number of cases in which 'hand' occurs, it is used in the ordinary literal sense ; there is no need to give references for these. Not infrequently there is the expression 'at hand' in the EV where in the original χείρ does not occur : *e.g.* 'the kingdom of heaven is at hand' (ἤγγικεν); such passages do not properly belong to this article, and are not taken into account.

1. All those things which are done by means of the hand, or in which the visible part is done by the hand (such as the working of miracles, or taking hold of a person or thing) are described as being performed διὰ χειρός, διὰ τῶν χειρῶν, διὰ χειρῶν τινος, Mk 6² etc.; ἐπὶ χειρῶν, Mt 4⁶, Lk 4¹¹; εἰς τὴν χεῖρα, Lk 15²². 'Hand' is used frequently as a synonym for 'power' (Mt 17²², Mk 9³¹, Lk 1⁷⁴ 9⁴⁴); in the slightly different sense of 'protecting power' (Lk 23⁴⁶); still in the sense of power but coupled with the idea of 'possession' (Jn 10²⁸·²⁹); as used in Lk 1⁶⁶ it contains the idea of God's 'furtherance'; then, again, it is used loosely,** in the sense of 'finger,' in Lk 15²² ('put a ring on his hand'); lastly, it is referred to (in a peculiarly Oriental manner) as though it had, metaphorically speaking, sense : 'if thine hand offend thee' (σκανδαλίσῃ),

---

* See art. 'Hand' in Hastings' *DB.*
† *Oxford Heb. Lexicon, s.v.*
‡ For the proof of this statement see Nielsen, *Die Altarabische Mondreligion und die Mosaische Ueberlieferung* (Strassburg, 1904), pp. 111, 154 ff., where illustrations of S. Arabian cylinder seals are also given, showing 'the hand of God' with the planet Venus above it ; the Divine hand has seven fingers.
§ On this idiom see *Encyc. Bibl.* ii. col. 1951.
‖ A later custom was to place the left hand on a tomb and quote Is 58¹¹.
¶ *Das Leben nach dem Tode*, p. 58, note. See also *CIS*, No. 199 ff.
** This is quite in accordance with OT usage, cf. *e.g.* Gn 24²² 'hands' used for 'wrists.'

---

and the same idea is conveyed in Mt 6³ 'let not thy left hand know what thy right hand doeth.'

2. But the most interesting use of 'hand' in the Gospels, as in the OT, is seen in idiomatic phrases in which it occurs ; these may be briefly enumerated as follows :—'To wash the hands' (ἀπονίπτειν τὰς χ.) was a symbolic action denoting a repudiation of responsibility or a declaration of innocence (Mt 27²⁴, cf. Ps 26⁶ 73¹³); the same phrase, very nearly, νίπτειν τὰς χ., refers to the washing before meals in obedience to tradition * (Mt 15²). To 'lay hands on' is used in several senses ; ἐπιβάλλειν τὰς χ. ἐπί τινα (or simply with the dat.) means to take hold of with violent intent (Mk 14⁴⁶); ἐπιτιθέναι τὰς χ. (or τὴν χ.) ἐπί τινα (or with dat.)† is synonymous with healing (Mt 9¹⁸, Mk 5²³); τιθέναι τὰς χ. ἐπί τινα is used of blessing children (Mk 10¹⁶); 'to put the hand to the plough' (ἐπιβάλλειν τὴν χ. ἐπ' ἄροτρον) is a metaphoric expression denoting the undertaking of some duty (Lk 9⁶²); different meanings attach to the phrase 'to stretch forth the hands' : ἐκτείνειν τὰς χ. ἐπί τινα is used of taking someone prisoner (Lk 22⁵³), or (with the same construction) to indicate a person (Mt 12⁴⁹); ἐκτ. τὴν χ. in Mt 14³¹ means to save from harm ; the same expression in Jn 21¹⁸ seems to be used in reference to the stretching out of the hands (in the sense of arms) on the cross. 'To lift up the hands' (ἐπαίρειν τὰς χ.) is the attitude of blessing (Lk 24⁵⁰); 'to take by the hand' (κρατεῖν τῆς χ.) means to take hold of someone with the purpose of helping (Mk 1³¹); 'to deliver up into the hands of' (παραδιδόναι εἰς χ. τινος) is to give into the power of, with evil intent (Mt 17²²), while διδόναι τι ἐν τῇ χ. τινος means to commit to the care of (Jn 3³⁵); 'to commend [the spirit] into the hands of' (παρατιθέναι τὸ πνεῦμα εἰς χ. τινος) is to place oneself under God's protection (Lk 23⁴⁶).

3. Lastly, there are many words in connexion with which 'hand' is not expressed, but implied ; all these convey one or other, or both, of the root conceptions of this word, viz. strength and activity.   W. O. E. OESTERLEY.

HANDMAID. — 'Handmaid' (Lk 1³⁸; 'handmaiden,' v.⁴⁸; in the American Standard RV 'handmaid' in both passages) answers to the Gr. δούλη, which means literally, as the RVm shows, 'slave.' In the LXX rendering of Hannah's vow (1 S 1¹¹), which is clearly echoed, almost cited, in Lk., δούλη represents the Hebrew *āmāh*, which, with the Aramaic equivalent *'amta* and the Bab. *amtu*, seems to have been a common Semitic designation of a female slave in Canaan and the neighbouring countries. It was sometimes used in courteous self-depreciation (1 K 1¹⁷, 1 S 25²⁴f·²⁸·³¹·⁴¹; the letter of an Assyrian lady in Johns' *Babylonian and Assyrian Laws, Contracts, and Letters,* p. 378), and then was naturally applied to relation to God (the above-mentioned vow, also Ps 86¹⁶ 116¹⁶). In the Aram. text, which probably underlay the Song of the Virgin, 'handmaiden' would be *'amta* with suffix (*Pal. Lect. of Gospels*, 1899, p. 234). The use of the word in the Gospels illustrates the Oriental habit of describing man as the slave of God, of which there are so many examples in the OT (Ps 19¹¹·¹³, Neh 1⁶·¹¹ etc.), in the so-called Babylonian Penitential Psalms, in ancient Semitic names— *Obadiah* found both in the Bible and on an ancient seal, *Abdeel* (Jer 36²⁶), *Abdiel* (1 Ch 5¹⁵), *Abednego* (Dn 1⁷), *Abd Ninip* (*Tell el-Amarna Letters*, No. 53, Winckler), '*Abd Ashtoreth* (*KAT*[*ZW*] 129); and in names current in the Holy Land at the present

---

* It is probable that the origin, of which this custom was a remnant, is to be sought in a ceremonial purifying before partaking of the sacrificial meal, at which the Deity was conceived of as being present ; cf. W. R. Smith, *RS* ² p. 229.
† The same phrase with the same construction='to ordain' in Ac 6⁶ 8¹⁷.

time, such as *Abdallah* (for many examples from southern and central Palestine cf. *PEFSt*, 1904, p. 155, and 1905, p. 48 f.). These illustrations, however, refer mainly if not entirely to men. In connexion with a list of personal names collected from various Moslem villages in the south of Palestine (*PEFSt*, 1904, p. 155), it is remarked that female names of the type of *Abdallah* have not been found. Still it must always have been easy for an Oriental woman to call herself 'the handmaid' of Deity. The transition from the courteous to the religious use would be readily effected.

W. TAYLOR SMITH.

HAPPINESS.—i. PAGAN AND CHRISTIAN IDEALS COMPARED. — Happiness was much discussed among the Greeks under the term 'well-being' (εὐδαιμονία). Aristotle said : 'For on the subject of happiness and what conduces to it, and of its opposites, exhortation or discussion is always conversant, and this because we needs do the things which procure it or any of its constituents, and refrain from doing the things which destroy or impede it' (*Rhet.* i. 5). The differences of the philosophic schools arose from the question wherein this well-being consisted. Was it in knowledge, pleasure, virtue, freedom from pain, wealth, or well-doing? The record of the answers to this forms the history of ancient Ethics. Jesus did not use the word 'happiness' (εὐδαιμονία), or propound any theory of the relation between duty and pleasure ; but absence of the word is no proof that the subject was foreign to His mind. It is inconceivable that the 'Son of Man' should neglect in His system so universal an instinct as the desire after happiness ; for in the final summation joy must be a part of the perfect state. The comparison between ancient and Christian Ethics must not be made on verbal or literary lines, but the systems must be judged by their actual contribution to well-being or happiness.

(1) *The failure of Paganism.* The systems of Plato and Aristotle did not bring any large satisfaction with them, nor did they discover any permanent refuge for the race. Of all the products of Greek speculation, Stoicism survived longest, and had the largest influence upon the civilization of the world ; but while, by its stern grandeur, it shaped a few noble characters which remained as a protest against the lax manners of the Empire, it failed to open up any fountain of joy for man. The Stoic sage was powerless to convert his theories into conduct, as he himself confessed ; and the *passionlessness* of soul which he advocated was a poor match for the strong impulses of the human heart. Where reliance upon human reason was undermined, it was met with an impotent religiousness ; and where reverence for the natural order was impaired, there was no message of a future life in which compensations would atone for present inequalities. Also the examples of the earlier leaders created a preference for suicide, which was a confession of failure to procure the well-being of life. Paganism withdrew from the struggle to provide happiness. It despaired, and was therefore defeated.

(2) *The success of Christianity.* The characteristic word of Christianity is *Life* ; for while the moral code and example of Christ are superior to others, it is not on this that His supremacy rests. Christ's *Person* is the vital force of the new religion. 'As the Father hath life in himself, so hath he given to the Son to have life in himself' (Jn 5²⁶). This same blessing is bestowed upon all who believe in Christ ; and so rich is this gift, that each believer becomes a constant source of life (Jn 6⁵⁷ 7³⁸). Life is imparted to the believer in many ways, but chiefly through Christ's words (6⁶³· ⁶⁸ 15³). This life is the realization of all human aspiration,

enabling the Christian to hold on with courage and hope in the face of temptation and doubts ; and the history of our civilization is the evidence that Jesus has succeeded where all others failed. To an age that was exhausted and desponding, that had failed to satisfy the deep desires of human nature, Christ came with convincing and converting power. When He spoke, men believed and lived again. Through Him rose

'One common wave of thought and joy,
    Lifting mankind again.'

Stoicism and Neo-Platonism produced thoughts of great beauty and purity. 'Yet neither of them could enable artisans and old women to lead a truly philosophic life. Christianity could and did ; the apologists point triumphantly to the realization of the moral ideal among Christians of every standing. That was due to the power which issued from Jesus Christ and actually transformed man. The certainty and confidence of faith based on Him, with reliance on God's grace in Jesus Christ, begat in Christians a matchless delight in doing good' (von Dobschütz, *Christian Life in the Primitive Church*, p. 329).

ii. THE TEACHING OF JESUS.—The NT verbal equivalent for 'happiness' is 'blessedness' (which see), but it is not conceived in terms of pleasure. It is a religious idea, drawing its worth from the blessing which God imparts. The adjective 'blessed' occurs frequently in Mt 5³⁻¹². This representative discourse may be entitled 'Christ's way to happiness.' Here Jesus describes how people become happy, but refrains from all abstract definition. Each of these Beatitudes falls into two parts. In the first half those virtues are mentioned the possession of which constitutes people happy ; in the second part the reward or result of each virtue is given. The following statements may be made as to Christ's teaching on this *way* : (1) The joy begins immediately on the commencement of the journey, and is not reserved for the future. Thus, all who are pure in heart *are* happy. (2) More depends upon the traveller than upon the outward conditions. Happiness rests in dispositions, such as purity, meekness, righteousness, peace, and not in possessions, such as wealth, health, fame. The happy man makes his own scenery. Christian joy, like other Christian graces, is inward ; and the OT conception of blessedness, in so far as it consisted in prosperity and length of days, yields to a more spiritual ideal. All who go Christ's way are like the *Happy Warrior*,

'Whose high endeavours are an inward light
    That makes the path before him ever bright.'
                            (Wordsworth).

(3) This happiness is not a passivity, but an activity, coinciding with some function of the will or mind. It cannot rise of itself as a mere state of emotion, but accompanies an act of service either for God or man. Happiness is associated with piety (Mt 5³⁻⁶) and probity (vv.⁷⁻¹¹). It follows upon doing the will of God, or upon seeking the well-being of others. Socrates also regarded happiness as εὐπραξία, well-doing. (4) This way, unlike the world's way, is endless, for the joy that begins on earth is an anticipation of the full joy of heaven (vv.³ᵇ ¹⁰ᵇ). (5) The pursuit of this way is a duty. All who walk with Christ not only will but ought to rejoice. Happiness is an imperative, 'Rejoice and be exceeding glad' (v.¹²). The ethical ideal of Jesus differs from Hedonism, in which morality and happiness are synonymous terms, because with Him blessedness is the associate of virtue. Christ neither confuses nor separates these two. Happiness and virtue are twin stars. The further use of the Beatitude in Christ's teaching continues to emphasize the spiritual ingredients of happiness. In Lk 11²⁸, Jn 13¹⁷, blessedness and

obedience are associated; in Mt 16[17] blessedness and *knowledge* are united; in Jn 20[29] blessedness and *faith* are joined. In many places blessedness is reserved for the future (Lk 7[23] 12[37-43] 14[15]). In the Fourth Gospel Jesus distinctly offers fulness of joy (Jn 16[24]).

iii. HAPPINESS AS REVEALED IN CHRIST'S PERSON.—The birth of Jesus was a proclamation of joy (Lk 2[10]). Though called the 'Man of sorrows,' He was not unhappy. Sorrows never distorted His soul, nor left the faintest shadow of melancholy or accidie. He was 'still cheerful and helpful and firm.' His first miracle contributed to the innocent pleasure of social intercourse (Jn 2[1-11]). The impression left by His address was pleasing; nor was His voice the voice of grief (Lk 4[22]). His gospel was a joyous prize (Mt 13[44. 45]). He delighted in healing pain (Lk 4[18]). Instead of reflecting the sadness of households, Jesus removed it (Jn 11[23], Lk 8[52]). He spoke of a joy that was His own peculiar and characteristic possession (Jn 15[11]), and promised entrance into His own joy as a supreme reward (Mt 25[21]). This joy He offered all who followed Him (Jn 16[24]), and He was anxious to complete the joy of His disciples (Jn 15[11] 17[13]). Christ shunned the moroseness of asceticism (Mt 11[19]), as He turned from the selfish happiness of the epicurean (Mt 20[28]). The joy of Christ arose from several causes—(1) He was free from sin, that root of sorrow and bitterness: 'For by sinning we kept neither piety nor felicity' (Augustine). (2) He had the intense joys of a Saviour (Lk 15[7]). His was the happiness that comes from being the creator of another's good (Lk 19[10]). The keen pleasure of rescue work filled His soul (Lk 15[5. 9. 23]). The thought of the countless hosts who would obtain eternal rest through His death was a secret potion to sweeten His bitter cup. For the joy set before Him He endured the cross. (3) The self-sacrifice of Jesus issued out of pure love (Jn 15[13]). Jesus was happy as a lover. (4) He rejoiced in the sense of Divine sonship. This was His earliest thought (Lk 2[49]). To do the will of God was better than food (Jn 4[34]). The knowledge of His Father was life (Jn 17[3]). It was an incomparable ecstasy for Him to dwell upon the love of God (Jn 17). This relieved Him of fear (Lk 23[46], Mt 6[34]); also it freed Him from the distracting care of false ambition (Jn 18[36]). Being thus free from many of the vexing thoughts and struggles that disturb our peace of mind, He was able to find comfort in Himself and His cause. He was the first citizen in the Kingdom of Heaven, which is righteousness and peace and joy in the Holy Ghost. Though tempted in all points like as we are, and acquainted with grief, Christ was nevertheless a man of joy.

Christ gives happiness by giving Himself. 'He that hath the Son hath life,' and the causes which led to His peace act in measure in all those who turn to Jesus. The first and last Beatitude of the Gospels is to those who believe in Him (Lk 1[45], Jn 20[29]). All life culminates in God, and man's *summum bonum* is God as He is revealed in Christ. Partnership with Him, even when joined with personal suffering and sacrifice, is more valuable than all worldly prosperity (Mt 10[39]). Plato had climbed to a lofty place when he declared that man's happiness was to be found in a supernatural good, in the knowledge of ideas, especially the idea of God. But Christianity rises higher. Jesus leads us up from imitation of God and acquaintance with Divine ideas to the sublime fact that we may know God personally. Not a resemblance, but a partnership; not a certainty that God is good, true, and wise, but a certainty that He loves us, and that we may love Him in return—this is the new faith (Jn 15[9]). Jesus is the Christian's joy. Into our restlessness of soul, due in

part to imperfect ideas, Christ comes with a fellowship and an ambition grand enough to supply man with the peace after which he is ever struggling (Mt 11[28]). Through Christ our sins are forgiven, our anxieties removed, our sorrows softened, our hopes revived, while He alone imparts that supreme gift of fellowship with God which is our highest good. Thus purest happiness comes, which some will still prefer to call blessedness, as more appropriate to such intimate and spiritual relationships.

LITERATURE.—Hastings' *DB*, artt. 'Beatitude,' 'Happiness,' 'Sermon on the Mount'; Hort, *The Way, The Truth, The Life* (Macmillan, 1894); Hilty, *Glück* (J. C. Hinrichs, Leipzig); *PRE*[3], art. 'Glückseligkeit'; Coleridge, *Aids to Reflection* : 'Prudential Aphorisms'; Shairp, *Studies*, 362; Seeley, *Ecce Homo* [15], 114, 195; Carlyle, *Sartor*, 112, 132, *Heroes*, 64.

JAMES W. FALCONER.

HARDENING OF HEART.—(*a*) The relation in Scripture between the blood and the life (Lv 17[11]) is such that the heart is naturally 'the typical centre of personal life' (cf. Westcott on He 4[12] and 1 Jn 1[7] Add. Notes); the seat of understanding (1 K 3[9. 12]), affection (Dt 6[5]), will (Jer 5[23]), character (1 K 9[4], Ezk 11[21]); the fountain at which all issues (Pr 4[23]) may receive a Divine direction. (*b*) It is described as tender (2 K 22[18f.]), hard (Ex 8[19]), of flesh or of stone (Ezk 11[19ff.]), not in the popular sense of merciful or cruel, but according to its receptivity (or otherwise) of Divine impressions. Of the Greek words employed to express such hardness the two more remarkable (see below) represent the heart as callous (*i.e.* ossified) or fat. (*c*) An important distinction is to be made between two expressions:—(i.) **'Hardness of heart.'** To a certain extent this is an unavoidable infirmity of man's natural condition. As such, it is the object of Divine condescension, which (as Christ directly asserts) is the explanation of much OT legislation (Mt 19[8] ‖). It is referred to in the Gospels as (1) σκληροκαρδία, Mt 19[8] ‖ Mk 10[5] [16[14]]; as (2) καρδ. πεπωρωμένη, Mk 6[52] 8[17]. (ii.) **'Hardening of heart.'** This is a voluntary process: the object therefore of Divine condemnation (cf. Mt 11[20ff.] 13[15] 23[37ff.], Ro 2[5]). Its active nature, as distinguished from passive infirmity, is indicated by the form πώρωσις, Mk 3[5] (cf. Ro 11[25], Eph 4[18]), in contrast to the pf. pt. pass. Mk 6[52] 8[17]. (*d*) Hardening is represented, alternatively with conversion, as a direct consequence of contact with grace and the gospel (Mt 13[15], Jn 3[19f.] 9[39]; cf. 2 Co 2[16]). The origin of the process is variously stated, according to the side from which it is viewed. Thus—(1) The heart *is hardened*, as though by the action of a mechanical law: Mt 13[15] = Is 6[10] LXX (cf. Ac 19[9], Ro 11[7. 25], 2 Co 3[14]). (2) Man *hardens his heart*. This aspect, though necessarily involved in man's responsibility and often stated in the OT (Ex 9[34], 1 S 6[6], 2 Ch 36[13]), is not expressly referred to in the NT, except in He 3[8] = Ps 95[8]. (3) *God hardens it*: Jn 12[40] = a paraphrase of Is 6[10]; see Westcott, *ad loc.*, and cf. Ro 9[18]. This is often known as 'judicial hardening': it is 'the inexorable law of moral consequence' (Westcott on He 3[8]). It comes to pass that 'he who *will not* turn at last *cannot*. And God, who established that law of man's nature, is said in Scripture to *do* that which occurs under it or results from it' (Vaughan on Ro 9[18]). (*e*) In the OT the typical case is that of Pharaoh; in which all three statements are remarkably exemplified (Ex 7[14] 8[15] 9[12]). Bunyan's 'Man in the iron cage' is a powerful picture of hardening in its final stage: at the same time, the man who is past repentance is usually past feeling (Eph 4[18f.]).

F. S. RANKEN.

HARLOT.—This is the term usually employed in AV as tr. of πόρνη, the only other tr. being 'whore.'

The practice of prostitution dates from the earliest times. While in Egypt, the Israelites must have been familiar with the fact that prostitution prevailed in connexion with Egyptian cults. No sooner were they settled in Canaan than the purity both of their morality and their religion was endangered by the contaminating influence of Semitic rites, in which the consecrated harlot (*ḳĕdēshāh*) played no small part. From glimpses of social life afforded us by the prophets (*e.g.* Jer 5⁷, Hos 4¹⁴), we can perceive the prevalence of ordinary prostitution in their day. One of the blessings of the Exile was the extinction among the Jews both of idolatry and of religious prostitution. The Apocrypha, however, witnesses to the continuance of the common harlot. She haunts the streets (Sir 9⁷), and employs singing as one of her seductive arts (9⁴). In the time of the Maccabees the Gentiles in Palestine 'dallied with harlots,' and had to do 'with women within the circuit of the holy places (2 Mac 6⁴). Cf. also Pr 7¹⁰.

The Gospels supply us with little information as to the extent of prostitution in Palestine during the time of Christ. In Mt 21³² our Lord refers to harlots as a class. The woman of Lk 7, 'who was a sinner in the city' (v.³⁷ *v.l.*), probably belonged to the class. In the parable of the Prodigal Son, the far country in which he devoured his living with harlots (Lk 15³⁰) might be supposed to be possibly within Palestine. Again, our Lord's reference to the sin of fornication (Mt 19⁹) suggests the existence of immoral women. The popular idea of Mary Magdalene as a woman of evil life is rejected by many of the best exegetes.

In Christ's day, Palestine was in many ways demoralized by Greek and Roman influences. Wherever the Greeks and Romans went, the ἑταίρα and the *meretrix* abounded. Religious prostitution reappeared in connexion with the Mysteries of Aphrodite, which culminated in vicious orgies, and these rites were not confined to Greece. Pagan gods and goddesses 'had their due secret solemnities whithersoever Greek (and partly Roman) colonists took their Lares and Penates' (Baring-Gould in Chambers' *Encyc.* vii. 369). Nor would the immorality of women employed in shameless rites be confined to religious ceremonies, any more than is the case to-day amongst similar women attached to Indian temples. In cities upon the coast of Asia Minor immoral cults prevailed in NT times.

To the Christian mind the matter of chief interest is the attitude of Jesus towards this class of sinners, and the significance of His gospel in respect of them. Here we cannot fail to contrast the harsh temper of the Pharisees towards such women with the holy and redemptive sympathy of Jesus. Even the austere John the Baptist had evidently welcomed them as penitents and as candidates for baptism (Mt 21³²),—a fact of which Jesus reminded His Pharisaic hearers. Our Lord plainly indicated that sins of fleshly frailty are less heinous and less likely to prove fatal than lovelessness, spiritual pride, and hypocrisy; for 'the publicans and the harlots go into the kingdom of God before you' (Mt 21³¹). His compassionate tenderness in this connexion appears very beautifully in St. Luke's story of the sinful woman, whose newness of heart was intensified by the love and gratitude consequent upon the pity and pardon experienced at the Saviour's hands. It may be added in respect of guilt of this description, that the peace of conscience begotten of faith in the Redeemer's atoning blood is oftentimes as deep as the sense of guilt was poignant. Nor should it be forgotten that the general effect of the way in which the Master admitted women to His intimate fellowship is to raise the status of woman in such a manner as to render her degradation through prostitution unthinkable.   ROBERT M. ADAMSON.

HARVEST.—See AGRICULTURE.

HATING, HATRED.—Although the noun does not occur in the Gospels, yet the verb (μισεῖν) is often found. The passages may be grouped as follows: (1) those which speak of the world's

hatred to Christ and His people; (2) those dealing with the Old Law, and Christ's hatred of sin; (3) those which prescribe hate; (4) some remaining passages.

1. The world being opposed, according to St. John's use of the term, to 'all that is of the Father' (1 Jn 2¹⁶), it was inevitable that the holy and sinless Jesus should arouse its antipathy; and this is specially noted in the Fourth Gospel. The world hated Him because He testified that its deeds were evil (Jn 7⁷). Its instinctive opposition to the light as manifested in Him was immediately aroused (3²⁰). Thus He said 'the world hath hated me' (μεμίσηκεν, 15¹⁸), the perfect tense expressing 'a persistent abiding feeling, not any isolated manifestation of feeling' (Westcott); and it was 'without a cause' (δωρεάν, 15²⁵), cf. Ps 35¹⁹ 69⁴; no reason could be found for such hostility except that He condemned its wickedness. This hatred carried with it hatred of the Father also (Jn 15²³), in which character He had revealed God to men, cf. 15²⁴ 'they have both seen and hated both me and my Father'; therefore they had no excuse for their sin, perhaps here the special sin of hatred to Him and His (Alford). Cf. in the parable of the Pounds, 'his citizens hated him' (Lk 19¹⁴).

Christ's disciples consequently may expect to experience the same hatred in proportion as they truly follow their Lord (Jn 15¹⁸⁻²⁰). 'When they came before the world, it showed at once and decisively its position of antagonism to the gospel' (ἐμίσησε, 'hated,' RV 17¹⁴) (Westcott), the ultimate cause being that men had no true knowledge of Him who sent Jesus (15²¹). He foretold that they should be 'hated of all men' for His Name's sake (Mt 10²² ‖), more precisely 'of all nations' (24⁹); cf. for its fulfilment Ac 12³ 28²², 1 Th 2¹⁴. ¹⁵, 1 P 2¹²; Tacitus, *Ann.* xv. 44, 'quos per flagitia invisos vulgus Christianos appellabat'; Suetonius, *Nero*, xvi., 'Christiani, genus hominum superstitionis novæ et maleficæ.' In so far as the world-spirit crept in among the disciples, there would be similar exhibitions of hatred among themselves (Mt 24¹⁰); cf. Gal 5¹⁵, 1 Jn 3¹⁵, the deadly hatred of the Judaizers towards St. Paul, and the name ὁ ἐχθρὸς ἄνθρωπος apparently given to him in the Pseudo-Clementines. The world's hatred, however, should be a cause of rejoicing (Lk 6²²), and not of wonder (1 Jn 3¹³, where 'if,' as in Jn 15¹⁸, implies no doubt of the fact). The disciples might well suspect their loyalty if they escaped the enmity of those who hated their Lord (Jn 7⁷), while their experience of it was a proof that they had been chosen out and united to Him (15¹⁹. ²⁰), as also a pledge of their future glory (Ro 8¹⁷, 2 Ti 2¹², 1 P 4¹³); 'Christianos quoque aut summo amore prosequuntur homines aut summo odio. Qui omnibus semper placent, sibi merito suspecti esse debent' (Bengel).

Groups (2) and (3) raise an apparent difficulty: the feeling which is forbidden in the one seems commanded in the other. Westcott has a valuable note on 1 Jn 2⁹ which suggests the solution: 'there is a certain ambiguity in the word "hate," for it serves as the opposite both to the love of natural affection (φιλεῖν) and to the love of moral judgment (ἀγαπᾷν). In the former case hatred, which may become a moral duty, involves the subjection of an instinct; in the latter case hatred expresses a general determination of character.' Thus μισεῖν as opposed to ἀγαπᾷν is condemned (Mt 5⁴³ᶠ, Eph 5²⁸. ²⁹, 1 Jn 2⁹. ¹⁰ 3¹⁴. ¹⁵ 4²⁰), while as opposed to φιλεῖν it may become a duty (Lk 14²⁶, Mt 10³⁷, Jn 12²⁵).

2. 'Ye have heard that it was said, Thou shalt love thy neighbour and hate thine enemy: but I say unto you, Love your enemies' (Mt 5⁴³); 'do good to them that hate you' (Lk 6²⁷, omitted by best authorities in Mt.). The first part of the maxim is found in Lv 19[18] ; but in the latter clause Jesus 'is not quoting precisely any OT or extra-Biblical utterance on record (cf. Sir 18[13])' (Hastings' *DB*, Extra Vol. p. 30). The question then arises—Is it a fair deduction from, and does it represent the spirit of, the OT, or is it an unwarranted extension and addition of the scribes ? In favour of the latter it is urged that this hatred is not conceived of as following in Lv 19[18], and that passages much nearer the Christian standard are found. The utmost consideration was to be shown even to an enemy's beast (Ex 23[4]) ; the fact that the owner cherished hate was no reason why help should be refused to him in his trouble (23[5]). Cf. as to rejoicing over an enemy in calamity, Job 31[29] ; as to returning evil for evil, Pr 24[29] ; and as to the better spirit often shown in OT, Gn 45[1f.], 1 S 24[7], 2 K 6[22], Ps 7[4] 35[13]. Jewish sages ordained that 'if a man finds both a friend and an enemy in distress, he shall first assist his enemy,' in order to subdue his evil inclination ; and held that it is not permitted to 'hate any one except only sinners who, having been duly warned and admonished, do not repent' (Kalisch on Leviticus, quoted in Alexander, *The Witness of the Psalms to Christ and Christianity*, p. 274). Pr 24[17] 25[21. 22] are sometimes quoted as approaching the Christian spirit, but the reason given in each case militates considerably against their force ('lest the LORD see it and it displease him, and he turn away his wrath from him,' 'and the LORD shall reward thee'). Hence some suppose that 'hate thine enemy' was an illegitimate inference ('pessima glossa,' Bengel) drawn by Rabbis from the precepts laid down concerning the Amalekites and other nations under the curse (Ex 23[23f.], Dt 7[1f.] 23[6] 25[17f.]) ; by giving to 'neighbour' the sense of 'friend,' and taking 'enemy' as meaning a 'private enemy,' they were easily turned into a justification of private hatred. On the other hand, it is held by many that this clause was really implied in Lv 19[18] and truly expressed the spirit of OT. The election of Israel, taken with the rules concerning the above nations, would foster an aversion to foreigners which was ever increasing in intensity ; cf. Ps 83, Jon 3[10]–4[11], Est. In time the Jews came to have such a profound contempt and disregard for all others as caused them to be charged with being enemies of the human race ('apud ipsos fides obstinata, misericordia in promptu, sed adversus omnes alios hostile odium,' Tac. *Hist.* v. 5. 2 ; 'non monstrare vias eadem nisi sacra colenti,' Juv. *Sat.* xiv. 103). Therefore Bp. Gore holds (*Sermon on Mount*, p. 97) that we must accept Mozley's conclusions, which are as follows,— The whole precept, as it stands, undoubtedly represents, and is a summary of, the sense of the Law ; nor is there any occasion to refer 'it hath been said' to the Law in the case of 'Love thy neighbour,' and to the tradition of the scribes in the case of 'Hate thine enemy' : all the other precepts which the Lord takes as instances of an inferior morality are precepts out of the Law, and there is no reason to distinguish this particular one from the rest with respect to its source. In the first place, it applied to 'neighbour' and 'enemy' in a national sense, and tended to strengthen the union of Israelites ; it was the inculcation of an *esprit de corps* which was the very bond of, and incentive to, union in the early ages. But it also referred to a private enemy, and was conceived in the general spirit of retaliation (cf. Mt 5[38] and such Psalms as 109).

It is evident from Mt 5[44] that Jesus took 'enemy' as meaning a 'private enemy,' who in the new Kingdom is to be loved, and to whom good is to be done. He used ἀγαπᾶν, not φιλεῖν, on which

Tittmann (see Alford) says, ' φιλεῖν, amare, pessimum quemque vir honestus non potest ; sed poterit eum tamen ἀγαπᾶν, i.e. bene ei cupere et facere quippe homo homini, cui etiam Deus benefaciat. Amor imperari non potest, sed dilectio.' Cf. Clem. Alex. τὸ ἀγαπᾶν τοὺς ἐχθροὺς οὐκ ἀγαπᾶν τὸ κακὸν λέγει, and Aug. 'sic dilige inimicos ut fratres optes, sic dilige inimicos ut in societatem tuam vocentur, sic enim dilexit ille qui in cruce pendens ait, Pater ignosce illis, quia nesciunt quid faciunt.' According to the teaching of Christ, therefore, the hatred of sin only is permissible, which is the necessary corollary of the Gospel of Love, and is according to His own example ; cf. He 1[9], Rev 2[6], where Lyra remarks (see Alford), 'non dixit Nicolaitas, sed facta : quia personæ sunt ex charitate diligendæ, sed eorum vitia odio sunt habenda.'

3. Lk 14[25. 26], Jesus turned and said unto the multitude, 'If any man cometh unto me, and hateth not his own father, and mother, and wife (peculiar to Luke), and children, and brethren, and sisters, yea, and his own life also, he cannot be my disciple'; cf. Mt 10[37] 'He that loveth father or mother more than me is not worthy of me' ; and Jn 12[25] 'He that loveth his life loseth it, and he that hateth his life in this world shall keep it unto life eternal.' We may at once dismiss such an interpretation as Renan put forward, viz. that Christ was here 'despising the healthy limits of man's nature,' 'warring against the most legitimate cravings of the heart,' and 'preaching a total rupture with the ties of blood.' The whole tenor of His life and teaching is against such an idea. He forbade hatred even of an enemy (Lk 6[27]) ; He condemned evasion of the Fifth Commandment (Mk 7[9-12]), and taught the sanctity of the marriage bond (Mk 10[2-9]) ; He showed tender thought for His mother (Jn 19[25f.]), and loved children (Mk 10[13f.]) ; His new commandment was 'that ye love one another, as I have loved you' (Jn 13[34]). St. John certainly did not understand Lk 14[26] in Renan's sense (1 Jn 2[9. 11] 3[15. 17] 4[16. 20]) ; nor St. Paul (Eph 5[28], 1 Ti 5[8], Tit 2[4], Ro 13[8]), who would regard those acting in such a way as ἄστοργοι 'without natural affection,' a vice of the heathen (Ro 1[31]).

Some have given to 'hate' in these passages the meaning of 'love less,' comparing Gn 29[30. 31], Dt 21[15] ; but it follows from the above that Jesus cannot have intended to condemn *any* degree of right affection as if it amounted to loving others more than Him. 'The love which Christ condemneth differs not in degree, but in kind, from rightful affection. It is one which takes the place of love to Christ, not which is placed by the side of that of Christ. For, rightly viewed, the two occupy different provinces. Wherever and whenever the two affections come into comparison, they also come into collision' (Edersheim, *Life and Times*, i. 650). There is a foolish affection which would do injury both to the giver and the receiver (cf. Pr 13[24]), and then hate is not only consistent with, but absolutely necessary for, the highest kind of love. It is 'that element in love which makes a wise and Christian friend not for time only, but for eternity.'

The words had special application to the time when they were spoken, and must have sounded strange to the multitude, which, for the most part, was following because of that very love of life which is condemned, desiring to get material benefits (cf. Jn 6[26]). Jesus' enemies were becoming more violent, divisions in families would take place (Mt 10[34-36] ; cf. Ex 32[26f.], Dt 33[9]), and discipleship would in many cases be impossible without the renunciation of the dearest ties. The mission field affords a parallel nowadays, where the hostility of relatives is often the greatest hindrance to the confession of Christ. The statement is made in the most startling form to arrest attention ; conditions must be supplied as in Mt 5²⁹ᶠ. Even where renunciation is not outwardly necessary, there must be potential alienation and the acknowledgment of Christ's claims as paramount. The key to the true explanation lies in 'yea and his own life also' (cf. Jn 12²⁵), it is presupposed that friendship is a source of enjoyment for ourselves ; 'Jesus does not indicate a course of action whereby we do evil to others, but such as constitutes a painful sacrifice for ourselves' (Wendt). At bottom our own life only, the last citadel (Job 2⁴), is to be hated, and everything else only in so far as it partakes of this principle of sin and death (Godet) ; 'secundum eam partem, secundum quam *se ipsum* odisse debet, a Christo aversam' (Bengel). 'He that so prizes his life that he cannot let it out of his own hand or give it up to good ends, checks its growth, and it withers and dies ; whereas he who treats it as if he hated it, giving it up freely to the needs of others, shall keep it to life eternal' (Dods, *Expositor's Greek Test.*). 'Nec tamen sufficit nostra relinquere, nisi relinquamus et nos' (Gregory, *Hom.* xxxii.).

Westcott on He 7³ quotes a striking passage from Philo which throws light on Lk 14²⁶ ; he describes the Levites as being in some sense 'exiles who to do God's pleasure had left parents and children and brethren and all their mortal kindred, and continues—ὁ γοῦν ἀρχηγέτης τοῦ θιάσου τούτου λέγων εἰσάγεται τῷ πατρὶ καὶ τῇ μητρί, Οὐχ ἑώρακα ὑμᾶς καὶ τοὺς ἀδελφοὺς οὐ γινώσκω καὶ τοῖς υἱοῖς ἀπογινώσκω ὑπὲρ τοῦ δίχα μεθολκῆς θεραπεύειν τὸ ὄν.' For the abstraction of the sinful desire to injure from the word 'hate,' leaving in it nothing but an aversion of a purely moral kind, Wendt compares the use of 'violence' and 'force' in Mt 11¹², where 'they are used only so far as they denote energetic seizure and appropriation, but not the unlawfulness of this seizure.'

4. Other passages—Mt 6²⁴ = Lk 16¹³ 'No man can serve two masters : for either he will *hate* the one and love (ἀγαπήσει) the other ; or else he will hold to the one and despise the other.' Here also 'hate' must get its full meaning in order to bring out the opposition and the division of the man's nature who attempts to serve both God and mammon. The change of words in the second part is remarkable (καταφρονήσει for. μισήσει, and ἀνθέξεται for ἀγαπήσει), 'non dixit *odiet* sed *contemnet*: sicut solent minas ejus postponere cupiditatibus suis, qui de bonitate ejus ad impunitatem sibi blandiuntur' (Aug.) ; to which Trench adds—'No man actually and openly professes to hate God and love the devil ; and therefore in the second clause, when the Lord is putting the converse case, He changes both words, which would be no longer the most appropriate ; the sinner '*holds to*' Satan when he follows his rewards ; he practically '*despises*' God when he heeds not His promises and His threatenings ; however little he may acknowledge to himself or to others that he is doing either this or the other.'

Lk 1⁷¹, 'salvation from our enemies and from the hand of all that hate us,' exhibits a parallelism with no particular distinction between the clauses, cf. Ps 18¹⁷ 106¹⁰.

LITERATURE.—Bethune-Baker's art. 'Hatred' in Hastings' *DB* ; Votaw's art. 'Sermon on the Mount,' *ib.* Extra Vol. ; Trench, *Exposition of the Sermon on the Mount*, also *Studies in the Gospels* (No. 12) ; Wendt, *Teaching of Jesus*, ii. 65–70 ; Mozley, *Lectures on the Old Testament* (Lect. viii.) ; Finlayson, *Expositor*, i. ix. [1879] 420 f. ; Dykes, *Manifesto of the King*, p. 311 ff. ; Butler, *Serm.* viii. ix. ; Seeley, *Ecce Homo*, ch. xxi. ; Martensen, *Chr. Eth.* ii. 118 ff. ; Gardner, *Conflict of Duties*, 133–148.

W. H. DUNDAS.

HEAD (κεφαλή).—**1.** *Natural importance.*—The relationship of the head to the body is that of master to servant. In this service the body is expected to ignore its own wants, and homelessness is to be without a resting-place for the head (Mt 8²⁰). The anointing of the head was an accompaniment of festive happiness (Mt 26⁷, Mk 14³, Lk 7⁴⁶), and this mark of joy was to be borrowed by Christian self-denial (Mt 6¹⁷). A crown of thorns on the head was part of the mock dignity thrust upon Christ as King of the Jews (Jn 19²).

The importance thus attached to the head gave a higher significance to the gestures which, among an emotional people, often emphasized or took the place of words. Such movements of the head are practised to-day in Palestine alike by young and old, and are resorted to on occasions similar to those described in the OT and NT. Thus a rapid shaking of the head from side to side, with a similar twirling of the open hand on the wrist, indicates that one is perplexed by some mystery, as when the owner of the garden asked why that useless fig-tree was still there (Lk 13⁷). It also indicates that the hearer has not heard distinctly, or grasped the meaning of what has been said. An abrupt jerk of the head backward does duty, especially when at some distance away, for an emphatic 'No.' The bending of the head downward is the attitude of the inferior in the presence of his superior (Is 58⁵, Lk 18¹³). The slow turning of the head once in one direction means that the words just heard or the scene witnessed pass all description. Such a gesture would be common among those who looked upon Christ's miracles of healing power. This motion, repeated several times, along with a dissociating wave of the hand, means contempt or disgust towards some action, or the abandonment of hope in the case of some party referred to (Jer 18¹⁶, Zeph 2¹⁵). The movement of the head up and down is the soliloquy of one speaking to himself and saying, 'It is as I expected ; I knew it must come to this' (La 2¹⁵, Mt 27³⁹). The head laid to one side, with a slight protrusion of the underlip, means, 'Causes must have consequences, you may do as you please' (Ps 22⁷). Such a gesture seems to fill the gap in the debate over the fig-tree in the garden (Lk 13⁹).

2. *Figurative authority.*—The connexion thus recognized between head and body was used to express all situations involving a relationship of authority and submission. The patriarchal East, with regard to both secular and sacred matters, has always attached more importance to the sceptre than to the statute. It does not understand impersonal edicts, and gives its homage to the official who can enforce his decrees. Its conception of life is of graded authority rather than of democratic equality. It was not so much in disapproval of this as by way of supplying a new line of action to the familiar instinct, that Christ said that in the coming Kingdom of God the way to honour would have to be sought through abundant and self-humbling service (Mt 20²⁶ᶠ· 23¹¹). The customs of swearing by the head and of appealing to heaven and earth and Jerusalem, are condemned, because, while such a habit of appealing under distress to the name of some one who could and must come to deliver and punish was a protection to the oppressed under primitive conditions of life, it was here diverted from its original meaning when the appeal was made to that which was not free, but already belonged to another. The practice was at once foolish and idolatrous. The true help is from the Lord which made heaven and earth ; and this help is for those whose speech is 'Yea, yea ; nay, nay' (Mt 5³³⁻³⁷).

For the *headship of Christ* see following article.

G. M. MACKIE.

HEADSHIP.—i. IN THE GOSPELS.—**1.** The word 'head' (κεφαλή), as applied to the relation of Christ to His Church, occurs only three times in the Gospels, and there in the passages in the Synoptics (Mt 21⁴² ‖ Mk 12¹⁰ ‖ Lk 20¹⁷) in which, applying the lesson of the parable of the Wicked Husbandmen, Jesus quotes Ps 118²² in the Septuagint version, 'The stone which the builders rejected, the same is become the head of the corner' (οὗτος ἐγενήθη εἰς κεφαλὴν γωνίας), where the expression κεφαλὴν γωνίας is an exact rendering of the Hebrew פִּנָּה רֹאשׁ. The meaning of the passage is clear. The building of which the Psalmist speaks is the theocracy, Israel as the people of God. The corner-stone, a stone fitted into an angle of the building and binding together the walls which meet at that point, and without which the structure must collapse, represents the Messiah, through whom the theocracy finds its realization.

What the Psalmist says about the rejection of the stone on the part of the builders has been explained by some as an allusion to an alleged incident in the building of the Second Temple.

'Some stone, a fragment, we may conjecture, of the Old Temple, rescued from its ruins, had seemed to the architects unfit for the work of binding together the two walls that met at right angles to each other. They would have preferred some new blocks of their own fashioning. But the priests, it may be, more conversant with the traditions of the Temple, knew that that was the right place for it, and that no other stone would answer half as well. The trial was made, and the issue answered their expectations' (Plumptre, *Biblical Studies*, quoted by Perowne, *Psalms, in loc.*).

It is more likely, however, that this story was suggested by Ps 118 than *vice versa*. Probably what was in the Psalmist's mind was Is 28^{16} 'Behold I lay in Zion for a foundation a stone, a tried stone, a precious corner-stone.' Ps 118^{22} was applied by Christ to His relation to the Church as uniting Jew and Gentile, and to His approaching rejection by Israel. Thus quoted and applied, the words of the Psalm speak of the Messiah as of Him 'upon whom depend the maintenance and development of the theocracy, without whom it would fall to pieces, as the corner-stone is the upholder and stay of a building' (Meyer). They speak of Christ as representing the principle of unity, that which constitutes the Church a grand whole. If we compare with this application by our Lord of Ps 118^{22} the use made of the same figure by St. Peter in the Acts of the Apostles (4^{11}) and in his First Epistle (2$^{4-8}$), where he speaks of the Church as a temple built of living stones, and by St. Paul when he describes Jesus Christ Himself as the chief corner-stone of a holy temple (Eph 2^{20}), we find the connecting link between the idea of the Headship of Christ as it is expressed in the Gospels and the similar conception of St. Paul in his Epistles to the Ephesians and Colossians (compare also 1 Co 11^3).

St. Peter, while keeping to the architectural figure suggested by the passages quoted from the Psalms and Isaiah, and speaking of Christ as 'head stone of the corner' (κεφαλὴ γωνίας), adds the thought of life to that of unity. St. Paul, still further working out the same idea, adopts a different figure, that of the head as the seat of life in the body, that which controls and regulates the action of each individual member (Eph 1$^{22, 23}$ 4$^{15, 16}$ 5$^{23, 28-30}$, Col 1^{18} 2^{19}). See § ii.

2. The idea of Headship is suggested in the Gospels in connexion with another figure, in our Lord's similitude of the Vine (Jn 15$^{1ff.}$), in which He illustrates and works out in detail the thought that He is the source of life and fruitfulness for the whole Church and for each individual member of the Church, the vital principle which unites all in one. As the head no less than the heart is the seat of life in the human body, inasmuch as the brain is the centre of the nervous system, and the nerves radiating from the brain and spinal cord are the source of the healthy activity of every part, the beautiful description which St. Paul gives (Col 2^{19})—'the head, from which all the body by joints and bands having nourishment ministered and knit together, increaseth with the increase of God'—corresponds to what Christ says in His parable of the Vine of the source of life and fruitfulness, with the thought of the healthy flow of life-giving sap which His words suggest: 'As the branch cannot

bear fruit of itself except it abide in the vine, no more can ye except ye abide in me. I am the vine, ye are the branches : he that abideth in me and I in him, the same bringeth forth much fruit ; for without me (χωρὶς ἐμοῦ—marg. 'severed from me') ye can do nothing' (Jn 15$^{4, 5}$).

3. Again, the thought of Headship is involved in that view of the Church's relation to Christ which our Lord presents in the blessing pronounced on St. Peter at Cæsarea Philippi (Mt 16$^{18, 19}$), and in a passage from the same Gospel, in many respects similar, in which He repeats His promise of power to bind and to loose (Mt 18$^{18-20}$). These passages are the more worthy of note in this connexion, that they are the only instances in which the Gospels represent Jesus as using the expression 'Church' (ἐκκλησία). According to the first, that which constitutes the being and the strength of the Church is her faith in Jesus as the Christ, the Son of the living God. Jesus speaks of the community which is founded upon faith in the Christ as 'My church' (μου τὴν ἐκκλησίαν), and then promises to invest this Church in the person of her representatives (in this case St. Peter as spokesman of the Twelve) with the power to bind and to loose. The other passage occurs in connexion with our Lord's injunction to make 'the church' the final court of appeal in cases of disputes among brethren. In it Jesus repeats the promise of power to bind and to loose, and states, in more universal terms than He employs in His promise to St. Peter, what constitutes the Church, or what entitles any body of believers to the name of 'Church.' That is the presence of Christ Himself in the midst of them. ' Where two or three are gathered together in my name, there am I in the midst of them.' That which constitutes the Church and invests her with authority and power, that which is the source of her life and energy, is the presence with her of Christ as her living Head, in whose name and guided by whose Spirit she discharges her spiritual functions.

LITERATURE :—Cremer, *Bib.-Theol. Lex. s.v.* κεφαλή ; Grimm-Thayer, *Lex. Novi Testamenti, s.vv.* κεφαλή, ἀνακεφαλαιόω ; *Comm.* of Meyer and Alford ; Baethgen, *Psalmen, ad loc.* ; Perowne, *The Psalms*, ii. p. 338 ; Beyschlag, *NT Theol.* i. 165 ff.

HUGH H. CURRIE.

ii. IN THE PAULINE EPISTLES.—The Headship of Christ, suggested in the teaching of our Lord Himself, is expressly taught in the Pauline Epp., and is applied, moreover, to a much wider sphere than that of Christian discipleship. For while emphasis is especially laid on Christ's Headship over the Church, suggestions are given for a doctrine of His Headship over the human race and even over the whole created universe.

1. *Christ's Headship over the Church.*—In 1 Co 12^{27} (cf. Ro 12^5) we find St. Paul, in his desire to impress his readers with a sense of their unity and mutual dependence, describing the local church as 'a body of Christ' (σῶμα Χριστοῦ)—conceiving of it *i.e.* under the figure of a body whose several members (eye, hand, head, feet, v.^{21}) are individual Christians. In Eph. and Col. this figure is elaborated at more points than one. In the first place, Christ is no longer thought of as Himself the whole body, of which individuals are the members—the head being a particular member like the rest. The Church is now the body, from which He is distinguished as the Head (Eph 1$^{22f.}$ 4$^{15f.}$ 5^{23}, Col 1^{18} 2^{19}). He is the vital centre, the ruling and directing power of the whole organism. Moreover, as the use of the art. before σῶμα (absent in 1 Co 12^{27}) now shows, it is the writer's intention that the figure should be applied not to any local church merely, but to the Church universal, and to this Church ideally conceived—the actual Church, no doubt, but regarded *sub specie æternitatis*, so that

the radiance of the heavenly antitype shines through the earthly form. To this Church, Christ is 'head over all things'; while it is 'his body, the fulness of him that filleth all in all' (Eph 1²²ᶠ·). See, further, art. BODY, ii. (3).

2. *Christ's Headship over the human race.*—In 1 Co 11³ the Apostle writes, 'The head of every man is Christ.' Here we have a doctrine of Headship stretching out beyond the limits even of the universal Church. The statement, as Hort points out (*Chr. Ecclesia*, p. 151), is a natural application of St. Paul's view of Christ as the Second Adam (1 Co 15²²· ⁴⁵ᶠᶠ·, cf. Ro 5¹²ᶠᶠ·). The Incarnation not only reveals the kinship of the 'man from heaven' with all the sons of men; it sets Him before them as the true spiritual Head of humanity, in whom the race is ideally summed up.

3. *Christ's Headship over the universe.*—In Eph 1¹⁰ we read that it is God's purpose 'to gather together all things under a head (ἀνακεφαλαιώσασθαι τὰ πάντα) in Christ, the things in the heavens and the things upon the earth.' And in Col 2¹⁰ Christ is expressly called 'the head of all principality and power'— words which are explained in 1¹⁵· ¹⁶, where He is declared to be 'the firstborn of all creation,' in whom 'were all things created, in the heavens and upon the earth, things visible and things invisible, whether thrones or dominions or principalities or powers; all things have been created through him and unto him; and he is before all things, and in him all things consist.' In these passages there is affirmed of Christ a relation of Headship to the universe alike for the past, the present, and the future. In Him all things were created at the first. In Him they even now consist as their vital Head, the underlying ground of their very being. And unto Him from whom they had their origin they shall all finally return, in the day of that great consummation when God shall 'gather together all things under a head in Christ.'

With this Pauline doctrine of the Headship of Christ over (1) the Church, (2) the human race, (3) the universe, it is interesting to compare the teaching of the Fourth Gospel regarding (1) the union of Christ as the living Vine with His people as the branches (Jn 15¹ᶠᶠ·); (2) the true Light which lighteth every man that cometh into the world (1⁹); (3) the creative Logos 'without [whom] was not anything made that hath been made' (1³).

LITERATURE.—The Comm. and NT Theologies on the passages referred to; Hort, *Chr. Ecclesia*, 144–152; Dale, *Eph.*, Lecture VI.; Bruce, *St. Paul's Conception of Christianity*, 331 ff.

J. C. LAMBERT.

HEALING.—See CURES.

HEARING.—**1.** There are two Gr. verbs (ἀκούω, εἰσακούω) used for 'hear' in the Gospels, and they are sometimes rendered in the EV by 'hearken,' 'listen' (RV), 'come to the ears of,' 'to be noised.' Another verb (παρακούω) is used, Mt 18¹⁷, and translated 'refuse to hear' (RV), and Mk 5³⁶ where the RV is 'not heeding' (mg. 'overhearing'). The noun (ἀκοή) also occurs, and is rendered 'hearing,' 'fame,' 'report,' 'rumour.'

2. The most obvious meaning of 'hear' is, of course, *to be endowed with the faculty of hearing, as opposed to deafness*; and in this sense it is used in Mt 11⁵ (Lk 7²²), Mk 7³⁷. (See CURES, DEAF AND DUMB).

Next, perhaps, in order of common usage are such meanings of the word as (*a*) *to have immediate perceptual experience through the organ of hearing* —the object being either personal, as Mt 2⁹ 'Having heard the king,' or impersonal, as Mt 11⁴ 'Tell John the things which ye do hear'; (*b*) *to find out (by hearsay), to have information about, learn* (*i.e. hear of mediately*)—the object again being either personal, as Mk 7²⁵ 'A woman . . . having heard

of him,' or impersonal, as Mk 6⁵⁵ 'where they heard he was.' In connexion with (*a*) and (*b*) it is interesting to note the passages in which the experience of Jesus is referred to: *e.g.* (*a*) Mt 8¹⁰ (Lk 7⁹) 21¹⁶ 27¹³, Mk 5³⁶, Lk 8⁵⁰ 18²²; (*b*) Mt 4¹² 9¹² (Mk 2¹⁷), Jn 9³⁵ 11⁴· ⁶.

3. The suggestive uses of the word, however, are those in which *more complex experiences* than the previous ones are signified by it. (*a*) The first usage to be named under this head is where the verb 'to hear' is used to mean *the receiving of inward communications.* For example, Jesus predicts the coming of the hour 'when the dead shall hear the voice of the Son of God' (Jn 5²⁵· ²⁸). Again He uses the word to describe *His own experience in relation to the revelation of the truth which He received from the Father and made known to men*, 'As I hear, I judge' (5³⁰); 'The things which I have heard from him (that sent me), these speak I unto the world' (8²⁶)—these as well as 8⁴⁰ and 15¹⁵ are instances in point. The Evangelist John, speaking of Jesus, says, similarly, 'What he hath seen and heard, of that he beareth witness' (3³²). In two places Jesus refers to *the occurrence of this experience in the case of others*: 'Ye have neither heard his voice at any time,' He says to His Jewish audience, 'nor seen his form' (5³⁷); 'Every one that hath heard from the Father, and hath learned, cometh unto me' (6⁴⁵). Finally, the inward communication may be far otherwise than Divine in its source. To the Jews, Jesus is reported by the Evangelist John as having said, 'Ye do the things which ye heard from your father' (8³⁸), and later on in the same chapter (v. ⁴⁴) their father is declared by Him to be the devil. It is characteristic that all the above usages are found in the Fourth Gospel. (*b*) In a few contexts the word 'hear' is used *with reference to God's attitude to prayer.* For example, we read that at the grave of Lazarus 'Jesus lifted up his eyes, and said, Father, I thank thee that thou heardest me. And I knew that thou hearest me always' (11⁴¹· ⁴²). In His teaching with regard to prayer Jesus warns His hearers against using vain repetitions, 'as the Gentiles do: for they think that they shall be heard for their much speaking' (Mt 6⁷). To Zacharias the angel Gabriel is reported as having said, 'Fear not, because thy supplication is heard' (Lk 1¹³). [εἰσακούω is the verb used in both the preceding contexts]. The man, blind from his birth, whom Jesus cured on the Sabbath, thus addressed the Jews, 'We know that God heareth not sinners; but if any man be a worshipper of God and do his will, him he heareth' (Jn 9³¹). (*c*) Another context may be noticed here, viz. that one in which Jesus, *describing the function of the Spirit, says of Him*, 'He shall not speak from himself; but what things soever he shall hear, these shall he speak' (16¹³). (*d*) In certain passages *emphasis is placed on the privilege of 'hearing' or 'becoming acquainted with'* the gospel. 'Blessed are your eyes,' said Jesus to the disciples, 'for they see; and your ears, for they hear. For verily I say unto you, that many prophets and righteous men desired to see the things which ye see, and saw them not; and to hear the things which ye hear, and heard them not' (Mt 13¹⁶· ¹⁷, Lk 10²⁴). The *duties attached to this privilege* may be grouped in the following way—(1) in respect to the exercise as such: 'He that hath ears to hear, let him hear' (Mt 11¹⁵ 13⁹· ⁴³, cf. Mk 4⁹· ²³ 7¹⁶, Lk 8⁸ 14³⁵); (2) in respect to that which the attention is given to: 'Take heed what ye hear' (Mk 4²⁴); (3) in respect to the manner of hearing: 'Take heed therefore how ye hear' (Lk 8¹⁸). (*e*) In a large number of passages, especially in the parable of the Sower, 'hearing' *either implies one or other of certain richer experiences, or it is ex-*

plicitly connected therewith as a prefatory experience. (1) Sometimes the experience implied, or mentioned as that in which 'hearing' fulfils itself (or does not fulfil itself), is *understanding or learning.* For example, referring to the multitude generally, Jesus said to the disciples, 'Therefore speak I to them in parables : because seeing they see not, and hearing they hear not, neither do they understand' (Mt 13¹³, Mk 4¹², Lk 8¹⁰). (See art. SEEING). 'Hear and understand, Not that which entereth into the mouth defileth the man ; but that which proceedeth out of the mouth, this defileth the man' (Mt 15¹⁰, Mk 7¹⁴). 'With many such parables spake he the word unto them, as they were able to hear it' (Mk 4³³), etc. (2) Sometimes the experience is *believing.* For example, some of the Samaritans are reported as having said to the woman who conversed with Jesus at the well, 'Now we believe, not because of thy speaking : for we have heard for ourselves' (Jn 4⁴²). 'Verily, verily, I say unto you,' said Jesus to the Jews, when they were seeking to kill Him, 'He that heareth my word, and believeth him that sent me, hath eternal life' (5²⁴). 'This is an hard saying,' said many of the disciples after Jesus had spoken of Himself as the bread which came down from heaven, 'who can hear it?' (6⁶⁰). Cf. also the references in Jn 10 to the sheep 'hearing' the voice of the Good Shepherd. (3) Sometimes the experience is *doing, bearing fruit,* or *keeping.* For example, the verses at the close of the Sermon on the Mount, 'Every one which heareth these sayings of mine and doeth them . . . Every one that heareth these sayings of mine and doeth them not' (Mt 7²⁴·²⁶, Lk 6⁴⁷·⁴⁹).* 'He that was sown upon the good ground, this is he that heareth the word, and understandeth it ; who verily beareth fruit and bringeth forth,' etc. (Mt 13²³, Mk 4²⁰, Lk 8¹⁵). When it was told Jesus that His mother and His brethren stood without desiring to see Him, He said, 'My mother and my brethren are these which hear the word of God and do it' (Lk 8²¹). When a certain woman out of the multitude said to Jesus, 'Blessed is the womb that bare thee, and the breasts which thou didst suck,' He answered, 'Yea rather, blessed are they that hear the word of God and keep it' (Lk 11²⁸, cf. Jn 12⁴⁷).

The above divisions represent the main usages of the word 'hearing.' It is interesting to notice the contexts in which (i.) the interest displayed in anticipation of hearing is described, and these may be collected together without further remark : Mt 12⁴² (Lk 11³¹), 13¹⁷ (Lk 10²⁴), Mk 3⁸ (cf. Mt 4²⁵, Mk 3²⁰ etc.), Lk 5¹·¹⁵ 6¹⁷ 15¹ 19⁴⁸ 21³⁸ 23⁸ ; and (ii.) those in which certain emotional results are described as resulting from 'hearing.' *e.g.* wonder, astonishment, amazement, etc., joy, rejoicing, gladness, etc., indignation, wrath, etc., sorrow, fear, trouble, perplexity, offence (see articles on most of these subjects).

In conclusion, it may be pointed out that the antinomy which is found throughout Scripture and is testified to by the human consciousness in connexion with religious experience, viz. between 'man's working out and God's working in,' appears in what is said about 'hearing' in the Gospels. For along with exhortations addressed to men to 'hear' and to fulfil that experience in understanding, believing, and doing, there occurs a saying of Jesus like this, 'Every one that hath heard from the Father and hath learned, cometh unto me' (Jn 6⁴⁵). The 'ability to hear' (Mk 4³³, Jn 6⁶⁰) implies an inward communication from God and an exercise of man's natural faculties.

LITERATURE.—Grimm - Thayer's *Gr. Lex. s.vv.* ; Moulton-Geden's *Gr. Concordance,* etc. ; see also Literature appended to art. SEEING.   A. B. MACAULAY.

---

* In connexion with this passage it is worth noting that the point of difference between the 'rock' and the 'sand' as foundations is just that between 'hearing and doing' and 'hearing and not doing.' The basal element is the same in both cases—'hearing,' but that which gives it the cohesiveness and permanence of 'rock' is 'doing'—habitual obedience

HEART.—In the NT 'heart' (καρδία) is the word most commonly used to denote the inner nature of man, the secret core of his being, where the springs of his intellectual and moral activity reside. In this, its general significance, it is the equivalent of the Hebrew term לֵב or לֵבָב in the OT. Originally employed to designate the bodily organ which is the centre of the animal life, it came by a natural process of thought to be applied to the invisible centre of the thinking and responsible life. In this sense it occurs with notable frequency in the Gospels ; but there, like the corresponding word in the OT, whilst always referring to man's interior nature, it is used in a variety of applications, according to the particular functions or aspects of that nature which are meant to be expressed. This is the case also in the other NT writings.

i. SHADES OF MEANING IN THE GOSPELS.— Heart in the Gospels is variously regarded—**1.** *As the faculty of thought, intelligence, and memory.*— Persons are spoken of as pondering (Lk 2¹⁹), musing (3¹⁵), reasoning (5²²), having thoughts arising (Mt 9⁴, Lk 9⁴⁷ 24³⁸) in their heart ; understanding or not with their heart (Mt 13¹⁵, Mk 6⁵² 8¹⁷) ; keeping, or laying up, things said or done, in their heart (Lk 1⁶⁶ 2⁵¹).

2. *As the seat of the affections, emotions, and passions :—e.g.* of love for God (Mt 22³⁷, Lk 10²⁷), for earthly or heavenly treasure (Mt 6¹⁹⁻²¹) ; of joy (Jn 16²², Lk 24³²) ; of sorrow (Jn 14¹ 16⁶) ; of forgivingness (Mt 18³⁵), purity (5⁸), humility (11²⁹) ; of good or evil dispositions (12³⁴·³⁵), perverse inclination (5²⁸ 24⁴⁸), luxurious tastes and desires (Lk 21³⁴).

3. *As the source of purpose and volition.*—The disciples are enjoined to settle in their hearts not to meditate what they shall say (Lk 21¹⁴) ; the fell design of Judas was put into his heart by Satan (Jn 13²) ; the adulterous act is virtually done in the intention of the heart (Mt 5²⁸).

4. *As the organ of moral discernment and religious belief, i.e. of conscience and faith.*—Reproofs are given for the hardness of heart which prevents the reception of the truth (Mt 19⁸, Mk 3⁵ 16¹⁴), and for slowness of heart to believe (Lk 24²⁵) ; there is an exhortation not to doubt in the heart, but believe (Mk 11²³) ; and the pure in heart have the promise of Divine illumination (Mt 5⁸).

In one passage only we find the phrase 'the heart of the earth' (Mt 12⁴⁰).

ii. CHRIST'S EMPHASIS ON THE HEART.—The superlative importance which Christ attached to the heart and its right condition was one of the pre-eminent characteristics of His teaching. He possessed an unrivalled insight into the workings of the heart (Jn 2²⁴·²⁵), and could read what was going on there with a penetration and accuracy often startling (Mt 9⁴ 12²⁵ 22¹⁸, Mk 2⁸, Lk 9⁴⁷). But His unique peculiarity was the seriousness and persistency with which He dealt with the heart, and laboured for its purification as the one concern vital to the well-being of men. To the heart He always appealed, and on its deepest instincts He sought to bring His influence to bear ; and although in many of His utterances the heart is not expressly named, it is still obvious that He had it directly in view. This was the 'inwardness' which constituted His great secret. The main points on which He insisted were :

1. *The heart as the source of all the good or the evil in men's lives.*—He dwelt on this with special earnestness—*e.g.* in His reply to the tradition-bound objectors, 'Out of the heart proceed evil thoughts, murders, adulteries,' etc., 'the things which defile a man' (Mt 15¹⁹ᶠ·) ; and in that suggestive saying, 'A good man out of the good treasure of his heart bringeth forth that which is good, and an evil man out of the evil treasure of his heart bringeth forth that which is evil' (Lk

6[45]); and the idea is to be found running through all His teaching.

2. *The dispositions and motives of the heart as determining the religious value of actions.*—Jesus unfailingly taught that the test of a man's worth before God was not the outward propriety of his conduct, but the heart-inclinations and purposes by which he was swayed (Lk 16[15]). Even a correctly decorous Pharisee like Simon did not stand so high in the Divine estimation as the frail woman who had erred sadly, because, while he was proud and self-satisfied in his moral respectability, she, amid all her failings, was melted into heartfelt penitence and gratitude (7[36-39]). A man's conduct may be free from all formal commission of impurity, but if he lust after a woman in his heart, the stain of impurity is already incurred (Mt 5[28]). Many things outwardly right and proper were done by the religionists of His day—seasons of prayer duly observed, alms given, etc.—which yet He pronounced to be of little moral value because done from a false motive, the desire for social credit, 'to be seen of men' (6[2. 5]). On the other hand, humble and obscure actions, like the widow's offering and the publican's supplication, He declared to be of inestimable worth in the eye of Heaven, by reason of the genuine heart-feeling from which they sprang (Mk 12[41-44], Lk 18[13. 14]). And in the great Judgment-picture (Mt 25[31-46]), He made it clear that it is the frank, unaffected generosity of the heart, finding expression in deeds of simple dutifulness, that ranks high in the Father's sight and secures the reward of immortal blessedness. Always and everywhere He pierced below surface appearances, and demanded inner rectitude as the criterion of worth.

3. *The regeneration of the heart as essential both to a right relation to God and to true happiness.*— The repentance Jesus preached meant a change of heart (Mt 4[17] 9[13], Lk 13[3]); the conversion He urged as a necessity was a turning of the heart to God as the source of life and grace (Mt 13[15], Mk 4[12], Jn 12[40]), a restoration of the childlike spirit (Mt 18[3]), a new birth within, apart from which it is impossible to enjoy the blessings of the heavenly Kingdom (Jn 3[3-7]).

iii. EVILS COUNTERACTED BY CHRIST'S TEACHING. — Of these, four at least may be specially noted:

1. *A pretentious ecclesiasticism.*—Men's minds were drawn away from dependence on the mere institutional aspects of religion, and confronted with the absolute necessity of internal righteousness. When orthodox Jews took a stand on their connexion with an ancient religious organization with its high covenanted privileges, and boasted of being children of Abraham, Christ flatly challenged their right to such a title, because of the vile purposes they cherished in their hearts, which proved that they did not possess Abraham's spirit (Jn 8[39]). He avowed that a scorned publican like Zacchæus, who was outside the pale of ecclesiastical recognition, was more truly a son of Abraham, in virtue of the higher dispositions which had been stirred in his heart, and which placed him in the line of moral and spiritual descent (Lk 19[9]). Again, in face of the arrogant presumption that restricted Divine blessing and salvation to those within the bounds of Judaism and its religious system, He held up the kind services of a generous heart as sufficient to raise even a Samaritan to a level of equal worth before God (10[30-37]).

2. *An external ceremonialism.*—Jesus attacked, sometimes with fiery indignation, the superficiality of that righteousness which was based on a punctilious attention to certain prescribed observances, —the tithing of mint and cummin, when justice, mercy, and the faith of the heart were neglected

(Mt 23[23], Lk 11[42]); the fastings which had no genuine penitence behind them (Mt 6[17. 18]); the careful washing of hands, while the heart was inwardly defiled (15[2. 3]). It was His dominant idea that on the disposition of the heart the spiritual value of worship depends (Jn 4[24]), and He had strong warnings to utter against the offerings at the altar when sinister feelings were nursed within (Mt 5[23]), and the ascription of honour to God with the lips while the heart was far from Him (15[8]). With scathing rebukes He exposed the pretensions of those who claimed peculiar sanctity on the ground of their ceremonial scrupulousness, characterizing them as whited sepulchres, outwardly fair, but inwardly full of uncleanness (23[27]). Thus He represented all external acts of righteousness which do not spring out of an upright, pious heart as a mere hypocritical show, and not real righteousness (6[1-6]).

3. *A legalistic moralism.*—In view of the fact that the great spiritual ideas inculcated by the prophets had been hardened into fixed laws and rules, in formal obedience to which righteousness was made to consist, Christ's endeavour to recall men to the supreme importance of inner motive was calculated to exert a powerful effect. The confidence which many had in their moral respectability was necessarily shaken when they found themselves forced to look within, and judge themselves by something higher than a legal standard; as, *e.g.*, in the case of the young man who had great possessions, and whose conduct outwardly was without reproach (Mt 19[16-22]). And there can be little doubt that the uneasiness and irritation created among the professedly religious classes by Christ's teaching was largely due to the consciousness it wakened in them of the insufficiency of the grounds on which their claim to righteousness was based. In the light of the stress He laid on the hidden springs of action in the heart, their moral regularity of life, founded on mere conformity to laws and rules, was bound to appear unsatisfactory and poor.

4. *A self-sufficient secularism.*—Such teaching, setting the renewed dispositions of the heart far above the riches and honours of the world in value, supplied a potent counteractive which prosperous security and self-assumption worldliness is apt to beget. It forced home the sense of something wanting within, even when the outward fortunes were flourishing. The parable of the Rich Fool is a vivid picture of the real poverty of the man who trusts in his worldly success and is not rich in the things that belong to the inner life (Lk 12[16-21]); while in the parable of the Rich Man and Lazarus there is another picture, fitted to break down the self-confidence of the prosperous, showing that the day will come when conditions may be reversed, and when heart-qualities alone will determine the status and happiness of men (Lk 16[19-31]).

iv. THE REVIVIFYING EFFECT ON RELIGION.— By His insistence on the heart as the vital element in righteousness, Christ transformed the whole character of religion. He made it (1) *living*,—not mechanical, a matter of prescribed and outwardly imposed form, but dynamical, a free, spontaneous spring of high purpose and feeling; not something put on, but a bent and impulse of the spirit within. Thus He gave religion an elasticity and perpetual vitality which prophesy for it permanence and power,—'a well of water springing up unto everlasting life' (Jn 4[14]). He made it (2) *effectually operative*,—an energizing force, working itself out in practical life, impressing its hallowed ideas and aims on the world of affairs, and proving its reality by the heightened quality of the actions to which it leads. And He made it (3) *a gracious influence,*—commending itself to the general conscience, winning reverence, inspiring self-devotion, and transmitting from heart to heart fervours of aspiration after the things of God.

LITERATURE.—Cremer, *Bib.-Theol. Lex. s.v. καρδία* ; art. 'Herz' in *PRE*[3] ; Wendt, *Teaching of Jesus*, i. 265 ff. ; Martensen, *Christian Ethics* (Individual), 80 ff. ; Weiss, *Bib. Theol. of NT*, i. 124.   G. M'HARDY.

HEAT (καύσων), Mt 20[12], Lk 12[55] ; RV 'scorching heat,' with marg. 'hot wind.' καύσων in. LXX has both meanings : (1) scorching heat (Gn 31[40], Is 49[10], Sir 18[16] 43[22]) ; (2) the east wind (קָדִים), hot, dry, dust-laden, withering up all vegetation, and blowing from the desert, like the simoom (Job 27[21], Jer 18[17], Ezk 17[10] 19[12], Jon 4[8], Hos 13[15]), usually ἄνεμος or πνεῦμα καύσων. AV gives 'burning heat,' and RV 'scorching wind' in Ja 1[11].

The first meaning seems preferable in Mt 20[12], though Trench (*Parables*) and others incline to RVm. 'Onus intrinsecus, a labore ; æstum extrinsecus, a sole' (Bengel). Lk 12[55] belongs to a class of passages based on the observation of natural phenomena ; cf. Mt 5[45] 7[24f.] 24[27], Lk 10[18], Jn 3[8] 12[24]. Here also the rendering 'scorching heat' is the more usual, and seems to agree better than 'hot wind' or 'east wind' with the mention of the south wind (νότος) which immediately precedes. Possibly, however, the distinction was not so clearly marked between these two winds, since in Ezk 27[26] קָדִים (east wind) is translated in LXX by τὸ πνεῦμα τοῦ νότου.

The only reference in the Gospels to heat for the purpose of warmth is Jn 18[18] 'a fire of coals' (ἀνθρακιάν), *i.e.* 'of charcoal' RVm, coals having probably still this meaning at the time of the AV. See WIND.

LITERATURE.—Grimm-Thayer, *Lex. s.v. καύσων* ; Hastings' *DB*, and *Encyc. Bibl.* art. 'Wind' ; Thomson, *Land and Book*, pp. 295, 536 f.   W. H. DUNDAS.

HEATHEN. — The Anglo-Saxon *haethen*, 'one who lives on the heaths and in the woods,' as opposed to a town-dweller ; cf. 'pagan,' from *paganus*, 'a countryman *or* villager.' This word is an indication of the fact that, as a rule, country-dwellers were Christianized later than those living in towns and cities. 'Heathen' occurs in AV of the Gospels in Mt 6[7] 18[17], and not at all in RV, which gives 'Gentiles' and 'Gentile' respectively in these two places (see GENTILES).

It has been pointed out that *paganus* also means 'a civilian' in opposition to 'a soldier,' and that thus a pagan would also mean one who was not a soldier of Christ. This secondary meaning of pagan probably came into use through a contemptuous designation by soldiers of non-military persons as 'countrymen.'

LITERATURE.—Murray, *New English Dictionary* ; and *Encyc. Bibl. s.v.* ; Bigg, *The Church's Task under the Roman Empire*, Lect. ii. p. 42, note 2 ; Trench, *Study of Words*.   ALBERT BONUS.

HEAVEN (οὐρανός, sing. and plur. ; in Mt. plur. chiefly, and always in ὁ πατὴρ ὁ ἐν τοῖς οὐρανοῖς, and ἡ βασιλεία τῶν οὐρανῶν).

Three uses of the word may be classified, omitting parallel passages—

(*a*) *Cosmological.*

'Heaven and earth' as constituting the entire Universe : as in the phrases 'till heaven and earth pass away' (Mt 5[18] 24[35], Lk 16[17]) ; 'Lord of heaven and earth' (Mt 11[25]). Heaven is 'the firmament,' where are fixed the stars and 'the powers' (Mt 24[29]), the sky (Mt 16[2] AV), the air (Mt 6[26] 8[20] 13[32], Lk 8[5], AV in each), the treasury of the clouds (Mt 24[30] 26[64]), the winds (Mt 24[31]), the lightning (Lk 17[24]), the rain (Lk 4[25]) ; and from whence are signs and portents (Mt 24[30], Lk 21[11]).

(*b*) *The abode of God and angels.*

Heaven is 'the throne of God' (Mt 5[34] 23[22], cf. 'Our Father which art in heaven,' Mt 6[9] ; 'your Father . . . in heaven,' Mt 5[16. 45] 6[1] 7[11] 18[14] 23[9] ; 'My Father . . . in heaven,' Mt 7[21] 10[32. 33] 12[50] 16[17] 18[10. 19] ; so also 'Heavenly (οὐράνιος) Father,' Mt 5[48]

RV, 6[14. 26. 32] 15[13] 18[35] (ἐπουράνιος)). Angels come from Heaven (Mt 28[2], Lk 22[43], cr. Mt 26[53]), and return to Heaven (Lk 2[15]), and are 'the heavenly host' (Lk 2[13]), beholding God (Mt 18[10], cf. Lk 15[10]), and doing perfectly His will (Mt 6[10]).

(*c*) *As a synonym for 'God.'*

The use of 'Heaven' for 'God' is put beyond question by Lk 15[18. 21], where 'sinned against heaven' can only mean 'against God.' There are other uses only less certain—thus 'from heaven or from men' (Mt 21[25]) is clearly 'from God or from men' (cf. Ac 5[38f.]) ; so also 'given him from heaven' (Jn 3[27]) must be 'from God.' But the most striking instance of this use of 'Heaven' as a synonym for 'God' is in the phrase 'the Kingdom of Heaven,' almost uniformly in Mt. for 'the Kingdom of God' of Mk. and Lk., and this in exactly parallel passages. It is quite possible to make a distinction between these titles, but it seems best to accept them as synonymous.*

Admitting the use of this metonymy, there can be no objection to its use in other instances where a clear meaning follows. Thus, 'bound, loosed in heaven' (Mt 16[19] 18[18]) = 'of God' ; 'The keys of the kingdom of heaven' (Mt 16[19]) = the authority of God ; 'names written in heaven' (Lk 10[20]) = acceptance with God, cf. Ex 32[32]. The demand for 'a sign from heaven' (Mt 16[1], Lk 11[16]), while it may refer to the expectation of some visible wonder out of the sky, has ultimate reference to some direct act of God. Anything 'from heaven' is an act of God, cf. the judgment upon the cities of the Plain (Lk 17[29]), also the request of the disciples (Lk 9[54]). Even the phrase 'treasure in heaven' has its exact equivalent in 'rich toward God' (Lk 12[21]). Additional instances of the use of periphrasis are seen in 'joy in the presence of the angels of God' (Lk 15[10]) for the joy of God ; confess 'before the angels of God' (Lk 12[8], cf. Mt 10[32]) ; power 'from on High' (Lk 24[49]) ; Dayspring 'from on High' (Lk 1[78]) ; 'from above' (Jn 19[11]) ; 'in thy sight' (Mt 11[26]) ; 'the Most High' (Lk 1[32. 76] 6[35], cf. Mk 57).

The transition from Heaven as the abode of God to 'Heaven' as a synonym for 'God' is illustrated in the custom of uplifting the eyes to Heaven when God is addressed. The thought of the Temple as the dwelling-place of God led to the habit in prayer of turning the face towards Jerusalem and towards the Temple (see 1 K 8[44. 48], Dn 6[10], Ps 28[2] 138[2]). With the higher faith of God's transcendence, as One dwelling in the Heaven of Heavens, came the custom of lifting up the eyes to the Heavens (Ps 123[1]). The publican 'would not lift up so much as his eyes unto heaven' (Lk 18[13], cf. Ezr 9[6]). So in prayer, Jesus 'lifted up his eyes' (Jn 11[41]), 'to heaven' (Jn 17[1]) ; 'looking up to heaven' (Mt 14[19], Mk 7[34]). There are several passages which present difficulty, but whatever conclusion may be come to as to the objective occurrences in the opening of the heavens (Mt 3[16]), and the voice 'out of the heavens' (Mt 3[17], Jn 12[28]), or 'out of the cloud' (Mt 17[5]), the subjective experience is the vital matter, the attestation to Jesus of His commission from and fellowship with God.

It is this which is symbolically represented in 'Ye shall see the heaven opened and the angels of God ascending and descending upon the Son of man' (Jn 1[51]). Here, in a figure, the mediatorship of Jesus is declared, His revelation of God to man and intercession for man with God. The striking saying, 'No man hath ascended into heaven but he that descended out of heaven, even the Son of man which is in heaven' (Jn 3[13]), has additional difficulty. The weight of MS authority is against the last clause, and the words may have been added as a gloss after the Ascension. If, with the RV, we retain them as the words of Jesus, they must be taken as qualifying the preceding utterance, which then becomes a declaration of His perfect fellowship with God (cf. Jn 1[18]) rather than as a reference to Heaven as a place. The 'heavenly things' (Jn 3[12]) are without doubt the things of God, the new revelation of His grace in Jesus Christ.

In what has been said above there is little that is distinctively Christian. The threefold use of the word 'Heaven' is common alike to the OT and Jewish thought of the time. But after this preliminary study we ought to be in a better position to consider the characteristic teaching of Jesus and the Christian faith.

1. The Kingdom of God finds its perfect realization in a future state, *a world above and beyond earth*, the Kingdom *in* Heaven. This is the reiterated lesson alike of parable and of direct discourse. All the judgment parables, where separation between the righteous and the wicked is declared, clearly teach a future inheritance of bliss or of woe. So the parables of the Tares (Mt 13[37f.]), the Virgins (Mt 25[1f.]), the Talents (Mt 25[14f.]), and the Unjust Steward (Lk 16[1f.], where under the figure of 'eternal tents' the future Canaan is 'the

---

* See Schürer, *HJP* II. ii. 171 ; Wendt, *Teaching of Jesus*, i. 371 n. ; Dalman, *Words of Jesus*, p. 93 ; Bruce, *Expos. Gr. Test.* on Mt 3[2] n., cf. also his *Kingdom of God*, p. 58, where a distinction is suggested ; also Beyschlag, *NT Theol.*, Eng. tr. i. 42, where identity of meaning is granted, but 'a mere paraphrase for God' denied ; and Stevens, *Theol. of the NT*, p. 27 f. : 'interchangeably in Mt,' but 'of Heaven' denotes 'origin and attributes.'

past idealized'). In accommodation to Jewish thought and hope, the reward is ' to sit down with Abraham and Isaac and Jacob in the kingdom of heaven' (Mt 8^11, Lk 13^28), a hope which reaches beyond the life of earth. The final consummation must be where Jesus Himself is, and He, who came from heaven (Jn 3^13. 31 6^33. 38. 41f.), was 'received up into heaven' (Mk 16^19, Lk 24^51, Jn 20^17. The MS uncertainty here in Mk. and Lk. does not affect the argument, which has the testimony of the Apostolic writings). This is the final reward of the faithful, the inheritance of the Kingdom prepared before the foundation of the world (Mt 25^34 26^29, Jn 14^1f.).

2. *The nature of Heaven.*—As the life of the Kingdom is fundamentally ethical (Mt 5^20 7^21), so is the nature of Heaven itself. It is the fulness of the eternal life, which in the Fourth Gospel is the synonym of the Kingdom. Then it is, and there, that 'the righteous shine forth as the sun' (Mt 13^43), a glory certainly of character whatever else may be implied. There, too, is the perfect vision of God (Mt 5^8).

It cannot be doubted that Jesus meant to localize the thought of Heaven. The sharp contrast between Heaven and earth (Mt 6^19-21) can have no other meaning. In His teaching God is no mere all-pervading Spirit, lost in negative infinitude. God, as transcendent, immanent, infinite, alone, does not satisfy His revelation of 'the Father in heaven.' That name implies that in some world beyond there is a supreme manifestation of His Presence,—a Father's House, an enduring Holy of Holies. This, for Christian faith, is the Glory of Christ (Jn 17^5), and to be with Him where He is and to behold His glory is the hope set before us in the gospel (Jn 17^24).

What the activities of Heaven may be is told only in part. They that are accounted worthy to attain to that world 'are as angels' (Mk 12^25, Lk 20^36), and the ministry of angels enters into the Gospel story. The faithful are to be 'set over many things,' and to 'enter into the joy' of their Lord (Mt 25^21, 23), which, in the light of the gospel, can only mean higher service.

As to *when* this inheritance is entered upon, very different conclusions are drawn even from the words of Jesus. The question is considered, for the most part, from the standpoint of retribution. So far as the reward is considered, it may be said definitely that the doctrine of an Intermediate State finds no support in Christ's gospel. The 'farewell discourses' of the Fourth Gospel would lose all their force by the introduction of this doctrine. So for Christian faith the highest hope of Heaven finds its confident expression in the words of St. Paul : 'absent from the body . . . at home with the Lord' (2 Co 5^8).

LITERATURE.—This is chiefly of a devotional or sermonic character, but the authors referred to above should be consulted ; also Salmond, *Christian Doctrine of Immortality* ; and Alger, *Doctrine of a Future Life.* On the general subject, which lies outside the scope of the present article, and especially for the Jewish conceptions of Heaven, see the works on Biblical Theology ; Morfill-Charles, *Book of the Secrets of Enoch* ; art. 'Heaven' in Hastings' *DB.*   W. H. DYSON.

HEAVENLY THINGS. — See EARTHLY AND HEAVENLY.

HEDGE.—This word belongs to the vocabulary of the parables of Jesus. It occurs in that of the Vineyard (Mt 21^33, Mk 12^1), and in that of the Great Supper (Lk 14^23).

1. *Literal application.*—The hedge is a detail in the outfit of a vineyard, one of many other properties (Mt 21^33 ||) in such a possession. It is a feature in the landscape of Palestine in the other case ('highways and hedges,' Lk 14^23). There is a connexion between the uses and the associations of the word. The contour of the land is controlled by the tillage of the soil. Vines need hedges. The word (φραγμός) used for a hedge in the Gospels 'denotes a fence of any kind, whether hedge, or wall, or palings' (Hastings, *DB* ii. 340^a). Another word might rather have called up a stone wall. φραγμός includes all the different kinds of hedges to be found in a country so furrowed with hills and valleys as is Palestine.

2. The *parabolical* use of the 'hedge' is rooted in the education of Israel. God made sea and desert a hedge of Palestine. Cf. Ellerton's hymn—

'Praise to our God, whose bounteous hand
    Prepared of old our glorious land,
    A garden fenced with silver sea.' . . .

He hedged the people. He gave them individuals, institutions, the whole national economy, as hedges to protect their life and to restrain it. Enemies raided the land and broke down the hedges (Ps 79. 80). Patriots and prophets saw and sang their gaps, and did their best to repair the historic institutional hedges. The tragedy of Jesus and the hedges was that He wanted them rooted up, while the chief priests hated the idea of their removal (Mt 21^45). Through the tragedy gleams the *philanthropic* import of the hedge (Lk 14^23). The eye of love sees humanity submerged. 'Them also he would bring.' He would make hedge-row people happy. He had seen their misery as He stole to silent midnight prayer, up the hillsides with their mosaic of fields, along whose hedges and through the gaps of which He passed to pray to the Father in secret. It is humanity's ragged regiment whom He would see housed by the compulsion of 'the love (Lk 14^23) that will not let them go.'

LITERATURE.—Geikie, *Life of Christ*, i. ch. 17 ; Thomson, *Land and Book*, ch. 14 ; *Philochristus*, chs. 1-3 for 'Hedge of the Law.'   JOHN R. LEGGE.

HEIR.—The heir (κληρονόμος) is one who enters on a position of privilege different from that of servants (Mt 21^38), through no personal exertion of his own, but as the result of filial relationship. This position is a thoroughly right and legal one, and absolutely valid. The thought of succession to a title upon the death of the present holder is not insisted upon. The son is naturally the heir, and the title is one of present privilege as well as the assurance of fuller possession in the future.

Christ, the Son, is the heir of all things (He 1^2 ; cf. our Lord's application of the term to Himself in the parable of the Wicked Husbandman, Mt 21^38). The complete lordship over Creation was given to Adam (Gn 1^28, Ps 8^6). The land of Canaan, again, was promised to Abraham and his seed (Gn 13^14. 15). These assurances given to Adam and to Abraham were absolutely fulfilled in Christ, who, as the firstborn of all creation, Himself both the Agent of the Creator's work and summing up in His own Person all created objects (Col 1^15-17), enjoys an eternal and incorruptible inheritance. 'The heirship of the Son was realised in the Incarnation, and in its essence is independent of the Fall (Westcott on He 1^2), though conditioned by it as to its circumstances.' It was the sin of man which caused the suffering and humiliation through which Christ, after the work of redemption was complete, won a name which is above every name (Ph 2^9). He had inherited in the eternal purpose of God (ἔθηκεν, He 1^2) a name more excellent than the angels (1^4).

The title of 'heir,' then, passes on to those who have obtained the blessing of Divine sonship in Baptism or Regeneration, corresponding spiritually to the promise made to Abraham. The Old Covenant (Testament) could not make men perfect, therefore God provided them with more strength, and in place of a worldly inheritance gave them a spiritual and eternal one. This title of heirship may be forfeited, if those who are called to it are not worthy of their inheritance. So Christ speaks in the Apocalypse : 'He that overcometh shall inherit these things ; and I will be his God, and he shall be my son' (Rev 21⁷). We, then, being made children of God through faith in Christ, are heirs according to the promise made to Abraham, who was accepted through faith in God's word against all appearances. No longer servants, but heirs, we are entitled to the Divine privilege of sonship through adoption. We are called to inherit a blessing as all true servants of God through Baptism.

It remains to be seen who are specially mentioned in the Gospels as heirs to this privilege : (1) 'The meek shall inherit the earth' (Mt 5⁵). (2) Those who have given up houses, lands, earthly relationships, etc., shall receive an hundred-fold and inherit eternal life, Mt 19²⁹, Mk 10¹⁷, Lk 18¹⁸. (3) The sheep in the parable of the Sheep and the Goats (Mt 25³⁴), *i.e.* those who have shown mercy to the weak and suffering, and whose service has been accepted by Christ as done to Himself, shall inherit the Kingdom prepared for them from the beginning of the world. But, on the other hand, no fornicator or unclean person or covetous man, who is an idolater, hath any inheritance in the Kingdom of God and of Christ (Eph 5⁵). See also INHERITANCE.

C. H. PRICHARD.

HELL.—See ESCHATOLOGY, GEHENNA, and the following article.

HELL (DESCENT INTO).—During the 16th cent. the Descent of Christ into Hades was made the subject of acrimonious debates. Though commentators still differ, they discuss the subject in a more peaceable spirit, and offer some hope of future agreement on the main question. We must review—(1) the evidence of the NT, (2) early Christian tradition, to explain (3) the insertion of such teaching in Creeds and Articles of Religion. We may then (4) summarize the history of the controversy in modern times.

1. The evidence of the NT.—It is important to distinguish between the bare statement of the Descent as a fact in the history of our Lord as the Son of Man, which is acknowledged by all who believe that He truly died, and any theory of His mission in the unseen world, which can claim acceptance only after careful scrutiny of incidental references to it in the NT supported by the independent testimony of the earliest Christian tradition.

Hades (Ἄιδης), corresponding to the Heb. *Sheol*, which in the AV of the OT is rendered by 'hell,' means both in the LXX and in the NT the abode of departed spirits. This was the general meaning of the word 'hell,' the *unseen, hidden* place which is the abode of the dead.

In the OT a sense of gloom and unreality was felt about the lot of the spirits of men taken away from the light and activity of earthly life. At first no distinction was supposed to exist in that shadowy realm between good and bad any more than between king and subject. But in NT times such ideas had grown up, and our Lord sanctioned current belief when in the parable of Dives and Lazarus (Lk 16¹⁹⁻³¹) He contrasted happiness in the society of Abraham with misery 'in torments.' This agrees with His promise to the penitent thief (23⁴³) : 'To-day shalt thou be with me in Paradise.' St. Peter in his first sermon (Ac 2²⁴⁻³¹) quotes Ps 16¹⁰ and explains the words, 'Thou wilt not leave my soul in Hades,' as a prophecy of the Resurrection of Christ, which received no fulfilment in the

case of David. He distinctly implies that Christ's soul passed into Hades at His death.

St. Paul (Ro 10⁷), adapting Dt 30¹³, teaches the same truth inferring that it is not necessary to search the depth, since Christ is risen from the dead. He regards the Descent as the preparation for the Ascension, Eph 4⁹ ' Now this, He ascended, what is it but that he also descended into the lower parts of the earth ?' In the LXX rendering of Ps 62¹⁰ (63⁹), this phrase, τὰ κατώτατα τῆς γῆς, is referred to Hades. It is therefore probable that St. Paul uses it in the same sense.* Obedience even unto death secured for the Lord the sovereignty of the underworld ; His descent was the pledge of His lordship over it (Ph 2¹⁰).

The famous passage 1 P 3¹⁸⁻²⁰ (cf. 4⁶) introduces the question of the object of the Descent : ' Because Christ also suffered for sins once, the righteous for the unrighteous, that he might bring us to God ; being put to death in the flesh, but quickened in the spirit ; in which also he went and preached unto the spirits in prison, which aforetime were disobedient, when the long-suffering of God waited in the days of Noah, while the ark was a preparing'; 4⁶ ' For unto this end was the gospel preached even to the dead, that they might be judged according to men in the flesh, but live according to God in the spirit.'

The earliest Christian tradition, which was probably independent of this passage, certainly supports the interpretation that Christ preached to the spirits of the men and women who were drowned in the Flood. Not until the time of St. Augustine was any other interpretation offered. The Apostle is endeavouring to encourage his readers in Christlike patience under persecution. Christ died, the just for the unjust, but His death in the flesh was followed by quickening in the spirit. Therefore we need not fear death, which will bring us freedom from sin and increase of spiritual energy. The reference which follows (v. ²²) to the Ascension suggests that this preaching took place after Christ's death, and not that Christ in Noah preached to the men of Noah's time.

In view of modern interpretations, however, we must enter further into detail. πνεύματα in the NT generally refers to angels (Ac 23⁸), but it refers also to spirits of the dead (He 12²³, cf. Lk 24³⁷⁻³⁹). And 1 P 4⁶ proves that this is the sense here.†

Some critics suppose that the preaching was to the fallen angels mentioned in 2 P 2⁴, Jude ⁶ ; according to Baur, after Christ's death ; according to Spitta, before the Incarnation. This view is regarded by Charles (art. ' Eschatology' in *Encyc. Bibl.*) as the only possible alternative. But Charles holds that Christ preached a gospel of redemption between His death and His resurrection. Salmond thinks that the key may be found in a non-canonical Jewish book. Others, again, think that Enoch was regarded as an incarnation of the Messiah, and that the passage refers to his preaching. But as Clemen says (*Niedergefahren*, p. 131), while we hear in the Book of Enoch (12⁴ff· 13⁸ 14¹ff·) of a preaching of punishment to fallen angels, we hear nothing of a preaching of salvation to the souls of men.

Perhaps the most extraordinary interpretation of all is that which Clemen quotes from Cramer. An unknown person, in possession of 1 and 2 Pet., is supposed to have been reminded by v. ²² of a former ὑποταγή of angels, and therefore on the basis of 2 P 2⁴· with which he compared Jude ⁶· ¹⁴ and

---

* Some commentators explain the words as contrasting the earth beneath with the heavens above, and refer them to the Incarnation when Christ descended to the earth.

† The tense of εὐαγγελίσθη shows that the preaching was regarded as a completed act in the past.

also the Book of Enoch, is supposed to have written in the margin: Ἐνὼχ τοῖς ἐν φυλακῇ πνεύμασιν πορευθεὶς ἐκήρυξεν, κ.τ.λ., understanding πνεύμασιν of angels and ἐκήρυξεν of a *concio damnatoria*. Some one else at a later time, referring the first word to the souls of the departed and the latter to the preaching of salvation, reading ΕΝΩΚ for ΕΝΩΧ, and this again for ἐν ᾧ καί, took the whole into the text after v.[18]!

Such speculations are absurd. On the other hand, it is reasonable to explain the ἐκήρυξεν of the one passage by the εὐαγγελίσθη of the other, to maintain that repentance was offered, rejecting the suggestion that Christ preached only to the righteous, or to those who had repented at the moment of death, or to some the gospel and to others damnation.

If it is asked, Why should only the generation of Noah profit by it? we can say that they were typical sinners, cut off in their sins, whose fate was questioned at that time. Bigg shows that 'it is possible that St. Peter is here expressing in a modified form a belief which was current in the Jewish schools.' Certain passages in the Book of Enoch seem to mean that the antediluvian sinners have a time of repentance allowed them between the first judgment (the Deluge) and the final judgment; *e.g.* 69[26] 'There was great joy among them because the name of the Son of Man was revealed unto them,' *Bereshith Rabba*: (a) 'But when they that are bound, they that are in Gehinnom, saw the light of the Messiah, they rejoiced to receive Him'; (b) 'This is that which stands written: "We shall rejoice and exult in Thee." When? When the captives climb up out of hell, and the Shekinah at their head.'

We may hope that research will yet further enlighten us on these points. Enough has been said to prove that, in the words of Professor Charles (art. cited):

'These passages in 1 Peter are of extreme value. They attest the achievement of the final stage in the moralization of Shĕōl. The first step in this moralization was taken early in the 2nd cent. B.C., when it was transferred into a place of moral distinctions, having been originally one of merely social or national distinctions. This moralization, however, was very inadequately carried out. What they were on entering Shĕōl, that they continued to be till the final judgment. From the standpoint of a true theism can we avoid pronouncing this conception mechanical and unethical? It precludes moral change in moral beings who are under the rule of a perfectly moral being.'

2. Early Christian tradition.—The belief that Christ's descent into Hades changed in some way the condition of the faithful departed meets us in the earliest Christian tradition.

Ignatius (A.D. 115), writing to the Magnesians (c. ix.), says: 'Even the prophets, being His disciples, were expecting Him as their teacher through the Spirit. And for this cause He whom they rightly awaited, when He came, raised them from the dead.'

Justin Martyr, in his *Dialogue with Trypho* (c. 72) accuses the Jews of cutting out the following passage from Jeremiah: 'The Lord God remembered His dead people of Israel, who lay in the graves, and descended to preach to them His own salvation.' Irenæus quotes this passage both from Isaiah (in iii. 22) and from Jeremiah (in iv. 36), and (in iv. 55) without naming the author. It is probably a fragment from some Jewish Apocalypse. Irenæus (iv. 42) also quotes a presbyter 'who had heard it from those who had seen the Apostles and from those who had been their disciples,' as saying that 'the Lord descended to the underworld, preaching His advent there also, and declaring remission of sins received by those who believe in Him.'

Tertullian (*de Anima*, c. 55) taught that Christ 'in Hades underwent the law of human death; nor did He ascend to the heights of heaven, until He descended to the lower parts of the earth, that there He might make patriarchs and prophets sharers of His life.'

We may even claim the heretic Marcion as a witness to this widespread tradition, though in his view, according to Irenæus (I. xxvii. 3), it was Cain and the Sodomites and other sinners who were released by the Lord from Hades.

The apocryphal *Gospel of Peter*, which may be dated possibly from about A.D. 165, contains the following passage: 'They see three men coming forth from the tomb, two of them supporting the other, and a cross following them; and the head of the two reached to heaven; but that of Him who was led by them overpassed the heavens. And they heard a voice from the heavens

saying, Hast thou preached to them that sleep? and a response was heard from the cross, Yea.'

The apocryphal *Gospel of Nicodemus*, a name given in the 13th cent. to two much older books, the *Acts of Pilate* and the *Descent into Hell*, tells the same story of the two brothers with a considerable amount of dramatic power.

Clement of Alexandria is the first Christian writer who brings the passage in 1 Peter into connexion with the tradition that Christ's Descent benefited OT saints. He taught that the heathen, as well as the Jews, shared in the revelation made to the souls in Hades. He quotes Hermas (*Sim.* ix. 16), who taught that the Apostles and first teachers of the gospel, when they entered into rest, preached to the souls in Hades. Clement (*Strom.* ii. 9, p. 452) explains the passage as including righteous heathens as well as Jews, though it is not clear that Hermas himself contemplated such an application of his words. The example quoted by St. Peter appeared to him to be only one example of a far-reaching law (*Strom.* vi. 6).

Origen seems to have been the first to suggest that, since the coming of Christ, the souls of the faithful can go at once to Paradise instead of Hades, regarding Paradise as an intermediate state (*in Reg. Hom.* 2). In his treatise against Celsus (ii. 43), to the scoff, 'You will not surely say that Christ, when He failed to persuade the living, went down to Hades to persuade those who dwell there?' he replies: 'His soul, stript of the body, did there hold converse with other souls that were in like manner stript, that He might there convert those who were capable of instruction, or were otherwise in ways known to Him fit for it.'

Athanasius speaks of the warders at the gates of Hell 'cowering in fear at the presence of the Lord,' quoting in this connexion Mt 27[54]. He thinks (*de Sal. Aduent.* 9) of 'the soul of Adam as held fast under the sentence of death, and crying to his Lord evermore, and of those who had pleased God, and had been justified by the law of nature, as mourning and crying with him,' till God in His mercy revealed the mystery of redemption. He quotes 1 P 3[19] in connexion with the Descent (*Ep. ad Epict.* 5).

The later Fathers, while they regarded Hades as a place of rest for the just, regarded Paradise as something better. Both Ambrose (*de Fide ad Gratian.* iv. 1) and Jerome (*Com. in Eccles.* c. iii.) followed Origen on this line of thought. This notion became the germ of the mediæval doctrine of the *Limbus Patrum*.

Cyril of Jerusalem (*Cat.* iv.) classed the doctrine of the Descent among the ten necessary dogmas, interpreting it as designed for the redemption of the just. 'Could you wish,' he asks, 'that the living should enjoy His grace, and that the holy dead should not share in freedom?' Having named OT saints, he explains John the Baptist's question 'Art thou he that should come?' as referring to the Descent. In this opinion he was followed by Rufinus.

Hilary of Poitiers (on Ps 119[82]) speaks of the souls of the faithful as knowing, on the witness of the Apostle Peter, that when the Lord went down into Hades, words of comfort were preached even to those who were in prison and were formerly unbelieving in the days of Noah. It is interesting to add that the Venerable Bede quoted the words, without naming the author, in order to condemn them, on the ground that the Catholic faith taught only the release of the faithful.

It was reserved for Augustine to give a new interpretation to St. Peter's words. In his earlier books he accepts the current teaching, but confuses Hades and Gehenna. In *de Gen. ad litt.* xii. 63, he says that there is reason for believing that the soul of Christ descended to the regions where sinners are punished, that He might release from torment those whom He, in His righteous judgment, which is hidden from us, found worthy to be loosed.

In his letter to Euodius, Bp. of Uzala, on the right interpretation of 1 P 3[19], as Bp. Horsley puts it, 'he perplexes himself with questions.' Why, out of all the tens of thousands who had died before the coming of Christ, some at least, though heathen, penitent and believing, did He bestow the knowledge of the gospel on those only who had perished in the Flood? He accepts the common belief that Adam was released. He notes that some believed this of Abel, Seth, Noah, and other patriarchs. Still confusing Hades with Gehenna, he asks, How could Abraham's bosom be a synonym for Paradise? Were the patriarchs worse off than Abraham? If they were at rest, how could they be benefited by Christ's descent into Hades? What was done for the disobedient of Noah's time should be done for all who died in ignorance before or since. But the idea that a man might believe after death would weaken the appeal of Christian preaching to the 'terrors of the Lord.' Not able to believe in salvation without Baptism, he cuts the knot of the difficulty by denying that the words of St. Peter had anything to do with the descent of Christ into Hades. Christ preached in spirit in the days of Noah as in Galilee in the days of His flesh. Plumptre truly says: 'he leaves all the questions which he had started as to the descent itself unanswered.' Finally (*de Heres.* 79), he reckoned it a heresy to believe that Christ cleared Hell of all the souls that were then in torment.

3. Creeds and Articles of Religion.—At the end of the 4th cent., Rufinus, commenting on the clause 'descended into hell' in the Creed of his native city of Aquileia, noted that it was not contained in the Creed of the Church of Rome or in Eastern Creeds. This is true of Baptismal Creeds, but not of others. The words had found a place in three confessions of faith put forward by Arian Synods at Sirmium, Nice, and Constantinople.

Sirmium, A.D. 359.	Nice, A.D. 359.	Constantinople, A.D. 360.
καὶ εἰς τὰ καταχθόνια κατελθόντα, καὶ τὰ ἐκεῖσε οἰκονομήσαντα· ὃν πυλωροὶ ᾅδου ἰδόντες ἔφριξαν.	καὶ ταφέντα καὶ εἰς τὰ καταχθόνια κατελθόντα· ὃν αὐτὸς ὁ ᾅδης ἐτρόμαξε.	καὶ ταφέντα καὶ εἰς τὰ καταχθόνια κατεληλυθότα· ὅντινα καὶ αὐτὸς ὁ ᾅδης ἔπτηξεν.

It is interesting to compare also the recently discovered 'Faith of St. Jerome,' which contains the words 'descended into hell, trod down the sting of death.' It has been found by Dom G. Morin, O.S.B., in some four MSS, and is probably the Confession of Faith which Jerome notes in one of the letters he had drawn up for Cyril of Jerusalem. This 'Faith' contains elements which may have been drawn from his Baptismal Creed of Pannonia. In like manner it is possible that the Sirmium Creed, quoted above, at this point quoted the Baptismal Creed of the district, since Sirmium is in the south-east corner of Pannonia. But it seems that the Creed was drawn up mainly by Mark, Bp. of Arethusa in Palestine; and there are traces of the influence of Cyril of Jerusalem elsewhere in this document. The doctrine was one on which he felt strongly; and, therefore, in default of further evidence as to the Pannonian Creed, it is safer to trace to his influence the occurrence of the words in the Creed of Sirmium, on which the Creeds of Nice and Constantinople are dependent.

As regards the interpretation put on the clause in the Creed of Aquileia, Pearson is incorrect when he suggests that Rufinus merely regarded it as equivalent to 'buried,' which was omitted. The Creed certainly contained the word 'buried,' and Rufinus was at pains to show that this word in the Eastern Creeds, as in the Roman, included the idea of a descent into Hades. Swete (p. 61) suggests that Rufinus had lost the clue to the interpretation of the clause, and that the addition was made long before his time, possibly to meet the Docetic tendency of the latter part of the 2nd century. The difficulty about this suggestion is that the Docetic apocryphal Gospel of Peter, as we have seen, distinctly teaches belief in the descent. The present writer would rather regard pseudo-Peter as witnessing to the common belief of the 2nd cent., and explain the addition in the Aquileian Creed as derived from the ordinary catechetical teaching, of which it may have been as 'necessary a dogma' then in Aquileia as in Jerusalem in the 4th century.

In the time of Rufinus it might seem more necessary to insist on such teaching in view of the rise of the heresy of Apollinaris, who denied that the Lord had a human soul. But Rufinus himself gives no hint of this. There is more reason to connect the occurrence of the clause in the so-called Athanasian writing of the 5th cent., with opposition to Apollinarianism, because the author obviously had that heresy in view. There is no proof, however, that the clause had yet passed into any Gallican Creed. By the end of the century we find it in the Creed of Cæsarius of Arles, and in the century following in the Creeds of Venantius Fortunatus of Poitiers and of the Spanish Bishop Martin of Bracara. Thus it passed into the Received Text of the Western Creed.

During the Middle Ages the idea of the 'Harrowing of Hell' was made popular by the Gospel of Nicodemus, and as the theme of Mystery Plays, and at a later time by Christian Art. Discussion seldom arose. But the opinion of Abelard that the soul of Christ entered the underworld only virtually and not substantially, was condemned by the Council of Sens (1140) and Pope Innocent II. It found favour with Durandus and Pico della Mirandola, whose names may suffice to show that the debate was not extinct in the 15th century. During the Reformation period, controversy began to wax fierce, and was reflected in some of the more famous Articles of Religion. In the Confession of Augsburg the bare fact of the Descent is stated, but the Geneva Catechism taught that the Descent meant only the terrible anguish with which the soul of Christ was tried. The Catechism of the Church of the Palatinate explained that Christ descended in order that the Christian in all his mental and spiritual agonies might know that there was One who had borne them and could sympathize with them. These Catechisms reflect the opinion of prominent leaders of thought. Luther, in his Table Talk (ccvi.), spoke of the laying of the devil in chains as the purpose of the Descent. His view fluctuated, but in his Com. on Hos 6[1] he wrote that Peter clearly teaches that Christ preached to some who, in the time of Noah, had not believed, and who waited for the long-suffering of God—that is, who hoped that God would not enter into so strict a judgment with all flesh—to the intent that they might acknowledge that their sins were forgiven through the sacrifice of Christ.

It was Calvin (Institut. ii. 16) who taught the revolting doctrine that the Descent means that in His suffering on earth, in Gethsemane and on the Cross, Christ suffered all the horrors of hell. To which Pearson's words are a sufficient reply: 'There is a worm that never dieth which could not lodge within His breast; that is, a remorse of conscience, seated in the soul, for what that soul hath done; but such a remorse of conscience could not be in Christ.' Zwingli (Fidei chr. exp., art. 'de Christo,' 7) taught that when Christ died the weight of His Redemption penetrated to the Underworld.

The Westminster Standards practically ignore the question of the Descent. The Confession of Faith is wholly silent, and so is the Shorter Catechism. The only allusion to the subject is in the Larger Catechism, where the answer to Question 50 runs: 'Christ's humiliation after His death consisted in His being buried, and continuing in the state of the dead, and under the power of death till the third day; which hath been otherwise expressed in these words, He descended into hell.'

Bishop Alley of Exeter, in a paper drawn up for the Convocation of 1553 wrote: 'There have been in my diocese great invections between the preachers.' He asked th t some certainty might be set concerning this doctrine. Perhaps this explains the form which was given to the third of the Forty-two Articles of 1553.

'As Christ died and was buried for us: so also it is to be believed that He went down into hell. For the body lay in the sepulchre until the resurrection: but His ghost departing from Him was with the ghosts that were in prison or in hell, and did preach to the same, as the place of St. Peter doth testify.'

Bishop Alley's 'hope of certainty' was not fulfilled, and in 1563 the Elizabethan revisers, with rare wisdom, struck out the last clause.

The Roman Catechism * speaks of the release of holy and just men as the purpose of the Descent, of the imparting of the fruit of the Passion, and of the Beatific Vision.

4. Summary of the controversy in modern times.—We may begin this section with the names of Pearson and Hammond, who agreed in teaching that the only meaning of St. Peter's words was that Christ by His Holy Spirit inspired the preaching of Noah.

Hammond (ad loc.) writes: 'The spirits in the prison are those souls of men that lay so sheathed, so useless and unprofitable in their bodies, im-

---

* Cat. Rom. 95.

mersed so deep in calamity as not to perform any service to God, who inspired and placed them there.' He quotes Is 42⁷ 49⁹ 61¹ to prove that elsewhere it is 'a figurative speech to express wicked men.' 'By His Spirit is evidently meant that Divine power by which He was raised from the dead after His crucifixion.' We have already noted the objections to this interpretation, and also the fact that Pearson on this point confuses Hades and Gehenna. He writes, indeed, 'less lucidly than is his wont,' but in regard of the Descent regarded as a fact his final summary strikes no uncertain note.

'I give a full and undoubting assent unto this as to a certain truth, that when all the sufferings of Christ were finished on the Cross, and His soul was separated from His body, though His body were dead, yet His soul died not; and though it died not, yet it underwent the condition of the souls of such as die; and being [i.e. since] He died in the similitude of a sinner, His soul went to the place where the souls of men are kept who die for their sins, and so did wholly undergo the law of death.'

Barrow taught to the same effect (Serm. xxviii.): 'If we do thus interpret our Saviour's *descent into hell*, for His soul's going into the common receptacle and mansion of souls, we shall so doing be sure not substantially to mistake.' He adds: 'I cannot well be at the pain to consider or examine those conceits, which pretend to acquaint us why and to what effect our Saviour descended into hell.' This almost contemptuous refusal to discuss the passages in St. Peter is partly explained by the gaps in the line of evidence of early Christian tradition which was known at that time. Coming from a man of Barrow's calibre, it has probably had great weight.

On the other hand, Jeremy Taylor,[*] while he avoids any explanation of St. Peter's reference to the Deluge, maintains the Patristic view that Christ improved the condition of holy souls.

'And then it was that Christ made their condition better: for though still it be a place of relation in order to something beyond it, yet the term and object of their hope is changed: they sate in the regions of darkness, expecting that great promise made to Adam and the patriarchs, the promise of the Messias; but when He that was promised came, He "preached to the spirits in prison," He communicated to them the mysteries of the gospel, the secrets of the kingdom, the things hidden from eternal ages, and taught them to look up to the glories purchased by His passion, and made the term of their expectation be His second coming, and the objects of their hope the glories of the beatific vision. . . . But now it was that in the dark and undiscerned mansions there was a scene of the greatest joy and the greatest horror represented, which yet was known since the first falling of the morning stars. Those holy souls, whom the prophet Zechariah calls "prisoners of hope," lying in the lake where there is no water, that is, no constant stream of joy to refresh their present condition (yet supported with certain showers and gracious visitations from God and illuminations of their hope); now that they saw their Redeemer come to change their condition, and to improve it into the neighbourhoods of glory and clearer revelations, must needs have the joy of intelligent and beatified understandings, of redeemed captives, of men forgiven after the sentence of death, of men satisfied after a tedious expectation, enjoying and seeing their Lord, whom, for so many ages, they had expected. But the accursed spirits, seeing the darkness of their prison shine with a new light, and their empire invaded, and their retirements of horror discovered, wondered how a man durst venture thither, or, if he were a God, how he should come to die.'

Bishop Horsley's sermon on 1 P 3¹⁹ at the end of the 18th cent. is the next important contribution to the subject. He regretted the alteration of the Third Article of 1563. He found it difficult to believe that 'of the millions who died in the Flood all died impenitent.' He taught that Christ 'certainly preached neither repentance nor faith, for the preaching of either comes too late for the departed soul.' He faced the great difficulty why only this one class of penitents should be mentioned, having 'observed in some parts of Scripture an anxiety, if the expression may be allowed, of the sacred writers to convey distinct intimations that the antediluvian race is not uninterested in the redemption and the final retribution.' The following words also deserve quotation, for they go to

[*] ed. Eden, ii. 718, 720.

the root of the matter. 'If the clear assertions of Holy Writ are to be discredited on account of difficulties which may seem to the human mind to arise out of them, little will remain to be believed in revealed or even in what is called natural religion.'

About the same time, Dr. Hey, Norrisian Professor at Cambridge, gave in his lectures a succinct account of the history of the doctrine, and discussed the difficulty of using the metaphor of descent in popular language (3rd ed. p. 654).

There is an excellent survey of the literature of the subject down to the middle of the last century in Dean Alford's *Greek Testament*. Both he and Bishop Wordsworth accepted the Patristic view that Christ preached salvation to the disembodied spirits of those drowned in the Flood if found penitent. Thus light is thrown on 'one of the darkest enigmas of Divine justice.' Bishop Harold Browne expounded the Article to the same effect, and has been followed recently by Bishop Gibson. But not all writers were equally bold. Bishop Harvey Goodwin was content with what was practically Pearson's position. Bishop Westcott (*Historic Faith*, p. 77) feared to say more on 'a mystery where our thought fails us and Scripture is silent.' Surely this is too dogmatic in face of the great consensus of opinion which interprets 1 P 3¹⁹ literally.

There is a full account of modern German literature on this subject in Clemen's *Niedergefahren zu den Toten*. He interprets 1 P 3¹⁹ as referring to human spirits, and builds on it an argument in favour of 'the larger hope,' though he does not commit himself to any theory of Universal Restitution. He makes much use of English books, especially Dean Plumptre's *The Spirits in Prison*.

This survey of the whole course of the controversy leads to the conclusion that eventually agreement will be reached as to the exegesis of the passage in 1 Peter. The weighty authority of Professor Charles may be invoked to prove that the interpretation which accepts Christ's mission to the dead fits in with our fuller knowledge of contemporary Jewish literature. It throws light on one of the darkest enigmas of the Divine justice. At the same time full justice will be done to the early Christian tradition that in some way or other Christ benefited the souls of the faithful departed. But it must be admitted that the bare statement of the Apostles' Creed asserts only that Christ's soul passed into the condition which our souls will enter at death, sanctifying every condition of human existence. Harnack writes that 'the clause is too weak to maintain its ground beside the others, as equally independent and authoritative,' but, as Swete (p. 62) says, he fails to point out in what the weakness lies, while 'to us it appears to possess in a very high degree the strength which comes from primitive simplicity and a wise reserve.'

Thus the consensus of theological opinion justifies the teaching of the poet of the Christian Year:[*]

'Sleep'st Thou indeed? or is Thy spirit fled　
　At large among the dead?　
Whether in Eden bowers Thy welcome voice　
　Wake Abraham to rejoice,　
Or in some drearier scene Thine eye controls　
　The thronging band of souls;　
That, as Thy blood won earth, Thine agony　
　Might set the shadowy world from sin and sorrow free.'

LITERATURE.—C. Bigg, *Com. on Epistles of St. Peter and St. Jude*, Clark, 1901; C. Clemen, *Niedergefahren zu den Toten*, Giessen, 1900; Bishop Gibson, *The Thirty-nine Articles*[2], Methuen, 1898; Bishop Harold Browne, *The Thirty-nine Articles*[2], 1854; Bishop Pearson, *Expos. of the Apostles' Creed*, ed. Burton[3], 1847; E. H. Plumptre, *The Spirits in Prison*, Isbister, 1885; S. D. F. Salmond, *Christian Doct. of Immortality*[5], Clark, 1903; F. Spitta, *Christi Predigt an die Geister*, 1890; H. B. Swete, *The Apostles' Creed*, Cambridge, 1899.　　A. E. BURN.

[*] J. Keble, *Easter Eve*.

HELLENISTS.—See GRECIANS.

HEM OF GARMENT.—This is the AV translation of κράσπεδον in Mt 9²⁰ 14³⁶ (of touching the hem of Jesus' garment with a view to healing). In these places, as on its occurrence elsewhere (Mt 23⁵, Mk 6⁵⁶, Lk 8⁴⁴), RV adopts the rendering 'border.' See art. BORDER.

HEN.—See ANIMALS, p. 64ᵃ.

HERB.—In modern botanical science, 'herb' is a well-defined term, and is applied to plants whose stem dies down annually. In the Bible it is used in a popular sense, being employed to translate several Hebrew and Greek words of varying significance. In the NT it is (except in He 6⁷, where the original has βοτάνη) the rendering of λάχανα (Mt 13³², Mk 4³², Ro 14²) or λάχανον (Lk 11⁴²), which denotes garden-herbs or vegetables. Many of these, such as lettuce, parsley, mint, etc., are in constant use to the present day. Delitzsch (*Heb. NT*) renders this word by ירק, which means 'green herbs' (cf. Dt 11¹⁰, Pr 15¹⁷). The other term, βοτάνη, means 'pasture,' but is evidently used (*l.c.*) of herbage in general, including cereals. Delitzsch's translation is עֶשֶׂב, 'ēsebh, which has the same signification.   HUGH DUNCAN.

HERMON.—A mountain on the north-eastern border of Palestine, the culminating point of the range of Anti-Lebanon, rising to an elevation of 9200 ft. above the sea. Its dome-like summit, usually covered with snow till late in summer, can be seen from almost every part of Palestine. Jesus in His youth must have often seen it from the hill west of Nazareth, and, during His ministry, from the Sea of Galilee. It is not mentioned by name in the Gospels, but is generally believed to be the 'high mountain' of Mt 17¹, Mk 9², and the 'mountain' of Lk 9²⁸ where the Transfiguration took place. This was probably not on the summit, which could be reached only by long and hard climbing, but on one of the elevated platforms on the southern slope. That Hermon, rather than Tabor (on which there was then a fortified city), is the 'high mountain' referred to, seems clear from the fact that the conversation (Mt 16²¹⁻²⁸) which preceded the Transfiguration by six days was closely connected with Peter's confession ; and this occurred at Cæsarea Philippi (Mt 16¹³⁻¹⁶), which stood just at the base of Hermon by the springs of Jordan. See also art. TRANSFIGURATION.

LITERATURE.—For description of Hermon, see Robinson, *BRP* iii. 344, 357 ; Stewart, *Land of Israel*, 296–301 ; Conder, *Tent-Work*, ch. viii.; *SWP* ('Jerusalem' Volume, Appendix, and Volume of Special Papers).   W. W. MOORE.

HEROD (Ἡρῴδης).—The rise of the Herodian dynasty * to the throne of the Hasmonæan priest-kings, begun by Antipater the Idumæan, and realized by his second son, Herod the Great,† was closely connected with the ascendency of Roman power in Palestine. Antipas or Antipater, the grandfather of Herod, had indeed been appointed governor of Idumæa by Alexander Jannæus (*Ant.* XIV. i. 3), but it was not until after the death of Alexandra (B.C. 67) that Antipater, who had succeeded his father Antipas in Idumæa, found opportunity to advance his interests in the dissensions between Hyrcanus, the legal but weak heir to the throne in Jerusalem, and the younger but more vigorous Aristobulus. Allying himself with Hyr-

* On the origin of the Herodian family, cf. *Ant.* XIV. i. 3 ; *BJ* I. vi. 2 ; Strabo, xvi. 2 ; Euseb. *HE* i. 7. 11, *Chron.*, ed. Schoene, ii. 134, 138 ; Epiph. *Hær.* xx. 1 ; Derenbourg, *Hist. de la Pal.* 154 ; and Schürer, *GJV* ³ i. 292, n. 3.

† On the title ὁ μίγας cf. Ewald, *HI* v. 418, n. 4 ; Madden, *Coins*, 105, n. 1.

canus, Antipater secured the aid of the Arabian king Aretas to establish his candidate in the government. Thereupon appeals were made by Hyrcanus and Aristobulus to the Roman general Scaurus, who had been sent by Pompey to Damascus. The Roman power, thus appealed to, at first favoured Aristobulus, but eventually, after Pompey had taken Jerusalem in B.C. 63, made Hyrcanus high priest (*Ant.* XIV. iv. 4 ; *BJ* I. vii. 6), and committed the administration to Scaurus, who in turn was succeeded by Gabinius. Antipater, however, proved himself useful to the Romans, both in the government and in their military operations against the Arabs, and also against the Hasmonæans, Aristobulus and his sons Alexander and Antigonus. He thus acquired considerable political influence (*Ant.* XIV. vi. 4, viii. 1 ; *BJ* I. viii. 7 ; cf. Schürer, *GJV* ³ i. 343, n. 14). After the battle of Pharsalus (B.C. 48) and the death of Pompey, Cæsar confirmed Hyrcanus in the high priesthood, and made him ethnarch. Upon Antipater he conferred Roman citizenship and constituted him procurator of Judæa (*Ant.* XIV. viii. 3, 5, ἐπίτροπος in the sense of ἐπιμελητής ; cf. Wellhausen, *IJG*⁴ 316, n. 2). Soon afterwards (B.C. 47) Antipater appointed his eldest son Phasael governor of Jerusalem, and committed the administration of Galilee to his second son Herod, á young man about twenty-five years of age (*Ant.* XIV. ix. 2 ; the transmitted text reads πέντε καὶ δέκα, but is conjecturally emended by Dindorf and Bekker to read πέντε καὶ εἴκοσι ; cf. Schürer, i. 348, n. 30 ; Grätz, *Hist.* 77, reads 'twenty'). The present article is concerned only with the Herods of the Gospels.

1. Herod the Great.—Among the first acts of Herod's administration of Galilee was the suppression of a band of robbers * that harassed his country and parts of Syria (*Ant.* XIV. ix. 2 ; *BJ* I. x. 5). These he captured, and their captain, a certain Hezekias, he slew, along with many of the robbers, —revealing in the energy with which he suppressed disorders a trait of character that even at this time attracted the attention of the Roman governor of Syria, Sextus Cæsar, and that subsequently made him an acceptable ally of the Romans. This act, however, brought Herod under the suspicion of the leaders at Jerusalem, who persuaded Hyrcanus that Herod should be summoned before the Sanhedrin for trial for violation of the national law in putting Hezekias to death without trial. Herod obeyed the summons, but took care to have a sufficient bodyguard to accompany him. At first the members of the Sanhedrin were overawed by such a show of force. They were recalled to a proper sense of their duty by the courageous words of scornful rebuke spoken by Sameas the Pharisee (*Ant.* XIV. ix. 4 ; *BJ* I. x. 5).† When the Sanhedrin was about to condemn Herod, Hyrcanus, who had received instructions from Sextus Cæsar to have him acquitted, adjourned the sitting and advised Herod to withdraw from Jerusalem. This he did, returning to Damascus. When he had been appointed governor of Cœle-Syria by Sextus Cæsar, he threatened Jerusalem with an army ; but, having so far satisfied his anger, he withdrew, on the advice of his father Antipater and his brother Phasael.

After the murder of Cæsar (15 Mar. B.C. 44), and

* Grätz (*Hist.* 78, less distinctly, 'All true patriots mourned ') and Derenbourg (160 ff.) regard these robbers as patriots, the predecessors of the Zealots, Judas the Galilæan being the son of Hezekias (*Ant.* XVII. x. 5 ; *BJ* II. iv. 1 ; Ac 5³⁷). I. Broydé (*Jewish Encyc.* vi. 356) calls them 'a band of fanatics, who had attacked heathen cities and robbed caravans' (cf. also Wellhausen⁴, 317).

† Cf. *Ant.* xv. i. 1, where Pollio is said to have made this speech, and Sameas is called his disciple. In Talmudic tradition (cf. Derenbourg, 147 ff.) Sameas is called Simeon ben Shetah, identified by Derenbourg with Shemaia, who, with Abtalion (Pollio), was, he thinks, at that time at the head of the Sanhedrin (similarly Gratz, *Hist.* 79, and I. Broydé. *Jewish Encyc.* vi. 356 ; cf. also Schürer³, ii. 358 f.).

the poisoning of Antipater (43),—apparently with the knowledge, if not the consent and participation, of Hyrcanus (*Ant.* XIV. xi. 3, 6; cf. Wellhausen[4], 319, n. 1, 327, n. 3),—Herod's fortunes reached their lowest ebb. Antony, indeed, while he was in the East, made Herod and Phasael tetrarchs (*Ant.* XIV. xiii. 1; *BJ* I. xii. 5); but not long afterwards, Antigonus, with the help of the Parthians, gained possession of Jerusalem, capturing Phasael and Hyrcanus. Phasael killed himself; and Hyrcanus, after his ears had been cut off, was taken by the Parthians to Babylon. Herod, who with his family was in Jerusalem, escaped by night, and, after many difficulties, in the midst of which he was on the point of taking his life, came to the fortress Masada. Here he left his family in charge of his brother Joseph and hastened to Rome. Antigonus, in the meantime, had established himself in Jerusalem, where he reigned for three years (B.C. 40–37) as Matthias, the coins of Antigonus bearing the inscription BACIΛEΩC ANTIΓONOU מתתיה כהן נדל חבר יה (cf. Madden, *Coins*, 99 ff.).

In Rome, Herod had little difficulty, with the aid of Antony and the concurrence of Octavius, in convincing the Senate that they would be serving their own interests by making him king of Judæa instead of Antigonus, who had been placed on the throne by the Parthians (*Ant.* XIV. xiv. 4; *BJ* I. xiv. 4). Appointed king by a decree of the Senate (B.C. 40), Herod now had before him the difficult task of conquering his kingdom. He returned to Palestine, raised an army, subdued Joppa, relieved Masada, and was eager to invest Jerusalem. The assistance of the Roman forces under Ventidius and Silo was far from effective; Galilee had to be conquered; it was not until the spring of 37 B.C. that the siege of Jerusalem could be seriously begun. It was during this siege that Herod, having put away his wife Doris and her son Antipater, celebrated in Samaria his marriage with Mariamne,* daughter of Alexander (son of Aristobulus) and Alexandra (daughter of Hyrcanus) (*Ant.* XIV. xv. 14; *BJ* I. xvii. 8; cf. *Ant.* XIV. xii. 1; *BJ* I. xii. 3).

Three months after the siege began, Jerusalem fell (*Ant.* XIV. xvi. 4; *BJ* I. xviii. 2; cf. Sieffert, *PRE*[3] vii. 762, l. 24 ff.). The city was saved from plunder and desecration only by a plentiful use of money on Herod's part. Antigonus surrendered himself to the Romans (*Ant.* XIV. xvi. 2; *BJ* I. xviii. 2), and at Herod's urgent request was beheaded in Antioch (*Ant.* XIV. xvi. 4; *BJ* I. xviii. 3). Herod also had forty-five members of the Sanhedrin slain, but passed over Pollio and Sameas because during the siege they had advised the city to yield to him (*Ant.* XV. i. 2).

Established in his kingdom by force of the Roman arms, and occupying the status of a *rex socius*, Herod fully understood that his continuance in power was dependent on the good-will of Rome and her rulers. Hence, throughout his reign of thirty-four years, he did not fail to cultivate in every possible way friendly relations with his overlords. His government, however, though not without some following among the people, never obtained the cordial support or willing consent of the great majority of its subjects. At the beginning of his reign he treated the Sadducæan aristocracy with severity, made the high priesthood subject to his own appointment, and deprived the Sanhedrin of all political influence. The Essenes and many of the Pharisees refused to

take the oath of allegiance to him or to the Roman emperor. The incipient Zealots or patriotic nationalists, whether gathered in the robber bands of Galilee or cherishing more quietly the old Hasmonæan ideals, were his natural and determined enemies. Herod, moreover, had no natural claims to his throne. Of Idumæan descent, he was in the eyes of his subjects but half-Jew (*Ant.* XIV. xv. 2), and had to endure, not only from his enemies but within the circle of his own family, taunts upon his low origin. Careful though he was not to offend the religious prejudices of the people in some respects,—for Herod was wiser and more cautious than Antiochus Epiphanes,—his whole reign breathed the spirit of Hellenism and pagan secularization so offensive to the Jews. Even his self-denying and efficient provision for the country when visited by famine, or his remission in part of a burdensome taxation, or his magnificent restoration of the Temple, called forth only momentary gratitude in the hearts of the people. Successful at Rome, unsuccessful in Jerusalem, Herod greatly increased the material interests of his country, and by the favour of Rome enlarged its borders. But while he rebuilt the Temple and dedicated it with great splendour and large sacrifices — boasting that he had done what the Hasmonæans were not able to accomplish—he placed above the Temple gate a golden eagle in honour of the Romans, built a theatre, amphitheatre, and hippodrome in or near Jerusalem for Greek plays and heathen games, and in other places erected temples for the cult of the emperor Augustus. He built or restored many cities and fortresses throughout his territory, and constructed a splendid harbour (*Sebastus*) at Strato's Tower, which he enlarged and called Cæsarea. He colonized restless Trachonitis with Jewish warriors from Babylon, and extended his munificence far beyond the bounds of his own country, to Syria, Asia Minor, Rhodes, Greece, and Macedonia. Antony, Cleopatra, Agrippa, and Augustus were entertained by him with royal honours, and in his will he made handsome bequests to his friends of the imperial household in Rome.

It is customary to divide the reign of Herod into three periods. The first extends from his accession in B.C. 37 to the death of the sons of Babas in B.C. 25, when the last male representatives of the Hasmonæan family were removed from his pathway. This period was characterized by the establishment and extension of Herod's power. The principal forces that he had to combat came from the royal family he had supplanted and to which he was allied by marriage. Alexandra, the mother of Mariamne, knew how to enlist the interest of Cleopatra, and Cleopatra had the ear of Antony. The measures adopted by Herod to meet the situation were not of the gentlest kind. He recalled Hyrcanus from Babylon, and though he treated him with every consideration, Josephus attributes to Herod the motive of wishing to get Hyrcanus in his power.* In view of the fact that Hyrcanus could not be appointed to the high priesthood, and that Aristobulus, the brother of Mariamne, was only about seventeen years of age, Herod made Ananel, a Babylonian Jew of priestly family, high priest. This did not please Alexandra, and she appealed to Cleopatra on behalf of her son. Thereupon Herod deposed Ananel and appointed Aristobulus in his stead. But the popularity of the young Hasmonæan aroused Herod's suspicion, and Aristobulus was drowned soon after the feast of Taber-

---

* This conventional spelling is retained here, although Μαριαμμή is adopted in the Greek text, both of Naber and of Niese (though Niese reads in the text of *BJ* I. § 241, Μαριαμήν). The spelling Μαριαμνή is given as a variant by Niese in *Ant.* xv. § 207, but in *BJ* I. § 433 Μαριάμην. In *Ant.* the MS E spells consistently Μαριαμή (except in XVII. § 335, where Μαρίας occurs) as M does in *BJ*.

* Mathews (*Hist. of NT Times*, 118, n. 1) rejects Josephus' account of Herod's motive (cf. also Schürer[3], i. 378; Wellhausen[4], 324; and Woodhouse, *Encyc. Bibl.* ii. 2206, n. 4). On the other hand, cf. Sieffert, *PRE*[3] vii. 762, l. 48 ff., and the indications given above that Hyrcanus was implicated in the death of Antipater.

nacles in the year B.C. 35. At the instance of Cleopatra, who learned of the event from Alexandra, Herod was summoned before Antony to give an account of the death of Aristobulus. Before answering the summons, Herod gave instructions to his uncle Joseph, in whose hands he left the government, that Mariamne should be put to death in the event of an unfavourable issue of his mission. Herod regained the favour of Antony, but had eventually to surrender to Cleopatra one of the most fruitful parts of his territory, the famous palm- and balsam-growing country about Jericho, together with the coast cities from the river Eleutherus to Egypt, with the exception of Tyre and Sidon. On his return from the conference with Antony at Laodicæa (Syrian), Herod learned through his sister Salome, the evil genius of his family troubles, that Joseph had revealed his command to Mariamne. Joseph was put to death, but a fruitful soil for suspicion against Mariamne remained. When Cleopatra, who had accompanied Antony on his expedition to Armenia, returned through Judæa, Herod entertained her; and, although he successfully withstood her charms, he was compelled to rent from her the territory about Jericho, and to guarantee similar payments due to her from the king of Arabia. The debt thus contracted proved to be a bad one, for the king of Arabia was slow in meeting his financial obligations. Hence, when war broke out between Antony and Octavius, and Herod was desirous of giving aid to Antony, Cleopatra, never doubting that Antony would be victor, thwarted Herod's purpose and sent him instead against the Arabians, in the hope that the two kings would destroy one another. Herod at first defeated the Arabians, but finally suffered a severe reverse, through the treacherous intervention of Cleopatra's general Athenio. About this time an earthquake brought great suffering on the people, and Herod's soldiers were discouraged. The Jewish ambassadors sent to the Arabians had been slain, and Herod's condition seemed desperate. His own courage, however, inspired his troops, and a decisive victory was gained over the enemy.

But Herod had scarcely re-established his power when news of the battle of Actium (2nd Sept. B.C. 31) brought him face to face with the crisis of his reign. Before going to Octavius to learn his fate, Herod had the aged Hyrcanus put to death for plotting with the Arabian governor Malchus to escape from Jerusalem.* Placing the government in charge of his brother Pheroras, and leaving his mother and sister at Masada, but Mariamne and Alexandra at Alexandrinum in care of Sohemus, with instructions that Mariamne and her mother should be killed if disaster overtook him,† Herod went to meet Octavius in Rhodes. He appeared before the emperor in royal apparel, laying aside only his diadem. His appeal for favour was based on a frank avowal of his friendship for Antony, and of his desire to aid him at Actium. But Antony had refused to take his advice about Cleopatra, and had fallen. He now offered Octavius the same loyalty and support that he had given Antony. Moreover, Herod had already had opportunity of proving his loyalty to his new master by preventing

Antony's gladiators from passing through his territory to join Antony in Egypt. At the close of the interview Octavius restored Herod's diadem, and confirmed him in his kingdom. In a short time Octavius even enlarged Herod's kingdom, restoring the territory taken from it by Antony for Cleopatra, and a number of cities, such as Gadara, Hippos, Samaria, Gaza, Anthedon, Joppa, and Strato's Tower. This was done in recognition of Herod's aid to the imperial army as it passed into Egypt.

When Herod returned from Rhodes, his old suspicions against Mariamne were aroused by discovering that Sohemus had repeated the folly of Joseph. Sohemus was executed, and soon afterwards Mariamne was tried on the charge of attempting to poison Herod, and put to death about the year B.C. 29. But Herod had loved her with a wild passion. After her death his remorse and an uncontrollable yearning for her (which Byron has finely expressed in one of his *Hebrew Melodies*) quickly brought him to the verge of insanity (cf. also Stephen Phillips, *Herod*). At length, when he fell sick in Samaria, Alexandra sought to gain possession of the fortresses in Jerusalem. But Herod, rousing himself from his stupor, had her put to death (B.C. 28). Costobar also and the sons of Babas were put to death on the evidence of Salome, who revealed the hiding-place of these men of Hasmonæan descent* and partizanship, and the part played by her husband in their protection (B.C. 25). Herod was now well established on his throne, in favour with Augustus, and triumphant over his enemies.

The second period of Herod's reign, extending from B.C. 25 to B.C. 13, was characterized by extension of his kingdom and great building operations. Trachonitis, Batanæa, and Auranitis were given to him by Augustus about B.C. 23 (*Ant.* xv. x. 1; *BJ* I. xx. 4), and to these the tetrarchy of Zenodorus together with the country of Ulatha and Panias was added about three years later (*Ant.* xv. x. 3; *BJ* I. xx. 4; Dio Cass. xlv. 9). During this period many cities were built or beautified by Herod, both in his own territory and in surrounding countries. Fortresses were constructed, and temples in honour of Augustus adorned Samaria (Sebaste), Panias (Cæsarea Philippi), and Strato's Tower (Cæsarea). But the greatest of Herod's works of construction were the harbour at Strato's Tower and the Temple at Jerusalem. The latter, begun about B.C. 19, was partially completed in a year and a half (the inner temple), and the whole brought to a temporary completion in about eight years, when it was formally dedicated, although work was continued on it until the time of Albinus (procurator A.D. 62–64, cf. *Ant.* xv. xi. 5, 6, xx. ix. 7; Jn 2[20]). Herod also built himself a magnificent palace in Jerusalem. Theatre, amphitheatre, and hippodrome were the scenes of plays and games not only in Cæsarea and Jericho, but in Jerusalem. Mercenary troops, aided by spies and strict police regulations, kept the people in subjection. Outlying districts such as Trachonitis were colonized to suppress disturbances. Herod's power was at its height. In his court were men of Greek learning, such as Nicolaus of Damascus and his brother Ptolemy. As a *rex socius*, Herod had the right to issue copper coinage. His friendship with Rome was firmly established. He interested himself in the Jews of the Dispersion, and helped to secure them their rights in Asia Minor. He also made generous provision from his private means to alle-

---

viate the suffering caused by a famine (B.C. 25), and on two occasions remitted part of the people's taxes, one-third in B.C. 20 and one-fourth in B.C. 14. But the glory of his reign and the material splendour of his works were offensive to the religious consciousness of his subjects, and his sporadic acts of unselfishness failed to arouse any permanently cordial response in the people.

The last period of Herod's reign, from B.C. 13 to B.C. 4, was one of family intrigue which formed, as Wellhausen aptly puts it, 'a chapter of court history in true Oriental style.' After the death of Mariamne, Herod had married another Mariamne, daughter of a certain Simon, a priest whom Herod had made high priest. He had also other wives, seven in number. His first wife had been recalled to court. His sister Salome and his mother Cypros had already shown some ability in the gentle art of false suggestion. Herod's brother Pheroras, whom he had made tetrarch of Peræa and Idumæa, was at hand with his wife. There were present also the two heirs to the throne, Alexander and Aristobulus, sons of Mariamne I., both proud of their Hasmonæan descent, possibly a little haughty in their manner, certainly a little unwise in their confidential conversations; having a grievance in the unjust death of their mother, but no protection against its misuse by their enemies; holding their mother's opinion of Herod's kindred,—an opinion shared by Glaphyra, wife of Aristobulus and daughter of Archelaus, king of Cappadocia, and fully reciprocated in kind by Salome and Cypros. If to this we add the villainy of a scoundrel like Euryclus, the presence of Antipater, Herod's eldest son, recalled to court for the purpose of checking presumptuous hopes of succession on the part of Alexander and Aristobulus; and, finally, the suspicious nature of Herod, now made more so by age, and the use of an absolute power over the lives of his subjects to extort evidence by torture,—under such conditions as these, 'where many things were done and more were believed and repeated,' intrigue could hardly fail to ripen into tragedy.

Soon after the return of Alexander and Aristobulus from Rome, where they had been educated, they were suspected of plotting vengeance on Herod for their mother's death, and of entertaining premature hopes of succession to the throne. Herod himself preferred charges against them before the Emperor at Aquileia, but Augustus succeeded in effecting a temporary reconciliation. Subsequently Alexander was arrested, but released through the influence of Archelaus. Gradually, however, the meshes of intrigue closed around the Hasmonæan brothers. Permission was obtained from Augustus to bring them to trial, but the Emperor's suggestions about the constitution of the court were not strictly adhered to. Herod himself appeared as a witness against his sons, and the court condemned them by a majority vote, Saturninus and his sons dissenting. They were strangled at Sebaste (Samaria), and buried at Alexandrinum about the year B.C. 7. Finally, on the death of his brother Pheroras, Herod discovered that Antipater, who had gone to Rome bearing the will of his father, which named him as successor to the throne, was himself implicated in a patricidal plot. Thereupon Herod wrote to Antipater, urging with great solicitude and paternal affection his speedy return. On arriving in Jerusalem, Antipater was brought to trial before Varus, Nicolaus of Damascus appearing to prosecute the case for Herod. And when Antipater failed to clear himself, he was cast into prison, while Herod awaited permission from Augustus to put him to death.

Herod was now grown old. His physical constitution, naturally powerful and robust, began to give way. The hot baths of Callirhoë gave little or no relief to his disorders. It soon became known that he was suffering from an incurable disease, and the signs of popular rejoicing only embittered the last hours of his despotic reign. The stirring of his anger, as on a former occasion, seemed to rouse his waning energy. When the disciples of two popular teachers of the Law in Jerusalem, Judas and Matthias, cut down the golden eagle from the gate of the Temple, Herod promptly returned, and had forty-two of the participants, including their teachers, burned to death. His sufferings now became more intense. A bath in warm oil ordered by his physicians almost killed him, and in a fit of despair he even attempted to take his own life. Josephus also reports that he gave orders that at the moment of his death all the principal men of the country, whom he had gathered in the hippodrome at Jericho, should be put to death, in order that the people might have cause to sorrow at his departure. But this order was never carried out (cf. Wellhausen [4], 345, n. 2). The imprisoned Antipater about this time, thinking that his father was dead, sought to escape; but Herod, learning of it, and having just received authority for his execution from Rome, gave the order for his death. On the fifth day after the death of Antipater, Herod died at Jericho, in March or April of the year B.C. 4, being about seventy years of age, and having reigned thirty-seven years since his appointment by the Roman Senate and thirty-four since the taking of Jerusalem. His body was carried to Herodium, and interred with military honours.

Herod had received from Augustus at Aquileia the right to dispose of his kingdom as he willed, and apparently at that time contemplated abdication in favour of his sons, but was restrained by the Emperor (*Ant.* XVI. iv. 5). When he returned to Jerusalem, he made public announcement of his intention that the succession should go to Antipater first, and then to Alexander and Aristobulus. Before his death he made three wills. In the first, made about B.C. 6, Antipater was named to succeed to the throne, or, in case of his death, Herod (Philip) the son of Mariamne the high priest's daughter (*Ant.* XVII. iii. 2; *BJ* I. xxix. 2). In the second, made after the treachery of Antipater had been discovered, Antipas was named as his heir (*Ant.* XVII. vi. 1; *BJ* I. xxxii. 7). In the third, made shortly before his death, Archelaus was appointed to succeed to Judæa and Samaria, with the title of king; Antipas was given Peræa, with the title of tetrarch; and Philip, with a similar title, received Trachonitis, Auranitis, and Batanæa (*Ant.* XVII. viii. 1; *BJ* I. xxxiii. 7).

Although Josephus gives a very detailed account of Herod's reign, depending to a far greater extent on Nicolaus of Damascus than his occasional citations would indicate (cf. Schürer [3], i. 82 ff.), it is not historically probable that he has recorded every incident found in his sources, much less every incident that occurred during this period. For, while his representation has in its main features and even in most of its details the appearance of a faithful and trustworthy narrative, it is not unlikely that he has misunderstood or misrepresented some movements, such as the character of the robbers in Galilee; others he has neglected for some reason, such as the Messianic ideas of the time, and their popular influence witnessed by the Psalms of Solomon and the NT (cf. Mt 2[ff.]; and Mathews, *Hist.* 126, *The Messianic Hope in the NT*, 13 ff.). It is possible also that Josephus misrepresented some details of the history through misunderstanding his sources, such, for example, as the day of the fall of Jerusalem, or, again, assigned wrong motives for actions, and even narrated as fact what did not happen. There are some descriptions of different events which reveal striking similarities, and there are some apparent inconsistencies. The narrative in *BJ* is closely parallel with that in *Ant.*, but in some instances the one contains what the other omits. However highly, therefore, we may estimate the trustworthiness of Josephus as an historian, his silence can be used as an argument against the historicity of an event, otherwise attested, only in case it can be shown that Josephus or his source could not have been in ignorance of the event, and would have had good reason to mention it had it occurred, and no good reason for omitting it if known. But even should this be established, the argument from silence would have only secondary value in confirming a negative judgment, since any judgment in such a case must depend primarily upon the character of the source in which the event is recorded.

Both St. Matthew and St. Luke assign the birth of Jesus to a time shortly before the death of Herod (Mt 2[1ff.], Lk 1[5. 26. 56] 2[1ff.]). This event, although not mentioned by Josephus, could not have taken place later than the spring of B.C. 4. St. Luke, indeed, brings the event more directly into connexion with the emperor Augustus by mentioning the imperial decree of enrolment, which caused the journey of Joseph and Mary from Nazareth to Bethlehem. St. Matthew, on the other hand, by narrating the visit of the Wise Men from the East (μάγοι ἀπὸ ἀνατολῶν, Mt 2[1]), gives us a glimpse of Jerusalem and Herod wonderfully true to the historical and psychological probabilities that may be inferred from Josephus and other sources. The arrival of the Magi in Jerusalem, the form of their question revealing the fact that they were not Jews, the Messianic significance of their question and its appreciation by the people and by Herod, the consequent effect on the city and on the king, Herod's questioning of the scribes where the Christ, *i.e.* the Messiah, should be born, the answer according well not only with OT prophecy, but with the Messianic ideas of the time (cf. Zahn, *Matth.* 94, n. 86; Bousset, *Religion des Jud.* 214), and, finally, the character of Herod, suspicious, dissimulating, treacherous,— the whole description vividly reflects the historical conditions of the closing years of Herod's reign. The local colouring betrays no false touch. The ideas and scenes are appropriate to the times, and the character of Herod is quite his own. When St. Matthew tells us that Herod in his anger at being deceived by the Magi slew all the children of two years and under in Bethlehem and its borders, we still recognize perfectly the man whose closing years were filled with passion and bloodshed. Josephus, indeed, does not mention the incident. What he does narrate of Herod, however, bears indirect testimony to a fact so entirely consistent with Herod's character. If the fact therefore be denied, the denial will rest on subjective rather than historical grounds.

Grätz, indeed, remarks (*Hist. of the Jews*, ii. 116): ' A legend of later date tells how Herod was not satisfied with shedding the blood of his own children, but how, in a passion, he ordered all children under two years of age in Bethlehem and the surrounding country to be massacred, because he had heard that the Messiah of the house of David had been born in that place. But Herod, criminal as he was, was innocent of this crime.' Similarly I. Broydé (*Jewish Encyc.* vi. 360), who, however, makes appeal to the fact that ' the massacre of the Innocents as related in the NT is now generally admitted by independent Christian thinkers to be legendary.' For this opinion, however, no historical evidence is advanced. The asserted legendary character of St. Matthew's narrative and its later date, even when strengthened by appeal to independent Christian thinkers, is only subjective and dogmatical. In the latter case, indeed (cf. Holtzmann, *Handcom.*[3] 41), the attempt is made to ground such a judgment historically by comparing Mt. and Lk., and inferring from their differences the untrustworthy character of each. The fundamental objection to the historicity of the Gospel narratives is, however, not so much the differences between them, which simply prove their relative independence, as

the supernatural facts which they record, and in particular, in this part of St. Matthew's narrative, the star of the Magi. Dr. Zahn (*Matth.* 98 f.) has suggested an interpretation of this phenomenon as a purely natural occurrence, described, however, not in terms of scientific precision but in popular language, and from the point of view of the Magi. But even should such an explanation be thought exegetically inadequate, the historicity of the narrative could be denied, and the narrative itself justly described as legendary, only on principles of interpretation whose ' independence,' by reason of their dependence on naturalistic premises, logically excluded from the sphere of history all miraculous events, and necessarily explained the narratives of such events as legendary in character and origin.

For an account of Herod's son Archelaus see ARCHELAUS.

2. Antipas.—The second son of Herod and Malthake, the full brother of Archelaus, is called by Josephus ᾽Αντίπας (*Ant.* XVII. vii. 1) or ῾Ηρῴδης (XVIII. ii. 1). In the NT and on the coins only the name ῾Ηρῴδης appears. Under his father's last will, as ratified by Augustus, Antipas received Peræa and Galilee, with the title τετράρχης (see TETRARCH). He is commonly designated by this title in the NT, although the popular ὁ βασιλεύς occurs in Mk 6[14ff.], Mt 14[9].

We know little concerning the events of Antipas' long reign (B.C. 4–A.D. 39). The narrative given by Josephus is very meagre after the death of Herod the Great.* Having little to tell of Archelaus, Josephus introduced very interesting digressions about the Pharisees, Sadducees, Zealots, and Essenes (*Ant.* XVIII. i.–vi. ; *BJ* II. viii. 1–14). But, having equally little to tell of Antipas, he filled in his narrative in *Ant.* with an account of the Parthians and their relations with Rome — with which, indeed, Antipas was incidentally connected (cf. *Ant.* XVIII. ii. 4, iv. 4 ; Schürer[3], i. 447). We learn from Josephus, however, that Antipas rebuilt and strongly fortified Sepphoris and Betharamphtha for the protection of Galilee and Peræa. He also built and colonized Tiberias on the Sea of Galilee. On one occasion, when in Rome at the house of his brother Herod Philip (*Ant.* XVIII. v. 1 ; cf. Mk 6[17]), son of Mariamne the high priest's daughter, Antipas secured the consent of Herodias, his brother's wife, to leave her husband and marry him, on condition that he put away his own wife, the daughter of Aretas, king of the Nabatæans. When Antipas returned, his wife, who had learned of his understanding with Herodias, asked permission to go to Machærus, a fortress near the border of her father's territory. Without suspecting her purpose, Antipas granted her request ; but she continued her journey to Arabia, and enlightened her father concerning the dutiful intentions of his son-in-law. Because of this and certain boundary disputes, enmity arose between Aretas and Antipas, which eventually issued in war, and a crushing defeat for Antipas.

It is difficult to determine just how soon after the marriage with Herodias the war between Antipas and Aretas broke out. Vitellius, although harbouring an old grudge against Antipas, and thus naturally disposed to make haste slowly in coming to his assistance, was, nevertheless, under orders from Rome, marching against Aretas to punish him for his rough treatment of Antipas, and had got as far as Jerusalem when news came of the death of Tiberius (A.D 37). The defeat of Antipas can hardly have been later than the year 36. Josephus, however, remarks (*Ant.* XVIII. v. 2) that the defeat of Antipas was popularly regarded as a Divine punishment for the murder of John the Baptist. Hence it has been inferred by Keim and others that neither the death of John nor the marriage with Herodias can have preceded this event by many years. Keim advocated the year 34 as the date of John's death, and assigned the death of Jesus to the year 35 (*Jesus of Nazara*, ii. 387 ff.). Sieffert dates the journey of Antipas to Rome, when he gained the consent of Herodias to their marriage, in the year 34 (*PRE*[3] vii. 769, l. 49). The concise character of Josephus' narrative, however, as well as the condition of the text in this section of *Ant.*, renders it precarious to infer, from the order of events, close chronological sequence (cf. Schürer[3], i. 443 ff. ; Wellhausen[4], 354). Equally

---

* This meagreness, as compared with the detailed account of the life and reign of Herod the Great, is due doubtless to the failure, after Herod's death, of one of the principal sources upon which Josephus depended, Nicolaus of Damascus (cf. Schürer[3]. i. 53 ; Mathews, *Hist.* 134, n. 1).

uncertain is the chronological inference from the popular connexion of Antipas' defeat with the death of John, since such a judgment is too flexible to furnish any very definite chronological datum.

The arrest, imprisonment, and death of John the Baptist are narrated in the Gospels and in Josephus (cf. Mt 4[12] 11[2ff.] 14[3ff.], Mk 1[14] 6[17ff.], Lk 3[19f.] 7[18ff.] 9[7ff.], Jn 3[24]; *Ant.* XVIII. v. 2). Both sources give an account of John's preaching and baptism. Josephus mentions a political motive for John's arrest ; but, while such a motive is not unlikely in view of the popularity of John's ministry (Mk 1[5], Mt 3[5], Lk 3[21], cf. Jn 5[35]) and the Messianic character of his preaching (Mk 1[9ff.], Mt 3[11f.], Lk 3[15ff.], cf. Jn 1[15. 19ff. 37] 3[28ff.]), it does not fully explain his death. We learn also from Josephus that John was imprisoned in the fortress of Machærus, but nothing is said concerning the length of the imprisonment. The Gospels, however, give a personal motive for the arrest of John, indicate that the imprisonment lasted for some time,—probably about a year,[*]—and attribute his death to the enmity of Herodias (Mk 6[17-29], Mt 14[3-12], Lk 3[19. 20]). For John had rebuked Herod for his marriage with Herodias, and for this had been imprisoned. The imprisonment seems to have been moderated by the free access of his disciples to him, and Herod himself heard John from time to time. At length, however, on the occasion of a birthday feast,[†] celebrated by Herod with the chief men of his government, probably at the palace in Machærus, a favourable opportunity presented itself for Herodias to be avenged on John for his attack on her marriage. Salome, the daughter of her former marriage,[‡] danced before Herod and his guests. Herod was pleased, and promised to do for her what she might ask. At the suggestion of her mother, her request took an unexpected form ; but because of his promise Herod granted her the death of the prophet, who, like his predecessor in the days of Ahab, had been bold to arraign immorality in high places.

The boyhood of Jesus and most of His public ministry were spent within the territory of Antipas. It was not, however, until the mission of the Twelve that Herod's attention was attracted to Jesus ; for, though labouring on the shores of the Sea of Galilee, and from Capernaum as a centre extending His work into the surrounding country, Jesus apparently did not visit Tiberias. Shortly after Jesus learned that Herod had heard of Him, He withdrew from Galilee, going into the region of Tyre and Sidon (part of the Roman province of Syria). On one occasion Jesus warned His disciples against the leaven of Herod (Mk 8[15]) ; on another the Pharisees, manifesting an unwonted interest in Jesus' safety, brought Him word that Herod was planning His death (Lk 13[31]). The reply of Jesus on the latter occasion—'Go tell that fox' —shows that He saw through the cunning design of Herod to be rid of Him. True to His own word,— 'for it cannot be that a prophet perish out of Jerusalem,'—it was not at the hand of Herod that the Saviour of the world suffered, but at the hands of the Roman world-rulers and their procurator,

---

[*] Jesus' Galilæan ministry began just after the imprisonment of John (Mk 1[14], Mt 4[12]). John's ministry was looked back upon as past at the feast of Jn 5[1], cf. 5[35]. Messengers came from the imprisoned John to Jesus in the midst of the early Galilæan ministry. News of Jesus reached Herod about the time of the mission of the Twelve, and in this connexion the Gospels mention the fears of Herod that John was risen from the dead. The inference is not improbable that John's death was a matter of recent occurrence.

[†] On the meaning of γενέσια in Mk 6[21], Mt 14[6], cf. Schürer[3], i. 439, n. 27 ; Zahn, *Matth.* 504, n. 81 ; Jos. *Ant.* XIX. vii. 1 ; Oxyr. Pap. i. 112. 4, iii. 494. 24, 521, iv. 736. 56, 57 ; Fay. Pap. i. 114. 20, 115. 6, 119. 30.

[‡] The reading Mk 6[22] αὐτοῦ in אBDLΔ, adopted by WH, is probably a corruption for αὐτῆς (cf. Swete, *The Gosp. acc. to St. Mk.* 118 ; Schürer[3], i. 441, n. 29).

Pontius Pilate. At the trial of Jesus, Herod's wish to see Him was at length gratified. For Pilate, when he learned that Jesus was of Galilee, and thus subject to Herod's jurisdiction, at once sent him to Herod, who was in Jerusalem at that time. This act of consideration, prompted possibly by the strained relations between the two rulers (Lk 23[12], cf. 13[1]), proved an effectual peace-offering, and cemented anew the bonds of friendship between them. Herod, however, had no desire to assume responsibility for the death of Jesus. His desire to see Jesus sprang from simple curiosity, stimulated by the hope that He would perform some miracle in His presence. But Jesus was silent before Herod and His accusers. Herod, therefore, when he had mocked Him, sent Him back to Pilate arrayed in fine garments. [The part taken by Herod in the trial of Jesus is the subject of legendary elaboration in the apocryphal *Gospel of Peter*].

Stirred by envy at the advancement of her brother Agrippa to royal dignity, Herodias persuaded Herod, against his better judgment, to seek from Caligula a similar honour. When he came to Rome, however, Agrippa preferred charges against him, and called attention to the military supplies that had been collected by Herod. Herod was unable to deny the existence of the supplies, and was banished by Caligula to Lyons in Gaul, probably in the summer of A.D. 39 (cf. Schürer[3], i. 448, n. 46 ; Madden, however, *Coins*, 122, gives the year 40). Herodias proudly refused the Emperor's generosity, and accompanied her husband in his banishment (*Ant.* XVII. vii. 2 ; *BJ* II. ix. 6). Herod's tetrarchy was given to Agrippa.

3. Philip.—Philip was son of Herod the Great and Cleopatra of Jerusalem. When Archelaus went to Rome to secure the ratification of his father's will, he left Philip in Jerusalem in charge of his affairs. Later, when Varus gave the Jews of Jerusalem permission to send an embassy to Rome to oppose Archelaus, Philip went also, at the suggestion of Varus, to profit by whatever course events might take. When Augustus ratified Herod's will, Philip received Batanæa, Trachonitis, Auranitis, Gaulanitis, and the territory of Panias (*Ant.* XVII. viii. 1, xi. 4, XVIII. iv. 6 ; *BJ* II. vi. 3). In Lk 3[1] the territory of Philip is described by the phrase, 'the region of Ituræa and Trachonitis' (τῆς Ἰτουραίας καὶ Τραχωνίτιδος χώρας ; cf. Schürer[3], i. 425, n. 23). The Trachonitis had on two occasions been colonized by Herod the Great—once with three thousand Idumæans, and again with Jewish warriors from Babylon (*Ant.* XVI. ix. 2, XVII. ii. 1–3). But the population of Philip's territory was chiefly Gentile, his coins, unlike those of his brothers, bearing the image of the Emperor. Philip rebuilt Panias, and called it *Cæsarea* in honour of Augustus, and also Bethsaida on the Sea of Galilee, calling it *Julias* after the Emperor's daughter. His reign was a mild and peaceful one. He lived in his own country and administered justice as he travelled from place to place (*Ant.* XVIII. iv. 6). He married his niece Salome, daughter of Herodias and Herod Philip (*Ant.* XVIII. v. 4). The Gospels narrate a journey of Jesus into the territory of Philip when He went north from Galilee into the region of Cæsarea Philippi (Mk 8[27], Mt 16[13] ; cf. CÆSAREA PHILIPPI). Philip died in the year 33 or 34, in the twentieth year of Tiberius, having reigned thirty-seven years. His territory was added to the province of Syria, but was given shortly afterwards by Caligula to Agrippa. See also art. HERODIAS.

LITERATURE.—Josephus ; Derenbourg, *Hist. de la Palestine* ; Madden, *Coins of the Jews* ; Schürer, *GJV*[3] (Eng. tr. of 2nd ed.) i. 338 ff. and Index [very full citation of literature] ; Hausrath, *Hist. of NT Times*, i. 207 ff. ; O. Holtzmann, *Neutest. Zeitgeschichte*, 71 ff. ; Riggs, *Hist. of the Jewish People*, 143 ff. ; Muirhead, *Times of Christ* ; Farrar, *The Herods* ; S. Mathews, *Hist.*

of NT Times, 100 ff. ; Mommsen, *Roman Provinces*, ii. 189 ff. ; Ewald, *HI* v. 395 ff. ; Grätz, *Hist. of the Jews*, ii. 57 ff. ; de Saulcy, *Hist. d'Hérode* ; Wellhausen, *IJG⁴* 323 ff. ; Keim in Schenkel's *Bibel-lexikon*, iii. 27 ff. ; Westcott in Smith's *DB²*, ii. 1048 ff. ; Sieffert, art. 'Herodes' in *PRE³* ; Hausleiter, art. 'Antipas,' *ib.* ; von Dobschütz, art. 'Philippus der Tetrarch,' *ib.* ; Woodhouse in *Encyc. Bibl.* ii. 2023 ff. ; Headlam in Hastings' *DB* ii. 353 ff. ; J. D. Davis, *DB*, artt. 'Herod,' 'Philip' ; W. Milwitzky, art. 'Antipas' in *Jewish Encyc.* ; I. Broydé, art. 'Herod,' *ib.* ; S. Ochser, art. 'Philip,' *ib.*

W. P. ARMSTRONG.

HERODIANS ('Ηρῳδιανοί). — Apart from the weakly attested reading in Mk 8¹⁵, the Herodians are mentioned but three times in the NT and on only two occasions, Mt 22¹⁶ being parallel with Mk 12¹³. The name 'Ηρῳδιανοί does not occur in Josephus. In *BJ* I. xvi. 6 the form 'Ηρῴδειοι is used of the party of Herod, and in *Ant.* XIV. xv. 10 the phrase οἱ τὰ 'Ηρῴδου φρονοῦντες occurs (cf. also *Ant.* XIV. vii. 4). (For the formation in -ιανος like Χριστιανός, cf. Blass, *Acta Apos.* 136, *Gram. of NT Greek*, § 27, 4 ; Harnack, *Mission u. Ausb. d. Christ.* 294 ff. ; *Etym. Magn. s.v.* 'Ηρῳδιανός).

If the party of Herod in Josephus be the same as the Herodians of the NT (cf. O. Holtzmann, *Neutest. Zeitgesch.* 157 f., but, on the other hand, Cheyne, *Encyc. Bibl.* ii. 2034), then the origin of the party must be sought in the time of Herod the Great. This view of the origin of the party will also determine our conception of its nature. It cannot have been a religious sect or party like the Pharisees or Sadducees, but was most probably a political party composed of the adherents and supporters of the Herodian dynasty. From the combination of the Pharisees with the Herodians (Mk 3⁶), and their common action in Jerusalem (Mt 22¹⁶, Mk 12¹³), it is not unlikely that the Herodian party was composed principally of Sadducees (cf. Lk 20¹⁹ and Mk 8¹⁵ with Mt 16⁶). After the death of Herod the Great, the deposition of Archelaus, and the establishment of Roman rule in Judæa, the aims and purposes of the party would naturally centre in Antipas. The presence of the Herodians in Galilee, indicated in Mk 3⁶, cannot be set aside with the remark of Cheyne : 'This, however, is evidently a mistake. In the country of the tetrarch Antipas there could not be a party called the Herodians' (*op. cit.* ii. 2043). Members of a party which wished to see Antipas sit upon the throne of his father may have been in Galilee as well as in Jerusalem ; for their ideal was a national one, differing from the ideal of the Zealots as royalist from democratic. Their union with the strong Pharisaic party, and their attempt to entrap Jesus with the question about tribute to Cæsar, find explanation not in any sympathy with the Pharisees or fondness for the traditions which Jesus' activity imperilled, but in their readiness to oppose and suppress any Messianic agitation of the people.

Other views attach some religious significance to the party, connect them with the Bœthusians or with the court of Antipas as members of the Herodian family, officers or servants, and attribute to them a friendly or hostile attitude towards the Roman sovereignty (cf. Tert. *ad Omn. Hær.* i. ; Epiph. *Hær.* xx. ; Steph. *Thesaur. s.v.* ; Ewald, *HI* v. 409 f. ; Renan, *Vie de Jésus*, 226 ; Edersheim, *Life and Times*, i. 237 ff., ii. 384 ; Bleek, *Syn.* ii. 327 ; Zahn, *Matth.* 528, n. 44, 632, n. 45).

LITERATURE. — Keim in Schenkel's *Bibel-lexikon*, iii. 65 ff. ; B. F. Westcott in Smith's *DB²*, ii. 1054 f. ; Sieffert in *PRE³*, vii. 769 ; T. K. Cheyne in *Encyc. Bibl.* ii. 2043 ; D. Eaton in Hastings' *DB* ii. 362 ; K. Kohler, *Jewish Encyc.* vi. 360 ; J. D. Davis, *DB* 293.

W. P. ARMSTRONG.

HERODIAS ('Ηρῳδιάς). — Herodias was the daughter of Aristobulus (son of Herod the Great and Mariamne the Hasmonæan) and Bernice (daughter of Salome, Herod's sister, and Costobar), and thus the full sister of Herod, king of Chalcis,

and Agrippa I. (*Ant.* XVIII. v. 4). She married first her half-uncle Herod, son of Herod the Great and Mariamne, the high priest's daughter. In Mk 6¹⁷ and Mt 14³ the first husband of Herodias is called **Philip**, the brother of Herod (Antipas). This Philip, therefore, most probably bore also the name 'Herod' (as did also his brothers Archelaus and Antipas), and is to be distinguished from Philip the tetrarch (Lk 3¹ ; cf. Mt 16¹³, Mk 8²⁷), who married Salome, the daughter of Herod Philip and Herodias (*Ant.* XVIII. v. 4). In Mk 6¹⁷ the reading Φιλίππου is given by Tisch. (ed. maj. viii.) without citation of a variant. In Mt 14³ Φιλίππου has the support of אBCL, etc., but is omitted in D a c e ff' g' k vg. In Lk 3¹⁹ Φιλίππου is inserted by ACK, etc., cop syr^utr. arm^edd aeth, but omitted by אBDL, etc. The reading thus appears to be original in Mk., probably original in Mt., and derivative in Luke. The statement (*Encyc. Bibl.* ii. 2032), 'In spite of Mk 6¹⁷ we cannot hold that he ever really bore the name Philip,' as well as the remark of Schürer³ (i. 435, n. 19), 'Since, according to Josephus, not the tetrarch but the above-named Herod was the first husband of Herodias, the statement of Mark and Matthew is evidently a mistake' (*ein entschiedenes Versehen*) are too positive. They do not rest on any more substantial evidence than the fact that Josephus calls this son of Herod the Great simply Herod. The argument that two sons of Herod would not have borne the same name Philip is weakened by the fact that even according to Josephus two sons of Herod bore the same name— Herod, son of Mariamne, the high priest's daughter, and Herod, son of Cleopatra (*Ant.* XVII. i. 3, XVIII. v. 4). Herod Philip had been designated in the first will of Herod the Great as the alternate of Antipas in succession to the throne (*Ant.* XVII. iii. 2 ; *BJ* I. xxix. 2), but was subsequently omitted because of his mother's connexion with the plot of Antipater (*Ant.* XVII. iv. 2 ; *BJ* I. xxx. 7). He continued in private life in Rome, where Antipas, while guest in his brother's house, persuaded Herodias to desert her husband and marry him. This second marriage of Herodias was especially offensive to the Jews, because her husband, to whom she had borne a child, was still alive (cf. Lv 18¹⁶, Dt 25⁵ ; also *Ant.* XVII. xiii. 1). John the Baptist rebuked Antipas for his action, and paid the penalty with his life for rousing the anger of an ambitious and unscrupulous woman. Her connexion with the downfall of Antipas has been mentioned (cf. art. HEROD under 'Antipas'). In the last recorded incident of her life, when Herodias voluntarily followed Antipas into exile and haughtily refused the Emperor's bounty, she displayed, like her grandmother Mariamne when unjustly sentenced to death, the proud fortitude and fine dignity of the old Hasmonæan house now brought so low through its union with the Herods (*Ant.* XVIII. vii. 2 ; cf. xv. ix. 5).

LITERATURE. — Schürer, *GJV³* i. 435–449 (Eng. tr., cf. Index) ; E. S. Ffoulkes in Smith's *DB²* ii. 1055 f. ; Sieffert in *PRE³* vii. 769 f. ; Woodhouse in *Encyc. Bibl.* ii. 2033 ; Headlam in Hastings' *DB* ii. 360 ; I. Broydé in *Jewish Encyc.* vi. 360 f. ; J. D. Davis, *DB* 293 f.

W. P. ARMSTRONG.

HEZEKIAH. — One of the kings of Judah, mentioned in Mt.'s (1⁹ᶠ.) genealogy of our Lord.

HEZRON. — A Judahite ancestor of Jesus (Mt 1³, Lk 3³³).

HIGH PRIEST. — The terms 'high priest' and 'chief priest' in the NT represent the same original (ἀρχιερεύς), varied in translation to correspond with the uses of the term as explained below. The office of high priest in the Jewish nation can be traced back to the early years of post‑exilic times. The priestly writings then adopted as authoritative assign its origin to the time of Moses, but the earlier writings contain no suggestion of the existence of the office, and cultural conditions before the Exile preclude an early date for its establishment. Immediately after the Return the office was a religious one, the secular power being in the hands of the 'prince'; for, great as was the emphasis in the new community upon law and ceremony, there seems to have been an equal emphasis upon the hoped for restoration of the State to a dignified and independent position. It very soon became evident that this hope was impossible of fulfilment, and the secular functions, so far as they were exercised by the Jews, were merged in the duties of the high priest. At first the position was for life and hereditary. In practice the principle was often violated, the violations being occasioned not so much by deliberate purpose as by the turmoils of Greek and Roman times. Moreover, internal conditions in the Jewish community were of themselves sufficient to have unsettled the principle. At the time of the Hasmonæan uprising, the assumption of high priestly functions and title by this family was essential to the success of the revolt. Under the Roman supremacy, the fortunes of the political parties in Rome added to the tendencies that made for the disappearance of the last vestige of permanence in the high priestly office, and at the time of Christ we find it entirely at the will of Rome, both as to appointment and tenure. Under these conditions there had grown up a caste of high priestly families, descended from high priests and otherwise connected with them; these formed a high aristocracy in Judaism, which was possessed of considerable authority, however difficult it may be to define the limits and extent of that influence. Very naturally the selection of the high priest was made from these families. The numerous references in the Gospels are ordinarily to this high priestly class, and when the Greek is so used it is translated 'chief priests' (see art. CHIEF PRIESTS).

As far as concerns the high priest proper, he occupied the position of chief political authority among the Jews, as head of the Sanhedrin. Josephus declares (*Ant.* xx. 10) that there were 28 high priests from the time of Herod to the destruction of Jerusalem. Of these, the Gospels mention the tenth, Annas, appointed by Quirinius (A.D. 6), and the fourteenth, Joseph, surnamed Caiaphas, who was in office at the time of the crucifixion of Jesus and presided over the Sanhedrin at His trial. Previous to this trial there was a preliminary trial or hearing, whether with or without legal right, before Annas, father-in-law of Caiaphas. The Gospel narrative of these events, so far from being confused or improbable, is confirmed as entirely consistent and probable by the records of Jewish practice of those days. Annas was a man of long continued influence among his people. No fewer than six of the high priests of the Herodian period are known to have been of his family. Other high priests after the end of their term of service are stated to have held high positions at home and abroad, and it is possible that some of the Gospel references to high or chief priests are to this group of ex-high priests together with the officiating priest.

The high priest was also at the head of the sacerdotal system, as the title, of course, implies. But although historically this was his chief claim to authority, his religious influence in the time of Christ was far less than his political power. The religion of the Jew was a matter quite distinct from the rites and ceremonies of the temple, though he might observe these with care. The

very success of the high priests centuries before, in uniting the two offices of religious and secular ruler, had operated to foster the development of a religion of a different sort. It was now a religion of the scribes.

The high priest conducted the sacrifices only on special occasions. He was required to officiate on the yearly Day of Atonement; and on other festival days, such as New Moons and Sabbaths, he officiated at his pleasure. These distinctively priestly duties do not come into consideration in the Gospel narratives. The Epistle to the Hebrews, on the other hand, makes much mention of the office in order by that means to portray more clearly the work of Jesus in behalf of men; but one will be disappointed who goes to this Epistle to discover what were the high priestly functions at the time of Christ, or even to discover the theory of sacrifice and priesthood current in those days. The author does not describe the ceremonial as he and his readers knew it from daily observation or participation. He does not allude to it because it was something vital in the religious experience of the Jew. He describes it as he knew it out of the Jewish Scriptures, and he reflects upon it as dispassionately as a philosopher or a theologian. The OT priesthood and sacrifice did not really make atonement for sin; to the author they typified that atonement. In the real atonement Christ had a part similar to that played by the high priest in the sensuous, temporary, typical atonement of the earlier dispensation. He made reconciliation for the sins of the people (2^{17}); He was faithful, the recipient of a greater glory than Moses (3^{1-6}); sought not the office, but was chosen as was Aaron (5^4); He was of the order of Melchizedek (5^{10} 6^{20}); was competent to sympathize with men (2^{18} 4^{15}). He possessed an unchanging priesthood, sacrificing once for all (7), and the sacrifice was Himself. He has passed through the heavens, through the veil (4^{14}), and serves in a perfect tabernacle. As the work wrought by Him for men surpassed that of the high priest, so the terminology of the older dispensation is insufficient, and breaks down under the burden of the description. Jesus is not only the Mediator of the new covenant, the High Priest, but He is also the sacrifice itself. The author will not say that the death on the cross fitted into the OT sacrificial system, any more than he brings Jesus into that system as priest. It was in the new order of things, in the spiritual atonement, which was the real one, with spiritual agencies and results, that His perfect humanity, His perfect obedience and sinlessness, found place. The temple is in the heavens whither He has gone to consummate the service of which His earthly career was an incident. See, further, art. PRIEST.

LITERATURE.—Schürer, *GJV* ³ §§ 23, 24; Beyschlag, *NT Theol.* ii. 315–331; Westcott, *Ep. to Hebrews*; Briggs, *Messiah of the Apostles*, 242–283; Ménégoz, *Théol. de l'Épître aux Hébreux*, 102 ff., 197 ff.   OWEN H. GATES.

HIGHWAY.—In the parable (Mt 22^9) where the invited guests all made excuse, the king sent his servants out ἐπὶ τὰς διεξόδους τῶν ὁδῶν, 'into the highways' (AV), to gather as many as they could find, and bid them to the feast. The Gr. phrase means literally 'the partings of the highways' (so RV), *exitus viarum* (Vulg.). This is the only occurrence of διέξοδοι in the NT, and it is impossible to determine with certainty what is meant by the expression. It may signify either the roads leading out of the town into the country, or the crossings of such, or the streets leading into the open spaces or square in front of the town. The idea is clear—where men both good and bad, Jew and Gentile, are most likely to be found. God's purpose cannot be frustrated; and if the invited guests neglect the call, then others who have hitherto been looked down upon will take their place. The invitation is to all and sundry, which leads Whedon to say, 'The good are not too good to need the gospel, nor the bad so bad as to have no hope if they will accept it.' It was the poor, the outcast, the hopeless that were to be found on the high-ways: blind Bartimæus (Mk 10⁴⁶) shouting, 'Have mercy on me,' and such as the lepers who stood afar off (Lk 17¹³) uttering the same miserable cry. See, further, art. ROADS.   R. LEGGAT.

HILL.—In Lk 3⁵ 23³⁰ ὄρος is distinguished from βουνός, which in LXX commonly stands for גִּבְעָה, and as representing the lesser eminence, is properly rendered 'hill.' Language like that of 23³⁰ is used in hyperbole to-day by Easterns, of preparing a highway for royalty through a practically roadless country. In two cases (Mt 5¹⁴, Lk 4²⁹) RV retains AV rendering of ὄρος, 'hill.' In Lk 9³⁷ RV rightly substitutes 'mountain.' Perhaps we should read 'mountain' also in Mt 5¹⁴. There is nothing to show that any particular city was referred to, but if the words were spoken on any height west of the Lake, Ṣafed, with white walls gleaming in the sun, must have been a striking feature in the landscape. It stands literally 'on a mountain,' to the north, nearly 3500 ft. above the Sea of Galilee. Ancient Nazareth, however, was built on the slope of a hill to which 'mountain' could hardly apply.

Hill country (ἡ ὀρεινή, Lk 1³⁹. ⁶⁵). ἡ ὀρεινη is a frequent LXX equivalent of הָהָר. The use of Heb. הר closely resembles that of Arab. jebel, which denotes a single height, but also a whole range, as Jebel Libnân; or a definite part of a range, as Jebel Nâblus—this indicating that portion of 'the mountain' which is under the government of Nâblus. This expression and Jebel el-Ḳuds the present writer has often heard on Palestinian lips, without any sense of vagueness or confusion. הָהָר was 'the mountain'—the central range as dis-tinguished from the plain and the Shephelah on the west, and the 'Arabah on the east. Jebel el-Ḳuds, 'mountain of Jerusalem,' is perhaps the nearest modern equivalent of ἡ ὀρεινὴ τῆς Ἰουδαίας, that part of 'the mountain' associated with the tribe of Judah. See, further, art. MOUNTAIN.
                                              W. EWING.

HINDRANCE.—The life of communion with God and of obedience to His revealed will is regarded as the normal state and right relationship of man made in God's image and for His glory. All defect and deflection from this standard are the result of external and internal hindrances. The world is an environment of hindrances and causes of stumbling (Mt 18⁷). Such is the pressure of opposing influ-ences that the entrance into life has to be by a narrow gate (7¹³). Instances of these outward and inward difficulties are given in the parable of the Sower (13¹⁸⁻²³), and in that of the Tares their final elimination is predicted (v.⁴¹).

1. The following hindrances are specially em-phasized: (1) prosperity and power (Mt 4⁸ 19²⁴, Lk 16³¹ 18²³); (2) self-righteousness and the arresting effect of an inferior standard (Mt 5²⁰ 6². ⁵. ¹⁶ 23⁵⁻⁷, Lk 18¹⁴); (3) family claims and their displacing power (Mt 8²¹ 10³⁷); (4) want of faith (Mt 14³¹ 17²⁰ 25²⁵, Lk 22³²); (5) blindness of heart in its pro-gressive stages of (a) ignorance (Mt 13¹⁵, Lk 18¹⁸ 23³⁴, Jn 17²⁵, repeated in Ac 3¹⁷, 1 Co 2⁸), (b) in-difference (Lk 7³²),—being the interval of apathy and discouragement that succeeds when ideals once regarded as final cease to fill the imagination and satisfy the heart, and institutions once held to be sacred fail to yield the expected results,—(c) inability to discern and feel (Mt 16³ 23³⁷), and lastly (d) conscious malignity towards the King-dom of God (Mt 23¹³ 27¹⁸, Mk 7⁸, Lk 11¹⁵. ⁵². cf. Ro 1³²).

2. Comparative moral values are attached to these hindrances (Mt 8¹⁰ 11²¹⁻²⁴ 12⁴¹. ⁴², Mk 12⁴¹⁻⁴⁴, Lk 7⁴⁷ 17¹⁶). Prayer may be offered for their removal (Mt 26³⁹, similarly 2 Co 12⁸).

3. Christ's relationship to the world-spirit is one of complete opposition (Jn 16³³ 18³⁶). The victory that can be obtained over all hindrances makes a sanctified cross the emblem of the Christian life (Mt 16²⁴, Mk 8³⁴, Lk 9²³). This power to overcome, promised to those who abide in Christ (Jn 15⁷), is referred to in the Epistles as already a verified fact in Christian experience (Ro 8³⁵⁻³⁹, Ph 4¹³).

Stumbling - block, stumbling - stone (πρόσκομμα, προσκοπή, also σκάνδαλον, 'trap' or 'snare' [Ro 11⁹], and frequently tr. 'offence,' 'offend' [Mt 16²³ 18⁶⁻⁹ 26³¹, Lk 17¹]). The root-idea is that of encounter-ing an obstacle where such ought not to be, as on a public road. In its fig. sense the offence is most blameworthy where the trust is most implicit and unreserved, as in the confidence of children (Mt 18⁶).

In the East the bridle-path is seldom repaired. Stones may be cast out upon it in clearing the neigh-bouring fields; squared stones for building, collected at the road-side for transport, are often scattered over the path; if a bed of sand suitable for mixing with lime be found near it, the path may be dug into and the cavity left unfilled. No harm can arise from it, men say, except to those for whom it is decreed. The people of the village soon come to know of it, and they are under no obligation to strangers. The better prepared roads have gener-ally been constructed for Government purposes and by forced labour, so that the people of the locality take little civic interest in their condition and pre-servation. Hence stumbling-blocks are frequently met with, and cause little surprise or comment.

In modern Palestine criminals and men of de-praved life are called mu'aththârîn, 'those who have been made to stumble'; and the same epithet is applied to such as are in trouble through mis-fortune.

The Cross that made God the sacrificer and suppliant, and called for faith in a Saviour who could not save Himself, was a stumbling-block or offence to the wisdom of the world, and to all its religious traditions (Ro 9³³, 1 Co 1²³, 1 P 2⁸).
                                          G. M. MACKIE.

HIRE.—'Hire' (μισθός) occurs in two passages as the regular payment given for service rendered. In the parable of the Labourers in the Vineyard (Mt 20⁸) it is spoken of the day's wage, the denarius, owing by agreement to the workers. The proverbial phrase, 'The labourer is worthy of his hire' (Lk 10⁷), is used by Christ in connexion with the mission of the Seventy. In Mt 10¹⁰ τροφή, 'food,' is substituted for μισθός. The latter Greek word occurs again (Jn 4³⁶) as the wages of the reaper. It is used in a good sense as the reward of devotion and service to God (Mt 5¹² 6¹ 10⁴¹, Mk 9⁴¹, Lk 6²³), as well as to describe the 'empty popu-larity' attaching to the religious ostentation of the hypocrites (Mt 6². ⁵. ¹⁶). It is employed (Rev 22¹²) of Christ's reward to His faithful followers: 'My reward is with me.'

The term 'hired servant' or 'hireling' (μισθωτός) is used in speaking of Zebedee's servants (Mk 1²⁰), and of the false shepherd who deserts his flock at the approach of danger (Jn 10¹². ¹³). A similar derivative (μίσθιος) describes the father's servants in the parable of the Prodigal Son (Lk 15¹⁹). The verb 'to hire' (μισθόω) occurs (Mt 20¹) of the house-holder who engaged the labourers for his vineyard. See also next article.   C. H. PRICHARD.

HIRELING.—A hireling is one who works for

wages, an employé. Originally synonymous with 'hired servant,' it did not necessarily imply venal motive. Ben Sira was acquainted with devoted hirelings : 'Entreat not evil thy servant that worketh, nor a hireling that giveth thee his life' (Sir 7[20]). Hireling now denotes a wage-earner who manifests certain baser qualities of human nature. Christ's use of the word in Jn 10[12. 13] to signify one who, because he cares more for his wages than for his work, proves unfaithful under trial, has determined its evolution into meaning an untrustworthy employé.

Calvin, who defines hirelings as 'those who retain the pure doctrine, and who proclaim the truth, as Paul says, to serve a purpose rather than from pure zeal,' discusses a question wont to be debated in times of persecution, viz.—Has that man to be reckoned a hireling who for any reason shrinks from encountering the wolves ? He agrees with Augustine that parties may flee ' if the public advantage of the flock be thereby promoted' (Calvin on *John*, vol. i. p. 403 f., Edinburgh, 1847).

D. A. MACKINNON.

HISTORICAL. — **1.** The word 'history' is ambiguous. It may mean (1) the course of events; or (2) any record of the events—*a* history ; or (3) the science, History, which understands the whole. Scientific history is comparatively a young thing; but already educated mankind are tending to refuse the name of 'a history' to anything under the second head which does not try to fulfil the requirements of science. What fails in that may be a chronicle, or may furnish useful materials to the true historian, but is not really history.

2. The aims of the science of history are twofold. (1) It must get at the facts ; and to do that it must secure, as far as possible, first-hand evidence ; (2) it must study the facts in their development or causation or connexion upon all sides. (1) In its search for first-hand evidence, the science of history has different kinds of material to work with. (*a*) The oldest material for history is tradition. All knowledge of past events lived at first in human memory before it assumed any more permanent shape. But tradition, unsupported or unassisted, is a bad witness. And in our own region there is no real historical tradition apart from the Christian records, etc. What is pretended by Catholicism in that sense is a make-believe, to cover over unwarranted innovations. The furthest admission we can make is that scraps of historical recollection, otherwise lost to us, may survive in Church legends, which were reduced pretty early to writing (the Thekla legend ?). (*b*) The best of all witnesses is epigraphy. Biblical learning owes something to this, and may come to owe a good deal more—no one can say. (*c*) The main source of historical knowledge is literature, —human speech reduced to the ordinary forms of writing. Less durable (as well as less stiff) than inscriptions, books are more numerous—so much more numerous, that they enjoy probably a better chance of survival. In our own field the Bible writings, though not absolutely isolated, stand head and shoulders above all other materials in point of importance. This is true on purely historical principles, theories of inspiration apart. (*d*) At the risk of making a cross-division, we must mention the importance of *foreign testimony*. The amount of this is increasing with modern study and research ; and the significance generally attached to affinities between primitive Christianity and other civilizations or religions is also on the increase. (2) The most manifest result of study in the field of history is to give a better knowledge of detail. But we must not allow ourselves to suppose that events occur disconnectedly, one by one, and that the mind of the scientific thinker imposes connexions upon them. Science does not create, it elicits the hidden law ; and anything that gives us greater knowledge of events increases

our knowledge of the relations in which they stand to each other. Facts without theory are 'blind,' if theories without fact are 'empty.' The ideal goal of historical study, never, of course, to be reached, would be a scientific grasp of every past event in its full significance—reality completely reproduced in the historian's intelligence. For the facts with which history deals are intelligent acts and intelligible processes. True, the unconscious tendency of the times may count for more than the conscious, perhaps selfish, effort of the great man. Or what he does unwillingly, as the executive of Providence and the *Zeitgeist*, may be the most significant and durable of all his acts. Yet history is man's story ; surely, then, man can read it !

3. The Christian study of Bible documents moves for great part of its way, though hardly to the very end [see below], upon historical lines. (1) Its admitted hermeneutical principle, since the days of Ernesti (*Institutio Interpretis NT*, 1761), is the 'grammatico-historical'—*i.e. literal* and *historical* —method. Strictly, each sentence has one meaning, and only one—the meaning its human author designed ; the meaning its first readers would naturally apprehend. This principle had to be laid down in face of the Church's age-long hankering after 'mystical' interpretation. If the Scriptures may be allegorized, theology and faith itself rest upon a quicksand. (2) Criticism of the text, by all its methods, aims at discovering, with as much probability as can be attained, the original form of words used by the writer in each passage. It has nothing to do— unless with supreme caution, as *possible* evidence to the fact—with the question, which words appear to the student most seemly or most telling. Nay, there is a recognized principle that 'the harder reading is probable' ; though we must be able to discriminate the sort of 'difficult' reading which suggests a powerful while perhaps erratic mind, from that which rather suggests a blundering copyist. (3) Careful study of the text leads to a further set of inferences, chiefly or entirely drawn from internal evidence, regarding probable date and probable authorship. This is the Higher Criticism—'higher' because dealing with larger questions than those of the text. (4) Even in Biblical Theology we are still occupied with the historian's business. Before all things, we are reproducing past facts. Scripture includes great masses of doctrinal teaching ; the Biblical Theologian seeks to put these in shape, as they stand— the affirmations of such and such books, or teachers, or ages. The result aimed at is not Divine truth as such, but various Biblical teachings about the truth ; not a normative statement regarding realities which are real, but a historical statement regarding what was held or announced to be spiritual reality ; historical, *not dogmatic*.

4. An attempt was made by a great theological leader, Schleiermacher, to bring even dogmatic theology under the same rubric. It was to be a branch of Historical Theology. Ceasing to be (primarily) a statement of truth, it was to be a statement of what a certain Church in a certain age has come to hold for true. The suggestion was ingenious, and avoided certain difficulties ; but it led to other and worse difficulties. If Christian theology, in its central department, cannot pretend to set forth *truth*, it proclaims itself bankrupt. It can live upon nothing less than the truths regarding God and His purposes which He has been pleased to make known to us.

5. What shall we say, then, of the remainder of the Biblical territory ? We were dealing, until the last paragraph, with stages in a process of historical study. We found that even doctrine was treated in Biblical Theology as a historical study, although on the systematic or dogmatic side it required us to occupy a different point of view from the historian's. But what are we to say regarding the history of Israel? Or—coming closer to our ground —regarding the life as distinct from the teaching of Jesus? Or, in general, regarding the origins of Christianity? That which was higher than man or than history has appeared once for all upon the plane of human history. *The Word became flesh.* Unless this be denied, we have come to a point where the contents of our study burst the bonds of ordinary historical investigation. Difficulty arises in two forms. First, there is the minor difficulty connected with physical miracles. Can history adjust itself to them? If so, how? If not, what are we to conclude? But, in the second place, substantially the same question, issuing in substantially the same alternatives, repeats itself as regards the very kernel of the Christian faith. Have we in Christ, and, to a lesser degree, in His antecedents and environment, a unique Divine revelation, a unique Divine redemption? Then how is the historian to deal with Christ?

6. The question is more familiar in its less formidable shape, as regards miracles. (1) It may be held that facts convince us of miracle. History makes its investigation, and bears witness. It cannot demonstrate, but it announces a satisfactory probability. This is the attitude generally taken up by British scholars, *e.g.* in Dr. Sanday's recent *Criticism of the Fourth Gospel* (though he has the wider as well as the narrower problem before him). (2) Secondly, there is the claim of dogmatic naturalism—'miracles do not happen'; for history, the miracle narrative is an interesting and instructive problem, the miracle itself a hallucination *a priori*, be the alleged evidence what it may. This mood of mind is sometimes confessed, but much oftener is silently at work behind a disguise. (3) There is an attempt by Harnack to strike out a *tertium quid*: 'The historian cannot regard a miracle as a sure given historical event; for in doing so he destroys the mode of consideration on which all historical investigation rests.' Belief in miracle is due to the 'unique impression' of Christ's person, though 'there has seldom been a strong religious faith which would not have drawn the conclusion' that Christ wrought miracles (*Hist. of Dogma*, vol. i. Eng. tr. p. 65, note). This seems to mean that history is prevented from dealing with miracles by limitations of its own,—limitations which do not necessarily imply the absence of miracle from the world of real events. (4) Against the point of view which excludes miracles *a priori*, we might set a point of view which welcomes them *a priori* as congruous to a Divine revelation and Divine redemption. They are only signs — not the Divine content itself; but are they not fit signs?

7. On a first inspection, none of the views named is definitely anti-Christian unless the second. Naturalism, which refuses miracle out and out, is plainly pledged in logic to deny revelation. But, as we have said, the importance of the whole matter lies in its further implications. The same difficult decision is called for—not face to face with miracle, but face to face with the Christ. And the logic of the *third* position—the logic which leads Harnack, while believing in revelation, to ban miracle as a thing the historian must not touch—will inevitably be applied by others to Jesus Himself. They will repeat or extend the claim to be historians, thorough historians, nothing but historians. They will describe the teacher of Nazareth, the martyr of Calvary; but the Christ of God will be a magnitude as inaccessible to them as physical miracle is to Dr. Harnack (cf. art. 'Jesus' in *Encyc. Bibl.*). And

if he is in the right, who can say that they are wrong? Analysis must go on to the end, and that great stumbling-block, the supernatural, be revealed plain in our path. Even if not formally declared an impossibility, supernatural revelation or redemption will be politely waved aside as irrelevant to the *historian*.

8. There is no question more important at the present moment than this. What is, *e.g.*, a 'historical' view of the NT? Is it a view of the NT in its historical actuality, looked at round and round? Or is it a view hampered by the limitations of one of the special sciences? Ambiguity is always dangerous. People omit the Divine 'Word' under pretext of the second definition—That lies beyond the historian's province! But presently they are found implying the *first* definition. History tells us everything! There is no Divine 'Word' at all—no supernatural salvation.

9. If history does not give full truth, what does? We shall probably be told, Metaphysics. The only court of appeal from 'scientific fact' is 'metaphysical reality.' Metaphysics is certainly pledged to many-sidedness, to all-sidedness. But the question remains, How far can metaphysics discharge its task? And, again, Can it do justice to the Christian origins? Idealistic interpreters of Christianity are very willing to undertake the championship of the Christ idea (*e.g.* Pfleiderer), but their patronage is not extended to the Christ fact. At any rate the majority, and those who know their business best, are found reducing Jesus of Nazareth to a *symbol*, very vaguely connected with any abiding spiritual reality. To a philosophical interpreter it remains 'foolishness' that the Divine Word literally and in deed *became flesh.* If the professional historian verges upon Ebionism, his philosophical colleague rarely escapes Docetism. Neither of these positions amounts to historical Christianity, which, amid increasing uncertainty in detail, may and ought to have increasing certainty in the fundamental outlines.

10. In the present writer's judgment the attempt to make history a special science, too coy or too scientific to deal with a (possibly real) supernatural, is hopelessly artificial. Scientific history must deal with all the demonstrable, nay, with all the probable, events of the real past. This may interfere with the rounded symmetry of the science; small loss, if it gives us wider and truer knowledge! Further, the writer's own belief is that (not a Christian *bias*, but) a Christian interpretation is indispensable; or, that experience bears its witness (cf. the fourth position, § **6,** as against the first; still, he recognizes that many Christians and many useful theological workers will find themselves able to maintain the first position, and will prefer it). It is perfectly true that faith misleads and over-idealizes (Dr. Moffatt); yet that is a half-truth, or rather it is much less than the half. Better a dazzled faith than 'blind unbelief.' Amid superficial errors, Christian faith grasps the essential truth. Amid superficial accuracies, non-Christian historians (and non-Christian philosophers no less) throw away the kernel. The *vraie vérité* —to a Christian—lies neither in metaphysics nor in the abstract findings of historical science, but in the fellowship of Jesus Christ the living Saviour. 'This is the true God and eternal life.'

11. One form of putting this appeal sets the evidence of later Christian history, with its known developments, against the academic modern study of Christian origins. Christ has founded, and must have meant to found, a worshipping Church! The Germans can put this in a phrase—'der geschichtliche Christus' *versus* 'der sogenannte historische Jesus' (Kähler). There is a measure of truth in this. Indeed, it is bad *history* to forget, in studying origins, whereunto the origins grew. On the other hand, the appeal, put forward without qualification, helps the High Churchmen, if not the Ultramontanes. The Church of history is sacerdotal! Protestant evangelical Christians are forced by their faith, by their experience, into a fruitful alliance with sober all-round history. Like the Reformers, we must go back to the primary revelation. Christianity, as the world knows it, is not the measure of Christ, nor His worthy interpreter. 'Hear ye Him!' ROBERT MACKINTOSH.

HOLINESS.—The word 'holy' is etymologically connected with 'whole,' 'hale,' 'healthy,' etc. (cf. Ger. *heilsam, heilig*). Modern lexicographers hesitate to speak with certainty in regard to the primitive meaning of the root whence this group of words is derived. Murray's *Eng. Dict.* is content to equate 'holy' with the Lat. *sanctus, sacer*, on the ground that 'we cannot in Old English get behind the Christian sense.' It is probable that the sense-development is either from *hailo, i.e.* inviolate, inviolable, that which must be preserved *whole*; or from *hail* in the sense of *health*, wellbeing.

In all the passages to which reference will be made, the Greek word is ἅγιος or one of its derivatives, with the exception of Ac 2²⁷ 13³⁵, Lk 1⁷⁵, He 7²⁶, where ὅσιος or ὁσιότης is found. In Acts the words of Ps 16¹⁰ are quoted twice; 'thy Holy One' is a title of the Messiah to whom pre-eminently belongs the OT designation of the theocratic nation,—οἱ ὅσιοι τοῦ θεοῦ, God's pious ones. 'The ὅσιος, the German *fromm*, is one who reverences the everlasting sanctities and owns their obligation' (Trench, *Synonyms of the NT*, § lxxxviii.). In Lk 1⁷⁵ 'holiness' and 'righteousness' are closely associated, as is frequently the case both in classical and biblical usage. The words are complementary, though the sharp distinction drawn by Plato (*Gorgias*, 507 B) cannot be maintained: in the NT 'righteousness' cannot be limited to duties toward men, nor can 'holiness' be restricted to duties toward God. Righteousness is the manward, as holiness is the Godward aspect of pious character and conduct. Hence Jesus, our High Priest, is 'holy' (He 7²⁶); in His filial reverence and in His devotion to His Father's will there is no flaw; He is, therefore, fitted to appear in the presence of God to do priestly service on our behalf. The LXX usually renders חָסִיד ('godly' or 'beloved') by ὅσιος (Dt 33⁸, 2 S 22²⁶, Ps 4⁴ etc.), but קָדוֹשׁ is generally translated ἅγιος (Ex 19⁶, Nu 6⁵, Ps 15¹, etc.).

Both ἅγιος and קָדוֹשׁ are used when holiness is ascribed to God as well as to persons and things. The question, therefore, arises—What is the primary meaning which underlies and connects these different applications of the word? If the fundamental idea is *separation*, the progress of thought is from the negative to the positive, from men and things to God, from the cleansing which is an essential qualification for use in the service of God to purity as the central attribute of God Himself. But if the fundamental idea is *essential Divinity*, separation becomes a derivative conception; the progress of thought is then from the positive to the negative, from God to external things and persons. Every *thing* devoted to God must be separated from profane or common uses; and every *person* devoted to God is not only thus set apart, but is also under moral obligation to fit himself for drawing near to God by separating himself from all that is sinful.

Those who regard *separation* as the radical meaning of ἅγιος make it almost synonymous with ἁγνός, which signifies *pure*, and sets forth a negative conception of holiness. Stevens (Hastings' *DB*

ii. 399) follows Trench, and interprets 1 Jn 3³—ἐκεῖνος ἁγνός ἐστιν—of God. But, as Westcott (*Com. in loc.*) points out, ἐκεῖνος in this Epistle always refers to Christ; it is in respect of His true humanity that it can be said 'He *is* pure,' and not only 'He *was* pure.' In His glorified state 'the result of the perfection of His earthly discipline (He 5⁷ᶠᶠ·) still abides.' According to St. John, a 'hope set on' (RV) Christ is a constant incentive to strive after holiness; and the standard by which the disciple will always measure his attainments is the perfect purity of his Lord. Few will doubt the soundness of the inference which Westcott bases on his exposition of this verse and on his study of the words:

'Both ἁγνός and καθαρός differ from ἅγιος in that they admit the thought or the fact of temptation or pollution; while ἅγιος describes that which is holy absolutely, either in itself or in idea. God can be spoken of as ἅγιος but not as ἁγνός, while Christ can be spoken of as ἁγνός in virtue of the perfection of His humanity. A man is ἅγιος in virtue of his Divine destination (He 10¹⁰) to which he is gradually conformed (ἁγιάζεται, He 10¹⁴); he is ἁγνός in virtue of earthly, human discipline.'

This clear and helpful distinction assumes that the primary meaning of ἅγιος must be sought in the revelation of the essential nature of God; the various meanings of ἅγιος may thus be traced in orderly sense-development from its root τὸ ἄγος, 'religious awe,' 'reverence.' 'Holy is his name' (Lk 1⁴⁹) is the starting-point; things and persons are holy by reason of their being destined for Divine uses; the secondary meaning of separation from defilement arises at a later stage, as clearer perception of the nature of God also reveals the need of preparation for His service by cleansing from all impurity.

This conclusion must be tested by a brief study of the Jewish conception of holiness. The etymology of קָדוֹשׁ (LXX generally ἅγιος, sometimes καθαρός, never ὅσιος) is disputed. Little can be learnt from the use of cognate words by non-Israelitish peoples. The profound and indeed unique meaning of holiness in the religion of revelation can be ascertained only from a careful investigation of the phraseology of the OT writers. An excellent sketch of the probable history of the word, which assumes that its fundamental idea is separation, is given in Sanday-Headlam's *Romans* (note on 17); but it is acknowledged that 'there is a certain element of conjecture . . . which is inevitable from the fact that the earlier stages in the history of the word had been already gone through when the Hebrew literature begins.' There is, therefore, scope for further inquiry. Kittel (*PRE* ³ vii. 566 ff.) maintains that the root-idea of the word is positive. Things are not holy because they are separated from other things; they are separated from other things because they are holy. When holiness is ascribed to vessels, animals for sacrifice, etc., either order of thought is suitable. But this is not the case when, *e.g.*, the temple, Zion, and heaven are called holy; they are holy because they are the abode of God. If the primary meaning of holy is *that which belongs to God and is devoted to His service*, persons may be called holy who stand in a close relation to God, inasmuch as they are in a special sense His servants. Very instructive is Nu 16⁵ 'In the morning the Lord will show who are his, and who is holy.' As applied to persons and to the nation, holiness acquired a deeper significance. In the Law of Holiness (Lv 17 ff.) the command, 'Ye shall be holy; for I the Lord your God am holy' (Lv 19²), is seen to involve both external requirements referring to ritual, and inward requirements referring to moral character. The holiness of God means, if the positive idea is primary, His 'essential Divinity.' Kittel's exposition accords with Bengel's saying that God's glory (כָּבוֹד) is His disclosed holiness, and His holiness (קֹדֶשׁ) is His inner glory. God's holiness is 'that which proves Him to be God; that which is worthy of God.' Cf. 'The Lord God hath sworn *by his holiness*' (Am 4²), with 'The Lord God hath sworn *by himself*' (Am 6⁸). If it be said that this definition is vague, the reply is that 'the Divine essence cannot be expressed in a single formula which is suitable for all stages in the development of the OT idea of God.' It is a manifest advantage of this view that the evolution of the idea of holiness finds its explanation in the historical evolution of the idea of God. An early stage is seen in 1 S 6²⁰ 'Who is able to stand before the Lord, this holy God?' None may approach Him save those who have complied with the prescribed regulations (cf. 1 S 21⁵). As the moral nature of God was more clearly apprehended, the conception of His holiness was spiritualized; in Hos 11⁹ 'I am God, and not man; the Holy One in the midst of thee,' the Divine holiness is the ethical motive of the resolve, 'I will not come in wrath (RVm) into the city.' Kittel rightly distinguishes God's glory from His holiness: 'Glory' is a cosmic predicate of God, and refers to the outshining of His attributes, which may be metaphysical or moral; but 'holiness' has always a tendency to acquire an ethical significance, and becomes at last solely His moral glory.

The fact that the conception of holiness varies with the conception of God explains the occasional deterioration of the idea. When stress was laid upon the transcendence of God, stress was also laid upon ritual purity. But, in general, later Jewish teaching has insisted upon moral as well as ceremonial purity as being essential qualifications for the service of the Holy One of Israel. Rightly to understand the meaning of 'holy' as used by our Lord and His contemporaries, it is needful to remember that for rabbinical Judaism holiness became 'synonymous with purity of life, purity of action, and purity of thought' (see *Jewish Encyc.* vi. 441b). Holiness is 'an ideal state of perfection attained only by God' (Jerus. *Ber.* ix. 13a); but 'man grows in holiness the more he aspires to the Divine will, rising above the sensual' (*Yoma*, 39a). Dalman says (*Words of Jesus*, p. 202) that 'the Holiness' (חַקֹּדֶשׁ) became a Divine title (*Siphre*, Num. 112, ed. Friedm. 33a).

The NT passages which fall within the limits of this article may be classified according as (1) holiness is ascribed to things, places, or persons by (a) the Evangelists, (b) our Lord; (2) holiness is ascribed to Christ (a) in the Acts, (b) in the Epistles.

1. Holiness in the Gospels.—(a) The Evangelists speak of 'the holy city' (Mt 4[5] 27[53]), 'the holy place' (Mt 24[15]), 'his holy covenant' (Lk 1[72]): Jerusalem and the temple are holy, as being the abode of God; the covenant made with Abraham is holy, as being a revelation of the gracious purpose of God in choosing a people to serve Him in holiness (Lk 1[75]; see above on ὁσιότης). Persons are described as holy, because they are devoted to God's service: in the Gospels mention is made of 'the holy angels' (Mk 8[38], Lk 9[26]), 'his holy prophets' (Lk 1[70]), and Herod is said to have recognized the holiness of John the Baptist (Mk 6[20]); in such uses of the word there is included an assertion of the moral purity which is an essential qualification for the service of God. In Lk 2[23] an OT quotation (Ex 13[2]) explains that the offering of the parents of Jesus, when they presented their child to the Lord in the temple, was a recognition of the fact that every firstborn son was holy as belonging to God. The ascription of holiness to the Divine Spirit (Mt 1[18] etc.) will be considered in paragraph (b); but here it may be noted that in the story of the Annunciation (Lk 1[35]), Mary is told that the Holy Spirit shall come upon her with the result that her child shall be holy (τὸ γεννώμενον ἅγιον); and that once (4[1]) Jesus is described as 'full of the Holy Spirit.' In Mk 1[24] = Lk 4[34] the man with an unclean spirit calls Christ 'the Holy One of God,' and according to the true text Simon Peter uses the same title (Jn 6[69]). The phrase is a designation of the Messiah, described by John (10[36]) as 'him whom the Father consecrated' (ἡγίασε. For this and other uses of ἁγιάζειν see art. CONSECRATION). Finally, holiness is ascribed to God in the *Magnificat*, and the whole context ('his mercy,' etc.) shows that 'holy is his name' (Lk 1[49]) is a declaration of the moral glory of God.

(b) Our Lord never speaks of any *person*, save the Father and the Spirit, as holy; and only once does He describe any *thing* as holy. His command, 'Give not that which is holy to the dogs' (Mt 7[6]), is a proverbial expression whose origin is probably some Jewish exclamation of horror at the thought of profaning altar-flesh, which had been offered in sacrifice to God (Lv 23[6ff.] LXX τὰ ἅγια). A similar saying is quoted from Aristotle: 'Do not fling wisdom into the street' (μήτε ῥῖψαι σοφίαν εἰς τοὺς τριόδους, *ap.* Themist. p. 234).

The application of our Lord's words need not be limited to preachers of the gospel; and it is certain that they do not sanction any doctrine of reserve in the statement of truth; their obvious meaning seems to be that holy themes are not to be exposed to the contempt of the profane. John Wesley's comment (*Sermon* xxx.) is both pithy and pertinent: 'Beware of thinking that any deserve this appellation till there is full and incontestable proof.' But 'great and glorious truths' are not to be forced upon those who 'contradict and blaspheme.' 'Do not begin a discourse with these upon remission

of sins and the gift of the Holy Ghost. . . . The most probable way to make Felix tremble is to reason with him of righteousness, temperance, and judgment to come.'

In each of the four Gospels there are passages in which our Lord speaks of the Holy Spirit, viz. Mt 12[32] 28[19], Mk 3[29] 12[36] 13[11], Lk 12[10. 12], Jn 14[26] 20[22]. In so speaking He definitely ascribes essential Divinity to the Spirit. Not in this way could He have spoken of 'a created Intelligence above the angels' but inferior to Himself. Moreover, this Divine agent is distinguished both from the Father who sends Him, and from the Son in whose name He is sent; and in the NT the phrase which normally describes Him—'the Holy Spirit' —ascribes to Him the essential attributes of Deity, the moral glory of God.

In this sense Dalman's words (*op. cit.* p. 202 f.) must be understood when he says, 'As regards content, there is no difference between "Spirit of God" and "Holy Spirit."' He is careful to point out that, as 'the Holiness' had become a Divine title, 'it might readily be supposed that in the term רוּחַ קָדְשָׁא "the Holy Spirit," the word קָדְשָׁא became in reality a name for God, so that τὸ πνεῦμα τοῦ θεοῦ would represent it more accurately than τὸ πνεῦμα τὸ ἅγιον. But in that case terms like רוּחַ קָדְשֵׁךְ "thy holy spirit" (Ps 51[11]), רוּחָא דְקָדְשִׁי "my holy spirit" (*Targ.* Is 42[1]), would be impossible. And yet it must be maintained that the addition of קָדְשָׁא is expressly meant to specify Divinity as an attribute of the Spirit.' See, further, HOLY SPIRIT.

The last recorded example of our Lord's use of the word 'holy' is in His intercessory prayer. He who never called any human being 'holy' prays that His disciples may attain unto holiness. His petitions are both negative and positive: from the corruptions of the world He asks that they may be kept in the name (Jn 17[11] RV) which in its fulness it had been His mission to reveal. But it is not enough for them to be kept from entering the domain of the Evil One (Jn 17[15] ἐκ τοῦ πονηροῦ, cf. 1 Jn 5[19] 'the whole world lieth in the evil one'). If they are to continue Christ's work, they must be partakers of His holiness, for only in complete devotion of all their powers to the service of God can they share their Master's joy. Hence He also asks, as in absolute self-sacrifice He consecrates Himself, that 'they themselves also may be consecrated in truth' (Jn 17[19]). In these petitions the love of Christ for His own finds full expression, and they are fitly introduced by the unique phrase 'Holy Father' (cf. 'Father,' v.[1], and 'righteous Father,' v.[25]). In this glorious name of God 'all excellences meet'; purity and tenderness unite, majesty and pity combine. Christ regards this all-sufficient knowledge of God as 'an ideal region of security,' in which His disciples will be safe from harm. As long as they are 'in the name,' it will be impossible for thoughts of God's holiness to suggest that it is dangerous to approach the Holy *Father* (cf. 1 S 6[20] 21[5], and see above). Nor can the revelation in Christ of His 'pitying tenderness Divine' lead to sinful presuming on His grace, and to neglect of moral purity, without which none may hold communion with the Holy Father. Therefore, as in the OT the conception of holiness varies with the conception of God, so in the NT the climax of the revelation of the Father in the Son is reached in the harmonizing of the 'many-hued' manifestations (cf. πολυποίκιλος, Eph 3[10]) of His glory in the pure, white light of His holy love. The opening petitions of the Lord's Prayer teach that His Kingdom will come and His will be done 'as in heaven, so on earth,' when in His Church on earth as in heaven the name of the Holy Father is hallowed (Mt 6[10] Ἁγιασθήτω τὸ ὄνομά σου . . . ὡς ἐν οὐρανῷ καὶ ἐπὶ γῆς).

2. The holiness of Christ.—Outside the Gospels holiness is ascribed to Christ in the Acts and the Epistles.—(a) *The Acts.* St. Peter (2[27]) and St. Paul (13[35]) see in the resurrection of Jesus proof that He is God's 'Holy One,' in whom is fulfilled the Messianic promise that He should not see corruption (Ps 16¹⁰; RVm renders חָסִיד 'godly or beloved,' see above on ὅσιος). In the prayer of the early Church, Jesus is twice described as Jehovah's 'Holy Servant' (4²⁷·³⁰), and it is probable that St. Peter has in mind Is 53 when he speaks of Jesus as 'the Holy and Righteous One' (3¹⁴, cf. v.¹³). In these passages ἅγιος is applied to the ideal Servant, in whose consecration, even unto death, God's moral glory was revealed.—(b) *The Epistles.* Our High Priest, for ever 'separated from sinners,' is 'holy' (He 7²⁶). Here ὅσιος is a comprehensive summary of those inward qualities which were manifested by our Lord's dutiful submission to His Father's will; pre-eminently He was 'pure in heart,' fitted to exercise, in the presence of God, His ministry of intercession. In Ro 1⁴ 'the spirit of holiness' is not a synonym of Holy Spirit; holiness is ascribed to the spirit of the Incarnate Son. The πνεῦμα of Christ was human; in this respect He was 'made like unto his brethren' (He 2¹⁷); but His spirit was holy, and in that He was 'without sin' (4¹⁵), He was unique among men. His 'spirit of holiness' was 'the seat of the Divine nature'; He was filled with the Holy Spirit, and being 'essentially filled with God' was 'full of Divine unpolluted life' (cf. Meyer, *Com. in loc.*). St. Paul declares that it was in complete accord (κατά) with the transcendent holiness which was the characterizing quality of the spirit of Christ that His Divine Sonship should be visibly manifested in the miracle of His resurrection. In 1 Jn 2²⁰ 'Ye have an anointing (χρίσμα) from the Holy One,' the reference may possibly be to God the Father; but almost certainly the Holy One is Christ (cf. 3³ 'He is pure,' and see above). The true reading in v.²⁷ (αὐτοῦ not τὸ αὐτό), 'His anointing,' seems to remove all ambiguity. St. John says that Christians have a chrism from the Christ; and there can be little doubt that the predominant reference in chrism is to the Holy Spirit. It is 'a faint prelusive note,' and in 3²⁴ 'the full distinct mention of the Holy Spirit comes like a burst of the music of the "Veni Creator," carrying on the fainter prelude' (*Expos. Bible*, p. 170).

The chief contributions to the formal exposition of the NT doctrine of holiness lie beyond the limits of this article. It need occasion no surprise that even to His disciples our Lord should not speak directly concerning holiness until in His farewell prayer He asked that the men called to continue His mission might share His consecration. The reason for His reticence is that 'in Him, and for them, holiness imported something—far more and other than it did in the religion of the day. . . . Only as they saw their Lord devote His person in the consummating sacrifice would they be prepared to realize what their Christian consecration involved' (Findlay, *Expositor*, VI. [1901] iv. 5). It is also significant that the prayer for His disciples' holiness should immediately follow the discourse in which our Lord expounds in welcome detail what is involved in the promise of the Spirit whose gracious indwelling is the secret of holiness.

The Gospels are, however, the supreme revelation of holiness. The imitation of Christ is the royal road to holiness; His teaching concerning union with Himself and the bestowment of the Holy Spirit reveals the secret of holiness. The writers of the Epistles, under the guidance of the promised Teacher, unfolded the implications of their own experience and the purpose of the Incarnation, the Passion, and the abiding Priesthood of the Son of God.

The stress laid on the positive idea, which is probably the primary conception of holiness, may serve to guard Christians against the error of supposing that holiness may be acquired by withdrawals and negations, or by compliance with external regulations. Holiness means the attainment of the Divine likeness, and this consists in moral qualities which are all comprised in holy love. The motive to holiness increases in strength as God is more perfectly known. In proportion as the Holy Father is known as He is, will be the gladness of our response to His claims, and the ardour of our desire to be like Him in this world. Into the world Christ sent the men for whose consecration He prayed, and His promise, 'Ye shall know that ye are in me' (Jn 14²⁰), conveyed to them His assurance that 'in the world' they should attain to holiness. Life in Christ is holiness.

LITERATURE.—In addition to the books mentioned in the body of the article, see the *Comm.* on the various passages, and works on *Theol. of NT*; also Grimm-Thayer and Cremer, *svv.* ἅγιος, ὅσιος; art. 'Holiness' in Hastings' *DB*; Issel, *Der Begriff d. Heiligkeit im NT*; Askwith, *Christian Conception of Holiness.*

J. G. TASKER.

HOLY ONE.—The expression 'the Holy One,' or 'the Holy One of God,' is used several times in the NT to describe our Lord. It is in itself so remarkable, and used in a manner so calculated to arrest attention, that it has been surmised that we have here a characteristic designation of the Messiah (Meyer on Mk 1²⁴). While it may be doubted if so positive an assertion can be justified, the expression is sufficiently striking to require a careful examination into its origin and its significance.

A scrutiny of the passages in which the AV has rendered the Greek expression by 'the Holy One,' will show that for the word 'holy' we have two Greek words, ὅσιος and ἅγιος. Now, since the two passages in which ὅσιος occurs are in a quotation from the LXX, and the signification of the term is most likely to be derived from a Hebrew original, it will be necessary to ask if these two words are uniformly used to represent corresponding Hebrew ones, or used indiscriminately to tr. different Heb. words in different places.

In the OT there are two distinct words used for 'holy,' חָסִיד and קְדוֹשׁ, and it is to be carefully noted that in the LXX, although ὅσιος tr. חָסִיד about 30 times, and ἅγιος tr. קְדוֹשׁ 100 times, in no single instance is ὅσιος used for קְדוֹשׁ, or ἅγιος for חָסִיד. (See Trench, *NT Synonyms*).

It is reasonable, then, to look for the signification of ὅσιος in חָסִיד, and ἅγιος in קְדוֹשׁ. See art. HOLINESS.

A. Passages in which our Lord is described as 'Holy One,' ὅσιος being used. As a substantive expression it occurs only in Ac 2²⁷ 13³⁵—in both cases a quotation from Ps 16¹⁰—used first by St. Peter and afterwards by St. Paul,—οὐδὲ δώσεις τὸν ὅσιόν σου ἰδεῖν διαφθοράν. Without a reference to the Hebrew, it might appear that such an expression, taken from the OT and applied by Apostles to Christ, would carry with it peculiar significance; but beyond the fact that the Apostles so used the expression, there is nothing in the words themselves to justify any unique position in which our Lord was described as 'holy.'

B. Passages in which our Lord is described as 'Holy One,' ἅγιος being used. If the examination of the foregoing passages prevents us giving to the word ὅσιος any peculiar significance which would make it describe our Lord as a being of peculiar holiness, the case is quite otherwise when we come to the expression ὁ ἅγιος.

1. *Use of the title.*—We find it first on the lips of the demoniac (Mk 1²⁴, Lk 4³⁴), who, in declaring his knowledge of Christ, describes Him as 'the Holy One of God' (οἶδά σε τίς εἶ, ὁ ἅγιος τοῦ Θεοῦ). The words probably made a deep impression on the disciples. We know how vague and uncertain were their views about their Master, and it would seem as if they seized on the demoniac's confession as a revelation of His claims ; for, the next time the title is ascribed to Him, it is by St. Peter himself, when striving to find words to answer our Lord's question if they too intended to abandon Him : 'Lord, to whom shall we go ? Thou hast the words of eternal life. And we have believed and know that thou art the Holy One of God' (ὅτι σὺ εἶ ὁ ἅγιος τοῦ Θεοῦ [so correct reading], Jn 6⁶⁹).

St. Peter, in his speech to the people in Solomon's porch (Ac 3¹⁴), charges them with denying 'the Holy and Righteous One' (τὸν ἅγιον καὶ δίκαιον). St. John (1 Jn 2²⁰) tells his readers that they have 'an anointing from the Holy One' (ἀπὸ τοῦ ἁγίου). In Rev 3⁷ our Lord so describes Himself in the address to the Church of Philadelphia : 'These things saith he that is holy' (τάδε λέγει ὁ ἅγιος).

2. *Derivation of the title.*—We have seen that the significance of ἅγιος is naturally to be looked for in the Heb. קָדוֹשׁ, which, like חָסִיד, is freely employed of places, things, and persons. Yet, while חָסִיד is used of God only in Jer 3¹² (LXX ἐλεήμων) and Ps 145¹⁷ (LXX ὅσιος), where it is joined with a reference to His works ('holy in all thy works'), קָדוֹשׁ is used very frequently to describe God Himself. It is so found in the Books of Job, Psalms, Isaiah, Hosea, and Habakkuk, קָדוֹשׁ 'the Holy One,' LXX ὁ ἅγιος. Besides the simple title 'the Holy One,' God is 24 times called by Isaiah 'the Holy One of Israel' ; elsewhere only in Ps 71²² 78⁴¹ 89¹⁸, Jer 50²⁹ 51⁵ [2 K 19²² = Is 37²³] קְדוֹשׁ יִשְׂרָאֵל.

3. *Its significance as applied to our Lord.*—To men familiar with the OT expressions 'the Holy One' and 'the Holy One of Israel,' as describing God Himself, it would seem almost impossible that the expression could have been used of Christ without a distinct desire to connect His title with that of Jehovah. Every male firstborn was indeed 'holy to the Lord' (Lk 2²³). But on the lips of St. Peter and the demoniac it must be felt to have that special and distinct significance such as Jesus Himself implies in Jn 10³⁶, when speaking of Himself as one 'whom the Father sanctified (ἡγίασε) and sent into the world.' Spoken by our Saviour of His Father (Jn 17¹¹), it signifies that which He is absolutely ; spoken of Christ Himself, it means both this and also His special dedication to the work of man's salvation (e.g. in Ro 12¹ it is used with the force of a sacrificial metaphor, the victim consecrated to God). Christ was indeed the Holy One of God above all others, but that which He was He came in a measure to make His people, so that, in the language of the NT, those who through Him were consecrated and set apart were also οἱ ἅγιοι. See, further, art. HOLINESS.

LITERATURE.—Trench, *NT Synonyms*, § lxxxviii.; Westcott on He 7²⁶ ; Lightfoot on 1 Th 11¹⁰ ; Jennings and Lowe, *Psalms* ; *Jewish Encyc.* vol. vi. *s.vv.* 'God' and 'Holiness' ; Dalman, *Words of Jesus*, p. 202.   J. B. BRISTOW.

HOLY SPIRIT.—With the exception of the 2nd and 3rd Epistles of John, every book in the NT mentions the Spirit. On a comprehensive view, indeed, it may be said that to understand what is meant by the Spirit is to understand these two things—the NT and the Christian Church. Not that the two can be precisely co-ordinated ; yet in them and in their mutual relations we have the only adequate witness to what the Spirit means for Christians. To the men who wrote the NT and to those for whom they wrote, the Spirit was not a doctrine but an experience ; they did not speak of believing in the Holy Spirit, but of receiving the Holy Spirit when they believed (Ac 19²). In some sense this covered everything that they included in Christianity. The work of the Christ was summed up in the words : 'He shall baptize with holy spirit' (Mk 1⁸). The acceptance of the

gospel is the subject of the question : 'Was it by works of law or by the hearing of faith that you received the Spirit?' (Gal 3²). The entire equality of Jews and Gentiles in the Christian community is asserted in the words : 'God who knows the heart bore them witness in that he gave the Holy Spirit to them even as he did to us' (Ac 15⁸). After this, there was no more to be said. Yet the very fact that all who speak to us in the NT are familiar with experiences of the Holy Spirit does not always make it easier for us to understand them. It is clear that very various experiences are described in this way, and sometimes we cannot refrain from asking whether experiences which one writer recounts without any reference to the Spirit would not have been explained as 'pneumatic' by another ; or *vice versa*, whether experiences ascribed to the Spirit by one writer would not in another have found a different interpretation. Further, there is the difficulty raised by the fact that while the experiences thus explained are represented, broadly speaking, as the work of the Risen Saviour, and as dependent somehow on His death and resurrection, the Spirit appears also in His life on earth. Was this the same thing? When we read that Jesus was baptized with the Holy Spirit, are we to suppose that He had experiences in consequence which were analogous to those of Christians in the Apostolic age? The purpose of this article is to bring out the facts as they are presented in the oldest Gospel to begin with, and to show from later stages in the history the relation between the Spirit and Jesus the Christ.

1. The earliest reference to the Spirit is in the preaching of the Baptist. To the end John was conscious of the impotence and inadequacy of all his efforts : the true Helper of Israel, whatever else he might be, must be 'One mightier than I.' 'I baptize you with water, he shall baptize you with holy spirit' (Mk 1⁸). A Christian Evangelist, like the author of the Gospel, might interpret such words in the light of his own post-Pentecostal experiences ; and when we find the later Evangelists (Mt 3¹¹, Lk 3¹⁶) add to 'holy spirit' the words 'and fire,' it is nearly certain that they have done so.* But it is not clear that for the Baptist the Holy Spirit of which he spoke was so clearly defined. He had not the Christian experience to put meaning into his words, and he can only have intended something which could be understood through its OT antecedents, or through experiences with which he had been in contact at an earlier period. The earliest form of the Gospel says nothing of such experiences, and when we look backward we cannot but be struck by the almost total disappearance of the Spirit from the apocalyptical literature of Judaism. 'First and Second Maccabees and Daniel are each in a different way witnesses for a very profound religious feeling of exactly the sort that in other ages, either earlier or later, would have been ascribed to the Spirit' (Wood, *The Spirit of God in Biblical Literature*, p. 71 ; cf. Gunkel, *Die Wirkungen des heiligen Geistes*, p. 50 f.). Yet the Spirit is not appealed to in explanation. When we come to the Hebrew OT, however, the one idea which is dominant in connexion with the Spirit is the one which is wanted here to explain the prophecy of the Baptist—the idea of power as opposed to impotence. The inability of Egypt to help Israel is expressed by Isaiah in the words : 'The Egyptians are men and not God, and their horses flesh and not spirit' (31³).

---

* The reference of the 'fire' in this connexion to the fire of Gehenna seems to the present writer (in spite of Mt 3¹², Lk 3¹⁷) simply incredible. The true key to it is Ac 2³, and the many passages in which the same or a similar figure recurs, *e.g.* 1 Th 5¹⁹, Ro 12¹¹, Ac 18²⁵.

Men and flesh are the impotent things, in contrast with the omnipotent, God and spirit. As A. B. Davidson puts it (*Theology of the OT*, 126), 'the Spirit of God *ab intra* is God active, showing life and power . . . the Spirit of God *ab extra* is God in efficient operation, whether in the cosmos or as giving life, reinforcing life, exerting efficiency in any sphere.' John the Baptist was a worker for God, but he never claims for himself either to have the Spirit or to be able to give it; he has the sense, however, that when the Mightier than himself comes, He will be distinguished in precisely these ways. He will baptize with 'holy spirit' in virtue of being full of the Spirit himself.

2. When Jesus comes to be baptized in Jordan, the remarkable phenomenon is that what for others is a baptism with water coincides for Him with a baptism in the Holy Spirit. According to Mk 1^{10}, as Jesus ascends from the water, He sees the heavens cleaving and the Spirit as a dove descending upon Him. In the earliest Evangelist this is the experience of Jesus only: it is He who sees the Spirit descending, He to whom the heavenly voice is addressed. The later Evangelists may have conceived it otherwise, and extended the vision and the hearing of the voice to John the Baptist or even to the bystanders: it is indifferent here. All agree that on this occasion Jesus received the Holy Spirit, and in it the attestation of His Sonship, the call to His unique task, and the endowments needed to discharge it.

Critics have suggested that the curiously indirect way in which the baptism of Jesus and the descent of the Spirit are mentioned in Lk $3^{21f.}$ is due to the writer's desire to slur over something which is really inconsistent with his account of Jesus' birth; but even if Luke had difficulty in adjusting these two things, as the Fourth Evangelist may have had difficulty in adjusting the incarnation of the Eternal Logos in Jesus with the descent of the Spirit upon Him in manhood, it is clear that for both the baptism was so securely fixed in the Gospel testimony that they had no alternative but to set it unambiguously down (cf. Jn 1^{31-34}).

Have we any means of saying what is meant by such words as the Evangelists employ in this connexion? Can we interpret Jesus' experience by what we read of spiritual gifts or states in the Primitive Church? Is it right to look in His life for such phenomena as we find, *e.g.*, in Acts or in 1 Cor. ascribed to the Spirit? May we look for such sudden accesses of feeling as we connect with scenes like Ac 2^4 4^{31} 13^9? Can there be such a thing as the rapture or ecstasy which seems to be meant by being 'in the Spirit' in Rev 1^{10} 4^2 17^3 21^{10}? These are not questions to be answered *a priori*. There must have been something in the life of Jesus as determined by the great experience of His baptism akin to the experiences which Christians subsequently ascribed to the Spirit, or they would hardly have traced both to the same source ; and the more closely we look into the Gospels, the less does the emotionally colourless Saviour of popular art seem to correspond to the historical reality. The experiences of Jesus at the Baptism and the Transfiguration were not those of everyday life; they belong to 'pneumatic' as contrasted with normal conditions. So again it might be said that if the cleansing of the temple (Mk $11^{15ff.}$), the cursing of the fig-tree (11^{14}), the excitement (apparently) with which, on the way to Jerusalem, Jesus took the lead of His disciples, to their bewilderment and fear (10^{32}), had been told of anybody else, that other would have been described, on each occasion, as 'filled with the Holy Spirit.' However this may be (see J. Weiss, *Die Predigt Jesu vom Reiche Gottes*, p. 54 n. ; O. Holtzmann, *War Jesus Ekstatiker ?*), the Evangelist makes no reference to the Spirit in this connexion. He leaves us to infer from the life which Jesus lived in the Spirit what the Spirit itself was. But it may fairly be said that some of the ideas which Chris-

tians subsequently connected with their own baptism were not without relation to the baptism of Jesus and to the interpretation which they put upon it. It was the facts of His baptism which led them to believe (*a*) in a normal coincidence of baptism with the Spirit and water-baptism, instead of in the displacement of the latter by the former ; (*b*) in the Spirit received in baptism as specifically the spirit of sonship ; and (*c*) in that same Spirit as one consecrating them to God and to service in His kingdom.

3. The first light is thrown on the nature of the Spirit as received by Jesus in the narrative of the Temptations. It is the Spirit which sends Him out to the wilderness, there to engage in conflict with the power of evil. The word ἐκβάλλει (Mk 1^{12}), though it must not be forced, suggests a Divine impulse which could not be resisted. Jesus was Divinely constrained — for the Spirit is always Divine—to face the ultimate issues of His work from the very beginning, to contemplate all the plausible but morally unsound ways of aiming at ascendency over men for God, and to turn from them ; to face the Prince of this world, and to demonstrate that that Prince had nothing in Him. The most elementary notion of the Spirit may be that of Divine power, but where we see it first at work in Jesus it is Divine power which is at the same time holy ; it is at war, in principle, with everything which is unworthy of God ; the kingdom which the Son of God is to found in the power of the Spirit is one which can make no kind of compromise with evil. It must be spiritual (in the complete Christian sense) in its nature—not based on bread ; spiritual in its methods—not appealing to miracles which only dazzle the senses or confound the mind ; and spiritual in its resources—not deriving any of its strength from alliance with Satan, from borrowing the help of the evil which wields such vast power among men, or from recognizing that it has a relative or temporary right to exist. 'The spirit,' as Mk. calls it ($1^{10.\ 12}$), while Mt. has 'God's spirit' (3^{16}), and Lk. 'the holy spirit' (3^{22}) or 'holy spirit' (4^1), is the Divine power with which Jesus was endowed at His baptism, and which committed Him to an irreconcilable conflict with evil. It is the conscious and victorious antagonist of another spirit, of which all that need be said is that it is not of God.

4. St. Luke tells us that Jesus returned from the Jordan 'in the power of the Spirit' into Galilee (4^{14}), and St. Peter in Ac ($10^{38f.}$) tells how God anointed Him (in the Baptism) 'with holy spirit and power' ; and it is under these conditions that the Evangelists conceive His whole ministry to be fulfilled. If they do not mention the Spirit at every step, it is because they think of Him as in full possession of it continually. It probably agrees, *e.g.*, with the Evangelist's own idea, to say that the passage in Mk. which immediately succeeds the Temptations illustrates first by Jesus' power over men (1^{16-20}), next by His power or authority in teaching ($1^{21f.}$), and, finally, by His power over demons ($1^{23ff.}$), what is involved in His possession of the Spirit. A Divine power accompanied all His words and deeds, and made them effective for God and for His kingdom. The allusion in 1^{35} to His rising early and going away to a desert place to pray suggests that, Divine as this power was, it wrought in, and in accordance with the laws of, a human nature which was capable of spiritual exhaustion, and had to recruit its strength with God. We do not find till we come to 3^{21} ('they said, He is beside himself,' ἐξέστη) any further indication of how His work in the Spirit affected Jesus. It is clear from this impatient word, in which the same charge is brought against the Lord as was afterwards brought against Paul (see

2 Co 5¹³, where ἐξέστημεν is opposed to σωφρονοῦμεν), that the tension of His spirit seemed at times abnormal: He was 'rapt' or 'carried away' by His earnestness, and became for the time unconscious of bodily needs or indifferent to them (cf. the fast in the wilderness, and Jn 4³¹ᶠᶠ·). Possibly even the charge brought against Him by the scribes, that He cast out devils by Beelzebub, in other words, that He was possessed Himself by a demon,—a charge mentioned in this connexion by Mk.,—appealed for support to this tension or rapture. If the character of Jesus' teaching and healing had been that of emotionless placidity, it would not have been even plausible to say δαιμόνιον ἔχει καὶ μαίνεται (Jn 8⁴⁸·⁵² 10²⁰: these passages from the Fourth Gospel are guaranteed by their agreement with Mk 3²¹ᶠ·). There is no trace in the Gospel of any want of self-control,—no such frenzy as is ascribed to the Spirit in 1 S 19²³ᶠ·, or in the description of the glossolalists in 1 Co 14,—but there is a superhuman intensity implied which was felt throughout the life in word and deed.

5. The main interest of the passage Mk 3²⁰⁻³⁵ lies in the word of Jesus Himself about the Holy Spirit: 'Verily I say unto you, All things shall be forgiven to the sons of men, the sins and the blasphemies, all that they have blasphemed: but whoso shall have blasphemed the Holy Spirit hath never forgiveness, but is guilty of eternal sin: because they said, He hath an unclean spirit' (v.²⁸ᶠ·). It is hardly doubtful that this is the true form of this much discussed saying of Jesus. The Holy Spirit is not here set in any contrast with Jesus, as though to blaspheme Jesus were a venial fault, but to blaspheme the Spirit an unpardonable one; on the contrary, the Holy Spirit is blasphemed when malignant hearts harden themselves to say of *Jesus*, 'He has an unclean spirit.' The Divine power which works through Jesus with such intensity, healing all who are under the tyranny of the devil, is in point of fact God's supreme and final appeal to men. It is such an exercise of power as is possible only for one who has already vanquished Satan, and is engaged in liberating his captives (Mk 3²⁷). No person with any sense for God in him can help being attracted by it to begin with. But if the other manifestations of this power should happen to provoke resentment,—if its ethical demands (as in the teaching of Jesus) should threaten seriously the reputation or the self-complacency of the insincere,—it is fearfully possible that they may set themselves against it, and so resist the Holy Spirit. Such resistance, once begun, may go to any length, even to the length of defiantly misinterpreting the life of Jesus, and affirming it to be from beneath, not from above. This is the sin against the Holy Spirit. In principle, it is the everyday sin of finding bad motives for good actions; carried to its unpardonable height, it is the sin of confronting the Divine holy power which wrought so irresistibly and so intensely in Jesus, and saying anything—the maddest, most wanton, most malignant thing—rather than acknowledge it for what it is. The people who said, 'He has Beelzebul' (3²²), 'He has an unclean spirit' (v.³⁰), were not giving expression to their first, but to their last thoughts of Christ. This was the depth which malignity in them had reached. The Holy Spirit receives here a certain interpretation from being contrasted with an 'unclean' spirit. 'Unclean' is a religious rather than an ethical word; the unclean spirit is one which has not and cannot have relations with God: it can only be excluded from His presence, as it excludes those who are possessed by it. The Holy Spirit is specifically God's; it brings Him in His power to men, it is the very token and reality of His presence with them. But it is interpreted

more precisely—and this is the point of Jesus' argument as it is brought out in the parallel passage in Mt. and Lk.—by the works which it does. 'If I in the spirit of God am casting out the demons, then the kingdom of God has come upon you' (Mt 12²⁸, cf. Lk 11²⁰, where for ἐν πνεύματι θεοῦ we have ἐν δακτύλῳ θεοῦ, the Divine power being the essential idea; cf. Ex 8¹⁹ ⁽¹⁵⁾). When the superhuman power which displays itself with such intensity is manifested in works of this sort, it is clear that it is not merely superhuman, but specifically Divine. To withstand what is so unambiguously the redeeming power of God, and to do so deliberately and malignantly, in the spirit which will kill Jesus rather than acknowledge Him as what He is, is the unpardonable sin.

The form of this saying which appears in Mt 12³¹ᶠ· and Lk 12¹⁰ has almost certainly been deflected in tradition. Mt. really has it in two forms, v.³¹ by itself corresponding to what we have in Mk., and v.³² to what we have in Luke. That is, Mt 12³¹ᶠ· is a doublet, in which the same saying is found, first as it appeared in the Gospel of Mk., and then as it appeared in the collection of discourses generally allowed to have been used by Mt. and Luke. What is meant in the second form, where a word spoken against the Son of Man is contrasted with blasphemy against the Holy Spirit, is not very clear. Mk., who puts the odious charge, 'He has an unclean spirit,' into connexion with the word of Jesus' friends, 'He is beside himself,' might be regarded as giving a key to the meaning, were it not for the fact that 'the Son of Man' does not occur in his text at all. An impatient, petulant word, like 'He is crazy,' bursting in a moment of anxiety or irritation or misunderstanding from hearts that at bottom loved Him, was no doubt a sin; His friends ought to have been more capable of doing Him justice. But it was not a sin which committed the whole nature blindly and finally against God; it could be repented of, and when it was, then, like other sins, it would be forgiven. This would be the word spoken against the Son of Man. In contrast with such a momentary petulance on the part of His friends stands the hideous expression in which hatred of God's present saving power reveals its utter antagonism: 'He has an unclean spirit.' Here the nature is finally committed against God; such a word blasphemes His Spirit—that is, it blasphemes God as He is actually here, working in Christ for man's salvation; as such it is sin absolutely, αἰώνιον ἁμάρτημα, *i.e.* sin which has the character of finality, and can never be anything but what it is—sin past which one cannot see so as to infer the possibility of forgiveness either in this world or in the next.

6. The expulsion of evil spirits from the possessed is regarded in the Gospel as a chief manifestation of the possession by Jesus of the Holy Spirit. But all His miracles are to be understood in this connexion. Without going so far as to say that in the Temptation narratives He is represented as tempted to put to selfish uses the power just conferred through the Spirit in baptism for the ends of God's kingdom, it is a mark of historicity in the canonical Gospels that until He is baptized with the Spirit, Jesus works no miracle. It is the Spirit in which the power is given for all His mighty works (δυνάμεις). It is not likely, however, that when we read of power as having gone forth from Him (which in Mk 5³⁰ and Lk 6¹⁹ may be only the Evangelist's reading of the facts, but in Lk 8⁴⁶ is distinctly ascribed to Jesus Himself), any reference to the Spirit is intended. The wisdom and the mighty works which astonished the Nazarenes (Mk 6²) would no doubt be referred to this source by the Evangelist; and when in 6⁷ Jesus sends out the Twelve, giving them authority over the unclean spirits, it can only have been conceived as due to the transference to them of a part in that Divine power which had been so wonderfully operative in Him (cf. Nu 11¹⁷). The idea, however, that it was the Risen Saviour by whom the Spirit was given to the Apostles so dominated the Evangelists, that none of them refers to the Spirit in connexion with this mission of the Twelve during Jesus' lifetime. The Spirit of Jesus in Mk 8¹² is no doubt, as in 2⁸, His human spirit; but if we admit that it is to this that the Spirit of God is most akin, or most immediately attached, it is perhaps not fanciful to suppose that the sigh (ἀναστενάξας, cf. in a similar situation 7³⁴) represents the grieving of the Spirit of God by the unbelief and hard-heartedness of man (cf. Eph 4[30], Is 63[10]). It is more hazardous to argue that only in 'pneumatic' and abnormal conditions—only in a psychological state extraordinarily and violently elevated above the level of common experience—did Jesus identify Himself with the Son of Man, who after a tragic career on earth was to rise again on the third day, or to come on the clouds of heaven (Mk 8[31] 9[31] 10[32ff.] 14[62]). Abnormal conditions such as are here supposed do not persist in sane minds, and to call Jesus an 'ecstatic' or a 'pneumatic' in this sense is only to avoid calling Him a fanatic by using a natural instead of a moral term to describe Him. Certainly the Gospel suggests in this period of His life accesses of intense emotion (Mk 8[33]) and phenomena both in His aspect (9[15]) and in His conduct (10[32]) which must have struck people as unusual, and due to something overpowering within, which it would have been natural to call the Spirit; but in point of fact there is no reference to the Spirit in this period. Perhaps the nearest approach to it is in Mk 10[38], where Jesus asks James and John, 'Are ye able to be baptized with the baptism with which I am baptized?' There is no doubt that Jesus speaks throughout this scene with unusual elevation of tone; and the figure of baptism, which He could hardly use without recalling the experience at the Jordan and all that His consecration there involved, lifts us into the region where the thought of the Spirit is near. Still, it is not expressed. The Triumphal Entry, the Cleansing of the Temple, and the Blighting of the Fig-tree are all acts implying intensity and elevation of feeling transcending common human limits: often other persons, visited by such impulses with startling suddenness, are said to be 'filled with holy spirit,' but in Jesus they do not seem to have made the same impression on bystanders. They did not apparently stand in relief in His life as they would have done in the life of others; little in it is specifically assigned to the Spirit, because the spiritual baptism at the beginning impelled and controlled it throughout. It does not really cast any light on Jesus' experience of the Spirit, when in Mk 12[36] He quotes Ps 110 by 'David himself said in the Holy Spirit': this merely represents the Jewish belief in the Divine inspiration of Scripture, a belief most distinctly preserved in the Epistle to the Hebrews, where OT quotations are introduced by 'as saith the Holy Spirit,' etc. (3[7] 9[8] 10[15]; cf. 2 P 1[21], 2 Ti 3[16], Ac 1[16]). More important is Mk 13[11], which contains the only promise of the Holy Spirit in the earliest Evangelist. Referring to the persecutions which will come upon the Apostles after His death, Jesus says: 'When they lead you to judgment and deliver you up, be not anxious beforehand what ye shall speak, but whatever is given to you in that hour, that speak; for it is not you that speak, but the Holy Spirit.' The Spirit is here conceived as a Divine reinforcement in the very crisis of need. If fidelity to the gospel brings men to extremity, they will not be left there, but will have experience of superhuman help. It is important to notice that the precise character in which the Spirit which comes to the help of the disciples is here conceived as acting is that of a παράκλητος or advocatus—an idea of which ampler use is made in the Gospel and 1st Epistle of John. The term παράκλητος may be due to the Evangelist, but the conception of the Spirit's function goes back to the Lord. It is not the Holy Spirit which is referred to in Mk 14[38]; and in 16[16-20], although mention is made, as is natural in a late passage based on other NT writings, of most of what are usually called spiritual gifts, the Spirit itself is not expressly named.

If, then, we try to sum up the oldest Evangelic

representation, we can hardly say more than that the Holy Spirit is the Divine power which from His baptism onward wrought in Jesus, making Him mighty in word and deed—a power the character of which is shown by the teaching and by the saving miracles of Jesus—a power to which the sanctity of God attached, so that it is Divine also in the ethical sense, and to blaspheme it is the last degree of sin—a power in which Jesus enabled His disciples to some extent to share, and which He promised would be with them in the emergencies of their mission—a power, however, which (contrary to what we might have anticipated) the Evangelist does not bring into prominence at any of the crises or intense moments of Jesus' life. It takes nothing less than that life itself, from beginning to end, to show us what the Spirit means. If the last Evangelist tells us that the Spirit interprets Jesus, the inference from the first is that Jesus also interprets the Spirit, and that only through Him can we know what it means.

7. If we turn from Mark to the other Evangelic source common to Mt. and Lk., we find little to add to this. Both our First and our Third Evangelists have everything which Mk. has, and their variations (e.g. Mt 3[11], Lk 3[16] as opp. Mk 1[8]; Mt 12[31f.], Lk 12[10] as opp. Mk 3[28ff.]; Mt 10[20], Lk 12[12] 21[15] as opp. Mk 13[11]) have been noticed already, or are of no consequence. But when we look at what is peculiar to Mt. and to Lk. respectively, there is more to say. Omitting for the moment the first two chapters in each, we notice these points.

(a) It is a mark of historicity in Mt. that in recording the Sermon on the Mount he nowhere alludes to the distinction of 'letter' and 'spirit' which occurs so spontaneously to the modern interpreter of the words of Jesus. On the other hand, in 7[22] we have an utterance of Jesus reproduced in terms which have almost certainly been influenced by post-Pentecostal experiences of the Spirit. It was only then that men 'prophesied' in the name of Jesus, etc., and till they had done so, such language as this could not have been used. Comparison with Lk 13[25ff.] justifies us in saying that we have here the word rather than the words of the Lord. But in any case, the idea that the most amazing gifts of the Spirit are worthless apart from common morality—the idea expanded in 1 Co 13—is here traced back to Jesus Himself. It is difficult to understand a Divine power, the action of which, so to speak, elevates and reinforces the nature, without raising the character; yet this is undeniably what is contemplated both by Jesus and by St. Paul. Perhaps the underlying truth is that the moral nature is the deepest and the hardest to penetrate by the Divine power, and may remain unaffected by it when other elements of our being have been subdued to its service. The unnaturalness of such a result is reflected on by Jesus in Mt 11[21f.], where woes are pronounced on the cities which had seen so many of His mighty works, yet had not repented. It is implied that these mighty works, the works of the Spirit in Him, were of such a character—that is, so holy and gracious—that they ought to have evoked penitence, and brought a new moral life into being. An interesting light is thrown on the Evangelist's own conception of the Spirit in relation to Jesus, by his application to our Lord of the prophecy in Is 42[1-4] 'I will put my spirit upon him, and he shall bring forth judgment to the Gentiles,' etc. (Mt 12[18-21]). Here not only the power of Jesus, which gives Him assurance of final victory (Mt 12[20]), but His method and His temper—His meekness, patience, constancy—are ascribed to the Spirit. The presence and power of God are felt in His superhuman renunciation of the ordinary ways and tempers of men as much as in the superhuman resources which He wielded. It is again a mark of historicity in Mt. that we find no mention of the Spirit where in a writer dominated by the consciousness of a later time we should certainly have expected it—that is, in the passages which speak of what are sometimes called ecclesiastical prerogatives or functions ($16^{18\text{ff.}}$ $18^{15\text{-}20}$). Contrast with these Jn $20^{22\text{f.}}$, Ac 15^{28}. The Trinitarian baptismal formula, however it be explained, throws no light on the Spirit as an experience in the life of Jesus (Mt 28^{19}).

(*b*) St. Luke's interest in the Spirit, as the most conspicuous phenomenon in primitive Christianity, is well known, and it is apparent in his Gospel. Thus he describes Jesus, as the result of His baptism, as πλήρης πνεύματος ἁγίου (4^1), where the adjective seems intended to describe a permanent condition, as opposed to the verb (used of sudden and transient accesses of the Spirit in $1^{41. \, 67}$). Similarly he says that in the wilderness ἤγετο ἐν τῷ πνεύματι (4^1), which seems to signify an intense, rapt, and absorbed state of feeling, in which He was carried up and down the desert. The form of words is used elsewhere to describe either possession by an evil spirit (Mk 1^{23} ἄνθρωπος ἐν πνεύματι ἀκαθάρτῳ) or ecstasy in the Divine (Rev 1^{10} ἐγενόμην ἐν πνεύματι). More instructive is the way in which St. Luke puts the whole ministry of Jesus under the heading of the Spirit. He returns from the Jordan to Galilee ἐν τῇ δυνάμει τοῦ πνεύματος, and it is this power which is the key to all the marvellous life which follows (4^{14}, cf. the summary account of Jesus' life by the same writer from the lips of St. Peter in Ac 10^{38}). But though power—that is, the presence of God, who can do what men cannot do—is the fundamental note of the Spirit, it is not power undefined. St. Luke has no sooner spoken of Jesus as entering on His work in the power of the Spirit, than he interprets this by the scene at Nazareth where Jesus applies to Himself the prophecy of Is $61^{1\text{f.}}$ 'The spirit of the Lord is upon me, because he hath anointed me to preach glad tidings to the poor,' etc. (Lk $4^{18\text{f.}}$). 'The words of grace which proceeded out of his mouth' on this occasion (v.^{22}), and the spiritual healings which He wrought, were as unmistakably tokens of the Spirit as the 'mighty works' which the Nazarenes had heard of as wrought at Capernaum.

If the reading of the TR in 9^{55} (οὐκ οἴδατε οἵου πνεύματός ἐστε ὑμεῖς) has any authority, it is to the same intent: the spirit in which Jesus came, to seek and save the lost, was the very opposite of that which wished to call down fire from heaven on the inhospitable Samaritans. There is an approach here to the sense of 'temper' or 'disposition' for spirit, but it is temper or disposition regarded in relation to the power which produces it; the Divine power which works in Jesus makes Him a Saviour, and it is therefore quite different from that other power, whatever it be, which has found its instruments in James and John.

One of the most interesting singularities in Lk. is his reference to the Spirit in 10^{21} ‖ Mt 11^{25} 'In that hour Jesus rejoiced in the Holy Spirit, and said, I thank thee, O Father,' etc. Both Evangelists, in giving the one passage in the Synoptic tradition which has the Johannine ring, are conscious of its peculiar elevation of thought and feeling, but only Lk. interprets it in this way. The authority on which he depended must have preserved for him the remembrance of a joyful excitement thrilling Jesus as He spoke. The context, too, favours this. The Seventy return to Jesus (10^{17}) exulting that even the demons are subject to them in His name. In a sudden flash Jesus reveals to them what He had seen in their absence, and through their little successes: ἐθεώρουν τὸν Σατανᾶν ὡς ἀστραπὴν ἐκ τοῦ οὐρανοῦ πεσόντα (v.^{18}). It is in the consciousness of this final victory, and of His power to make even His feeble followers more than conquerors, that, after warning them not to trust in what they can do for God, but rather in God's faithful love to them, He breaks into what

Lk. evidently regarded as His rapturous utterance. It is not with resignation, but with Divine exultant gladness, that Jesus accepts the Father's will as revealed in the results of His work. The Spirit is not connected with revelation either here or anywhere else in the life of Jesus, but only with the overpowering, joyful emotion of the hour. And the connexion of the Spirit and of joy is one of the most striking characteristics of the NT all through (see Lk $1^{14\text{f.}}$, Ro 14^{17}, Gal 5^{22}, Ac 13^{52}, 1 Th 1^6). No authority can be claimed for the *v.l.* in Lk 11^2, according to which, instead of 'Thy kingdom come,' or 'Hallowed be thy name,' we should read, 'Thy Holy Spirit come upon us and cleanse us.' Yet it is in keeping with St. Luke's interest in the Spirit that this reading is found here and not in Mt.'s version of the prayer (see Plummer's *St. Luke*, p. 295 n.). It is another proof of this interest that in Lk 11^{13} πνεῦμα ἅγιον replaces the 'good things' of Mt 7^{11}: for St. Luke, all 'good things' which Christians could ask from the Father were summed up in the Spirit. This is a clear case of later experience interpreting the words of Jesus and giving the sense of them in its own terms. Perhaps if another than Jesus had been in question, we might have read that the passionate words of $12^{49\text{f.}}$ broke from His lips when He was 'filled with holy spirit'; but to the Evangelist Jesus is always 'full of the Holy Spirit,' and no such points stand in relief in His career. Oddly enough, Lk. omits any mention of the Spirit in connexion with Ps 110 ($20^{41\text{ff.}}$), though both Mt. and Mk. seem to emphasize it, and in 21^{15} he replaces the express promise of the Spirit, which he has already used in 12^{12}, by a more general promise of an irresistible power of speech such as he ascribes in Ac 6^{10} to a man full of the Holy Spirit. There is no reference to the Holy Spirit in 23^{46}. The last light the Evangelist throws on it is in 24^{49}, where the Risen Saviour describes it as 'the promise of my Father,' and as 'power from on high.' The last word, therefore, brings us back to the first. The fundamental idea to be associated with the Spirit is that of Divine power: how the Divine power is to be further characterized, what it is ethically, and to what issues or in what temper it works, we can see only in the life of Jesus. He is the key to the interpretation of a term which of itself is indefinite indeed.

8. From the life of Jesus, as covered by the Apostolic testimony (Ac $1^{21\text{f.}}$), we now turn to the chapters of Mt. and Lk. which tell the story of His birth. If Mk. is the earliest form of the Evangelic tradition, it is natural to say (whatever the Evangelist's own Christology may be) that the Divine sonship of Jesus was originally connected with His baptism. It was there He received the Holy Spirit and heard the heavenly voice which said, 'Thou art my Son.' It would be all the more natural for Christians to say this who read in their Gospel of Luke (3^{22}), with *Codex Bezæ*, "Thou art my Son, *this day have I begotten thee*.' But as soon as reflexion woke, it would be apparent that Jesus could not suddenly, at the age of thirty or thereabouts, begin to be what He had in no sense been, or been destined and prepared for, before. This is the conviction which—not to speak of historical evidence—sustains the stories of the birth of Christ. He must always have been what Christians eventually knew Him in their own experience to be: He must always have been Son of God. If it is the Spirit which makes Him Son, then behind the baptism with the Spirit must lie a birth in which the Spirit is equally important: not only the equipment of this personality, but its origination, must be traced directly to God. And it *is* the origination of the personality of Jesus with which both Mt. and Lk. are concerned. Neither of them betrays any idea that the Son of God pre-existed, and that they are only narrating the mode in which He came from another order of being into this; and, difficult as it may be to understand how a companion and friend of St. Paul could ignore such an idea, we must abide by the facts as they are before us. No act of man, but only the power of God, lies behind and explains the existence of Jesus Christ in the world. In Mt. the story is told simply and briefly: Mary was found with child ἐκ πνεύματος ἁγίου (1[18. 20]). It is this which makes the Child to be *Immanuel*, 'God with us.' In Luke, though the setting is much more elaborate, the place and significance of the Spirit in the story are the same. The angel of the Annunciation says to Mary (1[35]): πνεῦμα ἅγιον ἐπελεύσεται ἐπὶ σέ, καὶ **δύναμις ὑψίστου** ἐπισκιάσει σοι· **διὸ** καὶ τὸ γεννώμενον ἅγιον κληθήσεται, **υἱὸς θεοῦ**. It is in virtue of this mode of origination that the future child is ἅγιον, Son of God. It is important to notice here the parallelism of πνεῦμα ἅγιον and δύναμις ὑψίστου. The two expressions are precisely equivalent. In the life and work of Jesus, the Divine power can reveal itself ethically (as the Gospel story shows in detail), but in the origination of His personality there is no room for anything to appear but bare power. The action of the Spirit is to be conceived not as sexual but as creative. This marks the truth as well as the purity of the NT. In the OT, where the gender of רוּחַ can be determined, the feminine instances are to the masculine as more than two to one; but in the NT this is irrelevant. πνεῦμα is of no gender. Few will be persuaded by O. Holtzmann (*Leben Jesu* and *War Jesus Ekstatiker?* p. 41) that the Gospel according to the Hebrews, in which Jesus is introduced as speaking of the Holy Spirit as His mother, represents anything more primitive or original on that account. To call the Spirit either 'mother' or 'father' is equally inept and un-Christian: the Spirit is the power of the Highest, to which the presence of the Son of God in the world is due. In other words, the Divine Sonship of Jesus does not date from His baptism, as that of Christians; it is not with Him as with us an affair of re-birth, but of birth simply; it is native and original, with roots as deep as His being; He is not only υἱὸς θεοῦ, but μονογενής.

9. But it is not only the birth of Jesus which in Lk 1 and 2 is connected with the Spirit: all the events of this period are transacted, so to speak, in an atmosphere agitated by the Spirit. The representation is conditioned partly by OT conceptions of the Spirit, and partly, no doubt, by primitive Christian experiences of it. Thus in 1[15] the angel says of John: πνεύματος ἁγίου πλησθήσεται ἔτι ἐκ κοιλίας μητρὸς αὐτοῦ, words in which we can think only of a Divine energy or intensity of life which was to characterize the child from the first. Possibly the juxtaposition of this with the prohibition of wine and strong drink (cf. Ac 2[13], Eph 5[18]) suggests the excitement or stimulation of the nature by God as opposed to any natural intoxicant. Yet the work which John is to do in consequence ('many of the children of Israel shall he turn to the Lord their God,' 1[16]), shows that the Divine power is conceived as working to ethical issues, and therefore as itself ethical. In the OT 'the spirit is never used as a cause except of those things which have to do with the affairs of the people of Israel' (Wood, *op. cit.* p. 9); and this is the point of view maintained throughout these chapters in Luke. The Spirit is connected with the Messianic age (this is universally the case in the NT), and with the preparations for the coming of the Messiah. In John, who comes 'in the spirit and power of Elijah' (1[17]), it is a prophetic spirit, yet rather in the OT than in the NT sense: indeed, it is the outstanding feature in the consciousness of

John that he neither has nor can impart holy spirit. When it is said that Elisabeth 'was filled with holy spirit, and lifted up her voice with a loud cry' (1[42]), we must think of a sudden and overpowering access of feeling referred to God as its source. The same remark applies to Zacharias (1[67]) as he utters the *Benedictus*: in both cases the emotion is one of joy (see above, § 7). More significant are the references to the Spirit in connexion with Simeon (2[25ff.]). He was a just and devout man, cherishing the Messianic hope, and it was probably conditioned by this character that πνεῦμα ἦν ἅγιον ἐπ᾽ αὐτόν. Yet this can hardly mean that he had an abiding possession of the Spirit. No such possession of the Spirit is contemplated anywhere in these chapters, and Simeon is presented to us only in relation to this one scene from the infancy of Jesus. All through his action here he is a Divinely impelled, Divinely illuminated man. This is what is meant by the words quoted. It is 'in the Spirit'—that is, under a Divine impulse—that he comes into the temple; it has been revealed to him 'by the Holy Spirit'—that is, he has had a Divine assurance granted him—that he will see the Christ before he dies. How this impulse or this revelation was imparted to Simeon the Evangelist does not tell, and it is vain to ask. But we need not say that it was not mediated at all, but blankly supernatural. The words in 2[34f.] could not have been spoken by a young man; here 'old experience doth attain to something of prophetic strain.' Perhaps we may say as much of the ancient prophetess Anna (v.[36ff.]). προφῆτις implies the Spirit, yet apart from this one occasion, at the presentation of the Child Jesus in the temple, when she gave thanks to God—no doubt in such an outburst of inspired feeling as is seen in the *Nunc dimittis*—we have no means of knowing how the Spirit expressed itself through her. For this sudden and eager outburst of thanksgiving (so much is implied in αὐτῇ τῇ ὥρᾳ ἐπιστᾶσα ἀνθωμολογεῖτο τῷ θεῷ) we may perhaps compare St. Luke's account of the first Spirit-given utterances at Pentecost: 'We do hear them speak in our tongues the mighty works of God' (Ac 2[11]).

10. In the Synoptic Gospels, what is said of the Spirit no doubt bears the impress, here and there, of experiences which were familiar to the writers under that name, but these experiences do not come independently into view. It is otherwise when we pass beyond the Synoptics. Writers like St. Luke in Acts, and St. Paul in many of his Epistles, deal directly and formally with this subject. In the Gospel of John there is reached even a stage of conscious reflexion upon it which may almost be called a doctrine of the Spirit. And everywhere in the NT there are casual lights thrown upon it in which we can see its place in Christian thought and life. It is not intended here to follow out these in detail, but to indicate in outline the main features of the post-Pentecostal experience and conception of the Spirit, keeping especially in view their relation to Christ and the Gospels.

11. Although there might be reasons for beginning with St. Paul, it is more convenient to follow up Lk.'s Gospel by Acts. The first reference of this book to the Spirit is one of the most singular: Jesus is spoken of as having 'given commandment through the Holy Spirit unto the apostles whom he had chosen' (1[2]). Though Jesus in the Gospel speaks and acts from beginning to end as one anointed with Holy Spirit and power, there is no parallel to this expression. It seems to suggest that with the Resurrection the dispensation of the Holy Spirit began, and that the disciples were conscious, as they listened to the new and final charge of their Lord, that they were in contact, as they had never been before, with the powers of the world to come (He 6[5]), the Divine inspiration of the Messianic age. This power with which the Risen Saviour is invested He bids the disciples themselves expect within a few days (1[5]). It is the promise of the Father : ' Ye shall receive power when the Holy Spirit is come upon you, and ye shall be my witnesses ' (1[8]). This promise was made good at Pentecost, when ' all were filled with the Holy Spirit, and began to speak with other tongues as the Spirit gave them utterance ' (2[4]). The representation of the tongues in Ac 2 as foreign languages has to be controlled by St. Paul's description in 1 Co 14. The miracle of Pentecost is not that the disciples spoke in foreign languages, which, in spite of the narrator, is meaningless and incredible, but that they spoke at all, that they spoke with tongues of fire, and that their speech was a testimony to Jesus, delivered with overwhelming Divine power. The whole Pentecostal phenomenon, including the emotional disturbance which suggested drunkenness (2[13]), and expressed itself in joyful if inarticulate thanksgivings (2[11], cf. 1 Co 14[18]), has the character of a testimony to Jesus. The central thought of the whole is that of 2[33] ' Having received from the Father the promise of the Holy Spirit, he hath poured forth this which ye both see and hear.' Pentecost, or the gift and possession of the Spirit, is the proof to the world of the exaltation of Jesus. It is His Divine power which is behind this incalculable elevation and reinforcement of the natural life. This is the NT point of view throughout. There is such a thing as a spirit which is not of God, but *the* Spirit which Christians have and of which they speak is never anything else than the Spirit of Jesus. It is never an undefined impulse or stimulus —a vague excitement originating anyhow and tending anywhither : it is always referred specifically to Jesus, and it is fundamentally a token that He is there in power (5[32]). That there is an abnormal or pathological side to speaking with tongues need not be questioned ; the equilibrium of a weak and sinful nature may easily be disturbed by the sudden irruption into it of such incalculable realities as the resurrection of Jesus, the redeeming love and the coming judgment of God ; but any degree of disturbance is better than indifference and insensibility. The only question is how the disturbance is to settle—whether men are to rise out of it into the balance of a renewed nature at a higher level, or to sink out of it into the old torpor again. The disturbance itself is the work of God through His Spirit—the Spirit of the Risen Saviour—whatever the issue be. For other references in Acts to speaking with tongues as the most conspicuous sign of having the Spirit, see 10[46] 19[6] : probably this is what is meant when we read of the Spirit *falling* on (ἐπιπίπτειν) people as in 8[15f.].

More important than speaking with tongues, even in Acts, is prophecy. St. Peter's sermon in Ac 2 is a specimen of Christian prophecy ; the Spirit enables him to read the OT (Joel and the Psalms) in a Christian sense, and to find in it Jesus and the Messianic age. It is similarly inspired men—' by the παράκλησις of the Holy Spirit ' (9[31])— under whose ministry the Church is multiplied. Five such men are mentioned by name as working in the Church at Antioch (13[1f.]). The seven at Jerusalem (6[3]) are chosen as men full of the Spirit and faith. The daughters of Philip, who prophesied, were women who shared in this gift (21[c.]). Sometimes the prophecy had the character of prediction : *e.g.* Agabus (11[28]) signified ' through the Spirit ' an impending famine, just as at a later date (21[11]) he foretold what awaited Paul at Jerusalem : ' thus saith the Holy Spirit.' It is no doubt the utterances of such ' inspired ' men that

are in view when St. Paul himself says (20[23]) : ' The Holy Spirit testifieth unto me in every city, saying that bonds and afflictions abide me ' (cf. 21[4]). It is important to note that St. Paul did not find it necessary to obey when Christian men said to him ' through the Spirit that he should not set foot in Jerusalem.' In some way he could urge the Spirit within him against this spirit without : ' I go bound in the spirit to Jerusalem ' (20[22], cf. 19[21]). He felt a Christian obligation to go at all hazards, and went against all omens. Akin to these warnings is the general guidance of the Church and the Apostles by the Spirit, especially at important crises. For example, in chs. 8 and 10, where it is important to represent that the extension of the Church beyond the Jews was Divinely authorized, the whole story is told at the supernatural level, and the Spirit appears at every turn : ' the Spirit said to Philip ' (8[29], cf. 8[26]) ; ' the Spirit of the Lord snatched Philip away ' (8[39]) ; ' while Peter was pondering the vision, the Spirit said, Behold two men seek thee . . . I have sent them ' (10[19f.]) ; ' the Spirit bade me go with them, nothing doubting ' (11[12]). How the Spirit made such communications we need not inquire : but it is important to notice that they are not about indifferent things. There is nothing of the pagan oracle which deals with any question proposed to it : the Spirit gives direction only in the concerns of the Kingdom of the Messiah. For other and striking illustrations connected with this guidance of the Church in the preaching of the gospel see 13[2] (where, no doubt, the Spirit spoke through an inspired man), 13[4] 15[28] 16[6. 7. 10]. The last verse probably shows that too hard and fast a line is not to be drawn between the voice of the Spirit and inferences drawn from facts by Christian intelligence.

One point of interest in Acts is the relation of the Spirit to baptism. The gift of the Spirit is itself represented beforehand *as* a baptism (1[5] ' ye shall be baptized with holy spirit not many days hence '). After Pentecost, instead of displacing and annulling water-baptism, as we might have anticipated, the baptism with the Spirit is regarded as normally coincident with the other : ' Repent and be baptized . . . and ye shall receive the gift of the Holy Spirit ' (2[38], cf. 9[17ff.]). When people believed and were baptized, and the Holy Spirit did not fall on any of them, it was abnormal and disconcerting,—at least on St. Luke's theory (8[14-17]),—and steps were taken to remedy it. It must be remembered that the only baptism spoken of in Acts is that of adult penitent believers, and that for such persons the public confession of their faith, in a ritual act, was naturally the occasion of profoundly moving experiences—experiences which, as rising into higher ranges of thought and feeling than usual, were ascribed by the early Church to the Spirit. To find in Ac 8[14-17] or 19[1-7] an analogue of ' confirmation,' a sacrament supplementary to baptism, and capable of being conferred only by an Apostle or by a bishop as his successor, is an anachronism. The gifts of the Holy Spirit bestowed on these two occasions when Apostles prayed and laid their hands on the baptized, were what may be called spiritual gifts falling within the sphere of the senses ; ' they spoke with tongues and prophesied ' (19[6]). In confirmation, this is neither asked nor wanted, but this and nothing else is what is desiderated by St. Luke. The emotional stimulation, which liberates the hidden powers of human nature, is itself the gift of the Holy Spirit in virtue of which people become glossolalists or prophets. But though, for the reason already stated, the gift of the Spirit is the normal accompaniment of baptism, the order of the two things may be reversed. Cornelius and his household are baptized, not in order to receive, but

because they have received, the Spirit (10^{44-48}).
And more important than any single observation
is the fact that in Acts, as elsewhere in the NT,
the reception of the Spirit is the whole of Christianity. 'They received the Holy Spirit even as
we did' (10^{47} 11^{15} $15^{8f.}$). All that makes a man a
Christian is in this, and where this is there can be
no distinction of Jew or Gentile more. The
Church is one in the unity of the Spirit.

12. In St. Paul's Epistles the Holy Spirit is mentioned nearly 120 times, and may be said to have
a prominence and importance which it has nowhere
else in the NT. It is impossible to discuss it in
detail here. On the one hand, we have representations of the Spirit, and of the effects produced
by its reception, entirely similar to those in Acts :
St. Paul's whole ministry, in word and deed, has
been accomplished in the power of the Holy Spirit
(Ro $15^{13f.}$) ; those who receive his gospel receive
the Spirit ; the chief χαρίσματα, or spiritual gifts,
are speaking with tongues and prophesying (1 Th
5^{19-22}, 1 Co 12–14). Though St. Paul was distinguished himself, above everyone at Corinth, by
his experiences of the glossolalic ecstasy, and
thanked God for it (1 Co 14^{18}), and though he discouraged the sober - minded Thessalonians who
would have hastily repressed it (this is what is
meant by 'Quench not the Spirit' in 1 Th 5^{19}), he
was not insensible to its dangers. There was
something morbid in it ; it might be tainted with
vanity and self-indulgence ; there was nothing in
it to edify the Church. Good Christians might
even be conceived as thanking God that they did
not speak with tongues. Even the higher gift of
prophecy needs criticism and control. The man
who comes to the church with a 'teaching' or a
'revelation' may come in the Spirit,—he may be
an inspired man,—but he is not irresponsible, nor
is he exempt from the criticism and control of the
Church. 'Prophets' spirits are subject to prophets'
(1 Co 14^{32}) : the Divine impulse under which the
prophet in each case speaks is not an uncontrollable force which must have its way irrespective of
order or decorum. Neither does it guarantee infallibility : the human individuality counts for
something in every utterance, and when two or
three 'prophets' have spoken the others are to
judge (1 Co 14^{29}). The Christian common sense of
the community, so to speak, is felt to be more
inspired than the most ardent utterance of any
individual. St. Paul even mentions among χαρίσματα one which he calls διακρίσεις πνευμάτων –the
faculty of deciding on each occasion what is the
true character of the impulse under which a
man speaks, and in particular whether it is of
God or not. The conception of a spiritual gift of
this kind—an instinctive sense for what is or is
not in keeping with the gospel—is peculiar. It
brings us within sight of what is characteristically
Pauline in the conception of the Spirit, namely,
a possession of the Spirit which is beyond all particular 'gifts' or 'operations' of a spiritual kind,
which is, in short, identical with Christian life.
To quote from Mr. Wood (*op. cit.* 268) : 'Paul
grasped the idea of the unity of the religious life,
and spoke of the spirit not merely as God acting
in an occasional extraordinary and emotional experience, but as being the Divine source and basis
of all the Christian life. For him the Holy Spirit
is the cause not only of religious experiences, but of
religious experience. The test of the Spirit of God
in a man is no longer subjective emotion, but the
objective value of his life for the progress of the
will of God as working itself out in the Church.'
In comparison with the Spirit in this large sense,
the particular manifestations or gifts of the Spirit
which are discussed at length in Ro 12, 1 Co 12–14,
Eph 4, have a subordinate though a vital import-

ance. The main point is that for St. Paul Christian life and life in the Spirit are one thing. All
Christian graces are the fruit of the Spirit (Gal
5^{22}). The Christian God is He who supplies the
Spirit (3^5). To become a Christian is to receive the
Spirit (3^2). To live as a Christian is to walk in or
by the Spirit (5^{16}). The Spirit and faith are correlative terms, and each of them covers, from a
different point of view, all that is meant by Christianity. Regarded from the side of God and His
grace and power in initiating and maintaining it,
Christianity is the Spirit ; regarded from the side
of man and his action and responsibility in relation to God, it is faith. The two are coextensive, and all Christianity is in each. This is
vividly expressed in one of those sentences in
which St. Paul concentrates his whole mind on
the greatest things : ἡμεῖς γὰρ πνεύματι ἐκ πίστεως
ἐλπίδα δικαιοσύνης ἀπεκδεχόμεθα (5^5). Here is everything that enters into Christianity and determines
it to be what it is. Like the old religion, it has
in δικαιοσύνη its hope or goal ; but in its attitude
to this, nothing is determined by law, in any sense
of that word ; there are only two powers of which
St. Paul is conscious as counting for anything in
his soul—the one is Divine (the Spirit), the other
is human (faith) ; and though these are distinguishable, they cannot be known apart. Cf. 2 Th 2^{13}
ἐν ἁγιασμῷ πνεύματος καὶ πίστει ἀληθείας, where 'in
consecration wrought by God's Spirit, and belief
of the truth,' is to be interpreted in the same way.

Without going into details, it is pertinent to
point out the connexions between this Pauline
conception of the Spirit and what we find in the
life of Jesus. (*a*) To begin with, the Spirit is for
St. Paul specifically Christian. It is not the power
or the life of God *simpliciter*, but the power or the
life of God as God has been manifested in Christ,
and especially in His resurrection and exaltation.
He calls it expressly the Spirit of Christ (Ro 8^9) ;
it is an epistle of Christ that is written on men's
hearts by the Spirit of the living God (2 Co 3^3) ; he
even goes so far as to say, the Lord is the Spirit
(3^{17}), and he who is joined to the Lord is one spirit
(1 Co 6^{17}). The presence of the Spirit is, it may
be said, the spiritual presence of the Lord ; it is
not an indefinite power of God, but the last Adam
who has become life-giving spirit (15^{45}). When a
criterion of 'spiritual' utterances is sought, it is
found in Jesus (12^3) : to say Jesus is anathema proves
that it is not God's Spirit in which one speaks ;
but only in the Holy Spirit can one say 'Jesus is
Lord.' To confess the exaltation, not of an unknown person, but of Jesus, and to live in the
acknowledgment of Jesus at the right hand of the
Father, is to be a genuine Christian. Passages
like these prove that if there was any danger in
the Pauline churches of an ecstatic enthusiasm
doing less than justice to the historical character
of Christianity, it was a danger to which St. Paul
was alive from the first, and which he did his best
to obviate. That St. Paul and the members of his
churches had such an acquaintance with the historical tradition of Jesus as gave definite meaning
to His name, the writer has no doubt. — (*b*) A
further point in St. Paul's conception of the Spirit,
which connects it essentially with Jesus, is seen in
this : it is a spirit of adoption or sonship, breaking
out in the loud and joyful cry, 'Abba, Father.'
All who are led by it are sons of God. Because
they are sons, God has sent forth the Spirit of His
Son into their hearts (Ro $8^{14ff.}$, Gal 4^6). It is not a
spirit of δουλεία or δειλία (2 Ti 1^7), but of trust and
joy. (*c*) Especially as a spirit of sonship is it a
spirit of freedom : ὁ δὲ κύριος τὸ πνεῦμα· οὗ δὲ τὸ
πνεῦμα κυρίου, ἐλευθερία (2 Co 3^{17}). Ἐλεύθερος, ἐλευθερία, and ἐλευθεροῦν are great Pauline words in
this connexion. What they suggest is the emanci-

pation of the Christian life from everything statutory, whatever its origin. The Christian is not under law, but under grace; no statute contributes in the least degree to make him what he is, or to give him the experiences which he has; it is as he stands in the presence of the crucified and risen Christ, and abandons himself in faith to the Divine love there revealed, that the Divine power descends into his heart which annuls all the statutes and conventions he has ever known, and is itself *everything* to him henceforth. It is under the inspiration of this power, and of this power alone, that he now lives and acts; not conformity to any external standard, however high, but moral originality like that of Jesus, because inspired by the consciousness of Jesus and of all he owes to Him, is what is required of him at every step. That such a conception is not without moral perils, and that it is capable of being abused, St. Paul was well aware (Gal 5¹³, Ro 6¹⁴); but it is in one respect the fundamental truth of his gospel, and he would never compromise upon it. That it has its basis in the teaching of Jesus—as its supreme illustration in the whole life of Jesus—we may see from the Sermon on the Mount, or from Mt 17²⁴⁻²⁷, Jn 8³¹⁻³⁶.—(d) Again, the Pauline idea of the earnest of the Spirit (ἀρραβών 2 Co 1²² 5⁵, Eph 1¹⁴), or of the first-fruits of the Spirit (ἀπαρχή, Ro 8²³), according to which the Spirit is a guarantee of eternal life, is continuous with the teaching of Jesus. The Spirit is such a guarantee because it is a quickening spirit, 'the Spirit of him that raised Jesus from the dead' (8¹¹); it brings to men the life of God, the same life that was manifested in Jesus, and that made it impossible that He should be holden of death (Ac 2²⁴). The argument, or rather the assumption of the Apostle, in all these passages is the same as that of Jesus in His answer to the Sadducees. When God has pledged His friendship to men as He did to the patriarchs in ancient days, or as He does to Christians now in making them, through the Spirit, partakers of His own life, He has entered into a relation to them to which death can make no difference. His love outwardly, His Spirit inwardly, both mean immortality. They both say of God's flock: 'They shall never perish; none can pluck them out of the Father's hand' (Jn 10²⁹). The only difference is that when immortality is deduced from the possession of the Spirit (that is, the life of God), it is referred, so to speak, to a natural or supernatural law, and we see it as part of a constitution of things; whereas when it is deduced from the friendship of God, we see it purely as a gift of His grace.—(e) Formally, there is one great contrast which brings out the meaning of spirit in St. Paul, but which cannot be directly connected with Jesus, the contrast of spirit and flesh. This pervades the Apostle's writings, and is conspicuous in such passages as Ro 8, Gal 5. The flesh represents for him sin in its virulent and constitutional character; the Spirit is the Divine power given to the believer in Jesus, which enables him to do what the Law could not do—to vanquish or put to death the flesh. Yet when St. Paul learned the lesson that only the Spirit could overcome the flesh, he merely learned what Jesus taught the rich ruler—'There is none good but one, that is God' (Mk 10¹⁸)—with its necessary inference, that for any goodness we can ever attain we must be absolutely dependent on God. St. Paul's gospel means not only that we must be so dependent, but that by God's mercy such dependence is made possible for us: God puts His Holy Spirit in those who believe in Jesus, with their sanctification expressly in view (1 Th 4⁷ᶠ·). There is, of course, a reference here to the OT conception of the Spirit in Ezk 36²⁷ 37¹⁴.

The passages in which the Spirit is regarded by St. Paul as a source of knowledge or revelation are among the most difficult in his writings, and have nothing analogous to them in the Synoptic words of Jesus. Besides 1 Co 12⁸ (where the 'word of wisdom' and the 'word of knowledge' are mediated through the Spirit) and 14²⁶ (where it explains διδαχή, ἀποκάλυψις, etc.), there are the longer passages in 1 Co 2 and Eph 1¹⁷ᶠ·. In both these passages a wisdom is spoken of which is imparted by the Spirit to believers (though ἡμῖν in 1 Co 2¹⁰ may refer only to the Apostles or other inspired teachers). The Spirit can impart this wisdom because it searches all things, even the depths of God. The contents of the wisdom in question are in both cases, apparently, eschatological. It is wisdom which God has foreordained 'for our glory' (not in honour of us, but with that glory in view which we are to share with the Lord of glory), 1 Co 2⁷. It speaks of the things 'which eye has not seen nor ear heard . . . all that God has prepared for those who love him' (2⁹), or, in the words of Eph 1¹⁸, of 'the hope attached to God's calling, of the riches of the glory of his inheritance in the saints.' Only the man who has the Spirit himself, who has had the eyes of his heart illumined, can receive, teach, or appreciate this wisdom. If we should say that we have a notable specimen of it in 1 Co 15, then its Christian character is thoroughly safeguarded: it speaks not merely of the things that are freely given to us by God (2⁸), but of the things that are freely given to us by God *in Christ*. It is *in Him* that all shall be made alive, and put on the body of glory (1 Co 15²², Ph 3²¹). It is *Christ* in us who is the hope of the glory contemplated for us in God's wisdom (Col 1²⁷, 1 Co 2⁵). The power with which God wrought in Christ when He raised Him from the dead and set Him at His right hand in the heavenly places (Eph 1¹⁸ᶠ·), is the same as 'the power which worketh in us' through the Spirit (3²⁰), and it works in us to the same glorious issue. It is perhaps impossible for us to appreciate as revelation all the forms in which St. Paul's thought and imagination clothed themselves as he laid hold of the hope of glory and immortality in Christ; but, judging from the combination of these passages, this seems to have been the substance of his Spirit-taught wisdom. On its agreement in substance with the mind of Christ see under (d) above. The truth of passages like 1 Co 2¹⁴⁻¹⁶ is generalized in such Johannine words of Jesus as '*My sheep* hear my voice . . . you do not believe because you are *not of my sheep* . . . every one that is *of the truth* heareth my voice' (Jn 10²⁷·²⁶ 18³⁷). This again unites with Jesus the Pauline conception of the Spirit.

13. The NT books which were written under Pauline influence scarcely call for independent consideration. Hebrews has one reference (2⁴) and perhaps a second (6⁴) to the 'gifts' of the Spirit, the first alluding to them as God's testimony to Christ; elsewhere it refers to the Spirit only as the speaker in the OT (3⁷ 9⁸ 10¹⁵). In 1 P 1² the striking expression ἐν ἁγιασμῷ πνεύματος, standing as it does between the 'foreknowledge of God the Father' and 'obedience and sprinkling of the blood of Jesus Christ,' is, no doubt, to be rendered, as in 2 Th 2¹³, 'in a consecration wrought by the Spirit'; it is in this that God's eternal purpose of redemption is realized. Probably in both places (1 P 1², 2 Th 2¹³) there is an allusion to baptism. In 1 Pt 1¹¹ the idea that the Spirit in the OT (?) prophets was Christ's Spirit must be connected with the belief in the pre-existence of Christ; in 1¹² the Holy Spirit sent from heaven is the power which attends the Christian evangelist and makes his words effective. This idea, of course, pervades the NT, and goes back to such words of Jesus as Mk 13¹¹, Lk 24⁴⁸ᶠ·. 'The Spirit of glory and of God' in 1 P 4¹⁴ recalls St. Paul's conception of the Spirit as the earnest of immortality; it is the spirit of the glory to be revealed because it opens men's eyes to the reality of it (1 Co 2, Eph 1¹⁷ᶠ·), and ensures their entrance into it (2 Co 5⁵). In 2 Ti 1¹⁴ it is the indwelling Holy Spirit which enables one to guard the Christian deposit — a Christian inference from 1 Co 2¹², Jn 18³⁷. In Tit 3⁵ the thought of 1 P 1², 2 Th 2¹³, is more articulately expressed: side by side with 'the laver of regeneration' we have 'renewal wrought by the Holy Spirit.' There is nothing more here than a fulfilment of the Baptist's words—'He shall baptize you with holy spirit' (Mk 1⁸).

14. The Johannine books cover all the literary forms known to the NT,—Gospel, Epistle, Apocalypse,—and the Spirit is prominent in all. To understand them it is necessary to remember that all the experience of the Pauline churches lies behind them, and that the circumstances in which they originated have exercised a decided influence on their presentation of the facts and ideas with which they deal.

(a) To begin with *the Apocalypse*, the writer speaks four times of being, or being carried off, ἐν πνεύματι (1¹⁰ 4² 17³ 21¹⁰), an expression which, whether it is literary artifice or a description of remembered experience, suggests the condition of prophetic ecstasy in which he saw his visions. If St. Paul had spoken of the Spirit in that connexion, we should have referred for interpretation to 2 Co 12¹ff·. The seven spirits before God's throne, whatever their connexion in the history of religion with the seven *Amshaspands* of Persia, are not numerically seven. In the Apocalypse they are treated as a unity; they are the Spirit of God in the completeness of its powers (1⁴ 3¹ 4⁵ 5⁶); and when Christ is spoken of as *having* the seven spirits of God, the meaning is the same as when we read in the Gospel (3³⁴) that God does not give the Spirit by measure to Him. This close connexion of Jesus with the Spirit (He first receives and then bestows it) is strikingly brought out in the Epistles to the Seven Churches. In all of them it is the Risen Christ who speaks; but at the end of each we read : 'He that hath an ear, let him hear what the Spirit saith to the Churches' (2⁷· ¹¹· ¹⁷· ²⁹ 3⁶· ¹³· ²²). In St. Paul's phrase, here too 'the Lord is the Spirit.' It is no other than Christ who speaks through the inspired prophet. And although ἐν πνεύματι probably means 'in an ecstasy,' it must be noted that there is nothing inarticulate or unbalanced about these searching letters. They are terrible in their calm as in their passion. Cf. the utterance of the Spirit in 14¹³. In 11¹¹ and 13¹⁵ we are really on OT ground, and the Spirit is not specifically Christian, but, as in OT *passim*, the principle of life. But the most striking utterance on the Spirit is 19¹⁰ ἡ γὰρ μαρτυρία Ἰησοῦ ἐστιν τὸ πνεῦμα τῆς προφητείας. This means that the Spirit, which, as we have already seen, is possessed by Jesus and bestowed by Him, has also Him as its object. In all the prophets—in all inspired men —what it does is to bear a testimony to Him. All the prophets, who are prophets simply through having the Spirit, are witnesses to Jesus. This agrees not only with the Gospel (15²⁶ 16¹⁴), but with such other words of Jesus as Ac 1⁸.

(b) Proceeding to the *Gospel* of John, we find, as in the Synoptics, that the Spirit is first mentioned in connexion with the baptism of Jesus. 'I have seen,' says the Baptist, 'the Spirit descending as a dove out of heaven, and it abide upon him. And I did not know him, but he who sent me to baptize in water, the same said unto me, On whomsoever thou seest the Spirit descending and abiding on him, the same is he who baptizeth in holy spirit. And I have seen and borne witness that this is the Son of God' (1³²ff·). What strikes us here is the assumption that every reader will know what is meant by 'the Spirit' or by 'holy spirit.' The Gospel is meant for Christians to whom the Spirit is an experience, an experience which they owe to Jesus (for it is He who baptizes with holy spirit); an experience, however, which Jesus in His turn had had (He had been baptized with holy spirit).

It is often said that this idea of the descent of the Spirit on Jesus is only a piece of the Christian tradition, too firmly established for the Evangelist to be able to discard it, but really inconsistent with the conception of Christ in the Prologue. The Word incarnate (it is argued) cannot need to be baptized with the Holy Spirit. To say so is to assume that we know what is meant by the 'Word incarnate' without looking at the story of Jesus. The assumption cannot be justified. A great spiritual experience, according to all the Gospels, is connected with the baptism of Jesus; according to all the Gospels, also, it is the experience of receiving the Holy Spirit. If the Evangelist sets this down without embarrassment side by side with his pro-

logue, the presumption is that he felt no inconsistency between them, and that there is none. His idea may rather be that it is the measureless gift of the Spirit in virtue of which Jesus *is* the Word incarnate. If He had not had this experience at His baptism, and all that flowed from it, He would not have been (or been recognizable as) the Son of God (Jn 1³³), as God manifest in the flesh, Immanuel.

Possibly part of the Evangelist's interest in the baptism of Jesus lay in this, that in it the symbol and the thing signified coincided. Ordinarily, in the Baptist's preaching, water and the Spirit are contrasted : here the one accompanies the other. This is the type of the Christian baptism with which the author and his readers are familiar. In it water and the Spirit normally coincide. This may seem a not very real idea to us; but we have to consider that even within the first century Christianity was assuming some of the features of a sacramental system, that much in the mental sympathies of the early centuries found this congenial, and that it might seem not unimportant to find at the very beginning of its history its fundamental rite undergone by the Founder, and proved to be not only a form, but a power.

The turning of the water into wine is no doubt a symbol of the whole work of Jesus,—the raising of religion to a higher power, or, more specifically, the elevation of water-baptism into baptism with holy spirit. The Spirit, however, is not mentioned in this connexion, and we get into closer quarters with the subject in ch. 3. There the decisive word is v.⁵ 'Except a man be born ἐξ ὕδατος καὶ πνεύματος, he cannot enter into the kingdom of God.' It is not the mind of Jesus with which we are immediately dealing, but the mind of Jesus as interpreted in the mind of the Evangelist and in the circumstances of his time. Granting this, it seems to the present writer quite impossible to question either a reference to Baptism here or one to the Supper in ch. 6. Nor is the meaning of the reference doubtful. As in the baptism of Jesus, so in Christian baptism, water and spirit are not thought of as in contrast, but as in conjunction. No question is raised as to the conditions under which baptism was administered —conditions of penitence and of faith in Christ on the part of the baptized. These are assumed as familiar to everyone. But under these conditions the new birth is connected unequivocally with the Spirit and with the rite in the administration of which the Spirit is normally present. One of the great words and ideas of the Gospel is 'life.' Sometimes it is spoken of simply as the gift of God. The Father has given to the Son to have life in Himself, and the Son gives life to whom He will (5²¹· ²⁶). Here, however, the life is conceived on the analogy of natural life, and the entrance into it is by a birth which depends on the act of God through His Spirit. The life with which we are here concerned is nothing less than the eternal life of God Himself (1 Jn 1²), and only God can beget it in the soul. To be born of God and born of the Spirit are the same thing (1 Jn 2²⁹ 3⁹ 5¹⁸). When Jesus says, 'That which is born of the flesh is flesh, and that which is born of the Spirit is spirit' (Jn 3⁶), He means that it is not anything we owe to our fathers and mothers, but only something we owe to God, which quickens the life of God in us. Put with this generality, it might seem as though the Spirit here had no connexion, or no particular connexion, with Christ; it is almost as though we were at the OT stage, at which the Spirit is merely a synonym for God acting. But to say this is to forget the connexion here asserted of the Spirit and the Christian sacrament of baptism. It is through baptism in the name of Jesus that the Spirit is received; and just as the πνεῦμα ζωοποιοῦν of St. Paul is the Spirit of the Risen Saviour, so here, in the sense of the

Evangelist, it is the same Spirit, acting in and through the ordinance of the Risen Saviour, that is the source of all Divine life. As the conversation goes on, too, while the water, as merely symbolical, drops out (it only appears in v.[5]), and the Spirit remains by itself (v.[8]), attention is directed to the Son of Man, lifted up as Moses lifted up the serpent in the wilderness, that whosoever believes may in Him have eternal life. Here we have the ideas introduced which define the Spirit —the experiences through which the experience of the Spirit comes to us with life-giving power. The new birth is mysterious, indeed, in all its aspects; it is like the wind which blows where it will. We cannot tell how it originates or in what it will end. But it is not blankly mysterious, and there is nothing magical in its connexion with the sacrament. It comes into experience along with other things which form part of the same system of reality with it,—the sin-bearing death of Christ, the proclamation of that death, and believing surrender to it. All this is concentrated and symbolized in baptism; and it is because of this that baptism and being born of the Spirit are represented as coincident. Baptism is a kind of focal point in which all the quickening powers of God in Christ crucified tell upon the soul under the conditions of penitence and faith which make them effective. The life that comes to us in this experience is the life of the Spirit, the Divine life; but quite definitely also it is a life which we owe to the death of Christ. (To apply this conception of baptismal regeneration to the case of infants is to desert the ground of experience, on which the Apostle speaks throughout, for what is to us an unconditioned void. In this adventure the NT gives us no assistance whatever).

At the close of ch. 3 we revert, apparently in words of the Baptist, really in words of the Evangelist, to the idea of the Spirit as bestowed on Jesus by God. He whom God sent speaks the words of God; He does this, and can do it, because God gives not the Spirit by measure to Him (3[34]). Here the idea is like that in 1 Co 2[11]: 'As no man knows the things of a man save the spirit of a man which is in him, even so the things of God no man knows, but the Spirit of God.' It is in virtue of having this Spirit, not partially but completely, that Jesus speaks the words of God; in distinction from those who had only partial and transient illumination, He has received the Spirit in its fulness and is the Word incarnate. To have the Spirit in this sense and measure, to be the Word made flesh, and to have all things put into His hand by the Father (3[34f.] 5[20]), are one and the same thing.

The absence of any allusion to the Spirit in ch. 4 (where Jesus offers the 'living water') and in ch. 5 (where we are told that the Son gives life to whom He will: with ζωοποιεῖν, v.[21], cf. St. Paul's πνεῦμα ζωοποιοῦν, 1 Co 15[45], and Jn 6[63]) is very remarkable; but it has an exact parallel in the complete absence of the Spirit from Ro 6. When we come to ch. 6 it is different. The reference here to the Supper is as unmistakable as that to Baptism in ch. 3. The discourse starts from the bread of life, but the general idea of feeding on Christ or living on Him by faith, is specified as it proceeds, in agreement with the ritual of the Supper, into eating His flesh and drinking His blood. In the most intense and vehement expressions of this kind, indeed, there is never anything more than in v.[47] ('He that believeth hath eternal life') or in v.[57] ('He that *eateth me* shall live by me'). It is not only conceivable, but highly probable, especially in view of a passage like 1 Co 10, that when this chapter was written materialistic and superstitious ideas about the sacrament of the Supper were already current in

the Church, and that the Evangelist has the express design of correcting them. He has no hesitation in using the boldest liturgical language: he speaks of eating the flesh and drinking the blood of the Son of Man in a tone which seems almost intended to challenge, if not to defy, intelligence; he recognizes by doing so that only language of poetic intensity like this, to which it is absurd to *say* that a symbol is only a symbol, is appropriate in worship; yet just as in ch. 3 water is mentioned only once, and the Spirit afterwards spoken of independently, so here any risk of religious materialism is swept away in the words, 'It is the *spirit* which gives life . . . the words that I have spoken to you are *spirit* and are *life*' (v.[63]). There is no depreciation of the sacrament here any more than in ch. 3, and no exaltation of the words of Jesus as opposed to it; but there is a safeguard against the superstitious abuse of it. It is nothing material, no *res sacramenti*, on which the believer depends for eternal life. No doubt Christ, the Christ who speaks of His flesh as true food and His blood as true drink (v.[55]), is, in all the truth of His humanity and His Passion, the meat and drink of the soul, and the believer realizes this in the sacrament; but it is not through the material elements that Christ sustains spiritual life; if His words are read in this sense, their character is misconceived; they are taken out of the region of spirit and life to which they belong, and in which alone Christ vivifies men.

One of the most characteristic passages on the Spirit is 7[37ff.]. On the last day of the Feast of Tabernacles, Jesus stands in the Temple and cries, 'If any man thirst, let him come unto me and drink.' The words are on a level with those in ch. 4, in which He promises the living water to the woman at the well. But here Jesus goes further. 'He that believeth in me,' He adds, 'as said the Scripture, Out of his belly shall flow rivers of living water.' Without discussing the reference to 'Scripture,' what does this mean? The Evangelist himself interprets the words: 'This he said of the Spirit which those who believed on him were to receive, for as yet there was no Spirit (οὔπω γὰρ ἦν πνεῦμα), for Jesus was not yet glorified.' This is clearly written from the standpoint of experience and fulfilment. *After* Jesus was glorified through death and resurrection, those who believed had experience of His power such as they had never had before. They had owed Him much while they were with Him on earth; He had in a sense satisfied their own spiritual needs (6[68f.]); He had given them the bread of life to eat and the living water to drink. But now He did more. He came to them in a power which enabled them to be witnesses to Him; others obtained the Spirit through them; the living water which He had given them overflowed from them as from an inexhaustible spring. Whether this is what Jesus meant or not, it is true; it answers to the facts of the case as the whole of the NT reveals them. Pentecost was inconceivable to the Evangelist except as the sequel to the Passion and Exaltation of Jesus; the possession of the Spirit which is the characteristic of the new era is determined in point of fact by these antecedents. We have seen the same connexion of ideas already in the chapters on the sacraments: the Passion of Christ is as unmistakably present in 3[15] and 6[52-59] as in 7[39]. It seems very gratuitous, then, to argue with Wendt that the Evangelist has mistaken Jesus, and that our Lord means no more here than in ch. 4.

The Johannine conception of the Spirit comes out most fully in chs. 14–16. The Spirit may be said to be the main subject in the discourses in which Jesus prepares the disciples for His departure. All the difficulties connected with the words of Jesus in the Fourth Gospel have to be allowed for here; to draw the line between what was literally said by Jesus at the moment and what is due to the commentary of experience interpreting His remembered words, might have seemed to the Evangelist himself not only unreal but unspiritual. The following points may be noted.

(1) The first hint of the future suggests the surpassing greatness of the experiences which the Spirit was to bring. 'He that believeth on me, the works that I do shall he do also; and greater works than these shall he do; because I go to the Father. And whatsoever ye shall ask in my name, that will I do, that the Father may be glorified in the Son' (14$^{12f.}$). The Spirit is not yet named, but we can see that it is in the writer's mind. The overwhelming experiences of the Apostolic age, the great movement then inaugurated, the new sense of the power of prayer as it takes hold of the name of Jesus, cast beforehand the shadow of their coming in these amazing words. This *is* a promise of the Spirit, though the name is not mentioned; and indeed nothing short of their fulfilment in the Apostolic age could have enabled the writer to recall such words, or to believe them, or to have any idea of what they might mean.

(2) Immediately after, the language becomes more precise, and the Spirit is expressly mentioned 14$^{15ff.}$. 'If you love me, you will keep my commandments. And I will ask the Father, and he shall give you another Comforter, that he may be with you for ever; even the Spirit of truth; which the world cannot receive, because it does not see or know it (αὐτό). You know it; for it dwells with you, and shall be in you. I will not leave you desolate: I come unto you.' What strikes us first here is the new name given to the Spirit, ἄλλον παράκλητον. It is indeed only the name which is new: in idea it answers closely to the only promise of the Spirit which we find in the Synoptic Gospels. These older writers (apart from Lk 11^{13}, which is no real exception) only speak of the Spirit as a future possession of the disciples in Mk 13^{11}, Lk 12^{12}, Mt 10^{19}. The situation contemplated is that in which the disciples are brought before judges and kings to bear testimony to their Master. That is the hour in which they need an *advocatus*, a counsel, a παράκλητος; and Jesus promises that they will have one in the Spirit. The expression '*another* advocate' implies that the disciples have already had experience of *one*, namely, of Jesus Himself. As long as He was with them their strength was reinforced from *Him*; and when He goes, then, in response to His intercession, His place is taken by the Spirit. There is another power with them now which does for them what Jesus did before. Yet is it really another? In 1 Jn 2^1 it is Jesus who is the παράκλητος, even after Pentecost; and even here (Jn 14^{18}) He says, '*I* come unto you.' The presence of the Spirit is Jesus' own presence in spirit; we are reminded again of 2 Co 3^{17} and of Mt 28^{20}. In the spirit Jesus will be with His own for ever, will dwell by them and be in them. What is meant at this point by calling the Spirit the Spirit of truth (Jn 14^{17}) is not quite clear, but some contrast is implied between it and the world (cf. 1 Co 2^{12}). The world, as Plato might have said, is the great sophist; it is a realm of deceits and illusions, by which the mind of the disciple, were he left to himself, might easily be put at fault; but in the Spirit the disciple has a safeguard against its subtleties and sophistications; he is kept in the truth which sanctifies because it is one with God, truth as truth is in Jesus (17^{17}, Eph 4^{21}). There is no definition here of the relation of the Spirit to Jesus or to the Father, though it might be said that the Spirit is the *alter ego* of Jesus. Only, it is the Son who asks the Father

and the Father who gives the Spirit; the three are one as they confront the disciples, co-operating for their salvation. In this Gospel, as everywhere in the NT, the Spirit belongs to the same region as the Father and the Son; it is included in what a Christian means when he speaks of 'God.' This is the Catholic doctrine of the Trinity; no man means all that a Christian means by 'God' unless he puts into 'God' all that is meant by the separate terms 'Father,' 'Son,' and 'Spirit.' This is a proposition which is securely based on experience, and which is implied in NT experience from the day of Pentecost onward (see Ac 2^{33}, 1 Co 12$^{4-6}$, Eph 2^{18}, Jn 14^{26}). More particularly, too, it may be said that the Spirit in the Fourth Gospel belongs to the Kingdom of God and to the religion of revelation: to the world it is unknown. And within the Messianic realm the full experience of it is ethically conditioned: 'If ye love me, ye will keep my commandments, and I will ask the Father,' etc.

(3) The next reference to the Spirit (14^{26}) is still more definite. 'The Paraclete, the Holy Spirit, which the Father shall send in my name, he (ἐκεῖνος) shall teach you all things, and shall bring to your remembrance all things that I said unto you.' Both the masculine pronoun (ἐκεῖνος) and the function ('he shall teach') represent the Spirit as personal, with a definiteness hitherto unnoticed. Not that suggestions of this are wanting elsewhere (cf. esp. 1 Co 12^{11}), and, of course, it must be in the last resort meaningless to speak of the spirit of a personal God as itself impersonal; but very often the meaning is covered by the idea of an impulse communicated by God, whereas here the personalizing is much more definite and conscious. The function of teaching or revealing, which, as we have seen above, has but a small space and a mainly eschatological reference in St. Paul, is far more prominent in St. John, and far more decisively defined by relation to the historical Saviour. The Spirit does not teach independently, but brings to remembrance all things that Jesus said to the Twelve. ὑπομνήσει is a word on which it is worth while to dwell. The Evangelist gives us two illustrations of things which the disciples remembered after the Spirit came, and which received a new meaning as they rose in the spiritual light. When He rose from the dead, they remembered the word that He spoke about destroying the temple and rebuilding it in three days; it had slept in their memories, an inert, meaningless, and therefore forgotten thing; now it leapt into meaning, and they had a vivid recollection of it (2^{22}). Cf. 12^{11} of the circumstances of the Triumphal Entry. We cannot think of these two illustrations without asking, What is involved in the spiritually quickened action of memory in such cases? Something is recalled, but it is not only recalled, it is for the first time understood; it is remembered because a key to it has been found; it is not only the dream, so to speak, which is recalled, but the dream and its interpretation together. Where events have deeply interested and impressed men, as the words and works of Jesus did the disciples, and especially where they have initiated great spiritual movements in which their significance has become apparent, memory cannot be insulated so as to perceive them in a purely neutral or 'objective' fashion. They are remembered in the heart as well as in the brain; they are remembered with an ardour which contemplates, explores, makes discoveries, worships; and when they are reproduced in the Spirit, it is not the unintelligent and misleading truth of an amateur photograph with which we are confronted, but something like the work of a great painter, something which is truer in a manner than the most literal recollection would be. It is not open

to question that the Fourth Gospel is, in this sense, a 'spiritual' Gospel; it is the decisive proof that the words of Jesus in 14²⁶ have been fulfilled. On the relation of Father, Son, and Spirit, this passage only confirms what has been said above under (2).

(4) In 15²⁶ many have sought for more than it contains. Here it is the Son who sends the Spirit from the Father, and the Spirit is described as that which proceeds from the Father. To pretend that we can distinguish between the 'procession' of the Spirit from the Father and the 'generation' of the Son by the Father, is only to invite Gibbon's sneer about 'the science, or rather the language of metaphysics.' The really important point here is that which has already emerged in Rev 19¹⁰ (see above): ἐκεῖνος μαρτυρήσει περὶ ἐμοῦ. Christ is the Spirit's subject. The Spirit is the Spirit of truth because it bears witness to Him who can say, 'I am the truth' (14⁶). The truth with which it deals is that which is incarnate in Christ, the very same truth to which the Apostles also are to bear witness, because they have been with Him from the beginning (15²⁷).

(5) The climax of our Lord's teaching in this line is reached in 16⁷ᶠᶠ. Here Jesus announces the paradoxical truth that it is expedient for the disciples that He should leave them, because the coming of the Paraclete is dependent on His departure. There are natural analogies to this: often there is a truer appreciation, even of a person who has been intimately known and loved, after death than before, a more adequate possession in memory than there was in actual intercourse. But more is meant here than that the disciples will get a better view of Jesus from a distance. It is Jesus Himself who is to send them the Paraclete, and He can do it, as He has already said (7³⁹), only on the ground of His death and exaltation. When He does do it, they have not lost Him, they really possess Him in the power in which He lives and reigns. The functions of the Spirit are here twofold, according as they have for their object (a) the world (vv.⁸⁻¹¹), (β) the Apostles themselves (vv.¹³⁻¹⁵). As for (a), it is the Spirit's function to convict the world, to reach its conscience with demonstration, in regard to certain subjects. This conviction is not wrought in an immediate supernatural way, but through the ministry of the Apostles; it is to them the Spirit comes, and through their preaching the world is convicted. It is convicted of sin, because men do not believe in Christ. This is perhaps the most general statement on sin in Scripture: it consists at bottom in refusing to believe in Christ. If men did believe in Him, sin in all its kinds would disappear. Conviction of sin cannot be produced by denunciation, or satire, or clever exposures, or by what is miscalled knowledge of human nature; it can be produced only by witnessing to Christ in the power of the Spirit. The Spirit also produces in the world a conviction of conscience with regard to righteousness. This is connected with the exaltation of Jesus: 'I go to the Father and ye see me no longer.' When this exaltation is brought home to men's minds with the power of the Spirit (Ac 4³³), they realize that there is such a thing as righteousness, and that the supreme power in the world is on its side. In a sense it might be said that it was easier to believe in righteousness when men saw it present in the world, incarnate in Jesus Christ the Righteous; but it is a more solemn sense of its reality and supremacy that rises in the heart when, through the power of the Spirit, we realize that that righteous One is seated at the right hand of the Father. The third point in regard to which the Spirit convicts the world is judgment. This may be said to combine the other two. Sin and righteousness are

at issue with each other, and the Apostolic ministry, in the power of the Spirit, convinces men that in Christ a final judgment has been pronounced upon the issue. The protagonists in the great cause—Christ and the Prince of this world—have confronted each other decisively, and the Prince of this world has been judged (16¹¹, cf. 12³¹). A mind unenlightened or unconvinced by the Spirit might easily hold the opposite, and, looking to the life and death of Jesus, infer the impotence of the good, its condemnation, as futile and ineffective, by the nature of things; but even in the Cross of Jesus what the Spirit-taught man sees is the condemnation of evil, the sentence which God has passed and will finally execute on the Prince of this world, the verdict of the supreme tribunal on behalf of the good. Sin, righteousness, and judgment are abstract ideas, and come home to men in their reality only when in the power of the Spirit they are interpreted in their connexion with Christ. In these verses (16⁸⁻¹¹) the main idea involved in the Spirit is that of power: it is what is required to make the Apostles' message effective (cf. Ac 4³³, 1 Th 1⁵, 1 Co 2⁴, 2 Co 6⁶ᶠ·). But when we pass to (β) vv.¹²⁻¹⁵, the main idea is that of illumination. The Spirit is conceived as giving the disciples the comprehension of Christ which, according to St. Paul also (see 2 Co 3), is necessary to make a man a fit minister of the new covenant, not of letter but of spirit. Both kinds of sufficiency—that of power and that of illumination—are of God, and specifically of the Spirit. If vv.⁸⁻¹¹ state the dependence of the Evangelist on the Spirit, vv.¹²⁻¹⁵ state the dependence of the theologian on the Spirit. The idea underlying the latter passage is that of v.¹²: Jesus is greater than His words. When the time comes for Him to leave His disciples, many things remain unuttered. Many things are involved in His presence in the world, and especially in His impending Passion, which He understands, but they do not and cannot: are these things to be lost for ever? Is the significance of Jesus to be so far thrown away? This is not what Jesus contemplates. On the contrary, the Spirit which He promises as the Spirit of truth will have this as His very task, to initiate them into the whole meaning of Jesus. He will lead them, not into all truth, but into all the truth—that is, the truth which is embodied in Him in all its dimensions. The new point which is emphasized here about the Spirit is that He shall not speak of Himself (ἀφ' ἑαυτοῦ, i.e. of His own motion, self-prompted or independently). Many scholars, in reading what is told of spiritual gifts in Acts or the Pauline Epistles, have felt that the early Church ran a real risk. Who could tell whether the Spirit, under the impulse of which men uttered themselves, did not sometimes speak of itself, and say things which may have been in a vague sense πνευματικά, but were not in any true sense Christian? We have seen already how St. Paul met this danger. Partly (as in 1 Th 5¹⁹⁻²², 1 Co 14) he provides for the control of 'spiritual' utterances by the gift of discernment or by the common sense of the Christian society. Partly (as in 1 Co 12³) he lays down a dogmatic criterion of what is genuinely Christian. This latter course is followed also in 1 Jn. (4²): the spirit which is really of God is that which confesses Jesus Christ as come in flesh, in contrast with a more 'spiritual' kind of spirit which did not allow the heavenly Christ to ally Himself permanently, and especially by birth and death, to our humanity. But what we have here in the Gospel is really more searching, and goes to the root of the matter. The Spirit, personally as it is here conceived, is not a pure spontaneity; it is always historically prompted and historically controlled. What vindicates any utterance as spiritual is that it is a testimony to the historical Saviour. What the Spirit hears—all that He hears—He shall speak. It is not easy to say how the Spirit is conceived as hearing, but the main point is clear : hearing precedes speaking, and limits and controls it. In particular, it is said of the Spirit, ' He shall announce to you the things that are coming.' Westcott, interpreting τὰ ἐρχό-μενα on the analogy of the Messianic ὁ ἐρχόμενος, and thinking of the needs of the Apostles at the stage of transition between the old and the new era, finds the main reference in this to be to the constitution of the Christian Church : the Spirit will enable the Apostles to understand (by antici-pating?) the new age on which they are about to enter. Godet is inclined to render the words in a more prophetic sense, and regards them as having their fulfilment in the Apocalypse. This is too precise : perhaps if we said 'in apocalypses' (such as are suggested by 1 Co 2⁹ᶠ· 14⁶· ²⁶, Eph 1¹⁷ᶠ·) it would be nearer the mark. It is a special function of the Spirit to animate hope by unveiling the future (H. Holtzmann, *Handcom. ad loc.*). But whatever the special reference in τὰ ἐρχόμενα may be, the work of the Spirit on this side is summed up in the words ἐκεῖνος ἐμὲ δοξάσει. In every sense of the terms the Spirit's work is to testify to Christ—to what He is, to His words, to what He has done and suffered, to what He is to achieve. In this His function, if not His being, as the Spirit of truth is exhausted. And to say that He uses only what is Christ's is not to narrow the range or the means of His action ; for, as the Speaker goes on to say, ' All that the Father hath is mine.' All that belongs to the truth of God's Fatherhood is revealed in the Son, and all that is revealed in the Son is interpreted and vivified by the Spirit. The most striking feature of this passage is, after all, that with which it opens : ' I have many things to say unto you, but ye cannot bear them now,' with the implicit promise that they should hear the Spirit say them when they were able to bear it. The Apostolic reading of the truth, as truth is in Jesus, is perfectly conscious that it goes beyond the *ipsissima verba* which Jesus spoke on earth ; but the Apostles would have felt it strangely un-real if they had been asked to cut down their testi-mony to Jesus to what Jesus Himself had expressly put into words. There were many things which circumstances made it impossible for Him to put into words—many things which it was rather for them to say about Him than for Him to say about Himself ; but when they said these things, under the guiding and quickening impulse of His Spirit, they had no doubt that they were declaring the truth of Christ. It was a proof of ' Christ speak-ing in them,' as St. Paul puts it (2 Co 13³). Once they had listened to His voice on earth, now they heard Him in their hearts interpret all He had been, and between the voices they made no dis-tinction. A great part of the peculiarity of the Fourth Gospel is covered if we say that the word of the Risen Saviour, speaking by His Spirit in the heart of the Apostle, is presented as though it had been actually spoken on earth. And, little as this may agree with our ideas of a purely historical narrative, it is a precarious operation to set aside such a testimony, based on Christian experience and contemplated by Christ, as though it could be merely irrelevant to the Christian religion.

(*c*) The Spirit in the *First Epistle* of John does not call for separate treatment. One important passage has been already mentioned (4²) : another (5⁶⁻⁸) in which the Spirit and the sacraments are again mentioned in conjunction is to be interpreted on the analogy of ch. 3 and ch. 6 in the Gospel (see the present writer's *Death of Christ*, p. 277 ff.). The NT hardly invites to any discussion of the

metaphysics of the Spirit. Of course, it is the Spirit of God, and Divine. It is part of the one Divine causality which—as Father, Son, and Spirit —confronts the sinful world, and works in unison for its redemption. It belongs unmistakably to the sphere of the Divine, not of the human. Yet there is something in man which is akin to it, and it is through it that God dwells in man, and makes him partaker of the Divine nature. As the Spirit of God, it cannot be truly thought of as im-personal, and yet it is far more frequently spoken of in a way which is satisfied by the conception of a Divine impulsion to or stimulation of human thought, feeling, oraction, than as a distinct per-sonality. This is so even in writers who, like St. Paul (1 Co 12¹¹) and St. John (16¹⁴), distinctly have the latter mode of representing the Spirit. Cer-tainly the Spirit is not so unmistakably thought of as a person as is the Father or the Son. We never, for example, find the Spirit in the salutations of the Epistles : ' Grace to you and peace from God the Father and the Lord Jesus Christ ' is never supplemented by ' and from the Holy Spirit.' Neither do we ever find the Spirit united with the Father and the Son in prayer, as, *e.g.*, in 1 Th 3¹¹ ' Now our God and Father himself and our Lord Jesus Christ direct our way to you.' Even in the Apostolic benediction (2 Co 13¹⁴) it may fairly be questioned whether the Spirit is conceived as per-sonally as the Lord Jesus Christ and God. As for attempts to distinguish within the Trinity the relation of the Spirit to the Father from that of the Son to the Father as 'procession' from 'genera-tion,' the present writer can only repeat that they have no reality which he can apprehend. But the NT and Christian experience are at one in teach-ing that the Christian conception of God includes all that is meant by Father, Son, and Spirit ; and as the omission of what is meant by any of these terms leaves the Christian conception unsatisfied, it may fairly be said that the doctrine of the Trinity is the fundamental doctrine of our faith. The Father, the Son, and the Spirit in their unity constitute the God whom we know as the God of our salvation.

Literature.—Gloel, *Der heilige Geist in der Heilsverkündi-gung des Paulus*, 1888 ; Gunkel, *Die Wirkungen des heiligen Geistes* ², 1899 ; Irving F. Wood, *The Spirit of God in Biblical Literature*, 1904 ; Weinel, *Die Wirkungen des Geistes u. der Geister*, 1899 ; Kähler, *Dogmatische Zeitfragen*, i. 167 ff. ; Schmiedel, art. 'Spiritual Gifts' in *Encyc. Bibl.* ; the books on NT Theology ; also literature mentioned under ' Holy Spirit' in Hastings' *DB*.　　　　　　　　JAMES DENNEY.

HOLY THING (τὸ ἅγιον).—**1.** Lk 1³⁵ AV ' There-fore also that holy thing which shall be born of thee shall be called the Son of God.' RV prefers to render, ' Wherefore also that which is to be born shall be called holy, the Son of God.' On the expression τὸ γεννώμενον cf. Mt 1²⁰ τὸ . . . γεννηθέν, and for the use of ἅγιος applied to our Lord, see artt. HOLY ONE, HOLINESS.

2. Mt 7⁶ μὴ δῶτε τὸ ἅγιον τοῖς κυσί.—τὸ ἅγιον is usually taken to refer here to sacrificial meat or the provision of the priests. So Lange, Alford, and most Comm. ; but Meyer objects to this as requiring to be more precisely designated, and urges that Christ has in view ' the holy ' in general, and that what is meant by this is the *holy*, because *Divine*, evangelic truth by which men are converted. The fundamental idea of ἅγιος is consecration : τὸ ἅγιον, that which is consecrated or set apart to the service of God ; its general opposite would be βέβηλος, ' profane.' (See Westcott on He 7²⁶ and literature of HOLY ONE generally).

In Christian writings we find τὰ ἅγια used for the gifts as offered in the offertory or prothesis, *i.e.* the act of setting forth the oblation, and also for the consecrated gifts ; thus in the Liturgy of the Nestorians we find the direction : 'And when the people have received the holy thing, the priest,' etc. (See Brightman, *Liturgies Eastern and Western*, pp. 122, 301, 379, 398).   J. B. BRISTOW.

HOME.—

1. The expressions bearing the sense of 'home' are : (1) οἰκία (Mt 8⁶ ; also Jn 14², where we may prefer 'home' to 'house,' the rendering of the EV) ; (2) οἶκος (Mk 5¹⁹, Lk 1²³· ⁵⁶ 9⁶¹ 15⁶ ; also Jn 7⁵³ EV, in the section concerning the adulteress) ; (3) τὰ ἴδια (Jn 19²⁷, cf. also 1¹¹ and 16³²). As for (1) and (2), where we have the ordinary term = 'house' employed, it is to be noted that a house naturally becomes a 'home' under the associations of family life and affection ; cf. the corresponding use of בַּיִת. (3), as a use of ἴδιος, illustrates a tendency to abbreviation and attenuation of phrasing in such connexions as this. ἴδιος, with the force of the possessive pronoun (= ἑαυτοῦ, ἑαυτῶν), appears in NT as in the LXX, the OT, Apocrypha, and in such writers as Philo and Josephus (Deissmann, *Bible Studies*, Eng. tr., p. 123 f.). Cf., in this particular use, our expression 'at his father's,' and the attenuated Fr. phrase *chez lui.* The Vulg. in Jn 19²⁷ has the strict parallel *in sua.*

2. The Gospels afford us a few glimpses of domestic interiors, forming a part of the simple background of the life of Jesus. We see the common domestic shadows of sickness and death beclouding the home of Simon Peter (Mk 1³⁰), of Jairus (Mk 5²²), of the Roman officer (Mt 8⁵· ⁶), of Lazarus and his sisters (Jn 11), and of others. Homely joys are illustrated in the marriage at Cana (Jn 2), in the sojourn of Jesus as a guest in the home at Bethany (Lk 10³⁸, Jn 12¹· ²). Hospitality and entertaining are again exemplified in the case of Levi (Lk 5²⁹) and of Simon the Pharisee (Lk 7³⁶). The ever-fresh interest attendant on the birth of a child as a notable incident in home life finds illustration in the story of the birth of John the Baptist (Lk 1⁵⁷· ⁵⁸). We have sight, too, of the sumptuous domestic establishments of the luxurious rich (Lk 16¹⁹· ²⁰), in contrast with the simple abodes of the mass of the people and the condition of the homeless poor.

No people ever prized the sanctities and blessings of the home more than the Jews. Their wonderful legislation bearing on domestic affairs, the sentiments that find expression in Pss 127. 128, and in the panegyric of the Good Wife (Pr 31¹⁰⁻³¹), the importance attaching to the family as the unit of national life, all bear witness to this. The whole system of feasts and fasts, joyous and solemn, including the weekly Sabbaths and the yearly commemorations and seasons,—a system imparting so much colour and interest to the life of the people —also strongly tended to deepen the domestic sentiment, the home being to so large an extent the theatre for the prescribed rites and observances.

The general conditions of Jewish home life in our Lord's day offered marked points of contrast with what largely obtains among Western peoples. The greatest simplicity in the matter of meals and clothing, and the fewness of other wants, contributed to an easier condition of life in general. Grinding poverty was by no means common. Every man had a trade, and every father had to teach his son a trade ; but a man was not obliged to toil long hours for a bare living. There was considerable leisure, and the Palestinian Jew had much time for contemplation, like the Arab of to-day. The man was often abroad in public places, frequenting discussions in the Temple and elsewhere, and mingling with his fellows. He was also charged with certain religious duties and observances from which women were exempt. The place of the woman, on the other hand, was preeminently in the home. (Note that one of the things desiderated for women in Tit 2⁵ is that they should be οἰκουργοί). In this respect the Jews shared the sentiment of other Oriental peoples ; but the lot of the Jewish woman was much superior

to that of non-Jewish women in the East, and her position in the home was better than that of the Roman matron of that period. A serious menace to the home, however, existed in the conditions obtaining as regards divorce. We know how Jesus dealt with this great abuse of easy divorce (Mk 10²⁻¹² = Mt 19³⁻⁹). Some of the Jewish Rabbis also (as Shammai) set themselves against the laxity that had grown up. On the whole, it is probable that general practice was much better than current precepts. A Talmudic saying is significant—'The altar itself weeps over the man who puts away his wife' (*Giṭṭin* 10*b*, *Sanhed.* 22*a*).

The home as a factor in education was of the greatest importance. In our Lord's time there was probably in addition only a school at the synagogue, taught by the *hazzan*. A religious atmosphere surrounded the Jewish child from the first, and the mother was the earliest teacher. As soon as the child could speak, his mother taught him a verse of the Torah (on the unity of God ; and on the election of Israel). See art. CHILDHOOD.

3. All interest in this subject, so far as the Gospels are concerned, is focussed in the home at Nazareth, where Jesus spent nearly the whole of His life. Actual information as to the life in that home is of the scantiest ; but there can be no question that the best traditions of the Jewish home at its best were all exemplified there. There could never have been a better mother-teacher than Mary. The round of religious observances and duties would not fail of scrupulous performance. The conditions of the home itself were no doubt of the simplest and lowliest kind ; but an abundance of human affection was an ample compensation. There was nothing to cripple or blight in any way the wonderful young life that was there unfolding. There is room also for interesting reflexion as to the history and experience of that family circle at Nazareth during all the years that Jesus was a member of it. The great crises of all domestic life—births, marriages, deaths—must surely, some or all of them, have marked the history of the home of Jesus during those years. As we think of Joseph, who, as it is commonly agreed, appears to have died at an early period, and of our Lord's 'brothers' and 'sisters' (Mk 3³¹ 6³), there is every reason to conclude that within the circle of the home Jesus had the experience of human bereavement and sorrow, and also of rejoicing, as His very own.

4. From the day of His leaving Nazareth for the Jordan, Jesus ceased to have any settled home. 'The Son of Man,' He once said, 'hath not where to lay his head' (Mt 8²⁰ ‖ Lk 9⁵⁸). It is true that this saying is not to be taken too literally (see Bruce, *With Open Face*, ch. ix.), for Jesus would be welcome in the houses of many friends, as He was notably in the home at Bethany. Still, during His public ministry He surrendered all the quiet joys of the old home life at Nazareth, and often in the course of His constant journeys must have had to endure the hardships and privations of a wanderer. When He called His first disciples to follow Him (Mt 4¹⁸ff. ‖ Mk 1¹⁶f., Lk 5²⁷f.), He was summoning them to a life of homelessness resembling His own. He made readiness to leave home, with all its possessions and endearments, a test of fitness to be His true disciple (Lk 9⁵⁷⁻⁶² ‖ Mt 8¹⁹⁻²², cf. Mt 19²¹ ‖). And though He sent one home who wished to follow Him (Mk 5¹⁹ ‖ Lk 8³⁹), He taught that, in principle at least, His disciples should be willing to forsake not only house and lands, but parents and brethren and sisters, and even wife and children, for the Kingdom of God's sake (Lk 18²⁸ff. ‖ Mt 19²⁹, Mk 10²⁹f.). See, further, art. FAMILY.

LITERATURE.—See the works cited at end of art. CHILDHOOD, and add E. Stapfer, *Palestine in the Time of Jesus Christ*, Eng.

tr., chs. vii. and viii. ; Stalker, *Imago Christi*, ch. ii. ; Dale, *Laws of Christ*, ch. xi.

J. S. CLEMENS.

HONESTY (the subst. does not occur in the Gospels ; the adj. 'honest' is found in both AV and RV of Lk 8[15] as a rendering of καλός = Lat. *honestus*, 'noble,' 'excellent.' See Hastings' *DB s.vv.*).—This virtue does not take the prominent place in the teaching of Jesus Christ that it assumes in most systems of ethics. Our Lord never discusses or enjoins it. The reasons for His seeming neglect of the subject may be (1) that there was no dispute about it in His day, the Sixth commandment being taken for granted as universally binding, (2) that He went beneath the precept to the principles underlying it when (*a*) He discouraged covetousness (Mk 7[22], Lk 12[15]), and (*b*) He bade His disciples do to others as they would that others should do to them (Mt 7[12] = Lk 6[31]), and (3) that He treated considerations of property as of secondary importance, so that when it was a question of suffering from dishonesty—not committing it, He advised submission (Mt 5[40]) ; and when the question of the division of an inheritance was submitted to Him, He dismissed it as not within His province, and that with a tone of contempt, as though such a matter had not the importance people usually attached to it (Lk 12[13f.]). In life we see that dishonesty generally indicates a radical rottenness of character. It cannot be dealt with on prudential lines such as are indicated by the proverb, 'Honesty is the best policy.' By creating the Christian character, Jesus cuts out the roots of dishonesty in deceit, treachery, and greed ; and implants those principles of truth and honour of which honesty is one of the natural fruits. The word rendered 'honest' in Lk 8[15] (καλῇ) really means 'fair,' 'sound,' 'excellent.' In the Synoptics, when Jesus speaks of a thief (κλέπτης), it is not to denounce his wickedness, but in one place (Mt 6[19, 20], cf. Lk 12[33]) to warn His disciples against making 'treasures of earthly things which thieves may steal or moths corrupt ; and in another place (Mt 24[43], cf. Lk 12[33]) to compare the suddenness and unexpectedness of His advent with the way in which a thief breaks into a house at night. In Jn 10[8ff.] the false leaders of the people are compared to 'thieves and robbers' who ravage the flock, in contrast to the Good Shepherd who tends it. In the parable of the Good Samaritan the subject of neighbourly kindness had fallen among robbers (Lk 10[30]), whose excessive cruelty is described ; but the point of the parable is not in their conduct, which is referred to only in order to show the depth of misery in which their victim was found. Jesus also refers to robbers, *i.e.* brigands (λησταί), when He denounces the Jews for making God's house 'a den of robbers' (Mk 11[17] RV ; cf. Mt 21[13], Lk 19[46]), quoting Jer 7[11]. Here it is not common dishonesty that rouses our Lord's anger so much as the desecration of the house of God.

When the Jewish authorities came with an armed troop to take Jesus, He expostulated with them, asking if they had come out against a robber (λῃστής, Mk 14[48] ; cf. Mt 26[55], Lk 22[52]). In none of these cases does Jesus lay any stress on the question of dishonesty, the occasion not bringing it into discussion. His merciful words to one of the malefactors crucified with Him (Lk 23[43]) cannot be taken as throwing light on His views of dishonesty and its pardonableness, because the man was probably a brigand insurgent and a follower of Barabbas, not a mere thief. Still it does indicate that gross sins, among which stealing may be included, can be forgiven in those who turn to Christ. The one strong condemnation of theft in the Gospels is St. John's scornful description of Judas as 'a thief'

(Jn 12[6]), indicative of the vile hypocrisy of the man's character.

In the parable of the Unjust Steward it might appear that Jesus was commending an act of dishonesty. This man having wasted his master's goods and being called to account, foresees that he will lose his situation. Accordingly, in order to have some homes to go to for a refuge, he buys the friendship of his master's debtors by reducing the amount of their debts (Lk 16[1-9]). On the surface, at all events, this appears to be a fraudulent action ; and yet the steward is commended for it, and held up to the disciples as an example for them to follow. It is to be observed, however, that the commendation comes from the rich man, not from Christ. The master in the parable commends his steward. Wellhausen—in opposition to Jülicher—ascribes v.[8] to Jesus, citing as parallel Lk 18[6]. According to this view, ὁ κύριος here means 'the Lord'—*i.e.* Christ, not 'his Lord,' as in AV and RV. But against that rendering is the fact that the rich man is called the steward's 'lord' throughout the parable. The natural conclusion is that the 'lord' referred to in v.[8] is the 'lord' previously mentioned in vv.[3, 5]. Thus, as Dr. Plummer remarks, the argument, like that implied by the parable of the Unjust Judge, is *a fortiori*. Even a worthless, dishonest steward is commended by his master, at least for shrewdness ; much more, then, should a true servant of Christ act wisely. Of course, it is only the prudence, not the dishonesty, that is commended. This parable is an extreme instance for the rule that in any parable the main lessons only should be sought, and not its details allegorized. Possibly we should accept the suggestion that the estate was farmed to the steward, who rack-rented the tenants and dishonestly appropriated the excess, so that his hasty reduction of their debts was only bringing them down to the right amount, that which the owner had been receiving ; but of this there is no evidence. Mr. Latham put forward the view that the steward had been too scrupulous in studying the interests of his employer, to the neglect of the rights of the tenants, whom he ground down cruelly ; and he took the parable as a warning against unwise zeal for God at the cost of unkindness to men, on whom in the name of God too heavy requirements are laid (*Pastor Pastorum*, pp. 386–398).   W. F. ADENEY.

HONEY.—Honey is mentioned very frequently in the OT : twenty times in the proverbial expression 'a land flowing with milk and honey' (Ex 3[8, 17] 13[5] 33[3], Lv 20[24], Nu 13[27] 14[8] 16[13f.], Dt 6[3] 11[9] 26[9, 15] 27[3] 31[20], Jos 5[6], Jer 11[5] 32[22], Ezk 20[6, 15]) ; or in other connexions, either literally, as a product of the soil and as food (Gn 43[11], Dt 8[8] 32[13], Jg 14[8f, 18], 1 S 14[25f. 29. 43], 2 S 17[29], 1 K 14[3], 2 K 18[32], 2 Ch 31[5], Job 20[17], Ps 81[16], Is 7[15. 22], Jer 41[8], Ezk 16[13. 19], Sir 11[3] 39[26]) ; or figuratively, as a term of comparison for sweetness (Ex 16[31], Ps 19[10] 119[103], Pr 5[3] 16[24] 24[13f.] 25[16. 27], Ca 4[11] 5[1], Ezk 3[3], Sir 24[20] 49[1]). On the other hand, it is very rarely named in the NT, and especially in the Gospels. There is no direct evidence that the Jews were acquainted with any other honey than that of wild bees. Yet the fact that in 2 Ch 31[5] honey is included among the products of which the first-fruits were to be offered, would appear to represent it as an object of culture, and the mention of 'wild honey' as part of the food of John the Baptist (Mt 3[4], Mk 1[6] [Syr. Sin., perhaps under the influence of Dt 32[13] and Ps 81[16], has 'honey of the mountains']) appears to point by way of contrast to the existence of honey derived from domesticated bees. As to artificial honey, made from boiled fruits (dates, raisins, figs), and to which the Arabs give the name of *dibs* (the phonetic equivalent of Heb. שְׁבַד 'honey' [of bees], it is not impossible that it was known to the Israelites and the Jews ; but we have no decisive Biblical proof of this (cf. Jos. *BJ* IV. viii. 3 ; Urquhart, *The Lebanon*, 1860, i. p. 393 ; Berggren, *Guide Français-Arabe*, col. 266, Nr. 94 and 95).

The two parallel passages cited above, relating to the food of John the Baptist, are the only ones in the Gospels in which the word μέλι, 'honey,' is found. Wild honey (μέλι ἄγριον) is named along with locusts as forming the very simple and frugal sustenance of an ascetic, a Nazirite, such as John was.[*] Further, in another Gospel passage (Lk

---

[*] One might be tempted, however, following a hint of Diodorus Siculus (xix. 94), to see in the 'wild honey' the designation of a vegetable and nutritive substance, such as the resin of the tamarisks or some other sweet and savoury exudation

24^{42}) there is mention, at least in the TR and AV, of a piece 'of a honeycomb' (ἀπὸ μελισσίου κηρίου) as having been offered along with 'a piece of broiled fish' to Jesus after His resurrection. But a number of the most ancient MSS of the NT (אABDLII) do not contain the former phrase, and the disposition of modern commentators, almost without exception, is to consider it as an addition. 'A singular interpolation, evidently from an extraneous source, written or oral,' say Westcott and Hort. The RV omits it. But this method of solving the problem cannot be regarded as satisfactory and final. In fact, if it is very hard to imagine, to use the language of Dean Burgon, 'that such a clause as that established itself universally in the sacred text, if it be spurious,' it is much less difficult to explain 'how such a clause became omitted from any manuscript, if it be genuine.' One can discover no possible motive for the surreptitious introduction of these words into the text. On the other hand, if they are regarded as an integral part of the primitive and authentic text, it is not impossible to disentangle the reason of their suppression in some MSS. With a view to this we must place the narrative of Lk 24$^{41-43}$ alongside of Jn 21$^{9-13}$, compare these two descriptions of a meal, and note that in many of the writings of the Fathers, and probably in various attempts to establish 'harmonies of the Four Gospels' (but not in the *Diatessaron* of Tatian), these two scenes are in fact identified (although they differ in all their essential features). Now, perhaps, we may be able to explain how the mention of the honeycomb came to disappear. The influence of Lv 2$^{11f.}$, which forbids the use of honey (probably because easily subject to fermentation) in any kind of sacrifice; that of the allegorical interpretation of Ca 5^1 (especially in the LXX version) applied to Christ; an ascetic tendency to proscribe sweet foods; the possible intervention of the Valentinians with their *Veritatis Evangelium*; and, finally, the proneness to polemize against the Gnostics, who made large use of honey in their solemn 'mysteries' (cf. Carl Schmidt, *Gnostische Schriften in koptischer Sprache*, Leipzig, 1892, pp. 203, 508), and who may have appealed for support to this text;—such are the motives which, either singly or all combined, may have brought about the removal of the disputed words. The present writer is strongly inclined, in common with the three authors cited below in the Literature, to retain them as authentic.

Literature.—Burgon-Miller, *The Traditional Text of the Holy Gospels*, London, 1896, Appendix I. 'Honeycomb,' pp. 240–252; Merx, *Evang. des Markus und Lukas*, Berlin, 1905, pp. 540–543; Nestle, *ThLZ*, 1906, col. 40. See also, for bees, Bochart, *Hieroz.* ii. 502 ff.; J. G. Wood, *Bible Animals*, 1869, pp. 605–612; Tristram, *Nat. Hist. of the Bible*[8], 1889, pp. 322–326.

LUCIEN GAUTIER.

HONOUR.—The codes of technical 'honour' are largely opposed to the teaching of Christ (Mt 5, Lk 6^{29}). Therefore such conceptions of 'honour' must be regarded as briers choking the word (Mk 4^{19}); for whatever justification codes of 'honour' may claim (as from Mt 7^{12}), they are impatient of the spirit of meekness inculcated by Christ in precept (Mt 5^{39}) and in example (Mt 27). So the Sons of Thunder would have vindicated summarily the honour of their Master (Lk 9^{54}). More generally, in the quest of honour, it is honour from God and not from men that is to be sought by the Christian —the glory of God rather than of men (Jn 12^{43}). Worldly honour may be a source of severest temptation (Lk 4^7), for the disciple is not greater than his Master whose sinlessness was thus brought

from a tree. To collect nourishment of this kind in the thickets along the Jordan would have been an easier task for the Baptist, and would have required less time, than to hunt for the honey of bees (cf. Berggren, *op. cit.* col. 564).

to view (Mt 10^{24}). Honour from God the Christian disciple will have: 'If any man will serve me, him will my Father honour' (Jn 12^{26}). And to be invited to the marriage-supper of the King's Son is a greater honour than any this world affords (Mt 22). But this honour and blessing from God contrasts with the dishonour and scorn that the world is ready to shower upon followers of One who was despised and rejected. The wicked husbandmen did not honour the son of the lord of the vineyard (Mk 12^6); they killed him and put him to shame (Mk 15). The Christian therefore must not be found

'Seeking an honour which they gave not Thee.'

Nay, even the most sacred honour is not the right goal for the follower of Christ, as James and John were taught (Mk 10^{37}). Service, not honour, is the true aim for the life of self-sacrifice,—not to be honoured of all, but to be servant of all (Mk 10^{44}). Honour is included in the all-things left to follow Christ (Mt 19^{27}), and it is worth while to abandon all worldly things in exchange for the true life (Mt 16^{26}). Still further, the *tradition of men* must give place to the *commandment of God* (Mk 7^8). Dishonour now will give place to eternal and Divine honour in due season (Mt 19^{28}).

W. B. FRANKLAND.

HOOK.—See FISH.

HOPE.—In considering the relation of hope to Christ and the Gospels, we are at once met with the fact that in the Gospels the word ἐλπίς does not occur at all, and ἐλπίζω only five times, viz. once in Mt (12^{21}), where the Evangelist quotes the LXX, three times in Lk (6^{34} 23^8 24^{21}), and once in Jn (5^{45}); and in none of these instances does it refer to the theological virtue.

This absence of the word is the more remarkable, when we remember not only that Judaism, the religion in which our Lord and His disciples were reared, was essentially a religion of hope, but also that the result of the teaching of Jesus was vastly to enlarge and deepen that hope, by imparting to it the riches of the Christian faith. Great as was the religious hope inspired by the older dispensation, it was small when compared with that 'better hope' (He 7^{19}) which rested on the unchangeable kingly Priesthood of Christ.

The disciples doubtless were too fully absorbed in the *present* to have felt deeply expectations for the future. They were held captive by the greatness of His personality and the depth of His love, and ultimately came to realize that they had in Him the Hope of Israel itself. And if Simeon, having received the Messiah into his arms, felt his greatest hopes realized, then the disciples, having found the Christ, must have been so absorbed by Him as to have had little room and little need for longings regarding the future.

But why did Jesus, who taught the necessity of *faith* (Mk 11^{22}, Jn 3^{16}) and the pre-eminence of *love* (Mt 22^{40}), remain silent as regards *hope*. It was due to the fact that in training His followers, the first necessity was to concentrate their attention on *Himself* as their present possession. Had He taught them fully of the fruition that awaited them at the end of the age, and had He thus made hope a distinctly prominent portion of His teaching, He would have dissipated their attention and diverted it from that which they most required to learn. St. Paul could teach, 'Christ our hope' (1 Ti 1^1). Jesus had to lay the foundation by teaching, 'Come unto me' (Mt 11^{28}).

But if He did not give direct teaching on the point, He nevertheless laid deeply the basis upon which the Church's doctrine of hope was to be built; for He pointed the disciples, in His promises, to the blessings which they ultimately would enjoy. The promises of His resurrection, of His perpetual spiritual presence, and of His final return in glory, were sure foundations upon which the Church could build her doctrine, and on this basis the developed teaching of the Epistles rests. And if the death of Jesus rudely shattered the Messianic hope of the disciples, His resurrection, followed by the illumination of the Holy Spirit, restored it to them in a purified and spiritual form.

As we study in the Epistles the doctrine of hope, which was thus awakened and became an integral part of Christian life, we find it vitally connected by the Church with her faith in Christ risen and glorified. (1) His resurrection is regarded as the *ground* of the Christian's hope : by it Christians are begotten 'unto a living hope,' and through it their hope in God is established (1 P 1$^{3.\ 21}$). (2) *All* Christian hopes are realized in Him. Various objects worthy of hope are mentioned, such as salvation (1 Th 5^8), eternal life (Tit 1^2 3^7), the glory of God (Ro 5^2, Col 1^{27}), the resurrection of the dead (Ac 24^{15} 23^6) ; but all these different blessings are summed up in Jesus Christ. When they hope for Him, they hope for them all ; for in Him all the scattered yearnings of the human heart are united and find their fulfilment. Thus it is that St. Paul calls Him 'our hope' (1 Ti 1^1). (3) The Church therefore fixes her gaze on the heavens ; for her Hope is there. She is ever 'looking for the blessed hope and appearing of the glory of our great God and Saviour Jesus Christ' (Tit 2^{13}), for then she shall be like Him, for she shall see Him as He is ; 'and every one that hath this hope set on him purifieth himself' (1 Jn 3$^{2.\ 3}$). Even inanimate nature groans for its coming redemption at the Parousia, having been subjected to vanity 'in hope' (Ro 8^{20}). (4) But while the full realization of Christian hope will not be reached until the return of Christ, yet even now the Church has a foretaste of the bliss that ultimately will be hers. For Christ now dwells in the Church and in the hearts of her members, and thus grants an earnest of final fulfilment. Christ in the Church and in the individual is 'the hope of glory' (Col 1^{27}), and therefore to be without Christ is to be without hope (Eph 2^{12}).

See, further, the following article.

CHARLES T. P. GRIERSON.

HOPEFULNESS (CHRIST'S).—Knowing that all our possessions of grace come from Christ, in whom we believe all fulness dwells, and believing that He alone among the sons of men possessed perfect knowledge, we might be led to doubt whether we could justly attribute hope to Him. As regards His perfect knowledge, we must remember that uncertainty is no essential element in hope. Human hope may be proverbially disappointing, but that is due to the uncertainty of temporal things, and not to the nature of hope itself. Indeed, the glory of the Christian hope consists in the moral certainty of its grounds. It is a 'better hope' in part as being 'sure and steadfast' (He 7^{19} 6^{19}). The fact, then, that our Lord's faith rendered future objects of desire almost a present possession in no way prevented Him from experiencing this grace.* As regards His possessing 'all fulness' as the God-man, and so being thought incapable of feeling hopefulness, it may be said that we clearly start our thoughts on a wrong line if we commence an investigation of this kind with our own *a priori* views of what the incarnate Son of God must have felt or not felt. We can in ourselves be no ade-

---

* Westcott (*Life*, vol. i. p. 41) writes in his diary : 'The fact of our Lord never mentioning His own faith or hope is a proof of His Divinity.' This, however, can hardly be looked upon as a careful statement, but rather as a passing thought, and it was noted down early in his life (æt. 21).

quate judges of the limitations which Deity might set upon itself when taking our flesh. Our duty is to study the NT, and especially the Gospels, with the view of discovering what is there revealed as to the true nature of this act of Divine condescension. And such a study teaches us that in our Lord's Person we have not only a revelation of the Father, but also a revelation of humanity at its highest. He loved to call Himself 'Son of Man,' because He thereby taught us to see in Him the ideal Man, and therefore we must expect to see in Him every truly human emotion (and hope is one of them) purified and perfected.

No teacher of mankind ever so frequently pointed to Himself in His teaching as Jesus did, and yet it is remarkable that He rarely revealed His own personal emotions. When He disclosed Himself it was as the source of all grace, so that men might be saved and nourished by His life. He was so absolutely *selfless* that He rarely sought sympathy by speaking of His heart's desires. It is not He but the Evangelists who tell us that He was weary, wept, exulted, marvelled. Thus it happens that He never definitely mentions His own hope. Indeed, strangely enough, the word ἐλπίς does not occur in the Gospels (see art. HOPE). But as hope is a necessary element of Christian character, being one of the 'abiding' graces (1 Co 13^{13}), Christ, if He be true man, must have experienced it. It is not *said* that He had faith, but must we not believe that His whole human career was sustained from the first consciousness of childhood to Calvary by faith, perfect in its range and steadfastness? The long nights of prayer surely tell us not only of a general attitude of dependence, but also of a definite trustful belief in the love and presence of His Father, which found its expression in petition. What habitual strength of faith is shown in such words as 'Thinkest thou that I cannot beseech my Father, and he shall even now send me more than twelve legions of angels?' (Mt 26^{53}).

No doubt His faith and hope are so raised above ours by their perfection, that they may no longer seem to be what to us are faith and hope. But He raised *all* human attributes to their perfection ; not thereby altering their essential character, but rather exhibiting them as they ought to be in ourselves. And if He felt no hope, never rejoiced in coming good, never was upborne when wearing the cross by anticipation of the crown, but lived His life in the cold calm of duty, then the Stoic is the ideal of our race.

Not a few evidences, more or less indirect, of Christ's hopefulness are found in the Gospels. In one case its object was of a temporal nature, namely, when being 'hungry' He approached the fig tree, 'if haply he might find anything thereon.' (Mk 11$^{12ff.}$)

Little reverence would be shown by interpreting this incident as feigned for the purpose of teaching a moral lesson. 'If He only pretended not to know that the tree was barren, we should expect the hunger also to have been pretended' (Mason, *Conditions of our Lord's Life*, p. 152). Rather have we an example of hope in the mind of Jesus for a desired good, which circumstances disappointed, and which He turned to a moral purpose.

Evidence of His being cheered during His ministry by hope of the results of His spiritual labours may probably be seen in His words to the disciples when the Samaritan woman had left (Jn 4$^{27-38}$). He had gained one soul, and with prophetic vision saw the land filled with ripened souls ready for the spiritual reaper. His followers, too, would receive wages in the joy of souls won, and ultimately they, with the earlier workers of God who had sown the seed, would rejoice together.

So full was His soul with joy of hope already realized, and with the prospect of still greater harvesting, that He was raised above the sense of hunger. The whole passage seems full of the deepest emotion of our Lord; and if so, hope was its strongest element. A similar anticipation of coming joy in the salvation of those He came to save may be felt in the words, 'Rejoice with me; for I have found my sheep which was lost' (Lk 15[6]). Further, may we not see that hope realized was the cause of the strong movement of His soul, when He exulted ($\dot{\eta}\gamma\alpha\lambda\lambda\iota\dot{\alpha}\sigma\alpha\tau o$, Lk 10[21]) in Satan's fall from heaven? It was a rejoicing of His innermost soul, because already He saw potentially accomplished the object of His mission. Similarly must we account for the deep feeling displayed by Him when visited by the inquiring Greeks (Jn 12[20-33]). Here again is hope anticipative. He sees the uttermost parts of the world potentially present in the persons of these Gentiles, and He declares that 'the hour is come that the Son of Man should be glorified' (v.[23]); and yet, foreknowing the terrible fate that awaited Him before the achievement of His desire, He alternated between the joy of hope and the sorrow of human dread, and prayed to be saved from that hour (v.[27]).

In His teaching to His disciples there is the oft-repeated lesson of His return to His Father (Jn 7[33] 8[14] 16[28]). Doubtless His chief object was to explain His heavenly origin and to prepare them for His departure, but not a little pathos and increased depth may be recognized in such words if we see in them also a longing hope for the time when the bitter trials of His voluntary humiliation would cease. Thus in His High-Priestly prayer, now that He has finished His work, He pleads for the renewal of the glory which He had with His Father before the world was (17[1-5]). And thinking of the loved ones to whom His parting would be so bitter a trial, He prays for the realization of the hope that they might ultimately be granted the beatific vision, beholding Him in His glory (v.[24]); then would He drink with them the fruit of the vine new in His Father's kingdom (Mt 26[29]).

Perhaps the most clearly expressed example of hope on the part of our Lord, an example which unequivocally shows His feeling of the emotion, is to be found in the words with which He commenced the Paschal meal. 'With desire I have desired to eat this passover with you before I suffer' (Lk 22[15]). Here we have a distinct statement, that He held ardently an expectation of a future good before its realization.

We further find that His ministry was exercised in a spirit of intense *optimism* as regards both the community and the individual. This is the more remarkable when we recall that He more than any other saw the reality of human corruption. The hidden disease of society, with its outward religiousness and inward godlessness, led Him to predict the overthrow of the ecclesiastical and national life, like Jeremiah of old. But, unlike that prophet, He, notwithstanding His clear view of coming judgment, looked to the future with a splendid hopefulness. His kingdom would yet fill the world (Mt 13); His gospel would be universally preached (Mk 13[10]); and ultimately *all* men would be drawn unto Him (Jn 12[32]).

The same optimism is to be seen in His dealings with individual sinners. In the most corrupt He saw germs of good; and thus could win sinful women from their ways (Lk 7[50], Jn 8[11]), and publicans from their grasping worldliness (Mk 2[14], Lk 19[9]); and He could discover sufficient moral worth in a dying thief and murderer to be able to promise him rest in Paradise (Lk 23[43]). The hopefulness of Christ in His message to mankind is fully embodied in His saying, 'Be of good cheer; I have overcome

the world' (Jn 16[33]). Thus we see that our Lord was in hope, as in all else save sin, 'like as we are' (He 4[15]). And if we in our trials are upborne by the hope of future bliss, He also was upborne to endure the cross and despise the shame by 'the joy that was set before him' (12[2]).

                 CHARLES T. P. GRIERSON.

HORN.—The expression 'a horn of salvation' in the song of Zacharias (Lk 1[69]) is undoubtedly a reference to the promised Messiah. A similar combination of words is found in Ps 18[2], but the conception is more probably due to 132[17], 1 S 2[10].

1. In the OT the word 'horn' is figuratively used in poetical and allegorical language: (*a*) for abstract notions of *strength* (Nu 23[22], Ps 89[17, 24]), and hence of dignity (112[9]) or pride (75[4ff.]); also, (*b*) in a concrete sense, to represent *kings and empires* (Dn 7[24] 8[20f.], Zec 1[18ff.]). The rendering 'a mighty salvation,' Lk 1[69] (Pr. Bk.), paraphrases the sense but obliterates the associations. Hor. *Od.* iii. 21. 18 is quoted as an instance of the metaphor in ordinary literature, in which it is rare.

2. Inasmuch as the horn in animals is a weapon of attack rather than of defence, some have regarded it as a symbol of *aggressive* strength (see Delitzsch, Perowne, etc., on Ps 18[2]): possibly *combative* strength, in which both ideas are included, would be a better definition. There are two classes of symbols expressive of such strength : (*a*) natural weapons (*e.g.* horn, right hand, arm, etc.), and (*b*) artificial weapons (arrows, axe, shield, etc.). When any distinction is to be made, the former class tends to represent that strength which is personal, inherent, immediate; the latter, to represent that strength in which second causes, instruments, agents appear (Is 10[5, 15]).   F. S. RANKEN.

HOSANNA (אנשְׁעָוה, Gr. $\dot{\omega}\sigma\alpha\nu\nu\dot{\alpha}$).—One of the Hebrew words which (like *Amen, Hallelujah, Sabbath, Sabaoth*) have passed, transliterated and not translated, from the vocabulary of the Jewish to that of the Christian Church. In the NT it occurs only in three Gospels: in them it is found six times (Mt 21[9 bis. 15], Mk 11[9, 10], Jn 12[13]), but only in the history of our Lord's triumphant entry to Jerusalem on Palm Sunday, and only as a vocal cry uttered, either by the palm-bearing multitude who met Him, or by the children who hailed Him thereafter in the Temple (Mt 21[15]). Among the Jews, however, the word came to designate not alone the cry, but also the *branches* of palms, myrtle, or willow which on their joyous feast of Tabernacles, and especially on its seventh day, the people were accustomed—for the Law did not enjoin this ceremony—to carry in procession with the priests to the fountain of Shiloah and thence again to the Temple, where these 'hosannas' were piled up and beaten against the altar. It is only with 'Hosanna' as a cry that we are here concerned; but we cannot forget that when, in honour of our Lord, the multitude raised the cry, they 'took branches of palm trees' (Jn 12[13]) as well; and therefore, besides expounding the meaning of the cry, we must consider how a ceremony customary at the feast of Tabernacles came to be adopted, popularly, on an occasion when the worshippers were assembling at Jerusalem to celebrate a feast of a widely different character, that of the Passover.

Philologically, the word *Hosanna* is explained as a derivation from or contraction of Ps 118[25] (Heb.): *ānnā Jahweh hôshî'āh-nnā* ('I beseech thee, O Lord, save now'). This Psalm was sung, and this verse of it used as a refrain by the people, at the feast of Tabernacles; and the refrain was abbreviated, through constant popular repetition, into *Hôsha'nā*, just as the old Canaanitish cry *Hoi Dod* (= 'Ho Adonis') was turned into a common interjection, *Hedad*.

The vocal 'Hosanna' was used by the Jews at the feast of Tabernacles when the branches also were employed; and on this account it has been asserted by Mr. Lewis N. Dembitz (in the *Jewish Encyc.* vol. vi. p. 276, s.v. 'Hosh'ana Rabbah') that 'the Gospels by a mistake place the custom in the season shortly before the Passover, instead of in the feast of Booths.' To this it may be answered, (1) that, according to another writer in the same *Encyclopedia*, Rabbi Kaufmann Kohler (vol. vi. p. 272), *Hosanna* 'became a popular cry used in solemn processions wherewith was connected the carrying of palm branches as described in 1 Mac 13⁵¹ and 2 Mac 10⁷.' But (2) the procession in 1 Mac 13⁵¹ was *not* at the feast of Tabernacles, which was kept on the 15th day of the 7th month (Lv 23³⁴), but at a wholly different season, 'on the three and twentieth day of the second month'; while the celebration in 2 Mac 10⁷, though 'the procession was *after the manner* of the feast of Tabernacles' (v.⁶), was somewhat later in the year. Thus there was historical and uninspired (for the Jews did not hold the Books of Maccabees to be inspired) precedent for the employment both of the palm-bearing and the shout on other suitable occasions besides the feast of Tabernacles. And (3) was not the occasion of Christ's entry into Jerusalem one that must have seemed eminently suitable alike to His disciples who began it (Lk 19³⁷) and to the candid (Mt 21¹⁵) and grateful (Jn 12¹⁷) Israelites who joined them in the celebration of it? The Jews, we know, were accustomed to associate with the feast of Tabernacles the highest of those blessings which Messiah was to bring. It was as Messiah that Jesus now presented Himself. He had chosen to ride that day upon the ass's colt, in accordance with Zechariah's prophecy (Zec 9⁹), just on purpose to make an offer of Himself to Jerusalem as her promised King (Mt 21⁴, Jn 12¹⁴). What, accordingly, would the people look for at His hands? What would they ask from Him? Salvation; but salvation not on its negative side alone, of deliverance, but on its positive side as well, of fruition. If the approaching feast of the Passover would remind them of the former, how their Egyptian oppressor had been smitten (Ex 12²⁹), it was the feast of Tabernacles which pre-eminently supplied illustrations of the latter: its branches and its booths were redolent of that first night of freedom which their fathers had enjoyed under the cool booths of Succoth (Ex 12³⁷), so refreshing after the dust and heat of the brickfield and the furnace. Both sides—the negative and the positive, the smiting and the booths—were in one chapter (Ex 12): they could hardly remember the one without the other. The form, therefore, which the celebration of our Lord's entry into Jerusalem is described by the Four Evangelists as assuming, is not such as to require us to suppose that they made a mistake in placing it at the season of the Passover. On the contrary, it was neither unprecedented nor unnatural; and the fact that it was not a legally prescribed but only a popular ceremony, left them quite free to use it when they thought fit. It is not as if the Evangelists had transferred the unleavened bread of the Passover to the Feast of Tabernacles.

Hosanna is rendered in both AV and RV (cf. Ps 118²⁵, whence it is taken) 'Save now.' The *now* is not here an adverb of time, but an interjection of entreaty, as in 'Come now': the word means 'Oh! save' (*Jewish Encyc.*), or 'Save, we beseech Thee.' As given (1) absolutely, as in Mk 11⁹ and Jn 12¹³, the natural meaning of this would be an address to Christ, as Messiah, asking Him to bestow the salvation expected of Him; or, as our English hymn expresses it, 'Bring near Thy great salvation.' We can understand how, in this sense, 'Hosanna' should be followed by salutations or acclamations, 'Blessed is he that cometh in the name of the LORD' (Ps 118²⁶, Mt 21⁹, Mk 11⁹), 'Blessed is the kingdom of our father David, that cometh in the name of the Lord' (Mk 11¹⁰), or 'Blessed is the King of Israel that cometh in the name of the Lord' (Jn 12¹³). All the different forms may have been used, for there was a multitude of speakers. The sequence of the thoughts is natural: for if Jesus be once conceived of as able to save (either by His own power or by that of Him that sent Him), the next thing, obviously, for His people to do, after asking Him to exert His power in their behalf, is to rejoice that He has come, and to bless Him for coming.

But (2) it is not only in this absolute construction that the Evangelists use the word *Hosanna*. St. Matthew employs it with a dative, 'Hosanna to the Son of David' (Mt 21⁹); and both St. Matthew and St. Mark give us 'Hosanna in the highest.' Both these variations have been censured by Dr. Kaufmann Kohler (*Jewish Encyc. l.c. supra*) as 'corruptions of the original version': the addition 'in the highest,' he declares to be 'words which no longer give any sense.' But in a connexion which

seems to justify St. Matthew, the dative is used alike in the OT (Ps 3⁸ 'Salvation belongeth unto the Lord') and in the NT in a passage based upon that Psalm (Rev 7¹⁰ 'Salvation unto our God; and unto the Lamb'); while there is surely nothing 'senseless' in the thought that the salvation which God gives, or sends, to men should fill the highest heaven with rejoicings in His praise. We have the idea in the OT (*e.g.* Ps. 8¹) and in the NT (Lk 2¹⁴, Eph 3¹⁰). To some Christian commentators, however, and those of no mean weight,—*e.g.* Cornelius à Lapide and Dean Alford,—St. Matthew's use of *Hosanna* with the dative has seemed to render requisite a different interpretation of the word. *Hosanna* was, says Alford (on Mt 21⁹), 'originally a formula of supplication, but [became] conventionally [one] of gratulation, so that it is followed by a dative, and by "in the highest,"—meaning "may it also be ratified in heaven,"'—and he cites 1 K 1³⁶, where Benaiah answers David, saying, 'Amen: the Lord, the God of my lord the king, say so too.' Cornelius à Lapide takes 'Hosanna to the Son of David' as a prayer for Christ, offered by the people 'asking all prosperous things for Him from God.' Now, this would, in itself, be admissible enough. Of Messiah, even when thought of as Divine and reigning, the Scripture says, 'prayer also shall be made for him continually' (Ps 72¹⁵). But it seems unnatural to postulate so violent an alteration in the meaning of the word—from 'supplication' to 'gratulation,' when, taken in its original meaning, it yields a sufficient sense: 'Save now, for it is to thee, O Son of David, that the power to save us has been given.' It was not unnatural that the people should speak in this sense: as Jews they knew already that 'salvation belongeth unto God' (Ps 3⁸). This view derives considerable confirmation from the parallel passage in the Apocalypse, where the whole scene in ch. 7¹⁴, and even the very words—'the multitude before the throne and before the Lamb . . . with palms in their hands' (Rev 7⁹, cf. Jn 12¹³), who cry with a loud voice (cf. Lk 19³⁷), saying, 'Salvation to our God . . . and to the Lamb'—seems to be based on what happened at Jerusalem on that first Palm Sunday; as if the Seer were beholding the salvation come which that day was asked, and recognized that the palm-bearers of the earthly Jerusalem were precursors of the hosts of the redeemed. St. John, it will be remembered, has, in his Gospel (12¹⁶), the remark, 'These things understood not his disciples at the first, but after he was risen they remembered,' etc. If, as seems clear, the vision is expressed in figures drawn from that event, then the acclaim in heaven must be held to settle the meaning of those Hosannas upon earth: the dative of the Apocalypse is the dative of the Gospel: it is the dative not of a prayer for Jesus, but of an ascription of salvation to Him as its Mediator and Bestower.

It remains only to be added that the Third Evangelist, while recording the same Triumphal Entry, and mentioning the acclamations of the people, omits alike the palm-branches and the word 'Hosanna.' The explanation, no doubt, of both omissions lies in the fact that St. Luke wrote especially for Gentiles: his readers would not have understood the Hosanna, and would have misunderstood the palms. To Greeks the palm-branch would have been, inevitably, the palm of pride and victory: not, as to the Hebrew mind, an emblem of peaceful rest, and freedom, and household joy. 'Hosanna' would have meant nothing at all. Therefore the Evangelist to the Greeks paraphrases the word, and paraphrases with it St. Matthew's and St. Mark's addition to it, 'in the highest'; rendering the whole by 'Peace in heaven, and glory in the highest' (Lk 19³⁸). And, as St.

Matthew had the dative of ascription, 'Hosanna to the Son of David'—as looking for salvation to Him who had come to Jerusalem in this capacity; so St. Luke, in his paraphrase of the Hosanna, employs what we may call a dative clause: his 'Peace in heaven, and glory in the highest,' are introduced so as to show us these as the result of Christ's coming as King in the name of the Lord: it is for these ends that He has come; and on this account the people call Him blessed. It was for these ends that He was born: wherefore the angels sang the same strain over Him at His Nativity (Lk 2¹⁴); it is for these ends now that He paces forward to His cross: and therefore men, though as yet they understand it not (Jn 12¹⁶), are moved, by a Power they know not, to bear Him record.

LITERATURE.—Art. 'Hosanna' in Hastings' *DB* and in *Encyc. Bibl.*; *Jewish Encyc.*, *loc. cit.*; Milligan, *Com. on Gospel of St. John* and *Revelation*; Westcott, *St. John's Gospel*; Cornelius à Lapide, Neale and Littledale, and Perowne, on Ps 118.

JAMES COOPER.

HOSPITALITY.—This marked Oriental virtue prevailed in Palestine in Christ's day. Our Lord assumes its exercise, rather than directly enjoins it. His Apostles, later, however, prescribed hospitality as a reflexion of the Christ spirit (Ro 12¹³, 1 Ti 3², Tit 1⁸, He 13², 1 P 4⁹), even towards an enemy (Ro 12²⁰). Because of the widespread prevalence of hospitality, inns (wh. see) were comparatively few; and even in *khans* or places of lodgment for strangers there were unfurnished rooms which were at the disposal of travellers, without cost. The innkeeper or **host** usually received remuneration for such extra service as the stranger might require, as in a case like that of the wounded man cared for at the Samaritan's expense (Lk 10³⁵). Since Jesus Himself 'had not where to lay his head' (Mt 8²⁰), He depended much upon the hospitality of the friendly disposed, as of Andrew and Peter at Capernaum (Mt 8¹⁴), and of Mary, Martha, and Lazarus at Bethany (Jn 11¹⁻⁵); and frequently accepted the hospitality of householders (Mt 26⁶, Lk 5²⁹ 7³⁶ff. 19⁵). On occasions of the great feasts at Jerusalem, guest-chambers were freely put at the disposal of visiting worshippers (Mk 14¹⁴). When the Master sent out the Seventy, they were to take no purse, but to rely upon the hospitality of the people of the towns into which they might go (Lk 10⁴ff.); a blessing being left with the hospitable (v.⁵), while a woe is pronounced upon the inhospitable city (vv.¹⁰⁻¹²). Christ said of His messengers that those who received them were in truth receiving Him (Jn 13²⁰). So incensed were two of His disciples at being refused entertainment in a Samaritan village, that they would have called down fire from heaven to destroy the people. But this spirit Jesus rebuked (Lk 9⁵²⁻⁵⁶). The spirit of hospitality was manifested in giving not only lodging and food, but also water for the feet (Lk 7⁴⁴, cf. Jn 13⁵); a servant usually unloosing and taking charge of the sandals (Lk 3¹⁶). Sometimes a kiss characterized the hospitable reception (Lk 7⁴⁵).

The emphasis that Jesus laid upon the virtue of hospitality may be discovered in His description of the Last Judgment, in which the righteous are commended because 'I was a stranger and ye took me in' (Mt 25³⁵). See also art. INN.

LITERATURE.—Thomson, *LB*, *passim*; Edersheim, *Sketches of Jewish Social Life*; Trumbull, *Oriental Social Life*; Hastings' *DB*, *s.v.*
E. B. POLLARD.

HOST.—See (1) ANGELS; (2) HOSPITALITY, INN, INVITATION.

HOUR.—**1.** In several of their accounts of Christ's healings, the Evangelists indicate the instantaneousness of the cures by some such expression as,

'He was healed in the selfsame hour' (Mt 8¹³, cf. 9²² 15²⁸ 17¹⁸, Jn 4⁵³). More definitely the word is used as a division of the day (Mt 20³. ⁵. ⁶. ¹² 27⁴⁵. ⁴⁶, cf. Mk 15³³. ³⁴, Lk 23⁴⁴, Jn 1³⁹ 4⁶. ⁵² 19¹⁴). The usual system of reckoning time was from 6 a.m. to 6 p.m., and again from 6 p.m. to 6 a.m. 'In the 1st cent. of our era the day was divided, in popular language, into twelve equal parts or hours, which varied in length according to the season. . . . The expression, "the first hour," indicated the time when the shadow on the dial reached the mark which showed that ₁¹₂ of the day had elapsed' (Ramsay, *Expositor*, March 1893, p. 216 f.). The question has been raised, because of the apparent divergence between Jn 19¹⁴ and Mk 15²⁵, whether St. John adopted another method of reckoning in the Fourth Gospel, viz. from midnight to midday, and from midday to midnight. Prof. Ramsay maintains that, though the Roman civil day was reckoned in this way, it was not divided into hours; and that the note of time when the martyrdom of Polycarp took place, ὥρᾳ ὀγδόῃ, does not prove its use in Asia Minor (*l.c.*). But the internal evidence of the Fourth Gospel points strongly to this mode of reckoning on the part of St. John. The tenth hour (Jn 1³⁹) is more probably 10 a.m. than 4 p.m., if the two disciples lodged with Jesus 'that day.' It harmonizes with the custom of Eastern women of drawing water in the evening, and accounts for the weariness of Jesus, if we take 'the sixth hour' of Jn 4⁶ not as noon, but as 6 p.m. And although we cannot look for precision in point of time in Oriental writers, the divergence between the Synoptists and St. John as to the hour of Christ's condemnation and crucifixion is too wide to be intelligible on any other hypothesis than that they used different systems of reckoning. But if the 'sixth hour' of Jn 19¹⁴ means 6 a.m., there is no divergence (see Westcott, *St. John*, p. 282; Smith, *The Days of His Flesh*, pp. 528–529; and for the opposite view, Dods, *Expos. Gr. Test.* i. 698, 855, 856). See, further, artt. DAY, TIME.

2. But Jesus, living 'in feelings, not in figures on a dial,' and 'counting time by heart-throbs,' gave the word an intense significance. To Him days and hours were moral magnitudes. The appointed span was not small, but spacious ('Are there not twelve hours in the day?' Jn 11⁹), to be employed in strenuous and loving obedience to the Divine will (cf. Jn 9⁴). Until the sunset, He knew He had no reason to fear the hostility of men. Life would be as long as duty, and in the path of God's service there are no tragic foreshortenings (Jn 11⁸. ⁹). But the twelfth hour of the day was that to which He so pathetically refers as 'Mine hour.' At the marriage feast in Cana, when appealed to by His mother with a suggestion for His help, He replied, 'Woman, what have I to do with thee? Mine hour is not yet come' (Jn 2⁴). This may simply mean that the time for giving such relief was not opportune, or that the opportunity for miracle-working, or the moment for self-manifestation, had not arrived. But the whole utterance produces the impression that the appeal had aroused strong feelings, and created a critical situation for Him.

'He was standing on the threshold of His ministry, conscious of His miraculous power, and He was questioning whether that were the hour to put it forth. . . . The supplying of wine to a company of peasants seemed so trivial, so unworthy of the Messiah, so insufficient for the inauguration of the kingdom of heaven' (Smith, *The Days of His Flesh*, p. 55).

But is there not even here a reference to what He calls peculiarly His hour—'the hour when the Son of Man should be glorified' (Jn 12²³, cf. 17¹); the hour when He should be betrayed into the hands of sinners (Mt 26⁴⁵); the hour when the Father's will gave Him over to the power of darkness (Lk 22⁵³)? If Jesus went down to the Jordan in order to participate in the Baptism of Repentance, conscious that His vocation as Messiah was to be that of the Suffering Servant, and to take upon Himself the sins of His brethren, then the thought of His hour as the hour of His sacrifice could never be absent from His mind. And the simple suggestion of His mother, involving, as it did, for Him the first exercise of a power which came to Him as Messiah, raised suddenly and vividly before Him the issue of suffering, and called forth the intense feeling in the words, 'Mine hour is not yet come.'

A similar tumult of emotion was produced towards the end of His ministry, by the request of the Greeks to see Him (Jn 12²⁰). The reply of Jesus, 'The hour is come, that the Son of man should be glorified. . . . Except a corn of wheat fall into the ground and die, it abideth alone,' is relevant to a prospect of possible exemption from the cross which the request raised in Him, rather than to the request itself. Once more an apparently innocent intrusion upon His thoughts had brought before Him the vision of His hour. He saw that the glory would be won at a great cost, and the prospect of it brought distress of soul, and wrung from Him the cry, 'Father, what shall I say? Save me from this hour.' But immediately He saw through the pain the holy purpose of God realizing itself, and recovered His poise of soul and unflinching devotion. 'But for this cause came I unto this hour. Father, glorify thy name.' It was by this simple word, therefore, that He expressed the conviction that His death was the climax of His life, and that the time of its accomplishment was with God. He would not forestall it by any premature manifestation of Himself to the world (Jn 7⁶); and until His hour came, His enemies were powerless against Him (v.³⁰ 8²⁰). But when it came, He was not reluctant to recognize it. Though it was a dark hour, the hour of men with sinister purpose and in league with Satan (Lk 22⁵³), He knew it as the hour when He should depart out of this world unto the Father (Jn 13¹), the hour when God should glorify His Son (17¹).

With the approach of that hour which marked the climax and close of His earthly ministry, a wider horizon opens. A new day of God dawns, and in it also there is a critical hour—'the hour when the Son of Man cometh' (Mt 25¹³). Even to Him the precise point of time was not disclosed (Mt 24³⁶). Of one thing He was sure, and gave repeated warning,—it would come upon men with startling suddenness : ' and in an hour when ye think not' (Mt 24⁴². ⁴⁴. ⁵⁰ 25¹³, cf. Lk 12³⁹. ⁴⁰. ⁴⁶) ; and He enforces therewith His command to 'watch,' 'be ready,' so that, though it come suddenly, it may be a glad surprise.　　　　　JOSEPH MUIR.

HOUSE (οἰκία, οἶκος).—The word 'house' is used in the Gospels, in accordance with ancient Hebrew usage, in a twofold sense, as referring either to the dwelling, or to the family living in it. Thus we have (1) 'the house of Israel' (Mt 10⁶), 'the house of David' (Lk 1²⁷), etc.; (2) 'built his house upon a rock' (Mt 7²⁴), 'the house of the ruler' (Mk 5³⁸), etc.

The 'house,' as a building, plays no such part in Oriental as in Western life and civilization. Climatic conditions in the East permit people to live much in the open. Accordingly we find artisans and merchants plying their trades in the street, or in open shops looking out on the street. Then the domestic life of the Oriental requires little beyond a sheltered place for sleeping and a quiet place for eating. The ordinary house of the ancient Hebrew, we may be sure, was much like that found in Palestine to-day—it could hardly be cruder, or more primitive. As to Hebrew architecture, of either OT or NT times, the Bible has little to say. Architecture proper can hardly be said to have arisen among the Hebrews before the time of the kings, say, about B.C. 1000. Then, it would seem, it differed little from that of the Phœnicians, Assyrians, and Egyptians. The style of the house would naturally be determined largely by the location, the materials at hand, and the purpose to be served. Palestine, as known to history, has had few great forests, and little timber of any kind suited for building. (Solomon had to import materials for palace and temple, 1 K 5²⁰). Houses built in the plains were usually constructed of mud, clay, or sun-dried bricks (cf. Job 4¹⁹). 'Houses of clay,' or those built of sun-dried bricks, could be easily broken into—a fact that gives point to our Lord's allusion in the Sermon on the Mount, when He would dissuade from laying up treasures 'where thieves break through and steal' (Mt 6¹⁹), where it is literally '*dig through*' (RVm). Great care needed to be taken with the foundations. In a limestone country like Palestine, if one dig deep enough, he finds almost anywhere a stratum of solid rock. It is still true that the wise man builds his house upon the rock (Mt 7²⁴). It is common there now to dig down to the rock and lay the foundation of even the 'house of clay' upon it. Mt 7²⁵ 'It was *founded*,' might well be rendered, 'It was *foundationed*' upon the rock,' if we had such a word in English. St. Luke (6⁴⁸) says, 'dug, and went deep, and laid a foundation upon the rock.'

In the mountainous regions limestone rock was the building material chiefly used, as it was abundant, easily quarried, and readily worked. The house of stone was, probably, modelled after, or developed from, the cave. The nature of the country invited to this. First the natural cave would be used, and, as there was demand, artificially enlarged. Then, occasionally, in some inviting place, a cave would be hewn out of the rock, *de novo*. Finally, a wall would be built in front for protection, or privacy, and so the cave would be converted into a sheltered dwelling. Henceforth it would serve as a model for detached stone houses. As a matter of fact, in the ancient village of Siloam are found all these kinds of houses, and they illustrate this process of development. (See *Jewish Encyc.* art. 'House'). Bricks were sometimes used even in the mountain regions, though counted inferior to hewn stone (2 S 12³¹). Many stone houses were unpretentious and rude, being built of rough, unhewn stones ; but some, then as now, were built of hewn stones, with vaulted stone roofs, *e.g.* the palaces of the rich, or of the ruling class (cf. 'the house of the ruler,' Mk 5³⁸, 'the high priest's house,' Lk 22⁵⁴). Sometimes space for walking was left around the dome, but often all the space between the dome and the battlement (Dt 22⁸) would be filled in, so as to give the much-desired flat **roof**—the favourite resort of the Oriental in the cool of the evening (2 S 11²), and an inviting sleeping-place in summer (1 S 9²⁵). Such a house will often have a hut of branches, or of vine-covered trellis-work, on the roof (cf. 2 S 16²², Neh 8¹⁶), and sometimes a more substantial room, where guests of honour are lodged (1 K 17¹⁹, 2 K 4¹⁰). For 'summer parlour,' cf. Jg 3²⁰, RVm has rightly 'upper chamber of cooling.' (See Mk 14¹⁵, and cf. 'upper room' elsewhere). From the roof one could easily see what was going on in the street, or on a neighbouring housetop (cf. 1 S 9²⁵) ; indeed, could even step from roof to roof, and thus walk the whole length of a street, as the present writer once did in Damascus (cf. Mk 13¹⁵ ; Jos. *Ant.* xiii. 140 [ed. Niese]).

The humbler house of the plain was very simple, having usually only one apartment, which sometimes sheltered both man and beast. The walls were sometimes smeared with clay (Lv 14⁴¹), sometimes plastered (Ezk 13¹⁰, Dt 27⁴). The roof was made, no doubt, as that of the common Arab house is made to-day, by laying rough beams about three feet apart, then laying reeds or brushwood close and thick across, covering it with something like the thickly matted thorn-bush called *bellan*, and then spreading over the whole, first a coat of thick mortar, and then one of marl or earth, and rolling it. Such roofs would require frequent repairing and rolling to keep out the rain, and, if neglected, would get so soaked with the tropical rains that they would cave in. In this way whole villages have had to be abandoned, and their houses left desolate. It was probably one of the simplest of such roofs that was 'broken up' (Mk 2⁴) when the paralytic was let down from the housetop at Capernaum into the presence of Jesus to be healed. The whole affair would seem to have been the extemporaneous device of plain peasants, accustomed to open their roofs and let down grain, straw, and other articles, as they still do in that country (Thomson, *Land and Book*, ii. 6 ff.). The furniture of such a house would be very simple,—a few mats, or pallets, spread on the ground floor for sleeping on at night, then rolled up and put aside in the day; latterly a 'divan' set against the wall on one side, a small table, a few rude chairs, a niche in the wall for the primitive little lamp, unless it was of a sort to hang from a rafter, and a few large jugs for grain, water, wine, or oil.

The palace of the rich would differ from such a house, of course, in having more rooms, and richer and more varied furniture. The numerous rooms, often preferably arranged in a suite on the ground floor around one or more open courts, were often built in storeys. Fine woods, olive, cedar, etc., were used for the doors and windows, and the floors were sometimes made of wood, but often of cement or stone, or even of rich mosaics; while the walls in rare instances were inlaid with ivory and beaten gold (cf. Am 5¹¹, 1 K 22³⁹ 6¹⁸·²⁰).

The Græco-Roman architecture of the Hellenistic period did not exert any very marked or lasting influence upon the architecture of Palestine, partly because of the Jewish antipathy to the Hellenizing tendency, and partly because it was confined to the larger buildings, such as palaces, baths, theatres, temples, etc. See, further, Hastings' *DB*, art. 'House.'

LITERATURE. — The Heb. Archæologies of Keil, Benzinger, Nowack; Edersheim, *Jewish Social Life*; Tristram, *Eastern Customs in Bible Lands*; Mackie, *Bible Manners*, etc.

GEO. B. EAGER.

HOUSEHOLD.—In Mt 24⁴⁵ (οἰκετεία), Lk 12⁴² (θεραπεία)=servants, *i.e.* the dependants on an estate to whom the steward was bound in our Lord's parable to serve out rations at intervals of a day, a week, or a month. It was their dependent and helpless condition which was the test of the steward's faithfulness to his trust. The same English word translates οἰκιακοί in Mt 10²⁵·³⁶, *i.e.* the inmates of a house, subordinate indeed to the master, but attached to him by ties of relationship or marriage. In v.²⁵ there is a contrast and comparison between the οἰκιακοί (Christ's disciples) and the οἰκοδεσπότης (the Lord Himself), and Christ warns the Twelve that if He has been called Beelzebul (or Beelzebub) by His enemies (cf. Mt 9³⁴ 12²⁴, Jn 8⁴⁸), those who belong to His household cannot expect to be free from this 'reproach of Christ.' In v.³⁶ the contrast is between some members of a household and the rest. Here He warns them of the inevitable opposition that will arise when some in a house love Christ supremely, while others are hostile or indifferent to Him. The words of ancient

prophecy (Mic 7⁶) then receive a fulfilment. The very closeness of association emphasizes the antagonism, and 'a man's foes shall be they of his own household.'

C. H. PRICHARD.

HOUSEHOLDER.—This term as well as 'goodman of the house,' 'master of the house,' are different translations of the same Greek word οἰκοδεσπότης. It is rendered 'householder' in the parables of the Tares and the Wheat (Mt 13²⁷), of the Owner bringing forth his treasures new and old (Mt 13⁵²), of the Labourers in the Vineyard (Mt 20¹), of the Vineyard let out to husbandmen (21³³), with special application to Christ as Head of the Church. The phrase 'goodman of the house' is applied (Mk 14¹⁴, Lk 22¹¹) to the owner of the house in which the Last Supper was to be prepared. The translation 'master of the house' is found in Lk 12³⁹ RV (AV 'goodman'), Mt 24⁴³, of the owner or overseer whose duty it is to protect his property against the thief in the night. It occurs also in the parable of the Great Supper, Lk 14²¹ (corresponding to the king of Mt 22²·⁷), also as denoting the head of the house whose persecution involves that of his subordinates, Mt 10²⁵ (see HOUSEHOLD); and once more in the parable of the Unfaithful, against whom the door was shut, Lk 13²⁵ (cf. parable of the Ten Virgins, Mt 25).

C. H. PRICHARD.

HULEH.—See JORDAN.

HUMANITY OF CHRIST. — The simplest fact about Jesus Christ, as we see Him pictured in the Gospels, is that He was a man. Whatever there was peculiar about His person, it did not destroy the reality of His humanity or take Him out of the *genus* 'man.' But this simple fact, seen in all its relations, admits of varied consideration, and indeed demands it.

1. *His human body.*—Jesus had a body, visible to the eye, giving the natural impression, as other bodies do, of reality. It came into life by the natural channel of birth (Mt 1²⁵ 2¹, Lk 2⁷); it grew as others do (Lk 2⁴⁰); was nourished by food as others are (Lk 7³⁴⁻³⁶, cf. 24⁴¹⁻⁴³); slept (Lk 8²³); was restricted by space as ordinary men are, and thus laboriously travelled about (Lk 8¹, Jn 4¹); was weary (Jn 4⁶); suffered under the inhumanities attending the Trial and Execution (Jn 19²⁸·³³), although, in the restraint of the Gospel narrative, no express mention is made of this fact; and truly died (as is made evident by the peculiar character of the phenomenon related in Jn 19³⁴, an unconscious testimony, by one not acquainted with the principles of anatomy, as to the reality of His death). See BODY.

With the reality of His body is closely associated the fact of the temptability of Jesus. The Epistle to the Hebrews lays emphasis upon this fact as a part of His qualification for the work of Saviour (2¹⁸ 4¹⁵). The Gospel history contains a narrative of temptation (Mt 4¹⁻¹¹ ‖) in which Jesus is assailed by solicitations addressed to His physical appetite, to His love of display, and to His ambition. As the reality of the human body is the presupposition of the reality of the temptation, so the character of the temptation confirms the proof of that body. Shrinking from physical pain may have been a part of the agony of the Garden (Lk 22⁴²·⁴⁴, cf. the interpretation given in He 5⁷·⁸). Naturally the sacred history, which is engaged with things done rather than with inner processes which are concealed from human observation, and which finds no occasion to trace the course of inner temptations which never result in outward sin, makes no mention of the appeal which alluring objects must have made to the sensibilities of the man Jesus Christ. But the Epistle to the Hebrews ('·in all points tempted like as we are,' 4[15]) sustains the inference which must necessarily follow from the possession of a human nature, that there were such appeals to the humanity of Jesus. See TEMPTATION.

2. *His human soul.*—Had Jesus a true human soul? The answer to such a question is to be obtained only by observing the phenomena of His recorded life, and drawing the necessary inferences from what we see. The statement of fact is, fortunately, very clear and copious. The moment we study the account of His independent life we find the evidences accumulating that in its inward, as well as its outward, processes it is a truly human life. In the temple we find the exercise of a desire—curiosity—and the acknowledgment of mental processes both like those of other men and commanding their respect (His 'understanding,' Lk 2[46. 47]). In His home in Nazareth He followed a life of obedience (Lk 2[51] 'subject'). As He grew in stature, so He did in 'wisdom' (Lk 2[52] σοφία, 'varied knowledge of things human and Divine,' Grimm-Thayer). At His temptation He showed an intellectual knowledge of the Scriptures (Mt 4[4. 7. 10]). His discourses moved along according to the laws of human address, idea suggesting idea according to the laws of natural association. The lower ranges of reasoning are pursued by Him as by others, and once He even expresses His thought syllogistically (Jn 8[47]). But the higher ranges of reason, the intuitive knowledge of the meaning of great truths, were peculiarly His, as is seen in the wider interpretation of the OT (Mt 5[17. 21-48]), and in the lofty ethical standard which He sets up, itself another instance of the larger interpretation of the OT, forming the still unsurpassed ideal of human conduct, more and more insisted upon in the social struggles for progress in our own time, the binding force and universal validity of the law of love (Mt 22[37-40]). To this standard He held Himself (Jn 10[30] 17[21], Mt 15[32] 20[34]). Thus He manifested at every essential point the possession of an *intellect* characterized by the same faculties and working by the same laws as our own. The same was no less true of the *sensibilities*, even those which we are inclined to view as trivial, the undue indulgence of which we stigmatize as weakness. Traces may be found of the operation of every one of the distinct emotions. Thus, for example, He had a love for esteem, manifested in His notice of the omission of certain acts of courtesy in Lk 7[44-46]; He displayed the natural affections, such as love of friends (Jn 15[15]), of family (Jn 19[26]), of country (Mt 23[37-39]); He exercised complacent love (Mk 14[8]), moral indignation (Lk 11[46], Jn 8[44]); His spiritual background was that of joy and peace (Jn 14[27], Lk 10[21]). The *will* was moved by appropriate considerations as ours is (Jn 7[1. 10]), and displays the same sort of activities, being sustained by the operation of the same forces as in ordinary men. Thus the struggle in time of temptation is to maintain His spiritual ideals (Mt 4[1-11], Jn 12[27]), and Jesus concentrates His attention, as men who will be victorious in time of temptation must, upon the proper object of human attention, upon the great purpose for which He has come into the world (Jn 18[37] and 19[11]). The virtues which may be particularly called the virtues of the will are exemplified, such as persistence, shown in His repeated healing upon the Sabbath (Jn 5[16], Mk 3[2. 3]), in His teaching sustained amid the constant evidence that the Jews were inclined decisively to reject Him (cf. the discourses in Jn 5 and foll. chapters). Even the more mysterious operations of the sub-conscious, or better of the supra-conscious, self are to be noted in Him, not merely in the displays of genius which He, as no other man, possessed, but in the manifestations of a power the operations of which first brought it to His

empirical consciousness (Mk 5[30] RV). In fact, the better psychologist a man is, the more clearly he can see, in the simple narratives of the Gospels, the operations of every fundamental faculty and law of the human soul.

3. *The necessity of Christ's humanity.*—To one who sees no Divinity in Christ, the question of the necessity of His humanity is meaningless, not to say impertinent. Of course, He must be human, says such a one, since this is the only path to leadership. God has committed His work for men in the world to men. Apart from those mysterious communications of revelation which selected teachers of men have had, the only possible teacher of men is a man who can approach them with messages which they can understand, in words appropriate to their nature. However true these general principles are, the standpoint here assumed is not that of the Gospels. To them, Christ 'came' to the earth (see DIVINITY OF CHRIST); and the question arises why this is so, why He took upon Himself humanity and 'became flesh' (Jn 1[14]). Did this question arise in the minds of the Apostles? and is there trace of speculation, or of interest as to it, in the Gospels? There are indisputable traces of both in the Epistles, especially in that to the Hebrews. It is represented in this Epistle that the object of Christ's coming in the flesh was particularly to offer His body a sacrifice (10[5. 10], cf. 2[9. 14]); but not merely this, for the possession of humanity itself affords Him a spiritual qualification for His priestly work, in that He shares the lot of men, and learns thereby how to sympathize with them in their temptations and their failures (2[17. 18] 4[15. 16] 5[2]). There is also the suggestion of an idea which is brought out more clearly in the Fourth Gospel,—the same as that suggested above,—that the humanity was the necessary medium of the revelation of God, since it is through Jesus that God 'speaks' (Jn 1[1] 3[11]). This form of presentation covers the point why the humanity was a necessity when once God had determined to enter upon the stage of human history as Redeemer. But St. John pushes the matter a little farther back. He begins with the eternal 'Word,' which was in the beginning with God and was God, and sets forth His appearing in the world under the figure of light shining into darkness (1[9] 3[19] 8[12]), and needed because of the darkness. The ground of the Incarnation is found in this need, in the existence of sin, and the necessity of salvation through faith (3[16]). It is to produce 'children of God' (1[12]) that Christ comes. The coming is the manifestation of the glory of God (1[14]), but that glory is the moral glory of 'grace and truth.' The culmination of the whole work of redemption is, however, the cross (3[14] 10[17. 18] 15[13], cf. He 10[5. 10]), and it is the human body and soul of Christ that suffered there (19[28]). This is the central idea of the Fourth Gospel; but other elements are not lacking, as the necessity of the humanity to the work of instruction, which was a main element of Jesus' work (3[11. 19. 31. 32]), and which culminated in the revelation of the Father, which needed humanity as the medium of communication to human beings (14[9] 12[45] 16[15]). Union with the Father was also essential to Christ's work (14[11] etc.), because this consisted in the manifestation of God's name (17[6]). The necessary spiritual sustenance, finally, was gained through the body and blood of Christ (6[35. 50. 51]), that is, through what His humanity alone was capable of doing for man.

4. *Unique elements of this humanity.* — The humanity of Christ, in order to satisfy the conditions now before us, must be a reality. No 'phantom,' or merely phenomenal body, could perform the offices required in these Scripture passages of the humanity. But other elements also appear which give a new aspect to the human nature. Among these need not be reckoned the origin of the body of Jesus by miraculous conception, as related in the First and Third Gospels; for however the process of development from the first cell might be initiated, the resulting development must be in any case that of a human body. Side by side with evident human limitations, such as ignorance (as of the day and hour of His own return to the earth, Mt 24³⁶), there exist phenomena of a like nature altogether transcending humanity, such as the knowledge by which He not only 'knew what was in man' (Jn 2²⁵), read the thoughts of men often as an open book (Mt 9⁴ 12²⁵, Lk 6⁸ 9⁴⁷), but, above all, knew perfectly the will of the Father and the mysteries of Divine truth. He walked laboriously from Judæa to Galilee (Jn 4⁴), but He could suddenly appear upon the surface of the sea in the storm, walking upon the water (Mt 14²⁵ ‖). These and other such considerations (see DIVINITY OF CHRIST) raise the question how these things could consist in Him, that is, the question of the nature of the Person of Christ, a question belonging to dogmatics, and thus lying outside of the scope of this article. But — this is the main point — whatever *more* than humanity there was in Christ, the evidence already cited is decisive as to the reality of His humanity.

5. *The unity of Jesus' consciousness.* — Christ was, then, a man. Does this word comprehensively express the Gospel teaching as to His person? He had a personality as men are persons. He had a consciousness which expressed itself by the pronoun 'I.' Was this a human consciousness, so that when asked as to Himself Jesus would have replied: '*I* am a man'? There are two elements in the answer to this question. (*a*) Jesus' consciousness was a unity. He passes easily from the consideration of earthly to heavenly things, from walking upon the water to sitting quietly in the boat, as if both of these things belonged to Him equally. The impression made upon the unsophisticated reader of the Gospels is that of a single consciousness. In fact, in order to be explicable at all, the Gospels must convey such an impression. But pivotal passages, even those which have seemed to give a basis for the idea that He spoke now 'as God' and now 'as man,' do not justify such an inference when carefully considered. He did not mean in Mt 4¹⁰ 'Thou (Satan) shalt worship the Lord thy God (me),' and not I thee. He meant that the law of worship for any one, and for Him as bound to fulfil all righteousness (Mt 3¹⁵), was the worship of the Lord only. In Mt 8²³⁻²⁷ and parallels He was not in one capacity asleep in the boat and in another watching over the disciples in that storm, but He was totally asleep as He appeared. He did not chide them for lack of faith in such a waking providence of His own, of which they had no knowledge, but for their lack of faith in God (cf. Mk 4⁴⁰), whose messenger Christ was, and who would care for both Him and them. In Mk 5³⁰ and parallels it is not Jesus in one personality healing the woman and in another inquiring what had happened, that is brought before us; but God the Father made use of Him to answer the petition, unknown to Him but known to God, and He became conscious in this use of Himself that He was so used ('having come to perceive that the power which [often, on other occasions] went forth from him had [on this occasion] gone forth,' cf. RV). (*b*) The centre of this personality, the Ego of this undivided consciousness, is God. Whenever He speaks of His coming into the world, it is always God that speaks, not less in Mt 10⁴⁵ and

parallels than in Jn 3¹³ 10¹⁰. This fact stands side by side with such facts as the confession of ignorance. They are never allowed to get far apart. When we have the passage Mt 24³⁶ confessing ignorance, it is preceded by the glorious description of the return of the Son of Man in Divine majesty (v.³⁰), and followed by the Judgment scene of 25³¹⁻⁴⁶. There is no trace of a sense of transition or of shock in passing from one form of consciousness to the other, because there is no such shock, no transition (see KENOSIS). The solution of this problem, of the unity of the consciousness in the midst of such apparent contradictions in the contents of consciousness, is, again, a problem of dogmatics.

6. *The significance of the humanity of Christ for religion.* — The interest of dogmatics in the humanity of Christ lies in the doctrine of a true Incarnation, which is the foundation of the doctrines of Atonement and Forgiveness. The interest of religion in Christ's humanity is the interest of believers in the forgiveness of sins, who need to feel the identification of their Redeemer with themselves. It is not without profound significance that it is said that judgment is committed to the Son of Man (Jn 5²²). Whatever else of deepest truth there may be in it, there is this, that the sinner needs to feel the identification of his Judge with himself by the possession of a common human nature. When the Judge knows both the persistency and depth of sin on the one hand, and the weakness and temptations of man on the other, —then only will the sinner be assured that the proffered forgiveness is for him. It is, again, the interest of believers in God, who get higher ideas of God's goodness from the greatness of the condescension involved in His 'becoming flesh.' It is, further, the interest of believers in Jesus, who, when they understand that Jesus is identified with us by the possession of our common humanity, feel a new confidence; are stimulated to more frequent prayer; become conscious that He truly draws near to them; regard their varied lot in life, which He has shared, as sanctified thereby; bear with greater equanimity their sorrows, which He also bore; find in Him their pattern of life (see OBEDIENCE, § ii.); and thus see in Him not an abstraction, but a real, objective, and personal Redeemer and object of faith, a Captain, and the Head of the Church. See, further, INCARNATION, SON OF MAN.

LITERATURE.—Dale, *Christian Doctrine*, 45–73; Stalker, *Imago Christi, passim*; Ullmann, *Sinlessness of Jesus*, 52 ff.; Wendt, *Teaching of Jesus*, i². 136 ff.; Fairbairn, *Christ in Modern Theology*, 347 ff.; F. W. Robertson, *Sermons*, i. 99 ff.; *Expositor*, v. iv. [1896] 388 ff. On the union of the human with the Divine in the Person of Christ see the Christological sections of standard works on Christian Doctrine.

FRANK HUGH FOSTER.

HUMILIATION OF CHRIST.—1. *Incarnation.*— Jesus Christ is a problem. And yet He is not so much a problem as man would be without Him. Indeed He is, in a true sense, the solution of the problem of man. Nevertheless, to the intellect, demanding that everything in the heavens above and on the earth beneath be reduced to 'the measure of man's mind,' He remains a problem. The expressions of His consciousness of pre-existence constitute one of the chief elements of that problem. But, taken in connexion with two facts of His history, even this aspect of His person is not so dense a problem as when it is considered by itself. These two facts are (1) the expressions of His self-consciousness, direct and incidental, as to His relation to God on the one hand, and to total humanity on the other; and (2) His effects in the world and on the world. Even the pre-existence of Jesus Christ, when taken in connexion with these two outstanding facts, is, on the whole, a less problem and a smaller difficulty than the world of humanity would be without Him.

Furthermore, it would be more difficult to believe that a being who had the consciousness that Jesus had, who has done for humanity what Jesus has done, and who is to humanity what Jesus is, should have had the absolute beginning of His existence at a late point in time, than to believe that He came out of eternity and is of the eternal order. In other words, assuming and accepting the pre-existence of Jesus Christ, mystery though it be, it is easier to understand His unique earthly history, His character, His consciousness, His revelations, His work, His actual effects on the world and on men, both in the past and at the present, than it would be without that assumption. At all events, He has in several instances expressed the consciousness of having existed in a previous state before His advent into this world (Jn 3^{13} 6^{62} 8^{58} 16^{28} 17$^{5.\ 24}$). This pre-existent state was one of intimate association and intercommunion with God and participation in the glory of the Eternal Father. It is also one of the underlying presuppositions in St. Paul's Epistles (1 Co 8^6, 2 Co 8^9, Ph 2$^{5-8}$, Col 1$^{15-17}$). It is found also in an original setting in Hebrews (1$^{2.\ 3}$).

Now, whatever may be the meaning of these great passages, whatever the pre-incarnate riches and glory of Christ, He voluntarily submitted to the surrender of the resources of a Divine state for the lowliness of a human lot and the extreme of human poverty, and to the relinquishment of His equal participation in the Divine glory in exchange for the nethermost depth of human humiliation. Exactly what was involved in His self-humiliation from the Divine to the human is treated specifically under the articles on PRE-EXISTENCE, KENOSIS, and INCARNATION. Confining our attention, then, in this article to His earthly history, we find that His whole life, His entire sojourn on earth, was a humiliation. His incarnation was but the first stage in His humiliation, which continued by a deepening descent to the very end of His earthly life. His whole career in this world was a protracted humiliation or succession of humiliations between the humiliation of His incarnation and the humiliation of His crucifixion. It is worthy of note that the words of St. Paul, 'he humbled himself' (in Ph 2^7), refer to experiences of His earthly life and not to the process of His incarnation.

2. *His earthly life to the assumption of the Messianic mission.*—The circumstances of His birth were most painful. It occurred, not in the sheltered privacy, and amid the comforts, of home, but while His mother was on a humiliating and painful pilgrimage, and among the feeding beasts, surrounded by the filth of a stable, and possib'y under the observation of strange and uncouth men. But the child Jesus was not a year old before He became the object of jealousy and persecution, and had to be taken on a long and painful journey into a foreign land to save His life—a baby fugitive on the face of the earth. Showing at the age of twelve a wisdom which astonished the wisest men of the nation, and which would have secured for Him recognition, position, power, and renown, He yet willingly returned to the obscure and humble home at Nazareth; and there for the space of nearly twenty years He submitted Himself, day after day, to the control of two plain peasant people, and to the occupation and drudgery of common manual labour.

3. *Humiliations of the Messianic ministry.*—He knew from the beginning what the Messianic mission meant and how it would end. It was not to Him an honour to be enjoyed; it was a burden to be borne. It cost Him a struggle to submit and adjust Himself to that which He knew was so fraught with difficulty, persecution, humiliation, loneliness, suspense, and suffering, ending with the final agonies and the death of abandonment and shame. This is the reason why He needed—and received—the expression of His Father's approval at the moment of His self-dedication to the work of Messiah (Mk 1^{11}, Lk 3^{22}). This was the meaning of His temptation in the wilderness. This was why at the sharp turning-point in His ministry, when He looked out on the dark and lonely way of obedience unto death and deliberately chose to walk in it alone, He needed again—and again received—the assurance of His Father's recognition, approval, and sympathy (Mk 9^7, Lk 9^{35}).* It was the burden of the Messianic task that made Him, beyond all men, a man of sorrows. More than once we are told that He wept; but never that He laughed. Almost from the beginning of His ministry He was looked on with jealousy and suspicion by the powerful leaders of the people, from whom He had a right to expect encouragement and support. They kept a watch on Him, they found fault with Him, they misconstrued His actions, they perverted His sayings, they dogged His steps, they nagged Him at every turn, they accused Him of being a law-breaker, a blasphemer, an impostor, a lunatic, a demoniac, an emissary of the powers of darkness (Lk 11^{15}). They laid plots to catch Him and to kill Him; and they never ceased until they succeeded. Not only so, but little by little He lost His early popularity and was abandoned by the people. He came to those whom He had the right to claim as His own; they refused to receive Him, turned against Him. His personal ministry was comparatively a failure, and He practically an outcast. He did not even have a refuge among the friends of His youth, the people of His old home at Nazareth. They also turned against Him, rejected His claims, drove Him out of their village, made a desperate attempt to kill Him (Mk 6^3, Lk 4^{28}). The members of His own family failed to understand Him, refused to accept Him, were alienated from Him (Jn 7^3). Probably they thought Him either a fanatic or a fraud. Probably on account of His strangeness and growing unpopularity they were ashamed of Him. He was subjected to the humiliation and pain of constant misunderstanding and sometimes even criticism on the part of His own disciples. He was rebuked (Mt 16^{22}) and denied (26$^{69-74}$) by one of them, sold and delivered into the hands of His enemies and murderers for a few pounds by another (26$^{14-16}$), deserted by all (Mt 26^{56}, Mk 14^{50}). Added to these things, He suffered the humiliations of a painful poverty. Rejected at home, ejected from home, He had no place of His very own where He could feel that He might retire when weary or lonely or heart-sore, and enjoy rest without the fear of intrusion or molestation. He was dependent on charity, He was supported by charity (Lk 8^3). He had to borrow a room for His last meal with His disciples (22^{11}). He had to borrow an ass to ride into Jerusalem on the day of His triumphal entry (19$^{33.\ 34}$). Another man's stable was borrowed for Him to be born in (2^7); another man's grave for Him to be buried in (Mt 27$^{59.\ 60}$).

4. *Trials and crucifixion.* — His implacable enemies brought Him at last to bay. Deep in that memorable night when He was in the depths of the impenetrable gloom of Gethsemane, the sacred privacy of His last hours and His last prayer was invaded by a howling mob of underlings, hangers-on, and soldiers of the temple guard, guided by one of His own disciples (Mt 26^{47}, Lk 22^{47}). They took Jesus, and when they had bound

* See chapters on the Baptism, the Temptation, and the Transfiguration in the present writer's *Son of Man*.

Him with ropes (Jn 18[12]), they led Him by the halter, as if He were a desperado, to the house of the high priest. He had a keen sense of this humiliation, and protested against it (Mk 14[48]). Nevertheless, conscious though He was of His innocence of any evil deed or design, of His absolute purity, yea, even of His Divine dignity and mission, He submitted to the humiliation of being put on trial before the corrupt and conscienceless occupant of the high-priestly office and the white-washed hypocrites who, for the most part, constituted the governing body of the nation. After the solemn mockery was enacted and they had condemned Him to death (14[64]), they heaped on Him the most humiliating insults their malicious ingenuity could devise. They spat in His face (ἐνέπτυσαν εἰς τὸ πρόσωπον αὐτοῦ, Mt 26[67]); they threw a cloth over Him and then beat Him on the head, mockingly demanding that He should tell them who it was that struck each blow (26[67. 68]). When it was morning, they bound Him again with ropes, and led Him thus to the Prætorium to secure sentence of death from the Roman Procurator (Mk 15[1], Mt 27[1]). Pilate, though convinced of His innocence, did not care to involve himself in the trouble and annoyance of taking His part, and he was glad to shirk his duty and get rid of the embarrassment by turning Him over to Herod Antipas, who was at that time in Jerusalem (Lk 23[7]). The poor prisoner, whom no one was found to befriend or defend, was dragged through the streets to another tribunal in the hope of finding some one who had the courage as well as the power to rid the earth of Him, and He had to suffer the humiliation of appearing as a culprit before this abandoned wretch. Herod was delighted to come face to face with Jesus, and now at last he was to have the long-coveted opportunity of having Him show off with a few miracles in his presence. But, though he plied Him with all sorts of requests and importunities, Jesus answered him not a single word. But Herod was not to be baulked. If he could not induce Jesus to entertain him in one way, he could at least force Him to furnish entertainment for him in another way. And this Herod, this creature of low cunning, this unwashed hog of a sensualist, this seducer of his own brother's wife, this cowardly murderer of the other of the two great prophets of the day, gratified his brutal instincts by joining his soldiers in putting Jesus to scorn. They dressed Him up in a gorgeous and glaring red mantle of mock royalty, and sent Him thus through the streets back to the Prætorium of Pilate (23[7-11]). Pilate, overcome by the persistence of the Jewish leaders and by his own selfish and cowardly fears, decided at last to deliver Jesus up to the tender mercies of the human bloodhounds who could be appeased by nothing but His death. But before doing so, he made his soldiers strip Him and inflict on Him the terrible Roman flagellation (Mk 15[15], Mt 27[26]), a punishment so severe that the victim often died under it. This bitter torture and bitterer humiliation Jesus endured in submission and silence. While the preparation is being made for the crucifixion, He is left in the hands of the soldiers, the whole cohort is invited in to enjoy the sport, and now for the third time He is made the amusement of a band of ruffians, for it is now their turn to have a little entertainment with the Nazarene fanatic. They torment Him as a cat teases and tortures a wounded bird before devouring it. They put on Him a scarlet military robe, and having twisted branches of thorn bushes into a sort of crown, they place it on His patient brow, put a mock sceptre in His unresisting hand, and then go down on their knees before Him, shouting, 'Long live the king of the Jews!'

They too indulged in the sport of spitting on Him, and, yielding to the wild beast instinct which their opportunity had aroused in them, they kept beating Him over the head (ἔτυπτον εἰς τὴν κεφαλὴν αὐτοῦ, Mt 27[30]; ἔτυπτον αὐτοῦ τὴν κεφαλὴν καλάμῳ, Mk 15[19]). While He was dressed up as a mock king, His face stained with blood and marred with spittle, Pilate, moved with pity, led Him out to the view of the clamorous mob, hoping that the spectacle of so abject an object might move them to pity (Jn 19[4. 5]). But it seemed the more to inflame their rage (v.[6]). His crucifixion was then finally decided on. And now a new humiliation was inflicted on Him. He leaves the Prætorium, and is led or driven along the crowded streets through the avenue of onlookers, bearing on His back the heavy wooden beam that was to be the instrument of His execution (v.[17]). It was the symbol of His degradation and the advertisement of His disgrace.

It may be well for us to stop and try to imagine what was passing in the mind of Jesus while all these horrors were heaped upon Him. We know He was accustomed, during the course of His ministry, to dwell, both in thought and in speech, on the horrors that He knew awaited Him (Mt 16[21] ὅτι δεῖ αὐτὸν . . . πολλὰ παθεῖν). If He so dreaded it from afar, how keen must have been the anguish of passing through it!

But these things were slight in comparison with what yet awaited Him; for the great humiliation was yet to come. He was to be subjected to the accursed and infamous death of crucifixion. When soldiers are to be put to death for desertion or treason, they are shot. The lowest of criminals, those upon whom we wish to heap disgrace in inflicting death, we hang on the gallows. What the gallows is to-day, the cross was in the days of Jesus. It was the method of execution that secured publicity, while it insured the utmost prolongation of the victim's misery. When the procession had reached the place, the cross was laid upon the ground, Jesus was denuded of all His clothing, He was stretched out upon the cross, long iron nails were driven through His hands and feet, the cross bearing His naked body was lifted up and dropped into its socket, and there, looking out on the sea of angry faces and suffering the infamous fate of the most abandoned criminal, hung Jesus, who, though He had the consciousness of having come from God and of being the sinless Son of God, yet willingly endured this humiliation that He might become the Redeemer of men. Wherefore all the ages and the highest of all the races of men have united with God in giving Him the name that is above every name, and with one accord agree in crowning Him Lord of all.

The descending scale of His humiliation, from the estate of conscious equality with God past all grades and levels down to the humiliation of the cross, has been grasped and, with a few master strokes, graphically portrayed by St. Paul in the great passage of Ph 2[6. 7]: the humiliation of the Divine to the level of the human, the humiliation of the human to the level of the servant, to the level of the outcast and condemned criminal, and, lastly, to the degradation of a punishment the most humiliating, the most shameful, the most bitter, the most revolting, the most horrible then or ever known among men.

LITERATURE.—Works like those of Weiss, Beyschlag, Stevens on *Biblical Theology*; Gore's *Bampton Lectures*; Gifford, *The Incarnation*; Mason, *Conditions of our Lord's Life on Earth*; Bruce, *The Humiliation of Christ* [giving on pp. 388-412 and 419-424 fine discussions of Kenotic literature]; Zöckler, *Das Kreuz Christi*; Nebe and Steinmeyer, *Leidensgeschichte*; Stalker, *The Trial and Death of Christ*; the chapters of Keim and Edersheim on the Passion and Death.

GROSS ALEXANDER.

HUMILITY.—This virtue or grace distinguished

the leaders of OT history like Abraham and Moses (Gn 18[27], Nu 12[3]), and was inculcated by the prophets as a chief duty (Mic 6[8]). It belongs even to the earlier revelation of God's character ('that humbleth himself,' Ps 113[6]), and is the key to man's communion with Him (Is 57[15]). In Judaism and the Rabbinical literature we meet with a variety of examples and maxims enforcing the truth that 'God is the highest type of humility.' These anticipations prepare us for the new and enlarged conception of humility which fills the NT, and was embodied in the teaching, example, and character of Jesus Christ. The moral quality of our Saviour's personality lies here (Mt 11[29]), and on this foundation of astonishing humility, exemplified on the cross, St. Paul bases his great ethical appeal (Ph 2[5ff.]). It may be claimed that the gospel alone has popularized humility, but the temper of Christ's disciples in every age proves that it is an excellence of rare and difficult attainment.

i. USE AND MEANING OF THE WORD.—The noun (ταπεινοφροσύνη, Heb. עֲנָוָה, Vulg. humilitas, Germ. Demut) does not occur till it is employed commonly in the NT (Lightfoot on Ph 2[3]); it is 'a birth of the Gospel' (Trench, Syn. of the NT, § 42). In contrast to the low and servile sense attaching to it in classical writings, humility in the LXX, Apocr., and NT becomes the designation 'of the noblest and most necessary of all virtues' (Cremer's Lex.). It rests on a lowly and unpretending view of one's self, and is opposed to the workings of the ambitious spirit (μεγαλοφροσύνη, ὑψηλοφροσύνη). The term refers mainly to inward character, and sometimes to outward condition. Of humility as the animating principle of Christian character, Jesus Himself was the great example, being 'lowly in heart' (Mt 11[29]), not merely in appearance like the professional religious leaders of the time. Pharisaism is the deadly enemy of humility or the religion of healthy-mindedness. The moral temper that inspired Christ's life and service is echoed by St. Paul, when he singles out the motive that prompted his labours ('serving the Lord with all lowliness of mind,' Ac 20[19]). Elsewhere humility is enjoined, along with kindred graces, as the means of averting unholy disputes and of promoting co-operation in the Church and among the members of the Christian society (Mt 18[4] 23[12], Eph 4[2], Ph 2[3], Col 3[12]). An exceptional use of the term occurs in Col 2[18. 23], where the Apostle guards his readers against the counterfeit of this virtue ('a voluntary humility'). In some instances the humble are viewed in the light of their earthly condition, which God may wonderfully raise and alter (Lk 1[52]), and which, notwithstanding its indignities and trials, should be borne submissively and cheerfully (Ja 1[9]). This class of sufferers corresponds to the afflicted and meek of the OT (עָנִי, עָנָו), and would be numerous among the peasantry or fellahin of an oppressed and lawless country (Hatch, Essays in Biblical Greek, s.v.). The 'poor in spirit' spoken of in the first of the Beatitudes (Mt 5[3], cf. Lk 6[20]) are probably best understood as placed in such circumstances. In agreement with this, Ritschl (op. cit. infra) defines ταπεινοφροσύνη as 'that temper inclining to the service of God which accepts resignedly an oppressed and wretched condition.' The term, therefore, as one of deep import, is freshly coined in the NT.

ii. CONTRAST BETWEEN GREEK AND CHRISTIAN ETHICS.—The rise of this grace creates an epoch. 'Humility is a vice with heathen moralists, but a virtue with Christian apostles' (Lightfoot on Col 2[18]). In particular, it marks the opposition to the Greek idea of 'high-mindedness' (art. 'Ethics,' by H. Sidgwick in Ency. Brit.[9]), and the advance in ethical sentiment and the standard of judgment

due to Christianity. A presentiment of the Christian virtue may be met with in Greek writers (see examples in Neander's Church History, vol. i. p. 26 [Eng. tr.], and in Trench, NT Syn.), but their use of ταπεινός in any noble sense is rare. The Greeks undoubtedly had their distinguishing qualities, but this was not one of them.

Cf. interesting note of conversation in Morley's Life of Gladstone, iii. p. 466. 'Mr. G.—I admit there is no Greek word of good credit for the virtue of humility. J. M.—ταπεινοτης? But that has an association of meanness. Mr. G.—Yes; a shabby sort of humility. Humility as a sovereign grace is the creation of Christianity.'

Greek Ethics, as expressed and systematized by Aristotle, the ancient master of moral analysis and definition, fostered pride, the genius of later Stoicism, and regarded the humble as contemptible, mean-spirited, and without force or aspiration. Aristotle's picture of the 'great-souled' man and his exaggerated sense of self-importance have a certain air of loftiness (μεγαλοψυχία), but fall below the standard which obliges the Christian to recognize his duty to others, and to treat with consideration those who are intellectually and socially inferior. The conception of humility, therefore, as it controls the Christian, lies outside the system of Aristotle (see Nic. Eth. bk. iv. ch. 3 [Sir A. Grant's ed. vol. ii. pp. 72–78]). This difference between Greek and Christian ideas of greatness and humility is fundamental, and the change was brought about by Christ's revelation of the character of God. Of Aristotle's great-souled man it is said—'his movements are slow, his voice is deep, and his diction stately' (Grant, vol. ii. p. 77, note). This measured efflorescence of pride reappears in Christ's portraiture of the Pharisee in the temple; but the Publican, the opposite and acceptable type, shows how influential, in Christian experience, is the thought of God, and how closely connected are humility, prayer, and confession of sin. In accordance with Augustine's well-known saying (quoted by Calvin, Institutio, bk. ii. ch. 2), humility comes first, second, third, and always, among the precepts of the Christian religion, and it marks the cleavage between Greek and Christian ideals. The magnificent figure drawn by the Greek philosopher disappears, and, instead, Christ presents the image of the little child (Mt 18[2]).

iii. OUR LORD'S EXAMPLE AND TEACHING.—1. The great saying which goes to the root of the matter—'I am meek and lowly in heart' (Mt 11[29]), has been variously interpreted (see art. by Herrmann, mentioned below), and even called in question as authentic. Martineau asks—'What meek and lowly soul was ever known to set itself forth as such and commend its own humility as the model for others?' and adds, 'did a Saviour bear such testimony of himself, his testimony would not be true' (Seat of Authority in Religion[2], p. 583). But the mode of speaking Christ adopted and the claim He put forward would not really seem incongruous in a 'Teacher of Israel' (Bruce, Expos. Gr. Test. note ad loc.); and, besides, the objection reads a false tone into the original utterance, and ignores the special nature of Christ's consciousness. Our Lord was more than a 'meek and lowly soul,' and had reason for presenting Himself as a model and a winning type to humanity. His humility clothed and concealed His essential dignity, and in speaking as He did He was conscious at the same time of standing in a unique relation to God (Mt 11[27], cf. Jn 13[3]). Indeed, the union on Christ's part of 'unbounded personal pretensions' with an unconscious humility that regarded His importance to the world as 'an objective fact with which his own opinion of himself had nothing to do' (Ecce Homo, ch. 15) is undeniable, and reminds us that majesty and meekness were the two poles of His mysterious yet harmonious character. Christ's humility, however, does not rest on a phrase, but was carried out in the lowly setting of His earthly life. His cradle in the manger at Bethlehem and His subjection in the home at Nazareth, His quiet entrance, at the hands of the Baptist, on public life, His restraint in the use of His supernatural powers, and His dislike of consequent honour and fame, His frequent periods of retirement, His choice of followers and friends, His sympathies with little children and humble suppliants (Mk 10$^{13\text{-}16}$ and 7$^{24\text{-}30}$), His appreciation of the smallest offering and the simplest service (Lk 21$^{1\text{-}4}$, Mt 10^{42}), and, finally, His submission to the experiences concentrated in the week of His Passion and Crucifixion, all attest the consistency of His character as One who was 'meek and lowly in heart,' and who, at every step of His career, plainly and profoundly 'humbled himself' (Ph 2^8).

2. Passing from Christ's example, the main lines of His teaching are two—

(1) *Humility in relation to God, or the Law of Grace.*—We are introduced here to the most powerful among the motives to humility, and to a relation deeper than any that influences us in the society of our fellow-men. In Wendt's language—'Humility is the conscious lowliness we feel before God in view of His superabundant love and holy majesty, and in contrast to our own unworthiness, guilt, and entire dependence on His grace' (*The Teaching of Jesus*, vol. i. p. 341, note [Eng. tr.]). We cannot therefore exaggerate our worth or assert our claims before God : the part we play is that of 'unprofitable servants' who, after all their performances, should be filled neither with the sense of merit nor the spirit of boasting (Lk 17^{10}). In the parable, which is a gem of teaching on this point, Jesus enforces on us the duty of humility towards God, the need of genuine self-abasement and confession of sin, as we see and feel our unworthiness in the Divine presence (Lk 18$^{9\text{-}14}$). He represents God as turning away from the shallow and sounding words of the Pharisee, but giving His mercy freely to the penitent publican who could not look up. For, as a fine Jewish saying puts it, 'While God despises what is broken among the animals, He loves in man a broken heart.' This is a fundamental law of the Kingdom of heaven and the indispensable condition of grace : 'for every one that exalteth himself shall be humbled, but he that humbleth himself shall be exalted' (cf. Pr 3^{34}, 1 P 5^5).

Prof. Dowden, in writing of Milton's view of the intercourse between God and the soul, remarks—'There are two humilities —that which bows and that which soars, the humility of a servant who looks down, the humility of a son who gazes up. Milton's humility invigorates itself in the effort to ascend. He would not prostrate himself in the presence of material symbols, but would enter as a glad child into the courts of heaven' (*Puritan and Anglican*, p. 167). This is the humility that Christ welcomes, and that makes religion not stiff and heavy with ceremonial, but simple, reverent, glad, and pleasing to God. On no other terms is grace given or fellowship with God possible. 'Whosoever shall not receive the kingdom of God as a little child, he shall in nowise enter therein' (Lk 18^{17}).

(2) *Humility in relation to men, or the Law of Service.*—While it is true that humility 'is not primarily concerned with our relation to other men, but with our relation to God, and springs from an intellectually true view of that relation' (Illingworth, *Christian Character*, 1905, p. 27), yet its importance in regulating men's ordinary conduct and intercourse did not escape Christ's notice. His striking lessons on this subject were called for at the time, and are far from being exhausted, for it is still true that 'the really humble man is as great in the moral world as he is rare' (Bruce, *Expos. Gr. Test.* on Mt 18^4).

(a) *The child, the unconscious type of humility* (Mt 18$^{1\text{-}4}$, Mk 9$^{33\text{-}37}$).—This was Christ's object-

lesson on the question that caused frequent heart-burning among the disciples, 'Who then is greatest?' etc. Their assimilation of their Master's mind proceeded slowly. As He went on absorbed in the thought of His approaching cross, His followers walked behind and stirred each other's worst passions by raising questions of place and precedence. At their next interview the Master of men set a child in the midst of His disciples, and shamed them out of their unworthy temper. This is our Lord's rebuke of pride, rivalry, and ambition in their thousand forms, His reversal of our ordinary and selfish ideas of greatness, and His warning against the world's spirit of exclusiveness, intolerance, and class distinctions. The truly great is he who considers the claims of others and is slow to give offence (Mt 18^6), and who on all occasions appears simple, teachable, unpretending, indifferent to questions of rank and superiority, and willing to humble himself 'as this little child.' It is only the childlike heart that is capable of knowing God (Mt 11^{25}), and of finding the way into His kingdom. This image has stamped itself on the mind of Christendom, and this pattern of greatness is still fresh. Human character is once for all taught to mould itself after this original and lovely type. Christ first saw the hatefulness and unworkableness of a world without a child !

(b) *The servant, the practical example of humility* (Mt 20$^{20\text{-}28}$ 23$^{1\text{-}12}$, Mk 10$^{35\text{-}45}$, Lk 22$^{24\text{-}27}$, Jn 13$^{1\text{-}17}$).— This ideal of service was presented on two distinct occasions : the one when the sons of Zebedee came forward with their request for the leading places in the Kingdom ; and the other when the same love of dignity, and the jealous exclusion of each other's claims, gave rise to the strife that marred the Last Supper. In rebuking this spirit, Christ had in view not merely the mistaken tendencies of His disciples, who were already fired by the promise of individual 'thrones' (Lk 22^{30}) dear to the Israelitish imagination, but also the popular and prevailing standards of the time. The rulers of the Gentiles aimed at supremacy, and, in the exercise of a harsh authority, delighted to 'lord it over them' ; and equally the scribes and Pharisees, in their fondness for places and titles of honour, coveted influence and recognition as the 'great ones' of Jewish society. Christ required a new standard and line of conduct from His followers. 'Not so shall it be among you.' Henceforth, greatness lies in conformity to a higher than the heathen or Jewish type : 'but whosoever would become great among you shall be your minister,' etc. The principle of this law is not impersonal, but personal ; and the seat of authority in the Christian religion and in Christian morals is Christ : 'even as the Son of Man came,' etc. (Mt 20^{28}). Finally, in one concrete act, Christ gave an illustration of the great principle He enunciated, when, at the Passover meal, He rose and 'took a towel and girded himself,' and washed the disciples' feet. This astonishing incident left an ineffaceable impression (1 P 5^5), and warranted the literal saying : 'I am in the midst of you as he that serveth' (Lk 22^{27}). Such an ideal and example of service have slowly effected a revolution in the moral sentiment and practice of mankind. We may add, if Christ's setting forth of the child was evidence of His originality as a teacher, the substitution of the servant for the ruler was a no less striking proof of the uniqueness of His insight and methods.

'It is one of the achievements of Jesus that He introduced into the world a new ideal of greatness, such an ideal as men had never dreamed of' (D. Smith, *The Days of His Flesh*, 1905, p. 442. Cf. Herrmann in art. below : 'Im NT ist ohne Zweifel der Eindruck wiedergegeben dass Jesus in dieser Beziehung seinen Jüngern etwas völlig Neues gegeben hat').

Some ideals are too airy and remote to come into touch with actual experience and practice, but

Christ's Law of Service is capable of daily realization, and is within the reach of every one. It is open to all to do some simple deed of kindness, helpfulness, and self-denial, and no action inspired by Christ-like love and humility will pass unnoticed or unrewarded by the gracious Master and great Servant of all (Mt 25⁴⁰).

iv. CHARACTERISTICS AND RELATIONSHIPS.—A few further points of general and practical interest are suggested by this subject, and may be briefly touched on.

1. *Humility and character.*—In ordinary experience, humility is related to sin and penitence, and marks the feeling of unworthiness in the light of the illimitable moral ideal. In presence of the holy revelation of the Son of God, conscience becomes sensitive, and the sense of guilt, as in the case of Peter (Lk 5⁸), weighs men down. 'This, however, is not one of the essential conditions of humility, for we know that humility was also an element in Christ's character' (Ritschl). The greatness of the Baptist was rooted in his humility and utter freedom from jealousy (Jn 3²⁷· ³⁰), and this grace has been the soil and safety of saints ever since. Keble treated others with a 'humbling humility' (Lock's *Life*, p. 233. Cf. MacEwen's *Life of Cairns*, p. 600 : 'The first personal impression that he made on all who met him was one of wonder at his humility'). The child, to which Christ pointed, represents humility as part of the essence and permanence of Christian character, and remains an immortal type, preserving the wonder and bloom of the moral world.

2. *Humility and kindred virtues.*—No Christian grace is isolated or thrives alone. Humility is 'part of a great moral whole. Instead of proscribing, it promotes the growth of virtues unlike yet not unfriendly to itself' (Liddon on 'Humility and Action' in *University Sermons*). Thus it is closely connected with *Truth*, for humility or confession that does not rest on the recognition of facts is insincere and worthless. It is inspired by *Love* ; ministering love appears always in the guise of humility. *Meekness* rests on humility as its foundation (Trench), and *Patience* expresses along with humility the practical virtue of the Christian religion, especially called for and tested in the world (Ritschl).

3. *Humility and self-consciousness.*—It has been the tendency of certain schools of theology and piety to make humility the result of self-contemplation, arrived at by the soul's reaction upon itself. This gives rise to artificial and extreme methods of discipline, and misses the healthy objectivity of the life that forgets self in the consideration and service of others (see Herrmann's art. for vigorous criticism of this tendency and ideal of asceticism, derived from Augustine and Bernard. Cf. Harnack's *History of Dogma* [Eng. tr.], vi. p. 10, note). Humility is 'the eye which sees everything except itself' (quoted in Ritschl). Work and the school of life are the best discipline of humility, as of the other virtues.

'We are to respect our responsibilities,' wrote Mr. Gladstone, 'not ourselves. We are to respect the duties of which we are capable, but not our capabilities simply considered. There is to be no complacent self-contemplation, beruminating upon self. When self is viewed, it must always be in the most intimate connexion with its purposes' (Morley's *Life*, i. 214).

On the other hand, the externalizing of humility and the danger of parading it in rules and ceremonies that lead to self-humiliation must equally be avoided. Christ and His Apostles discountenanced all needless self-consciousness and show of virtue (Mt 6¹ff·, Col 2²³. Cf. Ritschl : 'Even in ascetic forms of worship there is no particular form of expression necessary to humility').

4. *Humility and individuality.*—This virtue is not to be cultivated to the neglect of manliness or at the expense of loyalty to religious and moral principle (Mt 10³²). Christ honours the spirit of energy and enterprise in us, and blames the hiding of our talents and the misuse of our opportunities through diffidence or cowardice (Mt 25¹⁴ff·). The manly and energetic character of the centurion, as shown in his faith, was doubtless as pleasing to Jesus as the soldier's reverence and humbleness of address (Lk 7⁶). Humility or the fear of God should banish all unworthy fear. Christ's unflinching exposure of the scribes and Pharisees (Mt 23) calls us to be courageous in adherence to truth and righteousness, and in view of evil and opposition, however powerful. It was a wholesome saying of the Rabbis : 'The disciple of the wise should have sufficient pride to stand in defence of the Law he represents. Self-assertion has therefore its legitimate sphere, and the 'salt' of individuality in religion and in society should in nowise be lost. There is the danger, however, of exaggerating our own view and importance : 'it always needs much grace to see what other people are, and to keep a sense of moral proportion' (Denney, *Expos. Gr. Test.* on Ro 12³). In the adaptation of the Christian Church to society, and to reconcile conflicting interests, it requires humility 'to adjust men in due order for the purposes of life' (T. B. Strong's *Christian Ethics*, Bampton Lect. 1895, p. 127).

5. *Humility and science.*—Christ's interview with Nicodemus teaches that the assumption of knowledge ('we know,' Jn 3²) may cover only ignorance and confusion. The 'wise and understanding' (Mt 11²⁵) receive no new light : self-satisfied pride and prejudice are the foes of spiritual enlightenment and intellectual advance. The true student and investigator of nature must still feel, like Newton, that, notwithstanding his progress and attainments, the great ocean of truth lies undiscovered before him. Docility, not dogmatism, is the mark of the inquirer, and the means of intellectual development. In this important and ever-changing region of science, R. H. Hutton has well observed that humility 'means the docility of learners towards a teacher infinitely above them,' and that it requires wisdom to see the true relations between different kinds of knowledge, and to keep physical knowledge from being turned to a false and dangerous use in the sphere of moral truth. Here also the master of truth and knowledge must take the place of a servant, and illustrate his greatness by his humility—' and science is humble only when it uses its knowledge and its ignorance alike to help other men and not to lord it over them' (Essay on 'The Humility of Science' in *Aspects of Religious and Scientific Thought*, 1901). So manifold is the function of this indispensable and crowning grace.

LITERATURE.—Besides works above named, Grimm-Thayer's *Lex.*; Moulton-Geden's *Concord. to Greek Test.*; art. 'Humility' in Hastings' *DB* vol. ii.; Herrmann in *PRE*³ (' Demut, Demütig' —an art. characteristic in its Ritschlian standpoint and criticism); E. Schreiber, art. in *Jewish Encyc.* 1904 (interesting and suggestive); B. Weiss, *Bib. Theol. of NT*, pp. 116, 117, and Ritschl, *The Christian Doctrine of Justif. and Reconcil.* ch. ix. § 65 (both in Clark's tr.); A. B. Bruce, *Training of the Twelve*, chs. xiv. xxi.; Professor J. Seth, *A Study of Ethical Principles*⁴, p. 264 ; Rothe, *Sermons* ('The Humility of the Lord'—Clark's tr.); Liddon, *Some Words of Christ* ('True Greatness'); Church, *Cathed. and Univ. Sermons* ('The Condescension of our Lord'); Dante, *Purgatory*, Cantos 10–12 ; R. Browning's exquisite little poem, 'Humility' (*Asolando*); Kipling's *Recessional*.　　　　W. M. RANKIN.

HUMOUR.—Humour in its highest form is the sign of a mind at peace in itself, for which the contrasts and contradictions of life have ceased to jar, though they have not ceased to be ; which accepts them as necessary and not without meaning and value, indeed as giving an added charm to life, because it looks at them from a point above them. In other words, humour is the faculty which lets a man see what Plato calls 'the whole tragedy and comedy of life' (*Philebus*, 50 B)—the one in the other, comedy in tragedy, tragedy in comedy.

The Gospels make it plain that the environment of Jesus was quite a normal one. He had lived among men, worked, played, and talked with men from infancy to manhood, and was familiar with the language of men and with their habits of mind. Hence it may be noticed that in speaking to men He uses the language of reality and experience. His words are stamped as His own by their delicate ease, which implies sensibility to every real aspect of the matter in hand, a sense of mastery and peace. There lay a broad contrast between the common sense His hearers had gathered from experience and the moral ideals which He propounded, and it is quite clear that this contrast did not escape Him, nor can He have failed to see that, judged by the ordinary common sense of men, His sayings were absurd. With this consciousness of the superficial absurdity and the underlying value of what He said, He bade men when smitten on the one cheek 'turn the other' (Mt 5³⁹), go 'two miles' with the man who exacted one (v.⁴¹), yield the cloak to him who took the coat (v.⁴⁰),—in fact, His followers were asked to be 'lambs,' missionaries 'among wolves' (Mt 10¹⁶, Lk 10³), and to 'leap for joy' when they were ill treated (Lk 6²³). In all these sayings there is obvious contradiction between the surface value and the thought beneath.

Again, there is abundant evidence of the use of the grotesque by Jesus—a use natural to homely and friendly talk. Would a father, for example, offer a hungry child a stone instead of bread, a snake instead of a fish, a scorpion instead of an egg (Mt 7⁹·¹⁰, Lk 11¹¹·¹²)? The Pharisee, He says, is like a man who cleans the *outside* of his cup and forgets that he drinks from the inside (Mt 23²⁶). Do men, He asks, 'gather grapes of thorns, or figs of thistles'? (Mt 7¹⁶). He urges His hearers not to cast their 'pearls before swine' (Mt 7⁶). The idea of having 'a beam in one's own eye' is grotesque, as He meant it to be (Mt 7³⁻⁵). When He bade His hearers take no care for the morrow, because caring for the morrow was the distinguishing mark of the *Gentile* as contrasted with the Jew (Mt 6³²), He spoke with full knowledge of Jewish character, and must have known that His hearers would smile. 'Do not even the publicans so?' (Mt 5⁴⁷), is an instance of *reductio ad absurdum*. 'Is it lawful on the Sabbath days to do evil or to do good?' (Lk 6⁹), was, His critics on the spot would feel, an absurd question, except that it caught them in a dilemma. Similarly, to ask the rich young ruler if he had kept the commandments, 'Thou shalt not kill,' etc., must have struck the onlooker as odd, and Jesus can hardly have failed to feel this (Mk 10¹⁹). The simile that follows, of the camel and the needle's eye, shows recourse to the grotesque again (Mk 10²⁵). It should be remembered that Jesus' hearers were not unfamiliar with religious teaching given in ironic form.

There is humour in the appeal to the practice of the Egyptians and Syrians of calling their tyrannic and worthless rulers *Euergetes*, 'Benefactor' (Lk 22²⁵); and in the accompanying suggestion that the real chief among Christ's followers is 'he that doth serve' (Lk 22²⁶), there is a conscious reversal of ordinary notions, which would make the hearers smile even while they realized the serious meaning. There is a hint of playfulness in the promise that Peter shall 'catch men' (Lk 5¹⁰). The question put to the rich fool, 'Then whose shall those things be?' (Lk 12²⁰), has a grim touch,—there is a suggestion in it of reckonings grievously wrong; and something of the kind lurks in the tale of the man who built his house on the sand—a tale told, it

must be remembered, by one who had been a τέκτων (Mt 7²⁶). There are other stories, too, of people of pretension who are ludicrously out in their reckonings, *e.g.* the king who went to war with a light heart (Lk 14³¹), and the man who could not finish his tower (v.²⁸). There is surely grim humour also in the words, 'It cannot be that a prophet perish *out of Jerusalem*' (Lk 13³³).

In conclusion, there are in the recorded sayings of Jesus many traces of their origin in conversation. He is a man speaking to men in the language of men, and pathos, contrast, humour, and spontaneity are the natural and pleasant marks of that language. He, like all great teachers, speaks from the abundance of His heart (Mt 12³⁴), and a smile is felt in His words, as in the words of all who see contradiction without loss of inner peace. See also art. LAUGHTER.

LITERATURE.—Martensen, *Christian Ethics*, i. 186.

T. R. GLOVER.

HUNGER.—The substantive 'hunger' (EV) is the equivalent of a Greek word (λιμός) which in the NT is used either of the suffering of an individual (Lk 15¹⁷, cf. 2 Co 11²⁷), or, more generally, of the widespread plague of famine (cf. Mk 13⁸, Lk 4²⁵ etc.; see Blass' *Gram. of NT Greek*, p. 299, for the combination λοιμοὶ καὶ λιμοί [*parechesis*]). The more frequently occurring verb is an altogether different word (πεινᾶν), and it is sometimes found where we might expect λιμός or its cognates (Mt 5⁶ and Lk 6²¹). The latter occurs in but 6 places in the Gospels, while the former is found no fewer than 17 times.

There is, perhaps, no feature of Jesus' human experience so vividly instructive as that which is portrayed for us in the simple incidental expression 'He hungered' (Mt 4²=Lk 4², Mt 21¹⁸=Mk 11¹²). This is noted twice by the Synoptists; and though we have no such direct statement by St. John, we are not left by the latter without a reference to this side of 'the humiliation of Christ.' The story of Jesus' conversation with the woman of Samaria conveys the same impression as to the physical limitations to which He was subject with which we are struck in the Synoptic writings. The anxiety of the disciples for the satisfaction of their Master's needs (Jn 4³¹ 'Ραββεί, φάγε) explains at least one cause of the bodily weariness which compelled Him to rest 'thus by the well.'

It is of the greatest interest to notice that, on the two occasions when it is definitely stated that Jesus suffered the pangs of hunger, the writer has pointedly attached to the narrative a lesson of psychological and spiritual value. St. Matthew and St. Luke both inform us not only that on the completion of His forty days' fast 'he hungered'; they also tell us that the Tempter attacked Him on the side of His consequent weakness. 'If thou art the Son of God, command that these stones become bread' (Mt 4³, cf. the stronger and more graphic mould in which St. Luke casts the narrative by adopting the singular τῷ λίθῳ τούτῳ for οἱ λίθοι οὗτοι and ἄρτος for ἄρτοι, Lk 4³), expresses the subtle nature of this temptation in a manner which is profoundly in keeping with all human experience (see F. W. Robertson's sermon on 'Elijah,' second series).

<small>It is surely more rational to accept the Synoptic statement that this was, in point of fact, the first of the three temptations, for the reason given above, than to adopt the order given in the *Gospel according to the Hebrews*, as O. Holtzmann is inclined to do (cf. his *Leben Jesu*, Eng. tr. pp. 94 and 140–150). The author of this *Gospel* places the temptation by hunger after that on the high mountain, which he puts first in the series. Holtzmann, moreover, argues that the first temptation, according to the First and Third Evangelists, occurred last of all. Among other reasons for this inversion, he bases his statement on the fact that Jesus met the suggestion to convert the stone into a loaf by a quotation taken from Dt 8³, whereas His answers to the other two are quotations from an earlier part of the same book (Dt 6¹³ and 6¹⁶). To the present writer this looks like</small>

trifling with the evidence, and seems to expose this author to the charge of adopting any statement as having *prima facie* claims to being historical provided it be a contradiction of the sacred books. The very simplicity of the narratives as we have them forbids us to assume that the writers manufactured an order by means of 'a gradation as regards localities,' or by presenting a series of grand climacterics—'satisfaction of hunger, miraculous action, and sovereignty of the world.' [For the curious passage in the *Gospel according to the Hebrews* (. . . ἔνθα αὐτός ὁ Σωτήρ φησιν· ἄρτι ἔλαβέ με ἡ μήτηρ μου τὸ ἅγιον πνεῦμα ἐν μιᾷ τῶν τριχῶν μου, καὶ ἀπήνεγκέ με εἰς τὸ ὄρος τὸ μέγα Θαβώρ) which makes Mt. Tabor the scene of the Temptation, see Origen, *in Joann.* tom. ii. § 6 f., given in Nestle's *Græcum Supplementum*, p. 77. The same passage is quoted more than once by Jerome, who each time refers it to the *Evangelium quod secundum (juxta) Hebræos (e.g. in Is* 15¹¹)].

The other recorded occasion on which Jesus suffered from hunger was at the end of His ministry, and during that week when His last conflict with the religious authorities of His nation culminated in His Passion and Death. The incident affords an example of the way in which the Evangelists, in their choice of literary material, were guided to subordinate the selection of historical facts to the moral and spiritual importance attaching to them. Neither St. Matthew nor St. Mark was deterred from relating the story of the fruitless fig-tree by a fear lest the appearance of harshness and petulance should detract from the moral dignity of their Master. Their portrait of Him was too faithful and their insight too keen to permit any suggestion, to themselves at least, of an unworthy display, in an angry moment, of thaumaturgical energy. See art. FIG-TREE.

The union between Christ and His people, so repeatedly insisted on by Jesus as indispensable to their higher life (see, *e.g.*, Jn 15⁴ff.), is postulated in His great eschatological discourse. The sufferings of redeemed humanity are His sufferings, and the loving service, which clothes the naked and feeds the hungry, is hallowed because it is done, not merely in His cause, but for Himself (Mt 25³⁵ff., cf. 10⁴⁰ff.). There is something more in these words than an expression of sympathy by a brother who has himself experienced deprivation and suffering (cf. He 4¹⁵), and who feels for one who is passing through similar stages. We have in them a vivid portraiture of that essential and spiritual oneness upon which the writer of the Fourth Gospel lays such emphasis (cf. Jn 14²⁰ 17²¹·²³·²⁶ etc.; see also Ac 9⁵ Ἐγώ εἰμι Ἰησοῦς ὃν σὺ διώκεις).

It is not without significance that not only have we this mystic union adumbrated by the Synoptists which is elaborated and, inchoatively at least, systematized by St. John; we have also recorded in the writings of all three an incident illustrative of that complete companionship in privations as well as in privileges which He demanded as the essence of discipleship from the scribe who would follow Him whithersoever He went (Lk 9⁵⁸ = Mt 8²⁰; cf. Mt 10³⁸ 16²⁴, Lk 9²³, Mk 8³⁴ etc.). The fact that the disciples suffered hunger is specifically mentioned by St. Matthew, though it is only to be inferred from the parallel passages in the other two Synoptists (cf. Mk 2²³ff· = Mt 12¹ff· = Lk 6¹ff·). On this occasion Jesus takes advantage of the opportunity afforded by the carping criticism of the Pharisees to emphasize, by an appeal to the case of the hungry David, His teaching on the Sabbath question. A fine touch is added by each of the Synoptists which beautifully illustrates the spirit of *camaraderie* existing between Jesus and His disciples. The touch is incidental, and therefore the more effective. Each of the writers expressly states that it was the disciples who were plucking the ears of corn and not Jesus, though each commences the narrative by making Jesus the subject of the story (ἐπορεύθη ὁ Ἰησοῦς, κ.τ.λ., Mt 12¹; . . . αὐτὸν διαπορεύεσθαι, Mk 2²³, Lk 6¹). It was through the disciples that the Pharisees attacked Him (cf., however, Lk 6²); and it was in their defence that

Jesus met them with the unanswerable argument taken from their own armoury—the OT.

It will not surprise us to find Jesus transferring the idea of physical hunger to the spiritual life and experience, as this habit of transposition forms one of the most attractive and powerful features in His teaching. Just as in man's physical life hunger is a sign of health, and becomes an evil only when its cravings cannot be satisfied, so Jesus counts those blessed whose soul's health is robust enough to cause them to cry out from hunger after righteousness (note the peculiar construction which has the accusative τὴν δικαιοσύνην after πεινῶντες instead of the genitive of classical writers; cf. *Od.* xx. 137; Xen. *Cyr.* VIII. iii. 39; Plato, *Rep.* 521 A; see Blass' *Grammar of NT Greek*, p. 89 f.; and Liddell and Scott's *Lexicon*). That need, because it is felt, shall be met in the fullest possible way, hence their blessedness (ὅτι αὐτοὶ χορτασθήσονται, Mt 5⁶; cf. Lk 6²¹).

On the other hand, they are to be pitied whose spiritual appetite is so deranged that they feel no need at all, because the day shall come when they must feel, and the pangs of hunger shall remain without hope of alleviation (ὅτι πεινάσετε, Lk 6²⁵). That He possessed the power of permanently satisfying the deepest needs of the human soul, Jesus categorically asserts on more than one occasion (Jn 6³⁵, cf. 4¹⁴ and 7³⁷. In these express assurances we may see the profoundest explanation of the words of the *Magnificat* : 'The hungry he hath filled with good things; and the rich he hath sent empty away' (Lk 1⁵³), which are but the echo of the words in which the Psalmist long before had clothed his experience (Ps 107⁹). J. R. WILLIS.

HUSBAND (ἀνήρ).—Betrothal and marriage were virtually one among the Jews. The former consisted in the simple act, on the part of the bridegroom or his deputy, of giving to the bride or her representative a written engagement, in the presence of two witnesses, or a piece of money, large or small, with the words, 'Be thou consecrated unto me.' Like marriage itself, of which it was the initiatory step, it could be dissolved only by death or divorce. Under the Mosaic Law, the marriage tie was comparatively easily broken, and divorces seem to have been quite common. During the period of the later prophets the ethical standard was considerably advanced ('God hates putting away,' Mal 2¹⁶). Christ Himself utterly set aside the law of Moses, and limited the dissolution of the marriage tie to the one cause of adultery; and in this respect He apparently put the two sexes on the same plane (Mk 10¹¹f·). The mercy of Christ towards sinners against the law of sexual morality as laid down by Himself is, however, beautifully illustrated in His treatment of the Samaritan woman (Jn 4¹⁶⁻¹⁸), and in that of the woman taken in adultery (8⁴⁻¹¹). *

In Mt 1¹⁶·¹⁹ Joseph is called 'the husband' of Mary, indicating, in connexion with v.²⁵, that true marital relations existed between them. This is in evident conflict with the Apocrypha, which assigns to Joseph the place of a guardian rather than that of a true husband, in order to uphold the perpetual virginity of Mary. See, further, artt. MARRIAGE, WIFE. HENRY E. DOSKER.

HUSBANDMAN (γεωργός).—Jesus knew well the life of the fields. His keen eye for illustrations fell readily on the most fundamental of occupations; one universal since the primeval days when simple patriarchs began to be husbandmen, and princes digged at the up-springing well ('which the nobles of the people delved, with the sceptre

---

* This passage, whether genuine or not, is certainly a true reflexion of our Lord's mind and character.

and with their staves,' Nu 21^{18} RV). Agriculture, in Israel's best days, had been the chief employment, and still from out the scattered villages men were to be seen at work upon the croftlike patches. As sure token of happy and successful labours, the plain was verdant with the growing grain, the vines hung graceful from the terraced slope. The human mind never fails to be arrested in religious mood by the mystic forces of nature; and in the case of the Jews there was this added discipline, that Scripture, read statedly in their hearing, teemed with references to the tilling of the soil. Ready to the lips of Jesus, therefore, was an allusive speech which should prove powerful in appeal to educated and uneducated alike. The way into the popular sentiment was clear for Him. People were at least grounded in the elements of literary thought. On the principles and growth of the great Kingdom He could discourse profitably under the familiar images of seed-time and harvest, tree or plant culture in their gardens, or the ongoings in their season of the workers in the vineyard on the hill.

What probably commended this line of teaching to Jesus, however, was the fact that husbandry suggests, in singular fashion, the co-ordination of man's activity with God's. Without, on the one hand, what is graciously supplied to us—soil and seed, rain and sunshine—man's labour could be of no avail; yet, on the other hand, without that labour well directed, mankind would perish. The lesson is writ large in cultivated fields that faith and hope, zeal and patience, have a reward assured which comes immediate from the hand of God. Further, this rural imagery of Jesus met the fact that the minds hearing Him were not all equally ready to see the truth in His light. For such persons, pictures from the outer and familiar realm stored up material for self-culture in the future. And nothing better certifies the supreme instinct of the Master than this, that the thousand revelations of the natural science of to-day illustrate only the more those spiritual principles and universal laws of the unseen which He was wont to enforce by reference to phenomena around Him as He spoke.

The slighter glances recorded of Jesus in this realm are fairly numerous. Compare the references to plants and trees (Mt 7$^{16-20}$ 12^{33}, Lk 6$^{43-45}$), the putting of the hand to the plough (Lk 9^{62}), the application of salt to the land (Mt 5^{13}, Lk 14^{35}), the ox fallen into the pit (Lk 14^{5}), the action of the airs of heaven (Lk 12^{55}, Jn 3^{8}), the glowing or beclouded sky (Mt 16$^{2, 3}$, Lk 12^{54}), the buyer gone to survey his piece of ground (Lk 14^{18}), or busy testing his new teams (v.^{19}), the deeply-suggestive corn of wheat (Jn 12^{24}), the sifting of the same (Lk 22^{31}), the tenant counting up his measures (Lk 16^{7}), labourers needed for the plenteous harvest (Mt 9$^{57, 38}$, Lk 10^{2}), the growing whiteness of the crops (Jn 4^{35}), the fated twain of field workers (Mt 24^{40}, Lk 17^{36}), and the beautiful picture of the fig-tree at the approach of summer putting forth leaves upon its tender branch (Mt 24^{32}, Lk 21^{29}).

But chiefly in the exquisite parables do we see that power of observation in the material world which makes Jesus so engaging as a child of nature, who lived much, and lived free, in the open air of Palestine. As we move with Him by the highways and the hedges, we descry in one field the servant ploughing or feeding cattle (Lk 17^{7}), in another the well-remembered spot where gleams of joy lit up the rustic's eyes who happed upon hid treasure (Mt 13^{44}). Here we have the corn-lands green with the sprouting of the tiny blade (Mk 4$^{26-29}$), tangled betimes with the tares (Mt 13^{25}); there the rocky and the thorn-choked patches (Mk 4$^{5-7}$); and over

all the hovering birds (v.^{4}), ready to devour the precious seed. We see the labourers standing in the market-place for hire (Mt 20^{3}), the prosperous farmer critical about his barns (Lk 12^{18}), the shepherd searching the grassy plateau for his sheep (Mt 18^{12}). Men are working in the clumps of vines (Mt 21^{28}), from which the wine-press peeps (Mk 12^{1}), and where the watch-tower stands upon its bolder coign (v.^{1}). See the garden where the tall mustard grows (Lk 13^{19}), and yonder the forlorn fig-tree (v.^{6}) threatened with the axe. The whole world of nature, the varied scenes of toil, are laid amply under contribution, made the emblems and the witness of the highest things of the Spirit. (See art. VINE (ALLEGORY OF) for discourse upon the Vine and the Branches, Jn 15$^{1-8}$, where the Father is the Husbandman; cf. also art. AGRICULTURE).

One parable must be specially noted—the story of the Wicked Husbandmen (Mt 21$^{33-43}$, Mk 12$^{1-9}$, Lk 20$^{9ff.}$), which is an incisive review of God's relations with His people. Endless pains had been taken (Mk 12^{1}) with the vineyard of the Kingdom, yet when messenger after messenger came seeking fruit in the Divine name, they had been sent empty away, and contumeliously treated —one beaten, another wounded, a third killed (vv.$^{2-5}$). Nowhere does Jesus put Himself more clearly in line with the prophets. As the gloomy night is gathering fast around His own head, He feels full affinity of fate with them. In the passage He carries, indeed, the history of Israel's shameful conduct not only to the days of the Baptist, but even a little beyond the moment of utterance. We have insight into the marvellous composure of the heart of Jesus as He pictures His own case in the person of the one son, well beloved, who was cast out, bruised and bleeding, his body soon to be cold in death upon the highway (v.^{8}). Thus, in tragic fashion, He broadens the charge against His opponents, with their complacent jealousy (v.^{7}), by proving their conduct to be of a piece with Israel's cruel treatment of speakers for God in the past. The note of severity and moral indignation is unmistakable, but it is blended with one of wistful sadness. Not that His own approaching death troubles Him; He fears not as He enters into the cloud, and is ready to give His life as covenant blood for the setting up of the Kingdom. But His countrymen's wayward folly, and the terrible crisis at hand for the Jewish State, weigh heavy on His spirit. Their doom, He concludes, is written with God's own finger on the wall, for those who had the eyes to see: 'He will come, and destroy the husbandmen, and will give the vineyard unto others' (v.^{9}).

GEORGE MURRAY.

HUSKS.—The only mention of husks (κεράτια, so called from their shape, which resembles 'horns') occurs in Lk 15^{16}. Husks were the pods of the carob-tree, which is also known as the locust-tree (*Ceratonia siliqua*). This tree, which is common in Palestine, belongs to the order Leguminosæ, and is an evergreen. It attains to a height of about 30 feet, and has a dense foliage. Its leaves are of a dark, glossy green. The pods are from 6 to 10 inches in length and 1 in breadth. They contain a thick, sweet pulp, not unpleasant to the palate, and are used as food for pigs, cattle, and horses. They are also, because of their cheapness, eaten by the very poor.

Some have identified the pods of the carob with the 'locusts' (ἀκρίδες) which John the Baptist ate (Mt 3^{4}). It is true they are sometimes called 'St. John's bread,' this name having been given to them by the monks of Palestine or by 'pious pilgrims' (Thomson, *LB* p. 655), but there can be little doubt that the Baptist's food was not carob-pods, but the insect, which is still eaten by the wandering Arabs. See Locust.　　　　　　　　HUGH DUNCAN.

HYMN.—1. *Introductory.*—In the earliest period the terms 'hymn' ($ὕμνος$) and 'to hymn' ($ὑμνεῖν$) seem to have covered practically every kind of composition which was sung or rhythmically recited in Christian worship or the Christian assemblies.

In Col 3[16] and Eph 5[19] the three terms $ὕμνος$ ('hymn'), $ψαλμός$ ('psalm'), and $ᾠδή$ ('song') are found together as descriptive of the acts of praise offered to God in the early Christian assemblies. 'While the leading idea of $ψαλμ.$ is a musical accompaniment, and that of $ὕμν.$ praise to God, $ᾠδή$ is the general word for a song, whether accompanied or unaccompanied, whether of praise or on any other subject. Thus it was quite possible for the same song to be at once $ψαλμός$, $ὕμνος$, and $ᾠδή$' (Lightfoot on Col 3[16]).

Specifically hymns came in course of time to be distinguished from psalms (*i.e.* the canonical Bk. of Psalms[*]) and canticles ('poetical extracts from Holy Scripture which are incorporated among the Psalms in the Divine office'[†]). This, of course, applies to the period subsequent to the fixing of the Canon. But the earliest ecclesiastical hymns, in this sense, were not metrical.

The *ecclesiastical canticles* under the title of $ᾠδαί$ immediately follow the Psalter in certain of the Greek uncials and in a large number of the Greek cursive MSS. Nine of them are now sung at Lauds in the office of the orthodox Greek Church. Codex A gives the following in the following order:[‡]
(1) Ex 15[1-19] ('Song of Moses in Exodus'); (2) Dt 32[1-43] ('Song of Moses in Deut.'); (3) 1 S 2[1-10] ('Prayer of Hannah'); (4) Is 26[9-20] ('Prayer of Isaiah'); (5) Jon 3[5-10] ('Prayer of Jonah'); (6) Hab 3[1-19] ('Prayer of Habakkuk'); (7) Is 38[10-20] ('Prayer of Hezekiah'); (8) The Prayer of Manasseh; (9) Dn 3[26-45]; (10) Dn 3[52-88]; (11) *Magnificat*; (12) *Nunc Dimittis*; (13) *Benedictus*; (14) *Morning Hymn* (= full form of *Gloria in Excelsis*).

2. *Jewish Liturgical usage.*—In the Temple services the Psalms naturally played a great part. For the daily service the order of the Psalms, which were sung to a musical accompaniment by the Levitical choir,[§] was as follows: 1st day of the week, Ps 24; 2nd, Ps 48; 3rd, Ps 82; 4th, Ps 94; 5th, Ps 81; 6th, Ps 93; Sabbath, Ps 92. Special Psalms were also used for special occasions.

It has been questioned whether psalmody formed an element in the early synagogue-service (see esp. Gibson, *Expositor*, July 1890, pp. 25–27). It is true that in the Mishna‖ the only elements explicitly recognized in the synagogue-service are: (1) the Shema'; (2) prayer; (3) the reading of the Law; and (4) the reading of the Prophets, and the benediction. But we know from the NT that in addition to this the practice of translating and expounding the Scripture-lection was also in vogue; and it may be inferred that on certain special occasions the 'Hallel,' at any rate, was recited in the synagogues (see Hallel).¶ But it is difficult to believe that other parts of the Psalter were not also recited there. The internal evidence of the Psalms suggests that some at least were specially intended for synagogue use: esp. the 'Hallelujah' Psalms (105, 106, 107, 111, 112, 114, 116, 117, 118, 135, 136, 146–150).[**] However this may be, it is practically certain that a part, at least, of the sacred poetry of the OT, such as the Red Sea Song (Ex 15), the special Psalms for the days of the week, the Hallel, and possibly, also, the 'Psalms of Degrees,' would be known in Palestine in their Hebrew form in the time of Christ from their liturgical use in public worship, esp. in the Temple.[††] Examples of post-biblical poetry (Hebrew) of the early period (before the destruction of the Temple) are very rare. For an instance cf. Mishna, *Sukkā* v. 4 (a liturgical piece).

3. *The Evangelical Canticles.*—The poetical pieces which we know as the *Magnificat, Benedictus,*

---

[*] It is possible that in Col 3[16], Eph 5[19] the term $ψαλμός$ is similarly restricted in meaning.
[†] *Dict. Chr. Ant.* i. 284.
[‡] Cf. Swete, *Introd. to the OT in Greek*, p. 253 f.
[§] Cf. Edersheim, *Temple*, etc. p. 143 f.
[‖] Cf. esp. *Meg.* iv. 3.
[¶] It is worth noting that the regular term employed in the Mishna is to 'read' (קרא) the Hallel. In the Temple-service it was sung. Cf. also the benediction said before Hallel, which was probably the composition of the Pharisees ('who hast commanded us to read the Hallel').
[**] Cf. Cheyne, *Origin of the Psalter*, p. 14, note g, and p. 363 f. Pss. 146–150 form a well-defined group in the synagogue-liturgy, and are used in the daily morning service (cf. Singer, *Heb.-Eng. Prayer-Book*, p. 29 f.). Compare with this the custom in certain parts of the early Church of reciting the 'Hallelujah' Psalms daily. See Grünwald, *Ueber den Einfluss der Psalmen auf die Katholische Liturgie*, Heft iii. p. 23.
[††] Cf. also the so-called *Psalter of Solomon*, which may have been intended 'for public or even liturgical use,' and which almost certainly goes back to a Hebrew original. See ed. by Ryle and James, p. xci.

Nunc Dimittis, and *Gloria in Excelsis* (Angels' song), and which are embodied in the first two chapters of the Third Gospel, are probably the earliest examples of Christian hymns. They are ascribed to the Virgin Mary, Simeon, Zacharias, and the Angels respectively; but it is more probable that they are to be regarded as original liturgical compositions, reflecting the piety and devotion of the early Jewish-Christian community in Palestine. Probably, too, they are translations from Hebrew originals, and were at first sung or chanted in Hebrew.[*] The hymns themselves are obviously modelled on the psalm-poetry of the OT, some of which, as has been pointed out, would be generally familiar *in its Hebrew form* to the Aramaic-speaking Jews of Palestine in the time of Christ.[†]

For details as to the dependence of these hymns on the OT see the commentaries (in particular, Plummer, *Intern. Crit. Com.* on 'St. Luke'). Notice the prominence of the idea of a Messianic redemption from sin, which is characteristically Jewish-Christian (cf. Lk 1[77] with Plummer's note; and cf. Mt 1[21]). For the poetical form and structure cf. esp. Briggs, *The Messiah of the Gospels* (1894), ch. ii., and *New Light on the Life of Jesus* (1904), ch. xiii. (the latter esp. valuable). The present writer finds himself in independent agreement with Briggs in regarding Mt 1.[0b. 21] as a translation from a Hebrew poetical piece.[‡] According to the same scholar, the full number of poetical pieces given in Luke is seven, viz.: (1) The Annunciation to Zacharias (Lk 1[13-17]); (2) the Annunciation to Mary (4 parts: 1[28. 30-33. 35-37. 38]); (3) the Annunciation to the Shepherds (2 parts: 2[10-12. 14]); (4) the Song of Elisabeth (1[42-45]); (5) the Song of Mary (= *Magnificat*, 1[46-55]); (6) the Song of Zacharias (= *Benedictus*, 1[68-79]); (7) the Song of Simeon (= *Nunc Dimittis*, 2[29-32], to which should be appended vv.[34. 35]). Of these all but No. (5) are trimeter poems; (5) is a pentameter poem, as is also Mt 1[20b. 21]. Probably all go back to two long poems (a trimeter and pentameter), from which the above are extracts.

4. *Other Hymns and Hymn-pieces.*—(*a*) It has been suggested with some plausibility that the Prologue of the Fourth Gospel 'is a hymn to the Logos, composed independently of the Gospel and prefixed to it.'[§] Here also Professor Briggs detects a trimeter poem originally arranged in three parts.‖ For other possible extracts from early Christian hymns in the NT, reference may here be made to 'Hymn' in Hastings' *DB* ii. p. 440 f.

In the Apocalypse, also, there are a number of songs ($ᾠδαί$) which may, perhaps, be regarded as traditional Jewish-Christian hymns (cf. 4[11] 5[9f. 12f.] 11[17f.] 15[3f.]).

It is possible that the curious phrase, 'Amen, come' (Rev 22[20]), may be an acrostic reference to a Jewish hymn which is still sung in the synagogue (*'En Kēlōhēnū*, 'There is none like our God,' Singer, p. 167). This composition, in its present form, consists of 5 verses of 4 lines each. The initial letters of the lines of the 5 verses form the words אמן בא = '*Amen, come.*'‖ A Hebraized form (הִמְנוֹן) of the Greek term $ὕμνος$ occurs in the Midrash (cf. *Ber. Rabba* viii. 9 = a hymn to a king).

(*b*) *The Hosanna-hymn,* or cry of praise of Palm Sunday, with which Jesus was greeted on His last entry into Jerusalem,¶ is given in various forms in the Gospels. In its simplest form it occurs in Mk 11[9] and Jn 12[13], which really give the cry of the multitude: הושע נא ברוך הבא בשם יהוה. The additions that occur in the other passages ($τῷ υἱῷ Δαυείδ$, Mt 21[9. 15]; and $ἐν τοῖς ὑψίστοις$, Mt 21[9], Mk 11[10])[**] seem really to be later amplifications

---

[*] See an article by the present writer in *ZNTW* vi. p. 80 f. (Feb. 1905), on 'The Gospel Narratives of the Nativity,' etc.
[†] Cf. *op. cit.* p. 95.
[‡] That a *Hebrew* original underlies these two verses is shown by the fact that the play upon words in v.[21] (*Jesus shall save*) can be elucidated only by Hebrew—not Aramaic—phraseology (יֵשׁוּעַ, יֹשִׁיעַ).
[§] Cf. for details Briggs, *The Messiah of the Apostles* (1895), pp. 495–515; he compares the above to the 'credal hymn' in 1 Ti 3[14].
[‖] Cf. Schiller-Szinessy in the *Ency. Brit.*, *s.v.* 'Midrash' (p. 286), and C. Taylor, *Teaching of the Twelve Apostles*, p. 78 f.; also an art. by the present writer in *Church and Synagogue*, iii. p. 41 f. (Jan. 1901).
[¶] Also afterwards by the children in the Temple, Mt 21[15].
[**] Mk 11[10] will thus be a later addition. It is noteworthy that the original form *without these additions* occurs only in the Fourth Gospel. Lk. (19[38]) omits 'Hosanna' and alters the Psalm-verse into, 'Blessed be the King that cometh in the name of the Lord.' See art. Hosanna.

due to liturgical influence, when ὡσαννά (which in its Hebrew form הושיענא is really a cry addressed to God, 'Save now!') was misunderstood as a shout of homage or greeting = 'Hail!' or 'Glory to.' See Dalman, *Words of Jesus* (Eng. tr.), p. 220 f.

Cheyne's explanation, *Encyc. Bibl. s.v.* 'Hosanna,' is hardly convincing. Lightfoot, in his interesting note on Mt 21¹² (*Horæ Heb.* ed. Gandell, ii. 274 f.), ingeniously paraphrases, 'Save us, we beseech Thee, O Thou [who dwellest] in the highest,' taking ἐν τοῖς ὑψίστοις as a substitute for the Divine name. This is barely possible.

The Hosanna-cry (cf. Ps 118²⁵ᶠ·) and the palm branches naturally suggest the Feast of Tabernacles, with the ceremonies of which they were most closely associated (esp. in the 'Hosanna' processions of the Festival).* It seems, however, that such processions might be extemporized for other occasions of a joyous character (cf. 1 Mac 13⁵¹, 2 Mac 10⁷), and this was the case in the scene described in the Gospels.

Wünsche, indeed (*Erläuterungen der Evangelien aus Talmud und Midrash*, p. 241), supposes that a confusion has arisen in the Gospel accounts between Tabernacles and Passover; but this is unnecessary. It is noteworthy that there seem to be traces in the Midrash on the Psalms of the Messianic interpretation of Ps. 118²⁵.†

LITERATURE.—The most important contributions to the subject of NT hymnody are the works of Briggs above cited. Reference may also be made to artt. 'Hosanna' in the *Jewish Encyc.* and *Encyc. Bibl.* respectively; also to 'Hymns' in *Encyc. Bibl.*; 'Hymn' in Hastings' *DB₁*; 'Hymn,' 'Canticle,' in *Dict. Chr. Ant.*, and to 'Kirchenlied i. (in der alten Kirche)' and 'Liturgische Formeln' in *PRE³*. Other references have been given in the body of the article.

G. H. Box.

HYPOCRISY.—

'Hypocrisy' (ὑπόκρισις), 'hypocrite' (ὑποκριτής), 'act the hypocrite' (ὑποκρίνομαι). In the NT the verb appears only in Lk 20²⁰; ὑποκριτής only in the Synopp., but fifteen times in Mt. alone; ὑπόκρισις once in Mt. (23²⁸), once in Mk. (12¹⁵), once in Lk. (12¹), and also in Gal 2¹³, 1 Ti 4², and 1 P 2¹. The root meaning of the word is *to distinguish between things.* From this it early came to mean to answer, and to interpret, dreams. By what link of association it came to be applied to *declamation* is less easy to determine. In this sense it is used by the Attic writers of orators and rhapsodists as well as of actors. Soon it was restricted to declamation on the stage, and then, by a process repeated in other languages, was used for acting a part, and so for acting a part for a base end, for giving oneself out to be what one knew one ought to be, but had no intention of becoming.

In the Apocr. the word is found in this sense of acting a part, of feigning, and with varying shades of moral obliquity. In 2 Mac 6²¹⁻²⁵, Eleazar is urged to eat his own meat while *feigning* to eat the swine's flesh appointed by the king. Though the deception is urged as legitimate, Eleazar's reply shows that the word already had bad associations. Similarly 4 Mac 6¹⁷. In Sir 32¹⁵, as the opposite to fearing God and seeking the law, it is used almost exactly as in the NT. The LXX uses the word in Job 34³⁰ and 36¹³, to translate חָנֵף. In the first passage, it is an impiety which lays snares; in the second, it is an impiety of the heart which cherishes an inward bitterness against God. Here we have the true ancestry of the NT usage, which always includes the idea of impiety, of shutting out God and resolutely living in the darkness apart from Him. But the NT usage is also influenced by חָלָק, though the LXX translates that word by δολιοῦν or δολοῦν. From the root idea of smoothness it came to be employed for flattery, and so for all kinds of evil deception. The kinship of the two words חָנֵף and חָלָק may be seen in Dn 11³², where those who are basely disloyal to the covenant expose themselves to the danger of being led into a false position towards God by smooth deceits.

Yet the conception of this vice in the popular mind of His time, to which our Lord appealed, was less determined by any particular Hebrew word than by the general teaching of the OT. The hypocrites speak with a double heart (Ps 12²). They have smooth lips, and their profession is far beyond their performance (12³). They imagine that wickedness can be shut up in the heart. They are brazen towards God, and deceitful towards men. They cease to hate evil and take to planning it (36¹⁻⁴). Above all, they attempt to deceive God (78³⁶). Hypocrisy is a thing God cannot tolerate (Job 22¹⁶), and which He is continually exposing (5¹³). Idolatry is a sort of hypocrisy from which a man can keep by being perfect, *i.e.* whole-hearted, with the Lord his God (Dt 18¹³). The classical passage for a hypocrisy that practises the ceremonies and knows none of the duties of religion is Is 1, but nearly every prophet has occasion to speak against the evil. All false prophecy was hypocrisy—the saying

of the thing that pleased, and not of the thing that was true. The person most deceived was the hypocrite himself (Is 33¹⁴·¹⁵, Job 27⁸), but he was also a danger to the society in which he lived (Job 15³⁴). To all the true prophets he was the supreme danger to the State.

The Talmud lays the same stress upon hypocrisy, as the opposite of faith in God. 'There are four who cannot appear before God—the scoffer, the hypocrite, the liar, and the slanderer'—all vices of falsehood. 'God hates him who speaks one way with the mouth and another way with the heart.' 'A society which has hypocrites for its members is abominable and falls into exile.'

Hypocrisy was plainly no new vice in our Lord's time, but an ancient heritage into which the Pharisees entered. How, then, are we to account for the sudden prominence to which it is raised? No vice is held up to such unenviable notoriety in the Synoptics, no other combated with the same direct denunciation, while in John τὸ ψεῦδος is a conception only a little wider than ὑπόκρισις, and has the same condemnation. First of all, just because it is a sin of deception, it is mercilessly exposed, as if our Lord would give a practical demonstration that there is nothing hidden that shall not be made known. A sin which glories in misleading an opponent by smooth flatteries (Mt 22¹⁶), which goes about in long robes and seeks to be reverenced by public salutations, which takes its honour for granted and cloaks oppressive avarice with long prayers (Mk 12³⁸⁻⁴⁰), which cleanses the outside of the cup and platter while leaving them full of extortion and wickedness, which makes men hidden tombs, fair without and foul within (Lk 11⁴⁴), is met, as no other sin can be, by exposure.

Then the sin which lives by corrupting the conscience has cut itself off from the usual appeal of holiness and love by which our Lord seeks to win men from other sins. It substitutes traditional practices for living duties (Mt 15⁶); it uses minutiæ of ecclesiastical rule as a substitute for judgment and the love of God (Lk 11⁴²); it cannot receive the truth, because its eye is on man and not on God (Jn 5⁴⁴); it makes inquiries not in order to believe the truth, but in order to refute it (9²⁷·²⁸); and it is chained to its error by a confident assurance that it alone is right (9⁴¹). The only way of appeal left is direct denunciation.

Further, sin is, in a pre-eminent degree, the foe of all truth. The hypocrite is in a special sense the child of the father of lies (Jn 8⁴⁴). Hypocrisy is not a mere sin of impulse, but is the opposite of everything by which we may lay hold of truth and be delivered. As surely as faith reaches out towards truth, hypocrisy struggles against it. Not being able to live with truth, it can defend itself only by persecution. 'Ye seek to kill me because my word hath not free course in you' (8³⁷). The same spirit made their fathers kill the prophets as a natural consequence of rejecting their message, and it is only another hypocrisy which makes the descendants repudiate their fathers' deeds while cherishing their fathers' spirit. The justification for the terrible assault on the Pharisees in Mt 23, is that, sitting in Moses' seat, they show a spirit with which truth cannot dwell. The deep shadow is always in the bright sunlight, and the deep corruption is always in the place of opportunity. The Pharisees neither enter the Kingdom nor suffer others to enter. They are abundantly zealous, but in a bad cause. They pervert truth, debase it, fight against it. No appeal can touch them, and in the end their house is left to them desolate.

Then the evil of hypocrisy is more than negative. It does not stop with pretending to need signs, while it pays no attention to the evidence it has, and would be convinced by no evidence (Mt 16³·⁴). Hypocrisy is also an active leaven—a dangerous assimilative principle—against the corruption of which no warning can be too ample. It is more

---

* For a description of these see Dembitz, *Jewish Services*, etc., p. 323 f.

† Cf. also the citation of v.²²ᶠ· of the same Psalm in Mt 21⁴².

than the shadow of truth, the absence of faith. It definitely works to debase the whole man, just as faith works to regenerate him. In addition to refusing to enter in, it takes away the key of knowledge (Lk 11[52]). Against everything connected with the Kingdom of Heaven it is actively hostile.

In the Sermon on the Mount (Mt 6[1ff.]) hypocrisy is set over against the Kingdom of Heaven as its opposite and its negation. In the realm of hypocrisy appearances meet every requirement ; in the Kingdom of Heaven all is judged by the heart. Christ says, the issues of life are out of the heart alone ; hypocrisy says, they are mainly out of ceremonies. Of the whole standard of the Kingdom of Heaven hypocrisy is the daily practical denial—its broad result being the external righteousness of the Scribes and Pharisees, without exceeding which we shall in no wise enter into the Kingdom of Heaven. So alien is the whole unreal pretence of religion, that there is a good secrecy at the other extreme from it. Deliberate care must be taken that one's righteousness be not done in the public eye. Not only is no trumpet to be sounded before us in the street ; our praise is not even to find an echo in our own heart. Not only may prayer never be used for show ; true prayer is with ourselves and our Father in secret alone. Not only may we not fast with a sad countenance ; the head is to be anointed and the face washed as on a day of festival. Hypocrisy is the opposite of that singleness of eye which fills the whole body with light ; it turns the light that is in a man to darkness. It attempts to serve two masters while serving none. It sees motes in its brother's eye while ignoring beams in its own. It is in sheep's clothing without, and a ravening wolf within. It is the shadow of the light, the enemy of the truth. It is most of all hostile to the Kingdom of Heaven, just because it is the fullest light and the highest truth. Nor is that all. Hypocrisy, as the opposite and negation of the Kingdom of Heaven, is as ready to corrupt Christianity as it was to corrupt Judaism. Even Christ's name it is capable of turning into a substitute, not a synonym, for the will of the Father.

From all other vices men are delivered by the life of faith. For this reason our Lord never directly assails vices of impulse. The publican and the harlot He treated as the lost sheep He had come to seek. For them He set wide the door of the Kingdom. But the door, He knew, could never be made so narrow that the hypocrites would not at least appear to enter. The new hypocrisy will be to come in Christ's name, saying, 'I am he' (Mk 13[6]). Under that guise it will hide itself so dexterously as almost to deceive the elect ; and it will use its opportunity, as hypocrisy has always done, to strangle truth by persecution. Just because hypocrisy is thus an enemy in the camp poisoning the wells, our Lord deals with it openly, directly, negatively, by the method of denunciation, as with no other form of evil.

The supreme evil of hypocrisy, as the negation of the life of faith, appears still more clearly in what our Lord says about the eternal sin. In John unbelief is spoken of as the abiding sin. 'For if ye believe not that I am he, ye shall die in your sins' (8[24]). Yet, from the context, it is apparent that the abiding evil is not the act of unbelief, but the absence of all love of the truth, of which the unbelief is the evidence. Christ came that the thoughts of many hearts should be revealed (Lk 2[35]), and those who had cherished evil were as conspicuously displayed as those who had cherished good. The publican and the harlot who had secretly thirsted after righteousness came to be shown to have faith, though all appear-

ances were against them ; the Pharisee who had used his religious position to cover worldly ends was shown to want it, though all appearances were in his favour. While the publican came to the light, the Pharisee hated the truth and sought to repress it, and to do so sought to destroy Him who spoke the truth. Thus he showed himself of his father the devil, who from the beginning was a murderer as well as the father of lies. Here in John then we have juggling with truth, hypocrisies before God and the world and one's own soul, set forth as the cardinal sin which relates us as certainly to the spirit of evil as faith does to the spirit of good, and which works in hate, as surely as goodness works in love, and which leaves men to die in their sins, because it is hostile to all that could lead to penitence and pardon.

All this is in essential agreement with what the Synoptics say of blasphemy against the Holy Ghost (Mt 12[22-37], Mk 3[20-30], Lk 12[1-12]). The Pharisees had reached a turning-point in their opposition. They believed in miracles, they looked for signs. The miracle could no longer be questioned, but they could call it a sign of Beelzebub. Though unable to deny either the power or the beneficence of Christ's work, being resolved not to accept the practical consequences of belief, they call light darkness and good evil. The actual sin against the Holy Ghost, therefore, is possible only when face to face with the highest thing in religion and its clearest evidence, but the danger of coming to that point is present in all hypocrisy. Hypocrisy is ever an overweening pride, denying to other men the right to truth, and to God His power to see ; and the eternal sin is only the finished result of what is always present in it. This connexion is most evident in the narrative of Luke, which begins with a warning against the leaven of the Pharisees which is hypocrisy. Nothing, it is said, can be covered, and the hypocrite has power to do only one great evil—to associate others in his spiritual destruction. Faith in the God who cares even for the sparrow can alone preserve from this fatal vice, a clear indication that hypocrisy is the negation of faith, or at least that faith is the negation of hypocrisy. The natural outcome of faith is confession before men, and the accompaniment of that is Divine protection until the day of the final award. On the other hand, to follow hypocrisy is to go the road that leads to the blasphemy against the Holy Ghost—the state of mind that has so juggled with good and evil that good has no power over it, the sin which no change of dispensation, or perhaps nothing in eternity any more than in time, can modify. This may be most apparent in Luke, but in Mark and Matthew also the Holy Spirit is the Spirit of truth, and the sin which is eternal is not an act of oversight or passion, but an irremediable state which could be reached only by a finished, proud, and tyrannical hypocrisy. See UNPARDONABLE SIN.

In every form of evil, as Martensen rightly affirms, hypocrisy is present in a partial form. All sin is egoistic, yet every man depends on society—the sinner not least. Under some pretence of goodness alone can the egoist enter society. The seducer must swear false oaths, the deceiver feign friendship, the tyrant profess care for the commonweal. A finished life of wickedness would be one great lie, which would be the only ultimate form of atheism. And just because a God of truth cannot for ever be denied, hypocrisy comes to be more and more a spirit of hatred and opposition to truth. Thus it is, more even than *habit*, the cumulative element in devotion to evil. It is not only the greatest practical denial of God, it is also the greatest practical alienation from God. To be reconciled to God is primarily to be restored to truth. Wherefore hypocrisy may be taken not only as the negation of all Christ taught of God, but also as the negation of all Christ did to reconcile men to the Father, the negation of His work as a Saviour as well as of His work as a Revealer.

Throughout all the Christian centuries, wherever there has been a lively sense of the reality of Christianity, there has also been a lively sense of this shadow following the sun. The classical example of lying to the Holy Ghost found its occasion in the first flush of the Church's faith and love (Ac 5). The first great division of parties arose through the same vice, and arose almost with the Church's beginnings. The extreme bitterness of the Judaistic party was nourished by that external view of religion which could regard a ceremony as essential, and hatred as if it were godliness. Even Barnabas was almost carried away by their hypocrisy (Gal 2^{13}), showing how the vice seeks to deceive, if possible, the elect ; while their attempts to suppress Paul were limited only by their power and never by their scruples—showing that it is a vice which always persecutes as well as perverts. All the errors which cause men to fall away from the faith are, already in the NT, ascribed to the hypocrisy of men that speak lies (1 Ti 4^2). Regarding this root of error in moral falsehood, and not in mere intellectual mistake, much might be said, but it must suffice to mention what Augustine says of Manichæism. Long his difficulties seemed to him intellectual perplexity about the origin of evil. When, however, he saw that wickedness was no substance, but a perversity of the will, he discovered the true root of the error.

'They preferred to think Thy substance did suffer ill, than that their own did commit it' (*Conf.* vii. 4).

That, as our Lord predicted, hypocrisy has continued to work under the New Dispensation as under the Old, may be seen from the state of things in the Eastern Church as pictured by Eustathius, in the Western as drawn by Dante and Chaucer, and in later times as reflected in a literature too abundant and familiar to require to be named.

LITERATURE.—Hamburger, *RE*, 1884, art. 'Heuchelei,' vol. i. p. 515 ; Cremer, *Bibl.-Theol. Wörterbuch*^{3}, p. 527 ; L. Lemme, *Die Sünde wider den Heiligen Geist*, 1883, and art. ' Heuchelei' in *PRE*^{3} ; J. M. Schulhof, *The Law of Forgiveness as presented in the NT*, 1901, pp. 43–48 ; Martensen, *Christian Ethics*, 1st Div. 'Individual Ethics,' 1881 [Eng. tr.], pp. 114–118 ; *Eustathii Opuscula*, ed. by Tafel ; *Exiles of Eternity*, by J. S. Carroll, 1903 ; Mozley, *Univ. Serm.* Serm. ii. ; Seeley, *Ecce Homo*, 116 ff., 253 ff.   JOHN OMAN.

HYSSOP (אֵזוֹב, ὕσσωπος) is twice mentioned in the NT (Jn 19^{29}, He 9^{19}). We know that it was used for sprinkling (Ex 12^{22}), and that it grew on walls (1 K 4^{33}). By Tristram it is identified with the caper-plant (*Capparis spinosa*) ; and this view is very generally accepted. It is open, however, to the serious objection that the caper is not well adapted for use as a sprinkler. Many still favour the opinion of Maimonides that it was the ṣa tar of the Arabs. This plant, which 'springs out of the walls, those of the garden especially' (Thomson, *LB* p. 112), is a species of Satureia. In Morocco, the name ṣa'tar is given to marjoram (*Origanum*). Carruthers (*Bible Educator*, iv. 226) suggests that hyssop was a name applied to various plants of the genera Thymus, Origanus, and others nearly allied in form and habit. The balance of probability is in favour of this view.   HUGH DUNCAN.

I

IDEAL.—The word 'ideal' does not occur in EV of the NT, nor is there any term in the Gr. text which exactly corresponds to the general notion of the English word.* The subject of the highest good or moral ideal, however, is one that is constantly present in the teaching of Christ, and is wonderfully illuminated by His own character and life and influence in human history. An ideal may be defined as a mental conception taken as a standard of absolute perfection. The word is used with regard to various kinds of excellence. There are intellectual and æsthetic ideals as well as those which are properly to be described as moral. But it is to the realm of moral worth that the notion of the ideal is peculiarly appropriated, and it is with the moral ideal alone that we are at present concerned.

In the history of Ethics, discussion has always centred in this question of the ideal, the *summum bonum*, the 'chief end of man.' Aristotle begins his *Nicom. Ethics* (I. i. 1) by describing the good as that at which all aim, and he goes on to say (I. ii. 2) : ' And, like archers, shall we not be more likely to attain what is right if we have a mark (σκοπός) ?' This σκοπός, the target or goal of human endeavour, is just the ideal. Aristotle takes the human σκοπός to be happiness, which he defines as 'the active exercise of man's living powers, according to their highest virtue, in a life affording full room

for their development' (I. vii. 15). It is a striking coincidence that the only occasion on which the word σκοπός is found in the NT is in the saying of St. Paul, ' I press toward the mark (σκοπός) for the prize of the high calling of God in Christ Jesus' (Ph 3^{14}). The Christian ideal of St. Paul was very different from the pagan one of the Stagirite. But the Apostle, no less than the philosopher, recognized the necessity of an ideal, and its power to shape the whole conduct of life.

It would be interesting to discriminate the various ideals or ultimate moral aims which, in the progress of the world's history, have been advocated by the representatives of the leading religious or philosophical systems. These ideals, however, do not directly concern us here. It will be sufficient in the course of the article to refer to them in passing, when they serve, by way of contrast, to bring more clearly into view the distinctive features of the Christian ideal. Applying ourselves to a special consideration of the latter, we shall deal with it (1) as it is set forth in the teaching of Christ, (2) as it is embodied historically in His own person, (3) as it is made real in human experience through His constraining power.

i. THE IDEAL AS SET FORTH IN THE TEACHING OF CHRIST.—One great fault of all non-Christian, or pre-Christian, or imperfectly Christian ideals is their narrowness or one-sidedness : they ignore whole departments of the kingdom of moral worth, and do justice to one part of human nature at the expense of the rest. In contrast with this, the Christian ideal, as we meet it in Christ's teaching, strikes us by its comprehensiveness and perfect

---

* The translators of the *Twentieth Cent. NT* render Eph 4^{13b} 'until we reach the perfection of manhood and that degree of development of which the ideal to be found in the Christ is the standard.' But this is a paraphrase rather than a translation of the original.

balance. A consideration of the following particulars may serve to bring out this rounded symmetry of the Christian conception of the highest good.

1. *It is an ideal of blessedness attained through perfection of character.*—Pope invokes happiness as 'our being's end and aim . . . for which we bear to live, or dare to die' (*Epistle*, iv. 1 ff.). And Herbert Spencer, in his *Data of Ethics* (p. 46), affirms that 'no school can avoid taking for the ultimate moral aim a desirable state of feeling, called by whatever name—gratification, enjoyment, happiness.' Newman Smyth criticises Spencer's statement as a confusion between the form and the substance of the moral intuition (*Christian Ethics*, p. 86 f.). But if the conception of happiness is enlarged so as to include the appropriate Christian contents, if blessedness (wh. see), in other words, is taken as the NT synonym of happiness, little fault can be found with the language of either the poet or the philosopher. The Westminster Divines were very far from being mere Eudæmonists, but in the first question of the *Shorter Catechism* they define 'man's chief end' as consisting in this—'to glorify God, and to enjoy Him for ever.' If happiness is not the very substance of the Christian ideal, it is none the less, as Dr. Smyth himself says, 'its natural result and its necessary form' (*op. cit.* p. 119). By beginning His Sermon on the Mount with His great series of Beatitudes (Mt 5[1ff.], cf. Lk 6[20ff.]), Jesus places the ideal of blessedness in the forefront of His teaching. So far, therefore, we may say He is on the side of the Eudæmonists as against all who have sought to set up a hard abstract ideal of duty as the moral aim. But note at once the content of Christ's ideal, and it will be seen at once how far removed it is from ordinary Utilitarianism. The blessedness of which He speaks belongs to a character distinguished by meekness, mercy, purity of heart, and similar spiritual qualities (Mt 5[3-12])—a character which finds its standard not in human perfection merely, but in nothing less than the perfection of the Heavenly Father Himself (v. [48]). In its form of blessedness, happiness is to be desired by Christ's disciples; but only through perfection of character can this happiness come. No man will find delight in that vision of God which Jesus promises (v.[8]), no man will 'enjoy God,' unless a resemblance to the perfection of the 'Father which is in heaven' has been growing up within his heart.

2. *It is an ideal of natural as well as spiritual good.*—Even when it is fully recognized that blessedness belongs to the Christian ideal, this blessedness is sometimes conceived of too narrowly. Not only is the spiritual set above the natural, as it ought to be, but the natural is ignored or despised and then refused its proper rights. This is the inherent fault of all ascetic ideals, whether pagan or Christian. Now Christ certainly exalted the spiritual above the natural. He made blessedness depend, as we have seen, upon inward qualities. Moreover, He taught that His disciples must be ready to make any sacrifice—to cut off hand or foot, or to pluck out the right eye—for the sake of entering into life (Mt 5[29. 30] 18[8. 9] ‖ Mk 9[43ff.]), and that a man was nothing profited if he gained the whole world and lost his own soul (Mt 16[26]). But the blessedness He holds before His followers is by no means a purely spiritual thing. The Beatitude of the meek is that they shall inherit the earth (Mt 5[5]). The petition for daily bread is enshrined in the very heart of the Lord's Prayer (6[10. 11]). And when Jesus comes to speak more particularly of food and raiment, the very things which are most fundamental to our natural life in this world, while He forbids anxiety regarding them, the reason given is not that they are unworthy of a Christian's thought and care, but that 'all these things shall

be added' unto those who seek first the Kingdom of God and His righteousness (6[25-33]).

3. *It is an ideal of social well-being attained through individual worth.*—That the ideal of Jesus was a social one it is impossible to doubt. Deeply as He impressed upon His hearers the unspeakable value of the individual life or soul (Mt 10[30f.] 16[26], Lk 15[4ff.] etc.), He never said anything to justify a religious individualism which concerns itself only with personal salvation. The very fact that 'the kingdom of God' (wh. see) is the phrase by which He most frequently refers to His moral ideal, shows that it was an ideal of social good. In this He was coming, so far, into touch with the prevalent Jewish conceptions of His time; for it was a social, not an individual good for which Israel looked. But whereas the Jews conceived of this social good on purely national lines, Jesus enlarged the bounds of the blessed society so as to make room in it for men of all nations. 'They shall come,' He said, 'from the east and west, and from the north and south, and shall sit down in the kingdom of God' (Lk 13[29], Mt 8[11]). Yet while His moral ideal takes not only a social form, but one of universal breadth, He always taught that it must be through making its power felt in the individual heart that the Kingdom of God would be realized upon earth. This was where His teaching differed so greatly from the contemporary Jewish expectation, and from the thoughts of many in modern times who have been seized by the greatness of Christ's social purposes without grasping the individuality and spirituality of His methods. The Kingdom of God in popular Jewish hope was an exaltation of Israel brought about by deeds like those of Judas Maccabæus. The Kingdom of God in the vision of many earnest dreamers and workers of our own days is the result of a social revolution brought about by political activity. According to Christ's teaching, the Kingdom of God can come only through the regeneration of individual hearts. 'The kingdom of God cometh not with observation,' He said, '. . . for, behold, the kingdom of God is within you' (Lk 17[20. 21]). That this, and not the marginal readings 'among you' [AV], 'in the midst of you' [RV], is the proper rendering, seems to be confirmed by the second of the 'New Sayings of Jesus' discovered by Grenfell and Hunt (cf. p. 770[b] below). And He summed up the whole matter when He set a little child in the midst and said, 'Except ye turn and become as little children, ye shall in no wise enter into the kingdom of heaven' (Mt 18[3] ‖ ; cf. Jn 3[3]).

4. *The ideal is at once a reality in the present and a promise for the future.*—There are those who look for their *summum bonum* in the present hour, and whose philosophy of life was long ago summed up in the saying, 'Let us eat and drink; for to-morrow we die' (1 Co 15[32], cf. Is 22[13]). There are others again who have, not unjustly, incurred the charge of 'other-worldliness,' because they have despised God's present mercies and neglected their own urgent duties, while fixing their thoughts upon the hope of future blessings and rewards. But in the teaching of Jesus the ideal good is at once realized in the present and consummated in the future. On the one hand, He proclaims that the Kingdom of God is not merely coming, but already come (Mt 12[28], cf. Mk 1[15]); it is set up here and now within the individual heart (Lk 17[21]); its Beatitudes are present realities (Mt 5[3-11]; note not only the recurring 'Blessed are they, ye,' etc., but vv. [3. 10] 'theirs is [ἐστὶν] the kingdom of heaven'). On the other hand, He constantly taught His disciples to look to the future for the complete and perfect form of the Kingdom and its blessedness. His use of the phrase 'kingdom of heaven' as an alternative expression for 'kingdom of God' (and the evidence of the First Gospel points to the former as being the more habitual term on His lips, though it refers primarily, no doubt, to the spirituality of the Kingdom as coming from above and having its true home in the supersensible world, is surely not without its future reference. This Kingdom, which is heavenly in its origin and aims, is and must be heavenly also in its end. Christ's whole eschatological teaching, and especially everything that gathers round the thought of the Parousia, when all that is evil shall be cast out of the Kingdom (Mt 13[41f. 49f.] 22[13] 25[30]), and the faithful servant shall enter into the joy of his Lord (25[21. 23]), points to the same conclusion. And if we are not to reject the evidence of the Fourth Gospel, with respect even to its testimony as to the leading ideas in our Lord's teaching, the fact that in it 'eternal life' takes the central place which in the Synoptics is held by 'the kingdom of God' points once more to a future reference in Christ's ideal. For though futurity and everlastingness are not the fundamental conceptions in the category of eternal life, they are certainly necessary for the completeness of that life which Jesus promised to His disciples as their highest good.

ii. THE IDEAL AS EMBODIED HISTORICALLY IN THE PERSON OF CHRIST.—So far, we have been thinking of the Christian ideal as set forth in our Lord's teaching. But now we must notice the fact that Jesus not only expounded an ideal, but realized it historically in His own person. It is here that the Christian ideal differs specifically from the loftiest ideals of the philosophers and moralists; it is an ideal which was once made actual in a human life. Jesus not only taught, but *was*. He brought down the ideal out of the region of dreams, and hopes, and words into the world of positive realities. In His own history He showed how blessedness might be attained through moral perfection; how the life of highest spirituality might prove to be the life of widest social beneficence; how it was possible, while enjoying all natural blessings as gifts from the heavenly Father's hand, to place obedience to the Father's will above everything else; how the narrow path of present duty might be illuminated by the splendours of the eternal world, while the assurance of something yet more glorious than now appeared might thrill the heart of the faithful wayfarer.

1. *Jesus Christ is the Ideal Man.*—His character is not merely perfect in some aspects, but perfect in all—so rounded and complete as to become an ideal for the woman as well as for the man, for the Greek as well as for the Jew, for the modern as well as for the ancient world. He is not merely free from flaws, but full of vital and creative forces; His perfection is that not of a marble image, but of a living spirit. This is the verdict of history, the verdict of all who simply read and ponder the records of His life. Even those who do not believe Him to be more than man join without demur in the universal chorus of acclamation. They acknowledge that Jesus stands alone in His moral grandeur as the incarnation of personal human worth, and that the historical Christ is the ideal of humanity.

2. *As an Ideal, Christ becomes an Example* (wh. see).—For whatever it may be in other spheres, in the moral world, at all events, ideals, from the nature of the case, are not merely standards of an abstract perfection, but goals after which we must strive,—targets, to use Aristotle's figure, at which we aim and shoot those arrows of the soul which are the living energies of our moral being. Jesus never set Himself before men's eyes as a beautiful but impossible ideal. He claimed to be an example (Mt 11[29] 20[26-28] || Lk 22[27], Jn 13[15. 34] 15[12]). As such He was taken by His first disciples (1 P 2[21]). And

St. Paul, who saw the perfect and ideal man in the measure of the stature of the fulness of Christ (Eph 4[13]), never doubted that the perfection of manhood which was found in Christ was something to be personally striven after. That was the σκοπός of the long race. On that the Christian must fix his eyes, towards that he must constantly press, if he would attain to the prize of the high calling of God in Christ Jesus (Ph 3[13f.]). See also PERFECTION (OF JESUS).

iii. THE REALIZATION OF THE IDEAL THROUGH THE CONSTRAINING POWER OF CHRIST.—We have seen that Christ in His teaching holds up an ideal, that He embodies this ideal historically in His own person, and sets it before us as an example which we must strive to follow. But to weak and sinful men and women this presentation by word and deed of a perfect moral ideal would be little else than a mockery, if Christ did nothing more than offer us an outward standard after which we were to strive. It is in a far deeper sense than this that He is the Christian ideal. In his famous theory of Ideas, Plato conceived of the Ideal Good as an archetypal essence which becomes an efficient cause, imparting to individuals a share of its own being, as the sun imparts 'vitality, growth, and nutriment' to the creatures on which its rays fall (*Rep.* vi. 509). And it is in this vital and archetypal manner that Jesus becomes the moral ideal of the human race. He gives what He commands, and so has a right to command what He wills. We have constant illustrations in the Gospels of this constraining power of the Ideal Goodness as it is presented to men and women in the person of Christ. The sinful woman in the house of Simon the Pharisee (Lk 7[36-50]), Zacchæus, the grasping publican of Jericho (19[1-10]), Matthew, leaving the receipt of custom to become an Apostle (Mt 9[9] ||), may serve as examples. The author of the Fourth Gospel sums up the whole matter for us when he says: 'As many as received him, to them gave he power to become the sons of God' (Jn 1[12]). And to St. Paul, who brooded much over this mystery of Christ as it had been revealed to him in a profound personal experience, the secret of spiritual life and growth presented itself as an unfolding of the Christ-nature implanted by the agency of the Holy Spirit in the believer's soul. 'Christ in you,' he says, 'the hope of glory' (Col 1[27]); and again, 'I live; and yet no longer I, but Christ liveth in me' (Gal 2[20]). And when in another place he describes believers as 'foreordained to be conformed to the image of his Son, that he might be the firstborn among many brethren' (Ro 8[29]), he suggests a figure which helps us to understand how Christ the ideal is not merely an outward type but an inward archetype. The younger brothers of a house are conformed to the likeness of the firstborn not so much by personal imitation as by the operation of secret and vital forces which spring from the very fact of their birth as members of a particular family, and which lie far deeper than the workings of the individual will. And so it is as between Christ and His people. 'For both he that sanctifieth,' says another NT writer, 'and they that are sanctified are all of one: *for which cause he is not ashamed to call them brethren*' (He 2[11]).

LITERATURE.—Besides the particular references given in the art., mention may be made of Newman Smyth, *Chr. Ethics*, pt. i. chs. i.–vi.; Martensen, *Chr. Ethics*, i. 147–343; Green, *Prolegomena*, bks. iii.–iv.; Shairp, essay on 'The Moral Motive Power' in *Studies in Poetry and Philosophy*.

J. C. LAMBERT.

IDEAS (LEADING).—The leading ideas of our Lord may be divided into two classes, Moral and Religious. This is not an artificial division: it corresponds to two stages in His public teaching which are very clearly marked in the Gospels. The earlier stage is prevailingly ethical, and finds its most characteristic utterance in the Sermon on the Mount. The later is, in comparison, distinctively religious, and deals with the relation of God to man. Yet we are not to separate the two elements, for they inter-penetrate one another. They are inter-dependent, and form together an organic whole.

i. MORAL IDEAS.
    1. The Kingdom.
    2. The Pure Heart.
    3. The Infinite Value of the human Soul.
    4. The Law of Love.
    5. The Universality of Love.
    6. The Great Example.
    7. Self-renunciation.
ii. RELIGIOUS IDEAS.
    1. The Fatherhood of God.
    2. The Son.
    3. Faith.
    4. The Coming of the Kingdom.
    5. The Paraclete.

i. MORAL IDEAS.—**1. The Kingdom.**—This idea must be placed first on account of its position in our Lord's teaching. 'Repent ye; for the kingdom of heaven is at hand,' was the message of the Baptist and the first public utterance of Jesus (Mt 4[17], Mk 1[15]). From the beginning the idea of the Kingdom may be traced throughout the Gospels, and everywhere it will be found to indicate the supreme blessing which comes to man from God. In Mt. it is usually termed the Kingdom of Heaven. Elsewhere the phrase Kingdom of God is uniformly employed.

The idea of a Kingdom of God does not appear first in the NT. In the OT, the sovereignty of God is a fundamental conception. Jehovah was regarded as King over His chosen people. Israel was a theocracy. Always, whether under judges, kings, prophets, or priests, the human leaders were looked upon as representatives or agents of Jehovah, the true King. The natural tendency was to regard this as the exclusive privilege of the chosen people. Nevertheless, in the OT is to be found the vision of a great world-wide Kingdom of God. In the Book of Daniel especially we find how, to the prophetic mind, there was opened the glorious prospect of a universal Divinely-established sovereignty. Dn 2[44] and 7[13. 14] are the clearest. The latter of these two passages is especially important, because from it, most probably, our Lord adopted the title 'Son of Man' by which He usually described Himself. It was therefore a passage much in His thoughts, and it is scarcely possible to believe that, as He proclaimed 'the kingdom,' He had not clearly in mind the words 'His dominion is an everlasting dominion, which shall not pass away, and his kingdom that which shall not be destroyed.'

It is plain that among the Jews in our Lord's time there was a widely spread expectation of some great person who was to be leader of the chosen people, and through whom that people were to be established as a great world-power. The Jews of that age were looking for a kingdom. And to them came John the Baptist and then Jesus of Nazareth, proclaiming the coming of a Kingdom. As our Lord's ministry and teaching developed, He made it quite clear that the Kingdom He proclaimed was very different from the kingdom of popular expectations. Yet the two conceptions cannot be wholly unrelated. Our Lord would not have used the popular language if His meaning had no relation to the ideas of the popular mind.

This consideration is important, because of late years there have been efforts to show that the Kingdom, as conceived by our Lord, had no social content whatever; that, by the Kingdom of God, He meant a spiritual illumination in the heart of the individual (Harnack, *What is Christianity?* Lect. iii. He holds that our Lord shared the eschatological ideas of the Jews of His time, but that the essence of His teaching is that the Kingdom is the rule of God in the heart of the individual). This view rests mainly on a single text, Lk 17[21] 'The kingdom of God is within you,' and is supported by the consideration that the primary meaning of the word which is translated 'kingdom,' βασιλεία, is 'rule' or 'dominion.'

The sentence (Lk 17[21]) 'The kingdom of God is within you' (ἐντὸς ὑμῶν) is capable of being translated, 'The kingdom of God is in the midst of you,' and this rendering suits the context better than any other, for the saying was addressed to the Pharisees. But it must be granted that the 'New Sayings of Jesus,' recently discovered by Grenfell and Hunt, have thrown fresh light on this question. The words occur in the Second Saying, and in a connexion which precludes the translation 'in the midst of you.' 'The kingdom of heaven is within you, and whoever shall know himself shall find it.' This is, at least, a very early witness to the sense attached to the words in primitive times.

But we cannot found our interpretation of our Lord's teaching on a single passage, especially when we are dealing with a leading conception which was always more or less in His mind. Some of the parables which were intended to throw light on the nature of the Kingdom, e.g. the Mustard Seed, the Tares and the Wheat, the Draw-net, seem explicable only on the understanding that the Kingdom was regarded as a visible community. The only way of combining the two elements which seems to be truly satisfactory, is to regard the Kingdom as the rule of God, whether in the individual or in the community. It is then the *Summum Bonum*, the Absolute Good in which both the individual and the community find their realization. It is thus both a present blessing and an ideal to guide all future development. It is realized here and now whenever man stands in a right relation to God and to his fellows. Its perfect realization belongs to the great future: it is the end to which all creation and all history are tending. The Kingdom as a conception is thus at once moral, social, religious, and eschatological. All these aspects are distinctly visible in our Lord's teaching, and all are harmonized by the view which has just been adopted. We are now concerned with the moral aspect of this great idea.

The Sermon on the Mount, as we have it in Mt., must be taken as the fullest statement of our Lord's moral teaching. Whether it be accepted as a single discourse, or be regarded as a collection of sayings, the unity which pervades it and its perfect harmony with the rest of our Lord's utterances are manifest. Its place in the gospel of the Kingdom, as proclaimed by our Lord, is clearly defined. The Sermon is a statement of the *Law of the Kingdom*.

This is evident from Mt 5[17-20], in which a general principle concerning the ethical relation of the gospel to the Mosaic Law is laid down, and from vv.[21-48], in which several important illustrations of the practical application of this new principle are given. Mt 6[1-33] and 7[21-27] agree with this view of the nature of the Sermon. In the former passage, the whole subject of rewards and motives is dealt with, and the end which is to govern our religious life (vv.[1-18]) and our secular life (vv.[19-34]) is declared to be, not the praise of men (vv.[2. 5. 16]), not earthly rewards (vv.[19. 25]), but God's Kingdom and God's righteousness (v.[33]). This end includes all necessary goods (v.[33]). It therefore lifts the soul above anxiety (v.[34]). It is an eternal treasure (v.[20]). It must be pursued with whole-hearted devotion (v.[24]). In the latter passage (7[21-27]) the importance of doing the will of God, as contrasted with mere profession, is insisted on as a condition of entering into the Kingdom.

It is thus perfectly clear that the whole Sermon on the Mount regards human life from the point of view of the Kingdom, and lays down the moral principles which belong to that point of view. It may therefore be fitly described as the Law of the Kingdom.

At the same time, it is necessary to observe that the Sermon on the Mount is not a new Decalogue. Our Lord did not issue commandments like those of the old Law. On the contrary, He laid down principles, and taught His disciples how to apply them.

This is an important distinction. Commandments which classify actions, forbidding some and enjoining others, however necessary they may be for purposes of moral education, have always this defect, that they are sure, sooner or later, to come into conflict, and so give rise to perplexity and to casuistry. Principles, on the other hand, are truly universal, and therefore cannot conflict. There are parts of our Lord's moral teaching which have seemed perplexing to many, e.g. Mt 5[34. 39. 40. 41. 42]. But the perplexity vanishes when it is seen that these sayings contain not laws but examples, illustrations of the application of a principle (see v.[20]), which has been already laid down. As examples or illustrations, they must be considered in relation to circumstances, which inevitably limit every particular case.

Among moral principles laid down by our Lord, the Kingdom stands first and supreme. The passage which presents this truth most clearly has been already noticed. It occupies the whole of Mt 6, which fills the central space in the moral teaching of Jesus as we have it in St. Matthew's report of the Sermon. Here we have the motives of conduct dealt with. First, the prevailing wrong motives are pointed out : the praise of men which too often destroys the reality of the religious life (vv.[2. 5. 16. 18]) ; greed of gain, the laying up of earthly treasures (vv.[19-24]), which makes the 'single eye' impossible ; anxiety for the necessaries of life, food and clothing, things that will surely be given us if we live a true life (vv.[25-34]).

It is characteristic of our Lord that it is in connexion with this last subject that He reveals the true motive. He contemplates the life of the average man toiling for his daily bread and filled with anxiety lest that bread should fail. There is an extraordinary tenderness and sympathy in our Lord's language here. The passage is perhaps the most beautiful in all His teaching. And the lesson reaches the highest heights of spiritual vision. 'Seek first the kingdom of God and His righteousness, and all these things (the necessaries of life) shall be added unto you' (v.[33]).

It is singularly impressive that this teaching should be given in connexion with those common everyday duties at which the vast majority of human beings must spend their lives. To the great mass of the world's toilers our Lord says : Be not anxious about your bodily needs. In doing your daily work, seek the Highest, and the necessaries of life will not fail. And what is that Highest ? It is the Kingdom and righteousness of God. The answer presents both sides of the truth, the external and the internal, the objective aim and the quality of character which corresponds to it.

When we come to consider more carefully what is the nature of this highest objective aim which is termed the Kingdom, we are met by the difficulty that our Lord nowhere gives a formal definition of it. His manner of referring to it is rather an indication that He desired in the first instance to convince His hearers of its existence, and for the rest to approach it in many different ways, so as to exhibit different aspects of a thing too great for its nature to be made evident by any one statement. But certain characteristics emerge with sufficient clearness. What these characteristics are will be seen as we examine the other leading ideas of our Lord's moral teaching. See also art. KINGDOM OF GOD.

2. The Pure Heart.—'Blessed are the pure in heart,' said the Lord ; 'for they shall see God.' The idea expressed in this Beatitude is one of the most fundamental in the interpretation of the Law in terms of the gospel. Our Lord insisted upon the inwardness of all true goodness. An external morality had no value in His eyes. This teaching was not altogether new. Great prophets and psalmists had seen it (Jer 31[33], Ps 51[10]). Greek philosophers had taught the priority of *being* to *doing*. But Jesus gave to the world as a whole what had hitherto been the possession of select souls. By showing the power of this principle to deepen the received code, He was able to alter the popular conception of the moral ideal. He taught that within the Kingdom the only goodness which would be recognized would be goodness of heart. All the examples which He gave to show that the righteousness of the Kingdom must exceed the

righteousness of the scribes and Pharisees, display the operation of this principle. See Mt 5[22. 28. 34-37. 44-48], Lk 6[45]. Our Lord did not abolish the old Law. He fulfilled it (Mt 5[17]). He penetrated to the inner meaning and deeper truth which underlay it. And what is true of the good is true also of the evil : its nature is spiritual, it proceeds from the heart, and is not merely concerned with the outward action (Mt 15[18-20], Mk 7[21], Lk 6[45], see also Mt 12[34. 35]).

There is a tendency to regard this purity of heart as concerned only with the negation of one class of fleshly appetites. Our Lord did indeed apply the principle most impressively with that reference (Mt 5[27ff.]). But, as all the illustrations show, the principle is one of universal application, and concerns the very essence of all goodness. It is the principle which the philosopher Kant stated in the terms : 'Nothing can possibly be conceived in the world, or even out of it, which can be called *good* without qualification, except a *Good Will*.' It is the doctrine which modern Ethics expresses when it declares that the goodness or badness of conduct depends upon the motive. In the last resort, the 'single eye' and the 'pure heart' are the same. They both express the inward determination to do the good just because it is the good, and for no other reason. The former regards this moral attitude from the point of view of the end which is aimed at, the second contemplates the disposition of the heart, the moral condition of soul, out of which the good inevitably springs.

3. The Infinite Value of the human Soul.—This idea is very frequent in the teaching of our Lord. Explicitly or implicitly, it occurs everywhere. See Mt 6[26ff.] 10[29ff. 40. 42] 12[11. 12] 16[26] 18[5ff.], Mk 8[36. 37] 9[37. 42], Lk 9[25. 48] 10[29ff.] 12[7ff. 24. 28] 14[5] 15[4ff. 8ff. 11ff.] 19[10], Jn 3[16] 4[7ff.] 10[11ff.]. All passages which tell of the love of God for the individual soul or of the sacrifice by which the salvation of the soul was effected, are witnesses to the same truth. Every person, no matter how poor, wretched, sinful or degraded, is of infinite value when compared with any mere thing. The gospel was preached to the poor. The Christ received the publicans and sinners who came to Him. None were too miserable or too lowly for His compassion. The Great Father in heaven is ever watching over His human children. The very hairs of their heads are all numbered. Better to die a miserable death than be the cause of injury to one of His little ones. God so cares for even the most sinful among His children, that He is compared to the shepherd seeking the lost sheep, to the woman searching for her lost piece of money. There is joy in heaven over one sinner that repenteth. God is like a loving father who rejoices over the returning prodigal. As we have it in St. John, 'God so loved the world, that he gave his only-begotten Son' (3[16]).

Apart from the religious value of these teachings, their ethical importance is incalculable. They conveyed to mankind one of the greatest gifts which even Christianity had to bestow : the belief that each human soul is of absolute value, above all price or estimation. It is the doctrine which philosophical Ethics expresses, when it declares that every person is to be regarded as an end in himself, never as a means only. This is the doctrine which underlies the mission of the Church to go and make disciples of all the nations (Mt 28[19]). It is the principle which has overthrown tyrannies, abolished slavery, and justified all our modern enthusiasms for liberty and for the welfare of humanity.

This doctrine, combined with that of the Fatherhood of God, affords the true proof of individual immortality. Our Lord's teaching is quite clear on this subject. There must be a future life for men because God calls Himself their God. 'He is not the God of the dead, but of the living' (Mt 22[31ff.], Mk 12[27], Lk 20[37ff.]). That is, God cares for men, they are precious in His sight, therefore He cannot permit them to perish. The great Father will never forsake His children.

4. The Law of Love.—Christianity teaches us to think of love as the nature of God and as the highest law of human life. We owe this noble teaching to our Lord Himself. By precept and example He taught His followers to think of the

Almighty as their Father in heaven. While never ignoring the justice, the righteousness of God, He made His hearers realize the supremacy of the Divine Love. Out of this great love of God should flow a human love of the same nature, a beneficent love (Mt 5$^{44. 45}$, Lk 6$^{27-36}$), a love which embraces even those who are bitterly hostile. Not only so, but our Lord teaches that the Law of Love is the supreme law of conduct. It includes all the commandments (Mt 22$^{37-39}$, Mk 12$^{30ff.}$). In strict accordance with this teaching is the Law of Service. He is greatest who serves best (Mt 20$^{25ff.}$, Mk 10$^{43ff.}$, Lk 22$^{24-27}$, Jn 13$^{5-17}$). Loving service is the true test of the life (Mt 25$^{35ff.}$).

This teaching shows clearly that our Lord designed to give to men a blessing which should be, not merely an illumination for the soul of the individual, but a social bond. He set free a principle which would bless all in the blessing of each. That principle may be described as the family principle exalted to heaven for the good of all the earth. If God is 'Our Father,' then all we 'are brethren' (Mt 23^8). The kingdom of God is thus the kingdom of Love in which each is blessed in the blessing of all. And this is the true *Summum Bonum*, the ideal end, which finds its partial realization in every instance of genuine goodness in the individual life as well as in the life of the community, and which is the highest principle of all moral and social progress. Its perfect realization is the great hope of the future, the coming of the Kingdom in glory.

5. The Universality of Love.—The Law of Love in its relation to our duty to one another is expressed by the command, 'Thou shalt love thy neighbour as thyself.' But the question arises, What is the scope of this love? Or, as it was put to our Lord Himself, 'Who is my neighbour?' (Lk 10^{29}). The answer to this question is contained in the passage already referred to (Mt 5$^{43-48}$). Our love is to be, like God's, a blessing for all who need it, the evil as well as the good, the just as well as the unjust, our enemies as well as our friends. In the parable of the Good Samaritan (Lk 10$^{30ff.}$), the same answer is given in a way which makes its meaning even more distinct. To enforce the lesson, our Lord selected as the hero of His parable a man belonging to a race which was hated and despised by the Jews. There was an exquisite wisdom in this choice. Why not have made a Jew assist a Samaritan, or even a Gentile, in order to illustrate the principle? But our Lord wished to teach by an example appealing rather to the *humanity* than to the national feelings of His hearer. Had the act of mercy been shown by a Jew to a Samaritan it might have seemed condescension, a work of supererogation. Shown by a Samaritan to a Jew, the true character of the goodness it reveals becomes, from the Jewish point of view, far more evident. We are taught that love should be universal in its nature. It should break down the barriers erected by race, or privilege, or religion.

It is impossible to exaggerate the importance of this teaching. Ancient civilizations were for the most part founded on slavery or on the subjection of races or classes. Underlying the whole Jewish system was the idea of a privileged people. Our Lord broke through the most inveterate of prejudices, and taught the universal obligation to love and to bless. He laid the foundation of liberty and of philanthropy.

6. The Great Example.—In Mt 6^{33}, the ideal is set before us in two ways, as an objective aim and as a type of character: 'Seek ye first his kingdom and his righteousness.' The righteousness of God is the standard. There is, and must be, a correspondence between the outward and the inward, between the Kingdom of God as a universe of souls bound together by the great love of their Father in Heaven and their love one to another, and the moral condition of each individual soul. When the latter side is considered, we ask, What is its quality? what is its standard? The answer is—the character of God. This is implied in the

very name 'Father' (Mt 5^{45}). The teaching is, 'Be sons of your Father,' be like unto God. Even more explicit is the statement in Mt 5^{48} 'Ye therefore shall be perfect as your heavenly Father is perfect.' This standard may seem too high. It may seem unreal to say to ordinary men and women, 'Be perfect as God.' But all realization of good character in human creatures is, so far as it goes, an imitation of God, a reproduction of the Divine. Goodness is always a following of God, though it be a very long way off. What we have here is the absolute standard, the highest possible ideal of character. Our Lord will set nothing lower before us. But the ideal is brought near to us in a way which is characteristic of Christianity. Jesus Christ Himself is the incarnation of the ideal. See Mt 11^{29} 20$^{25-28}$, Mk 10$^{42-45}$, Lk 6^{40} 22^{27}, Jn 13$^{15. 34. 35}$ 15^{12}. In these passages our Lord holds Himself up as an example. And there can be no doubt that the influence of His character has been as potent a moral force as His words. He elevated humanity by being what He was. It is very hard to realize how vast was the change effected by the teaching and example of Christ. The conception of the ideal of character was altered. To see this truth we have but to compare Aristotle's picture of the 'great-souled man' with our Lord. Noble and virtuous with the splendid but imperfect nobility and virtue of pagan Greece, the great-souled man is proud, self-satisfied and pompous. His very 'greatness,' as conceived by Aristotle, makes him a poor creature when placed beside Jesus of Nazareth. Above all, our Lord's example shows us the principle of love at work in human life.

7. Self-renunciation.—When dealing with the lofty principles of absolute morality, our Lord's teaching is characterized by the most extraordinary sweetness. With joyous confidence His thought lingers on the sunny heights of truth. But when He comes to speak of the struggle through which the soul must pass in its upward progress, His manner changes. There is an awful force in the language and imagery with which He teaches the necessity of self-sacrifice. From this we learn His attitude towards sin. See Mt 5$^{29. 30}$ 18$^{6-9}$, Mk 9$^{42-48}$ 10$^{37-39}$. Such passages show that His tenderness towards the repentant sinner involved no condoning of sin. Our Lord received sinners, but He never regarded their sins with complaisance. The following passages are important: Mt 10$^{37ff.}$ 16$^{24-27}$, Mk 8$^{34ff.}$, Lk 9$^{23ff.}$ 14$^{25-35}$ 17^{33}, Jn 12^{25}, also Mt 7$^{13. 14}$, Lk 13$^{24ff.}$. In these passages the necessity of self-renunciation is expressed in terms of the most vivid intensity. Yet the denial of self is nowhere represented as an end in itself. It is a means, or rather the inevitable means. It is the way, not the goal. Yet it is a way which cannot be avoided if the goal is to be reached.

Our Lord clearly sets before us the reward of goodness and the punishment which awaits unrepented sin. The subject is a puzzling one, because of the ambiguities of language. But our thoughts will be set free from confusion if we consider our Lord's teaching as it stands, apart from certain popular misconceptions. It will be found that, in His teaching, the Kingdom is itself the reward. To gain this is to gain all, to lose it is to lose all. Sometimes it is described as 'the joy of thy Lord' (Mt 25^{21}), sometimes plainly as 'the kingdom' (v.^{34}), sometimes as 'eternal life' (v.^{46}). But all alike are ways of describing that one glorious end which is the *Summum Bonum*, the true and final good, that end in which God Himself with all His children shall have one undivided blessedness. To live for this reward is to live for the good itself. The goodness or badness of working for rewards depends altogether on the nature of the rewards which are sought. To work for selfish ends is always wrong, to seek as a reward that great end which is the supreme and universal blessing is always right; it is indeed the essence of all goodness.

ii. RELIGIOUS IDEAS.—We have considered the leading ethical ideas of our Lord's teaching. But, as must now be quite apparent, it is impossible to separate the ethical element from the religious. Though our Lord Himself advanced from a prevailingly ethical stage of instruction to a stage which was more distinctively religious, yet in His thought the two are united. Indeed, the religious side of the truth is the more fundamental. It deals with the underlying principles. For example, when speaking of the ordinary work of human life, and giving the great rule, 'Seek first the kingdom,' He led His hearers on to the thought of the Fatherhood of God as the reason why they should renounce all anxiety and live for the higher ends (Mt 6[26. 30. 32]).

1. The Fatherhood of God.—This idea stands first among those which belong to the distinctively religious side of our Lord's teaching. He gave it a fundamental position, and conveyed it in every possible way to the minds of His hearers. By word, by manner, by the manifestation of His own spiritual experience, and, above all, by being what He was, and at the same time declaring Himself to be a revelation of the mind and will of God (see Mt 11[27] 25[31ff.], Jn 5[19ff.] 8[12ff.] 10[5ff.] 12[44ff.] 14–16), our Lord taught men to think of God as 'the Father,' and to attribute to Him all the benignity and bountifulness of the fatherly character. Here it is impossible to separate the teaching from the life of Christ. It is through the Christ Himself that man learns to know God as the Father. Jesus was intensely conscious of God's presence and relation to Himself. He saw into the heart of God with a clearness of vision unparalleled in human experience. He speaks of God out of a perfect knowledge, and whenever a human soul is able truly to hear, belief follows. The revelation of God made by Him carries conviction with it. It is so great a thing that it cannot but be true. When once man has grasped it, no other account of God can be accepted.

The idea of the Fatherhood of God occurs in the OT (Dt 1[31] 8[5] 32[6], Ps 103[13]; see also Is 63[16] 64[8], Jer 3[4. 19], Hos 11[1] etc.). It was not unknown to pagan thought; see Ac 17[28]. But, as taught by our Lord, the Fatherhood of God became a new thing. Fatherhood is not, in all states of society, suggestive of watchful, loving affection. It has sometimes connoted a very harsh rule. The fulness of meaning and the spiritual value which now belong to the idea as connected with our relation to God, are very largely derived from the teaching and influence of our Lord.

In the teaching of our Lord the Fatherhood of God is presented in three ways: (1) Jesus speaks of God as 'My Father.' This name was very dear to Jesus. It sprang from His consciousness of relationship to God. Clearly, it bore a special meaning. He was Son of God in a unique sense. This truth is emphasized by the manner in which the expression 'My Father' is frequently used (Mt 10[32. 33] 11[27], Lk 2[49] 22[29], Jn 5[17] 10[29. 30] 17[5] 20[17]; see also Mt 7[21] 16[17] 18[10. 19. 35] 20[23], Mk 8[38], Lk 24[49], Jn 5[20-45] 6[32ff.] 8[19ff.] 14–16). These passages fully carry out the idea expressed in the announcements at His baptism and on the Mount of Transfiguration (Mk 1[11] and 9[7]). (2) Our Lord taught His disciples to think of themselves as a family, with God above them as their Father. They were called into a specially close relationship to God, and became in that special sense His children. In the Sermon on the Mount, Jesus addresses His disciples, and continually speaks to them of God, calling Him 'your Father' (Mt 5[16. 45. 48] 6[1. 8. 14. 15. 32] 7[11]). 'Fear not,' He says, 'little flock; for it is your Father's good pleasure to give you the kingdom' (Lk 12[32]). In the Lord's Prayer the address 'Our Father' has reference to the disciples as the family of God. Perhaps we dare not limit the 'our,' but the prayer was given to the disciples for their own use, and the word was surely meant to have the effect of uniting them as a family under the headship of their Father in Heaven. (3) Our Lord's

teaching regards God as the Father of all men. Mt 6[45], Lk 6[35] imply this great extension of the Divine Fatherhood. But clearer still are the parables of the Lost Sheep, the Lost Piece of Silver, and the Prodigal Son (Lk 15). The parable of the Good Samaritan extends the sphere of love beyond the bounds of Judaism, and throws light on such passages as Mt 6[45] and Lk 6[35]. Its principle corresponds, in the human sphere, to that expressed by the words, 'God so loved the world' (Jn 3[16]).

Our Lord, then, teaches us to think of God as the Father, and at the same time as Sovereign over the greatest of all kingdoms. The characteristic attribute of this paternal Sovereignty is love. His love is so wide that it includes the unthankful and evil, those who have turned their backs upon their Father's house and renounced His authority. It is the source from which springs all that is described as *Salvation*. It explains the mission of the Christ (Jn 3[16]). It is the inner truth of the life of Him who came to seek and to save the lost. It is that Divine characteristic from which proceed 'joy in heaven over one sinner that repenteth' (Lk 15[7]). And when this love has won the sinner, it introduces him into a circle in which he is brought more immediately under the Divine Fatherhood. He becomes a member of the family, the Kingdom, that great order of things in which men feel and experience the love of the Great Father. Finally, there is that supreme degree of Divine Fatherhood which belongs to the relation between the Father and Him who is in a unique sense the Son. The life and death of Christ reveal the love of God to man because of this relation. God's love appears because He gave His only-begotten Son. See also art. FATHER.

2. The Son.—The second stage of our Lord's teaching is concerned mainly with Himself and His work for man. It is one of the great paradoxes of His personality, that while humility was one of His most marked characteristics, He yet preached Himself as none else ever dared to do. Sometimes the humility and the self-assertion occur side by side, expressed in a single utterance. 'Come unto me, all ye that labour and are heavy laden, and I will give you rest. Take my yoke upon you, and learn of me; for I am meek and lowly in heart: and ye shall find rest unto your souls' (Mt 11[28. 29]). The invitation and promise here constitute a great claim. Yet He adds, 'I am meek and lowly in heart'; and the story of His life proves the truth of the assertion. Furthermore, these words follow one of the greatest statements ever made of the dignity of our Lord's person, and the extent of His authority: 'All things have been delivered unto me of my Father: and no one knoweth the Son, save the Father; neither doth any know the Father, save the Son, and he to whomsoever the Son willeth to reveal him' (Mt 11[27]). This passage is but one out of many. Jesus continually asserted His right to the absolute devotion of the hearts of men. No sacrifice is too great to be made in His service. Even the dearest of human relationships must be counted as nothing in comparison with Him. He claims, as His right, the utmost allegiance (Mt 10[37-39] 16[24-26] 19[28. 29] 25[31ff.], Mk 8[34-38] 9[37. 41] 10[29] 13[13] 14[7-9], Lk 9[23ff. 48. 57ff.] 10[22] 12[8ff.] 14[26ff.] 18[29], and throughout St. John's Gospel. See, especially, Jn 5[17ff.] 8[12ff.] 10[30] 14[6ff.]).

The only adequate explanation of these facts is that which the NT supplies, and which the Christian Church has always held: Jesus is Divine; He is the Incarnate Word of God (Jn 1[14]). No other doctrine can justify the claim which He makes, and explain the life, work, and teaching by which that claim is sustained. Our Lord did not declare Himself Divine, nor did He even make open proclamation of His Messiahship. That was not His method. He avoided anything which would have inflamed the minds of the multitude (Mk 1[37. 38. 43. 44] 3[12], Lk 4[42. 43] 5[16] 8[56], Jn 6[15]). Further, He knew that faith springs into being not from names and titles, but from the recognition by the soul of that which is alone worthy to be the object of faith. Therefore He chose to reveal Himself gradually in His daily intercourse with His followers, and so lead them to discover the great truth for themselves (Mt 16[13-20]). That our Lord deliberately followed this method is shown by the terms which He used when referring to Himself. For example, He habitually called Himself the **Son of Man.** The name presented a problem to all who heard it. It suggested a reference to Dn 7[13], but was not so definitely Messianic as to constitute a claim. It evoked the question, 'Who is this Son of Man?' (Jn 12[34]). The name occurs about eighty times in the Gospels, and always as used by our Lord of Himself. It is so characteristic of His own point of view that it is not used by others. It clearly implies His humiliation, yet it is employed by Him pointedly in those passages in which His glory is described. See Mt 13[41] 19[28] 25[31ff.], Lk 21[36], Jn 5[27] 6[62] etc.

The title Son of Man expresses the *humanity* of our Lord. It is His own testimony to His perfect Brotherhood with men. It marks His sympathy with human infirmity, and is used impressively in connexion with His mission of salvation (*e.g.* Mt 20[28], Lk 19[10]). It presents Him as the *Ideal Man.* This has been questioned as not in accordance with the thought of the time, but the OT had its ideal figures. Abraham, Moses, David, Elijah came to be regarded as typical representatives of whole peoples or classes. In the latter Isaiah this mode of thought reaches its most perfect development. The ideal Israel is depicted as the 'Servant of Jehovah,' and, as the prophet proceeds, the conception grows, until in Is 53 there rises into view the wonderful form of the Suffering Servant who is contrasted with, yet is one with, the people of God. There is therefore no anachronism in supposing that when our Lord styled Himself the Son of Man He intended to set Himself forth as the representative of the human race, the Ideal Man. See, further, art. SON OF MAN.

The title **Son of God** was not often used by Jesus Himself (see Mt 27[43], Jn 5[25] 9[35]), yet in many ways He implied His right to it. His constant and peculiar use of the expression 'My Father' (see above), and the frequent occurrence of the title 'Son of God,' as attributed to Him by others and not disclaimed by Himself, show what was His position in regard to this question (Mt 4[3] 8[29] 14[33] 27[40. 54], Mk 3[11], Lk 4[41] 22[70], Jn 1[34. 49] 3[18] 9[35] 11[27] etc.). This title was naturally seized upon by His disciples as the simplest way of expressing the mystery of His person. The essence of that mystery, as manifested in every instance in which He disclosed His inner mind, was the close relationship in which He stood to the Father (see Mt 11[27]). And so it was by means of this title that His *Divinity* was represented to the minds of His first followers. And for the practical purposes of the religious life, as distinguished from the definitions of theology, no mode of expression could have been so useful; the critical faculties were held in suspense while the needs of the soul were satisfied. See also art. SON OF GOD.

The two titles 'Son of God' and 'Son of Man' modify and explain one another. Taken together they constitute our Lord's own most characteristic way of expressing the nature of His person. It was in this way that He chose to teach men His humanity and His Divinity and the miracle of

their union. Thus the Incarnation is found to be implied in our Lord's attitude towards His own consciousness of Himself in relation to God and man. For a deeper insight into this profound subject we must turn to those passages in which that consciousness is most fully revealed: Mt 11[27] 25[31ff.], Mk 8[34ff.], Lk 10[21ff.], Jn 5[17ff.] 8[25-29] 10[30] 17[1-5] etc. With this is connected our Lord's consciousness of Himself as the bond of union among His disciples, uniting them to God and to one another: Jn 14[20] 15[1-11] 17[22. 23]. Also He presents Himself as the means of communication between God and man: Jn 10[7] 14[6]. These truths are aspects of His Incarnation.

Our Lord represented the work of His life as a work of *salvation*: Lk 19[9. 10]; cf. Mt 15[24], Lk 15[1-10]. This idea, though prominent in the Gospels from the first (see Mt 1[21], Lk 2[11], Jn 1[29]), and implied in all our Lord's language about Himself and His relation to men, yet remains undeveloped in His teaching until the end of His ministry. As the Gospels proceed, however, and His death approaches, sudden gleams of light are thrown upon the deeper meaning of salvation. In Jn 6[51ff.], the thought of Christ as the Bread of Life passes into that of the Paschal Lamb by whose death and blood-shedding the people of God are delivered. In Jn 10[11ff.], He is the Good Shepherd who lays down His life for the sheep. On the last journey to Jerusalem our Lord's mind was much occupied by the dreadful events which He knew were awaiting Him (Mk 10[33. 34], also Mt 20[17ff.], Lk 18[31-33]). Before this He had told His disciples of the facts (Mt 16[21], Mk 8[31] 9[31], Lk 9[22]), but now He declares something of their meaning and purpose. The occasion of the declaration was the ambitious petition of the sons of Zebedee. In reply to the two brothers, our Lord promises, in veiled language, participation in His sufferings; and to the whole body of the disciples He gives this teaching: 'Whosoever would become great among you shall be your minister; and whosoever would be first among you, shall be servant of all. For verily the Son of Man came not to be ministered unto, but to minister, and to give His life a ransom for many.' It is the first clear statement in our Lord's own language of the purpose of His death. With this passage must be connected Jn 12[23-27], in which, contemplating the terror of His cross, He lays down the law of sacrifice. But clearer still is the declaration which He made at the Last Supper. There are four accounts in the NT (Mt 26[26-28], Mk 14[22-24], Lk 22[19. 20], 1 Co 11[23-25]). No two of these correspond exactly. But all agree that our Lord connected the rite with the conception of His death as a sacrifice on behalf of men. He gave His body over to death, His blood to be shed 'for many unto the remission of sins.' And, as St. John tells us (chs. 14–16), that very night our Lord addressed His disciples at length on His love and His relation to the Father and to them, and said, 'Greater love hath no man than this, that a man lay down his life for his friends.'

In the teaching of our Lord, then, the atonement is the redemption of men from sin by the giving of His life. It is the remission of sins through His death and the shedding of His blood. It is the work of love. It is the corn of wheat falling into the ground that it may perish and, through perishing, bear much fruit. The impressiveness of this teaching is greatly increased when it is taken in connexion with certain events and fragmentary utterances which give the testimony of our Lord's own inner consciousness to the fact that, in His Passion and Death, He engaged in a great conflict with evil, a work given Him by His Father, a work which He was bound to accomplish. The following passages are the most important: Mt 16[22ff.],

Lk 22^{53}, Jn 12^{27} 14^{30}, Mt 26$^{38ff.}$, Mk 14$^{34ff.}$, Lk 22$^{41ff.}$, Mt 27^{46}, Mk 15^{34}. Most impressive of all is the Agony in the garden. It supplies the key to all the rest.

3. Faith.—But though the fuller explanation of the purpose of our Lord's life and death took place only towards the end, He had from the beginning made a demand which implied all that afterwards became explicit. He insisted on a faith which found its supreme object in Himself. The greatness of His personal claim has been already pointed out (see list of passages given above). We have been able to discern something of the meaning of this claim in relation to the doctrine of our Lord's person. But it is necessary also to observe that there is involved a very clear doctrine of the nature of faith. Jesus taught the supreme necessity of faith in God, the great Father. He also taught the necessity of faith in Himself. By the demands which He made, the promises He gave, the blessings He bestowed, He made it clear that He sought for a faith which should take the form of an absolute trust directed towards Himself. See Mt 8$^{2.\ 3.\ 10}$ 9$^{2.\ 22.\ 29}$ 15^{28}, Mk 1$^{40.\ 41}$ 2^5 4^{40} 5$^{34.\ 36}$ 6$^5.$ 6 7^{29} 8$^{12.\ 17-21}$ 10^{52} 14$^{6-9}$, Lk 5$^{12.\ 13.\ 20}$ 7$^{9.\ 50}$ 8$^{25.\ 48.\ 50}$ 10^{42} 17^{19} 18^{42} 19$^{39.\ 40}$. In the Gospel of St. John, faith of this kind is presented everywhere as the spiritual condition which enables man to become receptive of the highest blessing. See Jn 1$^{12.\ 50}$ 2$^{11.\ 23}$ 3$^{16.\ 18.\ 36}$ 4$^{41.\ 42.\ 50}$ 5^{24} 6$^{29.\ 35.\ 40}$ 8^{12} 9$^{35-38}$ 10$^{9.\ 16.\ 27}$ 11$^{25.\ 26}$ 12$^{46.\ 48}$ 14$^{9.\ 12}$ etc. In these passages and throughout the Fourth Gospel, Christ Himself, in His relation to God the Father on the one hand, and to those who believe on the other, sums up all spiritual blessing. He is the source of Eternal Life, the giver of the living water, the Bread of Life, the Light of the World, the Good Shepherd, the Resurrection and the Life, the Way, the Truth, and the Life, etc. All these images imply some attitude or act of reception on the part of those who benefit. Therefore we read of the New Birth, the drinking of the Living Water, the eating of the Bread of Life, the following of the Light, etc. And whatever else may be involved, there is, in all these, the teaching that faith on the part of the human recipient corresponds to the gifts which are bestowed in Christ. See, further, art. FAITH.

Our Lord's first teaching as to preparation for the Kingdom was a call to repentance (Mk 1^{15}). To this we must now add faith, as the subjective means by which the Kingdom is realized, a faith which, when developed, becomes faith in Jesus Christ.

4. The Coming of the Kingdom.—Our Lord came to found a kingdom, a great spiritual and social order of things, based on the principle of love, under the Fatherhood of God, and creating a Brotherhood among men. Its members were to enter into this new life through repentance and faith, and in it to realize a righteousness of heart and life far exceeding the righteousness of the scribes and Pharisees. The possibility of such a thing in a world like this would have been incredible, but for the way in which our Lord presented and manifested Himself to men. In Him resided the power which would realize the Kingdom. By His death He overcame the forces which opposed the Kingdom, by His life He established it.

But though the Kingdom was a present fact from the moment that Christ brought human souls into a right relation to God, we are taught by Him to think of the Kingdom as yet to come. In the Lord's Prayer we have the petition, 'Thy kingdom come.' And there are many passages which show that these words refer to a great future realization: Mt 8^{11} 13^{41} 25^{31}, Mk 8^{38} 14^{25}, Lk 21^{31} 22^{16}, Ac 1$^{6.\ 7}$ etc. But clearest of all are the parables of growth: the Tares, the Mustard Seed, the Leaven, the Draw-net, the Seed Growing in Secret. These parables deal with the development of the Kingdom in history and its relation to the world at large. They connect the conception of the Kingdom as a spiritual fact here and now with that conception which is distinctively eschatological and regards the Kingdom as a perfected state of things in the future. It is plain that our Lord never lost sight of the great final realization of the Ideal. He constantly looked at the present in the light of the future, and taught His followers to live and work with the great end in view (Lk 12$^{37ff.}$).

5. The Paraclete.—In the Fourth Gospel we find recorded a very distinct and detailed promise of a special gift by which the disciples of our Lord were to be fitted to do their Master's work after His departure. It occurs in the solemn address of the night before the Passion (Jn 14–16). 'I will pray the Father, and he shall give you another Comforter (Paraclete), that he may be with you for ever; even the Spirit of truth' (14$^{16.\ 17}$). Again and again in this great discourse our Lord returns to this promise, and dwells upon various aspects of the Spirit's work (14$^{18.\ 26}$ 15^{26} 16$^{7-15}$). The presence of the Spirit involves the presence of Christ Himself. The Spirit is to teach the Apostles, to guide them into all truth, to bear witness of Christ. He has also a mission to the world (16^8). It is good for the disciples that our Lord should leave them, because the Spirit's coming is dependent on His going. It is plain that the meaning is that the Spirit was to be given as a source of illumination and spiritual power for the people of Christ during the development of the Kingdom in the world. Thus the Spirit carries on the work of Christ.

In the Synoptic Gospels there is nothing as clear in regard to the office of the Holy Spirit. Yet there are passages which, though much less definite, agree perfectly with the teaching in Jn 14–16. Thus the connexion of the Spirit's work with the future of the Church is implied in Mt 10^{20}, Lk 12^{12}. See also Lk 4^{18}, Mt 12$^{28ff.}$, Mk 3^{29}, Lk 11^{13}, Mt 28^{19}. See, further, artt. HOLY SPIRIT and PARACLETE.

In Ac 1^4 we find an important corroboration by St. Luke of the promise recorded by St. John: Christ charges His disciples 'not to depart from Jerusalem, but to wait for the promise of the Father, which, said he, ye heard from me.' In Lk 24^{49} the promise is mentioned but not given.

The work of the Holy Ghost is therefore connected with the extension and development of the Kingdom. He is the inner regenerating power in the individual and the community. He is the Master of the movements of thought, guiding into all truth. The movements of thought are governed by ruling ideas,—ideas which present certain great ends as supremely desirable, and so become, in the true sense, ideals. Chief among all such is the idea of the Kingdom. It is the great ideal which is to be realized in and through the love of the Father, by the submission of human hearts to the Son, and under the superintending influence of the Holy Ghost. Thus the aims of men are to be subordinated to the one supreme end, that at last the Kingdom may come in its fulness.

LITERATURE.—It is not easy to supply a list of books dealing with this subject, as all commentaries on the Gospels and every 'Life of Christ' may be consulted. The most useful perhaps are: Weiss, *Life of Christ*; Edersheim, *Life and Times of Jesus the Messiah*; Dalman, *The Words of Jesus*. The last mentioned is most important. Wendt's *Teaching of Jesus* is not so useful as it should be. Sanday's art. 'Jesus Christ' in Hastings' *DB* is important. Orr's art. 'Kingdom of God,' *ib.*, should be consulted. The writer's *Ruling Ideas of our Lord* deals with the subject. Among works of a more general kind may be mentioned Seeley's *Ecce Homo*, Harnack's *What is Christianity?* (*Das Wesen des Christentums*), Liddon's *Divinity of our Lord*, and Latham's *Pastor Pastorum*. Archbishop Alexander's *Leading Ideas of the Gospels* deals with the ideas which guided the minds of the Evangelists. It will, however, be found suggestive on the subject of this article.

CHARLES F. D'ARCY.

IDUMÆA (NT Ἰδουμαία, which is also used in the LXX for the Heb. *Ĕdōm*).—This land is mentioned once only in the NT (Mk 3⁸), but is also notable as the native land of Herod and his family. The Edom of the OT lay between the Dead Sea and the Gulf of Aḳabah. In the early part of the Jewish exile many of the Edomites overran the south of Judæa, and when the Nabatæans, at some time during the Persian period, conquered their own land, many more joined the earlier settlers in South Judæa, and that district became known as Idumæa. Thus Idumæa at the time of Christ was 'practically the Southern Shephelah with the Negeb' (G. A. Smith, *HGHL* p. 239), *i.e.* roughly, all south of a line from Beth-sur to Gaza. Judas Maccabæus fought against the Idumæans with much success (1 Mac 5³) in 164. Fifty-five years later, John Hyrcanus conquered the country, and compelled the people to be circumcised (Jos. *Ant.* XIII. ix. 1 ; *BJ* I. ii. 6). By the law of Dt 23⁷·⁸ they thus became full Jews in the third generation, though Herod himself was sometimes reproached as a 'half-Jew' (Jos. *Ant.* XIV. xv. 2). Although the Idumæans were 'sons of Esau,' their interests from this time were entirely merged with those of the Jews, and their country was reckoned to Judæa, Idumæa being counted one of the eleven toparchies of Judæa in Roman times (Jos. *BJ* III. iii. 5).

G. W. THATCHER.

IGNORANCE.—1. *Religious ignorance* is uniformly regarded in the Bible as a moral and spiritual, and not merely as an intellectual, defect. Religious ignorance is always culpable, because the true light 'lighteth *every man*' (Jn 1⁹). The light of reason and of conscience shines even in the darkness of heathenism, and the heathen are plainly in fault if they 'apprehend' it not (v.⁵). To put the matter in another way, the truths of Natural Religion carry their own evidence with them, and those who worship the creature instead of the Creator, or who deny that there is a God, or who think that there is no essential difference between virtue and vice, wilfully blind themselves to the truth (cf. Ro 1¹⁹·²⁰, Ac 14¹⁷). Yet the culpability of the heathen, great as it is, is less than that of those who have received the light of revelation (Mt 10¹⁵ 12⁴¹). Our Lord specially blames the Samaritans because, having received the Law, they nevertheless remained in ignorance of its Author (Jn 4²² RV), and neglected to worship Him in the place which He had chosen. But far more culpable than the half-heathen Samaritans were the Jews, who had behind them a long religious ancestry of patriarchs and prophets (Ro 9⁵), who inherited the promises, and to whom were committed the oracles of God (3² 9⁴). The chosen race, wilfully blinding themselves to the true meaning of the Scriptures (Jn 5⁴⁵) and to the signs of the times (Mt 16³), especially the testimony of the Baptist (Jn 3²⁶·³²) and the words and works of Jesus (Mt 11²⁰, Jn 10³⁸ 14¹¹ 15²⁴), were punished by having the truth hidden from them in parables (Mt 13¹³), and by having their spiritual understanding darkened (Mt 13¹⁵, 2 Co 3¹⁴). Of the Jews the most culpable were the leaders—*the Sadducees*, because they were ignorant of the resurrection and the future life, truths inculcated by Moses himself (Mt 22²⁹) ; and *the Pharisees and scribes*, those blind leaders of the blind, who led their unwary followers into a pit (15¹⁴). The case of the Pharisees was particularly hopeless, because, being ignorant, they thought themselves wise : 'If ye were blind [and acknowledged it], ye would have no sin ; but now ye say, We see : your sin remaineth' (Jn 9⁴¹).

Ignorance of Jesus is treated in the Gospels as equivalent to ignorance of God : 'Ye know neither me nor my Father ; if ye knew me, ye would know my Father also' (8¹⁹) ; 'No man cometh to the Father but by me. If ye had known me, ye would have known my Father also' (14⁷). If men do not come to a knowledge of Christ in this world, Christ will profess Himself ignorant of them in the next, and this will exclude them from the joys of heaven (Mt 25¹² 7²³). Yet the obligation to know Christ in this world applies only to those to whom the gospel has been actually preached (Mk 16¹⁵·¹⁶).

The reason why ignorance of Christ is regarded as a sin is that the truth as it is in Jesus is spiritually discerned (1 Co 2¹⁴). Lovers of truth, whose lives are virtuous and holy, perceive intuitively that the teaching of Jesus comes from God : 'Every one that doeth ill hateth the light, and cometh not to the light. . . . But he that doeth the truth cometh to the light,' etc. (Jn 3²⁰).

Among the 'Seven Words' spoken by Jesus from the Cross there is one which bears upon this sin of ignorance : 'Father, forgive them ; for they know not what they do' (Lk 23³⁴). In saying this He renewed that condemnation which He had often passed upon religious ignorance, for He implied that those who slew Him had need of the Father's forgiveness—His own forgiveness the words themselves express. But what the saying immediately proclaims is that the sin of ignorance is not beyond forgiveness, even when it has led to the darkest of crimes ; nay, that ignorance itself may be pleaded in extenuation (γάρ) before Him who knoweth all. (On the genuineness of the saying see Meyer, Alford, WH [Appendix]).

2. *Christ's ignorance, or limitation of knowledge.* —See CONSCIOUSNESS, KENOSIS.

LITERATURE.—Müller, *Chr. Doct. of Sin*, i. 209 ; Paget, *Stud. in Chr. Character*, p. 154.　　　　C. HARRIS.

ILLUSTRATIONS.—The use of illustrations is a noticeable mark of Jesus' teaching. He spoke in similes and metaphors and parables ; general rules He illustrated by examples or stated in concrete instances. His aim may be gathered from observing what uses the method actually served.

Stories and similes, concrete facts and instances, catch the ear of the people. He who would win their attention must trick out his message in pictorial garb ; he must weave in his truth with earthly fact and incident on the loom of fancy. Such teaching also remains in the memory. Truth pictured makes vivid appeal to the eye, and what the eye sees the memory retains, store for mind and heart to brood over. Jesus knew what was in man, and, desiring His message to be current coin for all, treasure of life for the simplest, He spoke in pictures and similitudes.

Illustrative examples serve also to make abstract truth more easily understood. A tale may enter in at lowly doors, bearing its load of truth and suggestion, when a truth stated abstractly would remain without. The concreteness of the poet, his vision of truth and symbol wedded together, of principle incarnated in fact, is closely akin to the ordinary man's ways of thinking and speaking. It is primary ; the abstractness of thought, the language of reflexion and analysis, is secondary. Jesus spake to the people after their own fashion.

These uses are obvious ; but they are only surface explanations ; they hardly touch the main purpose. When Jesus said (Mt 7⁹⁻¹¹), 'What man is there of you, who, if his son ask a loaf, will give him a stone? If ye then, being evil, know how to give good gifts unto your children, how much more shall your Father which is in heaven give good things to them that ask him?', He was aiming at something more than a clear and striking presentation of His truth. He was speaking from the heart to the heart, appealing to their feeling for what is highest and best, for what is reasonable to faith in goodness. His illustration was an argument addressed to the heart. 'In theology,' it is said to be an axiom that 'parables do not act as arguments' (Trench[15], p. 40 n.); but they may in the sphere of faith. The parable of the Unmerciful Servant (Mt 18[21ff.]) was an answer to Peter's question, 'How often shall we forgive?' It gives no direct answer to that question. It is spoken not to the discursive intelligence busy about problems, but straight to the indignations of the generous spirit. The better nature is enlisted against the man forgiven who was not made thereby tender-hearted and pitiful. When the lawyer put the searching question, 'But who is my neighbour?' (Lk 10[29]), Jesus told the story of the Good Samaritan. That parable also does not answer the question directly. It rather sets before the heart the beauty of kindness, and its power to break down barriers between men which the neighbourhoods of race and religion may leave standing. An idea, such as that all men are potentially brothers, is apt to be barren, without conviction, without power of intellectual or spiritual inspiration; a story such as this appeals to the human heart by which we live, that tenderness in us which leaps up in admiration of a good man's deed.

The aim of our Lord's teaching was not enlightenment, the bringing of clear ideas to the mind : it was to create faith and sustain it. And the form of His teaching—His parables, similes, metaphors, concrete instances—was a means to serve that end. 'After all,' says Newman (*Gram. of Assent*, 94), 'man is not a reasoning animal; he is a seeing, feeling, contemplating, acting animal.' It is by the heart that man believes unto salvation. There is the seat of the emotions, the joy we have in things, the intuitions of faith, the admirations which rule conduct and fashion character and shape our beliefs. The heart has its own reasons : visions of what is noble and fair, spells mighty there. And Jesus' illustrations are mostly pictures painted for that inward eye, music played that the ear of faith there may hear.

Many of Jesus' parables and pictures are more than mere illustrations ; they have in them the imagination's power of interpretation, the revealing vision of the poet. The parable of the Pharisee and the Publican (Lk 18[9ff.]) is more than an illustrative example, it is as Jülicher classes it, 'an example of the spiritual worth of humility before God.' It reveals, as in a transparency, the essential and hidden evil of a religious class. Our Lord's controversy with the Pharisees sums itself up in this revealing picture where the inner spirit and tendency of Pharisaism is brought to a luminous point. The parable has the force of a revelation, suddenly illumining a whole spiritual world. The same quality is in the illustrations of hypocrisy in Mt 6. These kindle a light in the spiritual imagination. Jesus takes the cases of almsgiving, prayer, fasting. These are not chosen as representing the three spiritual worlds, or spheres of duty—neighbour, God, self (Gore). That activity of the schematizing intellect is foreign to the whole method of Jesus. These were the fashionable religious virtues of the day, and therefore the chosen theatre of hypocrisy : self-seeking in religion leaves the humble sequestered virtues alone ; and Christ's pictures of ostentatious service there, have that direct illumination of the religious and ethical imagination which sets it free from the bondage of all externalism. Many of the parables have this quality, such as the Seed Growing in Secret, the Good Samaritan, the Unmerciful Servant, the Prodigal Son, the Two Debtors.

In the Synoptic Gospels there is an explanation of Jesus' use of parables which is a startling paradox.

It is that He spake to those without in parables, and that He did so to hide His meaning (Mt 13[10-15], Mk 4[11, 12], Lk 8[10]). It is easy to show that these words are not universally true, and that the aim of Jesus generally was to make Himself understood. So Jülicher (*Encyc. Bibl.* art. 'Parables') rejects this conception, placed on the lips of Jesus, as quite unhistorical. But we find that in all these Gospels this explanation occurs at one place, namely, between the parable of the Sower as spoken to those without and its interpretation to the disciples. And there the words have a real significance. The parable did not convey its meaning on the face of it. In the circumstances in which it was spoken, it was largely an utterance of the ironic spirit. Jesus was looking on the multitudes, drawn together by curiosity and various motives, caring so little, most of them, for the truths He had to tell them ; and He gave utterance to the pathetic thoughts of His spirit. He spoke this parable which tells the disappointments of a prophet and the hope that sustains him, the faith that some, his sheep, will know his voice. It is a simple enough parable ; and yet a veil does rest upon it for the careless unspiritual many who are listening, though not any veil of subtle allegory. Jesus is speaking of hopes and fears they comprehend not ; and, looking on them in their ignorance, it was natural that the words of old prophecy, with their kindred pathos and irony, should come to His lips, and He should speak about those who hearing understood not and whose hearts were darkened. That explanation has in it a hint of wider suggestiveness. Clearness and directness of speech are not the only sources of enlightenment. 'Art may tell a truth obliquely, do the thing shall breed the thought.' A truth stated objectively, indirectly, in the form of a story, may not compel the understanding ; careless ones may hear it as though they heard it not ; but it has greater effectiveness with those who receive it. That is exemplified in Jesus' latest parables. These are parables of judgment ; the shadow of the Cross rests on them. In them, by their very form, the meaning is veiled somewhat. The intention and the value of that stand out strongly in this contrast. When Stephen stood before the Sanhedrin, he said : 'Ye stiff-necked and uncircumcised in heart and ears, ye do always resist the Holy Ghost : as your fathers did, so do ye' . . . (Ac 7[51ff.]). There is no mistaking that accusation, or evading it ; but there is no persuasion there. No wonder the bold truth-speaker was stoned. Jesus says to His enemies, 'Hear another parable' ; and after the parable of the Two Sons, He tells the parable of the Householder and his Vineyard. It is the same charge, but spoken indirectly ; the reference is left to their own thoughts. That is a way of persuasion ; sympathy and love, which are the sources of persuasiveness, have woven a vesture for the truth that, through the imagination, it may reach the heart. See art. PARABLES.

One great, though indirect, value of Jesus' illustrations must not be missed, *i.e.* their witness to the man He was, their revealing of His mind and heart. (1) His figurative method of teaching reveals the fashion of His mind. Farrar speaks of 'that kind metaphorical method of expression which our Blessed Lord adopted.' The thought there is of a stress put upon His mind through a sympathetic accommodation to His simple unlearned hearers, as though He first had a thought, and then searched for some simple familiar picture to express it. But a man's customary method of speech shows his manner of thinking. Our Lord 'reasoned in figures, because He had an eye for nature.' Thought and image were born together in His seeing ; His was the poet's mind, with its concreteness and beauty, its outlook of the whole personality, its individual vision of things flushed with emotion ; and the pictures He set in the light give joy to the generations as they pass, because they first of all gave joy to Himself as they arose in His imagination. (2) The illustrations He uses reveal also the simplicity and fulness of His interest in life. It is amazing how the common life of His day passes in procession through His words ! The sower in the fields, the merchant on his travels, the fisherman on the beach looking over his catch, the labourers waiting to be hired in the market-place, the beggar at the rich man's gate and the dogs licking his sores, the clamorous woman with her wrongs at the unjust judge's door, the poor woman turning her house upside down for her lost coin, the play of the little children in the streets ; and even the faults and follies of men, the Pharisee with his broad phylacteries and wide fringes praying ostentatiously at the street corners, the craft of the dishonest steward, the son who says 'I go, sir,' and goes not, the anxious host begging for a loaf at midnight, and the grumbling friend in bed with his children—all speak of the interest with which Jesus looked on life. 'The learned eye is still the loving one.' He was no thinker whose mind ranged among ideas, no dreamer living in a world of ideals. His heart was amid the pell-mell of ordinary life, ordinary men, and ordinary duties ; His thoughts of religion found their sphere there.

(3) Jesus' outlook on Nature was full of joy. That is shown, not so much by the abundance of His references, as by the light in which He places them, the thoughts they brought to Him. He speaks of the hen gathering her chickens under her wings, symbol of His own protecting love for Jerusalem ; the sparrows, objects of God's care ; the grass in its beauty and the lilies outvying the splendour of Solomon, symbols of the Creator's joy in the work of His hands, seeing He thus clothes these casual flowers of a day with such loveliness and grace. He touches also the common things of our life with the sudden glory of poetry—the growing of the corn, symbol of the upspringing of life in human souls ; the care of parents in the home, symbol of the sleepless providence of the Heavenly Father over all His children ; servants waiting for their lord, symbol of our duty to an unseen Master. When Jesus looked on Nature and the universal order of man's life, something great shone through—a Divine and beautiful mystery. It all spake of the Father in heaven who made and loves it all ; it was all instinct with the presence of God's Spirit. The beauty of religion, its tenderness and grace, is there ; and the spiritual glory of life. That is an outlook of the fullest joy.

LITERATURE.—Books on the Parables, by Trench, Arnot, Dods, Bruce ; Steinmeyer, *Die Parabeln des Herrn* ; Jülicher, *Die Gleichnisreden Jesu* ; Fiebig, *Altjüdische Gleichnisse und die Gleichnisse Jesu* ; Wendt, *The Teaching of Jesus*, Eng. tr. vol. i. § 2 ; Plummer, art. 'Parables' in Hastings' *DB* ; Sanday, *Outlines of the Life of Christ*, or art. 'Jesus Christ' in *DB* ; the various Lives of Christ.　　　　　　　　　　RICHARD GLAISTER.

IMAGE.—This is the tr. in AV and RV of εἰκών. In the Gospels it occurs only in Mt 22²⁰ ‖ Mk 12¹⁶ ‖ Lk 20²⁴, where, in Christ's answer as to the legality of the Roman tribute, it refers to the likeness of the emperor Tiberius.

IMAGINATION.—

Imagination is the faculty by which we are able to reproduce mentally the images or 'copies' of past elements of sense-experience. This may be done in three ways : (1) passively, as when we reproduce our mental pictures in the form or order in which we experienced them as sensations ; or (2) actively, as when we combine the images of past sensations into fresh groups for purposes of our own, as in the telling of an imaginary story ; or (3) creatively, as when these images are used to symbolize abstract ideas, or to illustrate the teaching of moral and spiritual truth. There are great differences in the endow-

ments of individual men and women in these respects. Many have but a faint power of mentally reproducing past events and objects, and among those in whom the power is well developed, some are able best to reproduce visual images (artists), others auditory impressions (musicians), others the images of movement (those possessing the dramatic gift). The poetic or creative temperament is richly endowed with all these aptitudes, and makes a free use of its resources in the presentation of ideal scenes and events as a medium for inculcating its message.

Students of our Lord's personality will at once recognize that He possessed the creative temperament in its noblest development. He was psychically endowed with a rich and varied imagination, which was disciplined, like all His human gifts, to the finest pitch of efficiency, and consecrated to the highest uses. His discourses are crowded with bright and vivid pictures, symbolic of the great truths which He had come to reveal. They are expressed in language that is rich, musical, and full of verbal colour and rhythmic phrases. In the narrative portions and the parables there is also a striking dramatic element, which gives them wonderful life and movement.

1. *Characteristics of the imagination of Jesus.*— It is the last feature—the *dramatic*—which is the most prominent quality in the imagination of our Lord. If the form of His teaching can be relied on as an indication of His mental endowments, it is clear that truth naturally clothed itself for Him in the form of concrete pictures and symbolic events. This is probably the key to the Temptation scenes so vividly described in Mt 4¹⁻¹¹. The temptations of His public life became visualized in these typical scenes, and in fighting them thus prophetically, He rehearsed the long drama of His future spiritual conflicts, and overcame them beforehand. The same dramatic way of dealing with the critical facts of His life and work may be seen in such incidents as are detailed in Mt 9³⁶⁻³⁸ 21³¹ 26³⁹, ⁵³, Lk 10¹⁸, and many others. This instinctive love of a dramatic situation as the vehicle of imparting spiritual truth, is illustrated also in the frequent use of object-lessons full of incident and movement. Sometimes He made a sudden and skilful use of opportunities offered to Him in the course of social intercourse, as in Mk 5³⁰ 10¹⁵ 12⁴¹, Lk 5²⁴ 7⁴⁴ 14¹⁻⁶ 17¹⁷ etc. In other cases He deliberately created the situation, and then drew the lesson with which He desired to impress the spectators, as in Mk 9³³⁻³⁷, Mt 18²⁻⁵, Lk 22¹⁷⁻²⁰, and Jn 13²⁻¹². (The incident of the Blasted Fig-tree, if understood as a simple but vivid action-parable, loses all the ethical difficulties which have hidden its meaning from so many commentators).

The *pictorial* side of our Lord's imagination is scarcely less obvious than the *dramatic*. He was temperamentally as well as spiritually in the deepest sympathy with Nature in all her varying moods, her wealth of life, her process of growth ; and He was a keen and accurate observer of her ways, showing a vivid interest in the life of plants and animals (Mt 6²⁸ 7¹⁶ 6²⁶ 8²⁰) and in the common experiences of human life. These impressions were all stored up, as He watched them, in the treasure-house of a faultless memory, to be afterwards used as drapery for the everlasting truths of the Kingdom in a way which makes many of His discourses a perfect arabesque of beautiful imagery. His predominating love, however, was for images drawn from the incidents of human life and experience. He seldom used imagery of a purely natural kind, *i.e.* drawn from the impersonal action of physical or vital forces : there is nearly always some human agent or sufferer in view whose action or suffering invests the simile with a sympathetic as well as an intellectual aspect. Thus He was fond of drawing His word-pictures from the occupations of such familiar folk as shepherds, husbandmen, fishermen ; from social customs in the home,—marriage ceremonies, feasts, salutations, journeyings; and even from bodily life and sensations,—the eye, ear, bones, feet, hunger and thirst, laughing, mourning, sickness, sleep, etc. Our Lord's use of natural imagery may be put into words written elsewhere by the present writer :

'Nature is interesting to Him only as the handiwork of God, and the mirror of His perfections or providential care for His creatures, or of Him as the Creator of human joys and sorrows. The cold impersonal attitude of the modern scientist towards the creation was impossible to the Lover of Souls. Nature with Him is the vehicle of truth as applied to conduct : she is a bundle of analogies in the sense of the poet :

"Two worlds are ours ; 'tis sin alone
        Forbids us to descry
The mystic earth and heaven within
        Plain as the earth and sky."

In this way our view of Nature is beautifully enriched and impregnated with higher meanings : and her operations resolve themselves into a series of delightful reminders of human duty and of Divine love' (*The Master and His Method*, p. 67).

The imaginative side of our Lord's mind is seen, finally, in the *artistic use of language*. Whether He spoke in the dialect of the common people, or (occasionally at least) in that form of Greek which was commonly known in Palestine, in which the Gospels have come down to us, it is unquestionable that even if we have His discourses only in translation, they are full of characteristic qualities of vividness, terseness, and colour. His use of popular proverbs in fresh applications (Mt $9^{12.\ 13}$ 7^{16} 5^{14} 6^{21} 11^{15} 12^{37} 16^{25}, Mk $10^{23.\ 27}$ etc.); His love of paradox (see Mt 5^{38-42} for four striking instances of this; also Mk 10^{23} and Jn 6^{53}); the exquisite grace of some of His descriptions of natural processes (Mt $6^{28ff.}$ $7^{24ff.}$), and of social functions (Mt 25^{1-12}), together with the symmetrical build of many of His sentences and discourses (esp. Mt 25^{31-46}), show a mastery over the resources of language to which only a poet whose natural gift had been carefully disciplined to high uses could attain. The more the form of our Lord's teaching is studied, the more does this verbal skill impress the reader as complete and minute.

2. *Practical uses of this imaginative element in our Lord's discourses.*—The method of Jesus being exclusively *oral*, it is easy to see how valuable is this pictorial, dramatic, vividly expressed quality that runs through them all. In order that this method should be effective under the circumstances of the time, it was essential that it should have the marks of *simplicity, concreteness, vividness*, and *brevity*. It must be *simple*, as it was meant to become current not amongst scholars, disciplined in the use of complicated trains of thought, well used to abstract lines of reasoning, and capable of retaining these in their memory for a long time, but amongst the common crowd of listeners who had had only an elementary education, and were incapable of giving a close and sustained attention to any train of thought. It must be *concrete*, because such people always thought and spoke in such terms as were closely allied to their daily experience. It must be *vivid*, because otherwise no deep or lasting impression could be made on such occasional and unstudied opportunities as our Lord habitually used to disseminate His teaching. And it must be *brief* and *portable*, for it was meant not merely for those who listened to Him at the time, but also for those who should afterwards 'believe in his name' through the 'preaching and teaching' of the eye-witnesses and auditors of His earthly ministry. All these ends were perfectly served by the imaginative method of presenting truth chosen by the Great Teacher, and consistently followed by Him throughout His public life. His wisdom is shown by the event. It was probably many years before any large portion of His discourses and life-story was committed

to writing. But there are clear indications that great care was taken to give the general outlines of the teaching accurately and without admixture, and that the utmost reverence was felt for the *ipsissima verba* of their Lord's utterances by the Apostles and their first pupils. Converts were carefully taught from the earliest times in *catechumen* classes in the 'doctrine of Christ' (cf. 1 Co 15^{11}, Col 2^6, Lk $1^{1.\ 2}$), and they were counselled to be specially careful to retain and transmit the exact form in which the teaching (the 'fair deposit' of truth) had been delivered to them (cf. 2 Ti 1^{13}, a very significant passage). It was only as these first witnesses were one by one removed by death, or so scattered as to be beyond the reach of appeal, that any need for a written version of the Gospel began to be felt. Then the immediate disciples of the Apostles would endeavour to perpetuate their record of the words and deeds of Christ by committing it to writing. In this way the first two Synoptic Gospels may have taken shape, using the common basis of the oral Gospel as a foundation on which to build. In time various versions would arise, which were collated and welded together into a more accurate whole by scholarly men such as St. Luke (1^{1-3}). Finally, as the last survivor of the original group passed away, his followers would have a strong desire to rescue his personal reminiscences from oblivion ere it was too late, and thus the Fourth Gospel arose as a supplement to the others.

, If the Gospels and the Epistles are compared as to their form, further light is shed on the wisdom of our Lord in using the imaginative style of speech as a vehicle for His oral teaching. St. Paul's involved literary style, full as it is of technical terms, long sentences, and abstract trains of reasoning, could not possibly have served as the vehicle of a spoken Gospel, though, as a supplementary commentary and exposition of the truths enshrined in that Gospel, it is admirably adapted for its purpose ; and the same is true, with qualifications, of the other NT writers.

3. *A lesson for preachers.*—The example of the Great Teacher still applies to those whose business it is to carry on the Christian function of preaching. In more illiterate periods, preachers naturally followed this method of putting their discourses into a concrete, illustrative, and vivid style ; but as books have spread, and the habit of reading has become general, there has been a growing tendency to throw sermons into a more literary form. While this has been partly inevitable and is so far justifiable, it is certain that the pulpit has lost much of its influence because of this unconscious change of method. All *spoken* discourse should aim at the qualities of simplicity, concreteness, vividness, and brevity of expression, which are so remarkable a feature in the discourses and parables of Christ. The very plethora of books makes this specially needful in an age when the human mind is overburdened with the rushing details of daily experience, and the evanescent appeal of ephemeral literature. Unique as are many of the qualities that belong to Christ as a preacher, and making due allowance for the contrast between the Oriental environment in which He lived and that of our own day, there is nothing that more needs to be built into our training of young preachers than a close study of the method of the Master with a view to adapt it to our own day and circumstances.

LITERATURE.—Wendt, *Teaching of Jesus*, i. 106–151 ; Stalker, *Imago Christi*, ch. xiii.   E. GRIFFITH-JONES.

IMITATION.—1. Christian Ethics was roughly constituted in the early centuries by the recognition of two moralities—common morality, requiring a minimum of obedience to law from those living in the world, and first-class morality, the super-legal or supererogatory goodness of those who practised asceticism. Into the service of the latter, with its 'counsels of perfection' (1 Co 7^{25} with Mt 19^{21}—these texts are very early applied in this fashion), all Christian enthusiasm tended to pour itself. This more exacting life is praised as *making men resemble the angels.* Christ had described the angels as unwedded (Mt 22^{30} ‖) ; an age, preoccupied with problems of sex, fastened upon this as the leading truth in regard to those exalted beings. But it is in point of fact a mere external—and therefore, of course, it is imitable ! The essential thing is, that angels 'fulfil God's word' (Ps 103^{20}). To our Lord Himself this was the essential about them : 'Thy will be done, *as in heaven,* so on earth' (Mt 6^{10}). And, when we think of that truth, we see that our proper pattern is not the angels, but the Son. About angels we know little, if anything, that is certain. They are supernatural, almost unnatural beings. The Son came into this world that we might know Him, and has obeyed God's will under our own conditions, in their extremest and most burdensome type.

2. This reinterpretation—imitation of Christ rather than of angels—took place within Catholic ethics, with a great gain in the direction of living Christian truth. The most conspicuous leader was St. Francis of Assisi (1182–1226), 'that child of nature and child of God, half angel and half nightingale' (C. Bigg). Long before his time, the pattern of asceticism had been summed up in three virtues, Poverty, Chastity (*i.e.* celibacy), and Obedience. There may have been pre-Christian influences at work in so moulding Christian monasticism. But the pattern of Christ could also be recognized in these virtues. He had 'become poor' (2 Co 8^9) ; He had 'made himself a eunuch *for the kingdom of heaven's sake*' (Mt 19^{12}) ; He had been 'obedient even unto death, yea, the death of the cross' (Ph 2^8). Of course, historical knowledge and Christian insight—but the Middle Ages were weak in both — see differences as well as similarities. Above all, Christ, who was persecuted and slain as a revolutionary, can hardly serve in fairness as a pattern of blind obedience to constituted human authorities. But, to St. Francis, the requirements of obedience—a rule for his 'Order,' and unhesitating submission to the Pope—were established conditions, which he never thought of criticising. Much the same may be said in regard to 'chastity.' The really important features of St. Francis' character, and of the movement it gave rise to, were as follows. (1) By the idea of imitating the behaviour of Jesus Christ, St. Francis cut his way direct to the centre of things, unhindered, if unhelped, by the overgrown and often corrupt Church system of his time, and restored new life to personal religion and personal Christianity. (2) His enthusiasm for poverty was a living contribution to religious progress. Poverty to him was no inherited conventional virtue. He joyed in it. And, in this joy, he penetrated beyond externals, and showed that he had drunk from deep and full fountains. Poverty may be acquired by imitation ; joy cannot. If there was something of extravagance in St. Francis' love of poverty, there was also a permanent moral idea — the 'simple life.' We cannot here discuss the claims or conditions or limitations of that virtue ; but we greet it with reverence in so great a genius as our Saint. Still further, we must recognize in St. Francis' joy the influences of romance. 'Poverty' was his dear 'bride.' It was not for nothing that he lived in the days of chivalry. We recognize, too, the buoyancy of youth ; St. Francis 'entered religion'

at 25, and died at 44. These are accessories—innocent and touching accessories—at which Christianity may smile, but certainly will not frown. The centre lies deeper. Who can doubt that Christ's own joy dwelt in St. Francis ? (3) He was a servant of his fellow-men. Here in part he inherited from the Church. The first ascetics were hermits, living in solitude ; but the social instinct, guided by the sagacity of Church rulers, crept after the solitaries, drew them into union, placed them under rule, and in many cases set them to useful work. The two great orders of friars, Dominicans as well as Franciscans, were preachers. But, besides preaching, St. Francis and all his followers who really shared his spirit were helpers of men in their needs and miseries ; a very genuine part of the pattern set by Christ. (4) The order of *Tertiaries*—semi-Franciscans, men or women, living in the world ; *not even pledged to celibacy*—was a gallant attempt to minimize the distinction between the two moralities, and to make personal Christianity, as St. Francis had discovered it, available for non-ascetics. Here then we see the Christianity of imitation at its very best (but, as we have noted, it is more than imitation). St. Francis' Christianity is an all-round thing—living, attractive, strong, serviceable, joyous. Why could he not reform the Church by his indirect influence? Perhaps he was too sweet. Perhaps the lingering taint of the theory of two castes and two moralities frustrated him. Again, external poverty might not be in others what it was in St. Francis, the vehicle of simplicity and spiritual joy. Most obviously, external poverty broke down—even Franciscans evaded the full sacrifice. It is little shame to have failed in a region where no one wholly succeeds. Yet we must note that where St. Francis failed, Luther triumphed.

3. Monasticism has left us a literary monument of a kindred type of Christianity ; one of the Church's and one of the world's classics ; à Kempis' work known by the [historically doubtful] name, *The Imitation of Christ.* As long as human sorrow endures, and faith is not dead among men, this book will be treasured and held in reverence. Christ died on the cross ; we must accept a crucifying, a denying, an abnegation of self and self-will. There the message of the book stops. Our fellow-men, even our Christian brethren, are only thought of as hindrances to Divine communion, tempters who threaten to impede our sanctification. À Kempis falls far below St. Francis, who served men for Christ's sake with eager loyalty. The dangerous one-sidedness of this glorious book is not due to externalizing Christ's example. Externally even, the Gospels rebuke it with a loud voice. And the book is not external. It has mystical depth and inwardness. Mysticism touched with the Christian spirit is its strength. But the defects which mar it lie no less deep.

4. The Reformation abolished the 'higher' morality of asceticism, with its imitation of such outward circumstances in the life of our Lord as His poverty or His celibacy. Ordinary lay Christianity was seen to involve a 'more perfect' obedience than the will-worship of the monk. (Recent study of Luther has called in question his insight on such points ; but there can be no doubt that he grasped the principle, however his remarks in detail may show the distorting influence of the mediæval tradition). It is also to be recognized that Protestant Christianity, with its emphasis on the Pauline Gospel of the cross—*Christ died for us* — had less receptiveness for the thought of Christ's example, in several of its forms. Ritschl and some other modern Protestants even assert that Christ's example amounts to no more than *faultless fulfilment of vocation*—a vocation very different from ours. This paradox belongs to the art. 'Example' rather than to the present article. What we have to insist upon is this—Christ cannot be truly followed by *imitating* Him in *externals*. But has the NT erred? He who was greatest humbled Himself; the Master of all served; the one perfectly innocent sufferer in all history forgave ungrudgingly; He laid down His life for us, that we might lay down our lives for others (Ph 2⁵⁻⁸, Jn 13¹⁴, Mt 20²⁸, 1 P 2²¹, Lk 23³⁴, 1 Jn 3¹⁶). Can this wonderful many-sided example be exchanged for a dry scholastic formula like 'fidelity to a vocation'? We have to be on our guard lest Protestantism, with its rediscovery of the gospel of God's love, and with its repudiation of false (monastic) conceptions of the higher life, should blur at some points that moral claim which is, in truth, high as heaven—high as Christ Himself.

5. Asceticism is an obsolete danger in modern Protestant circles; yet it is possible that the tendency to 'imitation' may take other forms. The socialistic reading of Christ's words—socialism crossed with crazy altruism; anarchistic socialism or socialistic anarchism; extremes meet!—is primarily a wooden way of conceiving Christ's teaching, just as imitation is a wooden way of following Christ's example. If we rise into the region of Christian principle, both dangers vanish. But there is a more subtle connexion between ideas of imitation and a false programme for the Christian life. Many schemes of the Atonement (*e.g.* the late Dr. Moberly's) tell us in substance that Christ initiated a process—to Dr. Moberly, a penitential process of self-mortification; to others, a process of world-redeeming love—which Christians must prolong. This is substantially imitation over again. We are to be saved by 'being such men as He was, too.' The Pauline and Protestant gospel tells us that Christ offered and finished the great sacrifice. We may well recoil from the old vulgar train of thought described by M'Leod Campbell: 'He suffered—I shall not suffer'; but God forbid we should dream that we share, in all respects and for every purpose, the lot of Christ. We fill up remaining suffering—if we are found worthy—but we do not fill out an uncompleted Atonement; that was 'finished,' once and for all, in mysterious anguish, in agony out of which springs our new life. We have not fully unlearned the dreary external programme of imitation till we confess Christ unambiguously as our life and our only hope. We are to resemble Him, partly as the younger born resemble the elder brother, partly as the saved resemble the Saviour. Confessing this, we are prepared to learn those further things He has to teach us about the ways of conformity to His image. Protestantism is to be developed or supplemented, but must not be abolished. Christian ethics presuppose the Christian gospel. They can never take its place.

LITERATURE.—The best recent book on the general subject is Stalker's *Imago Christi*, with its thoughtful criticism of the *Imitatio*. Early Christian literature is well summarized in Luthardt's *Hist. of Christian Ethics* (Eng. tr.). For St. Francis, see P. Sabatier's *Life* and other writings. For the Reformers, see Charles Beard's *Martin Luther*, also his *Hibbert Lecture*. (Luther, that great religious genius, is the Reformer to study).

ROBERT MACKINTOSH.

IMMANENCE (Lat. *in*, 'in,' and *manere*, 'to remain') means *abiding* or *dwelling in*. In general it denotes the existence and operation of one thing within another. In *Philosophy* it expresses the identity of the originating and causal principle, involved in the genesis of the universe, with the universe itself in its progressive history. In *Theology* it denotes the indwelling and operation of God within the entire universe, of which He is the first cause and the abiding ground. It stands in contrast with 'transcendence,' which implies that God is prior to, and not limited by, the universe, which depends upon Him for its origin and continued existence. But immanence and transcendence are not exclusive of each other. A correct theistic philosophy gives a place to each of these principles in its exposition of the relations of God to the universe.

The history of the principle of immanence is interesting. It is perhaps first suggested by the νοῦς of Anaxagoras, as the principle of operative intelligence in the universe. In the idealistic system of Plato, according to which the *ideas* that are supposed to be archetypal in God become ectypal in the universe, and constitute its real essence, order, and intelligibility, the immanence of Deity is involved. The same suggestion is also implied in the *eternal forms* of Aristotle, according to which the framer of the world moulded it into a harmonious whole. The Aristotelian distinction between the immanent acts of the soul in forming a purpose and its transient acts in making the purpose effective, illustrates the principle of immanence in a general way.

In the later Platonic philosophy of the School of Alexandria the principle of the λόγος, especially in the hands of Philo the Jew, also suggests the idea of immanence. Philo perhaps borrowed the term from the Wisdom literature, where it was used in the sense of σοφία or *ratio*, and applied to denote what Plato had called ἰδίαι. This usage of the term λόγος is interesting in itself and on account of its bearing upon the usage of the same term in the Fourth Gospel.

In modern philosophy the dictum of Malebranche, that we know things truly only when we see them in relation to God, and the monadology of Leibnitz, according to which a vital principle is supposed to lie at the heart of all things, both involve the idea of immanence. Spinoza's pantheism, as, indeed, all pantheism, so emphasizes immanence that transcendence has no place. The absolute idealism of the Hegelian type of philosophy and the Hindu theosophy both make so much of the immanence of the Deity that His transcendence is quite obscured. In the philosophy of our own time there is a tendency towards a fuller recognition of the immanence of God, and this tendency is affecting theology in a wholesome way. The result is a sound theistic philosophy, as the basis for a more vital theology.

This article has to do mainly with the idea of immanence as it appears in the Gospel narratives, and specially as it is exhibited in the teachings of Jesus Christ. The Synoptics do not give as much prominence to the Divine immanence as does the Fourth Gospel. It might be too much to say that transcendence prevails in the former and immanence in the latter; yet it is true that one of the points of difference between the Synoptics and the Fourth Gospel is the way in which the relations between God and the universe are construed.

1. In the *Synoptics* there are hints of the Divine immanence in *nature* which resemble the OT utterances upon this point, *e.g.* Mt 5⁴⁵ 6³⁰, Mk 6⁵¹, Lk 21²⁹. Transcendence is not excluded in these passages. God's immanence in *man* is also suggested by Mt 6⁸ 10²⁰, Mk 13¹¹, Lk 1⁶⁷ 2²⁶ 11¹⁷. The fact of the immanence of God in *Christ* is alluded to in Mt 3¹⁶ 4¹ 12¹⁸ 27⁴⁶, Mk 1¹² 9², Lk 4¹. That God is immanent in some sense in the *subjects* of His Kingdom is implied in Mt 10⁴⁰ 13³³ 18² 28²⁰, Mk 1¹⁵, Lk 13²¹. It may be added that demoniacal immanence in men is often expressed in the Synoptics, *e.g.* Mt 8²⁸ 12⁴⁵, Mk 3²² 9¹⁷, Lk 8³⁰.

We can scarcely conclude from these and similar passages that special stress is laid upon the idea of immanence in the Synoptics. The fact that God is constantly in vital and operative contact with the entire universe of being is very evident; but God's being and activity are not necessarily limited by the universe. He is the First Cause of all things, yet second causes have their place and dependent efficiency in the universe. Hence it is that God's transcendence is clearly recognized.

2. In the *Fourth Gospel* immanence has a larger place. Some interpreters suppose that St. John borrowed many of his ideas, especially that of the λόγος, from the Platonic philosophy, as represented by Philo of Alexandria, who combined some OT ideas with the philosophy of Plato. But there are differences between the λόγος doctrine of St. John and that of Philo which entirely exclude the supposition that St. John was a mere borrower.

The fact that he makes no allusion to Philo or to Alexandria, but rather assumes that he gathered his ideas from the teaching of Jesus, fully justifies this view.

The immanence of God in *nature* is implied in Jn 3[8] 4[24] 11[24]. His immanence in *man* is suggested in 1[1-14] 8[12] 14[6]. Here God, in some active way, is operative in nature and in the soul of man as its Divine light.

But it is in *Jesus Christ* that the Fourth Gospel finds the immanence of God in a special manner. For this see 1[1-14] 5[26] 7[33] 8[38. 43] 10[30] 12[24. 45. 50] 13[32] 14[11. 16. 26] 15[23] 16[27. 28] 17[5. 21. 23]. In several of these passages the term λόγος is used concerning Jesus Christ. In this term the idea of immanence is involved; but as this topic is fully treated in art. LOGOS it need not be discussed at length here. Suffice it to say that Jesus Christ, as the eternal Logos, is regarded by many as the Divine principle by whose agency the operative intelligence of God is manifested and made effective in the entire universe. Care is needed here not to give too much of the colour of the Alexandrian philosophy to the teaching of the Fourth Gospel upon this point.

This Gospel also lays stress upon the fact that God is immanent in *believers*, as the subjects of His spiritual Kingdom. See 3[27] 4[14] 6[53] 7[37. 38] 11[25] 15[1-10] 17[8. 23. 24]. In passages like these the fact is presented that there is such a union with, and participation in, Christ on the part of believers, that He is said to be the source of a spiritual life which is Divine. In a deep mystical sense God may be regarded as immanent in believers by virtue of this union, and their partaking of the Divine nature thereby.

As against Deism, the Gospels very plainly teach that God is in constant and vital contact with the universe. As against Pantheism, they also teach that God is vaster than the universe, and is in no way conditioned by it. Hence they present a sound Theism, which gives a proper place alike to the immanence and transcendence of God in the relations which He sustains to the universe. It may be added that the fact of this immanent and transcendent relation, rather than the mode of it, is set forth in the Gospels. The Epistles expand some of these things (cf. Ro 1[20] 5[5] 8[11], 1 Co 1[30] 2[10] 6[19] 8[6], Gal 1[16] 4[19], Eph 6[10], Ph. 2[13], Col 1[19], He 1[3] 2[16], 1 Jn 3[24] 4[15]; see also St. Paul in Ac 17[25. 28]).

LITERATURE. — Plato, *Phædrus*; Philo, *de Opif. Mundi*; Spinoza, *Ethica*; Hegel, *Logic*; Caird, *The Evolution of Religion*; Royce, *God and the Individual*; Illingworth, *Divine Immanence*; Thomas à Kempis, *Imitatio Christi*; Eckhart, *Writings*; Allan, *Continuity of Christian Thought*; Flint, *Anti-Theistic Theories*, p. 339; *Agnosticism*, p. 592; Martensen, *Chr. Dogmatics*, pp. 103–106; Orr, *Chr. View of God and the World*, p. 318.

FRANCIS R. BEATTIE.

IMMANUEL ('Εμμανουήλ) occurs once only in the NT (Mt 1[23], in the quotation from Is 7[14] where the name is given in the form עִמָּנוּאֵל). It is necessary, first of all, to examine the original prophecy before discussing the Evangelist's application of it to Jesus.

1. The circumstances which led to the prediction were as follows. Probably under the influence of a wish to force Judah into a coalition against Assyria, an attack was made on the southern kingdom by Syria and Ephraim about 735–734 (Is 7[1ff.]). The attack was specially directed against the Davidic dynasty, and it was the object of the allies to dethrone Ahaz and set the son of Tabeel in his place (v.[6]). The invasion filled Ahaz with panic, and he resolved to call in the aid of Tiglath-pileser, the king of Assyria (2 K 16[7ff.]). Between the great Empire of Assyria and the petty State of Judah there could be no talk of equal alliance, Judah must forfeit its independence and become a vassal of Assyria. This involved heavy taxation and the loss of all power of independent action. Taxation

would only aggravate the social misery and ruthless oppression from which the poor were suffering, and make it more difficult than ever to carry through those social reforms which the prophets regarded as most necessary. Accordingly, Isaiah vehemently opposed the king's project. He made light of the danger from Syria and Ephraim, and stigmatized the allies as fag-ends of smoking firebrands, which might cause considerable annoyance, but had lost all power for serious mischief. He bade Ahaz be quiet and fearless, assuring him that God would frustrate the designs of his foes (Is 7[4ff.]), but warning him that his stability depended on his faith (v.[9]). Possibly our present text is somewhat abbreviated, but at any rate Isaiah, either on that or possibly another occasion, offered him a sign in confirmation of his assurance, placing the universe from Sheol to Heaven at his disposal. Ahaz refused, since he had already made up his mind, but pretended that his unwillingness was prompted by reluctance to tempt God. The prophet passionately cries out against the conduct which, not content with wearying men, goes on to weary God. Then he proceeds to give the king a sign from God Himself, namely, the sign of Immanuel (v.[10ff.]).

The translation of the Hebrew is itself somewhat uncertain. It may now be taken for granted that the word עַלְמָה translated 'virgin' in the EV should be more correctly rendered 'young woman.' The proper Heb. term for 'virgin' is בְּתוּלָה, though even this is used in Jl 1[8] for 'young widow.' All that can with certainty be said of the word used by Isaiah is that it indicates a young woman of marriageable age, but says nothing as to whether she is married or not. Accordingly the terms of the prophecy do not warrant us in interpreting the sign as the prodigy of a virgin conception. The natural interpretation to put on the prophecy is that a young woman, either married at the time or soon to be married, would give birth to a son and call him by this name. It is also uncertain whether we should translate with RV 'shall conceive' or with RVm 'is with child.' The former is, however, perhaps the more probable. The third question is whether we should translate 'a virgin' or 'the virgin.' The Hebrew has the article, which is correctly rendered 'the virgin,' in which case some definite person is in the prophet's mind. But Hebrew idiom often uses the definite article where in English we should translate indefinitely, so that 'a virgin' is equally correct as a rendering of the Hebrew.

These uncertainties as to the precise meaning of the words themselves naturally leave much room for difference of opinion, and this is largely increased by other uncertainties. It is therefore desirable to narrow the range of possible interpretation as much as possible. It is clear, in the first place, that the prophet is referring to something in the near future, otherwise the sign could have conveyed no message to the king, all the more that his difficulty was urgent. In the next place, we must beware of supposing that anything extraordinary is necessarily intended by the sign. Isaiah walked in captive's dress for a sign and a wonder upon Egypt and Ethiopia (Is 20[3]), certainly not because of any miraculous character attached to his conduct (cf. also 8[18]). With these considerations in mind we may approach the question, What message was the sign intended to convey? When Ahaz had been bidden ask a sign, the object was to convince him that his enemies would be overthrown and their alliance against him come to nought. We naturally expect that the sign volunteered by the prophet will have the same significance. Yet there are objections to this view. It may be argued that Ahaz' refusal to ask a sign introduced a new element into the situation, especially after the warning in 7[9]; and if he rejected a sign assuring him of deliverance, it would not be strange if he received one that was ominous of disaster. And such a sign, according to our present text, we seem to possess. For the prediction in v.[15], that Immanuel should eat curdled milk and honey, implies that Judah would have reverted from the agricultural to the pastoral state, in other words, would have suffered a devastation at the hands of an enemy. And this is confirmed by v.[17], wherein a terrible invasion bringing a disaster unprecedented since the days of Rehoboam is predicted. On the other hand, this is difficult to harmonize with v.[16], at any rate in its present form, for that gives as the meaning of the sign that before the child knows to refuse the evil and choose the good, the land whose two kings Ahaz abhors will be forsaken. In other words, v.[16] interprets the sign as the desolation of Syria and Ephraim. It is therefore a sign, not of disaster to Judah, but of deliverance. We are accordingly confronted with the problem whether the original text is here preserved. It would suffice to bring v.[16] into harmony with vv.[15. 17] if the former were to read simply 'for before the child shall know to refuse the evil and choose the good, thy land shall be forsaken'; and several scholars have adopted this expedient. In that case the sign is simply one of disaster for Judah. Nevertheless there are serious difficulties in the way of accepting this solution, and the question is forced upon us whether more radical measures are not necessary. Even with the suggested abbreviation of v.[16] it does not connect so well with v.[15] as with v.[14]. But apart from that, there are other arguments for treating the sign as favourable. The name *Immanuel* itself, expressing the conviction that God was with His people, might, of course, be harmonized with either verse. It gains significance only on account of the distress in which the name was given, the mother's faith is a sign only when experience seems to contradict it. The name might therefore be given in the midst of the trouble caused by the Syrian invasion or in the greater distress that was to follow from Assyria. But Isaiah certainly anticipated the overthrow of Syria and Ephraim. Not only so, but a little later, in the public exhibition on a tablet of the word *Maher-shalal-hash-baz*, and nearly a year later in the giving of this name to his new-born son, he expressed his faith in the overthrow of the coalition. It is indeed urged that the sign of Immanuel would thus be only a duplication of the sign of Maher-shalal-hash-baz, but there seems to be no reason why such a duplication should be objectionable. Moreover, there is a significant parallelism between the two which points to such an identification of meaning. The time limit in both cases is very similar. In the one case it is before the child shall know to say 'my father and my mother'; in other words, the events described are to happen before the infant who has just been born has learnt to utter the first things that a child says. The other time limit is precisely similar, 'before the child knows to refuse the evil and choose the good.' By this the prophet need not mean before he comes to years of moral discretion, but before he learns to distinguish between good and harmful food. And the very fact that a year later Isaiah was still concerned mainly with the invasion of the allies and in asserting his conviction of their overthrow, surely makes it probable that the same question preoccupies his attention here. Nor is there any reason to suppose that the obstinacy of Ahaz would make any difference to the character of the sign. Unless we are explicitly warned to the contrary, it is natural to assume that the sign given possessed the same significance as the sign offered. The present writer accordingly takes the view that the sign is of a favourable character. This involves, it is true, the elimination of v.[15] (and perhaps of v.[17], though this may belong to another prophecy), but in any case something has to be struck out of the passage to secure consistency. It might, of course, seem easier to eliminate a few words in v.[16] than to strike out a whole verse. Nevertheless, when we look at v.[15] we see that it is practically compounded of part of v.[22] and part of v.[16], whereas the words 'whose two kings thou abhorrest' make a much greater impression of originality.

The question accordingly arises, In what precisely did the sign consist? The stress may lie either on the עַלְמָה, or the son, or the name given to him, or a combination of these. The traditional interpretation has, of course, thrown the stress on the first of these; for it the sign lay in the virgin-conception. But when the true sense of עַלְמָה is understood, this interpretation becomes impossible. If she were one of the king's wives, then the child would be the king's son, and the possibility of an identification with the Messiah would have to be considered. It would be possible to accept, with McCurdy, the identification of Immanuel with Hezekiah, the chronological difficulties not being altogether insuperable. A third possible alternative would be to accept the view taken by several scholars, most recently by Whitehouse in the *Century Bible*, and identify the עַלְמָה with the community in Zion. We have no evidence, however, that this term was used at that time for the Jewish community, and the identification with one of the king's wives must also be pronounced improbable, in spite of the fact that the trouble was dynastic even more than national, directed against the Davidic house rather than against Judah as a whole. Nor is there any reason for identifying Immanuel with the Messianic king mentioned in 9[1-7] and 11[1-9]. It is true that, according to the present text of 8[8], the land of Judah is represented as Immanuel's land, but it is probable that the text should be corrected in harmony with 8[10].* We may then set aside the

* Probably instead of 'thy land, O Immanuel,' we should read 'the land, for God is with us,' thus getting a refrain at the end of v.[8] to match that at the end of v.[10]. In that case the figure of the bird with wings spread over the land is a symbol of God's protecting care of Judah, shielding her from the combination of all earthly foes. The extreme abruptness of the transition from threat to promise makes it highly probable that 8[8b-10] is a fragment not connected with the preceding verses. It must even be granted that Marti may be right in regarding it as a later addition; for although the prophecy may be explained as Isaiah's, on the supposition that he is addressing the forces of Assyria as composed of various nationalities, yet taken by itself the reference to the coalition of the far nations against Judah recurs as a standing feature of the later apocalyptic.

Messianic identification. With the correction of 8[8] no reason remains for considering that the personality of Immanuel is an important element in the sign; it is in harmony with similar cases that it is the name and not the person who bears it that is important. This is true, for example, of Hosea's children, and, what is still more to the point, of Isaiah's children. The prophetic significance both of *Shear-jashub* and *Maher-shalal-hash-baz* lies not in the children themselves, but exclusively in their names. We expect the same to be true in this case. Just as the names of Isaiah's two children express, the one his doctrine of the remnant, the other his certainty that Syria and Ephraim would be overthrown, so the name *Immanuel* expresses the mother's conviction that God is with His people. The sign is no prodigy in this case. For against the king's unbelief and his obstinate refusal to accept a sign there arises the mother's impressive faith, which confronted danger without dismay, and uttered her conviction of God's presence with His people in the name she gave her son. The personality of the mother is equally with that of the son of no importance for the sign; that consists in the mother's faith and the son's name. Accordingly it is better to translate 'a young woman' instead of 'the young woman.' Isaiah, however, does not mean precisely that any young woman, who is shortly about to conceive and give birth to a son, may call his name Immanuel. While he has no definite young woman in his mind, he predicts that some young woman will, in the future, conceive and bear a son, to whom she will give the name Immanuel. His language is not that of hypothesis but of prediction.*

2. The way is now clear to discuss St. Matthew's use of the passage. This is not the place to examine the subject either of the Virgin-conception of Christ or of the early Christian interpretation of prophecy. It is quite plain that this interpretation was in general very little controlled by the original sense of the OT passage quoted. It was of a largely polemical character, since it was necessary, against the cavilling of the Jews, to prove the Messiahship of Jesus from the OT. Accordingly the Hebrew Scriptures were ransacked to find parallels with the life of Christ; and it is not unlikely that, at a quite early period, collections of these passages were drawn up for controversial use. The First Gospel is peculiarly rich in Messianic proof-texts, and it is therefore not surprising that for two facts so important to the author as the Virgin-conception and the Incarnation the writer should allege an OT prophecy. But the fact that he has done so creates a very interesting problem, which, however, will be approached differently by those who accept the Virgin-conception as a fact and by those who dispute it. For the former, the fact itself is the starting-point, and the author had to find in the OT a text appropriate to it. The only question that would really arise would be as to the part played by the LXX in suggesting Is 7[14]. In this passage the LXX renders עַלְמָה by παρθένος, which suggests virginity much more strongly than the Hebrew word. At the same time, the fact that the LXX so translated shows that the author of the First Gospel may independently have taken the word in the same sense. That he did so is rendered not improbable by the fact that his translation differs in some points from that of the LXX.† The significance for the doctrine of the Incarnation of the name *Immanuel*, which might be translated 'God with us' as well as 'God is with us,' probably first drew his attention to the passage, and then the translation of עַלְמָה by παρθένος would

* The connexion of v.[16] with v.[14] is as follows. A young woman will bear a son and call his name Immanuel. This will be a sign, for it will express a faith which triumphs over the appearance of imminent disaster. And it is truly God-inspired faith, for it will be splendidly vindicated. Ere the child thus born in days of darkness knows how to distinguish between hurtful and proper food, the hostile power will be crushed, and thus God's presence with His people will be clearly manifested. Immanuel will be a standing rebuke to the king's scepticism.

† The LXX of Is 7[14] reads in B : διὰ τοῦτο δώσει Κύριος αὐτὸς ὑμῖν σημεῖον· ἰδοὺ ἡ παρθένος ἐν γαστρὶ λήμψεται καὶ τέξεται υἱόν, καὶ καλέσεις τὸ ὄνομα αὐτοῦ Ἐμμανουήλ. For λήμψεται, however, אAQ read ἕξει, which is the same rendering as that in Matthew. For καλέσεις we have in א καλέσει; neither B nor א here coincide with Matthew. The text in Mt 1[23] reads ἰδοὺ ἡ παρθένος ἐν γαστρὶ ἕξει καὶ τέξεται υἱόν, καὶ καλέσουσιν τὸ ὄνομα αὐτοῦ Ἐμμανουήλ.

readily be suggested by his belief in the Virgin-conception.

Among those, however, who regard the belief in the Virgin-birth as a piece of primitive Christian mythology, there has been a controversy as to what led the author to quote this passage, and the relation between that belief and the passage in Isaiah. Many think that the former was created by the latter,* and probably in the form given to it by the LXX translation. The Hebrew, it is thought, would not naturally have lent itself to this purpose apart from the definite use of παρθένος in the LXX. Several recent scholars, on the other hand, consider that the use of παρθένος is quite insufficient to account for St. Matthew's quotation. They consider that even before the birth of Jesus there had been formed a doctrine of the Messiah, which included among other things His supernatural birth. This was ultimately derived from the pagan stories of children of the gods, but was not taken over directly from paganism by Jewish Christianity. It had arisen on the soil of Judaism itself, and it is in the Judæo-pagan syncretism, with its doctrine that the Messiah must be born of a virgin, that the origin of the belief is to be sought. What was said of Christ was subsequently transferred to Jesus, when Jesus and the Christ were identified. A quotation from Gunkel will make this position clear. After saying that the mythological representations did not make their first appearance in the later Gentile Christianity, he proceeds: 'But this would have been impossible if Judaism itself had not previously possessed this or similar representations. The birth of Christ from the Virgin through the Divine Spirit had, we may assume, already belonged to the Christological dogma before Jesus, just as His birth in Bethlehem and from David's race, and has been transferred to Jesus only at a later time. What we have to learn then, and what will subsequently be shown again, is that this Judaism which found its way into primitive Christianity must have been strongly inclined to syncretism' (Zum religionsgeschichtlichen Verständnis des NT, p. 69). Similarly, Cheyne, in his Bible Problems, considers that the historical explanation of the statement of the Virgin-birth is that it arose 'in the story of non-Jewish origin current in Jewish circles and borrowed from them by certain Jewish Christians.' He interprets 'virgin' in a peculiar sense. In its original meaning 'it expresses the fact that the great mythic mother-goddess was independent of the marriage tie' (p. 75). For him the passage in Mt. 'is a Jewish-Christian transformation of a primitive story, derived ultimately, in all probability, from Babylonia, and analogous to the Jewish trans-

* Cf. Harnack: 'Even the belief that Jesus was born of a virgin sprang from Is 7¹⁴. . . . The conjecture of Usener, that the idea of the birth from a virgin is a heathen myth which was received by the Christians, contradicts the entire earliest development of Christian tradition, which is free from heathen myths, so far as these had not already been received by wide circles of Jews (above all, certain Babylonian and Persian myths), which in the case of that idea is not demonstrable. Besides, it is in point of method not permissible to stray so far when we have near at hand such a complete explanation as Is 7¹⁴' (History of Dogma, i. p. 100, n. 1). Harnack, it is true, does not assert that it was the LXX rendering which created the belief, though it may be presumed that this is his view. He is not divided in principle from Gunkel and Cheyne, since he admits that heathen myths had come into Christianity through Judaism, but he considers that the Virgin-birth does not as a matter of fact belong to these, and that an extra-Jewish source should not be sought when a Jewish source is at hand. Lobstein characterizes the method applied to the documents of the Bible by Usener as 'supremely defective,' and, after admitting the 'remarkable likenesses to our Gospel tradition' in the pagan parallels he has accumulated, says: 'Yet the conclusions which he draws from them go singularly beyond his premisses: the Jewish and Christian factors suffice to explain the genesis of the myth of the Nativity' (The Virgin Birth of Christ, pp. 128, 129, cf. pp. 75, 76). He thinks the LXX translation responsible for ' the religious construction adopted by the Evangelist' (pp. 74, 75).

formation of the Babylonian cosmogony in the opening section of Genesis' * (p. 93). On the other hand, a good many scholars take the view that the story was created, not simply out of pagan materials, but on pagan soil and among Gentile Christians. This is the view of Usener, Schmiedel, Soltau, Pfleiderer, and others (see references below). It does not fall within the scope of this article to discuss this question further, since it is concerned simply with the bearing of the LXX translation of עַלְמָה by παρθένος on the development of the belief in the Virgin-conception of Christ. To rebut the Christian use of Is 7¹⁴ as a prediction of the supernatural birth of Christ, later Jewish translators substituted νεᾶνις for παρθένος. See VIRGIN BIRTH.

LITERATURE.—In addition to commentaries on Isaiah and Matthew, and articles on 'Immanuel' in Dictionaries of the Bible, reference may be made to the articles 'Mary' and 'Nativity' in the Encyc. Bibl.; Giesebrecht, SK, 1888; Porter, JBL, 1895; McCurdy, HPM, vol. i. pp. 368–371, 417–420; Soltau, The Birth of Jesus Christ, pp. 50–52; Lobstein, The Virgin Birth of Christ, pp. 73–75, 128–130; Cheyne, Bible Problems, pp. 67–100, 191–195; Pfleiderer, Das Urchristentum², i. pp. 551, 694; Harnack, History of Dogma, i. p. 100, n. 1; Box, 'The Gospel Narratives of the Nativity and the alleged Influence of Heathen Ideas' in ZNTW, 1905, p. 80 ff.

A. S. PEAKE.

IMMORTALITY.—In the ordinary acceptation of the term 'immortality' connotes 'endlessness.' It has ceased to express merely or solely a denial of physical death, in its incidence or its consequences, and has been extended to include the possibility or actuality of death, considered as putting an end to conscious existence either now or in the limitless future. Whether these two alternatives really mean the same thing, whether to be capable of dying is always and ultimately to die, and so that only is immortal which by its very nature and constitution is not liable to death, while all else perishes,—as is probably the case,—is a question that hardly comes within the scope of the present article. It will, however, be just, and will conduce to clearness, to separate these two considerations,—to seek to determine, in the first instance, the teaching of Christ with regard to immortality in the limited sense of a denial of cessation of existence at death; and, secondly, to review the much wider and more perplexed question of the permanence of this 'immortal' state. 'Does death end all?', according to the mind and teaching of the Founder of Christianity, is an inquiry that needs to be twice raised,—once as it concerns the terminus of the present life upon earth, and again as it refers or may refer to a future to which human thought can set no limit. It is obvious that the first question is comparatively simple and uninvolved; and that upon its answer in the affirmative depends the possibility of opening the second, which is highly complicated, and involves the most far-reaching and important problems that can present themselves for human consideration.

By some writers the terms used in the NT, and especially by Christ Himself, with reference to a life after death have been further understood to imply

* Cf. also the important remarks on pp. 193–195. He thinks the translation παρθένος is so far from accounting for the belief in the Virgin-birth that it needs to be explained itself. 'In Is 7¹⁴ the translator must have had some special motive, and that motive must have been not philological, but, if I may say so, ideological.' 'As for the quotation in Mt 1²²ᶠ· it is perfectly well accounted for as one of the subsidiary Biblical proofs which were habitually sought for by the evangelists. The real supports of their statements were traditions of one kind or another, but their belief in the written word of prophecy led them to look for a justification of these traditions in the prophetic scriptures, and with this amount of justice, that sometimes the traditions and the prophecies had a common origin.' The same view is taken by the scholars who regard the doctrine as purely pagan in origin. See, e.g., Pfleiderer, Das Urchristentum², i. pp. 551, 694, where he affirms that Mt.'s use of Is 7¹⁴ was possible only for one who had already quite other grounds for ascribing that origin to Jesus.

blessedness. Life immortal would thus be not only life in the ordinary acceptation of conscious existence, but it would be life *plus* felicity. It is perhaps hardly right or wise to saddle the doctrine with this additional connotation. It will, however, be necessary to examine how far the words of Christ suggest or imply that He regarded happiness as an essential and inseparable part of the life to come, or a future existence of misery more or less prolonged as inconceivable unless it were terminated by restoration to bliss or annihilation of consciousness.

There is, however, a further preliminary consideration which must be taken into account. An examination of the whole teaching of Christ upon so momentous a theme, as it is transmitted by the Evangelists, may be expected to yield results not only positive but negative. Positive, inasmuch as upon a subject that concerns the deepest interests of men no great religious teacher can do other than afford some guidance to those who seek knowledge and truth at his lips; and negative, since the revelation which he may venture or see fit to make of his own thoughts will obviously be determined and limited by the character and capacity of his contemporaries. In a sense neither derogatory nor contemptuous towards his hearers, he will refuse to cast his pearls before swine. Environment naturally and inevitably plays a large part in moulding the form into which doctrine shall be cast, and in assigning the bounds beyond which it shall not move. Teaching appropriate and welcome to the keen-witted and philosophic circles of Athens will fall on dull and inappreciative ears by the waterside or in the fields of Galilee. And of the confessedly greatest Teacher that the world has ever known this may be expected to be pre-eminently true; He will make His sayings accord both as to form and substance with the receptive ability of those to whom they are delivered. There will be many things within the compass of His own knowledge which they cannot now bear (Jn 16^{12}). And though He will at times give utterance to sayings hard to be understood (6$^{50ff.\ 60}$), of a depth and significance beyond their comprehension, foreshadowing truths into the full understanding of which only after-generations will be able to grow, the major part of His instruction will not be concerned with these; else would that instruction be barren and profitless to the hearers, no fruitful seed germinating to new spiritual and intellectual life. Moreover, it is precisely these sayings, dealing with the higher, more abstract and supra-sensible side of things, that would be most likely to be lost upon ordinary disciples, to fail to find a place in their memory, and in their subsequent reproductions, whether written or oral, of the Master's teaching. Only by the choicer natures, the more refined and contemplative spirits among His followers, such as we conceive the Apostle John to have been, would this aspect of His discourse and doctrine be caught up and treasured, to be afterwards faithfully delivered as words φωνᾶντα συνετοῖσιν, although for the moment they may have soared far above the care or comprehension of those who first heard them with their outward ears.

Upon *a priori* grounds, therefore, bearing in mind the character of the people among whom Christ lived and with whom He had to deal, we should expect to find the speculative and philosophic side of doctrine but slightly represented, while stress is laid more upon ethics and the practical conduct of life. The supernatural will be stated, as it were, in terms of the natural, the heavenly of the earthly, and with a constant recognition of the actual needs and circumstances and possibilities of His hearers. Whether and how far this

is so in fact only an examination of the texts can show. Such an examination of the more or less direct references in the Gospels to a future life will be most conveniently conducted under the three divisions suggested, viz.—(1) a renewed life after death, (2) the permanence of this life, (3) its comprehensiveness, whether it is to be conceived as embracing the entire race of mankind or limited to a part thereof. It will be necessary to take separately the evidence of the Synoptic Gospels and of St. John.

A. The Synoptists.—(1) With regard to the first point little need be said, for indeed there is nothing in dispute. That the teaching of Christ assumes from first to last *a conscious life beyond the grave* for Himself and His hearers lies upon the surface of His words and permeates His entire rule of life. The whole tone of His speech, the implications of His parables, the sanctions with which He surrounds His encouragements and warnings, the comparative value which He teaches men to set upon heavenly and earthly things, the gravity and seriousness of His outlook into the future, all show that here at least to Him and to His hearers there was common ground; that He did not need to begin by proving to them that death was not the end of all, but that the universal postulate of religious thought of His day anticipated a renewal of personal and conscious existence after death. In this respect He was but adopting, assuming, and making the basis of impressive exhortation and warning what the majority at least of His contemporaries believed.

The repeated references to the coming of the Kingdom of God or of the heavens (Mt 3^2 4^{17} 10^7 12^{28}, Mk 1^{15}, Lk 9^{27} 10^9 *al.*), into which not everyone who professes loyalty will enter (Mt 7^{21}); to the Day of Judgment or 'that day' (Mt 10^{15} 11$^{22.\ 24}$, Lk 10^{14}, Mt 7^{22} *al.*); to His own Resurrection (Mt 17$^{9.\ 28}$ 26^{32}, Mk 9^{31} 10^{34}, Lk 18^{33} *al.*) and the Coming of the Son of Man (Mt 10^{23} 16$^{27t.}$, Mk 13^{26} 14^{62} *al.*), when those who have confessed or denied Him upon earth will reap as they have sown, in a public confession or denial of them before His Father and the holy angels (Mt 10$^{32t.}$, Lk 9^{26} 12$^{8t.}$),—all presuppose and rest upon the foundation of a belief in another life after this. The disciples are to lay up treasure in heaven (Mt 6^{20}, Lk 12^{33}), the enjoyment of which is clearly not designed for the present. 'In the regeneration' these disciples shall sit upon thrones in the capacity of judges (Mt 19^{28}, Lk 22^{30}). Even His enemies, who hound Him to death, shall 'see' the Son of man sitting on the right hand of power (Mt 26^{64}, Mk 14^{62}; cf. Mt 24^{30}, Mk 13^{26}, Lk 21^{27}). The robber, after death, shall be with Christ in Paradise (Lk 23^{43}). More than one parable bears emphatic witness to the same belief, for example that of the King and the Wedding Feast (Mt 22$^{1ff.}$), of the Talents (25$^{14ff.}$), of the Rich Man and Lazarus (Lk 16$^{19ff.}$). These and other expressions which might be cited, figurative as some of them undoubtedly are, sufficiently emphasize the form and substance of a teaching which is not limited to the present, but always and consistently presupposes a life of active consciousness beyond the grave.

It is doubtful whether even the reputed scepticism of the Sadducees (Mt 22$^{23-33}$, Mk 12$^{18-27}$, Lk 20$^{27-40}$) is any real exception to this. The scope and articles of the creed that they professed remain very uncertain. And their famous apologue is perhaps rather directed against the conception of a joint and common resurrection at one time and place, at which the relationships of this life would be resumed, than implies disbelief in any sequel after death to the life lived upon earth. The incident gives occasion at least to a most emphatic assertion on the part of Christ of the reality of the life that succeeds the present, and an equally emphatic repudiation of the idea that those who have died have ceased to be—'God is not the God of the dead, but of the living; for all live unto him.'

(2) The question of *the duration of this new life,*

the permanence or impermanence of the state after death, presents greater difficulties. Once again it may be said in anticipation that the probabilities of the case are strongly in favour of the former hypothesis. A teacher of the elevation and spirituality of Christ would hardly be likely to suggest to His hearers as a reward for following Him a prolonged existence indeed, but one which closed in the thick darkness of oblivion; and if He wished to convey the thought that in this respect a sharp distinction prevailed between those who loved and obeyed Him and those who did not,—the former are to be immortal, the latter entirely cease to be,—He would do so very clearly and emphatically, as presenting a further powerful and almost overwhelming incentive to hearken to His words. Moreover, it is to be noted also that the conception of 'endlessness' in the abstract is not one easily formulated or grasped, and that a doctrine of this character, assuming it to be present in His teaching, may very well prove to have been set forth in the simplest terms, rather by way of suggestion and illustration that would appeal to His hearers, than in the rigorous language of a scheme of metaphysics. The more important terms that bear upon this point are collected and will be conveniently examined together at a later stage. A few expressions only from the Synoptic Gospels call here for notice.

One of the most important passages, rather, perhaps, on the ground of what it implies than of what it directly states, is the declaration recorded in St. Matthew's Gospel (16[18]) of the permanence and inviolability of Christ's Church, founded and built up as it is upon Himself.* The Speaker can hardly be conceived as thinking of a mere temporary duration of that Church, united as it is with Him in the closest of all bonds; the destruction or annihilation of the one would involve a like fate for the other; 'the gates of Hades shall not prevail against it' now or henceforth. And if the Church is to remain, then necessarily its members collectively; for the Church *is* the members.

It may be said also that the abiding nature of Christ's words (Mt 24[35], Mk 13[31], Lk 21[33]), under the circumstances of their utterance, presupposes the continued existence of intelligent receptive hearers and doers. The permanence of His words is contrasted with that which in the universe appears most permanent and unchanged, 'Heaven and earth shall pass away, but my words shall not pass away' (Mk 13[31], cf. Mt 5[18], Lk 16[17]); in no part or degree shall their accomplishment fail to be achieved. But this complete fulfilment does not imply the cessation of their effect upon and in those for whom they are spoken. Rather is it the beginning of a new life, which is only then perfected.

The literal demands of these passages would be satisfied by what has sometimes been termed 'racial' or 'collective' immortality; in which the race might be supposed to persist, while the individuals, each and all in turn, perished. Such an interpretation could not be ruled out of court on the ground that it is not suggested elsewhere in Christ's teaching. But a conception so remote and unusual would seem to require much more clear and definite exposition, and is hardly consistent with the numerous references to a personal and individual survival.

In a negative sense also phrases like τὸ τέλος

* It is strange that ἐπὶ ταύτῃ τῇ πέτρᾳ is still sometimes referred to Peter. The Speaker, or the Evangelist who reports Him, is playing upon the name in a characteristically Oriental manner. The similarity of the sound forms to Oriental thought a real bond of connexion between the persons. The whole point of the play is lost, and the expression reduced to meaninglessness and absurdity, if Πέτρος and πέτρα are identified (cf. 1 Co 10[4], and in the OT, Gn 2[23], Ex 2[10] etc.).

(Mt 24[6], Mk 13[7], Lk 21[9]), εἰς τέλος (Mt 10[22] 24[13], Mk 13[13]), ἡ συντέλεια τ. αἰῶνος (Mt 13[40. 49] 24[3]) clearly do not imply an absolute end, involving annihilation or the like. They do not, of course, assert survival in any universalistic sense; but they are not altogether neutral in the matter (cf. Mt 13 *ll.cc.*, and the interpretation that is given by Christ Himself of the parable of the Sower). The end of one era is the beginning of another, and for some at least ushers in a period of supreme blessedness (Mt 10[22] 24[13], Mk 13[13]).

The indications which the Synoptic Gospels afford on the subject of the comparative duration of the existence of the righteous and the wicked after death are almost wholly concerned with the significance of words like αἰώνιος (κόλασις αἰ. Mt 25[46], πῦρ αἰώνιον 18[8] 25[41], αἰώνιον ἁμάρτημα Mk 3[29], εἰς τὸν αἰῶνα *ib*.), and will be more conveniently examined together (see below). Here it need only be said that parables such as those of the Rich Man and Lazarus, the Wise and Foolish Virgins, or the Wedding Feast, do not in themselves suggest or demand any inequality of treatment as regards the mere duration of the allotted punishment or reward; and that references to the Judgment, the Day of Judgment, or the Last Day are equally neutral, as far as direct statement is concerned. While the burning of the tares in the parable of the Wheat and the Tares (Mt 13[30]), if the detail is to be pressed as anything more than the natural and appropriate setting of the story,—the legitimate and necessary end of weeds,—rather points in the direction of permanence and indestructibility. Burning is not annihilation of matter, but transformation of form. And this particular feature of the parable might admit of interpretation as implying renovation through suffering, but is hardly satisfied by any theory of absolute cessation of being. Similarly, it might be urged that the πῦρ ἄσβεστον of Mk 9[43] (cf. v.[48]) implies the permanence of the fuel on which it feeds. It is clear, however, that no secure or decisive argument can be based on what are obviously allusive and metaphorical expressions.

B. **St. John.**—Within the Fourth Gospel, where, if anywhere in the record of our Lord's teaching, we might expect to find a reasoned and philosophical doctrine of a future life, that teaching is so entirely, or almost entirely, conveyed in connexion with a special phraseology, the leading terms of which are ζωή, ζωὴ αἰώνιος, and εἰς τ. αἰῶνα, that little need be said by way of anticipation of the special investigation of these terms. It is worth noting, however, at once, in view of the interpretation of these expressions which will be urged below, that every reference in St. John to a definite termination or close of a world-period is, as we saw was the case in the Synoptics, such as to presuppose and assume a continuation beyond. The conception of an absolute end, beyond which there is nothing, is as foreign to the thought of this Gospel as to that of the others. There is a 'last day' (ἡ ἐσχάτη ἡμέρα, 6[39f. 44. 54] 11[24] 12[48], a phrase not found in the Synoptists); but it terminates one age only to usher in another more glorious. Judgment (κρίσις) again in St. John does not ordinarily await the setting up of a future tribunal; it is immediate conviction, wrought by the presence of the light. And in the one passage where it is definitely relegated to the future (5[29]) the parallelism of the phraseology (ἀνάστασις κρίσεως—ἀνάστασις ζωῆς) shows that whatever threatening of suffering or retribution may lie behind the word, there is no thought of extinction, or of a final end, in the mind of the Speaker, — they that have practised ill (RVm) come to the resurrection equally with those that have done good. He cannot be conceived to mean that they are raised merely that forthwith, or after a longer or shorter period, they may be destroyed.

It is in St. John also that the most emphatic assertions are found — apart from the special phraseology to which reference has been made — of the abiding blessedness and freedom from ill of those who believe in Christ. ' He that believeth in me οὐ μὴ ἀποθάνῃ ' (11^{26}); he that drinks of the Christ-given water ' οὐ μὴ διψήσει ' (4^{14}); ' he that cometh unto me οὐ μὴ πεινάσῃ, and he that believeth on me οὐ μὴ διψήσει πώποτε ' (6^{35}). The ' many mansions ' and the prepared place of 14^2 are clearly intended to convey the assurance of more than merely temporary resting-places. Finally, the prayer that all His followers may be one, as He is one with the Father ($17^{11.\ 21}$), and may be with Him where He is (v.^{24}), implies for those who are thus united a coequal duration of existence with Himself.

For the believer, therefore, the future, thus conditioned and defined, is a life of blessedness. But there is nothing to suggest, much less to show, that the continuance of the life is dependent upon its felicity; or that these two features are other than completely independent, no necessary connexion subsisting between them which would make an eternal but unblessed life a contradiction in terms.

αἰών, αἰώνιος, εἰς τὸν αἰῶνα or τοὺς αἰῶνας. — The primary significance of the term αἰών is not seriously in question. ' Age ' or ' period ' suggests a limited stretch of time marked by a definite close. In this sense the word is found in the Gospels, with reference to the present era under which the speaker is living, either simply or as ethically characterized by degeneracy and corruption. The cares τοῦ αἰῶνος choke the word (Mt 13^{22} ‖ Mk 4^{19}); the sons of this αἰών are wiser than the sons of light (Lk 16^8); οὗτος ὁ αἰών is contrasted with the αἰών that is to follow it as ὁ μέλλων (Mt 12^{32}), or ἐκεῖνος (Lk $20^{34f.}$); and the latter appears again as ὁ ἐρχόμενος αἰών in Mk 10^{30} ‖ Lk 18^{30}, where the present is οὗτος ὁ καιρός. It is worthy of notice that in one of the above passages (Lk 20^{35}) the future αἰών is something to be gained (τυχεῖν); its nature or characteristic, therefore, was more prominent to the writer's mind than any mere question of duration. In one context, the parable of the Tares in St. Matthew, the end of the present age is definitely indicated (ἡ) συντέλεια (τοῦ) αἰῶνος (Mt $13^{39f.\ 49}$), and the same phrase is twice employed later in the Gospel, once by the disciples with reference to the Parousia, which they assume to be synchronous with the end of the αἰών (24^3), and again by Christ Himself, when He asserts His presence with His disciples ἕως τῆς συντελείας τοῦ αἰῶνος (28^{20}).

In the last two passages especially it is clear that in no shape or form is there attached by the Speaker or His hearers to the phrase ' end of the age ' the thought of a termination of personality or conscious life. The close of the one epoch marks the opening of another, into which pass without interruption the actors and participators in the present. The pledge given to the disciples of personal association with Himself, or rather of His personal association with them—an association which is already subsisting (ἐγὼ μεθ' ὑμῶν εἰμί, Mt 28^{20}), could hardly have been couched in more emphatic or significant terms, or in words less suggestive of a possible severance, however clearly they may admit or even require the thought of a change of the conditions under which it is maintained.

αἰών is also twice used in the Gospels with reference to the past, ἀπ' αἰῶνος Lk 1^{70}, ἐκ τοῦ αἰῶνος Jn 9^{32}. In neither case are the words those of Christ Himself. And all, perhaps, that need be

said is that the speakers, Zacharias and the man born blind respectively, employ the phrase to denote in an indefinite kind of way the whole antecedent period of human history during which the conditions of life upon the earth have been such as they now know them to be, or believe them to have been in former times.

Elsewhere in the Gospels, the word under consideration is found only in the phrase εἰς τὸν αἰῶνα, or εἰς τοὺς αἰῶνας. The latter occurs in Lk 1^{33} and in the inserted doxology of Mt 6^{13} (retained in the margin of the Revised Version). It may fairly be regarded as merely a strengthened form of the other, intermediate between that and the yet more emphatic expression εἰς τοὺς αἰῶνας τῶν αἰώνων employed especially in the Apocalypse, and by St. Paul in doxologies. Εἰς τὸν αἰῶνα occurs once in St. Matthew and St. Luke (Mt 21^{19}, Lk 1^{55}), twice in St. Mark (3^{29} 11^{14}), and twelve times in St. John (4^{14} $6^{51.\ 58}$ 8^{35} bis. $51f.$ 10^{28} 11^{26} 12^{34} 13^8 14^{16}), constituting indeed this Evangelist's sole use of the word αἰών, with the exception of the phrase above noted (9^{32}). Setting aside Mt 21^{19} ‖ Mk 11^{14}, which condemns the fig-tree to perpetual barrenness, and where μηκέτι εἰς τὸν αἰῶνα is a strong negation of any possible or prospective fruitfulness at any time; and the passages from St. Luke, of which the first is Messianic and expressly asserts the endlessness of the Messiah's kingdom, and the second has reference to the Divine attitude or action towards men, which also can hardly be thought of as subject to termination or change; the remainder may be classified as positive or negative. In the former, the phrase εἰς τὸν αἰῶνα qualifies some verb expressive of continuance or life (ζῆν Jn $6^{51.\ 58}$, μένειν 8^{35} 12^{34}, εἶναι 14^{16}); in the latter it is joined with a more or less emphatic negative, and denies the possibility of the contingency to which the passage refers (οὐκ Mk 3^{29}, Jn 8^{35}; οὐ μή Jn 4^{14} $8^{51f.}$ 10^{28} 11^{26} 13^8).

Of all these passages it may be said at once that the Speaker clearly has in mind a state of things of which no reversal is by Him conceived as possible, either now or at any future time. In presence of natural death, the solemn declaration that he who believes οὐ μὴ ἀποθάνῃ εἰς τὸν αἰῶνα (Jn 11^{26}) does not merely defer the date, but repudiates the possibility of anything that deserves to be called death for the believer. The bond-servant, again, whose sojourn in the house of his master comes to an end, is expressly contrasted with the son who μένει εἰς τὸν αἰῶνα (Jn 8^{35}); and the same expression is used of the Christ (12^{34}), with the same associated ideas of permanence and perpetuity. Peter rejects his Master's offer of service in washing his feet (13^8)—a rejection which he immediately after gladly retracts—not certainly with the idea that he may accept the offer on some or any future occasion, but sincerely, and as far as his present thought is concerned, finally. And life εἰς τὸν αἰῶνα ($6^{51.\ 58}$) is not limited, terminable life, merely lengthened out as compared with the present, but is a life that needs no artificial and bodily sustenance to enable it uninterruptedly to endure. The connotation of the phrase, whether on the lips of Christ Himself or employed by another, evidently implies an outlook into a future to which the thought of the writer or speaker neither assigns nor conceives it possible to assign a limit.

The same considerations will apply to the adjective αἰώνιος, and especially as it is used to qualify ζωή in a phrase which becomes a distinctive feature of St. John's Gospel and First Epistle. For the word itself the somewhat question-begging rendering ' age-long ' has been offered. In such a rendering it is evident that all depends on the conception the writers had formed of the ' age,' and the associations it bore to their minds. If they thought of it as definitely terminated or terminable, then 'age-long' is equivalent to 'temporary.' If they regarded it and wrote of it without any associated idea of a limit or end, or if the context clearly intimates that no such idea would have been admitted, then so far 'age-long' is synonymous with 'immortal,' 'everlasting,' or 'eternal.' And it appears undesirable to introduce a new and ambiguous term. Apart, however, from the phrase ζωὴ αἰώνιος, the adjective is of rare occurrence in the Synoptic Gospels, and is not used by St. John. It is found three times in St. Matthew in association with terms expressive of suffering or retribution to be endured in the future (τὸ πῦρ τὸ αἰώνιον, 18⁸ 25⁴¹; κόλασις αἰώνιος, 26⁴⁶). St. Luke has a reference (16⁹) to τὰς αἰωνίους σκηνάς, 'the eternal tabernacles,' open to those who have been far-sighted enough to secure to themselves friends while it was in their power, from whom in their own day of need they may claim favours and return in kind. And a significant and unique phrase in Mk 3²⁹ ὃς δ' ἂν βλασφημήσῃ . . . ἔνοχός ἐστιν αἰωνίου ἁμαρτήματος, suggests far-reaching conclusions, with regard to which all that perhaps need be said in this place is that it stands here as an explanatory addition to an emphatic affirmation that blasphemy against the Holy Spirit hath not forgiveness εἰς τὸν αἰῶνα. The context, therefore, precludes an interpretation in a sense contrary to the implications of the preceding words, as though the writer might be thinking of an act of sin committed once for all, and then with all that it entailed definitely and finally set aside.

The reading ἁμαρτήματος is sufficiently decisively attested by the witness of אBLΔ 28. 33, the Latin and other versions, and is adopted by all editors. It is supported also by the Sinaitic Syriac, mutilated, however, in this verse, if the transcript (1894) may be trusted. The TR κρίσεως is found in אC²Γ and the cursives, with one or two Latin manuscripts, and the Peshiṭta Syriac. The various reading ἁμαρτίας, C*D 13. 69. 346, would seem to be a correction of ἁμαρτήματος designed to introduce into the text the meaning of 'sinfulness' as distinguished from 'a sin.' Cf. H. B. Swete, in loc., a not wholly satisfactory note. The true exposition seems to be given by E. P. Gould in his commentary :* ' An eternal sin may be one subjecting the person to an eternal punishment, eternal in its consequences, that is. But certainly it is equally allowable to suppose that it describes the sin itself as eternal, accounting for the impossibility of the forgiveness by the permanence of the sin,—endless consequences attached to endless sin. This is the philosophy of endless punishment. Sin reacts on the nature, an act passes into a state, and the state continues. That is, eternal punishment is not a measure of God's resentment against a single sin. . . . It is the result of the effect of any sin, or course of sin, in fixing the sinful state beyond recovery.'

With regard to the phrase ζωὴ αἰώνιος, there is a striking difference in its associations in the few passages in which it is found in the Synoptists, and in the more frequent use of St. John; a difference which seems to reflect the varying attitude of the writers towards the teaching of Christ. In the Synoptists the sphere of ζωὴ αἰώνιος is in the future. It is to be inherited (Mt 19²⁹), and to be received in the coming αἰών (Mk 10³⁰, Lk 18³⁰) in recompense for that which the disciples of Christ forego in this; which the ruler (ἄρχων, Lk 18¹⁸ ‖ Mt 19¹⁶, Mk 10¹⁷), or lawyer (νομικός, Lk 10²⁵) conceives that he may inherit or attain (σχῶ, Mt. l.c.) by virtue of good deeds in the present. In St. John, on the contrary, ζωὴ αἰώνιος is a present possession. The believer has or may have it (Jn 3³⁶ 5²⁴ 6⁴⁷, 3¹⁵· ¹⁶ 6⁴⁰); and the bestowal of this gift is described as the express aim and purpose of the coming of the Son to the world and of His death, the fruit of the Father's love (3¹⁶) and will (6⁴⁰), but conferred by the Son Himself (10²⁸ 17²). In one passage also where the same phrase is used, the closeness of the fellowship with Himself implied in the possession

* Intern. Critical Commentary, 'St. Mark,' T. & T. Clark, 1896.

of ζωὴ αἰώνιος is mystically described as an eating of His flesh and drinking of His blood, and is associated with the resurrection at the last day (6⁵⁴). This last passage would by itself prove, what the others assume, that ζωὴ αἰώνιος, though present, is not limited by the present. Elsewhere there is an approach to the Synoptic standpoint of a future life over against or following on that now lived, although sight seems never to be entirely lost of the conception of ζωὴ αἰώνιος as subsisting already and now attainable. He that hateth his soul (ψυχή) in this world will keep it εἰς ζωὴν αἰώνιον (12²⁵); the meat (βρῶσις), the gift of the Son of Man, abideth unto eternal life (6²⁷). The same thought recurs in Christ's words to the woman of Samaria; there it is the water, His gift, which becomes a well of water springing up unto eternal life (4¹⁴). And, finally, in connexion with the same incident, the harvest, the ripeness of which the disciples are bidden to recognize, is laid up unto a future which is undefined in time and place; the reaper gathereth together fruit εἰς ζωὴν αἰώνιον, and shares with the sower in a common joy (4³⁶).

Once also Christ appeals to the knowledge or belief of His hearers in the present reality of this eternal life; they think that they have it in the OT Scriptures, missing the spirit there, and the testimony of these Scriptures to Himself, and ascribing life to the letter (5³⁹). A somewhat similar thought underlies the answer of Simon Peter to Christ's question whether he and the Twelve intend to follow the example of others, and be repelled by 'hard sayings'; ' Thou hast the words of eternal life' (6⁶⁸),—words, that is to say, which in their spirit and teaching bring ζωὴν αἰώνιον to the hearers. Finally, lest, as it were, any lingering possibility or suggestion should remain of a time-limit to be understood in the phrase, or of its being confined under a merely temporal category, it is twice expressly defined in terms which are ethical and spiritual, and transcend all limitations of time or change; the Divine ἐντολή, committed by the Father to the Son and by Him transmitted to the world, is eternal life (12⁵⁰); and in similar pregnant words (17³) ζωὴ αἰώνιος is the learning to know the only true God, and Jesus Christ whom He has sent.

All the passages in which this phrase is found in the Gospels have now been passed in review. An extension of the examination to the remaining books of the New Testament would not modify the conclusions reached, or throw fresh light upon its meaning. It is used twice by St. Luke in the Acts (13⁴⁶· ⁴⁸); by St. Paul in the Romans (2⁷ 5²¹ 6²²ᶠ·), Galatians (6⁸), and Pastoral Epistles (1 Ti 1¹⁶ 6¹², Tit 1² 3⁷); by St. John himself in his First Epistle (1² 2²⁵ 3¹⁵ 5¹¹· ¹³· ²⁰; the adjective not elsewhere), and by St. Jude (v.²¹). These conclusions are entirely in harmony with the results obtained from a consideration of the term αἰών, or of the adjective αἰώνιος standing by itself. ζωὴ αἰώνιος is in its significance independent of time-limits, and may be described indifferently as either present or future. When, moreover, the occasion offers to indicate its characteristics and meaning by definition, that definition is framed not on the lines of time and space, as here, there, or elsewhere, now or then, but is wholly ethical, supranatural, belonging to the realm of the mind and spirit, and lifting up ζωὴ αἰώνιος beyond the touch of change or end, into the region of the changeless, the immortal.

At the risk, therefore, of repetition, it must again be pointed out that words and phrases which are crucial for any doctrine of immortality as taught by Christ in the Gospels, so far from implying or suggesting an absolute termination, whether nearer or more distant, to that future which the speakers or writers have in mind, seem to indicate that no such idea was ever present to them; and in some passages, which are neither isolated nor unimportant, a fair interpretation of the writer's thought in the light of the context appears to exclude the possibility of any such limit being found at any definite point or place in the 'age' towards which his gaze is directed.

ζωή, εἰσελθεῖν εἰς τὴν ζωήν, σώζεσθαι, σωτηρία.

There remains a group of words and phrases to be referred to, which with more or less distinctness characterize the future, or contrast it with the conditions of the present. All of them, when used in their fullest sense, imply *non-mortality*, but they do not bear directly upon the question of the duration of existence after death, which, as we have seen, has come to be the chief element in the connotation of the term 'immortality.' The chief of these is ζωή with its derivatives, including the phrases of which it forms a part. ζωή in the Gospels is not mere physical life, but is an expression for the higher life, the life which is life indeed, life in its fullest, richest aspects. Such life was in the Word (Jn 1⁴); it is Christ's gift to His disciples (10²⁸, cf. 6³³); nay, He is Himself 'the life' (11²⁵ 14⁶). It is so good a possession that to 'enter into life' is worth the sacrifice of an eye or a limb (Mt 18⁸ᶠ· ‖ Mk 9⁴³· ⁴⁵). It begins after death (Jn 5²⁴)—not in a temporal sense, but when θάνατος as a state ceases to be; and it is a 'resurrection of life' to which the well-doers will come forth from the tomb (v.²⁹). 'To have life in himself' is an attribute of the Father, and is His gift to the Son (v.²⁶); and this 'life' or 'eternal life' is repeatedly stated to be the present possession of the believer (Jn 3¹⁵ᶠ· ³⁶ 6⁴⁷· ⁵⁴), the gift of Christ which some of them wilfully refuse (5⁴⁰), and which the unbelieving will not see (3³⁶), but which is emphatically declared to be the final end of His coming into the world (10¹⁰, cf. 20³¹). The words which He has spoken are life (6⁶³), and His commandment is ζωὴ αἰώνιος (12⁵⁰). None of these passages suggests that the thought of a termination of the 'life' was present to the mind of the Speaker; some are hardly compatible with such a thought, and others absolutely forbid it (*e.g.* Jn 1⁴ 5²⁶). This ζωή, therefore, is fittingly represented as αἰώνιος.

A similar absence of limitation will be found to characterize expressions such as σώζεσθαι, σωτηρία, etc., which describe the future from the point of view of deliverance from the present, its calamities and its evils. These terms, however, are not in themselves suggestive of duration, except so far as their results are involved; and, as doctrinal terms, belong in the New Testament rather to the Epistles than to the Gospels. In the eschatological discourses, however, of the Synoptic Gospels, 'salvation' is described as a state to be attained by those who endure εἰς τέλος (Mt 10²² 24¹³ ‖ Mk 13¹³); the saving of the life or soul (ψυχή, cf. Lk 6⁹) is strikingly said to be the result of willingness to lose it for Christ's sake (Mk 8³⁵ ‖ Lk 9²⁴, cf. εὑρήσει αὐτήν, Mt 16²⁵); and in St. John the salvation of the κόσμος is the purpose of the Divine mission of the Son (Jn 3¹⁷), the salvation of His hearers, the end of the words and teaching which He imparts (5³⁴). Hence 'salvation' is contemplated as beyond an 'end'; τέλος is rather a crisis than a final close, the entrance into new conditions and a more gracious environment. Both thought and phraseology become meaningless if the subjects of the change are conceived as either annihilated or reduced to unconsciousness.

Agrapha. Of the 'unwritten' Sayings, few have interest or importance for the present subject. The most noteworthy and authentic is that which is embodied in St. Paul's argument of 1 Th 4¹⁵⁻¹⁷.

Whether all or any of this is intended to be a direct citation of Christ's words must remain uncertain. The teaching of the passage is, however, founded upon a λόγος Κυρίου. And though it has in view only 'the dead in Christ,' and their position of privilege and priority as compared with those alive at the time of the Lord's descent from heaven, it distinctly asserts of these that they will be 'for ever' (πάντοτε) with the Lord. The writer therefore contemplates for them an eternal co-existence with the Lord; and he claims that for this doctrine he has the authority of Christ Himself.

Of the Logia from Oxyrhynchus the mystical Saying, 'Except ye fast to the world, ye shall in no wise find the kingdom of God; and except ye keep the Sabbath, ye shall not see the Father' (*Log.* 2; Grenfell and Hunt, p. 10), may be said to imply that those who do so fast and truly keep the Sabbath will see the Father, and therefore live with Him. Of the later Logia also, which were discovered in 1903 (*Oxyrhynchus Papyri*, iv. p. 1 ff.), the Introduction, as it is named by the editors, apparently quotes Jn 8⁵²—the hearer of these words 'shall not taste of death.' And the first and second Sayings both make reference to the Kingdom which shall be a place of rest to him who seeks and finds. These indications are all of them slight, and do not add anything to the teaching of the Gospels. But as far as they go they are in harmony with what we have found to be the constant implications in Scripture of the words of Christ and His disciples.

The most striking and suggestive feature, therefore, of all these references in the Gospels to the future, and of the doctrine which they may be understood to imply, is the absence of any indication of a termination of the new conditions which they introduce. In some instances, indeed, the writer's statement might be regarded as colourless in this respect, and the thought and context of his words would not be directly contradicted by an assumption that these conditions were themselves temporary, and at some indefinite period superseded by others. Elsewhere the tone and context strongly support, if they do not compel, the view that the state of things contemplated was contemplated, as far as the forecast of the speaker was concerned, as permanent. In a third and most important series of passages, the same expressions and phrases are directly applied to the Divine Being and to His Kingdom in such a manner as to show that no thought of a cessation or close could by any possibility have entered into the mind of the Speaker, or have been regarded by Him as conceivable.

Moreover, the change of circumstances thus introduced involves no interference with the conscious life, not, at least, to the extent of reducing it to unconsciousness. The subjects of the change are represented as speaking, feeling, and willing, with all their faculties under control and in action. Nor is there any suggestion that this condition is occasional or temporary; it is, on the other hand, tacitly assumed to be usual and a matter of course.

Further, also, most prominent and characteristic examples of this manner of regarding the future were found to be associated with the terms αἰών and its derivatives. This word, originally apparently denoting a definite age, marked off by beginning and end, had come to be regularly employed to denote an 'age,' the beginning of which was, indeed, sometimes more or less obscurely indicated, but to which the Speaker did not assign a further limit, and, in some instances, would clearly have rejected the idea of a limit as contradictory and impossible. The thought underlying these expressions is not that of a terminable period, but of a limitless progression.

The only adequate rendering of such a thought in English is by the words 'eternal,' 'immortal,' or the like. For there lies implicit in these words precisely what we have found to be the implication of αἰώνιος, etc., in the Gospels ; viz. that the speaker rejects the idea of a bound or limit beyond which there is nothing, or nothing for the subject of whom he is speaking ; that however far off the boundary fence is in thought set up, he immediately insists that it shall be taken down, and removed farther away,—only to repeat the process as often as an attempt is made to assign a limit or define an end. This is, indeed, the only real conception which we seem able to frame of the meaning and content of such terms as immortality, eternity, etc., as they are ordinarily employed. They connote not a positive and comprehensive idea, which the mind distinctly outlines to itself as a whole, but rather the negative and indefinite one of the absence of an end ; looking forth into the future, we find ourselves unable to discern a point beyond which there is an absolute blank as far as the conditions under consideration are concerned. The association of the thought of a final end with the conditions or state supposed would involve a self-contradiction, or, if we prefer to use the phrase, would be impossible. Such a conception is entirely logical and consistent, and amounts practically to defining immortality as the summation of an infinite number of intervals or spaces of time, succeeding one another without break, and receding into dim, fathomless distance.

The precise words 'endless,' 'immortal,' or 'immortality' do not occur in the Gospels ; cf., however, Lk 1³³ 'Of his kingdom there shall be no end,' οὐκ ἔσται τέλος. The omission, if omission it be, is partly supplied by St. Paul, who describes the after-state of the Christian as ἀφθαρσία and ἀθανασία, 'incorruption' and 'deathlessness' (1 Co 15⁵³ᶠ.). The latter term is shown by its use in 1 Ti 6¹⁶ (the blessed and only Potentate . . . ὁ μόνος ἔχων ἀθανασίαν) to have moved far in the direction of a positive connotation.

Similar considerations apply generally to the references to this doctrine in the remaining books of the New Testament, a detailed examination of which lies outside the range of the present article. Such an examination would strengthen in detail, but would not change the character of the argument. In no instance is there a suggestion of absolute finality. The conclusion of every αἰών, for example, marks the commencement of another, accompanied by changed conditions, indeed, but not, as far as the statements and apparent train of thought carry us, by annihilation in any sense, or a destruction which involves loss of personal consciousness or life. And while the writers do not in so many words define that future into which their thought projects itself as 'immortal' or 'endless,' their attitude towards it and the phrases and descriptions which they employ are such as to negative the idea that they would or could have admitted of the drawing of a line here, there, or anywhere, beyond which absolute oblivion and death should reign. Compare Ro 1²⁵ ad fin. 6²² ad fin. 9⁵ 16²⁶ τοῦ αἰωνίου θεοῦ, 2 Co 4¹⁸ᵇ 11³¹, Philem ¹⁵, He 1⁸ 7³ 13⁸, 1 P 5¹⁰, Rev 1¹⁸.

(3) In passing to the third part of our inquiry, which relates to *the comprehensiveness of the life beyond the grave*, whether it is contemplated as equally endless for all, or whether a distinction is drawn as regards duration between the after-existence of the evil-doer and that of the righteous man, we are conscious of a certain reserve in description and expression on the part of the Evangelists, of a delicacy which certainly reflects the mind and teaching of the Master. The passages which refer to the future of the wicked are comparatively few in number ; and the outline, as it were, of the picture presented is drawn, not, indeed, waveringly or hesitatingly, but with a light hand,

as though the subject were one to which detail or elaboration were inappropriate. Reticence and brevity characterize all the utterances of Christ that bear upon the share which the evil-doers have in the life after death. Thus, while the righteous man and believer enters beyond the grave upon a renewed life, to the duration of which no limit is set, and which the hearers of Christ's words understood in this sense to be eternal, the question is justly raised whether the same statement may be made, and the same inference drawn, with regard to the future existence of those who are not righteous and do not believe. Do those who—to adopt the language of the parable—go away into the outer darkness, pass into oblivion, suffer extinction, or experience any other of the conjectural fates which have from time to time been assumed to be the lot of the wicked ? or, as an alternative, may 'outer darkness' be paraphrased into 'purgatory,' on the further side of which there is light ?

It may be said *in limine* that the presumption is against any such limitation of the duration of life beyond the grave in the case of one class or section only of humanity. It would require very strong evidence to enforce the acceptance of the view that terms or expressions which disown the idea of a boundary, an end, when used of the future state of the righteous, actually and of set purpose connote such an idea when they describe the lot of the wicked : or that the Speaker would confuse His audience with antitheses which were merely verbal, and possessed no underlying significance or reality. Upon this issue, again, only an examination and fair interpretation of the passages which bear upon the subject can decide. It will be found that such passages in the Gospels are few in number, though not wanting in suggestiveness.

The most significant and important passage is perhaps Mk 3²⁹, to which reference has already been made ; and its significance does not altogether depend upon the closing words, in which the variation of text occurs. Assuming that the reading αἰωνίου ἁμαρτήματος is correct, as we are justified in doing (see above, p. 788ᵃ), it is difficult to see what other meaning can be attached to the phrase than that of a sin the results of which are permanent. An 'act of sin' cannot be permanent or endless in execution, though it may be ceaselessly repeated ; it is only in its fruits that it endures. And if ἁμαρτήματος can be supposed to describe 'sinfulness' in any sense, the meaning is practically the same ; for endless sinfulness necessarily involves endless retribution. The earlier part of the verse has its parallels in the two other Synoptists—

Mt 12³² ὃς δ' ἂν εἴπῃ κατὰ τοῦ πνεύματος τοῦ ἁγίου οὐκ ἀφεθήσεται αὐτῷ οὔτε ἐν τούτῳ τῷ αἰῶνι οὔτε ἐν τῷ μέλλοντι.

Mk 3²⁹ ὃς δ' ἂν βλασφημήσῃ εἰς τὸ πνεῦμα τὸ ἅγιον οὐκ ἔχει ἄφεσιν εἰς τὸν αἰῶνα, ἀλλὰ ἔνοχός ἐστιν αἰωνίου ἁμαρτήματος.

Lk 12¹⁰ τῷ δὲ εἰς τὸ ἅγιον πνεῦμα βλασφημήσαντι οὐκ ἀφεθήσεται.

The simplest form is that of St. Luke ; but it is hardly less pregnant or decisive than those of the other Evangelists. The blasphemy is *personal*, the conscious and wilful act of a conscious and responsible being ; and therefore — unless the words are to be emptied of their force, and reduced to meaninglessness — the consequences are personal also, falling not on someone else, but on the blasphemer himself, for whom there is no place for forgiveness either in this 'age' or in that which is to come. The reason is supplied by St. Mark, and by St. Mark only,—he ' is guilty of an eternal sin,' is liable to its penalty, and subject to its consequences. The permanence of sin implies and necessitates the permanent impossibility of forgiveness. On the central and essential point the three reports are at one.

The significance for the doctrine of immortality of the parable or apocalypse of Mt 25[31-46], with the sentences pronounced on the 'sheep' and 'goats' and the penalties incurred, lies in the application of identical words and phrases to describe the duration of that future into which both pass from the judgment-seat. If the ζωή of the righteous is αἰώνιος, so is the κόλασις of the wicked (v.[46]); the fire into which the latter depart is αἰώνιον also (v.[41]), although this word is not applied to the Kingdom prepared for the righteous (v.[34]). It is surely an abuse of language to maintain that the Speaker designed to convey a different meaning in the two instances. If, as we have seen reason to believe, the term αἰώνιος carried with it the thought of the absence of an assigned or assignable end to that vista of the future contemplated by the Speaker, or, in other words, was practically identical in significance with our 'immortal,' 'eternal,' it cannot justly be shorn of this connotation when it is applied to the 'punishment' which overtakes those on the left hand of the Judge.

An expression is found in Jn 5[29] which has some bearing upon this subject. Its importance for a doctrine of universal immortality must not be overestimated; for the stress lies again upon the parallelism; but by implication, though not directly, it appears to assert the same equality of lot for all as regards the duration of the revived existence. It would not be difficult, indeed, to draw out at length a similar proof for the words ἀναστῆναι and ἀνάστασις to that which has been attempted above for αἰών and αἰώνιος; and to show that these expressions never, on the lips of Christ and in the Gospels, denote a resurrection which is the prelude to a new life leading only to a new death. On the contrary, ἀνάστασις ushers in another period and fresh conditions of existence, of which no termination is contemplated or conceivable. 'All that are in the tombs . . . shall come forth.' And as the 'resurrection of life,' the portion of those who have done good, can hardly be understood to indicate a merely temporary restoration or perpetuation of existence, so no interpretation of the difficult phrase 'resurrection of judgment' will be satisfactory which postulates a distinction in this respect between the righteous and those upon whom the judgment falls.

A similar argument might not unfairly be based upon the parable of the Rich Man and Lazarus (Lk 16[19ff.]), or the King and the Wedding Guests (Mt 22[2-14]), viz. that the conditions, the data of the parable, do not in either case suggest, but rather by their tone deprecate the idea of absolute annihilation awaiting those who, on the one hand, find no place in Abraham's bosom, or, on the other, have failed to fitly provide themselves with raiment meet for the wedding feast. It would, however, be at the best no more than an *argumentum e silentio*, to which no great value could be attached. The declaration of Christ also to the Sadducees, as reported in St. Luke's Gospel, that 'all live to him' (Lk 20[38]), though from one point of view susceptible of a universalistic interpretation, does seem on any construction to exclude the idea that there are some who finally cease to live in any real or intelligible sense of the word.

Ἀπολλύναι, ἀποθνήσκειν, etc. It remains to consider briefly the significance and implication of the terms employed in the Gospels to denote 'death,' 'perishing,' or 'destruction.' The principal of these are the verbs ἀπολλύναι and ἀποθνήσκειν, with the cognate nouns ἀπώλεια and θάνατος.

The uncompounded verb θνήσκειν occurs but rarely in the Gospels (Mt 2[20], Mk 15[44], Lk 7[12] 8[49], Jn 11[44] 19[33]), and is always

employed of mere physical death regarded as the termination of the activities, good or evil, of the present life. There is no thought of a future, either affirmed or denied, in the minds of the speakers; and in none of the passages is the word on the lips of Christ or reported as used by one of His disciples. Neither is the simple verb ὀλλύναι found in NT Greek. And the adjective θνητός is used only by St. Paul (twice as an epithet of σῶμα, Ro 6[12] 8[11], once of σάρξ, 2 Co 4[11], and in antithesis to ἀθανασία, 1 Co 15[53f.], or to ζωή, 2 Co 5[4]).

Ἀπώλεια is found only four times in the Gospels. In Mt 26[8] ‖ Mk 14[4] it is the 'waste' of the ointment. For its real purpose, as conceived by the Speaker, the ointment 'perishes,' is lost; but it is clearly not annihilated, only diverted from its proper use. In Mt 7[13] the way that leads εἰς τὴν ἀπώλειαν, 'to destruction,' is described as broad; no indication, however, is given as to the fate of those who traverse this way when they reach ἀπώλεια, and it is fair, therefore, to interpret the phrase in the light of the other passages where the word occurs (in the parallel passage Lk 13[24] no mention is made of the broad way). Jn 17[12] 'not one of them is lost but the son of perdition,' employs a Hebraistic mode of expression. ὁ υἱὸς τῆς ἀπωλείας is one who shares the qualities, is like in character to ἀπώλεια, cf. υἱὸν γεέννης, Mt 23[15]; but though he ἀπώλετο, and nothing is directly stated as to his present condition or future destiny, the son of perdition is certainly not conceived as either unconscious or extinct, nor is there any suggestion that this is to be his ultimate fate.

In the Synoptic Gospels ἀποθνήσκειν, like θνήσκειν, uniformly expresses merely physical death as the cessation of physical activities. Two passages in St. Luke, however, call for special notice. In the parable referred to above, both Lazarus and the rich man 'die' (ἀποθανεῖν, 16[22]); but their conscious activity does not terminate, it is merely transferred to other spheres. And of the sons of God, the sons of the resurrection, it is emphatically said (20[36]) that recurrence of death is for them impossible. Death, therefore, passes upon them once, but leaves them ἰσάγγελοι, 'equal to angels,' in an exalted and privileged state, no more subject to its power. The word is more common in St. John (28 times), and in accordance with the more contemplative and spiritual character of his Gospel is employed also metaphorically, though its predominant use is literal and physical. Thus the grain of wheat falls into the ground and dies (ἀποθάνῃ, 12[24]), but by and through death rises to a newer and richer life, and 'bears much fruit.' And for the believer death is but the beginning of life (11[25]), a life that is permanent and exposed to no return of death (πᾶς ὁ ζῶν . . . οὐ μὴ ἀποθάνῃ εἰς τὸν αἰῶνα, v.[26]).

Of the word θάνατος, 'death,' a similar account must be given. It is usually physical death, with no reference to or thought of that which is beyond. By the Synoptists it is employed more or less metaphorically in Mt 4[16], Lk 1[79] (quotations from Isaiah), Mt 26[38] ‖ Mk 14[34]. In Mt 20[18] ‖ Mk 10[33] θάνατος is for Christ Himself the prelude to life. So in Jn 5[24] he that believeth . . . 'hath passed out of death into life'; and later in the same Gospel Christ declares that he who keeps His word shall not see (8[51]), or taste of (v.[52]) death εἰς τὸν αἰῶνα (cf. 11[26]).

Finally, there is the term ἀπολλύναι, perhaps the most significant of all the expressions that describe dissolution and the cessation of a worldly estate. It is apparently employed by the Sacred Writers with a weaker as well as a stronger association. The former meaning, to 'lose,' to 'find to be missing,' is illustrated by Mt 15[24], Lk 15[4. 8f.], Jn 6[12] 18[9] and other passages. The predominant sense of the word, however, is that of 'ruin,' the precise nature or degree of which will be indicated by the context; but which consists essentially in the loss or withdrawal of capacity for the due discharge of function or duty. Thus the wine-skins 'perish' in St. Matthew (9¹⁷), both the wine and the skins in St. Mark (2²²) ; but the substance of both survives, though they have become wasted and useless. So also in Jn 6²⁷, where the βρῶσις that 'perishes' loses its nutritive power, and ceases to be able to perform the part of food. Applied to persons the word is equivalent to 'ruined,' 'undone,' succumbing to present or prospective emergency or pressure, e.g. Mt 8²⁵ ‖ Mk 4³⁸, Lk 8²⁴ ; Lk 15¹⁷, Jn 11⁵⁰. In the passages most pertinent to the present inquiry a definitely spiritual 'ruin' is contemplated, the object of which is usually the ψυχή, Mt 10²⁸·³⁹ 16²⁵ ‖ Mk 8³⁵, Lk 9²⁴ 17³³ ; Lk 6⁹, Jn 12²⁵ ; but the loss or ruin of the soul here is distinctly said to be preliminary to finding, saving, or (Lk 17³³) quickening it (ζωογονεῖν). The idea conveyed is again, therefore, not annihilation or destruction of being, but change of state. Here, also, the highest form of teaching is found in St. John. Every believer in Christ, or the sheep who hear His voice, are expressly declared to be permanently exempt from ruin (3¹⁶ 10²⁸) ; and while the man who 'loveth his life' (ὁ φιλῶν τὴν ψυχὴν αὐτοῦ) is the active cause of its ruin (ἀπολλύει αὐτήν), he who hates it in this world will keep it 'unto life eternal' (12²⁵). Passages in which the word is used of mere physical destruction, in which usually no thought of the future is involved, must be interpreted in accordance with this general conception (Mt 2¹³ 12¹⁴ 26⁵², Mk 9²², Lk 17²⁹ al.).

In the passages referred to above, Mt 10³⁹ and parallels, the antithesis ὃς ἀπολέσῃ or ὁ ἀπολέσας τὴν ψυχὴν αὐτοῦ is hardly to be weakened or explained away as mere *willingness* to lose. There is an actual loss incurred and completed. And the 'ruin' consists in the stripping off from the ψυχή of all those qualities and connexions which have bound it to the present, and have made it what it is, material and sensual. The essential ψυχή, the soul transformed, is 'saved' by the process, and enters upon a new life. Thus the phrase is practically equivalent to St. John's 'loving' and 'hating' (Jn 12²⁵).

In attempting to estimate the value of these indications with regard to the future life of the wicked, few and slight as they seem to be compared with the fulness and frequency of the references to the blessed lot of the righteous, two preliminary conditions which are essential to their right interpretation need to be borne in mind. In the first place, it was clearly far from the intention of the Teacher to lay down or elaborate any metaphysical doctrine of a future existence, such as we might reasonably expect from formal systems of philosophy. Written across His words and actions is their immediate and practical aim ; and to have mystified His plain and unlettered hearers with definitions and metaphysics would have been to repel them, and defeat His own purpose. That task He must leave to successors, who in other times, and with other surroundings, will enter into His labours. To expect to find, for example, in the Gospels a well-ordered and articulated defence of natural immortality, so called, is unreasonable. Any such expectation is by the conditions of the case doomed to disappointment. Hints, pre-intimations, there will naturally be, the elucidation and development of which will be the care of after ages ; but completeness, finality, from a logical or philosophic point of view, will not be found ; nor a series of statements which, however fitted they might be to meet the requirements of some one or other of the later centuries, were out of touch with the thought of His own day and generation.

Again, the reticence observed as to the fate of the wicked, and the comparative infrequency of mention thereof, are entirely in harmony with what is found to be the case in the early literatures of the other great religions of the world. To expatiate on a destiny of woe and pain, or upon the duration of the sufferings of the lost, is, judging from all analogy, evidence not of an early but of a late position in the history of religious thought ; and were this a marked feature of the Gospels, it would justly have laid them open to the suspicion of having at least undergone modification in the interests of later and more developed forms of belief. The hymns of the Rig-Veda, for example, dwell much upon the blessed estate of the good who do that which is acceptable to the gods, and accordingly go hereafter to dwell with them ; but they contain only slight and passing references to the lot of the evil-doers, who are hurled by Indra into darkness. The Egyptian Book of the Dead relates the varying trials and fortunes of the deceased in the nether world, through which he passes successfully by the aid of talismanic formulæ and the favour of the gods ; but complete silence is observed with regard to the man who at the bar of Osiris fails to pass the prescribed tests. And it is characteristic also not of primitive but of mature, if not decadent, Buddhism to set forth in vivid description and with luxuriant art the series of hells in which carefully graduated torments on an ascending scale of horror are apportioned with precision to the heinousness of the sinner's crimes. It was not otherwise in early Christianity. There, too, it was left to later ages to elaborate descriptions and to revel in details of a future life, the real circumstances of which neither human language is capable of defining nor human thought, tied down as it is to categories belonging essentially to present conditions, able to conceive. The comparative silence of the earliest authoritative documents, and of the earliest teaching so far as it has come down to us, is more eloquent and convincing than the most exhaustive and graphic statement of doctrine could ever have been.

Mohammedanism, it may be said, is an exception to this rule, and from the very beginning lavishes its descriptive powers on the torments that await the unbeliever. Islâm, however, sprang adult and full-armed from the mind of its founder, and was stereotyped in the Korân. Its doctrines have already a long history of development behind them, and, if we could trace them back to the starting-point, would probably be found in all instances to conform to the prevailing type of historic growth.

The results to which we have been led may be briefly summarized as follows :—

(1) The reality of a conscious life beyond the grave is uniformly assumed and taught by Christ Himself and by the writers of the Gospels.

(2) To this future life there is assigned no terminus or end. Rather do the phrases used suggest that the thought of a final end never presented itself to Speaker or writer as either actual or possible. And where words like τέλος, ἐσχάτη ἡμέρα, etc., are employed, the 'end' or 'last day' is obviously and patently not absolute, but marks and introduces a new beginning. No philosophical theory of immortality is formulated ; such a theory is not to be expected, and was, indeed, under the circumstances hardly possible. The doctrine of the Gospels, however, of a renewed life after death to which no limit is set, and for which by virtue of the very terms employed no limit appears to be conceivable, is in the last analysis all that we mean, or can mean, by 'eternity,' 'immortality.'

(3) The writers give no countenance whatever to any theory which in respect of its duration separates the lot of the righteous from that of the wicked. Slight and indefinite, overlaid with metaphor and parable, as are the indications of the conditions under which the future life of the latter will be lived, the guarded statements made and the hints allowed to fall consistently imply that in this respect equality of treatment is meted out to all. If the ζωή of the one is αἰώνιος, and he is not

to die εἰς τὸν αἰῶνα, the κόλασις of the other is αἰώνιος likewise, and he is or may be guilty of a ἁμάρτημα, the fruits of which are gathered in no less a period of time than is described by the same phrase. Theories of universal restoration, of final extinction, or of any modification or combination of these find no support in the words of Christ or of His disciples as recorded in the Gospels.

The present writer shares the convictions which have been very widely felt and expressed, that the final demonstration of immortality, if and when it is given, will have to be based on broader than any merely literal or narrowly expository grounds. Christ spoke to His own age ; and necessarily spoke such truths and in such a form as that age could receive and assimilate. That He exhausted the whole range of truth in His statement, or formulated both in shape and substance all doctrine that the mind of man could ever appreciate, is as impossible to believe as it is contrary to His own express words (Jn 16¹²). Nor can we doubt that if He had lived in our day, He would have delivered truths expanded and recast to meet the needs and tendencies and capacities with which He found Himself brought into touch.

That the Christian Church has been on the whole on right lines, and has justified generally in her interpretation of the teaching of her Founder and His immediate disciples with respect to this particular doctrine, the foregoing exposition has attempted to show. The end, however, is not yet. And the ferment of thought, not less, perhaps more, characteristic of our age than of any that have preceded it, is not destined to be stilled into unconcern, or to have its efforts paralyzed, by any dogmatic creed or pronouncement of whatever authority. It claims the right to work out its own doctrinal freedom not only in the light of the Sacred Records, but under the guidance of that reason which it holds no less certainly than revelation to be an element and gift of the Divine.

LITERATURE.—The treatises on NT Theology, or Theology in general, and the History of Doctrine contain little that is relevant. See the article on ' Eschatology ' by S. D. F. Salmond in Hastings' *DB*, vol. i. p. 749 ff., and the literature there cited. Add W. N. Clarke, *Outline of Christian Theology*, Edinburgh, 1898, p. 192 ff. ; William James, *Human Immortality*⁵, London, 1903 ; J. Royce, *Conception of Immortality*, London, 1904.

A. S. GEDEN.

IMPEDIMENT.—See DISEASE.

IMPORTUNITY.—The only passage in the EV where this word is found is Lk 11⁸ 'Because of his importunity he will arise and give him as many as he needeth.' This rendering dates from Tindale (1526). Wyclif (1380) has 'his contynuel axynge.' Good modern translations are 'persistency' (Weymouth), 'persistence' (*Twentieth Century NT*). Murray's *New English Dict.* gives the definition 'troublesome pertinacity in solicitation' ; as early as 1460 the word has this meaning, 'Through ymportunite off thair suyttes.' In the companion parable, Coverdale (1535) uses the cognate adjective, Lk 18⁵ 'yet seynge this weddowe is so importune vpon me, I will delyuer her.' The original meaning of 'importune' was 'inopportune,' 'untimely' ; in Sir 32⁴ 'display not thy wisdom out of season,' Coverdale has 'at an importunyte.' Intermediate stages in the growth of the later signification of the word from this root idea are marked by the now obsolete meanings 'troublesome' and 'urgent.'

'Importunity' (Lk 11⁸) is the translation of the Gr. ἀναίδεια, which signifies 'the absence of αἰδώς,' 'shamelessness.' In Biblical Greek it occurs only in Sir 25²², and is rendered 'impudence.' The Lat. *importunitas*, 'unfitness,' is found with the stronger meaning 'insolence' (Cic. *de Sen.* iii. 7),

and is therefore a more accurate translation of ἀναίδεια than its English equivalent. But persistent asking soon becomes insolent asking. The word contains, as Trapp says, 'a metaphor from beggars, that will not be said Nay, but are impudently importunate' (*Com. in loc.*). Cowper uses the word (*Task*, iv. 414) in an instructive context :

'Knaves . . . liberal of their aid
To clam'rous importunity in rags.'

To bring out the striking contrast which our Lord's parable suggests, it is necessary to show that persistence in asking becomes those who know that prayer is never troublesome to God, and never out of season. He who 'will not be said Nay,' and he alone, has learnt the secret of prevailing prayer. Wright notes (*Synopsis of the Gospels in Greek*, p. 243) that St. Luke 'three times uses bad men to represent God, or to be examples to us : (1) here, (2) the unjust steward, (3) the unjust judge.'

J. G. TASKER.

IMPOSSIBILITY.—The modern mind flatters itself upon its frank recognition of impossibility in the world of nature. There is also an impotence of faith which is content to allow impossibility in the sphere of grace. Both these tendencies to a lazy acquiescence in a fancied inevitable are out of touch with the gospel of Christ. There is, of course, such essential impossibility as that of a good tree bearing bad fruit (Mt 7¹⁸). And there is the practical impossibility of a house divided against itself escaping ruin (Mk 3²⁵). But the range of impossibility in the world of nature and in the sphere of grace is narrowed to evanescence by the faith of the Christian disciple. A mustard-seed of faith will remove a mountain (Mt 17²⁰). God is able to save to the uttermost (Lk 18²⁷), though it seems like the passage of a camel through a needle's eye for a rich man to enter the Kingdom of heaven (Mt 19²⁴, Mk 10²⁵). It is through Christ, the Son of God become the Son of Man, that all is possible and nothing impossible (Jn 15⁵, Mk 9²³). He Himself showed it in the supreme triumph of the Resurrection, when the tomb had been sealed so that escape might be impossible (Mt 27⁶⁶). The command over nature displayed in the stilling of the storm (Mk 4³⁹) and in the healing of the woman with the issue of blood (Mt 9²¹, Mk 5²⁸) is at the service of faith and prayer. The poor leper lost his despair in faith, and was rewarded (Lk 5¹²). The blind received sight, because through their faith human impossibility was swallowed up by Divine omnipotence (Mt 9²⁸). Infinite resources, acknowledging no bounds of impossibility, are within reach of the earnest childlike faith the Lord approves (Mk 11²³, Lk 17⁶). Such bright and uplifting lessons are remote from the gloomy and depressing problem of evil. There is, indeed, an undercurrent of impossibility in the stream of this world's development. 'It is impossible but that occasions of stumbling should come' (Lk 17¹). But this species of impossibility we are not to dwell upon too long. 'The redemption draws nigh' (Lk 21²⁸).

LITERATURE.—Trench, *Miracles*¹⁰, p. 9 ff. ; *Expos. Times*, iv. [1892] p. 1 ff. ; *Expositor*, I. ix. [1879] p. 307 ff., II. viii. [1884] p. 207 ff. ; Martensen, *Christian Dogmatics*, p. 220 ff. ; Clarke, *Outline of Christian Theology*, p. 85 ff.

W. B. FRANKLAND.

IMPOTENCE.—The single instance of our Lord's miracles specifically classified under this head is recorded in Jn 5²⁻⁹, where the sufferer is described as ὁ ἀσθενῶν (AV 'the impotent man,' RV 'the sick man'). The features of the case are its long continuance (for thirty-eight years) ; and the association of the man with the multitude of infirm and diseased people gathered round the Pool of

Bethesda (wh. see). Of the nature of the ailment we have no evidence. It has been thought to be palsy, but Bennett (*Diseases of the Bible*) considers this doubtful. The long duration of the disease is against its being identified with *locomotor ataxia*. It may have been some chronic wasting disease having its origin in an enfeebled or disorganized nervous system.

The chief feature of the healing is the fact that Jesus begins the process of restoration by dealing with the hopeless condition induced and established by thirty-eight years of suffering, and by the repeated dashing to the ground of slowly-rising hopes. ' Wouldest thou be made whole ? ' our Lord asked, appealing to the last flicker of expectation evinced by his remaining still at the healing pool, and calling it out into new vigour and consciousness.

Another significant feature is the apparent association in the mind of Jesus of this infirmity with sin, either the sin of the sufferer or the sinfulness of the race (Jn 5¹⁴). A similar association is found in the case recorded in Mt 9¹⁻⁸, Mk 2¹⁻¹², Lk 5¹⁷⁻²⁶ (see art. PARALYSIS). It cannot be definitely asserted that Jesus marked personal sin as the root-cause of disease in these cases, though the inference is not altogether unwarranted from the narratives. But it is at least evident that our Lord did habitually recognize the close connexion between personal and racial sinfulness and all manner of disease and sickness. While carefully guarding Himself from attributing all sickness and weakness to sin (Jn 9¹⁻³), He yet declared the essential alliance of sin with all kinds of bodily disorder. ' Sins of the flesh,' as commonly understood, are notoriously responsible for many of mankind's worst diseases and infirmities ; and the Apostolic catalogue of these sins includes not only adultery, uncleanness, murder, drunkenness, and revellings, but also hatred, variance, wrath, strife, envyings, and covetousness (Gal 5¹⁹⁻²¹, Col 3⁵, Eph 5³). Our Lord's list of sins that defile and destroy the body begins with ' evil thoughts ' and ends with moral stupidity or foolishness (Mk 7²², ἀφροσύνη).

Another case which must probably be included here is that of the woman with a spirit of infirmity (Lk 13¹¹⁻¹⁷). The features here are the Evangelist's description of the ailment as πνεῦμα ἔχουσα ἀσθενείας, the lengthened prevalence of the trouble (for eighteen years), and the completeness of the inability to raise herself. The description is evidently from a competent hand. The woman was bowed and crouched together (ἦν συγκύπτουσα), and was in no wise able to lift herself up. The inability was εἰς τὸ παντελές (cf. He 7²⁵, where the ability of the ever-living Christ to save mankind is also εἰς τὸ παντελές). The infirmity, however, did not debar the sufferer from attending the synagogue. The ailment may have been surgical —a gradual distortion and permanent bending, increased by old age, of the spinal column, such as in many cases is due to continual bending in field labour or in the bearing of heavy burdens. Bennett suggests ' the gradual wasting and relaxation of muscles and ligaments of the back by which the trunk is held erect, so that the body falls forward without any disease of brain or cord or mental impairment.' But it may not improperly be rather classified as due at least in part to some morbid mental condition such as hysteria. This seems to be indicated not obscurely by the description given, as a *spirit of infirmity*.

The reference of our Lord to Satan as binding the woman is not to be understood as pointing to possession, although it may have been a reflexion of the current idea that all bodily deformity was due to demonic agency—in which case the description is due to the Evangelist rather than to Jesus. But most probably it indicates our Lord's view of the infirmity as being part of that widespread calamity and curse that lies upon the whole race, of which complex coil Satan is the summary and representative.

The features of the healing are : (1) The Divine compassion expressed in our Lord's laying His hand upon the woman as He spoke the word of hope and deliverance ; (2) His profound sense that this suffering and weakness, this crouching spirit, were completely foreign to the will of God (v.¹⁶) ; and (3) His stedfast refusal to allow any pedantic Sabbath rules to stand in the way of His relief of suffering humanity. The last fact is dominant in the whole narrative, and consequently the other features and the healing are only casually reported.

T. H. WRIGHT.

IN (ἐν, εἰς, κατά, ἐπί, πρός, διά, ἔσω).—The word is prevailingly used in its primary meaning of position in place, but it frequently follows the Greek ἐν in its more or less figurative ramifications of meaning. It is also employed more or less accurately to translate various other prepositions which convey a slightly different *nuance* of significance. In the present article we shall follow the rendering of the RV, where the use of the prepositions is more consistent and precise, as well as more conformed to the modern usage, than in the AV. (For illustration of the wider use of ' in ' common in the Elizabethan period, cf. Hastings' *DB*, art. ' In ').

I. As translation of ἐν, the word indicates :

1. *Local* relations : (*a*) ' in,' ' at,' or ' on,' of simple locality (Mt 2¹ ' in Bethlehem,' 24⁴⁰ ' in the field,' Jn 4²⁰ ' in this mountain ') ; (*b*) that with which one is covered or clothed (Mk 12³⁸ ' walk in long robes,' Mt 7¹⁵ ' in sheep's clothing,' 11²¹ ' repented in sackcloth and ashes,' Jn 20¹² ' two angels in white ') ; (*c*) direct cohesion (15⁴ ' except it abide in the vine ') ; (*d*) position in a writing or book (Mt 21⁴² ' in the scriptures,' Mk 1² ' in Isaiah,' Lk 20⁴² ' in the book of Psalms ').

2. *Temporal* relations—the point or space of time when, or within which, anything occurs (Mt 22²⁸ ' in the resurrection,' 10¹⁵ etc. ' in the day of judgment'—the AV has also ' at the day of judgment,' Lk 9³⁶ ' in those days,' Jn 2¹⁹ ' in three days I will raise it up ').

3. *Figurative and personal* relations :

(*a*) Indicating a *person* : (α) conceived as the sphere where a certain quality or state of mind is found (Mt 6²³ ' the light that is in thee,' Mk 9⁵⁰ ' have salt in yourselves,' and similarly Mt 21⁴² ' marvellous in our eyes,' 5²⁸ ' committed adultery in his heart,' Mk 11²³ ' doubt in his heart ') ; or (β) in reference to whom another stands in a certain attitude (Mt 3¹⁷ ' in whom I am well pleased,' 11⁶ ' whosoever shall not be offended in me ').

(*b*) *Of the state or condition, manner or circumstance, range or sphere in which a person is or acts* : (α) state or condition (Mt 4¹⁶ ' the people which sat in darkness,' Lk 1⁷⁵ ' serve him in holiness and righteousness,' Jn 4²³ ' worship in spirit and truth,' Mt 21²² ' ask in prayer ') ; (β) manner (13³ ' in parables ') ; (γ) occasion (22¹⁵ ' ensnare him in talk,' Lk 23³¹ ' if they do this in the green tree,' 24³⁵ ' in the breaking of bread ') ; (δ) surrounding accompaniment (Mt 6²⁹ ' Solomon in all his glory,' 16²⁸ ' coming in his kingdom,' 16²⁷ ' in the glory of his Father ') ; (ε) range or sphere (Jn 8²¹ ' die in your sins,' Mk 1¹⁵ ' believe in the gospel ' will also belong to this head, unless we admit that this is an exceptional use of πιστεύω with ἐν. The LXX almost invariably construes the verb with the dative, the NT writers with εἰς or ἐπί. Probably therefore the verb is used here absolutely, and ἐν τῷ εὐαγγελίῳ marks the sphere within which faith is to be exercised. The only other instance of πιστεύω followed by ἐν in the NT is Jn 3¹⁵, which the RV translates 'that whosoever believeth *may in him* have eternal life'). For ἐν with ὄνομα see below.

(c) Of the *means or instrument*, or *personal agency* employed, where a simple dative might have been used instead of ἐν (Mt 3¹¹ 'I baptize you with [RVm 'in'] water'; cf. Lk 3¹⁶, where the simple dative is used; Mk 9³⁴ 'By [RVm 'In'] the prince of the devils casteth he out devils'; in other cases 'with' is used as translation, as Lk 22⁴⁹ 'shall we smite with (ἐν) the sword?').

(d) Of *persons inherently joined and connected*, where the completest intimacy conceivable is expressed; employed with noticeable frequency in the writings of St. Paul and the Fourth Gospel, to mark the close fellowship between the Christian and Christ (ἐν Χριστῷ Ἰησοῦ, ἐν Κυρίῳ, ἐν Χριστῷ, Ro 8¹ 16¹¹ 12⁵ 16⁷; μένειν ἐν ἐμοί, Jn 6⁵⁶ 15⁴ ⁵; cf. 1 Jn 2⁵ ⁶ ²⁴ ²⁷ ²⁸ ἐν αὐτῷ εἶναι, ἐν τῷ υἱῷ, ἐν αὐτῷ μένειν), between the Christian or Christ and God (ἐν θεῷ, ἐν τῷ πατρί, 1 Th 1¹, Col 3³, Jn 3²¹ 10³⁸ 14²⁰), or between the Christian and the Spirit (ἐν πνεύματι εἶναι, Ro 8⁹, 1 Co 12¹³; cf. Mt 22⁴³, Lk 2²⁷). The very repetition of such unusual expressions indicates that the thought was a favourite one in Pauline and Johannine theology. For the determination of the meaning, special weight should be attached to the fact that complementary expressions are used repeatedly—Χριστὸς ἔν τινι, πνεῦμα ἔν τινι, πατὴρ ἔν τινι (Ro 8⁹ 8¹⁰, 2 Co 13⁵, Gal 2²⁰, Jn 10³⁸ 14²⁰ 15⁴ ⁵ 17²¹⁻²³). The employment of these parallel expressions points to a relation of the most intimate communion; and the only question is how this spiritual communion is to be conceived. Deissmann, who has carefully sifted the material relating to the phrase ἐν Χριστῷ, insists that the translation 'in fellowship with Christ' does not quite adequately convey the concrete thought of St. Paul. He favours the view that the ἐν here retains its literal and local significance; the Christian lives in the element Christ, somewhat in the same way as animals live in the air, or fishes in the water, or the roots of plants in the earth. He notices the parallel use of ἐν Χριστῷ and Χριστὸς ἔν τινι with ἐν πνεύματι and πνεῦμα ἔν τινι, and argues that as the last phrase would be naturally understood in the most literal local sense, of one within whom the invisible powers of the Spirit resided, so in the phrases relative to Christ, the living pneumatic Christ of faith, the same local reference is implied. Or, again, the phrase ἐν θεῷ (1 Th 1¹, Col 3³, Ac 17²⁸ 'In him we live and move and have our being') expresses the thought that God is the element in which we live, implying the local conception of a Divine περιχώρησις. From such analogies Deissmann is inclined to accept the most literal and local interpretation of St. Paul's favourite phrase; and he believes that if we keep in mind the equation Χριστός = πνεῦμα, Christ the everliving Divine Spirit, the conception of real locality will not appear improbable. This interpretation certainly presses the literal meaning of ἐν too far; it tends to dissolve St. Paul's mystic idea of union into a semi-physical relation, and so to destroy the moral and spiritual basis of faith. The spiritual presence of Christ is indeed *pictured* as a local nearness of relation; yet St. Paul elsewhere clearly distinguishes between the spiritual nearness of present fellowship with Christ and the future local fellowship with (σύν or πρός) Christ in the life to come (1 Th 4¹⁷, Ph 1²³, 2 Co 5⁸). Even while 'absent from the Lord,' St. Paul is ἐν Χριστῷ, i.e. in spiritual but not local union. The implied ἐν θεῷ in Ac 17²⁸ 'In him we live and move and have our being,' is scarcely adducible as an analogy, since it refers rather to the natural basis of existence than to the spiritual ground. The Johannine

phrases already cited (μένειν ἐν ἐμοί; ἐγὼ ἐν τῷ πατρί μου, καὶ ὑμεῖς ἐν ἐμοί, κἀγὼ ἐν ὑμῖν) contain substantially the same thought as the Pauline ἐν Χριστῷ; and in these, in spite of the local figure employed, the idea is clearly not that of local inherence, but of spiritual inherence or communion. The mystic realism of the Pauline and Johannine phrases is rather to be found in the fact that they approach the thought of a *real identification* with the Logos or the pneumatic Christ. The life Divine incorporates itself in the Christian; the Spirit of Christ or of God takes the place of the human spirit, and is *individualized* in the life of believers. This idea of essential spiritual (*mystica, hypostatica*) union alone does justice to those passages where the union of believers with Christ, and even with one another, finds sublimest expression (Jn 17²¹⁻²³, 1 Co 6¹⁷ 12¹³). But while this thought of vital union is the central and original conception of the phrase used by St. Paul, the context often indicates some variety in the shades of meaning. Thus Ro 14¹⁴ 'I am persuaded in the Lord Jesus,' i.e. *in virtue of that fellowship*; Ph 2²⁹ 'Receive him in the Lord,' i.e. *in the spirit* of such fellowship; it is often used as a favourite expression for 'Christian'—Ro 16⁹· ¹⁰· ¹¹; while in other cases the relationship referred to is that between Christ and the Father; 1 Th 5¹⁸ 'this is the will of God in Christ Jesus'; 2 Co 5¹⁹ 'God was in Christ reconciling the world.'

II. The word is also used to translate other prepositions in the following senses:

διά, 'within' a space of time (Mt 26⁶¹ 'build it in three days').

κατά, 'throughout,' 'according to' (Lk 15¹⁴ 'a famine in that land,' Mt 1²⁰ 'in a dream').

πρός, 'towards,' *direction* (Lk 12³ 'spoken in the ear').

ἔσω, adverb, *within* (Mt 26⁵⁸ 'entered in').

ἐπί, 'on,' 'upon,' 'over.' The RV has followed the more restricted use of 'in' in many cases, and substituted 'on,' 'upon,' 'at,' 'over,' 'by,' 'unto,' 'to' (Mt 6¹⁰ 'thy will be done in earth' [RV 'on earth'], 18¹⁶ 'in [RV 'at'] the mouth of two or three witnesses,' 2²² 'reigning in [RV 'over'] Judæa,' 21¹⁹ 'in [RV 'by'] the way,' 13¹⁴ 'in [RV 'unto'] them is fulfilled the prophecy,' Mk 5³³ 'knowing what was done in [RV 'to'] her'); but in some cases 'in' is retained, where English idiom requires it, and where the sense is not liable to be mistaken (with the genitive, Mk 8⁴ 'in the wilderness' [RV 'in a desert place'], 11⁴ 'in a place where two ways met' [RV 'in the open street'], and, with the dative, Mt 14⁸ 'in a charger,' Mk 10²⁴ 'trust in riches,' Lk 18⁹ 'trusted in themselves that they were righteous,' i.e. rested their confidence of being righteous upon themselves. For ἐπί with ὄνομα see below.

εἰς, 'into,' 'with reference to,' 'with a view to': (a) = 'into,' locally or figuratively, often after verbs of rest, where previous motion and direction are implied (Mt 2²³ 'came and dwelt in a city,' Jn 9⁷ 'go wash in the pool,' Mt 10²⁷ 'what ye hear in the ear,' 13³³ 'hid in three measures of meal,' Mk 1⁹ 'baptized in the Jordan,' 5³⁴ 'go in peace,' Jn 1¹⁸ 'which is in the bosom of the Father'—εἰς τὸν κόλπον—i.e. placed in the Father's bosom and there abiding); (b) = 'with respect to,' 'with a view to' (Lk 22¹⁹ 'in remembrance of me,' 16⁸ 'wiser in their generation' [RV 'for their generation']). After πιστεύω, 'believe,' εἰς is largely used (Mt 18⁶, Jn 1¹² 2²³ 3¹⁸ etc.) = 'in' or 'on' in AV, in RV invariably 'on'; it implies the direction in which the believing soul turns, the fellowship into which it enters. Specially noteworthy is the use of εἰς, ἐπί, and ἐν with ὄνομα. While the Synoptists commonly employ ἐπί or εἰς or the simple dative, and rarely use ἐν except in the phrase, 'Blessed is he that cometh in the name of the Lord' (Mt 21⁹ 23³⁹, Mk 11⁹, Lk 13³⁵ 19³⁸), St. Paul and the Fourth Gospel prevailingly employ ἐν, and use εἰς only after πιστεύω or βαπτίζω. The prepositions have their own *nuance* of meaning ; the Synoptic ἐπὶ τῷ ὀνόματί μου (Mt 18⁵ 24⁵, Mk 9³⁷·³⁹ etc.) indicates *dependence* of some one on another, the authority on which one leans ; εἰς τὸ ὄνομα, *in reference to*, or *in view of*, what the name imports (Mt 10⁴¹ ' receive a prophet in the name of a prophet' = in view of his prophetic character or function, 18²⁰ ' two or three gathered together in my name' = not, *by My authority*, but, *in view of My name*, with the view of honouring Me ; and ἐν τῷ ὀνόματι, *by authority*, clothed with the commission, of some one (Mt 21⁹ ' cometh in the name of the Lord '), or even *by the use of the name*, as contrasted with the authority (Mk 9³⁸ ' we saw one casting out devils in thy name,' *i.e.* using the name of Jesus as a Jewish exorcist might). The very obvious preference which St. Paul and the Fourth Gospel show for ἐν and the corresponding εἰς may well be connected with the idea of *intimate mystic communion* which influences all their religious thought. In the great majority of cases ἐν ὀνόματι indicates not so much the authority, as the *union and fellowship* on which the authority is founded (Jn 17¹² ' I kept them in thy name,' 20³¹ ' that believing ye may have life in his name,' 1 Co 6¹¹ ' justified in the name of the Lord Jesus,' where ἐν has the same pregnant meaning as in the phrase ἐν Χριστῷ Ἰησοῦ) ; and εἰς τὸ ὄνομα after πιστεύω and βαπτίζω likewise indicates the communion into which the baptized believer enters (Jn 2²³ ' many believed εἰς τὸ ὄνομα αὐτοῦ,' Ro 6³, Gal 3²⁷ ' baptized into Christ' ; so probably Mt 28¹⁹ ' baptizing them into the name of the Father,' etc.).

In one or two cases ' in ' is used to translate ἐκ and μετά, but the RV renders these more precisely ' from ' and ' with.' It is also used as part-translation where a single Greek word is rendered by a phrase (Jn 8⁴ 2²⁰, Lk 10³⁴ 16¹⁹ etc.).

LITERATURE. — Besides commentaries on the Gospels, see Moulton, *Grammar of NT Greek* ; Grimm-Thayer, *Greek-English Lexicon of the NT* ; H. Cremer, *Bibl.-Theol. Lex. of the NT*, *s.vv.* ὄνομα, βαπτίζω, πιστεύω ; Abbot, *Shakespearian Grammar* ; A. Deissmann, *Die NT Formel 'in Christo Jesu.'*

J. DICK FLEMING.

INCARNATION.—

Introduction.—The idea of union with God : (1) in the ethnic faiths ; (2) in Greek philosophy—(a) the Stoics, (b) Philo ; (3) in the religion of Israel.
   The message of Christianity—Union with God in the Person of Christ.
A. THE CHARACTER OF CHRIST.—
   1. Perfect goodness.
      (1) Relation to God : (a) perfect knowledge, (b) perfect love.
      (2) Relation to men : perfect knowledge and love.
   2. Absolute sinlessness : evidence of contemporaries ; His own consciousness ; inference as to His Person.
B. THE SELF-WITNESS OF JESUS : the method of His self-disclosure.
   i. His claims :
      1. Teacher : (1) the solitariness of the office, (2) the note of authority, (3) the originality of the teaching, (4) the future of the teaching.
      2. Legislator.
      3. Messiah : His conception of Messiahship. Illustrative passages : (1) the Baptism, (2) the sermon at Nazareth, (3) the reply to John the Baptist, (4) the estimate of John the Baptist, (5) the threefold call of the disciples, (6) the answer to Peter, (7) later or more explicit announcements.
      4. Saviour : (1) the function, bestowal of forgiveness and of life ; (2) the response, personal trust.
      5. Lord.
      6. Worker of Miracles.
      7. Creator of the New Israel.
      8. Judge.
   ii. His self-designations.
      1. Son of Man : (1) Whence did Jesus derive the title? (2) How did He use it? (3) What does He reveal as to His own Person in it?
      2. Son of God : (1) use by demoniacs, (2) use by high priest, (3) ascription by Peter, (4) our Lord's use, (5) Divine attestation.
      Inference as to the constitution of our Lord's Person.

C. THE WITNESS OF THE APOSTLES.
      The primary fact, a living experience.   Then, the Christologies.
   i. The earlier chapters in the Acts of the Apostles.
   ii. The minor Christologies :
      1. James.
      2. First Epistle of Peter.
      3. Jude and 2 Peter.
      4. Apocalypse.
   iii. The Christology of St. Paul : (a) its origin in his experience, (b) its relation to the common belief of the Church, (c) its development.
      1. Christ in His relation to God.
      2. Christ in His relation to men.
      3. Christ in His relation to the Cosmos.
   iv. Hebrews.
   v. Fourth Gospel : Prologue, use of the term Logos.
Conclusion and Outlook : Christ known in history and experience as God and Man.
   1. The Person of Christ, the solution of the problem of union with God.
   2. The Person of Christ, a problem for faith. The knowableness of Christ.
      (1) Christ known as God
      (2) Christ known as Man.
         (a) The origin of His earthly life.
         (b) The relation of the human and Divine aspects of His personality. Theories under control of dualism. Psychological theories.
      Literature.

Introduction.—Christian theology has employed many ruling ideas in order that, by means of them, it might harmonize and systematize the mass of material presented in Scripture and in experience. Each of these, *e.g.* ' the Fatherhood of God,' or ' the Kingdom of God,' has meaning and value ; but they all lie within the supreme and commanding truth, which is the declaration of Christianity, viz. union with God.   This truth has both a *personal* and a *cosmic* aspect. God is *the life of man.* Only as man thinks the Divine thoughts, wills the Divine will, and acts in the Divine strength, does he reach the truth of his own nature, or realize his ideal self. When man is most truly himself, he finds himself to be a partaker of the Divine nature ; and what he is most profoundly conscious of is not himself, but the God in whom he lives, who is the source of all that is most truly human in his personal activities.   The end, in attaining which life and satisfaction for the individual and for the race are to be found, is God. God is also *the life of the universe.*   Christian theology has thrown off the blight of the old Deism, listens with delight to the expositions of Science, and names the thought, reason, law, life, force, whose operations science can trace, but whose essence she can never define, God, the same God who is the life of man. Between the power manifest in the physical universe and the power operative in the spiritual sphere there is no opposition.   Both are expressions of the same Divine energy.

(1) What is thus stated as a Christian doctrine is found to be present either implicitly or explicitly in all the great productions of the human spirit, which are also, most surely, productions of the Divine Spirit, as it impels and quickens the mind of man.   Union with God is at once the presupposition and the promise of the great religions, which have awakened the emotions and determined the aspirations of men.

Therianthropic polytheism, as in the religion of Egypt, however gross and repulsive it may seem to be, finds its strength in the demand for vital union with the Divine source of life. Anthropomorphic polytheism, as in the religion of Greece, even though its religious aspect may be overlaid by its æsthetic beauty, has yet its roots in the elemental demand for union with the Divine principle of being.   In those religions which for good or evil have recoiled from all contact with space and time, as in the pantheism which is the substratum even to-day of the Hindu consciousness, the demand has become clear and passionate.   For this purpose shrines are multiplied and austerities practised, that the soul of the worshipper may be united with the God, and so be carried on the tide of a lesser Divine life to the Diviner ocean of absolute Being.   The whole field of Comparative Religion, from polydemonism up to the highest ethical and universal religions, might be laid under contribution to illustrate and confirm the conclusion that the deepest passion of the human heart has ever been union with God.

(2) The idea of union with God is, further, the presupposition and the ruling category of philosophic thought. To think at all, implies that there is present to the mind the ideal of a unity *in* and *to* which the manifold details of the universe exist. Philosophy is simply the verification and application of this ideal. Philosophy, accordingly, however great its quarrel may be with any existing religion, is itself fundamentally religious. It seeks to accomplish, in thought and for thinkers, the harmonizing of all reality in and with God.

This is the effort of early Greek thought, though as yet the distinction of spiritual and material had scarcely emerged. From Xenophanes, with his assertion that nothing is save Being, and Heraclitus, with his counter assertion that all is flux, the problem of the higher synthesis is handed on to thinkers who, philosophizing imperially, seek to exhibit the ultimate unity of the universe as 'the Good,' or 'Thought of Thought.' From them, again, it has descended, in ever deepening complexity, to the days when the absolute idealism of Hegel is met by the demand to do justice to the reality and independence of the Self. And, in general, union with God is the need and aspiration of the human spirit. The deepest fact regarding human personality is that it is imperfect even in the broadest-minded, largest-hearted specimens of our race, and that consequently, in spite of its intense consciousness of itself, the human self is ill at ease till it enters into the life of the universal Self, and becomes its organ and its reproduction. This fact forces its way to intense conviction and impassioned utterance in every human family which has reached a certain stage of spiritual culture. In India the date may be picturesquely fixed in Buddha's 'great renunciation.' For the Western world the hour had come in the 1st cent. of our era. Two systems, the one born on Greek soil, the other on Jewish, occupied the minds of educated men, and supplied them with the instruments of thought.

(*a*) One was Stoicism. The systems of Plato and Aristotle had been pierced by dualism, which these masters had sought in vain to overcome. Their supreme merit is, that they did not disguise the intensity of the opposition between the rational and the irrational, between form and matter. In Stoicism, speculation is growing weary of the effort to heal this schism of the universe, and is hoping to make things easy for itself by seizing one of the opposing elements, and making that supreme. The Universal, the Rational, is the ultimate principle. Differences, the obstinate facts of a world which contains so much that is evil and irrational, are not so much resolved or harmonized with the supreme good, as resolutely denied or ignored. Stoicism begins at the furthest extreme from the universal, in an intense individualism. It directs the individual to turn away from a political sphere which has no longer a true, satisfying life to offer him, and to turn inward on himself. It promises, however, that there, in the inner world of his spirit, he will find a rational universal element which is identical with the life and being of the universe. Thus, as the Master of Balliol has pointed out (*Theol. in Gr. Philos.*, Lect. xvii.), Stoicism passed by one step from individualism to pantheism. It laid passionate hold on the conception of one all-embracing principle, one all-comprehensive, ever victorious good. High above the world, with its evil and its irrationality, is the realm of truth and goodness. To it the good belong. The message of Stoicism accordingly is, 'Live in accordance with this Reason, or Logos, which is immanent in the universe and germinally present in every man.' Such a faith as this was bound to have great issues, both in lives made sublime by cherishing it, and in noble achievements. The benefits conferred by Stoicism on civilization are patent and imperishable. At the same time, simply because it was no more than faith in an idea, it was bound to fail. Its most strenuous exponents toiled at what they knew was a hopeless task, and though they carried their burden nobly, their hearts were pierced with the sorrow of their failure. Belief in a purpose which links all the discords of the world into one plan, conquers all things evil, and makes them subservient to good, requires some surer basis than the meditations of a philosopher, however true or noble these may be. The failure of Stoicism is obvious now; but in the Hellenic world, in the early years of the Roman Empire, it permeated educated society like an atmosphere, and supplied thinking men with a point of view whence they might look out on life not wholly dismayed or despairing.

(*b*) The other system, which expresses the demand of the age for union with God, and which helps us to understand the attitude of the Greek mind toward Christianity, when it came forth with its great message of reconciliation accomplished, was that which originated with Philo, and which at a later stage, as elaborated by Plotinus, presented itself as a rival to Christianity. Philo's idea of God is Jewish only in name. It is essentially Greek; and yet it is Greek with a difference. The 'idea' of Plato and the 'pure form' of Aristotle have alike proved incapable of gathering into one the diverse elements of the universe. Philo rises not only above the anthropomorphism of the OT, but even above the intellectualism of Greek philosophy. God is indescribable by any forms of thought. Everything which could determine His being must be laid aside, for

to determine is to limit. God is thus the indeterminable. To Him no predicates apply. Philo's dualism is thus wider and deeper than that of the Greek thinkers. It is a dualism, not between God conceived as pure thought and the world condemned as material, but between the transcendent God who is too high to be expressed in the loftiest category of thought and the realm of the finite as such. His problem, accordingly, is to find a medium of transition from this remote transcendent God to the time and space world. This bridge, if we may so describe it, Philo built of elements borrowed both from Judaism and from Greek philosophy. In Jewish theology, as the ethical qualities of God are subordinated to the supposed majesty of His transcendence, Divine acts are attributed to personified metaphysical properties. In particular, there is a tendency to hypostatize the Word of God and to ascribe to it almost as to a person the functions of creation and of judgment. At the same time Philo, as a student of Greek philosophy, found in Stoicism the conception of the Logos or immanent reason of the universe. From this twofold attitude of mind, Jewish and Greek, Philo reached the conception of a principle which is Divine and yet distinct from God, which serves as mediator between the transcendent God and the material world. To this principle he gave the name Logos, which thus gathered to itself the import of the double lineage of thought from which it is descended, and thus to Jew and Greek alike came laden with not entirely dissimilar associations. This famous designation stands as the symbol of the highest effort the mind of man has ever made to reach a synthesis of the seemingly discordant elements of the universe, and to discover a medium whereby the spirit of man can ascend into union with the distant incomprehensible Deity. The situation in the 1st cent. is not adequately described by saying that a great many individuals were adherents of the Stoic philosophy, or of the Alexandrian theology; rather must we imagine an intellectual atmosphere full of the speculations which find a shorthand expression in the term Logos. This phrase is continually on the lips of men. It tells at once of what they sought and of what they thought they had found. Any new message coming to such a world must reckon with this phrase and all it stood for. That the Logos doctrine, whether in its Stoic or Philonic aspect, failed to solve the problem which awakened self-consciousness was stating so fully, and failed to regenerate either the individual or society, is the obvious fact. The reason of its failure is that the reconciliation which it offers is in idea merely, not in historic fact; in thought, and not in life. The opposition between God and the world is so stated as to make the conquest of it not merely difficult, but impossible. On the one side is God, conceived as pure thought, or as something still more remote, ethereal, indescribable. On the other is the universe of matter, in which man is immersed, finding in his body and its relations with the material world his sepulchre and his shame. How shall these two ever meet? The Logos bridge which God throws across the gulf cannot reach to the other, the lower side. The Logos is too ethereal, too Divine, to take to itself any particle of the material world, or to redeem any life which is bound up with matter. Man, for his part, cannot reach, stretch or leap as he will, even the extremity of that gleaming bridge. Matter will not be so easily got rid of. In the semi-physical ecstasy, which was man's last effort to reach the confines of the spiritual world, the flesh found itself still the victor. God and man belong to too disparate universes. They cannot be at one.

(3) In order to complete even so hasty a sketch of the spiritual situation in the Hellenic-Roman world at the advent of Christianity, it is necessary to note the fresh and more hopeful point of view presented by the religion of Israel. (*a*) Its presupposition is not the contrast, but the affinity of God and man. On the one hand, God is like man. Anthropomorphism is not false, for human nature is the reflex of the Divine, and the attributes of man do therefore, inadequately but not falsely, represent the attributes of God. On the other hand, man is like God, capable of communion with Him, as one person is with another, finding in that fellowship his true life. The Greek dualism of God and the universe, of form and matter, is unknown to the OT. Whatever mediation is wanted is found in man himself, who is creation's crown, to whom nature is bound by community of substance, in whose destiny, for weal or woe, nature is profoundly implicated. (*b*) Its analysis is wholly different from, and far deeper than, the Greek. It lays bare, not distance between God and man, as between two disparate natures, but a breach, as between two persons who ought to have been at one, but are now, through the action of the dependent personality, woefully opposed. The gulf to be bridged, therefore, is not that between form and matter, but between will and will. To overcome this, no one of the Divine attributes, but God Him-

self alone, will suffice. (c) The goal of the religion of Israel, accordingly, is the indwelling of God in man. The coming of Jehovah in His fulness is the end to which the prophets of Israel look. When He comes, Israel will be restored, and the universe, sharing the blessing, will itself be renovated. They conceived this coming of the Lord without perspective, and in the forms belonging to the world of their own day. In this way alone could the hope of the coming of the Lord have sustained and comforted their own spirits ; only in such forms could they have proclaimed it to others who, like themselves, waited for the consolation of Israel. The spiritual history of the devout in Israel, accordingly, is one of continual disillusionment. Form after form broke like mist ; and still the perfect form in which the presence of Jehovah would be fully realized did not come. It is little wonder, therefore, that the hope of Israel did not retain its purity and spirituality, save in the hearts of an inner circle of whom the theologians and politicians of the time took no account,—the poor in spirit, the mourners, the meek, the pure in heart. Comparison between the two lines of development, that of Greek philosophy and that of the religion of Israel, shows that the ruling idea of both was union with God, and, through this, the unifying of all the elements of the life of man and of nature. On neither line had the goal been reached. In the one there was at best an occasional and intermittent experience of ecstasy. In the other there was, in the deepest natures, a hoping against hope, that God would yet visit His people.

Into such a world, Jewish and Hellenic, Christianity entered, with the declaration that what men had been seeking had come to pass, that union with God was no longer a mere dream or a wistful hope, but an accomplished fact. God, so the announcement runs, has united Himself with one Man, so that all men may, in this Man, who is both Christ and Logos, become one with God. The reconciliation of God and man is effected not merely in idea, but in a historic Person. He is both God and man, through Him men have access to God, in Him man and the universe are gathered into unity, and are perfected in their being. He is, with respect to the Divine purpose, at once ἀρχή and τέλος, the active cause of its fulfilment, and the goal of its accomplishment. It is plain that the heart of this announcement is the Person of Christ. Do the facts regarding Him warrant the transcendent claim made on His behalf ? Is this man Divine as well as human ? Does He indeed meet the demand for union with God ? These questions must not be approached with any dogmatic presuppositions. The answer to them must be sought in the portraiture of the historic Christ, and in the impression which His personality made on those who came under its influence.

A. *THE CHARACTER OF CHRIST.*—It is remarkable that all study of Christ necessarily begins with His character. It is not so with other great men, even the founders of religions. What primarily drew adherents to them was not the goodness of their characters, but some gift or power which they possessed. Believers in the greatness of these heroes have been able to retain their faith, even while admitting the moral defects of those to whom they prostrated both intellect and will. It is not so with Jesus Christ. He rules the minds of men by the impression of His personality, and in this impression His character forms an integral part. Prove Him guilty of sin, and at once the spell is broken. He has achieved nothing, if He can be classed among other frail, failing, sinful mortals. All Christology, therefore, must begin with a character study of Jesus. An attempt at

such a study has been made in the article CHARACTER OF CHRIST, the details of which need not be repeated here. We may, however, restate the results of that article—the results, as we believe, to which the study of His character must necessarily lead. Contemplating Him as He is presented to us in the Gospels, two features of His character stand out supreme and unmistakable.

1. The first is positive, His *perfect goodness.* This quality is to be sought, and is found, in all the relations in which Jesus stood to His fellow-men and to God. (1) Between Him and God the relations were such as never existed in the case of any other man. They include : (a) perfect knowledge, (b) perfect love. Jesus knew God directly and fully, with the complete intimacy of a Son, nay, of one who, in comparison with all other men, is *the* Son (Mt 11²⁷). He beheld Divine realities with immediate vision, and reported what He had seen and heard (Jn 1¹⁸ 6⁴⁶ 8³⁸ 15¹⁵). We see in Jesus one whose vision of God was absolutely undimmed, whose intercourse with God was unhindered by any incapacity on His part to receive, or to respond to, the communications of God to Him. Jesus, moreover, loved God with the strength of a nature which had never been injured by any breach with God. In His love for God there is no trace of the compunctions, the heart-breaking memories, which make the love of the redeemed a thing compounded of tears and pain, as well as of adoration and gladness. It shows itself in serene and unbroken trust, which continually depends on the Father's gifts (Jn 5²⁰·³⁰ 7¹⁶ 14¹⁰·²⁴), and in perfect and comprehensive obedience, which owned no other will than the Father's (Lk 2⁴⁹, Jn 4³⁴ 6³⁸). Thus loving God, He was aware that God loved Him, and did continually pour upon Him the fulness of a Divine love which found no limitations in the spiritual receptivity of its object. The Divine love, which returns from every other object restrained by incapacity or wounded by misunderstanding, is concentrated upon Christ, abides and has free course in Him, and returns to its source in God completely satisfied and rejoicing with eternal joy. Nothing less than complete mutual indwelling and perfect mutual joy of fellowship are unveiled to us in the communings between Jesus and God, to which the narratives reverently admit us.

(2) Between Jesus and His fellow-men the relations are no less perfect. It is true, He could not realize in His own case all possible circumstances in which a man might be placed. But He could, and did, hold such an attitude to men as would enable Him to enter with perfect sympathy and entire appropriateness into any situation into which Divine Providence might conduct a man. In a word, He loved men. It is abundantly evident that He knew them, both in the broad qualities of humanity and in the individual features of the lives which came before Him. The amazing fact, accordingly, is, that, in spite of such knowledge, He loved men, believed in their high destiny, yearned to save them, and was ready to give the supreme proof of His love by dying for them.

We conclude, then, that Jesus was good, not merely as being one of a class of men upon whom we may pass this verdict without setting them thereby apart from their fellows, but as standing alone in the completeness of His ethical achievement. His character bears the mark of attainment and finality. All other goodness is to be estimated by the measure in which it approximates to His. This is not matter of dogma but of observation. It is a clear inference from the moral history of the race subsequent to His appearing. It is a fact that He is the ethical head of humanity. To say this, however, is to define Him as more than man. However we may construe His person, it will be impossible to confine ourselves to a merely humanitarian interpretation of it. 'He who alone stands in this universal relation to humanity cannot be merely a member of it' (Forrest, *Christ of History*, etc. p. 66).

2. The second is negative, His *absolute sinlessness*. The evidence of the portrait constrains us to conclude, not merely that Jesus was a very good man, in whom there was 'the *minimum* of sinfulness' and 'the *maximum* of holiness,' but that in Him was no sin. The testimony of His contemporaries might not suffice to establish this result, though it is, indeed, most impressive to note how those who knew Him intimately bear unanimous and most solemn testimony to His sinlessness, and ascribe to Him an office which could be held only by an absolutely holy person (1 P 1¹⁹ 2²² 3¹⁸, 1 Jn 2¹ 3⁵, Ac 3¹⁴ 7⁵² 22¹⁴). The weight of proof lies in His own consciousness. It is beyond question that in that consciousness there was no sense of personal unworthiness, of shortcomings or failures, even the slightest. He who taught others to pray for forgiveness, and never besought it of the Divine mercy for Himself; He who proclaimed the necessity of regeneration for all men, and Himself never passed through any such phase of experience; He who in tenderest sympathy drew close to the sinner's side, and yet always manifested a singular aloofness of spirit, and never included Himself among the objects of the Divine compassion; He who made it His vocation to die for the remission of sins, must have been, in actual fact, sinless :— either that, or He must have been sunk in a moral darkness more profound than sin ordinarily produces, even in the worst of men. The sinlessness of Jesus is a fact whose possibility ought not to be questioned through mere unwillingness to admit the inferences which follow from it. If Jesus is sinless, He stands alone in the moral history of the race. He cannot be classed along with other men, however good and great. They are approximations to an ideal. He is the Ideal. This uniqueness, moreover, cannot be interpreted as that of a *lusus naturæ*, or a special product of creative power. The difference between Jesus and other good men is this, that while He has produced a conviction of sin immeasurably more profound than they have evoked among their admirers, He has also awakened a confidence and a peace which they have never wrought in their closest imitators. Unnumbered multitudes of human souls have come under regenerative and sanctifying influences, which, without doubt, have emanated from His personality, and which have wrought in them a type of character which is the reflex of His. There is only one place in which a reverent and open-minded study of the character of Christ can set Him, and that is beside God, as essentially Divine. He is certainly human. The closer we draw to Him, the more clearly do we discern His humanity. There is nothing, sin excepted, to divide us from Him. Pain and sorrow, temptation and conflict, discipline and growth,—He knows them all. In His universality all the endless variety of human experiences is comprehended; so that He is kinsman of every family on earth, contemporary of every generation, neighbour and friend of every soul that breathes and suffers. Yet this very humanity is the unveiling of Divinity. If, because of His humanity, we have been inclined to draw Him into our ranks, we soon find that He will not be thus classified. He is man, yet more than man—the Holy One of God. He was born a man, yet His birth was not the inevitable product of physiological and racial conditions; it was the entrance into humanity of one whose home and native air were elsewhere. They were within the circle of Divinity. See, further, art. SIN, § 7.

A study of the character of Christ does not provide us with a ready-made dogma of the constitution of His person. Two things, however, it does effect : (*a*) it sets the person of Christ in the centre of Christianity as its main declaration and its most cogent proof; (*b*) it makes a merely humanitarian construction of His personality for ever impossible. We are constrained to conceive of the sinless Christ, not as the bloom and efflorescence of humanity, but rather as One who has entered into humanity on an errand of profound significance for the moral history of the race. We turn, therefore, once more to the portrait in the Gospels, to see if the consciousness of Jesus reveals any traces of a uniqueness of personal constitution corresponding to the uniqueness of His character. If such there be, they will both sustain the impression of His sinlessness, and derive from it their true interpretation. Supernatural functions and gifts would mean nothing for mankind apart from ethical perfection.

B. *THE SELF-WITNESS OF JESUS.*—It is noteworthy that Jesus does not discuss the constitution of His Person, and gives none of the definitions with which theology has been rife. This is an indication of the truthfulness of the narrative, and shows that it has been to a wonderful degree untouched by the doctrinal development which we know had preceded its earliest written form. It suggests, moreover, that the very highest construction that can be put on the words of Christ is no more than the truth. If, in truth, Jesus *be* the highest that is said of Him, this is precisely the method which He would adopt in order to disclose the transcendent aspect of His being. He would make no categorical statements regarding it, but would leave it to be apprehended through the total impression of His personality.

i. HIS CLAIMS.—As soon as we return to the portrait, we are impressed by the extraordinary claims which Jesus makes on His own behalf. He is perfect in humility; and yet, combined with the utmost gentleness, the most winning loveliness, there is an assertion of His own supreme importance, which is at once profound and sublime. These claims are sometimes stated explicitly; more frequently they are implied in what He says and does. In any case, they are inseparable from what He believes Himself to be. They enter into the very texture of the narrative. They are wrought of the very fibre of the personality of Him who makes them. Whatever quality of being is required to make them valid, we must impute to Him who deliberately advances them. Without presuming to make a complete enumeration, we note the following among the offices and functions which Jesus avowedly claims to hold and fulfil.

1. Teacher.—In Jesus' discharge of this office, certain features at once attract attention.—(1) *The solitariness of the office.* There were in Jesus' day many teachers of religion, and the title of Rabbi, commonly given to them, He accepted (Mk 14¹⁴, Jn 13¹³·¹⁴). These others, however, were prepared to be followed by successors who might wear their title and inherit their honours. But Jesus claimed to be a teacher in a sense in which He could not be followed by any of His disciples, however learned and pious (Mt 23⁸). He did not aim at raising up men who should succeed Him in this office. His office of teacher is His alone. No doubt there came to be in the Church certain men upon whom the Spirit of God conferred a special gift of knowledge, who were accordingly recognized as 'teachers' (1 Co 12²⁸). But teachers after the pattern of Christ were not to be instituted, and were not needed in the new Society (1 Th 4⁹, 1 Jn 2²⁷). This solitariness of His office is a remarkable fact. He was, then, the bearer of a message which could not be pronounced by other lips than His, which originated in the depths of His consciousness, and owed all its significance and value to the personality of Him who declared it.

(2) *The note of authority.*—This could not be missed, and, in one who had not received the special training of a school Rabbi, it was profoundly impressive. When the people heard His first sermon in Capernaum, 'they were astonished at his teaching : for he taught them as having authority, and not as the scribes' (Mk 1²²). The source of this authority lies in the quality of His mind, which directly sees things Divine. His teaching is not the issue of a dialectic process ; it is of the nature of a report, and implies that the Teacher lives in a habitual intercourse with God, such as no other man ever enjoyed (Jn 3¹¹). His authority, therefore, is His own absolutely. He quotes no other Rabbi, leans on no human opinion, however sound and wise. More amazing still, He does not use the formula which marks the supernatural authority of a prophet, 'Thus saith the Lord.' For this He substitutes the simpler, more astounding phrase, 'I say unto you.' 'He speaks at all times with the same absolute conviction and consciousness of His Divine right. There is majesty in His least utterance, and it is nowhere more easily recognized than in the unvarnished record of the Gospel according to St. Mark' (Swete, *Studies in the Teaching of our Lord*, p. 64). Many men have been intoxicated by their own conceit ; but the swelling vanity of their tone has easily been detected. When Jesus employs the note of authority, He is simply being true to His own inner consciousness, which, to its inmost core, is clear, genuine, and reliable.

(3) *The originality of the teaching.*—It would be a mistake to attribute to Jesus the independence of a mind which excluded all possible sources of information or instruction, and operated only in a medium of its own imaginations or conceptions. Relations may be traced between the teaching of Jesus and ideas which found lodgment in other minds than His ; yet His originality is not thereby infringed. Thus, for instance, His teaching was couched in the terminology and in the forms of thought common to the religious teaching of His day. A parallel might easily be drawn to illustrate this (cf. Shailer Mathews, *The Messianic Hope in the NT*, p. 71 ff.). This, however, in no way lowers the value of the teaching of Jesus. Ideas are not necessarily valueless, because found in Rabbinical theology. By taking them up into His larger and loftier thought, Jesus has placed upon them the stamp of His authority. The central idea of the teaching, moreover, is not borrowed from contemporary thought. The spirituality of the Kingdom of God is Jesus' special contribution to the religious life of His day. This conception is all His own, and is the organizing power of all His teaching. Attempts to set aside certain parts of His teaching as derived from external sources, and as being, therefore, of no permanent value, wreck themselves upon the fact that He was certainly no eclectic, and that His teaching has none of the features of a patchwork. His originality consists in the synthetic, transforming power of His mind. Again, His teaching is not independent of, rather is it rooted in, the OT. He Himself repudiated the idea that He was breaking with the religion of Israel. He does claim, however, to 'fulfil' the Law and the Prophets (Mt 5¹⁷).

Law and Prophets, which are thus conjoined in Jesus' speech (Mt 7¹² 11¹³ 22³⁵⁻⁴⁰), are equivalent to the OT taken as a whole, and viewed, in its ethical and spiritual significance, as the utterance of the Divine mind regarding the relations of God and man. *This*, therefore, *i.e.* the inspired record of God's revelation, Jesus claims to fulfil, to preserve and perfect, to retain and develop. We are not to water down the implicit

claim. Who can undertake to give the true inwardness of the Divine thought, and carry to completion the eternal purpose? Through the prophets God speaks 'by divers portions.' When He speaks finally and fully, His spokesman can be none other than His Son (He 1¹).

Once more, the originality of Jesus appears most strikingly in the fact that He traces all His teaching to His Father (Jn 7¹⁶). The very refusal of the claim to be independent of God is itself a claim of the most stupendous kind. He whose words and deeds are entirely the speaking and acting of God in Him, between whom and God there is complete intimacy and uninterrupted reciprocity of thought and purpose, stands apart from all human teachers, even the most brilliant and the most original. His teaching is not His own. It is the message of Another, even of Him who sent Him to carry it to the human race.

(4) *The future of the teaching.*—Teachers die ; their great thoughts perish not. Socrates passed from the market-place ; but Plato and Aristotle, those real Socratics, took up the threads of thought, and wove them into systems which have dominated the intellectual world ever since. It is noticeable, however, that this has not been the history of the ideas of Jesus. He uttered them, and then passed from the scene of His labours. But no disciple took them and expanded them into a system. No philosophical or theological system to-day can claim to be His. He Himself predicted a much more remarkable future for His teaching. He would have a successor, indeed, but not St. Peter with his vigour, or St. John with his speculative gift. The successor of Jesus in the teaching office is none other than the Spirit of God (Jn 16¹²⁻¹⁵). He will take the thoughts of Jesus and unfold their meaning, and apply their vitalizing power to the questionings of all successive generations of men, till, finally, all uncertainties are resolved in the light of the eternal day. It is certain that He who 'sat thus by the well' and talked with a woman, who preached in synagogues, and taught in the Temple, had this consciousness of Himself as initiating a teaching which was destined to continue, through the power of the Spirit of God, unfailing, imperishable, and indefeasible. In respect of this also, Jesus stands apart from and superior to all other teachers of men.

2. Legislator.—Jesus is more than a teacher, whether of the type of a Jewish Rabbi or of that of a Greek philosopher. The disciple band is more than a group of docile souls, who may be expected to assimilate and propagate the ideas of their Master. The analogy of the Schools fails to give us Jesus' point of view. He has before Him the Kingdom of God, which has existed throughout the past ages of Israel's history, and is now about to pass into a new stage of realization. He speaks, accordingly, not so much in the character of a communicator of new ideas, as in that of a legislator laying down principles upon which the community of God shall be built or rebuilt, delivering laws which shall guide it in its future history. The tone of Jesus is not that of a prophet who, standing within the Kingdom, a member of it, like those whom he addresses, speaks out of the circumstances of his age, and addresses to his fellow-citizens words of warning, of counsel, of rebuke, and of hope. Jesus stands consciously on a far higher platform, and does not class Himself with those whom He addresses, as though He and they bore the same relation to the Law. They are not His fellow-citizens. They are His subjects, citizens of the community of which He is head and lawgiver. The laws of the Kingdom He promulgates by His own personal authority. Six times in the Sermon on the Mount He sets aside 'that which was spoken to them of old time,' and substitutes a rule of His own. In doing so, however, He is no mere revolutionary. He is taking the inner spiritual principle of the old

Law, and liberating it from the restrictions which had protected it in the time of man's pupilage. After the same manner He interprets and applies the Sabbath law (Mk $2^{27.\ 28}$). In dealing with perversions of the Law He is still more peremptory and drastic; *e.g.* as to fasting ($2^{18ff.}$) and ceremonial purification ($7^{5ff.}$). The consciousness of One who thus legislates for the Kingdom is not that of a prophet, not even of the greatest of the prophets, who was God's instrument in the first founding of the community, and received the law at His hands. It is rather that of One in whom God comes to His people, who is the Divinely appointed King in Israel, whose relation to God is closer than any mere man's can be, who speaks, therefore, with the very authority of God Himself.

3. Messiah.—The sense in which Jesus claimed the title of Messiah is certainly not to be gathered from any views regarding the Messiah entertained by His contemporaries. The clue is to be sought in Jesus' attitude towards the OT. (*a*) He regards the OT as a unity. Critical questions are not before His mind, and upon them He pronounces no judgment. 'David,' 'Moses,' 'Isaiah' are simply terms of reference. What He does lay hold of is the unity of the revelation. One mind is revealed. One self-consistent purpose moves amid these varied scenes and ages. (*b*) He conceives the Divine purpose in the OT to be redemptive. The heart of the OT is union with God, the formation of a spiritual fellowship in which God is fully known and men enter upon the position and privilege of sons. In this connexion He preaches the Kingdom not merely as at hand (Mk 1^{15}), but as present in commanding power (Mt 12^{28}). Thus He appropriates to Himself as descriptive of His own work the picture language of Is 61^{1-4}. So also in the most solemn hour of His life, when He was on the verge of laying it down, He claimed redemptive efficacy for His death in accordance with the oracle of the new covenant (Mt 26^{28}, Jer 31^{31}). This was central in the consciousness of Jesus. An eschatology, no doubt, He had; but it was subordinate to the spiritual conception of redemption, and represented in terms of current thought the consummation of redemption in the world to come. Messiahship, accordingly, meant for Jesus the vocation in which the redemptive purpose of God, which had been growing to completion through the history of Israel, would be fulfilled. We can understand, therefore, how unwilling He would be to receive such a title, when its meaning in the minds of those who used it differed widely from His own conception of it; how glad He would be to accept it when it was applied to Him, not because of His supposed fulfilment of popular requirements, but in spite of His obvious non-fulfilment of these demands; and how careful He would be to train those who clung to Him as Messiah in the apprehension of His own transformed idea of it.

The passages which may be adduced as proof of the Messianic consciousness of Jesus all exhibit His own interpretation of Messiahship, as the calling of the agent of a Divine work of redemption. (1) *The Baptism.*—(For discussion of Baptism and Temptation, see art. CHARACTER OF CHRIST, p. 285 f.) This is evidently much more than installation into a prophetical office. It was the solemn acceptance by Jesus of the vocation of Messiah interpreted with reference to the taking away of sin. For such an office, a personal rank superior to that of all other men, and a personal endowment of the Spirit in a measure which no other man could receive, were essential.—(2) *The sermon at Nazareth.* Here the Messianic era is described in terms of intense spirituality; and the Speaker claims to be the Messiah in a sense which identifies Him with the Servant of the Lord (Lk 4^{16-30}).—

(3) *The reply to John the Baptist.* To the question 'Art thou he that cometh?' He makes a reply which is at once an affirmation and an interpretation. He is the Messiah, not after a political sort, employing external or catastrophic instrumentality, but of a far higher order, employing means which reach to the depth of man's necessity (Mt 11^{2-6}, cf. Is $35^{5.\ 6}$).—(4) *The estimate of John the Baptist.* In Mt 11^{10} John is the messenger of Mal 3^1 who prepares the way for Jehovah, or for the Angel of the Covenant, who is identified with Jehovah. In Mk $9^{12.\ 13}$ John is Elijah, the precursor of the Messiah; while in $1^{2.\ 3}$ he is identified with the 'voice' of Is 40^{3-5}. The implied claim on the part of Jesus, which the Evangelist repeats, is to a personal dignity not less than that of One whose coming is, at the same time, the coming of Jehovah to His people.—(5) *The threefold call of the disciples.* The call mentioned in the Fourth Gospel (Jn 1^{35-41}) is necessary to render intelligible that which is mentioned first by the Synoptists (Mk 1^{16-20}, Mt 4^{18-22}, Lk $5^{10.\ 11}$). The third call in the ordination to Apostleship (Mk $3^{13.\ 14}$) is the culmination of the series. Messiahship and Apostleship thus receive progressive interpretation. The Kingdom, the King, and high rank even like that of prince in a tribe of Israel, are all to be interpreted in a manner that confounds and contradicts popular theory.—(6) *The answer to Peter.* Into one moment of intense emotional strain and profound spiritual instruction are compressed (*a*) joyous recognition of faith's insight and grasp (Mt 16^{17}); (*b*) solemn illumination of the truth which faith had thus, with little intelligent apprehension, made its own (Mk 8^{27-31}). The Messianic calling has an aim which is reached through death and resurrection. He who is competent to carry out such a scheme does not stand in the same rank of being with other men. Jesus' doctrine of His person is never dogmatically announced. It is none the less, rather all the more, impressively taught, because He allows it to grow upon the minds of believers as an irresistible inference.—(7) It is significant that Jesus' claims to Messiahship become more explicit toward the close of His career. No doubt the explanation is that misapprehension was scarcely now possible. If He be—as He is—a King, it is through humiliation He passes to His glory (Mk $11^{1-11.\ 15-19}$ $13^{5.\ 6}$ $14^{61.\ 62}$ 15^2).

4. Saviour.—(1) Jesus' view of sin, in respect of its guilt, and power, and pollution, was the very gravest. Yet He did not hesitate to announce Himself as able to save men from an evil for which the OT provided no institute of deliverance. He forgave sin (Mt 9^6). He restored the outcast (Lk 7^{48-50} 19^{10}). He died to make good His claims as Redeemer (Mt 26^{28}). This negative form of salvation, however, is not that upon which alone, or even usually, He dwells. He dwells rather on the positive aspect of salvation, and claims to be able to bestow upon men the highest blessing of which the OT revelation can conceive, viz. life. Not merely does He promise it in the future, but He bestows it in the present. He possesses life (Jn 5^{26}). He bestows life (6^{57}). His words convey life (6^{63}). Those who believe in Him are media of life to others (7^{38}). Life consists fundamentally in knowledge of God, and of Himself as the Christ (17^3). If we admit that the Fourth Gospel has reproduced the teaching of Jesus with substantial accuracy, it is impossible not to recognize the superhuman nature of Jesus' self-consciousness. The Jews might well strive with one another (6^{52}) as to what His words meant. They certainly conveyed a claim which no mere man could offer in his own behalf.

(2) There is only one possible response on the part of men to the Divine saving act, viz. faith, as personal trust. There can be no doubt that Jesus did require faith in Himself, and, in so doing,

consciously stood toward men in a place that can be filled by God only. It is true that the words 'believe in me' occur but rarely in the Synoptics (Mk 9[42], Mt 18[6]). But if they have not the phrase, they have the fact. In Beyschlag's well-known words, 'the conduct of those who sought His help, to whom He says so often "thy faith hath saved thee," is, at bottom, a faith in Christ.' So also, confessing Him (Mt 10[32]), praying in His name (18[20]), coming to Him and learning of Him (11[28-30]), are, in essence, religious acts. What is implicit in the Synoptics becomes explicit in the Fourth Gospel (Jn 11[25] 12[46] 14[1] 16[9], in which cases the use of εἰς implies trustful giving up of self to the personal object of faith. Surely there is only one justification for the man who speaks in such phrases and adopts such an attitude toward His fellows, viz. that, human though He be, He consciously occupies a relation to God radically distinct from that which can be held by any mere man. Jesus accepted a worship that can be rendered to God only. Yet He never by a breath suggested that He was a rival to Jehovah in the faith and love of men. Whom, then, did He conceive Himself to be? Whom must they, who thus worship Him, believe Him to be, if they are to be free from the error of man-worship?

5. Lord.—He who is Saviour has the right of absolute lordship. Such sovereignty Jesus claims, unhesitatingly, unceasingly. (1) He commands rather than invites discipleship (e.g. Mt 4[19] 8[22] 9[9] 19[21]). (2) He enjoins on His representatives a similar usage (10[12-15]). (3) He demands entire surrender, placing Himself first in the regard of the human heart (e.g. Mt 10[37. 38], Lk 9[59-62]). (4) He decides infallibly on the spiritual cases set before Him, and deals with them in a manner which would be an invasion of elemental human rights, if it were not warranted by a unique function, which, in turn, is rooted in a unique personality. (5) He appoints the whole future of His disciples, both here and hereafter (Mt 10[16-20], Jn 14[2. 3]). In all this there is implied a sovereignty over man which cannot be wielded by one who is no more than man.

6. Worker of Miracles.—If we take the standpoint of monism, that there is only one substance, and only one set of laws appropriate to it, or that of dualism or parallelism, that spiritual and material facts belong to two distinct and incommunicable orders of being, we shall find it impossible to believe in miracle; and we shall condemn, as mistaken, Jesus' evident belief that He was able to seal His redemptive activities by works of superhuman power in the realm of physical nature. If, however, we hold the theistic position, which Jesus Himself held, that between God and the universe there is neither pantheistic identification nor dualistic separation, but that God maintains constant contact with the world which He has made, and directs the activities of which He is the source, towards ends in harmony with His own nature, then we shall find it possible to believe in those interventions of spiritual power in the domain of physical nature, which we call miracle. The only question we shall ask—apart from that of evidence—is that of need. In a perfect universe there might be no need for miracle. In the universe as we know it there is abundant need. Redemption is needed, at once ethical and cosmical. The Kingdom of God is miraculous in its very nature. Miracles, therefore, naturally will attend its advent into the realm of time and space. They are altogether congruous with the mission of Jesus. They are 'signs' of the Kingdom, the characteristic 'works' of Him in whom the Kingdom comes. Such, in any case, was the conviction of Jesus. Before the forces of nature, and of the obscure

spirit-world that borders on the physical, in presence of disease and death, He did not own Himself conquered. He bore Himself as Master, as One to whom God's universe lay open, so that its powers were at His disposal for the furtherance of the cause committed to Him. This commanding authority of His was an element in that impression of supernatural greatness which He made on those who came under His influence (Mk 1[27], Lk 5[8]).

7. Creator of the New Israel.—The word ἐκκλησία is but once heard on the lips of Jesus in its special significance; but the occasion is one of solemn import (Mt 16[18]). Peter has made his inspired confession, and Jesus makes reply, 'Thou art Petros, and on this Petra I will build my Ecclesia; and the gates of Hades shall not prevail against it.' Those who heard could not fail to identify Ecclesia with Israel, as though Jesus had said, 'on this Rock will I build my Israel' (Hort, *The Christian Ecclesia*, p. 11). This claim has reference to the *past*. That community, which originated at the first Passover, which endured through the vicissitudes of Israel's history, which cannot be identified with the nation which has rejected Christ, is now rebuilt, or built, by Jesus in His capacity as Messiah. It has reference to the *future*. To the Ecclesia, or community of believers in Jesus, He gives the seals of the Supper and Baptism; to it He gives the commission to carry on His work; in it He promises to dwell by His Spirit. Regarding it He predicts that it will prove invincible in face of the powers of Hades. He, Jesus of Nazareth, undertakes to erect on the bed-rock of that group of loyal disciples a new Israel, a spiritual dominion which shall not pass away while time endures. It is vain to characterize a consciousness such as this as merely human. Jesus, in His own belief, stands above humanity, Revealer and Representative of the everlasting God, superior to the lapse of time.

8. Judge.—Our view of eschatology will depend on our conception of history. If we believe in the progressive accomplishment of a Divine purpose we shall anticipate a climax, in which the whole movement will be complete. In that case we shall not be able to set aside 'Messianism' as irrelevant to the essence of religion. Our Lord certainly regarded redemption as a process to be continued through a lapse of time, whose culmination would form the completion of the world's history; and, at the highest point of that culmination, He placed Himself. Amid the many difficulties, textual and other, which surround the eschatology of Jesus, it seems clear that He keeps close to the OT representations, without committing Himself to the details elaborated in later literature. In one all-important point, however, He modifies the OT representation; where the OT placed Jehovah, Jesus places Himself as Judge (Mt 7[21-23] 13[30. 41] 16[27] 25[11. 12. 31ff.], Lk 13[25-27]).

In the Fourth Gospel there is another judgment, one which belongs to the present time, and is carried out through the presence or the word of Christ (Jn 3[17-21] 12[47. 48]). This, however, is not inconsistent with a final judgment, but is rather its precursor; while the final judgment itself is not absent from the representations of the Fourth Gospel (Jn 12[48] 5[27. 28]; cf. 1 Jn 2[28] 4[17]).

Here, then, is the climax of our Lord's self-assertion. There is manifest in this claim a consciousness which we should pronounce insane were it not that of the humblest and sanest man the world ever saw. Nothing can warrant such a claim, nothing justify such a consciousness, save the hypothesis that Jesus had a higher being than appertains to men, and that, as arising from this constitution of His person, He had universal functions which none other than Himself could exercise.

ii. His Self-Designations.—The claims of Jesus, accordingly, direct us to conclude that He believed Himself to be human indeed, yet at the same time One who was related to God, in the ground and origin of His being, as no other man could be. From this consciousness the functions He claimed relative to humanity must have been derived. It must have been on the ground of what He was, and knew Himself to be, in the inherent quality of His being, that He set Himself forth as called and enabled to do certain acts in and for mankind.

It was impossible for men to listen to His claims without inquiring as to His person. Nay, He Himself stimulated the inquiry, and displayed, if one may so say, an anxiety to know what men were thinking of Him. What help, if any, does He give us in seeking for an answer? It is certain that He will not give us definitions after the style of the creeds, or analytic descriptions in the manner of a modern handbook of psychology. The most, and the best, He can do for us, is to grant such unveilings of what was and must remain His secret, as shall enable us, under the requisite spiritual conditions, to know Him and to trust Him. Christ is not a proposition to be proved, or an object to be dissected. He is a Person to be known. By what names, then, does He will to be known? Among the titles or descriptive phrases by which He designates Himself, two are of supreme importance. The discussions regarding their meaning form a kind of register of the history of modern Christology. If the Person of Christ be the centre of the Church's faith, and the apprehension of it be the note of the Church's growth, these discussions cannot be expected to reach scientific finality. The titles stand for all that Christ means in the experience of His disciples, and their wealth of meaning is, therefore, too rich for our exegetical skill to tabulate.

1. The Son of Man.—Three questions are pertinent to our present purpose.

(1) *Whence did Jesus derive the title?*—It would not have been necessary to ask this question—the title might have been at once accepted as invented by Jesus Himself—were it not that a phrase, suggestive of it, occurs both in the later apocalyptic literature and in the OT, in unmistakably Messianic connexions. It is inconceivable that Jesus should have adopted this title, and *not* have meant it to designate Himself, as the personal realization of what was but vaguely suggested in the indefinite phrase of Dn 7[13]. We infer, therefore, that the title 'Son of Man' stood on Jesus' lips as equivalent to the title 'Messiah,' which He would not use unless and until His use of it could not be misapprehended.

The title, moreover, is not arbitrary or empty. It suggests the type of Messiah which Jesus believed Himself to be, and the kind of actions through which He intended to fulfil His Messianic vocation. The passage in Daniel, taken as a whole, turns on the contrast between two kinds of sovereignty—that which is won by brute force, and that which belongs to a being not brutal but human. But this is precisely Jesus' conception of His Messiahship, viz. a sovereignty to be won through service. There is another passage which ought not to be forgotten when we ask for the sources of Jesus' idea of the Son of Man, viz. Is 53. It may be too much to say that Jesus intended 'Son of Man' to be a synonym for 'Servant of the Lord,' though His use of the title in Mk 9[12] is significant. But it is certain that He filled the phrase 'Son of Man' with the contents of that other conception, and meant by 'Son of Man' to identify 'Messiah' with the Servant who, in the prophetic vision, passed through suffering to glory.

(2) *How did He use it?*—Let the relative passages be placed before us, as is done in Driver's great art. 'Son of Man' in Hastings' *DB*, and at once a twofold use reveals itself. One class of passages describes the work which Messiahship entails upon Him, His manner of effecting it, and His relation to those for whom it is done. It is a redemptive work; it is performed in lowliest service and profoundest suffering; its motive is deep, true sympathy with men in their needy condition. The other class contains references to the sovereignty which is now hidden by the lowliness, though in no sense inconsistent with it (Mk 10[42ff.]), which, when the ends of humiliation are achieved, will be demonstrated in the face of the universe. Together these passages set forth a Messiah whose work is the redemption of men, through a life of service and suffering, and a death which has in it the quality of an atonement, a Messiah whose faithfulness to His vocation will be crowned with royal honours.

(3) *What does He reveal as to His own Person in it?*—The interpretation of the title as 'representa-

tive' or 'ideal' man is surely too modern to be an accurate reflexion of Jesus' own mode of thinking. We shall not be in error, however, if we read in the title Jesus' identification of Himself with men, His profound insight into their condition and His acceptance of it as His own, His taking upon Himself the griefs from which they suffer, and His achieving, in the depths of His suffering, their deliverance. The title, accordingly, sums up the relations in which Jesus stands to men. He touches human nature at every point. It is true He is sinless; but this fact, so far from hindering His perfect sympathy with men, is its necessary pre-condition. Just because He is sinless, His identification with men can be complete, and He can be to men what no other can be. He can do for men what not one of themselves can do. The fulness of His humanity distinguishes Him from all individual members of the race. He is not 'a man'; He is 'the Son of Man,' the kinsman of every man, the Head and King of redeemed and reconstituted humanity.

Here is a gracious fact, verifiable in the experience of every man who will yield his heart to this Saviour and Lord. This very fact, however, opens depths of mystery within itself. Who is He who is perfect man? What is the basis of this human sonship? It cannot be a Personality, limited as ours is, needing, as ours does, some bond beyond itself to connect it with God. He who can stand in this unique relation to men must stand also in a unique relation to God. See also art. SON OF MAN.

2. The Son of God.—This title, as Jesus used it or accepted it, is plainly derived from the OT, where it is applied to the theocratic people (Ex 4[22], Hos 11[1]), to the theocratic King (2 S 7[14], Ps 89[26. 27]), and to the Messiah (Ps 2[7]). The OT usage evidently is not barely official, but shows a growth in spirituality of connotation and in definiteness of application. It would be too much to suppose that any OT prophet clearly discerned the Divinity of the Messiah; but at least the prophetic vision catches sight of One who should stand in a spiritual relation to God closer than that which can possibly be occupied by any member of the theocracy. The title, accordingly, as it applies to the Messiah, does not express barely His office, but rather some quality of His person which is superhuman, and is the source of reverent awe in the minds of those who contemplate the thought of Him. There is a vagueness in it which excludes either a dogmatic definition of His Divinity, or a merely humanitarian view of His person. When it occurs in the NT, we cannot get rid of it by pointing out that it simply means 'the Messiah.' No doubt it means the Messiah; but it connotes that in the man who claims to be the Messiah which lifts Him above the level of mankind.

(1) We cannot draw any definite inference from *the use of it* by demoniacs, or by Satan in the Temptation narrative. Probably, however, as the idea of the 'subliminal' sphere which engirdles our conscious life makes its way into psychology, men will be more likely to give weight to narratives which imply that between such unhappy beings and Jesus there existed mutual knowledge, and that He exerted over them a peculiar and direct authority. In that case the title on their lips would certainly be a description of the superhuman dignity and power which He possessed.

(2) Neither can we base a doctrinal proposition on the expression *used by the high priest* (Mk 14[61], Mt 26[63]), for the charge of claiming to be 'the Christ' did not carry with it the verdict of capital punishment. The addition 'Son of God' or 'Son of the Blessed' looks like a climax. In St. Luke's narrative (22[66-71]) the question, 'If thou art the Christ' (v.[67]), is separated from the second, 'Art thou then the Son of God?' (v.[70]), by Jesus' claim to Divine honours (v.[69]). The impression made by the scene is that our Lord's judges understood Him to be claiming superhuman dignity. This claim they regarded as blasphemous, and it formed *ipso facto* the warrant of the death sentence.

(3) *Peter's ascription* in Mt 16[16] has some doubt thrown on it by the absence of the clause 'the Son of the living God' from the parallel passages in Mark and Luke. Yet an argument

based on omissions is precarious. St. Matthew had access to special sources. His version has the ring of genuineness; and it is to be noted that the benediction upon Peter is not found in Mark and Luke, where the ascription of Sonship is also awanting. If, then, we may accept the genuineness of the saying, we cannot, indeed, attribute to Peter a doctrine of his Master's person which he could reach only through momentary experience of the risen Christ; but, certainly, we note that he is far in advance of the momentary impression of Mt 14^{33}. He cannot mean less than that He to whom he speaks is the Son of Jehovah, having an intimacy with Him possessed by no other man, revealing Him as no other can, not even the greatest of the prophets. Peter knows nothing of dogma, but he has flung the plummet of his faith far into the depths of his Master's being. In that moment of supreme spiritual uplift a revelation has been made to him which will carry him far in after days, of which the opening verses in Hebrews and the prologue to the Fourth Gospel will be no more than the adequate expression.

(4) When we turn to *our Lord's own testimony* as to His Sonship toward God, we are at once lifted high above the merely official aspect of the designation. In the Synoptic Gospels He never uses the title 'Son of God'; but His filial relation toward God is not for a moment in question. A son's devotion to his father, a son's utter trust in his father, a son's joyful intercourse with his father —all these, raised to an immeasurable degree, are the characteristics of Jesus' bearing toward God. If the phrase had never occurred in the OT, or fallen from any human lips regarding Him, none the less would any sympathetic view of the Figure portrayed have yielded the inference: Here is a man who in very deed is Son of God, in a sense to which no other man ever attained or could attain. The unique Sonship which Jesus knew Himself to possess gains express utterance in three great sayings (Mk 13^{32} 14^{36} [cf. Lk 23$^{34.\ 46}$] and Mt 11^{27}). The first of these sets the rank of the Son in a more conspicuous light, because Jesus is disclaiming a knowledge which, on the supposition that He was God's Son, it might have been expected that He would possess. The second unveils the mystery of the Passion, the profound acceptance of the Father's purpose in the midst of a suffering which the Father Himself appoints. The third, with its strongly Johannine phrasing, brings Jesus and the Father together in unique mutual knowledge. The loftiest Christology lies implicit in these words; and, in the consciousness which they express, the invitation which follows, addressed to all the weary and heavy laden, promising them rest, can alone find its warrant. In the Fourth Gospel Jesus is represented as using the exact phrase, 'Son of God' (Jn 5^{25} 9^{35} 10^{36} 11^{4}). In one of these passages, however, there is uncertainty as to the correct reading, and in the others the possibility that the author may have imported into the narrative phraseology of later date, may be admitted. But the correlative terms 'the Father' and 'the Son' abound; and no reader of the Fourth Gospel, whatever his critical views or theological prejudices may be, doubts that the deep consciousness of Jesus, revealed in such utterances (*e.g.* 5^{18} 10$^{30.\ 38}$ 14^{11} 17^{21}), is that of a Sonship toward God which belongs to Himself alone of all the human race. Few, also, will be found to deny that the representations of the Fourth Gospel are not in excess of the portraiture of the Synoptic Gospels.

(5) *The Divine attestation.* — At the Baptism and the Transfiguration God solemnly attested the Divine Sonship of Jesus in words which reproduce the language of the OT (Ps 2^{7}, Is 42^{1}). It is needless to discuss the 'objective' aspect of the communication. In any case, the attestation was made direct to the consciousness of Jesus. The language is that of Messianic prophecy; but as it fell on Jesus' inward ear, it was not a mere certification of His Messiahship, but rather a gracious assurance of that which interpreted for Him Messiahship, and made its achievement possible, *viz.* a relation toward God which lay deep in His

being, and was the primary element in His self-knowledge.

How, then, are we to conceive the Sonship of Jesus toward God? Let us avoid modern abstractions, which were certainly not present to the mind of our Lord, or to any of those who came under His influence and have recorded their convictions. In particular, let us not be coerced by the supposed contrast between 'ethical' and 'metaphysical,' and by the alternative, which some Divine writers would force upon us, of regarding the Divine Sonship of Jesus as being ethical merely, or of imputing to Him a metaphysical Sonship which is an importation from Greek philosophy. Ethical the Sonship of Jesus undoubtedly was. It manifested itself in knowledge of God and love to God, together with trust and obedience and other lovely qualities and experiences. The Sonship to which believers in Him are introduced is of this type, and is marked by the same characteristics. He Himself claims them as His brethren (Mk 3^{35}). But does this mean that He and they are of one class? Does His Sonship differ from theirs merely in degree? Is He unique only in the measure in which He realized the privileges of a filial standing, which, however, belongs to men simply as men? Is this the utmost impression that the whole portrait makes upon us? It certainly was not all that His Jewish auditors inferred from His self-witness. They declared that He was making Himself equal to God, and they would have killed Him for His blasphemy (Jn 5^{18} 8^{59} 10$^{31-33}$). Were they mistaken? He does not say so. His retort (10$^{34ff.}$) is no earnest disclaimer; rather is it a reassertion of His essential unity with God. Surely this is the impression we gain from the record, that along with His intense nearness to men, there is a note of aloofness from them as of a Being of another order. Surely there are qualities in His Sonship that are incommunicable to men, aspects of it which can never be found in theirs. Could any of them ever say, 'I and the Father are one?' Could it be said of any one of them, that 'to see him was to see the Father'? It is noteworthy, and ought to be final on this subject, that Jesus never classes Himself along with His disciples as if He and they were alike children of the Heavenly Father. He distinguishes Himself as *the* Son from all other sons of God (cf. Mt 6^{32} 10^{29} with 18^{35} 20^{23}). They *become* sons, He *is* the Son. The correlation between 'the Father' and 'the Son' is absolute, and excludes any other son of God from that unique and perfect fellowship. When we weigh these things, the distinction between ethical and metaphysical becomes meaningless. The Sonship of Jesus has an ethical uniqueness which carries with it essential relations to God. His self-witness carries us to equality of being with God. As 'Son of Man' means humanity in the broadest, truest sense, so 'Son of God' means Divinity in the deepest signification of the term, which will require for its statement and defence the utmost range of reverent thought, while yet it cannot be comprehended or set forth in any formula.

This is the self-witness of Jesus. He is a Divine Being. His life in time under the conditions of humanity is not His whole life. He has come from a sphere wherein He dwelt with God, a conscious Person in equality with God. He entered into this world to execute a purpose which involved His complete oneness with humanity, and a sympathetic appropriation of a complete human experience; He had before Him, throughout His experience as a man, His return to the abode which He had left, His regaining the glory which, for purposes of infinite love, He had laid aside. He knew 'that he came forth from God, and goeth unto God' (Jn 13^{3}). These were facts which, in the nature of the case, could not be proved by any external evidence. Sympathetic hearts and open minds would be prepared for them. Narrow-minded, unspiritual, and prejudiced persons would reject them. The truth regarding His Personality stands or falls by His own self-witness : 'Even if I bear witness of myself, my witness is true ; for I know whence I came, and whither I go.' Or, if another witness is wanted, there is Another who witnesses along with Him, even the Father in whom He abides (Jn 8¹²⁻¹⁹). Of a mode of being which He had with God antecedent to His earthly life He could not speak freely. Necessarily, He could not but observe the utmost reticence regarding it. Nevertheless, His recollection of it was continually with Him, and occasionally, in great moments, for example in conflict with His critics, or in communion with His Father (Jn 6⁶² 8⁵⁸ 17⁵⋅ ²⁴).

It will be said that this highest reach of the self-witness of Jesus opens out into sheer mystery ; and attempts are continually being made to bring down the teaching of Jesus regarding Himself to the terms of mere humanity, with the view of making the record more intelligible, and making Jesus Himself more accessible to our imaginations. Such attempts wreck themselves through over-strenuousness of criticism and over-ingenuity of exegesis. Moreover, they defeat their own end. If Jesus is no more than man, the Gospel narrative is for ever unintelligible ; and Jesus Himself remains behind in the past, at best a pathetic memory, at worst a mere enigma. The faith which regards Jesus as 'the only-begotten Son,' or 'God only-begotten' (Jn 1¹⁸), is a just deduction from the narrative of His life and from His own self-witness. It supplies, moreover, the explanation which is wanted for the whole representation as it is given not merely in the Fourth Gospel, but in the Synoptic Gospels as well. The humanity of Jesus, with its completeness and universality, could belong only to One who was Son of God as well as Son of Man. The Messianic redemptive work of Jesus, in its efficacy, as sealing the new covenant, could be undertaken and discharged only by One who was, and knew Himself to be, the Son of God.

C. *THE WITNESS OF THE APOSTLES.*—The disciples of Jesus, even when He was with them as their Master and Teacher, were not a mere school. They were a community, enjoying the unexampled privilege of fellowship with the most wonderful Personality which ever impressed itself on human souls. For a brief space, which must have seemed an eternity of pain, they thought He had left them. Then He astounded, rebuked, and blessed them by His risen presence. Thus the disciples were reconstituted as a community, the secret of whose unity and vitality was fellowship with the unseen yet living Lord. This is their experience : Christ is risen ; no hallucination, dream, or vision, but the Lord Himself as they had begun to know Him, and now know Him as they could never have known Him had He tarried through lapse of years in flesh among them. Now that He is risen they are less than ever a school ; they are an Ecclesia, His Ecclesia, as He had said Himself (Mt 16¹⁸), a fellowship of human beings, the hidden source of whose privileges and gifts is fellowship with the ever present Saviour and Head. To Him they owed that 'loosing' from sin which the elaborate institutes of the OT had failed to accomplish (Rev 1⁵). From Him they derived that life which was the choicest privilege of the OT, but which could not be perfectly possessed till God was fully known (Jn 17³). Christianity as it is presented in the NT is life in fellowship with Jesus Christ. Such an experience cannot be stationary. It must be a growth in the grace and the knowledge of Jesus Christ. The NT throbs and thrills with life, exultant, buoyant, hopeful ; expanding, deepening, increasing in energy ; not without weaknesses, relapses, defects ; but ever correcting its faults, cleansing its stains, renewing its vitality through fellowship with Christ, who is its unfailing source. It is important to remind ourselves that the primary fact in the NT is an experience living and increasing ; lest we be tempted to go to it as

to a volume of philosophy, or a systematic statement of theology, demanding from it intellectual completeness, and feel proportionately disappointed if it provide not an answer to every question which may rise in our minds. Such a *doctrinaire* view, whether held by the destructive critic or the constructive theologian, is erroneous and misleading. The NT is experimental to its core, and is fundamentally a witness borne to Him with whom believers are united in an ever-increasing fellowship. 'That which we have seen and heard declare we unto you also, that ye also may have fellowship with us : yea, and our fellowship is with the Father, and with his Son Jesus Christ' (1 Jn 1³). When, accordingly, we approach the records of this testimony, we anticipate that the notes of experience will be found in it, viz. (*a*) variety, created by differences in the spiritual history of the individual writers, as well as by differences in the occasion and circumstances of their writing ; (*b*) development throughout the whole period covered by the NT literature, the earlier stages being marked by attention mainly to the conspicuous activities of the risen Saviour, the later being characterized by a deeper insight into the personal relations of Christ to God and to man and to the world ; (*c*) unity, fundamentally the same view of Christ being present in all the writings, earlier and later, inasmuch as all Christian experience, in its origin as well as in its progress, is rooted and grounded in the same almighty Saviour, the same exalted Lord. The witness may be briefly summarized as follows.

i. THE EARLIER CHAPTERS IN THE ACTS OF THE APOSTLES.—In the midst of much critical discussion of these chapters, it can scarcely be questioned that they reproduce, with substantial truth, the type of life and teaching in the primitive Church ; and give us 'a Christology which must have come from a primitive source' (Knowling, *Testimony of St. Paul to Christ*, p. 171). How, then, did Peter and his associates preach Christ?

Three points seem plain. (1) They lay the basis of the gospel in the humanity of Christ. They do not grudgingly admit His humanity, as though it presented an intellectual difficulty ; nor do they dogmatically insist on it, as though it had been denied by some Docetic scheme. They use His human name. They dwell on His human life and character. He whom they preach as the Christ is the Jesus of that historic past which is so fresh in their memories, so lovely in their hearts. Upon what He had been and done as a man, all that He now is and accomplishes is founded (2²² 3⁶ 4¹⁰ 10³⁸).—(2) They set the fact of the Resurrection in the forefront of their preaching. That event carries the weight of the greatest doctrines of the faith. This is the message which conveys the glory of God's accomplished purpose of mercy : 'He is risen ; we are witnesses' (2²⁵⁻³²). The Resurrection is not merely the miracle of a dead man raised. It is a great historic act on the part of God, who hereby authenticates the mission and vindicates the claims of Jesus. It is not merely that Jesus survives a tragedy. Through death He passes to a higher seat than that of His father David, even the throne of the Divine Majesty (2³⁴ 5³¹ 7⁵⁵). In doing this for Jesus, God did not take a mere man and make Him what a man cannot be, or set Him where a man could not breathe. Jesus is placed in the position which is His by right, to which His person perfectly corresponds. The earliest preaching is in complete harmony with Ro 1⁴. The idea of pre-existence, though not explicitly stated, is one of the implications of this teaching, even as it is of the Synoptic portraiture.—(3) They apply to Him titles which describe Him as the fulfilment of the highest reach of OT prophecy, and carry with them, in some instances, a distinctly Divine rank of being : *Messiah*, in Jesus' own interpretation of Messiah and His mission (3¹⁸⁻²⁰ 4²⁵⁻²⁸) ; *Lord* (1²¹ 2³⁴⁻³⁶ 10³⁶), *i.e.* the OT name of Jehovah, which could be borne only by a Divine being, though, it may well be, the theological bearings of such ascription were not fully present to their minds ; *Prophet* (3²²), *Saviour* (5³¹ 4¹²), *Prince* (ἀρχηγός, 5³¹ 3¹⁵), *Servant* (3¹³⋅ ²⁶ 4²⁷⋅ ³⁰, cf. 8³²⋅ ³³), with evident reference to the Servant of the Lord in Deutero-Isaiah ; *Holy* or *Righteous One* (2²⁷ 4²⁷⋅ ³⁰ 3¹⁴ 7⁵²), *Son of God* (9²⁰), a title used in this place only, yet significantly, as a current description of preaching the gospel.—(4) They dwell on certain present functions and activities, exercised by the exalted Saviour. He bestows the Spirit (2³³⋅ ³⁸). He grants the forgiveness of sins (2³⁸ 3¹⁹ 5³¹). He operates in miracles of healing (3¹⁶ 4¹⁰), the condition on the human side being faith in His name. He is the Source of Salvation (4¹²). To Him, therefore, the preachers invite their hearers to come. They insist, however, on repentance, not merely of sin in general, but of the specific guilt of His death (3¹³⁻¹⁵), and they require faith as an act of personal trust in Him (10⁴³).—(5) They announce His return, at the completion of the Messianic period, for judgment (3²¹ 10⁴²). This announcement gave a distinctive character to the preaching ; and rendered it not so much 'an argument as to certain truths,' as 'the proclamation of a message' (S. Mathews, *The Messianic Hope in the NT*, p. 145). None the less it bore, as its heart and centre, the truth of the Lord's superhuman personal dignity.

The Divinity of Christ is not discussed by these missionary preachers. They are concerned with the facts regarding Christ, His power, His promises, His benefits. They do not unfold the doctrine of His person which is implied in their statements : their own conceptions of it were, probably, at a very early stage of development. They held and taught such things regarding Him as implied that conception of Christ which was set forth by later teachers. Those brethren who wrote at a later date, and more explicitly, were not moving away from the historic Christ. They were, rather, getting nearer to Him, and seeing Him more clearly, than had been possible to those who bore their witness at an earlier period.

ii. THE MINOR CHRISTOLOGIES.—Some NT writings have scarcely advanced beyond the point of view of the Acts. They are mainly occupied with the saving functions of the Messiah, and do not enter deeply into the consideration of His Person. With respect to the simplest of them, however, it remains true that the place of Jesus in religious experience is central and supreme. He is the object of faith, the source of every spiritual blessing.

1. James.—His Epistle has sometimes been animadverted on as though it were little better than Jewish-Christian. We may content ourselves with Hort's more generous estimate : 'Unlike as it is to the other books of the NT, it chiefly illustrates Judaistic Christianity by total freedom from it' (*Judaistic Christianity*, p. 151). We may refer also to Dr. Patrick's recent volume, *James, the Lord's Brother*, p. 98 ff.

The doctrinal scheme of the Epistle is very simple, and deeply religious. God is the absolutely good One (1⁵· ¹³· ¹⁷). Man is made in His image (3⁹), and is meant to be separate from the world (1²⁷), and wholly given up to God (1¹⁸). Sin is the forswearing of this allegiance, and the choice of the world instead of God, and leads to death (1¹⁴· ¹⁵). For men, under the power of sin, deliverance lies in the act of God, who quickens them into a new life. This He effects by His word (1¹⁸· ²¹) ; and this word comes through the mediation of Christ, by whom the old law is transformed into a new law, a royal law, a law of liberty (2⁸· ¹²). Christ, accordingly, is the Saviour to whom we owe our salvation. He is the object of saving faith, which we must not belie by any inconsistent life (2¹).

To St. James, as to all Christians, Jesus is also Lord, ranked along with Jehovah in honour and dignity (1¹ 2¹). To Him belongs 'the honourable name' (2⁷). He will shortly come for judgment (5⁸· ⁹). Dorner's summary is borne out by the whole Epistle : 'Both in soteriological and in Christological form, James acknowledges the absoluteness of the Christian religion' (*System*, vol. iii. p. 159).

2. The First Epistle of Peter.—There is distinct advance in this Epistle beyond the statements in St. Peter's speeches reported in the Acts, though even yet the Christology is not so rich and full as in St. Paul or St. John. The sinlessness of Jesus is clearly stated (1¹⁹ 2²²) ; and this gives an impression of the Personality of Christ which is inconsistent with a merely humanitarian view of His person. The death of Christ, which had once offended Peter, but which in his preaching he had declared to be part of Messiah's redemptive work, he now glories in as the ground of salvation, and he describes it in its atoning efficacy with rich variety of phrase—covenant blood (1²), ransom (1¹⁸ᶠ·), sin-bearing (2²⁰ᶠᶠ·), substitution (3¹⁸). One who ascribed such efficacy to the death of Christ must

have taken an exalted view of His Person. Lordship in the usual Christian sense is ascribed to Him (1³ 2¹³ 3¹⁵). Sonship toward God is implied in 1³. Resurrection, exaltation, supremacy have their wonted place in St. Peter's thoughts, as in all Christian faith (1²¹ 3²²). The wording of 1¹¹ and 1²⁰ scarcely allows us to regard these passages as distinctly teaching a *personal* pre-existence of Christ, although such an interpretation of them is certainly legitimate, and is, besides, much more characteristic of St. Peter's non-speculative cast of mind than the *ideal* pre-existence which is held by some interpreters to be the meaning. In any case, Christ is to St. Peter a Being far more than man or angel ; and this means, since the thought of a demi-god is impossible to a Jewish monotheist, that St. Peter placed his Lord side by side with Jehovah, sharer with God in Divine rank and worship. This he did with the memory full and clear within him of his Master's human life. That St. Peter, who so often spoke frankly and plainly to Jesus, and once rebuked Him and once denied Him, should have come to adore Him as Divine, is a fact most wonderful, and fraught with far-reaching consequences.

3. Jude and 2 Peter.—In these brief and, from many points of view, difficult writings, there is no Christological discussion. Both Epistles, however, assume the Lordship of Christ, and look forward to His coming as Judge. In 2 P 1², He is conjoined with the Father as the object of religious knowledge ; and in the previous verse He is described as 'our God and Saviour Jesus Christ.'

4. Apocalypse.—Whatever view we take of the composition of this book, the key to which has so long been mislaid, there is no doubt that its pages glow with the glory of Jesus. It contains abundant recollections of the human life of Jesus (*e.g.* 5⁵ 22¹⁶ 21¹⁴ 11⁸). It is the exalted, glorified, victorious Lord, however, who chiefly fills the seer's gaze. To Him the writer desires the eyes of the persecuted Church to turn, that she may be certified of her vindication and reward at the hand of Him whom she adores.

He is included in the sacred Threefold source of blessing (1⁴⁻⁶). The radiant Figure of the vision in 1¹²⁻²⁰, whose self-designations are 'the first and the last' and 'the Living one,' to whom belong 'the keys of death and of Hades,' is no mere earthly Being who has undergone apotheosis. He is a Divine being, who came out of eternity, entered into time, and on earth suffered and died, and now, within the unseen world, lives and reigns as God ; who, also, will one day return for judgment (14¹⁴⁻¹⁶ 22²⁰). He is on the Throne (3²¹ 7¹⁷ 12⁵ 22¹· ³). Worship is paid to Him as God (7¹⁰ 5¹²· ⁸). He is the Son of God, as none other can be (1⁶ 2²⁷ 3²¹). He is a pre-existent and eternal Being (1¹⁷· ¹⁸ 3¹⁴ 21⁶ 22¹³) ; such is the interpretation which is required by these passages in view of the Christology of the book as a whole. See discussion in Stevens, pp. 538–540. To Him belongs the incommunicable Name (3¹² 19¹²). It is impossible to exaggerate the significance of the adoration of Jesus which pervades all the NT literature, and is so intense and sincere in this book. 'Although the writer is plainly a Jew of Jews, his mind saturated with Hebrew literature and Hebrew modes of thought, a true son of the race with which monotheism had become a passion, and the ascription of Divine honour to any other than the supreme God a horror and a 'blasphemy, he nevertheless sets Jesus, the man whom he had known in the flesh, side by side with God' (C. A. Scott, *The Book of the Revelation*, p. 27).

The NT books are not efforts of solitary thinkers evolving schemes out of their inner consciousness. The Christian Ecclesia, the fellowship of Christ, the communion of saints lived by such thoughts and spiritual activities as these. Its members knew nothing of the subtleties of post-Nicene Christology ; but they knew Jesus, the Lamb of God, who died for them, the Living Lord in whose right hand were seven stars, who walked amid the candlesticks.

iii. THE CHRISTOLOGY OF ST. PAUL.—

Amid the manifold discussions of this topic, three positions seem to be attracting to themselves an increasing volume of consentient opinion.

(*a*) St. Paul's Christology is the outcome of his experience.

He had seen the Risen Christ. The simplest, most obvious, interpretation of 1 Co 9¹ 15⁵⁻⁹ is surely the truest. Attempts to assimilate St. Paul's sight of Christ on the road to Damascus with ecstatic experiences, which he also records, betray, by their very ingenuity, the *a priori* assumption that a fully objective revelation of the kind alleged is impossible. St. Paul's sight of Christ was of the same nature as that by which the faith of the Eleven was first established. If the 'vision hypothesis' does not do justice to the facts in their case, neither will it account for the sudden and complete revolution which took place in the life of St. Paul. That he had seen the Risen Christ, in the same sense, with the same convincing 'objectivity,' as St. Peter had seen Him, is the source of Paul's authority as an Apostle. It is the source, also, of his Christian faith. It warrants the utmost and the greatest which Paul can ever say regarding the wonderful being of his Lord. From that date, the hour when he heard the words 'I am Jesus,' he had been 'in Christ.' Christ had been a present reality to him, and out of his fellowship with Christ had come every grace of his character, every privilege of his soul, every activity of his career. 'That I may know him' (Ph 3¹⁰) is the passion of his life, and his so-called 'Christology' is not a philosophy of the 'logos,' or 'avatar,' or any other type. It is the testimony he bears, incidentally, as the needs of his converts demand, to the Christ whom he knows.

(*b*) St. Paul's conception of Christ does not stand wholly apart from the views entertained by the primitive Church. His experience, remarkable as it was, did not differ in kind from that of other believers. The Church was from the beginning a fellowship with Christ. Every member of it is united to Christ by faith. There were others who had been 'in Christ' before St. Paul had gained that blessed privilege (Ro 16⁷). The knowledge which he possessed of Christ was common to the fellowship of believers, and had been theirs while Paul was raging against the Church in persecuting fury. In fact, it was precisely the lofty claims advanced by the disciples of the Nazarene on behalf of their Master, which called the young zealot to destroy a movement which he saw clearly was an invasion of the supremacy, not of Cæsar, but of Jehovah. When, in later days, he himself is glorying in the lofty attributes and Divine dignity of Christ, he is well aware that he is setting forth no novelties, but is speaking out of the fulness of a personal knowledge possessed by his readers as well as by himself. Dr. Sanday's words, commenting on 1 Th 1¹, are most memorable: 'An elaborate process of reflexion, almost a system of theology, lies behind those familiar terms.' Dr. Knowling's weighty and balanced statement ought to be borne in mind by every student of St. Paul's thought: 'The evidence to be gathered from the Apostle's own writings is not to be judged as if it was only of a reflective character upon the events of the life of Jesus seen through a long retrospect of years : in some particulars it carries us up to the earliest period of the existence of the Christian Church; in other particulars it is plainly incidental, it is used as occasion demands, and it justifies the inference that it has behind it a large reserve of early teaching and tradition' (*Testimony*, etc., p. 211).

(*c*) To say that St. Paul's Christology is more developed in his later Epistles than in his earlier, is only to note the fact that his personal acquaintance with Christ grew richer as the years of his inner life and of his missionary activity passed over him. But this advance was not determined by accretions from without. He had not to wait till theosophical speculation suggested it to him before he ascribed the loftiest, most comprehensive position and dignity to Christ. Such ascription belongs to his earlier as well as to his later writings. Prof. Bacon has strongly emphasized the presence of Paul's later thoughts 'in a partly developed form in the earlier Epistles' (*Story of St. Paul*, p. 208); and Dr. Knowling's great work, already referred to, is largely devoted to an illustration of this fact (*e.g.* pp. 48, 90 f., 206, 211 f., 502).

1. Christ in His relation to God.

—(1) *He is a Divine Being.*—St. Paul is an OT believer, utterly removed from polytheism, and wholly incapable of believing in demi-gods. He is not a Greek philosopher; impersonal abstractions or principles have no meaning for him. He of whom he speaks is 'Christ,' which with St. Paul is a proper name, the official designation being lost in the personal appellative. If, then, he ascribes to Christ the qualities which a Jewish monotheist, a member of the Old Covenant, attributed to Jehovah, he can mean nothing else than that this same person, Jesus Christ, is a Divine Being, equal with God and one with God.

(*a*) He attributes Lordship to Christ (2 Co 4⁵); and uses the title 'Lord' habitually in connexion with the historic and personal names 'Jesus' and 'Christ.' It is no courtesy title; it is used in the sense in which the LXX uses it of God, and it has the 'connotation of Godhead.' Passages of the OT, accordingly, which belong to Jehovah are applied to Christ (Ro 10¹³, 1 Co 10²²). To the Lord, therefore, as to God, worship is offered, and prayers are addressed by St. Paul and by all Christians (2 Co 12⁸, 1 Co 1², Ro 10¹³). (*b*) He designates Christ as 'the Son of God.' The teaching of St. Paul on this subject is in harmony with the other NT representations.

Believers in Christ enter upon the status of sons of God, and St. Paul even calls them υἱοί, while St. John uses only the term τέκνα. But among such sons of God Christ is not one. He stands alone. They *become* sons. He *is* the Son (Ro 8³·³², Gal 4⁴). This Sonship is the very essence of Christ's being. It means Divinity in the fullest sense, in most complete reality. St. Paul testifies to the Divinity of Christ while fully recognizing His humanity. On one side of His being He is linked to humanity ; and St. Paul has ample knowledge of the facts of Christ's human life, and shows no want of interest, and still less any reluctance, in referring to them. How should he, when it was his main business as a missionary to prove that this very Jesus was the Son of God? On the other side of His being, Christ possesses Godhead as the only Son of the Father. Of this Divine Sonship the Resurrection is declaration and proof (Ro 1¹⁻⁴). St. Paul's Christianity centres in this Divine Sonship of Christ (Gal 2²⁰, Eph 4¹³). It was no invention of his brain, no borrowing from pagan adulation of the Emperor. It was the centre of Christianity as such, and belongs to the very earliest period of which we have literary record, being implied in 1 Th 1¹. The faith in Christ as Son of God is the *differentia* of Christianity. They are Christians who think of Jesus Christ 'as of God' (ὡς περὶ θεοῦ); and so thinking they name Him, as St. Paul did, 'God' (Ro 9⁵).

(2) *He is one with the Father.*—The relation of the Divine Christ to the Godhead became an insoluble problem for subsequent thought. Let the presupposed conception of God be abstract simplicity and unity. Let Him be conceived as Pure Being, Pure Form, Pure Thought, the Idea, or Substance. Then let the claim be advanced on behalf of a historic person that he is God. The result will be a problem which, in the nature of the case, must be insoluble. With such a Deity, the Divinity of the historic Christ is utterly incompatible. Christ must be lowered to the rank of a demi-god, or He must be etherialized into an impersonal principle.

Suppose, however, that God be differently conceived; in that case the claim of Divinity advanced on behalf of one who lived a human life may not lead to intellectual impossibilities. It is certain, however, that neither St. Paul nor any other NT writer held any such speculative idea of God as was prevalent in Greek Philosophy. To the men of the NT, God was the God of the OT, the living God, a Person, loving, energizing, seeking the accomplishment of an everlasting purpose of mercy, the satisfaction of His own loving nature. When, accordingly, the facts of the character and claims and resurrection of an historic person compelled them to recognize Him as Divine, they were constrained greatly to enlarge their thought of God ; but they were saved the labour of stretching a logical formula to cover facts wholly irreconcilable with it, for the simple reason that no such formula had any place in their thoughts. They set the Divine Christ side by side with the Divine Father, and thus found a manifoldness in the being of God which did not destroy its unity. St. Paul, therefore, includes Christ in the Divine (1 Th 3¹¹⁻¹³, 2 Th 2¹⁶·¹⁷, 1 Co 8⁶, 2 Co 13¹⁴). 'Abstract monotheism' has ceased, and has been 'replaced by a Theism which finds within the one Godhead room for both Father and Son' (Fairbairn, *Place of Christ*, p. 309). Perhaps it would be more correct to say that the monotheism of the OT was never abstract, because the God of the OT was never a conception, or a substance, but always a Person. Personality, indeed, has never been the bare unity of a monad. It always makes room for distinctions ; and reaches its greatest wealth of meaning in the fellowship of person with person. Between an abstraction and a historic person there can be no unity. Between two historic persons there may be unity of the profoundest kind. St. Paul, moreover, is not thinking of a mere quantitative equivalence between the Divine Christ and God. He is true to the conception of Sonship. The relation of Christ to the Father is that of a real son, including dependence and subordination (1 Co 3²³ 11³ 15²⁴⁻²⁸). To the Son, as reward of obedience, is given a glory and a fulness which enable Him to fulfil His mediatorial function

(Ph 2^{9-11}, Ro 14^9, Col 1^{19}). This, however, in no sense lowers the Divine being of the Son, or shuts Him out of the Godhead. The glory He had with the Father from eternity, and the glory gained as He returns to the Father, are not inconsistent. Without the former, indeed, the latter would be impossible.

2. Christt in His relation to mankind.—(1) *Pre-incarnate.* —The Being who thus existed from eternity as God has affinities in His very nature with men. Had He been a demi-god, a *tertium quid*, the passage from Him to us and from us to Him would have been impossible. It may seem an ingenious plan to effect the union of God and man by inserting between them a being who is neither God nor man. Really, it makes the problem insoluble. St. Paul knows nothing of the supposed differences between the Divine and the human natures which make a *tertium quid* appear necessary to bring them together. God and man resemble one another in their constitution as personal beings. The problem at once of religion and of philosophy is to bring *two persons* together, not to force two disparate natures into an unreal unity. This problem, the problem of the human spirit, is solved in the Person of Christ. The heart of His eternal being is Sonship. He lives in a filial relation toward God, and upon the model of that relationship ours is formed (Gal 4^{4-6}, Ro 8^{29}). Our very existence depends on Him (1 Co 8^6). What we are to be is determined by what He is (Eph 1^4 2^{10}). The deepest relations of man to man find their guarantee in the relations in which He stands to God and to man (1 Co 11^3, Eph 5^{22-31}). Even before the fulness of time He was not utterly unconnected with the problem of redemption. So, at least, we may interpret the mystic utterance of 1 Co 10^4 ἡ πέτρα δὲ ἦν ὁ Χριστός. This Rock, the fountain of life for the Church of the wilderness, was the Christ, not as an idea but as a person. Thus St. Paul conceives of Christ as existing in these past centuries, fulfilling the functions for the Church which then was, which He now fulfils for the new Ecclesia (cf. Jn 7^{37}).

(2) *Incarnate.*—The Son is a real person, who conceives, purposes, acts. 'Before the foundation of the world' He had assumed the vocation of Redeemer, constrained thereto by the love which is the essence of the Divine nature. When the time comes, in God's discipline of the race, He takes up His task, which requires for its fulfilment incarnation, the complete identification of Himself with men in life and in death. In two pregnant passages St. Paul sets forth this deed of wonder, in whose depths thought and feeling lose themselves, Ph 2^{5-11}, 2 Co 8^9. Three stages of the history of Christ are indicated, so far as human imagination can frame to itself a record so amazing:—(i.) A person, Divine in His being, enjoying the form and circumstance of Godhead, rich in the glory which is the manifestation of the Divine nature; cf. Jn 17^5, He 1^3. (ii.) This Divine Being surrendering that form and that wealth, assuming a form the most opposite conceivable, that of a servant, revealing Himself to men in their likeness, so that His humanity is no phantom, while yet it is not His by mere accident of birth, but is acquired in an act of will which extends to the assumption of man's condition as a sinner, exposed to sin's sign and seal, even death. (iii.) This same person raised from the dead, and receiving as a gift from the Father what He had not grasped at, namely, equality with God in form and circumstance, and the name which corresponds to that rank and honour, so that to this Being, known now through His humanity as Jesus, there should be rendered the worship of all intelligent creatures throughout the universe of God.

It is in connexion with the incarnate stage of Christ's career that the problem of the constitution of His Person presses most acutely. Questions press as to the relation of His Divinity to His humanity, of His knowledge as God to His knowledge as man, of His personality as a Divine Being to His personality as a human being, of His activities in the flesh to His contemporaneous activities in the Cosmos and in the circle of the Godhead. It is noteworthy that St. Paul does not discuss these questions, seems, indeed, to be scarcely conscious of them. He wonders and adores as he thinks of the love which led Christ to that stupendous sacrifice. He contemplates with delight and worship the Person of his glorified Lord, and throws his being open to the gracious influences of His Spirit. He has no other ambition on earth save to know Christ; but when he speaks of knowing, he means such spiritual intimacy as person has with person, and in particular a growing appreciation of, and entrance into, the power of Christ's resurrection, the fellowship of His sufferings, and conformity to His death (Ph 3^{10}). But to dissect the Person of Christ, to lay out the Divinity on one side and the humanity on the other, and to discuss a *communicatio idiomatum*, does not lie within the four corners of Pauline thought. This fact may suggest the doubt whether questions such as the above are rightly conceived. They evidently proceed from the point of view of dualism, according to which one nature is contrasted with another; whereas Paul's views of God and of man and of the God-man, are all synthetic. Personal unity, and not logical dualism, is the key to the thought of St. Paul. Between God and man, there is the unity of moral likeness; between the Father and the Son, the unity of being and fellowship; between the pre-incarnate and the incarnate periods of Christ's experience and action, the unity of one continuous life; between Christ and those whom He saves, the unity of reciprocal indwelling.

(3) *Post-incarnate.*—Having become man, Christ remains human. In the Kingdom whose Lord He is, He is Jesus who was so named in His earthly life. Mediator between God and man, He is Himself man (1 Ti 2^5). From Him, as the Head, life streams down to all members of the body (Col 1^{18}, 1 Co 12^{27}, Eph $4^{12. 13}$). In Him the members are 'complete,' receive fulness of satisfaction (Col 2^{10}). In Him human nature finds itself raised to its highest perfection, hence in Him there can be none of the barriers that divide man from man (Col 3^{11}, Gal 3^{28}). This is the point of the comparison in Ro 5^{12-21} and 1 Co 15^{45-47} between the first Adam and the Second. In one sense Adam is the head of the race, in another the Risen and Exalted Christ is the Head, and from Him all life comes. This is the very heart of St. Paul's experience, and therefore also of His Christology. Christ is living. St. Paul presupposes the pre-existent Christ; his Christ could not begin to be in time. He is acquainted with the historic life through which Christ gained His glory. But that which St. Paul gazes upon with endless adoration is the Person of the Risen and Glorified Lord. Between the living Christ and him there is such union as surpasses power of language to express. Christ dwells in the believer in His complete human-Divine personality, and imparts Himself in growing fulness to the believer; and there is thus developed identity of experience and identity of character, which will ultimately be crowned by identity of outward condition (Gal 2^{20}, 2 Co 3^{18}, Ph 3^{21}).

3. Christ in His relation to the Cosmos.—The intellect of the time was much occupied with speculations regarding the relation of God to the world. To Greek dualism this was really an insoluble problem. The gulf between God and the universe yawned impassable. The place of a solution was taken by a mythology of 'powers,' 'principalities,' and the like supposititious beings, who existed only in the jargon of the philosophical sects. On Jewish soil this mythology was changed into a hierarchy of angels. Wild as these dreams are, they represent a real need of thought and of religious experience. The problems of creation and redemption cannot be held apart. The creative purpose must include redemption, and redemption must have cosmic bearings. We cannot rest in a harmony with God which leaves the universe outside, unreconciled, possibly the abode of forces against which the redeeming agency would be powerless to defend us. St. Paul's view is that the universe has a part in the history of man. Injured by human sin, it will come to its completion when the children of God enter on their heritage (Ro 8[21]). Christ, the Redeemer of men, accordingly, is Lord of the universe. Nothing lies outside His gracious sway. The clumsy machinery of angels, or powers, or whatever these needless creations are named, is replaced by the one Person, who is the Agent of God alike in creation and in redemption (Col 1[15-17]). Christ, who is the manifestation of God, is of infinitely higher rank than all the creatures. All things, whatever their place and dignity, owe to Him their existence, and find in Him their goal. This exalted Person is also Head of the Church, and Agent in reconciliation (vv.[18-20]). That is to say, the work of redemption can be accomplished only by One who is also the Creator. The Redeemer must be God absolutely, else there will be needed a Mediator for Him also. The Redeemer cannot have, in our apprehension, the value of God, unless He is God in His own proper being.

The testimony of St. Paul to Christ contains great heights and depths, but it exhibits no inconsistency with Jesus' self-witness. It is not a mosaic of Jewish and Hellenic clements. It is the product of experience, developed under the conditions of that Divine assistance which Jesus Himself described, Jn 16[12-15].

iv. HEBREWS. — In this Epistle the Christian faith is defended against any attempt to belittle the person and office of the Redeemer. However glorious other agents of the Divine purpose might have been, 'this man' is more glorious by far in the dignity of His person and in the vastness and finality of His redemptive work. To Him, therefore, is applied the familiar Christian designation of Lord (2[3] 7[14] 13[20]). The characteristic name applied to Him, however, is *Son* (1[1. 2] 7[28] 5[8] 1[8] 6[6] 7[3] 10[29] 4[14]). This title expresses His Divine and eternal being. The author of this Epistle follows the example of the Apostle Paul in describing the Christian salvation under the aspect of a history of the Son of God. This history moves in three stages.

(1) *The pre-existent state.*—Not much is said on this mysterious topic. The NT writers are concerned to allude to it only in order that, in the light of it, the earthly life of Jesus may be discerned in its marvellous condescension as an act of self-sacrifice, and in order that His present position of equality with God may be intellectually credible. In this pre-existent state the Son is the effulgence of God's glory, the very image of His substance (1[3]). Without formally discussing the question of the being of God, the writer has already surpassed any mere monadism. God is not bare abstract unity. With God there is One who exactly corresponds to Himself, who gives back to Him the glory which is His. Between Him and God there is perfect oneness. Between these two there is no room for a mediator. The functions of the Son in this state are not described further than to indicate that no department of the universe is outside the scope of His power (1[3]). There is no room, accordingly, for any being, other than the Son of God, to whom worship or gratitude is due.

(2) *The incarnate life.*—This writer, like the Apostle Paul, passes by all the questions, so abundantly discussed in later theology, as to 'two natures,' etc. His whole interest is concerned with the heart-subduing fact that the birth of Christ is the descent of a Divine Being from heaven to earth, the definite assumption by Him of a complete and true humanity (2[9] 10[5] 2[14]). To this writer the humanity of Jesus is wonderful and glorious. A Being truly Divine has become man, and has entered fully into human experience. There is nothing human that is not His, sin excepted. Temptation, suffering, death—He passed through them all. All this He endured in pursuance of the

vocation with which He entered humanity. Before Him lay His task. Beyond shone the glory. Not once, for so great a glory, would He evade one human sorrow. It was all wanted to perfect Him in His vocation (2[10] 5[8. 9]). The resemblance to St. Paul's line of thought in Ph 2[5-11] is obvious.

(3) *The exaltation.* — The position of majesty which the Son now occupies is described in two aspects. (*a*) Its *possibility* is due to what He was in Himself, antecedently to His human experiences. He has been appointed heir of all things, both because He is the Son of God and because, through Him, God made the worlds (1[2]). He has sat down on the right hand of the majesty on high, because He is, in His very nature, the effulgence of God's glory and the very image of His substance. No being less than God, in His own person, could occupy such a place. (*b*) Its *attainment* is due to His discharge of His redemptive mission, and is of the nature of a reward for His fidelity. His present position presupposes His pre-existent place and function, and yet is distinct from them. It is that of King in God's realm of redemption.

Here, just as in connexion with the incarnate condition, questions arise which this writer does not discuss. 'The relation of this rule to the primary rule of God, or to His own primary upholding of all things by the word of His power, is not indicated' (A. B. Davidson's *Com.* p. 78). It is enough for faith that, in the universe of being, there is no other power than that of the exalted Redeemer.

v. THE FOURTH GOSPEL. — St. John's Christology, like that of St. Paul, is the transcript of his experience. He makes plain his object in telling the story of the life of Christ (20[30f.]). Out of all the mass of material which his memory provides, he selects those incidents which may be most useful in proving to generations which had not the privilege of direct vision, that Jesus is the Christ, the Son of God. The principles of selection, and the insight into the meaning of words and deeds which are reproduced, are due to a lifetime of thought and communion, as well as to the continual illumination of the Spirit of Christ. St. John's conception of Christ is summarily set forth in the Prologue to the narrative (1[1-18]). No doubt these much-debated verses are meant to provide the point of view which the reader of the narrative is to occupy; but equally without doubt they do not present an idea, formed in speculation, and then employed to determine the narrative, to invent the incidents, and to create the discourses. The narrative, with the words and signs, logically precedes the Prologue, which presents us with the extracted meaning of the history. The Person portrayed in the narrative is One of whose history, in the wider sense, the earthly career is but a part. He had a being with God before He was seen on earth. He had a Divine mode of existence and exercised Divine functions, before He appeared as a man and wrought His deeds through human organs of action. At the set time He entered into humanity, and, through living intercourse with men, revealed to them the glory of His person, and interpreted for them the character of the invisible God. The remarkable feature of the Prologue is its use of the term Logos to designate Him whom the narrative leads us to know as the Son. It is certainly not the key to the narrative, which is to be read from the point of view of the Divine Sonship, which it reveals. It is not used in the narrative, though it reappears in the First Epistle of John. It is certainly not taken over from Philo, and intended to create a new religious philosophy. Probably its presence is to be explained, as are the references in St. Paul's letters, by the technicalities of prevalent philosophy or theosophy. Christianity appeared when the problem of the relation of God to the world had reached its fullest statement ; when, also, the utmost that human thought could do had been done in the way of a solution. The last and most strenuous effort of human thought to meet the demand of the human spirit had found expression in Philo's Logos speculation, which owed its origin partly to developments of Hebrew thought as to the word and wisdom of God, and partly to ideas which had been the motive power of the whole history of Greek philosophy. It was not possible for Christianity to ignore the problem. Christianity is more immediately concerned with the problem of the redemption of man ; but this cannot be dissociated from the wider problem of the relation of God to the world. The key to the one must unlock the other also. St. Paul and St. John, accordingly, take up the technical terms most in vogue, with whatever they stand for, and say in effect: What human thought has endeavoured to achieve by its machinery of angels or powers, or by its hypostatization of the Logos, has been accomplished in the Person of the Son of God. He is the life of the redeemed. He is the life also of the whole universe of God. There is but one purpose in creation and redemption, and that is summed up in Christ. He is the Logos.

The term Logos, accordingly, is used by St. John to express the identity of Him whom we know as Jesus Christ, with the personal Wisdom and Power of God, who is God's agent in creation, who alone could redeem men, and who achieved this in the only way possible, by Himself assuming human nature, and dwelling for a space with men. The term, having served the purpose of presenting Christ as the goal of the immemorial quest of the human spirit for union with God, is not again employed in the Gospel.

It is not necessary to attempt here a detailed analysis of the Prologue (see Westcott's *Com.* ; Dods in *Expos. Gr. Test.* ; and a valuable paper by Principal Falconer in *Expositor*, v. v. [1897] 222). The leading ideas are plain—(1) *The eternity of the Logos* (1[1. 2], cf. 17[5] 8[58], 1 Jn 1[1]). The Logos had a being coeval with God, and did not come into existence at a point in time, and therefore is not a creature. (2) *The fellowship of the Logos with God*. The Logos is personal, has a life of His own, which yet is directed toward God, so that He finds His life in God, and is 'in the bosom of the Father' (v.[18]). (3) *The Divine nature of the Logos*, as identical in being with God, while yet distinct as a person. (4) *The creative function of the Logos* (vv.[3. 10], cf. Col 1[16], He 1[2. 3]). (5) *The revealing function of the Logos* (v.[4f.]). (6) *The historical manifestation of the Logos* (vv.[6-13]). (7) *The incarnation of the Logos* (vv.[14-18]). This is the climax to which the Prologue has led up. This is the event of which the whole Gospel narrative is the record and description. The Logos, the same Being who had dwelt in the circle of the Godhead, left the glory which He had with God (17[5]), and, retaining His personal identity, became 'flesh,' *i.e.* became man, assumed human nature in its fulness, and dwelt among men as a man.

The problems with regard to the life of the incarnate Logos, which press so heavily on our minds, are not discussed by St. John any more than by St. Paul. He is wholly occupied with the glorious fact. It is amazing, but it has happened ; and in that great event the whole purpose of God, creative as well as redemptive, has reached its consummation. Revelation is complete. No one can declare God save One who is God, and this is He, Jesus Christ, 'God only-begotten' (v.[18]).

From the simple missionary preaching of the Acts to the high intense thinking of the Prologue to the Fourth Gospel is a long movement. It is a movement, however, not away from the facts, but toward their inward, spiritual, universal, and eternal meaning. This movement, moreover, has not been dependent on unaided human reflexion, nor are its results mere guesses or inferences. It has been conducted under the guidance of Christ's own self-witness and the illumination of Christ's own Spirit ; and its conclusions express the wealth of Christian experience, and in experience find their ultimate demonstration.

Conclusion and Outlook.—A study of the character of Christ, and a close and reverent attention to His self-witness, compel the inference that His Person, completely and really human though He is, is not constituted like that of other men. It is to

be admitted, however, or rather it is to be urged, that what the facts suggest and demand cannot be fully apprehended by any merely intellectual process whatever. What Christ is, in His own Person, can be known only by those who know Him ; and personal knowledge has conditions which are not satisfied in any exercise of the mere understanding, however careful and exact. Such conditions are an attitude or direction of the human spirit, and an immediate operation, at once illuminating and quickening, of the Divine Spirit. When these conditions meet and interact, in that profound region where the Spirit of God and the spirit of man touch and interpenetrate one another, there is produced that knowledge of God and of Christ which our Lord describes as life. There is *no other* knowledge of Christ ; and if Christology is supposed to be an intellectual process, governed by forms of discursive thought, and issuing in propositions for which is claimed the cogency of a logical demonstration, it stands condemned as being out of all relation to Christian experience. But this personal experience *is* knowledge of Christ. He is as really known in this spiritual fellowship as one human person is known by another, and is known more closely and fully than one man can be known by another. Christianity, accordingly, presents to the world the solution of its problem, the answer to its need ; while, at the same time, it has before itself a constant problem, the answer to which it seeks, not with ever-growing weariness and sense of defeat, but with ever-renewed energy of faith and love.

1. The problem of the world, the more or less conscious and articulate demand of the human spirit, is, as we noted at the outset, union with God. This union is, primarily, *personal*—an ethical fellowship, in which God shall fully disclose His character, and impart Himself, to man ; in which man shall freely open his being to the communications of God, and find in God his life and development. Such personal union, however, carries with it *cosmical union* also, or the harmonizing of all those differences from God which are implied in the existence of the created universe, and find their most acute expression in the self-assertion of man against God. The reconciling of man is the reconciling of all things. The solution of a problem, thus fundamentally personal, must be itself personal. Christianity, accordingly, met the problem of the early centuries, as it meets the same problem in the twentieth century, by the preaching of the personal Christ. He is the Son of God ; and therefore, also, He is the Son of Man. In Christ, God is fully present ; through Him, God is perfectly known ; with Him, God is one. In Christ, human nature is fully realized in all that it was meant to be, both in respect of its complete dependence upon God and of its complete fulfilment of spiritual function. In Christ, accordingly, the history of creation is complete. He stands at the head of a universe reconciled to God. He *is* its reconciliation. Wherever the problem of union with God takes expression in concrete facts—in the sense of guilt in the individual conscience ; in death, which closes human life with a pall of impenetrable darkness ; in the antagonism of man to man, manifested in personal animosities, or the war of nation with nation and class with class—in facts whose gloom no pessimism can exaggerate : there, the knowledge of Christ supplies the solution. To know Christ is to be at one with God and with man. Christianity is thus both religion and ethic. It is an intense individual experience, which is the impulse of boundless social service. And when the same problem finds the precision and articulateness of philosophical expression—as it did, for instance, in that Neo-Platonism which had such strange affinities to Christianity while it was also its bitterest opponent ; or as it does to-day,

in that Absolute Idealism which, in some aspects, is the noblest ally of the Christian faith, and, in others, its proudest and least sympathetic rival—the key to its solution will still be found in the conception of a Personality at once Divine and human, a life lived under historic conditions, which was at once the life of God in man and the life of man in and through God. The words of the Master of Balliol apply to the present as well as to the primitive position of Christianity :

'It contained implicitly the key to all the antagonisms of thought that had been developed in Greek philosophy — the antagonism of the material and the spiritual, the antagonism of the phenomenal and the ideal or intelligible world, the antagonism of the finite and the infinite, the antagonism of the temporal and the eternal. In a word, it contained in itself the principle of an optimism which faces and overcomes the deepest pessimism, of an idealism which has room in itself for the most realistic consciousness of all the distinctions and relations of the finite' (*Evolution of Theology in the Greek Philosophers*, vol. ii. p. 351).

2. The Incarnation of the Son of God is therefore the article of a standing Church. It is, at the same time, the abiding problem of a living Church. It is not, however, a problem which is suggested by one faculty to be handed over to another for solution. Faith does not receive Christ, and then appeal to intellect to tell us who He is, and how His Person is constituted. It has been the profound error of Scholasticism, both before and since the Reformation, to suppose that faith supplies a mass of crude amorphous facts and experiences, upon which the intellect exercises its analytic, systematizing genius, distinguishing, defining, separating, and then tying into bundles by means of formulæ. The result of such a method, applied to the problem of the Person of Christ, is a Christology in whose dogmatic construction the living Christ of history and experience is wholly unrecognizable. The Reformation was the protest of Christian faith against this attempt to rob it of the personal Saviour, whom it appropriates, whom the believer knows directly and truly. Ritschlianism, however incomplete its constructive work may be, is nevertheless, as a protest against formalism, in harmony with the spirit of the Reformation.

The value of such a protest, however, will be greatly lessened if it lend colour to the supposition that our knowledge of Christ is confined to His benefits, while He Himself, in the secret of His being, belongs to some supposed noumenal sphere, inaccessible to human knowledge, so that it is impossible either to affirm or deny His Divinity. 'Hoc est Christum cognoscere, beneficia ejus cognoscere' is a proposition true if it mean that no one can know Christ who is not vitally one with Him, and therefore a partaker of His benefits ; but certainly false if it mean that, beyond His benefits, there is a supposed substratum of being, about which nothing can be known, which may or may not be Divine (cf. Martensen, *Christian Dogmatics*, p. 63). Thus does the misapplied category of substance take revenge upon the critical method, which, while denying its validity, retains it as a kind of metaphysical phantom. To know the benefits of Christ, to live in fellowship with Him, to carry out His commission, is to know Himself. No shadow of unreality lies upon that knowledge, any more than it lies upon the knowledge we have of the friend whom we know better than we know ourselves. This does not mean, of course, that any believer, or the whole community of believers, now knows, or ever will know, all about Christ. Personality, even human personality, is a great deep ; and the joy of friendship is the progressiveness which is the mark of personal knowledge. Much more is this true of the personality of Christ. Knowledge of Christ is boundlessly progressive ; what more is to be known of Him than the Church at present apprehends, depends on those conditions

belonging to the whole personal life which make any knowledge of Him possible. In short, the problem of the Person of Christ is presented by that faith, which is already knowledge, to that knowing power, which is simply faith itself, as it grows in apprehension of Christ. Christ is not divided ; and there is no division in the faculty which apprehends Him, though the stages of its exercise and its acquisition advance endlessly from less to more. It follows that Christology, which is simply the reflective expression of the knowledge of Christ gained in actual experience, must not subject the fulness of its material to any form of thought borrowed from an alien sphere ; or if, in the exigencies of a defensive statement, it uses loan-words derived from philosophy, it must never for a moment imagine that these explain or exhaust the living reality with which it is dealing. These words float, like derelicts, on the ocean of the Church's thought, and many a promising speculation has struck thereon and foundered. Especially ought modern Christology to be on its guard against that dualistic mode of thought, with the terminology which it employs, which is the *damnosa hœreditas* bequeathed to theology by Greek Philosophy, the shadow of which fell upon Kant, and has not departed from the new Kantians of recent times. The task of Christology at the present day is to restate and to defend two certainties of Christian experience.

(1) To Christian experience, educated and informed by Scripture and by the Spirit of truth, *Christ is known as God*. The problem of the relation of the Divine Christ to the Divine Father is thus necessarily raised, and will not be evaded. If, however, the conception of absolute Godhead be modelled upon the forms of Greek dualism, the mystery becomes an insoluble problem, confounding thought and troubling faith. Within a Godhead conceived as abstract unity there is no room for the Divine Christ. The best that thought can do is to place the Son outside God, though as near to Him as possible. But this is straightway to deprive faith of its object, and to imperil the fact of reconciliation. The Church, accordingly, would have none of the Arian honorific titles applied to Christ on the presupposition that He was less than God, and would be content with nothing less than the consubstantiality of the Son with the Father. The term ὁμοούσιος, borrowed not without reluctance from philosophy, was probably inevitable, and served sufficiently to utter the Church's faith-knowledge of the true Divinity of its Lord. The danger lay in supposing that οὐσία, or the category of substance, is adequate to express the infinite wealth of the Divine Personality, or, worse still, in directing men's minds to conceive of God as Substance rather than as Personality. From the baleful effects of this point of view, theology has not yet shaken itself free. The only category which can apply to the mystery of the relation of the Father to the Son is that of organic union, whose highest illustration is in the domain of personal life. There are deep and living relations which subsist between persons even within the human family. If one person not only *may*, but *must* live in another person in order to be a person, and if between these two there is such community of life that each finds his life in the other, and these two are not so much two as one, we may find ourselves on the verge of a greater mystery and a far deeper unity : the abiding of the Father in the Son and the Son in the Father, and these two, along with the Spirit of both, forming the One God of redemption and of creation. By such a path as this must Christology move to a fuller grasp of the truth, which the Nicene Creed asserted, but did not adequately or finally set forth.

(2) To Christian experience, maintained in fellowship with the living Christ, *He is known as man*. Faith apprehends Him as incarnate, *i.e.* as a Divine Being, who became man, entered into the sphere and conditions of human life, and passed through a complete human experience. Humanity, therefore, reaches its consummation in His Person ; and human beings, divided though they may be from one another, find no impassable barriers between themselves and Christ. Christian experience, accordingly, is vitally concerned with the earthly life of Christ, as recorded in the Gospels. Docetism and Ebionism are both false to the conviction of faith. Between the Divinity and the humanity of Jesus Christ, faith finds no abstract opposition. Christ is known as at once Divine and human.

As soon, however, as faith seeks to make clear to itself its convictions, and to state and defend them in view of inquiry or attack, certain questions regarding the human-Divine life of the Lord inevitably arise.

(*a*) The problem of the origin of this life presented itself very early to the minds of those who had learned to see in Jesus Christ the Son of God. He is man, yet He is related to God as no other man can be. Is it possible that He could have come into the world, as other men do, as a child of a human father and mother ? The answer to be found in two of the Gospels is that He did not ; that the Holy Ghost came upon His mother, and the power of the Most High overshadowed her ; that her Son had no human father. The truth of the narrative of the supernatural birth is challenged, in many quarters, on critical and on metaphysical grounds. In view of these objections, it ought to be freely admitted that the Incarnation *might* have taken place under normal human conditions. We are not in a position to determine *a priori* what course Infinite Power and Love shall take. It is impossible, therefore, to place the *mode* of the Incarnation, through a virgin-birth, on the same footing of religious or theological importance as the great *fact* of the Incarnation itself. If, however, from a study of the data presented in the NT, *i.e.* from a consideration of the character of Christ, of His claims and self-witness, as well as of the testimony of His disciples, *apart from* the narratives of His infancy, we have arrived at the conviction of His unequalled and supreme greatness ; and if we *then* return to a study of these narratives, we cannot fail to find in them an ethical purity and a spiritual fitness which command our glad acceptance. Their value for Christian thought lies in their providing a physical fact, correspondent to the conviction which a study of the person of Christ has wrought in us, viz. that He is not the product of a natural evolution from humanity, but is a Divine Being who has entered into the conditions and experiences of human nature.

The supernatural birth of Jesus is not our warrant for belief in His Divinity and His sinlessness. But belief in His Divinity and His sinlessness is our warrant for regarding the supernatural birth as being not merely possible or credible, but as being wholly congruous with the uniqueness of His personality, and, therefore, as serving as a welcome illustration and confirmation of the contents of Christian experience.

(*b*) In studying the record of the life of Christ, many questions arise in connexion with the relation of the Divine to the human aspects of His personality. Are not the notes of Godhead absoluteness, finality, completeness, independence of all the means by which human character is developed ? How, then, are we to understand the evident facts of our Lord's life on earth, that He

inquired, and learned, and was ignorant ; that He passed through the stages of a temporal development, moving toward His goal through conflict and suffering ; and that, in His communion with His Father, He employed the means of grace which are ordained for men—reading the Sacred Scriptures, and being much in prayer ?

In considering such problems, Christian thought has been much 'hindered by the domination of metaphysical conceptions such as 'nature,' and by the controlling influence of a dualism which has opposed the Divine and human natures, regarding them as possessed of contrary attributes. The history of Christology consists, mainly, in a series of attempts to bring into harmony with one another, in the unity of the person, 'natures' which, it is presupposed, are fundamentally opposed in their characteristics and activities. *Eutychianism* brings them so close together as to confound them in a result which is a compound of Divine and human. *Nestorianism* holds them so far apart as to make them almost the seats of independent personalities. *The formula of Chalcedon* can scarcely be called a theory ; it is rather an enumeration of the contrasted elements and a mere assertion of the unity which comprehends them. The *Lutheran Christology* seeks to reduce the dualism of Divine and human to the lowest possible degree by the deification of Christ's human nature. The *Kenotic theories* of more recent times have sought to reach the same result by the idea of a depotentiation of His Divine nature. However remarkable these schemes may be as intellectual efforts, and whatever value they may have in directing attention to one or another element in the complex fact, it is certain that they all fall under a threefold condemnation. (i.) They are dominated by metaphysical conceptions which are profoundly opposed to the ideas which prevail throughout Scripture ; being dualistic to the core, whereas the ruling ideas of Scripture are synthetic, and are far removed from the distinctions which mark the achievements of the Greek mind. (ii.) They do not correspond with, or do justice to, the knowledge which faith has of the personal Christ ; separating, as they do, what faith grasps as a unity, while their attempted harmonies are artificial, and not vital. (iii.) They fail to reproduce the portrait of Christ presented in the Gospels ; they utterly fail to give adequate utterance to the impression which the Christ of the Gospels makes upon the minds which contemplate Him. This is true even of the Chalcedonian scheme, which, in substance, is repeated in many modern creeds and confessions.

'A Being who combines in an inscrutable fashion Divine with human properties, and of whom, consequently, contradictory assertions may be made, while His dual natures hold an undefined relation to one another. This is not a scheme to satisfy either head or heart' (Principal Dykes, papers on 'The Person of our Lord' in *Expos. Times*, Oct. 1905–Jan. 1906).

Christian thought, accordingly, must abandon the dualism which has so long impeded its efforts. It can never, indeed, emphasize too strongly the lowliness of man, both as creature and as sinful creature, and must never, even in its most spiritual exercises, forget the reverence that is due from man to God. But it must reject as misleading all theories which presuppose a generic difference between the Divine and the human natures. It must, therefore, reject the 'two-natures' doctrine of the Person of Christ, in the form in which it has hitherto prevailed ; and must start in its study of Christ from the Biblical point of view of the essential affinity of the Divine and the human natures.

In recent literature the influence of Psychology upon Christological study is deeply marked. Instead of two natures, two consciousnesses are suggested as giving the adequate conception of our Lord's life on earth. The Son of God became the Son of Man; and had a true human experience in respect of knowledge, will, and every other aspect of normal human life; while at the same time He remained the Logos, retaining the attributes of Deity, such as omniscience. He lived, so to speak, in two universes at once, the macrocosm of creation at large and the microcosm of human life. This double life and double consciousness, it is suggested, are to be interpreted in the light of recent psychological experiments, which seem to establish the conclusion that there is a vast subliminal sphere, where the larger part of our life is lived, that which emerges in consciousness being but a section of the greater whole.

It may well be that such psychological hints are not to be thrown away. Yet it may be doubted whether success on this line is surer than under the old metaphysical control. There are curiosities of Psychology as well as of Metaphysics; and the idea of a subliminal sphere may prove as inadequate to explain the mystery of the Incarnation as the old 'bloodless' categories of 'substance' or 'nature.' The soul of Jesus is not on the dissecting table, and a psychology of it is impossible. In particular, it must be asked whether the representation of Jesus as being ordinarily absorbed in His human experiences, while having occasional visitations of His own Logos consciousness, is true to the portrait of Christ in the Gospels. Is there any suggestion in the narrative of a movement on the part of Jesus, to and fro, between the sub-conscious and the conscious spheres? Is not the deepest note in His character the continuousness of His conscious fellowship with God as of the Son with the Father? Is there a hint anywhere of a shutting off of His Divine consciousness during the greater part of His human experience? There is certainly no indication of the shock which a *merely* human consciousness would receive if it were suddenly invaded by a Divine consciousness. Is not the dualism of two consciousnesses as fatal to the harmony of the life and character of Christ as that of the 'two natures' ever was? Or, at least, are not the two consciousnesses really coincident, the Divine being the root of the human, the human being penetrated, formed, and inspired by the Divine?

In any case, whatever value we may attach to theories of the Person of Christ, whether metaphysical or psychological, and whatever may be our forecast of the issues of future Christological study, certain conclusions have established themselves as of permanent importance for Christian thought and experience. (i.) It is possible for a Divine Being to have a truly human experience. There is nothing in the nature of God or of man to forbid this. Scripture knows nothing of such disparity between the Divine and human natures as to make the idea of Incarnation an intellectual impossibility. Without doubt, the fact of Incarnation must be a theme of unending wonder and praise: but our view of it ought not to be confounded by the intrusion of speculative difficulties which do not belong to the actual situation. The Son of God became man. He was born, grew, thought, willed, prayed, rejoiced, suffered, died; and in and through all these perfectly human experiences He was, and was conscious of being, the Son of the Father. This Divine consciousness would, no doubt, profoundly modify, in His case, these experiences. The effect, for instance, of His sinlessness and of His filial relation to God upon the exercise of His intellectual faculties must have been such as to raise His knowledge high above that of other men, and would give to it what has been called 'intensive infinitude.' But the Divine consciousness would not make the human

experiences other or less than human. Surely it ought to be admitted, once for all, that humanity, as we know it, is not complete, and that it gains completeness only as it approximates to the Divine nature. It is not so correct to say that Jesus Christ was Divine and *yet* human, as to say He was Divine and *therefore* human.

(ii.) It follows that the human experiences of such a Being constitute at once a veiling and a manifestation of the Divine glory. In the thinking, feeling, acting, suffering of the Son, the Father is drawing near to His creatures, and achieving for them the purpose both of creation and of redemption. We are to look for the Divinity of Christ, not apart from His humanity, but within it, in the facts of His character, and in those actions which He performs and those sufferings which He endures in closest fellowship with men. His human experiences, so far from casting doubt on His Divinity, or seeming to be inconsistent with it, will be its chief demonstration, and will constitute God's mightiest work for us, His most moving appeal to us. This Man is the Word of God incarnate.

(iii.) Knowledge of Christ, accordingly, is personal, and, like all personal knowledge, is ethically-conditioned. All constructive statements regarding the Person of Christ, accordingly, must be, to a degree not attained in the older formularies of the Church, synthetic and concrete. We rise from a study of the life and character of Jesus, and of the experience of those who have come under His saving influence, with the conviction of His essential Godhead. We confess Him to be the Son of God. But His Godhead is not to be regarded in abstract separation from His humanity. It is the Godhead of One who is profoundly and truly human.

It is Godhead, as it discloses itself in humanity, which presents itself for our reverent study, and our no less reverent doctrinal statement.

From this point of view alone can the facts of the life of Christ be apprehended. In this light alone can Christ be presented to this generation as the answer to its need, the age-long need of the human spirit, for personal union with God.

LITERATURE.—(a) Greek Philosophy: Caird, *Evolution of Theology in the Greek Philosophers* (1894); Zeller, *Stoics and Epicureans*; Lightfoot, *Dissertations on the Apostolic Age*, 'St. Paul and Seneca'; Drummond, *Philo Judæus*, and art. 'Philo' by same author in Hastings' *DB*, Extra Vol.

(b) Religion of Israel: *Theol. of the OT*, by Schultz, Davidson, Oehler; Drummond, *Jewish Messiah*; Stanton, *Jewish and Christian Messiah*; Kautzsch's art. in Hastings' *DB*, Extra Vol.

(c) Character and self-witness of Jesus: *NT Theol.* of Weiss, Beyschlag, Reuss, Stevens; Wendt, *Teaching of Jesus*; Dalman, *Words of Jesus*; Forrest, *Christ of History and of Experience*, and *Authority of Christ*; Shailer Mathews, *Messianic Hope in the NT* (1905); Adamson, *Mind in Christ*; Bruce, *Training of the Twelve*, *Kingdom of God*, *Galilean Gospel*; Swete, *Studies in the Teaching of our Lord* (1904); Zöckler's art. 'Jesus Christus' in *PRE*[3]; Sanday's art. 'Jesus Christ' in Hastings' *DB*; Driver's art. 'Son of Man,' and Sanday's 'Son of God,' *ib.*; Westcott, *Revelation of the Father*, *Christus Consummator*.

(d) Testimony of the Apostles: *NT Theol.* as above; also Shailer Mathews as above; Bacon, *Story of St. Paul: a Comparison of Acts and Epistles* (1904); Knowling, *Testimony of St. Paul to Christ* (1905), note copious literature of recent date referred to in Lecture xxiv.; Patrick, *James, the Lord's Brother* (1906).

(e) Development of Doctrine: Harnack, *Hist. of Dogma*; Loofs, *Leitfaden*[4] (1906); Gwatkin, *Studies of Arianism*; Dorner, *Doctrine of the Person of Christ*; Ottley, *Doctrine of the Incarnation*; Réville, *Hist. du dogme de la divinité de Jésus Christ*; Schultz, *Die Lehre von der Gottheit Christi* (1881); Herm. Schmidt, *Zur Christologie*; Loofs' art. 'Christologie' in *PRE*[3]; Kunze, *Die ewige Gottheit Jesu Christi* (1904); Orr, *Christian View of God and the World*, *Progress of Dogma*, *God's Image in Man* (1905); Bruce, *Humiliation of Christ*; T. C. Edwards, *The God-Man*; Liddon, *Divinity of our Lord*; Gore, *Bampton Lecture*, and *Dissertations*; Walker, *The Spirit and the Incarnation*; Dods, *Incarnation of the Eternal Word* (1849); Illingworth, *Personality Human and Divine*, *Divine Immanence*; D'Arcy, *Idealism and Theology*; Sturt and others, *Personal Idealism*; Fairbairn, *Christ in Modern Theology*, *Philosophy of Christian Religion*. **T. B. KILPATRICK.**

INCENSE.—The English word comes from the Lat. *incensus*, 'burnt' (*incendere*, 'to burn'), and is applied to the materials used for making a perfume which was emitted by the materials being burned. These materials consist of fragrant gums, spices, and scents.

'Incense' is the usual tr. of θυμίαμα, which occurs in the NT 6 times only : Lk 1$^{10. 11}$, Rev 5^8 8$^{3. 4}$ 18^{13}. In the passages in Rev. it is always in the plural, and in 18^{13} is rendered in AV by 'odours.' θυμίαμα is the LXX equivalent of Heb. קְטֹרֶת, which comes from קְטַר 'to raise an odour by burning,' and so 'to burn incense.' Cognate Gr. words are θυμιάω, 'to burn incense,' Lk 1^9 (ἄπ. λεγ. in NT) ; and θυμιατήριον, He 9^4 'censer,' or 'altar of incense.' The root of these words is θύω = (1) 'to be in heat,' (2) 'to burn,' (3) 'to sacrifice (by burning)' ; see Grimm-Thayer, *s.v.*, and cf. θυμός and θυμόω. The word θυμίαμα is to be carefully distinguished from λίβανος, 'frankincense' (Heb. לְבֹנָה). The latter was an ingredient of the former. λίβανος is found twice in NT (Mt 2^{11} and Rev 18^{13}, in the latter together with θυμιάματα).

Incense came to be used in connexion with the Levitical worship in the Temple. Special care was to be taken in the making of it (Ex 30$^{34f.}$ P). Several passages in the OT indicate that the Israelites came to regard it (as they did other ceremonies) *per se*, apart from its spiritual meaning. Hence the denunciations of the prophets (Is 1^{13} etc.). In the NT it is referred to only in connexion with the daily service of the Temple (Lk 1), and also as part of the symbolical heavenly worship in the Apocalypse. In Rev 5^8 and 8$^{3. 4}$ it is associated with the prayers of the saints ; in 5^8 apparently being identified with the prayers, and in 8$^{3. 4}$ added to the prayers (cf. ταῖς προσευχαῖς in both verses), as though to render them acceptable. RV 'with' in Rev 8^4 seems impossible.

The symbolism seems to be generally that of worship, which, like incense, *ascends* from earth to heaven. In Ps 141^2 prayer is thus likened to incense. Godet (on Lk 1^{10}) thinks there was a close connexion between the two acts of burning incense and offering prayer.

'The one was the typical, ideal, and therefore perfectly pure prayer ; the other the real prayer, which was inevitably imperfect and defiled. The former covered the latter with its sanctity, the latter communicated to the former its reality and life. Thus they were the complement of each other.'

Incense is used in worship in the Greek and Roman Catholic Churches, and by some congregations in the Anglican Church. Its earliest use in the Christian Church seems to have been as a fumigant (so Tertullian). No liturgical use is known for at least 4 if not 5 centuries. Up till then it was regarded as a relic of heathenism. As the Holy Communion came to be regarded as a sacrifice, and in some respects analogous to the Jewish sacrifices, incense became gradually associated with Christian worship. It is at least noteworthy that there is an entire absence of any reference to incense in the Christian Church of the NT in Acts and the Epistles, the only allusions being those in the symbolism of the Apocalypse. May not this be rightly regarded as an *argumentum e silentio*? Having the substance, what need is there of the shadow? (Jn 4$^{23. 24}$).

LITERATURE.—Artt. 'Incense,' 'Frankincense' in Hastings' *DB* ; 'Incense' in Smith's *DCA* ; Godet and Plummer on Lk 1$^{9-11}$; *Speaker's Com.* on Rev 5^8 8^3 18^{13}.

W. H. GRIFFITH THOMAS.

INDEPENDENCE.—See ORIGINALITY.

INDIGNATION.—See ANGER, and FIERCENESS.

INDIVIDUAL.—It has almost become a commonplace of Apologetics that the significance of the individual is first recognized in Christianity. In Antiquity the idea that the individual might stand over against the State, either through the sense of duty or the sense of truth, was not entertained. Most ancient civilizations were based on slavery, which at once refused to recognize a large section of the members of the State as individuals, and placed the individuality of the others not on an equal moral basis, but on a basis of social inequality.

Yet the Christian conception of the individual did not descend upon the earth without any indication of its coming. Socrates had instructed men to know themselves, and, though his greatest disciple did not consider this teaching inconsistent with a Republic in which the family and the most sacred rights of the individual are sacrificed to the interests of the State, the real significance of the Greek Philosophy was the growing clearness with which it went on to bring out the importance of man to himself. Stoicism insisted that a man's dignity should not be at the mercy of events, and even Epicureanism taught that man's surest ground of happiness is within. Baur's contention, that the chief preparation for Christianity was a growing need for a universal, a moral religion, is only another way of saying that the individual, not as a free man, or a cultured man, or a member of a Greek State, but as an individual, was slowly coming to his rights.

This progress in the Gentile world, however, was not in any strict sense a preparation for our Lord's teaching, but, at most, of the world for receiving it. His true foundations are in the OT, and more particularly in the prophets. Here again it is a commonplace of theological thinking that the religion of the OT does not concern itself about the individual at all in the same sense as the religion of the NT. Worship is a social and even a civil act. The God men worship is the God of their fathers, *i.e.* the God of their race. The great body of the ritual exalts not the covenant person, but the covenant people. Even the prophets have very little to say about individual piety, but concern themselves with the rulers and the conduct of society and the destiny of the nation. We cannot be sure, even in what seem the most personal Psalms, that it is not the voice of a nation rather than of an individual that confesses sin and implores help. This uncertainty regarding the place of the individual is made greater by the indistinctness, at least in the earlier books, of the hope of individual immortality, which, however we may try to get round it, is essential to any high estimate of the worth of the individual.

No book, nevertheless, compares with the OT for the boldness with which the individual stands out in contrast and, if need be, in opposition to, the community, and that on spiritual, not social considerations. The standard of its teaching is personal responsibility, and that ultimately sets a man alone as an individual with his God. If it is a national and not an individual hope the prophets contend for, they place it on an individual not a communistic foundation. They are not concerned to reform institutions or demand new laws. The reform they seek is of personal action and manners, and the law they wish to see obeyed is God's. For this law it is the individual that signifies—the pressure of his personal call being so great that his duty to follow it is never questioned, even though it should bring him into conflict with both the State and the people. Ezekiel may have been the first to recognize the full significance of this attitude, but he was by no means the first to take it up. Of every prophet it could be said, 'Behold, I have made thy face hard against their faces, and thy forehead against their foreheads' (Ezk 3^8). To each of them the Spirit of God was a power to help him to be true to himself. It set each of them on his feet before speaking to him (Ezk 2^2). The very mark of a true prophet was to hear God's voice only, and not man's, and to be true to the individuality God had given him, and not to be an echo of the party cries around. To have that most selfish kind of individualism which consists in agreeing with the majority of the powers that be, was the mark of the false prophet (Jer 20).

Such an attitude of independence could not be taken up without a very strong sense of the significance of the individual for God. The significance of the solitary figure of Jeremiah could not be less because he lived for the welfare of his people, and their ingratitude left him in isolation. Ezekiel naturally followed with the application. Were Noah, Daniel, and Job in a wicked land, they could but deliver their own souls by their righteousness (14¹⁴). God deals equally with all, and every act is weighed, without prejudice either from a man's own past or from the doings of his fathers (18². ²³⁻³⁰). The soul that sinneth, it shall die (v.⁴).

Of other OT writings the two most important are the Psalms and Job. The eye of the writers may at times be on the nation, but even that is part of their personal piety, and to our day the unfailing interest of the Psalms is in the experience of the individual walking with his God. The Book of Job is wholly occupied with the problem of the individual, even if this individual be supposed to stand for the nation; and no one has ever stated with greater splendour of imagination or intellectual daring his right to fair dealing, not only from his fellow-men but from his God.

The OT conception of the relation of the moral individual to God, moreover, necessarily reached out toward the hope of immortality,—and that not merely as an extension of man's desires beyond time, but as the just requirement of an individuality that defied time and lived by the eternal.

That our Lord entered upon this heritage and accepted the estimate of each individual which we indicate by calling him an immortal soul, and that on the ground of the OT conception of the blessedness of the man whom God hears, appears from His argument with the Sadducees (Mt 22³², Mk 12²⁷, Lk 20³⁸), and is a postulate of His whole teaching. The saying, ' What shall it profit a man, if he gain the whole world and lose his own soul?' (Mk 8³⁶), may only indicate a man's value to himself, and the other, ' How much then is a man better than a sheep!' (Mt 12¹²), may not seem to go very far. Christ's true conception of the individual rather appears in the *belief* He offers for man's acceptance and the *duty* He requires that man should perform.

Of this *belief* the centre of everything is the manifestation of the Father. As revealed through the Son, He is a Father, which means that He does not, as a mere Ruler, deal with men in groups, but that each man has to Him the distinctiveness, the importance, the whole significance he can have to himself. The side of God's infinity which our Lord insists on, is the infinity of His care for the individual. In God's sight also, nothing can be given in exchange for a soul. By His care and guidance, that frail thing, an individual spirit, can walk without anxiety amid all the forces which might threaten his destruction, not only sure of protection, but sure that everything will be used to serve his true welfare. This attitude toward earthly cares is not sustained by hardness or indifference, but by a belief that God regards these things as the servants of His children, whose individual well-being He sets far above material things. It is not a low view of the world, but a high view of the spiritual individual, which our Lord teaches.

Speaking, as He always does, with this thought of God towards man in the foreground, Jesus is led to dwell rather on the worth of the insignificant and imperfect individual in the concrete than on the general worth of the individual in the abstract. Hard-hearted religious people spoke lightly of 'this multitude' being 'accursed' (Jn 7⁴⁹). He called none accursed, and warned His followers against calling any one *Raca* (Mt 5²²); and when He used the word 'lost,' it became in His mouth tender and compassionate and full of the heart of God. The parables of the Lost Sheep, the Lost Piece of Money, and above all of the Prodigal Son (Lk 15), speak of God's unwillingness to let anything so precious as an individual be lost. The little child is the type of what is greatest (Mt 18¹. ²), and the little one in moral stature, whom to offend is worse than death, is guarded by the very angels of the Presence (18¹⁰).

The same estimate of the worth of the individual appears in the ideal of human *duty*. There is no one, however poor or humble, who should not set before him the goal of being perfect as our Father in heaven (Mt 5⁴⁸). It is better to cut off the right hand than use another individual for our lusts, or to put out an eye than purpose such a thing (5²⁷⁻³⁰). Most distinctive is the duty of forgiveness. Our Lord takes for granted that it will be difficult. We shall have so much respect for our own individuality that we must be hurt, and for the individuality of others that we cannot pass over their faults easily. Only by rising to the height of God's thought can we hope to attain to God's way of dealing with the unthankful and evil. We are to understand that God also does not pardon lightly. He does not regard the whole mass of good and bad indifferently. On the contrary, He sets each individual before Him as something of great significance to Him, something whereby He can be deeply hurt and grieved, and then, out of the same love that can be hurt, He pardons him. It is the significance of the individual that gives its whole importance to the doctrine of pardon, whether on God's part or on man's.

But the very greatness of this relation to God might seem to withdraw something from the distinctiveness of man as an individual. The worth of the individual is not ultimately from himself but from God. ' If a man abide not in me, he is cast forth as a branch, and is withered' (Jn 15⁶). This might almost seem to be a denial that there is such a thing as an individual. The individual would then be a mere manifestation of God. Spinoza's formula, *omnis determinatio est negatio*, would obtain, and the assertion of one's own individuality would only be as cutting off a certain portion of the air with a knife. But the inalienable secret of the gospel is that it enables a man to find God and himself at the same time. It does not deal with the endless substance, but with a Father. That He is an individual is not His limitation, but the condition of all His greatness; for it is the condition of His working by love, and love is greater than power. Conversion is thus not only a turning to God, but a finding of oneself (Lk 15¹⁷), and a coming to one's true home and to one's right possession. While no succour of God fails a man who will have it, it remains a necessity of God's love to set a man by himself in the task of working out his own destiny. He is allowed to go into the far country and waste his substance. In all the descriptions which glance out into the future there is a strange aloneness of the individual who has gone his own way, into which God Himself cannot intrude. Just because every human personality is so definitely an individual, we cannot be sure that, in the end, there may not be a lost individual. A relation of love in Christ's sense necessarily means a relation of individuals, and that means such a marking off of a man from God that even God cannot enter that personality again, except the door is opened to Him, as it were, from the inside.

This high gift of being an individual with the possibility of being a child of God, carries with it also the possibility of such exclusion of good as can make him a child of the wicked one (Mt 13³⁸). Nor does the closest relation to God absorb the individual. Whatever ordinances there may be for public worship, the distinctive position is to enter into our closet and shut to the door, and be with our Father who sees in secret (Mt 6⁶). There is an individual hearing and an individual answering, which, however little our minds may compass it, are essential both in God's giving and in man's receiving. Just as there is a strange pitiful isolation of the individual who rejects God, so there is a strange saving of his own individuality in losing it, in the soul that finds God. That we remain individuals is as essential to the relationship as that we find our joy in another individual. The revelation of the Father in the Son must preclude all idea of absorption in God.

This is the ground of Ritschl's contention not only against a catholicism which bears down the individual by the weight of the institution, but also against a mysticism which reduces all individuals to mere personality, upon which a Spirit, Himself mere personality, operates not as individual with individual, but as abstract spiritual force upon abstract spiritual substance. The influences of grace we must, on the contrary, interpret through Christ, the Spirit having come in His place to bring His words to our remembrance (Jn 14²⁶). Ritschl argues that God only uses His revelation in the Scriptures on the one hand, and His dealings with us by the experiences and duties of life on the other. The tendency with him is, not only to limit God, but also to ignore possibilities in man ; yet his main contention is of great value, and it helps us to understand the patient humanness of God's revelation, if we take it to be a dialogue in which God could not speak the next word till man had responded to the last.

The only influences our Lord used were the appeals of wisdom and love. In every case He respected the individuality of another, and sought to make men realize how much they were to themselves as well as to God. When any influence appeared as a substitute for personal choice, He sternly repressed it. He trusted no general movement, and appealed to nothing occult. He was always willing to leave a crowd for an individual (Mk 1³⁷, Lk 4⁴², Jn 6¹⁵). The only miracle He ever wrought for the multitude He used for sifting them and for gathering individuals from among them (Jn 6²⁷). And when a crowd did gather to hear Him preach, He gave them most individual teaching. He never departed from the method of being an individual dealing with individuals, and from requiring of them the most individual of actions—repentance and obedience to one's own call.

Nor is the individual overborne by the society (see artt. CHURCH, KINGDOM OF GOD, INDIVIDUALISM). Here it suffices to say that it is just the distinctive place Christ assigned to the individual that marks His Church off from the world, and His kingdom as a Kingdom of Heaven, a Kingdom of God. A kingdom which treats its subjects as mere pawns in a great game, is, in that very act, marked as temporal. Other-worldliness, indeed, is not the mind of Christ, and the attempt to derive everything from the far-sighted selfishness which does ' good according to the will of God and for the sake of everlasting happiness,' leaves no room for the highest things of Christianity. But it is not true, as is argued, that we reach a higher stage when we are able calmly to recognize that the individual passes and the society remains, that everyone should be content to live on in the lives of others, and that the Kingdom of God is everything and the individual nothing. The Kingdom of God is not thereby exalted. Nay, there can be no Kingdom of God, but a mere fleeting earthly Utopia. If the individual is obliterated, then, in view of the endless ages, but a moment more, and the society is obliterated as well. It becomes the

Kingdom of God only when it deals with the eternal, and that must always be the individual. It is of God and not of mere human regulation just because it respects the individual—his choice, his peace, his freedom ; because it is a society of persons not constrained by force to a common purpose, but attuned to it by love and wisdom. All our Lord says of His society speaks of an association in which its members will realize what the Apostle calls the glorious liberty of the children of God, and, so long as the Church is content to stand over against men as an institution claiming external authority, Christ's great problem of how men were at once to live wholly for the Kingdom of God, and not surrender their Christian freedom, their rights as individuals, remains unsolved. (For the general philosophical questions regarding the individual, see art. PERSONALITY).

One question yet remains. Can a person whose isolation has been thus defined to himself, ever again pass into the great undistinguishable mass ? According to the orthodox conception, individuality, though a mere containing wall, is so adamantine, that, whatever it may contain, it must abide. Ritschl, for one, argues that an alienation from God which the highest love cannot overcome, must mean annihilation. The very idea of a reality so important as to be inextinguishable, while all its manifestations demand its extinction, he would ascribe to the pernicious influence of the abstract Platonic idea of the soul. Nor can it be said that in the Gospels, or anywhere else in Scripture, there is any metaphysical basis of a Platonic kind for a necessary individual immortality. The Scripture hope is not in man, but in the character of God, and we cannot suppose Him under any necessity to continue evil for its own sake. On the other hand, if, as Ritschl maintains, the personality of God and man is individual, and pantheism is wholly an abandonment of the religious problem, which is how to maintain the spiritual personality against the whole material universe, through belief in the exalted Power that rules above it, it remains a problem whether evil can ever attain such power as to be able to blot out for God an individual.

LITERATURE.—The whole of modern philosophy is concerned with the problem of the individual, but special mention may be made of : Spinoza, *Ethics* ; Hume, *Human Nature* ; Leibnitz, *de Principio Individui* ; Kant, *Anthropologie* ; J. H. Fichte, *Die Idee der Persönlichkeit und der individuellen Fortdauer* ; Nathaniel Southgate Shaler, *The Individual : A Study of Life and Death*, 1902 ; Doud, *Évolution of the Individual*, 1901 ; Beyschlag, *NT Theol.*, esp. vol. i. 125–187 (Eng. tr.) ; Lemme, *Christliche Ethik*, esp. § 10 ; Kretschmar, *Das Christliche Persönlichkeits Ideal*, 1898 ; J. R. Illingworth, *Personality*.   JOHN OMAN.

INDIVIDUALISM.—The word individualism is used in two senses, and the difference of meaning is constantly employed in order to discredit one set of ideas by arguing against the other. In a general way the uses may be distinguished by calling the one philosophical and the other political. Individualism, in the philosophical sense, attempts to derive everything from the intellect and the interests of the individual. However much a man derives from others, he ultimately depends, it argues, on his own judgment and his five senses ; and, however benevolent he may be, all his motives have their source in self-love. Descartes started to reconstruct our whole knowledge from the individual's knowledge of himself, and his successors naturally sought to construct our whole activity from the individual's love to himself. Shaftesbury and Butler had to affirm almost as a discovery that benevolence is as true and real a part of human nature as self-love. Only after Hume had reduced this kind of individualism to sensationalism, leaving the individual himself a mere series of sensations, and after Spinozism began to be poured into the waters of speculation, was it seen that man could not be understood alone, but only in his whole context.

It is needless to prove that this kind of individualism is not maintained by the Scriptures. And still less is it necessary to show that it is not our Lord's reading of human nature. The creature that is made in the image of God is not made for himself. The creed that says, 'If any man will come after me, let him deny himself' (Mt 16[24]), believes that it finds something more in man than even the wisest self-love to which it can appeal. The individual does not, it is true, lose in Christ's service. On the contrary, he will receive an hundredfold, and, over and above, life everlasting (Mt 19[29]). But that is only after he has learned the secret of forsaking all, after he has been taught, not of his own self-interest, but after he has been drawn by the Father from all self-regard (Jn 6[44]). This possibility in man, our Lord recognizes, was also taught by the prophets, who wrote, 'And they shall all be taught of God' (v.[45]). To be taught of God means to be saved from this kind of individualism, to discover that it is not our right position and not our true selves, but is alienation from our true life and our true home; it is to learn that not only is love part of our nature, but that we have never found ourselves at all till it takes us out of ourselves (Lk 17[33], Mt 10[39]).

Philosophical Individualism, however, is not only perfectly consistent with the appeal to authority which the other kind of individualism rejects, but it is almost entirely dependent upon such an authority for any explanation of the social order. On the other hand, what we have called Political Individualism is frequently maintained precisely on the ground that man is not, in the sense of belonging only to himself, individualistic, but has his true social quality within himself. 'Individualism' in this other sense means the rights of the individual over against authority, a position which does not, as is usually assumed, involve logically the other individualism, the individualism of every man for himself. It is not a denial of the necessity of a corporate existence or of the value of society. Its real opposite is Communism, and the real point at issue is whether society depends on the individual or the individual on society. Both Individualism and Communism, of course, would admit a mutual inter-relation, but the question is which is first, the individual or the social institution, and which is to be our chief reliance, the good-will of the individual or the control of the social machinery. So far is this kind of individualism from involving individualism in the other sense, that it rather assumes that all the elements for the highest social state exist in each man, and would come to fruition, if only the external hindrances could be removed. On this latter question, it must be admitted, our Lord's attitude is much more difficult to determine.

Of this practical individualism there are several types. First, there is the individualism of Nietzsche, to whom every altruistic feeling is the mere unreasoning instinct of the herd. That kind of individualism stood at the foot of the Cross, and said, 'He saved others, himself he cannot save,' and saw in the position the height of absurdity. Then there is the vigorous Philistine individualism of Herbert Spencer. It conceives man as a creature with five senses and ten fingers, who needs nothing on earth but a free field and no favour, whose chief duty to the human race is to secure its progress by making the weakest go to the wall. The text it most firmly believes in, in the whole Bible, is, 'He becometh poor that dealeth with a slack hand'; and what it cannot away with in Jesus is that He told people to give to everyone who asked, and to sell all, and give to the poor,—a frightful encouragement to laziness and mendicancy, and a most hurtful interference with the law of the survival of the fittest. Again, there is the individualism of Mr. Auberon Herbert and the *Free Life*. In its eyes men are quite free to part with everything they have, and it is believed they would part with it for the best purposes, if it were not that they are robbed and also debased by being blackmailed under the name of taxes. 'Bumble' is the true name and nature of all authorities, it having been their way in all time to muddle everything, doing it

wastefully and doing it badly. Freedom, on the other hand, is man's highest privilege, and would, if it could get a chance, be his surest guidance. Force, which is the sole instrument of the State, has only one right application. It has a right to resist force, to suppress violence. The State is, when it keeps to its own sphere, simply the big policeman, 'a terror to evil-doers,' and also, in so far as it kindly lets them alone, 'a praise to them that do well.' With less hesitation regarding consequences, this individualism reasserts J. S. Mill's principle, 'that the sole end for which mankind are warranted, individually or collectively, in interfering with the liberty of action of any of their number, is self-protection.' Finally, there is the individualism of Count Tolstoi, the basis of which he finds in the Gospels themselves. 'Judge not, that ye be not judged,' applies as much to a man in his official capacity as in his private, and 'Resist not evil' is required from the community as much as from the individual. No man is ever so much wiser and better than his fellows that he can have the right in any capacity to take over the regulation of their lives, and the very goal of history is to teach the folly and wickedness of any body of men trying to bear rule over others,—a philosophy of history somewhat akin to St. Paul's conception of the dispensation of the Law as meant to shut all up unto disobedience (Ro 11[32]).

The kindliness of the Socialists towards Tolstoi seems at first sight inexplicable, for nothing could be more opposed to their method than this rejection of all visible authorities. The Socialist, moreover, has the same sympathy with Christ's teaching. Take, *e.g.*, Headlam's *Fabian Tract*, No. 42. The teaching of Jesus, he affirms, had hardly anything to do with a life after death, but a great deal to do with a Kingdom of God, which is a righteous society to be established upon earth. Christ's works were secular, socialistic works. Whatever may be said of His miracles of raising the dead, they show that the death of a young person was a monstrous, disorderly thing to Him. If men would live in a rational, organized, orderly brotherhood, they would be clothed as beautifully as the lily. His denunciations were for those who oppressed the poor; and the man whom He spoke of as in hell, was the man who calmly accepted the difference between the rich and the poor; while the persons who were on the right hand at the Judgment, were those who had taken pains to know that people were properly clothed and fed. The Christian society was meant to do on a large scale the social work which Jesus had done on a small. Jesus ordained Baptism to receive every human child as equal into His Church, and the Eucharist to be a sacrament of equal brotherhood; and He made the first word in His prayer the recognition of a common Father, which must involve the equality of brethren. The Song of Mary describes Him as putting down the mighty from their seats and sending the rich empty away, and His Apostles insist on every man labouring, and on the labourer, not the capitalist, being first partaker of the fruits. If, therefore, 'you want to be a good Christian, you must be something very much like a good Socialist.' The Church, we are told, is fettered, and ineffective for carrying out this task, but much 'may be done by those Churchmen who remember that the State is a sacred organization as well as the Church,' and who are willing to help to seize it for the good of the people. Their first task, strangely, will be to free the Church from the fetters of the State, for one would rather have imagined that the logical conclusion should have been Rothe's position, that it is the business of the Church so to labour that ultimately it may be absorbed in the Christian State.

This exposition clearly shows the reason for sympathy with Tolstoi. It is a case of extremes meeting. Extreme Individualism and extreme Socialism are both alike conscious of the present distress. Individualism is as little satisfied as Socialism with twelve millionaires dining at one end of London and finding the cultivated globe too small to please their palates, and at the other a million and a half of their fellow-creatures not knowing whether they will have any dinner at all. Than this, both are a great deal nearer the position of Him who said, 'Sell that ye have, and give alms' (Lk 12[33]), 'Woe unto you who are rich' (6[24]), who denounced the robbery of the widow and the orphan, and no doubt included every form of ruthless competition whereby the strong get advantage of the weak. Competition has become a sacred word in these days, but it never has been a Christian word, and if some higher law does not rule above it, the fittest that will survive by it will not be the best but only the most rapacious.

Extreme Socialism and extreme Individualism, moreover, have this in common, that both carry on their propaganda in the interests of the individual and in the hope of arriving at a better state of society. The Individualist thinks a better society can be formed only out of better individuals, and regards force as the great obstacle; whereas the Socialist thinks the individual will never have a chance in the present kind of social conditions. That Christ aimed both at creating a better individual and a better society needs no proof, and it must further be recognized that the society He Himself created, considered a voluntary community of goods at least in agreement with the spirit of His teaching (see art. WEALTH). The emphasis which the leaders put on this voluntary aspect of communism distinguishes Christianity clearly from Socialism, but still the experiment indicates that, in a more Christian society, the Socialist ideal might be accomplished in another way. With our present concentration on material well-being, the end of competition would be almost the end of individuality; but if our real life were less lived by bread alone, if our true individuality were dependent on higher concerns, we might come to cultivate together the soil of the earth and enjoy together all it produces as much in common as we use the air that moves on its surface and the water that comes down its hills, and we should then be enabled to accept many of Christ's commands as literal which we can only now live with as figures of speech.

One feels in reading the Gospels that what is more alien to them than either Individualism or Socialism, is the current amalgam of both, which defends all the Individualism that means personal profit and all the Socialism that means personal security and dignity, which finds all our Lord's concessions literal and all His demands figurative. The typical attitude, though not usually expressed so bluntly, is Loisy's. Christ, he says, conceived the Kingdom of God, which He thought was at hand, as the great social panacea. Though He enforced it with the enthusiasm and excess which are necessary to implant any great ideal, it was quite unworkable in this rough world. There rose up in place of it, therefore, the Church with its authorities for belief and for conduct, that useful, practical, enduring compromise between the individual and the religious society. It is this combination which most of our countrymen who love compromise as the oil, if not the water, of life, are concerned to maintain ; and when they welcome the passing of Individualism, they mean to hail the revival of the power of the visible authorities ; and when they object to Socialism, they only mean that they do not approve of the purposes for which the power is to be used.

The method of Socialism, nevertheless, is not the method of the gospel, and the usual course of the Socialist is that which Mr. Headlam follows,—to prove that the aims of Socialism are Christ's, and then take for granted that He would approve of the means proposed for attaining them. Even supposing we make the large concession of granting the exegesis, we still do not find the slightest attempt to show that our Lord ever in any way trusted to the State as the instrument for accomplishing His design. The usual way of avoiding this difficulty is to say that He could not be expected to look to a Pagan State as we are justified in looking to the Christian State. To this there are two very evident replies. First, Is the State ever Christian in our Lord's sense ? Second, It was not the Pagan but the Theocratic State our Lord dealt with nearly all His days. It was there waiting to be adopted ; yet He lived chiefly in conflict with it, and He never attempted to reform it or work through it. He certainly expected His followers to have a good deal to do with States and kings and governors, but it would be in an extremely individualistic position (Mt 10[18]), and all that was expected of them was not to fear them that kill the body, but are not able to kill the soul (v.[28]). Our Lord's action was not revolutionary in the sense of actually overthrowing existing institutions, but He cannot be said to have cherished them. A certain regard was to be paid to the Scribes and Pharisees who sat in Moses' seat (Mt 23[2]), but He also subjected them to such criticism as must have sapped their power. He Himself so far honoured the religious institutions as not to oppose them ; but the only evil He ever put His hand to the task of reforming, was that which disturbed the private worshipper (Mt 21[12-16], Jn 2[13-17]), and His entire indifference to ceremonial purity rejected a great deal of the institution to the advantage of the individual. All this might seem to refer rather to the Church than the State ; but if He distrusted the leadership of the former, He would not be likely any more to trust the leadership of the latter, if it took over the guidance of life. It also would be the blind leading the blind. What our Lord manifestly expects to see, is what He calls the seed of the Kingdom (Mt 13[38]), those who in every place are worthy, who are prepared to be as lights shining in a dark place. Why

should He speak of the result as a Kingdom of God at all, if, in the final issue, it is only of man's regulation ? The meaning certainly lies very near, that it was a kingdom of souls regulated only by love, a kingdom of souls bent on a direct service and obedience to God, and requiring no other rule. This fundamental distinction between it and all other earthly kingdoms would seem to be the very reason for calling it *of God*.

This view is confirmed by what seems the most convincing explanation of our Lord's temptations. To suppose that He was tempted merely by His own hunger and love of success and love of praise, is to ascribe to Him motives which had no power over Him at other times. But if they are temptations of His work, the temptation to provide a kingdom with fulness of bread and to rule by accepting the methods of force in the State and of display in the Church, we see how He could be touched in His deepest interests. When He turned from that way to the road that led by a solitary path to Calvary, to call many, but to choose only the few who also would be prepared to walk in it, He surely decided to look to the individual to save the institution, and not to the institution to save the individual. In view of all this, it cannot be questioned that the aristocrat in his peasant's dress, digging his bread out of the earth, and living as if the social revolution had come, in the high conviction that the Divine way is personal surrender and not social supervision, represents Christ's attitude better than the respectable persons who meantime take all the present system of competition will give, while they wait for salvation from the action of the State.

But Socialism only makes a pretence of being workable through the State, by ignoring the bearing which its action would have on the whole life of the individual, and it is with this larger question that our Lord is concerned. His Kingdom is not of this world, and its treasures are not upon earth, and it only concerns itself with the things upon earth as they have to do with the great treasure in heaven, which is character, and the great rule of the Kingdom, which is love. That He expected this idea to be embodied in an earthly society is plain, for the beginnings of it arose in His own lifetime. But it was to be a very singular society, in which none was to exercise authority on one hand, and none to call any man master on the other. The only dignity was to be service ; and the higher the position, the lowlier one should serve. Nothing can reconcile this with the ecclesiastical embodiment of it in all ages, wherein the true succession has been placed in the officials, who determined not only action but belief, and who have penetrated further into the inner sanctuary of the individual life than any earthly government that ever existed. But no one recognized more fully than Christ Himself that the channels by which His influence would go down would intermingle their clay with the pure waters ; and to assume that any organization is more than a dim human attempt at reaching out towards His ideal, is to neglect His own warnings. As the believer must be in the world, so he must be in the institution—in it but not of it, always retaining his right to consider whether Christ is there or not when men say, ' Lo, here, or Lo, there.' In so far as the institution serves this Kingdom of God, this kingdom of souls, whose only authority is God the Father as revealed in the Son, and whose only rule is love, it is to be honoured ; but it must ever be prepared to be judged by that standard.

The great end of all progress, therefore, is not to subject the individual, but to call him to the realization of his own heritage of freedom. It is in the crowd that men have done all the great iniquities. The multitude come to take Christ; the disciples all in a body forsake Him; the rulers come together to judge Him; the whole band of soldiers is called together to buffet Him; the crowd cry, 'Crucify Him'; the chief priests mock Him among themselves. Even those that were crucified with Him stilled their pain by falling in with the cry of the multitude. Whatever institution, therefore, we may submit to, we can only belong to the true Church by first of all having 'salt in ourselves' (Mk 9⁵⁰), by being of the truth and hearing Christ's voice (Jn 18³⁷).

It is argued that the full meaning and claim of Christianity can never be explicable on the basis of Individualism, because 'from first to last it deals with minds which are in relation with actual truth in regard to the soul, the world, and God, and which have not fully attained even the limits of their own nature till they are united in the Spirit-bearing Body, through Christ to the Father' (Strong). Possibly Hume contends for the Individualism here refuted. Nobody else does. Why Christianity is so individualistic is precisely that the soul is so directly, or, at all events, can, through God's revelation and grace, be so directly in contact with actual truth, the world and God, as to make it only a distraction for another man, on merely official grounds, to come in between as a necessary channel; that the possession of such a personal relation to truth is a common bond of more power than any external tie; and that the visible organization is only vital and useful as it expresses this union. The usual way is to say the Kingdom of God is a purely spiritual condition on the one hand, and has a place and effect in the world on the other; to seek no common basis; to avoid deriving one from the other; to ascribe methods of worldly rule to the visible society, and then to transfer to it the attributes of love and truth and holiness that belong to the invisible, and so to claim for it, in subjection, the obedience which belongs to the other, in freedom. It is quite true that a person in a state of salvation is one called and admitted into a society; but, just because it is a society of saved persons, it is different in its relation to its members from all visible societies. Instead of more submission to their teachers and more obedience to their rulers, the Scripture hope of progress is still what it was of old, 'Would that the Lord's people were all prophets,'—would that each man were less concerned about his neighbour and more about his own message and his own call! Men are always ready to organize others; the fruitful and difficult task is to organize one's own soul.

LITERATURE.—Butler's *Sermons*, and, in contrast, Paley's *Moral Philosophy*. For the extensive literature for and against Socialism, see *Fabian Tract*, No. 29, 'What to Read: A List of Books for Social Reformers.' For individual freedom, J. S. Mill, *On Liberty*; Herbert Spencer, *Man versus the State*, and *Sociology*; Tolstoi, *Essays*, and many smaller works. On the relation of the individual to the Church, reference may be made to Loisy, *L'Évangile et l'Église* [tr. *The Gospel and the Church*, 1903]; Newman, *The Development of Christian Doctrine*, 1878; and T. B. Strong, *God and the Individual*, 1903.

JOHN OMAN.

INDIVIDUALITY. — The word 'individuality' may be used merely for the quality of being an individual, but its common use is to indicate the special characteristics which distinguish one individual from another, that which, as it has been expressed, marks each one as a particular thought of God. Only in this latter sense is the word considered here.

Both in morals and in religion it has always been a difficult matter to determine the due place of individual differences. The great weakness of Deism, *e.g.*, was that, while it abundantly exalted the individual, it had no place for individuality. Its natural religion and utilitarian ethic had, as its very standard of excellence, that it excluded everything whereby one man was different from another. Even Kant, the highest

product of Rationalism, with his view of religion as an appendage to a moral law, and his supreme test of a moral law by its fitness to be a law universal, only accentuated this limitation. The Romantic reaction had as its characteristic note the glory of individuality. The marvel of the universe was just its variety, and the glory of man that he was the most varied thing in the universe. The whole duty of man was to be himself and admit no law except the law of his own nature. Then unfortunately it too frequently appeared that what man took to be his nature was only self-pleasing, and what he thought was religion was only satisfaction of the artistic sense. There was also another very strange result. This excessive insistence upon individuality came to obliterate the individual. So much stress was laid upon what was changing and varied, that nothing was thought of what is one and unchanging. Hence everything was reduced to the great World-Spirit whose artistic pleasure in unfolding His variety constituted the history of the world.

This insistence on the importance of individuality by Romanticism, nevertheless, bore large fruit in both ethics and religion. Indeed, all modern study at least of the historical religions may be dated from Schleiermacher's insistence on the marked individuality of all the great founders of religion. Nor is it possible to question his right to point in particular to Jesus. The supreme human interest in all the Scriptures is their immense gallery of persons who gave scope to their individuality. For the most part they are very far from being perfect, but none of them is fashioned on the common worldly type, none of them is rolled like smooth stones on the beach, in the continual social attrition. Yet, even in this great gallery of the children of nature and of God, Jesus stands out pre-eminent. Whatever may be said of the stories of His birth, they mark the profoundest impression made on His contemporaries by a great, a striking, an unforgetable individuality. Though the many attempts at painting His human individuality, from the Apocryphal Gospels downwards, cannot be regarded as nearer a true likeness than the attempts at portraying His human features, every reader of the Gospels feels that, amid all the things He surrendered, He never surrendered His own marked human individuality. On the contrary, it continued to be a prominent thing that forced itself on everyone. He went His own way, thought His own thoughts, lived His own life, and never accorded anything to that tyranny of fashion to which, in our weak regard for others, we continually sacrifice what is greatest and best in our natures.

Our Lord's regard for the individuality of the persons He dealt with might be used as a key for understanding large portions of the Gospels. He took special care to bring out the individuality of each one's faith. He brings the modesty of the woman with the issue of blood into prominence, to give her the assurance she needed for her comfort (Mt 9²⁰ff.). He rejects roughly the prayer of the Canaanitish woman, to show more clearly her right to be heard (Mt 15²¹⁻²⁸). He sits at meat in the publican's house, to create self-respect in the social outcast (Mk 2¹⁵). He meets the centurion, the man of command, by working through a command (Lk 7¹⁻¹⁰); and He answers John, the man who had required action, by action (v.²²). He justified wisdom both in John the ascetic and in Himself who came eating and drinking, and only blamed the narrow censoriousness which could appreciate neither (Mt 11¹⁹).

In the Fourth Gospel, in particular, the key to almost everything Jesus says or does is that He knew what was in man (Jn 2²⁵). Nicodemus, the man dried to parchment and swathed in conventional considerations, needs to be born again into a new and fresh life (3¹⁻¹⁵). The woman of Samaria, no longer able to command the protection of even the poorest marriage tie, and too disreputable to appear at the well except when the midday sun kept the other women at home, is offered living water to refresh her soul parched for sympathy, and is so interpreted to herself that she said, 'He told me all that ever I did' (4¹⁻²⁶). Because the nobleman has the aristocratic spirit of his class, he is simply told to go his way, his son lives (4⁵⁰); because his bed has for thirty-eight years been the centre of all his interest, the cripple at Bethesda is told to take it up (5⁸). All the Gospels are full of persons of vivid individuality. A striking feature of our Lord's whole ministry is the way in which, in His presence, a man's true qualities inevitably come to light. The respectable convention behind which men hide inevitably falls away, and men appear in all their real characteristics, often with the unhonoured to their honour, and with the highly esteemed to their shame. Even the Pharisee, the type in all ages in which individuality is most suppressed by creed and custom, cannot keep the curtain drawn in His presence. At first sight this definiteness seems to be lost in the strange, vague atmosphere of the Fourth Gospel, which is so strongly irradiated by one individuality—that of the writer. But in life it is not the persons who are themselves colourless who do most justice to the individuality of others. So it is that in John we see, more than in any other Gospel, the vivid individuality, in particular, of the disciples, and how Jesus recognized it and dealt with it. Andrew and Nathanael, Philip and Thomas are mere names and shadows in the other Gospels, while in John they have each one his own characteristic note. Even Peter, in the other Gospels, is little more than an inexplicable mixture of insight and error; but in John he is drawn in a phrase by the Master Himself, 'When thou wast young thou girdedst thyself and walkedst whither thou wouldest' (21[18]). This enterprising but impetuous character appears in the whole presentation of him in John, till, in the days of heaviness, he flung off the slackness which had fallen upon all the disciples, and said with his old grip at his girdle, 'I go a fishing' (21[3]). In considering the question of the authenticity of John, this, at all events, deserves consideration, that it leaves us with such a sense of the strong individuality of the Apostles, both as children of nature and as children of grace, as to make it not incredible that a handful of poor men should start to conquer the world. In this Gospel, moreover, faith is not only an individual act, which it must always be, but also an attitude which brings out a man's deepest individuality. Men do not believe, because they trust only what they see (4[48]). They cannot believe in Christ, because already they have not believed in the highest they knew (5[47]). It is a certain preparedness for Christ which makes men believe in Him (6[35. 37]). Belief is a special word to oneself, a hearing from the Father (6[45]). Unbelief arises from being from beneath (8[23]), from being of one's father the devil (8[44]). There is, throughout, a family likeness in unbelief; while belief, in the consciousness of its own special needs, finds its own call. It does not lean on Abraham, or fashion itself on the accepted model, but, like Nathanael, it seeks God under the fig-tree, like Philip is ready to say to conventional questions, 'Come and see.' This faith, moreover, issues in an eternal life, the present effect of which is to give us possession of our own souls, to know God in such a way as not to be greatly concerned about men, to be in the world yet not of it (17[15]).

Though less prominent in the Synoptics, our Lord's regard to individuality is not less significant. To enter the Kingdom, so pronounced an individuality is required that it can take by itself the narrow way, while the common course is the broad road (Mt 7[13]); it is to be one in so characteristic a fashion as to cause more joy in heaven than the ninety and nine who, satisfied with the received standard, need no repentance (Mt 18[13], Lk 15[7]). This strong insistence that many are called and only few chosen, indicates not arbitrariness in dealing with individuals, but the rarity of the individuality God requires (Mt 22[14]). His true disciples must be of so pronounced a type that, while they shun the poor glory of self-display (Mt 6[2]), they must yet be the salt of the earth, and not even fear the prominence of being as a city set on a hill. They must shun the all-pervasive, all-assimilative creed of the time, the leaven of the Pharisees; nor will the accepted Christian formula,

the saying of 'Lord, Lord,' be any more approved (Mt 7[21]).

Our Lord does not really differ from the pagan view that the worth of the individual depends upon his individuality. The difference is in the estimate of that wherein this individuality consists, and of the possibilities in each man of attaining it. Even to Aristotle individuality meant something aristocratic. The qualities in a person worth considering are liberality (ἐλευθεριότης), magnificence (μεγαλοπρέπεια), and magnanimity (μεγαλοψυχία). These all require a certain social station, a certain aloofness from the petty concerns of life, which could be possible for all men only when the great mechanical slave whom Aristotle dreamt of could be made to do the drudgery. With Christ, on the other hand, a man could have true individuality in the lowest seats and at the lowliest services.

Nor is Christ's conception that of modern culture, which, indeed, is much nearer Aristotle than Jesus. He does not seek, with Goethe, to build up as high as possible the pyramid of his nature. A man does not fail of that individuality which the Kingdom of God requires, even though he have to cut off an offending hand or pluck out an offending eye, and enter blind and maimed (Mt 5[29]).

The classical presentation of the type of individuality permitted and required in the Kingdom of God is in the Beatitudes. Too often they are read as a suppression of individuality, which they are if a man's chief characteristics are possessions, popularity, self-assertion, self-indulgence. But in Christ's eyes this should not be the way of showing a man's true nature. The description, taken as a whole, presents an energetic type which, just because of its superiority both to society and to nature, is bound to be of marked individuality. To be poor in spirit is not to be poor-spirited, not to bend and break under every trial, but is to be rich in a faith which accepts poverty or anything else in the assurance of never being broken or bent. The mourner is not one given to tears, but one in energetic opposition to wrong and in energetic sympathy with suffering. The meek is not the meek and mild, not the soft, timid person, but one who has too high a faith in a wiser power than his own to strive and cry. To hunger and thirst after righteousness is necessarily to take an independent and difficult course in the world; while to be merciful requires decided strength of character, most of the cruel things on earth being done not in self-will and malice, but in thoughtlessness and weakness. Purity of heart never could survive in this world as mere innocence and ignorance of evil; the soft people who seek to shun everything disagreeable are the chief makers of dispeace; and only persons of determined character and decided principles ever run any risk of being persecuted for righteousness' sake. Were there no other condition but this last, it would mark the contrast with the accepted type, with the person whose first motive is prudence, whose guiding star is agreement with the authorities, who feels an obtrusive individuality to be in bad taste, and who regards a somewhat colourless membership of the Church and of Society as the hall-mark of the Divine approval. Instead we see one who is the odd man in the hundred, one who will not walk with the crowd in the broad way, one who has something of the singularity of the prophet which will ensure for him the singularity of the prophet's reward.

This large scope for individuality is maintained chiefly by resting the guidance of life not on a rule, but on a relation to God, revealed not in a code, but in a Person. This was the basis of a rule of love to God and to man to which all the Law and the Prophets could be reduced. Love is the way of at once giving scope to our own individuality and cherishing the individuality of others. Not that love can be without law. As it has been well said, What is love at the centre is always law at the circumference. But love at the centre will always keep law mindful of human differences. It will be a law in accordance with the Apostle's interpretation of his Master's meaning when he enjoins us to be true to our own highest individuality, *i.e.* the special demands of our own conscience, to do nothing that is not of faith (Ro 14[23]); to attend so far to the weakness of our own individuality as not to be enslaved to anything; and to regard the individuality of our neighbour so far as to take heed to what edifies (1 Co 10[23]). Nevertheless it is no true development of Christian faith or morals, as Newman (in his *Development*) and countless others have argued, that the faith has been elaborated into a creed that omits no detail of doctrine, and the morality into a code that lays down every detail of duty. Nor can it ever be true humility to surrender our individuality to any other man made like to ourselves.

Yet a free Protestant code and a smaller creed do not necessarily give us a true and characteristic faith, or save us from a mainly negative standard of duty, and perhaps there is no kind of consideration for others more needed at the present day than to have courage to be ourselves.

To leave room for this individuality is one of the most difficult and most neglected tasks of theology, and to leave scope for it in the Church is a task that has never been very anxiously pursued by the ecclesiastic. Yet if the true manifestation of faith is power to become sons of God in spite of society and circumstances, a very important element of it should be the maintenance of our true individuality; and though truth can only be one, there should be something characteristic in each man's faith. The preservation of this difference among the Scripture writers is the real task of Biblical Theology, which should not aim at evaporating truth into what each man thinks, but at showing how important every man is for his faith.

Literature.—Goethe, *Wilhelm Meister*; Schleiermacher, *Reden* [tr. *On Religion: Speeches to its Cultured Despisers*, 1893] and *Monologen* [tr. *Monologues*]; Hegel, *Philosophie der Geschichte* [tr. *Philosophy of History*, 1857]; Carlyle, *Heroes*; Emerson, *Essays*; J. S. Mill, *On Liberty*; Lüdemann, *Persönlichkeit und Individualität*, 1900; Lemme, *Christliche Ethik*, § 56, 1905; Schian, 'Glaube und Individualität' (*Zeitschr. für Theol. u. Kirche*, 1898); A. Breithaupt, *Rechte und Pflichten der Individualität im Christlich-sittlichen Leben*, 1901.

JOHN OMAN.

INDIVIDUALITY (OF CHRIST).—Regarded simply as a historical character, or as a subject of a visible career among men, Christ undoubtedly presents as distinct an aspect of individuality, or concrete reality, as can be affirmed of any historical personage. On the other hand, when we pass from the historical point of view to that of Christological construction, we can hardly fail to raise the question whether it is possible to escape from qualifying the category of individuality as applied to Christ on the side of His humanity. Proceeding from the latter point of view, and deferring to the Catholic postulates respecting the union of our Lord's manhood with the pre-existent Logos or Son of God, we are confronted with the task of explaining how a real concrete manhood can be taken into veritable union with the Logos without effecting a heterogeneous and double personality. The task is a very difficult one, and in wrestling with it a temptation easily arises to strip the manhood of concreteness or individuality, and thus to accommodate it more fully to the demands of personal unity. But a resort to this alternative has its own difficulty, and that by no means a slight one, since the thought of an Incarnation which means the union of the Son of God with a mutilated manhood, or with a mere semblance of manhood, is far from being satisfactory. Indeed, there is little hazard in affirming that the mind and heart of Christendom would sooner tolerate an element of unresolved dualism in the person of Christ, than sacrifice in any appreciable degree the reality and perfection of His manhood.

1. Among the prominent theories involving a sacrifice of this kind the *Apollinarian* is the most explicit and intelligible. By its supposition that the Logos took the place of the rational soul in the Redeemer, so that the Incarnation involved only the assumption of a human body with its principle of animal life, it evidently simplifies very much the problem of Christ's person. But the simplification takes place at too great a cost. The immutable Logos clothed in a fleshly garment is obviously no proper subject for temptation or for a real implication in human experiences generally. He cannot be brought into accord with the Gospel representations, except by resort to an artificial, Docetic interpretation. As lacking the most essential factor of manhood, He is destitute of the most apprehensible bond of brotherhood and ground of companionship. In short, the advantage which pertains to the Apollinarian theory, on the score of simplicity and intelligibility, is overmatched by the disadvantage which it incurs by its incompatibility with Gospel facts and by its abridgment of Christ's competency to enter into the life of men, and thus to fulfil the complete office of mediation. In effect it abolishes the Son of Man; for the archetypal manhood, which Apollinaris supposed to be resident in the eternal Logos, is a far off thing in comparison with the concrete reality which naturally is present to our thought when we use the term 'manhood.'

2. A second historic theory which has a distinct bearing upon our theme is that of *Monophysitism*. This differs from Apollinarism in its formal acknowledgment that by the incarnation of the Son of God is to be understood the assumption of a complete human nature. This acknowledgment, however, turns out to be rather verbal than substantial. The Monophysite assertion of a single nature in the incarnated Christ involved the compounding of the human nature in Him with the Divine; and this, in connexion with the vast preponderance assigned to the Divine in post-Nicene thinking, meant virtually the reduction of the human to the rank of an accident, a secondary and contingent property or group of properties, superinduced upon a Divine subject. Such an outcome, it is needless to say, runs very close to the submergence of the human side of Christ. It leaves no place for the thought of a real ethical manhood; for a proper ethical character is not predicable of a selfless accident. And with this deficit is conjoined a serious metaphysical difficulty, since fundamental thinking insists upon a relation of commensurability between attributes and their subject, and does not approve the notion that attributes appropriate to a finite personality can be made properly to inhere in an infinite subject.

3. A theory favoured with more orthodox associations than the Monophysite, but having a somewhat questionable bearing on the Christological problem, is the theory of *the impersonality of Christ's manhood*, or more specifically, the theory that His manhood, being devoid of a personality of its own, obtained from the first moment of subsistence its personal subject in the Ego of the pre-existent Logos (the so-called doctrine of *enhypostasis*). This theory was broached by Leontius in the 6th cent., was advocated by John of Damascus in the 8th cent., and has had in later times considerable currency among theologians of reputed orthodoxy, though never receiving any distinct œcumenical sanction. As handled by John of Damascus, the notion of the impersonality of Christ's manhood cannot be said to have been suitably reconciled with the full reality of that manhood. While formally he assigned to the Redeemer the full complement of human faculties, he felt obliged in one connexion or another to deny to them their characteristic forms of activity. It would not do, as he conceived, to admit progress in knowledge on the part of Christ, as this would contravene the truth that the hypostatic union of the human with the Divine in Him was complete from the start. For a like reason it was considered inadmissible to impute real prayer to Him. Divinity needs nothing, and a humanity that is perfectly united with Divinity shares in its sufficiency. In relation to the will also the Damascene considered it necessary to retrench from the proper human mode. The logical issue of his representations is to deny to the human will in Christ all power of initiative, and to reduce it entirely to the office of a 'medium through which the Logos moved the man Jesus.' Quite possibly John of Damascus does not afford the best specimen of what can be done in Christological construction with the notion that the human nature of Christ, being without personality of its own, derived such personal character as pertained to it from its relation to the person of the Logos. But certainly it is difficult in the light of his exposition to discover the real Son of Man. The image of a genuine and living manhood does not stand forth in his representation of the Redeemer.

It has sometimes been concluded that a special advantage belongs to the doctrine of the impersonality of the human nature of Christ, as helping to explain the atoning efficacy of His work. The inference is made that human nature in this character is not a concrete, limited entity, such as is the human nature of the individual man, but rather generic or universal. It is then argued that Christ in perfecting His own human nature sanctified human nature in general. Again, it is claimed that, in virtue of His literal community with men, His doing was in the proper sense a transaction within, as well as for, the whole body of humanity. As an eminently spiritual writer has expressed the thought, 'every man was a part of Him, and He felt the sins of every man, not in sympathy, but in sorrow and abhorrence' (Thomas Erskine). To such representations it is legitimate to reply, that what needs to be sanctified is not human nature in itself, but myriads of human beings; that the sanctification of human nature in Christ cannot rationally be conceived to have any immediate effect upon its sanctification elsewhere, inasmuch as human nature in Christ cannot be regarded as a stuff out of which men universally are fashioned; and that a generic or universal human nature belongs purely to the realm of the conceptual, and cannot possibly have any place in the sphere of real being. In short, the line of representation in question rests upon a fiction which modern philosophy for the most part has discountenanced—the fiction of the real existence of universals.

4. While it is impossible to be satisfied with any one of these historic theories, as respects its bearing on the integrity or concrete reality of Christ's manhood, it is far from easy to offer a definite substitute which is not open to exception. Indeed, an attempt at strict construction is certain to miscarry. The extraordinary as such rebels against complete elucidation, and by supposition the union of the Divine and the human in Christ is an extraordinary fact. Any one who accepts the Incarnation must admit that the individuality of Christ's manhood was specially conditioned; but equally, any one who admits the extraordinary character of the Incarnation must grant the impossibility of giving a full explanation of the mode and measure of this special conditioning. We cannot fully construe our own relation to the Divine; how then should we expect to gain clear insight into the relation of the human to the Divine in the person of our Lord? Probably the best that can be done is to form an ideal picture of the normal relation of perfected manhood to the Divine, and then beyond this to postulate *the mystery of a special bond* between Christ's manhood and His Divinity. The forming of the ideal picture will be distinctly helpful. For, having clearly apprehended the great truth that manhood loses nothing of its proper character by intimate union with the Divine, that the human spirit is never more itself than when it is possessed by and insphered in the Divine Spirit, that freedom is never so complete as when the human will by its own consent passes under the absolute direction of the Divine will, we shall be prepared to believe that manhood in Christ suffered no retrenchment by its extraordinary union with the Divine, but rather is to be accounted the full-orbed specimen of manhood as respects ethical worth and all tender and beautiful traits.

Taken in a popular sense, rather than in relation to Christological theory, the subject of individuality suggests a discussion of those characteristics which may be regarded as specially distinctive of Christ as a historic personage. This discussion, however, is reserved for the art. UNIQUENESS.

LITERATURE.—J. A. Dorner, *History of the Doctrine of the Person of Christ*; Adolf Harnack, *History of Dogma*; R. L. Ottley, *The Doctrine of the Incarnation*; John Caird, *The Fundamental Ideas of Christianity*, Lectures xiii.-xv.; *Contentio Veritatis*, ch. ii.; Illingworth, *Personality Human and Divine.*   HENRY C. SHELDON.

INDOLENCE.—The spirit of Christ's religion is inimical to indolence in the sphere of business (Lk 16[11], Mt 24[48] 25[26]), but more especially indolent Christianity is *salt without savour* (Mt 5[13]). Not only is a state of salvation hard to maintain (Mt 7[14]), but perfection is to be aimed at (5[48]). An enemy sows tares while we sleep (13[25]). The oil in our lamps consumes as we rest (25[5]). Watchfulness is the very opposite of indolence (26[41]). The hid talent will reproach the indolent in the day of reckoning (25[18]). Most deadly is the spiritual indolence which is satisfied to have Abraham for father (Lk 3[8], Jn 8[39]), or Christ for Saviour, without response to the impulses of the Holy Spirit, the source of life and motion and progress.

A signal judgment may be executed upon the indolent soul, either after a period of further probation (Lk 13[6-9]), or suddenly and unexpectedly when that day comes as a snare (Lk 21[34]), and the Judge pronounces the sentence (Mk 11[14]). The conscience must be kept awake and intelligent (Mt 5[23. 24]). The beginnings of evil must be checked (v.[18f.]). The ears must be open to learn, and the heart ready to believe (11[15]). The rock foundation to build the house upon may need much toil to reach it (7[24]). And continually the servant of Christ must be ready for his Master's coming, with loins girded and lights burning (Lk 12[35]).—Love is not indolent in seeking the lost sheep (Mt 18[12]). Hope is not indolent in running to the sepulchre (Jn 20[4]), or hastening to the manger (Lk 2[16]). Faith is not indolent in pressing through the crowd to be healed (Mk 5[27]). 'The zeal of thine house shall eat me up' (Jn 2[17]). See also art. SLOTHFULNESS.

W. B. FRANKLAND.

INFANCY.—

1. The period of infancy, properly speaking, may be taken as lying between the birth of a child and its being weaned; and Hebrew children were usually weaned at two years of age or thereabouts. Quite a number of terms are used in Heb. to describe childhood and youth at various stages; and in this earliest period before a child has become a *gāmūl* (נָמֻל 'weaned'), there are three different terms that may be applied to him. The infant is יֶלֶד (f. יַלְדָּה), the (new-) *born* (cf. 'bairn,' 'barn'), יִנֵק (the suckling), and עוֹלָל (or עוּל), also indicating dependence for nourishment. In NT, apart from the general use of παῖς or παιδίον, the terms used are (1) βρέφος (applying to the unborn child as well [Lk 1⁴¹]), and (2) νήπιος. The aspect of infancy connoted by νήπιος, as contrasted with the Heb. terms, is inability to speak (= Lat. infans). In Mt 21¹⁶, in the quotation from Ps 8³, LXX, the Greek translators use νήπιος as= עוֹלֵל, and the ptcp. θηλάζων as= יוֹנֵק. With the exception of Lk 18¹⁵, βρέφος occurs in the Gospels only in Lk.'s account of the birth of Christ; and νήπιος, in addition to Mt 21¹⁶, only in a figurative use in Mt 11²⁵ = Lk 10²¹.

2. All that the Gospels have to tell concerning the infancy of Jesus is found in Lk 2 and Mt 2. Excluding the story of the Birth, we have the following series of events :—the Circumcision, the Presentation, the Visit of the Magi, the Flight into Egypt, the Slaughter of the Innocents, the Return and Settlement at Nazareth. The insuperable difficulties in the way of weaving these narratives into a coherent and harmonious whole are now generally recognized. Harmonists have not been able to agree even as to the time-order in which the events should be placed. (Andrews, in his *Life of Our Lord*, p. 91 f., conveniently shows the diversity that has obtained). If it were a matter of supreme importance to settle such order, Wieseler's view (*Chron. Synopsis*, i. ch. iii.) seems the most reasonable, arranging as follows :—Circumcision, Presentation (or Purification of Mary), Visit of the Magi, Flight into Egypt and Slaughter of the Innocents, Return to Nazareth. So far, however, as the narrative in Mt 2 is concerned, it is evidently unrelated to Lk.'s account of the infancy of Jesus; it stands as a story by itself, detached from its own context ; the opening (τοῦ δὲ Ἰησοῦ γεννηθέντος, κ.τ.λ.) is quite indefinite as a time-expression, and anything like chronological interest is at a minimum.

The accounts of the Infancy comprise : (*a*) normal features—the Circumcision, the Presentation (= Purification of Mary and Redemption of the Firstborn) ; and (*b*) peculiar features—the Visit of the Magi and connected incidents.

As for (*a*), it is noticeable that we have these particulars given in Lk. alone. The rites appointed to be performed on the birth of a Hebrew boy, a firstborn, were duly carried out. The Circumcision took place on the eighth day (Lk 2²¹), *i.e.* at the time prescribed by ancient law and usage (Lv 12³). Again, after the proper interval (Lv 12⁴) the Purification of Mary with all due rites took place at the Temple (Lk 2²²).

The αὐτῶν ('*their* purification') cannot without strain be made to refer to any but both Joseph and Mary who brought the child to Jerusalem (see also v.³³). This, as well as the interpretation making αὐτῶν refer to mother and child (see, *e.g.*, rendering of the *Twentieth Cent. NT*), is in conflict with the ritual law (Lv 12) ; and the reading followed by AV ('*her* purification'), which has practically no MS authority, is an evident correction to remove the discrepancy.

The offering brought was that prescribed for persons in humble circumstances (Lv 12⁸), though the regulation is so quoted in Lk 2²⁴ that this does not explicitly appear. The Presentation of the infant Jesus involved at the same time the ancient ceremony of the Redemption of the firstborn son, as the reference to Ex 13². ¹⁵ shows. In our Lord's day a rabbinical regulation had added to the Mosaic rule the condition that the child thus presented and redeemed should be free from physical defect and blemish.

In the Pentateuch this devotion of the male firstborn of both man and beast to Jahweh, carrying with it the necessity of redemption in the case of sons, is traced as to its institution to the smiting of the firstborn in Egypt at the Exodus (Ex 13¹⁵, Nu 3¹³). There can be little doubt, however, that there is an affinity between this Hebrew custom and the sacrifice of firstlings amongst the Arabs, and that they have a common source in ideas of taboo as associated with the firstborn—ideas belonging to a remote Semitic antiquity (see W. R. Smith, *RS*² p. 462 ff.).

Yet in connexion with these ordinary incidents of infancy among the Jews we have touches of the unusual, though the forecast of a great destiny thus indicated is not *per se* an incredible feature of the dawn of such a life. At the Circumcision the name Jesus was given, we are told (Lk 2²¹), in accordance with an angelic intimation to Mary prior to conception (1³¹), a matter in which, it may be noted, a marked contrast with the representation in Mt 1¹⁸⁻²⁵ appears. At the Presentation the part played by Simeon and Anna (Lk 2²⁵⁻³⁸) forms an unwonted accompaniment of the ceremonies of the occasion, and wonderfully breaks in upon the even recital of customary proceedings (cf. vv.²⁴. ³⁹). The close parallel, however, which exists here with the story of John the Baptist's birth cannot be overlooked. Cf. Lk 1¹³. ⁵⁹⁻⁶³ and 1³¹ 2²¹ ; also 1⁶⁵⁻⁷⁹ and 2²⁷⁻³⁸. The character of the narratives as a whole, and especially as regards such elements as these, suggests that we have thus conveyed to us 'the traditional Jewish-Christian views of Jesus,' and argues a special Jewish-Christian (Palestinian) source (see Moffatt, *Historical NT*, p. 651 ff.).

(*b*) The more peculiar features are furnished by the narrative in Mt 2. It is quite unnecessary to give an outline of the stories themselves ; but some notice must be taken of the considerable problems to which they give rise. Did they form from the very first an integral part of Mt.'s Gospel? Considerations of style and general structure favour the probability of their being from another hand than that which furnished the main body of the Gospel. The stories are not therefore to be rejected as without historic basis ; nor are we to cast them aside on the arbitrary ground of intrinsic incredibility. But we cannot ignore the striking features of the narrative that raise the question as to what the nature of the narrative precisely is. Consider, *e.g.*, the use made of dream-warnings (vv.¹². ¹³. ¹⁹. ²²) ; the peculiarities in the leading of the 'star' (seen first in the East, then lost sight of —else they had not gone to Jerusalem instead of Bethlehem—only to reappear and go before them to Bethlehem, moving in the heavens, and at last stopping 'over where the young child was') ; the symbolic character of the threefold offering (v.¹¹) ; and, lastly, the dominant interest in the element of prophetic fulfilment, making each turn in the story answer to some passage from the prophets (vv.⁶. ¹⁵. ¹⁷. ²³), the correspondence in some cases being but remote and obscure. We at once characterize as legendary such embroidery of the story of the Magi as makes them 'three kings of Orient,' gives them names, and elaborates their after history, and such features as the ox and the ass incessantly adoring the Child (*Gosp. of pseudo-Mt.*) ; but is the story as it stands in Mt. absolutely free from elements of the same order? The narrative is so naïve, *e.g.*, that it seems superfluous and beside the mark to venture seriously on calculations to prove that some astronomical phenomenon, such as a conjunction of planets, really explains what is said of the star.

The story of the Massacre of the Innocents cannot be said to be inherently improbable. Herod was not the man to hesitate at such a measure if occasion arose for it. Absence of confirmatory references in history also goes for little when all the circumstances are considered. Macrobius (*Saturn.* ii. 4), writing in the 5th cent., states that Augustus, hearing that some baby boys of less than two years of age had been put to death at Herod's command, and that the king's own child was amongst those killed, said 'Melius est Herodis porcum esse quam filium.' This looks like a reference ; but how strange, if it were so, that the Mt. narrative should fail to notice such a notable circumstance ! It is a curious passage, but evidently all its interest is in the Emperor's *bon mot*, playing on the Gr. terms for 'pig' ($\hat{v}s$) and 'son' ($v\iota\acute{o}s$). It has often been pointed out that the number of little ones slain must have been comparatively small (Edersheim says 'probably 20 at most,' i. 214), in correction of later exaggerations (perhaps helped by the vivid language of v.[18]); but this does not destroy the pathetic element in such an association with the infancy of our Lord in Christian tradition. But, all things considered, though it is plausible to suggest that we have here a designed Messianic parallel to the deliverance of the infant Moses, the parallel is not so close as to suggest pure invention, and it is difficult to imagine all substratum of fact to be wanting.

Suggestions, also, which see in the 'Repose in Egypt,' as it used to be called, only a typical indication of Jesus as the vine of Israel 'brought out of Egypt' (art. 'Gospels' in *Encyc. Bibl.* ii. 1780), are not wholly convincing and satisfactory. At the same time, as regards the whole narrative in Mt 2, we must be content to say that the state of our knowledge affords no solution of the difficulties to which it gives rise when compared with the representations of Lk., especially, *e.g.*, in the implication that Joseph and Mary were continuously resident at Bethlehem probably until Jesus was nearly two years old, and that they went to Nazareth to live only after their return from Egypt.

3. The sources of the Infancy narratives remain a subject of debate. Speaking of the Mt. document in particular, Sanday says 'we are in the dark' (art. 'Jesus Christ' in Hastings' *DB* ii. 644). Resch's well-known attempt to establish an original Hebrew 'Childhood-Gospel,' having as parts of its contents both the Lk. and Mt. stories, has failed to carry conviction. An important problem, however, is presented by a comparison of these narratives with the conspicuous features of certain of the Apocryphal Gospels, particularly the *Protevangelium of James*, the *Gospel according to Thomas*, and the *Arabic Gospel of the Childhood*. It may be said that it is just at such a point as this that the apocryphal writings come most noticeably into contact with our Canonical Gospels, as also it is in the ministry and teaching of Jesus that they depart most widely from them. A superabundance of fantastic elements in these Christian Apocrypha is at once revealed on the most superficial comparison: still there are elements in common, and here and there points of close contact. In the *Gospel of the Childhood*, *e.g.*, we have the story of the Magi woven into the narrative, and Mt 2[1] is almost literally paralleled, as also the adoration and offering of the threefold gift (see H. Sike's edition of 1697, with Lat. tr. p. 17), though at the same time the most curious divergences appear. It is most improbable that our narratives were directly borrowed from any of these apocryphal works and finally incorporated in the Canonical Gospels. It seems also unlikely that our Gospels were used specifically in the production of any of the Apocrypha, and that out of our Gospels the narratives in Mt 1. 2 and Lk 1. 2 were simply taken for expansion into the extraordinary congeries of marvels of which these extra-canonical writings mostly consist. Why may not canonical and apocryphal accounts have alike originated in a common early tradition, though they have flowed so far apart? It is well to remember that those who promulgated and those who received most of the Apocryphal Gospels sincerely believed themselves to be Christians. Pseudo-Matthew indeed openly professes to be actuated by the love of Christ in writing his wonder-crowded account of the infancy and boyhood of our Lord. Our narratives, however, are characterized by a wonderful simplicity and restraint when compared with such accounts as his; they proclaim themselves so much nearer what the

facts must have been. But one source of apocryphal developments appears to have been the deep-seated fondness of Jews for *haggādôth* (see Donehoo, *The Apocryphal and Legendary Life of Christ*, p. xix); and one great feature of such *haggādôth* was the interest shown in connecting OT prophecies with fulfilments. The question suggests itself whether haggadic elements may not even have found their way into our brief canonical narratives. If it be so, it cannot detract from the supreme value of the portraiture of Christ in the Gospels. G. H. Box (in *ZNTW*, 1905, p. 80 ff.) suggests that Mt 1. 2 are to be regarded as a *midrāsh*, which means much the same thing, though otherwise expressed. The historical basis, that is to say, is treated in subservience to edification and the expression of a Messianic faith. See also artt. BABE, CHILDHOOD.

LITERATURE. — Lives of Christ; Supplemental section of Sanday's art. 'Jesus Christ' in Hastings' *DB*; Ramsay, *Was Christ born at Bethlehem?*; Resch, 'Das Kindheits-evangelium' (*TU* iv. Heft 3, 1897); Gore, *Dissertations*, p. 12 ff.

J. S. CLEMENS.

INFLUENCE.—1. THE INFLUENCE OF CHRIST DURING HIS LIFE. — (*a*) *On His disciples.* — This from the very first was remarkable. The short interview that John and Andrew had with Jesus after He had been pointed out by their old master as the Lamb of God that taketh away the sin of the world, seems to have carried them away at once. Andrew has no misgivings, but goes off to his brother with the great news that they have found the Messiah (Jn 1[37ff.]). The disciples, spiritually minded though they were, must have felt all the prejudices that widely existed against the appearance of the Messiah as a poor and undistinguished person from a northern village of no reputation, and yet they were at once conquered. One evening's conversation convinced them that He was their Prince. A like instantaneous recognition is recorded of Bartholomew, if he be, as seems likely, the same as Nathanael. He has difficulties to overcome which he had frankly stated to Philip when he ran in with the same great news that Andrew had told Peter. But they vanish before the presence and words of his Lord. The encouraging description of his own character set Nathanael wondering, and when this was followed by news which showed that He knew of some secret passage in his life, he confesses His greatness in the fullest terms, 'Rabbi, thou art the Son of God, thou art the King of Israel' (1[49]). In all these cases it is to be noted that the impression is made not by any miracle or sign, but by what Christ was and what He said. A little later there follows the first sign, — the changing of water into wine, — and with it the natural deepening of the hold Christ had on His disciples (2[ff.]). All their previous hopes were confirmed ('crediderunt amplius,' Bengel). Up to this time there are no hostile influences at work. As simple-minded men they probably supposed that all the world would share their sanguine hopes. The cleansing of the Temple, followed as it was by public questioning as to His right to take that bold step (2[13ff.]), was probably the first indication that He would not be able to influence all men alike.

From that time onward the attempt to break down our Lord's influence becomes much more definite and decided. His supposed birthplace, — Nazareth, — His humble parentage, His lack of a really good education, all these and many other objections were constantly urged (Jn 7[15]), and must have caused some difficulty in the disciples' minds. His great assertions that He was the Bread of Life and the Light of the world (Jn 6[35. 48] 8[12] 9[5]), aroused great opposition and lost Him many friends. But when after eighteen months of criticism, obloquy, and insult, He asked His disciples definitely as to their opinion about Him, they replied through Peter without hesitation: 'Thou art the Christ, the Son of the Living God' (Mt 16[16]). It is true that this was the conviction they had had at the outset, but it had not been tested, it had not been held against the whole world. The disciples were not fanatics, they were not indifferent to the opinion of their own Church and nation; they felt keenly the opposition and hatred which their view everywhere encountered, and yet they held it. It is a striking proof of our Lord's personal influence. That He knew their difficulties is plain from the fact that He prayed for them before He asked the question (Lk 9[18]). That He rejoiced in their loyalty is also plain from the great words spoken to Peter (Mt 16[17-19]). The Transfiguration followed quickly (Mt 17[1ff.] ||), in order that the three disciples who knew Him best might have something to fall back upon in the greater difficulties that lay before them. Soon our Lord became a proscribed person, not only excommunicated from all the synagogues of the land, but bringing under that ban all His friends (Jn 9[22]). Their loyalty, however, remained unbroken except in one case, that of Judas. This man must have felt our Lord's influence at one time, and indeed been always more or less under it. He could not tear himself away from it, though he was feeling more and more uncomfortable in the barren prospects that Christ's language and the hostility of the world seemed to suggest. Only little by little he stifled it, and we may well believe that it was not till the very last, even after he had promised to betray Him, that it failed. Then St. John (13[27]) adds the significant words, 'After the sop, then entered Satan into him,' and the disciple was lost.

The severest test was felt after the arrest. That the Prince and Messiah should be betrayed by His own people into the hands of the heathen, and that they should clamour for His death, was the greatest trial that a faithful friendship has ever had to bear. It is true the disciples ought to have known their Scriptures; but, like good people to-day, they followed current interpretations instead of searching the Holy Writings for themselves. That our Lord's influence would have remained with them had He not risen again is, of course, certain; but it would have been the influence of a holy life and a great example, not of an abiding Presence and a magnificent hope. This was given them by the Resurrection, which at once illuminated all the perplexities of the past and made His Messiahship a felt reality. And after Pentecost they found their minds and imaginations extraordinarily stimulated by the presence of the Holy Ghost who witnessed to every word and act of the Crucified and Risen Christ.

(b) *On the people.*—This was as surprising in its own way as His influence on the disciples. 'They heard Him gladly' (Mk 12[37]). They would have taken Him 'by force and made him king' (Jn 6[15]). They prevented any open act of hostility against Him on the part of the rulers, who were afraid of them (Lk 20[19] 22[2]). They never could make up their minds who He was, but yet were convinced He was no ordinary person. He was either Elijah, or the great expected Prophet, or Jeremiah, or even the Baptist risen again (Mt 16[14] ||). That they turned completely round at the last was no doubt due to the malign influence of the Pharisees joined to the great disappointment experienced when nothing followed the events of Palm Sunday. Like the people of Lystra, they were enraged at having openly declared themselves on the side of a movement which seemed to have no result. Our Lord's influence on the people was just what we should expect, as we shall see when we consider its particular character.

(c) *On His enemies.*—At first it strikes us strangely that One who not only did no harm, but always went about doing good, One who refused to be entrapped into any political movement, One who observed fasts and festivals, attended synagogue and temple, should have excited such bitter hostility. He had none of the marks of a great social reformer, disliked crowds and great cities, refused to take advantage of any excitement caused by His words or deeds, chose for His intimate friends plain middle-class men who had no particular mark about them except their religiousness. All His teaching was constructive rather than destructive. He did not speak of the Gentiles as His servant Paul did, nor of the Temple as Stephen did. He was indignant at the abuses of the time, and was unsparing in His condemnation of Pharisees and scribes, but the hostility had set in before that, and its only explanation is the hatred of bad men to a holy life.

(d) *On individuals.*—(α) The visit of *Nicodemus* shows something of the power Jesus exercised in public. Although Nicodemus was a person of some importance, he treats our Lord, in spite of His humble circumstances, as not only a great but a Divine teacher from whom he would gladly learn (Jn 3[2]). And the conversation with Him on that occasion bore fruit. (β) *Pilate*, too, was evidently greatly impressed by Jesus. With his inborn contempt for the Jews he would have decided the matter the Sanhedrin brought before him very quickly, had it not been for the majesty of Jesus' presence and the brief but striking words He spoke. That he should have been afraid when the Jews told him that the prisoner had claimed to be the Son of God and at once sought another interview, shows that there was a mysterious influence about our Lord which made the governor feel uncomfortable; and this fear was only increased when his question, 'Whence art thou?' received no answer (Jn 19[8f.]). (γ) Even *Caiaphas* treats Christ with a respect which he would have gladly dispensed with. His continued silence led the high priest to take the very unusual step of forcing some statement out of Him by solemn adjuration (Mt 26[63]). (δ) The most touching illustrations of Christ's influence are found amongst *the sinful.* They were drawn to Him as steel to the magnet. He was their friend (Mt 11[19]), to whom they could give their confidences. Tired of life they turned instinctively to Him, and gladly gave Him their all. Matthew, Zacchæus, Mary Magdalene, the woman that was a sinner, are only typical of hundreds of men and women who came to Him because they were sure of His love, and recognized that He had power to forgive.

2. SECRET OF CHRIST'S INFLUENCE. — (a) *Not the influence of His position as Son of God.*—When we remember who He was, the Word made flesh, the eternal Son of God, we are perhaps surprised that our Lord never used the influence of His unique position. Had He chosen, He could have done what He was tempted to do, forced men to believe by some plain unmistakable wonder like that of throwing Himself from the pinnacle of the Temple (Mt 4[5]). He could have appeared as the great I AM attended by legions of angels (26[53]). He could have declared authoritatively that He was the great God, and proved it by the destruction of the towns and villages which denied it (Lk 9[52ff.]). He could have used His position and forced men to recognize it. And again and again, as the above references show, He was tempted to do it. But He rejected the temptation. It is a method, as we know, freely employed in the world, and widely popular. People prefer the influence of the

direct to the indirect. They like to have some sign from heaven which will save them the trouble of thinking, and be a short cut to a difficult conclusion. And the Jews were always seeking this (Mt 12³⁸); always hoping that He would either show that His claims were invalid and that He was unable to give a sign, or satisfy their curiosity by some miracle. Our Lord tells them that, even if He gave them a sign, the sign of a man risen from the dead, it would have no effect in changing their lives (Lk 16³²). It may be asked—But what about His miracles? In the first place, they were never done as a proof of His claims. He never proclaimed a great truth and then worked a miracle to show it was true. They were all in obedience to an earnest call for help; and faith, where it could be had, was a condition essential to His working (Mk 6⁵). When done, they were evidences, but only secondary to the evidence of His own personality. If men were too dull to believe in Him for what He was, then there was still the sign of His works. 'Though ye believe not me, believe the works' (Jn 10³⁸); 'Believe me that I am in the Father, and the Father in me; or else believe me for the very works' sake' (14¹¹).

(b) *Not the influence of popularity.*—In the next place, Jesus did not seek influence through flattering people or rulers. Satan recognized in Christ extraordinary attractive powers. His love and manners were such that He could, had He chosen, have won over the whole world to His side. Never in anyone had there been such rich human gifts, such wide sympathies, such intimate knowledge of men's ways and hearts. Satan's attempt to persuade Christ to do him homage (Mt 4⁹ ‖ Lk 4⁷) was more subtle than is often supposed. It was the temptation to win, through flattery of the world-power, —a path that has again and again been pursued by great men. It is needless to point out that Christ never sought influence that way. The Pharisees and Herodians only expressed the general feeling in saying, 'Master, we know that thou art true, and teachest the way of God in truth, and carest not for anyone: for thou regardest not the person of men' (Mt 22¹⁶).

(c) *The influence of personality.* — Christ influenced men not by the majesty of His position nor by His marvellous works, but by His personality. It was what He *was* more than what He said or did. Men felt about Him that He was always infinitely greater than anything He said. And it was because of the tremendous force that sprang forth from His personality that He could say the most amazing things without amazing. It must be remembered that the disciples were, during His lifetime, feeling their way towards the mystery of His Person. They did not know at first what they knew afterwards. And yet they could feel thankful for teaching which placed Him before wife and child, before brother or sister (Mt 10³⁷). They welcomed Him as the Way, the Truth, and the Life. He did not point it out, for He was it. He did not give it as something apart from Himself. All this, which would have been intolerable from anyone else, was a relief from Him, as it expressed in words their own feelings (7²⁹). So, too, the weight of His authority was not that of the scribes, dependent on others, but that derived from His own personality. It was this that astonished the people, who were accustomed in their teachers to quotations from others and to second-hand information. With Him it was always personal: 'We speak that we do know, and testify that we have seen' (Jn 3¹¹). Now and again it flashed forth in a way that dazzled and overpowered, as when the men of Nazareth wished to fling Him over the cliff, as when those of Jerusalem would have stoned Him, as when those sent to arrest Him fell back when He declared who He was (Lk 4²⁹, Jn 8⁵⁹ 18⁶).

(d) *Power of the Holy Ghost.*—Beyond all this there is something far more difficult to explain, viz. the effect of the descent of the Holy Ghost at His Baptism. When the Baptist was asked to account for the influence of Christ, he replied, 'A man can receive nothing except it be given him from heaven,' and went on to say that not only was the Christ above all as coming from above, but that He was endowed with the Spirit beyond all measure (Jn 3²⁷·³⁴). It would seem, though the passage is not clear, that part of His influence was due to the co-operation of the Holy Ghost with His own spirit. The Holy Ghost given to man in such measure as man's limitations allow, was given to the infinite heart and mind of Christ fully, infinitely, without bound. And in the power of that Divine Spirit He began His ministry (Lk 4¹⁸⁻²¹), not only teaching men's minds, but by the 'finger of God' (11²⁰)—an expression interpreted by some of the Holy Ghost—casting out devils. But whatever may be the mystery of the union of the Holy Spirit with Christ, it is certain that He laid stress on this Power as being that which would be the source of the influence His disciples should exercise.

3. INFLUENCE OF THE DISCIPLES.—All Christ's disciples, without exception, were to be influential. The words, 'Ye shall receive power, when the Holy Ghost is come upon you' (Ac 1⁸), were probably spoken to the 120 disciples, numbering some women amongst them. They were to rely upon Him. He had told them previously that in the difficult situations which persecutions would create, they were not to be anxious as to how best to answer the accusations of their adversaries: He Himself would give them 'a mouth and wisdom,' and then further explained by saying, 'for it is not ye that speak, but the Holy Spirit' (Lk 21¹⁴ᶠ·). They were then to influence the world not primarily by intellectual power or by wonderful signs, but by that which is deeper than thought or gifts, namely, their own personality. It would be what they *were*, not what they had, the power of their own inner spirit, not that of cleverness; and this through the power of the Eternal Spirit. Spirit can be touched only by spirit, personality can be developed only by personality. When, then, the Holy Spirit came down upon them on the Day of Pentecost, it was the depths, not the surface of their lives, that were stirred. It was not the development of mere intellectual gifts which enabled them to communicate with others, but such an enlargement of their own spirits that they felt in touch with the whole world, and in their struggle to express this rush of sympathy, found a language suitable for each person with whom they came in contact. So afterwards we do not find the gift of tongues a new language, but rather an endeavour to express the new enlargement of their own spirit. They felt more than they could express, more sometimes than their minds could recognize (1 Co 14¹³). And this growth of personality is what we see even in the brief records of the NT: Simon becomes Peter; Levi, Matthew; Bartholomew, Nathanael; Joseph, Barnabas; and Saul, Paul. Their characters are not only stronger, but fuller and larger, and through them they built up churches, and changed the face of the world in which they lived. Our Lord never supposes they will be effective through education or culture or the presence of gifts. 'Apart from me ye can do nothing' (Jn 15⁴). But the co-operation which He promises as the secret of their success is not that of a master who gets over his pupil's difficulty by solving it for him, but that of one who by his sympathy, power, and skill enables him to meet it for himself. Christ dwelt in them through

faith by the power of the Holy Spirit, and worked in them and through them in every painful task they had to accomplish.

LITERATURE.—Phillips Brooks, *Influence of Jesus*; Dale, *The Living Christ*, ch. iii.; Stalker, *Imago Christi*, ch. xvii.; Newman, *Gram. of Assent*[5], 463 ff.

G. H. S. WALPOLE.

INHERITANCE (Mt 21[38], Mk 12[7], Lk 20[14]; Lk 12[13] : κληρονομία, derived from κλῆρος, 'lot,' 'portion,' 'possession,' and νέμειν, 'to own or administer').—The ordinary Biblical idea of inheritance is 'the enjoyment by a rightful title of that which is not the fruit of personal exertion. The heir being what he is in relation to others, enters upon a possession which corresponds with his position; but there is no necessary thought of succession to one who has passed away' (Westcott, *Epistle to the Hebrews*, p. 168). In the Gospels, however, the idea of succession to a deceased person is the prominent one, as with ourselves. The chief difference between the ordinary ancient and the ordinary modern conception of inheritance is this : We have more regard to the mere change in the ownership of certain property which takes place : the ancient civilized races looked rather to the position of the heir as executor and administrator of the deceased's property, and as the person who, being clothed, so to speak, with the personality of the deceased, took upon himself all the obligations of the testator, as well as the continuance of his race and the perpetuation of his family religion. The last considerations were the most prominent, and account for the prevalence of adoption in ancient society. An adopted son, or a relative compelled to marry the deceased's daughter, could carry on the family and its rites as well as a real son. (See Maine's *Ancient Law*, ch. vi., and artt. 'Heir' and 'Inheritance' in Hastings' *DB*). See also art. HEIR.

ALEX. SOUTER.

INN.—Inns in the time of Christ were neither so infrequent nor so ill-equipped as many writers have represented.

Thus Stapfer (*Palestine in the Time of Christ*, 1866, p. 232), quoting from the Talmud a story of some Levites, who, travelling from Zoar, left at an inn one of their number who had fallen ill upon the road (*Yeb.* xvi. 7), adds the comment, 'Such hostelries were rare, and were found only in very remote places.' Other writers convey the impression that the only inns existing in Palestine were a few *khans*, as bare and comfortless as those now found in many parts of the East, and often described by modern travellers (see, *e.g.*, Burckhardt, *Travels in Syria*, 1822, p. 36; Layard, *Nin. and Bab.* 1853, p. 498; Kinglake, *Eothen*, ch. xvii.; also Kitto's *Cyc.*, art. 'Caravanserais'; and Vigouroux's *Dict.*, art. 'Caravansérail').

This seems to the present writer a mistaken inference, arising partly from exaggerated notions of Oriental hospitality, and partly from attributing to the 1st cent. A.D. social conditions which prevailed, it is true, in patriarchal times, and are found even now on the great trade and pilgrim routes across the desert, but did not obtain to anything like the same degree in the busy, populated, and prosperous country of the Herods. The customary hospitality of the East (see Hastings' *DB*, *s.v.*, and art. 'Gast' in Hamburger's *RE*) may, of course, be a reason why inns in the modern sense of the word should be less needed than in Western countries; but the statement that 'the warm commendations of hospitality in the NT show that even in the Roman period the buildings set apart for strangers to lodge in were of a simple character in Palestine' (*Encyc. Bibl.* art. 'Inn'), requires considerable modification.

Some of these commendations obviously refer to the interchange of courtesies among members of the Christian community only (*e.g.* Ro 12[13a], 1 P 4[9], 3 Jn [5]), while others which definitely mention 'strangers' and 'enemies' are not necessarily any indication of the rarity and poverty of existing places of entertainment, but a sign of the new Christian spirit (Ro 12[20], He 13[2]). Ramsay argues (Hastings' *DB*, Ext. Vol. p. 394ᵃ) that the motive of this urging of hospitality was the desire to pre-serve Christian converts from the corrupting influences among which they would be thrown at the public inns.

Numerous passages are cited from the Talmud to prove the extent to which hospitality prevailed among the Jews; but this traditional virtue was probably more praised than practised in the 1st century. The conditions peculiar to a nomad life came to be very materially modified when the countryside was covered with populous villages and towns. It is true that, at the Passover, if a Jew came up to Jerusalem from any part of the empire, he would find entertainment at a private house. It was the boast of the Rabbis that, notwithstanding the crowds, no man could say, 'I have not found a bed in Jerusalem to lie in' (Lightfoot, *Works*, 1823, ix. p. 128); but what if the Jew came at some other time than at one of the great national feasts? What if a Samaritan came? Moreover, there was a large population of heathen; and even if Jewish habits of hospitality to Jews were equal in practice to the theory, no provision was made for the Gentile. Even to a Jew a Jew would shut his door. When Jesus is sending out His disciples to preach, He does not take it for granted that they will always find a ready welcome or free entertainment (Mt 10[11-14], Mk 6[10. 11], Lk 10[10. 11]).

Nor is it safe to argue from the comparative silence of contemporary records that inns were rare. It would not be guessed by a reader of the Gospels that in Jerusalem there were many synagogues.[*] It is quite possible that there were almost as many inns in Jerusalem. At any rate, it is misleading to make the general statement, as though it applied to all periods of Jewish history, that 'inns in our sense of the term were, as they still are, unknown in the East' (M'Clintock and Strong, *Cyc. s.v.*). A truer view is given in the *Jewish Encyc.* (art. 'Caravanserai') : 'By NT times the Holy Land had been sufficiently developed to afford opportunity for real inns.'

The influx of Greeks into Palestine, the constant presence of a large Roman element, civil and military, the mixed retinue attached to the Herodian court, the increase of trade, the importation of foreign workmen, the presence in several towns of companies of gladiators, actors, and the like, —would necessitate not only inns, but various kinds and grades of inns.

There were inns built on a large scale, comfortable and elegant, suited for high officials (see *CIL* iii. 6123, where Mommsen explains *prætoria* as 'diversoria nobiliora magistratibus iter facientibus reliquisque honestioribus destinata'). Epictetus draws a picture of a traveller lingering at a fine hotel because he finds everything agreeable there (*Diss.* ii. xxiii. 36). Josephus (*Ant.* xv. v. 1) relates that when Herod the Great was celebrating games at Cæsarea, he entertained a number of ambassadors and other visitors at the public inns (καταγωγαῖς). On the other hand, there were inns of the lowest description. At the same port of Cæsarea there would doubtless be a number of taverns for sailors (cf. Jos. *BJ* i. xxi. 7). The numerous Talmudic references to inns (which, of course, must be used with some degree of caution) indicate that they were a distinct feature of social life, *e.g.* 'a public inn in which Israelites come and go' (*Aboda Zara*, v. 3); 'An Israelite and a heathen were once at an inn drinking wine' (*ib.*); 'R. Papa used to stand outside the store of the heathen and drink his beer' (ii. 4). R. Ishmael bar Jose declared that his father used to pray in an inn (*Ber.* iv. 7); 'Cattle must not be placed in the inns of heathen' (*Aboda Zara*, ii. 1).

There can be little doubt that there were numerous taverns where food as well as drink could be obtained (cf. Franz Delitzsch, *Jewish Artizan Life in the Time of Christ*, p. 47). Not only heathen were innkeepers, but Jews; not only men, but women. 'A Jewish woman dealing in wine once left her keys in charge of a heathen, and the question came up whether her wine she has in the tavern is allowed' (*Aboda Zara*, v. 3).

Jülicher (*Gleichnisreden*, ii. p. 590; cf. Bertholet,

[*] See Talm. Bab. *Kethub.* 105a; Jerus. *Megilla*, 73d (although, of course, the 400 is a characteristic exaggeration).

Die Stellung der Israeliten und der Juden zu den Fremden, p. 24) rightly maintains that the inn of Lk 10[34], to which the good Samaritan took his patient, was a hostelry ('nicht blos Caravanserai sondern Gasthaus'). The word used in this passage (πανδοχεῖον) is significant. It was taken over into Rabbinic Hebrew, and is the usual word (פונדקא) for 'inn' in the Talmud. The Greek name shows that inns were largely a product of the Hellenistic period (see Schürer, *HJP* II. i. 33). Other Rabbinic terms, אשפיזא and אכסניא, are equivalents of *hospitium* and ξενία; and as these replace the OT terms מָלוֹן and גֵּרוּת, they seem to indicate that something is intended quite different from the *khan* of the lonely road or the 'lodging-place of wayfaring men in the wilderness' (Jer 9[2]).

It is difficult to fix the exact significance of κατάλυμα, the other word used in the Gospels for 'inn.' Etymologically, it means 'the place where burdens were loosed for the night.' In Lk 2[7] it is generally taken to mean an inn of the *khan* type. Polybius uses it in the plural form (II. xxxvi. 1). Diodorus (xiv. 93) relates that the Romans, in gratitude for the services of one Timasitheus, granted him δημόσιον κατάλυμα.* The κατάλυμα of Mk 14[14] and Lk 22[11], where the Last Supper was eaten, is generally supposed to have been a private house (Hastings' *DB*, art. 'Inn'); and the use of the verb καταλύω, as in Lk 19[7], is quite in keeping with this. Nothing very definite, however, can be deduced from these names as to the precise character of the place of lodging.

Did Jesus Himself ever enter or stay at inns? It is usually assumed that His disciples always provided hospitality for Him. Yet the only recorded cases in which He accepted it are those of Peter's house at Capernaum and the house at Bethany. The words, 'the Son of Man hath not where to lay his head' (Mt 8[20], Lk 9[58]), suggest that hospitality was not always forthcoming. We know that it was not in Samaria (Lk 9[52]) and among the Gerasenes (8[37]). During a considerable part of the year it would be no hardship to spend the night in the open air, and apparently Jesus often preferred this, that He might have opportunity for quiet prayer, and more privacy than would be possible in a house or an inn. (Cf. J. L. Porter, *Giant Cities of Bashan*, 1866, pp. 157–159; also, for the habits of St. Francis and his followers, P. Sabatier, *Vie*, 1894, p. 88 f.). There is, however, no reason against His having resorted upon occasion to places of public entertainment. These were sometimes kept by Jews; but, if kept by a Gentile, this would not necessarily deter Him from going in. Strict Jews objected to entering the house of a Gentile, lest they should incur defilement (Jn 18[28], cf. Hausrath, *Hist. NT Times*, ii. 85); but Jesus, while recognizing that His mission was to Jews primarily, never allowed His action to be limited by ceremonial considerations. For instance, He did not hesitate, in spite of protest, to visit the house of Zacchæus, and the freedom of His intercourse with all kinds of people brought on Him the charge of being a 'wine-bibber,' and of consorting with the lowest classes (Mt 11[19], Lk 7[34]). His desire to seek 'the lost' suggests that He would not avoid the places where these were most likely to be found.

In this connexion it is interesting to note that the Talmud has the following passage: 'In the time of the Messiah the people will be impudent, and be given to drinking; publichouses will flourish, and the vine will be dear' (*Soṭa*, quoted in M'Clintock and Strong's *Cyc.*, art. 'Inn').

The reputation of inns seems to have been generally bad; they were very often houses of ill-fame, and hostesses were looked upon with suspicion.

* In inscriptions in the Hauran we find δημόσιον πανδοχεῖον (Le Bas and Waddington, vol. iii. n. 2462).

Yet some of the larger inns would bear a better character and be centres of influence, and there is no reason why Jesus should not have visited them. In most countries and periods the itinerant preacher has found the public inn to be a soil where the word might readily take root. (Cf. Fox, *Journal*, 1901, vol. i. pp. 118, 261, 258; Wesley, *Journal*, under March 1738; Borrow, *Bible in Spain, passim*).

LITERATURE.—Ramsay, art. 'Roads and Travel (in NT)' in Hastings' *DB*, Ext. Vol., under *Inns and Entertainment*.

J. ROSS MURRAY.

INNOCENCE.—Innocence, strictly speaking, denotes the entire absence of sin in a human soul. As such, in its primary meaning, we have no personal experience of it in ourselves or in others. 'For all have sinned and come short of the glory of God' (Ro 3[23]). We can, therefore, have no actual knowlege of what would be the effect of this quality upon a human character. In this sense it is an attribute of Jesus Christ alone among men, who 'was in all points tempted like as we are, yet without sin' (He 4[15]); 'who knew no sin' (2 Co 5[21]); who could address to His watchful foes the challenge, 'Which of you convicteth me of sin?' (Jn 8[46]). The gulf between innocence and the state of the soul that has once committed sin can be realized only as we comprehend the nature of sin and its immeasurable depravity and consequences. See art. SINLESSNESS. (For the subject of our Lord's innocence of the charges which led to His crucifixion, see art. TRIAL OF JESUS CHRIST).

Innocence in a comparative sense may be attributed to men who, though fallen, are yet, in respect of particular sins, innocent, or who from circumstances of upbringing, or by the special grace of God, are shielded from that knowledge of sin by personal experience which is the common lot of men. Such a man was John the Baptist, who 'was in the deserts until the day of his showing unto Israel' (Lk 1[80]). It has been said that there are only two states of life open to the man who wishes to serve God. The one is the state of innocence, the other of penitence. John the Baptist may be taken as a type of the one, St. Peter of the other. It must not be supposed that innocence implies ignorance or weakness. If John the Baptist, in whose life no fall is recorded, the essence of whose career is one unbroken record of devotion to the service of God, be taken as a type of innocence, he is pre-eminently the stern masculine type of character, and he displays great knowledge of men and power of dealing with the varied temptations of soldiers, publicans, and professors of religion.

The temptation specially addressed to innocence is the knowledge of evil as well as good (Gn 3[5]), but the experience of evil which entails the irrecoverable loss of innocence is not wisdom in the true sense of the word. 'The knowledge of wickedness is not wisdom' (Sir 19[22]). Innocence possesses an intuitive perception of right and wrong, observable in the child, which becomes blunted by the indulgence of sin; it also implies a strength which is lost by a fall. Each successive lapse from innocence makes the soul weaker in that particular direction in which the fall has taken place.

For further treatment of this subject the reader may be referred to a sermon on the subject in Illingworth's *University and Cathedral Sermons*, p. 99 ff.

M. R. NEWBOLT.

INNOCENTS.—In Mt 2[16-18] we find the narrative of what is called the Massacre of the Innocents. Adopting the language of Jer 31[15], the Evangelist represents Rachel, the ancestral mother of the people of Israel, as weeping over the cruel death of her children. Herod the Great, hearing from the Magi about the birth of a king of the Jews, foreshadowed by the star in the East which they had followed, inquired of the chief priests and scribes where this promised prince should be born. They quoted to him the words of Micah (5²), who speaks of the governor ruling Israel, who is to come out of Bethlehem in Judah, the city of David. When the Magi, having offered their gifts before the young child at Bethlehem, refused to inform Herod, but returned to their own country another way, the enraged king gave orders that all the children from two years old and under should be slain. This was done with much cruelty, so that in Bethlehem and the surrounding country there was great lamentation.

The truth of this story has been questioned. The chief ground is the silence of Josephus on the subject. While he speaks of many cruel deeds of Herod, he passes this one by. But it is plainly quite of a piece with Herod's well-known character, and, indeed, compared with his other deeds of monstrous cruelty, it would easily escape notice. The whole number of victims, probably not more than twenty or thirty, would not make a very great sensation at that time. Besides, the whole of Josephus' statements in regard to the Messianic expectations and doings of his time are to be looked upon with some suspicion, for he seems to have been afraid to make many clear and direct allusions to those matters. See INFANCY.

The deed illustrates well Herod's general character for bloodthirsty cruelty and short-sighted folly. But all his efforts to defeat the purposes of God with His people turn out to be vain. Joseph, warned in a dream by the angel, took Mary and the young child hastily down to Egypt, where they could calmly await the death of the tyrant. Heaven's vengeance soon fell on the blood-stained usurper, dyed with so many inhuman crimes, and he passed away from earth under the maledictions of his down-trodden people.

LITERATURE.—Hastings' *DB*, art. 'Herod'; Schaff-Herzog, *Encyc. of Rel. Knowl.*, art. 'Innocents' Day'; Farrar, *Christ in Art*, p. 268 ff.; C. Rossetti, *Verses*, p. 57.

D. M. W. LAIRD.

INSCRIPTION.—See TITLE ON CROSS.

INSECTS.—See ANIMALS, p. 67ᵃ.

INSIGHT.—In ordinary literary usage the word 'insight' is employed to signify the intellectual apprehension of the cause or processes to which an object or event owes its origin, as distinguished from the mere perception of the object or event itself. We get an insight into the working of a steam-engine, *e.g.*, when we have mastered the principles of engineering; or into some great political crisis, when the various motives that acted upon the minds of the statesmen who took part in it are revealed to us. Insight is also used to designate the faculty that penetrates into the causes that lie behind appearances. A man of practical insight is a man of quick discernment of the principles that determine the appearance of the objects or events that are recurrent in the business or intercourse of life. A man of political insight is a man who instinctively understands what the community will think, desire, or do at any particular period or special conjunction of circumstances.

In the spiritual or metaphysical sphere, 'insight' has the same double meaning. It is the immediate apprehension of the spiritual significance of truths that can be stated as objective facts. It is also the faculty of the higher reason which intuitively grasps this spiritual significance. Goethe says: 'There are men who put their knowledge in the place of insight.' Here the word is used in the first sense of intuitive apprehension of spiritual truth. 'Jealousy to resist metaphor,' says Francis Newman, 'does not testify to depth of insight.' Here it is the faculty that is referred to. The limits or even the precise nature of this faculty of insight have never been adequately defined. It is used of those subtle processes of thought that elude the syllogistic reason, but with which all are more or less familiar in experience. It is used also to designate that higher faculty of the soul through which the mystic claims to attain to the immediate cognition of the Absolute in its pure being.

Generally it may be said that, in the religious meaning of the word, insight is direct perception of, or the faculty of the soul that perceives, the spiritual order that lies behind phenomena. Sight sees the visible, the phenomenal; insight grasps the invisible, the noumenal. The very definition involves a theory. It implies that there is in the universe a spiritual order, of which man is a constituent element, to perceive; that the noumenal is real, and that what is called immediate cognition of it conveys genuine knowledge, knowledge that can be relied upon as a safe guide to action. It is clear that this theory cannot be proved by any of the ordinary processes of reasoning, seeing it is the result of an immediate cognition which is valid only for the individual. Sight carries its own evidence; and insight, which is the higher sight, must do the same. Truths which come to us through insight, and which press themselves home to the soul with irresistible conviction, must prove themselves in experience by their power of explaining the facts and solving the problems of life. Experience must be the ultimate test of reality. Truths of insight are the postulates of experience. The soul recognizes its immediate cognitions as corresponding with reality, because they are necessary to make its experience rational.

It is a characteristic of Jesus that with Him sight is insight. The spiritual vision is to Him so clear that it is unnecessary to designate the faculty or its object by another term. Jesus is the only-begotten Son which is in the bosom of the Father (Jn 1¹⁸)—the Logos which was with God and which was God (v.¹). Jesus sees God as no man can see Him, for human vision of God can only be through the light with which He illumines the soul (v.¹⁸). Because of this unique relation with the ultimate spiritual Reality, His insight into the nature of God is a clear and open vision. The claims He makes, therefore, as to His intimate union with God are the outcome of a personal consciousness which is part of His essential being. It is similar to our own assurance of selfhood. When Jesus says, 'I and the Father are one' (10³⁰), He is as certain of the fact as when we say, 'I am I.' For Jesus is living in a realm where the object of consciousness is not deflected and refracted by the illusions of sense or the distortions of passion, but where the spirit sees things as they are. It is the realm of pure Reality. There the soul sees what is, not what seems to be. And, further, Jesus thus living in the Absolute and Eternal, sees the lives of men and the processes of history purely in the light of their spiritual issues. What touches His consciousness in the great human drama is the hidden movement that is working out human destiny. With Him the fact is merely the symbol, and the symbol has become so luminous that His vision is always of the spiritual processes of which it is an indication. Browning in the *Epistle of Karshish, the Arab Physician*, has made a daring attempt to get into a consciousness similar to that of Jesus, by trying to imagine how a man whose soul had assimilated the pure spiritual environment of heaven, would feel and act were he permitted to come back to earth and to envisage life from the standpoint of the new experience. It would be—

'Heaven opened to a soul while yet on earth,
Earth forced on a soul's use while seeing heaven.'

The attempt is strikingly suggestive, but Lazarus remains a man with a finite soul, who cannot find his true function in what is now an alien environment. With Jesus this spiritual consciousness was so perfect that it mastered its alien environment and moved through it calmly and serenely, indicating its true place in the Divine purpose, and giving the right interpretation to all its manifestations. The teaching of Jesus is thus a key to the meaning of life, because He sees life in its essence, and has a sure insight into those hidden processes that are evolving the visible order of existence.

And again, from His very nature, the insight of Jesus into the individual souls of men is no less sure and unerring. He reads the human soul like an open book. He needed not that any should testify of man, for He knew what was in man (Jn 2^{25}). He could trace accurately the working of the ideas He was instilling into the minds of His disciples, as they mingled with their own crude religious conceptions (6^{61}). He understood perfectly the feeling of instinctive resistance that arose within the minds of the Pharisees at the impact of spiritual truth upon the hard crust of an artificial religionism which had become part of their very nature (Lk 6^8, Mt 12^{25}). And He recognized the uprising of a pure spiritual emotion in the hearts even of the most degraded when it was spontaneous and genuine (Lk 7^{47}), while He could repress and discourage the most fervent offer of devotion when He detected in it a vein of insincerity (9$^{57.58}$). It was this insight into human nature which was the secret of His amazing power over men in the days of His flesh. It is a faculty possessed by men in very varying degrees. Its accuracy and intensity depend upon the richness of a man's nature—upon his knowledge of and sympathy with the gamut of human emotion. There have been many men of wonderful insight, and therefore of strong personal magnetism. But man's insight is always obscured by individual bias and by the obstruction of the medium of sense which conceals the soul's working. Men are always more or less deceived, and even men of the keenest insight often break down in their reading of character at the point where it is most essential for them to be right. Jesus was perfect man, and therefore His sympathy with men was full and entire, and touched human nature at every point. For Jesus, who viewed human life in the light of eternity, the sense-medium did not exist. It was the spirit that was always before His vision, and therefore His knowledge of the human heart was instinctive and unerring. Hence it was that the method of Jesus in dealing with diverse types of character is so full of suggestiveness and instruction.

This conception of the consciousness of Jesus must be kept clearly in mind when we study His sayings. His is a consciousness that moves freely in the realm of pure Reality, and visualizes God, human destiny, and the individual soul in the light of their eternal relations. Hence those marvellous revelations of the essence of the Divine Nature in its correspondence to human needs and human aspirations. Hence, too, it results that it is the spiritual meaning of human actions alone that gives them value to Him, and the measure of their value is the degree of spiritual vitality they indicate. Thus Jesus continually reverses the valuations of the world, which are based on the theory of the reality of the objects of sense-perception. He that is greatest among men is he that is the servant of all (Mk 9^{35}). The two mites thrown by the widow into the Temple treasury are a more munificent offering than the costly gifts of the Pharisees, because they represent a greater degree of sacrifice (12$^{43.44}$). The action of Mary in breaking over the head of Jesus the alabaster box of very precious ointment, is one of the memorable events of history, because it indicates a fine perception of what is due to the Lord of life at the supremely critical moment of world-development (Mk 14^3, Jn 12^3). Jesus gives to the penitent thief the assurance of immediate entry into Paradise, because full and adequate penitence for sin is itself the crossing of the threshold of the spiritual realm (Lk 23^{43}). If this clue be rigorously applied, it solves many of the difficulties that beset a literal exegesis of the words of Jesus. It is especially significant when we study His apocalyptic utterances. Here the difficulty of interpretation frequently lies in the fact that the commentator often attempts to force upon them a materialistic meaning that was never intended. Language is material, and has been constructed primarily to indicate the phenomena of sense-perception. When it is used to describe spiritual processes, the ideas conveyed must be detached from the medium of conveyance, if they are to be rightly understood. Jesus lived in the noumenal world. What He saw there He could convey to the souls of His hearers only by the use of words that had been coined to connote totally different conceptions. When Nathanael, struck by Jesus' recognition of him under the fig-tree, hails Him as the Son of God, Jesus says: 'Because I said unto thee, I saw thee under the fig-tree, believest thou? . . . Verily, verily, I say unto you, *Henceforth* ye shall see heaven open, and the angels of God ascending and descending upon the Son of man' (Jn 1$^{50.51}$). It is significant that the AV translates ἀπ' ἄρτι 'hereafter.' The translators were evidently dominated by the idea that Jesus is describing a physical marvel which Nathanael will witness in the distant future. But Jesus clearly means that the intercourse of Nathanael with Himself will bring heaven to his soul, and enable him to realize that a living link of communication has been established between God and man.

The words of Jesus regarding death, judgment, His second coming, and the life to come, can be interpreted with rigorous precision, even although they clothe spiritual conceptions with a material garb. They are not mere metaphors, for a metaphor is rarely, if ever, the exact counterpart of the idea it illustrates. Jesus is dwelling in eternity and contemplating the processes of the spiritual world, and He conveys to the receptive soul by the only medium at His command the impression He Himself receives from His direct vision of the truth He is envisaging. The medium is of value only in so far as it serves its purpose. To the irresponsive soul it has no meaning or value at all. To the soul that has the faculty of vision the words are luminous, and reveal God's secrets. There is no question here of metaphor except in so far as nine-tenths of spoken words are metaphorical. There is nothing overstrained or untrue.

The bearing of this on the doctrine of Revelation cannot here be overlooked. Revelation is insight in its intensest form. The revelation granted to the prophets in OT times was their insight into the meaning of God's ways, their vision of the spiritual processes through which the higher life of humanity is evolved. The revelation granted to the Apostles was their response to the brilliancy of the light that streamed from the Eternal Word during the brief period of His Incarnation. Jesus reveals because He is the Light of the world. He never argues. He knows nothing of the dialectic process in pressing home the higher truths to the soul. He sees and He would have others to see, and only in so far as they see is He capable of blessing them (Jn 12⁴⁴· ⁴⁶). It follows that all revelation is personal, and incommunicable from one man to another. Only the Triune God is the Revealer of the spiritual mystery. A written revelation is thus, in the strict meaning of the words, a contradiction in terms. The Bible is not a revelation, but a record of a series of revelations that were given to men of insight, men who possessed the faculty of vision. Its purpose is not to reveal, but to put the soul in an attitude of expectancy by telling what other men have seen. It is the Holy Spirit that quickens the soul and conveys the gift of vision to which alone Divine Truth can be revealed. This is everywhere the doctrine of Scripture, and has never been more clearly or beautifully stated than in the *Westminster Confession of Faith* (ch. i. par. 5).

Jesus invariably attaches a knowledge of the Divine mysteries to a certain spiritual attitude apart from which nothing can be known. It is the pure in heart who see God (Mt 5⁸). It is the doer of God's will who alone can judge of the truth of His doctrine (Jn 7¹⁶· ¹⁷). The sin of the Pharisees is that they are blind while they think they see (9⁴¹). No matter with what brilliancy the light may shine, so long as the spiritual orb is darkened it can reveal nothing of the wonders of the spirit-land (1¹²). And St. Paul says that no man knoweth the things of God; it is the Spirit of God alone who knoweth them; and only in so far as the spirit of man is illumined by the Spirit of God can they be revealed to him (1 Co 2¹¹). Only when the Divine in man meets and mingles with the Divine that is without and around him can there result that spiritual certainty which is revelation.

Insight, then, in the spiritual sense of the term (which is the sense in which it is generally used), links itself on to the doctrine of the Holy Spirit (wh. see). It is the Light that lighteth every man coming into the world; for we must assume that the capacity, in germ at least, is universal as humanity, otherwise there would be some to whom religion is impossible. But it is given in varying degrees, and is conditioned by varying environments. The visions it sees are not always of reality, for the medium through which it looks is often obscured by earthly passions and prejudices. But when it does see right into the heart of things, it enunciates truths to which the soul clings as essential to its very life.

Literature.—Knight, *Aspects of Theism; Maxims and Reflections of Goethe* (tr. by Bailey Saunders); Gilchrist, *Life of William Blake*; F. W. Newman, *The Soul*; Hibbert Lectures on *Basis of Religious Belief,* by C. B. Upton; James, *Varieties of Religious Experience*; Ewald, *Revelation, its Nature and its Record*; Oman, *Vision and Authority*; W. P. du Bose, *The Ecumenical Councils*; Herrmann, *Verkehr des Christen mit Gott*; Meister Eckhart, *Schriften und Predigten,* Leipzig, 1903.

A. Miller.

INSPIRATION.—The term employed to denote the action of the Divine Spirit upon the writers of Scripture. Literally signifying *a breathing into,* it has the secondary meaning of breathing a certain spirit into the mind or soul, and is therefore naturally employed to express the influence of God upon the sacred writers. ' Inspiration in general is the influence of one person upon another; Divine inspiration is the influence of the Divine Person upon the human ' (Wood, *A Tenable Theory of Insp.* p. 10). In Scripture itself we find the idea in Hos 9⁷ (LXX) expressed by the word πνευματοφόρος — though in this case the inspiration was not Divine. In the NT (2 P 1²¹) similarly ὑπὸ πνεύματος ἁγίου φερόμενοι. In non-Christian literature inspired men are spoken of as θεοδίδακτοι, θεόφοροι, θεοφορούμενοι, θεόδοχοι, θεόπνευστοι, ἔνθεοι, ἐπίπνοοι, βακχευόμενοι, μαινόμενοι, *divino numine afflati, inspirati, furentes.* The use of the word ' inspiration ' to express the

Divine factor in Scripture is probably derived from the fact that the words of 2 Ti 3¹⁶ πᾶσα γραφὴ θεόπνευστος are rendered in the Vulgate 'omnis Scriptura divinitus inspirata.' The definition given by Lee (*Insp.* p. 27 f.) is sufficient as conveying the general idea attached to the word. ' By inspiration I understand that actuating energy of the Holy Spirit, in whatever degree or manner it may have been exercised, guided by which the human agents chosen by God have *officially* proclaimed His will by word of mouth, or have committed to writing the several portions of the Bible.' Sanday's explanation of the word is excellent : ' Just as one particular branch of one particular stock was chosen to be in a general sense the recipient of a clearer revelation than was vouchsafed to others, so within that branch certain individuals were chosen to have their hearts and minds moved in a manner more penetrating and more effective than their fellows, with the result that their written words convey to us truths about the nature of God and His dealings with man which other writings do not convey with equal fulness, power, and purity. We say that this special moving is due to the action upon those hearts and minds of the Holy Spirit. And we call that action Inspiration' (*Bampton Lect.* p. 127). Or we may say that as God revealed Himself in creation, in the history of His people, and especially in Jesus Christ, He also enabled certain persons to perceive and express the significance of that revelation; and this ability is what we mean by inspiration.

Inspiration is claimed not only for our Scriptures, but for the other sacred books of the world. The Vedas, the books of Zoroaster and of the Buddhists, the Koran, all rest their claim to be received on the belief that they proceed from a Divine source. Even where tribes are too uncivilized to possess sacred writings, there exists a belief that God makes known His mind through dreams, oracles, or inspired individuals; and the presence and influence of God is frequently spoken of as an afflatus, the blowing of a breath or wind upon the inspired person. To the idea that knowledge is supernaturally conveyed to persons who are not in the historic line of Scriptural revelation, sanction is given in the OT by the instances of Abimelech, Pharaoh, and Balaam. And while in the sacred books of the world there is a great deal that is superstitious, contemptible, and degrading, there is also much that illustrates man's thirst for God, and much also to show that God responds to that thirst. We naturally expect to find a fuller inspiration in those who were in touch with, and were called to record, the great progressive historical revelation which culminated in Christ; but we need not therefore deny all Divine response and assistance to those who on other lines were setting their faces Godwards.

1. The claim of Scripture to be inspired.— The OT was accepted as inspired both by the NT writers and by all their Jewish contemporaries. At that date certain of the books eventually included in the OT had not been definitely admitted to canonical authority; but, speaking generally, the writings of the OT were universally held to be Divine, sacred, in some true sense the word of God. Of this there is abundant evidence.

(*a*) Our Lord Himself appeals to the OT as a final authority (Mt 19⁴, Jn 5⁴⁶). He refers to it as the prophetic index to, and justification of, the providential dealings of God (Lk 24⁴⁴, Jn 10³⁵). Expressly, in citing Ps 110, He introduces the quotation with the words, ' David himself by the Holy Spirit said ' (αὐτὸς Δαυεὶδ εἶπεν ἐν τῷ πνεύματι τῷ ἁγίῳ), Mk 12³⁶. And significantly in adducing the Law in contrast to the traditions of the elders, the highest human authority, He altogether neglects the human mediation of the writer, and simply says, 'For God said' (Mt 15⁴). His personal reliance upon Scripture is visible in His use of it as His defence in the stress of temptation (Mt 4⁴. ⁷. ¹⁰) and as the authentication of His ministry (Lk 4¹⁷⁻²¹). It was the OT which preserved the knowledge of the marvellous history of which He recognized Himself to be the culmination. In it He met all that was Divine in the past, and acknowledged the regulating Divine Spirit throughout.

(b) As with the Master, so with the disciples. In the First Gospel the writer has ever in his eye τὸ ῥηθὲν ὑπὸ κυρίου διὰ τοῦ προφήτου (1²²). In their first independent action the disciples were determined by their belief that they must fulfil the Scripture ἣν προεῖπεν τὸ πνεῦμα τὸ ἅγιον διὰ στόματος Δαυείδ (Ac 1¹⁶, cf. 28²⁵). For St. Paul as for St. Peter the utterances of the OT are the λόγια θεοῦ (Ro 3², 1 P 4¹¹). 'It is written' is the ultimate authority. The Scripture is identified with God, so that St. Paul can say (Ro 9¹⁷) 'the scripture saith unto Pharaoh'; and it is God who speaks in the prophets (9²⁵). In the Epistle to the Hebrews the same conception of Scripture prevails. Quotations are introduced with the formula, 'the Holy Spirit saith'; and the revelation of Christ is but the completion of the revelation of the OT. It was God who spoke in the prophets (He 1¹). The very titles under which the OT Scriptures are designated sufficiently manifest the belief that they were written under the inspiration of God. (For these titles, see Ryle, Canon of OT, p. 302).

(c) As representative of contemporary Jewish thought it is enough to cite Philo and Josephus. The former explicitly affirms the inspiration of Moses, speaking of him as 'that purest mind which received at once the gift of legislation and of prophecy with Divinely inspired wisdom' (θεοφορήτῳ σοφίᾳ, de Congr. Erud. c. 24, ed. Mangey, i. 538) and as καταπνευσθεὶς ὑπ᾽ ἔρωτος οὐρανίου (de Vita Mos., Mangey, ii. 145). To Isaiah and Jeremiah 'as members of the prophetic choir,' he expressly ascribes inspiration (τοῦ προφητικοῦ θιασώτης χοροῦ, ὃς καταπνευσθεὶς ἐνθουσιῶν ἀνεφθέγξατο, de Conf. Ling. c. 12, Mangey, i. 411). Josephus is equally explicit. Vying with Philo in reverential esteem for the OT, he bases this esteem on the belief that the authors of the various books wrote under the influence of the Divine Spirit (Ant. IV. viii. 49, III. v. 4, X. ii. 2; cf. c. Apion. i. 7).

No belief of later Judaism was more universal or constant than this acceptance of the OT Scriptures as inspired. 'Die heilige Schrift ist entstanden durch Inspiration des heiligen Geistes, stammt also von Gott selbst ab, der in ihr redet.' This statement of Weber's (Lehren d. Talmud, p. 78) is amply justified by the passages he cites, as, e.g., 'He who affirms that the Thora is not from heaven, has no part in the future world' (Sanhed. x. 1). Bousset (Die Religion d. Judentums, p. 125) reaches the same conclusion : 'Die heiligen Schriften sind nach spätjüdischem Dogma inspiriert.'

This belief in the inspiration of the OT was the natural and inevitable result of the phenomena it presented ; and was not, as has sometimes been suggested, the mere reflexion of the vague idea that all ancient writings, especially if poetical, were inspired.* Moses is represented as speaking face to face with God and as receiving the Law from Him. The prophets demand attention to their words by prefacing them with the announcement, 'Thus saith the Lord.' In Ex 4¹⁰⁻¹², Is 59²¹, Jer 1⁷⁻⁹ the equipment of the prophet is described by the expression, 'I have put my words in thy mouth.' From these two phenomena it was

* Cf. Hatch, Hibbert Lect. p. 51.

a necessary inference that at any rate the Law and the Prophets were inspired. Prof. Sanday (Insp. p. 128) justly remarks that 'the prophetic inspiration seems to be a type of all inspiration. It is perhaps the one mode in which the most distinctive features of Biblical inspiration can be most clearly recognized.' It must, however, also be borne in mind that among the Jews themselves it was the Law, rather than the Prophets, which satisfied, and perhaps suggested, their idea of inspiration. Latterly they went so far as to say that, had the Law found in Israel recipients worthy of it, nothing beyond would have been required. The Law itself was a perfect and complete revelation, and neither Prophets nor Hagiographa were indispensable (see passages in Weber, Lehren d. Talm. p. 79). The response of conscience to the Law confirmed the traditional accounts of its origin, and the belief in its inspiration was inevitable. Possibly it was the belief that the whole OT was normative that prompted the usage by which even the Prophets and the Psalms were cited in the NT as 'the Law' (see Jn 15²⁵ 10³⁴, 1 Co 14²¹, Ro 3¹⁹).

The inspiration of the NT stands on a somewhat different footing. The supreme instance of inspiration is our Lord Himself (Lk 4¹⁷⁻²¹); and He is also its source to His followers. At His Baptism, Jesus was formally called to, and equipped for, His ministry; and His equipment consisted in His receiving the fulness of the Holy Spirit. Under the influence of this Spirit all His works were done and all His words spoken. 'He whom God hath sent speaketh the words of God, for he giveth not the Spirit by measure' (Jn 3³⁴) ; 'My teaching is not mine, but his that sent me' (7¹⁶) ; 'as the Father hath taught me, I speak these things' (8²⁸). And it is His words, spoken under the influence of the Divine Spirit, that form the nucleus of the NT Canon. They were the first portion of that Canon to be recognized as authoritative, and however difficult certain writings found it to gain access to the Canon, the words of our Lord were from the first, and universally, regarded as Divine by all Christians.

But those whom He appointed to be His witnesses and to explain to the world the significance of His manifestation, required above all else the inspiration of the Author of salvation. This was emphatically and reiteratedly promised to them. The presence of the Divine Spirit was promised not only to prompt and support them on critical occasions, as when they were summoned before magistrates (Mk 13¹¹, Mt 10²⁰, Lk 12¹¹), but as the Spirit of truth He was promised as the very substitute of Christ Himself : 'He shall teach you all things, and bring to your remembrance all that I said unto you' (Jn 14²⁶ 16¹³). This promise cannot be understood as meant to assure the disciples that they would be able to recall every word their Lord had said ; as little as this assurance is conveyed to all Christians by the words of St. John (1 Jn 2²⁷), 'His anointing teacheth you concerning all things.' At the same time it was meant to encourage them to believe that their sympathy with their Lord and their acceptance of His Spirit would give them a sufficient remembrance and understanding of His teaching.

That this promise was fulfilled is certain. The relation of the risen Lord to His Church, His presence with those who represented Him, and the aid He afforded them in accomplishing His purposes, compel the conclusion that His Spirit dwelt in those who taught and built up the Church by word and letter. Those who preached the gospel discharged their function 'with the Holy Ghost sent down from heaven' (1 P 1¹²). Of this the outpouring of the Spirit at Pentecost was the earnest. In guiding the Church the aid of this

Spirit was experienced (Ac 13² 15²⁸ etc.). In writing to the Galatians, St. Paul claims to have been instructed by the Lord in the gospel he preached. In 2 Co 13³ he is prepared to give 'a proof of Christ that speaketh in me.' And even in less essential matters regarding which he can claim no definite instructions or revelation, he yet in the exercise of his own judgment believes himself to be guided by the Spirit of God (1 Co 7⁴⁰). In his enumeration of the various manifestations of the Spirit, the writing of sacred books, it is true, finds no place, neither do the writers of the Gospels claim to be inspired. But 'the word of wisdom,' 'the word of knowledge,' the charism of the prophet and the teacher, may quite reasonably, if not even necessarily, be supposed to include written as well as spoken discourse.

2. THE SIGNIFICANCE OF THE CLAIM TO BE INSPIRED, OR THE MEANING AND EFFECTS OF INSPIRATION.—Several opinions or theories present themselves. And in determining which of these is correct, we must be guided not by *a priori* ideas of the results which must flow from inspiration, but only by the phenomena presented in the Bible; in other words, by the actual effects of inspiration as these are seen in the writings of inspired men. 'What inspiration is must be learned from what it does. . . . We must not determine the character of the books from the inspiration, but must rather determine the nature of the inspiration from the books' (Bowne's *Christian Revelation*, p. 45).

(1) *The 'mechanical' or 'dictation' theory, or theory of verbal inspiration.*—This is the theory that in writing the books of Scripture the human author was merely the mouthpiece of the Divine, and that therefore every word in the Bible as truly represents the mind of God as if He had dictated it. 'Facts, doctrines, precepts, references to history or chronology, quotations from writers sacred or profane, allusions to scientific truth, visions or prophetic declarations, mere references to the most ordinary actions of life, according to this view, are not the work of man but of Omniscience. The only use which has been made of human agency in the book has been to copy down with pen, ink, and paper what has been dictated by the Divine Spirit.' Absolute inerrancy is on this theory presumed to be the accompaniment of inspiration. As one of its defenders says: 'God employed men in writing. But these men were so controlled by Him, that He is the Author of the writing; and so the Author, that any charge of inaccuracy against the record, or Scripture, as originally given, must be preferred against Him' (Kennedy, *The Doctrine of Insp.* 1878, p. 6). To use the common way of putting it, the writers were 'the pens, not the penmen' of God. They were possessed by God, so that it was not so much their own mind and their own experience, but the mind of God that was represented in their writings.*

This theory has all the prestige which antiquity can give it, for it runs back to those primitive stages of civilization in which possession by a deity was produced by inhaling fumes, or by violent dancings and contortions. This frenzied state being induced, the words spoken were believed to be Divine. The theory has also the prestige which

is conferred by the advocacy of great names. Plato countenanced the idea that the inspired man is so possessed by the Divine that his words and thoughts are not his own. In the *Timæus* (p. 71) and in the *Phædrus* (p. 244) he maintains that when a man receives the inspired word, either his intelligence is enthralled in sleep, or he is demented by some distemper or possession. The relation of the Divine to the human is viewed quantitatively. As the Divine comes in, the human must go out and make room for it. It was probably through Philo that this view gained currency in the Church. Philo's account of Inspiration is quite explicit. 'A prophet,' he says, 'gives forth nothing of his own, but acts as interpreter at the prompting of another in all his utterances; and as long as he is under inspiration he is in ignorance, his reason departing from its place and yielding up the citadel of his soul, when the Divine Spirit enters into it and dwells in it, and strikes at the mechanism of his voice, sounding through it to the clear declaration of that which he prophesieth' (*de Sp. Legg.* ii. 343, quoted in Sanday's *Insp.* p. 74). Again (in the tract *Quis rer. div.* i. 511) Philo explains that 'so long as we are masters of ourselves we are not possessed; but when our own mind ceases to shine, inspiration and madness lay hold on us. For the understanding that dwells in us is ousted on the arrival of the Divine Spirit, but is restored to its own dwelling when that Spirit departs; for it is unlawful that mortal dwell with immortal.' A theory identical with or similar to this of Philo's has been largely held in the Church.

There are also expressions in the NT which seem, at first sight, to countenance such a theory. In Mt 5¹⁸ our Lord is reported as saying: 'Till heaven and earth pass away, one jot or one tittle shall in nowise pass from the law, till all things be accomplished.' But, as the context shows, that which our Lord intimates in these words is that it was in Himself the Law and the Prophets were to find their fulfilment. Immediately upon giving utterance to this saying He Himself proceeds to repeal commandments of the Law, substituting for them His own better principles, and thus showing that what He had in view was not Scripture as Scripture. Another passage which to the superficial reader might seem to countenance this theory is that in which St. Paul contrasts the wisdom of God with the wisdom of men (1 Co 2¹⁻¹⁶). After speaking of the things revealed by the Spirit of God, he says, 'which things we also speak, not in words which man's wisdom teacheth, but which the Spirit teacheth' (v.¹³). But a consideration of the passage makes it apparent that what he means is that he had arrived at the conclusion that his style of address should be in keeping with his subject, and that 'the mystery of God' did not require the garnishing of meretricious ornament or anything which the world might esteem as 'excellency of wisdom,' but such simplicity and directness as the Holy Spirit prompted. He is contrasting two methods, two styles, the worldly and the spiritual, and he is justifying the style he himself adopted. To conclude from this that St. Paul considered that every word he spoke was dictated by infallible wisdom is quite illegitimate.

This mechanical theory is beset by grave difficulties. (*a*) Inspiration and dictation are, as has more than once been pointed out, two different, even mutually exclusive, operations. Dictation precludes inspiration, leaving no room for any spiritual influence. Inspiration precludes dictation, making the prompting of words unnecessary by the communication of the right spirit.

(*b*) It is irreconcilable with the phenomena presented in Scripture. The authors, instead of being passive recipients of information and ideas and

---

* 'Omnes et singulæ res quæ in S. Scriptura continentur, sive illæ fuerint S. Scriptoribus naturaliter incognitæ, sive naturaliter quidem cogniscibiles, actu tamen incognitæ, sive denique non tantum naturaliter cogniscibiles, sed etiam actu ipso notæ, vel aliunde, vel per experientiam, et sensuum ministerium, non solum per assistentiam et directionem divinam infallibilem literis consignatæ sunt, sed singulari Spiritus S. suggestioni, inspirationi, et dictamini acceptæ ferendæ sunt' (Quenstedt, cited with other similar dicta, in *Hutterus Redivivus, s.v.* 'Inspiratio').

feelings, represent themselves as active, deliberating, laborious, intensely interested. The material used by the historical writers has been derived from written sources, or, as in the case of the Third Gospel, from careful critical inquiry at the most reliable witnesses. They do not tell us that their knowledge of events had been supernaturally imparted, but either that they themselves had seen what they relate, or that they had it from trustworthy sources. The Apostles were inspired witnesses of Christ, and proclaimed what they had seen and heard. But if supernatural information was even more trustworthy, why should they have been chosen only from those who had been with our Lord during His ministry? 'If they did not really remember those facts or discourses when they asserted their reality, they are found false witnesses of God. If they were the mere dictation of the Spirit to their minds, St. Peter's declaration which he made to the Jewish Council, "We cannot but speak the things which we have seen and heard," would have to be corrected into, "We cannot but speak the things which the Spirit has introduced into our minds"' (Row, *Insp.* p. 154). Similarly, if the intense emotions expressed in the Psalms or in the Epp. of St. Paul are not the outpouring of human sorrow and human experience, they at once become artificial and false. When St. Paul in 2 Co 11[17] says, 'That which I speak, I speak not after the Lord, but as in foolishness, in this confidence of boasting,' it is intelligible to say that an inspired man is speaking, it is not intelligible to say that this is God speaking. The mind of God is discernible through the words, but it is not the mind of God we are directly in contact with.

(c) Another class of phenomena presented by Scripture is inconsistent with this theory. For if God be the sole Author, then it is impossible to account for errors in grammar, imperfections of style, discrepancies between one part and another. But such errors, imperfections, and discrepancies exist. The sayings of our Lord are variously reported in the several Gospels. Even in reporting the Lord's Prayer the Evangelists differ. It is impossible to remove from the Book of Acts all disagreement with the Pauline Epistles. And in the disagreement between Peter and Paul at Antioch, we see how possible it was that men equally inspired should hold divergent and even antagonistic opinions upon matters essential to the well-being of the Church. In the face of these discrepancies, it is impossible to suppose that inspiration carries with it literal accuracy of expression.

(d) The manner in which the NT writers quote the OT books proves that while they believed these books to be authoritative and their writers inspired, they did not consider that their inspiration rendered every word they uttered infallible. Taking 275 quotations from the OT in the NT, it has been found that there are only 53 in which the Hebrew, the LXX, and the NT writer agree : while there are 99 passages in which the NT quotation differs both from the Hebrew and from the LXX, which also differ from one another, and 76 in which the correct rendering of the LXX has been erroneously altered.* No doubt when the correct citation of a single word serves the writer's purpose, as in the insistence by St. Paul on the singular instead of the plural (Gal 3[16]), there stress is laid upon the very word ; but in the face of the general style of quotation above indi-

* These statistics are taken from D. M'Calman Turpie's *OT in the NT*, 1868. There are many more quotations than those here given, but these give a fair sample of the whole. A full list of quotations is given in the 2nd vol. of Westcott and Hort's *Greek Testament*. And Dittmar in his *Vetus T. in Novo* gives the NT text, the LXX, and the Hebrew.

cated, it is impossible to believe that inspiration was supposed to make each word infallible.

(2) To escape the psychological and other difficulties of a mechanical, verbal inspiration, other theories have been devised. Observing the different values of the various books of Scripture, the Jews themselves supposed that there were *three degrees of inspiration* corresponding to the tripartite division of the OT. Attempts were made by the Rabbis, by the schoolmen, and by some modern writers to differentiate between suggestion, direction, superintendence, and elevation. Thus Bishop Daniel Wilson (*Evidences of Christianity*, i. 506, quoted by Lee) defines as follows : 'By the inspiration of *suggestion* is meant such communication of the Holy Spirit as suggested and dictated minutely every part of the truths delivered. The inspiration of *direction* is meant of such assistance as left the writers to describe the matter revealed in their own way, directing only the mind in the exercise of its powers. The inspiration of *elevation* added a greater strength and vigour to the efforts of the mind than the writers could otherwise have attained. The inspiration of *superintendency* was that watchful care which preserved generally from anything being put down derogatory to the Revelation with which it was connected.' Obviously this theory is very open to criticism. That there are different degrees of inspiration is true, but it is very questionable whether any such classification is complete. In this theory there are hints of truth, but not the whole truth.

(3) The so-called *dynamical theory* brings us somewhat nearer the truth, though it too falls short. This theory is a reaction against the mechanical, and affirms that the human qualities of the writers are not superseded, but are cleansed, strengthened, and employed by the Divine Author. 'The Divine influence acted upon man's faculties in accordance with their natural laws' ; classical expression is given to this theory in the words of Augustine (*in Joan.* I. i. 1), 'inspiratus a Deo, sed tamen homo.' The Divine Agent selects suitable media for His communications, and does not try 'to play lyre-music on flutes, and harp-music on trumpets.' The imperfections and weaknesses found in Scripture are human, the truths uttered are Divine. The theory in its most acceptable form, and as held by Erasmus, Grotius, Baxter, Paley, and many modern writers, suggests that the Biblical writers were so inspired as to secure accuracy in all matters of conduct and doctrine, while it declines to pledge itself to their perfect accuracy in non-essentials or subsidiary particulars. Hence it is sometimes called the 'essential' theory.

This theory, while it endeavours to recognize the facts of Scripture and to account for them, yet fails to give us an understanding of inspiration. It does not explain, or even attempt to explain, how writers should be possessed of supernatural knowledge while inditing one sentence, and in the next be dropped to a lower level. It fails to give us the psychology of that state of mind which can infallibly pronounce on matters of doctrine while it is astray on the often simpler facts of history. It makes no attempt to analyze the relation subsisting between the Divine mind and the human which produces such results. Nor does it explain how we are to distinguish essentials from non-essentials, or disentangle the one from the other.

(4) Constructively we may make the following affirmations regarding Inspiration, derived from the facts presented in the Bible :

(a) It is the *men*, not directly the writings, that were inspired. 'Men spake from God, being moved by the Holy Ghost' (2 P 1[21]). Inspiration does not mean that one inspired thought is magically communicated to a man in the form in which he is to declare it to his fellows, and in no connexion with the previous contents and normal action of his mind. As he sits down to write, he continues in that state of mind and spirit in which he has been living and to which the Spirit of God has brought him. The book he produces is not the abnormal, exceptional product of a unique condition of mind and spirit, but is the natural and spontaneous outflow from the previous experience and thought of the writer. All his past training and knowledge, all his past strivings to yield himself wholly to the Spirit of Christ, enter into what he now produces.

(b) When we say that a writer of Scripture is Divinely inspired, we mean that *as he writes he is under the influence of the Holy Spirit*. All Christians possess this same Spirit, and are by Him being led into a full knowledge of the truth that is in Christ, to a full perception of that whole revelation of God which is made in Christ; and when some of their number are *characterized* as inspired, this means that such persons are distinguished above their fellow-Christians by a special readiness and capacity to perceive the meaning of Christ as the revelation of God and to make known what they see.

(c) Inspiration is primarily a *spiritual* gift, and only secondarily a mental one. The Spirit of God may dwell richly in a man and yet not render him infallible even in matters of religion. In 1 Th 4⁹ St. Paul speaks of his converts as θεοδίδακτοι, but to one end, and that a spiritual not a mental end. Our Lord (Jn 6⁴⁵) applies to all those who come to Him in Spirit the prophetic words, 'They shall be all taught of God,' but no one can suppose that this involves infallible knowledge. It cannot be summarily argued that because God dwells in a man, all that the man speaks partakes of the Divine omniscience. Inspiration operates as any newborn passion, such as maternal love, operates. It does not lift the person out of all limitations, but it seizes upon and uses all the faculties, elevating, refining, and directing to one purpose. It illuminates the mind as enthusiasm does, by stimulating and elevating it; it enriches the memory as love does, by intensifying the interest in a certain object, and by making the mind sensitive to its impressions and retentive of them. It brings light to the understanding and wisdom to the spirit, as purity of intention or a high aim in life does. It brings a man into sympathy with the nature and purposes of God, enables him to see God where others do not see Him, and to interpret His revelations in the same Spirit in which they are given.

LITERATURE.—The history of opinion may partly be traced in Westcott's *Introd. to Study of Gospels*, Appendix on 'Primitive Doctrine of Insp.'; in Hagenbach's *Hist. of Doctrine*; and in Sanday's *Bampton Lectures*. Lutheran teaching is represented and traced in *Hutterus Redivivus*, and Anglican in Fitzjames Stephens' *Defence of the Rev. Rowland Williams* (1862).—From the mass of literature one or two representative books may be named: *The Insp. of Holy Scrip.*, by William Lee, 1854; *The Nature and Extent of Divine Insp.*, by Rev. C. A. Row, M.A., 1864; *Plenary Insp. of Holy Scrip.*, by Gaussen; *Insp. and the Bible*, by R. F. Horton; *A Tenable Theory of Insp.*, by Professor Wood; cf. also the present writer's *The Bible: its Origin and Nature*. Schleiermacher's interesting statement of his views occurs in *Der christliche Glaube*, iv. §§ 128–132. Weiss gives an excellent specimen of moderate opinion in *Die Religion d. NT*, p. 31 ff.
MARCUS DODS.

INSURRECTION (στάσις, Mk 15⁷, and Lk 23¹⁹·²⁵ where AV gives 'sedition') is defined by Plato (*Rep.* v. 470 B) thus: ἐπὶ γὰρ τῇ τοῦ οἰκείου ἔχθρᾳ στάσις κέκληται, ἐπὶ δὲ τῇ τῶν ἀλλοτρίων πόλεμος. Its use in these passages is important as showing that Barabbas was not merely a robber (λῃστής, Jn 18⁴⁰), but also a leader in one of those fierce fanatical outbursts which were so common in the last years of the Jewish nation, especially from the accession

of Herod. Josephus tells of notable leaders such as Ezekias, his son Judas, and his four grandsons, all of whom were put to death (*Ant.* XIV. ix. 2, XVII. x. 5, XVIII. i. 1; *BJ* II. iv. 1, viii. 1, xiii. 5, etc.; cf. Ac 5³⁶ᶠ· 21³⁸). Josephus in his account of the final troubles uses ζηλωτής and λῃστής almost as convertible terms. Nothing further is known of this particular στάσις, unless, as Ewald (*HI* vi. 67 f.) suggests, it may have arisen on account of the aqueduct which Pilate had built with money taken from the Temple treasury (Josephus, *BJ* II. ix. 4; cf. Lk 13⁴). Barabbas may have been moved by patriotic ideas at the first, becoming an outlaw and notorious robber when his rising was suppressed; or he may have used aspirations after freedom merely as a cloak for brigandage (see Westcott, *Some Lessons of the Revised Version of the NT*, p. 74 f.).* He was 'lying bound with them that had made insurrection' (στασιαστῶν, v.l. συστασιαστῶν, Mk 15⁷), including probably the two robbers who were crucified; for him the third cross may have been intended. Such men had a deep hold on the popular sympathy, which goes to explain the strong demand of the people for the release of their hero, and the interest which the priests showed on behalf of Barabbas, notwithstanding their pretence to holiness. But the hollowness of their new-found zeal for Cæsar was thereby exposed, seeing that Barabbas was admittedly guilty of the crime which they alleged against Jesus. See, further, BARABBAS.

LITERATURE.—Edersheim, *Life and Times of Jesus the Messiah*, ii. 576 ff.; Trench, *Studies in the Gospels* (No. 15).
W. H. DUNDAS.

INTERCESSION (the act of one who goes between) is generally taken to mean that part of prayer in which we approach God on behalf of others. The corresponding word in NT, ἔντευξις, which occurs only at 1 Ti 2¹ 4⁵, does not necessarily mean what we now understand by intercession, but rather, as its connexion with ἐντυγχάνω implies, drawing close to God in free and familiar prayer (see Trench, *Syn.* p. 190, where, however, it is added, 'In justice to our translators it must be observed that intercession had not in their time that limited meaning of prayer for others which we now ascribe to it').

Intercession has always been regarded as a characteristic duty and privilege of believers in Christ. There is no fact or aspect of prayer more distinctive of the Christian religion than this, in which the Christian heart, rising above all consideration of self, expands with a Christ-like benevolent desire for the welfare of every living soul, and prays for all mankind. Accordingly, we find that from the beginning intercession has been looked upon as a specific and characteristic part of the vocation of the Christian Church as a whole as well as of its individual members. The practice was enjoined by Christ, He Himself setting the example to His disciples. As prayer, in the general sense of the word, is essential to the Christian life, so intercessory prayer has always been looked upon as an essential part of Christian prayer.

Christ, when on earth, prayed for His followers, and still continues to plead for them beyond the veil, though in thinking of this aspect of His intercession it is a mistake to confine it merely to prayer. This has been admirably and convincingly pointed out by Milligan in *The Ascension and Heavenly Priesthood of our Lord* (pp. 149–153), and though this aspect of Christ's intercession belongs to a subsequent heading (§ 2 below), yet, because the intercession of Christians must always be based upon the Lord's intercession, it may be

* There is no reference to the insurrection in the Sin. Syr. Gospels: see Mrs. Lewis in *Exp. Times*, xii. (1901), pp. 118, 271.

premised here that in the intercessions we offer to God the idea is wider than mere petition on behalf of others. 'Intercession and giving of thanks' are to be made for all men (1 Ti 2[1]). It is a commonplace that prayer is more than mere petition; and so even in prayer on behalf of others mere asking of benefits for them cannot be the whole of prayer. Intercession, then, would appear to embrace thanksgiving for benefits bestowed on others as well as imploring favours for them. Further, intercession also seems to imply that in praying for others, if we pray sincerely, we place ourselves with our means and our energies at God's disposal for His purposes of grace towards those for whom we pray. Intercession thus leads up to and necessitates self-dedication. In proceeding now to examine our Lord's teaching, we note:

1. *The duty of intercession.*—The duty of intercession is explicitly and frequently taught by Christ in the Gospels. It has often been remarked about His teaching as to prayer that He seldom, if ever, gives a direct command to His followers to pray, but, taking it for granted that they do pray and do not need to be told to pray, He simply gives them directions how to pray, and shows them what are the essential elements, characteristics, and conditions of prayer (cf. *e.g.* Mt 6[5, 9], Mk 11[24, 25], Lk 18[1]).

It hardly needs to be remarked that the Christian religion, being a social religion, implies that prayer on behalf of others is an essential and distinguishing element in its devotions. It would have been surprising if Christ had not taught the duty of intercession. This, of course, must not be taken as meaning that He taught it for the first time. Under the OT dispensation God's people were admitted to the privilege of intercession, and their prayers for others were availing. In particular, 'the prophets were intercessors in virtue of their calling. The ground of this was twofold. The prophet was an acceptable person; but, further, he had the Spirit, and the possession of it enabled him not only to interpret the mind of God to man, but also the mind of man to God' (Bernard in Hastings' *DB*, vol. iv. p. 40[b]). But in the Gospels we might have expected to find, as we do find, that the duty and privilege of intercession is advanced and developed. In Christ's teaching, intercession takes a wider range and a higher view than under the OT dispensation, for no section of mankind is excluded from the scope of His redemption. Jewish prayers, even of intercession, had been offered to 'the Lord God of Israel' or 'the God of our Fathers,' but in our Lord's pattern prayer, as well as throughout His teaching, every human being is invited to call upon God as his Father, and in so doing to regard all mankind as his brethren. 'When His disciples ask to be taught to pray, He gives them a prayer very unlike what John would have given, for it contains not a word of that petition for blessing upon Israel which, in any prayer that an Israelite offered, contained, to his mind, the gist of the whole' (Latham, *Pastor Pastorum*, p. 416).

The Incarnation has furnished a new motive and a new power for intercession. The man who is in Christ is no longer an isolated unit: he is a member of the Body of Christ, and therefore prays for all mankind as Christ did; for, knowing that God has loved him in Christ, he loves others for whom as for himself Christ came, and in the power of that love he prays for all men living.

When we come to our Lord's express teaching as to intercession, we are at once arrested by the fact that in the Lord's Prayer—given to the disciples in response to their request to be taught how to pray—intercession not only holds the first place, but the spirit of intercession pervades it all.

This prayer, which is the peculiar prayer of the Christian believer, the use of which marks him out from all others (witness the fact that in the early Church it was not taught to the catechumens till they were *competentes* and on the eve of their baptism), is a prayer of intercession. 'Our Father, which art in heaven, hallowed be Thy name. Thy kingdom come. Thy will be done on earth as it is in heaven.' Here the disciples are taught to pray that all mankind may be brought into the Kingdom of God, that they may reverence His name, that they may learn to do His will and submit themselves to His rule. Here all limits of space and time are transcended, and he who prays the Lord's Prayer prays for all mankind, even for the generations yet unborn. It would hardly, therefore, be an exaggeration to say that in Christ's teaching upon prayer, intercession holds the first place. This is in keeping with the whole tenor of His teaching and with the genius of His religion, who all His life took thought for others, and whose first utterance on the cross was a prayer for His murderers (Lk 23[34]). Following upon this, it is noteworthy that, according to Lk 11[5-13], it was in direct sequence to and by way of commentary upon the Lord's Prayer that Christ spoke the parable of the Friend at Midnight, in which He teaches the necessity of importunate prayer, the importunity inculcated being the importunity of one for his friend. Intercession, therefore, according to Christ's teaching, is not only to be offered, but it is to be offered with importunity.

2. *Christ's personal example.*—Besides His great prayer of intercession recorded in Jn 17, the Gospels afford several instances of our Lord's personal example in intercession. His prayer on the eve of the ordination of the Twelve, when He continued all night in prayer (Lk 16[12f.]), was, it is highly probable, largely occupied with intercession for them. He prayed for St. Peter (22[32]). His first word from the cross was a prayer for His enemies. There is also the prayer recorded in Mt 11[25-27], and His prayer at the grave of Lazarus (Jn 11[41f.]), both of which are intercessory.

Christ teaches that, as He is the Mediator between God and man, intercession must be offered through Him. He is the Intercessor, and our intercessions can avail only because He intercedes, presenting our prayers to the Father. He prayed for His disciples and for all who through their word might believe, and now He prays within the veil, carrying forward the intercession begun on earth. This comes out clearly in His 'Intercessory Prayer' (Jn 17), or, as it has perhaps been more fittingly designated, His 'High Priestly Prayer.' Reading it in the light of the happily correct rendering of RV, we see that He is speaking as if He had already entered into the glory, and were looking back upon His earthly course. In the joy of His anticipated triumph He presents Himself before the Father and pleads for the fulfilment of the Father's will. Christ's intercession for mankind which was begun on earth is continued in heaven, and our prayers for others are presented by Him in virtue of His mediation. At the same time, this prayer affords an unfailing guide to our prayers of intercession, teaching us that prayer is to be offered for the ingathering of men into the Kingdom, for the unity of the Church of God, for the perseverance of believers, and for the sanctification, for all these ends, of those who are engaged in the Church's work.

3. *The scope of intercession.*—Our Lord is careful to tell His disciples to pray for their enemies (Mt 5[44]), and in so doing He bids them remember in prayer those whom they might not have thought of including, assuming that they would, without being specially directed, pray for all others. He thus teaches both by direct precept and by implication that intercession is to be full and universal. The only other special direction He gives in this connexion is that they are to pray for labourers to be sent into the Lord's harvest (Mt 9[38], Lk 10[2]). Christ gives these few general directions as to the scope of intercession, leaving it to time and growing experience to suggest their amplification. The scope of Christian intercession must always be widening.

'It grows with the growth of the Church and her needs; it grows with the growing complexity of human society as new classes and new objects rise up to claim its help. . . . Intercession is also an ever widening element in each individual life; as a man's interest and experiences widen, so must his prayers' (Frere, *Sursum Corda*, p. 1).

4. *The conditions of intercession.*—Two distinct, though sometimes confused, conditions of acceptable intercession are laid down by Christ. (1) In Mk 11[25] He shows that effectual intercession presupposes a forgiving spirit. Those who pray for others through Christ must have the spirit of Christ. (2) In Mt 5[23. 24] the disciples are taught that a condition of acceptable prayer is that they must seek reconciliation with any one who regards them (rightly or wrongly) as having done him a wrong (see Zahn, *ad loc.*). There must be a removal of the sense of injury from his mind as well as forgiveness to those who have wronged themselves. He who prays for others must be in peace and charity with all men.

LITERATURE.—Most of the modern popular books on Prayer are astonishingly silent as to Intercession. In many of the so-called 'divisions of prayer' Intercession does not even find a place. But in Matthew Henry's *Method of Prayer*, a book little used now, Intercession is prominent. Of the few modern books in which the subject is dealt with, mention may be made of Worlledge on 'Prayer' in the *Oxford Library of Practical Theology*; Frere and Illingworth's *Sursum Corda*; Reid's *Christian Prayer*; Rendel Harris' *Union with God*, pp. 41–64.

J. CROMARTY SMITH.

INTEREST.—'Interest,' found twice in RV of the Gospels (Mt 25[27], Lk 19[23]) instead of 'usury' of AV, represents the Greek τόκος which in the LXX is the equivalent of the Heb. *neshekh* in the whole of the eleven passages in which the latter occurs (Ex 22[25], Lv 25[36] etc.). Now *neshekh* is rightly rendered 'usury,' the reference being to the interest, often exorbitant, charged by money-lenders in the ancient East. In the NT τόκος, though often used in contemporary Greek in the sense just defined, clearly signifies 'interest on deposit paid by a banker.' There were many banks in the Roman period scattered over the Græco-Roman world, some called 'public banks' and others private firms (*e.g.* 'Theon & Co.,' 'Herodes & Co.,' at Oxyrhynchus). These, however, seem, from a lately discovered text, to have farmed from the government, in Egypt at any rate, the right of administering business; the Roman authorities, it would appear, following in some degree Ptolemaic precedent (*Papyri of Oxyrhynchus*, No. 513, vol. iii.: cf. the note on p. 248 f.). Not much seems to be known about the deposit department of ancient banking. The technical term for a deposit on which interest was paid was *creditum*. The amounts lodged in Roman banks towards the end of the Republic and under the Empire must have been, in some instances, very large. About the rate of interest paid to depositors there seems to be little or no information. The statement of Suetonius, that Augustus branded some people with infamy (*notavit*) because they borrowed at low interest and invested at high (*Octavius*, 39), may hint how the bankers made money out of the funds entrusted to their care. The usual rate of interest on loans under the Empire seems to have been one per cent. per month, or twelve per cent. per annum. This rate is repeatedly mentioned in the *Papyri of Oxyrhynchus* (No. 243 of A.D. 79, and No. 270 of A.D. 94, etc.). The rate paid to deposi-

tors will have been much lower. A considerable banking business was also done in ancient temples. So in ancient Babylonia (Johns, *Babylonian and Assyrian Laws, Contracts, and Letters*, 211), and in the Greek world, at the temple of the Ephesian Artemis, for instance (*Anabasis*, v. iii. 6 f.). That the temple of Jerusalem was used in this way is expressly stated by Josephus (*BJ* VI. v. 2), and in the legend about Heliodorus (2 Mac 3[10-12. 15]). About the management of this temple bank nothing seems to be known. Our Lord's references are probably to local τραπεζίται, the Eastern representatives of the Roman *argentarii*. See also BANK.

LITERATURE.—Besides the authorities mentioned above, see Hastings' *DB*, art. 'Usury'; *Encyc. Bibl.*, art. 'Trade and Commerce,' § 78; Smith, *Dict. of Ant.*, artt. 'Fenus' and 'Argentarii; Winer, *RWB*, art. 'Hinterlage'; Schürer, *GJV*[3] ii. 268.

W. TAYLOR SMITH.

INTERMEDIATE STATE.—See DEAD, p. 426[a].

INVITATION.—The method of public teaching adopted by our Lord being exclusively oral, it was necessary that two features difficult to combine should be prominent in the form of His instruction, —an immediate impression, and a firm grip on the memory. This He secured by mingling freely in the social life of the time, and by an abundant use of similes and illustrations drawn from facts in the daily life and social customs of the people whom He addressed. This is one of the reasons why He clothed so many of His doctrines in parables and figures centred in the idea of hospitality.

The Hebrews were an eminently sociable people. In the earliest times, the laws of hospitality were specially sacred; strangers were made heartily welcome at the door of the patriarch's tent (Gn 18[3], cf. He 13[2]); and in later times a surly attitude towards travellers needing refreshment was considered a serious offence against good manners (1 S 25[4-10]). Many strict injunctions were laid down in the Mosaic Law (Lv 19[33. 34], Dt 14[29] etc.) as to the duty of kindness to strangers. At a still later period, when the community was settled in towns and cities, an elaborate code of manners grew up, both as to giving and receiving hospitality. There was much entertainment of friends, relations, and strangers among the Jews in the time of our Lord; social meetings were frequent, and religious gatherings frequently took on a festive character.

Jesus freely accepted such opportunities of social intercourse as were offered to Him; He was fond of being entertained by His friends (Lk 10[38] etc.), and distinguished Himself from the outset of His public career as an eminently sociable man (Mt 9[10]), often accepting invitations from quarters that gave offence to those who considered themselves leaders of society (v.[11], cf. Lk 19[7]). This, however, He did, not merely because He delighted in the fellowship of men and women, but mainly because of the unexampled opportunity it afforded Him of spiritual instruction (Mt 9[12. 13], Lk 7[41-50]), and of bringing His influence to bear on those around Him, whether they were His personal friends (Lk 10[41. 42]), or secret enemies (7[36]), or the general public (Jn 12[9]), or individuals who were denied entrance into recognized society (Lk 18[10]). It was a sign of His insight and wisdom as well as of His broad sympathies, that in a community so eminently sociable as that in which He moved, He should make such free use of the machinery of hospitality for His Messianic purpose, and devise many parables and illustrations drawn from the customs of the day, and from the etiquette that ruled the relations of hosts and guests, from the highest circles of life to the lowest.

It is partly from this point of view that we are to understand His frequent habit of representing the gospel of grace as God's invitation to the soul to partake of the blessings of salvation. It made an instant appeal to the sympathies of His audience; it brought spiritual realities within reach of the intelligence of the humblest and most ordinary people, and it predisposed them to receive His message willingly; and, as the similes and illustrations in which He clothed His teaching represented recurrent facts and exigencies in their lives, it helped to drive home deep into their memory the lessons which He taught, and to bring them back frequently to their recollection. In this way the method of His teaching helped to perpetuate its substance till the time when it took a written form. But the parables of invitation have a wider appeal, for the relationships from which they were drawn are universal, and belong to all nations and communities where the customs of social life are honoured. These customs vary in detail in different ages and lands, but the root-relations of hosts and guests are permanent. These parables are a kind of *Esperanto* of the spiritual life, and appeal to the universal intelligence and sympathies of mankind. Thus the human side of Christ's teaching forms an ideal channel for its Divine contents.

When we pass from the form to the substance of the teaching, which represents the gospel as an invitation, the simile is further justified by its appropriateness and its beauty.

1. It emphasizes the bright and genial aspects of religion, which shine with so clear a lustre in the teaching of Jesus. It has been a recurrent and baneful feature of theological learning that it has tended to envelop religion in an atmosphere of gloom, by making so much of the horror and mischief of sin, and dwelling so exclusively on the need of repentance, atonement, and justification. Religious ritual introduced another baneful element into the spiritual life by representing its duties too much as a series of sacerdotal observances, which by frequent recurrence became mechanical and wearisome. Ethical writers have likewise been prone to dwell exclusively on the responsibilities of religion, to the obscuration of its privileges. In the teaching of Jesus there is nothing of this mischievous tendency. His parables are full of the sound of wedding-bells, of the voice of laughter, of the joy of a great deliverance, of the discovery of a precious and unsuspected happiness. There are clouds on the horizon, and the echo of distant thunders; but the foreground is full of happy figures intent on celebrating the marriage of the soul to its Divine Lover and Friend, and on enjoying the new-found fellowship of God as the Giver of life and salvation. Without in any way obscuring the evils from which the soul is delivered by the gracious ministries of the gospel, preachers should follow their great Model in placing greater emphasis on the sunny joys and holy privileges brought within our reach in Jesus Christ. One reason why the common people heard Him so gladly was, that He took them away from the word-splitting and elaborate discussions of the Rabbis, and transported them into that circle of happy human relationships from which He mainly drew His illustrations. What was true then is just as true to-day.

2. The presentation of the gospel as a Divine invitation throws emphasis on another of its essential features,—that it embodies a free gift of grace from God to man. The central idea of hospitality is that one gives freely what the many receive and enjoy 'without money and without price.' Jesus in the 'parables of grace' teaches us that the gospel contains something infinitely precious which is given to us, but which we could never deserve or buy. Religion is not a bargain between man

and God; it is a boon, a largess bestowed by God on man. It is not commerce, it is reconciliation and friendship. It is thus represented not as an exchange of commodities in a market-place, but as a feast where the one side gives all and receives nothing back, save in realizing the happiness and loyal gratitude of the invited guests. Jesus justifies this idea of a one-sided benefit by nearly always making use of a simile of feasting in which a superior invites his inferior to a banquet. It is a king inviting his subjects to the wedding-feast of his son (Mt 22²⁻¹⁴); it is a great man entertaining a miscellaneous assemblage of guests from all quarters (Lk 14¹⁵⁻²⁴); it is a father welcoming home a renegade son with the best of the flock. In all these cases there could be no question of a return in kind. The conditions were satisfied by the coming of the guests, and their happy enjoyment of the good things provided. 'The gospel is ever a gospel of grace.'

3. A third significant aspect suggested by the simile of an invitation is its voluntariness on both sides. There can be no compulsion in the invitation to a feast of rejoicing. Unwilling guests have no place at a banquet. Religion has no room for the idea of spiritual compulsion. The invitation is free to all: acceptance must be as free. Thus is the sacred function of spiritual liberty, of the freedom of the will, safeguarded by the gospel. Those who refuse or neglect a social invitation may be incurring a grave responsibility; but they can do so if they choose. The spiritual appeal of religion may also be refused; it lies with the soul whether it will respond to the call of God or reject it.

The word translated 'compel' in Lk 14²³ (ἀνάγκασον) must be read in its secondary meaning of 'constrain by persuasion.' It 'reflects in the first place the urgent desire of the master to have an absolutely full house, in the second the feeling tha', pressure will be needed to overcome the incredulity of country people as to such an invitation to them being meant seriously. They would be apt to laugh in the servant's face' (Bruce in *Expositor's Gr. Test., in loco*).

4. The idea of an invitation thus merges into that of response; and it is important to notice that great stress is laid on this side of the question in the parables. In not a few it is clearly the pivot on which the teaching turns. There is one way in which an invitation may be worthily accepted; there are several in which it may be rejected: *e.g.* it may be (1) openly scorned, (2) accepted and then rejected or ignored, (3) accepted in a wrong spirit, or with an imperfect realization of its privileges and value. Each of these situations is dealt with by Christ to typify the attitude of men to His gospel. In the parable of the Marriage of the King's Son, the first guests invited treat the offer with scorn (Mt 22³), and 'make light' of it, preferring to find their satisfaction in their own way, and even maltreating the king's messengers. By this Jesus exposed the attitude of the Pharisees and scribes towards His gospel, and in a wider sense that of all those who in a thoroughly worldly spirit have since treated His offer of salvation with derision or disrespect. In the parable of the Great Supper, the guests first accepted the invitation, and then, finding other more absorbing interests, sent various excuses for not attending. These represent the fickle multitude, who at first thronged to hear the 'gracious words that proceeded out of his mouth,' and afterwards left Him, having exhausted the sensational aspect of His ministry and wonderful works, and having no love for His higher message. Returning to the parable of the Marriage, we find a final episode in which the man without a 'wedding-garment' is dealt with. Clearly he stands for those who, having heard and accepted the invitation of the gospel, show that they have failed to realize the lofty and decorous spirit in which the soul should respond to it, and who treat it as a common thing, with no sense of its high privilege. The care with which Jesus developed these situations in His parables, and proclaimed the doom that followed, shows how deeply He felt the importance of a right attitude towards spiritual realities. It is as though He were repeating in many tones and accents the fact that God offers man His best in the invitations of the gospel, and expects man to be at his best in responding to them, otherwise he perils his soul (cf. Mt 22[7. 13], Lk 14[24]).

When we turn from the teaching to the practice of Christ, the same attitude of appeal and invitation is manifested, and the same spirit of loyal and worthy acceptance is expected in turn. Everywhere in His dealings with men we find Him acting as God's messenger of goodwill, and urging them to respond to heavenly grace with grateful hearts and willing service. Where men do so He promises them a great reward (Mt 19[27-30]); where they fail to do so He shows a Divine and touching sorrow (23[37. 38]); and though He is clear in revealing His own disappointment at such a result, He lays the chief stress on the loss and misery which rejection must bring on those who are guilty of spurning or ignoring His ever-renewed appeal.

The heart of the gospel is found in the central invitation given by Christ to all men in the words, 'Come unto me, all ye that labour and are heavy laden, and I will give you rest' (Mt 11[28]).

Literature.—Wendt, *Teach. of Jesus*, i. 148 ff.; Stalker, *Imago Christi*, ch. vii.; Bruce, *Galilean Gospel*, ch. xii.; *Expositor*, I. xi. [1880] 101 ff. See, further, art. Coming to Christ.

E. Griffith-Jones.

IRONY.—See Humour, and Laughter.

ISAAC.—Named (1) in our Lord's genealogy, Mt 1[2], Lk 3[34]; (2) in such collocations as 'sit down with Abraham and Isaac and Jacob' (Mt 8[11]), 'see Abraham and Isaac and Jacob' (Lk 13[28]), 'the God of Abraham and of Isaac and of Jacob' (Mt 22[32], Mk 12[26], Lk 20[37]). See Abraham, and Fathers. The sacrifice of Isaac came at an early date to be used by Christian writers as a type of the sacrifice on the cross (cf. *e.g.* Ep. of Barn. ch. 7). It is just possible that some such thought underlies Ro 8[32] 'He that spared not his own Son.'

ISAIAH.—There are seven instances recorded in the Gospels in which Jesus quotes from the prophecies of Isaiah, besides numerous other cases in which His language is more or less manifestly reminiscent of expressions in the book. The most notable passages are two in which our Lord applies to Himself the terms used by the prophet of the Exile with regard to the Servant of Jehovah, viz. Lk 4[16-22], where Jesus reads and expounds the words of Is 61[1. 2]; and Lk 22[37], where He adopts as a prediction of His own experience a clause of Is 53[12]. Our Lord thus plainly taught that, alike in the mission and in the vicarious suffering of the ideal Servant of Deutero-Isaiah, His own person and work were typified and foreshadowed. More general is the application of Is 6[9. 10] to the people of His own time (Mt 13[14. 15], Mk 4[12], Lk 8[10]); and also His use of Is 29[13] of the Pharisees and scribes (Mt 15[7-9], Mk 7[6. 7]). All three Synoptists record the quotation from Is 56[7] with which He rebuked the temple-traders (Mt 21[13] ||). St. John alone gives the quotation of a general character from Is 54[13] (Jn 6[45]), while St. Mark records an expression which manifestly comes from Is 66[24] (Mk 9[48]). In only three of the above seven cases is Isaiah mentioned by name, and in no case is there any indication that bears in the slightest degree upon the question as to the authorship of the various parts of the book.

In addition to these more direct references, there are many expressions in the discourses of Jesus in which we have echoes of Isaiah's language. Our Lord's mind was filled with the OT, and it was to be expected that His utterances should be cast in the mould, and often expressed in the very words, of psalm and prophecy. In Mt 5[34. 35] we perceive a reminiscence of Is 66[1]; Mt 21[33ff.] || at once suggests Is 5[1. 2]. Other less obvious instances are probably to be found in Mt 11[23] (cf. Is 14[13. 15]) 16[19] (Is 22[22]) 6[6] (Is 26[20]); and various expressions in the eschatological discourses of Mt 24 and Lk 21. To these others might possibly be added; but it is not warrantable to find in every case of verbal similarity a reference to, or even a reminiscence of, the words of the OT. But apart from doubtful cases, it will be seen that the Book of Isaiah, both in its earlier and in its later portions, is fully acknowledged and used in the teaching of Jesus.

It is not less so with the Evangelists themselves. All four quote Is 40[3] with regard to the mission of John the Baptist (Mt 3[3] and ||); while Mt., who uses the OT so largely in connexion with the ministry of Jesus, applies to His coming and mission the passages Is 7[14] (Mt 1[23]) 9[1. 2] (Mt 4[14-16]) 53[4] (Mt 8[17]) 42[1-4] (Mt 12[18-21]). St. John (12[38-41]) quotes Is 53[1] 6[10] in reference to the rejection of Christ by the people; and the Synoptists all record the voice heard at the Baptism and the Transfiguration as using the language of Is 42[1].

As with the words of Jesus Himself, so, in the case of the Evangelists, no theory with regard to the actual authorship of any part of the book can claim to be supported by the manner of the references. 'Isaiah,' even when named, stands manifestly for the reputed author, and (as in Jn 12[38]) the mode of expression is naturally and rightly that popularly used and understood. No critical conclusions can be drawn from any of the references.

With regard to the original Messianic import of the passages applied in the Gospels to Jesus Christ and His work, there is no difficulty in those cases where the 'Servant of Jehovah' is identified with the Messiah. And even in such passages as Is 7[14] 9[1. 2] quoted by Mt., we must recognize, beneath and beyond the immediate prophetic reference, an *ideal* element which permitted and justified the specific application by the Evangelist. Especially is this so with the prophetic conception of 'Immanuel,' an ideal figure in whom we find the earliest portraiture of the Messianic King (Is 7[14] 8[8. 10] 9[6. 7]). Though it might in some cases be without historical or critical exactitude (as in Mt 4[15. 16] from Is 9[1. 2]), it was quite legitimate to find unexpected correspondences between the earlier and the later stages of Providence and Revelation, based on the deep underlying unity and consistency of the Divine purpose and methods.

J. E. M'Ouat.

ISCARIOT.—See Judas Iscariot.

ISRAEL, ISRAELITE.—1. The former name occurs 30 times in the Gospels, and the latter once (Jn 1[47]). The following expressions are found: 'Israel,' with or without the article (Mt 8[10] 9[33], Lk 1[54. 80] 2[25. 34] 4[25. 27] 7[9] 24[21], Jn 1[31] 3[10]; also Mk 12[29] vocative); 'people (λαός) Israel' (Mt 2[6], Lk 2[32]); 'house of Israel' (Mt 10[6] 15[24]); 'sons of Israel' (Mt 27[9], Lk 1[16]); 'tribes of Israel' (Mt 19[28], Lk 22[30]); 'land of Israel' (Mt 2[20f.]); 'God of Israel' (Mt 15[31], Lk 1[68]); 'King of Israel' (Mt 27[42], Mk 15[32], Jn 1[49] 12[13]). The force of the name is best understood by comparing it with two others used in the NT. 'Hebrew' (Ἑβραῖος) is one who speaks the Hebrew language—*i.e.* the vernacular Aramaic dialect (Ac 6[1]; cf. Lk 23[38], Jn 19[13. 17. 20]). 'Jew' (Ἰουδαῖος) implies national descent; originally used for those who were members of the tribe of Judah, and lived in the country of Judah, it became a wider term, after the return from Babylon, for all who were members of the Hebrew race. 'Israel' differed from both of these as being the name of privilege given by God to Jacob, the ancestor of the race (Gn 32²⁸ 35¹⁰), and the thought of the theocratic privileges of the chosen people and of God's covenant with them always underlies the term. See esp. Mt 2⁶, Lk 1⁵⁴· ⁶⁸ 2²⁵· ³² 24²¹, Ac 1⁶, all of which reveal the national conviction that the Messiah would come for the benefit of Israel, and that to Israel were God's attention and love especially given. But in marked contrast to such passages are those which imply that the theocratic nation has failed to fulfil the Divine purposes for it:—a Roman centurion exhibits greater faith than was to be found in the holy nation (Mt 8¹⁰ ‖ Lk 7⁹); the house of Israel are as a whole 'lost sheep' (Mt 10⁶ 15²⁴); they need some-one to turn them to the Lord their God (Lk 1¹⁶); an honoured and official teacher of Israel is shown to be ignorant of the fundamental principles of the spiritual life (Jn 3¹⁰); incidents in the OT prove that some Gentiles received God's care and blessing, and were preferred to Israelites (Lk 4²⁵⁻²⁷); and a mysterious intimation is given of the supremacy of the Church of Christ hereafter (Mt 19²⁸ ‖ Lk 22³⁰); it is character, and not theocratic privileges, that makes a man 'truly an Israelite' (Jn 1⁴⁷). See NATHANAEL. Thus the Gospels teach incidentally what St. Paul lays down categorically: (a) that Israel does not comprise all who are of Israel (Ro 9⁶); (b) that the privileged position of Israel is to be taken by Christians, for the latter are 'the Israel of God' (Gal 6¹⁶, cf. Eph 2¹¹⁻¹⁹); (c) that this is for the purpose of ultimately restoring Israel to spiritual communion and salvation (Ro 9-11).

2. The status of the chosen people before God is to be taken by Christians. But that does not mean that Christianity is merely to be substituted for Judaism. Christianity is not a completely new creation fallen from heaven, but rather a growth from the religion of Israel—a growth far surpassing the germ from which it sprang, as an oak surpasses an acorn, but yet composed of elements which are discernible in the earlier dispensation in a rudimentary form. In order, therefore, to estimate the relation in which the Gospels, and particularly our Lord's teaching, stood towards Israel, it is necessary to estimate broadly how much the New was indebted to the Old, and how much it discarded in rising out of it with its Divine and potent growth.

(a) *Monotheism* was the chiefest glory of Judaism. Part of the inspiration of the people of Israel is seen in its 'genius for religion,' the capacity for realizing the supreme and only existence of God. A step towards this had been monolatry, the national adhesion to one Deity only, which was compatible with the recognition that other nations and lands were under the protection of other deities (Jg 11²⁴, 1 S 26¹⁹). But it was not long before the Hebrew prophets taught that Jehovah was the God of all the nations of the earth, a spiritual Being whose service was incumbent upon all mankind, that service consisting not primarily in ritual but in morality. And this truth is the very fibre of Christianity; a Christian is in the truest sense a Unitarian. 'Jesus answered, "The chief [commandment] is—Hear O Israel, the Lord our God is one Lord; and thou shalt love the Lord thy God"' (Mk 12²⁹). But even in the OT there are not wanting intimations that the Godhead is not a 'monotonous unity,' but that there are distinctions within It; *e.g.* 'the Angel of Jahweh or of God,' *i.e.* His presence manifesting itself in outward act (Ex 3² 14¹⁹ 22²³); 'the Captain of

Jahweh's host,' who is also called Jahweh (Jos 5¹⁴ᶠ· 6²); 'His Holy Spirit' (Is 63¹⁰ᶠ·); see also the thrice repeated name (Nu 6²⁴⁻²⁶), and the *Tersanctus* (Is 6³).* According to the reports of His teaching as contained in the Gospel records, our Lord expressly formulated the truth of the unity of God, but never that of the Holy Trinity; and yet the latter pervades the whole record. 'In the gradual process of intercourse with Him, His disciples came to recognize Father, Son, and Holy Spirit as included in their deepening and enlarging thought of God.' But the truth is definitely implied in the discourses in the Upper Room (Jn 14-17), and in the baptismal formula (Mt 28¹⁹). See Gore's *Bampton Lectures*, pp. 134 ff.; Illingworth's *do.* pp. 67 ff.; Gibson, *The Thirty-nine Articles*, vol. i. pp. 93-101.

(b) *Covenant.*—The monolatry which preceded monotheism was calculated to give birth to the idea that between Jahweh and His people there was a close and mutual agreement. If He was exclusively their God and Protector, they were bound to do Him service. It is not easy to say at what period the conception arose. But the earlier prophets, though they do not expressly mention a covenant—except Hosea (6⁷ doubtful, 8¹)—all teach the truth that Jahweh requires moral, ethical service from His people. And in the JE compilations of the national traditions the covenant relationship with God is firmly established in the religious thought of Israel. The covenant with Abraham (Gn 15) is the starting-point. The covenant at Sinai (Ex 24¹⁻¹¹· 34¹⁰⁻²⁸) opens the second stage of the history. D has yet another covenant, based on the contents of the Deut. law, and made on the borders of Moab (Dt 29¹· ⁹· ¹²· ¹⁴· ²¹; cf. 26¹⁶⁻¹⁹, 2 K 23²· ²¹). But when Israel was carried into Babylon, the Old Covenant was in reality at an end; they had broken it by their sins. Jeremiah, therefore, speaks of a New Covenant (31³¹ᶠᶠ·), forgiveness of sins, righteousness, peace and joy. It had been foreshadowed in the life story of Hosea, and was to be the fulfilment of the dreams and longings of all the prophets. 'In the visions of the new covenant the OT becomes Christian.' And the thought is the inspiration of Ezekiel and of Deutero-Isaiah. But there were two other crises in Israel's history where the idea of a covenant is prominent. God gave a covenant, *i.e.* a promise, to Levi of a perpetual priesthood in the tribe (Dt 33⁸, Jer 33¹⁸· ²¹ᶠ·, Mal 2⁴⁻⁶), and to David of a perpetual lineage on the throne (2 S 7. 23⁵, Ps 89³· ³⁴ᶠ·, Jer 33¹⁷· ²¹ᶠ·). Thus there were several factors which went to make up the fulness of the Christian covenant. In the Gospels, with the exception of Lk 1⁷², where the Abrahamic covenant is referred to, the only occurrence of the word is at the Last Supper (Mt 26²⁸ ‖ Mk 14²⁴, Lk 22²⁰); our Lord uses Jeremiah's term, 'the new covenant,' but at the same time the words 'This is my blood' refer to the covenant at Sinai (Ex 24⁴⁻⁸). This application of the word to the results of His own Person and work served as a starting-point for the fuller working out of the thought by the Apostolic writers. The analogy of the Abrahamic covenant is drawn out chiefly by St. Paul (Ro 4, Gal 3), while the Ep. to the Hebrews deals with the kingship (ch. 1; cf. Mt 22⁴⁴), the priesthood (7-10), and, closely connected with the latter, the spiritual covenant of the forgiveness of sins (10¹⁵⁻¹⁸).

(c) *Law.*—A study of the passages in the Gospels which speak of the Mosaic Law shows in a striking manner the relation of Christ's teaching to the religion of Israel. On the one hand, He recognized the Divine authority of the Law, *in its true meaning and spirit*, and not as interpreted and em-

* On the use of the indefinite plural 'they,' see Taylor on *Pirḳe Aboth*, ii. 2.

bodied in the 'deformed righteousness' of the scribes and Pharisees (Mt 5[17-20] 12[5] 19[17] 23[3], Lk 16[17]). But, on the other hand, in order to 'fulfil' ($\pi\lambda\eta\rho\hat{\omega}$-$\sigma\alpha\iota$) the Law He was obliged to take a negative or critical attitude. 'The Law and the Prophets,' as a dispensation, have had their day, and have given place to 'the kingdom of heaven' (Mt 11[12f.] ‖ Lk 16[16]), and to 'grace and truth' (Jn 1[17]; and see Mt 9[17] ‖ Mk 2[21f.], Lk 5[37]). Even the Law and the Prophets meant something deeper than they had hitherto been understood to mean (Mt 7[12] 22[34-40]); and this deeper meaning is contained in a 'new commandment' which Jesus gives to the disciples (Jn 13[34]). The Law had generally been considered as a compendium of positive commands bearing on the details of life; but the only parts of it that mattered were 'the weightier things,' judgment, mercy and faith (Mt 23[23] ‖ Lk 11[42]). Other criticisms of the Law are found in Mt 5[21-48] 19[8] (divorce) 12[1-12], Lk 13[10-17] 14[1-6], Jn 5[9-17] 9 (Sabbath). Our Lord took care to avoid causing offence (Mt 18[6f.]), though showing at the same time that He was raised above bondage to purely ritual and non-ethical enactments: e.g. in the payment of the Temple tax (Mt 17[24-27]); in *touching* the leper, but at the same time telling him to offer the requisite sacrifices (Mt 8[1-4]). The one decisive breach that He made with Jewish legalism was in dealing with the distinction between clean and unclean foods, and with ceremonial washings (Mt 15[1-20], Mk 7[1-23] [note RV of v. [19]], Lk 10[7] 11[38-41]).

(d) *Sacrifice.*—The Jewish ordinances of sacrifice formed part of the 'Law,' and were also in intimate connexion with the covenant idea; this section, therefore, must to some extent overlap the two preceding. Our Lord accorded to sacrifices the same recognition that He accorded to the Law as a whole; He accepted them as of Divine authority, and binding upon the Jews. He told the recovered leper to offer the prescribed gift (Mt 8[4]); He assumed that His hearers offered them as an ordinary practice (5[23f.]). But the latter passage also shows that He relegated them to a subordinate place as compared with the higher moral duties. He twice quoted the saying of Hosea that God desires 'mercy and not sacrifice' (Mt 9[13] 12[7]). And by the inauguration of the New Covenant in His own blood, the whole Jewish system was by implication abrogated by being transcended. The thought of sacrifice seems also to underlie the words in Mt 20[28] ‖ Mk 10[45]. Christ gave His life as a 'ransom' ($\lambda\acute{v}\tau\rho\sigma\nu$) —a means of redemption or release. The word is used in the LXX as a rendering of כֹּפֶר a 'covering' or 'atonement.' But such a passage as Nu 35[31] shows that it does not necessarily imply the death of an animal; and it is precarious to press our Lord's words to support any *theory* of the Atonement, as has been done with disastrous results by widely differing schools of thought. Further, Jn 19[36] refers to the Passover lamb; and possibly also Jn 1[29. 36], but it is safer to regard the Baptist's words as an allusion to Is 53[6. 7], where the sufferings and death of the Servant of Jahweh are described as being in some sense vicarious, and availing to 'take away the sin of the world'; this truth was depicted symbolically by the 'scapegoat' on the Day of Atonement. The words of our Lord at the institution of the Eucharist were, as has been said above, the starting-point for the fuller teaching of the Apostolic writers. Of the debts which Christianity owes to Israel, none is more fundamental than the conception of sacrifice. The references to the subject in St. Paul's writings, though not numerous, are quite enough to show that he had a deep and firm belief in the sacrificial and propitiatory character of Christ's death (Sanday-Headlam, *Romans*, pp. 91 f.). See also 1 P 1[2] (an allusion to the covenant sacrifice at

Horeb), 1[19] (the Passover lamb), 2[24] (a general description of an atoning sacrifice). And it is the paramount thought in Hebrews, which shows how Christ's sacrifice and priesthood were analogous to, but infinitely surpassed, the Jewish sacrifices and the Levitical priesthood (see art. DAY OF ATONEMENT).

(e) *Messianic expectations.*—(i.) The universal expectation in Israel in our Lord's time that One was to come who should be a national deliverer, had its roots as far back as the Divine promises to Abraham; but the focussing of all hopes on a *King* was due to the promise made to David that his line should have perpetual possession of the throne. The hopes of national peace and glory under a king reach a climax in Isaiah and Micah. But they received a terrible reverse at the Captivity, and in subsequent OT writings the idea largely disappeared. It was revived, however, to a certain extent in apocryphal and especially in apocalyptic literature. In two of the earlier portions of the Sibylline Oracles, in parts of the Ethiopic Enoch and in the Psalms of Solomon, there are indications of the hope, though the title 'Messiah' is not used. The Christian belief that Jesus was the Messiah (though the truth was guessed by the first disciples, Jn 1[41. 49]) was due to His own claims, which were not, however, put forward even to the Twelve till near the close of His ministry. He pronounced Simon Peter blessed because the truth had been Divinely revealed to him (Mt 16[16f.]); and He acknowledged to Pilate that He was a king (Mt 27[11] ‖ Mk 15[2], Lk 23[3], Jn 18[36f.]). But while He declared the fact, He raised it into a new sphere of thought—'My kingdom is not of this world; if my kingdom were of this world, then would my servants fight . . . but now is my kingdom not from hence.' And in conversing with the Twelve He linked with it the clear announcement of His approaching sufferings (Mk 8[27-31] and parallels; cf. Mt 20[20-28]).

(ii.) The kingship of the Messiah was the only conception which had been entertained by the Jews themselves. But 'in the minds of the first members of the Christian Church the experiences of the Cross, the Resurrection and Pentecost, together with the impression which the character and work, the life and teaching of Jesus had made upon them, led to a rapid transformation, pregnant with important consequences, of the idea of the Messiah which they held as Jews' (Hastings' *DB* iii. 356[a]). As they studied the OT Scriptures in the light of these experiences, 'they found scattered there the elements of a relatively complete ideal, which had been perfectly fulfilled in Jesus' (*ib.* 356[b]). The very mode of life and teaching which He had adopted drew their attention to the promise of a 'true *prophet*' (Dt 18[15], Ac 3[22f.] 7[37]). And in the miracles which He performed He appeared to be a counterpart of OT prophets. This working of miracles formed part of the current Messianic conception, as is implied by John the Baptist (Mt 11[2f.]), and in the questionings of the Jews (Jn 7[31]). Another trait in the prophetic office of the Messiah—that of the revealer of unknown truths—is implied by the Samaritan woman (Jn 4[25]). This had formed no definite part of the earlier Messianic expectations, though the nation had looked forward to a true prophet (1 Mac 14[41]). In our Lord's time men hoped for the return of one of the old prophets (Mk 6[15] 8[27f.]), or the coming of one who was called 'the prophet' (Jn 1[21. 25] 6[14]); but there is no indication that 'the prophet' was identified with the Messiah.

(iii.) The more clearly the atoning value of Christ's death was realized, the more completely was He seen to be the ideal Priest foreshadowed by the Levitical priesthood. His own words would form the starting-point for this conception; He 'laid down' His life, He 'gave' His life as a ransom (see above). The double thought of Christ as Victim and Priest is fully worked out in Hebrews on the basis of Ps 110⁴.

(iv.) The OT contains many passages which teach that Divine purposes are accomplished through the sufferings of the righteous; and in the later chapters of the Book of Isaiah the righteous portion of the nation merges into the vision of one representative *Servant* of Jahweh, whose preaching was to bring the whole nation, and even Gentiles, to the light, and whose sufferings were to have a vicarious value. This representation does not appear to have exercised any influence on the later Jewish expectations of the Messiah. The inspired utterance of John the Baptist (Jn 1²⁹·³⁶) pointed towards the truth, though his hearers do not seem to have understood his words. The Twelve could not realize the necessity for Christ's sufferings until He had suffered, when the great truth dawned upon them (Mt 12¹⁸⁻²¹, Ac 3¹³·²⁶ 4²⁷·³⁰). It has been suggested that the servant (δοῦλος) of Lk 14¹⁶ᶠ· may be an allusion to the same figure of prophecy.

(*f*) *Eschatology.* — The Jewish and Christian Messianic beliefs were closely bound up with eschatological teaching as a whole. In the OT the expectations with regard to a hereafter consisted mainly of the aspirations of saints who felt certain that righteousness is eternal, and that God's power and dominion are infinite. This intuitive assurance that the present life with its inequalities and anomalies cannot be the whole of life, maintained itself in some minds side by side with the popular notions held by the Hebrews in common with the Babylonian and other Semitic peoples, that Sheol was a state in which man would continue to exist, but only in a shadowy, nerveless, purposeless reproduction of his present personality. In apocalyptic literature an advance was made to some extent. The 'last things' began to be detailed in a great variety of forms—some of them, indeed, sensuous, and marred by narrow Jewish exclusiveness, but others more spiritual and universal; in some the Messianic kingdom is to be on this earth, in others in a transformed heaven and earth; in some the enemies of Israel are punished at death in Sheol or Hades, which thus becomes equivalent to Hell, while the righteous (*i.e.* Israel) attain to a resurrection; in others the resurrection is universal, and a prelude to a final spiritual judgment. And Christian teaching borrowed much, both from the OT and from later Jewish writings; but it rose to a spiritual height and certainty far beyond the former, while at the same time it discarded the gross, exaggerated, and unspiritual elements which marred the latter. Christ's own eschatological teaching centres round the *Kingdom of God.* He, like the OT writers, does not discuss theoretical or speculative questions, but deals with broad moral issues. His teaching 'unfolds the course of the Divine kingdom' which had been the object of OT faith and the centre of OT hope. It presents that kingdom as a thing of the actual present, brought to men in and by the Teacher Himself, but also as a thing of the future which looks through all historical fulfilments to a completer realization—a thing, too, of gradual, unobtrusive growth, yet destined to be finally established by a great conclusive event' (Hastings' *DB* i. 750ᵇ). Our Lord, as reported by the Synoptists, gave a large place to the promise of His own *Return*, an objective event, the time of which was not yet revealed even to the Son. In some passages this is closely connected with a quite distinct occurrence—the destruction of Jerusalem (Mt 24 ∥ Mk 13; cf. Mt 10²³ 16²⁷ᶠ·, Mk 8³⁸ 9¹, Lk 9²⁶ᶠ· 21³²). Connected with the Parousia, and

the cause of it, is the *Final Judgment*, which will occur at the end of the world, a judgment of individuals, and of universal scope, in which Christ the Son of Man will be Himself the Judge. The Fourth Gospel, while not without indications (cf. 12⁴⁸) of this final judgment, lays stress rather on a present judgment, 'fulfilling itself in a probation of character and a self-verdict which proceed now' (3¹⁷ᶠ· 12⁴⁷ᶠ·). With the teaching of Jesus on the Parousia and Judgment is connected the doctrine of a *Resurrection.* In the OT this was not a doctrine, but a vague longing of a few great minds for a deliverance from Sheol, a life superior to death. It was only gradually and at a late date that the conception became more distinct. At first it was a re-animation of Israel as a whole, but Is 26¹⁹ seems to breathe the more individual hope; and the clearest statement is reached in Dn 12²ᶠ·, the latest OT utterance on the subject. Nowhere in the OT is a resurrection thought of as extending beyond the case of Israel; but the doctrine of a resurrection of all men was gradually evolved, and had been accepted before the Christian era by the Pharisees and the mass of the people, though rejected by the Sadducees, in accordance with their principle of rejecting all traditions and accretions later than the OT. Our Lord's teaching holds a course between the two; it is based on the great principles of the OT, but is coloured, as to some details, by the eschatology of later writings, being at the same time free from the crudeness and extravagances of the popular beliefs. See Mt 22²³⁻³³ ∥ Mk 12¹⁸⁻²⁷, Lk 20²⁷⁻⁴⁰; Mt 8¹¹, Lk 13²⁸ᶠ·; Mt 10²⁸, Lk 14¹⁴, Jn 5²⁵ᶠ· ²⁸ᶠ· 11²¹⁻²⁶.

(*g*) *Angelology.*—The NT belief with regard to angels is taken over almost entire from the later phases of Judaism. Angels are innumerable (Mt 26⁵³, Lk 2¹³), and glorious in appearance (Mt 28³, Lk 2⁹; cf. δόξαι 2 P 2¹⁰); they minister to God's people (Mt 2¹³ 4¹¹, Lk 22⁴³), and carry the saints to Paradise (Lk 16²²). As Jahweh, in the OT, was surrounded by them, so the Son of Man will be accompanied by them at His Parousia (Mt 16²⁷ 25³¹); and they are charged with duties connected with the Last Day (Mt 13⁴¹·⁴⁰ 24³¹). In OT and NT alike only two angelic names are recorded, Michael and Gabriel (Dn 10¹³·²¹ 8¹⁶ 9²¹, Jude⁹, Rev 12⁷, Lk 1¹⁹·²⁶). Satan is an individual being (Mk 1¹³, Lk 10¹⁸). In a few points Christian conceptions show an advance upon the Jewish. In the Book of Daniel angels are guardians or patrons of particular countries (10¹³·²⁰·²¹ 12¹); in Mt 18¹⁰ they appear to be guardians of individual human beings, especially of children. Satan is attended by a company of angels (Mt 25⁴¹, Rev 12⁷), an idea not found in earlier writings. Angels are spirits (He 1¹⁴). Christ, and men in union with Him, are better than angels (He 2⁵, 1 Co 6³).

(*h*) *Scripture.*—This has been placed at the end, and not at the beginning, of the series, because the growth of Christianity out of the religion of Israel would remain a fact even if all the Jewish records had been destroyed. But it is true that the possession of, and devotion to, the OT Scriptures had an enormous effect on the formation of Christian thought and teaching and phraseology. The direct quotations from the OT in the NT are very many; and there are, besides, a mass of more or less distinct allusions and reminiscences which must be studied in their OT context if their meaning in the NT is to be understood. See artt. OLD TESTAMENT, and QUOTATIONS.

LITERATURE.—In addition to the works on OT Theology and on the Life of Christ, the following are among the more useful English works which are easily obtainable. They are arranged according to the sections in the article—

1. Sanday-Headlam, *Romans*, on chs. 9-11.
2. (*a*) Gore, *Bampton Lectures*; Illingworth, *do.*; Gibson, *The Thirty-nine Articles*, vol. i. 91-118; E. Caird, *The Evolu-*

tion of Religion. The doctrine of God from the Jewish side is treated in Montefiore's *Hibbert Lectures.*

(*b*) Westcott, *Hebrews*, 298–302 ; Candlish, *Expos. Times*, 1892 (Oct.-Nov.).

(*c*) Hort, *Judaistic Christianity* ; M'Giffert, *History of Christianity in the Apostolic Age* ; Bruce, *The Kingdom of God*, and *St. Paul's Conception of Christianity* ; Sand.-Headl., *Romans*, 187 ff.

(*d*) Cave, *The Scriptural Doctrine of Sacrifice* ; Maurice, *The Doctrine of Sacrifice* ; Milligan, *The Ascension and Heavenly Priesthood of our Lord* ; Westcott, *Hebrews* ; Sand.-Headl., *Romans*, 91 f. ; Driver, *Deuteronomy*, note on כָּפַר, 425 f.

(*e*) (*f*) Edersheim, *Life and Times of Jesus the Messiah* ; Drummond, *The Jewish Messiah* ; Stanton, *The Jewish and the Christian Messiah* ; Dalman, *The Words of Jesus* (Eng. tr.); Driver-Neubauer, *The Jewish Interpreters of Is. liii.* ; Charles, *Eschatology Hebrew Jewish and Christian* ; Salmond, *The Christian Doctrine of Immortality* ; Thackeray, *The Relation of St. Paul to Contemporary Jewish Thought* ; Enoch (ed. Charles) ; Psalms of Solomon (ed. Ryle-James).

(*g*) Fuller, Excursus on ' Angelology and Demonology,' in *Speaker's Apocrypha*, vol. i. ; Comm. on Dan., Zech., and Revelation.

(*h*) See art. SEPTUAGINT with the literature there.

Besides the above, a mass of useful information is contained in the following articles in Hastings' *DB* :—' Israel,' ' God,' ' Jesus Christ,' ' Covenant,' ' Law (in N.T.),' ' Sacrifice,' ' Atonement,' ' Messiah,' ' Eschatology,' ' Resurrection,' ' Angel,' ' Satan,' ' Development of Doctrine ' (Extra Vol.)

A. H. M'NEILE.

ISSUE OF BLOOD.—One peculiarly distressing case of this ailment is mentioned in the Gospels (Mt 9²⁰ αἱμορροοῦσα, Mk 5²⁵, and Lk 8⁴³ οὖσα ἐν ῥύσει αἵματος). The description indicates a very severe and obstinate form of uterine hæmorrhage possibly arising from internal growth, for the patient had suffered many things of many physicians and only grew worse for the treatment ; and she had endured the complaint for twelve years. The malady was in general regarded as incurable by medical treatment, and was handed over to be dealt with by magic charms and amulets. Its painful character, apart from its enfeebling and prostrating effects, was increased by the fact that it involved a rigorous isolation from society, and was looked upon with particular horror. All female discharges, even the normal monthly occurrences, were peculiarly repugnant to the Semitic mind, and came under the cycle of custom and legislation to which the Polynesian term *taboo* has been applied. The terror arose from the dread of supernatural penalties and of malignant agencies which were supposed to emanate from women at such times. Supernatural powers were believed to reside in the blood of the *menses*, on account of which it was itself held to be efficacious as a charm. The idea may have been modified before NT times, and yet would remain at least as a vague undefined repugnance and fear (see W. R. Smith, *RS*, Note on ' Holiness, Uncleanness, and Taboo '). The sufferer would further be compelled to perpetual celibacy.

Among Talmudic cures of this malady we find the following : ' Let the patient sit at the parting of the ways with a cup of wine in her hand, and let some one coming up behind startle her by calling out, Be healed of thine issue of blood.' And, ' Take three measures of onions, boil in wine and give the patient to drink, at the same time calling out suddenly, Be healed of thine issue.'—An interesting anticipation of certain familiar features of modern therapeutics.

That our Lord's healing of the sufferer was regarded as memorable and attained to a considerable vogue apart from the NT record, is evidenced by the legend that the votive figure at Bâniâs, supposed to be that of Christ, was erected by this woman out of gratitude to her Deliverer, and other kindred legends.

The chief feature of the miracle was the fact that the healing was gained surreptitiously, apart from the will and initiative of Jesus. Our Lord was pressing through the crowd on His way to the house of Jairus, when the woman, moved by a great expectation of healing, drew near to touch at least the fringe of His garment (in which special sanctity resided), assured that even this slight

contact would remove her trouble. Having accomplished her object, ' immediately she felt in her body that she was healed of the plague,' and our Lord became conscious that ' virtue ' had gone out of Him. The idea that healing power was resident in the body of Jesus, comparable to a charge of electric energy, is not to be entertained. The casual touching of His body by any sick person would have had no such result. We must emphasize (1) *the touch of faith.* The whole nature of the woman had been roused to activity and hopefulness. No labour of Jesus to create and evoke this essential condition of being healed was necessary or possible. The expectation existed at full tension, and she was prepared mentally and therefore physically to receive the healing power. And (2) corresponding to this exercise of faith is a *Divinely great capacity for sympathy resident in the spirit and life of Jesus.* While this capacity infinitely transcends the forces of human sympathy which exist in humanity, it still may be believed to operate on the same plane and to be not alien but kindred. The possibility of sympathetic relations being in existence between ' mind and mind,' quite irrespective of consciousness or will on the part of both or of either, is an ascertained fact, however it may be explainable. Various theories are put forward to account for the phenomena, but meanwhile the fact must be recognized—the power of mind to affect mind by other than the channels of sense. Moreover, (3), our Lord's own teaching must be duly weighed, that His works were due to *the indwelling Divine power.* The nature of Jesus was strung to sympathy with the whole complex coil of human suffering and need. At the very moment of this occurrence His heart was full of intensest sympathy with the sorrowing ruler. Such a nature then would present, quite apart from the immediate exercise of will, a fitting instrument for the Divine healing energy. The Divine power utilized and made more efficacious these already powerful sympathies and expectations; but while this is to be freely recognized, the chief emphasis is to be laid on the holy will of the unseen Father, with whom our Lord was morally and essentially one.

LITERATURE.—The Comm.,and standard works on the *Miracles*; Ker, *Serm.* 1st ser. p. 186 ff.; Maclaren, *Serm. pr. in Manchester*, 2nd ser. p. 294 ff. On the telepathic powers of the subliminal consciousness see the relevant sections of F. W. Myers' *Human Personality.*

T. H. WRIGHT.

ITURÆA.—This term is used in Lk 3¹ among other designations of political and geographical districts, the identification of whose rulers is intended to give a fixed chronological starting-point for the ministry of John the Baptist. It does not occur as a substantive in any pre-Christian writer. Neither does it occur again in post-Christian literature until the days of Eusebius, and doubtfully then. The term ' Ituræans,' however, as the name of a people, is frequently mentioned. The first mention among Greek writers of the Ituræans is that of Eupolemus (B.C. 150) as quoted by Eusebius (*Præp. Evan.* ix. 30). Cicero (*Philip.* ii. 112) speaks of them as a predatory people, and Cæsar (*Bell. Afr.* 20) calls them skilful archers (cf. Jos. *Ant.* XIII. xi. 3 [Dindorf reads Ἰτουραίαν ; but it is commonly agreed that this is incorrect, and Naber's and Niese's reading, Ἰτουραίων, is preferred]; Strabo XVI. ii. 10, 18, 20 ; Dio Cass. xlix. 32. 5 ; Appian, *Civ.* v. 7 ; also Virgil, *Georg.* ii. 448 ; Lucan, *Pharsal.* vii. 230, 514).

The most important fact brought into view by the history of the Ituræans, so far as the understanding of Lk 3¹ is concerned, is their migratory character. They first appear as the sons of Jetur (Gn 25¹⁵, 1 Ch 1³¹), a branch of the race of Ishmael (cf. artt. 'Jetur' and 'Ishmael' in Hastings' *DB*). Their original home was the territory to the S.E. of Palestine. In the course of their wanderings they drifted northward, and some time before the Exile reached the country adjacent to Israel, east of the Jordan. Late in the 2nd cent. B.C., Aristobulus I. conquered certain bands of non-Israelites who had settled in Galilee, and compelled them either to submit to circumcision or leave the country. It has been conjectured that among these there were some Ituræans, who moved still farther north. At any rate, in the next generation the Ituræans are definitely located in the region of Lebanon. Strabo (XVI. ii. 10) speaks of them as inhabiting the 'mountain country' which with Chalcis and Marsyas was ruled by Ptolemy the son of Mennæus (B.C. 85–40). He further describes them in association with the Arabs as 'all lawless men dwelling in the mountain region of the Libanus and anti-Libanus territory,' and harassing the agricultural population of the adjacent plain. D. Æmilius Secundus, a millitary commander under Quirinius, reports that in a campaign against the Ituræans in the Lebanon range, he had stormed a fortress of theirs (Mommsen, *Ephemeris Epigr.* iv. 1881, p. 538). With the death of Ptolemy, the government of this entire region passed into the hands of his son Lysanias, whom accordingly Dio Cassius calls 'king of the Ituræans' (xlix. 32). Lysanias was put to death by Mark Antony in B.C. 34, and a little over ten years later (B.C. 23) this territory came, by way of a lease, under the control of a chief named Zenodorus (Jos. *Ant.* XV. x. 1 ; *BJ* I. xx. 4) ; but in B.C. 20, upon the death of Zenodorus, Augustus gave a portion of it to Herod the Great ; and when Herod's kingdom was broken up among his heirs into tetrarchies, it fell to the lot of Philip to possess it (Jos. *Ant.* XV. x. 3 ; *BJ* II. vi. 3). Subsequently to the mention of Ituræa by St. Luke, the emperor Caligula bestowed it upon a certain Soemus (A.D. 38), entitled by Tacitus (*Ann.* xii. 23) and Dio Cassius (lix. 12) 'king of the Ituræans.' From A.D. 49, the date of the death of Soemus, and onwards, the country appears as a part of the province of Syria, furnishing a quota of soldiers for the Roman army (*Ephem. Epigr.* 1884, p. 194).

The mention of Ituræa by St. Luke raises the following questions : (1) Did he use the term as a noun or as an adjective ? This is partly a question of correct Greek usage. A noun 'Ituræa' would be a linguistic anachronism at the time of St. Luke. It is unknown until the 4th cent. ; but that the Evangelist fell into the error of using it as such is maintained by Schürer and H. Holtzmann, while Ramsay (*Expos.*, Feb. 1894, p. 144 ff., Apr. p. 288 ff.), contends against this position.*

(2) Out of this linguistic question grows the historical one : Did St. Luke speak accurately when he enumerated the Ituræan country as a

---

part of the tetrarchy of Philip? For even if the Evangelist did use the word 'Ituræa' as an adjective, it does not follow that he has correctly located the country. H. Holtzmann (*Hand-Com.* 'Syn. Gosp.' p. 58) calls it an error that Ituræa should be included with Trachonitis in Philip's tetrarchy, and explains that St. Luke probably had in mind a later arrangement of the territory under Agrippa. As a matter of fact, Josephus describes the tetrarchy of Philip as consisting of 'Batanea, Trachonitis, Auranitis, and certain parts of the house of Zeno (Zenodorus) about Paneas yielding a revenue of one hundred talents' (*Ant.* XVII. xi. 4 ; *BJ* II. vi. 3). Ituræa is not given in this description. But it does not seem probable that St. Luke, who is writing with so much regard for historical details, should have failed at this point. Hence efforts have been made to account for his statement as it stands. Of these it is easy to set aside as futile (*a*) the identification of Ituræa with *Jedur* (a region S.W. of Damascus), as etymologically unsound, and as not corresponding geographically to the descriptions given by Strabo. According to these, the Ituræans lived in a mountainous region. (*b*) Cheyne (art. 'Ituræa' in *Encyc. Bibl.*) proposes an interesting emendation of the text of Luke. Instead of Ἰτουραίας he would read Αὐρανίτιδος. But in order to get this substitution he assumes that by a transcriptional error ιδ was dropped from Αὐρανίτιδος, and the remainder of the word, thus left in confusion, was by another transcriptional manipulation converted into Ἰτουραίας. Evidently this is too elaborate and too purely conjectural a proceeding to be accepted. (*c*) Statements of Eusebius (*OS*² p. 268, Ἰτουραία ἡ καὶ Τραχωνῖτις, and p. 298, Τραχωνῖτις χώρα ἡ καὶ Ἰτουραία ; cf. also Jerome's translation of the same, 'Trachonitis regio sive Ituræa,' *Lib. de Situ*, etc., p. 238) definitely identify Ituræa and Trachonitis, and have been accepted as satisfactorily removing the difficulty. The terms 'Trachonitis' and 'Ituræa' do not, however, seem to be used by the Evangelist with the exact equivalency that the phraseology of Eusebius suggests. Hence (*d*) it is best not to identify Ituræa with Trachonitis as a whole, but to assume a certain overlapping of the two, giving a fairly painstaking writer good ground for connecting them together in the attempt to present the situation broadly. This conclusion is supported by the constantly changing character of the territory occupied by the Ituræans, as exhibited in the sketch of their history above given, as well as the repeated shifting of the boundary lines in this general region during the centuries before and after Christ.

LITERATURE.—Münter, *de Rebus Ituræorum*, 1824 ; Schürer, *GJV*³ i. 707 ff. [*HJP* I. ii. App. i.] ; Krenkel, *Josephus u. Lukas*, 1894, pp. 90–95 ; G. A. Smith, art. 'Ituræa' in Hastings' *DB*, and *Expos.* March 1894, pp. 231–238 ; Ramsay, *Expos.* Jan. 1894, p. 43 ff., Feb. p. 144 ff., Apr. p. 288 ff.

A. C. ZENOS.

---

* The importance of this conclusion by Professor Ramsay, apart from the purely academic vindication of St. Luke as a master of good Greek, is that it establishes an analogy for the South-Galatian theory so strenuously advocated by himself.

J

JACOB.—**1.** According to the genealogical list in Matthew, Jacob (Ἰακώβ) is the father of Joseph the husband of Mary (Mt 1¹⁵. ¹⁶).

2. One of the reputed progenitors of the Jewish nation. Apart from the reference to Jacob's well

---

(πηγὴ τοῦ Ἰακώβ, see next art.), in Jn 4⁶, and his place in the genealogies of Matthew and Luke (Mt 1², Lk 3³⁴), Jacob is mentioned in the Gospels only as one of the three patriarchs (Mt 8¹¹ 'Many shall come from the east and the west ; and shall sit down with Abraham and Isaac and Jacob . . .' cf. Lk 13²⁸ᶠ·, Mt 22³² ∥ Mk 12²⁶, Lk 20³⁷ 'I am the God of Abraham, and the God of Isaac, and the God of Jacob'). These three were grouped from early times (Ex 2²⁴ 3⁶· ¹⁵· ¹⁶, Lv 26⁴², 1 K 18³⁶, 2 K 13²³, Jer 33²⁶, 1 Ch 29¹⁸, 2 Ch 30⁶), and occupied a place apart in Jewish thought. According to the Rabbis, they alone were entitled to be called אָבוֹת 'fathers.' To them was traced not only the origin of the nation, but also the beginning of true worship. As a descendant of these three, a Jew might claim nobility and a special relationship to God. This claim was recognized as זְכוּת אָבוֹת 'righteousness of the fathers,' and was based on Ex 32¹³. It was denounced by John the Baptist (see ABRAHAM, and cf. Mt 3⁹, Lk 3⁸), and it figured prominently in the conflicts between Jesus and the Pharisees (cf. Jn 8³³· ³⁷). Apparently in the time of Jesus it was liable to be abused, and on this account later Rabbis refused to lay stress upon it, declaring it no longer valid. In Rabbinic literature, Jacob is recognized as the most important of the three patriarchs (cf. Lv 26⁴²). He prevails with God (Gn 32²⁸). He names the sanctuary the house of God (28²²), and, in contrast to Abraham the father of Ishmael, and Isaac the father of Esau, Jacob inherits the promise in *all* his children (49).

LITERATURE.—A most suggestive analysis of the character of Jacob, and a full discussion of the problems of the narrative in Genesis, including the names 'Jacob' and 'Israel,' is given by Driver in Hastings' *DB* ii. 526–535; cf. also Stanley, *Jewish Church*, i. pp. 46–66; Gore, *Studia Biblica*, iii. 37 f.; Ph. Berger, 'La Signification Historique des Noms des Patriarches Hébreux' in *Mémoires de la Société Linguistique*, vi. 150.

G. GORDON STOTT.

JACOB'S WELL.—On the arrest of John the Baptist by Herod Antipas, Jesus left Judæa and returned with His loosely-attached followers to Galilee (Mk 1¹⁴). He travelled by 'the great north road' through Samaria. This road, after skirting the W. edge of the plain of Mukhneh, and passing under the slopes of Gerizim, enters the wide bay forming the approach to the Vale of Nâblus. Here it divides, one branch striking west, the other going north across the bay, past the ruins and spring of 'Askar. In the fork of these roads is Jacob's Well (*Bîr Yâḳûb*), where Jesus, being wearied with His journey,—it was about the hour of noon,—sat down and rested (Jn 4⁶).

The well is described (Jn 4⁵) as in the neighbourhood of 'a city of Samaria called Sychar, near to the parcel of ground that Jacob gave to his son Joseph.' This parcel of ground (χωρίον) is evidently the plot referred to in Gn 33¹⁸· ¹⁹ as lying 'before' (or 'to the east of') Shechem, which Jacob purchased from the native Shechemites for 100 *ḳesîṭahs*. Somewhere within its borders the bones of Joseph were afterwards buried (Jos 24³², cf. Ac 7¹⁶): and the plot came to have for the N. Kingdom the kind of sanctity that Machpelah had for the Kingdom of Judah. It is nowhere recorded that Jacob dug a well here; but the fact had become a matter of common and well-established belief by the time of Jesus, and no serious doubt has since been raised as to the origin or locality of the well. The traditional sites of Jacob's Well and Joseph's Tomb (a little to the N.) are acknowledged by Jews, Samaritans, Christians, and Moslems alike. The tradition for the well goes back to Eusebius (*OS*, *s.v.* 'Sychar'). See also art. SYCHAR.

In v.⁶ the well is called πηγή ('fountain') τοῦ Ἰακώβ: in v.¹¹ the woman refers to it as τὸ φρέαρ ('the cistern *or* pit') which Jacob gave. The latter is the more exact description, inasmuch as it 'is not an *'ain*, a well of living water, but a *ber*, a cistern to hold water' (*PEFSt*, 1897, p. 197). Rainwater probably formed the greater part of its supply, though another smaller portion may have been due to infiltration from the surrounding strata. This would partly account for the 'great local reputation' of the water 'for purity and flavour among the natives of El 'Askar and Nâblus.' The neighbouring springs were 'heavy' (or hard),

being strongly impregnated with lime, while Jacob's Well contained 'lighter' (or softer) water, 'cool, palatable, and refreshing' (G. A. Smith, *HGHL* p. 676). The woman's presence at the well *at noon* may have been due to the fact that she was seeking water for workmen on the adjacent cornlands, rather than for domestic use (*PEFSt*, 1897, p. 149). The sacred associations of the spot, together with the 'real excellence' of the water, probably drew visitors regularly both from 'Askar (¾ mile away) and from Nâblus (1¾ miles distant), in spite of nearer and more copious supplies.

The true mouth of the well is several feet below the surface, and beneath a ruined vault, which once formed part of the ancient cruciform church mentioned by Arculph (A.D. 700), and referred to by Jerome (*OS*, *s.v.* 'Sychar'). This narrow opening, 4 ft. long and just wide enough to admit the body of a man, broadens out into the cylindrical tank or well itself, which is about 7½ ft. in diameter and over 100 feet deep (G. A. Smith, *l.c.* p. 373). The interior appears to have been lined throughout with masonry, and thick layers of débris cover the bottom.*

If the uniform tradition as to the well's origin be correct, probably the incomer Jacob sank this 'deep' pit to avoid collision with the natives among whom he settled. A well of his own, on his own ground, would make him secure and independent.

LITERATURE.—Hastings' *DB* ii. ᴅ35 f.; *Encyc. Bibl.* iv. 4829; Robinson, *BRP*² ii. 283 f.; Thomson, *LB* ii. 146 f.; Baedeker-Socin, *Pal.* 215 f.; Stanley, *SP* 241; G. A. Smith, *HGHL* 367 f., 676; Sanday, *Sacred Sites*, 31 ff., 91; *PEFMem.* ii. 172 f.; *PEFSt*, 1897, pp. 96, 149, 196; *Expos. Times*, v. [1893] 97 f.

A. W. COOKE.

JAIRUS.—**1.** The name Ἰάειρος occurs in Mk 5²² and in the Lukan parallel (8⁴¹), but not in Mt. (9¹⁸). Such variants as Ἰάηρος, Ἰάιρος, Ἰάϊρος (as Cod. א) are also to be met with in the MSS. It cannot be positively identified with the Heb. name יָאִיר (as in Jg 10³,=prob. 'Jahweh enlightens'), the LXX equivalent of which is variously Ἰαείρ, Ἰαήρ, Ἰαΐρ, by simple transcription. In favour of regarding Ἰάειρος as the Grecized form of the Heb. name is the fact that this form occurs in LXX in Est 2⁵ for יָאִיר, the father of Mordecai (Cod. A, by a curious slip, has Ἰαιρός), as also in the Apocrypha (Est 11²), where the EV has 'Jairus' as the name of the same person. In any case, however, analogy permits the adoption of 'Jair' as the English equivalent of Ἰάειρος; and were the name in familiar vogue, like such names as 'Paul,' this would naturally be its form. The AV 'Jairus' follows the Vulg. (Wyclif, 'Jayrus'). Note the RV 'Jaïrus,' fixing it as a trisyllable; and cf. other modes of transcription, as *e.g.* 'Jaeirus' (*Twentieth Cent. NT*, ed. 1904).

Cheyne (*Ency. Bibl.* ii. s.v.) regards the name as unauthentic, 'the spontaneous invention of a pious and poetic imagination.' He rejects its identification with OT יָאִיר, and yet he does not hesitate to explain it by reference to יָעִיר, simply because the meaning of the latter term, as he gives it ('he will awaken'), suits his theory of a fanciful creation to fit the drift of the story. This is quite arbitrary and precarious. (Note, the name יָעִיר occurs in 1 Ch 20⁵ as the *Ḳᵉrê*; EV 'Jair').

2. Jairus is described in Mk. as εἷς τῶν ἀρχισυναγώγων (5²²) and similarly afterwards as ἀρχισυνάγωγος. Lk.'s ἄρχων τῆς συναγωγῆς (8⁴¹) is perhaps simply explanatory of this term which he himself uses later (v.⁴⁹). Mt. has ἄρχων alone (9¹⁸); but there is no need to suppose that this is intended to represent Jairus as a member of the Sanhedrin, or in any other capacity than that indicated in the other Gospels. The brevity and conciseness of the

---

* Robinson (in 1838) gives the depth as 105 feet; Anderson (in 1866) and Conder (in 1875) measured 75 feet. Evidently débris from the surface accumulated rather quickly.

form in which Mt. gives the story probably explain this loose use of ἄρχων. Wyclif's 'prince' here is due to the Vulg. *princeps*, and elsewhere he invariably uses 'prince of the synagoge' as = ἀρχισυνάγωγος. The Vulg., however, uses *archisynagogus* in the Markan passage, whilst in Lk 8⁴⁹ it has *principem synagogæ*, perhaps through the influence of the phrase in v.⁴¹. The Gr. term exactly = the Heb. title רֹאשׁ הַכְּנֶסֶת, and the office held by Jairus had well-defined functions. Pre-eminently the 'ruler' (*al.* 'president' or 'leader') was the director of public worship. Schürer holds that generally there was 'but one archisynagogus for each synagogue' (*HJP* II. ii. 65). The expression used in Mk 5²² quite agrees with this, as it describes the *class* to which Jairus belonged (one of the 'synagogue-rulers' or 'synagogue-presidents') rather than a particular body of 'rulers' of which he was a member. The locality of the synagogue in which he held office is not definitely indicated. See artt. RULER and SYNAGOGUE.

3. In the triple narrative in which Jairus figures, Mk 5²¹⁻⁴³ = Mt 9¹⁸⁻²⁶ = Lk 8⁴⁰⁻⁵⁶, the condensed form of Mt.'s account is most noticeable. In addition to the omission of the ruler's name and the loose use of ἄρχων (see above), there is no mention of the servant who met our Lord and Jairus on the way with the news that the child was dead (Mk 5³⁵ = Lk 8⁴⁹). In harmony with this, whilst Mk. says she was *in extremis* (ἐσχάτως ἔχει), and Lk. that she 'was dying' (ἀπέθνησκεν), when her father came to Jesus, Mt. represents her as already dead (ἄρτι ἐτελεύτησεν). Perhaps, as a matter of structure, the prefatory link in Mt 9¹⁸ may be compared with the phrase in Mk 5³⁵ (= Lk 8⁴⁹) ἔτι αὐτοῦ λαλοῦντος, with a bearing on this point.

Cheyne thinks the Mt. form of the story the most original, and explains the representation in Mk. on this point as due to the feeling of a later time that no one would have had a sufficiently bold faith to ask Jesus to restore one who was already dead. So far as that goes, however, the Markan account is parallel with the situation in the story of Lazarus (Jn 11); and we have no other instance in the Gospels besides this in Mt. of a request that one dead should be restored to life. Compression still best accounts for the form in Matthew. The account of the actual restoration to life is also given with the greatest brevity.

The effort to explain this incident as a case of restoration from trance is not quite successful. Mk.'s narrative would admit of such an interpretation, but Lk.'s definite phrases in vv.⁵³· ⁵⁵ distinctly fix the sense otherwise. In the primitive tradition the daughter of Jairus was believed to have been brought back from death to life. The story as a whole is full of grace and beauty, and 'belongs to the earliest stratum of the Gospel tradition' (Cheyne, *Ency. Bibl. ut supra*).

J. S. CLEMENS.

JAMES (Heb. יַעֲקֹב, Gr. Ἰακώβ, Ἰάκωβος. The English name *James* is analogous to the Portuguese *Xayme* and Gael. *Hamish*).—The name does not occur in the OT except in the case of the patriarch, but had become common in NT times, and is borne by several persons mentioned in the Gospels. Passing over the father of Joseph the husband of the Virgin Mary, according to St. Matthew's genealogy (Mt 1¹⁶ where the form is Ἰακώβ), we have—
1. James the father (AV 'brother') of Judas, Lk 6¹⁶ ('not Iscariot,' Jn 14²²), the Thaddæus of Mt. and Mk.). The AV translation is derived from the Latin of Beza, and is due to a confusion of this Judas with a quite different person, Judas (Jude) the 'brother of James' (Jude¹, Mt 13⁵⁵). The older English versions have either 'Judas of James' (Wyclif = Vulg. *Iudam Iacobi*) or 'Judas James' sonne' (Tindale, etc.). Further, St. Luke's practice is to insert ἀδελφός when he means 'brother' (Lk 3¹ 6¹⁴, Ac 12²). Nothing more is known of this James.

2. James the brother of John (Mt 10², Mk 3¹⁷, Lk 6¹⁴, Ac 1¹³), elder * son of Zebedee, a well-to-do † Galilæan fisherman, most probably a native of Capernaum. The call of James to Apostleship is related in Mt 4²¹· ²², Mk 1¹⁹· ²⁰ and (perhaps) Lk 5¹⁰.‡ The two sons of Zebedee appear to have been partners (κοινωνοί, μέτοχοι) with Peter in the fishing industry. Their mother's name was Salome, who was probably a sister of the Virgin Mary (see art. SALOME). The two brothers received from our Lord the name *Boanerges* ('sons of thunder'), perhaps because of their impetuous zeal for their Master's honour, shown by incidents like the wish to call down fire to consume certain Samaritans who refused Him a passage through their country (Lk 9⁵⁴; cf. Mk 9³⁸, Lk 9⁴⁹⁻⁵⁰). James is specially mentioned as present at the healing of Peter's wife's mother (Mk 1²⁹), at the raising of Jairus' daughter (Mk 5³⁷), at the Transfiguration (Mk 9²), at the Mount of Olives during the great 'eschatological' discourse (Mk 13³), and at the agony in the Garden of Gethsemane (Mk 14³³). On two of these occasions, the first and the fourth, Andrew is associated with the three; but on all the others, Peter, James, and John are alone with Christ. The special favour accorded to the two brothers (and perhaps their kinship to Jesus) probably prompted the ambitious request of Salome that they might sit as assessors to Him in His kingdom (Mk 10³⁵⁻⁴⁰, Mt 20²⁰⁻²³). James was called upon to 'drink the cup' of suffering (Mk 10³⁸· ³⁹) first of all the Apostolic band, being beheaded by Herod Agrippa I. in A.D. 44 (Ac 12²). An untrustworthy tradition represents him as preaching the gospel in Spain, of which country he is patron saint. Eusebius (*HE* ii. 9) relates, on the authority of Clement of Alexandria, that, when he was tried for his life, his accuser was so greatly affected by his constancy that he declared himself a Christian, and died with him after obtaining his forgiveness and blessing. See, further, Hastings' *DB* ii. 541.

3. James the son of Alphæus, one of the Twelve (Mt 10³, Mk 3¹⁸, Lk 6¹⁵, Ac 1¹³). In each list he stands at the head of the third group along with Simon Zelotes (with whom he is coupled by St. Luke), Judas of James (= Thaddæus, with whom he is coupled by Mt. and Mk.), and Judas Iscariot. The Gospels tell us nothing more about him, but he was most likely a brother of Matthew, who also was a 'son of Alphæus' (cf. Mt 9⁹ with Mk 2¹⁴). He has been identified with (4) and (5); but the probabilities seem to the present writer to be against the former identification, while the latter is almost certainly wrong.

4. James ὁ μικρός § (Mk 15⁴⁰; cf. Mt 27⁵⁶, Jn 19²⁵). He is mentioned as the son of a Mary, probably the wife of Clopas, one of the four women, of whom the other three were Mary the Lord's mother, Mary Magdalene, and Salome, present at the crucifixion. This Mary, with Mary Magdalene, re-

---

* The usual order is 'James and John.' St. Luke sometimes inverts it (8⁵¹ 9²⁸, Ac 1¹³), probably because of the early death of James and the subsequent prominence of John.

† He had 'hired servants' (Mk 1²⁰). His wife was one of those who ministered to Christ 'of their substance' (Mk 15⁴¹, Lk 8³).

‡ The question whether the Lukan narrative refers to the same incident as that related by Mt. and Mk. is not easy to decide. Hammond, Trench, Wordsworth, and other commentators answer it in the affirmative; Alford, Greswell, etc., in the negative. Plummer ('St. Luke' in *Internat. Crit. Com.*) is doubtful. A. Wright regards it as a conflation of the Markan narrative with that found in Jn 21¹⁻⁶. The characteristic features of the Lukan account are: (1) there is no mention of Andrew or Zebedee; (2) St. Peter is the prominent figure; (3) there is no command to follow Christ; (4) the fishermen are washing (not casting or mending) their nets; (5) there is a miraculous draught of fishes.

§ St. Jerome's rendering *minor* (Vulg. *Maria Jacobi minoris*), on which he founds an argument for the identification of this James with (3) and (5), takes no account of the fact that the Greek is positive, not comparative.

mained to see where Jesus was buried. She had another son Joseph. Those who identify this James with (3) argue that Alphæus (Ἀλφαῖος, חֵלֶף) and Clopas (Κλωπᾶς) are two forms of the same name (Meyer, Alford). Philologically this is improbable. The extant Syriac Versions render 'Alphæus' by *Chalpai*, while 'Clopas' is rendered by *Kleopha*. Nor can it be said to be absolutely certain that ἡ τοῦ Κλωπᾶ of Jn 19²⁵ means the *wife* of Clopas. It may mean '*daughter* of Clopas.' And it is unlikely that St. Mark would describe James *the son of Alphæus* by a new designation, James '*the Little*' (in stature).* Moreover, it is hard to see why St. John, writing for readers acquainted with the Synoptic Gospels, should introduce into his Gospel the name Clopas if he meant Alphæus. On the whole, therefore, we must conclude with Ewald (*Hist. of Israel*, vi. 305, note 4) that the identification is unlikely.† Of this James we know nothing further.

5. James the Lord's brother. He is mentioned by name twice in the Gospels (Mt 13⁵⁵, Mk 6³). He is the eldest of four brothers, James, Joseph, Judas, and Simon (Simon and Judas, Mt 13⁵⁵). Other references to the Brethren of the Lord are found in Mt 12⁴⁶⁻⁵⁰, Mk 3³¹⁻³⁵, Lk 8¹⁹⁻²¹, Jn 7³⁻⁵. From these passages we learn that they thought Him mad, and opposed His work. St. John tells us plainly that His brethren did not believe in Him.

The following passages outside the Gospels have to do with this James: 1 Co 15⁷, Ac 1¹³ 12¹⁷ 15 (*passim*) 21¹⁸⁻²⁵, Gal 1¹⁸. ¹⁹ 2¹⁻¹⁰; Jos. *Ant.* XX. ix. 1; Eusebius, *HE* ii. 1 (quotation from Clement of Alexandria), ii. 23 (quotation from Hegesippus), vii. 19; Jerome, *de Vir. Illus.* (quotation from the Gospel according to the Hebrews); *Clementine Homilies* (ad init.); *Apostolic Constitutions*, viii. 35. From these passages we learn that he was converted to a full acknowledgment of Christ (probably by the Resurrection), that the Lord appeared to him specially, that he became head of the Church of Jerusalem, and that he was put to death by the Jews either just before the siege (Hegesippus) or some ten years earlier (Josephus). He was surnamed the Just by his fellow-countrymen, and was greatly respected by all classes in Jerusalem.

The Epistle bearing his name, which is almost universally attributed to the brother of the Lord, is of the greatest interest to students of the Gospels. There is no Epistle which contains in a small compass so many allusions to the teaching of Christ subsequently contained in the Gospels as we have them. The following list includes all the more striking parallels: Mt 5³. ⁷. ⁹. ¹¹. ²². ³⁴⁻³⁷ = Ja 2⁵. ¹³ 3¹⁸ 1². ¹⁹ 5¹²; Mt 6¹⁹. ²⁴ = Ja 5² 4⁴; Mt 7¹. ⁷⁻⁸. ¹². ¹⁶. ²⁴ = Ja 4¹¹⁻¹² 1⁵ 2⁸ 3¹¹. ¹² 1²² (all these are from the Sermon on the Mount). Cf. also Mt 12³⁶ with Ja 3¹. ², Mt 18⁴ with Ja 4⁶; Lk 6²⁴ = Ja 5¹; Lk 12¹⁶⁻²¹ = Ja 4¹⁴; Lk 8¹⁵ 21¹⁹ (ὑπομονή, used by Lk. only in the Gospels) = Ja 1³. ⁴ 5¹¹; Jn 3³ = Ja 1¹⁷; Jn 8³¹⁻³³ = Ja 1²⁵; Jn 13¹⁷ = Ja 4¹⁷.‡ On these passages it may be remarked (1) that, while some of the parallels may be explained as coincidences, there remain others which even Renan (*l'Antéchrist*³, p. 54) admits to be reminiscences of the words of Jesus; (2) that the evidence is cumulative, and includes correspondence in teaching (*e.g.* on riches, formalism, prayer) as well as in language; (3) that the most striking parallels are with the Gospel according to St. Matthew, and with the earlier parts of that, suggesting the possibility that James may at first

have been a hearer of our Lord, and making it fairly certain that he was acquainted with the special Matthæan 'source.'

A second point to be noticed is that the Epistle of James is clearly the work of one trained in the strict observance of the Law, while at the same time his obedience to it is the obedience of zealous love, as far removed as possible from the Pharisaic formalism denounced by our Lord (Ja 1²²⁻²⁷ 2⁸⁻¹² 4⁵⁻⁷ 5¹⁰. ¹¹). Both in his case and in that of St. Paul, although they developed on somewhat different lines, the Law was a παιδαγωγὸς εἰς Χριστόν. This view of the training of James, and consequently of our Lord his Brother, is confirmed by the Gospels. The names of the four brothers, James, Joseph, Simon (= Simeon), and Jude (= Judah), are those of patriarchs. The parents are careful to observe the Law in our Lord's case (Lk 2²²⁻²⁴. ³⁹. ⁴¹. ⁴²).

The Western Church, in regarding James the Lord's brother as identical with James the son of Alphæus, seems to have been influenced by the authority of Jerome, who, in replying to Helvidius (*circa* 383 A.D.), urges that, as James the Lord's brother is called an Apostle by St. Paul (Gal 1¹⁸. ¹⁹), he must be identified with James the son of Alphæus, since James the son of Zebedee was dead; and, further, that he was our Lord's first cousin. (Jerome does not identify Alphæus with Clopas). But it may be observed (1) that Jerome himself seems to have abandoned this view (*Ep.* cxx. *ad Hedibiam*); (2) that ἀδελφός never = ἀνεψιὸς in the NT; (3) that James the brother of the Lord is always distinguished from the Twelve (Jn 2¹², Ac 1¹⁴; cf. Mt 12⁴⁷⁻⁵⁰); (4) that 'His brethren did not believe in him' (Jn 7³. ⁵); (5) that the word ἀπόστολος, on which Jerome relies, is not confined to the Twelve (Ac 14⁴. ¹⁴, 1 Co 15⁴⁻⁷).* [For a fuller discussion of the question see the article BRETHREN OF THE LORD].

LITERATURE. — Besides the authorities quoted above, see articles in Hastings' *DB* (by J. B. Mayor), *Encyc. Bibl.* (by Orello Cone), Smith's *DB* ² (by Meyrick, with full list of the views of British theologians); Herzog, *PRE* ³ (by Sieffert, with Bibliography); Commentaries of Swete (on Mk.), Alford, Meyer (Eng. tr., Edin. 1882), Plumptre (*Cambridge Bible*), von Soden (*Hand-Commentar*, Freiburg, 1890), Plummer (in *Expositor's Bible*, 1891); W. Patrick, *James the Lord's Brother*, 1906.

H. W. FULFORD.

JANNAI. — One of the links in the Lukan genealogy of our Lord (Lk 3²⁴).

JARED. — Father of Enoch, named in our Lord's genealogy (Lk 3³⁷).

JEALOUSY. — This word is not used in the Gospels, though Jn 2¹⁷ has ὁ ζῆλος τοῦ οἴκου σου = קִנְאַת בֵּיתְךָ (Ps 69¹⁰) = 'jealousy for thy house'; and one of Jesus' disciples was Simon ὁ ζηλωτής (Lk 6¹⁵, Ac 1¹³) = Simon ὁ Καναναῖος (Mk 3¹⁸), a man who had belonged to that party in the Jewish State which was so jealous for the sole sovereignty of God in Israel that it regarded the recognition of any other (*e.g.* by paying tribute to Cæsar) as a form of treason. But the thing which the OT means by קִנְאָה, in all its aspects, is everywhere present in the NT, and especially in the Gospels.

1. The jealousy of God in the OT is connected with the truth that He is God alone, and it is expressed mainly in two ways. First, *in the exclusive claims which He makes for Himself*: 'Thou shalt have no other gods before me' (Ex 20³); 'Thou shalt love the Lord thy God with all thy

---

* μικρός may also mean 'young' (Deissmann, *Bible Studies*, Eng. tr. 144).

† Ewald, however, identifies Clopas with Cleopas (a Greek name), Lk 24¹⁸.

‡ Fuller lists will be found in Mayor, *Epistle of St. James* (2nd ed.), lxxxv-lxxxviii; Salmon, *Introduction to NT*, 455 (5th ed.); Zahn, *Einleitung*, i. p. 87; Knowling, *St. James*, xxi-xxiii.

* In favour of the identification of (3), (4), and (5) it is sometimes urged that it is unlikely there would be four persons, all named James, closely connected with our Lord. But it must be remembered (1) that the name was certain to be popular among patriotic Jews; and (2) that 'Jewish names in ordinary use at that time were very few' (Lightfoot, *Galatians*, p. 268). Twelve persons are mentioned in the NT as bearing the name Simon (Simeon), and nine that of Joseph (Joses).

heart,' etc. (Dt 6⁵); 'I am the Lord, that is my name; and my glory will I not give to another, neither my praise unto graven images' (Is 42⁸). This exclusiveness or intolerance of God—His jealousy *for Himself*, as it may be called—pervades the OT. It is the source of that compulsion which He puts upon the human race to learn the most important lesson which the mind is capable of receiving, that there is one only, the living and true God. This is the presupposition not only of all uplifting religion, but of all science, and of all morality which rises above caste and convention; and what we see in the OT is the jealousy of God working monotheism into the constitution of a race who should impart it to the world. In this sense the jealousy of God is represented in the mind of Christ by the exclusive claims which He makes for Himself, and in the rest of the NT by the reiteration of these claims through the lips of His disciples. Sometimes the expression of it is informal: *e.g.* 'He that loveth father or mother more than me is not worthy of me' (Mt 10³⁷); or, 'Blessed is he whosoever shall find none occasion of stumbling in me' (11⁶). Sometimes, again, it is quite explicit: 'No one knoweth the Son save the Father; neither doth any know the Father save the Son, and he to whomsoever the Son willeth to reveal him' (11²⁷). In the Fourth Gospel this tone predominates, and there could not be more precise and formal expressions of the jealousy of God, as God is revealed in Christ, than are found, *e.g.*, in Jn 1¹⁸ 8²⁴ 14⁶ (see art. PREACHING CHRIST). This jealousy of God for Himself is echoed in passages like Ac 4¹² ('There is none other name,' etc.), 1 Co 3¹¹ ('Other foundation can no man lay,' etc.), Gal 1⁸ᶠ· ('Though we or an angel from heaven should preach unto you any other gospel,' etc.: the peculiarity of the Pauline as opposed to the Judaizing gospel being that it ascribed the whole of salvation to Christ *alone*, and did not share His glory with the Law), and 2 Jn 9ᶠ·.

The second way in which the jealousy of God expresses itself in the OT is in *God's unreserved identification of Himself with His people*. It is a jealousy *for them*, in which their cause is His, in which His honour (if such a word can be used in such a connexion) is touched if they are wronged, in which His love rises into passion, and takes on itself responsibilities for them of which they would not have dared to think. Sometimes this, too, is informally expressed: *e.g.* 'He that toucheth you toucheth the apple of his eye' (Zec 2⁸). Sometimes it is quite explicit: *e.g.* the great Messianic promises of Is 9¹ᶠ· are sealed in v.⁷ by 'The jealousy of Jahweh of hosts shall do this.' Cf. also the striking passage Zec 8²ᶠᶠ· All this is reproduced in the mind and words of Jesus. He is jealous for His people, especially for 'the little ones' (who, however, are not so much a class of Christians, as Christians generally—a weak and inconsiderable folk in ordinary eyes), and nothing that concerns them is alien to Him. The very slightest service done them has a reward solemnly assured to it (Mt 10⁴²); the sin of causing one of them to stumble is denounced with a passion which startles us still as we read (18⁶); cf. art. ANGER, 2 (*a*). The most thrilling illustration of this jealousy of Jesus for His 'little ones' is given in the Final Judgment: 'Inasmuch as ye did it (*or*, did it not) to one of these least, my brethren, ye did it (*or*, did it not) unto me' (25⁴⁰· ⁴⁵). Jealous love can go no further than this.

2. Since God, especially God revealed in Christ, is in this twofold sense a jealous God, it is clear that there must be in the Christian religion and character a corresponding intensity and passion. Christians ought to be jealous for Christ, sensitive to all that dishonours Him, and especially to all that degrades Him from the place which He claims, and which belongs to Him alone. The NT gives Him what He demands, the name which is above every name; and it is inconsistent with jealousy for Him to give Him only a name alongside of other names—to classify Him, as is often done, with prophets or religious heroes or founders of religions. Jealousy, no doubt, is apt to be a turbid virtue; the OT examples of it—Phinehas, Elijah, and Jehu —all illustrate this; and even in Christian history jealousy for Jesus as sole Lord and Saviour has often been confounded with zeal for a definition of one's own making, or for the predominance of one's own ecclesiastical or political faction. Of all virtues, it is the one which most readily calls the old man into the field to reinforce the new, a process which always ends in disaster. Nevertheless, it is the primary virtue of a Christian, just as the keeping of the first commandment was the primary virtue of a Jew.

3. Apart from their use in the sense of an ardent and exclusive devotion to God in Christ, and to the cause of Christ in His people (2 Co 11²), the associations of the words ζῆλος, ζηλοῦν in the NT are rather repellent. Sometimes ζῆλος is *anger* (Ac 5¹⁷), the Heb. קִנְאָה being at least once rendered θυμός in LXX; often it is *envy* (Ac 13⁴⁵: so the verb 7⁹ 17⁵); in this sense, too, it is frequently combined with ἔρις (Ro 13¹³, 1 Co 3³, 2 Co 12²⁰, Gal 5²⁰); only rarely does it denote a keen and affectionate interest (2 Co 7⁷· ¹¹). But this last sense is the one which is really congruous with the fundamental import of jealousy as the sense of self-respect and of honour in the God who is revealed in Christ as Love.

JAMES DENNEY.

JECHONIAH.—Also called in OT *Jehoiachin* and *Coniah*; mentioned in Mt 1¹¹ᶠ· as a link in our Lord's genealogy.

JEHOSHAPHAT.—A king of Judah, named in our Lord's genealogy (Mt 1⁸).

JERICHO was situated in the valley of the Jordan, about 5 miles west of the river and about 6 north of the Dead Sea. The distance between Jerusalem and Jericho was about 17 miles. The immediate vicinity enjoyed the advantage of abundant springs (2 K 2¹⁹⁻²²), and showed great fertility. It was the 'city of palms' (Dt 34³, 2 Ch 28¹⁵), and Josephus gives an enthusiastic account of the abundance and variety of its products (*BJ* IV. viii. 2, 3).

The Jericho which was destroyed by Joshua was a considerable town, characterized by the wealth of its inhabitants and the strength of its fortifications (Jos 6 and 7). The rebuilding of the city is described in 1 K 16³⁴, but the place is referred to at earlier dates (Jos 18²¹, 2 S 10⁵, 1 Ch 19⁵). A school of prophets was established at Jericho (2 K 2⁵), and it was from Jericho that Elijah and Elisha went down to Jordan. Other references are found in 2 Ch 28¹⁵, 2 K 25⁵, Jer 39⁵, Ezr 2³⁴, Neh 3² 7³⁶.

In the time of our Lord, Jericho was a large and important town. Antony granted the revenues of Jericho and the surrounding district to Cleopatra, and these were farmed from her by Herod the Great. Afterwards Herod received Jericho by gift from Augustus, and erected a citadel, which he called *Cypros*, above the town. He also built within the city a palace, in which he died. This palace was rebuilt by Herod Archelaus after it had been burned down by Simon during the troubles which followed upon the death of Herod the Great (Jos. *Ant.* XVII. x. 6 and xiii. 1). After the deposition of Herod Archelaus as tetrarch of Judæa, Jericho was held directly by the Roman procurator, who farmed out its revenues.

Modern Jericho (*er-Rîḥa*) is a miserable village of 300 inhabitants; the forest of palms has entirely disappeared, and only here and there can traces of the former fertility of the district be seen. The exact site of the Canaanite Jericho does not correspond with that of the modern village, and probably there were two towns, a little apart from one another, which, during the prosperity of the Roman occupation, may have been united by continuous building.

By tradition, Jericho has been closely associated with the Baptism of Jesus and the Temptation. The site of Bethany or Bethabara (wh. see), however, cannot be fixed with certainty, and some (*e.g.* Conder) maintain that the ford east from Jericho cannot be the place, but rather a ford farther north, lying east from Cana of Galilee. The traditional scene of the Temptation is a mountain called from this association *Quarantania*, lying to the west of Jericho. But the uncertainty of the scene of the Baptism and the vagueness of the phrase 'the wilderness' (Mt 4^1 ‖) make this a matter of tradition only.

From Jericho to Jerusalem there are three roads. The central one of these is the most direct, and was that used by pilgrims going from Galilee to Jerusalem, who took the circuitous route in order to avoid entering Samaria. It is an extremely arduous path, and wayfarers were much exposed to the attacks of robbers, who easily found secure concealment among the bare and rugged hills which it traversed : a fact which gives vividness to the parable of the Good Samaritan (Lk 10^{30}). This road was that which Jesus took on His last journey to Jerusalem. After the raising of Lazarus, Jesus and His disciples withdrew 'into a city called Ephraim' (Jn 11^{54}). (On its site see art. EPHRAIM). From this place Jesus could see the pilgrim bands from Galilee going down to Jericho on their way to Jerusalem. And in all probability, when 'the Passover was nigh at hand,' He joined one of these bands, and so paid that visit to Jericho with which the names of Bartimæus and Zacchæus are associated. See artt. BARTIMÆUS and ZACCHÆUS.[*]

LITERATURE.—Stanley, *SP* ch. vii. pp. 305, 316 ; G. A. Smith, *HGHL* 264, 268, 493, 496 ; Hastings' *DB*, artt. 'Jericho, 'Ephraim,' 'Bethabara'; Farrar, *Life of Christ*, ii. 178–186.

ANDREW N. BOGLE.

JERUSALEM.—

  1. Name.
  2. Natural site.
  3. Climate and Diseases
  4. Water supply.
  5. Topography.
  6. History of the city during period of the Gospels.
  7. Jerusalem in the Gospels.
      Literature.

1. NAME.—This appears in the Gospels as Ἱεροσόλυμα and Ἱερουσαλήμ. The former of these names, and the more used, appears to have come into common vogue a century or so before the commencement of the Christian era. It occurs in 2 Maccabees (3^9), in the *Letter of Aristeas*, and in Strabo, and it is the form always employed by Josephus. In Latin Pagan writers, *e.g.* Cicero, Pliny, Tacitus, it is employed transliterated as *Hierosolyma*. Ἱερουσαλήμ unquestionably is much nearer to the Hebrew םִלָשׁוּרְי, however this was vocalized, and is therefore the more primitive. St. Luke specially employs this both in his Gospel and in the Acts. It is noticeable that it is the form put into the mouth of Jesus when His words are professedly reported verbatim (Mt 23^{37}, Lk 13^{34} 23^{28}). The name *Jerusalem*, as used throughout the Western world, and the Arabic form used in Palestine to-day, *Yerusalim*, are both derived from this Greek form. In Mt 4^5 27^{53} we have the expression, used previously too in the OT, 'the

holy city.' This is familiar to us in Western lands, but it is also, for other reasons, the name for Jerusalem throughout the Moslem world. *El-Ḳuds*, or, more classically, *el-Mukaddas*, 'the sanctuary' or 'holy place,' is the common name for this city in the East.

2. NATURAL SITE.—Modern Jerusalem occupies a situation which is defined geographically as 31° 46′ 45″ N. lat. by 35° 13′ 25″ long. E. of Greenwich, and lies at levels between 2300 and 2500 feet above the Mediterranean. It is overlooked by somewhat higher ground to the N., to the E., and the South. On the West the outlook is somewhat more open, but even here the view is not very extensive ; only along a narrow line to the S.E. a gap in the mountains exposes to view a long strip of the beautiful mountains of Moab across the Dead Sea, itself invisible in its deep basin. Although the exact situation of the city has varied considerably during historical times, yet the main natural features which gave Jerusalem its strength— and its weakness— both as a fortress and as a sanctuary, may be easily recognized to-day. Built, as it has been, in a peculiarly bare and ill-watered region, off the natural lines of communication, it could never have enjoyed its long and famous history but for certain compensating advantages.

The city's site lies slightly to the east of the great mountainous backbone of Palestine, upon a tongue-shaped ridge running from N.W. to S.E. This 'tongue' is the central of three branches given off at this point. The N.E. one terminates opposite the city as the Mount of Olives, while a southern branch, given off near the highest point before the modern Jaffa road commences to descend to the city, runs almost due south, and terminates near the commencement of the *Wady el-Wurd*, at a point on which is situated to-day the summer residence of the Greek Patriarch, known as *Katamûn*. The whole mountain group is isolated from its neighbours on the N.W. and W. by the deep *Wady beit Hanîna*, to the S.W. by the roots of the *Wady es-Surâr*, and to the E. and S.E. by the *Wady en-Nâr* and other steep valleys running down towards the Jordan and the Dead Sea. To the north and south, where the ancient caravan road from Hebron and the Negeb runs towards Samaria and Galilee, it is separated from the main backbone by only shallow and open valleys. The special ridge of land on which Jerusalem stands is roughly quadrilateral in shape, but merges itself into higher ground towards the N. and N.W. The surface direction is generally downwards from N. to S., with a slight tilt towards the E. ; this is due to the dip of the strata, which run E.S.E. Like all this part of the country, the rocky formation is grey chalky limestone, deposited in beds of varying hardness. The least durable, which still lies on the surface of the Mount of Olives, having been denuded here, the top layer over the city's site, is a hard limestone with flinty bands, known locally as the *Mezzeh*. This is the formation most suitable for building-stone, though the hardest to work upon. Under this are thick strata of a soft white stone of uniform consistence, known locally as *Meleki*. These softer layers have been of the greatest importance in the history of the city, as in them have been excavated the countless caves, cisterns, and tombs which cover the whole district, and from them in ancient times most of the building-stones were taken. In many places this *Meleki* rock when first excavated is quite soft and easily worked with the most primitive tools, but on exposure to the air it rapidly hardens. The stones from this soft layer, however, never have the durability of those from the *Mezzeh* ; and doubtless it is because of the poor material used that so

---

[*] The statement is frequently met with, in connexion with our Lord's treatment of Zacchæus and also in connexion with the parable of the Good Samaritan, that Jericho was a sacerdotal city. In regard to this, it is certain that the priests and Levites did not all reside in Jerusalem, but were scattered throughout the towns and villages of Judæa. Jericho, as within easy reach of Jerusalem and an important place, may have been a favourite residence for the priests (see Schürer, *HJP* ii. i. 229).

few relics of real antiquity have survived till to-day. Under the *Meleki* is a layer of dolomite limestone which comes to the surface in the valley to the south of the city, and is of importance, because along its non-porous surface the water, which percolates through the other layers, is conducted upwards to the one spring—the Virgin's Fountain.

The enormous accumulation of débris over the ancient site renders it difficult to picture to-day its primitive condition. The extensive investigations made here during the past fifty years, as well as the examination of many kindred sites in other parts of Palestine, lead to the conclusion that the whole area before human habitation consisted of an irregular, rocky surface, broken up by a number of small shallow valleys in which alone there was sufficient soil for vegetation. To-day the rock is everywhere covered with débris of a depth varying from 40 to 70 or more feet. Only those who understand how much this vast accumulation has blotted out the ancient natural landmarks can realize how very difficult are even the essential and elementary questions of Jerusalem topography.

Of the broad natural features that survive, most manifest are the two great valleys which demark the before-mentioned tongue of land. The Eastern Valley commences a mile north of the city wall in a shallow depression near the watershed, a little to the N. of the highest point on the Jaffa road. It at first runs S.E., and is shallow and open : it is here known as the *Wady el-Jôz*. It then turns due south, and soon becomes a ravine with steep sides, called by the Moslems the *Wady Sitti Miriam*, and by Christians since the 4th cent. the Valley of Jehoshaphat * (a name very probably connected originally with the neighbouring village of *Sk̲afat*, and corrupted to Jehoshaphat because of Jl 3². ¹²). This ravine, on reaching the northern extremity of the village of Silwan, turns S.W. and joins the Western Valley near the well now called *Bir Eyyûb*. In ancient times this part of the valley with its steep and, in places, precipitous sides, must have formed a most efficient protection to the whole E. and S.E. sides of the city. It is mentioned in the NT as the 'brook' (χείμαρρος) Ḳidron (Jn 18¹). The valley is almost all the year quite dry, but after a sudden heavy storm quite a considerable torrent may pour down its centre. The present writer has traversed the road along the lower parts of the valley immediately after such rain, with the water half-way to his knees.

The Western Valley—known to-day as the *Wady er-Rabābi*—is shorter and more crooked than that on the East. It commences to the S. of the modern Jaffa road close to the *Birket Mamilla*, its head being now occupied by a large Moslem burying-ground. After running E. towards the Jaffa Gate—near which it has been extensively filled up with rubbish during recent years—it curves south, and some 300 yards down is crossed by the arched, though now half-buried, 'low-level aqueduct.' A little further on it is transformed by the erection of a barrier across its breadth into a great pool—the *Birket es-Sultân*. Below the barrier it rapidly deepens and curves S.E., until at *Bîr Eyyûb* it joins the Ḳidron Valley; the new valley formed by their union runs, under the name of the *Wady en-Nâr* (the Valley of Fire), down to the Dead Sea. The *Wady er-Rabābi* is very generally considered to be the Valley of Hinnom. Several good authorities are against this identification, but for the present purpose there is no need to enter into this discussion, and here it may be provisionally accepted. Although not

so steep a valley as the Eastern one, the *Wady er-Rabābi* presented a much more effective protection to the walls in ancient days than present conditions suggest. In NT times it must have made attack along the whole W. and S.W. sides almost impracticable. Only to the N. and N.W. was the city without natural defence, and it was from these points that she always proved vulnerable.

The quadrilateral plateau enclosed by these valleys, about half a mile in breadth and some 1000 acres in extent, was subdivided by several shallow natural valleys. Of these the most important, and the only one which to-day is clearly seen, is a valley known as *el-Wad*. This, commencing near the present Damascus Gate, runs S. in a somewhat curved direction, dividing the modern city into two unequal halves, and after passing out near the Dung Gate joins the Ḳidron Valley at the Pool of Siloam. Although extensively filled up in places, the outline of the valley may still be clearly seen from any high point in the city near the Damascus Gate, and its bed is to-day traversed by one of the two carriage roads in the city. Though crossed near the *Bab es-Silsileh* by an artificial causeway in which was discovered 'Wilson's Arch,' it again appears near the Jews' Wailing-place, much of its bed being even to-day waste ground. At this point the W. hill still preserves something of its precipitous face,* but on its E. side it is largely encroached upon by the S.W. corner of the Ḥaram. This valley is evidently that described as the Tyropœon or Cheesemongers' Valley, and by it the whole natural site of Jerusalem is divided into Western and Eastern hills.

The broader and loftier Western hill is without doubt that called by Josephus the Upper Marketplace and the Upper City, and it is the one which since the 4th cent. has been known as **Zion**. Josephus (*BJ* v. iv. 1) mentions that in his day it was called the Citadel of David, and this tradition survives in the name the 'Tower of David,' given to the fortress at the Jaffa Gate. This is not the place to discuss the position of Zion, but it is now fairly generally admitted that the tradition which placed the Citadel of David and Zion on this Western spur was wrong, and that these sites lay on the Eastern hill south of the Temple. Josephus (*BJ* v. iv. 1) describes the Western hill as 'much higher' and 'in length more direct' than the other hill opposite to it. The buildings on it extended southward to the Valley of Hinnom, but to the north it is bounded by a valley which runs eastward from near the modern Jaffa Gate to join the Tyropœon Valley opposite the Western wall of the Temple area. It is to-day largely filled up, but its direction is preserved by David Street. The first wall ran along the S. edge of this valley, and the suburbs which grew up to its north were enclosed by the second wall.

Regarding the Eastern hill, or, rather, regarding the name for part of this Eastern hill, there is much more dispute. Josephus (*BJ* v. iv. 1) wrote of the 'other hill, which was called Akra, and sustains the lower city': it 'is the shape of a moon when she is horned; over against this there was a third hill'—evidently, from the description, that covered by the Temple—'but naturally lower than Akra, and parted formerly from the other by a deep valley.' He narrates how Simon Maccabæus, after capturing the fortress which stood there, set his followers to work night and day for three years levelling the mountain, so that it should no longer be able to support a fortress which could overlook the Temple. As a result of this work, the valley between this hill and the Temple was filled up.

---

* Eusebius, *Onomasticon*², 193. 20.

* Robinson, *BRP* i. 390.

The conclusion is therefore that this hill, which we learn was the 'City of David' at the time of the Maccabees, formed in the days of Josephus one hill with the Temple hill, and further that it was separated from the Western hill, whereon was the Upper City, by the valley which 'extended as far as Siloam.' All this points to the Eastern hill south of the Temple as the site of Akra * and of the Lower City. Akra cannot have lain north of the Temple, for here lay the Antonia (*Ant.* XV. xi. 4; *BJ* V. v. 8), the ancient Baris or tower, a fortress distinct from the Akra, indeed largely its successor; and north of this again was Bezetha, the New City.

There is much to confirm this view of the position of the Akra. The Akra was built on the 'City of David,' and this is identical with the Jebusite Zion. On quite other grounds Zion has been placed on this hill by many modern authorities. Then Akra is associated, in the description of the taking of Jerusalem, with 'the fountain,' *i.e.* the Virgin's Fountain, and Siloam (*BJ* V. vi. 1).† The appropriateness of the name 'Lower City' for the part of Jerusalem which sloped down south from the Temple is as evident as 'Upper City' is for that which actually overlooked the Temple on the west. If this, the most ancient part of Jerusalem, is not that described by Josephus as Akra and Lower City, what name did it have? It must have contained a very large share of the ordinary dwellings of the people. *Ophlas* (the Ophel of the OT) seems in Josephus' (*BJ* V. iv. 2) time, at any rate, to have been only a particular knoll near the S.E. corner of the Temple.

The topographical difficulties are not insurmountable if the history is borne in mind. It is highly probable that a valley does exist either south of the present Temple area or even on a line between the present Temple platform and the *el-Aḳsa* mosque. The name may have remained associated with the highest parts of the hill, even though the wall of the Temple at the time of Josephus may have encroached on the hill, and even have covered part of the site of the ancient fortress. The Lower City seems to have extended up the Tyropœon Valley at least to the first wall, and hence the descent by steps from one of the W. gates of the Temple described by Josephus presents no real difficulty to the view of the position of Akra here maintained.

The older view of Robinson, Warren, Conder, and others, that Akra was the hill now sustaining the *Muristan* and the Church of the Sepulchre, north of the W. branch of the Tyropœon Valley, presents many difficulties. This was the area enclosed by the second wall, and Josephus calls it not the Lower City, but 'the northern quarter of the city.' Then the condition of neither the hill nor the valley tallies with the description of Josephus, and in his day the valley between this and the Temple must have been very much deeper than it is to-day. Josephus is more likely to be wrong in stating that the hill had once been higher than the Temple and was separated from it by a deep valley—a statement which depended on tradition—than in describing the hill as lower in his time and the valley as filled up—facts which he must have seen with his own eyes.

3. CLIMATE AND DISEASES. — The climate of Jerusalem, while bearing the broad characteristics common to the land, presents in some respects marked features of contrast to that of the Jordan Valley and other low-lying places which were the scenes of the ministry of Jesus. There is

every reason for believing that the general climatic features are the same to-day as then. On the whole, Jerusalem must be considered healthy, and what disease there is, is largely due to preventable causes. The marked changes of season, the clear pure atmosphere, with frequent winds, and the cool nights even in midsummer, combine to give Jerusalem a climate superior to the lower parts of Palestine. In winter the cold is considerable but never extreme, the lowest temperature recorded in 20 years being only 25° F. As a rule, a frost occurs on some half a dozen nights in each year. January, February, and December are, in this order, the three coldest and wettest months, though the minimum temperature has occurred several times in March, and a night temperature as low as 40° at the end of May (cf. Jn 18[18]). Snow falls heavily at times, but only in exceptionally severe winters. The average rainfall is about 26 inches, a lower mean than at Hebron, but higher than in the plains and the Jordan Valley. The maximum fall recorded (1847) was 41·62 inches, the minimum (1870) was 13·39. So low a fall as this, especially if preceded by a scanty fall, means considerable distress in the succeeding dry season. During the summer no rain falls, and the mean temperature steadily rises till August, when it reaches 73·6, though the days of maximum heat (near or even over 100°) are often in September. It is not, however, the seasons of extreme heat or cold that are most trying to the health, but the intermediate spring and autumn, especially the months of May and October. This is largely due to the winds. Of all the winds the most characteristic is the S.E. — the sirocco — which in midwinter blows piercingly cold, and in the spring and autumn (but not at all in the summer) hot, stifling, and often laden with fine dust from the deserts whence it comes. On such days all Nature suffers, the vegetation droops, and man not only feels debilitated and depressed, but is actually more liable to illness, especially 'fever' and ophthalmia. The N.W. is the cold refreshing wind which, almost every summer afternoon and evening, mitigates the heat. The S.W. wind blows moist off the sea, and in the later summer brings the welcome copious clouds and, in consequence, the refreshing 'dews.' In the early mornings of September and October thick mists often fill the valleys till dispersed by the rising sun. The onset of the rains, in late October, is not uncommonly signalized by heavy thunderstorms and sudden downpours of rain, which fill with raging and destructive floods the valleys still parched by seven months' drought. As much as 4 inches of rain has fallen in one day.

The diseases of Jerusalem are preventable to a large extent under proper sanitary conditions. Malarial fevers, ophthalmia, and smallpox (in epidemics) are the greatest scourges. Enteric fever, typhus, measles, scarlet fever, and cholera (rarely) occur in epidemics. Tubercular diseases, rheumatism, erysipelas, intestinal worms, and various skin diseases are all common.

4. WATER SUPPLY.—The water supply of Jerusalem has in all its history been of such importance and, on account of the altitude of the city, has involved so many elaborate works, which remain to-day as archæological problems, that it will be well to consider it separately. The city never appears to have seriously suffered from want of water in sieges, but probably at no period was Jerusalem more lavishly supplied with water than it was during the Roman predominance, and most of the arrangements were complete before the time of Christ.

Of springs we know of only one to-day, and there is no reason to believe there were ever any

---

* This view was apparently first put forward by Olshausen, and has been recently revived by Benzinger, G. A. Smith, and Sanday.

† Cf. *BJ* V. iv. 1, VI. vi. 3, and V. vii. 2.

more. This spring is that known to the Christians as '*Ain Sitti Miriam*—the spring of the Lady Mary—or the Virgin's Fountain (from a tradition that the Virgin washed the clothes of the infant Jesus there), to the Moslem fellahin as '*Ain umm ed-deraj*—' the spring of the mother of the steps,' and to the eastern Jews as ' Aaron's (or ' the priests'') bath.' The water arises in a small cave reached by 30 steps, some 25 feet underground, in the Kidron Valley, due south of the Temple area. Though to-day lying so deep, there are ample evidences that originally the mouth of the cave opened out on the side of the valley, and that the water flowed out thence. It has become buried through the accumulated débris in the valley bed. At the back of the cave—some 30 feet from the entrance—is a tunnel mouth, the beginning of the famous Siloam aqueduct (see SILOAM). The flow is intermittent, about two or three times a day on an average. This fact is recorded by Jerome, and is by many authorities considered a reason for locating here the Pool of Bethesda (see BETHESDA). The water is brackish to the taste, and chemical examination shows that, to-day at any rate, it is contaminated with sewage. It is undoubtedly unfit for drinking purposes : it is used chiefly by the people of the village of *Silwan*, especially at the Siloam-pool end of the aqueduct, for watering their gardens.

Further down the valley, at its junction with the Valley of Hinnom, there is a well, 125 feet deep, known as *Bîr Eyyûb*, or Job's Well. This, though rediscovered by the Crusaders, is almost certainly ancient and may have been the En-rogel of the OT. From here great quantities of water are drawn all the year round, much of which is carried in skins and sold in Jerusalem, but it is in no way of better quality than that from the Virgin's Fountain. After a spell of heavy rain the water rises up like a genuine spring, and overflowing underground a little below the actual well mouth, it bursts forth in a little stream and runs down the *Wady en-Nâr*. Such an outflow may last several days, and is a great source of attraction to the people of Jerusalem, who, on the cessation of the rain, hasten out to sit by the ' flowing Kidron ' and refresh themselves beside its running waters. During the unusually heavy rains of the winter 1904–5 the ' Kidron' ran thus four times. A little farther down the valley there occurs, at the same time and under the same circumstances, another apparent ' spring '—the '*Ain el-Lôz*—due to the water of *Bîr Eyyûb* finding its way along an ancient rock-cut aqueduct and bursting up through the ground where the conduit is blocked.

The *Hammâm esh-Shefa* (bath of healing) under the W. wall of the Haram area has by many been considered an ancient spring. To-day the water collects in an extensive underground rocky chamber at the bottom of a well 86 feet deep. Quite possibly before the area to the north was so thickly inhabited, when, for example, this well was outside the walls, a certain amount of good water may have been obtainable here, but now what collects is a foul and smelling liquid which percolates to the valley bottom from the neighbouring inhabited area, and it is unfit for even its present use—in a Turkish bath.

More important than springs or wells are the innumerable cisterns with which, from the earliest times, the hill of Jerusalem has been honeycombed. It has already been pointed out that the rainfall of this region is considerable, and rain-water collected on a clean roof and stored in a well-kept cistern is good for all domestic purposes. There are private cisterns under practically every house, but there are in addition a number of larger reservoirs for

public use. In the Haram—the ancient Temple area—there are 37 known excavations, of which one, the ' great sea,' it is calculated, can hold about 2,000,000 gallons.

In other parts the more important cisterns are— the *Birket Mamilla*, *Hammâm el-Batrak*, *Birket Israël*, *Birket es-Sultân*, ' The Twin Pools,' the so-called ' Pool of Bethesda,' and the two Siloam pools—*Birket Silwan* and *Birket el-Hamra*. The last three are dealt with in the special articles BETHESDA and SILOAM respectively. The *Birket es-Sultân*, the misnamed ' Lower Pool of Gihon ' in the Valley of Hinnom, was probably first constructed by German knights in the 12th cent., and was repaired by the Sultan Suleiman ibn Selim in the 16th cent., while the Twin Pools near the ' Sisters of Zion ' were made in the moat of the Antonia fortress after the destruction of the city in A.D. 70 ; so neither of these needs description here. The other three require longer notice. The *Birket Mamilla*, incorrectly called the ' Upper Pool of Gihon,' lies at the head of the Valley of Hinnom, about 700 yards W. N. W. of the Jaffa Gate, and used to collect all the surface water from the higher ground around ; in recent years the Moslem cemetery in which it lies has been surrounded by a wall, which has largely cut off the supplies. After a spell of heavy rain it often used to fill to overflowing. It is 97 yards long, 64 yards wide, and 19 feet deep. It appears to be 'the Serpents' Pool ' of Josephus (*BJ* v. iii. 2). The outlet on the E. side leads to a conduit which enters the city near the Jaffa Gate and empties itself into the great rock-cut pool—*Birket Hammâm el-Batrak* (the pool or bath of the Patriarch), commonly known as the Pool of Hezekiah. The pool, 80 yards long by 48 yards wide, is largely rock-cut, and lies across the W. arm of the Tyropœon Valley ; there are indications that it extended at one time further north than it does at present. Josephus apparently refers to this as the Pool Amygdalon (κολυμβήθρα Ἀμύγδαλον), a name perhaps derived from *Berekat ha-migdalim* (Pool of the Towers) on account of the near proximity of some of the great fortresses on the neighbouring walls. As the pool is not mentioned in Josephus until after the second wall had been captured, it may be presumed that it was within that wall (*BJ* v. xi. 4).

The *Birket Israël* is built across the width of a natural valley which runs from N.W. to S.E., and passes under the N.E. course of the Haram at this point. It is supposed by some authorities that the pool itself did not exist at the period of Christ's ministry, but as a defence to the Temple enclosure and to the neighbouring Castle of Antonia (wh. see) it may well have been the Pool Struthius mentioned by Josephus (*ib.*). He says the fifth legion raised a bank at the tower of Antonia ' over against the middle of the pool that is called Struthius.' It must, however, be stated that M. Ganneau and others propose to identify the ' Twin Pools ' with Struthius.

Constructed for Jerusalem, though seven miles from the city, are the three great reservoirs known as 'Solomon's Pools,' or *el-Buruk*. They lie one below the other down a valley ; their floors are made of the valley bed, deepened in places, and they are naturally deepest at their lower or eastern ends ; they increase in size from above downward. The largest and lowest is nearly 200 yards long, 60 yards wide, and 50 feet deep. To-day they are useless, but when kept in repair and clean were no doubt valuable as storeplaces of surplus supplies of surface water from the surrounding hills and of water from the springs. Regarding the question when these pools were made there are most contrary opinions. It is highly improbable that they go back anything like as far as Solomon's time, and the association of his name with any great and wise work is so common in the East that the name 'Solomon's Pools' means nothing. On the whole, it is likely the work was not later than Roman times.

The system of aqueducts which centre round these pools has a special interest. Two were constructed to carry water from the four springs in the Valley of the Pools to Jerusalem, and two others

PLAN

OF THE

ENVIRONS OF JERUSALEM

TO ILLUSTRATE THE

WATER SUPPLY

The "Low Level" Aqueduct thus	————
The "High Level" Aqueduct "	- - - - - -
The Wady Biar "Khariz" "	o—o—o—
Aqueduct to the Herodium "	··········
Modern Iron-Pipe Conduit "	·—·—·—·

(Modified from Schick)

to supplement this supply. The first two are the well-known high- and low-level aqueducts. The former appears to have reached the city somewhere about the level of the Jaffa Gate, and may also have supplied the *Birket Mamilla*. It is specially remarkable for the way it crossed a valley on the Bethlehem road by means of an inverted syphon. Large fragments of this great stone tube have been found, and from inscriptions carved on the limestone blocks the date of its construction or repair must have been in Roman times and, according to some authorities, as late as about A.D. 195. Unless, however, the account given of the royal palace gardens of Herod is greatly exaggerated, the aqueduct must have been in use in Herod's days, as it is the only conduit by which *running* water could have reached the city at a level high enough to have supplied these gardens. The low-level aque-

duct, still in use along a good part of its course, may easily be followed to-day along its whole length of 11½ miles. It brought water from the springs into the Temple area. It is very probably the source of the 'spring' which is said by Tacitus (*Hist.* v. 12) to have run perpetually in the Temple. Of the two supplementary aqueducts, one, of exactly the same construction as the last mentioned, brought water from the copious springs at *Wady Arrúb*—two-thirds of the way from Jerusalem to Hebron—along an extraordinarily winding conduit 28 miles long. The other, built on an altogether different principle, is a four-mile channel which gathers water from a long chain of wells in the *Wady Biár* on the plan of a Persian *kharíz*, such as is extensively used in Northern Syria. This, pronounced by Sir C. Wilson 'one of the most remarkable works in Palestine,' is probably comparatively late. It seems to have been used to supplement the water of the springs in the Valley of the Pools.

The special interest of the great 'low-level aqueduct' described above, with its total length of 40 miles, lies in the historical fact that it, or some part of it, was one of the causes of the recall of Pontius Pilate. 'Pilate (*Ant.* XVIII. iii. 2) undertook to bring a current of water to Jerusalem, and did it with the sacred money, and derived the origin of the stream from the distance of two hundred furlongs.' A riot took place, and a 'great number' of people were slain. This may be the incident referred to in Lk 13¹ᵗ. If Josephus is correct in saying that Pilate was bringing water a distance of 200 stadia (=26 miles), then this must apply to the extension of the aqueduct to *Wady Arrúb*. In any case, it is highly improbable that his was the initiation of the whole work. The very absence of inscriptions and of contemporary references makes it probable that the conduit was at least older than Roman times. If we allow that the high-level aqueduct goes back to the days of Herod the Great, then the low-level aqueduct may well go back some centuries earlier.

5. TOPOGRAPHY OF THE CITY IN THE TIME OF CHRIST.—The city walls.—At the time of Christ, Jerusalem had two walls which had been restored by order of Julius Cæsar (*Ant.* XIV. x. 5). In A.D. 43, Agrippa I. commenced a third one of great magnificence, which, however, seems never to have been properly finished.

(*a*) The *first wall* had 60 towers; it encompassed the ancient and most important secular buildings of the city. Though some minor details are yet unknown, its general course is perfectly clear. The tower Hippicus, at which it arose—one of those magnificent towers built by Herod—was situated close to the present so-called 'Tower of David,' in which indeed its remains may even be incorporated. From here it ran along the S. edge of the W. arm of the Tyropœon Valley. It then passed the Xystus, joined on to the Council House near the present *Mehkemeh* or Town Hall, and ended at the Western Cloister. It probably crossed the Tyropœon Valley, where to-day there is the causeway leading to the *Bab es-Silsileh* of the Ḥaram. The western wall commenced at the tower Hippicus, and probably followed the line of the present western wall to the great corner tower, the rocky foundations of which are now included in the C.M.S. Boys' School. Somewhere near this part of its course it passed 'a place called Bethso'—unidentified ; it then bent S.E. 'to the gate of the Essenes, and went thence southward along the steep edge of the Valley of Hinnom down to the Pool of Siloam.' It had 'its bending above the fountain Siloam,' which probably implies that it surrounded the pool on the W., N., and E., but did not enclose it, as a wall at another period undoubtedly did. It then ran on the edge of the steep rocks above the Virgin's

Fountain—called, apparently, by Josephus 'Solomon's Pool'—and thence to 'a certain place which they called Ophlas, where it joined to the eastern cloister of the Temple' (*BJ* v. iv. 2).

Extensive remains of this wall have been traced. Those of the great tower at the S.W. corner were examined by Maudslay in 1874. He found the base of a tower 20 feet high hewn out of the native rock. It was nearly square, and projected 45 feet from the scarp to which it was attached—altogether a great work, and at a point which must have always been specially well fortified.* A little to the east is another great scarp, and here Bliss † began to trace out the buried remains of the south wall. He found near the commencement of his excavations a gate which may very probably be the Gate of the Essenes. In tracing the wall towards Siloam, foundations belonging to two distinct periods were excavated. Bliss considered that the higher of these belonged to the wall of the period between Herod and Titus. A little to the W. of Siloam he found the remains of a fine gateway showing three periods of use—the sill lying at different heights in each period—and a fine rock-cut underground drain, almost certainly Roman work, which he traced for a great distance up the W. side of the Tyropœon Valley, where it came to lie under a paved street ascending the valley in the direction of the Temple. After leaving the before-mentioned gate, there were indications—not, it must be admitted, decisive—that the wall at one period surrounded the pool on three sides, as Josephus apparently describes, while at another period it crossed the mouth of the Tyropœon Valley on an elaborate dam. To the east of the pool the rock scarp is exposed, and almost every trace of the wall has been removed. As regards the E. section of this southern wall, Sir Charles Warren in 1875 traced the buried remains of a wall 14½ feet thick and, in places, 70 feet high from the S.E. corner of the Temple southwards for 90 feet, and then S.W. for 700 feet. Two hundred feet from the end he unearthed the remains of a massive tower standing to the height of 66 feet and founded upon rock. The wall itself had been built, not on rock, but on virgin soil. The course of the wall, as described by Josephus, thus appears to be very fully verified by modern discoveries.

(*b*) With regard to the *second wall* a great deal of uncertainty prevails. There are few more hotly disputed problems in Jerusalem topography. This second wall appears to have been on the line of that made by the later kings of Judah, to have been repaired by Nehemiah, and used by the Hasmonæans. It is dismissed by Josephus (*BJ* v. iv. 2) in a very few words; it 'took its beginning from that gate which they call Gennath, which belonged to the first wall; it only encompassed the northern quarter of the city and reached as far as the tower of Antonia.' It had 40 towers on it. No remains of the gate Gennath have been found, but the configuration of the ground makes it improbable that the wall could have taken its rise very far to the E. of the present Jaffa Gate, as here there exists a narrow neck of high ground, but a little to the E. the level abruptly descends into the W. arm of the Tyropœon. In 1886 some 30 yards of the remains of what seemed a city wall were discovered 15 feet below the street, where the foundations of the Grand New Hotel were dug. They were supposed by Messrs. Merrill and Schick to be part of the second wall at its W. end, but too short a piece was examined to allow of positive conclusions. The other supposed traces of the second wall are even more ambiguous. In the N. part of the

Muristan, where to-day stands the German church, Schick found remains of which he said, 'I am convinced that these are traces of the second wall': these would fall in line with a wall 10 or 12 feet thick, which, according to Robinson (*BRP* i. 408), was found N. of the Pool of Hezekiah, when the foundations of the Coptic Convent were laid. Again, just to the N. of the German church and E. of the Church of the Holy Sepulchre were found extensive ruined walls, which are to-day treasured by the Russian ecclesiastical authorities as sure evidences that the site of the traditional Holy Sepulchre was outside the ancient walls. It is, however, much more probable that these remains, which are quite unlike city walls, are really fragments of Constantine's Great Basilica.

The question is thus quite an open one, but the argument that the second wall *cannot*, on military grounds, have followed a course S. of the site of the Sepulchre is an unsafe one. As Sir C. Wilson * points out : 'There are several Greek towns in Asia Minor where the city walls or parts of them are quite as badly traced according to modern ideas. In ancient towns the Acropolis was the principal defence, the city wall was often weak.' It may indeed be suggested that this very weakness made Agrippa undertake his new wall along a better line for defence.

(*c*) The whole question of the second wall depends largely on what view is taken of the course of the *third wall* constructed by Agrippa I. The most widely accepted opinion to-day is that this followed much the same course as the present N. wall. It was begun upon the most elaborate plan, but was never apparently finished on the scale designed, because Agrippa feared Claudius Cæsar, 'lest he should suspect that so strong a wall was built in order to make some innovation in public affairs' (*BJ* v. iv. 2). It was, however, at the time of the siege, over 18 feet wide and 40 feet high, with 90 massive towers. It began at the tower Hippicus, and had its N.W. corner at a great octagonal tower, called Psephinus, 135 feet high and overlooking the whole city.† From here was an extensive view of Arabia, *i.e.* the Land of Moab, at sunrise, 'as well as of the utmost limits of the Hebrew possessions at the sea westwards' (*BJ* v. iv. 3). The foundations of this tower are supposed to survive to-day just inside the N.W. angle of the modern city, under the name *Kalât el-Jalud*, or Goliath's Castle. From this corner the wall 'extended till it came over against the monuments of Helena, queen of Adiabene, the daughter of Izates' (*BJ* v. iv. 2). This, however, 'must be read in the light of the statement of Josephus in another place (*Ant.* xx. iv. 3) that this tomb is 'distant no more than three furlongs from the city of Jerusalem.' The so-called 'Tombs of the Kings' are now very generally identified as the very notable tomb of Queen Helena, and, that being so, the distance given, 3 stadia or furlongs (700 yards), is a fair description of the distance of this monument from the present north wall near the Damascus Gate. He next states that 'it extended further to a great length, and passed by the sepulchral caverns of the kings'—these last may very well be the extensive caves known as 'Solomon's Quarries.' The wall 'bent again at the tower of the corner,' which then may have been where the present Stork Tower at the N.E. corner of the city is, 'at the monument which is called the monument of the fuller'—probably destroyed—'and joined the old wall at the valley called the Valley of the Ḳidron.' This was probably near the present St. Stephen's Gate. The

---

* *PEFSt*, 1875, p. 83.

† See 'Excavations at Jerusalem, 1894–97,' Bliss and Dickie, *PEFSt*.

* *PEFSt*, 1903, p. 247 footnote.

† It does not appear whether this tower was one of Herod's constructions or of later date, but the latter now seems the more probable.

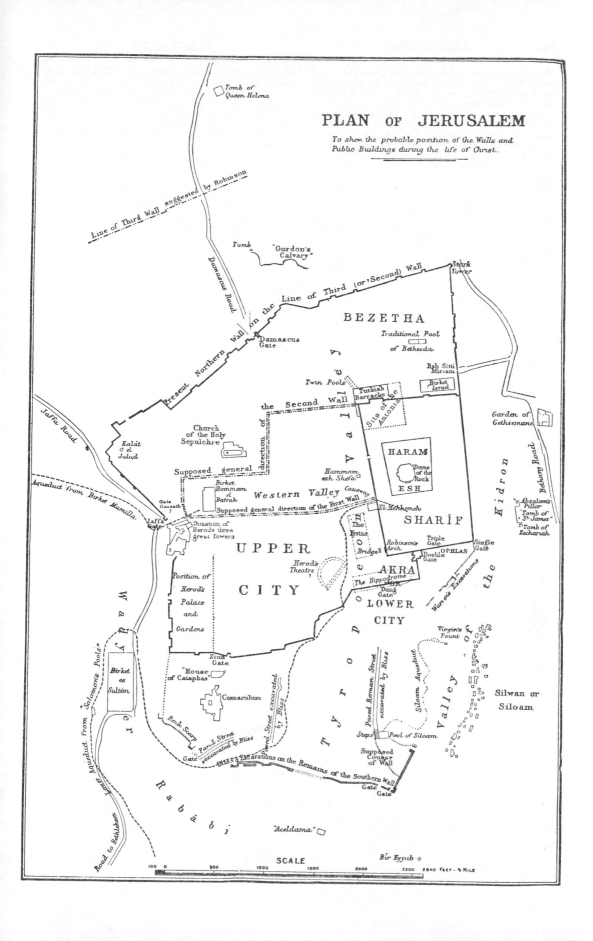

PLAN of JERUSALEM

To shew the probable position of the Walls and Public Buildings during the life of Christ.

□ *Tomb of Queen Helena*

Line of Third Wall suggested by Robinson

Damascus Road

Tomb □   "*Gordon's Calvary*"

on the Line of Third (or? Second) Wall

Stork Tower

BEZETHA

Present Northern Wall

Damascus Gate

Traditional Pool of Bethesda

Bab Sitti Miriam

Birket Israel

Twin Pools

Turkish Barracks

Site of the Antonia

Garden of Gethsemane

the Second Wall

Valley

Jaffa Road

Church of the Holy Sepulchre

HARAM

Dome of the Rock

ESH

Bethany Road

Kalât el Jalud

Supposed general

direction of

Hammam esh Shefa

Absalom's Pillar

Tomb of St James

Aqueduct from Birket Mamilla

Birket Hammam el Batrak

Western Valley

Causeway

El Mekhemeh

SHARÎF

Tomb of Zechariah

Gate Gennath

Supposed general direction of the First Wall

Situation of Herod's three great Towers

Jaffa Gate

The Xystus

Bridge

Robinson's Arch

Triple Gate

Single Gate

the Kidron

Double Gate

OPHLAS

UPPER CITY

Herod's Theatre?

AKRA

The Hippodrome

LOWER CITY

Dung Gate

Position of Herod's Palace and Gardens

Warren's Excavations

Virgin's Fount

Zion Gate

Wady

"House of Caiaphas"

Silwan or Siloam

Birket es Sultan

Coenaculum

Rock Scarp

Paved Roman Street

Paved Street excavated by Bliss

Siloam Aqueduct

Aqueduct from "Solomon's Pools"

Rabâbi

Gate

Paved Street excavated by Bliss

Steps

Pool of Siloam

Valley of

Bliss's Excavations on the Remains of the Southern Wall

Supposed Course of Wall

Gate   *Gate*

Road to Bethlehem

Tyropoeon

"Aceldama" □

SCALE

Bir Eyyub ○

100 0   500   1000   1500   2000   2500   2640 Feet = ½ Mile

exact course at the N.E. corner is very doubtful; it is quite possible that it turned S.E. near 'Herod's Gate.' It will be observed that the description fits in very well with the course followed by the existing N. wall. At the Damascus Gate there are unmistakable evidences that a gate at least as ancient as Roman times stood there. The supporters of the view that the second wall ran here lay stress on certain supposed remains of the third wall further north. A candid examination of such of these as survive, and of the accounts, both verbally and in publications, of those that have been removed, does not seem very convincing. One of the best marked pieces, forming the side of a cistern near Helena's Tomb, proved on recent examination to be but a piece of smooth scarp facing towards the city, and not remains of a building at all.

As is clear from the history of the taking of the city, there was another wall, no doubt greatly inferior in strength to those before mentioned, which ran along the western side of the Tyropœon, bounding in that direction the 'Upper City' (Tacitus, *Hist.* v. 11), and it is probable that some kind of wall, though doubtless only a temporary one, ran along the opposite or eastern side of the valley.

Towers.—Of the great towers the three erected by Herod the Great yet remain to be described. Josephus, in his usual exaggerated manner, says they 'were for largeness, beauty, and strength beyond all that were in the habitable earth' (*BJ* v. iv. 3). They were dedicated to Herod's friend Hippicus, his brother Phasael, and his wife Mariamne, whom he had murdered. Each of these towers was of solid masonry at the base. The base of Hippicus was about 44 feet square and 50 high, over which was a reservoir and several rooms, and, surmounting all, battlements with turrets: the total height was 140 feet. The second tower, Phasael, was 70 feet square at the base and nearly 160 feet high, and, it is said, 'wanted nothing that might make it appear to be a royal palace.' The Mariamne tower was smaller and less lofty, but 'its upper buildings were more magnificent.' As to the position of these towers, the present 'Tower of David' is generally considered to contain the remains of Phasael, with various Crusading and Saracenic additions. Hippicus must have been near this spot, perhaps where the Jaffa Gate now stands, and Mariamne probably a little more to the east on higher ground. The three are all described as being 'on the north side of the wall,' and from a distance they all appeared to be of the same height. The N.W. corner of the city, where they stood, was one without much natural defence, and they bore the same important relation to the King's Palace as the other fortress, the Antonia, did to the Temple.

Of the other great architectural works of the period we have but scanty description and still scantier remains, with the exception, of course, of the Temple, for which see art. TEMPLE.

Herod's great *palace*, built on the site of the palace of the Hasmonæans (*Ant.* XX. viii. 11), evidently adjoined the before-mentioned towers on the south, and occupied an area of land now covered by the English church and schools and the Armenian quarter, probably extending also to the Patriarch's house and gardens—the greater part, indeed, of the area between the present David Street (along the line of which the first wall ran) to the N. and the modern city walls as far east as the Zion Gate to the south. It is quite possible that the present course of the southern wall was determined by the remains of the S. wall of this palace. From the walls an extensive view could be seen, and at a later time Agrippa II. gave great offence when he

added a lofty dining-room from which he could watch all the doings in the Temple. To frustrate this, the Jews raised a wall upon the 'uppermost building which belonged to the inner court of the Temple towards the west.' This gave annoyance not only to Agrippa but also to Festus, who ordered it to be removed. On appeal, however, Nero gave his verdict in favour of the Jews. The palace had walls, in parts over 50 feet high, with many towers, and was internally fitted with great luxury. Around it were numerous porticos, with 'curious pillars' buried among groves of trees, and gardens well irrigated and 'filled with brazen statues through which the water ran out.'

Between the palace grounds and the Temple lay the *Xystus*, a gymnasium surrounded with columns, for Greek games. Connecting the W. wall of the Temple with the W. hill and the 'Upper City,' was a *bridge* which had been broken down when Pompey (*Ant.* XIV. iv. 4; *BJ* I. vii. 2) besieged the Temple in B.C. 65, but had been repaired. The projecting arch of this bridge was first recognized by Robinson, and the *PEF* excavations not only uncovered the central pier, but beneath the early Roman pavement found an old voussoir of the earlier bridge of Pompey's time, which had fallen through into an ancient drain below the street. No remains of this bridge have, however, so far been recovered further to the west.

The *hippodrome* apparently lay somewhat to the south, on the borders, perhaps, of the Tyropœon Valley near the present Dung Gate; this was very probably the 'place of exercise' of 2 Mac 4[12] (cf. 1 Mac 1[15]), and the description 'under the very castle' would well suit this place if Akra was where it is here proposed to locate it. Of the position of Herod's *theatre* nothing at all is known.

Next to the Temple, perhaps the most famous building in Jerusalem was **Antonia**, the great fortress of the Temple, and the acropolis of the city, which from its lofty height is described by Tacitus (*Hist.* v. 11) as pre-eminently conspicuous. It had received the name *Antonia* from Herod after Mark Antony, but it had in Hasmonæan times been known as *Baris*. Nehemiah (2[8] RV) mentions a castle (*birah*) as being here—to the north of the Temple: this the high priest Hyrcanus (*BJ* I. vi. 1) made his headquarters. It is interesting that at least a portion of the site with so great a reputation as a military stronghold should even to-day be occupied by troops—the Turkish garrison. A great rock scarp on which part of the ancient fortress stood is still clearly visible from the Haram, and in the moat cut to protect its northern aspect lie the 'Twin Pools.' The fortress lay at the N.W. corner of the Temple enclosure, and is described by Josephus as being built on a rock over 87 feet high, 'on a great precipice'; the rock was covered with smooth stones, and upon the rocky platform was a building 70 feet high fitted up with great magnificence. At the four corners were towers 87 feet high, except that at the S.E. corner, which was over 120 feet high; from it the whole Temple was overlooked, but a considerable space separated it from the Temple itself (*BJ* VI. ii. 5–7). At the W. corner there were passages into the W. and the N. cloisters by which the Temple guards could obtain access to the Temple. The Western boundary was probably on the line of the present W. wall of the Haram, and the moat (*BJ* v. iv. 2) to the N. appears to have been demonstrated, but the S. and E. boundaries are unknown. The total area must have been large, as it held a whole Roman legion, and it is clear from history that it was a powerful fortress. Even before its extension by Herod, Antigonus could not capture it until after the city and the Temple had been taken by storm, and in A.D. 70 the capture of Antonia is recorded as one of the fiercest of the fights of the siege (*BJ* VI. i. and ii.). It is commonly believed that the *Prætorium* (Mk 15[16ff.]) was in part of Antonia, for there undoubtedly was the Roman garrison (Ac 21[34]). See PRÆTORIUM.

Near the W. wall of the Temple where is now the Turkish Town Hall (*el-Mehkemeh*) was the *Town Council House*. Possibly it was here the high priest held his court.

The palaces of Monobazus, king of Adiabene, and of his mother Queen Helena appear to have been on the southern slopes of the Eastern hill, the former probably due east of the Pool of Siloam.

Of the great number of **tombs** around Jerusalem the majority of the most conspicuous and notable belong to a later period than Christ's life. The monuments of Queen Helena, known as the 'Tombs of the Kings,' and probably almost all the tombs in the valley in which the 'Tombs of the Judges' are situated, are of a date very soon after Christ's death. The same is probably true of the famous group of tombs near the S.E. corner of the Temple, the so-called 'Pillar of Absalom,' the 'Tomb of Jehoshaphat,' the 'Grotto of St. James,' and the 'Pyramid of Zacharias.' It is very tempting to connect these highly ornamented tomb structures with the words of Jesus (Mt 23[27. 35]), spoken as they probably were almost within sight of this spot. If so, the indications of work of a later period may be additions to earlier constructions of the Herodian era. The so-called Tombs of Joseph of Arimathæa and of Nicodemus, to the W. of the shrine of the Holy Sepulchre, though only by a late tradition associated with these NT characters, are undoubtedly old tombs, probably much before Christ's time. The traditional tomb of Christ has been treated in a separate article. See GOLGOTHA.

A general view of the city in the time of Christ from such a height as Olivet must have been an impressive sight. In the foreground lay the great Temple in a grandeur and beauty greater than it had ever had in all its long history, its courts all day crowded with throngs of worshippers from every corner of the known world. To the north of this, Antonia, with its four massive towers, stood sentinel over the city and the Temple. Behind these lay the Upper City crowned by the magnificent palace-fortress of Herod, with its great groves of trees and well-watered gardens. To the right of this lay the great towers Hippicus, Phasael, and Mariamne. Then between these buildings and the Temple lay the central valley with the Xystus and its many columns, the lofty bridge, and, a little to the south, the great Hippodrome. Then somewhere among the houses, which rose tier above tier from the valley, very probably in that part of the city which is described by Josephus (*Ant.* XV. viii. 1) as like an amphitheatre itself, lay the theatre of Herod, doubtless facing the distant mountains of Moab. Then southward, covering both the hills as they descended into the deep valleys towards Siloam, were the thick built houses of the common folk, with other palaces such as those of Monobazus and Helena rising like islands from among them. Enclosing all were the mighty walls of the Temple and of the city—these latter alone with a hundred towers—rising up, in many places precipitously, from deep valleys, suggestive at once of strength and security. To the north lay the New City, yet unwalled, where, doubtless, countless villas rose amid the fresh greenness of gardens and trees.

'The devil taketh him up into an exceeding high mountain, and sheweth him all the kingdoms of the world, and the glory of them' (Mt 4[8]). Did they not all lie beneath the gaze of the Man of Galilee if He were brought from the neighbouring

wilderness into the blaze of material glory—Greek, Roman, and Hebrew—spread out beneath Him in the Holy City?

The city over which the Son of Man wept (Lk 19[41]) must have been a city representing, in small area, more extravagant display, more intense contrasts of materialism and religious zeal, of Rome's iron discipline and seething rebellion, of the East and the West, and more seeds of that fanatic hatred that spells murder than the world has ever seen. Elements were here gathered that made the city a miniature of the whole world, of a world, too, hastening to destruction.

The total *population* of the city cannot have been large, and the numbers given by Josephus (*BJ* II. xiv. 2, v. vi. 1, VI. ix. 3) and Tacitus (*Hist.* v. 13) are manifestly exaggerated. The present permanent population of modern Jerusalem, which covers a considerably larger area than the city in the time of Christ, is about 65,000. However closely the people were packed in the ancient city, it is hardly possible that there could have been so many as this, and many put the estimate at one-half this number. At the time of the Passover, when numbers were camped on the Mount of Olives and at other spots around, it is possible to believe that the population may have been considerably higher than that of to-day.

6. HISTORY OF JERUSALEM DURING THE PERIOD OF THE GOSPELS.—For a few short years before the birth of Jesus, Jerusalem enjoyed a time of extraordinary material prosperity, during which the great architectural works of Herod the Great were completed. It is evident, as has often been the case in the East, that this work was carried out only by means of great oppression, so that the king, while he left behind him vast monuments in stone, left also a memory execrated in the hearts of the common people. Some twenty years before the birth of Jesus the magnificent palace of Herod was finished ; * the three great towers, the theatre, the Xystus, and the Hippodrome (these last two adorned, if not initiated, by Herod) were completed early in his reign. Several years (B.C. 19-11) were also spent in adorning and extending the Temple, a work which was being continued during the life of Christ (Jn 2[20]). At this time the Temple must have attained a grandeur and beauty exceeding all previous eras. Yet the declining days of Herod the Great found the city seething with rebellion, which, just before his death, found vent in the public destruction of the golden eagle (*BJ* I. xxxiii.) which he had erected over the gate of the Temple. In revenge for this forty persons were burnt alive, and others were executed in less terrible ways. When the king considered that his last hour was imminent, he shut into the Hippodrome the most illustrious of the Jews, with orders that they should be executed when he died, so that the city might on his death be filled with mourning, even if not for him.

Herod's death in B.C. 4, the year of the Nativity, let loose on all sides the disorderly elements. Archelaus, the heir by Herod's will, advertised his accession by ascending a golden throne in the Temple on a 'high elevation made for him,' and hastened to ingratiate himself by promising all kinds of good things to the expectant and worshipping crowds. He was, however, unable to satisfy the excessive and exacting demands of the unruly crowds, who had been deeply stirred by the heavy punishment meted out by Herod in the affair of the golden eagle, and at the approach of the Passover a riot followed which ended in the massacre of three thousand Jews—mainly visitors to the feast, who were encamped in tents outside the Temple. Archelaus forthwith hastened to Rome to have his ap-

---

* Palace built B.C. 24 ; Temple restored B.C. 19–11.

pointment confirmed, leaving the city in utter confusion. As soon as he had taken ship, Sabinus, the Roman procurator, hastened to the city, seized and garrisoned the king's palace and all the fortified posts of which he could get possession, and laid hands on all the treasures he could find. He endeavoured to assert his authority with a view to opposing the absent Archelaus, for he at the same time sent to Rome a letter accusing him to Cæsar. At the succeeding feast of Pentecost the crowds of Galilæans, Idumæans, and trans-Jordan Jews, with recruits from the more unrestrained elements from Jerusalem, rose in open rebellion, and commenced to besiege Sabinus in the palace. One party assembled along the whole W. wall of the Temple to attack from the east, another towards the south at the Hippodrome, and a third to the west— apparently outside the W. walls of the city. Sabinus, who seems to have been an arrant coward, sent an appeal for help to Varus, the governor of Syria, who was then in Antioch, and shut himself up in the tower Phasael. From there he signalled to the troops to fall upon the people. A terrible fight ensued, at first in the city itself and then in the Tyropœon Valley, from which the Roman soldiers shot up at the rioters assembled in the Temple cloisters. Finding themselves at great disadvantage from their position in the valley, the soldiers in desperation set fire to the cloisters, and their Jewish opponents, crowded within and upon the roof, were either burnt to death or were slaughtered in attempting to escape. Some of the soldiers pursuing their victims through the flames burst into the Temple precincts and seized the sacred treasures; of these Sabinus is stated to have received 400 talents for himself. Upon this, other parties of Jews, exasperated by these affairs, made a counter attack upon the palace and threatened to set it on fire. They first offered a free pass to all who would come out peaceably, whereupon many of Herod's soldiers came out and joined the Jews; but Rufus and Gratus with a band of horsemen went over to the Romans with three thousand soldiers. Sabinus continued to be besieged in the palace, the walls of which the Jews commenced to undermine, until Varus arrived, after which he slunk away to the seacoast. The Jerusalem Jews excused themselves to the governor by laying all the blame on their fellow-countrymen from other parts. Varus suppressed the rebellion with ruthless firmness, crucifying two thousand Jews; and then, leaving a legion in the city to maintain order, he returned to Antioch. Archelaus returned some months later as ethnarch, and ruled for ten years, until, being accused to Cæsar of oppression, he was banished to Vienne.

During the rule of Coponius (6–10), the procurator who succeeded, another Passover disturbance occurred. This was due to the extraordinary and defiant conduct of a party of Samaritans, who threw some dead bodies into the cloisters of the Temple just after midnight,—a step which must, without doubt, have deepened the smouldering hatred between Jews and Samaritans (Jn 4⁹). Marcus Ambivius (11–12) and Annius Rufus (13) after short and uneventful terms of office were succeeded by Valerius Gratus (14–25), whose eleven years were marked only by the many changes he made in the high priesthood. His successor, Pontius Pilate (26–37), left the stamp of his character on secular history by making a great show of authority, in constituting Jerusalem the military headquarters, and introducing Cæsar's effigies into the city, but entirely reversing this policy when it was vigorously opposed by the more fanatic elements of the Jews. On this occasion a great gathering of Jews assembled in, apparently, the

Xystus (ἐν τῷ μεγάλῳ σταδίῳ), and preferred to bare their necks to Pilate's soldiers to withdrawing their demands (Ant. XVIII. iii. 1). Mention has already been made of the 'current of water' Pilate brought to Jerusalem, and the riot which followed because he used for the work 'sacred money' of the Temple. When persuasions had failed to quell the tumult, Pilate gave a signal to the soldiers, whom he had distributed in disguise through the crowd, and many were killed and wounded (Ant. XVIII. iii. 2).

The whole secular history as given by Josephus shows in what an excitable and unstable condition the Jews were, specially at the time of the feasts, when the city was filled by outsiders. In such a city it is not wonderful that twice (Jn 8⁵⁹ 10³¹) Jesus was threatened with stoning. The histories of past Passovers in the Holy City may have made Pilate acutely anxious as to whither the commotion connected with the arrest of Jesus was tending; the leaders of the Jews, on the other hand, had doubtless learnt by their victory in the matter of Cæsar's effigies to anticipate that, if they blustered and threatened enough, Pilate was unlikely finally to withstand their demands.

7. JERUSALEM IN THE GOSPELS. — The earliest Gospel incident connected with the city is the foretelling to Zacharias in the Temple of the birth of John the Baptist (Lk 1⁵⁻²³); the second, the arrival of the Magi to inquire in the city where the 'king of the Jews' was born (Mt 2¹⁻¹⁰). Shortly after this occur the purification of the Virgin Mary and the presentation of Jesus in the Temple (Lk 2²²⁻³⁹); and some twelve years later the first (?) Passover of Jesus in the Holy City and the incident of His staying behind to discuss with the doctors in the Temple (Lk 2⁴¹⁻⁴⁹). After this, with the exception of one brief scene in the Temptation (Mt 4⁵), the Synoptics are silent regarding any events in the city until the last week of His life. It is clear that Jesus rather avoided the city, and that the city was hostile to Him. It was Jerusalem as the centre of Jewish religious life which alone drew Jesus there; almost exclusively His being there was connected with attendance at a feast; and, with the single exception of the incident at the Pool of Bethesda, all His doings were, till the last week, in the courts of the Temple. In the Fourth Gospel there is mention of a Passover at which Jesus cleansed the Temple, and later had His discourse with Nicodemus (Jn 2¹³ 3¹⁻²¹). Then a year and a half later, while He was attending the Feast of Tabernacles, occurred the incidents of the adulteress and the blind man (Jn 7² 8³ff. 9¹ff.), ending in an attempt to arrest Him and a threatened stoning. A little later in the year, at the Feast of Dedication, He appeared in the Temple and was again threatened with stoning (Jn 10²²⁻³⁹). After the raising of Lazarus at Bethany, Jesus deliberately avoided entering the city, but shortly afterwards He determinately turned His face towards it, with the consciousness that suffering and death inevitably awaited Him there (Mk 10³²⁻³⁴).

When at last the step of return to the metropolis had been taken and the triumphal entry into the city (Mt 21¹⁻¹¹, Mk 11¹⁻¹⁰, Lk 19²⁹⁻⁴⁴, Jn 12¹²⁻¹⁹) and the second cleansing of the Temple (Mt 21¹²⁻¹⁶, Mk 11¹¹, Lk 19⁴⁵·⁴⁶) had occurred, Jesus seems to have gladly withdrawn Himself night after night from the turmoil of the city to the quiet of the village life of Bethany, out of sight of the sad and tragic city over which He could but weep (Lk 19⁴¹⁻⁴⁴). The night of His arrest seems to have been the first in that fateful week He spent in the immediate environs of the city. Then during the closing days came teaching by the miracle of the fig-tree (Mt 21²⁰⁻²², Mk 11²⁰⁻²⁵) and by parable (the Wicked Husbandmen, the Ten Virgins, the

Sheep and the Goats), as well as by direct prediction, to enforce the lesson that judgment on the city and the nation was nigh at hand. The wickedness and hypocrisy of the city led to the sterner denunciations of the scribes and Pharisees by One who considered that their doom was practically sealed (Mt 23). Only in the incidents of the widow's mite (Mk 12[41-44], Lk 21[1-4]) and in the coming of the Greek strangers to Jesus (Jn 12[20-33]) is there any sign of this lifting of the heavy clouds of approaching tragedy. The efforts of Pharisees, Sadducees, and lawyers to catch Him in some political indiscretion or unorthodoxy in His teaching were alike foiled, and at length the leaders of the Jews made their unholy compact with the traitor Judas.

As the first day of Unleavened Bread drew nigh, the disciples were sent into the city to prepare the Passover. The scene of this incident is to-day pointed out as an upper room (50 feet by 30 feet) near the modern Zion gate of the city; tradition, according to Epiphanius, records that this was one of the few buildings which escaped destruction by Titus. It is certainly on the *site*, even if it is not the actual room, referred to by Bishop Cyril of Jerusalem in the middle of the 4th cent. as the place where the disciples were assembled on the day of Pentecost. Arculf is the first (about A.D. 685) to point it out as the *Cœnaculum*. Since 1561 the buildings, with the traditional tomb of David adjoining, have been in the hands of the Moslems.

After the Supper, Jesus withdrew with His disciples to the Garden of Gethsemane. The fact that He crossed the Kidron points to some spot on the lower slopes of the Mount of Olives, and tradition since the 4th cent. has fixed on one which is now preserved as a garden by the Franciscans. If the site of the *Cœnaculum* is correct, it is probable that Jesus reached Gethsemane along the line of the paths now running outside the S. wall of the city, leaving the city south of the Temple.

After arrest, Jesus was taken by the soldiers to the palace of the high priest in the Temple precincts. Probably the procession followed the general direction of the road which to-day runs from Gethsemane to St. Stephen's gate, though there are indications that in ancient times this road was more direct than it now is. In the early morning He was brought before Pilate in the Prætorium, and he in turn sent Him (Lk 23[7-11]) to Herod Antipas, tetrarch of Galilee, who happened to be in Jerusalem at the time. The natural place where Herod would have his quarters would be in some part of his father's palace on the W. hill, and it may well be argued by those who think it more likely that the Prætorium was in the same enclosure, that it is hardly probable that Pilate would have lightly risked sending Jesus twice through the streets when so many Galilæans were about the city.

After the condemnation came the procession to Golgotha. The traditional route of this, known as the *Via Dolorosa*, has been selected on very slender grounds; indeed, all the 'stations of the cross' on the way have varied greatly from time to time. Even the first station, the site of the Prætorium, has been placed in many parts of the city. In the 4th cent. it was near the present *Bab el-Kattanin*, two centuries later it was marked by the basilica of St. Sophia. During the Crusading period it was placed first on the W. hill, under the idea that Pilate's house must have been near the Royal Palace, as several good modern authorities think it was; but at a later period it was transferred to the present Turkish barracks, indisputably on some part of the site of Antonia, as the more probable. The starting-point of the Via Dolorosa being so arbitrarily fixed, it necessarily follows that the various 'stations of the cross' are the flimsiest traditions. The *second* station—where the cross was laid on Jesus—is below the steps descending from the barracks. Near this is the well-known Ecce Homo arch—a construction of the 2nd cent.; and inside the adjoining institution of the Sisters of Zion is shown a large sheet of pavement belonging to the Roman period (and identified by the Latin authorities as the Gabbatha of Jn 19[13]), which may quite possibly have been in position at the time of the Crucifixion: part of its surface belongs to a street. The *third* station is shown where the street from the barracks—*Tarik bâb Sitti Miriam*—joins the carriage road from the Damascus Gate, running along the ancient Tyropœon Valley; the spot is marked by a broken, prostrate column. Here Jesus sank under the weight of the cross. A few yards farther down the carriage road, the *fourth* station—where Jesus met His mother—lies on the right. At the next turning to the right is the *fifth* station, where Simon of Cyrene took the cross from Jesus; and if we ascend this street by a series of steps, the *sixth* station—the scene of the incident of St. Veronica's handkerchief—is found, near where the road becomes arched over. When the Via Dolorosa crosses the central street of the city, *Suk es-Semany*, the procession is supposed to have left the city walls. This is the *seventh* station. The *eighth* station, where Jesus admonished the women not to weep for Him but for themselves (Lk 23[27, 28]), lies up the ascent towards the Church of the Sepulchre; and the *ninth* station, where Jesus is said to have fallen a second time under the weight of the cross, is in front of the Coptic monastery. The remaining five stations are included in the Church of the Sepulchre, for which see art. GOLGOTHA.

The last mention of Jerusalem in the Gospels is in the injunction to the disciples to begin preaching the gospel there (Lk 24[47]). The full force of this, and the necessity for their being specially commanded, is fully realized only when it is seen what a unique position Jerusalem held in the mind of Jesus, as was recognized by His regular attendance at the Temple services and the periodical feasts; how deep was His pity for its close approaching doom; how bitter had been the hostility to His teaching and His claims; and, lastly, how extraordinarily important was Jerusalem at that time as a meeting-place of many intensely held religious ideals.

LITERATURE.—This is enormous, and to attempt an exhaustive analysis would here be out of place. The authorities mentioned below are only some of those of which the writer has himself made use, and in the great majority of instances the references are only to modern writers.—

The Bible, the Apocrypha, the works of Josephus, and the *History* of Tacitus; the volume 'Jerusalem' in the Memoirs of the *PEF* (1884); Rev. W. F. Birch in *PEFSt*; Bliss and Dickie, *Excavations in Jerusalem* (1894–1897); Dr. T. Chaplin on the Climate of Jerusalem in *PEFSt*, 1883; Conder, art. 'Jerusalem' in Hastings' *DB*, and many other works and papers; Glaisher, 'Meteorological observations in Jerusalem' in *PEF* special pamphlet; Richard Gottheil, art. 'Jerusalem' in *Jewish Encyclopedia* (1904); Rev. E. Hanauer and Dr. Merrill of Jerusalem, various papers in the *PEFSt*; Lewin, *Siege of Jerusalem by Titus* (1863); Prof. Mitchell, art. on the Walls of Jerusalem in *JBL* (1903); Porter in Murray's *Guide Book*[1]; Robinson's *BRP* (1858); Sanday, *Sacred Sites of the Gospels* (1903); Schick, 'Die Wasserversorgung der Stadt Jerusalem' in the *ZDPV* (1878), and many papers in the *PEFSt* and elsewhere; Geo. Adam Smith, artt. 'Jerusalem' in *Encyc. Bibl.* and *Expositor*, 1903 and 1905; W. R. Smith, part of art. 'Jerusalem' in *Encyc. Bibl.*; Socin and Benzinger in Baedeker's *Handbook to Palestine*; Sir Charles Warren, *Underground Jerusalem* (1876); Andrew Watt on Climate in *Jour. of Scot. Meteor. Society*, 1900–1901; Williams, *Holy City*, 1849; Sir Charles Wilson, art. 'Jerusalem' in Smith's *DB*[2] (1893), also on 'Golgotha and the Holy Sepulchre' in *PEFSt*, 1902-3-4-5, and many other articles.

E. W. G. MASTERMAN.

JESSE.—The father of king David, named in our Lord's genealogy (Mt 1[5f.], Lk 3[32]).

JESUS (the name).—It is strange that even this

name has not yet been explained with certainty. ᾿Ιησοῦς (gen., dat., voc. ᾿Ιησοῦ; acc. ᾿Ιησοῦν, Mt 1¹ 8³⁴, Mk 1²⁴, Mt 1²¹ [on ᾿Ιησοῖ as gen. and dat. see Winer-Schmiedel, § 10, note 6]) is the Greek form of the Hebrew יֵשׁוּעַ or יְהוֹשֻׁעַ. Aquila has for the latter (Dt 1³⁸) ᾿Ιησουά; in some passages ᾿Ιησουέ is found (1 Ch 7²⁷, 2 Es 2⁶· ⁴⁰); see Redpath's *Concordance*.

No satisfactory explanation has yet been offered of the varying forms יְהוֹשֻׁעַ and יֵשׁוּעַ The high priest, for instance, who led the Jews back from Babylon with Zerubbabel, is constantly called יְהוֹשֻׁעַ in the prophetical books of Haggai and Zechariah (RV Joshua,' not ' Jehoshua, as in the name of his father ' *Jehozadak* '), and with equal constancy יֵשׁוּעַ in the historical books of Ezra and Nehemiah (where also the name of his father is written in the abbreviated form ' Jozadak '). Were, then, both forms used at the same time? Or is this a hint that the difference is due to later recensions, and that the form ' Jeshua ' is later than the time of the Exile? Again, how did ' *Jehoshua* ' become ' *Jeshua* '? The question is the more difficult as *nowhere* is the intermediate form ' *Joshua* ' found, as in the other names formed with ' Jeho-,' *e.g.* יוֹאָב side by side with יְהוֹאָב, etc. The nearest parallel seems to be the name of the king of Moab, who is called ' *Mesha*' ' (מֵישַׁע) in the MT of 2 K 3⁴, but Μωσά in the LXX; or the name ' *Moab*,' which is explained as if =*mē-ʼab* in Gn 19³⁷. The reason for the vowel change has been sought in the analogy of names beginning with *el*, or merely on phonetical principles (differentiation, as *rishôn* from *rôsh*, etc.). (For quite a different explanation, which will hardly stand examination, see Fr. Prätorius in *ZDMG* lix. 342) The difficulty is increased by the fact that the name is spelt יְהוֹשׁוּעַ (with ו) but twice (Dt 3²¹, Jg 27); and יֵשׁוּעַ may therefore have been originally ' Jehoshaʼ,' like אֱלִישׁוּעַ alongside of אֱלִישָׁע.

Hitherto it has generally been presupposed that the name was formed from the root יָשַׁע ' to save' (or rather ' to be safe'), like יְהוֹשֻׁעַ, which, according to Nu 13⁸· ¹⁶ and Dt 32⁴⁴, was the earlier name of ' Joshua '; cf. the name הושע on a Palestinian jar-handle, combined by Macalister with the name ישע 1 Ch 4²⁹ (*PEFSt*, 1905, p. 330). But the dropping of the first letter is not easily explained on this theory. And the analogy of the names שׁוּעַ, אֱלִישׁוּעַ, בַּתְשׁוּעַ side by side with בַּת־שֶׁבַע, אֱלִישֶׁבַע, שֶׁבַע, points to the possibility that יְהוֹשֻׁעַ is related to שֶׁבַע, as שׁוּעַ is to שֶׁבַע As to the meaning of these names nothing is certain. That to popular sentiment the name recalled the idea of *salvation* is proved for the OT by Nu 13⁸· ¹⁶, and for the NT by Mt 1²¹ ' Thou shalt call his name *Jesus*; for he shall *save* his people from their sins.' Perhaps also in 1 Th 1¹⁰ ᾿Ιησοῦν τὸν ῥυόμενον ἡμᾶς, we have an allusion to this etymology. Greek Christians were reminded by the name of the root ἰάομαι, ' to heal'; cf. *Sib. Or.* i. 351 καὶ τότε δὴ νοσεροὺς ἰήσεται; Clem. Al. *Pædag.* i. 7. 61 τοιοῦτον ἡμῖν ὄνομα σωτηρίου προφητεύει παιδαγωγοῦ . . . ἵν᾿ οὓς ὁ λόγος ὁ πειθήνιος οὐκ ἰᾶται, ἀπειλὴ ἰάσεται, κ.τ.λ., *ib.* iii. 12. 98 ὁ ἰώμενος ἡμῶν καὶ σῶμα καὶ ψυχήν, τὸν ἀΐδιον ἄνθρωπον, ᾿Ιησοῦς; Cyril of Jerusalem, *Cateches.* x. p. 88 ᾿Ιησοῦς τοίνυν ἐστὶ κατὰ τὴν ῾Ελλάδα γλῶσσαν ὁ ἰώμενος. ᾿Επειδὰν ἰατρός ἐστι ψυχῶν καὶ σωμάτων, καὶ θεραπευτὴς πνευμάτων, τυφλῶν μὲν αἰσθητῶν θεραπευτὴς . . . χωλῶν φαινομένων ἰατρός; Epiphanius, *Hær.* 29, Nazar. § 4 ᾿Ιησοῦς γὰρ κατὰ τὴν ῾Εβραϊκὴν διάλεκτον θεραπευτὴς καλεῖται, ἤτοι ἰατρὸς καὶ σωτήρ. Epiphanius betrays in these last words also a knowledge of the Hebrew root; and the same is the case with Chrysostom, who expressly states (*Hom. 2 in Matth.* p. 23), τὸ γὰρ ᾿Ιησοῦς τοῦτο ὄνομα οὐκ ἔστιν ῾Ελληνικόν, ἀλλὰ τῇ ῾Εβραίων φωνῇ οὕτω λέγεται ᾿Ιησοῦς· ὅ ἐστιν εἰς τὴν ῾Ελλάδα γλῶτταν ἑρμηνευόμενον, σωτήρ· σωτὴρ δέ, ἀπὸ τοῦ σῶσαι τὸν λαὸν αὐτοῦ. To the same effect is the statement of Eusebius (*Dem. Ev.* iv. 17, p. 199), who compares Christ with the high priest of the Return, and writes on their names, § 23, Εἰκότως οὖν τῆς εἰκόνος ἕνεκα καὶ οὗτος τῆς τοῦ σωτῆρος προσηγορίας ἠξιοῦτο . . . ἐπειδὴ σωτήριον θεοῦ εἰς τὴν ῾Ελλάδα φωνὴν τὸ τοῦ ᾿Ιησοῦ μεταληφθὲν ὄνομα σημαίνει· ᾿Ιησουά μὲν γὰρ ῾Εβραίοις σωτηρία, υἱὸς δὲ Ναυῆ παρὰ τοῖς αὐτοῖς ᾿Ιωσουέ

ὀνομάζεται· ᾿Ιωσουὲ δέ ἐστιν ᾿Ιάω σωτηρία, τοῦτ᾿ ἔστι θεοῦ σωτήριον. εἰκότως εἴ που θεοῦ σωτήριον ἐν τοῖς ῾Ελληνικοῖς ἀντιγράφοις ὠνόμασται, οὐδ᾿ ἄλλο τι ἢ τὸν ᾿Ιησοῦν κατὰ τὴν ῾Εβραίων φωνὴν πέπεισο δηλοῦσθαι; cf. also Theodoret, ii. 385, on Is 61¹⁰, ἐν τῇ ῾Εβραίων φωνῇ τὸ ' ἱμάτιον σωτηρίου' ἱμάτιον ἰεσσουὰ κεῖται, τοῦτ᾿ ἔστι Χριστοῦ. Lagarde (*Übersicht*, p. 97) concludes from this that ܝܶܫܽܘܥ, the Syriac form of the name, had a double *š*.

Already in the oldest MSS of the Gr. Test. the name is written with abbreviations ΙC, ΙΥ, ΙΝ; but occasionally in some MSS, and regularly in the Codex Bezæ, ΙΗΥ is found (in the Codex Sinaiticus ΙΗΥ and ΙΥ in consecutive lines in Rev 22²⁰· ²¹). The Epistle of Barnabas seems to have known the abbreviation ΙΗ, because the number 318 (=ΤΙΗ) in Gn 14¹⁴ is explained there of the cross of Jesus; and the same inference may be drawn for Irenæus from a comparison of the texts of Irenæus, Hippolytus, and Epiphanius on the Marcosians (see *ExpT* xvii. [1905] pp. 44, 139).

H. Leclercq, in art. ' Abréviations' in Cabrol's *Dict. d'Archéol. Chrétienne*, has a special paragraph ' de l'abréviation ΙΗV, ΙΗS' (col. 177–180). The earliest coins exhibiting the symbol ΙΗS are of Justinian II. (685–695, and 705–711). In the legend ΙΗSVS XPISTVS NICA found on coins of Constantine II. (780–791), the second letter is pronounced to be the Greek η, despite the C in NICA. On the story that the monogram of Christ was found written on the heart of Ignatius (θεοφόρος), when at his martyrdom it was laid bare by the claws of the lions, see A. Bell, *The Saints in Christian Art*, i. [1901] p. 205.

On the power of the name ᾿Ιησοῦς, which cannot be translated, see Origen, *c. Cels.* i. 25 : like the names Michael, Gabriel, Raphael, καὶ ὁ ἡμέτερος ᾿Ιησοῦς, οὗ τὸ ὄνομα μυρίους ἤδη ἐναργῶς ἑώραται δαίμονας ἐξελάσαν ψυχῶν καὶ σωμάτων, ἐνέργησαν εἰς ἐκείνους ἀφ᾿ ὧν ἀπηλάθησαν.

We have as yet no explanation of the statement of Irenæus : ' Jesus autem nomen secundum propriam Hebræorum linguam litterarum est duarum ac dimidiæ, sicut periti eorum dicunt, significans dominum eum, qui continet cœlum et terram, quia Jesus secundum antiquam Hebraicam linguam cœlum est : terra autem iterum SURA USSER dicitur' (= SMA UERS) ' heaven and earth '). In another passage Irenæus writes : ' Nihilominus autem et unigenitus et maxime autem super omnia nomen, quod dicitur Deus, quod et ipsum hebraice *Baruch* dicitur, et duas et dimidium habet literas.'

The Jews now write ישׁו, which is explained by Händler (*Lexicon der Abbreviaturen*, 1897) ימח שמו, by Lagarde (*Mitteilungen*, ii. 290) וזכרנו, '*ש*' ויתאבד, ' may his name (and memory) be wiped out (and perish)'; Jastrow's *Dictionary* explains it as an abbreviation of ישׁו; Reuchlin and other Christian Hebraists wrote the name יהשׁוה, as a combination of the tetragrammaton יהוה, with ש. wherein they found deep mysteries.

The first letter of the Greek ᾿Ιησοῦς seems to be treated as a consonant in the hexameter

᾿Ισαακ | ἠδ ᾿Ια | κωβ ᾿Ιη | σους Δανι | ηλ τ᾿ ῾Ηλίας,

Sib. Or. ii. 247; also in the verse of Theodorus Prodromus: τοῦ δ᾿ ᾿Ιησοῦ θανόντος ᾿Ιούδας μένει. On its numerical value (10) and its straight form see speculations in Clement's *Pædag.* i. 9. 25 ἡ εὐθεῖα καὶ κατὰ φύσιν, ἣν αἰνίττεται τὸ ᾿Ιῶτα τοῦ ᾿Ιησοῦ, ἡ ἀγαθωσύνη αὐτοῦ, and ii. 43. 3, the psalter of ten strings; in Epiphanius, *Hær.* l. 3 = the 10th of Nisan, on which the Paschal lamb was chosen; the tithes (δεκάται σωτηρίου ἀρχὴ ὀνόματος ᾿Ιησοῦ) in *Apost. Const.* ii. 25; in the *Opus imperf. in Mt.* (Migne, lvi. 618).

On the spelling of the name in the Latin MSS of the Bible, Iesus, Ihesus, Hiesus, see Wordsworth-White on Mt 1¹ and p. 776; H. J. Lawlor, *Chapters on the Book of Mulling*, p. 76; the letter of Amalarius to Bp. Jonas of Orleans and to Abp. Jeremias of Sens ' de nomine dñi Iesu,' whether ΙΗC or ΙΗS is the correct spelling, whether the middle letter is the Greek η or the Latin *h*, whether the last letter is Greek or Latin. In the Russian Church there was at one time a violent dispute about this orthographical question. In mediæval poetry, for instance in Ekkehart IV. of St. Gall, *Isus* is made to rhyme with *visus*, etc. :

'Virgo prior visum cunctis agnoverat Isum . . .
Sed nec ab his volumus nudetur laudibus Isus.'

Damasus formed the lines :

'In rebus tantis Trina conjunctio mundI
Erigit humanum sensum laudare venustE,
Sola salus nobis et mundi summa potestaS
Venit peccati nodum dissolvere fructU
Summa salus cunctis nituit per secula terriS.'

The Mohammedan form '*Isā* was certainly adapted to get an assonance with *Mūsa* (like *Ibrahim* with *Ismail*, *Kabil* with *Habil*), and not to identify the name with Esau. This was the more easy because the Nestorians pronounced the name *Ishố*, not *Jeshu*' like the Jacobites. On the proposal to introduce the Mohammedan form '*Isā* instead of '*Gisū*' into the Urdu NT, see *Bible House* Papers, No. iii. p. 28.

That the name contains 4 vowels and one consonant doubled, and has the numerical value 888 (10+8+200+70+400+200), is shown by *Sib. Or.* i. 326 ff. and by the speculations of the Marcosians (Iren. xv. 2 ; Hippol. vi. 50).
On the monograms for the name of Jesus see *PRE*[3] xii. esp. p. 371 f. ; Jerome, 'de monogramma XPI' in *Anecdota Maredsolana*, iii. 3 (1903), pp. 195–198 ; P. Cafaro, *l'ebreo nome Gesù*, Napoli, 1890, p. 390.

In the Ethiopian Church the name Jesus is avoided as a proper name (*ZDMG* xxviii. 309) ; in the Syriac Church it is 'still very commonly used as a man's name' (Maclean, *Dict. of the Dialects of Vernacular Syriac*, 1901). It would be an interesting task to collect the proper names formed with Jesus as first or second part ; they seem especially frequent in the Syriac and Persian Churches.   EB. NESTLE.

JEWS.—This term, originally perhaps applied only to men of the tribe of Judah, 'men of Judæa,' is employed in the Gospels (1) in opposition to Gentiles, proselytes, or Samaritans : Mk 7[3], Jn 2[6. 13] 4[9. 22] 5[1] 6[4] 7[2] 19[40. 42] ; (2) specially of Jews as antagonistic to our Lord, a usage which is characteristic of Jn. as distinguished from the Synoptics : Mt 28[15], Jn 6[41. 52] 8[48-57] 9[18] 10[19] 11[19. 31. 33. 36] 12[9. 11]. On the inferences that have been drawn from this usage as to the authorship and date of the Fourth Gospel, see art. JOHN (GOSPEL OF). 'The Jews' in this sense were blind followers of the Pharisees, and bitter opponents of Christ. Scrupulous about all the practices sanctioned by the elders,—washing of hands, of cups and pots and brazen vessels, Sabbath observance, etc. (Mk 7[3. 4], Jn 5[10] etc.),—they had forsaken the 'old paths' trodden by their fathers, and the things commanded by God. 'For fear of the Jews' men hesitated to confess Christ (Jn 7[13] 9[22]).

For customs of the Jews see art. SOCIAL LIFE. See also artt. ISRAEL and JERUSALEM.

LITERATURE.—Westcott, *Gospel of St. John*, Introd. p. viii ff. ; Andrews, *Life of our Lord* [ed. 1893], p. 470 ; Fairbairn, *Studies in the Life of Christ*, ch. x.   J. SOUTAR.

JOANAN.—A link in our Lord's genealogy (Lk 3[27]).

JOANNA ('Ιωάννα, Tisch. and Revisers' Text ; but 'Ιωάνα, WH and Nestle ; from Aram. אןחוי, Heb. יהוחנה).—The wife of Chuza, the 'steward' of Herod Antipas. In Lk 8[1-3] she appears as one of certain women who had been healed, and in gratitude ministered to Jesus and His disciples. The passage reads as though she had herself derived physical benefit from Jesus ; but it is possible, as Godet suggests *in loc.*, that the 'nobleman' or king's officer of Jn 4[46-53] was Chuza. If so, Joanna may have been led to attach herself to Christ through the restoration of her son's health, or even of his life if the Johannine narrative is to be identified with Mt

8[5-13] and Lk 7[1-10]. The latter identification, as early as Irenæus (*adv. Hær.* ii. 33), and not without distinguished support (Wetstein, Ewald, de Wette, Baur), is attractive but precarious. Joanna is mentioned again in Lk 24[10] as one of the women who went to the sepulchre to embalm the body of Jesus. She is almost certainly the same person as in 8[3], though her husband's name does not occur in the later passage. There is no need to explain the omission by a suggestion that he was dead, or had become obscure through dismissal from his office by Antipas because of the relations of his household with Jesus. The Evangelist had already sufficiently marked the identity of Joanna, who through her own devotion would be well known to the disciples. See also CHUZA.
                    R. W. MOSS.

JODA.—A link in our Lord's genealogy (Lk 3[26]).

JOHN.—The father of Simon Peter (Jn 1[42] 21[15. 16. 17] RV ; AV *Jonas*). See PETER.

JOHN THE BAPTIST.—

    i. John's Importance, and Sources for his History.
    ii. Birth, Youth, and Pre-Prophetic Life.
    iii. The Public Ministry.
    iv. John's Baptism of Jesus and Witness regarding Him.
    v. Imprisonment and Death.
    vi. John and his Disciples.
    vii. Our Lord's Estimate of John.

i. JOHN'S IMPORTANCE, AND SOURCES FOR HIS HISTORY.—The significance of John the Baptist for the history of Christianity is shown by the place given him in the Gospel records by every one of the four Evangelists. St. Mark describes John's mission in the very first words of his narrative as 'the beginning of the gospel of Jesus Christ, the Son of God' (1[1]). St. Luke makes the story of John's birth the prelude to his wonderful narrative of the greater birth at Bethlehem (1[5ff.]). The three Synoptists are agreed in representing his mission as the necessary preparation, in accordance with OT prophecy, for the manifestation of the Christ (Mk 1[2. 3], Mt 3[3], Lk 3[4ff.]), while in all the Gospels his baptism of Jesus becomes the moment of the Lord's equipment with the Spirit for His Messianic office (Mk 1[9ff.], Mt 3[16f.], Lk 3[21f.] ; cf. Jn 1[32ff.]). In the Prologue to his Gospel the Fourth Evangelist describes John as 'a man sent from God,' who 'came for a witness, to bear witness of the light, that all men through him (*i.e.* Jesus) might believe' (1[6. 7]). In accordance with this general sense of John's great importance for Christ and Christianity is the space devoted to him in the Gospel narratives as a whole. It is true that Lk. alone furnishes any information about him previous to the moment when he suddenly issued from his retirement in the wilderness and began to preach the baptism of repentance in the Jordan Valley, and true also that in the case of the Fourth Gospel it is difficult often to distinguish between the Evangelist's statements as a historian and his own subjective exposition. But when we put together all the references to John's ministry and history and character which we find either in the form of historical narrative, or testimony from the lips of Jesus, or reflexion on the part of an Evangelist, and when we make use besides of one or two sidelights which fall from the book of Acts and the pages of Josephus, we find that for knowledge regarding the Baptist's mission, his character, his relation to Jesus Christ, and his place in the history of both the old and the new dispensations, we are in no lack of plentiful and trustworthy sources of information.

ii. BIRTH, YOUTH, AND PRE-PROPHETIC LIFE.—

The fact that Lk. alone of the Gospels gives an account of John's earlier life, together with the artistic nature of the narrative and its presumed discrepancy with the representation of the Fourth Gospel in respect of a connexion between John and Jesus previous to the baptism of the latter (cf. Lk 1³⁶·⁵⁶ with Jn 1³¹·³³), has frequently been supposed to reduce this exquisite story to the level of pure legend. In view, however, of St. Luke's claims to historical accuracy (1¹·⁴), and of the vindication of these claims at so many points by modern research (cf. W. M. Ramsay, *St. Paul the Traveller*, ch. i., *Was Christ born at Bethlehem?*; Chase, *The Credibility of Acts*), it is impossible to set his narrative aside as if it rested on no basis of historical fact. It is full of poetry, no doubt, but it is the kind of poetry which bursts like a flower from the living stem of actual truth. Any attempt to dissolve the narrative into fictions of a later growth must reckon with the fact that the Evangelist is evidently making use at this point of an early Aramaic source steeped in the colours of the OT—'the earliest documentary evidence respecting the origins of Christianity which has come down to us, evidence which may justly be called contemporary' (Plummer, 'St. Luke' in *Internat. Crit. Com.*, p. 7). This document, which, if it is historical, must have rested in large part upon the authority of the Virgin Mary, St. Luke, 'as a faithful collector of evangelic *memorabilia*, allows to speak for itself, with here and there an editorial touch' (Bruce, *Expositor's Gr. Test., ad loc.*). To appreciate the historical sobriety and manifestly primary character of this early Jewish-Christian source, we have only to compare the first chapter of Lk. with the relative sections of the *Protevangelium Jacobi*, and especially with those chapters (22–24) which Harnack calls the *Apocryphum Zachariæ* (see Hastings' *DB*, Extra Vol. p. 431).

According to Lk., John was the son of Zacharias, a priest of the course of Abijah (see art. ZACHARIAS), and his wife Elisabeth who belonged to the family of Aaron (1⁵ᶠᶠ·). Elisabeth was a kinswoman (not 'cousin,' see Plummer, *op. cit.* p. 25) of the Virgin Mary (1³⁶), who paid her a three months' visit immediately before the birth of John (v.⁵⁶, cf. vv.³⁶·³⁹·⁴⁰). John was the senior of Jesus by six months (1³⁶·⁵⁷, cf. 2⁶). The name John, properly Johanan (Ἰωάννης = יוֹחָנָן, cf. Heb. text and LXX of 1 Ch 3²⁴, 2 Ch 28¹²), was given to the child by his parents in obedience to a Divine direction (1¹³), and in spite of the opposition of neighbours and kinsfolk (vv.⁵⁸⁻⁶³).

Regarding the place of John's birth there has been much discussion. Lk. describes the house of Zacharias as in 'a city of Judah' which lay in 'the hill country' (vv.³⁹·⁴⁰). A number of commentators have assumed, without any warrant, that this must have been Hebron, as being a priestly town in that region. Others have suggested that πόλις Ἰούδα is a corruption for πόλις Ἰούτα (Reland, *Pal.* p. 870; Robinson, *BRP²* ii. 206), so that the Baptist's birthplace would be Jutah or Juttah, to the south of Hebron (Robinson, *op. cit., ib.*, and i. 495), which is mentioned in Joshua as having been allotted to the priests (21¹⁶). A tradition as early as the Crusades assigns the honour to '*Ain Karim*, a village which lay between Jerusalem and Bethlehem. All this, however, is purely conjectural, and it is best to be content to say that John was born in a town unknown, in the hill country of Judah. See, further, art. JUDAH.

Of the external incidents of John's childhood and youth Lk. gives no information. All that is told us bears upon his spiritual growth. According to an announcement of the angel Gabriel, he was to be 'filled with the Holy Ghost from his mother's womb' (1¹⁵). That a peculiar Divine blessing did rest upon him from the first is implied in the words, 'the hand of the Lord was upon him' (v.⁶⁶); that this Divine presence made itself manifest in the development of his character is evident when the Evangelist adds, 'and the child grew, and waxed strong in spirit' (v.⁸⁰).

But whatever the outward tenor of John's way in that priestly house in the hill country of Judah, a great crisis must have come at last, followed by a sudden break in his manner of life. A priest's son, he would naturally, according to all Jewish traditions, have stepped into the priestly office, and enjoyed the honours, abundance, and comparative ease that were parts of his birthright. But spiritual instincts and powers which had long been unknown in Israel began to make themselves felt in the young man's heart, and this son of a priest went forth into the deserts to be shaped in solitude into a prophet mightier than Elijah or Isaiah. Of the precise nature of the impulse which first led him to withdraw himself from his fellows, the duration of his stay in the wilderness, and the

fashion of his life while there, no Evangelist has anything to tell us. But it is certainly a grotesque mistake to suppose that he left his home and the haunts of men in order to become an Essene (see the excellent remarks of Godet on this point, *Com. on Lk.* i. p. 117 f.).*

There was absolutely no resemblance between John, the desert solitary, as he is described to us in the pages of the Gospels (Mt 3⁴ ‖ 11⁷ᶠᶠ· ‖ 11¹⁸ ‖), and the Essenes with their white garments and their cenobitic establishments, as we come across them in the pages of Josephus (*BJ* II. viii. 2–13, *Ant.* XVIII. i. 5). All that can be said is that John was an ascetic as the Essenes were, and that in both cases the revolt against prevailing luxury and corruption sprang out of the deep seriousness which marked the more earnest spirits of the time (see Rüegg, art. 'Johannes der Täufer' in *PRE³*). John's withdrawal into the wilderness indicated his disapproval of society as he found it, it signified more especially an absolute break with the prevalent Pharisaic type of piety. But in his case it meant much more than this, much more even than the adoption of severely ascetic habits in the interests of his own spiritual life. It was as one who was conscious that he was set apart for the office of a prophet (cf. Lk 1¹⁴⁻¹⁷· ⁷⁶ᶠᶠ·), and who felt himself called in particular to take up in Israel a work of reformation similar to that of Elijah (Lk 1¹⁷; cf. Mt 11¹⁴ 17¹², Jn 1²¹), that John betook himself to the deserts (Lk 1⁸⁰) and there lived the life of one who hides himself from men that he may the better see the face of God. Locusts and wild honey were his food, while his clothing was a loose cloak (ἔνδυμα) of woven camel's hair and a leathern girdle about his loins (Mt 3⁴, Mk 1⁶; cf. 2 K 1⁸).†

How long John remained in 'the deserts, by which is doubtless meant the awful solitudes of the Wilderness of Judæa, and how he grew into the full sense of the precise nature of his prophetic vocation as the forerunner and herald of the Messiah, we cannot tell. But the Holy Ghost who had been working in him, and the hand of the Lord which had been laid upon him from the first, his own constant brooding over words of ancient prophecy (Jn 1²³, cf. Mt 3³ ‖), and a deep intuitive reading of the signs of the times, would gradually bring him to a clear knowledge both of his function as a prophet and of the time when he must begin to exercise it. And so came at last the day of his 'shewing' (ἀνάδειξις) unto Israel (Lk 1⁸⁰).

iii. THE PUBLIC MINISTRY.—It was in the 15th year of the reign of Tiberius Cæsar that the word of God came to John in the wilderness summoning him to enter upon his work as a prophet (Lk 3¹·²). Immediately he obeyed the summons (v.³). The scene of his ministry, according to Mk., was 'the wilderness' (1⁴), according to Mt. 'the wilderness of Judæa' (3¹), according to Lk. 'all the country about Jordan' (3³). Probably, as hitherto, the Wilderness of Judæa continued to be his home— that wild region which stretches westwards from the Dead Sea and the Jordan to the edge of the central plateau of Palestine; but when he preached he must have done so in some place not too far removed from the haunts of men, while, owing to

* This theory, put forth by Grätz (*Gesch. der Juden*, iii. p. 100) and adopted by many since, has been repeated once more in the art. 'Essenes' in *Jewish Encyc.*, where it is added that the silence of the NT about the Essenes 'is perhaps the best proof that they furnish the new sect (*i.e.* Christianity) with its main elements as regards personnel and views'—as striking an illustration as could well be discovered of a fallacious use of the *argumentum e silentio*. On John's relations to the Essenes see Lightfoot, *Colossians*, Dissert. iii.
† That he ate locusts, as the Bedawin still do, not carob-beans, is now the prevalent opinion of scholars (cf. art. LOCUST, and in Hastings' *DB, s.v.*). Cheyne, however, holds out for carob-beans (*Encyc. Bibl.*, artt. 'Husks' and 'John the Baptist'). See also *Expos. Times*, xv. [1904] pp. 285, 335, 429, xvi. [1905] p. 382.

his practice of baptism (almost certainly by immersion), the Jordan necessarily marked the central line of his activity (Mt 3⁶·¹³·¹⁶, Mk 1⁵·⁹). To Jn. we owe the information that he baptized on both sides of the river (1²⁸ 3²³ 10⁴⁰). John's work may be considered under two aspects, (1) his preaching, (2) his baptism.

1. John's Preaching.—According to Mt. the essence of John's preaching, the text as we might say of all his sermons, was this : 'Repent ye, for the kingdom of heaven is at hand' (3²). The second part of this text was the fundamental part. It shows that John was fully conscious that the long-expected Messianic age was now about to dawn, and that it was his mission to proclaim the fact. By his trumpet-voiced proclamation of this fact he thrilled the nation to its heart and drew forth the multitude into the wilderness to hear him (Mt 3⁵, Lk 3⁷; cf. Jos., *Ant.* XVIII. v. 2)—men from Jerusalem and men from Galilee (Jn 1¹⁹·³⁵ff.), civilians and soldiers (Lk 3¹⁰·¹⁴), Pharisees and publicans side by side (Mt 3⁷, Lk 3¹²).

But while the preacher's fundamental message was the announcement of the near approach of the Messianic Kingdom, he combined with these glad tidings of good a stern summons to repentance. Repentance, he said, μετάνοια, a change of mind and heart, were indispensable as a preparatory condition for all who would share in the privileges of the new order about to be set up. To the Jewish mind this was an unexpected and unwelcome note in a herald of the Messiah; and John's utterance of it and strenuous emphasis upon it form one of the marks of his profound originality as a prophet. According to the popular conviction, all Israel would have a lot and a part in the blessings of the Messianic age, and that specifically because of their descent from Abraham. It was recognized that judgments would accompany the appearance of the Christ, but these judgments were to fall upon the Gentiles, while Abraham's children would be secure and happy in that day of the Lord. The Talmud explains the cry of the prophetic watchman, 'The morning cometh, and also the night' (Is 21¹²), by saying, 'The night is only to the nations of the world, but the morning to Israel' (Jerus. *Taan.* 64a, quoted by Edersheim, *Life and Times*, i. 271). Not so, said John. Repentance is the prime requisite for all who would enter the Kingdom of heaven. Descent from Abraham counts for nothing (Mt 3⁹). Every fruitless or worthless tree must be hewn down and cast into the fire (v¹⁰). The very leaders of the nation themselves, the Pharisees and Sadducees, must bring forth fruit worthy of repentance if they are to escape from the wrath to come (vv.⁷·⁸).

2. John's Baptism.—Alongside of the spoken word John set that great distinctive symbol of his ministry from which his title 'the Baptist' (ὁ Βαπτιστής) was derived. He came not only preaching but baptizing, or rather, so closely was the symbol interwoven with the word, he came 'preaching the baptism of repentance' (Mk 1⁴, Lk 3³). To understand John's baptismal doctrine it is necessary to think of the historical roots out of which it sprang. For though he gave to the rite a depth of meaning it had never had in Israel before, he evidently appealed to ideas on the subject which were already familiar to the Jewish people. In particular, three moments in the preceding history of the religion of Israel appear to be gathered up in the baptism of John as it meets us in the Gospels.

(a) *The theocratic washings of the Jews* (Lv 11–15, Nu 19). That a religious intention underlay those 'divers washings' of the ceremonial law is evident (cf. Lv 14³² 15¹³, Mk 1⁴⁴, Lk 2²² 5¹⁴, Jn 2⁶), while the historical connexion of John's baptism with them is proved by the fact that in NT times

βαπτίζειν had come to be the regular term alike for those ceremonial washings and for the Messianic baptism of the Forerunner (for detailed proof and reff. on these points see the present writer's *Sacraments in the NT*, p. 56 f.). And yet, though John's baptism finds its earliest historical roots in the Levitical washings, it is far from finding its complete explanation there. It was essentially an ethical rite, and thus very different from an outward ceremony to which some value could be attached apart from the moral and spiritual condition of the recipient. In the case of all who came to him John insisted upon repentance; and they 'were baptized of him in Jordan, confessing their sins' (Mt 3²·⁶).

(b) *The Messianic lustration foretold by the prophets.*—Long before the time of John, prophetic souls in Israel had seen that for a true cleansing the nation must look to those Messianic days when God should open a fountain for sin and for uncleanness, sprinkling His people with clean water, and putting a new heart and a new spirit within them (Jer 33⁸, Ezk 36²⁵·²⁶, Zec 13¹). It was John's function to declare that those great Messianic promises were now going to receive their fulfilment at the hands of the Messiah Himself. His baptism, we have said, was a baptism of preparation for the Kingdom, preparation which took the form of repentance and confession. But even more than a baptism of preparation it was a baptism of promise, promise both of the Kingdom and the King, being a promissory symbol of a perfect spiritual cleansing which the Messiah in person should bestow—'I indeed baptize you with water unto repentance; but he that cometh after me . . . shall baptize you with the Holy Ghost and with fire' (Mt 3¹¹∥).

(c) Another historical moment which should not be lost sight of is *the proselyte baptism of the Jewish Church.* It may now be regarded as certain that the baptism of proselytes had been the rule in Israel long before NT times (see especially Schürer, *HJP* II. ii. 319; Edersheim, *Life and Times*, ii. 745 ff.); and proselyte baptism helps us to understand the baptism of John in certain of its aspects. When a Gentile 'sought shelter under the wings of the Shekinah,' it was understood that he was utterly renouncing his past. And John insisted on a like renunciation in the case of candidates for his baptism. The danger of the proclamation that the Kingdom of heaven was at hand lay in the fact that multitudes would claim to enter that Kingdom as a matter of course, without being prepared to submit to the necessary conditions. Not so, said John. God does not depend upon Israel alone for the peopling of His Kingdom. He 'is able of these stones to raise up children unto Abraham' (Mt 3⁹). Even a Jew, if he is to be received, must come as a humble penitent who casts himself upon the Divine grace. He must come like a stranger and a proselyte renouncing the past, not as one who claims an inalienable right, but as one who seeks by fruits of repentance to flee from the wrath to come (Mt 3⁷·⁸, Lk 3⁷·⁸). For the baptism of the Coming One is a baptism of judgment. His winnowing-fan is in His hand; and while He will gather His wheat into the garner, He will burn up the chaff with unquenchable fire (Mt 3¹², Lk 3¹⁷). On the baptism of John see, further, art. BAPTISM.

iv. JOHN'S BAPTISM OF JESUS AND WITNESS REGARDING HIM.—1. The baptism of Jesus by John is recorded in all the Synoptics (Mt 3¹³ff., Mk 1⁹·, Lk 3²¹), but is not mentioned in the Fourth Gospel. The author, however, makes the Baptist refer to the descent of the Spirit upon Jesus in the form of a dove (Jn 1³²ff.) as an authenticating sign which he received that He was the Messiah; and this incident is represented by the other three as following immediately upon the baptism, though the first two, and probably the third also, describe the visible sign as bestowed upon Jesus Himself along with the approving voice from heaven (Mt 3[16], Mk 1[10f.], Lk 3[22]). If the scene of the baptism was the same as that of John's subsequent witness to Jesus recorded in the Fourth Gospel, it took place at 'Bethany beyond Jordan' (Jn 1[28]), a site which has been much discussed, but cannot be said to have been certainly identified (see art. BETHABARA).

It was here, then, in all likelihood, that Jesus met John when He came from Galilee to be baptized of him (Mt 3[13]). At first John was unwilling to perform the rite upon such an applicant, but Jesus insisted. 'Thus it becometh us to fulfil all righteousness' (v.[15]). He recognized John's baptism as an appointment of the Divine righteousness which it was proper that He should accept. If the fitness of that baptism in the case of Jesus is called in question, we must remember that it had an initiatory aspect which would commend to Him as He saw in it an opportunity of consecrating Himself definitely and openly to the Messianic kingdom and its tasks. But if John's words of protest (v.[14]) imply that even in the baptism of Christ the cleansing aspect of the rite was in view, was it not proper that the 'Lamb of God' (Jn 1[29, 36]), who had no sense of personal guilt, nothing to repent of or confess, should even now begin to bear upon His heart the burden of the sins of others, even as on a coming day He was to bear them 'in his own body on the tree' (1 P 2[24])?

2. Of the intercourse of John with Jesus, the Fourth Gospel gives an account which differs widely from that presented in the Synoptics; but apart from the Johannine colouring of the later narrative, the difference is sufficiently explained on the ordinary view that the Synoptists describe the meeting between the two at the time of our Lord's baptism, while the Fourth Evangelist concerns himself only with John's subsequent testimony to the now recognized Messiah (cf. Jn 1[7f.]). There is no real discrepancy between John's 'I knew him not,' reported in the Fourth Gospel (1[31]), and the representation of Mt. (3[13ff.]), that when the Man from Nazareth presented Himself at the Jordan, John declined at first to baptize Him, on the ground of his own unworthiness in comparison. Even if we suppose that in spite of their kinship and the friendship between their mothers the two had not met before, the fact that John's baptism was a baptism of repentance and confession seems to imply a personal interview with applicants previous to the performance of the rite—an interview which in the case of Jesus must have revealed to one with the Baptist's insight the beauty and glory of His character. On the other hand, the 'I knew him not' of the last Gospel, as the context shows, only means that John did not know that Jesus was indeed the Messiah until he received the promised sign (1[32f.]).

It is true that in the Fourth Gospel John is made to bear a witness to Jesus by the banks of the Jordan (1[15-36]) which finds no parallel in the earlier narratives; but if we follow the ordinary view of students of the chronology of our Lord's life—that the narrative of the Fourth Evangelist comes in after the forty days of the Temptation have intervened, and that John now sees Jesus in the light not only of the authenticating sign given at the baptism, but of his own reflexion ever since upon the subject of the character of Jesus and the fulfilment of the Messianic promise—the fulness and explicitness of his testimony upon this later occasion appear perfectly natural. The twice-repeated ἔμπροσθέν μου γέγονεν (vv.[15, 30]), it is true, cannot be understood, so far as the Baptist himself

is concerned, as referring to pre-existence, though this was probably involved in the thought of the Evangelist. But the designation of Jesus as 'the Lamb of God' (vv.[29, 36]), and especially the phrase 'which taketh away the sin of the world' (v.[29]), reveals a conception of the Saviour's Messianic functions which is certainly profound, but which, in spite of the objections which have been taken to it, cannot surprise us in the case of one who had brooded like John over the utterances of OT prophecy (cf. especially Is 53).

The Fourth Evangelist records a further witness regarding Jesus which John bore to his own disciples on a later occasion, when he was baptizing in Ænon (wh. see), near to Salim (3[23ff.]). In this passage the difficulty of discriminating between the original words and facts of history and the Johannine setting and atmosphere is even greater than usual, but the figure of the Bridegroom 'that hath the bride' and the Bridegroom's friend who rejoices in the other's joy (v.[29]), and the saying, 'He must increase, but I must decrease' (v.[30]), are so thoroughly in keeping with other utterances of the Baptist recorded in the Synoptics as well as in the Fourth Gospel regarding the relations between the Messiah and himself (Mt 3[3, 11], Jn 1[15, 27]), that it is difficult to resist the impression of historical reality which they make upon the reader.

v. JOHN'S IMPRISONMENT AND DEATH (Mt 14[3-12], Mk 6[17-29], Lk 3[19, 20]; cf. Jos. Ant. XVIII. v. 1, 2). —According to the Synoptists, the arrest and execution of John were due to the spiteful hatred of Herodias (wh. see), because he had rebuked Herod for making her his wife in flagrant defiance of the law of Israel (Lv 18[16] 20[21]). Josephus, on the other hand, says that Herod put the prophet to death because he 'feared lest the great influence John had over the people might put it in his power and inclination to raise a rebellion; for they seemed ready to do anything he should advise.' The two statements, however, are not irreconcilable; and certainly the evidence of Josephus, whose interests as a historian lay altogether in the political direction, is not such as to cast any suspicion on the trustworthiness of the more detailed and more intimate Gospel narrative. It may very well have been the case that, while John's death was really due to the implacable hate of Herodias, Herod felt that this was hardly an adequate ground, or one that he would care to allege, for the execution of the Baptist, and so made political reasons his excuse. Assuredly there was nothing of the political revolutionary about John; yet his extraordinary influence over the people and the wild hopes raised among certain classes by his preaching might make it easy for Herod to present a plausible justification of his base deed by representing John as a politically dangerous person.

There may seem to be a contradiction within the Evangelic narratives themselves, when we find Mt. saying that Herod would have put John to death but that he feared the multitude (14[5]), while Mk. alleges that Herod 'feared John, knowing that he was a righteous man and an holy, and kept him safe . . . and heard him gladly' (6[20]). But the contradiction lies in Herod's character rather than in the testimonies of the two writers, and the words πολλὰ ἠπόρει, 'he was much perplexed' (Mk 6[20] WH and RV), explain adequately enough a moral situation of which we have the final revelation in Herod's weakly vacillating behaviour, 'letting I dare not wait upon I would,' when Herodias through her daughter Salome (Mt 14[6], Mk 6[22]; cf. Jos. Ant. XVIII. v. 4) presented her horrible request. That Herod did not really regard John as a political fanatic is suggested by all that the Gospels tell us as to the way in which he treated him while he lay in prison; by the personal audiences he granted him (Mk 6[20]), and by the fact that he allowed him to have intercourse with his disciples (Mt 11[2], Lk 7[18. 19]), and through them to exchange messages with Jesus (Mt 11[2-6], Lk 7[19-23]).

The message which John sent to Jesus has often been regarded as exceedingly strange on the part of one who had previously borne so signal a witness that Jesus was the Christ, and it has even been suggested that he sent his messengers not because there was any wavering of his own faith, but for the sake of his disciples, to whom he wished some confirmation of the Messiahship of Jesus to be given (see Bebb in Hastings' *DB* ii. 680[a]). But the more simple explanation is also the one which is truer to human nature. The depression wrought by imprisonment on one accustomed to the freedom of the wilderness, together with his disappointment at the seeming delay of Jesus to assert His power and authority as the Christ of Israel, had resulted in an hour of the power of darkness in the soul of the great prophet, when he began to wonder whether after all he had not made a great mistake. That in spite of his doubts he had not lost his faith in Jesus is shown by the very fact that it was to Jesus Himself that he applied to have these doubts removed, as well as by that message of encouragement and 'strong consolation' which the Bridegroom sent back to His sorely tried friend : 'Blessed is he whosoever shall not be offended in me' (Mt 11[6], Lk 7[23]).

From Josephus we learn that the Castle of Machærus (wh. see) was the scene of the Baptist's imprisonment (*Ant.* XVIII. v. 1, 2). Machærus was a powerful stronghold, at once a fortress and a palace (*BJ* VII. vi. 1-3; cf. Pliny, *Hist. Nat.* V. xvi. 72), situated on the eastern shores of the Dead Sea (G. A. Smith, *HGHL* p. 569 f.). Within these gloomy walls, then, the death of John took place, one of 'those awful tragedies for which nature has provided here so sympathetic a theatre' (*op. cit. in loc.*). Of this tragedy St. Mark has furnished us with the fullest account (6[21-29]) in a narrative which is not more thrilling in its dramatic vividness than it is instinct with the elements of what might almost be described as self-evidencing moral and historical truth.

vi. JOHN AND HIS DISCIPLES. — Besides the crowds that came to him to be baptized, John appears to have drawn around him a circle of closer followers, who are referred to in all the Gospels as his 'disciples' (Mt 9[14] [‖ Mk 2[18], Lk 5[33]] 11[2] [‖ Lk 7[18. 19]], Mk 6[29], Lk 11[1], Jn 1[35. 37] 3[25] 4[1]; cf. Ac 18[25] 19[1ff.]). It appears that, unlike Jesus, he enjoined regular fasts upon his disciples (Mt 9[14] ‖), and that he also gave them forms of prayer (Lk 11[1]) which they were in the habit of employing frequently (Lk 5[33]). Possibly he utilized them as assistants in the work of baptizing, for which he could hardly have sufficed personally when his movement was at its height.

It was from the circle of these disciples of the Baptist that the disciples of Jesus were immediately drawn (Jn 1[28-51]), and that not only with John's full consent, but through his own express witness both in public (Jn 1[19ff. 29ff.]) and in private (v.[35f.]) to the superior worth of Jesus and to his own function as the mere herald and forerunner of the latter. And yet he did not, as we might have expected, decline, after Christ's baptism, to stand any longer to others in the relation of a master to his disciples. Perfectly loyal as he was to Him whom he recognized as the Messiah, he evidently felt, as Jesus also did previous to John's imprisonment (Jn 3[22. 24] 4[1. 2]), that there was still need for a work of preparation, and room therefore for a discipleship to the Forerunner. But when his disciples grew jealous of the rapidly growing popularity of Jesus,

and came to him with their complaint, he proclaimed to them once more the true relation between that Other and himself,—'He must increase, but I must decrease,'—and reminded them how he had said from the first that he was not the Christ, but was sent before Him (Jn 3[28] ; cf. Mt 3[11] ‖).

The fidelity of John's disciples to their master is shown by their holding together and continuing to observe his prescriptions after he was cast into prison (cf. Mt 4[12] ‖ with 9[14] ‖), by their attendance upon him during his captivity (Mt 11[2ff.], Lk 7[18. 19ff.]), and by their loving and reverent treatment of his corpse (Mk 6[29]). The vital impression he made upon them, and the self-propagating power of the baptism of repentance in the absence of a higher teaching, is proved by the fact that more than 20 years afterwards, and in the far-off city of Ephesus, St. Paul found certain disciples, including no less a personage than Apollos, the Alexandrian Jew, who knew no other baptism than that of John (Ac 19[1ff.], cf. 18[24ff.]). Before the growing light of Christianity John's baptism as a baptism of preparation for the Messiah soon vanished away, but the traces of his memory and influence are found lingering long afterwards in the name, doctrines, and practices of the Hemerobaptists, who claimed John as one of themselves (*Clem. Hom.* ii. 23 ; cf. Hegesippus in Euseb. *HE* iv. 22 ; Justin Martyr, *Dial. c. Tryph.* On the relation of the Hemerobaptists to John, see Lightfoot, *Colossians*, p. 402 ff.).

vii. OUR LORD'S ESTIMATE OF JOHN.—The task of appreciating the character and activity of John the Baptist is rendered easy for us by the frequent utterances of Jesus Himself. If the worth of praise is to be measured by the lips from which it falls, no mortal man was ever praised so greatly as he whom Jesus described as 'a burning and a shining light' (Jn 5[35]), as one who was 'much more than a prophet' (Mt 11[9] RV, Lk 7[26]), as the Elijah who by his coming was to 'restore all things' (Mt 11[14] 17[10ff.], Mk 9[11ff.]) ; and of whom He said : 'Among them that are born of women there hath not risen a greater than John the Baptist' (Mt 11[11] ; see the whole passage, and cf. Lk 7[24ff.]). That John had his limitations Jesus made clear (Mk 2[18ff.]), but He attributed these not to any personal shortcomings, but to the fact that he belonged to the time of preparation, and so stood by a dispensational necessity outside of the realized Kingdom of God (Mt 11[11b], Lk 7[28b]).

Again and again Jesus revealed His sense of the Divine value that attached to the baptism of John. He showed it when He insisted on submitting to that baptism Himself, and by the words He used on the occasion (Mt 3[15]). He showed it when He asked the question, 'The baptism of John, whence was it? from heaven, or of men ?' (Mt 21[25] ‖), a question to which His own answer was self-evident, and which St. Luke answers for us when he says that 'all the people when they heard, and the publicans, justified God, being baptized with the baptism of John. But the Pharisees and the lawyers rejected for themselves the counsel of God, being not baptized of him' Lk 7[29f.]. And may we not say that in His words to a certain Pharisee (Jn 3[1]) about the necessity of a birth 'of water and the Spirit' (v.[5]), He was indicating once more the deep religious value of John's water-baptism, while insisting at the same time on the indispensableness of that spiritual birth which comes only from above (v.[3]) ? Time after time, too, even to the closing days of His ministry, words which Jesus let fall reveal to us that He carried about with Him continually the thought of His predecessor's career, and perceived the bearing of its lessons upon His own ministry and earthly lot and fate (see Mt 9[15ff.]

11^{12ff. 18f.} 17^{9ff.} 21³², Lk 16¹⁶). And, finally, after His resurrection, we find that as He had justified John at the first by taking up his baptism of preparation, so now He crowns the work of the Forerunner by instituting the baptism of the Kingdom itself (Mt 28¹⁹). John had adopted the rite as the distinctive symbol of his reforming activity and the gateway into the sphere of Messianic preparation. Jesus transformed it into a sacrament of the Christian Church—at once the token of the gospel of forgiveness and the sign and seal of discipleship to Himself.

LITERATURE.—Relative sections in works on Life of Christ by Neander, Keim, Renan, Weiss, Beyschlag, and Edersheim; Ewald, *HI* vi. 160-200; Reynolds, *John the Baptist*; Feather, *John the Baptist*; Hastings' *DB*, artt. 'John the Baptist,' 'Baptism,' and vol. ii. 610 f.; *PRE*³, art. 'Johannes der Täufer'; Haupt, *Johannes der Täufer*; Bornemann, *Die Taufe Christi durch Johannes*; Seeley, *Ecce Homo*, ch. i.; *Expos. Times*, xiii. [1902] 483 f., xv. [1903] 5 ff.; *Expositor*, I. v. [1877] 11 ff., 98 ff., viii. [1878] 23 ff., III. i. [1885] 267 ff., v. i. [1895] 201 ff., vi. [1897] 139 ff., vii. [1898] 187 ff.; Wilkinson, *A Johannine Document in the First Chapter of St. Luke's Gospel*; the earlier sections of Althaus, *Die Heilsbedeutung der Taufe*.

J. C. LAMBERT.

JOHN (THE APOSTLE).—As the Gospels are but memorabilia of Jesus, giving relatively but meagre accounts of His life and works, it is to be expected that they can afford us only glimpses of the Apostles. Such is the case; and, while a few more references are made to Peter, James, and John than to the others, we have no such material as allows any more than a fragmentary account of any one. Tradition has, in the case of each Apostle, added to the Scripture narrative a story of subsequent activity and fate. For convenience of reference, therefore, to all that is known of John we may group the materials under the following heads: (1) those found in the Scriptures; (2) those given us by tradition. To the account thus obtained we shall add a brief delineation of his character.

i. THE TESTIMONY OF SCRIPTURE.—Preliminary to giving the facts in their chronological order, it is well to call attention to the almost universal identification of the unnamed disciple of the Fourth Gospel with John.*

John is first introduced to us as a disciple of John the Baptist (Jn 1³⁵). How long he had been with this stern preacher of the desert we do not know, but the time was one of preparation for the higher discipleship soon to follow. After the Temptation Jesus returned to the Jordan. Then and there John first met Jesus, and, with Andrew, showed such deep interest in Him that He invited them to go with Him to His abode. So critical was the hour when they went—four o'clock in the afternoon—that it was remembered long years after (1³⁶⁻⁴⁰). John's home was in Galilee (probably at Bethsaida), where his father, Zebedee, a man apparently of means (Mk 1²⁰), was busy as a fisherman on the Lake. His mother was Salome (cf. Mt 27⁵⁶ with Mk 15⁴⁰). On the next day after his first meeting with Jesus, John accompanied Him to Galilee, and was present at the marriage feast at Cana (Jn 2¹⁻¹¹). From Cana they went to Capernaum, in order, perhaps, to make ready for going up to Jerusalem to the Passover. At this first Passover Jesus cleansed the Temple, and also 'did signs' which awakened popular interest. Here also He conversed with Nicodemus (2¹³-3²¹). The capital had not shown itself ready for the work He wished to do, so Jesus withdrew into the country of Judæa and summoned the people to the baptism of repentance, just as the Baptist himself was doing.

* Dr. Delff has with considerable force advanced and defended the theory that 'the disciple whom Jesus loved' was not the Apostle John, but a younger disciple, who shared all the privileges of the Twelve, but who was a native of Jerusalem and a member of the higher aristocracy. While this theory explains satisfactorily some of the facts given in the Gospels, it is beset with grave difficulties.

John was with Him all through this sojourn of over seven months in Judæa, and doubtless assisted in the administering of the baptismal rite, for Jesus did not Himself baptize (4²). At the end of this period Jesus returned by way of Samaria to Galilee. On the way occurred the incident of the Samaritan woman, so fully depicted for us in the Fourth Gospel (4¹⁻⁴²). Once more the Master came to Cana, and while there cured the nobleman's son (vv. ⁴⁶⁻⁵⁴). For a brief time John seems now to have been at home, and to have engaged in his customary business of fishing; but the Baptist's imprisonment was the signal to Jesus for more vigorous work, and He appeared at the Lake-side to call to be His permanent escort the men who had already acknowledged Him and given Him some service (Mk 1¹⁶⁻²⁰, Mt 4¹⁸⁻²², Lk 5¹⁻¹¹). John now entered upon that second stage of discipleship which was to prepare him for his life-work. The record of events which shows Jesus performing miracles and preaching in the towns and villages of Galilee is the record of John's training (see Mk 1²¹-2²²). When, some time afterwards, John was chosen to the Apostolate (Mk 3^{13-19a}, Mt 10²⁻⁴, Lk 6¹²⁻¹⁹), it was but to confirm him in the position he had already occupied, and to make more definite his mission. At this time Jesus called him and his brother Boanerges, that is, 'sons of thunder' (Mk 3¹⁷). See BOANERGES.

As from this time onwards the most of John's experiences were common to all the Apostles, it is necessary to mark only those which were in any way exceptional for him. They are sufficient to show that he was among the most prominent of the little band, and that he was especially close in friendship to the Master. With Peter and James he saw the raising of Jairus' daughter (Mk 5³⁷, Lk 8⁵¹). These three were with Jesus upon the Mount of Transfiguration (Mk 9², Mt 17¹, Lk 9²⁸). It was John who 'answered and said, Master we saw one casting out devils in thy name: and we forbade him, because he followeth not with us' (Mk 9³⁸, Lk 9⁴⁹). It was he and James who wished to call down fire upon an inhospitable Samaritan village (Lk 9⁵⁴). His mistaken ambition for high place at the side of his Master is recorded in Mk 10³⁷, Mt 20²¹. He took part in the questioning about the time for the fulfilment of the solemn prophecies concerning Jerusalem (Mk 13³). He and Peter were sent to make ready the Passover (Lk 22⁸). At the supper itself he reclined 'in Jesus' bosom' (see art. BOSOM), and asked Him who it was that was to be the betrayer (Jn 13²³⁻²⁵). In the garden of Gethsemane he was, with Peter and James, near his Master (Mk 14³³, Mt 26³⁷). Panic-stricken, he fled with all the other disciples at the time of the arrest (Mt 26⁵⁶), but soon recovered himself, and followed the procession to the palace of the high priest (Jn 18¹⁵). Being known to the high priest, he was admitted to the court of the palace, and secured entrance for Peter (v. ¹⁶). Faithful now to the last, he stood near the cross, and there received the commission to care for the mother of Jesus (19^{26. 27}). On the morning of the resurrection Mary Magdalene tells him and Peter of the empty grave, and they hasten together to the spot (20^{2. 3}). In the account of the appearance of the risen Lord in Galilee (21²⁻⁷) the 'sons of Zebedee' have special mention, and again in the closing scene and words of the Fourth Gospel the impression that he should not die before the Lord's coming is corrected, and the truthfulness of his witness as given in this Gospel confirmed (21²⁰⁻²⁴).

Outside of the Gospels there are but few references to him in the NT. In the Acts he appears twice in the company of Peter. As they were going together, at the hour of prayer, to the Temple, they met a man, lame from birth, at the

Beautiful Gate, and cured him. The deed caused great excitement, and a large crowd gathered around them in Solomon's porch. While they were speaking to the people the authorities came, and 'being sore troubled because they taught the people,' arrested them, and on the following day brought them before the Sanhedrin (Ac 4³). Later, he and Peter were sent to Samaria to those who had received the word of God under Philip's ministry, and 'they prayed for these that they might receive the Holy Ghost' (8¹⁴. ¹⁵). About A.D. 50 we find John in Jerusalem, for at that time Paul meets him there and consults with him regarding his work among the Gentiles (Gal 2¹⁻⁹). He was at this time one of the pillars of the Church. The only other mention of him in the NT is in Rev 1⁴. ⁹.

ii. THE TESTIMONY OF TRADITION.—1. *Regarding John's residence in Ephesus.*—From the time of his meeting with Paul in Jerusalem until his activity in later life at Ephesus, we have no certain knowledge of the Apostle. Nicephorus (*HE* ii. 2) tells us that Mary lived with John in Jerusalem for eleven years after the death of the Lord. There is nothing unlikely in this story, unless it be, as Godet suggests, that 'his own home' (Jn 19²⁷) was in Galilee rather than in the capital, in which case there would be an explanation of the Apostle's absence at the time of Paul's first visit to the city (Gal 1¹⁸. ¹⁹). It is but conjecture, however, which fixes the date of his final departure from Jerusalem, though we know that he was not there when Paul came for the last time (Ac 21¹⁸ff.), and that the signs of the impending destruction of the city caused all the Christians to retire to Pella, *c.* 68 A.D. (Eus. *HE* iii. 5. 3). It is of more moment to inquire why he should go to Ephesus, and in answer two reasons may be given : (*a*) the importance of this city as a centre for missionary activity ; and (*b*) the necessity of carrying on and developing the work of Paul. In the latter part of the 1st cent. 'the Church's centre of gravity was *no longer* at Jerusalem ; it was *not yet* at Rome ; it *was* at Ephesus' (Thiersch, quoted by Godet, *Com. on John*, vol. i. p. 45). Not only within the borders of this city had Christianity made a marked impression, but all about were cities in which the Church had been established. The seven letters in the Apocalypse enable us to see what ceaseless vigilance and intelligent care were needed to protect these Churches from error in doctrine, and to keep them faithful in life. No louder call for Apostolic service could be given than this part of the world was then giving, and, as far as tradition is concerned, there can be little doubt that John responded to this call. Just at this point, however, criticism, in the interest of its discussions regarding the authorship of the Fourth Gospel, has taken its stand, and tried to make it appear that tradition is untrustworthy. The Ephesian residence of John is therefore a critical matter, and as such must be given somewhat extended attention. The main witnesses for the common tradition are Irenæus, Polycrates (Bishop of Ephesus), and Clement of Alexandria.

(*a*) *Irenæus* bears repeated testimony to the Apostle's presence in Asia, and says explicitly :

'Afterwards' (*i.e.* after the first three) 'John the disciple of the Lord, who also lay on His breast, likewise published a Gospel while dwelling at Ephesus' (*adv. Hær.* iii. 1). Polycarp was not only instructed by the Apostles, and had intercourse with many who had seen Christ, but he was also installed by the Apostles as Bishop in Asia in the Church at Smyrna. 'We also saw him (Polycarp) in our earliest youth, for he lived very long, and left this life at a great age, having suffered a glorious and brilliant martyrdom, and having always taught what he had learned from the Apostles.' Also the Church at Ephesus, founded by Paul, and with which John lived till Trajan's time (98–117), 'is a truthful witness to the tradition of the Apostles' (*ib.* iii. 3, 4). In a letter to Florinus, a part of which has been

preserved by Eusebius (*HE* v. 20), Irenæus tells of his vivid recollections of Polycarp. The way of the venerable martyr's life, his bodily form, the discourses he gave to the people, and the account which he gave of his intercourse with John and with the rest who had seen the Lord, were clearer to him (Irenæus) in memory than many recent experiences. Again, when Victor the Bishop of Rome excommunicated the Quartodeciman Churches, Irenæus wrote admonishing the Bishop, and, in the course of what he had to say, referred to the difference between Anicetus and Polycarp over the Paschal question, in these words : 'Anicetus could not persuade Polycarp not to observe what he had always observed with John the disciple of our Lord and the other Apostles with whom he had associated' (Eus. *HE* v. 24).

The value of all this testimony is enhanced when one marks the overlapping of lives which is here evident. Polycarp suffered martyrdom in the year A.D. 155 at the age of 86. He was born, therefore, in the year 69. If John lived until Trajan's time, it were easily possible for the two to have associated with each other. Irenæus while a boy (12–18 years of age) listened with peculiar and observant attentiveness to Polycarp. These three names cover over a century. They link together in such a manner the experiences of personal associations and reverent memories that the evidence for John's presence in Ephesus seems well-nigh conclusive. Its cogency, however, is supposed to be greatly weakened by two important considerations : (*a*) the silence among older writers regarding the Ephesian residence, and (*b*) the possible confusion, on the part of Irenæus, of John the Apostle with John the Presbyter. At first sight the silence of Polycarp and Ignatius is surprising, but it is not beyond explanation. Polycarp's letter is to the Philippian Church, and calls for no reference to John. The absence of all mention of the Apostle in the Epistle of Ignatius to the Ephesians is not so easy to account for, but an argument from silence is precarious when one considers how sparingly he brings in even the name of Paul. It is apparently the similarity of their fortunes which leads him to speak of this Apostle at all, for just as Paul had sent for the elders of the Ephesian Church to meet him at Miletus on his way to imprisonment in Rome, so Ignatius at Smyrna received a delegation from Ephesus (*Ephes.* 12). This would exclude any reference to John ; and in view of all other evidence, it can be as certainly affirmed, as it can be denied, that the general reference in the previous section covers the name of John. This reference is, 'May I be found in the lot of the Christians of Ephesus, who have always been of the same mind with the Apostles through the power of Jesus Christ' (*Ephes.* 11). When, moreover, one takes into account the scantiness of the remains of this early period, the probable growth of John's reputation during the 2nd century, and the prevalence in the Ignatian Epistles themselves of a Johannine type of teaching (see von der Goltz's 'Ignatius von Antiochien als Christ und Theolog' in *TU*, Bd. xii. [1894]), the argument from silence loses much of its force. The other consideration urged against the testimony of Irenæus is really a seconding of the correction made by Eusebius of the declaration of Irenæus that 'Papias was a hearer of John and a companion of Polycarp' (*adv. Hær.* v. 33. 4).[*] The words of Eusebius are found in his *History*, iii. 39. After quoting the above words from Irenæus, he says, 'But Papias himself by no means declares that he was himself a hearer and eye-witness of the holy Apostles'; and then he goes on to infer that it was the Presbyter John who was meant in the statement of Irenæus. This brings us to the examination of the witness of Papias in its bearing upon the whole question. In his preface to his *Expositions of the Oracles of the Lord* he says :

[*] This objection is urged by Keim, Harnack, Holtzmann, and other modern critics in their discussion of the authorship of John's Gospel.

'But I shall not hesitate also to put down for you along with my interpretations whatsoever things I have at any time learned carefully from the elders and carefully remembered, guaranteeing their truth. For I did not, like the multitude, take pleasure in those that speak much, but in those that speak the truth ; not in those that relate strange commandments, but in those that deliver the commandments given by the Lord to faith and springing from the truth itself. If, then, anyone came who had been a follower of the elders, I questioned him in regard to the words of the elders—what Andrew or what Peter said, or what was said by Philip, or by Thomas, or by James, or by John, or by Matthew, or by any other of the disciples of the Lord, and what things Aristion and the presbyter John, the disciples of the Lord, say. For I did not think that what was to be gotten from the books would profit me as much as what came from the living and abiding voice' (Eus. *HE* iii. 39).

A just interpretation of these words must allow for a distinction between the Apostle John and the Presbyter John, but the inference based on the tense of the verb in the sentence, 'What things Aristion and the Presbyter John, the disciples of the Lord, *say*,'—that Papias was actually a hearer of the Presbyter,—is very questionable. Much discussion has been given to the import of this latter part of Papias' preface. A thoroughly satisfactory understanding is, however, that which makes these words we have just quoted refer not to the spoken witness, but to the *written* testimony of Aristion and the Presbyter John.[*] In his search for enlightenment Papias inquired after the unwritten sayings of all referred to except Aristion and John the Presbyter. In their case his inquiry was concerning their written sayings about which there might be some doubt. 'The books,' bearing possibly such titles as 'Narratives of Aristion,' or 'Traditions of the Presbyter John,' needed confirmation by competent witnesses. Papias had not the same confidence in them as in oral reports. Points which confirm this understanding are (1) the hesitation of Eusebius about his own inference that Papias was an actual hearer of John the Presbyter ['at least he mentions them frequently by name, and gives their traditions in writing' (*HE* iii. 39)]; (2) the suggested antitheses in the phrases 'his own writing' and 'unwritten tradition,' which are found in the accounts of the sources of Papias later on in the same section (*HE* iii. 39 : 'The same author has communicated also other things that came to him as from unwritten tradition'; 'but he also commits to his own writing other narratives of the sayings of the Lord of the aforesaid Aristion and traditions of the Presbyter John'). 'His own writing' suggests somebody else's writing; the 'unwritten tradition' suggests written tradition. If this interpretation of the words of Papias be true, then it affords no evidence that Papias was a hearer of the Presbyter John. Indeed, it does not require us to think that he was living at the time the words of Papias were written, or that he was even ever in Ephesus at all. The only support we have for this last supposition is Dionysius of Alexandria, who in the interests of the authorship of the Apocalypse by some other John than the Apostle cites the tradition that 'there are two monuments in Ephesus, each bearing the name of John.'

We come back now to Irenæus. The statement which he makes regarding the relationship of Papias to the Apostle John and to Polycarp is not derived from the preface of Papias (see above), and if there is no possible confusion in the two Johns, we need only ask what value the positive statement of Irenæus really has. Recall for a moment his reference to Polycarp. If these words are true, and there is no reason to doubt them, then it was no mere passing acquaintance which Irenæus had with Polycarp. He had carefully observed him, and attentively listened to his discourses. Can it be possible that he understood him, whenever he

[*] See Drummond, *The Character and Authorship of the Fourth Gospel*, pp. 199–204.

spoke of John, to be referring to John the Presbyter, and was Polycarp himself talking of his intercourse with John the Presbyter? Such confusion as this on the part of men so intimately related is quite improbable. Certainly it is equally improbable that, at the early time of Polycarp, John the Presbyter should have become such a figure in Ephesus that Polycarp could speak of him exactly as if he were John the Apostle. There is therefore no sufficient reason for doubting the testimony of Irenæus.

(*b*) In turning to the witness of *Polycrates*, it is well to note that he was Bishop of Ephesus, had seven relatives who were bishops, and was at the time of his letter to Victor, Bishop of Rome, an old enough man to have been living at the time of Polycarp. He was therefore in a position to know fully whereof he wrote. This fact of the continuity of experiences as lying behind these several testimonies needs repeated emphasis. In his letter to Victor (see Eus. *HE* v. 24) he is writing upon the Quartodeciman question, and citing his authorities for the observance of the 'fourteenth day of the Passover according to the Gospel.' Among these he places 'John, who was both a witness and a teacher who reclined upon the bosom of the Lord, and being a priest wore the sacerdotal plate. He fell asleep at Ephesus.'

The reference to one 'who reclined upon the bosom of the Lord' seems to point unmistakably to the Apostle, but two statements of Polycrates seem to some to run counter to this : (1) That he was a priest and wore the sacerdotal plate (τὸ πέταλον). From the fact that Epiphanius (*Hær.* xxvii. 14) says the same of James the brother of the Lord, it is probably a purely figurative statement, indicating the exalted and revered position of these men among their Christian brethren. (2) The other counter-statement is derived from the notice given of Philip in this same letter. It is claimed that Polycrates has clearly confused the Apostles and Evangelists, hence he may have in the same way confused John the Apostle with John the Presbyter. The whole question turns upon the allusion to the daughters of Philip. Briefly stated, the disputed evidence is this. Papias, the earliest witness, places Philip among the Apostles (*HE* iii. 39). Then he goes on to relate a wonderful tale which he heard from the daughters of Philip. There is no indication whatever that this is not the same Philip just referred to. Polycrates now follows with his testimony that among those who had died in Asia was 'Philip, one of the Twelve Apostles, who sleeps in Hierapolis, and his two virgin daughters and another daughter who lived in the Holy Spirit and now rests at Ephesus' (*HE* iii. 31). Again the reference to the Apostle is clear. Clement of Alexandria declares that the Apostles Peter and Philip had children, and that Philip gave his daughters to husbands (*Strom.* iii. 6). From all this it is clear that the Apostle Philip had daughters. So far there seems to be no confusion. If this comes in at all, it appears in a statement of Proclus, who speaking of the death of Philip and his daughters, says : 'After this arose four prophetesses, the daughters of Philip, at Hierapolis in Asia. Their tomb is there, and the tomb of their father' (*HE* iii. 31). The close resemblance of this record to the statement in Ac 21[9] makes it appear that the Evangelist is referred to ; but even if the identification of the two Philips be here allowed, it is made comparatively late, and need not involve Polycrates. 'The report of Polycrates deserves our credence rather than that of Proclus, because, in the first place, Polycrates was earlier than Proclus ; in the second place, because his report is more exact, and it is hard to imagine how, if all four were buried in one place, the more detailed report of Polycrates could have arisen, while on the other hand it is quite easy to explain the rise of the more general but inexact account of Proclus' (McGiffert on Eusebius, *in loco*). It should be noted also that we have in Polycrates, as a contemporary of Irenæus, an independent witness.

(*c*) It is in connexion with the story of the young convert who subsequently became a robber that *Clement of Alexandria* speaks of John's residence in Asia. The value of this testimony lies in the fact that Clement, in gathering memoranda to be 'stored up against old age as a remedy against forgetfulness,' had collected traditions handed down 'from the holy Apostles Peter, James, John, and Paul, the sons receiving it from the father.' As Drummond says of this witness, 'It seems probable that we have here a distinct line of tradition which affords independent confirmation of the statements of Irenæus and Polycrates.' The clearness, positiveness, and fulness of the witness of these three, taken together with the personal relations involved, affords adequate basis for the general belief of the Church that in the latter part of his life John made his home in Ephesus.

2. *Regarding John's banishment to Patmos.*— The discussion of the deliverances of tradition in regard to John's exile in Patmos is vitally connected with the authorship of the Apocalypse (see art. 'John, Gospel of,' in Hastings' *DB* ii. 707 ff.). The references to this fact are quite numerous in the Fathers, and begin with Clement of Alexandria (A.D. 190). Tertullian, Origen, Eusebius, Epiphanius, Jerome all speak of it, but do not agree as to the time of it. Epiphanius (*Hær.* 12) assigns it to the reign of Claudius, while Clement of Alexandria, Eusebius, and Jerome place it in the reign of Domitian. Internal evidence from the Apocalypse itself favours an early time, while tradition is explicit about the later date. All testimonies to the exile are probably based upon the statement found in Rev 1[9], and this gives no real foundation for any banishment at all. If John was in Patmos, it may be that he went thither, as Weiss supposes, to find a religious retreat, or, as others think, to avoid persecution.

3. *Regarding John's death.*—In accord with the statement of Irenæus that 'John remained among them (the disciples) in Asia up to the time of Trajan' (*adv. Hær.* ii. 22), it has been generally believed that the Apostle lived to a ripe old age, and died quietly at Ephesus. Of late this opinion has been earnestly disputed, on the basis of a statement found in the *Chronicle* of Georgius Hamartolos (9th cent.), which reads, 'Papias, Bishop of Hierapolis, declares in the second book of the Oracles of the Lord that John was put to death by the Jews.' This testimony has been confirmed by the de Boor Fragment, which expressly says that Papias tells in his second book of the death of James and John at the hands of the Jews. Of course, if John the Apostle died in this way, there is nothing left but to take some other John as the John of Ephesus; and all the testimony of Irenæus, Polycrates, and Clement of Alexandria has a confusion of names underlying it; also the John of the Apostolic council (Gal 2[9]) was not the son of Zebedee. All this is by no means likely. Various attempts have been made to account for the record of Georgius—such as Lightfoot's supposition of a lacuna, which was later filled in as we now have it (see Essay on *Supernatural Religion*, p. 211 ff.); or Zahn's (*Forsch.* vi. 147–151) of an interpolation, and that Papias was really referring to the Baptist; but the more probable explanation is that the statement arose from a desire to find a fulfilment of Mk 10[38. 39], and a mistaken interpretation of the word μαρτυρῶν, which in its earlier sense did not necessarily involve death. It is certainly not easy to understand why Eusebius and others ignored the fact, if such it was.

Thus far we have sought to get at the real facts of tradition. It will surprise no one to know that the life of one so eminent as John was embellished with all manner of legends, such as his meeting with Cerinthus in the bath-house at Ephesus (*adv. Hær.* iii. 3, 4); his being carried in extreme old age to the church, and saying, 'Little children, love one another' (Jerome, *Com. ad Gal.* vi. 11); his recovery of the young robber from his life of shame (Eus. *HE* iii. 23); his immersion in a caldron of boiling oil (Tert. *Præscript. Hær.* ch. xxvi.); and a number of others. Some of them may have germs of truth in them. They all seek in some way to illustrate the noble character of the man, or to interpret the prophecy of the Gospels regarding his earthly destiny.

iii. THE CHARACTER OF JOHN.—It is commonly thought that John was of a gentle, contemplative nature, and almost effeminate in character. Contemplative he was, and the Gospel is but an expression of his profound meditation upon the character and work of his Master; but a moment's reflexion upon some of the scenes of the Gospels (see Mt 20[20-24], Lk 9[49. 54]), in correspondence with which are some of the legends regarding his later life, will show that this Apostle was, at least in earlier life, impetuous, intolerant, and ambitious. Doubtless he was effectively moulded by the Spirit of Christ during his long discipleship, but he was always stern and uncompromising in his hatred of evil and in his defence of truth. He loved with a strong, passionate devotion, and he hated all wrong and untruth as only one can who understands as profoundly as he did the significance of his Lord and His teaching. Because of his profound understanding, he writes as one who has an immediate perception of truth. He does not reason as does Paul. He *saw* 'the King in his beauty,' or, to use his own words, 'the glory of the only-begotten of the Father' (Jn 1[14]). His strength and devotion made him courageous; his affection and sympathy made him tender and abundantly helpful. His was the finest type of strong manhood made beautiful by spiritual purity.

LITERATURE.—Among the more recent works which discuss the Ephesian residence of John, we would call attention to the following: James Drummond, *The Character and Authorship of the Fourth Gospel*; V. H. Stanton, *The Gospels as Historical Documents*; W. Sanday, *The Criticism of the Fourth Gospel*; A. C. McGiffert, *The Apostolic Age*; *Encyc. Bibl.* art. 'John, Son of Zebedee'; Hastings' *DB*, art. 'John, the Apostle'; Harnack, *Chronol. der Altchrist. Lit. bis Eusebius*, pp. 320–340, 656–680; Keim, *Gesch. Jesu von Nazara*, Eng. tr. i. pp. 211–232.

JAMES S. RIGGS.

JOHN, GOSPEL OF (I. : Critical article).—

Introduction.
i. External evidence for the authorship of the Fourth Gospel.
 1. Writers of the last quarter of the 2nd century.
 2. Justin Martyr.
 3. Tatian.
 4. The Apostolic Fathers.
 5. Evidence derived from Opponents of the Church doctrine.
 6. Evidence afforded by the Quartodeciman controversy.
 7. The Alogi.
ii. Internal evidence of authorship.
 1. The author is a Jew.
 2. The author is a Jew of Palestine.
 3. A contemporary of the events and persons.
 4. Relationship to Jesus and the Apostolic circle.
 5. Is John the Apostle the author?
iii. The divergences from the Synoptic narrative.
iv. The problem of the historicity of the Gospel.
 Literature.

Introduction.—It is important to remember that the Kingdom of Christ was in being before the Gospel records were written. They did not originate the institution, but are themselves the expression of it. Previous to the publication of the Johannine Gospel, which is the latest of the four, St. Paul had completed his mission to the Gentiles; and in Ephesus, where the Gospel was written, his doctrine had already an assured place in the Christian Church. It is therefore historically untrue to say that faith in the Divine Person and work of Jesus is destroyed if the authenticity of the Fourth Gospel cannot be proved. For the basis of our faith we must dig deeper than the results of critical investigation.

The question, however, of the authorship of this Gospel is more than a merely academic one. It occupies a unique position. None of the other three claims to be written by the man whose name it bears, but the Fourth Gospel is issued with an explicit statement to that effect (21[24]). Moreover, its contents are vitally connected with the individuality of the author. The very way in which his identity is studiously concealed shows that the writer is himself conscious that the Gospel contains a personal testimony, which he does not hesitate to present as objective and impersonal. We desire to know who it is that claims to be an eye-witness ; who it is that narrates events and discourses of Jesus so distinct in character from the Synoptics, and yet meant to occupy a place alongside these without contradiction ; who it is that has so boldly mingled historic fact and ideal conceptions, that has given to the Person of Christ a timeless cosmic significance, and has represented our Lord in His acts and in His words as Himself justifying that impression and those claims. If, as is certain, the work is influenced by developed theological conceptions, and reflects the contemporary historical situation of the Christian Church, we desire to be certain that the writer was in a position not seriously to misrepresent the actual facts. This is no merely antiquarian question. There can be no doubt that the Gospel is intended to be read as the work of the Apostle, and it would seriously detract from its value, if, as extreme critics are more and more inclined to allow, that claim means only that it contains a nucleus of Johannine tradition. The same objection applies to all partition theories of the Gospel (*e.g.* Wendt's), and it is assumed in this article that their authors have failed to prove their case. If, on the other hand, the writer was the beloved disciple, an eye-witness possessing a specially intimate knowledge of the mind and character of Jesus, we have an assurance that when, for example, he wrote the opening sentences of the Gospel, he felt himself in touch not merely with current theological thought, but with the historic fact of the consciousness of Jesus of Nazareth. So far from being a stumbling-block to the Johannine authorship, the Prologue even gains in value and significance with the acceptance of the traditional view. The striking juxtaposition in the Prologue of the timeless Logos idea and the historical witness of the Baptist, to whom the conception was unfamiliar, and the frequent mention of the Baptist throughout the Gospel, even at times when the situation scarcely demands it (*e.g.* 10⁴⁰⁻⁴²), are saved from abruptness only if the writer is developing an impression made on him by his earliest teacher, who led him to Christ. His experience stretches in one continuous whole from that time to this when he begins to write.

I. *EXTERNAL EVIDENCE FOR THE AUTHORSHIP OF THE FOURTH GOSPEL.*—The face of the Johannine problem has greatly changed since the days of Baur and his school. The prophecy of Lightfoot, that 'we may look forward to the time when it will be held discreditable to the reputation of any critic for sobriety and judgment to assign to this Gospel any later date than the end of the first century or the very beginning of the second,' has been amply fulfilled. 80–110 A.D. may be regarded as the *termini a quo* and *ad quem* for the date of the writing, and the trend of modern opinion is towards the end of the 1st century. This result makes it desirable to throw the emphasis in a less degree on the external evidence for an early date, and in a greater degree on the evidence for the Apostolic authorship. If, however, the problem of external evidence be presented in this form, we must guard ourselves against a certain feeling of disappointment at the meagre results. In the first place, there is no evidence that the Apostolic authorship was contested in the 2nd cent. except by the Alogi ; and none that it was ever debated. The questions that agitated the mind of the Church in this period seem to have been entirely doctrinal (Gnosticism and Montanism). Again, it is not until the latter part of the century that there are indications of a distinct value attached to each separate Gospel. Εὐαγγέλιον was the term employed to denote the general contents of those books that embodied the facts concerning the life and teaching of our Lord, and we first find the term εὐαγγέλια in Justin

(*Apol.* I. lxvi.). The contrast between the Synoptics and John in this period arose entirely from the differences in subject-matter, and there is no indication that the Fourth Gospel was set on a lower plane of authority.

One remarkable fact in connexion with the external evidence is that none of the writers in question ever actually calls St. John an Apostle. This fact is never lost sight of by opponents of the Apostolic authorship. It is true that Irenæus speaks of 'John and the other Apostles' ; but in referring to St. John alone he always calls him 'the disciple.' This is in accordance with the usage of the Fourth Gospel itself, where the title ἀπόστολος is only once used (13¹⁶), and there is a sense that seems to deprecate any presumptuous or mercenary claim to official position. If such claims were rife in Ephesus, perhaps St. John himself preferred to be known as 'disciple.' (Cf. H. T. Purchas, *Johann. Problems and Modern Needs*, ch. iii.).

We shall now proceed to examine in detail, working backwards from the end of the 2nd cent., the evidence of those Ecclesiastical writers who have made direct or indirect reference to the Fourth Gospel.

1. *A group of writers in the last quarter of the 2nd cent. whose geographical distribution over the Christian Church gives evidence of a widespread tradition.*

(1) **Irenæus** was bishop of Lyons in Gaul. His work entitled *Against Heresies* has come down to us, and in the writings of Eusebius we possess other fragments. An important letter to Florinus has also been preserved. The date of his literary activity may be put within the limits 173–190. He explicitly attributes the Fourth Gospel to the Apostle, and gives it a place alongside Matthew, Mark, and Luke. He says that 'John, the disciple of the Lord, who leaned upon His breast,' wrote it 'while dwelling in Ephesus, the city of Asia' (*adv. Hær.* III. i. 1). Stress is also to be laid on the fact that Irenæus speaks of the Gospels not merely as Apostolic, but also as inspired by the Holy Spirit. For him the tradition of the fourfold Gospel, which he supports strongly, has passed into a deep spiritual fact, which he seeks to establish, not by bringing forward proofs of authorship, but in his well-known mystic fashion. 'The gospel is the Divine breath or word of life for men ; there are four chief winds ; therefore four Gospels.' He brings forward other analogies, all of which are equally fanciful, but serve to show that this firm belief in the fourfold Gospel as a Divine arrangement could not have been a creation of his own mind, but represents a tradition of considerable antiquity. The opinion of Irenæus is corroborated by a contemporary letter written by the members of the Churches at Vienne and Lyons to the brethren in Asia Minor during the time of persecution in 177. Thus Irenæus is in touch with the living Church around him.

(2) **Clement of Alexandria** is the author of a statement preserved by Eusebius (*HE* vi. 14), which professes to represent ' the tradition of the Presbyters from the first (παράδοσιν τῶν ἀνέκαθεν πρεσβυτέρων) that John, last, having observed that the bodily things [σωματικά, *i.e.* the simple facts relating to the life and teaching of Christ] had been set forth in the Gospels, on the exhortation of his friends (γνώριμοι), inspired by the Spirit, produced a spiritual Gospel.' From about 189, Clement was head of the celebrated catechetical school at Alexandria. His great reverence for his teacher Pantænus, who also preceded him in office, may fairly be regarded as indicating that he represents the ecclesiastical tradition at Alexandria. He was also in living touch with opinion at other centres. He travelled in Greece, Magna Græcia, Syria, and the East, expressly for the purpose of collecting information about the Apostolic tradition. In his extant writings he quotes words from all the four Gospels, regards them as possessing Divine authority, and lays great emphasis on the differences between them and other writings professing to be Gospels.

(3) **Tertullian** was a famous theologian of the Western Church, and was born at Carthage about 160. The style of his writing suggests that he was trained as an advocate. He was reputed a man of great learning. Jerome speaks of his ' eager and vehement disposition,' and his habit of mind is in striking contrast to the philosophic temper of Clement. It is needless to quote passages from his writings, as he undoubtedly assumes without question the genuineness of the Gospel, and lays under contribution every chapter. Little is known of his personal life, but he was certainly in touch with theological opinion, not only at Carthage, but also at Rome. In the line of argument that he adopts in his reply to Marcion he is concerned above all else to show that the doctrine of the Church is in line with Apostolic tradition. He makes appeal in another writing, *de Præscriptione Hæreticorum*, to the testimony of those Churches that were founded by Apostles, or to whom Apostles declared their mind in letters. Among these he mentions Ephesus, evidently in connexion with the name of St. John. His term for the fourfold Gospel is a legal term, *Evangelicum Instrumentum, i.e.* a valid document finally declaring the mind of the Church with regard to spiritual truth. He became a distinguished leader of the Montanists, and would on that account be predisposed to combat any objection, if it had been urged, against the authenticity of the Gospel. At the same time, he is not indifferent to questions of literary criticism, applied to the Gospels. In his reply to Marcion he makes careful and scholarly investigation into the text of St. Luke, and is able to prove that Marcion's Gospel is a mutilated copy.

(4) **The Muratorian Fragment on the Canon.** —This fragment contains the earliest known list of the books that were regarded at the date at which it was written as canonical. It was published in the year 1740 by an Italian scholar, Muratori.

Lightfoot, Westcott, and others argue for a date 150–175 ; but Salmon, Zahn, and Harnack agree in placing its date, from internal evidence, not earlier than A.D. 200. Sanday, in his *Gospels in the Second Century* (pp. 264–266), suggests 170–180, and perhaps within ten years later. Stanton, in *The Gospels as Historical Documents* (p. 247, n. 1), inclines to the later date.

The writer gives an account of the origin of the Fourth Gospel which is plainly legendary. The important statement in it is that the Gospel is the work of St. John (*Johannes ex discipulis*), who is also the author of at least two of the Epistles (*in suis epistolis*). The further statement is made that he resolved to write it after a fast had been held, and at the request of contemporary Christians (*cohortantibus condiscipulis et episcopis suis*), and the concurrence is also claimed of the rest of the Apostles (*recognoscentibus cunctis*). The second statement seems, like the γνώριμοι of Clement, to be founded on Jn 1[14] and 21[24], and possesses no independent value, except as an interpretation of internal evidence.

The object of the author was clearly controversial, ' to draw a broad line of separation between the inspired writings of the Apostolic age and modern additions' (Salmon, *Introduction*, p. 46). He strongly protests, for example, against the inclusion of *Hermas* in the Canon, though he has no objection to its being ' read.' Bacon (*Hibbert Journal*, April 1903) has interpreted the Muratorian Fragment as indicating the existence of controversy in the Church at that date as to the Apostolic authorship ; but the emphasis on that question might easily be explained by the fact that the historicity —the *varia principia* of the Gospels—was alone in question. There is no attempt to *harmonize* the statements in the various Gospels ; but it is sought to secure for the contents of the Fourth Gospel a place of equal authority with the other three.

Throughout the whole history of the NT Canon the admission of a book was not decided solely on the question of authorship, but far more on the general consideration whether its teaching was congruent with the received doctrine of the Church. Salmon thinks that the writer of the Muratorian Fragment is arguing against the Montanists, and Zahn and Drummond that he is opposing the Alogi (see below). The legendary account of the origin of the Gospel would seem to indicate that the fact of the Apostolic authorship was already well established and well known. An additional confirmation of the view that the historicity alone is within the purview of the writer is that the words of the First Epistle (it is true in a somewhat inaccurate rendering), ' What we have seen with our eyes, and heard with our ears, and our hands have handled, these things we have written' (*hæc scripsimus*), are quoted as a reference by the author to his Gospel.

(5) **Theophilus**, bishop of Antioch (*c.* A.D. 180), wrote, among other works, a defence of Christianity, addressed to Autolycus, ' a real or imaginary heathen friend of wide learning and high culture' (Watkins). He is the earliest writer of the 2nd cent., who, while quoting a passage from the Gospel (1[13]), also refers to St. John by name. His words are, ' We are taught by the Holy Scriptures and all Spirit-bearing men, among whom John says' ; and then follow *verbatim* quotations from the Prologue to the Gospel. There are also other sentences in his work that recall the Fourth Gospel. It is significant also, as belying any appearance of controversy as to the authorship of the Gospel, that he introduces the name of St. John in this quite incidental fashion. Commentaries on the Gospels are also attributed to him, but their genuineness, upheld by Zahn, is assailed by Harnack. This part of his evidence must at present be set aside.

2. Justin Martyr.—The works of Justin that are relevant in this connexion are the two *Apologies* and the *Dialogue with Trypho the Jew*. They may be set within the limits A.D. 140–161. Palestine was his birthplace, and he was brought up in the religion of his father, who was a heathen. He was an ardent student of philosophy, and after an unsatisfying experience of various teachers he ultimately became a Platonist. After his conversion to Christianity, of which he gives a full account in *Trypho*, ii.–viii., he was ' kindled with love to Christ,' and consecrated his philosophic attainments to the defence of the Christian religion.

Among the authorities to which Justin refers in the course of his writings, he gives an important place to ' The Memoirs of Christ, composed by the Apostles and those who followed them.' The battle of criticism still rages around the question whether Justin includes in these Memoirs only the four Gospels. It may now, at least, be regarded as settled amongst all classes of critics that Justin makes use of the Gospel (cf. Schmiedel, *Encyc. Bibl.*, art. ' John, Son of Zebedee,' ii. 2546). It is not so generally admitted that he includes it among his Memoirs of the Apostles. Those, however, who deny that Justin regarded the Gospel as the work of the Apostle are laid under the necessity of explaining how his contemporary Irenæus could be so assured that the Gospel is a genuine Apostolic work.

(1) *Quotations.*—The *locus classicus* in Justin is the passage on Baptism (*Apol.* I. lxi.). He describes how those who are about to make a Christian profession—

' are brought by us where there is water, and are born again in the same manner in which we ourselves were born again. For in the name of God the Father and Lord of the universe, and of our Saviour Jesus Christ, and of the Holy Spirit, they then receive the washing with water. For Christ also said, " Except ye be born again, ye shall not enter into the kingdom of heaven " (ἂν μὴ ἀναγεννηθῆτε, οὐ μὴ εἰσέλθητε εἰς τὴν βασιλείαν τῶν οὐρανῶν).

Now that it is impossible for those who have once been born to enter into their mother's wombs, is manifest to all.'

This passage immediately recalls Jn 3³⁻⁵. The language, however, reveals some striking variations from the text of the Gospel. No one would now endorse the verdict of the author of *Supernatural Religion*, that 'there does not exist a single linguistic trace by which the passage in Justin can be connected with the Fourth Gospel.' It may be conceded that some of his expressions have more than an accidental relationship with Mt 18³. Justin certainly uses ἀναγεννηθῆτε ('born again') instead of γεννηθῇ ἄνωθεν ('born from above') of the Fourth Gospel, but this variation is at least a possible rendering of the Johannine expression. There are, however, other linguistic differences. The difficulty is increased by the discovery that in the *Clementine Homilies* (xi. 26) there is a passage containing similar linguistic deviations from the Gospel. Has their author copied Justin, or does the similarity point to the use by both of a common source other than the Gospel? The fact that the context in each is quite different excludes the first hypothesis, and the second may well be viewed as improbable, until the alleged common source—that 'ghost-like' Gospel of which Volkmar speaks—has emerged from the place of shades, and embodied itself in a MS (cf. Drummond, *Character and Authorship*, pp. 88–96).

It ought to be sufficient to establish the high probability, amounting to certainty, that Justin quotes Jn 3³⁻⁵, that, giving due weight to linguistic differences, the Fourth Gospel is the only source known to us from which he could have derived such ideas. The idea of birth as applied to spiritual change is found in none of the Gospels but St. John; and it is significant that both Justin and St. John expressly connected this thought with the rite of Baptism. As regards the impossibility of a second physical birth, it is to be noted that this somewhat wistful, and, at the same time, wilfully absurd, objection of Nicodemus—which in the Gospel is the symptom of a heart profoundly moved, and has a living place in the context—is prosaically reproduced by Justin. This is evidently the result of a familiar association of ideas derived from the passage in Jn 3. The words, 'for Christ also said,' introduce the quotation, and the document from which it is taken is clearly looked upon as an authoritative source for the words of Christ.

Justin has other correspondences with the peculiar thought of the Fourth Gospel. He uses the title μονογενής of Christ, and in the next sentence speaks of the Virgin-Birth (*Dialogue* 105), adding the words, 'as we have learned from the Memoirs.' This seems to point to a combination of St. John and the Synoptics. Justin has also made much use of the thought of the Logos Gospel in his doctrine of the Logos, and his teaching on that subject is influenced by the theology of the Gospel. It is sometimes urged as an objection that Justin does not make more use of the authority of the Gospel in his teaching about the Logos, but this is to presuppose that the thought was first suggested to him by that source. Justin's philosophy is filled with Alexandrine ideas, but the thought of the Incarnation of the Logos of which Justin makes use is found only in St. John (*Apol.* i. 32). The Johannine expressions φῶς, σάρξ are also found in Justin.

On the question of the relationship between Justin and the fragment of the *Gospel of Peter*, discovered in 1892, see Hastings' *DB* iii. 535ᵇ; Drummond, *Character and Authorship*, pp.151-155. The evidence is insufficient to prove that this Gospel is one of Justin's Memoirs. Loisy and Harnack hold that the *Gospel of Peter* is dependent on the Fourth Gospel, to whose existence it would therefore be the most ancient witness. The date of the *Gospel of Peter* is put c. 110-130 by Loisy (*Le Quatrième Évangile*, p. 16) and Harnack (*Chron.* i. 623).

(2) *His use of the Gospel.*—Another consideration is adduced to prove that Justin did not regard the Gospel as an authority on the same level as the Synoptics, and therefore viewed it as non-Apostolic. Schmiedel (*Encyc. Bibl.*, art. 'John, Son of Zebedee,' ii. 2546) states that 'his employment of it is not only more sparing but also more circumspect' than his use of the Synoptics. There are occasions on which it would be open to him to use it in proof of his doctrine of the Logos and of the pre-existence of Christ. Why has Justin not used the Fourth Gospel more? It is perfectly relevant to reply that we do not know, and perhaps never shall know, with complete certainty. At the same time, there are certain considerations that ought to be borne in mind. Justin is certainly the first writer who displays the tendency to attach a separate value to the four Gospels; he is the first to speak of εὐαγγέλια instead of εὐαγγέλιον; but he can scarcely be expected to have completely emancipated himself, at this transition stage, from the older conception of the gospel as embracing equally the contents of the four. Justin's purpose and his audience must be borne in mind, and these would insensibly lead him to rely mostly on the Synoptic Gospels. It is specially noticeable that the witness of Christ to Himself, so prominent in the Fourth Gospel, is nowhere used by Justin as an argument, and in one place in the *Dialogue with Trypho* (ch. 18) he even apologizes for citing the words of Christ alongside the words of the prophets. His *Apologies* are addressed to the Emperor, Senate, and People of Rome, and to quote to them the Christian writings in proof of Christian doctrine would have been to reason in a circle. Moreover, it may be suggested that not even at that date was the Gospel regarded as, strictly speaking, historical, and its spiritual or reflective character rendered it hardly so suitable for Justin's purpose as the Synoptics.

(3) *Evidence as to Apostolic authorship.*—Is there any evidence in Justin that he attributed the authorship to St. John the Apostle? In the first place, if the Memoirs are composed of our four Gospels, we may answer the question with certainty in the affirmative. Justin describes them as composed by 'the Apostles and those that followed them,' a description which tallies completely with the four Evangelists. The plural 'Apostles' could be used only if he believed in the Apostolic authorship of the Fourth Gospel. Again, the strongest argument adduced against Justin's evidence is still the argument from his silence as to the name of the author. It seems, however, to have been the custom among apologists not to mention the Evangelists by their names, which would carry no weight with unbelievers. Moreover, it has been pointed out that Justin never mentions the name of St. Paul, although it is certain that at least four of his Epistles from which he quotes are of undoubted authenticity. Justin once names St. John as the author of Revelation (*Dialogue* 81), but 'he nowhere quotes this work, which he regarded as inspired, apostolic, prophetic, though it contains so much which might seem to favour his view of the person of Christ' (Ezra Abbot, p. 61). In the passage he speaks of the author as one whose name is not likely to carry weight ('a certain man with us, whose name was John'), but it is essential to his argument, in thus making use of a Revelation or Vision, that he should mention the recipient. (Cf. Stanton, *Gospels as Historical Documents*, i. p. 89).

3. Tatian was a native of Syria, and, like Justin, travelled as a wandering philosopher. His conversion to Christianity took place at Rome about A.D. 150. He became a disciple of Justin, during whose lifetime he wrote the *Oratio ad Græcos*. After Justin's death in 166, Tatian taught in Rome, and ultimately adopted a heretical position. He died about A.D. 180.

Tatian clearly quotes the Gospel in his *Oratio*,

which was written perhaps as early as 153 (so Zahn and Harnack), although he does not refer to the author by name. The important work, however, for our purpose is the *Diatessaron*. It is a compendium of the Life and Teaching of our Lord, founded on our four Gospels, and containing also some material taken from the Apocryphal Gospels. The book had apparently an ancient place in the worship of the Syrian Churches. Theodoret, bishop of Cyrrhus, near the Euphrates, in 453, tells how he found more than 200 copies of the work in the churches of his district. These he collected and, with considerable difficulty, put away, substituting for them the *four* Gospels.

The *Diatessaron* includes the whole of the Fourth Gospel, except 1⁶, the first half of 2²³, the *Pericope Adulteræ*, and some other passages that are common to the Synoptics.

The significance of Tatian's work lies in the fact that an authoritative value is attached to the contents of our four Gospels, and that the Fourth Gospel is placed on a level with the Synoptics. Moreover, Tatian's use of the Fourth Gospel renders it very difficult to doubt that it was also one of the Memoirs of his contemporary, Justin.

4. The Apostolic Fathers.—(1) **Papias** was bishop of Hierapolis in Phrygia. Unfortunately his testimony has given rise to more questions about the Gospel than it solves. Only one or two fragments of his work preserved by Eusebius have come down to us. We know that in the time of Eusebius the only writing of Papias to which he had access was a work in five books, entitled 'Exposition(s) of the Oracles of the Lord' (Λογίων κυριακῶν ἐξήγησις [or -εις]). Cf. Drummond, *op. cit.* note 4, p. 195.

The 'Oracles' were probably a collection of sayings of our Lord, together with some kind of historical setting.

There is a tendency among modern critics to fix a later date than formerly for the writings of Papias. His written work seems not to have been produced till about the age of sixty. The change in the date is owing to the discovery of a fragment, purporting to contain statements by Papias, that was published by De Boor in 1888. It dates from the 7th or 8th cent., and is in turn probably based on the *Chronicle* of Philip of Sidé (c. A.D. 430). Among other matters it relates that those individuals who had been raised from the dead by Christ survived 'till the time of Hadrian.' Hadrian reigned 117-138, which compels us to fix a date for Papias' work not earlier than 140-160 (so Harnack, Drummond, and Schmiedel. Sanday in his most recent work, *The Criticism of the Fourth Gospel*, includes the date of Papias among the 'unsolved problems'). The date of his martyrdom is also very uncertain.

Eusebius says that Papias 'evidently was a man of very mean capacity, as one may say, judging from his statements' (*HE* iii. 39). This judgment must be considered strictly in connexion with the context. Eusebius is speaking of his millenarian notions, and of the unimaginative way in which he interpreted the figurative language of the Apostolic writings. These defects do not reflect on his accuracy in matters of fact, but rather indicate a literalness and exactness which may at times be painful, but are yet a source of strength in the present discussion.

(i.) Papias is best known by the famous extract from the Preface to his work which is preserved by Eusebius :

'I will not hesitate to place before you, along with my interpretations (of the Oracles of the Lord), everything that I carefully learned, and carefully remembered in time past from the elders, and I can guarantee its truth. For I take no pleasure, as do the many, in those who have so very much to say, but in those who teach the truth : nor in those who relate commandments foreign (to the mind of the Lord), but in those (who record) such as were given to the faith by the Lord, and found on the truth itself. Moreover, if I met with anyone on any occasion who had attended the elders, I used to inquire about the words of the elders; what Andrew or what Peter said, or what Philip, or what Thomas, or James or John or Matthew, or any other of the disciples of the Lord said, and what Aristion and the elder John, disciples of the Lord, say. For I was not inclined to suppose that statements made by the books would

help me, so much as the utterances of a living and abiding voice' (*HE* iii. 39).

Several questions of moment are raised by these words of Papias.

(*a*) *Who are the elders or presbyters of whom he speaks?*—They clearly include the Apostles themselves, and Papias derives his information from their friends, *i.e.* those who not merely 'had followed them' in the literal sense, but had 'attended to' (παρηκολουθηκώς) their words. He is in search of direct oral tradition about the 'Oracles.' At the same time he mentions two, Aristion and John, who are not Apostles, and whom he regards as 'presbyters' or elders. He also designates the whole group as 'disciples of the Lord.' In the case of Aristion and the Presbyter John, οἱ μαθηταί is found only in one MS, and the preferable reading is to omit the article. In the first case, the use of the article with μαθητῶν means 'the disciples' specially known as such, and the key to the use of the term 'disciple' in the second case, is found in the statement of Ac 6⁷, where all those who were members of the first Christian community are called 'disciples.' The 'Elders,' then, signify all those men who were members of the primitive Christian Church who may or may not have followed the Lord Himself.

Irenæus has said that Papias was 'a hearer of John,' by whom he evidently means the Apostle. This would place him in immediate contact with the Apostolic circle. If, however, we are to rely only on the statements in the Preface, it is plain that Eusebius must be right when, in opposition to Irenæus, he says that 'Papias certainly does not declare that he himself was a hearer and eye-witness to the holy Apostles.' Yet even with the later date assigned to Papias, there is no chronological impossibility in his having known the Apostle ; and it must not be forgotten that Irenæus was not necessarily dependent solely on the words of the Preface, but may have had other statements of Papias, or the living tradition of the Church, on which to found his assertion. If the position has to be surrendered that Papias was a 'hearer of John,' it is at least certain that he put himself in the most favourable position to hear clearly 'the living and abiding voice' of Apostolic times, conveyed to him through the 'friends' of the Elders.

(*b*) *What can we determine regarding the nature and purpose of the work of Papias?*—He contrasts his sources with 'those who have so very much to say' (τοῖς τὰ πολλὰ λέγουσιν), with 'those who relate commandments foreign to the mind of the Lord' (τοῖς τὰς ἀλλοτρίας ἐντολὰς μνημονεύουσιν) and with 'the contents of the books' (τὰ ἐκ τῶν βιβλίων). 'The books' which he mentions have been interpreted as meaning some form of 'the Gospels' (Jülicher, *Introd.*, Eng. tr. p. 487), and also as 'writings of Aristion and the Elder John' (Drummond and Bacon). In regard to the former interpretation, it seems out of the question that Papias should oppose 'the living and abiding voice' to the sources of his Logia. On the other hand, it is hardly likely that Papias would minimize the value of the oral evidence of Aristion and the Presbyter John by disparaging their written work. The simplest explanation is that given by Lightfoot (followed by Schwarz, *Ueber den Tod der Söhne Zebedæi*, p. 11), that the exegetical commentaries on the Gospels written by Gnostics like Basilides are meant. It is to these also that he refers when he speaks of 'foreign commandments' and of 'those who have so very much to say.' Papias himself seems to have been a commentator on the 'Oracles of the Lord,' and seeks to support his own explanations (ἐξηγήσεις) by direct oral tradition from those who were in touch with the first Christian community.

(*c*) *What position does the Presbyter John hold in Papias' view?*—It is noticeable that while the past tense 'said' (εἶπεν) is used of the first group of Apostles, as though they were dead at the time of writing, the present tense 'say' (λέγουσιν) is used of Aristion and the Presbyter John. The entirely unconvincing explanation of Lightfoot, that the tense should probably be regarded as an historic present, introduced 'for the sake of variety,' must be rejected. On the other hand, the present tense seems rather meagre evidence on which to rear the hypothesis that *books* written by these two men were before Papias (so Drummond, *Character and Authorship*, p. 200), especially as he distinctly tells us that it is oral evidence of which he is in search. There is evidence in the writing of Papias that some literary productions of these men were extant, but the intention of Papias in his Preface seems to be to convey the impression that they were alive at the time he wrote. Papias had begun, at a much earlier time ('in time past'), to collect information from the elders, and had gone on doing so up to the time of writing. He means that Aristion and John are still available for any-one who wishes to check the authority of the explanations he gives.

The foregoing establishes the reality of the second John. It is no longer possible to regard the existence of the Presbyter 'as due to a confusion of Eusebius,' or to accuse Papias of 'slovenliness of composition,' which would lead us to suppose that two Johns are mentioned, while all the time he is only referring to the same man a second time. The question is debated by modern critics whether this Presbyter John has any connexion with the authorship of the Gospel. It is necessary only to indicate the grounds on which the suggestion is based. Eusebius, in the passage from which we have quoted (*HE* iii. 39), suggests that he is the author of Revelation. He controverts the statement of Irenæus that Papias means to be looked upon as a hearer of the Apostle John, and gathers from the use of the present tense (λέγουσιν) that he is really a hearer of Aristion and the Elder John. We have seen that in the time of Papias these two men were still alive, but the evidence as to his relationship with them rather suggests that he had not himself met them. Papias seems to have had to collect information about what they 'say,' and Eusebius himself puts forward his statement about an oral relationship merely as a suggestion. It does not follow that Eusebius, in attributing the authorship of Revelation to the Presbyter, even hints at the idea that he is also the author of the Gospel. He may have regarded it as an advantage to assign another authorship to the book, that the Apostle John might not be held responsible for the millenarian ideas of Papias. Papias accords the Presbyter no special place of honour in his list, and indeed places him last, after Aristion. If Papias had recorded anything of importance about him, no doubt Eusebius would have noted it, in order to support his view of the authorship of Revelation. See also artt. ARISTION and PAPIAS.

(ii.) We have next to inquire *whether there is any evidence in the writing of Papias that he used the Fourth Gospel.* (a) A passage occurs in the writings of Irenæus which contains a quotation of Jn 14² 'Our Lord has said, that in the abode of my Father are many mansions.' The passage is introduced, like many others in Irenæus, as a quotation from the words of 'the Elders.' Is Irenæus here quoting from the sayings of 'the Elders' as reported by Papias? By the way in which the Johannine quotation is prefaced, it is fair to suppose that 'the Elders' are here referring to a written record, and not reproducing merely oral tradition, and that some well-known and accepted source for the words of our Lord is meant.

An additional confirmation of the position that Irenæus quotes *verbatim* from the Elders of Papias is found in another portion of his work. He is speaking of the fruitfulness of the earth at the millennium, and inserts a fanciful passage about vines with ten thousand shoots. He says that he received it from 'the Elders who saw John, the disciple of the Lord.' After quoting the passage, he adds: 'Papias also, a hearer of

John and companion of Polycarp, an ancient man, confirms these things in writing.' Harnack contends that the words 'also' and 'confirms in writing' 'certainly ought not to be pressed' to mean that Irenæus is giving a confirmation from Papias of the words of the Elders, but that he only means to indicate the written source from which he takes them. (This position is stoutly opposed by Schmiedel, *op. cit.* ii. 2549, where see a statement of the whole controversy and its issues).

If Papias quotes 14² we have here an important clue to an early date for the Gospel. The Elders of Papias belonged to the early Christian community.

(b) There are indications in the Preface of Papias that the Gospel permeates his thought, and that the references would be apparent to his readers. He speaks of 'those who teach the truth' (τοῖς τἀληθῆ διδάσκουσιν), and he also applies the term 'the Truth' to Christ. It is also not without significance that St. Andrew and St. Peter and St. Philip are named in the exact order in which the names occur in the first chapter of St. John, while St. Philip and St. Thomas are prominent only in the Fourth Gospel.

(c) Eusebius (*HE* iii. 39) says that 'Papias has used testimonies from the former Epistle of John and from that of Peter similarly.' If 1 John and the Gospel are by the same author, we have here additional confirmation that Papias knew and used the Fourth Gospel. This item of evidence, however, can have weight only in connexion with the rest of the evidence. Formerly the fact that Eusebius, while mentioning his use of the Epistle, is silent as to any use of the Gospel by Papias, was relied upon as a strong argument for the non-existence of the Gospel before 160–170 (*e.g.* in *Supernatural Religion*). After Lightfoot's complete answer to this position (*Essays on Supernatural Religion*, ii.), it is not now possible to deny a much earlier date for the Gospel. Modern opponents of the traditional view now rely on the argument from the silence of Eusebius, as proving that Papias nowhere appeals to the Gospel as of Apostolic authority (*e.g.* Bacon). It is therefore necessary to examine anything in Papias which seems to indicate that he regarded the Gospel as the work of St. John the Apostle.

(iii.) *The evidence of Papias as to the authorship of the Gospel.*—(a) Eusebius, in the often quoted passage, says that Papias distinguishes the Presbyter John from John the Apostle, 'evidently meaning the Evangelist.' The words in inverted commas would seem to point to some indication that Eusebius found in Papias' writing that he spoke of St. John the Apostle as the Evangelist. To this may be added the naming of St. John immediately after the Evangelist St. Matthew in the Preface.

(b) A Vatican MS of the 9th cent. contains the statement: 'Evangelium Johannis manifestatum et datum est ecclesiis ab Johanne adhuc in corpore constituto: sicut Papias nomine Hierapolitanus, discipulus Johannis carus, in exotericis—id est in extremis—quinque libris retulit. Descripsit vero evangelium dictante Johanne recte.' The words are part of a translation of an early Greek *argumentum* or proof that the Gospel was written by John the Apostle. As the passage stands, the words *exotericis* and *extremis* are unintelligible, and the conjecture of Lightfoot may be accepted that the former should read *exegeticis* and *extremis* should read *externis*, which was an explanation of the false reading *exotericis*. Again, it is nonsense to say that the Gospel was published 'by John while he was yet alive'; and Harnack suggests (*Chron.* i. 665) that the preposition *ab* should be deleted. With these changes it is possible to make sense of the words. The statement 'Johanne adhuc in corpore constituto' would then imply that there was an interval between the writing and the publication of the Gospel, and has reference to Jn 21²⁵. This would explain why Papias had found it necessary to say that the Gospel was published 'in the lifetime of the Apostle.' The statement at the end, that Papias wrote the Gospel at the dictation of St. John, may safely be set aside. At the same time, apart from the fact that it is necessary so to edit the fragment, there are serious difficulties in the way of accepting it as reliable evidence. For one thing, it is strange that Eusebius does not mention such a statement in Papias, although he mentions similar statements of his with regard to St. Matthew and St. Mark. Moreover, in view of the modern question of the Presbyter authorship, there is nothing to indicate which John is meant. (For discussion of the alleged statement of Papias recorded by Philip of Sidé, that John died a martyr in Jerusalem, see art. JOHN [THE APOSTLE]).

If the direct testimony of Papias must be regarded as inconclusive, it may fairly be asked whether we have a right to expect more. There is a very high probability that the Gospel was one of the sources of the 'Oracles' which he expounded, and his silence as to the author, so far from displaying any uncertainty on the question, may quite as easily be interpreted as meaning that the personality of St. John was eclipsed in the mind of Papias by the desire to hear the living voice of the Lord Himself in the Gospel. It is probable that in Papias we are in the presence of a certain conservatism which marked with some regret the dying out of those who were in possession of the oral tradition about the life and teaching of Jesus, and the gradual substitution of the written word as the authority for the Christian life which, of necessity, was taking place. It was his aim from an early period in his activity to collect the oral tradition. One thing at least is practically certain, that if Papias knew and quoted the Gospel, it must have been for him an authentic record. If the Gospel emerged at the close of the 1st cent. or the very beginning of the 2nd, as it undoubtedly did, and did not bring with it the strongest credentials and most unmistakable indications that it was in complete accord with the accredited oral teaching so much valued by Papias, it is difficult to think that in a mind of such simplicity as his it could have raised, as it appears to have done, only the merest ripple on the surface.

(2) **Ignatius** was bishop of Antioch in Syria. A number of letters have come down to us under his name, of which only seven are genuine. The writer was at the time on his way from Antioch to Rome under sentence of death. The date 110–117, the closing years of Trajan's reign, may be assigned to them.

In *Romans* vii. 2, Ignatius says, 'There is not in me a fire fed by fleshly motive, but water living and speaking in me, saying within me, Come to the Father.' These words inevitably recall Jn 4¹⁰· ¹⁴ (cf. also 4²³ 'the Father seeketh such to worship him'). Not only the ideas, but the coincidence of ideas, seem to point to the story of the woman of Samaria as to a passage in the Gospel which is affording him comfort in his trial. Again, in *Philad.* vii. 1, he says, 'The Spirit is not deceived, being from God; for it knoweth whence it cometh and whither it goeth, and searcheth out the hidden things' (cf. Jn 3⁸ 8¹⁴, 1 Jn 2¹¹). There are some striking differences in the thought of the parallel passages; but it is difficult to resist the conclusion that the words of Ignatius are due to the influence of these Johannine passages 'floating in his mind' (*New Test. in Apost. Fathers*, Oxford Society of Historical Theology, 1905, p. 82, where see other parallelisms). Both in expression and in doctrine there is an undoubted affinity between Ignatius and the Evangelist. Loisy admits that Ignatius, in his Christology, is dependent on the Gospel (*Le Quatrième*

Évangile, p. 7). Von der Goltz holds that the affinity of thought is so deep that it cannot be explained by the influence of a book, and that the writer of the letters must have been imbued with the tradition and thought of a school (quoted by Sanday, *Crit. of Fourth Gospel*, p. 243). Sanday himself 'doubts whether there is any other instance of resemblance between a Biblical and patristic book that is really so close' (*ib.*).

Two arguments, taken from the writings of Ignatius, are relied upon by opponents of the Apostolic authorship. (*a*) It is urged that he nowhere quotes the Gospel as of Apostolic authority, although there are occasions (notably *Smyrn.* iii. 2) where it would have been exceedingly apposite to do so. It may be pointed out as having a bearing on this objection, that, although it is quite evident that Ignatius knew 1 Cor. 'almost by heart,' he has 'no quotations (in the strictest sense, with mention of the source) from that Epistle' (*NT in Apost. Fathers*, p. 67). This is only another instance of the precariousness of the argument from silence, considered apart from the idiosyncrasies of a writer. (*b*) Again, it is also objected that in writing to the Ephesian community in which St. John is said to have laboured, Ignatius mentions St. Paul as a hero of the faith, whom he sets before himself and them for imitation, but makes no mention of St. John (*Ephes.* xii.). To this argument it must be admitted that no very satisfactory answer has yet been given. Ignatius is, indeed, predisposed to mention St. Paul's name, through his evident desire to compare his own experience and the Apostle's in calling together the elders of Ephesus. Again, the writings of St. Paul, which have more clearly in view the various heresies of the time, would perhaps suit his purpose better.

It cannot be regarded as certain that Ignatius used the Gospel. His evidence is on the border-line between evidence for the existence of the Gospel and proof of the influence of a *milieu* of Johannine teaching and thought. It is probable that Ignatius had access to some document containing Johannine teaching (cf. *e.g.* his reference to the narrative of the woman of Samaria); on the other hand, that might easily have been a story told orally by the Apostle in the course of his preaching and teaching, and embedded in the hearts and minds of those who heard him.

(3) **Polycarp** was bishop of Smyrna. His writing has come down to us in the form of an *Epistle to the Philippians*. The date of his martyrdom was long uncertain, but the investigations of Lightfoot and Harnack have led to the almost certain conclusion that he died in 155 at the age of 86.

As regards the Gospel, we have two sources from which we may derive evidence as to his opinions, viz. the *Epistle* and some reminiscences of Irenæus.

(*a*) In the *Epistle*, Polycarp makes no reference to any document, except that he refers to St. Paul's Ep. to the Philippians immediately after mentioning his name, and in another passage again quotes the Epistle without remark. There is also a sentence which, though not verbally accurate, bears every trace of having been taken from the First Epistle of St. John: 'Everyone who shall not confess that Jesus Christ is come in the flesh is Antichrist' (cf. 1 Jn 4². ³). He has also a passage that recalls at once words of Christ in the Gospel and the thought of the Epistle: 'He that raised Him from the dead will raise us also, if we do His will and walk in His commandments, and love the things which He loved' (cf. Jn 7¹⁷ 14¹⁵, 1 Jn 2⁶· ¹⁷ 5¹· ²). We also find in Polycarp, v. 2, 'As He hath promised to raise us from the dead.' This promise is found only in Jn 6⁴⁴. These parallelisms at least show that he was familiar with a circle of Johannine thought. He does not once mention the name of St. John ; but the Church at Philippi had not been directly in contact with that Apostle. Moreover, his habits of quotation hardly lead us to expect any other result (cf. *NT in Apost. Fathers*, p. 84).

(*b*) Irenæus gives Polycarp a foremost place among the elders whom he quotes. He says that he 'had not only been instructed by Apostles, and associated with many who had seen the Christ, but had also been placed by Apostles in Asia in the Church at Smyrna as a bishop, whom we also saw in our early life' (ἐν τῇ πρώτῃ ἡλικίᾳ) (*Hær.* III. iii. 4). Eusebius has preserved for us a letter of his to Florinus, in which he gives an account of his listening with peculiar attention to Polycarp, and vividly recalls the very place where he sat when he discoursed, his manner of life, and his personal appearance, 'and how he would describe his intercourse with John, and with the rest who had seen the Lord, and how he would relate their words. And whatsoever things he had heard from them about the Lord, and about His miracles, and about His teaching, Polycarp, as having received them from eye-witnesses of the life of the Word, would relate them in accordance with the Scriptures' (*ap.* Euseb. *HE* v. xx. 6). Again, Irenæus also, in a letter to Victor, bishop of Rome, on the Paschal controversy, uses as an argument the fact that Polycarp followed the example of 'John the disciple of the Lord, and the rest of the Apostles with whom he consorted.' Irenæus is undoubtedly referring to the Apostle John ; and if that be so, there can be little doubt that 'the Scriptures' to which Polycarp referred contained the Fourth Gospel in some form. Thus the silence of Polycarp, in the solitary writing that has come down to us, is balanced by the explicit statement of Irenæus that Polycarp knew St. John, and referred to him in his discourse.

Opponents of the Johannine authorship of the Gospel have cast doubt on the trustworthiness of Irenæus in this matter. They allege that he made a mistake in regarding Papias as a hearer of John, and that he has possibly done the same in the case of Polycarp. The John to whom Polycarp referred may have been the Presbyter. Irenæus was still a boy (ἐκ παιδων) when he heard his teacher. At the same time, it is hardly likely that the vivid personal impression he has of Polycarp contains a mistake of this kind. Polycarp evidently mentioned the name of John with some frequency, and there is no evidence that the Presbyter John was a man of such note in Asia as to be thus referred to in Polycarp's lectures. It is inconceivable that, if there had been any prospect of confusion in the mind of a youth who was listening to him, Polycarp would not have guarded against it (see Stanton, *Gospels as Hist. Doct.* pp. 214–218).

(4) We have still to deal with a group of writings classed among the Apostolic Fathers, whose evidence on the subject is rendered vague and inconclusive, inasmuch as they contain no definite quotations from the Gospel, and there is also uncertainty as to their dates. (*a*) **The Epistle of Barnabas** reflects the condition of thought in Egypt, and the date may lie anywhere between 79 and 132. The theory that Barnabas used the Fourth Gospel found strangely a strong champion in Keim, who assigned the date 120–130 (*Jesus of Naz.* i. 192–195). Loisy, on the other hand, accepting the date *c.* 130, urges complete ignorance of the Gospel on the part of Barnabas, and uses the argument to prove that the Johannine writings had not yet taken complete possession of ecclesiastical usage (*Le Quatrième Év.* p. 5). In *Barnabas*, use is made of the idea of the Brazen Serpent ; and the conceptions of 'eternal life,' which often occurs, and of 'feeding upon the words of life,' seem to point to the influence of a Johannine current of thought. (*b*) Only one of the epistles known under the name of **Clement of Rome** is genuine. It was written from the Roman community to the Corinthian, *c.* 100. Here, again, the writer seems to be influenced by Johannine teaching (cf. Clem. xlix.

and Jn 14[15. 23], 1 Jn 5[1-3]). (*c*) **The Didache, or Teaching of the Twelve Apostles**, is a composite document, and is the earliest manual of Church procedure extant. The elements of which it is composed may have been in use at the end of the 1st cent., but the work in its present form was published much later. It contains a specimen of a prayer of thanksgiving for use after the Eucharist, in which there is a very remarkable parallel to the anti-sacramentarian treatment of the ideas of the Supper in the Fourth Gospel (ch. 6) : 'Thou, Almighty Master, didst create all things for thy name's sake, and didst give food and drink unto men for enjoyment, that they might render thanks unto thee ; but didst bestow upon us spiritual food and drink and eternal life through thy Son' (*Did.* x. 3). (*d*) **The Shepherd of Hermas** (*c.* 100 Zahn, 135–145 Harnack) displays a Johannine colouring of thought.

5. *Evidence derived from Opponents of Church doctrine in the 2nd century.*—(1) **The Clementine Homilies.** — These are the work of a Jewish Christian, and were published at Rome not earlier than A.D. 160–170. In one of the *Homilies* (discovered by Dressel in 1837) there is an undoubted quotation (xix. 22) from Jn 9[2. 3]. There are also in the *Homilies* other apparent references to the Gospel.

(2) **The Gnostics.**—There were two great schools of Gnostics—the Valentinians and the Basilidians. The date of the literary activity of *Valentinus* is uncertain, but we know that there existed a school of his followers before A.D. 150. . *Heracleon* was a pupil of Valentinus ; and it is exceptionally strong evidence, not only for the early existence but also for the authenticity of the Fourth Gospel, that he composed a Commentary on it which is quoted by Origen. Tertullian contrasts Valentinus and Marcion as to the way in which they use Scripture. He says that Marcion used the 'knife,' while Valentinus 'accepted the whole instrument' (*i.e.* the four Gospels), but with an ability not less than Marcion's 'laid hands upon the truth.' We hear of a school of *Basilides c.* 133, and his own period of activity was A.D. 117–138. Hippolytus in his *Refutatio* quotes Basilides, and in the quotations there are undoubted extracts from the Gospel. The question discussed by modern criticism is whether these are quotations from Basilides or from the representative of a school (cf. Drummond, *op. cit.* 296–301). There is a strong preponderance of evidence in favour of Basilides himself as the source.

So far as the earlier Gnostics are concerned—the Naasseni, Peratæ, Ophites, and Docetæ—it is generally admitted that the Gospel is earlier than these controversies ; and Hippolytus tells us that they made abundant use of the Gospel.

(3) **Marcion** was a contemporary of Valentinus. —The principle of his work is to secure a Gospel that shall represent the pure doctrine of Christ, unmixed with Jewish prejudices, which he regarded as inherent in the minds of the primitive Apostles. We find him rejecting all others in favour of St. Luke, which was written under Pauline influence ; and he mutilated even that Gospel to suit his purpose. We cannot expect to find in his writing any reference to the Gospel of John, but, from his action in rejecting the writings of the early Apostles, we may draw the negative conclusion that if the Gospel was regarded as written by St. John it would be sufficient reason for its rejection. He made use of the passage in Galatians where St. Paul rebukes 'Apostles themselves' 'who walked not uprightly according to the truth of the gospel' (2[14]). His silence as to the Fourth Gospel is all the more striking because of its anti-Judaic tendency, which would have predisposed him in its favour had it not been written by a primitive Apostle.

6. The Quartodeciman controversy. — In the latter part of the 2nd cent. a controversy was rife between certain Asiatic Christians and the Church with regard to their Paschal observance on the 14th Nisan. They appealed to the example of the Apostle John in defence of their practice. In the Gospel the Paschal meal falls on the 13th, and it was contended by Bretschneider, followed by the Tübingen School, that therefore the Apostle could not be the author of the Gospel. A fuller investigation, however, into the rationale of the Quartodeciman controversy goes far to remove the difficulty. In opposition to the Tübingen School, it was held that the 14th was kept not in commemoration of the Passover, but in commemoration of the death of Christ, which would be in accord with the Fourth Gospel. This still leaves the difficulty unsolved, that in the Synoptics the death of Christ falls on the 15th. Accordingly, Bleek (followed by Schürer) and Stanton maintain that the observance in question was neither of the institution of the Supper, nor of the death of Christ alone, but that the Christian Jews gave to the Passover day a new meaning which made it a commemoration of the entire fact of redemption, including the Supper, the Death, and the Resurrection of Christ. This interpretation seems to be the correct one. At the same time, while it surmounts the difficulty caused by the chronology of the Fourth Gospel, there still remains the fact that the Quartodecimans of the latter half of the century appealed to the example of Christ as eating the Passover on the 14th. If such an appeal was made in the earlier part of the controversy, and at the same time the example of St. John was quoted in support, we should be face to face with a strong argument against the Apostolic authorship of the Gospel. There is no proof, however, that the argument from the example of Christ was used before the time of Apollinaris. Apollinaris distinctly assumes that the Synoptics and St. John must not be made to contradict one another ; and Polycrates as distinctly holds the Apostolic authorship, although he is a Quartodeciman (cf. Schmiedel, *op. cit.* ii. 2552–2553, who regards the Quartodeciman argument as still valid against the Apostolic authorship. The question is fully discussed by Stanton, *op. cit.* i. pp. 173–197, with a result favourable to the traditional view).

7. The Alogi. — These were a party in Asia Minor (*c.* A.D. 180) who rejected the Johannine authorship of the Gospel and the Apocalypse. They are first mentioned by Epiphanius and Philaster (4th cent.), but it may now be safely admitted that Irenæus opposes their views in *Hær.* III. xi. 12 (Zahn and Harnack). They attributed the authorship to Cerinthus, and founded their argument chiefly on the chronological disparity with the Synoptics. The main interest in the Alogi centres round the question whether they betoken uncertainty in the ecclesiastical tradition. Epiphanius ranks them among heretics, but it is certain that they were a party in the Church (Schürer and Harnack). The name 'Alogi' is a jest of Epiphanius, and indicates merely that they rejected the Logos Gospel, with more than a hint at their stupidity (ἄλογος = ' unreasonable '). It gives no clue to their doctrinal position. Epiphanius, himself very orthodox, says ' that they seem to believe as we do.' Probably they were opposed to some form of the Montanist heresy, and in their zeal sought to get rid of the teaching of the Gospel on the Holy Spirit by rejecting the whole. This step they strove to justify by the chronological disparities with the Synoptics and other internal discrepancies. Irenæus says of them that 'they frustrate the gift of the Spirit.' The millenarian views of the Montanists may have directed their first attack on the Apocalypse, which they extended to the Gospel ' by a piece of sheer bravado' (Sanday, *Crit. of Fourth Gospel*, p. 65). Their influence seems to have been small. Irenæus and Epiphanius refer to them slightingly, and Schwarz (*op. cit.* p. 33), in common with Salmon, although from a different motive, narrows them down to a single individual with perhaps a coterie behind him. We may admit that the presence of the Alogi in the Church indicates that the belief in the Johannine authorship had not reached that stage of clear definition and regular acceptance which only controversy and time could give. They 'came upon the tradition unawares' (Loisy). The Church was not yet in a position either to challenge with critical weapons, or to expel as heretics those who differed from her traditional beliefs about authorship (Irenæus could only defend the fourfold Gospel mystically), especially when they were fighting, as in this case, a common foe in Montanism. Indeed, the Alogi can really be pressed into the service of tradition. ' Its ascription to Cerinthus, an impossible author, betrays the recklessness of the judgment pronounced ; while the naming of a contemporary and fellow - townsman of the Apostle may be accepted as an indication of the true date of the Gospel ' (Dods, *Expos. Gr. Test.* i. p. 659).

II. *THE INTERNAL EVIDENCE.* — No text of the Gospel that we possess is without the categorical statement of 21²⁴ that the book contains the witness of the Apostle John and is written by him. It seems the more probable view that this whole chapter was composed by friends of the Evangelist, either towards the end of his life, or after his death, in order to remove a misinterpretation of a saying of Jesus about him. The position assigned to St. Peter in the chapter might be explained by the desire to show that, although the Gospel leaves him weighted with the guilt of his denial, he was restored to his place in the Apostolic circle, and that no disparagement or supersession is intended of the Petrine Gospel that lies at the basis of the Synoptics. We have no moral right to regard the statement of 21²⁴ as anything but a *bona fide* statement of the earliest view of the authorship, and in the internal evidence we have to consider how far the book itself corresponds with this suggested view.

1. The author is a Jew. — (1) *His attitude towards the OT* shows unmistakably that it was for him a valuable aid to faith and a deep source of religious experience. The opening words of the Gospel are reminiscent of Gn 1¹; 3¹³ recalls Dt 30¹². ' His own ' in 1¹¹ can betray only the tragic consciousness of a Jew that the chosen nation rejected the Christ. The words in 10³⁵ ' the Scripture cannot be broken,' may be taken as expressing the Evangelist's own conviction. He sees in certain incidents in the life of Jesus that would otherwise cause perplexity, especially some connected with the Passion, the fulfilment of the OT. Twice the conduct of Judas is explained by Scripture (13¹⁸ 17¹²). The mournful sight of the garments of Jesus distributed among the rough soldiers brings to mind a prophecy (19²⁴). The thirst of Jesus, who Himself had the gift of the living water, is a fulfilment of Scripture (19²⁸). It is in Scripture that he finds a solution for the problem of the failure of Christ's ministry and teaching (12³⁷). The very spear-thrust has a place in the counsels of God (19³⁶· ³⁷), and becomes an aid to faith (19³⁵). While the Evangelist rarely cites incidents from the OT, and the great majority of the OT references are contained in the discourses of Christ, it has to be borne in mind that the Gospel was written for Gentile readers, to whom only the outlines of the history would be familiar.

(2) The writer is familiar *not only with the Messianic expectation, but also with the limitations that it suffered in the popular mind.* The hope is current in Galilee (1⁴¹· ⁴⁶· ⁴⁹ 6¹⁵· ²⁸· ³⁰ᶠ·), in Samaria (4²⁵· ²⁹· ⁴²)

in Judæa ($5^{39.\ 45f.}$ $7^{26f.\ 40-43}$ $8^{30f.}$ 10^{24}). 'Among friends, among foes, among neutrals alike, it is discussed.' The purpose of the Gospel is to induce belief that Jesus is the Christ (20^{31}). Not only so, but the limitations and misconceptions of the idea of the Christ in the popular mind are familiar to him. Elijah and the Prophet are not yet come (1^{21}); the outlook is unspiritual ($6^{14.\ 15}$); the Messiah will never die (6^{60} 12^{34}); Jesus does not satisfy their conventional ideas ($7^{27.\ 42}$).

(3) The writer is familiar with *the ideas and customs of the Jews.* We have a picture of a Jewish marriage feast (2^{1-10}), of pastoral life (10^{1-14}), of burial customs ($11^{38.\ 44}$ 19^{40}), the estimate of women (4^{27}), the disparagement of the Dispersion (7^{35}), the heredity of sin (9^2). The religious observances of the people are known to him, and he displays great familiarity with the Temple and its services. The Synagogue and the Temple are places of resort (18^{20}); he knows the side of the Temple where shelter is to be had in inclement weather ($10^{22.\ 23}$); it was forty-six years in building (2^{20}); he speaks of the treasury (8^{20}). The two feasts of Tabernacles and of Dedication are familiar to him, even to the implied ritualistic details (Westcott, vi.). He speaks of the 'great day' of the feast of Tabernacles. He is familiar with the narrow Sabbatarian views of the Jews (5^{10} 9^{14} 7^{21-23}). In the last passage a subtle argument is founded on the knowledge that circumcision is allowable on the Sabbath.

Does the statement that Caiaphas was 'high priest that same year' (11^{49}, repeated 11^{51} 18^{13}) imply that the writer imagined that the office was tenable only for a year? The repetition after the manner of the Evangelist is meant to impress more than a chronological fact. Either the words may have an ironical significance, arising from the fact that the three predecessors of Caiaphas had been deposed after a year's tenure, and would be an allusion to the present uncertainty of the office (Delff, *Gesch. des Rabbi Jesus von Nazareth*, pp. 85, 86); or the Evangelist seeks to connect emphatically the office of the high priest with the part that he took in accomplishing the death of Christ. The high priest entered alone once a year into the Holy of Holies, where he offered atonement for the sins of the people (He 9⁷), and in 'that memorable year' Caiaphas is but an unconscious instrument in bringing about the great and final sacrifice (Westcott, vi.; cf. also B. Weiss, *Com. ad loc.*).

(4) It has been contended against these indications that *when the writer mentions the Jews he seems to speak of them as a foreigner would speak.* They are throughout represented as the bitter enemies of Christ (2^{18} $5^{10ff.}$ 6^{41} $7^{11ff.}$ $8^{22ff.}$ $10^{24ff.}$ 11^{36} 13^{33} 20^{19}). The term οἱ Ἰουδαῖοι is sometimes used to denote the Jews as a nation, in distinction from other nations: sometimes as Judæans distinguished from Galilæans or Peræans: and sometimes the leaders of the Jewish people alone are meant. This somewhat indefinite mode of speech has a sufficient explanation if the Evangelist wrote as he used to speak (Drummond, *op. cit.* 416, note). There is no indication in his tone of national antagonism. Rather his attitude is like that of St. Paul to his countrymen. The Jews are 'His own' (1^{11}); Jesus Himself is a Jew (4^9); salvation is of the Jews (4^{22}); Nathanael is an 'Israelite indeed' (1^{47}); there are believing Jews (8^{31} etc.). This Gospel also preserves words of Christ that trace the subsequent persecution by the Jews to its roots in their ignorance of the Father and the Son ($16^{2.\ 3}$). In this Gospel Jesus never denounces the leaders of the people in as strong terms as He uses in the Synoptics. That He expressly distinguishes His disciples from the Jews (13^{33}), and also speaks of 'your law' (8^{17} 10^{34}), 'their law' (15^{25}), implies that this external attitude adopted by the writer was not unknown during the ministry on earth (cf. Dods, *Expos. Gr. Test.* i. 666).

2. The author is a Jew of Palestine.—Many of the preceding characteristics are already indications that the writer is a native of Palestine. (1)

He is also familiar with *sites and places.* Jacob's well is deep (4^{11}); the mountain and the ripening cornfields are suggested in the most natural fashion (vv.$^{20.\ 21.\ 35}$); it is a *descent* from the high ground where Cana stood to the shores of Gennesaret at Capernaum (v.^{47}). Ch. 6 contains some minute information as to the district. Bethsaida (1^{44} 12^{21}) and Bethany (11^1) are not merely localities, but connected with the names of friends. He carefully distinguishes Bethany 'nigh unto Jerusalem about fifteen furlongs' (11^{18}) from 'Bethany beyond Jordan' (1^{28}). Nazareth is mentioned not only as the home of Jesus, but as a place so well known to Nathanael that he considered it unlikely that 'any good thing' could spring from such commonplace surroundings (1^{46}); cf. the details as to Sychar (4^5), Ænon (3^{23}), Ephraim (11^{54}). A very striking feature is the accurate knowledge displayed of the topography of Jerusalem and its environs (cf. 5^2 18^1): the Kidron; which is a ravine on the way from the city to the Mount of Olives, and a torrent only in winter (χειμάρρου, 18^1); the Pavement (Gabbatha) in the Prætorium (19^{13}); Golgotha (19^{17}). The acclaiming multitude carried in their hands '*the* branches of *the* palm trees' which grew on the Mount of Olives (12^{13}).

(2) It has been customary to regard the *so-called Hebraisms* of the Fourth Gospel, which it was supposed to share with the other NT writings, as an indication that the writer was a Palestinian. The study of the papyri has revolutionized this idea. It is now no longer permissible to speak of Hebraistic Greek. The papyri are written in the vernacular Greek, and range in date from the 3rd cent. B.C. to the 7th cent. A.D. The earlier specimens furnish a convincing parallel in language to the Greek of the NT. Where there are Hebraic modes of expression, these must be traced to direct translation from the Aramaic, or to those causes that operate in the introduction of foreign elements into the vernacular of any language (Moulton, *Grammar of NT Greek*, Prolegomena, vol. i. pp. 18, 19). At the same time, while we must attribute the simple structure of this Evangelist's sentences and the absence of connecting particles to his use of the vernacular, we are not left without evidence that he knew Hebrew. In his quotations from the OT he made use of the LXX (2^{17} 12^{38} 19^{24} 10^{34}); but he is also independent of it (19^{36} 7^{38} 1^{23} 6^{31}); and there is an interesting group of cases where the LXX seems to be corrected by reference to the Hebrew (6^{45} 13^{18} 19^{37}; cf. Westcott, *Gospel of John*, xiii–xiv; Drummond, *op. cit.* p. 364).

(3) Can *the Logos conception* of the Gospel be shown to have greater affinity with Alexandrian than with Hebrew thought? It is noteworthy that the term λόγος is not used throughout the Gospel, either in the discourses or in the narrative parts, except in the ordinary sense of 'word'; but we must not neglect other passages where the Logos idea is in the background. The lofty and undefined sense of the plural subject in such passages as 3^{11-13}, the well-known pre-existence passages, the assertion by Christ of what He had seen with the Father (6^{46} 8^{38}, cf. 1^{18}), His teaching which is not of Himself (7^{14-17}), His complete unity of existence with the Father (14^{7-11}), are all expressions of the Logos consciousness (cf. Grill, *Untersuchungen über die Entstehung des vierten Evangeliums*, i. pp. 32, 33). On the other hand, in order to prove that the Evangelist had either a literary acquaintance with the works of Philo, or was deeply influenced by his thought, it would be necessary to discover a much closer correspondence between them than is actually to be found. In the Stoic philosophy with which Philo closely identifies himself, the term 'Logos' has the double significance of 'reason' (λόγος ἐνδιάθετος) and 'word' (λόγος προφορικός), and

in the Fourth Gospel there is not a trace of the former sense. Jesus is the manifestation of God, the uttered Word. Again, in the Gospel the Logos is identified with the Messiah, and in Philo there is no such identification. It is doubtful whether Philo attributes personality to the Logos; but there can be no doubt of the personal existence of the Logos in the Gospel. At the same time, the author of the Fourth Gospel, like every Hebrew thinker, is no metaphysician, and he simply projects the conception of personality, which he derived from the knowledge of the Incarnate One, into the Word in its pre-incarnate existence. The Angel of the Lord and the personified Wisdom in the OT are not so much independent existences as immanent determinations of the Divine Being. Moreover, the Incarnation of the Logos is an idea quite foreign to the mind of Philo, not because with him matter is essentially corrupt, but because it is 'regarded as a principle purely negative, arresting, limiting, restraining the penetration of the Divine action, in proportion to its thickness and opacity' (Réville, *Le Quatrième Évangile*, p. 87). For Alexandrian thought an Incarnation of the Logos could only be Docetic; and this may have given rise to the heresy of 1 Jn 2²².

There are, however, *some very striking affinities of expression between Philo and the Fourth Gospel.* Philo speaks of 'a second God' (δεύτερος θεός); the Word Himself is God and the Son of God (ὁ υἱὸς τοῦ θεοῦ); the Word is the agent or instrument in creation (δι' οὗ ὁ κόσμος κατεσκευάσθη); Light and Life are conceptions of Philo as applied to the Logos; he uses the term 'Paraclete,' but applies it to the 'cosmos' and not to the 'Logos.' The Logos exists in heaven; reveals the name of God; possesses supernatural knowledge and power; is continually at work; is eternal; is free from sin; instructs and convinces; dwells in the souls of men; is high priest towards God; is the source of unity, joy, and peace; imparts eternal life; is bridegroom, father, guide, steersman, shepherd, physician; imparts manna; is the food of the soul (Grill, pp. 115–128). For a discussion of the whole question see Sanday, *l.c.* pp. 185–200. These coincidences cannot be overlooked in deciding the question of authorship. We must bear in mind that 'Logos' was the word by which the Hebrew idea of the Word of God is translated in the LXX, and that there are passages in the OT, the Apocrypha, and in the Jewish Targums that afford equally important coincidences of thought (Ps 33⁶ 107²⁰ 147¹⁵, Is 40⁸ 55¹⁰.¹¹, Wis 9¹ 16¹² 18¹⁵.¹⁶. For the *Memra* of the Targums, see Edersheim, *Life and Times*, i. pp. 46–48). The Evangelist would meet with these ideas nowhere more readily than in Ephesus, which was also the home of the Logos philosophy of Heraclitus. He would be disposed to keep in view his Greek readers, among whom these expressions were current. Again, we find similar coincidences of thought with Philo in the writings of St. Paul and in the Epistle to the Hebrews. If, indeed, we were to isolate the Prologue to the Gospel, which may be regarded as containing all that was in the author's mind essential to the Logos idea, and to rid ourselves of all associations of the word 'Logos' derived from Greek philosophy, we should find that the thought remains within the limits of the OT, except in the case of vv.¹⁻¹⁴.

3. The writer is a contemporary of the events and persons in his narrative.—(1) *His knowledge of the ecclesiastical situation and feeling of the time.*—A deputation is sent to the Baptist from the ecclesiastical authorities in Jerusalem consisting of priests and their attendant Levites (1¹⁹ff.), and the writer breaks the narrative of the deputation to insert the remark, evidently meant to explain the question that follows, that the deputation included some Pharisees (v.²⁴). Their inquiry betrays an interest in ritual and in the orderly observance of the Law which is characteristic of that party, as distinct from the Sadducees. The Sadducees seem to have applied rationalist principles to the old religion, and were distinguished by dogmatic differences not only regarding the rule of faith, but in connexion with such questions as the life after death, and the question of free-will and predestination (Edersheim, *Life and Times*, i. pp. 310–324). The writer does not speak of Pharisees and Sadducees, but of Chief Priests and Pharisees, showing that he is acquainted with the fact that the Sadducees held the offices in the time of Christ. The passage 11⁴⁷⁻⁵³ is full of ecclesiastical knowledge. The discussion in the Sanhedrin is occasioned by the

influence on the people of the raising of Lazarus, and we can clearly distinguish the attitude of the two parties. The Pharisees are represented as in touch with the people (11⁴⁶, cf. Jos. *Ant.* XIII. x. 6), and they are afraid lest a tumult should arise, and thereby the ecclesiastical influence (τόπος) and the national existence be destroyed by Rome. The reply of Caiaphas is characteristic. He scornfully sets aside the question of the miracle, and urges an opportunist policy to deal with the actual situation (vv.⁴⁹·⁵⁰). It can scarcely be without meaning that the Evangelist, who knew the Sadducæan disbelief in predestination, should represent Caiaphas as the unconscious prophet and instrument of the death of Christ (vv.⁵¹·⁵²). In 7⁴⁵⁻⁵² there is displayed a similar knowledge of ecclesiastical circles. After the triumphal entry the Pharisees seem to have been filled with dismay at their loss of influence with the people, and at the popularity of Christ (12¹⁹), and it is the ruling Sadducæan party who plot the death of Lazarus (v.¹⁰). Again, it is the Fourth Evangelist who tells us of the informal trial before Annas, who, though still wielding much power, had been deposed in favour of his son-in-law (18¹²⁻²⁴).

These indications of an acquaintance with opinion in ecclesiastical circles are in complete correspondence with the statement in 18¹⁵ about the disciple 'who was known to the high priest.' In this Gospel alone are we told the name (Malchus) of the servant of the high priest whose ear was cut off by Peter. It is noteworthy, also, that the Evangelist is acquainted with Nicodemus, and with Joseph of Arimathæa, who belonged to the Pharisaic party. In this connexion may be mentioned the tradition of Polycrates that 'John, who leaned on Jesus' breast,' also wore 'the frontlet' (πέταλον) of the high priest (Eus. *HE* III. xxxi. 3).

Delff has propounded the theory that the author of the Fourth Gospel was an unnamed native of Jerusalem, not of the number of the Twelve, but a man of high-priestly family, and a member of the higher aristocracy. He founds on 18¹⁵, on the statement of Polycrates, and on the other indications in the Gospel. He identifies the author with 'the disciple whom Jesus loved,' and describes him as a kind of 'supernumerary disciple.' Sanday (*Crit. of Fourth Gospel*, 99–108) has discussed this theory with great generosity, but it necessitates a further theory of interpolations, and itself presents some insuperable difficulties. This disciple and Peter are close friends (20²), and in the other Gospels, Peter and John are often named together (cf. Ac 3¹·¹¹ 4¹³ 8¹⁴, Gal 2⁹). We cannot suppose that within the Apostolic circle there were two pairs of friends, one identical in each. Again, if Delff is right, the Apostle John is not once referred to in the Gospel, and, on the other hand, this unknown disciple has completely vanished from history, unless he be the timorous man who fled at the arrest, leaving his linen cloth behind him, or the shadowy Presbyter John of Papias. It will be admitted that Delff's conclusion goes considerably beyond the evidence, but we must be prepared, in assigning the authorship, to recognize the undoubted insight of the Evangelist into the ecclesiastical situation.

(2) *His knowledge of the opinions of the populace* (ὄχλος).—He knows their varying verdicts about Christ (7¹¹⁻¹³); the wonder of the 'Jerusalemites' at the immunity Jesus enjoys from injury, notwithstanding His fearless speaking (7²⁵⁻²⁷); the belief of some of the crowd (7³¹, cf. v.⁴⁰); the fickleness of the *popularis aura* is graphically described (7⁴⁰⁻⁴⁴); the excitement among the people in view of the request of the Sanhedrin for information as to the whereabouts of Jesus, and the possibility of His appearance at the feast, is vividly portrayed (11⁵⁶·⁵⁷). The climax of popular acclamation is reached in 12¹²⁻¹⁹.

(3) *The writer speaks as one to whom the men and women of his narrative are personally familiar.*—Nicodemus is introduced somewhat suddenly into the narrative, but that is in the manner of the Evangelist, and presupposes that his readers are aware, either from the other Gospels, or from the oral tradition, or from personal acquaintance, of his historical existence. Nicodemus is introduced almost in the same words as John the Baptist (cf. 1⁶ and 3¹), a

fact which must not be forgotten in view of the tendency to find allegorical meanings in the characters (cf. 1[29] and 4[7]). It would be strange if the Evangelist should take so little pains to distinguish between characters known to be historical, and those that are allegorical. The reality of the characters is witnessed by the words they utter. It is not stupidity, but a profound emotion that makes Nicodemus speak as he does in 3[4], when he discovers that all that he has learned must be unlearned, and that he must begin the process of human experience anew. He is on the threshold of a world of facts as yet unrealized by him (3[9]). The woman of Samaria is introduced upon the scene, amid real surroundings, at Jacob's well, on the road from Judæa to Galilee. Her character is revealed in her nonchalant air and bantering mood, behind which she conceals an aching and guilty heart, and is much too true to life for allegory. How *can* the woman of Samaria be an allegory of the Samaritan Church, and her five husbands symbolize her idolatrous worship? (so, *e.g.*, Keim, *Jesus of Naz.* i. 159, note 1 ; Loisy, *Le Quat. Évangile*, p. 354). It is not necessary to suppose that the Evangelist was present at these interviews. It is enough to remember that Christ was present, and that the Evangelist is the 'disciple whom Jesus loved,' with whom confidences of that kind would be exchanged. Leaving for the moment the lifelike characters of the Apostolic circle, we are confronted in the closing scenes with a group of men that could have been painted only by a contemporary hand. The writer knows Caiaphas so well that he is able to reveal the man in a single sentence that fell from his lips (11[49]). Pilate is depicted, irresolute, and fettered by a guilty past of oppressive and cruel government. At the critical moment, the Evangelist places in the hands of the people the powerful weapon of a covert threat to denounce him to the Emperor (19[12]).

4. Relationship of the Evangelist to Jesus and the Apostolic circle.—It is evident that the author was able in a peculiar degree to interpret the mind of our Lord. He tells us of His emotions, thoughts, and motives (11[33] 13[21] 2[24] 4[1-3] 6[15] 13[1] 18[4]). Is the writer identical with 'the disciple whom Jesus loved'? Jn 21[20. 24] leaves us in no doubt. It is an entirely inadequate interpretation to say that the phrase is meant to stand for 'the type of the perfect Gnostic, the spiritual witness of Jesus' (so Loisy, *Le Quat. Év.* p. 125). It is a strong argument against the view that a purely ideal figure is meant, when we note the variety of the references. His existence is implied in 1[40] : in 13[23] he is described as leaning on Jesus' breast ; in 18[15] he is mentioned as 'another disciple who was known to the high priest.' It would also be necessary to interpret the scene in 19[26] as allegorical, if the disciple is not a historical figure. The variety of the situations shows that the author had a real person in his mind.

We have, however, to explain the difficulty that when the personality of the Evangelist is obtruded, he describes himself as 'the disciple whom Jesus loved.' If there is an apparent lack of modesty in the use of the phrase, it may be questioned whether this charge would not be equally relevant in those passages where the Evangelist confidently interprets the inmost thoughts of our Lord. The fact that he should describe himself in this indirect fashion at all will be matter for discussion under the question of the historicity of the Gospel. In the meantime it is sufficient to point out that in every case where the phrase is used, the writer is laid under the necessity of referring to himself individually. In 13[23] he explains the fact that he is lying on Jesus' breast. And in 19[26] Jesus addresses him directly. Perhaps in 20[2] there is the

suggestion of a thought in Mary's mind that the disciple would tell the mother of Jesus. The only alternative in these cases is to use the personal pronoun or to mention his own name, a course which the Evangelist systematically avoids. If ch. 21 is an appendix by another hand, there is no difficulty about the use of the phrase in vv.[7. 20].

It is also apparent that the author of the Gospel stood in a very intimate relationship to the Apostolic circle. We have miniature portraits of several of the Apostles, conveyed often through questions they put. Philip throughout appears as a man of somewhat practical and business-like turn of mind (1[46] 6[5] 14[8]). Andrew is wise, helpful, and unobtrusive (1[41] 6[8. 9] 12[22]). Thomas is despondent : his moods colour his outlook, and he experiences violent reaction (11[16] 14[5] 20[24ff. 27ff.]). Peter is over-confident and impulsive, and at a time cowardly (13[6ff. 36ff.] 18[10ff. 16ff.]). The scandal of Judas' presence among the Twelve is referred to as if by one who felt the shame of it and was eager to clear the situation (12[4-6] 13[2. 26-30] 18[2]). He knows also their places of resort (11[54] 18[2] 20[19]), and the thoughts of the disciples at critical moments (2[11. 17. 22] 4[27] 6[19. 60] 12[15] 13[22. 28] 20[9]).

5. Is St. John the Apostle the author of the Gospel?—Is he the unnamed disciple who is identified with the writer? This unnamed disciple is called among the earliest disciples, and remembers even the hour of the day (1[39]). He is closely associated with St. Peter in the closing scenes. We know from the Synoptics that St. Peter and the two sons of Zebedee were in specially close relationship with Jesus. St. Peter is out of the question ; St. James died early ; only St. John is left. Unless John be the beloved disciple, one of the 'pillar' Apostles (Gal 2[9]) is never once mentioned in the Gospel, except indirectly in 21[2]. A very strong argument for supposing that St. John is meant may also be founded on the fact that nowhere does the author refer to 'the Baptist,' but always to 'John.' Elsewhere he is very careful to distinguish names (*e.g.* 14[22]), but in this case he seems to have thought that no confusion was possible.

If St. John is the writer of the Gospel, why does he so studiously conceal his identity? The Fourth Gospel is distinguished from the Synoptics by the fact that, while in them we have a purely impersonal narrative except in the preface to St. Luke, in St. John we have a narrative where individual experience ('testimony') is prominent. Is it solely because St. John is himself the author and writer of the Gospel, that he sedulously veils his own name? Why was it not possible for him to incorporate his own testimony in the Gospel without keeping himself in the background in such a way as really to attract attention? There must be some reason for this conduct other than a modesty which thus defeats its own end. It is quite evident that the authority of the Gospel for the Church is regarded as depending on the fact that St. John the Apostle wrote it. It is permissible to see in 21[24] an indication that it was felt necessary, even at that early date, to authenticate the position that the Apostle John made himself responsible for the statements contained in this Gospel. This is not because there was doubt as to the Johannine authorship, but because the Gospel differs so much in character, subject, and content from the Synoptics, which already held the ground as authorities for the life and teaching of the Lord.

We shall be able to find an answer to these questions if we consider the two passages in the Gospel itself that have been most relied on as direct statements of Johannine authorship. (*a*) 1[14]. In what sense is 'we beheld' to be taken? It has been contended that a seeing with the bodily eye is not meant, but spiritual vision. If we compare the parallel passage in 1 Jn 1¹, there can be little doubt that the 'hearing' and the 'handling' there mentioned demand the sense that the 'seeing' is also literal. The presumption is in favour of applying the same interpretation to the passage in the Gospel. By 'we' is meant a group of eye-witnesses who are associated with St. John in the statement. Who these were it is impossible actually to determine, but perhaps it is unnecessary to limit the range of 'we' to the circle of the Twelve. The Gospel shows that the writer is interested in the testimony, however imperfect it may sometimes be, of many others besides his fellow-Apostles. Clement of Alexandria says that 'last of all, John, perceiving that the bodily facts had been set forth in the other Gospels, at the instance of his disciples and with the inspiration of the Spirit composed a spiritual Gospel.' With this may be compared the statement in the Muratorian Canon : 'It was revealed to Andrew, one of the Apostles, that John should narrate everything in his own name, subject to the revision of the rest' (*ut recognoscentibus cunctis Johannes suo nomine cuncta describeret*). While these statements may not have independent historical value, and may themselves be based on the internal evidence of the Gospel, and especially on 21²⁴, surely they must be regarded as the simplest and most direct interpretation of the facts. A group of eye-witnesses was concerned in the origin of the Gospel. We may therefore offer the hypothesis that, while St. John wrote the Gospel and impressed upon it his own personality, the form in which he expresses himself, the philosophical mould in which the writing is cast, the Philonic phraseology, and the extraordinary power of analyzing situations and characters, would owe much to the intellectual environment of Ephesus, and in some cases to direct suggestion on the part of some fellow-disciple, not necessarily one of the Twelve. The value of the Gospel and its authenticity are confirmed by the fact that it is the expression of St. John's own experience, attested by that of his fellow-disciples who had seen the Lord. The purpose of the Gospel is to treat the facts of the life and teaching of Jesus in such a way as to advance faith in the hearts of those who had *not* been eye-witnesses, and were therefore all the more inclined to regard their position in relation to the 'bodily facts' as a loss and a hindrance to faith. So far from this, the climax of faith is not to have seen and yet to believe (20²⁹). There would, no doubt, be men like Thomas in the early Church, easily cast down, and satisfied only by the bodily presence of Christ, to whom all else was unreal. No personal assurance was sufficient to convince them. St. John, therefore, veiled his identity, and emphasized the joint-testimony of the group of eye-witnesses to which he also belonged. This is also the origin of the impersonal reference in 20³¹ 'These things are written,' etc.

(*b*) 19³⁵⁻³⁷. Here is an instance where the Evangelist is compelled to distinguish his own personality from the circle in whose name he speaks. St. John alone of that group was present at the Cross (19²⁶). In this case he has to find, in accordance with his principle, some means of authenticating his testimony. It is interesting to notice how this is done, and the character of the Gospel as not dependent on the evidence of a single testimony alone vindicated. A threefold corroboration is adduced. (*a*) 'His witness is true' (ἀληθινός), *i.e.* confirmed by the 'Spirit of truth' (14¹⁷· ²⁶). (β) Reference is made to One who 'knoweth that he saith true.' It is possible, but awkward, to refer ἐκεῖνος to the Evangelist. Rather it is meant to denote Christ Himself (cf. 1¹⁸, 1 Jn 3¹⁶ 4¹⁷). It is

so taken by Sanday (*op. cit.* p. 78) and Schmiedel (*Encyc. Bibl.* ii. 1809). This interpretation is as old as Erasmus. (γ) The Scriptures are adduced as a witness, *i.e.* the witness of God Himself (vv.³⁶· ³⁷). The fact of the flow of blood and water from the pierced side can be explained medically, and the emphasis is laid not on the fact, but on the interpretation to be put upon it. It is a 'sign,' and the writer must have regarded it as of peculiar value to his readers. Perhaps some form of the Docetic heresy is aimed at (cf. Haussleiter, *Zwei Apost. Zeugen*, p. 29).

In conclusion, the Gospel is a genuine Johannine work from the pen of the Apostle, who wrote from Ephesus.* We cannot, however, overlook the undoubted fact that the writer is concerned to hide his own identity, and thereby to impress the fact that the Gospel is not the work of a single individual, but the testimony of a group of eye-witnesses. With John's as the guiding mind, they conjointly made themselves responsible for the statements contained in the book. This is at once the oldest and simplest solution of the problem of authorship.

Two objections, on general grounds, to the traditional authorship may here be mentioned.

1. *Can a Galilæan fisherman have written this Gospel?*—There is no question of NT criticism where the need is more imperative to rid ourselves of prejudice than this question of the Johannine authorship of the Fourth Gospel. It is possible to have a completely mistaken conception of the connexion between letters and handicraft in the days of the Apostles. St. Peter and St. John are described in Ac 4¹³ as 'unlearned and ignorant men' (ἀγράμματοι καὶ ἰδιῶται). ἰδιώτης marks a caste distinction, in opposition to the learned or academic classes. The use of the vernacular tongue by the Apostles would be sufficient to suggest the expression. The Pharisaic objection is, as Delitzsch reminds us, a decline from the traditional honourable connexion between the Rabbi and the hand-worker (*Jewish Artisan Life*, p. 54). Zebedee owned his own fishing vessel, and the presumptuous request of the mother of Zebedee's sons betrays a somewhat overweening sense of social position. St. John was 'known to the high priest.' Moreover, we too must take knowledge that he 'had been with Jesus,' and it would not be easy to estimate, in addition to the spiritual training, the purely educative influence of companionship with Jesus of Nazareth. The over-ardent spirit that sought to call down fire on a hostile Samaritan village, finds a nobler expression in the withering exposure of Judas (12⁶) and of Caiaphas (11⁴⁹⁻⁵²). He who with such insight lets us into the spiritual incapacity of Nicodemus, must have been himself born again into a new world, and have gained a new outlook.

2. *Is it impossible that John, a 'pillar' Apostle* (*Gal* 2⁹), *who so favoured the claims of the circumcision, should also have written such an anti-Judaic Gospel?* — Yet even then he cordially recognized, by the giving of the right hand of fellowship, St. Paul's mission to the Gentiles. Does the love for his own nation not breathe in the emphasis he lays in the Fourth Gospel on the tragedy of their rejection of Christ? The effect of the destruction of Jerusalem must have been very great on a mind like John's, and the Gospel was written forty years after that event. None of the other Evangelists lays such stress on the teaching of events as the Fourth. In Ephesus also he would breathe the atmosphere of the Pauline gospel, full of thoughts of the sovereignty of God, the condescension of the Divine grace, and the universality of the gospel message. He who

* For arguments against the Ephesian residence, see Drummond, Sanday, Stanton, and art. JOHN THE APOSTLE.

beheld the awe-inspiring vision of the Risen Christ in Patmos, might well, in the calm of later years, write the majestic words of the Prologue.

III. *RELATION TO THE SYNOPTIC GOSPELS.*— It is impossible to doubt that the Fourth Evangelist presupposes that his readers are acquainted with the contents of the first three Gospels, or that he himself is acquainted with them. We shall confine ourselves in this discussion to *certain points of divergence* between John and the Synoptics.

1. The scene of the ministry of Christ is for the most part confined to Jerusalem. The Galilæan ministry is referred to in 2^{12} $6^{1.\ 59}$ 7^1 21^1. We are not now concerned with the demand for chronological correspondence with the Synoptic account. It will be sufficient to show that there is no inconsistency in the prominence given in this Gospel to the events in Jerusalem. The Judæan ministry is presupposed in Lk 4^{44}, but the reading is doubtful. Scribes and Pharisees came from Jerusalem to attend on the Galilæan ministry (Lk 5^{17}, Mk 3^{22} 7^1). Judas was a native of Kerioth, in Judæa. The friendship of Joseph of Arimathæa, who in all probability resided in Jerusalem, has to be explained. The relations with Martha and Mary point to frequent visits to Bethany. We have also the 'How often'! of Mt 23^{37} and Lk $13^{22.\ 33.\ 34}$, which indicates not merely unfulfilled desire, but baffled effort. After the Ascension the disciples make their headquarters in Jerusalem. It is well-nigh impossible to explain the attitude of the authorities, and many incidents of the closing days (*e.g.* the friend at whose house the Supper was eaten), unless by the Johannine accounts of the visits to Jerusalem. The Synoptics tell us of only one Passover, but events could hardly have ripened there as they did unless Jesus had been previously known in Jerusalem.

2. Certain incidents are omitted in St. John which in the Synoptics are crises in the life of Christ.— The omission of the *Temptation* narrative is perhaps not strange in one who knew the mind of Jesus so intimately. The beloved disciple would be well qualified to understand the parabolic nature of the story. The essence of the Temptation narrative is the possession of Divine power and the refusal to use it for selfish ends. Similarly, Christ's freedom of action, especially in regard to His death, is frequently emphasized in the Fourth Gospel (cf. $10^{17.\ 18}$). The outward glory of the *Transfiguration* is merged in a higher glory, which is seen in the communicating of Life and Light to men (1^4). As regards the omission of the narrative of the institution of the *Lord's Supper*, it was no doubt unnecessary, at the time at which the Gospel was written, to repeat words that were in common use in the Church. The inner meaning of the sacrament is perhaps displayed in ch. 6, and throughout chs. 13–17, as an abiding union with Christ, and the redemptive death is emphasized elsewhere in the Gospel. It is possible that there had been creeping into the Church superstitious views of the ordinance, and the author is concerned both to bring out the spiritual meaning and to show that the ideas usually connected solely with the institution, of eating and drinking the flesh and blood of Christ, were already familiar to His disciples. It is the washing of the disciples' feet in the Fourth Gospel to which a symbolic meaning is attached (13^{6-10}). The Fourth Evangelist omits the *Agony in the Garden*. It is suggested that he would regard it as incompatible with the dignity of the Logos, and damaging to his conception of the Person of Christ. Certainly the Christ of the Fourth Gospel retains no trace of the Agony when at His word the Roman soldiers fall back on the ground. The Intercessory Prayer also preserves 'an imperial calm.' Yet we must take into account such statements as $12^{27.\ 28}$,

and the recalling of the very words of the Agony in 18^{11}. Moreover, it is untrue to say that the Fourth Evangelist regards bodily weakness as incompatible with the Logos. Jesus sits at Jacob's well tired and weary (4^6), He weeps at the grave of Lazarus, and thirsts on the cross (19^{28}). The last passage gives us a key to the author's attitude in reference to the person of Christ. Jesus spoke the words in full consciousness ('knowing,' etc., *i.e.* they were not *wrung* from Him), and in speaking them fulfils a great Divine purpose ('that the scripture might be fulfilled'). In his picture of Jesus upon earth, the Evangelist brings out in strong relief attributes of His Person which presented themselves to him in their full significance only through his experience of the Risen Christ. The two conceptions of Christ's humanity and Divinity are naïvely set side by side (cf. 6^6 12^{30} $11^{5.\ 6.\ 41.\ 42}$).

The reverse side of the question is presented in the miracle of the *Raising of Lazarus*. Here the Fourth Evangelist inserts an occurrence which is also a crisis in the last days, and yet the Synoptics do not mention it. The contradiction is partly resolved if we remember that the Synoptic account may really be reduced to one original document closely corresponding to our Gospel of St. Mark, and containing recollections of the preaching of St. Peter. Again, the mere fact that a miracle of raising from the dead has been omitted need excite no surprise. Jairus' daughter also was dead. The difficulty is that the miracle should be one of such central importance in the working out of the end. It may be that in the preaching of the early Apostles, which is the basis for the oral tradition of the Synoptics, the incident would not be dwelt on, considering the hatred provoked against Lazarus himself (12^{10}). At all events, the extraordinary knowledge displayed by the Fourth Evangelist of the situation, in the closing days at Jerusalem, leads to the presumption that he is right in the place he gives to the miracle.

3. The date of the Last Supper.— All the Synoptics agree in putting the Last Supper on the evening of 'the first day of unleavened bread,' *i.e.* on the evening which began Passover day, according to Jewish reckoning (Mt $26^{17.\ 20}$, Mk $14^{12.\ 17}$, Lk $22^{7.\ 14}$). Thus the day of the Crucifixion is the Passover day, or 15th Nisan. On the other hand, the Fourth Gospel regards the day of the Crucifixion as identical with the day of Preparation for the Passover ($19^{14.\ 31.\ 42}$). The rulers would not enter the Prætorium lest they be prevented by defilement from eating the Passover (18^{28}). Jn 13^1 puts the Supper 'before the feast of the Passover.' Elaborate and ingenious attempts have been made to bring either the Synoptics into harmony with the Fourth Gospel or *vice versa*. No successful attempt has yet been made to reconcile the two accounts chronologically, and it does not appear probable that any solution can be found in that direction. The only points on which all four are agreed are that our Lord suffered on a Friday (but see Westcott, *Introd. to Study of Gospels*, p. 322), and rose again on the following Sunday. We must choose between the Crucifixion on the 14th Nisan (John) or on 15th Nisan (Synoptics).

There are two questions that call for answer. (1) Is this Friday Passover day (*i.e.* 15th Nisan according to Jewish reckoning from sunset to sunset)? (2) Is the Supper held on the evening of Friday the regular Paschal meal?

(1) There are various internal contradictions in the Synoptic account. Chwolson has challenged the accuracy of the expression 'the first day of unleavened bread' as applied to the day of preparation. He holds that the words can strictly be used only of the first day of the Passover week, *i.e.* of Passover day itself. It was the case, however, that the leaven began to be removed from Jewish houses in the daytime of the 14th Nisan, and this would be sufficient to account for the phrase. Again, we are told that the Sanhedrin determined to avoid putting Jesus to death during the feast (Mk 14^2). Did they change their plans? (Mk $14^{12.\ 17}$ and $^{43-46}$). Peter is armed, and

the servants of the high priest are accompanied by an armed band. This was, strictly speaking, contrary to Jewish law on the Passover days ; but the situation might well be regarded as exceptional. It is not so easy to believe that a hurried meeting of the Sanhedrin would be held immediately after partaking of the Paschal meal. Simon of Cyrene is coming up out of the country (Mk 15²¹)—not necessarily from his work, which would, of course, indicate that it was not yet Passover, but more probably to purify himself for the Passover (Jn 11⁵⁵). Again, it is not easy to account for the haste with which it was sought to take down the body of Christ (Mk 15⁴²), unless the Passover was imminent. Joseph buys fine linen, and lays the body in the tomb, which could scarcely be done on Passover day. These considerations serve to show that the Synoptic account is at least uncertain. Thus there are also indications in the Synoptic story that go to confirm the clear statement of the Fourth Gospel that Jesus ate the Supper and was crucified on the day of Preparation for the Passover. The only argument against the Johannine position is that urged by Baur and his school, that an attempt is made, in a theological interest, to show that Jesus died on the day on which the Passover lamb was slain.

(2) If we accept the Johannine view, it follows that the Last Supper was not the regular Paschal meal. It is remarkable that in none of the Gospels is there mention of the lamb. John expressly distinguishes the Supper from the Passover (13¹ᶠ·). At the same time it must not be forgotten that in Lk. Christ speaks of the meal as a Passover (22¹⁵), and in such a way as to imply that there was some foreboding in His mind that they would not celebrate the Passover together on the legal day. The *Chronicon Paschale*, quoting Clement of Alexandria, says that the disciples learned that Jesus was Himself the Lamb, the food and the wine of the feast. St. Paul seems to imply that he identified in his mind the Crucifixion with the sacrifice of the Paschal lamb (1 Co 5⁷). If the Supper is meant by Jesus to anticipate the Passover meal, the shifting of the day would have as its secondary cause the haste with which the final preparations for arrest were made. At the same time it is hardly correct to say that the Fourth Evangelist is himself conscious of discrepancy with the Synoptics. Otherwise the phrase in 13¹ would have been more exact. His references (13¹ 19¹⁴·³¹·⁴²) rather imply that a definite tradition is before him.

(An exhaustive discussion of the question will be found in Hastings' *DB* ii. p. 711 ; Drummond, *op. cit.* pp. 47-59. See also artt. DATES, LAST SUPPER, LORD'S SUPPER).

4. The conception of miracles.—In the Fourth Gospel the miracles are interpreted as manifestations of Christ's glory, with the view of calling attention to His Person. In the Synoptics they are performed as the outcome of His compassion. St. John certainly lays stress on the evidential aspect of the miracles, but he cannot be said to overlook the motive of compassion. Jesus created wine to add to the happiness of a perplexed marriage party (2¹·¹¹). 'Whence shall we buy bread, that these may eat?' is a question full of tender feeling (6⁵). After their discouraging and chilling interviews with the Jews, Jesus 'found' both the sick man of Bethesda and the man born blind (5¹⁴ 9³⁵), and spoke further words of spiritual healing. The allegory of the Good Shepherd is spoken for the sake of the excommunicated man, and breathes compassion (10¹⁻¹⁸). The Evangelist guards against the delay of two days being interpreted as a want of compassionate love for the sisters of Lazarus (11⁵). There is nothing in the high claims of Jesus inconsistent with the Synoptic account. Compare the lofty claim that is implied in the sending forth of the Apostles in Mt 10, and the impression produced by His calming of the storm (Mk 4⁴¹). Note the tenderness and solicitude for the troubled and sorrowful disciples in the valedictory discourses (cf., further, 5⁴⁰ 6²⁷ 10⁹ and Mt 11²⁵⁻³⁰, Lk 10²¹⁻²²). We may admit that there is 'a certain heightening of the effect,' as, for example, when we are told that the man at Bethesda had been a cripple for thirty-eight years, and that Lazarus was four days in the tomb. On the other hand, this Gospel is alone in declaring that the miraculous is an inferior kind of evidence (14¹⁰⁻¹⁴, cf. 2²³⁻²⁵).

5. The picture of the Baptist has been regarded as inconsistent with the Synoptics. Sometimes, indeed, the Baptist speaks in the manner of the Evangelist, but it has to be remembered that only one aspect of the Baptist, viz. his witness to the Person of Christ, is emphasized. Baldensperger has contended (*Prolog des vierten Evangelium*) that the Gospel is written with the purpose of combating

a sect in Asia Minor who were inclined to exalt the claims of the Baptist above those of Jesus. If we modify his statement so far as to admit that this is *one* of the aims of the Gospel, and that it has in view such a sect as we are told of in Ac 18²⁴-19⁷, we are provided with the means of explaining the striking introduction of the Baptist as 'a man' sent from God (1⁶) ; his being contrasted with the Logos in the Prologue ; why he is represented in the Fourth Gospel solely as directing his disciples to Jesus (1³⁶) ; why it is stated that the Baptist's work and Christ's went on simultaneously, and that Jesus did not merely take up John's work where he left it (3²²⁻³⁰); why the baptism of Jesus is mentioned in such a way as to exclude the conferring of any charism on Him by the Baptist (1³¹⁻³³).

6. It is urged as an objection to the Fourth Gospel that there is **a lack of development in connexion with the claims of Jesus.** At the very beginning He is hailed as the Messiah (1⁴¹·⁴⁵), and as Son of God (1³⁴·⁴⁹). He reveals Himself as Messiah to the Samaritan woman (4²⁶). A process of development, however, is represented (*e.g.* 2²²) as going on in the minds of the disciples, and the transition is easy, from remembering what Jesus had said, to unconsciously mingling with the actual narrative the expansion of the meaning of words and events through time. Moreover, the narrative moves in growing cycles of belief and disbelief. His reply to His mother (2⁴), His brethren's insinuation (7³·⁴), His own words in 7¹⁷, the reproof of Philip (14⁹), and the speculations of the crowd (7¹²·²⁶·²⁷), all indicate that the understanding of men did not keep pace with His own declarations. In this Gospel we still find the echo of the *Messiasgeheimniss* (10²⁴; cf. Sanday, *op. cit.* pp. 162-165). Again, is it not to be expected that if a Fourth Gospel was thought necessary, it would present a somewhat different aspect of Christ's claims and teaching? The Synoptics tell us how Jesus taught the audiences of Galilæan peasants. The Fourth Gospel deals largely with the experience of individuals, and of the inner group of disciples, and the way in which Christ's claims were met by the authorities at Jerusalem (cf. Dods, *Expos. Gr. Test.* Introduction, pp. 671-676).

IV. *HISTORICITY OF THE GOSPEL.*—Clement of Alexandria described the Gospel as 'spiritual,' in contrast to the Synoptics, which relate the 'bodily facts' concerning Christ. In the Prologue itself we have an example of the way in which statements of spiritual truth and historical fact are characteristically interwoven, and the Evangelist tells us that he aims at presenting, out of the fulness of his knowledge, such an impression of Christ and of His teaching 'that ye may believe' (20³⁰·³¹). Can we understand more clearly from the character of the Gospel itself the impulses that actuated his mind? Can we in any measure detach the ideal element from the historical in the Gospel?

1. The narrative of events.—(1) *There are many signs in the Gospel that the author is narrating facts in which he himself had a personal interest.* He claims to be an eye-witness (1¹⁴). He gives us exact notes of time (1²⁹ 2¹ 4⁴⁰ 6²² 7¹⁴ 11⁶ 12¹ 19³¹ 20¹). The hour of the day is mentioned (1³⁹ 4⁶ 19¹⁴). Similarly, exact numbers are given (1³⁵ 2⁶ 6⁹·¹⁰·¹⁹ 4¹⁸ 19²³·³⁹). The significance of these marks of real recollection is increased by the fact that they occur chiefly in connexion with incidents of critical importance in the life of Jesus or in the experience of His followers. Note the accurate chronology dealing with the rise of faith in the Apostolic circle (1-2¹¹), and with the Passion week (18-20). This Evangelist alone tells us of 'the *barley* loaves' (6⁹·¹³), that Mary 'fell down at his feet'(11³²), of 'the house filled with the fragrance of the ointment' (12³). Note also such personal impressions as 13²⁴ 18⁶ 19⁵. These touches are introduced spontaneously, forming an integral part of the consciousness of the writer.

Again, it is evident that a selection has been made out of a number of incidents that were available ($20^{30.\ 31}$). Incidents related in detail in the Synoptics are implied (7^{42} 3^{24} $1^{32.\ 33}$). Barabbas is mentioned without introduction, and the single comment, 'Now Barabbas was a robber,' is full of suppressed meaning (18^{40}). The trial before Caiaphas is not described. Two great miracles are related substantially as in the Synoptics (6^{1-21}). Compare also the Anointing (12) and the Triumphal Entry (12^{12-15}). The Trial scenes and the Crucifixion correspond in the main with the Synoptics. The Denial of Peter gains in verisimilitude by being broken up into separate incidents. The Baptist's words in 3^{29} are confirmed by Mt 9^{15}. The Baptist's ministry is implied in $10^{40.\ 41}$.

(2) *The Evangelist describes himself not as a biographer, but as a 'witness.'* He brings forward others as witnessing. In 21^{24}, if the order is significant, 'witnessing' is looked upon as of prior importance to 'writing.' A governing idea in the writer's mind is 'the truth,' which consists not in historical fact, but in having the mind brought into tune with the Divine facts of love and self-sacrifice. The miracles are not only actualities ($\check{\epsilon}\rho\gamma a$), they are also signs ($\sigma\eta\mu\epsilon\hat{\iota}a$). The Evangelist's mind is specially open to any suggestion of spiritual truth conveyed by the actual facts (*e.g.* $2^{11.\ 17}$). Siloam is 'sent,' the sending forth of the waters being typical, perhaps, of the Christ sent of God (9^7). Judas goes out of the light of the upper room 'into the night' (13^{30}). 'It was winter' at the Feast of the Dedication (10^{22}), symbolizing the storm of hatred and the chill of indifference that met the warmth of Jesus' love. The use made of the sign in $19^{35\text{ff.}}$ is also typical of the Evangelist's mind. The reflective character of the writing is seen in the frequent use of $\check{\iota}\nu a$ and $o\mathring{\upsilon}\nu$ as connective particles. He emphasizes on various occasions the doctrine of a higher purpose running through the history (*e.g.* 11^{51}; cf. 'the hour,' 2^4 etc. 3^{27} 19^{28}). This idea of the sovereignty of God in events is found also in St. Paul, and is not represented in the Christian tradition solely by the Fourth Evangelist. There is also the frank confession that the disciples failed to understand some sayings and incidents at the time, and that only the Spirit, mediated through the teaching of events, revealed the hidden meaning (*e.g.* 2^{22} 12^{16}). This is in accordance with the abstract expression of the same idea in 14^{26}.

It is impossible fully to understand the author's conception of history without taking into account his clear consciousness that the gift of the Spirit of Truth must be part of the equipment for writing such a narrative as this Gospel (14^{17}, cf. 19^{35} and the use of $\mathring{a}\lambda\eta\theta\iota\nu\acute{o}s$). The theory of history that is exemplified in the Gospel is summed up in 15^{24-27}. Even the situation of distress in the Church at the time he wrote finds its interpretation only in the prophetic words of Christ (14^{29} 16^4).

With a conception of history so far removed from that of the mere chronicler, it is not surprising that the perspective of certain incidents (*e.g.* the Cleansing of the Temple) has been disturbed. There was a careful selection of those events in the life of Christ that were best fitted to illustrate in all their varying phases the belief and unbelief called forth by the Person and teaching of Jesus, but the Evangelist always starts with what he has seen (1^{14}). There are some difficulties of sequence that would be removed by giving a different order to the narrative; *e.g.* 'Arise, let us go hence' (14^{31}), where the discourse is resumed in ch. 15. Again, the discourse in 7^{15-24} would be eminently in place at the end of ch. 5. These transpositions might have taken place through various causes after the

document had left the writer's hands (see Bacon, *Introduction*, pp. 271-274).

2. The discourses. — There are differences in style and in length between the discourses of Christ in the Fourth Gospel and those in the Synoptics. At first sight they seem far removed in character. Yet nothing could be farther from the truth than to say that the personal contribution of the Evangelist in the discourses is more apparent than his desire to reproduce the exact words of Jesus, or that he makes use of the Synoptics in mechanical fashion. He has preserved one or two isolated sayings (1^{43} 5^8 6^{20} $13^{21.\ 38}$ 20^{19}) which are also found in the Synoptics, and the discourse in 5^{19-47} contains many coincidences of word and thought with Mt 11^{2-19}. (For other coincidences see Westcott, lxxxi.). Yet there is no sufficient evidence to warrant the hypothesis that even in these cases the Evangelist was entirely dependent on the Synoptic narratives, although it is probable that he had them before him. Even the discourses of the Fourth Gospel, when reduced to their elements, are full of short and pregnant sayings, such as we are accustomed to connect with Christ (see a most suggestive collection in Drummond, *op. cit.* p. 16 ff.). Discourses much longer than any that are found in John are to be found in the Synoptics. It is true that the style of the discourses and the style of the Evangelist are practically identical, but that may be partly due to the fact that the words of Jesus have been translated from the Aramaic. The dialogue form is more fully represented in the Fourth Gospel than in the others, which would rather make for authenticity.

There are indications in the Gospel that the Evangelist is concerned to keep his own ideas separate from those of Christ. The actual Logos idea outlined in the Prologue is never put into the mouth of Christ except as underlying His words in certain cases. He keeps separate his own explanations of words of Christ (2^{19-21} 12^{33} 7^{39}). What can only be an actual saying of Christ is represented as haunting the minds of the disciples in 16^{14-19}. Again, in 12^{44-50}, in the midst of a passage containing his own reflexions, there is a summary containing a free rendering of words of Christ that are repeated elsewhere in the Gospel; 14^2 would seem to indicate that the same ideas had been expressed before, and would be familiar to the disciples.

On the other hand, it is clear that it is not the concern of this Evangelist to record the precise phrase that 'once for a moment ruffled the air of Palestine.' 'The words that I speak unto you, they are spirit, and they are life' (6^{63}). At one point the disciples think they understand clearly the words they hear, but Jesus shows them their ignorance still ($16^{29\text{ff.}}$). The teaching by parables appears only as transformed into allegory. In 10^{1-18} the image and the interpretation are inextricably intermingled. In some of the discourses the meaning is carried up to a certain point, and is then repeated like a *motif*, as though the Evangelist sought to express himself more clearly (*e.g.* the valedictory discourses). There are some cases where there is doubt as to where the words of Jesus end and the words of the Evangelist begin. It is conceivable that a more exact study of his language would afford us critical appliances more capable of detaching the two elements than those we now possess. Abbott, in his *Johannine Grammar* (2066*b*), has suggested that where $\gamma\acute{a}\rho$ is used as a connective it is an indication that the Evangelist is entering on his own words. This would certainly suit such cases as 3^{15} 4^9 $5^{21-23.\ 26.\ 27}$. At the same time, whatever further grammatical study may reveal, we must be prepared to regard the Johannine tradition of the words of Christ as differing in many aspects from that of the Synoptics. On the other hand, affinities are found in earlier NT writings with the words of Christ as reported in the Fourth Gospel (cf. 1 P 5$^{2-4}$ and Jn 10^1, 1 P 2^{25} and Jn 10^{16} ; also 1 P 1$^{8, 23}$, Ro 6^{16} and Jn 8^{34} ; Gal 5^{17} and 5^{36}, Eph 2$^{13ff.}$ and Jn 10^{16} ; Ph 2^5 and Jn 10^{17}), and in all probability the question of the historicity of the words of Christ is not a problem peculiar to the Fourth Gospel (see P. Ewald, *Das Hauptproblem der Evangelienfrage*). The dialogues with the Jews in this Gospel have taken on the abstract form that we should expect if they had often been orally repeated by the Evangelist in his preaching, before they were written down. The discourses themselves are definitely connected with historical situations, and may, in some cases, be the expansion of fragmentary reminiscences. On the other hand, the gaps in the thought seem sometimes to point to abridgement. The problem is the same as in the case of the Sermon on the Mount. The valedictory discourses have no doubt taken their continuous form through the welding together of recollections of the closing days, suggested by the desire to make plain to the early Church that her present condition of anxiety and distress was anticipated with solicitous forethought in the prophetic words of the Saviour. The prayer in ch 17 is the prayer of One who has become the Great High Priest of His Church and of humanity. There is no reason for denying that the mind of the writer had a place in the composition of these. The spiritual equipment of the Evangelist is the guarantee for the fidelity of his psychological attitude as a 'witness,' and we must be prepared to trust not only the man himself, but above all his peculiar and intimate knowledge of the mind of Christ. We may thus reverently examine the material of which his unique spiritual experience is composed, but may well refrain from dividing a seamless robe.

LITERATURE.—Full bibliographies will be found in Luthardt, *St. John the Author of the Fourth Gospel* (by C. P. Gregory); Reynolds in Hastings' *DB* ii. pp. 721–722 ; a survey of modern literature in Loisy, *Le Quatrième Évangile*, p. 36 ff. ; a critical account of recent literature in Sanday, *Criticism of the Fourth Gospel*, pp. 1–32.

1. The most important works hostile to the traditional view of the authorship are : Bretschneider, *Probabilia*, 1820 ; Strauss, *Leben Jesu*, 1835–1840 [mythical view]; Baur, *Die Kanonischen Evangelien*, 1847 [date A.D. 170, tendency criticism]; Keim, *Jesu von Nazara*, 1867 [written by a Jewish Christian, 110–115, under name of Apostle John]; J. J. Tayler, *An Attempt to ascertain the Character of the Fourth Gospel*, 1867 ; *Supernatural Religion*, 1874 [replied to by Lightfoot, *Cont. Rev.*, Dec. 1874, Jan. 1875 ; Sanday, *Gospels in Second Century*; Luthardt, *St. John the author of Fourth Gospel*, 1875]; Albrecht Thoma, *Die Genesis der Johann. Evang.* 1882 [Gospel an Alexandrian allegory of Philonic character]; Oscar Holtzmann, 1887 [specially valuable for Jewish element in Gospel]; H. J. Holtzmann, *Handcom. zum NT*, 1893 ; Jean Réville, *Le Quatrième Évangile*, 1901 [unknown author; 'beloved disciple' not an individual but an ideal type]; Moffatt, *Historical NT*, 1901 ; Schmiedel in *Encyc. Bibl.* ii. art. 'John, son of Zebedee,' and 'Die Johann. Schriften' in *Religionsgeschichtliche Volksbücher*; Wrede, *Charakter und Tendenz*, 1903 ; Loisy, *Le Quatrième Évangile*, 1903.

2. A mediating position is represented by : Weisse, *Ev. Geschichte*, 1838, *Die Evangelische Frage*, 1856 [discourses and prologue Apostolic]; C. Weizsäcker, *Untersuchungen*, 1864, reprinted 1901 [written by disciple of John; narratives and discourses in substance historical, but contains a large ideal element]; Renan, *Vie de Jésus*, 1863 [practically abandons the historicity of discourses, but retains narrative as fundamentally Johannine]; Hugo Delff, *Grundzüge des Entwickelungs-Geschichte d. Religion*, 1883, *Das vierte Evangelium*, and *Neue Beiträge*, 1890 ; Jülicher, *Einleitung*, 1901 (tr. 1904); B. W. Bacon, *Introduction*, 1902 ; Wendt, *Lehre Jesu*, 1886, i. 215–342, *Das Johannesevangelium*, 1900 (translated) [a development of the partition theory of Weisse ; criticised by Wauchope Stewart in *Expositor*, Jan., Feb. 1903, and Drummond, *Character and Authorship*, pp. 399–404]; Harnack, *Chronologie d. altchrist. Litteratur*, vol. i.

3. The Apostolic authorship is maintained by : Neander, *Life of Christ* ; Luthardt, *op. cit.* ; Andrews Norton, *Genuineness of the Four Gospels* [all three in answer to Strauss]; Bleek, *Einleitung*, 1862, tr. [in answer to Baur]; Pressensé, *Jésus Christ : son Temps, sa Vie*, etc.; Sabatier, *Essai sur les sources de la Vie de Jésus* ; Godet, *Introd. and Com.* (1864, tr. 1896, posthumous edition, 1901) [still most valuable in every direction]; R. H. Hutton in *Essays Theological and Literary*, 1871 [defending historical credibility against Baur]; Sanday, *Authorship and Historical*

Character of the Fourth Gospel, 1872 ; M. Arnold, *God and the Bible* (from *Contemp. Review*, 1875); Willibald Beyschlag, *Zur johann. Frage*, 1876, *NT Theol.* (Eng. tr. i. 216–221); Salmon, *Historical Introduction*, 1885 ; Westcott, *Introd. and Com.* 1881 [classical]; Reynolds, *Pulpit Commentary*, and art. in Hastings' *DB* ; Watkins, *Bampton Lectures*, 1890 [specially valuable for external evidence]; P. Ewald, *Das Hauptproblem der Evangelienfrage*, 1890 [seeks to show that the Johannine element has a fundamental place in the entire Evangelic tradition of four Gospels]; Gloag, *Introd. to the Johann. Writings*, 1891 [containing valuable summary of positions]; Volume of Essays by Ezra Abbot, A. P. Peabody, J. B. Lightfoot, 1892 ; B. Weiss, *Einleitung* (tr. 1888), *Das Johann. Evang.* 1897 ; Marcus Dods, *Expos. Gr. Test.* vol. i. 1897 ; Zahn, *Einleitung*[2], 1899 ; Drummond, *Character and Authorship of the Fourth Gospel*, 1903 [very significant owing to the theological position of the writer ; especially suggestive in treatment of external evidence ; displays tendency towards allegorical interpretation]; Stanton, *Gospels as Historical Documents*, i. 1903 [external evidence]; Sanday, *Criticism of the Fourth Gospel*, 1905 [containing surveys and estimates of recent theories, and valuable criticism of critical methods]; Barth, *Biblischen Zeit- und Streitfragen*, 'Das Johann. evang. und die Synopt. Evang.' 1903.

The series of volumes by Edwin Abbott, entitled 'Diatessarica' (esp. *From Letter to Spirit*, 1903 ; *Johannine Vocabulary*, 1905 ; *Johannine Grammar*, 1906), contains much fresh matter, suggested by an elaborate study of the language of the Fourth Gospel.

Among articles in magazines may be mentioned W. Milligan in *Contemp. Review* (Sept. 1867, Aug. and Nov. 1868), and *British and Foreign Evangelical Review* (Oct. 1871) [directed against Baur and his school]; Schürer, *Contemp. Review*, 1891 [a review of the position of the problem ; replied to by Sanday, Oct. 1891]; Bacon, *Hibbert Journal*, April 1903, Jan. 1904, 1905 [has developed theory of editorship by author of 1–3 Jn. and ch. 21]; three important articles on conservative side by an anonymous writer in the *Church Quarterly Review*, 1905–1906. The monograph by Schwarz, *Ueber den Tod der Söhne Zebedæi*, 1904, while completely hostile to the traditional view, is valuable for certain portions of the external evidence.

R. H. STRACHAN.

JOHN, GOSPEL OF (II.: Contents).—**1. Character of the Gospel.**—The interesting fragment of Eusebius (*HE* vi. 14), quoted from the lost 'Outlines' of Clement of Alexandria, gives us the earliest view which was taken of the Fourth Gospel. 'John, last, having observed that the bodily things had been set forth in the [earlier] Gospels, and exhorted thereto by his friends, and inspired by the Spirit, produced a *spiritual* Gospel.' The word 'spiritual,' or 'pneumatic,' is here, as usually with the Alexandrians, opposed to 'bodily,' or 'somatic.' And what the difference was, as regards the records of the past, is shown admirably by Origen's comment on Jn 2^{12}. He says that if all the four Gospels are to be believed, the truth of them cannot be in their 'bodily characters,' but in their spiritual meaning. The Gospels, he says elsewhere (*de Princ.* 4), contain many things which are said to have happened, but which did not happen literally ; and in one place of his Commentary on St. John he says that when the writers of Holy Scripture were unable to speak the truth 'at once spiritually and bodily' (*i.e.* at once literally and with a deeper symbolical or allegorical meaning), it was their practice to prefer the spiritual to the corporeal, 'the true spiritual meaning being often preserved in the corporeal falsehood' (σωζομένου πολλάκις τοῦ ἀληθοῦς πνευματικοῦ ἐν τῷ σωματικῷ ψευδεῖ). So Epiphanius says of St. John's Gospel : 'most of the things spoken by him were spiritual, the fleshly things having been already attested' (*Hær.* li. 19).

These passages are very important for the study of the Fourth Gospel. They are evidence, not, of course, for the author's method of composition, but for what was thought of the Gospel in the latter part of the 2nd cent. and the first half of the 3rd, that is to say, as soon as it was widely known. It was accepted as 'a spiritual Gospel,' and by spiritual was meant, not devotional, ethical, and philosophical, but allegorical as opposed to barely historical.

The distinction between the two modes of treatment was familiar at Alexandria, and had been familiar long before the Fourth Gospel was written. Philo compares the literal mean ing to the body, and the spiritual to the soul. He applies this exegetical principle to the OT narratives with great thoroughness. To the literal truth of ancient sacred history he is very indifferent. Particular events are important only in proportion to their universal significance. To grasp the truth of a narrative is to see its relation to universal spiritual law or fact. He would have considered the laborious investigation of historical detail to be merely learned trifling, worthy only of a grammarian or a pedant. Moral edification and gnosis were the only objects for which it was at all worth while to trouble about the records of the past.

We have, of course, no right to assume that the 2nd cent. was right in classing the Fourth Gospel as a 'spiritual' work. We shall have to consider its allegorism in detail before we can pronounce on its relation to history. But it should be perfectly obvious that its author did not mean it to be studied as a plain historical narrative. He would probably have said that he had a higher aim than to record trivial details, some of which had no spiritual meaning. The Gospel is, and claims to be, an *interpretation* of our Lord's Person and ministry, an ideal construction which aims at producing a certain impression about the Person of Christ. This impression is to be the *true* interpretation of the historical Jesus—the author is infinitely anxious about this. He is writing no mere historical romance, like the Life of Apollonius of Tyana, which was afterwards concocted as a rival to the Gospels. He is no Docetist, as is shown by several passages in the Gospel, and more categorically in 1 John, which, if not by the same author, is in closest connexion with the Gospel. But a very slight critical investigation is enough to show that he allows himself a free hand in manipulating the facts on which he is working. It is perfectly honest history, as history was understood by the ancients. But even the most scientific of ancient historians did not scruple to put his own views of the political situation into the mouths of the chief characters in his period; and among the Jews the composer of a *haggādah* had no fear of being branded as a romancer or a forger.

The plan of the Gospel is clearly stated in 20[30. 31], an impressive passage which was intended to be the conclusion of the book, and was so until the appendix was added. The object here avowed is strictly adhered to throughout. No other book of the NT is so entirely dominated by one conception. The theology of the Incarnation, taught in the form of a historical narrative, with an underlying framework of symbolism and allegory, which, though never obtruded, determines the whole arrangement and selection of incidents—this is the topic of the Fourth Gospel. And unless it is read in the light of this purpose, and with a due recognition of the peculiar method, the seven seals of the Apocalypse will remain set upon the 'spiritual Gospel.'

Different opinions have been held as to the readers whom the writer has mainly in view. Réville thinks that 'the author has wished to prove to his contemporaries who had remained in the liberal and philosophical Judaism of the Diaspora, that, in Jesus Christ, the revelation of the Logos, admitted by them in the OT, has its full and definitive fulfilment.' But the Gospel is not an *apologia* written for the Jews. The extremely unconciliatory tone, used throughout in speaking of them, is enough to disprove this hypothesis. There is a subordinate element of apologetic, but the main object is clearly to edify and teach the faithful, not to convert the unbeliever. The author never descends to his opponents' ground, but remains throughout on his own. His aim is didactic, but not exactly dogmatic. He wishes, not to prove a theological thesis, but to confirm and perfect the believer in his adhesion to Christ as the Incarnate Word, the principle of spiritual regeneration, and the nourishment of 'eternal' life. This is the

foundation of his own faith, and the characteristic Johannine ideas are the intellectual form of this faith, which is centred in the *unio mystica*. There is no sign of a polemic against Docetism, Ebionism, or against Cerinthus. Still less is he writing against liberalized Judaism, as Réville seems to suggest. Whatever was his attitude towards Philo (and the question is not an easy one to answer), it was not one of conscious antagonism.

The author, then, is writing for Christians. But for what Christians? It has often been maintained or assumed that his object is to teach a philosophy of religion—that he is, in fact, the author of the formula 'Jesus Christ, the promised Messiah of the Jews, is the Incarnate Logos of God.' But this view is untenable. There is no systematic philosophy in the Gospel—not even in the Prologue. And besides, the Logos theology was not new. It is not propounded as new in the Gospel; and it exists in substance in St. Paul's Epistles, as well as in the Hebrews. There can be little doubt that Apollos, the learned Jew of Alexandria, made this identification in his preaching, which was so mightily convincing. For at this time 'Logos' was as familiar a term to all educated persons as 'Evolution' is to our own generation.

The Gospel is not a philosophical treatise. Is it, then, an attempt to *mediate* between two parties in the Church, between the advocates of 'Faith' and 'Knowledge,' of Gnosis and Pistis? The conflict between these two parties was acute at the end of the 2nd cent., as we see from the caution imposed upon Clement of Alexandria by conservative prejudice, and on the other side by the diatribes of the obscurantist Tertullian against philosophy. At that period Gnosticism had gained a footing within the Church, and orthodoxy had become alive to the dangers which threatened the Christian religion from this side. The intellectualists were even strong enough to drive Montanism out of the Church. During the first quarter of the 2nd cent. the great Gnostics were outside the Church, and the chief danger was that the party of $\psi\iota\lambda\dot{\eta}$ $\pi\iota\sigma\tau\iota\varsigma$, ignorant and superstitious, with materialistic notions of religion and hopes of a coming reign of the saints, might make the position of the Christian philosopher impossible, and drive him into the arms of the Gnostics. Moreover, at the time when the Gospel was written, the inadequacy of *both* presentations of Christianity was becoming apparent. The primitive revivalism was decaying; the hopes of a Parousia were growing faint; while, on the other hand, Docetism and the fantastic schemes of the Gnostic party were visibly tending to discard the Gospel in favour of a barbarized Platonism. The author of this Gospel interposed his powerful influence to save Christianity from being either swamped in a mythology or sublimated into a theosophy. 'The Jews' demanded miracles, 'the Greeks' a philosophy; this Gospel, like St. Paul, presents both with 'Christ the power of God and the wisdom of God' (1 Co 1[22-24]). The author addresses himself chiefly to the Faith-party, who most needed teaching. He tries to recall them to real history, by subtly spiritualizing the miraculous narratives, to which they attributed too much importance, and bringing out their ethical and spiritual significance. He never makes the slightest attempt to rationalize a miracle,—on the contrary, the miracles which he records are more startling than anything in the Synoptics,—but no stress is laid on any physical portent as momentous in and for itself, or as evidence, apart from its symbolical value as a type of the Person, work, and office of Christ. This design of spiritualizing the tradition is kept in view throughout; but it is carried out so subtly and quietly that it has often been overlooked.

A glance at one of the old-fashioned 'Harmonies' of the four Evangelists makes us realize how few of the events of our Lord's life, before the last few days, are recorded by the Synoptists and also by St. John. And even the few common elements are employed differently, and in different settings. There are notable and irreconcilable differences in the chronology, including, as is well known, a discrepancy as to the date of the Crucifixion. The development of Christ's mission is differently conceived, the Johannine Christ making the most exalted claims to equality with the Father near the beginning of His career, and in the presence of His enemies (2^{19} 6^{40} 8^{58} etc.), whereas in the Synoptics the question and answer at Cæsarea Philippi are clearly intended to be of crucial importance (Mt $16^{13\mathrm{ff.}}$ ||). The form and substance of the discourses are also very different, the Christ of the Synoptics speaking as a man to men, as a Jew to Jews ; conveying His message in pithy aphorisms, easily understood and remembered, and in homely parables, adapted to the comprehension of country folk. These discourses are directed rather to bringing men to the Father, and to righteousness and consistency of life, than to inculcating any doctrines about His own Person ; sometimes He expresses His attachment to the Law, and repudiates any intention of abrogating it. Our Evangelist, on the other hand, represents Jesus as taking part in long polemical disputations with 'the Jews,' who are as much His enemies as they were the enemies of the Christian Church 80 years later ; the parables have disappeared, and their place is taken by 'proverbs' or symbolic language ; and, above all, His whole teaching is centred upon faith in and devotion to Himself. The emphatic ἐγώ occurs 15 times in St. Matthew, 117 times in St. John. Many facts to which our Evangelist attaches great importance are completely strange to the Synoptic tradition. Such are : the marriage in Cana of Galilee, with which the public ministry opens ; the conversation with the Samaritan woman ; the healing of the paralytic at the pool of Bethesda ; the incident of the man born blind ; the raising of Lazarus, which in St. John's Gospel appears to have been the immediate cause of the plot against the life of Jesus ; the washing of the disciples' feet at the Last Supper ; the conversation with Pilate at the trial ; the presence of the beloved disciple and Mary at the Cross ; the appearance to Thomas after the Resurrection. On the other hand, the writer of the Fourth Gospel omits the genealogy and the birth from a virgin, because it could be of no interest to him to prove that Jesus (or rather Joseph) was descended from king David, and the Incarnation of the Logos is a far grander conception than a miraculous birth. by the operation of the Holy Ghost ; he omits the Baptism of Jesus, of which notwithstanding he shows knowledge, because, again, the true Baptism is the Incarnation of the Logos in Jesus, and also partly, perhaps, because he is anxious to discountenance the Adoptionist views of the Person of Christ which were prevalent at the time when he wrote ; he omits the Temptation, because it is no part of his plan to exhibit Jesus as experiencing any temptation or weakness ; he omits the Transfiguration, because in his view the whole life of Christ on earth is a manifestation of His glory, not by visible light but to the spiritual eye ; he omits the institution of the Eucharist, because he has already given his sacramental doctrine in his discourse about the Bread of Life (Jn $6^{26\mathrm{ff.}}$), following the miracle of the 5000, and does not wish the truth of the mystical union to be bound up too closely with the participation in an ecclesiastical rite ; he omits the Agony in the Garden of Gethsemane, and the cry, 'Eli, Eli, lama sabachthani,' because the impression which he

wishes to convey of the complete voluntariness of Christ's sufferings and death, and of the 'glory' which was manifested by His humiliation as well as by His triumph over death, might be impaired by incidents which seem to indicate human weakness and hesitation ; and, lastly, he omits the Ascension and the descent of the Paraclete, because he does not wish the withdrawal of Christ's bodily presence, and the continuation of the Incarnation in another more spiritual form, to be associated with physical portents, or to be assigned to particular days.

There can be no question that these omissions are deliberate, and not the result of ignorance. Those who wish to discredit any of the narratives which appear in the Synoptics, cannot rightly draw any inferences from St. John's silence. Such features of the Christian tradition as the Birth at Bethlehem and the Ascension must have been well known by any well-instructed Christian at the beginning of the 2nd cent., and there are no signs that our Evangelist wishes to correct his predecessors from the standpoint of one who has had access to better information. Not only are incidents like the Baptism referred to incidentally (1^{32}), but an attempt is made to provide substitutes for several of the omitted narratives. Instead of the Davidic ancestry of Joseph, we have the eternal generation of the μονογενής ; instead of the Lord's Prayer, taught to the disciples, we have the High-Priestly prayer of ch. 17, in which almost every clause of the Lord's Prayer is represented, though in each case, except the last ('Deliver us from the evil one'), the petition is changed into a statement that the work has been done, the boon conferred. The institution of Baptism is represented by the discourses with Nicodemus and the Samaritan woman ; that of the Eucharist by the miracle in ch. 6 and the discourse on the Bread of Life which follows it. The Transfiguration is represented by the voice from heaven in $12^{7.\,28}$; while the preceding verse (which should be printed as a question, 'Shall I say, Father, save me from this hour ?') is intended to compensate us for the loss of the Agony in the Garden. Lastly, the words to Thomas in 20^{29}—the last beatitude—more than reconcile us to the loss of any description of the Ascension.

The number of miracles is much reduced ; but those which are given are representative, and in some cases are more tremendous than those of the Synoptics. The healing of the son of Herod's official ($4^{46\mathrm{ff.}}$) is the only miracle which has the true Synoptic ring ; in the others no 'faith' is required in those who are to benefit by the sign, and the object seems to be to manifest some aspect of Christ's Person and work. In the marriage at Cana, the feeding of the multitude, the healing of the blind man, and the raising of Lazarus, the Evangelist himself tells us the spiritual meaning of the miracle, in words spoken either by the Lord Himself or by some one else.

There is, however, a great deal of symbolism in the Gospel which is unexplained by the author, and unnoticed by the large majority of his readers. The method is strange to us, and we do not look out for allegories which would be at once understood by Alexandrians in the 2nd century. A few examples are necessary, to justify the view here taken that symbolism or allegorism pervades the whole Gospel. In 1^{29} John the Baptist designates Christ 'the Lamb of God,' with clear reference to the Paschal sacrifice. The prophetic type of the Paschal lamb dominates the whole of the Passion narrative in St. John. Even the date, it would appear, is altered, in order that Christ may die on the day when the Paschal lambs were killed. The change of the 'reed' of the Synoptics to 'hyssop' seems to have been made with the same object, when we remember the ritual use of hyssop at the Passover. The Gospel abounds in enigmatic utterances, such as 'Thou hast kept the good wine until now' (2^{10}); 'It is expedient that one man should die for the people' (11^{50}); 'Judas went immediately out, and it was night' (13^{30}); in which the reader is plainly meant to see a double meaning. The symbolism is often in three stages. The text presents an apparent sense, which is in figure a second, which in turn points to a third and still deeper signification. Especially in the narrative, a prophetic utterance quoted from the OT is sometimes the intermediate stage in this allegorical construction. The type of the Paschal lamb comes as it were between the literal feeding of the 5000 and the idea that Christ gives His life to take away the sin of the world, and that He may be our spiritual food and sustenance. The words quoted from the Psalms, 'the zeal of thy house shall eat me up,' come in like manner between the cleansing of the Temple at Jerusalem and the idea of the glorification of Jesus as the building of the true Temple, the body of Christ, the Church. There are, we might venture to say, three temples in the mind of the Evangelist—the material temple built by Herod, the temple of Christ's natural body, which was to be destroyed and raised up 'in three days,' and the temple which is the spiritual body of Christ—namely, the Church. Similarly, in 7^{38}, the quotation, 'out of his belly shall flow rivers of living water,' comes, as it were, between the thrust of the lance and the effusion of the Holy Spirit on the disciples and the Church.

But the most remarkable part of the allegoric method is that connected with *numbers*. There can be no doubt, in the opinion of the present writer, that the Philonic method of playing with numbers had a strong fascination for our Evangelist. The examples are far too numerous to be accidental. The number 7 recurs in the number of the miracles (omitting ch. 21 from our calculations), in the number of solemn declarations beginning 'I am'; in the number of 'witnesses' borne to Christ, and perhaps in other places. The officer's son is healed at the seventh hour; the paralytic on the seventh day. It is thoroughly in accordance with the method of the Evangelist, that he avoids the word ἑπτά, just as he avoids the two crucial words γνῶσις and πίστις, which had become watchwords of parties. As for the number 3, perhaps too much ingenuity has been shown in cutting up the whole Gospel into arrangements of 3; but unquestionably the book does lend itself very readily to such classification, and the fact that it is concealed rather than obtruded is in accordance with what seems to have been the method and design of the writer. With regard to higher numbers, the extreme precision of the Evangelist must excite suspicion of an allegorical motive; and when we find that 38, 46, and 153 can be plausibly explained on Philonic principles, the suspicion becomes almost a certainty. For example, the 153 fish may be the 'fulfilment' of $10+7$; $1+2+3+\ldots+17=153$; or, as Bishop Wordsworth suggests, it may be the square of $12+$ the square of 3. It is said that 200 (Peter is 200 cubits from the land) signifies, in the Philonian lore, repentance. The 'forty-six years' since the beginning of the building of the Temple may possibly be connected with the age assigned to Jesus ('not yet fifty years old'); it has been suggested that the Evangelist wishes to make Him seven times seven years old at the Crucifixion; but this is very doubtful. The frequent use of number-symbolism in the Gospel is more certain than the correctness of particular interpretations. These interpretations would occur readily to the 'Gnostic' of the 2nd cent.; to us they must be guesswork.

Some critics, such as Renan, have objected to this discovery of allegorism in the Fourth Gospel, that the allegorist always tries to attract attention to his symbols, whereas St. John clearly does not, but conceals them so carefully that the large majority of his readers do not even suspect their existence. This sounds plausible. But the question really is whether the Evangelist has not done all that he need have done in order to be understood by those among his first readers who knew his method. It is not suggested that the Johannine symbolism was meant for all to understand. There is abundant evidence that those who valued the 'Gnosis' were agreed that it must not be profaned by being explained to all. We find this conviction in Philo, and very strongly in Clement of Alexandria, who, as a Christian, is important evidence. He says that to put the spiritual exegesis before the common people is like giving a sword to a child to play with. He will not write all that he knows, because of the danger that it may get into wrong hands. There are some religious truths which can only be safely imparted orally. There is reason to think that he abandoned his project of putting the coping-stone on his theological works by a book of an esoteric character, because a published treatise cannot be confined to those who ought to read it. Since, then, the existence of the symbolic method, and the obligation of concealing it from the ordinary reader, are both proved, there is nothing strange in the veiled symbolism which we have found to characterize this Gospel.

The Evangelist writes throughout for two classes of readers—for the *simpliciores*, who would be satisfied by the narrative in its plain sense, and for the 'Gnostic,' who could read between the lines without difficulty. And yet he *wishes* all his readers to rise towards a spiritual understanding. Again and again he puts the key in the lock—in such solemn utterances as 'I am the Bread of Life —the Light of the World—the Resurrection and the Life.' His own word for the allegoric method is 'proverb' (παροιμία). Up to the end of the last discourse, Jesus has spoken to His disciples in proverbs; but the time was coming (after the withdrawal of His bodily presence) in which, through the medium of the Paraclete, He should no more speak to them in proverbs, but should show them plainly of the Father. The proverb is different from the Synoptic παραβολή, which is a story with a religious and moral application—a story which has a complete sense in itself, apart from the lesson, which is generally conveyed by the story as a whole, and not by the details. St. John, however, tries to keep the historical parabolic form in which Jesus actually taught. Yet, in spite of himself, he half substitutes the Alexandrian and Philonic allegory for the Synoptic parable. The double sense runs all through the narrative. Whenever the Johannine Christ begins to teach— whether His words are addressed to Nicodemus, the Samaritan woman, 'the Jews,' or His own disciples—He nearly always begins by enunciating a proposition which contains, under a sensible and symbolic image, a religious truth. The auditor regularly misunderstands Him, interpreting literally what should have been easily perceived to be a metaphor. This gives Jesus an opportunity to develop His allegory, and, in so doing, to instruct the reader, if not the original hearer of the discourse, whom once or twice (as in ch. 3) the Evangelist seems to have quite forgotten. The Johannine Christ loves words which, at any rate in Greek, have a double sense, such as ἄνωθεν, πνεῦμα, λόγος (cf. esp. 10^{31-38}). Whether the very numerous cases where a verb may be indicative or imperative are intentionally ambiguous, it is not easy to say. The symbolism reaches its height in some of the discourses to the Jews; the last discourses to the disciples are more plain; and in ch. 17, which is the climax of the teaching of the Gospel, the mystical union is expounded with much directness.

One of the most difficult problems in connexion with the classes of readers for whom the Gospel was intended is presented by certain explanations introduced by the Evangelist. The chief of these are 2^{21} $6^{64.\ 65}$ 7^{39} 8^{27} 12^{33} 18^9. These explanations seem to us at times superficial and unworthy of their context. We cannot be surprised that they have given force to partition-theories like that of Wendt, who maintains that the discourses are on a higher intellectual and spiritual level than could be within the compass of the author of parts of the narrative. The difficulties in the way of partition-theories seem to be insuperable. A more plausible hypothesis is that the Evangelist deliberately introduced these childlike observations for the benefit of the *simpliciores*, trusting to the educated reader being able to divine his purpose. But this theory is not very satisfactory. We have seen that St. John is able to see as many as three meanings in a simple occurrence. And so he may have felt that 'the Temple' might mean Christ's natural body as well as the stone building and the Church of Christ, which last must have been mainly in his mind when he foresaw the downfall of the Jewish sanctuary and all which it represented.

The *style* of the Fourth Gospel is as different from that of the Synoptics as the matter. Instead of the variety which we find in them, we have a small number of essential thoughts repeated again and again under a small number of images. From this results a strange impressiveness, common in mystical writings, which often share this peculiarity, though to some readers the monotony appears tedious and inartistic. The discourses of Christ have a sweet and melancholy charm, with an indescribable dignity and grandeur; over them all hangs the luminous haze of mysticism, in which mystery seems clear, and clearness itself is mysterious. The phraseology is Hebraic, not Greek; in the Prologue we have a species of rhythm which recalls the old prophets, and in many places we find the parallelism of Hebrew poetry. The arrangement is that of the writer's own thought, not chronological. The appearance of detailed accuracy is not, as has often been seriously argued, a proof of first-hand knowledge, but is due to the vividness of the Evangelist's mental images. The numbers, as has been said, seem often to have a symbolic meaning; the figures, such as Nicodemus and the Greeks who asked for an introduction to Jesus, disappear from the writer's mind as soon as the point is made. No difference can be detected between the style of the various speakers, or between the discourses of Christ and the Evangelist's own comments.

2. Theology of the Gospel.—The first question which meets us is the relation of the Prologue to the rest of the Gospel. Harnack, whose antipathy to the Logos theology apparently influences his judgment, suggests that the Prologue was merely prefixed to the narrative in order to predispose the Greeks in favour of the views which the author was about to propound, views which do not really at all correspond with the Logos philosophy as they understood it.

'The Prologue brings in conceptions which were familiar to the Greeks, and enters into these more deeply than is justified by the presentation which follows; for the notion of the incarnate Logos is by no means the dominant one in the Gospel. Though faint echoes of this idea may possibly be met with here and there in the Gospel,—I confess I do not notice them,—the predominating thought is essentially that of Christ as the Son of God, who obediently executes what the Father has shown and appointed Him' (*ZThK* ii. 189 ff.).

This strangely perverse judgment has evoked protests from several critics who understand the Gospel better than Harnack, among others from Réville, who has certainly no bias in favour of traditional views. It would be easy to show that every one of the dogmatic statements in the Prologue is reasserted in the body of the Gospel. For the pre-existence of the Logos, beyond time, in personal relation to, and in essential union with, God, cf. 6^{62} 8^{58} 14^{10} 17$^{5.\ 24}$. For the Logos as the Agent in creation, and its life-giving and sustaining principle, cf. 5^{26} 8^{12} 9^5. (From the nature of the

subject-matter, there is not *much* cosmological teaching in the Gospel; but what there is, is in full accordance with the Prologue). For manifestations of the Logos before the Incarnation, by revelations and by His immanent presence, cf. 8^{56} and 9^5, 'whenever I am in the world,' etc. There is thus chapter and verse in the Gospel, and in Christ's own words, for every statement in the Prologue; and though Jesus never calls Himself the Logos, this sublime conception of His personality pervades the whole narrative. The stumbling-block to Harnack and others has been what some critics (*e.g.* Beyschlag and Réville) have called the 'contradictory double theology' of the Gospel. By the side of a conception of Christ's Person which seems to class the Evangelist as a speculative mystic or Gnostic, we have statements which seem to belong to the school of Christianity which was dominated by Jewish positivism. Such doctrines are the actual 'becoming flesh' of the Logos, as opposed to a theophany under human form; and the repeated mention of 'the Last Day,' a conception with which, as Reuss says, 'mystical theology has no concern.' But the Evangelist does not write or think as a philosopher. The supreme merit of his book as a Gospel is that he does not write the life of Christ as a Christian Platonist might have been tempted to write it, but keeps a firm hold on the historical Jesus, and on the concrete facts in His teaching. There is, undoubtedly, a double thread of the kind indicated. In some parts of the narrative we feel that 'tabernacled among us' is a truer description of the character of the Johannine Christ than 'became flesh.' There is an aloofness, a solitary grandeur, about the central figure which prevents Him from seeming fully human; while in other places there is an approximation to the Synoptic portrait. But it is only to the minute critic that these difficulties become apparent. To the religious consciousness of Christendom there has never been any hesitation in recognizing the profound agreement between the Synoptic and the Johannine presentations of Jesus Christ. See, further, art. LOGOS.

The intense ethical dualism of the Fourth Gospel is another perplexing phenomenon to those who look for philosophical consistency in a religious treatise. Christian Platonism, into which the Logos theology passed as its most important ingredient, seems to leave no room for a personal devil, or for human beings who are children of the devil. It seems rather to favour the conception of evil as mere *privatio boni*. St. John, however, is quite unconscious of any such difficulty. Although the Logos is the immanent cause of all life, so that 'without him nothing whatever came into being,' the 'darkness' in which the light shines is no mere absence of colour, but a positive malignant thing, a rival kingdom which has its own subjects and its own sphere. Some critics have even been reminded of the metaphysical dualism of Manichæan speculation. This last, however, is in too flagrant contradiction with the Logos theology to effect a lodgment in the Evangelist's mind. The Logos is the true light which lighteth every man as it comes into the world. But since the philosophical problem is not present to the mind of the writer, he is not careful to draw the line between the ethical dualism which was part of his religious experience, and the metaphysical dualism which would have subverted the foundations of his intellectual system. The sources of this ethical dualism may be found partly in the spiritual struggles of an intensely devout nature, but to a greater extent, probably, in the furious antagonism of Judaism to nascent Christianity, a hostility which, to a Christian, must have seemed really diabolical. The temper of his own age was unconsciously transferred to the ministry of Jesus, who certainly could not have adopted the attitude of uncompromising antagonism to 'the Jews' which we find in this Gospel. But it is worthy of note that some of the devotional literature of later times, which shows the closest affinity with Johannine ideas,—the *Theologia Germanica* is a particularly good example,—displays the same extreme ethical dualism as the Gospel. Stöckl, in criticising the *Theologia Germanica* from the standpoint of modern Romanism, finds in it the 'Gnostic dualism' which, with equal justice, he might have detected in parts of the Fourth Gospel. In neither the one nor the other does the distinction correspond with the Gnostic division of mankind into pneumatic and psychic, with an impassable gulf between them. Compare, *e.g.*, the Evangelist's use of 'the world' in 15¹⁹.

(1) *Doctrine of God the Father.*—According to the logic of the system, it has often been said, God should always manifest Himself through the Logos. No man hath seen or heard God at any time (1¹⁸ 5³⁷ 6⁴⁶). So Philo holds that there can be no immediate communication between God, who is transcendent and unknowable, and the world. Nevertheless, it is impossible to impose this philosophical idea upon St. John. His God is not the unknowable 'One' of the later Platonism. He is Spirit (4²⁴), that is, on the negative side, He is non-material, not appreciable by sense, spaceless and timeless. Yet He is not darkness, but Light ; and light includes the ideas of radiation and illumination. Further yet, He is Love. He loves the world. As loving the world, He is the principle of *action*, the principle of the activity of the Logos. He is the *Father*, who 'draws' men to Himself. Several other passages (*e.g.* 5¹⁷· ²¹ 9²⁹) imply independent direct action by the Father. Still, we must not over-emphasize this as a proof of the Evangelist's disagreement with Philo. Philo, no doubt, could not acknowledge an Incarnation ; but the idea of theophanies was naturally very familiar to him from his OT studies. There is nothing un-Philonic in the 'voice from heaven' (12³⁸). Philo, too, speaks of 'a voice formed in the air, not coming from any animate body.'

(2) *Doctrine of the Holy Spirit.*—The dualism of Flesh and Spirit in St. John is one expression of the ethical dualism of which we have spoken above. It is very clearly set forth in the conversation with Nicodemus, when Christ says that no one can see the Kingdom of God unless he be born from above (*or* afresh). This He explains by repeating that unless a man be born of water and the Spirit, he cannot see the Kingdom of God. 'That which is born of the flesh is flesh, and that which is born of the Spirit is spirit.' This regeneration by water and the Spirit is the birth from above, not a simple moral renovation, but a real communication of the Divine Spirit. Natural generation is only a feeble image of this supernatural generation, which, says Loisy (perhaps too boldly, in the absence of any expression of this thought in the Gospel), 'is attached to the same order as the Incarnation of the Word.' St. John does not draw this comparison ; but he says of the elect that they 'were born, not of blood, nor of the will of the flesh, nor of the will of man, but of God' (1¹³). The sphere of the Spirit forms a world absolutely opposed to the world of the flesh. What, then, is the content of this world of the Spirit? Since God is Spirit, the world of Spirit is the world of God, and partakes of the Divine attributes. It is absolute and indestructible ; the Father 'hath life in himself,' and has given this absolute life to the Son also. Even so the Son can transmit it, 'quickening whom he will.' The Spirit quickeneth, the flesh profiteth nothing : it was to com-

municate to men a life which they have not naturally, that the Word became incarnate. This gift of spiritual life is figured as 'the bread from heaven' and 'the living water,' symbols which, as the Evangelist was far from forgetting, are the outward and visible signs in the two great Sacraments. The Divine gift is also typified as Light and Truth, words which imply an illumination of the intellect. So in 17³ life eternal is defined as the knowledge of (or rather, the process of knowing) the only true God, and Jesus Christ, whom He sent. This advancing knowledge is the highest form of life. Those who 'are of the truth' listen to the words of Christ ; but the contemptuous or careless question of Pilate, 'What is truth?' receives no answer. The truth also 'makes us free' ; it breaks the yoke of sin. In opposition to this higher world, St. John develops the idea of the *cosmos*, which is the direct opposite of the Spirit. It has only the appearance of life ; he who has been redeemed from it 'has passed from death into life' (5²⁴). It is therefore possible to call the devil the prince of this world ; although the passage from the kingdom of the world to that of the Spirit is open (3¹⁷ and 17). Jesus Christ, who has full possession of the Spirit, is come to raise men from the sphere of the world into that of the Spirit. Thus, the Johannine soteriology contemplates an enrichment, not a restoration, of human nature. The Evangelist regards sin as essentially a failure to recognize the Divine in the world. Those to whom the light has not been brought are blind, but not guilty : those to whom it has appeared, and who turn their backs upon it, are the typical sinners. From henceforth, these lovers of darkness are doomed to destruction (ἀπώλεια), when Jesus shall 'overcome the world' as a triumphant conqueror.

The relations of the Spirit to the Logos are difficult to define. What, for example, was the office of the Spirit in the world before the Incarnation? Life, as we know, was immanent in the Logos : there seems to be no room for another πνεῦμα ζωοποιοῦν. The descent of the Holy Spirit upon Jesus at His baptism is referred to in St. John, but not described. To him, the Baptism could have no such importance as it appears to have in the Synoptic record. The Spirit was given to Christ 'without measure' from the first.

During the ministry we do not hear much of the Spirit. St. John tells us bluntly (7³⁹) that 'There was as yet no Spirit, because Jesus was not yet glorified.' Instead of the Spirit, we have a *quasi*-independent power ascribed to the *words* of the Lord Jesus, which are spoken of in the same sort of way in which Philo speaks of the λόγοι and δυνάμεις. Jesus insists that the words are not His own, but come from God (3³⁴ and several other places). The words are, of course, inoperative, unless they are received and taken into the heart : but if they are so received, they will abide in the heart as a living and spiritual principle (15⁷ 6⁶³). 'He that keepeth my words shall never see death,' says Jesus (8⁵¹) ; and St. Peter exclaims, 'Lord, to whom shall we go? Thou hast the words of eternal life' (6⁶⁸) : that is to say, not words about eternal life, but words which confer eternal life, as in 8⁵¹. Of the disobedient, He says, 'The word which I have spoken will judge him at the last day' (12⁴⁸) ; and to His disciples, 'He that heareth my words hath passed from death unto life' (5²⁴) ; 'Now ye are clean through the word that I have spoken unto you' (15³). The word or words would thus seem to exercise all the functions of the Paraclete. But they must not be identified ; for the words were addressed to all who heard them ; the Paraclete was given only to the faithful disciples. Moreover, the ministry of the Spirit, properly speaking, begins only after the glorification of

Jesus Christ. Remembering that the Johannine theology implies a Trinitarian doctrine of equality and oneness between the three Persons of the Trinity, we may still say that the office of the Son, during the period of His sojourn on earth, was to reveal the Father, while the office of the Holy Spirit was, and is, to reveal the Son.

St. John takes no interest in purely speculative or dogmatic questions, and therefore he does not trouble himself about such questions as the office of the Holy Spirit, as distinguished from that of the Logos, before the Incarnation. From the practical point of view it is possible to say, as he does, that 'there was as yet no Spirit' before Jesus was glorified. After this glorification, although the action of the Holy Spirit is often represented as that of Christ Himself returning to His own, there is a difference between the mode of action of the Incarnate Christ and that of the Holy Spirit. Not only is the former external, the latter internal ; but the Incarnate Christ addressed Himself to all who came into contact with Him, and was obliged to adapt His teaching to the limited intelligence of His auditors. The Paraclete is a principle of spiritual life in the hearts of believers, on whom He acts directly and without intermediary. His work consists in glorifying Christ, bearing witness to Him and continuing His work of revelation. It is quite useless to ask whether, for St. John, the Paraclete is a distinct hypostasis in the Godhead. The category of personality is quite foreign to the Evangelist, as to his whole school, and no answer to such a question can be drawn from his words. The Evangelist does not speculate about the relation of the Spirit to the Father, who 'sends' Him. The expression 'God is Spirit' (not 'the Spirit') expresses, so to speak, the *quality* of the Divine nature ; it does not assert the identity of the Father and the Holy Ghost, any more than θεὸς ἦν ὁ λόγος in the Prologue asserts such an identity between the First and Second Persons. The Evangelist is much more concerned with the relation of the Paraclete to Christ. This indeed is one of the dominating thoughts of the Fourth Gospel. Jesus 'baptizes with the Holy Ghost' (1^{33}) ; that is to say, the gift of the Holy Ghost is an end of the ministry of Jesus. A very important passage is 14^{17}, in which Jesus says that the world cannot receive the Paraclete 'because it seeth him not, neither knoweth him : but ye know him ; because he dwelleth with you, and shall be in you.' The words 'dwelleth with you' must refer to the presence of Jesus Himself, who has received the Spirit in absolutely full measure, in the midst of His disciples : after His departure the Spirit 'shall be in you,' a condition which did not yet exist at the time when the words were spoken. This gift was, in a manner, communicated when, after the Resurrection, Jesus breathed on the disciples and said, 'Receive ye the Holy Ghost.' But it would be quite foreign to the thought of the Gospel to attach importance to the physical 'insufflation' as the vehicle of the gift of the Holy Ghost. The gift would follow in response to the prayer of Christ (14^{16}). He would be sent in Christ's name (14^{26}). Jesus Himself will send Him (15^{26}). After the gift has come, when the disciples have entered into the sphere of the Spirit, they will still look to Christ as the principle of their life. He will still be the true Vine, of which they are the branches. It is even possible for Him to promise, 'I will see you again'—certainly not with reference to the appearances after the Resurrection, but to the spiritual vision which has nothing to do with bodily presence (16^{16-23}). So when He says, 'I have declared unto them thy name, and will declare it' (17^{26}), the intention does not refer to any future discourses with the disciples on earth, before or after His Passion, but to the relations which will exist between Him and them under the dispensation of the Spirit. The expressions 'we will come unto him, and make our abode with him' (14^{23}) ; and 'I will come again and receive you unto myself' (14^3), have the same meaning, though in the latter passage there may be a special reference to the 'coming' of Christ at the death of each believer. There is no reference in St. John to such a picture as that drawn by St. Paul in 1 Co 15. In Jn $16^{13f.}$ there is a remarkable statement about the Paraclete, that 'he shall not speak of himself . . . he shall take of mine and shall show it unto you.' The relation of the Paraclete to Christ is thus exactly the same as that between Christ and the Father (cf. 5^{30} 6^{38} etc.).

But the special office of the Spirit in the world begins with Christ's departure from earth. The death of Christ, in St. John, has not the same significance as in the Pauline theology. St. John even shrinks from the idea of death in connexion with the incarnate Logos. 'The death of Christ,' says Reuss, 'in the Johannine theology, is an exaltation, not an abasement.' 'The end of the ministry of Christ,' says Réville, 'is not, properly speaking, His death. His death is in reality a deliverance.' The redemptive element in the death of Christ is not His suffering, but His glorification. And yet we must not forget that the idea of sacrifice, and of Christ as the true Paschal Lamb, is frequently in the mind of the Evangelist. It appears not only in the 'testimony' of John the Baptist ($1^{29. 36}$), but in the High-Priestly prayer, where the words 'for their sakes I consecrate myself' (17^{19}), have a definitely sacrificial meaning. This doctrine was part of the Christian tradition, which St. John accepts heartily without attempting to bring it into line with his own dominant ideas. It is, however, true to say that it is by His life, and not by His death, that the Johannine Christ gives life to the world. 'Because I live, ye shall live also' (14^{19}). The principle of life within them will be the Holy Spirit. As Paraclete, He will be their defender and helper against all adversaries, ghostly and bodily. He will also be their Comforter (we cannot wonder that some have defended this meaning of Paraclete) ; He will change their sorrow into joy, as a grain of wheat dies only to live again, or as a woman, when she is in travail, exchanges her pain for joy that a man is born into the world ; He will guide them into all truth—a word which in St. John has a predominantly moral significance. His action on the unbelieving 'world' is one of 'conviction' (ἐλέγχειν, 16^8), a Philonic expression, of somewhat obscure meaning. St. John does not seem to contemplate any direct action of the Holy Spirit, except in the hearts of the faithful : the office assigned to Him in the Anglican Catechism, as the 'sanctifier of all the elect people of God,' is quite Johannine ; but indirectly He will show in their true colours, and condemn, those who are the enemies of Jesus Christ. See, further, art. HOLY SPIRIT, **14** (*b*).

3. Scheme of the Fourth Gospel.—After the Prologue begins a section of the Gospel which may be called 'The Testimony.' We have first the testimony of John the Baptist, then of the disciples, then of 'signs'—the miracle at Cana. The Evangelist next describes how Jesus manifests Himself, first in Judæa, then in Samaria, and thirdly in Galilee. But another thread seems to run through these chapters, which also lends itself to the arrangement in triplets. We might call these first chapters the doctrine of *Water*. First we have the water of the Law superseded by the wine of the Gospel, typified by the changing of the water into wine at the marriage-feast ; next we have the water of purification mentioned in the discourse with

Nicodemus; and thirdly, the water of life, the nature of which is expounded in the dialogue with the woman of Samaria. In ch. 5 begins the second of the three great divisions of the book, which should be called the *Conflict* or κρίσις. After two more 'signs' a prolonged controversy with the Jews is described, in which the divergence between Christ and the hierarchy becomes more and more acute, till the final catastrophe is seen to be inevitable. The tension comes to breaking point after the final 'sign,' and the end of Christ's public ministry. It is at this point that the unstable 'multitude' quits the scene with the significant question, unanswered like that of Pilate, 'Who is this Son of Man?' (12^{34}). In these chapters also a subordinate thread may be discovered in the doctrine of *Bread* (ch. 6), the doctrine of *Light* (ch. 8), and the doctrine of *Life* (the transit through death into life a spiritual law). The third part of the Gospel may be called the *Glorification* (δόξα). Jesus reveals Himself to His disciples in a series of esoteric discourses, addressed to them only, in view of His approaching departure from them. This section culminates in the High-Priestly prayer (ch. 17). Then follows the narrative of the Passion, conceived throughout as the glorification of Christ through self-chosen suffering. The humiliation and sacrifice, no less than the triumph of death, are part of the δόξα. This part of the Gospel ends with the appearance to Thomas, and the 'last beatitude.' Ch. 21 is an epilogue.

4. Characteristic Words in the Fourth Gospel. —(1) *Life* (ζωή).—In the Prologue an interesting and rather important question of punctuation arises in connexion with this word. Ought we to read with AV χωρὶς αὐτοῦ ἐγένετο οὐδὲ ἕν ὃ γέγονεν. ἐν αὐτῷ ζωὴ ἦν, or, with ACD and nearly all the Ante-Nicene Fathers who comment on it, should we put the full stop at ἕν? The former view, which is supported by Chrysostom, has prevailed in modern times, though several authorities, such as WH, put the stop at ἕν. The latter theory seems to give a richer and deeper meaning, and one more completely in accordance with the religious philosophy of the Gospel. 'All things were made by Him (as the Instrument), and without Him nothing came into being. That which has come into being was, in Him, life.' The Logos is the vital principle from whom all that lives derives its life. Whatever life exists in the world *was*, eternally, timelessly, in Him. To have 'life in Himself' is an eternal attribute of God the Son; all that appears on this fleeting scene exists, so far as it exists, by participation in His life. In short, the Logos, as life, is a cosmic principle. The idea that all things pre-existed eternally in the mind of God, and are, as it were, unrolled as the ages go on, was familiar to Jewish thought. But St. John's doctrine is more *Greek*—that the things of time derive whatever reality they possess from a sphere of higher reality beyond time and place. With this accord the other passages in the Gospel where Life is mentioned. In 6^{33-56} Christ is declared to be the Bread of God which cometh down from heaven to give life to the world. Whoso eateth His flesh and drinketh His blood hath eternal life. He who is closely united to Christ—who makes the life of Christ his own—has the principle of life within him. In 17^3 the knowledge of the Father and of the Son is said to constitute eternal life. This knowledge can be possessed only through the indwelling of Him who is the principle of life. The same idea recurs in 11^{25}, and in 14^6 Christ, 'in whom all things consist,' as St. Paul says (Col 1^{17}), is Himself the Resurrection and the Life, and the Way, the Truth, and the Life. Accordingly, the Life is a present possession rather than a future hope. He that believeth on the Son hath everlasting life (3^{36} 5^{24}).

Christ came that we might have life, and have it abundantly (10^{10}). See LIFE.

(2) *Truth* (ἀλήθεια).—St. John's use of this word cannot be paralleled in the Synoptics, but it occurs in the Epistles of St. James, St. Peter, and St. Paul. Typical examples of the use of the word in this Gospel are 1^{17} 'grace and truth came by Jesus Christ'; 8^{32} 'the truth shall make you free'; 14^6 'I am the truth'; 16^{13} 'the Spirit of truth shall guide you into all truth'; 17^{17} 'thy word is truth.' Christ, however, came 'to bear witness to the truth' (18^{37}), so that it must have been in the world before the Incarnation. Those that 'are of the truth' heard and accepted Him. From these passages we gather that 'the truth' is all that *really exists* in every sphere, and this is why Jesus Christ, as the Logos, calls Himself the Truth (cf. Scotus Erigena: 'certius cognoscas Verbum naturam omnium esse'). Recognition of this brings freedom, because truth corresponds with the law of our being. For those who have eyes to see, all experience is a commentary on, and witness to, Christ's religion. But the children of the evil one, who was a liar from the beginning, cannot hear the words of truth ($8^{44f.}$).

(3) Closely akin to Truth is *Witness* (μαρτυρία). This idea is never absent from St. John's mind, particularly in the earlier part of his Gospel. Every event in history, every experience, is valuable as a witness to the truth. Christ is the centre, to whose Person and claims everything testifies. The Father bears witness concerning Christ. Christ bears, and yet does not bear, witness concerning Himself (5^{31} contrasted with 8^{14}); the Spirit will bear witness concerning Him (15^{26}; cf. 1 Jn 5^6 'it is the Spirit that beareth witness, because the Spirit is truth'); John the Baptist and the disciples bear witness (1^7 15^{27}); especially the Evangelist himself (19^{35} 21^{24}); the Scriptures bear witness ($5^{39.40}$); and lastly, the 'works' of Christ bear witness (10^{25} 14^{11}). The 'witness,' therefore, is found in every avenue through which the truth can reach us. Converging from all sides upon the Person of Christ, it is the means of progressive initiation (ἵνα γνῶτε καὶ γιγνώσκητε, 10^{38}) into the whole truth—that is to say, into the knowledge and love of Christ. The contradiction in 5^{31} and 8^{14} is only partially explained. Christ makes a unique claim for Himself (in 8^{14}), as having full knowledge of past, present, and future.

(4) *Light* (φῶς).—When the First Epistle, putting into terse and definite phrases the teaching of the Gospel, says that 'God is light' (1 Jn 1^5), it means, in modern language, that it is the nature of God to communicate Himself. This self-communication is effected through the Logos as the principle of life. 'The life was the light of men' (1^4). Christ is 'the true light which lighteth every man as it comes into the world.' There is not much room for doubt that this is the right translation of 1^9. The 'coming' is repeated or continues; cf. 9^5 'whenever (ὅταν) I am in the world, I am the light of the world.' The Evangelist certainly asserts that there were earlier partial Christophanies, as there will be later and even greater Christophanies through the Spirit. And yet there is a sense in which Jesus could say, 'Yet a little while is the light with you' (12^{35}).

(5) The Light converges upon one point, where it shines forth as *Glory* (δόξα), another very characteristic word. Christ was in glory with the Father before the world was (17^5); an important passage as negativing the pantheistic conception that the Word is *only* the life and light of the world—that the world is the complete and only expression of His being. He was incarnate to 'glorify' the Father on the earth (17^5), and thereby was also glorified Himself (13^{31} 14^{13}). The Spirit, too, will

glorify Christ by making Him more fully known (16¹⁴). It has been said that in St. John the universe is the poem of the Word to the glory of the Father.

(6) *Judgment* (κρίσις).—As at the creation God divided the light from the darkness, so the Incarnation necessarily and naturally divided mankind, condemning those who would not receive the light. This is 'the judgment' (3¹⁹). With regard to Christ's own function as Judge, we have another formal contradiction (cf. 12⁴⁸ 3¹⁷ 12⁴⁷ with 5²². ²⁷ 9³⁹ 5³⁰). The contrast is striking, but the Evangelist's meaning is clear. The coming of Christ disclosed an actual relation ; He made no new, more severe laws ; He only revealed, in all its unfathomable depth, the gulf that yawns between God and the devil, and between their respective servants. The 'one that seeketh and judgeth' (8⁵⁰) is the eternal power of righteousness which is symbolized in the Law (5⁴⁵), and expressed in the Gospel (12⁴⁸ᶠ). At the same time, the judgment is a *personal* one, and is committed to Christ as *a* son of man (5²⁷). Mankind is judged by a human standard, though by the standard of humanity at its best.

(7) *World* (κόσμος).—It is remarkable that St. John uses κόσμος, while the Synoptics use αἰών. The former is the Greek, the latter the Jewish way of envisaging reality ; for the Greeks pictured it more readily under the form of space, the Jews under that of time. The 'world' is the sum-total of existence viewed (by abstraction) without the spiritual world. It is 'the things below' (8²³), as opposed to 'the things above.' The concept is therefore an abstraction for certain purposes, and has no real existence, for the world is upheld in being only by the Logos, who is 'not of the world.' It comprises all that belongs to the categories of time and place. Christ 'came into the world' at His incarnation, and He is 'in the world' till His death and glorification. He prays not that His disciples may be taken out of the world, but that they may be kept from the evil. From this idea comes that of the world as human society as it organizes itself apart from God, hence the severe judgments passed upon the world ; *e.g.* 1 Jn 5¹⁹ 'the whole world lieth in the wicked one,' and similar phrases in the Gospel. Thus the world is that which is external, transitory, and corrupt. The Evangelist, it need hardly be said, does not follow up the thought of the unreality of the world apart from God, into acosmistic speculations. Thinkers who have done so have been driven into a purely negative conception of evil, and have often drifted into a dreamy pantheism. But St. John, as we have seen, presents us with an intense ethical dualism, including a belief in a personal or *quasi*-personal devil, who is the *de facto* prince of this world.

(8) *To believe* (πιστεύειν).—This, and not the substantive πίστις, is St. John's chosen expression. The verb has two constructions : (1) with the dative (5²⁴ 8³¹, both mistranslated in AV), to believe a person or statement—accept the veracity of the former, or the truth of the latter ; and (2) π. εἰς τινα—a construction characteristically Johannine, which occurs only once in the Synoptics (Mt 18⁶ = Mk 9⁴²). In the Synoptics generally faith is relative to a particular object—the condition of obtaining some special miraculous benefit. But in St. John faith is allegiance to Jesus Christ, and, as such, a condition of eternal life (1¹² 6⁴⁰), which is also a progressive state, depending on knowledge (17³) as well as faith. The Evangelist studiously avoids γνῶσις as well as πίστις, using in both cases the verbs only.

(9) *Love* (ἀγάπη).—This is the new commandment (13³⁴). Love is the bond which unites the Son to the Father, the disciples to the Son, and the dis-

ciples to each other. 'As the Father hath loved me, so have I loved you' (15⁹). 'That the love wherewith thou hast loved me may be in them, and I in them.' The virtue of love is no vague sentiment, but shows itself necessarily in action. 'He that hath my commandments and keepeth them, he it is that loveth me' (14²¹. ²³). Love is not to be sharply distinguished from faith, though the former is a state mainly of the affections, the latter of the will and the intellect. Theologians who developed the Johannine ideas further, like Clement of Alexandria, agree that faith is the beginning, love the crown, of the spiritual life. Faith and love are both *simple* states, and, as Clement says, 'are not taught.' The soul passes out of the simplicity of faith, through the multiplicity of strenuous interests in the life of duty, into a second and more Divine simplicity, and immediacy of intercourse with God. St. John's teaching about love culminates in ch. 17, in which our Lord seems to imply that the 'name' of the Father, which He has declared to His disciples, is Love.

5. The miracles of the Fourth Gospel.—The miracles in St. John are either 'signs' (σημεῖα), in which case their abnormal and also their symbolic character is emphasized, or 'works' (ἔργα), in which case no distinction between natural and supernatural is thought of, and the 'works' are only component parts of the one 'work,' to do which Jesus came into the world. The Johannine Christ does not wish faith in His person to rest on the signs, though He allows them a legitimate weight in fortifying a weak faith. It is better to·believe for the sake of the words than of the works, He implies in 14¹¹ ; and the last beatitude (20²⁹) is a reproof of Thomas, who believed only when he had ocular testimony to the Resurrection. The seven miracles selected by the Evangelist have the value of acted parables, and in some cases the symbolical significance is clearly indicated.

(1) *The miracle at Cana in Galilee* (2¹ᶠ).—Christ is represented as beginning His public ministry at a wedding. Unlike the Essenes, and unlike John the Baptist, Jesus was not personally an ascetic. He drank wine, and ate what was put before Him. There was, indeed, a special appropriateness in this festivity at the beginning of His ministry, when He had just called together His family of Apostles, whom He loved to compare to a bridal party (cf. Mt 9¹⁵ ‖). The miracle may have taken place on the last of the seven days usually given up to bridal festivities. The occasion gives Christ an opportunity to assert the superior sacredness of His mission to any family ties (His words to His mother convey an unmistakable rebuke), and also (through the mouth of the master of the ceremonies) to indicate symbolically the supersession of the water of the Law by the good wine of the Gospel.

(2) *The healing of the official's son* (4⁴⁶ᶠ).—The miracle of healing, performed for the benefit of a court·official (βασιλικός) of Herod Antipas, is the only 'sign' of the Synoptic type recorded in St. John. The miracle is conditioned by the faith of the father ; it is a work of mercy, pure and simple, and no symbolic meaning can easily be detected in it.

(3) *The paralytic at Bethesda* (5¹ᶠ).—This work of healing at first sight resembles the last, and it introduces the situation, familiar in the Synoptics, of a quarrel with the strict legalists about Sabbath observance. But the Evangelist has a deeper lesson to convey by this work of healing on the Sabbath, one which profoundly modifies the whole conception of the way in which that day should be kept. 'My Father worketh hitherto, and I work' (v.¹⁷). That is to say, the Sabbath rest of God is unimpeded activity, and that is the true notion of

rest, as opposed to inertia. It follows that a mere negative abstinence from exertion of every kind is not an intelligent or acceptable mode of honouring God. The verse is also theologically important, as separating the Christian idea of God the Father from the Neo-Platonic Absolute, and from the God of such speculative mystics as Eckhart and Silesius. Lastly, by co-ordinating His own activity with that of the Father, Jesus claims to be Himself Divine.

(4) *The feeding of the five thousand* (6[5ff.]).—This miracle is also recorded by the Synoptists, but St. John tells it with a very different purpose. In no other miracle is the didactic purpose, referred to by St. Augustine, more apparent. 'Interrogemus ipsa miracula quid nobis loquantur de Christo; habent enim, si intellegantur, linguam suam. Nam quia ipse Christus Verbum Dei est, etiam factum Verbi verbum nobis est.' How much this miracle is an acted parable is shown by v.[30], where, in answer to the challenge of the Jews, Christ does not make any appeal to the miracle as a 'sign.' His answer is, 'My Father *giveth* you the true bread from heaven'—not only in one miraculous act, but always. In v.[34] the metaphor is misunderstood by the hearers (a favourite literary device of the Evangelist), and then comes the great saying in v.[35]. The device recurs in vv.[52-54]. The discourse on the Bread of Life does not refer directly to the Eucharist, which had not yet been instituted; but the Evangelist undoubtedly wishes, by narrating it, to spiritualize and generalize the Eucharistic doctrine current when he wrote, and to check the tendency to formality and materialism (cf. esp. v.[63]). In v.[51ff.] there is clearly an allusion to the Paschal lamb, the blood of which was sprinkled on the lintels and doorposts; and therefore the thought of *sacrifice* was already in the mind of Jesus. But the leading idea is that of identifying ourselves with the life of Christ, being reborn into His spirit: this union constitutes eternal life. Christ is Himself the gift which He brings; even through apparent failure He fulfils His work (vv.[34-38]). A *spiritual* preparation is needed to understand how a *man* can thus unite earth and heaven (vv.[43. 44]); but in part the question is answered in the OT (vv.[45. 46]), and in part the believer must co-operate (vv.[47-50]). Man lives only by participation in the virtues of Christ's life and death, which brings with it a personal union between the believer and Christ (vv.[53-56]). The whole discourse (λόγος, not 'saying,' v.[60]) seemed 'harsh' (σκληρός) to those who heard it: it pointed to self-devotion, and surrender even to death. Accordingly, many even of His *disciples* left Him. Christ thereupon said (v.[61]), 'Does this offend you? What if ye shall see the Son of Man ascend where he was before?' When the bodily presence is withdrawn, and the flesh entirely disappears, the meaning of the 'harsh discourse' will be made manifest—viz. that the union with Christ is spiritual, and therefore a truth for all times and' places. Unlike the eating of manna by 'the fathers,' which only nourished their bodily frames for a few hours, the bread from heaven confers eternal life. The flesh profiteth nothing; the *words* which He spoke to them were spirit and life. This language would bring great comfort to the disciples of the Evangelist's own day, when the 'hope deferred' of the Second Coming was making many hearts sick. It can hardly be an accident that the designation of the traitor, which in the Synoptics occurs at the same hour as the institution of the Eucharist, in this Gospel follows immediately the discourse on the bread of life. The whole passage *represents*, under another form, the narrative of the Last Supper.

(5) *The walking on the sea* (6[16f.]) is closely connected with the more important miracle, and merely illustrates the power of Christ over another element.

(6) *The man born blind* (ch. 9).—The disciples are confronted by one of the most perplexing problems of life—that of a *vie manquée*. A beggar lies before them, who has been blind from his birth. Was this crippling infirmity a punishment for his own sins, either in a previous state of existence or in anticipation of those which he was going to commit, or for the sins of his parents? Jesus says that neither explanation is the right one; the reason is 'that the works of God might be made manifest in him.' He adds that for all alike 'the night cometh, when no man can work.' The moral difficulty about the justice of human suffering receives no direct answer. The most significant verses in the discourse about the Light of the world are [25. 39. 41]. Jesus has come into the world for judgment, not only for a *discernment* of good and bad people, but (as a necessary result) to procure for the first eternal life, and to pardon the last. The blind man typifies humanity converted to Christianity, coming out of darkness and made to see by Christ; while the representatives of Judaism, proud of their enlightenment, are struck with blindness—'blind leaders of the blind.'

(7) *The raising of Lazarus* (ch. 11).—The narrative of this, the last and greatest of the seven 'signs,' contains several characteristic features. The suggestion implied in v.[3] does not induce Jesus to hurry His action at all. He deliberately waits two days before starting for Judæa. Similarly in 2[3f.] the Evangelist is anxious to· show that He did not act upon His mother's suggestion. Still more instructive is the misunderstanding of Christ's words in v.[12], and the conversation of Martha (v.[21ff.]). She makes a half request, which she does not dare to put directly (v.[22]), to which Christ answers: 'Thy brother shall rise again.' Martha *misunderstands* this to refer to the resurrection at the last day. But Christ did not mean either this or that He intended to bring Lazarus to life again. Just as in ch. 6 He refuses to mention the miracle, in reply to the question 'What sign showest thou?' (v.[30]), but gives as the sign the declaration, 'I am the bread of life'; so here He does not invite attention to what He is about to do, but to His own Person. 'I am the resurrection and the life.' The deep significance of this is often missed. If the words referred only to the approaching miracle, they would convey but hollow comfort to the Christian mourner, for whom no miracles are wrought; if we take them to refer to the future resurrection at the last day, we are forgetting that the words were spoken as a *correction* of that thought. The words bid us concentrate our thoughts upon the Person of Christ. 'He that believeth on me, though he die, yet shall he live; and he that liveth and believeth on me shall never die.' This is not a promise of resurrection; it is a denial of death. The resurrection is a personal communication of the Lord Himself, not a gift to be obtained from another. Martha had spoken of a gift to be obtained from God and dispensed by Christ. Jesus answers that He Himself *is* (not 'will give or procure') the Resurrection and the Life. By taking humanity upon Himself He has revealed the permanence of man's individuality and its indestructibility. The Incarnation brought life and immortality to *light*. Death is abolished; the grave has been robbed of its victory by the fact that Christ lives, and is the life of the individual believer. In Him all that belongs to the completeness of personal being finds its permanence and consummation. Because He is the Life, He must also be the Resurrection; in other words, our true life is hid with Him in God. The dead in Christ are alive, in virtue of their union with Him

who is the Resurrection and the Life. After this sublime lesson, the physical miracle seems almost an anti-climax, a thing to be half regretted, like the restitution of Job's large fortune and his flourishing family by his second marriage. But not only is the miracle a parallel in act to the verbal revelation which precedes it, but it emphasizes the very deep lesson that though life in its highest sense is indestructible, we must pass through the gate of death in order to reach it. This is one of the profoundest and most characteristic doctrines of Christianity. Those who have found in the maxim 'Die to live' the kernel of Christ's religion, have penetrated a large part at least of His 'secret.' This, and the lesson that it is the Person of Christ Himself, revealed as the Resurrection and the Life, rather than the hopes of a gift to be one day conferred by Him, that should be the truest consolation for mourners, are the two main points in the narrative of the raising of Lazarus.

Conclusion.— The Fourth Gospel gives us an answer to the question, 'What think ye of Christ?' Moreover, it maintains that the answer to this question is the dividing-line between light and darkness. To know Christ is to know the Father; and no man cometh to the Father except by Him. The Christ 'whom to know is to live' is not, of course, merely the human Jesus, but the eternal Word who tabernacled among us in human form. The Evangelist would have accepted Bengel's dictum, that '*conversio fit ad Dominum ut Spiritum.*' But he regards the identification of this spiritual power with Jesus of Nazareth as essential. The vigorous words of 1 John (1[1-3] 4[1-3]) unquestionably express the Christological position of the author of the Gospel, even if some doubts exist as to the common authorship of the two books. It is the peculiarity of the Johannine theology that we pass backwards and forwards between the universal and the particular, between time and eternity, present and future, outward and inward. To the philosopher this oscillation is most perplexing; but it is the true normal pulsation of the spiritual and moral life, in which we may always trace a double movement of expansion and concentration. On the one hand, we must lose our souls in order to find them, we must die daily in order to live. We must continually pass out of ourselves, forget ourselves, and identify ourselves with interests of which we are not the centre. We must enlarge our life till there is nothing selfish, personal, or limited about it. And, on the other hand, exactly in proportion as we succeed in doing this, we shall enrich our lives and become more keenly conscious of the worth and value of our own souls in God's sight. There will be no blurring of individual distinctions, no Buddhist absorption in the Infinite, but a growing sense that the soul of man is the throne of the Godhead, and his body the temple of the Holy Ghost.

LITERATURE.—See at end of preceding article.

W. R. INGE.

JONAH ('Ιωνᾶς, Heb. יוֹנָה 'dove,' AV of NT *Jonas*).—A prophet, the story of whose mission to Nineveh is related in the Book of Jonah, and who is probably to be identified with the Jonah of 2 K 14[25]; referred to by our Lord twice at least (see below) in the Gospels (Mt 12[39-41] || Lk 11[29-32] and Mt 16[4]).

Certain of the scribes and Pharisees, not content with our Lord's many miracles or signs (cf. Jn 12[37]), some of which were, after all, like those performed by their 'sons' (Mt 12[27], Lk 11[19]), demanded of Him a special sign, most probably, as in Mt 16[1] || Mk 8[11], from heaven, since such a sign would at once attest His Divine mission (cf. Jn 6[30-32]). He replied: 'An evil and adulterous generation seeketh after a sign; and there shall no sign be given to

it [and we must naturally understand such a sign as they demanded] but the sign of Jonah the prophet: for as Jonah was three days and three nights in the belly of the whale, so shall the Son of Man be three days and three nights in the heart of the earth. The men of Nineveh shall stand up in the judgment with this generation, and shall condemn it: for they repented at the preaching of Jonah; and behold, a greater than Jonah is here.' The parallel account in Lk. has the appearance of being a summary report of that in Mt., and there are some notable differences. In place of the reference to the three days, Lk. has, 'For even as Jonah became a sign unto the Ninevites, so shall also the Son of Man be to this generation,'—words which many think refer only to Jonah's preaching. Again, the verse concerning the rising up of the men of Nineveh in the judgment follows that referring to the queen of the south instead of preceding it as in Mt. The reference to Jonah in Mt 16[4] was obviously made on another occasion; it contains only the words, 'An evil and adulterous generation seeketh after a sign [here plainly from heaven, cf. v.[1]]; and there shall no sign be given unto it, but the sign of Jonah.'

Although it is not the purpose of this article to discuss the difficulties connected with the story of Jonah as told in the OT, or to consider the arguments advanced for and against the historicity of the book, it will yet be necessary to allude to some of them in connexion with the problems arising out of our Lord's references to the prophet. Those who maintain the historicity of the Book of Jonah, and who hold that it contains a record of facts, find no special difficulties in our Lord's allusions to it,—He referred to Jonah and to facts in his history, just as He referred to other historical personages and to facts in their history, as to Abraham, for instance, to Moses, or to the queen of Sheba; for such persons the only difficulties are the subordinate ones belonging to the exegesis and application of the passages in question. On the other hand, those who deny the historicity of the book, and who hold, with whatever modifications, that the story is a fictitious symbolic narrative with a didactic purpose, like some others in the OT and in the Apocrypha, find many grave difficulties in our Lord's use of the book—difficulties which perhaps do not admit of an absolutely certain solution. Before, however, adverting to them there is a preliminary point to be considered.

It has been maintained by some that Mt 12[40] is no part of our Lord's original utterance, but is either an amplification by the Evangelist of 12[39] (and cf. Lk 11[30], Mt 16[4]), or at least a very early interpolation. Against the verse it is said: (1) It runs counter to the Gospel history, for according to that history Jesus had wrought many signs, and could not therefore say, 'No sign shall be given.' (2) The resurrection was not a sign to the men of that generation, *i.e.* such as they demanded (cf. Ac 10[41]). (3) The clause is unnecessary, and interferes with the balance which without it exists in Mt 12[41. 42] || Lk 11[31. 32], for it was Jonah's preaching and the consequent repentance of the Ninevites, in contrast with His own preaching and the indifference of the men of His generation, to which Jesus especially alluded; His words without v.[40] are a complete answer to their demand for a sign: the repentance-preaching Jonah was a sign to the Ninevites of God's mercy; the repentance-preaching Jesus of Nazareth was a sign, though a greater one, to the Jews. (4) Add that (3) harmonizes well with Lk 11[30], which was perhaps the original out of which Mt 12[40] was evolved. (5) There is the difficulty about the reckoning of the three days and three nights in the case of our Lord's resurrection.

To these objections it may be replied : (1) There is no contradiction of the Gospel story, for the scribes and Pharisees plainly demanded a sign of a different character from those which they had so far witnessed (see above).   (2) The resurrection *was* a sign, since the Apostles proclaimed it (Acts and Epistles *passim*), and made it the corner-stone of their teaching about the Christ.   (3) V.[40] is unnecessary only on the gratuitous assumption that Jonah's preaching was the only way in which he was to be a sign to the men of Christ's generation ; the introduction in v.[40] of another particular in which Jonah was to be a sign does not weaken or interfere with what our Lord says about the prophet's preaching.   (4) Lk 11[30], instead of being the original, may well be a summary report of Mt 12[40] as suggested above,—an explanation rendered not improbable by the whole form and tenor of the passage in Lk. referring to Jonah.   (5) This difficulty, such as it is, makes rather for than against the authenticity of the verse (see below). To these replies it may be added : (6) There is some ground for the conjecture that allusion was made on another occasion by our Lord, and also by St. Paul, to Jonah's deliverance after three days from the 'whale' as typifying the resurrection (Lk 24[46], 1 Co 15[4]), it being much more unlikely that the reference in these places is to Hos 6[2] or Gn 22[4] ; and this may be thought to add some strength to the probability that our Lord did utter the words recorded in v.[40] (cf. also Mt 27[63], Mk 8[31], Jn 2[19]).   (7) There is no textual authority for the rejection of the verse.   On the whole, the conclusion that this verse is really part of our Lord's original utterance can be fully justified.

We have now to consider briefly the difficulties connected with our Lord's use of the story of Jonah on the supposition that the book is not historical, but a fictitious narrative with a didactic purpose.   (1) Did our Lord cite details from the story of Jonah as facts, He Himself thinking them to be facts?   If we reply in the affirmative, we must admit that our Lord was not completely omniscient, and that on a point of literary knowledge He was and could be in error.   Into a discussion of the great question of the limitation of our Lord's human knowledge we cannot, of course, enter here ; it must suffice to point out that the most earnest maintainers of our Lord's Divinity have in all ages recognized, in view of such passages as Mt 24[36] (RV) ‖ Mk 13[32], Lk 2[40. 52], Ph 2[7], not only a gradual growth of His human knowledge, but even a mysterious limitation of His knowledge of Divine things ; and however difficult it may be to understand the union of the Divine and the human in one Person, we must not, in maintaining His Divinity, forget that He was 'perfect man.'   'Is it,' asks Dr. Sanday, 'inconsistent with our Christian belief to suppose that He who called Himself the Son of Man, along with the assumption of human flesh and a human mind, should also have assumed the natural workings of such a mind, even in its limitations?' (*Bamp. Lect.* viii. p. 415).   (2) But did our Lord know in Himself that the story of Jonah was fiction and yet cite details from it as though they were such, His hearers thinking them to be such?   Here, again, we might reply in the affirmative, and that without detracting from our Lord's honesty as a moral and religious teacher, for He would have been but speaking according to the beliefs of His hearers, as many other teachers in all ages have done.   Speaking to children in knowledge, He spoke to them as such.   In this way, it is nearly universally agreed, we are to explain His words about Hades and Abraham's bosom in the graphic parable of the

Rich Man and Lazarus ; *i.e.* in warning and in inculcating truth He spoke according to the beliefs of His hearers and of His age, without necessarily endorsing those beliefs as true.   (3) Or did both our Lord and His hearers, the scribes and Pharisees, regard the story of Jonah as a parable or fictitious narrative, like others in the OT and in the Apocrypha, and did He thus refer to it? Although in view of To 14[4. 8], 3 Mac 6[8], Jos. *Ant.* IX. x. it is not very probable that our Lord's hearers regarded the book as fictitious, we might yet admit without hesitation that part of our Lord's reference could be thus explained.   Even so firm a maintainer of the historicity of Jonah as Huxtable writes in the *Speaker's Commentary* : 'The reference to Jonah's experiences, as yielding an illustrative pa...lel to what would be seen in His own case, or even as predictive of it, seems as cogent on the supposition of the book being an inspired parable, as on that of its being authentic narrative.'   And in fact a teacher might, without doing any violence to right teaching, cite well-known fiction (*The Pilgrim's Progress, Rasselas,* Shakespeare's characters) to enforce warnings or moral truth, and so could our Saviour have done. There is, however, an objection to this explanation, besides that referred to above, which, if it be not a fatal one, is at least of considerable force, viz. that our Lord would not naturally have said of persons whom a *fiction* represented as repentant, that they would rise up in the Judgment ; nor would He have put as a parallel case to a fiction the facts of the queen of Sheba's visit to Solomon.

It does not seem possible to pronounce a decided verdict in favour of any one of these hypotheses to the exclusion of the others, though it may be allowed that (3) contains more of difficulty than (1) or (2) ; and whilst of these latter (2) is perhaps the more attractive, (1) can certainly be held without belittling our Lord's Divinity or detracting from His authority as a moral and religious Teacher, and without weakening the force of the lessons for all generations derivable from the use He made of the story of Jonah for the edification and warning of the men of His own day.

It remains to notice the difficulty connected with the reckoning of the *three days and three nights.*   It is certain that this length of time did not literally elapse between the burial and the resurrection of Christ, and the commentaries in explanation usually follow the lead of St. Jerome and of St. Augustine, who point out that we must understand the passage on the principle that the part is taken for the whole ; and accordingly it is usually said that our Lord was in the 'heart of the earth' on three day-night periods or νυχθήμερα (reference is made to Gn 1[5. 8] etc., Lv 23[32], 1 S 30[12. 13], 2 Ch 10[5. 12], Dn 8[14] margin).   It must be confessed, however, that this explanation seems somewhat forced, in view of the peculiar form of the sentence in v.[40], and there is not a little to be said against it ; and it is perhaps more satisfactory to suppose that our Lord was speaking only in general terms. At any rate the difficulty, such as it is, lends support to the arguments for the authenticity of the verse, since if it were an amplification by the Evangelist, or an interpolation, the Evangelist or the interpolator would hardly have made our Lord utter a prediction expressed in a form not in literal and precise accord with the facts of the resurrection as related in the Gospels.

It is worth noticing that the story of Jonah had a peculiar interest for the early Christians ; his deliverance from a strange sea-monster is depicted many times in the Roman catacombs as typifying the resurrection.

LITERATURE.—Jerome, *Com. in Jonam,* ii. 405, also in *Evang. Matth.* ii. 12. 83 ; Augustine, *de Consensu Evang.* iii. 24, 66 ;

'The Book of Jonah, How far is it Historical?' by M. P. in *JSL*, Oct. 1865; Liddon, *Bampton Lectures*, on 'Our Lord's Divinity,' Lect. viii.; Introduction to 'Jonah' in *Speaker's Commentary*; C. H. H. Wright, *Biblical Essays*, 1886, pp. 34–98; Farrar, *The Minor Prophets*, 1890; *Lux Mundi*, pref. to the 10th edition; J. Kennedy, *A Monograph on the Book of Jonah*, 1895; Gore, *Bampton Lectures*, on 'The Incarnation,' Lects. vi., vii.; Sanday, *Bampton Lectures*, on 'Inspiration,' Lect. viii.; G. A. Smith, *The Book of the Twelve Prophets*, vol. ii., 1898; Driver, *LOT*[6], pp. 321–325; art. 'Jonah' in Hastings' *DB*, in the *Encyc. Bibl.* 1901, and in the *Jewish Encyclopedia*, 1904.

ALBERT BONUS.

JONAM.—A link in our Lord's genealogy (Lk 3[30]).

JORAM.—Son of Jehoshaphat, named in our Lord's genealogy (Mt 1[8]).

JORDAN.—**1.** *Name.*—The name of this river is in the OT יַרְדֵּן; LXX Ἰορδάνης, Ἰόρδανος, Ἰορδάννης; NT always Ἰορδάνης; Jos. Ἰορδάνης, Ἰόρδανος.

The form of the word *Yardēn* is difficult to explain. To say, with Ewald (*Ausf. Lehrbuch der heb. Sprache*[8], p. 426), or with Olshausen (*Lehrbuch der heb. Sprache*, p. 405), that the primitive form is *Yardān* or *Yardān*, does not help us much; and we can hardly suppose, like Stade (*Lehrbuch der heb. Grammatik*, p. 176) or Winckler (*Altorient. Forsch.* i. p. 422 f.), that it is a word borrowed from another language, seeing that it is accompanied by the article. It might be better to hold, with Seybold (*MNDPV*, 1896, p. 10 f.), that the LXX has preserved the real vocalization, *Yordan*, formed on the analogy of *ḳorban, shulḥan.* The name of the Jordan has not yet been found in the cuneiform inscriptions; but it figures in an Egyptian text (Anast. I. xxiii. 1) in the form of *Y-ira-du-na* (W. M. Müller, *As. u. Eur.* pp. 97 f., 196).

The word יַרְדֵּן is a common noun, and is therefore always accompanied by the article (הַיַּרְדֵּן), with a few exceptions, which will be pointed out below. Yet it is worthy of note that we have not a single passage in which *Yardēn* is treated with certainty as a common noun.

From the point of view of etymology, it is most natural to connect this word with the verb יָרַד, 'to descend,' and this is how it is treated by the prevalent opinion, found, however, more frequently among geographers than among philologists, according to which the Jordan is 'the descending,' 'the flowing,' a name which might, of course, be applicable to any stream of water, and which, in a single particular case, would have become a proper name, just as the Hebrews called the Euphrates הַנָּהָר, 'the river.' But it is more probable that, while retaining the root יָרַד as our starting-point, we should interpret *Yardēn* as the place to which one goes down, *sc.* to drink, *i.e.* 'the watering-place.' Two authors, Seybold (*MNDPV*, 1896, *l.c.*) and Cheyne (*Encyc. Bibl.* ii. col. 2575), have, independently of each other, suggested this explanation. If this derivation is correct, the modern Arabic name of the Jordan would be a literal translation of the old name, for they call it *esh-Sherī'a*, 'the watering-place,' and more fully *esh-Sherī'a el-Kebireh*, 'the great watering-place,' to distinguish it from another stream, its tributary, the *Sherī'at el-Manadireh* (Yarmuk). However, there is found also among the Arabs the name *el-Urdunn*, an approximate transcription of the Hebrew name (cf. Kampffmeyer, in *ZDPV* xv. [1892] p. 27; Ed. König, *Lehrgebäude der heb. Sprache*, ii. i. p. 461).

We must mention one other way of explaining the name of the Jordan, which used to be in great favour with the Fathers of the Church as well as the Jewish teachers. According to this interpretation, the name Jordan may be divided into *Jor* and *Dan*, and these two monosyllables denote the two sources of the river. *Dan*, that is to say, is the name of the city of Dan, formerly Laïsh or Leshem (Jos 18. 19[47]), and consequently that of the branch of the river issuing from it; *Jor* is the name of the other stream, and Jordan is the final name of the river from the point where the two branches unite. This explanation was given by St. Jerome, and accepted by many writers after him. An attempt has been made to support it by

interpreting *Jor* as a contraction of *Ye'ōr* (יְאֹר), a Heb. word meaning 'watercourse,' and used especially in reference to the Nile. This strange etymology has now no interest except that of curiosity, and is not upheld by anybody, any more than another found in the Talmud (*Bekhoroth*, 55), which takes *Yardēn* to be a contraction of *Yered-dan* or *Yored-dan*, and thus brings in both the verb 'to descend' and the name of the city of Dan.

The only passages in which *Yardēn* is used without the article are: (*a*) Job 40[23], where it may be equally well translated by 'the Jordan' or 'a river'; but several commentators doubt whether the text is reliable; Budde suggests deleting this word as a gloss; Gunkel and Winckler change it into *Ye'ōr* (יְאֹר), because in the same passage reference is made to the Nile; Cheyne into *Giḥōn* (גִּיחוֹן) for the same reason. (*b*) Ps 42[7], where *'ereç hay-Yardēn* (אֶרֶץ הַיַּרְדֵּן) seems to denote 'the country of the Jordan,' *i.e.* probably the region round about the sources of the river, which is confirmed by the mention of Hermon or rather the Hermons (in the plural) in the same verse. It must be observed, however, that, according to the Talmud, the river bore the name of Jordan only between the Lake of Tiberias and the Dead Sea, a statement which is neither confirmed nor contradicted by the Bible, and cannot be proved in any way; we may add that, according to some writers, the present custom is exactly the opposite, for it is alleged—has the claim any foundation?—that at the present day only the part of the river above the lake is called *Urdunn*, and the part below, *Sherī'a.*

The word *Jordan* in the rôle of common noun is further proved by the expression 'Jordan of Jericho' (יַרְדֵּן יְרֵחוֹ), in the construct state. The meaning of this will be examined below, in connexion with the lower course of the river near where it falls into the Dead Sea.

2. *General geography and geology.*—The total length of the valley of the Jordan, from its source to its mouth at the Dead Sea, is about 120 miles. It stretches from north to south in a practically straight line. It begins as a continuation of the *Beḳa'a* (Cœle-Syria), that valley which stretches between the Lebanon on the west and the Anti-Lebanon on the east, but whose waters run towards the north. Almost immediately after leaving Lake Ḥuleh, which is 7 feet above the level of the Mediterranean, the Jordan begins to fall below the level of the sea; the Lake of Tiberias is 682 feet, the Dead Sea 1292 feet, below it. There is not another example of such a marked depression on the surface of our globe, except with tracts covered by the seas; the other cases which may be cited attain much less depths; the greatest is about 300 feet in the Sahara, while, taking into account the depth of the Dead Sea (1300 feet), we get a total of almost 2600 feet. G. A. Smith has well said (*HGHL* p. 407): 'Among the rivers of the world the Jordan is unique by a twofold distinction of Nature and History. . . . The Nile and the Jordan, otherwise so different, are alike in this, that the historical singularity of each has behind it as remarkable a singularity of physical formation. . . . Every one knows the incomparableness of the Nile. . . . In its own way the Jordan is as solitary and extreme an effect of natural forces. There may be something on the surface of another planet to match the Jordan Valley; there is nothing in this.'

As regards the geological explanation of this remarkable phenomenon, we may say that it was supplied in the 19th cent. in a very satisfactory manner by the experts who made a study of Palestine, and the valley of the Jordan and the Dead Sea in particular: Fraas, Hull, Lartet, and Blanckenhorn. The following is briefly the result of their labours. When, during the Eocene period, and even before it, during the Cretaceous period, successive strata of limestone had been deposited, there was produced towards the end of the Eocene epoch, by the action of lateral (east and west) pressure, a falling away, *i.e.* a 'fault' or fracture was formed in the earth's crust. This movement, however, was not of a convulsive nature, it was not a sudden cataclysm, but a slow and gradual process, extending over a long period of time. The result of it was the formation of the parallel chains of Lebanon and Anti-Lebanon, and further south that of the two ranges of hills which skirt the Jordan valley. The southern end of this depression is, from the point of view of the flow of water, a transverse ridge reaching 650 feet above the Red Sea and the Mediterranean, and situated about 46 miles from Aḳabah and more than 73 miles from the Dead Sea.

At the end of the Miocene and the beginning of the Pliocene period, the waters in the Jordan valley must have been just about at their present level. But the pluvial period (Pliocene) brought about a considerable raising of the aqueous surface enclosed ; the Jordan valley became a lake which must have been about 200 miles long and more than 2000 feet deep. The glacial period (post-Pliocene), during which the temperature sank considerably and the rainfall increased, only served to accentuate this state of affairs still more. Then, at the close of this period, the streams of water diminished, and also the lake, until things once more arrived at their present state. On the lateral slopes of the valley traces of the heights to which the waters rose are still distinguishable ; some of the most notable of these traces are 1180, others 347, feet above the present level of the Dead Sea.

Alongside of this theory, held in common by those who have studied this question, we must mention, as worthy of attention, the one which W. Libbey, Professor of Physical Geography in the University of Princeton, has recently published (Libbey and Hoskins, *The Jordan Valley and Petra*, ii. pp. 251–260).

The ancients were completely ignorant of the fact that the bottom of the Jordan valley lay below the level of the Mediterranean Sea. Nor were they aware at that time that the depression between the Dead Sea and the Gulf of Aḳabah was intersected by a sort of natural barrier, forming two anticlinal slopes and making a dividing line for the waters. And even in the first part of the 19th cent. it was held by Carl Ritter, W. M. Leake, de Hoff, Léon de Laborde, etc., that formerly— perhaps even in historical times before the catastrophe of Sodom and Gomorrah—the Jordan passed through the Dead Sea, continued its southward course, and flowed into the Red Sea. Those are ideas which have had to be given up. It was in 1836–37 that two German scholars, von Schubert and Roth, and at the same time two Englishmen, G. H. Moore and W. G. Beke, discovered that the Jordan valley sank far down below the level of the sea. The Austrian Russegger, the Frenchman Jules de Bertou, and the Englishman Symonds soon confirmed this sensational discovery, as a consequence of explorations carried on in quite an independent way. Before them, famous travellers, such as Seetzen (1806–07), Burckhardt (1810–12), Irby and Mangles (1817–18), had visited those same parts without any suspicion of the strange phenomenon regarding the altitude.

The course of the Jordan is interrupted twice— first by the Lake of Ḥuleh, a description of which occurs later in the course of the present article, then by the Lake of Tiberias or Sea of Galilee (which see) ; we have not to examine this here. These interruptions quite naturally cause us to divide the next part of this article into three sections : (*a*) the sources of the Jordan, (*b*) the Upper Jordan as far as Lake Tiberias, (*c*) the Lower Jordan from the Lake of Tiberias to the Dead Sea.

3. *The sources of the Jordan.*—Just as in the Alps the traditional opinion of mountaineers does not always show as the principal source of a river the one which tourists or even geographers would denote as such, so is it with the Jordan. The most northerly of its sources, the one which gives rise to

the stream which covers the longest distance, is found near Ḥasbeya, at 1846 feet above the sea, at the foot of the Great Hermon. The name *Ḥasbani* is given to the river which starts there and flows towards the south, following a course parallel at first to that of the Liṭani ; between these twin valleys there is only a short distance and a ridge of mountains of moderate height ; so that one might quite well imagine the Ḥasbani rejoining the Liṭani, and falling along with it into the Mediterranean. But, on the contrary, it remains faithful to its course from north to south, and is joined by a tributary, which some modern scholars would include among the sources of the Jordan—the *Nahr-Bareighit* (Flea River), 'the smallest of the four sources of the Jordan' (Libbey and Hoskins, i. p. 89), but which is usually left aside, so that attention may be given only to the three other more important ones. These are, besides the Ḥasbani, the one which springs forth at Tell el-Ḳadi, and the one which emerges from the grotto of Banias. The Tell el-Ḳadi source is called the *Leddan*. This unexplained name is interpreted by some as containing an allusion to the city of Dan, situated in this region, and generally (G. A. Smith, however, is an exception, *HGHL* pp. 480, 678) identified with Tell el-Ḳadi, Ḳadi, 'judge,' being considered the exact equivalent of the Heb. *Dan*. The source of Tell el-Ḳadi is double, in the sense that it streams forth, at 500 feet above the sea, in two places close together under a hillock which is about 300 feet broad and covered with tall trees, and rises in a very striking manner from the plain, over which it towers about 60 feet. The stream which flows from it is the shortest but most copious of the sources of the Jordan ; it is not, therefore, on account of its abundance, but because of its short length, that Josephus calls it 'the little Jordan' (*BJ* IV. i. 1 ; *Ant.* VIII. viii. 4), or 'the lesser Jordan' (*Ant.* v. iii. 1). Lastly, we find the 'river of Banias,' *Nahr-Banias*, which starts at 1200 feet above the sea from a grotto, the ancient shrine of the Semitic, and then of the Græco-Roman, gods, well known under the name of *Paneion*, and round which arose the city known under the names of Cæsarea Philippi and Paneas, and now called Banias, a corruption of the latter name. Josephus mentions, under the name of Paneas, both the town and the district of which it was the centre ; he also mentions the Paneion, and speaks of 'the famous fountain' (cf. *BJ* I. xxi. 3, III. x. 7 ; *Ant.* XV. x. 3, XVIII. ii. 1). He adds that the water of the source comes from Lake Phiala, situated 120 stades from Cæsarea ; this is, undoubtedly, the small lake nowadays called *Birket-Ram* (cf. Schumacher in *ZDPV* ix. [1886] p. 256 f.), but it is only 60 stades distant. There is, however, no subterranean communication between this lake, an ancient volcanic crater, and the Paneion source.

The Leddan and the river of Banias meet at an altitude of 148 feet, after the Leddan has flowed 5 miles. A little farther down, the Ḥasbani, in its turn, becomes united with them : whence the Jordan is formed.

4. *The Upper Jordan.*—From the confluence, which we have just mentioned, to the Lake of Tiberias the course of the Jordan is unimportant from a historical point of view. The books of the Bible do not speak of it, and later writers very seldom. Nor, from a specifically geographical point of view, has this part of the river any great importance. Its chief interest lies in the fact that at 10 miles distance from the confluence it forms a lake or lagoon, the *Baḥr* or *Buḥeirat* (lake or small lake) **Ḥuleh,** triangular in shape, the level of which is 7 feet above the Mediterranean, and which is rich in papyrus plants. The size of this sheet of water varies very much according to the seasons :

at one time it is a considerable limpid stretch, at another it is simply a kind of huge morass. Its traditional identification with 'the waters of Merom' (Jos 11[5. 7]) must be regarded with caution (cf. *ZDPV* ix. [1886] p. 252); the evidence of Josephus is not favourable. He gives this lake another name, that of 'the lake of the Semechonites' (*BJ* iv. i. 1; cf. *ZDPV l.c.* and p. 348 f.). As regards the modern name *Ḥuleh*, it is perhaps derived from the word *Ulatha*, by which Josephus denotes a district near Banias. For the description of the whole upper course of the Jordan from its sources to the Lake of Tiberias, including Lake Ḥuleh, see Macgregor, *The Rob Roy on the Jordan*, 1869, 5th ed. 1880.

As soon as it leaves Lake Ḥuleh, the Jordan begins to flow below the level of the sea, and falls almost 700 feet in a distance of 10 miles. We must here notice a bridge, the *Jisr Benât-Ya'ḳub*, 'bridge of Jacob's Daughters,' sometimes wrongly called 'bridge of Jacob' or 'bridge of Jacob's Sons'; the name itself is really difficult to explain; see on this subject an ingenious solution suggested in *PEFSt*, 1898, p. 29 f., by B. Z. Friedmann.

5. *The Lower Jordan.*—The Jordan issues from the Lake of Tiberias at a place called *Bab et-Tum*, leaving on the east the little modern village of Semakh, which has no bridge connecting it with the right bank, and as the river is not fordable at this place, the passage, naturally of frequent occurrence, is accomplished by means of boats. A little farther down there are the remains of an ancient bridge called at the present day *Umm el-Ḳanatir*, and again at a short distance below, the ruins of another bridge, *Umm es-Sidd*. There the Jordan begins to assume a very sinuous course, describing endless meanders; Pliny spoke of it as an *annis ambitiosus*, i.e. a winding river. The distance in a straight line from the Lake of Tiberias to the Dead Sea is about 65 miles, but if we take into account all the sinuosities of the river it reaches a total of 200 miles.

The Jordan valley at this part is now called the *Ghôr*, i.e. 'depression,' 'valley.' Even in the OT it was designated (Jos 13[19. 27]) by the name *ha-'ēmek*, 'the valley,' in opposition to the neighbouring heights. But a name much more frequent in the OT is '*Arabah*, which was applied to the valley to the north as well as that to the south of the Dead Sea; nowadays the name '*Arabah*, which has been preserved, is applied only to the valley to the south of the Dead Sea. In Greek, not in the LXX, but in Jos., Eusebius, etc., 'Arabah is rendered Αὐλών. Josephus also uses the expressions 'wide wilderness' and 'the great plain' (*BJ* iii. x. 7, iv. viii. 2; *Ant.* iv. vi. 1).

The *Ghôr* is hemmed in on either side by chains of mountains, or at least hills, of variable height, but sometimes rising 1500 or even 1800 feet above the bed of the river. The slopes are generally somewhat steep, but not to such an extent as to prevent their being scaled. Especially at the spots where the wadis come down from one of the side mountains, means of access are opened up. The soil of the valley is fertile, especially in the northern and middle parts. As to the river itself, it flows in a bed which it has hollowed out for itself, called the *Zôr*. This bed is somewhat variable in breadth, and it may be easily seen that the river has frequently changed its course. Thus at Damieh, of which we shall speak below, and where we find the half-ruined arches of a bridge of the Middle Ages, the Jordan actually no longer passes under the bridge, but at some distance from it. The ground bordering either side of the river is covered with very thick brushwood; this is undoubtedly what is called in Jer 12[5] 49[19] 50[44], Zec 11[3] the גְּאוֹן הַיַּרְדֵּן, i.e. 'the majesty (RV 'pride') of Jordan' (AV 'the swelling of Jordan' [in the Jer. passages] arises

from a wrong interpretation, as if the reference here was to the floods of Jordan; these do exist; they are sometimes sudden and very violent, rendering the fords impassable; cf. Jos 3[15], Sir 24[26 (36)]).

The vegetation, especially as we go further south, becomes very nearly tropical, and the fauna resembles that of Africa. The lion, which abounded in ancient times, and continued to be encountered even in the Middle Ages, has completely disappeared. But other carnivorous animals are found here, leopards and hyænas, as well as wild boars, porcupines, etc. In Palestine 58 species of birds are met with, which are also N. African: nearly all of them belong to the *Ghôr*. The flora has the same character, it recalls that of Nubia, Abyssinia, the Sahara, and the region of the great African lakes. Great heat prevails throughout this whole region, a fact which is quite naturally explained when we remember that it is a valley shut in between high walls, at its highest point 682 and at its lowest 1292 feet below the sea-level. The temperature varies from 77° to 130° Fahr. This circumstance undoubtedly accounts largely for the fact that there are not and never have been any towns on the banks of the Jordan. But another reason for the latter important fact may be found in the danger to which the inhabitants would be exposed, owing to the impossibility of effectually fortifying themselves against attacks. The few towns of the *Ghôr* at one time populated, *e.g.* Phasaël and Jericho, are on the height at some distance from the river, near protecting mountains. The other inhabited places are only wretched villages.

The Jordan forms a very large number of rapids; about thirty may be counted, apart from the whirl-pools, which are numerous. There is also a considerable number of fords; the majority of them—22—are in the northern part, to the north of *Ḳarn Sarṭabeh*; there are 5 more in the south. A little to the north of Beisan there is a bridge, which dates from the Middle Ages, the *Jisr el-Mujamieh*, on the way—an ancient Roman road—leading from the plain of Jezreel to Gadara and Damascus. Further south is the ruined bridge of Damieh; and lastly, near Jericho, a modern bridge, the *Jisr el-Ghoranieh*, at the place where the mosaic map of Madaba indicates a ferry-boat. For information regarding the fords of the Jordan, see G. A. Smith, *HGHL* p. 336 f.

The configuration of the Jordan valley is remarkable for its formation into terraces (in Arabic *ṭabaḳât*), the river flowing between the lowermost of these. There is no comparatively equal and continuous incline from the mountain to the river, but a succession of horizontal platforms, with sudden and very steep slopes, which form what are called the steep banks or cliffs of Jordan. They are marly, and have a tendency to become worn, and even to give way. The *Zôr* itself is bordered by them, and the Jordan often flows, at least at one side, along the foot of a declivity impossible of ascent. This is the case, *e.g.*, in front of the so-called place of the Baptism at the latitude of Jericho. These terraces correspond to the different levels attained by the waters of the great lake which at one time filled the whole valley, and which first increased and then sank down again.

The Jordan is fed by numerous tributaries. The most important of these are on the left bank. One of them, the *Hieromax* of the Greeks, the *Yarmuk* of the Rabbis, the *Sherî'at el-Manadireh* of the Arabs, already mentioned above, flows down from the high plateau on the east of Lake Tiberias, and passes between the warm springs of el-Ḥammah and the ancient Gadara (modern *Umm Ḳeis*). Further south, also on the eastern bank, the Jordan receives the *Zerḳa* (blue river), the *Yabboḳ* of ancient times, which, after passing *'Amman* (Rabbath-Ammon, Philadelphia), describes an immense semi-circle towards the east, resumes its westward course, passes to the south of *Jerash* (Gerasa), and at last empties itself into the Jordan; the position of its mouth has considerably changed in the course of the centuries. On the right bank, we must mention the *Nahr-Jalud*, which springs from the fountain of Ḥarod at the foot of Mt. Gilboa and passes to Beisan; then, close to Jericho, the *Wadi el-Ḳelt*, which tradition, probably wrongly, identifies with the Cherith of the Bible.

It is scarcely necessary to say that the Jordan is not navigable. Yet on three occasions the attempt has been made to sail down its course from the Lake of Tiberias to the Dead Sea. The first time it was an Irishman, Costigan, who, in 1835, accomplished this daring feat alone in a boat for one oarsman; the second time it was Lieutenant Molyneux, of the British Navy, in 1847. Both succeeded in reaching the Dead Sea, but both died soon after from the strain which they had undergone. Lastly, in 1848, an American expedition, under Lieutenant Lynch, sailed all the way down in two boats specially built for the purpose, reached the Dead Sea, and were able to record a whole series of very useful observations. Other travellers have also made a careful study of the Jordan valley, but from the land; besides those whom we have already mentioned, we may recall the names of Robinson, Guérin, and Conder. Long before there was any question of scientific explorations, pilgrims had followed the course of the Jordan through the whole of the *Ghôr*, *e.g.* Antonius Martyr in the 6th cent., Willibald in the 8th; we may add to these the name of King Baldwin I., who passed up from Jericho to the Lake of Tiberias.

While the northern part of the *Ghôr* is fertile, and more especially the environs of Beisan, it is very different in the south, near Jericho. This town, it is true, and its immediate neighbourhood, form a kind of oasis; but the rest of this region is not nearly so rich, the soil being impregnated with salt substances; one is reminded of the nearness of the Dead Sea.

It is this district that is referred to in the passages of the OT where the 'Jordan of Jericho' is spoken of. This does not mean a particular branch of the river, far less another stream of the same name (as, *e.g.*, they say in Valais, 'the Visp of Saas' and 'the Visp of Zermatt'). It is simply 'the Jordan in the district of Jericho.' See Nu 22¹ 26³. ⁶³ 31¹² 33⁴⁸. ⁵⁰ 34¹⁵ 35¹ 36¹³, Jos 13³² 16¹ 20⁸, 1 Ch 6⁶³ (⁷⁸). We must correct the AV and RV in this respect, and remember that Jordan is originally a common noun.

Another Biblical expression referring to this particular region is *Kikkar hay-Yardēn* (כִּכַּר הַיַּרְדֵּן), Gn 13¹⁰ᶠ, or *hak-Kikkār* (Gn 13¹² 19¹⁷. ²⁵. ²⁸ᶠ, Neh 3²² 12²⁸), lit. 'the circle' (*i.e.* the basin) of the Jordan, or, more briefly, 'the circle'; in Greek ἡ περίχωρος τοῦ Ἰορδάνου (LXX, Mt 3⁵, Lk 3³). It may seem at first sight that this expression should apply to the whole valley, but it is more probable, considering the passages in which it is used, that it is only a designation of the broader part lying to the north of the Dead Sea, with Jericho as centre (cf. Dt 34³) and stretching northwards until near Sarṭabeh (cf. 2 S 18²³, 1 K 7⁴⁶, 2 Ch 4¹⁷), and perhaps also including the basin of the Dead Sea. This latter point depends on the position assigned to the cities of the *Kikkār* (Cities of the Plain), and to Zoar in particular; the present writer thinks their site ought to be sought to the north of the Dead Sea, and this frees him from the necessity of extending the term *Kikkār* to embrace the region of the Dead Sea. We also find as a designation of the region of Jericho, the phrase '*arboth Yerichô* (Jos 5¹⁰, 2 K 25⁵), and for the district facing it, to the east of the Jordan, '*arboth Moab* (Nu 22¹ 26³. ⁶³ 31¹² 33⁴⁸·⁵⁰ 35¹ 36¹³, Dt 34¹. ⁸, Jos 13³²). The Hebrew word used here is the plural of '*Arabah*.

6. *Historical and political rôle.*—It is a commonplace to say that the Jordan separates E. Palestine from W. Palestine. But one often yields to the temptation to over-estimate the importance of this separation. The Jordan has been called 'the great Divider.' We should not exaggerate. The separation does exist, but it is not so great as people think. And if separation there is, it is not the river itself, with its narrow breadth—45 to 90 feet

on an average, at places perhaps as broad as 180 (?) feet—and its numerous fords, that constitute it; it is rather the valley as a whole, the *Ghôr* enclosed between its lateral ramparts, with its intolerable heat, and its want of security. The stream itself is so little of an obstacle that it is constantly being crossed, easily, too easily.

In ancient times it kept back neither armies nor raids. The pilgrims of Galilee, who in the times of Judaism made their way to Jerusalem, had so little dread of passing the river that they chose to cross it twice and make their journey by way of Peræa rather than pass through the territory of the Samaritans. John the Baptist baptized beyond the Jordan, and that did not prevent crowds from going to him. Later on, the river was again crossed at all times and with great ease, and down to the most recent epochs the incursions of trans-Jordan Bedawîn have not been prevented by the river, any more than the expeditions sent forth in pursuit of them. And this was as little the case when the Midianites invaded the territory of the Israelites, and Gideon put them to rout and pursued them, while the Ephraimites held the fords. The mountain-slopes are here and there quite accessible; it is easy to descend and ascend the lateral wadis. The valley which stretches down from Jezreel to Beisan is the most convenient of the great routes, and there are many others. G. A. Smith has admirably shown the close connexion between Samaria and the country of Gilead (*HGHL* p. 335 ff.).

The Jordan valley is so ineffectual a barrier, that at all times the possessors of the western district have felt the necessity of establishing themselves on the eastern bank for the sake of safety. The 2½ tribes of Israel quartered on the left bank were a rampart guarding their western brethren from the invaders and pillagers of the east. The Romans realized the need of occupying the country across the Jordan in a strong and unassailable manner. And in our day security was not really re-established on the west of the Jordan until the Turkish Government imposed its authority in a firm and permanent fashion in the provinces east of the river.

7. *OT references.*—It has been well said (*Jewish Encyc.* vii. p. 239), 'There is no regular description of the Jordan in the Bible; only scattered and indefinite references to it are given.' There are 176 references to the Jordan in the OT, the majority of which are found in the narrative books of Jos. (67), Deut. (26), Nu. (20), Sam. (17 : 2+15), Kings (12 : 3+9), Jg. (12), Ch. (7 : 1+6), Gn. (5). But by far the greater number of those have to do with topographical expressions such as 'on this side Jordan,' 'beyond Jordan,' 'to go over Jordan,' 'by Jordan.' If those cases are deducted, all that remain are very few. Besides, as the present Dictionary is devoted to the Gospels, we have not to enter into details as we should have to do if it treated of the OT. We shall confine ourselves therefore to noting the following. (*a*) The crossing of the Jordan by the Israelites (Jos 3–4 : cf. Ps 114³· ⁵). This narrative must be compared with what happened on the 8th of December 1267 at the bridge of Damieh, in the reign of the Sultan Beibars I. (1260–77), according to the Arabic historian Nowairi (*PEFSt*, 1895, pp. 253–261, 334–338), and the mention of a similar fact in the Val Blenio, in Tessin, when in 1512 a landslip stopped the flow of a stream for 14 months, after which a clearance was effected by the bursting of the barrier which had been formed. (*b*) The seizing of the fords of the Jordan by Ehud after the murder of Eglon (Jg 3²⁸). (*c*) The campaign of Gideon (Jg 7–8) against Midian. (*d*) That of Jephthah against the Ephraimites (Jg 12). (*e*) The flight of David before Absalom, the battle which followed it and the return of David to Jerusalem (2 S 17$^{22. 24}$ 19$^{16-43}$) [on this point the Hebrew text speaks (19$^{18(19)}$) of a עֲבָרָה for enabling the king to cross from the other side of the river; Jos. (*Ant.* VII. xi. 2) renders this word by γέφυρα, 'bridge,' but it more probably refers to a ferry-boat]. (*f*) The crossing of Elijah with Elisha, and the return of the latter alone (2 K 2). (*g*) Two other narratives referring to Elisha: Naaman (2 K 5$^{10ff.}$), and the adventure of the lost axe (2 K 6^{5}). (*h*) The reference in 1 Mac 5$^{24. 52}$ 9$^{35-49}$ to certain incidents of war, relating to the struggles of the Jews with the Syrians. In the poetical and prophetic books, the Jordan is scarcely mentioned; we have already had occasion to quote the few texts where it occurs.

8. *NT references.*—Here again, several times, the Jordan is mentioned in the phrase 'beyond Jordan.' See Mt 4^{15} (which quotes Is 9^{1}) 4^{25} 19^{1}, Mk 3^{8} 10^{1}. All the other passages of the Gospels which mention the Jordan are connected with the ministry of John the Baptist, and the baptism of Jesus, or make a retrospective allusion to them. Thus Mt 3^{5}, Mk 1^{5}, Lk 3^{3} describe John at work, preaching and baptizing; and on this point Mt. and Lk. mention the περίχωρος of the Jordan, a word which we explained when speaking of the *Kikkār* of the OT (see above, § 5). Others (Mt 3^{13}, Mk 1^{9}) show us Jesus baptized 'in the Jordan,' and then leaving the banks of the river (Lk 4^{1}) in order to go away to the desert. The Gospel of John is the only one which defines more precisely the place where John baptized and where Jesus was baptized. Jn 1^{28} tells us that 'these things were done in Bethany beyond Jordan, where John was baptizing,' and two later passages in the same Gospel recall the same fact; 3^{26} 'He that was with thee beyond Jordan,' and 10^{40} 'He went away again beyond Jordan to the place where John at first baptized.' See art. BETHABARA. Without entering here into the discussion of the problem which is raised by the substitution (by Origen) of *Bethabara* for *Bethany*, we may say that the latter is infinitely better attested, and ought to be preferred (this does away with the topographical hypotheses based on *Bethabara*). As regards Bethany, the knowledge at our disposal does not enable us to determine its site. It must be (*a*) beyond Jordan, which excludes the traditional so-called 'place of the Baptism' near Jericho; and (*b*) near Jordan, which renders improbable the suggestions of Grove, Wilson, and Cheyne, who would combine Bethany and Bethabara into Bethanabra, and the view of Furrer ('Das Geog. im Ev. nach Joh.' in *ZNTW*, 1902, p. 257 f.), put forward also by Zahn (*Einl. NT* ii. p. 561), and noted by Sanday (*Sacred Sites of the Gospels*, p. 94), which identifies Bethany with Betaneh = Betonim (Jos 13^{26}). See on this special question Lagrange, 'Béthanie et Béthabara' in *RB* iv. [1895] pp. 502–522; G. A. Smith, *HGHL* p. 496; C. Mommert, *Aenon und Bethania*, 1903, pp. 1–19, 30–56.

LITERATURE.—*SWP* i. pp. 85, 97, 109–113, 139–142, ii. pp. 76–79, 380–388, iii. 169 ff., 232; Saunders, *Introduction to the Survey of W. P.*, 1881, pp. 62–97, 143–170; *PEFSt*, almost every volume [see Indexes]; Reland, *Palästina*, pp. 261–266, 270–279; Seetzen, *Reisen*, i. pp. 323–343, ii. 259–271, 296–323; Burckhardt, *Travels*, pp. 342–347; Irby and Mangles, *Travels*, p. 91 ff.; Buckingham, *Travels in Palestine*, ii. p. 92 ff., *Travels among the Arub Tribes*, pp. 6 15; von Schubert, *Reise in das Morgenland*, iii. pp. 67–94; de Bertou, 'Voyage depuis les sources du Jourdain jusqu' à la Mer Rouge' in *Bulletin de la Société de Géographie*, 1839, pp. 114–168; Molyneux, 'Expedition to the Jordan and the Dead Sea' in *Jour. R. Geog. Soc.* xviii. [1848] pp. 104–130, cf. p. xxxvi; Lynch, *Narrative of the United States Expedition to the River Jordan and the Dead Sea*, 1849, the same author's *Official Report*, 1852; Robinson, 'Depression of the Dead Sea and of the Jordan Valley' in *Jour. R. Geog. Soc.* xviii. [1848] pp. 77–88, the same author's *Physical Geography of the Holy Land*, pp. 66–95, 116–139, and his *BRP* i. 537–568, iii. 390–418; Petermann, 'On the Fall of the Jordan' in *Jour. R. Geog. Soc.* xviii. [1848] pp. 89–104; Ritter, *Erdkunde*, xv. pp. 152–238, 266–281, 358–556, 698–723, the same author's *Der Jordan*

und die Beschiffung des Todten Meeres, 1850; Tobler, *Topographie*, ii. pp. 669–719; Lartet, *Exploration géologique de la Mer Morte*, 1878; Reclus, *Géographie universelle*, ix. pp. 727–736; Lortet, *La Syrie d'aujourd'hui*, pp. 443–470, 543–553; Guérin, *Samarie*, i. pp. 97–109, 239–240, *Galilée*, i. 133, 282–285, 342, ii. 297, 308–310, 338, 450 f.; G. A. Smith, *HGHL* pp. 465–496; Buhl, *GAP* pp. 35–39, 111–113, 115 f.; Thomson, *LB* i. pp. 359–370, ii. pp. 447–459, 468–473; Hull, 'Memoir on the Geology and Geography of Arabia Petræa, Palestine,' etc., in *SWP*, 1889, pp. 3–20, 29 ff., 103–120, the same author's *Mount Seir, Sinai, and Western Palestine*, 1889, pp. 75–143, 159–169; Conder, *Tent Work*[6], pp. 214–235; MacCoun, *The Holy Land in Geography and History*, 1897, i. pp. 1–3, 47–50, ii. p. 30; Newbold, 'The Lake Phiala, the Jordan and its Sources' in *JRAS* xvi. [1856] pp. 8–31; J. L. Porter, *Through Samaria to Galilee and the Jordan*, 1889, pp. 114–142, 266–298; Dawson, *Modern Science in Bible Lands*, pp. 313–319, 338–354; Libbey and Hoskins, *The Jordan Valley and Petra*, 1905; Fraas, *Aus dem Orient*, 1867, pp. 72–78, 204–206; Blanckenhorn, 'Entstehung und Geschichte des Todten Meeres' in *ZDPV* xix. [1896] pp. 1–59.

LUCIEN GAUTIER.

JORIM.—Named in our Lord's genealogy (Lk 3^{29}).

JOSECH (AV *Joseph*).—Named in our Lord's genealogy (Lk 3^{26}).

JOSEPH ('Ιωσήφ).—**1.** The patriarch, mentioned only in the description of the visit of Jesus to Sychar (Jn 4^{5}).—**2. 3.** Joseph son of Mattathias and Joseph son of Jonam are both named in the genealogy of Jesus given in Lk. (3$^{24. 30}$).*—**4.** One of the brethren of the Lord, Mt 13^{55} (AV **Joses**, the form adopted in both AV and RV in Mt 27^{56}, Mk 6^{3} 15$^{40. 47}$. See JOSES).

5. Joseph, the husband of Mary and the reputed father of Jesus (Lk 3^{23}), is not mentioned in Mk., and only indirectly in Jn. (1^{45} 6^{42}). He was of Davidic descent; and, though Mt. and Lk. differ in the genealogical details, they connect Jesus with Joseph and through him with David (Mt 1$^{1ff.}$, Lk 3$^{23ff.}$). Joseph, who was a carpenter (Mt 13^{55}) and a poor man, as his offering in the temple showed (Lk 2^{24}), lived in Nazareth (2^{4}) and was espoused to Mary, also of Nazareth (1^{26}). By their betrothal they entered into a relationship which, though not the completion of marriage, could be dissolved only by death or divorce. Before the marriage ceremony Mary was 'found with child of the Holy Ghost,' but the angelic annunciation to her was not made known to Joseph. He is described as a just man (Mt 1^{19}), a strict observer of the Law. The law was stern (Dt 22$^{23. 24}$), but its severity had been mitigated and divorce had taken the place of death. Divorce could be effected publicly, so that the shame of the woman might be seen by all; or it could be done privately, by the method of handing the bill of separation to the woman in presence of two witnesses.† Joseph, not willing to make Mary a public example, 'was minded to put her away privily' (Mt 1^{19}). An angel, however, appeared to him in a dream, telling him not to fear to marry Mary, as the conception was of the Holy Ghost, and also that she would bring forth a son, whom he was to name Jesus (v.$^{20f.}$). The dream was accepted as a revelation,‡ as a token of Divine favour, and Joseph took Mary as his wife, but did not live with her as her husband till she had brought forth her firstborn son (v.$^{24f.}$).

Before the birth of Christ there was an Imperial decree that all the world should be taxed, and Joseph, being of the house and lineage of David, had to leave Nazareth and go to Bethlehem, to be taxed with Mary.§ In Bethlehem Jesus was born;

* Joseph the son of Juda in v.^{26} (AV) becomes Josech the son of Joda in RV.

† Cf. Edersheim, *The Life and Times of Jesus the Messiah*, i. 154. Dalman asserts that Edersheim is incorrect in stating that public divorce was possible (see Hastings' *DB*, art. 'Joseph').

‡ *Op. cit.* i. 155.

§ On the question of the visit to Bethlehem see Ramsay's *Was Christ born at Bethlehem?*

and there the shepherds, to whom the angel had announced the birth of the Saviour, found Mary and Joseph and 'the babe lying in a manger' (Lk 2¹⁶). At the circumcision, on the eighth day after the birth, the child received the name 'Jesus' which Joseph had been commanded to give Him; and on a later day, when Mary's purification was accomplished (cf. Lv 12²·³·⁴), she and Joseph took Jesus to the temple in Jerusalem (Lk 2²²), to 'present him to the Lord'* and to offer a sacrifice, according to the requirements of the law (Ex 13², Lv 12⁸). Joseph fulfilled the law as if he were the father of Jesus; and after the ceremonies in the temple he must have returned with Mary and her son to Bethlehem, which was 6 miles distant from Jerusalem. In Bethlehem the Wise Men who had come from the East saw Mary and 'the young child' and worshipped Him; and after their departure the angel of the Lord appeared again to Joseph, bidding him take Mary and the child and flee into Egypt on account of Herod, who would seek to destroy Him (Mt 2¹³). Joseph was quick to obey, and rising in the night he took the young child and His mother and departed for Egypt, where Herod had no authority (v.¹⁴). In Egypt they were to remain till the angel brought word to Joseph (v.¹³); and there they dwelt, possibly two or even three years, till the death of Herod, when the angel again appeared in a dream to Joseph. The angel commanded him to take the young child and His mother and go into the land of Israel. Obedience was at once given by Joseph, but he became afraid when he learned that Archelaus was reigning in Judæa. Again the angel appeared in a dream, and after a warning Joseph proceeded to Nazareth, which was not under the rule of Archelaus, who had an evil reputation, but under that of the milder Antipas (vv.¹⁴⁻²³).

It is recorded of Joseph that he and Mary went every year, at the Passover, to Jerusalem, and that when Jesus was twelve years of age He accompanied them. On that occasion Jesus tarried in Jerusalem, after Joseph and Mary, thinking He was with them in the company, had left the city. When they had gone a day's journey they found He was not with them, and they turned back to Jerusalem. After three days they found Him in the temple among the doctors, and they were amazed. Mary's words, 'Son, why hast thou thus dealt with us?' behold, thy father and I have sought thee sorrowing,' called forth an answer which Joseph and Mary did not understand. But after the incident in Jerusalem, Jesus went with them to Nazareth and 'was subject unto them' (Lk 2⁴¹⁻⁵¹). Mary's words and the record of the subjection of Jesus to her and Joseph indicate that Joseph stood to Jesus in the place of an earthly father. How long that relationship continued is unknown, since the time of the death of Joseph is not stated in the Gospels. It may be accepted as a certainty that he was not alive throughout the period of the public ministry of Jesus, seeing that he is not directly or indirectly mentioned along with His mother and brothers and sisters (Mk 3³¹ 6³).

6. Joseph of Arimathæa ('Ιωσὴφ ὁ ἀπὸ 'Αριμαθαίας, see ARIMATHÆA).—A rich and pious Israelite (Mt 27⁵⁷), a member of the Sanhedrin (Mk 15⁴³), who, secretly for fear of the Jews, was Jesus' disciple (Jn 19³⁸). He had not consented to the death of Jesus (Lk 23⁵¹), and could not therefore have been present at the Council, where they all condemned Him to be guilty of death (Mk 14⁶⁴). The timidity which prevented him from openly avowing his discipleship, and perhaps from defending Jesus in the Sanhedrin, fled when he beheld the death of

* 'The earliest period of presentation was thirty-one days after birth, so as to make the legal month quite complete' (Edersheim, *The Life and Times of Jesus the Messiah*, i. 193).

the Lord. Jewish law required that the body of a person who had been executed should not remain all night upon the tree, but should 'in any wise' be buried (Dt 21²²·²³). This law would not bind the Roman authorities, and the custom in the Empire was to leave the body to decay upon the cross (cf. Hor. *Ep.* I. xvi. 48; Plautus, *Mil. Glor.* II. iv. 19). But at the crucifixion of Jesus and of the two malefactors, the Jews, anxious that the bodies should not remain upon the cross during the Sabbath, besought Pilate that the legs of the crucified might be broken and death hastened, and that then the bodies might be taken away (Jn 19³¹). According to Roman law, the relatives could claim the body of a person executed (*Digest*, xlviii. 24, 'De cadav. punit.'). But which of the relatives of Jesus had a sepulchre in Jerusalem where His body might be placed? Joseph, wishing the burial not to be 'in any wise' (cf. Jos 8²⁹), but to be according to the most pious custom of his race, went to Pilate and craved the body. The petition required boldness (Mk 15⁴³), since Joseph, with no kinship in the flesh with Jesus, would be forced to make a confession of discipleship, which the Jews would note. Pilate, too, neither loved nor was loved by Israel, and his anger might be kindled at the coming of a Jew, and the member of the Sanhedrin be assailed with insults. Pilate, however, making sure that Jesus was dead, gave the body. Perhaps he had pity for the memory of Him he had condemned, or perhaps the rich man's gold, since Pilate, according to Philo (*Op.* ii. 590), took money from suppliants, secured what was craved. Joseph, now with no fear of the Jews, acted openly, and had to act with speed, as the day of preparation for the Sabbath was nearly spent. Taking down the body of Jesus from the cross (and other hands must have aided his), he wrapped it in linen which he himself had bought (Mk 15⁴⁶). In the Fourth Gospel it is told how Nicodemus, bringing a mixture of myrrh and aloes, about an hundred pound weight, joined Joseph, and how they took the body and wound it in linen clothes with the spices (Jn 19⁴⁰). Near the place of crucifixion was a garden, and in the garden a new sepulchre, which Joseph had hewn out in the rock, doubtless for his own last resting-place; and in that sepulchre, wherein was never man yet laid, was placed the body of Jesus prepared for its burial (Mt 27⁶⁰, Jn 19⁴¹). In the court at the entrance to the tomb, the preparation would be made. All was done which the time before the Sabbath allowed reverent hands to do; and then Joseph, perhaps thinking of the pious offices that could yet be done to the dead, rolled a great stone to the door of the sepulchre and departed (Mt 27⁶⁰). On late legends regarding Joseph of Arimathæa see Hastings' *DB*, vol. ii. p. 778.

J. HERKLESS.

JOSES ('Ιωσῆς, יוֹסֵי, a shortened form of יוֹסֵף, 'he adds'; cf. Gn 30²⁴. The identity of the two names is doubted by Lightfoot [*Gal.*³ 261, note 1], chiefly on the ground of the use of different forms in the Peshiṭta; but Dalman [*Gram. Aram.* 75] rightly views יוסי as a dialectical, and probably Galilæan, abbreviation of יוסי. The names are apparently interchangeable [cf. Mt 13⁵⁵ with Mk 6³]; in Mt 27⁵⁶ WH and Nestle with Tisch. read 'Ιωσήφ, and in all the passages there is textual evidence, sufficiently strong not to be overlooked, for the name rejected).—**1.** A brother of Jesus (Mk 6³). This brother is not mentioned anywhere else except in the above passage of Matthew (27⁵⁶). For views as to his real relationship see Hastings' *DB* i. 320 ff., and art. BRETHREN OF THE LORD in present work. **2.** The brother of James the Little (Mt 27⁵⁶, Mk 15⁴⁰·⁴⁷). The name of Joses stands alone in the last passage, but that of his better known brother is substituted by the 'Western' text.

The father was Clopas (Jn 19²⁵); but of him, as of his son Joses, nothing certain is known. Both must have been familiar to the members of the early Christian community; but the Syriac versions are against the identification of Clopas with Alphæus, and Hegesippus does not say enough (Eus. *HE* iii. 11) to warrant the conclusion that Joses was a nephew of Joseph of Nazareth.

R. W. Moss.

JOSIAH. — The well - known king of Judah, named in our Lord's genealogy (Mt 1¹⁰ᶠ·).

JOT.—This modern spelling of the AV, followed by RV, which has discarded the 16th cent. 'iote' (in Tindale, Coverdale, Cranmer 'iott') of Rhemish, Bishops', AV (1611), somewhat obscures the etymology of the word, which is simply a transliteration of the Greek term (ἰῶτα = 'i'). Wyclif's translation and paraphrase ('oon i, *that is lest lettre*') was not adopted by any of the subsequent English versions. The Greek trisyllable being pronounced 'jota' (cf. Spanish 'jota,' German 'jota,' 'jodt,' 'jott,' 'jot'), the reduction to the monosyllable 'iote' (pronounced 'jote') with its variants 'ioyt,' 'ioit' (Scots form : see J. Knox, *Hist. Ref.* 1572, Wks. 1846, i. 107; and Davidson, *Commend. Vprichtnes*, 152 (1573), in Satir. P. Ref. xl.) and 'iott,' was natural and normal. The German authorized version is still Luther's paraphrase : 'der kleinste Buchstabe' for which Weizsäcker prefers the transliteration : 'ein Jota,' while the French versions also transliterate : ' un (seul) iota.'

The proverbial phrase ἰῶτα ἓν ἢ μία κεραία (Mt 5¹⁸ only) derives its point from the fact that ἰῶτα in the Greek alphabet, like its equivalent letter and original *yod* in the Hebrew, is the smallest character. In fact, as Dr. Hastings notes (*s.v.* in *DB*), the *yod* being more distinctively the smallest, provides an argument in favour of those who regard Aramaic as the language of Jesus.

After Tindale's introduction of the word (1526), its meaning, derived from the passage above cited, was not so much 'the least letter or written part of any writing,' as in a more general application 'the very least,' 'a whit,' and was usually preceded by a negative expressed or implied. Thus : Bale (1538), *God's Promises*, iii. in Dodsley O. Pl. i. 1 : 'I wyll not one iote, Lord, from thy wyll dyssent'; Shakspeare (1596), *Merch. of Ven.*: 'This bond doth giue thee here no iot of bloud'; Spenser (1595), *Sonnets*, lvii.: 'That wonder is how I should liue a iot.'

P. Henderson Aitken.

JOTHAM.—A king of Judah, named in our Lord's genealogy (Mt 1⁹).

JOURNEY.—See Travel.

JOY.—In the Greek of the NT there are two verbs, with their corresponding nouns, used to express the idea of joy. These are ἀγαλλιᾶν, ἀγαλλίασις, and χαίρειν, χαρά.

The word ἀγαλλιᾶν conveys rather the idea of exultation or exuberant gladness, and is a favourite with St. Luke, who has been called the 'most profound psychologist among the Evangelists.' It is in the pages of his Gospel also that we find the most frequent mention of circumstances of joy attending the proclamation and reception of the gospel message, and the whole character of his writing reveals our Lord in the most joyous relation to His own disciples and to the world at large. The Gr. word for 'gospel' (εὐαγγέλιον) means 'good tidings,' or, as it is described in Lk 2¹⁰, in the message of the angel to the shepherds, 'good tidings of great joy' (εὐαγγελίζομαι ὑμῖν χαρὰν μεγάλην). In the case of the angel messenger to Zacharias, the two words are combined in his greeting. Thus at the very outset the idea of joy attends the prophecy of even the harsher ministry of John the Baptist. 'Thou shalt,' says the angel, 'have joy and gladness (χαρὰ καὶ ἀγαλλίασις), and many shall rejoice (χαρήσονται) at his birth' (Lk 1¹⁴). Another strange attendant circumstance of the joy of these days that preceded our Lord's incarnation is the utterance of Elisabeth, who, when Mary, the predestined mother of the Messiah, comes to visit her, cries out in an ecstasy of wonder and joy, 'Behold, when the voice of thy salutation came into mine ears, the babe leapt in my womb for joy' (v.⁴⁴). In the same scene there immediately follows the song of thanksgiving known in the Church as the *Magnificat* (wh. see), which is pervaded by the spirit of joy, and in which the word 'rejoiced' occurs at the very outset (v.⁴⁷).

When we turn to the historical account of the beginnings of the proclamation of the gospel, we find that, according to Jn.'s narrative, when John the Baptist declared the coming of the Greater than himself, he heralded His advent in the words, 'He that hath the bride is the bridegroom: but the friend of the bridegroom, which standeth and heareth him, rejoiceth greatly because of the bridegroom's voice: this my joy therefore is fulfilled' (Jn 3²⁹).

This statement is rather remarkable in the light of the accounts of the Baptist's ministry given in the Synoptics. There the ascetic note is much more prominent, and it is our Lord who says that, because John came 'neither eating nor drinking,' the people supposed he had a devil (Mt 11¹⁸ ‖ Lk 7³³). Whether we are to think that the Fourth Evangelist had carried back the conception of his Lord's ministry into the prophetic description of it given by His forerunner or not, it is difficult to decide. In any case, the statement here attributed to John the Baptist stands alone, and is not characteristic of his general attitude or of the question which, according to Mt. and Lk., he addressed at a later time to our Lord Himself.

In the parables in which the secret of the Kingdom is itself set forth by our Lord, we meet the word 'joy' several times. In the interpretation of the parable of the Sower we are told : 'He that was sown upon the rocky places, this is he that heareth the word, and straightway with joy receiveth it' (Mt 13²⁰), a striking characterization of the temper of those who eagerly adopt a new idea, but are just as ready to exchange it for some more recent fashion. It is a temper that our Lord describes in another place, when, discussing the ministry of His forerunner, He says : 'He was the lamp that burneth and shineth, and ye were willing to rejoice for a season in his light' (Jn 5³⁵). Joy of a deeper and more permanent character is that of the man who found a treasure hidden in his field, and 'in his joy he goeth and selleth all that he hath and buyeth that field' (Mt 13⁴⁴). This is the true and evangelical temper of a proper reception of the gospel message. In Lk 15 joy is given a higher place and a yet more spiritual significance. In the three famous parables that fill that chapter, the joy of God's own heart is set forth under the images of the shepherd with his sheep, the woman with her precious coin, and the father with his restored son. Joy, says our Lord, in the two former cases, fills all heaven, even increasing the gladness of the angels in sympathy with their King ; while the exuberant picture of the joy of the household at the prodigal's return gives a still more tender and touching picture of the Divine Fatherhood. The reward promised to the faithful servant in the parable of the Talents is to enter into 'the joy of his Lord' (Mt 25²¹). The meaning of this is obviously that the servant should be partaker in the richer and fuller joy that is his Lord's portion, which may probably be the joy that comes from the exercise of higher responsibilities, and the opportunities of fuller usefulness (see the Comm. *in loco*).

In the narrative in Lk. descriptive of the return of the seventy disciples from their mission in Galilee, we read (10^{17}) that they 'returned with joy, saying, Lord, even the devils are subject unto us in thy name.' It may be that our Lord regarded this as too much akin to the shallow joy which He had exposed in the parable of the Sower, or, at any rate, as detrimental to the more serious thought with which He wished their minds to be filled; for He replied (v. [20]): 'Howbeit in this rejoice not that the spirits are subject unto you, but rejoice that your names are written in heaven.' The keynote thus given to the real joy of the disciple is the assurance of his belonging to the Kingdom of God, a joy, therefore, that is 'with trembling.' According to Lk.'s account, it is at the same moment that we read of Christ's rejoicing, but the parallel in Mt. does not bear out the same historical connexion (cf. Lk 10^{21} and Mt 11^{25}).

In Lk.'s narrative also there is the unique expression, 'He rejoiced in the Holy Spirit.' What exactly is meant by this phrase it is most difficult to say, and some have even supposed it to be a forestalling of the strange experiences of the Christian Church after Pentecost. This does not seem very probable, and it may be that Lk. is only expressing with greater fulness and exactitude the truth that it was through the inspiration of the Spirit that our Lord was able clearly to thank His Father for the manner in which His mighty works were done, as well as to perform these works themselves.

In the passage in which Lk. gives his setting of the Beatitudes, he puts very strongly the blessing of suffering for righteousness' sake, the words being, 'Rejoice in that day, and leap: for, behold, your reward is great in heaven' (Lk 6^{23}).

In Jn. there is a very striking use of the verb 'rejoice' in a passage of great difficulty (8^{56}). It occurs in the reported controversy of our Lord with the Jews, where He tells them, 'Your father Abraham rejoiced (ἠγαλλιάσατο) to see my day: and he saw it, and was glad' (ἐχάρη). The force of the Greek implies that Abraham 'exulted that he should see,' that is, presumably, in the promises that were made to him, while the actual seeing of it, of which the Lord speaks, is possibly an assertion of Abraham's living with God, as in Christ's similar use of the text, 'I am the God of Abraham, of Isaac, and of Jacob,' to prove the reality of the doctrine of the resurrection.

We must next turn to a class of passages contained in the closing addresses of our Lord to His disciples, as recorded in the Fourth Gospel, where much stress is laid upon our Lord's own joy and the disciples' share in it. The clear declaration of His commandments is to effect the purpose of their partaking in His own joy of obedience, and to secure the permanence and completeness of their own glad following of the Divine will (Jn 15^{11}). Again, the natural sorrow at His approaching departure is to be a sorrow like that of a woman in her birth-pangs,—a sorrow, that is, which is not only full of purpose, but is a necessary element in a great deliverance; and the joy that will succeed not only causes forgetfulness of the previous suffering, but abides, while the pain is only a passing and comparatively unimportant experience ($16^{20\text{-}24}$).

And, finally, in the great prayer of intercession contained in Jn 17, our Lord requests that the joy which was His own peculiar possession should find its full accomplishment in the hearts of His disciples (v. [13]). The joy thus foretold and interceded for is noted by the Evangelist as a possession of the disciples immediately after the resurrection. In Mt 28^8 we are told that the women departed from the tomb 'with fear and great joy,' while the effect of the gladness is noted by Lk., with a truthfulness to human experience that is most remarkable, as being itself a ground of scepticism (see Lk 24^{41}). This joy was not only the possession, but

the abiding possession of- the early Church, as frequent notes in the Book of Acts prove; and many passages in St. Paul's Epistles speak of joy as one of the true fruits of the indwelling of the Holy Spirit (see Ac 13^{52} and Gal 5^{22}).

While the passages above examined contain most of the instances in which the words 'joy' or 'rejoice' are used in the Gospels, there remain very many passages in which the idea is prominent. Our Lord's own description of Himself, for instance, as the Bridegroom when He is vindicating the liberty of His disciples to abstain from the ascetic practices of the Pharisees, shows how He conceived His mission and ministry (see Mk $2^{18\text{-}22}$). Many of the parables, other than those already named, set forth the inherent joy of the Kingdom, as, for example, those of the Wedding Supper and the Ten Virgins. The Lord's Supper itself was a feast of joy, for, according to Lk.'s account (22^{15}), our Lord said, 'With desire I have desired to eat this Passover with you before I suffer,' thus indicating that He had eagerly and gladly anticipated it; and in the further words that He speaks on that occasion He indicates that there is only to be a pause in the joy which will be resumed and heightened in other surroundings. 'I will not,' He continues, 'drink from henceforth of the fruit of the vine until the kingdom of God shall come,' or, as Mt. phrases it (26^{29}), 'until that day when I drink it new with you in my Father's kingdom.'

There must have been much in our Lord's intercourse with the people that led them to see in Him a helper of their joys rather than a restraint upon their merriment. He was, for example, an honoured guest at a wedding feast (Jn 2^1), and at many a social meal (cf. Lk 14^1 and Jn 12^2); and when He decided to abide at the house of Zacchæus, we are told that the latter 'received him joyfully.' In His triumphal entry into Jerusalem the people gladly welcomed Him (Lk 19^{37}), and the children cried joyfully in the Temple, 'Hosanna to the Son of David' (Mt 21^{15}). All these more or less exuberant outbursts of spontaneous joy greatly offended the Pharisees and other formal religionists; and while it would not be correct to say that our Lord designedly arranged circumstances in which the contrasts would be clearly manifested, still the conditions in which they were so displayed were admirable parables in action of some of the deepest truths of His kingdom.

There is much beauty, as well as truth, in the imaginary description of Renan: 'He thus traversed Galilee in the midst of a continual feast. When He entered a house it was considered a joy and a blessing. He halted in the villages and at the large farms, where He received open hospitality. In the East when a stranger enters a house it becomes at once a public place. All the village assembles there, the children invade it, they are put out by the servants, but always return. Jesus could not suffer these innocent auditors to be treated harshly. He caused them to be brought to Him and embraced them. . . . He protected those who wished to honour Him. In this way children and women came to adore Him' (Life of Jesus, ch. xi.).

The joy that emanated from our Lord's person and presence during His earthly ministry was without question a great part of its power. His attitude stood in such clear contrast to the general character of the religious people round about Him, that the consciousness of it must have been felt by all the onlookers; but in addition to this fact was the whole teaching about His kingdom, which, as set forth in parable and precept, was to be a kingdom of gladness. In this latter respect it came into line with what the prophets had described as the marked characteristic of the Kingdom of God, and also with what the Jewish apocalypses pictured as the outcome of the Messiah's advent. That a more earthly conception of joy filled the hearts of many of the disciples there is little reason to question, but a great deal of our Lord's teaching was directed to spiritualize their hopes and to deepen their insight into the true character of spiritual joy.

LITERATURE.—The Comm. on the passages referred to, esp. the Introductions to Lk. by Plummer and Adeney ; art. 'Joy' in Hastings' *DB* ; Bruce, *Galilean Gospel*, chs. vii. xii. ; Farrar, *Life of Christ*, new ed. 1894, 225 ff. ; J. W. Diggle, *Short Studies in Holiness*, 1900, 111 ff. ; G. Matheson, *Studies in the Portrait of Christ*, 1st series, 272 ff. ; J. Moffatt in *Expos. Times*, ix. (1898) 334.

G. CURRIE MARTIN.

JUDÆA.—**1.** In its earlier signification the term 'Judæa' ('Ιουδαία) was applied to a limited district, of which Jerusalem was the centre, occupied by the captives who returned from Babylon after the decree of Cyrus. The scattered remnants of the Israelites who availed themselves of this opportunity, representing most, if not all, of the several tribes, joined forces with the men of Judah in rebuilding the Temple and its defences ; and from this date, except on the lists of the genealogical and tribal records, they were not distinguished from them. Hence the tribe of Judah, which, according to Josephus, arrived first in those parts, gave name both to the inhabitants and the territory, the former being designated as Jews and the latter as 'Judæa' or 'Jewry' (*Ant.* XI. v. 7). At a later date both names were used in a wider sense, including all the Israelites who returned, and also their settlements or possessions in other sections of the land. Under Persian rule the land of Judah was designated as a province of the Empire, and was administered by a governor, who resided at Jerusalem (Ezr 5[8. 14], Neh 11[3], Hag 1[1. 14]). During the period of the Roman occupation the term was sometimes used as a general expression for Palestine as a whole (*BJ* I. viii. 2 ; Strabo, xvi. 2. 21 ; Tacitus, *Hist.* v. 6 ; Lk 1[5], Ac 28[21]), also to include a portion, apparently, of the trans-Jordanic country (*Ant.* XII. iv. 11 ; Mt 19[1], Mk 10[1] ; Ptol. v. 16. 9). Apart from this exceptional usage, the name ordinarily—as we find it in the NT and the writings of Josephus—is applied to the southernmost of the three districts — Galilee, Samaria, Judæa — into which Western Palestine was divided in the time of Christ. With some variations on the north and west borders at different periods, Judæa covered all of the territory south of the *Wady Ishar* and the village of *Akrabbeh* (*PEFSt*, 1881, p. 48), from the Mediterranean to the Jordan Valley and the Dead Sea. According to Josephus, its limits extended from a village on the north called Anuath, or Borkeos, identified with '*Aina Berkit*, to Iardas (possibly *Tell Arad*), on the edge of the desert, to the south. Its breadth he defines, in general terms, as extending from the river Jordan to Joppa (*BJ* III. iii. 5). In other words, its area practically corresponded with the area of the kingdom of Judah in the period of its greatest enlargement. As thus defined it included the tribal possessions of Simeon, Judah, Benjamin, Dan, and, to some extent at least, of Ephraim.

A distinction should be noted here between the use of the word Judæa to designate *strictly Jewish* territory, from which the outlying Hellenistic or Gentile towns were excluded, and the Roman usage of the word to designate a political division, which for administrative purposes included all the coast towns south of Mt. Carmel, the chief of which in the time of Christ was Cæsarea, the residence of its Procurator. In the one case its northern limit was Antipatris, on the plain of Sharon ; in the other it extended to Acre (Ptolemais) beyond Mt. Carmel. The S.E. portion of Judæa has sometimes been designated as a separate district under the name *Idumæa*, but this term properly describes a settlement of the Edomites in Judæa, and not a separate division of the country. Idumæa, according to Josephus, was one of the eleven toparchies into which Judæa proper was

divided for administrative purposes under Roman rule (*BJ* III. iii. 5). See IDUMÆA.

2. When our Lord was born, Judæa constituted a part of the dominion of Herod the Great, who accordingly is called by the Evangelists 'king of Judæa' (Lk 1[5], cf. Mt 2[1]). After the death of Herod, the Roman emperor assumed the right to settle the dispute which had arisen among his sons concerning the division of the kingdom, and by his decree Judæa and Samaria were in the partition assigned to Archelaus. The sovereignty of Rome was more fully asserted also at this time in refusing to any of Herod's sons the title 'king.' When by the same authority Archelaus was deposed (A.D. 6), the territory over which he held rule was attached to the province of Syria, and thus for the first time came under immediate Roman rule. From this date it was administered by a governor or procurator, who was chosen from the equestrian order. Following Archelaus the province was administered by five procurators during the life and ministry of Jesus, viz. Coponius (*c*. A.D. 6–9), Marcus Ambivius (*c*. 9–12), Annius Rufus (*c*. 12–15), Valerius Gratus (15–25), Pontius Pilate (26–36). It was during Pilate's rule that the word of God came to John the Baptist in the wilderness, and some years later this Roman procurator made his name for ever infamous by giving sentence that the Christ, whom he had openly declared to be innocent of crime, should be led away to be crucified.

3. The *physical features of Judæa* are sharply outlined and singularly diversified. Its distinctive characteristics fall naturally into five subdivisions, originally suggested by the OT writers, viz. the 'Plain of the Coast,' the 'Shephelah' or region of the low hills, the 'Hill country,' the 'Negeb' or dry country, and the 'Wilderness.'

The Maritime Plain varies in width from 10 to 16 miles. It is for the most part flat or rolling, and rises gradually toward the base of the mountains. The upper portion (Sharon) is noted for its rich pasturage ; the lower (Philistia) for its vast grain-fields, which have yielded enormous crops without the use of fertilizers, except such as nature has distributed over its surface from the wash and waste of the mountains, for forty centuries. The international highway which follows the line of the coast inside the region of the sand-dunes is one of the oldest caravan and military roads in the world. Most of the noted towns of the Plain are on or near this ancient highway. This section of Judæa has no associations with the life or ministry of Jesus, but in the Acts there are several references to visits which were made, or events which took place, in its towns, in connexion with the work of the Apostles or their associates (chs. 8–10 and 18–21).

The 'Shephelah' belongs to the plain rather than to the central ridge of the mountains, from which it is distinctly separated by a series of almost continuous breaks or depressions. It has been aptly described as 'a loose gathering of chalk and limestone hills, round, bare, and featureless, but with an occasional bastion flung well out in front of them.' There are several noted valleys, which begin their courses as wadis in the central range, and cut their way through the Shephelah to the plain. Each of these affords a passage-way into the heart of the mountain stronghold of Judæa, and each has its distinct characteristics and historical associations. Apostles and evangelists entered this region soon after the dispersion of the believers at Jerusalem, and in its limestone grottoes, in the days of the persecutions, multitudes of hunted and outlawed Christians found refuges and hiding-places (*HGHL*, ch. xi.).

The 'Hill country' or highland region fills most of the space between the Jordan Valley and the sea, and gives character to the district as a whole. In its present condition it is the most rugged and desolate section of the Lebanon range. In former times its hillsides were terraced, and every available break in its table-lands was carefully cultivated ; and yet in every period of its history it has been regarded as a rough, stony land, more suitable for pastoral than for agricultural pursuits. Its watershed is an irregular, undulating plateau, which varies in width from 12 to 18 miles. The general direction of the numerous ravines or torrent-beds which diversify, and in some sections deeply corrugate, its sides, is east and west. On the east side they are short, direct, and deeply cleft ; on the west, comparatively long and shallow, reaching the coast often by circuitous routes. The highest elevation (3564 ft.) is *er-Ramah*, a short distance north of Hebron. The general average of the plateau on which Jerusalem is located is about 2500 ft. South of Hebron there is a gradual descent by steps or terraced slopes to the region which for many centuries has borne the distinctive name 'Negeb' or dry country.

The 'Wilderness' includes the whole of the eastern slope or declivity of the Judæan mountains. It is a barren, uncultivated region, unique in its setting, and notable above all other sections of the land for its desolation, its loneliness, and its scenes of wild and savage grandeur. The variation in levels from the edge of the plateau to the surface of the Dead Sea is but little short of 4000 ft., nearly one half of which is a precipitous descent from sea-level to the margin of the deeply depressed basin amid the silent hills. In this 'land not inhabited' John the Baptist sought seclusion while preparing for his ministry as the forerunner of the Messiah ; and here the Holy One, concerning whom he bore record, abode 'forty days tempted of Satan ; and was with the wild beasts ; and the angels ministered unto him' (Mt 3¹⁻⁶ ǁ Lk 3², Mt 4¹⁻¹¹ ǁ Mk 1¹²˙¹³).

4. The sacred memories and thronging events which have been, and for ever shall be, associated with these holy hills cannot be fittingly expressed by voice or pen. In the long ages past the highways of this Judæan plateau have been trodden by the feet of patriarchs, prophets, priests, and kings, and for centuries its sanctuary on Mt. Zion was the dwelling-place of Jehovah ; but, more than all else in its wonderful history, it was the place of the incarnation, the self-denying ministry, the agony, the death, the resurrection, and the ascension of the Son of God, the Saviour of the world.

LITERATURE.—Stanley, *SP* pp. 227–233 ; Conder, *Pal.* ch. i. p. 221 ; Schürer, *HJP*, index ; G. A. Smith, *HGHL*, chs. xii.–xv. ; Neubauer, *Géog. du Talm.* p. 52 ff. ; *PEF Memoirs*, vol. iii. ; C. W. Wilson in Hastings' *DB*, vol. ii. p. 791 ; Smith, *DB²*, vol. ii. p. 1488 ; Hastings' *DB*, art. 'Palestine' ; Baedeker, *Pal. and Syria*, lvi.   ROBERT L. STEWART.

JUDAH.—The eponymous ancestor of the tribe to which our Lord belonged (Mt 1²ᶠ·, Lk 3³³, He 7¹⁴ ; cf. art. GENEALOGIES).

JUDAH ('Ιούδα).—Two passages in the Gospels mention 'Judah' (RV), or 'Juda' (AV), which is orthographically distinct from 'Judæa' ('Ιουδαία) as well as geographically smaller. The one is Mt 2⁶. 'And thou Bethlehem, land of Judah, art in no wise least among the princes of Judah,' etc., alluding to Bethlehem, the birthplace of Christ, in the heart of the hill country. The other is Lk 1³⁹ 'And Mary arose in these days and went into the hill country with haste, into a city of Judah' ; which also probably alludes to some town in the centre of the hill country, the birthplace of John the Baptist. In the latter passage, however, instead of εἰς πόλιν Ἰούδα, Reland in 1714 (*Pal.* p. 870), endorsed by Robinson in 1841 (*BRP²* ii. 206) and

others of more recent date, emend to read εἰς πόλιν Ἰούτα, *i.e.* 'Juttah' in lieu of 'Judah.' But there is no good philological reason for thinking that the latter is a corruption or softer pronunciation of the former ; and, as the context would indicate, the word 'Judah' in v.³⁹ seems to be parallel to the 'hill country' of v.⁶⁵ (cf. Cheyne, art. 'Juttah' in *Encyc. Bibl.*, also Plummer, *Int. Crit. Com. ad* Lk 1³⁹). It is, therefore, probably better to treat the passage as a reference to that portion of the hill country of Judah round about Hebron, or to the south of it. Tradition has fixed upon '*Ain Kârim*, a little west of Jerusalem, as the birthplace of John the Baptist. See, further, artt. JUDÆA, HILL, etc.   GEORGE L. ROBINSON.

JUDAS.—1. Judas the son of James. The eleventh name in two lists of the Apostles (Lk 6¹⁶, Ac 1¹³) is Ἰούδας Ἰακώβου. RV 'Judas *the son* of James' is a better rendering than AV 'Judas *the brother* of James.' The note in RVm is 'Or *brother*. See Jude¹' ; but in Jude¹ there is no ambiguity ; the Gr. text is ἀδελφὸς Ἰακώβου. The AV rendering is grammatically possible ; but it is improbable that the genitive has two different meanings in one short list of names (cf. AV and RV 'James *the son* of Alphæus'), and it is noteworthy that in Lk 3¹ 6¹⁴ ἀδελφός is expressed. The AV rendering may have been caused by Jude¹ ; certainly it has led to the erroneous identification of these two Judases. The evidence of Versions is in favour of RV. Syr ᵖᵉˢʰ and Theb. have 'son of' ; 'none suggests the exceptional rendering "the brother of"' (Plummer in Smith's *DB*, vol. i. pt. 2). Syr ˢⁱⁿ has 'Judas son of James' instead of Thaddæus or Lebbæus in Mt 10⁴.

In two lists of the Apostles (Mt 10⁴, Mk 3¹⁸) 'Judas *the son* of James' has no place ; the other names correspond in all four lists. In Mt. and Mk. **Thaddæus** (*v.l.*, in Mt., **Lebbæus**) is one of the Twelve. There is little doubt that 'Judas *the son* of James' had a second name 'Thaddæus,' and perhaps a third name 'Lebbæus.' Jerome (*Com. in loc.*) calls him *trinomius.* Cf. Nestle in Hastings' *DB* iv. 741.

It is significant that on the only occasion when this obscure Apostle is referred to in the Gospels, he is distinguished from his notorious namesake as 'Judas, not Iscariot' (Jn 14²²). All that we know of 'Judas Thaddæus' is that he asked the question, 'Lord, what is come to pass that thou wilt manifest thyself unto us, and not unto the world ?' He could not understand how the kingdom was to come unless the Messiah would make a public disclosure (ἐμφανίζω) of His glory. The answer of Jesus explains that in the very nature of the case it is not possible for Him to reveal His glory to unloving and disobedient hearts. The question of Judas Thaddæus expressed the thought not only of other members of the Apostolic band, but also of many who have since believed in Christ. Our Lord's words have a message for all disciples whose impatience is an evidence of the influence of the spirit of the world. Well may St. Paul claim to 'have the mind of Christ' when he affirms that 'the natural man' is not only unable to 'receive' and to 'know' spiritual things, but is also incompetent to 'interpret' and to 'judge' them (cf. 1 Co 2¹³ᶠᶠ·).

Concerning the name of this Apostle, who is little more than a name to us, there has been much discussion. In Jn 14²² Syr ˢⁱⁿ has 'Thomas,' Syr ᶜᵘʳ has 'Judas Thomas.' Plummer (*op. cit.*) is probably right in regarding the latter as 'a corrupt reading arising from the fact that the Syrian Christians called Thomas the Apostle, Judas.' Eusebius (*HE* i. 13. 10) refers, in his narrative concerning Abgar, king of Edessa, to 'Judas who was also called Thomas.' McGiffert (*Nicene and Post-Nicene Fathers*, i. 562) suggests that 'it is possible that Eusebius, or the translator of the document, made a mistake, and applied to Thomas a name which in the original was given to Thaddæus.'

But Thomas is also called Judas Thomas in *Acts of Thomas*, c. 11 f., 31, 39, and in the Syriac *Doctrina Apostolorum.* Preuschen (Hennecke, *Handbuch zu den NT Apokryphen*, p. 562) says : 'In regard to the name Judas-Thomas, *i.e.* Judas the Twin, cf. *Doctrine of Addai* (p. 5, ed. Phillips), Bar-Hebræus, *Chronicon Ecc.* iii. 2. The Syriac translation of Eusebius, *Ch. Hist.* i. 13. 10, renders the Gr. 'Ιούδας ὁ καὶ Θωμᾶς by יהודא תאומא which, according to the Nestorian pronunciation of the Syriac, must have been understood to mean Judas the Twin.' It is possible that these Syriac traditions preserve the personal name of Thomas 'the Twin'; it is impossible to believe that in the Fourth Gospel the Judas of 14[22] and the doubting Apostle are the same.

2. Judas the brother of James.—In two Gospels (Mt 13[55], Mk 6[3]) 'James and Joseph and Simon and Judas' are named as brothers of Jesus. In Jude[1] the author of that Epistle is described as 'Judas . . . the brother of James' (RV). The AV has 'Jude'; and in Mk 6[3] 'Juda.' 'Judas the brother of James' is, therefore, a designation both Scriptural and simple, yet sufficient to distinguish the person so named from 'Judas the son of James,' who was an Apostle. The use of the full expression ἀδελφὸς 'Ιακώβου in the Epistle of Jude, and the statement (Mt 13[55]) that Judas and James were οἱ ἀδελφοὶ ['Ιησοῦ], justifies the limiting of the title 'the brother of James' to the Judas who was also a 'brother of Jesus.' Much confusion has been caused by the erroneous AV rendering of 'Ιούδας 'Ιακώβου (cf. No. 1 above).

Of 'Judas the brother of James' as an individual we know nothing ; but account should be taken of what is said collectively of our Lord's brothers. He was probably a son of Joseph and Mary, and a younger brother of Jesus (cf. 'Brethren of the Lord' in Hastings' *DB*) ; he misunderstood the popularity of Jesus (Mt 12[46ff.]), who was, in his estimation, a foolish enthusiast (Mk 3[21]) ; before the resurrection of Jesus he did not acknowledge his Brother as the Messiah (Jn 7[3ff.]), but after the resurrection he is found 'in prayer' in the upper room (Ac 1[14]) ; his doubts, like those of his brother James (1 Co 15[7]), may have vanished in the presence of the risen Lord. The distinct mention of the brothers of Jesus (Ac 1[14]) after the Eleven have been named, is another reason for rejecting the tradition which identifies 'Judas the brother of James' with Judas Thaddæus the Apostle.

The authorship of the Epistle of Jude is much disputed. Harnack regards the words 'brother of James' as an interpolation added towards the end of the 2nd cent. to enhance the value of the Epistle 'as a weapon against Gnosticism.' But 'the simplest interpretation of the salutation, which identifies the writer . . . with the brother of the Lord, is the best' (Chase, Hastings' *DB* ii. 804[a]). Eusebius (*HE* iii. 19. 20[1-8]. 32) quotes from Hegesippus the account of an accusation brought against the grandchildren of Judas ; they are described as 'descended from one of the so-called brothers of the Saviour, whose name was Judas'; it is further said that 'after they had borne testimony before Domitian in behalf of faith in Christ . . . they took the lead of every church as witnesses and as relatives of the Lord.' If 'Judas the brother of James' presided over the Church in the city where he lived, he may well have been the author of an Epistle. Mrs. Lewis conjectures that 'Thomas, the doubting disciple, is identical with Jude, the youngest brother of our Lord'; but this theory involves his exclusion from the statement in Jn 7[5] that our Lord's brothers did not believe that He was the Messiah (cf. *ExpT* xiv. 398 ; also Rendel Harris, *The Dioscuri in the Christian Legends*).

3. Judas Iscariot.—See following article.

J. G. TASKER.

JUDAS ISCARIOT.—
    i. The NT sources.
    ii. Name and Designations :
       (*a*) Judas.
       (*b*) Iscariot.
       (*c*) One of the Twelve.
       (*d*) A thief.
       (*e*) Betrayer or traitor.
       (*f*) A devil.
       (*g*) Son of perdition.
    iii. Other NT references to Judas :
       (*a*) Before the Betrayal ;
       (*b*) Describing the Betrayal ;
       (*c*) After the Betrayal.
    iv. The character of Judas :
       (*a*) The good motives theory ;
       (*b*) The Satan incarnate theory ;
       (*c*) The mingled motives theory ; he was (*α*) covetous, (*β*) ambitious, (*γ*) jealous.
    v. References to Judas in post-Biblical literature :
       (*a*) Apocryphal works ;
       (*b*) Early Christian writings.
       (*c*) Folk-lore.
           Literature.

i. THE NT SOURCES.—The basis of any satisfactory solution of the fascinating and perplexing problem of the personality of Judas must be a comprehensive and careful study of the words of Jesus and the records of the Evangelists. Interest in his life and character may have been unduly sacrificed to dogmatic discussions of 'fix'd fate, free will, foreknowledge absolute,' but the reaction in favour of psychological methods of study may be carried to excess. Conclusions arrived at by the use of these methods are not always consistent with the historical data furnished by the Gospels. In psychological as well as theological investigations, speculation may prove an unsafe guide ; at least it should always move in a path made by prolonging the lines laid down in the documents which are the main sources of our information. Theories framed by induction from a critical comparison of the narratives may claim to be attempts to untie the knot, but theories involving excisions from, and conjectural emendations of, the text of the Gospels and Acts are mere cuttings of the knot. A frank acknowledgment that there are difficulties at present inexplicable is preferable to the adoption of such violent methods of removing them. The NT material available for the investigation of the subject in its manifold aspects is found in the following passages :

1. The lists of the Apostles : Mk 3[16ff.], Mt 10[2ff.], Lk 6[13ff.].
2. Early allusions to Judas : Jn 6[64ff.] 12[4ff.] 17[12], Lk 22[3] (cf. Mk 14[4f.], Mt 26[8f.]).
3. The narratives of the Betrayal : Mk 14[10f.], Mt 26[14ff.], Lk 22[4ff.] ; Jn 13[2ff.] ; Mk 14[18ff.], Mt 26[21ff.], Lk 22[21ff.], Jn 13[21f.] ; Mk 14[43ff.], Mt 26[47ff.], Lk 22[47f.], Jn 18[2ff.].
4. The two accounts of the death of Judas : Mt 27[3ff.], Ac 1[16ff.].

From this classification it will be seen that, with the exception of Lk 22[3], the Synoptists say nothing about Judas before the Betrayal ; their account of the Betrayal also differs in many details from that given in the Fourth Gospel. Some divergent traditions it is difficult, and perhaps impossible, to harmonize ; assumptions that the one is an intentional modification of the other, or that they are contradictory, must be carefully examined ; suggestions that they are supplementary, or mutually explanatory, must be fairly considered. Statements in the Fourth Gospel which are said to show John's bias against Judas will be investigated in due course.

ii. NAME AND DESIGNATIONS.—(*a*) *Judas.*—In all the lists of the Twelve this is the name of the Apostle mentioned last. Another Apostle (see preced. art. No. 1) bore this common Jewish name, but 'Judas' now means the Betrayer of Jesus. His sin has stamped the word with such evil significance that it has become the class-name of perfidious friends, who are 'no better than Judases' (cf. 'Judas-hole,' 'Judas-trap,' etc.).

'Ιούδας is the Gr. form of the Heb. *Judah* (יְהוּדָה), which in Gn 29[35] is derived from the verb 'to praise' (יָדָה), and is taken as meaning 'one who is the subject of praise' (cf. Gn 49[8]). The etymology is disputed, but in its popular sense it suggests a striking paradox, when used of one whose name became a synonym for shame.

(*b*) *Iscariot* : the usual surname of Judas. 'Ισκαριώθ, a transliteration from Heb., is the best attested reading in Mk 3[19] 14[10], Lk 6[16] ; 'Ισκαριώτης, the Græcized form in Mt 26[14], Lk 22[3], Jn 6[71] 13[2. 26] ; ὁ 'Ισκαριώτης in Mt 10[4], Jn 12[4] 14[22]. Eight of these passages refer to Judas ; in two (Jn 6[71] 13[26]) his father Simon is called Iscariot ; once (Jn 14[22]) his fellow-Apostle is distinguished from his more famous namesake as 'not the Iscariot.' Only in Jn 13² does the full phrase occur—'Judas Iscariot, the son of Simon.' Nestle thinks that ἀπὸ Καριώτου, a reading of Codex Bezæ, found four times in Jn instead of Ἰσκαριώτης, is a paraphrastic rendering of Iscariot by the author of the Fourth Gospel. Chase furnishes other evidence for this reading (*The Syro-Latin Text of the Gospels*, p. 102 f.), but argues that it cannot be part of the original text. His conclusion is that an early Syriac translator represented Ἰσκαριώτης by this paraphrase (cf. *ExpT* ix. pp. 189, 240, 285).

Two facts already mentioned have an important bearing on the interpretation of Ἰσκαριώτης: (1) the true reading, 'Simon Iscariot,' shows that the epithet was equally applicable to the father and the son, and this twofold use of the word suggests that it is a local name; (2) the paraphrase ἀπὸ Καριώτου confirms the view that Judas is named after his place of abode (cf. Zahn, *Das Evangelium des Matthäus*, p. 393). Cheyne says 'we should have expected ἀπο κεριωθ,' yet admits that 'it is a plausible view' that Ἰσκαριώτης is derived from Ish-Kerioth (אִישׁ קְרִיוֹת), 'a man of Kerioth' (*Ency. Bibl.* ii. 2624). Dalman (*The Words of Jesus*, p. 51 f.) thinks that Ἰσκαριώθ was the original reading, and points back to the Hebrew, whilst ὁ ἀπὸ Καριώτου corresponds to the equivalent Aramaic דְּקְרִיוֹת or דְּמִן קְרִיוֹת. Hence the surname *Iscariot* probably means 'a Kariothite.'

It is impossible to say with certainty where the **Kerioth** was situate of which Judas was a native. (1) On account of this difficulty, Cheyne conjectures that Ἰεριχωτής, 'a man of Jericho,' is the true reading. (2) The majority of scholars incline to the view that Kerioth is the Kerioth-Hezron or Hazor of Jos 15²⁵ (Vulg. *Carioth*); Buhl identifies the place with the modern *Karjaten* in South Judah (*GAP* p. 182). (3) Others suggest the Kerioth mentioned in Am 2², Jer 48²⁴ (LXX Καριώθ),—an important city, either Kir-Moab, or Ar, the capital of Moab. Harper ('Am. and Hos.,' *Int. Crit. Com.* p. 42) says that 'the reference in the Moabite stone (l. 13) favours Ewald's view that it is another name for Ar.' A less probable opinion is that the town referred to is Κορέαι or Kurawa (Jos. *BJ* I. vi. 5, IV. viii. 1; *Ant.* XIV. iii. 4) in North Judæa (Buhl, *GAP* p. 181). If any one of these towns was the birthplace of Judas, he was not a Galilæan.

(c) '*One of the Twelve*.'—In the Synoptic Gospels this phrase is found only in the narrative of the Betrayal, and it is applied only to Judas. It marks the mingled sorrow and indignation of the Evangelists, that within that select circle there could be a single treacherous heart. The simple formula is once changed by St. Luke (22³), who adds to his statement that 'Satan entered into Judas' these significant words: 'being of the number of the twelve'—*i.e.* counted among those whom Jesus called His friends, but about to become an ally of His foes, because in spirit he was 'none of his' (cf. Mt 26¹⁴. ⁴⁷, Mk 14¹⁰. ²⁰. ⁴³, Lk 22³. ⁴⁷). In the Fourth Gospel the phrase is used once of another than Judas; like a note of exclamation, it expresses surprise that Thomas, a member of the Apostolic band, was absent when the risen Saviour appeared to His disciples (Jn 20²⁴). But St. John also applies the phrase to Judas, giving it a position in which its tragic and pathetic emphasis cannot be mistaken: 'You—the twelve, did not I choose? and of you one is a devil. Now he spake of Judas, the son of Simon Iscariot; for it was he that was about to betray him—one of the twelve' (6⁷⁰. ⁷¹). St. John's phrase (εἷς ἐκ τῶν δώδεκα) differs slightly from that used by the Synoptists (εἷς τῶν δώδεκα); Westcott suggests that it marks 'the unity of the body to which the unfaithful member belonged' (*Com. in loc.*).

That Judas was 'one of the twelve' is an important factor in the problem presented by his history. It implies that Jesus saw in him the material out of which an Apostle might have been made,—the clay out of which a vessel unto honour might have been shaped; it implies that Judas, of free-will, chose to follow Jesus and to continue with Him; and it implies that Judas heard from the Master's lips words of gracious warning against the peril of his besetting sin. On the other hand, the fact that Judas was 'one of the twelve' does not imply that Jesus had the betrayal in view when He chose this Apostle and entrusted him with the common purse; it does not imply that even in that most holy environment Judas was exempted from the working of the spiritual law that such 'evil things' as 'thefts . . . covetings, . . . deceit . . . proceed from within, and defile the man' (Mk 7²²ᶠ.); and it does not imply that there were no good impulses in the heart of Judas when he became a disciple of Jesus. Of Judas in his darkest hour the words of Lavater are true: he 'acted like Satan, but like a Satan who had it in him to be an Apostle.'

In Mk 14¹⁰ the best supported reading (אBCLM) is ὁ εἷς τῶν δώδεκα, with a note in RVm—'Gr. the one of the twelve.' Wright (*Synopsis of the Gospels in Greek*, p. 31, cf. p. 147) is of opinion that Mk. distinctly calls Judas 'the chief of the twelve.' He takes ὁ εἷς as equal to ὁ πρῶτος, as in τῇ μιᾷ τῶν σαββάτων (Mk 16²). But the definite article is not found with this phrase in any other passage in the Gospels; moreover, it is almost impossible to believe that when the Gospels were written the assertion that Judas was 'the chief' or even *primus inter pares* had a place in the original text. On the other hand, Field (*Notes on the Translation of the NT, in loc.*) is scarcely justified in saying 'ὁ εἷς τῶν δ. can mean nothing but "the first (No. 1) of the twelve," which is absurd.'* The unique reading may, however, preserve a genuine reminiscence of a time in the earlier ministry of Jesus when Judas, the treasurer of the Apostolic company, had a kind of priority. If this were so, there would come a time when, as Wright suggests, the supporters of Judas would become 'jealous of the honour bestowed on Peter.'† Jealousy would account not only for the dispute about rival claims to be the greatest, but also for the respective positions of Judas and Peter at the supper-table. The most probable explanation of the details given (Mt 26²³, Jn 13²³. ²⁶) is that John was reclining on the right of Jesus; but Judas 'claimed and obtained the chief seat at the table' next Jesus, and was reclining on His left, whilst 'the lowest place was voluntarily taken by Peter, who felt keenly the Lord's rebuke of this strife for precedence' (cf. Andrews, *The Life of our Lord*, p. 485; Edersheim, *Life and Times*, ii. 493).

(d) '*A thief*.'—The meaning of the statement that 'Judas was a thief' (Jn 12⁶) is quite plain, if the RV correctly renders the following sentence: 'and having the bag, *took away* (ἐβάσταζεν) what was put therein.' βαστάζω means (1) to bear, (2) to bear away, as in Jn 20¹⁵ (cf. 'cattle-lifting'). Its use in the sense of bearing away secretly or pilfering is established (cf. Field, *op. cit. in loc.*). In this context the statement that Judas carried the money put into the bag which was in his possession seems singularly tame, if it is not mere repetition. On the other hand, to say that Judas had formed the habit of pilfering is a natural explanation of

---

* Swete (*Com. in loc.*) explains the phrase as a contrast with οἱ λοιποί, 'the rest'; Judas was 'the only one of the twelve' who turned traitor.

† There is force in Edersheim's remark (*Life and Times*, ii. 536), that 'viewed in its primary elements (not in its development) Peter's character was, among the disciples, the likest to that of Judas.'

the assertion that he had been guilty of theft. Weiss (*Leben Jesu*, ii. 443) thinks that 'John had found out thefts committed by the greedy Judas'; this does not necessarily imply that the thefts were known to John at the time of Mary's anointing, for they may have come to light after that act, but before the narrative was shaped in this form.

The rendering of ἐβάσταζεν by the neutral word 'bare' is adopted by some, who hold that John's words do not imply more than that Judas had a thievish disposition. Ainger adopts this interpretation in a finely-wrought study of the character of Judas (*The Gospel and Human Life*, p. 231). It is true in a sense that 'he may have been a thief long before he began to steal,' but this exposition involves the unlikely assumption that the betrayal of Jesus was the 'first act by which he converted his spirit of greed into actual money profit.' If Judas had not formed the habit of pilfering, it is more difficult to understand how the thirty pieces of silver could be a real temptation to him.

Cheyne gets rid of the difficulty by assuming that the text is corrupt. In his conjectural emendation the word 'thief' has no place; he reads 'because he was a harsh man, and used to carry the common purse' (ὅτι χαλετὸς ἦν καὶ τὸ κοινὸν βαλλαντιον ἐβάσταζε). 'The statement about Judas' in this hypothetical text is then naively said to be 'worthy of more credit than it has sometimes received from advanced critics' (*Ency. Bibl.* ii. 2625).

(e) '*Betrayer*' or '*traitor*.'—In the list of the Apostles given in Lk 6[16] there is a variation from the phrase by which Judas is usually described. Instead of ὃς καὶ παρέδωκεν αὐτόν ('who also betrayed him,' *lit.* 'delivered him up') St. Luke has ὃς ἐγένετο προδότης, well rendered by Field—'who turned traitor' (cf. Amer. RV 'became a traitor'; Weymouth, 'proved to be a traitor'). The translation in the EV—'which was the traitor'—neither brings out the force of γίνομαι, nor the significance of the omission of the article.

The statement that Judas 'turned traitor' should be remembered in framing or estimating theories to account for his history; it confirms what has been said on this subject under (c). From this point of view the various phrases used in the Gospels will repay careful discrimination: most frequent is the simple statement of the tragic deed as a historic fact—'who betrayed him' (Mk 3[19] παρέδωκεν); but there is also the prophecy, 'The Son of Man is about to be betrayed' (Mt 17[22] μέλλει παραδίδοσθαι), and the statement, when the time was drawing nigh, that the process had already begun, 'The Son of Man is being betrayed' (Mt 26[2] παραδίδοται). Similarly, Judas is described as 'he who would betray him' (Jn 6[64] ὁ παραδώσων), 'he who is betraying me' (Mt 26[46] ὁ παραδιδούς), and as 'he who had betrayed him' (Mt 27[3] ὁ παραδούς). In this connexion Jn 6[64] deserves special attention: 'Jesus knew from the beginning . . . who it was that should betray him.' Needless difficulties are occasioned when 'from the beginning' is regarded as referring to any period before the call of Judas; the thought seems to be that Jesus perceived 'from the beginning' of His intercourse with Judas the spirit that was in him. Hence the statement is wrongly interpreted in a fatalistic sense. The rendering, 'Jesus knew who it was that would betray him' has the advantage of suggesting that Jesus discerned the thoughts and intents of His unfaithful Apostle, and knew that 'the germ of the traitor-spirit was already in the heart of Judas' (cf. W. F. Moulton in Schaff's *Popular Commentary, in loc.*).*

(f) '*A devil.*'—In Jn 6[70] there is a contrast between the hopes of Jesus when He chose (ἐξελ-

* Our Lord's words to Pilate, 'He that delivered me unto thee hath greater sin' (Jn 19[11]), are sometimes applied to Judas; but the reference is almost certainly to Caiaphas.

ἐξάμην) the Twelve, and His present grief over the moral deterioration of one whose nature is now devilish (διάβολός ἐστιν). Our Lord's spiritual discourse to the multitude brought all who heard it to the parting of the ways; it shattered the hopes of those who were eager to share in the glories of an earthly kingdom. On the inner circle of the Apostles that teaching also cast its searching light; to Jesus, though not to Peter (v.[69]), it was plain that Judas was at heart a deserter,—in sympathy with those who 'went back and walked no more with him.' What Jesus detected in Judas was 'a sudden crystallization of evil, diabolic purpose, which made him a very adversary of the one whom he called friend' (Wright, *op. cit. in loc.*). But an adversary is not an irreconcilable foe; the assertion taken in its full strength of meaning is a message of conciliation as well as of warning. It involved no lowering of the position of Judas among the Twelve, for his name is not mentioned; and it assuredly involved no relaxing of our Lord's efforts to scatter with the light of love the gloom which was creeping into the heart of one whom He had chosen 'to be with him.' A strained interpretation of the saying underlies the statement that it 'appears to be inconsistent with the equal confidence in all the disciples shown by Jesus according to the Synoptic tradition' (*Ency. Bibl.* ii. 2624). 'No man,' says Pressensé, 'could be more akin to a devil than a perverted apostle' (*Jesus Christ*, p. 324).

(g) '*Son of perdition.*'—The Gr. word rendered 'perdition' in this phrase (Jn 17[12]) is ἀπώλεια, which signifies *the state of being lost*. It is the substantive derived from the same root as the main verb of the sentence (ἀπώλετο). The connexion of thought is not easy to reproduce in English. Ainger (*op. cit.* p. 227) brings out the sense of the passage in a paraphrase: 'None of them is lost, but he whose very nature it was to be lost—he (that is to say) whose insensibility to the Divine touch, whose irresponsiveness to the heavenly discipline, made it a certainty that he should fall away.' The apostasy of Judas is traced to the 'natural gravitation' of his character. By a well-known Hebraism Judas is described as the 'son of' that which stamps his nature; he is of such a character that his proper state is one of loss (cf. 2 Th 2[3]). The same word (ἀπώλεια) is rendered 'waste' in the Synoptic accounts of Mary's anointing (Mt 26[9], Mk 14[4]). 'To what purpose is this waste?' was the expression of indignation of 'some' (Mk.) of the disciples; perhaps it was originally the question of Judas, though St. John does not say so. It may well be, however, that he whose audible murmur, 'Why this loss or waste?' was echoed by the other disciples is himself described by Jesus as 'the son of loss'—'the waster.'

This verse (Jn 17[12]) is often appealed to by rival champions of Calvinism and Arminianism. In Bishop Sanderson's *Works* (v. 324 f.) there is a letter to him from H. Hammond, who affirms that 'here it is expressly said that Judas, though by his apostasy now become the son of perdition, was by God given to Christ.' But the true reading is, 'I kept them in thy name which thou hast given me' (RV), and the thought (cf. v.[9] 'those whom thou hast given me') is rather that 'they in whom the Father's object is attained' are those 'given' to the Son; Judas, therefore, was not so given. 'To suppose that Judas is now brought before us as one originally doomed to perdition, and that his character was but the evolving of his doom, would contradict not only the meaning of the Hebraic expression "son of" (which always takes for granted moral choice), but the whole teaching of this Gospel. In no book of the NT is the idea of will, of choice on the part of man, brought forward so repeatedly and with so great an emphasis' (W. F. Moulton, *op. cit. in loc.*).

iii. OTHER NT REFERENCES TO JUDAS.—(a) *Before the Betrayal.*—The obscurity which rests upon the early history of Judas accounts to a large extent for the difficulty of estimating his character. But for occasional allusions in the Fourth Gospel, all that is related of him before the Betrayal is that he was one of the chosen Twelve, and that he turned traitor. There is, however, a statement peculiar to St. Luke among the Synoptists, which is obviously intended to furnish an explanation of the act of Betrayal—'Satan entered into Judas' (22³). It finds a fitting place in the introduction to the narrative of the Betrayal in the psychological Gospel which so often gives internal reasons; 'the Gospel of the *physician* is also the Gospel of the *psychologist*' (Alexander, *Leading Ideas of the Gospels*, p. 107). The same phrase, 'Satan entered into him' (εἰσῆλθεν εἰς ἐκεῖνον ὁ Σατανᾶς), is also found in Jn 13²⁷, and it is preceded by the statement (13²) that the devil had 'already put into the heart (ἤδη βεβληκότος εἰς τὴν καρδίαν) of Judas' the thought of betrayal. It is true, as Cheyne says (*Ency. Bibl.* ii. 2625), that in Jn. we have 'a modification of the Synoptic tradition,' but that is not equivalent to 'quite a different account.' So far from asserting that 'it was at the Last Supper that the hateful idea occurred to Judas,' St. John prefaces his description of the proceedings at the Supper (δείπνου γινομένου) by the emphatic assertion that 'already' (ἤδη), *i.e.* at some time other than the Supper, the suggestion of the devil had been entertained by Judas. In St. Luke's brief account it is said, once for all, that 'Satan entered into Judas.' In the Fourth Gospel the genesis of the foul purpose is distinguished from its consummation; the Satanic influences were not irresistible; the devil had not full possession of the heart of Judas until, 'after the sop,' he acted on the suggestion which had then become his own resolve.

The Fourth Gospel also makes the Anointing at Bethany (12⁴ᶠ·) a definite stage in the process which is sometimes called the 'demonizing' of Judas, but is better described as his 'giving place to the devil' (Eph 4²⁷). St. Luke does not mention Mary's anointing. St. Matthew and St. Mark have full accounts of it, but Judas is not named; yet immediately after the narrative of the Anointing both Mt. and Mk. place Judas' offer to the chief priests to betray Jesus for money, thus clearly recognizing an intimate connexion between the two events. St. John explains this sequence by adding the significant detail that the murmuring against Mary's waste of ointment had its origin in the heart of Judas. Our Lord's defence of Mary's beautiful deed implied a rebuke to Judas, and unmasked his hypocrisy; moreover, our Lord's plain references to His coming death involved the disillusionment of His ambitious Apostle. The reproof would rankle; the disappointment would be acute. The angry spirit engendered by such emotions is closely akin to the spirit of treachery and revenge. On insufficient grounds, therefore, Gould speaks of 'John's evident attempt to belittle Judas' (*Int. Crit. Com.*, note on Mk 14⁴). No more likely origin of the murmuring, which was not confined to Judas (Mk 14⁵, Mt 26⁸), is suggested. On the other hand, there seems to be no reason for belittling St. John; his addition to the Synoptic Gospels justifies their association of Mary's anointing with Judas' desertion of Christ; it also furnishes a link between the Anointing of which St. Luke gives no account and his statement 'Satan entered into Judas,'—that statement is the psychological explanation of the actions of Judas recorded in the narratives of the Anointing and the Last Supper.

(*b*) *Describing the Betrayal.*—In the Passion narratives all the Gospels refer to our Lord's consciousness of His approaching Betrayal; all record His announcement, at the beginning of the Supper, of the presence of the Betrayer; and all mention the consternation and self-questioning of the Apostles to which that statement gave rise (Mk

14¹⁸ᶠᶠ·, Mt 26²¹ᶠᶠ·, Lk 22²¹ᶠᶠ·, Jn 13²¹ᶠᶠ·). There is no reason to suppose (Weiss) that Judas was definitely indicated by our Lord's words, 'He that dipped his hand with me in the dish, the same shall betray me' (Mt 26²³). Before the lamb was placed on the table, each guest dipped his own bread into the bitter sauce and ate the sop. The aorist participle (ὁ ἐμβάψας) refers to this act, but does not necessarily fix its time; as thus interpreted, the phrase is in harmony with the vague expression 'that man,' used twice in v.²⁴, with the passage quoted (Jn 13¹⁸) from Ps 41⁹ ('He that eateth my bread'; cf. 'messmate'), and with the parallel passage in Mk 14²⁰ where the present participle is used (ὁ ἐμβαπτόμενος). An addition to the Synoptic tradition is found in the Fourth Gospel, which describes Jesus as giving a sop to Judas (13²⁶). At Eastern meals this was a mark of special attention (cf. Macmillan, 'A Mock Sacrament,' in *ExpT* iii. 107 f.); our Lord's action would indicate the traitor to the disciple who was 'leaning back' on His breast, though it left John, like the rest, in ignorance of the meaning of the words with which Jesus urged Judas to hasten the work he was already doing (v.²⁷). To the traitor himself the words of Jesus, gradually narrowing in their range and therefore increasing in intensity, were at once a tender appeal and a final warning. St. Matthew alone records the question of Judas, 'Is it I, Rabbi?' and our Lord's answer, 'Thou hast said' (26²⁵). If Judas had the chief seat at the table next to Jesus (cf. above, ii. (*c*)), the assent conveyed, perhaps in a whisper and certainly not in the ordinary form (cf. Dalman, *The Words of Jesus*, 308 f.), must have had for him a tragic significance. As Zahn points out (*op. cit. in loc.*), the prefixed pronoun in σὺ εἶπας heightens the contrast between the questioner and the speaker, and conveys the meaning, 'What *thou* hast said, there is no need for *me* to say.' St. Matthew does not state that at this juncture Judas left the Supper-table, but the next allusion to Judas (v.⁴⁷) implies an absence of some duration. The probable solution of the much-discussed problem, 'Did Judas eat the Passover?' is that, although he ate the sop given to him by Jesus at the beginning of the Supper, he had gone out into the darkness (Jn 13³⁰) before Jesus gave the bread and the wine to His disciples. It is true that in Lk 22 the narrative of the Supper precedes our Lord's announcement of the Betrayer's presence, but the 'order' (1³) characteristic of this Gospel does not imply chronological sequence in every detail; Wright (*op. cit.* p. 132) accounts for the variation from the parallel passages by the suggestion that St. Luke was influenced by the language of St. Paul in 1 Co 11²⁹.

In their accounts of the actual Betrayal of our Lord the Synoptics state that the kiss of Judas was the prearranged signal for His arrest (Mk 14⁴⁵, Mt 26⁴⁹; cf. Lk 22⁴⁷). In the Fourth Gospel nothing is said of the kiss, but a graphic account is given of our Lord's unexpected declaration to His foes that He was the Nazarene for whom they were seeking (18⁴ᶠ·). The silence of St. John is no proof that the kiss was not given; nor is the fact which he records any evidence that the kiss was superfluous. A sufficient motive for the self-manifestation of Jesus is mentioned: 'let these go their way' (v.⁸); such a request is appropriate whether the kiss of Judas be placed before or after the question of Jesus, 'Whom seek ye?' If *before*, our Lord supplemented the Betrayer's signal owing to the hesitancy of the awestruck soldiers, who shrank from arresting Him. If *after*, Judas must have been disconcerted by our Lord's action; the kiss would not be given until later, when, as his courage returned, he did not scruple to kiss his Master with the unnecessary demonstration of a feigned affection ($\kappa\alpha\tau\epsilon\phi\iota\lambda\eta\sigma\epsilon\nu$, Mk 14[45], Mt 26[49]). Our Lord's discernment of the evil purpose underlying this emotional display is indicated by His question, 'Judas, betrayest thou the Son of Man with a kiss?' (Lk 22[48]). In Mt 26[50] Jesus is reported to have also said (RV), 'Friend, *do* that for which thou art come' (cf. AV 'Friend, wherefore art thou come?').

> Bruce (*Expos. Gr. Test. in loc.*) takes the laconic phrase $\dot\epsilon\phi'$ $\ddot{o}$ $\pi\acute\alpha\rho\epsilon\iota$ as a 'question in effect, though not in form'; its probable meaning is 'Comrade, and as a comrade here?' (cf. Bengel, *in loc.* '*Hoccine illud est cujus causa ades?*'). Blass unnecessarily (cf. 22[12]) changes $\dot\epsilon\tau\alpha\hat\iota\rho\epsilon$ into $\alpha\hat\iota\rho\epsilon$, which yields the meaning 'take away that for which thou art come,' or 'art here,' according as $\pi\acute\alpha\rho\epsilon\iota$ is taken from $\pi\alpha\rho\epsilon\hat\iota\nu\alpha\iota$ or $\pi\alpha\rho\iota\acute\epsilon\nu\alpha\iota$. Cheyne (*Ency. Bibl.* ii. 2626) conjectures that the true reading is $\dot\upsilon\pi\sigma\kappa\rho\acute\iota\nu\epsilon\iota$, 'thou actest a part,' or 'thou art no friend of mine'; $\dot\epsilon\tau\alpha\hat\iota\rho\epsilon$ is got rid of as a dittograph.

(*c*) *After the Betrayal.*—In three of the Gospels (Mk., Lk., Jn.) there is no mention of the Betrayer after the arrest of Jesus; but Mt 27[3ff.] relates the after-history and fate of Judas as the fulfilment of prophecy. The ascription to Jeremiah of Zec 11[13] is probably due to a failure of memory; the passage is freely quoted, and may include reminiscences of the language of Jeremiah (cf. 18[2ff.] 19[1ff.] 32[6ff.]). The absence of Ἰερεμίου from some of the Old Lat. and ancient Syr. VSS shows that the name was a stumbling-block to early translators of the NT. Zahn (*Gesch. des NT Kanons,* ii. 696) says that the Nazarenes had a Hebrew MS ascribed to Jeremiah, in which the passage is found *verbatim,*—'manifestly an Apocryphon invented to save the honour of Matthew.' The variations from the Heb. and LXX are not consistent with the theory that the Evangelist's narrative is a legend evolved from the passage in Zechariah; they are explicable on the supposition that the facts suggested the prophecy. J. H. Bernard (*Expositor,* 6th series, ix. 422 ff.) shows that St. Matthew's account must be based upon 'a tradition independent of the prophecy cited.' The 'salient features' of this tradition are thus summarized—'(*a*) Judas, stricken by remorse, returned the money paid him; (*b*) he hanged himself in despair; (*c*) the priests with the money bought a field called the "Potter's Field," which was henceforth called Ἀγρὸς Αἵματος; (*d*) the field was used as a cemetery for foreigners.' The point of connexion between the fact and the prophecy is the exact correspondence between the amount paid for the prophet's hire and for the prophet of Nazareth's betrayal. In both cases the paltry sum was the expression of the nation's ingratitude; the thirty pieces of silver was the price of a slave (Ex 21[32]). Meditating on the details of the Betrayal, the Evangelist called to mind the experience of Zechariah, and saw in it the foreshadowing of the treatment of Jesus in which the sin of a thankless people reached its climax.

In Ac 1[18. 19] a different account of the death of Judas is given. Plummer regards the tradition preserved in the Gospel as 'nearer in time to the event, and probably nearer to the truth' (Hastings' *DB* ii. 798[a]). Bartlet holds that the Lukan tradition 'represents the actual facts most nearly' ('Acts' in *Cent. Bible,* Note A). The chief argument for the latter view is a saying of Papias which resembles the statement in Acts, though it adds repulsive details (Cramer, *Catena on Mt.*). Dr. Rendel Harris, *AJTh* iv. 490 ff., thinks that the Papias tradition is 'the fountainhead of the Judas legends, to which fountainhead Luke lies nearer than Matthew.' The difficulties involved in this supposition are, (1) that it treats the account in Matthew as 'a mere substitution'; (2) that it involves the conjecture of an original reading in Acts, 'he swelled up and burst asunder.' It is more probable that the Papias story contains later

additions from folk-lore than that the present text of Acts omits essential details. Dr. Harris points out striking coincidences between the Judas narratives and the accounts of the death of Nadan, the traitorous nephew of Aḥikar, Sennacherib's grand vizier; but the parallel does not prove that the Aḥikar stories are 'the literary parent' of the Judas stories. Knowling (*Expos. Gr. Test. in loc.*) rightly says: 'Whatever may be alleged as to the growth of popular fancy and tradition in the later account in Acts of the death of Judas, it cannot be said to contrast unfavourably with the details given by Papias, *Fragment* 18, which Blass describes as "insulsissima et foedissima."' See, further, AKELDAMA.

iv. THE CHARACTER OF JUDAS.—(*a*) *The good motives theory.*—Many have attempted to explain the action of Judas as arising not from treachery and avarice, but from an honest endeavour to arouse Jesus to action and to hasten His Messianic triumph. Modern writers reproduce, with slight modifications, the theory to which the charm of De Quincey's literary style has imparted a fascination out of all proportion to its probability (*Works,* vi. 21 ff.; cf. Whately, *Essays on Dangers to the Christian Faith,* Discourse iii.). The theory assumes (1) that Jesus, like Hamlet, was 'sublimely over-gifted for purposes of speculation, . . . but not correspondingly endowed for the business of action'; (2) that Judas was alive to the danger resulting from this morbid feature in the temperament of Jesus, and acted not from perfidy, but with a genuine conviction that if Christ's kingdom was to be set up on earth, He 'must be compromised before doubts could have time to form.' This theory implies that the judgment of Judas was at fault, but that he had no evil intent; it finds no support in the Gospel history, and it is inconsistent with our Lord's stern words of condemnation.

(*b*) *The Satan incarnate theory.*—Dante (*Inferno,* xxxiv. 62) places Judas in the Giudecca, the lowest circle of the frozen deep of Hell, accounting him a sharer in the sin of Satan, inasmuch as his treachery was aggravated by ingratitude towards his benefactor. A similar tendency to set Judas apart as the arch-villain is manifest in works which reflect the popular imagination. Critics of the Ober-Ammergau Passion-play complain that the Betrayer is represented as a low, cunning rascal, and is often made to look ridiculous. But the comic personifications of Judas, as of Satan himself, in folk-lore are really tokens of popular abhorrence (cf. Büttner, *Judas Ischarioth,* p. 11 f.); they are the result of regarding him as an incarnation of Satanic wickedness. Daub, in the Introduction to a speculative work on the relation of good to evil (*Judas Ischarioth, oder Betrachtungen über das Böse im Verhältniss zum Guten*), conceives Judas as the Satanic kingdom personified in contrast with Jesus who is the Divine kingdom personified; Judas is 'an incarnation of the devil.' Dr. Fairbairn, who gives (*Studies in the Life of Christ,* p. 264 f.) a succinct summary of Daub's 'gruesome book,' truly says that he is 'unjust to Judas, sacrificing his historical and moral significance to a speculative theory.' The practical effect of such exaggerations of the innate vice of Judas is to place him outside the pale of humanity; but they are as untrue to the Evangelists' delineation of his character as are the attempts to explain away his sin. The same objection may be urged against theories which portray Judas as a mere compound of malice and greed, uninfluenced by any high impulse or noble ambition. In the Gospels he appears as a man 'of like nature with ourselves'; he was both tempted of the devil and 'drawn away by his own lust'; Satan approached his soul along avenues by which he draws near to us; he was not 'twofold more a son of hell' than ourselves (Mt 23[15]); he went to 'his own place' in the 'outer darkness,' because he turned away from the 'light of life'; the darkness 'blinded his eyes' because he would not abide in the light, though 'the true light' was shining upon him (cf. 1 Jn 2[8ff.]).

(c) *The mingled motives theory.*—The key to the complex problem of the character of Judas is not to be found in a single word. The desire to simplify his motives has led, on the one hand, to an attempt to exonerate him from guilt; and, on the other hand, to a description of him as the devil incarnate. The truth lies between the two extremes; in Judas, possibilities of good were unrealized because he 'gave place to the devil.' It is a mistake to set one motive over against another, as though a man of *covetous* disposition may not also be *ambitious*, and as though an ambitious man may not also be *jealous*. The references to Judas in the Gospels, to which attention has already been called in this article, furnish reasons, it is believed, for saying that Judas was swayed by all three motives, one being sometimes more prominent than another, and the one reacting upon the other. It may well be that ambition would, for a time, restrain covetousness, and yet revive it in the hour of disappointment; whilst, in turn, jealousy would embitter, and covetousness would degrade ambition.

(a) Violence is done to the statements of the Evangelists when *covetousness* is eliminated from the motives which influenced Judas. His covetous disposition is not incompatible either with the fact that he was a disciple of Jesus of his own free will, or with his position of trust, or with his remorse at the consequences of his perfidy. (1) The call of Jesus would arouse 'a new affection,' powerful enough to expel for a time all selfish greed, even though Judas, like the rest of the disciples, cherished the hope of attaining to honour in the Messianic kingdom. (2) His appointment by Jesus to a position of trust scarcely 'proves that he was no lover of money' (Fairbairn, *op. cit.* p. 266); to entrust a man possessing more than ordinary business gifts with the common cash-box is to provide him with an opportunity of honourable service which may become the occasion of his downfall; it was along the line of his capacity to handle moneys that the temptation came to Judas to handle them to his own gain. (3) The objection that the remorse of Judas discredits the idea of his being actuated by greed of money has force only when covetousness is regarded as the sole motive of the betrayal. What we know of the conduct of Judas towards the close of his career suggests that covetousness—the sin against which Jesus had so earnestly warned His disciples —was once more gaining the upper hand.

(β) To say that Judas was *ambitious* is not to differentiate him from his fellow-Apostles. The contrast between him and them was gradually brought to light as together they listened to the spiritual teaching of Jesus; that contrast is definitely marked by St. John when he first mentions Judas (6[71]). It was a time of crisis; the Apostles had been severely tested (1) by the refusal of Jesus to accept the homage of the Galilæan crowd, who had been impressed by His recent miracles and desired perforce to make Him king; (2) by the searching question, 'Would ye also go away?' (v.[67]) put by Jesus to the Twelve, when Master and disciples were alike saddened by the desertion of the many. St. Peter thought he was speaking for all the Twelve when he made his confession of faith; but within that select circle

there was one who had not found in Christ all that he was seeking. Jesus saw that already in spirit Judas was a deserter, and, as Westcott points out, a man who regards Christ 'in the light of his own selfish views' is 'turning good into evil' (διαβάλλειν), and is, therefore, a partaker of 'that which is essential to the devil's nature' (*Speaker's Com. in loc.*). It was in the light of the Betrayal that St. John came not only to recognize in Judas the disloyal Apostle to whom Christ referred without mentioning his name, but also to perceive the significance of the words of Jesus, 'One of you is a devil' (6[70]). The whole incident shows that the words and actions of Jesus had proved a disillusionment to Judas; when he joined the disciples of Christ, he hoped for more than 'words of eternal life'; baffled ambition was one of the motives which prompted him to do the devil's work of betrayal.

(γ) Reasons for believing that *jealousy* was one of the motives which led Judas to turn traitor have been given above (cf. ii. (c)). An ambitious man is peculiarly susceptible to this temptation. It would embitter Judas to realize that he was in a false position owing to his misconception of the aims of Christ, that his chances of advancement in the coming kingdom were dwindling, and that some of the least of his brethren would be greater than he. In proportion as others gained a higher place than himself in the esteem of Christ, the expectations he had been cherishing would fade. 'Trifles light as air are to the jealous confirmation' of their fears. Fuller knowledge of the life of Judas would probably enable us to see this sin in germ. It may also be, as Ainger suggests (*op. cit.* p. 234), that the Evangelists are silent because 'there was so little to tell.' Judas is described as 'a sullen and silent person . . . dwelling ever on himself—how *he* should profit if the cause were victorious, how *he* might suffer if the cause should fail.' Such a man would be prone to jealousy and 'fit for treasons.'

Whether covetousness, ambition, or jealousy was the basal motive of Judas when he betrayed Jesus, it is difficult, perhaps impossible, to say. It is probable that the flame of resentment, kindled by baffled ambition, was fanned by malign jealousy and base desire to snatch at paltry gain when all seemed lost. That the thirty pieces of silver tormented Judas does not prove that they had never attracted him; that he keenly suffered from the pangs of remorse makes neither his evil deed nor his evil motives good. All that we are warranted in saying is well expressed by Bruce (*The Training of the Twelve*, p. 367): 'He was bad enough to do the deed of infamy, and good enough to be unable to bear the burden of its guilt. Woe to such a man! Better for him, indeed, that he had never been born!'

v. REFERENCES TO JUDAS IN POST-BIBLICAL LITERATURE. — (a) *Apocryphal works.* — In the *Gospel of the Twelve Apostles* Judas Iscariot is mentioned (§ 2). In the *Arabic Gospel of the Childhood* (§ 35) Judas is represented as possessed by Satan at the birth of Jesus; he tried to bite Jesus, but could not; he did, however, strike Jesus, and immediately Satan went forth from him in the shape of a mad dog. In the *Gospel of Judas* (Iren. *adv. Hær.* i. 31; cf. Epiph. xxxviii. 1. 3) the Cainites—an important Gnostic sect—are said to have declared 'that Judas the traitor . . . knowing the truth as no others did, alone accomplished the mystery of the betrayal.' In the *Acts of Peter* (§ 8), Peter speaks of Judas as his 'fellow-disciple and fellow-apostle'; he also refers to his 'godless act of betrayal.' In the *Acts of Thomas* (§ 32) the dragon or serpent says, 'I am he who inflamed and bribed Judas to deliver the Messiah to death.' Later (§ 84), there is a warning against 'theft, which enticed Judas Iscariot and caused him to hang himself.' The account of the death of the serpent (§ 32) probably contains reminiscences of the story of the death of Judas; after sucking the poison the serpent 'began to swell,' and ultimately 'burst.' Dr. Rendel Harris (*op. cit.* p. 508) quotes from Solomon of Bassora, *The Book of the Bee*, the interesting comparison: 'Judas Iscariot, the betrayer, . . . was like unto the serpent, because he dealt craftily with the Lord.'

(*b*) *Early Christian writings.*—Clement of Rome (1 *Ep. ad Cor.* xlvi. 8) combines 'the words spoken by our Lord with regard to Judas' (Mt 26²⁴ = Mk 14²¹) with 'a saying recorded in another connexion in the three Synoptic Gospels' (cf. Mt 18⁶ᶠ· etc.). Hermas (*Vis.* IV. ii. 6) probably borrows the same saying from the Synoptists, 'the change being no greater than we may expect when there is no express quotation' (cf. *The NT in the Apostolic Fathers*, pp. 61, 121).

Papias refers to the horrible end of Judas (cf. above, iii. (*c*)) in the fourth book of his 'Expositions of the Oracles of the Lord' (Cramer, *Catena in Mat.* 27). From the same book Irenæus (*adv. Hær.* v. 33³ᶠ·) quotes an 'unwritten' saying of Jesus, foretelling days when the earth shall be marvellously fruitful, and the animals shall be at peace. Papias further says that 'when the traitor Judas did not give credit to these things, and put the question, "How then can things about to bring forth so abundantly be wrought by the Lord?" the Lord declared, "They who shall come to these [times] shall see."'

Tertullian, like Irenæus (cf. above, v. (*a*)), condemns the Cainites because they held the conduct of Judas to be meritorious; he represents them as saying (*adv. omnes Hæreses*, ii.): 'Judas, observing that Christ wished to subvert the truth, betrayed Him.' Tertullian also (*adv. Marcionem*, iv. 40) refers to the treachery of Judas as predetermined by prophecy.

Origen (*contra Celsum*, ii. 11 f.) replies to the 'childish objection that no good general was ever betrayed'; Celsus is reminded that he had learnt of the betrayal from the Gospels, and that he had called 'the one Judas many disciples,' thus unfairly stating his accusation (cf. also *Tract. in Mat.* 35).

(*c*) *Folk-lore.*—Some of the wild fables about Judas may be traced to the legend of the Wandering Jew (cf. Moncure D. Conway, art. 'Jew' in *Ency. Brit.*⁹ xiii. 674). Another source of popular tradition is a 17th cent. work by Ulrich Megerle, a Vienna priest, generally known as Abraham a Santa Clara. His *Judas der Erzschelm, oder eigentlicher Entwurf und Lebensbeschreibung des Ischariotischen Bösewichts* was translated into several European languages; the English edition bears the title, *The Arch-Knave, or the History of Judas from the cradle to the gallows.* From the *Polychronicon* (14th cent.) and the *Golden Legend* (13th cent.) many stories of Judas, current as folk-lore, are supposed to be derived. Many curious allusions to Judas and quaint customs connected with his name are mentioned in *Notes and Queries*, ii. 5, 6, 7, iii. 7, iv. 1, v. 6. Cholevius, *Geschichte der deutschen Poesie nach ihren antiken Elementen*, compares the Judas legend with the Œdipus story.

LITERATURE.—It is superfluous to name Lives of Christ, Commentaries on the Gospels, and articles in Encyclopædias. Mention has already been made of the most important works which deal with the NT narratives of the life of Judas, to which may now be added *Expositor*, III. x. [1889] 161 ff.; Ker, *Sermons*, i. 282 ff.; Stalker, *Trial and Death of Jesus Christ*, 110 ff. Interesting studies of or references to Judas will be found in the following poems: Story, *A Roman Lawyer in Jerusalem*; Matthew Arnold, *St. Brandan*; Robert Buchanan, *The Ballad of Judas Iscariot*; Keble, *Judas's Infancy* ('Cradle Songs' 13 in; *Lyra Innocentium*). Dr. A. B. Grosart mentions Gianni,

Sonnet on Judas; a few German poems may be added: Klopstock, *Messias*, 3rd Aufzug; Geibel, *Judas Ischarioth*; Max Crone, *Judasrätsel* and *Der Sohn des Verderbens.*

J. G. TASKER.

JUDGING (by men).—

In the NT 'to judge' is always a tr. of κρίνειν or its compounds, although κρίνω is frequently rendered by other words than 'judge.' The primary meaning of κρίνω is *to separate, put asunder.* Through the derivative signification *to search into, to investigate*, it came to mean *to choose, prefer, determine, to decide moral questions or disputes after examination, to judge.* In this last sense it is used of the authoritative decisions Christ will declare as to conduct and destiny at the general judgment of the last day. When κρίνω is not rendered by 'judge' in the NT, it always involves the kindred meaning of reaching a decision, or of action consequent upon a decision. In a number of instances it means *to determine to pursue the course decided upon as best.* St. Paul had determined (κεκρίκει) to sail past Ephesus (Ac 20¹⁶); he determined (ἔκρινα) not to know anything among the Corinthians save Jesus Christ and Him crucified (1 Co 2²); not to come to them in sorrow (2 Co 2¹). The Jews denied Jesus before Pilate wʰ en he was determined (κρίναντος) to let Him go (Ac 3¹³, see also 24²¹ 25²⁵, 1 Co 7³⁷). In Mt 5⁴⁰ κριθῆναι is rendered 'go to law' in RV, and other forms are rendered 'condemn' (Ac 13²⁷), 'called in question' (24²¹), 'ordained' (16⁴), 'esteemeth' (Ro 14⁵).

1. *Judging by men permitted and commended.*—The right to pass judgment upon both the actions of men and their characters as manifested in their conduct is implied in the power of rational and moral discrimination which all possess. Its exercise is also made imperative by the very nature of things. Men must form an opinion not only of the quality of deeds, but also of those who do them, if there is to be the prudent and wise action in our necessary relations to others, which shall be best for us and for them. St. Paul recognizes this power of moral judgment in even the heathen (Ro 2¹⁴⁻¹⁶). To this, truth and right conduct may confidently appeal (2 Co 4²). He commends those who exercise it upon all moral questions, and hold fast the good it approves, and abstain from the evil it condemns (1 Th 5²¹· ²²). It is to this moral judgment that all true teaching and preaching appeal. Our Lord assumes that all have the power to know the quality of outward deeds of men, and lays down the principle that the quality of the man corresponds with that of his deeds (Mt 7¹⁵⁻¹⁹), and, therefore, that we can form a right judgment of men, when the fruitage of their lives matures, however much they may seek to hide under false pretences. To this great principle of judging our Lord made frequent appeal in His controversies with the Pharisees. The Satanic conduct of these leaders proved them the children of the devil,—as having his nature (Jn 8³⁸⁻⁴⁴),—while His own works made it plain He was from God (Jn 5³⁶ 10²⁵ etc.). Even in Mt 7¹⁻⁵, in connexion with our Lord's strongest condemnation of judging, it is implied (vv.²· ⁵) that men may judge others guilty of faults and help to cure them of the failings discovered, if they but be free enough from faults themselves to have the clearest discernment. He also censures the Jews (Lk 12⁵⁷) because they do not judge what is right as to the Messianic time of His preaching, as they do the signs of the sky, and are therefore in danger of arraignment and condemnation at the highest tribunal.

2. *The judging which is condemned.*—(*a*) That prompted by a wrong spirit. Of this kind is that forbidden by our Lord in Mt 7¹⁻⁴. It is prompted by *a critical and censorious spirit.* The man possessed by this disposition subjects others to searching scrutiny to find out faults. Where even the smallest defects are discovered, he becomes so absorbed in them that he is oblivious alike of his own greater faults and the greater virtues which may be associated with the minor faults of others. Those who are critical of others in order to find something to blame, instead of being critical of themselves in order to become fitted to help them, will but bring upon themselves from God as well as from men the condemnation they are so ready to mete out to others (see also Lk 6[37]).

(b) Judging according to false or inadequate principles or standards. In Jn 7[23. 24], cf. 5[8], our Lord condemns *judging upon superficial principles* —mere literal conformity to outward rules. Had the Jews seen the deeper intent of the Sabbath law, they would not have condemned Him for apparently breaking it by healing a man on that day. It was this superficial standard of judging— on literal and mere legal grounds rather than upon the deeper underlying principles—which constituted judging after the flesh rather than after the spirit. It is only the judging after the spirit that is righteous and to be commended (Jn 8[15]). It is for this reason that the natural ($\psi v \chi \iota \kappa \acute{o} s$) man receiveth not the things of the Spirit, but he that is spiritual ($\pi \nu \epsilon v \mu \alpha \tau \iota \kappa \acute{o} s$) judgeth ($\dot{\alpha} \nu \alpha \kappa \rho \acute{\iota} \nu \epsilon \iota$) all things (1 Co 2[14]). The one has in his nature only that to which the mere outward and superficial appeals—the other has in him that in which the deepest inner principles of life and action find a response. The latter, through this sensitive response of his nature to the deepest truths, can give strict judgment as to their character.

LITERATURE.—Dale, *Laws of Christ*, p. 93, *Week Day Sermons*, p. 32; Dykes, *Manifesto of the King*, p. 621; Mozley, *Univ. Sermons*, p. 72; Wendt, *Teaching of Jesus*, i. 274.

C. GOODSPEED.

JUDGMENT.—The Synoptic Gospels differ from the Gospel of John in their view of a judgment. The former set forth a multitude of external tests which furnish ground for continuous judgment in this life. The 'deeds' or 'works' of a man are a measure of his attitude toward Jesus Christ. The Gospel of John is more especially concerned with the inner and hidden judgment which is being pronounced continually in man's soul. The sensuous and external aspects are little emphasized. All the Gospels hint unmistakably at a final crisis or judgment.

Mt. is pre-eminently the Gospel of judgment, for, throughout, Jesus appears as the Judge of men, and is always discriminating and separating the good from the bad, the sheep from the goats, the wheat from the tares, the grain from the chaff, the sincere man from the hypocrite (13[38] 25[33] 13[25-30] 3[12] 6[5. 6]). The predominance of this special aspect of Jesus' teaching, selected from among His varied utterances, in this Gospel, may arise from Matthew's Hebrew predisposition to consider Israel as a people separated from the Gentile world. Almost every utterance carries within it an unmistakable voice of judgment which separates men into two classes. The judgment which eventuates in blessedness, as in the Beatitudes (Mt 5[3-10]) or as 'Come, ye blessed of my Father' (25[34]), is as notable as that which leads to separation from Christ and to eternal wretchedness (25[46]).

1. *Jesus is the Judge.*—This is the view of all the Gospels. The Father gives all judgment to the Son (Jn 5[22-27]). Jesus came into the world for judgment (9[39]). He separates men under moral tests (Mt 25[31-46], cf. 7[23]). He pronounces judgment on the Pharisees (2.2[15-46]). He judges Satan (16[23]). He imparts the authority for judgment to men (16[19]). (Cf. Ac 10[42], Ro 14[10], 2 Co 5[10], 2 Ti 4[1]). His judgment-seat is at the same time the throne of His glory (Mt 25[31]), as it marks the culmination of the work which He has mediated in creation and in redemption. The judgment will be glorious, because then will be the final enthronement of holiness among men, and the deposition of evil. It is to be noted that He associates with Himself the twelve disciples (like the Roman assessors of judgment) who are to judge the twelve tribes of Israel (Mt 19[28], Lk 22[30]; cf. 1 Co 6[2. 3]). This exhibits the vital union of righteous souls with Christ, for the new life which His disciples obtain through Him would dispose them to pronounce judgment upon the same principles of justice as does their Lord. It is fitting that He who has mediated creation, maintenance, and redemption, should pronounce judgment upon man with regard to his attitude

and responsibility toward each of these sovereign acts and relations. All judgment is determined by the attitude which men hold towards Christ. He is set forth as a perpetual challenge to men to live a right thinking and right acting life.

2. *The Judgment.*—Jesus in the Gospels presents an almost numberless series of tests by which men may judge themselves in this present age. Their 'works' or 'deeds' are reviewed (Mt 16[27] 25[31]; cf. Ro 2[6], Rev 20[12]). Every kindness to a disciple will be rewarded (Mk 9[41], Mt 10[42]). Every cause of stumbling to one of these little ones (Lk 17[2]) will be punished. Jesus presents Himself as the supreme and personal test. What is man's attitude towards Him as proved by 'his deeds and works'? This kind of judgment is continuous and cumulative here, and comes to a conclusion at the final crisis or judgment. These are some of the tests:

Following Him (Mt 4[18-22] 10[38] 19[28], Mk 8[34]); confessing Him (Mt 10[32], Lk 12[8]); failure to appreciate His presence and work (Mt 11[21]); failure to come to Him (Jn 5[40]); failure to believe Him (Jn 3[18]); failure to obey Him (Jn 3[36]); failure to honour Him (Jn 5[23]); failure to stand with Him (Mt 12[30]); failure of right fruitage (Mt 21[31-42] 7[16], Lk 6[44]); failure in outward conduct (Mt 22[11-13]); failure to help men (Mt 25[31-46]); failure to repent (Jn 5[40]); failure to use the gifts of God (Mt 25[14-30]); making light of His personal invitations (Mt 22[1-7]); unwillingness to hear His words (Mt 12[41. 42]); unwillingness to forgive an injury (Mt 6[15] 18[28-30]); being ashamed of Him (Mk 8[38]); breaking a commandment (Mt 5[19]); the spirit of our judgment on others (Mt 7[2]); faith or lack of it (Mt 8[10] 9[22. 29] 15[28], Mk 5[34]); heart unreceptive to His words (Mt 10[14. 15]); hypocrisy (Mt 23[13-36]); idle words (Mt 12[36]); lip service without the heart (Mt 15[7]); selfish conceit (Mt 6[2]); wicked pride (Mk 12[38]); love of darkness (Jn 3[19]); rejection of His disciples (Lk 10[16]); adultery (Mt 19[9]); commercialism in worship (Mt 21[13]); blasphemy against the Spirit (Mt 12[31-32]); loving others more than God (Mt 10[37]); hearing, seeing the Son, with belief or with failure to believe (Mt 7[24] 13[23], Jn 5[24. 640]); the cup of cold water given to a disciple (Mt 10[42]); mercifulness (Lk 6[36]); love to Christ (Lk 7[47], Jn 21[16]); love to enemies (Lk 6[27]); humble-mindedness as a child (Mt 18[4]); fidelity of service (Mt 20[14] 24[45-51]); endurance in well-doing (24[13]); doing will of God (12[50]); deeds in general (16[27]); inward thoughts and motives (Mk 7[21], Lk 5[22. 23]).

These are clear, varied, and concrete tests which men may apply daily to conduct and character, and which bring them into continual judgment. They cover almost every phase of human life, both inward and outward. The great first and second commandments in the law which our Lord enunciated to the lawyer (Mt 22[37-39]) are in the nature of a judgment, for men know whether or not they have been kept. Judgments are continuous in the sphere of moral life, as conscience persistently affirms. They are continuous in the religious life, and the principles upon which they are based are found in these teachings and in the character of Jesus. No man can plead ignorance of the grounds on which judgment is pronounced on him, because these varied tests cover clearly and openly so much of his life. Jesus always holds Himself forth ('I am the way and the truth and the life,' Jn 14[6]) as the supreme standard of life; and the invitation to come to Him leads to a comparison and judgment of likeness or unlikeness. The work of the Holy Spirit (whom Jesus sends, Jn 16[7]) is to convict men of sin, righteousness, and judgment (v.[9]), and He accomplishes this by showing men their unlikeness to Christ. The character of Jesus is thus continually a challenge to men, and the measure of the judgment which they must pass on themselves. In all the Gospels, judgment is determined by the relation which a man holds to Jesus Christ. But the Gospels also teach that this continuous judgment will culminate in a crisis or Final Judgment. The inadequacy and inequalities of punishment here seem to demand a final adjusting of the accounts of all men on principles of eternal equity. The parable of Dives and Lazarus (Lk 16[20-25]) exhibits this final accounting and the equitable readjustment of their respective conditions. Lazarus had wretchedness. Dives had luxury. The continuous judgment in this life did not result in the proper rewards and penalties, hence the balances are struck after death. Final judgment and penalty are then reached.

3. *The time of this Final Judgment* is set forth in the Synoptics as at 'the end of the world' (Mt 13[39]). Some have held that this means at the end of eacn man's life, but the more obvious meaning is the end of this time-order of race, life, and things (cf. He 9[27]). The words 'the time' (Mt 8[29]), and 'then' (16[27] 25[1]), point to a time which follows the Lord's appearing in glory with His angels after the resurrection from the dead. 'That day and hour' (24[36]), 'the resurrection of life' and 'the resurrection of judgment' (Jn 5[29]), are the antithetical statements of what takes place after the resurrection, which to one class of men is entrance into life, and to the other entrance into judgment followed by spiritual death. The Gospels do not give information as to whether or not the Final Judgment follows immediately on the general resurrection. The weight of impression is that judgment does follow immediately, but it would be by no means an entire misinterpretation of the sayings of Jesus if one held that there was a considerable period of intervening time.

4. *All mankind and all evil spirits are to be judged.*—'All nations' (Mt 25[32]) and all men (12[36], Jn 5[29]) shall be judged (cf. Ro 14[10], 2 Co 5[10], Rev. 20[12-15]). It is implied in Mt 8[29] that evil spirits also are to stand in the judgment. But it is clear that the holy angels do not come into judgment, for they accompany and serve the holy Judge (Mt 16[27] 25[31]). Judgment would not be necessary for men if it were not for their sin. Wherever there has been need of a redemption, there will be need of a Final Judgment.

5. *Some characteristics.*—Jesus Christ the Judge in His glory (Mt 16[27] 19[28], Mk 8[38], Lk 9[26]) [the glory of Jesus will be as manifest in His judgments as in His forgiveness]; 'the throne of his glory' (Mt 25[31]); the surrounding holy angels as His servitors (cf. Mt 13[41]); mankind gathered before Him; evil spirits awaiting their final doom; the sharp separations; the openness of the facts upon which judgment proceeds; the uncovered moral life of every man; the irrevocableness of the decision (Mt 25[46]),—all these, together with the manifestly diverse feelings of the righteous and the wicked, present a scene of surpassing grandeur, extent, and interest. Judgment stands in the Gospels as the natural terminus of an æon in the life of the race which began with Creation, was continued under a purpose and revelation of Redemption, and demands a Judgment as its proper culmination.   NATHAN E. WOOD.

JUST and 'righteous' in AV represent the same word, δίκαιος, which, however, has usually the wider meaning of 'righteous, observing Divine and human laws, one who is such as he ought to be, prop. the Heb. צדּיק' (Grimm-Thayer), and comprehends duty both to God and to man. The Vulg. had no word available except *justus*, which strictly means 'what is according to *jus*, the rights of man,' hence 'just' in many places in AV. In the Gospels it is used of Joseph (Mt 1[19]), Simeon (Lk 2[25]), John the Baptist (Mk 6[20]), Joseph of Arimathæa (Lk 23[50]), and Christ (Mt 27[19. 24]). In Ac 3[14] 7[52] 22[14] (cf. 1 P 3[18], and possibly Ja 5[6]) 'the Just One' is a Messianic name corresponding to the prophecies of the Righteous Servant of Jehovah (Is 53[11]; cf. 11[3f.], Jer 23[5]); its use 'affords in itself a marvellous proof of the impression made by the human life of Jesus upon those who knew Him best, or who, at all events, like St. Stephen, had ample opportunities of learning' (*Expos. Gr. Test.*). In nearly every case RV uniformly gives 'righteous,' excep-

tions being Mt 5[45] ('rain on the just and the unjust'), Lk 1[17] ('wisdom of the just') 14[14] ('resurrection of the just'). In Lk 2[25] 'just' might perhaps have been retained with advantage to bring out the difference in the same verse between δίκαιος and εὐλαβής, which latter means 'reverencing God, devout' ('δίκαιος, *justus*, in officiis; εὐλαβής, Vulg. *timoratus*, in habitu animæ erga Deum'—Bengel). For full discussion of δίκαιος see art. RIGHTEOUS.
                                            W. H. DUNDAS.

JUSTICE.—

In the AV of NT the word 'justice' does not occur, δικαιοσύνη being always translated 'righteousness.' For the adj. δίκαιος we have 'just' and 'righteous' used interchangeably. God is *just* (1 Jn 1[9], Rev 15[3]), *righteous* (Jn 17[25], 2 Ti 4[8]); Christ is the *Just* One (Ac 3[14] 7[52]), and *righteous* (1 Jn 2[1]). Men, both as individuals and collectively, are *just* or *righteous* (Mt 1[19] 5[45] 10[41] 13[43], Ac 10[22] 24[15]). In Jn 5[30] we have *just*, and in Rev 16[7] *righteous* judgment. In Col 4[1] τὸ δίκαιον refers to what is due by masters to their slaves; and in Mt 20[4] to a money payment for work done. This haphazard rendering of δίκαιος is partially rectified in the RV. In classical Greek the noun and the adj. are sometimes used in the wider sense of moral rectitude in general; but under the influence of the Platonic and Aristotelian philosophy its later usage inclines to the narrower sense of political and social justice. Aristotle (*Nic. Eth.* v. 1. 15) qualifies the general idea by making it refer to what is due to one's neighbour; and Plato (*Republic*, Bks. i. ii. iv.) deals with δικαιοσύνη at great length but almost exclusively in the sense of political and individual justice, though he does attempt to give the idea a wider scope by connecting it with that of the Absolute Good. In Biblical Greek, both in the LXX and the NT, the wider meaning is restored, and is the common one. In Lk 1[6] Zacharias and Elisabeth are said to be δίκαιοι; and this is explained, if not defined, by the words πορευόμενοι ἐν πάσαις ταῖς ἐντολαῖς καὶ δικαιώμασι τοῦ Κυρίου ἄμεμπτοι. This is the general idea of righteousness; but our word 'justice' must be taken as signifying the recognition and fulfilment of what is due from one to another, righteous dealing between persons, each rendering to others what is their right and due. See also art. RIGHTEOUS.

1. The justice of God.—The justice of God is an aspect of His righteousness, and belongs, therefore, to His essential nature. It may be shown to have significance for the Divine life, even apart from His relation to others. God's attributes are not all of co-ordinate worth. His omnipotence, *e.g.*, is subordinate to His ethical attributes; it does not use them as a means to accomplish its ends, but they use it. Omnipotence is not a power to do what *it* wills, but to do what God wills; and as His will is holy, it can be only ethically determined. If in God's nature mere power were supreme, and holiness and love subordinate, this would be as contrary to justice as when, in a kingdom, the rule of right has been overturned by irresponsible violence. As in the State, justice is the controlling principle which preserves the body politic for the discharge of its several functions, so, in the Divine justice, we have the regulative principle of order in the Divine nature and life.

(1) *God's justice in His relations with men.*—He shows favour to the righteous. He could not withhold His approval of that in them which is the object of complacency and delight in Himself. This does not mean that they have a claim on God for a happy earthly lot, and exemption from earthly troubles. This doctrine of recompense was the prevalent one during the early and non-reflective stage of Israel's religious progress; but it did not bear the strain put on it by the national calamities. In the teaching of Christ it is repudiated: Mt 5[45] 13[28. 29], Lk 16[25] 18[1-5], Jn 9[2. 3]; and in Ro 8[18-39] and He 12[11] an explanation of the sufferings of the righteous is given which goes far to remove their seeming variance with the justice of God. They are part of His fatherly discipline by which His children are prepared for their heavenly inheritance (2 Co 4[16. 17], He 5[8]). Even here they have their great reward in the favour and friendship of God (Mt 5[10-12], 1 P 2[19. 20] 3[12-14]).

(2) *God's justice in relation to sin.*—God is just, and will therefore punish sin. This is one of the Christian certainties (Gal 6[7]). Different views.

however, have been held as to the nature of the punishment and its object. Some think (and this is Ritschl's opinion) that the true punishment of sin consists in the sense of guilt and alienation from God which a persuasion of the Divine displeasure awakens ; and that the outward evils which are regarded as punishments are really due to natural causes that have no relation to human guilt (Ritschl, *Justification and Reconciliation*, 47 ff., 257 ff.). Now, the sense of God's displeasure must always be a most important part of punishment, and might almost stand for the whole of it, if we could suppose the sinner as responsive to it as he ought to be, as, *e.g.*, a saint made perfect in holiness would be. To such a saint the sense of alienation from God would be harder to bear than the most untoward outward calamity. But sin increasingly blunts the sinner's susceptibility to suffering from this source ; and if no effective provision has been made to bring God's displeasure home to him, he would at last work out his term of punishment. There may be no link of causation between our sin and most of the outward evils of life. Maeterlinck may be right in saying that nature knows nothing of justice ; but in that case we should have to believe with him that neither can nature be regarded as the creation of a Being in whom ethical attributes are supreme (Maeterlinck, *Buried Temple*, Essay on the 'Mystery of Justice').

God's justice in relation to sin is at once retributive, educative, and protective. It is *retributive* because it punishes sin simply as sin ; it is *educative* or reformatory because the punishment is also intended for the moral improvement of the transgressor ; it is *protective* because by the punishment others are restrained from wrong-doing, and are themselves guarded against the evils which would result from the prevalence of unpunished sin. That the Scripture view of God's justice implies retribution may be shown from many passages : Mt 16[27] 24. 25, Lk 12[45-48], Ro 2[6. 16] 6[23], 2 Co 5[10], Col 3[25], 2 Th 1[9], He 2[2] 10[27]. One could scarcely gather from these passages that God's sole aim in punishment is the reformation of the offender. Yet this is the popular view with many modern theologians. As a protest against the once prevalent opinion that God, in punishing, desires merely to exact vengeance without any regard to the sinner's repentance, it has its justification. But, like other reactionary views, it carries us too far in the opposite direction. The whole drift of Biblical teaching is that God punishes sinners because they deserve it. Punishment is the reaction of His holy nature against wrong-doing, and without it the moral order of the world could not be maintained. If sin did not arouse His displeasure, He would not be holy ; and if He did not manifest His displeasure objectively by punishment, men could not know that He is holy. But it is said that God is love, and that what love inflicts is chastisement, not punishment in the retributive sense. Holy love, however, cannot accomplish its end unless the sinner is brought to feel that he deserves punishment. How could punishment benefit him if, while undergoing it, he believed that it had not been merited ? Retribution does tend to the offender's improvement, and this is part of God's purpose in it ; but its reformatory influence never takes effect until the sinner acknowledges its justice. His improvement begins only when he is brought into this state of mind and feeling. If, indeed, God's sole aim were reformation, it would follow that, if rewards carried with them the same benefits as punishments, as in many cases they do, then the offender would deserve them, and this because of his sin. In like manner it would be very difficult to persuade people that it is right

that they should be protected from the spread of violence by the punishment of those to whom punishment was not justly due.

God's justice is also shown in the forgiveness of sins on condition of repentance. Repentance is a sign that the disciplinary purpose which accompanies retribution has not missed its mark ; and if now God withheld forgiveness, it would imply a failure of justice. According to 1 Jn 1[9], 'God is faithful and just (δίκαιος) to forgive.' Forgiveness and punishment are alike connected with the justice of God. The justice of forgiveness further appears from this, that the man who repents is a different moral person from the man who had sinned. His relation to his sin has been reversed ; for whereas formerly his will was identified with sin, it is now identified with the mind and will of God regarding it. In proportion to the depth and sincerity of his repentance, we feel that he is a changed man, and should no longer be treated as if sin still formed part of the texture of his being. He has separated from, and now unsparingly condemns, his past sinful self ; and, having thus come over to the side of righteousness, he is no longer a fit object of the Divine displeasure. Theologians, who first make logical distinctions between the Divine attributes and then reason from these as if they were real distinctions, say that justice cannot, but love alone can, forgive ; as if love and justice were two contending powers in God's nature. In reality, it is holy love that forgives ; and this means that love and justice are joined hand in hand in forgiveness as they are in punishment. From a non-moral love gifts would come, but they might not be blessings ; and justice without love never could be perfectly just, for love is part of the tribute which justice demands. The OT and NT writers never attempt to reconcile love and justice, because they were not conscious of any contrariety between them (see Mt 6[12. 14. 15] 12[31. 32] 18[15-17. 21-35], Lk 6[37] 7[37-50] 13[3. 5] 15[11-32] 17[3. 4] 18[10-14] 22[61. 62] ; cf. Jn 21[15-17], Ac 2[39] 3[19] 5[31], 2 P 3[9], 1 Jn 1[9]). Of course, imperfection clings to all human repentance, because past sin disqualifies even the sincerest penitent for that godly sorrow for sin 'which worketh repentance not to be repented of' (2 Co 7[10]). Hence the need for the work of Christ and the regenerating influence of the Spirit, by which imperfect repentance is atoned for and made perfect.

2. Justice in man.—If man has been created in the image of God, we should expect to find reflected in him the same supremacy of the ethical attributes as exists in God. Thus for him also justice or righteousness will be the supreme law of his being, obligatory, not through any human convention, but in virtue of man's Godlikeness. As supreme, it will be regulative of his whole life, determining his use of his freedom, the outflow of his emotions and thoughts, his activity in all human relations. Justice will regulate his life Godward, for God has definite claims on man for devotion and service ; and as in Christ He has made Himself known as a Father and Saviour, these claims are, for the Christian, raised to a higher sphere of obligation. These are duties which man owes to God, and, when they are withheld, justice is violated. God is robbed when that which is His due is not rendered (Mal 3[8]). Hence the just or righteous (δίκαιος) man is represented as walking 'in all the commandments of the Lord blameless' (Lk 1[6]), and of these the first and greatest is, 'Thou shalt love the Lord with all thy heart' (Mt 22[37]). Not until we give God this wholehearted love do we give Him His due. We are *then* 'just before God' ; and from 1 Jn 3[10. 17] 4[20. 21] 5[1] we learn that only when man responds to God's claim can he fulfil the obligations of love and justice to his fellow-men. That man can be just or unjust in relation to God appears also from passages in which sin is spoken of as a state of indebtedness—God being the creditor and man the debtor (Mt 5²⁶ 6¹² 18²³⁻³⁵, Lk 7⁴¹⁻⁴³) ; and from those parables in which God and man are related as Master and servant, or King and subject (Mt 20¹⁻¹⁶ 21³³⁻⁴¹ 25¹⁴⁻³⁰, Mk 12¹⁻¹²).

One characteristic of the NT doctrine of justice, as compared with the views current in the Jewish and classical worlds, is a noteworthy enlargement of its sphere. Justice to man as man was a subject of speculation among the Stoics, but in the popular morality its obligation was ignored and even repudiated. The Jew hated the Samaritan (Lk 9⁵⁴) and despised the Gentile, with whom he would not share his privileges (Ac 21²⁷⁻³⁰). Why should they show favour to those whom God had not honoured? The Greek was bound by moral ties to his fellow-citizens, but between him and the barbarians there was no moral reciprocity; if he was conscious of any obligation, it was an obligation to do them all the injury he could. Then again there was the slave class, who were regarded as incapable of virtue, and, therefore, like the lower animals, outside the ethical sphere. Thus Jew and Gentile alike acknowledged no moral relationship between themselves and the vast majority of the race. It was, therefore, a great step in advance when Christ proclaimed a universal Kingdom of justice and love, and taught that, since God was the Father of all, they were due to all men, on the ground not of citizenship or nationality, but of humanity and of their common relationship to God (Mt 5⁴³⁻⁴⁸ 28¹⁹, Lk 10³⁰⁻³⁷, Jn 3¹⁶ 12³²).

There was also a subjective enlargement of its sphere. Under the influence of Pharisaic teaching and example, the moral law had come to be regarded as merely an external rule of conduct; the inner world of thought and motive and feeling being overlooked or regarded as of only secondary importance. All the virtues had thus suffered deterioration, and justice among them. But in the Sermon on the Mount, Christ claimed this neglected sphere for the moral law. Its authority was extended so as to cover the entire life of men, for in the spiritual realm of being, thoughts and feelings are accounted as deeds, as acts of the moral self. And this was an infinite extension of the sway of justice. 'Out of the heart proceed adulteries, fornications, murders, thefts' (Mk 7²¹). Sin is not confined to outward acts; it begins the moment evil thoughts and desires arise in the heart; and a régime of justice is necessary there. To be angry with our brother without cause is to do him wrong (Mt 5²²); and the man is accounted guilty who, while refraining from actual murder, yet thinks in his heart, 'I would, if I dared.' Our neighbour has a claim on us, that we should think and feel justly regarding him; and when this is withheld, we fail to give him his due. Again, the sin of adultery may be begun and completed by simply looking on a woman to lust after her (Mt 5²⁸). Before the tribunal of the Kingdom, the man is adjudged to have wronged the woman. The Christian law of justice is embodied in the Golden Rule, 'All things whatsoever ye would that men should do to you, do ye even so to them' (Mt 7¹²); and also in the second of the great commandments, 'Thou shalt love thy neighbour as thyself' (Mk 12³¹). According to the Golden Rule, we are to regard our fellow-man as an *alter ego*, to put ourselves in his place, and judge his claims or needs and our duties from his point of view (Ph 2⁴⁻⁸). Then the commandment tells us positively what our obligation is. 'Thou shalt love him as thyself,' not with a non-moral love, which seeks

nothing higher than the happiness of its objects. We are to care for him with that holy love which attaches itself to that in him which in ourselves is the legitimate object of our self-love,—the moral self or soul which was created in, and can be restored to, the image of God. It is for His moral perfections that we love God; and the claims of Christian justice are met, only when our love for others has as its aim their restoration to Godlikeness (Mt 16²⁶, Ja 5²⁰, He 13¹⁷). The Christian law requires us not merely to refrain from doing our neighbour wrong, but to promote, even at the cost of self-sacrifice, his highest well-being as we would our own. For a Christian man to say, 'I have done my neighbour justice, and he has no claim on me for more,' is to prove false to the Christian ideal; for, in the Kingdom of righteousness, benevolence is not something that may be withheld, but is simply justice made perfect.

LITERATURE. — For meaning of δίκαιος and δικαιοσύνη see Grimm-Thayer, *Lex.*; Cremer, *Bib.-Th. Lex.*; Westcott, *Ep. of Jn.* 24 f.; Sanday-Headlam, *Rom.* 28 ff. See also T. Aquinas, *Sum.* i., Qu. xxi. ii. 2, Qu. LVIII.-LXXXI.; Hodge, *Syst. Theol.* vol. i.; the *Dogmatics* of Martensen and Dorner; Ritschl, *Justification and Reconciliation*; Moberly, *Atonement and Personality*, esp. i.-iv.; Clarke, *Outline of Theol.*; Stevens, *Chr. Doct. of Salvation*; the *Christian Ethics* of Martensen (Social), Dorner, Newman Smyth; Luthardt, *Hist. of Chr. Ethics*; Wendt, *Teaching of Jesus*, vol. i.; C. Wagner, *Justice*; Seeley, *Ecce Homo.* In the following works on General Ethics, 'Justice' is, in the main, treated from the Christian standpoint: Hegel, *Phil. of Right*; Bradley, *Eth. Studies*; Green, *Proleg. to Ethics*, also *Principles of Polit. Obligation*; M'Kenzie, *Introd. to Social Phil.*; Seth, *Ethical Principles*; Maeterlinck, Essay on the 'Mystery of Justice' in his *Buried Temple* [contains some fine thoughts, but Agnostic in tone and tendency].

A. BISSET.

JUSTIFICATION.—

I. Biblical doctrine.
   1. The OT and Pharisaic doctrines.
   2. The Pauline doctrine.
II. Historical.
   1. The Catholic doctrine.
   2. The Protestant doctrine.
   3. Modern theories.
III. Constructive treatment.

I. BIBLICAL DOCTRINE.—**1.** *The OT and Pharisaic doctrines.*—The doctrine of justification through faith in Christ owes its origin to St. Paul, and is the outcome of two factors, his Jewish training on the one hand, and his Christian experience on the other. The idea of justification itself was derived by the Apostle from the Rabbinic theology, whose doctrine of justification by the works of the Law is at once the antithesis and the necessary background of his own. The Rabbinic doctrine again rested upon an OT basis. We can trace the development of the idea of righteousness before God in the prophets, who from the first judge Israel by the standard of the absolutely righteous demands of Jahweh. In the time of Jeremiah and Ezekiel the idea is brought into connexion with the individual (Jer 20¹², Hab 1⁴· ¹³ 2⁴, Ezk 3²⁰· ²¹ 18¹⁹ff. 33¹²ff·). Further, this age being also that of the development of the Law, whose authors aimed at embodying the demands of Jahweh in a practical form, we find the idea connected with the fulfilment either of the Law as a whole (Dt 6²⁵), or of a single commandment contained in it (24¹³). Finally, in the post-exilic period the idea receives a great development. God is characterized as the righteous Judge (Ps 9⁷· ⁸ 50⁶ 94² 96¹⁰· ¹³ etc.), whose righteousness results in the punishment of sinners (1⁵· ⁶ 9¹⁶ 11⁵· ⁶ etc.). The actual positive recognition of the righteousness of the righteous is said in Ps 62¹² to depend on the Divine grace; the latter term, however, is practically synonymous with righteousness in its beneficent aspect (33⁵ 36⁶· ⁷ 48⁹· ¹⁰ 145¹⁷). Sinners God can justify so far as they are at bottom righteous (Job 33²⁶). But the godless He may not justify (Ps 69²⁷). The general idea is, further, that the recognition of righteousness by God is manifested by outward good fortune ; just as His displeasure is shown by outward calamity (Is 65¹². ¹⁴, Mal 4². ³, Ps 37¹⁹. ²⁰ etc. ; cf. Wellhausen, *IJG*⁵ p. 220, n. 1). In the later post-exilic literature, however, the idea that the righteous is always rewarded and the wicked always punished in this life, is abandoned, and there appears the conception that the final justification or condemnation takes place after death (Job 19²⁵. ²⁶, Dn 12². ³). This conception is henceforth predominant, as in the Pharisaic theology, to which we now turn.

The Pharisaic conception of the relation of man to God was purely legal, and based upon the idea of the Law as a contract between God and man. The idea of grace which qualifies the legalism of the OT sinks altogether into the background. The Pharisaic doctrine implies that the Divine demands expressed in the Law can be satisfied, and that the fulfilment of them gives a claim to reward. It is the recognition of this claim that is now meant by 'justification.' The conception is further carried out into detail in that the Law is regarded atomically as the sum of the commandments it contains (cf., however, Dt 6²⁵). Every act of obedience is entered by God in the heavenly books, as is also every act of transgression. The decision is according to the preponderance. If this is on the side of the good, the Divine sentence of justification follows, which consists in the declaration that the man is righteous. The account is finally made up at death (Weber, *Jüd. Theol.*² 1897, p. 277 ff.).

It will be apparent that the whole idea, both in the OT and still more distinctly in the Pharisaic theology, is forensic. With this, again, agrees the derivation of the group of technical terms used in the OT in connexion with the idea of justification (צְדָקָה, צֶדֶק 'righteousness,' צַדִּיק 'righteous,' הִצְדִּיק 'justify'). This group has almost universally a forensic sense. The words are so used secularly, and are therefore naturally applied with this meaning in religion (Smend, *Alttest. Religionsgeschichte*², 1899, p. 388 f.). In the LXX the equivalents are δικαιοσύνη,, δίκαιος, δικαιόω. On the constant forensic use of δικαιόω in the LXX (OT and Apocr.), also in the pseudepigraphic books, see Sanday-Headlam, ' Romans ' in *Internat. Crit. Com.* p. 31. In Talmudic theology צְדָק is replaced by זְכוּת 'innocence,' and הִצְדִּיק by זִכָּה ; זָכָה also appears for צַדִּיק, but the latter is maintained in use along with it (Weber, p. 277 f.).

It is finally to be observed that, both in the OT and in the Rabbinic theology, righteousness before God and justification, whether looked for from the Divine grace or on the ground of human merit, are *religious* ideas. Righteousness is not sought for its own sake, as a moralist might seek it, but always as the condition of acceptance with God, and the blessings which flow from this, in this world or the next. It is at this point that the Pauline conception of justification by faith links itself on to the older theologies. What St. Paul has in view is always the question of acceptance with God, and his doctrine is the answer of his Christian experience to a problem set in the terms of the Pharisaic theology.

2. *The Pauline doctrine.*—There is no doubt that St. Paul's idea of justification is essentially the same as the Pharisaic, and, like it, forensic. In the fundamental passage Ro 3¹⁹ff. the whole setting is forensic. Note the words ἵνα πᾶν στόμα φραγῇ, ὑπόδικος (v.¹⁹) ; ἐνώπιον αὐτοῦ (v.²⁰). Mankind is arraigned before the judgment-bar of God, and the justification which follows must be forensic. So in Ro 4⁵ justification is connected with imputation, a distinctly legal conception : λογίζεται = ' is reckoned,' *i.e.* in the heavenly account-books. See, further, Sanday-Headlam, *l.c.* p. 30, who decide on general

philological grounds that δικαιοῦν means *to pronounce righteous* : ' It has relation to a verdict pronounced by a judge. . . . It cannot mean to make righteous.' So far, then, St. Paul is in agreement with the Pharisees. But the deeper insight of his conscience will not allow him to suppose that God can be satisfied with a mere preponderance of performance over transgression. For him to attain righteousness by the works of the Law would involve the complete fulfilment of it. But this is impossible ; for all are sinners (Ro 3²³). Hence St. Paul concludes that ' by the works of the law shall no flesh be justified in God's sight ' (3²⁰).

Here is the point where St. Paul introduces his doctrine, based on his own personal experience, of a new method of justification (3²¹ff.), of which the principle on God's side is grace (χάρις), *i.e.* the free unmerited love of God (3²⁴), and on man's side faith (1¹⁷ 4⁵). As proceeding from the Divine grace, justification by faith is totally opposed to justification by works, which depends on merit (4⁴). Instead of attaining a righteousness by his own efforts, the believer submissively receives a righteousness which is wholly of God, and His gift (5¹⁷ 10³, Ph 3⁹). This casts light upon the Pauline conception of faith. It is the method by which the grace of God is subjectively appropriated. In so far as the believer, instead of acting on his own initiative, allows himself to be determined by God (Ro 10³), faith is a species of obedience ; thus St. Paul speaks of the obedience of faith (1⁵). But as correlative to grace, or the free love of God, faith is psychologically trust, a believing ' on God ' (4²⁴).

The revelation of the Divine grace which awakens faith takes place, according to St. Paul, in the Person of Christ (2 Co 5¹⁹) and in His work, more especially in His death, but also in His resurrection. Christ's death was the work of the Divine grace in that God ordained it as an expiatory sacrifice for sin, Christ dying instead of sinners, that in the act of justification He might not appear indulgent of sin (Ro 3²⁵ ; cf. 2 Co 5²¹, Ro 5⁸). Christ's resurrection is also included in the revelation by which God's grace to sinners is made known (Ro 4²⁵ 8³⁴ 10⁹, 1 Co 15¹⁷), but St. Paul does not define its exact place in it. In fact, Christ's resurrection, as the object of faith, is hardly separable from the Risen Christ. It is God's act by which He presents Christ alive, in spite of His death (Ro 4²⁴ 10⁹), as the object of faith.

It is to be observed, finally, that justification requires for its complete explanation both sides of the correlation, grace and faith, which in St. Paul's mind are associated in the closest possible manner. Thus he speaks of the revelation of the righteousness of God through faith (1¹⁷ 3²²) : the whole is really one idea. Only thus can we explain the remarkable interchange of language which the Apostle uses with respect to the two sides of the correlation. Justification is generally associated more closely with faith, or the subjective side (3²⁶ 5¹). But in 2 Co 5¹⁹ St. Paul says that God was in Christ, not imputing to men their trespasses, which last phrase is synonymous with ' justifying men '; so that here justification is associated with the *objective* side, or the revelation of grace (cf. Ro 3²⁴). So also in Ro 5¹⁶, if δικαίωμα be rightly translated ' sentence of justification ' (so Sanday-Headlam, *l.c.* p. 141), then St. Paul here represents this sentence as falling once for all at the death of Christ. On the other hand, the sacrifice of Jesus Christ belongs to the objective side of the correlation ; yet St. Paul speaks of Christ in Ro 3²⁵ as propitiatory through faith in His blood. Evidently, then, grace and faith are so organically related that the one implies the other, and is properly understood only through its correlative.

We must now return to the form in which St.

Paul has expressed his doctrine of justification. It is, as we have seen, determined by his Pharisaic training, and is that of a forensic judgment. But the *form* is all that the Apostle has in common with the Pharisaic idea. The judgment of justification in his conception is extra-judicial, *i.e.* God has regard in it to considerations outside the Law. The righteousness of faith is '*apart from law*' ($\chi\omega\rho\lambda s$ $\nu\delta\mu\nu\nu$, Ro 3^{21}). The Law as such takes account only of merit, as St. Paul himself testifies : ' He that doeth them shall live in them ' (Gal 3^{12}). But the Divine sentence of justification takes account of faith, which is a consideration beyond the purview of the Law : 'The law is not of faith ' (*ib.*). In fact, in justification the Law is transcended by grace, which reckons faith for righteousness (Ro $4^{4.5}$). St. Paul does not mean that faith is a work, and that grace simply reckons the work of faith instead of the works of the Law. This would be, after all, half legalism. With the Apostle, as we have seen, faith is not a work, but a receiving ; not a second principle of justification over against grace, but simply the reflex of Divine grace in man. Grace therefore sees in faith simply this reflex of itself, and in justifying the sinner by faith in reality justifies on the ground of itself (cf. Is 43^{25}).

What, then, is the essential point in the Pauline presentation of justification as forensic ? It is, to use philosophic language, that justification is a synthetic, not an analytic judgment. It is not based on anything in the believer—not even on his faith, which comes into view only so far as the Divine grace is reflected in it. In justification God 'justifies the ungodly ' (Ro 4^5) : the words are evidently chosen by St. Paul with a clear sense of the paradox involved, as the deliberate opposition of language to the OT shows (cf. Ex 23^7, Dt 25^1, Pr 17^{15}, Is 5^{23}). God does not, in justification, recognize the presence of any attribute in the sinner ; on the contrary, He adds to him an attribute while he is still a sinner, viz. that of righteousness. It is evident that the paradoxical character of this doctrine created misunderstanding even in St. Paul's time (Ro 3^8; cf. 6^1) ; and it has done so ever since. The paradox, however, resolves itself at once as soon as we remember that it is 'righteousness,' not in the ethical, but in the religious sense, as the condition of acceptance with God, which is meant. The OT taught that righteousness was the condition of acceptance with God ; the Pharisees sharpened this into the doctrine that the performance of the Law was the condition. St. Paul's language is determined by this form in which he found the problem of acceptance with God stated ; his meaning simply is that God accepts the sinner on the ground of His mere grace, apart from all question of merit. It is consequently ' only another, though less difficult, expression for the same act of the Divine judgment' when St. Paul speaks of adoption ($\nu\iota\omega\theta\epsilon\sigma\iota\alpha$, Gal 4^5), or the reception of the sinner into the position of a child of God (Holtzmann, *Neutest. Theol.* ii. p. 134). Adoption is also formally a judicial act, and really a synthetic act of the Divine judgment. The possible objection to this identification of justification and adoption, viz. that justification is the act of God as Judge, but adoption His act as Father, falls to the ground as soon as it is remembered that justification is really an extra-judicial judgment, proceeding from the Divine grace (Ritschl, *Justification and Reconciliation*[3], iii., Eng. tr. p. 86 ff.).

Finally, we get still further light on St. Paul's meaning as to justification from the fact that in Ro 4^7 he introduces, as synonymous with the imputation of righteousness or justification, the OT idea of the forgiveness of sins (cf. also Eph 1^7),

which links his teaching on at once to that of Christ Himself ; and it appears that the Pauline conceptions of justification and adoption are simply the equivalent of the Fatherly forgiveness taught by Jesus (Kaftan, *Dogmatik*[3. 4], p. 523). The idea that forgiveness is something merely negative, while justification conveys a positive status, turns on an inadequate conception of the Biblical idea of forgiveness.

So far we have considered justification as a Divine operation ; it now remains to consider its practical issues, when it takes effect in the admission of the sinner to fellowship with God. Faith now comes into view, not simply as the reflexion of grace, but in its psychological nature as trust, including the submission of the will to God ; and the practical effects of justification appear as the unfolding of this trust in its various aspects. The first of these is the sense of present peace with God (Ro 5^1), or the consciousness of acceptance with Him. Here appears a strong contrast with the Pharisaic theology, which, teaching not the justification of the sinner, but only of him who has kept the precepts, defers justification till the hour of death, and consequently demands in the present a condition of anxious fear lest in the end justification should not be attained (Weber, *l.c.* pp. 284, 334 ff. ; cf. Ro 8^{15}). Along with present peace goes patience in all present suffering (Ro $5^{2. 3. 5}$), in the belief that it is Divinely ordered for the best ends (8^{28}), while there is at the same time a consciousness of the Divine love (5^5 8^{35-39}). Here appears a contrast to the OT point of view, from which temporal sufferings appeared as signs of Divine displeasure. This contrast is strikingly brought out by comparing St. Paul's triumphant use of the quotation in Ro 8^{36} with its original despondent meaning in Ps 44^{22}. While St. Paul finds it impossible that persecution should separate the believer from the love of God, the Psalmist sees in it a proof that God has cast off His people (cf. Ps 44^9). Finally, there is no fear of final punishment (Ro 5^9), but rather a joyful hope, nay certainty, of ultimate salvation ($5^{2. 10}$ 6^{23} $8^{30. 38. 39}$). The sum of all these things, in fact the whole consequence of justification, St. Paul expresses by saying that, for the believer, 'There is now no condemnation' (8^1), or that he is not under law, but under grace (6^{15}). From this point of view the work of Christ appears as a redemption from the curse of the Law. Christ, in His death, bore its curse, and its power is therefore at an end (Gal 3^{13}). St. Paul refers in this passage to the Jewish Law, as the antithesis with v.[14] shows : 'Christ redeemed us [Jews] from the curse of the law . . . that upon the Gentiles might come the blessing of Abraham in Christ Jesus.' But his idea of freedom from the Law is not to be limited to freedom from the Jewish Law. Though, historically, this special case was of the greatest importance, St. Paul means that the Christian religion is a religion not of law, but of grace. He also expresses the same idea in terms of the parallel conception of adoption, by saying that the believer has received, in place of the spirit of bondage, leading to fear, the spirit of adoption, ' whereby we cry, Abba, Father' (Ro 8^{15}).

The doctrine of the Epistle of James on justification, whether the author has the Pauline doctrine or abuses of it in view or not [on the critical question connected with the Epistle see Moffatt, *Historical NT*[2], p. 576, for a good statement of the alternatives ; also Sanday-Headlam, 'Romans,' p. 104 ; and W. Patrick, *James the Lord's Brother*], raises an important problem in connexion with it. It is to be noted, first, that the idea of faith in the Epistle is quite different from St. Paul's. When the author teaches that justification is not by faith only, but by works also, the faith he has in view is a mere intellectual assent to Christian truth, especially to the doctrine of the Divine unity (Ja 2^{19}). Further, his idea of works is not that of meritorious performance deserving reward, but of practical morality. He solves the problem of justification in reality by going back behind the legalism of the Pharisees, and behind the Law altogether, to the position of the OT prophets, in so far as they demanded practical righteousness as the condition of acceptance with God. His doctrine and St. Paul's, therefore, touch nowhere except in language; in thought they are altogether apart. At the same time, the Epistle of James serves forcibly to raise the question, which St. Paul's doctrine is always liable to provoke, viz. what safeguard it offers, while satisfying the religious needs of man, for his moral interests. Reference has already been made to the passage in which St. Paul speaks of opposition to his teaching; it was its apparent antinomianism that provoked this opposition (Ro 3[8], cf. 6[1]).

We have thus to return to St. Paul, and ask how he met this difficulty. He does it by opening a new line of argument, in which he presents a fresh view of the death and resurrection of Christ, where these acts appear in the ethical sense of a death to sin and a resurrection to a new life unto God (Ro 6[10]), and where, further, Christ in His death and resurrection appears as inclusive of all for whom He died (2 Co 5[14]). In correspondence with this view, faith also takes on a new significance. It is still a receptivity and an obedience; but as that which it receives is different, it appears with new powers, as establishing a mystic union with Christ in His death and resurrection, the outward symbol of which is baptism (Gal 2[20], Ro 6[1-6], Col 2[11]), from which union St. Paul draws the ethical consequence, that the believer being dead with Christ to sin, and alive with Him to God, should live accordingly (Ro 6[4. 11-13], Col 3[1. 5]). A parallel line of argument presents the view of the Risen Christ as the Spirit (2 Co 3[17]), and faith correspondingly as involving the endowment of the Spirit (Gal 3[2], cf. Ro 8[1-11]), by which the believer is transformed into the likeness of Christ (2 Co 3[18]). But again, the possession of the Spirit demands a life according to the Spirit (Ro 5[25], Ro 8[12. 13]). Along these lines, then, St. Paul makes provision for Christian morality. He presents, as we see, his total thought on the salvation of the individual through the work of Christ in two hemispheres—the former doctrine of justification and this further doctrine which corresponds to the ecclesiastical doctrines of regeneration and sanctification. St. Paul passes continually from the one hemisphere to the other in a way that shows that he feels them to be vitally related; and there are not wanting points of contact between them, amongst which we may note especially the fact that the idea of faith is common to both hemispheres, as is also that of the Spirit, who appears in connexion with justification and adoption as diffusing the consciousness of the love of God (Ro 5[5]) and as witnessing to our adoption (8[16]), as well as in connexion with regeneration and sanctification as the potency of the new life. Further, there is a cycle of passages in which there appears a tendency to the unification of the two hemispheres of thought, by making justification conditional on regeneration and sanctification, and thus still future and the object of effort (Ro 8[17], Gal 2[17], 1 Co 4[4. 9]24. 27, Ph 3[10-14]). See on the whole subject Holtzmann, *Neutest. Theol.* ii. p. 137 ff. In the main, however, St. Paul keeps the two hemispheres apart. Holtzmann (p. 137, n. 1) quotes Pfleiderer, who, using another figure, speaks of 'the two streams which unite in Paulinism in one bed, without, however, inwardly blending.'

II. HISTORICAL.—**1.** *The Catholic doctrine.*—St. Paul's doctrine of justification remained after his death in practical abeyance, until it was revived at the Reformation. There is little trace of it in the NT outside of his own Epistles (*i.e.* of the specific Pauline form of the doctrine of forgiveness). Only uncertain echoes of it are found in the post-Apostolic age, and under the régime of Catholicism, both ancient and mediæval, it remained practically a dead letter. Common Catholicism, in fact, returned substantially to the Pharisaic doctrine of salvation by merit, against which St. Paul had fought, with its accompanying atmosphere of fear of coming short at last. According to Gregory the Great, who is here typical, assurance is the mother of indolence, and the fear of Divine judgment is the only fit attitude for the Christian till his last day on earth (Harnack, *Dogmengeschichte*[3], iii. p. 250, n. 1). In such an atmosphere the words of the Pauline vocabulary necessarily lost their original meaning, and took on a new significance. Faith came to mean, not trust, but intellectual assent to revealed truth; grace, not the unmerited love of God, but the Holy Spirit, as sacramentally communicated or infused (so Tertullian; see Loofs, *Leitfaden*, p. 104). It was the work of Augustine to create a new doctrine of justification by the combination of these ideas. First he interpreted the word 'justification' itself to mean not 'a declaring righteous,' but 'a making righteous'; what else is *justificati* than *justi facti*? (*de Sp. et Litt.* 26, 45). Then, further, he combined the idea of justification in this sense with that of 'infused' grace. Augustine teaches that it is this

infused grace which justifies or makes righteous by renewing the nature. He is able thus, with St. Paul, to conceive righteousness as a gift; the gift, however, is not of forensic, but of inherent righteousness. This idea of justification by infused grace, it is to be noted, lacks that immediate and necessary connexion with the work of Christ which lies at the base of the Pauline doctrine. Augustine, indeed, regards the forgiveness of sins as an effect of grace, parallel with the renewal of the nature; but faith is not brought into the connexion. The idea of faith remains with Augustine simply the common Catholic idea of assent to revealed truth; so that faith is no more than a presupposition of salvation. Only as it is completed by hope and love through the infusion of grace, is it Christian and saving faith (Seeberg, *Dogmengeschichte*, i. 276). It is obvious how far Augustine is here from St. Paul, though he constantly uses the Apostle's formula 'justification by faith' (Seeberg, p. 277). The climax of his departure from Pauline doctrine, however, is reached when the idea of merit is drawn into the scheme. The combination is thus effected. Grace alone renders merit possible. God in His condescension accepts as meritorious the works which are really His own gifts: 'what are called our merits are His gifts' (*de Trinitate*, xiii. 10, 14).

In Western Catholicism the doctrine of justification remains substantially that of Augustine. The Roman Catholic doctrine was finally formulated in opposition to Protestantism at the Council of Trent. It is necessary to refer to two points only. The first is that, in the Middle Ages, Duns Scotus taught a modification of the Augustinian doctrine, which makes still wider room for the idea of merit. He avails himself of a distinction already found in Thomas Aquinas between merit of congruity (*meritum de congruo*) and condign merit (*meritum de condigno*). The former is based upon the idea of the Divine equity, to which it is congruous to reward every one who works according to his power after the excellency of the Divine power. The latter is based on the idea of strict justice, which rewards according to desert (Seeberg, *l.c.* ii. 105). According to Duns, the first grace itself can be merited *de congruo* by attrition, *i.e.* such repentance as is possible without grace. The second point to be observed is that the Council of Trent draws a natural consequence from the Augustinian idea of justification, by teaching that justification is progressive, and can and ought to receive continual increment (Sess. VI. cap. x.).

The great contrast between the Catholic doctrine and that of St. Paul is obvious at the first glance. A second look, however, might suggest that perhaps the contrast was not so great after all. For the Catholic doctrine of justification corresponds, though by no means exactly, to St. Paul's doctrine of regeneration and sanctification. It might, therefore, appear as if the difference were really one of language. Nevertheless, in the end the contrast remains unmitigated by this seeming possibility of reconciliation; as Ritschl has acutely observed (*op. cit.*[3] iii. 36). Catholicism still remains in opposition to St. Paul's idea of justification. What the Apostle calls 'justification,' viz. acceptance with God, including the assurance of eternal life (Ro 5[10] 6[23] 8[30. 33. 39]), Catholic doctrine includes under the conception of hope. So Conc. Trid. Sess. VI. cap. xiii. : Christians 'ought to fear, knowing that they are regenerated unto the hope of glory, and not yet unto glory. . . .' No one, indeed, can be absolutely certain even of present grace (cap. ix.). It is true that within Catholicism the practical attitude of trust for salvation to the Divine mercy alone, apart from all merits, and the consequent sense of assurance, are to be found, as to some extent in Augustine (Harnack, *op. cit.* iii. p. 85 f.), but preeminently in Bernard of Clairvaux. In this attitude is the true harbinger of the return to St. Paul at the Reformation (Ritschl, *op. cit.*[3] i. 109 ff.). But we are now concerned with the Catholic doctrine, not with an attitude maintained in spite of it.

2. *The Protestant doctrine.*—With the Reformation we have a return to the Pauline idea of justification. The absolutely fundamental character for the Christian religion of the Pauline conception is firmly seized. As is well known, Luther called justification by faith 'the article of a standing and falling Church.' The Protestant doctrine, however, assumes a special form, in antithesis to the interim Catholic development, and St. Paul's formula is sharpened into the still more definite shape 'justification by faith alone.'

We have to note, first of all, a reversion to the original Pauline ideas of grace, faith, and justification. Luther, indeed, especially in his earlier period, remained somewhat entangled with the Catholic conception of the last, making the term include both a forensic and a real justification. This, however, was merely a matter of terminology, and has only a historical significance. Practically Luther held the Pauline view : the emphasis with him falls on the forensic aspect of justification. Moreover, the somewhat confused terminology of Luther was corrected by Melanchthon, who says decidedly that justification with the Hebrews was a forensic word, and opposes the idea of a real justification (*Loci Theologici* : 'De gratia et justificatione').

The Protestant theology, further, like St. Paul, found the revelation of the Divine grace in Christ, and His work for sinners. Here, however, a considerable development takes place, based upon the mediæval development of the doctrine of the Atonement due to Anselm. The latter had viewed the death of Christ in the first place as a satisfaction to God's honour, which liberated Him from the necessity of punishing sinners, and in the second place as a merit or work of supererogatory obedience, which could be made available for His followers. The Protestant theology accepted both these ideas, but with such modifications as made it possible to combine them with the forensic idea of justification. The death of Christ was viewed not as a satisfaction to God's honour, but to the penal sanctions of His Law. To this was added His active obedience to the Law in His life as a satisfaction to its positive requirements. The whole was summed up as Christ's active and passive obedience or merit, and regarded as a provision of the Divine grace with a view to the justification of sinners. Justification consists in the gracious imputation of this twofold merit or obedience to the sinner on the sole condition of faith, so that he becomes not only guiltless before the Law, but also totally free from its claims. This conception is common to both the Lutheran and the Reformed Churches. It did not grow up all at once ; but the roots of it can be traced in the earlier Reformers, and it finally established itself firmly in both Churches. It is completely stated in the *Formula of Concord* (pars ii. Solida Declaratio, iii. 14, 15).

The change from the Pauline doctrine is marked by the alteration of his formula, the imputation of faith for righteousness, into that of the imputation of Christ's righteousness. It is not merely one of language. The conception of Christ's death as a satisfaction to the penal sanctions of the Divine law, on the ground of which God forgives sinners, may, indeed, be accepted as a natural interpretation of the Pauline conception of Christ's death as an expiatory sacrifice for sin, if this conception is to be translated into terms of law. Whether, however, such translation is desirable, is questionable ; as we saw that the forensic point of view is only formally and not materially regulative for the Pauline conception of justification. Thus, instead of seeking to translate related conceptions into legal terminology, we ought rather to seek such an explanation (or, if need be, modification) of them as accords with the material element

in St. Paul's idea of justification, viz. that it is entirely the work of grace, 'apart from law.' The Protestant theology, in fact, misinterprets Paul by taking his legal phraseology as essential, and seeking to systematize his whole view of justification and its presuppositions under legal ideas. The attempt of the Protestant doctors to conceive the whole process of salvation in legal forms, made them introduce into theology a number of axioms which are in no way part of the Christian view of the world. Such an axiom is that all sin must be punished ; whereas the Christian religion teaches that it can be forgiven, and forgiveness and punishment are mutually exclusive (cf. W. N. Clarke, *Christian Theology*, p. 330). Another axiom is that the punishment of sin may be transferred from one person to another ; whereas the very essence of the idea of punishment is its connexion with guilt. The vicarious suffering of the innocent for the guilty is not punishment. A third axiom is that merit may similarly be transferred from one person to another ; whereas the moral result of a life, which is what is meant, is personal, and while it may result in the good of others, cannot possibly be separated from the person of its author, and treated as a commercial asset. That the Protestant doctors had to base their theology on axioms like these, plainly shows that they were on the wrong line in attempting to translate the doctrine of salvation into legal terms. We may no doubt recognize behind the forms of the Protestant theology the intention to show that the Divine grace itself is the grace of a Holy and a Righteous God. But the immediate identification of the Divine Righteousness with its expression in law is fatal to a full and complete view of grace. St. Paul might have taught a better conception of law as a temporary and preparatory manifestation of the Divine righteousness, whose end is fulfilled in a higher way by grace (Gal 3²⁴).

This defect in the view of the revelation of the Divine grace in Christ does not, however, prevent the Protestant theology from being true in the main to the Pauline conception of justification. Over against Catholicism, Protestant theology teaches justification by God's grace appropriated by faith alone, and apart from all question of human merit. Moreover, in the total view the emphasis, at any rate with the earlier Reformers, does not fall on the supposed legal forms of the Divine revelation in Christ, but on the idea of grace itself. A remarkable proof of this is to be found in the fact that in Melanchthon's *Loci Theologici* there is no *locus* devoted to the doctrine of Christ's satisfaction. Even so late as Gerhard in the early part of the 17th cent., the doctrine is treated by him simply as a part of the *locus de justificatione.*

After this critical excursus we return to the Protestant theology itself, in order next to describe the positions by which it further defined its conception of justification as over against Catholicism. As regards what the Catholics call 'justification,' but the Protestants 'regeneration,' it is taught that the latter is the necessary accompaniment and logical (the later Lutheran theology says, temporal) consequence of justification. Its objective principle is the gift of the Holy Spirit, its subjective manifestation the activity of faith in good works.

On some further points the two Evangelical Churches diverge not only from Catholicism, but from one another. The first of these has to do with the question of assurance. The Lutherans teach that the believer's consciousness of justification is in itself an immediate certainty of the reality of justification, operated by the Holy Ghost (*fides divina*). Where, however, doubt enters, recourse must be had to the Word and the Sacraments, that the Holy Ghost, who works through the Word, may rekindle faith. The Reformed theologians teach that the guarantee of the reality of justification is God's eternal predestination to salvation, which manifests itself subjectively in perseverance in the state of grace. Hence the assurance of justification cannot be gathered directly from faith itself, but by a reference to its evidence in its fruits (*syllogismus practicus*). [See Lipsius, *Dogmatik*[3], p. 675 f.].

The second difference between the Protestant Churches is that the Lutherans make the moment of justification, alike in earth and heaven, the moment when saving faith comes into being. The Reformed, on the other hand, regard justification as accomplished in the resurrection of Christ for the whole Church as His mystical body (*justificatio activa*), but as regards individual believers based on the decree of justification, which accompanies their eternal election, and realized when saving faith arises (*justificatio passiva*). It is to be noted that the objective justification, which is accomplished for believers in Christ's resurrection, depends only upon their *ideal* incorporation in His mystical body. The Reformed doctrine does not therefore, as has sometimes been said, make justification dependent on regeneration. Christ's resurrection is regarded as the acceptance of His satisfaction, made for believers, and thus as ideally their justification in Him (cf. Lipsius, *Dogmatik*, p. 677 f.; Ritschl, *op. cit.*[3] i. 293 ff.).

The third difference is as to the doctrine of perseverance. The Lutherans teach that a man may fall from faith, and thus from grace, but that he may regain his position by renewed repentance and faith. On the contrary, the Reformed teach that the members of Christ's body cannot fall, but must persevere in faith to the end. A faith that does not endure, is not real faith; and the consciousness of justification it may bring is only self-deception (Lipsius, p. 679).

Reference must now be made to certain views within Protestantism which deviate from the orthodox conception. The first of these is that of Osiander, who, attaching himself to many expressions in the teaching of Luther, attempted once more to teach a real justification, and yet avoid introducing the Catholic conception of salvation by merit. In opposition to the idea of justification by the mere external imputation of Christ's righteousness, he taught that the essential ground of justification is Christ's righteousness as really communicated to us; though at the same time he regards this indwelling righteousness of Christ not as our own, but as an alien righteousness, and in so far as an imputed righteousness (Lipsius, p. 668).

Another line of thought is opened by the Socinian theology. A criticism of the legal forms of the ecclesiastical doctrine of reconciliation leads to the complete rejection of it. Socinus, however, retains a doctrine of justification by faith, regarded as including not only trust in God as revealed by Christ, but consequent obedience to His will. There is no justification by works without faith; but, on the other hand, works are not merely the fruit of faith, but its execution and perfection, and in so far the works which follow faith justify (Socinus, *de Fide et Operibus*, Bibliotheca Fratrum Polonorum, 1656, tom. i. p. 623). But as works done in faith are not perfect, justification is also said to be by faith in opposition to works, because the mercy of God imputes righteousness to the believer (*de Jesu Christo Servatore*, p. iv, c. 11). In other words, faith is here considered as the principle of active righteousness, and the doctrine of justification comes to mean that God judges not by the outward work, but by the inward disposition. This conclusion is distinctly drawn by the Rationalism of the German Illumination (Lipsius, p. 684).

3. *Modern theories.*—The most important forms in which the doctrine of justification has been stated in modern theology, so far as that does not simply repeat older points of view, owe their origin chiefly to Kant and Schleiermacher, particularly the latter. Kant took up the subject where it had been left by the Illumination, but in view of his deeper ethics stated it as an ethico-religious problem, viz. how a man conscious of guilt could obtain power to live a new life. The solution is to be found in the conception of faith in the ideal. On the one hand, this appears as the principle of a good life; on the other, it affords the principle of acceptance with God, in so far as God judges men by the ideal they follow, though their realization of it may be imperfect. The Kantian theologian Tieftrunk further pointed out that from a psychological point of view the operation of the Divine grace is absolutely necessary, if a man, in spite of

his consciousness of guilt, is to be able joyfully to fulfil the moral law; so that it is required from the point of view of the law itself, in so far as it looks for fulfilment (Lipsius, p. 685; Ritschl[3], i. p. 429 ff.).

The defect of the Kantian conception, from the point of view of the Christian religion, is its lack of organic connexion with the historical revelation of God in Jesus Christ. In the system of Schleiermacher, however, the fundamental character for Christianity of this revelation is fully recognized, while at the same time, instead of a return to the standpoint of the older Protestant dogmatics, there is introduced a new and fruitful theological principle. Schleiermacher demands that all conceptions concerning Divine operations shall be verified by their correspondence with Christian experience, not indeed the experience of an individual, but of the Christian community as a whole (*Der christliche Glaube*[5], i. § 30. p. 162).

From this point of view Schleiermacher treats justification. He begins with the Christian consciousness of redemption and reconciliation through Christ. 'The Redeemer receives believers into the power of His God-consciousness, and this is His redeeming activity' (ii. § 100. p. 94). 'The Redeemer receives believers into the fellowship of His undisturbed happiness, and this is His reconciling activity' (ii. § 101. p. 102). Schleiermacher thus views the work of Christ through the total impression of His character and life. Only as a part of the latter do His sufferings come into question (ii. § 101. 4, p. 108). In accordance with this groundwork follows the doctrine of justification. Justification and conversion are the two inseparable parts of regeneration or assumption into union with Christ. 'Assumption into union with Christ is, viewed as an altered relation of man to God, his justification; viewed as an altered form of life, his conversion' (ii. § 107. p. 165). Justification is by faith, and includes the forgiveness of sins and adoption into Divine sonship (ii. § 109. p. 190). All these things flow naturally and inseparably from union with Christ, which alters alike the will and the contemplative consciousness. In particular, the consciousness of forgiveness follows from the fact that the new man in Christ has no relation to the sins of the old man or their penalties. Present suffering he regards simply as evil, not as punishment, and of future suffering he has no fear (ii. § 109. 2, p. 193). Finally, when passing over from our own consciousness we view justification as a Divine act, it is not to be separated from the effective working of Christ in conversion. The Divine act of justification, moreover, is one with the sending of Christ into the world. There is no 'declaratory act' apart from this: only figuratively can such be spoken of. As regards the justification of the individual, the case is simply that the one Divine decree of justification in Christ is realized in successive points of time. Finally, faith is not to be described as the instrumental cause, or the ὄργανον ληπτικόν of justification. We bring nothing to the Divine grace in Christ but our mere receptivity (ii. § 109. 3, p. 195 f.). Faith is awakened wholly by the operation of Christ (ii. § 108. 6, p. 186).

The influence of the Reformed theology is plainly visible in the position of Schleiermacher, that justification is, as a Divine act, to be viewed as realized first of all in Christ, and then successively in believers. Compare what is said above, also Turretin (*Inst. Theol. Elencticæ*, Loc. xvi. Qu. ix. 12), who says that justification is one from the point of view of God, though from our point of view it appears in successive acts, viz. God's eternal decree of justification, the realization of it in Christ's work, the application of it in experience, and the declaration of it at the last day. But, further, the correspondence of this point of view with the tendency previously noted in St. Paul to bring the objective and subjective sides of justification into close and indeed inseparable relation, may also be remarked. Schleiermacher, however, brings the principle which underlies this tendency to clear consciousness, and bases on it his theological method, for which, as we saw, the continuity of Divine operation and human experience is fundamental.

Schleiermacher's doctrine of justification has been differently understood. Most theologians have considered that he means to make justification conditional on a real union with Christ (cf. Lipsius, p. 686 ff.). Ritschl, however, thinks that only an ideal union is referred to (iii.[3] p. 559). Two different developments, therefore, have taken place, starting from either view of Schleiermacher's position.

In the first place, one of the commonest views in modern theology makes justification dependent on a real union with Christ, breaking down the sharp distinction between justification and regeneration, and treating them simply as aspects of the same process. Faith, on this view, is to be regarded in justification not simply as the reflex of Divine grace, but as comprehending the spiritual content of union with Christ, and of the gift of the Spirit, which is the basis of the ethical life of the Christian. Hence this view of justification is claimed to be 'ethical'; justification according to it being a recognition of what really is in the believer his new life, as well pleasing to God. A reconciliation with the forensic view is found in the Kantian thought that God judges by the ideal; so that justification appears as a prophetic judgment, which sees in the first germ of the new life its whole fruit.

This view is closely akin to Osiander's. It has undoubtedly points of contact with the broader use of the word 'faith' in St. Paul, who, as Pfleiderer points out, often uses it as practically equivalent to the whole of Christianity (*Urchristenthum*[2], i. p. 250; cf. 1 Co 12[9f.] 16[13]). It is further along the line developed in the cycle of passages like Ro 8[17], Gal 2[17], 1 Co 4[4] 9[24. 27], Ph 3[10-14], as previously explained. But it does not represent St. Paul's main line of thought with respect to justification, and the objection to it further is that in the end it bases justification either upon the imperfect realization of Christ in us, or, in so far as the imperfection is counterbalanced by a reference to the ideal, upon what is still future, thus resembling the Catholic view. This view does not, therefore, meet the *religious* need of a firm and unshakable ground of trust as to acceptance with God.

In opposition to it, therefore, Ritschl develops the doctrine of Schleiermacher along the other line, which he takes to be its real meaning, giving in his theology also prominence to a conception which with Schleiermacher is in the background—that of revelation. The idea of justification is consequently construed directly through the idea of the Divine grace as revealed in Christ, and faith is thought of as of a piece with this revelation and the realization of it in human lives. Justification is thus in the first instance through grace, but by faith. Ritschl's way of expressing this is by saying that justification is the act of God as Father, and further that the sentence of justification falls in the first instance on the religious community founded by Christ as a whole, to which God imputes the position towards Him of Christ its Founder, and on individuals as by faith in the Gospel they attach themselves to this community; justification thus becoming effective for them. Faith is simply obedience to God and trust in the revelation of His grace in Christ. Its functions are religious, not moral (iii.[3] p. 139; cf. also p. 70). As regards the effects of justification, the comprehensive description of them is that it is 'the acceptance of sinners into fellowship with God, in which their salvation is to be realized and carried out into eternal life.' In particular, the consciousness of guilt is removed, in so far as the element of mistrust of God, which is the essence of it, is removed (p. 85). Assurance of justification can be obtained only by the exercise of faith in patience or 'lordship over the world.' Finally, the course of moral action is conditioned by justification; but the direct aim of the latter is not the product of moral action, but the bestowal of eternal life, which is realized here and now in lordship over the world (pp. 192, 534 f., 670).

III. CONSTRUCTIVE TREATMENT.—It appears to the present writer that a correct modern interpretation of the Pauline conception of justification must move generally along the lines suggested by Ritschl. Perhaps it may be necessary to observe that such an interpretation is required, and that it is not sufficient simply to rest in the Pauline statement as it stands. In the first place, we have seen that St. Paul suggests more than one point of view, and we have to settle which is to be regarded as determinative. Then, again, there are gaps in the Pauline presentation which require to be filled up, especially in view of the points raised by later theological controversies. Finally, the Pauline theology is only one among the early Christian presentations of the Christian salvation, and it is necessary in some points to modify his conceptions in order to do justice to other NT points of view, especially those presented in the Gospels. We proceed, then, to present the doctrine of justification along the general lines of Ritschl, but with regard also to the treatment of other theologians, who have, as it seems to the writer, dealt more satisfactorily than Ritschl with particular points. Reference is made particularly to Ritschl's own followers, Kaftan and Häring, but also to Lipsius and Kähler, and finally to W. N. Clarke.

Instead of beginning with St. Paul's technical term 'justification,' we shall first make use of its material equivalent, the idea of *forgiveness*, having already established our right to do this. We thus, as Kaftan says (*Dogmatik*[3. 4], p. 523), present the issue in a simpler and less equivocal form, with the advantage also of keeping before the mind the connexions of the subject in the teaching of Jesus. What Paul calls grace is to Jesus the Fatherly forgiving love of God.

We begin, then, with the analysis of forgiveness as a Divine act, and consider, after Paul, first the objective side of this act—revelation, — and then the subjective side—faith, by which the revelation is appropriated and forgiveness fully realized. The revelation of forgiveness is in Jesus Christ, His Person and Work; not merely, however, as St. Paul teaches, in His death and resurrection, but as the Gospels clearly show, and as Schleiermacher, after them, recognized, in His whole life, including these culminating acts. Forgiveness is revealed by the whole of Christ's activity as well as by His sufferings. In fact, His sufferings reveal forgiveness because of the activity expressed in the endurance of them. Jesus further makes this revelation as the unique and perfect representative of God in the world, absolutely one with the Father in thought and feeling; so that by every word and deed and by His whole attitude He incarnates God in the world, to do which is His earthly mission and vocation.

The Fatherly forgiveness of God, which Jesus reveals, is no mere good-natured indulgence; on the contrary, the Father is the Holy Father, the Righteous Father (Jn 17[11. 25]), and His forgiveness is holy and righteous forgiveness. Jesus guarantees this by His revelation not only of the Divine forgiveness, but also of the Divine holiness in its stern condemnation of sin. A holy hatred of sin is evident in His whole attitude.

But, finally, Jesus reveals the holy forgiving love of God not only in these two separate moments, but in its entirety, by His bearing in love the sins of men upon His soul. We can explain His sorrow over Jerusalem only as the pain of One who, full of love to men, felt their sin as the heaviest burden. We can explain the agony in Gethsemane and the cry of desolation on the cross only along the same lines, as caused by the pressure of the sin of the world upon the loving heart of the Saviour. In this bearing of sin, however, Jesus was still revealing the attitude of God towards sinners. The fact that the burden of sin upon His soul broke in upon the peace and bliss of His personal communion with the Father, makes no difference as to this point. Christ's actual communion with the Father had to be maintained, indeed, by an act of supreme self-surrender (Mk 14[36]), or of faith, unaided by any evidence of the Divine presence (15[34]). It was necessary that the holy love of God should come to complete self-expression in the world, which could only be by the revelation of the depth of suffering caused to sinless love by sin; and this revelation could not be made except by the Revealer proceeding along a path which brought upon His human spirit the sense of separation from God. This path was, however, not a new one; it was but the continuation, to the end of the path, of Christ's vocation as Revealer of God. To reveal the holy love of God in a world of sin could have but one issue, that which it historically had, viz. to rouse up the opposition of sin, as much to the love as to the holiness (Lk 15[2]), to the uttermost. The final act of self-surrender and faith, therefore, by which Jesus gave Himself to the death at the hands of sinners, which was inevitable, if He persevered in His vocation, was simply the climax of the self-surrender and faith by which as man He gave Himself at every moment to the work of His vocation. The whole revelation of God made by Jesus being a revelation within humanity, was made at every point by the offering up of the human will of Jesus to the Father. His whole life and death together constituted a sacrifice, which He offered up to God as the necessary means of the revelation in the world of His holy love. And this He did for the sake of men, that they might come to know the holy forgiveness of the Father.

Such, then, would seem to be the necessary restatement of the Pauline doctrine of the revelation of the grace of God in Christ in view of the historical statements of the Gospels. To complete it, however, it is necessary to add that the function of the resurrection is to make the historical revelation permanent and abiding, by presenting Christ as the perpetual object of faith. This leads to the next point, which is that of the doctrine of faith, or the subjective appropriation of the revelation. There St. Paul's conception of faith as in the first place, on the side of the will, a species of obedience or submission to God, remains fundamental. It is in essential agreement, it may be observed, with the teaching of Jesus Himself, in which μετάνοια, or turning to God, is made the subjective principle of forgiveness. But in order that the subjective appropriation may correspond in all points with the objective revelation, faith must not be limited psychologically to trust, but must include penitence also, in this way appearing as the proper correlative of both the love and the holiness of forgiveness. When the revelation of forgiveness in Christ awakens this faith in the heart, then the Divine act of forgiveness is completed, and forgiveness is fully realized.

We turn next to forgiveness as an experience, where St. Paul gives ample guidance, and all that is necessary is to explain some points in reference to the problems raised by later theologians. The first practical effect of justification is peace with God, or the removal of the consciousness of guilt which separated the sinner from God. This is removed by the appropriation of the Divine forgiveness, which is realized as the removal of guilt. Nor does conscience offer any obstacle to the realization of the removal of guilt in the consciousness of the believer; since the holiness of the Divine forgiveness is assured by the very revelation which brings the knowledge of it. In fact, the penitence which accompanies trust in the

Divine forgiveness as the result of the revelation in Christ, is an inward appropriation of the Divine condemnation of sin. Thus there is peace with God as the result of faith, and that upon the sure and certain basis of the knowledge of God's holy love, in which both the conscience and the heart find rest.

Forgiveness is also realized as the remission of the penalties of sin. The chief penalty of sin is eternal death, or separation from God. But further, of physical evils some are clearly the effects of sin; and the rest, to the sinner conscious of separation from God, also tend to appear as the tokens of His displeasure. Forgiveness removes the fear of eternal death by the establishment of communion with God; while, so far as physical evils are concerned, though the consequences of former sins may continue to abound, yet all these appear no longer as tokens of God's displeasure, but as fatherly chastisements, so that the believer's communion with God remains unbroken by them. Finally, the positive expression of the whole experience is that the believer enjoys the privilege of Divine sonship, and has, in his communion with God, here and now, the gift of eternal life; while his trust in God enables him confidently to leave to Him the maintenance of this privilege in the future. The negative statement of this experience is that the standing of the believer with God is not on terms of law or merit. In other words, to sum up the whole matter, the Christian religion is not a religion of law but a religion of grace. This is the real meaning of the article of justification by faith, which shows at once why it is so fundamental for Christianity, and why it is so necessary to maintain that justification is by faith alone.

We have now reached the end of the exposition of the subject-matter of the doctrine; some necessary questions, however, remain to be discussed. The first is formal. *With what point in time is the Divine act of justification to be connected?* If the exposition above has been followed, it will be seen that the question is one of definition. Forgiveness is revealed in Christ, and realized in faith. We may, therefore, connect the Divine act more particularly with the death of Christ as the climax of the revelation, as Kaftan does (*Dogmatik*[3, 4], p. 523), which is, perhaps, most logical; or we may, with Lipsius (*Dogmatik*, p. 696), connect it with the awakening of faith in the sense that then God by His Spirit speaks pardon to the soul. The one is the *justificatio activa*, the other the *justificatio passiva* of Reformed theology; each is simply an aspect of one process.

The next question is that of *assurance*. The view of Lipsius here seems most in accordance with the spirit of Paul, viz. that 'when faith becomes uncertain, there remains to us nothing but ever to return anew in believing trust to the objective message of grace, which meets us in the gospel or in the historical revelation in Christ, till the lost consciousness of salvation revives again.'

There remains the most difficult question of all, as Lipsius calls it, 'the master question of theology' (*Dogmatik*, p. 699), viz. the question of *the relation of justification to regeneration and the Christian life*. The Pauline answer to this question is, as we have seen, that the same Divine revelation in Christ by which forgiveness is revealed, is also the revelation of an ethical ideal as an energizing spirit; and that, as faith receives the revelation of grace in forgiveness, so it receives also at the same time the revelation of the ideal as a quickening influence upon the life. It is still an act of obedience or submission to God, but, in this latter aspect, the act of obedience or submission to the Christian ideal, or the reception of the Spirit of Christ as the principle of life. It is one and the same revelation in both cases, and one and the same faith or receptivity in both cases. Justification and regeneration are therefore vitally connected, and it is impossible to experience one without the other. Nevertheless Christian theology is compelled to treat them as separate articles, in order to do justice to each. In spite of the oneness of the revelation in Christ, and of the faith of the Christian, it remains true that justification has its ground simply in the Divine grace, and that faith comes into view in the matter, not in its general reference to the Christian life as a whole, but as it reflects the Divine revelation of God's holy forgiveness.

LITERATURE.—Only a representative selection can be given. It falls into three divisions, corresponding to those of the article. First, however, must be named a work covering all three divisions, viz. Ritschl's great work, *Rechtfertigung und Versöhnung*[3], 3 vols. 1889 [Eng. tr. (*Justification and Reconciliation*) of 1st vol. from 1st ed. 1872, of 3rd vol. from 3rd ed. 1902].
I. *BIBLICAL THEOLOGY.*—(*a*) Art. 'Justification' in Hastings' *DB*, vol. ii.; R. Smend, *Alttest. Religionsgeschichte*[2], 1899; Weber, *Jüd. Theol.*[2] 1897; Bousset, *Religion des Judenthums im Neutest. Zeitalter*, 1903.—(*b*) The various NT Theologies, especially that of Holtzmann, 1897; the general works on Paulinism; further, Ménégoz, *Le péché et la rédemption d'après St. Paul*, 1882; Riggenbach, *Die Rechtfertigungslehre des Apostels Paulus*, 1897; H. Cremer, *Die paulin. Rechtfertigungslehre*[2], 1900; the Comm. on St. Paul's Epistles, esp. Sanday-Headlam, *Romans*, 1895.
II. *HISTORY OF THE DOCTRINE.*—(*a*) The general works on the History of Doctrine, esp. Seeberg, *Dogmengesch.* 1895–1898; Baur, *Lehre von der Versöhnung*, 1838.—(*b*) The Catholic doctrine: Aquinas, *Summa Theologica* [many editions]; *Canones et Decreta Concilii Tridentini*, ed. Tauchnitz, 1846; Möhler, *Symbolik*[8], 1872 [also in Eng. tr.]; Newman, *Lectures on Justification*[6], 1892.—(*c*) The Protestant doctrine: the various Symbols of the Lutheran and Reformed Churches, esp. *Formula Concordiæ*, 1589, and Berlin, 1857. (*a*) Lutheran: Köstlin, *Luthers Theologie*[2], 1901; Th. Harnack, *Luthers Theologie*, 1862–1886; Melanchthon, *Loci Theologici*, 1561, Erlangen, 1828; Gerhard, *Loci Theologici*, 1610–1625, also ed. by Frank, 1885; Frank, *System der Christlichen Wahrheit*[3], 1894. (?) Reformed: Calvin, *Inst. Relig. Christ.* 1559, and Edin. 1874; Turretin, *Inst. Theol. Elencticæ*, 1688, and Edin. 1847; Owen, *On Justification*, 1677 and Edin. 1851; Hodge, *Systematic Theology*, 1872.—(*d*) The Socinian criticism: Faustus Socinus, *de Jesu Christo Servatore*, in Bibliotheca Fratrum Polonorum, 1656.
III. *MODERN THEORIES.*—Kant, *Die Religion innerhalb der Grenzen der blossen Vernunft*, 1793; Schleiermacher, *Der Christliche Glaube*[2], 1830; Rothe, *Theol. Ethik*[2], 1867–1871; Dorner, *System der Christlichen Glaubenslehre*, 1879–1881 [also Eng. tr. *System of Christian Doctrine*, 1880–1883]; Lipsius, *Dogmatik*[3], 1893; Kähler, *Die Wissenschaft der Christlichen Lehre*[3], 1905; Kaftan, *Dogmatik*[3, 4], 1901; W. N. Clarke, *Outline of Christian Theology*, 1903; Stevens, *The Christian Doctrine of Salvation*, 1905.

ROBERT S. FRANKS.

JUSTIFYING ONE'S SELF.—When our Lord

told the lawyer that loving God with all the heart and one's neighbour as one's self was the way to inherit eternal life, the man, 'willing to justify himself, said unto Jesus, And who is my neighbour?' (Lk 10[29]). And on a later occasion, in opposition to the Pharisees who derided Him, our Lord said to them, 'Ye are they which justify yourselves before men' (16[15]). The English word 'justify' always means 'to show to be just,' and in the different passages the idea of the Greek also is that of showing one's self to be just or righteous. In the first case the lawyer wished to justify either his past neglect of the command to love his neighbour, or else his having asked the question, by seeking to be told to whom the term 'neighbour' was to be applied. He would thereby suggest the impossibility of fulfilling the command until he knew for certain to whom the term was rightly applicable. In the case of the Pharisees in the latter passage, the emphasis is clearly laid upon the fact that they were endeavouring (with apparent success) to show themselves to be righteous persons in the judgment of men, though God's idea of them was entirely different. With reference to the lawyer's question, 'Who is my neighbour?' the precise form of the inquiry is noteworthy. Just as if a man could pick and choose after being told who and what constitutes a neighbour. The question really comes from a self-centred man who meant, 'Who is neighbour to me?' Bishop Lightfoot once preached a sermon on this subject, in which he pointed out that the true question is, 'Who my neighbour is,' that is, 'What is he like? what are his characteristics?' It does not call attention to this or that person as a possible neighbour, but concentrates thought on my getting to know all about the man who is 'nigh' me, my neighbour in every sense. Thus by his very question the man, so far from justifying himself, that is, showing himself to be just, really condemned himself. The character of the question reveals a selfish man whose one thought was about some one being neighbour to him instead of inquiring as to whom he could be a neighbour. Our Lord's parable of the Good Samaritan and its application, 'Which of these was *neighbour unto him?*' revealed the true aspect and attitude. This is but one instance of the great law that no man can justify himself before God. 'By the deeds of the law shall no flesh living be justified' (Ro 3[20]).

W. H. GRIFFITH THOMAS.

K

KEEPING.—The Eng. verb 'keep,' with its equivalents 'watch,' 'beware of,' 'preserve,' 'observe,' is a tr. of several Gr. words: τηρέω (and its compounds διατηρέω, συντηρέω), φυλάσσω (and its compound διαφυλάσσω), ποιέω, ἔχω (and its compounds κατέχω, συνέχω), κρατέω, ἄγω.

The most important of these words are τηρέω and φυλάσσω with their respective compounds, and for a discussion of the difference in meaning between them the reader is referred to Grimm-Thayer's *Gr. Lex.*, and Westcott's *St. John* (note on 8[51]).

1. Two common usages of the word have to be noticed first. (*a*) It is=*exercise watchful care.* The participle tr. in AV 'the keepers' (Mt 28[4]) is a part of the same verb (τηρέω) as is rendered 'watch' in Mt 27[36] 'and they sat and watched him there' (RV), and in v.[54] 'The centurion and they that were with him watching . . . feared

exceedingly' (RV). It is a compound of that verb, too (συντηρέω), which is used to describe the action of putting 'new wine into new bottles'—'both are preserved,' *i.e.* properly cared for (Mt 9[17]). And the same compound occurs again in the passage in Mk. (6[20]), where it is said that Herod 'observed' (AV) John, or 'kept' him 'safe' (RV). (*b*) It is= *guard*, the direct implication being that this action is necessary in view of possible assaults. For instance, 'There were shepherds in the same country abiding in the field, and keeping watch (φυλάσσοντες φυλακάς) by night over their flocks' (Lk 2[8]); 'It is written, He shall give his angels charge over thee to keep (RV guard) thee' (Lk 4[10], where the verb used is διαφυλάσσω). Other instances of the same usage of the word are to be found in Lk 8[29] 11[21] 12[15].

2. *Retain* may be taken as another general

synonym for 'keep' as it is used in the Gospels. For example, at the marriage in Cana the ruler of the feast is reported as having said to the bridegroom, 'Thou hast kept (τηρέω) the good wine until now' (Jn 2¹⁰).

Retention (κατέχω) is described as a stage in the process whereby 'an honest and good heart' brings to the fulfilment of fruitfulness the experience of 'hearing the word' (Lk 8¹⁵). It is opposed to 'hearing with joy, but having no root,' and to 'hearing and going on one's way, and being choked with cares and riches and pleasures of this life.'

But, apart from Mk 9¹⁰, where the disciples are said to have 'kept (κρατέω) the saying' which Jesus spoke to them on their way down from the Mount of Transfiguration [Luke says, 9³⁶, they 'held their peace' (ἐσίγησαν) about the things they had seen on the Mount], the two most striking contexts in which the word is used with this meaning are found in Luke's Gospel. When the shepherds made known concerning the saying which had been spoken to them about the child in Bethlehem, 'all that heard it wondered. . . . But Mary kept (συνετήρει) all these sayings (or things), pordering them in her heart' (Lk 2¹⁸ᶠ·). She kept them to herself, and did not allow the impression of them to dissipate in mere astonishment. 'The wonder of the many was a transient emotion; this recollecting and brooding of Mary was an abiding habit' (Bruce, *Expos. Gr. Test.*). Again, referring to what took place on the occasion of the visit to Jerusalem, the narrative goes on to say that Jesus went down with His parents 'and came to Nazareth; and he was subject unto them; and his mother kept (διετήρει) all these sayings (or things) in her heart' (Lk 2⁵¹). She kept them continually and carefully. They were never absent from her consciousness. They were always the subject of her thought. Motherhood, in all its pathos and beauty, in all its self-forgetfulness, and devoted intentness, and jealous vigilance, is revealed in these simple words —'*His mother kept* all these sayings in her heart.'

3. Two further usages of the word may be grouped together here. (*a*) In certain contexts it means to *celebrate*. For example, we read that Herod 'exercised a watchful care' over the Baptist, '*but* when his birthday was kept' (ἄγω, AV), he was found off his guard (Mt 14⁶). Again, the verb used to describe the celebration of the Passover (26¹⁸) is 'keep' (ποιέω—a most appropriate term to use in connexion with an ordinance which largely consisted in representing ancient events by means of symbolic actions). Once more, in the report given in John's Gospel of the anointing by Mary in Bethany, we read that Jesus said of Mary's action, 'Suffer her to keep (τηρέω) it against the day of my burying' (Jn 12⁷ RV)—the meaning of 'keep it' evidently being to 'celebrate this as a rite.' (*b*) In several contexts it means generally to *observe* or *conform to*. For instance, we read that when the Pharisees and scribes asked Jesus why His disciples walked not according to the tradition of the elders, but ate their bread with defiled hands, He replied, 'Full well do ye reject the commandment of God, that ye may keep (τηρέω) your tradition' (Mk 7⁹). Again, the conclusion to which some of the Pharisees are reported to have come with regard to our Lord's action in healing a man blind from his birth on the Sabbath, was, 'This man is not from God, because he keepeth (τηρέω) not the Sabbath' (Jn 9¹⁶).

4. But 'keep' has the more precise meanings of: (*a*) *believe*, in such passages as 'Blessed are they that hear the word of God and keep (φυλάσσω) it' (Lk 11²⁸), and 'If any man hear my sayings, and keep (φυλάσσω) them not, I judge him not' (Jn 12⁴⁷); and (*b*) *obey*, in such passages as that in which the rich young ruler is reported as having

said with reference to the commandments cited by Jesus, 'All these things have I kept (φυλάσσω) from my youth up' (Mt 19²⁰ AV, cf. Mk 10²⁰, Lk 18²¹), and that in which Jesus is reported as having taxed the Jews with failure to 'keep' (AV) or 'do' (RV; ποιέω) the Law of Moses (Jn 7¹⁹).

But the significant passages in this connexion are those which (with the exception of Mt 19¹⁷ and 28²⁰) occur in the Fourth Gospel, and in which the verb to 'keep' (τηρέω in every instance) is associated with the terms λόγος (sing. or plur. 'word' or 'words') and ἐντολαί (plur. 'commandments'). (i.) Westcott points out (note to Jn 8⁵¹) that the phrase 'keeping Christ's word' (or 'words') refers to 'the observance of the whole revelation in its organic completeness.' The opposite of 'to keep' in this connexion is 'to *disregard* or *disbelieve.*' He who 'keeps' Christ's 'word' (or 'words') is he who first attends to it, and lets the wonder and significance of the message it conveys sink into his mind, and who then appropriates and makes his own by faith the revelation it brings. To pay no heed to Christ's 'word' (or 'words'), to be at no pains to think out the purport of His appearance in history, and of the tidings of salvation He proclaimed; or, the meaning and worth of the gospel having in some measure been realized, to set it aside, to neglect it, to occupy one's self seriously with other things only —that is the attitude to Himself which Christ describes when He speaks of a man *not* 'keeping His word.' To 'keep' Christ's word, in short, is to take Christ at His word—to believe in Him (cf. Jn 8⁵¹· ⁵² 14²³· ²⁴ 15²⁰ 17⁶). The word of Christ is the word of the Father (14²⁴ 17⁶), and it is the word which the disciples are to proclaim (15²⁰). (ii.) The phrase 'keeping Christ's commandments' refers to 'the observance of definite precepts' (Westcott, *ib.*). The opposite of 'to keep' in this connexion is clearly '*to disobey.*' He that 'keeps Christ's commandments' is he who recognizes their supremacy over his will, and seeks to regulate his inward and his outward life by them. To slight the obligations which Christ imposes, to look upon the principles of conduct which He enjoins on men as subject to qualification and as mere alternatives to other possible and perhaps more congenial maxims, or, their authority being acknowledged, to limit one's conformity to them to an external and superficial obedience, an obedience that is only a travesty of active Christian discipleship—that is the attitude to Christ which is described when it has to be said of a man that he '*keeps not*' His commandments. 'To keep Christ's commandments' is to own Him as the sole sovereign of one's life, and to bring one's whole self—mind and will and heart—into captivity to the obedience of Christ (cf. 14¹⁵· ²¹ 15¹⁰).

Love for Christ is described by Him as being the condition that ensures both *belief* in His word or words (14²³· ²⁴), and *obedience* to His commandments (v.¹⁵); and *obedience* to His commandments, on the other hand (v.²¹), is described by Him as being the evidence that bears witness to the reality of that love. Further, to *believing* in His word He attaches two promises. 'If a man love me, he will keep my word: and my Father will love him, and we will come unto him and make our abode with him' (v.²³), and 'If a man keep my word, he shall never see death' (8⁵¹)—a combination of passages which shows what 'death' involves. Similarly with *obedience* to His commandments Christ connects this promise, 'If ye keep my commandments, ye shall abide in my love; even as I . . . abide in my Father's love' (15¹⁰); and with the love to Him that is borne witness to by *obedience* to His commandments, this other: 'He that loveth me shall be loved of my Father, and I will love him, and will manifest myself unto him' (14²¹).

Finally, Christ describes Himself as standing in this twofold relation to the Father, viz. of 'keeping his word,' and 'keeping his commandments'; 'I know him, and keep his word' (8⁵⁵); 'I have kept my Father's commandments, and abide in his love' (15¹⁰).

5. The last usage of the word 'keep' refers to the *Divine care of men*, and occurs in our Lord's Intercessory Prayer (17). (*a*) V.¹¹ lets us see one aspect of the meaning of this 'keeping': 'Holy Father, keep (τηρέω) them [*i.e.* 'those whom thou hast given me' (v.⁹)] in thy name which thou hast given me, that they may be one, even as we are.' This was the work which Christ had wrought for the disciples while He was with them. He had kept (τηρέω) them in the Father's name, and guarded (φυλάσσω) them (v.¹²). In these two phrases — the former of which suggests positive communication of truth and solicitude that the recipients might not be dispossessed of it, and the latter protection against the assaults of temptation — the 'educative care' which Christ spent on the disciples is summed up (see *Expos. Gr. Test. ad loc.*). And now that He is to be 'no more in the world,' He prays the Father to keep them in the name of Himself as Father. 'To be kept in the name' means not only 'to be kept in the knowledge,' but 'to be kept in the experience'—there being other modes of relation and sensibility to God on man's part besides that of knowledge. That the disciples' faith in God as Father might be characterized by assurance, is the burden of Christ's prayer (see Westcott, *ad loc.*, on the title 'Holy Father'). (*b*) V.¹⁵ shows us another aspect of the meaning of the Divine 'keeping': 'I pray not that thou shouldest take them out of the world, but that thou shouldest keep them from (Gr. 'out of') the evil' (RV 'evil one'). Whether 'evil' should be interpreted as masculine or neuter need not be discussed here. The point to notice is that the experience, and the only experience, of Divine 'keeping' which Christ by His example encourages men to pray for and anticipate, consists not in immunity from adversity, injuries, suffering, sorrow, and death, but in maintenance in a condition of certitude with regard to the Father's love and of perseverance in the path and practice of goodness—freedom from evil. The man who does not lend himself and the man who does lend himself to this keeping are described in 12²⁵: 'He that loveth his life loseth it; and he that hateth his life in this world shall keep (φυλάσσω) it unto life eternal' RV).

LITERATURE.—Moulton-Geden, *Concord. to Gr. Test.*; Grimm-Thayer, *Gr. Lex.*; Westcott, *Com. on John*; *Expos. Gr. Test.* and works referred to there.   A. B. MACAULAY.

KENOSIS.—The word κένωσις is not itself found in the NT, but the verb κενόω *to empty, to make empty*, occurs in Ph 2⁷, where AV renders 'made himself of no reputation,' but the RV correctly 'emptied himself' (see Lightfoot's Com. *in loc.*, and Grimm-Thayer's *Greek-English Lexicon*). It is disputed among theologians as to the extent to which the Son of God stripped Himself of His Divine prerogatives, but it is not necessary here to discuss these differences, as the purpose of this article is only to collect the evidences the Gospels afford of the actual conditions of the Incarnation. But two questions may here be very briefly touched on before we pass to this subject.

(1) We may glance at the description of this *Kenosis* of the Son of God found in the Apostolic writings. The passage in Philippians (2⁶⁻⁸) lays stress on the surrender, on the one hand, of the form of God ('the glories, the prerogatives of deity,' Lightfoot), of equality with God; and the assumption, on the other hand, of the form of a servant,

the likeness of man, self-humiliation and obedience 'even unto death, yea, the death of the cross.' In 2 Co 8⁹ St. Paul describes the *Kenosis* as the abandonment of wealth for poverty (the Divine for the human mode of existence). In four pregnant statements, in which the Christian salvation is brought into most intimate relation with the humiliation of the Son of God, this *Kenosis* is more fully defined: 'God, sending his own Son in the likeness of sinful flesh [He shared the flesh, but not the sin], condemned sin in the flesh' (Ro 8³); 'God sent forth his Son, born of a woman, born under the law' (Gal 4⁴); 'Him who knew no sin he made to be sin on our behalf' [the penalty of sin was endured by the sinless for the sinful (2 Co 5²¹)]; 'Christ redeemed us from the curse of the law, having become a curse for us' [Christ as the sacrificial victim 'became in a certain sense the impersonation of the sin and of the curse,' Lightfoot on Gal 3¹³]. The writer of the Epistle to the Hebrews lays emphasis on the participation of the Son of God in *flesh* and *blood*, in order that He might be capable of dying (2¹⁴); on His experience of temptation as enabling Him to sympathize with and succour the tempted (2¹⁸ 4¹⁵); on the obedience He learned by suffering (5⁸). The prologue to John's Gospel may be regarded as Apostolic interpretation; and there the *Kenosis* is described in the words 'and the Word became flesh' (1¹⁴, see Westcott *in loco*). It is the intention of all these statements to affirm the complete reality of the manhood of Jesus.

(2) We may glance at the attempts to define theologically the process of the Incarnation in the Kenotic theory, 'which seeks to make the manhood of Christ real by representing the Logos as contracting Himself within human dimensions and literally becoming man' (Bruce's *The Humiliation of Christ*, p. 136. This lecture contains the best account in English of the modern Kenotic theories. Bruce distinguishes four types, the *absolute dualistic*, the *absolute metamorphic*, the *absolute semi-metamorphic*, the *real but relative*. The differences in these theories concern two points, the degree in which the Logos laid aside the Divine attributes of omnipresence, omnipotence, and omniscience in order to become man, and the relation between the Logos and the human soul of Christ, as retaining distinctness, or as becoming identical. As regards the first point, the theories are absolute or relative; as regards the second, dualistic, metamorphic, semimetamorphic). Of the speculative attempts to formulate the doctrine of the Incarnation, Ritschl says that 'what is taught under the head of the Kenosis of the Divine Logos is pure mythology' (*Justification and Reconciliation*, pp. 409–411). Without endorsing the terms of this condemnation, the present writer may repeat what he has elsewhere written on this matter. 'The Kenotic theories are commendable as attempts to do justice to the historical personality of Jesus, while assuming the ecclesiastical dogma; but are unsatisfactory in putting an undue strain on the passages in the New Testament which are supposed to teach the doctrine, and in venturing on bold assertions about the constitution of deity, which go far beyond the compass of our intelligence in these high matters' (*The Ritschlian Theology*, p. 271 note). The study of the facts of the life of Jesus proves undoubtedly the *Kenosis*, of which none of these theories offers a satisfactory explanation, as partly the *data*—the inner life of the Godhead—lie beyond our reach. We now confine ourselves to the *data* offered in the Gospels. (A useful summary of the data, although by no means exhaustive, will be found in Gore's *Dissertations*, 'The Consciousness of our Lord in His Mortal Life.' Adamson in *The Mind in Christ* deals very thoroughly with all the data bearing on the knowledge of Christ).

The Kenotic theories concern themselves specially with the three metaphysical attributes of God, manifest in His transcendent, yet immanent, relation to the world — omnipresence, omnipotence, omniscience. The Gospels show that Jesus possessed none of these. He was localized in a body (Jn 1[14] 'tabernacled among us'), and moved from place to place as His mission required. The cure of the nobleman's son (Jn 4[50]) does not prove omnipresence, but is explicable as an act of faith in God. In the absence of their Master the disciples become faithless (Mk 9[19]), and He has to return to them to restore their confidence. In His farewell discourse He promises His constant presence as a future gift (Jn 14[18. 19]), and fulfils His promise after the Resurrection (Mt 28[20]). His miracles do not prove omnipotence, as they were wrought in dependence on, with prayer to, God (Mk 9[29], Jn 11[41. 42]), were restrained by unbelief (Mt 13[58]), seemingly involved physical strain (Mk 5[30]), and sometimes were accompanied by means of cure (Mk 7[33-34]; see The Expositor, 6th series, vol. vi., 'The Function of the Miracles'). Jesus never claimed omniscience. He claimed to know the Father as no other knew Him (Mt 11[27]), but, on the other hand, He confessed that His knowledge as Son was limited in so important a matter as the time of His Return (Mt 24[36] RV, Mk 13[32]). The express distinction between the knowledge of the Son and of the Father made in this utterance disproves the view sometimes advanced, that the Son's perfect knowledge of the Father must include a knowledge of all the Father knows. It is the character, purpose, and activity of God as Father that the Son knows and reveals. When Jesus Himself thus confesses ignorance in a matter affecting Himself so closely, it is not reverence to claim for Him universal knowledge regarding such matters as the date and authorship of Old Testament writings, the causes of disease, the course of events in the remote future; nor is it any lack of homage and devotion to acknowledge the other evidences of limitation of knowledge the Gospels offer. He made a mistake regarding the barren fig-tree (Mk 11[13]); He was sometimes surprised and disappointed [see art. SURPRISE] (Mt 8[10] 26[40], Mk 1[45] 2[1. 2] 6[6] 7[24. 25. 36] 8[12], Lk 2[49]); information came to Him by the ordinary channels of hearing and seeing (Mt 4[12. 17] 14[12. 13], Mk 1[37. 38] 2[17], Jn 4[1-3]), and He sought it in this way (Jn 1[38] 9[35], Mk 5[30-32], Lk 4[17]). He asked questions not rhetorically, but because He desired an answer (Mt 16[13. 15], Lk 8[30], Jn 11[34]). He developed mentally (Lk 2[52]), and during His ministry learned by experience (Jn 2[21]; the verb used is γινώσκειν, see Westcott in loco). He sought guidance from God in prayer (Lk 5[16] 6[12] 9[18. 28] 10[21]). The necessity of the cup offered by His Father's will was not at first evident to Him (Mt 26[39]), and, when convinced that His Father's will required it, He was not sure that His strength to drink it would endure (v.[42]; cf. He 5[7. 8]). His cry of desolation (Mt 27[46]) on the cross was not only the culmination of His Passion, but in being this it was also the temporary obscuration of His knowledge of the Father, who in that moment had not forsaken Him. Instances of supernatural knowledge are found in the Gospels. Some of these: the getting of the ass (Mt 21[2]), and of the upper room (26[17-19]), the finding of the money in the fish's mouth (17[27]), are only apparent, and allow another explanation. The statement to the woman of Samaria about the number of her husbands (Jn 4[17. 18]) is very perplexing; and possibly, as the conversation was probably reported by the woman, may have been made more definite by her guilty conscience than it actually was, even as she exaggerates in her account of what Christ had told her (v.[29]). The command to the disciples about casting their net (Lk 5[5]) was probably an act of faith in God, even as the command to the storm (Mk 4[39]). The other cases fall into two classes: prophetic anticipations (His own death and resurrection, the doom of Jerusalem), or exercises of an exceptional moral insight and spiritual discernment. We may admit occasionally, for the fulfilment of His vocation, miraculous knowledge as well as power, without the constant possession of omniscience or omnipotence.

We cannot dissever the intellectual from the moral life; and the development of the latter involves necessarily some limitations in the former. Omniscience cannot be 'tempted in all points even as we are,' nor can it exercise a childlike faith in God such as Jesus calls us to exercise along with Him. Moral and religious reality is excluded from the history of Jesus by the denial of the limitation of His knowledge. He was tempted (see articles on TEMPTATION and STRUGGLES OF SOUL). In the Wilderness the temptation was possible, because He had to learn by experience the uses to which His miraculous powers might legitimately be put, and the proper means for the fulfilment of His vocation. Without taint or flaw in His own nature, the expectations of the people regarding the Messiah, and the desires they pressed upon Him, afforded the occasions of temptation to Him. The necessity of His own sacrifice was not so certain to Him as to exclude the possibility of the temptation to escape it. That Jesus was Himself conscious of being still the subject of a moral discipline is suggested by His refusal of the epithet 'good' (Mk 10[18]). Although morally tempted and developing, Jesus betrays no sign of penitence for sin or failure, and we are warranted in affirming that He was tempted without sin, and in His development knew no sin. But that perfection would have been only a moral semblance had there been no liability to temptation and no limitation of knowledge. As Son of God, He lived in dependence on God (Mt 11[27a]) and submission to Him (v.[26], Mt 26[39]). It is the Fourth Gospel that throws into special prominence this feature (Jn 3[34] 5[19. 20] 8[28] 15[15] 17[1. 8]). The Son delivers the words and performs the deeds given by the Father. There are a few utterances given in this Gospel which express a sense of loss for Himself and His disciples in the separation from the Father that His earthly life involves (Jn 14[28]), a desire for the recovery of the former conditions of communion (17[5]), and an expectation of gain in His return to the Father (14[19. 20]). Jesus was subject to human emotion: He groaned (Jn 11[33. 38]), sighed (Mk 7[34] 8[12]), wept at the grave of Lazarus (Jn 11[35]) and over Jerusalem (Lk 13[34] 19[41], Mt 23[37]). He endured poverty (Mt 8[20], Lk 9[58]), labour (Mk 6[3]), weariness (Jn 4[6], Mt 21[7]), weakness (Mt 27[32]), hunger (Mt 4[2] 21[18]), thirst (Jn 4[7] 19[28]), pain (Mt 27[34-35]), and death (Mt 27[50], Jn 19[30]). Some have conjectured from the evidence of Jn 19[34] that He died literally of a broken heart (see Farrar's Life of Christ, note at the end of chap. lxi.). This Kenosis did not obscure His moral insight and spiritual discernment; did not involve any moral defect or failure, any religious distrust; did not weaken or narrow His love, mercy, or grace; did not lower His authority, or lessen His efficiency as Revealer of God and Redeemer of men; but, on the contrary, it was necessary, for only under such human conditions and limitations could He fulfil His mission, deliver His message, present His sacrifice, and effect His salvation. That He might receive the name of Saviour and Lord, which is above every other name, He must empty Himself.

LITERATURE.—Works referred to in the art.; Liddon, BL; Gore, BL; Gifford, The Incarnation; Wendt, Teaching of Jesus, on the various passages quoted; Stalker, Christology of Jesus.
ALFRED E. GARVIE.

KERIOTH.—See JUDAS ISCARIOT.

KEYS.—The word (κλείς) occurs 6 times in the New Testament, twice in the Synoptic Gospels, and 4 times in Revelation. In Lk 11[52] Jesus upbraids the lawyers on the ground that they have 'taken away the key of knowledge,' the instrument by which entrance into knowledge could be obtained, and thereby hindered the people from the privilege which should have been theirs. This they had done by substituting a false confidence in the wrong kind of knowledge, with the result that the right kind was ignored and forgotten. The knowledge from which the people are thus excluded is 'that of the way of salvation' (Plummer), or, more profoundly, that knowledge of the Lord, for lack of which the 'people perish' (Hos 4[6]), to seek which they had been urged by the prophets (cf. Jn 17[3]).

In Mt 16[19] the word is used again metaphorically, in the address to Peter : 'I will give unto thee the keys of the kingdom of heaven.' The apparent limitation of the promise to one Apostle is to be controlled by the repetition of the following and interpretive clause addressed to the Apostles in general in Mt 18[18]. The keys are to be intrusted to Peter as to a steward of the house (and in like manner to the Apostles in general), to whom might be given the power of locking and unlocking, but not of deciding who did or did not belong to the household (Weiss). The significance of this promise would be fully met if it announced the effectual proclamation, through the Apostles, of the gospel by means of which the believer obtains entrance into the kingdom. On the passage as a whole see artt. CÆSAREA PHILIPPI, p. 249, and PETER.

In Rev 1[18] the Son of Man in John's vision says : 'I have the keys of death and of Hades,' i.e. control over the entrance to the realm of the dead. The figure of death as a realm with portals comes down from Ps 9[13], and was freely developed in the Rabbinic writings. The 'key of death' was one of the three (four) keys which were said to be in the hand of God alone. Thus in *Sanhedrin*, 113, 'Elijah desired that there should be given to him the key of rain ; he desired that there should be given to him the key of resurrection of the dead : they said to him, "Three keys are not given into the hand of a representative, the key of birth, the key of rain, and the key of resurrection of the dead."' There is therefore strong significance in the claim here made by the Risen Messiah.

In like manner a claim to at least Messianic dignity is involved in the phrase in Rev 3[7] 'he that hath the key of David.' The allusion is clearly to the promise in Is 22[22] 'I will give to him (Eliakim) the key of the house of David upon his shoulder,' a passage which, according to Zullich, was commonly referred by Jewish commentators to the Messiah.

In the two remaining passages (Rev 9[1] 20[1]) the use of the word ('the key of the pit of the abyss,' 'the key of the abyss') depends on the idea familiar in Jewish cosmogony, viz. that there was a communication between the upper world and the under world or abyss by means of a pit or shaft, the opening to which might be conceived as covered and locked. According to Rabbinic tradition, this opening was placed beneath the foundations of the Temple, as the Moslems hold to this day that it is to be found beneath the Dome of the Rock, or Mosque of Omar (see Gunkel, *Schöpfung und Chaos*, pp. 91–98).   C. ANDERSON SCOTT.

KHAN.—See INN.

KID.—See ANIMALS, p. 64[a].

KIDRON.—See BROOK.

KIN, KINDRED, KINSHIP.—'The antique conception of kinship is participation in one blood, which passes from parent to child, and circulates in the veins of every member of the family. The unity of family or clan is viewed as a physical unity ; for the blood is the life,—an idea familiar to us from the OT,—and it is the same blood, and therefore the same life, that is shared by every descendant of the common ancestor. The idea that the race has a life of its own, of which individual lives are only parts, is expressed even more clearly by picturing the race as a tree, of which the ancestor is the root or stem and the descendants the branches' (W. R. Smith, *RS*[2] 40 f.). This conception underlies the words 'kin' (συγγενής, Mk 6[4]) and 'kindred' (συγγένεια, Lk 1[61]). But it was Christ's purpose to organize society according to another conception of the basis of unity. He made kinship depend not upon physical but spiritual affinities (Mt 12[48] etc.). 'Already, in the spiritual religion of the Hebrews, the idea of Divine fatherhood is entirely dissociated from the basis of natural fatherhood. Man was created in the image of God, but he was not begotten ; God-sonship is not a thing of nature, but of grace' (*RS*[2] 41). There, however, the sonship of the *nation* is emphasized : in Christ's teaching the *personal* relationship is brought into prominence. Sonship depends on personal faith (Jn 1[12]), and its evidence is individual submission to the will of God (Mt 12[48ff.]). In His allegory of the Vine (Jn 15[1]), Jesus practically adopts the old figure. He Himself takes the place of stem or root, but the branches share the common life only on condition of an abiding faith (cf. St. Paul's figure of the olive-tree, Ro 11[17] etc.). The ancient kindred of blood, with its narrow physical limits, gives place in the NT to a fellowship of faith which is open to all mankind. See also art. FAMILY.   W. EWING.

KINDNESS.—The NT term χρηστότης, which is rendered in the EV both by 'kindness' and by 'goodness' (once in Ro 3[12] as 'good,' following the LXX of Ps 13 (14)[1. 3], there quoted, in which χρηστότητα = טוֹב), nowhere occurs in the Gospels. The quality it denotes, however, is an evangelical virtue. Like its OT counterpart חֶסֶד, it is attributable both to God (as in Ro 2[4] *et al.*) and to man (as in 2 Co 6[6] *et al.*). The adj. χρηστός, EV 'kind,' is found once in the Gospels as referring to God (Lk 6[35]). The other instances of its use in very different connexions, as applied to a yoke (Mt 11[30]) and to wine (Lk 5[39]), though such use is a natural outgrowth of its root-meaning, need only be mentioned.

1. The Kindness of God in the Teaching of Jesus. —The passage in which God is explicitly represented as 'kind' occurs in Lk.'s version of the *logion* of Jesus concerning love of friends and hatred of foes (Lk 6[27-36] ‖ Mt 5[43-48]). The highest reward attendant upon a love that extends to both friends and foes and is ready to show kindness to all men without distinction, is that thereby men become 'sons of the Most High.' 'Sons of your Father which is in heaven,' as it runs in Mt 5[45], would appear to be the primitive phrase, but 'the Most High' (ὕψιστος) is quite a favourite name for God with Lk., and its substitution here is probably due to this preference (see Dalman, *The Words of Jesus*, Eng. tr. p. 199). God is kind to the ungrateful and wicked. In the Mt. parallel this benign goodness is expressed in the concrete picture of sunshine and rain bestowed equally upon the evil and the good, the just and the unjust. Clearly the expression of an all-embracing benignity can go no further so far as extent is concerned. The only enhancing possible is in connexion with the gift which betokens that benignity, and this we have in the great saying of Jn 3[16], along with the same sweep of reference, 'God so loved *the world*, that he gave *his only-begotten Son*.' That fontal love is manifested in the kindness (cf. Tit 3[4]) on which Jesus lays so much stress in His presentment of God as our Father, a kindness going far beyond the providential bounties and mercies of this life, and concerning itself with the profoundest needs of sinful men.

If explicit statements of the character of that now considered are not multiplied in our Lord's teaching, it is to be pointed out that the same conception of God is necessarily implied in a considerable group of the parables—those, in particular, that illustrate the Divine grace. The great trilogy of Lk 15, exhibiting the Divine concern for man as τὸ ἀπολωλός; the parables which show how royally and wonderfully God pities and forgives, whether that forgiveness is gratefully realized (the Two Debtors, Lk 7[36-50]) or is strangely disregarded (the Unmerciful Servant, Mt 18[23-35]); the parable of the Great Supper (Lk 14[16-24]), with its comprehensive 'welcome for the sinner'—these and other such are full of the wide-reaching kindness of God.

An OT basis for this conspicuous feature in Jesus' representation of God undoubtedly exists. Whilst God was supremely known in Israel as King, His fatherly relation to Israel is not obscurely dwelt upon in OT writings, particularly in the prophets (*e.g.* Isaiah, Jeremiah, Hosea). God's goodness and graciousness are gratefully celebrated in the Psalms; witness the refrain of Ps 107, 'Oh that men would praise the Lord for his goodness (חַסְדּוֹ)!' Stress on this Divine quality is the great characteristic of Hosea. Ḥeṣed is the bond uniting Jahweh and Israel in one covenant relation: the *ḥeṣed* of J″ to Israel being His grace, of Israel to J″, piety or dutiful love, and of Israelite to Israelite, love and mutual consideration. Love to J″ and love to one's brethren are identical (cf. Hos 4[1] and 6[4. 6]), and both are made imperative by a right sense of J″'s fatherly affection and kindness towards His people (see W. R. Smith, *The Prophets of Israel*, p. 160 ff.). This line of thought, however, regarding God was arrested in later Judaism; God's transcendent kingly greatness was emphasized in Jewish thought in our Lord's time, and His grace and loving-kindness had fallen into the background. Jesus deliberately chose this conception of fatherly kindness as the one predominant characteristic in His revelation of God, and, what is more, proclaimed this gracious God as the Father of all mankind.

No difficulty need be raised as to the reconciliation of such a conception of God with His character as 'Rex tremendæ majestatis,' or as the holy God who cannot regard wickedness with indifference. That God is gracious does not mean that He is an easy-going God. Moral distinctions cannot be obliterated. Though in Christ's simple language God sends sunshine and rain upon the unjust, though He is kind to the ungrateful and wicked and they enjoy great prosperity, it cannot be other than an evil thing to be unjust, ungrateful, and wicked. And even though such blessings should appear to be withheld from the just and good, it still must be an altogether good thing to be just and good. Is it not significant that Jesus declares God's kindness without any qualification whatever, and shows Himself all unconscious that any difficulties are thereby occasioned, that there is anything requiring to be explained and adjusted? The parable of the Unmerciful Servant displays God's benignity; but the truculence which shows itself unaffected by an amazing experience of forgiving mercy must needs lose the boon which that benignity bestowed. The conclusion of the parable (Mt 18[35]) expresses what must needs be; and Jesus presents the doom of the 'wicked servant' as a picture of God's dealings with men just as directly and simply as He sets forth the kindness of our Father in heaven. The one presentation is perfectly consistent with the other.

Similarly, the problem of suffering and misery, which times without number has evoked the cry 'Is God good?', is not allowed by Jesus to qualify in any way His declaration of the kindness of God. It is not because He ignored the problem; He is Himself conspicuous as the Sufferer. And with our Lord the Divine kindness is not involved in doubt, because, as we say, God permits so much suffering amongst men, but rather that kindness is represented by Him as specially called forth by human misery. God is particularly set forth as viewing the sufferings and sorrows of men with compassion and pity; and pity is simply kindness brought into relation to suffering and distress. God declares Himself 'most chiefly in shewing mercy and pity' (Collect for 11th Sunday after Trinity). So also it is significant that in enforcing the lesson of Lk 6[35], Christ does not say, 'Be ye kind, as your Father is kind,' but (v.[36]), 'Be ye compassionate, as your Father is compassionate' (οἰκτίρμων). And what a vast deduction from the sum of human misery would result, and how the problem would be simplified, if everywhere 'man's inhumanity to man' gave place to such a spirit!

2. *Kindness as the Law of Human Life.*—'Love one another' is the new commandment of Jesus (Jn 13[34]); and kindness is love in its practical manifestation. From what has been said above, we see that this great law of life is directly enforced by the exhibition of the loving-kindness of God our Father. This is the case notably in the comment of our Lord on the dictum, 'Thou shalt love thy neighbour and hate thine enemy' (Mt 5[43-48]).

The ideal of a relation of kindness between man and man is, however, not altogether an original and peculiar feature in our Lord's teaching. In the OT (as, *e.g.*, in Hosea) *ḥeṣed* is presented as the right characteristic of human relationships, even as it denotes God's graciousness to men; and as a term belonging to common life it indicates that 'those who are linked together by the bonds of personal affection, or of social unity, owe to one another more than can be expressed in the forms of legal obligation' (W. R. Smith, *op. cit.* p. 161). And Jesus quotes Hos 6[6] with approval, 'I desire mercy (*ḥeṣed*) and not sacrifice' (Mt 12[7])—a passage which makes that quality of kindness of greater importance than worship, and worship vain without it. In heathen religions and philosophies, too, ideas are found corresponding more or less to such a conception of the social bond.

Further, it is true that our Lord very emphatically insisted on the application of the principle of kindness as a law of life to relations of men with men in general, and not merely those of co-religionists and people of the same tribe or country. What can equal the parable of the Good Samaritan as helping to a definition of the 'neighbour' to whom the service of kindness is due?

Yet the OT and other forms of teaching are not without traces of a wider view than the scribes of Christ's day would allow. The duty of kindness to the stranger in the land (as in Lv 19[9f.], Dt 10[18f.] *et al.*), and of kindness to enemies, with readiness in forgiving injuries (as in Ex 23[4f.], Pr 24[29] 25[21f.] *et al.*), is explicitly set forth in the OT. We get one glimpse (among many) of this wider humane feeling, from a very different quarter, in the Indian saying, 'I met a hundred men going to Delhi, and every one of them was my brother.'

Our Lord's exposition of this law of kindness is pre-eminent and *sui generis*. And the newness of His teaching in this respect appears in His having established this duty on a firm religious basis and given it 'an essential place in the moral consciousness of men' (Wendt, *Teaching of Jesus*, i. p. 332). It is significant that the judgment of men in Mt 25[31ff.] is made to turn on the performance or neglect of the acts of mercy or kindness. The kindness inculcated, also, extends to all creatures: and it is to express itself in the little courtesies of life (Mt 5[47] 10[12]).

A view of Christ's ethical teaching as a whole makes it clear that the stress thus laid on the duty of kindness favours no loosening of obligation to justice and fidelity in the manifold relationships of men, nor does it do away with the duty and need of punishment when that obligation is violated. The maintenance of just and faithful dealing does not necessarily involve severity and harshness; rather it is itself part of the law of kindness rightly considered. Love of neighbour and of enemy is as truly reconcilable with the claims of justice on the human plane as is God's benignity with His righteous government. And Christ makes us see once for all that love is the only satisfactory basis for human relationships, and indeed the only possible bond in the perfected social state. See also artt. LOVE, NEIGHBOUR.

3. *The Kindness of Jesus.*—The perfect embodiment of this kindness in human life is seen in Jesus Himself. 'As I have loved you' is the Johannine counterpart (Jn 13[34] 15[12]) of the Synoptic 'as your Father is compassionate' in the enforcement of the Law of Love. The whole Gospel portraiture shows us that in Jesus the kindness and pity of God fully dwelt. His dealing with sickness and suffering in all forms, His attitude towards sin, His sense of social disorder, His regard for men as men and indifference to class distinctions, His whole demeanour, His gracious speech (Lk 4[22])—all proclaimed the Divine kindness. His fiery denunciation of scribes and Pharisees (see Mt 23) presents no exception; for His wrath is the wrath of love, and the denunciation must be read in the light of the yearning lament over Jerusalem (Mt 23[37ff.]).— Jerusalem in which Pharisaism and scribism were specially entrenched. The key to this perfect life of kindness and love is found in His own words— 'The Son of Man came not to be ministered unto, but to minister, and to give His life a ransom for many' (Mk 10[45]). The declaration of vivid and loving remembrance is that He 'went about doing good, and healing all that were oppressed of the devil' (Ac 10[38]).   J. S. CLEMENS.

KING.—The primitive Christian Church regarded herself as the vassal of Jesus Christ, her exalted Lord and King, under whose regal sway she had been brought by Divine grace (Col 1[13]). The current belief was that Jesus had been installed in His royal office by the Resurrection; in that event God had made Him both Lord and Christ (Ac 2[36]), and in it had been fulfilled the prophecy regarding the Messianic King, 'Thou art my son; this day have I begotten thee' (Ps 2[7], cf. Ac 13[33]), as also another prophetic utterance, 'Sit thou at my right hand' (Ps 110[1]; cf. Ac 2[34], Rev 3[21]). This sovereignty is indeed temporary; it will come to an end with the final overthrow of the enemies of God: 'Then shall he deliver up the kingdom to God, even the Father' (1 Co 15[24. 28]). It was the conviction of the primitive community that the idea of a Messianic kingdom upon earth — whether eternal (Lk 1[33]) or of limited duration (Rev 20[4ff.])— as it gleams through the Jewish Apocalyptic and in the earlier Messianic hope, had at last been realized in the Kingdom of Christ, *i.e.*, the Church as subject to her exalted King.

Now the question which we seek to answer in the present article is this :—*Did Jesus Himself in His lifetime put forward a claim to be the Messianic King?* Here we light upon a problem which is vigorously canvassed among theologians, particularly at the present day. While there are scholars of high repute, such as Wellhausen and Wrede,* who deny that Jesus thought of Himself as the Messiah at all, there are others who are convinced that He was in possession of some kind of 'Messianic consciousness'; and among the latter the controversy turns upon the peculiar significance and the specific colouring of the implied claims and expectations. It is impossible in the space at our disposal to discuss the problem in all its bearings; for the details reference must be made to other works of the present writer.† The task of

determining the sense in which Jesus assumed the title of King is all that meanwhile concerns us.

The prophecy regarding Jesus uttered by the angel Gabriel : 'The Lord shall give unto him the throne of his father David, and he shall reign over the house of Jacob for ever, and of his kingdom there shall be no end' (Lk 1[32f.]), was not brought to fulfilment in the lifetime of Jesus. But the writer of the Gospel of the Infancy in Lk. would hardly have recorded the prediction, had he not entertained the hope that its fulfilment was but a matter of time. It is beyond question that the earliest Jewish - Christian communities believed that Jesus would come again in kingly glory, as is acknowledged by the repentant thief upon the cross (Lk 23[42], reading ὅταν ἔλθῃς ἐν τῇ βασιλείᾳ σου as preferable to εἰς τὴν βασιλείαν σου). This belief appears also in the emphasis which the early churches laid upon the descent of Jesus from David (Ro 1[3]), and in the endeavours which were made to substantiate it by the construction of genealogical tables (Mt 1[1-16], Lk 3[23-38]). These tables were not constructed for merely academic or theological purposes; they were designed to support the contention with which the Jewish Christians confronted their unbelieving compatriots, viz. that Jesus was the King of Israel. It is true, indeed, that in the primitive tradition of the life of Jesus, His Kingship is not explicitly asserted. The acclamations of the multitude on the occasion of the Triumphal Entry into Jerusalem, 'Hosanna to the son of David' (Mt 21[9]), 'Blessed is the kingdom that cometh, the kingdom of our father David' (Mk 11[10]), cannot have been more than a bold anticipation of the future. The crown of thorns (15[17]) was an act of derision, to the true significance of which the soldiers were blind; while the inscription on the cross (15[26]) was a prediction which Pilate, in opposition to the wishes of the Jews and in ignorance of what he was doing (Jn 19[19f.]), was constrained to set forth in all the great languages of the world. In point of fact the primitive tradition makes it perfectly clear that Jesus deprecated and even disclaimed the ascription of royalty, or at all events that He thought of the dignity as something to become His only in the future.

To the question of Pilate, 'Art thou the King of the Jews?' Jesus answers, according to Mk 15[2], neither *yea* nor *nay*, but replies only in the words 'Thou sayest it.' Is this an affirmative? St. Mark certainly regarded it as such (cf. 14[62]), but St. Luke shows unmistakably that the words were not so understood by Pilate, since, if he had regarded them as equivalent to *yea*, he could not have said, 'I find no fault in this man' (23[4]): a claimant to the throne must necessarily have been convicted of sedition. St. John also indicates that Jesus at first replied evasively to the question (18[33f.]), but that afterwards He frankly avowed His claim to the title of King, though with the reservation that His Kingdom was 'not of this world' (18[36]). Even more clearly than in the Synoptists we see in St. John's account a definite purpose : he aims at showing that Jesus was no political usurper, no pretender to the crown, who designed by force of arms to deliver His people from the thraldom of Rome, and to reinstall the dynasty of David. Notwithstanding the obvious tendency of the writer of the Fourth Gospel, we must grant that in this instance his narrative, equally with those of the earlier Evangelists, is essentially faithful to fact.

That Jesus harboured no design of restoring the Davidic monarchy may be asserted without misgiving. To the policy of the violent, who would take the Kingdom by force (Mt 11[12]), He lent no countenance, and when, after the feeding of the multitude, they wanted to make Him a King, he betook Himself elsewhere (Jn 6¹⁵). We shall be asked, however, if He did not, on the occasion of His Triumphal Entry into Jerusalem, carefully organize and carry through a demonstration designed to further His royal claims. In answer to this it is to be said that St. Mark's account of the episode (11¹ᶠ·) cannot be taken as historical; and we must either accept the narrative of Jn. (12¹²ᶠᶠ·), according to which the demonstration emanated from His supporters among the people and was only *permitted* by Him, and which weakens the impression of the incident by its quotation from Zec 9⁹;* or else we must abandon the hope of winning from the event any light for our theme at all. Had the Triumphal Entry been of such capital importance and of such a striking character as St. Mark represents, the authorities would certainly have intervened, and the matter would have figured in the trial of Jesus as a count in the indictment [but see ENTRY INTO JERUSALEM].

In the discourses of Jesus we find telling arguments, both positive and negative, in favour of the view that He either made no claim whatever to the title of Messianic King, or that He did so in a most unobtrusive way. To His descent from David, if He gave it credence at all, He did not attach the slightest importance; indeed, He even sought to convince the scribes that in regarding the coming Messiah as the Son of David they fell far short of the truth. To all appearance He desired to eradicate from the minds of His hearers the prevailing idea of a Davidic ruler, and to substitute for it another Messianic figure, viz. the 'Son of Man,' the 'Man' who, as Daniel (7¹³ᶠ·) had prophesied, was to come in the clouds of heaven at the end of the age. This 'Son of Man' is no earthly monarch, but a Being of Divine and heavenly nature; not one who by means of a revolution rises from his native obscurity to a throne, but one who descends from heaven to earth. With such a figure dominating the outlook of Jesus, there is no place for a Messianic King. It is thus quite in keeping with these facts that He announces, not that God is about to send forth the Messiah, the Son of David, not that the kingdom of David is at hand, but that 'the kingdom of *God* is at hand.' The purport of this message has been dealt with elsewhere:† suffice it to say here, that the announcement of a cosmical catastrophe, of a new æon, in which the existing sway of Satan shall be destroyed, and God shall be all in all, is intrinsically incompatible with the idea of a Messianic King standing side by side with the Most High. Nor do the prophecies of Daniel, when rightly interpreted, present us with the figure of a Messiah. Hence it is by no mere accident that in the utterances of Jesus the title 'King' is applied to God alone: cf. Jerusalem 'the city of the great king' (Mt 5³⁵), the parable of the Unmerciful Servant (18²³); and in particular, the parable of the Marriage Feast (22¹ᶠᶠ·), where the Messiah appears as the King's son. It is only in the description of the Last Judgment (25³¹) that the 'Son of Man' appears as King—note the abrupt change vv.³⁴·⁴⁰; probably, however, we have in this passage reminiscences of some older parable, which had to do with a king and not with the Messiah at all. Only on one recorded occasion (Lk 22²⁹) does Jesus invest Himself with the βασιλεία, but that is *for the future*. This occurred, according to Lk., during the Last Supper,—a circumstance which leads us to infer that Jesus did not in any sense regard Himself as being a king in the days of His flesh. What He has in prospect here is simply a participation in the Divine Sovereignty, a prerogative guaranteed also to those who accept Him.

* Op. cit. i. i. 163.
† J. Weiss, *Die Predigt Jesu vom Reiche Gottes* ² (1900).

He believes, indeed, that He will occupy the chief place among them that are His; that He will take the seat of honour at table, having them on His right hand and on His left (Mt 20²¹); but of a Messianic Kingship in the ordinary sense of the word there is no suggestion at all. If Jesus deemed Himself to be the predestined Messiah in any sense whatsoever, He certainly thought of the Messianic office as being different from that of a king. See, further, art. MESSIAH.   JOHANNES WEISS.

KING OF THE JEWS.—See preceding art., DIVINITY OF CHRIST (p. 477ᵇ), NAMES AND TITLES OF CHRIST.

KINGDOM OF GOD (or HEAVEN).—To learn what Jesus meant by the term 'kingdom of heaven,' or 'kingdom of God,' we must go first and chiefly to His own words. The simple fact that He employed a term which was in common use, and which had parallels also in the Jewish Scriptures (*e.g.* 1 Ch 28⁵, Dn 2⁴⁴ 4³), does not justify one in assuming that His conception can be defined by the current view of His day, or by a study of the OT. It is plain that He might make use of the familiar term, but might put into it a new and higher meaning. Indeed, it is quite certain that Jesus, as a wise teacher, started from the beliefs and longings of those whom He sought to help, and that He aimed at fulfilling rather than destroying. We should expect, then, to find Him using old terms, but pouring into them new meanings. Moreover, the thought of Jesus in regard to the kingdom of heaven is presented to us more fully and clearly than is that of His Jewish contemporaries. Hence there is no occasion for approaching our topic indirectly, either by the way of the OT or that of the Rabbinic usage. It will be best to go at once to the main source of information, and seek the thought of Jesus from His own words, though availing ourselves of any light that can be found in other quarters.

1. *Survey of the data.*—According to Mk. and Mt., the memorable word in the first preaching of Jesus in Galilee was the announcement of the nearness of the kingdom of God [or of heaven] (ἤγγικεν ἡ βασιλεία τοῦ θεοῦ [or τῶν οὐρανῶν], Mk 1¹⁵, Mt 4¹⁷); and in the last interview with His disciples, on the evening before His death, He still spoke of the kingdom, anticipating a union with them there (Mk 14²⁵). In all the interval between these events the term was frequently on His lips both in public and in private. St. Mark records 13 instances of its use by Jesus, St. Luke 34, and St. Matthew 48. Its central importance in the teaching of Jesus is frequently apparent. Thus the gospel itself is spoken of as the gospel of the kingdom (Mt 9³⁵); the Twelve and the Seventy are sent out to announce that the kingdom is at hand (Mt 10⁷, Lk 10⁹); more than a third of the parables are explicitly said to be an unfolding of the truth of the kingdom;* the disciples are taught to pray for the coming of the kingdom (Mt 6¹⁰); it is the preaching of the kingdom of heaven that terminates the period of the Law and the Prophets (Mt 11¹², Lk 16¹⁶); the kingdom is presented as the *summum bonum* (Mt 13⁴⁴·⁴⁵); and the kingdom is the great fact of the future (*e.g.* Mt 25³⁴).

But while the kingdom is thus seen to be of great significance in the teaching of Jesus, it is equally obvious that its meaning varies widely in different passages. Thus Jesus says that the kingdom is to be entered at once by those to whom He is speaking (7¹³·¹⁴), and again, that the righteous

* The use of the formula ὁμοία ἐστὶν ἡ βασιλεία τῶν οὐρανῶν, or ὡμοιώθη ἡ βασιλεία τῶν οὐρανῶν, cannot be at once attributed to Jesus. In some instances it has no manifest connexion with the thought of the parable (*e.g.* Mt 20¹ 22²).

are to enter it when the Son of Man shall have come in His glory (25³⁴). At one time Jesus says to the Pharisees, 'The kingdom of heaven is among you' (ἐντὸς ὑμῶν),* and at another He teaches that it is the place where Abraham, Isaac, and Jacob, with all the prophets, rest and are blessed (Lk 17²¹ 13²⁸). Now the kingdom is thought of as something that can be taken away from the Jews and be given to the Gentiles (Mt 21⁴³), and again, it is that for whose coming the disciples are instructed to pray (6¹⁰). The kingdom is thought of at one time as a good that can be obtained by seeking (6³³), and as something to be slowly developed from within the soul (Mk 4²⁶); at another time, as an event of the future, realized suddenly and by Divine power (8³⁸ 9¹).

From this survey it is readily seen that the term 'kingdom of God (or heaven)' in the usage of Jesus is not easy to be defined; that it appears to be an elastic, poetic symbol rather than the vehicle of a single sharply-bounded conception.

2. *The original form of the expression.*—With the exception of two passages in Mt. which speak of the kingdom without any qualifying word (Mt 8¹² 13³⁸), and three passages in which the kingdom (always thought of as future) is spoken of by Jesus as '*His*' [or '*My*'] kingdom (Mt 13⁴¹ 16²⁸, Lk 22³⁰), His usage fluctuates between 'kingdom of heaven' and 'kingdom of God,' the former greatly predominating in Matthew, and the latter being the exclusive term in Mark and Luke. It seems probable that the term ordinarily used by Jesus was 'kingdom of heaven,' and that for the following reasons. (1) It is the prevailing term in the *Logia* of Matthew, and the *Logia*, unlike the Gospels of Mark and Luke, are regarded as directly Apostolic. (2) The presumption is that Jesus used a current Jewish term, and 'kingdom of heaven' has a distinctly Jewish colouring, which does not belong to the term 'kingdom of God.' For the Greek word for 'heaven' in this phrase is a plural (τῶν οὐρανῶν) in accordance with the Hebrew usage (מַלְכוּת שָׁמַיִם), but contrary to the Greek. And, further, the expression 'kingdom of heaven' accords better with the popular Jewish belief that the kingdom of the Messiah was to come *from above*. (3) The originality of the term 'kingdom of heaven' is favoured by the consideration that the Second and Third Evangelists, since they wrote for Gentile readers, may more readily be thought to have modified a Jewish expression than that the author of the *Logia*, who wrote for Jews, modified the term used by Jesus.†

But, while there is therefore every reason to conclude that Jesus ordinarily used the term 'kingdom of heaven,' we certainly are not justified in saying that He did this to avoid speaking the Divine name (cf. O. Holtzmann, *The Life of Jesus*, pp. 163, 164; Dalman, *Die Worte Jesu*, p. 92, Eng. tr.). It is impossible to suppose that the man who called God His Father, and who felt that God was always with Him, the man who brought God near to His disciples and convinced them that He numbered the hairs of their heads, that they could approach Him at any time without priest or outward sacrifice,—that such a man shared the superstitious regard for the Holy Name. If Jesus habitually used the term 'kingdom of heaven,' which we believe to have been the case, He probably did so because that was the name in common use among His hearers.

3. *Fundamental thought of the term.*—To ascertain the central idea of the term 'kingdom of heaven,' as used by Jesus, we may well begin with a passage in which He seems to give a general

interpretation of it, viz. the second and third petitions of the Lord's Prayer, 'Thy kingdom come, Thy will be done, as in heaven, so on earth' (Mt 6¹⁰). The second of these petitions appears to explain the first. It seems to imply that, where the will of God is done, there the kingdom of God has come. That will is thought of as being done perfectly in heaven; and when it is done thus on earth, then the kingdom of heaven is realized. Accordingly this passage suggests that the fundamental idea of 'kingdom of heaven' is the *rule of God*.

Another passage which, though not using the word 'kingdom,' seems to throw light on the conception of Jesus, is that which records His answer to those who, while He was teaching on a certain occasion, told Him that His mother and brothers desired to see Him (Mk 3³¹⁻³⁵). He said, 'Whosoever shall do the will of God, the same is my brother, and sister, and mother.' But if these people who sat around Him, listening to His word, were owned as His *kindred*, it is reasonable to think that what made them His kindred made them also members of His kingdom. And that which brought them near to Him was the doing of God's will—the very thing which in the Lord's Prayer seems to explain the term 'kingdom.'

In line with the thought of these two passages which have been considered, is the conception of a considerable number of important sayings of Jesus concerning the kingdom. Thus, in the Sermon on the Mount, He told His hearers to seek the kingdom and the righteousness of their heavenly Father (Mt 6³³). Here, as in the Lord's Prayer, the kingdom is something to be desired and sought. It is contrasted with food and drink and clothing,—things that the Gentiles seek,—and is thus characterized as an inward and spiritual good. We may then regard the word 'righteousness' as giving here the dominant thought of that kingdom which is to be sought. Not otherwise are we to understand the word in that passage which deals with the young scribe who answered Jesus discreetly (Mk 12³⁴). The Master told him that he was not far from the kingdom of God. Now, in these words He was obviously characterizing the moral and spiritual state of the young man; and thus the content of the term 'kingdom' is here moral and spiritual. So in the parable of the Automatic Earth. As it is the function of the earth to carry forward the development of the seed lodged in it, so by analogy it is the function of the heart to develop the kingdom of heaven (4²⁶⁻²⁹). Manifestly, then, the kingdom is here thought of as a spiritual principle to be received into the heart.

Another passage in which the content of the term is virtually indicated by Jesus is the reply which He gave to the question of certain Pharisees. They asked Him when the kingdom of God should come, and He replied: 'The kingdom of God is in the midst of you' (Lk 17²¹). That is to say, the kingdom is already present, already an accomplished fact. It had not come with outward show and noise, but quietly and naturally. There seems to be only one way of understanding this remarkable utterance, for the view that it refers to the future, and means that the kingdom will come as a surprise, rests on the identification of the coming of the kingdom with the Parousia of the Son of Man (see Wernle, *The Beginnings of Christianity*, i. 62). But this identification cannot be made, for the Parousia will have the very characteristic which Jesus here denies to the coming of the kingdom. It will be 'with observation' (μετὰ παρατηρήσεως; see, e.g., Mk 13²⁴⁻²⁶· ²⁹). We must hold, then, that the utterance of Jesus had a present force, and must find the justification of it in His own experience. He was conscious that the kingdom was realized in His own heart, and was be-

---

* See below, § 3.

† Note the bearing of the words ὁ ἐν τοῖς οὐρανοῖς, which frequently modify 'Father.'

ginning to be realized in His disciples. Thus this passage falls into line with those in which Jesus suggests that He meant by the term 'kingdom of heaven' an inner spiritual fact, viz. the rule of God in the heart.[*]

Now these passages which have been considered present a conception of the kingdom of heaven which Jesus unquestionably entertained. That this conception was central in His usage, and must be called the fundamental content of the term 'kingdom of heaven,' is seen from the following considerations. (a) It is the only explanation of a number of most important passages which is suggested by Jesus Himself. (b) It is an explanation in perfect harmony with the other teaching of Jesus. For that teaching, as seen, for instance, in the Sermon on the Mount, is inward and spiritual ; and such is the thought of the 'kingdom of heaven' as the rule of God in the heart of man. (c) The Fourth Gospel, with the exception of two passages (3³⁻⁵ 18³⁶), does not employ the term 'kingdom of heaven'; but the term which it does employ, where the Synoptics have 'kingdom of heaven,' is the equivalent of 'kingdom' in the sense of God's rule. This term is 'eternal life.' That is the *summum bonum* in John, as the kingdom of heaven is in the early Gospels (Jn 4¹⁴ 5²⁴ 6⁴⁰ 10²⁸). This eternal life, like the kingdom of heaven, is bound up with the personality and mission of Jesus (4¹⁴ 6²⁷). Again, like the rule of God in the Synoptics, the gift of eternal life in John is both for the present and for the future (4³⁶ 12²⁵). Therefore we say that this early interpretation of the Gospel which we have in John helps to confirm the view that the fundamental conception of the term 'kingdom of heaven' in the mind of Jesus was the rule of God. (d) And, finally, the correctness of this view is established by the fact that, while the Synoptics use the term 'kingdom of heaven' in various other senses, these are all secondary to the thought of God's rule, and are derived from it. This will be shown in the next section.

4. Special uses of the term.—(a) There is a group of passages in which the term 'kingdom of heaven' evidently denotes *a company of men*. This is the prominent thought of the expression when Jesus says that he who is least in the kingdom of heaven is greater than John the Baptist (Mt 11¹¹); also in the parables of the Tares and the Drag-net (13²⁴⁻³⁰·⁴⁷⁻⁵⁰). The tares are the sons of the evil one, and at the end of the present age they are to be gathered *out* of the kingdom. They are therefore *in* the kingdom up to that time. To be gathered out of the kingdom means to be separated from the sons of the kingdom. The interest of the parable centres in the teaching that these two classes—the sons of the kingdom and the sons of the evil one—must remain intermingled until the end of the age. Hence it is obvious that the kingdom out of which the 'stumbling-blocks' are to be taken is the company of those who inwardly belong to God.

Now, while the foremost thought in these passages is that of a certain company of persons, these persons cannot be defined without the aid of the thought of God's rule. They are the persons who are under that rule, or at least claim to be under it.

(b) A second special use of the term 'kingdom of heaven' is presented in the parable of the Labourers in the Vineyard (21⁴³). Jesus said to

the Jews at the close of the parable, 'The kingdom of God shall be taken away from you, and shall be given to a nation bringing forth the fruits thereof.' In this case 'kingdom' cannot mean the *rule* of God, for these Jews were hostile to this, and obviously it cannot mean those who are under the Divine rule. We take it in the sense of *the high privilege and blessing which the Jews had enjoyed as God's peculiar people*. It was these things which were actually taken from the Jews when the gospel of Jesus was freely proclaimed to the Gentiles. Another passage which may well be assigned to the same category is the first Beatitude (5³). The poor in spirit are blessed because 'theirs is the kingdom of heaven.' It *is* now theirs. They experience its blessing by virtue of the fact that they *are* poor in spirit. They will doubtless experience it in much larger measure in the future, but they have a foretaste of the experience now. In like manner they who hungered after righteousness began to be 'filled' by Jesus at once : the satisfaction of their longing was not deferred to a distant future. Again, as purity of heart brought a vision of God to Jesus, even in His earthly life, we cannot doubt that the promise of His beatitude for the pure in heart was a promise not merely of a future good, but of a good to be enjoyed in some measure here and now.

(c) Another special use of the term 'kingdom of heaven,' and yet one that is easily derived from its fundamental idea, is found in a considerable number of passages. Thus Jesus said, 'It is better to enter into the kingdom of God with one eye, than having two eyes to be cast into Gehenna' (Mk 9⁴⁷). Since Gehenna stands here in contrast to the kingdom of God, it is obvious that the latter term denotes the place to which the righteous go at death. Again we read, 'Not every one that saith unto me, Lord, Lord, shall enter into the kingdom of heaven ; but he that doeth the will of my Father who is in heaven' (Mt 7²¹). It is plain from the following verse that Jesus is thinking of the end of the present age, and therefore the kingdom of heaven is here a synonym for heaven as the abode of the blessed. It is used in the same sense when Jesus says that many shall come from the east and the west, and sit down with Abraham, Isaac, and Jacob in the kingdom of heaven (8¹¹) ; and again, in the parable of the Tares, when it is said that the righteous, *after* the judgment of the wicked, shall shine forth as the sun in the kingdom of their Father (13⁴³).

The prominent thought in these passages is the place to be occupied by those who are under the rule of God, rather than that rule itself. The kingdom of heaven in this sense alone is wholly eschatological. It belongs entirely to the future. Yet it is by no means the Jewish apocalyptic kingdom even in these passages. It is open to Gentiles as well as Jews (8¹¹·¹²), and it is not a kingdom for this earth. It is where the spirits of the patriarchs are now.

Such are the special uses of the term 'kingdom of heaven' in the words of Jesus. No one of them furnishes a conception that binds the various uses together as does the idea of the rule of God.

5. The ideal of Jesus and that of the scribes.—Jesus' conception of the kingdom of heaven was not developed out of that of the scribes. It was the antithesis of that. The story of the Temptation marks the definite rejection of the popular idea. For there would have been no ground for the temptation of Jesus, in regard to the Messianic office, if that ideal which He put away as fundamentally evil had not been the ideal of His people. His ideal was born out of His own inner experience of the rule of God. Hence for Him the kingdom in its fundamental idea was something

---

[*] The AV and RV rendering of ἐντὸς ὑμῶν, viz. 'within you,' is sanctioned by general usage and by the context (see Godet, *Com. in loc.*) equally with the marginal 'among you,' 'in the midst of you,' and possibly receives some confirmation from the 2nd of Grenfell and Hunt's 'New Sayings of Jesus' (see art. IDEAS [LEADING], p. 770b). But, if adopted, it falls even more readily than the other into line with Christ's teaching as to the spirituality of the kingdom

to be realized from within, quietly and gradually, by spiritual means. The scribes, on the contrary, looked for a kingdom to be realized from without, in a spectacular and supernatural manner. This is plain from certain references in the Gospel itself. Thus, when Jesus entered Jerusalem riding on an ass, and all the crowds shouted Hosanna, His disciples thought that He was now at last to set up a visible Messianic banner, and they hailed the *coming* kingdom of their father David (Mk 11[10]). Thus the establishment of the kingdom was associated in their minds with outward pomp. The disciples of Jesus, even after the resurrection, seem to have thought that the kingdom was to be set up in some miraculous manner, at any rate it was not to come *through them* (Ac 1[6]).

This idea of the kingdom is common also in other Jewish writings. Thus, *e.g.*, in the *Psalms of Solomon* we read that the Messiah will destroy the ungodly nations by the breath of His mouth, and He alone will establish the kingdom (17[23-25]). Of the same purport is the teaching of the Talmud. Deliverance by the Messiah, like the deliverance of Israel by Moses, is to come from without, miraculously, and not at all from within. The Jews who are alive at the coming of the Messiah seem to have no more to do with the establishment of the kingdom than the Jews who are dead, and who at the beginning of the Messianic age are raised up to enjoy the kingdom (see Weber, *Jüd. Theol.*[2] pp. 347–354; Hilgenfeld, *Die jüd. Apokalyptik*, p. 86).

Again, the popular conception of the kingdom of heaven in the time of Jesus was thoroughly *political* and *national*. This is made plain by the Gospel. Thus, *e.g.*, the third temptation of Jesus presupposes that people thought of the kingdom as a political organism. For the suggestion that Jesus might secure all the kingdoms of the world and their glory—He a carpenter from the little town of Nazareth, poor and as yet without a follower—would have been psychologically impossible, had not the popular view associated world-wide political dominion with Messiahship; and it would not have been a temptation of any power to the mind of Jesus, had it not been deeply rooted in the Jewish heart, and had it not seemed to have strong support in the OT itself.

The Fourth Evangelist tells us that after the miracle of feeding the five thousand, Jesus perceived that the people were about to make Him *king* (Jn 6[15]). This word is capable only of a political meaning in this place, and therefore shows that the Galilæan idea of the kingdom was political. The character and strength of the popular view are seen in the request of Salome, seconded by James and John (Mk 10[37]), and in the question of the disciples who, after the resurrection, asked the Lord if He would now *restore* the kingdom to Israel (Ac 1[6]).

In utter contrast to this view, the fundamental conception of Jesus was, from the first, non-political and universal. The rule which He contemplated was, primarily, the rule of God in the heart, a rule which He doubtless thought of as transforming the entire outward life, social and political, and as bringing it into harmony with the Divine rule, though on this consequence of the inner rule of God He gave no explicit teaching. He dwelt on the fundamental spiritual fact of God's rule in the heart. If at times He used the word 'kingdom' in the sense of the company of men who were under the rule of God, He did so without a suggestion of any political organization. And when by the 'kingdom of heaven' Jesus meant the full realization of His ideal in the future age, it is manifest that His conception is wholly religious in character and universal in its scope. Men enter the kingdom from the east and the west—all who have shown the spirit of Jesus; and what they inherit is eternal life (Mt 8[11. 12] 25[34]).

We conclude, then, that just as Jesus derived His conception of God from His own experience, so it was from His experience of the rule of God that He developed His teaching about the kingdom of heaven. This teaching was akin to the spiritual views of the great prophets, but was wholly unlike that of the scribes of His day. See also art. ESCHATOLOGY, p. 528 ff.

LITERATURE.—Wendt, *Die Lehre Jesu* [*Teaching of Jesus*], 1886; V. II. Stanton, *The Jewish and the Christian Messiah*, 1886; J. Weiss, *Die Predigt Jesu vom Reiche Gottes*, 1892; W. Baldensperger, *Das Selbstbewusstsein Jesu*[2], 1892; C. H. Toy, *Judaism and Christianity*, 1892; J. Drummond, *Hibbert Lectures*, 1894; Beyschlag, *NT Theol.*, Eng. tr. 1895; L. Paul, *Die Vorstellungen vom Messias und vom Gottesreich bei den Synoptikern*, 1895; W. Lütgert, *Das Reich Gottes nach den Evangelien*, 1895; A. Titius, *Jesu Lehre vom Reiche Gottes*, 1895; H. J. Holtzmann, *Lehrbuch der NT Theol.* 1897; Stevens, *Theol. of NT*, 1899; Gould, *Bibl. Theol. of NT*, 1900; G. Dalman, *Die Worte Jesu*, Eng. tr. 1902; W. Bousset, *Rel. des Judenthums*, 1903; Wernle, *Beginnings of Christianity*, Eng. tr. 1903; Candlish, *Kingdom of God*; Bruce, *Kingdom of God*; Orr, *Chr. View of God and the World*, p. 401 ff., and his art. in Hastings' *DB* ii. 844; Denney, *Stud. in Theol.*, ch. viii.; *ExpT* iv. [1893] pp. 248, 464.

GEORGE HOLLEY GILBERT.

KISS.—Originally a token of affection belonging to the intimate conditions of family life, but extended to more general relationships.

1. To *kiss the hands* is the expression of respect towards seniority and higher rank. Children in Oriental homes are taught to rise at the entrance of visitors and salute in this way. It is also their first form of greeting to parents and adult relatives before being kissed on the lips and cheek by them. When two sheikhs meet they kiss each other's hands in recognition of the rank held by each. Kissing the hand, or making an attempt to do so, often occurs when one person receives a commission from another or undertakes to do some work for him. The feeling of respect originating in the relationship of child to parent is extended to that of employed and employer.

With regard to the salutation of Judas Iscariot (Lk 22[47. 48]), to have kissed the hand of Christ after the interval of absence caused by his conference with the chief priests would have been but an ordinary tribute of respect, and as such would have escaped the notice of the disciples, while giving the required information to those who had come with him. If, on the other hand, the kiss was on the face, it was an act of presumption for an Oriental disciple to take the initiative in offering to his master the salutation of equal friendship. The prodigal son, in meeting his father, would be described as kissing his hands before being embraced and kissed by the latter (Lk 15[20]).

2. Among those of the same age, and where the relationships of life permitted it, the salutation is given sometimes on the *lips*, but more frequently on the *cheek* or *neck*. For intimate relatives or acquaintances of the same sex to part for a time, or to meet after a period of separation without such salutation, would seem strained and unnatural (Lk 15[20]). In this form of greeting all thought of superior and inferior is lost in the equality of affection and identity of interest (Ac 20[37]). Such was the kiss of peace or salutation of good-will that prevailed for a time in the congregations of the early Church. It testified to the new bond of fellowship in the family of the firstborn, and was called a *holy* kiss (Ro 16[16]) as a reminder of Christian sainthood, and also a kiss of *love* (1 P 5[14]) made possible by the love that had given them such discipleship and communion.

G. M. MACKIE.

KNEELING.—A comparison of the passages that refer to bodily posture seems to prove that kneeling is nowhere intended unless the word 'knee' ($\gamma \acute{o} \nu \nu$) forms part of the expression. The word $\pi \rho o \sigma \kappa \nu \nu \acute{e} \omega$, usually tr. 'worship,' always denotes prostration, not kneeling. Kneeling is referred to as—(a) A posture of *homage*. In this sense it was rendered to Christ in awe of His person (Mk 10[17], Lk 5[8]), and in mockery of His claims (Mt 27[29]). There is no instance of Christ Himself paying this homage to any man. (b) The posture of a *suppliant* (Mt 17[14], Mk 1[40]). In classical literature the suppliant kneels and touches the knees, or beard, of the person applied to. (c) A posture of *prayer*. Lk 22[41] is the only instance of this in the Gospels. Among the Jews the usual custom (and in the Temple and synagogues at ordinary times the invariable custom) was to stand at prayer (Mt 6[5], Mk 11[25], Lk 9[28-32] 18[11ff.] 22[46] etc.). The prayers of Solomon (1 K 8[54] = 2 Ch 6[13]) and Ezra (Ezr 9[5]), both offered kneeling in the Temple, are altogether exceptional. Beyond general (and ambiguous) expressions, *e.g.* Ps 95[6], Is 45[23], any references to particular cases of kneeling are very rare in the OT (cf. Dn 6[10]). In the Jewish Church, Solomon's prayer is the only instance prior to the Captivity. In the Christian Church, instances multiply after Pentecost (Ac 7[60] 9[40] 20[36] 21[5]). This may have been due in some measure to Hellenistic and Gentile influences. In 1 Ch 29[20] LXX there is an alteration of 'heads' to 'knees' bowed. The description given in Lk 22[41] (not supported by ||) occurs in a Gospel of Gentile authorship; and Gentile connexions are found in all except one (Ac 9[40]) of the NT passages already quoted. If this supposition is correct, the spread of kneeling as a posture of prayer has an interesting association with the change from a national to a universal religion.

F. S. RANKEN.

KNOCKING. — The guarding of the Oriental house-door led to the more elaborate precautions with regard to entrance by the city gate.

1. During the daytime any unannounced approach is felt to be unneighbourly, and open to suspicion. It is regarded as an act of thoughtlessness or implied contempt to ride up to a Bedawî tent from behind. The privacy of domestic life forbids a visitor from entering even the walled enclosure round the house, without first knocking and asking permission. He must wait until his call is heard, and the bar of the door or gate, if closed, has been removed by a member or servant who can conduct him into the house.

2. It is, however, at night that the difficulty is greatest. The family have retired together into a room with closed doors, and on account of the habit of sleeping with the coverlet drawn over the head they usually are unable for a time to hear the sound of knocking at the door. In the still, elastic air it is also difficult to localize the sound. In this way one is often disturbed by the loud persistent knocking and summoning by name resorted to by a neighbour who has returned late at night to his house (Lk 12[36]). The large wooden key of ancient times was too cumbersome to carry about, so that even one who had the right to enter, or was sure of being welcome, had to wait outside until the door was opened (Ac 12[16]). It was to those already familiar with such obstacles and the way of overcoming them that Christ said with regard to a higher entrance, 'Knock, and it shall be opened unto you' (Mt 7[7.8]); cf. Rev 3[20] 'Behold, I stand at the door, and knock.'

G. M. MACKIE.

KNOWLEDGE. — See CONSCIOUSNESS, IGNORANCE, KENOSIS, TEACHING OF JESUS.